Y0-DOM-681

Holy Bible

PRESENTED TO

Adam Weiss

by Mom & Dad

We love you & are

proud of you. Serve

Jesus always!

on 19

Certificate of Marriage

THIS CERTIFIES THAT

____

AND

____

WERE UNITED IN

Holy Matrimony

on ______________________________ 19 ________

at ______________________________________

____

____

Officiant

Witness: ___________________________________

Witness: ___________________________________

Born on 19

at

Born on 19

at

Born on 19

at

Born on 19

at

Born on 19

at

Born on 19

at

Born on 19

at

Born on 19

at

Born on 19

at

Born on 19

at

Born on 19

at

Born on 19

at

Born on 19

at

to

on 19

to

on 19

to

on 19

to

on 19

to

on 19

to

on 19

Occasions to Remember

____

on ______________________ 19 ______

____

on ______________________ 19 ______

____

on ______________________ 19 ______

____

on ______________________ 19 ______

____

on ______________________ 19 ______

____

on ______________________ 19 ______

____

on ______________________ 19 ______

____

on ______________________ 19 ______

____

on ______________________ 19 ______

The
HOLY BIBLE

The

HOLY BIBLE

containing the
Old and New Testaments

AUTHORIZED KING JAMES VERSION

Broadman and Holman Publishers
Nashville, Tennessee

Published by
Broadman and Holman Publishers
Nashville, Tennesee 37234

Color	*Binding*	*ISBN*
Black	Bonded Leather	1-55819-824-5
Black	Genuine Leather	1-55819-827-X
Burgundy	Bonded Leather	1-55819-826-1
Burgundy	Genuine Leather	1-55819-828-8
White	Bonded Leather	1-55819-825-3

Printed in Belgium
1 2 3 4 5 6   02 01 00 99 98

Books of the Bible

Old Testament

New Testament

Books of the Bible
in
Alphabetical Order

The books in the New Testament are indicated by *italics*.

The
OLD TESTAMENT

THE FIRST BOOK OF MOSES COMMONLY CALLED

GENESIS

Life's Questions

How did the world get in this condition?
Do we have reason to hope for something better?
How is God involved in this world? How does He expect me to be involved?

God's Answers

The Bible's first book provides answers to life's fundamental questions. In many ways Genesis gives the starting point for every teaching God has for you in Scripture.

Genesis' teachings come in two parts: the beginnings (chs. 1 to 11) and the fathers or patriarchs (chs. 12 to 50). The first section shows how our world began and then got into the condition we find it. The second shows how God 's promises lead people He calls to His life of blessing and hope.

Genesis presents a continued contrast between the Creator's goodness and grace and humanity's sin and rebellion.

God creates a very good world and establishes the family in it (chs. 1—2).
Humanity's repeated sin leads to God's discipline of the flood (chs. 3—7).
God began over with his covenant with Noah (8:1—9:17).
Noah's sin steamrolled to the universal rebellion at Babel (9:18—11:32).
God called Abraham to expect blessing and be a blessing (12:1—25:10).
Isaac passes the blessing to Jacob, not Esau (25:11—28:9).
Deceitful Jacob wrestles with God and people to become Israel and continue the blessing (28:10—36:43).
God does good for faithful Joseph who overcomes repeated obstacles to save his family and the world's most powerful nation (chs. 37—50).

Genesis sees a family prosper in a foreign country and prepare to become God's nation of blessing. Genesis thus showed God's people who they are, a people of covenant blessing expected to bless the nations. It showed the world what they were: proud rebels trusting themselves rather than God and creating chaos rather than peace. Most of all Genesis shows who God is: the all-powerful Creator who in grace and love created people for a loving relationship with Him and whose promises and leadership give hope for the future even when the present seems darkest. Genesis thus says life is a love relationship with God, listening to His promises and in faith obeying His commands.

1 In [a]the beginning [b]God created the
heaven and the earth.
2 And the earth was [c]without form,
and void; and darkness *was* upon the
face of the deep. [d]And the Spirit of
God moved upon the face of the waters.
3 ¶ [e]And God said, Let there be light:
and there was light.
4 And God saw the light, that *it was*
good: and God divided [1]the light from
the darkness.
5 And God called the light [f]Day, and
the darkness he called Night. [2]And the
evening and the morning were the first
day.
6 ¶ And God said, [g]Let there be a
[3]firmament in the midst of the waters,
and let it divide the waters from the
waters.
7 And God made the firmament, and
divided the waters which *were* under
the firmament from the waters which
were above the firmament: and it was
so.
8 And God called the firmament
Heaven. And the evening and the
morning were the second day.
9 ¶ And God said, [h]Let the waters
under the heaven be gathered together
unto one place, and let the dry *land*
appear: and it was so.

CHAPTER 1
1 [a]John 1.1-3
[b]Job 38.4;
2 [c]Jer. 4.23
[d]Isa. 40.12
3 [e]Ps. 33.9
4 [1]between the light and between the darkness
5 [f]Ps. 74.16
[2]And the evening was, and the morning was
6 [g]Job 37.18; Jer. 10.12
[3]expansion
9 [h]Job 26.10; Ps. 33.7
11 [i]Heb. 6.7
[4]tender grass
[j]Luke 6.44
14 [k]Deut. 4.19;
[5]between the day and between the night
16 [6]for the rule of the day, etc.
17 [l]Ps. 8.1

10 And God called the dry *land*
Earth; and the gathering together of
the waters called he Seas: and God
saw that *it was* good.
11 And God said, [i]Let the earth bring
forth [4]grass, the herb yielding seed,
and the fruit tree yielding fruit [j]after
his kind, whose seed *is* in itself, upon
the earth: and it was so.
12 And the earth brought forth
grass, *and* herb yielding seed after his
kind, and the tree yielding fruit, whose
seed *was* in itself, after his kind: and
God saw that *it was* good.
13 And the evening and the morning
were the third day.
14 ¶ And God said, [k]Let there be
lights in the firmament of the heaven
to divide [5]the day from the night; and
let them be for signs, and for seasons,
and for days, and years:
15 And let them be for lights in the
firmament of the heaven to give light
upon the earth: and it was so.
16 And God made two great lights;
the greater light [6]to rule the day, and
the lesser light to rule the night: *he
made* the stars also.
17 And God [l]set them in the firmament of the heaven to give light upon
the earth,
18 And to rule over the day and over
the night, and to divide the light from

the darkness: and God saw that *it was*
good.
19 And the evening and the morning
were the fourth day.
20 And God said, [m]Let the waters
bring forth abundantly the [7]moving
creature that hath [8]life, and [9]fowl *that*
may fly above the earth in the [10]open
firmament of heaven.
21 And God created great whales,
and every living creature that moveth, which the waters brought forth
abundantly, after their kind, and every
winged fowl after his kind: and God
saw that *it was* good.
22 And God blessed them, saying,
Be fruitful, and multiply, and fill the
waters in the seas, and let fowl multiply in the earth.
23 And the evening and the morning
were the fifth day.
24 ¶ And God said, [n]Let the earth
bring forth the living creature after his
kind, cattle, and creeping thing, and
beast of the earth after his kind: and it
was so.
25 And God made the beast of the
earth after his kind, and cattle after
their kind, and every thing that creepeth upon the earth after his kind: and
God saw that *it was* good.
26 ¶ And God said, [o]Let us make
man [p]in our image, after our likeness:
and let them have [q]dominion over the
fish of the sea, and over the fowl of the
air, and over the cattle, and over all the
earth, and over every creeping thing
that creepeth upon the earth.
27 So God created man in his *own*
image, in the [r]image of God created
he him; [s]male and female created he
them.
28 And [t]God blessed them, and God
said unto them, Be [u]fruitful, and multiply, and replenish the earth, and subdue it: and have dominion over the fish
of the sea, and over the fowl of the air,
and over every living thing that [11]mov-
eth upon the earth.
29 ¶ And God said, Behold, I have
given you every herb [12]bearing seed,
which *is* upon the face of all the earth,
and every tree, in the which *is* the fruit
of a tree yielding seed; [v]to you it shall
be for meat.
30 And [w]to every beast of the earth,
and [x]to every fowl of the air, and
to every thing that creepeth upon the
earth, wherein *there is* [13]life, *I have
given* every green herb for meat: and it
was so.
31 And [y]God saw every thing that
he had made, and, behold, *it was* very
good. And the evening and the morning were the sixth day.

2 Thus the heavens and the earth
were finished, and all the host of
them.
2 And [a]on the seventh day God
ended his work which he had made;
and he rested on the seventh day from
all his work which he had made.
3 And God [b]blessed the seventh day,
and sanctified it: because that in it he

20 [m]Ps. 104.24
[7]Or, creeping
[8]soul
[9]let fowl fly
[10]face of the firmament of heaven
24 [n]Ps. 104.18-23
26 [o]Ps. 100.3
[p]Eph. 4.24; Jas. 3.9
[q]Ps. 8.6
27 [r]1 Cor. 11.7; Eph. 4.24; Col. 3.10
[s]Mal. 2.15; Matt. 19.4; Mark 10.6
28 [t]Ps. 127.3; 1 Tim. 4.3
[u]ch. 9.1-7; Lev. 26.9; Ps. 128.3-4
[11]creepeth
29 [12]seeding seed
[v]Job 36.31; Ps. 104.14-15; Ps. 136.25; Ps. 146.7; Acts 14.17
30 [w]Ps. 145.15-16; Ps. 147.9
[x]Job 38.41
[13]a living soul
31 [y]Ps. 104.24; 1 Tim. 4.4
CHAPTER 2
2 [a]Ex. 31.17; Heb. 4.4
3 [b]Ex. 16.22-30
[1]created to make
5 [c]Ps. 104.14
[d]Ps. 65.9-11
6 [2]Or, a mist which went up
7 [3]the dust of, etc
8 [e]ch. 13.10
9 [f]Ezek. 31.8
[g]ch. 3.22; Rev. 22.2-14
10 [h]Ps. 46.4
11 [i]ch. 25.18
13 [4]Cush
14 [j]Dan. 10.4
[5]Or, eastward to Assyria
15 [6]Or, Adam
16 [7]eating thou shalt eat
17 [8]dying thou shalt die
18 [9]as before him
19 [k]Ps. 8.6
[10]Or, the man
20 [11]called
21 [l]ch. 15.12
22 [12]builded

had rested from all his work which God
[1]created and made.
4 ¶ These *are* the generations of the
heavens and of the earth when they
were created, in the day that the LORD
God made the earth and the heavens,
5 And [c]every plant of the field before it was in the earth, and every
herb of the field before it grew: for the
[d]LORD God had not caused it to rain
upon the earth, and *there was* not a
man to till the ground.
6 But [2]there went up a mist from the
earth, and watered the whole face of
the ground.
7 And the LORD God formed man [3]*of*
the dust of the ground, and breathed
into his nostrils the breath of life; and
man became a living soul.
8 ¶ And the LORD God planted a
[e]garden eastward in Ē'dĕn; and there
he put the man whom he had formed.
9 And out of the ground made the
LORD God to [f]grow every tree that
is pleasant to the sight, and good for
food; [g]the tree of life also in the midst
of the garden, and the tree of knowledge of good and evil.
10 And [h]a river went out of Ē'dĕn
to water the garden; and from thence
it was parted, and became into four
heads.
11 The name of the first *is* Pī'son:
that *is* it which compasseth the whole
land of [i]Hăv'ĭ-lah, where *there is* gold;
12 And the gold of that land *is* good:
there *is* bdellium and the onyx stone.
13 And the name of the second river
is Gī'hon: the same *is* it that compasseth the whole land of [4]Ē-thĭ-ō'pĭ-a.
14 And the name of the third river *is*
[j]Hĭd'de-kel: that *is* it which goeth [5]to-
ward the east of Ăs-sўr'ĭ-ȧ. And the
fourth river *is* Eū-phrā'tēs.
15 And the LORD God took [6]the man,
and put him into the garden of Ē'dĕn to
dress it and to keep it.
16 And the LORD God commanded
the man, saying, Of every tree of the
garden [7]thou mayest freely eat:
17 But of the tree of the knowledge
of good and evil, thou shalt not eat
of it: for in the day that thou eatest
thereof [8]thou shalt surely die.
18 ¶ And the LORD God said, *It is* not
good that the man should be alone; I
will make him an help [9]meet for him.
19 And out of the ground the LORD
God formed every beast of the field,
and every fowl of the air; and [k]brought
them unto Ăd'ăm to see what he would
call them: and whatsoever [10]Ăd'ăm
called every living creature, that *was*
the name thereof.
20 And Ăd'ăm [11]gave names to all
cattle, and to the fowl of the air, and to
every beast of the field; but for Ăd'ăm
there was not found an help meet for
him.
21 And the LORD God caused a deep
[l]sleep to fall upon Ăd'ăm, and he slept:
and he took one of his ribs, and closed
up the flesh instead thereof;
22 And the rib, which the LORD God
had taken from man, [12]made he a

woman, and [m]brought her unto the
man.
23 And Ăd'ăm said, This *is* now bone
[n]of my bones, and flesh of my flesh:
she shall be called [13]Woman, because
she was taken out of [14]Man.
24 Therefore [o]shall a man leave his
father and his mother, and shall cleave
unto his wife: and [p]they shall be one
flesh.
25 And they were both naked, the
man and his wife, and were not
[q]ashamed.

CHAPTER 3

3 Now the serpent was more subtil
[a]than any beast of the field which
the LORD God had made. And he said
unto the woman, Yea, [1]hath God said,
Ye shall not eat of every tree of the
garden?
2 And the woman said unto the serpent, We may eat of the fruit of the
trees of the garden:
3 [b]But of the fruit of the tree which
is in the midst of the garden, God hath
said, Ye shall not eat of it, neither shall
ye touch it, lest ye die.
4 And the serpent said unto the
woman, [c]Ye shall not surely die:
5 For God doth know that in the day
ye eat thereof, then your eyes shall be
opened, and ye shall be as gods, knowing good and evil.
6 And when the woman saw that the
tree *was* good for food, and that it *was*
[2]pleasant to the eyes, and a tree to be
desired to make *one* wise, she took of
the fruit thereof, and did eat, and gave
also unto her husband with her; [d]and
he did eat.
7 And the eyes of them both were
opened, and they knew that they *were*
naked; and they sewed fig leaves together, and made themselves [3]aprons.
8 And they heard [e]the voice of the
LORD God walking in the garden in the
[4]cool of the day: and Ăd'ăm and his
wife [f]hid themselves from the presence of the LORD God amongst the
trees of the garden.
9 And the LORD God called unto
Ăd'ăm, and said unto him, [g]Where *art*
thou?
10 And he said, I heard thy voice in
the garden, and [h]I was afraid, because
I *was* naked; and I hid myself.
11 And he said, Who told thee that
thou *wast* naked? Hast thou eaten of
the tree, whereof I commanded thee
that thou shouldest not eat?
12 And the man said, [i]The woman
whom thou gavest *to be* with me, she
gave me of the tree, and I did eat.
13 And the LORD God said unto the
woman, What *is* this *that* thou hast
done? And the woman said, The serpent beguiled me, and I did eat.
14 And the LORD God said unto the
serpent, Because thou hast done this,
thou *art* cursed above all cattle, and
above every beast of the field; upon
thy belly shalt thou go, and [j]dust shalt
thou eat all the days of thy life:
15 And I will put [k]enmity between
thee and the woman, and between thy
seed and her seed; [l]it shall bruise thy
head, and thou shalt bruise his heel.
16 Unto the woman he said, I will
greatly multiply thy sorrow and thy
conception; [m]in sorrow thou shalt
bring forth children; and thy desire
shall be [5]to thy husband, and he shall
rule over thee.
17 And unto Ăd'ăm he said, Because
thou hast hearkened unto the voice of
thy wife, and hast eaten of the tree, of
which I commanded thee, saying, Thou
shalt not eat of it: cursed *is* the ground
for thy sake; [n]in sorrow shalt thou eat
of it all the days of thy life;
18 Thorns also and thistles shall it
[6]bring forth to thee; and thou shalt eat
the herb of the field;
19 In the sweat of thy face shalt thou
eat bread, till thou return unto the
ground; for out of it wast thou taken:
for dust thou *art*, and [o]unto dust shalt
thou return.
20 And Ăd'ăm called his wife's name
[7]Ēve; because she was the mother of all
living.
21 Unto Ăd'ăm also and to his wife
did the LORD God make coats of skins,
and clothed them.
22 ¶ And the LORD God said, [p]Be-
hold, the man is become as one of us,
to know good and evil: and now, lest
he put forth his hand, [q]and take also of
the tree of life, and eat, and live for
ever:
23 Therefore the LORD God sent him
forth from the garden of Ē'dĕn, to till
the ground from whence he was taken.
24 So he drove out the man; and
he placed [r]at the east of the garden
of Ē'dĕn [s]Chĕr'u-bĭms, and a flaming
sword which turned every way, [t]to
keep the way of the tree of life.

CHAPTER 4

4 And Ăd'ăm knew Ēve his wife; and
she conceived, and bare [1]Cāin, and
said, I have gotten a man from the
LORD.
2 And she again bare his brother
[2]Ā'bĕl. And Ā'bĕl was [3]a keeper of
sheep, but Cāin was a tiller of the
ground.
3 And [4]in the process of time it came
to pass, that Cāin brought of the fruit
of the ground an offering unto the
LORD.
4 And Ā'bĕl, he also brought of [a]the
firstlings of his [5]flock and of the fat
thereof. And the LORD had [b]respect
unto Ā'bĕl and to his offering:
5 But [c]unto Cāin and to his offering
he had not respect. And Cāin was very
wroth, and his countenance fell.
6 And the LORD said unto Cāin, Why
art thou wroth? and why is thy countenance fallen?
7 If thou doest well, shalt thou not
[6]be accepted? and if thou doest not
well, sin lieth at the door. And [7]unto
thee *shall be* his desire, and thou shalt
rule over him.
8 And Cāin talked with Ā'bĕl his
brother: and it came to pass, when
they were in the field, that Cāin rose up
against Ā'bĕl his brother, and [d]slew
him.

[m]Prov. 18.22; Heb. 13.4
23 [n]ch. 29.14; Eph. 5.30
[13]Isha
[14]Ish; 1 Cor. 11.8
24 [o]Ps. 45.10; 1 Cor. 6.16
[p]Eph. 5.28-31
25 [q]Ex. 32.25; Isa. 47.3

CHAPTER 3
1 [a]Matt. 10.16; Rev. 20.2
[1]because, etc
3 [b]ch. 2.16-17
4 [c]2 Cor. 11.3;
6 [2]a desire
[d]Rom. 5.12-19
7 [3]Or, things to gird about
8 [e]Job 38.1
[4]wind
[f]Job 31.33;
9 [g]ch. 4.9
10 [h]Job 23.15;
12 [i]Prov. 28.13;
14 [j]Isa. 65.25;
15 [k]Num. 21.6-7
[l]Rom. 16.20;
16 [m]John 16.21;
[5]Or, subject to thy husband
17 [n]Job 5.7;
18 [6]cause to bud
19 [o]1 Cor. 15.21-22
20 [7]Chavah, or, living
22 [p]verse 5
[q]ch. 2.9
24 [r]ch. 2.8
[s]Ps. 104.4;
[t]John 14.6

CHAPTER 4
1 [1]That is, gotten, or, acquired
2 [2]Hebel
[3]feeder
3 [4]at the end of days
4 [a]Ex. 13.12;
[5]sheep, or, goats
[b]Judg. 6.21
5 [c]Heb. 11.4
7 [6]Or, have the excellency; Heb. 11.4
[7]Or, subject unto thee; ch. 3.16
8 [d]Matt. 23.35;

9 ¶ And the LORD said unto Cāin,
Where *is* Ā'bĕl thy brother? And he
said, I know not: *Am* I my brother's
keeper?
10 And he said, What hast thou
done? the voice of thy brother's [8]blood
[e]crieth unto me from the ground.
11 And now *art* thou [f]cursed from
the earth, which hath opened her
[g]mouth to receive thy brother's blood
from thy hand;
12 When thou tillest the ground, it
shall not henceforth yield unto thee
her strength; a fugitive and a vagabond shalt thou be in the earth.
13 And Cāin said unto the LORD,
[9]My punishment *is* greater than I can
bear.
14 Behold, thou hast driven me out
this day from the face of the earth; and
from thy face shall I be hid; and I shall
be a fugitive and a vagabond in the
earth; and it shall come to pass, *that*
every one that findeth me shall slay
me.
15 And the LORD said unto him,
Therefore whosoever slayeth Cāin,
vengeance shall be taken on him sevenfold. And the LORD [h]set a mark
upon Cāin, lest any finding him should
kill him.
16 ¶ And Cāin went out from the
[i]presence of the LORD, and dwelt in the
land of Nŏd, on the east of Ē'dĕn.
17 And Cāin knew his wife; and she
conceived, and bare [10]Ē'nŏch: and he
builded a city, [j]and called the name of
the city, after the name of his son,
Ē'nŏch.
18 And unto Ē'nŏch was born Ī'răd:
and Ī'răd begat Me-hū'ja-el: and Me-
hū'ja-el begat Me-thu'sa-el: and Me-
thu'sa-el begat [11]Lā'mech.
19 ¶ And Lā'mech took unto him two
wives: the name of the one *was* Ā'dah,
and the name of the other Zĭl'lah.
20 And Ā'dah bare Jā'băl: he was
the father of such as dwell in tents, and
of such as have cattle.
21 And his brother's name *was* Jū'-
bal: he was the father of all such as
handle the harp and organ.
22 And Zĭl'lah, she also bare Tu'-
bal–cāin, an [12]instructer of every artificer in brass and iron: and the sister of
Tu'bal–cāin *was* Nā'a-mah.
23 And Lā'mech said unto his wives,
Ā'dah and Zĭl'lah, Hear my voice; ye
wives of Lā'mech, hearken unto my
speech: for [13]I have slain a man to my
wounding, and a young man [14]to my
hurt.
24 If Cāin shall be avenged sevenfold, truly Lā'mech seventy and sevenfold.
25 ¶ And Ăd'ăm knew his wife again;
and she bare a son, and called his name
[15]Seth: For God, *said she,* hath appointed me another seed instead of
Ā'bĕl, whom Cāin slew.
26 And to Sĕth, to him also there
was born a son; and he called his name
[16]Ē'nos: then began men [17]to call upon
the name of the LORD.

10 [8]bloods
[e]Heb. 12.24; Rev. 6.10
11 [f]Deut. 28.15-20; Gal. 3.10
[g]Job 16.18
13 [9]Or, Mine iniquity is greater than that it may be forgiven
15 [h]Ezek. 9.4-6
16 [i]2 Ki. 13.23; Jer. 52.3
17 [10]Chanoch
[j]Ps. 49.11 116.17; 1 Cor. 1.2
18 [11]Lemech
22 [12]whetter
23 [13]Or, I would slay a man in my wound, etc
[14]Or, in my hurt
25 [15]Sheth, that is, appointed, or, put
26 [16]Enosh
[17]Or, to call themselves by the name of the LORD; ch. 6.2; 1 Ki. 18.24; Ps. 18.3
CHAPTER 5
1 [a]1 Chr. 1.1; Luke 3.38
[b]ch. 1.26-27; Col. 3.10
5 [c]ch. 3.19; Heb. 9.27
9 [1]Kenan
12 [2]Maleleel, that is, Praiser of God
15 [3]Jered, that is, descending
18 [d]1 Chr. 1.3
21 [4]Or, Mathusala, that is, at his death the sending forth of waters
22 [e]ch. 6.9;
24 [f]2 Ki. 2.11;
25 [5]Lemech

5 This *is* the [a]book of the generations
of Ăd'ăm. In the day that God created man, in [b]the likeness of God made
he him;
2 Male and female created he them;
and blessed them, and called their
name Ăd'ăm, in the day when they
were created.
3 ¶ And Ăd'ăm lived an hundred
and thirty years, and begat a *son* in
his own likeness, after his image; and
called his name Sĕth:
4 And the days of Ăd'ăm after he
had begotten Sĕth were eight hundred
years: and he begat sons and daughters:
5 And all the days that Ăd'ăm lived
were nine hundred and thirty years:
[c]and he died.
6 And Sĕth lived an hundred and
five years, and begat Ē'nos:
7 And Sĕth lived after he begat Ē'nos
eight hundred and seven years, and
begat sons and daughters:
8 And all the days of Sĕth were nine
hundred and twelve years: and he died.
9 ¶ And Ē'nos lived ninety years,
and begat [1]Ca-i'nan:
10 And Ē'nos lived after he begat Ca-
i'nan eight hundred and fifteen years,
and begat sons and daughters:
11 And all the days of Ē'nos were
nine hundred and five years: and he
died.
12 ¶ And Ca-i'nan lived seventy
years, and begat [2]Ma-hā'la-lē-el:
13 And Ca-i'nan lived after he begat
Ma-hā'la-lē-el eight hundred and forty
years, and begat sons and daughters:
14 And all the days of Ca-i'nan were
nine hundred and ten years: and he
died.
15 ¶ And Ma-hā'la-lē-el lived sixty
and five years and begat [3]Jā'red:
16 And Ma-hā'la-lē-el lived after he
begat Jā'red eight hundred and thirty
years, and begat sons and daughters:
17 And all the days of Ma-hā'la-lē-el
were eight hundred ninety and five
years: and he died.
18 ¶ And Jā'red lived an hundred
sixty and two years, and he begat
[d]Ē'nŏch:
19 And Jā'red lived after he begat
Ē'nŏch eight hundred years, and begat
sons and daughters:
20 And all the days of Jā'red were
nine hundred sixty and two years: and
he died.
21 ¶ And Ē'nŏch lived sixty and five
years, and begat [4]Me-thu'se-lah:
22 And Ē'nŏch [e]walked with God
after he begat Me-thu'se-lah three hundred years, and begat sons and daughters:
23 And all the days of Ē'nŏch were
three hundred sixty and five years:
24 And [f]Ē'nŏch walked with God:
and he *was* not; for God took him.
25 And Me-thu'se-lah lived an hundred eighty and seven years, and begat
[5]Lā'mech:
26 And Me-thu'se-lah lived after he
begat Lā'mech seven hundred eighty

and two years, and begat sons and
daughters:
27 And all the days of Me-thu'se-
lah were nine hundred sixty and nine
years: and he died.
28 ¶ And Lā'mech lived an hundred
eighty and two years, and begat a son:
29 And he called his name [6]Nō'ah,
saying, This *same* shall comfort us
concerning our work and toil of our
hands, because of the ground [g]which
the LORD hath cursed.
30 And Lā'mech lived after he begat
Nō'ah five hundred ninety and five
years, and begat sons and daughters:
31 And all the days of Lā'mech were
seven hundred seventy and seven
years: and he died.
32 And Nō'ah was five hundred
years old: and Nō'ah begat Shĕm,
Hăm, and Jā'pheth.

6 And it came to pass, when men began to multiply on the face of the
earth, and daughters were born unto
them,
2 That [a]the sons of God saw the
daughters of men that they *were* fair;
and they [b]took them wives of all which
they chose.
3 And the LORD said, [c]My spirit shall
not always strive with man, [d]for that
he also *is* flesh: yet his days shall be an
hundred and twenty years.
4 There were giants in the earth in
those days; and also after that, when
the sons of God came in unto the
daughters of men, and they bare *children* to them, the same *became* mighty
men which *were* of old, men of renown.
5 ¶ And [e]GOD saw that the wickedness of man *was* great in the earth,
and *that* [1]every [f]imagination of the
thoughts of his heart *was* only evil
[2]continually.
6 And [g]it repented the LORD that he
had made man on the earth, and it
[h]grieved him at his heart.
7 And the LORD said, I will destroy
man whom I have created from the
face of the earth; [3]both man, and beast,
and the creeping thing, and the fowls
of the air; for it repenteth me that I
have made them.
8 But Nō'ah [i]found grace in the eyes
of the LORD.
9 ¶ These *are* the generations of
Nō'ah: Nō'ah was a just man *and*
[4]perfect in his generations, *and* Nō'ah
walked with God.
10 And Nō'ah begat three sons,
Shĕm, Hăm, and Jā'pheth.
11 The earth also was corrupt before God, and the earth was filled with
violence.
12 And God [j]looked upon the earth,
and, behold, it was corrupt; for all
flesh had corrupted his way upon the
earth.
13 And God said unto Nō'ah, [k]The
end of all flesh is come before me;
for the earth is filled with violence
through them; and, behold, I will destroy them [5]with the earth.

29 [6]that is, rest, or, comfort
[g]ch. 3.17; ch. 4.11

CHAPTER 6
2 [a]2 Cor. 6.18
[b]Deut. 7.3-4
3 [c]Luke 19.42; Gal. 5.16-17; 1 Pet. 3.20
[d]Ps. 78.39
5 [e]Rom. 1.28-31
[1]the whole imagination, with the purposes and desires of the heart
[f]ch. 8.21; Deut. 29.19; Prov. 6.18; Matt. 15.19
[2]every day
6 [g]Num. 23.19; 1 Sam. 15. 11, 29
[h]Isa. 63.10; Eph. 4.30
7 [3]from man unto beast
8 [i]ch. 19.19; Ex. 33.12; Luke 1.30; Acts 7.46
9 [4]Or, upright
12 [j]Ps. 14.2; Ps. 33.13
13 [k]Ezek. 7.2; Amos 8.2; 1 Pet. 4.7
[5]Or, from the earth
14 [6]nests
17 [l]2 Pet. 2.5
[m]Rom. 5.12-14
21 [n]ch. 1.29-30
22 [o]Heb. 11.7
[p]ch. 7.5

CHAPTER 7
1 [a]Ps. 91.1-10; Heb. 11.7; 1 Pet. 3.20; 2 Pet. 2.5
[b]ch. 6.9; Ps. 33.18-19; 2 Pet. 2.9
2 [c]Lev. 11
[1]seven seven
4 [d]Job 22.16; 2 Pet. 2.5
[2]blot out
5 [e]ch. 6.22; Ps. 119.6
7 [f]Heb. 11.7
10 [3]Or, on the seventh day

14 ¶ Make thee an ark of gopher
wood; [6]rooms shalt thou make in the
ark, and shalt pitch it within and without with pitch.
15 And this *is the fashion* which thou
shalt make it *of:* The length of the
ark *shall be* three hundred cubits, the
breadth of it fifty cubits, and the height
of it thirty cubits.
16 A window shalt thou make to the
ark, and in a cubit shalt thou finish it
above; and the door of the ark shalt
thou set in the side thereof; *with* lower,
second, and third *stories* shalt thou
make it.
17 [l]And, behold, I, even I, do bring a
flood of waters upon the earth, to destroy all flesh, wherein *is* the breath
of life, from under heaven; *and* every
thing that *is* in the earth [m]shall die.
18 But with thee will I establish my
covenant; and thou shalt come into the
ark, thou, and thy sons, and thy wife,
and thy sons' wives with thee.
19 And of every living thing of all
flesh, two of every *sort* shalt thou bring
into the ark, to keep *them* alive with
thee; they shall be male and female.
20 Of fowls after their kind, and of
cattle after their kind, of every creeping thing of the earth after his kind,
two of every *sort* shall come unto thee,
to keep *them* alive.
21 And take thou unto thee of all
[n]food that is eaten, and thou shalt
gather *it* to thee; and it shall be for
food for thee, and for them.
22 [o]Thus did Nō'ah; [p]according to
all that God commanded him, so did
he.

7 And the LORD said unto Nō'ah,
[a]Come thou and all thy house into
the ark; [b]for thee have I seen righteous
before me in this generation.
2 Of every [c]clean beast thou shalt
take to thee by [1]sevens, the male and
his female: and of beasts that *are* not
clean by two, the male and his female.
3 Of fowls also of the air by sevens,
the male and the female; to keep seed
alive upon the face of all the earth.
4 For yet seven days, and [d]I will
cause it to rain upon the earth forty
days and forty nights; and every living
substance that I have made will I [2]de-
stroy from off the face of the earth.
5 And Nō'ah did according unto all
[e]that the LORD commanded him.
6 And Nō'ah *was* six hundred years
old when the flood of waters was upon
the earth.
7 ¶ [f]And Nō'ah went in, and his sons,
and his wife, and his sons' wives with
him, into the ark, because of the waters
of the flood.
8 Of clean beasts, and of beasts that
are not clean, and of fowls, and of every thing that creepeth upon the earth,
9 There went in two and two unto
Nō'ah into the ark, the male and the
female, as God had commanded Nō'ah.
10 And it came to pass [3]after seven
days, that the waters of the flood were
upon the earth.

11 ¶ In the six hundredth year of Nō'ah's life, in the second month, the seventeenth day of the month, the same day were all [g]the fountains of the great deep broken up, and the [h4]windows of heaven were opened.

12 And the rain was upon the earth forty days and forty nights.

13 In the selfsame day entered Nō'ah, and Shĕm, and Hăm, and Jā'pheth, the sons of Nō'ah, and Nō'ah's wife, and the three wives of his sons with them, into the ark;

14 They, and every beast after his kind, and all the cattle after their kind, and every creeping thing that creepeth upon the earth after his kind, and every fowl after his kind, every bird of every [5]sort.

15 And they went in unto Nō'ah into the ark, two and two of all flesh, wherein *is* the breath of life.

16 And they that went in, went in male and female of all flesh, as God had commanded him: and the LORD [i]shut him in.

17 And the flood was forty days upon the earth; and the waters increased, and bare up the ark, and it was lift up above the earth.

18 And the waters prevailed, and were increased greatly upon the earth; [j]and the ark went upon the face of the waters.

19 And the waters prevailed exceedingly upon the earth; [k]and all the high hills, that *were* under the whole heaven, were covered.

20 Fifteen cubits upward did the waters prevail; and the mountains were covered.

21 [l]And all flesh died that moved upon the earth, both of fowl, and of cattle, and of beast, and of every creeping thing that creepeth upon the earth, and every man:

22 All in [m]whose nostrils *was* [6]the breath of life, of all that *was* in the dry *land,* died.

23 And every living substance was destroyed which was upon the face of the ground, both man, and cattle, and the creeping things, and the fowl of the heaven; and they were destroyed from the earth: and [n]Nō'ah only remained *alive,* and they that *were* with him in the ark.

24 [o]And the waters prevailed upon the earth an hundred and fifty days.

8 And God [a]remembered Nō'ah, and every living thing, and all the cattle that *was* with him in the ark: [b]and God made a wind to pass over the earth, and the waters asswaged;

2 [c]The fountains also of the deep and the windows of heaven were stopped, and [d]the rain from heaven was restrained;

3 And the waters returned from off the earth [1]continually: and after the end [e]of the hundred and fifty days the waters were abated.

4 And the ark rested in the seventh month, on the seventeenth day of the month, upon the mountains of Ar'ărat.

5 And the waters [2]decreased continually until the tenth month: in the tenth *month,* on the first *day* of the month, were the tops of the mountains seen.

6 ¶ And it came to pass at the end of forty days, that Nō'ah opened [f]the window of the ark which he had made:

7 And he sent forth [g]a raven, which went forth [3]to and fro, until the waters were dried up from off the earth.

8 Also he sent forth a dove from him, to see if the waters were abated from off the face of the ground;

9 But the dove [h]found no rest for the sole of her foot, and she returned unto him into the ark, for the waters *were* on the face of the whole earth: then he put forth his hand, and took her, and [4]pulled her in unto him into the ark.

10 And he stayed yet other seven days; and again he sent forth the dove out of the ark;

11 And the dove came in to him in the evening; and, lo, in her mouth *was* an [i]olive leaf pluckt off: so Nō'ah knew that the waters were abated from off the earth.

12 And he stayed yet other seven days; and sent forth the dove; which returned not again unto him any more.

13 ¶ And it came to pass in the six hundredth and first year, in the first *month,* the first *day* of the month, the waters were dried up from off the earth: and Nō'ah removed the covering of the ark, and looked, and, behold, the face of the ground was dry.

14 And in the second month, on the seven and twentieth day of the month, was the earth dried.

15 ¶ And God spake unto Nō'ah, saying,

16 Go [j]forth of the ark, thou, and thy wife, and thy sons, and thy sons' wives with thee.

17 Bring forth with thee every living thing that *is* with thee, of all flesh, *both* of fowl, and of cattle, and of every creeping thing that creepeth upon the earth; that they may breed abundantly in the earth, and [k]be fruitful, and multiply upon the earth.

18 And Nō'ah went forth, and his sons, and his wife, and his sons' wives with him:

19 Every beast, every creeping thing, and every fowl, *and* whatsoever creepeth upon the earth, after their [5]kinds, went forth out of the ark.

20 ¶ And Nō'ah builded an altar unto the LORD; and took of [l]every clean beast, and of every clean fowl, and offered burnt offerings on the altar.

21 And the LORD smelled [6]a sweet savour; and the LORD said in his heart, I will not again [m]curse the ground any more for man's sake; [7]for the [n]imagination of man's heart *is* evil from his youth; [o]neither will I again smite any more every thing living, as I have done.

11 [g]ch. 8.2; Prov. 8.28; Ezek. 26.19
[h]Ps. 78.23; Mal. 3.10
[4]Or, floodgates
14 [5]wing
16 [i]Ps. 91; 1 Pet. 1.5
18 [j]Ps. 104.26
19 [k]Ps. 104.6
21 [l]ch. 6.13-17; 2 Pet. 3.6
22 [m]ch. 2.7
[6]the breath of the spirit of life
23 [n]Ezek. 14.14; 2 Pet. 2.5
24 [o]ch. 8.3-4; compared with verse 11 of this chapter

CHAPTER 8
1 [a]ch. 19.29; Ps. 136.23
[b]Ex. 14.21; Ps. 104.7
2 [c]ch. 7.11
[d]1 Ki. 8.35; Job 38.37
3 [1]in going and returning
[e]ch. 7.24
5 [2]were in going and decreasing
6 [f]ch. 6.16
7 [g]1 Ki. 17.4
[3]in going forth and returning
9 [h]Deut. 28.65
[4]caused her to come
11 [i]Luke 2.14
16 [j]ch. 7.13; Ps. 121.8
17 [k]ch. 1.22
19 [5]families
20 [l]Lev. 11
21 [6]savour of rest; Lev. 1.9; Ex. 29.41; 2 Cor. 2.15; Eph. 5.2
[m]ch. 3.17; Isa. 54.9
[7]Or, though
[n]ch. 6.5; Eph. 2.1-3
[o]ch. 9.15

22 [8]While the earth remaineth, seed-
time and harvest, and cold and heat,
and summer and winter, and [p]day and
night shall not cease.

9 And [a]God blessed Nō'ah and his
sons, and said unto them, Be fruitful, and multiply, and replenish the
earth.
2 [b]And the fear of you and the dread
of you shall be upon every beast of the
earth, and upon every fowl of the air,
upon all that moveth *upon* the earth,
and upon all the fishes of the sea; into
your hand are they delivered.
3 [c]Every moving thing that liveth
shall be meat for you; even as the green
herb have I given you all things.
4 [d]But flesh with the life thereof,
which is the blood thereof, shall ye not
eat.
5 And surely your blood of your
lives will I require; [e]at the hand of every beast will I require it, and [f]at the
hand of man; at the hand of every
[g]man's brother will I require the life of
man.
6 [h]Whoso sheddeth man's blood, by
man shall his blood be shed: [i]for in the
image of God made he man.
7 And you, be ye fruitful, and multiply; bring forth abundantly in the
earth, and multiply therein.
8 ¶ And God spake unto Nō'ah, and
to his sons with him, saying,
9 And I, behold, I establish my covenant with you, and with your seed after you;
10 And with [j]every living creature
that *is* with you, of the fowl, of the cattle, and of every beast of the earth with
you; from all that go out of the ark, to
every beast of the earth.
11 And I will establish my covenant
with you; neither shall all flesh be cut
off any more by the waters of a flood;
neither shall there any more be [k]a
flood to destroy the earth.
12 And God said, This *is* [l]the token
of the covenant which I make between
me and you and every living creature
that *is* with you, for perpetual generations:
13 I do set my bow in the cloud, and
it shall be for a token of a covenant
between me and the earth.
14 And it shall come to pass, when I
bring a cloud over the earth, that the
bow shall be seen in the cloud:
15 And I will remember my covenant, which *is* between me and you
and every living creature of all flesh;
[m]and the waters shall no more become
a flood to destroy all flesh.
16 And the bow shall be in the cloud;
and I will look upon it, that I may remember [n]the everlasting covenant between God and every living creature of
all flesh that *is* upon the earth.
17 And God said unto Nō'ah, This *is*
the token of the covenant, which I
have established between me and all
flesh that *is* upon the earth.
18 ¶ And the sons of Nō'ah, that
went forth of the ark, were Shĕm, and

22 [8]As yet all the days of the earth
[p]Jer. 33.20-25
CHAPTER 9
1 [a]ch. 1.28
2 [b]Hos. 2.18; Jas. 3.7
3 [c]Deut. 12.15; Deut. 14.3
4 [d]Lev. 17.10; Acts 15.20-29
5 [e]Ex. 21.28-29
[f]Num. 35.31
[g]Acts 17.26
6 [h]Ex. 21.12-14; Rev. 13.10
[i]ch. 1.27; 1 Cor. 11.7
10 [j]ch. 8.1
11 [k]2 Pet. 3.5
12 [l]Matt. 26.26-28
15 [m]Ex. 28.12; Isa. 54.9
16 [n]ch. 17.13-19; 2 Sam. 23.5
18 [o]ch. 10.6
[1]Chenaan
19 [p]ch. 10.32; 1 Chr. 1.4
20 [q]ch. 3.19; Eccl. 5.9
21 [r]ch. 19.32-36;
23 [s]Ex. 20.12;
25 [t]Deut. 27.16;
[u]Josh. 9.23;
26 [v]Ps. 144.15;
[2]Or, servant to them
27 [3]Or, persuade
[w]Eph. 2.13-14;
29 [x]ch. 3.19;
CHAPTER 10
2 [a]1 Chr. 1.5-7
4 [1]Or, Chittim
[2]Or, Rodanim
9 [b]ch. 6.11
10 [c]Mic. 5.6
[3]Or, Babylon
11 [4]Or, he went out into Assyria
[5]Or, the streets of the city

Hăm, and Jā'pheth: [o]and Hăm *is* the
father of [1]Cā'năan.
19 These *are* the three sons of Nō'ah:
[p]and of them was the whole earth over-
spread.
20 And Nō'ah began *to be* [q]an husbandman, and he planted a vineyard:
21 And he drank of the wine, [r]and
was drunken; and he was uncovered
within his tent.
22 And Hăm, the father of Cā'năan,
saw the nakedness of his father, and
told his two brethren without.
23 [s]And Shĕm and Jā'pheth took a
garment, and laid *it* upon both their
shoulders, and went backward, and
covered the nakedness of their father;
and their faces *were* backward, and
they saw not their father's nakedness.
24 And Nō'ah awoke from his wine,
and knew what his younger son had
done unto him.
25 And he said, [t]Cursed *be* Cā'năan;
[u]a servant of servants shall he be unto
his brethren.
26 And he said, [v]Blessed *be* the
LORD God of Shĕm; and Cā'năan shall
be [2]his servant.
27 God shall [3]enlarge Jā'pheth, and
[w]he shall dwell in the tents of Shĕm;
and Cā'năan shall be his servant.
28 ¶ And Nō'ah lived after the flood
three hundred and fifty years.
29 And all the days of Nō'ah were
nine hundred and fifty years: and he
[x]died.

10 Now these *are* the generations of
the sons of Nō'ah, Shĕm, Hăm,
and Jā'pheth: and unto them were sons
born after the flood.
2 [a]The sons of Jā'pheth; Gō'mer,
and Mā'gŏg, and Măd'a-ī, and Jā'văn,
and Tṳ'bal, and Mē'shech, and Tī'ras.
3 And the sons of Gō'mer; Ăsh'ke-
năz, and Rī'phath, and To-gär'mah.
4 And the sons of Jā'văn; E-lī'shah,
and Tär'shish, [1]Kĭt'tĭm, and [2]Dŏd'a-
nĭm.
5 By these were the isles of the Gĕn-
tīles divided in their lands; every one
after his tongue, after their families, in
their nations.
6 ¶ And the sons of Hăm; Cŭsh, and
Mĭz'ra-ĭm, and Phŭt, and Cā'năan.
7 And the sons of Cŭsh; Sē'bȧ, and
Hăv'ĭ-lah, and Săb'tah, and Rā'a-mah,
and Săb'te-chah: and the sons of Rā'a-
mah; Shē'bȧ, and Dē'dan.
8 And Cŭsh begat Nĭm'rŏd: he began to be a mighty one in the earth.
9 He was a mighty hunter before the
LORD: wherefore it is said, Even as
Nĭm'rŏd the mighty hunter before [b]the
LORD.
10 And the beginning of his [c]king-
dom was [3]Bā'bel, and Ē'rĕch, and Ăc'-
căd, and Căl'neh, in the land of Shī'när.
11 Out of that land [4]went forth Ăs'-
shṳr, and builded Nĭn'e-veh, and [5]the
city Rē-hō'both, and Cā'lah,
12 And Rē'sen between Nĭn'e-veh
and Cā'lah: the same *is* a great city.
13 And Mĭz'ra-ĭm begat Lṳ'dĭm, and
Ăn'a-mĭm, and Lē'ha-bĭm, and Năph'-
tu-hĭm,

14 And Păth-ru̥'sĭm, and Căs'lu̥-hĭm,
([d]out of whom came Phĭ-lĭs'tĭm,) and
Căph'tō-rĭm.
15 ¶ And Cā'năan begat [6]Sī'dŏn his
firstborn, and Hĕth,
16 And the Jĕb'u-site, and the Ăm'-
ôr-īte, and the Gĭr'ga-sīte,
17 And the Hī'vīte, and the Ärk'īte,
and the Sĭn'īte,
18 And the Är'vad-īte, and the Zĕm'-
a-rīte, and the Hā'math-īte: and afterward were the families of the Cā'năan-
ītes spread abroad.
19 [e]And the border of the Cā'năan-
ītes was from Sī'dŏn, as thou comest to
Gē'rär, unto [7]Gā'zȧ; as thou goest, unto
Sŏd'om, and Go-mŏr'rah, and Ăd'-
mah, and Ze-bō'im, even unto Lā'shȧ.
20 These *are* the sons of Hăm, after
their families, after their tongues, in
their countries, *and* in their nations.
21 ¶ Unto Shĕm also, the father of
all the children of Ē'bĕr, the brother of
Jā'pheth the elder, even to him were
children born.
22 The [f]children of Shĕm; Ē'lăm,
and Ăs'shur, and [8]Är'phăx'ăd, and
Lŭd, and Ā'ram.
23 And the children of Ā'ram; Ŭz,
and Hŭl, and Gē'thĕr, and Măsh.
24 And Är'phăx'ăd begat [9g]Sā'lah;
and Sā'lah begat Ē'bĕr.
25 [h]And unto Ē'bĕr were born two
sons: the name of one *was* [10]Pē'leg; for
in his days was the earth divided; and
his brother's name *was* Jŏk'tan.
26 And Jŏk'tan begat Ăl-mō'dăd,
and Shē'leph, and Hā'zar–mā'veth,
and Jē'räh,
27 And Ha-dō'ram, and Ū'zal, and
Dĭk'lah,
28 And Ō'bal, and A-bĭm'ă-el, and
Shē'bȧ,
29 And Ō'phĭr, and Hăv'ĭ-lah, and
Jō'băb: all these *were* the sons of Jŏk'-
tan.
30 And their dwelling was from Mē'-
shȧ, as thou goest unto Sē'phar a
mount of the east.
31 These *are* the sons of Shĕm, after
their families, after their tongues, in
their lands, after their nations.
32 [i]These *are* the families of the sons
of Nō'ah, after their generations, in
their nations: [j]and by these were the
nations divided in the earth after the
flood.

11 And the whole earth was [a]of one
[1]language, and of one [2]speech.
2 And it came to pass, as they journeyed [3]from the east, that they found a
plain in the land of [b]Shī'när; and they
dwelt there.
3 And [4]they said one to another, Go
to, let us make brick, and [5]burn them
throughly. And they had brick for
stone, and slime had they for morter.
4 And they said, Go to, let us build us
a city and a tower, [c]whose top [6]*may*
reach unto heaven; and let us make [d]us
a name, lest we be [e]scattered abroad
upon the face of the whole earth.
5 [f]And the LORD came down to see
the city and the tower, which the children of men builded.

14 [d]1 Chr. 1.12
15 [6]Tzidon
19 [e]ch. 13.12-14, 15; ch. 15.18-21; Num. 34.2-12; Josh. 13.4
[7]Azzah
22 [f]1 Chr. 1.17
[8]Arpachshad
24 [9]Shelah
[g]ch. 11.12
25 [h]1 Chr. 1.19
[10]That is, Division
32 [i]1 Chr. 1.4
[j]ch. 9.19
CHAPTER 11
1 [a]Acts 2.6
[1]lip
[2]words
2 [3]Or, eastwards, as ch. 13.11
[b]Dan. 1.2
3 [4]a man said to his neighbour
[5]burn them to a burning
4 [c]Deut. 1.28
[6]may be very high
[d]John 5.44
[e]Luke 1.51
5 [f]ch. 18.21; Ps. 33.13; Ps. 53.2
6 [g]Ps. 2.1-4
7 [h]ch. 1.26
[i]ch. 42.23; Deut. 28.49; 1 Cor. 14.2, 11-23
8 [j]ch. 10.25-32; Luke 1.51
9 [7]That is, Confusion
[k]1 Cor. 14.23
10 [l]1 Chr. 1.17-27
12 [m]Luke 3.35
16 [n]1 Chr. 1.19
[8]Or, Phalec, Luke 3.35
18 [9]Or, Ragau, Luke 3.35
20 [10]Or, Saruch, Luke 3.35
24 [11]Or, Thara, Luke 3.34
26 [o]ch. 12.1; 1 Chr. 1.26
27 [p]ch. 12.4; 2 Pet. 2.7
29 [q]ch. 17.15
[r]ch. 22.20

6 And the LORD said, Behold, the
people *is* one, and they have all one
language; and this they begin to do:
and now nothing will be restrained
from them, which they have [g]imag-
ined to do.
7 Go to, [h]let us go down, and there
confound their language, that they may
[i]not understand one another's speech.
8 So the LORD scattered them abroad
from thence [j]upon the face of all the
earth: and they left off to build the city.
9 Therefore is the name of it called
[7]Bā'bel; [k]because the LORD did there
confound the language of all the earth:
and from thence did the LORD scatter
them abroad upon the face of all the
earth.
10 ¶ [l]These *are* the generations of
Shĕm: Shĕm *was* an hundred years
old, and begat Är'phăx'ăd two years
after the flood:
11 And Shĕm lived after he begat
Är'phăx'ăd five hundred years, and
begat sons and daughters.
12 And Är'phăx'ăd lived five and
thirty years, [m]and begat Sā'lah:
13 And Är'phăx'ăd lived after he
begat Sā'lah four hundred and three
years, and begat sons and daughters.
14 And Sā'lah lived thirty years, and
begat Ē'bĕr:
15 And Sā'lah lived after he begat
Ē'bĕr four hundred and three years,
and begat sons and daughters.
16 [n]And Ē'bĕr lived four and thirty
years, and begat [8]Pē'leg:
17 And Ē'bĕr lived after he begat
Pē'leg four hundred and thirty years,
and begat sons and daughters.
18 And Pē'leg lived thirty years, and
begat [9]Rē'u:
19 And Pē'leg lived after he begat
Rē'u two hundred and nine years, and
begat sons and daughters.
20 And Rē'u lived two and thirty
years, and begat [10]Sē'rug:
21 And Rē'u lived after he begat Sē'-
rug two hundred and seven years, and
begat sons and daughters.
22 And Sē'rug lived thirty years, and
begat Nā'hor:
23 And Sē'rug lived after he begat
Nā'hor two hundred years, and begat
sons and daughters.
24 And Nā'hor lived nine and twenty
years, and begat [11]Tē'rah:
25 And Nā'hor lived after he begat
Tē'rah an hundred and nineteen years,
and begat sons and daughters.
26 And Tē'rah lived seventy years,
and [o]begat Ā'brăm, Nā'hor, and Hā'-
ran.
27 ¶ Now these *are* the generations
of Tē'rah: Tē'rah begat Ā'brăm, Nā-
'hor, and Hā'ran; and Hā'ran begat
[p]Lŏt.
28 And Hā'ran died before his father Tē'rah in the land of his nativity,
in Ŭr of the Chăl'dees.
29 And Ā'brăm and Nā'hor took
them wives: the name of Ā'brăm's wife
was [q]Sā'răi; and the name of Nā'hôr's
wife, [r]Mĭl'cah, the daughter of Hā'ran,

the father of Mĭl'cah, and the father of
Ĭs'cah.
30 But [s]Sā'rāi was barren; she *had*
no child.
31 And Tē'rah took Ā'brăm his son,
and Lŏt the son of Hā'ran his son's son,
and Sā'rāi his daughter in law, his son
Ā'brăm's wife; and they [t]went forth
with them from Ŭr of the Chăl'dees, to
go into [u]the land of Cā'năan; and they
came unto [12]Hā'ran, and dwelt there.
32 And the days of Tē'rah were two
hundred and five years: and Tē'rah
died in Hā'ran.

12 Now the [a]LORD had said unto
Ā'brăm, Get thee out of thy country, and from thy kindred, and from
thy father's house, unto a land that I
will shew thee:
2 [b]And I will make of thee a great
nation, and I will bless thee, and make
thy name great; and thou shalt be a
blessing:
3 [c]And I will bless them that bless
thee, and curse him that curseth thee:
[d]and in thee shall all families of the
earth be blessed.
4 So Ā'brăm departed, as the LORD
had spoken unto him; and Lŏt went
with him: and Ā'brăm *was* seventy
and five years old when he departed
out of Hā'ran.
5 And Ā'brăm took Sā'rāi his wife,
and Lŏt his brother's son, and all their
substance that they had gathered, and
the souls that they had gotten [e]in Hā'-
ran; and they went forth to go [f]into the
land of Cā'năan; and into the land of
Cā'năan they came.
6 ¶ And Ā'brăm passed through the
land unto the place of [1]Sī'chem, [g]unto
the plain of Mō'reh. And the Cā'năan-
īte *was* then in the land.
7 [h]And the LORD appeared unto
Ā'brăm, and said, [i]Unto thy seed will I
give this land: and there builded he an
[j]altar unto the LORD, who appeared
unto him.
8 And he removed from thence unto
a mountain on the east of Bĕth'–el, and
pitched his tent, *having* Bĕth'–el on the
west, and [2]Hā'ī on the east: and there
he builded an altar unto the LORD, and
called upon the name of the LORD.
9 And Ā'brăm journeyed, [3]going on
[k]still toward the south.
10 ¶ And there was [l]a famine in the
land: and Ā'brăm [m]went down into
Ē'ġypt to sojourn there; for the famine
was [n]grievous in the land.
11 And it came to pass, when he was
come near to enter into Ē'ġypt, that he
said unto Sā'rāi his wife, Behold now, I
know that thou *art* [o]a fair woman to
look upon:
12 Therefore it shall come to pass,
when the E-ġўp'tians shall see thee,
that they shall say, This *is* his wife: and
they [p]will kill me, but they will save
thee alive.
13 Say, [q]I pray thee, [r]thou *art* my
sister: that it may be well with me for
thy sake; and my soul shall live because of thee.

30 [s]ch. 16.1
31 [t]Neh. 9.7; Acts 7.4; Heb. 11.8
[u]ch. 10.19
[12]Or, Charan

CHAPTER 12
1 [a]ch. 15.7; Acts 7.3
2 [b]ch. 17.6; ch. 18.18; ch. 46.3; Num. 23.10; Deut. 26.5; 1 Ki. 3.8
3 [c]ch. 24.35; Num. 24.9
[d]ch. 22.18; Gal. 3.8
5 [e]ch. 11.31
[f]Heb. 11.8
6 [1]Or, Sychar; John 4.5
[g]Deut. 11.30; Judg. 7.1
7 [h]ch. 17.1
[i]Deut. 34.4; Ps. 105.9-12
[j]ch. 13.4
8 [2]Or, Ai, or Aija
9 [3]in going and journeying
[k]ch. 13.3
10 [l]ch. 26.1
[m]Ps. 105.13
[n]ch. 43.1
11 [o]ch. 26.7
12 [p]ch. 20.11
13 [q]Ps. 25.21; Eph. 4.25
[r]ch. 20.5-13
15 [s]Esth. 2.16
17 [t]ch. 20.18; Heb. 13.4
18 [u]ch. 20.9; Prov. 21.1

CHAPTER 13
2 [a]ch. 24.35; Prov. 10.22
4 [b]ch. 12.7-8
6 [c]ch. 36.7; Luke 12.17-18
7 [d]ch. 26.20
8 [e]Phil. 2.14-15
[1]men brethren; Ex. 2.13; Ps. 133.1
9 [f]ch. 20.15
[g]Rom. 12.18; Jas. 3.13-18
10 [h]Num. 32.1
[i]Deut. 34.3; Ps. 107.34
[j]ch. 19.24; Ps. 107.34
[k]ch. 14.2; ch. 19.22

14 ¶ And it came to pass, that, when
Ā'brăm was come into Ē'ġypt, the E-
ġўp'tians beheld the woman that she
was very fair.
15 The [s]princes also of Phā'raōh
saw her, and commended her before
Phā'raōh: and the woman was taken
into Phā'raōh's house.
16 And he entreated Ā'brăm well
for her sake: and he had sheep, and
oxen, and he asses, and menservants,
and maidservants, and she asses, and
camels.
17 And the LORD [t]plagued Phā'raōh
and his house with great plagues because of Sā'rāi Ā'brăm's wife.
18 And Phā'raōh called Ā'brăm, and
said, [u]What *is* this *that* thou hast done
unto me? why didst thou not tell me
that she *was* thy wife?
19 Why saidst thou, She *is* my sister? so I might have taken her to me to
wife: now therefore behold thy wife,
take *her*, and go thy way.
20 And Phā'raōh commanded *his*
men concerning him: and they sent
him away, and his wife, and all that he
had.

13 And Ā'brăm went up out of
Ē'ġypt, he, and his wife, and all
that he had, and Lŏt with him, into the
south.
2 And Ā'brăm *was* [a]very rich in cattle, in silver, and in gold.
3 And he went on his journeys from
the south even to Bĕth'–el, unto the
place where his tent had been at the
beginning, between Bĕth'–el and Hā'ī;
4 Unto the place of the [b]altar, which
he had made there at the first: and
there Ā'brăm called on the name of the
LORD.
5 ¶ And Lŏt also, which went with
Ā'brăm, had flocks, and herds, and
tents.
6 And the [c]land was not able to bear
them, that they might dwell together:
for their substance was great, so that
they could not dwell together.
7 And there was [d]a strife between
the herdmen of Ā'brăm's cattle and the
herdmen of Lŏt's cattle: and the Cā'-
năan-īte and the Pĕr'ĭz-zīte dwelled
then in the land.
8 And Ā'brăm said unto Lŏt, [e]Let
there be no strife, I pray thee, between
me and thee, and between my herdmen
and thy herdmen; for we *be* [1]brethren.
9 *Is* [f]not the whole land before thee?
separate thyself, I pray thee, from me:
[g]if *thou wilt take* the left hand, then I
will go to the right; or if *thou depart* to
the right hand, then I will go to the left.
10 And Lŏt lifted up his eyes, and
[h]beheld all the [i]plain of Jôr'dan, that it
was well watered every where, before
the LORD [j]destroyed Sŏd'om and Go-
mŏr'rah, *even* as the garden of the
LORD, like the land of Ē'ġypt, as thou
comest [k]unto Zō'ar.
11 Then Lŏt chose him all the plain
of Jôr'dan; and Lŏt journeyed east:
and they separated themselves the one
from the other.

12 Ā'brăm dwelled in the land of
Cā'năan, and Lŏt dwelled in the cities
[l]of the plain, and pitched *his* tent toward Sŏd'om.
13 But [m]the men of Sŏd'om *were*
wicked and [n]sinners before the LORD
exceedingly.
14 ¶ And the LORD said unto Ā'brăm,
after that Lŏt was separated from him,
[o]Lift up now thine eyes, and look
from the place where thou art [p]north-
ward, and southward, and eastward,
and westward:
15 For all the land which thou seest,
to thee will I give it, and to thy [q]seed
for ever.
16 And I will make thy seed as the
[r]dust of the earth: so that if a man
can number the dust of the earth, *then*
shall thy seed also be numbered.
17 Arise, walk through the land in
the length of it and in the breadth of it;
for I will give it unto thee.
18 Then Ā'brăm removed *his* tent,
and came and dwelt in the [2]plain of
Măm're, which *is* in Hē'bron, and built
there an altar unto the LORD.
14 And it came to pass in the days
of Ăm'ra-phel king of [a]Shī'när,
Ā'rĭ-ŏch king of Ĕl'la-sär, Chĕd-ŏr-lā'-
o-mēr king of [b]Ē'lăm, and Tī'dal king
of nations;
2 *That these* [c]made war with Bē'rȧ
king of Sŏd'om, and with Bĭr'sha king
of Go-mŏr'rah, Shī'năb king of [d]Ăd'-
mah, and Shĕm'e-ber king of Ze-
bōi'ĭm, and the king of Bē'lȧ, which is
[e]Zō'ar.
3 All these were joined together in
the vale of Sĭd'dim, [f]which is the salt
sea.
4 Twelve years they served Chĕd-
ŏr-lā'o-mēr, and in the thirteenth year
they rebelled.
5 And in the fourteenth year came
Chĕd-ŏr-lā'o-mēr, and the kings that
were with him, and smote the Rĕph'a-
ĭms in Ăsh'tĕ-rŏth Kär-nā'im, and the
Zū'zims in Hăm, and the Ē'mĭms in
[1]Shā'veh Kĭr-ī-a-thā'im,
6 And the Hō'rītes in their mount
Sē'ïr, unto [2]Ĕl–pā'ran, which *is* by the
wilderness.
7 And they returned, and came to
Ĕn–mĭsh'pat, which *is* Kā'desh, and
smote all the country of the Ăm'a-lĕk-
ītes, and also the Ăm'ôr-ītes, that dwelt
[g]in Hăz'e-zon–tā'mar.
8 And there went out the king of
Sŏd'om, and the king of Go-mŏr'rah,
and the king of Ăd'-mah, and the king
of Ze-bōi'ĭm, and the king of Bē'lȧ (the
same *is* Zō'ar;) and they joined battle
with them in the vale of Sĭd'dim;
9 With Chĕd-ŏr-lā'o-mēr the king of
Ē'lăm, and with Tī'dal king of nations,
and Ăm'ra-phel king of Shī'när, and
Ā'rĭ-ŏch king of Ĕl'la-sär; four kings
with five.
10 And the vale of Sĭd'dim *was full*
of [h]slimepits; and the kings of Sŏd'om
and Go-mŏr'rah fled, and fell there;
and they that remained fled to the
[i]mountain.

12 [l]ch. 19.29
13 [m]ch. 18.20; Ezek. 16.49; 2 Pet. 2.7
[n]ch. 6.11
14 [o]Isa. 49.18
[p]ch. 28.14
15 [q]2 Chr. 20.7
16 [r]ch. 26.4; Ex. 32.13; Num. 23.10; Deut. 1.10; 1 Chr. 27.23; Jer. 33.22; Rom. 4.16; Heb. 11.12
18 [2]plains

CHAPTER 14
1 [a]ch. 10.10
[b]Isa. 11.11
2 [c]Jas. 4.1
[d]Deut. 29.23
[e]ch. 19.22
3 [f]Deut. 3.17; Num. 34.12; Josh. 3.16; Ps. 107.34
5 [1]Or, the plain of Kiriathaim
6 [2]Or, the plain of Paran
7 [g]2 Chr. 20.2
10 [h]ch. 11.3
[i]ch. 19.17-30
12 [j]ch. 11.31
[k]ch. 13.12; Jer. 2.17-19
13 [l]ver. 24
14 [m]ch. 13.8
[3]Or, led forth
[4]Or, instructed
[n]ch. 17.27; Eccl. 2.7
[o]Deut. 34.1; Isa. 41.2
16 [p]1 Sam. 30.8, 18-19
17 [q]2 Sam. 18.18
18 [r]Heb. 7.1-2
[s]Ps. 110.4; Heb. 7.10-22
20 [t]Heb. 7.4
21 [5]souls
22 [u]Dan. 12.7; Rev. 10.5
[v]Ps. 24.1; Matt. 11.25
23 [w]Esth. 9.15; 2 Cor. 11.9-12

CHAPTER 15
1 [a]ch. 46.2
[b]Isa. 41.10
[c]Ps. 58.11; Heb. 11.6
4 [d]ch. 17.16; 2 Sam. 7.12

11 And they took all the goods of
Sŏd'om and Go-mŏr'rah, and all their
victuals, and went their way.
12 And they took Lŏt, [j]Ā'brăm's
brother's son, [k]who dwelt in Sŏd'om,
and his goods, and departed.
13 ¶ And there came one that had
escaped, and told Ā'brăm the Hē'brew;
for he dwelt in the plain of Măm're
the Ăm'ôr-īte, brother of Ĕsh'cŏl, and
brother of Ā'nēr: and these [l]*were* confederate with Ā'brăm.
14 And when Ā'brăm heard that his
[m]brother was taken captive, he [3]armed
his [4]trained *servants*, [n]born in his own
house, three hundred and eighteen,
and pursued *them* [o]unto Dăn.
15 And he divided himself against
them, he and his servants, by night,
and smote them, and pursued them
unto Hō'bah, which *is* on the left hand
of Da-măs'cus.
16 And [p]he brought back all the
goods, and also brought again his
brother Lŏt, and his goods, and the
women also, and the people.
17 ¶ And the king of Sŏd'om went
out to meet him after his return from
the slaughter of Chĕd-ŏr-lā'o-mēr, and
of the kings that *were* with him, at the
valley of Shā'veh, which *is* the [q]king's
dale.
18 And [r]Mĕl-chĭz'e-dĕk king of Sā'-
lem brought forth bread and wine: and
he *was* the priest of [s]the most high
God.
19 And he blessed him, and said,
Blessed *be* Ā'brăm of the most high
God, possessor of heaven and earth:
20 And blessed be the most high
God, which hath delivered thine enemies into thy hand. And he gave him
tithes [t]of all.
21 And the king of Sŏd'om said unto
Ā'brăm, Give me the [5]persons, and
take the goods to thyself.
22 And Ā'brăm said to the king of
Sŏd'om, [u]I have lift up mine hand unto
the LORD, the most high God, [v]the possessor of heaven and earth,
23 That I [w]will not *take* from a
thread even to a shoelatchet, and that I
will not take any thing that *is* thine,
lest thou shouldest say, I have made
Ā'brăm rich:
24 Save only that which the young
men have eaten, and the portion of the
men which went with me, Ā'nēr, Ĕsh'-
cŏl, and Măm're; let them take their
portion.
15 After these things the word of
the LORD came unto Ā'brăm in
[a]a vision, saying, [b]Fear not, Ā'brăm:
I *am* thy shield, *and* thy exceeding
[c]great reward.
2 And Ā'brăm said, Lord GOD, what
wilt thou give me, seeing I go childless,
and the steward of my house *is* this E-
li-ē'zēr of Da-măs'cus?
3 And Ā'brăm said, Behold, to me
thou hast given no seed: and, lo, one
born in my house is mine heir.
4 And, behold, the word of the LORD
came unto him, saying, This shall not
be thine heir; but he that shall [d]come

forth out of thine own bowels shall be thine heir.

5 And he brought him forth abroad, and said, Look now toward heaven, and [e]tell the stars, if thou be able to number them: and he said unto him, [f]So shall thy seed be.

6 And [g]he believed in the LORD; and he [h]counted it to him for righteousness.

7 And he said unto him, I *am* the LORD that [i]brought thee out of Ûr of the Chăl'dees, to give thee this land to inherit it.

8 And he said, Lord GOD, [j]whereby shall I know that I shall inherit it?

9 And he said unto him, Take me an heifer of three years old, and a she goat of three years old, and a ram of three years old, and a turtledove, and a young pigeon.

10 And he took unto him all these, and divided them in the midst, and laid each piece one against another: but the birds divided he not.

11 And when the fowls came down upon the carcases, Ā'brăm drove them away.

12 And when the sun was going down, a [k]deep sleep fell upon Ā'brăm; and, lo, an horror of great darkness fell upon him.

13 And he said unto Ā'brăm, Know of a surety that [l]thy seed shall be a stranger in a land *that is* not theirs, and shall serve them; and they shall [m]afflict them [n]four hundred years;

14 And also [o]that nation, whom they shall serve, will I judge: and afterward shall they come out with great substance.

15 And thou shalt go to thy fathers in peace; thou shalt be buried [p]in a good old age.

16 But in the fourth generation they shall come hither again: for the iniquity of the Ăm'ôr-ītes [q]*is* not yet full.

17 And it came to pass, that, when the sun went down, and it was dark, behold a smoking furnace, and [1]a burning lamp that passed between those pieces.

18 In the same day the LORD made a covenant with Ā'brăm, saying, Unto thy seed [r]have I given this land, from the river of Ē'gypt unto the great river, the river Eū-phrā'tēs:

19 The Kĕn'ītes, and the Kĕn'iz-zītes, and the Kăd'mŏn-ītes,

20 And the Hĭt'tītes, and the Pĕr'ĭz-zītes, and the Rĕph'a-ĭms,

21 And the Ăm'ôr-ītes, and the Că'năan-ītes, and the Gĭr'ga-shītes, and the Jĕb'u-sītes.

16 Now Sā'rāi Ā'brăm's wife [a]bare him no children: and she had an handmaid, an E-gȳp'tian, whose name *was* [1]Hā'gar.

2 And Sā'rāi said unto Ā'brăm, Behold now, the LORD [b]hath restrained me from bearing: I pray thee, go in unto my maid; it may be that I may [2]obtain children by her. And Ā'brăm hearkened to the voice of Sā'rāi.

5 [e]Ps. 147.4 [f]Ex. 32.13; Heb. 11.12
6 [g]Rom. 4.3-6-20-25 [h]Ps. 106.31; Gal. 3.6
7 [i]Acts 7.2
8 [j]Judg. 6.36-40; 1 Sam. 14.9-10; 2 Ki. 20.8; Luke 1.18
12 [k]ch. 2.21
13 [l]Ex. 1.1 [m]Ex. 1.11 [n]Ex. 12.40
14 [o]Ex. 6.6; Ex. 7.14
15 [p]ch. 25.8; Job 5.26; Heb. 11.13
16 [q]Matt. 23.32; 2 Pet. 3.8-9
17 [1]a lamp of fire
18 [r]ch. 17.8; Ps. 105.11

CHAPTER 16

1 [a]Judg. 13.2; Luke 1.7 [1]Or, Agar; Gal. 4.24
2 [b]ch. 30.2 [2]be builded by her; Ruth 4.11
4 [c]Prov. 30.23
5 [d]Ex. 5.21
6 [3]that which is good in thine eyes [4]afflicted her
7 [e]ch. 25.18
9 [f]Eph. 6.5-9
10 [g]ch. 22.15-18; Mal. 3.1 [h]ch. 25.12
11 [5]That is, God shall hear [i]Ex. 2.23-24
12 [j]ch. 25.18
13 [k]Ps. 139.1-12
14 [6]That is, The well of him that liveth and seeth me

CHAPTER 17

1 [a]ch. 5.22 [b]Job 1.1 [1]Or, upright, or, sincere
2 [c]Gal. 3.17-18
3 [d]Ex. 3.6
4 [2]multitude of nations
5 [3]That is, Father of a great multitude

3 And Sā'rāi Ā'brăm's wife took Hā'gar her maid the E-gȳp'tian, after Ā'brăm had dwelt ten years in the land of Că'năan, and gave her to her husband Ā'brăm to be his wife.

4 ¶ And he went in unto Hā'gar, and she conceived: and when she saw that she had conceived, her mistress was [c]despised in her eyes.

5 And Sā'rāi said unto Ā'brăm, My wrong *be* upon thee: I have given my maid into thy bosom; and when she saw that she had conceived, I was despised in her eyes: [d]the LORD judge between me and thee.

6 But Ā'brăm said unto Sā'rāi, Behold, thy maid *is* in thy hand; do to her [3]as it pleaseth thee. And when Sā'rāi [4]dealt hardly with her, she fled from her face.

7 ¶ And the angel of the LORD found her by a fountain of water in the wilderness, by the fountain in the way to [e]Shûr.

8 And he said, Hā'gar, Sā'rāi's maid, whence camest thou? and whither wilt thou go? And she said, I flee from the face of my mistress Sā'rāi.

9 And the angel of the LORD said unto her, Return to thy mistress, and [f]submit thyself under her hands.

10 And [g]the angel of the LORD said unto her, [h]I will multiply thy seed exceedingly, that it shall not be numbered for multitude.

11 And the angel of the LORD said unto her, Behold, thou *art* with child, and shalt bear a son, and shalt call his name [5]Ĭsh'ma-el; because [i]the LORD hath heard thy affliction.

12 And he will be a wild man; his hand *will be* against every man, and every man's hand against him; and [j]he shall dwell in the presence of all his brethren.

13 And she called the name of the LORD that spake unto her, [k]Thou God seest me: for she said, Have I also here looked after him that seeth me?

14 Wherefore the well was called [6]Bē'er–la-hāi'-roi; behold, *it is* between Kā'desh and Bē'red.

15 ¶ And Hā'gar bare Ā'brăm a son: and Ā'brăm called his son's name, which Hā'gar bare, Ĭsh'ma-el.

16 And Ā'brăm *was* fourscore and six years old, when Hā'gar bare Ĭsh'ma-el to Ā'brăm.

17 And when Ā'brăm was ninety years old and nine, the LORD appeared to Ā'brăm, and said unto him, I *am* the Almighty God; [a]walk before me, and be thou [b][1]perfect.

2 And I will make my [c]covenant between me and thee, and will multiply thee exceedingly.

3 And Ā'brăm [d]fell on his face: and God talked with him, saying,

4 As for me, behold, my covenant *is* with thee, and thou shalt be a father of [2]many nations.

5 Neither shall thy name any more be called Ā'brăm, but thy name shall be [3]Ā'brā-hăm; for a father of many nations have I made thee.

6 And I will make thee exceeding fruitful, and I will make nations of thee, and kings shall come out of thee.

7 And I will establish my covenant between me and thee and thy seed after thee in their generations for an everlasting covenant, [e]to be a God unto thee, and to thy seed after thee.

8 And I will give unto thee, and to thy seed after thee, the land [4]wherein thou art a stranger, all the land of Cā'năan, for an everlasting possession; and [f]I will be their God.

9 ¶ And God said unto Ā'bră-hăm, [g]Thou shalt keep my covenant therefore, thou, and thy seed after thee in their generations.

10 This *is* my covenant, which ye shall keep, between me and you and thy seed after thee; Every man child among you shall be circumcised.

11 And [h]ye shall circumcise the flesh of your foreskin; and it shall be a token of the covenant betwixt me and you.

12 And [5]he that is eight days old shall be circumcised among you, every man child in your generations, he that is born in the house, or bought with money of any stranger, which *is* not of thy seed.

13 He that is born in thy house, and he that is bought with thy money, must needs be circumcised: and my covenant shall be in your flesh for an everlasting covenant.

14 And the uncircumcised man child whose flesh of his foreskin is not circumcised, that soul shall be [i]cut off from his people; he hath broken my covenant.

15 ¶ And God said unto Ā'bră-hăm, As for Sā'rāi thy wife, thou shalt not call her name Sā'rāi, but [6]Sā'rah *shall* her name *be*.

16 And I will bless her, and [j]give thee a son also of her: yea, I will bless her, and [7]she shall be a *mother* of nations; kings of people shall be of her.

17 Then Ā'bră-hăm fell upon his face, and [k]laughed, and said in his heart, Shall a *child* be born unto him that is an hundred years old? and shall [l]Sā'rah, that is ninety years old, bear?

18 And Ā'bră-hăm said unto God, O that Ĭsh'ma-el might live before thee!

19 And God said, [m]Sā'rah thy wife shall bear thee a son indeed; and thou shalt call his name Ī'saac: and I will establish my covenant with him for an everlasting covenant, *and* with his seed after him.

20 And as for Ĭsh'ma-el, I have heard thee: Behold, I have blessed him, and will make him fruitful, and will [n]multiply him exceedingly; [o]twelve princes shall he beget, and I will make him [p]a great nation.

21 But my covenant will I establish with Ī'saac, which [q]Sā'rah shall bear unto thee at this set time in the next year.

22 And he left off [r]talking with him, and God went up from Ā'bră-hăm.

23 ¶ And Ā'bră-hăm took Ĭsh'ma-el his son, and all that were born in his house, and all that were bought with his money, every male among the men of Ā'bră-hăm's house; and circumcised the flesh of their foreskin in the selfsame day, as [s]God had said unto him.

24 And Ā'bră-hăm *was* ninety years old and nine, when he was circumcised in the flesh of his foreskin.

25 And Ĭsh'ma-el his son *was* thirteen years old, when he was circumcised in the flesh of his foreskin.

26 In [t]the selfsame day was Ā'bră-hăm circumcised, and Ĭsh'ma-el his son.

27 And all the men of [u]his house, born [v]in the house, and bought with money of the stranger, were circumcised with him.

18 And the LORD [a]appeared unto him in the plains of Măm're: and he sat in the tent door in the heat of the day;

2 And he lift up his eyes and looked, and, lo, [b]three men stood by him: and when he saw *them,* he ran [c]to meet them from the tent door, and bowed himself toward the ground,

3 And said, My Lord, if now I have found favour in thy sight, pass not away, I pray thee, from thy servant:

4 Let a little water, I pray you, be fetched, and [d]wash your feet, and rest yourselves under the tree:

5 And I will fetch a morsel of bread, and [1]comfort ye your hearts; after that ye shall pass on: for therefore [2]are ye come to your servant. And they said, So do, as thou hast said.

6 And Ā'bră-hăm hastened into the tent unto Sā'rah, and said, [3]Make ready quickly three measures of fine meal, knead *it,* and make cakes upon the hearth.

7 And Ā'bră-hăm ran unto the herd, and fetcht a calf tender and good, and gave *it* unto a young man; and he hasted to dress it.

8 And he took butter, and milk, and the calf which he had dressed, and set *it* before them; and he stood by them under the tree, and they did eat.

9 ¶ And they said unto him, Where *is* Sā'rah thy wife? And he said, Behold, [e]in the tent.

10 And he said, I will certainly return unto thee according to the time of life; and, lo, Sā'rah thy wife shall have a [f]son. And Sā'rah heard *it* in the tent door, which *was* behind him.

11 Now Ā'bră-hăm and Sā'rah *were* [g]old *and* well stricken in age; *and* it ceased to be with Sā'rah after the [h]manner of women.

12 Therefore Sā'rah laughed within herself, saying, [i]After I am waxed old shall I have pleasure, my [j]lord being old also?

13 And the LORD said unto Ā'bră-hăm, Wherefore did Sā'rah laugh, saying, Shall I of a surety bear a child, which am old?

14 Is any thing [k]too hard for the LORD? At the time appointed I will re-

7 [e]ch. 26.24; ch. 28.13; Heb. 11.16; Rom. 9.7-9
8 [4]of thy sojournings; ch. 23.4; ch. 28.4
[f]Ex. 6.7; Ex. 29.45; Lev. 26.12; Deut. 4.37; Deut. 14.2; Deut. 26.18; Deut. 29.13; Ps. 48.14; Rev. 21.7
9 [g]Ps. 25.10
11 [h]Acts 7.8; Rom. 4.11; Gal. 6.15
12 [5]a son of eight days; Luke 2.21; John 7.22
14 [i]Ex. 4.24; Josh. 5.2-7
15 [6]That is, Princess
16 [j]ch. 18.10; ch. 21.1
[7]she shall become nations
17 [k]ch. 18.12; ch. 21.6
[l]ch. 21.7
19 [m]ch. 18.10; ch. 21.2; Gal. 4.28-31
20 [n]ch. 16.10
[o]ch. 25.12-16
[p]ch. 21.18
21 [q]ch. 21.2
22 [r]ch. 18.33; ch. 35.9-15
23 [s]ver. 9
26 [t]Ps. 119.60
27 [u]ch. 18.19
[v]ch. 14.14

CHAPTER 18
1 [a]ch. 13.18; ch. 14.13; Acts 7.2
2 [b]ver. 22; ch. 19.1
[c]Heb. 13.2; 1 Pet. 4.9
4 [d]ch. 24.32; ch. 43.24
5 [1]stay
[2]you have passed
6 [3]Hasten
9 [e]ch. 24.67; Tit. 2.5
10 [f]ch. 21.2; Luke 1.13; Rom. 9.9
11 [g]Rom. 4.19
[h]Heb. 11.11
12 [i]ch. 17.17; Luke 1.18
[j]1 Pet. 3.6
14 [k]Ps. 115.3; Jer. 32.17; Zech. 8.6; Heb. 11.17-19

turn unto thee, according to the time of life, and Sā'rah shall have a son.

15 Then Sarah denied, saying, I laughed not; for she was afraid. And he said, Nay; but thou didst laugh.

16 ¶ And the men rose up from thence, and looked toward Sŏd'om: and Ā'brā-hăm went with them to bring them on the way.

17 And the LORD said, [l]Shall I hide from Ā'brā-hăm that thing which I do;

18 Seeing that Ā'brā-hăm shall surely become a great and mighty nation, and all the nations of the earth shall [m]be blessed in him?

19 For I know him, that he [n]will command his children and his household after him, and they shall keep the way of the LORD, to do justice and judgment; that the LORD may bring upon Ā'brā-hăm that which he hath spoken of him.

20 And the LORD said, Because the [o]cry of Sŏd'om and Go-mŏr'rah is great, and because their sin is very grievous;

21 I will go down now, [p]and see whether they have done altogether according to the cry of it, which is come unto me; and if not, I will know.

22 And the men turned their faces from thence, and went toward Sŏd'om: but Ā'brā-hăm stood yet before the [q]LORD.

23 ¶ And Ā'brā-hăm drew near, and said, [r]Wilt thou also destroy the righteous with the wicked?

24 Peradventure there be [s]fifty righteous within the city: wilt thou also destroy and not spare the place for the fifty righteous that *are* therein?

25 That be far from thee to do after this manner, to slay the righteous with the wicked: and [t]that the righteous should be as the wicked, that be far from thee: Shall [u]not the Judge of all the earth do right?

26 And the LORD said, [v]If I find in Sŏd'om fifty righteous within the city, then I will spare all the place for their sakes.

27 And Ā'brā-hăm answered and said, [w]Behold now, I have taken upon me to speak unto the Lord, which *am* [x]*but* dust and ashes:

28 Peradventure there shall lack five of the fifty righteous: wilt thou destroy all the city for *lack of* five? And he said, If I find there forty and five, I will not destroy *it*.

29 And he spake unto him [y]yet again, and said, Peradventure there shall be forty found there. And he said, I will not do *it* for forty's sake.

30 And he said *unto him*, [z]Oh let not the Lord be angry, and I will speak: Peradventure there shall thirty be found there. And he said, I will not do *it*, if I find thirty there.

31 And he said, Behold now, [a]I have taken upon me to speak unto the Lord: Peradventure there shall be twenty found there. And he said, I will not destroy *it* for twenty's sake.

32 And he said, [b]Oh let not the Lord be angry, and I will speak yet but this once: Peradventure ten shall be found there. And he said, [c]I will not destroy *it* for ten's sake.

33 And the LORD went his way, as soon as he had left communing with Ā'brā-hăm: and Ā'brā-hăm returned unto his place.

19 And there came [a]two angels to Sŏd'om at even; and Lŏt sat in the gate of Sŏd'om: and Lŏt seeing *them* rose up to meet them; and he bowed himself with his face toward the ground;

2 And he said, Behold now, my lords, [b]turn in, I pray you, into your servant's house, and tarry all night, and wash your feet, and ye shall rise up early, and go on your ways. And they said, Nay; [c]but we will abide in the street all night.

3 And he pressed upon them greatly; and they turned in unto him, and entered into his house; and [d]he made them a feast, and did bake unleavened bread, and they did eat.

4 ¶ But before they lay down, the men of the city, *even* the men of Sŏd'om, compassed the house round, both old and young, all the people from every quarter:

5 And [e]they called unto Lŏt, and said unto him, [f]Where *are* the men which came in to thee this night? bring them out unto us, that we may know them.

6 And [g]Lŏt went out at the door unto them, and shut the door after him,

7 And said, I pray you, brethren, do not so wickedly.

8 Behold now, I have two daughters which have not known man; let me, I pray you, bring them out unto you, and do ye to them as *is* good in your eyes: only unto these men do nothing; for [h]therefore came they under the shadow of my roof.

9 And they said, Stand back. And they said *again*, [i]This one *fellow* came in to sojourn, and he will needs be a judge: now will we deal worse with thee, than with them. And they pressed sore upon the man, *even* Lŏt, and came near to break the door.

10 But the men put forth their hand, and pulled Lŏt into the house to them, and shut to the door.

11 And they smote the men that *were* at the door of the house [j]with blindness, both small and great: so that they wearied themselves to find the door.

12 ¶ And the men said unto Lŏt, Hast [k]thou here any besides? son in law, and thy sons, and thy daughters, and whatsoever thou hast in the city, [l]bring *them* out of this place:

13 For we will destroy this place, because the cry of them is waxen great before the face of the LORD; and the LORD hath [m]sent us to destroy it.

14 And Lŏt went out, and spake unto his sons in law, which married [n]his daughters, and said, Up, [o]get you out of this place; for the LORD will destroy

17 [l]Ps. 25.14; Amos 3.7; John 15.15
18 [m]ch. 12.3; ch. 22.18; Ps. 72.17; Acts 3.25; Gal. 3.8-9-10, 18
19 [n]Deut. 6.6-7; Josh. 24.15; Eph. 6.4
20 [o]ch. 4.10; ch. 19.13; Jas. 5.4
21 [p]ch. 11.5; Ex. 3.8; Ps. 14.2; Heb. 4.13
22 [q]verses 1-2
23 [r]Num. 16.22; 2 Sam. 24.17; Ps. 11.4-7
24 [s]Matt. 7.13-14
25 [t]Isa. 3.10-11
[u]Job 8.3-20; Job 34.17; Ps. 58.11; Ps. 94.2; Rom. 3.5-6
26 [v]Jer. 5.1; Ezek. 22.30; Matt. 11.23
27 [w]Luke 18.1
[x]Ps. 8.4
29 [y]1 Thess. 5.17
30 [z]Isa. 55.8-9
31 [a]Heb. 4.16
32 [b]Judg. 6.39
[c]Ex. 34.6-7; Jas. 5.16
CHAPTER 19
1 [a]ch. 18.2-22
2 [b]Heb. 13.2
[c]Luke 24.28
3 [d]ch. 18.8
5 [e]Isa. 3.9
[f]ch. 4.1; Jude 7
6 [g]Judg. 19.24
8 [h]ch. 18.5
9 [i]Ex. 2.14; 2 Pet. 2.7-8
11 [j]2 Ki. 6.18; Acts 13.11
12 [k]Josh. 6.22
[l]ch. 7.1; 2 Pet. 2.9
13 [m]1 Chr. 21.15
14 [n]Matt. 1.18
[o]Num. 16.21-45; Rev. 18.4

this city. But he seemed [p]as one that mocked unto his sons in law.

15 ¶ And when the morning arose, then the angels hastened Lŏt, saying, Arise, take thy wife, and thy two daughters, which [1]are here; lest thou be consumed in the [2]iniquity of the city.

16 And while he lingered, the men laid hold upon his hand, and upon the hand of his wife, and upon the hand of his two daughters; [q]the LORD being merciful unto him: and they brought him forth, and set him without the city.

17 ¶ And it came to pass, when they had brought them forth abroad, that he said, [r]Escape for thy life; [s]look not behind thee, neither stay thou in all the plain; escape to the mountain, lest thou be consumed.

18 And Lŏt said unto them, Oh, not so, my Lord:

19 Behold now, thy servant hath found grace in thy sight, and thou [t]hast magnified thy mercy, which thou has shewed unto me in saving my life; and I cannot escape to the mountain, lest some evil take me, and I die:

20 Behold now, this city *is* near to flee unto, and it *is* a little one: Oh, let me escape thither, (*is* it not a little one?) and my soul shall live.

21 And he said unto him, See, I have accepted [3]thee concerning this thing also, that I will not overthrow this city, for the which thou hast spoken.

22 Haste thee, escape thither; for I cannot do any thing till thou be come thither. Therefore the name of the city was [u]called [4]Zō'ar.

23 ¶ The sun was [5]risen upon the earth when Lŏt entered into Zō'ar.

24 Then [v]the LORD rained upon Sŏd'om and upon Go-mŏr'rah brimstone and fire from the LORD out of heaven;

25 And he overthrew those cities, and all [w]the plain, and all the inhabitants of the cities, and that which grew upon the ground.

26 ¶ But his wife [x]looked back from behind him, and she became a pillar of salt.

27 ¶ And Ā'bră-hăm gat up early in the morning to the place where he [y]stood before the LORD:

28 And he looked toward Sŏd'om and Go-mŏr'rah, and toward all the land of the plain, and beheld, and, lo, [z]the smoke of the country went up as the smoke of a furnace.

29 ¶ And it came to pass, when God destroyed the cities of the plain, that God [a]remembered Ā'bră-hăm, and sent Lŏt out of the midst of the overthrow, when he overthrew the cities in the which Lŏt dwelt.

30 ¶ And Lŏt went up out of Zō'ar, and [b]dwelt in the mountain, and his two daughters with him; for he feared to dwell in Zō'ar: and he dwelt in a cave, he and his two daughters.

31 And the firstborn said unto the younger, Our father *is* old, and *there is* not a man in the earth [c]to come in unto us after the manner of all the earth:

32 Come, [d]let us make our father drink wine, and we will lie with him, [e]that we may preserve seed of our father.

33 And they made their father drink wine that night: and the firstborn went in, and lay with her father; and he perceived not when she lay down, nor when she arose.

34 And it came to pass on the morrow, that the firstborn said unto the younger, Behold, I lay yesternight with my father: let us make him drink wine this night also; and go thou in, *and* lie with him, that we may preserve seed of our father.

35 And they made their father drink wine that night also: and the younger arose, and lay with him; and he perceived not when she lay down, nor when she arose.

36 Thus were both the daughters of Lŏt with child by their father.

37 And the firstborn bare a son, and called his name Mō'ab: the same [f]*is* the father of the Mō'ab-ītes unto this day.

38 And the younger, she also bare a son, and called his name Bĕn–ăm'mī: the [g]same *is* the father of the children of Ăm'mŏn unto this day.

20 And Ā'bră-hăm journeyed from thence [a]toward the south country, and dwelled between Kā'desh and Shûr, and sojourned in [b]Gē'rär.

2 And [c]Ā'bră-hăm said of Sā'rah his wife, She *is* my sister: and A-bĭm'ĕ-lech king of Gē'rär sent, and took [d]Sā'rah.

3 But God [e]came to A-bĭm'ĕ-lech in [f]a dream by night, and said to him, Behold, thou *art but* [g]a dead man, for the woman which thou hast taken; for she *is* [1]a man's wife.

4 But A-bĭm'ĕ-lech had not come near her: and he said, Lord, [h]wilt thou slay also a righteous nation?

5 Said he not unto me, She *is* my sister? and she, even she herself said, He *is* my brother: in the [2]integrity of my heart and innocency of my hands have I done this.

6 And God said unto him in a dream, Yea, I know that thou didst this in the integrity of thy heart; for I also [i]withheld thee from sinning against me: therefore suffered I thee not to touch her.

7 Now therefore restore the man *his* wife; for he *is* a prophet, and he [j]shall pray for thee, and thou shalt live: and if thou restore *her* not, know thou that thou shalt surely die, thou, and all that *are* thine.

8 Therefore A-bĭm'ĕ-lech rose early in the morning, and called all his servants, and told all these things in their ears: and the men were sore afraid.

9 Then A-bĭm'ĕ-lech called Ā'bră-hăm, and said unto him, What hast thou done unto us? and what have I offended thee, that thou hast brought on me and on my kingdom [k]a great sin? thou hast done deeds unto me that ought not to be done.

[p]Ex. 9.21; Luke 24.11
15 [1]are found [2]Or, punishment
16 [q]Ex. 34.7; Eph. 2.4-5
17 [r]Heb. 2.3
[s]verse 26
19 [t]1 Tim. 1.14-16
21 [3]thy face; Job 42.9; 1 Sam. 25.35; Ps. 145.19
22 [u]ch. 13.10; ch. 14.2 [4]That is, little
23 [5]gone forth
24 [v]Deut. 29.23; Jude 7
25 [w]ch. 14.3;
26 [x]Luke 17.31
27 [y]ch. 18.22
28 [z]Rev. 18.9
29 [a]ch. 8.1;
30 [b]verses 17.19
31 [c]ch. 16.2-4;
32 [d]Luke 21.34;
[e]Mark 12.19
37 [f]Deut. 2.9
38 [g]Deut. 2.19
CHAPTER 20
1 [a]ch. 18.1
[b]ch. 26.6
2 [c]ch. 12.11-13;
[d]ch. 12.15
3 [e]Ps. 105.14
[f]Job 4.12;
[g]verse 7 [1]married to an husband
4 [h]ch. 18.23-25
5 [2]Or, simplicity, or, sincerity
6 [i]ch. 35.5;
7 [j]1 Sam. 7.5;
9 [k]ch. 39.9;

10 And A-bĭm'ĕ-lech said unto Ā'bră-
hăm, What sawest thou, that thou hast
done this thing?
11 And Ā'bră-hăm said, Because I
thought, [l]Surely the fear of God *is* not
in this place; and they will slay me for
my wife's sake.
12 And [m]yet indeed *she is* my sister;
she *is* the daughter of my father, but
not the daughter of my mother; and
she became my wife.
13 And it came to pass, when God
[n]caused me to wander from my father's house, that I said unto her, This
is thy kindness which thou shalt shew
unto me; at every place whither we
shall come, say of me, [o]He *is* my
brother.
14 And A-bĭm'ĕ-lech took [p]sheep,
and oxen, and menservants, and womenservants, and gave *them* unto Ā'bră-
hăm, and restored him Sā'rah his wife.
15 And A-bĭm'ĕ-lech said, [q]Behold,
my land *is* before thee: dwell [3]where it
pleaseth thee.
16 And unto Sā'rah he said, Behold,
I have given thy [r]brother a thousand
pieces of silver: behold, he *is* to thee a
covering of the eyes, unto all that *are*
with thee, and with all *other:* thus she
was reproved.
17 ¶ So Ā'bră-hăm [s]prayed unto
God: and God healed A-bĭm'ĕ-lech,
and his wife, and his maidservants;
and they bare *children.*
18 For the LORD had [t]fast closed up
all the wombs of the house of A-bĭm'ĕ-
lech, because of Sā'rah Ā'bră-hăm's
wife.

21 And the LORD [a]visited Sā'rah as
he had said, and the LORD did
unto Sā'rah [b]as he had spoken.
2 For Sā'rah conceived, [c]and bare
Ā'bră-hăm a son in his old age, at the
set time of which God had spoken to
him.
3 And Ā'bră-hăm [d]called the name
of his son that was born unto him,
whom Sā'rah bare to him, Ī'saac.
4 And Ā'bră-hăm [e]circumcised his
son Ī'saac being eight days old, as God
had commanded him.
5 And Ā'bră-hăm was an hundred
years old, when his son Ī'saac was
born unto him.
6 ¶ And Sā'rah said, [f]God hath made
me to laugh, *so that* all that hear will
laugh [g]with me.
7 And she said, Who would have
said unto Ā'bră-hăm, that Sā'rah
should have given children suck? for
[h]I have born *him* a son in his old age.
8 And the child grew, and was
weaned: and Ā'bră-hăm made a great
feast the *same* day that Ī'saac was
weaned.
9 ¶ And Sā'rah saw the [i]son of Hā'-
gar the E-ġўp'tian, which she had born
unto Ā'bră-hăm, [j]mocking.
10 Wherefore she said unto Ā'bră-
hăm, [k]Cast out this bondwoman and
her son: for the son of this bondwoman
shall not be heir with my son, *even*
with Ī'saac.

11 And the thing was very [l]grievous
in Ā'bră-hăm's sight because of his
son.
12 ¶ And God said unto Ā'bră-hăm,
Let it not be grievous in thy sight because of the lad, and because of thy
bondwoman; in all that Sā'rah hath
said unto thee, hearken unto her voice;
for [m]in Ī'saac shall thy seed be called.
13 And also [n]of the son of the bondwoman will I make a nation, because
he *is* thy seed.
14 And Ā'bră-hăm rose up early in
the morning, and took bread, and a bottle of water, and gave *it* unto Hā'gar,
putting *it* on her shoulder, and the
child, and [o]sent her away: and she departed, and wandered in the wilderness of Bē'er–shē'bȧ.
15 And [p]the water was spent in the
bottle, and she cast the child under one
of the shrubs.
16 And she went, and sat her down
over against *him* a good way off, as it
were a bowshot: for she said, [q]Let me
not see the death of the child. And she
sat over against *him,* and lift up her
voice, and wept.
17 And [r]God heard the voice of the
lad; and the angel of God called to
Hā'gar out of heaven, and said unto
her, What aileth thee, Hā'gar? fear not;
for God hath heard the voice of the lad
where he *is.*
18 Arise, lift up the lad, and hold
him in thine hand; for [s]I will make him
a great nation.
19 And God [t]opened her eyes, and
she saw a well of water; and she went,
and filled the bottle with water, and
gave the lad drink.
20 And [u]God was with the lad; and
he grew, and [v]dwelt in the wilderness,
and became an archer.
21 And he dwelt in the wilderness of
Pā'ran: and his mother took him a wife
out of the [w]land of Ē'ġўpt.
22 ¶ And it came to pass at that time,
that [x]A-bĭm'ĕ-lech and Phī'chol the
chief captain of his host spake unto
Ā'bră-hăm, saying, [y]God *is* with thee
in all that thou doest:
23 Now therefore [z]swear unto me
here by God [1]that thou wilt not deal
falsely with me, nor with my son, nor
with my son's son: *but* according to
the kindness that I have done unto
thee, thou shalt do unto me, and to the
land wherein thou hast sojourned.
24 And Ā'bră-hăm said, I will swear.
25 And Ā'bră-hăm reproved A-bĭm'-
ĕ-lech because of a well of water, which
A-bĭm'ĕ-lech's servants had violently
[a]taken away.
26 And A-bĭm'ĕ-lech said, I wot not
who hath done this thing: neither didst
thou tell me, neither yet heard I *of it,*
but to day.
27 And Ā'bră-hăm took sheep and
oxen, and gave them unto A-bĭm'ĕ-
lech; and both of them [b]made a covenant.
28 And Ā'bră-hăm set seven ewe
lambs of the flock by themselves.

11 [l]ch. 42.18; Neh. 13:8 Prov. 16.6
12 [m]ch. 11.29
13 [n]ch. 12.1-9-11
[o]ch. 12.13
14 [p]ch. 12.16
15 [q]ch. 13.9; ch. 47.6
[3]as is good in thine eyes
16 [r]verse 5
17 [s]Job 42.8; Jas. 5.16
18 [t]ch. 12.17

CHAPTER 21
1 [a]1 Sam. 2.21
[b]ch. 17.19; ch. 18.10-14; Gal. 4.23
2 [c]Acts 7.8; Heb. 11.11
3 [d]ch. 17.19
4 [e]ch. 17.10-12
6 [f]Ps. 126.2; Isa. 54.1
[g]Luke 1.14-58
7 [h]ch. 18.11
9 [i]ch. 16.1-4-15
[j]Gal. 4.29
10 [k]ch. 25.6; ch. 36.6-7; Gal. 4.30-31
11 [l]ch. 17.18
12 [m]Rom. 9.7; Heb. 11.18
13 [n]ch. 16.10; ch. 17.20; ch. 25.12
14 [o]John 8.35
15 [p]Num. 20.5; Ps. 63.1
16 [q]ch. 44.34
17 [r]Ex. 3.7; 2 Ki. 13.4-23
18 [s]verse 13; ch. 25.12; Judg. 8.24
19 [t]Num. 22.31; 2 Ki. 6.17; Luke 24.16
20 [u]ch. 39.2-3
[v]ch. 16.12
21 [w]ch. 24.4
22 [x]ch. 20.2
[y]ch. 26.28; Isa. 8.10
23 [z]Josh. 2.12; 1 Sam. 24.21
[1]if thou shalt lie unto me
25 [a]ch. 26.15-22
27 [b]ch. 26.28-31

29 And A-bĭm'ĕ-lech said unto Ā'bră-
hăm, [c]What *mean* these seven ewe
lambs which thou hast set by themselves?
30 And he said, For *these* seven ewe
lambs shalt thou take of my hand, that
[d]they may be a witness unto me, that I
have digged this well.
31 Wherefore he [e]called that place
[2]Bē'er–shē'bȧ; because there they
sware both of them.
32 Thus they made a covenant at
Bē'er–shē'bȧ: then A-bĭm'ĕ-lech rose
up, and Phī'chol the chief captain of
his host, and they returned into the
[f]land of the Phĭ-lĭs'tĭnes.
33 ¶ And *Ā'bră-hăm* planted a [3]grove
in Bē'er–shē'bȧ, and called there on
the name of the LORD, the [g]everlasting
God.
34 And Ā'bră-hăm sojourned in the
Phĭ-lĭs'tĭnes' land many days.

22 And it came to pass after these
things, that [a]God did tempt
Ā'bră-hăm, and said unto him, Ā'bră-
hăm: and he said, [1]Behold, *here* I *am.*
2 And he said, [b]Take now thy son,
thine only *son* Ī'saac, whom thou lovest, and get thee into the land [c]of Mo-
rī'ah; and offer him there for a burnt
offering upon one of the mountains
which I will tell thee of.
3 ¶ And Ā'bră-hăm [d]rose up early in
the morning, and saddled his ass, and
took two of his young men with him,
and Ī'saac his son, and clave the wood
for the burnt offering, and rose up, and
went unto the place of which God had
told him.
4 Then on the third day Ā'bră-hăm
lifted up his eyes, and saw the place
afar off.
5 And Ā'bră-hăm said unto his
young men, Abide ye here with the
ass; and I and the lad will go yonder
and worship, and come again to you.
6 And Ā'bră-hăm took the wood of
the burnt offering, and [e]laid *it* upon
Ī'saac his son; and he took the fire in
his hand, and a knife; and they went
both of them together.
7 And Ī'saac spake unto Ā'bră-hăm
his father, and said, My father: and
he said, [2]Here *am* I, my son. And he
said, Behold the fire and the wood: but
where *is* the [3]lamb for a burnt offering?
8 And Ā'bră-hăm said, My son, God
will provide himself [f] a lamb for a burnt
offering: so they went both of them together.
9 And they came to the place which
God had told him of; and Ā'bră-hăm
built an altar there, and laid the wood
in order, and [g]bound Ī'saac his son,
and laid him on the altar upon the
wood.
10 And Ā'bră-hăm [h]stretched forth
his hand, and took the knife to slay his
son.
11 And the angel of the LORD called
unto him out of heaven, and said,
Ā'bră-hăm, Ā'bră-hăm: and he said,
Here *am* I.

29 [c]ch. 33.8
30 [d]ch. 31.48
31 [e]ch. 26.33 [2]That is, the well of the oath
32 [f]Josh. 13.2
33 [3]Or, tree
[g]Deut. 33.27; Rev. 15.7
CHAPTER 22
1 [a]Jas. 1.12-14; Heb. 11.17 [1]Behold me
2 [b]John 3.16
[c]2 Chr. 3.1
3 [d]Heb. 11.17-19
6 [e]John 19.17; 1 Pet. 2.24
7 [2]Behold me [3]Or, kid
8 [f]1 Pet. 1.19
9 [g]John 10.17-18; Heb. 11.17
10 [h]Isa. 53.6-12
12 [i]1 Sam. 15.22
[j]ch. 26.5; Jas. 2.22
13 [k]1 Cor. 5.7-8
14 [4]That is, the Lord will see, or, provide
16 [l]Ps. 105.9; Heb. 6.13-14
17 [m]ch. 15.5; Jer. 33.22
[n]ch. 13.16 [5]lip; Ps. 2.8
[o]ch. 24.60; Mic. 1.9
18 [p]ch. 12.3; Gal. 3.8-9-16-18
[q]verses 3-10;
20 [r]ch. 11.29
21 [s]Job 1.1
[t]Job 32.2
23 [u]ch. 24.15
CHAPTER 23
2 [a]John 11.31-35
4 [b]ch. 17.8;
[c]ch. 49.30
6 [1]a prince of God
[d]ch. 13.2;

12 And he said, [i]Lay not thine hand
upon the lad, neither do thou any thing
unto him: for now [j]I know that thou
fearest God, seeing thou hast not withheld thy son, thine only *son* from me.
13 And Abraham lifted up his eyes,
and looked, and behold behind *him* a
ram caught in a thicket by his horns:
and Ā'bră-hăm went and took the ram,
and offered him up for a burnt offering
[k]in the stead of his son.
14 And Ā'bră-hăm called the name
of that place [4]Je-hō'vah–jī'reh: as it is
said *to* this day, In the mount of the
LORD it shall be seen.
15 ¶ And the angel of the LORD called
unto Ā'bră-hăm out of heaven the second time,
16 And said, [l]By myself have I
sworn, saith the LORD, for because
thou hast done this thing, and hast not
withheld thy son, thine only *son:*
17 That in blessing I will bless thee,
and in multiplying I will multiply thy
seed as the [m]stars of the heaven, and
as the [n]sand which *is* upon the sea
[5]shore; and thy seed shall [o]possess the
gate of his enemies;
18 And [p]in thy seed shall all the nations of the earth be blessed; because
[q]thou hast obeyed my voice.
19 So Ā'bră-hăm returned unto his
young men, and they rose up and went
together to Bē'er–shē'bȧ; and Ā'bră-
hăm dwelt at Bē'er–shē'bȧ.
20 ¶ And it came to pass after these
things, that it was told Ā'bră-hăm, saying, Behold, [r]Mĭl'cah, she hath also
born children unto thy brother Nā'hor;
21 Hŭz [s]his firstborn, and Bŭz his
brother, and Ke-mŭ'el the father of
[t]Ā'ram,
22 And Chē'sed, and Hā'zō, and Pĭl'-
dăsh, and Jĭd'laph, and Bĕth-ū'el.
23 And [u]Bĕth-ū'el begat Re-bĕk'ah:
these eight Mĭl'cah did bear to Nā'hor,
Ā'bră-hăm's brother.
24 And his concubine, whose name
was Reū'mah, she bare also Tē'bah,
and Gā'hăm, and Thā'hăsh, and Mā'a-
chah.

23 And Sā'rah was an hundred and
seven and twenty years old:
these were the years of the life of
Sā'rah.
2 And Sā'rah died in Kĭr'jath–är'bȧ;
the same *is* Hē'bron in the land of Cā'-
năan: and Ā'bră-hăm came [a]to mourn
for Sā'rah, and to weep for her.
3 ¶ And Ā'bră-hăm stood up from
before his dead, and spake unto the
sons of Hĕth, saying,
4 I *am* [b]a stranger and a sojourner
with you: give me a possession of a
[c]buryingplace with you, that I may
bury my dead out of my sight.
5 And the children of Hĕth answered
Ā'bră-hăm, saying unto him,
6 Hear us, my lord: thou *art* [1]a
mighty [d]prince among us: in the choice
of our sepulchres bury thy dead; none
of us shall withhold from thee his sepulchre, but that thou mayest bury thy
dead.

7 And Ā'brā-hăm stood up, and bowed [e]himself to the people of the land, *even* to the children of Hĕth.

8 And he communed with them, saying, If it be your mind that I should bury my dead out of my sight; hear me, and intreat for me to Ē'phron the son of Zō'har,

9 That he may give me the cave of Măch-pē'lah, which he hath, which *is* in the end of his field; for [2]as much money as it is worth he shall give it me for a possession of a buryingplace amongst you.

10 And Ē'phron dwelt among the children of Hĕth: and Ē'phron the Hĭt'-tīte answered Ā'brā-hăm in the [3]audience of the children of Hĕth, *even* of all that went in at the [f]gate of his city, saying,

11 Nay, [g]my lord, hear me: the field give I thee, and the cave that *is* therein, I give it thee; in the presence of the sons of my people give I it thee: bury thy dead.

12 And Ā'brā-hăm bowed down himself before the people of the land.

13 And he spake unto Ē'phron in the audience of the people of the land, saying, But if thou *wilt give it,* I pray thee, hear me: [h]I will give thee money for the field; take *it* of me, and I will bury my dead there.

14 And Ē'phron answered Ā'brā-hăm, saying unto him,

15 My lord, hearken unto me: the land *is worth* four hundred shekels [i]of silver; what *is* that betwixt me and thee? bury therefore thy dead.

16 And Ā'brā-hăm hearkened unto Ē'phron; and Ā'brā-hăm [j]weighed to Ē'phron the silver, which he had named in the audience of the sons of Hĕth, four hundred shekels of silver, current *money* with the merchant.

17 ¶ And [k]the field of Ē'phron, which *was* in Măch-pē'lah, which *was* before Măm're, the field, and the cave which *was* therein, and all the trees that *were* in the field, that *were* in all the borders round about, were made sure

18 Unto Ā'brā-hăm for a possession in the presence of the children of Hĕth, before all that went in at the gate of his city.

19 And after this, [l]Ā'brā-hăm buried Sā'rah his wife in the cave of the field of Măch-pē'lah before Măm're: the same *is* Hē'bron in the land of Cā'năan.

20 And the field, and the cave that *is* therein, were [m]made sure unto Ā'brā-hăm for a possession of a buryingplace by the sons of Hĕth.

24 And Ā'brā-hăm [a]was old, *and* [1]well stricken in age: and the LORD had [b]blessed Ā'brā-hăm in all things.

2 And Ā'brā-hăm said [c]unto his eldest servant of his house, that ruled [d]over all that he had, [e]Put, I pray thee, thy hand under my thigh:

3 And I will make thee swear by the LORD, the God of heaven, and the God of the earth, that thou shalt [f]not take a

7 [e]Rom. 13.7
9 [2]full money
10 [3]ears
[f]ch. 34.20-24; Ruth 4.4
11 [g]2 Sam. 24.20-24
13 [h]Phil. 4.5-8
15 [i]Ex. 30.13; Ezek. 45.12
16 [j]Jer. 32.9-12
17 [k]ch. 25.9; ch. 40.30-32; ch. 50.13; Acts 7.16
19 [l]ch. 35.29
20 [m]Ruth 4.7-10; Jer. 32.10-11

CHAPTER 24

1 [a]ch. 18.11
[1]gone into days
[b]ch. 13.2; Gal. 3.9
2 [c]ch. 15.2
[d]verse 10; ch. 39.4-6
[e]ch. 47.29; Lam. 5.6
3 [f]Ex. 34.16; Deut. 7.3; 2 Cor. 6.14-17
4 [g]ch. 28.2
6 [h]2 Pet. 2.20-22
7 [i]ch. 12.1-7
[j]ch. 13.15; Ex. 32.13
[k]Ex. 23.20; Ps. 34.7; Isa. 63.9
8 [l]Josh. 2.17-20
10 [2]Or, and
[m]ch. 27.43
11 [3]women which draw water go forth
[n]Ex. 2.16; 1 Sam. 9.11
12 [o]verse 27; ch. 26.24; Ex. 3.6-15
[p]Phil. 4.6
14 [q]Prov. 19.14
[r]Judg. 6.17-37; 1 Sam. 6.7
15 [s]Ps. 34.15
[t]ch. 11.29
16 [u]ch. 26.7
[4]good of countenance
17 [v]John 4.7
18 [w]1 Pet. 3.8; 1 Pet. 4.9

wife unto my son of the daughters of the Cā'năan-ītes, among whom I dwell:

4 But thou shalt go [g]unto my country, and to my kindred, and take a wife unto my son Ī'saac.

5 And the servant said unto him, Peradventure the woman will not be willing to follow me unto this land: must I needs bring thy son again unto the land from whence thou camest?

6 And Ā'brā-hăm said unto him, Beware [h]thou that thou bring not my son thither again.

7 ¶ The LORD God of heaven, which took [i]me from my father's house, and from the land of my kindred, and which spake unto me, and that sware unto me, saying, [j]Unto thy seed will I give this land; he shall send [k]his angel before thee, and thou shalt take a wife unto my son from thence.

8 And if the woman will not be willing to follow thee, then thou shalt [l]be clear from this my oath: only bring not my son thither again.

9 And the servant put his hand under the thigh of Ā'brā-hăm his master, and sware to him concerning that matter.

10 ¶ And the servant took ten camels of the camels of his master, and departed; [2]for all the goods of his master *were* in his hand: and he arose, and went to Mĕs-o-po-tā'mĭ-ȧ, unto the [m]city of Nā'hor.

11 And he made his camels to kneel down without the city by a well of water at the time of the evening, *even* the time that [3]women [n]go out to draw *water.*

12 And he said, [o]O LORD God of my master Ā'brā-hăm, [p]I pray thee, send me good speed this day, and shew kindness unto my master Ā'brā-hăm.

13 Behold, I stand *here* by the well of water; and the daughters of the men of the city come out to draw water:

14 And let it come to pass, that the damsel to whom I shall say, Let down thy pitcher, I pray thee, that I may drink; and she shall say, Drink, and I will give thy camels drink also: *let the same be* she [q]*that* thou hast appointed for thy servant Ī'saac; and [r]thereby shall I know that thou hast shewed kindness unto my master.

15 ¶ And it came to pass, [s]before he had done speaking, that, behold, Rebĕk'ah came out, who was born to Bĕth-ū'el, son of [t]Mĭl'cah, the wife of Nā'hor, Ā'brā-hăm's brother, with her pitcher upon her shoulder.

16 And the damsel *was* [u]very [4]fair to look upon, a virgin, neither had any man known her: and she went down to the well, and filled her pitcher, and came up.

17 And the servant ran to meet her, and said, [v]Let me, I pray thee, drink a little water of thy pitcher.

18 And she said, [w]Drink, my lord: and she hasted, and let down her pitcher upon her hand, and gave him drink.

19 And when she had done giving him drink, she said, I will draw *water* for thy camels also, until they have done drinking.

20 And she hasted, and emptied her pitcher into the trough, and ran again unto the well to draw *water*, and drew for all his camels.

21 And the man [x]wondering at her held his peace, to wit whether the LORD had made his journey prosperous or not.

22 And it came to pass, as the camels had done drinking, that the man took a golden [5]earring of [y]half a shekel weight, and two bracelets for her hands of ten *shekels* weight of gold;

23 And said, Whose daughter *art* thou? tell me, I pray thee: is there room *in* thy father's house for us to lodge in?

24 And she said unto him, I *am* the daughter of Bĕth-u̯'el the son of Mĭl'cah, which she bare unto Nā'hor.

25 She said moreover unto him, We [z]have both straw and provender enough, and room to lodge in.

26 And the man [a]bowed down his head, and worshipped the LORD.

27 And he said, [b]Blessed *be* the LORD God of my master Ā'bră-hăm, who hath not left destitute my master of [c]his mercy and his truth: I *being* in the way, [d]the LORD led me to the house of my master's brethren.

28 And the damsel ran, and told *them of* her mother's house these things.

29 ¶ And Re-bĕk'ah had a brother, and his name *was* [e]Lā'ban: and Lā'ban ran out unto the man, unto the well.

30 And it came to pass, when he saw the earring and bracelets upon his sister's hands, and when he heard the words of Re-bĕk'ah his sister, saying, Thus spake the man unto me; that he came unto the man; and, behold, he stood by the camels at the well.

31 And he said, Come in, [f]thou blessed of the LORD; wherefore standest thou without? for I have prepared the house, and room for the camels.

32 ¶ And the man came into the house: and he ungirded his camels, and [g]gave straw and provender for the camels, and water to wash his feet, and the men's feet that *were* with him.

33 And there was set *meat* before him to eat: but he said, [h]I will not eat, until I have told mine errand. And he said, Speak on.

34 And he said, I *am* Ā'bră-hăm's servant.

35 And the LORD hath [i]blessed my master greatly; and he is become great: and he hath given him [j]flocks, and herds, and silver, and gold, and menservants, and maidservants, and camels, and asses.

36 And Sā'rah my master's wife bare [k]a son to my master when she was old: and [l]unto him hath he given all that he hath.

37 And my master [m]made me swear, saying, Thou shalt not take a wife to my son of the daughters of the Cā'năan-ītes, in whose land I dwell:

38 But thou shalt go unto my father's house, and to my kindred, and take a wife unto my son.

39 And I said unto my master, Peradventure the woman will not follow me.

40 And [n]he said unto me, The LORD, before whom [o]I walk, will send his [p]angel with thee, and prosper thy way; and thou shalt take a wife for my son of my kindred, and of my father's house:

41 Then [q]shalt thou be clear from *this* my oath, when thou comest to my kindred; and if they give not thee *one*, thou shalt be clear from my oath.

42 And I came this day unto the well, and said, [r]O LORD God of my master Ā'bră-hăm, if now thou [s]do prosper my way which I go:

43 Behold, [t]I stand by the well of water; and it shall come to pass, that when the virgin cometh forth to draw *water*, and I say to her, Give me, I pray thee, a little water of thy pitcher to drink;

44 And she say to me, [u]Both drink thou, and I will also draw for thy camels: *let* the same *be* the woman whom the LORD hath appointed out for my master's son.

45 And [v]before I had [w]done speaking in mine heart, behold, Re-bĕk'ah came forth with her pitcher on her shoulder; and she went down unto the well, and drew *water*: and I said unto her, Let me drink, I pray thee.

46 And she made haste, and let down her pitcher from her *shoulder*, and said, Drink, and I will give thy camels drink also: so I drank, and she made the camels drink also.

47 And I asked her, and said, Whose daughter *art* thou? And she said, The daughter of Bĕth-u̯'el, Nā'hôr's son, whom Mĭl'cah bare unto him: and I put the [x]earring upon her face, and the bracelets upon her hands.

48 And I [y]bowed down my head, and worshipped the LORD, and blessed the LORD God of my master Ā'bră-hăm, which had [z]led me in the right way to take my master's brother's daughter unto his son.

49 And now [a]if ye will deal kindly and truly with my master, tell me: and if not, tell me; that I may turn to the right hand, or to the left.

50 Then Lā'ban and Bĕth-u̯'el answered and said, [b]The thing proceedeth from the LORD: we cannot speak unto thee bad or good.

51 Behold, Re-bĕk'ah *is* [c]before thee, take *her*, and go, and let her be thy master's son's wife, as the LORD hath spoken.

52 And it came to pass, that, when Ā'bră-hăm's servant heard their words, he worshipped the LORD, *bowing himself* to the earth.

53 And the servant brought forth jewels [d]of silver, and [6]jewels of gold, and raiment, and gave *them* to Re-bĕk'ah: he gave also to her brother and to her mother [e]precious things.

21 [x]Luke 2.19-51
22 [5]Or, jewel for the forehead
[y]Ex. 32.2-3; Isa. 3.19-20; 1 Pet. 3.3
25 [z]1 Pet. 4.9
26 [a]verse 52; Ex. 4.31
27 [b]Ex. 18.10; Ruth 4.14; 1 Sam. 25.32; 2 Sam. 18.28; Luke 1.68
[c]ch. 32.10; Ps. 98.3
[d]verse 48; Prov. 3.6
29 [e]ch. 29.5
31 [f]ch. 26.29; Judg. 17.2; Ruth 3.10; Ps. 115.15
32 [g]ch. 43.24; Judg. 19.21
33 [h]Job 23.12; John 4.34; Eph. 6.5-7
35 [i]verse 1; ch. 13.2
[j]Job 1.3
36 [k]ch. 21.2
[l]ch. 21.10; ch. 25.5
37 [m]verse 3
40 [n]verse 7
[o]ch. 5.22-24; ch. 17.1
[p]Ex. 23.20
41 [q]verse 8
42 [r]1 Ki. 1.37; Acts 10.7-8-22
[s]Neh. 1.11; Ps. 90.17; Rom. 1.10
43 [t]verse 13
44 [u]Heb. 13.2
45 [v]verse 15
[w]1 Sam. 1.13; Isa. 65.24
47 [x]Ezek. 16.11-12
48 [y]verse 26
[z]Ps. 32.8; Ps. 48.14; Ps. 107.7; Isa. 48.17
49 [a]ch. 47.29; Josh. 2.14
50 [b]Ps. 118.23; Matt. 21.42; Mark 12.11
51 [c]ch. 20.15
53 [d]Ex. 3.22; Ex. 11.2; Ex. 12.35
[6]vessels
[e]2 Chr. 21.3; Ezra 1.6

54 And they did eat and drink, he
and the men that *were* with him, and
tarried all night; and they rose up in
the morning, and he said, [f]Send me
away unto my master.
55 And her brother and her mother
said, Let the damsel abide with us [7]*a*
few days, at the least ten; after that she
shall go.
56 And he said unto them, Hinder
me not, seeing the [g]LORD hath prospered my way; send me away that I
may go to my master.
57 And they said, We will call the
damsel, and inquire at her mouth.
58 And they called Re-bĕk'ah, and
said unto her, Wilt thou go with this
man? And she said, I will go.
59 And they sent away Re-bĕk'ah
their sister, and her [h]nurse, and Ā'bră-
hăm's servant, and his men.
60 And they blessed Re-bĕk'ah, and
said unto her, Thou *art* our sister, be
thou [i]*the mother* of thousands of mil-
lions, and let thy [j]seed possess the
gate of those which hate them.
61 ¶ And Re-bĕk'ah arose, and her
damsels, and they rode upon the camels, and followed the man: and the servant took Re-bĕk'ah, and went his way.
62 And Ī'saac came from the way of
the well [k]La-hāi'roi; for he dwelt in the
south country.
63 And Ī'saac went out [8][l]to meditate
in the field at the eventide: and he
lifted up his eyes, and saw, and, behold, the camels *were* coming.
64 And Re-bĕk'ah lifted up her eyes,
and when she saw Ī'saac, she lighted
[m]off the camel.
65 For she *had* said unto the servant,
What man *is* this that walketh in the
field to meet us? And the servant *had*
said, It *is* my master: therefore she
took a [n]veil, and covered herself.
66 And the servant told Ī'saac all
things that he had done.
67 And Ī'saac brought her into his
mother Sā'rah's tent, and took Re-
bĕk'ah, and she became his wife; and
he loved her: and [o]Ī'saac was comforted after his mother's *death*.

25 Then again Ā'bră-hăm took a
wife, and her name *was* Ke-tū'-
rah.
2 And she bare him [a]Zĭm'răn, and
Jŏk'shan, and Mē'dan, and Mĭd'ĭ-an,
and Ĭsh'băk, and Shu'ah.
3 And Jŏk'shan begat Shē'bȧ, and
Dē'dan. And the sons of Dē'dan were
Ăs-shu'rim, and Le-tū'shim, and Le-
ŭm'mim.
4 And the sons of Mĭd'ĭ-an; Ē'phah,
and Ē'phĕr, and Hā'noch, and A-bī'-
dah, and Ĕl'da-ah. All these *were* the
children of Ke-tū'rah.
5 ¶ And Ā'bră-hăm [b]gave all that he
had unto Ī'saac.
6 But unto the sons of the concubines, which Ā'bră-hăm had, Ā'bră-
hăm gave gifts, and [c]sent them away
from Ī'saac his son, while he yet lived,
eastward, unto the [d]east country.
7 And these *are* the days of the years
of Ā'bră-hăm's life which he lived, an
hundred threescore and fifteen years.
8 Then Ā'bră-hăm gave up the ghost,
and died in [e]a good old age, an old
man, and full *of years;* and was [f]gath-
ered to his people.
9 And his sons [g]Ī'saac and Ĭsh'ma-
el buried him [h]in the cave of Măch-
pē'lah, in the field of Ē'phron the son
of Zō'har the Hĭt'tīte, which *is* before
Măm're;
10 The [i]field which Ā'bră-hăm purchased of the sons of Hĕth: there was
Ā'bră-hăm buried, and Sā'rah his wife.
11 ¶ And it came to pass after the
death of Ā'bră-hăm, that God blessed
his son Ī'saac; and Ī'saac dwelt by the
well [j]La-hāi'roi.
12 ¶ Now these *are* the [k]generations
of Ĭsh'ma-el, Ā'bră-hăm's son, whom
Hā'gar the Ē-gyp'tian, Sā'rah's handmaid, bare unto Ā'bră-hăm:
13 And these *are* the names of the
sons of Ĭsh'ma-el, by their names, according to their generations: the firstborn of Ĭsh'ma-el, Ne-bā'joth; and Kē'-
där, and Ăd'be-el, and Mĭb'sam,
14 And Mĭsh'mȧ, and Du'mah, and
Măs'sȧ,
15 [1]Hā'där, and Tē'mȧ, Je'tŭr, Nā'-
phish, and Kĕd'e-mah:
16 These *are* the sons of Ĭsh'ma-el,
and these *are* their names, by their
towns, and by their castles; [l]twelve
princes according to their nations.
17 And these *are* the years of the life
of Ĭsh'ma-el, an hundred and thirty
and seven years: and he gave [m]up the
ghost and died; and was gathered unto
his people.
18 And they dwelt from [n]Hăv'ĭ-lah
unto Shûr, that *is* before Ē'gypt, as
thou goest toward Ăs-syr'ĭ-ȧ: *and* he
[2]died in the [o]presence of all his brethren.
19 ¶ And these *are* the generations
of Ī'saac, Ā'bră-hăm's son: Ā'bră-hăm
[p]begat Ī'saac:
20 And Ī'saac was forty years old
when he took [q]Re-bĕk'ah to wife, the
[r]daughter of Bĕth-u'el the Syr'ĭ-an of
Pā'dan-ā'ram, the [s]sister to Lā'ban
the Syr'ĭ-an.
21 And Ī'saac [t]intreated the LORD
for his wife, because she *was* barren:
and the LORD was [u]intreated of him,
and Re-bĕk'ah his wife [v]conceived.
22 And the children struggled together within her; and she said, If *it be*
so, why *am* I thus? And she went to
[w]inquire of the LORD.
23 And the LORD said unto her, Two
nations *are* in thy womb, and two
[x]manner of people shall be separated
from thy bowels: and *the one* people
shall be stronger than *the other* people; and the elder shall serve the younger.
24 ¶ And when her days to be delivered were fulfilled, behold, *there were*
twins in her womb.
25 And the first came out red, all
[y]over like an hairy garment; and they
called his name Ē'sau.

54 [f]verses 56-59
55 [7]Or, a full year, or, ten months
56 [g]verse 40
59 [h]ch. 35.8
60 [i]ch. 17.16; Ruth 4.11
[j]ch. 22.17
62 [k]ch. 16.14; ch. 25.11
63 [8]Or, to pray
[l]Josh. 1.8; Ps. 1.2; Ps. 35.17; Ps. 77.12; Ps. 119.15; Ps. 143.5; Dan. 6.10; Matt. 6.5-6; Matt. 14.23; Mark 1.35; Mark 6.46; Luke 5.16; Luke 6.12; Acts 10.9
64 [m]Josh. 15.18; 1 Sam. 25.23
65 [n]1 Cor. 11.3-6-7-10
67 [o]1 Thess. 4.13

CHAPTER 25
2 [a]1 Chr. 1.32
5 [b]ch. 24.36
6 [c]ch. 21.14
[d]Judg. 6.3
8 [e]ch. 15.15; ch. 47.8-9
[f]ch. 35.29; ch. 49.33; Acts 13.36
9 [g]ch. 50.13
[h]ch. 49.29-30
10 [i]ch. 23.16
11 [j]ch. 16.14; ch. 24.62
12 [k]1 Chr. 1.29
15 [1]Or, Hadad; 1 Chr. 1.30
16 [l]ch. 17.20
17 [m]verse 8; ch. 49.33; Mark 15.37
18 [n]1 Sam. 15.7
[2]fell
[o]ch. 16.12
19 [p]Matt. 1.2
20 [q]ch. 24.67
[r]ch. 22.23
[s]ch. 24.29
21 [t]1 Sam. 1.11
[u]1 Chr. 5.20; 2 Chr. 33.13; Ezra 8.23
[v]Rom. 9.10
22 [w]1 Sam. 9.9; 1 Sam. 10.22
23 [x]ch. 24.60
25 [y]ch. 27.11

26 And after that came his brother
out, and [z]his hand took hold on Ē'sa̤u's
heel; and [a]his name was called Jā'cob:
and Ī'saac *was* threescore years old
when she bare them.
27 And the boys grew: and Ē'sa̤u
was a [b]cunning hunter, a man of the
field; and Jā'cob *was* [c]a plain man,
[d]dwelling in tents.
28 And Ī'saac loved Ē'sa̤u, because
[3]he did [e]eat of *his* venison: [f]but Re-
bĕk'ah loved Jā'cob.
29 ¶ And Jā'cob sod pottage: and
Ē'sa̤u came from the field, and he *was*
faint:
30 And Ē'sa̤u said to Jā'cob, Feed
me, I pray thee, [4]with that same red
pottage; for I *am* faint: therefore was
his name called [5]Ē'dom.
31 And Jā'cob said, Sell me this day
thy birthright.
32 And Ē'sa̤u said, Behold, I *am* [6]at
the point to die: and what profit shall
this birthright do to me?
33 And Jā'cob said, Swear to me
this day; and he sware unto him: and
he [g]sold his birthright unto Jā'cob.
34 Then Jā'cob gave Ē'sa̤u bread
and pottage of lentiles; and [h]he did eat
and drink, and rose up, and went his
way: thus Ē'sa̤u despised *his* birthright.

26

26 And there was a famine in the
land, beside [a]the first famine
that was in the days of Ā'bră-hăm.
And Ī'saac went unto [b]A-bĭm'ĕ-lech
king of the Phĭ-lĭs'tĭnes unto Gē'rär.
2 And the LORD appeared unto him,
and said, Go not down into Ē'gypt;
dwell in the [c]land which I shall tell
thee of:
3 Sojourn [d]in this land, and [e]I will
be with thee, and [f]will bless thee; for
unto thee, and unto thy seed, [g]I will
give all these countries, and I will perform [h]the oath which I sware unto
Ā'bră-hăm thy father;
4 And [i]I will make thy seed to multiply as the stars of heaven, and will give
unto thy seed all these countries; and
[j]in thy seed shall all the nations of the
earth be blessed;
5 Because [k]that Ā'bră-hăm obeyed
my voice, and kept my charge, my commandments, my statutes, and my laws.
6 ¶ And Ī'saac dwelt in Gē'rär:
7 And the men of the place asked
him of his wife; and he said, [l]She *is* my
sister: for [m]he feared to say, *She is* my
wife; lest, *said he,* the men of the place
should kill me for Re-bĕk'ah; because
she *was* [n]fair to look upon.
8 And it came to pass, when he had
been there a long time, that A-bĭm'ĕ-
lech king of the Phĭ-lĭs'tĭnes looked out
at a window, and saw, and, behold,
Ī'saac *was* sporting with Re-bĕk'ah his
wife.
9 And A-bĭm'ĕ-lech called Ī'saac,
and said, Behold, of a surety she *is* thy
wife: and how saidst thou, She *is* my
sister? And Ī'saac said unto him, Because I said, Lest I die for her.
10 And A-bĭm'ĕ-lech said, What *is*
this thou hast done unto us? one of
the people might lightly have lien with
thy wife, and [o]thou shouldest have
brought guiltiness upon us.
11 And A-bĭm'ĕ-lech charged all *his*
people, saying, He that [p]toucheth this
man or his wife shall surely be put to
death.
12 Then Ī'saac sowed in that land,
and [1]received in the same year an [q]hun-
dredfold: and the LORD blessed [r]him.
13 And the man [s]waxed great, and
[2]went forward, and grew until he became very great:
14 For he had possession of flocks,
and possession of herds, and great
store of [3]servants: and the Phĭ-lĭs'tĭnes
[t]envied him.
15 For all the wells [u]which his father's servants had digged in the days
of Ā'bră-hăm his father, the Phĭ-lĭs'-
tĭnes had stopped them, and filled them
with earth.
16 And A-bĭm'ĕ-lech said unto Ī'saac,
Go from us; for [v]thou art much mightier than we.
17 ¶ And Ī'saac departed thence, and
pitched his tent in the valley of Gē'rär,
and dwelt there.
18 And Ī'saac digged again the wells
of water, which they had digged in the
days of Ā'bră-hăm his father; for the
Phĭ-lĭs'tĭnes had stopped them after the
death of Ā'bră-hăm: [w]and he called
their names after the names by which
his father had called them.
19 And Ī'saac's servants digged in
the valley, and found there a well of
[4]springing water.
20 And the herdmen of Gē'rär did
[x]strive with Ī'saac's herdmen, saying,
The water *is* ours: and he called the
name of the well [5]Ē'sĕk; because they
strove with him.
21 And they digged another well,
and strove for that also: and he called
the name of it [6]Sĭt'nah.
22 And he removed from thence, and
digged another well; and for that they
strove not: and he called the name of it
[7]Rē-hō'both; and he said, For now the
LORD hath made room for us, and we
shall be [y]fruitful in the land.
23 And he went up from thence to
Bē'er–shē'bȧ.
24 And the LORD appeared unto him
the same night, and said, [z]I *am* the
God of Ā'bră-hăm thy father: [a]fear
not, for [b]I *am* with thee, and will bless
thee, and multiply thy seed for my servant Ā'bră-hăm's sake.
25 And he [c]builded an altar there,
and [d]called upon the name of the
LORD, and pitched his tent there: and
there Ī'saac's servants digged a well.
26 ¶ Then A-bĭm'ĕ-lech went to him
from Gē'rär, and A-hŭz'zath one of his
friends, and Phī'chol the chief captain
of his army.
27 And Ī'saac said unto them, Wherefore come ye to me, seeing ye [e]hate me,
and have sent me away from you?
28 And they said, [8]We saw certainly
that the LORD [f]was with thee: and we
said, Let there be now an oath betwixt

26 [z]Hos. 12.3
[a]ch. 27.36
27 [b]ch. 27.3-5
[c]Job 1.1-8; Job 2.3
[d]Heb. 11.9
28 [3]venison was in his mouth
[e]ch. 27.19
[f]ch. 27.6
30 [4]with that red, with that red pottage
[5]That is, Red
32 [6]going to die
33 [g]Heb. 12.16
34 [h]1 Cor. 15.32

CHAPTER 26
1 [a]ch. 12.10
[b]ch. 20.2
2 [c]ch. 12.1; Ps. 37.3
3 [d]ch. 20.1; Heb. 11.9
[e]ch. 28.15
[f]ch. 12.2
[g]ch. 13.15
[h]Ps. 105.9
4 [i]ch. 15.5
[j]ch. 22.18; Ps. 72.17
5 [k]ch. 22.16
7 [l]ch. 12.13
[m]Prov. 29.25
[n]ch. 24.16
10 [o]ch. 20.9
11 [p]Ps. 105.15
12 [1]found
[q]Matt. 13.8; Mark 4.8
[r]ch. 24.1;
13 [s]Prov. 10.22
[2]went going
14 [3]Or, husbandry
[t]ch. 37.11;
15 [u]ch. 21.30
16 [v]Ex. 1.9
18 [w]ch. 21.31
19 [4]living
20 [x]ch. 21.25
[5]That is, Contention
21 [6]That is, Hatred
22 [7]That is, Room
[y]ch. 17.6;
24 [z]ch. 24.12;
[a]ch. 15.1
[b]verses 3-4;
25 [c]ch. 12.7;
[d]Ps. 116.17
27 [e]Judg. 11.7
28 [8]Seeing we saw
[f]ch. 21.22-23

us, *even* betwixt us and thee, and let us make a covenant with thee;

29 [9]That thou wilt do us no hurt, as we have not touched thee, and as we have done unto thee nothing but good, and have sent thee away in peace: [g]thou *art* now the blessed of the LORD.

30 And [h]he made them a feast, and they did eat and drink.

31 And they rose up betimes in the morning, and [i]sware one to another: and Ī'saac sent them away, and they departed from him in peace.

32 And it came to pass the same day, that Isaac's servants came, and told him concerning the well which they had digged, and said unto him, We have found water.

33 And he called it [10]Shē'bah: therefore [j]the name of the city *is* [11]Bē'er-shē'bȧ unto this day.

34 ¶ And [k]Ē'sạu was forty years old when he took to wife Jū'dith the daughter of Be-e'rī the Hĭt'tīte, and Băsh'ĕ-măth the daughter of Ē'lon the Hĭt'tīte:

35 Which [l]were [12]a grief of mind unto Ī'saac and to Re-bĕk'ah.

27

And it came to pass, that when Ī'saac was old, and [a]his eyes were dim, so that he could not see, he called Ē'sạu his eldest son, and said unto him, My son: and he said unto him, Behold, *here am* I.

2 And he said, Behold now, I am old, [b]I know not the day of my death:

3 Now [c]therefore take, I pray thee, thy weapons, thy quiver and thy bow, and go out to the field, and [1]take me *some* venison;

4 And make me savoury meat, such as I love, and bring *it* to me, that I may eat; that my soul [d]may bless thee before I die.

5 And Re-bĕk'ah heard when Ī'saac spake to Ē'sạu his son. And Ē'sạu went to the field to hunt *for* venison, *and* to bring *it*.

6 ¶ And Re-bĕk'ah spake unto Jā'cob her son, saying, Behold, I heard thy father speak unto Ē'sạu thy brother, saying,

7 Bring me venison, and make me savoury meat, that I may eat, and bless thee before the LORD before my death.

8 Now therefore, my son, [e]obey my voice according to that which I command thee.

9 Go now to the flock, and fetch me from thence two good kids of the goats; and I will make them savoury [f]meat for thy father, such as he loveth:

10 And thou shalt bring *it* to thy father, that he may eat, and that he [g]may bless thee before his death.

11 And Jā'cob said to Re-bĕk'ah his mother, Behold, [h]Ē'sạu my brother *is* a hairy man, and I *am* a smooth man:

12 My father peradventure [i]will feel me, and I shall seem to him as a deceiver; and I shall bring [j]a curse upon me, and not a blessing.

13 And his mother said unto him, Upon [k]me *be* thy curse, my son: only obey my voice, and go fetch me *them*.

14 And he went, and fetched, and brought *them* to his mother: and his mother [l]made savoury meat, such as his father loved.

15 And Re-bĕk'ah took [2]goodly raiment [m]of her eldest son Ē'sạu, which *were* with her in the house, and put them upon Jā'cob her younger son:

16 And she put the skins of the kids of the goats upon his hands, and upon the smooth of his neck:

17 And she gave the savoury meat and the bread, which she had prepared, into the hand of her son Jā'cob.

18 ¶ And he came unto his father, and said, My father: and he said, Here *am* I; who *art* thou, my son?

19 And Jā'cob said unto his father, I *am* Ē'sạu thy firstborn; [n]I have done according as thou badest me: arise, I pray thee, sit and eat of my venison, [o]that thy soul may bless me.

20 And Ī'saac said unto his son, How *is it* that thou hast found *it* so quickly, my son? [p]And he said, Because the LORD thy God brought *it* [3]to me.

21 And Ī'saac said unto Jā'cob, Come near, I pray thee, that [q]I may feel thee, my son, whether thou *be* my very son Ē'sạu or not.

22 And Jā'cob went near unto Ī'saac his father; and he felt him, and said, The voice *is* Jā'cob's voice, but the hands *are* the hands of Ē'sạu.

23 And he discerned him not, because [r]his hands were hairy, as his brother Ē'sạu's hands: so he blessed him.

24 And he said, *Art* thou my very son Ē'sạu? And he said, [s]I *am*.

25 And he said, Bring *it* near to me, and I will eat of my son's venison, [t]that my soul may bless thee. And he brought *it* near to him, and he did eat: and he brought him wine, and he drank.

26 And his father Ī'saac said unto him, Come near now, and kiss me, my son.

27 And he came near, and kissed him: and he smelled the smell of his raiment, and blessed him, and said, See, [u]the smell of my son *is* as the smell of a field which the LORD hath blessed:

28 Therefore [v]God give thee of the [w]dew of heaven, and [x]the fatness of the earth, and [y]plenty of corn and wine:

29 Let [z]people serve thee, and nations bow down to thee: be lord over thy brethren, and [a]let thy mother's sons bow down to thee: cursed [b]*be* every one that curseth thee, and blessed *be* he that blesseth thee.

30 ¶ And it came to pass, as soon as Ī'saac had made an end of blessing Jā'cob, and Jā'cob was yet scarce gone out from the presence of Ī'saac his father, that Ē'sạu his brother came in from his hunting.

31 And he also had made savoury meat, and brought it unto his father, and said unto his father, Let my father

29 [9]If thou shalt, etc [g]ch. 24.31; Ps. 115.15
30 [h]ch. 19.3
31 [i]ch. 21.31
33 [10]That is, An oath [j]ch. 21.31 [11]That is, The well of the oath
34 [k]ch. 36.2
35 [l]ch. 27.46; ch. 28.1-8 [12]bitterness of spirit

CHAPTER 27
1 [a]ch. 48.10; 1 Sam. 3.2; Eccl. 12.3
2 [b]Prov. 27.1; Jas. 4.14
3 [c]ch. 25.27-28 [1]hunt
4 [d]verse 27; ch. 48.9-15; ch. 49.28; Deut. 33.1; Heb. 11.20
8 [e]verse 13
9 [f]verse 4
10 [g]ch. 48.15
11 [h]ch. 25.25
12 [i]verse 22 [j]ch. 9.25; Deut. 27.18
13 [k]ch. 43.9; 1 Sam. 25.24; 2 Sam. 14.9; Matt. 27.25
14 [l]verses 4-9
15 [2]desirable [m]verse 27
19 [n]1 Ki. 13.18; 1 Ki. 14.2; Isa. 28.15; Zech. 13.4 [o]verse 4
20 [p]Ex. 20.7 [3]before me
21 [q]verse 12
23 [r]verse 16
24 [s]Rom. 3.7-8; Eph. 4.25
25 [t]verse 4
27 [u]Hos. 14.6; Song 2.13; Heb. 6.7
28 [v]Heb. 11.20 [w]Deut. 33.13; 2 Sam. 1.21 [x]Num. 18.12 [y]Deut. 33.28; Ps. 65.9; Zech. 9.17
29 [z]ch. 9.25; ch. 25.23 [a]ch. 49.8 [b]ch. 12.3; Num. 24.9

arise, and [c]eat of his son's venison,
that thy soul may bless me.
32 And Ī'saac his father said unto
him, Who *art* thou? And he said, I *am*
thy son, thy firstborn Ē'sa̤u.
33 And Ī'saac [4]trembled very exceedingly, and said, Who? where *is* he
that hath [5]taken venison, and brought
it me, and I have eaten of all before
thou camest, and have blessed him?
yea, [d]*and* he shall be blessed.
34 And when Ē'sa̤u heard the words
of his father, [e]he cried with a great and
exceeding bitter cry, and said unto his
father, Bless me, *even* me also, O my
father.
35 And he said, Thy brother came
with [f]subtilty, and hath taken away
thy blessing.
36 And he said, [g]Is not he rightly
named [6]Jā'cob? for he hath supplanted
me these two times: [h]he took away my
birthright; and, behold, now he hath
taken away my blessing. And he said,
Hast thou not reserved a blessing for
me?
37 And Ī'saac answered and said
unto Ē'sa̤u, [i]Behold, I have made him
thy lord, and all his brethren have I
given to him for servants; and [j]with
corn and wine have I [7]sustained him:
and what shall I do now unto thee, my
son?
38 And Ē'sa̤u said unto his father,
Hast thou but one blessing, my father?
bless me, *even* me also, O my father.
And Ē'sa̤u lifted up his voice, [k]and
wept.
39 And Ī'saac his father answered
and said unto him, Behold, [l]thy dwelling shall be [8]the fatness of the earth,
and of the dew of heaven from above;
40 And by thy sword shalt thou live,
and [m]shalt serve thy brother; and [n]it
shall come to pass when thou shalt
have the dominion, that thou shalt
break his yoke from off thy neck.
41 ¶ And Ē'sa̤u [o]hated Jā'cob because of the blessing wherewith his father blessed him: and Ē'sa̤u said in his
heart, [p]The days of mourning for my
father are at hand; [q]then will I slay my
brother Jā'cob.
42 And these words of Ē'sa̤u her elder son were told to Re-bĕk'ah: and
she sent and called Jā'cob her younger son, and said unto him, Behold,
thy brother Ē'sa̤u, as touching thee,
doth [r]comfort himself, *purposing* to
kill thee.
43 Now therefore, my son, obey my
voice; and arise, flee thou to Lā'ban
my brother to [s]Hā'ran;
44 And tarry with him a few days,
until thy brother's fury turn away;
45 Until thy brother's anger turn
away from thee, and he forget *that*
which thou hast done to him: then I
will send, and fetch thee from thence:
why should I be deprived also of you
both in one day?
46 And Re-bĕk'ah said to Ī'saac, [t]I
am weary of my life because of the
daughters of Hĕth: [u]if Jā'cob take a
wife of the daughters of Hĕth, such as

31 [c]verse 4
33 [4]trembled with a great trembling greatly
[5]hunted
[d]ch. 28.3-4; Rom. 11.29
34 [e]Heb. 12.17
35 [f]1 Thess. 4.6
36 [g]ch. 25.26
[6]That is, a supplanter
[h]ch. 25.33
37 [i]Fulfilled, 2 Sam. 8.14
[j]verse 28
[7]Or, supported
38 [k]Heb. 12.17
39 [l]Heb. 11.20
[8]Or, of the fatness
40 [m]ch. 25.23; Obad. 18-20
[n]Fulfilled, 2 Ki. 8.20
41 [o]ch. 37.4-8
[p]ch. 50.3-4-10
[q]Obad. 10;
42 [r]Ps. 64.5
43 [s]ch. 11.31
46 [t]ch. 26.35;
[u]ch. 24.3

CHAPTER 28

1 [a]ch. 27.33
3 [b]ch. 17.1-6
[1]an assembly of people
4 [c]ch. 12.2;
[2]of thy sojournings
[d]ch. 17.8;
8 [e]ch. 24.3
[3]were evil in the eyes, etc
9 [f]ch. 36.3-she is called Bashemath
[g]ch. 25.13
10 [h]Called, Acts 7.2-Charran
12 [i]ch. 41.1;
[j]John 1.51;
13 [k]ch. 35.1;
[l]ch. 26.24
[m]ch. 13.15
14 [n]ch. 13.16
[4]break forth
[o]ch. 13.14;
[p]ch. 12.3
15 [q]ch. 26.24;
[r]ch. 48.16;
[s]ch. 35.6
[t]Deut. 31.6
[u]Num. 23.19

these *which are* of the daughters of the
land, what good shall my life do me?

28 And Ī'saac called Jā'cob, and
blessed [a]him, and charged him,
and said unto him, Thou shalt not take
a wife of the daughters of Cā'năan.
2 Arise, go to Pā'dan–ā'ram, to the
house of Bĕth-u̧'el thy mother's father;
and take thee a wife from thence of
the daughters of Lā'ban thy mother's
brother.
3 And [b]God Almighty bless thee,
and make thee fruitful, and multiply
thee, that thou mayest be [1]a multitude
of people;
4 And give thee [c]the blessing of
Ā'brā-hăm, to thee, and to thy seed
with thee; that thou mayest inherit the
land [2]wherein thou art a [d]stranger,
which God gave unto Ā'brā-hăm.
5 And Ī'saac sent away Jā'cob: and
he went to Pā'dan–ā'ram unto Lā'ban,
son of Bĕth-u̧'el the Sȳr'ĭ-an, the
brother of Re-bĕk'ah, Jā'cob's and
Ē'sa̤u's mother.
6 ¶ When Ē'sa̤u saw that Ī'saac had
blessed Jā'cob, and sent him away to
Pā'dan–ā'ram, to take him a wife from
thence; and that as he blessed him he
gave him a charge, saying, Thou shalt
not take a wife of the daughters of
Cā'năan;
7 And that Jā'cob obeyed his father
and his mother, and was gone to Pā'-
dan–ā'ram;
8 And Ē'sa̤u seeing [e]that the daughters of Cā'năan [3]pleased not Ī'saac his
father;
9 Then went Ē'sa̤u unto Ĭsh'ma-el,
and took unto the wives which he had
[f]Mā'ha-lath the daughter of Ĭsh'ma-el
Ā'brā-hăm's son, the [g]sister of Ne-bā'-
joth, to be his wife.
10 ¶ And Jā'cob went out from Bē'-
er–shē'bȧ, and went [h]toward Hā'ran.
11 And he lighted upon a certain
place, and tarried there all night, because the sun was set; and he took of
the stones of that place, and put *them*
for his pillows, and lay down in that
place to sleep.
12 And he [i]dreamed, and behold a
ladder set up on the earth, and the top
of it reached to heaven: and behold
[j]the angels of God ascending and descending on it.
13 And, [k]behold, the LORD stood
above it, and said, [l]I *am* the LORD God
of Ā'brā-hăm thy father, and the God
of Ī'saac: [m]the land whereon thou liest,
to thee will I give it, and to thy seed;
14 And [n]thy seed shall be as the dust
of the earth, and thou shalt [4]spread
abroad to the [o]west, and to the east,
and to the north, and to the south: and
in thee and [p]in thy seed shall all the
families of the earth be blessed.
15 And, behold, [q]I *am* with thee, and
will [r]keep thee in all *places* whither
thou goest, and will [s]bring thee again
into this land; for [t]I will not leave thee,
[u]until I have done *that* which I have
spoken to thee of.

16 ¶ And Jā'cob awaked out of his
sleep, and he said, Surely the LORD is
in [v]this place; and I knew *it* not.
17 And he was afraid, and said, How
dreadful *is* this place! this *is* none other
but the house of God, and this *is* the
gate of heaven.
18 And Jā'cob rose up early in the
morning, and took the stone that he
had put *for* his pillows, and set it up *for*
a pillar, and poured oil upon the top of
it.
19 And he called the name of that
[w]place [5]Bĕth'–el: but the name of that
city *was called* Lŭz at the first.
20 And [x]Jā'cob vowed a vow, saying, If [y]God will be with me, and will
keep me in this way that I go, and will
give me [z]bread to eat, and raiment to
put on,
21 So that [a]I come again to my father's house in peace; [b]then shall the
LORD be my God:
22 And this stone, which I have set
for a pillar, [c]shall be God's house: [d]and
of all that thou shalt give me I will
surely give the tenth unto thee.
29 Then Jā'cob [1]went on his journey, [a]and came into the land of
the [2]people of the east.
2 And he looked, and behold a well
in the field, and, lo, there *were* three
flocks of sheep lying by it; for out of
that well they watered the flocks: and a
great stone *was* upon the well's mouth.
3 And thither were all the flocks
gathered: and they rolled the stone
from the well's mouth, and watered the
sheep, and put the stone again upon the
well's mouth in his place.
4 And Jā'cob said unto them, My
brethren, whence *be* ye? And they said,
Of Hā'ran *are* we.
5 And he said unto them, Know ye
Lā'ban the son of Nā'hor? And they
said, We know *him*.
6 And he said unto them, [3b]*Is* he
well? And they said, *He is* well: and,
behold, Rā'chel his daughter cometh
with the sheep.
7 And he said, Lo, [4]*it is* yet high
day, neither *is it* time that the cattle
should be gathered together: water ye
the sheep, and go *and* feed *them*.
8 And they said, We cannot, until all
the flocks be gathered together, and
till they roll the stone from the well's
mouth; then we water the sheep.
9 ¶ And while he yet spake with
them, Rā'chel came with her father's
sheep: [c]for she kept them.
10 And it came to pass, when Jā'cob
saw Rā'chel the daughter of Lā'ban his
mother's brother, and the sheep of Lā'-
ban his mother's brother, that Jā'cob
went near, and [d]rolled the stone from
the well's mouth, and watered the flock
of Lā'ban his mother's brother.
11 And Jā'cob [e]kissed Rā'chel, and
lifted up his voice, and wept.
12 And Jā'cob told Rā'chel that he
was [f]her father's brother, and that he
was Re-bĕk'ah's son: [g]and she ran and
told her father.

16 [v]Ex. 3.5; Josh. 5.15
19 [w]Judg. 1.23; Hos. 4.15
[5]That is, The house of God
20 [x]ch. 31.13; Judg. 11.30; 2 Sam. 15.8
[y]verse 15
[z]1 Tim. 6.8
21 [a]Judg. 11.31; 2 Sam. 19.24
[b]Deut. 26.17; 2 Sam. 15.8; 2 Ki. 5.17
22 [c]ch. 35.7
[d]Lev. 27.30
CHAPTER 29
1 [1]lift up his feet
[a]Num. 23.7; Hos. 12.12
[2]children
6 [3]Is there peace to him?
[b]ch. 43.27
7 [4]yet the day is great
9 [c]Ex. 2.16
10 [d]Ex. 2.17
11 [e]ch. 33.4; ch. 45.14; Rom. 16.16; 1 Cor. 16.20; 2 Cor. 13.12; 1 Pet. 5.14
12 [f]ch. 13.8; ch. 14.14
[g]ch. 24.28
13 [5]hearing
[h]ch. 24.29
14 [i]ch. 2.23; Judg. 9.2; 2 Sam. 5.1; 2 Sam. 19.12-13
[6]a month of days
18 [j]ch. 31.41; 2 Sam. 3.14
20 [k]ch. 30.26
[l]Song 8.7
21 [m]Judg. 15.1
22 [n]Judg. 14.10; John 2.1
26 [7]place
27 [o]Judg. 14.12
30 [p]ch. 30.26; ch. 31.41; Hos. 12.12
31 [q]Ps. 127.3
[r]ch. 30.1
32 [8]That is, See a son
[s]Ex. 3.7; Ex. 4.31; Deut. 26.7; Ps. 25.18; Ps. 106.44

13 And it came to pass, when Lā'ban
heard the [5]tidings of Jā'cob his sister's
son, that [h]he ran to meet him, and
embraced him, and kissed him, and
brought him to his house. And he told
Lā'ban all these things.
14 And Lā'ban said to him, Surely
[i]thou *art* my bone and my flesh. And
he abode with him [6]the space of a
month.
15 ¶ And Lā'ban said unto Jā'cob,
Because thou *art* my brother, shouldest thou therefore serve me for nought?
tell me, what *shall* thy wages *be?*
16 And Lā'ban had two daughters:
the name of the elder *was* Lē'ah, and
the name of the younger *was* Rā'chel.
17 Lē'ah *was* tender eyed; but Rā'-
chel was beautiful and well favoured.
18 And Jā'cob loved Rā'chel; and
said, [j]I will serve thee seven years for
Rā'chel thy younger daughter.
19 And Lā'ban said, *It is* better that I
give her to thee, than that I should give
her to another man: abide with me.
20 And Jā'cob [k]served seven years
for Rā'chel; and they seemed unto him
but a few days, for [l]the love he had to
her.
21 ¶ And Jā'cob said unto Lā'ban,
Give *me* my wife, for my days are fulfilled, that I may [m]go in unto her.
22 And Lā'ban gathered together all
the men of the place, and made a
[n]feast.
23 And it came to pass in the evening, that he took Lē'ah his daughter,
and brought her to him; and he went in
unto her.
24 And Lā'ban gave unto his daughter Lē'ah Zĭl-pah his maid *for* an handmaid.
25 And it came to pass, that in the
morning, behold, it *was* Leah: and he
said to Lā'ban, What *is* this thou hast
done unto me? did not I serve with thee
for Rā'chel? wherefore then hast thou
beguiled me?
26 And Lā'ban said, It must not be
so done in our [7]country, to give the
younger before the firstborn.
27 [o]Fulfil her week, and we will give
thee this also for the service which
thou shalt serve with me yet seven
other years.
28 And Jā'cob did so, and fulfilled
her week: and he gave him Rā'chel his
daughter to wife also.
29 And Lā'ban gave to Rā'chel his
daughter Bĭl'hah his handmaid to be
her maid.
30 And he went in also unto Rā'chel,
and he loved also Rā'chel more than
Lē'ah, and served with him yet [p]seven
other years.
31 ¶ And when the LORD [q]saw that
Lē'ah *was* hated, he [r]opened her
womb: but Rā'chel *was* barren.
32 And Lē'ah conceived, and bare
a son, and she called his name [8]Reu'-
ben: for she said, Surely the LORD hath
[s]looked upon my affliction; now therefore my husband will love me.
33 And she conceived again, and
bare a son; and said, Because the LORD

hath heard that I *was* hated, he hath
therefore given me this *son* also: and
she called his name [9]Sĭm'e-on.
34 And she conceived again, and
bare a son; and said, Now this time will
my husband be joined unto me, because I have born him three sons: therefore was his name called [10]Lē'vī.
35 And she conceived again, and
bare a son: and she said, Now will I
praise the LORD: therefore she called
his name [11]Jū'dah; and [12]left bearing.

30 And when Rā'chel saw that [a]she
bare Jā'cob no children, Rā'-
chel [b]envied her sister; and said unto
Jā'cob, Give me children, [c]or else I die.
2 And Jā'cob's anger was kindled
against Rā'chel: and he said, [d]*Am* I in
God's stead, who hath withheld from
thee the fruit of the womb?
3 And she said, Behold [e]my maid
Bĭl'hah, go in unto her; [f]and she shall
bear upon my knees, [g]that I may also
[1]have children by her.
4 And she gave him Bĭl'hah her
handmaid [h] to wife: and Jā'cob went
in unto her.
5 And Bĭl'hah conceived, and bare
Jā'cob a son.
6 And Rā'chel said, God hath [i]judged
me, and hath also heard my voice, and
hath given me a son: therefore called
she his name [2]Dăn.
7 And Bĭl'hah Rā'chel's maid conceived again, and bare Jā'cob a second
son.
8 And Rā'chel said, With [3]great
wrestlings have I wrestled with my
sister, and I have prevailed: and she
called his name [j][4]Năph'ta-lī.
9 When Lē'ah saw that she had left
bearing, she took Zĭl-pah her maid,
and gave her Jā'cob to wife.
10 And Zĭl-pah Lē'ah's maid bare
Jā'cob a son.
11 And Lē'ah said, A troop cometh:
and she called his name [5]Găd.
12 And Zĭl-pah Lē'ah's maid bare
Jā'cob a second son.
13 And Lē'ah said, [6]Happy am I, for
the daughters [k]will call me blessed:
and she called his name [7]Ăsh'ēr.
14 ¶ And Reu̧'ben went in the days of
wheat harvest, and found mandrakes
[l]in the field, and brought them unto his
mother Lē'ah. Then Rā'chel said to Lē-
'ah, [m]Give me, I pray thee, of thy son's
mandrakes.
15 And she said unto her, [n]*Is it*
a small matter that thou hast taken
my husband? and wouldest thou take
away my son's mandrakes also? And
Rā'chel said, Therefore he shall lie
with thee to night for thy son's mandrakes.
16 And Jā'cob came out of the field
in the evening, and Lē'ah went out to
meet him, and said, Thou must come in
unto me; for surely I have hired thee
with my son's mandrakes. And he lay
with her that night.
17 And God hearkened unto Lē'ah,
and she conceived, and bare Jā'cob the
fifth son.
18 And Lē'ah said, God hath given
me my hire, because I have given my
maiden to my husband: and she called
his name [8]Ĭs'sa-char.
19 And Lē'ah conceived again, and
bare Jā'cob the sixth son.
20 And Lē'ah said, God hath endued
me *with* a good dowry; now will my
husband dwell with me, because I have
born him six sons: and she called his
name [9]Zĕb'u-lun.
21 And afterwards she bare a daughter, and called her name [10]Dī'nah.
22 ¶ And God [o]remembered Rā'-
chel, and God hearkened to her, and
[p]opened her womb.
23 And she conceived, and bare a
son; and said, God hath taken away
[q]my reproach:
24 And she called his name [11]Jō'-
seph; and said, [r]The LORD shall add to
me another son.
25 ¶ And it came to pass, when Rā'-
chel had born Jō'seph, that Jā'cob said
unto Lā'ban, [s]Send me away, that I
may go unto [t]mine own place, and to
my country.
26 Give *me* my wives and my children, [u]for whom I have served thee,
and let me go: for thou knowest my
service which I have done thee.
27 And Lā'ban said unto him, I pray
thee, if I have found favour in thine
eyes, *tarry: for* [v]I have learned by experience that the LORD hath blessed me
[w]for thy sake.
28 And he said, [x]Appoint me thy
wages, and I will give *it.*
29 And he said unto him, [y]Thou
knowest how I have served thee, and
how thy cattle was with me.
30 For *it was* little which thou hadst
before I *came,* and it is *now* [12]increased
unto a multitude; and the LORD hath
blessed thee [13]since my coming: and
now when shall I [z]provide for mine
own house also?
31 And he said, What shall I give
thee? And Jā'cob said, Thou shalt not
give me any thing: if thou wilt do this
thing for me, I will again feed *and* keep
thy flock.
32 I will pass through all thy flock
to day, removing from thence all the
speckled and spotted cattle, and all the
brown cattle among the sheep, and the
spotted and speckled among the goats:
and [a]*of such* shall be my hire.
33 So shall my [b]righteousness answer for me [14]in time to come, when it
shall come for my hire before thy face:
every one that *is* not speckled and
spotted among the goats, and brown
among the sheep, that shall be counted
stolen with me.
34 And Lā'ban said, Behold, I would
it might be according to thy word.
35 And he removed that day the he
goats that were ringstraked and spotted, and all the she goats that were
speckled and spotted, *and* every one
that had *some* white in it, and all
the brown among the sheep, and gave
them into the hand of his sons.

33 [9]That is, Hearing
34 [10]That is, Joined; Num. 18.2-4
35 [11]That is, Praise
[12]stood from bearing

CHAPTER 30
1 [a]ch. 29.31
[b]ch. 37.11
[c]Job 5.2
2 [d]ch. 16.2; 1 Sam. 1.5
3 [e]ch. 16.2
[f]ch. 50.23; Job 3.12
[g]ch. 16.2
[1]be built by her
4 [h]ch. 35.22
6 [i]Ps. 35.24; Lam. 3.59
[2]That is, Judging
8 [3]wrestlings of God
[j]Called, Nephthalim; Matt. 4.13
[4]That is, My wrestling
11 [5]That is, A troop, or, company; Isa. 65.11
13 [6]In my happiness
[k]Prov. 31.28; Luke 1.48
[7]That is, Happy
14 [l]Song 7.13; Precious fruits, or sweet flowers
[m]ch. 25.30
15 [n]Num. 16.9
18 [8]That is, An hire
20 [9]That is, Dwelling
21 [10]That is, Judgment
22 [o]ch. 8.1;
[p]ch. 29.31
23 [q]1 Sam. 1.6;
24 [11]That is, Adding
[r]ch. 35.17
25 [s]ch. 24.55
[t]ch. 18.33;
26 [u]ch. 29.20
27 [v]ch. 39.3-5;
[w]ch. 26.24
28 [x]ch. 29.15
29 [y]ch. 31.6;
30 [12]broken forth
[13]at my foot
[z]1 Tim. 5.8
32 [a]ch. 31.8
33 [b]Ps. 37.6
[14]to morrow

36 And he set three days' journey betwixt himself and Jā'cob: and Jā'cob fed the rest of Lā'ban's flocks.

37 ¶ And [c]Jā'cob took him rods of green poplar, and of the hazel and chesnut tree; and pilled white strakes in them, and made the white appear which *was* in the rods.

38 And he set the rods which he had pilled before the flocks in the gutters in the watering troughs when the flocks came to drink, that they should conceive when they came to drink.

39 And the flocks conceived before the rods, and brought forth cattle ringstraked, speckled, and spotted.

40 And Jā'cob did separate the lambs, and set the faces of the flocks toward the ringstraked, and all the brown in the flock of Lā'ban; and he put his own flocks by themselves, and put them not unto Lā'ban's cattle.

41 And it came to pass, whensoever the stronger cattle did conceive, that Jā'cob laid the rods before the eyes of the cattle in the gutters, that they might conceive among the rods.

42 But when the cattle were feeble, he put *them* not in: so the feebler were Lā'ban's, and the stronger Jā'cob's.

43 And the man [d]increased exceedingly, and [e]had much cattle, and maidservants, and menservants, and camels, and asses.

31 And he [a]heard the words of Lā'ban's sons, saying, Jā'cob hath taken away all that *was* our father's; and of *that* which *was* our father's hath he gotten all this [b]glory.

2 And Jā'cob beheld [c]the countenance of Lā'ban, and, behold, it *was* not [d]toward him [1]as before.

3 And the LORD said unto Jā'cob, [e]Return unto the land of thy fathers, and to thy kindred; and I will be with thee.

4 And Jā'cob sent and called Rā'chel and Lē'ah to the field unto his flock,

5 And said unto them, [f]I see your father's countenance, that it *is* not toward me as before; but the God of my father [g]hath been with me.

6 And [h]ye know that with all my power I have served your father.

7 And your father hath deceived me, and [i]changed my wages [j]ten times; but God [k]suffered him not to hurt me.

8 If he said thus, [l]The speckled shall be thy wages; then all the cattle bare speckled: and if he said thus, The ringstraked shall be thy hire; then bare all the cattle ringstraked.

9 Thus God hath [m]taken away the cattle of your father, and given *them* to me.

10 And it came to pass at the time that the cattle conceived, that I lifted up mine eyes, and saw in a dream, and, behold, the [2]rams which leaped upon the cattle *were* ringstraked, speckled, and grisled.

11 And [n]the angel of God spake unto me in a dream, *saying*, Jā'cob: And I said, Here *am* I.

12 And he said, Lift up now thine eyes, and see, all the rams which leap upon the cattle *are* ringstraked, speckled, and grisled: for [o]I have seen all that Lā'ban doeth unto thee.

13 I *am* the God of Běth'–el, [p]where thou anointedst the pillar, *and* where thou vowedst a vow unto me: now [q]arise, get thee out from this land, and return unto the land of thy kindred.

14 And Rā'chel and Lē'ah answered and said unto him, [r]*Is there* yet any portion or inheritance for us in our father's house?

15 Are we not counted of him strangers? for [s]he hath sold us, and hath quite devoured also our money.

16 For all the riches which God hath taken from our father, that *is* ours, and our children's: now then, whatsoever God hath said unto thee, do.

17 ¶ Then Jā'cob rose up, and set his sons and his wives upon camels;

18 And he carried away all his cattle, and all his goods which he had gotten, the cattle of his getting, which he had gotten in Pā'dan–ā'ram, for to go to Ī'saac his father in the land of Cā'năan.

19 And Lā'ban went to shear his sheep: and Rā'chel had stolen the [3][t]images that *were* her father's.

20 And Jā'cob stole away [4]unawares to Lā'ban the Sȳr'ĭ-an, in that he told him not that he fled.

21 So he fled with all that he had; and he rose up, and passed over the river, and [u]set his face *toward* the mount Gĭl'e-ăd.

22 And it was told Lā'ban on the third day that Jā'cob was fled.

23 And he took his [v]brethren with him, and pursued after him seven days' journey; and they overtook him in the mount Gĭl'e-ăd.

24 And God [w]came to Lā'ban the Sȳr'ĭ-an in a dream by night, and said unto him, Take heed that thou [x]speak not to Jā'cob [5]either good or bad.

25 ¶ Then Lā'ban overtook Jā'cob. Now Jā'cob had pitched his tent in the mount: and Lā'ban with his brethren pitched in the mount of Gĭl'e-ăd.

26 And Lā'ban said to Jā'cob, What hast thou done, that thou hast stolen away unawares to me, and [y]carried away my daughters, as captives *taken* with the sword?

27 Wherefore didst thou flee away secretly, and [6]steal away from me; and didst not tell me, that I might have sent thee away with mirth, and with songs, with tabret, and with harp?

28 And hast not suffered me [z]to kiss my sons and my daughters? [a]thou hast now done foolishly in *so* doing.

29 It is in the power of my hand to do you hurt: but the [b]God of your father spake unto me [c]yesternight, saying, Take thou heed that thou speak not to Jā'cob either good or bad.

30 And now, *though* thou wouldest needs be gone, because thou sore longedst after thy father's house, *yet* wherefore hast thou [d]stolen my gods?

37 [c]ch. 31.9
43 [d]verse 30; Ezek. 39.10
[e]ch. 13.2; ch. 26.13
CHAPTER 31
1 [a]Job 5.2; Jas. 3.8
[b]Ps. 49.16
2 [c]ch. 4.5
[d]Deut. 28.45
[1]as yesterday and the day before; 1 Sam. 19.7
3 [e]ch. 28.15; ch. 32.9
5 [f]verse 2
[g]ch. 21.22; Heb. 13.5
6 [h]ch. 30.29
7 [i]verse 41
[j]Num. 14.22; Zech. 8.23
[k]ch. 15.1; Prov. 30.5
8 [l]ch. 30.32
9 [m]verses 1-16
10 [2]Or, he goats
11 [n]ch. 48.16
12 [o]Ex. 3.7; Eph. 6.9
13 [p]ch. 28.18
[q]verse 3; ch. 32.9
14 [r]ch. 2.24
15 [s]ch. 29.15
19 [3]teraphim; Judg. 17.5; 1 Sam. 19.13; Hos. 3.4
[t]ch. 35.2
20 [4]the heart of Laban
21 [u]ch. 46.28; Luke 9.51
23 [v]ch. 13.8
24 [w]ch. 20.3; Matt. 1.20
[x]ch. 24.50
[5]from good to bad
26 [y]1 Sam. 30.2
27 [6]hast stolen me
28 [z]Ruth 1.9; Acts 20.37
[a]1 Sam. 13.13; 2 Chr. 16.9
29 [b]ch. 28.13; Ps. 115.9
[c]verse 24
30 [d]verse 19; Acts 19.26

31 And Jā'cob answered and said to Lā'ban, Because I was afraid: for I said, Peradventure thou wouldest take by force thy daughters from me.

32 With whomsoever thou findest thy gods, [e]let him not live: before our brethren discern thou what *is* thine with me, and take *it* to thee. For Jā'cob knew not that Rā'chel had stolen them.

33 And Lā'ban went into Jā'cob's tent, and into Lē'ah's tent, and into the two maidservants' tents; but he found *them* not. Then went he out of Lē'ah's tent, and entered into Rā'chel's tent.

34 Now Rā'chel had taken the images, and put them in the camel's furniture, and sat upon them. And Lā'ban [7]searched all the tent, but found *them* not.

35 And she said to her father, Let it not displease my lord that I cannot [f]rise up before thee; for the custom of women *is* upon me. And he searched, but found not the [g]images.

36 ¶ And Jā'cob [h]was wroth, and chode with Lā'ban: and Jā'cob answered and said to Lā'ban, What *is* my trespass? what *is* my sin, that thou hast so hotly pursued after me?

37 Whereas thou hast [8]searched all my stuff, what hast thou found of all thy household stuff? [i]set *it* here before my brethren and thy brethren, that they may judge betwixt us both.

38 This twenty years *have* I *been* with thee; thy ewes and thy she goats have not cast their young, and the rams of thy flock have I not eaten.

39 That [j]which was torn *of beasts* I brought not unto thee; I bare the loss of it; of [k]my hand didst thou require it, *whether* stolen by day, or stolen by night.

40 *Thus* I was; in the day the drought consumed me, and the frost by night; and my sleep departed from mine eyes.

41 Thus have I been twenty years in thy house; I [l]served thee fourteen years for thy two daughters, and six years for thy cattle: and [m]thou hast changed my wages ten times.

42 Except [n]the God of my father, the God of Ā'brā-hăm, and [o]the fear of Ī'saac, had been with me, surely thou hadst sent me away now empty. [p]God hath seen mine affliction and the labour of my hands, and [q]rebuked *thee* yesternight.

43 ¶ And Lā'ban answered and said unto Jā'cob, *These* daughters *are* my daughters, and *these* children *are* my children, and *these* cattle *are* my cattle, and all that thou seest *is* mine: and what can I do this day unto these my daughters, or unto their children which they have born?

44 Now therefore come thou, [r]let us make a covenant, I and thou; and [s]let it be for a witness between me and thee.

45 And Jā'cob [t]took a stone, and set it up *for* a pillar.

46 And Jā'cob said unto his brethren, Gather stones; and they took stones, and made an heap: and they did eat there upon the heap.

47 And Lā'ban called it [9]Jē'gar–sā-ha-dū'thȧ: but Jā'cob called it [10]Găl'ĕ-ed.

48 And Lā'ban said, [u]This heap *is* a witness between me and thee this day. Therefore was the name of it called Găl'ĕ-ed;

49 And [v][11]Mĭz'pah; for he said, The LORD watch between me and thee, when we are absent one from another.

50 If thou shalt afflict my daughters, or if thou shalt take *other* wives beside my daughters, no man *is* with us; see, God *is* witness betwixt me and thee.

51 And Lā'ban said to Jā'cob, Behold this heap, and behold *this* pillar, which I have cast betwixt me and thee;

52 This heap *be* witness, and *this* pillar *be* witness, that I will not pass over this heap to thee, and that thou shalt not pass over this heap and this pillar unto me, for harm.

53 The God of Ā'brā-hăm, and the God of Nā'hor, the God of their father, [w]judge betwixt us. And Jā'cob [x]sware by the fear of his father Ī'saac.

54 Then Jā'cob [12]offered sacrifice upon the mount, and called his brethren to eat bread: and they did eat bread, and tarried all night in the mount.

55 And early in the morning Lā'ban rose up, and kissed his sons and his daughters, and [y]blessed them: and Lā'ban departed, and returned unto his place.

32 And Jā'cob went on his way, and [a]the angels of God met him.

2 And when Jā'cob saw them, he said, This *is* God's [b]host: and he called the name of that place [1]Mā-ha-nā'im.

3 And Jā'cob sent messengers before him to Ē'sạu his brother unto [c]the land of Sē'ĭr, [d]the [2]country of Ē'dom.

4 And he commanded them, saying, [e]Thus shall ye speak unto my lord Ē'sạu; Thy servant Jā'cob saith thus, I have sojourned with Lā'ban, and stayed there until now:

5 And [f]I have oxen, and asses, flocks, and menservants, and womenservants: and I have sent to tell my lord, that [g]I may find grace in thy sight.

6 ¶ And the messengers returned to Jā'cob, saying, We came to thy brother Ē'sạu, and also [h]he cometh to meet thee, and four hundred men with him.

7 Then Jā'cob was greatly afraid and [i]distressed: and he [j]divided the people that *was* with him, and the flocks, and herds, and the camels, into two bands;

8 And said, If Ē'sạu come to the one company, and smite it, then the other company which is left shall escape.

9 ¶ And [k]Jā'cob said, [l]O God of my father Ā'brā-hăm, and God of my father Ī'saac, the LORD [m]which saidst unto me, Return unto thy country, and to thy kindred, and I will deal well with thee:

10 [3]I am not [n]worthy of the least of all the [o]mercies, and of all the truth, which thou hast shewed unto thy ser-

32 [e]ch. 44.9
34 [7]felt
35 [f]Ex. 20.12; Lev. 19.32; Eph. 6.1
[g]verse 19
36 [h]Eph. 4.26
37 [8]felt
[i]1 Sam. 12.3; 1 Cor. 6.5
39 [j]Ex. 22.10
[k]Ex. 22.12
41 [l]ch. 29.27
[m]verse 7
42 [n]Ps. 124.1
[o]verse 53; Isa. 8.13
[p]ch. 29.32; Ex. 3.7
[q]1 Chr. 12.17; Jude 9
44 [r]ch. 26.28
[s]Josh. 24.27
45 [t]ch. 28.18
47 [9]That is, The heap of witness. Chald.
[10]That is, The heap of witness. Heb.
48 [u]Josh. 24.27
49 [v]Judg. 11.29; 1 Sam. 7.5
[11]That is, A beacon, or, watch-tower
53 [w]ch. 16.5
[x]ch. 21.23
54 [12]Or, killed beasts
55 [y]ch. 28.1; 2 Sam. 6.20

CHAPTER 32
1 [a]Ps. 91.11; Heb. 1.14
2 [b]Josh. 5.14; 2 Ki. 6.16; Ps. 103.21; Ps. 148.2; Luke 2.13
[1]That is, Two hosts, or camps
3 [c]ch. 33.14
[d]ch. 36.6-8; Deut. 2.5; Josh. 24.4
[2]field
4 [e]Prov. 15.1
5 [f]ch. 30.43
[g]ch. 33.8
6 [h]ch. 33.1
7 [i]ch. 35.3
[j]Prov. 2.11; Eph. 5.15
9 [k]Ps. 50.15
[l]ch. 28.13
[m]ch. 31.3
10 [3]I am less than all, etc
[n]2 Sam. 9.8
[o]ch. 24.27

vant; for with [p]my staff I passed over
this Jôr'dan; and now I am become
two bands.
11 [q]Deliver me, I pray thee, from
the hand of my brother, from the hand
of Ē'sa̤u: for I fear him, lest he will
come and smite me, *and* the [r]mother
[4]with the children.
12 And [s]thou saidst, I will surely do
thee good, and make thy seed as the
sand of the sea, which cannot be numbered for multitude.
13 ¶ And he lodged there that same
night; and took of that which came
to his hand a [t]present for Ē'sa̤u his
brother;
14 Two hundred she goats, and
twenty he goats, two hundred ewes,
and twenty rams,
15 Thirty milch camels with their
colts, forty kine, and ten bulls, twenty
she asses, and ten foals.
16 And he delivered *them* into the
hand of his servants, every drove by
themselves; and said unto his servants,
Pass over before me, and put a space
betwixt drove and drove.
17 And he commanded the foremost, saying, When Ē'sa̤u my brother
meeteth thee, and asketh thee, saying,
Whose *art* thou? and whither goest
thou? and whose *are* these before
thee?
18 Then thou shalt say, *They be* thy
servant Jā'cob's; it *is* a present sent
unto my lord Ē'sa̤u: and, behold, also
he *is* behind us.
19 And so commanded he the second, and the third, and all that followed the droves, saying, On this manner shall ye speak unto Ē'sa̤u, when ye
find him.
20 And say ye moreover, Behold, thy
servant Jā'cob *is* behind us. For he
said, I will [u]appease him with the present that goeth before me, and afterward I will see his face; peradventure
he will accept [5]of me.
21 So went the present over before
him: and himself lodged that night in
the company.
22 And he rose up that night, and
took his two wives, and his two womenservants, and his eleven sons, and
[v]passed over the ford Jăb'bok.
23 And he took them, and [6]sent them
over the brook, and sent over that he
had.
24 ¶ And Jā'cob was left alone; and
there wrestled a man with him until
the [7]breaking of the day.
25 And when he saw that he prevailed not against him, he touched the
hollow of his thigh; and [w]the hollow of
Jā'cob's thigh was out of joint, as he
wrestled with him.
26 And [x]he said, Let me go, for the
day breaketh. And he said, [y]I will not
let thee go, except thou bless me.
27 And he said unto him, What *is*
thy name? And he said, Jā'cob.
28 And he said, Thy name shall be
called no more Jā'cob, but [8]Ĭs'ra-el: for
as a prince hast thou power [z]with God
and [a]with men, and hast prevailed.

[p]Job 8.7
11 [q]Ps. 59.1-2
[r]Hos. 10.14
[4]upon
12 [s]ch. 28.13-15
13 [t]ch. 43.11
20 [u]Prov. 21.14
[5]my face
22 [v]Deut. 3.16
23 [6]caused to pass
24 [7]ascending of the morning
25 [w]Matt. 26.41; 2 Cor. 12.7
26 [x]Luke 24.28
[y]Hos. 12.4
2 Ki. 17.34
28 [8]That is, A prince of God
[z]Hos. 12.3-4
[a]ch. 25.31; ch. 27.33
29 [b]Judg. 13.18
30 [9]That is, The face of God
[c]ch. 16.13; Ex. 24.11; Ex. 33.20; Deut. 5.24; Judg. 6.22; Judg. 13.22; Isa. 6.5

CHAPTER 33
1 [a]ch. 32.6
3 [b]ch. 18.2; ch. 42.6; ch. 43.26
4 [c]ch. 32.28; Prov. 16.1; Prov. 21.1; Jer. 10.23
[d]ch. 45.14
5 [1]to thee
5 [e]ch. 48.9; Ps. 127.3; Isa. 8.18
8 [2]What is all this band to thee?
[f]ch. 32.16
[g]ch. 32.5
9 [3]be that to thee that is thine
10 [h]ch. 43.3; 2 Sam. 3.13; 2 Sam. 14.24-28-32; Matt. 18.10
11 [i]Judg. 1.15; 1 Sam. 25.27; 2 Ki. 5.15
[4]all things; Phil. 4.18
[j]2 Ki. 5.23

29 And Jā'cob asked *him*, and said,
Tell *me*, I pray thee, thy name. And he
said, [b]Wherefore *is* it *that* thou dost
ask after my name? And he blessed
him there.
30 And Jā'cob called the name of
the place [9]Pe-nī'el: for [c]I have seen
God face to face, and my life is preserved.
31 And as he passed over Pe-nū'el
the sun rose upon him, and he halted
upon his thigh.
32 Therefore the children of Ĭs'ra-el
eat not *of* the sinew which shrank,
which *is* upon the hollow of the thigh,
unto this day: because he touched the
hollow of Jā'cob's thigh in the sinew
that shrank.

33 And Jā'cob lifted up his eyes,
and looked, and, behold, [a]Ē'sa̤u
came, and with him four hundred men.
And he divided the children unto Lē-
'ah, and unto Rā'chel, and unto the
two handmaids.
2 And he put the handmaids and
their children foremost, and Lē'ah and
her children after, and Rā'chel and
Jō'seph hindermost.
3 And he passed over before them,
and [b]bowed himself to the ground
seven times, until he came near to his
brother.
4 And [c]Ē'sa̤u ran to meet him, and
embraced him, [d]and fell on his neck,
and kissed him: and they wept.
5 And he lifted up his eyes, and saw
the women and the children; and said,
Who *are* those [1]with thee? And he said,
The children which [e]God hath graciously given thy servant.
6 Then the handmaidens came near,
they and their children, and they bowed
themselves.
7 And Lē'ah also with her children
came near, and bowed themselves: and
after came Jō'seph near and Rā'chel,
and they bowed themselves.
8 And he said, [2]What *meanest* thou
by [f]all this drove which I met? And he
said, *These are* [g]to find grace in the
sight of my lord.
9 And Ē'sa̤u said, I have enough, my
brother; [3]keep that thou hast unto thyself.
10 And Jā'cob said, Nay, I pray thee,
if now I have found grace in thy sight,
then receive my present at my hand:
for therefore I [h]have seen thy face, as
though I had seen the face of God, and
thou wast pleased with me.
11 Take, I pray thee, [i]my blessing
that is brought to thee; because God
hath dealt graciously with me, and because I have [4]enough. [j]And he urged
him, and he took *it*.
12 And he said, Let us take our journey, and let us go, and I will go before
thee.
13 And he said unto him, My lord
knoweth that the children *are* tender,
and the flocks and herds with young
are with me: and if men should over-
drive them one day, all the flock will
die.

14 Let my lord, I pray thee, pass
over before his servant: and I will lead
on softly, [5]according as the cattle that
goeth before me and the children be
able to endure, until I come unto my
lord [k]unto Sē'ĭr.
15 And Ē'sạu said, Let me now
[6]leave with thee *some* of the folk that
are with me. And he said, [7]What needeth it? [l]let me find grace in the sight of
my lord.
16 ¶ So Ē'sạu returned that day on
his way unto Sē'ĭr.
17 And Jā'cob journeyed to [m]Sŭc'-
coth, and built him an house, and made
booths for his cattle: therefore the
name of the place is called [8]Sŭc'coth.
18 ¶ And Jā'cob came to [n]Shā'lem,
a city of [9]Shē'chem, which *is* in the
land of Cā'năan, when he came from
Pā'dan–ā'ram; and pitched his tent before the city.
19 And [o]he bought a parcel of a
field, where he had spread his tent,
at the hand of the children of [10]Hā'-
mor, Shē'chem's father, for an hundred [11]pieces of money.
20 And he erected there an altar,
and [p]called it [12]Ēl–e-lō'he–Ĭs'ra-el.
34 And [a]Dī'nah the daughter of Lē-
'ah, which she bare unto Jā'cob,
[b]went out to see the daughters of the
land.
2 And when Shē'chem the son of
Hā'mor the Hī'vīte, prince of the country, [c]saw her, he [d]took her, and lay
with her, and [1]defiled her.
3 And his soul clave unto Dī'nah the
daughter of Jā'cob, and he loved the
damsel, and spake [2]kindly unto the
damsel.
4 And Shē'chem [e]spake unto his father Hā'mor, saying, Get me this damsel to wife.
5 And Jā'cob heard that he had defiled Dī'nah his daughter: now his sons
were with his cattle in the field: and
Jā'cob held his peace until they were
come.
6 ¶ And Hā'mor the father of Shē'-
chem went out unto Jā'cob to commune with him.
7 And the sons of Jā'cob came out of
the field when they heard *it:* and the
men were grieved, and they [f]were very
wroth, because he [g]had wrought folly
in Ĭs'ra-el in lying with Jā'cob's daughter; [h]which thing ought not to be done.
8 And Hā'mor communed with them,
saying, The soul of my son Shē'chem
longeth for your daughter: I pray you
give her him to wife.
9 And [i]make ye marriages with us,
and give your daughters unto us, and
take our daughters unto you.
10 And ye shall dwell with us: and
[j]the land shall be before you; dwell
and [k]trade ye therein, and get [l]you
possessions therein.
11 And Shē'chem said unto her father and unto her brethren, Let me find
grace in your eyes, and what ye shall
say unto me I will give.
12 Ask me never so much [m]dowry
and gift, and I will give according as ye
shall say unto me: but give me the damsel to wife.
13 And the sons of Jā'cob answered
Shē'chem and Hā'mor his father [n]de-
ceitfully, and said, because he had defiled Dī'nah their sister:
14 And they said unto them, We cannot do this thing, to give our sister to
one that is uncircumcised; for [o]that
were a reproach unto us:
15 But in this will we consent unto
you: If ye will be as we *be,* that every
male of you be circumcised;
16 Then will we give our daughters
unto you, and we will take your daughters to us, and we will dwell with you,
and we will become one people.
17 But if ye will not hearken unto us,
to be circumcised; then will we take
our daughter, and we will be gone.
18 And their words pleased Hā'mor,
and Shē'chem Hā'mor's son.
19 And the young man deferred not
to do the thing, because he had delight in Jā'cob's daughter: and he *was*
[p]more honourable than all the house
of his father.
20 ¶ And Hā'mor and Shē'chem his
son came unto the [q]gate of their city,
and communed with the men of their
city, saying,
21 These men *are* peaceable with
us; therefore let them dwell in the land,
and trade therein; for the land, behold
it is large enough for them; let us take
their daughters to us for wives, and let
us give them our daughters.
22 Only herein will the men consent
unto us for to dwell with us, to be one
people, if every male among us be circumcised, as they *are* circumcised.
23 *Shall* not their cattle and their
substance and every beast of theirs *be*
ours? only let us consent unto them,
and they will dwell with us.
24 And unto Hā'mor and unto Shē'-
chem his son hearkened all that [r]went
out of the gate of his city; and every
male was circumcised, all that went
out of the gate of his city.
25 ¶ And it came to pass on the third
day, when they were sore, that two
of the sons of Jā'cob, [s]Sĭm'e-on and
Lē'vī, Dī'nah's brethren, took each
man his sword, and came upon the city
boldly, and slew all the males.
26 And they slew Hā'mor and Shē'-
chem his son with the [3]edge of the
sword, and took Dī'nah out of Shē'-
chem's house, and went out.
27 The sons of Jā'cob came upon
the slain, and spoiled the city, because
they had defiled their sister.
28 They took their sheep, and their
oxen, and their asses, and that which
was in the city, and that which *was* in
the field,
29 And all their wealth, and all their
little ones, and their wives took they
captive, and spoiled even all that *was*
in the house.
30 And Jā'cob said to Sĭm'e-on and
Lē'vī, [t]Ye have [u]troubled me [v]to make
me to stink among the inhabitants of
the land, among the Cā'năan-ītes and

14 [5]according to the foot of the work, etc., and according to the foot of the children
[k]ch. 32.3
15 [6]set, or, place
[7]Wherefore is this?
[l]Ruth 2.13
17 [m]Josh. 13.27; Judg. 8.5
[8]That is, booths
18 [n]John 3.23
[9]Called, Sychem; Acts 7.16; Josh. 24.1
19 [o]Josh. 24.32; John 4.5
[10]Acts 7.16- Called, Emmor
[11]Or, lambs
20 [p]ch. 35.7
[12]That is, God the God of Israel

CHAPTER 34
1 [a]ch. 30.21
[b]Tit. 2.5
2 [c]ch. 6.2; Judg. 14.1
[d]ch. 20.2
[1]humbled her; Deut. 22.29
3 [2]to the heart of the damsel; Isa. 40.2; Hos. 2.14
4 [e]Judg. 14.2
7 [f]ch. 49.7; 2 Sam. 13.21
[g]Josh. 7.15; Judg. 20.6
[h]Deut. 23.17; 2 Sam. 13.12
9 [i]Ex. 23.32
10 [j]ch. 13.9; ch. 20.15
[k]ch. 42.34
[l]ch. 47.27
12 [m]Ex. 22.16; Deut. 22.29; 1 Sam. 18.25
13 [n]2 Sam. 13.24
14 [o]Josh. 5.9
19 [p]1 Chr. 4.9
20 [q]2 Sam. 15.2; Ruth 4.1
24 [r]ch. 23.10
25 [s]ch. 49.5-7
26 [3]mouth
30 [t]ch. 49.6
[u]Josh. 7.25
[v]Ex. 5.21; 1 Sam. 13.4

the Pĕr'ĭz-zītes: and [w]I *being* few in
number, they shall gather themselves
together against me, and slay me; and I
shall be destroyed, I and my house.
31 And they said, [x]Should he deal
with our sister as with an harlot?
35 And God said unto Jā'cob, Arise,
go up to [a]Bĕth'–el, and dwell
there: and make there an altar unto
God, [b]that appeared unto thee [c]when
thou fleddest from the face of Ē'sạu
thy brother.
2 Then Jā'cob said unto his [d]house-
hold, and to all that *were* with him, Put
away [e]the strange gods that *are* among
you, and [f]be clean, and change your
garments:
3 And let us arise, and go up to
Bĕth'–el; and I will make there an altar
unto God, [g]who answered me in the
day of my distress, [h]and was with me
in the way which I went.
4 And they gave unto Jā'cob all the
strange gods which *were* in their hand,
and *all their* [i]earrings which *were* in
their ears; and Jā'cob hid them under
[j]the oak which *was* by Shē'chem.
5 And they journeyed: and [k]the terror of God was upon the cities that
were round about them, and they did
not pursue after the sons of Jā'cob.
6 ¶ So Jā'cob came to [l]Lŭz, which *is*
in the land of Cā'năan, that *is*, Bethel,
he and all the people that *were* with
him.
7 And he [m]built there an altar, and
called the place [1]Ĕl-bĕth'el: because
[n]there God appeared unto him, when
he fled from the face of his brother.
8 But [o]Dĕb'o-rah Re-bĕk'ah's nurse
died, and she was buried beneath
Bĕth'–el under an oak: and the name
of it was called [2]Ăl'lŏn–băch'uth.
9 ¶ And [p]God appeared unto Jā'cob
again, when he came out of Pā'dan–
ā'ram, and blessed him.
10 And God said unto him, Thy
name *is* Jā'cob: [q]thy name shall not be
called any more Jā'cob, [r]but Ĭs'ra-el
shall be thy name: and he called his
name Ĭs'ra-el.
11 And God said unto him, [s]I *am*
God Almighty: be fruitful and multiply; a [t]nation and a company of nations shall be of thee, and kings shall
come out of thy loins;
12 And the land [u]which I gave
Ā'brā-hăm and Ī'saac, to thee I will
give it, and to thy seed after thee will I
give the land.
13 And God [v]went up from him in
the place where he talked with him.
14 And Jā'cob [w]set up a pillar in the
place where he talked with him, *even* a
pillar of stone: and he poured a drink
offering thereon, and he poured oil
thereon.
15 And Jā'cob called the name of
the place where God spake with him,
[x]Bĕth'–el.
16 ¶ And they journeyed from
Bĕth'–el; and there was but [3]a little
way to come to Ĕph'răth: and Rā'chel
travailed, and she had hard labour.
17 And it came to pass, when she
was in hard labour, that the midwife
said unto her, Fear not; [y]thou shalt
have this son also.
18 And it came to pass, as her soul
was in departing, (for she died) that
she called his name [4]Bĕn-ō'nī: but his
father called him [5]Bĕn'ja-min.
19 And [z]Rā'chel died, and was buried in the way to [a]Ĕph'răth, which *is*
Bĕth'–lĕ-hĕm.
20 And Jā'cob set a pillar upon her
grave: that *is* the pillar of Rā'chel's
grave [b]unto this day.
21 ¶ And Ĭs'ra-el journeyed, and
spread his tent beyond [c]the tower of
Ē'där.
22 And it came to pass, when Ĭs'ra-el
dwelt in that land, that Reụ'ben went
and [d]lay with Bĭl'hah his father's concubine: and Ĭs'ra-el heard *it*. Now the
sons of Jā'cob were twelve:
23 The sons of Lē'ah; [e]Reụ'ben,
Jā'cob's firstborn, and Sĭm'e-on, and
Lē'vī, and Jū'dah, and Ĭs'sa-char, and
Zĕb'u-lun:
24 The sons of Rā'chel; Jō'seph, and
Bĕn'ja-min:
25 And the sons of Bĭl'hah, Rā'chel's
handmaid; Dăn, and Năph'ta-lī:
26 And the sons of Zĭl-pah, Lē'ah's
handmaid; Găd, and Ăsh'ēr: these *are*
the sons of Jā'cob, which were born to
him in Pā'dan–ā'ram.
27 ¶ And Jā'cob came unto Ī'saac
his father unto [f]Măm're, unto the [g]city
of Ăr'bah, which *is* Hē'bron, where
Ā'brā-hăm and Ī'saac sojourned.
28 And the days of Ī'saac were an
hundred and fourscore years.
29 And Ī'saac [h]gave up the ghost,
and died, and [i]was gathered unto his
people, *being* old and full of days: and
[j]his sons Ē'sạu and Jā'cob buried him.
36 Now these *are* the generations of
Ē'sạu, [a]who *is* Ē'dom.
2 [b]Ē'sạu took his wives of the daughters of Cā'năan; Ā'dah the daughter of
Ē'lon the Hĭt'tīte, and [c]A-hō-lĭb'ă-mah
the daughter of Ā'nah the daughter of
Zĭb'e-on the Hī'vīte;
3 And [d]Băsh'ĕ-măth Ĭsh'ma-el's
daughter, sister of Ne-bā'joth.
4 And [e]Ā'dah bare to Ē'sạu Ĕl'ĭ-
phăz; and Băsh'ĕ-măth bare Reụ'el;
5 And A-hō-lĭb'ă-mah bare Jē'ush,
and Ja-ā'lam, and Kō'rah: these *are*
the sons of Ē'sạu, which were born
unto him in the land of Cā'năan.
6 And Ē'sạu took his wives, and his
sons, and his daughters, and all the
[1]persons of his house, and his cattle,
and all his beasts, and all his substance, which he had got in the land of
Cā'năan; and went into the country
from the face of his [f]brother Jā'cob.
7 For [g]their riches were more than
that they might dwell together; and
the land [h]wherein they were strangers
could not bear them because of their
cattle.
8 Thus dwelt Ē'sạu in [i]mount Sē'īr:
[j]Ē'sạu *is* Ē'dom.
9 ¶ And these *are* the generations of
Ē'sạu the father of [2]the Ē'dom-ītes in

[w]Deut. 4.27;
31 [x]Prov. 6.34
CHAPTER 35
1 [a]ch. 28.19
[b]ch. 28.13
[c]ch. 27.43
2 [d]ch. 18.19;
[e]ch. 31.19-34;
[f]Ex. 19.10
3 [g]ch. 32.7-24;
[h]ch. 28.20;
4 [i]Hos. 2.13
[j]Josh. 24.26
5 [k]Ex. 15.16;
6 [l]ch. 28.22
7 [m]Eccl. 5.4
[1]That is, The God of Beth-el
[n]ch. 28.13
8 [o]ch. 24.59
[2]That is, The oak of weeping
9 [p]Hos. 12.4
10 [q]ch. 17.5
[r]ch. 32.28
11 [s]ch. 17.1;
[t]ch. 17.5-6;
12 [u]ch. 12.7;
13 [v]ch. 17.22
14 [w]ch. 28.18
15 [x]ch. 28.19
16 [3]a little piece of ground
17 [y]ch. 30.24
18 [4]That is, The son of my sorrow
[5]That is, The son of the right hand
19 [z]ch. 48.7
[a]Ruth 1.2;
20 [b]1 Sam. 10.2
21 [c]Mic. 4.8
22 [d]ch. 49.4;
23 [e]ch. 46.8;
27 [f]ch. 13.18
[g]Josh. 14.15
29 [h]Eccl. 12.7
[i]ch. 15.15;
[j]ch. 25.9;
CHAPTER 36
1 [a]ch. 25.30
2 [b]ch. 26.34
[c]verse 25
3 [d]ch. 28.9
4 [e]1 Chr. 1.35
6 [1]souls
[f]Deut. 23.7
7 [g]ch. 13.6-11
[h]ch. 17.8;
8 [i]ch. 32.3
[j]verse 1
9 [2]Edom

mount Sē'ïr:
10 These *are* the names of Ē'sau's
sons; [k]Ĕl'ĭ-phăz the son of Ā'dah the
wife of Ē'sau, Reu'el the son of Băsh'ĕ-
măth the wife of Ē'sau.
11 And the sons of Ĕl'ĭ-phăz were
Tē'man, Ō'mar, [3]Zē'pho, and Gā'tam,
and Kē'năz.
12 And Tĭm'nȧ was concubine to Ĕl'-
ĭ-phăz Ē'sau's son; and she bare to Ĕl'ĭ-
phăz [l]Ăm'a-lĕk: these *were* the sons of
Ā'dah Ē'sau's wife.
13 And these *are* the sons of Reu'el;
Nā'hăth, and Zē'rah, Shăm'mah, and
Mĭz'zah: these were the sons of Băsh'-
ĕ-măth Ē'sau's wife.
14 ¶ And these were the sons of A-
hō-lĭb'ă-mah, the daughter of Ā'nah
the daughter of Zĭb'e-on, Ē'sau's wife:
and she bare to Ē'sau Jē'ush, and Ja-
ā'lam, and Kō'rah.
15 ¶ These *were* dukes of the sons of
Ē'sau: the sons of Ĕl'ĭ-phăz the firstborn *son* of Ē'sau; duke Tē'man, duke
Ō'mar, duke Zē'pho, duke Kē'năz,
16 Duke Kō'rah, duke Gā'tam, *and*
duke Ăm'a-lĕk: these *are* the dukes
that came of Ĕl'ĭ-phăz in the land of
Ē'dom; these *were* the sons of Ā'dah.
17 ¶ And these *are* the sons of Reu'el
Ē'sau's son; duke Nā'hăth, duke Zē'-
rah, duke Shăm'mah, duke Mĭz'zah:
these *are* the dukes *that came* of Reu'el
in the land of Ē'dom; these *are* the sons
of Băsh'ĕ-măth Ē'sau's wife.
18 ¶ And these *are* the sons of A-
hō-lĭb'ă-mah Ē'sau's wife; duke Jē'-
ush, duke Ja-ā'lam, duke Kō'rah: these
were the dukes *that came* of A-hō-lĭb'-
ă-mah the daughter of Ā'nah, Ē'sau's
wife.
19 These *are* the sons of Ē'sau, who
is Ē'dom, and these *are* their dukes.
20 ¶ [m]These *are* the sons of Sē'ïr the
[n]Hō'rīte, who inhabited the land; Lō'-
tan, and Shō'bal, and Zĭb'e-on, and
Ā'nah,
21 And Dī'shon, and Ē'zēr, and Dī'-
shan: these *are* the dukes of the Hō'-
rītes, the children of Sē'ïr in the land of
Ē'dom.
22 And the children of Lō'tan were
Hō'rī and [4]Hē'mam; and Lō'tan's sister *was* Tĭm'nȧ.
23 And the children of Shō'bal *were*
these; [5]Ăl'văn, and Măn'a-hăth, and
Ē'bal, [6]Shē'pho, and Ō'nam.
24 And these *are* the children of Zĭb'-
e-on; both Ā'jah, and Ā'nah: this *was*
that Ā'nah that found [o]the mules in the
wilderness, as he fed the asses of Zĭb'e-
on his father.
25 And the children of Ā'nah *were*
these; Dī'shon, and A-hō-lĭb'ă-mah the
daughter of Ā'nah.
26 And these *are* the children of Dī'-
shon; [7]Hĕm'dan, and Ĕsh'ban, and Ĭth'-
ran, and Chē'ran.
27 The children of Ē'zēr *are* these;
Bĭl'hăn, and Zā'a-văn, and [8]Ā'kan.
28 The children of Dī'shan *are* these;
Ŭz, and Ā'răn.
29 These *are* the dukes *that came* of
the Hō'rītes; duke Lō'tan, duke Shō'-
bal, duke Zĭb'e-on, duke Ā'nah,

10 [k]1 Chr. 1.35-etc
11 [3]Or, Zephi
12 [l]Ex. 17.8; Num. 24.20; Deut. 25.17-19; 1 Sam. 15.2-3
20 [m]1 Chr. 1.38
[n]ch. 14.6; Deut. 2.12-22. 1 Chr. 1.38
1 Chr. 1.39
1 Chr. 1.40
22 [4]Or, Homam,
23 [5]Or, Alian, [6]Or, Shephi,
24 [o]Lev. 19.19 1 Chr. 1.40 1 Chr. 1.41
26 [7]Or, Amram,
27 [8]Or, Jakan,
31 [p]1 Chr. 1.43
[q]1 Sam. 10.24
39 [r]1 Chr. 1.50, Hadad Pai. After his death was an Aristocracy, Ex. 15.15
40 [s]1 Chr. 1.51
[9]Or, Aliah
43 [10]Edom
CHAPTER 37
1 [1]of his father's sojournings; ch. 17.8; ch. 23.4; ch. 28.4; ch. 36.7; ch. 47.9; 1 Chr. 29.15; Ps. 39.12; Ps. 105.12; Ps. 119.19; 2 Cor. 5.6-7; Heb. 11.9; 1 Pet. 1.17; 1 Pet. 2.11
2 [a]1 Sam. 2.22-24
3 [b]ch. 44.20
[2]Or, pieces; Judg. 5.30; 2 Sam. 13.18; Ps. 45.14; Ezek. 16.16
4 [c]ch. 27.41; ch. 49.23; 1 Sam. 17.28; John 7.3-5; 1 John 2.11; 1 John 3.10-12
7 [d]ch. 42.6-9; ch. 43.26; ch. 44.14

30 Duke Dī'shon, duke Ē'zēr, duke
Dī'shan: these *are* the dukes *that came*
of Hō'rī, among their dukes in the land
of Sē'ïr.
31 ¶ And [p]these *are* the kings that
reigned in the land of Ē'dom, before
there reigned any [q]king over the children of Ĭs'ra-el.
32 And Bē'lȧ the son of Bē'or reigned
in Ē'dom: and the name of his city *was*
Dĭn'hā-bah.
33 And Bē'lȧ died, and Jō'băb the
son of Zē'rah of Bŏz'rah reigned in his
stead.
34 And Jō'băb died, and Hū'sham of
the land of Tĕm'a-nī reigned in his
stead.
35 And Hū'sham died, and Hā'dăd
the son of Bē'dăd, who smote Mĭd'ĭ-an
in the field of Mō'ab, reigned in his
stead: and the name of his city *was*
Ā'vĭth.
36 And Hā'dăd died, and Săm'lah of
Măs're-kah reigned in his stead.
37 And Săm'lah died, and Saul of
Rē-hō'both *by* the river reigned in his
stead.
38 And Saul died, and Bā'al–hā'nan
the son of Ăch'bôr reigned in his stead.
39 And Bā'al–hā'nan the son of
Ăch'bôr died, and [r]Hā'där reigned in
his stead: and the name of his city *was*
Pā'u; and his wife's name *was* Me-
hĕt'a-bel, the daughter of Mā'tred, the
daughter of Mĕz'a-hab.
40 And these *are* the names of the
[s]dukes *that came* of Ē'sau, according
to their families, after their places, by
their names; duke Tĭm'nah, duke [9]Ăl'-
vah, duke Jē'theth,
41 Duke A-hō-lĭb'ă-mah, duke Ē'lah,
duke Pī'non,
42 Duke Kē'năz, duke Tē'man, duke
Mĭb'zar,
43 Duke Măg'dĭ-el, duke Ī'ram: these
be the dukes of Ē'dom, according to
their habitations in the land of their possession: he *is* Ē'sau the father of [10]the
Ē'dom-ītes.

37 And Jā'cob dwelt in the land
[1]wherein his father was a
stranger, in the land of Cā'năan.
2 These *are* the generations of Jā'-
cob. Jō'seph, *being* seventeen years
old, was feeding the flock with his
brethren; and the lad *was* with the sons
of Bĭl'hah, and with the sons of Zĭl-pah,
his father's wives: and Jō'seph brought
unto his father [a]their evil report.
3 Now Ĭs'ra-el loved Jō'seph more
than all his children, because he *was*
[b]the son of his old age: and he made
him a coat of *many* [2]colours.
4 And when his brethren saw that
their father loved him more than all his
brethren, they [c]hated him, and could
not speak peaceably unto him.
5 ¶ And Jō'seph dreamed a dream,
and he told *it* his brethren: and they
hated him yet the more.
6 And he said unto them, Hear, I
pray you, this dream which I have
dreamed:
7 For, [d]behold, we *were* binding
sheaves in the field, and, lo, my sheaf

arose, and also stood upright; and, behold, your sheaves stood round about,
and made obeisance to my sheaf.
8 And his brethren said to him, Shalt
thou indeed reign over us? or shalt thou
indeed have dominion over us? And
they hated him yet the more for his
dreams, and for his words.
9 ¶ And he dreamed yet another
dream, and told it his brethren, and
said, Behold, I have dreamed a dream
more; and, behold, [e]the sun and the
moon and the eleven stars made obeisance to me.
10 And he told *it* to his father, and to
his brethren: and his father rebuked
him, and said unto him, What *is* this
dream that thou hast dreamed? Shall I
and thy mother and [f]thy brethren indeed come to bow down ourselves to
thee to the earth?
11 And [g]his brethren envied him:
but his father [h]observed the saying.
12 ¶ And his brethren went to feed
their father's flock in Shē'chem.
13 And Ĭs'ra-el said unto Jō'seph,
Do not thy brethren feed *the flock* in
Shē'chem? come, and I will send thee
unto them. And he said to him, Here
am I.
14 And he said to him, Go, I pray
thee, [3]see whether it be well with thy
brethren, and well with the flocks; and
bring me word again. So he sent him
out of the vale [i]of Hē'bron, and he
came to Shē'chem.
15 ¶ And a certain man found him,
and, behold, *he was* wandering in the
field: and the man asked him, saying,
What seekest thou?
16 And he said, I seek my brethren:
[j]tell me, I pray thee, where they feed
their flocks.
17 And the man said, They are departed hence; for I heard them say, Let
us go to Dō'than. And Jō'seph went
after his brethren, and found them in
[k]Dō'than.
18 And when they saw him afar off,
even before he came near unto them,
they [l]conspired against him to slay
him.
19 And they said one to another, Behold, this [4]dreamer cometh.
20 Come [m]now therefore, and let us
slay him, and cast him into some pit,
and we will say, Some evil beast hath
devoured him: and we shall see what
will become of his dreams.
21 And [n]Reu̯'ben heard *it*, and he
delivered him out of their hands; and
said, Let us not kill him.
22 And Reu̯'ben said unto them,
Shed no blood, *but* cast him into this
pit that *is* in the wilderness, and lay no
hand upon him; that he might rid him
out of their hands, to deliver him to his
father again.
23 ¶ And it came to pass, when Jō'-
seph was come unto his brethren, that
they stript Jō'seph out of his coat, *his*
coat of *many* [5]colours that *was* on him;
24 And they took him, and cast him
into a pit: and the pit *was* empty, *there*
was no water in it.

9 [e]ch. 46.29
10 [f]ch. 27.29
11 [g]Acts 7.9
[h]Dan. 7.28;
14 [3]see the peace of thy brethren, etc; ch. 29.6;
1 Sam. 17.17
[i]ch. 13.18;
16 [j]Song 1.7
17 [k]2 Ki. 6.13
18 [l]1 Sam. 19.1;
19 [4]master of dreams
20 [m]Prov. 1.11;
21 [n]ch. 42.22
23 [5]Or, pieces
25 [o]Prov. 30.20;
[p]verses 28-36
[q]Jer. 8.22
26 [r]ch. 4.10;
27 [s]1 Sam. 18.17
[t]ch. 42.21
[u]ch. 29.14
[6]hearkened
28 [v]ch. 39.1;
[w]ch. 45.4-5;
[x]Matt. 27.9
29 [y]Job 1.20
30 [z]ch. 42.13-36;
31 [a]verse 23
33 [b]verse 20;
34 [c]verse 29
35 [d]2 Sam. 12.17
[e]ch. 42.38
36 [f]ch. 39.1 officers
[7]eunuch: But the word doth signify not only eunuchs, but alsochamberlains, courtiers, and
[8]chief of the slaughtermen, or, executioners. Or, chief marshal

CHAPTER 38
1 [a]2 Ki. 4.8
2 [b]ch. 34.2
[c]1 Chr. 2.3
3 [d]Num. 26.19
4 [e]ch. 46.12
5 [f]Num. 26.20
6 [g]ch. 24.4
7 [h]ch. 46.12
[i]1 Chr. 2.3
8 [j]Matt. 22.24

25 And [o]they sat down to eat bread:
and they lifted up their eyes and looked,
and, behold, a company of [p]Ĭsh'me-
el-ītes came from Gĭl'e-ăd with their
camels bearing spicery and [q]balm and
myrrh, going to carry *it* down to Ē'ġypt.
26 And Jū'dah said unto his brethren, What profit *is it* if we slay our
brother, and [r]conceal his blood?
27 Come, and let us sell him to the
Ĭsh'me-el-ītes and [s]let not our hand be
upon him; for he *is* [t]our brother *and*
[u]our flesh. And his brethren [6]were content.
28 Then there passed by [v]Mĭd'ĭ-an-
ītes merchantmen; and they drew and
lifted up Jō'seph out of the pit, [w]and
sold Jō'seph to the Ĭsh'me-el-ītes for
[x]twenty *pieces* of silver: and they
brought Jō'seph into Ē'ġypt.
29 ¶ And Reu̯'ben returned unto the
pit; and, behold, Jō'seph *was* not in the
pit; and he [y]rent his clothes.
30 And he returned unto his brethren, and said, The child [z]*is* not; and I,
whither shall I go?
31 And they took [a]Jō'seph's coat,
and killed a kid of the goats, and
dipped the coat in the blood;
32 And they sent the coat of *many*
colours, and they brought *it* to their
father; and said, This have we found:
know now whether it *be* thy son's coat
or no.
33 And he knew it, and said, *It is*
my son's coat; an [b]evil beast hath devoured him; Jō'seph is without doubt
rent in pieces.
34 And Jā'cob [c]rent his clothes,
and put sackcloth upon his loins, and
mourned for his son many days.
35 And all his sons and all his daughters [d]rose up to comfort him; but he
refused to be comforted; and he said,
[e]For I will go down into the grave unto
my son mourning. Thus his father wept
for him.
36 And [f]the Mĭd'ĭ-an-ītes sold him
into Ē'ġypt unto Pŏt'ĭ-phar, an [7]offi-
cer of Phā'raōh's, *and* [8]captain of the
guard.
38 And it came to pass at that time,
that Jū'dah went down from his
brethren, and [a]turned in to a certain A-
dŭl'lăm-īte, whose name *was* Hī'rah.
2 And Jū'dah [b]saw there a daughter
of a certain Cā'năan-īte, whose name
was [c]Shu̯'ah; and he took her, and
went in unto her.
3 And she conceived, and bare a son;
and he called his name [d]Ēr.
4 And she conceived again, and bare
a son; and she called his name [e]Ō'nan.
5 And she yet again conceived, and
bare a son; and called his name [f]Shē'-
lah: and he was at Chē'zĭb, when she
bare him.
6 And Jū'dah [g]took a wife for Ēr his
firstborn, whose name *was* Tā'mar.
7 And [h]Ēr, Jū'dah's firstborn, was
wicked in the sight of the LORD; [i]and
the LORD slew him.
8 And Jū'dah said unto Ō'nan, Go in
unto [j]thy brother's wife, and marry
her, and raise up seed to thy brother.

9 And Ō'nan knew that the seed should not be [k]his; and it came to pass, when he went in unto his brother's wife, that he spilled *it* on the ground, lest that he should give seed to his brother.

10 And the thing which he did [1]displeased the LORD: wherefore he slew [l]him also.

11 Then said Jū'dah to Tā'mar his daughter in law, [m]Remain a widow at thy father's house, till Shē'lah my son be grown: for he said, Lest peradventure he die also, as his brethren *did*. And Tā'mar went [n]and dwelt in her father's house.

12 ¶ And [2]in process of time the daughter of Shu̮'ah Jū'dah's wife died; and Jū'dah was [o]comforted, and went up unto his sheepshearers to Tĭm'nath, he and his friend Hī'rah the A-dŭl'lăm-īte.

13 And it was told Tā'mar, saying, Behold thy father in law goeth up [p]to Tĭm'nath to shear his sheep.

14 And she put her widow's garments off from her, and covered her with a veil, and wrapped herself, and [q]sat in [3]an open place, which *is* by the way to Tĭm'nath; for she saw [r]that Shē'lah was grown, and she was not given unto him to wife.

15 When Jū'dah saw her, he thought her *to be* an harlot; because she had covered her face.

16 And he turned unto her by the way, and said, Go to, I pray thee, let me come in unto thee; (for he knew not that she *was* his daughter in law.) And she said, What wilt thou give me, that thou mayest come in unto me?

17 And he said, [s]I will send *thee* [4]a kid from the flock. And she said, Wilt [t]thou give *me* a pledge, till thou send *it?*

18 And he said, What pledge shall I give thee? And she said, Thy [u]signet, and thy bracelets, and thy staff that *is* in thine hand. And he gave *it* her, and came in unto her, and she conceived by him.

19 And she arose, and went away, and [v]laid by her veil from her, and put on the garments of her widowhood.

20 And Jū'dah sent the kid by the hand of his friend the A-dŭl'lăm-īte, to receive *his* pledge from the woman's hand: but he found her not.

21 Then he asked the men of that place, saying, Where *is* the harlot, that *was* [5]openly by the way side? And they said, There was no harlot in this *place*.

22 And he returned to Jū'dah, and said, I cannot find her; and also the men of the place said, *that* there was no harlot in this *place*.

23 And Jū'dah said, Let her take *it* to her, lest we [6]be shamed: behold, I sent this kid, and thou hast not found her.

24 ¶ And it came to pass about three months after, that it was told Jū'dah, saying, Tā'mar thy daughter in law hath [w]played the harlot; and also, behold, she *is* with child by whoredom. And Jū'dah said, Bring her forth, [x]and let her be burnt.

25 When she *was* brought forth, she sent to her father in law, saying, By the man, whose these *are, am* I with child: and she said, [y]Discern, I pray thee, whose *are* these, the signet, and bracelets, and staff.

26 And Jū'dah [z]acknowledged *them*, and said, [a]She hath been more righteous than I; because that [b]I gave her not to Shē'lah my son. And he knew her again [c]no more.

27 ¶ And it came to pass in the time of her travail, that, behold, twins *were* in her womb.

28 And it came to pass, when she travailed, that *the one* put out *his* hand: and the midwife took and bound upon his hand a scarlet thread, saying, This came out first.

29 And it came to pass, as he drew back his hand, that, behold, his brother came out: and she said, [7]How hast thou broken forth? *this* breach *be* upon thee: therefore his name was called [8]Pharez.

30 And afterward came out his brother, that had the scarlet thread upon his hand: and his name was called [9]Zā'rah.

39 And Jō'seph was brought down to Ē'ġypt; and [a]Pŏt'ĭ-phar, an officer of Phā'raōh, captain of the guard, an E-ġy̆p'tian, [b]bought him of the hands of the Ĭsh'me-el-ītes, which had brought him down thither.

2 And [c]the LORD was with Jō'seph, and he was a prosperous man; and he was in the house of his master the E-ġy̆p'tian.

3 And his master saw that the LORD *was* with him, and that the LORD [d]made all that he did to prosper in his hand.

4 And Jō'seph [e]found grace in his sight, and he served him: and he made him [f]overseer over his house, and all *that* he had he put into his hand.

5 And it came to pass from the time *that* he had made him overseer in his house, and over all that he had, that [g]the LORD blessed the E-ġy̆p'tian's house for Jō'seph's sake; and the blessing of the LORD was upon all that he had in the house, and in the field.

6 And he left all that he had in Jō'seph's hand; and he knew not ought he had, save the bread which he did eat. And Jō'seph was [h]*a* goodly *person*, and well favoured.

7 ¶ And it came to pass after these things, that his master's wife cast her eyes upon Jō'seph; and she said, [i]Lie with me.

8 But he refused, and said unto his master's wife, Behold, my master wotteth not what *is* with me in the house, and he hath committed all that he hath to my hand;

9 *There is* none greater in this house than I; neither hath he kept back any thing from me but thee, because thou *art* his wife: [j]how then can I do this great wickedness, and [k]sin against God?

9 [k]Deut. 25.6
10 [1]was evil in the eyes of the LORD
[l]Num. 26.19
11 [m]Ruth 1.13
[n]Lev. 22.13
12 [2]the days were multiplied
[o]2 Sam. 13.39
13 [p]Josh. 15.10-57; Judg. 14.1
14 [q]Prov. 7.12
[3]the door of eyes, or, of Enajim
[r]verses 11-26
17 [s]Ezek. 16.33
[4]a kid of the goats
[t]verse 20
18 [u]verse 25
19 [v]verse 14
21 [5]Or, in Enajim
23 [6]become a contempt
24 [w]Judg. 19.2
[x]Lev. 21.9; Deut. 22.21
25 [y]ch. 37.32
26 [z]ch. 37.33
[a]1 Sam. 24.17
[b]verse 14
[c]Job 34.31
29 [7]Or, wherefore hast thou made this breach against thee?
[8]That is, A breach; ch. 46.12; Num. 26.20; 1 Chr. 2.4; Matt. 1.3
30 [9]That is, East, or, Brightness

CHAPTER 39
1 [a]ch. 37.36; Ps. 105.17
[b]ch. 37.28
2 [c]ch. 21.22; ch. 26.24-28; Acts 7.9
3 [d]Ps. 1.3; Prov. 28.20
4 [e]ch. 18.3; ch. 19.19
[f]ch. 24.2
5 [g]ch. 30.27
6 [h]1 Sam. 16.12
7 [i]2 Sam. 13.11
9 [j]Prov. 6.29-32
[k]ch. 20.6; Ps. 51.4

10 And it came to pass, as she spake
to Jō'seph day by day, that he hearkened not unto her, to lie by her, *or* to
be with her.
11 And it came to pass about this
time, that *Joseph* went into the house
to do his business; and *there was* none
of the men of the house there within.
12 And [l]she caught him by his garment, saying, Lie with me: and he left
his garment in her hand, and fled, and
got him out.
13 And it came to pass, when she
saw that he had left his garment in her
hand, and was fled forth,
14 That she called unto the men of
her house, and spake unto them, saying, See, he hath brought in an Hē'-
brew unto us to mock us; he came in
unto me to lie with me, and I cried with
a [1]loud voice:
15 And it came to pass, when he
heard that I lifted up my voice and
cried, that he left his garment with me,
and fled, and got him out.
16 And she laid up his garment by
her, until his lord came home.
17 And she [m]spake unto him according to these words, saying, The Hē'-
brew servant, which thou hast brought
unto us, came in unto me to mock me:
18 And it came to pass, as I lifted up
my voice and cried, that he left his garment with me, and fled out.
19 And it came to pass, when his
master heard the words of his wife,
which she spake unto him, saying, After this manner did thy servant to me;
that his [n]wrath was kindled.
20 And Jō'seph's master took him,
and [o]put him into the [p]prison, a place
where the king's prisoners *were* bound:
and he was there in the prison.
21 ¶ But the LORD was with Jō'seph,
and [2]shewed him mercy, and [q]gave
him favour in the sight of the keeper of
the prison.
22 And the keeper of the prison
[r]committed to Jō'seph's hand all the
prisoners that *were* in the prison; and
whatsoever they did there, he was the
doer *of it*.
23 The keeper of the prison looked
not to any thing *that was* under his
hand; because [s]the LORD was with
him, and *that* which he did, the LORD
made *it* to prosper.

40

40 And it came to pass after these
things, *that* the [a]butler of the
king of Ē'ġypt and *his* baker had offended their lord the king of Ē'ġypt.
2 And Phā'raōh was [b]wroth against
two *of* his officers, against the chief of
the butlers, and against the chief of the
bakers.
3 And [c]he put them in ward in the
house of the captain of the guard, into
the prison, the place where Jō'seph
was bound.
4 And the captain of the guard
charged Jō'seph with them, and he
served them: and they continued a season in ward.
5 ¶ And they dreamed a dream both
of them, each man his dream in one

12 [l]Prov. 7.13-etc
14 [1]great
17 [m]Ex. 23.1; Prov. 30.23
19 [n]Prov. 6.34
20 [o]Ps. 105.18; 1 Pet. 2.19
[p]ch. 40.3; ch. 41.14
21 [2]extended kindness unto him
[q]Ex. 3.21; Acts 7.9
22 [r]ch. 40.3-4
23 [s]verses 2-3; Prov. 11.11
CHAPTER 40
1 [a]Neh. 1.11
2 [b]Prov. 16.14
3 [c]ch. 39.20 Neh. 2.2
7 [1]are your faces evil?
8 [d]ch. 41.15
[e]ch. 41.16; Dan. 2.11
12 [f]Judg. 7.14; Dan. 4.19
13 [2]Or, reckon
[g]Ps. 3.3; Jer. 52.31
14 [3]remember me with thee
[h]Luke 23.42
[i]Josh. 2.12;
15 [j]ch. 39.20
16 [4]Or, full of holes
17 [5]meat of Pharaoh, the work of a baker, or, cook
19 [6]Or, reckon thee, and take thy office from thee
20 [k]Matt. 14.6
[l]Mark 6.21
[7]Or, reckoned
[m]Matt. 25.19
21 [n]verse 13
[o]Neh. 2.1
22 [p]Esth. 7.10
23 [q]Job 19.14;

night, each man according to the interpretation of his dream, the butler and
the baker of the king of Ē'ġypt, which
were bound in the prison.
6 And Jō'seph came in unto them in
the morning, and looked upon them,
and, behold, they *were* sad.
7 And he asked Phā'raōh's officers
that *were* with him in the ward of his
lord's house, saying, Wherefore [1]look
ye *so* sadly to day?
8 And they said unto him, [d]We have
dreamed a dream, and *there is* no interpreter of it. And Jō'seph said unto
them, [e]*Do* not interpretations *belong*
to God? tell me *them,* I pray you.
9 And the chief butler told his dream
to Jō'seph, and said to him, In my
dream, behold, a vine *was* before me;
10 And in the vine *were* three
branches: and it *was* as though it budded, *and* her blossoms shot forth; and
the clusters thereof brought forth ripe
grapes:
11 And Phā'raōh's cup *was* in my
hand: and I took the grapes, and
pressed them into Phā'raōh's cup, and
I gave the cup into Phā'raōh's hand.
12 And Jō'seph said unto him, [f]This
is the interpretation of it: The three
branches *are* three days:
13 Yet within three days shall Phā'-
raōh [2g]lift up thine head, and restore
thee unto thy place: and thou shalt deliver Phā'raōh's cup into his hand, after the former manner when thou wast
his butler.
14 But [3h]think on me when it shall
be well with thee, and [i]shew kindness,
I pray thee, unto me, and make mention of me unto Phā'raōh, and bring
me out of this house:
15 For indeed I was stolen away out
of the land of the Hē'brews: and [j]here
also have I done nothing that they
should put me into the dungeon.
16 When the chief baker saw that
the interpretation was good, he said
unto Jō'seph, I also *was* in my dream,
and, behold, *I had* three [4]white baskets
on my head:
17 And in the uppermost basket
there was of all manner of [5]bakemeats
for Phā'raōh; and the birds did eat
them out of the basket upon my head.
18 And Jō'seph answered and said,
This *is* the interpretation thereof: The
three baskets *are* three days:
19 Yet within three days shall Phā'-
raōh [6]lift up thy head from off thee,
and shall hang thee on a tree; and the
birds shall eat thy flesh from off thee.
20 ¶ And it came to pass the third
day, *which was* [k]Phā'raōh's birthday,
that he [l]made a feast unto all his servants: and he [7m]lifted up the head of
the chief butler and of the chief baker
among his servants.
21 And he [n]restored the chief butler
unto his butlership again; and he [o]gave
the cup into Phā'raōh's hand:
22 But he [p]hanged the chief baker:
as Jō'seph had interpreted to them.
23 Yet did not the chief butler remember Jō'seph, but [q]forgat him.

41 And it came to pass at the end of two full years, that Phā'raōh dreamed: and, behold, he stood by the river.
2 And, behold, there came up out of the river seven well favoured kine and fatfleshed; and they fed in a meadow.
3 And, behold, seven other kine came up after them out of the river, ill favoured and leanfleshed; and stood by the *other* kine upon the brink of the river.
4 And the ill favoured and leanfleshed kine did eat up the seven well favoured and fat kine. So Phā'raōh awoke.
5 And he slept and dreamed the second time: and, behold, seven ears of corn came up upon one stalk, [1]rank and good.
6 And, behold, seven thin ears and blasted with the east wind sprung up after them.
7 And the seven thin ears devoured the seven rank and full ears. And Phā'raōh awoke, and, behold, *it was* a dream.
8 And it came to pass in the morning [a]that his spirit was troubled; and he sent and called for all [b]the magicians of Ē'ġypt, and all the [c]wise men thereof: and Phā'raōh told them his dream; but *there was* none that could interpret them unto Phā'raōh.
9 ¶ Then spake the chief butler unto Phā'raōh, saying, I do remember my faults this day:
10 Phā'raōh was [d]wroth with his servants, [e]and put me in ward in the captain of the guard's house, *both* me and the chief baker:
11 And [f]we dreamed a dream in one night, I and he; we dreamed each man according to the interpretation of his dream.
12 And [g]*there was* there with us a young man, an Hē'brew, [h]servant to the captain of the guard; and we told him, and he [i]interpreted to us our dreams; to each man according to his dream he did interpret.
13 And it came to pass, [j]as he interpreted to us, so it was; me he restored unto mine office, and him he hanged.
14 ¶ Then [k]Phā'raōh sent and called Jō'seph, and they [l2]brought him hastily [m]out of the dungeon: and he shaved *himself*, and changed his raiment, and came in unto Phā'raōh.
15 And Phā'raōh said unto Jō'seph, I have dreamed a dream, and *there is* none that can interpret it: [n]and I have heard say of thee, *that* [3]thou canst understand a dream to interpret it.
16 And Jō'seph answered Phā'raōh, saying, [o]*It is* not in me: [p]God shall give Phā'raōh an answer of peace.
17 And Phā'raōh said unto Jō'seph, In my dream, behold, I stood upon the bank of the river:
18 And, behold, there came up out of the river seven kine, fatfleshed and well favoured; and they fed in a meadow:

CHAPTER 41
5 [1]fat
8 [a]Dan. 4.5
[b]Ex. 7.11; Isa. 29.14; Dan. 1.20; Dan. 2.2
[c]Matt. 2.1
10 [d]ch. 40.2-3
[e]ch. 39.20
11 [f]ch. 40.5
12 [g]2 Ki. 5.4
[h]ch. 37.36
[i]ch. 40.12
13 [j]ch. 40.22
14 [k]Ps. 105.20
[l]Dan. 2.25
[2]made him run
[m]1 Sam. 2.8; Ps. 113.7-8
15 [n]Ps. 25.14; Dan. 5.16
[3]Or, when thou hearest a dream thou canst interpret it
16 [o]Ps. 25.14; Prov. 3.32; Dan. 2.30; Amos 3.7; John 15.15; Acts 3.12; 2 Cor. 3.5
[p]ch. 40.8; Deut. 29.29; Dan. 2.22-28-47; Dan. 4.2
21 [4]come to the inward parts of them
23 [5]Or, small
24 [q]Ps. 60.11; Ps. 118.8; Ps. 146.3; Isa. 8.19; Dan. 4.7
25 [r]Dan. 2.28-29-45; Rev. 4.1
27 [s]2 Ki. 8.1
30 [t]ch. 47.13; 1 Ki. 17.1; Ps. 105.16
31 [6]heavy
32 [7]Or, prepared of God
34 [8]Or, overseers
36 [9]be not cut off
38 [u]Num. 27.18; Job 32.8; Prov. 2.6; Dan. 4.8; Dan. 5.11

19 And, behold, seven other kine came up after them, poor and very ill favoured and leanfleshed, such as I never saw in all the land of Ē'ġypt for badness:
20 And the lean and the ill favoured kine did eat up the first seven fat kine:
21 And when they had [4]eaten them up, it could not be known that they had eaten them; but they *were* still ill favoured, as at the beginning. So I awoke.
22 And I saw in my dream, and, behold, seven ears came up in one stalk, full and good:
23 And, behold, seven ears, [5]withered, thin, *and* blasted with the east wind, sprung up after them:
24 And the thin ears devoured the seven good ears: and [q]I told *this* unto the magicians; but *there was* none that could declare *it* to me.
25 ¶ And Jō'seph said unto Phā'raōh, The dream of Phā'raōh *is* one: [r]God hath shewed Phā'raōh what he *is* about to do.
26 The seven good kine *are* seven years; and the seven good ears *are* seven years: the dream *is* one.
27 And the seven thin and ill favoured kine that came up after them *are* seven years; and the seven empty ears blasted with the east wind shall be [s]seven years of famine.
28 This *is* the thing which I have spoken unto Phā'raōh: What God *is* about to do he sheweth unto Phā'raōh.
29 Behold, there come seven years of great plenty throughout all the land of Ē'ġypt:
30 And there shall arise after them seven years of famine; and all the plenty shall be forgotten in the land of Ē'ġypt; and the famine shall [t]consume the land;
31 And the plenty shall not be known in the land by reason of that famine following; for it *shall be* very [6]grievous.
32 And for that the dream was doubled unto Phā'raōh twice; *it is* because the thing *is* [7]established by God, and God will shortly bring it to pass.
33 Now therefore let Phā'raōh look out a man discreet and wise, and set him over the land of Ē'ġypt.
34 Let Phā'raōh do *this*, and let him appoint [8]officers over the land, and take up the fifth part of the land of Ē'ġypt in the seven plenteous years.
35 And let them gather all the food of those good years that come, and lay up corn under the hand of Phā'raōh, and let them keep food in the cities.
36 And that food shall be for store to the land against the seven years of famine, which shall be in the land of Ē'ġypt; that the land [9]perish not through the famine.
37 ¶ And the thing was good in the eyes of Phā'raōh, and in the eyes of all his servants.
38 And Phā'raōh said unto his servants, Can we find *such a one* as this *is*, a man [u]in whom the Spirit of God *is*?

39 And Phā′raōh said unto Jō′seph, Forasmuch as God hath shewed thee all this, *there is* none so discreet and wise as thou *art:*

40 Thou shalt be over my house, and according unto thy word shall all my people [10]be ruled: only in the throne will I be greater than thou.

41 And Phā′raōh said unto Jō′seph, See, I [v]have set thee over all the land of Ē′ġypt.

42 And Phā′raōh [w]took off his ring from his hand, and put it upon Jō′-seph's hand, and arrayed him in vestures of [11]fine linen, and [x]put a gold chain about his neck;

43 And he made him to ride in the second chariot which he had; and they cried before him, [12]Bow the knee: and he made him *ruler* over all the land of Ē′ġypt.

44 And Phā′raōh said unto Jō′seph, I *am* Phā′raōh, and without thee shall no man lift up his hand or foot in all the land of Ē′ġypt.

45 And Phā′raōh called Jō′seph's name [13]Zăph′nath–pā-a-nē′ah; and he gave him to wife Ās′e-năth the daughter of Po-tĭ′phe-rah [14]priest of Ōn. And Jō′seph went out over *all* the land of Ē′ġypt.

46 ¶ And Jō′seph *was* thirty years old when he [y]stood before Phā′raōh king of Ē′ġypt. And Jō′seph went out from the presence of Phā′raōh, and went throughout all the land of Ē′ġypt.

47 And in the seven plenteous years the earth brought forth by handfuls.

48 And he gathered up all the food of the seven years, which were in the land of Ē′ġypt, and laid up the food in the cities: the food of the field, which *was* round about every city, laid he up in the same.

49 And Jō′seph gathered corn [z]as the sand of the sea, very much, until he left numbering; for *it was* without number.

50 And [a]unto Jō′seph were born two sons before the years of famine came, which Ās′e-năth the daughter of Po-tĭ-′phe-rah [15]priest of Ōn bare unto him.

51 And Jō′seph called the name of the firstborn [16]Ma-năs′seh: For God, *said he,* hath made me forget all my toil, and all my father's house.

52 And the name of the second called he [17]Ē′phră-ĭm: For God hath caused me to be fruitful in the land of my affliction.

53 ¶ And the seven years of plenteousness, that was in the land of Ē′ġypt, were ended.

54 And [b]the seven years of dearth began to come, according as Jō′seph had said: and the dearth was in all lands; but in all the land of Ē′ġypt there was bread.

55 And when all the land of Ē′ġypt was famished, the people cried to Phā′-raōh for bread: and Phā′raōh said unto all the E-ġy̆p′tians; Go unto Jō′seph; what he saith to you, do.

56 And the famine was over all the face of the earth: And Jō′seph opened [18]all the storehouses, and sold [c]unto the E-ġy̆p′tians; and the famine waxed sore in the land of Ē′ġypt.

57 And [d]all countries came into Ē′ġypt to Jō′seph for to buy *corn;* because that the famine was [e]*so* sore in all lands.

42 Now when [a]Jā′cob saw that there was corn in Ē′ġypt, Jā′cob said unto his sons, Why do ye look one upon another?

2 And he said, Behold, I have heard that there is corn in Ē′ġypt: get you down thither, and buy for us from thence; that we may [b]live, and not die.

3 ¶ And Jō′seph's ten brethren went down to buy corn in Ē′ġypt.

4 But Bĕn′ja-min, Jō′seph's brother, Jā′cob sent not with his brethren; for he said, [c]Lest peradventure mischief befall him.

5 And the sons of Ĭs′ra-el came to buy *corn* among those that came: for the famine was [d]in the land of Cā′-năan.

6 And Jō′seph *was* the governor [e]over the land, *and* he *it was* that sold to all the people of the land: and Jō′-seph's brethren came, and [f]bowed down themselves before him *with* their faces to the earth.

7 And Jō′seph saw his brethren, and he knew them, but made himself strange unto them, and spake [1]roughly unto them; and he said unto them, Whence come ye? And they said, From the land of Cā′năan to buy food.

8 And Jō′seph knew his brethren, but they knew not him.

9 And Jō′seph [g]remembered the dreams which he dreamed of them, and said unto them, Ye *are* spies; to see the nakedness of the land ye are come.

10 And they said unto him, Nay, my lord, but to buy food are thy servants come.

11 We *are* all one man's sons; we *are* true *men,* thy servants are no spies.

12 And he said unto them, Nay, but to see the nakedness of the land ye are come.

13 And they said, Thy servants *are* twelve brethren, the sons of one man in the land of Cā′năan; and, behold, the youngest *is* this day with our father, and one [h]*is* not.

14 And Jō′seph said unto them, That *is it* that I spake unto you, saying, Ye *are* spies:

15 Hereby ye shall be proved: [i]By the life of Phā′raōh ye shall not go forth hence, except your youngest brother come hither.

16 Send one of you, and let him fetch your brother, and ye shall be [2]kept in prison, that your words may be proved, whether *there be any* truth in you: or else by the life of Phā′raōh surely ye *are* spies.

17 And he [3]put them all together into ward three days.

18 And Jō′seph said unto them the third day, This do, and live; *for* [j]I fear God:

40 [10]be armed, or, kiss
41 [v]Ps. 105.21; Prov. 14.35; Eccl. 4.13-14; Dan. 6.3; Acts 7.10
42 [w]Esth. 3.10; Esth. 8.2 [11]Or, silk [x]Dan. 5.29 revealed.
43 [12]Abrech, or, Tender father
45 [13]Which in the Coptic signifies, A revealer of secrets, or, The man to whom secrets are [14]Or, prince; Ex. 2.16; 2 Sam. 20.26
46 [y]1 Sam. 16.21; 1 Ki. 12.6-8; Dan. 1.19
49 [z]ch. 22.17; Ps. 78.27
50 [a]ch. 46.20; ch. 48.5 [15]Or, prince
51 [16]That is, Forgetting
52 [17]That is, Fruitful
54 [b]Ps. 105.16; Acts 7.11
56 [18]all wherein was [c]ch. 42.6; Prov. 11.26
57 [d]Deut. 9.28 [e]ch. 12.10; 2 Ki. 8.1

CHAPTER 42
1 [a]Acts 7.12
2 [b]ch. 43.8; Isa. 38.1
4 [c]verse 38
5 [d]ch. 12.10; Acts 7.11
6 [e]ch. 41.41 [f]ch. 27.29; Isa. 60.14
7 [1]hard things with them
9 [g]ch. 37.5-9
13 [h]ch. 37.30; Lam. 5.7
15 [i]1 Sam. 1.26; 1 Sam. 17.55
16 [2]bound
17 [3]gathered
18 [j]Lev. 25.43; Neh. 5.15

19 If ye *be* true *men,* let one of your brethren be bound in the house of your prison: go ye, carry corn for the famine of your houses:

20 But [k]bring your youngest brother unto me; so shall your words be verified, and ye shall not die. And they did so.

21 ¶ And they said one to another, [l]We *are* verily guilty concerning our brother, in that we saw the anguish of his soul, when he besought us, and we would not hear; [m]therefore is this distress come upon us.

22 And Reu̧'ben answered them, saying, [n]Spake I not unto you, saying, Do not sin against the child; and ye would not hear? therefore, behold, also his blood is [o]required.

23 And they knew not that Jō'seph understood *them;* for [4]he spake unto them by an interpreter.

24 And he turned himself about from them, and wept; and returned to them again, and communed with them, and took from them Sĭm'e-on, and bound him before their eyes.

25 ¶ Then Jō'seph commanded to fill their sacks with corn, and to restore every man's money into his sack, and to give them provision for the way: and [p]thus did he unto them.

26 And they laded their asses with the corn, and departed thence.

27 And as [q]one of them opened his sack to give his ass provender in the inn, he espied his money; for, behold, it *was* in his sack's mouth.

28 And he said unto his brethren, My money is restored; and, lo, *it is* even in my sack: and their heart [5]failed *them,* and they were afraid, saying one to another, What *is* this *that* God hath done unto us?

29 ¶ And they came unto Jā'cob their father unto the land of Cā'năan, and told him all that befell unto them; saying,

30 The man, *who is* the lord of the land, [r]spake [6]roughly to us, and took us for spies of the country.

31 And we said unto him, We *are* true *men;* we are no spies:

32 We *be* twelve brethren, sons of our father; one *is* not, and the youngest *is* this day with our father in the land of Cā'năan.

33 And the man, the lord of the country, said unto us, [s]Hereby shall I know that ye *are* true *men;* leave one of your brethren *here* with me, and take *food for* the famine of your households, and be gone:

34 And bring your youngest brother unto me: then shall I know that ye *are* no spies, but *that* ye *are* true *men: so* will I deliver you your brother, and ye shall [t]traffick in the land.

35 ¶ And it came to pass as they emptied their sacks, that, behold, [u]every man's bundle of money *was* in his sack: and when *both* they and their father saw the bundles of money, they were afraid.

36 And Jā'cob their father said unto them, Me have ye [v]bereaved *of my children:* Jō'seph *is* not, and Sĭm'e-on *is* not, and ye will take Bĕn'ja-min *away:* all these things are against me.

37 And Reu̧'ben spake unto his father, saying, Slay my two sons, if I bring him not to thee: deliver him into my hand, and I will bring him to thee again.

38 And he said, My son shall not go down with you; for his [w]brother is dead, and he is left alone: [x]if mischief befall him by the way in the which ye go, then shall ye [y]bring down my gray hairs with sorrow to the grave.

43 And the famine *was* [a]sore in the land.

2 And it came to pass, when they had eaten up the corn which they had brought out of Ē'gypt, their father said unto them, Go again, buy us a little food.

3 And Jū'dah spake unto him, saying, The man [1]did solemnly protest unto us, saying, Ye shall not see my face, except [b]your brother *be* with you.

4 If thou wilt send our brother with us, we will go down and buy thee food:

5 But if thou wilt not send *him,* we will not go down: for the man said unto us, Ye shall not see my face, except your brother *be* with you.

6 And Ĭs'ra-el said, Wherefore dealt ye *so* ill with me, *as* to tell the man whether ye had yet a brother?

7 And they said, The man [2]asked us straitly of our state, and of our kindred, saying, *Is* your father yet alive? have ye *another* brother? and we told him according to the [3]tenor of these words: [4]could we certainly know that he would say, Bring your brother down?

8 And Jū'dah said unto Ĭs'ra-el his father, Send the lad with me, and we will arise and go; that we may live, and not die, both we, and thou, *and* also our little ones.

9 I will be surety for him; of my hand shalt thou require him: [c]if I bring him not unto thee, and set him before thee, then let me bear the blame for ever:

10 For except we had lingered, surely now we had returned [5]this second time.

11 And their father Ĭs'ra-el said unto them, If *it must be* so now, do this; take of the best fruits in the land in your vessels, and [d]carry down the man a present, a [e]little balm, and a little honey, spices, and myrrh, nuts, and almonds:

12 And take double money in your hand; and the money [f]that was brought again in the mouth of your sacks, carry *it* again in your hand; peradventure it *was* an oversight:

13 Take also your brother, and arise, go again unto the man:

14 And [g]God Almighty give you mercy before the man, that he may send away your other brother, and Bĕn'ja-min. [6]If I be bereaved *of my children,* I am bereaved.

20 [k]verse 34; ch. 43.5; ch. 44.23
21 [l]Job 36.8-9; Hos. 5.15
[m]Ps. 107.17; Prov. 5.22; Prov. 11.21; Prov. 21.13; Matt. 7.2
22 [n]ch. 37.21
[o]ch. 9.5; 1 Ki. 2.32; 2 Chr. 24.22; Ps. 9.12; Luke 11.50-51
23 [4]an interpreter was between them
25 [p]Matt. 5.44; Rom. 12.17-20-21; 1 Pet. 3.9
27 [q]ch. 43.21
28 [5]went forth
30 [r]verse 7
[6]with us hard things
33 [s]verses 15-19-20
34 [t]ch. 34.10
35 [u]ch. 43.21
36 [v]ch. 43.14
38 [w]verse 13; ch. 44.28
[x]verse 4; ch. 44.29
[y]ch. 37.35; ch. 44.31

CHAPTER 43
1 [a]ch. 12.10; Lam. 5.10
3 [1]protesting protested
[b]ch. 42.20; ch. 44.23
7 [2]asking asked us
[3]mouth
[4]knowing could we know
9 [c]ch. 44.32; Philem. 18-19
10 [5]Or, twice by this
11 [d]ch. 32.20; Prov. 18.16
[e]ch. 37.25; Ezek. 27.17
12 [f]ch. 42.25-35
14 [g]1 Sam. 14.6; Nah. 1.7
[6]Or, and I, as I have been, etc; Esth. 4.16

15 ¶ And the men took that present, and they took double money in their hand, and Bĕn'ja-min; and rose up, and went down to Ē'ġypt, and stood before Jō'seph.

16 And when Jō'seph saw Bĕn'jamin with them, he said to [h]the ruler of his house, Bring *these* men home, and [7]slay, and make ready; for *these* men shall [8]dine with me at noon.

17 And the man did as Jō'seph bade; and the man brought the men into Jō'seph's house.

18 And the men were afraid, because they were brought into Jō'seph's house; and they said, Because of the money that was returned in our sacks at the first time are we brought in; that he may [9]seek occasion against us, and fall upon us, and take us for bondmen, and our asses.

19 And they came near to the steward of Jō'seph's house, and they communed with him at the door of the house,

20 And said, O sir, [10]we came indeed down at the first time to buy food:

21 And [i]it came to pass, when we came to the inn, that we opened our sacks, and, behold, *every* man's money *was* in the mouth of his sack, our money in full weight: and we have brought it again in our hand.

22 And other money have we brought down in our hands to buy food: we cannot tell who put our money in our sacks.

23 And he said, Peace *be* to you, fear not: your God, and the God of your father, hath given you treasure in your sacks: [11]I had your money. And he brought Sĭm'e-on out unto them.

24 And the man brought the men into Jō'seph's house, and [j]gave *them* water, and they washed their feet; and he gave their asses provender.

25 And they made ready the present against Jō'seph came at noon: for they heard that they should eat bread there.

26 ¶ And when Jō'seph came home, they brought him the present which *was* in their hand into the house, and [k]bowed themselves to him to the earth.

27 And he asked them of *their* [12]welfare, and said, [13]*Is* your father well, the old man of [l]whom ye spake? *Is* he yet alive?

28 And they answered, Thy servant our father *is* in good health, he *is* yet alive. [m]And they bowed down their heads, and made obeisance.

29 And he lifted up his eyes, and saw his brother Bĕn'ja-min, [n]his mother's son, and said, *Is* this your younger brother, [o]of whom ye spake unto me? And he said, God be gracious unto thee, my son.

30 And Jō'seph made haste; [p]for his bowels did yearn upon his brother: and he sought *where* to weep; and he entered into *his* chamber, and [q]wept there.

31 And he washed his face, and went out, and refrained himself, and said, Set on [r]bread.

32 And they set on for him by himself, and for them by themselves, and for the E-ġy̆p'tians, which did eat with him, by themselves: because the E-ġy̆p'tians might not eat bread with the Hē'brews; for that *is* an [s]abomination unto the E-ġy̆p'tians.

33 And they sat before him, the firstborn according to his birthright, and the youngest according to his youth: and the men marvelled one at another.

34 And he took *and sent* messes unto them from before him: but Bĕn'ja-min's mess was [t]five times so much as any of theirs. And they drank, and [14]were merry with him.

44 And he commanded [1]the steward of his house, saying, Fill the men's sacks *with* food, as much as they can carry, and put every man's money in his sack's mouth.

2 And put my cup, the silver cup, in the sack's mouth of the youngest, and his corn money. And he did according to the word that Jō'seph had spoken.

3 As soon as the morning was light, the men were sent away, they and their asses.

4 *And* when they were gone out of the city, *and* not *yet* far off, Jō'seph said unto his steward, Up, follow after the men; and when thou dost overtake them, say unto them, Wherefore have ye rewarded evil for good?

5 *Is* not this *it* in which my lord drinketh, and whereby indeed he [2]divineth? ye have done evil in so doing.

6 ¶ And he overtook them, and he spake unto them these same words.

7 And they said unto him, Wherefore saith my lord these words? God forbid that thy servants should do according to this thing:

8 Behold, [a]the money, which we found in our sacks' mouths, we brought again unto thee out of the land of Cā'năan: how then should we steal out of thy lord's house silver or gold?

9 With whomsoever of thy servants it be found, [b]both let him die, and we also will be my lord's bondmen.

10 And he said, Now also *let* it *be* according unto your words: he with whom it is found shall be my servant; and ye shall be blameless.

11 Then they speedily took down every man his sack to the ground, and opened every man his sack.

12 And he searched, *and* began at the eldest, and left at the youngest: and the cup was found in Bĕn'ja-min's sack.

13 Then they [c]rent their clothes, and laded every man his ass, and returned to the city.

14 ¶ And Jū'dah and his brethren came to Jō'seph's house; for he *was* yet there: and they [d]fell before him on the ground.

15 And Jō'seph said unto them, What deed *is* this that ye have done? wot ye not that such a man as I can certainly [3]divine?

16 And Jū'dah said, [e]What shall we say unto my lord? what shall we speak?

16 [h]ch. 24.2; ch. 39.4; ch. 44.1 [7]kill a killing; 1 Sam. 25.11 [8]eat
18 [9]roll himself upon us; Job 30.14
20 [10]coming down we came down; ch. 42.3-10
21 [i]ch. 42.27-35
23 [11]your money came to me
24 [j]ch. 18.4; ch. 24.32; Luke 7.44; John 13.5; 1 Tim. 5.10
26 [k]ch. 27.29; ch. 33.6; ch. 37.7-10; Ruth 2.10
27 [12]peace; ch. 37.14 [13]Is there peace to your father? [l]ch. 42.11-13
28 [m]ch. 37.7-10; Prov. 14.19
29 [n]ch. 35.17-18 [o]ch. 42.13
30 [p]1 Ki. 3.26; Jer. 31.20 [q]ch. 42.24; 2 Sam. 18.33
31 [r]verse 25
32 [s]ch. 46.34; Ex. 8.26
34 [t]ch. 45.22 [14]drank largely; Hag. 1.6; John 2.10
CHAPTER 44
1 [1]him that was over his house
5 [2]Or, maketh trial
8 [a]ch. 43.21
9 [b]ch. 31.32
13 [c]ch. 37.29-34; Num. 14.6; 2 Sam. 1.11
14 [d]ch. 37.7
15 [3]Or, make trial; verse 5
16 [e]Job 40.4

or how shall we clear ourselves? God hath found out the iniquity of thy servants: behold, [f]we *are* my lord's servants, both we, and *he* also with whom the cup is found.

17 And he said, [g]God forbid that I should do so: *but* the man in whose hand the cup is found, he shall be my servant; and as for you, get you up in peace unto your father.

18 ¶ Then Jū'dah came near unto him, and said, Oh my lord, let thy servant, I pray thee, speak a word in my lord's ears, and [h]let not thine anger burn against thy servant: for thou *art* [i]even as Phā'raōh.

19 My lord asked his servants, saying, Have ye a father, or a brother?

20 And we said unto my lord, We have a father, an old man, and [j]a child of his old age, a little one; and his brother is dead, and he alone is left of his mother, and his father loveth him.

21 And thou saidst unto thy servants, [k]Bring him down unto me, that I may set mine eyes upon him.

22 And we said unto my lord, The lad cannot leave his father: for *if* he should leave his father, *his father* would die.

23 And thou saidst unto thy servants, [l]Except your youngest brother come down with you, ye shall see my face no more.

24 And it came to pass when we came up unto thy servant my father, we told him the words of my lord.

25 And [m]our father said, Go again, *and* buy us a little food.

26 And we said, We cannot go down: if our youngest brother be with us, then will we go down: for we may not see the man's face, except our youngest brother *be* with us.

27 And thy servant my father said unto us, Ye know that [n]my wife bare me two *sons:*

28 And the one went out from me, and I said, [o]Surely he is torn in pieces; and I saw him not since:

29 And if ye [p]take this also from me, and mischief befall him, ye shall bring down my gray hairs with sorrow to the grave.

30 Now therefore when I come to thy servant my father, and the lad *be* not with us; seeing [q]that his life is bound up in the lad's life;

31 It shall come to pass, when he seeth that the lad *is* not *with us,* that he will die: and thy servants shall bring down the gray hairs of thy servant our father with sorrow to the grave.

32 For thy servant became surety for the lad unto my father, saying, If [r]I bring him not unto thee, then I shall bear the blame to my father for ever.

33 Now therefore, I pray thee, [s]let thy servant abide instead of the lad a bondman to my lord; and let the lad go up with his brethren.

34 For how shall I go up to my father, and the lad *be* not with me? lest peradventure I see the evil that shall [4]come on my father.

45

Then Jō'seph could not refrain himself before all them that stood by him; and he cried, Cause every man to go out from me. And there stood no man with him, while Jō'seph made himself known unto his brethren.

2 And he [1]wept aloud: and the Eġy̆p'tians and the house of Phā'raōh heard.

3 And Jō'seph said unto his brethren, [a]I *am* Jō'seph; doth my father yet live? And his brethren could not answer him; for they were [2]troubled at his presence.

4 And Jō'seph said unto his brethren, Come near to me, I pray you. And they came near. And he said, I *am* Jō'seph your brother, [b]whom ye sold into Ē'ġypt.

5 Now therefore [c]be not grieved, [3]nor angry with yourselves, that ye sold me hither: for [d]God did send me before you to preserve life.

6 For these two years *hath* the famine *been* in the land: and yet *there are* five years, in the which *there shall* neither *be* earing nor harvest.

7 And God sent me before you [4]to preserve you a posterity in the earth, and to save your lives by a great deliverance.

8 So now *it was* not you *that* sent me hither, but God: and he hath made me a [e]father to Phā'raōh, and lord of all his house, and a ruler throughout all the land of Ē'ġypt.

9 Haste ye, and go up to my father, and say unto him, Thus saith thy son Jō'seph, God hath made me lord of all Ē'ġypt: come down unto me, tarry not:

10 And [f]thou shalt dwell in the land of Gō'shen, and thou shalt be near unto me, thou, and thy children, and thy children's children, and thy flocks, and thy herds, and all that thou hast:

11 And there will I nourish thee; for [g]yet *there are* five years of famine; lest thou, and thy household, and all that thou hast, come to poverty.

12 And, behold, your eyes see, and the eyes of my brother Bĕn'ja-min, that *it is* [h]my mouth that speaketh unto you.

13 And ye shall tell my father of all my glory in Ē'ġypt, and of all that ye have seen; and ye shall haste and [i]bring down my father hither.

14 And he fell upon his brother Bĕn'ja-min's neck, and wept; and Bĕn'ja-min wept upon his neck.

15 Moreover he kissed all his brethren, and wept upon them: and after that his brethren talked with him.

16 ¶ And the fame thereof was heard in Phā'raōh's house, saying, Jō'seph's brethren are come: and it [5]pleased Phā'raōh well, and his servants.

17 And Phā'raōh said unto Jō'seph, Say unto thy brethren, This do ye; lade your beasts, and go, get you unto the land of Cā'năan;

18 And take your father and your households, and come unto me: and I will give you the good of the land of Ē'ġypt, and ye shall eat [j]the fat of the land.

[f]verse 9
17 [g]Josh. 22.29; Gal. 6.14
18 [h]ch. 18.30-32; Ex. 32.22
[i]ch. 41.40; Prov. 19.12
20 [j]ch. 37.3
21 [k]ch. 42.15-20
23 [l]ch. 43.3-5
25 [m]ch. 43.2
27 [n]ch. 46.19
28 [o]ch. 37.33
29 [p]ch. 42.36-38
30 [q]1 Sam. 18.1
32 [r]ch. 43.9
33 [s]Ex. 32.32
34 [4]find my father; Ex. 18.8; Job 31.29; Ps. 116.3; Ps. 119.143

CHAPTER 45
2 [1]gave forth his voice in weeping; Num. 14.1
3 [a]Acts 7.13 [2]Or, terrified; Job 4.5; Job 23.15; Ps. 77.4; Zech. 12.10; Matt. 14.26; Mark 6.50
4 [b]ch. 37.28
5 [c]Isa. 40.2; [3]neither let there be anger in your eyes
[d]ch. 50.20;
7 [4]to put for you a remnant
8 [e]ch. 41.43;
10 [f]ch. 47.1
11 [g]1 Tim. 5.4
12 [h]ch. 42.23
13 [i]Acts 7.14
16 [5]was good in the eyes of Pharaoh; ch. 41.37
18 [j]ch. 27.28

19 Now thou art commanded, this do ye; take you wagons out of the land of Ē′ġypt for your little ones, and for your wives, and bring your father, and come.

20 Also [6]regard not your stuff; for the good of all the land of Ē′ġypt *is* yours.

21 And the children of Ĭs′ra-el did so: and Jō′seph gave them wagons, according to the [7]commandment of Phā′raōh, and gave them provision for the way.

22 To all of them he gave each man changes of raiment; but to Bĕn′ja-min he gave three hundred *pieces* of silver, and five changes of raiment.

23 And to his father he sent after this *manner;* ten asses [8]laden with the good things of Ē′ġypt, and ten she asses laden with corn and bread and meat for his father by the way.

24 So he sent his brethren away, and they departed: and he said unto them, See that ye fall not out by the way.

25 ¶ And they went up out of Ē′ġypt, and came into the land of Cā′năan unto Jā′cob their father,

26 And told him, saying, Jō′seph *is* yet alive, and he *is* governor over all the land of Ē′ġypt. [k]And [9]Jā′cob's heart fainted, for he believed them not.

27 And they told him all the words of Jō′seph, which he had said unto them: and when he saw the wagons which Jō′seph had sent to carry him, the spirit of Jā′cob their father revived:

28 And Ĭs′ra-el said, *It is* enough; Jō′seph my son *is* yet alive: I will go and see him before I die.

46 And Ĭs′ra-el took his journey with all that he had, and came [a]to Bē′er–shē′bȧ, and offered sacrifices unto [b]the God of his father Ī′saac.

2 And God spake unto Ĭs′ra-el [c]in the visions of the night, and said, Jā′cob, Jā′cob. And he said, Here *am* I.

3 And he said, I *am* God, [d]the God of thy father: fear not to go down into Ē′ġypt; for I will there make [e]of thee a great nation:

4 [f]I will go down with thee into Ē′ġypt; and I will also surely [g]bring thee up *again:* and [h]Jō′seph shall put his hand upon thine eyes.

5 And [i]Jā′cob rose up from Bē′er–shē′bȧ: and the sons of Ĭs′ra-el carried Jā′cob their father, and their little ones, and their wives, in the wagons which Phā′raōh had sent to carry him.

6 And they took their cattle, and their goods, which they had gotten in the land of Cā′năan, and came into Ē′ġypt, [j]Jā′cob, and all his seed with him:

7 His sons, and his sons' sons with him, his daughters, and his sons' daughters, and all his seed brought he with him into Ē′ġypt.

8 ¶ And [k]these *are* the names of the children of Ĭs′ra-el, which came into Ē′ġypt, Jā′cob and his sons: [l]Reu′ben, Jā′cob's firstborn.

9 And the sons of Reu′ben; Hā′noch, and Phăl′lū, and Hĕz′ron, and Cär′mī.

10 ¶ And [m]the sons of Sĭm′e-on; [1]Je-mū′el, and Jā′min, and Ō′hăd, and [2]Jā′chin, and [3]Zō′har, and Shā′ul the son of a Cā′năan-īt-ish woman.

11 ¶ And the sons of Lē′vī; [4]Gēr′shŏn, Kō′hath, and Me-rā′rī.

12 ¶ And the sons of Jū′dah; Ēr, and Ō′nan, and Shē′lah, and Phā′rĕz, and Zā′rah: but [n]Ēr and Ō′nan died in the land of Cā′năan. And [o]the sons of Phā′rĕz were Hĕz′ron and Hā′mŭl.

13 ¶ And the sons of Ĭs′sa-char; Tō′lȧ, and [5]Phū′vah, and Jōb, and Shĭm′ron.

14 ¶ And the sons of Zĕb′u-lun; Sē′red, and Ē′lon, and Jăh′lĕ-el.

15 These *be* the sons of Lē′ah, which she bare unto Jā′cob in Pā′dan–ā′ram, with his daughter Dī′nah: all the souls of his sons and his daughters *were* thirty and three.

16 ¶ And the sons of Găd; [p]Zĭph′ĭ-on, and Hăg′gī, Shu′nī, and [6]Ĕz′bŏn, Ē′rī, and [7]Ăr′ŏ-dī, and A-rē′lī.

17 ¶ And [q]the sons of Ăsh′ēr; Jĭm′nah, and Ĭsh′u-ah, and Ĭs′u-ī, and Be-rī′ah, and Sē′rah their sister: and the sons of Be-rī′ah; Hē′bēr, and Măl′chī-el.

18 These *are* [r]the sons of Zĭl-pah, whom Lā′ban gave to Lē′ah his daughter, and these she bare unto Jā′cob, *even* sixteen souls.

19 The sons of Rā′chel Jā′cob's wife; Jō′seph, and Bĕn′ja-min.

20 ¶ And [s]unto Jō′seph in the land of Ē′ġypt were born Ma-năs′seh and Ē′phră-ĭm, which Ăs′e-năth the daughter of Po-tī′–phe-rah [8]priest of Ōn bare unto him.

21 ¶ And [t]the sons of Bĕn′ja-min *were* Bē′lah, and Bē′chēr, and Ash′bel, Gē′rȧ, and Nā′a-man, [u]Ē′hī, and Rŏsh, [v]Mŭp′pim, and [9]Hŭp′pim, and Ȧrd.

22 These *are* the sons of Rā′chel, which were born to Jā′cob: all the souls *were* fourteen.

23 ¶ And [w]the sons of Dăn; [10]Hū′shim.

24 ¶ And [x]the sons of Năph′ta-lī; Jăh′zē-el, and Gū′nī, and Jē′zēr, and Shĭl′lem.

25 These [y]*are* the sons of Bĭl′hah, which [z]Lā′ban gave unto Rā′chel his daughter, and she bare these unto Jā′cob: all the souls *were* seven.

26 [a]All the souls that came with Jā′cob into Ē′ġypt, which came out of his [11]loins, besides Jā′cob's sons' wives, all the souls *were* threescore and six;

27 And the sons of Jō′seph, which were born him in Ē′ġypt, *were* two souls: [b]all the souls of the house of Jā′cob, which came into Ē′ġypt, *were* threescore and ten.

28 ¶ And he sent Jū′dah before him unto Jō′seph, [c]to direct his face unto Gō′shen; and they came into the land of Gō′shen.

29 And Jō′seph made ready his chariot, and went up to meet Ĭs′ra-el his father, to Gō′shen, and presented himself unto him; and he fell on his neck, and wept on his neck a good while.

20 [6]let not your eye spare, etc
21 [7]mouth
23 [8]carrying
26 [k]Job 29.24; Ps. 126.1; Luke 24.11-41 [9]his

CHAPTER 46

1 [a]ch. 21.31 [b]ch. 26.24; ch. 31.42
2 [c]ch. 15.1; Job 33.14-15
3 [d]ch. 28.13 [e]ch. 12.2; Ex. 1.9
4 [f]ch. 28.15; ch. 48.21 [g]ch. 15.16; Ex. 3.8 [h]ch. 50.1
5 [i]ch. 15.13; Acts 7.15
6 [j]Deut. 26.5; Isa. 52.4
8 [k]Ex. 1.1; Ex. 6.14 [l]Num. 26.5; 1 Chr. 5.1
10 [m]Ex. 6.15; 1 Chr. 4.24 [1]Or, Nemuel [2]Or, Jarib [3]Or, Zerah, 1 Chr. 4.24
11 [4]Or, Gershom
12 [n]ch. 38.3 [o]ch. 38.29; 1 Chr. 2.5
13 [5]Or, Puah, and Jashub
16 [p]Num. 26.15-Zephon [6]Or, Ozni [7]Or, Arod
17 [q]1 Chr. 7.30
18 [r]ch. 30.10
20 [s]ch. 41.50 [8]Or, prince
21 [t]1 Chr. 7.6 [u]Num. 26.38-Ahiram [v]Num. 26.39-Shupham; 1 Chr. 7.12-Shuppim [9]Hupham
23 [w]1 Cor. 7.12 [10]Or, Shuham
24 [x]1 Chr. 7.13
25 [y]ch. 30.5-7 [z]ch. 29.29
26 [a]Ex. 1.5 [11]thigh
27 [b]Deut. 10.22; Acts 7.14
28 [c]ch. 31.21

30 And Ĭs'ra-el said unto Jō'seph, Now [d]let me die, since I have seen thy face, because thou *art* yet alive.

31 And Jō'seph said unto his brethren, and unto his father's house, I will go up, and shew Phā'raōh, and say unto him, My brethren, and my father's house, which *were* in the land of Cā'năan, are come unto me;

32 And the men *are* shepherds, for [12]their trade hath been to feed cattle; and they have brought their flocks, and their herds, and all that they have.

33 And it shall come to pass, when Phā'raōh shall call you, and shall say, [e]What *is* your occupation?

34 That ye shall say, Thy servants' trade hath been about cattle [f]from our youth even until now, both we, *and* also our fathers: that ye may dwell in the land of Gō'shen; for every shepherd *is* [g]an abomination unto the Ē-ġȳp'tians.

47 Then Jō'seph [a]came and told Phā'raōh, and said, My father and my brethren, and their flocks, and their herds, and all that they have, are come out of the land of Cā'năan; and, behold, they *are* in the [b]land of Gō'shen.

2 And he took some of his brethren, *even* five men, and [c]presented them unto Phā'raōh.

3 And Phā'raōh said unto his brethren, [d]What *is* your occupation? And they said unto Phā'raōh, [e]Thy servants *are* shepherds, both we, *and* also our fathers.

4 They said moreover unto Phā'raōh, [f]For to sojourn in the land are we come; for thy servants have no pasture for their flocks; [g]for the famine *is* sore in the land of Cā'năan: now therefore, we pray thee, let thy servants [h]dwell in the land of Gō'shen.

5 And Phā'raōh spake unto Jō'seph, saying, Thy father and thy brethren are come unto thee:

6 The [i]land of Ē'ġypt *is* before thee; in the best of the land make thy father and brethren to dwell; in [j]the land of Gō'shen let them dwell: and if thou knowest *any* men of activity among them, then make them [k]rulers over my cattle.

7 And Jō'seph brought in Jā'cob his father, and set him before Phā'raōh: and Jā'cob blessed Phā'raōh.

8 And Phā'raōh said unto Jā'cob, [1]How old *art* thou?

9 And Jā'cob said unto Phā'raōh, The [l]days of the years of my pilgrimage *are* an hundred and thirty years: [m]few and evil have the days of the years of my life been, and have [n]not attained unto the days of the years of the life of my fathers in the days of their pilgrimage.

10 And Jā'cob [o]blessed Phā'raōh, and went out from before Phā'raōh.

11 ¶ And Jō'seph placed his father and his brethren, and gave them a possession in the land of Ē'ġypt, in the best of the land, in the land of [p]Ra-mē'sēs, as [q]Phā'raōh had commanded.

12 And Jō'seph nourished his father, and his brethren, and all his [r]father's household, with bread, [2]according to *their* families.

13 ¶ And *there was* no bread in all the land; for the famine *was* very sore, [s]so that the land of Ē'ġypt and *all* the land of Cā'năan fainted by reason of the famine.

14 And [t]Jō'seph gathered up all the money that was found in the land of Ē'ġypt, and in the land of Cā'năan, for the corn which they bought: and Jō'seph brought the money into Phā'raōh's house.

15 And when money failed in the land of Ē'ġypt, and in the land of Cā'năan, all the E-ġȳp'tians came unto Jō'seph, and said, Give us bread: for [u]why should we die in thy presence? for the money faileth.

16 And Jō'seph said, Give your cattle; and I will give you for your cattle, if money fail.

17 And they brought their cattle unto Jō'seph: and Jō'seph gave them bread *in exchange* for horses, and for the flocks, and for the cattle of the herds, and for the asses: and he [3]fed them with bread for all their cattle for that year.

18 When that year was ended, they came unto him the second year, and said unto him, We will not hide *it* from my lord, how that our money is spent; my lord also hath our herds of cattle; there is not ought left in the sight of my lord, but our bodies, and our lands:

19 Wherefore shall we die before thine eyes, both we and our land? buy us and our land for bread, and we and our land will be servants unto Phā'raōh: and give *us* seed, that we may live, and not die, that the land be not desolate.

20 And Jō'seph bought all the land of Ē'ġypt for Phā'raōh; for the E-ġȳp'tians sold every man his field, because the famine prevailed over them: so the land became Phā'raōh's.

21 And as for the people, he removed them to cities from *one* end of the borders of Ē'ġypt even to the *other* end thereof.

22 Only [v]the land of the [4]priests bought he not; for the priests had a portion *assigned them* of Phā'raōh, and did eat their portion which Phā'raōh gave them: wherefore they sold not their lands.

23 Then Jō'seph said unto the people, Behold, I have bought you this day and your land for Phā'raōh: lo, *here is* seed for you, and ye shall sow the land.

24 And it shall come to pass in the increase, that ye shall give the fifth *part* unto Phā'raōh, and four parts shall be your own, for seed of the field, and for your food, and for them of your households, and for food for your little ones.

25 And they said, Thou hast saved our lives: [w]let us find grace in the sight of my lord, and we will be Phā'raōh's servants.

30 [d]Luke 2.29
32 [12]they are men of cattle
33 [e]ch. 47.2-3
34 [f]ch. 30.35; ch. 34.5; ch. 37.12
[g]Ex. 8.26

CHAPTER 47
1 [a]ch. 46.31
[b]ch. 45.10; ch. 46.28
2 [c]Acts 7.13
3 [d]ch. 46.33
[e]ch. 46.34
4 [f]ch. 15.13; Deut. 26.5; Ps. 105.23; Isa. 52.4
[g]ch. 43.1; Acts 7.11
[h]ch. 46.34
6 [i]ch. 20.15
[j]verse 4
[k]1 Ki. 11.28; Prov. 12.24; Prov. 22.29
8 [1]How many are the days of the years of thy life?
9 [l]Ps. 39.12; Ps. 119.19; 2 Cor. 5.6-7; Heb. 11.9-13; 1 Pet. 2.11
[m]Job 7.7; Job 14.1; Ps. 102.3; Eccl. 2.23; Jas. 4.14; 1 Pet. 1.24
[n]ch. 25.7; ch. 35.28
10 [o]verse 7
11 [p]Ex. 1.11; Ex. 12.37
[q]verse 6
12 [r]Ex. 20.12; Prov. 10.1
[2]Or, as a little child is nourished; according to the little ones; ch. 50.21
13 [s]ch. 41.30; Acts 7.11
14 [t]ch. 41.56
15 [u]verse 19
17 [3]led them
22 [v]Ezra 7.24
[4]Or, princes; ch. 41.45; 2 Sam. 8.17
25 [w]ch. 33.15

26 And Jō'seph made it a law over
the land of Ē'ġypt unto this day, *that*
Phā'raōh should have the fifth *part;*
[x]except the land of the [5]priests only,
which became not Phā'raōh's.
27 ¶ And Ĭs'ra-el [y]dwelt in the land
of Ē'ġypt, in the country of Gō'shen;
and they had possessions therein, and
[z]grew, and multiplied exceedingly.
28 And Jā'cob lived in the land of
Ē'ġypt seventeen years: so [6]the whole
age of Jā'cob was an hundred forty
and seven years.
29 And the time [a]drew nigh that Ĭs'-
ra-el must die: and he called his son
Jō'seph, and said unto him, If now I
have found grace in thy sight, [b]put, I
pray thee, thy hand under my thigh,
and [c]deal kindly and truly with me;
[d]bury me not, I pray thee, in Ē'ġypt:
30 But [e]I will lie with my fathers,
and thou shalt carry me out of Ē'ġypt,
and [f]bury me in their buryingplace.
And he said, I will do as thou hast said.
31 And he said, Swear unto me.
And he sware unto him. And [g]Ĭs'ra-el
bowed himself upon the bed's head.

48 And it came to pass after these
things, that *one* told Jō'seph, Behold, thy father *is* sick: and he took
with him his two sons, Ma-năs'seh and
Ē'phră-ĭm.
2 And *one* told Jā'cob, and said,
Behold, thy son Jō'seph cometh unto
thee: and Ĭs'ra-el strengthened himself, and sat upon the bed.
3 And Jā'cob said unto Jō'seph, God
Almighty appeared unto me at [a]Lŭz in
the land of Cā'năan, and blessed me,
4 And said unto me, Behold, I will
make thee fruitful, and multiply thee,
and I will make of thee a multitude of
people; and will give this land to thy
seed after thee [b]*for* an everlasting possession.
5 ¶ And now thy [c]two sons, Ē'phră-
ĭm and Ma-năs'seh, which were born
unto thee in the land of Ē'ġypt before I
came unto thee into Ē'ġypt, *are* mine;
as Reū'ben and Sĭm'e-on, they shall be
mine.
6 And thy issue, which thou begettest after them, shall be thine, *and* shall
be called after the name of their brethren in their inheritance.
7 And as for me, when I came from
Pā'dan, [d]Rā'chel died by me in the
land of Cā'năan in the way, when yet
there was but a little way to come unto
Ĕph'răth: and I buried her there in the
way of Ĕph'răth; the same *is* Bĕth'–lĕ-
hĕm.
8 And Ĭs'ra-el beheld Jō'seph's sons,
and said, Who *are* these?
9 And Jō'seph said unto his father,
[e]They *are* my sons, whom God hath
given me in this *place.* And he said,
Bring them, I pray thee, unto me, and
[f]I will bless them.
10 Now [g]the eyes of Ĭs'ra-el were
[1]dim for age, *so that* he could not see.
And he brought them near unto him;
and he [h]kissed them, and embraced
them.

26 [x]verse 22 [5]Or, princes
27 [y]verse 11
[z]ch. 12.2; Acts 7.17
28 [6]the days of the years of his life
29 [a]Deut. 31.14; 1 Ki. 2.1
[b]ch. 24.2
[c]ch. 24.49
[d]ch. 50.25
30 [e]2 Sam. 19.37
[f]ch. 23.2-17-20;
31 [g]ch. 48.2;
CHAPTER 48
3 [a]ch. 28.13-19;
4 [b]ch. 17.8
5 [c]ch. 41.50;
7 [d]ch. 35.19
9 [e]ch. 33.5
[f]ch. 27.4
10 [g]ch. 27.1 [1]heavy; Isa. 6.10; Isa. 59.1
[h]ch. 27.27
11 [i]ch. 45.26
15 [j]Heb. 11.21
16 [k]ch. 28.15
[l]Amos 9.12; [2]as fishes do increase
17 [m]verse 14 [3]was evil in his eyes
19 [n]Num. 2.19; [4]fulness
20 [o]Ruth 4.11
21 [p]ch. 50.24
22 [q]Josh. 24.32;
[r]ch. 34.28;
CHAPTER 49
1 [a]Deut. 33.6-25
[b]Num. 24.14;
2 [c]Ps. 34.11
3 [d]Deut. 21.17
4 [1]do not thou excel
[e]Deut. 27.20; [2]Or, my couch is gone
5 [f]Prov. 18.9 [3]Or, their swords are weapons of violence
[g]ch. 34.25

11 And Ĭs'ra-el said unto Jō'seph, [i]I
had not thought to see thy face: and, lo,
God hath shewed me also thy seed.
12 And Jō'seph brought them out
from between his knees, and he bowed
himself with his face to the earth.
13 And Jō'seph took them both,
Ē'phră-ĭm in his right hand toward
Ĭs'ra-el's left hand, and Ma-năs'seh in
his left hand toward Ĭs'ra-el's right
hand, and brought *them* near unto
him.
14 And Ĭs'ra-el stretched out his
right hand, and laid *it* upon Ē'phră-
ĭm's head, who *was* the younger, and
his left hand upon Ma-năs'seh's head,
guiding his hands wittingly; for Ma-
năs'seh *was* the firstborn.
15 ¶ And [j]he blessed Jō'seph, and
said, God, before whom my fathers
Ā'brā-hăm and Ī'saac did walk, the
God which fed me all my life long unto
this day,
16 The Angel [k]which redeemed me
from all evil, bless the lads; and let
[l]my name be named on them, and the
name of my fathers Ā'brā-hăm and
Ī'saac; and let them [2]grow into a multitude in the midst of the earth.
17 And when Jō'seph saw that his
father [m]laid his right hand upon the
head of Ē'phră-ĭm, it [3]displeased him:
and he held up his father's hand, to
remove it from Ē'phră-ĭm's head unto
Ma-năs'seh's head.
18 And Jō'seph said unto his father,
Not so, my father: for this *is* the firstborn; put thy right hand upon his head.
19 And his father refused, and said,
I know *it,* my son, I know *it:* he also
shall become a people, and he also
shall be great: but truly his [n]younger
brother shall be greater than he, and
his seed shall become a [4]multitude of
nations.
20 And he blessed them that day,
saying, [o]In thee shall Ĭs'ra-el bless, saying, God make thee as Ē'phră-ĭm and
as Ma-năs'seh: and he set Ē'phră-ĭm
before Ma-năs'seh.
21 And Ĭs'ra-el said unto Jō'seph,
Behold, I die: but [p]God shall be with
you, and bring you again unto the land
of your fathers.
22 Moreover [q]I have given to thee
one portion above thy brethren, which
I took out of the hand of the [r]Ăm'ôr-īte
with my sword and with my bow.

49 And Jā'cob called unto his sons,
and said, Gather yourselves together, that I may [a]tell you *that* which
shall befall you [b]in the last days.
2 Gather yourselves together, and
hear, ye sons of Jā'cob; and [c]hearken
unto Ĭs'ra-el your father.
3 ¶ Reū'ben, thou *art* my firstborn,
my might, [d]and the beginning of my
strength, the excellency of dignity, and
the excellency of power:
4 Unstable as water, [1][e]thou shalt not
excel; because thou wentest up to thy
father's bed; then defiledst thou *it:* [2]he
went up to my couch.
5 ¶ Sĭm'e-on and Lē'vī *are* [f]breth-
ren; [3][g]instruments of cruelty *are in*

their habitations.
6 O my soul, [h]come not thou into
their secret; [i]unto their assembly, mine
honour, be not thou united: for in their
anger they slew a man, and in their
selfwill they [4]digged down a wall.
7 Cursed *be* their anger, for *it was*
fierce; and their wrath, for it was cruel:
[j]I will divide them in Jā'cob, and scatter them in Ĭs'ra-el.
8 ¶ Jū'dah, thou *art he* whom thy
brethren shall praise: thy hand *shall be*
in the neck of thine enemies; thy father's children shall bow down before
thee.
9 Jū'dah *is* a lion's whelp: from the
prey, my son, thou art gone up: [k]he
stooped down, he couched as a lion,
and as an old lion; who shall rouse him
up?
10 The [l]sceptre shall not depart
from Jū'dah, nor a [m]lawgiver from between his feet, [n]until Shī'lōh come;
[o]and unto him *shall* the gathering of
the people *be*.
11 Binding his foal unto the vine,
and his ass's colt unto the choice vine;
he washed his garments in wine, and
his clothes in the blood of grapes:
12 His eyes *shall be* red with wine,
and his teeth white with milk.
13 ¶ [p]Zĕb'u-lun shall dwell at the
haven of the sea; and he *shall be* for an
haven of ships; and his border *shall be*
unto Zī'dŏn.
14 ¶ Ĭs'sa-char *is* a strong ass couch-
ing down between two burdens:
15 And he saw that rest *was* good,
and the land that *it was* pleasant; and
bowed his shoulder to bear, and became a servant unto tribute.
16 ¶ [q]Dăn shall judge his people, as
one of the tribes of Ĭs'ra-el.
17 [r]Dăn shall be a serpent by the
way, [5]an adder in the path, that biteth
the horse heels, so that his rider shall
fall backward.
18 [s]I have waited for thy salvation,
O LORD.
19 ¶ [t]Găd, a troop shall overcome
him: but he shall overcome at the last.
20 ¶ Out of Āsh'ēr his bread *shall be*
fat, and he shall yield royal dainties.
21 ¶ Năph'ta-lī *is* a hind let loose: he
giveth goodly words.
22 ¶ Jō'seph *is* a fruitful bough, *even*
a fruitful bough by a well; *whose*
[6]branches run over the wall:
23 The archers have [u]sorely grieved
him, and shot *at him,* and hated him:
24 But his [v]bow abode in strength,
and the arms of his hands were made
strong by the hands of the [w]mighty
God of Jā'cob; (from thence [x]*is* the
shepherd, [y]the stone of Ĭs'ra-el:)
25 *Even* by the God of thy father,
who shall help thee; and by the Almighty, [z]who shall bless thee with
blessings of heaven above, blessings
of the deep that lieth under, blessings
of the breasts, and of the womb:
26 The blessings of thy father have
prevailed above the blessings of my
progenitors unto the utmost bound of
the everlasting hills: they shall be on

6 [h]Prov. 1.15
[i]Ps. 26.9
[4]Or, houghed oxen
7 [j]Josh. 19.1; 1 Chr. 4.24
9 [k]Num. 24.9
10 [l]Num. 24.17
[m]Ps. 60.7
[n]1 Chr. 5.2; Luke 1.32
[o]Isa. 2.2; Luke 2.30
13 [p]Deut. 33.18
16 [q]Judg. 15.16-20; Judg. 18.2
17 [r]Judg. 18.23-27
[5]an arrowsnake
18 [s]Ps. 25.3-5; Tit. 2.13
19 [t]Deut. 33.20
22 [6]daughters
23 [u]ch. 37.24
24 [v]Job 29.20
[w]Ps. 132.2-5
[x]Ps. 80.1
[y]Isa. 28.16
25 [z]Deut. 33.13
27 [a]Judg. 20.21-25
[b]Num. 23.24; Zech. 14.1-7
29 [c]ch. 15.15; ch. 25.8
[d]ch. 47.30; 2 Sam. 19.37
[e]ch. 50.13
30 [f]ch. 23.16
31 [g]ch. 23.19; ch. 25.9
[h]ch. 35.29
CHAPTER 50
1 [a]ch. 46.4
[b]2 Ki. 13.14
2 [c]2 Chr. 16.14; John 19.39-40
3 [1]wept
[d]Num. 20.29; Deut. 34.8
4 [e]Esth. 4.2
5 [f]2 Chr. 16.14;

the head of Jō'seph, and on the crown
of the head of him that was separate
from his brethren.
27 ¶ Bĕn'ja-min shall [a]ravin *as* a
wolf: in the morning he shall devour
the prey, [b]and at night he shall divide
the spoil.
28 ¶ All these *are* the twelve tribes of
Ĭs'ra-el: and this *is it* that their father
spake unto them, and blessed them; every one according to his blessing he
blessed them.
29 And he charged them, and said
unto them, I [c]am to be gathered unto
my people: [d]bury me with my fathers
[e]in the cave that *is* in the field of
Ē'phron the Hĭt'tīte,
30 In the cave that *is* in the field of
Măch-pē'lah, which *is* before Măm're,
in the land of Cā'năan, which [f]Ā'bră-
hăm bought with the field of Ē'phron
the Hĭt'tīte for a possession of a buryingplace.
31 [g]There they buried Ā'bră-hăm
and Sā'rah his wife; [h]there they buried
Ī'saac and Re-bĕk'ah his wife; and
there I buried Lē'ah.
32 The purchase of the field and of
the cave that *is* therein *was* from the
children of Hĕth.
33 And when Jā'cob had made an
end of commanding his sons, he gathered up his feet into the bed, and
yielded up the ghost, and was gathered
unto his people.
50 And Jō'seph [a]fell upon his father's face, and [b]wept upon him,
and kissed him.
2 And Jō'seph commanded his servants the physicians to [c]embalm his
father: and the physicians embalmed
Ĭs'ra-el.
3 And forty days were fulfilled for
him; for so are fulfilled the days of
those which are embalmed: and the
E-ġȳp'tians [1d]mourned for him threescore and ten days.
4 And when the days of his mourning were past, Jō'seph spake unto [e]the
house of Phā'raōh, saying, If now I
have found grace in your eyes, speak, I
pray you, in the ears of Phā'raōh, saying,
5 My father made me swear, saying,
Lo, I die: in my grave [f]which I have
digged for me in the land of Cā'năan,
there shalt thou bury me. Now therefore let me go up, I pray thee, and bury
my father, and I will come again.
6 And Phā'raōh said, Go up, and
bury thy father, according as he made
thee swear.
7 ¶ And Jō'seph went up to bury his
father: and with him went up all the
servants of Phā'raōh, the elders of his
house, and all the elders of the land of
Ē'ġȳpt,
8 And all the house of Jō'seph, and
his brethren, and his father's house:
only their little ones, and their flocks,
and their herds, they left in the land of
Gō'shen.
9 And there went up with him both
chariots and horsemen: and it was a
very great company.

10 And they came to the threshingfloor of Ā'tad, which *is* beyond Jôr'-
dan, and there they [g]mourned with a
great and very sore lamentation: [h]and
he made a mourning for his father
seven days.
11 And when the inhabitants of the
land, the Cā'năan-ītes, saw the mourning in the floor of Ā'tad, they said, This
is a grievous mourning to the E-ġўp'-
tians: wherefore the name of it was
called [2]Ā'běl–mĭz'ră-im, which *is* beyond Jôr'dan.
12 And his sons did unto him according as he commanded them:
13 For [i]his sons carried him into
the land of Cā'năan, and buried him in
the cave of the field of Măch-pē'lah,
which Ā'bră-hăm bought with the field
for a possession of a buryingplace of
Ē'phron the Hĭt'tīte, before Măm're.
14 ¶ And Jō'seph returned into
Ē'ġypt, he, and his brethren, and all
that went up with him to bury his father, after he had buried his father.
15 ¶ And when Jō'seph's brethren
saw that their father was dead, [j]they
said, Jō'seph will peradventure hate
us, and will certainly requite us all the
evil which we did unto him.
16 And they [3]sent a messenger unto
Jō'seph, saying, Thy father did command before he died, saying,
17 So shall ye say unto Jō'seph, Forgive, I pray thee now, the trespass of
thy brethren, and their sin; for [k]they
did unto thee evil: and now, we pray
thee, forgive the trespass of the servants of [l]the God of thy father. And
Jō'seph wept when they spake unto
him.
18 And his brethren also went and
[m]fell down before his face; and they
said, Behold, we *be* thy servants.
19 And Jō'seph said unto them, Fear
not: [n]for *am* I in the place of God?
20 But [o]as for you, ye thought evil
against me; *but* [p]God meant it unto
good, to bring to pass, as *it is* this day,
to save much people alive.
21 Now therefore fear ye not: [q]I will
nourish you, and your little ones. And
he comforted them, and spake [4]kindly
unto them.
22 ¶ And Jō'seph dwelt in Ē'ġypt,
he, and his father's house: and Jō'seph
lived an hundred and ten years.
23 And Jō'seph saw Ē'phră-ĭm's
children [r]of the third *generation:* the
children also of Mā'chĭr the son of Ma-
năs'seh [s]were [5]brought up upon Jō'-
seph's knees.
24 And Jō'seph said unto his brethren, I die: and [t]God will surely visit
you, and bring you out of this land
unto the land [u]which he sware to
Ā'bră-hăm, to Ī'saac, and to Jā'cob.
25 And [v]Jō'seph took an oath of the
children of Ĭs'ra-el, saying, God will
surely visit you, and ye shall carry up
my bones from hence.
26 So Jō'seph died, *being* an hundred and ten years old: and they embalmed him, and he was put in a coffin
in Ē'ġypt.

10 [g]Acts 8.2 [h]1 Sam. 31.13; Job 2.13
11 [2]That is, The mourning of the Egyptians
13 [i]ch. 23.16; Acts 7.16
15 [j]Job 15.21
16 [3]charged
17 [k]Prov. 28.13 [l]ch. 49.25
18 [m]ch. 37.7-10
19 [n]Deut. 32.35; Rom. 12.19; Heb. 10.30
20 [o]Ps. 56.5; Isa. 10.7 [p]ch. 45.5-7; Acts 3.13-15
21 [q]ch. 47.12; Matt. 5.44 [4]to their hearts
23 [r]Job 42.16 [s]ch. 30.3 [5]borne
24 [t]Ex. 3.16-17; Heb. 11.22 [u]ch. 26.3
25 [v]ch. 47.29; Ex. 13.19; Josh. 24.32

THE SECOND BOOK OF MOSES COMMONLY CALLED

EXODUS

Life's Questions

Can God deliver on His promises?
What kind of relationship does God want from me?
How do I respond to what God has done for me?

God's Answers

Exodus is the heart of the Old Testament, the Book of salvation and identity for God's people.

Exodus features God, His work and His expectations for the people with whom He is present. Exodus has four major parts: God elects a leader (1:1—7:2); God delivers a people (7:3—18:27); God makes a covenant with His people (19:1—24:18); and God shows His presence even with a sinful people (25:1—40:38).

Exodus highlights the saving grace of God contrasted with the unbelieving murmuring of His people.

God preserves a deliverer for an oppressed people (1:1—4:17).
God sends His leader on an impossible mission (4:18—7:2).
God shows His sovereignty in punishing Egypt's Pharaoh (7:3—12:30).
God shows His power and faithfulness at the Red Sea (12:31—15:21).
God provides for a doubting, complaining people (15:22—18:27).
God starts His kingdom with a covenant people (19:1—20:21).
God gives civil, ceremonial, and criminal identification to the covenant (20:22—23:33).
God and people ratify the covenant (24:1–18).
God plans for His continual presence with His people (25:1—31:17).
God restores a rebellious, sinful people (31:18—34:35).
God is present with an obedient people (35:1—40:38).

Exodus sees a slave people in a foreign empire become an obedient people in a loving relationship with the God whose name they know, whose delivering love and power they have seen, and whose covenant they have entered. They have learned that idols have no power before Yahweh of Israel. Israel has learned God can and will fulfill His promises to the fathers. Individuals and nation have learned the identifying life-style that marks them as God's covenant people. God has placed His presence among His people even after they have sinned. Exodus thus says life is an obedient covenant relationship with the God who showed His power and love in the Exodus and who expects their covenant obedience and worship.

1 Now [a]these *are* the names of the
children of Ĭs'ra-el, which came into
Ē'ġypt; every man and his household
came with Jā'cob.
2 Reṷ'ben, Sĭm'e-on, Lē'vī, and Jū'-
dah,
3 Ĭs'sa-char, Zĕb'u-lun, and Bĕn'ja-
min,
4 Dăn, and Năph'ta-lī, Găd, and
Ăsh'ēr.
5 And all the souls that came out of
the [1]loins of Jā'cob were seventy
[b]souls: for Jō'seph was in Ē'ġypt *already*.
6 And [c]Jō'seph died, and all his
brethren, and [d]all that generation.
7 ¶ And [e]the children of Ĭs'ra-el
were fruitful, and increased abundantly, and multiplied, and waxed exceeding mighty; and the land was
filled with them.
8 Now there arose up a new king
over Ē'ġypt, which knew not Jō'seph.
9 And he said unto his people, Behold, [f]the people of the children of
Ĭs'ra-el *are* more and mightier than
we:
10 Come [g]on, let us [h]deal wisely
with them; lest they multiply, and it
come to pass, that, when there falleth
out any war, they join also unto our
enemies, and fight against us, and *so*
get them up out of the land.
11 Therefore they did set over them
taskmasters [i]to afflict them with their
[j]burdens. And they built for Phā'raōh
treasure cities, Pī'thom [k]and Ra-ăm'-
sēs.
12 [2]But the more they afflicted them,
the more they multiplied and grew.
And they were grieved because of the
children of Ĭs'ra-el.
13 And the E-ġy̆p'tians made the
children of Ĭs'ra-el to serve with rigour:
14 And they [l]made their lives bitter
with hard bondage, [m]in morter, and in
brick, and in all manner of service in
the field: all their service, wherein they
made them serve, *was* with rigour.
15 ¶ And the king of Ē'ġypt spake to
the Hē'brew midwives, of which the
name of the one *was* Shĭph'rah, and
the name of the other Pū'ah:
16 And he said, When ye do the
office of a midwife to the Hē'brew
women, and see *them* upon the stools;
if it *be* a son, then ye shall kill him: but
if it *be* a daughter, then she shall live.
17 But the midwives [n]feared God,
and did not [o]as the king of Ē'ġypt commanded them, but saved the men children alive.
18 And the king of Ē'ġypt called
for the midwives, and said unto them,
Why have ye done this thing, and have
saved the men children alive?
19 And [p]the midwives said unto
Phā'raōh, Because the Hē'brew women
are not as the E-ġy̆p'tian women; for
they *are* lively, and are delivered ere the
midwives come in unto them.
20 Therefore [q]God dealt well with
the midwives: and the people multiplied, and waxed very mighty.
21 And it came to pass, because the
midwives feared God, [r]that he made
them houses.
22 And Phā'raōh charged all his people, saying, Every son that is born ye
shall cast into the river, and every
daughter ye shall save alive.

2 And there went [a]a man of the house
of Lē'vī, and took *to wife* a daughter
of Lē'vī.
2 And the woman conceived, and
bare a son: and [b]when she saw him
that he *was a* goodly *child*, she hid him
three months.
3 And when she could not longer
hide him, she took for him an ark of bulrushes, and daubed it with slime and
with pitch, and put the child therein;
and she laid *it* in the flags by the river's
brink.
4 And [c]his sister stood afar off, to
wit what would be done to him.
5 ¶ And the [d]daughter of Phā'raōh
came down to wash *herself* at the river;
and her maidens walked along by the
river's side; and when she saw the ark
among the flags, she sent her maid to
fetch it.
6 And when she had opened *it*, she
saw the child: and, behold, the babe
wept. And she had compassion on him,
and said, This *is one* of the Hē'brews'
children.
7 Then said his sister to Phā'raōh's
daughter, Shall I go and call to thee a
nurse of the Hē'brew women, that she
may nurse the child for thee?
8 And Phā'raōh's daughter said to
her, Go. And the maid went and called
the child's mother.
9 And Phā'raōh's daughter said unto
her, Take this child away, and nurse it
for me, and I will give *thee* thy wages.
And the woman took the child, and
nursed it.
10 And the child grew, and she
brought him unto Phā'raōh's daughter, and he became her son. And she
called his name [1]Moses: and she said,
Because I drew him out of the water.
11 ¶ And it came to pass in those
days, [e]when Mō'ses was grown, that
he went out unto his brethren, and
looked on their burdens: and he spied
an E-ġy̆p'tian smiting an Hē'brew, one
of his brethren.
12 And he looked this way and that
way, and when he saw that *there was*
no man, he slew the E-ġy̆p'tian, and
hid him in the sand.
13 And when he went out the second
day, behold, two men of the Hē'brews
strove together: and he said to him that
did the wrong, Wherefore smitest thou
thy fellow?

CHAPTER 1
1 [a]Gen. 46.8; ch. 6.14
5 [1]thigh
[b]Gen. 46.26; Deut. 10.22
6 [c]Gen. 50.26; Acts 7.15
[d]Eccl. 1.4
7 [e]Gen. 46.3; Deut. 26.5; Ps. 105.24; Acts 7.17
9 [f]Ps. 105.24
10 [g]Ps. 10.2; Ps. 83.3
[h]Job 5.13; Prov. 28.16; Acts 7.19
11 [i]Gen. 15.13; ch. 3.7
[j]ch. 2.11; ch. 5.4-5; Prov. 27.3; Ps. 81.6
[k]Gen. 47.11
12 [2]And as they afflicted them, so they multiplied, etc
14 [l]ch. 2.23; ch. 22.21; Lev. 25.14-17; Num. 20.15; Job 20.19; Ps. 10.17-18; Prov. 14.31
[m]Ps. 81.6
17 [n]Prov. 16.6
[o]Dan. 3.16-18; Dan. 6.13; Acts 5.29
19 [p]Josh. 2.4; 2 Sam. 17.19-20
20 [q]Prov. 11.18; Eccl. 8.12; Isa. 3.10; Heb. 6.10
21 [r]1 Sam. 2.35; 2 Sam. 7.11-13-27-29; 1 Ki. 2.24; 1 Ki. 11.38; Ps. 127.1

CHAPTER 2
1 [a]ch. 6.20; Num. 26.59; 1 Chr. 23.13-14
2 [b]Heb. 11.23
4 [c]ch. 15.20; Num. 26.59
5 [d]Acts 7.21
10 [1]That is, Drawn out
11 [e]Heb. 11.24-26

14 And he said, Who made thee [2]a prince and a judge over us? intendest thou to kill me, as thou killedst the E-ġȳp'tian? And Mō'ses feared, and said, Surely this thing is known.

15 Now when Phā'raōh heard this thing, he sought to slay Mō'ses. But Mō'ses fled from the face of Phā'raōh, and dwelt in the land of Mĭd'ĭ-an: and he sat down by [f]a well.

16 [g]Now the [3]priest of Mĭd'ĭ-an had seven daughters: [h]and they came and drew *water*, and filled the troughs to water their father's flock.

17 And the shepherds came and drove them away: but Mō'ses stood up and helped them, and watered their flock.

18 And when they came to [i]Reu̱'el their father, he said, How *is it that* ye are come so soon to day?

19 And they said, An E-ġȳp'tian delivered us out of the hand of the shepherds, and also drew *water* enough for us, and watered the flock.

20 And he said unto his daughters, And where *is* he? why *is* it *that* ye have left the man? call him, that he may [j]eat bread.

21 And Mō'ses was content to dwell with the man: and he gave Mō'ses Zĭp-pō'rah his daughter.

22 And she bare *him* a son, and he called his name [4k]Gẽr'shōm: for he said, I have been [l]a stranger in a strange land.

23 ¶ And it came to pass [m]in process of time, that the king of Ē'ġypt died: and the children of Ĭs'ra-el [n]sighed by reason of the bondage, and they cried, and their [o]cry came up unto God by reason of the bondage.

24 And God [p]heard their groaning, and God [q]remembered his [r]covenant with Ā'brā-hăm, with Ī'saac, and with Jā'cob.

25 And God [s]looked upon the children of Ĭs'ra-el, and God [5]had respect unto *them*.

3 Now Mō'ses kept the flock of Jē'thro his father in law, the priest of Mĭd'ĭ-an: and he led the flock to the backside of the desert, and came to [a]the mountain of God, *even* to Hō'reb.

2 And [b]the angel of the LORD appeared unto him in a flame of fire out of the midst of a bush: and he looked, and, behold, the bush burned with fire, and the bush *was* not consumed.

3 And Mō'ses said, I will now turn aside, and see [c]this great sight, why the bush is not burnt.

4 And when the LORD saw that he turned aside to see, God called unto [d]him out of the midst of the bush, and said, Mō'ses, Mō'ses. And he said, Here *am* I.

5 And he said, Draw not nigh hither: [e]put off thy shoes from off thy feet, for the place whereon thou standest *is* holy ground.

6 Moreover he said, [f]I *am* the God of thy father, the God of Ā'brā-hăm, the God of Ī'saac, and the God of Jā'cob. And Mō'ses hid his face; for [g]he was afraid to look upon God.

7 ¶ And the LORD said, I have surely seen the affliction of my people which *are* in Ē'ġypt, and have heard their cry by reason of their taskmasters; for [h]I know their sorrows;

8 And [i]I am come down to [j]deliver them out of the hand of the E-ġȳp'tians, and to bring them up out of that land [k]unto a good land and a large, unto a land [l]flowing with milk and honey; unto the place of the [m]Cā'năan-ītes, and the Hĭt'tītes, and the Ăm'ôr-ītes, and the Pĕr'ĭz-zītes, and the Hī'vītes, and the Jĕb'u-sītes.

9 Now therefore, behold, the cry of the children of Ĭs'ra-el is come unto me: and I have also seen the oppression wherewith [n]the E-ġȳp'tians oppress them.

10 Come [o]now therefore, and I will send thee unto Phā'raōh, that thou mayest bring forth my people the children of Ĭs'ra-el out of Ē'ġypt.

11 ¶ And Mō'ses said unto God, [p]Who *am* I, that I should go unto Phā'raōh, and that I should bring forth the children of Ĭs'ra-el out of Ē'ġypt?

12 And he said, [q]Certainly I will be with thee; and this *shall be* a token unto thee, that I have sent thee: When thou hast brought forth the people out of Ē'ġypt, ye shall serve God upon this mountain.

13 And Mō'ses said unto God, Behold, *when* I come unto the children of Ĭs'ra-el, and shall say unto them, The God of your fathers hath sent me unto you; and they shall say to me, [r]What *is* his name? what shall I say unto them?

14 And God said unto Mō'ses, I AM THAT I AM: and he said, Thus shalt thou say unto the children of Ĭs'ra-el, [s]I AM hath sent me unto you.

15 And God said moreover unto Mō'ses, Thus shalt thou say unto the children of Ĭs'ra-el, The LORD God of your fathers, the God of Ā'brā-hăm, the God of Ī'saac, and the God of Jā'cob, hath sent me unto you: this *is* [t]my name for ever, and this *is* my memorial unto all generations.

16 Go, and gather the elders of Ĭs'ra-el together, and say unto them, The [u]LORD God of your fathers, the God of Ā'brā-hăm, of Ī'saac, and of Jā'cob, appeared unto me, saying, [v]I have surely visited you, and *seen* that which is done to you in Ē'ġypt:

17 And I have said, [w]I will bring you up out of the affliction of Ē'ġypt unto the land of the Cā'năan-ītes, and the Hĭt'tītes, and the Ăm'ôr-ītes, and the Pĕr'ĭz-zītes, and the Hī'vītes, and the Jĕb'u-sītes, unto a land flowing with milk and honey.

18 And they shall hearken to thy voice: and thou shalt come, thou and the elders of Ĭs'ra-el, unto the king of Ē'ġypt, and ye shall say unto him, The LORD God of the Hē'brews hath [x]met with us: and now let us go, we beseech thee, three days' journey into

---

- 14 [2]a man, a prince; Gen. 13.8; Gen. 47.22-26; 1 Sam. 8.18; 2 Sam. 20.26
- 15 [f]Gen. 24.11; Gen. 29.2
- 16 [g]ch. 3.1 [3]Or, prince, as Gen. 41.45 [h]Gen. 29.10; 1 Sam. 9.11
- 18 [i]Num. 10.29; Called also Jethro, or Jether
- 20 [j]Gen. 31.54
- 22 [4]That is, A stranger here [k]ch. 18.3 [l]Heb. 11.13
- 23 [m]ch. 7.7 [n]Ps. 12.5 [o]Gen. 18.20; Jas. 5.4
- 24 [p]ch. 6.5 [q]Ps. 105.8 [r]Gen. 15.14
- 25 [s]2 Sam. 16.12; Luke 1.25 [5]knew

CHAPTER 3

- 1 [a]1 Ki. 19.8
- 2 [b]Deut. 33.16;
- 3 [c]Ps. 111.2
- 4 [d]Deut. 33.16
- 5 [e]Josh. 5.15
- 6 [f]Gen. 28.13; [g]Isa. 6.1-5;
- 7 [h]Gen. 18.21
- 8 [i]Gen. 11.5 [j]ch. 12.51 [k]Deut. 1.25 [l]Num. 13.27 [m]Gen. 15.18
- 9 [n]ch. 1.11
- 10 [o]Ps. 105.26;
- 11 [p]1 Sam. 18.18;
- 12 [q]Gen. 31.3;
- 13 [r]Gen. 32.29
- 14 [s]ch. 6.3;
- 15 [t]Ps. 135.13;
- 16 [u]Gen. 48.15 [v]Gen. 50.24;
- 17 [w]Gen. 15.14
- 18 [x]Num. 23.3

the wilderness, that we may sacrifice to the LORD our God.

19 ¶ And I am sure that the king of Ē'ġypt will not let you go, [1]no, not by a mighty hand.

20 And I will stretch out my hand, and smite Ē'ġypt with [y]all my wonders which I will do in the midst thereof: and [z]after that he will let you go.

21 And [a]I will give this people favour in the sight of the E-ġy̌p'tians: and it shall come to pass, that, when ye go, ye shall not go empty:

22 But [b]every woman shall borrow of her neighbour, and of her that sojourneth in her house, jewels of silver, and jewels of gold, and raiment: and ye shall put *them* upon your sons, and upon your daughters; [c]and ye shall spoil [2]the E-ġy̌p'tians.

4 And Mō'ses answered and said, But, behold, they will not believe me, nor hearken unto my voice: for they will say, The LORD hath not appeared unto thee.

2 And the LORD said unto him, What *is* that in thine hand? And he said, A rod.

3 And he said, Cast it on the ground. And he cast it on the ground, and it became a serpent; and Mō'ses fled from before it.

4 And the LORD said unto Mō'ses, Put forth thine hand, and take it by the tail. And he put forth his hand, and caught it, and it became a rod in his hand:

5 That they may [a]believe that the LORD God of their fathers, the God of Ā'bră-hăm, the God of Ī'saac, and the God of Jā'cob, hath appeared unto thee.

6 ¶ And the LORD said furthermore unto him, Put now thine hand into thy bosom. And he put his hand into his bosom: and when he took it out, behold, his hand *was* leprous [b]as snow.

7 And he said, Put thine hand into thy bosom again. And he put his hand into his bosom again; and plucked it out of his bosom, and, behold, [c]it was turned again as his *other* flesh.

8 And it shall come to pass, if they will not believe thee, neither hearken to the voice of the first sign, that they will believe the voice of the latter sign.

9 And it shall come to pass, if they will not believe also these two signs, neither hearken unto thy voice, that thou shalt take of the water of the river, and pour *it* upon the dry *land:* and [d]the water which thou takest out of the river [1]shall become blood upon the dry *land.*

10 ¶ And Mō'ses said unto the LORD, O my Lord, I *am* not [2]eloquent, neither [3]heretofore, nor since thou hast spoken unto thy servant: but [e]I *am* slow of speech, and of a slow tongue.

11 And the LORD said unto him, [f]Who hath made man's mouth? or who maketh the dumb, or deaf, or the seeing, or the blind? have not I the LORD?

12 Now therefore go, and I will be [g]with thy mouth, and teach thee what thou shalt say.

13 And he said, O my Lord, [h]send, I pray thee, by the hand *of him whom* thou [4]wilt send.

14 And the anger of the LORD was kindled against Mō'ses, and he said, *Is* not Aâr'on the Lē'vīte thy brother? I know that he can speak well. And also, behold, he cometh forth to meet thee: and when he seeth thee, he will be glad in his heart.

15 And [i]thou shalt speak unto him, and put words in his mouth: and I will be with thy mouth, and with his mouth, and [j]will teach you what ye shall do.

16 And he shall be thy spokesman unto the people: and he shall be, *even* he shall be to thee instead of a mouth, and [k]thou shalt be to him instead of God.

17 And thou shalt take this rod in thine hand, wherewith thou shalt do signs.

18 ¶ And Mō'ses went and returned to [5]Jē'thro his father in law, and said unto him, Let me go, I pray thee, and return unto my brethren which *are* in Ē'ġypt, and see whether they be yet alive. And Jē'thro said to Mō'ses, Go in peace.

19 And the LORD said unto Mō'ses in Mĭd'ĭ-an, Go, return into Ē'ġypt: for [l]all the men are dead which sought thy life.

20 And Mō'ses took his wife and his sons, and set them upon an ass, and he returned to the land of Ē'ġypt: and Mō'ses took the [m]rod of God in his hand.

21 And the LORD said unto Mō'ses, When thou goest to return into Ē'ġypt, see that thou do all those wonders before Phā'raōh, which I have put in thine hand: but [n]I will harden his heart, that he shall not let the people go.

22 And thou shalt say unto Phā'raōh, Thus saith the LORD, [o]Ĭs'ra-el *is* my son, [p]*even* my firstborn:

23 And I say unto thee, Let my son go, that he may serve me: and if thou refuse to let him go, behold, I [q]will slay thy son, *even* thy firstborn.

24 ¶ And it came to pass by the way in the inn, that the [r]LORD met him, and sought to [s]kill him.

25 Then Zĭp-pō'rah took [t]a sharp [6]stone, and cut off the foreskin of her son, and [7]cast *it* at his feet, and said, Surely a bloody husband *art* thou to me.

26 So he let him go: then she said, A bloody husband *thou art,* because of the circumcision.

27 ¶ And the LORD said to Aâr'on, Go into the wilderness to meet Mō'ses. And he went, and met him in [u]the mount of God, and kissed him.

28 And Mō'ses told Aâr'on all the words of the LORD who had sent him, and all the signs which he had commanded him.

29 ¶ And Mō'ses and Aâr'on went and [v]gathered together all the elders of the children of Ĭs'ra-el:

19 [1]Or, but by strong hand
20 [y]ch. 7.3; Acts 7.36
[z]ch. 12.31
21 [a]ch. 11.3; Prov. 16.7
22 [b]Gen. 15.14; ch. 11.2
[c]Job 27.17; Ezek. 39.10
[2]Or, Egypt

CHAPTER 4
5 [a]ch. 19.9
6 [b]Num. 12.10; 2 Ki. 5.27
7 [c]Num. 12.13-14; Matt. 8.3
9 [d]ch. 7.19
[1]shall be and shall be
10 [2]a man of words
[3]since yesterday, nor since the third day
[e]ch. 6.12; Jer. 1.6
11 [f]Ps. 94.9
12 [g]Isa. 50.4; Luke 21.14
13 [h]Jon. 1.3
[4]Or, shouldest
15 [i]Num. 23.12; Jer. 1.9
[j]Deut. 5.31
16 [k]ch. 7.1; ch. 18.19
18 [5]Jether
19 [l]ch. 2.15-23; Matt. 2.20
20 [m]ch. 17.9; Num. 20.8
21 [n]Josh. 11.20; Jas. 1.13-17
22 [o]Hos. 11.1;
[p]Jer. 31.9;
23 [q]ch. 11.5;
24 [r]Num. 22.22
[s]Gen. 17.14
25 [t]Josh. 5.2-3
[6]Or, knife
[7]made it touch
27 [u]ch. 3.1
29 [v]verse 16

30 And Aâr'on spake all the words
which the LORD had spoken unto Mō'-
ses, and did the signs in the sight of the
people.
31 And the people [w]believed: and
when they heard that the LORD had
[x]visited the children of Ĭs'ra-el, and
that he had [y]looked upon their affliction, then [z]they bowed their heads and
worshipped.
5 And afterward Mō'ses and Aâr'on
went in, and told Phā'raōh, Thus
saith the LORD God of Ĭs'ra-el, Let my
people go, that they may hold [a]a feast
unto me in the wilderness.
2 And Phā'raōh said, [b]Who *is* the
LORD, that I should obey his voice to
let Ĭs'ra-el go? I know not the LORD,
[c]neither will I let Ĭs'ra-el go.
3 And they said, [d]The God of the
Hē'brews hath met with us: let us go,
we pray thee, three days' journey into
the desert, and sacrifice unto the LORD
our God; lest he fall upon us with pestilence, or with the sword.
4 And the king of Ē'gypt said unto
them, [e]Wherefore do ye, Mō'ses and
Aâr'on, let the people from their
works? get you unto your [f]burdens.
5 And Phā'raōh said, Behold, the
people of the land now *are* [g]many, and
ye make them rest from their burdens.
6 And Phā'raōh commanded the
same day the [h]taskmasters of the people, and their officers, saying,
7 Ye shall no more give the people
straw to make brick, as heretofore: let
them go and gather straw for themselves.
8 And the tale of the bricks, which
they did make heretofore, ye shall lay
upon them; ye shall not diminish *ought*
thereof: for they *be* idle; therefore they
cry, saying, Let us go *and* sacrifice to
our God.
9 [1]Let there more work be laid upon
the men, that they may labour therein;
and let them not regard vain words.
10 ¶ And the [i]taskmasters of the
people went out, and their officers,
and they spake to the people, saying,
Thus saith Phā'raōh, I will not give
you straw.
11 Go ye, get you straw where ye
can find it: yet not ought of your work
shall be diminished.
12 So the people were scattered
abroad throughout all the land of
Ē'gypt to gather stubble instead of
straw.
13 And the taskmasters hasted *them,*
saying, Fulfil your works, [2]*your* daily
tasks, as when there was straw.
14 And [j]the officers of the children
of Ĭs'ra-el, which Phā'raōh's taskmasters had set over them, were beaten,
and demanded, Wherefore have ye not
fulfilled your task in making brick both
yesterday and to day, as heretofore?
15 ¶ Then the officers of the children
of Ĭs'ra-el came and cried unto Phā'-
raōh, saying, Wherefore dealest thou
thus with thy servants?
16 There is no straw given unto thy
servants, and they say to us, Make
brick: and, behold, thy servants *are*
beaten; but the fault *is* in thine own
people.
17 But he said, Ye *are* idle, *ye are*
idle: therefore ye say, Let us go *and* do
sacrifice to the LORD.
18 Go therefore now, *and* work; for
there shall no straw be given you, yet
shall ye deliver the tale of bricks.
19 And the officers of the children of
Ĭs'ra-el did see *that* they *were* in evil
case, after it was said, Ye shall not
minish *ought* from your bricks of your
daily task.
20 ¶ And they met Mō'ses and
Aâr'on, who stood in the way, as they
came forth from Phā'raōh:
21 And [k]they said unto them, The
LORD look upon you, and judge; because ye have made our savour [3]to be
abhorred in the eyes of Phā'raōh, and
in the eyes of his servants, to put a
sword in their hand to slay us.
22 And Mō'ses [l]returned unto the
LORD, and said, Lord, wherefore hast
thou *so* evil entreated this people? why
is it *that* thou hast sent me?
23 For since I came to Phā'raōh to
speak in thy name, he hath done evil to
this people; [4]neither [m]hast thou delivered thy people at all.
6 Then the LORD said unto Mō'ses,
Now shalt thou see what I will do to
Phā'raōh: for with a strong hand shall
he let them go, and with a strong hand
[a]shall he drive them out of his land.
2 And God spake unto Mō'ses, and
said unto him, I *am* [1]the LORD:
3 And I appeared unto Ā'brā-hăm,
unto Ī'saac, and unto Jā'cob, by *the
name of* [b]God Almighty, but [c]by my
name JE-HŌ'VAH was I not known to
them.
4 And [d]I have also established my
covenant with them, [e]to give them the
land of Cā'năan, the land of their pilgrimage, wherein they were strangers.
5 And [f]I have also heard the groaning of the children of Ĭs'ra-el, whom
the E-ġȳp'tians keep in bondage; and I
have remembered my covenant.
6 Wherefore say unto the children
of Ĭs'ra-el, I *am* the LORD, and [g]I will
bring you out from under the burdens
of the E-ġȳp'tians, and I will rid you
out of their bondage, and I will [h]re-
deem you with a stretched out arm,
and with great judgments:
7 And I will [i]take you to me for a
people, and [j]I will be to you a God: and
ye shall know that I *am* the LORD your
God, which bringeth you out [k]from under the burdens of the E-ġȳp'tians.
8 And I will bring you in unto
the land, concerning the which I did
[2l]swear to give it to Ā'brā-hăm, to
Ī'saac, and to Jā'cob; and I will give it
you for an heritage: I *am* the LORD.
9 ¶ And Mō'ses spake so unto the
children of Ĭs'ra-el: but they hearkened not unto Mō'ses for [3]anguish of
spirit, and for cruel bondage.
10 And the LORD spake unto Mō'-
ses, saying,

31 [w]ch. 3.18 [x]ch. 3.16 [y]ch. 2.25; ch. 3.7 [z]Gen. 24.26; ch. 12.27; 1 Chr. 29.20

CHAPTER 5

1 [a]ch. 10.9
2 [b]2 Ki. 18.35; Job 21.15; Ps. 12.3-5; 2 Chr. 32.14 [c]ch. 3.19
3 [d]ch. 3.18
4 [e]Prov. 28.15 [f]ch. 1.11
5 [g]ch. 1.7-9
6 [h]ch. 1.11
9 [1]let the work be heavy upon the men
10 [i]ch. 1.11; Prov. 29.12
13 [2]a matter of a day in his day
14 [j]Gen. 15.13
21 [k]ch. 6.9 [3]to stink; Gen. 34.30; 1 Sam. 13.4; 2 Sam. 10.6; 1 Chr. 19.6
22 [l]Num. 11.11; 1 Sam. 30.6
23 [4]delivering thou hast not delivered [m]Matt 14.31; Heb. 10.23

CHAPTER 6

1 [a]ch. 11.1; ch. 12.31
2 [1]Or, JEHOVAH
3 [b]Gen. 17.1; Gen. 48.3 [c]ch. 3.14; Rev. 1.4
4 [d]Gen. 15.18; Gen. 17.4-7 [e]Gen. 17.8
5 [f]ch. 2.24
6 [g]ch. 3.17; Ps. 136.11-12 [h]ch. 15.13; Neh. 1.10
7 [i]Deut. 7.6; 2 Sam. 7.24 [j]Gen. 17.7-8; Rev. 21.7 [k]Ps. 81.6
8 [2]lift up my hand; Gen. 14.22 [l]Gen. 15.18; Gen. 26.3
9 [3]shortness, or, straitness

11 Go in, speak unto Phā'raōh king
of Ē'ġypt, that he let the children of
Ĭs'ra-el go out of his land.
12 And Mō'ses spake before the
LORD, saying, Behold, the children of
Ĭs'ra-el have not hearkened unto me;
how then shall Phā'raōh hear me,
[m]who *am* of uncircumcised lips?
13 And the LORD spake unto Mō'-
ses and unto Aâr'on, and gave them a
charge unto the children of Ĭs'ra-el,
and unto Phā'raōh king of Ē'ġypt, to
bring the children of Ĭs'ra-el out of the
land of Ē'ġypt.
14 ¶ These *be* the heads of their fathers' houses: [n]The sons of Reu̧'ben
the firstborn of Ĭs'ra-el; Hā'noch, and
Păl'lu, Hĕz'ron, and Cär'mī: these *be*
the families of Reu̧'ben.
15 And [o]the sons of Sĭm'e-on; Je-
mū'el, and Jā'min, and Ō'hăd, and Jă'-
chin, and Zō'har, and Shā'ul the son of
a Cā'năan-īt-ish woman: these *are* the
families of Sĭm'e-on.
16 ¶ And these *are* the names [p]of
the sons of Lē'vī according to their
generations; Ġēr'shŏn, and Kō'hath,
and Me-rā'rī: and the years of the life
of Lē'vī *were* an hundred thirty and
seven years.
17 The sons of Ġēr'shŏn; Lĭb'nī, and
Shĭ'mī, according to their families.
18 And [q]the sons of Kō'hath; Ăm'-
răm, and Ĭz'har, and Hē'bron, and Ŭz'-
zĭ-el: and the years of the life of Kō'-
hath *were* an hundred thirty and three
years.
19 And the sons of Me-rā'rī; Mā'ha-
lī and Mū'shī: these *are* the families of
Lē'vī according to their generations.
20 And [r]Ăm'răm took him Jŏch'e-
bed his father's sister to wife; and she
bare him Aâr'on and Mō'ses: and the
years of the life of Ăm'răm *were* an
hundred and thirty and seven years.
21 ¶ And [s]the sons of Ĭz'har; Kō'rah,
and Nē'pheg, and Zĭch'rī.
22 And [t]the sons of Ŭz'zĭ-el; Mĭsh'-
a-el, and Ĕl'za-phăn, and Zĭth'rī.
23 And Aâr'on took him E-lĭsh'e-bȧ,
daughter of [u]Ăm-mĭn'a-dab, sister of
Na-ăsh'on, to wife; and she bare him
[v]Nā'dăb, and A-bī'hū, Ē-le-ā'zar, and
Ĭth'a-mär.
24 And the [w]sons of Kō'rah; Ăs'sĭr,
and Ĕl'kă-nah, and A-bī'ă-săph: these
are the families of the Kôr'hītes.
25 And Ē-le-ā'zar Aâr'on's son took
him *one* of the daughters of Pū'tĭ-el to
wife; and [x]she bare him Phĭn'e-has:
these *are* the heads of the fathers of the
Lē'vītes according to their families.
26 These *are* that Aâr'on and Mō'-
ses, to whom the LORD said, Bring out
the children of Ĭs'ra-el from the land of
Ē'ġypt according to their [y]armies.
27 These *are* they which spake to
Phā'raōh king of Ē'ġypt, [z]to bring out
the children of Ĭs'ra-el from Ē'ġypt:
these *are* that Mō'ses and Aâr'on.
28 ¶ And it came to pass on the day
when the LORD spake unto Mō'ses in
the land of Ē'ġypt,
29 That the LORD spake unto Mō'-
ses, saying, I *am* the LORD: [a]speak
thou unto Phā'raōh king of Ē'ġypt all
that I say unto thee.
30 And Mō'ses said before the LORD,
Behold, [b]I *am* of uncircumcised lips,
and how shall Phā'raōh hearken unto
me?
7 And the LORD said unto Mō'ses, See,
I have made thee [a]a god to Phā'-
raōh: and Aâr'on thy brother shall be
thy prophet.
2 Thou shalt speak all that I command thee: and Aâr'on thy brother
shall speak unto Phā'raōh, that he send
the children of Ĭs'ra-el out of his land.
3 And I will harden Phā'raōh's heart,
and [b]multiply my [c]signs and my wonders in the land of Ē'ġypt.
4 But Phā'raōh shall not hearken
unto you, [d]that I may lay my hand
upon Ē'ġypt, and bring forth mine armies, *and* my people the children of
Ĭs'ra-el, out of the land of Ē'ġypt [e]by
great judgments.
5 And the E-ġy̆p'tians shall know
that [f]I *am* the LORD, when I [g]stretch
forth mine hand upon Ē'ġypt, and bring
out the children of Ĭs'ra-el from among
them.
6 And Mō'ses and Aâr'on did as the
LORD commanded them, so did they.
7 And Mō'ses *was* [h]fourscore years
old, and Aâr'on fourscore and three
years old, when they spake unto Phā'-
raōh.
8 ¶ And the LORD spake unto Mō'ses
and unto Aâr'on, saying,
9 When Phā'raōh shall speak unto
you, saying, [i]Shew a miracle for you:
then thou shalt say unto Aâr'on, [j]Take
thy rod, and cast *it* before Phā'raōh,
and it shall become a serpent.
10 ¶ And Mō'ses and Aâr'on went
in unto Phā'raōh, and they did so as
the LORD had commanded: and Aâr'on
cast down his rod before Phā'raōh,
and before his servants, and it [k]be-
came a serpent.
11 Then Phā'raōh also [l]called the
wise men and [m]the sorcerers: now the
magicians of Ē'ġypt, they also [n]did in
like manner with their enchantments.
12 For they cast down every man his
rod, and they became serpents: but
Aâr'on's rod swallowed up their rods.
13 And he hardened Phā'raōh's heart,
that he hearkened not unto them; [o]as
the LORD had said.
14 ¶ And the LORD said unto Mō'ses,
[p]Phā'raōh's heart *is* hardened, he refuseth to let the people go.
15 Get thee unto Phā'raōh in the
morning; lo, he goeth out unto the water; and thou shalt stand by the river's
brink against he come; and [q]the rod
which was turned to a serpent shalt
thou take in thine hand.
16 And thou shalt say unto him, The
LORD God of the Hē'brews hath sent
me unto thee, saying, Let my people go,
[r]that they may serve me in the wilderness: and, behold, hitherto thou wouldest not hear.
17 Thus saith the LORD, In this thou
[s]shalt know that I *am* the LORD: behold, I will smite with the rod that *is* in

12 [m]Jer. 1.6
14 [n]Gen. 46.9; 1 Chr. 5.3
15 [o]Gen. 46.10; 1 Chr. 4.24
16 [p]Gen. 46.11; 1 Chr. 6.1
18 [q]Num. 26.57; 1 Chr. 6.18
20 [r]ch. 2.1-2; Num. 26.59
21 [s]Num. 16.1; 1 Chr. 6.37-38
22 [t]Lev. 10.4; Num. 3.30
23 [u]Ruth 4.19-20; Matt. 1.4
[v]Lev. 10.1; 1 Chr. 24.1
24 [w]Num. 26.11
25 [x]Num. 25.7-11-12; Josh. 24.33
26 [y]ch. 7.4; Num. 33.1
27 [z]ch. 32.7; Ps. 77.20
29 [a]ch. 7.2
30 [b]ch. 4.10; Jer. 1.6

CHAPTER 7
1 [a]ch. 4.16; Jer. 1.10
3 [b]ch. 11.9
[c]ch. 4.7
4 [d]ch. 10.1; ch. 11.9
[e]ch. 6.6
5 [f]ch. 8.22; Ps. 83.18
[g]ch. 3.20
7 [h]Deut. 29.5; Acts 7.23-30
9 [i]Isa. 7.11; John 6.30
[j]ch. 4.2-17
10 [k]ch. 4.3
11 [l]Gen. 41.8; Dan. 2.2
[m]2 Tim. 3.8
[n]verse 22; Rev. 13.14
13 [o]ch. 4.21
14 [p]ch. 8.15; ch. 10.1-20-27
15 [q]ch. 4.2-3
16 [r]ch. 3.12-18;
17 [s]Ps. 9.16;

mine hand upon the waters which *are*
in the river, and [t]they shall be turned
[u]to blood.
18 And the fish that *is* in the river
shall die, and the river shall stink; and
the E-ġȳp'tians shall [v]loathe to drink
of the water of the river.
19 ¶ And the LORD spake unto Mō'-
ses, Say unto Aâr'on, Take thy rod,
and [w]stretch out thine hand upon the
waters of Ē'ġypt, upon their streams,
upon their rivers, and upon their
ponds, and upon all their [1]pools of water, that they may become blood; and
that there may be blood throughout all
the land of Ē'ġypt, both in *vessels of*
wood, and in *vessels of* stone.
20 And Mō'ses and Aâr'on did so, as
the LORD commanded; and [x]he lifted
up the rod, and smote the waters that
were in the river, in the sight of Phā'-
raōh, and in the sight of his servants;
and all the [y]waters that *were* in the
river were turned to blood.
21 And the fish that *was* in the river
died; and the river stank, and the E-
ġȳp'tians could not drink of the water of the river; and there was blood
throughout all the land of Ē'ġypt.
22 And the magicians of Ē'ġypt did
so with their enchantments: and Phā'-
raōh's heart was hardened, neither did
he hearken unto them; as the LORD
had said.
23 And Phā'raōh turned and went
into his house, neither [z]did he set his
heart to this also.
24 And all the E-ġȳp'tians digged
round about the river for water to
drink; for they could not drink of the
water of the river.
25 And seven days were fulfilled, after that the LORD had smitten the river.

8 And the LORD spake unto Mō'ses,
Go unto Phā'raōh, and say unto
him, Thus saith the LORD, Let my people go, [a]that they may serve me.
2 And if thou [b]refuse to let *them* go,
behold, I will smite all thy borders with
[c]frogs:
3 And the river shall bring forth
frogs abundantly, which shall go up
and come into thine house, and into
[d]thy bedchamber, and upon thy bed,
and into the house of thy servants, and
upon thy people, and into thine ovens,
and into thy [1]kneadingtroughs:
4 And the frogs shall come up both
on thee, and upon thy people, and upon
all thy servants.
5 ¶ And the LORD spake unto Mō'ses,
Say unto Aâr'on, [e]Stretch forth thine
hand with thy rod over the streams,
over the rivers, and over the ponds, and
cause frogs to come up upon the land of
Ē'ġypt.
6 And Aâr'on stretched out his hand
over the waters of Ē'ġypt; and [f]the
frogs came up, and covered the land of
Ē'ġypt.
7 And [g]the magicians did so with
their enchantments, and brought up
frogs upon the land of Ē'ġypt.
8 ¶ Then Phā'raōh called for Mō'-
ses and Aâr'on, and said, [h]Intreat the
LORD, that he may take away the frogs
from me, and from my people; and I
will let the people go, that they may do
sacrifice unto the LORD.
9 And Mō'ses said unto Phā'raōh,
[2]Glory over me: [3]when shall I intreat
for thee, and for thy servants, and for
thy people, [4]to destroy the frogs from
thee and thy houses, *that* they may remain in the river only?
10 And he said, [5]To morrow. And he
said, *Be it* according to thy word: that
thou mayest know that [i]*there is* none
like unto the LORD our God.
11 And the frogs shall depart from
thee, and from thy houses, and from
thy servants, and from thy people; they
shall remain in the river only.
12 And Mō'ses and Aâr'on went out
from Phā'raōh: and Mō'ses cried [j]unto
the LORD because of the frogs which
he had brought against Phā'raōh.
13 And the LORD did according to
the word of Mō'ses; and the frogs died
out of the houses, out of the villages,
and out of the fields.
14 And they gathered them together
upon heaps: and the land stank.
15 But when Phā'raōh saw that there
was [k]respite, [l]he hardened his heart,
and hearkened not unto them; as the
LORD had said.
16 ¶ And the LORD said unto Mō'ses,
Say unto Aâr'on, Stretch out thy rod,
and smite the dust of the land, that it
may become lice throughout all the
land of Ē'ġypt.
17 And they did so; for Aâr'on
stretched out his hand with his rod,
and smote the dust of the earth, and
[m]it became lice in man, and in beast;
all the dust of the land became lice
throughout all the land of Ē'ġypt.
18 And [n]the magicians did so with
their enchantments to bring forth lice,
but they [o]could not: so there were lice
upon man, and upon beast.
19 Then the magicians said unto
Phā'raōh, This *is* [p]the finger of God:
and Phā'raōh's heart was hardened,
and he hearkened not unto them; as
the LORD had said.
20 ¶ And the LORD said unto Mō'ses,
[q]Rise up early in the morning, and
stand before Phā'raōh; lo, he cometh
forth to the water; and say unto him,
Thus saith the LORD, Let my people go,
that they may serve me.
21 Else, if thou wilt not let my people
go, behold, I will send [6]swarms *of flies*
upon thee, and upon thy servants, and
upon thy people, and into thy houses:
and the houses of the E-ġȳp'tians shall
be full of swarms *of flies*, and also the
ground whereon they *are*.
22 And [r]I will sever in that day the
land of Gō'shen, in which my people
dwell, that no swarms *of flies* shall be
there; to the end thou mayest know
that I *am* the LORD in the midst of the
earth.
23 And I will put [7]a division between
my people and thy people: [8]to morrow
shall this sign be.

[t]ch. 4.9
[u]Rev. 16.4-6
18 [v]verse 24
19 [w]ch. 8.5; ch. 9.22; ch. 10.12-21; ch. 14.21-26
[1]gathering of their waters
20 [x]ch. 17.5
[y]Ps. 78.44; Ps. 105.29
23 [z]Prov. 29.1
CHAPTER 8
1 [a]ch. 3.12
2 [b]ch. 7.14; ch. 9.2
[c]Rev. 16.13
3 [d]Ps. 105.30
[1]Or, dough
5 [e]ch. 7.19
6 [f]Ps. 78.45; Ps. 105.30
7 [g]ch. 7.11
8 [h]ch. 9.28; ch. 10.17; Num. 21.7; 1 Ki. 13.6; Acts 8.24
9 [2]Or, have this honour over me, etc
[3]Or, against when
[4]to cut off
10 [5]Or, against to morrow
[i]ch. 9.14; Deut. 33.26; 2 Sam. 7.22; 1 Chr. 17.20; Ps. 86.8; Isa. 46.9; Jer. 10.6-7
12 [j]ch. 9.33; ch. 10.18; ch. 32.11; Jas. 5.16-18
15 [k]Eccl. 8.11
[l]Prov. 21.29
17 [m]Ps. 105.31
18 [n]ch. 7.11
[o]Luke 10.18; 2 Tim. 3.8-9
19 [p]1 Sam. 6.3-9; Job 27.11; Ps. 8.3; Matt. 12.28; Luke 11.20; Acts 13.11
20 [q]ch. 7.15
21 [6]Or, a mixture of noisome beasts, etc
22 [r]ch. 9.4-6-26
23 [7]a redemption
[8]Or, by to morrow

24 And the LORD did so; [s]and there
came a grievous swarm *of flies* into the
house of Phā'raōh, and *into* his servants' houses, and into all the land of
Ē'ġypt: the land was [9]corrupted by reason of the swarm *of flies*.
25 ¶ And Phā'raōh called for Mō'ses
and for Aâr'on, and said, Go ye, sacrifice to your God in the land.
26 And Mō'ses said, It is not meet so
to do; for we shall sacrifice the abomination [t]of the E-ġȳp'tians to the LORD
our God: lo, shall we sacrifice the
abomination of the E-ġȳp'tians before
their eyes, and will they not stone us?
27 We will go [u]three days' journey
into the wilderness, and sacrifice to the
LORD our God, as [v]he shall command
us.
28 And Phā'raōh said, I will let you
go, that ye may sacrifice to the LORD
your God in the wilderness; only ye
shall not go very far away: [w]intreat for
me.
29 And Mō'ses said, Behold, I go out
from thee, and I will intreat the LORD
that the swarms *of flies* may depart
from Phā'raōh, from his servants, and
from his people, to morrow: but let not
Phā'raōh deal deceitfully any more in
not letting the people go to sacrifice to
the LORD.
30 And Mō'ses went out from Phā'-
raōh, and intreated the LORD.
31 And [x]the LORD did according to
the word of Mō'ses; and he removed
the swarms *of flies* from Phā'raōh,
from his servants, and from his people;
there remained not one.
32 And Phā'raōh [y]hardened his heart
at this time also, neither would he let the
people go.

9 Then the LORD said unto Mō'ses,
Go [a]in unto Phā'raōh, and tell him,
Thus saith the LORD God of the Hē'-
brews, Let my people go, that they
may serve me.
2 For if thou [b]refuse to let *them* go,
and wilt hold them still,
3 Behold, the [c]hand of the LORD is
upon thy cattle which *is* in the field,
upon the horses, upon the asses, upon
the camels, upon the oxen, and upon
the sheep: *there shall be* a very grievous murrain.
4 And [d]the LORD shall sever between the cattle of Is'ra-el and the cattle of Ē'ġypt: and there shall nothing
die of all *that is* the children's of Is'-
ra-el.
5 And the LORD appointed a set time,
saying, To morrow the LORD shall do
this thing in the land.
6 And the LORD did that thing on the
morrow, and [e]all the cattle of Ē'ġypt
died: but of the cattle of the children of
Is'ra-el died not one.
7 And Phā'raōh sent, and, behold,
there was not one of the cattle of the
Is'ra-el-ītes dead. And [f]the heart of
Phā'raōh was hardened, and he did
not let the people go.
8 ¶ And the LORD said unto Mō'ses
and unto Aâr'on, Take to you handfuls
of ashes of the furnace, and let Mō'ses
sprinkle it toward the heaven in the
sight of Phā'raōh.
9 And it shall become small dust in
all the land of Ē'ġypt, and shall be [g]a
boil breaking forth *with* blains upon
man, and upon beast, throughout all
the land of Ē'ġypt.
10 And they took ashes of the furnace, and stood before Phā'raōh; and
Mō'ses sprinkled it up toward heaven;
and it became [h]a boil breaking forth
with blains upon man, and upon beast.
11 And the [i]magicians could not
stand before Mō'ses because of the
boils; for the boil was upon the magicians, and upon all the E-ġȳp'tians.
12 And [j]the LORD hardened the heart
of Phā'raōh, and he hearkened not unto
them; as [k]the LORD had spoken unto
Mō'ses.
13 ¶ And the LORD said unto Mō'ses,
[l]Rise up early in the morning, and
stand before Phā'raōh, and say unto
him, Thus saith the LORD God of the
Hē'brews, Let my people go, that they
may serve me.
14 For I will at this time send all my
plagues upon thine heart, and upon thy
servants, and upon thy people; [m]that
thou mayest know that *there is* none
like me in all the earth.
15 For now I will [n]stretch out my
hand, that I may smite thee and thy
people with pestilence; and thou shalt
be cut off from the earth.
16 And in very deed for [o]this *cause*
have I [1]raised thee up, for to shew *in*
thee my power; and that my name may
be declared throughout all the earth.
17 As yet exaltest thou thyself against
my people, that thou wilt not let them
go?
18 Behold, to morrow about this time
I will cause it to rain a very grievous
hail, such as hath not been in Ē'ġypt
since the foundation thereof even until
now.
19 Send therefore now, *and* gather
thy cattle, and all that thou hast in the
field; *for upon* every man and beast
which shall be found in the field, and
shall not be brought home, the hail
shall come down upon them, and they
shall die.
20 He that feared the word of the
LORD among the servants of Phā'raōh
made his servants and his cattle flee
into the houses:
21 And he that [2]regarded not the
word of the LORD left his servants and
his cattle in the field.
22 ¶ And the LORD said unto Mō'ses,
Stretch forth thine hand toward heaven,
that there may be [p]hail in all the land of
Ē'ġypt, upon man, and upon beast, and
upon every herb of the field, throughout
the land of Ē'ġypt.
23 And Mō'ses stretched forth his
rod toward heaven: and [q]the LORD sent
thunder and hail, and the fire ran along
upon the ground; and the LORD rained
hail upon the land of Ē'ġypt.
24 So there was hail, and fire mingled with the hail, very grievous, such

24 [s]Ps. 78.45 [9]Or, destroyed **26** [t]Gen. 46.34; Deut. 7.25-26; Deut. 12.31 **27** [u]ch. 3.18 [v]ch. 3.12 **28** [w]ch. 9.28; 1 Ki. 13.6; Ezra 6.10; Acts 8.24 **31** [x]Jas. 5.17 **32** [y]ch. 4.21; Prov. 28.14; Rom. 9.17-23; Jas. 1.13-17

CHAPTER 9
1 [a]ch. 8.1; Jer. 22.1 **2** [b]ch. 8.2; Rom. 2.5 **3** [c]ch. 7.4; 1 Sam. 5.6; 1 Sam. 6.3-5; Job 27.11; Ps. 39.10; Luke 11.20; Acts 13.11 **4** [d]ch. 8.22 **6** [e]Ps. 78.50 **7** [f]ch. 8.32 **9** [g]Rev. 16.2 **10** [h]Deut. 28.27 **11** [i]2 Tim. 3.9 **12** [j]ch. 4.21; ch. 7.14; ch. 8.32; ch. 10.1-20; ch. 14.8; Deut. 2.30; Josh. 11.20; Isa. 63.17; John 12.40; Rom. 9.18; Jas. 1.13-17 [k]ch. 4.21 **13** [l]ch. 8.20 **14** [m]Deut. 3.24; Deut. 33.26; 2 Sam. 7.22; 1 Chr. 17.20; Ps. 71.19; Ps. 86.8; Isa. 45.5-25; Isa. 46.9; Jer. 10.6-7 **15** [n]ch. 3.20 **16** [o]Prov. 16.4; Rom. 9.17; 1 Pet. 2.9 [1]made thee stand **21** [2]set not his heart unto **22** [p]Rev. 16.21 **23** [q]Josh. 10.11; Ps. 18.13; Ps. 78.47; Ps. 105.32; Ps. 148.8; Isa. 30.30; Ezek. 38.22; Rev. 8.7

as there was none like it in all the land of Ē'ġypt since it became a nation.

25 And the hail smote throughout all the land of Ē'ġypt all that *was* in the field, both man and beast; and the hail [r]smote every herb of the field, and brake every tree of the field.

26 Only [s]in the land of Gō'shen, where the children of Ĭs'ra-el *were*, was there no hail.

27 ¶ And Phā'raōh sent, and called for Mō'ses and Aâr'on, and said unto them, [t]I have sinned this time: [u]the LORD *is* righteous, and I and my people *are* wicked.

28 [v]Intreat the LORD (for *it is* enough) that there be no *more* [3]mighty thunderings and hail; and I will let you go, and ye shall stay no longer.

29 And Mō'ses said unto him, As soon as I am gone out of the city, I [w]will spread abroad my hands unto the LORD; *and* the thunder shall cease, neither shall there be any more hail; that thou mayest know how that the [x]earth *is* the LORD'S.

30 But as for thee and thy servants, [y]I know that ye will not yet fear the LORD God.

31 And the flax and the barley was smitten: [z]for the barley *was* in the ear, and the flax *was* bolled.

32 But the wheat and the rie were not smitten: for they *were* [4]not grown up.

33 And Mō'ses went out of the city from Phā'raōh, and [a]spread abroad his hands unto the LORD: and the thunders and hail ceased, and the rain was not poured upon the earth.

34 And when Phā'raōh saw that the rain and the hail and the thunders were ceased, he sinned yet more, and hardened his heart, he and his servants.

35 And the heart of Phā'raōh was hardened, neither would he let the children of Ĭs'ra-el go; as the LORD had spoken [5]by Mō'ses.

10 And the LORD said unto Mō'ses, Go in unto Phā'raōh: [a]for I have hardened his heart, and the heart of his servants, that [b]I might shew these my signs before him:

2 And that [c]thou mayest tell in the ears of thy son, and of thy son's son, what things I have wrought in Ē'ġypt, and my signs which I have done among them; that ye may know how that I *am* the LORD.

3 And Mō'ses and Aâr'on came in unto Phā'raōh, and said unto him, Thus saith the LORD God of the Hē'brews, How long wilt thou refuse to [d]humble thyself before me? let my people go, that they may serve me.

4 Else, if thou refuse to let my people go, behold, to morrow will I bring the [e]locusts into thy coast:

5 And they shall cover the [1]face of the earth, that one cannot be able to see the earth: and [f]they shall eat the residue of that which is escaped, which remaineth unto you from the hail, and shall eat every tree which groweth for you out of the field:

6 And they [g]shall fill thy houses, and the houses of all thy servants, and the houses of all the E-ġȳp'tians; which neither thy fathers, nor thy fathers' fathers have seen, since the day that they were upon the earth unto this day. And he turned himself, and went out from Phā'raōh.

7 And Phā'raōh's servants said unto him, How long shall this man be [h]a snare unto us? let the men go, that they may serve the LORD their God: knowest thou not yet that Ē'ġypt is destroyed?

8 And Mō'ses and Aâr'on were brought again unto Phā'raōh: and he said unto them, Go, serve the LORD your God: [2]*but* who *are* they that shall go?

9 And Mō'ses said, [i]We will go with our young and with our old, with our sons and with our daughters, with our flocks and with our herds will we go; for [j]we *must hold* a feast unto the LORD.

10 And he said unto them, Let the LORD be so with you, as I will let you go, and your little ones: look *to it;* for evil *is* before you.

11 Not so: go now ye *that are* men, and serve the LORD; for that ye did desire. And they were driven out from Phā'raōh's presence.

12 ¶ And the LORD said unto Mō'ses, [k]Stretch out thine hand over the land of Ē'ġypt for the locusts, that they may come up upon the land of Ē'ġypt, [l]and eat every herb of the land, *even* all that the hail hath left.

13 And Mō'ses stretched forth his rod over the land of Ē'ġypt, and the LORD brought an east wind upon the land all that day, and all *that* night; *and* when it was morning, the east wind brought the locusts.

14 And [m]the locusts went up over all the land of Ē'ġypt, and rested in all the coasts of Ē'ġypt: very grievous *were they;* [n]before them there were no such locusts as they, neither after them shall be such.

15 For they [o]covered the face of the whole earth, so that the land was darkened; and they [p]did eat every herb of the land, and all the fruit of the trees which the hail had left: and there remained not any green thing in the trees, or in the herbs of the field, through all the land of Ē'ġypt.

16 ¶ Then Phā'raōh [3]called for Mō'ses and Aâr'on in haste; and he said, [q]I have sinned against the LORD your God, and against you.

17 Now therefore forgive, I pray thee, my sin only this once, [r]and intreat the LORD your God, that he may take away from me this death only.

18 And he [s]went out from Phā'raōh, and intreated the LORD.

19 And the LORD turned a mighty strong west wind, which took away the locusts, and [4]cast them into [t]the Red sea; there remained not one locust in all the coasts of Ē'ġypt.

25 [r]Ps. 105.33
26 [s]ch. 9.4-6; ch. 11.7; Isa. 32.18-19
27 [t]ch. 10.16 [u]2 Chr. 12.6; Ps. 129.4; Ps. 145.17; Lam. 1.18; Dan. 9.14
28 [v]ch. 8.8-28; ch. 10.17; Acts 8.24 [3]voices of God; Ps. 29.3-4
29 [w]1 Ki. 8.22-38; Ps. 143.6; Isa. 1.15 [x]Ps. 24.1; 1 Cor. 10.26
30 [y]Isa. 26.10
31 [z]Ruth 1.22; Ruth 2.23
32 [4]hidden, or, dark
33 [a]ch. 8.12
35 [5]by the hand of Moses; ch. 4.13

CHAPTER 10
1 [a]ch. 7.14; Deut. 2.30; Josh. 11.20; John 12.40; Rom. 9.18 [b]ch. 7.4
2 [c]Deut. 4.9; Ps. 44.1; Ps. 71.18; Joel 1.3
3 [d]1 Ki. 21.29; 2 Chr. 34.27; Jas. 4.10; 1 Pet. 5.6
4 [e]Prov. 30.27; Rev. 9.3
5 [1]eye [f]Joel 2.25
6 [g]ch. 8.3-21
7 [h]ch. 23.33; Josh. 23.13; 1 Cor. 7.35
8 [2]who, and who, etc
9 [i]Prov. 3.9 [j]ch. 5.1
12 [k]ch. 7.19 [l]verses 4-5
14 [m]Deut. 28.38; Rev. 9.2-4 [n]Joel 2.2
15 [o]verse 5 [p]Ps. 105.35
16 [3]hastened to call [q]ch. 9.27
17 [r]ch. 9.28; Job 34.31
18 [s]ch. 8.30
19 [4]fastened [t]Joel 2.20

20 But the LORD [u]hardened Phā′raōh's heart, so that he would not let the children of Ĭs′ra-el go.

21 ¶ And the LORD said unto Mō′ses, [v]Stretch out thine hand toward heaven, that there may be darkness over the land of Ē′ġypt, [5]even darkness *which* may be felt.

22 And Mō′ses stretched forth his hand toward heaven; and there was a [w]thick darkness in all the land of Ē′ġypt three days:

23 They saw not one another, neither rose any from his place for three days: [x]but all the children of Ĭs′ra-el had light in their dwellings.

24 ¶ And Phā′raōh called unto Mō′ses, and said, Go ye, serve the LORD; only let your flocks and your herds be stayed: let your [y]little ones also go with you.

25 And Mō′ses said, Thou must give [6]us also sacrifices and burnt offerings, that we may sacrifice unto the LORD our God.

26 Our cattle also shall go with us; there shall not an hoof be left behind; for thereof must we take to serve the LORD our God; and we know not with what we must serve the LORD, until we come thither.

27 ¶ But the LORD [z]hardened Phā′raōh's heart, and he would not let them go.

28 And Phā′raōh said unto him, Get thee from me, take heed to thyself, see my face no more; for in *that* day thou seest my face thou shalt die.

29 And Mō′ses said, Thou hast spoken well, [a]I will see thy face again no more.

11 And the LORD said unto Mō′ses, Yet will I bring one plague *more* upon Phā′raōh, and upon Ē′ġypt; afterwards he will let you go hence: [a]when he shall let *you* go, he shall surely thrust you out hence altogether.

2 Speak now in the ears of the people, and let every man [1]borrow of his neighbour, and every woman of her neighbour, [b]jewels of silver, and jewels of gold.

3 And [c]the LORD gave the people favour in the sight of the E-ġȳp′tians. Moreover the man [d]Mō′ses *was* very great in the land of Ē′ġypt, in the sight of Phā′raōh's servants, and in the sight of the people.

4 And Mō′ses said, Thus saith the LORD, [e]About midnight will I go out into the midst of Ē′ġypt:

5 And [f]all the firstborn in the land of Ē′ġypt shall die, from the firstborn of Phā′raōh that sitteth upon his throne, even unto the firstborn of the maidservant that *is* behind the mill; and all the firstborn of beasts.

6 And [g]there shall be a great cry throughout all the land of Ē′ġypt, such as there was none like it, nor shall be like it any more.

7 But against any of the children of Ĭs′ra-el shall [h]not a dog move his tongue, against man or beast: that ye may know how that the LORD doth put [i]a difference between the E-ġȳp′tians and Ĭs′ra-el.

8 And all these thy servants shall come down unto me, and bow down themselves unto me, saying, Get thee out, and all the people [2]that follow thee: and after that I will go out. And he went out from Phā′raōh in [3]a great anger.

9 And the LORD said unto Mō′ses, Phā′raōh shall not hearken unto you; that my wonders may be multiplied in the land of Ē′ġypt.

10 And Mō′ses and Aâr′on did all these wonders before Phā′raōh: and [i]the LORD hardened Phā′raōh's heart, so that he would not let the children of Ĭs′ra-el go out of his land.

12 And the LORD spake unto Mō′ses and Aâr′on in the land of Ē′ġypt, saying,

2 This [a]month *shall be* unto you the beginning of months: it *shall be* the first month of the year to you.

3 ¶ Speak ye unto all the congregation of Ĭs′ra-el, saying, In the tenth *day* of this month they shall take to them every man a [1]lamb, according to the house of *their* fathers, a lamb for an house:

4 And if the household be too little for the lamb, let him and his neighbour next unto his house take *it* according to the number of the souls; every man according to his eating shall make your count for the lamb.

5 Your lamb shall be [b]without blemish, a male [2]of the first year: ye shall take *it* out from the sheep, or from the goats:

6 And ye shall keep it up until the [c]fourteenth day of the same month: and the whole assembly of the congregation of Ĭs′ra-el shall kill it [3]in the evening.

7 And they shall take of the blood, and strike *it* on the two side posts and on the upper door post of the houses, wherein they shall eat it.

8 And they shall eat the flesh in that night, roast with fire, [d]and unleavened bread; *and* with bitter *herbs* they shall eat it.

9 Eat not of it raw, nor sodden at all with water, but roast *with* fire; his head with his legs, and with the purtenance thereof.

10 And [e]ye shall let nothing of it remain until the morning; and that which remaineth of it until the morning ye shall burn with fire.

11 ¶ And thus shall ye eat it; *with* your loins girded, your shoes on your feet, and your staff in your hand; and ye shall eat it in haste: it [f]*is* the LORD'S passover.

12 For I [g]will pass through the land of Ē′ġypt this night, and will smite all the firstborn in the land of Ē′ġypt, both man and beast; and [h]against all the [4]gods of Ē′ġypt I will execute judgment: I *am* the LORD.

13 And [i]the blood shall be to you for a token upon the houses where ye *are*: and when I see the blood, I will pass

20 [u]ch. 4.21; ch. 11.10; Deut. 2.30; Jas. 1.13-17
21 [v]ch. 9.22 [5]that one may feel darkness
22 [w]Ps. 105.28
23 [x]ch. 8.22
24 [y]verse 10
25 [6]into our hands
27 [z]verse 20; ch. 14.4-8
29 [a]Heb. 11.27

CHAPTER 11
1 [a]ch. 12.31
2 [1]Or, demand [b]ch. 3.22; ch. 12.35
3 [c]ch. 3.21; Ps. 106.46 [d]2 Sam. 7.9; Esth. 9.4
4 [e]ch. 12.12-23-29; Amos 5.17
5 [f]Amos 4.10
6 [g]Amos 5.17
7 [h]Josh. 10.21; Hos. 2.18 [i]Mal. 3.18
8 [2]that is at thy feet; Judg. 4.10; Judg. 8.5; 1 Ki. 20.10; 2 Ki. 3.9 [3]heat of anger
10 [i]ch. 7.3-13; Rom. 9.22

CHAPTER 12
2 [a]ch. 13.4; Deut. 16.1
3 [1]Or, kid
5 [b]Lev. 22.19; 1 Pet. 1.19 [2]son of a year; Lev. 23.12
6 [c]Lev. 23.5; Deut. 16.1-6 [3]between the two evenings; ch. 16.12
8 [d]Num. 9.11; 1 Cor. 5.8
10 [e]ch. 23.18
11 [f]Deut. 16.5
12 [g]ch. 11.4-5; Amos 5.17 [h]Num. 33.4 [4]Or, princes; ch. 22.28; Ps. 82.1-6; John 10.34
13 [i]Heb. 11.28

over you, and the plague shall not be upon you [5]to destroy *you*, when I smite the land of Ē'ġypt.

14 And this day shall be unto you for a memorial; and ye shall keep it a [j]feast to the LORD throughout your generations; ye shall keep it a feast by an ordinance for ever.

15 [k]Seven days shall ye eat unleavened bread; even the first day ye shall put away leaven out of your houses: for whosoever eateth leavened bread from the first day until the seventh day, [l]that soul shall be cut off from Ĭs'ra-el.

16 And in the first day *there shall be* an holy convocation, and in the seventh day there shall be an holy convocation to you; no manner of work shall be done in them, save *that* which every [6]man must eat, that only may be done of you.

17 And ye shall observe *the feast of* unleavened bread; for [m]in this selfsame day have I brought your armies out of the land of Ē'ġypt: therefore shall ye observe this day in your generations by an ordinance for ever.

18 ¶ In [n]the first *month*, on the fourteenth day of the month at even, ye shall eat unleavened bread, until the one and twentieth day of the month at even.

19 [o]Seven days shall there be no leaven found in your houses: for whosoever eateth that which is leavened, [p]even that soul shall be cut off from the congregation of Ĭs'ra-el, whether he be a stranger or born in the land.

20 Ye shall eat nothing leavened; in all your habitations shall ye eat unleavened bread.

21 ¶ Then Mō'ses called for all the elders of Ĭs'ra-el, and said unto them, [q]Draw out and take you a [7]lamb according to your families, and kill the passover.

22 And ye shall take a bunch of hyssop, and dip *it* in the blood that *is* in the bason, and strike the lintel and the two side posts with the blood that *is* in the bason; and none of you shall go out at the door of his house until the morning.

23 For the LORD will pass through to smite the E-ġy̆p'tians; and when he seeth the blood upon the lintel, and on the two side posts, the LORD will pass over the door, and will not [r]suffer [s]the destroyer to come in unto your houses to smite *you*.

24 And ye shall observe this thing for an ordinance to thee and to thy sons for ever.

25 And it shall come to pass, when ye be come to the land which the LORD will give you, according as he hath promised, that ye shall keep this service.

26 And [t]it shall come to pass, when your children shall say unto you, What mean ye by this service?

27 That ye shall say, It *is* the sacrifice of the LORD'S passover, who passed over the houses of the children of Ĭs'ra-el in Ē'ġypt, when he smote the E-ġy̆p'tians, and delivered our houses. And the people bowed the head and worshipped.

28 And the children of Ĭs'ra-el went away, and did as the LORD had commanded Mō'ses and Aâr'on, so did they.

29 ¶ And it came to pass, that at midnight the [u]LORD smote all the firstborn in the land of Ē'ġypt, from the firstborn of Phā'raōh that sat on his throne unto the firstborn of the captive that *was* in the [8]dungeon; and all the firstborn of cattle.

30 And Phā'raōh rose up in the night, he, and all his servants, and all the E-ġy̆p'tians; and there was a [v]great cry in Ē'ġypt; for *there was* not a house where *there was* not one dead.

31 ¶ And he called for Mō'ses and Aâr'on by night, and said, Rise up, *and* get you forth from among my people, [w]both ye and the children of Ĭs'ra-el; and go, serve the LORD, as ye have said.

32 Also take your flocks and your herds, as ye have said, and be gone; and [x]bless me also.

33 And [y]the E-ġy̆p'tians were urgent upon the people, that they might send them out of the land in haste; for they said, [z]We *be* all dead *men*.

34 And the people took their dough before it was leavened, their [9]kneadingtroughs being bound up in their clothes upon their shoulders.

35 And the children of Ĭs'ra-el did according to the word of Mō'ses; and they [10]borrowed of the E-ġy̆p'tians [a]jewels of silver, and jewels of gold, and raiment:

36 And the LORD gave the people favour in the sight of the E-ġy̆p'tians, so that they lent unto them *such things as they required*. [b]And they spoiled the E-ġy̆p'tians.

37 ¶ And [c]the children of Ĭs'ra-el journeyed from [d]Ra-mē'sēs to Sŭc'-coth, about [e]six hundred thousand on foot *that were* men, beside children.

38 And [11]a mixed multitude went up also with them; and flocks, and herds, *even* very much cattle.

39 And they baked unleavened cakes of the dough which they brought forth out of Ē'ġypt, for it was not leavened; because [f]they were thrust out of Ē'ġypt, and could not tarry, neither had they prepared for themselves any victual.

40 ¶ Now the sojourning of the children of Ĭs'ra-el, who dwelt in Ē'ġypt, *was* [g]four hundred and thirty years.

41 And it came to pass at the end of the four hundred and thirty years, even the selfsame day it came to pass, that all [h]the hosts of the LORD went out from the land of Ē'ġypt.

42 It *is* [12]a night to be much observed unto the LORD for bringing them out from the land of Ē'ġypt: this *is* that night of the LORD to be observed of all the children of Ĭs'ra-el in their generations.

---

[5]for a destruction
14 [j]Lev. 23.4-5; 2 Ki. 23.21
15 [k]Num. 28.17; 1 Cor. 5.7
[l]Gen. 17.14; Num. 9.13
16 [6]soul
17 [m]ch. 13.3
18 [n]Lev. 23.5
19 [o]ch. 23.15; ch. 34.18
[p]Num. 9.13
21 [q]Num. 9.4; Luke 22.7
[7]Or, kid
23 [r]Ezek. 9.6; Rev. 9.4
[s]2 Sam. 24.16; Heb. 11.28
26 [t]ch. 13.8-14; Ps. 78.6
29 [u]Num. 8.17; Isa. 37.36
[8]house of the pit
30 [v]ch. 11.6; Jas. 2.13
31 [w]ch. 10.9
32 [x]Gen. 27.34
33 [y]ch. 11.8; Ps. 105.38
[z]Gen. 20.3
34 [9]Or, dough; ch. 8.3
35 [10]Or, demanded
[a]ch. 3.22; ch. 11.2
36 [b]Gen. 15.14; ch. 3.22
37 [c]Num. 33.3-5
[d]Gen. 47.11
[e]Gen. 12.2; Num. 11.21
38 [11]a great mixture, Num. 11.4
39 [f]ch. 6.1; ch. 11.1
40 [g]Gen. 15.13;
41 [h]ch. 7.4
42 [12]a night of observations

43 ¶ And the LORD said unto Mō'ses and Âar'on, This *is* [i]the ordinance of the passover: There shall no stranger eat thereof:

44 But every man's servant that is bought for money, when thou hast [j]circumcised him, then shall he eat thereof.

45 A [k]foreigner and an hired servant shall not eat thereof.

46 In one house shall it be eaten; thou shalt not carry forth ought of the flesh abroad out of the house; [l]neither shall ye break a bone thereof.

47 All the congregation of Ĭs'ra-el shall [13]keep it.

48 And when a stranger shall sojourn with thee, and will keep the passover to the LORD, let all his males be circumcised, and then let him come near and keep it; and he shall be as one that is born in the land: for no uncircumcised person shall eat thereof.

49 [m]One law shall be to him that is homeborn, and unto the stranger that sojourneth among you.

50 Thus did all the children of Ĭs'ra-el; as the LORD commanded Mō'ses and Âar'on, so did they.

51 And it came to pass the selfsame day, *that* the LORD did bring the children of Ĭs'ra-el out of the land of Ē'ġypt by [n]their armies.

13 And the LORD spake unto Mō'ses, saying,

2 Sanctify [a]unto me all the firstborn, whatsoever openeth the womb among the children of Ĭs'ra-el, *both* of man and of beast: it *is* mine.

3 ¶ And Mō'ses said unto the people, [b]Remember this day, in which ye came out from Ē'ġypt, out of the house of [1]bondage; for by [c]strength of hand the LORD brought you out from this *place*: there shall no leavened bread be eaten.

4 This [d]day came ye out in the month Ā'bĭb.

5 ¶ And it shall be when the LORD shall bring thee into the land of the Cā'năan-ītes, and the Hĭt'tītes, and the Ăm'ôr-ītes, and the Hī'vītes, and the Jĕb'u-sītes, which he sware unto thy fathers to give thee, a land flowing with milk and honey, that thou shalt keep this service in this month.

6 [e]Seven days thou shalt eat unleavened bread, and in the seventh day *shall be* a feast to the LORD.

7 Unleavened bread shall be eaten seven days; and there shall no leavened bread be seen with thee, neither shall there be leaven seen with thee in all thy quarters.

8 ¶ And thou shalt [f]shew thy son in that day, saying, *This is done* because of that *which* the LORD did unto me when I came forth out of Ē'ġypt.

9 And it shall be for a [g]sign unto thee upon thine hand, and for a memorial between thine eyes, that the LORD'S law may be in thy mouth: for with a strong hand hath the LORD brought thee out of Ē'ġypt.

10 Thou shalt therefore keep this ordinance in his season from year to year.

11 ¶ And it shall be when the LORD shall bring thee into the land of the Cā'năan-ītes, as he [h]sware unto thee and to thy fathers, and shall give it thee,

12 That [i]thou shalt [2]set apart unto the LORD all that openeth the matrix, and every firstling that cometh of a beast which thou hast; the males *shall be* the LORD'S.

13 And every firstling of an ass thou shalt redeem with a [3]lamb; and if thou wilt not redeem it, then thou shalt break his neck: and all the firstborn of man among thy children [j]shalt thou redeem.

14 ¶ And [k]it shall be when thy son asketh thee [4]in time to come, saying, What *is* this? that thou shalt say unto him, By strength of hand the LORD brought us out from Ē'ġypt, from the house of bondage:

15 And it came to pass, when Phā'raōh would hardly let us go, that the LORD slew all the firstborn in the land of Ē'ġypt, both the firstborn of man, and the firstborn of beast: therefore I sacrifice to the LORD all that openeth the matrix, being males; but all the firstborn of my children I redeem.

16 And it shall be for [l]a token upon thine hand, and for frontlets between thine eyes: for by strength of hand the LORD brought us forth out of Ē'ġypt.

17 ¶ And it came to pass, when Phā'raōh had let the people go, that God led them not *through* the way of the land of the Phĭ-lĭs'tīnes, although that *was* near; for God said, Lest peradventure the people repent [m]when they see war, and they [n]return to Ē'ġypt:

18 But [o]God led the people about, *through* the way of the wilderness of the Red sea: and the children of Ĭs'ra-el went up [5]harnessed out of the land of Ē'ġypt.

19 And Mō'ses took the bones of Jō'seph with him: for he had straitly sworn the children of Ĭs'ra-el, saying, [p]God will surely visit you; and ye shall carry up my bones away hence with you.

20 ¶ And they took their journey from Sŭc'coth, and encamped in Ē'tham, [q]in the edge of the wilderness.

21 And [r]the LORD went before them by day in a pillar of a cloud, to lead them the way; and by night in a pillar of fire, to give them light; to go by day and night:

22 He [s]took not away the pillar of the cloud by day, nor the pillar of fire by night, *from* before the people.

14 And the LORD spake unto Mō'ses, saying,

2 Speak unto the children of Ĭs'ra-el, that they turn and encamp before [a]Pī-ha-hī'roth, between [b]Mĭg'dol and the sea, over against Bā'al-zē'phon: before it shall ye encamp by the sea.

3 For Phā'raōh will say of the children of Ĭs'ra-el, [c]They *are* entangled

43 [i]Num. 9.14
44 [j]Gen. 17.12-13
45 [k]Lev. 22.10
46 [l]Ps. 34.20; John 19.33
47 [13]do it
49 [m]Num. 9.14; Gal. 3.28
51 [n]Acts 7.36
CHAPTER 13
2 [a]ch. 22.29-30; Luke 2.23
3 [b]ch. 12.42; Deut. 16.3 [1]servants [c]ch. 6.1
4 [d]ch. 23.15; Deut. 16.1
6 [e]ch. 12.15-16
8 [f]Ps. 44.1
9 [g]ch. 12.14; Matt. 23.5
11 [h]Gen. 15.18; Ps. 105.42-45
12 [i]ch. 22.29; Ezek. 44.30 [2]cause to pass over
13 [3]Or, kid [j]Num. 3.46
14 [k]ch. 12.26; Josh. 4.6-21 [4]to morrow
16 [l]Deut. 6.8
17 [m]ch. 14.11; Num. 14.1-4 [n]Deut. 17.16
18 [o]ch. 14.2; Num. 33.6 [5]Or, by five in a rank
19 [p]Gen. 50.25; Acts 7.16
20 [q]Num. 33.6
21 [r]Deut. 1.33;
22 [s]Ps. 121.5-8
CHAPTER 14
2 [a]Num. 33.7 [b]Jer. 44.1
3 [c]Ps. 35.21;

in the land, the wilderness hath shut
them in.
4 And [d]I will harden Phā'raōh's
heart, that he shall follow after them;
and I [e]will be honoured upon Phā'-
raōh, and upon all his host; that the E-
ġy̆p'tians may know that I *am* the
LORD. And they did so.
5 ¶ And it was told the king of Ē'ġypt
that the people fled: and the heart
of Phā'raōh and of his servants was
turned against the people, and they
said, Why have we done this, that we
have let Is'ra-el go from serving us?
6 And he made ready his chariot,
and took his people with him:
7 And he took six hundred chosen
chariots, and all the chariots of Ē'ġypt,
and captains over every one of them.
8 And [f]the LORD hardened the heart
of Phā'raōh king of Ē'ġypt, and he pursued after the children of Is'ra-el: and
the children of Is'ra-el went out with
an high hand.
9 But the [g]E-ġy̆p'tians pursued after
them, all the horses *and* chariots of
Phā'raōh, and his horsemen, and his
army, and overtook them encamping
by the sea, beside Pī–ha-hī'roth, before Bā'al–zē'phon.
10 ¶ And when Phā'raōh drew nigh,
the children of Is'ra-el lifted up their
eyes, and, behold, the E-ġy̆p'tians
marched after them; and they were
sore afraid: and the children of Is'ra-el
[h]cried out unto the LORD.
11 And [i]they said unto Mō'ses, Because *there were* no graves in Ē'ġypt,
hast thou taken us away to die in the
wilderness? wherefore hast thou dealt
thus with us, to carry us forth out of
Ē'ġypt?
12 [j]*Is* not this the word that we did
tell thee in Ē'ġypt, saying, Let us alone,
that we may serve the E-ġy̆p'tians? For
it had been better for us to serve the
E-ġy̆p'tians, than that we should die in
the wilderness.
13 ¶ And Mō'ses said unto the people, [k]Fear ye not, stand still, and see
the salvation of the LORD, which he
will shew to you to day: [1]for the
E-ġy̆p'tians whom ye have seen to day,
ye shall see them again no more for
ever.
14 The [l]LORD shall fight for you,
and ye shall [m]hold your peace.
15 ¶ And the LORD said unto Mō'ses,
Wherefore criest thou unto me? speak
unto the children of Is'ra-el, that they
go forward:
16 But [n]lift thou up thy rod, and
stretch out thine hand over the sea,
and divide it: and the children of Is'ra-
el shall go on dry *ground* through the
midst of the sea.
17 And I, behold, I will [o]harden the
hearts of the E-ġy̆p'tians, and they shall
follow them: and I will get me honour
upon Phā'raōh, and upon all his host,
upon his chariots, and upon his horsemen.
18 And the E-ġy̆p'tians shall know
that I *am* the LORD, when I have gotten
me honour upon Phā'raōh, upon his
chariots, and upon his horsemen.
19 ¶ And [p]the angel of God, which
went before the camp of Is'ra-el, removed and went behind them; and the
pillar of the cloud went from before
their face, and stood behind them:
20 And it came between the camp of
the E-ġy̆p'tians and the camp of Is'ra-
el; and [q]it was a cloud and darkness *to*
them, but it gave light by night *to*
these: so that the one came not near
the other all the night.
21 And Mō'ses stretched out his
hand over the sea; and the LORD
caused the sea to go *back* by a strong
east wind all that night, and made the
sea dry *land,* and the waters were [r]di-
vided.
22 And [s]the children of Is'ra-el went
into the midst of the sea upon the dry
ground: and the waters *were* [t]a wall
unto them on their right hand, and on
their left.
23 ¶ And the E-ġy̆p'tians pursued,
and went in after them to the midst of
the sea, *even* all Phā'raōh's horses, his
chariots, and his horsemen.
24 And it came to pass, that in the
morning watch the LORD looked unto
the host of the E-ġy̆p'tians through the
pillar of fire and of the cloud, and troubled the host of the E-ġy̆p'tians,
25 And took off their chariot wheels,
[2]that they drave them heavily: so that
the E-ġy̆p'tians said, Let us flee from
the face of Is'ra-el; for the LORD fighteth for them against the E-ġy̆p'tians.
26 ¶ And the LORD said unto Mō'ses,
Stretch out thine hand over the sea,
that the waters may come again upon
the E-ġy̆p'tians, upon their chariots,
and upon their horsemen.
27 And Mō'ses stretched forth his
hand over the sea, and the sea [u]re-
turned to his strength when the morning appeared; and the E-ġy̆p'tians fled
against it; and the LORD [3]overthrew
the E-ġy̆p'tians in the midst of the sea.
28 And [v]the waters returned, and
covered the chariots, and the horsemen, *and* all the host of Phā'raōh that
came into the sea after them; there remained not so much as one of them.
29 But [w]the children of Is'ra-el
walked upon dry *land* in the midst of
the sea; and the waters *were* a wall
unto them on their right hand, and on
their left.
30 Thus the LORD [x]saved Is'ra-el
that day out of the hand of the E-ġy̆p'-
tians; and Is'ra-el saw [y]the E-
ġy̆p'tians dead upon the sea shore.
31 And Is'ra-el saw that great [4]work
which the LORD did upon the E-ġy̆p'-
tians: and the people feared the LORD,
and [z]believed the LORD, and his servant Mō'ses.

15

Then sang [a]Mō'ses and the children of Is'ra-el this song unto the
LORD, and spake, saying, I will sing
unto the LORD, for he hath triumphed
gloriously: the horse and his rider hath
he thrown into the sea.

4 [d]Jas. 1.13-17 [e]ch. 9.16; Rom. 9.17-23
8 [f]ch. 6.1; ch. 13.9; Num. 33.3
9 [g]ch. 15.9; Josh. 24.6
10 [h]Josh. 24.7; Neh. 9.9; Ps. 34.17; Ps. 107.6
11 [i]Ps. 106.7
12 [j]ch. 6.9
13 [k]2 Chr. 20.15-17; Isa. 41.10-13-14 [1]Or, for whereas ye have seen the Egyptians to day, etc
14 [l]Deut. 20.4; Josh. 10.14-42; Josh. 23.3; 2 Chr. 20.29; Neh. 4.20; Isa. 31.4 [m]Isa. 30.15
16 [n]ch. 7.19
17 [o]Prov. 29.1
19 [p]Gen. 48.16
20 [q]Isa. 8.14; 2 Cor. 4.3
21 [r]Josh. 3.16; Josh. 4.23; Neh. 9.11; Ps. 74.13; Ps. 106.9; Ps. 114.3
22 [s]ch. 15.19; Num. 33.8; Ps. 66.6; Ps. 78.13; 1 Cor. 10.1; Heb. 11.29 [t]Hab. 3.10
25 [2]Or, and made them to go heavily
27 [u]Josh. 4.18 [3]shook off; Deut. 11.4; Neh. 9.11; Ps. 78.53
28 [v]Hab. 3.8
29 [w]Ps. 77.20; Ps. 78.52-53
30 [x]Ps. 106.8-10 [y]Ps. 58.10; Ps. 59.10
31 [4]hand [z]ch. 19.9; John 2.11; John 11.45
CHAPTER 15
1 [a]Judg. 5.1; 2 Sam. 22.1

2 The LORD *is* my strength [b]and
song, and he is become my salvation:
he *is* my God, and I will prepare him
an habitation; my father's God, and I
[c]will exalt him.
3 The LORD *is* a man of [d]war: the
LORD *is* his [e]name.
4 Phā'raōh's chariots and his host
hath he cast into the sea: his chosen
captains also are drowned in the Red
sea.
5 The depths have covered them:
they sank into the bottom as a stone.
6 Thy [f]right hand, O LORD, is become glorious in power: thy right hand,
O LORD, hath dashed in pieces the enemy.
7 And in the greatness of thine excellency thou hast overthrown them that
rose up against thee: thou sentest forth
thy wrath, *which* [g]consumed them [h]as
stubble.
8 And [i]with the blast of thy nostrils
the waters were gathered together, [j]the
floods stood upright as an heap, *and*
the depths were congealed in the heart
of the sea.
9 The enemy said, I will pursue, I
will overtake, I will [k]divide the spoil;
my lust shall be satisfied upon them; I
will draw my sword, my hand shall [1]de-
stroy them.
10 Thou didst blow with thy wind,
the sea covered them: they sank as
lead in the mighty waters.
11 Who [l]*is* like unto thee, O LORD,
among the [2]gods? who *is* like thee, glorious in holiness, fearful *in* praises, doing wonders?
12 Thou stretchedst out thy right
hand, the earth swallowed them.
13 Thou in thy mercy hast led forth
the people *which* thou hast redeemed:
thou hast guided *them* in thy strength
unto [m]thy holy habitation.
14 The [n]people shall hear, *and* be
afraid: [o]sorrow shall take hold on the
inhabitants of Păl-es-tī'nȧ.
15 Then the dukes of Ē'dom shall be
amazed; [p]the mighty men of Mō'ab,
trembling shall take hold upon them;
all the inhabitants of Cā'năan shall
melt away.
16 [q]Fear and dread shall fall upon
them; by the greatness of thine arm
they shall be *as* still [r]as a stone; till thy
people pass over, O LORD, till the people pass over, [s]*which* thou hast purchased.
17 Thou shalt bring them in, and
[t]plant them in the mountain of thine inheritance, *in* the place, O LORD, *which*
thou hast made for thee to dwell in,
in the Sanctuary, O Lord, *which* thy
hands have established.
18 The LORD shall reign for ever and
ever.
19 For the horse of Phā'raōh went in
with his chariots and with his horsemen into the sea, and the LORD brought
again the waters of the sea upon them;
but the children of Ĭs'ra-el went on dry
land in the midst of the sea.
20 ¶ And Mĭr'ĭ-am the prophetess,
the sister of Aâr'on, [u]took a timbrel
in her hand; and all the women went
out after her with timbrels and with
dances.
21 And Mĭr'ĭ-am answered them,
Sing ye to the LORD, for he hath triumphed gloriously; the horse and his
rider hath he thrown into the sea.
22 So Mō'ses brought Ĭs'ra-el from
the Red sea, and they went out into the
wilderness of Shûr; and they went three
days in the wilderness, and found no
water.
23 ¶ And when they came [v]to Mā'-
rah, they could not drink of the waters
of Mā'rah, for they *were* bitter: therefore the name of it was called [3]Mā'rah.
24 And the people murmured against
Mō'ses, saying, What shall we drink?
25 And he [w]cried unto the LORD;
and the LORD shewed him a tree,
[x]*which* when he had cast into the
waters, the waters were made sweet:
there he [y]made for them a statute and
an ordinance, and there [z]he proved
them,
26 And said, [a]If thou wilt diligently
hearken to the voice of the LORD thy
God, and wilt do that which is right in
his sight, and wilt give ear to his commandments, and keep all his statutes, I
will put none of these [b]diseases upon
thee, which I have brought upon the
E-ġȳp'tians: for I *am* the LORD [c]that
healeth thee.
27 ¶ And [d]they came to E'lĭm, where
were twelve wells of water, and threescore and ten palm trees: and they encamped there by the waters.

16

16 And they took their journey from
E'lĭm, and all the congregation of
the children of Ĭs'ra-el came unto the
wilderness of [a]Sĭn, which *is* between
E'lĭm and Sī'nāi, on the fifteenth day of
the second month after their departing
out of the land of Ē'ġypt.
2 And the whole congregation of the
children of Ĭs'ra-el [b]murmured against
Mō'ses and Aâr'on in the wilderness:
3 And the children of Ĭs'ra-el said
unto them, Would to God we had died
by the hand of the LORD in the land of
Ē'ġypt, when [c]we sat by the flesh pots,
and when we did eat bread to the full;
for ye have brought us forth into this
wilderness, to kill this whole assembly
with hunger.
4 ¶ Then said the LORD unto Mō'ses,
Behold, I will rain [d]bread from heaven
for you; and the people shall go out
and gather [1]a certain rate every day,
that I [e]may prove them, whether they
will walk in my law, or no.
5 And it shall come to pass, that on
the sixth day they shall prepare *that*
which they bring in; and [f]it shall be
twice as much as they gather daily.
6 And Mō'ses and Aâr'on said unto
all the children of Ĭs'ra-el, [g]At even,
then ye shall know that the LORD
hath brought you out from the land of
Ē'ġypt:
7 And in the morning, then ye shall
see the [h]glory of the LORD; for that he
heareth your murmurings against the

2 [b]Isa. 12.2
[c]2 Sam. 22.47; Ps. 99.5
3 [d]Rev. 19.11
[e]Ps. 83.18
6 [f]Ps. 118.15
7 [g]Deut. 4.24; Heb. 12.29
[h]Isa. 5.24
8 [i]Job 4.9
[j]Hab. 3.10
9 [k]Isa. 53.12; Luke 11.22
[1]Or, repossess
11 [l]2 Sam. 7.22;
[2]Or, mighty ones
13 [m]Ps. 78.54
14 [n]Josh. 2.9
[o]Ps. 48.6
15 [p]Hab. 3.7
16 [q]Deut. 2.25
[r]1 Sam. 25.37
[s]Deut. 32.9;
17 [t]Ps. 44.2
20 [u]Judg. 11.34;
23 [v]Num. 33.8
[3]That is, Bitterness, Ruth 1.20
25 [w]ch. 14.10;
[x]2 Ki. 2.21;
[y]Josh. 24.25
[z]ch. 16.4;
26 [a]Deut. 7.12
[b]Deut. 28.27
[c]ch. 23.25;
27 [d]Num. 33.9

CHAPTER 16
1 [a]Ezek. 30.15
2 [b]ch. 15.24;
3 [c]Num. 11.4
4 [d]Ps. 78.24-25;
[1]the portion of a day in his day, Prov. 30.8; Matt. 6.11
[e]ch. 15.25;
5 [f]Lev. 25.21
6 [g]ch. 6.7;
7 [h]Isa. 35.2;

LORD: and what *are* we, that ye murmur against us?

8 And Mō'ses said, *This shall be,* when the LORD shall give you in the evening flesh to eat, and in the morning bread to the full; for that the LORD heareth your murmurings which ye murmur against him: and what *are* we? your murmurings *are* not against us, but [i]against the LORD.

9 ¶ And Mō'ses spake unto Aâr'on, Say unto all the congregation of the children of Ĭs'ra-el, Come near before the LORD: for he hath heard your murmurings.

10 And it came to pass, as Aâr'on spake unto the whole congregation of the children of Ĭs'ra-el, that they looked toward the wilderness, and, behold, the glory of the LORD [j]appeared in the cloud.

11 ¶ And the LORD spake unto Mō'ses, saying,

12 I [k]have heard the murmurings of the children of Ĭs'ra-el: speak unto them, saying, [l]At even ye shall eat flesh, and [m]in the morning ye shall be filled with bread; and ye [n]shall know that I *am* the LORD your God.

13 And it came to pass, that at even [o]the quails came up, and covered the camp: and in the morning [p]the dew lay round about the host.

14 And when the dew that lay was gone up, behold, upon the face of the wilderness *there lay* [q]a small round thing, *as* small as the hoar frost on the ground.

15 And when the children of Ĭs'ra-el saw *it,* they said one to another, [2]It *is* manna: for they wist not what it *was.* And Mō'ses said unto them, [r]This *is* the bread which the LORD hath given you to eat.

16 ¶ This *is* the thing which the LORD hath commanded, Gather of it every man according to his eating, [s]an omer [3]for every man, *according to* the number of your [4]persons; take ye every man for *them* which *are* in his tents.

17 And the children of Ĭs'ra-el did so, and gathered, some more, some less.

18 And when they did mete *it* with an omer, [t]he that gathered much had nothing over, and he that gathered little had no lack; they gathered every man according to his eating.

19 And Mō'ses said, Let no man leave of it till the morning.

20 Notwithstanding they hearkened not unto Mō'ses; but some of them left of it until the morning, and it bred worms, and stank: and Mō'ses was wroth with them.

21 And they gathered it every morning, every man according to his eating: and when the sun waxed hot, it melted.

22 ¶ And it came to pass, *that* on the sixth day they gathered twice as much bread, two omers for one *man:* and all the rulers of the congregation came and told Mō'ses.

23 And he said unto them, This *is* *that* which the LORD hath said, To morrow *is* [u]the rest of the holy sabbath unto the LORD: bake *that* which ye will bake *to day,* and seethe that ye will seethe; and that which remaineth over lay up for you to be kept until the morning.

24 And they laid it up till the morning, as Mō'ses bade: and it did not [v]stink, neither was there any worm therein.

25 And Mō'ses said, Eat that to day; for to day [w]*is* a sabbath unto the LORD: to day ye shall not find it in the field.

26 [x]Six days ye shall gather it; but on the seventh day, *which is* the sabbath, in it there shall be none.

27 ¶ And it came to pass, *that* there went out *some* of the people on the seventh day for to gather, and they found none.

28 And the LORD said unto Mō'ses, How long [y]refuse ye to keep my commandments and my laws?

29 See, for that the LORD hath given you the sabbath, therefore he giveth you on the sixth day the bread of two days; abide ye every man in his place, let no man go out of his place on the seventh day.

30 So the people rested on the seventh day.

31 And the house of Ĭs'ra-el called the name thereof Manna: and [z]it *was* like coriander seed white; and the taste of it *was* like wafers *made* with honey.

32 ¶ And Mō'ses said, This *is* the thing which the LORD commandeth, Fill an omer of it to be kept for your generations; that they may see the bread wherewith I have fed you in the wilderness, when I brought you forth from the land of Ē'gypt.

33 And Mō'ses said unto Aâr'on, Take [a]a pot, and put an omer full of manna therein, and lay it up before the LORD, to be kept for your generations.

34 As the LORD commanded Mō'ses, so Aâr'on laid it up [b]before the Testimony, to be kept.

35 And the children of Ĭs'ra-el did eat manna [c]forty years, [d]until they came to a land inhabited; they did eat manna, until they came unto the borders of the land of Cā'năan.

36 Now an omer *is* the tenth *part* of an ephah.

17 And [a]all the congregation of the children of Ĭs'ra-el journeyed from the wilderness of Sĭn, after their journeys, according to the commandment of the LORD, and pitched in Rĕph'ĭ-dim: and *there was* no water for the people to drink.

2 [b]Wherefore the people did chide with Mō'ses, and said, Give us water that we may drink. And Mō'ses said unto them, Why chide ye with me? wherefore do ye [c]tempt the LORD?

3 And the people thirsted there for water; and the people [d]murmured against Mō'ses, and said, Wherefore *is* this *that* thou hast brought us up out of Ē'gypt, to kill us and our children and our cattle with thirst?

8 [i]1 Sam. 8.7; Luke 10.16; Rom. 13.2; 1 Thess. 4.8
10 [j]1 Ki. 8.10
12 [k]Num. 14.27 [l]verse 6 [m]verse 7 [n]ch. 6.7; 1 Ki. 20.28; Joel 3.17
13 [o]Num. 11.31; Ps. 78.27-28; Ps. 105.40 [p]Num. 11.9
14 [q]Num. 11.7; Deut. 8.3; Neh. 9.15; Ps. 78.24; Ps. 105.40
15 [2]Or, What is this? or, It is a portion [r]Isa. 25.6; John 6.31-49-58; 1 Cor. 10.3
16 [s]verse 36 [3]by the poll, or, head [4]souls
18 [t]2 Cor. 8.15
23 [u]Gen. 2.3; ch. 20.8; ch. 31.15; ch. 35.3; Lev. 23.3
24 [v]verse 20
25 [w]Matt. 12.12; Matt. 24.20; Heb. 4.4
26 [x]ch. 20.9-10
28 [y]2 Ki. 17.14; Ps. 78.10-22; Ps. 106.13; Jer. 4.14
31 [z]Num. 11.7-8
33 [a]Heb. 9.4
34 [b]ch. 25.16-21; ch. 40.20; Num. 17.10; Deut. 10.5; 1 Ki. 8.9
35 [c]Num. 33.38; Deut. 8.2-3; Neh. 9.20-21; John 6.31-49 [d]Josh. 5.12; Neh. 9.15

CHAPTER 17
1 [a]ch. 16.1; ch. 19.2; Num. 33.12-14
2 [b]Num. 20.3 [c]Deut. 6.16; Ps. 78.18-41; Isa. 7.12; 1 Cor. 10.9
3 [d]ch. 16.2

4 And Mō'ses cried unto the LORD,
saying, What shall I do unto this people? they be almost ready to [e]stone
me.
5 And the LORD said unto Mō'ses,
[f]Go on before the people, and take
with thee of the elders of Ĭs'ra-el; and
thy rod, wherewith [g]thou smotest the
river, take in thine hand, and go.
6 [h]Behold, I will stand before thee
there upon the rock in Hō'reb; and
thou shalt smite the rock, and there
shall come water out of it, that the people may drink. And Mō'ses did so in
the sight of the elders of Ĭs'ra-el.
7 And he called the name of the
place [1]Măs'sah, and [2]Mĕr'ĭ-bah, because of the chiding of the children of
Ĭs'ra-el, and because they tempted the
LORD, saying, Is the LORD among us,
or not?
8 ¶ Then [i]came Ăm'a-lĕk, and fought
with Ĭs'ra-el in Rĕph'ĭ-dim.
9 And Mō'ses said unto [j]Jŏsh'u-ȧ,
Choose us out men, and go out, fight
with Ăm'a-lĕk: to morrow I will stand
on the top of the hill with the rod of
God in mine hand.
10 So Jŏsh'u-ȧ did as Mō'ses had
said to him, and fought with Ăm'a-lĕk:
and Mō'ses, Aâr'on, and Hûr went up
to the top of the hill.
11 And it came to pass, when Mō'-
ses [k]held up his hand, that Ĭs'ra-el prevailed: and when he let down his hand,
Ăm'a-lĕk prevailed.
12 But Mō'ses' hands *were* heavy;
and they took a stone, and put *it* under
him, and he sat thereon; and Aâr'on
and Hûr stayed up his hands, the one
on the one side, and the other on the
other side; and his hands were steady
until the going down of the sun.
13 And Jŏsh'u-ȧ discomfited Ăm'a-
lĕk and his people with the edge of the
sword.
14 And the LORD said unto Mō'ses,
[l]Write this *for* a memorial in a book,
and rehearse *it* in the ears of Jŏsh'u-ȧ:
for [m]I will utterly put out the remembrance of Ăm'a-lĕk from under heaven.
15 And Mō'ses built an altar, and
called the name of it [3]Je-hō'vah–nĭs'sī:
16 For he said, [4]Because [5]the LORD
hath sworn *that* the LORD *will have*
war with Ăm'a-lĕk from generation to
generation.

18

When Jē'thro, the priest of Mĭd'-
ĭ-an, Mō'ses' father in law, heard
of all that God had done for Mō'ses,
and for Ĭs'ra-el his people, *and* that
the LORD had brought Ĭs'ra-el out of
Ē'ġypt;
2 Then Jē'thro, Mō'ses' father in law,
took Zĭp-pō'rah, Mō'ses' wife, after he
had sent her back,
3 And her two sons; of which the
name of the one *was* [1]Gĕr'shŏm; for he
said, I have been an alien in a strange
land:
4 And the name of the other *was* [2]El-
i-ē'zĕr; for the God of my father, *said
he, was* mine help, and delivered me
from the sword of Phā'raōh:

4 [e]1 Sam. 30.6; John 10.31
5 [f]Ezek. 2.6
[g]Num. 20.8
6 [h]Ps. 105.41; 1 Cor. 10.4
7 [1]That is, Tentation, Ps. 95.8; Heb. 3.8
[2]That is, Chiding, or, Strife
8 [i]Gen. 36.12; 1 Sam. 15.2
9 [j]Called, Jesus, Acts 7.45; Heb. 4.8
11 [k]Jas. 5.16
14 [l]ch. 34.27
[m]Deut. 25.19;
15 [3]That is, The LORD my banner, Judg. 6.24
16 [4]Or, Because the hand of Amalek is against the throne of the LORD, therefore, etc
[5]the hand upon the throne of the LORD

CHAPTER 18
3 [1]That is, A stranger there
4 [2]That is, My God is an help
7 [3]peace, Gen. 43.27; 2 Sam. 11.7
8 [4]found them
11 [a]2 Chr. 2.5;
[b]ch. 1.10
[c]Job 40.11
12 [d]Deut. 12.7;
16 [e]2 Sam. 15.3;
[5]a man and his fellow
[f]Num. 36.6
18 [6]Fading thou wilt fade
[g]Num. 11.14;
19 [h]Deut. 5.5
[i]Num. 27.5
20 [j]Deut. 4.1-5
[k]Ps. 143.8
[l]Deut. 1.18
21 [m]Deut. 16.18;
[n]Gen. 42.18;
[o]Ezek. 18.8

5 And Jē'thro, Mō'ses' father in law,
came with his sons and his wife unto
Mō'ses into the wilderness, where he
encamped at the mount of God:
6 And he said unto Mō'ses, I thy father in law Jē'thro am come unto thee,
and thy wife, and her two sons with
her.
7 ¶ And Mō'ses went out to meet his
father in law, and did obeisance, and
kissed him; and they asked each other
of *their* [3]welfare; and they came into
the tent.
8 And Mō'ses told his father in law
all that the LORD had done unto Phā'-
raōh and to the E-ġўp'tians for Ĭs'ra-
el's sake, *and* all the travail that had
[4]come upon them by the way, and *how*
the LORD delivered them.
9 And Jē'thro rejoiced for all the
goodness which the LORD had done to
Ĭs'ra-el, whom he had delivered out of
the hand of the E-ġўp'tians.
10 And Jē'thro said, Blessed *be* the
LORD, who hath delivered you out of
the hand of the E-ġўp'tians, and out of
the hand of Phā'raōh, who hath delivered the people from under the hand of
the E-ġўp'tians.
11 Now I know that the LORD *is*
[a]greater than all gods: [b]for in the thing
wherein they dealt [c]proudly *he was*
above them.
12 And Jē'thro, Mō'ses' father in
law, took a burnt offering and sacrifices for God: and Aâr'on came, and all
the elders of Ĭs'ra-el, to eat bread with
Mō'ses' father in law [d]before God.
13 ¶ And it came to pass on the morrow, that Mō'ses sat to judge the people: and the people stood by Mō'ses
from the morning unto the evening.
14 And when Mō'ses' father in law
saw all that he did to the people, he
said, What *is* this thing that thou doest
to the people? why sittest thou thyself
alone, and all the people stand by thee
from morning unto even?
15 And Mō'ses said unto his father
in law, Because the people come unto
me to inquire of God:
16 When they have [e]a matter, they
come unto me; and I judge between
[5]one and another, and I do [f]make *them*
know the statutes of God, and his laws.
17 And Mō'ses' father in law said
unto him, The thing that thou doest *is*
not good.
18 [6]Thou wilt surely wear away, both
thou, and this people that *is* with thee:
for this thing *is* too heavy for thee; [g]thou
art not able to perform it thyself alone.
19 Hearken now unto my voice, I
will give thee counsel, and God shall
be with thee: be thou [h]for the people to
God-ward, that thou mayest [i]bring the
causes unto God:
20 And thou shalt [j]teach them ordinances and laws, and shalt shew them
[k]the way wherein they must walk, and
[l]the work that they must do.
21 Moreover thou shalt provide out
of all the people [m]able men, such as
[n]fear God, [o]men of truth, hating covetousness; and place *such* over them, *to*

be rulers of thousands, *and* rulers of hundreds, rulers of fifties, and rulers of tens:

22 And let them judge the people at all seasons: [p]and it shall be, *that* every great matter they shall bring unto thee, but every small matter they shall judge: so shall it be easier for thyself, and they shall bear *the burden* with thee.

23 If thou shalt do this thing, and God command thee *so,* then thou shalt be able to endure, and all this people shall also go to their place in peace.

24 So Mō′ses hearkened to the voice of his father in law, and did all that he had said.

25 And [q]Mō′ses chose able men out of all Ĭs′ra-el, and made them heads over the people, rulers of thousands, rulers of hundreds, rulers of fifties, and rulers of tens.

26 And they judged the people at all seasons: the [r]hard causes they brought unto Mō′ses, but every small matter they judged themselves.

27 ¶ And Mō′ses let his father in law depart; and [s]he went his way into his own land.

19

In the third month, when the children of Ĭs′ra-el were gone forth out of the land of Ē′gypt, the same day came they *into* the wilderness of Sī′nāi.

2 For they were departed from Rĕph′ĭ-dim, and were come *to* the desert of Sī′nāi, and had pitched in the wilderness; and there Ĭs′ra-el camped before the mount.

3 And [a]Mō′ses went up unto God, and the LORD called unto him out of the mountain, saying, Thus shalt thou say to the house of Jā′cob, and tell the children of Ĭs′ra-el;

4 Ye have seen what I did unto the E-gȳp′tians, and *how* [b]I bare you on eagles' wings, and brought you unto myself.

5 Now therefore, if ye will obey my voice indeed, and keep my covenant, then [c]ye shall be a peculiar treasure unto me above all people: for [d]all the earth *is* mine:

6 And ye shall be unto me [e]a kingdom of priests, and an [f]holy nation. These *are* the words which thou shalt speak unto the children of Ĭs′ra-el.

7 ¶ And Mō′ses came and called for the elders of the people, and laid before their faces all these words which the LORD commanded him.

8 And [g]all the people answered together, and said, All that the LORD hath spoken we will do. And Mō′ses returned the words of the people unto the LORD.

9 And the LORD said unto Mō′ses, Lo, I come unto thee [h]in a thick cloud, [i]that the people may hear when I speak with thee, and believe thee for ever. And Mō′ses told the words of the people unto the LORD.

10 ¶ And the LORD said unto Mō′ses, Go unto the people, [j]and sanctify them to day and to morrow, and let them [k]wash their clothes,

11 And be ready against the third day: for the third day the [l]LORD will come down in the sight of all the people upon mount Sī′nāi.

12 And thou shalt set bounds unto the people round about, saying, Take heed to yourselves, *that ye* go *not* up into the mount, or touch the border of it: [m]whosoever toucheth the mount shall be surely put to death:

13 There shall not an hand touch it, but he shall surely be stoned, or shot through; whether *it be* beast or man, it shall not live: when the [1]trumpet soundeth long, they shall come up to the mount.

14 ¶ And Mō′ses went down from the mount unto the people, and sanctified the people; and they washed their clothes.

15 And he said unto the people, Be ready against the third day: come [n]not at *your* wives.

16 ¶ And it came to pass on the third day in the morning, that there were thunders and lightnings, and a thick cloud upon the mount, and the voice of the trumpet exceeding loud; so that all the people that *was* in the camp trembled.

17 And [o]Mō′ses brought forth the people out of the camp to meet with God; and they stood at the nether part of the mount.

18 And [p]mount Sī′nāi was altogether on a smoke, because the LORD descended upon it [q]in fire: and the smoke [r]thereof ascended as the smoke of a furnace, and the whole [s]mount quaked greatly.

19 And when the voice of the trumpet sounded long, and waxed louder and louder, Mō′ses spake, and [t]God answered him by a voice.

20 And the LORD came down upon mount Sī′nāi, on the top of the mount: and the LORD called Mō′ses *up* to the top of the mount; and Mō′ses went up.

21 And the LORD said unto Mō′ses, Go down, [2]charge the people, lest they break through unto the LORD to [u]gaze, and many of them perish.

22 And let the priests also, which come near to the LORD, [v]sanctify themselves, lest the LORD [w]break forth upon them.

23 And Mō′ses said unto the LORD, The people cannot come up to mount Sī′nāi: for thou chargedst us, saying, Set bounds about the mount, and sanctify it.

24 And the LORD said unto him, Away, get thee down, and thou shalt come up, thou, and Aâr′on with thee: but let not the priests and the people break through to come up unto the LORD, lest he break forth upon them.

25 So Mō′ses went down unto the people, and spake unto them.

20

And God spake all these words, [a]saying,

2 I [b]*am* the LORD thy God, which have brought thee out of the land of Ē′gypt, [c]out of the house of [1]bondage.

22 [p]Lev. 24.11; Num. 15.33; Deut. 17.8
25 [q]Deut. 1.15; Acts 6.5
26 [r]Job 29.16
27 [s]Num. 10.29

CHAPTER 19
3 [a]Acts 7.38
4 [b]Deut. 32.11; Isa. 63.9; Rev. 12.14
5 [c]Deut. 32.8; 1 Ki. 8.53; Ps. 135.4; Isa. 43.1; Tit. 2.14
[d]Deut. 10.14; Job 41.11; Ps. 50.12; 1 Cor. 10.26
6 [e]1 Pet. 2.5-9; Rev. 20.6
[f]Lev. 20.24; Deut. 7.6; Isa. 62.12; 1 Thess. 5.27
8 [g]ch. 24.3-7; Deut. 26.17
9 [h]Deut. 4.11; Ps. 97.2; Matt. 17.5
[i]Deut. 4.12; John 12.29
10 [j]Heb. 10.22
[k]Lev. 15.5
11 [l]ch. 34.5; Deut. 33.2
12 [m]Heb. 12.20
13 [1]Or, cornet
15 [n]1 Cor. 7.5; Rev. 3.2
17 [o]Deut. 4.10
18 [p]Judg. 5.5; Ps. 68.7-8
[q]2 Chr. 7.1
[r]Gen. 15.17; Ps. 144.5; Rev. 15.8
[s]Ps. 68.8; Ps. 114.7; Jer. 4.24
19 [t]Neh. 9.13; Ps. 81.7
21 [2]contest
[u]1 Sam. 6.19
22 [v]Lev. 10.3
[w]2 Sam. 6.7

CHAPTER 20
1 [a]Deut. 5.22
2 [b]Lev. 26.1; Deut. 5.6; Ps. 81.10; Hos. 13.4
[c]ch. 13.3
[1]servants

3 [d]Thou shalt have no other gods before me.

4 [e]Thou shalt not make unto thee any graven image, or any likeness *of any thing* that *is* in heaven above, or that *is* in the earth beneath, or that *is* in the water under the earth:

5 [f]Thou shalt not bow down thyself to them, nor serve them: for I the LORD thy God *am* [g]a jealous God, [h]visiting the iniquity of the fathers upon the children unto the third and fourth *generation* of them that hate me;

6 And [i]shewing mercy unto thousands of them that love me, and keep my commandments.

7 [j]Thou shalt not take the name of the LORD thy God in vain; for the LORD [k]will not hold him guiltless that taketh his name in vain.

8 [l]Remember the sabbath day, to keep it holy.

9 [m]Six days shalt thou labour, and do all thy work:

10 But the [n]seventh day *is* the sabbath of the LORD thy God: *in it* thou shalt not do any work, thou, nor thy son, nor thy daughter, thy manservant, nor thy maidservant, nor thy cattle, [o]nor thy stranger that *is* within thy gates:

11 For *in* six days the LORD made heaven and earth, the sea, and all that in them *is*, and rested the seventh day: wherefore the LORD blessed the sabbath day, and hallowed it.

12 ¶ [p]Honour thy father and thy mother: that thy days may be long upon the land which the LORD thy God giveth thee.

13 [q]Thou shalt not kill.

14 [r]Thou shalt not commit adultery.

15 [s]Thou shalt not steal.

16 Thou shalt not bear false witness against thy neighbour.

17 [t]Thou shalt not covet thy neighbour's house, [u]thou shalt not covet thy neighbour's wife, nor his manservant, nor his maidservant, nor his ox, nor his ass, nor any thing that *is* thy neighbour's.

18 ¶ And [v]all the people saw the thunderings, and the lightnings, and the noise of the trumpet, and the mountain smoking: and when the people saw *it*, they removed, and stood afar off.

19 And they said unto Mō'ses, [w]Speak thou with us, and we will hear: but let not God speak with us, lest we die.

20 And Mō'ses said unto the people, Fear not: [x]for God is come to prove you, and [y]that his fear may be before your faces, that ye sin not.

21 And the people stood afar off, and Mō'ses drew near unto the thick darkness where God *was*.

22 ¶ And the LORD said unto Mō'ses, Thus thou shalt say unto the children of Is'ra-el, Ye have seen that I have talked with you from heaven.

23 Ye shall not make with me gods of silver, neither shall ye make unto you gods of gold.

24 ¶ An altar of earth thou shalt make unto me, and shalt sacrifice thereon thy burnt offerings, and thy peace offerings, thy sheep, and thine oxen: in all [z]places where I record my name I will come unto thee, and I will [a]bless thee.

25 And [b]if thou wilt make me an altar of stone, thou shalt not [2]build it of hewn stone: for if thou lift up thy tool upon it, thou hast polluted it.

26 Neither shalt thou go up by steps unto mine altar, that thy nakedness be not discovered thereon.

21

Now these *are* the judgments which thou shalt [a]set before them.

2 If [b]thou buy an Hē'brew servant, six years he shall serve: and in the seventh he shall go out free for nothing.

3 If he came in [1]by himself, he shall go out by himself: if he were married, then his wife shall go out with him.

4 If his master have given him [c]a wife, and she have born him sons or daughters; the wife and her children shall be her master's, and he shall go out by himself.

5 And [d]if the servant [2]shall plainly say, I love my master, my wife, and my children; I will not go out free:

6 Then his master shall bring him unto the [e]judges; he shall also bring him to the door, or unto the door post; and his master shall [f]bore his ear through with an aul; and he shall serve him for ever.

7 ¶ And if a man [g]sell his daughter to be a maidservant, she shall not go out as the menservants do.

8 If she [3]please not her master, who hath betrothed her to himself, then shall he let her be redeemed: to sell her unto a strange nation he shall have no power, seeing he hath dealt deceitfully with her.

9 And if he have betrothed her unto his son, he shall deal with her after the manner of daughters.

10 If he take him another *wife*: her food, her raiment, [h]and her duty of marriage, shall he not diminish.

11 And if he do not these three unto her, then shall she go out free without money.

12 ¶ He [i]that smiteth a man, so that he die, shall be surely put to death.

13 And [j]if a man lie not in wait, but God [k]deliver *him* into his hand; then [l]I will appoint thee a place whither he shall flee.

14 But if a man come [m]presumptuously upon his neighbour, to slay him with guile; [n]thou shalt take him from mine altar, that he may die.

15 ¶ And he that smiteth his father, or his mother, shall be surely put to death.

16 ¶ And [o]he that stealeth a man, and [p]selleth him, or if he be [q]found in his hand, he shall surely be put to death.

17 ¶ And [r]he that [4]curseth his father, or his mother, shall surely be put to death.

---

3 [d]Deut. 6.14; Jer. 25.6
4 [e]Lev. 26.1; Deut. 4.16
5 [f]Josh. 23.7; Isa. 44.14-15
[g]Josh. 24.19; Nah. 1.2
[h]Num. 14.18; Ezek. 18.19
6 [i]Deut. 7.9; Rom. 11.28
7 [j]Ps. 15.4; Matt. 5.33
[k]Mic. 6.11
8 [l]ch. 31.13; Deut. 5.12
9 [m]Ezek. 20.12; Luke 13.14
10 [n]Gen. 2.2
[o]Neh. 13.16
12 [p]Lev. 19.3
13 [q]Rom. 13.9
14 [r]Matt. 5.27
15 [s]Lev. 19.11;
17 [t]Mic. 2.2;
[u]Prov. 6.29
18 [v]Heb. 12.18
19 [w]Gal. 3.19
20 [x]Gen. 22.1
[y]Prov. 3.7
24 [z]2 Chr. 6.6
[a]Gen. 12.2
25 [b]Josh. 8.31
[2]build them with hewing

CHAPTER 21

1 [a]ch. 24.3-4;
2 [b]Lev. 25.39
3 [1]with his body
4 [c]Lev. 25.44
5 [d]Deut. 15.16
[2]saying shall say
6 [e]ch. 12.12;
[f]Ps. 40.6
7 [g]Neh. 5.5
8 [3]be evil in the eyes of, etc
10 [h]1 Cor. 7.5
12 [i]Gen. 9.6
13 [j]Deut. 19.4-5
[k]1 Sam. 24.4-10-18
[l]Num. 35.11
14 [m]Num. 15.30;
[n]1 Ki. 2.28-34;
16 [o]Deut. 24.7
[p]Gen. 37.28
[q]ch. 22.4
17 [r]Lev. 20.9;
[4]Or, revileth

18 ¶ And if men strive together, and
one smite [5]another with a stone, or with
his fist, and he die not, but keepeth *his*
bed:
19 If he rise again, and walk abroad
[s]upon his staff, then shall he that smote
him be quit: only he shall pay *for* [6]the
loss of his time, and shall cause *him* to
be thoroughly healed.
20 ¶ And if a man smite his servant,
or his maid, with a rod, and he die under his hand; he shall be surely [7]pun-
ished.
21 Notwithstanding, if he continue a
day or two, he shall not be punished:
for [t]he *is* his money.
22 ¶ If men strive, and hurt a woman
with child, so that her fruit depart *from
her,* and yet no mischief follow: he
shall be surely punished, according as
the woman's husband will lay upon
him; and he shall [u]pay as the judges
determine.
23 And if *any* mischief follow, then
thou shalt give life for life,
24 [v]Eye for eye, tooth for tooth, hand
for hand, foot for foot,
25 Burning for burning, wound for
wound, stripe for stripe.
26 ¶ And [w]if a man smite the eye of
his servant, or the eye of his maid, that
it perish; he shall let him go free for his
eye's sake.
27 And if he smite out his manservant's tooth, or his maidservant's
tooth; he shall let him go free for his
tooth's sake.
28 ¶ If an ox gore a man or a woman,
that they die: then [x]the ox shall be
surely stoned, and his flesh shall not
be eaten; but the owner of the ox *shall
be* quit.
29 But if the ox were wont to push
with his horn in time past, and it hath
been testified to his owner, and he
hath not kept him in, but that he hath
killed a man or a woman; the ox shall
be stoned, and his owner also shall be
put to death.
30 If there be laid on him a sum of
money, then he shall give for the [y]ran-
som of his life whatsoever is laid upon
him.
31 Whether he have gored a son, or
have gored a daughter, according to
this judgment shall it be done unto
him.
32 If the ox shall push a manservant
or a maidservant; he shall give unto
their master [z]thirty shekels of silver,
and the ox shall be stoned.
33 ¶ And if a man shall open a pit, or
if a man shall dig a pit, and not cover it,
and an ox or an ass fall therein;
34 The owner of the pit shall make *it*
good, *and* give money unto the owner
of them; and the dead *beast* shall be
his.
35 ¶ And if one man's ox hurt another's, that he die; then they shall sell the
live ox, and divide the money of it; and
the dead *ox* also they shall divide.
36 Or if it be known that the ox
hath used to push in time past, and his
owner hath not kept him in; he shall
surely pay ox for ox; and the dead
shall be his own.

22 If a man shall steal an ox, or a
[1]sheep, and kill it, or sell it; he
shall restore five oxen for an ox, and
[a]four sheep for a sheep.
2 ¶ If a [b]thief be found breaking up,
and be smitten that he die, *there shall*
[c]no blood *be shed* for him.
3 If the sun be risen upon him, *there
shall be* blood *shed* for him; *for* he
should make full restitution; if he have
nothing, then he shall be [d]sold for his
theft.
4 If the [2]theft be certainly [e]found in
his hand alive, whether it be ox, or ass,
or sheep; he shall [f]restore double.
5 ¶ If a man shall cause a field or
vineyard to be eaten, and shall put in
his beast, and shall feed in another
man's field; of the best of his own field,
and of the best of his own vineyard,
shall he make restitution.
6 ¶ If fire break out, and catch in
thorns, so that the stacks of corn, or
the standing corn, or the field, be consumed *therewith;* he that kindled the
fire shall surely make restitution.
7 ¶ If a man shall deliver unto his
neighbour money or stuff to keep, and
it be stolen out of the man's house; if
the thief be found, let him pay double.
8 If the thief be not found, then the
master of the house shall be brought
unto the judges, *to see* whether he
have put his hand unto his neighbour's
goods.
9 For all manner of trespass, *whether
it be* for ox, for ass, for sheep, for raiment, *or* for any manner of lost thing,
which *another* challengeth to be his, the
[g]cause of both parties shall come before
the judges; *and* whom the judges shall
condemn, he shall pay double unto his
neighbour.
10 If a man deliver unto his neighbour an ass, or an ox, or a sheep, or
any beast, to keep; and it die, or be
hurt, or driven away, no man seeing *it:*
11 *Then* shall an [h]oath of the LORD
be between them both, that he hath
not put his hand unto his neighbour's
goods; and the owner of it shall accept
thereof, and he shall not make *it* good.
12 And [i]if it be stolen from him, he
shall make restitution unto the owner
thereof.
13 If it be torn in pieces, *then* let
him bring it *for* witness, *and* he shall
not make good that which was torn.
14 ¶ And if a man borrow *ought* of
his neighbour, and it be hurt, or die,
the owner thereof *being* not with it, he
shall surely make *it* good.
15 *But* if the owner thereof *be* with
it, he shall not make *it* good: if it *be* an
hired *thing,* it came for his hire.
16 ¶ And [j]if a man entice a maid that
is not betrothed, and lie with her, he
shall surely endow her to be his wife.
17 If her father utterly refuse to give
her unto him, he shall [3]pay money according to the [k]dowry of virgins.
18 ¶ [l]Thou shalt not suffer a witch to
live.

18 [5]Or, his neighbour

19 [s]2 Sam. 3.29
[6]his ceasing

20 [7]avenged, Gen. 4.15-24; Lev. 25.43; Rom. 13.4; Eph. 6.9; 1 Tim. 3.3; Jas. 3.1

21 [t]Lev. 25.45

22 [u]Deut. 22.18-19

24 [v]Lev. 24.20; Deut. 19.21; Matt. 5.38; Matt. 7.2

26 [w]Col. 4.1

28 [x]Gen. 9.5

30 [y]Num. 35.31

32 [z]Zech. 11.12-13; Matt. 26.15; Phil. 2.7

CHAPTER 22

1 [1]Or, goat
[a]2 Sam. 12.6; Prov. 6.31; Luke 19.8

2 [b]Ex. 20.15; Lev. 19.11; Deut. 5.19; Matt. 6.19; Matt. 19.18; Matt. 24.43; Luke 18.20; Rom. 13.9; 1 Cor. 6.10; Eph. 4.28; 1 Pet. 4.15
[c]Num. 35.27

3 [d]ch. 21.2; Matt. 18.25

4 [2]thing stolen
[e]ch. 21.16
[f]Prov. 6.31

9 [g]Deut. 25.1; 2 Chr. 19.10

11 [h]Heb. 6.16

12 [i]Gen. 31.39

16 [j]Deut. 22.28

17 [3]weigh, Gen. 23.16
[k]1 Sam. 18.25

18 [l]Deut. 18.10

19 ¶ Whosoever lieth with a beast shall surely be put to death.

20 ¶ [m]He that sacrificeth unto *any* god, save unto the LORD only, he shall be utterly destroyed.

21 ¶ [n]Thou shalt neither vex a stranger, nor oppress him: for ye were strangers in the land of Ē′gypt.

22 ¶ [o]Ye shall not afflict any widow, or fatherless child.

23 If thou afflict them in any wise, and they [p]cry at all unto me, I will surely [q]hear their cry;

24 And my [r]wrath shall wax hot, and I will kill you with the sword; and [s]your wives shall be widows, and your children fatherless.

25 ¶ If [t]thou lend money to *any of* my people *that is* poor by thee, thou shalt not be to him as an usurer, neither shalt thou lay upon him usury.

26 If [u]thou at all take thy neighbour's raiment to pledge, thou shalt deliver it unto him by that the sun goeth down:

27 For that *is* his covering only, it *is* his raiment for his skin: wherein shall he sleep? and it shall come to pass, when he crieth unto me, that I will hear; for I *am* gracious.

28 ¶ Thou [v]shalt not revile the [4]gods, nor curse the ruler of thy people.

29 ¶ Thou shalt not delay *to offer* [5]the first of thy ripe fruits, and of thy liquors: the firstborn of thy sons shalt thou give unto me.

30 Likewise shalt thou do with thine oxen, *and* with thy sheep: seven days it shall be with his dam; on the eighth day thou shalt give it me.

31 ¶ And ye shall be holy men unto me: neither shall ye eat *any* flesh *that is* torn of beasts in the field; ye shall cast it to the dogs.

23

Thou [a]shalt not [1]raise a false report: put not thine hand with the wicked to be an [b]unrighteous witness.

2 ¶ Thou [c]shalt not follow a multitude to *do* evil; [d]neither shalt thou [2]speak in a cause to decline after many to wrest *judgment*:

3 ¶ Neither shalt thou [e]countenance a poor man in his cause.

4 ¶ If [f]thou meet thine enemy's ox or his ass going astray, thou shalt surely bring it back to him again.

5 If thou see the ass of him that hateth thee lying under his burden, [3]and wouldest forbear to help him, thou shalt surely help with him.

6 [g]Thou shalt not wrest the judgment of thy poor in his cause.

7 Keep [h]thee far from a false matter; and the innocent and righteous slay thou not: for [i]I will not justify the wicked.

8 ¶ And [j]thou shalt take no gift: for the gift blindeth [4]the wise, and perverteth the words of the righteous.

9 ¶ Also [k]thou shalt not oppress a stranger: for ye know the [5]heart of a stranger, seeing ye were strangers in the land of Ē′gypt.

10 And [l]six years thou shalt sow thy land, and shalt gather in the fruits thereof:

11 But the seventh *year* thou shalt let it rest and lie still; that the poor of thy people may eat: and what they leave the beasts of the field shall eat. In like manner thou shalt deal with thy vineyard, *and* with thy [6]oliveyard.

12 Six [m]days thou shalt do thy work, and on the seventh day thou shalt rest: that thine ox and thine ass may rest, and the son of thy handmaid, and the stranger, may be refreshed.

13 And in all *things* that I have said unto you be circumspect: and make [n]no mention of the name of other gods, neither let it be heard out of thy mouth.

14 ¶ Three [o]times thou shalt keep a feast unto me in the year.

15 Thou shalt keep the feast of unleavened bread: (thou shalt eat unleavened bread seven days, as I commanded thee, in the time appointed of the month Ā′bĭb; for in it thou camest out from Ē′gypt: and none shall appear before me empty:)

16 And [p]the feast of harvest, the firstfruits of thy labours, which thou hast sown in the field: and the feast of ingathering, *which is* in the end of the year, when thou hast gathered in thy labours out of the field.

17 Three times in the year all thy males shall appear before the Lord GOD.

18 Thou shalt not offer the blood of my sacrifice with leavened bread; neither shall the fat of my [7]sacrifice remain until the morning.

19 The [q]first of the firstfruits of thy land thou shalt bring into the house of the LORD thy God. Thou shalt not seethe a kid in his mother's milk.

20 ¶ Behold, I send an Angel before thee, to keep thee in the way, and to bring thee into the place which I have prepared.

21 Beware of him, and obey his voice, provoke [r]him not; for he will [s]not pardon your transgressions: for [t]my name *is* in him.

22 But if thou shalt indeed obey his voice, and do all that I speak; then [u]I will be an enemy unto thine enemies, and [8]an adversary unto thine adversaries.

23 For mine Angel shall go before thee, and [v]bring thee in unto the Ăm′ôr-ītes, and the Hĭt′tītes, and the Pĕr′ĭz-zītes, and the Cā′năan-ītes, and Hī′vītes, and the Jĕb′u-sītes: and I will cut them off.

24 Thou shalt not [w]bow down to their gods, nor serve them, nor do after their works: but thou shalt utterly overthrow them, and quite break down their images.

25 And ye shall [x]serve the LORD your God, and he [y]shall bless thy bread, and thy water; and [z]I will take sickness away from the midst of thee.

26 ¶ There [a]shall nothing cast their young, nor be barren, in thy land: the number of thy days I will [b]fulfil.

---

20 [m]Num. 25.2
21 [n]Lev. 19.33
22 [o]Deut. 10.18
23 [p]Deut. 15.9; [q]Job 34.28;
24 [r]Job 31.23 [s]Ps. 109.9
25 [t]Lev. 25.35
26 [u]Job 24.3
28 [v]Eccl. 10.20; [4]Or, judges, Ps. 82.6
29 [5]thy fulness

CHAPTER 23

1 [a]Prov. 10.18 [1]Or, receive [b]1 Ki. 21.10
2 [c]1 Ki. 19.10; [d]Ps. 72.2 [2]answer
3 [e]Lev. 19.15
4 [f]Prov. 25.21
5 [3]Or, wilt thou cease to help him? or, and wouldest cease to leave thy business for him; thou shalt surely leave it to join with him
6 [g]Job 31.13
7 [h]Eph. 4.25 [i]Rom. 1.18
8 [j]Prov. 17.8 [4]the seeing
9 [k]Ps. 94.6 [5]soul
10 [l]Lev. 25.3
11 [6]Or, olive trees
12 [m]Luke 13.14
13 [n]Hos. 2.17
14 [o]Deut. 16.16
16 [p]Lev. 23.10
18 [7]Or, feast
19 [q]Neh. 10.35
21 [r]Eph. 4.30 [s]Josh. 24.19; [t]Isa. 9.6
22 [u]Gen. 12.3 [8]Or, I will afflict them that afflict thee
23 [v]Josh. 24.8
24 [w]ch. 20.5
25 [x]Deut. 10.12; [y]Deut. 28.5 [z]Deut. 7.15
26 [a]Job 21.10 [b]Gen. 25.8

27 I will send [c]my fear before thee,
and will destroy all the people to whom
thou shalt come, and I will make all
thine enemies turn their [9]backs unto
thee.
28 And I [d]will send hornets before
thee, which shall drive out the Hī'vīte,
the Cā'năan-īte, and the Hĭt'tīte, from
before thee.
29 I [e]will not drive them out from
before thee in one year; lest the land
become desolate, and the beast of the
field multiply against thee.
30 By little and little I will drive them
out from before thee, until thou be increased, and inherit the land.
31 And [f]I will set thy bounds from
the Red sea even unto the sea of the
Phĭ-lĭs'tĭnes, and from the desert unto
the river: for I [g]will deliver the inhabitants of the land into your hand; and
thou shalt drive them out before thee.
32 Thou shalt make no covenant
with them, nor with their gods.
33 They shall not dwell in thy land,
lest they make thee sin against me: for
if thou serve their gods, [h]it will surely
be a snare unto thee.

24 And he said unto Mō'ses, Come
up unto the LORD, thou, and
Aâr'on, [a]Nā'dăb, and A-bī'hū, [b]and
seventy of the elders of Ĭs'ra-el; and
worship ye afar off.
2 And Mō'ses alone shall come near
the LORD: but they shall not come nigh;
neither shall the people go up with him.
3 ¶ And Mō'ses came and told the
people all the words of the LORD, and
all the judgments: and all the people
answered with one voice, and said, All
the words which the LORD hath said
will we do.
4 And Mō'ses [c]wrote all the words
of the LORD, and rose up early in the
morning, and builded an altar under
the hill, and twelve [d]pillars, according
to the twelve tribes of Ĭs'ra-el.
5 And he sent young men of the children of Ĭs'ra-el, which offered burnt offerings, and sacrificed peace offerings
of oxen unto the LORD.
6 And Mō'ses [e]took half of the blood,
and put *it* in basons; and half of the
blood he sprinkled on the altar.
7 And he took the book of the covenant, and read in the audience of the
people: and they said, All that the LORD
hath said will we do, and be obedient.
8 And Mō'ses took the blood, and
sprinkled *it* on the people, and said, Behold [f]the blood of the covenant, which
the LORD hath made with you concerning all these words.
9 ¶ Then went up Mō'ses, and Aâr'on,
Nā'dăb, and A-bī'hū, and seventy of the
elders of Ĭs'ra-el:
10 And they [g]saw the God of Ĭs'ra-el: and *there was* under his feet
as it were a paved work of [h]a sapphire stone, and as it were the [i]body
of heaven in *his* clearness.
11 And upon the nobles of the children of Ĭs'ra-el he [j]laid not his hand:
also [k]they saw God, and did [l]eat and
drink.

27 [c]Gen. 35.5; Deut. 2.25; Josh. 2.9-11; 1 Sam. 14.15 [9]neck, Ps. 18.40
28 [d]Deut. 7.20
29 [e]Deut. 7.22
31 [f]1 Ki. 4.21 [g]Josh. 21.44
33 [h]ch. 34.12-15; Deut. 7.2; Deut. 12.30; Josh. 23.13; Judg. 2.3; 1 Sam. 18.21; Ps. 106.36-37

CHAPTER 24
1 [a]ch. 28.1; Lev. 10.1-2 [b]Num. 11.16
4 [c]Deut. 31.9 [d]Gen. 28.18; Gen. 31.45
6 [e]Heb. 9.18
8 [f]Heb. 9.20; Heb. 13.20; 1 Pet. 1.2
10 [g]Gen. 32.30; ch. 3.6; ch. 33.20-23; Judg. 13.22; Isa. 6.1-5; John 1.18; 1 Tim. 6.16; 1 John 4.12 [h]Ezek. 1.26; Ezek. 10.1; Rev. 4.3 [i]Matt. 17.2
11 [j]ch. 19.21 [k]Gen. 16.13; Deut. 4.33 [l]Gen. 31.54; ch. 18.12; 1 Cor. 10.18
12 [m]ch. 32.15; Deut. 5.22
13 [n]ch. 33.11
15 [o]ch. 19.9; Matt. 17.5
16 [p]ch. 16.10; Num. 14.10
17 [q]Heb. 12.18
18 [r]Deut. 9.9

CHAPTER 25
2 [1]take for me [2]Or, heave offering [a]1 Chr. 29.3; 2 Cor. 9.7
4 [3]Or, silk, Gen. 41.42
7 [b]ch. 28.15
8 [c]Lev. 4.6 [d]Heb. 3.6; Rev. 21.3
10 [e]ch. 37.1; Deut. 10.3; Heb. 9.4

12 ¶ And the LORD said unto Mō'ses,
Come up to me into the mount, and be
there: and I will give thee [m]tables of
stone, and a law, and commandments
which I have written; that thou mayest
teach them.
13 And Mō'ses rose up, and [n]his
minister Jŏsh'u-ȧ: and Mō'ses went up
into the mount of God.
14 And he said unto the elders, Tarry
ye here for us, until we come again unto
you: and, behold, Aâr'on and Hûr *are*
with you: if any man have any matters
to do, let him come unto them.
15 And Mō'ses went up into the
mount, and [o]a cloud covered the
mount.
16 And [p]the glory of the LORD abode
upon mount Sī'nāi, and the cloud covered it six days: and the seventh day he
called unto Mō'ses out of the midst of
the cloud.
17 And the sight of the glory of the
LORD *was* like [q]devouring fire on the
top of the mount in the eyes of the children of Ĭs'ra-el.
18 And Mō'ses went into the midst
of the cloud, and gat him up into the
mount: and [r]Mō'ses was in the mount
forty days and forty nights.

25 And the LORD spake unto Mō'ses, saying,
2 Speak unto the children of Ĭs'ra-el,
that they [1]bring me an [2]offering: [a]of
every man that giveth it willingly with
his heart ye shall take my offering.
3 And this *is* the offering which ye
shall take of them; gold, and silver,
and brass,
4 And blue, and purple, and scarlet,
and [3]fine linen, and goats' *hair,*
5 And rams' skins dyed red, and badgers' skins, and shittim wood,
6 Oil for the light, spices for anointing oil, and for sweet incense,
7 Onyx stones, and stones to be set
in the ephod, and in the [b]breastplate.
8 And let them make me a [c]sanctuary; that [d]I may dwell among them.
9 According to all that I shew thee,
after the pattern of the tabernacle,
and the pattern of all the instruments
thereof, even so shall ye make *it.*
10 ¶ And [e]they shall make an ark *of*
shittim wood: two cubits and a half
shall be the length thereof, and a cubit
and a half the breadth thereof, and a
cubit and a half the height thereof.
11 And thou shalt overlay it with
pure gold, within and without shalt
thou overlay it, and shalt make upon it
a crown of gold round about.
12 And thou shalt cast four rings of
gold for it, and put *them* in the four
corners thereof; and two rings *shall be*
in the one side of it, and two rings in
the other side of it.
13 And thou shalt make staves *of*
shittim wood, and overlay them with
gold.
14 And thou shalt put the staves into
the rings by the sides of the ark, that
the ark may be borne with them.

15 The [f]staves shall be in the rings
of the ark: they shall not be taken from
it.
16 And thou shalt put into the ark
[g]the testimony which I shall give thee.
17 And [h]thou shalt make a mercy
seat *of* pure gold: two cubits and a half
shall be the length thereof, and a cubit
and a half the breadth thereof.
18 And thou shalt make two cherubims *of* gold, *of* beaten work shalt thou
make them, in the two ends of the
mercy seat.
19 And make one cherub on the one
end, and the other cherub on the other
end: *even* [4]of the mercy seat shall ye
make the cherubims on the two ends
thereof.
20 And [i]the cherubims shall stretch
forth *their* wings on high, covering the
mercy seat with their wings, and their
faces *shall look* one to another; toward
the mercy seat shall the faces of the
cherubims be.
21 [j]And thou shalt put the mercy
seat above upon the ark; and in the ark
thou shalt put the testimony that I shall
give thee.
22 And [k]there I will meet with thee,
and I will commune with thee from
above the mercy seat, from [l]between
the two cherubims which *are* upon
the ark of the testimony, of all *things*
which I will give thee in commandment unto the children of Is'ra-el.
23 ¶ Thou [m]shalt also make a table
of shittim wood: two cubits *shall be* the
length thereof, and a cubit the breadth
thereof, and a cubit and a half the
height thereof.
24 And thou shalt overlay it with
pure gold, and make thereto a crown
of gold round about.
25 And thou shalt make unto it a border of an hand breadth round about,
and thou shalt make a golden crown to
the border thereof round about.
26 And thou shalt make for it four
rings of gold, and put the rings in the
four corners that *are* on the four feet
thereof.
27 Over against the border shall the
rings be for places of the staves to bear
the table.
28 And thou shalt make the staves *of*
shittim wood, and overlay them with
gold, that the table may be borne with
them.
29 And thou shalt make [n]the dishes
thereof, and spoons thereof, and covers
thereof, and bowls thereof, [5]to cover
withal: *of* pure gold shalt thou make
them.
30 And thou shalt set upon the table
[o]shewbread before me alway.
31 ¶ And [p]thou shalt make a candlestick *of* pure gold: *of* beaten work shall
the candlestick be made: his shaft, and
his branches, his bowls, his knops, and
his flowers, shall be of the same.
32 And [q]six branches shall come out
of the sides of it; three branches of the
candlestick out of the one side, and
three branches of the candlestick out of
the other side:

15 [f]1 Ki. 8.8
16 [g]ch. 16.34; ch. 31.18; ch. 40.20; Num. 17.10; Deut. 10.2; Deut. 31.26; 1 Ki. 8.9; 2 Ki. 11.12
17 [h]ch. 37.6; Rom. 3.25; Heb. 9.5
19 [4]Or, of the matter of the mercy seat
20 [i]1 Ki. 8.7; 1 Chr. 28.18
21 [j]ch. 26.34; ch. 40.20
22 [k]ch. 29.42-43; ch. 30.6-36; Lev. 16.2; Num. 17.4; Ezek. 9.3; Jas. 2.13
[l]Num. 7.89; 1 Sam. 4.4; 2 Sam. 6.2; 2 Ki. 19.15; Isa. 37.16
23 [m]ch. 37.10; Heb. 9.2
29 [n]ch. 37.16; Num. 4.7
[5]Or, to pour out withal
30 [o]Lev. 24.5
31 [p]ch. 37.17; Rev. 4.5
32 [q]ch. 37.18-19; Num. 8.4
37 [r]Rev. 1.12
[s]ch. 27.21; 2 Chr. 13.11
[6]Or, cause to ascend
[t]Num. 8.2
[7]the face of it
40 [u]ch. 26.30; Heb. 8.5
[8]which thou wast caused to see
CHAPTER 26
1 [a]ch. 25.9; Rev. 21.3
[b]1 Cor. 12.28; Heb. 1.14
[1]the work of a cunning workman, or, embroiderer
3 [c]1 Cor. 12.4-5-6-12
4 [d]Eph. 4.13; Col. 2.2-19
7 [e]ch. 36.14

33 Three bowls made like unto almonds, *with* a knop and a flower in one
branch; and three bowls made like almonds in the other branch, *with* a knop
and a flower: so in the six branches that
come out of the candlestick.
34 And in the candlestick *shall be*
four bowls made like unto almonds,
with their knops and their flowers.
35 And *there shall be* a knop under
two branches of the same, and a knop
under two branches of the same, and a
knop under two branches of the same,
according to the six branches that proceed out of the candlestick.
36 Their knops and their branches
shall be of the same: all it *shall be* one
beaten work *of* pure gold.
37 And thou shalt make the [r]seven
lamps thereof: and [s]they shall [6]light
the lamps thereof, that they may [t]give
light over against [7]it.
38 And the tongs thereof, and the
snuffdishes thereof, *shall be of* pure
gold.
39 *Of* a talent of pure gold shall he
make it, with all these vessels.
40 And [u]look that thou make *them*
after their pattern, [8]which was shewed
thee in the mount.

26 Moreover thou shalt make the
[a]tabernacle *with* ten curtains *of*
fine twined linen, and blue, and purple,
and scarlet: [b]*with* cherubims of [1]cun-
ning work shalt thou make them.
2 The length of one curtain *shall*
be eight and twenty cubits, and the
breadth of one curtain four cubits: and
every one of the curtains shall have
one measure.
3 The five curtains shall be coupled
[c]together one to another; and *other*
five curtains *shall be* coupled one to
another.
4 And thou shalt make [d]loops of
blue upon the edge of the one curtain
from the selvedge in the coupling; and
likewise shalt thou make in the uttermost edge of *another* curtain, in the
coupling of the second.
5 Fifty loops shalt thou make in the
one curtain, and fifty loops shalt thou
make in the edge of the curtain that *is*
in the coupling of the second; that the
loops may take hold one of another.
6 And thou shalt make fifty taches
of gold, and couple the curtains together with the taches: and it shall be
one tabernacle.
7 ¶ And [e]thou shalt make curtains *of*
goats' *hair* to be a covering upon the
tabernacle: eleven curtains shalt thou
make.
8 The length of one curtain *shall be*
thirty cubits, and the breadth of one
curtain four cubits: and the eleven curtains *shall be all* of one measure.
9 And thou shalt couple five curtains by themselves, and six curtains
by themselves, and shalt double the
sixth curtain in the forefront of the tabernacle.
10 And thou shalt make fifty loops
on the edge of the one curtain *that is*
outmost in the coupling, and fifty loops

in the edge of the curtain which coupleth the second.
11 And thou shalt make fifty taches
of brass, and put the taches into the
loops, and couple the [2]tent together,
that it may be one.
12 And the remnant that remaineth
of the curtains of the tent, the half curtain that remaineth, shall hang over
the backside of the tabernacle.
13 And a cubit on the one side, and a
cubit on the other side [3]of that which
remaineth in the length of the curtains
of the tent, it shall hang over the sides
of the tabernacle on this side and on
that side, to cover it.
14 And [f]thou shalt make a covering
for the tent *of* rams' skins dyed red, and
a covering above *of* badgers' skins.
15 ¶ And thou shalt make boards for
the tabernacle *of* shittim wood standing up.
16 Ten cubits *shall be* the length of a
board, and a cubit and a half *shall be*
the breadth of one board.
17 Two [4]tenons *shall there be* in one
board, set in order one against another: thus shalt thou make for all the
boards of the tabernacle.
18 And thou shalt make the boards
for the tabernacle, twenty boards on
the south side southward.
19 And thou shalt make forty [g]sock-
ets of silver under the twenty boards;
two sockets under one board for his
two tenons, and two sockets under another board for his two tenons.
20 And for the second side of the tabernacle on the north side *there shall be*
twenty boards:
21 And their forty sockets *of* silver;
two sockets under one board, and two
sockets under another board.
22 And for the sides of the tabernacle [5]westward thou shalt make six
boards.
23 And two boards shalt thou make
for the corners of the tabernacle in the
two sides.
24 And they shall be [6]coupled together beneath, and they shall be coupled together above the head of it unto
one ring: thus shall it be for them both;
they shall be for the two corners.
25 And they shall be eight boards,
and their sockets *of* silver, sixteen sockets; two sockets under one board, and
two sockets under another board.
26 ¶ And thou shalt make [h]bars *of*
shittim wood; five for the boards of the
one side of the tabernacle,
27 And five bars for the boards of the
other side of the tabernacle, and five
bars for the boards of the side of the
tabernacle, for the two sides westward.
28 And the middle bar in the midst
of the boards shall reach from end to
end.
29 And thou shalt overlay the boards
with gold, and make their rings *of* gold
for places for the bars: and thou shalt
overlay the bars with gold.
30 And thou shalt rear up the tabernacle according [i]to the fashion thereof
which was shewed thee in the mount.
31 ¶ And [j]thou shalt make a vail *of*
blue, and purple, and scarlet, and fine
twined linen of cunning work: with
cherubims shall it be made:
32 And thou shalt hang it upon four
pillars of shittim *wood* overlaid with
gold: their hooks *shall be of* gold, upon
the four sockets of silver.
33 ¶ And thou shalt hang up the
vail under the taches, that thou mayest
bring in thither within the vail [k]the ark
of the testimony: and [l]the vail shall
divide unto you between [m]the holy
place and the most holy.
34 And [n]thou shalt put the mercy
seat upon the ark of the testimony in
the most holy *place*.
35 And [o]thou shalt set the table without the vail, and the [p]candlestick over
against the table on the side of the tabernacle toward the south: and thou
shalt put the table on the north side.
36 And [q]thou shalt make an hanging for the door of the tent, *of* blue, and
purple, and scarlet, and fine twined
linen, wrought with needlework.
37 And thou shalt make for the hanging five [r]pillars *of* shittim *wood*, and
overlay them with gold, *and* their hooks
shall be of gold: and thou shalt cast five
sockets of brass for them.

27 And thou shalt make [a]an altar *of*
shittim wood, five cubits long,
and five cubits broad; the altar shall
be foursquare: and the height thereof
shall be three cubits.
2 And thou shalt make [b]the horns of
it upon the four corners thereof: his
horns shall be of the same: and [c]thou
shalt overlay it with brass.
3 And thou shalt make his pans to
receive his ashes, and his shovels, [d]and
his basons, and his fleshhooks, and his
firepans: all the vessels thereof thou
shalt make *of* brass.
4 And thou shalt make for it a [1]grate
of network *of* brass; and upon the net
shalt thou make four brasen rings in
the four corners thereof.
5 And thou shalt put it under the
compass of the altar beneath, that the
net may be even to the midst of the
altar.
6 And thou shalt make staves for the
altar, staves *of* shittim wood, and overlay them with brass.
7 And the staves shall be put into
the rings, and the staves shall be upon
the two sides of the altar, to [e]bear it.
8 Hollow with boards shalt thou
make it: [f]as [2]it was shewed thee in the
mount, so shall they make *it*.
9 ¶ And [g]thou shalt make the court
of the tabernacle: for the south side
southward *there shall be* hangings for
the court *of* fine twined linen of an hundred cubits long for one side:
10 And the twenty pillars thereof
and their twenty sockets *shall be of*
brass; the hooks of the pillars and their
fillets *shall be of* silver.
11 And likewise for the north side in
length *there shall be* hangings of an
hundred *cubits* long, and his twenty

11 [2]Or, covering
13 [3]in the remainder, or, surplusage
14 [f]ch. 36.19; Num. 24.5
17 [4]hands
19 [g]ch. 38.27
22 [5]seaward, Gen. 12.8
24 [6]twinned, Ps. 133.1; 1 Cor. 1.10; Col. 3.2-19
26 [h]ch. 36.31; Num. 3.36; Rom. 15.1; 1 Cor. 9.19; 2 Cor. 13.11; Gal. 6.2
30 [i]ch. 25.9-40; ch. 27.8; Acts 7.44; Heb. 8.5
31 [j]Lev. 16.2; 2 Chr. 3.14; Matt. 27.51; Mark 15.38; Luke 23.45; Heb. 9.3
33 [k]ch. 25.16; ch. 37.1; ch. 40.21; Num. 3.31; Josh. 4.11; 1 Sam. 4.6; 1 Sam. 6.19; 1 Ki. 8.6; 1 Chr. 15.1; Ps. 132.8; Heb. 9.4; Rev. 11.19
[l]2 Chr. 3.14
[m]Lev. 16.2; Matt. 24.15; Heb. 9.2-3
34 [n]ch. 25.21; ch. 40.20; Lev. 16.2; Heb. 9.5
35 [o]ch. 40.22; Heb. 9.2
[p]ch. 40.24
36 [q]ch. 36.37
37 [r]ch. 36.38

CHAPTER 27
1 [a]ch. 38.1; Ezek. 43.13
2 [b]1 Ki. 1.50; 1 Ki. 2.28; Ps. 118.27
[c]Num. 16.38
3 [d]1 Sam. 2.13-14
4 [1]Or, sieve, Amos 9.9
7 [e]Num. 4.15; Isa. 52.11
8 [f]ch. 25.40; ch. 26.30; Acts 7.44; Heb. 8.5
[2]he shewed
9 [g]ch. 38.9; Ps. 100.4

pillars and their twenty sockets *of*
brass; the hooks of the pillars and their
fillets *of* silver.
12 ¶ And *for* the breadth of the court
on the west side *shall be* hangings of
fifty cubits: their pillars ten, and their
sockets ten.
13 And the breadth of the court on
the east side eastward *shall be* fifty cubits.
14 The hangings of one side *of the*
gate shall be fifteen cubits: their pillars
three, and their sockets three.
15 And on the other side *shall be*
hangings fifteen *cubits:* their pillars
three, and their sockets three.
16 ¶ And for the gate of the court
shall be an hanging of twenty cubits,
of blue, and purple, and scarlet, and
fine twined linen, wrought with needlework: *and* their pillars *shall be* four,
and their sockets four.
17 All the pillars round about the
court *shall be* filleted with silver; their
hooks *shall be of* silver, and their sockets *of* brass.
18 ¶ The length of the court *shall be*
an hundred cubits, and the breadth
[3]fifty every where, and the height five
cubits *of* fine twined linen, and their
sockets *of* brass.
19 All the vessels of the tabernacle
in all the service thereof, and all the
pins thereof, and all the [4]pins of the
court, *shall be of* brass.
20 ¶ And [h]thou shalt command the
children of Ĭs'ra-el, that they bring thee
pure oil olive beaten for the light, to
cause the lamp [5]to burn always.
21 In the tabernacle of the congregation without [i]the vail, which *is* before
the testimony, [j]Aâr'on and his sons
shall order it from evening to morning
before the LORD: [k]*it shall be* a statute
for ever unto their generations on the
behalf of the children of Ĭs'ra-el.

CHAPTER 28

28 And [a]take thou unto thee Aâr'on
thy brother, and his sons with
him, from among the children of Ĭs'ra-
el, that he may minister unto me in
the priest's office, *even* Aâr'on, Nā'-
dăb and A-bī'hū, Ē-le-ā'zar and Ĭth'a-
mär, Aâr'on's sons.
2 And [b]thou shalt make holy garments for Aâr'on thy brother for glory
and for beauty.
3 And [c]thou shalt speak unto all
that are wise hearted, [d]whom I have
filled with the spirit of wisdom, that
they may make Aâr'on's garments to
consecrate him, that he may minister
unto me in the priest's office.
4 And these *are* the garments which
they shall make; a breastplate, and an
ephod, and a robe, and a broidered
coat, a mitre, and a girdle: and they
shall make holy garments for Aâr'on
thy brother, and his sons, that he may
minister unto me in the priest's office.
5 And they shall take gold, and blue,
and purple, and scarlet, and fine linen.
6 ¶ And [e]they shall make the ephod
of gold, *of* blue, and *of* purple, *of* scarlet, and fine twined linen, with cunning
work.
7 It shall have the two shoulderpieces thereof joined at the two edges
thereof; and *so* it shall be joined together.
8 And the [1]curious girdle of the
ephod, which *is* upon it, shall be of the
same, according to the work thereof;
even of gold, *of* blue, and purple, and
scarlet, and fine twined linen.
9 And thou shalt take two onyx
stones, and grave on them the names
of the children of Ĭs'ra-el:
10 Six of their names on one stone,
and *the other* six names of the rest
on the other stone, according to their
birth.
11 With the work of an engraver
in stone, *like* the engravings of a signet, shalt thou engrave the two stones
with the names of the children of Ĭs'-
ra-el: thou shalt make them to be set
in ouches of gold.
12 And thou shalt put the two stones
upon the shoulders of the ephod *for*
stones of memorial unto the children
of Ĭs'ra-el: and [f]Aâr'on shall bear their
names before the LORD upon his two
shoulders [g]for a memorial.
13 ¶ And thou shalt make ouches *of*
gold;
14 And two chains *of* pure gold at
the ends; *of* wreathen work shalt thou
make them, and fasten the wreathen
chains to the ouches.
15 ¶ And [h]thou shalt make the breastplate of judgment with cunning work;
after the work of the ephod thou shalt
make it; *of* gold, *of* blue, and *of* purple,
and *of* scarlet, and *of* fine twined linen,
shalt thou make it.
16 Foursquare it shall be *being* doubled; a span *shall be* the length thereof,
and a span *shall be* the breadth thereof.
17 And [i]thou shalt [2]set in it settings
of stones, *even* four rows of stones: *the*
first row *shall be* a [3]sardius, a topaz,
and a carbuncle: *this shall be* the first
row.
18 And the second row *shall be* an
emerald, a sapphire, and a diamond.
19 And the third row a ligure, an ag-
ate, and an amethyst.
20 And the fourth row a beryl, and
an onyx, and a jasper: they shall be set
in gold in their [4]inclosings.
21 And the stones shall be with the
names of the children of Ĭs'ra-el, twelve,
according to their names, *like* the engravings of a signet; every one with his
name shall they be [j]according to the
twelve tribes.
22 ¶ And thou shalt make upon
the breastplate chains at the ends *of*
wreathen work *of* pure gold.
23 And thou shalt make upon the
breastplate two rings of gold, and shalt
put the two rings on the two ends of
the breastplate.
24 And thou shalt put the two
wreathen *chains* of gold in the two
rings *which are* on the ends of the
breastplate.
25 And *the other* two ends of the
two wreathen *chains* thou shalt fasten

18 [3]fifty by fifty
19 [4]Or, nails, or, stakes, Ezra 9.8; Isa. 33.20; Zech. 10.4
20 [h]Lev. 24.2 [5]to ascend up
21 [i]ch. 26.31-33
[j]ch. 30.8; 1 Sam. 3.3; 2 Chr. 13.11
[k]ch. 28.43; ch. 29.9-28; Lev. 3.17; Lev. 16.34; Lev. 24.9; Num. 18.23; Num. 19.21; 1 Sam. 30.25
CHAPTER 28
1 [a]Num. 16.1-3; Num. 17.1-3-8; Num. 18.7; Heb. 5.1-4
2 [b]ch. 29.5-29; Num. 20. 26-28
3 [c]ch. 31.6; Acts 6.3
[d]ch. 35.30-31; Eph. 1.17
6 [e]ch. 39.2; Lev. 8.7
8 [1]Or, embroidered
12 [f]ch. 39.7; Zech. 6.13
[g]Gen. 9.12-17; 1 Cor. 11.24-25
15 [h]ch. 39.8; 1 Thess. 5.8
17 [i]ch. 39.10; Mal. 3.17 [2]fill in it fillings of stone [3]Or, ruby
20 [4]fillings, Jas. 1.3
21 [j]Num. 1.5; Rev. 21.12

in the two ouches, and put *them* on the
shoulderpieces of the ephod before it.
26 ¶ And thou shalt make two rings
of gold, and thou shalt put them upon
the two ends of the breastplate in the
border thereof, which *is* in the side of
the ephod inward.
27 And two *other* rings of gold thou
shalt make, and shalt put them on the
two sides of the ephod underneath, toward the forepart thereof, over against
the *other* coupling thereof, above the
curious girdle of the ephod.
28 And they shall bind the breastplate by the rings thereof unto the rings
of the ephod with a lace of blue, that *it*
may be above the curious girdle of the
ephod, and that the breastplate be not
loosed from the ephod.
29 And Aâr'on shall [k]bear the names
of the children of Is'ra-el in the breastplate of judgment upon his heart, when
he goeth in unto the holy *place*, [l]for a
memorial before the LORD continually.
30 ¶ And [m]thou shalt put in the
breastplate of judgment the U'rim and
the Thŭm'mim; and they shall be upon
Aâr'on's heart, when he goeth in before the LORD: and Aâr'on shall bear
the judgment of the children of Is'ra-el
upon his heart before the LORD continually.
31 ¶ And [n]thou shalt make the robe
of the ephod all *of* blue.
32 And there shall be an hole in the
top of it, in the midst thereof: it shall
have a binding of woven work round
about the hole of it, as it were the hole
of an habergeon, that it be not rent.
33 ¶ And *beneath* upon the [5]hem of it
thou shalt make pomegranates *of* blue,
and *of* purple, and *of* scarlet, round
about the hem thereof; and bells of gold
between them round about:
34 A golden bell and a pomegranate, a golden bell and a pomegranate,
upon the hem of the robe round about.
35 And it shall be upon Aâr'on to
minister: and his sound shall be heard
when he goeth in unto the holy *place*
before the LORD, and when he cometh
out, that he die not.
36 ¶ And [o]thou shalt make a plate *of*
pure gold, and grave upon it, *like* the
engravings of a signet, HOLINESS TO
THE LORD.
37 And thou shalt put it on a blue
lace, that it may be upon the mitre;
upon the forefront of the mitre it shall
be.
38 And it shall be upon Aâr'on's
forehead, that Aâr'on may [p]bear the
iniquity of the holy things, which the
children of Is'ra-el shall hallow in all
their holy gifts; and it shall be always
upon his forehead, that they may be
[q]accepted before the LORD.
39 ¶ And thou shalt embroider the
coat of fine linen, and thou shalt make
the mitre *of* fine linen, and thou shalt
make the girdle *of* needlework.
40 ¶ And [r]for Aâr'on's sons thou
shalt make coats, and thou shalt make
for them girdles, and bonnets shalt
thou make for them, for glory and for
beauty.
41 And thou shalt put them upon
Aâr'on thy brother, and his sons with
him; and shalt [s]anoint them, and [6][t]con-
secrate them, and sanctify them, that
they may minister unto me in the
priest's office.
42 And thou shalt make them linen
[u]breeches to cover [7]their nakedness;
from the loins even unto the thighs
they shall [8]reach:
43 And they shall be upon Aâr'on,
and upon his sons, when they come in
unto the tabernacle of the congregation, or when they come near [v]unto the
altar to minister in the holy *place;* that
they [w]bear not iniquity, and die: [x]*it
shall be* a statute for ever unto him and
his seed after him.

29 And this *is* the thing that thou
shalt do unto them to hallow
them, to minister unto me in the priest's
office: [a]Take one young bullock, and
two rams without blemish,
2 And [b]unleavened bread, and
cakes unleavened tempered with oil,
and wafers unleavened anointed with
oil: *of* wheaten flour shalt thou make
them.
3 And thou shalt put them into one
basket, and bring them in the basket,
with the bullock and the two rams.
4 And Aâr'on and his sons thou shalt
bring unto the door of the tabernacle
of the congregation, and [c]shalt wash
them with water.
5 And [d]thou shalt take the garments,
and put upon Aâr'on the coat, and the
robe of the ephod, and the ephod, and
the breastplate, and gird him with [e]the
curious girdle of the ephod:
6 And thou shalt put the mitre upon
his head, and put the holy crown upon
the mitre.
7 Then shalt thou take the anointing
[f]oil, and pour *it* upon his head, and
anoint him.
8 And thou shalt bring his sons, and
put coats upon them.
9 And thou shalt gird them with girdles, Aâr'on and his sons, and [1]put the
bonnets on them: and the [g]priest's office shall be theirs for a perpetual statute: and thou shalt [2]consecrate Aâr'on
and his sons.
10 And thou shalt cause a bullock
to be brought before the tabernacle of
the congregation: and [h]Aâr'on and his
sons shall put their hands upon the
head of the bullock.
11 And thou shalt kill the bullock before the LORD, *by* the door of the tabernacle of the congregation.
12 And thou [i]shalt take of the blood
of the bullock, and put *it* upon [j]the
horns of the altar with thy finger, and
pour all the blood beside the bottom of
the altar.
13 And [k]thou shalt take all the fat
that covereth the inwards, and [3]the
caul *that is* above the liver, and the
two kidneys, and the fat that *is* upon
them, and burn *them* upon the altar.

29 [k]Song 8.6; Isa. 49.15-16; Heb. 9.24
[l]verse 12
30 [m]Lev. 8.8; Num. 27.21; Deut. 33.8; 1 Sam. 28.6; Ezra 2.63; Neh. 7.65
31 [n]ch. 39.22; Lev. 8.7; 2 Sam. 6.14; Hos. 3.4
33 [5]Or, skirts
36 [o]ch. 39.30; Lev. 8.9; 1 Chr. 16.29; Heb. 12.14
38 [p]Lev. 10.17; 1 Pet. 2.24
[q]Lev. 1.4; Isa. 56.7
40 [r]ch. 39.27; Ezek. 44.17-18
41 [s]ch. 29.7; Lev. 10.7
[6]fill their hand
[t]Lev. 8; Heb. 7.28
42 [u]Lev. 6.10; Ezek. 44.18
[7]flesh of their nakedness
[8]be
43 [v]ch. 20.26
[w]Lev. 20.19-20; Num. 18.22
[x]Lev. 17.7

CHAPTER 29
1 [a]Lev. 8.2
2 [b]Lev. 6.20-22
4 [c]ch. 40.12; Heb. 10.22
5 [d]Lev. 8.7
[e]ch. 28.8
7 [f]ch. 30.25; Isa. 61.1
9 [1]bind
[g]Num. 18.7
[2]fill the hand of
10 [h]Lev. 1.4; Lev. 8.14
12 [i]Lev. 8.15
[j]ch. 27.2; ch. 30.2
13 [k]Lev. 3.3
[3]It seemeth by anatomy, and the Hebrew doctors, to be the midriff

14 But [l]the flesh of the bullock, and his skin, and his dung, shalt thou burn with fire without the camp: it *is* a sin offering.

15 ¶ Thou [m]shalt also take one ram; and Âr'on and his sons shall put [n]their hands upon the head of the ram.

16 And thou shalt slay the ram, and thou shalt take his blood, and sprinkle *it* round about upon the altar.

17 And thou shalt cut the ram in pieces, and wash the inwards of him, and his legs, and put *them* unto his pieces, and [4]unto his head.

18 And thou shalt burn the whole ram upon the altar: it *is* a burnt offering unto the LORD: it *is* [o]a sweet savour, an offering made by fire unto the LORD.

19 ¶ And [p]thou shalt take the other ram; and Âr'on and his sons shall put their hands upon the head of the ram.

20 Then shalt thou kill the ram, and take of his blood, and put *it* upon the tip of the right ear of Âr'on, and upon the tip of the right ear of his sons, and upon the thumb of their right hand, and upon the great toe of their right foot, and sprinkle the blood upon the altar round about.

21 And thou shalt take of the blood that *is* upon the altar, and of [q]the anointing oil, and sprinkle *it* upon Âr'on, and upon his garments, and upon his sons, and upon the garments of his sons with him: and [r]he shall be hallowed, and his garments, and his sons, and his sons' garments with him.

22 Also thou shalt take of the ram the fat and the rump, and the fat that covereth the inwards, and the caul *above* the liver, and the two kidneys, and the fat that *is* upon them, and the right shoulder; for it *is* a ram of consecration:

23 And [s]one loaf of bread, and one cake of oiled bread, and one wafer out of the basket of the unleavened bread that *is* before the LORD:

24 And thou shalt put all in the hands of Âr'on, and in the hands of his sons; and shalt [5]wave them *for* a wave offering before the LORD.

25 And [t]thou shalt receive them of their hands, and burn *them* upon the altar for a burnt offering, for a sweet savour before the LORD: it *is* an offering made by fire unto the LORD.

26 And thou shalt take [u]the breast of the ram of Âr'on's consecration, and wave it *for* a wave offering before the LORD: and [v]it shall be thy part.

27 And thou shalt sanctify [w]the breast of the wave offering, and the shoulder of the heave offering, which is waved, and which is heaved up, of the ram of the consecration, *even* of *that* which *is* for Âr'on, and of *that* which is for his sons:

28 And it shall be Âr'on's and his sons' by [x]a statute for ever from the children of Is'ra-el: for it *is* an heave offering: and [y]it shall be an heave offering from the children of Is'ra-el of the sacrifice of their peace offerings, *even* their heave offering unto the LORD.

29 ¶ And the holy garments of Âr'on shall [z]be his sons' after him, [a]to be anointed therein, and to be consecrated in them.

30 *And* [6]that son that is priest in his stead shall put them on [b]seven days, when he cometh into the tabernacle of the congregation to minister in the holy *place*.

31 ¶ And thou shalt take the ram of the consecration, and [c]seethe his flesh in the holy place.

32 And Âr'on and his sons shall eat the flesh of the ram, and the bread [d]that *is* in the basket, *by* the door of the tabernacle of the congregation.

33 And [e]they shall eat those things wherewith the atonement was made, to consecrate *and* to sanctify them: but [7]a stranger shall not eat *thereof*, because they *are* holy.

34 And if ought of the flesh of the consecrations, or of the bread, remain unto the morning, then thou shalt burn the remainder with fire: it shall not be eaten, because it *is* holy.

35 And thus shalt thou do unto Âr'on, and to his sons, according to all *things* which I have commanded thee: [f]seven days shalt thou consecrate them.

36 And thou shalt [g]offer every day a bullock *for* a sin offering for atonement: and thou shalt cleanse the altar, when thou hast made an atonement for it, [h]and thou shalt anoint it, to sanctify it.

37 Seven days thou shalt make an atonement for the altar, and sanctify it; [i]and it shall be an altar most holy: [j]whatsoever toucheth the altar shall be holy.

38 ¶ Now this *is that* which thou shalt offer upon the altar; [k]two lambs of the first year [l]day by day continually.

39 The one lamb thou shalt offer in [m]the morning; and the other lamb thou shalt offer at even:

40 And with the one lamb a tenth deal of flour mingled with the fourth part of an hin of beaten oil; and the fourth part of an hin of wine *for* a drink offering.

41 And the other lamb thou shalt [n]offer at even, and shalt do thereto according to the meat offering of the morning, and according to the drink offering thereof, for a sweet savour, an offering made by fire unto the LORD.

42 *This shall be* [o]a continual burnt offering throughout your generations *at* the door of the tabernacle of the congregation before the LORD: [p]where I will meet you, to speak there unto thee.

43 And there I will meet with the children of Is'ra-el, and [8]*the tabernacle* [q]shall be sanctified by my glory.

44 And I will sanctify the tabernacle of the congregation, and the altar: I will [r]sanctify also both Âr'on and his sons, to minister to me in the priest's office.

14 [l]Lev. 4.11-12-21; Heb. 13.11
15 [m]Lev. 8.18 [n]Lev. 1.4; Isa. 53.6; Gal. 4.3-5
17 [4]Or, upon
18 [o]Gen. 8.21
19 [p]Lev. 8.22
21 [q]ch. 30.25; Lev. 8.30 [r]Heb. 9.22
23 [s]Lev. 8.26
24 [5]Or, shake to and fro
25 [t]Lev. 8.28
26 [u]Lev. 7.31-34; Lev. 8.29; Num. 18.11-18 [v]Ps. 99.6
27 [w]Deut. 18.3
28 [x]Lev. 10.15 [y]Lev. 7.34
29 [z]Num. 20.26 [a]Num. 18.8; Num. 35.25
30 [6]he of his sons [b]Lev. 8.35
31 [c]Lev. 8.31
32 [d]Matt. 12.4
33 [e]Lev. 10.14 [7]every one not a Levite
35 [f]Lev. 8.33
36 [g]Heb. 10.11 [h]ch. 30.26
37 [i]ch. 40.10 [j]ch. 30.29; Matt. 23.19
38 [k]Num. 28.3; 1 Chr. 16.40; 2 Chr. 2.4; 2 Chr. 13.11; 2 Chr. 31.3; Ezra 3.3 [l]Dan. 9.27; Dan. 12.11
39 [m]Ezek. 46.13
41 [n]1 Ki. 18.29; 2 Ki. 16.15; Ezra 9.4-5; Ps. 141.2; Ezek. 4.3-5; Dan. 9.21
42 [o]Dan. 8.11 [p]Num. 17.4
43 [8]Or, Israel [q]1 Ki. 8.11; Hag. 2.7-9; Matt. 3.1
44 [r]Lev. 21.15

45 ¶ And [s]I will dwell among the children of Is'ra-el, and will be their God.

46 And they shall know that I *am* the LORD their God, that brought them forth out of the land of E'gypt, that I may dwell among them: I *am* the LORD their God.

30

And thou shalt make [a]an altar [b]to burn incense upon: *of* shittim wood shalt thou make it.

2 A cubit *shall be* the length thereof, and a cubit the breadth thereof; foursquare shall it be: and two cubits *shall be* the height thereof: the horns thereof *shall be* of the same.

3 And thou shalt overlay it with pure gold, the [1]top thereof, and the [2]sides thereof round about, and the horns thereof; and thou shalt make unto it a crown of gold round about.

4 And two golden rings shalt thou make to it under the crown of it, by the two [3]corners thereof, upon the two sides of it shalt thou make *it;* and they shall be for places for the staves to bear it withal.

5 And thou shalt make the staves *of* shittim wood, and overlay them with gold.

6 And thou shalt put it before the vail that *is* by the ark of the testimony, before the mercy seat that *is* over the testimony, where I will meet with thee.

7 And Aâr'on shall burn thereon [4c]sweet incense every morning: when he dresseth the lamps, he shall burn incense upon it.

8 And when Aâr'on [5]lighteth the lamps [6]at even, he shall burn incense upon it, a perpetual incense before the LORD throughout your generations.

9 Ye shall offer no [d]strange incense thereon, nor burnt sacrifice, nor meat offering; neither shall ye pour drink offering thereon.

10 And [e]Aâr'on shall make an atonement upon the horns of it once in a year with the blood of the sin offering of atonements: once in the year shall he make atonement upon it throughout your generations: it *is* most holy unto the LORD.

11 ¶ And the LORD spake unto Mō'ses, saying,

12 When [f]thou takest the sum of the children of Is'ra-el after [7]their number, then shall they give every man [g]a ransom for his soul unto the LORD, when thou numberest them; that there be no [h]plague among them, when *thou* numberest them.

13 This [i]they shall give, every one that passeth among them that are numbered, half a shekel after the shekel of the sanctuary: ([j]a shekel *is* twenty gerahs:) an half shekel *shall be* the offering of the LORD.

14 Every one that passeth among them that are numbered, from twenty years old and above, shall give an offering unto the LORD.

15 The [k]rich shall not [8]give more, and the poor shall not [9]give less than half a shekel, when *they* give an offering unto the LORD, to make an atonement for your souls.

16 And thou shalt take the atonement money of the children of Is'ra-el, and shalt appoint it for the service of the tabernacle of the congregation; that it may be [l]a memorial unto the children of Is'ra-el before the LORD, to make an atonement for your souls.

17 ¶ And the LORD spake unto Mō'ses, saying,

18 [m]Thou shalt also make a laver *of* brass, and his foot *also of* brass, to wash *withal:* and thou shalt put it between the tabernacle of the congregation and the altar, and thou shalt put water therein.

19 For Aâr'on and his sons [n]shall wash their hands and their feet thereat:

20 When they go into the tabernacle of the congregation, they shall wash with water, that they die not; or when they come near to the altar to minister, to burn offering made by fire unto the LORD:

21 So they shall wash their hands and their feet, that they die not: and [o]it shall be a statute for ever to them, *even* to him and to his seed throughout their generations.

22 ¶ Moreover the LORD spake unto Mō'ses, saying,

23 Take thou also unto [p]thee principal spices, of pure [q]myrrh five hundred *shekels,* and of sweet cinnamon half so much, *even* two hundred and fifty *shekels,* and of sweet [r]calamus two hundred and fifty *shekels,*

24 And of [s]cassia five hundred *shekels,* after the shekel of the sanctuary, and of oil olive an [t]hin:

25 And thou shalt make it an oil of holy ointment, an ointment compound after the art of the [10]apothecary: it shall be [u]an holy anointing oil.

26 And [v]thou shalt anoint the tabernacle of the congregation therewith, and the ark of the testimony,

27 And the table and all his vessels, and the candlestick and his vessels, and the altar of incense,

28 And the altar of burnt offering with all his vessels, and the laver and his foot.

29 And thou shalt sanctify them, that they may be most holy: whatsoever toucheth them shall be holy.

30 And thou shalt anoint Aâr'on and his sons, and consecrate them, that *they* may minister unto me in the priest's office.

31 And thou shalt speak unto the children of Is'ra-el, saying, This shall be an holy anointing oil unto me throughout your generations.

32 Upon man's flesh shall it not be poured, neither shall ye make *any other* like it, after the composition of it: it *is* holy, *and* it shall be holy unto you.

33 Whosoever compoundeth *any* like it, or whosoever putteth *any* of it upon [11]a stranger, [w]shall even be cut off from his people.

34 ¶ And the LORD said unto Mō'ses, [x]Take unto thee sweet spices,

45 [s]Ex. 25.8; Lev. 26.12; Rev. 21.3

CHAPTER 30

1 [a]ch. 37.25; ch. 40.5

[b]Rev. 8.3

3 [1]roof [2]walls

4 [3]ribs

7 [4]incense of spices

[c]1 Sam. 2.28; Luke 1.9

8 [5]causeth to ascend, or, setteth up [6]between the two evens

9 [d]Lev. 10.1

10 [e]Lev. 23.27

12 [f]ch. 38.25; 2 Sam. 24.2 [7]them that are to be numbered

[g]Num. 31.50; 1 Pet. 1.18

[h]2 Sam. 24.15

13 [i]Matt. 17.24

[j]Lev. 27.25; Ezek. 45.12

15 [k]Job 34.19; 1 Pet. 1.17 [8]multiply [9]diminish

16 [l]Num. 16.40

18 [m]1 Ki. 7.38

19 [n]Isa. 52.11; Heb. 10.22

21 [o]ch. 28.43

23 [p]Song 4.14; Ezek. 27.22

[q]Ps. 45.8

[r]Jer. 6.20

24 [s]Ps. 45.8

[t]ch. 29.40

25 [10]Or, perfumer

[u]Num. 35.25; Ps. 133.2

26 [v]Lev. 8.10; Num. 7.1

33 [11]One not a priest, Lev. 22.10-12-13; Num. 1.51; Num. 3.10

[w]Gen. 17.14; Lev. 7.20-21

34 [x]ch. 25.6; ch. 37.29

stacte, and onycha, and galbanum;
these sweet spices with pure frankincense: of each shall there be a like
weight:
35 And thou shalt make it a perfume, a confection after the art of the
apothecary, [12]tempered together, pure
and holy:
36 And thou shalt beat *some* of it
very small, and put of it before the testimony in the tabernacle of the congregation, [y]where I will meet with thee:
[z]it shall be unto you most holy.
37 And *as for* the perfume which
thou shalt make, ye shall not make to
yourselves according to the composition thereof: it shall be unto thee holy
for the LORD.
38 Whosoever shall make like unto
that, to smell thereto, shall even be cut
off from his people.

31 And the LORD spake unto Mō'-
ses, saying,
2 See, [a]I have called by name Be-
zăl'ĕ-el the [b]son of Ū'ri, the son of
Hûr, of the tribe of Jū'dah:
3 And I have [c]filled him with the
spirit of God, in wisdom, and in understanding, and in knowledge, and in all
manner of workmanship,
4 To devise cunning works, to work
in gold, and in silver, and in brass,
5 And in cutting of stones, to set
them, and in carving of timber, to work
in all manner of workmanship.
6 And I, behold, I have given with
him [d]A-hō'lĭ-ab, the son of A-hĭs'a-
mach, of the tribe of Dăn: and in the
hearts of all that are [e]wise hearted I
have put wisdom, that they may make
all that I have commanded thee;
7 The [f]tabernacle of the congregation, and the ark of the testimony, and
the mercy seat that *is* thereupon, and
all the [1]furniture of the tabernacle,
8 And the table and his furniture,
and the pure candlestick with all his
furniture, and the altar of incense,
9 And the altar of burnt offering with
all his furniture, and the laver and his
foot,
10 And the cloths of service, and the
holy garments for Aâr'on the priest,
and the garments of his sons, to minister in the priest's office,
11 And the anointing oil, and sweet
incense for the holy *place:* according to
all that I have commanded thee shall
they do.
12 ¶ And the LORD spake unto Mō'-
ses, saying,
13 Speak thou also unto the children of Ĭs'ra-el, saying, [g]Verily my sabbaths ye shall keep: for it *is* a sign between me and you throughout your
generations; that *ye* may know that I
am the LORD that doth sanctify you.
14 [h]Ye shall keep the sabbath therefore; for it *is* holy unto you: every one
that defileth it shall surely be put to
death: for [i]whosoever doeth *any* work
therein, that soul shall be cut off from
among his people.
15 Six days may work be done; but
in the [j]seventh *is* the sabbath of rest,

35 [12]salted, Lev. 2.13
36 [y]ch. 29.42; Lev. 16.2
[z]ch. 29.37; Lev. 2.3
CHAPTER 31
2 [a]ch. 35.30
[b]1 Chr. 2.20
3 [c]ch. 35.31; 1 Ki. 7.14; Isa. 28.26; 1 Cor. 12.4-8
6 [d]ch. 35.34
[e]ch. 28.3; ch. 36.1
7 [f]ch. 36.8
[1]vessels
13 [g]Lev. 19.3; Lev. 26.2; Ezek. 20.12; Ezek. 44.24
14 [h]Deut. 5.15; Neh. 9.14; Isa. 56.6; Isa. 58.13; Ezek. 20.12
[i]ch. 35.2; Num. 15.35
15 [j]Gen. 2.2; ch. 16.23; ch. 20.10
[2]holiness, ch. 28.36
17 [k]Ezek. 20.12
[l]Gen. 1.31
18 [m]ch. 24.12; ch. 32.15; ch. 34.28-29; 2 Cor. 3.3
CHAPTER 32
1 [a]ch. 24.18; Deut. 9.9
[b]Isa. 46.6-7; Acts 7.40
2 [c]Judg. 8.24
4 [d]ch. 20.23; Rom. 1.23
5 [e]Lev. 23.2; 2 Ki. 10.20
6 [f]1 Cor. 10.7
7 [g]Deut. 9.12
[h]Gen. 6.11; Hos. 9.9
8 [i]ch. 20.3-4-23; Deut. 9.16
[j]1 Ki. 12.28
9 [k]ch. 33.3-5; Acts 7.51
10 [l]Deut. 9.14
[m]Num. 14.12
11 [n]Deut. 9.18-26-29; Ps. 106.23
[1]the face of the LORD

[2]holy to the LORD: whosoever doeth
any work in the sabbath day, he shall
surely be put to death.
16 Wherefore the children of Ĭs'ra-
el shall keep the sabbath, to observe
the sabbath throughout their generations, *for* a perpetual covenant.
17 It *is* [k]a sign between me and the
children of Ĭs'ra-el for ever: for *in* [l]six
days the LORD made heaven and earth,
and on the seventh day he rested, and
was refreshed.
18 ¶ And he gave unto Mō'ses, when
he had made an end of communing
with him upon mount Sī'nāi, [m]two tables of testimony, tables of stone, written with the finger of God.

32 And when the people saw that
Mō'ses [a]delayed to come down
out of the mount, the people gathered
themselves together unto Aâr'on, and
said unto him, [b]Up, make us gods,
which shall go before us; for *as for* this
Mō'ses, the man that brought us up out
of the land of Ē'gypt, we wot not what
is become of him.
2 And Aâr'on said unto them, Break
off the [c]golden earrings, which *are* in
the ears of your wives, of your sons,
and of your daughters, and bring *them*
unto me.
3 And all the people brake off the
golden earrings which *were* in their
ears, and brought *them* unto Aâr'on.
4 And [d]he received *them* at their
hand, and fashioned it with a graving
tool, after he had made it a molten calf:
and they said, These *be* thy gods, O
Ĭs'ra-el, which brought thee up out of
the land of Ē'gypt.
5 And when Aâr'on saw *it*, he built
an altar before it; and Aâr'on made
[e]proclamation, and said, To morrow *is*
a feast to the LORD.
6 And they rose up early on the morrow, and offered burnt offerings, and
brought peace offerings; and the [f]peo-
ple sat down to eat and to drink, and
rose up to play.
7 ¶ And the LORD said unto Mō'ses,
[g]Go, get thee down; for thy people,
which thou broughtest out of the land
of Ē'gypt, [h]have corrupted *themselves:*
8 They have turned aside quickly
out of the way which I [i]commanded
them: they have made them a molten
calf, and have worshipped it, and have
sacrificed thereunto, and said, [j]These
be thy gods, O Ĭs'ra-el, which have
brought thee up out of the land of
Ē'gypt.
9 And the LORD said unto Mō'ses, [k]I
have seen this people, and, behold, it *is*
a stiffnecked people:
10 Now therefore [l]let me alone, that
my wrath may wax hot against them,
and that I may consume them: and [m]I
will make of thee a great nation.
11 And [n]Mō'ses besought [1]the LORD
his God, and said, LORD, why doth
thy wrath wax hot against thy people,
which thou hast brought forth out of
the land of Ē'gypt with great power,
and with a mighty hand?

12 Wherefore should the E-ġy̆p'tians
speak, and say, For mischief did he
bring them out, to slay them in the
mountains, and to consume them from
the face of the earth? Turn from thy
fierce wrath, and repent of this evil
against thy people.
13 Remember Ā'brā-hăm, Ī'saac, and
Is'ra-el, thy servants, to whom thou
[o]swarest by thine own self, and saidst
unto them, [p]I will multiply your seed as
the stars of heaven, and all this land
that I have spoken of will I give unto
your seed, and they shall inherit *it* for
ever.
14 And the LORD [q]repented of the
evil which he thought to do unto his
people.
15 ¶ And [r]Mō'ses turned, and went
down from the mount, and the two tables of the testimony *were* in his hand:
the tables *were* written on both their
sides; on the one side and on the other
were they written.
16 And the [s]tables *were* the work of
God, and the writing *was* the writing
of God, graven upon the tables.
17 And when Jŏsh'u-ȧ heard the
noise of the people as they shouted, he
said unto Mō'ses, *There is* a noise of
war in the camp.
18 And he said, *It is* not the voice of
them that shout for mastery, neither *is*
it the voice of *them that* cry for [2]being
overcome: *but* the noise of *them that*
sing do I hear.
19 ¶ And it came to pass, as soon as
he came nigh unto the camp, that he
saw the calf, and the dancing: and Mō'-
ses' anger waxed hot, and he cast the
tables out of his hands, and brake them
beneath the mount.
20 And he took the calf which they
had made, and burnt *it* in the fire, and
ground *it* to powder, and strawed *it*
upon the water, and made the children
of Is'ra-el drink *of it*.
21 And Mō'ses said unto Aâr'on,
[t]What did this people unto thee, that
thou hast brought so great a sin upon
them?
22 And Aâr'on said, Let not the anger of my lord wax hot: [u]thou knowest
the people, that they *are set* on mischief.
23 For they said unto me, Make us
gods, which shall go before us: for *as*
for this Mō'ses, the man that brought
us up out of the land of Ē'gypt, we wot
not what is become of him.
24 And I said unto them, Whosoever
hath any gold, let them break *it* off. So
they gave *it* me: then I cast it into the
fire, and there came out this calf.
25 ¶ And when Mō'ses saw that the
people *were* [v]naked; (for Aâr'on had
[w]made them naked unto *their* shame
among [3]their enemies:)
26 Then Mō'ses stood in the gate of
the camp, and said, Who *is* on the
LORD'S side? *let him come* unto me.
And all the sons of Lē'vī gathered themselves together unto him.
27 And he said unto them, Thus saith
the LORD God of Is'ra-el, Put every man
his sword by his side, *and* go in and out
from gate to gate throughout the camp,
and [x]slay every man his brother, and
every man his companion, and every
man his neighbour.
28 And the children of Lē'vī did according to the word of Mō'ses: and
there fell of the people that day about
three thousand men.
29 [4][y]For Mō'ses had said, [5]Conse-
crate yourselves to day to the LORD,
even every man upon his son, and upon
his brother; that he may bestow upon
you a blessing this day.
30 ¶ And it came to pass on the morrow, that Mō'ses said unto the people,
[z]Ye have sinned a great sin: and now I
will go up unto the LORD; [a]peradven-
ture I shall make an atonement for
your sin.
31 And Mō'ses returned unto the
LORD, and said, Oh, this people have
sinned a great sin, and have made
them gods of gold.
32 Yet now, if thou wilt forgive their
sin—; and if not, [b]blot me, I pray thee,
[c]out of thy book which thou hast written.
33 And the LORD said unto Mō'ses,
[d]Whosoever hath sinned against me,
him will I blot out of my book.
34 Therefore now go, lead the people unto *the place* of which I have
spoken unto thee: [e]behold, mine Angel shall go before thee: nevertheless
[f]in the day when I visit I will visit their
sin upon them.
35 And the LORD plagued the people,
because [g]they made the calf, which
Aâr'on made.

33 And the LORD said unto Mō'-
ses, Depart, *and* go up hence,
thou and the people which thou hast
brought up out of the land of Ē'gypt,
unto the land which I sware unto
Ā'brā-hăm, to Ī'saac, and to Jā'cob,
saying, [a]Unto thy seed will I give it:
2 And [b]I will send an angel before
thee; and I will drive out the Cā'năan-
īte, the Ăm'ôr-īte, and the Hĭt'tīte, and
the Pĕr'ĭz-zīte, the Hī'vīte, and the Jĕb'-
u-site:
3 Unto a land flowing with milk and
honey: for I will not go up in the midst
of thee; for thou *art* [c]a stiffnecked people: lest I consume thee in the way.
4 ¶ And when the people heard these
evil tidings, they mourned: and [d]no
man did put on him his ornaments.
5 For the LORD had said unto Mō'-
ses, Say unto the children of Is'ra-el,
Ye *are* a stiffnecked people: I will come
up into the midst of thee in a moment,
and consume thee: therefore now put
off thy ornaments from thee, that I
[e]may know what to do unto thee.
6 And the children of Is'ra-el stripped
themselves of their ornaments by the
mount Hō'reb.
7 And Mō'ses took the tabernacle,
and pitched it without the camp, afar
off from the camp, and called it the
Tabernacle of the congregation. And it
came to pass, *that* every one which
[f]sought the LORD went out unto the

13 [o]Gen. 22.16; Heb. 6.13
[p]Gen. 12.7; Gen. 13.15; Gen. 35.12
14 [q]Num. 23.19; Jon. 3.10
15 [r]Deut. 9.15
16 [s]ch. 31.18
18 [2]weakness
21 [t]Gen. 20.9
22 [u]ch. 15.24
25 [v]ch. 33.4-5
[w]2 Chr. 28.19
[3]those that rose up against them
27 [x]Deut. 33.9
29 [4]Or, And Moses said, Consecrate yourselves to day to the LORD, because every man hath been against his son, and against his brother, etc
[y]Num. 25.11; Zech. 13.3
[5]fill your hands
30 [z]1 Sam. 12.20
[a]2 Sam. 16.12; Amos 5.15
32 [b]Deut. 9.14; Rom. 9.3
[c]Ps. 56.8; Rev. 22.19
33 [d]Lev. 23.30; Ezek. 18.4
34 [e]Num. 20.16
[f]Amos 3.14; Rom. 2.5-6
35 [g]2 Sam. 12.9
CHAPTER 33
1 [a]Gen. 12.7
2 [b]Deut. 7.22; Josh. 24.11
3 [c]ch. 32.9; Deut. 9.6
4 [d]2 Sam. 19.24
5 [e]Ps. 139.23
7 [f]2 Sam. 21.1

tabernacle of the congregation, which
was without the camp.
8 And it came to pass, when Mō′ses
went out unto the tabernacle, *that* all
the people rose up, and stood every
man [g]*at* his tent door, and looked after
Mō′ses, until he was gone into the tabernacle.
9 And it came to pass, as Mō′ses entered into the tabernacle, the cloudy pillar descended, and stood *at* the door of
the tabernacle, and *the* LORD [h]talked
with Mō′ses.
10 And all the people saw the cloudy
pillar stand *at* the tabernacle door: and
all the people rose up and worshipped,
every man *in* his tent door.
11 And [i]the LORD spake unto Mō′-
ses face to face, as a man speaketh
unto his friend. And he turned again
into the camp: but [j]his servant Jŏsh′-
u-ȧ, the son of Nŭn, a young man, departed not out of the tabernacle.
12 ¶ And Mō′ses said unto the LORD,
See, thou sayest unto me, Bring up this
people: and thou hast not let me know
whom thou wilt send with me. Yet
thou hast said, [k]I know thee by name,
and thou hast also found grace in my
sight.
13 Now therefore, I pray thee, [l]if I
have found grace in thy sight, [m]shew
me now thy way, that I may know thee,
that I may find grace in thy sight: and
consider that this nation *is* [n]thy people.
14 And he said, [o]My presence shall
go *with thee,* and I will [p]give thee rest.
15 And he said unto him, [q]If thy
presence go not *with me,* carry us not
up hence.
16 For wherein shall it be known
here that I and thy people have found
grace in thy sight? [r]*is it* not in that
thou goest with us? so [s]shall we be
separated, I and thy people, from all
the people that *are* upon the face of the
earth.
17 And the LORD said unto Mō′ses,
[t]I will do this thing also that thou hast
spoken: for thou hast found grace in
my sight, and I know thee by name.
18 And he said, I beseech thee, shew
me [u]thy glory.
19 And he said, [v]I will make all my
goodness pass before thee, and I will
proclaim the name of the LORD before
thee; [w]and will be gracious to whom I
will be gracious, and will shew mercy
on whom I will shew mercy.
20 And he said, Thou canst not see
my face: for [x]there shall no man see
me, and live.
21 And the LORD said, Behold, *there*
is a place by me, and thou shalt stand
upon a rock:
22 And it shall come to pass, while
my glory passeth by, that I will put
thee [y]in a clift of the rock, and will
[z]cover thee with my hand while I pass
by:
23 And I will take away mine hand,
and thou shalt see my back parts: but
my face shall [a]not be seen.

8 [g]Num. 16.27
9 [h]Ps. 99.7
11 [i]Gen. 32.30; Deut. 5.24; Deut. 34.10
[j]ch. 24.13
12 [k]Ps. 1.6; 2 Tim. 2.19
13 [l]ch. 34.9
[m]Ps. 25.4; Ps. 119.33
[n]Deut. 9.26; Joel 2.17
14 [o]ch. 40.34-38; Isa. 63.9
[p]Deut. 3.20; Ps. 95.11
15 [q]ch. 34.9
16 [r]Num. 14.14
[s]Deut. 4.34; Tit. 2.14
17 [t]Gen. 19.21; Jas. 5.16
18 [u]1 Tim. 6.16
19 [v]Jer. 31.14
[w]Rom. 4.4; Rom. 9.15
20 [x]Gen. 32.30; Rev. 1.16
22 [y]Isa. 2.21
[z]Ps. 91.1-4
23 [a]John 1.18; 1 John 4.12
CHAPTER 34
1 [a]Deut. 10.1
[b]Deut. 10.2-4
6 [c]Neh. 9.17; Joel 2.13
[d]Rom. 2.4
[e]Ps. 108.4
7 [f]Jer. 32.18; Dan. 9.4
[g]Eph. 4.32; 1 John 1.9
[h]Josh. 24.19; Job 10.14
9 [i]Ps. 94.14; Zech. 2.12
10 [j]Deut. 29.12
[k]2 Sam. 7.23; Ps. 147.20
[l]Isa. 64.3
11 [m]Deut. 12.28
12 [n]Judg. 2.2
13 [1]statues
[o]2 Ki. 18.4
14 [p]Isa. 57.15
[q]ch. 20.5
15 [r]Ezek. 6.9
[s]1 Cor. 10.27
[t]1 Cor. 8.4
16 [u]Ezra 9.2

34 And the LORD said unto Mō′ses,
[a]Hew thee two tables of stone
like unto the first: and [b]I will write
upon *these* tables the words that were
in the first tables, which thou brakest.
2 And be ready in the morning, and
come up in the morning unto mount
Sī′nāi, and present thyself there to me
in the top of the mount.
3 And no man shall come up with
thee, neither let any man be seen
throughout all the mount; neither let
the flocks nor herds feed before that
mount.
4 ¶ And he hewed two tables of stone
like unto the first; and Mō′ses rose up
early in the morning, and went up unto
mount Sī′nāi, as the LORD had commanded him, and took in his hand the
two tables of stone.
5 And the LORD descended in the
cloud, and stood with him there, and
proclaimed the name of the LORD.
6 And the LORD passed by before
him, and proclaimed, The LORD, The
LORD [c]God, merciful and gracious,
longsuffering, and abundant in [d]good-
ness and [e]truth,
7 [f]Keeping mercy for thousands,
[g]forgiving iniquity and transgression
and sin, and that [h]will by no means
clear *the guilty;* visiting the iniquity
of the fathers upon the children, and
upon the children's children, unto the
third and to the fourth *generation.*
8 And Mō′ses made haste, and bowed
his head toward the earth, and worshipped.
9 And he said, If now I have found
grace in thy sight, O Lord, let my Lord,
I pray thee, go among us; for it *is* a
stiffnecked people; and pardon our iniquity and our sin, and take us for
[i]thine inheritance.
10 ¶ And he said, Behold, [j]I make a
covenant: before all thy people I will
[k]do marvels, such as have not been
done in all the earth, nor in any nation:
and all the people among which thou
art shall see the work of the LORD: for
it *is* [l]a terrible thing that I will do with
thee.
11 [m]Observe thou that which I command thee this day: behold, I drive out
before thee the Ăm′ôr-īte, and the Cā′-
năan-īte, and the Hĭt′tīte, and the Pĕr′-
ĭz-zīte, and the Hī′vīte, and the Jĕb′u-
site.
12 [n]Take heed to thyself, lest thou
make a covenant with the inhabitants
of the land whither thou goest, lest it
be for a snare in the midst of thee:
13 But ye shall destroy their altars,
break their [1]images, and [o]cut down
their groves:
14 For thou shalt worship no other
god: for the LORD, whose [p]name *is* Jealous, *is* a [q]jealous God:
15 Lest thou make a covenant with
the inhabitants of the land, and they
[r]go a whoring after their gods, and do
sacrifice unto their gods, and *one* [s]call
thee, and thou eat [t]of his sacrifice;
16 And thou take of their [u]daugh-
ters unto thy sons, and their daughters

go [v]a whoring after their gods, and
make thy sons go a whoring after their
gods.
17 [w]Thou shalt make thee no molten
gods.
18 ¶ The feast of [x]unleavened bread
shalt thou keep. Seven days thou shalt
eat unleavened bread, as I commanded
thee, in the time of the month Ā'bĭb:
for in the month Ā'bĭb thou camest out
from Ē'ġypt.
19 [y]All that openeth the matrix *is*
mine; and every firstling among thy
cattle, *whether* ox or sheep, *that is*
male.
20 But [z]the firstling of an ass thou
shalt redeem with a [2]lamb: and if thou
redeem *him* not, then shalt thou break
his neck. All the firstborn of thy sons
thou shalt redeem. And none shall appear before me [a]empty.
21 ¶ [b]Six days thou shalt work, but
on the seventh day thou shalt rest: in
earing time and in harvest thou shalt
rest.
22 ¶ And [c]thou shalt observe the
feast of weeks, of the firstfruits of
wheat harvest, and the feast of ingathering at the [3]year's end.
23 ¶ [d]Thrice in the year shall all
your men children appear before the
Lord GOD, the God of Ĭs'ra-el.
24 For I will [e]cast out the nations
before thee, and [f]enlarge thy borders:
[g]neither shall any man desire thy land,
when thou shalt go up to appear before
the LORD thy God thrice in the year.
25 [h]Thou shalt not offer the blood of
my sacrifice with leaven; neither [i]shall
the sacrifice of the feast of the passover be left unto the morning.
26 The [j]first of the firstfruits of thy
land thou shalt bring unto the house
of the LORD thy God. Thou shalt not
seethe a kid in his mother's milk.
27 And the LORD said unto Mō'ses,
Write thou [k]these words: for after the
tenor of these words I have made a
covenant with thee and with Ĭs'ra-el.
28 And [l]he was there with the LORD
forty days and forty nights; he did neither eat bread, nor drink water. And
[m]he wrote upon the tables the words
of the covenant, the ten [4]command-
ments.
29 ¶ And it came to pass, when Mō'-
ses came down from mount Sī'nāi with
the [n]two tables of testimony in Mō'ses'
hand, when he came down from the
mount, that Mō'ses wist not that [o]the
skin of his face shone while he talked
with him.
30 And when Aâr'on and all the children of Ĭs'ra-el saw Mō'ses, behold,
the skin of his face shone; and they
were afraid to come nigh him.
31 And Mō'ses called unto them; and
Aâr'on and all the rulers of the congregation returned unto him: and Mō'ses
talked with them.
32 And afterward all the children of
Ĭs'ra-el came nigh: [p]and he gave them
in commandment all that the LORD had
spoken with him in mount Sī'nāi.

[v]Num. 25.1-2
17 [w]Lev. 19.4
18 [x]ch. 23.15
19 [y]ch. 22.29; Luke 2.23
20 [z]Num. 18.15
[2]Or, kid
[a]Deut. 16.16; 2 Sam. 24.24
21 [b]Deut. 5.12; Luke 13.14
22 [c]ch. 23.16
[3]revolution of the year
23 [d]Deut. 16.16
24 [e]Lev. 18.24; Ps. 80.8
[f]Deut. 19.8
[g]Gen. 35.5; Prov. 16.7
25 [h]ch. 23.18
[i]ch. 12.10
26 [j]Deut. 26.2-10; Prov. 3.9
27 [k]Deut. 31.9; Isa. 30.8
28 [l]Deut. 9.9-18
[m]ch. 31.18; Deut. 10.2-4
[4]words
29 [n]ch. 32.15
[o]Matt. 17.2
32 [p]ch. 24.3
33 [q]2 Cor. 3.13
CHAPTER 35
1 [a]ch. 34.32
2 [b]ch. 31.14-15; Luke 13.14
[1]holiness
3 [c]ch. 16.23
4 [d]ch. 25.1-2
5 [e]ch. 25.2; 2 Cor. 9.7
10 [f]ch. 31.6; Isa. 28.26
11 [g]ch. 25.9; Rev. 21.3
12 [h]ch. 25.10
13 [i]ch. 25.23
[j]ch. 25.30; Lev. 24.5-6
14 [k]ch. 25.31
15 [l]ch. 30.1; ch. 40.5
[m]ch. 30.23
[n]ch. 30.34;
16 [o]ch. 27.1
17 [p]ch. 27.9
19 [q]ch. 31.10

33 And *till* Mō'ses had done speaking with them, he put [q]a vail on his
face.
34 But when Mō'ses went in before
the LORD to speak with him, he took
the vail off, until he came out. And he
came out, and spake unto the children
of Ĭs'ra-el *that* which he was commanded.
35 And the children of Ĭs'ra-el saw
the face of Mō'ses, that the skin of
Mō'ses' face shone: and Mō'ses put the
vail upon his face again, until he went
in to speak with him.

35 And Mō'ses gathered all the congregation of the children of Ĭs'ra-
el together, and said unto them, [a]These
are the words which the LORD hath
commanded, that *ye* should do them.
2 [b]Six days shall work be done, but
on the seventh day there shall be to
you [1]an holy day, a sabbath of rest
to the LORD: whosoever doeth work
therein shall be put to death.
3 [c]Ye shall kindle no fire throughout your habitations upon the sabbath
day.
4 ¶ And Mō'ses spake unto all the
congregation of the children of Ĭs'ra-
el, saying, [d]This *is* the thing which the
LORD commanded, saying,
5 Take ye from among you an offering unto the LORD: [e]whosoever *is* of a
willing heart, let him bring it, an offering of the LORD; gold, and silver, and
brass,
6 And blue, and purple, and scarlet,
and fine linen, and goats' *hair*,
7 And rams' skins dyed red, and badgers' skins, and shittim wood,
8 And oil for the light, and spices for
anointing oil, and for the sweet incense,
9 And onyx stones, and stones to be
set for the ephod, and for the breastplate.
10 And [f]every wise hearted among
you shall come, and make all that the
LORD hath commanded;
11 The [g]tabernacle, his tent, and his
covering, his taches, and his boards,
his bars, his pillars, and his sockets,
12 The [h]ark, and the staves thereof,
with the mercy seat, and the vail of the
covering,
13 The [i]table, and his staves, and all
his vessels, and the [j]shewbread,
14 The [k]candlestick also for the light,
and his furniture, and his lamps, with
the oil for the light,
15 And [l]the incense altar, and his
staves, and [m]the anointing oil, and
[n]the sweet incense, and the hanging
for the door at the entering in of the
tabernacle,
16 The [o]altar of burnt offering, with
his brasen grate, his staves, and all his
vessels, the laver and his foot,
17 The [p]hangings of the court, his
pillars, and their sockets, and the hanging for the door of the court,
18 The pins of the tabernacle, and
the pins of the court, and their cords,
19 The [q]cloths of service, to do
service in the holy *place*, the holy

garments for Aâr'on the priest, and
the garments of his sons, to minister
in the priest's office.
20 ¶ And all the congregation of the
children of Ĭs'ra-el departed from the
presence of Mō'ses.
21 And they came, every one [r]whose
heart stirred him up, and every one
whom his spirit made willing, *and* they
brought the LORD'S offering to the work
of the tabernacle of the congregation,
and for all his service, and for the holy
garments.
22 And they came, both men and women, as many as were willing hearted,
and brought bracelets, and earrings,
and rings, and tablets, all jewels of
gold: and every man that offered *of-*
fered an offering of gold unto the LORD.
23 And [s]every man, with whom was
found blue, and purple, and scarlet,
and fine linen, and goats' *hair*, and
red skins of rams, and badgers' skins,
brought *them*.
24 Every one that did offer an offering of silver and brass brought the
LORD'S offering: and every man, with
whom was found shittim wood for any
work of the service, brought *it*.
25 And all the women that were
[t]wise hearted did spin with their hands,
and brought that which they had spun,
both of blue, and of purple, *and* of scarlet, and of fine linen.
26 And all the women whose heart
stirred them up in wisdom spun goats'
hair.
27 And [u]the rulers brought onyx
stones, and stones to be set, for the
ephod, and for the breastplate;
28 And [v]spice, and oil for the light,
and for the anointing oil, and for the
sweet incense.
29 The children of Ĭs'ra-el brought a
[w]willing offering unto the LORD, every
man and woman, whose heart made
them willing to bring for all manner
of work, which the LORD had commanded to be made by the hand of
Mō'ses.
30 ¶ And Mō'ses said unto the children of Ĭs'ra-el, See, [x]the LORD hath
called by name Be-zăl'ĕ-el the son of
Ū'ri, the son of Hûr, of the tribe of
Jū'dah;
31 And he hath filled him with the
[y]spirit of God, in wisdom, in understanding, and in knowledge, and in all
manner of workmanship;
32 And to devise curious works, to
work in gold, and in silver, and in
brass,
33 And in the cutting of stones, to
set *them*, and in carving of wood, to
make any manner of cunning work.
34 And he hath put in his heart that
he may teach, *both* he, and [z]A-hō'lĭ-
ab, the son of A-hĭs'a-mach, of the
tribe of Dăn.
35 Them hath he [a]filled with wisdom of heart, to work all manner of
work, of the engraver, and of the cunning workman, and of the embroiderer, in blue, and in purple, in scarlet,
and in fine linen, and of the weaver,

21 [r]ch. 25.2; ch. 36.2; 1 Chr. 28.2-9; 1 Chr. 29.9; Ezra 7.27; 2 Cor. 8.12; 2 Cor. 9.7
23 [s]1 Chr. 29.8
25 [t]ch. 28.3; ch. 31.6; ch. 36.1; 2 Ki. 23.7; Prov. 31.19-22-24
27 [u]1 Chr. 29.6; Ezra 2.68
28 [v]ch. 30.23
29 [w]1 Chr. 29.9
30 [x]ch. 31.2
31 [y]Gen. 41.38; Job 32.8; Prov. 2.6
34 [z]ch. 31.6
35 [a]verse 31; ch. 31.3-6; ch. 36.1-2; 1 Ki. 7.14; 2 Chr. 2.14; Isa. 28.26; Jas. 1.5
CHAPTER 36
1 [a]ch. 28.3; ch. 31.6; ch. 35.10-35; Job 32.8; Isa. 28.26; Prov. 2.6
[b]ch. 25.8; Lev. 4.6; Lev. 19.30; Num. 3.8; Num. 18.5; 1 Ki. 6.16; Ps. 96.6; Ps. 134.2; Ps. 150.1; Isa. 63.18; Lam. 1.10; Lam. 2.20; Lam. 4.1; Ezek. 5.11; Dan. 8.13-14; Heb. 9.1-2
2 [c]ch. 35.21-26; 1 Chr. 29.5
3 [d]ch. 35.27
5 [e]2 Cor. 8.2-3
8 [f]ch. 26.1; Job 32.8; Prov. 10.8; Prov. 15.14; Prov. 16.1; Prov. 18.15; Prov. 21.1
[g]Gen. 3.24; 1 Ki. 6.23; 2 Chr. 3.10; Ezek. 1.5-28; Ezek. 10.1
12 [h]ch. 26.5
14 [i]ch. 26.7

even of them that do any work, and of
those that devise cunning work.
36 Then wrought Be-zăl'ĕ-el and A-
hō'lĭ-ab, and every [a]wise hearted
man, in whom the LORD put wisdom
and understanding to know how to
work all manner of work for the service
of the [b]sanctuary, according to all that
the LORD had commanded.
2 And Mō'ses called Be-zăl'ĕ-el and
A-hō'lĭ-ab, and every wise hearted
man, in whose heart the LORD had put
wisdom, *even* every one [c]whose heart
stirred him up to come unto the work
to do it:
3 And they received of Mō'ses all
the offering, which the children of Ĭs'-
ra-el [d]had brought for the work of the
service of the sanctuary, to make it
withal. And they brought yet unto him
free offerings every morning.
4 And all the wise men, that wrought
all the work of the sanctuary, came every man from his work which they
made;
5 ¶ And they spake unto Mō'ses, saying, [e]The people bring much more than
enough for the service of the work,
which the LORD commanded to make.
6 And Mō'ses gave commandment,
and they caused it to be proclaimed
throughout the camp, saying, Let neither man nor woman make any more
work for the offering of the sanctuary.
So the people were restrained from
bringing.
7 For the stuff they had was sufficient for all the work to make it, and
too much.
8 ¶ [f]And every wise hearted man
among them that wrought the work of
the tabernacle made ten curtains *of*
fine twined linen, and blue, and purple,
and scarlet: *with* [g]cherubims of cunning work made he them.
9 The length of one curtain *was*
twenty and eight cubits, and the breadth
of one curtain four cubits: the curtains
were all of one size.
10 And he coupled the five curtains
one unto another: and *the other* five
curtains he coupled one unto another.
11 And he made loops of blue on the
edge of one curtain from the selvedge
in the coupling: likewise he made in
the uttermost side of *another* curtain,
in the coupling of the second.
12 [h]Fifty loops made he in one curtain, and fifty loops made he in the
edge of the curtain which *was* in the
coupling of the second: the loops held
one *curtain* to another.
13 And he made fifty taches of gold,
and coupled the curtains one unto another with the taches: so it became one
tabernacle.
14 ¶ And [i]he made curtains *of* goats'
hair for the tent over the tabernacle:
eleven curtains he made them.
15 The length of one curtain *was*
thirty cubits, and four cubits *was* the
breadth of one curtain: the eleven curtains *were* of one size.

16 And he coupled five curtains by
themselves, and six curtains by themselves.
17 And he made fifty loops upon the
uttermost edge of the curtain in the coupling, and fifty loops made he upon the
edge of the curtain which coupleth the
second.
18 And he made fifty taches *of* brass
to couple the tent together, that it might
be one.
19 And [j]he made a covering for the
tent *of* rams' skins dyed red, and a covering *of* badgers' skins above *that.*
20 ¶ And [k]he made boards for the
tabernacle *of* [l]shittim wood, standing
up.
21 The length of a board *was* ten cubits, and the breadth of a board one
cubit and a half.
22 One board had two tenons, equally
distant one from another: thus did he
make for all the boards of the tabernacle.
23 And he made boards for the tabernacle; twenty boards for the south side
southward:
24 And forty sockets of silver he
made under the twenty boards; two
sockets under one board for his two
[1]tenons, and two sockets under another board for his two tenons.
25 And for the other side of the tabernacle, *which is* toward the north corner, he made twenty boards,
26 And their forty sockets of silver;
two sockets under one board, and two
sockets under another board.
27 And for the sides of the tabernacle [2]westward he made six boards.
28 And two boards made he for the
corners of the tabernacle in the two
sides.
29 And they were [3]coupled beneath,
and coupled together at the head
thereof, to one ring: thus he did to both
of them in both the corners.
30 And there were eight boards; and
their sockets *were* sixteen sockets of
silver, [4]under every board two sockets.
31 ¶ And he made [m]bars of shittim
wood; five for the boards of the one
side of the tabernacle,
32 And five bars for the boards of
the other side of the tabernacle, and
five bars for the boards of the tabernacle for the sides westward.
33 And he made the middle bar to
shoot through the boards from the one
end to the other.
34 And he overlaid the boards with
gold, and made their rings *of* gold *to be*
places for the bars, and overlaid the
bars with gold.
35 ¶ And he made [n]a vail *of* blue, and
purple, and scarlet, and fine twined
linen: *with* cherubims made he it of
cunning work.
36 And he made thereunto four pillars *of* shittim *wood,* and overlaid them
with gold: their hooks *were of* gold;
and he cast for them four sockets of
silver.
37 ¶ And he made an [o]hanging for
the tabernacle door *of* blue, and purple, and scarlet, and fine twined linen,
[5]of needlework;
38 And the five pillars of it with their
hooks: and he overlaid their chapiters
[p]and their fillets with gold: but their
five sockets *were of* brass.
37 And [a]Be-zăl'ĕ-el made [b]the ark
of shittim wood: two cubits and a
half *was* the length of it, and a cubit
and a half the breadth of it, and a cubit
and a half the height of it:
2 And he overlaid it with pure gold
within and without, and made a crown
of gold to it round about.
3 And he cast for it four rings of
gold, *to be set* by the four corners of it;
even two rings upon the one side of it,
and two rings upon the other side of it.
4 And he made [c]staves *of* shittim
wood, and overlaid them with gold.
5 And he [d]put the staves into the
rings by the sides of the ark, to bear
the ark.
6 ¶ And he made the [e]mercy seat *of*
pure gold: two cubits and a half *was*
the length thereof, and one cubit and a
half the breadth thereof.
7 And he made two cherubims *of*
gold, beaten out of one piece made he
them, on the two ends of the mercy
seat;
8 One cherub [1]on the end on this
side, and another cherub [2]on the *other*
end on that side: out of the mercy seat
made he the cherubims on the two
ends thereof.
9 And the [f]cherubims spread out
their wings on high, *and* covered with
their wings over the mercy seat, with
their faces one to another; *even* to the
mercy seatward were the faces of the
cherubims.
10 ¶ And he made [g]the table *of* shittim wood: two cubits *was* the length
thereof, and a cubit the breadth thereof,
and a cubit and a half the height thereof:
11 And he overlaid it with pure gold,
and made thereunto a crown of gold
round about.
12 Also he made thereunto a border
of an handbreadth round about; and
made a crown of gold for the border
thereof round about.
13 And he cast for it four rings of
gold, and put the rings upon the four
corners that *were* in the four feet
thereof.
14 Over against the border were the
rings, the places for the staves to bear
the table.
15 And he made the staves *of* shittim wood, and overlaid them with gold
to bear the table.
16 And he made the vessels which
were upon the table, his [h]dishes, and
his spoons, and his bowls, and his covers [3]to cover withal, *of* pure gold.
17 ¶ And he made the [i]candlestick
of pure gold: *of* beaten work made
he the candlestick; his shaft, and his
branch, his bowls, his knops, and his
flowers, were of the same:
18 And six branches going out of the
sides thereof; three branches of the
candlestick out of the one side thereof,

19 [j]ch. 26.14
20 [k]ch. 26.15
[l]ch. 25.5-10; Num. 25.1; Deut. 10.3; Josh. 2.1
24 [1]hands
27 [2]seaward, ch. 26.22
29 [3]twinned, ch. 26.24; Ps. 133.1; Acts 2.46; 1 Cor. 1.10
30 [4]two sockets, two sockets under one board
31 [m]ch. 26.26
35 [n]ch. 26.31; Matt. 27.51; Heb. 6.19; Heb. 10.20
37 [o]ch. 26.36
[5]the work of a needleworker, or, embroiderer
38 [p]1 Ki. 7.16; 2 Chr. 4.12; Jer. 52.22

CHAPTER 37
1 [a]ch. 35.30
[b]ch. 25.10
4 [c]Num. 4.6
5 [d]Num. 1.50; 2 Sam. 6.3
6 [e]ch. 25.17
8 [1]Or, out of, etc
[2]Or, out of, etc
9 [f]Gen. 3.24; ch. 25.22; 1 Ki. 6.23; 2 Chr. 3.10; Ps. 80.1; Ezek. 1.5-28; Ezek. 10.1; John 1.51; Phil. 2.10; 1 Tim. 3.16; Heb. 1.14; 1 Pet. 1.12
10 [g]ch. 25.23; Mal. 1.7-12
16 [h]ch. 25.29
[3]Or, to pour out withal
17 [i]ch. 25.31; Lev. 24.4; 1 Chr. 28.15; Zech. 4.2; Matt. 5.15-16; John 5.35; Phil. 2.15; 1 Pet. 2.9; Rev. 1.20

and three branches of the candlestick
out of the other side thereof:
19 Three bowls made after the fashion of almonds in one branch, a knop
and a flower; and three bowls made
like almonds in another branch, a knop
and a flower: so throughout the six
branches going out of the candlestick.
20 And in the candlestick *were* four
bowls made like [j]almonds, his knops,
and his flowers:
21 And a knop under two branches
of the same, and a knop under two
branches of the same, and a knop under two branches of the same, according to the six branches going out of it.
22 Their knops and their branches
were of the same: all of it *was* one
beaten work *of* pure gold.
23 And he made [k]his seven lamps,
and his snuffers, and his snuffdishes,
of pure gold.
24 *Of* a talent of pure gold made he
it, and all the vessels thereof.
25 ¶ And [l]he made the incense altar
of shittim wood: the length of it *was* a
cubit, and the breadth of it a cubit; *it*
was foursquare; and two cubits *was*
the height of it; the horns thereof were
of the same.
26 And he overlaid it with pure gold,
both the top of it, and the sides thereof
round about, and the horns of it: also
he made unto it a crown of gold round
about.
27 And he made two rings of gold
for it under the crown thereof, by the
two corners of it, upon the two sides
thereof, to be places for the staves to
bear it withal.
28 And he made the staves *of* shittim
wood, and overlaid them with gold.
29 ¶ And he made [4]the holy anointing oil, and the pure [m]incense of sweet
spices, according to the work of the
apothecary.

38 And he made the altar [a]of burnt
offering *of* shittim wood: five cubits *was* the length thereof, and five
cubits the breadth thereof; *it was* foursquare; and three cubits the height
thereof.
2 And he made the horns thereof on
the four corners of it; the horns thereof
were of the same: and he overlaid it
with brass.
3 And he made all the vessels of the
altar, the pots, and the shovels, and the
basons, *and* the fleshhooks, and the
firepans: all the vessels thereof made
he *of* [b]brass.
4 And he made for the altar a brasen
grate of network under the compass
thereof beneath unto the midst of it.
5 And he cast four rings for the four
ends of the grate of brass, *to be* places
for the staves.
6 And he made the staves *of* shittim
wood, and overlaid them with brass.
7 And he put the staves into the rings
on the sides of the altar, to bear it
withal; he made the altar hollow with
boards.
8 ¶ And he made [c]the laver *of* brass,
and the foot of it *of* brass, of the [1]look-

20 [j]Num. 17.8; Jer. 1.11
23 [k]Rev. 1.20; Rev. 4.5
25 [l]ch. 30.1; ch. 40.26; 1 Ki. 9.25; 2 Chr. 29.6-7; Isa. 60.6; Mal. 1.11; Heb. 7.25; 1 Pet. 2.5; Rev. 8.3
29 [4]unction of holiness, ch. 30.23-34; Ps. 133.2; Isa. 11.2; Isa. 61.1; 1 John 2.20
[m]Ps. 141.2; Song 4.14; Mal. 1.11; Heb. 5.7; Heb. 7.25; Rev. 5.8

CHAPTER 38
1 [a]ch. 27.1; 2 Chr. 29.23-24; Ps. 51.15-19; Isa. 61.8; Ezek. 44.11; Heb. 9.14; Heb. 13.10
3 [b]1 Ki. 7.45
8 [c]ch. 30.18; 2 Ki. 16.17; 2 Chr. 4.2; Ps. 26.6; Ezek. 36.25; Zech. 13.1; 2 Cor. 7.1; Heb. 10.22; 1 John 5.6
[1]Or, brasen glasses
[2]assembling by troops, as 1 Sam. 2.22
9 [d]ch. 27.9; Ps. 84.2-10; Ps. 92.13
18 [e]2 Chr. 3.14
20 [f]ch. 27.19; 2 Chr. 3.9; Isa. 22.23; Eph. 2.21-22
21 [g]Num. 1.50-53; 2 Chr. 24.6; Acts 7.44
[h]Num. 4.28-33
22 [i]ch. 31.2-6
24 [j]ch. 30.13; Lev. 5.15; Num. 18.16

ingglasses of *the women* [2]assembling,
which assembled *at* the door of the tabernacle of the congregation.
9 ¶ And he made [d]the court: on the
south side southward the hangings of
the court *were of* fine twined linen, an
hundred cubits:
10 Their pillars *were* twenty, and
their brasen sockets twenty; the hooks
of the pillars and their fillets *were of*
silver.
11 And for the north side *the hang-*
ings were an hundred cubits, their pillars *were* twenty, and their sockets of
brass twenty; the hooks of the pillars
and their fillets *of* silver.
12 And for the west side *were* hangings of fifty cubits, their pillars ten,
and their sockets ten; the hooks of the
pillars and their fillets *of* silver.
13 And for the east side eastward
fifty cubits.
14 The hangings of the one side *of*
the gate were fifteen cubits; their pillars three, and their sockets three.
15 And for the other side of the court
gate, on this hand and that hand, *were*
hangings of fifteen cubits; their pillars
three, and their sockets three.
16 All the hangings of the court
round about *were* of fine twined linen.
17 And the sockets for the pillars
were of brass; the hooks of the pillars
and their fillets *of* silver; and the overlaying of their chapiters *of* silver; and
all the pillars of the court *were* filleted
with silver.
18 And the hanging for the gate of
the court *was* needlework, *of* blue, [e]and
purple, and scarlet, and fine twined
linen: and twenty cubits *was* the length,
and the height in the breadth *was* five
cubits, answerable to the hangings of
the court.
19 And their pillars *were* four, and
their sockets *of* brass four; their hooks
of silver, and the overlaying of their
chapiters and their fillets *of* silver.
20 And all the [f]pins of the tabernacle, and of the court round about, *were*
of brass.
21 ¶ This is the sum of the tabernacle, *even* of [g]the tabernacle of testimony, as it was counted, according to
the commandment of Mō'ses, *for* the
service of the Lē'vītes, by [h]the hand of
Ĭth'a-mär, son to Aâr'on the priest.
22 And [i]Be-zăl'ĕ-el the son of Ū'ri,
the son of Hûr, of the tribe of Jū'dah,
made all that the LORD commanded
Mō'ses.
23 And with him *was* A-hō'lĭ-ab, son
of A-hĭs'a-mach, of the tribe of Dăn,
an engraver, and a cunning workman,
and an embroiderer in blue, and in purple, and in scarlet, and fine linen.
24 All the gold that was occupied for
the work in all the work of the holy
place, even the gold of the offering,
was twenty and nine talents, and seven
hundred and thirty shekels, after [j]the
shekel of the sanctuary.
25 And the silver of them that were
numbered of the congregation *was* an
hundred talents, and a thousand seven

hundred and threescore and fifteen
shekels, after the shekel of the sanctuary:
26 A [k]bekah for [3]every man, *that is,*
half a shekel, after the shekel of the
sanctuary, for every one that went to
be numbered, from twenty years old
and upward, for [l]six hundred thousand and three thousand and five hundred and fifty *men.*
27 And of the hundred talents of silver were cast [m]the sockets of the sanctuary, and the sockets of the vail; an
hundred sockets of the hundred talents, a talent for a socket.
28 And of the thousand seven hundred seventy and five *shekels* he made
hooks for the pillars, and overlaid their
chapiters, and filleted them.
29 And the brass of the offering *was*
seventy talents, and two thousand and
four hundred shekels.
30 And therewith he made the sockets to the door of the tabernacle of the
congregation, and the brasen altar, and
the brasen grate for it, and all the vessels of the altar,
31 And the sockets of the court round
about, and the sockets of the court gate,
and all the pins of the tabernacle, and
all the [n]pins of the court round about.
39 And of [a]the blue, and purple, and
scarlet, they made [b]cloths of service, to do service in the holy *place,* and
made the holy garments for Aâr'on;
[c]as the LORD commanded Mō'ses.
2 And [d]he made the ephod *of* gold,
blue, and purple, and scarlet, and fine
twined linen.
3 And they did beat the gold into
thin plates, and cut *it into* wires, to
work *it* in the blue, and in the purple,
and in the scarlet, and in the fine linen,
with cunning work.
4 They made shoulderpieces for it,
to couple *it* together: by the two edges
was it coupled together.
5 And the [e]curious girdle of his
ephod, that *was* upon it, *was* of the
same, according to the work thereof;
of gold, blue, and purple, and scarlet,
and fine twined linen; as the LORD commanded Mō'ses.
6 ¶ And [f]they wrought [g]onyx stones
inclosed in ouches of gold, graven, as
signets are graven, with the [h]names of
the children of Is'ra-el.
7 And he put them on the shoulders of the ephod, *that they should be*
stones for a [i]memorial to the children
of Is'ra-el; as the LORD commanded
Mō'ses.
8 ¶ And [j]he made the breastplate *of*
cunning work, like the work of the
ephod; *of* gold, blue, and purple, and
scarlet, and fine twined linen.
9 It was foursquare; they made the
breastplate double: a span *was* the
length thereof, and a span the breadth
thereof, *being* doubled.
10 And [k]they set in it four rows of
stones: *the first* row *was* a [1]sardius, a
[2l]topaz, and a [3m]carbuncle: this *was*
the first row.

26 [k]ch. 30.13-15
[3]a poll
[l]Num. 1.46
27 [m]ch. 26.19-21-25-32
31 [n]ch. 27.19; Eph. 2.21-22
CHAPTER 39
1 [a]ch. 35.23
[b]ch. 31.10; Ezek. 43.12
[c]ch. 28.4
2 [d]ch. 28.6; Lev. 8.7
5 [e]Isa. 11.5; Rev. 1.13
6 [f]ch. 28.9
[g]Job 28.16
[h]Isa. 49.16; Rev. 2.17
7 [i]ch. 28.12; Josh. 4.7
8 [j]ch. 28.15; Isa. 59.17
10 [k]ch. 28.17
[1]Or, ruby; Reuben's stone
[2]Simeon's stone
[l]Job 28.19; Rev. 21.19-20
[3]Levi's stone
[m]Isa. 54.12
11 [4]Judah's stone
[n]Ezek. 27.16; Rev. 4.3
[5]Issachar's stone
[o]Job 28.6; Isa. 54.11
[6]Zebulun's stone
[p]Jer. 17.1
12 [7]Dan's stone
[8]Naphtali's stone
[9]Gad's stone
13 [10]Asher's stone
[q]Dan. 10.6
[11]Joseph's stone
[r]Job 28.16
[12]Benjamin's stone
[s]Rev. 21.11
22 [t]ch. 28.31; 2 Sam. 6.14
25 [u]ch. 28.33; The pomegranates prevented the bells from striking against each other
27 [v]ch. 28.39-40; Gal. 3.27
28 [w]ch. 28.4-39; Ezek. 44.18
[x]ch. 28.42

11 And the second row, an [4n]emer-
ald, a [5o]sapphire, and a [6p]diamond.
12 And the third row, a [7]ligure, an
[8]agate, and an [9]amethyst.
13 And the fourth row, a [10q]beryl,
an [11r]onyx, and a [12s]jasper: *they were*
inclosed in ouches of gold in their in-
closings.
14 And the stones *were* according to
the names of the children of Is'ra-el,
twelve, according to their names, *like*
the engravings of a signet, every one
with his name, according to the twelve
tribes.
15 And they made upon the breastplate chains at the ends, *of* wreathen
work *of* pure gold.
16 And they made two ouches *of*
gold, and two gold rings; and put the
two rings in the two ends of the breastplate.
17 And they put the two wreathen
chains of gold in the two rings on the
ends of the breastplate.
18 And the two ends of the two
wreathen chains they fastened in the
two ouches, and put them on the shoulderpieces of the ephod, before it.
19 And they made two rings of gold,
and put *them* on the two ends of
the breastplate, upon the border of it,
which *was* on the side of the ephod
inward.
20 And they made two *other* golden
rings, and put them on the two sides
of the ephod underneath, toward the
forepart of it, over against the *other*
coupling thereof, above the curious girdle of the ephod.
21 And they did bind the breastplate
by his rings unto the rings of the ephod
with a lace of blue, that it might be
above the curious girdle of the ephod,
and that the breastplate might not be
loosed from the ephod; as the LORD
commanded Mō'ses.
22 ¶ And [t]he made the robe of the
ephod *of* woven work, all *of* blue.
23 And *there was* an hole in the
midst of the robe, as the hole of an habergeon, *with* a band round about the
hole, that it should not rend.
24 And they made upon the hems of
the robe pomegranates *of* blue, and
purple, and scarlet, *and* twined *linen.*
25 And they made [u]bells *of* pure
gold, and put the bells between the
pomegranates upon the hem of the
robe, round about between the pomegranates;
26 A bell and a pomegranate, a bell
and a pomegranate, round about the
hem of the robe to minister *in;* as the
LORD commanded Mō'ses.
27 ¶ And [v]they made coats *of* fine
linen *of* woven work for Aâr'on, and
for his sons,
28 And [w]a mitre *of* fine linen, and
goodly bonnets *of* fine linen, and [x]linen
breeches *of* fine twined linen,
29 And a girdle *of* fine twined linen,
and blue, and purple, and scarlet, *of*
needlework; as the LORD commanded
Mō'ses.

30 ¶ And they made the plate of the holy crown *of* pure gold, and wrote upon it a writing, *like to* the engravings of a signet, [y]HOLINESS TO THE LORD.

31 And they tied unto it a lace of blue, to fasten *it* on high upon the mitre; as the LORD commanded Mō'ses.

32 ¶ Thus was all the work of the tabernacle of the tent of the congregation finished: and the children of Is'ra-el did [z]according to all that the LORD commanded Mō'ses, so did they.

33 ¶ And they brought [a]the tabernacle unto Mō'ses, the tent, and all his furniture, his taches, his boards, his bars, and his pillars, and his sockets,

34 And the covering of rams' skins dyed red, and the covering of badgers' skins, and the vail of the covering,

35 The ark of the testimony, and the staves thereof, and the mercy seat,

36 The table, *and* all the vessels thereof, and the shewbread,

37 The [b]pure candlestick, *with* the lamps thereof, *even with* the lamps [c]to be set in order, and all the vessels thereof, and the oil for light,

38 And the golden altar, and the anointing oil, and [13]the sweet incense, and the hanging for the tabernacle door,

39 The [d]brasen altar, and his grate of brass, his staves, and all his vessels, the laver and his foot,

40 The hangings of the court, his pillars, [e]and his sockets, and the hanging for the court gate, his cords, and his pins, and all the vessels of the service of the tabernacle, for the tent of the congregation,

41 The cloths of service to do service in the holy *place*, and the holy garments for Aâr'on the priest, and his sons' garments, to minister in the priest's office.

42 According to all that the LORD commanded Mō'ses, so the children of Is'ra-el [f]made all the work.

43 And Mō'ses did look upon all the work, and, behold, they had done it as the LORD had commanded, even so had they done it: and Mō'ses [g]blessed them.

40 And the LORD spake unto Mō'ses, saying,

2 On the first day of the [a]first month shalt thou set up [b]the tabernacle of the tent of the congregation.

3 And [c]thou shalt put therein the ark of the testimony, and cover the ark with the vail.

4 And [d]thou shalt bring in the table, and set [e]in order [1]the things that are to be set in order upon it; and thou shalt bring in the candlestick, and light the lamps thereof.

5 And thou shalt set the [f]altar of gold for the incense before the ark of the testimony, and put the hanging of the door to the tabernacle.

6 And thou shalt set the altar of the burnt offering before the door of the tabernacle of the tent of the congregation.

7 And [g]thou shalt set the laver between the tent of the congregation and the altar, and shalt put water therein.

8 And thou shalt set up the court round about, and hang up the hanging at the court gate.

9 And thou shalt take [h]the anointing oil, and anoint the tabernacle, and all that *is* therein, and shalt hallow it, and all the vessels thereof: and it shall be holy.

10 And thou shalt anoint the altar of the burnt offering, and all his vessels, and sanctify the altar: and [i]it shall be an altar [2]most holy.

11 And thou shalt anoint the laver and his foot, and sanctify it.

12 And [j]thou shalt bring Aâr'on and his sons unto the door of the tabernacle of the congregation, and wash them with water.

13 And thou shalt put upon Aâr'on the holy garments, [k]and anoint him, and sanctify him; that he may minister unto me in the priest's office.

14 And thou shalt bring [l]his sons, and clothe them with coats:

15 And thou shalt anoint them, as thou didst anoint their father, that they may minister unto me in the priest's office: for their anointing shall surely be [m]an everlasting priesthood throughout their generations.

16 Thus did Mō'ses: according to all that the LORD commanded him, so did he.

17 ¶ And it came to pass in the first month in the second year, on the first *day* of the month, *that* the [n]tabernacle was reared up.

18 And Mō'ses reared up the tabernacle, and fastened his sockets, and set up the boards thereof, and put in the bars thereof, and reared up his pillars.

19 And he spread abroad the tent over the tabernacle, and put the covering of the tent above upon it; as the LORD commanded Mō'ses.

20 ¶ And he took and put [3][o]the testimony into the ark, and set the staves on the ark, and put the mercy seat above upon the ark:

21 And he brought the ark into the tabernacle, and [p]set up the vail of the covering, and covered the ark of the testimony; as the LORD commanded Mō'ses.

22 ¶ And [q]he put the table in the tent of the congregation, upon the side of the tabernacle northward, without the vail.

23 And he set the bread in order upon it before the LORD; as the LORD had commanded Mō'ses.

24 ¶ And [r]he put the candlestick in the tent of the congregation, over against the table, on the side of the tabernacle southward.

25 And [s]he lighted the lamps before the LORD; as the LORD commanded Mō'ses.

30 [y]Ps. 93.5; Zech. 14.20; Isa. 23.18
32 [z]ch. 25.40
33 [a]Heb. 9
37 [b]Rev. 1.13-20
[c]ch. 27.20; Matt. 5.14; Phil. 2.15
38 [13]the incense of sweet spices
39 [d]ch. 38.30; 1 Ki. 8.64
40 [e]Rev. 3.12
42 [f]ch. 35.10
43 [g]Gen. 14.19; Lev. 9.22; Num. 6.23; Josh. 22.6; 2 Sam. 6.18; 1 Ki. 8.14; 2 Chr. 30.27

CHAPTER 40
2 [a]ch. 12.2; ch. 13.4
[b]ch. 25.9; ch. 26.1-30; Num. 7.1; Acts 7.44-45; Heb. 8.2-5; Heb. 9.2-11; Rev. 21.3
3 [c]Num. 4.5
4 [d]ch. 26.35
[e]Lev. 24.5-6
[1]the order thereof
5 [f]Heb. 9.24; Heb. 10.19-22
7 [g]ch. 30.18
9 [h]ch. 30.23-26
10 [i]ch. 29.36
[2]holiness of holinesses
12 [j]Lev. 8.1-13
13 [k]ch. 28.41
14 [l]Ps. 133.2; Heb. 7.23
15 [m]Num. 25.13; Heb. 7.11; 1 Pet. 2.5-9; Rev. 1.6
17 [n]Num. 7.1
20 [3]tables of the law
[o]ch. 25.16; Ps. 78.5; Isa. 8.20
21 [p]ch. 35.12
22 [q]ch. 26.35
24 [r]ch. 26.35
25 [s]ch. 25.37

26 ¶ And [t]he put the golden altar in the tent of the congregation before the vail:

27 And [u]he burnt sweet incense thereon; as the LORD commanded Mō'ses.

28 ¶ And [v]he set up the hanging *at* the door of the tabernacle.

29 And he put the altar of burnt offering *by* the door of the tabernacle of the tent of the congregation, and [w]offered upon it the burnt offering and the meat offering; as the LORD commanded Mō'ses.

30 ¶ And [x]he set the laver between the tent of the congregation and the altar, and put water there, to wash *withal.*

31 And Mō'ses and Aâr'on and his sons washed their hands and their feet thereat:

32 When they went into the tent of the congregation, and when they came near unto the altar, they washed; [y]as the LORD commanded Mō'ses.

33 And [z]he reared up the court round about the tabernacle and the altar, and set up the hanging of the court gate. So Mō'ses finished the work.

34 ¶ Then [a]a cloud covered the tent of the congregation, and the glory of the LORD filled the tabernacle.

35 And Mō'ses [b]was not able to enter into the tent of the congregation, because the cloud abode thereon, and the glory of the LORD filled the tabernacle.

36 And [c]when the cloud was taken up from over the tabernacle, the children of Ĭs'ra-el [4]went onward in all their journeys:

37 But [d]if the cloud were not taken up, then they journeyed not till the day that it was taken up.

38 For [e]the cloud of the LORD *was* upon the tabernacle by day, and fire was on it by night, in the sight of all the house of Ĭs'ra-el, throughout all their journeys.

26 [t]ch. 30.6
27 [u]ch. 30.7
28 [v]ch. 26.36
29 [w]ch. 29.38
30 [x]ch. 30.18
32 [y]ch. 30.19
33 [z]ch. 27.9-16
34 [a]Lev. 16.2; Num. 9.15; 1 Ki. 8.10; 2 Chr. 5.13; 2 Chr. 7.2; Isa. 6.4; Ezek. 43.4; Hag. 2.7-9; Rev. 15.8
35 [b]1 Ki. 8.11; 2 Chr. 5.14; Ps. 78.14
36 [c]Num. 10.11; Neh. 9.19
[4]journeyed
37 [d]Num. 9.19-22
38 [e]ch. 13.21; Num. 9.15

THE THIRD BOOK OF MOSES COMMONLY CALLED

LEVITICUS

Life's Questions

How can a sinful person like I am be acceptable to God?
How do I respond to God out of the daily activities of life?
What is God's essential quality?

God's Answers

Leviticus is the Bible's worship manual. It ushers a sinful people into God's accepting presence and shows them what He expects of those who worship Him.

Leviticus has six parts: sacrifices (1:1—7:38), priests (8:1—10:20), purification (11:1—16:34), holiness (17:1—26:46), and vows (27:1-34). Israel thus knows the ceremonies of worship, the requirements of worship leaders and worshipers, ways to be qualified for God's presence, and the seriousness of acting out all promises.

Leviticus unfolds the seriousness of the contrast between sinful people and holy God.

God expects pleasing sacrifices for various purposes (1:1—6:7).

God expects priests to offer sacrifices in the ways commanded (6:8—7:38).

God expects priests to consecrate themselves to mediate between Him and His people (8:1—10:20).

God expects the community to obey His ways of being pure before Him in situations that cause impurity (11:1—15:33).

God expects yearly atonement for the sins of all (16:1-34).

God expects people, priests, and land to be holy before Him (17:1—25:55).

God expects people to remember His covenant curses and blessings (26:1-39).

God expects people to remember His faithfulness (26:40-46).

God expects people to keep the promises they make in His presence (27:1-34).

Before Israel marched through the wilderness to the promised land, they had to learn how to live in the presence of the God who led them. and whose living quarters they had built. God showed them what He expected in worship and in daily life that threatened to make them impure for worship. Leviticus revealed that Israel had to be like God: holy, pure, and faithful. When they were not, they had to follow God's instructions for worship and atonement to become pure and holy again. At the center of such purity and holiness stood the relationship of love.

1 And the LORD [a]called unto Mō'ses, and spake [b]unto him out of the tabernacle of the congregation, saying,

2 Speak unto the children of Ĭs'ra-el, and say unto them, [c]If any man of you bring an offering unto the LORD, ye shall bring your offering of the cattle, *even* of the herd, and of the flock.

3 If his offering *be* a burnt sacrifice of the herd, let him offer a male [d]without blemish: he shall offer it of his own voluntary will at the door of the tabernacle of the congregation before the LORD.

4 And [e]he shall put his hand upon the head of the burnt offering; and it

CHAPTER 1
1 [a]Ex. 19.3
[b]Num. 12.4-5
2 [c]ch. 22.18
3 [d]Ex. 12.5;
4 [e]Ex. 29.10;

shall be [f]accepted for him to [g]make
atonement for him.
5 And he shall kill the [h]bullock before the LORD: [i]and the priests, Aâr'-
on's sons, shall bring the blood, and
[j]sprinkle the blood round about upon
the altar that *is by* the door of the tabernacle of the congregation.
6 And he shall flay the burnt offering, and cut it into his pieces.
7 And the sons of Aâr'on the priest
shall put fire upon the altar, and [k]lay
the wood in order upon the fire:
8 And the priests, Aâr'on's sons,
shall lay the parts, the head, and the
fat, in order upon the wood that *is* on
the fire which *is* upon the altar:
9 But his inwards and his legs shall
he wash in water: and the priest shall
burn all on the altar, *to be* a burnt sacrifice, an offering made by fire, of a
[l]sweet savour unto the LORD.
10 ¶ And if his offering *be* of the
flocks, *namely,* of the sheep, or of the
goats, for a burnt sacrifice; he shall
bring it a male without blemish.
11 And he shall kill it on the side of
the altar northward before the LORD:
and the priests, Aâr'on's sons, shall
sprinkle his blood round about upon
the altar.
12 And he shall cut it into his pieces,
with his head and his fat: and the priest
shall lay them in order on the wood that
is on the fire which *is* upon the altar:
13 But he shall wash the inwards
and the legs with water: and the priest
shall bring *it* all, and burn *it* upon the
altar: it *is* a burnt sacrifice, an offering
made by fire, of a sweet savour unto
the LORD.
14 ¶ And if the burnt sacrifice for his
offering to the LORD *be* of fowls, then
he shall bring his offering of [m]turtle-
doves, or of young pigeons.
15 And the priest shall bring it unto
the altar, and [1]wring off his head, and
burn *it* on the altar; and the blood
thereof shall be wrung out at the side
of the altar:
16 And he shall pluck away his crop
with [2]his feathers, and cast it beside
the altar on the east part, by the place
of the ashes:
17 And he shall cleave it with the
wings thereof, *but* [n]shall not divide *it*
asunder: and the priest shall burn it
upon the altar, upon the wood that *is*
upon the fire: it *is* a burnt sacrifice, an
offering made by fire, of a sweet savour unto the LORD.
2 And when any will offer [a]a meat
offering unto the LORD, his offering shall be *of* fine flour; and he shall
pour oil upon it, and put frankincense
thereon:
2 And he shall bring it to Aâr'on's
sons the priests: and he shall take thereout his handful of the flour thereof, and
of the oil thereof, with all the frankincense thereof; and the priest shall burn
[b]the memorial of it upon the altar, *to be*
an offering made by fire, of a sweet
savour unto the LORD:
3 And [c]the remnant of the meat offering *shall be* Aâr'on's and his sons':
[d]*it is* a thing most holy of the offerings
of the LORD made by fire.
4 ¶ And if thou bring an oblation of a
meat offering baken in the oven, *it
shall be* unleavened cakes of fine flour
mingled with oil, or unleavened wafers
[e]anointed with oil.
5 ¶ And if thy oblation *be* a meat offering *baken* [1]in a pan, it shall be *of*
fine flour unleavened, mingled with
oil.
6 Thou shalt part it in pieces, and
pour oil thereon: it *is* a meat offering.
7 ¶ And if thy oblation *be* a meat offering *baken* in the fryingpan, it shall
be made *of* fine flour with oil.
8 And thou shalt bring the meat offering that is made of these things unto
the LORD: and when it is presented
unto the priest, he shall bring it unto
the altar.
9 And the priest shall take from the
meat offering a memorial thereof, and
shall burn *it* upon the altar: *it is* an
[f]offering made by fire, of a sweet savour unto the LORD.
10 And that which is left of the meat
offering *shall be* Aâr'on's and his sons':
it is a thing most holy of the offerings of
the LORD [g]made by fire.
11 No meat offering, which ye shall
bring unto the LORD, shall be made
with [h]leaven: for ye shall burn no
leaven, nor any honey, in any offering
of the LORD made by fire.
12 ¶ As [i]for the oblation of the firstfruits, ye shall offer them unto the
LORD: but they shall not [2]be burnt on
the altar for a sweet savour.
13 And every oblation of thy meat
offering shalt [j]thou season with salt;
neither shalt thou suffer the [k]salt of
the covenant of thy God to be lacking
from thy meat offering: with [l]all thine
offerings thou shalt offer salt.
14 And if thou offer a meat offering
of thy [m]firstfruits unto the LORD, thou
[n]shalt offer for the meat offering of thy
firstfruits green ears of corn dried by
the fire, *even* corn beaten out of [o]full
ears.
15 And thou shalt put oil upon it,
and lay frankincense thereon: it *is* a
meat offering.
16 And the priest shall burn the memorial of it, *part* of the beaten corn
thereof, and *part* of the oil thereof, with
all the frankincense thereof: *it is* an offering made by fire unto the LORD.
3 And if his oblation *be* a [a]sacrifice
of peace offering, if he offer *it* of the
herd; whether *it be* a male or female,
he shall offer it without blemish before
the LORD.
2 And [b]he shall lay his hand upon
the head of his offering, and kill it
at the door of the tabernacle of the
congregation: and Aâr'on's sons the
priests shall sprinkle the blood upon
the altar round about.
3 And he shall offer of the sacrifice
of the peace offering an offering made
by fire unto the LORD; the [1]fat that

[f]Isa. 56.7; Rom. 12.1; Phil. 4.18
[g]Num. 15.25; Rom. 5.11
5 [h]Mic. 6.6
[i]Heb. 10.11
[j]Heb. 12.24; 1 Pet. 1.2
7 [k]Gen. 22.9
9 [l]Gen. 8.21; Ezek. 20.28; 2 Cor. 2.15; Eph. 5.2; Phil. 4.18
14 [m]ch. 5.7; Luke 2.24
15 [1]Or, pinch off the head with the nail
16 [2]Or, the filth thereof
17 [n]Gen. 15.10

CHAPTER 2
1 [a]ch. 6.14; ch. 9.17; Num. 15.4
2 [b]ch. 5.12; ch. 6.15; ch. 24.7; Isa. 66.3; Acts 10.4
3 [c]ch. 7.9; ch. 10.12-13
[d]Ex. 29.37; Num. 18.9
4 [e]Ex. 29.2
5 [1]Or, on a flat plate, or, slice
9 [f]Ex. 29.18; Rom. 12.1
10 [g]Ex. 29.18-37
11 [h]ch. 6.17; Matt. 16.12; Mark 8.15; Luke 12.1; 1 Cor. 5.8; Gal. 5.9
12 [i]Ex. 22.29; ch. 23.10-11; Deut. 26.10
[2]ascend
13 [j]Mark 9.49; Col. 4.6
[k]Num. 18.19
[l]Ezek. 43.24
14 [m]Ex. 23.19; Prov. 3.9
[n]ch. 23.10-14
[o]2 Ki. 4.42

CHAPTER 3
1 [a]ch. 22.21
2 [b]Ex. 29.10; Num. 8.12; Isa. 53.4; 2 Cor. 5.21; Heb. 9.28; 1 Pet. 2.24; 1 Pet. 3.18
3 [1]Or, suet

covereth the inwards, and all the fat that *is* upon the inwards,

4 And the two kidneys, and the fat that *is* on them, which *is* by the flanks, and the [2]caul above the liver, with the kidneys, it shall he take away.

5 And Aâr'on's sons [c]shall burn it on the altar upon the burnt sacrifice, which *is* upon the wood that *is* on the fire: *it is* an offering made by fire, of a sweet savour unto the LORD.

6 ¶ And if his offering for a sacrifice of peace offering unto the LORD *be* of the flock; male or female, he shall offer it [d]without blemish.

7 If he offer a lamb for his offering, then shall he offer it before the LORD.

8 And he shall lay his hand upon the head of his offering, and kill it before the tabernacle of the congregation: and Aâr'on's sons shall sprinkle the blood thereof round about upon the altar.

9 And he shall offer of the sacrifice of the peace offering an offering made by fire unto the LORD; the fat thereof, *and* the whole rump, it shall he take off hard by the backbone; and the fat that covereth the inwards, and all the fat that *is* upon the inwards,

10 And the two kidneys, and the fat that *is* upon them, which *is* by the flanks, and the caul above the liver, with the kidneys, it shall he take away.

11 And the priest shall burn it upon the altar: *it is* [e]the food of the offering made by fire unto the LORD.

12 ¶ And if his offering *be* a goat, then he shall offer it before the LORD.

13 And he shall lay his hand upon the head of it, and kill it before the tabernacle of the congregation: and the sons of Aâr'on shall sprinkle the blood thereof upon the altar round about.

14 And he shall offer thereof his offering, *even* an offering made by fire unto the LORD; the fat that covereth the inwards, and all the fat that *is* upon the inwards,

15 And the two kidneys, and the fat that *is* upon them, which *is* by the flanks, and the caul above the liver, with the kidneys, it shall he take away.

16 And the priest shall burn them upon the altar: *it is* the food of the offering made by fire for a sweet savour: [f]all the fat *is* the LORD'S.

17 *It shall be* a [g]perpetual statute for your generations throughout all your dwellings, that ye eat neither [3]fat nor [h]blood.

4 And the LORD spake unto Mō'ses, saying,

2 Speak unto the children of Ĭs'ra-el, saying, [a]If a soul shall sin through ignorance against any of the commandments of the LORD *concerning things* which ought not to be done, and shall do against any of them:

3 If [b]the priest that is anointed do sin according to the sin of the people; then let him bring for his sin, which he hath sinned, a young [c]bullock without blemish unto the LORD for a sin offering.

4 [2]Or, midriff over the liver, and over the kidneys

5 [c]Ex. 29.13; 1 Sam. 2.15-16

6 [d]2 Cor. 5.21; Tit. 2.11-12; Heb. 7.26-27; 1 Pet. 1.19

11 [e]ch. 21.6-8-17-21-22; ch. 22.25; Ezek. 44.7; Mal. 1.7-12

16 [f]ch. 7.23; 1 Sam. 2.15; 2 Chr. 7.7

17 [g]ch. 6.18; ch. 7.36; ch. 17.7; ch. 23.14
[3]Compare Deut. 32.14, with Neh. 8.10
[h]Gen. 9.4; ch. 17.10; Deut. 12.16; 1 Sam. 14.33; Ezek. 44.7-15; Rom. 14.20-23

CHAPTER 4

2 [a]ch. 5.15-17; Num. 15.22; 1 Sam. 14.27; Ps. 19.12

3 [b]ch. 8.12; ch. 21.10-12; Heb. 5.3
[c]ch. 9.2

4 [d]ch. 1.3-4

5 [e]ch. 16.14; Num. 19.4; Heb. 9.13

6 [f]Isa. 42.21; Rev. 5.9

7 [g]ch. 8.15; Heb. 9.21-25
[h]ch. 5.9

11 [i]Ex. 29.14; Num. 19.5

12 [1]to without the camp
[j]ch. 6.11
[k]Heb. 13.11
[2]at the pouring out of the ashes

13 [l]Num. 15.24; Josh. 7.11
[m]ch. 5.2-3-4-17

15 [n]Ex. 29.10-15-19; 1 Pet. 2.24

16 [o]Heb. 9.12-14

4 And he shall bring the bullock unto [d]the door of the tabernacle of the congregation before the LORD; and shall lay his hand upon the bullock's head, and kill the bullock before the LORD.

5 And the priest that is anointed shall [e]take of the bullock's blood, and bring it to the tabernacle of the congregation:

6 And the priest shall dip his finger in the blood, and sprinkle of the blood seven times before the [f]LORD, before the vail of the sanctuary.

7 And the priest shall [g]put *some* of the blood upon the horns of the altar of sweet incense before the LORD, which *is* in the tabernacle of the congregation; and shall pour [h]all the blood of the bullock at the bottom of the altar of the burnt offering, which *is at* the door of the tabernacle of the congregation.

8 And he shall take off from it all the fat of the bullock for the sin offering; the fat that covereth the inwards, and all the fat that *is* upon the inwards,

9 And the two kidneys, and the fat that *is* upon them, which *is* by the flanks, and the caul above the liver, with the kidneys, it shall he take away,

10 As it was taken off from the bullock of the sacrifice of peace offerings: and the priest shall burn them upon the altar of the burnt offering.

11 And [i]the skin of the bullock, and all his flesh, with his head, and with his legs, and his inwards, and his dung,

12 Even the whole bullock shall he carry forth [1]without the camp unto a clean place, [j]where the ashes are poured out, and [k]burn him on the wood with fire: [2]where the ashes are poured out shall he be burnt.

13 ¶ And [l]if the whole congregation of Ĭs'ra-el sin through ignorance, [m]and the thing be hid from the eyes of the assembly, and they have done *somewhat against* any of the commandments of the LORD *concerning things* which should not be done, and are guilty;

14 When the sin, which they have sinned against it, is known, then the congregation shall offer a young bullock for the sin, and bring him before the tabernacle of the congregation.

15 And the elders of the congregation shall [n]lay their hands upon the head of the bullock before the LORD: and the bullock shall be killed before the LORD.

16 And [o]the priest that is anointed shall bring of the bullock's blood to the tabernacle of the congregation:

17 And the priest shall dip his finger *in some* of the blood, and sprinkle *it* seven times before the LORD, *even* before the vail.

18 And he shall put *some* of the blood upon the horns of the altar which *is* before the LORD, that *is* in the tabernacle of the congregation, and shall pour out all the blood at the bottom of the altar of the burnt offering, which *is at* the door of the tabernacle of the congregation.

19 And he shall take all his fat from
him, and burn *it* upon the altar.
20 And he shall do with the bullock
as he did with the bullock for a sin offering, so shall he do with this: [p]and
the priest shall make an atonement for
them, and it shall be forgiven them.
21 And he shall carry forth the bullock without the camp, and burn him as
he burned the first bullock: it *is* a sin
offering for the congregation.
22 ¶ When a [q]ruler hath sinned,
and done *somewhat* through ignorance *against* any of the commandments of the LORD his God *concerning*
things which should not be done, and
is guilty;
23 Or if his sin, wherein he hath
sinned, come to his knowledge; he shall
bring his offering, a kid of the goats, a
male without blemish:
24 And he shall lay his hand upon
the head of the goat, and kill it in the
place where they kill the burnt offering before the LORD: it *is* a sin offering.
25 And the priest shall take of the
blood of the sin offering with his finger, and put *it* upon the horns of the
altar of burnt offering, and shall pour
out his blood at the bottom of the altar
of burnt offering.
26 And he shall burn all his fat upon
the altar, as [r]the fat of the sacrifice of
peace offerings: [s]and the priest shall
make an atonement for him as concerning his sin, and it shall be forgiven him.
27 ¶ And [t]if [3]any one of the [4]com-
mon people sin through ignorance,
while he doeth *somewhat against* any
of the commandments of the LORD *con-*
cerning things which ought not to be
done, and be guilty;
28 Or [u]if his sin, which he hath
sinned, come to his knowledge: then
he shall bring his offering, a kid of the
goats, a female without blemish, for
his sin which he hath sinned.
29 And [v]he shall lay his hand upon
the head of the sin offering, and slay
the sin offering in the place of the
burnt offering.
30 And the priest shall take of the
blood thereof with his finger, and put *it*
upon the horns of the altar of burnt offering, and shall pour out all the blood
thereof at the bottom of the altar.
31 And [w]he shall take away all the
fat thereof, [x]as the fat is taken away
from off the sacrifice of peace offerings; and the priest shall burn *it* upon
the altar for a [y]sweet savour unto the
LORD; [z]and the priest shall make an
atonement for him, and it shall be forgiven him.
32 And if he bring a [a]lamb for a sin
offering, [b]he shall bring it a female
without blemish.
33 And he shall lay his hand upon
the head of the sin offering, and slay it
for a sin offering in the place where
they kill the burnt offering.
34 And the priest shall take of the
blood of the sin offering with his finger, and put *it* upon the horns of the
altar of burnt offering, and shall pour

20 [p]Num. 15.25; Dan. 9.24; Rom. 5.11; Heb. 2.17; Heb. 10.10-12; 1 John 1.7; 1 John 2.2
22 [q]Ex. 18.21; Num. 16.2; 2 Sam. 21.1-3; 2 Sam. 24.10-17; Ezra 9.2; Acts 3.17
26 [r]ch. 3.5
[s]Num. 15.28
27 [t]Num. 15.27; Eccl. 7.20
[3]any soul
[4]people of the land
28 [u]verse 23
29 [v]verses 4-24
31 [w]ch. 3.14
[x]ch. 3.3
[y]Ex. 29.18; ch. 1.9; Ezra 6.10
[z]verse 26
32 [a]Isa. 53.7; John 1.29; Acts 8.32; 1 Pet. 1.19; Rev. 5.6-14; Rev. 13.8
[b]verse 28
35 [c]ch. 3.5
[d]Dan. 9.24; 1 John 2.2
CHAPTER 5
1 [a]1 Ki. 8.31; Matt. 26.63
[b]Gen. 17.14; Num. 9.13
2 [c]ch. 11.24-28-31-39; Num. 19.11-13-16
3 [d]ch. 12.1-2; ch. 15.1-2
4 [e]That is, rashly, as 1 Sam. 14.24
[f]1 Sam. 25.22; Acts 23.12
[g]Mark 6.23
5 [h]ch. 26.40; Ezra 10.11
7 [i]ch. 14.21
[1]his hand cannot reach to the sufficiency of a lamb
8 [2]Or, pinch off the head with the nail
10 [j]ch. 1.14
[3]Or, ordinance
11 [k]Num. 5.15

out all the blood thereof at the bottom
of the altar:
35 And he shall take away all the
fat thereof, as the fat of the lamb is
taken away from the sacrifice of the
peace offerings; and the priest shall
burn them upon the altar, according to
[c]the offerings made by fire unto the
LORD: and the priest shall make an
[d]atonement for his sin that he hath
committed, and it shall be forgiven
him.

5

And if a soul sin, [a]and hear the
voice of swearing, and *is* a witness,
whether he hath seen or known *of it;* if
he do not utter *it,* then he shall [b]bear
his iniquity.
2 Or [c]if a soul touch any unclean
thing, whether *it be* a carcase of an unclean beast, or a carcase of unclean cattle, or the carcase of unclean creeping
things, and *if* it be hidden from him; he
also shall be unclean, and guilty.
3 Or if he touch the [d]uncleanness of
man, whatsoever uncleanness *it be*
that a man shall be defiled withal, and
it be hid from him; when he knoweth
of it, then he shall be guilty.
4 Or if a soul swear, [e]pronouncing
with *his* lips [f]to do evil, or [g]to do good,
whatsoever *it be* that a man shall pronounce with an oath, and it be hid from
him; when he knoweth *of it,* then he
shall be guilty in one of these.
5 And it shall be, when he shall be
guilty in one of these *things,* that he
shall [h]confess that he hath sinned in
that *thing:*
6 And he shall bring his trespass offering unto the LORD for his sin which
he hath sinned, a female from the flock,
a lamb or a kid of the goats, for a sin
offering; and the priest shall make an
atonement for him concerning his sin.
7 And [i]if [1]he be not able to bring
a lamb, then he shall bring for his
trespass, which he hath committed,
two turtledoves, or two young pigeons,
unto the LORD; one for a sin offering,
and the other for a burnt offering.
8 And he shall bring them unto the
priest, who shall offer *that* which *is* for
the sin offering first, and [2]wring off his
head from his neck, but shall not divide *it* asunder:
9 And he shall sprinkle of the blood
of the sin offering upon the side of the
altar; and the rest of the blood shall be
wrung out at the bottom of the altar: it
is a sin offering.
10 And he shall offer the second *for* a
burnt offering, according to the [j3]man-
ner: and the priest shall make an atonement for him for his sin which he hath
sinned, and it shall be forgiven him.
11 ¶ But if he be not able to bring
two turtledoves, or two young pigeons,
then he that sinned shall bring for his
offering the tenth part of an ephah of
fine flour for a sin offering; [k]he shall
put no oil upon it, neither shall he put
any frankincense thereon: for it *is* a sin
offering.
12 Then shall he bring it to the priest,
and the priest shall take his handful of

it, *even* a memorial thereof, and burn *it* on the altar, according [l]to the offerings made by fire unto the LORD: it *is* a sin offering.

13 And the priest shall make an atonement for him as touching his sin that he hath sinned in one of these, and it shall be forgiven him: and *the remnant* shall be the priest's, as a meat offering.

14 ¶ And the LORD spake unto Mō'ses, saying,

15 If [m]a soul commit a trespass, and sin through ignorance, in the holy things of the LORD; then [n]he shall bring for his trespass unto the LORD a ram without blemish out of the flocks, with thy estimation by shekels of silver, after [o]the shekel of the sanctuary, for a trespass offering:

16 And he shall make amends for the harm that he hath done in the holy thing, and [p]shall add the fifth part thereto, and give it unto the priest: [q]and the priest shall make an atonement for him with the ram of the trespass offering, and it shall be forgiven him.

17 ¶ And if a soul sin, and commit any of these things which are forbidden to be done by the commandments of the LORD; [r]though he wist *it* not, yet is he guilty, and shall bear his iniquity.

18 And he shall bring a ram without blemish out of the flock, with thy estimation, for a trespass offering, unto the priest: and the priest shall make an atonement for him concerning his ignorance wherein he erred and wist *it* not, and it shall be forgiven him.

19 It *is* a trespass [s]offering: [t]he hath certainly trespassed against the LORD.

6 And the LORD spake unto Mō'ses, saying,

2 If a soul sin, and [a]commit a trespass against the LORD, and [b]lie unto his neighbour in that [c]which was delivered him to keep, or in [1]fellowship, or in a thing taken away by violence, or hath [d]deceived his neighbour;

3 Or [e]have found that which was lost, and lieth concerning it, and [f]sweareth falsely; in any of all these that a man doeth, sinning therein:

4 Then it shall be, because he hath sinned, and is guilty, that he shall restore that which he took violently away, or the thing which he hath deceitfully gotten, or that which was delivered him to keep, or the lost thing which he found,

5 Or all that about which he hath sworn falsely; he shall even [g]restore it in the principal, and shall add the fifth part more thereto, *and* give it unto him to whom it appertaineth, [2]in the day of his trespass offering.

6 And he shall bring his trespass offering unto the LORD, a ram without [h]blemish out of the flock, with thy estimation, for a trespass offering, unto the priest:

7 And the priest shall make an atonement for him before the LORD: and it shall be forgiven him for any thing of all that he hath done in trespassing therein.

8 ¶ And the LORD spake unto Mō'ses, saying,

9 Command Aâr'on and his sons, saying, This *is* the law of the burnt offering: It *is* the burnt offering, [3]because of the burning upon the altar all night unto the morning, and the fire of the altar shall be burning in it.

10 And [i]the priest shall put on his linen garment, and his linen breeches shall he put upon his flesh, and take up the ashes which the fire hath consumed with the burnt offering on the altar, and he shall put them beside the altar.

11 And he shall put off his garments, and put on other garments, and carry forth the ashes without the camp unto a clean place.

12 And the fire upon the altar shall be burning in it; it shall not be put out: and the priest shall burn wood on it every morning, and lay the burnt offering in order upon it; and he shall burn thereon the fat of the peace offerings.

13 The [j]fire shall ever be burning upon the altar; it shall never go out.

14 ¶ And [k]this *is* the law of the meat offering: the sons of Aâr'on shall offer it before the LORD, before the altar.

15 And he shall take of it his handful, of the flour of the meat offering, and of the oil thereof, and all the frankincense which *is* upon the meat offering, and shall burn *it* upon the altar *for* a sweet savour, *even* the memorial of it, unto the LORD.

16 And the remainder thereof shall Aâr'on and his sons eat: [l]with unleavened bread shall it be eaten in the holy place; in the court of the tabernacle of the congregation they shall eat it.

17 It [m]shall not be baken with leaven. [n]I have given it *unto them for* their portion of my offerings made by fire; [o]it *is* most holy, as *is* the sin offering, and as the trespass offering.

18 [p]All the males among the children of Aâr'on shall eat of it. [q]*It shall be* a statute for ever in your generations concerning the offerings of the LORD made by fire: [r]every one that toucheth them shall be holy.

19 ¶ And the LORD spake unto Mō'ses, saying,

20 This [s]*is* the offering of Aâr'on and of his sons, which they shall offer unto the LORD in the day when he is anointed; the tenth part of an [t]ephah of fine flour for a meat offering perpetual, half of it in the morning, and half thereof at night.

21 In a pan it shall be made with oil; *and when it is* baken, thou shalt bring it in: *and* the baken pieces of the meat offering shalt thou offer *for* a sweet savour unto the LORD.

22 And the priest of his sons that is anointed in his stead shall offer it: *it is* a statute for ever unto the LORD; [u]it shall be wholly burnt.

12 [l]ch. 4.35
15 [m]ch. 22.14
[n]Ezra 10.19
[o]Ex. 30.13; ch. 27.25
16 [p]ch. 6.5; ch. 22.14; ch. 27.13-15-27-31; Num. 5.7
[q]ch. 4.26; Heb. 9.13-14
17 [r]Ps. 19.12; Luke 12.48; Heb. 5.2
19 [s]Isa. 53.10
[t]Ezra 10.2

CHAPTER 6

2 [a]Num. 5.6
[b]ch. 19.11; Acts 5.4; Col. 3.9
[c]Ex. 22.7-10
[1]putting of the hand, or, in dealing
[d]Prov. 24.28; Prov. 26.19
3 [e]Deut. 22.1
[f]Ex. 22.11; ch. 19.12; Jer. 7.9; Zech. 5.4
5 [g]ch. 5.16; Num. 5.7; 2 Sam. 12.6; Luke 19.8
[2]in the day of his trespass, or, in the day of his being found guilty
6 [h]Ex. 12.5; ch. 3.1; ch. 22.20-21; Deut. 15.21; Eph. 5.27; 1 Tim. 2.5-6; Heb. 9.14
9 [3]Or, for the burning
10 [i]Ex. 28.39-43; ch. 16.4; Ezek. 44.17
13 [j]Ps. 50.3; Isa. 33.14; Dan. 7.10
14 [k]Num. 15.4
16 [l]Num. 18.10
17 [m]ch. 2.11
[n]Num. 18.9-10
[o]Ex. 29.37
18 [p]Num. 18.10
[q]ch. 3.17
[r]Ex. 29.37; ch. 22.3-7
20 [s]Ex. 29.2
[t]Ex. 16.36
22 [u]Ex. 29.25; Isa. 53.10; Dan. 9.26; 1 Tim. 2.6

23 For every meat offering for the
priest shall be wholly burnt: it shall not
be eaten.
24 ¶ And the LORD spake unto Mō'-
ses, saying,
25 Speak unto Aâr'on and to his
sons, saying, This *is* the law of the sin
offering: [v]In the place where the burnt
offering is killed shall the sin offering
be killed before the LORD: [w]it *is* most
holy.
26 The [x]priest that offereth it for sin
shall eat it: in the holy place shall it be
eaten, in the court of the tabernacle of
the congregation.
27 [y]Whatsoever shall touch the flesh
thereof shall be holy: and when there is
sprinkled of the blood thereof upon any
garment, thou shalt wash that whereon
it was sprinkled in the holy place.
28 But the earthen vessel wherein it
is sodden [z]shall be broken: and if it be
sodden in a brasen pot, it shall be both
scoured, and rinsed in water.
29 [a]All the males among the priests
shall eat thereof: it *is* most holy.
30 And [b]no sin offering, whereof
any of the blood is brought into the
tabernacle of the congregation to reconcile *withal* in the holy *place*, shall be
eaten: it shall be burnt in the fire.

7 Likewise [a]this *is* the law of the trespass offering: [b]it *is* most holy.
2 In [c]the place where they kill the
burnt offering shall they kill the trespass offering: and the blood thereof
shall he sprinkle round about upon the
altar.
3 And he shall offer of it [d]all the
fat thereof; the rump, and the fat that
covereth the inwards,
4 And the two kidneys, and the fat
that *is* on them, which *is* by the flanks,
and the caul *that is* above the liver,
with the kidneys, it shall he take away:
5 And the priest shall burn them
upon the altar *for* an [e]offering made
by fire unto the LORD: it *is* a trespass
offering.
6 [f]Every male among the priests
shall eat thereof: it shall be eaten in the
holy place: [g]it *is* most holy.
7 As the sin offering *is*, so *is* [h]the
trespass offering: *there is* one law for
them: the priest that maketh atonement therewith shall have *it*.
8 And the priest that offereth any
man's burnt offering, *even* the priest
shall have to himself the skin of the
burnt offering which he hath offered.
9 And [i]all the meat offering that
is baken in the oven, and all that is
dressed in the fryingpan, and [1]in the
pan, shall be the [j]priest's that offereth
it.
10 And every meat offering, mingled with oil, and dry, shall all the sons
of Aâr'on have, one *as much* as another.
11 And [k]this *is* the law of the sacrifice of peace offerings, which he shall
offer unto the LORD.
12 If he offer it for a thanksgiving,
then he shall offer with the sacrifice of
thanksgiving unleavened cakes mingled with oil, and unleavened wafers
[l]anointed with oil, and cakes mingled
with oil, of fine flour, fried.
13 Besides the cakes, he shall offer *for* his offering [m]leavened bread
with the sacrifice of thanksgiving of
his peace offerings.
14 And of it he shall offer one out of
the whole oblation *for* an heave offering unto the LORD, [n]*and* it shall be the
priest's that sprinkleth the blood of the
peace offerings.
15 And [o]the flesh of the sacrifice of
his peace offerings for thanksgiving
shall be eaten the same day that it is
offered; he shall not leave any of it until the morning.
16 But [p]if the sacrifice of his offering *be* a vow, or a voluntary offering, it
shall be eaten the same day that he
offereth his sacrifice: and on the morrow also the remainder of it shall be
eaten:
17 But the remainder of the flesh of
the sacrifice on the third day shall be
burnt with fire.
18 And if *any* of the flesh of the sacrifice of his peace offerings be eaten at
all on the third day, it shall not be accepted, neither shall it be [q]imputed
unto him that offereth it: it shall be an
[r]abomination, and the soul that eateth
of it shall bear his iniquity.
19 And the flesh that toucheth any
unclean *thing* shall not be eaten; it
shall be burnt with fire: and as for the
flesh, all that be clean shall eat thereof.
20 But the soul that eateth *of* the
flesh of the sacrifice of peace offerings,
that *pertain* unto the LORD, [s]having
his uncleanness upon him, even that
soul [t]shall be cut off from his people.
21 Moreover the soul that shall
touch any unclean *thing, as* [u]the uncleanness of man, or *any* [v]unclean
beast, or any [w]abominable unclean
thing, and eat of the flesh of the sacrifice of peace offerings, which *pertain*
unto the LORD, even that soul shall be
cut off from his people.
22 ¶ And the LORD spake unto Mō'-
ses, saying,
23 Speak unto the children of Ĭs'ra-
el, saying, [x]Ye shall eat no manner of
fat, of ox, or of sheep, or of goat.
24 And the fat of the [2]beast that dieth
of itself, and the fat of that which is torn
with beasts, may be used in any other
use: but ye shall in no wise eat of it.
25 For whosoever eateth the fat of
the beast, of which men offer an offering made by fire unto the LORD, even
the soul that eateth *it* shall be cut off
from his people.
26 Moreover [y]ye shall eat no manner of blood, *whether it be* of fowl or of
beast, in any of your dwellings.
27 Whatsoever soul *it be* that eateth
any manner of blood, even that soul
shall be cut off from his people.
28 ¶ And the LORD spake unto Mō'-
ses, saying,
29 Speak unto the children of Ĭs'ra-
el, saying, [z]He that offereth the sacrifice of his peace offerings unto the LORD

25 [v]ch. 4.24-29
[w]ch. 21.22; Ps. 93.5
26 [x]Num. 18.9; Ezek. 44.27-28
27 [y]Ex. 29.37; Ex. 30.29
28 [z]ch. 11.33; ch. 15.12
29 [a]Num. 18.10
30 [b]ch. 16.27; Heb. 13.11

CHAPTER 7
1 [a]ch. 5.1-6; ch. 6.1-7
[b]Ex. 29.37; ch. 6.17; ch. 21.22
2 [c]ch. 4.24-29-33
3 [d]Ex. 29.13; ch. 3.4-9-10-14-15; ch. 4.8-9
5 [e]Tit. 2.14; Heb. 9.28
6 [f]ch. 6.16; Num. 18.9
[g]ch. 2.3; Ps. 93.5
7 [h]ch. 6.25; ch. 14.13
9 [i]ch. 2.3-10; Num. 18.9
[1]Or, on the flat plate, or, slice
[j]ch. 2.3-10; ch. 5.13; Num. 5.9; 1 Cor. 9.7-14
11 [k]ch. 3.1; ch. 22.18
12 [l]ch. 2.4; Num. 6.15
13 [m]Amos 4.5
14 [n]Num. 18.8
15 [o]ch. 22.30; Heb. 3.13-15
16 [p]ch. 19.6
18 [q]Gen. 4.4-5; Num. 18.27
[r]ch. 11.10; Prov. 15.8; Amos 5.22
20 [s]ch. 15.3
[t]Gen. 17.14
21 [u]ch. 12; ch. 22.4
[v]ch. 11.24-28
[w]ch. 11.10-13-20-41-42; Ezek. 4.14
23 [x]ch. 3.17; 1 Sam. 2.29
24 [2]carcase
26 [y]Gen. 9.4; Acts 15.20
29 [z]ch. 3.1

shall bring his oblation unto the LORD of the sacrifice of his peace offerings.

30 His own hands shall bring the offerings of the LORD made by fire, the fat with the breast, it shall he bring, that [a]the breast may be waved *for* a wave offering before the LORD.

31 And [b]the priest shall burn the fat upon the altar: but the breast shall be Aâr'on's and his sons'.

32 And [c]the right shoulder shall ye give unto the priest *for* an heave offering of the sacrifices of your peace offerings.

33 He among the sons of Aâr'on, that offereth the blood of the peace offerings, and the fat, shall have the right shoulder for *his* part.

34 For [d]the wave breast and the heave shoulder have I taken of the children of Is'ra-el from off the sacrifices of their peace offerings, and have given them unto Aâr'on the priest and unto his sons by a statute for ever from among the children of Is'ra-el.

35 ¶ This *is the portion* of the anointing of Aâr'on, and of the anointing of his sons, out of the offerings of the LORD made by fire, in the day *when* he presented them to minister unto the LORD in the priest's office;

36 Which the LORD commanded to be given them of the children of Is'ra-el, [e]in the day that he anointed them, *by* a statute [f]for ever throughout their generations.

37 This *is* the law [g]of the burnt offering, of the meat offering, [h]and of the sin offering, and of the trespass offering, [i]and of the consecrations, and of the sacrifice of the peace offerings;

38 Which the LORD commanded Mō'ses in mount Sī'nāi, in the day that he commanded the children of Is'ra-el to offer their oblations unto the LORD, in the wilderness of Sī'nāi.

8 And the LORD spake unto Mō'ses, saying,

2 Take [a]Aâr'on and his sons with him, and the garments, and [b]the anointing oil, and a bullock for the sin offering, and two rams, and a basket of unleavened bread;

3 And gather thou all the congregation together unto the door of the tabernacle of the congregation.

4 And Mō'ses did as the LORD commanded him; and the assembly was gathered together unto the door of the tabernacle of the congregation.

5 And Mō'ses said unto the congregation, This *is* the thing which the LORD commanded to be done.

6 And Mō'ses brought Aâr'on and his sons, and [c]washed them with water.

7 And he put upon him [d]the coat, and girded him with the girdle, and clothed him with the robe, and put the ephod upon him, and he girded him with the curious girdle of the ephod, and bound *it* unto him therewith.

8 And he put the breastplate upon him: also he put in the breastplate [e]the Ū'rim and the Thŭm'mim.

9 And [f]he put the mitre upon his head; also upon the mitre, *even* upon his forefront, did he put the golden plate, the holy crown; as the LORD [g]commanded Mō'ses.

10 And [h]Mō'ses took the anointing oil, and anointed the tabernacle and all that *was* therein, and sanctified them.

11 And he sprinkled thereof upon the altar seven times, and anointed the altar and all his vessels, both the laver and his foot, to sanctify them.

12 And he [i]poured of the anointing oil upon Aâr'on's head, and anointed him, to sanctify him.

13 And [j]Mō'ses brought Aâr'on's sons, and put coats upon them, and girded them with girdles, and [1]put bonnets upon them; as the LORD commanded Mō'ses.

14 And [k]he brought the bullock for the sin offering: and Aâr'on and his sons [l]laid their hands upon the head of the bullock for the sin offering.

15 And he slew *it;* [m]and Mō'ses took the blood, and put *it* upon the horns of the altar round about with his finger, and purified the altar, and poured the blood at the bottom of the altar, and sanctified it, to make reconciliation upon it.

16 And [n]he took all the fat that *was* upon the inwards, and the caul *above* the liver, and the two kidneys, and their fat, and Mō'ses burned *it* upon the altar.

17 But the bullock, and his hide, his flesh, and his dung, he burnt with fire without the camp; as the LORD [o]commanded Mō'ses.

18 ¶ And [p]he brought the ram for the burnt offering: and Aâr'on and his sons laid their hands upon the head of the ram.

19 And he killed *it;* and Mō'ses sprinkled the blood upon the altar round about.

20 And he cut the ram into pieces; and Mō'ses burnt the head, and the pieces, and the fat.

21 And he washed the inwards and the legs in water; and Mō'ses burnt the whole ram upon the altar: it *was* a burnt sacrifice for a sweet savour, *and* an offering made by fire unto the LORD; [q]as the LORD commanded Mō'ses.

22 ¶ And [r]he brought the other ram, the ram of consecration: and Aâr'on and his sons laid their hands upon the head of the ram.

23 And he slew *it;* and Mō'ses took of the blood of it, and put *it* upon [s]the tip of Aâr'on's right ear, and upon the thumb of his right hand, and upon the great toe of his right foot.

24 And he brought Aâr'on's sons, and Mō'ses put of the blood upon the tip of their right ear, and upon the thumbs of their right hands, and upon the great toes of their right feet: and Mō'ses [t]sprinkled the blood upon the altar round about.

25 And [u]he took the fat, and the rump, and all the fat that *was* upon the

30 [a]Ex. 29.24-27; ch. 8.27; Num. 6.20
31 [b]ch. 3.5-11
32 [c]ch. 9.21; Num. 6.20
34 [d]Ex. 29.28; ch. 10.14-15; Num. 18.18; Deut. 18.3
36 [e]Ex. 40.13-15; ch. 8.12-30 [f]Heb. 7.18-28; Heb. 8.1-13
37 [g]ch. 6.9 [h]ch. 6.25 [i]Ex. 29.1; ch. 6.20

CHAPTER 8
2 [a]Ex. 29.1 [b]Ex. 30.24-25
6 [c]Ex. 30.19; Ps. 26.6; Isa. 52.11; Ezek. 36.25; 1 Cor. 6.11; Eph. 5.26; Heb. 9.9-14; Rev. 1.5-6
7 [d]Ex. 28.4
8 [e]Num. 27.21; Deut. 33.8; 1 Sam. 28.6; Ezra 2.63; Neh. 7.65
9 [f]Ex. 29.6; Zech. 3.5 [g]Ex. 28.37
10 [h]Ex. 30.26-29
12 [i]Ex. 29.7; ch. 21.10-12; Ps. 133.2; Isa. 61.1
13 [j]Ex. 29.8-9; Ps. 132.9; Isa. 61.10 [1]bound
14 [k]Ex. 29.10; Ps. 51.19; Ps. 66.15; Ezek. 43.19; Heb. 9.13-14 [l]ch. 4.4
15 [m]Ex. 29.12-36; ch. 4.7; Heb. 9.22
16 [n]Ex. 29.13; ch. 4.8
17 [o]Ex. 29.14; ch. 4.11-12
18 [p]Ex. 29.15
21 [q]Ex. 29.18
22 [r]Ex. 29.19-31; ch. 7.37; Rev. 1.5-6
23 [s]Ex. 29.20; 1 Cor. 6.20
24 [t]Heb. 9.18-24
25 [u]Ex. 29.22

inwards, and the caul *above* the liver,
and the two kidneys, and their fat, and
the right shoulder:
26 And [v]out of the basket of unleavened bread, that *was* before the
LORD, he took one unleavened cake,
and a cake of oiled bread, and one wafer, and put *them* on the fat, and upon
the right shoulder:
27 And he put all [w]upon Aâr'on's
hands, and upon his sons' hands, and
waved them *for* a wave offering before
the LORD.
28 And [x]Mō'ses took them from off
their hands, and burnt *them* on the altar upon the burnt offering: they *were*
consecrations for [y]a sweet savour: it
is an offering made by fire unto the
LORD.
29 And Mō'ses took the breast, and
waved it *for* a wave offering before the
LORD: *for* of the ram of consecration it
was [z]Mō'ses' part; as the LORD commanded Mō'ses.
30 And [a]Mō'ses took of the anointing oil, and of the blood which *was*
upon the altar, and sprinkled *it* upon
Aâr'on, *and* upon his garments, and
upon his sons, and upon his sons' garments with him; and sanctified Aâr'on,
and his garments, and his sons, and his
sons' garments with him.
31 ¶ And Mō'ses said unto Aâr'on
and to his sons, [b]Boil the flesh *at* the
door of the tabernacle of the congregation: and there eat it with the bread
that *is* in the basket of consecrations,
as I commanded, saying, Aâr'on and
his sons shall eat it.
32 And [c]that which remaineth of the
flesh and of the bread shall ye burn
with fire.
33 And ye shall not go out of the
door of the tabernacle of the congregation *in* seven days, until the days of
your consecration be at an end: for
[d]seven days shall he consecrate you.
34 As he [e]hath done this day, *so* the
LORD hath commanded to do, to make
an atonement for you.
35 Therefore shall ye abide *at* the
door of the tabernacle of the congregation day and night seven days, and
[f]keep the charge of the LORD, that ye
die not: for so I am commanded.
36 So Aâr'on and his sons did all
things which the LORD commanded by
the hand of Mō'ses.
9 And [a]it came to pass on the eighth
day, *that* Mō'ses called Aâr'on and
his sons, and the elders of Ĭs'ra-el;
2 And he said unto Aâr'on, [b]Take
thee a young calf for a sin offering,
and [c]a ram for a burnt offering, without blemish, and offer *them* before the
LORD.
3 And unto the children of Ĭs'ra-el
thou shalt speak, saying, [d]Take ye a
kid of the goats for a sin offering; and a
calf and a lamb, *both* of the first year,
without blemish, for a burnt offering;
4 Also a bullock and a ram for peace
offerings, to sacrifice before the LORD;
and a [e]meat offering mingled with oil:
for [f]to day the LORD will appear unto
you.
5 ¶ And they brought *that* which
Mō'ses commanded before the tabernacle of the congregation: and all the
congregation drew near and stood before the LORD.
6 And Mō'ses said, This *is* the thing
which the LORD commanded that ye
should do: and [g]the glory of the LORD
shall appear unto you.
7 And Mō'ses said unto Aâr'on, Go
unto the altar, and [h]offer thy sin offering, and thy burnt offering, and make
an atonement for thyself, and for the
people: and [i]offer the offering of the
people, and make an atonement for
them; as the LORD commanded.
8 ¶ Aâr'on therefore went unto the
altar, and slew the calf of the sin offering, which *was* for himself.
9 And [j]the sons of Aâr'on brought
the blood unto him: and he dipped his
finger in the blood, and [k]put *it* upon
the horns of the altar, and poured out
the blood at the bottom of the altar:
10 But [l]the fat, and the kidneys, and
the caul above the liver of the sin offering, he burnt upon the altar; [m]as the
LORD commanded Mō'ses.
11 And [n]the flesh and the hide he
burnt with fire without the camp.
12 And he slew the burnt offering;
and Aâr'on's sons presented unto him
the blood, which he sprinkled round
about upon the altar.
13 And they presented the burnt offering unto him, with the pieces thereof,
and the head: and he burnt *them* upon
the altar.
14 And he did wash the inwards and
the legs, and burnt *them* upon the burnt
offering on the altar.
15 ¶ And [o]he brought the people's
offering, and took the goat, which *was*
the sin offering for the people, and
slew it, and offered it for sin, as the
first.
16 And he brought the burnt offering, and offered it according to the
[1]manner.
17 And he brought the meat offering, and [2]took an handful thereof, and
burnt *it* upon the altar, [p]beside the
burnt sacrifice of the morning.
18 He slew also the bullock and the
ram *for* a sacrifice of peace offerings, which *was* for the people: and
Aâr'on's sons presented unto him the
blood, which he sprinkled upon the altar round about,
19 And the fat of the bullock and
of the ram, the rump, and that which
covereth *the inwards*, and the kidneys,
and the caul *above* the liver:
20 And they put the fat upon the
breasts, and he burnt the fat upon the
altar:
21 And the breasts and the right
shoulder Aâr'on waved [q]*for* a wave offering before the LORD; as Mō'ses commanded.
22 And Aâr'on lifted up his hand toward the people, and [r]blessed them,
and came down from offering of the

26 [v]Ex. 29.23
27 [w]Ex. 29.24
28 [x]Ex. 29.25
[y]Gen. 8.21; Eph. 5.2
29 [z]Ex. 29.26
30 [a]Ex. 29.21; Ex. 30.30; Num. 3.3; 1 Pet. 1.2
31 [b]Ex. 29.31; Ezek. 46.20
32 [c]Ex. 29.34
33 [d]Ex. 29.30-35; ch. 14.8; Num. 19.12; Ezek. 43.25-26
34 [e]Heb. 7.16
35 [f]Num. 3.7; Num. 9.19; Deut. 11.1; 1 Ki. 2.3; Ezek. 48.11; 1 Tim. 1.18; 1 Tim. 5.21

CHAPTER 9
1 [a]ch. 14.10-23; ch. 15.14; Ezek. 43.27
2 [b]Ex. 29.1; ch. 4.3
[c]ch. 8.18
3 [d]ch. 4.23; Ezra 6.17; Ezra 10.19; Isa. 53.10; Rom. 8.3; 1 Pet. 2.24
4 [e]ch. 2.4
[f]Ex. 29.43
6 [g]Ex. 24.16; Ex. 40.34-35; 1 Ki. 8.10-12
7 [h]1 Sam. 3.14; Heb. 5.3; Heb. 7.27
[i]ch. 4.16-20; Heb. 5.1
9 [j]ch. 8.15
[k]ch. 4.7
10 [l]ch. 8.16
[m]ch. 4.8
11 [n]ch. 4.10-11; ch. 8.17
15 [o]Isa. 53.10; John 1.29; 1 Cor. 15.3; 2 Cor. 5.21; Eph. 5.2; Gal. 1.4; Heb. 1.3; Heb. 2.17; 1 Pet. 2.24; 1 John 2.2; Rev. 1.5
16 [1]Or, ordinance
17 [2]filled his hand out of it
[p]Ex. 29.38
21 [q]Ex. 29.24
22 [r]Deut. 21.5; Luke 24.50

sin offering, and the burnt offering, and peace offerings.

23 And Mō'ses and Aâr'on went into the tabernacle of the congregation, and came out, and [s]blessed the people: [t]and the glory of the LORD appeared unto all the people.

24 And [u]there came a fire out from [v]before the LORD, and consumed upon the altar the burnt offering and the fat: *which* when all the people saw, [w]they shouted, and fell on their faces.

10 And [a]Nā'dăb and A-bī'hū, the sons of Aâr'on, took either of them his censer, and put fire therein, and put incense thereon, and offered [b]strange fire before the LORD, which he commanded them not.

2 And there [c]went out fire from the LORD, and devoured them, and they died before the LORD.

3 Then Mō'ses said unto Aâr'on, This *is it* that the LORD spake, saying, I will be sanctified in them that [d]come nigh me, and before all the people I will be [e]glorified. And Aâr'on held his peace.

4 And Mō'ses called Mĭsh'a-el and Ĕl'za-phăn, the sons of [f]Ŭz'zĭ-el the uncle of Aâr'on, and said unto them, Come near, [g]carry your brethren from before the sanctuary out of the camp.

5 So they went near, and carried them in their coats out of the camp; as Mō'ses had said.

6 And Mō'ses said unto Aâr'on, and unto Ē-le-ā'zar and unto Ĭth'a-mär, his sons, [h]Uncover not your heads, neither rend your clothes; lest ye die, and lest [i]wrath come upon all the people: but let your brethren, the whole house of Ĭs'ra-el, bewail the burning which the LORD hath kindled.

7 And [j]ye shall not go out from the door of the tabernacle of the congregation, lest ye die: [k]for the annointing oil of the LORD *is* upon you. And they did according to the word of Mō'ses.

8 ¶ And the LORD spake unto Aâr'on, saying,

9 [l]Do not drink wine nor strong drink, thou, nor thy sons with thee, when ye go into the tabernacle of the congregation, lest ye die: *it shall be* a statute for ever throughout your generations:

10 And that ye may [m]put difference between holy and unholy, and between unclean and clean;

11 And [n]that ye may teach the children of Ĭs'ra-el all the statutes which the LORD hath spoken unto them by the hand of Mō'ses.

12 ¶ And Mō'ses spake unto Aâr'on, and unto Ē-le-ā'zar and unto Ĭth'a-mär, his sons that were left, Take the [o]meat offering that remaineth of the offerings of the LORD made by fire, and eat it without leaven beside the altar: for [p]it *is* most holy:

13 And ye shall eat it in the holy place, because it *is* thy due, and thy sons' due, of the sacrifices of the LORD made by fire: for so I am commanded.

14 And [q]the wave breast and heave shoulder shall ye eat in a clean place; thou, and thy sons, and thy daughters with thee: for *they be* thy due, and thy sons' due, *which* are given out of the sacrifices of peace offerings of the children of Ĭs'ra-el.

15 The heave shoulder and the wave breast shall they bring with the offerings made by fire of the fat, to wave *it for* a wave offering before the LORD; and it shall be thine, and thy sons' with thee, by a statute for ever; as the LORD hath commanded.

16 ¶ And Mō'ses diligently sought the [r]goat of the sin offering, and, behold, it was burnt: and he was angry with Ē-le-ā'zar and Ĭth'a-mär, the sons of Aâr'on *which were* left *alive*, saying,

17 [s]Wherefore have ye not eaten the sin offering in the holy place, seeing it *is* most holy, and *God* hath given it you to bear the iniquity of the congregation, to make atonement for them before the LORD?

18 Behold, the blood of it was not brought in within the holy *place:* ye should indeed have eaten it in the holy *place,* [t]as I commanded.

19 And Aâr'on said unto Mō'ses, Behold, this [u]day have they offered their sin offering and their burnt offering before the LORD; and such things have befallen me: and *if* I had eaten the sin offering to day, [v]should it have been accepted in the sight of the LORD?

20 And when Mō'ses heard *that,* he was content.

11 And the LORD spake unto Mō'ses and to Aâr'on, saying unto them,

2 Speak unto the children of Ĭs'ra-el, saying, [a]These *are* the beasts which ye shall eat among all the beasts that *are* on the earth.

3 Whatsoever parteth the hoof, and is clovenfooted, *and* cheweth the cud, among the beasts, that shall ye eat.

4 Nevertheless these shall ye not eat of them that chew the cud, or of them that divide the hoof: *as* the camel, because he cheweth the cud, but divideth not the hoof; he *is* unclean unto you.

5 And the coney, because he cheweth the cud, but divideth not the hoof; he *is* unclean unto you.

6 And the hare, because he cheweth the cud, but divideth not the hoof; he *is* [b]unclean unto you.

7 And the swine, though he divide the hoof, and be clovenfooted, yet he cheweth not the cud; [c]he *is* unclean to you.

8 Of their flesh shall ye not eat, and their carcase shall ye not touch; [d]they *are* unclean to you.

9 ¶ [e]These shall ye eat of all that *are* in the waters: whatsoever hath fins and scales in the waters, in the seas, and in the rivers, them shall ye eat.

10 And all that have not fins and scales in the seas, and in the rivers, of all that move in the waters, and of any living thing which *is* in the waters, they *shall be* an [f]abomination unto you:

23 [s]2 Sam. 6.18; 1 Chr. 16.2; 2 Chr. 6.3
[t]Num. 16.19
24 [u]Gen. 4.4; Gen. 15.17; 2 Chr. 7.1
[v]Ex. 29.18
[w]1 Ki. 18.39; Ezra 3.11

CHAPTER 10
1 [a]Num. 26.61
[b]Ex. 30.9
2 [c]Num. 16.35; 2 Sam. 6.7
3 [d]Ex. 19.22; Isa. 52.11; Ezek. 20.41
[e]Isa. 49.3; Ezek. 28.22; 2 Thess. 1.10
4 [f]Ex. 6.18; Num. 3.19
[g]Acts 5.6
6 [h]Num. 6.6-7
[i]2 Sam. 24.1
7 [j]ch. 21.12
[k]Ex. 28.41
9 [l]Prov. 31.5; Tit. 1.7
10 [m]Jer. 15.19; Ezek. 22.26
11 [n]Deut. 24.8; Jer. 18.18
12 [o]Ex. 29.2; Num. 18.9-10
[p]ch. 21.22
14 [q]Ex. 29.24; Num. 18.11
16 [r]ch. 9.3-15
17 [s]Ezek. 44.29
18 [t]ch. 6.26
19 [u]ch. 9.8-12
[v]Jer. 6.20; Hos. 9.4

CHAPTER 11
2 [a]Deut. 14.4; Col. 2.16
6 [b]1 Tim. 4.4-5
7 [c]Isa. 65.4; Isa. 66.3-17
8 [d]Isa. 52.11; Heb. 9.10
9 [e]Deut. 14.9-10
10 [f]ch. 7.18; Deut. 14.3

11 They shall be even an abomination unto you; ye shall not eat of their flesh, but ye shall have their carcases in abomination.

12 Whatsoever hath no fins nor scales in the waters, that *shall be* an abomination unto you.

13 ¶ And [g]these *are they which* ye shall have in abomination among the fowls; they shall not be eaten, they *are* an abomination: the eagle, and the [1]ossifrage, and the [2]ospray,

14 And the vulture, and the kite after his kind;

15 Every raven after his kind;

16 And the owl, and the night hawk, and the cuckow, and the hawk after his kind,

17 And the little owl, and the cormorant, and the great owl,

18 And the swan, and the [h]pelican, and the [3]gier eagle,

19 And the stork, the heron after her kind, and the lapwing, and the bat.

20 All [4]fowls that creep, going upon *all* four, *shall be* an abomination unto you.

21 Yet these may ye eat of every flying creeping thing that goeth upon *all* four, which have legs above their feet, to leap withal upon the earth;

22 *Even* these of them ye may eat; the [i]locust after his kind, and the bald locust after his kind, and the beetle after his kind, and the grasshopper [j]after his kind.

23 But all *other* flying creeping things, which have four feet, *shall be* an abomination unto you.

24 And for these ye shall be unclean: whosoever toucheth the carcase of them shall be unclean until the even.

25 And whosoever beareth *ought* of the carcase of them [k]shall wash his clothes, and be unclean until the even.

26 *The carcases* of every beast which divideth the hoof, and *is* not clovenfooted, nor cheweth the cud, *are* unclean unto you: every one that toucheth them shall be unclean.

27 And [5]whatsoever goeth upon his paws, among all manner of beasts that go on *all* four, those *are* unclean unto you: whoso toucheth their carcase shall be unclean until the even.

28 And he that beareth the carcase of them shall wash his clothes, and be unclean until the even: they *are* unclean unto you.

29 ¶ These also *shall be* [l]unclean unto you among the creeping things that creep upon the earth; the weasel, and [m]the mouse, and the [6]tortoise after his kind,

30 And the ferret, and the chameleon, and the lizard, and the [n]snail, and the [o]mole.

31 These *are* unclean to you among all that creep: whosoever doth touch them, when they be dead, shall be unclean until the even.

32 And upon whatsoever *any* of them, when they are dead, doth fall, it shall be unclean; whether *it be* any vessel of wood, or raiment, or skin, or sack, whatsoever vessel *it be*, wherein *any* work is done, [p]it must be put into water, and it shall be unclean until the even; so it shall be cleansed.

33 And every earthen vessel, whereinto *any* of them falleth, whatsoever *is* in it shall be unclean; and [q]ye shall break it.

34 Of all meat which may be eaten, *that* on which *such* water cometh shall be unclean: and all drink that may be drunk in every *such* vessel shall be unclean.

35 And every *thing* whereupon *any part* of their carcase falleth shall be unclean; *whether it be* oven, or ranges for pots, they shall be broken down: *for* they *are* unclean, and shall be unclean unto you.

36 Nevertheless a fountain or pit, [7]*wherein there is* plenty of water, shall be clean: but that which toucheth their carcase shall be unclean.

37 And if *any part* of their carcase fall upon any sowing seed which is to be sown, it *shall be* clean.

38 But if *any* water be put upon the seed, and *any part* of their carcase fall thereon, it *shall be* unclean unto you.

39 And if any beast, of which ye may eat, die; he that toucheth the carcase thereof shall be unclean until the even.

40 And [r]he that eateth of the carcase of it shall wash his clothes, and be unclean until the even: he also that beareth the carcase of it shall wash his clothes, and be unclean until the even.

41 And every creeping thing that creepeth upon the earth *shall be* an abomination; it shall not be eaten.

42 Whatsoever goeth upon the belly, and whatsoever goeth upon *all* four, or whatsoever [8]hath more feet among all creeping things that creep upon the earth, them ye shall not eat; for they *are* an abomination.

43 Ye [s]shall not make [9]yourselves abominable with any creeping thing that creepeth, neither shall ye make yourselves unclean with them, that ye should be defiled thereby.

44 For [t]I *am* the LORD your God: ye shall therefore sanctify yourselves, and [u]ye shall be holy; for I *am* holy: neither shall ye defile yourselves with any manner of creeping thing that creepeth upon the earth.

45 For [v]I *am* the LORD that bringeth you up out of the land of Ē'gypt, to be your God: [w]ye shall therefore be holy, for I *am* holy.

46 This *is* the law of the beasts, and of the fowl, and of every living creature that moveth in the waters, and of every creature that creepeth upon the earth:

47 To [x]make a difference between the unclean and the clean, and between the beast that may be eaten and the beast that may not be eaten.

12 And the LORD spake unto Mō'ses, saying,

2 Speak unto the children of Is'ra-el, saying, If a woman have conceived

13 [g]Deut. 14.12; Rom. 14
[1]A species of eagle
[2]The black eagle

18 [h]Ps. 102.6; Zeph. 2.14
[3]The golden vulture

20 [4]Supposed to mean all flying insects

22 [i]Matt. 3.4

[j]Judg. 6.5; Jer. 46.23; Nah. 3.17

25 [k]ch. 14.8; ch. 15.5; Num. 19.10-22

27 [5]Supposed to mean monkeys, bears, frogs, etc

29 [l]Heb. 9.10

[m]Isa. 66.17
[6]Supposed to mean the frog

30 [n]Ps. 58.8

[o]Isa. 2.20

32 [p]ch. 15.12

33 [q]ch. 6.28

36 [7]a gathering together of waters

40 [r]ch. 17.15; ch. 22.8; Deut. 14.21; Ezek. 4.14

42 [8]doth multiply feet

43 [s]ch. 20.25
[9]your souls

44 [t]Isa. 43.3; Isa. 51.15

[u]Ex. 19.6; ch. 19.2; 1 Thess. 4.7; 1 Pet. 1.15

45 [v]Gen. 35.1-2; Ex. 6.7; Rom. 14.17

[w]Rom. 12.1; 1 Cor. 6.11

47 [x]ch. 10.10; Jer. 15.19; Ezek. 22.26

seed, and born a man child: then [a]she shall be unclean seven days; [b]according to the days of the separation for her infirmity shall she be unclean.

3 And in the [c]eighth day the flesh of his foreskin shall be circumcised.

4 And she shall then continue in the blood of her purifying three and thirty days; she shall touch no hallowed thing, nor come into the sanctuary, until the days of her purifying be fulfilled.

5 But if she bear a maid child, then she shall be unclean two weeks, as in her separation: and she shall continue in the blood of her purifying threescore and six days.

6 And [d]when the days of her purifying are fulfilled, for a son, or for a daughter, she shall bring a [e]lamb [1]of the first year for a burnt offering, and a young pigeon, or a turtledove, for a sin offering, unto the door of the tabernacle of the congregation, unto the priest:

7 Who shall offer it before the LORD, and make [f]an atonement for her; and she shall be cleansed from the issue of her blood. This *is* the law for her that hath born a male or a female.

8 And [g]if [2]she be not able to bring a lamb, then she shall bring two turtles, or two young pigeons; the one for the burnt offering, and the other for a sin offering: and the [h]priest shall make an atonement for her, and she shall be clean.

13 And the LORD spake unto Mō'ses and Aâr'on, saying,

2 When a man shall have in the skin of his flesh a [1]rising, [a]a scab, or bright spot, and it be in the skin of his flesh *like* the plague of leprosy; [b]then he shall be brought unto Aâr'on the priest, or unto one of his sons the priests:

3 And the priest shall look on the plague in the skin of the flesh: and *when* the hair in the plague is turned white, and the plague in sight *be* deeper than the skin of his flesh, it *is* a plague of leprosy: and the priest shall look on him, and pronounce him unclean.

4 If the bright spot *be* white in the skin of his flesh, and in sight *be* not deeper than the skin, and the hair thereof be not turned white; then the priest shall shut up *him that hath* the plague seven days:

5 And the priest shall look on him the seventh day: and, behold, *if* the plague in his sight be at a stay, *and* the plague spread not in the skin; then the priest shall shut him up seven days more:

6 And the priest shall look on him again the seventh day: and, behold, *if* the plague *be* somewhat dark, *and* the plague spread not in the skin, the priest shall pronounce him clean: it *is* *but* a scab: and he shall [c]wash his clothes, and be clean.

7 But if the scab spread much abroad in the skin, after that he hath been seen of the priest for his cleansing, he shall be seen of the priest again:

8 And *if* the priest see that, behold, the scab spreadeth in the skin, then the priest shall pronounce him unclean: it *is* [d]a leprosy.

9 ¶ When the plague of leprosy is in a man, then he shall [e]be brought unto the priest;

10 And [f]the priest shall see *him:* and, behold, *if* the rising *be* white in the skin, and it have turned the hair white, and *there be* [2]quick raw flesh in the rising;

11 It *is* an old leprosy in the skin of his flesh, and the priest shall pronounce him unclean, and shall not shut him up: for he *is* unclean.

12 And if a leprosy break out abroad in the skin, and the leprosy cover all the skin of *him that hath* the plague from his head even to his foot, wheresoever the priest looketh;

13 Then the priest shall consider: and, behold, *if* the leprosy have covered all his flesh, he shall [3]pronounce *him* clean *that hath* the plague: it is all turned white: he *is* clean.

14 But when raw flesh appeareth in him, he shall be unclean.

15 And the [g]priest shall see the raw flesh, and pronounce him to be unclean: *for* the raw flesh *is* unclean: it *is* a leprosy.

16 Or if the raw flesh turn again, and be changed unto white, he shall [h]come unto the priest;

17 And the priest shall see him: and, behold, *if* the plague be turned into white; then the priest shall pronounce *him* clean *that hath* the plague: he [i]*is* clean.

18 ¶ The flesh also, in which, *even* in the skin thereof, was [j]a boil, and is healed,

19 And in the place of the boil there be a white rising, or a bright spot, white, and somewhat reddish, and it be shewed to the priest;

20 And if, when the priest seeth it, behold, it *be* in sight lower than the skin, and the hair thereof be turned white; the priest shall pronounce him unclean: it *is* a plague of leprosy broken out of the boil.

21 But if the priest look on it, and, behold, *there be* no white hairs therein, and *if* it *be* not lower than the skin, but *be* somewhat dark; then the priest shall shut him up seven days:

22 And if it spread much abroad in the skin, then the priest shall pronounce him unclean: it *is* a plague.

23 But if the bright spot stay in his place, *and* spread not, it *is* a burning boil; and the priest [k]shall pronounce him clean.

24 ¶ Or if there be *any* flesh, in the skin whereof *there is* [4]a hot burning, and the quick *flesh* that burneth have a white bright spot, somewhat reddish, or white;

25 Then the priest shall look upon it: and, behold, *if* the hair in the bright spot be turned white, and it *be in* sight deeper than the skin; it *is* a leprosy broken out of the burning: wherefore the

CHAPTER 12
2 [a]Luke 2.22 [b]ch. 15.19
3 [c]Gen. 17.12; Luke 1.59; John 7.22-23
6 [d]Luke 2.22 [e]Isa. 53.7; Luke 24.26-27; John 1.29-36; 1 Pet. 1.18-19; Rev. 5.6-8 [1]a son of his year
7 [f]Heb. 9.9-28; Heb. 10.1-12
8 [g]ch. 5.7; Luke 2.24; 2 Cor. 8.9 [2]her hand find not sufficiency of [h]ch. 4.26; ch. 13

CHAPTER 13
2 [1]Or, swelling [a]Deut. 28.27; Isa. 3.17 [b]ch. 10.10-11; Deut. 17.8-9; Deut. 24.8; Ezek. 22.26; Luke 17.11-16; John 13.8-10
6 [c]ch. 11.25; ch. 14.8
8 [d]2 Sam. 3.29
9 [e]2 Ki. 5.3
10 [f]Num. 12.10-12; 2 Ki. 5.27; 2 Chr. 26.19-20; Luke 5.14; Luke 17.14 [2]the quickening of living flesh
13 [3]make clean the plague, Ex. 15.26; Ps. 103.2-3
15 [g]Deut. 24.8
16 [h]Luke 5.12-14
17 [i]Deut. 32.36-39; Ps. 147.3
18 [j]Ex. 9.9; Ex. 15.26; Isa. 38.21
23 [k]Prov. 28.13; 1 Pet. 4.1-5
24 [4]a burning of fire

priest shall pronounce him unclean: it
is the [l]plague of leprosy.
26 But if the priest look on it, and,
behold, *there be* no white hair in the
bright spot, and it *be* no lower than
the *other* skin, but *be* somewhat dark;
then the priest shall shut him up seven
days:
27 And the priest shall look upon
him the seventh day: *and* if it be spread
much abroad in the skin, then [m]the
priest shall pronounce him unclean: it
is the plague of leprosy.
28 And if the bright spot stay in his
place, *and* spread not in the skin, but
it *be* somewhat dark; it *is* a rising of
the burning, and the priest shall pronounce him clean: for it *is* an inflammation of the burning.
29 ¶ If a man or woman have a
plague upon the head or the beard;
30 Then [n]the priest shall see the
plague: and, behold, if it *be* in sight
deeper than the skin; *and there be* in
it a yellow thin hair; then the priest
shall pronounce him unclean: it *is* a
dry [o]scall, *even* a leprosy upon the
head or beard.
31 And if the priest look on the
plague of the scall, and, behold, it *be*
not in sight deeper than the skin, and
that there is no black hair in it; then
the priest shall shut up *him that hath*
the plague of the scall seven days:
32 And in the seventh day the priest
shall look on the plague: and, behold,
if the scall spread not, and there be in it
no yellow hair, and the scall *be* not in
sight deeper than the skin;
33 He shall be [p]shaven, but the scall
shall he not shave; and the priest shall
shut up *him that hath* the scall seven
days more:
34 And in the seventh day the priest
shall look on the scall: and, behold, *if*
the scall be not spread in the skin, nor
be in sight deeper than the skin; then
the priest shall pronounce him clean:
and he shall wash his clothes, and be
clean.
35 But if the scall spread much in
the skin after his cleansing;
36 Then the priest shall look on him:
and, behold, if the scall be spread in
the skin, the priest shall not seek for
yellow hair; he *is* unclean.
37 But if the scall be in his sight at
a stay, and *that* there is black hair
grown up therein; the scall is healed,
he *is* clean: and the [q]priest shall pronounce him clean.
38 ¶ If a man also or a woman have
in the skin of their flesh bright spots,
even white bright spots;
39 Then the priest shall look: and,
behold, *if* the bright spots in the skin of
their flesh *be* darkish white; it *is* a
freckled spot *that* groweth in the skin;
he *is* clean.
40 And the man whose [5]hair is fallen
off his head, he *is* [r]bald; *yet is* he clean.
41 And he that hath his hair fallen
off from the part of his head toward his
face, he *is* forehead bald: *yet is* he
clean.

25 [l]Ex. 4.6-7; Num. 12.10; 2 Sam. 3.29; 2 Ki. 5.27; 2 Chr. 26.19; Luke 5.12-14

27 [m]ch. 10.10; Jer. 15.19; Ezek. 22.26

30 [n]Deut. 24.8; Mal. 2.7; 1 Cor. 12.9

[o]Deut. 28.27; Isa. 3.17

33 [p]Job 1.20; Rom. 8.13

37 [q]ch. 10.10; Jer. 15.19; Ezek. 22.26; Ezek. 44.23

40 [5]head is pilled

[r]Isa. 15.2; Amos 8.10

43 [s]ch. 10.10; Ezek. 22.26

45 [t]Ezek. 24.17-22; Mic. 3.7

[u]1 Ki. 8.37; Job 40.4; Job 42.6; Ps. 61; Ps. 72.12; Isa. 6.5; Lam. 4.15; Luke 17.12-13; Rev. 21.4

46 [v]Num. 5.2; Num. 12.14; 2 Ki. 7.3; 2 Chr. 26.21; Luke 17.12; 1 Cor. 5.5; 2 Thess. 3.6; Heb. 12.15

47 [w]Isa. 59.6; Ezek. 16.16; Zech. 3.4; Rom. 1.21-31; Rom. 13.12; Jude 23

48 [6]work of

49 [7]vessel, or, instrument

50 [x]Jer. 15.19; Ezek. 44.23

51 [y]ch. 14.44; Ezek. 16.43

55 [8]whether it be bald in the head thereof, or in the forehead thereof

42 And if there be in the bald head,
or bald forehead, a white reddish sore;
it *is* a leprosy sprung up in his bald
head, or his bald forehead.
43 Then [s]the priest shall look upon
it: and, behold, *if* the rising of the sore
be white reddish in his bald head, or in
his bald forehead, as the leprosy appeareth in the skin of the flesh;
44 He is a leprous man, he *is* unclean: the priest shall pronounce him
utterly unclean; his plague *is* in his
head.
45 And the leper in whom the plague
is, his clothes shall be rent, and his
head bare, and he shall put [t]a covering
upon his upper lip, and shall cry, [u]Un-
clean, unclean.
46 All the days wherein the plague
shall be in him he shall be defiled; he *is*
unclean: he shall dwell alone; [v]with-
out the camp *shall* his habitation *be*.
47 ¶ The [w]garment also that the
plague of leprosy is in, *whether it be* a
woollen garment, or a linen garment;
48 Whether *it be* in the warp, or
woof, of linen, or of woollen; whether
in a skin, or in any [6]thing made of skin;
49 And if the plague be greenish or
reddish in the garment, or in the skin,
either in the warp, or in the woof, or in
any [7]thing of skin; it *is* a plague of leprosy, and shall be shewed unto the
priest:
50 And [x]the priest shall look upon
the plague, and shut up *it that hath* the
plague seven days:
51 And he shall look on the plague
on the seventh day: if the plague be
spread in the garment, either in the
warp, or in the woof, or in a skin, *or* in
any work that is made of skin; the
plague *is* [y]a fretting leprosy; it *is* unclean.
52 He shall therefore burn that garment, whether warp or woof, in woollen or in linen, or any thing of skin,
wherein the plague is: for it *is* a fretting leprosy; it shall be burnt in the
fire.
53 And if the priest shall look, and,
behold, the plague be not spread in the
garment, either in the warp, or in the
woof, or in any thing of skin;
54 Then the priest shall command
that they wash *the thing* wherein the
plague *is*, and he shall shut it up seven
days more:
55 And the priest shall look on the
plague, after that it is washed: and, behold, *if* the plague have not changed his
colour, and the plague be not spread; it
is unclean; thou shalt burn it in the fire;
it *is* fret inward, [8]*whether* it *be* bare
within or without.
56 And if the priest look, and, behold, the plague *be* somewhat dark after the washing of it; then he shall rend
it out of the garment, or out of the skin,
or out of the warp, or out of the woof:
57 And if it appear still in the garment, either in the warp, or in the
woof, or in any thing of skin; it *is* a
spreading *plague*: thou shalt burn that
wherein the plague *is* with fire.

58 And the garment, either warp, or
woof, or whatsoever thing of skin *it be,*
which thou shalt wash, if the plague be
departed from them, then it shall be
washed the second time, and shall be
clean.
59 This *is* the law of the plague of
leprosy in a garment of woollen or
linen, either in the warp, or woof, or
any thing of skins, to pronounce it
clean, or to pronounce it unclean.

CHAPTER 14

14 And the LORD spake unto Mō'-
ses, saying,
2 This shall be the law of the leper in
the day of his cleansing: He [a]shall be
brought unto the priest:
3 And the priest shall go forth out of
the camp; and the priest shall look,
and, behold, *if* the plague of leprosy be
healed in the leper;
4 Then shall the priest command to
take for him that is to be cleansed
two [1]birds alive *and* clean, and [b]cedar
wood, [c]and scarlet, [d]and hyssop:
5 And the priest shall command that
one of the birds be killed in an earthen
vessel over running water:
6 As for the living bird, he shall take
it, and the cedar wood, and the scarlet,
and the hyssop, and shall dip them and
the living bird in the blood of the bird
that was killed over the running water:
7 And he shall [e]sprinkle upon him
that is to be cleansed from the leprosy
[f]seven times, and shall pronounce him
clean, and shall let the living bird loose
[2]into the open field.
8 And he that is to be cleansed [g]shall
wash his clothes, and shave off all his
hair, and [h]wash himself in water, that
he may be clean: and after that he shall
come into the camp, and [i]shall tarry
abroad out of his tent seven days.
9 But it shall be on the seventh day,
that he shall shave all his hair off his
head and his beard and his eyebrows,
even all his hair he shall shave off: and
he shall wash his clothes, also he shall
wash his flesh in water, and he shall be
clean.
10 And on the eighth day [j]he shall
take two he lambs without blemish,
and one ewe lamb [3]of the first year
without blemish, and three tenth deals
of fine flour *for* [k]a meat offering, mingled with oil, and one log of oil.
11 And the priest that maketh *him*
clean shall present the man that is to
be made clean, and those things, before the LORD, *at* the door of the tabernacle of the congregation:
12 And the priest shall take one he
lamb, and [l]offer him for a trespass offering, and the log of oil, and [m]wave
them *for* a wave offering before the
LORD:
13 And he shall slay the [n]lamb in
[o]the place where he shall kill the sin
offering and the burnt offering, in the
holy place: for [p]as the sin offering *is*
the priest's, *so is* the trespass offering:
[q]it *is* most holy:
14 And the priest shall take *some* of
the blood [r]of the trespass offering, and
the priest shall put *it* upon [s]the tip
of the right ear of him that is to be
cleansed, and upon the thumb of his
right hand, and upon the great toe of
his right foot:
15 And the priest shall take *some* of
the log of oil, and pour *it* into the palm
of his own left hand:
16 And the priest shall dip his right
finger in the oil that *is* in his left hand,
and shall sprinkle of the oil with his
finger seven times before the LORD:
17 And of the rest of the oil that *is* in
his hand shall the priest put upon the
tip of the right ear of him [t]that is to be
cleansed, and upon the thumb of his
right hand, and upon the great toe of
his right foot, upon the blood of the
trespass offering:
18 And the remnant of the oil that *is*
in the priest's hand he shall pour upon
the head of him that is to be cleansed:
and the priest shall make an [u]atone-
ment for him before the LORD.
19 And the priest shall offer the sin
offering, and make an atonement for
him that is to be cleansed from his uncleanness; and afterward he shall kill
the burnt offering:
20 And the priest shall offer the
burnt offering and the meat offering
upon the altar: and the priest shall
make an atonement for him, and he
shall be clean.
21 And [v]if he *be* poor, and [4]can-
not get so much; then he shall take
one lamb *for* a trespass offering [5]to be
waved, to make an atonement for him,
and one tenth deal of fine flour mingled with oil for a meat offering, and a
log of oil;
22 And [w]two turtledoves, or two
young pigeons, such as he is able to
get; and the one shall be a sin offering,
and the other a burnt offering.
23 And he shall bring them on the
eighth day for his cleansing unto the
priest, unto the door of the tabernacle
of the congregation, before the LORD.
24 And the priest shall take the lamb
of the trespass offering, and the log of
oil, and the priest shall wave them *for* a
wave offering before the LORD:
25 And he shall kill the lamb of the
trespass offering, and the priest shall
take *some* of the [x]blood of the trespass
offering, and put *it* upon the tip of the
right ear of him that is to be cleansed,
and upon the thumb of his right hand,
and upon the great toe of his right foot:
26 And the priest shall pour of the
oil into the palm of his own left hand:
27 And the priest shall sprinkle with
his right finger *some* of the oil that *is* in
his left hand seven times before the
LORD:
28 And the priest shall put of the oil
that *is* in his hand upon the tip of the
right ear of [y]him that is to be cleansed,
and upon the thumb of his right hand,
and upon the great toe of his right foot,
upon the place of the blood of the trespass offering:
29 And the rest of the oil that *is* in
the priest's hand he shall put upon the

2 [a]Jer. 15.19; Ezek. 44.23; Luke 5.12-14; Luke 17.14
4 [1]Or, sparrows
[b]Num. 19.6
[c]Heb. 9.19
[d]Ex. 12.22; Num. 19.18; Ps. 51.7
7 [e]Ezek. 36.25; Heb. 9.13; Heb. 10.22
[f]ch. 8.11; 2 Ki. 5.10-14
[2]upon the face of the field
8 [g]ch. 13.6
[h]ch. 11.25
[i]Num. 5.2-3; Num. 12.15; 2 Chr. 26.20-21
10 [j]Luke 5.14
[3]the daughter of her year
[k]ch. 2.1; Num. 15.4-15
12 [l]ch. 5.2-6-18; ch. 6.6-7
[m]Ex. 29.24
13 [n]Isa. 53.7; John 1.29; 1 Pet. 1.19; Rev. 5.6
[o]Ex. 29.11; ch. 1.5-11
[p]ch. 7.7
[q]ch. 2.3; ch. 7.6
14 [r]Eph. 1.7; Col. 1.14; Heb. 9.9-14; Rev. 12.11
[s]Ex. 29.20; ch. 8.23; Rom. 12.1; 2 Cor. 7.1
17 [t]Rom. 6.13-22; Rom. 12.1; 1 Cor. 6.20
18 [u]ch. 4.26; 1 John 1.7
21 [v]ch. 5.7; John 5.3
[4]his hand reach not
[5]for a waving
22 [w]ch. 12.8; Luke 2.24
25 [x]1 Thess. 5.23; Rev. 1.5
28 [y]1 Cor. 6.11

head of him that is to be cleansed, to
make an atonement for him before the
LORD.
30 And he shall offer the one of the
[z]turtledoves, or of the young pigeons,
such as he can get;
31 *Even* such as he is able to get, the
one *for* a sin offering, and the other *for*
a burnt offering, with the meat offering: and the priest shall make an atonement for him that is to be cleansed before the LORD.
32 This *is* the law *of him* in whom *is*
the plague of leprosy, whose hand is
not able to get *that which pertaineth*
to his cleansing.
33 ¶ And the LORD spake unto Mō'-
ses and unto Aâr'on, saying,
34 [a]When ye be come into the land
of Cā'năan, which I give to you for a
possession, and [b]I put the plague of
leprosy in a house of the land of your
possession;
35 And he that owneth the house
shall come and tell the priest, saying, It
seemeth to me *there is* as it were [c]a
plague in the house:
36 Then the priest shall command
that they [6]empty the house, before the
priest go *into it* to see the plague, that
[d]all that *is* in the house be not made
unclean: and afterward the priest shall
go in to see the house:
37 And he shall look on the plague,
and, behold, *if* the plague *be* in the
walls of the house with hollow strakes,
greenish or reddish, which in sight *are*
lower than the wall;
38 Then the priest shall go out of the
house to the door of the house, and
shut up the house seven days:
39 And the priest shall come again
the seventh day, and shall look: and,
behold, *if* the plague be spread in the
walls of the house;
40 [e]Then the priest shall command
that they take away the stones in which
the plague *is*, and they shall cast them
into an unclean place without the city:
41 And he shall cause the house to
be scraped within round about, and
they shall pour out the dust that they
scrape off without the city into an unclean place:
42 And they shall take other stones,
and put *them* in the place of those
stones; and he shall take other morter,
and shall plaister the house.
43 And if the plague come again,
and break out in the house, after that
he hath taken away the stones, and after he hath scraped the house, and after it is plaistered;
44 Then the priest shall come and
look, and, behold, *if* the plague be
spread in the house, it *is* [f]a fretting leprosy in the house: it *is* unclean.
45 And he shall break down the
house, the stones of it, and the timber
therof, and all the morter of the house;
and he shall carry *them* forth out of the
city into an unclean place.
46 Moreover he that goeth into the
house all the while that it is shut up
shall be unclean [g]until the even.
47 And he that lieth in the house
shall wash his clothes; and he that eateth in the house shall wash his clothes.
48 And if the priest [7]shall come in,
and look *upon it*, and, behold, the
plague hath not spread in the house,
after the house was plaistered: then
the priest shall pronounce the house
clean, because the plague is [h]healed.
49 And he shall take to cleanse the
house two birds, and cedar wood, and
scarlet, and hyssop:
50 And he shall kill the one of the
birds in an earthen vessel over running
water:
51 And he shall take the cedar wood,
and the [i]hyssop, and the scarlet, and
the living bird, and dip them in the
blood of the slain bird, and in the running water, and sprinkle the house
seven times:
52 And he shall cleanse the house
with the blood of the bird, and with
the running water, and with the living
bird, and with the cedar wood, and
with the hyssop, and with the scarlet:
53 But he shall let go the living bird
out of the city into the open fields, and
make an atonement for the house: and
it shall be clean.
54 This *is* the law for all manner of
plague of leprosy, and [j]scall,
55 And for the [k]leprosy of a garment, and of a house,
56 And [l]for a rising, and for a scab,
and for a bright spot:
57 To [m]teach [8]when *it is* unclean,
and when *it is* clean: this *is* the law of
leprosy.

15

And the LORD spake unto Mō'ses
and to Aâr'on, saying,
2 Speak unto the children of Ĭs'ra-el,
and say unto them, [a]When any man
hath a [1]running issue out of his flesh,
because of his issue he *is* unclean.
3 And this shall be his uncleanness
in his issue: whether his flesh run with
his issue, or his flesh be stopped from
his issue, it *is* his uncleanness.
4 Every bed, whereon he lieth that
hath the issue, is unclean: and every
[2]thing, whereon he sitteth, shall be unclean.
5 And whosoever toucheth his bed
shall wash his clothes, [b]and bathe *himself* in water, and be unclean until the
even.
6 And he that sitteth on *any* thing
whereon he sat that hath the issue shall
wash his clothes, and bathe *himself* in
water, and be unclean until the even.
7 And he that toucheth the flesh of
him that hath the issue shall wash his
clothes, and bathe *himself* in water,
and be unclean until the even.
8 And if he that hath the issue [c]spit
upon him that is clean; then he shall
wash his clothes, and bathe [d]*himself* in
water, and be unclean until the even.
9 And what saddle soever he rideth
upon that hath the issue shall be unclean.
10 And whosoever toucheth any
thing that was under him shall be
unclean until the even: and he that

30 [z]ch. 15.15; Rom. 8.3
34 [a]Gen. 17.8; Num. 32.22; Deut. 7.1; Deut. 19.1 [b]Deut. 32.49; Isa. 45.7; Amos 3.6
35 [c]Ps. 91.10; Prov. 3.33; Zech. 5.4
36 [6]Or, prepare [d]Num. 19.18; Ps. 51.7; Isa. 52.11; 1 Cor. 5.6-7; 2 Cor. 6.17; 2 Thess. 3.6; 1 Tim. 5.22; Rev. 18.4
40 [e]Jer. 15.19; Ezek. 22.26; Ezek. 44.23
44 [f]ch. 13.51; Zech. 5.4
46 [g]ch. 17.15; ch. 22.6; Num. 19.7-10-21-22; 1 Cor. 15.33
48 [7]in coming in shall come in, etc [h]Deut. 32.39; Job 5.18; Hos. 6.1; Luke 7.21
51 [i]1 Ki. 4.33; Ps. 51.7
54 [j]ch. 13.30
55 [k]ch. 13.47
56 [l]ch. 13.2
57 [m]Ex. 15.26; Deut. 4.9; Deut. 24.8; Ps. 78.5; Ps. 119.96; Prov. 6.23; Prov. 13.13; Eccl. 8.5; Ezek. 44.23 [8]in the day of the unclean, and in the day of the clean

CHAPTER 15
2 [a]ch. 22.4; Num. 5.2; 2 Sam. 3.29; Matt. 9.20; Mark 5.25; Luke 8.43 [1]Or, running of the reins
4 [2]vessel
5 [b]ch. 11.25; ch. 17.15; Heb. 9.10
8 [c]Num. 12.14; Job 30.10 [d]2 Cor. 7.1

beareth *any of* those things shall wash his clothes, and bathe *himself* in water, and be unclean until the even.

11 And whomsoever he [e]toucheth that hath the issue, and hath not rinsed his hands in water, he shall wash his clothes, and bathe *himself* in water, and be unclean until the even.

12 And the [f]vessel of earth, that he toucheth which hath the issue, shall be broken: and every vessel of wood shall be rinsed in water.

13 And when he that hath an issue is cleansed of his issue; then [g]he shall number to himself seven days for his cleansing, and wash his clothes, and bathe his flesh in running water, and shall be clean.

14 And on the eighth day he shall take to him [h]two turtledoves, or two young pigeons, and come before the LORD unto the door of the tabernacle of the congregation, and give them unto the priest:

15 And the priest shall offer them, [i]the one *for* a sin offering, and the other *for* a burnt offering; and the [j]priest shall make an atonement for him before the LORD for his issue.

16 And [k]if any man's seed of copulation go out from him, then he shall wash all his flesh in water, and be unclean until the even.

17 And every garment, and every skin, whereon is the seed of copulation, shall be washed with water, and be unclean until the even.

18 The woman also with whom man shall lie *with* seed of copulation, they shall *both* bathe *themselves* in water, and [l]be unclean until the even.

19 ¶ And [m]if a woman have an issue, *and* her issue in her flesh be blood, she shall be [3]put apart seven days: and whosoever toucheth her shall be unclean until the even.

20 And every thing that she lieth upon in her separation shall be unclean: every thing also that she sitteth upon shall be unclean.

21 And whosoever toucheth her bed shall wash his clothes, and bathe *himself* in water, and be unclean until the even.

22 And whosoever toucheth any thing that she sat upon shall wash his clothes, and bathe [n]*himself* in water, and be unclean until the even.

23 And if it *be* on *her* bed, or on any thing whereon she sitteth, when he toucheth it, he shall be unclean until the even.

24 And [o]if any man lie with her at all, and her flowers be upon him, he shall be unclean seven days; and all the bed whereon he lieth shall be unclean.

25 And [p]if a woman have an issue of her blood many days out of the time of her separation, or if it run beyond the time of her separation; all the days of the issue of her uncleanness shall be as the days of her separation: she *shall be* unclean.

26 Every bed whereon she lieth all the days of her issue shall be unto her as the bed of her separation: and whatsoever she sitteth upon shall be unclean, as the uncleanness of her separation.

27 And whosoever toucheth those things shall be unclean, and shall wash his clothes, and bathe *himself* in water, and be unclean until the even.

28 But if she be cleansed of her issue, then she shall number to herself seven days, and after that she shall be clean.

29 And on the eighth day she shall take unto her two turtles, or two young pigeons, and bring them unto the priest, to the door of the tabernacle of the congregation.

30 And the priest shall offer the one *for* a sin offering, and the other *for* a burnt offering; and the priest shall make [q]an atonement for her before the LORD for the issue of her uncleanness.

31 Thus shall ye [r]separate the children of Is'ra-el from their uncleanness; that they die not in their uncleanness, when they [s]defile my tabernacle that *is* among them.

32 This *is* the law of him that hath an issue, and *of him* whose seed goeth from him, and is defiled therewith;

33 And of her that is sick of her flowers, and of him that hath an issue, of the man, and of the woman, and of him that lieth with her that is unclean.

16 And the LORD spake unto Mō'ses after the [a]death of the two sons of Aâr'on, when they offered before the LORD, and died;

2 And the LORD said unto Mō'ses, Speak unto Aâr'on thy brother, that he [b]come not at all times into the holy *place* within the vail before the mercy seat, which *is* upon the ark; that he die not: for I [c]will appear in the cloud upon the mercy seat.

3 Thus shall Aâr'on [d]come into the holy *place:* [e]with a young bullock for a sin offering, and a ram for a burnt offering.

4 He shall put on [f]the holy linen coat, and he shall have the linen breeches upon his flesh, and shall be girded with a linen girdle, and with the linen mitre shall he be attired: these *are* [g]holy garments; therefore [h]shall he wash his flesh in water, and *so* put them on.

5 And he shall take of [i]the congregation of the children of Is'ra-el two kids of the goats for a sin offering, and one ram for a burnt offering.

6 And Aâr'on shall offer his bullock of the sin offering, which *is* for himself, and [j]make an atonement for himself, and for his house.

7 And he shall take the two goats, and present them before the LORD *at* the door of the tabernacle of the congregation.

8 And Aâr'on shall cast lots upon the two goats; one lot for the LORD, and the other lot for the [1]scapegoat.

11 [e]1 Cor. 15.33-34
12 [f]ch. 6.28; ch. 11.32-33
13 [g]ch. 14.8; Num. 12.14; Num. 19.11
14 [h]ch. 14.22-23; Num. 6.10; Heb. 10.10-12-14
15 [i]ch. 14.30-31
[j]ch. 14.19-31; Heb. 9.14; Heb. 10.1
16 [k]ch. 22.4; Deut. 23.10
18 [l]1 Sam. 21.4
19 [m]ch. 12.2; Ezek. 36.17
[3]in her separation
22 [n]2 Cor. 7.1; Heb. 10.22
24 [o]ch. 20.18
25 [p]Matt. 9.20; Mark 5.25; Luke 8.43
30 [q]Rom. 3.25; 2 Cor. 5.18-19; Eph. 1.7; Eph. 2.12-22; Col. 1.19-22; Heb. 2.17; Heb. 9.14; Heb. 10.1; Heb. 13.20; 1 John 1.2; 1 John 1.7; 1 John 2.1
31 [r]ch. 11.47; Deut. 24.8; Ezek. 22.26; Ezek. 44.23
[s]Num. 5.3; Num. 19.13-20; Ezek. 5.11; Ezek. 23.38; 1 Cor. 3.17

CHAPTER 16
1 [a]ch. 10.1-2
2 [b]Ex. 30.10; ch. 23.27-28; Heb. 10.19
[c]Ex. 25.22; 1 Ki. 8.10-11-12
3 [d]Heb. 9.7-25
[e]ch. 4.3
4 [f]Ex. 28.39; Heb. 2.14
[g]Ps. 93.5
[h]Ex. 30.20; Heb. 10.22
5 [i]ch. 4.14; Ezek. 45.22
6 [j]ch. 9.7; Heb. 7.27-28
8 [1]Azazel

9 And Aâr'on shall bring the goat
upon which the LORD'S [k]lot [2]fell, and
offer him *for* a sin offering.
10 But the goat, on which the lot fell
to be the scapegoat, shall be presented
alive before the LORD, to make [l]an
atonement with him, *and* to let him go
for a scapegoat into the wilderness.
11 And Aâr'on shall bring the bullock of the sin offering, which *is* for
himself, and shall make an atonement
for himself, and for his house, and
shall kill the bullock of the sin offering
which *is* for himself:
12 And he shall take [m]a censer full
of burning coals of fire from off the
altar before the LORD, and his hands
full of [n]sweet incense beaten small,
and bring *it* within the vail:
13 And [o]he shall put the incense
upon the fire before the LORD, that the
[p]cloud of the incense may cover the
[q]mercy seat that *is* upon the testimony,
that he die not:
14 And [r]he shall take of the blood of
the bullock, and sprinkle *it* with his
finger upon the mercy seat eastward;
and before the mercy seat shall he
sprinkle of the blood with his finger
seven times.
15 ¶ [s]Then shall he kill the goat of
the sin offering, that *is* for the people,
and bring his blood [t]within the vail,
and do with that blood as he did with
the blood of the bullock, and sprinkle
it upon the mercy seat, and before the
mercy seat:
16 And he shall [u]make an atonement for the holy *place*, because of the
uncleanness of the children of Is'ra-el,
and because of their transgressions in
all their sins: and so shall he do for the
tabernacle of the congregation, that
[3]remaineth among them in the midst of
their uncleanness.
17 And [v]there shall be no man in the
tabernacle of the congregation when
he goeth in to make an atonement in
the holy *place*, until he come out, and
have made an atonement for himself,
and for his household, and for all the
congregation of Is'ra-el.
18 And he shall go out unto the altar
that *is* before the LORD, and [w]make an
atonement for it; and shall take of the
blood of the bullock, and of the blood
of the goat, and put *it* upon the horns
of the altar round about.
19 And he shall sprinkle of the blood
upon it with his finger seven times, and
cleanse it, and [x]hallow it from the uncleanness of the children of Is'ra-el.
20 ¶ And when he hath made an end
of [y]reconciling the holy *place*, and the
tabernacle of the congregation, and the
altar, he shall bring the live goat:
21 And Aâr'on shall lay both his
hands upon the head of the live goat,
and confess over him all the iniquities
of the children of Is'ra-el, and all their
transgressions in all their sins, [z]put-
ting them upon the head of the goat,
and shall send *him* away by the hand
of [4]a fit man into the wilderness:
22 And the goat shall [a]bear upon
him all their iniquities unto a land [5]not
inhabited: and he shall let go the goat
in the wilderness.
23 And Aâr'on shall come into the
tabernacle of the congregation, and
[b]shall put off the linen garments,
which he put on when he went into the
holy *place*, and shall leave them there:
24 And he shall wash his flesh with
water in the holy place, and put on his
garments, and come forth, and offer
his burnt offering, and the burnt offering of the people, and make an atonement for himself, and for the people.
25 And [c]the fat of the sin offering
shall he burn upon the altar.
26 And he that let go the goat for the
scapegoat shall wash his clothes, [d]and
bathe his flesh in water, and afterward
come into the camp.
27 And [e]the bullock *for* the sin offering, and the goat *for* the sin offering,
whose blood was brought in to make
atonement in the holy *place*, shall *one*
carry forth without the camp; and they
shall burn in the fire their skins, and
their flesh, and their dung.
28 And he that burneth them shall
wash his clothes, and bathe his flesh in
water, and afterward he shall come
into the camp.
29 ¶ And *this* shall be a statute for
ever unto you: *that* [f]in the seventh
month, on the tenth *day* of the month,
ye shall afflict your souls, and do no
work at all, *whether it be* one of your
own country, or a stranger that sojourneth among you:
30 For on that day shall *the priest*
make an atonement for you, to [g]cleanse
you, *that* ye may be clean from all your
sins before the LORD.
31 [h]It *shall be* a sabbath of rest unto
you, and ye shall afflict your souls, by
a statute for ever.
32 And the priest, whom he shall
anoint, and whom he [i6]shall consecrate to minister in the priest's office
in his father's stead, shall make the
atonement, and shall put on the linen
clothes, *even* the holy garments:
33 And he shall make an atonement
for the holy sanctuary, and he shall
make an atonement for the tabernacle
of the congregation, and for the altar,
and he shall make an atonement for
the priests, and for all the people of the
congregation.
34 And [j]this shall be an everlasting
statute unto you, to make an atonement for the children of Is'ra-el for all
their sins [k]once a year. And he did as
the LORD commanded Mō'ses.

17

And the LORD spake unto Mō'-
ses, saying,
2 Speak unto Aâr'on, and unto his
sons, and unto all the children of Is'ra-
el, and say unto them; This *is* the thing
which the LORD hath commanded, saying,
3 What man soever *there be* of the
house of Is'ra-el, that killeth an ox, or
lamb, or goat, in the camp, or that
killeth *it* out of the camp,

9 [k]Prov. 16.33 [2]went up
10 [l]Isa. 53.4-10; Rom. 3.25; 2 Cor. 5.21; Heb. 7.26; Heb. 9.23-24; 1 John 2.2
12 [m]ch. 10.1; Num. 16.18; Rev. 8.5 [n]Ex. 30.34; Ex. 31.11; Ex. 37.29; Rev. 8.3-4
13 [o]Ex. 30.1-7-8; Num. 16.7-18-46; Rev. 8.3-4 [p]1 Tim. 6.16 [q]Ex. 25.21-22
14 [r]Heb. 10.4
15 [s]Heb. 2.17 [t]Heb. 6.19
16 [u]Ex. 29.36 [3]dwelleth
17 [v]Luke 1.10
18 [w]Heb. 9.22
19 [x]Ezek. 43.20
20 [y]Ezek. 45.19-20
21 [z]Isa. 53.6 [4]a man of opportunity
22 [a]Ps. 103.1-13; Matt. 8.17; Heb. 9.28; 1 Pet. 2.24 [5]of separation
23 [b]Ezek. 42.14; Phil. 2.6-11
25 [c]Ex. 29.13; ch. 4.10
26 [d]ch. 15.5; Heb. 9.10
27 [e]ch. 8.17; ch. 4.12-21; ch. 6.30; Heb. 13.11
29 [f]Ex. 30.10; ch. 23.27; Num. 29.7; Isa. 58.3-5; Dan. 10.3-12
30 [g]Ezek. 36.25; Jer. 33.8; Tit. 2.14; Eph. 5.26; Heb. 9.13-14
31 [h]Ex. 31.15; Ex. 35.2; ch. 23.32
32 [i]Ex. 29.29; Num. 20.26 [6]fill his hand
34 [j]ch. 23.31; Num. 29.7 [k]Ex. 30.10; Heb. 9.7-25

4 And [a]bringeth it not unto the door
of the tabernacle of the congregation,
to offer an offering unto the LORD before the tabernacle of the LORD; blood
shall be [b]imputed unto that man; he
hath shed blood; and that man [c]shall
be cut off from among his people:
5 To the end that the children of Ĭs'-
ra-el may bring their sacrifices, [d]which
they offer in the open field, even that
they may bring them unto the LORD,
unto the door of the tabernacle of the
congregation, unto the priest, and offer them *for* peace offerings unto the
LORD.
6 And the priest shall sprinkle the
blood upon the altar of the LORD *at* the
door of the tabernacle of the congregation, and [e]burn the fat for a sweet
savour unto the LORD.
7 And they shall no more offer their
sacrifices [f]unto devils, after whom they
[g]have gone a whoring. This shall be a
statute for ever unto them throughout
their generations.
8 ¶ And thou shalt say unto them,
Whatsoever man *there be* of the house
of Ĭs'ra-el, or of the strangers which sojourn among you, that offereth a burnt
offering or sacrifice,
9 And bringeth it not unto the door
of the tabernacle of the congregation,
to offer it unto the LORD; even that
man shall be cut off from among his
people.
10 ¶ And [h]whatsoever man *there be*
of the house of Ĭs'ra-el, or of the strangers that sojourn among you, that eateth
any manner of blood; [i]I will even set
my face against that soul that eateth
blood, and will cut him off from among
his people.
11 For the life of the flesh *is* in the
blood: and I have given it to you upon
the altar [j]to make an atonement for
your souls for [k]it *is* the blood *that*
maketh an atonement for the soul.
12 Therefore I said unto the children
of Ĭs'ra-el, No soul of you shall eat
blood, neither shall any stranger that
sojourneth among you eat blood.
13 And whatsoever man *there be* of
the children of Ĭs'ra-el, or of the strangers that sojourn among you, [1]which
hunteth and catcheth any beast or fowl
that may be eaten; he shall even [l]pour
out the blood thereof, and [m]cover it
with dust.
14 [n]For *it is* the life of all flesh; the
blood of it *is* for the life thereof: therefore I said unto the children of Ĭs'ra-el,
Ye shall eat the blood of no manner of
flesh: for the life of all flesh *is* the blood
thereof: whosoever eateth it shall be
cut off.
15 And [o]every soul that eateth [2]that
which died *of itself*, or that which was
torn *with beasts, whether it be* one of
your own country, or a stranger, he
shall both wash his clothes, and bathe
himself in water, and be unclean until
the even: then shall he be clean.
16 But if he wash *them* not, nor
bathe his flesh; then [p]he shall bear his
iniquity.

CHAPTER 17
4 [a]Deut. 12.5
[b]Ps. 32.2; Rom. 4.6
[c]Gen. 17.14
5 [d]Gen. 21.33; Ezek. 20.28
6 [e]Ex. 29.18; Num. 18.17
7 [f]Deut. 32.17; 1 Cor. 10.20
[g]Ex. 34.15; Deut. 31.16
10 [h]Gen. 9.4; 1 Sam. 14.33
[i]ch. 26.17; Ezek. 15.7
11 [j]Mark 14.24; Col. 1.14
[k]Heb. 9.22
13 [1]that hunteth any hunting
[l]Deut. 12.16; 1 Sam. 14.32-34
[m]Ezek. 24.7
14 [n]Gen. 9.4
15 [o]Ex. 22.31; Deut. 14.21
[2]a carcase
16 [p]Num. 19.20; Heb. 9.28

CHAPTER 18
2 [a]Ex. 6.7; Ezek. 20.5
3 [b]Ezek. 23.8
[c]Ex. 23.24
5 [d]Luke 10.28; Gal. 3.12
[e]Isa. 44.6; Mal. 3.6
6 [1]remainder of his flesh
8 [f]Gen. 49.4; 1 Cor. 5.1
9 [g]2 Sam. 13.12
15 [h]Gen. 38.26; Ezek. 22.11
16 [i]Matt. 14.3-4; Matt. 22.24
18 [2]Or, one wife to another, 1 Tim. 3.2
[j]Gen. 30.15;
19 [k]Ezek. 18.6
20 [l]Prov. 6.29;

18 And the LORD spake unto Mō'-
ses, saying,
2 Speak unto the children of Ĭs'ra-el,
and say unto them, [a]I am the LORD
your God.
3 After [b]the doings of the land of
Ē'ġypt, wherein ye dwelt, shall ye not
do: and after [c]the doings of the land of
Cā'năan, whither I bring you, shall ye
not do: neither shall ye walk in their
ordinances.
4 Ye shall do my judgments, and
keep mine ordinances, to walk therein:
I *am* the LORD your God.
5 Ye shall therefore keep my statutes, and my judgments: [d]which if a
man do, he shall live in them: [e]I *am* the
LORD.
6 ¶ None of you shall approach to
any that is [1]near of kin to him, to uncover *their* nakedness: I *am* the LORD.
7 The nakedness of thy father, or the
nakedness of thy mother, shalt thou
not uncover: she *is* thy mother; thou
shalt not uncover her nakedness.
8 The [f]nakedness of thy father's wife
shalt thou not uncover: it *is* thy father's
nakedness.
9 The [g]nakedness of thy sister, the
daughter of thy father, or daughter of
thy mother, *whether she be* born at
home, or born abroad, *even* their nakedness thou shalt not uncover.
10 The nakedness of thy son's daughter, or of thy daughter's daughter, *even*
their nakedness thou shalt not uncover:
for theirs *is* thine own nakedness.
11 The nakedness of thy father's
wife's daughter, begotten of thy father,
she *is* thy sister, thou shalt not uncover
her nakedness.
12 Thou shalt not uncover the nakedness of thy father's sister: she *is*
thy father's near kinswoman.
13 Thou shalt not uncover the nakedness of thy mother's sister: for she
is thy mother's near kinswoman.
14 Thou shalt not uncover the nakedness of thy father's brother, thou
shalt not approach to his wife: she *is*
thine aunt.
15 [h]Thou shalt not uncover the nakedness of thy daughter in law: she *is*
thy son's wife; thou shalt not uncover
her nakedness.
16 [i]Thou shalt not uncover the nakedness of thy brother's wife: it *is* thy
brother's nakedness.
17 Thou shalt not uncover the nakedness of a woman and her daughter,
neither shalt thou take her son's daughter, or her daughter's daughter, to uncover her nakedness; *for* they *are* her
near kinswomen: it *is* wickedness.
18 Neither shalt thou take [2]a wife to
her sister, [j]to vex *her*, to uncover her
nakedness, beside the other in her life
time.
19 [k]Also thou shalt not approach
unto a woman to uncover her nakedness, as long as she is put apart for her
uncleanness.
20 Moreover [l]thou shalt not lie carnally with thy neighbour's wife, to defile thyself with her.

21 And thou shalt not let any of thy
seed [m]pass through *the* [n]*fire* to Mō′-
lech, neither shalt thou [o]profane the
name of thy God: [p]I *am* the LORD.
22 [q]Thou shalt not lie with mankind, as with womankind: it *is* abomination.
23 Neither shalt thou lie with any
beast to defile thyself therewith: neither shall any woman stand before a
beast to lie down thereto: it *is* confusion.
24 [r]Defile not ye yourselves in any
of these things: [s]for in all these the
nations are defiled which I cast out before you:
25 And [t]the land is defiled: therefore I do [u]visit the iniquity thereof
upon it, and the land itself vomiteth
out her inhabitants.
26 Ye shall therefore keep my statutes and my judgments, and shall not
commit *any* of these abominations; *neither* any of your own nation, nor any
stranger that sojourneth among you:
27 (For all these abominations have
the men of the land done, which *were*
before you, and the land is defiled;)
28 That the land spue not you out
also, when ye defile it, as it spued out
the nations that *were* before you.
29 For whosoever shall commit any
of these abominations, even the souls
that commit *them* shall be cut off from
among their people.
30 Therefore shall ye keep mine ordinance, that *ye* commit not *any one*
of these abominable customs, which
were committed before you, and that
ye defile not yourselves therein: I *am*
the LORD your God.

19

And the LORD spake unto Mō′-
ses, saying,
2 Speak unto all the congregation of
the children of Is′ra-el, and say unto
them, [a]Ye shall be holy: for I the LORD
your God *am* holy.
3 ¶ Ye shall fear every man his
mother, and his father, and [b]keep my
sabbaths: I *am* the LORD your God.
4 ¶ [c]Turn ye not unto idols, nor make
to yourselves molten gods: I *am* the
LORD your God.
5 ¶ And if ye offer a sacrifice of
peace offerings unto the LORD, ye shall
offer it at your own will.
6 It shall be eaten the same day ye
offer it, and on the morrow: and if
ought remain until the third day, it
shall be burnt in the fire.
7 And if it be eaten at all on the third
day, it *is* abominable; it shall not be
accepted.
8 Therefore *every one* that eateth
it shall bear his iniquity, because he
hath profaned the hallowed thing of
the LORD: and that soul shall be cut off
from among his people.
9 ¶ And [d]when ye reap the harvest
of your land, thou shalt not wholly
reap the corners of thy field, neither
shalt thou gather the gleanings of thy
harvest.
10 And thou shalt not glean thy vineyard, neither shalt thou gather *every*
grape of thy vineyard; thou shalt leave
them [e]for the poor and stranger: I *am*
the LORD your God.
11 ¶ Ye shall not steal, neither deal
falsely, [f]neither lie one to another.
12 ¶ And ye shall not swear by my
name falsely, neither shalt thou profane the name of thy God: I *am* the
LORD.
13 ¶ Thou shalt not defraud thy
neighbour, neither rob *him*: [g]the wages
of him that is hired shall not abide with
thee all night until the morning.
14 ¶ Thou shalt not curse the deaf,
[h]nor put a stumblingblock before the
blind, but shalt [i]fear thy God: I *am* the
LORD.
15 ¶ [j]Ye shall do no unrighteousness
in judgment: thou shalt not respect the
person of the poor, nor honour the person of the mighty: *but* in righteousness
shalt thou judge thy neighbour.
16 ¶ Thou shalt not go up and down
as a talebearer among thy people:
neither shalt thou [k]stand against the
blood of thy neighbour: I *am* the LORD.
17 ¶ [l]Thou shalt not hate thy brother
in thine heart: [m]thou shalt in any wise
rebuke thy neighbour, [1]and not suffer
sin upon him.
18 ¶ [n]Thou shalt not avenge, nor
bear any grudge against the children
of thy people, [o]but thou shalt love thy
neighbour as thyself: I *am* the LORD.
19 ¶ Ye shall keep my statutes. Thou
shalt not let thy cattle gender with a
diverse kind: thou shalt not sow thy
field with mingled seed: neither shall a
garment mingled of linen and woollen
come upon thee.
20 ¶ And whosoever lieth carnally
with a woman, that *is* a bondmaid, [2]be-
trothed to an husband, and not at all
redeemed, nor freedom given her; [3]she
shall be scourged; they shall not be put
to death, because she was not free.
21 And he shall bring his trespass
offering unto the LORD, unto the door
of the tabernacle of the congregation,
even a ram for a trespass offering.
22 And the priest shall make an
atonement for him with the ram of the
trespass offering before the LORD for
his sin which he hath done: and the sin
which he hath done shall be forgiven
him.
23 ¶ And when ye shall come into
the land, and shall have planted all
manner of trees for food, then ye shall
count the fruit thereof as uncircumcised: three years shall it be as uncircumcised unto you: it shall not be
eaten of.
24 But in the fourth year all the fruit
thereof shall be [4]holy [p]to praise the
LORD *withal*.
25 And in the fifth year shall ye eat
of the fruit thereof, that it may yield
unto you the increase thereof: I *am* the
LORD your God.
26 ¶ Ye shall not eat *any thing* with
the blood: [q]neither shall ye use enchantment, nor observe times.

21 [m]2 Ki. 16.3; Jer. 19.5
[n]1 Ki. 11.7-33
[o]Ezek. 36.20; Mal. 1.12
[p]Isa. 42.8
22 [q]Rom. 1.27; 1 Tim. 1.10
24 [r]Matt. 15.18-19 1 Cor. 3.17
[s]Deut. 18.12
25 [t]Num. 35.34; Jer. 16.18
[u]Isa. 26.21; Jer. 9.9
CHAPTER 19
2 [a]Ex. 19.6; 1 Pet. 1.16
3 [b]Gen. 2.2; Heb. 4.9
4 [c]Ex. 20.3-5
9 [d]Ex. 23.11
10 [e]Ps. 41.1
11 [f]1 Ki. 13.18
13 [g]Deut. 24.14
14 [h]Rom. 14.13
[i]1 Pet. 2.17
15 [j]Ps. 82.2
16 [k]1 Ki. 21.13
17 [l]Gen. 27.41;
[m]Luke 17.3
[1]Or, that thou bear not sin for him, 1 Cor. 5.2
18 [n]Rom. 12.17
[o]Matt. 5.43-44
20 [2]reproached by, or, for man, or, abused by any
[3]there shall be a scourging, or, they shall be scourged
24 [4]holiness of praises, to the LORD
[p]Deut. 12.17-18
26 [q]2 Ki. 17.17

27 [r]Ye shall not round the corners of your heads, neither shalt thou mar the corners of thy beard.

28 Ye shall not [s]make any cuttings in your flesh for the dead, nor print any marks upon you: I *am* the LORD.

29 ¶ [t]Do not [5]prostitute thy daughter, to cause her to be a whore; lest the land fall to whoredom, and the land become full of wickedness.

30 ¶ [u]Ye shall keep my sabbaths, and [v]reverence my sanctuary: I *am* the LORD.

31 ¶ [w]Regard not them that have familiar spirits, neither seek after wizards, to be defiled by them: I *am* the LORD your God.

32 ¶ [x]Thou shalt rise up before the hoary head, and honour the face of the old man, and fear thy God: I *am* the LORD.

33 ¶ And [y]if a stranger sojourn with thee in your land, ye shall not [6]vex him.

34 *But* [z]the stranger that dwelleth with you shall be unto you as one born among you, and [a]thou shalt love him as thyself; for ye were strangers in the land of Ē'gypt: I *am* the LORD your God.

35 ¶ Ye shall do no unrighteousness in judgment, in meteyard, in weight, or in measure.

36 [b]Just balances, just [7]weights, a just ephah, and a just hin, shall ye have: I *am* the LORD your God, which brought you out of the land of Ē'gypt.

37 [c]Therefore shall ye observe all my statutes, and all my judgments, and do them: I *am* the LORD.

20 And the LORD spake unto Mō'ses, saying,

2 Again, thou shalt say to the children of Ĭs'ra-el, [a]Whosoever *he be* of the children of Ĭs'ra-el, or of the strangers that sojourn in Ĭs'ra-el, that giveth *any* of his seed unto Mō'lech; he shall surely be put to death: the people of the land shall stone him with stones.

3 And I will set my face against that man, and will cut him off from among his people; because he hath given of his seed unto Mō'lech, to [b]defile my sanctuary, and to profane my holy name.

4 And if the people of the land do any ways hide their eyes from the man, when he giveth of his seed unto Mō'lech, and kill him not:

5 Then I will set my face against that man, and [c]against his family, and will cut him off, and all that [d]go a whoring after him, to commit whoredom with Mō'lech, from among their people.

6 ¶ And [e]the soul that turneth after such as have familiar spirits, and after wizards, to go a whoring after them, I will even set my face against that soul, and will cut him off from among his people.

7 ¶ [f]Sanctify yourselves therefore, and be ye holy: for I *am* the LORD your God.

8 And ye shall keep my statutes, and do them: [g]I *am* the LORD which sanctify you.

9 ¶ For [h]every one that curseth his father or his mother shall be surely put to death: he hath cursed his father or his mother; [i]his blood *shall be* upon him.

10 ¶ And [j]the man that committeth adultery with *another* man's wife, *even he* that committeth adultery with his neighbour's wife, the adulterer and the adulteress shall surely be put to death.

11 And [k]the man that lieth with his father's wife hath uncovered his father's nakedness: both of them shall surely be put to death; their blood *shall be* upon them.

12 [l]And if a man lie with his daughter in law, both of them shall surely be put to death: they have wrought confusion; their blood *shall be* upon them.

13 If a man also lie with mankind, as he lieth with a woman, both of them have committed an abomination: they shall surely be put to death; their blood *shall be* upon them.

14 And [m]if a man take a wife and her mother, it *is* wickedness: they shall be burnt with fire, both he and they; that there be no wickedness among you.

15 And [n]if a man lie with a beast, he shall surely be put to death: and ye shall slay the beast.

16 And if a woman approach unto any beast, and lie down thereto, thou shalt kill the woman, and the beast: they shall surely be put to death; their blood *shall be* upon them.

17 And [o]if a man shall take his sister, his father's daughter, or his mother's daughter, and see her nakedness, and she see his nakedness; it *is* a wicked thing; and they shall be cut off in the sight of their people: he hath uncovered his sister's nakedness; he shall bear his iniquity.

18 And [p]if a man shall lie with a woman having her sickness, and shall uncover her nakedness; he hath [1]discovered her fountain, and she hath uncovered the fountain of her blood: and both of them shall be cut off from among their people.

19 And [q]thou shalt not uncover the nakedness of thy mother's sister, nor of thy father's sister: for he uncovereth his near kin: they shall bear their iniquity.

20 And if a man shall lie with his uncle's wife, he hath uncovered his uncle's nakedness: they shall bear their sin; they shall die childless.

21 And [r]if a man shall take his brother's wife, it *is* [2]an unclean thing: he hath uncovered his brother's nakedness; they shall be childless.

22 ¶ Ye shall therefore keep all my [s]statutes, and all my judgments, and do them: that the land, whither I bring you to dwell therein, spue you not out.

23 And ye shall not walk in the manners of the nation, which I cast out before you: for they committed all these things, and [t]therefore I abhorred them.

24 But [u]I have said unto you, Ye shall inherit their land, and I will give

27 [r]Jer. 9.26
28 [s]Deut. 14.1
29 [t]Deut. 23.17
[5]profane
30 [u]ch. 26.2
[v]Eccl. 5.1
31 [w]1 Sam. 28.7; Isa. 8.19
32 [x]1 Ki. 2.19; Prov. 20.29; Prov. 23.22; 1 Tim. 5.1
33 [y]Ex. 22.21
[6]Or, oppress
34 [z]Ex. 12.48
[a]Deut. 10.19
36 [b]Deut. 25.13-15; Prov. 20.10
[7]stones
37 [c]ch. 18.4-5; Deut. 5.1; Deut. 6.25

CHAPTER 20

2 [a]2 Ki. 17.17; 2 Ki. 23.10; 2 Chr. 33.6
3 [b]Ezek. 5.11; Num. 19.20
5 [c]Ex. 20.5
[d]ch. 17.7
6 [e]ch. 19.31; 2 Ki. 23.24
7 [f]Ex. 22.31; Matt. 5.48; Eph. 1.4; Col. 3.12; 1 Thess. 5.23; 1 Pet. 1.16
8 [g]Ex. 31.13
9 [h]Ex. 21.17; Deut. 27.16; Prov. 20.20; Matt. 15.4
[i]2 Sam. 1.16; 2 Sam. 11.2-3
10 [j]Deut. 22.22; Jer. 29.23; John 8.4-5; 1 Cor. 6.9; Heb. 13.4
11 [k]ch. 18.8; Deut. 27.23
12 [l]ch. 18.15; Deut. 23.17; Judg. 19.22; Rom. 1.27-32
14 [m]ch. 18.17
15 [n]Deut. 27.21
17 [o]Gen. 20.12
18 [p]ch. 15.24
[1]made naked
19 [q]ch. 18.12
21 [r]ch. 18.16
[2]a separation
22 [s]ch. 18.26; ch. 19.37
23 [t]Deut. 9.5
24 [u]Ex. 3.17; Ex. 6.8

it unto you to possess it, a land that
floweth with milk and honey: I *am* the
LORD your God, [v]which have separated you from *other* people.
25 [w]Ye shall therefore put difference between clean beasts and unclean, and between unclean fowls and
clean: and ye shall not make your
souls abominable by beast, or by fowl,
or by any manner of living thing that
[3]creepeth on the ground, which I have
separated from you as unclean.
26 And ye shall be holy unto me: for
[x]I the LORD *am* holy, and [y]have severed you from *other* people, that ye
should be mine.
27 ¶ A [z]man also or woman that
hath a familiar spirit, or that is a wizard, shall surely be put to death: they
shall stone them with stones: their
blood *shall be* upon them.
21 And the LORD said unto Mō'ses,
Speak unto the priests the sons
of Aâr'on, and say unto them, There
[a]shall none be defiled for the dead
among his people:
2 But for his kin, that is near unto
him, *that is*, for his mother, and for his
father, and for his son, and for his
daughter, and for his brother,
3 And for his sister a virgin, that is
nigh unto him, which hath had no husband; for her may he be defiled.
4 *But* [1]he shall not defile himself, *being* a chief man among his people, to
profane himself.
5 [b]They shall not make baldness
upon their head, neither shall they
shave off the corner of their beard, nor
make any cuttings in their flesh.
6 They shall be holy unto their God,
and [c]not profane the name of their
God: for the offerings of the LORD
made by fire, *and* the [d]bread of their
God, they do offer: therefore they shall
be holy.
7 [e]They shall not take a wife *that is*
a whore, or profane; neither shall they
take a woman [f]put away from her husband: for he *is* holy unto his God.
8 Thou shalt sanctify him therefore;
for he offereth the bread of thy God:
he shall be holy unto thee: [g]for I the
LORD, which sanctify you, *am* holy.
9 ¶ And [h]the daughter of any priest,
if she profane herself by playing the
whore, she profaneth her father: she
shall be burnt with fire.
10 And [i]*he that is* the high priest
among his brethren, upon whose head
the anointing oil was poured, and [j]that
is consecrated to put on the garments,
[k]shall not uncover his head, nor rend
his clothes;
11 Neither shall he [l]go in to any
dead body, nor defile himself for his
father, or for his mother;
12 [m]Neither shall he go out of the
sanctuary, nor profane the sanctuary
of his God; for [n]the crown of the anointing oil of his God *is* upon him: I *am* the
LORD.
13 And [o]he shall take a wife in her
virginity.

[v]Ex. 19.5; 1 Pet. 2.9
25 [w]ch. 11.47; Deut. 14.4
[3]Or, moveth
26 [x]ch. 19.2; Rev. 4.8
[y]Tit. 2.14
27 [z]Ex. 22.18; 1 Sam. 28.7
CHAPTER 21
1 [a]ch. 5.2;
4 [1]Or, being an husband among his people, he shall not defile himself for his wife, etc
5 [b]ch. 19.27-28
6 [c]Ex. 20.7;
[d]ch. 3.11
7 [e]Ezek. 44.22
[f]Deut. 24.1-2
8 [g]ch. 20.7-8
9 [h]Gen. 38.24
10 [i]Ex. 29.29;
[j]Ex. 28.2
[k]ch. 10.6
11 [l]Num. 19.14
12 [m]ch. 10.7;
[n]Ex. 28.36
13 [o]Ezek. 44.22
15 [p]Rom. 12.1
17 [q]Num. 16.5;
[2]Or, food
18 [r]ch. 22.22
20 [3]Or, too slender
[s]Deut. 23.1
22 [t]ch. 2.3-10;
[u]ch. 22.10
CHAPTER 22
2 [a]Num. 6.3
[b]Ex. 13.12
3 [c]ch. 7.20
4 [d]ch. 15.2
[1]running of the reins
[e]ch. 15.13
[f]Num. 19.11-22
5 [g]ch. 11.24
[h]ch. 15.7-19
6 [i]Heb. 10.22

14 A widow, or a divorced woman,
or profane, *or* an harlot, these shall he
not take: but he shall take a virgin of
his own people to wife.
15 Neither shall he profane his seed
among his people: for [p]I the LORD do
sanctify him.
16 ¶ And the LORD spake unto Mō'-
ses, saying,
17 Speak unto Aâr'on, saying, Whosoever *he be* of thy seed in their generations that hath *any* blemish, let him not
[q]approach to offer the [2]bread of his
God.
18 For whatsoever man *he be* that
hath a blemish, he shall not approach:
a blind man, or a lame, or he that hath
a flat nose, or any thing [r]superfluous,
19 Or a man that is brokenfooted, or
brokenhanded,
20 Or crookbackt, or a [3]dwarf, or
that hath a blemish in his eye, or be
scurvy, or scabbed, or [s]hath his stones
broken;
21 No man that hath a blemish of the
seed of Aâr'on the priest shall come
nigh to offer the offerings of the LORD
made by fire: he hath a blemish; he
shall not come nigh to offer the bread
of his God.
22 He shall eat the bread of his God,
both of the [t]most holy, and of the
[u]holy.
23 Only he shall not go in unto the
vail, nor come nigh unto the altar, because he hath a blemish; that he profane not my sanctuaries: for I the LORD
do sanctify them.
24 And Mō'ses told *it* unto Aâr'on,
and to his sons, and unto all the children of Is'ra-el.
22 And the LORD spake unto Mō'-
ses, saying,
2 Speak unto Aâr'on and to his sons,
that they [a]separate themselves from
the holy things of the children of Is'ra-
el, and that they profane not my holy
name *in those things* which they [b]hal-
low unto me: I *am* the LORD.
3 Say unto them, Whosoever *he be*
of all your seed among your generations, that goeth unto the holy things,
which the children of Is'ra-el hallow
unto the LORD, having his [c]unclean-
ness upon him, that soul shall be cut
off from my presence: I *am* the LORD.
4 What man soever of the seed of
Aâr'on *is* a leper, or hath [d]a [1]run-
ning issue; he shall not eat of the holy
things, [e]until he be clean. And [f]whoso
toucheth any thing *that is* unclean *by*
the dead, or a man whose seed goeth
from him;
5 Or [g]whosoever toucheth any creeping thing, whereby he may be made unclean, or [h]a man of whom he may take
uncleanness, whatsoever uncleanness
he hath;
6 The soul which hath touched any
such shall be unclean until even, and
shall not eat of the holy things, unless
he [i]wash his flesh with water.
7 And when the sun is down, he
shall be clean, and shall afterward eat

of the holy things; because [j]it *is* his food.

8 [k]That which dieth of itself, or is torn *with beasts*, he shall not eat to defile himself therewith: I *am* the LORD.

9 They shall therefore keep mine ordinance, [l]lest they bear sin for it, and die therefore, if they profane it: I the LORD do sanctify them.

10 [m]There shall no stranger eat *of* the holy thing: a sojourner of the priest, or an hired servant, shall not eat *of* the holy thing.

11 But if the priest buy *any* soul [2]with his money, he shall eat of it, and he that is born in his house: they shall eat of his meat.

12 If the priest's daughter also be *married* unto [3]a stranger, she may not eat of an offering of the holy things.

13 But if the priest's daughter be a widow, or divorced, and have no child, and [n]is returned unto her father's house, [o]as in her youth, she shall eat of her father's meat: but there shall no stranger eat thereof.

14 ¶ And [p]if a man eat *of* the holy thing unwittingly, then he shall put the fifth *part* thereof unto it, and shall give *it* unto the priest with the holy thing.

15 And [q]they shall not profane the holy things of the children of Ĭs'ra-el, which they offer unto the LORD;

16 Or [4]suffer them to bear the iniquity of trespass, when they eat their holy things: for I the LORD do sanctify them.

17 ¶ And the LORD spake unto Mō'ses, saying,

18 Speak unto Aâr'on, and to his sons, and unto all the children of Ĭs'ra-el, and say unto them, [r]Whatsoever *he be* of the house of Ĭs'ra-el, or of the strangers in Ĭs'ra-el, that will offer his oblation for all his vows, and for all his freewill offerings, which they will offer unto the LORD for a burnt offering;

19 *Ye shall offer* at your own will a male without blemish, of the beeves, of the sheep, or of the goats.

20 *But* [s]whatsoever hath a blemish, *that* shall ye not offer: for it shall not be acceptable for you.

21 And whosoever offereth a sacrifice of peace offerings unto the LORD [t]to accomplish *his* vow, or a freewill offering in beeves or [5]sheep, it shall be perfect to be accepted; there shall be no blemish therein.

22 Blind, or broken, or maimed, or having a wen, or scurvy, or scabbed, ye shall not offer these unto the LORD, nor make an offering by fire of them upon the altar unto the LORD.

23 Either a bullock or a [6]lamb that hath any thing [u]superfluous or lacking in his parts, that mayest thou offer *for* a freewill offering; but for a vow it shall not be accepted.

24 Ye shall not offer unto the LORD that which is bruised, or crushed, or broken, or cut; neither shall ye make *any offering thereof* in your land.

25 Neither [v]from a stranger's hand shall ye offer the bread of your God of any of these; because their [w]corruption *is* in them, *and* blemishes *be* in them: they shall not be accepted for you.

26 ¶ And the LORD spake unto Mō'ses, saying,

27 [x]When a bullock, or a sheep, or a goat, is brought forth, then it shall be seven days under the dam; and from the eighth day and thenceforth it shall be accepted for an offering made by fire unto the LORD.

28 And *whether it be* cow or [7]ewe, ye shall not kill it [y]and her young both in one day.

29 And when ye will [z]offer a sacrifice of thanksgiving unto the LORD, offer *it* at your own will.

30 On the same day it shall be eaten up; ye shall leave none of it until the morrow: I *am* the LORD.

31 [a]Therefore shall ye keep my commandments, and do them: I *am* the LORD.

32 Neither shall ye profane my holy name; but [b]I will be hallowed among the children of Ĭs'ra-el: I *am* the LORD which hallow you,

33 [c]That brought you out of the land of Ē'gypt, to be your God: I *am* the LORD.

23 And the LORD spake unto Mō'ses, saying,

2 Speak unto the children of Ĭs'ra-el, and say unto them, *Concerning* the feasts of the LORD, which ye shall [a]proclaim *to be* holy convocations, *even* these *are* my feasts.

3 [b]Six days shall work be done: but the seventh day *is* the sabbath of rest, an holy convocation; ye shall do no work *therein*: it *is* [c]the sabbath of the LORD in all your dwellings.

4 ¶ [d]These *are* the feasts of the LORD, *even* holy convocations, which ye shall proclaim in their seasons.

5 [e]In the fourteenth *day* of the first month at even *is* the LORD'S passover.

6 And on the fifteenth day of the same month *is* the feast of unleavened bread unto the LORD: seven days ye must eat unleavened bread.

7 [f]In the first day ye shall have an holy convocation: ye shall do no servile work therein.

8 But ye shall offer an offering made by fire unto the LORD seven days: in the seventh day *is* an holy convocation: ye shall do no servile work *therein*.

9 ¶ And the LORD spake unto Mō'ses, saying,

10 Speak unto the children of Ĭs'ra-el, and say unto them, [g]When ye be come into the land which I give unto you, and shall reap the harvest thereof, then ye shall bring a [1]sheaf of [h]the firstfruits of your harvest unto the priest:

11 And he shall [i]wave the sheaf before the LORD, to be accepted for you: on the morrow after the sabbath the priest shall wave it.

12 And ye shall offer that day when ye wave the sheaf an he lamb without blemish of the first year for a burnt offering unto the LORD.

7 [j]Num. 18.11
8 [k]Ex. 22.31; ch. 17.15
9 [l]Ex. 28.43; Num. 18.22
10 [m]One not a priest, Ex. 29.33; 1 Sam. 21.6
11 [2]with the purchase of his money
12 [3]a man a stranger
13 [n]Gen. 38.11
[o]Num. 18.11
14 [p]ch. 5.15-16
15 [q]Num. 18.32
16 [4]Or, lade themselves with the iniquity of trespass in their eating
18 [r]Num. 15.14
20 [s]Deut. 15.21; Heb. 9.14
21 [t]Num. 15.3-8; Ps. 65.1
[5]Or, goats
23 [6]Or, kid
[u]ch. 21.18
25 [v]Num. 15.15
[w]Mal. 1.14
27 [x]Ex. 22.30
28 [7]Or, she goat
[y]Deut. 22.6
29 [z]Ps. 107.22; Amos 4.5
31 [a]ch. 19.37; Deut. 4.40
32 [b]Isa. 6.3; Luke 11.2
33 [c]Ex. 6.7
CHAPTER 23
2 [a]Ex. 32.5; Ps. 81.3
3 [b]Ex. 20.9; Luke 13.14
[c]Neh. 13.22; Isa. 58.13
4 [d]Ex. 23.12
5 [e]Ex. 12.6; Deut. 16.1
7 [f]Ex. 12.16; Num. 28.18
10 [g]Ex. 23.16;
[1]omer, or, handful
[h]Prov. 3.9
11 [i]Ex. 29.24

13 And the meat offering thereof
shall be two tenth deals of fine flour
mingled with oil, an offering made by
fire unto the LORD *for* a sweet savour:
and the drink offering thereof *shall be*
of wine, the fourth *part* of an hin.
14 And ye shall eat neither bread,
nor parched corn, nor green ears, until
the selfsame day that ye have brought
an offering unto your God: *it shall be* a
statute for ever throughout your generations in all your dwellings.
15 ¶ And [j]ye shall count unto you
from the morrow after the sabbath,
from the day that ye brought the sheaf
of the wave offering; seven sabbaths
shall be complete:
16 Even unto the morrow after the
seventh sabbath shall ye number [k]fifty
days; and ye shall offer a new meat
offering unto the LORD.
17 Ye shall bring out of your habitations two wave loaves of two tenth
deals: they shall be of fine flour; they
shall be baken with leaven; *they are*
[l]the firstfruits unto the LORD.
18 And ye shall offer with the bread
seven lambs without blemish of the
first year, and one young bullock, and
two rams: they shall be *for* a burnt offering unto the LORD, with their meat
offering, and their drink offerings, *even*
an offering made by fire, of sweet savour unto the LORD.
19 Then ye shall sacrifice [m]one kid
of the goats for a sin offering, and two
lambs of the first year for a sacrifice of
peace offerings.
20 And the priest shall wave them
with the bread of the firstfruits *for* a
wave offering before the LORD, with
the two lambs: [n]they shall be [2]holy to
the LORD for the priest.
21 And ye shall proclaim on the selfsame day, *that* it may be an holy convocation unto you: ye shall do no servile work *therein: it shall be* a statute
for ever in all your dwellings throughout your generations.
22 ¶ And [o]when ye reap the harvest
of your land, thou shalt not make clean
riddance of the corners of thy field
when thou reapest, [p]neither shalt thou
gather any gleaning of thy harvest:
thou shalt leave them unto the poor,
and to the stranger: I *am* the LORD
your God.
23 ¶ And the LORD spake unto Mō′-
ses, saying,
24 Speak unto the children of Ĭs′ra-
el, saying, In the [q]seventh month, in
the first *day* of the month, shall ye
have a sabbath, a [r]memorial of blowing of trumpets, an holy convocation.
25 Ye shall do no servile work
therein: but ye shall offer an offering
made by fire unto the LORD.
26 ¶ And the LORD spake unto Mō′-
ses, saying,
27 Also on the tenth *day* of this seventh month [s]*there shall be* a day of
atonement: it shall be an holy convocation unto you; and ye shall afflict your
souls, and offer an offering made by
fire unto the LORD.
28 And ye shall do no work in that
same day: for it *is* a day of atonement,
to make an atonement for you before
the LORD your God.
29 For whatsoever soul *it be* that
shall not be afflicted in that same day,
[t]he shall be cut off from among his
people.
30 And whatsoever soul *it be* that
doeth any work in that same day, the
same soul will I destroy from among
his people.
31 Ye shall do no manner of work: *it*
shall be a statute for ever throughout
your generations in all your dwellings.
32 It *shall be* unto you a sabbath of
rest, and ye shall afflict your souls: in
the ninth *day* of the month at even,
from even unto even, shall ye [3]cele-
brate your sabbath.
33 ¶ And the LORD spake unto Mō′-
ses, saying,
34 Speak unto the children of Ĭs′ra-
el, saying, [u]The fifteenth day of this
seventh month *shall be* the feast of tabernacles *for* seven days unto the LORD.
35 On the first day *shall be* an holy
convocation: ye shall do no servile
work *therein.*
36 Seven days ye shall offer an offering made by fire unto the LORD: [v]on
the eighth day shall be an holy convocation unto you; and ye shall offer an
offering made by fire unto the LORD: it
is a [4]solemn assembly; *and* ye shall do
no servile work *therein.*
37 These *are* the feasts of the LORD,
which ye shall proclaim *to be* holy convocations, to offer an offering made by
fire unto the LORD, a burnt offering,
and a meat offering, a sacrifice, and
drink offerings, every thing upon his
day:
38 Beside the sabbaths of the LORD,
and beside your gifts, and beside all
your vows, and beside all your freewill
offerings, which ye give unto the LORD.
39 Also in the fifteenth day of the
seventh month, when ye have [w]gath-
ered in the fruit of the land, ye shall
keep a feast unto the LORD seven days:
on the first day *shall be* a sabbath, and
on the eighth day *shall be* a sabbath.
40 And [x]ye shall take you on the
first day the [5]boughs of goodly trees,
branches of palm trees, and the boughs
of thick trees, and willows of the brook;
[y]and ye shall rejoice before the LORD
your God seven days.
41 And ye shall keep it a feast unto
the LORD seven days in the year. *It*
shall be a statute for ever in your generations: ye shall celebrate it in the seventh month.
42 Ye shall dwell in booths seven
days; all that are Ĭs′ra-el-ītes born shall
dwell in booths:
43 [z]That your generations may know
that I made the children of Ĭs′ra-el to
dwell in booths, when I brought them
out of the land of Ē′gypt: I *am* the LORD
your God.
44 And Mō′ses declared unto the
children of Ĭs′ra-el the feasts of the
LORD.

15 [j]Ex. 34.22; ch. 25.8; Deut. 16.9
16 [k]Acts 2.1
17 [l]Ex. 23.16; Ex. 22.29; Num. 28.26; Deut. 26.1-2
19 [m]ch. 4.23-28; Num. 28.30
20 [n]ch. 7.31-34; ch. 8.29; Num. 18.12; Deut. 18.4 [2]most holy
22 [o]Ex. 23.11; Deut. 15.1-18; Job 20.19; Ps. 112.9; Prov. 14.31; Prov. 29.7; Eccl. 5.8; Isa. 58.7-8; Jas. 2
[p]ch. 19.9-10; Deut. 24.19; Ruth 2.15-16
24 [q]Num. 29.1
[r]ch. 25.9; Num. 10.10
27 [s]Ex. 30.10; ch. 16.30; Num. 29.7; Isa. 58.3-5; Dan. 10.3-12
29 [t]Gen. 17.14; ch. 13.46; Num. 5.2; 2 Chr. 26.21; 2 Thess. 3.6
32 [3]rest
34 [u]Ex. 23.16; Num. 29.12; Deut. 16.13; Neh. 8.14; Zech. 14.16; John 7.2; Heb. 11.9
36 [v]Num. 29.35; 2 Chr. 7.8-9; Neh. 8.18; John 7.37 [4]day of restraint
39 [w]Ex. 23.16; Deut. 16.13; Matt. 21.8
40 [x]Neh. 8.15 [5]fruit
[y]Deut. 16.14; Isa. 35.10; Isa. 66.10; Rom. 5.11
43 [z]Deut. 31.13; Ps. 78.5-6

24

And the LORD spake unto Mō'ses, saying,

2 Command [a]the children of Ĭs'ra-el, that they bring unto thee pure oil olive beaten for the light, [1]to cause the lamps to burn continually.

3 Without the vail of the testimony, in the tabernacle of the congregation, shall Aâr'on order it from the evening unto the morning before the LORD continually: *it shall be* a statute for ever in your generations.

4 He shall order the lamps upon the [b]pure candlestick before the LORD continually.

5 ¶ And thou shalt take fine flour, and bake twelve [c]cakes thereof: two tenth deals shall be in one cake.

6 And thou shalt set them in two rows, six on a row, [d]upon the pure table before the LORD.

7 And thou shalt put pure frankincense upon *each* row, that it may be on the bread for a memorial, *even* an offering made by fire unto the LORD.

8 [e]Every sabbath he shall set it in order before the LORD continually, *being taken* from the children of Ĭs'ra-el by an everlasting covenant.

9 And [f]it shall be Aâr'on's and his sons'; and [g]they shall eat it in the holy place: for it *is* most holy unto him of the offerings of the LORD made by fire by a perpetual statute.

10 ¶ And the son of an Ĭs'ra-el-īt-ĭsh woman, whose father *was* an E-ġy̆p'tian, went out among the children of Ĭs'ra-el: and this son of the Ĭs'ra-el-īt-ĭsh *woman* and a man of Ĭs'ra-el strove together in the camp;

11 And the Ĭs'ra-el-īt-ĭsh woman's son blasphemed the name *of the LORD*, and [h]cursed. And they [i]brought him unto Mō'ses: (and his mother's name *was* Shĕl'o-mĭth, the daughter of Dĭb'rī, of the tribe of Dăn:)

12 And they [j]put him in ward, [2]that the mind of the LORD might be shewed them.

13 And the LORD spake unto Mō'ses, saying,

14 Bring forth him that hath cursed without the camp; and let all that heard *him* [k]lay their hands upon his head, and let all the congregation stone him.

15 And thou shalt speak unto the children of Ĭs'ra-el, saying, Whosoever curseth his God [l]shall bear his sin.

16 And he that [m]blasphemeth the name of the LORD, he shall surely be put to death, *and* all the congregation shall certainly stone him: as well the stranger, as he that is born in the land, when he blasphemeth the name *of the LORD*, shall be put to death.

17 ¶ And [n]he that [3]killeth any man shall surely be put to death.

18 And he that killeth a beast shall make it good; [4]beast for beast.

19 And if a man cause a blemish in his neighbour; as [o]he hath done, so shall it be done to him;

20 Breach for breach, eye for eye, tooth for tooth: as he hath caused a blemish in a man, so shall it be done to him *again*.

21 And [p]he that killeth a beast, he shall restore it: and he that killeth a man, he shall be put to death.

22 Ye shall have [q]one manner of law, as well for the stranger, as for one of your own country: for I *am* the LORD your God.

23 ¶ And Mō'ses spake to the children of Ĭs'ra-el, that they should bring forth him that had cursed out of the camp, [r]and stone him with stones. And the children of Ĭs'ra-el did as the LORD commanded Mō'ses.

25

And the LORD spake unto Mō'ses in mount Sī'nāi, saying,

2 Speak unto the children of Ĭs'ra-el, and say unto them, When ye come into the land which I give you, then shall the land [1]keep a [a]sabbath unto the LORD.

3 Six years thou shalt sow thy field, and six years thou shalt prune thy vineyard, and gather in the fruit thereof;

4 But in the seventh year shall be a sabbath of rest unto the land, a sabbath for the LORD: thou shalt neither sow thy field, nor prune thy vineyard.

5 [b]That which groweth of its own accord of thy harvest thou shalt not reap, neither gather the grapes [2]of thy vine undressed: *for* it is a year of rest unto the land.

6 And the sabbath of the land shall be meat for you; for thee, and for thy servant, and for thy maid, and for thy hired servant, and for thy stranger that sojourneth with thee,

7 And for thy cattle, and for the beast that *are* in thy land, shall all the increase thereof be meat.

8 ¶ And thou shalt number seven sabbaths of years unto thee, seven times seven years; and the space of the seven sabbaths of years shall be unto thee forty and nine years.

9 Then shalt thou cause the trumpet [3]of the jubile to sound on the tenth *day* of the seventh month, in [c]the day of atonement shall ye make the trumpet sound throughout all your land.

10 And ye shall hallow the fiftieth year, and [d]proclaim liberty throughout *all* the land unto all the inhabitants thereof: it shall be a jubile unto you; and [e]ye shall return every man unto his possession, and ye shall return every man unto his family.

11 A jubile shall that fiftieth year be unto you: ye shall not sow, neither reap that which groweth of itself in it, nor gather *the grapes* in it of thy vine undressed.

12 For it *is* the jubile; it shall be holy unto you: ye shall eat the increase thereof out of the field.

13 [f]In the year of this jubile ye shall return every man unto his possession.

14 And if thou sell ought unto thy neighbour, or buyest *ought* of thy neighbour's hand, [g]ye shall not oppress one another:

15 According to the number of years after the jubile thou shalt buy of thy

CHAPTER 24
2 [a]Ex. 27.20; Ex. 39.37; Num. 8.2-4
[1]to cause to ascend
4 [b]Ex. 31.8
5 [c]Ex. 40.23
6 [d]1 Ki. 7.48; 2 Chr. 4.19; Heb. 9.2
8 [e]Num. 4.7; 1 Chr. 9.32; 2 Chr. 2.4
9 [f]1 Sam. 21.6; Matt. 12.4; Mark 2.26; Luke 6.4
[g]Ex. 29.33; ch. 8.31
11 [h]Job 1.5; Isa. 8.21
[i]Ex. 18.22
12 [j]Num. 15.34
[2]to expound unto them according to the mouth of the LORD
14 [k]Deut. 17.7
15 [l]ch. 5.1; Num. 9.13
16 [m]1 Ki. 21.10; Ps. 74.10-18; Matt. 12.31; Mark 3.28
17 [n]Gen. 9.6; Rev. 13.10
[3]smiteth the life of a man
18 [4]life for life
19 [o]Deut. 19.21; Matt. 5.38
21 [p]Ex. 21.33
22 [q]Ex. 12.49; Num. 15.16
23 [r]Deut. 13.6-10

CHAPTER 25
2 [1]rest
[a]ch. 26.34-35; 2 Chr. 36.21
5 [b]2 Ki. 19.29; Isa. 37.30
[2]of thy separation
9 [3]loud of sound
[c]ch. 23.24; ch. 16.20-30
10 [d]Ex. 20.2; Gal. 5.1
[e]Num. 36.4
13 [f]ch. 28.24; Num. 36.4
14 [g]ch. 19.13; Mic. 2.2

neighbour, *and* according unto the number of years of the fruits he shall sell unto thee:

16 According to the multitude of years thou shalt increase the price thereof, and according to the fewness of years thou shalt diminish the price of it: for *according* to the number *of the years* of the fruits doth he sell unto thee.

17 [h]Ye shall not therefore oppress one another; but thou shalt fear thy God: for I *am* the LORD your God.

18 ¶ Wherefore ye shall do my statutes, and keep my judgments, and do them; [i]and ye shall dwell in the land in safety.

19 And the land shall yield her fruit, and ye shall eat your fill, and dwell therein in safety.

20 And if ye shall say, [j]What shall we eat the seventh year? behold, we shall not sow, nor gather in our increase:

21 Then I will [k]command my blessing upon you in the sixth year, and it shall bring forth fruit for three years.

22 And [l]ye shall sow the eighth year, and eat *yet* of [m]old fruit until the ninth year; until her fruits come in ye shall eat *of* the old *store.*

23 ¶ The land shall not be sold [4]for ever: for [n]the land *is* mine; for ye *are* [o]strangers and sojourners with me.

24 And in all the land of your possession ye shall grant a redemption for the land.

25 ¶ [p]If thy brother be waxen poor, and hath sold away *some* of his possession, and if [q]any of his kin come to redeem it, then shall he redeem that which his brother sold.

26 And if the man have none to redeem it, and [5]himself be able to redeem it;

27 Then let him count the years of the sale thereof, and restore the overplus unto the man to whom he sold it; that he may return unto his possession.

28 But if he be not able to restore *it* to him, then that which is sold shall remain in the hand of him that hath bought it until the year of jubile: and in the jubile it shall go out, and he shall return unto his possession.

29 And if a man sell a dwelling house in a walled city, then he may redeem it within a whole year after it is sold; *within* a full year may he redeem it.

30 And if it be not redeemed within the space of a full year, then the house that *is* in the walled city shall be established for ever to him that bought it throughout his generations: it shall not go out in the jubile.

31 But the houses of the villages which have no wall round about them shall be counted as the fields of the country: [6]they may be redeemed, and they shall go out in the jubile.

32 Notwithstanding [r]the cities of the Lē′vītes, *and* the houses of the cities of their possession, may the Lē′vītes redeem at any time.

17 [h]Prov. 14.31; Jer. 7.6; 1 Thess. 4.6
18 [i]ch. 26.5; Deut. 12.10; Ps. 4.8; Prov. 1.33
20 [j]Matt. 6.25; Num. 11.4-13; 2 Ki. 6.15
21 [k]Deut. 28.8; Ps. 33.12; Ps. 119.2; Prov. 8.32; 1 Tim. 4.8
22 [l]2 Ki. 19.29
[m]Josh. 5.11
23 [4]for cutting off, or, to be quite cut off
[n]Deut. 32.43; 2 Chr. 7.20; Isa. 8.8
[o]Ps. 119.19; 1 Pet. 2.11
25 [p]Ruth 2.20
[q]Ruth 3.2-13
26 [5]his hand hath attained and found sufficiency
31 [6]redemption belongeth unto it
32 [r]Josh. 21.2
33 [7]Or, one of the Levites redeem them
34 [s]Acts 4.36
35 [8]his hand faileth
[9]strengthen
[t]Deut. 15.7; Rom. 12.10
36 [u]Ex. 22.25; Prov. 28.8
39 [v]Ex. 21.2; Jer. 34.14
[10]serve thyself with him with the service, etc
42 [w]Rom. 6.22; 1 Cor. 7.23
[11]with the sale of a bondman
43 [x]Ex. 1.13-14; Col. 4.1
[y]Ex. 1.17-21; Mal. 3.5
46 [12]ye shall serve yourselves with them
47 [13]his hand obtain, etc

33 And if [7]a man purchase of the Lē′vītes, then the house that was sold, and the city of his possession, shall go out in *the year of* jubile: for the houses of the cities of the Lē′vītes *are* their possession among the children of Is′ra-el.

34 But the [s]field of the suburbs of their cities may not be sold; for it *is* their perpetual possession.

35 ¶ And if thy brother be waxen poor, and [8]fallen in decay with thee; then thou shalt [9][t]relieve him: *yea, though he be* a stranger, or a sojourner; that he may live with thee.

36 [u]Take thou no usury of him, or increase: but fear thy God; that thy brother may live with thee.

37 Thou shalt not give him thy money upon usury, nor lend him thy victuals for increase.

38 I *am* the LORD your God, which brought you forth out of the land of Ē′ġypt, to give you the land of Cā′năan, *and* to be your God.

39 ¶ And [v]if thy brother *that dwelleth* by thee be waxen poor, and be sold unto thee; thou shalt not [10]compel him to serve as a bondservant:

40 *But* as an hired servant, *and* as a sojourner, he shall be with thee, *and* shall serve thee unto the year of jubile:

41 And *then* shall he depart from thee, *both* he and his children with him, and shall return unto his own family, and unto the possession of his fathers shall he return.

42 For they *are* [w]my servants, which I brought forth out of the land of Ē′ġypt: they shall not be sold [11]as bondmen.

43 [x]Thou shalt not rule over him with rigour; but [y]shalt fear thy God.

44 Both thy bondmen, and thy bondmaids, which thou shalt have, *shall be* of the heathen that are round about you; of them shall ye buy bondmen and bondmaids.

45 Moreover of the children of the strangers that do sojourn among you, of them shall ye buy, and of their families that *are* with you, which they begat in your land: and they shall be your possession.

46 And ye shall take them as an inheritance for your children after you, to inherit *them for* a possession; they [12]shall be your bondmen for ever: but over your brethren the children of Is′ra-el ye shall not rule one over another with rigour.

47 ¶ And if a sojourner or stranger wax [13]rich by thee, and thy brother *that dwelleth* by him wax poor, and sell himself unto the stranger *or* sojourner by thee, or to the stock of the stranger's family:

48 After that he is sold he may be redeemed again; one of his brethren may redeem him:

49 Either his uncle, or his uncle's son, may redeem him, or *any* that is nigh of kin unto him of his family may redeem him; or if he be able, he may redeem himself.

50 And he shall reckon with him
that bought him from the year that he
was sold to him unto the year of jubile:
and the price of his sale shall be according unto the number of years, according to the time of an hired servant shall
it be with him.
51 If *there be* yet many years *behind,* according unto them he shall
give again the price of his redemption
out of the money that he was bought
for.
52 And if there remain but few years
unto the year of jubile, then he shall
count with him, *and* according unto his
years shall he give him again the price
of his redemption.
53 *And* as a yearly hired servant
shall he be with him: *and the other*
shall not rule with rigour over him in
thy sight.
54 And if he be not redeemed [14]in
these *years,* then he shall go out in the
year of jubile, *both* he, and his children with him.
55 For unto me the children of Ĭs'ra-
el *are* servants; they *are* my servants
whom I brought forth out of the land of
Ē'gypt: I *am* the LORD your God.

26 Ye shall make you [a]no idols nor
graven image, neither rear you
up a [1]standing image, neither shall ye
set up *any* [2]image of stone in your land,
to bow down unto it: for I *am* the LORD
your God.
2 ¶ Ye shall keep my sabbaths, and
reverence my sanctuary: I *am* the LORD.
b3 ¶ If ye walk in my statutes, and
keep my commandments, and do them;
4 [b]Then I will give you rain in due
season, and the land shall yield her increase, and the trees of the field shall
yield their fruit.
5 And your threshing shall reach
unto the vintage, and the vintage shall
reach unto the sowing time: and [c]ye
shall eat your bread to the full, and
[d]dwell in your land safely.
6 And [e]I will give peace in the land,
and ye [f]shall lie down, and none shall
make *you* afraid: and I will [3]rid [g]evil
beasts out of the land, neither shall
[h]the sword go through your land.
7 And ye shall chase your enemies,
and they shall fall before you by the
sword.
8 And five of you shall chase an hundred, and an hundred of you shall put
ten thousand to flight: and your enemies shall fall before you by the sword.
9 For I will [i]have respect unto you,
and [j]make you fruitful, and multiply
you, and establish my covenant with
you.
10 And ye shall eat old store, and
bring forth the old because of the new.
11 And [k]I will set my tabernacle
among you: and my soul shall not [l]ab-
hor you.
12 And [m]I will walk among you, and
[n]will be your God, and ye shall be my
people.
13 I *am* the LORD your God, which
brought you forth out of the land of
Ē'gypt, that ye should not be their

54 [14]Or, by these means
CHAPTER 26
1 [a]Ex. 20.4-5; Ps. 97.7
[1]Or, pillar
[2]a stone of picture, or, figured stone
4 [b]Deut. 28.12; Isa. 30.23
5 [c]Deut. 11.15; Joel 2.19-26
[d]Job 11.18
6 [e]1 Chr. 22.9; Isa. 45.7
[f]Ps. 3.5; Jer. 30.10
[3]cause to cease
[g]2 Ki. 17.25
[h]Josh. 23.10
9 [i]Ex. 2.25; 2 Ki. 13.23
[j]Gen. 17.6-7
11 [k]Ezek. 37.26
[l]Deut. 32.19
12 [m]2 Cor. 6.16; Eph. 2.21
[n]Ezek. 11.20
13 [o]Ezek. 34.27
14 [p]Deut. 28.15
15 [q]2 Ki. 17.15
16 [4]upon you
[r]Deut. 28.22
[s]1 Sam. 2.33
[t]Job 31.8
17 [u]Judg. 2.14
[v]Ps. 106.41
[w]Ps. 53.5
18 [x]1 Sam. 2.5
19 [y]1 Sam. 4.10
20 [z]Ps. 127.1
[a]Deut. 28.18; Hag. 1.10
21 [5]Or, at all adventures with me
22 [b]Deut. 32.24; 2 Ki. 17.25
[c]Judg. 5.6; 2 Chr. 15.5
23 [d]Jer. 5.3
24 [e]2 Sam. 22.27
25 [f]Ezek. 6.3
[g]Deut. 28.21
26 [h]Isa. 3.1
[i]Mic. 6.14
28 [j]Isa. 59.18
29 [k]2 Ki. 6.29
30 [l]2 Chr. 34.3
[m]2 Ki. 23.20

bondmen; [o]and I have broken the
bands of your yoke, and made you go
upright.
14 ¶ But [p]if ye will not hearken unto
me, and will not do all these commandments;
15 And if ye shall [q]despise my statutes, or if your soul abhor my judgments, so that ye will not do all my
commandments, *but* that ye break my
covenant:
16 I also will do this unto you; I will
even appoint [4]over you terror, consumption, [r]and the burning ague, that
shall [s]consume the eyes, and cause sorrow of heart: and [t]ye shall sow your
seed in vain, for your enemies shall eat
it.
17 And I will set my face against you,
and ye [u]shall be slain before your enemies: [v]they that hate you shall reign
over you; and [w]ye shall flee when none
pursueth you.
18 And if ye will not yet for all this
hearken unto me, then I will punish
you [x]seven times more for your sins.
19 And I will [y]break the pride of
your power; and I will make your
heaven as iron, and your earth as
brass:
20 And your [z]strength shall be spent
in vain: for [a]your land shall not yield
her increase, neither shall the trees of
the land yield their fruits.
21 ¶ And if ye walk [5]contrary unto
me, and will not hearken unto me; I
will bring seven times more plagues
upon you according to your sins.
22 [b]I will also send wild beasts
among you, which shall rob you of
your children, and destroy your cattle,
and make you few in number; and
[c]your *high* ways shall be desolate.
23 And if [d]ye will not be reformed
by me by these things, but will walk
contrary unto me;
24 [e]Then will I also walk contrary
unto you, and will punish you yet seven
times for your sins.
25 And [f]I will bring a sword upon
you, that shall avenge the quarrel of
my covenant: and when ye are gathered together within your cities, [g]I will
send the pestilence among you; and ye
shall be delivered into the hand of the
enemy.
26 *And* [h]when I have broken the
staff of your bread, ten women shall
bake your bread in one oven, and they
shall deliver *you* your bread again by
weight: and [i]ye shall eat, and not be
satisfied.
27 And if ye will not for all this hearken unto me, but walk contrary unto
me;
28 Then I will walk contrary unto
you also [j]in fury; and I, even I, will
chastise you seven times for your sins.
29 And [k]ye shall eat the flesh of
your sons, and the flesh of your daughters shall ye eat.
30 And [l]I will destroy your high
places, and cut down your images, and
[m]cast your carcases upon the carcases

of your idols, and my soul shall [n]abhor
you.
31 And [o]I will make your cities
waste, and [p]bring your sanctuaries
unto desolation, and I will not smell
the savour of your sweet odours.
32 And [q]I will bring the land into
desolation: and your enemies which
dwell therein shall be astonished at it.
33 And [r]I will scatter you among the
heathen, and will draw out a sword after you: and your land shall be desolate, and your cities waste.
34 [s]Then shall the land enjoy her
sabbaths, as long as it lieth desolate,
and ye *be* in your enemies' land; *even*
then shall the land rest, and enjoy her
sabbaths.
35 As long as it lieth desolate it shall
rest; because it did not rest in your sabbaths, when ye dwelt upon it.
36 And upon them that are left *alive*
of you I [t]will send a faintness into their
hearts in the lands of their enemies;
and the [u]sound of a [6]shaken leaf shall
chase them; and they shall flee, as fleeing from a sword; and they shall fall
when none pursueth.
37 And [v]they shall fall one upon another, as it were before a sword, when
none pursueth: and [w]ye shall have no
power to stand before your enemies.
38 And ye shall perish among the
heathen, and the land of your enemies
shall eat you up.
39 And they that are left of you
[x]shall pine away in their iniquity in
your enemies' lands; and also in the
iniquities of their fathers shall they
pine away with them.
40 [y]If they shall confess their iniquity, and the iniquity of their fathers,
with their trespass which they trespassed against me, and that also they
have walked contrary unto me;
41 And *that* I also have walked contrary unto them, and have brought
them into the land of their enemies; if
then their [z]uncircumcised hearts be
[a]humbled, and they then accept of the
punishment of their iniquity:
42 Then will I [b]remember my covenant with Jā'cob, and also my covenant with Ī'saac, and also my covenant
with Ā'brā-hăm will I remember; and I
will [c]remember the land.
43 The land also shall be left of them,
and shall enjoy her sabbaths, while she
lieth desolate without them: and they
shall accept of the punishment of their
iniquity: because, even because they
despised my judgments, and because
their soul abhorred my statutes.
44 And yet for all that, when they be
in the land of their enemies, [d]I will not
cast them away, neither will I abhor
them, to destroy them utterly, and to
break my covenant with them: for I *am*
the LORD their God.
45 But I will [e]for their sakes remember the covenant of their ancestors,
whom I brought forth out of the land of
Ē'gypt [f]in the sight of the heathen, that
I might be their God: I *am* the LORD.

[n]Ps. 78.59
31 [o]Neh. 2.3
[p]Ps. 74.1-8; Jer. 22.5; Lam. 1.10
32 [q]Jer. 9.11; Jer. 25.11
33 [r]Deut. 4.27; Deut. 28.64; Ps. 44.11; Zech. 7.14
34 [s]ch. 25.2-4; 2 Chr. 36.21
36 [t]Gen. 35.5; Josh. 2.9-11
[u]Prov. 28.1
[6]driven
37 [v]Judg. 7.22; Isa. 10.4
[w]Judg. 2.14
39 [x]Neh. 1.9; Jer. 3.25
40 [y]1 Ki. 8.33; Job 34.31; Prov. 28.13; Jer. 3.12; Luke 15.18
41 [z]Jer. 9.25; Acts 7.51; Rom. 2.29
[a]1 Ki. 21.29; 2 Chr. 12.6
42 [b]Ex. 2.24; Ps. 106.45
[c]Ps. 136.23
44 [d]Deut. 4.31
45 [e]Rom. 11.28
[f]Ezek. 20.9
46 [g]Deut. 33.4

CHAPTER 27
2 [a]Gen. 28.20-22; Num. 6.2; Deut. 23.21-23; 1 Sam. 1.11-28; Job 22.27; Ps. 50.14-15; Eccl. 5.4-6; Jon. 1.16
3 [b]Ex. 30.13; Num. 3.47; Num. 18.16
8 [c]ch. 12.8; ch. 14.21-22; Luke 21.1; 2 Cor. 8.12
9 [1]shall be sacrificed
12 [2]according to thy estimation, O priest, etc
14 [d]ch. 25.29-31; Num. 18.14;
16 2 Cor. 9.10
[3]Or, the land of an homer, etc

46 [g]These *are* the statutes and judgments and laws, which the LORD made
between him and the children of Ĭs'ra-
el in mount Sī'nāi by the hand of Mō'-
ses.

27 And the LORD spake unto Mō'-
ses, saying,
2 Speak unto the children of Ĭs'ra-el,
and say unto them, [a]When a man shall
make a singular vow, the persons *shall*
be for the LORD by thy estimation.
3 And thy estimation shall be of the
male from twenty years old even unto
sixty years old, even thy estimation
shall be fifty shekels of silver, after
[b]the shekel of the sanctuary.
4 And if it *be* a female, then thy estimation shall be thirty shekels.
5 And if *it be* from five years old
even unto twenty years old, then thy
estimation shall be of the male twenty
shekels, and for the female ten shekels.
6 And if *it be* from a month old even
unto five years old, then thy estimation
shall be of the male five shekels of silver, and for the female thy estimation
shall be three shekels of silver.
7 And if *it be* from sixty years old
and above; if *it be* a male, then thy
estimation shall be fifteen shekels, and
for the female ten shekels.
8 But [c]if he be poorer than thy estimation, then he shall present himself
before the priest, and the priest shall
value him; according to his ability that
vowed shall the priest value him.
9 And if *it be* a beast, whereof men
bring an offering unto the LORD, all
that *any man* giveth of such unto the
LORD [1]shall be holy.
10 He shall not alter it, nor change
it, a good for a bad, or a bad for a good:
and if he shall at all change beast for
beast, then it and the exchange thereof
shall be holy.
11 And if *it be* any unclean beast, of
which they do not offer a sacrifice unto
the LORD, then he shall present the
beast before the priest:
12 And the priest shall value it,
whether it be good or bad: [2]as thou val-
uest it, *who art* the priest, so shall it be.
13 But if he will at all redeem it, then
he shall add a fifth *part* thereof unto
thy estimation.
14 ¶ And when a man shall [d]sanctify
his house *to be* holy unto the LORD, then
the priest shall estimate it, whether it be
good or bad: as the priest shall estimate
it, so shall it stand.
15 And if he that sanctified it will
redeem his house, then he shall add
the fifth *part* of the money of thy estimation unto it, and it shall be his.
16 And if a man shall sanctify unto
the LORD *some part* of a field of his
possession, then thy estimation shall
be according to the seed thereof: [3]an
homer of barley seed *shall be valued* at
fifty shekels of silver.
17 If he sanctify his field from the
year of jubile, according to thy estimation it shall stand.

18 But if he sanctify his field after
the jubile, then the priest shall [e]reckon
unto him the money according to the
years that remain, even unto the year
of the jubile, and it shall be abated
from thy estimation.
19 And if he that sanctified the field
will in any wise redeem it, then he
shall add the fifth *part* of the money of
thy estimation unto it, and it shall be
assured to him.
20 And if he will not redeem the
field, or if he have sold the field to another
man, it shall not be redeemed
any more.
21 But the field, [f]when it goeth out
in the jubile, shall be holy unto the
LORD, as a field devoted; the [g]possession
thereof shall be the priest's.
22 And if *a man* sanctify unto the
LORD a field which he hath bought,
which *is* not of the fields of his possession;
23 Then the priest shall reckon unto
him the worth of thy estimation, *even*
unto the year of the jubile: and he shall
give thine estimation in that day, *as* a
holy thing unto the LORD.
24 [h]In the year of the jubile the field
shall return unto him of whom it was
bought, *even* to him to whom the possession
of the land *did belong*.
25 And all thy estimations shall be
according to the shekel of the sanctuary:
[i]twenty gerahs shall be the shekel.
26 ¶ Only the [4]firstling of the beasts,
which should be the LORD'S firstling,
no man shall sanctify it; whether *it be*
ox, or sheep: it *is* the LORD'S.
27 And if *it be* of an unclean beast,
then he shall redeem *it* according to
thine estimation, and shall add a fifth
part of it thereto: or if it be not redeemed,
then it shall be sold according
to thy estimation.
28 [j]Notwithstanding no devoted
thing, that a man shall devote unto the
LORD of all that he hath, *both* of man
and beast, and of the field of his possession,
shall be sold or redeemed: every
devoted thing *is* most holy unto the
LORD.
29 None devoted, [5]which shall be devoted
of men, shall be redeemed; *but*
shall surely be put to death.
30 And [k]all the tithe of the land,
whether of the seed of the land, *or* of
the fruit of the tree, *is* the LORD'S: *it is*
holy unto the LORD.
31 And if a man will at all redeem
ought of his tithes, he shall add thereto
the fifth *part* thereof.
32 And concerning the tithe of the
herd, or of the flock, *even* of whatsoever
[l]passeth under the rod, the tenth
shall be holy unto the LORD.
33 He shall not search whether it be
good or bad, neither shall he change it:
and if he change it at all, then both it
and the change thereof shall be holy; it
shall not be redeemed.
34 These *are* the commandments,
which the LORD commanded Mō'ses
for the children of Is'ra-el in mount
Sī'nāi.

18 [e]ch. 25.15-16
21 [f]ch. 25.10-28-31 [g]Num. 18.14; Ezek. 44.29
24 [h]verses 27-29; ch. 25.28; Isa. 35.9-10; Jer. 32.15
25 [i]Ex. 30.13; Num. 3.47; Num. 18.16; Ezek. 45.12
26 [4]firstborn, etc., Ex. 13.2-12; Ex. 22.30; Num. 18.17; Deut. 15.19
28 [j]Josh. 6.17; Judg. 11.30-31
29 [5]Persons, Ex. 22.20; Num. 21.2; Deut. 7; Deut. 20.16; Deut. 25.19; Josh. 6.17; 1 Sam. 15.3
30 [k]Gen. 28.22; Num. 18.21; 2 Chr. 31.5; Neh. 13.12
32 [l]Jer. 33.13; Ezek. 20.37; Mic. 7.14

THE FOURTH BOOK OF MOSES COMMONLY CALLED

NUMBERS

Life's Questions

What does God do with rebels?
How does God respond to complainers?
What happens when God's leaders quarrel?
Can God face the challenges of a new land and new threats?

God's Answers

Numbers shows the love relationship between God and His people at work in real life situations. Crossing the wilderness and facing the reality of the Promised Land had already challenged Israel's faith. The people failed. Their leaders failed. What then? Numbers shows in four parts: preparations (1—10), rebellion and complaint (11:1—20:13), purposes achieved (20:14—25:18), and preparation for new situations (26:1—36:13).

In unfolding daily encounters with God, Israel learned His greatness and their own weakness. The experience finally prepared Israel to complete God's mission of taking the Promised Land. Numbers reveals God's dedication to His mission and Israel's self-centered fear that God will not succeed.

God prepares His people for war and worship with His presence (1:1—10:36).
God settles authority crises for His people (11:1—12:16).
Israel fears to take God's promised land (13:1—14:45).
God prepares the people for worship in the land (15:1–41).
God defends and punishes His chosen leaders (16:1—20:13).
God leads His rebels to victory (20:14—21:35).
God proves His sovereignty over other gods and kings (22:1—24:25).
God plagues teaches a sinful people (25:1–18).
God organizes a new generation to take the Promised Land (26:1—27:23).
God provides a way of worship in a new situation (28:1—29:40).
God expects obedience in love and war (30:1—31:54).
God lets Israel begin to settle beyond the Jordan (32:1–42).

God prepares His people to live in the Promised Land (33:1—36:13).

God's people did not trust Him to give them the land. They endured forty years of training as God raised a new generation to occupy the land. They learned God could defeat their enemies, provide for their needs, and forgive their sins. They also learned God did not take sin linghtly and would punish the sinner whatever status the person held in the community.

1 And the LORD spake unto Mō'ses [a]in the wilderness of Sī'nāi, [b]in the tabernacle of the congregation, on the first *day* of the second month, in the second year after they were come out of the land of Ē'ġypt, saying,

2 [c]Take ye the sum of all the congregation of the children of Ĭs'ra-el, after their families, by the house of their fathers, with the number of *their* names, every male by their polls;

3 From twenty years old and upward, all that are able to go forth to war in Ĭs'ra-el: thou and Aâr'on shall [1]number them by their armies.

4 And with you there shall [d]be a man of every tribe; every one head of the house of his fathers.

5 ¶ And these *are* the names of the men that shall stand with you: of *the* [e]*tribe of* Reu̱'ben; E-lī'zŭr the son of Shĕd'ĕ-ur.

6 Of Sĭm'e-on; She-lū'mĭ-el the son of Zū-rĭ-shăd'da-ī.

7 Of Jū'dah; [f]Näh'shon the son of Ăm-mĭn'a-dab.

8 Of Ĭs'sa-char; Ne-thăn'e-el the son of Zū'ar.

9 Of Zĕb'u-lun; E-lī'ab the son of Hē'lon.

10 Of the children of Jō'seph: of Ē'phră-ĭm; E-lĭsh'a-mȧ the son of Ăm-mī'hŭd: of Ma-năs'seh; Ga-mā'lĭ-el the son of Pe-däh'zur.

11 Of Bĕn'ja-min; Ăb'i-dăn the son of [2]Gĭd-e-ō'nī.

12 Of Dăn; Ā-hi-ē'zĕr the son of Ăm-mi-shăd'da-ī.

13 Of Ăsh'ĕr; Pā'ġi-el the son of Ŏc'-ran.

14 Of Găd; E-lī'a-săph the son of [g]Deū'el.

15 Of Năph'ta-lī; A-hī'rȧ the son of Ē'nan.

16 [h]These *were* the renowned of the congregation, princes of the tribes of their fathers, [i]heads of thousands in Ĭs'ra-el.

17 ¶ And Mō'ses and Aâr'on took these men which are expressed by *their* names:

18 And they assembled all the congregation together on the first *day* of the second month, and they declared their [j]pedigrees after their families, by the house of their fathers, according to the number of the names, from twenty years old and upward, by their polls.

19 As [k]the LORD commanded Mō'ses, so he numbered them in the wilderness of Sī'nāi.

20 And the children of Reu̱'ben, Ĭs'ra-el's eldest son, by their generations, after their families, by the house of their fathers, according to the number of the names, by their polls, every male from twenty years old and upward, all that were [l]able to go forth to war;

21 Those that were numbered of them, *even* of the tribe of Reu̱'ben, *were* forty and six thousand and five hundred.

22 ¶ Of the children of Sĭm'e-on, by their generations, after their families, by the house of their fathers, those that were numbered of them, according to the number of the names, by their polls, every male from twenty years old and upward, all that were able to go forth to war;

23 Those that were numbered of them, *even* of the tribe of Sĭm'e-on, *were* fifty and nine thousand and three hundred.

24 ¶ Of the children of [m]Găd, by their generations, after their families, by the house of their fathers, according to the number of the names, from twenty years old and upward, all that were able to go forth to war;

25 Those that were numbered of them, *even* of the tribe of Găd, *were* forty and five thousand six hundred and fifty.

26 ¶ Of the [n]children of Jū'dah, by their generations, after their families, by the house of their fathers, according to the number of the names, from twenty years old and upward, all that were able to go forth to war;

27 Those that were numbered of them, *even* of the tribe of Jū'dah, *were* threescore and fourteen thousand and six hundred.

28 ¶ Of the children of Ĭs'sa-char, by their generations, after their families, by the house of their fathers, according to the number of the names, from twenty years old and upward, all that were able to go forth to war;

29 Those that were numbered of them, *even* of the tribe of Ĭs'sa-char, *were* fifty and four thousand and four hundred.

30 ¶ Of the children of Zĕb'u-lun, by their generations, after their families, by the house of their fathers, according to the number of the names, from twenty years old and upward, all that were able to go forth to war;

31 Those that were numbered of them, *even* of the tribe of Zĕb'u-lun, *were* fifty and seven thousand and four hundred.

32 ¶ Of the children of Jō'seph, *namely*, of the [o]children of Ē'phră-ĭm, by their generations, after their families, by the house of their fathers, according to the number of the names, from twenty years old and upward, all that were able to go forth to war;

33 Those that were numbered of them, *even* of the tribe of Ē'phră-ĭm, *were* forty thousand and five hundred.

34 ¶ Of the children of Ma-năs'seh, by their generations, after their families, by the house of their fathers,

CHAPTER 1

1 [a]Ex. 19.1 [b]Ex. 25.22

2 [c]Ex. 30.12; 2 Sam. 24.2; 1 Chr. 21.2

3 [1]muster

4 [d]ch. 2.2; 1 Chr. 27.1

5 [e]Gen. 29.32; Deut. 33.6; Rev. 7.5

7 [f]ch. 7.12; Ruth 4.20; 1 Chr. 2.10; Luke 3.32

11 [2]That is, a cutter down

14 [g]ch. 2.14, he is called Reuel

16 [h]Gen. 6.4; Ex. 18.21; ch. 7.2; Judg. 6.15; 1 Chr. 5.24; Mic. 5.2 [i]Ex. 18.21-25; Deut. 1.15; 1 Sam. 22.7

18 [j]Neh. 7.61; Heb. 7.3

19 [k]ch. 26.1-2; 2 Sam. 24.1

20 [l]2 Sam. 22.35; Ps. 44.3; Ps. 60.12; Ps. 144.1; 1 Cor. 16.13; 2 Cor. 3.5; Eph. 6.12

24 [m]Gen. 30.11; Gen. 49.19; Josh. 4.12; Jer. 49.1; Rev. 7.5

26 [n]Gen. 29.35; Gen. 38.1-3; Gen. 49.8, with ch. 2.3-4; Deut. 33.7; 2 Sam. 24.9; 1 Chr. 5.2; Ps. 78.68; Matt. 1.2; Heb. 7.14; Rev. 5.5

32 [o]Gen. 30.24; Gen. 48.19-20, with ch. 2.18-19; Judg. 12.6; Ps. 60.7; Jer. 7.15; Obad. 19

according to the number of the names,
from twenty years old and upward, all
that were able to go forth to war;
35 Those that were numbered of
them, *even* of the tribe of Ma-năs'seh,
were thirty and two thousand and two
hundred.
36 ¶ Of the [p]children of Bĕn'ja-min,
by their generations, after their families, by the house of their fathers, according to the number of the names,
from twenty years old and upward, all
that were able to go forth to war;
37 Those that were numbered of
them, *even* of the tribe of Bĕn'ja-min,
were thirty and five thousand and four
hundred.
38 ¶ Of the [q]children of Dăn, by
their generations, after their families,
by the house of their fathers, according to the number of the names, from
twenty years old and upward, all that
were able to go forth to war;
39 Those that were numbered of
them, *even* of the tribe of Dăn, *were*
threescore and two thousand and seven
hundred.
40 ¶ Of the children of Ăsh'ēr, by
their generations, after their families,
by the house of their fathers, according to the number of the names, from
twenty years old and upward, all that
were able to go forth to war;
41 Those that were numbered of
them, *even* of the tribe of Ăsh'ēr, *were*
forty and one thousand and five hundred.
42 ¶ Of the children of Năph'ta-lī,
throughout their generations, after
their families, by the house of their fathers, according to the number of the
names, from twenty years old and upward, all that were able to go forth to
war;
43 Those that were numbered of
them, *even* of the tribe of Năph'ta-lī,
were fifty and three thousand and four
hundred.
44 [r]These *are* those that were numbered, which Mō'ses and Aâr'on numbered, and the princes of Ĭs'ra-el, *being*
twelve men: each one was for the house
of his fathers.
45 So were all those that were numbered of the children of Ĭs'ra-el, by
the house of their fathers, from twenty
years old and upward, all that were
able to go forth to war in Ĭs'ra-el;
46 Even all they that were numbered
were [s]six hundred thousand and three
thousand and five hundred and fifty.
47 ¶ But [t]the Lē'vītes after the tribe
of their fathers were not numbered
among them.
48 For the LORD had spoken unto
Mō'ses, saying,
49 [u]Only thou shalt not number the
tribe of Lē'vī, neither take the sum of
them among the children of Ĭs'ra-el:
50 But [v]thou shalt appoint the Lē'-
vītes over the tabernacle of testimony,
and over all the vessels thereof, and
over all things that *belong* to it: they
shall bear the tabernacle, and all the
vessels thereof; and they shall minis-

36 [p]Gen. 35.16-18; Gen. 44.20; ch. 26.41; Judg. 20.44-46; 2 Chr. 17.17; Ps. 68.27; Rev. 7.8
38 [q]Gen. 30.5-6; Gen. 46.23, with ch. 2.25
44 [r]ch. 26.64
46 [s]Gen. 13.16; Ex. 12.37; ch. 26.51; Deut. 10.22; 1 Ki. 4.20
47 [t]ch. 2.33; ch. 3; 1 Chr. 6.1; 1 Chr. 21.6
49 [u]ch. 26.62
50 [v]Ex. 31.18; ch. 3.7-8; ch. 4.15-25-26-27-33
[w]ch. 3.23-29-35-38
51 [x]ch. 10.17-21
[3]Every one not a Levite
52 [y]ch. 2.2-34
53 [z]Lev. 10.6; ch. 8.19; ch. 16.46; 1 Sam. 6.19
[a]ch. 8.24; ch. 18.3-4; 1 Chr. 23.32; 2 Chr. 13.11
CHAPTER 2
2 [a]ch. 1.52
[b]ch. 24.2-9
[1]over against
3 [c]ch. 10.14; Ruth 4.20; 1 Chr. 2.10; Matt. 1.4; Luke 3.32-33
5 [d]ch. 7.18-23
6 [e]ch. 26.25
7 [f]Gen. 49.13; Deut. 33.18
9 [g]ch. 10.14; 1 Chr. 5.2; Ps. 78.52
10 [h]Deut. 33.6; 1 Chr. 5.1

ter unto it, [w]and shall encamp round
about the tabernacle.
51 And [x]when the tabernacle setteth forward, the Lē'vītes shall take it
down: and when the tabernacle is to be
pitched, the Lē'vītes shall set it up: and
the [3]stranger that cometh nigh shall be
put to death.
52 And the children of Ĭs'ra-el shall
pitch their tents, [y]every man by his
own camp, and every man by his own
standard, throughout their hosts.
53 But the Lē'vītes shall pitch round
about the tabernacle of testimony, that
there be no [z]wrath upon the congregation of the children of Ĭs'ra-el: [a]and the
Lē'vītes shall keep the charge of the
tabernacle of testimony.
54 And the children of Ĭs'ra-el did
according to all that the LORD commanded Mō'ses, so did they.

2

And the LORD spake unto Mō'ses
and unto Aâr'on, saying,
2 [a]Every man of the children of Ĭs'-
ra-el shall [b]pitch by his own standard,
with the ensign of their father's house:
[1]far off about the tabernacle of the congregation shall they pitch.
3 And on the east side toward the
rising of the sun shall they of the standard of the camp of Jū'dah pitch
throughout their armies: and
[c]Näh'shon the son of Ăm-mĭn'a-dab
shall be captain of the children of
Jū'dah.
4 And his host, and those that were
numbered of them, *were* threescore
and fourteen thousand and six hundred.
5 And those that do pitch next unto
him *shall be* the tribe of Ĭs'sa-char:
[d]and Ne-thăn'e-el the son of Zū'ar
shall be captain of the children of Ĭs'sa-
char.
6 And his host, and those that were
numbered thereof, *were* [e]fifty and four
thousand and four hundred.
7 *Then* the tribe of [f]Zĕb'u-lun: and
E-lī'ab the son of Hē'lon *shall be* captain of the children of Zĕb'u-lun.
8 And his host, and those that were
numbered thereof, *were* fifty and seven
thousand and four hundred.
9 All that were numbered in the
camp of Jū'dah *were* an hundred thousand and fourscore thousand and six
thousand and four hundred, throughout their armies. [g]These shall first set
forth.
10 ¶ On the south side *shall be* the
standard of the camp of [h]Reu'ben according to their armies: and the captain of the children of Reu'ben *shall be*
E-lī'zŭr the son of Shĕd'ĕ-ur.
11 And his host, and those that were
numbered thereof, *were* forty and six
thousand and five hundred.
12 And those which pitch by him
shall be the tribe of Sĭm'e-on: and the
captain of the children of Sĭm'e-on
shall be She-lū'mĭ-el the son of Zū-rĭ-
shăd'da-ī.
13 And his host, and those that were
numbered of them, *were* fifty and nine
thousand and three hundred.

14 Then the tribe of Găd: and the captain of the sons of Găd *shall be* E-lī'a-săph the son of [2]Reu̯'el.

15 And his host, and those that were numbered of them, *were* forty and five thousand and six hundred and fifty.

16 All that were numbered in the camp of Reu̯'ben *were* an hundred thousand and fifty and one thousand and four hundred and fifty, throughout their armies. And [i]they shall set forth in the second rank.

17 ¶ [j]Then the tabernacle of the congregation shall set forward with the camp of the Lē'vītes in the midst of the camp: as they encamp, so shall they set forward, every [k]man in his place by their standards.

18 ¶ On the west side *shall be* the standard of the camp of [l]Ē'phră-ĭm according to their armies: and the captain of the sons of Ē'phră-ĭm *shall be* E-lĭsh'a-mȧ the son of Ăm-mī'hŭd.

19 And his host, and those that were numbered of them, *were* forty thousand and five hundred.

20 And by him *shall be* the tribe of Ma-năs'seh: and the captain of the children of Ma-năs'seh *shall be* Ga-mā'lī-el the son of Pe-dāh'zur.

21 And his host, and those that were numbered of them, *were* thirty and two thousand and two hundred.

22 Then the tribe of [m]Bĕn'ja-min: and the captain of the sons of Bĕn'jamin *shall be* Ăb'i-dăn the son of [3]Gĭd-e-ō'nī.

23 And his host, and those that were numbered of them, *were* thirty and five thousand and four hundred.

24 All that were numbered of the camp of Ē'phră-ĭm *were* an hundred thousand and eight thousand and an hundred, throughout their armies. And [n]they shall go forward in the third rank.

25 ¶ The standard of the camp of [o]Dăn *shall be* on the north side by their armies: and the captain of the children of Dăn *shall be* Ā-hi-ē'zēr the son of Ăm-mi-shăd'da-ī.

26 And his host, and those that were numbered of them, *were* threescore and two thousand and seven hundred.

27 And those that encamp by him *shall be* the tribe of Ăsh'ēr: and the captain of the children of Ăsh'ēr *shall be* Pā'gĭ-el the son of Ŏc'ran.

28 And his host, and those that were numbered of them, *were* forty and one thousand and five hundred.

29 ¶ Then the tribe of [p]Năph'ta-lī: and the captain of the children of Năph'ta-lī *shall be* A-hī'rȧ the son of Ē'nan.

30 And his host, and those that were numbered of them, *were* fifty and three thousand and four hundred.

31 All they that were numbered in the camp of Dăn *were* an hundred thousand and fifty and seven thousand and six hundred. [q]They shall go hindmost with their standards.

32 ¶ These *are* those which were numbered of the children of Ĭs'ra-el by the house of their fathers: [r]all those that were numbered of the camps throughout their hosts *were* six hundred thousand and three thousand and five hundred and fifty.

33 But [s]the Lē'vītes were not numbered among the children of Ĭs'ra-el; as the LORD commanded Mō'ses.

34 And the children of Ĭs'ra-el did according to all that [t]the LORD commanded Mō'ses: so [u]they pitched by their standards, and so they set forward, every one after their families, according to the house of their fathers.

3

These also *are* the generations of Aâr'on and Mō'ses in the day *that* the LORD spake with Mō'ses in mount Sī'nāi.

2 And these *are* the names of the sons of Aâr'on; Nā'dăb the [a]firstborn, and A-bī'hū, Ē-le-ā'zar, and Ĭth'a-mär.

3 These *are* the names of the sons of Aâr'on, [b]the priests which were anointed, [1]whom he consecrated to minister in the priest's office.

4 And [c]Nā'dăb and A-bī'hū died before the LORD, when they offered strange fire before the LORD, in the wilderness of Sī'nāi, and they had no children: and Ē-le-ā'zar and Ĭth'a-mär ministered in the priest's office in the sight of Aâr'on their father.

5 ¶ And the LORD spake unto Mō'ses, saying,

6 [d]Bring the tribe of Lē'vī near, and present them before Aâr'on the priest, that they may minister unto him.

7 And they shall keep his charge, and the charge of the whole congregation before the tabernacle of the congregation, to do the [e]service of the tabernacle.

8 And they shall keep all the instruments of the tabernacle of the congregation, and the charge of the children of Ĭs'ra-el, to do the service of the tabernacle.

9 And [f]thou shalt give the Lē'vītes unto Aâr'on and to his sons: they *are* wholly given unto him out of the children of Ĭs'ra-el.

10 And thou shalt appoint Aâr'on and his sons, [g]and they shall wait on their priest's office: and [2]the stranger that cometh nigh shall be put to death.

11 And the LORD spake unto Mō'ses, saying,

12 And I, behold, [h]I have taken the Lē'vītes from among the children of Ĭs'ra-el instead of all the firstborn that openeth the matrix among the children of Ĭs'ra-el: therefore the Lē'vītes shall be mine;

13 Because [i]all the firstborn *are* mine; [j]*for* on the day that I smote all the firstborn in the land of Ē'gypt I hallowed unto me all the firstborn in Ĭs'ra-el, both man and beast: mine shall they be: I *am* the LORD.

14 ¶ And the LORD spake unto Mō'ses in the [k]wilderness of Sī'nāi, saying,

15 Number the children of Lē'vī after the house of their fathers, by their

---

14 [2]Deuel
16 [i]ch. 10.18; Gen. 49.3; 1 Chr. 5.1
17 [j]Acts 7.44; Heb. 8.2
[k]1 Cor. 14.40
18 [l]Gen. 48.14-20; ch. 10.22; Deut. 33.17; Ps. 80.2; Jer. 31.9-18-21; Hos. 11.3; Zech. 9.9-17
22 [m]Ps. 68.27; Rev. 7.8
[3]That is, A cutter down
24 [n]ch. 10.22
25 [o]Deut. 33.22
29 [p]Gen. 30.8; Gen. 49.21; 2 Ki. 15.29; Rev. 7.6
31 [q]ch. 10.25
32 [r]Ex. 12.37; ch. 1.46; ch. 11.21
33 [s]ch. 1.47; ch. 3.5-51; ch. 26.57-62; 1 Chr. 6
34 [t]Ex. 39.42; ch. 24.2; Ps. 119.6; Isa. 45.12; Luke 1.6
[u]ch. 24.2-9; Song 6.10; 1 Cor. 14.40

CHAPTER 3
2 [a]Ex. 6.23; ch. 26.61; 1 Chr. 6.3
3 [b]Ex. 28.41; Lev. 8.1
[1]whose hand he filled
4 [c]Lev. 10.1; 1 Chr. 24.2; Isa. 66.15; 2 Thess. 1.8; Heb. 12.29
6 [d]Ex. 32.26; ch. 8.6
7 [e]ch. 1.50
9 [f]ch. 8.19
10 [g]ch. 18.7; 1 Chr. 6.49; Acts 6.3-4; Rom. 12.7
[2]Every one not a Levite
12 [h]ch. 8.16; ch. 18.6
13 [i]Ex. 13.2; Lev. 27.26; ch. 8.16; Neh. 10.36; Luke 2.23
[j]Ex. 13.12-15
14 [k]Ex. 19.1

families: [l]every male from a month old and upward shalt thou number them.

16 And Mō'ses numbered them according to the [3]word of the LORD, as he was commanded.

17 And [m]these were the sons of Lē'vī by their names; Gẽr'shŏn, and Kō'hath, and Me-rā'rī.

18 And these *are* the names of the sons of Gẽr'shŏn by their families; [n]Lĭb'nī, and Shĭm'e-ī.

19 And the sons of Kō'hath by their families; Ăm'răm, and Ĭz'e-här, Hē'bron, and Ŭz'zĭ-el.

20 And the sons of Me-rā'rī by their families; Mäh'lī, and Mū'shī. These *are* the families of the Lē'vītes according to the house of their fathers.

21 Of Gẽr'shŏn *was* the family of the Lĭb'nītes, and the family of the Shĭm'ītes: these *are* the families of the Gẽr'shon-ītes.

22 Those that were numbered of them, according to the number of all the males, from a month old and upward, *even* those that were numbered of them *were* seven thousand and five hundred.

23 The [o]families of the Gẽr'shon-ītes shall pitch behind the tabernacle westward.

24 And the chief of the house of the father of the Gẽr'shon-ītes *shall be* E-lī'a-săph the son of Lā'el.

25 And [p]the charge of the sons of Gẽr'shŏn in the tabernacle of the congregation *shall be* [q]the tabernacle, and [r]the tent, [s]the covering thereof, and [t]the hanging for the door of the tabernacle of the congregation,

26 And [u]the hangings of the court, and [v]the curtain for the door of the court, which *is* by the tabernacle, and by the altar round about, and [w]the cords of it for all the service thereof.

27 ¶ And [x]of Kō'hath *was* the family of the Ăm'răm-ītes, and the family of the Ĭz'e-har-ītes, and the family of the Hē'bron-ītes, and the family of the Ŭz'zĭ-el-ītes: these *are* the families of the Kō'hath-ītes.

28 In the number of all the males, from a month old and upward, *were* eight thousand and six hundred, keeping the charge of the sanctuary.

29 The [y]families of the sons of Kō'hath shall pitch on the side of the tabernacle southward.

30 And the chief of the house of the father of the families of the Kō'hath-ītes *shall be* E-lĭz'a-phan the son of Ŭz'zĭ-el.

31 And [z]their charge *shall be* [a]the ark, and [b]the table, and [c]the candlestick, and [d]the altars, and the vessels of the sanctuary wherewith they minister, and [e]the hanging, and all the service thereof.

32 And Ē-le-ā'zar the son of Aâr'on the priest *shall be* [f]chief over the chief of the Lē'vītes, *and have* the oversight of them that keep the charge of the sanctuary.

33 ¶ Of Me-rā'rī *was* the family of the Mäh'lītes, and the family of the Mū'shītes: these *are* the families of Me-rā'rī.

34 And those that were numbered of them, according to the number of all the males, from a month old and upward, *were* six thousand and two hundred.

35 And the chief of the house of the father of the families of Me-rā'rī *was* Zū'rĭ-el the son of Ăb-i-hā'il: [g]*these* shall pitch on the side of the tabernacle northward.

36 And [4]*under* the custody and charge of the sons of Me-rā'rī *shall be* the boards of the tabernacle, and the bars thereof, and the pillars thereof, and the sockets thereof, and all the vessels thereof, and all that serveth thereto,

37 And the pillars of the court round about, and their sockets, and their pins, and their cords.

38 ¶ [h]But those that encamp before the tabernacle toward the east, *even* before the tabernacle of the congregation eastward, *shall be* Mō'ses, and Aâr'on and his sons, keeping [i]the charge of the sanctuary [j]for the charge of the children of Ĭs'ra-el; and [5]the stranger that cometh nigh shall be put to death.

39 [k]All that were numbered of the Lē'vītes, which Mō'ses and Aâr'on numbered at the commandment of the LORD, throughout their families, all the males from a month old and upward, *were* twenty and two thousand.

40 ¶ And the LORD said unto Mō'ses, Number [l]all the firstborn of the males of the children of Ĭs'ra-el from a month old and upward, and take the number of their names.

41 And [m]thou shalt take the Lē'vītes for me (I *am* the LORD) instead of all the firstborn among the children of Ĭs'ra-el; and the cattle of the Lē'vītes instead of all the firstlings among the cattle of the children of Ĭs'ra-el.

42 And Mō'ses numbered, as the LORD commanded him, all the firstborn among the children of Ĭs'ra-el.

43 And all the firstborn males by the number of names, from a month old and upward, of those that were numbered of them, were twenty and two thousand two hundred and threescore and thirteen.

44 ¶ And the LORD spake unto Mō'ses, saying,

45 Take the Lē'vītes instead of all the firstborn among the children of Ĭs'ra-el, and the cattle of the Lē'vītes instead of their cattle; and the Lē'vītes shall be [n]mine: I *am* the LORD.

46 And for those that are to be [o]redeemed of the two hundred and threescore and thirteen of the firstborn of the children of Ĭs'ra-el, [p]which are more than the Lē'vītes;

47 Thou shalt even take [q]five shekels apiece by the poll, after the shekel of the sanctuary shalt thou take *them:* ([r]the shekel *is* twenty gerahs:)

48 And thou shalt give the money, wherewith the odd number of them is

15 [l]ch. 26.62
16 [3]mouth
17 [m]Gen. 46.11; Ex. 6.16; ch. 26.57; 1 Chr. 23.6
18 [n]Ex. 6.17
23 [o]ch. 1.53
25 [p]ch. 4.24-26; 1 Chr. 9.14-33; 1 Chr. 23.32
[q]Ex. 25.9
[r]Ex. 26.1
[s]Ex. 26.7-14
[t]Ex. 26.36
26 [u]Ex. 27.9
[v]Ex. 27.16
[w]Ex. 35.18
27 [x]1 Chr. 26.23
29 [y]ch. 1.53
31 [z]ch. 4.15
[a]Ex. 25.10
[b]Ex. 25.23
[c]Ex. 25.31
[d]Ex. 27.1; Ex. 30.1
[e]Ex. 26.31
32 [f]ch. 20.25-28; 2 Ki. 25.18; 1 Chr. 9.20
35 [g]ch. 1.53
36 [4]the office of the charge
38 [h]ch. 1.53; ch. 2.3
[i]ch. 18.5; 1 Chr. 6.48-49
[j]verses 7-8
[5]Every one not a Levite
39 [k]ch. 4.46-48; ch. 26.62
40 [l]verse 15
41 [m]verses 12-45
45 [n]verses 12-41; 1 Sam. 1.28
46 [o]ch. 18.15
[p]verses 39-43
47 [q]Lev. 27.6; ch. 18.16
[r]Lev. 27.25; ch. 18.16

to be redeemed, unto Aâr'on and to his
sons.
49 And Mō'ses took the [s]redemp-
tion money of them that were over and
above them that were redeemed by the
Lē'vītes:
50 Of the firstborn of the children of
Ĭs'ra-el took he the money; [t]a thousand
three hundred and threescore and five
shekels, after the shekel of the sanctuary:
51 And Mō'ses gave the money of
them that were redeemed unto Aâr'on
and to his sons, according to the word
of the LORD, as the LORD commanded
Mō'ses.
4 And the LORD spake unto Mō'ses
and unto Aâr'on, saying,
2 Take the sum of the sons of Kō'-
hath from among the sons of Lē'vī, after their families, by the house of their
fathers,
3 [a]From thirty years old and upward even until fifty years old, all that
enter into the [1]host, to do the work in
the tabernacle of the congregation.
4 [b]This *shall be* the service of the
sons of Kō'hath in the tabernacle of
the congregation, *about* the most holy
things:
5 ¶ And when the camp setteth forward, Aâr'on shall come, and his sons,
and they shall take down [c]the covering vail, and cover the [d]ark of testimony with it:
6 And shall put thereon the covering
of badgers' skins, and shall spread over
it a cloth wholly of blue, and shall put
in [e]the staves thereof.
7 And upon the [f]table of shewbread
they shall spread a cloth of blue, and
put thereon the dishes, and the spoons,
and the bowls, and covers to [2]cover
withal: and the continual bread shall
be thereon:
8 And they shall spread upon them a
cloth of scarlet, and cover the same
with a covering of badgers' skins, and
shall put in the staves thereof.
9 And they shall take a cloth of blue,
and cover the [g]candlestick of the light,
[h]and his lamps, and his tongs, and
his snuffdishes, and all the oil vessels
thereof, wherewith they minister unto
it:
10 And they shall put it and all the
vessels thereof within a covering of
badgers' skins, and shall put *it* upon a
bar.
11 And upon [i]the golden altar they
shall spread a cloth of blue, and cover
it with a covering of badgers' skins,
and shall put to the staves thereof:
12 And they shall take all the instruments of ministry, wherewith they minister in the sanctuary, and put *them* in
a cloth of blue, and cover them with a
covering of badgers' skins, and shall
put *them* on a bar:
13 And they shall take away the
ashes from the altar, and spread a purple cloth thereon:
14 And they shall put upon it all the
vessels thereof, wherewith they minister about it, *even* the censers, the
fleshhooks, and the shovels, and the
[3]basons, all the vessels of the altar; and
they shall spread upon it a covering of
badgers' skins, and put to the staves of
it.
15 And when Aâr'on and his sons
have made an end of covering the sanctuary, and all the vessels of the sanctuary, as the camp is to set forward; after
that, the [j]sons of Kō'hath shall come to
bear *it*: [k]but they shall not touch *any*
holy thing, lest they die. [l]These *things*
are the burden of the sons of Kō'hath
in the tabernacle of the congregation.
16 ¶ And to the office of Ē-le-ā'zar
the son of Aâr'on the priest *pertaineth*
[m]the oil for the light, and the [n]sweet
incense, and the [o]daily meat offering,
and the [p]anointing oil, *and* the oversight of all the tabernacle, and of all
that therein *is*, in the sanctuary, and in
the vessels thereof.
17 ¶ And the LORD spake unto Mō'-
ses and unto Aâr'on, saying,
18 Cut ye not off the tribe of the families of the Kō'hath-ītes from among the
Lē'vītes:
19 But thus do unto them, that they
may live, and not die, when they approach unto the [q]most holy things:
Aâr'on and his sons shall go in, and
appoint them every one to his service
and to his burden:
20 [r]But they shall not go in to see
when the holy things are covered, lest
they die.
21 ¶ And the LORD spake unto Mō'-
ses, saying,
22 Take also the sum of the sons
of Gēr'shŏn, throughout the houses of
their fathers, by their families;
23 [s]From thirty years old and upward until fifty years old shalt thou
number them; all that enter in [4]to perform the service, to do the work in the
tabernacle of the congregation.
24 This *is* the service of the families
of the Gēr'shon-ītes, to serve, and for
[5]burdens:
25 And [t]they shall bear the curtains
of the tabernacle, and the tabernacle of
the congregation, his covering, and the
covering of the badgers' skins that *is*
above upon it, and the hanging for the
door of the tabernacle of the congregation,
26 And the hangings of the court,
and the hanging for the door of the gate
of the court, which *is* by the tabernacle
and by the altar round about, and their
cords, and all the instruments of their
service, and all that is made for them:
so shall they serve.
27 At the [6u]appointment of Aâr'on
and his sons shall be all the service
of the sons of the Gēr'shon-ītes, in
all their burdens, and in all their service: and ye shall appoint unto them
in charge all their burdens.
28 This *is* the service of the families
of the sons of Gēr'shŏn in the tabernacle of the congregation: and their
charge *shall be* under the hand of Ĭth'-
a-mär the son of Aâr'on the priest.

49 [s]Gal. 4.4-5; 1 Tim. 2.6; Tit. 2.14; Heb. 9.12; 1 Pet. 1.18
50 [t]verses 46-47; Acts 20.33
CHAPTER 4
3 [a]Gen. 41.46; ch. 3.40; 1 Chr. 23.3-24-27; Luke 3.23
[1]Or, warfare
4 [b]verse 15
5 [c]Ex. 26.31; Lev. 16.2; 2 Chr. 3.14; Matt. 27.51; Heb. 9.3
[d]Ex. 25.10-16
6 [e]Ex. 25.13
7 [f]Lev. 24.6-8
[2]Or, pour out withal
9 [g]Ex. 25.31
[h]Ex. 25.37-38
11 [i]Ex. 30.1
14 [3]Or, bowls
15 [j]ch. 7.9; Deut. 31.9; 2 Sam. 6.13
[k]2 Sam. 6.6-7
[l]ch. 3.31
16 [m]Ex. 25.6; Lev. 24.2
[n]Ps. 141.2; Mal. 1.11; Rev. 5.8
[o]Ex. 29.40; ch. 28.3; Dan. 9.27
[p]Ex. 30.23
19 [q]verse 4
20 [r]1 Sam. 6.19
23 [s]1 Chr. 23.3-24-27
[4]to war the warfare
24 [5]Or, carriage
25 [t]Ex. 26.1-14; ch. 3.25-26
27 [6]mouth
[u]Luke 1.70

29 ¶ As for the sons of Me-rā'rī, thou shalt number them after their families, by the house of their fathers;

30 [v]From thirty years old and upward even unto fifty years old shalt thou number them, every one that entereth into the [7][w]service, to do the work of the tabernacle of the congregation.

31 And [x]this *is* the charge of their burden, according to all their service in the tabernacle of the congregation; the boards of the tabernacle, and the bars thereof, and the pillars thereof, and sockets thereof,

32 And the pillars of the court round about, and their sockets, and their pins, and their cords, with all their instruments, and with all their service: and by name ye shall reckon [y]the instruments of the charge of their burden.

33 This *is* the service of the families of the sons of Me-rā'rī, according to all their service, in the tabernacle of the congregation, under the hand of Ĭth'a-mär the son of Âr'on the priest.

34 ¶ And [z]Mō'ses and Âr'on and the chief of the congregation numbered the sons of the Kō'hath-ītes after their families, and after the house of their fathers,

35 [a]From thirty years old and upward even unto fifty years old, every one that entereth into the service, for the work in the tabernacle of the congregation:

36 And those that were numbered of them by their families were two thousand seven hundred and fifty.

37 These *were* they that were numbered of the families of the Kō'hath-ītes, all that might do service in the tabernacle of the congregation, which Mō'ses and Âr'on did number according to the commandment of the LORD by the hand of Mō'ses.

38 And those that were numbered of the sons of Gēr'shŏn, throughout their families, and by the house of their fathers,

39 From thirty years old and upward even unto fifty years old, every one that entereth into the service, for the work in the tabernacle of the congregation,

40 Even those that were numbered of them, throughout their families, by the house of their fathers, were two thousand and six hundred and thirty.

41 These *are* they that were numbered of the families of the sons of Gēr'shŏn, of all that might do service in the tabernacle of the congregation, whom Mō'ses and Âr'on did number according to the commandment of the LORD.

42 ¶ And those that were numbered of the families of the sons of Me-rā'rī, throughout their families, by the house of their fathers,

43 [b]From thirty years old and upward even unto fifty years old, every one that entereth into the service, for the work in the tabernacle of the congregation,

44 Even those that were numbered of them after their families, were three thousand and two hundred.

45 These *be* those that were numbered of the families of the sons of Me-rā'rī, whom Mō'ses and Âr'on numbered according to the word of the LORD by the hand of Mō'ses.

46 All those that were numbered of the Lē'vītes, whom Mō'ses and Âr'on and the chief of Ĭs'ra-el numbered, after their families, and after the house of their fathers,

47 [c]From thirty years old and upward even unto fifty years old, every one that came to do the service of the ministry, and the service of the burden in the tabernacle of the congregation,

48 Even those that were numbered of them, were eight thousand and five hundred and fourscore.

49 According to the commandment of the LORD they were numbered by the hand of Mō'ses, [d]every one according to his service, and according to his burden: thus were they numbered of him, as the LORD commanded Mō'ses.

5 And the LORD spake unto Mō'ses, saying,

2 Command the children of Ĭs'ra-el, that they put out of the camp every [a]leper, and every one that hath an [b]issue, and whosoever is defiled by the [c]dead:

3 Both male and female shall ye put out, without the camp shall ye put them; that they defile not their camps, [d]in the midst whereof I dwell.

4 And the children of Ĭs'ra-el did so, and put them out without the camp: as the LORD spake unto Mō'ses, so did the children of Ĭs'ra-el.

5 ¶ And the LORD spake unto Mō'ses, saying,

6 Speak unto the children of Ĭs'ra-el, [e]When a man or woman shall commit any sin that men commit, to do a trespass against the LORD, and that person be guilty;

7 [f]Then they shall confess their sin which they have done: and he shall recompense his trespass [g]with the principal thereof, and add unto it the fifth *part* thereof, and give *it* unto *him* against whom he hath trespassed.

8 But if the man have no kinsman to recompense the trespass unto, let the trespass be recompensed unto the LORD, *even* to the priest; beside [h]the ram of the atonement, whereby an atonement shall be made for him.

9 And every [1]offering of all the holy things of the children of Ĭs'ra-el, which they bring unto the priest, shall be his.

10 And every man's hallowed things shall be his: whatsoever any man giveth the priest, it shall be [i]his.

11 ¶ And the LORD spake unto Mō'ses, saying,

12 Speak unto the children of Ĭs'ra-el, and say unto them, If any man's [j]wife go aside, and commit a trespass against him,

13 And a man [k]lie with her carnally, and it be hid from the eyes of

30 [v]verse 3; Gen. 41.46; ch. 4.23; ch. 8.24-26; 1 Chr. 28.12-13
[7]warfare
[w]Ps. 110; 1 Tim. 6.11; 2 Tim. 2.4; 2 Tim. 4.7
31 [x]ch. 3.36-37
32 [y]Ex. 25.9; ch. 3.8; ch. 7.1; 1 Chr. 9.29
34 [z]verse 2; ch. 3.19-27
35 [a]ch. 8.24-26; 1 Chr. 23.24; Luke 3.23; 1 Tim. 3.6
43 [b]verses 35-40; Deut. 33.8-11 2 Cor. 12.9
47 [c]Rom. 12.6-8
49 [d]1 Cor. 12.4-28

CHAPTER 5
2 [a]Lev. 13.3-46; ch. 12.14; Deut. 23.10; 2 Ki. 5.27; 2 Chr. 26.20; Isa. 52.11; Luke 17.12
[b]Lev. 15.2
[c]Lev. 21.1; ch. 9.6-10
3 [d]Ex. 25.8; Lev. 26.11-12; Deut. 32.9; Josh. 22.19; Ps. 76.2; Zech. 2.10; 2 Cor. 6.16; Rev. 21.3
6 [e]Lev. 6.2-3
7 [f]Lev. 5.5; Josh. 7.19
[g]Lev. 6.5
8 [h]Lev. 6.7
9 [1]Or, heave offering
10 [i]Lev. 10.13
12 [j]Prov. 2.16; Prov. 7.10-27; Hos. 4.13
13 [k]Lev. 18.20; Prov. 30.20

her husband, and be kept close, and
she be defiled, and *there be* no witness against her, neither she be taken
with the manner;
14 And [l]the spirit of jealousy come
upon him, and he be jealous of his
wife, and she be defiled: or if the spirit
of jealousy come upon him, and he be
jealous of his wife, and she be not defiled:
15 Then shall the man bring his wife
unto the priest, and he shall bring her
[m]offering for her, the tenth *part* of an
ephah of barley meal; he shall pour
no oil upon it, nor put frankincense
thereon; for it *is* an offering of jealousy, an offering of memorial, [n]bring-
ing iniquity to remembrance.
16 And the priest shall bring her
near, and [o]set her before the LORD:
17 And the priest shall take holy water in an earthen vessel; and of the dust
that is in the floor of the tabernacle the
priest shall take, and put *it* into the
water:
18 And the priest shall set the woman
before the LORD, and uncover the woman's head, and put the offering of memorial in her hands, which *is* the jealousy offering: and the priest shall have
in his hand the bitter water that causeth
the curse:
19 And the priest shall charge her
by an oath, and say unto the woman,
If no man have lain with thee, and if
thou hast not gone aside to uncleanness [2]*with another* instead of thy husband, be thou free from this bitter water that causeth the curse:
20 But if thou hast gone aside *to another* instead of thy husband, and if
thou be defiled, and some man have
lain with thee beside thine husband:
21 Then the priest shall [p]charge the
woman with an oath of cursing, and the
priest shall say unto the woman, [q]The
LORD make thee a curse and an oath
among thy people, when the LORD doth
make thy thigh to [3]rot, and thy belly to
swell;
22 And this water that causeth the
curse [r]shall go into thy bowels, to
make *thy* belly to swell, and *thy* thigh
to rot: [s]And the woman shall say,
Amen, amen.
23 And the priest shall write these
curses in a book, and he shall blot
them out with the bitter water:
24 And he shall cause the woman to
drink the bitter water that causeth the
curse: and the water that causeth the
curse shall enter into her, *and become*
bitter.
25 Then the priest shall take the jealousy offering out of the woman's hand,
and shall [t]wave the offering before the
LORD, and offer it upon the altar:
26 And [u]the priest shall take an
handful of the offering, *even* the memorial thereof, and burn *it* upon the altar,
and afterward shall cause the woman
to drink the water.
27 And when he hath made her to
drink the water, then it shall come
to pass, *that,* if she be defiled, and
have done trespass against her husband, that the water that causeth the
curse shall enter into her, *and become*
bitter, and her belly shall swell, and
her thigh shall rot: and the woman
[v]shall be a curse among her people.
28 And if the woman be not defiled,
but be clean; then she [w]shall be free,
and shall conceive seed.
29 This *is* the law of jealousies, when
a wife goeth aside *to another* instead of
her husband, and is defiled;
30 Or when the spirit of jealousy
cometh upon him, and he be jealous
over his wife, and shall set the woman
before the LORD, and the priest shall
execute upon her all this law.
31 Then shall the man be guiltless
from iniquity, and this woman [x]shall
bear her iniquity.

6 And the LORD spake unto Mō'ses,
saying,
2 Speak unto the children of Ĭs'ra-el,
and say unto them, When either man
or woman shall [1]separate *themselves*
to vow a vow of a Năz'a-rīte, to separate *themselves* unto the LORD:
3 [a]He shall separate *himself* from
wine and strong drink, and shall drink
no vinegar of wine, or vinegar of strong
drink, neither shall he drink any liquor
of grapes, nor eat moist grapes, or
dried.
4 All the days of his [2]separation shall
he eat nothing that is made of the [3]vine
tree, from the kernels even to the husk.
5 All the days of the vow of his separation there shall no [b]razor come upon
his head: until the days be fulfilled, in
the which he separateth *himself* unto
the LORD, he shall be holy, *and* shall let
the locks of the hair of his head grow.
6 All the days that he separateth
himself unto the LORD [c]he shall come
at no dead body.
7 [d]He shall not make himself unclean for his father, or for his mother,
for his brother, or for his sister, when
they die: because the [4]consecration of
his God *is* upon his head.
8 All the days of his separation he *is*
holy unto the LORD.
9 And if any man die very suddenly
by him, and he hath defiled the head of
his consecration; then he shall [e]shave
his head in the day of his cleansing, on
the seventh day shall he shave it.
10 And [f]on the eighth day he shall
bring two turtles, or two young pigeons, to the priest, to the door of the
tabernacle of the congregation:
11 And the priest shall offer the one
for a sin offering, and the other for a
burnt offering, and make an atonement for him, for that he sinned by the
dead, and shall hallow his head that
same day.
12 And he shall consecrate unto the
LORD the days of his separation, and
shall bring a lamb of the first year for
a trespass offering: but the days that
were before shall [5]be lost, because his
separation was defiled.
13 ¶ And this *is* the law of the Năz'a-
rīte, when [g]the days of his separation

14 [l]Prov. 6.34; Song 8.6; Isa. 19.14
15 [m]Lev. 5.11; Isa. 53.4-5
[n]1 Ki. 17.18
16 [o]Lev. 10.3; 1 Chr. 28.9; Jer. 17.10; Mal. 3.5; Heb. 13.4
19 [2]under thy husband, or, being in the power of thy husband
21 [p]Gen. 9.25; Josh. 6.26; Neh. 10.29; Mal. 4.6; Matt. 26.74
[q]Isa. 65.15; Jer. 29.22
[3]fall
22 [r]Ps. 109.18; Prov. 1.31
[s]Deut. 27.15
25 [t]Lev. 8.27
26 [u]Lev. 2.2-9
27 [v]Deut. 28.37; Ps. 83.9; Eccl. 7.26; Isa. 65.15; Jer. 24.9; Zech. 8.13
28 [w]Job 17.8-9; Ps. 37.5-6; Rom. 5.3-5
31 [x]Lev. 20.17; Rom. 2.8-9
CHAPTER 6
2 [1]Or, make themselves Nazarites
3 [a]Lev. 10.9; Judg. 13.4; Amos 2.12; Luke 1.15
4 [2]Or, Naza-riteship
[3]vine of the wine
5 [b]Judg. 13.5; 1 Sam. 1.11; Lam. 4.7
6 [c]Lev. 19.28; Lev. 21.11; Jer. 16.5-6; Matt. 8.21-22
7 [d]ch. 9.6
[4]separation
9 [e]Acts 18.18
10 [f]Lev. 5.7
12 [5]fall
13 [g]Acts 21.26

are fulfilled: he shall be brought unto
the door of the tabernacle of the congregation:
14 And he shall offer his offering
unto the LORD, one he lamb of the first
year without blemish for a burnt offering, and one ewe lamb of the first
year without blemish [h]for a sin offering, and one ram without blemish [i]for
peace offerings,
15 And a basket of unleavened
bread, [j]cakes of fine flour mingled
with oil, and wafers of unleavened
bread [k]anointed with oil, and their
meat offering, and their [l]drink offerings.
16 And the priest shall bring *them*
before the LORD, and shall offer his sin
offering, and his burnt offering:
17 And he shall offer the ram *for* a
sacrifice of peace offerings unto the
LORD, with the basket of unleavened
bread: the priest shall offer also his
meat offering, and his drink offering.
18 And [m]the Năz'a-rīte shall shave
the head of his separation *at* the door
of the tabernacle of the congregation,
and shall take the hair of the head of his
separation, and [n]put *it* in the fire which
is under the sacrifice of the peace offerings.
19 And the priest shall take the [o]sod-
den shoulder of the ram, and one unleavened cake out of the basket, and
one unleavened wafer, and [p]shall put
them upon the hands of the Năz'a-
rīte, after *the hair of* his separation is
shaven:
20 And the priest shall wave [q]them
for a wave offering before the LORD:
this *is* holy for the priest, with the
wave breast and heave shoulder: and
[r]after that the Năz'a-rīte may drink
wine.
21 This *is* the law of the Năz'a-rīte
who hath vowed, *and of* his offering
unto the LORD for his separation, beside *that* that his hand shall get: according to the vow which he vowed, so
he must do after the law of his separation.
22 ¶ And the LORD spake unto Mō'-
ses, saying,
23 Speak unto Aâr'on and unto his
sons, saying, On this wise [s]ye shall
bless the children of Ĭs'ra-el, saying
unto them,
24 The LORD [t]bless thee, and [u]keep
thee:
25 The LORD [v]make his face shine
upon thee, and [w]be gracious unto thee:
26 The [x]LORD lift up his countenance upon thee, and [y]give thee peace.
27 And [z]they shall put my name
upon the children of Ĭs'ra-el; and [a]I
will bless them.

7 And it came to pass on the day
that Mō'ses had fully set up the
tabernacle, and had anointed it, and
[a]sanctified it, and all the instruments
thereof, both the altar and all the vessels thereof, and had anointed them,
and sanctified them;
2 That the princes of Ĭs'ra-el, heads
of the house of their fathers, who *were*

14 [h]Lev. 4.2
[i]Lev. 3.6
15 [j]Lev. 2.4; Lev. 8.2; John 6.50-53
[k]Ex. 29.2
[l]ch. 15.5-7; Isa. 62.9; Joel 1.9-13; 1 Cor. 10.3
18 [m]Acts 21.24
[n]Luke 17.10; Rom. 6.6; Col. 3.9
19 [o]Lev. 8.31
[p]Ex. 29.23-24
20 [q]Lev. 9.21
[r]Eccl. 9.7; Isa. 35.10; John 17.4-5; Rev. 14.13
23 [s]1 Chr. 23.13
24 [t]Ps. 134.3
[u]Ps. 121.7; John 17.11; 1 Pet. 1.5
25 [v]Ps. 67.1; Dan. 9.17
[w]Gen. 43.29; Rom. 5.21
26 [x]Ps. 21.6; Acts 2.28
[y]Ps. 85.10; 2 Thess. 3.16
27 [z]Deut. 28.10; 2 Chr. 7.14
[a]Ps. 115.12

CHAPTER 7
1 [a]Gen. 32.26-29; Eph. 1.3
2 [1]who stood
[b]Ex. 35.27; Neh. 7.70-72
9 [c]2 Sam. 6.13; 1 Chr. 23.26
10 [d]Deut. 20.5; Ezra 6.16
11 [e]1 Cor. 15.23
13 [f]Ex. 25.29; Jer. 52.19
[2]There were three shekels: the royal shekel, value 1*s.* 3*d.*, the shekel of the sanctuary, value 2*s.* 6*d.*, and the common shekel, about 1*s*
14 [g]2 Ki. 25.14-15
[h]Ex. 30.34; Rev. 5.8
16 [i]Lev. 4.23
17 [j]Luke 3.32

the princes of the tribes, [1]and were
over them that were numbered, [b]of-
fered:
3 And they brought their offering before the LORD, six covered wagons,
and twelve oxen; a wagon for two of
the princes, and for each one an ox:
and they brought them before the tabernacle.
4 And the LORD spake unto Mō'ses,
saying,
5 Take *it* of them, that they may be
to do the service of the tabernacle of
the congregation; and thou shalt give
them unto the Lē'vītes, to every man
according to his service.
6 And Mō'ses took the wagons and
the oxen, and gave them unto the Lē'-
vītes.
7 Two wagons and four oxen he
gave unto the sons of Gēr'shŏn, according to their service:
8 And four wagons and eight oxen
he gave unto the sons of Me-rā'rī, according unto their service, under the
hand of Ĭth'a-mär the son of Aâr'on
the priest.
9 But unto the sons of Kō'hath he
gave none: because the service of the
sanctuary belonging unto them [c]*was*
that they should bear upon their shoulders.
10 ¶ And the princes offered [d]for
dedicating of the altar in the day that it
was anointed, even the princes offered
their offering before the altar.
11 And the LORD said unto Mō'ses,
They shall offer their offering, each
prince [e]on his day, for the dedicating
of the altar.
12 ¶ And he that offered his offering
the first day was Näh'shon the son of
Ăm-mĭn'a-dab, of the tribe of Jū'dah:
13 And his offering *was* one silver
charger, the [f]weight thereof *was* an
hundred and thirty *shekels,* one silver
bowl of seventy shekels, after [2]the
shekel of the sanctuary; both of them
were full of fine flour mingled with oil
for a meat offering:
14 One [g]spoon of ten *shekels* of gold,
full of [h]incense:
15 One young bullock, one ram, one
lamb of the first year, for a burnt offering:
16 One kid of the goats for [i]a sin
offering:
17 And for a sacrifice of peace offerings, two oxen, five rams, five he
goats, five lambs of the first year: this
was the offering of Näh'shon [j]the son
of Ăm-mĭn'a-dab.
18 ¶ On the second day Ne-thăn'e-el
the son of Zū'ar, prince of Ĭs'sa-char,
did offer:
19 He offered *for* his offering one silver charger, the weight whereof *was*
an hundred and thirty *shekels,* one silver bowl of seventy shekels, after the
shekel of the sanctuary; both of them
full of fine flour mingled with oil for a
meat offering:
20 One spoon of gold of ten *shekels,*
full of incense:

21 One young bullock, one ram, one
lamb of the first year, for [k]a burnt offering:
22 One kid of the goats for a sin offering:
23 And for a sacrifice of [l]peace offerings, two oxen, five rams, five he
goats, five lambs of the first year: this
was the offering of Ne-thăn'e-el the
son of Zū'ar.
24 ¶ On the third day E-lī'ab the son
of Hē'lon, prince of the children of
Zĕb'u-lun, *did offer:*
25 His offering *was* one silver
charger, the weight whereof *was* an
hundred and thirty *shekels,* one silver
bowl of seventy shekels, after the shekel of the sanctuary; both of them full of
fine flour mingled with oil for a meat
offering:
26 One golden spoon of ten *shekels,*
full of incense:
27 One young bullock, one ram, one
[m]lamb of the first year, for a burnt offering:
28 One kid of the goats for a sin offering:
29 And for a sacrifice of peace offerings, two oxen, five rams, five he
goats, five lambs of the first year: this
was the offering of E-lī'ab the son of
Hē'lon.
30 ¶ On the fourth day E-lī'zŭr the
son of Shĕd'ĕ-ur, prince of the children
of Reu'ben, *did offer:*
31 His offering *was* one silver
charger of the weight of an hundred
and thirty *shekels,* one silver bowl of
seventy shekels, after the shekel of the
sanctuary; both of them full of fine
flour mingled with oil for a meat offering:
32 One golden spoon of ten *shekels,*
full of incense:
33 One young bullock, one ram, one
lamb of the first year, for a burnt offering:
34 One kid of the goats for a sin offering:
35 And for a sacrifice of peace offerings, two oxen, five rams, five he
goats, five lambs of the first year: this
was the offering of E-lī'zŭr the son of
Shĕd'ĕ-ur.
36 ¶ On the fifth day She-lū'mĭ-el
the son of Zū-rĭ-shăd'da-ī, prince of
the children of Sĭm'e-on, *did offer:*
37 His offering *was* one silver
charger, the weight whereof *was* an
hundred and thirty *shekels,* one silver
bowl of seventy shekels, after the shekel of the sanctuary; both of them full of
fine flour mingled with oil for a meat
offering:
38 One golden spoon of ten *shekels,*
full of incense:
39 One young bullock, one ram, one
[n]lamb of the first year, for a burnt offering:
40 One kid of the goats for a sin offering:
41 And for a sacrifice of peace offerings, two oxen, five rams, five he
goats, five lambs of the first year: this
was the offering of She-lū'mĭ-el the
son of Zū-rĭ-shăd'da-ī.
42 ¶ On the sixth day [o][3]E-lī'a-săph
the son of Deŭ'el, prince of the children of Găd, *offered:*
43 His offering *was* one silver
charger of the weight of an hundred
and thirty *shekels,* a silver bowl of seventy shekels, after the shekel of the
sanctuary; both of them full of fine
flour mingled with [p]oil for a meat offering:
44 One golden spoon of ten *shekels,*
full of incense:
45 One [q]young bullock, one ram,
one lamb of the first year, for a burnt
offering:
46 One kid of the goats for a sin offering:
47 And for a sacrifice of [4]peace offerings, two oxen, five rams, five he
goats, five lambs of the first year: this
was the offering of E-lī'a-săph the son
of Deŭ'el.
48 ¶ On the seventh day [r]E-lĭsh'a-
mȧ the son of Ăm-mī'hŭd, prince of the
children of Ē'phră-ĭm, *offered:*
49 His offering *was* one silver
charger, the weight whereof *was* an
hundred and thirty *shekels,* one silver
bowl of seventy shekels, after the shekel of the sanctuary; both of them full of
fine flour mingled with oil for a meat
offering:
50 One golden spoon of ten *shekels,*
full of [s]incense:
51 One [t]young bullock, one ram,
one lamb of the first year, for a burnt
offering:
52 One kid of the goats for a sin offering:
53 And for a sacrifice of peace offerings, two oxen, five rams, five he
goats, five lambs of the first year: this
was the offering of E-lĭsh'a-mȧ the son
of Ăm-mī'hŭd.
54 ¶ On the eighth day *offered* Ga-
mā'lĭ-el [u]the son of Pe-dăh'zur, prince
of the children of Ma-năs'seh:
55 His offering *was* one silver
charger of the weight of an hundred
and thirty *shekels,* one silver bowl of
seventy shekels, after the shekel of the
sanctuary; both of them full of fine
flour mingled with oil for a meat offering:
56 One golden spoon of ten *shekels,*
full of [v]incense:
57 One young bullock, one ram, one
[w]lamb of the first year, for a burnt offering:
58 One kid of the goats for a sin offering:
59 And for [x]a sacrifice of peace offerings, two oxen, five rams, five he
goats, five lambs of the first year: this
was the offering of Ga-mā'lĭ-el the son
of Pe-dăh'zur.
60 ¶ On the ninth day [y]Ăb'i-dăn the
son of Gĭd-e-ō'nī, prince of the children of Bĕn'ja-min, *offered:*
61 His offering *was* one silver
charger, the weight whereof *was* an
hundred and thirty *shekels,* one silver
bowl of seventy shekels, after the

21 [k]Gen. 8.20; Lev. 6.9; Ps. 20.1-3; Ps. 51.19; Ezek. 45.17; Eph. 5.2; Heb. 9.13

23 [l]Lev. 7.11-13; 1 Ki. 8.63; Prov. 7.14; Col. 1.20

27 [m]Isa. 53.7; John 1.29; Acts 8.32; Gal. 1.4; 1 Pet. 1.19; Rev. 5.6-14

39 [n]Ex. 12.5; Isa. 53.7; John 1.29; Acts 8.32; Heb. 9.28; 1 Pet. 1.19; Rev. 5.6

42 [o]ch. 1.14; ch. 2.14; ch. 10.20
[3]Son of Reuel

43 [p]Lev. 2.5; Lev. 14.10; Heb. 1.9; 1 John 2.27

45 [q]Ps. 40.6; Ps. 50.8-14; Ps. 51.16; Isa. 1.11; Jer. 7.22; Amos 5.22; 2 Cor. 5.21

47 [4]A sacrifice of payment, or, of perfections

48 [r]ch. 1.10; ch. 2.18; 1 Chr. 7.26

50 [s]Deut. 33.10; Ps. 66.15; Ps. 141.2; Ezek. 8.11; Mal. 1.11; Luke 1.10; Rev. 5.8; Rev. 8.3

51 [t]Mic. 6.6-8

54 [u]ch. 1.10; ch. 2.20

56 [v]Ex. 30.7

[w]Ex. 12.5; John 1.29; Acts 8.32; 1 Pet. 1.19; Rev. 5.6

59 [x]Lev. 3.1; Mic. 5.5; 2 Cor. 5.19-21; Eph. 2.14

60 [y]ch. 1.11; ch. 2.22

shekel of the sanctuary; both of them full of fine flour mingled with oil for a meat offering:

62 One golden spoon of ten *shekels*, full of [z]incense:

63 One [a]young bullock, one ram, one lamb of the first year, for a burnt offering:

64 One kid of the goats for a sin offering:

65 And for a sacrifice of [b]peace offerings, two oxen, five rams, five he goats, five lambs of the first year: this *was* the offering of Ăb'i-dăn the son of Gĭd-e-ō'nī.

66 ¶ On the tenth day [c]Ā-hi-ē'zĕr the son of Ăm-mi-shăd'da-ī, prince of the children of Dăn, *offered:*

67 His offering *was* one silver charger, the weight whereof *was* an hundred and thirty *shekels*, one silver bowl of seventy shekels, after the [d]shekel of the sanctuary; both of them full of fine flour mingled with oil for a meat offering:

68 One golden spoon of ten *shekels*, full of [e]incense:

69 One young bullock, one ram, one lamb of the first year, for a burnt offering:

70 One kid of the goats for a sin offering:

71 And for a sacrifice of peace offerings, two oxen, five rams, five he goats, five lambs of the first year: this *was* the offering of Ā-hi-ē'zĕr the son of Ăm-mi-shăd'da-ī.

72 ¶ On the eleventh day [f]Pā'gi-el the son of Ŏc'ran, prince of the children of Ăsh'ĕr, *offered:*

73 His offering *was* one silver charger, the weight whereof *was* an hundred and thirty *shekels*, one silver bowl of seventy shekels, after the shekel of the sanctuary; both of them full of fine flour mingled with oil for a meat offering:

74 One golden spoon of ten *shekels*, full of [g]incense:

75 One young bullock, one ram, one lamb of the first year, for a burnt offering:

76 One kid of the goats for a sin offering:

77 And for a sacrifice of peace offerings, two oxen, five rams, five he goats, five lambs of the first year: this *was* the offering of Pā'gi-el the son of Ŏc'ran.

78 ¶ On the twelfth day [h]A-hī'rȧ the son of Ē'nan, prince of the children of Năph'ta-lī, *offered:*

79 His offering *was* one [i]silver charger, the weight whereof *was* an hundred and thirty *shekels*, one silver bowl of seventy shekels, after the shekel of the sanctuary; both of them full of fine flour mingled with oil for a meat offering:

80 One golden spoon of ten *shekels*, full of incense:

81 One young bullock, one ram, one lamb of the first year, for a burnt offering:

62 [z]Isa. 66.20; Ps. 141.2; Dan. 9.27; Rom. 15.16; Phil. 4.18; Heb. 13.15; Rev. 5.8
63 [a]Ps. 40.6; Isa. 53.4; 2 Cor. 5.21
65 [b]Lev. 3.1; 1 Ki. 8.63; Prov. 7.14; Col. 1.20
66 [c]ch. 1.12; ch. 2.25
67 [d]Lev. 27.25; ch. 3.47
68 [e]Ex. 30.7-9; Ps. 141.2; Isa. 66.20; Dan. 9.27; Heb. 13.15
72 [f]ch. 1.13; ch. 2.27
74 [g]Mal. 1.11; Luke 1.11
78 [h]ch. 1.15; ch. 2.29
79 [i]Ezra 1.9-10; Matt. 14.8-11
84 [j]1 Chr. 29.6; Rev. 21.14
[k]Josh. 22.13-14; Hos. 13.10
86 [l]Ex. 30.13
87 [m]Rom. 12.1
[n]Lev. 2.1; ch. 15.4
89 [o]Ex. 31.18; ch. 12.8
[5]That is, God
[p]Ex. 25.22; Heb. 4.16
[q]Gen. 3.24; Heb. 1.14
CHAPTER 8
2 [a]Ex. 40.25; John 1.9
4 [b]Ex. 25.31
[c]Ex. 25.18
[d]Ex. 25.40
6 [e]Ps. 26.6; Heb. 7.26
7 [1]sin water, ch. 19.9-17
[2]let them cause a razor to pass over, etc
[f]Lev. 14.8-9
8 [g]Lev. 2.1
9 [h]Ex. 29.4
[i]Lev. 8.3

82 One kid of the goats for a sin offering:

83 And for a sacrifice of peace offerings, two oxen, five rams, five he goats, five lambs of the first year: this *was* the offering of A-hī'rȧ the son of Ē'nan.

84 This *was* [j]the dedication of the altar, in the day when it was anointed, by [k]the princes of Is'ra-el: twelve chargers of silver, twelve silver bowls, twelve spoons of gold:

85 Each charger of silver *weighing* an hundred and thirty *shekels*, each bowl seventy: all the silver vessels *weighed* two thousand and four hundred *shekels*, after the shekel of the sanctuary:

86 The golden spoons *were* twelve, full of incense, *weighing* ten *shekels* apiece, after the [l]shekel of the sanctuary: all the gold of the spoons *was* an hundred and twenty *shekels*.

87 All the oxen for the [m]burnt offering *were* twelve bullocks, the rams twelve, the lambs of the first year twelve, with their [n]meat offering: and the kids of the goats for sin offering twelve.

88 And all the oxen for the sacrifice of the peace offerings *were* twenty and four bullocks, the rams sixty, the he goats sixty, the lambs of the first year sixty. This *was* the dedication of the altar, after that it was anointed.

89 And when Mō'ses was gone into the tabernacle of the congregation [o]to speak with [5]him, then he heard [p]the voice of one speaking unto him from off the mercy seat that *was* upon the ark of testimony, from between [q]the two cherubims: and he spake unto him.

8 And the LORD spake unto Mō'ses, saying,

2 Speak unto Aâr'on, and say unto him, When thou [a]lightest the lamps, the seven lamps shall give light over against the candlestick.

3 And Aâr'on did so; he lighted the lamps thereof over against the candlestick, as the LORD commanded Mō'ses.

4 And [b]this work of the candlestick *was of* beaten gold, unto the shaft thereof, unto the flowers thereof, *was* [c]beaten work: [d]according unto the pattern which the LORD had shewed Mō'ses, so he made the candlestick.

5 ¶ And the LORD spake unto Mō'ses, saying,

6 Take the Lē'vītes from among the children of Is'ra-el, and [e]cleanse them.

7 And thus shalt thou do unto them, to cleanse them: Sprinkle [1]water of purifying upon them, and [2]let them [f]shave all their flesh, and let them wash their clothes, and *so* make themselves clean.

8 Then let them take a young bullock with [g]his meat offering, *even* fine flour mingled with oil, and another young bullock shalt thou take for a sin offering.

9 And [h]thou shalt bring the Lē'vītes before the tabernacle of the congregation: [i]and thou shalt gather the whole

assembly of the children of Ĭs'ra-el together:
10 And thou shalt bring the Lē'vītes
before the LORD: and the children of
Ĭs'ra-el [j]shall put their hands upon the
Lē'vītes:
11 And Aâr'on shall [3]offer the Lē'-
vītes before the LORD *for* an [4]offering
of the children of Ĭs'ra-el, that [5]they
may execute the service of the LORD.
12 And [k]the Lē'vītes shall lay their
hands upon the heads of the bullocks:
and thou shalt offer the one *for* a sin
offering, and the other *for* a burnt offering, unto the LORD, to make an atonement for the Lē'vītes.
13 And thou shalt set the Lē'vītes before Aâr'on, and before his sons, and
offer them *for* an offering unto the
LORD.
14 Thus shalt thou separate the Lē'-
vītes from among the children of Ĭs'ra-
el: and the Lē'vītes shall be [l]mine.
15 And after that shall the Lē'vītes
go in to do the service of the tabernacle
of the congregation: and thou shalt
cleanse them, and [m]offer them *for* an
offering.
16 For they *are* wholly given unto
me from among the children of Ĭs'ra-el;
[n]instead of such as open every womb,
even instead of the firstborn of all the
children of Ĭs'ra-el, have I taken them
unto me.
17 [o]For all the firstborn of the children of Ĭs'ra-el *are* mine, *both* man
and beast: on the day that I smote every firstborn in the land of Ē'gypt I
sanctified them for myself.
18 And I have taken the Lē'vītes for
all the firstborn of the children of Ĭs'ra-
el.
19 And [p]I have given the Lē'vītes *as*
[6]a gift to Aâr'on and to his sons from
among the children of Ĭs'ra-el, to do the
service of the children of Ĭs'ra-el in the
tabernacle of the congregation, and to
make an atonement for the children
of Ĭs'ra-el: [q]that there be no plague
among the children of Ĭs'ra-el, when
the children of Ĭs'ra-el come nigh unto
the sanctuary.
20 And Mō'ses, and Aâr'on, and all
the congregation of the children of Ĭs'-
ra-el, did to the Lē'vītes according unto
all that the LORD commanded Mō'ses
concerning the Lē'vītes, so did the children of Ĭs'ra-el unto them.
21 And the Lē'vītes were purified,
and they washed their clothes; and
[r]Aâr'on offered them *as* an offering
before the LORD; and Aâr'on made an
atonement for them to cleanse them.
22 And [s]after that went the Lē'vītes
in to do their service in the tabernacle
of the congregation before Aâr'on, and
before his sons: as the LORD had commanded Mō'ses concerning the Lē'-
vītes, so did they unto them.
23 ¶ And the LORD spake unto Mō'-
ses, saying,
24 This *is it* that *belongeth* unto the
[t]Lē'vītes: from twenty and five years
old and upward they shall go in [7]to

10 [j]Lev. 1.4
11 [3]wave
[4]wave offering
[5]they may be to execute, etc
12 [k]Ex. 29.10; Lev. 1.4; Lev. 8.14; Lev. 16.21
14 [l]ch. 3.45; ch. 16.9; Mal. 3.17
15 [m]Ex. 29.24
16 [n]ch. 3.12-45
17 [o]Ex. 13.2-12-13-15; Luke 2.23
19 [p]ch. 3.9
[6]given
[q]ch. 1.53; ch. 16.46
21 [r]Rom. 15.16
22 [s]2 Chr. 30.15; 2 Chr. 31.2
24 [t]ch. 4.3; 1 Chr. 23.3-24-27
[7]to war the warfare of, etc
25 [8]return from the warfare of the service
26 [u]ch. 1.53; 1 Chr. 23.28-32; Ezek. 44.8-11

CHAPTER 9
2 [a]Ex. 12.12; Lev. 23.5; ch. 28.16; Deut. 16.1-2; Heb. 10.1
3 [1]between the two evenings
5 [b]Josh. 5.10
6 [c]ch. 5.2; ch. 6.6-7; John 18.28
[d]Ex. 18.15
7 [e]1 Cor. 5.7-8
8 [f]Ps. 25.14; Ps. 85.8; Prov. 3.5-6; John 7.17; Eph. 1.9-18; Heb. 3.5-6
11 [g]2 Chr. 30.2-15
[h]Ex. 12.8
12 [i]Ex. 12.10
[j]John 19.36
[k]Ex. 12.43
13 [l]Gen. 17.14; Ex. 12.15; Lev. 17.4-10-14-16; Heb. 6.6; Heb. 12.25
[m]ch. 5.31; Heb. 10.26

wait upon the service of the tabernacle
of the congregation:
25 And from the age of fifty years
they shall [8]cease waiting upon the service *thereof*, and shall serve no more:
26 But shall minister with their brethren in the tabernacle of the congregation, [u]to keep the charge, and shall do
no service. Thus shalt thou do unto the
Lē'vītes touching their charge.
9 And the LORD spake unto Mō'ses in
the wilderness of Sī'nāi, in the first
month of the second year after they
were come out of the land of Ē'gypt,
saying,
2 Let the children of Ĭs'ra-el also
keep [a]the passover at his appointed
season.
3 In the fourteenth day of this month,
[1]at even, ye shall keep it in his appointed season: according to all the
rites of it, and according to all the ceremonies thereof, shall ye keep it.
4 And Mō'ses spake unto the children of Ĭs'ra-el, that they should keep
the passover.
5 And [b]they kept the passover on
the fourteenth day of the first month
at even in the wilderness of Sī'nāi:
according to all that the LORD commanded Mō'ses, so did the children of
Ĭs'ra-el.
6 ¶ And there were certain men, who
were [c]defiled by the dead body of a
man, that they could not keep the passover on that day: and [d]they came before Mō'ses and before Aâr'on on that
day:
7 And those men said unto him, We
are defiled by the dead body of a man:
wherefore are we kept back, that we
may [e]not offer an offering of the LORD
in his appointed season among the children of Ĭs'ra-el?
8 And Mō'ses said unto them, Stand
still, and [f]I will hear what the LORD
will command concerning you.
9 ¶ And the LORD spake unto Mō'-
ses, saying,
10 Speak unto the children of Ĭs'ra-
el, saying, If any man of you or of your
posterity shall be unclean by reason of
a dead body, or *be* in a journey afar off,
yet he shall keep the passover unto the
LORD.
11 The [g]fourteenth day of the second month at even they shall keep it,
and [h]eat it with unleavened bread and
bitter *herbs*.
12 [i]They shall leave none of it unto
the morning, [j]nor break any bone of it:
[k]according to all the ordinances of the
passover they shall keep it.
13 But the man that *is* clean, and is
not in a journey, and forbeareth to
keep the passover, even the same soul
[l]shall be cut off from among his people: because he brought not the offering of the LORD in his appointed season, that man shall [m]bear his sin.
14 And if a stranger shall sojourn
among you, and will keep the passover
unto the LORD; according to the ordinance of the passover, and according
to the manner thereof, so shall he do:

[n]ye shall have one ordinance, both for
the [2]stranger, and for him that was
born in the land.
15 ¶ And on the day that the tabernacle was reared up the cloud covered the
tabernacle, *namely,* the tent of the testimony: and [o]at even there was upon the
tabernacle as it were the appearance of
fire, until the morning.
16 So it was alway: the cloud covered it *by day,* and the appearance of
fire by night.
17 And when the [p]cloud [q]was taken
up from the tabernacle, then after that
the children of Ĭs'ra-el journeyed: and
in the place where the cloud abode,
there the children of Ĭs'ra-el pitched
their tents.
18 At the commandment of the LORD
the children of Ĭs'ra-el journeyed, and
at the commandment of the LORD they
pitched: [r]as long as the cloud abode
upon the tabernacle they rested in their
tents.
19 And when the cloud [3]tarried long
upon the tabernacle many days, then
the children of Ĭs'ra-el kept the charge
of the LORD, and journeyed not.
20 And *so* it was, when the cloud
was a few days upon the tabernacle;
according to the commandment of the
LORD they abode in their tents, and according to the commandment of the
LORD [s]they journeyed.
21 And *so* it was, when the cloud
[4]abode from even unto the morning,
and *that* the cloud was taken up in the
morning, then they journeyed: whether
it was by day or by night that the cloud
was taken up, they journeyed.
22 Or *whether it were* two days, or
a month, or a year, that the cloud tarried upon the tabernacle, remaining
thereon, the children of Ĭs'ra-el abode
in their tents, and journeyed not: [t]but
when it was taken up, they journeyed.
23 At the commandment of the LORD
they rested in the tents, and [u]at the commandment of the LORD they journeyed:
they kept the charge of the LORD, at the
commandment of the LORD by the hand
of Mō'ses.

10 And the LORD spake unto Mō'-
ses, saying,
2 Make thee two trumpets of silver;
of a whole piece shalt thou make them:
that thou mayest use them for the [a]call-
ing of the assembly, and for the journeying of the camps.
3 And when [b]they shall blow with
them, all [c]the assembly shall assemble
themselves to thee at the door of the
tabernacle of the congregation.
4 And if they blow *but* with one
trumpet, then the princes, *which are*
[d]heads of the thousands of Ĭs'ra-el,
shall gather themselves unto thee.
5 When ye blow an alarm, then the
[e]camps that lie on the east parts shall
go forward.
6 When ye blow an alarm the second time, then the camps that lie on
the south side shall take their journey:
they shall blow an alarm for their journeys.
7 But when the congregation is to be
gathered together, ye shall blow, but
ye shall not [f]sound an alarm.
8 And [g]the sons of Âar'on, the
priests, shall blow with the trumpets;
and they shall be to you for an ordinance for ever throughout your generations.
9 And if ye go to war in your land
against the enemy that [h]oppresseth
you, then ye shall blow an alarm with
the trumpets; and ye shall be [i]remem-
bered before the LORD your God, and
ye shall be saved from your enemies.
10 Also [j]in the day of your gladness,
and in your solemn days, and in the
beginnings of your months, ye shall
blow with the trumpets over your burnt
offerings, and over the sacrifices of
your peace offerings; that they may be
to you [k]for a memorial before your
God: I *am* the LORD your God.
11 ¶ And it came to pass on the twentieth *day* of the second month, in the
second year, that the cloud was [l]taken
up from off the tabernacle of the testimony.
12 And the children of Ĭs'ra-el took
[m]their journeys out of the [n]wilderness
of Sī'nāi; and the cloud rested in the
[o]wilderness of Pā'ran.
13 And they first took their journey
[p]according to the commandment of
the LORD by the hand of Mō'ses.
14 ¶ In the first *place* went the standard of the camp of the children of
Jū'dah according to their armies: and
over his host *was* Näh'shon the son of
Ăm-mĭn'a-dab.
15 And over the host of the tribe
of the children of Ĭs'sa-char *was* Ne-
thăn'e-el the son of Zū'ar.
16 And over the host of the tribe of
the children of Zĕb'u-lun *was* E-lī'ab
the son of Hē'lon.
17 And [q]the tabernacle was taken
down; and the sons of Gĕr'shŏn and
the sons of Me-rā'rī set forward, [r]bear-
ing the tabernacle.
18 ¶ And the standard of the camp
of Reu'ben set forward according to
their armies: and over his host *was* E-
lī'zŭr the son of Shĕd'ĕ-ur.
19 And over the host of the tribe of
the children of Sĭm'e-on *was* She-lū'-
mĭ-el the son of Zū-rĭ-shăd'da-ī.
20 And over the host of the tribe of
the children of Găd *was* E-lī'a-săph the
son of Deu'el.
21 And the Kō'hath-ītes set forward,
bearing the [1]sanctuary: and [2]*the other*
did set up the tabernacle against they
came.
22 ¶ And the standard of the camp
of the children of Ē'phră-ĭm set forward according to their armies: and
over his host *was* E-lĭsh'a-mȧ the son
of Ăm-mī'hŭd.
23 And over the host of the tribe of
the children of Ma-năs'seh *was* Ga-
mā'lĭ-el the son of Pe-dāh'zur.
24 And over the host of the tribe of
the children of Bĕn'ja-min *was* Ăb'i-
dăn the son of Gĭd-e-ō'nī.

14 [n]Ex. 12.49 [2]proselyte
15 [o]Ex. 13.21
17 [p]Ex. 13.21-22; Deut. 1.33; Neh. 9.12 [q]Ex. 40.36-37; ch. 10.11-33-34; Ps. 78.14; Isa. 49.10; John 10.4
18 [r]1 Cor. 10.1
19 [3]prolonged
20 [s]Ps. 48.14; Prov. 3.5-6
21 [4]was
22 [t]Ex. 40.36-37; Ps. 73.24; Isa. 63.14
23 [u]Ps. 73.24; Isa. 63.14

CHAPTER 10
2 [a]Ps. 81.3; Ps. 89.15; Isa. 1.13; Hos. 8.1; Joel 1.14
3 [b]Jer. 4.5; Joel 2.15 [c]Ps. 22.22; Ps. 35.18; Ps. 36.7-8; Ps. 40.9-10; Isa. 55.1-4; Zech. 8.21-23; Rev. 22.17
4 [d]Ex. 18.21; ch. 1.16
5 [e]ch. 2.3
7 [f]Joel 2.1
8 [g]ch. 31.6; Josh. 6.4; 1 Chr. 15.24; 2 Chr. 13.12
9 [h]Judg. 2.18; Judg. 3.27; Ps. 106.42 [i]Gen. 8.1; Ps. 106.4
10 [j]Lev. 23.24; Ps. 81.3 [k]Ex. 28.29; 1 Cor. 11.24-26
11 [l]ch. 9.17
12 [m]Ex. 40.36 [n]ch. 1.1 [o]ch. 12.16; Hab. 3.3
13 [p]ch. 2.34
17 [q]ch. 1.51 [r]ch. 4.24-31
21 [1]The most holy furniture [2]That is, the Gershonites and the Merarites

25 ¶ And [s]the standard of the camp
of the children of Dăn set forward,
which was the rereward of all the
camps throughout their hosts: and over
his host *was* Ā-hi-ē'zēr the son of Ăm-
mi-shăd'da-ī.
26 And over the host of the tribe of
the children of Ăsh'ēr *was* Pā'gĭ-el the
son of Ŏc'ran.
27 And over the host of the tribe of
the children of Năph'ta-lī *was* A-hī'ră
the son of Ē'nan.
28 [3t]Thus *were* the journeyings of
the children of Ĭs'ra-el according to
their armies, when they set forward.
29 ¶ And Mō'ses said unto Hō-băb,
the son of [u]Ra-gū'el the Mĭd'ĭ-an-īte,
Mō'ses' father in law, We are journeying unto the place of which the LORD
said, [v]I will give it you: come thou with
us, and [w]we will do thee good: for [x]the
LORD hath spoken good concerning
Ĭs'ra-el.
30 And he said unto him, I will not
go; but I will depart to mine own land,
and to my kindred.
31 And he said, Leave us not, I pray
thee; forasmuch as thou knowest how
we are to encamp in the wilderness,
and thou mayest be to us [y]instead of
eyes.
32 And it shall be, if thou go with us,
yea, it shall be, that what goodness the
LORD shall do unto us, the same will
we do unto thee.
33 ¶ And they departed from [z]the
mount of the LORD three days' journey: and the ark of the covenant of the
LORD [a]went before them in the three
days' journey, to search out a resting
place for them.
34 And [b]the cloud of the LORD *was*
upon them by day, when they went out
of the camp.
35 And it came to pass, when the ark
set forward, that Mō'ses said, [c]Rise up,
LORD, and let thine enemies be scattered; and let them that hate thee flee
before thee.
36 And when it rested, he said, Return, [d]O LORD, unto the [4]many thousands of Ĭs'ra-el.

CHAPTER 11

11 And [a]*when* the people [1]com-
plained, [2]it displeased the LORD:
and the LORD heard *it;* and his anger was kindled; and the [b]fire of the
LORD burnt among them, and consumed *them that were* in the uttermost parts of the camp.
2 And the people cried unto Mō'ses;
and when Mō'ses [c]prayed unto the
LORD, the fire [3]was quenched.
3 And he called the name of the
place [4]Tăb'e-rah: because the fire of
the LORD burnt among them.
4 ¶ And the [d]mixt multitude that *was*
among them [5]fell a lusting: and the children of Ĭs'ra-el also [6]wept again, and
said, [e]Who shall give us flesh to eat?
5 [f]We remember the fish, which we
did eat in Ē'gypt freely; the cucumbers, and the melons, and the leeks,
and the onions, and the garlick:
6 But now our soul *is* dried away:
there is nothing at all, beside this manna, *before* our eyes.
7 And the manna *was* as coriander
seed, and the [7]colour thereof as the colour of [g]bdellium.
8 *And* the people went about, and
gathered *it*, and ground *it* in mills, or
beat *it* in a mortar, and baked *it* in
pans, and made cakes of it: and the
taste of it was as the taste of fresh oil.
9 And when the dew fell upon the
camp in the night, the manna fell upon
it.
10 ¶ Then Mō'ses heard the people
weep throughout their families, every
man in the door of his tent: and the
anger of the LORD was kindled greatly;
Mō'ses also was displeased.
11 And [h]Mō'ses said unto the LORD,
Wherefore hast thou afflicted thy servant? and wherefore have I not found
favour in thy sight, that thou layest the
burden of all this people upon me?
12 Have I conceived all this people?
have I begotten them, that thou shouldest say unto me, [i]Carry them in thy
bosom, as a [j]nursing father beareth
the sucking child, unto the land which
thou [k]swarest unto their fathers?
13 [l]Whence should I have flesh to
give unto all this people? for they weep
unto me, saying, Give us flesh, that we
may eat.
14 [m]I am not able to bear all this
people alone, because *it is* too heavy
for me.
15 And if thou deal thus with me,
[n]kill me, I pray thee, out of hand, if I
have found favour in thy sight; and let
me not [o]see my wretchedness.
16 ¶ And the LORD said unto Mō'ses,
Gather unto me [p]seventy men of the
elders of Ĭs'ra-el, whom thou knowest
to be the elders of the people, and officers over them; and bring them unto
the tabernacle of the congregation, that
they may stand there with thee.
17 And I will [q]come down and talk
with thee there: and [r]I will take of the
spirit which *is* upon thee, and will put
it upon them; and they shall bear the
burden of the people with thee, that
thou bear *it* not thyself alone.
18 And say thou unto the people,
[s]Sanctify yourselves against to morrow, and ye shall eat flesh: for ye have
wept [t]in the ears of the LORD, saying,
Who shall give us flesh to eat? [u]for *it*
was well with us in Ē'gypt: therefore
the LORD will give you flesh, and ye
shall eat.
19 Ye shall not eat one day, nor two
days, nor five days, neither ten days,
nor twenty days;
20 *But* even a [8]whole month, until
it come out at your nostrils, and it
be loathsome unto you: because that
ye have despised the LORD which *is*
among you, and have wept before him,
saying, Why came we forth out of
Ē'gypt?
21 And Mō'ses said, The people,
among whom I *am*, *are* six hundred
thousand footmen; and thou hast said,

25 [s]Josh. 6.9
28 [3]These
[t]Ps. 80.1; Song 6.10
29 [u]Ex. 2.18
[v]Gen. 12.7
[w]Judg. 1.16
[x]Gen. 32.12
31 [y]Job 29.15
33 [z]Ex. 3.1
[a]Deut. 1.33; Jer. 31.2
34 [b]Neh. 9.12-19; Ps. 105.39
35 [c]Ps. 68.1-2; Isa. 51.9
36 [d]Ps. 90.14-17; Ps. 132.8
[4]ten thousand thousands

CHAPTER 11
1 [a]Ex. 15.23-24; Lam. 3.39
[1]Or, were as it were complainers
[2]it was evil in the ears of, etc
[b]Lev. 10.2; 2 Ki. 1.12
2 [c]Jas. 5.16
[3]sunk
3 [4]That is, A burning
4 [d]Ex. 12.38
[5]lusted a lust
[6]returned and wept
[e]1 Cor. 10.6
5 [f]Ex. 16.3; Phil. 3.19
7 [7]eye of it as the eye of
[g]Gen. 2.12
11 [h]Ex. 17.4; 2 Cor. 11.28
12 [i]Isa. 40.11; Ezek. 34.23
[j]Isa. 49.23; 1 Thess. 2.7
[k]Gen. 22.16-17; Ex. 13.5
13 [l]2 Ki. 4.43; Mark 8.4
14 [m]Ex. 18.18
15 [n]1 Ki. 19.4; Jon. 4.3
[o]Zeph. 3.15
16 [p]Ex. 24.1-9
17 [q]Gen. 11.5
[r]1 Sam. 10.6;
18 [s]Ex. 19.10
[t]Ex. 16.7
[u]Acts 7.39
20 [8]month of days

I will give them flesh, that they may eat
a whole month.
22 [v]Shall the flocks and the herds
be slain for them, to suffice them? or
shall all the fish of the sea be gathered
together for them, to suffice them?
23 And the LORD said unto Mō'ses,
[w]Is the LORD'S hand waxed short? thou
shalt see now whether [x]my word shall
come to pass unto thee or not.
24 ¶ And Mō'ses went out, and told
the people the words of the LORD, and
gathered the seventy men of the elders
of the people, and set them round about
the tabernacle.
25 And the LORD [y]came down in a
cloud, and spake unto him, and took of
the spirit that *was* upon him, and gave
it unto the seventy elders: and it came
to pass, *that,* [z]when the spirit rested
upon them, they [a]prophesied, and did
not cease.
26 But there remained two *of the*
men in the camp, the name of the one
was Ĕl'dăd, and the name of the other
Mē'dăd: and the spirit rested upon
them; and they *were* of them that were
written, but [b]went not out unto the tabernacle: and they prophesied in the
camp.
27 And there ran a young man, and
told Mō'ses, and said, Ĕl'dăd and Mē'-
dăd do prophesy in the camp.
28 And Jŏsh'u-ȧ the son of Nŭn, the
servant of Mō'ses, *one* of his young
men, answered and said, My lord Mō'-
ses, [c]forbid them.
29 And Mō'ses said unto him, En-
viest thou for my sake? [d]would God
that all the LORD'S people were prophets, *and* that the LORD would put his
spirit upon them!
30 And Mō'ses gat him into the
camp, he and the elders of Ĭs'ra-el.
31 ¶ And there went forth a [e]wind
from the LORD, and brought quails
from the sea, and let *them* fall by the
camp, as it were [9]a day's journey on
this side, and as it were a day's journey
on the other side, round about the
camp, and as it were two cubits *high*
upon the face of the earth.
32 And the people stood up all that
day, and all *that* night, and all the next
day, and they gathered the quails: he
that gathered least gathered ten [f]ho-
mers: and they spread *them* all abroad
for themselves round about the camp.
33 And while the [g]flesh *was* yet between their teeth, ere it was chewed,
the wrath of the LORD was kindled
against the people, and the LORD smote
the people with a very great plague.
34 And he called the name of that
place [10]Kĭb'roth–hat-tā'a-vah: because
there they buried the people that lusted.
35 *And* [h]the people journeyed from
Kĭb'roth–hat-tā'a-vah unto Ha-zē'roth;
and [11]abode at Ha-zē'roth.

12 And Mĭr'ĭ-am and Aâr'on spake
against Mō'ses because of the [1]Ē-
thĭ-ō'pĭ-an woman whom he had married: for [a]he had [2]married an Ē-thĭ-
ō'pĭ-an woman.
2 And they said, Hath the LORD indeed spoken only by Mō'ses? [b]hath he
not spoken also by us? And the LORD
[c]heard *it.*
3 (Now the man Mō'ses *was* [d]very
meek, above all the men which *were*
upon the face of the earth.)
4 And [e]the LORD spake suddenly
unto Mō'ses, and unto Aâr'on, and unto
Mĭr'ĭ-am, Come out ye three unto the
tabernacle of the congregation. And
they three came out.
5 And [f]the LORD came down in the
pillar of the cloud, and stood *in* the door
of the tabernacle, and called Aâr'on
and Mĭr'ĭ-am: and they both came
forth.
6 And he said, Hear now my words:
If there be a prophet among you, *I* the
LORD will make myself known unto
him [g]in a vision, *and* will speak unto
him [h]in a dream.
7 [i]My servant Mō'ses *is* not so, [j]who
is faithful in all mine house.
8 With him will I speak [k]mouth to
mouth, even [l]apparently, and not in
dark speeches; and [m]the similitude of
the LORD shall he behold: wherefore
then [n]were ye not afraid to speak
against my servant Mō'ses?
9 And the anger of the LORD was kindled against them; and he departed.
10 And the cloud departed from off
the tabernacle; and, [o]behold, Mĭr'ĭ-am
became [p]leprous, *white* as snow: and
Aâr'on looked upon Mĭr'ĭ-am, and, behold, *she was* leprous.
11 And Aâr'on said unto Mō'ses,
Alas, my lord, I beseech thee, [q]lay not
the sin upon us, wherein we have done
foolishly, and wherein we have sinned.
12 Let her not be [r]as one dead, of
whom the flesh is half consumed when
he cometh out of his mother's womb.
13 And Mō'ses [s]cried unto the LORD,
saying, Heal her now, O God, I beseech
thee.
14 ¶ And the LORD said unto Mō'-
ses, [t]If her father had but spit in her
face, should she not be ashamed seven
days? let her be [u]shut out from the
camp seven days, and after that let her
be received in *again.*
15 And [v]Mĭr'ĭ-am was shut out from
the camp seven days: and the people
journeyed not till Mĭr'ĭ-am was brought
in *again.*
16 And afterward the people removed from Ha-zē'roth, and pitched in
the wilderness of Pā'ran.

13 And the LORD spake unto Mō'-
ses, saying,
2 [a]Send thou men, that they may
search the land of Că'n̦aan, which I
give unto the children of Ĭs'ra-el: of every tribe of their fathers shall ye send a
man, every one a ruler among them.
3 And Mō'ses by the commandment
of the LORD sent them from the wilderness of Pā'ran: all those men *were*
heads of the children of Ĭs'ra-el.
4 And these *were* their names: of the
tribe of Reu̧'ben, Shăm-mū'ȧ the son
of Zăc'cur.

22 [v]2 Ki. 7.2; Matt. 15.33; Mark 6.37
23 [w]Isa. 50.2 [x]Ezek. 12.25
25 [y]Ex. 34.5; ch. 12.5 [z]2 Ki. 2.15 [a]1 Sam. 10.5-6; Joel 2.28; Acts 2.17-18; 1 Cor. 14.1
26 [b]1 Sam. 20.26; Jer. 36.5
28 [c]Mark 9.38; John 3.26
29 [d]Acts 26.29; 1 Cor. 14.5
31 [e]Ps. 78.26 [9]the way of a day
32 [f]Ex. 16.36
33 [g]Ps. 78.30
34 [10]That is, The graves of lust
35 [h]ch. 33.17; Deut. 1.1 [11]they were in, etc

CHAPTER 12
1 [1]Or, Cushite [a]Ex. 2.21 [2]taken
2 [b]Ex. 15.20; Mic. 6.4 [c]Gen. 29.33; 2 Ki. 19.4; Ps. 94.9; Isa. 37.4
3 [d]Ps. 147.6; 1 Pet. 3.4
4 [e]Ps. 76.9
5 [f]Ex. 34.5; ch. 16.19
6 [g]Gen. 46.2; Luke 1.11-22 [h]Matt. 1.20
7 [i]Ps. 105.26 [j]Heb. 3.2-5
8 [k]Deut. 34.10 [l]1 Cor. 13.12 [m]Ex. 33.19 [n]2 Pet. 2.10
10 [o]Deut. 24.9 [p]2 Ki. 5.27; 2 Chr. 26.19
11 [q]2 Sam. 19.19
12 [r]Ps. 88.4; 1 Tim. 5.6
13 [s]Jas. 5.16
14 [t]Heb. 12.9 [u]Lev. 13.46; ch. 5.2-3
15 [v]Deut. 24.9; 2 Chr. 26.20

CHAPTER 13
2 [a]ch. 32.8; Deut. 1.22

5 Of the tribe of Sĭm'e-on, Shā'phat
the son of Hō'rī.
6 Of the tribe of Jū'dah, [b]Cā'leb the
son of Je-phŭn'neh.
7 Of the tribe of Ĭs'sa-char, Ī'găl the
son of Jō'seph.
8 Of the tribe of Ē'phră-ĭm, O-shē'ȧ
the son of Nŭn.
9 Of the tribe of Bĕn'ja-min, Păl'tī
the son of Rā'phu.
10 Of the tribe of Zĕb'u-lun, Găd'dĭ-
el the son of Sō'dī.
11 Of the tribe of Jō'seph, *namely,*
of the tribe of Ma-năs'seh, Găd'dī the
son of Su'sī.
12 Of the tribe of Dăn, Ăm'mĭ-el the
son of Ge-măl'lī.
13 Of the tribe of Ăsh'ēr, Sē'thur the
son of Mī'chaĕl.
14 Of the tribe of Năph'ta-lī, Näh'bī
the son of Vŏph'sī.
15 Of the tribe of Găd, Ge-ū'el the
son of Mā'chī.
16 These *are* the names of the men
which Mō'ses sent to spy out the land.
And Mō'ses called [c]O-shē'ȧ the son of
Nŭn [1]Je-hŏsh'u-ȧ.
17 ¶ And Mō'ses sent them to spy
out the land of Cā'năan, and said unto
them, Get you up this *way* [2]southward,
and go up into [d]the mountain:
18 And see the land, what it *is;*
and the people that dwelleth therein,
whether they *be* strong or weak, few or
many;
19 And what the land *is* that they
dwell in, whether it *be* good or bad;
and what cities *they be* that they dwell
in, whether in tents, or in strong holds;
20 And what the land *is,* whether it
be [e]fat or lean, whether there be wood
therein, or not. And [f]be ye of good
courage, and bring of the fruit of the
land. Now the time *was* the time of the
firstripe grapes.
21 ¶ So they went up, and searched
the land from the wilderness of Zĭn
unto Rē'hŏb, as men come to Hā'math.
22 And they ascended by the south,
and came unto Hē'bron; where [g]A-
hī'măn, Shē'shāi, and Tăl'māi, the children of Ā'năk, *were.* (Now Hē'bron
was built seven years before [h]Zō'an in
Ē'ġypt.)
23 And they came unto the [3]brook of
Ĕsh'cŏl, and cut down from thence a
branch with one cluster of grapes, and
they bare it between two upon a staff;
and *they brought* of the pomegranates, and of the figs.
24 The place was called the [4]brook
[5]Ĕsh'cŏl, because of the cluster of
grapes which the children of Ĭs'ra-el
cut down from thence.
25 And they returned from searching of the land after forty days.
26 ¶ And they went and came to
Mō'ses, and to Aâr'on, and to all the
congregation of the children of Ĭs'ra-
el, unto the wilderness of Pā'ran, to
Kā'desh; and brought back word unto
them, and unto all the congregation,
and shewed them the fruit of the land.
27 And they told him, and said, We
came unto the land whither thou sent-

6 [b]ch. 14.6-30; Josh. 14.6
16 [c]Ex. 17.9 [1]He shall save
17 [2]Into the south country
[d]Gen. 14.10; Judg. 1.9-19
20 [e]Deut. 8.7-8; Ezek. 34.14
[f]Deut. 31.6; Heb. 13.6
22 [g]Judg. 1.10; Josh. 15.13-14
[h]Ps. 78.12; Isa. 30.4
23 [3]Or, valley
24 [4]Or, valley [5]That is, A cluster of grapes
27 [i]Ex. 3.8; Deut. 1.25
[j]Deut. 1.25
28 [k]Deut. 1.28; Deut. 9.1-2
29 [l]Ex. 17.8; 1 Sam. 15.3
30 [m]Josh. 14.7; Heb. 11.33-34
32 [n]Matt. 23.13 [6]Perhaps a plague was then in the country
[o]Amos 2.9 [7]men of statures
33 [p]1 Sam. 17.4-7
[q]Isa. 40.22
CHAPTER 14
2 [a]Ps. 106.25
[b]Deut. 28.68
4 [c]Neh. 9.17; Heb. 11.15
8 [d]Deut. 10.15;
[e]ch. 13.27
9 [f]Deut. 9.7-23-24
[g]Deut. 20.3
[h]ch. 24.8 [1]shadow
[i]Gen. 48.21;
10 [j]Ex. 17.4
[k]Ex. 16.10;

est us, and surely it floweth with [i]milk
and honey; [j]and this *is* the fruit of it.
28 Nevertheless [k]the people *be*
strong that dwell in the land, and the
cities *are* walled, *and* very great: and
moreover we saw the children of Ā'năk
there.
29 The [l]Ăm'a-lĕk-ītes dwell in the
land of the south: and the Hĭt'tītes,
and the Jĕb'u-sītes, and the Ăm'ôr-
ītes, dwell in the mountains: and the
Cā'năan-ītes dwell by the sea, and by
the coast of Jôr'dan.
30 And [m]Cā'leb stilled the people before Mō'ses, and said, Let us go up at
once, and possess it; for we are well
able to overcome it.
31 But the men that went up with him
said, We be not able to go up against
the people; for they *are* stronger than
we.
32 And they [n]brought up an evil
report of the land which they had
searched unto the children of Ĭs'ra-el,
saying, The land, through which we
have gone to search it, *is* a land that
[6]eateth up the inhabitants thereof; and
[o]all the people that we saw in it *are*
[7]men of a great stature.
33 And there we saw the giants, [p]the
sons of Ā'năk, *which come* of the giants: and we were in our own sight [q]as
grasshoppers, and so we were in their
sight.

14 And all the congregation lifted
up their voice, and cried; and the
people wept that night.
2 And [a]all the children of Ĭs'ra-el
murmured against Mō'ses and against
Aâr'on: and the whole congregation
said unto them, [b]Would God that we
had died in the land of Ē'ġypt! or would
God we had died in this wilderness!
3 And wherefore hath the LORD
brought us unto this land, to fall by the
sword, that our wives and our children
should be a prey? were it not better for
us to return into Ē'ġypt?
4 And they said one to another, [c]Let
us make a captain, and let us return
into Ē'ġypt.
5 Then Mō'ses and Aâr'on fell on
their faces before all the assembly of
the congregation of the children of Ĭs'-
ra-el.
6 ¶ And Jŏsh'u-ȧ the son of Nŭn, and
Cā'leb the son of Je-phŭn'neh, *which*
were of them that searched the land,
rent their clothes:
7 And they spake unto all the company of the children of Ĭs'ra-el, saying,
The land, which we passed through to
search it, *is* an exceeding good land.
8 If the LORD [d]delight in us, then he
will bring us into this land, and give it
us; [e]a land which floweth with milk
and honey.
9 Only [f]rebel not ye against the
LORD, [g]neither fear ye the people of
the land; for [h]they *are* bread for us:
their [1]defence is departed from them,
[i]and the LORD *is* with us: fear them
not.
10 [j]But all the congregation bade
stone them with stones. And [k]the glory

of the LORD appeared in the tabernacle
of the congregation before all the children of Ĭs'ra-el.
11 ¶ And the LORD said unto Mō'ses,
How long will this people [l]provoke
me? and how long will it be ere they
[m]believe me, for all the signs which I
have shewed among them?
12 I will smite them with the pestilence, and disinherit them, and [n]will
make of thee a greater nation and
mightier than they.
13 ¶ And [o]Mō'ses said unto the
LORD, Then the E-ġy̆p'tians shall hear
it, (for thou broughtest up this people
in thy might from among them;)
14 And they will tell *it* to the inhabitants of this land: [p]*for* they have heard
that thou LORD *art* among this people, that thou LORD art seen face to
face, and *that* [q]thy cloud standeth over
them, and *that* thou goest before them,
by day time in a pillar of a cloud, and in
a pillar of fire by night.
15 ¶ Now *if* thou shalt kill *all* this
people as one man, then the nations
which have heard the fame of thee will
speak, saying,
16 Because the LORD was not [r]able
to bring this people into the land which
he sware unto them, therefore he hath
slain them in the wilderness.
17 And now, I beseech thee, let the
power of my Lord be great, according
as thou hast spoken, saying,
18 The LORD *is* [s]longsuffering, and
of great mercy, forgiving iniquity and
transgression, and by no means clearing *the guilty*, [t]visiting the iniquity of
the fathers upon the children unto the
third and fourth *generation*.
19 Pardon, I beseech thee, the iniquity of this people according unto the
greatness of thy mercy, and as thou
hast forgiven this people, from Ē'ġy̆pt
[2]even until now.
20 And the LORD said, I [u]have pardoned according to thy word:
21 But *as* truly *as* I live, [v]all the
earth shall be filled with the glory of
the LORD.
22 [w]Because all those men which
have seen my glory, and my miracles,
which I did in Ē'ġy̆pt and in the wilderness, and have tempted me now [x]these
ten times, and have not hearkened to
my voice;
23 [3y]Surely they shall not see the
land which I sware unto their fathers,
neither shall any of them that provoked me see it:
24 But my servant Cā'leb, because
he had another spirit with him, and
hath followed me fully, him will I bring
into the land whereinto he went; and
[z]his seed shall possess it.
25 (Now the Ăm'a-lĕk-ītes and the
Cā'năan-ītes dwelt in the valley.) To
morrow turn you, and get you into the
wilderness by the way of the Red sea.
26 ¶ And the LORD spake unto Mō'-
ses and unto Aâr'on, saying,
27 [a]How long *shall I bear with*
this evil congregation, which murmur
against me? [b]I have heard the murmur-

11 [l]Heb. 3.8
[m]Ps. 78.22; John 12.37
12 [n]Ex. 32.10
13 [o]Ezek. 20.9
14 [p]Ex. 15.14
[q]Neh. 9.12
16 [r]Josh. 7.9
18 [s]Ps. 103.8; Jon. 4.2
[t]Ex. 34.7
19 [2]Or, hitherto
20 [u]Jas. 5.16; 1 John 5.16
21 [v]Ps. 72.19; Rev. 11.15
22 [w]Deut. 1.31-34; Heb. 4.6-7
[x]Gen. 31.7
23 [3]If they see the land
[y]Deut. 1.35; Heb. 3.18
24 [z]Ps. 25.13; Matt. 5.5
27 [a]Ex. 16.28;
[b]Ex. 16.12;
28 [c]Heb. 3.17
29 [d]ch. 26.65
30 [4]lifted up my hand
[e]Deut. 1.36-38
31 [f]Ps. 106.24;
32 [g]1 Cor. 10.5
33 [5]Or, feed
[h]Ps. 107.40
[i]Deut. 2.14
34 [j]ch. 13.25
[k]Ps. 95.10
[l]1 Ki. 8.56;
[6]Or, interruption
35 [m]ch. 23.19
36 [n]ch. 13.31
37 [o]Jer. 28.16-17;
38 [p]Josh. 14.6
39 [q]Prov. 19.3;
40 [r]Deut. 1.41;
41 [s]2 Chr. 24.20
[t]Job 9.4;
42 [u]Deut. 1.42;
43 [v]Judg. 16.20

ings of the children of Ĭs'ra-el, which
they murmur against me.
28 Say unto them, [c]*As truly as* I live,
saith the LORD, as ye have spoken in
mine ears, so will I do to you:
29 Your carcases shall fall in this
wilderness; and [d]all that were numbered of you, according to your whole
number, from twenty years old and upward, which have murmured against
me,
30 Doubtless ye shall not come into
the land, *concerning* which I [4]sware to
make you dwell therein, [e]save Cā'leb
the son of Je-phŭn'neh, and Jŏsh'u-ȧ
the son of Nŭn.
31 But your little ones, which ye said
should be a prey, them will I bring in,
and they shall know the land which [f]ye
have despised.
32 But *as for* you, [g]your carcases,
they shall fall in this wilderness.
33 And your children shall [5h]wan-
der in the wilderness [i]forty years, and
bear your whoredoms, until your carcases be wasted in the wilderness.
34 [j]After the number of the days in
which ye searched the land, *even* [k]forty
days, each day for a year, shall ye bear
your iniquities, *even* forty years, [l]and
ye shall know my [6]breach of promise.
35 [m]I the LORD have said, I will
surely do it unto all this evil congregation, that are gathered together against
me: in this wilderness they shall be consumed, and there they shall die.
36 And [n]the men, which Mō'ses sent
to search the land, who returned, and
made all the congregation to murmur
against him, by bringing up a slander
upon the land,
37 Even those men that did bring up
the evil report upon the land, [o]died by
the plague before the LORD.
38 [p]But Jŏsh'u-ȧ the son of Nŭn, and
Cā'leb the son of Je-phŭn'neh, *which
were* of the men that went to search the
land, lived *still*.
39 And Mō'ses told these sayings
unto all the children of Ĭs'ra-el: and
[q]the people mourned greatly.
40 ¶ And they rose up early in the
morning, and gat them up into the top
of the mountain, saying, Lo, [r]we *be
here*, and will go up unto the place
which the LORD hath promised: for we
have sinned.
41 And Mō'ses said, Wherefore now
do ye transgress [s]the commandment
of [t]the LORD? but it shall not prosper.
42 [u]Go not up, for the LORD *is* not
among you; that ye be not smitten before your enemies.
43 For the Ăm'a-lĕk-ītes and the Cā'-
năan-ītes *are* there before you, and ye
shall fall by the sword: [v]because ye
are turned away from the LORD, therefore the LORD will not be with you.
44 But they presumed to go up unto
the hill top: nevertheless the ark of the
covenant of the LORD, and Mō'ses, departed not out of the camp.
45 Then the Ăm'a-lĕk-ītes came
down, and the Cā'năan-ītes which

dwelt in that hill, and smote them, and
discomfited them, *even* unto Hôr'mah.
15 And the LORD spake unto Mō'-
ses, saying,
2 [a]Speak unto the children of Ĭs'ra-
el, and say unto them, When ye be
come into the land of your habitations,
which I give unto you,
3 And [b]will make an offering by fire
unto the LORD, a burnt offering, or a
sacrifice [c]in [1]performing a vow, or in a
freewill offering, [d]or in your solemn
feasts, to make a [e]sweet savour unto
the LORD, of the herd, or of the flock:
4 Then [f]shall he that offereth his offering unto the LORD bring [g]a meat offering of a tenth deal of flour mingled
[h]with the fourth *part* of an hin of oil.
5 And [i]the fourth *part* of an hin of
wine for a drink offering shalt thou prepare with the burnt offering or sacrifice, for one lamb.
6 Or for a ram, thou shalt prepare
for a meat offering two tenth deals of
flour mingled with the third *part* of an
hin of oil.
7 And for a drink offering thou shalt
offer the third *part* of an hin of wine,
for a sweet savour unto the LORD.
8 And when thou preparest a bull-
ock *for* a burnt offering, or *for* a sacrifice in performing a vow, or [j]peace offerings unto the LORD:
9 Then shall he bring with a bullock
a meat offering of three tenth deals of
flour mingled with half an hin of oil.
10 And thou shalt bring for a drink
offering half an hin of wine, *for* an offering made by fire, of a sweet savour
unto the LORD.
11 Thus shall it be done for one bullock, or for one ram, or for a lamb, or a
kid.
12 According to the number that ye
shall prepare, so shall ye do to every
one according to their number.
13 All that are born of the country
shall do these things after this manner,
in offering an offering made by fire, of
a sweet savour unto the LORD.
14 And if a stranger sojourn with
you, or whosoever *be* among you in
your generations, and will offer an offering made by fire, of a sweet savour
unto the LORD; as ye do, so he shall do.
15 [k]One ordinance *shall be both* for
you of the congregation, and also for
the stranger that sojourneth *with you,*
an ordinance for ever in your generations: as ye *are,* so shall the stranger be
before the LORD.
16 One law and one manner shall be
for you, and for the stranger that sojourneth with you.
17 ¶ And the LORD spake unto Mō'-
ses, saying,
18 Speak unto the children of Ĭs'ra-
el, and say unto them, When ye come
into the land whither I bring you,
19 Then it shall be, that, when ye eat
of the [l]bread of the land, ye shall offer
up an heave offering unto the LORD.
20 [m]Ye shall offer up a cake of the
first of your dough *for* an heave offering: as *ye do* [n]the heave offering of the
threshingfloor, so shall ye heave it.
21 Of the first of your dough ye shall
give unto the LORD an heave offering
in your generations.
22 ¶ And [o]if ye have erred, and
not observed all these commandments,
which the LORD hath spoken unto Mō'-
ses,
23 *Even* all that the LORD hath commanded you by the hand of Mō'ses,
from the day that the LORD commanded *Mō'ses,* and henceforward
among your generations;
24 Then it shall be, [p]if *ought* be
committed by ignorance [2]without the
knowledge of the congregation, that
all the congregation shall offer one
young bullock for a burnt offering, for
a sweet savour unto the LORD, with his
meat offering, and his drink offering,
according to the [3]manner, and [q]one
kid of the goats for a sin offering.
25 And [r]the priest shall make an
atonement for all the congregation of
the children of Ĭs'ra-el, and it shall be
forgiven them; for it *is* ignorance: and
they shall bring their offering, a sacrifice made by fire unto the LORD, and
their sin offering before the LORD, for
their ignorance:
26 And it shall be forgiven all the
congregation of the children of Ĭs'ra-
el, and the stranger that sojourneth
among them; seeing all the people *were*
in ignorance.
27 ¶ And [s]if any soul sin through ignorance, then he shall bring a she goat
of the first year for a sin offering.
28 And [t]the priest shall make an
atonement for the soul that sinneth ignorantly, when he sinneth by ignorance before the LORD, to make an
atonement for him; and it shall be forgiven him.
29 Ye shall have one law for him
that [4]sinneth through ignorance, *both
for* him that is born among the children
of Ĭs'ra-el, and for the stranger that sojourneth among them.
30 ¶ But [u]the soul that doeth *ought*
[5]presumptuously, *whether he be* born
in the land, or a stranger, the same reproacheth the LORD; and that soul shall
be cut off from among his people.
31 Because he hath [v]despised the
word of the LORD, and hath broken his
commandment, that soul shall utterly
be cut off; [w]his iniquity *shall be* upon
him.
32 ¶ And while the children of Ĭs'ra-
el were in the wilderness, [x]they found
a man that gathered sticks upon the
sabbath day.
33 And they that found him gathering sticks brought him unto Mō'ses
and Aâr'on, and unto all the congregation.
34 And they put him [y]in ward, because it was not declared what should
be done to him.
35 And the LORD said unto Mō'ses,
[z]The man shall be surely put to death:
all the congregation shall [a]stone him
with stones without the camp.

CHAPTER 15
2 [a]Lev. 23.10
3 [b]Ex. 29.18-25-41; Lev. 1.2-3
[c]Lev. 7.16; Lev. 22.18-21
[1]separating
[d]Lev. 23.8-12; ch. 28.19-27; ch. 29.2-8-13; Deut. 16.10
[e]Gen. 8.21; Lev. 1.9; Ezek. 20.41; 2 Cor. 2.15; Eph. 5.2; Phil. 4.18
4 [f]Lev. 2.1; Isa. 66.20
[g]Ex. 29.40
[h]Lev. 14.10
5 [i]ch. 28.7
8 [j]Lev. 7.11
15 [k]Lev. 24.22; Col. 3.11
19 [l]Josh. 5.11-12
20 [m]Ex. 23.19; Prov. 3.9
[n]Lev. 2.14; Lev. 23.10
22 [o]Lev. 4.2; 1 John 2.1
24 [p]Lev. 4.13
[2]from the eyes
[3]Or, ordinance
[q]Lev. 4.23; Ezra 6.17
25 [r]Lev. 4.20; 1 John 1.7
27 [s]Lev. 4.27-28; Luke 12.48
28 [t]Lev. 4.35
29 [4]doth
30 [u]Deut. 17.12; 2 Pet. 2.10
[5]with an high hand
31 [v]2 Sam. 12.9; Heb. 10.28
[w]Ezek. 18.20
32 [x]Ex. 35.2-3
34 [y]Lev. 24.12
35 [z]Ex. 31.14-15; Gal. 3.5
[a]1 Ki. 21.13; Acts 7.58

36 And all the congregation brought
him without the camp, and stoned him
with stones, and he died; as the LORD
commanded Mō'ses.
37 ¶ And the LORD spake unto Mō'-
ses, saying,
38 Speak unto the children of Ĭs'ra-
el, and bid [b]them that they make them
fringes in the borders of their garments
throughout their generations, and that
they put upon the fringe of the borders
a ribband of blue:
39 And it shall be unto you for a
fringe, that ye may look upon it, and
remember all the commandments of
the LORD, and do them; and that ye
[c]seek not after your own heart and
your own eyes, after which ye use [d]to
go a whoring:
40 That ye may remember, and do
all my commandments, and be [e]holy
unto your God.
41 I *am* the LORD your God, which
brought you out of the land of Ē'ġypt,
to be your God: I *am* the LORD your
God.
16 Now [a]Kō'rah, the son of Ĭz'har,
the son of Kō'hath, the son of
Lē'vī, and Dā'than and A-bī'răm, the
sons of E-lī'ab, and Ōn, the son of Pē'-
leth, sons of Reu'ben, took *men:*
2 And they rose up before Mō'ses,
with certain of the children of Ĭs'ra-el,
two hundred and fifty princes of the
assembly, [b]famous in the congregation, men of renown:
3 And [c]they gathered themselves
together against Mō'ses and against
Aâr'on, and said unto them, [1]*Ye take*
too much upon you, seeing [d]all the congregation *are* holy, every one of them,
[e]and the LORD *is* among them: wherefore then lift ye up yourselves above
the congregation of the LORD?
4 And when Mō'ses heard *it,* [f]he fell
upon his face:
5 And he spake unto Kō'rah and
unto all his company, saying, Even to
morrow the LORD will shew [g]who *are*
his, and *who is* [h]holy; and will cause
him to come near unto him: even *him*
whom he hath [i]chosen will he cause to
[j]come near unto him.
6 This do; Take you censers, Kō'rah,
and all his company;
7 And put fire therein, and put incense in them before the LORD to morrow: and it shall be *that* the man whom
the LORD doth choose, he *shall be* holy:
ye take too much upon you, ye sons of
Lē'vī.
8 And Mō'ses said unto Kō'rah,
Hear, I pray you, ye sons of Lē'vī:
9 *Seemeth it but* [k]a small thing unto
you, that the God of Ĭs'ra-el hath [l]sepa-
rated you from the congregation of
Ĭs'ra-el, to bring you near to himself to
do the service of the tabernacle of the
LORD, and to stand before the congregation to minister unto them?
10 And he hath brought thee near *to*
him, and all thy brethren the sons of
Lē'vī with thee: and seek ye the priesthood also?
11 For which cause *both* thou and
all thy company *are* gathered together
against the LORD: [m]and what *is* Aâr'on,
that ye murmur against him?
12 ¶ And Mō'ses sent to call Dā'-
than and A-bī'răm, the sons of E-lī'ab:
which said, We will not come up:
13 *Is it* a small thing that thou hast
brought us up out of a land that floweth with milk and honey, to kill us in
the wilderness, except thou [n]make thyself altogether a prince over us?
14 Moreover thou hast not brought
us into [o]a land that floweth with milk
and honey, or given us inheritance of
fields and vineyards: wilt thou [2]put out
the eyes of these men? we will not
come up.
15 And Mō'ses was very wroth, and
said unto the LORD, [p]Respect not thou
their offering: [q]I have not taken one
ass from them, neither have I hurt one
of them.
16 And Mō'ses said unto Kō'rah, Be
thou and all thy company before the
LORD, thou, and they, and Aâr'on, to
morrow:
17 And take every man his censer,
and put incense in them, and bring ye
before the LORD every man his censer,
two hundred and fifty censers; thou
also, and Aâr'on, each *of you* his censer.
18 And they took every man his censer, and put fire in them, and laid incense thereon, and stood in the door
of the tabernacle of the congregation
with Mō'ses and Aâr'on.
19 And Kō'rah gathered all the congregation against them unto the door
of the tabernacle of the congregation:
and [r]the glory of the LORD appeared
unto all the congregation.
20 And the LORD spake unto Mō'ses
and unto Aâr'on, saying,
21 [s]Separate yourselves from among
this congregation, that I may [t]consume
them in a moment.
22 And they fell upon their faces,
and said, O God, [u]the God of the spirits
of all flesh, shall [v]one man sin, and
wilt thou be wroth with all the congregation?
23 ¶ And the LORD spake unto Mō'-
ses, saying,
24 Speak unto the congregation, saying, Get you up from about the tabernacle of Kō'rah, Dā'than, and A-bī'răm.
25 And Mō'ses rose up and went
unto Dā'than and A-bī'răm; and the elders of Ĭs'ra-el followed him.
26 And he spake unto the congregation, saying, [w]Depart, I pray you, from
the tents of these wicked men, and
touch nothing of theirs, lest ye be consumed in all their sins.
27 So they gat up from the tabernacle of Kō'rah, Dā'than, and A-bī'răm,
on every side: and Dā'than and A-
bī'răm came out, and stood [x]in the
door of their tents, and their wives,
and their sons, and their little children.
28 And Mō'ses said, [y]Hereby ye
shall know that the LORD hath sent me

38 [b]Deut. 22.12; Luke 8.43-44
39 [c]Deut. 29.19; Ezek. 6.9
[d]Ex. 34.15-16; Jas. 4.4
40 [e]Lev. 11.44-45; 1 Pet. 1.15
CHAPTER 16
1 [a]Jude 11
2 [b]ch. 26.9
3 [c]Ps. 106.16
[1]It is much for you
[d]Ex. 19.6
[e]Ex. 29.45
4 [f]ch. 20.6
5 [g]2 Tim. 2.19
[h]Lev. 21.6-12
[i]Ex. 28.1; Ps. 105.26
[j]Lev. 10.3
9 [k]1 Sam. 18.23; Isa. 7.13
[l]Deut. 10.8
11 [m]1 Cor. 3.5
13 [n]Acts 7.27-35
14 [o]Ex. 3.8; Lev. 20.24
[2]bore out, that is, blind with fair words
15 [p]Gen. 4.4-5
[q]1 Sam. 12.3; 2 Cor. 7.2
19 [r]Ex. 16.7-10; Lev. 9.6-23
21 [s]Gen. 19.17; Rev. 18.4
[t]Ex. 32.10; Isa. 37.36
22 [u]Job 12.10; Heb. 12.9
[v]2 Sam. 24.17; Ezek. 18.20
26 [w]Gen. 19.12; Rev. 18.4
27 [x]Job 9.4; Prov. 16.18
28 [y]Deut. 18.22;

to do all these works; for *I have* not *done them* [z]of mine own mind.

29 If these men die [3]the common death of all men, or if they be [a]visited after the visitation of all men; *then* the LORD hath not sent me.

30 But if the LORD [4]make [b]a new thing, and the earth open her mouth, and swallow them up, with all that *appertain* unto them, and they [c]go down quick into the pit; then ye shall understand that these men have provoked the LORD.

31 ¶ And [d]it came to pass, as he had made an end of speaking all these words, that the ground clave asunder that *was* under them:

32 And the earth opened her mouth, and swallowed them up, and their houses, and [e]all the men that *appertained* unto Kō'rah, and all *their* goods.

33 They, and all that *appertained* to them, went down alive into the pit, and the earth closed upon them: and they perished from among the congregation.

34 And all Ĭs'ra-el that *were* round about them fled at the cry of them: for they said, Lest the earth swallow us up *also*.

35 And there [f]came out a fire from the LORD, and consumed the two hundred and fifty men that offered incense.

36 ¶ And the LORD spake unto Mō'ses, saying,

37 Speak unto Ē-le-ā'zar the son of Aâr'on the priest, that he take up the censers out of the burning, and scatter thou the fire yonder; for they are hallowed.

38 The censers of these [g]sinners against their own souls, let them make them broad plates *for* a covering of the altar: for they offered them before the LORD, therefore they are hallowed: [h]and they shall be a sign unto the children of Ĭs'ra-el.

39 And Ē-le-ā'zar the priest took the brasen censers, wherewith they that were burnt had offered; and they were made broad *plates for* a covering of the altar:

40 *To be* a memorial unto the children of Ĭs'ra-el, [i]that no stranger, which *is* not of the seed of Aâr'on, come near to offer incense before the LORD; that he be not as Kō'rah, and as his company: as the LORD said to him by the hand of Mō'ses.

41 ¶ But on the morrow [j]all the congregation of the children of Ĭs'ra-el murmured against Mō'ses and against Aâr'on, saying, Ye have killed the people of the LORD.

42 And it came to pass, when the congregation was gathered against Mō'ses and against Aâr'on, that they looked toward the tabernacle of the congregation: and, behold, the [k]cloud covered it, and the glory of the LORD appeared.

43 And Mō'ses and Aâr'on came before the tabernacle of the congregation.

44 ¶ And the LORD spake unto Mō'ses, saying,

45 Get you up from among this congregation, that I may consume them as in a moment. And [l]they fell upon their faces.

46 ¶ And Mō'ses said unto Aâr'on, Take a censer, and put fire therein from off the altar, and put on incense, and go quickly unto the congregation, and make an atonement for them: [m]for there is wrath gone out from the LORD; the plague is begun.

47 And Aâr'on took as Mō'ses commanded, and ran into the midst of the congregation; and, behold, the plague was begun among the people: and he put on incense, and made an atonement for the people.

48 And he [n]stood between the dead and the living; and the plague was stayed.

49 Now they that died in the plague were fourteen thousand and seven hundred, beside them that died about the matter of Kō'rah.

50 And Aâr'on returned unto Mō'ses unto the door of the tabernacle of the congregation: and the plague was stayed.

17 And the LORD spake unto Mō'ses, saying,

2 Speak unto the children of Ĭs'ra-el, and take of every one of them a rod according to the house of *their* fathers, of all their princes according to the house of their fathers twelve rods: write thou every man's name upon his rod.

3 And thou shalt write Aâr'on's name upon the rod of Lē'vī: for one rod *shall be* for the head of the house of their fathers.

4 And thou shalt lay them up in the tabernacle of the congregation before the testimony, [a]where I will meet with you.

5 And it shall come to pass, *that* the man's rod, [b]whom I shall choose, shall blossom: and I will make to cease from me the murmurings of the children of Ĭs'ra-el, whereby they murmur against you.

6 ¶ And Mō'ses spake unto the children of Ĭs'ra-el, and every one of their princes gave him [1]a rod apiece, for each prince one, according to their fathers' houses, *even* twelve rods: and the rod of Aâr'on *was* among their rods.

7 And Mō'ses laid up the rods before the LORD in [c]the tabernacle of witness.

8 And it came to pass, that on the morrow Mō'ses went into the tabernacle of witness; and, behold, the rod of Aâr'on for the house of Lē'vī was [d]budded, and brought forth buds, and bloomed blossoms, and yielded almonds.

9 And Mō'ses brought out all the rods from before the LORD unto all the children of Ĭs'ra-el: and they looked, and took every man his rod.

10 ¶ And the LORD said unto Mō'ses, Bring [e]Aâr'on's rod again before the testimony, to be kept for [f]a token

[z]Jer. 23.16; Ezek. 13.17

29 [3]as every man dieth

[a]Ex. 20.5; Job 35.15; Isa. 10.3; Jer. 5.9; Lam. 4.22

30 [4]create a creature

[b]Job 31.3; Isa. 28.21

[c]Ps. 55.15; Rev. 9.2

31 [d]ch. 26.10; ch. 27.3; Deut. 11.6; Ps. 106.17

32 [e]1 Chr. 6.22

35 [f]Lev. 10.2; ch. 11.1; Ps. 106.18

38 [g]Prov. 20.2; Hab. 2.10

[h]ch. 17.10; ch. 26.10; Ezek. 14.8; 1 Cor. 10.11; 2 Pet. 2.6

40 [i]ch. 3.38; ch. 18.4-7; 1 Ki. 13

41 [j]ch. 14.2; Ps. 106.13-26; Matt. 5.11; Acts 21.28; 2 Cor. 6.8

42 [k]Ex. 16.7-10; Ex. 24.16; Ex. 40.34; Lev. 9.23; ch. 14.10

45 [l]ch. 20.6; 1 Chr. 21.16; Matt. 26.39

46 [m]Lev. 10.6; ch. 1.53; Ps. 106.29

48 [n]2 Sam. 24.16-17-25; Jas. 5.16

CHAPTER 17

4 [a]Ex. 25.22; 1 Ki. 8.10-12

5 [b]ch. 16.5

6 [1]a rod for one prince, a rod for one prince

7 [c]Ex. 38.21; Acts 7.44

8 [d]Gen. 40.10; Isa. 35.1-2

10 [e]Heb. 9.4

[f]Ex. 16.32; Deut. 31.19-26

against the [2]rebels; and thou shalt quite
take away their murmurings from me,
that they die not.
11 And Mō'ses did *so:* as the LORD
commanded him, so did he.
12 And the children of Ĭs'ra-el spake
unto Mō'ses, saying, Behold, we die,
we perish, we all perish.
13 [g]Whosoever cometh any thing
near unto the tabernacle of the LORD
shall die: shall we be consumed with
dying?

CHAPTER 18

18 And the LORD said unto Aâr'on,
[a]Thou and thy sons and thy father's house with thee shall [1]bear the
iniquity of the sanctuary: and thou and
thy sons with thee shall bear the iniquity of your priesthood.
2 And thy brethren also of the tribe of
Lē'vī, the tribe of thy father, bring thou
with thee, that they may be [b]joined unto
thee, and [c]minister unto thee: but thou
and thy sons with thee *shall minister*
before the tabernacle of witness.
3 And they shall keep thy charge,
and the [d]charge of all the tabernacle:
[e]only they shall not come nigh the vessels of the sanctuary and the altar,
[f]that neither they, nor ye also, die.
4 And they shall be joined unto thee,
and keep the charge of the tabernacle
of the congregation, for all the service
of the tabernacle: and a stranger shall
not come nigh unto you.
5 And ye shall keep [g]the charge of
the sanctuary, and the charge of the
altar: that there be no wrath any more
upon the children of Ĭs'ra-el.
6 And I, behold, I have [h]taken your
brethren the Lē'vītes from among the
children of Ĭs'ra-el: to you *they are*
given *as* a gift for the LORD, to do the
service of the tabernacle of the congregation.
7 Therefore thou and thy sons with
thee shall keep your priest's office for
every thing of the altar, and [i]within
the vail; and ye shall serve: I have
given your priest's office *unto you as* a
service of gift: and the [j]stranger that
cometh nigh shall be put to death.
8 ¶ And the LORD spake unto Aâr'on,
Behold, [k]I also have given thee the
charge of mine heave offerings of all
the hallowed things of the children of
Ĭs'ra-el; unto thee have I given them
[l]by reason of the anointing, and to thy
sons, by an ordinance for ever.
9 This shall be thine of the most holy
things, *reserved* from the fire: every oblation of theirs, every [m]meat offering
of theirs, and every [n]sin offering of
theirs, and every trespass offering of
theirs, which they shall render unto
me, *shall be* most holy for thee and for
thy sons.
10 In the [2]most holy *place* shalt thou
eat it; every male shall eat it: it shall be
holy unto thee.
11 And this *is* thine; [o]the heave offering of their gift, with all the wave
offerings of the children of Ĭs'ra-el: I
have given them unto thee, [p]and to thy
sons and to thy daughters with thee, by
a statute for ever: [q]every one that is
clean in thy house shall eat of it.
12 [r]All the [3]best of the oil, and all
the best of the wine, and of the wheat,
the firstfruits of them which they shall
offer unto the LORD, them have I given
thee.
13 *And* whatsoever is first ripe in
the land, which they shall bring unto
the LORD, shall be thine; every one that
is clean in thine house shall eat *of* it.
14 [s]Every thing devoted in Ĭs'ra-el
shall be thine.
15 Every thing that openeth [t]the
matrix in all flesh, which they bring
unto the LORD, *whether it be* of men
or beasts, shall be thine: nevertheless
[u]the firstborn of man shalt thou surely
redeem, and the firstling of unclean
beasts shalt thou redeem.
16 And those that are to be redeemed
from a month old shalt thou redeem,
[v]according to thine estimation, for the
money of five shekels, after the shekel
of the sanctuary, [w]which *is* twenty gerahs.
17 But [x]the firstling of a cow, or the
firstling of a sheep, or the firstling of a
goat, thou shalt not redeem; they *are*
holy: [y]thou shalt sprinkle their blood
upon the altar, and shalt burn their
fat *for* an offering made by fire, for a
sweet savour unto the LORD.
18 And the flesh of them shall be
thine, as the [z]wave breast and as the
right shoulder are thine.
19 All the heave offerings of the holy
things, which the children of Ĭs'ra-el offer unto the LORD, have I given thee,
and thy sons and thy daughters with
thee, by a statute for ever: it *is* [4]a covenant of salt for ever before the LORD
unto thee and to thy seed with thee.
20 ¶ And the LORD spake unto
Aâr'on, Thou shalt have no inheritance in their land, neither shalt thou
have any part among them: [a]I *am* thy
part and thine inheritance among the
children of Ĭs'ra-el.
21 And, behold, [b]I have given the
children of Lē'vī all the tenth in Ĭs'ra-el
for an inheritance, for their service
which they serve, *even* the service of
the tabernacle of the congregation.
22 Neither must the children of Ĭs'-
ra-el henceforth come nigh the tabernacle of the congregation, [c]lest they
bear sin, [5]and die.
23 But the Lē'vītes shall do the service of the tabernacle of the congregation, and they shall bear their iniquity:
it shall be a statute for ever throughout
your generations, that among the children of Ĭs'ra-el they have no inheritance.
24 But the tithes of the children of
Ĭs'ra-el, which they offer *as* an heave
offering unto the LORD, I have given to
the Lē'vītes to inherit: therefore I have
said unto them, [d]Among the children
of Ĭs'ra-el they shall have no inheritance.
25 ¶ And the LORD spake unto Mō'-
ses, saying,

[2]children of rebellion
13 [g]ch. 18.4-7
CHAPTER 18
1 [a]ch. 17.13
[1]be responsible for whatever is done about the sanctuary
2 [b]Gen. 29.34
[c]ch. 3.6-10
3 [d]ch. 3.25-31
[e]ch. 16.40
[f]ch. 4.15
5 [g]Ex. 27.21; 1 Chr. 24.5
6 [h]ch. 3.12-45
7 [i]Heb. 9.3-6
[j]1 Sam. 6.19
8 [k]Lev. 6.16-18; Lev. 10.14-15
[l]Ex. 40.13-15
9 [m]Lev. 2.2-3; Lev. 10.12-13
[n]Lev. 4.22-27; Lev. 6.25-26
10 [2]inner court
11 [o]Ex. 29.27-28; Lev. 7.30-34
[p]Lev. 10.14; Deut. 18.3
[q]Lev. 22.2
12 [r]Ex. 23.19; Deut. 18.4
[3]fat
14 [s]Lev. 27.28
15 [t]Ex. 13.2; ch. 3.13
[u]Ex. 13.13; Lev. 27.28
16 [v]Lev. 27.2-6; ch. 3.47
[w]Ex. 30.13; Ezek. 45.12
17 [x]Deut. 15.19
[y]Lev. 3.2-5
18 [z]Ex. 29.26-28;
19 [4]a perpetual covenant
20 [a]Deut. 10.9;
21 [b]Lev. 27.30-32;
22 [c]Lev. 22.9
[5]to die
24 [d]Deut. 10.9

26 Thus speak unto the Lē'vītes, and say unto them, When ye take of the children of Is'ra-el the tithes which I have given you from them for your inheritance, then ye shall offer up an heave offering of it for the LORD, *even* [e]a tenth *part* of the tithe.

27 And *this* your heave offering shall be reckoned unto you, as though *it were* the corn of the threshingfloor, and as the fulness of the winepress.

28 Thus ye also shall offer an heave offering unto the LORD of all your tithes, which ye receive of the children of Is'ra-el; and ye shall give thereof the LORD'S heave offering to Aâr'on the priest.

29 Out of all your gifts ye shall offer every heave offering of the LORD, of all the [6]best thereof, *even* the hallowed part thereof out of it.

30 Therefore thou shalt say unto them, When ye have heaved the best thereof from it, then it shall be counted unto the Lē'vītes as the increase of the threshingfloor, and as the increase of the winepress.

31 And ye shall eat it in every place, ye and your households: for it *is* [f]your reward for your service in the tabernacle of the congregation.

32 And ye shall [g]bear no sin by reason of it, when ye have heaved from it the best of it: neither shall ye pollute the holy things of the children of Is'ra-el, lest ye die.

19 And the LORD spake unto Mō'ses and unto Aâr'on, saying,

2 This *is* the ordinance of the law which the LORD hath commanded, saying, Speak unto the children of Is'ra-el, that they bring thee [a]a red heifer without spot, wherein *is* no blemish, *and* [b]upon which never came yoke:

3 And ye shall give her unto Ē-le-ā'zar the priest, that he may bring her [c]forth without the camp, and *one* shall slay her before his face:

4 And Ē-le-ā'zar the priest shall take of her blood with his finger, and [d]sprinkle of her blood directly before the tabernacle of the congregation seven times:

5 And *one* shall burn the heifer in his sight; [e]her skin, and her flesh, and her blood, with her dung, shall he burn:

6 And the priest shall take [f]cedar wood, and hyssop, and scarlet, and cast *it* into the midst of the burning of the heifer.

7 [g]Then the priest shall wash his clothes, and he shall bathe his flesh in water, and afterward he shall come into the camp, and the priest shall be unclean until the even.

8 And he that burneth her shall wash his clothes in water, and bathe his flesh in water, and shall be unclean until the even.

9 And a man *that is* clean shall gather up the [h]ashes of the heifer, and lay *them* up without the camp in a clean place, and it shall be kept for the congregation of the children of Is'ra-el [i]for a water of separation: it *is* a purification for sin.

10 And he that gathereth the ashes of the heifer shall wash his clothes, and be unclean until the even: and it shall be unto the children of Is'ra-el, and unto the stranger that sojourneth among them, for a statute for ever.

11 ¶ [j]He that toucheth the dead body of any [1]man shall be unclean seven days.

12 [k]He shall purify himself with it on the third day, and on the seventh day he shall be clean: but if he purify not himself the third day, then the seventh day he shall not be clean.

13 Whosoever toucheth the dead body of any man that is dead, and purifieth not himself, [l]defileth the tabernacle of the LORD; and that soul shall be cut off from Is'ra-el: because [m]the water of separation was not sprinkled upon him, he shall be unclean; [n]his uncleanness *is* yet upon him.

14 This *is* the law, when a man dieth in a tent: all that come into the tent, and all that *is* in the tent, shall be unclean seven days.

15 And every [o]open vessel, which hath no covering bound upon it, *is* unclean.

16 And whosoever toucheth one that is slain with a sword in the open fields, or a dead body, or a bone of a man, or a grave, shall be unclean seven days.

17 And for an unclean *person* they shall take of the [2]ashes of the burnt heifer of purification for sin, and [3]running water shall be put thereto in a vessel:

18 And a clean person shall take [p]hyssop, and dip *it* in the water, and sprinkle *it* upon the tent, and upon all the vessels, and upon the persons that were there, and upon him that touched a bone, or one slain, or one dead, or a grave:

19 And the clean *person* shall sprinkle upon the unclean on the third day, and on the seventh day: and [q]on the seventh day he shall purify himself, and wash his clothes, and bathe himself in water, and shall be clean at even.

20 But the man that shall be unclean, and shall not purify himself, that [r]soul shall be cut off from among the congregation, because he hath defiled the sanctuary of the LORD: the water of separation hath not been sprinkled upon him; he *is* unclean.

21 And it shall be a perpetual statute unto them, that he that sprinkleth the water of separation shall wash his clothes; and he that toucheth the water of separation shall be unclean until even.

22 And [s]whatsoever the unclean *person* toucheth shall be unclean; and the soul that toucheth *it* shall be unclean until even.

20 Then [a]came the children of Is'ra-el, *even* the whole congregation, into the desert of Zĭn in the first month: and the people abode in Kā'desh; and

26 [e]Neh. 10.38
29 [6]fat
31 [f]Matt. 10.10; Luke 10.7; 1 Cor. 9.13; 2 Cor. 12.13; Gal. 6.6; 1 Thess. 5.12-13; 1 Tim. 5.18
32 [g]Lev. 19.8; Lev. 22.16
CHAPTER 19
2 [a]Isa. 53.4-6; Gal. 4.4; Heb. 9.13-14; Rev. 1.5
[b]Deut. 21.3; 1 Sam. 6.7; John 10.17; Phil. 2.6-8
3 [c]Lev. 4.12-21; Lev. 13.46; Lev. 16.27; Lev. 24.14; Heb. 13.11
4 [d]Lev. 4.6-17; Lev. 16.14; Isa. 52.15; Ezek. 36.25; Heb. 9.13-14; 1 Pet. 1.2
5 [e]Ex. 29.14; Lev. 4.11-12; Isa. 53.10
6 [f]Lev. 14.4-6
7 [g]Lev. 11.25; Lev. 15.5
9 [h]Heb. 9.13
[i]ch. 31.23; 2 Cor. 7.1
11 [j]Lev. 21.1; Eph. 2.1
[1]soul of man
12 [k]ch. 31.19
13 [l]Lev. 15.31
[m]ch. 8.7
[n]Lev. 7.20; Lev. 22.3
15 [o]Lev. 11.32; ch. 31.20
17 [2]dust
[3]living waters shall be given
18 [p]Ps. 51.7; Heb. 9.14
19 [q]Lev. 14.9
20 [r]Gen. 17.14; Gal. 3.10
22 [s]Hag. 2.13
CHAPTER 20
1 [a]ch. 33.36

[b]Mĭr'ĭ-am died there, and was buried
there.
2 And [c]there was no water for the
congregation: [d]and they gathered themselves together against Mō'ses and
against Aâr'on.
3 And the people [e]chode with Mō'-
ses, and spake, saying, Would God that
we had died [f]when our brethren died
before the LORD!
4 And [g]why have ye brought up the
congregation of the LORD into this wilderness, that we and our cattle should
die there?
5 And wherefore have ye made us to
come up out of Ē'ġypt, to bring us in
unto this evil place? it *is* no place of
seed, or of figs, or of vines, or of pomegranates; neither *is* there any water to
drink.
6 And Mō'ses and Aâr'on went from
the presence of the assembly unto the
door of the tabernacle of the congregation, and [h]they fell upon their faces:
and the glory of the LORD appeared
unto them.
7 ¶ And the LORD spake unto Mō'-
ses, saying,
8 [i]Take the rod, and gather thou the
assembly together, thou, and Aâr'on
thy brother, and speak ye unto the
rock before their eyes; and it shall give
forth his water, and [j]thou shalt bring
forth to them water out of the rock: so
thou shalt give the congregation and
their beasts drink.
9 And Mō'ses took the rod [k]from before the LORD, as he commanded him.
10 And Mō'ses and Aâr'on gathered
the congregation together before the
rock, and he said unto them, [l]Hear
now, ye rebels; must we fetch you water out of this rock?
11 And Mō'ses lifted up his hand,
and with his rod he smote the rock
[m]twice: and the [n]water came out abundantly, and the congregation drank,
and their beasts *also*.
12 ¶ And the LORD spake unto Mō'-
ses and Aâr'on, Because [o]ye believed
me not, to [p]sanctify me in the eyes of
the children of Ĭs'ra-el, therefore ye
shall not bring this congregation into
the land which I have given them.
13 [q]This *is* the water of [1]Mĕr'ĭ-bah;
because the children of Ĭs'ra-el strove
with the LORD, and he was sanctified
in them.
14 ¶ [r]And Mō'ses sent messengers
from Kā'desh unto the king of Ē'dom,
[s]Thus saith thy brother Ĭs'ra-el, Thou
knowest all the travail that hath [2]be-
fallen us:
15 How our fathers went down into
Ē'ġypt, and we have dwelt in Ē'ġypt a
long time; and the E-ġȳp'tians vexed
us, and our fathers:
16 And [t]when we cried unto the
LORD, he heard our voice, and [u]sent an
angel, and hath brought us forth out of
Ē'ġypt: and, behold, we *are* in Kā'-
desh, a city in the uttermost of thy border:
17 [v]Let us pass, I pray thee, through
thy country: we will not pass through
the fields, or through the vineyards,
neither will we drink *of* the water of
the wells: we will go by the king's *high*
way, we will not turn to the right hand
nor to the left, until we have passed thy
borders.
18 And Ē'dom said unto him, Thou
shalt not pass by me, lest I come out
against thee with the sword.
19 And the children of Ĭs'ra-el said
unto him, We will go by the high way:
and if I and my cattle drink of thy
water, [w]then I will pay for it: I will
only, without *doing* any thing *else*, go
through on my feet.
20 And he said, [x]Thou shalt not go
through. And Ē'dom came out against
him with much people, and with a
strong hand.
21 Thus Ē'dom refused to give Ĭs'ra-
el passage through [y]his border: wherefore Ĭs'ra-el [z]turned away from him.
22 ¶ And the children of Ĭs'ra-el,
even the whole congregation, journeyed from [a]Kā'desh, and [b]came unto
mount Hôr.
23 And the LORD spake unto Mō'ses
and Aâr'on in mount Hôr, by the coast
of the land of Ē'dom, saying,
24 Aâr'on shall [c]be gathered unto
his people: for he shall not enter into
the land which I have given unto the
children of Ĭs'ra-el, because ye rebelled
against my [3]word at the water of Mĕr'ĭ-
bah.
25 [d]Take Aâr'on and Ē-le-ā'zar his
son, and bring them up unto mount
Hôr:
26 And strip Aâr'on of his garments,
and put them upon Ē-le-ā'zar his son:
and Aâr'on shall be gathered *unto his*
people, and shall die there.
27 And Mō'ses did as the LORD commanded: and they went up into mount
Hôr in the sight of all the congregation.
28 [e]And Mō'ses stripped Aâr'on of
his garments, and put them upon Ē-le-
ā'zar his son; and [f]Aâr'on died there
in the top of the mount: and Mō'ses
and Ē-le-ā'zar came down from the
mount.
29 And when all the congregation
saw that Aâr'on was dead, they
mourned for Aâr'on [g]thirty days, *even*
all the house of Ĭs'ra-el.

21

And *when* [a]king Ā'răd the Cā'-
năan-īte, which dwelt in the south,
heard tell that Ĭs'ra-el came by the way
of the spies; then he fought against Ĭs'-
ra-el, and took *some* of them prisoners.
2 And [b]Ĭs'ra-el vowed a vow unto
the LORD, and said, If thou wilt indeed
deliver this people into my hand, then
[c]I will utterly destroy their cities.
3 And the LORD hearkened to the
voice of Ĭs'ra-el, and delivered up
the Cā'năan-ītes; and they utterly destroyed them and their cities: and he
called the name of the place [1]Hôr'mah.
4 ¶ And they journeyed from mount
Hôr by the way of the Red sea, to compass the land of Ē'dom: and the soul of
the people was much [2]discouraged because of the way.

[b]ch. 26.59
2 [c]Ex. 17.1
[d]Ex. 16.2-7-12; 1 Cor. 10.10
3 [e]Ex. 17.2; ch. 14.2
[f]ch. 11.1-33; Lam. 4.9
4 [g]Ex. 5.21; Acts 7.35-40
6 [h]ch. 14.5
8 [i]Ex. 17.5
[j]Neh. 9.15; Isa. 43.20
9 [k]ch. 17.10
10 [l]Ps. 106.33
11 [m]Jas. 1.20
[n]Ex. 17.6; 1 Cor. 10.4
12 [o]ch. 27.14; Deut. 3.26
[p]Lev. 10.3; 1 Pet. 3.15
13 [q]Ps. 95.8
[1]That is, Strife
14 [r]Judg. 11.16-17
[s]Deut. 23.7; Obad. 10-12
[2]found us
16 [t]Ex. 2.23; Ex. 3.7
[u]Acts 7.35
17 [v]ch. 21.22
19 [w]Deut. 2.6-28
20 [x]Gen. 27.41; Amos 1.11
21 [y]Deut. 2.27-29
[z]Judg. 11.18; Heb. 12.14
22 [a]ch. 33.37
[b]ch. 21.4
24 [c]Gen. 25.8; Heb. 12.23
[3]mouth
25 [d]Deut. 32.50
28 [e]Ex. 29.29-30; Job 30.23
[f]ch. 23.10;
29 [g]Gen. 50.3-10;
CHAPTER 21
1 [a]ch. 33.40;
2 [b]Gen. 28.20;
[c]Lev. 27.28
3 [1]That is, Utter destruction
4 [2]shortened, or, grieved

5 And the people [d]spake against God, and against Mō'ses, [e]Wherefore have ye brought us up out of Ē'gypt to die in the wilderness? for *there is* no bread, neither *is there any* water; and [f]our soul loatheth this light bread.

6 And [g]the LORD sent [h]fiery serpents among the people, and they bit the people; and much people of Ĭs'ra-el died.

7 ¶ [i]Therefore the people came to Mō'ses, and said, We have sinned, for we have spoken against the LORD, and against thee; [j]pray unto the LORD, that he take away the serpents from us. And Mō'ses prayed for the people.

8 And the LORD said unto Mō'ses, Make thee a fiery serpent, and set it upon a pole: and it shall come to pass, that every one that is bitten, when he looketh upon it, shall live.

9 And [k]Mō'ses made a serpent of brass, and put it upon a pole, and it came to pass, that if a serpent had bitten any man, when he beheld the serpent of brass, he lived.

10 ¶ And the children of Ĭs'ra-el set forward, and pitched in Ō'both.

11 And they journeyed from Ō'both, and pitched at [3]Ĭj'e–ăb'a-rĭm, in the wilderness which *is* before Mō'ab, toward the sunrising.

12 ¶ From thence they removed, and pitched in the valley of Zā'red.

13 From thence they removed, and pitched on the other side of Ăr'nŏn, which *is* in the wilderness that cometh out of the coasts of the Ăm'ôr-ītes: for [l]Ăr'nŏn *is* the border of Mō'ab, between Mō'ab and the Ăm'ôr-ītes.

14 Wherefore it is said in the book of the wars of the LORD, [4]What he did in the Red sea, and in the brooks of Ăr'nŏn,

15 And at the stream of the brooks that goeth down to the dwelling of Ăr, and [5]lieth upon the border of Mō'ab.

16 And from thence *they went* to [m]Bē'er: that *is* the well whereof the LORD spake unto Mō'ses, Gather the people together, and [n]I will give them water.

17 ¶ [o]Then Ĭs'ra-el sang this song, [6]Spring up, O well; [7]sing ye unto it:

18 The princes digged the well, the nobles of the people digged it, by *the direction of* the [p]lawgiver, with their staves. And from the wilderness *they went* to Măt'ta-nah:

19 And from Măt'ta-nah to Na-ha'lĭ-el: and from Na-ha'lĭ-el to Bā'mŏth:

20 And from Bā'mŏth *in* the valley, that *is* in the [8]country of Mō'ab, to the top of [9]Pĭs'gah, which looketh [q]toward [10]Jĕsh'i-mŏn.

21 ¶ And [r]Ĭs'ra-el sent messengers unto Sī'hŏn king of the Ăm'ôr-ītes, saying,

22 [s]Let me pass through thy land: we will not turn into the fields, or into the vineyards; we will not drink *of* the waters of the well: *but* we will go along by the king's *high* way, until we be past thy borders.

5 [d]Ps. 78.19
[e]Ex. 16.3
[f]Prov. 27.7
6 [g]Amos 9.3-4;
1 Cor. 10.9
[h]Deut. 8.15
7 [i]Ps. 78.34;
Isa. 26.16;
Hos. 5.15
[j]Ex. 8.8-28;
Acts 8.24
9 [k]2 Ki. 18.4;
John 3.14-15
11 [3]Or, Heaps of Abarim
13 [l]ch. 22.36;
Judg. 11.18
14 [4]Or, Vaheb in Suphah
15 [5]leaneth
16 [m]Judg. 9.21
[n]Rev. 7.17
17 [o]Ex. 15.1;
Ps. 105.2
[6]Ascend
[7]Or, answer
18 [p]Deut. 33.4;
Isa. 33.22
20 [8]field
[9]Or, the hill
[q]ch. 23.28
[10]Or, the wilderness
21 [r]Deut. 2.26;
Judg. 11.19
22 [s]ch. 20.17
23 [t]Deut. 29.7
[u]Deut. 2.32-33
24 [v]Deut. 29.7;
Amos 2.9
25 [11]daughters
28 [w]Isa. 15.4;
Jer. 48.45-46
[x]Deut. 2.9;
Isa. 15.1
29 [y]Judg. 11.24;
2 Ki. 23.13
30 [z]Jer. 48.18-22
32 [a]Jer. 48.32
33 [b]Josh. 13.12
34 [c]Deut. 3.2
[d]Ps. 135.11;
Ps. 136.20
35 [e]Deut. 3.3-4

CHAPTER 22
1 [a]ch. 33.48;
Jer. 32.21
2 [b]Judg. 11.25
3 [c]Ex. 15.15
4 [d]ch. 31.8;
Josh. 13.21

23 And [t]Sī'hŏn would not suffer Ĭs'ra-el to pass through his border: but Sī'hŏn gathered all his people together, and went out against Ĭs'ra-el into the wilderness: and [u]he came to Jā'hăz, and fought against Ĭs'ra-el.

24 And [v]Ĭs'ra-el smote him with the edge of the sword, and possessed his land from Ăr'nŏn unto Jăb'bok, even unto the children of Ăm'mŏn: for the border of the children of Ăm'mŏn *was* strong.

25 And Ĭs'ra-el took all these cities: and Ĭs'ra-el dwelt in all the cities of the Ăm'ôr-ītes, in Hĕsh'bŏn, and in all the [11]villages thereof.

26 For Hĕsh'bŏn *was* the city of Sī'hŏn the king of the Ăm'ôr-ītes, who had fought against the former king of Mō'ab, and taken all his land out of his hand, even unto Ăr'nŏn.

27 Wherefore they that speak in proverbs say, Come into Hĕsh'bŏn, let the city of Sī'hŏn be built and prepared:

28 For there is [w]a fire gone out of Hĕsh'bŏn, a flame from the city of Sī'hŏn: it hath consumed [x]Ăr of Mō'ab, *and* the lords of the high places of Ăr'nŏn.

29 Woe to thee, Mō'ab! thou art undone, O people of [y]Chē'mŏsh: he hath given his sons that escaped, and his daughters, into captivity unto Sī'hŏn king of the Ăm'ôr-ītes.

30 We have shot at them; Hĕsh'bŏn is perished even [z]unto Dī'bŏn, and we have laid them waste even unto Nō'phah, which *reacheth* unto Mĕd'e-bȧ.

31 ¶ Thus Ĭs'ra-el dwelt in the land of the Ăm'ôr-ītes.

32 And Mō'ses sent to spy out [a]Ja-ā'zēr, and they took the villages thereof, and drove out the Ăm'ôr-ītes that *were* there.

33 ¶ And they turned and went up by the way of Bā'shăn: and Ōg the king of Bā'shăn went out against them, he, and all his people, to the battle [b]at Ĕd're-ī.

34 And the LORD said unto Mō'ses, [c]Fear him not: for I have delivered him into thy hand, and all his people, and his land; and [d]thou shalt do to him as thou didst unto Sī'hŏn king of the Ăm'ôr-ītes, which dwelt at Hĕsh'bŏn.

35 [e]So they smote him, and his sons, and all his people, until there was none left him alive: and they possessed his land.

22 And [a]the children of Ĭs'ra-el set forward, and pitched in the plains of Mō'ab on this side Jôr'dan *by* Jĕr'ī-chō.

2 ¶ And [b]Bā'lăk the son of Zĭp'por saw all that Ĭs'ra-el had done to the Ăm'ôr-ītes.

3 And [c]Mō'ab was sore afraid of the people, because they *were* many: and Mō'ab was distressed because of the children of Ĭs'ra-el.

4 And Mō'ab said unto the [d]elders of Mĭd'ĭ-an, Now shall this company lick up all *that are* round about us, as the ox licketh up the grass of the field.

And Bā'lăk the son of Zĭp'por *was* king of the Mō'ab-ītes at that time.

5 He sent messengers therefore unto [e]Bā'laam the son of Bē'or to [f]Pē'thôr, which *is* by the river of the land of the children of his people, to call him, saying, Be̱hold, there is a people come out from Ē'ġypt: behold, they cover the [1]face of the earth, and they abide over against me:

6 Come now therefore, I pray thee, [g]curse me this people; for they *are* too mighty for me: peradventure I shall prevail, *that* we may smite them, and *that* I may drive them out of the land: for I wot that he whom thou blessest *is* blessed, and he whom thou cursest is cursed.

7 And the elders of Mō'ab and the elders of Mĭd'ĭ-an departed with the [h]rewards of divination in their hand; and they came unto Bā'laam, and spake unto him the words of Bā'lăk.

8 And he said unto them, Lodge here this night, and I will bring you word again, as the LORD shall speak unto me: and the princes of Mō'ab abode with Bā'laam.

9 And [i]God came unto Bā'laam, and said, What men *are* these with thee?

10 And Bā'laam said unto God, Bā'lăk the son of Zĭp'por, king of Mō'ab, hath sent unto me, *saying,*

11 Be̱hold, *there is* a people come out of Ē'ġypt, which covereth the face of the earth: come now, curse me them; peradventure [2]I shall be able to overcome them, and drive them out.

12 And God said unto Bā'laam, Thou shalt not go with them; thou shalt not curse the people: for [j]they *are* blessed.

13 And Bā'laam rose up in the morning, and said unto the princes of Bā'lăk, Get you into your land: for the LORD refuseth to give me leave to go with you.

14 And the princes of Mō'ab rose up, and they went unto Bā'lăk, and said, Bā'laam refuseth to come with us.

15 ¶ And Bā'lăk sent yet again princes, more, and more honourable than they.

16 And they came to Bā'laam, and said to him, Thus saith Bā'lăk the son of Zĭp'por, [3]Let nothing, I pray thee, hinder thee from coming unto me:

17 For [k]I will promote thee unto very great honour, and I will do whatsoever thou sayest unto me: come therefore, I pray thee, curse me this people.

18 And Bā'laam answered and said unto the servants of Bā'lăk, If Bā'lăk would give me his house full of silver and gold, [l]I cannot go beyond the word of the LORD my God, to do less or more.

19 Now therefore, I pray you, tarry ye also here this night, that I may know what the LORD will say unto me more.

20 And God came unto Bā'laam at night, and said unto him, If the men come to call thee, rise up, *and* go with them; but [m]yet the word which I shall say unto thee, that shalt thou do.

21 And Bā'laam rose up in the morning, and saddled his ass, and went [n]with the princes of Mō'ab.

22 ¶ And God's anger was kindled because he went: [o]and the angel of the LORD stood in the way for an adversary against him. Now he was riding upon his ass, and his two servants *were* with him.

23 And [p]the ass saw the angel of the LORD standing in the way, and his sword drawn in his hand: and the ass turned aside out of the way, and went into the field: and Bā'laam smote the ass, to turn her into the way.

24 But the angel of the LORD stood in a path of the vineyards, a wall *being* on this side, and a wall on that side.

25 And when the ass saw the angel of the LORD, she thrust herself unto the wall, and crushed Bā'laam's [q]foot against the wall: and he smote her again.

26 And the angel of the LORD went further, and stood in a narrow place, [r]where *was* no way to turn either to the right hand or to the left.

27 And when the ass saw the angel of the LORD, she fell down under Bā'laam: [s]and Bā'laam's anger was kindled, and he smote the ass with a staff.

28 And the LORD [t]opened the mouth of the ass, and she said unto Bā'laam, What have I done unto thee, that thou hast smitten me these three times?

29 And Bā'laam said unto the ass, Because thou hast mocked me: I would there were a sword in mine hand, [u]for now would I kill thee.

30 And [v]the ass said unto Bā'laam, *Am* not I thine ass, [4]upon which thou hast ridden [5]ever since *I was* thine unto this day? was I ever wont to do so unto thee? And he said, Nay.

31 Then the LORD [w]opened the eyes of Bā'laam, and he saw the angel of the LORD standing in the way, and his sword drawn in his hand: and he [x]bowed down his head, and [6]fell flat on his face.

32 And the angel of the LORD said unto him, Wherefore hast thou smitten thine ass these three times? behold, I went out [7]to withstand thee, because *thy* way is [y]perverse before me:

33 And the ass saw me, and turned from me these three times: unless she had turned from me, surely now also I had slain thee, and saved her alive.

34 And Bā'laam said unto the angel of the LORD, [z]I have sinned; for I knew not that thou stoodest in the way against me: now therefore, if it [8]displease thee, I will get me back again.

35 And the angel of the LORD said unto Bā'laam, Go with the men: but only the word that I shall speak unto thee, that thou shalt speak. So Bā'laam went with the princes of Bā'lăk.

36 ¶ And when Bā'lăk heard that Bā'laam was come, [a]he went out to meet him unto a çity of Mō'ab, which *is* in the border of Ar'nŏn, which *is* in the utmost coast.

5 [e]Deut. 23.4; Mic. 6.5
[f]Deut. 23.4
[1]eye
6 [g]Gen. 12.3; Neh. 13.2
7 [h]Ex. 23.8; Mic. 3.11
9 [i]Gen. 20.3; Gen. 31.24
11 [2]I shall prevail in fighting against him
12 [j]Gen. 12.2; Rom. 11.29
16 [3]Be not thou letted from, etc
17 [k]Deut. 16.19; Matt. 16.26
18 [l]1 Ki. 22.14; 2 Chr. 18.13
20 [m]ch. 23.12-26; Isa. 46.10
21 [n]Prov. 15.27
22 [o]Ex. 4.24
23 [p]2 Ki. 6.17
25 [q]Isa. 47.12
26 [r]Isa. 26.11
27 [s]Prov. 14.16
28 [t]Matt. 19.26
29 [u]Prov. 12.10
30 [v]1 Cor. 1.27
[4]who hast ridden upon me
[5]Or, ever since thou wast, etc
31 [w]Gen. 21.19;
[x]Job 8.20;
[6]Or, bowed himself
32 [7]to be an adversary unto thee
[y]Deut. 23.4
34 [z]1 Sam. 26.21;
[8]be evil in thine eyes
36 [a]Gen. 14.17

37 And Bā'lăk said unto Bā'laam, Did I not earnestly send unto thee to call thee? wherefore camest thou not unto me? am I not able indeed to promote thee to honour?

38 And Bā'laam said unto Bā'lăk, Lo, I am come unto thee: have I now any power at all to say any thing? [b]the word that God putteth in my mouth, that shall I speak.

39 And Bā'laam went with Bā'lăk, and they came unto [9]Kĭr'jath–hū'zoth.

40 And Bā'lăk offered oxen and sheep, and sent to Bā'laam, and to the princes that *were* with him.

41 And it came to pass on the morrow, that Bā'lăk took Bā'laam, and brought him up into the [c]high places of Bā'al, that thence he might see the utmost *part* of the people.

23 And Bā'laam said unto Bā'lăk, Build me here seven altars, and prepare me here seven oxen and seven rams.

2 And Bā'lăk did as Bā'laam had spoken; and Bā'lăk and Bā'laam offered on *every* altar a bullock and a ram.

3 And Bā'laam said unto Bā'lăk, Stand by thy burnt offering, and I will go: peradventure the LORD will come to meet me: and whatsoever he sheweth me I will tell thee. And [1]he went to an high place.

4 And God met Bā'laam: and he said unto him, I have prepared seven altars, and I have offered upon *every* altar a bullock and a ram.

5 And the LORD [a]put a word in Bā'laam's mouth, and said, Return unto Bā'lăk, and thus thou shalt speak.

6 And he returned unto him, and, lo, he stood by his burnt sacrifice, he, and all the princes of Mō'ab.

7 And [b]he took up his parable, and said, Bā'lăk the king of Mō'ab hath brought me from [c]Ā'ram, out of the mountains of the east, *saying*, Come, curse me Jā'cob, and come, [d]defy Is'ra-el.

8 How shall I curse, whom God hath not cursed? or [e]how shall I defy, *whom* the LORD hath not defied?

9 For from the top of the rocks I see him, and from the hills I behold him: lo, [f]the people shall dwell alone, and [g]shall not be reckoned among the nations.

10 [h]Who can count the dust of Jā'cob, and the number of the fourth *part* of Is'ra-el? Let [2]me die the [i]death of the righteous, and let my last end be like his!

11 And Bā'lăk said unto Bā'laam, What hast thou done unto me? [j]I took thee to curse mine enemies, and, behold, thou hast blessed *them* altogether.

12 And he answered and said, Must I not take heed to speak that which the LORD hath put in my mouth?

13 And Bā'lăk said unto him, Come, I pray thee, with me unto another place, from whence thou mayest see them: thou shalt see but the utmost part of them, and shalt not see them all: and curse me them from thence.

14 ¶ And he brought him into the field of Zō'phim, to the top of [3]Pisgah, [k]and built seven altars, and offered a bullock and a ram on *every* altar.

15 And he said unto Bā'lăk, Stand here by thy burnt offering, while I meet *the* LORD yonder.

16 And the LORD met Bā'laam, and put a word in his mouth, and said, Go again unto Bā'lăk, and say thus.

17 And when he came to him, behold, he stood by his burnt offering, and the princes of Mō'ab with him. And Bā'lăk said unto him, What [l]hath the LORD spoken?

18 And he took up his parable, and said, [m]Rise up, Bā'lăk, and hear; hearken unto me, thou son of Zĭp'por:

19 [n]God *is* not a man, that he should lie; neither the son of man, that he should repent: hath he said, and shall he not do *it*? or hath he spoken, and shall he not make it good?

20 Behold, I have received *commandment* to bless: and [o]he hath blessed; and I cannot reverse it.

21 [p]He hath not beheld iniquity in Jā'cob, neither hath he seen perverseness in Is'ra-el: the [q]LORD his God *is* with him, [r]and the shout of a king *is* among them.

22 God brought them out of Ē'gypt; he hath as it were [s]the strength of an unicorn.

23 Surely *there is* no enchantment [4]against Jā'cob, neither *is there* any divination against Is'ra-el: according to this time it shall be said of Jā'cob and of Is'ra-el, [t]What hath God wrought!

24 Behold, the people shall rise up as a great lion, and lift up himself as a young lion: he shall not lie down until he eat *of* the prey, and drink the blood of the slain.

25 ¶ And Bā'lăk said unto Bā'laam, Neither curse them at all, nor bless them at all.

26 But Bā'laam answered and said unto Bā'lăk, Told not I thee, saying, All that the LORD speaketh, that I must do?

27 ¶ And Bā'lăk said unto Bā'laam, Come, I pray thee, I will bring thee unto another place; peradventure it will please God that thou mayest curse me them from thence.

28 And Bā'lăk brought Bā'laam unto the top of Pē'or, that looketh toward [5]Jĕsh'i-mŏn.

29 And [u]Bā'laam said unto Bā'lăk, Build me here seven altars, and prepare me here seven bullocks and seven rams.

30 And Bā'lăk did as Bā'laam had said, and offered a bullock and a ram on *every* altar.

24 And when Bā'laam saw that it pleased the LORD to bless Is'ra-el, he went not, as at other times, [1]to seek for enchantments, but he set his face toward the wilderness.

2 And Bā'laam lifted up his eyes, and he saw Is'ra-el abiding *in his tents*

38 [b]1 Ki. 22.14; 2 Chr. 18.13
39 [9]Or, A city of streets
41 [c]Deut. 12.2; Jer. 48.35

CHAPTER 23
3 [1]Or, he went solitary
5 [a]Deut. 18.18; Jer. 1.9
7 [b]Job 27.1; Matt. 13.35
[c]Gen. 10.22; Gen. 28.5
[d]1 Sam. 17.10
8 [e]Prov. 21.30; Isa. 47.12
9 [f]Lev. 20.24; 1 Ki. 8.53
[g]Ezra 9.2; Eph. 2.14
10 [h]Gen. 22.17
[2]my soul, or, my life
[i]Ps. 116.15; Isa. 57.1-2
11 [j]Josh. 24.10; Neh. 13.2
14 [3]Or, The hill
[k]Isa. 1.10-11; Hos. 12.11
17 [l]1 Sam. 3.17
18 [m]Judg. 3.20
19 [n]1 Sam. 15.29; Jas. 1.17
20 [o]Gen. 12.2; ch. 22.12
21 [p]Jer. 50.20;
[q]Ex. 13.21
[r]Ps. 89.15;
22 [s]Deut. 33.17
23 [4]Or, in
[t]Ps. 31.19
28 [5]Or, The wilderness
29 [u]2 Pet. 2.16

CHAPTER 24
1 [1]to the meeting of enchantments

according to their tribes; and [a]the
spirit of God came upon him.
3 And [b]he took up his parable, and
said, Bā'laam the son of Bē'or hath
said, and the man [2]whose eyes are
open hath said:
4 He hath said, which heard the
words of God, which saw the vision of
the Almighty, [c]falling *into a trance,*
but having his eyes open:
5 How goodly are thy tents, O Jā'-
cob, *and* thy tabernacles, O Ĭs'ra-el!
6 As the valleys are they spread
forth, as gardens by the river's side, as
the trees of lign aloes [d]which the LORD
hath planted, *and* as cedar trees beside
the waters.
7 He shall pour the water out of his
buckets, and his seed *shall be* in many
waters, and his king shall be higher
than [e]Ā'găg, and his [f]kingdom shall
be exalted.
8 God brought him forth out of
Ē'ġypt; he hath as it were the strength
of an unicorn: he shall eat up the nations his enemies, and shall break their
bones, and pierce *them* through with
his arrows.
9 He couched, he lay down as a lion,
and as a great lion: who shall stir him
up? [g]Blessed *is* he that blesseth thee,
and cursed *is* he that curseth thee.
10 ¶ And Bā'lăk's anger was kindled against Bā'laam, and he smote his
hands together: and Bā'lăk said unto
Bā'laam, I called thee to curse mine
enemies, and, behold, thou hast altogether blessed *them* these three times.
11 Therefore now flee thou to thy
place: I thought to promote thee unto
great honour; but, lo, the LORD hath
kept thee back from honour.
12 And Bā'laam said unto Bā'lăk,
Spake I not also to thy messengers
which thou sentest unto me, saying,
13 If Bā'lăk would give me his house
full of silver and gold, I cannot go beyond the commandment of the LORD,
to do *either* good or bad of mine own
mind; *but* what the LORD saith, that
will I speak?
14 And now, behold, I go unto my
people: come *therefore, and* I will advertise thee what this people shall do
to thy people in the latter days.
15 ¶ And he took up his parable, and
said, Bā'laam the son of Bē'or hath
said, and the man whose eyes are open
hath said:
16 He hath said, which heard the
words of God, and knew the knowledge of the most High, *which* saw the
vision of the Almighty, falling *into a
trance,* but having his eyes open:
17 [h]I shall see him, but not now: I
shall behold him, but not nigh: there
shall come [i]a Star out of Jā'cob, and [j]a
Sceptre shall rise out of Ĭs'ra-el, and
shall [3]smite the corners of Mō'ab, and
destroy all the children of Shēth.
18 And [k]Ē'dom shall be a possession, Sē'ïr also shall be a possession
for his enemies; and Ĭs'ra-el shall do
valiantly.

2 [a]ch. 11.25; 1 Cor. 12.8-10
3 [b]ch. 23.7 [2]who had his eyes shut, but now opened
4 [c]1 Sam. 19.24; Rev. 1.10-17
6 [d]Ps. 1.3; Jer. 17.8
7 [e]1 Sam. 15.32 [f]2 Sam. 5.12; Isa. 2.2
9 [g]Gen. 12.3; Matt. 25.40-45
17 [h]Job 19.25-27 [i]Jer. 23.5; Rev. 22.16 [j]Gen. 49.10; Ps. 110.2 [3]Or, smite through the princes of Moab
18 [k]Gen. 27.37; Amos 9.12
20 [4]Or, the first of the nations that warred against Israel [5]Or, shall be even to destruction
22 [6]Kain [7]Or, how long shall it be ere Asshur carry thee away captive?
24 [l]Gen. 10.4; [m]Gen. 11.14 [n]Lev. 26.28

CHAPTER 25
1 [a]ch. 33.49; [b]ch. 31.16
2 [c]Josh. 22.17; [d]Ex. 34.15 [e]Ex. 20.5
3 [f]Ps. 106.28
4 [g]Josh. 22.17 [h]Deut. 13.17
5 [i]1 Ki. 18.40
6 [j]Joel 2.17
7 [k]Ex. 6.25 [1]a spear, or, pike
9 [l]1 Cor. 10.8
11 [m]Ps. 106.30 [2]with my zeal [n]Ex. 20.5

19 Out of Jā'cob shall come he that
shall have dominion, and shall destroy
him that remaineth of the city.
20 ¶ And when he looked on Ăm'a-
lĕk, he took up his parable, and said,
Ăm'a-lĕk *was* [4]the first of the nations;
but his latter end [5]*shall be* that he perish for ever.
21 And he looked on the Kĕn'ītes,
and took up his parable, and said,
Strong is thy dwellingplace, and thou
puttest thy nest in a rock.
22 Nevertheless [6]the Kenite shall be
wasted, [7]until Ăs'shur shall carry thee
away captive.
23 And he took up his parable, and
said, Alas, who shall live when God
doeth this!
24 And ships *shall come* from the
coast of [l]Chĭt'tim, and shall afflict Ăs'-
shur, and shall afflict [m]Ē'bēr, and [n]he
also shall perish for ever.
25 And Bā'laam rose up, and went
and returned to his place: and Bā'lăk
also went his way.

25 And Ĭs'ra-el abode in [a]Shĭt'tim,
and [b]the people began to commit whoredom with the daughters of
Mō'ab.
2 And [c]they called the people unto
the [d]sacrifices of their gods: and the
people did eat, and [e]bowed down to
their gods.
3 And Ĭs'ra-el joined himself unto
Bā'al–pē'or: and [f]the anger of the
LORD was kindled against Ĭs'ra-el.
4 And the LORD said unto Mō'ses,
[g]Take all the heads of the people, and
hang them up before the LORD against
the sun, [h]that the fierce anger of the
LORD may be turned away from Ĭs'ra-
el.
5 And Mō'ses said unto the judges
of Ĭs'ra-el, [i]Slay ye every one his men
that were joined unto Bā'al–pē'or.
6 ¶ And, behold, one of the children
of Ĭs'ra-el came and brought unto his
brethren a Mĭd'ĭ-an-ĭt-ish woman in the
sight of Mō'ses, and in the sight of all
the congregation of the children of Ĭs'-
ra-el, [j]who *were* weeping *before* the
door of the tabernacle of the congregation.
7 And when Phĭn'e-has, [k]the son of
Ē-le-ā'zar, the son of Aâr'on the priest,
saw *it,* he rose up from among the congregation, and took [1]a javelin in his
hand;
8 And he went after the man of Ĭs'-
ra-el into the tent, and thrust both of
them through, the man of Ĭs'ra-el, and
the woman through her belly. So the
plague was stayed from the children of
Ĭs'ra-el.
9 And [l]those that died in the plague
were twenty and four thousand.
10 ¶ And the LORD spake unto Mō'-
ses, saying,
11 [m]Phĭn'e-has, the son of Ē-le-ā'-
zar, the son of Aâr'on the priest, hath
turned my wrath away from the children of Ĭs'ra-el, while he was zealous
[2]for my sake among them, that I consumed not the children of Ĭs'ra-el in
[n]my jealousy.

12 Wherefore say, [o]Behold, I give unto him my covenant of peace:

13 And he shall have it, and [p]his seed after him, *even* the covenant of [q]an everlasting priesthood; because he was [r]zealous for his God, and made an atonement for the children of Ĭs′ra-el.

14 Now the name of the Ĭs′ra-el-īte that was slain, *even* that was slain with the Mĭd′ĭ-an-īt-ish woman, *was* Zĭm′rī, the son of Sā′lu, a prince of a [3]chief house among the Sĭm′e-on-ītes.

15 And the name of the Mĭd′ĭ-an-īt-ish woman that was slain *was* Cŏz′bī, the daughter of Zûr; he *was* head over a people, *and* of a chief house in Mĭd′ĭ-an.

16 ¶ And the LORD spake unto Mō′ses, saying,

17 Vex the Mĭd′ĭ-an-ītes, and smite them:

18 For they vex you with their wiles, wherewith they have beguiled you in the matter of Pē′or, and in the matter of Cŏz′bī, the daughter of a prince of Mĭd′ĭ-an, their sister, which was slain in the day of the plague for Pē′or's sake.

26

26 And it came to pass after the plague, that the LORD spake unto Mō′ses and unto Ē-le-ā′zar the son of Aâr′on the priest, saying,

2 [a]Take the sum of all the congregation of the children of Ĭs′ra-el, from twenty years old and upward, throughout their fathers' house, all that are able to go to war in Ĭs′ra-el.

3 And Mō′ses and Ē-le-ā′zar the priest spake with them [b]in the plains of Mō′ab by Jôr′dan *near* Jĕr′ĭ-chō, saying,

4 *Take the sum of the people,* from twenty years old and upward; as the LORD commanded Mō′ses and the children of Ĭs′ra-el, which went forth out of the land of Ē′gypt.

5 ¶ [c]Reu′ben, the eldest son of Ĭs′ra-el: the children of Reu′ben; Hā′noch, *of whom cometh* the family of the Hā′noch-ītes: of Păl′lu, the family of the Păl′lu-ītes:

6 Of Hĕz′ron, the family of the Hĕz′ron-ītes: of Căr′mī, the family of the Căr′mītes.

7 These *are* the families of the Reu′ben-ītes: and they that were numbered of them were forty and three thousand and seven hundred and thirty.

8 And the sons of Păl′lu; E-lī′ab.

9 And the sons of E-lī′ab; Ne-mū′el, and Dā′than, and A-bī′răm. This *is that* Dā′than and A-bī′răm, *which were* [d]famous in the congregation, who strove against Mō′ses and against Aâr′on in the company of Kō′rah, when they strove against the LORD:

10 And the earth opened her mouth, and swallowed them up together with Kō′rah, when that company died, what time the fire devoured two hundred and fifty men: [e]and they became a sign.

11 Notwithstanding [f]the children of Kō′rah died not.

12 ¶ The sons of Sĭm′e-on after their families: of [g]Ne-mū′el, the family of the Ne-mū′el-ītes: of Jā′min, the family of the Jā′min-ītes: of [h]Jā′chin, the family of the Jā′chin-ītes:

13 Of [i]Zē′rah, the family of the Zär′hītes: of Shā′ul, the family of the Shā′ul-ītes.

14 These *are* the families of the Sĭm′e-on-ītes, twenty and two thousand and two hundred.

15 ¶ The children of Găd after their families: of [j]Zē′phon, the family of the Zē′phon-ītes: of Hăg′gī, the family of the Hăg′gītes: of Shu′nī, the family of the Shu′nītes:

16 Of [1]Ŏz′nī, the family of the Ŏz′nītes: of Ē′rī, the family of the Ē′rītes:

17 Of [k]Ā′rŏd, the family of the Ā′rŏd-ītes: of A-rē′lī, the family of the A-rē′lītes.

18 These *are* the families of the children of Găd according to those that were numbered of them, forty thousand and five hundred.

19 ¶ The [l]sons of Jū′dah *were* Ēr and Ō′nan: and Ēr and Ō′nan died in the land of Cā′năan.

20 And [m]the sons of Jū′dah after their families were; of Shē′lah, the family of the Shē′lan-ītes: of Phā′rĕz, the family of the Phär′zītes: of Zē′rah, the family of the Zär′hītes.

21 And the sons of Phā′rĕz were; of Hĕz′ron, the family of the Hĕz′ron-ītes: of Hā′mŭl, the family of the Hā′mŭl-ītes.

22 These *are* the families of Jū′dah according to those that were numbered of them, threescore and sixteen thousand and five hundred.

23 ¶ [n]*Of* the sons of Ĭs′sa-char after their families: *of* Tō′lȧ, the family of the Tō′lȧ-ītes: of [2]Pū′ȧ, the family of the Pū′nītes:

24 Of [3]Jăsh′ŭb, the family of the Jăsh′ŭb-ītes: of Shĭm′ron, the family of the Shĭm′ron-ītes.

25 These *are* the families of Ĭs′sa-char according to those that were numbered of them, threescore and four thousand and three hundred.

26 ¶ [o]*Of* the sons of Zĕb′u-lun after their families: of Sē′red, the family of the Sär′dītes: of Ē′lon, the family of the Ē′lon-ītes: of Jäh′lĕ-el, the family of the Jäh′lĕ-el-ītes.

27 These *are* the families of the Zĕb′u-lun-ītes according to those that were numbered of them, threescore thousand and five hundred.

28 ¶ The [p]sons of Jō′seph after their families *were* Ma-năs′seh and Ē′phrā-ĭm.

29 Of the sons of Ma-năs′seh: of [q]Mā′chĭr, the family of the Mā′chĭr-ītes: and Mā′chĭr begat Gĭl′e-ăd: of Gĭl′e-ăd *come* the family of the Gĭl′e-ăd-ītes.

30 These *are* the sons of Gĭl′e-ăd: *of* [r]Je-ē′zĕr, the family of the Je-ē′zĕr-ītes: of Hē′lek, the family of the Hē′lek-ītes:

---

12 [o]Mal. 3.1
13 [p]1 Chr. 6.4
[q]Ex. 40.15
[r]Acts 22.3
14 [3]house of a father

CHAPTER 26
2 [a]Ex. 30.12; ch. 1.2
3 [b]Deut. 4.46-49; ch. 35.1
5 [c]Gen. 29.32; Rev. 7.5
9 [d]ch. 16.1-2; Jude 11
10 [e]ch. 16.38; Jude 7
11 [f]Ex. 6.24; 1 Chr. 6.22
12 [g]Gen. 46.10; Ex. 6.15, Jemuel
[h]1 Chr. 4.24, Jarib
13 [i]Gen. 46.10, Zohar
15 [j]Gen. 46.16, Ziphion
16 [1]Or, Ezbon
17 [k]Gen. 46.16, Arodi
19 [l]Gen. 38.2; 1 Chr. 2.3
20 [m]Gen. 49.8; Rev. 7.5
23 [n]Gen. 46.13; 1 Chr. 7.1
[2]Or, Phuvah
24 [3]Or, Job
26 [o]Gen. 46.14;
28 [p]Gen. 41.51;
29 [q]ch. 32.39-40;
30 [r]Called Abiezer, Josh. 17.2

31 And *of* Ăs'rĭ-el, the family of the
Ăs'rĭ-el-ītes: and *of* Shē'chem, the family of the Shē'chem-ītes:
32 And *of* She-mī'dȧ, the family of
the She-mī'dȧ-ītes: and *of* Hē'phẽr, the
family of the Hē'phẽr-ītes.
33 ¶ And [s]Ze-lō'phe-hăd the son of
Hē'phẽr had no sons, but daughters:
and the names of the daughters of Ze-
lō'phe-hăd *were* Măh'lah, and Nō'ah,
Hŏg'lah, Mĭl'cah, and Tĭr'zah.
34 These *are* the families of Ma-năs'-
seh, and those that were numbered of
them, fifty and two thousand and seven
hundred.
35 ¶ These *are* the sons of Ē'phrā-ĭm
after their families: of Shu'the-lah, the
family of the Shu'thal-hītes: of [t]Bē'-
chẽr, the family of the Băch'rītes: of
Tā'hăn, the family of the Tā'han-ītes.
36 And these *are* the sons of Shu'-
the-lah: of Ē'răn, the family of the
Ē'răn-ītes.
37 These *are* the families of the sons
of Ē'phrā-ĭm according to those that
were numbered of them, thirty and
two thousand and five hundred. These
are the sons of [u]Jō'seph after their
families.
38 ¶ The [v]sons of Bĕn'ja-min after
their families: of Bē'lȧ, the family of
the Bē'lȧ-ītes: of Ash'bel, the family of
the Ăsh'bel-ītes: of [w]A-hī'ram, the family of the A-hī'ram-ītes:
39 Of [x]Shu'pham, the family of the
Shu'pham-ītes: of Hū'pham, the family of the Hū'pham-ītes.
40 And the sons of Bē'lȧ were [y]Ärd
and Nā'a-man: *of Ärd,* the family of
the Ärd'ītes: *and* of Nā'a-man, the family of the Nā'a-mītes.
41 These *are* the sons of Bĕn'ja-min
after their families: and they that were
numbered of them *were* forty and five
thousand and six hundred.
42 ¶ [z]These *are* the sons of Dăn after their families: of [4]Shu'ham, the family of the Shu'ham-ītes. These *are* the
families of Dăn after their families.
43 All the families of the Shu'ham-
ītes, according to those that were numbered of them, *were* threescore and
four thousand and four hundred.
44 ¶ [a]*Of* the children of Ăsh'ẽr after
their families: of Jĭm'nȧ, the family of
the Jĭm'nītes: of Jĕs'u-ī, the family of
the Jĕs'u-ītes: of Be-rī'ah, the family of
the Be-ri'-ites.
45 Of the sons of Be-rī'ah: of Hē'bẽr,
the family of the Hē'bẽr-ītes: of Măl'-
chĭ-el, the family of the Măl'chĭ-el-ītes.
46 And the name of the daughter of
Ăsh'ẽr *was* Sā'rah.
47 These *are* the families of the sons
of Ăsh'ẽr according to those that were
numbered of them; *who were* fifty and
three thousand and four hundred.
48 ¶ [b]*Of* the sons of Năph'ta-lī after
their families: of Jăh'zē-el, the family
of the Jăh'zē-el-ītes: of Gū'nī, the family of the Gū'nītes:
49 Of Jē'zẽr, the family of the Jē'-
zẽr-ītes: of [c]Shĭl'lem, the family of the
Shĭl'lem-ītes.

50 These *are* the families of Năph'-
ta-lī according to their families: and
they that were numbered of them *were*
forty and five thousand and four hundred.
51 [d]These *were* the numbered of the
children of Ĭs'ra-el, six hundred thousand and a thousand seven hundred
and thirty.
52 ¶ And the LORD spake unto Mō'-
ses, saying,
53 Unto [5]these the land shall be divided for an inheritance according to
the number of names.
54 [e]To many thou shalt [6]give the
more inheritance, and to few thou shalt
[7]give the less inheritance: to every one
shall his inheritance be given according to those that were numbered of
him.
55 Notwithstanding the land shall
be [f]divided by lot: according to the
names of the tribes of their fathers
they shall inherit.
56 According to the lot shall the possession thereof be divided between
many and few.
57 ¶ And [g]these *are* they that were
numbered of the Lē'vītes after their
families: of Gẽr'shŏn, the family of the
Gẽr'shon-ītes: of Kō'hath, the family
of the Kō'hath-ītes: of Me-rā'rī, the
family of the Me-rā'rītes.
58 These *are* the families of the Lē'-
vītes: the family of the Lĭb'nītes, the
family of the Hē'bron-ītes, the family
of the Măh'lītes, the family of the Mū'-
shītes, the family of the Kō'rath-ītes.
And Kō'hath begat Ăm'răm.
59 And the name of Ăm'răm's wife
was [h]Jŏch'e-bed, the daughter of Lē'vī,
whom *her mother* bare to Lē'vī in
Ē'gypt: and she bare unto Ăm'răm
Aâr'on and Mō'ses, and Mĭr'ĭ-am their
sister.
60 And unto Aâr'on was born Nā'-
dăb, and A-bī'hū, Ē-le-ā'zar, and Ĭth'a-
mär.
61 And [i]Nā'dăb and A-bī'hū died,
when they offered strange fire before
the LORD.
62 And [j]those that were numbered
of them were twenty and three thousand, all males from a month old and
upward: [k]for they were not numbered
among the children of Ĭs'ra-el, because
there was [l]no inheritance given them
among the children of Ĭs'ra-el.
63 ¶ These *are* they that were numbered by Mō'ses and Ē-le-ā'zar the
priest, who numbered the children of
Ĭs'ra-el in the plains of Mō'ab by Jôr'-
dan *near* Jĕr'ĭ-chō.
64 [m]But among these there was not
a man of them whom Mō'ses and
Aâr'on the priest numbered, when they
numbered the children of Ĭs'ra-el in the
wilderness of Sī'nāi.
65 For the LORD had said of them,
They [n]shall surely die in the wilderness. And there was not left a man of
them, [o]save Cā'leb the son of Je-phŭn'-
neh, and Jŏsh'u-ȧ the son of Nŭn.
27 Then came the daughters of [a]Ze-
lō'phe-hăd, the son of Hē'phẽr,

33 [s]ch. 27.1; Josh. 17.3
36 [t]1 Chr. 7.20, Bered
37 [u]Deut. 33.13-17
38 [v]Gen. 46.21; 1 Chr. 7.6; 1 Chr. 8.1
[w]Gen. 46.21, Ehi; 1 Chr. 8.1, Aharah
39 [x]Gen. 46.21, Muppim, and, Huppim
40 [y]1 Chr. 8.3, Addar
42 [z]Gen. 46.23; Gen. 49.16-17; ch. 1.38-39; Deut. 33.22
[4]Or, Hushim
44 [a]Gen. 46.17; 1 Chr. 7.30
48 [b]Gen. 46.24; 1 Chr. 7.13
49 [c]1 Chr. 7.13, Shallum
51 [d]ch. 1.46; ch. 2.32
53 [5]Thus each man's portion would be fifteen acres
54 [e]ch. 33.54
[6]multiply his inheritance
[7]diminish his inheritance
55 [f]ch. 34.13; Josh. 11.23; Josh. 14.2; Josh. 17.14; Josh. 18.6-10-11
57 [g]Gen. 46.11; Ex. 6.16; 1 Chr. 6.1-16
59 [h]Ex. 2.1-2
61 [i]Lev. 10.1-2; ch. 3.4; 1 Chr. 24.2
62 [j]ch. 3.39
[k]ch. 1.49
[l]ch. 18.20-23-24; ch. 35.2-8; Deut. 10.9; Josh. 14.3
64 [m]ch. 1.1; Deut. 2.14-15
65 [n]ch. 14.28; Jude 5
[o]ch. 14.30; Deut. 1.36-38
CHAPTER 27
1 [a]ch. 1.34-35; 1 Chr. 7.15

the son of Gĭl'e-ăd, the son of Mā'chĭr, the son of Ma-năs'seh, of the families of Ma-năs'seh the son of Jō'seph: and these *are* the names of his daughters; Māh'lah, Nō'ah, and Hŏg'lah, and Mĭl'cah, and Tĭr'zah.

2 And they stood before Mō'ses, and before Ē-le-ā'zar the priest, and before the princes and all the congregation, *by* the door of the tabernacle of the congregation, saying,

3 Our father [b]died in the wilderness, and he was not in the company of them that gathered themselves together against the LORD [c]in the company of Kō'rah; [d]but died in his own sin, and had no sons.

4 Why should the name of our father be [1]done away from among his family, because he hath no son? Give unto us *therefore* a possession among the brethren of our father.

5 And Mō'ses [e]brought their cause before the LORD.

6 ¶ And the LORD spake unto Mō'ses, saying,

7 The daughters of Ze-lō'phe-hăd speak right: [f]thou shalt surely give them a possession of an inheritance among their father's brethren; and thou shalt cause the inheritance of their father to pass unto them.

8 And thou shalt speak unto the children of Ĭs'ra-el, saying, If a man die, and have no son, then ye shall cause his inheritance to pass unto his daughter.

9 And if he have no daughter, then ye shall give his inheritance unto his brethren.

10 And if he have no brethren, then ye shall give his inheritance unto his father's brethren.

11 And if his father have no brethren, then ye shall give his inheritance unto his kinsman that is next to him of his family, and he shall possess it: and it shall be unto the children of Ĭs'ra-el [g]a statute of judgment, as the LORD commanded Mō'ses.

12 ¶ And the LORD said unto Mō'ses, [h]Get thee up into this mount Ăb'ă-rim, and see the land which I have given unto the children of Ĭs'ra-el.

13 And when thou hast seen it, thou also [i]shalt be gathered unto thy people, as Aâr'on thy brother was gathered.

14 For ye [j]rebelled against my commandment in the desert of Zĭn, in the strife of the congregation, to sanctify me at the water before their eyes: that *is* the [k]water of Mĕr'ĭ-bah in Kā'desh in the wilderness of Zĭn.

15 ¶ And Mō'ses spake unto the LORD, saying,

16 Let the LORD, the [l]God of the spirits of all flesh, set a man over the congregation,

17 [m]Which may go out before them, and which may go in before them, and which may lead them out, and which may bring them in; that the congregation of the LORD be not [n]as sheep which have no shepherd.

3 [b]ch. 26.64-65 [c]ch. 16.1-2 [d]ch. 14.22-37; Rom. 5.12
4 [1]diminished
5 [e]Ex. 18.15; Lev. 24.12-13; Prov. 3.5-6
7 [f]ch. 36.2
11 [g]ch. 35.29
12 [h]Deut. 3.27; Deut. 32.49
13 [i]ch. 20.24-28; ch. 31.2; Deut. 10.6
14 [j]Deut. 1.37; Ps. 106.32 [k]Ex. 17.7; ch. 20.1-13-24
16 [l]ch. 16.22; Heb. 12.9; Zech. 12.1
17 [m]Deut. 31.2; 1 Sam. 8.20; 2 Chr. 1.10 [n]1 Ki. 22.17; 2 Chr. 18.16; Matt. 9.36
18 [o]Gen. 41.38
19 [p]Deut. 31.7
20 [q]ch. 11.17; 1 Sam. 10.6; 2 Ki. 2.15 [r]Deut. 34.9; Josh. 1.16
21 [s]Josh. 9.14; Judg. 1.1; 1 Sam. 23.9; 1 Sam. 30.7 [t]Lev. 8.8; Deut. 33.8; 1 Sam. 28.6 [u]Josh. 9.14; 1 Sam. 22.10
23 [v]Deut. 3.28; Isa. 55.4

CHAPTER 28

2 [a]Lev. 3.11; Mal. 1.7-12 [1]a savour of my rest
3 [b]Ex. 29.38 [2]in a day
4 [3]between the two evenings
5 [c]Ex. 16.36; Lev. 2.1; ch. 15.4 [d]Lev. 2.1 [e]Ex. 29.40
7 [f]Ex. 29.42; Lev. 23.13; ch. 15.5-7-10; Isa. 57.6
10 [g]Ezek. 46.4
11 [h]ch. 10.10; Col. 2.16

18 ¶ And the LORD said unto Mō'ses, Take thee Jŏsh'u-ȧ the son of Nŭn, a man [o]in whom *is* the spirit, and lay thine hand upon him;

19 And set him before Ē-le-ā'zar the priest, and before all the congregation; and [p]give him a charge in their sight.

20 And [q]thou shalt put *some* of thine honour upon him, that all the congregation of the children of Ĭs'ra-el [r]may be obedient.

21 And [s]he shall stand before Ē-le-ā'zar the priest, who shall ask *counsel* for him [t]after the judgment of Ū'rim before the LORD: [u]at his word shall they go out, and at his word they shall come in, *both* he, and all the children of Ĭs'ra-el with him, even all the congregation.

22 And Mō'ses did as the LORD commanded him: and he took Jŏsh'u-ȧ, and set him before Ē-le-ā'zar the priest, and before all the congregation:

23 And he laid his hands upon him, [v]and gave him a charge, as the LORD commanded by the hand of Mō'ses.

28 And the LORD spake unto Mō'ses, saying,

2 Command the children of Ĭs'ra-el, and say unto them, My offering, *and* [a]my bread for my sacrifices made by fire, *for* [1]a sweet savour unto me, shall ye observe to offer unto me in their due season.

3 And thou shalt say unto them, [b]This *is* the offering made by fire which ye shall offer unto the LORD; two lambs of the first year without spot [2]day by day, *for* a continual burnt offering.

4 The one lamb shalt thou offer in the morning, and the other lamb shalt thou offer [3]at even;

5 And [c]a tenth *part* of an ephah of flour for a [d]meat offering, mingled with the fourth *part* of an [e]hin of beaten oil.

6 *It is* a continual burnt offering, which was ordained in mount Sī'nāi for a sweet savour, a sacrifice made by fire unto the LORD.

7 And the drink offering thereof *shall be* the fourth *part* of an hin for the one lamb: [f]in the holy *place* shalt thou cause the strong wine to be poured unto the LORD *for* a drink offering.

8 And the other lamb shalt thou offer at even: as the meat offering of the morning, and as the drink offering thereof, thou shalt offer *it*, a sacrifice made by fire, of a sweet savour unto the LORD.

9 ¶ And on the sabbath day two lambs of the first year without spot, and two tenth deals of flour *for* a meat offering, mingled with oil, and the drink offering thereof:

10 *This is* [g]the burnt offering of every sabbath, beside the continual burnt offering, and his drink offering.

11 ¶ And [h]in the beginnings of your months ye shall offer a burnt offering unto the LORD; two young bullocks,

and one ram, seven lambs of the first year without spot;

12 And [i]three tenth deals of flour *for* a meat offering, mingled with oil, for one bullock; and two tenth deals of flour *for* a meat offering, mingled with oil, for one ram;

13 And a several tenth deal of flour mingled with oil *for* a meat offering unto one lamb; *for* a burnt offering of a sweet savour, a sacrifice made by fire unto the LORD.

14 And their drink offerings shall be half an hin of wine unto a bullock, and the third *part* of an hin unto a ram, and a fourth *part* of an hin unto a lamb: this *is* the burnt offering of every month throughout the months of the year.

15 And one kid of the goats for a sin offering unto the LORD shall be offered, beside the continual burnt offering, and his drink offering.

16 And [j]in the fourteenth day of the first month *is* the passover of the LORD.

17 And [k]in the fifteenth day of this month *is* the feast: seven days shall unleavened bread be eaten.

18 In the [l]first day *shall be* an holy convocation; ye shall do no manner of servile work *therein:*

19 But ye shall offer a sacrifice made by fire *for* a burnt offering unto the LORD; two young bullocks, and one ram, and seven lambs of the first year: [m]they shall be unto you without blemish:

20 And their meat offering *shall be of* flour mingled with oil: three tenth deals shall ye offer for a bullock, and two tenth deals for a ram;

21 A several tenth deal shalt thou offer for every lamb, throughout the seven lambs:

22 And [n]one goat *for* a sin offering, to make an atonement for you.

23 Ye shall offer these beside the burnt offering in the morning, which *is* for a continual burnt offering.

24 After this manner ye shall offer daily, throughout the seven days, the meat of the sacrifice made by fire, of [o]a sweet savour unto the LORD: it shall be offered beside the continual burnt offering, and his drink offering.

25 And [p]on the seventh day ye shall have an holy convocation; ye shall do no servile work.

26 ¶ Also [q]in the day of the firstfruits, when ye bring a new meat offering unto the LORD, after your weeks *be out,* ye shall have an holy convocation; ye shall do no servile work:

27 But ye shall offer the burnt offering for a sweet savour unto the LORD; [r]two young bullocks, one ram, seven lambs of the first year;

28 And their meat offering of flour mingled with oil, three tenth deals unto one bullock, two tenth deals unto one ram,

29 A several tenth deal unto one lamb, throughout the seven lambs;

30 *And* one kid of the goats, to make an atonement for you.

31 Ye shall offer *them* beside the continual burnt offering, and his meat offering, (they shall be unto you without blemish) and their drink offerings.

29 And in the seventh month, on the first *day* of the month, ye shall have an holy convocation; ye shall do no servile work: [a]it is a day of blowing the trumpets unto you.

2 And ye shall offer a burnt offering for a sweet savour unto the LORD; one young bullock, one ram, *and* seven lambs of the first year without blemish:

3 And their meat offering *shall be of* flour mingled with oil, three tenth deals for a bullock, *and* two tenth deals for a ram,

4 And one tenth deal for one lamb, throughout the seven lambs:

5 And one kid of the goats *for* a sin offering, to make an atonement for you:

6 Beside [b]the burnt offering of the month, and his meat offering, and [c]the daily burnt offering, and his meat offering, and their drink offerings, [d]according unto their manner, for [1]a sweet savour, a sacrifice made by fire unto the LORD.

7 ¶ And [e]ye shall have on the tenth *day* of this seventh month an holy convocation; and ye shall [f]afflict your souls: ye shall not do any work *therein.*

8 But ye shall offer a burnt offering unto the LORD *for* a sweet savour; one young bullock, one ram, *and* seven lambs of the first year; [g]they shall be unto you without blemish:

9 And their meat offering *shall be of* flour mingled with oil, three tenth deals to a bullock, *and* two tenth deals to one ram,

10 A several tenth deal for one lamb, throughout the seven lambs:

11 One kid of the goats *for* a sin offering; beside [h]the sin offering of atonement, and the continual burnt offering, and the meat offering of it, and their drink offerings.

12 ¶ And [i]on the fifteenth day of the seventh month ye shall have an holy convocation; ye shall do no servile work, and ye shall keep a feast unto the LORD seven days:

13 And [j]ye shall offer a burnt offering, a sacrifice made by fire, of a sweet savour unto the LORD; thirteen young bullocks, two rams, *and* fourteen lambs of the first year; they shall be without blemish:

14 And their meat offering *shall be of* flour mingled with oil, three tenth deals unto every bullock of the thirteen bullocks, two tenth deals to each ram of the two rams,

15 And a several tenth deal to each lamb of the fourteen lambs:

16 And one kid of the goats *for* a sin offering; beside the continual burnt offering, his meat offering, and his drink offering.

17 ¶ And on the second day *ye shall offer* twelve [2]young bullocks, two rams,

12 [i]ch. 15.4; ch. 29.10
16 [j]Ex. 12.6; Lev. 23.5; Ezek. 45.21; Matt. 26.2-17; Luke 22.7
17 [k]Ex. 12.15-17; Lev. 23.6
18 [l]Lev. 23.7
19 [m]Lev. 22.20; ch. 29.8; Deut. 15.21
22 [n]Lev. 16.18; Rom. 8.3; Gal. 4.4; Heb. 9.12
24 [o]2 Cor. 2.15; Eph. 5.2
25 [p]Ex. 12.16; Lev. 23.8
26 [q]Ex. 23.16; Lev. 23.10-15; Deut. 16.10; Prov. 3.9; Acts 2.1
27 [r]Lev. 23.18-19

CHAPTER 29

1 [a]Lev. 23.24; Ps. 89.15; Isa. 27.13; Zech. 9.14; Mark 16.15; 1 Cor. 15.52; Rev. 8.6-13
6 [b]ch. 28.11 [c]Ex. 29.38; Lev. 6.9; ch. 28.3; Dan. 12.11 [d]ch. 15.11-12 [1]a savour of rest
7 [e]Lev. 16.29; Lev. 23.27 [f]Ezra 8.21; Ps. 35.13; Isa. 58.5; Matt. 5.4; Luke 13.3-4; 1 Cor. 9.27; 2 Cor. 7.9; Jas. 4.9
8 [g]Lev. 22.20; ch. 28.19; Deut. 15.21; Deut. 17.1
11 [h]Lev. 16.3-5
12 [i]Ex. 23.16; Ex. 34.22; Ezek. 45.25
13 [j]Ezra 3.4; Heb. 10.1-18
17 [2]Perhaps the gradual decrease of the bullocks denoted the gradual abolition of the ceremonies

fourteen lambs of the first year without spot:

18 And their meat offering and their drink offerings for the bullocks, for the rams, and for the lambs, *shall be* according to their number, [k]after the manner:

19 And one kid of the goats *for* a sin offering; beside the continual burnt offering, and the meat offering thereof, and their drink offerings.

20 ¶ And on the third day eleven bullocks, two rams, fourteen lambs of the first year without blemish;

21 And their meat offering and their drink offerings for the bullocks, for the rams, and for the lambs, *shall be* according to their number, after the manner:

22 And one goat *for* a sin offering; beside the continual burnt offering, and his meat offering, and his drink offering.

23 ¶ And on the fourth day ten bullocks, two rams, *and* fourteen lambs of the first year without blemish:

24 Their meat offering and their drink offerings for the bullocks, for the rams, and for the lambs, *shall be* according to their number, after the manner:

25 And one kid of the goats *for* a sin offering; beside the continual burnt offering, his meat offering, and his drink offering.

26 ¶ And on the fifth day nine bullocks, two rams, *and* fourteen lambs of the first year [l]without spot:

27 And their meat offering and their drink offerings for the bullocks, for the rams, and for the lambs, *shall be* according to their number, after the manner:

28 And one goat *for* a sin offering; beside the continual burnt offering, and his meat offering, and his drink offering.

29 ¶ And on the sixth day eight bullocks, two rams, *and* fourteen lambs of the first year without blemish:

30 And their meat offering and their drink offerings for the bullocks, for the rams, and for the lambs, *shall be* according to their number, after the manner:

31 And one goat *for* a sin offering; beside the continual burnt offering, his meat offering, and his drink offering.

32 ¶ And on the seventh day seven bullocks, two rams, *and* fourteen lambs of the first year without blemish:

33 And their meat offering and their drink offerings for the bullocks, for the rams, and for the lambs, *shall be* according to their number, after the manner:

34 And one goat *for* a sin offering; beside the continual burnt offering, his meat offering, and his drink offering.

35 ¶ On the eighth day ye shall have a [m]solemn assembly: ye shall do no servile work *therein:*

36 But ye shall offer a burnt offering, a sacrifice made by fire, of a sweet savour unto the LORD: one bullock, one ram, seven lambs of the first year without blemish:

37 Their meat offering and their drink offerings for the bullock, for the ram, and for the lambs, *shall be* according to their number, after the manner:

38 And one goat *for* a sin offering; beside the continual burnt offering, and his meat offering, and his drink offering.

39 These *things* ye shall [3]do unto the LORD in your [n]set feasts, beside your [o]vows, and your freewill offerings, for your burnt offerings, and for your meat offerings, and for your drink offerings, and for your peace offerings.

40 And [p]Mō'ses told the children of Is'ra-el according to all that the LORD commanded Mō'ses.

30 And Mō'ses spake unto [a]the heads of the tribes concerning the children of Is'ra-el, saying, This *is* the thing which the LORD hath commanded.

2 [b]If a man vow a vow unto the LORD, or [c]swear an oath to bind his soul with a bond; he shall not [1]break his word, he shall [d]do according to all that proceedeth out of his mouth.

3 If a woman also vow a vow unto the LORD, and bind *herself* by a bond, *being* in her father's house in her youth;

4 And her father hear her vow, and her bond wherewith she hath bound her soul, and her father shall hold his peace at her: then all her vows shall stand, and every bond wherewith she hath bound her soul shall stand.

5 But if her father disallow her in the day that he heareth; not any of her vows, or of her bonds wherewith she hath bound her soul, shall stand: and the LORD shall forgive her, because her father disallowed her.

6 And if she had at all an husband, when [2]she vowed, or uttered ought out of her lips, wherewith she bound her soul;

7 And her husband heard *it*, and held his peace at her in the day that he heard *it:* then her vows shall stand, and her bonds wherewith she bound her soul shall stand.

8 But if her husband [e]disallowed her on the day that he heard *it;* then he shall make her vow which she vowed, and that which she uttered with her lips, wherewith she bound her soul, of none effect: and the LORD shall forgive her.

9 But every vow of a widow, and of her that is [f]divorced, wherewith they have bound their souls, shall stand against her.

10 And if she vowed in her husband's house, or bound her soul by a bond with an oath;

11 And her husband heard *it*, and held his peace at her, *and* disallowed her not: then all her vows shall stand, and every bond wherewith she bound her soul shall stand.

12 But if her husband hath [3]utterly made them void on the day he heard

18 [k]ch. 15.12; ch. 28.7-14; Lev. 2

26 [l]Heb. 7.26; 1 Pet. 1.19; Rev. 5.6-14

35 [m]Lev. 23.36; Ps. 47.5-6; Isa. 11.10; Isa. 54; Isa. 60; Matt. 28; John 7.37; Heb. 1.3; Heb. 4.9; Rev. 7.9-17; Rev. 11.15

39 [3]Or, offer

[n]Lev. 23.2; 1 Chr. 23.31; Neh. 10.33; Isa. 1.14

[o]Lev. 7.11-16; Lev. 22.21-23; Lev. 23.38; ch. 6.21; Deut. 12.6; 1 Cor. 10.31

40 [p]Ex. 24.3; Deut. 5.27-31; John 1.17; Acts 7.37-38

CHAPTER 30

1 [a]ch. 1.4-16; Deut. 1.13-17

2 [b]Gen. 28.20; Lev. 27.2; Judg. 11.30-35; Ps. 56.12; Prov. 20.25; Eccl. 5.4

[c]Lev. 5.4; Matt. 14.9; Acts 23.14 [1]profane

[d]Job 22.27; Ps. 22.25; Ps. 50.14; Ps. 66.13-14; Nah. 1.15

6 [2]her vows were upon her

8 [e]Gen. 3.16; 1 Cor. 7.4; Eph. 5.22-24; Col. 3.18; 1 Pet. 3.1

9 [f]Lev. 21.7

12 [3]making void hath made them void

them; then whatsoever proceeded out
of her lips concerning her vows, or concerning the bond of her soul, shall not
stand: her husband hath made them
void; and the LORD shall forgive her.
13 Every vow, and every binding
oath to afflict the soul, her husband
may establish it, or her husband may
make it void.
14 But if her husband altogether
hold his peace at her from day to day;
then he establisheth all her vows, or
all her bonds, which *are* upon her: he
confirmeth them, because he held his
peace at her in the day that he heard
them.
15 But if he shall any ways make
them void after that he hath heard
them; then he shall [4]bear her iniquity.
16 These *are* the statutes, which the
LORD commanded Mō′ses, between a
man and his wife, between the father
and his daughter, *being yet* in her
youth in her father's house.
31 And the LORD spake unto Mō′-
ses, saying,
2 [a]Avenge the children of Ĭs′ra-el of
the Mĭd′ĭ-an-ītes: afterward shalt thou
[b]be gathered unto thy people.
3 And Mō′ses spake unto the people,
saying, Arm some of yourselves unto
the war, and let them go against the
Mĭd′ĭ-an-ītes, and [c]avenge the LORD of
Mĭd′ĭ-an.
4 [1]Of every tribe a thousand, throughout all the tribes of Ĭs′ra-el, shall ye
send to the war.
5 So there were delivered out of the
thousands of Ĭs′ra-el, a thousand of *every* tribe, twelve thousand armed for
war.
6 And Mō′ses sent them to the war,
a thousand of *every* tribe, them and
Phĭn′e-has the son of Ē-le-ā′zar the
priest, to the war, with the holy instruments, and the [d]trumpets to blow in
his hand.
7 And they warred against the Mĭd′-
ĭ-an-ītes, as the LORD commanded Mō′-
ses; and [e]they slew all the [f]males.
8 And they slew the kings of Mĭd′ĭ-
an, beside the rest of them that were
slain; *namely,* [g]Ē′vī, and Rē′kem, and
Zûr, and Hûr, and Rē′bȧ, five kings
of Mĭd′ĭ-an: [h]Bā′laam also the son of
Bē′or they slew with the sword.
9 And the children of Ĭs′ra-el took
all the women of Mĭd′ĭ-an captives,
and their little ones, and took the spoil
of all their cattle, and all their flocks,
and all their goods.
10 And they burnt all their cities
wherein they dwelt, and all their goodly
castles, with fire.
11 And [i]they took all the spoil, and
all the prey, *both* of men and of beasts.
12 And they brought the captives,
and the prey, and the spoil, unto Mō′-
ses, and Ē-le-ā′zar the priest, and unto
the congregation of the children of Ĭs′-
ra-el, unto the camp at the plains of
Mō′ab, which *are* by Jôr′dan *near* Jĕr′-
ĭ-chō.
13 ¶ And Mō′ses, and Ē-le-ā′zar the
priest, and all the princes of the congre-

15 [4]Or, take away

CHAPTER 31

2 [a]ch. 25.17; [b]Gen. 15.15;

3 [c]Deut. 32.35;

4 [1]A thousand of a tribe, a thousand of a tribe

6 [d]ch. 10.9

7 [e]Deut. 20.13; [f]Judg. 6.1-2-33

8 [g]Josh. 13.21 [h]ch. 22.10;

11 [i]Deut. 20.14

14 [2]host of war

15 [j]Deut. 2.34;

16 [k]ch. 25.2 [l]ch. 24.14;

17 [m]Judg. 21.11 [3]a male

19 [n]ch. 5.2; [o]ch. 9.6-10;

20 [4]instrument, or, vessel of skins

23 [p]ch. 8.7;

24 [q]Lev. 11.25;

26 [5]of the captivity

27 [r]Josh. 22.8;

28 [s]2 Sam. 8.11; [t]ch. 18.26

30 [6]Or, goats [u]ch. 3.7-8-25-31-36

gation, went forth to meet them without the camp.
14 And Mō′ses was wroth with the
officers of the host, *with* the captains
over thousands, and captains over hundreds, which came from the [2]battle.
15 And Mō′ses said unto them, Have
ye saved all [j]the women alive?
16 Behold, [k]these caused the children of Ĭs′ra-el, through the [l]counsel
of Bā′laam, to commit trespass against
the LORD in the matter of Pē′or, and
there was a plague among the congregation of the LORD.
17 Now therefore [m]kill every male
among the little ones, and kill every
woman that hath known man by lying
with [3]him.
18 But all the women children, that
have not known a man by lying with
him, keep alive for yourselves.
19 And [n]do ye abide without the
camp seven days: whosoever hath
killed any person, and whosoever
[o]hath touched any slain, purify *both*
yourselves and your captives on the
third day, and on the seventh day.
20 And purify all *your* raiment, and
all [4]that is made of skins, and all work
of goats' *hair,* and all things made of
wood.
21 ¶ And Ē-le-ā′zar the priest said
unto the men of war which went to the
battle, This *is* the ordinance of the law
which the LORD commanded Mō′ses;
22 Only the gold, and the silver, the
brass, the iron, the tin, and the lead,
23 Every thing that may abide the
fire, ye shall make *it* go through the
fire, and it shall be clean: nevertheless
it shall be purified with [p]the water of
separation: and all that abideth not the
fire ye shall make go through the water.
24 And [q]ye shall wash your clothes
on the seventh day, and ye shall be
clean, and afterward ye shall come into
the camp.
25 ¶ And the LORD spake unto Mō′-
ses, saying,
26 Take the sum of the prey [5]that
was taken, *both* of man and of beast,
thou, and Ē-le-ā′zar the priest, and the
chief fathers of the congregation:
27 And [r]divide the prey into two
parts; between them that took the war
upon them, who went out to battle, and
between all the congregation:
28 And levy a [s]tribute unto the LORD
of the men of war which went out to
battle: [t]one soul of five hundred, *both*
of the persons, and of the beeves, and
of the asses, and of the sheep:
29 Take *it* of their half, and give *it*
unto Ē-le-ā′zar the priest, *for* an heave
offering of the LORD.
30 And of the children of Ĭs′ra-el's
half, thou shalt take one portion of
fifty, of the persons, of the beeves, of
the asses, and of the [6]flocks, of all manner of beasts, and give them unto the
Lē′vītes, [u]which keep the charge of
the tabernacle of the LORD.

31 And Mō'ses and Ē-le-ā'zar the
priest did as the LORD commanded
Mō'ses.
32 And the booty, *being* the rest of
the prey which the men of war had
caught, was six hundred thousand and
seventy thousand and five thousand
sheep,
33 And threescore and twelve thousand beeves,
34 And threescore and one thousand
asses,
35 And thirty and two thousand persons in all, of women that had not
known man by lying with him.
36 And the half, *which was* the portion of them that went out to war, was
in number three hundred thousand and
seven and thirty thousand and five hundred sheep:
37 And the LORD'S [v]tribute of the
sheep was six hundred and threescore
and fifteen.
38 And the beeves *were* thirty and
six thousand; of which the LORD'S tribute *was* threescore and twelve.
39 And the asses *were* thirty thousand and five hundred; of which the
LORD'S tribute *was* threescore and one.
40 And the persons *were* sixteen
thousand; of which the LORD'S tribute
was thirty and two persons.
41 And Mō'ses gave the tribute,
which was the LORD'S heave offering, unto Ē-le-ā'zar the priest, [w]as the
LORD commanded Mō'ses.
42 And of the children of Ĭs'ra-el's
half, which Mō'ses divided from the
men that warred,
43 (Now the half *that pertained unto*
the congregation was three hundred
thousand and thirty thousand *and* seven
thousand and five hundred sheep,
44 And thirty and six thousand
beeves,
45 And thirty thousand asses and
five hundred,
46 And sixteen thousand persons;)
47 Even of the children of Ĭs'ra-el's
half, Mō'ses took one portion of fifty,
both of man and of beast, and gave
them unto the Lē'vītes, which kept the
charge of the tabernacle of the LORD;
as the LORD commanded Mō'ses.
48 ¶ And the officers which *were*
over thousands of the host, the captains of thousands, and captains of
hundreds, came near unto Mō'ses:
49 And they said unto Mō'ses, Thy
servants have taken the sum of the men
of war which *are* under our [7]charge,
and there lacketh not one [x]man of us.
50 We have therefore brought an oblation for the LORD, what every man
hath [8]gotten, of jewels of gold, chains,
and bracelets, rings, earrings, and tablets, [y]to make an atonement for our
souls before the LORD.
51 And Mō'ses and Ē-le-ā'zar the
priest took the gold of them, *even* all
wrought jewels.
52 And all the gold of the [9]offering
that they offered up to the LORD, of the
captains of thousands, and of the captains of hundreds, was sixteen thousand seven hundred and fifty shekels.
53 (*For* [z]the men of war had taken
spoil, every man for himself.)
54 And Mō'ses and Ē-le-ā'zar the
priest took the gold of the captains
of thousands and of hundreds, and
brought it into the tabernacle of the
congregation, [a]*for* a memorial for the
children of Ĭs'ra-el before the LORD.

32 Now the children of Reu'ben and
the children of Găd had a very
great multitude of cattle: and when
they saw the land of [a]Jā'zēr, and the
land of Gĭl'e-ăd, that, behold, the place
was a place for cattle;
2 The children of Găd and the children of Reu'ben came and spake unto
Mō'ses, and to Ē-le-ā'zar the priest,
and unto the princes of the congregation, saying,
3 Ăt'a-rŏth, and Dī'bŏn, and Jā'zēr,
and [b]Nĭm'rah, and Hĕsh'bŏn, and Ē-le-
ā'leh, and [c]Shē'bam, and Nē'bo, and
[d]Bē'ŏn,
4 *Even* the country [e]which the LORD
smote before the congregation of Ĭs'ra-
el, *is* a land for cattle, and thy servants
have cattle:
5 Wherefore, said they, if we have
found grace in thy sight, let this land
be given unto thy servants for a possession, *and* bring us not over Jôr'dan.
6 ¶ And Mō'ses said unto the children of Găd and to the children of Reu'-
ben, Shall your brethren go to war,
and shall ye sit here?
7 And wherefore [1]discourage ye the
heart of the children of Ĭs'ra-el from
going over into the land which the
LORD hath given them?
8 Thus did your fathers, [f]when I sent
them from Kā'desh–bär'ne-ȧ [g]to see
the land.
9 For [h]when they went up unto the
valley of Ĕsh'cŏl, and saw the land,
they discouraged the heart of the children of Ĭs'ra-el, that they should not
go into the land which the LORD had
given them.
10 And [i]the LORD'S anger was kindled the same time, and he sware, saying,
11 Surely none of the men that came
up out of Ē'gypt, [j]from twenty years
old and upward, shall see the land
which I sware unto Ā'brȧ-hăm, unto
Ī'saac, and unto Jā'cob; because [k]they
have not [2]wholly followed me:
12 Save Cā'leb the son of Je-phŭn'-
neh the Kĕn'ez-īte, and Jŏsh'u-ȧ the
son of Nŭn: [l]for they have wholly followed the LORD.
13 And the LORD'S anger was kindled against Ĭs'ra-el, and he made them
[m]wander in the wilderness forty years,
until [n]all the generation, that had done
evil in the sight of the LORD, was consumed.
14 And, behold, ye are risen up in
your fathers' stead, an increase of sinful men, to augment yet the [o]fierce anger of the LORD toward Ĭs'ra-el.
15 For if ye [p]turn away from after
him, he will yet again leave them in the

37 [v]Lev. 25.55; Deut. 10.14; Job 41.11; Ps. 24.1; Ps. 50.12; Prov. 3.9; Matt. 22.21; Mark 12.17; Luke 20.25; 1 Cor. 10.26-28
41 [w]ch. 5.9-10; ch. 18.8-19
49 [7]hand [x]Ex. 23.7; Lev. 26.7-9; 1 Sam. 30.19; Ps. 72.14; Ps. 116.15
50 [8]found [y]Ex. 30.12-16; Lev. 17.11; Matt. 26.28; Rom. 3.25
52 [9]heave offering
53 [z]Deut. 20.14
54 [a]Ex. 30.16; ch. 16.40; Zech. 6.14; Luke 22.19; Acts 10.4

CHAPTER 32
1 [a]ch. 21.32; Josh. 13.25; 2 Sam. 24.5; Isa. 16.8-9
3 [b]verse 36, Beth-nimrah [c]verse 38, Shibmah [d]verse 38, Baal-meon
4 [e]ch. 21.24-34
7 [1]break
8 [f]ch. 13.3 [g]Deut. 1.22
9 [h]ch. 13.23; Deut. 1.24
10 [i]ch. 14.11; Deut. 1.34; Ps. 95.11; Heb. 3.8-19
11 [j]Deut. 1.35 [k]ch. 14.24 [2]fulfilled after me
12 [l]Deut. 1.36; Josh. 14.8-9; Job 4.7; Ps. 37.29; Prov. 11.31
13 [m]ch. 14.33 [n]ch. 26.64
14 [o]Deut. 1.34
15 [p]Deut. 30.17; 2 Chr. 7.19; 2 Chr. 15.2

wilderness; and ye shall destroy all
this people.
16 ¶ And they came near unto him,
and said, We will build sheepfolds here
for our cattle, and cities for our little
ones:
17 But [q]we ourselves will go ready
armed before the children of Ĭs'ra-el,
until we have brought them unto their
place: and our little ones shall dwell in
the fenced cities because of the inhabitants of the land.
18 [r]We will not return unto our
houses, until the children of Ĭs'ra-el
have inherited every man his inheritance.
19 For we will not inherit with them
on yonder side Jôr'dan, or forward;
[s]because our inheritance is fallen to us
on this side Jôr'dan eastward.
20 ¶ And [t]Mō'ses said unto them, If
ye will do this thing, if ye will go armed
before the LORD to war,
21 And will go all of you armed over
Jôr'dan before the LORD, until he hath
driven out his enemies from before
him,
22 And [u]the land be subdued before
the LORD: then afterward [v]ye shall return, and be guiltless before the LORD,
and before Ĭs'ra-el; and [w]this land
shall be your possession before the
LORD.
23 But if ye will not do so, behold, ye
have sinned against the LORD: and be
sure [x]your sin will find you out.
24 [y]Build you cities for your little
ones, and folds for your sheep; and do
that which hath proceeded out of your
mouth.
25 And the children of Găd and the
children of Reu'ben spake unto Mō'-
ses, saying, Thy servants will do as my
lord commandeth.
26 [z]Our little ones, our wives, our
flocks, and all our cattle, shall be there
in the cities of Gĭl'e-ăd:
27 [a]But thy servants will pass over,
every man armed for war, before the
LORD to battle, as my lord saith.
28 So concerning them Mō'ses commanded Ē-le-ā'zar the priest, and
Jŏsh'u-ȧ the son of Nŭn, and the chief
fathers of the tribes of the children of
Ĭs'ra-el:
29 And Mō'ses said unto them, If the
children of Găd and the children of
Reu'ben will pass with you over Jôr'-
dan, every man armed to battle, before
the LORD, and the land shall be subdued before you; then ye shall give
them the land of Gĭl'e-ăd for a possession:
30 But if they will not pass over with
you armed, they shall have possessions among you in the land of Cā'-
năan.
31 And the children of Găd and the
children of Reu'ben answered, saying,
As the LORD hath said unto thy servants, so will we do.
32 We will pass over armed before
the LORD into the land of Cā'năan, that
the possession of our inheritance on
this side Jôr'dan *may be* ours.

17 [q]Josh. 4.12-13
18 [r]Josh. 22.4
19 [s]Josh. 12.1
20 [t]Deut. 3.18; Josh. 1.14
22 [u]Deut. 3.20; Josh. 11.23
[v]Josh. 22.4
[w]Deut. 3.12; Josh. 1.15; Josh. 13.8-32
23 [x]Gen. 4.7; Gen. 44.16; Ps. 140.11; Prov. 13.21; Isa. 3.11; Isa. 59.12; Rom. 2.9; 1 Cor. 4.5
24 [y]verses 16-34
26 [z]Josh. 1.14
27 [a]Josh. 4.12
33 [b]Deut. 3.12; Josh. 12.6
[c]ch. 21.24; Deut. 2.30-35; Deut. 3.1-8; Ps. 136.19-21
34 [d]ch. 33.45
[e]Deut. 2.36
35 [f]verses 1-3, Jazer
36 [g]verse 3, Nimrah
38 [h]Isa. 46.1
[i]ch. 22.41
[j]Ex. 23.13
[3]they called by names the names of the cities
39 [k]Gen. 50.23; Josh. 17.1
40 [l]Deut. 3.12; Josh. 17.1
41 [m]Deut. 3.14; 1 Chr. 2.21
[n]Judg. 10.4; 1 Ki. 4.13
42 [o]2 Sam. 18.18; Ps. 49.11

CHAPTER 33
3 [a]Gen. 47.11; Ex. 1.11
[b]Ex. 12.2; Mic. 2.13
[c]Ex. 14.8
4 [d]Ex. 12.12; Rev. 12.8
5 [e]Ex. 12.37
6 [f]Gen. 33.17; Ps. 60.6
7 [g]Ex. 14.2-9
8 [h]Ex. 14.22

33 And [b]Mō'ses gave unto them,
even to the children of Găd, and to the
children of Reu'ben, and unto half the
tribe of Ma-năs'seh the son of Jō'seph,
[c]the kingdom of Sī'hŏn king of the
Ăm'ôr-ītes, and the kingdom of Ŏg
king of Bā'shăn, the land, with the cities thereof in the coasts, *even* the cities
of the country round about.
34 ¶ And the children of Găd built
[d]Dī'bŏn, and Ăt'a-rŏth, and [e]Ăr'ō-ēr,
35 And Ăt'rŏth, Shō'phan, and [f]Ja-
ā'zēr, and Jŏg'-be-hah,
36 And [g]Bĕth-nĭm'rah, and Bĕth-
hā'ran, fenced cities: and folds for
sheep.
37 And the children of Reu'ben built
Hĕsh'bŏn, and Ē-le-ā'leh, and Kĭr-jath-
ā'im,
38 And [h]Nē'bo, and [i]Bā'al-mē'on,
([j]their names being changed,) and
Shĭb'mah: and [3]gave other names unto
the cities which they builded.
39 And the children of [k]Mā'chĭr the
son of Ma-năs'seh went to Gĭl'e-ăd,
and took it, and dispossessed the Ăm'-
ôr-īte which *was* in it.
40 And Mō'ses [l]gave Gĭl'e-ăd unto
Mā'chĭr the son of Ma-năs'seh; and he
dwelt therein.
41 And [m]Jā'īr the son of Ma-năs'seh
went and took the small towns thereof,
and called them [n]Hā'voth-jā'īr.
42 And Nō'bah went and took Kē'-
nath, and the villages thereof, and
called it Nō'bah, after [o]his own name.
33 These *are* the journeys of the children of Ĭs'ra-el, which went forth
out of the land of Ē'gypt with their armies under the hand of Mō'ses and
Aâr'on.
2 And Mō'ses wrote their goings out
according to their journeys by the commandment of the LORD: and these *are*
their journeys according to their goings out.
3 And they [a]departed from Ra-mē'-
sēs in the [b]first month, on the fifteenth
day of the first month; on the morrow
after the passover the children of Ĭs'ra-
el went out [c]with an high hand in the
sight of all the Egyptians.
4 For the E-gўp'tians buried all *their*
firstborn, which the LORD had smitten
among them: [d]upon their gods also the
LORD executed judgments.
5 And [e]the children of Ĭs'ra-el removed from Ra-mē'sēs, and pitched in
Sŭc'coth.
6 And they departed from [f]Sŭc'coth,
and pitched in Ē'tham, which *is* in the
edge of the wilderness.
7 And [g]they removed from Ē'tham,
and turned again unto Pī-ha-hī'roth,
which *is* before Bā'al-zē'phon: and
they pitched before Mĭg'dol.
8 And they departed from before Pī-
ha-hī'roth, and [h]passed through the
midst of the sea into the wilderness,
and went three days' journey in the wilderness of Ē'tham, and pitched in Mā'-
rah.
9 And they removed from Mā'rah,
and came unto Ē'lĭm: and in Ē'lĭm
were twelve fountains of water, and

threescore and ten palm trees; and
they pitched there.
10 And they removed from E'lĭm,
and encamped by the Red sea.
11 And they removed from the Red
sea, and encamped in the [i]wilderness
of Sĭn.
12 And they took their journey out of
the wilderness of Sĭn, and encamped in
Dŏph'kah.
13 And they departed from Dŏph'-
kah, and encamped in Ā'lush.
14 And they removed from Ā'lush,
and encamped at [j]Rĕph'ĭ-dim, where
was no water for the people to drink.
15 And they departed from Rĕph'ĭ-
dim, and pitched in the [k]wilderness of
Sī'nāi.
16 And they removed from the desert of Sī'nāi, and pitched [l]at [1]Kĭb'-
roth–hat-tā'a-vah.
17 And they departed from Kĭb'-
roth–hat-tā'a-vah, and encamped at
Ha-zē'roth.
18 And they departed from Ha-zē'-
roth, and pitched in [m]Rĭth'mah.
19 And they departed from Rĭth'-
mah, and pitched at Rĭm'mon–pā'rez.
20 And they departed from Rĭm'-
mon–pā'rez, and pitched in [n]Lĭb'nah.
21 And they removed from Lĭb'nah,
and pitched at Rĭs'sah.
22 And they journeyed from Rĭs'-
sah, and pitched in Ke-hĕl'a-thah.
23 And they went from Ke-hĕl'a-
thah, and pitched in mount Shā'pher.
24 And they removed from mount
Shā'pher, and encamped in Hăr'a-dah.
25 And they removed from Hăr'a-
dah, and pitched in Măk-hē'loth.
26 And they removed from Măk-hē'-
loth, and encamped at Tā'hăth.
27 And they departed from Tā'hăth,
and pitched at Tā'rah.
28 And they removed from Tā'rah,
and pitched in Mĭth'cah.
29 And they went from Mĭth'cah,
and pitched in Hăsh-mō'nah.
30 And they departed from Hăsh-
mō'nah, and [o]encamped at Mo-sē'-
roth.
31 And they departed from Mo-sē'-
roth, and pitched in Bĕn-e–jā'a-kăn.
32 And they removed from [p]Bĕn-e–
jā'a-kăn, and encamped at [q]Hôr–ha-
gĭd'gad.
33 And they went from Hôr–ha-gĭd'-
gad, and pitched in Jŏt'ba-thah.
34 And they removed from Jŏt'ba-
thah, and encamped at E-brō'nah.
35 And they departed from E-brō'-
nah, [r]and encamped at Ē'zĭ-on–gā'-
bĕr.
36 And they removed from Ē'zĭ-on–
gā'bĕr, and pitched in the [s]wilderness
of Zĭn, which *is* Kā'desh.
37 And they removed from [t]Kā'-
desh, and pitched in mount Hôr, in the
edge of the land of Ē'dom.
38 And [u]Aâr'on the priest went up
into mount Hôr at the commandment
of the LORD, and died there, in the fortieth year after the children of Ĭs'ra-el
were come out of the land of Ē'gypt, in
the first *day* of the fifth month.

39 And Aâr'on *was* an hundred and
twenty and three years old when he
died in mount Hôr.
40 And [v]king Ā'răd the Cā'năan-īte,
which dwelt in the south in the land of
Cā'năan, heard of the coming of the
children of Ĭs'ra-el.
41 And they departed from mount
Hôr, and pitched in Zal-mō'nah.
42 And they departed from Zal-mō'-
nah, and pitched in Pū'non.
43 And they departed from Pū'non,
and pitched in Ō'both.
44 And they departed from Ō'both,
and pitched in [2]Ĭj'e–ăb'a-rĭm, in the
border of Mō'ab.
45 And they departed from Ī'ĭm, and
pitched in [w]Dī'bon–gad.
46 And they removed from Dī'bon–
găd, and encamped in [x]Ăl'mŏn–dĭb-
la-thā'ĭm.
47 And they removed from Ăl'mŏn–
dĭb-la-thā'ĭm, [y]and pitched in the mountains of Ăb'ă-rim, before Nē'bo.
48 And they departed from the mountains of Ăb'ă-rim, and [z]pitched in the
plains of Mō'ab by Jôr'dan *near* Jĕr'ĭ-
chō.
49 And they pitched by Jôr'dan, from
Bĕth–jĕs'–ĭ-mŏth *even* unto [3]Ā'bĕl–
shĭt'tim in the plains of Mō'ab.
50 ¶ And the LORD spake unto Mō'-
ses in the plains of Mō'ab by Jôr'dan
near Jĕr'ĭ-chō, saying,
51 Speak unto the children of Ĭs'ra-
el, and say unto them, [a]When ye are
passed over Jôr'dan into the land of
Cā'năan;
52 [b]Then ye shall drive out all the
inhabitants of the land from before
you, and destroy all their pictures, and
destroy all their molten images, and
quite pluck down all their high places:
53 And ye shall dispossess *the inhabitants of* the land, and dwell therein:
[c]for I have given you the land to possess it.
54 And [d]ye shall divide the land by
lot for an inheritance among your families: *and* to the more ye shall [4]give the
more inheritance, and to the fewer ye
shall [5]give the less inheritance: every
man's *inheritance* shall be in the place
where his lot falleth; according to the
tribes of your fathers ye shall inherit.
55 But if ye will not drive out the
inhabitants of the land from before
you; then it shall come to pass, that
those which ye let remain of them *shall
be* [e]pricks in your eyes, and thorns in
your sides, and shall vex you in the
land wherein ye dwell.
56 Moreover it shall come to pass,
that I shall do unto you, as I thought to
do unto them.

34 And the LORD spake unto Mō'-
ses, saying,
2 Command the children of Ĭs'ra-el,
and say unto them, When ye come into
[a]the land of Cā'năan; (this *is* the land
that shall fall unto you for an inheritance, *even* the land of Cā'năan with
the coasts thereof:)
3 Then [b]your south quarter shall be
from the wilderness of Zĭn along by

11 [i]Ex. 16.1
14 [j]Ex. 17.1
15 [k]Ex. 16.1
16 [l]ch. 11.34 [1]That is, The graves of lust
18 [m]ch. 12.16; Deut. 1.1
20 [n]Deut. 1.1, Laban
30 [o]Deut. 10.6
32 [p]Gen. 36.27; Deut. 10.6; 1 Chr. 1.42 [q]Deut. 10.7, Gudgodah
35 [r]Deut. 2.8; 1 Ki. 9.26; 1 Ki. 22.48
36 [s]ch. 13.21; ch. 20.1; ch. 27.14; ch. 34.3-4; Deut. 32.51; Josh. 15.1
37 [t]ch. 20.22-23; ch. 21.4
38 [u]ch. 20.25-28; Deut. 10.6; Deut. 32.50
40 [v]ch. 21.1
44 [2]Or, Heaps of Abarim
45 [w]ch. 32.34
46 [x]Jer. 48.22
47 [y]ch. 21.20
48 [z]ch. 22.1
49 [3]Mournful Shittim, or, The plains of Shittim
51 [a]Deut. 7.1; Deut. 9.1
52 [b]Ex. 23.24; Ex. 34.12-17; Deut. 7.2-5-25-26; Deut. 12.2-3-30-31; Deut. 20.16-18; Josh. 11.12; Judg. 2.2
53 [c]Ps. 24.1; Deut. 10.14; Job 41.11; Dan. 4.35
54 [d]ch. 26.53 [4]multiply his inheritance [5]diminish his inheritance
55 [e]Josh. 23.13; Ps. 106.34

CHAPTER 34
2 [a]Gen. 17.8; Deut. 1.7; Ps. 78.55
3 [b]Josh. 15.1

the coast of Ē'dom, and your south border shall be the outmost coast of [c]the
salt sea eastward:
4 And your border shall turn from
the south [d]to the ascent of A-krăb'bim,
and pass on to Zĭn: and the going forth
thereof shall be from the south to Kā'-
desh–bär'ne-ȧ, and shall go on to Hā'-
zar–ăd'dar, and pass on to Ăz'mŏn:
5 And the border shall fetch a compass from Ăz'mŏn [e]unto the river of
Ē'gypt, and the goings out of it shall be
at the sea.
6 And *as for* the western border, ye
shall even have [1]the great sea for a border: this shall be your west border.
7 And this shall be your north border: from the great sea ye shall point
out for you mount [2]Hôr:
8 From mount Hôr ye shall point out
your border [f]unto the entrance of Hā'-
math; and the goings forth of the border shall be to [g]Zedad:
9 ¶ And the border shall go on to
Zĭph'rŏn, and the goings out of it shall
be at [h]Hā'zar–ē'nan: this shall be your
north border.
10 And ye shall point out your east
border from Hā'zar–ē'nan to Shē'-
pham:
11 And the coast shall go down from
Shē'pham [i]to Rĭb'lah, on the east side
of Ā'in; and the border shall descend,
and shall reach unto the [3]side of the
sea [j]of Chĭn'ne-rĕth eastward:
12 And the border shall go down to
Jôr'dan, and the goings out of it shall
be at the salt sea: this shall be your land
with the coasts thereof round about.
13 And Mō'ses commanded the children of Ĭs'ra-el, saying, [k]This *is* the
land which ye shall inherit by lot, which
the LORD commanded to give unto the
nine tribes, and to the half tribe:
14 [l]For the tribe of the children of
Reu'ben according to the house of their
fathers, and the tribe of the children of
Găd according to the house of their fathers, have received *their inheritance;*
and half the tribe of Ma-năs'seh have
received their inheritance:
15 The two tribes and the half tribe
have received their inheritance on this
side Jôr'dan *near* Jĕr'ĭ-chō eastward,
toward the sunrising.
16 And the LORD spake unto Mō'-
ses, saying,
17 These *are* the names of the men
which shall divide the land unto you:
[m]Ē-le-ā'zar the priest, and Jŏsh'u-ȧ the
son of Nŭn.
18 And ye shall take one prince of
every tribe, to divide the land by inheritance.
19 And the names of the men *are*
these: Of the tribe of [n]Jū'dah, Cā'leb
[o]the son of Je-phŭn'neh.
20 And of the tribe of the children of
[p]Sĭm'e-on, She-mū'el the son of Am-
mī'hŭd.
21 Of the tribe of [q]Bĕn'ja-min, E-
lī'dad the son of Chĭs'lon.
22 And the prince of the tribe of
the children of Dăn, Bŭk'kī the son of
Jŏg'lī.

[c]Gen. 14.3
4 [d]ch. 32.8
5 [e]Gen. 15.18; 1 Ki. 8.65; Isa. 27.12
6 [1]The Mediterranean
7 [2]Not the Mount Hor on the border of Edom, where Aaron died, but Mount Hor north of Lebanon
8 [f]ch. 13.21; Josh. 13.5-6; 2 Sam. 8.9; Jer. 39.5
[g]Ezek. 47.15
9 [h]Ezek. 47.17
11 [i]2 Ki. 23.33
[3]shoulder
[j]Deut. 3.17; Josh. 11.2
13 [k]Josh. 14.1-2
14 [l]ch. 32.33
17 [m]Ex. 6.23-25
19 [n]Gen. 29.35; Ps. 60.7
[o]ch. 13.6-30; Deut. 1.36
20 [p]Gen 29.33; Ezek. 48.24
21 [q]Gen. 35.18; Ps. 68.27
23 [r]Gen. 48.8-22; Ps. 80.1
29 [s]Deut. 32.8; Acts 17.26
CHAPTER 35
2 [a]Lev. 25.32-33; Ezek. 45.1
4 [1]Six hundred and eight yards
6 [b]Deut. 4.41; Isa. 4.6
[2]above them ye shall give
7 [c]1 Chr. 6.54-81
8 [d]Josh. 21.3
[e]Ex. 16.18; ch. 26.54
[3]they inherit
10 [f]Deut. 19.2
11 [g]Ex. 21.13
[4]by error

23 The prince of the [r]children of Jō'-
seph, for the tribe of the children of Ma-
năs'seh, Hăn'nĭ-el the son of Ē'phŏd.
24 And the prince of the tribe of the
children of Ē'phră-ĭm, Ke-mū'el the
son of Shĭph'tan.
25 And the prince of the tribe of the
children of Zĕb'u-lun, E-lĭz'a-phan the
son of Pär'nach.
26 And the prince of the tribe of the
children of Ĭs'sa-char, Păl'tĭ-el the son
of Ăz'zan.
27 And the prince of the tribe of the
children of Ăsh'ẽr, A-hī'hud the son of
Shĕl'o-mī.
28 And the prince of the tribe of the
children of Năph'ta-lī, Pĕd'a-hĕl the
son of Ăm-mī'hŭd.
29 These *are they* whom the LORD
commanded to divide the [s]inheritance
unto the children of Ĭs'ra-el in the land
of Cā'năan.

35 And the LORD spake unto Mō'ses
in the plains of Mō'ab by Jôr'dan
near Jĕr'ĭ-chō, saying,
2 [a]Command the children of Ĭs'ra-
el, that they give unto the Lē'vītes of
the inheritance of their possession cities to dwell in; and ye shall give *also*
unto the Lē'vītes suburbs for the cities
round about them.
3 And the cities shall they have to
dwell in; and the suburbs of them shall
be for their cattle, and for their goods,
and for all their beasts.
4 And the suburbs of the cities, which
ye shall give unto the Lē'vītes, *shall*
reach from the wall of the city and outward [1]a thousand cubits round about.
5 And ye shall measure from without the city on the east side two thousand cubits, and on the south side two
thousand cubits, and on the west side
two thousand cubits, and on the north
side two thousand cubits; and the city
shall be in the midst: this shall be to
them the suburbs of the cities.
6 And among the cities which ye
shall give unto the Lē'vītes *there shall*
be [b]six cities for refuge, which ye shall
appoint for the manslayer, that he may
flee thither: and [2]to them ye shall add
forty and two cities.
7 *So* all the cities which ye shall give
to the Lē'vītes *shall be* [c]forty and eight
cities: them *shall ye give* with their suburbs.
8 And the cities which ye shall give
shall be [d]of the possession of the children of Ĭs'ra-el: [e]from *them that have*
many ye shall give many; but from
them that have few ye shall give few:
every one shall give of his cities unto
the Lē'vītes according to his inheritance which [3]he inheriteth.
9 ¶ And the LORD spake unto Mō'-
ses, saying,
10 Speak unto the children of Ĭs'ra-
el, and say unto them, [f]When ye be
come over Jôr'dan into the land of
Cā'năan;
11 Then [g]ye shall appoint you cities
to be cities of refuge for you; that the
slayer may flee thither, which killeth
any person [4]at unawares.

12 And [h]they shall be unto you cities for refuge from the avenger; that
the manslayer die not, until he stand
before the congregation in judgment.
13 And of these cities which ye shall
give six cities shall ye have for refuge.
14 [i]Ye shall give three cities on this
side Jôr'dan, and three cities shall ye
give in the land of Cā'năan, *which* shall
be cities of refuge.
15 These six cities shall be a refuge,
both for the children of Ĭs'ra-el, and
[j]for the stranger, and for the sojourner
among them: that every one that killeth
any person unawares may flee thither.
16 And [k]if he smite him with an instrument of iron, so that he die, he *is* a
murderer: the murderer shall surely be
put to death.
17 And if he smite him [5]with throw-
ing a stone, wherewith he may die, and
he die, he *is* a murderer: the murderer
shall surely be put to death.
18 Or *if* he smite him with an hand
weapon of wood, wherewith he may
die, and he die, he *is* a murderer: the
murderer shall surely be put to death.
19 [6]The revenger of blood himself
shall slay the murderer: when he meeteth him, he shall slay him.
20 But [l]if he thrust him of hatred, or
hurl at him [m]by laying of wait, that he
die;
21 Or in enmity smite him with his
hand, that he die: he that smote *him*
shall surely be put to death; *for* he *is* a
murderer: the revenger of blood shall
slay the murderer, when he meeteth
him.
22 But if he thrust him suddenly
without enmity, or have cast upon him
any thing without laying of wait,
23 Or with any stone, wherewith a
man may die, seeing *him* not, and cast
it upon him, that he die, and *was* not
his enemy, neither sought his harm:
24 Then [n]the congregation shall
judge between the slayer and the
revenger of blood according to these
judgments:
25 And the congregation shall deliver the slayer out of the hand of the
revenger of blood, and the congregation shall restore him to the city of his
refuge, whither he was fled: and [o]he
shall abide in it unto the death of the
high priest, which [p]was anointed with
the holy oil.
26 But if the slayer shall at any time
come without the border of the city of
his refuge, whither he was fled;
27 And the revenger of blood find
him without the borders of the city of
his refuge, and the revenger of blood
kill the slayer; [7]he shall not be guilty of
blood:
28 Because he should have remained
in the city of his refuge until the death
of the high priest: but after the death of
the high priest the slayer shall return
into the land of his possession.
29 So these *things* shall be for [q]a
statute of judgment unto you throughout your generations in all your dwellings.
30 Whoso killeth any person, the
murderer shall be put to death by the
[r]mouth of witnesses: but one witness
shall not testify against any person *to
cause him* to die.
31 Moreover ye shall take no sat-
isfaction for the life of a murderer,
which *is* [8]guilty of death: but he shall
be surely put to death.
32 And ye shall take [s]no satisfac-
tion for him that is fled to the city of his
refuge, that he should come again to
dwell in the land, until the death of the
priest.
33 So ye shall not pollute the land
wherein ye *are*: for blood [t]it defileth the land: and [9]the land cannot
be cleansed of the blood that is shed
therein, but [u]by the blood of him that
shed it.
34 [v]Defile not therefore the land
which ye shall inhabit, wherein I dwell:
for [w]I the LORD dwell among the children of Ĭs'ra-el.

36

36 And the chief fathers of the families of the [a]children of Gĭl'e-ăd,
the son of Mā'chĭr, the son of Ma-
năs'seh, of the families of the sons of
Jō'seph, came near, and spake before
Mō'ses, and before the princes, the
chief fathers of the children of Ĭs'ra-el:
2 And they said, [b]The LORD commanded my lord to give the land for an
inheritance by lot to the children of
Ĭs'ra-el: and [c]my lord was commanded
by the LORD to give the inheritance
of Ze-lō'phe-hăd our brother unto his
daughters.
3 And if they be married to any of
the sons of the *other* tribes of the children of Ĭs'ra-el, then shall their inheritance be taken from the inheritance of
our fathers, and shall be put to the inheritance of the tribe [1]whereunto they
are received: so shall it be taken from
the lot of our inheritance.
4 And when [d]the jubile of the children of Ĭs'ra-el shall be, then shall their
inheritance be put unto the inheritance
of the tribe whereunto they are received: so shall their inheritance be
taken away from the inheritance of the
tribe of our fathers.
5 And Mō'ses commanded the children of Ĭs'ra-el according to the word
of the LORD, saying, The tribe of the
sons of Jō'seph [e]hath said well.
6 This *is* the thing which the LORD
doth command concerning the daughters of Ze-lō'phe-hăd, saying, Let them
[2]marry to whom they think best; only
to the family of the tribe of their father
shall they marry.
7 So shall not the [f]inheritance of the
children of Ĭs'ra-el remove from tribe
to tribe: for every one of the children of
Ĭs'ra-el shall [3]keep himself to the inheritance of the tribe of his fathers.
8 And [g]every daughter, that possesseth an inheritance in any tribe of
the children of Ĭs'ra-el, shall be wife
unto one of the family of the tribe of
her father, that the children of Ĭs'ra-el
may enjoy every man the inheritance
of his fathers.

12 [h]Deut. 19.6
14 [i]Deut. 4.41; 2 Cor. 8.13-14
15 [j]ch. 15.16
16 [k]Ex. 21.12-14; Deut. 19.11-12
17 [5]with a stone of the hand
19 [6]He was the nearest kinsman of the person slain
20 [l]Gen. 4.8; Luke 4.29
[m]Ex. 21.14; Ps. 10.7-10
24 [n]Josh. 20.6
25 [o]Eph. 1.7
[p]Ex. 29.7; Lev. 21.10
27 [7]no blood shall be to him
29 [q]ch. 27.11
30 [r]Deut. 17.6; Rev. 11.3
31 [8]faulty to die
32 [s]Acts 4.12; Gal. 2.21
33 [t]Gen. 4.9-12; Mic. 4.11
[9]there can be no expiation for the land
[u]Gen. 9.6
34 [v]Lev. 18.25; Deut. 21.23
[w]ch. 5.3;
CHAPTER 36
1 [a]ch. 26.29
2 [b]ch. 26.55;
[c]ch. 27.1-7
3 [1]unto whom they shall be
4 [d]Lev. 25.10
5 [e]ch. 27.7
6 [2]be wives
7 [f]1 Ki. 21.3
[3]cleave to the, etc
8 [g]1 Chr. 23.22

9 Neither shall the inheritance remove from *one* tribe to another tribe;
but every one of the tribes of the children of Ĭs′ra-el shall keep himself to
his own inheritance.
10 Even as the LORD commanded
Mō′ses, so did the daughters of Ze-
lō′phe-hăd:
11 [h]For Māh′lah, Tĭr′zah, and Hŏg′-
lah, and Mĭl′cah, and Nō′ah, the daughters of Ze-lō′phe-hăd, were married
unto their father's brothers' sons:
12 *And* they were married [4]into the
families of the sons of Ma-năs′seh the
son of Jō′seph, and their inheritance
remained in the tribe of the family of
their father.
13 These *are* the commandments and
the judgments, [i]which the LORD commanded by the hand of Mō′ses unto
the children of Ĭs′ra-el in [j]the plains of
Mō′ab by Jôr′dan *near* Jĕr′ĭ-chō.

11 [h]ch. 27.1
12 [4]to some that were of the families
13 [i]Deut. 33.4; Neh. 9.12-13-14; John 1.17
[j]ch. 22.1; ch. 26.3; ch. 31.12; ch. 33.50

THE FIFTH BOOK OF MOSES COMMONLY CALLED

DEUTERONOMY

Life's Questions

Since God loves me so much, what should I do?
Can my generation be different from our parents?
What exactly is a covenant love relationship with God?

God's Answers

Deuteronomy describes the love relationship between God and His people. It reminds a covenant people of what God has done and of what they must do.

Moses' three sermons give Deuteronomy three parts: the call of the past (1:1—4:43), the expectations for the present (4:44—28:68), the commitments to the future (29:1—34:12). From Deuteronomy God's people know how faithfully God has led in the past, how seriously He takes the covenant commands of the present, and how graciously He invites them into a covenant relationship of love for the future.

Deuteronomy describes God's covenant faithfulness and the choice Israel has to be a people of curse or of blessing.

God's saving acts of the past call His people to faithful obedience (1:6—3:29).
God's Word is the identifying mark for God's people (4:1–43).
The Ten Commandments form the center of God's love relationship with His people (4:44—6:25).
Total commitment to God's commands and God's people characterize the love relationship of God's people (7:1—11:32).
Love relationship involves proper worship (12:1–28).
Love relationship makes people different from their neighbors (12:29—16:17).
God requires leaders who are just and holy (16:18—18:22).
God's Word makes life holy and pure (19:1—23:19).
God's Word seeks justice for all (23:20—25:19).
God's people show commitment offerings and tithes (26:1–19).
God's love relationship offers a choice: blessing or curse (27:1—28:68).
God seeks to renew covenant love through repentance (29:1—30:20).
God calls leaders to serve His Word and His people (31:1—34:12).

Ready to attack the Promised Land, Israel needed review. Commitment to love God and follow His game plan for life in the new country came before war plans. Repentance, renewal of the love relationship, and recommitment to God's mission are God priorities for His people.

1 These *be* the words which Mō′ses
spake unto all Ĭs′ra-el [a]on this side
Jôr′dan in the wilderness, in the plain
over against [1]the Red *sea*, between Pā′-
ran, and Tō′phel, and Lā′ban, and Ha-
zē′roth, and Dĭz′a-hăb.
2 (*There are* eleven days' *journey*
from Hō′reb by the way of mount Sē′ïr
[b]unto Kā′desh–bär′ne-ȧ.)
3 And it came to pass [c]in the fortieth
year, in the eleventh month, on the first
day of the month, *that* Mō′ses spake
unto the children of Ĭs′ra-el, according
unto all that the LORD had given him in
commandment unto them;
4 [d]After he had slain Sī′hŏn the king
of the Ăm′ôr-ītes, which dwelt in Hĕsh′-
bŏn, and Ŏg the king of Bā′shăn, which
dwelt at Ăs′ta-rŏth [e]in Ĕd′re-ī:
5 On this side Jôr′dan, in the land of
Mō′ab, began Mō′ses to declare this
law, saying,
6 The LORD our God spake unto us
[f]in Hō′reb, saying, Ye have dwelt long
[g]enough in this mount:
7 Turn you, and take your journey,
and go to the mount of the Ăm′ôr-ītes,
and unto [2]all *the places* nigh thereunto,
in the plain, in the hills, and in the vale,
and in the south, and by the sea side, to
the land of the Cā′năan-ītes, and unto
Lĕb′a-non, unto the great river, the
river Eū-phrā′tēs.
8 Behold, I have [3]set the land before you: go in and possess the land
which the LORD sware unto your fathers, [h]Ā′brā-hăm, Ī′saac, and Jā′cob,
to give unto them and to their seed after them.

CHAPTER 1
1 [a]Num. 32.6-20-29; Josh. 9.1
[1]Or, Zuph
2 [b]Num. 13.26; ch. 9.23
3 [c]Num. 33.38
4 [d]Num. 21.24; Ps. 135.11
[e]Josh. 13.12
6 [f]Ex. 3.1
[g]Ex. 19.1;
7 [2]all his neighbours
8 [3]given
[h]Gen. 12.7;

9 ¶ And [i]I spake unto you at that
time, saying, I am not able to bear you
myself alone:
10 The LORD your God hath multiplied you, and, behold, [j]ye *are* this day
as the stars of heaven for multitude.
11 (The LORD God of your fathers
make you a thousand times so many
more as ye *are*, and bless you, [k]as he
hath promised you!)
12 [l]How can I myself alone bear
your cumbrance, and your burden, and
your strife?
13 [4]Take you wise men, and understanding, and known among your
tribes, and I will make them rulers
over you.
14 And ye answered me, and said,
The thing which thou hast spoken *is*
good *for us* to do.
15 So I took the chief of your tribes,
wise men, and known, and [5]made them
heads over you, captains over thousands, and captains over hundreds, and
captains over fifties, and captains over
tens, and officers among your tribes.
16 And I charged your judges at that
time, saying, Hear *the causes* between
your brethren, and [m]judge righteously
between *every* man and his [n]brother,
and the stranger *that is* with him.
17 [o]Ye shall not [6]respect persons in
judgment; *but* ye shall hear the small
as well as the great; ye shall [p]not be
afraid of the face of man; for the [q]judg-
ment *is* God's: and the cause that is too
hard for you, [r]bring *it* unto me, and I
will hear it.
18 And I commanded you at that
time all the things which ye should do.
19 ¶ And when we departed from
Hō'reb, [s]we went through all that great
and terrible wilderness, which ye saw
by the way of the mountain of the
Ăm'ôr-ītes, as the LORD our God commanded us; and [t]we came to Kā'desh–
bär'ne-ȧ.
20 And I said unto you, Ye are come
unto the mountain of the Ăm'ôr-ītes,
which the LORD our God doth give
unto us.
21 Behold, the LORD thy God hath
set the land before thee: go up *and* possess *it*, as the LORD God of thy fathers
hath said unto thee; [u]fear not, neither
be discouraged.
22 ¶ And ye came near unto me every one of you, and said, We will send
men before us, and they shall search
us out the land, and bring us word
again by what way we must go up, and
into what cities we shall come.
23 And the saying pleased me well:
and [v]I took twelve men of you, one of a
tribe:
24 And they turned and went up into
the mountain, and came unto the valley
of Ĕsh'cŏl, and searched it out.
25 And they took of the fruit of the
land in their hands, and brought *it*
down unto us, and brought us word
again, and said, *It is* a good land which
the LORD our God doth give us.

9 [i]Ex. 18.18
10 [j]Gen. 15.5; Gen. 22.17; Ex. 32.13; ch. 10.22; 1 Chr. 27.23
11 [k]Gen. 22.17; Ex. 32.13
12 [l]1 Ki. 3.8; 2 Cor. 11.28
13 [4]Give
15 [5]gave
16 [m]Ex. 23.2-3-7-8; John 7.24 [n]Lev. 24.22
17 [o]1 Sam. 16.7; Prov. 24.23; Jas. 2.1 [6]acknowledge faces [p]Prov. 28.21 [q]2 Chr. 19.6 [r]Ex. 18.22-26
19 [s]Num. 10.12; ch. 8.15 [t]Num. 13.26
21 [u]Num. 13.30; Josh. 1.9; Ps. 27.1-3; Ps. 46.1-7-11; Isa. 41.10; Isa. 43.1-2; Luke 12.32; Heb. 13.6
23 [v]Num. 13.3
26 [w]Num. 14.1-4; Ps. 106.24
27 [x]ch. 9.28
28 [7]melted [y]Num. 13.28-31-33; ch. 9.1-2 [z]Num. 13.28
30 [a]Ex. 14.14; Neh. 4.20
31 [b]Ex. 19.4; Acts 13.18
32 [c]Ps. 106.24; Jude 5
33 [d]Ex. 13.21; Ps. 78.14 [e]Num. 10.33; Ezek. 20.6
34 [f]ch. 2.14
35 [g]Num. 14.22; Ps. 95.11
36 [8]fulfilled to go after
37 [h]Num. 27.14; Ps. 106.32
38 [i]Ex. 24.13; 1 Sam. 16.22 [j]ch. 31.7-23
39 [k]Isa. 7.15-16; Ezek. 18.20

26 [w]Notwithstanding ye would not
go up, but rebelled against the commandment of the LORD your God:
27 And ye murmured in your tents,
and said, Because the LORD [x]hated us,
he hath brought us forth out of the land
of Ē'gypt, to deliver us into the hand of
the Ăm'ôr-ītes, to destroy us.
28 Whither shall we go up? our
brethren have [7]discouraged our heart,
saying, [y]The people *is* greater and
taller than we; the cities *are* great and
walled up to heaven; and moreover we
have seen the sons of the [z]Ăn'a-kĭms
there.
29 Then I said unto you, Dread not,
neither be afraid of them.
30 [a]The LORD your God which goeth
before you, he shall fight for you, according to all that he did for you in
Ē'gypt before your eyes;
31 And in the wilderness, where thou
hast seen how that the LORD thy God
[b]bare thee, as a man doth bear his son,
in all the way that ye went, until ye came
into this place.
32 Yet in this thing [c]ye did not believe the LORD your God,
33 [d]Who went in the way before
you, [e]to search you out a place to pitch
your tents *in*, in fire by night, to shew
you by what way ye should go, and in a
cloud by day.
34 And the LORD heard the voice
of your words, and was wroth, [f]and
sware, saying,
35 [g]Surely there shall not one of
these men of this evil generation see
that good land, which I sware to give
unto your fathers,
36 Save Cā'leb the son of Je-phŭn'-
neh; he shall see it, and to him will
I give the land that he hath trodden
upon, and to his children, because he
hath [8]wholly followed the LORD.
37 [h]Also the LORD was angry with
me for your sakes, saying, Thou also
shalt not go in thither.
38 *But* Jŏsh'u-ȧ the son of Nŭn,
[i]which standeth before thee, he shall
go in thither: [j]encourage him: for he
shall cause Ĭs'ra-el to inherit it.
39 Moreover your little ones, which
ye said should be a prey, and your children, which in that day [k]had no knowledge between good and evil, they shall
go in thither, and unto them will I give
it, and they shall possess it.
40 But *as for* you, turn you, and take
your journey into the wilderness by
the way of the Red sea.
41 Then ye answered and said unto
me, We have sinned against the LORD,
we will go up and fight, according to all
that the LORD our God commanded us.
And when ye had girded on every man
his weapons of war, ye were ready to
go up into the hill.
42 And the LORD said unto me, Say
unto them, Go not up, neither fight; for
I *am* not among you; lest ye be smitten
before your enemies.
43 So I spake unto you; and ye
would not hear, but rebelled against

the commandment of the LORD, [9]and went presumptuously up into the hill.

44 And the Âm'ôr-ītes, which dwelt in that mountain, came out against you, and chased you, [l]as bees do, and destroyed you in Sē'ĭr, *even* unto Hôr'-mah.

45 And ye returned and wept before the LORD; [m]but the LORD would not hearken to your voice, nor give ear unto you.

46 [n]So ye abode in Kā'desh many days, according unto the days that ye abode *there*.

2 Then we turned, and took our journey into the wilderness by the way of the Red sea, as the LORD spake unto me: and we compassed mount Sē'ĭr many days.

2 And the LORD spake unto me, saying,

3 Ye have compassed this mountain long enough: turn you northward.

4 And command thou the people, saying, Ye *are* to pass through the coast of your brethren the children of Ē'sąu, which dwell in Sē'ĭr; and they shall be afraid of you: take ye good heed unto yourselves therefore:

5 Meddle not with them; for I will not give you of their land, [1]no, not so much as a foot breadth; [a]because I have given mount Sē'ĭr unto Ē'sąu *for* a possession.

6 Ye shall buy meat of them for money, that ye may eat; and ye shall also buy water of them for money, that ye may drink.

7 For the LORD thy God hath blessed thee in all the works of thy hand: he knoweth thy walking through this great wilderness: these forty years the LORD thy God *hath been* with thee; thou hast lacked nothing.

8 And when we passed by from our brethren the children of Ē'sąu, which dwelt in Sē'ĭr, through the way of the plain from [b]Ē'lăth, and from Ē'zĭ-on–gā'bĕr, we turned and passed by the way of the wilderness of Mō'ab.

9 And the LORD said unto me, [2]Distress not the Mō'ab-ītes, neither contend with them in battle: for I will not give thee of their land *for* a possession; because I have given [c]Är unto [d]the children of Lŏt *for* a possession.

10 [e]The Ē'mĭms dwelt therein in times past, a people great, and many, and tall, as [f]the Ăn'a-kĭms;

11 Which also were accounted giants, as the Ăn'a-kĭms; but the Mō'ab-ītes call them Ē'mĭms.

12 [g]The Hō'rĭms also dwelt in Sē'ĭr beforetime; but the children of Ē'sąu [3]succeeded them, when they had destroyed them from before them, and dwelt in their [4]stead; as Ĭs'ra-el did unto the land of his possession, which the LORD gave unto them.

13 Now rise up, *said I*, and get you over the [5]brook Zē'red. And we went over the brook Zē'red.

14 And the space in which we came from Kā'desh–bär'ne-ȧ, until we were come over the brook Zē'red, *was* thirty and eight years; [h]until all the generation of the men of war were wasted out from among the host, [i]as the LORD sware unto them.

15 For indeed the [j]hand of the LORD was against them, to destroy them from among the host, until they were consumed.

16 ¶ So it came to pass, when all the men of war were consumed and dead from among the people,

17 That the LORD spake unto me, saying,

18 Thou art to pass over through Är, the coast of Mō'ab, this day:

19 And *when* thou comest nigh over against the children of Ăm'mŏn, distress them not, nor meddle with them: for I will not give thee of the land of the children of Ăm'mŏn *any* possession; because I have given it unto [k]the children of Lŏt *for* a possession.

20 (That also was accounted a land of giants: giants dwelt therein in old time; and the Ăm'mŏn-ītes call them [l]Zam-zŭm'mims;

21 A people great, and many, and tall, as the Ăn'a-kĭms; but the LORD destroyed them before them; and they succeeded them, and dwelt in their stead:

22 As he did to the children of Ē'sąu, [m]which dwelt in Sē'ĭr, when he [n]destroyed the Hō'rĭms from before them; and they succeeded them, and dwelt in their stead even unto this day:

23 And [o]the Ā'vĭms which dwelt in Ha-zē'rĭm, *even* unto [p]Ăz'zah, [q]the Căph'tŏ-rĭms, which came forth out of Căph'tôr, destroyed them, and dwelt in their stead.)

24 ¶ Rise ye up, take your journey, and [r]pass over the river Är'nŏn: behold, I have given into thine hand Sī'-hŏn the Ăm'ôr-īte, king of Hĕsh'bŏn, and his land: [6]begin to possess *it*, and contend with him in battle.

25 [s]This day will I begin to put the dread of thee and the fear of thee upon the nations *that are* under the whole heaven, who shall hear report of thee, and shall tremble, and be in anguish because of thee.

26 ¶ And I sent messengers out of the wilderness of Kĕd'e-mŏth unto Sī'-hŏn king of Hĕsh'bŏn [t]with words of peace, saying,

27 [u]Let me pass through thy land: I will go along by the high way, I will neither turn unto the right hand nor to the left.

28 Thou shalt sell me meat for money, that I may eat; and give me water for money, that I may drink: [v]only I will pass through on my feet;

29 ([w]As the children of Ē'sąu which dwell in Sē'ĭr, and the Mō'ab-ītes which dwell in Är, did unto me;) until I shall pass over Jôr'dan into the land which the LORD our God giveth us.

30 [x]But Sī'hŏn king of Hĕsh'bŏn would not let us pass by him: for the [y]LORD thy God [z]hardened his spirit, and made his heart obstinate, that he

43 [9]ye were presumptuous, and went up
44 [l]ch. 28.25; Isa. 7.18
45 [m]Job 27.9; Zech. 7.11
46 [n]Num. 13.25; Num. 20.1-22

CHAPTER 2

5 [1]even to the treading of the sole of the foot
[a]Gen. 36.8; Acts 17.26
8 [b]1 Ki. 9.26; 2 Ki. 14.22
9 [2]Or, use no hostility against Moab
[c]Num. 21.28
[d]Gen. 19.36; Ps. 83.8
10 [e]Gen. 14.5
[f]Num. 13.22; ch. 9.2
12 [g]Gen. 14.6; Gen. 36.20
[3]inherited them
[4]Or, room
13 [5]Or, valley
14 [h]Num. 14.33; Ps. 90.3-9
[i]ch. 1.34-35
15 [j]1 Sam. 5.6-9-11; Heb. 4.1-5
19 [k]Gen. 19.38
20 [l]Gen. 14.5- Zuzims
22 [m]Gen. 36.8
[n]Job 12.23
23 [o]Josh. 13.3
[p]Jer. 25.20; Zeph. 2.4
[q]Gen. 10.14; Amos 9.7
24 [r]Num. 21.13-14
[6]begin, possess
25 [s]Ex. 15.14; ch. 11.25
26 [t]ch. 20.10;
27 [u]Num. 21.21
28 [v]Num. 20.19
29 [w]ch. 23.3
30 [x]Num. 21.23
[y]Josh. 11.20
[z]Ex. 4.21

might deliver him into thy hand, as *appeareth* this day.

31 And the LORD said unto me, Behold, I have begun to give Sī'hŏn and his land before thee: begin to possess, that thou mayest inherit his land.

32 Then Sī'hŏn came out against us, he and all his people, to fight at Jā'hăz.

33 And [a]the LORD our God delivered him before us; and [b]we smote him, and his sons, and all his people.

34 And we took all his cities at that time, and [c]utterly destroyed the [7]men, and the women, and the little ones, of every city, we left none to remain:

35 Only the cattle we took for a prey unto ourselves, and the spoil of the cities which we took.

36 [d]From Ăr'ŏ-ēr, which *is* by the brink of the river of Ăr'nŏn, and *from* the city that *is* by the river, even unto Gĭl'e-ăd, there was not one city too strong for us: [e]the LORD our God delivered all unto us:

37 Only unto the land of the children of Ăm'mŏn thou camest not, *nor* unto any place of the river [f]Jăb'bok, nor unto the cities in the mountains, nor unto whatsoever the LORD our God forbad us.

3

Then we turned, and went up the way to Bā'shăn: and Ŏg the king of Bā'shăn came out against us, he and all his people, to battle at Ĕd're-ī.

2 And the LORD said unto me, Fear him not: for I will deliver him, and all his people, and his land, into thy hand; and thou shalt do unto him as thou didst unto [a]Sī'hŏn king of the Ăm'ôr-ītes, which dwelt at Hĕsh'bŏn.

3 So the LORD our God delivered into our hands Ŏg also, the king of Bā'shăn, and all his people: and we smote him until none was left to him remaining.

4 And we took all his cities at that time, there was not a city which we took not from them, threescore cities, [b]all the region of Ăr'gŏb, the kingdom of Ŏg in Bā'shăn.

5 All these cities *were* fenced with high walls, gates, and bars; beside unwalled towns a great many.

6 And we utterly destroyed them, as we did unto Sī'hŏn king [c]of Hĕsh'bŏn, utterly destroying the men, women, and children, of every city.

7 But all the cattle, and the spoil of the cities, we took for a prey to ourselves.

8 And we took at that time out of the hand of the two kings of the Ăm'ôr-ītes the land that *was* on this side Jôr'dan, from the river of Ăr'nŏn unto mount Hĕr'mŏn;

9 (*Which* [d]Hĕr'mŏn the Sī-dō'nĭ-ans call Sĭr'i-ŏn; and the Ăm'ôr-ītes call it [e]Shē'nir;)

10 [f]All the cities of the plain, and all Gĭl'e-ăd, and [g]all Bā'shăn, unto Săl'chah and Ĕd're-ī, cities of the kingdom of Ŏg in Bā'shăn.

11 [h]For only Ŏg king of Bā'shăn remained of the remnant of [i]giants; behold, his bedstead *was* a bedstead of iron; *is* it not in [j]Răb'bath of the children of Ăm'mŏn? nine cubits *was* the length thereof, and four cubits the breadth of it, after the cubit of a man.

12 And this land, *which* we possessed at that time, [k]from Ăr'ŏ-ēr, which *is* by the river Ăr'nŏn, and half mount Gĭl'e-ăd, and [l]the cities thereof, gave I unto the Reu'ben-ītes and to the Găd'ītes.

13 [m]And the rest of Gĭl'e-ăd, and all Bā'shăn, *being* the kingdom of Ŏg, gave I unto the half tribe of Ma-năs'seh; all the region of Ăr'gŏb, with all Bā'shăn, which was called the land of giants.

14 [n]Jā'īr the son of Ma-năs'seh took all the country of Ăr'gŏb [o]unto the coasts of Gĕsh'u-rī and Ma-ăch'a-thī; and called them after his own name, Bā'shăn–hā'voth–jā'īr, unto this day.

15 [p]And I gave Gĭl'e-ăd unto Mā'chĭr.

16 And unto the Reu'ben-ītes [q]and unto the Găd'ītes I gave from Gĭl'e-ăd even unto the river Ăr'nŏn half the valley, and the border even unto the river Jăb'bok, [r]*which is* the border of the children of Ăm'mŏn;

17 The plain also, and Jôr'dan, and the coast *thereof*, from [s]Chĭn'ne-rĕth [t]even unto the sea of the plain, [u]*even* the salt sea, [1]under Ăsh'doth–pĭs'gah eastward.

18 ¶ And I commanded you at that time, saying, The LORD your God hath given you this land to possess it: ye shall pass over armed before your brethren the children of Ĭs'ra-el, all *that are* [2]meet for the war.

19 But your wives, and your little ones, and your cattle, (*for* I know that ye have much cattle,) shall abide in your cities which I have given you;

20 Until the LORD have given rest unto your brethren, as well as unto you, and *until* they also possess the land which the LORD your God hath given them beyond Jôr'dan: and *then* shall ye [v]return every man unto his possession, which I have given you.

21 ¶ And I commanded Jŏsh'u-ȧ at that time, saying, Thine eyes have seen all that the LORD your God hath done unto these two kings: so shall the LORD do unto all the kingdoms whither thou passest.

22 Ye shall not fear them: for the [w]LORD your God he shall fight for you.

23 And I besought the LORD at that time, saying,

24 O Lord GOD, thou hast begun to shew thy servant [x]thy greatness, and thy mighty hand: for [y]what God *is there* in heaven or in earth, that can do according to thy works, and according to thy might?

25 I pray thee, let me go over, and see [z]the good land that *is* beyond Jôr'dan, that goodly mountain, and Lĕb'a-non.

26 But the LORD was wroth with me for your sakes, and would not hear me: and the LORD said unto me, Let it suffice thee; speak no more unto me of this matter.

33 [a]Ex. 23.31; Ps. 136.18-20
[b]ch. 29.7
34 [c]Lev. 27.28; 1 Sam. 15.3-8-9
[7]every city of men, and women, and little ones
36 [d]ch. 3.12; Josh. 13.9
[e]Ps. 44.3
37 [f]Gen. 32.22; ch. 3.16

CHAPTER 3
2 [a]Num. 21.34
4 [b]ch. 29.8
6 [c]ch. 2.24; Ps. 135.10-12
9 [d]Ps. 29.6; Ps. 133.3
[e]1 Chr. 5.23
10 [f]ch. 4.49
[g]Josh. 12.5
11 [h]Amos 2.9
[i]Gen. 14.5-Rephaims
[j]2 Sam. 12.26; Amos 1.14
12 [k]Num. 32.33-38; 2 Ki. 10.33
[l]Num. 32.33
13 [m]Num. 32.39-42; 1 Chr. 5.23
14 [n]1 Chr. 2.22
[o]2 Sam. 3.3; 2 Sam. 10.6
15 [p]Num. 26.29; Josh. 17.1
16 [q]2 Sam. 24.5
[r]Num. 21.24
17 [s]Num. 34.11
[t]Gen. 13.10; Josh. 12.3
[u]Gen. 14.3-The sea of Sodom
[1]Or, under the springs of Pisgah, or, the hill
18 [2]sons of power
20 [v]Josh. 22.4
22 [w]Ex. 14.14; ch. 1.30
24 [x]ch. 11.2; Ps. 145.3-6
[y]Ex. 15.11;
25 [z]ch. 4.22

27 Get thee up into the top of [3]Pĭs'-
gah, and lift up thine eyes westward,
and northward, and southward, and
eastward, and behold *it* with thine
eyes: for thou shalt not go over this
Jôr'dan.
28 But [a]charge Jŏsh'u-ȧ, and encourage him, and strengthen him: for
he shall go over before this people, and
he shall cause them to inherit the land
which thou shalt see.
29 So we abode in [b]the valley over
against Bĕth–pē'ôr.

4 Now therefore hearken, O Ĭs'ra-el,
unto [a]the statutes and unto the judgments, which I teach you, for to do
them, that ye may live, and go in and
possess the land which the LORD God
of your fathers giveth you.
2 [b]Ye shall not add unto the word
which I command you, neither shall ye
diminish *ought* from it, that ye may
keep the commandments of the LORD
your God which I command you.
3 Your eyes have seen what the
LORD did because of Bā-al–pē'or: for
all the men that followed Bā-al–pē'or,
the LORD thy God hath destroyed them
from among you.
4 But ye that did cleave unto the
LORD your God *are* alive every one of
you this day.
5 Behold, I have taught you statutes
and judgments, even as the LORD my
God commanded me, that ye should do
so in the land whither ye go to possess
it.
6 Keep therefore and do *them;* for
this *is* [c]your wisdom and your understanding in the sight of the nations,
which shall hear all these statutes, and
say, [d]Surely this great nation *is* a wise
and understanding people.
7 For [e]what nation *is there so* great,
who *hath* [f]God *so* nigh unto them, as
the LORD our God *is* in all *things that*
we call upon him *for?*
8 And what nation *is there so* great,
that hath statutes and judgments *so*
righteous as all this law, which I set
before you this day?
9 Only take heed to thyself, and
[g]keep thy soul diligently, [h]lest thou
forget the things which thine eyes have
seen, and lest they depart from thy
heart all the days of thy life: but [i]teach
them thy sons, and thy sons' sons;
10 *Specially* [j]the day that thou stoodest before the LORD thy God in Hō'reb,
when the LORD said unto me, Gather
me the people together, and I will make
them hear my words, that they may
learn to fear me all the days that they
shall live upon the earth, and *that* they
may teach their children.
11 And ye came near and stood under the mountain; and the mountain
burned with fire unto the [1]midst of
heaven, with darkness, clouds, and
thick darkness.
12 And the LORD spake unto you out
of the midst of the fire: ye heard the
voice of the words, but saw no similitude; [2]only *ye heard* a voice.

27 [3]Or, The hill
28 [a]Num. 27.18; ch. 1.38
29 [b]ch. 4.46
CHAPTER 4
1 [a]Ezek. 20.11; Rom. 10.5
2 [b]ch. 12.32; Josh. 1.7; Prov. 30.6; Matt. 15.9; Rev. 22.18
6 [c]Job 28.28; Ps. 19.7; Prov. 1.7; 2 Tim. 3.15
[d]1 Ki. 10.6-9; Dan. 1.20; Mal. 3.12; Acts 4.13
7 [e]2 Sam. 7.23
[f]Ex. 25.8; Lev. 26.12; Jas. 4.8
9 [g]Prov. 4.23
[h]Prov. 3.1-3
[i]Gen. 18.19; Eph. 6.4
10 [j]Ex. 19.9-16; Heb. 12.18
11 [1]heart
12 [2]save a voice
15 [k]Prov. 4.23-27; Mal. 2.15
[l]Isa. 40.18; Acts 17.24-29
16 [m]Rom. 1.23
19 [n]ch. 17.3; Job 31.26
[o]Gen. 2.1; 2 Ki. 17.16
[3]Or, imparted
22 [p]2 Pet. 1.13
24 [q]Ex. 24.17; Heb. 12.29
[r]Ex. 20.5; Isa. 42.8
25 [s]2 Ki. 17.17
26 [t]ch. 30.18-19; Mic. 6.2
27 [u]Lev. 26.33; Ezek. 12.15
28 [v]ch. 28.36-64; Acts 7.42

13 And he declared unto you his covenant, which he commanded you to perform, *even* ten commandments; and he
wrote them upon two tables of stone.
14 ¶ And the LORD commanded me
at that time to teach you statutes and
judgments, that ye might do them in
the land whither ye go over to possess
it.
15 [k]Take ye therefore good heed
unto yourselves; for ye saw no manner
of [l]similitude on the day *that* the LORD
spake unto you in Hō'reb out of the
midst of the fire:
16 Lest ye corrupt *yourselves,* and
make you a graven image, the similitude of any figure, [m]the likeness of
male or female,
17 The likeness of any beast that
is on the earth, the likeness of any
winged fowl that flieth in the air,
18 The likeness of any thing that
creepeth on the ground, the likeness of
any fish that *is* in the waters beneath
the earth:
19 And lest thou [n]lift up thine eyes
unto heaven, and when thou seest the
sun, and the moon, and the stars, *even*
[o]all the host of heaven, shouldest be
driven to worship them, and serve
them, which the LORD thy God hath divided [3]unto all nations under the whole
heaven.
20 But the LORD hath taken you, and
brought you forth out of the iron furnace, *even* out of Ē'ġypt, to be unto
him a people of inheritance, as *ye are*
this day.
21 Furthermore the LORD was angry
with me for your sakes, and sware that
I should not go over Jôr'dan, and that I
should not go in unto that good land,
which the LORD thy God giveth thee
for an inheritance:
22 But [p]I must die in this land, I
must not go over Jôr'dan: but ye shall
go over, and possess that good land.
23 Take heed unto yourselves, lest
ye forget the covenant of the LORD
your God, which he made with you,
and make you a graven image, *or* the
likeness of any *thing,* which the LORD
thy God hath forbidden thee.
24 For [q]the LORD thy God *is* a consuming fire, *even* [r]a jealous God.
25 ¶ When thou shalt beget children,
and children's children, and ye shall
have remained long in the land, and
shall corrupt *yourselves,* and make a
graven image, *or* the likeness of any
thing, and [s]shall do evil in the sight of
the LORD thy God, to provoke him to
anger:
26 [t]I call heaven and earth to witness against you this day, that ye shall
soon utterly perish from off the land
whereunto ye go over Jôr'dan to possess it; ye shall not prolong *your* days
upon it, but shall utterly be destroyed.
27 And the LORD [u]shall scatter you
among the nations, and ye shall be left
few in number among the heathen,
whither the LORD shall lead you.
28 And [v]there ye shall serve gods,
the work of men's hands, wood and

stone, which neither see, nor hear, nor
eat, nor smell.
29 [w]But if from thence thou shalt
seek the LORD thy God, thou shalt find
him, if thou seek him with all thy heart
and with all thy soul.
30 When thou art in tribulation, and
all these things [4]are come upon thee,
[x]*even* in the latter days, if thou [y]turn
to the LORD thy God, and shalt be obedient unto his voice;
31 (For the LORD thy God *is* [z]a merciful God;) he will not forsake thee, neither destroy thee, nor forget the covenant of thy fathers which he sware
unto them.
32 For [a]ask now of the days that are
past, which were before thee, since the
day that God created man upon the
earth, and *ask* [b]from the one side of
heaven unto the other, whether there
hath been *any such thing* as this great
thing *is,* or hath been heard like it?
33 Did *ever* people hear the voice of
God speaking out of the midst of the
fire, as thou hast heard, and live?
34 Or hath God assayed to go *and*
take him a nation from the midst of *another* nation, by temptations, by signs,
and by wonders, and by war, and by a
mighty hand, and by a stretched out
arm, and by great terrors, according to
all that the LORD your God did for you
in Ē'ġypt before your eyes?
35 Unto thee it was shewed, that
thou mightest know that the LORD he
is God; [c]*there is* none else beside him.
36 [d]Out of heaven he made thee to
hear his voice, that he might instruct
thee: and upon earth he shewed thee
his great fire; and thou heardest his
words out of the midst of the fire.
37 And because he loved thy fathers, therefore he chose their seed after them, and brought thee out in his
sight with his mighty power out of
Ē'ġypt;
38 To drive out nations from before
thee greater and mightier than thou
art, to bring thee in, to give thee their
land *for* an inheritance, as *it is* this
day.
39 Know therefore this day, and consider *it* in thine heart, that [e]the LORD
he *is* God in heaven above, and upon
the earth beneath: *there is* none else.
40 [f]Thou shalt keep therefore his statutes, and his commandments, which I
command thee this day, [g]that it may go
well with thee, and with thy children
after thee, and that thou mayest prolong *thy* days upon the earth, which the
LORD thy God giveth thee, for ever.
41 ¶ Then Mō'ses [h]severed three cities on this side Jôr'dan toward the
sunrising;
42 That the slayer might flee thither,
which should kill his neighbour unawares, and hated him not in times
past; and that fleeing unto one of these
cities he might live:
43 *Namely,* [i]Bē'zēr in the wilderness, in the plain country, of the Reu'-
ben-ītes; and Rā'moth in Ġĭl'e-ăd, of
the Găd'ītes; and Gō'lan in Bā'shăn, of
the Ma-năs'sītes.
44 ¶ And this *is* the law which Mō'-
ses set before the children of Ĭs'ra-el:
45 These *are* the testimonies, and
the statutes, and the judgments, which
Mō'ses spake unto the children of Ĭs'-
ra-el, after they came forth out of
Ē'ġypt,
46 On this side Jôr'dan, [j]in the valley over against Bĕth–pē'ôr, in the land
of Sī'hŏn king of the Ăm'ôr-ītes, who
dwelt at Hĕsh'bŏn, whom Mō'ses and
the children of Ĭs'ra-el smote, after they
were come forth out of Ē'ġypt:
47 And they possessed his land, and
the land [k]of Ŏg king of Bā'shăn, two
kings of the Ăm'ôr-ītes, which *were* on
this side Jôr'dan toward the sunrising;
48 [l]From Ăr'ō-ēr, which *is* by the
bank of the river Ăr'nŏn, even unto
mount Sī'ŏn, which *is* [m]Hĕr'mŏn,
49 And all the plain on this side Jôr'-
dan eastward, even unto the sea of the
plain, under the springs of Pĭs'gah.

5 And Mō'ses called all Ĭs'ra-el, and
said unto them, Hear, O Ĭs'ra-el, the
statutes and judgments which I speak
in your ears this day, that ye may learn
them, and [1]keep, and do them.
2 The [a]LORD our God made a covenant with us in Hō'reb.
3 The LORD [b]made not this covenant with our fathers, but with us, *even*
us, who *are* all of us here alive this day.
4 The [c]LORD talked with you face to
face in the mount out of the midst of
the fire,
5 ([d]I stood between the LORD and
you at that time, to shew you the word
of the LORD: for [e]ye were afraid by
reason of the fire, and went not up into
the mount;) saying,
6 ¶ [f]I *am* the LORD thy God, which
brought thee out of the land of Ē'ġypt,
from the house of [2]bondage.
7 [g]Thou shalt have none other gods
before me.
8 [h]Thou shalt not make thee *any* graven image, *or* any likeness *of any thing*
that *is* in heaven above, or that *is* in the
earth beneath, or that *is* in the waters
beneath the earth:
9 Thou shalt not bow down thyself
unto them, nor serve them: for I the
LORD thy God *am* a jealous God, [i]visit-
ing the iniquity of the fathers upon the
children unto the third and fourth *generation* of them that hate me,
10 And [j]shewing mercy unto thousands of them that love me and keep
my commandments.
11 [k]Thou shalt not take the name of
the LORD thy God in vain: for the LORD
will not hold *him* guiltless that taketh
his name in vain.
12 [l]Keep the sabbath day to sanctify it, as the LORD thy God hath commanded thee.
13 [m]Six days thou shalt labour, and
do all thy work:
14 But the seventh day *is* the [n]sab-
bath of the LORD thy God: *in it* thou
shalt not do any work, thou, nor
thy son, nor thy daughter, nor thy

---

29 [w]2 Chr. 15.4; Isa. 55.6
30 [4]have found thee
[x]Gen. 49.1; Jer. 23.20
[y]Jer. 4.1-2
31 [z]Ex. 34.6; Jon. 4.2
32 [a]Job 8.8
[b]Ex. 15.11; Mark 12.29
35 [c]ch. 32.39; Mark 12.29
36 [d]Ex. 19.9-19; Heb. 12.18
39 [e]Josh. 2.11; Dan. 4.35
40 [f]Lev. 22.31
[g]ch. 5.16; Eph. 6.3
41 [h]Num. 35.6
43 [i]Josh. 20.8
46 [j]ch. 3.29
47 [k]Num. 21.35; ch. 3.3-4
48 [l]ch. 2.36
[m]Ps. 133.3

CHAPTER 5
1 [1]keep to do them
2 [a]Ex. 19.5; Heb. 8.6-13
3 [b]Matt. 13.17; Heb. 8.9
4 [c]Ex. 19.9-19; ch. 34.10
5 [d]Ex. 19.16; Heb. 12.18-19
[e]Ex. 19.16
6 [f]Ex. 20.2; Ps. 81.10
[2]servants
7 [g]Ex. 20.3
8 [h]Ex. 20.4; Acts 17.29
9 [i]Ex. 34.7
10 [j]Jer. 32.18; 1 John 1.7
11 [k]Ex. 20.7; Matt. 5.33
12 [l]Ex. 20.8; Neh. 13.17
13 [m]Ex. 23.12
14 [n]Gen. 2.2

manservant, nor thy maidservant, nor
thine ox, nor thine ass, nor any of thy
cattle, nor thy stranger that *is* within
thy gates; that thy manservant and thy
maidservant may rest as well as thou.
15 And remember that thou wast a
servant in the land of Ē'gypt, and *that*
the LORD thy God brought thee out
thence through a mighty hand and by a
stretched out arm: therefore the LORD
thy God commanded thee to keep the
sabbath day.
16 ¶ [o]Honour thy father and thy
mother, as the LORD thy God hath commanded thee; [p]that thy days may be
prolonged, and that it may go well with
thee, in the land which the LORD thy
God giveth thee.
17 [q]Thou shalt not kill.
18 [r]Neither shalt thou commit adultery.
19 [s]Neither shalt thou steal.
20 [t]Neither shalt thou bear false witness against thy neighbour.
21 [u]Neither shalt thou desire thy
neighbour's wife, neither shalt thou
covet thy neighbour's house, his field,
or his manservant, or his maidservant,
his ox, or his ass, or any *thing* that *is*
thy neighbour's.
22 ¶ These words the LORD spake
unto all your assembly in the mount
out of the midst of the fire, of the cloud,
and of the thick darkness, with a great
voice: and he added no more. And he
[v]wrote them in two tables of stone,
and delivered them unto me.
23 And it came to pass, when ye
heard the voice out of the midst of the
darkness, (for the mountain did burn
with fire,) that ye came near unto me,
even all the heads of your tribes, and
your elders;
24 And ye said, Behold, the LORD
our God hath shewed us his glory and
his greatness, and we have heard his
voice out of the midst of the fire: we
have seen this day that God doth talk
with man, and he liveth.
25 Now therefore why should we
die? for this great fire will consume us:
if we [3]hear the voice of the LORD our
God any more, then we shall die.
26 [w]For who *is there of* all flesh,
that hath heard the voice of the living
God speaking out of the midst of the
fire, as we *have,* and lived?
27 Go thou near, and hear all that the
LORD our God shall say: and [x]speak
thou unto us all that the LORD our God
shall speak unto thee; and we will hear
it, and do *it.*
28 And the LORD heard the voice of
your words, when ye spake unto me;
and the LORD said unto me, I have
heard the voice of the words of this
people, which they have spoken unto
thee: they have well said all that they
have spoken.
29 [y]O that there were such an heart
in them, that they would fear me, and
[z]keep all my commandments always,
that it might be well with them, and
with their children for ever!

16 [o]Lev. 19.3; ch. 27.16; Eph. 6.2-3; Col. 3.20
[p]ch. 4.40
17 [q]Matt. 5.21
18 [r]Luke 18.20
19 [s]Rom. 13.9
20 [t]1 Ki. 21.10
21 [u]Mic. 2.2; Hab. 2.9; Luke 12.15; Rom. 7.7; Gal. 5.14
22 [v]Ex. 24.12
25 [3]add to hear
26 [w]ch. 4.33
27 [x]Heb. 12.19
29 [y]ch. 32.29; Ps. 81.13; Isa. 48.18; Matt. 23.37; Luke 19.42; 2 Cor. 5.20; Heb. 12.25
[z]ch. 11.1; Ps. 119.1-5; Luke 11.28; John 15.14; Rev. 22.14
31 [a]Mal. 4.4; Gal. 3.19
32 [b]ch. 17.20; Josh. 1.7; Prov. 4.27
33 [c]ch. 10.12; Ps. 119.6; Eccl. 8.12; Luke 1.6; 1 Tim. 4.8
[d]ch. 4.40; ch. 12.25-28; Eph. 6.3

CHAPTER 6
1 [1]pass over
2 [a]Ex. 20.20; Ps. 111.10; Ps. 128.1; Eccl. 12.13
[b]Prov. 3.1
4 [c]Isa. 9.6; Mark 12.29; John 1.1; Phil. 2.5-6
5 [d]ch. 30.6; Mark 12.30-32
6 [e]Isa. 51.7
7 [f]Eph. 6.4
[2]whet, or, sharpen
8 [g]Prov. 3.3; Prov. 7.3
9 [h]ch. 11.20; Isa. 57.8
10 [i]Josh. 24.13; Ps. 105.44
12 [3]bondmen, or, servants
13 [j]ch. 13.4; Luke 4.8
[k]Ps. 63.11

30 Go say to them, Get you into your
tents again.
31 But as for thee, stand thou here
by me, and [a]I will speak unto thee all
the commandments, and the statutes,
and the judgments, which thou shalt
teach them, that they may do *them* in
the land which I give them to possess
it.
32 Ye shall observe to do therefore
as the LORD your God hath commanded
you: [b]ye shall not turn aside to the right
hand or to the left.
33 Ye shall walk in [c]all the ways
which the LORD your God hath commanded you, that ye may live, [d]and
that it may be well with you, and *that*
ye may prolong *your* days in the land
which ye shall possess.
6 Now these *are* the commandments,
the statutes, and the judgments,
which the LORD your God commanded
to teach you, that ye might do *them* in
the land whither ye [1]go to possess it:
2 [a]That thou mightest fear the LORD
thy God, to keep all his statutes and
his commandments, which I command
thee, thou, and thy son, and thy son's
son, all the days of thy life; [b]and that
thy days may be prolonged.
3 ¶ Hear therefore, O Is'ra-el, and
observe to do *it;* that it may be well
with thee, and that ye may increase
mightily, as the LORD God of thy fathers hath promised thee, in the land
that floweth with milk and honey.
4 [c]Hear, O Is'ra-el: the LORD our
God *is* one LORD:
5 And [d]thou shalt love the LORD thy
God with all thine heart, and with all
thy soul, and with all thy might.
6 And [e]these words, which I command thee this day, shall be in thine
heart:
7 And [f]thou shalt [2]teach them diligently unto thy children, and shalt
talk of them when thou sittest in thine
house, and when thou walkest by the
way, and when thou liest down, and
when thou risest up.
8 And [g]thou shalt bind them for a
sign upon thine hand, and they shall
be as frontlets between thine eyes.
9 And [h]thou shalt write them upon
the posts of thy house, and on thy
gates.
10 And it shall be, when the LORD
thy God shall have brought thee into
the land which he sware unto thy fathers, to Ā'brā-hăm, to Ī'saac, and to
Jā'cob, to give thee great and goodly
cities, [i]which thou buildedst not,
11 And houses full of all good *things,*
which thou filledst not, and wells
digged, which thou diggedst not, vineyards and olive trees, which thou plantedst not; when thou shalt have eaten
and be full;
12 *Then* beware lest thou forget the
LORD, which brought thee forth out of
the land of Ē'gypt, from the house of
[3]bondage.
13 Thou shalt [j]fear the LORD thy
God, and serve him, and [k]shalt swear
by his name.

14 Ye shall not [l]go after other gods,
of the gods of the people which *are*
round about you;
15 (For the LORD thy God *is* a jealous God among you) lest the anger of
the LORD thy God be kindled against
thee, and destroy thee from off the face
of the earth.
16 ¶ [m]Ye shall not tempt the LORD
your God, [n]as ye tempted *him* in Măs'-
sah.
17 Ye shall [o]diligently keep the commandments of the LORD your God, and
his testimonies, and his statutes, which
he hath commanded thee.
18 And thou shalt do *that which is*
right and good in the sight of the LORD:
that it may be well with thee, and that
thou mayest go in and possess the good
land which the LORD sware unto thy
fathers,
19 To cast out all thine enemies from
before thee, as the LORD hath spoken.
20 *And* when thy son asketh thee [4]in
time to come, saying, What *mean* the
testimonies, and the statutes, and the
judgments, which the LORD our God
hath commanded you?
21 Then thou shalt say unto thy
son, We were Phā'raōh's bondmen in
Ē'gypt; and the LORD brought us out of
Ē'gypt with a mighty hand:
22 And the LORD shewed signs and
wonders, great and [5]sore, upon Ē'gypt,
upon Phā'raōh, and upon all his household, before our eyes:
23 And he brought us out from
thence, that he might bring us in, to
give us the land which he sware unto
our fathers.
24 And the LORD commanded us to
do all these statutes, to fear the LORD
our God, [p]for our good always, that
[q]he might preserve us alive, as *it is* at
this day.
25 And [r]it shall be our righteousness, if we observe to do all these commandments before the LORD our God,
as he hath commanded us.

7

When the LORD thy God shall bring
thee into the land whither thou goest to possess it, and hath cast out many
nations before thee, the Hĭt'tītes, and
the Gĭr'ga-shītes, and the Ăm'ôr-ītes,
and the Cā'năan-ītes, and the Pĕr'ĭz-
zītes, and the Hī'vītes, and the Jĕb'u-
sītes, seven nations greater and mightier than thou;
2 And when the LORD thy God shall
deliver them before thee; thou shalt
smite them, *and* [a]utterly destroy them;
[b]thou shalt make no covenant with
them, nor shew mercy unto them:
3 [c]Neither shalt thou make marriages with them; thy daughter thou
shalt not give unto his son, nor his
daughter shalt thou take unto thy son.
4 For they will turn away thy son
from following me, that they may serve
other gods: so will the anger of the
LORD be kindled against you, and destroy thee suddenly.
5 But thus shall ye deal with them;
ye shall [d]destroy their altars, and break
down their [1]images, and cut down their
groves, and burn their graven images
with fire.
6 [e]For thou *art* an holy people unto
the LORD thy God: [f]the LORD thy God
hath chosen thee to be a special people
unto himself, above all people that *are*
upon the face of the earth.
7 The LORD did not set his love upon
you, nor choose you, because ye were
more in number than any people; for
ye *were* the fewest of all people:
8 But because the LORD loved you,
and because he would keep the [g]oath
which he had sworn unto your fathers,
[h]hath the LORD brought you out with a
mighty hand, and redeemed you out of
the house of bondmen, from the hand
of Phā'raōh king of Ē'gypt.
9 Know therefore that the LORD thy
God, he *is* God, [i]the faithful God,
[j]which keepeth covenant and mercy
with them that love him and keep his
commandments to a thousand generations;
10 And [k]repayeth them that hate
him to their face, to destroy them: he
will not be slack to him that hateth
him, he will repay him to his face.
11 Thou shalt therefore keep the
commandments, and the statutes, and
the judgments, which I command thee
this day, to do them.
12 ¶ Wherefore it shall come to pass,
[2]if ye hearken to these judgments, and
keep, and do them, that the LORD thy
God shall keep unto thee the covenant
and the mercy which he sware unto
thy fathers:
13 And he will [l]love thee, and bless
thee, and multiply thee: he will also
bless the fruit of thy womb, and the
fruit of thy land, thy corn, and thy
wine, and thine oil, the increase of thy
kine, and the flocks of thy sheep, in the
land which he sware unto thy fathers
to give thee.
14 Thou shalt be blessed above all
people: there shall not be male or female barren among you, or among
your cattle.
15 And the LORD will take away
from thee all sickness, and will put
none of the evil [m]diseases of Ē'gypt,
which thou knowest, upon thee; but
will lay them upon all *them* that hate
thee.
16 And thou shalt consume all the
people which the LORD thy God shall
deliver thee; thine eye shall have no
pity upon them: neither shalt thou
serve their gods; for that *will be* [n]a
snare unto thee.
17 If thou shalt say in thine heart,
These nations *are* more than I; how
can I [o]dispossess them?
18 Thou shalt not be afraid of them:
but shalt well [p]remember what the
LORD thy God did unto Phā'raōh, and
unto all Ē'gypt;
19 The great temptations which thine
eyes saw, and the signs, and the wonders, and the mighty hand, and the
stretched out arm, whereby the LORD
thy God brought thee out: so shall the

14 [l]Jer. 25.6
16 [m]Matt. 4.7
[n]1 Cor. 10.9
17 [o]Ps. 119.4
20 [4]to mor-
row
22 [5]evil
24 [p]Job 35.7-
8
[q]Ps. 41.2;
Luke 10.28
25 [r]Rom.
10.3
CHAPTER 7
2 [a]Josh. 6.17
[b]Ex. 23.32;
Josh. 2.14;
Judg. 1.24
3 [c]Josh.
23.12; 1 Ki.
11.2;
Ezra 9.2
5 [d]Ex. 23.24
[1]statues, or,
pillars
6 [e]Ps. 50.5;
Jer. 2.3; Amos
3.2; Tit. 2.14;
1 Pet. 2.5
[f]Ps. 135.4;
Amos 3.2;
1 Pet. 2.9
8 [g]Ex. 32.13;
Ps. 105.8;
Luke 1.55
[h]Ex. 13.3
9 [i]Isa. 49.7;
1 Cor. 1.9;
2 Cor. 1.18;
1 Thess. 5.24;
2 Tim. 2.13;
Heb. 11.11
[j]Neh. 1.5;
Dan. 9.4
10 [k]Ps. 21.8;
Prov. 11.31;
Isa. 59.18;
Nah. 1.2;
Rom. 12.19
12 [2]because
13 [l]Ex. 23.25;
Ps. 1.3; Ps.
11.7; Ps. 63.3;
Ps. 146.8;
Prov. 15.9;
John 14.21
15 [m]Ex. 9.14;
ch. 28.27;
Ps. 105.37
16 [n]Judg.
8.27;
Ps. 106.36
17 [o]Num.
33.53
18 [p]Judg.
6.13; Ps.
77.11; Ps.
105.5; Ps.
135.8-10;
Isa. 63.11-15

LORD thy God do unto all the people of whom thou art afraid.

20 [q]Moreover the LORD thy God will send the hornet among them, until they that are left, and hide themselves from thee, be destroyed.

21 Thou shalt not be affrighted at them: for the LORD thy God *is* [r]among you, [s]a mighty God and terrible.

22 And the LORD thy God will [3]put out those nations before thee by little and little: thou mayest not consume them at once, lest the beasts of the field increase upon thee.

23 But the LORD thy God shall deliver them [4]unto thee, and shall destroy them with a mighty destruction, until they be destroyed.

24 And [t]he shall deliver their kings into thine hand, and thou shalt destroy their name from under heaven: [u]there shall no man be able to stand before thee, until thou have destroyed them.

25 The graven images of their gods [v]shall ye burn with fire: thou [w]shalt not desire the silver or gold *that is* on them, nor take *it* unto thee, lest thou be [x]snared therein: for it *is* [y]an abomination to the LORD thy God.

26 Neither shalt thou bring an abomination into thine house, lest thou be a cursed thing like it: *but* thou shalt utterly detest it, and thou shalt utterly abhor it; [z]for it *is* a cursed thing.

8 All the commandments which I command thee this day shall ye observe to do, that ye may live, and multiply, and go in and possess the land which the LORD sware unto your fathers.

2 And thou shalt remember all the way which the LORD thy God [a]led thee these forty years in the wilderness, to humble thee, *and* to prove thee, [b]to know what *was* in thine heart, whether thou wouldest keep his commandments, or no.

3 And he humbled thee, and [c]suffered thee to hunger, and fed thee with manna, which thou knewest not, neither did thy fathers know; that he might make thee know that man doth [d]not live by bread only, but by every *word* that proceedeth out of the mouth of the LORD doth man live.

4 [e]Thy raiment waxed not old upon thee, neither did thy foot swell, these forty years.

5 [f]Thou shalt also consider in thine heart, that, as a man chasteneth his son, *so* the LORD thy God chasteneth thee.

6 Therefore thou shalt keep the commandments of the LORD thy God, to walk in his ways, and to fear him.

7 For the LORD thy God bringeth thee into a good land, a land of brooks of water, of fountains and depths that spring out of valleys and hills;

8 A land of wheat, and barley, and vines, and fig trees, and pomegranates; a land [1]of oil olive, and honey;

9 A land wherein thou shalt eat bread without scarceness, thou shalt not lack any *thing* in it; a land whose

20 [q]Ex. 23.28; Josh. 24.12
21 [r]Num. 14.9
[s]ch. 10.17; Neh. 1.5
22 [3]pluck off
23 [4]before thy face
24 [t]Josh. 10.24
[u]ch. 11.25; Josh. 1.5
25 [v]Ex. 32.20; ch. 12.3; 1 Chr. 14.12
[w]Ex. 20.17; Josh. 7.1; Col. 3.5
[x]Judg. 8.27; Zeph. 1.3
[y]ch. 17.1
26 [z]Lev. 27.28

CHAPTER 8
2 [a]Ps. 136.16; Amos 2.10
[b]2 Chr. 32.31; John 2.25
3 [c]Ex. 16.2; 1 Cor. 10.3-4
[d]Ps. 104.29; Heb. 13.5-6
4 [e]ch. 29.5; Neh. 9.21
5 [f]Ps. 89.32; Rev. 3.19
8 [1]of olive tree of oil
10 [g]Ps. 103.2; 1 Tim. 4.3
12 [h]Prov. 30.9
14 [i]1 Cor. 4.7
[j]Ps. 106.21
15 [k]Isa. 63.12
[l]Num. 21.6; Hos. 13.5
[m]Num. 20.11
16 [n]Ex. 16.15
[o]Jer. 24.5-6; 1 Pet. 1.7
17 [p]ch. 9.4
18 [q]Prov. 10.22; Hos. 2.8
20 [r]Lam. 1; Zech. 1.6

CHAPTER 9
1 [a]ch. 4.38; ch. 7.1
[b]ch. 1.28
2 [c]Num. 13.22
3 [d]ch. 31.3; Rev. 19.11-15
[e]ch. 4.24; Heb. 12.29
[f]Ex. 23.31
4 [g]ch. 8.11-17; 1 Cor. 4.4

stones *are* iron, and out of whose hills thou mayest dig brass.

10 When [g]thou hast eaten and art full, then thou shalt bless the LORD thy God for the good land which he hath given thee.

11 Beware that thou forget not the LORD thy God, in not keeping his commandments, and his judgments, and his statutes, which I command thee this day:

12 [h]Lest *when* thou hast eaten and art full, and hast built goodly houses, and dwelt *therein;*

13 And *when* thy herds and thy flocks multiply, and thy silver and thy gold is multiplied, and all that thou hast is multiplied;

14 [i]Then thine heart be lifted up, and thou [j]forget the LORD thy God, which brought thee forth out of the land of Ē'ġypt, from the house of bondage;

15 Who [k]led thee through that great and terrible wilderness, [l]*wherein were* fiery serpents, and scorpions, and drought, where *there was* no water; [m]who brought thee forth water out of the rock of flint;

16 Who fed thee in the wilderness with [n]manna, which thy fathers knew not, that he might humble thee, and that he might prove thee, [o]to do thee good at thy latter end;

17 And [p]thou say in thine heart, My power and the might of *mine* hand hath gotten me this wealth.

18 But thou shalt remember the LORD thy God: [q]for *it is* he that giveth thee power to get wealth, that he may establish his covenant which he sware unto thy fathers, as *it is* this day.

19 And it shall be, if thou do at all forget the LORD thy God, and walk after other gods, and serve them, and worship them, I testify against you this day that ye shall surely perish.

20 As the nations which the LORD destroyeth before your face, [r]so shall ye perish; because ye would not be obedient unto the voice of the LORD your God.

9 Hear, O Ĭs'ra-el: Thou *art* to pass over Jôr'dan this day, to go in to possess nations [a]greater and mightier than thyself, cities great and [b]fenced up to heaven,

2 A people great and tall, [c]the children of the Ăn'a-kĭms, whom thou knowest, and *of whom* thou hast heard *say,* Who can stand before the children of Ā'năk!

3 Understand therefore this day, that the LORD thy God *is* he which [d]goeth over before thee; *as* a [e]consuming fire he shall destroy them, and he shall bring them down before thy face: [f]so shalt thou drive them out, and destroy them quickly, as the LORD hath said unto thee.

4 [g]Speak not thou in thine heart, after that the LORD thy God hath cast them out from before thee, saying, For my righteousness the LORD hath brought me in to possess this land: but

[h]for the wickedness of these nations the LORD doth drive them out from before thee.

5 [i]Not for thy righteousness, or for the uprightness of thine heart, dost thou go to possess their land: but for the wickedness of these nations the LORD thy God doth drive them out from before thee, and that he may perform [j]the word which the LORD sware unto thy fathers, Ā′brā-hăm, Ī′saac, and Jā′cob.

6 Understand therefore, that the LORD thy God giveth thee not this good land to possess it for thy righteousness; for thou *art* a stiffnecked people.

7 ¶ Remember, *and* forget not, how thou provokedst the LORD thy God to wrath in the wilderness: [k]from the day that thou didst depart out of the land of Ē′ġypt, until ye came unto this place, ye have been rebellious against the LORD.

8 Also [l]in Hō′reb ye provoked the LORD to wrath, so that the LORD was angry with you to have destroyed you.

9 When I was gone up into the mount to receive the tables of stone, *even* the tables of the covenant which the LORD made with you, then [m]I abode in the mount forty days and forty nights, I neither did eat bread nor drink water:

10 And the LORD delivered unto me two tables of stone written with the finger of God; and on them *was written* according to all the words, which the LORD spake with you in the mount out of the midst of the fire in the day of the assembly.

11 And it came to pass at the end of forty days and forty nights, *that* the LORD gave me the two tables of stone, *even* the tables of the covenant.

12 And the LORD said unto me, [n]Arise, get thee down quickly from hence; for thy people which thou hast brought forth out of Ē′ġypt have corrupted *themselves;* they are [o]quickly turned aside out of the way which I commanded them; they have made them a molten image.

13 Furthermore [p]the LORD spake unto me, saying, I have seen this people, and, behold, [q]it *is* a stiffnecked people:

14 Let me alone, that I may destroy them, and [r]blot out their name from under heaven: and I will make of thee a nation mightier and greater than they.

15 So I turned and came down from the mount, and the mount burned with fire: and the two tables of the covenant *were* in my two hands.

16 And I looked, and, behold, ye had sinned against the LORD your God, *and* had made you a molten calf: ye had turned aside quickly out of the way which the LORD had commanded you.

17 And [s]I took the two tables, and cast them out of my two hands, and brake them before your eyes.

18 And I [t]fell down before the LORD, as at the first, forty days and forty nights: I did neither eat bread, nor drink water, because of all your sins which ye sinned, in doing wickedly in the sight of the LORD, to provoke him to anger.

19 [u]For I was afraid of the anger and hot displeasure, wherewith the LORD was wroth against you to destroy you. [v]But the LORD hearkened unto me at that time also.

20 And the LORD was very angry with Aâr′on to have destroyed him: and I prayed for Aâr′on also the same time.

21 And [w]I took your sin, the calf which ye had made, and burnt it with fire, and stamped it, *and* ground *it* very small, *even* until it was as small as dust: and I cast the dust thereof into the brook that descended out of the mount.

22 And at [x]Tăb′e-rah, and at Măs′sah, and at [y]Kĭb′roth–hat-tā′a-vah, ye provoked the LORD to wrath.

23 Likewise [z]when the LORD sent you from Kā′desh–bär′ne-ȧ, saying, Go up and possess the land which I have given you; then ye rebelled against the commandment of the LORD your God, and ye [a]believed him not, nor hearkened to his voice.

24 [b]Ye have been rebellious against the LORD from the day that I knew you.

25 Thus I fell down before the LORD forty days and forty nights, as I fell down *at the first;* because the LORD had said he would destroy you.

26 [c]I prayed therefore unto the LORD, and said, O Lord GOD, destroy not thy people and thine inheritance, which thou hast redeemed through thy greatness, which thou hast brought forth out of Ē′ġypt with a mighty hand.

27 Remember thy servants, Ā′brā-hăm, Ī′saac, and Jā′cob; look not unto the stubbornness of this people, nor to their wickedness, nor to their sin:

28 Lest [d]the land whence thou broughtest us out say, [e]Because the LORD was not able to bring them into the land which he promised them, and because he hated them, he hath brought them out to slay them in the wilderness.

29 [f]Yet they *are* thy people and thine inheritance, which thou broughtest out by thy mighty power and by thy stretched out arm.

10 At that time the LORD said unto me, [a]Hew thee two tables of stone like unto the first, and come up unto me into the mount, and [b]make thee an ark of wood.

2 And I will write on the tables the words that were in the first tables which thou brakest, and thou shalt put them in the ark.

3 And I made an ark *of* [c]shittim wood, and hewed two tables of stone like unto the first, and went up into the mount, having the two tables in mine hand.

4 And [d]he wrote on the tables, according to the first writing, the ten [1]commandments, [e]which the LORD spake unto you in the mount out of the midst of

[h]Gen. 15.16; Lev. 18.24; ch. 18.12
5 [i]2 Tim. 1.9; Tit. 3.5
[j]Gen. 12.7; Gen. 13.15; Gen. 15.7; Gen. 17.8; Gen. 26.4; Gen. 28.13; Ex. 32.13; Luke 1.54-55; Acts 13.32-33; Rom. 15.8
7 [k]Ex. 14.11; Num. 11.4
8 [l]Ex. 32.4; Ps. 106.19
9 [m]Ex. 24.18; Luke 4.1
12 [n]Ex. 32.7
[o]ch. 31.29; Judg. 2.17
13 [p]Ex. 32.9
[q]ch. 10.16; ch. 31.27; 2 Ki. 17.14
14 [r]ch. 29.20; Ps. 9.5; Ps. 109.13
17 [s]Ps. 69.9; Ps. 119.139
18 [t]Ex. 34.28; Ps. 106.23
19 [u]Ex. 32.10-11; Heb. 12.29
[v]Ex. 32.14; ch. 10.10; Ps. 106.23; Amos 7.1-6; Jas. 5.15
21 [w]Ex. 32.20; Isa. 2.18-21; Isa. 30.22; Isa. 31.7; Hos. 8.11
22 [x]Num. 11.1
[y]Num. 11.4
23 [z]Num. 13.3
[a]Ps. 78.22; Ps. 106.24; Heb. 3.18-19; Heb. 4.2
24 [b]ch. 31.27
26 [c]1 Sam. 7.9; Prov. 15.29; Jer. 15.1
28 [d]Gen. 41.57; 1 Sam. 14.25
[e]Num. 14.16; ch. 32.26-27; Isa. 48.9-11
29 [f]ch. 4.20; Ps. 95.7

CHAPTER 10
1 [a]Ex. 34.1-2
[b]Ex. 25.10
3 [c]Ex. 25.5
4 [d]Jer. 31.33
[1]words
[e]Ex. 20.1

the fire [f]in the day of the assembly: and
the LORD gave them unto me.
5 And I turned myself and [g]came
down from the mount, and [h]put the
tables in the ark which I had made;
[i]and there they be, as the LORD commanded me.
6 ¶ And the children of Ĭs'ra-el took
their journey from Be-ē'rŏth [j]of the children of Jā'a-kăn to Mo-sē'rȧ: [k]there
Aâr'on died, and there he was buried,
and Ē-le-ā'zar his son ministered in the
priest's office in his stead.
7 From thence they journeyed unto
Gŭd'go-dah; and from Gŭd'go-dah to
Jŏt'băth, a land of rivers of waters.
8 ¶ At that time the LORD separated
the tribe of Lē'vī, to bear the ark of the
covenant of the LORD, to stand before
the LORD to minister unto him, and [l]to
bless in his name, unto this day.
9 [m]Wherefore Lē'vī hath no part
nor inheritance with his brethren; the
LORD *is* his inheritance, according as
the LORD thy God promised him.
10 And I stayed in the mount, according to the [2]first time, forty days
and forty nights; and the LORD hearkened unto me at that time also, *and*
the LORD would not destroy thee.
11 And the LORD said unto me, Arise,
[3]take *thy* journey before the people,
that they may go in and possess the
land, which I sware unto their fathers
to give unto them.
12 ¶ And now, Ĭs'ra-el, [n]what doth
the LORD thy God require of thee, but
to fear the LORD thy God, to walk in all
his ways, and [o]to love him, and to
serve the LORD thy God with all thy
heart and with all thy soul,
13 To keep the commandments of
the LORD, and his statutes, which I command thee this day for thy good?
14 Behold, [p]the heaven and the
heaven of heavens *is* the LORD'S thy
God, [q]the earth *also*, with all that
therein *is*.
15 Only the LORD had a delight in
thy fathers to love them, and he chose
their seed after them, *even* you above
all people, as *it is* this day.
16 Circumcise therefore [r]the foreskin of your heart, and be no more
stiffnecked.
17 For the LORD your God *is* [s]God of
gods, and [t]Lord of lords, a great God,
a mighty, and a terrible, which [u]re-
gardeth not persons, nor taketh reward:
18 [v]He doth execute the judgment
of the fatherless and widow, and loveth the stranger, in giving him food
and raiment.
19 Love ye therefore the stranger:
for ye were strangers in the land of
Ē'gypt.
20 [w]Thou shalt fear the LORD thy
God; him shalt thou serve, and to him
shalt thou cleave, [x]and swear by his
name.
21 [y]He *is* thy praise, and he *is* thy
God, that hath done for thee these great
and terrible things, which thine eyes
have seen.
22 Thy fathers went down into Ē'gypt
with threescore and ten persons; and
now the LORD thy God hath made thee
as the stars of heaven for multitude.
11 Therefore thou shalt love the
LORD thy God, and [a]keep his
charge, and his statutes, and his judgments, and his commandments, alway.
2 And know ye this day: for *I speak*
not with your children which have not
known, and which have not seen the
chastisement of the LORD your God,
his greatness, his mighty hand, and his
stretched out arm,
3 And his miracles, and his acts,
which he did in the midst of Ē'gypt
unto Phā'raōh the king of Ē'gypt, and
unto all his land;
4 And what he did unto the army of
Ē'gypt, unto their horses, and to their
chariots; how he made the water of the
Red sea to overflow them as they pursued after you, and *how* the LORD hath
destroyed them unto this day;
5 And what he did unto you in the
wilderness, until ye came into this
place;
6 And [b]what he did unto Dā'than
and A-bī'răm, the sons of E-lī'ab, the
son of Reu'ben: how the earth opened
her mouth, and swallowed them up,
and their households, and their tents,
and all the [1]substance that [2]*was* in
their possession, in the midst of all
Ĭs'ra-el:
7 But your eyes have seen all the
great acts of the LORD which he did.
8 Therefore shall ye keep all the
commandments which I command you
this day, that ye may [c]be strong, and
go in and possess the land, whither ye
go to possess it;
9 And [d]that ye may prolong *your*
days in the land, which the LORD sware
unto your fathers to give unto them and
to their seed, [e]a land that floweth with
milk and honey.
10 ¶ For the land, whither thou goest
in to possess it, *is* not as the land
of Ē'gypt, from whence ye came out,
[f]where thou sowedst thy seed, and wa-
teredst *it* with thy foot, as a garden of
herbs:
11 [g]But the land, whither ye go to
possess it, *is* a land of hills and valleys, *and* drinketh water of the rain of
heaven:
12 A land which the LORD thy God
[3]careth for: [h]the eyes of the LORD thy
God *are* always upon it, from the beginning of the year even unto the end of
the year.
13 ¶ And it shall come to pass, if ye
shall hearken [i]diligently unto my commandments which I command you this
day, [j]to love the LORD your God, and
to serve him with all your heart and
with all your soul,
14 That [k]I will give *you* the rain of
your land in his due season, [l]the first
rain and the latter rain, that thou mayest gather in thy corn, and thy wine,
and thine oil.

[f]ch. 9.10; ch. 18.16
5 [g]Ex. 34.29 [h]Ex. 40.20 [i]1 Ki. 8.9
6 [j]Num. 33.31 [k]Num. 20.28
8 [l]Lev. 9.22; Num. 6.23; ch. 21.5
9 [m]Num. 18.20-24; ch. 18.1-2; Ezek. 44.28
10 [2]Or, former days
11 [3]go in journey
12 [n]Mic. 6.8 [o]Matt. 22.37; 1 Tim. 1.5
14 [p]1 Ki. 8.27; Ps. 115.16 [q]Gen. 14.19; Ps. 24.1
16 [r]Lev. 26.41; Rom. 2.28; Eph. 4.22; Col. 2.11
17 [s]Ps. 136.2; Dan. 2.47 [t]Rev. 17.14 [u]2 Chr. 19.7; Acts 10.34; Rom. 2.11; Gal. 2.6; Eph. 6.9; Col. 3.25; 1 Pet. 1.17
18 [v]Ps. 68.5; Ps. 146.9
20 [w]Matt. 4.10 [x]Ps. 63.11
21 [y]Ps. 22.3
CHAPTER 11
1 [a]Zech. 3.7
6 [b]Num. 16.1; Ps. 106.17 [1]Or, living substance which followed them [2]was at their feet
8 [c]Josh. 1.6-7
9 [d]ch. 4.40; ch. 5.16; Prov. 3.1-26; Prov. 10.27 [e]Ex. 3.8
10 [f]Zech. 14.18
11 [g]ch. 8.7
12 [3]seeketh [h]1 Ki. 9.3
13 [i]ch. 6.17 [j]2 Thess. 3.5
14 [k]Lev. 26.4; ch. 28.12 [l]Joel 2.23; Jas. 5.7

15 And [m]I will [4]send grass in thy fields for thy cattle, that thou mayest [n]eat and be full.

16 Take heed to yourselves, [o]that your heart be not deceived, and ye turn aside, and serve other gods, and worship them;

17 And *then* [p]the LORD'S wrath be kindled against you, and he [q]shut up the heaven, that there be no rain, and that the land yield not her fruit; and *lest* ye perish quickly from off the good land which the LORD giveth you.

18 ¶ Therefore shall ye lay up these my words in your heart and in your soul, and bind them for a sign upon your hand, that they may be as frontlets between your eyes.

19 [r]And ye shall teach them your children, speaking of them when thou sittest in thine house, and when thou walkest by the way, when thou liest down, and when thou risest up.

20 [s]And thou shalt write them upon the door posts of thine house, and upon thy gates:

21 That [t]your days may be multiplied, and the days of your children, in the land which the LORD sware unto your fathers to give them, [u]as the days of heaven upon the earth.

22 ¶ For if [v]ye shall diligently keep all these commandments which I command you, to do them, to love the LORD your God, to walk in all his ways, and to cleave unto him;

23 Then will the LORD [w]drive out all these nations from before you, and ye shall [x]possess greater nations and mightier than yourselves.

24 [y]Every place whereon the soles of your feet shall tread shall be yours: [z]from the wilderness and Lĕb'a-non, from the river, the river Eū-phrā'tēs, even unto the uttermost sea shall your coast be.

25 [a]There shall no man be able to stand before you: *for* the LORD your God shall lay the fear of you and the dread of you upon all the land that ye shall tread upon, [b]as he hath said unto you.

26 ¶ [c]Behold, I set before you this day a blessing and a curse;

27 A [d]blessing, if ye obey the commandments of the LORD your God, which I command you this day:

28 And a [e]curse, if ye will not obey the commandments of the LORD your God, but turn aside out of the way which I command you this day, to go after other gods, which ye have not known.

29 And it shall come to pass, when the LORD thy God hath brought thee in unto the land whither thou goest to possess it, that thou shalt put [f]the blessing upon mount Gĕr'ĭ-zĭm, and the curse upon mount Ē'bal.

30 *Are* they not on the other side Jôr'dan, by the way where the sun goeth down, in the land of the Cā'năan-ītes, which dwell in the champaign over against Gĭl'găl, beside the plains of Mō'reh?

31 For ye shall pass over Jôr'dan to go in to possess the land which the LORD your God giveth you, and ye shall possess it, and dwell therein.

32 And ye shall observe to do all the statutes and judgments which I set before you this day.

12 These *are* the statutes and judgments, which ye shall observe to do in the land, which the LORD God of thy fathers giveth thee to possess it, [a]all the days that ye live upon the earth.

2 [b]Ye shall utterly destroy all the places, wherein the nations which ye shall [1]possess served their gods, [c]upon the high mountains, and upon the hills, and under every green tree:

3 And [d]ye shall [2]overthrow their altars, and break their pillars, and burn their groves with fire; and ye shall hew down the graven images of their gods, and destroy the [e]names of them out of that place.

4 Ye shall not do so unto the LORD your God.

5 But unto the place which the LORD your God shall [f]choose out of all your tribes to put his name there, *even* unto his habitation shall ye seek, and thither thou shalt come:

6 And [g]thither ye shall bring your burnt offerings, and your sacrifices, and your [h]tithes, and heave offerings of your hand, and your vows, and your freewill offerings, and the firstlings of your herds and of your flocks:

7 And [i]there ye shall eat before the LORD your God, and [j]ye shall rejoice in all that ye put your hand unto, ye and your households, wherein the LORD thy God hath blessed thee.

8 Ye shall not do after all *the things* that we do here this day, every man whatsoever *is* right in his own eyes.

9 For ye are not as yet come to the rest and to the inheritance, which the LORD your God giveth you.

10 But *when* ye go over Jôr'dan, and dwell in the land which the LORD your God giveth you to inherit, and *when* he giveth you rest from all your enemies round about, so that ye dwell in safety;

11 Then there shall be [k]a place which the LORD your God shall choose to cause his name to dwell there; thither shall ye bring all that I command you; your burnt offerings, and your sacrifices, your tithes, and the heave offering of your hand, and all [3]your choice vows which ye vow unto the LORD:

12 And ye shall rejoice before the LORD your God, ye, and your sons, and your daughters, and your menservants, and your maidservants, and the Lē'vīte that *is* within your gates; forasmuch as [l]he hath no part nor inheritance with you.

13 [m]Take heed to thyself that thou offer not thy burnt offerings in every place that thou seest:

14 But in the place which the LORD shall choose in one of thy tribes, there thou shalt offer thy burnt offerings,

15 [m]Ps. 104.14
[4]give
[n]Joel 2.19
16 [o]Job 31.27
17 [p]ch. 6.15
[q]1 Ki. 8.35; 2 Chr. 6.26; 2 Chr. 7.13
19 [r]Prov. 22.6
20 [s]Hab. 2.2
21 [t]Prov. 3.2; Prov. 4.10; Prov. 9.11
[u]Ps. 72.5; Ps. 89.29
22 [v]ch. 6.17
23 [w]ch. 4.38
[x]ch. 9.1
24 [y]Josh. 1.3; Josh. 14.9
[z]Gen. 15.18; Num. 34.3
25 [a]ch. 7.24
[b]Ex. 23.27
26 [c]ch. 30.1
27 [d]ch. 28.2
28 [e]ch. 28.15
29 [f]ch. 27.12

CHAPTER 12
1 [a]ch. 4.10; 1 Ki. 8.40; Gal. 6.9
2 [b]Ex. 34.13
[1]Or, inherit
[c]2 Ki. 16.4; 2 Ki. 17.10-11; Jer. 3.6
3 [d]Num. 33.52; Judg. 2.2
[2]break down
[e]Ps. 16.4; Zech. 13.2
5 [f]ch. 26.2; 1 Ki. 8.29; 2 Chr. 7.12; Ps. 78.68
6 [g]Lev. 17.3
[h]ch. 14.22
7 [i]ch. 14.26
[j]Lev. 23.40; Eccl. 3.12; Eccl. 5.18
11 [k]ch. 14.23; ch. 15.20; ch. 16.2; ch. 17.8; ch. 18.6; ch. 26.2; ch. 31.11; Josh. 18.1; 1 Ki. 8.29; Ps. 78.68; Ps. 87.2
[3]the choice of your vows
12 [l]ch. 10.9; ch. 14.29
13 [m]Lev. 17.4

and there thou shalt do all that I command thee.

15 Notwithstanding thou mayest kill and eat flesh in all thy gates, whatsoever [n]thy soul lusteth after, according to the blessing of the LORD thy God which he hath given thee: the unclean and the clean may eat thereof, [o]as of the roebuck, and as of the hart.

16 [p]Only ye shall not eat the blood; ye shall pour it upon the earth as water.

17 ¶ Thou mayest not eat within thy gates the tithe of thy corn, or of thy wine, or of thy oil, or the firstlings of thy herds or of thy flock, nor any of thy vows which thou vowest, nor thy freewill offerings, or heave offering of thine hand:

18 [q]But thou must eat them before the LORD thy God in the place which the LORD thy God shall choose, thou, and thy son, and thy daughter, and thy manservant, and thy maidservant, and the Lē′vīte that *is* within thy gates: and thou shalt [r]rejoice before the LORD thy God in all that thou puttest thine hands unto.

19 [s]Take heed to thyself that thou forsake not the Lē′vīte [4]as long as thou livest upon the earth.

20 ¶ When the LORD thy God shall enlarge thy border, [t]as he hath promised thee, and thou shalt say, I will eat flesh, because thy soul longeth to eat flesh; thou mayest eat flesh, whatsoever thy soul lusteth after.

21 If the place which the LORD thy God hath chosen to put his name there be too far from thee, then thou shalt kill of thy herd and of thy flock, which the LORD hath given thee, as I have commanded thee, and thou shalt eat in thy gates whatsoever thy soul lusteth after.

22 Even as the roebuck and the hart is eaten, so thou shalt eat them: the unclean and the clean shall eat *of* them alike.

23 Only [5]be sure that thou eat not the blood: [u]for the blood *is* the life; and thou mayest not eat the life with the flesh.

24 Thou shalt not eat it; thou shalt pour it upon the earth as water.

25 Thou shalt not eat it; [v]that it may go well with thee, and with thy children after thee, [w]when thou shalt do *that which is* right in the sight of the LORD.

26 Only thy [x]holy things which thou hast, and [y]thy vows, thou shalt take, and go unto the place which the LORD shall choose:

27 And [z]thou shalt offer thy burnt offerings, the flesh and the blood, upon the altar of the LORD thy God: and the blood of thy sacrifices shall be poured out upon the altar of the LORD thy God, and thou shalt eat the flesh.

28 Observe and hear all these words which I command thee, [a]that it may go well with thee, and with thy children after thee for ever, when thou doest *that which is* good and right in the sight of the LORD thy God.

29 ¶ When [b]the LORD thy God shall cut off the nations from before thee, whither thou goest to possess them, and thou [6]succeedest them, and dwellest in their land;

30 Take heed to thyself that thou be not snared [7]by following them, after that they be destroyed from before thee; and that thou inquire not after their gods, saying, How did these nations serve their gods? even so will I do likewise.

31 [c]Thou shalt not do so unto the LORD thy God: for every [8]abomination to the LORD, which he hateth, have they done unto their gods; for [d]even their sons and their daughters they have burnt in the fire to their gods.

32 What thing soever I command you, observe to do it: [e]thou shalt not add thereto, nor diminish from it.

13 If there arise among you a prophet, or a dreamer of dreams, and [a]giveth thee a sign or a wonder,

2 And [b]the sign or the wonder come to pass, whereof he spake unto thee, saying, Let us go after other gods, which thou hast not known, and let us serve them;

3 Thou shalt not hearken unto the words of that prophet, or that dreamer of dreams: for the LORD your God [c]proveth you, to know whether ye love the LORD your God with all your heart and with all your soul.

4 Ye shall [d]walk after the LORD your God, and fear him, and keep his commandments, and obey his voice, and ye shall serve him, and cleave unto him.

5 And [e]that prophet, or that dreamer of dreams, shall [f]be put to death; because he hath [1]spoken to turn *you* away from the LORD your God, which brought you out of the land of Ē′gypt, and redeemed you out of the house of bondage, to thrust thee out of the way which the LORD thy God commanded thee to walk in. [g]So shalt thou put the evil away from the midst of thee.

6 ¶ If thy brother, the son of thy mother, or thy son, or thy daughter, or [h]the wife of thy bosom, or thy friend, which *is* as thine own soul, entice thee secretly, saying, Let us go and serve other gods, which thou hast not known, thou, nor thy fathers;

7 *Namely*, of the gods of the people which *are* round about you, nigh unto thee, or far off from thee, from the *one* end of the earth even unto the *other* end of the earth;

8 Thou shalt [i]not consent unto him, nor hearken unto him; neither shall thine eye pity him, neither shalt thou spare, neither shalt thou conceal him:

9 But thou shalt surely kill him; [j]thine hand shall be first upon him to put him to death, and afterwards the hand of all the people.

10 And thou shalt stone him with stones, that he die; because he hath sought to thrust thee away from the LORD thy God, which brought thee out

15 [n]Gen. 9.4
[o]ch. 14.5; ch. 15.22
16 [p]Gen. 9.4; Acts 15.20-29
18 [q]ch. 14.23
[r]Eccl. 3.12-13; Eccl. 5.18-20
19 [s]ch. 14.27
[4]all thy days
20 [t]Gen. 15.18; ch. 19.8
23 [5]be strong
[u]Gen. 9.4; Lev. 17.11-14
25 [v]ch. 4.40; Isa. 3.10
[w]ch. 13.18; 1 Ki. 11.38
26 [x]Num. 5.9-10
[y]1 Sam. 21.22-24
27 [z]Lev. 1.5-9-13; Lev. 17.11
28 [a]Ps. 25.12-13; Eccl. 8.12
29 [b]Ex. 23.23; Ps. 78.55
[6]inheritest, or, possessest them
30 [7]after them
31 [c]Lev. 18.3-26-30; 2 Chr. 33.2
[8]abomination of the
[d]Jer. 32.35
32 [e]Josh. 1.7; Rev. 22.18

CHAPTER 13

1 [a]2 Thess. 2.9
2 [b]Jer. 28.9; Matt. 7.22
3 [c]Matt. 24.24; 2 Thess. 2.11
4 [d]2 Ki. 23.3; 1 John 1.7
5 [e]1 Ki. 18.40; Rev. 19.20
[f]1 Ki. 18.40; 2 Ki. 10.18-28
[1]spoken revolt against the LORD
[g]1 Cor. 5.13
6 [h]Job 2.9
8 [i]Prov. 1.10
9 [j]ch. 17.7

of the land of Ē′ġypt, from the house of
[2]bondage.
11 And [k]all Ĭs′ra-el shall hear, and
fear, and shall do no more any such
wickedness as this is among you.
12 ¶ [l]If thou shalt hear *say* in one of
thy cities, which the LORD thy God
hath given thee to dwell there, saying,
13 *Certain* men, [3]the children of Bē′-
lĭ-al, [m]are gone out from among you,
and have [n]withdrawn the inhabitants
of their city, saying, Let us go and
serve other gods, which ye have not
known;
14 Then shalt thou inquire, and
make search, and ask diligently; and,
behold, *if it be* truth, *and* the thing certain, *that* such abomination is wrought
among you;
15 Thou shalt surely smite the inhabitants of that city with the edge of the
sword, [o]destroying it utterly, and all
that *is* therein, and the cattle thereof,
with the edge of the sword.
16 And thou shalt gather all the spoil
of it into the midst of the street thereof,
and shalt burn with fire the city, and all
the spoil thereof every whit, for the
LORD thy God: and it shall be [p]an heap
for ever; it shall not be built again.
17 And [q]there shall cleave nought of
the [4]cursed thing to thine hand: that the
LORD may [r]turn from the fierceness of
his anger, and shew thee mercy, and
have compassion upon thee, and multiply thee, [s]as he hath sworn unto thy
fathers;
18 When thou shalt hearken to the
voice of the LORD thy God, [t]to keep all
his commandments which I command
thee this day, to do *that which is* right
in the eyes of the LORD thy God.

14 Ye *are* [a]the children of the LORD
your God: [b]ye shall not cut yourselves, nor make any baldness between your eyes for the dead.
2 [c]For thou *art* an holy people unto
the LORD thy God, and the LORD hath
chosen thee to be a peculiar people
unto himself, above all the nations that
are upon the earth.
3 ¶ [d]Thou shalt not eat any abominable thing.
4 [e]These *are* the beasts which ye
shall eat: the ox, the sheep, and the
goat,
5 The hart, and the roebuck, and the
fallow deer, and the wild goat, and the
[1]pygarg, and the wild ox, and the cham-
ois.
6 And every beast that parteth the
hoof, and cleaveth the cleft into two
claws, *and* cheweth the cud among the
beasts, that ye shall eat.
7 Nevertheless these ye shall not eat
of them that chew the cud, or of them
that divide the cloven hoof; *as* the camel, and the hare, and the coney: for
they chew the cud, but divide not the
hoof; *therefore* they *are* unclean unto
you.
8 And the swine, because it divideth
the hoof, yet cheweth not the cud, it *is*
unclean unto you: ye shall not eat of
their flesh, nor touch their dead carcase.
9 ¶ These ye shall eat of all that *are*
in the waters: all that have fins and
scales shall ye eat:
10 And whatsoever hath not fins and
scales ye may not eat; it *is* unclean unto
you.
11 ¶ *Of* all clean birds ye shall eat.
12 [f]But these *are they* of which ye
shall not eat: the eagle, and the ossi-
frage, and the ospray,
13 And the glede, and the kite, and
the vulture after his kind,
14 And every raven after his kind,
15 And the owl, and the night hawk,
and the cuckow, and the hawk after
his kind,
16 The little owl, and the great owl,
and the swan,
17 And the pelican, and the gier eagle, and the cormorant,
18 And the stork, and the heron after her kind, and the lapwing, and the
bat.
19 And every creeping thing that flieth *is* unclean unto you: they shall not
be eaten.
20 *But of* all clean fowls ye may eat.
21 ¶ [g]Ye shall not eat *of* any thing
that dieth of itself: thou shalt give it
unto the stranger that *is* in thy gates,
that he may eat it; or thou mayest sell it
unto an alien: for thou *art* an holy people unto the LORD thy God. [h]Thou shalt
not seethe a kid in his mother's milk.
22 [i]Thou shalt truly tithe all the increase of thy seed, that the field bringeth forth year by year.
23 And thou shalt eat before the
LORD thy God, in the place which he
shall choose to place his name there,
the tithe of thy corn, of thy wine, and of
thine oil, and the firstlings of thy herds
and of thy flocks; that thou [j]mayest
learn to fear the LORD thy God always.
24 And if the way be too long for
thee, so that thou art not able to carry
it; *or* [k]if the place be too far from thee,
which the LORD thy God shall choose
to set his name there, when the LORD
thy God hath blessed thee:
25 Then shalt thou turn *it* into money,
and bind up the money in thine hand,
and shalt go unto the place which the
LORD thy God shall choose:
26 And thou shalt bestow that money
for whatsoever thy soul lusteth after, for
oxen, or for sheep, or for wine, or for
strong drink, or for whatsoever thy soul
[2]desireth: and thou shalt eat there before the LORD thy God, and thou shalt
rejoice, thou, and thine household,
27 And [l]the Lē′vīte that *is* within
thy gates; thou shalt not forsake him;
for [m]he hath no part nor inheritance
with thee.
28 ¶ [n]At the end of three years thou
shalt bring forth all the tithe of thine
increase the same year, and shalt lay *it*
up within thy gates:
29 And the Lē′vīte, (because he hath
no part nor inheritance with thee,) and
[o]the stranger, and the fatherless, and
the widow, which *are* within thy gates,

10 [2]bondmen
11 [k]ch. 19.20
12 [l]Josh. 22.11
13 [3]Or, naughty men
[m]1 John 2.19
[n]2 Ki. 17.21
15 [o]Josh. 6.17
16 [p]Isa. 17.1; Isa. 25.2
17 [q]ch. 7.26
[4]Or, devoted
[r]Josh. 7.26
[s]Gen. 22.17; Gen. 26.4-24; Gen. 28.14
18 [t]ch. 12.25

CHAPTER 14

1 [a]Gen. 6.2-4; Ps. 82.6-7; Jer. 3.19; Hos. 1.10; Rom. 8.16; Gal. 3.26; 1 John 3.1
[b]Lev. 19.28; Lev. 21.5; Jer. 16.6; 1 Thess. 4.13
2 [c]Lev. 11.45; Lev. 19.2; Lev. 20.26; Isa. 62.12; Dan. 8.24; Rom. 12.1; 1 Pet. 2.9
3 [d]Isa. 65.4; Ezek. 4.14; Acts 10.13; Rom. 14.14
4 [e]Lev. 11.2
5 [1]dishon, or, bison
12 [f]Lev. 11.13
21 [g]Ex. 22.31; Lev. 17.15; Lev. 22.8; Ezek. 4.14
[h]Ex. 23.19
22 [i]Lev. 27.30; ch. 12.6-17; Neh. 10.37
23 [j]Ps. 2.11; Ps. 5.7; Ps. 111.10; Ps. 147.11; Prov. 3.13; Isa. 8.13; Jer. 32.38-41; Heb. 12.28
24 [k]ch. 12.21
26 [2]asketh of thee
27 [l]Rom. 13.4; Rom. 15.27; 1 Cor. 9.1-14
[m]Num. 18.20; ch. 18.1-2
28 [n]Amos 4.4
29 [o]ch. 10.18; Heb. 13.2

shall come, and shall eat and be satisfied; that the [p]LORD thy God may bless
thee in all the work of thine hand which
thou doest.

15 At the end of [a]*every* seven years
thou shalt make a release.
2 And this *is* the manner of the
release: Every [1]creditor that lendeth
ought unto his neighbour shall release
it; he shall not exact *it* of his neighbour,
or of his brother; because it is called the
LORD'S release.
3 [b]Of a foreigner thou mayest exact
it again: but *that* which is thine with
thy brother thine hand shall release;
4 [2]Save when there shall be no poor
among you; [c]for the LORD shall greatly
bless thee in the land which the LORD
thy God giveth thee *for* an inheritance
to possess it:
5 Only if thou carefully hearken unto
the voice of the LORD thy God, to observe to do all these commandments
which I command thee this day.
6 For the LORD thy God blesseth
thee, as he promised thee: and thou
shalt lend unto many nations, but thou
shalt not borrow; and [d]thou shalt reign
over many nations, but they shall not
reign over thee.
7 ¶ If there be among you a poor
man of one of thy brethren within any
of thy gates in thy land which the
LORD thy God giveth thee, thou [e]shalt
not harden thine heart, nor shut thine
hand from thy poor brother:
8 [f]But thou shalt open thine hand
wide unto him, and shalt surely lend
him sufficient for his need, *in that*
which he wanteth.
9 Beware that there be not a [3]thought
in thy [4]wicked heart, saying, The seventh year, the year of release, is at
hand; and thine [g]eye be evil against
thy poor brother, and thou givest him
nought; and [h]he cry unto the LORD
against thee, and [i]it be sin unto thee.
10 Thou shalt surely give him, and
[j]thine heart shall not be grieved when
thou givest unto him: because that [k]for
this thing the LORD thy God shall bless
thee in all thy works, and in all that
thou puttest thine hand unto.
11 For the poor shall never cease
out of the land: therefore I command
thee, saying, Thou shalt open thine
hand wide unto thy brother, to thy
poor, and to thy needy, in thy land.
12 ¶ *And* [l]if thy brother, an Hē'brew
man, or an Hē'brew woman, be sold
unto thee, and serve thee six years;
then in the seventh year thou shalt let
him go free from thee.
13 And when thou sendest him out
free from thee, thou shalt not let him
go away empty:
14 Thou shalt furnish him liberally
out of thy flock, and out of thy floor,
and out of thy winepress: *of that* wherewith the LORD thy God hath [m]blessed
thee thou shalt give unto him.
15 And thou shalt remember that
thou wast a bondman in the land of
Ē'gypt, and the LORD thy God re-

[p]ch. 15.10; 2 Cor. 9.6-11

CHAPTER 15

1 [a]Ex. 23.10; Jer. 34.14

2 [1]master of the lending of his hand

3 [b]ch. 23.20

4 [2]Or, to the end that there be no poor among you

[c]ch. 28.8

6 [d]Prov. 22.7

7 [e]Matt. 18.30; 1 John 3.17

8 [f]Lev. 25.35; Gal. 2.10

9 [3]word [4]Belial

[g]ch. 28.54; Matt. 20.15

[h]ch. 24.15; Jas. 5.4

[i]Matt. 25.41

10 [j]Matt. 25.40; 1 Pet. 4.11

[k]ch. 14.29; Prov. 29.7

12 [l]Ex. 21.2; Jer. 34.14

14 [m]Prov. 10.22

16 [n]Ex. 21.5-6

18 [o]Isa. 16.14; Isa. 21.16

19 [p]Ex. 13.2

20 [q]ch. 12.5; ch. 16.11

21 [r]Lev. 22.20; ch. 17.1

22 [s]ch. 12.15-22

23 [t]Gen. 9.4; ch. 12.16

CHAPTER 16

1 [a]Ex. 12.2; John 18.28

[b]1 Cor. 5.7-8; Heb. 11.28

2 [c]Ex. 12.5-7;

3 [d]Ex. 12.15-19-39

4 [e]Ex. 12.10

5 [1]Or, kill

6 [f]Matt. 27.46

7 [g]Ex. 12.8;

[h]2 Ki. 23.23;

deemed thee: therefore I command
thee this thing to day.
16 And it shall be, [n]if he say unto
thee, I will not go away from thee; because he loveth thee and thine house,
because he is well with thee;
17 Then thou shalt take an aul, and
thrust *it* through his ear unto the door,
and he shall be thy servant for ever.
And also unto thy maidservant thou
shalt do likewise.
18 It shall not seem hard unto thee,
when thou sendest him away free from
thee; for he hath been worth [o]a double
hired servant *to thee,* in serving thee
six years: and the LORD thy God shall
bless thee in all that thou doest.
19 ¶ [p]All the firstling males that
come of thy herd and of thy flock thou
shalt sanctify unto the LORD thy God:
thou shalt do no work with the firstling
of thy bullock, nor shear the firstling
of thy sheep.
20 [q]Thou shalt eat *it* before the LORD
thy God year by year in the place which
the LORD shall choose, thou and thy
household.
21 And [r]if there be *any* blemish
therein, *as if it be* lame, or blind, *or*
have any ill blemish, thou shalt not sacrifice it unto the LORD thy God.
22 Thou shalt eat it within thy gates:
the [s]unclean and the clean *person shall*
eat it alike, as the roebuck, and as the
hart.
23 Only thou shalt not eat [t]the blood
thereof; thou shalt pour it upon the
ground as water.

16 Observe the [a]month of Ā'bīb,
and keep the [b]passover unto the
LORD thy God: for in the month of
Ā'bīb the LORD thy God brought thee
forth out of Ē'gypt by night.
2 Thou shalt therefore sacrifice the
passover unto the LORD thy God, of
the flock and [c]the herd, in the place
which the LORD shall choose to place
his name there.
3 [d]Thou shalt eat no leavened bread
with it; seven days shalt thou eat unleavened bread therewith, *even* the
bread of affliction; for thou camest
forth out of the land of Ē'gypt in haste:
that thou mayest remember the day
when thou camest forth out of the land
of Ē'gypt all the days of thy life.
4 And there shall be no leavened
bread seen with thee in all thy coast
seven days; [e]neither shall there *any*
thing of the flesh, which thou sacri-
ficedst the first day at even, remain all
night until the morning.
5 Thou mayest not [1]sacrifice the
passover within any of thy gates, which
the LORD thy God giveth thee:
6 But at the place which the LORD
thy God shall choose to place his name
in, there thou shalt sacrifice the passover [f]at even, at the going down of the
sun, at the season that thou camest
forth out of Ē'gypt.
7 And thou shalt [g]roast and eat *it*
[h]in the place which the LORD thy God
shall choose: and thou shalt turn in the
morning, and go unto thy tents.

8 Six days thou shalt eat unleavened bread: and [i]on the seventh day *shall be* a [2]solemn assembly to the LORD thy God: thou shalt do no work *therein.*

9 ¶ [j]Seven weeks shalt thou number unto thee: begin to number the seven weeks from *such time as* thou beginnest *to put* the sickle to the corn.

10 And thou shalt keep the feast of weeks unto the LORD thy God with [3]a tribute of a freewill offering of thine hand, which thou shalt give *unto the LORD thy God,* [k]according as the LORD thy God hath blessed thee:

11 And thou shalt rejoice before the LORD thy God, thou, and thy son, and thy daughter, and thy manservant, and thy maidservant, and the Lē′vīte that *is* within thy gates, and [l]the stranger, and the fatherless, and the widow, that *are* among you, in the place which the LORD thy God hath chosen to place his name there.

12 And [m]thou shalt remember that thou wast a bondman in Ē′gypt: and thou shalt observe and do these statutes.

13 ¶ [n]Thou shalt observe the feast of tabernacles seven days, after that thou hast gathered in thy [4]corn and thy wine:

14 And [o]thou shalt rejoice in thy feast, thou, and thy son, and thy daughter, and thy manservant, and thy maidservant, and the Lē′vīte, the stranger, and the fatherless, and the widow, that *are* within thy gates.

15 Seven days shalt thou keep a solemn feast unto the LORD thy God in the place which the LORD shall choose: because the LORD thy God shall bless thee in all thine increase, and in all the works of thine hands, therefore thou shalt surely rejoice.

16 ¶ Three times in a year shall all thy males appear before the LORD thy God in the place which he shall choose; in the feast of unleavened bread, and in the feast of weeks, and in the feast of tabernacles: and they shall not appear before the LORD empty:

17 Every man *shall give* [5]as he is able, according to the blessing of the LORD thy God which he hath given thee.

18 ¶ Judges and officers shalt thou make thee in all thy gates, which the LORD thy God giveth thee, throughout thy tribes: and they shall judge the people with just judgment.

19 [p]Thou shalt not wrest judgment; [q]thou shalt not respect persons, [r]neither take a gift: for a gift doth blind the eyes of the wise, and pervert the [6]words of the righteous.

20 [7]That which is altogether just shalt thou follow, that thou mayest [s]live, and inherit the land which the LORD thy God giveth thee.

21 ¶ [t]Thou shalt not plant thee a grove of any trees near unto the altar of the LORD thy God, which thou shalt make thee.

22 Neither shalt thou set thee up *any* [8]image; which the LORD thy God hateth.

8 [i]Ex. 12.16; Lev. 23.8 [2]restraint
9 [j]Ex. 23.16; Lev. 23.15; Num. 28.26; Acts 2.1
10 [3]Or, sufficiency [k]Prov. 10.22; Joel 2.14; 1 Cor. 16.2
11 [l]Luke 14.12
12 [m]Gen. 15.13; ch. 15.15; ch. 25.6; Ps. 105.23-25
13 [n]Lev. 23.34; Num. 29.12 [4]floor, and thy winepress
14 [o]ch. 26.11; Isa. 30.29
17 [5]according to the gift of his hand
19 [p]Ex. 23.2; Isa. 1.17-23 [q]Prov. 24.23; Acts 10.34 [r]Ex. 23.8; Eccl. 7.7 [6]Or, matters
20 [7]Justice, justice [s]ch. 4.1; Ezek. 18.5
21 [t]Ex. 34.13; 2 Chr. 33.3
22 [8]Or, statue, or, pillar

CHAPTER 17
1 [1]Or, goat
3 [a]Job 31.26 [b]Jer. 7.22
5 [c]Lev. 24.14; Josh. 7.25
6 [d]Num. 35.30; Heb. 10.28
8 [e]2 Chr. 19.10; Mal. 2.7 [f]Ex. 21.13; Num. 35.11 [g]ch. 12.5; Ps. 122.5
9 [h]Jer. 18.18 [i]ch. 19.17 [j]Judg. 4.5; 1 Ki. 3.16
12 [k]Num. 15.30; Hos. 4.4 [2]not to hearken [l]ch. 18.5

17 Thou shalt not sacrifice unto the LORD thy God *any* bullock, or [1]sheep, wherein is blemish, *or* any evilfavouredness: for that *is* an abomination unto the LORD thy God.

2 ¶ If there be found among you, within any of thy gates which the LORD thy God giveth thee, man or woman, that hath wrought wickedness in the sight of the LORD thy God, in transgressing his covenant,

3 And hath gone and served other gods, and worshipped them, either the [a]sun, or moon, or any of the host of heaven, [b]which I have not commanded;

4 And it be told thee, and thou hast heard *of it,* and inquired diligently, and, behold, *it be* true, *and* the thing certain, *that* such abomination is wrought in Is′ra-el:

5 Then shalt thou bring forth that man or that woman, which have committed that wicked thing, unto thy gates, *even* that man or that woman, and [c]shalt stone them with stones, till they die.

6 [d]At the mouth of two witnesses, or three witnesses, shall he that is worthy of death be put to death; *but* at the mouth of one witness he shall not be put to death.

7 The hands of the witnesses shall be first upon him to put him to death, and afterward the hands of all the people. So thou shalt put the evil away from among you.

8 ¶ [e]If there arise a matter too hard for thee in judgment, [f]between blood and blood, between plea and plea, and between stroke and stroke, *being* matters of controversy within thy gates: then shalt thou arise, [g]and get thee up into the place which the LORD thy God shall choose;

9 And [h]thou shalt come unto the priests the Lē′vītes, and [i]unto the judge that shall be in those days, and inquire; [j]and they shall shew thee the sentence of judgment:

10 And thou shalt do according to the sentence, which they of that place which the LORD shall choose shall shew thee; and thou shalt observe to do according to all that they inform thee:

11 According to the sentence of the law which they shall teach thee, and according to the judgment which they shall tell thee, thou shalt do: thou shalt not decline from the sentence which they shall shew thee, *to* the right hand, nor *to* the left.

12 And [k]the man that will do presumptuously, [2]and will not hearken unto the priest [l]that standeth to minister there before the LORD thy God, or unto the judge, even that man shall die: and thou shalt put away the evil from Is′ra-el.

13 And all the people shall hear, and fear, and do no more presumptuously.

14 ¶ When thou art come unto the land which the LORD thy God giveth thee, and shalt possess it, and shalt

dwell therein, and shalt say, [m]I will set
a king over me, like [n]as all the nations
that *are* about me;
15 Thou shalt in any wise set *him*
king over thee, whom the LORD thy
God shall choose: *one* [o]from among
thy brethren shalt thou set king over
thee: thou mayest not set a stranger
over thee, which *is* not thy brother.
16 But he shall not multiply horses
[p]to himself, nor cause the people [q]to
return to Ē′ġypt, to the end that he
should multiply horses: forasmuch as
[r]the LORD hath said unto you, [s]Ye
shall henceforth return no more that
way.
17 Neither shall he multiply wives
to himself, that [t]his heart turn not
away: neither shall he greatly [u]multi-
ply to himself silver and gold.
18 And [v]it shall be, when he sitteth
upon the throne of his kingdom, that
he shall write him a copy of this law in
a book out of *that* [w]*which is* before the
priests the Lē′vītes:
19 And [x]it shall be with him, and he
shall read therein all the days of his
life: that he may learn to fear the LORD
his God, to keep all the words of this
law and these statutes, to do them:
20 That his heart be not lifted up
above his brethren, and that he [y]turn
not aside from the commandment, *to*
the right hand, or *to* the left: to the end
that he may prolong *his* days in his
kingdom, he, and his children, in the
midst of Is′ra-el.

18 The priests the Lē′vītes, *and* all
the tribe of Lē′vī, shall have no
part nor inheritance with Is′ra-el: they
[a]shall eat the offerings of the LORD
made by fire, and his inheritance.
2 Therefore shall they have no inheritance among their brethren: the
LORD *is* their inheritance, as he hath
said unto them.
3 ¶ And this shall be the priest's due
from the people, from them that offer a
sacrifice, whether *it be* ox or sheep;
and [b]they shall give unto the priest the
shoulder, and the two cheeks, and the
maw.
4 The [c]firstfruit *also* of thy corn, of
thy wine, and of thine oil, and the first
of the fleece of thy sheep, shalt thou
give him.
5 For the LORD thy God hath chosen
him out of all thy tribes, [d]to stand to
minister in the name of the LORD, him
and his sons for ever.
6 ¶ And if a Lē′vīte come from any
of thy gates out of all Is′ra-el, where he
[e]sojourned, and come with all the desire of his mind unto the place which
the LORD shall choose;
7 Then he shall minister in the name
of the LORD his God, as all his brethren
the Lē′vītes *do*, which stand there before the LORD.
8 They shall have like [f]portions to
eat, beside [1]that which cometh of the
sale of his patrimony.
9 ¶ When thou art come into the
land which the LORD thy God giveth
thee, [g]thou shalt not learn to do after
the abominations of those nations.
10 There shall not be found among
you *any one* that maketh his son or his
daughter to pass through the fire, [h]*or*
that useth divination, *or* an observer of
times, or an enchanter, or a witch,
11 Or a charmer, or a consulter with
familiar spirits, or a wizard, or a necro-
mancer.
12 For all that do these things *are* an
abomination unto the LORD: and [i]be-
cause of these abominations the LORD
thy God doth drive them out from before thee.
13 Thou shalt be [2]perfect with the
LORD thy God.
14 For these nations, which thou
shalt [3]possess, hearkened unto [j]ob-
servers of times, and unto diviners: but
as for thee, the LORD thy God hath not
suffered thee so *to do*.
15 ¶ [k]The LORD thy God will raise
up unto thee a Prophet from the midst
of thee, of thy brethren, like unto me;
unto him ye shall hearken;
16 According to all that thou desiredst of the LORD thy God in Hō′reb
in the day of the assembly, saying, Let
me not hear again the voice of the
LORD my God, neither let me see this
great fire any more, that I die not.
17 And the LORD said unto me, They
have well *spoken that* which they have
spoken.
18 [l]I will raise them up a Prophet
from among their brethren, like unto
thee, and [m]will put my words in his
mouth; [n]and he shall speak unto them
all that I shall command him.
19 And [o]it shall come to pass, *that*
whosoever will not hearken unto my
words which he shall speak in my
name, I will require *it* of him.
20 But [p]the prophet, which shall presume to speak a word in my name,
which I have not commanded him to
speak, or [q]that shall speak in the name
of other gods, even that prophet shall
die.
21 And if thou say in thine heart,
How shall we know the word which
the LORD hath not spoken?
22 [r]When a prophet speaketh in the
name of the LORD, if the thing follow
not, nor come to pass, that *is* the thing
which the LORD hath not spoken, *but*
the prophet hath spoken it presumptuously: thou shalt not be afraid of him.

19 When the LORD thy God hath cut
off the nations, whose land the
LORD thy God giveth thee, and thou
[1]succeedest them, and dwellest in their
cities, and in their houses;
2 [a]Thou shalt separate three cities
for thee in the midst of thy land, which
the LORD thy God giveth thee to possess it.
3 Thou shalt prepare thee a way, and
divide the coasts of thy land, which the
LORD thy God giveth thee to inherit,
into three parts, that every slayer may
flee thither.
4 ¶ And this *is* the case of the slayer,
which shall flee thither, that he may

14 [m]1 Sam. 10.19; Hos. 13.9
[n]1 Sam. 8.5
15 [o]Jer. 30.21
16 [p]1 Ki. 4.26; Ps. 20.7
[q]Isa. 31.1
[r]Ex. 13.17
[s]Hos. 11.5
17 [t]1 Ki. 11.3
[u]1 Ki. 10.21
18 [v]2 Ki. 11.12
[w]ch. 31.9; 2 Ki. 22.8
19 [x]Josh. 1.8; Ps. 119.97
20 [y]ch. 5.32; 1 Ki. 15.5

CHAPTER 18
1 [a]Num. 18.8-9; 1 Cor. 9.13
3 [b]Lev. 7.30
4 [c]Ex. 22.29
5 [d]ch. 10.8
6 [e]Num. 35.2-3
8 [f]2 Chr. 31.4
[1]his sales by the fathers
9 [g]Lev. 18.26; ch. 12.29
10 [h]Lev. 19.26
12 [i]Lev. 18.24
13 [2]Or, upright, or, sincere
14 [3]Or, inherit
[j]2 Ki. 21.6
15 [k]Num. 24.17; Isa. 11.1; Matt. 11.3; Matt. 21.11; Luke 2.25-34; Luke 4.16-22; Luke 7.16; Luke 24.19; John 4.19-25-26; John 6.14; Acts 3.22; Acts 7.37
18 [l]John 1.45
[m]Isa. 51.16; John 17.8
[n]John 4.25; John 8.28
19 [o]Acts 3.23
20 [p]ch. 13.5; Jer. 14.14; Zech. 13.3
[q]Jer. 2.8
22 [r]Jer. 28.9

CHAPTER 19
1 [1]inheritest, or, possessest
2 [a]Josh. 20.2

live: Whoso killeth his neighbour ignorantly, whom he hated not [2]in time
past;
5 As when a man goeth into the
wood with his neighbour to hew wood,
and his hand fetcheth a stroke with the
ax to cut down the tree, and the [3]head
slippeth from the [4]helve, and [5]lighteth
upon his neighbour, that he die; he
shall flee unto one of those cities, and
live:
6 Lest the avenger of the blood pursue the slayer, while his heart is hot,
and overtake him, because the way is
long, and [6]slay him; whereas he *was*
not worthy of death, inasmuch as he
hated him not [7]in time past.
7 Wherefore I command thee, saying, Thou shalt separate three cities for
thee.
8 And if the LORD thy God [b]en-
large thy coast, as he hath sworn unto
thy fathers, and give thee all the land
which he promised to give unto thy fathers;
9 If thou shalt keep all these commandments to do them, which I command thee this day, to love the LORD
thy God, and to walk ever in his ways;
[c]then shalt thou add three cities more
for thee, beside these three:
10 That innocent blood be not shed
in thy land, which the LORD thy God
giveth thee *for* an inheritance, and *so*
blood be upon thee.
11 ¶ But [d]if any man [e]hate his neighbour, and lie in wait for him, and rise
up against him, and smite him [8]mor-
tally that he die, and fleeth into one of
these cities:
12 Then the elders of his city shall
send and fetch him thence, and deliver
him into the hand of the avenger of
blood, that he may die.
13 Thine eye shall not pity him, [f]but
thou shalt put away *the guilt of* innocent blood from Is′ra-el, that it may go
well with thee.
14 ¶ [g]Thou shalt not remove thy
neighbour's landmark, which they of
old time have set in thine inheritance,
which thou shalt inherit in the land
that the LORD thy God giveth thee to
possess it.
15 ¶ [h]One witness shall not rise up
against a man for any iniquity, or for
any sin, in any sin that he sinneth: at
the mouth of two witnesses, or at the
mouth of three witnesses, shall the matter be established.
16 ¶ If a false witness [i]rise up against
any man to testify against him [9]*that
which is* wrong;
17 Then both the men, between
whom the controversy *is*, shall stand
before the LORD, before the priests and
the judges, which shall be in those
days;
18 And the judges shall make diligent inquisition: and, behold, *if* the witness *be* a false witness, *and* hath testified falsely against his brother;
19 [j]Then shall ye do unto him, as
he had thought to have done unto his

4 [2]from yesterday the third day
5 [3]iron [4]wood [5]findeth
6 [6]smite him in life [7]from yesterday the third day
8 [b]Gen. 15.18
9 [c]Josh. 20.7
11 [d]Ex. 21.12; Num. 35.16; Prov. 28.17 [e]Prov. 29.10; 1 John 3.15 [8]in life
13 [f]1 Ki. 2.31
14 [g]ch. 27.17; Job 24.2; Prov. 22.28; Hos. 5.10
15 [h]Matt. 18.16; John 8.17; 2 Cor. 13.1; 1 Tim. 5.19; Heb. 10.28
16 [i]Ps. 27.12; 1 Ki. 21.13 [9]Or, falling away
19 [j]Prov. 19.5; Dan. 6.24
20 [k]ch. 17.13; ch. 21.21
21 [l]Ex. 21.23; Lev. 24.20
CHAPTER 20
1 [a]Ps. 20.7; Isa. 31.1 [b]Num. 23.21; ch. 31.6-8; 2 Chr. 13.12; 2 Chr. 32.7-8; Ps. 23.4; Isa. 41.10
3 [1]be tender [2]make haste
4 [c]ch. 1.30; ch. 3.22; Josh. 23.10
5 [d]Neh. 12.27; See title of Ps. 30
6 [3]made it common
7 [e]ch. 24.5
8 [f]Judg. 7.3 [4]melt
9 [5]to be in the head of the people
10 [g]2 Sam. 20.18-20
11 [h]1 Ki. 9.21
13 [i]Num. 31.7
14 [j]Josh. 8.2 [6]spoil [k]Josh. 22.8

brother: so shalt thou put the evil away
from among you.
20 And [k]those which remain shall
hear, and fear, and shall henceforth
commit no more any such evil among
you.
21 And thine eye shall not pity; *but*
[l]life *shall go* for life, eye for eye, tooth
for tooth, hand for hand, foot for foot.

20 When thou goest out to battle
against thine enemies, and seest
[a]horses, and chariots, *and* a people
more than thou, be not afraid of them:
for the LORD thy God *is* [b]with thee,
which brought thee up out of the land
of E′gypt.
2 And it shall be, when ye are come
nigh unto the battle, that the priest
shall approach and speak unto the people,
3 And shall say unto them, Hear, O
Is′ra-el, ye approach this day unto battle against your enemies: let not your
hearts [1]faint, fear not, and do not [2]trem-
ble, neither be ye terrified because of
them;
4 For the LORD your God *is* he that
goeth with you, [c]to fight for you against
your enemies, to save you.
5 ¶ And the officers shall speak unto
the people, saying, What man *is there*
that hath built a new house, and hath
not [d]dedicated it? let him go and return to his house, lest he die in the battle, and another man dedicate it.
6 And what man *is he* that hath
planted a vineyard, and hath not *yet*
[3]eaten of it? let him *also* go and return
unto his house, lest he die in the battle,
and another man eat of it.
7 And [e]what man *is there* that hath
betrothed a wife, and hath not taken
her? let him go and return unto his
house, lest he die in the battle, and another man take her.
8 And the officers shall speak further unto the people, and they shall
say, [f]What man *is there that is* fearful
and fainthearted? let him go and return unto his house, lest his brethren's
heart [4]faint as well as his heart.
9 And it shall be, when the officers
have made an end of speaking unto the
people, that they shall make captains
of the armies [5]to lead the people.
10 ¶ When thou comest nigh unto a
city to fight against it, [g]then proclaim
peace unto it.
11 And it shall be, if it make thee
answer of peace, and open unto thee,
then it shall be, *that* all the people *that
is* found therein shall be [h]tributaries
unto thee, and they shall serve thee.
12 And if it will make no peace with
thee, but will make war against thee,
then thou shalt besiege it:
13 And when the LORD thy God hath
delivered it into thine hands, [i]thou
shalt smite every male thereof with the
edge of the sword:
14 But the women, and the little
ones, and [j]the cattle, and all that is in
the city, *even* all the spoil thereof, shalt
thou [6]take unto thyself; and [k]thou shalt

eat the spoil of thine enemies, which the LORD thy God hath given thee.

15 Thus shalt thou do unto all the cities *which are* very far off from thee, which *are* not of the cities of these nations.

16 But [l]of the cities of these people, which the LORD thy God doth give thee *for* an inheritance, thou shalt save alive nothing that breatheth:

17 But thou shalt utterly destroy them; *namely,* the Hĭt'tītes, and the Ăm'ôr-ītes, the Cā'năan-ītes, and the Pĕr'ĭz-zītes, the Hī'vītes, and the Jĕb'u-sītes; as the LORD thy God hath commanded thee:

18 That [m]they teach you not to do after all their abominations, which they have done unto their gods; so should ye [n]sin against the LORD your God.

19 ¶ When thou shalt besiege a city a long time, in making war against it to take it, thou shalt not destroy the trees thereof by forcing an ax against them: for thou mayest eat of them, and thou shalt not cut them down ([7]for the tree of the field *is* man's *life*) [8]to employ *them* in the siege:

20 Only the trees which thou knowest that they *be* not trees for meat, thou shalt destroy and cut them down; and thou shalt build bulwarks against the city that maketh war with thee, until [9]it be subdued.

21 If *one* be found [a]slain in the land which the LORD thy God giveth thee to possess it, lying in the field, *and* it be not known who hath slain him:

2 Then thy elders and thy judges shall come forth, and they shall measure unto the cities which *are* round about him that is slain:

3 And it shall be, *that* the city *which is* next unto the slain man, even the elders of that city shall take an heifer, which hath not been wrought with, *and* which hath not drawn in the yoke;

4 And the elders of that city shall bring down the heifer unto a rough valley, which is neither eared nor sown, and shall strike off the heifer's neck there in the valley:

5 And the priests the sons of Lē'vī shall come near; for [b]them the LORD thy God hath chosen to minister unto him, and to bless in the name of the LORD; and [c]by their [1]word shall every controversy and every stroke be *tried:*

6 And all the elders of that city, *that are* next unto the slain *man,* [d]shall wash their hands over the heifer that is beheaded in the valley:

7 And they shall answer and say, [e]Our hands have not shed this blood, neither have our eyes seen *it.*

8 Be merciful, O LORD, unto thy people Ĭs'ra-el, whom thou hast redeemed, [f]and lay not innocent blood [2]unto thy people of Ĭs'ra-el's charge. And the blood shall be forgiven them.

9 So [g]shalt thou put away the *guilt of* innocent blood from among you, when thou shalt do *that which is* right in the sight of the LORD.

10 ¶ When thou goest forth to war against thine enemies, and the [h]LORD thy God hath delivered them into thine hands, and thou hast taken them captive,

11 And seest among the captives a beautiful woman, and hast a desire unto her, that thou wouldest have her to thy wife;

12 Then thou shalt bring her home to thine house; and she shall shave her head, and [3]pare her nails;

13 And she shall put the raiment of her captivity from off her, and shall remain in thine house, [i]and bewail her father and her mother a full month: and after that thou shalt go in unto her, and be her husband, and she shall be thy wife.

14 And it shall be, if thou have no delight in her, then thou shalt let her go whither she will; but thou shalt not sell her at all for money, thou shalt not make merchandise of her, because thou [j]hast humbled her.

15 ¶ If a man have two wives, one beloved, and [k]another hated, and they have born him children, *both* the beloved and the hated; and *if* the firstborn son be hers that was hated:

16 Then it shall be, [l]when he maketh his sons to inherit *that* which he hath, *that* he may not make the son of the beloved firstborn before the son of the hated, *which is indeed* the firstborn:

17 But he shall acknowledge the son of the hated *for* the firstborn, by [m]giving him a double portion of all [4]that he hath: for he *is* [n]the beginning of his strength; [o]the right of the firstborn *is* his.

18 ¶ If a man have a stubborn and rebellious son, which will not obey the voice of his [p]father, or the voice of his mother, and *that,* when they have chastened him, will not hearken unto them:

19 Then shall his father and his mother lay hold on him, and bring him out unto the elders of his city, and unto the gate of his place;

20 And they shall say unto the elders of his city, This our son *is* stubborn and rebellious, he will not obey our voice; *he is* a glutton, and a drunkard.

21 And all the men of his city shall stone him with stones, that he die: [q]so shalt thou put evil away from among you; [r]and all Ĭs'ra-el shall hear, and fear.

22 ¶ And if a man have committed a sin [s]worthy of death, and he be to be put to death, and thou hang him on a tree:

23 [t]His body shall not remain all night upon the tree, but thou shalt in any wise bury him that day; (for [u]he that is hanged *is* [5]accursed of God;) that [v]thy land be not defiled, which the LORD thy God giveth thee *for* an inheritance.

22 Thou [a]shalt not see thy brother's ox or his sheep go [b]astray, and hide thyself from them: thou shalt in

16 [l]Num. 21.2-3-35; Josh. 11.14
18 [m]Ex. 34.12-17; 1 Cor. 15.33
[n]Ex. 23.33; Hos. 8.11
19 [7]Or, for, O man, the tree of the field is to be employed in the siege
[8]to go from before thee
20 [9]it come down

CHAPTER 21
1 [a]Ps. 9.12; Prov. 28.17
5 [b]1 Chr. 23.13
[c]ch. 17.8-9
[1]mouth
6 [d]Job 9.30; Heb. 9.10
7 [e]2 Sam. 3.28
8 [f]Jer. 26.15; 1 Thess. 2.15-16
[2]in the midst
9 [g]ch. 19.13
10 [h]Josh. 21.44; 2 Chr. 32.8
12 [3]make, or, dress, or, suffer to grow
13 [i]Ps. 45.10
14 [j]Gen. 34.2; Judg. 19.24
15 [k]Gen. 29.33
16 [l]2 Chr. 11.19; Rom. 8.29
17 [m]Gen. 25.5-6; 1 Chr. 5.1
[4]that is found with him
[n]Gen. 49.3
[o]Gen. 25.31
18 [p]Ex. 20.12; Eph. 6.1
21 [q]ch. 19.19
[r]ch. 13.11
22 [s]ch. 22.26; Acts 23.29
23 [t]Josh. 8.29;
[u]Gal. 3.13
[5]the curse of God
[v]Lev. 18.25

CHAPTER 22
1 [a]Ex. 23.4;
[b]Prov. 27.10

any case bring them again unto thy
brother.
2 And if thy brother *be* not nigh
unto thee, or if thou know him not,
then thou shalt bring it unto thine own
house, and it shall be with thee until
thy brother seek after it, and thou shalt
restore it to him again.
3 In like manner shalt thou do with
his ass; and so shalt thou do with his
raiment; and with all lost thing of thy
brother's, which he hath lost, and thou
hast found, shalt thou do likewise: thou
mayest not hide thyself.
4 ¶ Thou shalt not see thy brother's
ass or his ox fall down by the way,
and hide thyself from them: thou shalt
surely help him to lift *them* up again.
5 ¶ The [c]woman shall not wear that
which pertaineth unto a man, neither
shall a man put on a woman's garment: for all that do so *are* abomination unto the LORD thy God.
6 ¶ If a bird's nest chance to be before thee in the way in any tree, or on
the ground, *whether they be* young
ones, or eggs, and the dam sitting upon
the young, or upon the eggs, [d]thou
shalt not take the dam with the young:
7 *But* thou shalt in any wise let the
dam go, and take the young to thee;
[e]that it may be well with thee, and *that*
thou mayest prolong *thy* days.
8 ¶ When thou buildest a new house,
then thou shalt make a battlement for
thy roof, that thou bring not blood
upon thine house, if any man fall from
thence.
9 ¶ [f]Thou shalt not sow thy vineyard
with divers seeds: lest the [1]fruit of thy
seed which thou hast sown, and the
fruit of thy vineyard, be defiled.
10 ¶ [g]Thou shalt not plow with an
ox and an ass together.
11 ¶ [h]Thou shalt not wear a garment
of divers sorts, *as* of woollen and linen
together.
12 ¶ Thou shalt make thee [i]fringes
upon the four [2]quarters of thy vesture,
wherewith thou coverest *thyself.*
13 ¶ If any man take a wife, [j]and go
in unto her, and hate her,
14 And give occasions of speech
against her, and bring up an evil name
upon her, and say, I took this woman,
and when I came to her, I found her not
a maid:
15 Then shall the father of the damsel, and her mother, take and bring
forth *the tokens of* the damsel's virginity unto the elders of the city in the
gate:
16 And the damsel's father shall say
unto the elders, I gave my daughter
unto this man to wife, and he hateth
her;
17 And, lo, he hath given occasions
of speech *against her,* saying, I found
not thy daughter a maid; and yet these
are the tokens of my daughter's virginity. And they shall spread the cloth before the elders of the city.
18 And [k]the elders of that city shall
take that man and chastise him;
19 And they shall amerce him in an
hundred *shekels* of silver, and give
them unto the father of the damsel, because he hath brought up an evil name
upon a virgin of Is'ra-el: and she shall
be his wife; he may not put her away
all his days.
20 But if this thing [l]be true, *and the
tokens of* virginity be not found for the
damsel:
21 Then they shall bring out the damsel to the door of her father's house,
and the men of her city shall stone her
with stones that she die: because she
hath [m]wrought folly in Is'ra-el, to play
the whore in her father's house: [n]so
shalt thou put evil away from among
you.
22 ¶ [o]If a man be found lying with a
woman married to an husband, then
they shall both of them die, *both* the
man that lay with the woman, and the
woman: so shalt thou put away evil
from Is'ra-el.
23 ¶ If a damsel *that is* a virgin be
[p]betrothed unto an husband, and a
man find her in the city, and lie with
her;
24 Then ye shall bring them both out
unto the gate of that city, and ye shall
stone them with stones that they die;
the damsel, because she cried not, *being* in the city; and the man, because he
hath [q]humbled his neighbour's wife:
so thou shalt put away evil from among
you.
25 ¶ But if a man find a betrothed
damsel in the field, and the man [3]force
her, and lie with her: then the man
only that lay with her shall die:
26 But unto the damsel thou shalt do
nothing; *there is* in the damsel no sin
worthy of death: for as when a man
riseth against his neighbour, and slayeth him, even so *is* this matter:
27 For he found her in the field, *and*
the betrothed damsel cried, and *there
was* none to save her.
28 ¶ [r]If a man find a damsel *that is* a
virgin, which is not betrothed, and lay
hold on her, and lie with her, and they
be found;
29 Then the man that lay with her
shall give unto the damsel's father fifty
shekels of silver, and she shall be his
wife; because he hath humbled her, he
may not put her away all his days.
30 ¶ [s]A man shall not take his father's wife, nor [t]discover his father's
skirt.

23

He that is wounded in the stones,
or hath his privy member cut off,
shall not enter into the congregation of
the LORD.
2 A bastard shall not enter into the
congregation of the LORD; even to his
tenth generation shall he not enter into
the congregation of the LORD.
3 [a]An Ăm'mŏn-īte or Mō'ab-īte shall
not enter into the congregation of the
LORD; even to their tenth generation
shall they not enter into the congregation of the LORD for ever:
4 [b]Because they met you not with
bread and with water in the way, when

5 [c]1 Cor. 14.40
6 [d]Lev. 22.28; Neh. 9.6; Ps. 36.6; Ps. 145.9; Prov. 12.10; Matt. 10.29; Luke 12.6
7 [e]ch. 4.40
9 [f]Lev. 19.19; Matt. 6.24; Matt. 9.16; 2 Cor. 6.14-16; 2 Cor. 11.3 [1]fulness of thy seed
10 [g]2 Cor. 6.14-15-16
11 [h]Lev. 19.19
12 [i]Num. 15.38; Matt. 23.5 [2]wings
13 [j]Gen. 29.21; Judg. 15.1
18 [k]Ex. 18.21; ch. 1.9-18; Rom. 13.4
20 [l]ch. 17.4
21 [m]Gen. 34.7; Lev. 21.9; Judg. 20.6-10 [n]ch. 13.5; ch. 17.7
22 [o]Lev. 20.10; Prov. 6.22; Mal. 3.5; Matt. 5.27-28; John 8.5; 1 Cor. 6.9; Heb. 13.4
23 [p]Matt. 1.18-19
24 [q]ch. 21.14; Matt. 1.20-24
25 [3]Or, take strong hold of her
28 [r]Ex. 22.16-17
30 [s]Lev. 18.8; Lev. 20.11; ch. 27.20; 1 Cor. 5.1 [t]Gen. 9.22-27; Ruth 3.9

CHAPTER 23
3 [a]Ruth 4.5; Neh. 4.3-7; Neh. 13.1-2
4 [b]Gen. 14.18; ch. 2.29; 1 Sam. 25.11; 1 Ki. 18.4; Isa. 63.9; Matt. 10.40-42

ye came forth out of Ē'ġypt; and [c]because they hired against thee Bā'laam the son of Bē'or of Pē'thôr of Mĕs-o-po-tā'mĭ-ȧ, to curse thee.

5 Nevertheless the LORD thy God would not hearken unto Bā'laam; but the LORD thy God turned the [d]curse into a blessing unto thee, because the LORD thy God loved thee.

6 [e]Thou shalt not seek their peace nor their [1]prosperity all thy days for ever.

7 ¶ Thou shalt not abhor an Ē'dom-īte; [f]for he *is* thy brother: thou shalt not abhor an E-ġȳp'tian; because [g]thou wast a stranger in his land.

8 The children that are begotten of them shall enter into the congregation of the LORD in their third generation.

9 ¶ When the host goeth forth against thine enemies, then keep thee from every wicked thing.

10 ¶ [h]If there be among you any man, that is not clean by reason of uncleanness that chanceth him by night, then shall he go abroad out of the camp, he shall not come within the camp:

11 But it shall be, when evening [2]cometh on, he shall wash *himself* with water: and when the sun is down, he shall come into the camp *again*.

12 ¶ Thou shalt have a place also without the camp, whither thou shalt go forth abroad:

13 And thou shalt have a paddle upon thy weapon; and it shall be, when thou [3]wilt ease thyself abroad, thou shalt dig therewith, and shalt turn back and cover that which cometh from thee:

14 For the LORD thy God [i]walketh in the midst of thy camp, to deliver thee, and to give up thine enemies before thee; therefore shall thy camp be [j]holy: that he see no [4]unclean thing in thee, and turn away from thee.

15 ¶ [k]Thou shalt not deliver unto his master the servant which is escaped from his master unto thee:

16 He shall dwell with thee, *even* among you, in that place which he shall choose in one of thy gates, where it [5]liketh him best: [l]thou shalt not oppress him.

17 ¶ There shall be no [6]whore of [m]the daughters of Is'ra-el, nor [n]a sodomite of the sons of Is'ra-el.

18 Thou shalt not bring the hire of a whore, or the price of a dog, into the house of the LORD thy God for any vow: for even both these *are* abomination unto the LORD thy God.

19 ¶ [o]Thou shalt not lend upon usury to thy brother; usury of money, usury of victuals, usury of any thing that is lent upon usury:

20 [p]Unto a stranger thou mayest lend upon usury; but unto thy brother thou shalt not lend upon usury: [q]that the LORD thy God may bless thee in all that thou settest thine hand to in the land whither thou goest to possess it.

21 ¶ [r]When thou shalt vow a vow unto the LORD thy God, thou shalt not slack to pay it: for the LORD thy God will surely require it of thee; and it would be sin in thee.

22 But if thou shalt forbear to vow, it shall be no sin in thee.

23 [s]That which is gone out of thy lips thou shalt keep and perform; *even* a freewill offering, according as thou hast vowed unto the LORD thy God, which thou hast promised with thy mouth.

24 ¶ When thou comest into thy neighbour's vineyard, then thou mayest eat grapes thy fill at thine own pleasure; but thou shalt not put *any* in thy vessel.

25 When thou comest into the standing corn of thy neighbour, [t]then thou mayest pluck the ears with thine hand; but [u]thou shalt not move a sickle unto thy neighbour's standing corn.

24 When a [a]man hath taken a wife, and married her, and it come to pass that she find no favour in his eyes, because he hath found [1]some uncleanness in her: then let him write her a bill of [2]divorcement, and give *it* in her hand, and send her out of his house.

2 And when she is departed out of his house, she may go and be another man's *wife*.

3 And *if* the latter husband hate her, and write her a bill of divorcement, and giveth *it* in her hand, and sendeth her out of his house; or if the latter husband die, which took her *to be* his wife;

4 [b]Her former husband, which sent her away, may not take her again to be his wife, after that she is defiled; for that *is* abomination before the LORD: and thou shalt not cause the land to sin, which the LORD thy God giveth thee *for* an inheritance.

5 ¶ When a man hath taken a new wife, he shall not go out to war, [3]neither shall he be charged with any business: *but* he shall be free at home one year, and shall [c]cheer up his wife which he hath taken.

6 ¶ No man shall take the nether or the upper [d]millstone to pledge: for he taketh *a man's* life to pledge.

7 ¶ [e]If a man be found stealing any of his brethren of the children of Is'ra-el, and maketh merchandise of him, or selleth him; then that thief shall die; and thou shalt put evil away from among you.

8 ¶ Take heed in [f]the plague of leprosy, that thou observe diligently, and do according to all that the priests the Lē'vītes shall teach you: as I commanded them, *so* ye shall observe to do.

9 [g]Remember what the LORD thy God did [h]unto Mĭr'ĭ-am by the way, after that ye were come forth out of Ē'ġypt.

10 ¶ When thou dost [4]lend thy brother any thing, thou shalt not go into his house to fetch his pledge.

11 Thou shalt stand abroad, and the man to whom thou dost lend shall bring out the pledge abroad unto thee.

[c]Num. 22.5-6; Josh. 24.9
5 [d]Prov. 26.2
6 [e]Ezra 9.12 [1]good
7 [f]Gen. 25.24-25-26; Obad. 10-12 [g]Ex. 22.21; Lev. 19.34; ch. 10.19
10 [h]Lev. 15.16; Num. 5.2-3; 1 Cor. 5.11-13
11 [2]turneth toward
13 [3]sittest down
14 [i]Gen. 15.1; Lev. 26.12; Jer. 32.40; 2 Cor. 6.16 [j]Ex. 3.5 [4]nakedness of any thing
15 [k]1 Sam. 30.15
16 [5]is good for him [l]Ex. 22.21; Mal. 3.5
17 [6]Or, sodomitess [m]Prov. 2.16 [n]Gen. 19.5
19 [o]Lev. 25.36; Luke 6.34
20 [p]Lev. 19.34 [q]ch. 15.10
21 [r]Job 22.27; Eccl. 5.4-5
23 [s]Ps. 66.13
25 [t]Matt. 12.1 [u]Luke 12.15; Col. 3.5

CHAPTER 24

1 [a]Matt. 5.31; Mark 10.4 [1]matter of nakedness [2]cutting off
4 [b]Jer. 3.1
5 [3]not any thing shall pass upon him [c]Prov. 5.18
6 [d]Isa. 47.2
7 [e]Ex. 21.16
8 [f]Lev. 13.2; Luke 5.14
9 [g]Luke 17.32; 1 Cor. 10.6 [h]Num. 12.10
10 [4]lend the loan of any thing to, etc

12 And if the man *be* poor, thou shalt not sleep with his pledge:

13 [i]In any case thou shalt deliver him the pledge again when the sun goeth down, that he may sleep in his own raiment, [j]and bless thee: and [k]it shall be righteousness unto thee before the LORD thy God.

14 ¶ Thou shalt not [l]oppress an hired servant *that is* poor and needy, *whether he be* of thy brethren, or of thy strangers that *are* in thy land within thy gates:

15 At his day [m]thou shalt give *him* his hire, neither shall the sun go down upon it; for he *is* poor, and [5]setteth his heart upon it: [n]lest he cry against thee unto the LORD, and it be sin unto thee.

16 [o]The fathers shall not be put to death for the children, neither shall the children be put to death for the fathers: every man shall be put to death for his own sin.

17 ¶ [p]Thou shalt not pervert the judgment of the stranger, *nor* of the fatherless; nor [q]take a widow's raiment to pledge:

18 But thou shalt remember that thou wast a bondman in Ē'ġypt, and the LORD thy God redeemed thee thence: therefore I command thee to do this thing.

19 ¶ [r]When thou cuttest down thine harvest in thy field, and hast forgot a sheaf in the field, thou shalt not go again to fetch it: it shall be for the stranger, for the fatherless, and for the widow: that the LORD thy God may [s]bless thee in all the work of thine hands.

20 When thou beatest thine olive tree, [6]thou shalt not go over the boughs again: it shall be for the stranger, for the fatherless, and for the widow.

21 When thou gatherest the grapes of thy vineyard, thou shalt not glean *it* [7]afterward: it shall be for the stranger, for the fatherless, and for the widow.

22 And thou shalt remember that thou wast a bondman in the land of Ē'ġypt: therefore I command thee to do this thing.

25 If there be a controversy between men, and they come unto judgment, that *the judges* may judge them; then they shall justify the righteous, and condemn the wicked.

2 And it shall be, if the wicked man *be* [a]worthy to be beaten, that the judge shall cause him to lie down, [b]and to be beaten before his face, according to his fault, by a certain number.

3 [c]Forty stripes he may give him, *and* not exceed: lest, *if* he should exceed, and beat him above these with many stripes, then thy brother should [d]seem vile unto thee.

4 ¶ [e]Thou shalt not muzzle the ox when he [1]treadeth out *the corn*.

5 ¶ [f]If brethren dwell together, and one of them die, and have no child, the wife of the dead shall not marry without unto a stranger: her [2]husband's brother shall go in unto her, and take her to him to wife, and perform the duty of an husband's brother unto her.

6 And it shall be, *that* the firstborn which she beareth [g]shall succeed in the name of his brother *which is* dead, that his name be not put out of Ĭs'ra-el.

7 And if the man like not to take his [3]brother's wife, then let his brother's wife go up to the gate unto the elders, and say, My husband's brother refuseth to raise up unto his brother a name in Ĭs'ra-el, he will not perform the duty of my husband's brother.

8 Then the elders of his city shall call him, and speak unto him: and *if* he stand *to it*, and say, I like not to take her;

9 Then shall his brother's wife come unto him in the presence of the elders, and [h]loose his shoe from off his foot, and spit in his face, and shall answer and say, So shall it be done unto that man that will not build up his brother's house.

10 And [i]his name shall be called in Ĭs'ra-el, The house of him that hath his shoe loosed.

11 ¶ When men strive together one with another, and the wife of the one draweth near for to deliver her husband out of the hand of him that smiteth him, and putteth forth her hand, and taketh him by the secrets:

12 Then thou shalt cut off her hand, [j]thine eye shall not pity *her*.

13 ¶ [k]Thou shalt not have in thy bag [4]divers weights, a great and a small.

14 Thou shalt not have in thine house [5]divers measures, a great and a small.

15 *But* thou shalt have a perfect and just weight, a perfect and just measure shalt thou have: [l]that thy days may be lengthened in the land which the LORD thy God giveth thee.

16 For [m]all that do such things, *and* all that do unrighteously, *are* an abomination unto the LORD thy God.

17 ¶ [n]Remember what Ăm'a-lĕk did unto thee by the way, when ye were come forth out of Ē'ġypt;

18 How he met thee by the way, and smote the hindmost of thee, *even* all *that were* feeble behind thee, when thou *wast* faint and weary; and he [o]feared not God.

19 Therefore it shall be, [p]when the LORD thy God hath given thee rest from all thine enemies round about, in the land which the LORD thy God giveth thee *for* an inheritance to possess it, *that* thou shalt blot out the remembrance of Ăm'a-lĕk from under heaven; thou shalt not forget *it*.

26 And it shall be, when thou *art* come in unto the land which the LORD thy God giveth thee *for* an inheritance, and possessest it, and dwellest therein;

2 [a]That thou shalt take of the first of all the fruit of the earth, which thou shalt bring of thy land that the LORD thy God giveth thee, and shalt put *it* in a basket, and shalt [b]go unto the place which the LORD thy God shall choose to place his name there.

3 And thou shalt go unto the priest that shall be in those days, and say

13 [i]Ex. 22.26; Amos 2.8
[j]Job 29.11; 2 Tim. 1.18
[k]ch. 6.25; Dan. 4.27
14 [l]Prov. 14.31; Mal. 3.5
15 [m]Lev. 19.13
[5]lifteth his soul unto it
[n]Job 27.13; Jas. 5.4
16 [o]2 Ki. 14.6; Ezek. 18.20
17 [p]Ex. 22.21-22; Mal. 3.5
[q]Ex. 22.26
19 [r]Lev. 23.22
[s]Prov. 19.17
20 [6]thou shalt not bough it after thee
21 [7]after thee
CHAPTER 25
2 [a]Luke 12.48; Prov. 19.29
[b]Matt. 10.17
3 [c]2 Cor. 11.24
[d]Job 18.3
4 [e]Prov. 12.10; 1 Tim. 5.18
[1]thresheth
5 [f]Luke 20.28
[2]Or, next kinsman
6 [g]Gen. 38.9
7 [3]Or, next kinsman's wife
9 [h]Ruth 4.7;
10 [i]Prov. 6.33;
12 [j]ch. 19.13
13 [k]Lev. 19.35;
[4]a stone and a stone
14 [5]an ephah and an ephah
15 [l]Ex. 20.12
16 [m]Prov. 11.1;
17 [n]Ex. 17.8
18 [o]Neh. 5.9-15;
19 [p]1 Sam. 15.3
CHAPTER 26
2 [a]Ex. 23.19;
[b]ch. 12.5

unto him, I profess this day unto the
LORD thy God, that I am come unto the
country which the LORD sware unto
our fathers for to give us.
4 And the priest shall take the basket out of thine hand, and set it down
before the altar of the LORD thy God.
5 And thou shalt speak and say before the LORD thy God, [c]A Sȳr'ĭ-an
[d]ready to perish *was* my father, and he
went down into Ē'ġypt, and sojourned
there with a [e]few, and became there a
nation, great, mighty, and populous:
6 And [f]the E-ġȳp'tians evil entreated
us, and afflicted us, and laid upon us
hard bondage:
7 And [g]when we cried unto the LORD
God of our fathers, the LORD heard our
voice, and looked on our affliction, and
our labour, and our oppression:
8 And the LORD brought us forth out
of Ē'ġypt with a mighty hand, and with
an outstretched arm, and [h]with great
terribleness, and with signs, and with
wonders:
9 And he hath brought us into this
place, and hath given us this land, *even*
[i]a land that floweth with milk and
honey.
10 And now, behold, I have brought
the firstfruits of the land, which [j]thou,
O LORD, hast given me. And thou shalt
set it before the LORD thy God, and
worship before the LORD thy God:
11 And [k]thou shalt rejoice in every
good *thing* which the LORD thy God
hath given unto thee, and unto thine
house, thou, and the Lē'vīte, and the
stranger that *is* among you.
12 ¶ When thou hast made an end of
tithing all the [l]tithes of thine increase
the third year, *which is* [m]the year of
tithing, and hast given *it* unto the Lē'-
vīte, the stranger, the fatherless, and
the widow, that they may eat within
thy gates, and be filled;
13 Then thou shalt say before the
LORD thy God, I have brought away
the hallowed things out of *mine* house,
and also have given them unto the Lē'-
vīte, and unto the stranger, to the fatherless, and to the widow, according
to all thy commandments which thou
hast commanded me: I have not transgressed thy commandments, [n]neither
have I forgotten *them:*
14 [o]I have not eaten thereof in my
mourning, neither have I taken away
ought thereof for *any* unclean *use,* nor
given *ought* thereof for the dead: *but* I
have hearkened to the voice of the
LORD my God, *and* have done according to all that thou hast commanded
me.
15 [p]Look down from thy holy habitation, from heaven, and bless thy people Ĭs'ra-el, and the land which thou
hast given us, as thou swarest unto our
fathers, a land that floweth with milk
and honey.
16 ¶ This day the LORD thy God hath
commanded thee to do these statutes
and judgments: thou shalt therefore
keep and do them with all thine heart,
and with all thy soul.

5 [c]Gen. 26.5; Hos. 12.12
[d]Gen. 43.1-2
[e]Gen. 46.27; ch. 10.22
6 [f]Ex. 1.11
7 [g]Ex. 3.9; Ex. 4.31
8 [h]ch. 4.34; ch. 34.11-12
9 [i]Ex. 3.8
10 [j]ch. 8.18; Prov. 10.22
11 [k]ch. 12.7-12-18; ch. 16.11; Eccl. 3.12-13; Isa. 65.14; Acts 2.46-47; Phil. 4.4; 1 Tim. 6.17
12 [l]Lev. 27.30; Num. 18.24
[m]ch. 14.28-29
13 [n]Ps. 119.141-153-176
14 [o]Lev. 7.20; Hos. 9.4
15 [p]2 Chr. 6.26-27; Ps. 80.14; Ps. 102.19-20; Isa. 1.2; Isa. 57.15; Zech. 2.13; Acts 7.49
17 [q]Ex. 20.19; Ps. 48.14
18 [r]Ex. 6.7; ch. 7.6; ch. 14.2; ch. 28.9; ch. 29.13; 2 Sam. 7.23-24
19 [s]ch. 4.7-8; ch. 28.1; Ps. 148.14
[t]Ex. 19.6; Lev. 20.24-26; ch. 7.6; Ps. 50.5; Isa. 62.12; 1 Cor. 3.17; 1 Thess. 5.27; 1 Pet. 2.9

CHAPTER 27
2 [a]Josh. 4.1
[b]Josh. 8.32
4 [c]ch. 11.29; Josh. 8.30
5 [d]Ex. 20.25; Josh. 8.31
8 [e]Hab. 2.2
12 [f]ch. 11.29; Judg. 9.7
13 [1]for a cursing
14 [g]ch. 33.10; Josh. 8.33; Neh. 8.7-8; Mal. 2.7-9
15 [h]Ex. 20.4; Hos. 13.2

17 Thou hast [q]avouched the LORD
this day to be thy God, and to walk
in his ways, and to keep his statutes,
and his commandments, and his judgments, and to hearken unto his voice:
18 And [r]the LORD hath avouched
thee this day to be his peculiar people,
as he hath promised thee, and that
thou shouldest keep all his commandments;
19 And to make thee [s]high above all
nations which he hath made, in praise,
and in name, and in honour; and that
thou mayest be an [t]holy people unto
the LORD thy God, as he hath spoken.

27

And Mō'ses with the elders of
Ĭs'ra-el commanded the people,
saying, Keep all the commandments
which I command you this day.
2 And it shall be on the day [a]when
ye shall pass over Jôr'dan unto the
land which the LORD thy God giveth
thee, that thou [b]shalt set thee up great
stones, and plaister them with plaister:
3 And thou shalt write upon them all
the words of this law, when thou art
passed over, that thou mayest go in
unto the land which the LORD thy God
giveth thee, a land that floweth with
milk and honey; as the LORD God of
thy fathers hath promised thee.
4 Therefore it shall be when ye be
gone over Jôr'dan, *that* ye shall set up
these stones, which I command you
this day, [c]in mount Ē'bal, and thou
shalt plaister them with plaister.
5 And there shalt thou build an altar
unto the LORD thy God, an altar of
stones: [d]thou shalt not lift up *any* iron
tool upon them.
6 Thou shalt build the altar of the
LORD thy God of whole stones: and
thou shalt offer burnt offerings thereon
unto the LORD thy God:
7 And thou shalt offer peace offerings, and shalt eat there, and rejoice
before the LORD thy God.
8 And thou shalt write upon the
stones all the words of this law very
[e]plainly.
9 ¶ And Mō'ses and the priests the
Lē'vītes spake unto all Ĭs'ra-el, saying,
Take heed, and hearken, O Ĭs'ra-el;
this day thou art become the people of
the LORD thy God.
10 Thou shalt therefore obey the
voice of the LORD thy God, and do
his commandments and his statutes,
which I command thee this day.
11 ¶ And Mō'ses charged the people
the same day, saying,
12 These shall stand [f]upon mount
Gĕr'ĭ-zĭm to bless the people, when ye
are come over Jôr'dan; Sĭm'e-on, and
Lē'vī, and Jū'dah, and Ĭs'sa-char, and
Jō'seph, and Bĕn'ja-min:
13 And these shall stand upon mount
Ē'bal [1]to curse; Reu'ben, Găd, and
Ăsh'ēr, and Zĕb'u-lun, Dăn, and Năph'-
ta-lī.
14 ¶ And [g]the Lē'vītes shall speak,
and say unto all the men of Ĭs'ra-el
with a loud voice,
15 [h]Cursed *be* the man that maketh
any graven or molten image, an

abomination unto the LORD, the work
of the hands of the craftsman, and
putteth *it* in *a* secret *place.* [i]And all the
people shall answer and say, Amen.
16 [j]Cursed *be* he that setteth light
by his father or his mother. And all the
people shall say, Amen.
17 [k]Cursed *be* he that removeth his
neighbour's landmark. And all the people shall say, Amen.
18 [l]Cursed *be* he that maketh the
blind to wander out of the way. And all
the people shall say, Amen.
19 [m]Cursed *be* he that perverteth
the judgment of the stranger, fatherless, and widow. And all the people
shall say, Amen.
20 [n]Cursed *be* he that lieth with his
father's wife; because he uncovereth
his father's skirt. And all the people
shall say, Amen.
21 Cursed *be* he that lieth with any
manner of beast. And all the people
shall say, Amen.
22 [o]Cursed *be* he that lieth with his
sister, the daughter of his father, or the
daughter of his mother. And all the people shall say, Amen.
23 Cursed *be* he that lieth with his
mother in law. And all the people shall
say, Amen.
24 [p]Cursed *be* he that smiteth his
neighbour secretly. And all the people
shall say, Amen.
25 [q]Cursed *be* he that taketh reward
to slay an innocent person. And all the
people shall say, Amen.
26 [r]Cursed *be* he that confirmeth
not *all* the words of this law to do them.
And all the people shall say, Amen.

28

And it shall come to pass, [a]if thou
shalt hearken diligently unto the
voice of the LORD thy God, to observe
and to do all his commandments which
I command thee this day, that the LORD
thy God [b]will set thee on high above all
nations of the earth:
2 And all these blessings shall come
on thee, and [c]overtake thee, if thou
shalt hearken unto the voice of the
LORD thy God.
3 [d]Blessed *shalt* thou *be* in the city,
and blessed *shalt* thou *be* [e]in the field.
4 Blessed *shall be* [f]the fruit of thy
body, and the fruit of thy ground, and
the fruit of thy cattle, the increase of
thy kine, and the flocks of thy sheep.
5 Blessed *shall be* thy basket and
thy [1]store.
6 [g]Blessed *shalt* thou *be* when thou
comest in, and blessed *shalt* thou *be*
when thou goest out.
7 The LORD [h]shall cause thine enemies that rise up against thee to be smitten before thy face: they shall come out
against thee one way, and flee before
thee seven ways.
8 The LORD shall [i]command the
blessing upon thee in thy [2]storehouses,
and in all that thou [j]settest thine hand
unto; and he shall bless thee in the
land which the LORD thy God giveth
thee.
9 [k]The LORD shall establish thee an
holy people unto himself, as he hath

[i]Num. 5.22; 1 Cor. 14.16
16 [j]Ex. 20.12; Lev. 19.3
17 [k]Prov. 22.28
18 [l]Lev. 19.14; Rev. 2.14
19 [m]Ex. 22.21; Mal. 3.5
20 [n]Lev. 18.8; 1 Cor. 5.1
22 [o]2 Sam. 13.1
24 [p]Lev. 24.17; Num. 35.31
25 [q]Ex. 23.7; Ps. 15.5
26 [r]Ps. 119.21; Gal. 3.10
CHAPTER 28
1 [a]Ex. 15.26; Jer. 11.4
[b]1 Chr. 14.2; Rom. 2.10
2 [c]Zech. 1.6
3 [d]Ps. 128.1-4
[e]Gen. 39.5
4 [f]Gen. 22.17;
5 [1]Or, dough, or, kneading trough
6 [g]Ps. 121.8
7 [h]2 Sam. 22.38-41
8 [i]Lev. 25.21 [2]Or, barns
[j]ch. 15.10
9 [k]Gen. 17.7;
10 [l]2 Chr. 7.14
11 [m]Prov. 10.22 [3]Or, for good [4]belly
12 [n]Jas. 1.18
14 [o]Josh. 1.7;
15 [p]Lev. 26.14;
18 [q]Isa. 3.1;
20 [r]Prov. 3.33;
[s]Ps. 80.16; [5]which thou wouldest do
21 [t]Lev. 26.25;
22 [u]Lev. 26.16 [6]Or, drought

sworn unto thee, if thou shalt keep the
commandments of the LORD thy God,
and walk in his ways.
10 And all people of the earth shall
see that thou [l]art called by the name of
the LORD; and they shall be afraid of
thee.
11 And [m]the LORD shall make thee
plenteous [3]in goods, in the fruit of thy
[4]body, and in the fruit of thy cattle, and
in the fruit of thy ground, in the land
which the LORD sware unto thy fathers
to give thee.
12 The LORD [n]shall open unto thee
his good treasure, the heaven to give
the rain unto thy land in his season,
and to bless all the work of thine hand:
and thou shalt lend unto many nations,
and thou shalt not borrow.
13 And the LORD shall make thee
the head, and not the tail; and thou
shalt be above only, and thou shalt not
be beneath; if that thou hearken unto
the commandments of the LORD thy
God, which I command thee this day,
to observe and to do *them:*
14 [o]And thou shalt not go aside from
any of the words which I command
thee this day, *to* the right hand, or *to*
the left, to go after other gods to serve
them.
15 ¶ But it shall come to pass, [p]if
thou wilt not hearken unto the voice of
the LORD thy God, to observe to do all
his commandments and his statutes
which I command thee this day; that
all these curses shall come upon thee,
and overtake thee:
16 Cursed *shalt* thou *be* in the city,
and cursed *shalt* thou *be* in the field.
17 Cursed *shall be* thy basket and
thy store.
18 Cursed *shall be* the fruit of thy
body, and the [q]fruit of thy land, the
increase of thy kine, and the flocks of
thy sheep.
19 Cursed *shalt* thou *be* when thou
comest in, and cursed *shalt* thou *be*
when thou goest out.
20 The LORD shall send upon thee
cursing, [r]vexation, and [s]rebuke, in all
that thou settest thine hand unto [5]for to
do, until thou be destroyed, and until
thou perish quickly; because of the
wickedness of thy doings, whereby
thou hast forsaken me.
21 The LORD shall make [t]the pestilence cleave unto thee, until he have
consumed thee from off the land,
whither thou goest to possess it.
22 [u]The LORD shall smite thee with
a consumption, and with a fever, and
with an inflammation, and with an ex-
treme burning, and with the [6]sword,
and with blasting, and with mildew;
and they shall pursue thee until thou
perish.
23 And thy heaven that *is* over thy
head shall be brass, and the earth that
is under thee *shall be* iron.
24 The LORD shall make the rain
of thy land powder and dust: from
heaven shall it come down upon thee,
until thou be destroyed.

25 [v]The LORD shall cause thee to be smitten before thine enemies: thou shalt go out one way against them, and flee seven ways before them: and [w]shalt be [7]removed into all the kingdoms of the earth.

26 And thy carcase shall be meat unto all fowls of the air, and unto the beasts of the earth, and no man shall fray *them* away.

27 The LORD will smite thee with [x]the botch of Ē′gypt, and with [y]the emerods, and with the scab, and with the itch, whereof thou canst not be healed.

28 The LORD shall smite thee with madness, and blindness, and astonishment of heart:

29 And thou shalt grope at noonday, as the blind gropeth in darkness, and thou shalt not prosper in thy ways: and thou shalt be only oppressed and spoiled evermore, and no man shall save *thee.*

30 [z]Thou shalt betroth a wife, and another man shall lie with her: thou shalt build an house, and thou shalt not dwell therein: thou shalt plant a vineyard, and shalt not [8]gather the grapes thereof.

31 Thine ox *shall be* slain before thine eyes, and thou shalt not eat thereof: thine ass *shall be* violently taken away from before thy face, and [9]shall not be restored to thee: thy sheep *shall be* given unto thine enemies, and thou shalt have none to rescue *them.*

32 Thy sons and thy daughters *shall be* given unto another people, and thine eyes shall look, and fail *with longing* for them all the day long: and *there shall be* no might in thine hand.

33 [a]The fruit of thy land, and all thy labours, shall a nation which thou knowest not eat up; and thou shalt be only oppressed and crushed alway:

34 So that thou shalt be mad for the sight of thine eyes which thou shalt see.

35 The LORD shall smite thee in the knees, and in the legs, with a sore botch that cannot be healed, from the sole of thy foot unto the top of thy head.

36 The LORD shall [b]bring thee, and [c]thy king which thou shalt set over thee, unto a nation which neither thou nor thy fathers have known; and [d]there shalt thou serve other gods, wood and stone.

37 And thou shalt become [e]an astonishment, a proverb, [f]and a byword, among all nations whither the LORD shall lead thee.

38 [g]Thou shalt carry much seed out into the field, and shalt gather *but* little in; for [h]the locust shall consume it.

39 Thou shalt plant vineyards, and dress *them,* but shalt neither drink *of* the wine, nor gather *the grapes;* for the worms shall eat them.

40 Thou shalt have olive trees throughout all thy coasts, but thou shalt not anoint *thyself* with the oil; for thine olive shall cast *his fruit.*

41 Thou shalt beget sons and daughters, but [10]thou shalt not enjoy them; for [i]they shall go into captivity.

42 All thy trees and fruit of thy land shall the locust [11]consume.

43 The stranger that *is* within thee shall get up above thee very high; and thou shalt come down very low.

44 He shall lend to thee, and thou shalt not lend to him: [j]he shall be the head, and thou shalt be the tail.

45 Moreover all these curses shall come upon thee, and shall pursue thee, and overtake thee, till thou be destroyed; because thou hearkenedst not unto the voice of the LORD thy God, to keep his commandments and his statutes which he commanded thee:

46 And they shall be upon thee [k]for a sign and for a wonder, and upon thy seed for ever.

47 [l]Because thou servedst not the LORD thy God with joyfulness, and with gladness of heart, for the abundance of all *things;*

48 Therefore shalt thou serve thine enemies which the LORD shall send against thee, in hunger, and in thirst, and in nakedness, and in want of all *things:* and he [m]shall put a yoke of iron upon thy neck, until he have destroyed thee.

49 [n]The LORD shall bring a nation against thee from far, from the end of the earth, [o]*as swift* as the eagle flieth; a nation whose tongue thou shalt not [12]understand;

50 A nation [13]of fierce countenance, [p]which shall not regard the person of the old, nor shew favour to the young:

51 And he shall [q]eat the fruit of thy cattle, and the fruit of thy land, until thou be destroyed: which *also* shall not leave thee *either* corn, wine, or oil, *or* the increase of thy kine, or flocks of thy sheep, until he have destroyed thee.

52 And he shall [r]besiege thee in all thy gates, until thy high and fenced walls come down, wherein thou trustedst, throughout all thy land: and he shall besiege thee in all thy gates throughout all thy land, which the LORD thy God hath given thee.

53 And [s]thou shalt eat the fruit of thine own [14]body, the flesh of thy sons and of thy daughters, which the LORD thy God hath given thee, in the siege, and in the straitness, wherewith thine enemies shall distress thee:

54 *So that* the man *that is* tender among you, and very delicate, his eye shall be evil toward his brother, and toward the wife of his bosom, and toward the remnant of his children which he shall leave:

55 So that he will not give to any of them of the flesh of his children whom he shall eat: because he hath nothing left him in the siege, and in the straitness, wherewith thine enemies shall distress thee in all thy gates.

56 The tender and delicate woman among you, which would not adventure to set the sole of her foot upon the ground for delicateness and

25 [v]Lev. 26.17; ch. 32.30; Isa. 30.17
[w]Jer. 15.4; Ezek. 23.46
[7]for a removing
27 [x]Ex. 9.9
[y]1 Sam. 5.6; Ps. 78.66
30 [z]Job 31.10; Jer. 8.10
[8]profane, or, use it as common meat
31 [9]shall not return to thee
33 [a]Lev. 26.16; Jer. 5.17
36 [b]2 Ki. 17.4; 2 Ki. 25.7-11
[c]Jer. 39; 2 Chr. 33
[d]Jer. 16.13
37 [e]1 Ki. 9.7-8; Jer. 24.9; Zech. 8.13
[f]Ps. 44.14
38 [g]Mic. 6.15; Hag. 1.6
[h]Ex. 10.4; Joel 1.4
41 [10]they shall not be thine
[i]Jer. 52.28
42 [11]Or, possess
44 [j]Ezra 9.7; Lam. 1.5
46 [k]Num. 26.10; Isa. 8.18; Ezek. 5.15; Ezek. 14.8
47 [l]Neh. 9.35-36-37
48 [m]Isa. 47.6; Jer. 27.12; Jer. 28.14; Matt. 11.29
49 [n]Jer. 5.15; Jer. 6.22-23; Luke 19.43
[o]Jer. 48.40; Jer. 49.22; Hos. 8.1
[12]hear
50 [13]strong of face, Prov. 7.13; Eccl. 8.1
[p]2 Chr. 36.17; Isa. 47.6
51 [q]Isa. 1.7; Jer. 5.15-17
52 [r]2 Ki. 25.1; Matt. 22.7
53 [s]Lev. 26.29; Luke 21.23
[14]belly

tenderness, her eye shall be evil toward
the husband of her bosom, and toward
her son, and toward her daughter,
57 And [t]toward her [15]young one that
cometh out from between her feet,
and toward her children which she
shall bear: for she shall eat them for
want of all *things* secretly in the siege
and straitness, wherewith thine enemy
shall distress thee in thy gates.
58 If thou wilt not observe to do all
the words of this law that are written
in this book, that thou mayest fear
[u]this glorious and fearful [v]name, THE
LORD THY GOD;
59 Then the LORD will make thy
plagues [w]wonderful, and the plagues
of thy seed, *even* great plagues, and of
long continuance, and sore sicknesses,
and of long continuance.
60 Moreover he will bring upon thee
all the diseases of Ē'gypt, which thou
wast afraid of; and they shall cleave
unto thee.
61 Also every sickness, and every
plague, which *is* not written in the book
of this law, them will the LORD [16]bring
upon thee, until thou be destroyed.
62 And ye shall be left few in number,
whereas ye were [x]as the stars
of heaven for multitude; because thou
wouldest not obey the voice of the
LORD thy God.
63 And it shall come to pass, *that* as
the LORD [y]rejoiced over you to do you
good, and to multiply you; so the LORD
[z]will rejoice over you to destroy you,
and to bring you to nought; and ye shall
be plucked from off the land whither
thou goest to possess it.
64 And the LORD [a]shall scatter thee
among all people, from the one end of
the earth even unto the other; and there
thou shalt serve other gods, which neither
thou nor thy fathers have known,
even wood and stone.
65 And [b]among these nations shalt
thou find no ease, neither shall the sole
of thy foot have rest: [c]but the LORD
shall give thee there a trembling heart,
and failing of eyes, and sorrow of mind:
66 And thy life shall hang in doubt
before thee; and thou shalt fear day
and night, and shalt have none assurance
of thy life:
67 [d]In the morning thou shalt say,
Would God it were even! and at even
thou shalt say, Would God it were
morning! for the fear of thine heart
wherewith thou shalt fear, and for the
sight of thine eyes which thou shalt
see.
68 And the LORD [e]shall bring thee
into Ē'gypt again with ships, by the
way whereof I spake unto thee, Thou
shalt see it no more again: and [17]there
ye shall be sold unto your enemies
for bondmen and bondwomen, and no
man shall buy *you.*

29

These *are* the words of the covenant,
which the LORD commanded
Mō'ses to make with the children
of Ĭs'ra-el in the land of Mō'ab,
beside the covenant which he made
with them in Hō'reb.

57 [t]Lam. 4.10 [15]afterbirth
58 [u]Ex. 6.3; Mal. 1.14
[v]Ps. 20.1; Phil. 2.10
59 [w]1 Ki. 9.7-9; Dan. 9.12
61 [16]cause to ascend
62 [x]Neh. 9.23
63 [y]Isa. 62.5; Luke 15.6-10
[z]Prov. 1.26; Isa. 1.24
64 [a]Lev. 26.33; Neh. 1.8
65 [b]Gen. 8.9; Amos 9.4
[c]Lev. 26.36
67 [d]Job 7.4
68 [e]Jer. 43.7; Hos. 8.13
[17]Fulfilled at the destruction of Jerusalem by the Romans, A. D. 79
CHAPTER 29
3 [a]ch. 4.34; ch. 7.19
4 [b]Ps. 13.3; 2 Thess. 2.11
5 [c]ch. 1.3; ch. 8.2
6 [d]Ex. 16.12; Ps. 78.24
7 [e]Num. 21.23;
8 [f]Num. 32.33
9 [g]Josh. 1.7;
11 [h]Josh. 9.21
12 [1]pass
13 [i]Gen. 17.6-7
14 [j]Jer. 31.31;
15 [k]Acts 2.39;
17 [2]dungy gods
18 [l]Heb. 12.15
[3]rosh, or, a poisonful herb
19 [m]Ps. 14.1
[n]Num. 15.39;

2 ¶ And Mō'ses called unto all Ĭs'ra-
el, and said unto them, Ye have seen
all that the LORD did before your eyes
in the land of Ē'gypt unto Phā'raōh,
and unto all his servants, and unto all
his land;
3 [a]The great temptations which thine
eyes have seen, the signs, and those
great miracles:
4 Yet [b]the LORD hath not given you
an heart to perceive, and eyes to see,
and ears to hear, unto this day.
5 [c]And I have led you forty years in
the wilderness: your clothes are not
waxen old upon you, and thy shoe is
not waxen old upon thy foot.
6 [d]Ye have not eaten bread, neither
have ye drunk wine or strong drink:
that ye might know that I *am* the LORD
your God.
7 And when ye came unto this place,
[e]Sī'hŏn the king of Hĕsh'bŏn, and Ŏg
the king of Bā'shăn, came out against
us unto battle, and we smote them:
8 And we took their land, and [f]gave
it for an inheritance unto the Reu'ben-
ītes, and to the Găd'ītes, and to the half
tribe of Ma-năs'seh.
9 [g]Keep therefore the words of this
covenant, and do them, that ye may
prosper in all that ye do.
10 ¶ Ye stand this day all of you before
the LORD your God; your captains
of your tribes, your elders, and your
officers, *with* all the men of Ĭs'ra-el,
11 Your little ones, your wives, and
thy stranger that *is* in thy camp, from
[h]the hewer of thy wood unto the drawer
of thy water:
12 That thou shouldest [1]enter into
covenant with the LORD thy God, and
into his oath, which the LORD thy God
maketh with thee this day:
13 That he may [i]establish thee to
day for a people unto himself, and
that he may be unto thee a God, as he
hath said unto thee, and as he hath
sworn unto thy fathers, to Ā'bră-hăm,
to Ī'saac, and to Jā'cob.
14 Neither with you only [j]do I make
this covenant and this oath;
15 But with *him* that standeth here
with us this day before the LORD our
God, [k]and also with *him* that *is* not
here with us this day:
16 (For ye know how we have dwelt
in the land of Ē'gypt; and how we
came through the nations which ye
passed by;
17 And ye have seen their abominations,
and their [2]idols, wood and stone,
silver and gold, which *were* among
them:)
18 Lest there should be among you
man, or woman, or family, or tribe,
whose heart turneth away this day
from the LORD our God, to go *and*
serve the gods of these nations; [l]lest
there should be among you a root that
beareth [3]gall and wormwood;
19 And it come to pass, when he
heareth the words of this curse, that he
bless himself in his heart, saying, [m]I
shall have peace, though I walk [n]in the

[4]imagination of mine heart, [o]to add
[5]drunkenness to thirst:
20 [p]The LORD will not spare him,
but then [q]the anger of the LORD and
[r]his jealousy shall smoke against that
man, and all the curses that are written
in this book shall lie upon him, and the
LORD shall blot out his name from under heaven.
21 And the LORD [s]shall separate him
unto evil out of all the tribes of Is′ra-el,
according to all the curses of the covenant that [6]are written in this book of
the law:
22 So that the generation to come of
your children that shall rise up after
you, and the stranger that shall come
from a far land, shall say, when they
see the plagues of that land, and the
sicknesses [7]which the LORD hath laid
upon it;
23 *And that* the whole land thereof
is brimstone, [t]and salt, *and* burning,
that it is not sown, nor beareth, nor
any grass groweth therein, [u]like the
overthrow of Sŏd′om, and Go-mŏr′-
rah, Ăd′-mah, and Ze-bō′im, which the
LORD overthrew in his anger, and in
his wrath:
24 Even all nations shall say, [v]Where-
fore hath the LORD done thus unto this
land? what *meaneth* the heat of this
great anger?
25 Then men shall say, Because they
have forsaken the covenant of the LORD
God of their fathers, which he made
with them when he brought them forth
out of the land of Ē′gypt:
26 For they went and served other
gods, and worshipped them, gods whom
they knew not, and [8]*whom* he had not
[9]given unto them:
27 And the anger of the LORD was
kindled against this land, [w]to bring
upon it all the curses that are written in
this book:
28 And the LORD [x]rooted them out
of their land in anger, and in wrath, and
in great indignation, and cast them into
another land, as *it is* this day.
29 The [y]secret *things belong* unto
the LORD our God: but [z]those *things*
which are revealed *belong* unto us and
to our children for ever, that *we* may
do all the words of this law.

30

And [a]it shall come to pass, when
[b]all these things are come upon
thee, the blessing and the curse, which
I have set before thee, and [c]thou shalt
call *them* to mind among all the nations, whither the LORD thy God hath
driven thee,
2 And shalt [d]return unto the LORD
thy God, and shalt obey his voice according to all that I command thee this
day, thou and thy children, with all
thine heart, and with all thy soul;
3 [e]That then the LORD thy God will
turn thy captivity, and have compassion upon thee, and will return
and [f]gather thee from all the nations,
whither the LORD thy God hath scattered thee.
4 [g]If *any* of thine be driven out
unto the outmost *parts* of heaven, from
thence will the LORD thy God gather
thee, and from thence will he fetch
thee:
5 And the LORD thy God will bring
thee into the land which thy fathers
possessed, and thou shalt possess it;
and he will do thee good, and multiply
thee above thy fathers.
6 And [h]the LORD thy God will circumcise thine heart, and the heart of
thy seed, to love the LORD thy God
with all thine heart, and with all thy
soul, that thou mayest live.
7 And the LORD thy God will put all
these curses upon thine enemies, and
on them that hate thee, which persecuted thee.
8 And thou shalt return and obey the
voice of the LORD, and do all his commandments which I command thee this
day.
9 And the LORD thy God will make
thee plenteous in every work of thine
hand, in the fruit of thy body, and in
the fruit of thy cattle, and in the [i]fruit
of thy land, for good: for the LORD will
again [j]rejoice over thee for good, as he
rejoiced over thy fathers:
10 If thou shalt hearken unto the
voice of the LORD thy God, to keep his
commandments and his statutes which
are written in this book of the law, *and*
if thou turn unto the LORD thy God
with all thine heart, and with all thy
soul.
11 ¶ For this commandment which I
command thee this day, it *is* [k]not hidden from thee, neither *is* it far off.
12 [l]It *is* not in heaven, that thou
shouldest say, Who shall go up for us
to heaven, and bring it unto us, that we
may hear it, and do it?
13 Neither *is* it beyond the sea, that
thou shouldest say, Who shall go over
the sea for us, and bring it unto us, that
we may hear it, and do it?
14 But the word *is* very nigh unto
thee, in thy mouth, and in thy heart,
that thou mayest do it.
15 ¶ See, [m]I have set before thee this
day life and good, and death and evil;
16 In that I command thee this day
to love the LORD thy God, to walk in
his ways, and to keep his commandments and his statutes and his judgments, that thou mayest live and multiply: and the LORD thy God shall bless
thee in the land whither thou goest to
possess it.
17 But if thine heart turn away, so
that thou wilt not hear, but shalt be
drawn away, and worship other gods,
and serve them;
18 [n]I denounce unto you this day,
that ye shall surely perish, *and that* ye
shall not prolong *your* days upon the
land, whither thou passest over Jôr′-
dan to go to possess it.
19 I call heaven and earth to record
this day against you, *that* I have set
before you life and death, blessing and
cursing: therefore choose life, that both
thou and thy seed may live:
20 That thou mayest love the LORD
thy God, *and* that thou mayest obey his

[4]Or, stubbornness
[o]Job 15.16; Isa. 30.1; Eph. 4.19
[5]the drunken to the thirsty
20 [p]Ezek. 14.7
[q]Ps. 74.1
[r]Ps. 79.5
21 [s]Matt. 24.51
[6]is written
22 [7]wherewith the LORD hath made it sick
23 [t]Judg. 9.45; Ps. 107.34; Ezek. 47.11; Zeph. 2.9; Luke 14.34-35
[u]Gen. 19.24
24 [v]1 Ki. 9.8
26 [8]Or, who had not given to them any portion
[9]divided
27 [w]Ps. 11.6
28 [x]2 Chr. 7.20; Job 11.6-7; Ps. 52.5; Prov. 2.22
29 [y]Job 11.6-7; Prov. 3.32; Jer. 23.18; Amos 3.7; Acts 1.7
[z]Ps. 19.7; Luke 16.29; John 5.39; Acts 17.11; 2 Tim. 3.16
CHAPTER 30
1 [a]Lev. 26.40
[b]ch. 28
[c]1 Ki. 8.47-50; Luke 15.17
2 [d]Neh. 1.9
3 [e]Ps. 106.45; Jer. 29.14; Lam. 3.22
[f]Ps. 147.2; Ezek. 34.13
4 [g]ch. 28.64
6 [h]ch. 10.16
9 [i]Ezek. 34.27
[j]Jer. 32.41; Zeph. 3.17; Luke 15.6-10-32
11 [k]Isa. 45.19
12 [l]Prov. 30.4; John 3.13; Rom. 10.6
15 [m]ch. 11.26; Mark 16.16; John 3.16; Gal. 3.13-14
18 [n]ch. 4.26; Isa. 63.17-18

voice, and that thou mayest cleave unto
him: for he *is* thy [o]life, and the length of
thy days: that thou mayest dwell in the
land which the LORD sware unto thy
fathers, to Ā'brā-hăm, to Ī'saac, and to
Jā'cob, [p]to give them.

31 And Mō'ses went and spake these
words unto all Ĭs'ra-el.
2 And he said unto them, I [a]*am* an
hundred and twenty years old this day;
I can no more [b]go out and come in: also
the LORD hath said unto me, [c]Thou
shalt not go over this Jôr'dan.
3 The LORD thy God, [d]he will go
over before thee, *and* he will destroy
these nations from before thee, and
thou shalt possess them: *and* Jŏsh'u-à,
he shall go over before thee, as the
LORD hath said.
4 And the LORD shall do unto them
[e]as he did to Sī'hŏn and to Ōg, kings of
the Ăm'ôr-ītes, and unto the land of
them, whom he destroyed.
5 And [f]the LORD shall give them up
before your face, that ye may do unto
them according unto all the commandments which I have commanded you.
6 [g]Be strong and of a good courage,
[h]fear not, nor be afraid of them: for the
LORD thy God, [i]he *it is* that doth go
with thee; [j]he will not fail thee, nor
forsake thee.
7 ¶ And Mō'ses called unto Jŏsh'u-à,
and said unto him in the sight of all
Ĭs'ra-el, [k]Be strong and of a good courage: for thou must go with this people
unto the land which the LORD hath
sworn unto their fathers to give them;
and thou shalt cause them to inherit it.
8 And the LORD, [l]he *it is* that doth
go before thee; [m]he will be with thee,
he will not fail thee, neither forsake
thee: fear not, neither be dismayed.
9 ¶ And Mō'ses wrote this law, [n]and
delivered it unto the priests the sons of
Lē'vī, [o]which bare the ark of the covenant of the LORD, and unto all the elders of Ĭs'ra-el.
10 And Mō'ses commanded them,
saying, At the end of *every* seven years,
in the solemnity of the [p]year of release,
[q]in the feast of tabernacles,
11 When all Ĭs'ra-el is come to [r]ap-
pear before the LORD thy God in the
place which he shall choose, [s]thou
shalt read this law before all Ĭs'ra-el in
their hearing.
12 [t]Gather the people together, men,
and women, and children, and thy
stranger that *is* within thy gates, that
they may hear, and that they may
learn, and fear the LORD your God, and
observe to do all the words of this law:
13 And *that* their children, [u]which
have not known *any thing*, [v]may hear,
and learn to fear the LORD your God,
as long as ye live in the land whither ye
go over Jôr'dan to possess it.
14 ¶ And the LORD said unto Mō'-
ses, [w]Behold, thy days approach that
thou must die: call Jŏsh'u-à, and present yourselves in the tabernacle of the
congregation, that I may give him a
charge. And Mō'ses and Jŏsh'u-à went,

20 [o]Job 12.10; Acts 17.25-28
[p]Gen. 12.7; Acts 7.5

CHAPTER 31

2 [a]Ex. 7.7; ch. 34.7
[b]Num. 27.17; 1 Ki. 3.7
[c]Num. 20.12; ch. 3.27
3 [d]ch. 9.3
4 [e]Num. 21.24
5 [f]ch. 7.2
6 [g]1 Chr. 22.13
[h]ch. 1.29; ch. 7.18
[i]ch. 20.4; Ps. 118.6
[j]Heb. 13.5
7 [k]ch. 1.38
8 [l]Ex. 13.21; Rom. 8.31
[m]1 Chr. 28.20
9 [n]ch. 17.18
[o]Num. 4.15; 1 Chr. 15.12
10 [p]ch. 15.1
[q]Lev. 23.34
11 [r]ch. 16.16
[s]Josh. 8.34; 2 Ki. 23.2
12 [t]ch. 4.10
13 [u]ch. 11.2; Eph. 6.4
[v]Ps. 78.6-7
14 [w]Num. 27.13
15 [x]Ex. 33.9; Ps. 99.7
16 [1]lie down
[y]Ex. 32.6
[z]Judg. 2.17
[a]ch. 32.15; Isa. 1.4
17 [b]2 Chr. 15.2; 2 Chr. 24.20
[c]ch. 32.20; Ezek. 39.23
[2]find them
[d]Num. 14.42;
[e]Num. 14.42
20 [f]ch. 32.15
21 [3]before
[g]1 Chr. 28.9;
[h]Amos 5.25
[4]do
23 [i]Josh. 1.6
26 [j]1 Ki. 8.9
27 [k]ch. 9.24
[l]ch. 9.6

and presented themselves in the tabernacle of the congregation.
15 And [x]the LORD appeared in the
tabernacle in a pillar of a cloud: and
the pillar of the cloud stood over the
door of the tabernacle.
16 ¶ And the LORD said unto Mō'ses,
Behold, thou shalt [1]sleep with thy fathers; and this people will [y]rise up,
and [z]go a whoring after the gods of the
strangers of the land, whither they go
to be among them, and will [a]forsake
me, and break my covenant which I
have made with them.
17 Then my anger shall be kindled
against them in that day, and [b]I will
forsake them, and I will [c]hide my face
from them, and they shall be devoured,
and many evils and troubles shall [2]be-
fall them; so that they will say in that
day, [d]Are not these evils come upon
us, because our God *is* [e]not among us?
18 And I will surely hide my face in
that day for all the evils which they
shall have wrought, in that they are
turned unto other gods.
19 Now therefore write ye this song
for you, and teach it the children of
Ĭs'ra-el: put it in their mouths, that this
song may be a witness for me against
the children of Ĭs'ra-el.
20 For when I shall have brought
them into the land which I sware unto
their fathers, that floweth with milk
and honey; and they shall have eaten
and filled themselves, [f]and waxen fat;
then will they turn unto other gods,
and serve them, and provoke me, and
break my covenant.
21 And it shall come to pass, when
many evils and troubles are befallen
them, that this song shall testify [3]against
them as a witness; for it shall not be
forgotten out of the mouths of their
seed: for [g]I know their imagination
[h]which they [4]go about, even now, before I have brought them into the land
which I sware.
22 ¶ Mō'ses therefore wrote this
song the same day, and taught it the
children of Ĭs'ra-el.
23 And he gave Jŏsh'u-à the son of
Nŭn a charge, and said, [i]Be strong and
of a good courage: for thou shalt bring
the children of Ĭs'ra-el into the land
which I sware unto them: and I will be
with thee.
24 ¶ And it came to pass, when Mō'-
ses had made an end of writing the
words of this law in a book, until they
were finished,
25 That Mō'ses commanded the Lē'-
vītes, which bare the ark of the covenant of the LORD, saying,
26 Take this book of the law, [j]and
put it in the side of the ark of the covenant of the LORD your God, that it may
be there for a witness against thee.
27 [k]For I know thy rebellion, and
thy [l]stiff neck: behold, while I am yet
alive with you this day, ye have been
rebellious against the LORD; and how
much more after my death?
28 ¶ Gather unto me all the elders of
your tribes, and your officers, that I

may speak these words in their ears,
[m]and call heaven and earth to record
against them.
29 For I know that after my death ye
will utterly corrupt *yourselves,* and
turn aside from the way which I have
commanded you; and evil will befall
you in the latter days; because ye will
do evil in the sight of the LORD, to provoke him to anger through the work of
your hands.
30 And Mō'ses spake in the ears
of all the congregation of Is'ra-el the
words of this song, until they were
ended.

CHAPTER 32

32 Give [a]ear, O ye heavens, and I
will speak; and hear, O earth, the
words of my mouth.
2 [b]My doctrine shall drop as the
rain, my speech shall distil as the dew,
[c]as the small rain upon the tender
herb, and as the showers upon the
grass:
3 Because I will publish the name of
the LORD: ascribe ye greatness unto
our GOD.
4 *He is* the Rock, [d]his work *is* perfect: for [e]all his ways *are* judgment: [f]a
God of truth and [g]without iniquity,
just and right *is* he.
5 [1]They have corrupted themselves,
[2]their spot *is* not *the spot* of his children: *they are* a perverse and crooked
generation.
6 Do ye thus [h]requite the LORD, O
foolish people and unwise? *is* not he
[i]thy father *that* hath [j]bought thee?
hath he not made thee, and established
thee?
7 ¶ Remember the days of old, consider the years of [3]many generations:
ask thy father, and he will shew thee;
thy elders, and they will tell thee.
8 When the most High [k]divided to
the nations their inheritance, when he
[l]separated the sons of Ad'ăm, he set
the bounds of the people according to
the number of the children of Is'ra-el.
9 For [m]the LORD'S portion *is* his people; Jā'cob *is* the [4]lot of his inheritance.
10 He found him in a desert land,
and in the waste howling wilderness;
he [5]led him about, he [n]instructed him,
he [o]kept him as the apple of his eye.
11 As an eagle stirreth up her nest,
fluttereth over her young, spreadeth
abroad her wings, taketh them, beareth them on her wings:
12 *So* the LORD alone did lead him,
and *there was* no strange god with
him.
13 [p]He made him ride on the high
places of the earth, that he might eat
the increase of the fields; and he made
him to suck [q]honey out of the rock,
and oil out of the flinty rock;
14 Butter of kine, and milk of sheep,
with fat of lambs, and rams of the
breed of Bā'shăn, and goats, [r]with the
fat of kidneys of wheat; and thou didst
drink the pure [s]blood of the grape.
15 ¶ But Jĕsh'u-rŭn waxed fat, and
kicked: thou art waxen fat, thou art
grown thick, thou art covered *with
fatness;* then he [t]forsook God *which*

28 [m]ch. 30.19
CHAPTER 32
1 [a]Ps. 50.4
2 [b]2 Sam. 23.4; [c]Ps. 72.6
4 [d]2 Sam. 22.3 [e]Dan. 4.37 [f]Jer. 10.10 [g]Job 34.10
5 [1]He hath corrupted to himself [2]Or, that they are not his children, that is their blot
6 [h]Ps. 116.12 [i]Isa. 63.16 [j]2 Sam. 7.23
7 [3]generation and generation
8 [k]Zech. 9.2 [l]Gen. 11.8
9 [m]1 Sam. 10.1 [4]cord
10 [5]Or, compassed him about [n]ch. 4.36; [o]Ps. 17.8
13 [p]Isa. 58.14 [q]Job 29.6
14 [r]Ps. 147.14 [s]Gen. 49.11
15 [t]Isa. 1.4 [u]Ps. 89.26
17 [6]Or, which were not God
19 [7]Or, despised
20 [v]Matt. 17.17
21 [w]1 Sam. 12.21 [x]Rom. 10.19
22 [y]Lam. 4.11 [8]Or, hath burned [9]Or, hath consumed
24 [10]burning coals
25 [z]Lam. 1.20 [11]from the chambers [12]bereave
27 [a]Ps. 140.8 [13]Or, Our high hand, and not the LORD, hath done all this
29 [b]Ps. 81.13
30 [c]Josh. 23.10 [d]Ps. 44.12
31 [e]1 Sam. 4.8
32 [14]Or, is worse than the vine of Sodom, etc
34 [f]Job 14.17

made him, and lightly esteemed the
[u]Rock of his salvation.
16 They provoked him to jealousy
with strange *gods,* with abominations
provoked they him to anger.
17 They sacrificed unto devils, [6]not
to God; to gods whom they knew not, to
new *gods that* came newly up, whom
your fathers feared not.
18 Of the Rock *that* begat thee thou
art unmindful, and hast forgotten God
that formed thee.
19 And when the LORD saw *it,* he
[7]abhorred *them,* because of the provoking of his sons, and of his daughters.
20 And he said, I will hide my face
from them, I will see what their end
shall be: for they *are* a very froward
generation, [v]children in whom *is* no
faith.
21 They have moved me to jealousy
with *that which is* not God; they have
provoked me to anger [w]with their vanities: and [x]I will move them to jealousy
with *those which are* not a people; I
will provoke them to anger with a foolish nation.
22 For [y]a fire is kindled in mine anger, and [8]shall burn unto the lowest
hell, and [9]shall consume the earth with
her increase, and set on fire the foundations of the mountains.
23 I will heap mischiefs upon them;
I will spend mine arrows upon them.
24 *They shall be* burnt with hunger,
and devoured with [10]burning heat, and
with bitter destruction: I will also send
the teeth of beasts upon them, with the
poison of serpents of the dust.
25 [z]The sword without, and terror
[11]within, shall [12]destroy both the young
man and the virgin, the suckling *also*
with the man of gray hairs.
26 I said, I would scatter them into
corners, I would make the remembrance of them to cease from among
men:
27 Were it not that I feared the wrath
of the enemy, lest their adversaries
should behave themselves strangely,
and lest they should [a]say, [13]Our hand *is*
high, and the LORD hath not done all
this.
28 For they *are* a nation void of counsel, neither *is there any* understanding
in them.
29 [b]O that they were wise, *that* they
understood this, *that* they would consider their latter end!
30 How should [c]one chase a thousand, and two put ten thousand to
flight, except their Rock [d]had sold
them, and the LORD had shut them up?
31 For their rock *is* not as our Rock,
[e]even our enemies themselves *being*
judges.
32 For their vine [14]*is* of the vine of
Sŏd'om, and of the fields of Go-mŏr'-
rah: their grapes *are* grapes of gall,
their clusters *are* bitter:
33 Their wine *is* the poison of dragons, and the cruel venom of asps.
34 *Is* not this [f]laid up in store with
me, *and* sealed up among my treasures?

35 [g]To me *belongeth* vengeance, and recompence; their foot shall slide in *due* time: for the day of their calamity *is* at hand, and the things that shall come upon them make haste.

36 For the LORD shall judge his people, [h]and repent himself for his servants, when he seeth that *their* [15]power is gone, and *there is* none shut up, or left.

37 And he shall say, [i]Where *are* their gods, *their* rock in whom they trusted,

38 Which did eat the fat of their sacrifices, *and* drank the wine of their drink offerings? let them rise up and help you, *and* be [16]your protection.

39 See now that I, *even* I, *am* he, and [j]*there is* no god with me: [k]I kill, and I make alive; I wound, and I heal: neither *is there any* that can deliver out of my hand.

40 [l]For I lift up my hand to heaven, and say, I live for ever.

41 If I whet my glittering sword, and mine hand take hold on judgment; I will render vengeance to mine enemies, and will reward them that hate me.

42 I will make mine arrows drunk with blood, and my sword shall devour flesh; *and that* with the blood of the slain and of the captives, from the beginning of revenges [m]upon the enemy.

43 [17][n]Rejoice, O ye nations, *with* his people: for he will [o]avenge the blood of his servants, and [p]will render vengeance to his adversaries, and will be merciful unto his land, *and* to his people.

44 ¶ And Mō'ses came and spake all the words of this song in the ears of the people, he, and [18]Ho-shē'ȧ the son of Nŭn.

45 And Mō'ses made an end of speaking all these words to all Ĭs'ra-el:

46 And he said unto them, Set your hearts unto all the words which I testify among you this day, which ye shall command your children to observe to do, all the words of this law.

47 For it *is* not a vain thing for you; [q]because it *is* your life: and through this thing ye shall prolong *your* days in the land, whither ye go over Jôr'dan to possess it.

48 [r]And the LORD spake unto Mō'ses that selfsame day, saying,

49 Get thee up into this mountain Ăb'ă-rim, *unto* mount Nē'bo, which *is* in the land of Mō'ab, that *is* over against Jĕr'ĭ-chō; and behold the land of Cā'năan, which I give unto the children of Ĭs'ra-el for a possession:

50 And die in the mount whither thou goest up, and be gathered unto thy people; as Aâr'on thy brother died in mount Hôr, and was gathered unto his people:

51 Because [s]ye trespassed against me among the children of Ĭs'ra-el at the waters of [19]Mĕr'ĭ-bah–Kā'desh, in the wilderness of Zĭn; because ye sanctified me not in the midst of the children of Ĭs'ra-el.

35 [g]Ps. 94.1; Heb. 10.30
36 [h]Judg. 2.18; Ps. 106.45
[15]hand
37 [i]Judg. 10.14; 2 Ki. 3.13
38 [16]an hiding for you
39 [j]Isa. 41.4; Isa. 45.5
[k]1 Sam. 2.6; Hos. 6.1
40 [l]Ex. 6.8
42 [m]Job 13.24
43 [17]Or, Praise his people, ye nations: or, Sing ye
[n]Rom. 15.10
[o]Rev. 6.10
[p]Ps. 85.1
44 [18]Or, Joshua
47 [q]Prov. 3.2; Rom. 10.5
48 [r]Num. 27.12
51 [s]Num. 20.11
[19]Or, strife at Kadesh

CHAPTER 33
1 [a]Gen. 49.28; Luke 24.50-53
2 [b]Ex. 19.18; Hab. 3.3
[c]Dan. 7.10; Heb. 2.2
[1]a fire of law
3 [d]Hos. 11.1; Mal. 1.2
[e]1 Sam. 2.9; Ps. 50.5
[f]Luke 10.39; Acts 22.3
4 [g]John 7.19
5 [h]Job 29.25
7 [i]Gen. 49.8
8 [j]Ex. 28.30; Num. 27.21
9 [k]ch. 13.6; Luke 14.26
[l]Ex. 32.26
[m]Mal. 2.5
10 [2]Or, Let them teach, etc
[3]Or, let them put incense
[4]at thy nose
[n]Ps. 51.19
11 [o]Ps. 20.3
13 [p]Gen. 49.25
[q]Gen. 27.28
14 [5]thrust forth
[6]moons
15 [r]Hab. 3.6
16 [s]Ex. 3.2-4

52 Yet thou shalt see the land before *thee;* but thou shalt not go thither unto the land which I give the children of Ĭs'ra-el.

33

And [a]this *is* the blessing, wherewith Mō'ses the man of God blessed the children of Ĭs'ra-el before his death.

2 And he said, [b]The LORD came from Sī'nāi, and rose up from Sē'ĭr unto them; he shined forth from mount Pā'-ran, and he came with [c]ten thousands of saints: from his right hand *went* [1]a fiery law for them.

3 Yea, [d]he loved the people; [e]all his saints *are* in thy hand: and they [f]sat down at thy feet; *every one* shall receive of thy words.

4 [g]Mō'ses commanded us a law, *even* the inheritance of the congregation of Jā'cob.

5 And he was [h]king in Jĕsh'u-rŭn, when the heads of the people *and* the tribes of Ĭs'ra-el were gathered together.

6 ¶ Let Reu'ben live, and not die; and let *not* his men be few.

7 ¶ And this *is the blessing* of Jū'-dah: and he said, Hear, LORD, the voice of Jū'dah, and bring him unto his people: [i]let his hands be sufficient for him; and be thou an help *to him* from his enemies.

8 ¶ And of Lē'vī he said, [j]*Let* thy Thŭm'mim and thy Ū'rim *be* with thy holy one, whom thou didst prove at Măs'sah, *and with* whom thou didst strive at the waters of Mĕr'ĭ-bah;

9 Who said unto his [k]father and to his mother, I have not seen him; [l]neither did he acknowledge his brethren, nor knew his own children: for [m]they have observed thy word, and kept thy covenant.

10 [2]They shall teach Jā'cob thy judgments, and Ĭs'ra-el thy law: [3]they shall put incense [4]before thee, [n]and whole burnt sacrifice upon thine altar.

11 Bless, LORD, his substance, and accept [o]the work of his hands: smite through the loins of them that rise against him, and of them that hate him, that they rise not again.

12 ¶ *And* of Bĕn'ja-min he said, The beloved of the LORD shall dwell in safety by him; *and the* LORD shall cover him all the day long, and he shall dwell between his shoulders.

13 ¶ And of Jō'seph he said, [p]Blessed of the LORD *be* his land, for the precious things of heaven, for [q]the dew, and for the deep that coucheth beneath,

14 And for the precious fruits *brought forth* by the sun, and for the precious things [5]put forth by the [6]moon,

15 And for the chief things of the ancient mountains, and for the precious things [r]of the lasting hills,

16 And for the precious things of the earth and fulness thereof, and *for* the good will of [s]him that dwelt in the bush: let *the blessing* come upon the head of Jō'seph, and upon the top of the head of him *that was* separated from his brethren.

17 His glory *is like* the firstling of his bullock, and his horns *are like* the horns of [7]unicorns: with them [t]he shall push the people together to the ends of the earth: and they *are* the ten thousands of Ē'phră-ĭm, and they *are* the thousands of Ma-năs'seh.

18 ¶ And of Zĕb'u-lun he said, Rejoice, Zĕb'u-lun, in thy going out; and, Ĭs'sa-char, in thy tents.

19 They shall [u]call the people unto the mountain; there [v]they shall offer sacrifices of righteousness: for they shall suck *of* the abundance of the seas, and *of* treasures hid in the sand.

20 ¶ And of Găd he said, Blessed *be* he that [w]enlargeth Găd: he dwelleth as a lion, and teareth the arm with the crown of the head.

21 And [x]he provided the first part for himself, because there, *in* a portion of the lawgiver, *was he* [8]seated; and [y]he came with the heads of the people, he executed the justice of the LORD, and his judgments with Ĭs'ra-el.

22 ¶ And of Dăn he said, Dăn *is* a lion's whelp: [z]he shall leap from Bā'-shăn.

23 ¶ And of Năph'ta-lī he said, O Năph'ta-lī, satisfied with favour, and full with the blessing of the LORD: [a]possess thou the west and the south.

24 ¶ And of Ăsh'ēr he said, *Let* Ăsh'ēr *be* blessed with children; let him be acceptable to his brethren, and let him [b]dip his foot in oil.

25 [9]Thy shoes *shall be* iron and brass; and as thy days, *so shall* thy strength *be*.

26 ¶ *There is* [c]none like unto the God of Jĕsh'u-rŭn, [d]*who* rideth upon the heaven in thy help, and in his excellency on the sky.

27 The eternal God *is thy* [e]refuge, and underneath *are* the everlasting arms: and he shall thrust out the enemy from before thee; and shall say, Destroy *them*.

28 [f]Ĭs'ra-el then shall dwell in safety alone: the fountain of Jā'cob *shall be* upon a land of corn and wine; also his heavens shall drop down dew.

29 Happy [g]*art* thou, O Ĭs'ra-el: [h]who *is* like unto thee, O people saved by the LORD, the shield of thy help, and who *is* the sword of thy excellency! and thine enemies [10]shall be found liars unto thee; and thou shalt tread upon their high places.

34 And Mō'ses went up from the plains of Mō'ab unto the mountain of Nē'bo, to the top of [1]Pĭs'gah, that *is* over against Jĕr'ĭ-chō. And the LORD shewed him all the land of Gĭl'e-ăd, [a]unto Dăn,

2 And all Năph'ta-lī, and the land of Ē'phră-ĭm, and Ma-năs'seh, and all the land of Jū'dah, [b]unto the utmost sea,

3 And the south, and the plain of the valley of Jĕr'ĭ-chō, [c]the city of palm trees, unto Zō'ar.

4 And the LORD said unto him, This *is* the land which I sware unto Ā'bră-hăm, unto Ī'saac, and unto Jā'cob, saying, I will give it unto thy seed: I have caused thee to see *it* with thine eyes, but thou shalt not go over thither.

5 ¶ [d]So Mō'ses the servant of the LORD died there in the land of Mō'ab, according to the word of the LORD.

6 And he buried him in a valley in the land of Mō'ab, over against Bĕth-pē'ôr: but [e]no man knoweth of his sepulchre unto this day.

7 ¶ [f]And Mō'ses *was* an hundred and twenty years old when he died: [g]his eye was not dim, nor his [2]natural force abated.

8 ¶ And the children of Ĭs'ra-el wept for Mō'ses in the plains of Mō'ab [h]thirty days: so the days of weeping *and* mourning for Mō'ses were ended.

9 ¶ And Jŏsh'u-ȧ the son of Nŭn was full of the [i]spirit of wisdom; for Mō'ses [j]had laid his hands upon him: and the children of Ĭs'ra-el hearkened unto him, and did as the LORD commanded Mō'ses.

10 ¶ And there [k]arose not a prophet since in Ĭs'ra-el like unto Mō'ses, [l]whom the LORD knew face to face,

11 In all the signs and the wonders, which the LORD sent him to do in the land of Ē'gypt to Phā'raōh, and to all his servants, and to all his land,

12 And in all that mighty hand, and in all the great terror which Mō'ses shewed in the sight of all Ĭs'ra-el.

17 [7]an unicorn [t]1 Ki. 22.11
19 [u]Isa. 2.3 [v]Ps. 4.5
20 [w]1 Chr. 12.8
21 [x]Num. 32.16 [8]cieled [y]Num. 32.16-21
22 [z]Josh. 19.47
23 [a]Josh. 19.32
24 [b]Job 29.6
25 [9]Or, Under thy shoes shall be iron
26 [c]Ps. 86.8; Jer. 10.6 [d]Ps. 68.4-33-34; Hab. 3.8
27 [e]Ps. 90.1
28 [f]Num. 23.9; Jer. 23.6
29 [g]Ps. 144.15 [h]2 Sam. 7.23 [10]Or, shall be subdued

CHAPTER 34
1 [1]Or, the hill [a]Judg. 18.29
2 [b]Ex. 23.31; Num. 34.6; ch. 11.24
3 [c]Judg. 1.16; 2 Chr. 28.15
5 [d]ch. 32.50; Josh. 1.1-2; Mal. 4.4
6 [e]Jude 9
7 [f]ch. 31.2 [g]Gen. 27.1 [2]moisture fled
8 [h]Gen. 50.3; Num. 20.29
9 [i]Ex. 31.3; Num. 11.17; 1 Ki. 3.12; Isa. 11.2 [j]Num. 27.18
10 [k]ch. 18.15-18 [l]Ex. 33.11; Num. 12.6; ch. 5.4

THE BOOK OF

JOSHUA

Life's Questions

What happens when I join in God's mission?
How do I respond to the good times of life?
What is involved in renewing the love relationship with God?

God's Answers

Joshua shows God fulfills His promises and renews His expectations of His people. In three parts Joshua shows: God wins complete victory over the enemies (chs. 1—12); God divides the land among the people (chs. 13—23); and God calls His people to unity in covenant renewal (22:1—24:33).

Joshua centers attention on God's faithfulness and the faithfulness of a people behind a faithful leader.

God expects faithfulness to His Book (1:1–18).
God uses an unlikely example of faith to prepare His people to take the land (2:1—5:15).
God provides total victory when His people repent and obey (6:1—12:24).
God divides the land before rest is won (13:1—19:48).
God rewards a faithful leader (19:49–51; compare 14:1–15).
God provides justice for the accused in refuge cities (20:1–9),
God provides for the priests (21:1–42).
God fulfills all His promises (21:43–45).
God wants a unified people (22:-1–34).
God calls His people to choose the love relationship of covenant (23:1—24:33).

Joshua shows God using a leader dedicated to His word to fulfill the promise of land and to bring the people to unified commitment to His covenant. The people learn they must obey to gain the promise; God will be faithful to His promise; God works for justice; and God wants to be in a love relationship of covenant with His people.

1 Now after the death of Mō'ses the
servant of the LORD it came to pass,
that the LORD spake unto Jŏsh'u-ȧ the
son of Nŭn, Mō'ses' [a]minister, saying,
2 [b]Mō'ses my servant is dead; now
therefore arise, go over this Jôr'dan,
thou, and all this people, unto the land
which I do give to them, *even* to the
children of Ĭs'ra-el.
3 [c]Every place that the sole of your
foot shall tread upon, that have I given
unto you, as I said unto Mō'ses.
4 [d]From the wilderness and this
Lĕb'a-non even unto the great river,
the river Eū-phrā'tēs, all the land of
the Hĭt'tītes, and unto the great sea toward the going down of the sun, shall
be your coast.
5 [e]There shall not any man be able
to stand before thee all the days of thy
life: [f]as I was with Mō'ses, *so* I will be
with thee: [g]I will not fail thee, nor forsake thee.
6 Be strong and of a good courage:
for [1]unto this people shalt thou divide
for an inheritance the land, which I
sware unto their fathers to give them.
7 Only be thou strong and very courageous, that thou mayest observe to
do according to all the law, [h]which
Mō'ses my servant commanded thee:
turn not from it *to* the right hand or
to the left, that thou mayest [2]prosper
whithersoever thou goest.
8 [i]This book of the law shall not depart out of thy mouth; but [j]thou shalt
meditate therein day and night, that
thou mayest observe to do according
to all that is written therein: for [k]then
thou shalt make thy way prosperous,
and then thou shalt [3]have good success.
9 Have not I commanded thee? Be
strong and of a good courage; [l]be not
afraid, neither be thou dismayed: for
the LORD thy God *is* with thee whithersoever thou goest.
10 ¶ Then Jŏsh'u-ȧ commanded the
officers of the people, saying,
11 Pass through the host, and command the people, saying, Prepare you
victuals; for [m]within three days ye
shall pass over this Jôr'dan, to go in to
possess the land, which the LORD your
God giveth you to possess it.

CHAPTER 1
1 [a]Deut. 1.38
2 [b]Deut. 34.5
3 [c]Deut. 11.24
4 [d]Gen. 15.18; 1 Chr. 5.9
5 [e]Deut. 7.24; Rom. 8.31-37
[f]Ex. 3.12
[g]Deut. 31.6
6 [1]Or, thou shalt cause this people to inherit the land
7 [h]Num. 27.23; ch. 11.15
[2]Or, do wisely
8 [i]Deut. 17.18-19
[j]Ps. 1.2
[k]1 Chr. 22.13; Prov. 3.1
[3]Or, do wisely
9 [l]Ps. 27.1
11 [m]Deut. 9.1
13 [n]Num. 32.20
14 [4]marshalled by five: as Ex. 13.18
15 [o]ch. 22.4
17 [p]Gen. 21.22
CHAPTER 2
1 [1]Or, had sent
[a]Num. 25.1
[b]Heb. 11.31;
[c]Matt. 1.5;
[2]lay
2 [d]Ps. 127.1
4 [e]2 Sam. 17.19

12 ¶ And to the Reu̯'ben-ītes, and to
the Găd'ītes, and to half the tribe of
Ma-năs'seh, spake Jŏsh'u-ȧ, saying,
13 Remember [n]the word which Mō'-
ses the servant of the LORD commanded you, saying, The LORD your
God hath given you rest, and hath
given you this land.
14 Your wives, your little ones, and
your cattle, shall remain in the land
which Mō'ses gave you on this side
Jôr'dan; but ye shall pass before your
brethren [4]armed, all the mighty men of
valour, and help them;
15 Until the LORD have given your
brethren rest, as *he hath given* you,
and they also have possessed the land
which the LORD your God giveth them:
[o]then ye shall return unto the land of
your possession, and enjoy it, which
Mō'ses the LORD'S servant gave you
on this side Jôr'dan toward the sunrising.
16 ¶ And they answered Jŏsh'u-ȧ,
saying, All that thou commandest us
we will do, and whithersoever thou
sendest us, we will go.
17 According as we hearkened unto
Mō'ses in all things, so will we hearken unto thee: only the LORD thy God
[p]be with thee, as he was with Mō'ses.
18 Whosoever *he be* that doth rebel
against thy commandment, and will
not hearken unto thy words in all that
thou commandest him, he shall be put
to death: only be strong and of a good
courage.

2 And Jŏsh'u-ȧ the son of Nŭn [1]sent
[a]out of Shĭt'tim two men to spy secretly, saying, Go view the land, even
Jĕr'ĭ-chō. And they went, and [b]came
into an harlot's house, named [c]Rā'hăb,
and [2]lodged there.
2 And [d]it was told the king of Jĕr'ĭ-
chō, saying, Behold, there came men
in hither to night of the children of
Ĭs'ra-el to search out the country.
3 And the king of Jĕr'ĭ-chō sent unto
Rā'hăb, saying, Bring forth the men
that are come to thee, which are entered into thine house: for they be come
to search out all the country.
4 [e]And the woman took the two
men, and hid them, and said thus,
There came men unto me, but I wist
not whence they *were*:

5 And it came to pass *about the time*
of shutting of the gate, when it was
dark, that the men went out: whither
the men went I wot not: pursue after
them quickly; for ye shall overtake
them.
6 But [f]she had brought them up to
the roof of the house, and hid them
with the stalks of flax, which she had
laid in order upon the roof.
7 And the men pursued after them
the way to Jôr'dan unto the fords: and
as soon as they which pursued after
them were gone out, they shut the gate.
8 ¶ And before they were laid down,
she came up unto them upon the roof;
9 And she said unto the men, I know
that the LORD hath given you the land,
and that your [g]terror is fallen upon us,
and that all the inhabitants of the land
[3]faint because of you.
10 For we have heard how the LORD
[h]dried up the water of the Red sea for
you, when ye came out of Ē'gypt; and
[i]what ye did unto the two kings of the
Ăm'ôr-ītes, that *were* on the other side
Jôr'dan, Sī'hŏn and Ŏg, whom ye utterly destroyed.
11 And as soon as we had [j]heard
these things, [k]our hearts did melt, neither [4]did there remain any more courage in any man, because of you: for
[l]the LORD your God, he *is* God in
heaven above, and in earth beneath.
12 Now therefore, I pray you, [m]swear
unto me by the LORD, since I have
shewed you kindness, that ye will also
shew kindness unto [n]my father's house,
and give me a true token:
13 And *that* ye will save alive my
father, and my mother, and my brethren, and my sisters, and all that they
have, and deliver our lives from death.
14 And the men answered her, Our
life [5]for yours, if ye utter not this our
business. And it shall be, when the
LORD hath given us the land, that [o]we
will deal kindly and truly with thee.
15 Then she [p]let them down by a
cord through the window: for her house
was upon the town wall, and she dwelt
upon the wall.
16 And she said unto them, Get you
to the mountain, lest the pursuers meet
you; and hide yourselves there three
days, until the pursuers be returned:
and afterward may ye go your way.
17 And the men said unto her, We
will be [q]blameless of this thine oath
which thou hast made us swear.
18 Behold, *when* we come into the
land, thou shalt bind this line of scarlet
thread in the window which thou didst
let us down by: [r]and thou shalt [6]bring
thy father, and thy mother, and thy
brethren, and all thy father's household, home unto thee.
19 And it shall be, *that* whosoever
shall go [s]out of the doors of thy house
into the street, his blood *shall be* upon
his head, and we *will be* guiltless: and
whosoever shall be with thee in the
house, [t]his blood *shall be* on our head,
if *any* hand be upon him.
20 And if thou utter this our business, then we will be quit of thine oath
which thou hast made us to swear.
21 And she said, According unto
your words, so *be* it. And she sent
them away, and they departed: and
she bound the scarlet line in the window.
22 And they went, and came unto
the mountain, and abode there three
days, until the pursuers were returned:
and the pursuers sought *them* throughout all the way, but found *them* not.
23 ¶ So the two men returned, and
descended from the mountain, and
passed over, and came to Jŏsh'u-ȧ the
son of Nŭn, and told him all *things* that
befell them:
24 And they said unto Jŏsh'u-ȧ,
Truly [u]the LORD hath delivered into
our hands all the land; for even all the
inhabitants of the country do [7]faint because of us.

3 And Jŏsh'u-ȧ rose early in the morning; and they removed [a]from Shĭt'-
tim, and came to Jôr'dan, he and all the
children of Ĭs'ra-el, and lodged there
before they passed over.
2 And it came to pass [b]after three
days, that the officers went through
the host;
3 And they commanded the people,
saying, [c]When ye see the ark of the
covenant of the LORD your God, [d]and
the priests the Lē'vītes bearing it, then
ye shall remove from your place, and
go after it.
4 [e]Yet there shall be a space between you and it, about two thousand
cubits by measure: come not near unto
it, that ye may know the way by which
ye must go: for ye have not passed *this*
way [1]heretofore.
5 And Jŏsh'u-ȧ said unto the people,
Sanctify [f]yourselves: for to morrow
the LORD will do wonders among you.
6 And Jŏsh'u-ȧ spake unto the priests,
saying, [g]Take up the ark of the covenant, and pass over before the people.
And they took up the ark of the covenant, and went before the people.
7 ¶ And the LORD said unto Jŏsh'-
u-ȧ, This day will I begin to [h]magnify
thee in the sight of all Ĭs'ra-el, that
they may know that, as I was with
Mō'ses, *so* I will be with thee.
8 And thou shalt command the
priests that bear the ark of the covenant, saying, When ye are come to the
brink of the water of Jôr'dan, ye shall
stand still in Jôr'dan.
9 ¶ And Jŏsh'u-ȧ said unto the children of Ĭs'ra-el, Come hither, and hear
the words of the LORD your God.
10 And Jŏsh'u-ȧ said, Hereby ye
shall know that the [i]living God *is*
among you, and *that* he will without
fail [j]drive out from before you the Cā'-
năan-ītes, and the Hĭt'tītes, and the
Hī'vītes, and the Pĕr'ĭz-zītes, and the
Gĭr'ga-shītes, and the Ăm'ôr-ītes, and
the Jĕb'u-sītes.
11 Behold, the ark of the covenant
of [k]the Lord of all the earth passeth
over before you into Jôr'dan.

6 [f]Ex. 1.17
9 [g]Gen. 35.5; Ex. 15.15; Deut. 2.25
[3]melt
10 [h]ch. 4.23
[i]Num. 21.24-34-35
11 [j]Ex. 15.14-15
[k]ch. 5.1; ch. 7.5; Isa. 13.7
[4]rose up
[l]Deut. 4.39; 1 Ki. 8.60; Ps. 83.18; Dan. 4.34-35; Zech. 8.20-23
12 [m]1 Sam. 20.14-15-17
[n]Eph. 6.1-2; 1 Tim. 5.8
14 [5]instead of you to die
[o]Matt. 5.7
15 [p]Acts 9.25; Heb. 11.31
17 [q]Ex. 20.7
18 [r]Gen. 7.1; Gen. 19.12-17; ch. 6.23; Esth. 8.6; Acts 11.14; 2 Tim. 1.16
[6]gather
19 [s]Num. 35.26-27
[t]Matt. 27.25
24 [u]Ex. 23.31; ch. 6.2; ch. 21.44
[7]melt

CHAPTER 3
1 [a]Num. 25.1; ch. 2.1
2 [b]ch. 1.10-11
3 [c]Num. 10.33
[d]Deut. 31.9
4 [e]Ex. 19.12; Deut. 28.58; 1 Chr. 16.30; Ps. 2.11; Heb. 12.28
[1]since yesterday, and the third day
5 [f]Lev. 20.7; Num. 11.18; ch. 7.13; 1 Sam. 16.5
6 [g]Num. 4.15
7 [h]ch. 4.14; 2 Chr. 1.1
10 [i]Deut. 5.26; Matt. 16.16
[j]Ex. 33.2; Ps. 44.2
11 [k]Job 41.11; Zech. 4.14

12 Now therefore [l]take you twelve
men out of the tribes of Ĭs'ra-el, out of
every tribe a man.
13 And it shall come to pass, as soon
as the soles of the feet of the priests
that bear the ark of the LORD, the Lord
of all the earth, shall rest in the waters
of Jôr'dan, *that* the waters of Jôr'-
dan shall be cut off *from* the waters
that come down from above; and they
[m]shall stand upon an heap.
14 ¶ And it came to pass, when the
people removed from their tents, to
pass over Jôr'dan, and the priests bearing the [n]ark of the covenant before the
people;
15 And as they that bare the ark
were come unto Jôr'dan, and the feet
of the priests that bare the ark were
dipped in the brim of the water, (for
[o]Jôr'dan [2]overfloweth all his banks
[p]all the time of harvest,)
16 That the waters which came down
from above stood *and* rose up upon an
heap very far from the city Ȧ'dăm, that
is beside [q]Zăr'e-tăn: and those that
came down [r]toward the sea of the plain,
even [s]the salt sea, failed, *and* were cut
off: and the people passed over right
against Jĕr'ĭ-chō.
17 And the priests that bare the ark
of the covenant of the LORD stood firm
on dry ground in the midst of Jôr'dan,
[t]and all the Ĭs'ra-el-ītes passed over on
dry ground, until all the people were
passed clean over Jôr'dan.

4 And it came to pass, when all the
people were clean passed [a]over
Jôr'dan, that the LORD spake unto
Jŏsh'u-ȧ, saying,
2 [b]Take you twelve men out of the
people, out of every tribe a man,
3 And command ye them, saying,
Take you hence out of the midst of
Jôr'dan, out of the place where the
priests' feet stood firm, twelve stones,
and ye shall carry them over with you,
and leave them in the lodging place,
where ye shall lodge this night.
4 Then Jŏsh'u-ȧ called the twelve
men, whom he had prepared of the children of Ĭs'ra-el, out of every tribe a
man:
5 And Jŏsh'u-ȧ said unto them, Pass
over before the ark of the LORD your
God into the midst of Jôr'dan, and take
you up every man of you a stone upon
his shoulder, according unto the number of the tribes of the children of Ĭs'ra-
el:
6 That this may be a sign among
you, *that* [c]when your children ask
their fathers [1]in time to come, saying,
What *mean* ye by these stones?
7 Then ye shall answer them, That
[d]the waters of Jôr'dan were cut off before the ark of the covenant of the
LORD; when it passed over Jôr'dan, the
waters of Jôr'dan were cut off: and
these stones shall be for [e]a memorial
unto the children of Ĭs'ra-el for ever.
8 And the children of Ĭs'ra-el did so
as Jŏsh'u-ȧ commanded, and took up
twelve stones out of the midst of Jôr'-
dan, as the LORD spake unto Jŏsh'u-ȧ,

12 [l]ch. 4.2
13 [m]Ex. 15.8; Hab. 3.15
14 [n]Ex. 25.10; Heb. 9.4
15 [o]1 Chr. 12.15; Jer. 12.5
[2]Occasioned by the melting of the snow on Lebanon
[p]ch. 4.18; ch. 5.10-12
16 [q]1 Ki. 4.12; 1 Ki. 7.46
[r]Deut. 3.17
[s]Gen. 14.3; Num. 34.3
17 [t]Ex. 14.29; Heb. 11.29
CHAPTER 4
1 [a]Deut. 27.2; ch. 3.17
2 [b]Num. 13.2-16; 1 Ki. 18.31
6 [c]Ex. 12.26; Isa. 38.16
[1]to morrow
7 [d]ch. 3.13
[e]Ex. 12.14; 1 Cor. 11.24
9 [f]Gen. 28.18; 1 Sam. 7.12
[2]B. C. 1427
12 [g]Num. 32.20
13 [3]Or, ready armed
14 [h]ch. 3.7; 2 Chr. 1.1
16 [i]Ex. 25.16; Rev. 11.19
18 [4]plucked up
[5]went
19 [j]ch. 5.9; Mic. 6.5
21 [6]to morrow
23 [k]Ex. 14.21; Isa. 43.16
24 [l]Ex. 9.16; Dan. 3.26-29
[m]1 Chr. 29.12;
[n]Ex. 14.31;
[7]all days

according to the number of the tribes
of the children of Ĭs'ra-el, and carried
them over with them unto the place
where they lodged, and laid them down
there.
9 And Jŏsh'u-ȧ [f]set up twelve stones
in the midst of Jôr'dan, in the place
where the feet of the priests which bare
the ark of the covenant stood: and they
are there [2]unto this day.
10 ¶ For the priests which bare the
ark stood in the midst of Jôr'dan, until
every thing was finished that the LORD
commanded Jŏsh'u-ȧ to speak unto the
people, according to all that Mō'ses
commanded Jŏsh'-u-ȧ: and the people
hasted and passed over.
11 And it came to pass, when all the
people were clean passed over, that
the ark of the LORD passed over, and
the priests, in the presence of the people.
12 And [g]the children of Reu'ben,
and the children of Găd, and half the
tribe of Ma-năs'seh, passed over armed
before the children of Ĭs'ra-el, as Mō'-
ses spake unto them:
13 About forty thousand [3]prepared
for war passed over before the LORD
unto battle, to the plains of Jĕr'ĭ-chō.
14 ¶ On that day the LORD magnified
[h]Jŏsh'u-ȧ in the sight of all Ĭs'ra-el;
and they feared him, as they feared
Mō'ses, all the days of his life.
15 And the LORD spake unto Jŏsh'-
u-ȧ, saying,
16 Command the priests that bear
[i]the ark of the testimony, that they
come up out of Jôr'dan.
17 Jŏsh'u-ȧ therefore commanded
the priests, saying, Come ye up out of
Jôr'dan.
18 And it came to pass, when the
priests that bare the ark of the covenant of the LORD were come up out of
the midst of Jôr'dan, *and* the soles of
the priests' feet were [4]lifted up unto the
dry land, that the waters of Jôr'dan returned unto their place, and [5]flowed
over all his banks, as *they did* before.
19 ¶ And the people came up out of
Jôr'dan on the tenth *day* of the first
month, and encamped [j]in Ḡĭl'găl, in
the east border of Jĕr'ĭ-chō.
20 And those twelve stones, which
they took out of Jôr'dan, did Jŏsh'u-ȧ
pitch in Ḡĭl'găl.
21 And he spake unto the children
of Ĭs'ra-el, saying, When your children
shall ask their fathers [6]in time to come,
saying, What *mean* these stones?
22 Then ye shall let your children
know, saying, Ĭs'ra-el came over this
Jôr'dan on dry land.
23 For the LORD your God dried up
the waters of Jôr'dan from before you,
until ye were passed over, as the LORD
your God did to the Red sea, [k]which he
dried up from before us, until we were
gone over:
24 [l]That all the people of the earth
might know the hand of the LORD, that
it *is* [m]mighty: that ye might [n]fear the
LORD your God [7]for ever.

5 And it came to pass, when all the
kings of the Ăm'ôr-ītes, which *were*
on the side of Jôr'dan westward, and all
the kings of the Cā'năan-ītes, [a]which
were by the sea, [b]heard that the LORD
had dried up the waters of Jôr'dan
from before the children of Ĭs'ra-el, until we were passed over, that their heart
melted, [c]neither was there spirit in
them any more, because of the children
of Ĭs'ra-el.
2 ¶ At that time the LORD said unto
Jŏsh'u-ȧ, Make thee [1]sharp knives, and
circumcise again the children of Ĭs'ra-
el the second time.
3 And Jŏsh'u-ȧ made him sharp
knives, and circumcised the children
of Ĭs'ra-el at [2]the hill of the foreskins.
4 And this *is* the cause why Jŏsh'u-ȧ
did circumcise: [d]All the people that
came out of Ē'ġypt, *that were* males,
even all the men of war, died in the
wilderness by the way, after they came
out of Ē'ġypt.
5 Now all the people that came out
were circumcised: but all the people
that were born in the wilderness by the
way as they came forth out of Ē'ġypt,
them they had not circumcised.
6 For the children of Ĭs'ra-el walked
[e]forty years in the wilderness, till all
the people *that were* men of war, which
came out of Ē'ġypt, were consumed, because they obeyed not the voice of the
LORD: unto whom the LORD sware that
[f]he would not shew them the land,
which the LORD sware unto their fathers that he would give us, a land that
floweth with milk and honey.
7 And [g]their children, *whom* he
raised up in their stead, them Jŏsh'u-ȧ
circumcised: for they were uncircumcised, because they had not circumcised them by the way.
8 And it came to pass, [3]when they
had done circumcising all the people,
that they abode in their places in the
camp, [h]till they were whole.
9 And the LORD said unto Jŏsh'u-ȧ,
This day have I rolled away [i]the reproach of Ē'ġypt from off you. Wherefore the name of the place is called
[4]Gĭl'găl unto this day.
10 ¶ And the children of Ĭs'ra-el encamped in Gĭl'găl, and kept the passover [j]on the fourteenth day of the
month at even in the plains of Jĕr'ĭ-
chō.
11 And they did eat of the old corn of
the land on the morrow after the passover, unleavened cakes, and parched
corn in the selfsame day.
12 ¶ And the manna ceased on the
morrow after they had eaten of the old
corn of the land; neither had the children of Ĭs'ra-el manna any more; but
they did eat of the fruit of the land of
Cā'năan that year.
13 ¶ And it came to pass, when Jŏsh'-
u-ȧ was by Jĕr'ĭ-chō, that he lifted up
his eyes and looked, and, behold, there
stood [k]a man over against him with his
sword drawn in his hand: and Jŏsh'u-ȧ
went unto him, and said unto him, *Art*
thou for us, or for our adversaries?
14 And he said, Nay; but *as* [5]captain
of the host of the LORD am I now come.
And Jŏsh'u-ȧ [l]fell on his face to the
earth, and did worship, and said unto
him, What saith my lord unto his servant?
15 And the captain of the LORD'S
host said unto Jŏsh'u-ȧ, [m]Loose thy
shoe from off thy foot; for the place
whereon thou standest *is* holy. And
Jŏsh'u-ȧ did so.
6 Now Jĕr'ĭ-chō [1]was straitly shut up
because of the children of Ĭs'ra-el:
none went out, and none came in.
2 And the LORD said unto Jŏsh'u-ȧ,
See, [a]I have given into thine hand Jĕr'-
ĭ-chō, and the king thereof, *and* the
mighty men of valour.
3 And ye shall compass the city, all
ye men of war, *and* go round about the
city once. Thus shalt thou do six days.
4 And seven priests shall bear before the ark seven [b]trumpets of rams'
horns: and the seventh day ye shall
compass the city seven times, and [c]the
priests shall blow with the trumpets.
5 And it shall come to pass, that
when they make a long *blast* with
the ram's horn, *and* when ye hear the
sound of the trumpet, all the people
shall shout with a great shout; and the
wall of the city shall fall down [2]flat,
and the people shall ascend up every
man straight before him.
6 ¶ And Jŏsh'u-ȧ the son of Nŭn
called the priests, and said unto them,
Take up the ark of the covenant, and
let seven priests bear seven trumpets
of rams' horns before the ark of the
LORD.
7 And he said unto the people, Pass
on, and compass the city, and let him
that is armed pass on before the ark of
the LORD.
8 ¶ And it came to pass, when Jŏsh'-
u-ȧ had spoken unto the people, that
the seven priests bearing the seven
trumpets of rams' horns [d]passed on
[3]before the LORD, and blew with the
trumpets: and the ark of the covenant
of the LORD followed them.
9 ¶ And the armed men went before
the priests that blew with the trumpets,
[e]and the [4]rereward came after the ark,
the priests going on, and blowing with
the trumpets.
10 And Jŏsh'u-ȧ had commanded
the people, saying, Ye shall not shout,
nor [5]make any noise with your voice,
neither shall *any* word proceed out of
your mouth, until the day I bid you
shout; then shall ye shout.
11 So the ark of the LORD compassed
the city, going about *it* once: and they
came into the camp, and lodged in the
camp.
12 ¶ And Jŏsh'u-ȧ rose early in the
morning, [f]and the priests took up the
ark of the LORD.
13 And seven priests bearing seven
trumpets of rams' horns before the ark
of the LORD [g]went on continually, and
blew with the trumpets: and the armed
men went before them; but the rereward came after the ark of the LORD,

CHAPTER 5
1 [a]Num. 13.29 [b]Ex. 15.14; Ps. 48.6 [c]1 Ki. 10.5
2 [1]Or, knives of flints
3 [2]Or, Gibeah-haaraloth
4 [d]Num. 14.29; Num. 26.64
6 [e]Deut. 1.3; Ps. 95.10 [f]Heb. 3.11
7 [g]Num. 14.31
8 [3]when the people had made an end to be circumcised [h]Gen. 34.25
9 [i]Lev. 18.3; ch. 24.14; 1 Sam. 14.6; Ezek. 20.7 [4]That is, Rolling
10 [j]Ex. 12.6; Num. 9.5
13 [k]Gen. 18.2; Zech. 1.8; Acts 1.10
14 [5]Or, prince [l]Gen. 17.3; Lev. 9.24; Num. 16.22-45
15 [m]Ex. 3.5; Lev. 19.2; 1 Sam. 2.2; 1 Chr. 16.25-29; Ps. 22.3; Ps. 29.2; Ps. 33.8; Ps. 76.7-11; Ps. 89.7; Ps. 96.4-9; Isa. 6.3; Acts 7.33; Rev. 4.8

CHAPTER 6
1 [1]did shut up, and was shut up
2 [a]ch. 2.9; 2 Sam. 5.19; Neh. 9.24; Dan. 5.18-19
4 [b]Judg. 7.16 [c]Num. 10.8
5 [2]under it
8 [d]ch. 4.13 [3]That is, before the ark
9 [e]Num. 10.25; Isa. 52.12-13 [4]gathering host
10 [5]make your voice to be heard
12 [f]Deut. 31.25
13 [g]1 Chr. 15.26

the priests going on, and blowing with the trumpets.

14 And the second day they compassed the city once, and returned into the camp: so they did six days.

15 And it came to pass on the seventh day, that they rose early about the dawning of the day, and compassed the city after the same manner seven times: only on that day they compassed the city seven times.

16 And it came to pass at the seventh time, when the priests blew with the trumpets, Jŏsh'u-ȧ said unto the people, [h]Shout; for the LORD hath given you the city.

17 ¶ And the city shall be [6]accursed, *even* it, and all that *are* therein, to the LORD: only Rā'hăb the harlot shall live, she and all that *are* with her in the house, because [i]she hid the messengers that we sent.

18 And ye, [j]in any wise keep *yourselves* from the accursed thing, lest ye make *yourselves* accursed, when ye take of the accursed thing, and make the camp of Ĭs'ra-el a curse, [k]and trouble it.

19 But all the silver, and gold, and vessels of brass and iron, *are* [7]consecrated unto the LORD: they shall come into the treasury of the LORD.

20 So the people shouted when *the priests* blew with the trumpets: and it came to pass, when the people heard the sound of the trumpet, and the people shouted with a great shout, that [l]the wall fell down [8]flat, so that the people went up into the city, every man straight before him, and they took the city.

21 And they [m]utterly destroyed all that *was* in the city, both man and woman, young and old, and ox, and sheep, and ass, with the edge of the sword.

22 But Jŏsh'u-ȧ had said unto the two men that had spied out the country, Go into the harlot's house, and bring out thence the woman, and all that she hath, [n]as ye sware unto her.

23 And the young men that were spies went in, and brought out Rā'hăb, [o]and her father, and her mother, and her brethren, and all that she had; and they brought out all her [9]kindred, and left them without the camp of Ĭs'ra-el.

24 And they burnt the city with fire, and all that *was* therein: only the silver, and the gold, and the vessels of brass and of iron, they put into the treasury of the house of the LORD.

25 And Jŏsh'u-ȧ saved Rā'hăb the harlot alive, and her father's household, and all that she had; and [p]she dwelleth in Ĭs'ra-el *even* [10]unto this day; because she hid the messengers, which Jŏsh'u-ȧ sent to spy out Jĕr'ĭ-chō.

26 ¶ And Jŏsh'u-ȧ adjured *them* at that time, saying, [q]Cursed *be* the man before the LORD, that riseth up and buildeth this city Jĕr'ĭ-chō: he shall lay the foundation thereof in his firstborn, and in his youngest *son* shall he set up the gates of it.

27 [r]So the LORD was with Jŏsh'u-ȧ; and his [s]fame was *noised* throughout all the country.

7 But the children of Ĭs'ra-el committed a trespass in the accursed thing: for [a][1]Ā'chăn, the son of Căr'mī, the son of [2]Zăb'dī, the son of Zē'rah, of the tribe of Jū'dah, took of the accursed thing: and the anger of the LORD was kindled against the children of Ĭs'ra-el.

2 And Jŏsh'u-ȧ sent men from Jĕr'ĭ-chō to Ā'ī, which *is* beside Bĕth-ā'ven, on the east side of Bĕth'-el, and spake unto them, saying, Go up and view the country. And the men went up and viewed Ā'ī.

3 And they returned to Jŏsh'u-ȧ, and said unto him, Let not all the people go up; but let [3]about two or three thousand men go up and smite Ā'ī; *and* make not all the people to labour thither; for they *are but* few.

4 So there went up thither of the people about three thousand men: [b]and they fled before the men of Ā'ī.

5 And the men of Ā'ī smote of them about thirty and six men: for they chased them *from* before the gate *even* unto Shĕb'a-rĭm, and smote them [4]in the going down: wherefore [c]the hearts of the people melted, and became as water.

6 ¶ And Jŏsh'u-ȧ [d]rent his clothes, and fell to the earth upon his face before the ark of the LORD until the eventide, he and the elders of Ĭs'ra-el, and [e]put dust upon their heads.

7 And Jŏsh'u-ȧ said, Alas, O Lord GOD, [f]wherefore hast thou at all brought this people over Jôr'dan, to deliver us into the hand of the Ăm'ôr-ītes, to destroy us? would to God we had been content, and dwelt on the other side Jôr'dan!

8 O Lord, what shall I say, when Ĭs'ra-el turneth their [5]backs before their enemies!

9 For the Cā'năan-ītes and all the inhabitants of the land shall hear *of it,* and shall environ us round, and [g]cut off our name from the earth: and [h]what wilt thou do unto thy great name?

10 ¶ And the LORD said unto Jŏsh'u-ȧ, Get thee up; wherefore [6]liest thou thus upon thy face?

11 Ĭs'ra-el hath sinned, and they have also transgressed my covenant which I commanded them: [i]for they have even taken of the accursed thing, and have also stolen, and [j]dissembled also, and they have put *it* even among their own stuff.

12 [k]Therefore the children of Ĭs'ra-el could not stand before their enemies, *but* turned *their* backs before their enemies, because [l]they were accursed: neither will I be with you any more, except ye destroy the accursed from among you.

13 Up, [m]sanctify the people, and say, [n]Sanctify yourselves against to morrow: for thus saith the LORD God of Ĭs'ra-el, *There is* an accursed thing in

16 [h]Judg. 7.20; 2 Chr. 13.14
17 [6]Or, devoted, Lev. 27.28; Mic. 4.13
[i]Gen. 12.3; Heb. 6.10
18 [j]Deut. 7.26; 1 Thess. 5.22
[k]ch. 7.25; Jon. 1.12
19 [7]holiness
20 [l]Heb. 11.30
[8]under it
21 [m]Deut. 7.2; Rev. 18.21
22 [n]ch. 2.14; Heb. 11.31
23 [o]ch. 2.13
[9]families
25 [p]Matt. 1.5
[10]B. C. 1427
26 [q]1 Ki. 16.34; Mal. 1.4
27 [r]Gen. 39.2; Rom. 8.31
[s]ch. 9.1-3; 1 Sam. 2.30

CHAPTER 7
1 [a]ch. 22.20
[1]1 Chr. 2.7-Achar
[2]Or, Zimri, 1 Chr. 2.6
3 [3]about two thousand men, or about three thousand men
4 [b]Lev. 26.17; Isa. 59.2
5 [4]Or, in Morad
[c]ch. 2.9-11; Ps. 22.14
6 [d]Gen. 37.29; Acts 14.14
[e]1 Sam. 4.12; Job 2.12
7 [f]Ex. 5.22
8 [5]necks
9 [g]Ps. 83.4
[h]Ex. 32.12
10 [6]fallest
11 [i]ch. 6.17
[j]Acts 5.1
12 [k]Num. 14.45
[l]Deut. 7.26;
13 [m]Ex. 19.10
[n]ch. 3.5

the midst of thee, O Ĭs'ra-el: thou canst
not stand before thine enemies, until
ye take away the accursed thing from
among you.
14 In the morning therefore ye shall
be brought according to your tribes:
and it shall be, *that* the tribe which
[o]the LORD taketh shall come according to the families *thereof:* and the family which the LORD shall take shall
come by households; and the household which the LORD shall take shall
come man by man.
15 [p]And it shall be, *that* he that is
taken with the accursed thing shall be
burnt with fire, he and all that he hath:
because he hath transgressed the covenant of the LORD, and because he [q]hath
wrought [7]folly in Ĭs'ra-el.
16 ¶ So Jŏsh'u-ȧ rose up early in
the morning, and brought Ĭs'ra-el by
their tribes; and the tribe of Jū'dah
was taken:
17 And he brought the family of Jū'-
dah; and he took the family of the
Zär'hītes: and he brought the family of
the Zär'hītes man by man; and Zăb'dī
was taken:
18 And he brought his household
man by man; and [r]Ā'chăn, the son
of Cär'mī, the son of Zăb'dī, the son
of Zē'rah, of the tribe of Jū'dah, was
taken.
19 And Jŏsh'u-ȧ said unto Ā'chăn,
My son, [s]give, I pray thee, glory to the
LORD God of Ĭs'ra-el, [t]and make confession unto him; and tell me now what
thou hast done; hide *it* not from me.
20 And Ā'chăn answered Jŏsh'u-ȧ,
and said, Indeed I have sinned against
the LORD God of Ĭs'ra-el, and thus and
thus have I done:
21 When I saw among the spoils a
goodly Băb'ȳ-lō-nish garment, and two
hundred shekels of silver, and a [8]wedge
of gold of fifty shekels weight, then I
[u]coveted them, and took them; and, behold, they *are* hid in the earth in the
midst of my tent, and the silver under it.
22 ¶ So Jŏsh'u-ȧ sent messengers,
and they ran unto the tent; and, behold, *it was* hid in his tent, and the
silver under it.
23 And they took them out of the
midst of the tent, and brought them
unto Jŏsh'u-ȧ, and unto all the children of Ĭs'ra-el, and [9]laid them out before the LORD.
24 And Jŏsh'u-ȧ, and all Ĭs'ra-el with
him, took Ā'chăn the son of Zē'rah,
and the silver, and the garment, and the
wedge of gold, and his sons, and his
daughters, and his oxen, and his asses,
and his sheep, and his tent, and all that
he had: and they brought them unto
[v]the valley of Ā'chôr.
25 And Jŏsh'u-ȧ said, [w]Why hast
thou troubled us? the LORD shall trouble thee this day. [x]And all Ĭs'ra-el
stoned him with stones, and burned
them with fire, after they had stoned
them with stones.
26 And they [y]raised over him a great
heap of stones unto this day. So [z]the
LORD turned from the fierceness of
his anger. Wherefore the name of that
place was called, [a]The valley of [10]Ā'-
chôr, unto this day.

8 And the LORD said unto Jŏsh'u-ȧ,
[a]Fear not, neither be thou dismayed: take all the people of war with
thee, and arise, go up to Ā'ī: see, [b]I
have given into thy hand the king of
Ā'ī, and his people, and his city, and
his land:
2 And thou shalt do to Ā'ī and her
king as thou didst unto [c]Jĕr'ĭ-chō and
her king: only [d]the spoil thereof, and
the cattle thereof, shall ye take for a
prey unto yourselves: lay thee an ambush for the city behind it.
3 ¶ So Jŏsh'u-ȧ arose, and all the
people of war, to go up against Ā'ī:
and Jŏsh'u-ȧ chose out thirty thousand
mighty men of valour, and sent them
away by night.
4 And he commanded them, saying,
Behold, [e]ye shall lie [1]in wait against
the city, *even* behind the city: go not
very far from the city, but be ye all
ready:
5 And I, and all the people that *are*
with me, will approach unto the city:
and it shall come to pass, when they
come out against us, as at the first, that
[f]we will flee before them,
6 (For they will come out after us)
till we have [2]drawn them from the city;
for they will say, They flee before us,
as at the first: therefore we will flee
before them.
7 Then ye shall rise up from the ambush, and seize upon the city: for the
LORD your God will deliver it into your
hand.
8 And it shall be, when ye have taken
the city, *that* ye shall set the city on
fire: according to the commandment of
the LORD shall ye do. [g]See, I have commanded you.
9 ¶ Jŏsh'u-ȧ therefore sent them
forth: and they went to lie in ambush,
and abode between Bĕth'–el and Ā'ī,
on the west side of Ā'ī: but Jŏsh'u-ȧ
lodged that night among the people.
10 And Jŏsh'u-ȧ [h]rose up early in
the morning, and numbered the people, and went up, he and the elders of
Ĭs'ra-el, before the people to Ā'ī.
11 And all the people, *even the people* of war that *were* with him, went up,
and drew nigh, and came before the
city, and pitched on the north side of
Ā'ī: now *there was* a valley between
them and Ā'ī.
12 And he took about five thousand
men, and set them to lie in ambush [i]be-
tween Bĕth'–el and Ā'ī, on the west
side [3]of the city.
13 And when they had set the people, *even* all the host that *was* on the
north of the city, and [4]their liers in wait
on the west of the city, Jŏsh'u-ȧ went
that night into the midst of the valley.
14 ¶ And it came to pass, when the
king of Ā'ī saw *it,* that they hasted and
rose up early, and the men of the city
went out against Ĭs'ra-el to battle, he
and all his people, at a time appointed,
before the plain; but he [j]wist not that

14 [o]1 Sam. 10.19-21; Prov. 16.33; Jon. 1.7; Acts 1.24-26
15 [p]1 Sam. 14.38-39
[q]Gen. 34.7
[7]Or, wickedness
18 [r]Gen. 4.7; Num. 32.23; Prov. 13.21; Jer. 2.26; Acts 5.1-10
19 [s]1 Sam. 6.5; John 9.24
[t]Num. 5.6-7; 2 Chr. 30.22; Ps. 51.3; Dan. 9.4
21 [8]tongue
[u]Ex. 20.17; 1 Ki. 21; Prov. 15.27; Hab. 2.9; Luke 12.15; Rom. 7.7-8; Eph. 5.5; 1 Tim. 6.10
23 [9]poured
24 [v]ch. 15.7
25 [w]ch. 6.18; 1 Ki. 18.17; 1 Chr. 2.7; Gal. 5.12
[x]Deut. 17.5
26 [y]ch. 8.29; Lam. 3.53
[z]Deut. 13.17
[a]Isa. 65.10
[10]That is, Trouble

CHAPTER 8
1 [a]Deut. 1.21; ch. 1.9
[b]ch. 2.24; Ps. 44.3
2 [c]ch. 6.21
[d]Deut. 20.14
4 [e]Judg. 20.29
[1]Or, in ambush
5 [f]Judg. 20.32
6 [2]pulled
8 [g]ch. 1.16; 2 Sam. 13.28
10 [h]Gen. 22.3; Jer. 21.12
12 [i]Gen. 12.8; Judg. 1.22
[3]Or, of Ai
13 [4]their lying in wait
14 [j]Judg. 20.34; 2 Pet. 2.3

there were liers in ambush against him behind the city.

15 And Jŏsh′u-ȧ and all Ĭs′ra-el [k]made as if they were beaten before them, and fled [l]by the way of the wilderness.

16 And all the people that *were* in Ā′ī were called together to pursue after them: and they pursued after Jŏsh′u-ȧ, and were drawn away [m]from the city.

17 And there was not a man left in Ā′ī or Bĕth′–el, that went not out after Ĭs′ra-el: and they left the city open, and pursued after Ĭs′ra-el.

18 And the LORD said unto Jŏsh′u-ȧ, Stretch out the spear that *is* in thy hand toward Ā′ī; for [n]I will give it into thine hand. And Jŏsh′u-ȧ stretched out the spear that *he had* in his hand toward the city.

19 And the ambush arose quickly out of their place, and they ran as soon as he had stretched out his hand: and they entered into the city, and took it, and hasted and set the city on fire.

20 And when the men of Ā′ī looked behind them, they saw, and, behold, the smoke of the city ascended up to heaven, and they had no [5]power to flee this way or that way: and the people that fled to the wilderness turned back upon the pursuers.

21 And when Jŏsh′u-ȧ and all Ĭs′ra-el saw that the ambush had taken the city, and that the smoke of the city ascended, then they turned again, and slew the men of Ā′ī.

22 And the other issued out of the city against them; so they were in the midst of Ĭs′ra-el, some on this side, and some on that side: and they smote them, so that they [o]let none of them remain or escape.

23 And the king of Ā′ī they took alive, and brought him to Jŏsh′u-ȧ.

24 And it came to pass, when Ĭs′ra-el had made an end of slaying all the inhabitants of Ā′ī in the field, in the wilderness wherein they chased them, and when they were all fallen on the edge of the sword, until they were consumed, that all the Ĭs′ra-el-ītes returned unto Ā′ī, and smote it with the edge of the sword.

25 And *so* it was, *that* all that fell that day, both of men and women, *were* twelve thousand, *even* all the men of Ā′ī.

26 For Jŏsh′u-ȧ drew not his hand back, wherewith he stretched out the spear, until he had utterly destroyed all the inhabitants of Ā′ī.

27 [p]Only the cattle and the spoil of that city Ĭs′ra-el took for a prey unto themselves, according unto the word of the LORD which he commanded Jŏsh′u-ȧ.

28 And Jŏsh′u-ȧ burnt Ā′ī, and made it an [q]heap for ever, *even* a desolation unto [r]this day.

29 [s]And the king of Ā′ī he hanged on a tree until eventide: [t]and as soon as the sun was down, Jŏsh′u-ȧ commanded that they should take his carcase down from the tree, and cast it at the entering of the gate of the city, and [u]raise thereon a great heap of stones, *that remaineth* unto this day.

30 ¶ Then Jŏsh′u-ȧ [v]built an altar unto the LORD God of Ĭs′ra-el [w]in mount Ē′bal,

31 As Mō′ses the servant of the LORD commanded the children of Ĭs′ra-el, as it is written in the [x]book of the law of Mō′ses, an altar of whole stones, over which no man hath lift up *any* iron: and [y]they offered thereon burnt offerings unto the LORD, and sacrificed peace offerings.

32 ¶ And [z]he wrote there upon the stones a copy of the law of Mō′ses, which he wrote in the presence of the children of Ĭs′ra-el.

33 And all Ĭs′ra-el, and their elders, and officers, and their judges, stood on this side the ark and on that side before the priests the Lē′vītes, [a]which bare the ark of the covenant of the LORD, as well [b]the stranger, as he that was born among them; half of them over against mount Gĕr′ĭ-zĭm, and half of them over against mount Ē′bal; [c]as Mō′ses the servant of the LORD had commanded before, that they should bless the people of Ĭs′ra-el.

34 And afterward [d]he read all the words of the law, [e]the blessings and cursings, according to all that is written in the book of the law.

35 There was not a word of all that Mō′ses commanded, which Jŏsh′u-ȧ read not before all the congregation of Ĭs′ra-el, [f]with the women, and the little ones, and [g]the strangers that [6]were conversant among them.

9 And it came to pass, when all the kings which *were* on this side Jôr′dan, in the hills, and in the valleys, and in all the coasts of the [a]great sea over against Lĕb′a-non, [b]the Hĭt′tīte, and the Ăm′ôr-īte, the Cā′năan-īte, the Pĕr′ĭz-zīte, the Hī′vīte, and the Jĕb′u-site, heard *thereof;*

2 That they [c]gathered themselves together, to fight with Jŏsh′u-ȧ and with Ĭs′ra-el, with one [1]accord.

3 ¶ And when the inhabitants of Gĭb′e-on [d]heard [e]what Jŏsh′u-ȧ had done unto Jĕr′ĭ-chō and to Ā′ī,

4 They did work wilily, and went and made as if they had been ambassadors, and took old sacks upon their asses, and [f]wine bottles, old, and rent, and bound up;

5 And old shoes and clouted upon their feet, and old garments upon them; and all the bread of their provision was dry *and* mouldy.

6 And they went to Jŏsh′u-ȧ [g]unto the camp at Gĭl′găl, and said unto him, and to the men of Ĭs′ra-el, We be come from a far country: now therefore make ye a league with us.

7 And the men of Ĭs′ra-el said unto [h]the Hī′vītes, Peradventure ye dwell among us; and [i]how shall we make a league with you?

8 And they said unto Jŏsh′u-ȧ, [j]We *are* thy servants. And Jŏsh′u-ȧ said

15 [k]Judg. 20.36
[l]ch. 15.61; ch. 16.1; ch. 18.12
16 [m]Ex. 14.3-4; Judg. 20.31; Ps. 9.16
18 [n]Deut. 7.23-24; Deut. 9.3; Deut. 31.5-8; ch. 1.5; Jer. 49.3
20 [5]hand
22 [o]Lev. 27.29; Deut. 7.2; Job 20.5; 1 Thess. 5.3
27 [p]Num. 31.22-26; Matt. 20.15
28 [q]Deut. 13.16; Jer. 9.11
[r]B. C. 1427
29 [s]ch. 10.26; Ps. 107.40
[t]Deut. 21.23; ch. 10.27
[u]ch. 7.26; 2 Sam. 18.17
30 [v]Gen. 8.20; Ex. 20.24
[w]Deut. 27.4-5
31 [x]Deut. 27.5-6
[y]Ex. 20.25
32 [z]Deut. 27.2-8
33 [a]Deut. 31.9-25
[b]Lev. 24.22; Num. 15.16
[c]Deut. 11.29
34 [d]Deut. 31.11; Neh. 8.3
[e]Deut. 29.20-21
35 [f]Deut. 31.12
[g]Zech. 8.23
[6]walked

CHAPTER 9
1 [a]Num. 34.6
[b]Gen. 15.18-21; Deut. 7.1
2 [c]1 Chr. 20.1; Acts 4.26-28
[1]mouth
3 [d]ch. 10.2; 2 Sam. 21.1-2
[e]ch. 6.27
4 [f]Matt. 9.17; Luke 5.37-38
6 [g]ch. 5.10
7 [h]ch. 11.19
[i]Ex. 23.32; Deut. 7.2
8 [j]Deut. 20.11

unto them, Who *are* ye? and from
whence come ye?
9 And they said unto him, [k]From a
very far country thy servants are come
because of the name of the LORD thy
God: for we have [l]heard the fame of
him, and all that he did in Ē'ġypt,
10 And [m]all that he did to the two
kings of the Ăm'ôr-ītes, that *were* beyond Jôr'dan, to Sī'hŏn king of Hĕsh'-
bŏn, and to Ōg king of Bā'shăn, which
was at Ăsh'ta-rŏth.
11 Wherefore our elders and all the
inhabitants of our country spake to us,
saying, Take victuals [2]with you for the
journey, and go to meet them, and say
unto them, We *are* your servants: therefore now make ye a league with us.
12 This our bread we took hot *for*
our provision out of our houses on the
day we came forth to go unto you; but
now, behold, it is dry, and it is mouldy:
13 And these bottles of wine, which
we filled, *were* new; and, behold, they
be rent: and these our garments and
our shoes are become old by reason of
the very long journey.
14 And [3]the men took of their victuals, [n]and asked not *counsel* at the
mouth of the LORD.
15 And Jŏsh'u-ȧ [o]made peace with
them, and made a league with them, to
let them live: and the princes of the
congregation sware unto them.
16 ¶ And it came to pass at the end
of three days after they had made a
league with them, that they heard that
they *were* their neighbours, and *that*
they dwelt among them.
17 And the children of Ĭs'ra-el journeyed, and came unto their cities on
the third day. Now their cities *were*
[p]Ġĭb'e-on, and Che-phī'rah, and Be-
ē'rŏth, and Kĭr'jath–jē'a-rĭm.
18 And the children of Ĭs'ra-el smote
them not, [q]because the princes of the
congregation had sworn unto them by
the LORD God of Ĭs'ra-el. And all the
congregation murmured against the
princes.
19 But all the princes said unto all
the congregation, We have sworn unto
them by the LORD God of Ĭs'ra-el: now
therefore we may not touch them.
20 This we will do to them; we will
even let them live, lest [r]wrath be upon
us, because of the oath which we sware
unto them.
21 And the princes said unto them,
Let them live; but let them be [s]hewers
of wood and drawers of water unto all
the congregation; as the princes had
promised them.
22 ¶ And Jŏsh'u-ȧ called for them,
and he spake unto them, saying, Wherefore have ye beguiled us, saying, We
are very far from you; when ye dwell
among us?
23 Now therefore ye *are* [t]cursed,
and there shall [4]none of you be freed
from being bondmen, and hewers of
wood and drawers of water for the
house of my God.
24 And they answered Jŏsh'u-ȧ, and
said, Because it was certainly told thy
servants, how that the LORD thy God
[u]commanded his servant Mō'ses to
give you all the land, and to destroy all
the inhabitants of the land from before
you, therefore [v]we were sore afraid of
our lives because of you, and have
done this thing.
25 And now, behold, we *are* [w]in
thine hand: as it seemeth good and
right unto thee to do unto us, do.
26 And so did he unto them, and delivered them out of the hand of the children of Ĭs'ra-el, that they slew them
not.
27 And Jŏsh'u-ȧ [5]made them that
day hewers of wood and drawers of
water for the congregation, and for the
altar of the LORD, even unto this day,
[x]in the place which he should choose.

10 Now it came to pass, when A-
dŏn'i–zē'dec king of Je-ru'sa-
lĕm had heard how Jŏsh'u-ȧ had taken
Ā'ī, and had utterly destroyed it; [a]as he
had done to Jĕr'ĭ-chō and her king, so
he had done to [b]Ā'ī and her king; and
[c]how the inhabitants of Ġĭb'e-on had
made peace with Ĭs'ra-el, and were
among them;
2 That they [d]feared greatly, because
Ġĭb'e-on *was* a great city, as one of the
[1]royal cities, and because it *was* greater
than Ā'ī, and all the men thereof *were*
mighty.
3 Wherefore A-dŏn'i–zē'dec king of
Je-ru'sa-lĕm sent unto Hō'ham king of
[e]Hē'bron, and unto Pī'ram king of Jär'-
mŭth, and unto Ja-phī'ȧ king of Lā'-
chish, and unto Dē'bīr king of Ĕg'lŏn,
saying,
4 Come up unto me, and help me,
that we may smite Ġĭb'e-on: [f]for it
hath made peace with Jŏsh'u-ȧ and
with the children of Ĭs'ra-el.
5 Therefore the five kings of the
Ăm'ôr-ītes, the king of Je-ru'sa-lĕm,
the king of Hē'bron, the king of Jär'-
mŭth, the king of Lā'chish, the king
of Ĕg'lŏn, [g]gathered themselves together, and went up, they and all their
hosts, and encamped before Ġĭb'e-on,
and made war against it.
6 ¶ And the men of Ġĭb'e-on sent
unto Jŏsh'u-ȧ [h]to the camp to Ġĭl'găl,
saying, Slack not thy hand from thy
servants; come up to us quickly, and
save us, and help us: for all the kings of
the Ăm'ôr-ītes that dwell in the mountains are gathered together against us.
7 So Jŏsh'u-ȧ ascended from Ġĭl'-
găl, he, and [i]all the people of war with
him, and all the mighty men of valour.
8 ¶ And the LORD said unto Jŏsh'u-
a, [j]Fear them not: for I have delivered
them into thine hand; [k]there shall not
a man of them stand before thee.
9 Jŏsh'u-ȧ therefore came unto them
suddenly, *and* went up from Ġĭl'găl all
night.
10 And the LORD [l]discomfited them
before Ĭs'ra-el, and slew them with a
great slaughter at Ġĭb'e-on, and chased
them along the way that goeth up [m]to
Bĕth–hō'rŏn, and smote them to [n]A-
zē'kah, and unto Măk-kē'dah.

9 [k]Deut. 20.15
[l]Ex. 15.14
10 [m]Num. 21.24-33
11 [2]in your hand
14 [3]Or, they received the men by reason of their victuals
[n]Num. 27.21; Judg. 1.1; 1 Sam. 22.10; 1 Sam. 30.8; 2 Sam. 2.1; Isa. 30.1-2
15 [o]2 Sam. 21.2
17 [p]ch. 18.25; Ezra 2.25
18 [q]Ps. 15.4
20 [r]2 Sam. 21.1; Zech. 5.3-4; Mal. 3.5
21 [s]Deut. 29.11
23 [t]Gen. 9.25
[4]not be cut off from you
24 [u]Ex. 23.32; Num. 33.51-52-55-56; Deut. 7.1-2
[v]Ex. 15.14
25 [w]Gen. 16.6
27 [5]gave, or delivered to be
[x]Deut. 12.5; 1 Ki. 8.29; 1 Ki. 9.7; 2 Chr. 7.12-20; Ps. 78.68

CHAPTER 10
1 [a]ch. 6.21
[b]ch. 8.22
[c]ch. 9.15
2 [d]Ex. 15.14-16; Deut. 11.25; Ps. 48.4-6; Prov. 1.26-27; Heb. 10.27-31; Rev. 6.15-17
[1]cities of the kingdom
3 [e]Gen. 23.2
4 [f]ch. 9.15
5 [g]ch. 9.2
6 [h]ch. 5.10
7 [i]ch. 8.1
8 [j]Deut. 7.24; ch. 11.6; ch. 23.9
[k]ch. 1.5
10 [l]Judg. 4.15; 1 Sam. 7.10; 2 Chr. 14.12; Ps. 18.14; Isa. 28.21
[m]ch. 16.3-5
[n]ch. 15.35

11 And it came to pass, as they fled
from before Is'ra-el, *and* were in the
going down to Bĕth–hō'rŏn, [o]that the
LORD cast down great stones from
heaven upon them unto A-zē'kah, and
they died: *they were* more which died
with hailstones than *they* whom the
children of Is'ra-el slew with the sword.
12 ¶ Then spake Jŏsh'u-ȧ to the LORD
in the day when the LORD delivered up
the Am'ôr-ītes before the children of
Is'ra-el, and he said in the sight of Is'ra-
el, [p]Sun, [2]stand thou still upon Gĭb'e-
on; and thou, Moon, in the valley of
[q]Aj'a-lŏn.
13 And the sun stood still, and the
moon stayed, until the people had
avenged themselves upon their enemies. [r]*Is* not this written in the book of
[3]Jā'shĕr? So the sun stood still in the
midst of heaven, and hasted not to go
down about a whole day.
14 And there was [s]no day like that
before it or after it, that the LORD hearkened unto the voice of a man: for [t]the
LORD fought for Is'ra-el.
15 ¶ And Jŏsh'u-ȧ returned, and all
Is'ra-el with him, unto the camp to
Gĭl'găl.
16 But these five kings fled, and hid
themselves in a cave at Măk-kē'dah.
17 And it was told Jŏsh'u-ȧ, saying,
The five kings are found hid in a cave
at Măk-kē'dah.
18 And Jŏsh'u-ȧ said, Roll great
stones upon the mouth of the cave, and
set men by it for to keep them:
19 And stay ye not, *but* pursue after
your enemies, and [4]smite the hindmost
of them; suffer them not to enter into
their cities: for the LORD your God
hath delivered them into your hand.
20 And it came to pass, when Jŏsh'-
u-ȧ and the children of Is'ra-el had
made an end of slaying them with a
very great slaughter, till they were consumed, that the rest *which* remained of
them entered into fenced cities.
21 And all the people returned to the
camp to Jŏsh'u-ȧ at Măk-kē'dah in
peace: [u]none moved his tongue against
any of the children of Is'ra-el.
22 Then said Jŏsh'u-ȧ, Open the
mouth of the cave, and bring out those
five kings unto me out of the cave.
23 And they did so, and brought
forth those five kings unto him out of
the cave, the king of Je-ru'sa-lĕm, the
king of Hē'bron, the king of Jär'mŭth,
the king of Lā'chish, *and* the king of
Ĕg'lŏn.
24 And it came to pass, when they
brought out those kings unto Jŏsh'u-ȧ,
that Jŏsh'u-ȧ called for all the men of
Is'ra-el, and said unto the captains of
the men of war which went with him,
Come near, [v]put your feet upon the
necks of these kings. And they came
near, and put their feet upon the necks
of them.
25 And Jŏsh'u-ȧ said unto them,
[w]Fear not, nor be dismayed, be strong
and of good courage: [x]for thus shall
the LORD do to all your enemies against
whom ye fight.

11 [o]Ps. 18.13-14; Ps. 77.17; Isa. 28.2; Isa. 30.30; Rev. 16.21
12 [p]Deut. 4.19; Ps. 19.4; Isa. 28.21; Isa. 38.8; Isa. 60.20; Hab. 3.11
[2]be silent
[q]Judg. 12.12
13 [r]2 Sam. 1.18
[3]Or, The upright
14 [s]Isa. 38.8
[t]Ex. 14.14; Deut. 1.30; Deut. 3.22; ch. 23.3-10; 2 Chr. 20.29; Neh. 4.20; Ps. 33.8-12-20; Isa. 31.4; Isa. 42.13; Isa. 52.10-12; Zech. 14.3
19 [4]cut off the tail
21 [u]Ex. 11.7; Isa. 54.17
24 [v]Deut. 33.29; Ps. 2.8-12; Ps. 91.13; Ps. 107.40; Ps. 110.5; Isa. 26.5-6; Mal. 4.3; Rev. 2.26-27
25 [w]ch. 1.9; 1 Sam. 17.37; Ps. 63.7; 2 Cor. 1.10; 2 Tim. 4.17
[x]Deut. 3.21
26 [y]Num. 25.4; ch. 8.29; 2 Sam. 21.6-9; Esth. 2.23; Esth. 7.9-10; Ps. 149.7-9
27 [z]Deut. 21.23; ch. 8.29
28 [a]ch. 6.21
29 [b]ch. 15.42; ch. 21.13; 2 Ki. 8.22; 2 Ki. 19.8
31 [c]2 Ki. 14.19; Mic. 1.13
33 [d]ch. 16.3-10; 1 Ki. 9.16-17; 1 Chr. 20.4
35 [5]pulled down
36 [e]Num. 13.22; ch. 14.13; ch. 15.13; Judg. 1.10; 2 Sam. 5.1-3
38 [f]ch. 15.15; ch. 21.15

26 And afterward Jŏsh'u-ȧ smote
them, and slew them, and hanged them
on five trees: and they [y]were hanging
upon the trees until the evening.
27 And it came to pass at the time of
the going down of the sun, *that* Jŏsh'-
u-ȧ commanded, and they [z]took them
down off the trees, and cast them into
the cave wherein they had been hid,
and laid great stones in the cave's
mouth, *which remain* until this very
day.
28 ¶ And that day Jŏsh'u-ȧ took
Măk-kē'dah, and smote it with the
edge of the sword, and the king thereof
he utterly destroyed, them, and all the
souls that *were* therein; he let none remain: and he did to the king of Măk-
kē'dah [a]as he did unto the king of
Jĕr'ĭ-chō.
29 Then Jŏsh'u-ȧ passed from Măk-
kē'dah, and all Is'ra-el with him, unto
[b]Lĭb'nah, and fought against Lĭb'nah:
30 And the LORD delivered it also,
and the king thereof, into the hand of
Is'ra-el; and he smote it with the edge
of the sword, and all the souls that
were therein; he let none remain in it;
but did unto the king thereof as he did
unto the king of Jĕr'ĭ-chō.
31 ¶ And Jŏsh'u-ȧ passed from Lĭb'-
nah, and all Is'ra-el with him, unto
[c]Lā'chish, and encamped against it,
and fought against it:
32 And the LORD delivered Lā'chish
into the hand of Is'ra-el, which took it
on the second day, and smote it with
the edge of the sword, and all the souls
that *were* therein, according to all that
he had done to Lĭb'nah.
33 ¶ Then Hō'ram king of [d]Gē'zĕr
came up to help Lā'chish; and Jŏsh'u-ȧ
smote him and his people, until he had
left him none remaining.
34 ¶ And from Lā'chish Jŏsh'u-ȧ
passed unto Ĕg'lŏn, and all Is'ra-el
with him; and they encamped against
it, and fought against it:
35 And they took it on that day, and
smote it with the edge of the sword,
and all the souls that *were* therein he
utterly [5]destroyed that day, according
to all that he had done to Lā'chish.
36 And Jŏsh'u-ȧ went up from Ĕg'-
lŏn, and all Is'ra-el with him, unto [e]Hē'-
bron; and they fought against it:
37 And they took it, and smote it
with the edge of the sword, and the
king thereof, and all the cities thereof,
and all the souls that *were* therein; he
left none remaining, according to all
that he had done to Ĕg'lŏn; but destroyed it utterly, and all the souls that
were therein.
38 ¶ And Jŏsh'u-ȧ returned, and all
Is'ra-el with him, to [f]Dē'bĭr; and fought
against it:
39 And he took it, and the king
thereof, and all the cities thereof; and
they smote them with the edge of the
sword, and utterly destroyed all the
souls that *were* therein; he left none
remaining: as he had done to Hē'bron,
so he did to Dē'bĭr, and to the king

thereof; as he had done also to Lĭb'-
nah, and to her king.
40 ¶ So Jŏsh'u-ȧ smote [g]all the country of the hills, and of the south, and of
the vale, and of the springs, and all
their kings: he left none remaining, but
utterly destroyed all that breathed, as
the LORD God of Ĭs'ra-el [h]commanded.
41 And Jŏsh'u-ȧ smote them from
Kā'desh–bär'ne-ȧ [i]even unto [j]Gā'zȧ,
and [k]all the country of Gō'shen, even
unto Ğĭb'e-on.
42 And [l]all these kings and their
land did Jŏsh'u-ȧ take at one time, because the LORD God of Ĭs'ra-el fought
for Ĭs'ra-el.
43 And Jŏsh'u-ȧ returned, and all
Ĭs'ra-el with him, unto the camp to
Ğĭl'găl.

11 And it came to pass, when [a]Jā'-
bin king of Hā'zôr had heard
those things, that he [b]sent to Jō'băb
king of Mā'dŏn, and to the king [c]of
Shĭm'ron, and to the king of Ăch'-
shăph,
2 And to the kings that *were* on the
north of the mountains, and of the
plains south of [d]Chĭn'ne-rŏth, and in
the valley, and in the borders [e]of Dôr
on the west,
3 *And to* the Cā'năan-īte on the east
and on the west, and *to* the Ăm'ôr-īte,
and the Hĭt'tīte, and the Pĕr'ĭz-zīte,
and the Jĕb'u-site in the mountains,
[f]and *to* the Hī'vīte under [g]Hĕr'mŏn
[h]in the land of Mĭz'peh.
4 And they went out, they and all
their hosts with them, much people,
[i]even as the sand that *is* upon the sea
shore in multitude, with horses and
chariots very many.
5 And when all these kings were
[1]met together, they came and pitched
together at the waters of Mē'rom, to
fight against Ĭs'ra-el.
6 ¶ And the LORD said unto Jŏsh'-
u-ȧ, Be not afraid because of them: for
to morrow about this time will I deliver
them up all slain before Ĭs'ra-el: thou
shalt [j]hough their horses, and burn
their chariots with fire.
7 So Jŏsh'u-ȧ came, and all the people of war with him, against them by
the waters of Mē'rom suddenly; and
they fell upon them.
8 And the LORD delivered them into
the hand of Ĭs'ra-el, who smote them,
and chased them unto [2]great Zī'dŏn,
and unto [3]Mĭs're-photh–mā'im, and
unto the valley of Mĭz'peh eastward;
and they smote them, until they left
them none remaining.
9 And Jŏsh'u-ȧ did unto them as
the LORD bade him: he houghed their
horses, and burnt their chariots with
fire.
10 ¶ And Jŏsh'u-ȧ at that time turned
back, and took Hā'zôr, and smote the
king thereof with the sword: for Hā'zôr
beforetime was the head of all those
kingdoms.
11 And they smote all the souls that
were therein with the edge of the
sword, utterly destroying *them:* there

40 [g]ch. 15.21-63;
ch. 19.1-8
[h]Ex. 23.31-33;
Deut. 7.2
41 [i]Num. 13.17-26
[j]Gen. 10.19;
Acts 8.26
[k]ch. 11.16
42 [l]Ps. 44.2;
Isa. 43.4

CHAPTER 11

1 [a]Ps. 2.1-2;
Ps. 83
[b]ch. 10.3
[c]ch. 19.15
2 [d]Num. 34.11
[e]ch. 17.11;
1 Ki. 4.11
3 [f]Judg. 3.3
[g]ch. 13.11
[h]Gen. 31.49;
1 Ki. 15.22
4 [i]Gen. 22.17;
1 Sam. 13.5
5 [1]assembled by appointment
6 [j]2 Sam. 8.4
8 [2]Or, Zidon-rabbah
[3]Burnings of waters, or, Salt pits
11 [4]any breath
12 [k]Num. 33.52;
Deut. 7.2
13 [5]on their heap
15 [l]Ex. 34.11
[m]Deut. 7.2
[n]ch. 1.7
[6]he removed nothing
16 [o]ch. 12.8
[p]ch. 10.41
17 [q]ch. 12.7
[7]Or, the smooth mountain
[r]Deut. 7.24
18 [8]Till 1445; verse 23
19 [s]ch. 9.3-7
20 [t]Ex. 4.21;
[u]Deut. 20.16
21 [v]Num. 13.22;
22 [w]1 Sam. 17.4
[x]ch. 15.46
23 [y]Num. 34.2
[z]Num. 26.53
[a]ch. 14.15;

CHAPTER 12

1 [a]Num. 21.24;
[b]Deut. 3.8-9

was not [4]any left to breathe: and he
burnt Hā'zôr with fire.
12 And all the cities of those kings,
and all the kings of them, did Jŏsh'u-ȧ
take, and smote them with the edge of
the sword, *and* he utterly destroyed
them, [k]as Mō'ses the servant of the
LORD commanded.
13 But *as for* the cities that stood
still [5]in their strength, Ĭs'ra-el burned
none of them, save Hā'zôr only; *that*
did Jŏsh'u-ȧ burn.
14 And all the spoil of these cities,
and the cattle, the children of Ĭs'ra-el
took for a prey unto themselves; but
every man they smote with the edge of
the sword, until they had destroyed
them, neither left they any to breathe.
15 ¶ [l]As the LORD commanded Mō'-
ses his servant, so [m]did Mō'ses command Jŏsh'u-ȧ, and [n]so did Jŏsh'u-ȧ;
[6]he left nothing undone of all that the
LORD commanded Mō'ses.
16 So Jŏsh'u-ȧ took all that land, the
[o]hills, and all the south country, [p]and
all the land of Gō'shen, and the valley,
and the plain, and the mountain of
Ĭs'ra-el, and the valley of the same;
17 [q]*Even* from [7]the mount Hā'lăk,
that goeth up to Sē'ĭr, even unto Bā'al-
gad in the valley of Lĕb'a-non under
mount Hĕr'mŏn: and [r]all their kings
he took, and smote them, and slew
them.
18 [8]Jŏsh'u-ȧ made war a long time
with all those kings.
19 There was not a city that made
peace with the children of Ĭs'ra-el, save
[s]the Hī'vītes the inhabitants of Ğĭb'e-
on: all *other* they took in battle.
20 For [t]it was of the LORD to harden
their hearts, that they should come
against Ĭs'ra-el in battle, that he might
destroy them utterly, *and* that they
might have no favour, but that he
might destroy them, [u]as the LORD commanded Mō'ses.
21 ¶ And at that time came Jŏsh'u-ȧ,
and cut off [v]the Ăn'a-kĭms from the
mountains, from Hē'bron, from Dē'bĭr,
from Ā'nab, and from all the mountains of Jū'dah, and from all the mountains of Ĭs'ra-el: Jŏsh'u-ȧ destroyed
them utterly with their cities.
22 There was none of the Ăn'a-kĭms
left in the land of the children of Ĭs'ra-
el: only in Gā'zȧ, in [w]Găth, and [x]in
Ăsh'dŏd, there remained.
23 So Jŏsh'u-ȧ took the whole land,
[y]according to all that the LORD said
unto Mō'ses; and Jŏsh'u-ȧ gave it for
an inheritance unto Ĭs'ra-el [z]accord-
ing to their divisions by their tribes.
[a]And the land rested from war.

12 Now these *are* the kings of the
land, which the children of Ĭs'ra-
el smote, and possessed their land on
the other side Jôr'dan toward the rising of the sun, [a]from the river Ăr'-
nŏn [b]unto mount Hĕr'mŏn, and all the
plain on the east:
2 Sī'hŏn king of the Ăm'ôr-ītes, who
dwelt in Hĕsh'bŏn, *and* ruled from Ăr'-
ŏ-ēr, which *is* upon the bank of the
river Ăr'nŏn, and from the middle of

the river, and from half Gĭl'e-ăd, even unto the river Jăb'bok, *which is* the border of the children of Ăm'mŏn;

3 And [c]from the plain to the sea of Chĭn'ne-rŏth on the east, and unto the sea of the plain, *even* the salt sea on the east, [d]the way to Bĕth–jĕsh'ĭ-mŏth; and from [1]the south, under [2]Ăsh'doth–pĭs'gah:

4 ¶ And [e]the coast of Ŏg king of Bā'shăn, *which was* of [f]the remnant of the giants, that dwelt at Ăsh'ta-rŏth and at Ĕd're-ī,

5 And reigned in mount Hĕr'mŏn, and [g]in Săl'cah, and in all Bā'shăn, unto [h]the border of the Gĕsh'u-rītes and the Ma-ăch'a-thītes, and half Gĭl'e-ăd, the border of Sī'hŏn king of Hĕsh'bŏn.

6 Them did Mō'ses the servant of the LORD and the children of Ĭs'ra-el smite: and Mō'ses the servant of the LORD gave it *for* a possession unto the Reu'ben-ītes, and the Găd'ītes, and the half tribe of Ma-năs'seh.

7 ¶ And these *are* the kings of the country which Jŏsh'u-ȧ and the children of Ĭs'ra-el smote on this side Jôr'dan on the west, from Bā'al–gad in the valley of Lĕb'a-non even unto the mount Hā'lăk, that goeth up to [i]Sē'ĭr; which Jŏsh'u-ȧ gave unto the tribes of Ĭs'ra-el *for* a possession according to their divisions;

8 [j]In the mountains, and in the valleys, and in the plains, and in the springs, and in the wilderness, and in the south country; the Hĭt'tītes, [k]the Ăm'ôr-ītes, and the Cā'năan-ītes, the Pĕr'ĭz-zītes, the Hī'vītes, and the Jĕb'u-sītes:

9 ¶ [l]The king of Jĕr'ĭ-chō, one; [m]the king of Ā'ī, which *is* beside Bĕth'–el, one;

10 [n]The king of Je-ru'sa-lĕm, one; the king of Hē'bron, one;

11 The king of Jär'mŭth, one; the king of Lā'chish, one;

12 The king of Ĕg'lŏn, one; the king of Gē'zĕr, one;

13 The king of Dē'bĭr, one; the king of Gē'dĕr, one;

14 The king of Hôr'mah, one; the king of Ā'răd, one;

15 The king of Lĭb'nah, one; the king of A-dŭl'lăm, one;

16 The king of Măk-kē'dah, one; the king of Bĕth'–el, one;

17 The king of Tăp'pu-ah, one; [o]the king of Hē'phĕr, one;

18 The king of Ā'phek, one; the king of [3]La-shâr'on, one;

19 The king of Mā'dŏn, one; the king of Hā'zôr, one;

20 The king of [p]Shĭm'ron–mē'ron, one; the king of Ăch'shăph, one;

21 The king of Tā'a-năch, one; the king of Me-gĭd'do, one;

22 [q]The king of Kē'desh, one; the king of Jŏk''ne-ăm of Cär'mel, one;

23 The king of Dôr in the coast of Dôr, one; the king of [r]the nations of Gĭl'găl, one;

24 The king of Tĭr'zah, one: all the kings thirty and one.

3 [c]Deut. 3.17
[d]ch. 13.20
[1]Or, Teman
[2]Or, The springs of Pisgah, or, The hill
4 [e]Num. 21.35
[f]Deut. 3.11
5 [g]ch. 13.11
[h]Deut. 3.14; 2 Ki. 25.23
7 [i]Gen. 14.6; Gen. 32.3
8 [j]ch. 10.40
[k]Ex. 3.8
9 [l]ch. 6.2
[m]ch. 8.29
10 [n]ch. 10.23
17 [o]ch. 19.13; 1 Ki. 4.10
18 [3]Or, Sharon
20 [p]ch. 11.1; ch. 19.15
22 [q]ch. 19.37
23 [r]Gen. 14.1-2

CHAPTER 13
1 [a]Gen. 18.11; Luke 1.7
[1]to possess it, Deut. 31.3
2 [b]Ex. 23.29-31; Deut. 11.23-24
[c]Gen. 10.14; Gen. 26.1
[d]1 Sam. 27.8; 2 Sam. 13.37
3 [e]Jer. 2.18
[f]1 Sam. 6.4-16; Zeph. 2.5
[g]Deut. 2.23
4 [2]Or, The cave
[h]ch. 19.30
[i]Judg. 1.34
5 [j]1 Ki. 5.18; Ps. 83.7
[k]ch. 12.7
6 [l]ch. 11.8
[m]ch. 23.13
[n]ch. 14.1-2
8 [o]Num. 32.33; ch. 22.4
9 [p]Num. 21.30; Isa. 15.2
11 [q]ch. 12.5
12 [r]Deut. 3.11
[s]Num. 21.24
14 [t]Num. 18.20; ch. 14.3-4
16 [u]Num. 21.28-30;
[v]Num. 21.28

13 Now Jŏsh'u-ȧ [a]was old *and* stricken in years; and the LORD said unto him, Thou art old *and* stricken in years, and there remaineth yet very much land [1]to be possessed.

2 [b]This *is* the land that yet remaineth: all [c]the borders of the Phĭ-lĭs'tĭnes, and all [d]Gĕsh'u-rī,

3 [e]From Sī'hôr, which *is* before Ē'gypt, even unto the borders of Ĕk'rŏn northward, *which* is counted to the Cā'năan-īte: [f]five lords of the Phĭ-lĭs'tĭnes; the Gā'zăth-ītes, and the Ăsh'dŏth-ītes, the Ĕsh'ka-lŏn-ītes, the Gĭt'tītes, and the Ĕk'rŏn-ītes; also [g]the Ā'vītes:

4 From the south, all the land of the Cā'năan-ītes, and [2]Me-ā'rah that *is* beside the Sī-dō'nĭ-ans, [h]unto Ā'phek, to the borders of [i]the Ăm'ôr-ītes:

5 And the land of [j]the Gĭb'lītes, and all Lĕb'a-non, toward the sunrising, [k]from Bā'al–gad under mount Hĕr'mŏn unto the entering into Hā'math.

6 All the inhabitants of the hill country from Lĕb'a-non unto [l]Mĭs're-photh–mā'im, *and* all the Sī-dō'nĭ-ans, them [m]will I drive out from before the children of Ĭs'ra-el: only [n]divide thou it by lot unto the Ĭs'ra-el-ītes for an inheritance, as I have commanded thee.

7 Now therefore divide this land for an inheritance unto the nine tribes, and the half tribe of Ma-năs'seh,

8 With whom the Reu'ben-ītes and the Găd'ītes have received their inheritance, [o]which Mō'ses gave them, beyond Jôr'dan eastward, *even* as Mō'ses the servant of the LORD gave them;

9 From Ăr'ō-ĕr, that *is* upon the bank of the river Ăr'nŏn, and the city that *is* in the midst of the river, [p]and all the plain of Mĕd'e-bȧ unto Dī'bŏn;

10 And all the cities of Sī'hŏn king of the Ăm'ôr-ītes, which reigned in Hĕsh'bŏn, unto the border of the children of Ăm'mŏn;

11 [q]And Gĭl'e-ăd, and the border of the Gĕsh'u-rītes and Ma-ăch'a-thītes, and all mount Hĕr'mŏn, and all Bā'shăn unto Săl'cah;

12 All the kingdom of Ŏg in Bā'shăn, which reigned in Ăsh'ta-rŏth and in Ĕd're-ī, who remained of [r]the remnant of the giants: [s]for these did Mō'ses smite, and cast them out.

13 Nevertheless the children of Ĭs'ra-el expelled not the Gĕsh'u-rītes, nor the Ma-ăch'a-thītes: but the Gĕsh'u-rītes and the Ma-ăch'a-thītes dwell among the Ĭs'ra-el-ītes until this day.

14 [t]Only unto the tribe of Lē'vī he gave none inheritance; the sacrifices of the LORD God of Ĭs'ra-el made by fire *are* their inheritance, as he said unto them.

15 ¶ And Mō'ses gave unto the tribe of the children of Reu'ben *inheritance* according to their families.

16 And their coast was [u]from Ăr'ō-ĕr, that *is* on the bank of the river Ăr'nŏn, [v]and the city that *is* in the midst of the river, and all the plain by Mĕd'e-bȧ;

17 Hĕsh'bŏn, and all her cities that
are in the plain; Dī'bŏn, and [3]Bā'-
mŏth–bā'al, and Bĕth–bā'al–mē'on,
18 [w]And Ja-hā'zȧ, and Kĕd'e-mŏth,
and Mĕph'a-ăth,
19 [x]And Kĭr-jath-ā'im, and Sĭb'mah,
and Zā'reth–shā'har in the mount of
the valley,
20 And Bĕth–pē'ôr, and [4]Ăsh'doth–
pĭs'gah, and Bĕth–jĕsh'ĭ-mŏth,
21 [y]And all the cities of the plain,
and all the kingdom of Sī'hŏn king of
the Ăm'ôr-ītes, which reigned in Hĕsh'-
bŏn, [z]whom Mō'ses smote with [a]the
princes of Mĭd'ĭ-an, Ē'vī, and Rē'kem,
and Zûr, and Hûr, and Rē'bȧ, *which*
were dukes of Sī'hŏn, dwelling in the
country.
22 ¶ [b]Bā'laam also the son of Bē'or,
the [5]soothsayer, did the children of Ĭs'-
ra-el slay with the sword among them
that were slain by them.
23 And the border of the children of
Reu'ben was Jôr'dan, and the border
thereof. This *was* the inheritance of
the children of Reu'ben after their families, the cities and the villages thereof.
24 And Mō'ses gave *inheritance* unto
the tribe of Găd, *even* unto the children
of Găd according to their families.
25 [c]And their coast was Jā'zēr, and
all the cities of Ĝĭl'e-ăd, [d]and half the
land of the children of Ăm'mŏn, unto
Ăr'ŏ-ēr that *is* before [e]Răb'bah;
26 And from Hĕsh'bŏn unto Rā'-
math–mĭz'peh, and Bĕt'ŏ-nim; and
from Mā-ha-nā'im unto the border of
Dē'bīr;
27 And in the valley, Bĕth–ā'răm,
and Bĕth–nĭm'rah, [f]and Sŭc'coth, and
Zā'phŏn, the rest of the kingdom of
Sī'hŏn king of Hĕsh'bŏn, Jôr'dan and
his border, *even* unto the edge [g]of the
sea of Chĭn'ne-rĕth on the other side
Jôr'dan eastward.
28 This *is* the inheritance of the children of Găd after their families, the cities, and their villages.
29 ¶ And Mō'ses gave *inheritance*
unto the half tribe of Ma-năs'seh: and
this was *the possession* of the half
tribe of the children of Ma-năs'seh by
their families.
30 And their coast was from Mā-ha-
nā'im, all Bā'shăn, all the kingdom of
Ŏg king of Bā'shăn, and [h]all the towns
of Jā'īr, which *are* in Bā'shăn, threescore cities:
31 And half Ĝĭl'e-ăd, and [i]Ăsh'ta-
rŏth, and Ĕd're-ī, cities of the kingdom
of Ŏg in Bā'shăn, *were pertaining* unto
the children of Mā'chĭr the son of Ma-
năs'seh, *even* to the one half of the children of Mā'chĭr by their families.
32 These *are the countries* which
Mō'ses did distribute for inheritance in
the plains of Mō'ab, on the other side
Jôr'dan, by Jĕr'ĭ-chō, eastward.
33 [j]But unto the tribe of Lē'vī Mō'ses
gave not *any* inheritance: the [k]LORD
God of Ĭs'ra-el *was* their inheritance, as
he said unto them.

14 And these *are the countries* which
the children of Ĭs'ra-el inherited
in the land of Cā'năan, [a]which Ē-le-

17 [3]Or, The high places of Baal, and house of Baal-meon
18 [w]Num. 21.23
19 [x]Num. 32.37
20 [4]Or, Springs of Pisgah, or, The hill
21 [y]Deut. 3.10
[z]Num. 21.24
[a]Num. 31.8
22 [b]Num. 22.5; Rev. 2.14
[5]Or, diviner
25 [c]Num. 32.35
[d]Num. 21.26-28-29-with Deut. 2.19; Judg. 11.13
[e]2 Sam. 11.1; 2 Sam. 12.26
27 [f]Gen. 33.17; 1 Ki. 7.46
[g]ch. 11.2; Luke 5.1
30 [h]1 Chr. 2.23
31 [i]ch. 12.4
33 [j]ch. 18.7
[k]Num. 18.20; Ezek. 44.28
CHAPTER 14
1 [a]Num. 34.17
2 [b]Num. 26.55;
3 [c]Num. 32.29;
4 [d]Gen. 48.5;
5 [e]Num. 35.2;
6 [f]Num. 32.12;
[g]Deut. 1.36
[h]Num. 13.26;
8 [i]Deut. 1.36;
9 [j]ch. 1.3
[k]Num. 13.22
10 [l]Num. 14.30;
[1]walked
11 [m]Deut. 34.7
[n]Deut. 31.2
12 [o]1 Sam. 14.6;
[p]ch. 15.14;
13 [q]Gen. 47.7-10;
[r]ch. 10.37;
15 [s]Gen. 23.2;

ā'zar the priest, and Jŏsh'u-ȧ the son of
Nŭn, and the heads of the fathers of the
tribes of the children of Ĭs'ra-el, distributed for inheritance to them.
2 [b]By lot *was* their inheritance, as
the LORD commanded by the hand of
Mō'ses, for the nine tribes, and *for* the
half tribe.
3 [c]For Mō'ses had given the inheritance of two tribes and an half tribe on
the other side Jôr'dan: but unto the Lē'-
vītes he gave none inheritance among
them.
4 For [d]the children of Jō'seph were
two tribes, Ma-năs'seh and Ē'phră-ĭm:
therefore they gave no part unto the
Lē'vītes in the land, save cities to dwell
in, with their suburbs for their cattle
and for their substance.
5 [e]As the LORD commanded Mō'-
ses, so the children of Ĭs'ra-el did, and
they divided the land.
6 ¶ Then the children of Jū'dah came
unto Jŏsh'u-ȧ in Ĝĭl'găl: and Cā'leb
the son of Je-phŭn'neh the [f]Kĕn''ez-īte
said unto him, Thou knowest [g]the
thing that the LORD said unto Mō'ses
the man of God concerning me and
thee [h]in Kā'desh–bär'ne-ȧ.
7 Forty years old *was* I when Mō'ses
the servant of the LORD sent me from
Kā'desh–bär'ne-ȧ to espy out the land;
and I brought him word again as *it was*
in mine heart.
8 Nevertheless my brethren that
went up with me made the heart of the
people melt: but I wholly [i]followed the
LORD my God.
9 And Mō'ses sware on that day, saying, [j]Surely the land [k]whereon thy
feet have trodden shall be thine inheritance, and thy children's for ever, because thou hast wholly followed the
LORD my God.
10 And now, behold, the LORD hath
kept me alive, [l]as he said, these forty
and five years, even since the LORD
spake this word unto Mō'ses, while *the*
children of Ĭs'ra-el [1]wandered in the
wilderness: and now, lo, I *am* this day
fourscore and five years old.
11 [m]As yet I *am as* strong this day
as *I was* in the day that Mō'ses sent
me: as my strength *was* then, even so
is my strength now, for war, both [n]to
go out, and to come in.
12 Now therefore give me this mountain, whereof the LORD spake in that
day; for thou heardest in that day how
the Ăn'a-kĭms *were* there, and *that* the
cities *were* great *and* fenced: [o]if so be
the LORD *will be* with me, then [p]I shall
be able to drive them out, as the LORD
said.
13 And Jŏsh'u-ȧ [q]blessed him, and
[r]gave unto Cā'leb the son of Je-phŭn'-
neh Hē'bron for an inheritance.
14 Hē'bron therefore became the inheritance of Cā'leb the son of Je-phŭn'-
neh the Kĕn''ez-īte unto this day, because that he wholly followed the LORD
God of Ĭs'ra-el.
15 And [s]the name of Hē'bron before
was Kĭr'jath–är'bȧ; *which* Ăr'bȧ *was* a

great man among the Ăn'a-kĭms. [t]And
the land had rest from war.

15 This then was the lot of the tribe
of the children of Jū'dah by their
families; [a]*even* to the border of Ē'dom
the [b]wilderness of Zĭn southward *was*
the uttermost part of the south coast.
2 And their south border was from
the shore of the salt sea, from the [1]bay
that looketh southward:
3 And it went out to the south side
to [2]Ma-ăl'eh–a-crăb'bim, and passed
along to Zĭn, and ascended up on the
south side unto Kā'desh–bär'ne-ȧ, and
passed along to Hĕz'ron, and went up
to Ā'där, and fetched a compass to
Kär'ka-ȧ:
4 *From thence* it passed [c]toward Ăz'-
mŏn, and went out unto [d]the river of
Ē'gypt; and the goings out of that coast
were at the sea: this shall be your south
coast.
5 And the east border *was* the salt
sea, *even* unto the end of Jôr'dan. And
their border in the north quarter *was*
from the bay of the sea at the uttermost
part of Jôr'dan:
6 And the border went up to Bĕth–
hŏg'lȧ, and passed along by the north
of Bĕth–ăr'ă-bah; and the border went
up [e]to the stone of Bō'han the son of
Reu'ben:
7 And the border went up toward
Dē'bĭr from [f]the valley of Ā'chôr, and
so northward, looking toward Gĭl'găl,
that *is* before the going up to A-dŭm'-
mĭm, which *is* on the south side of the
river: and the border passed toward
the waters of Ēn–shē'mesh, and the goings out thereof were at [3]Ēn–rō'gel:
8 And the border went up [g]by the
valley of the son of Hĭn'nom unto the
south side of the [h]Jĕb'u-site; the same
is Je-ru'sa-lĕm: and the border went up
to the top of the mountain that *lieth*
before the valley of Hĭn'nom westward, which *is* at the end [i]of the [4]val-
ley of the giants northward:
9 And the border was drawn from
the top of the hill unto the fountain of
the water of Nĕph'to-ah, and went out
to the cities of mount Ē'phron; and the
border was drawn to [j]Bā'al-ah, which
is [k]Kĭr'jath–jē'a-rĭm:
10 And the border compassed from
Bā'al-ah westward unto mount Sē'ĭr,
and passed along unto the side of
mount Jē'a-rĭm, which *is* Chĕs'ă-lon,
on the north side, and went down
to Bĕth–shē'mĕsh, and passed on to
[l]Tĭm'nah:
11 And the border went out unto the
side of [m]Ĕk'rŏn northward: and the
border was drawn to Shī'crŏn, and
passed along to mount Bā'al-ah, and
went out unto Jăb'nĕ-el; and the goings out of the border were at the sea.
12 And the west border *was* [n]to the
great sea, and the coast *thereof*. This
is the coast of the children of Jū'dah
round about according to their families.
13 ¶ And [o]unto Cā'leb the son of Je-
phŭn'neh he gave a part among the
children of Jū'dah, according to the

[t]ch. 11.23
CHAPTER 15
1 [a]Num. 34.3
[b]Num. 33.36
2 [1]tongue
3 [2]Or, The going up to Acrabbim
4 [c]Num. 34.5
[d]Gen. 15.18; 1 Ki. 8.65
6 [e]ch. 18.17
7 [f]ch. 7.26; Isa. 65.10; Hos. 2.15
[3]Fuller's fountain
8 [g]ch. 18.16; 2 Ki. 23.10; Jer. 19.2-6
[h]ch. 18.28; Judg. 1.21; Judg. 19.10
[i]ch. 18.16
[4]Or, Rephaim
9 [j]1 Chr. 13.6
[k]Judg. 18.12
10 [l]Gen. 38.13
11 [m]ch. 19.43
12 [n]Deut. 11.24; Ezek. 47.20
13 [o]ch. 14.13
[5]Or, Kirjath-arba
14 [p]Judg. 1.10
[q]Num. 13.22
15 [r]ch. 10.38
17 [s]Judg. 3.9
[t]ch. 14.6
18 [u]Judg. 1.14
[v]Gen. 24.64; 1 Sam. 25.23
19 [w]Gen. 33.11
20 [x]Gen. 49. 8-12
21 [6]Jekabzeel
[y]Gen. 35.21
24 [z]1 Sam. 15.4
31 [a]ch. 19.5; 1 Sam. 27.6; 1 Chr. 12.1
32 [b]Neh. 11.29
33 [c]ch. 19.41
35 [d]ch. 10.3-5
[e]ch. 12.15
[f]1 Sam. 17.1
[g]ch. 10.10
36 [h]1 Sam. 17.52
[7]Or, or
38 [i]Not that in ch. 11.3, Gen. 31.49, or ch. 18.26
[j]2 Ki. 14.7
39 [k]ch. 10.3; 2 Ki. 18.14; 2 Chr. 11.9
[l]2 Ki. 22.1
[m]ch. 12.12

commandment of the LORD to Jŏsh'-
u-ȧ, *even* [5]the city of Är'bȧ the father
of Ā'năk, which *city is* Hē'bron.
14 And Cā'leb drove thence [p]the
three sons of Ā'năk, [q]Shē'shāi, and A-
hī'măn, and Tăl'māi, the children of
Ā'năk.
15 And [r]he went up thence to the
inhabitants of Dē'bĭr: and the name of
Dē'bĭr before *was* Kĭr'jath–sē'phĕr.
16 ¶ And Cā'leb said, He that smiteth Kĭr'jath–sē'phĕr, and taketh it, to
him will I give Ăch'sah my daughter to
wife.
17 And [s]Ŏth'nĭ-el the [t]son of Kē'-
năz, the brother of Cā'leb, took it: and
he gave him Ăch'sah his daughter to
wife.
18 And [u]it came to pass, as she came
unto him, that she moved him to ask of
her father a field: and [v]she lighted off
her ass; and Cā'leb said unto her, What
wouldest thou?
19 Who answered, Give me [w]a blessing; for thou hast given me a south
land; give me also springs of water.
And he gave her the upper springs,
and the nether springs.
20 [x]This *is* the inheritance of the
tribe of the children of Jū'dah according to their families.
21 And the uttermost cities of the
tribe of the children of Jū'dah toward
the coast of Ē'dom southward were
[6]Kăb'ze-el, and [y]Ē'dĕr, and Jā'gŭr,
22 And Kī'nah, and Di-mō'nah, and
Ăd'ă-dah,
23 And Kē'desh, and Hā'zôr, and
Ĭth'nan,
24 Zĭph, and [z]Tē'lem, and Bē'ă-lŏth,
25 And Hā'zôr, Ha-dăt'tah, and Kē'-
rĭ-ŏth, *and* Hĕz'ron, which *is* Hā'zôr,
26 Ā'măm, and Shē'mȧ, and Mŏl'a-
dah,
27 And Hā'zar–găd'dah, and Hĕsh'-
mŏn, and Bĕth–pā'let,
28 And Hā'zar–shu'al, and Bē'er–
shē'bȧ, and Bĭz-jŏth'jah,
29 Bā'al-ah, and Ī'ĭm, and Ā'zem,
30 And Ĕl'to-lăd, and Chē'sĭl, and
Hôr'mah,
31 And [a]Zĭk'lag, and Măd-măn'nah,
and Săn-săn'nah,
32 And Lĕb'a-ŏth, and Shĭl'him, and
Ā'in, and [b]Rĭm'mon: all the cities *are*
twenty and nine, with their villages:
33 *And* in the valley, [c]Ĕsh'tă-ŏl, and
Zō're-ah, and Ăsh'nah,
34 And Za-nō'ah, and Ĕn–găn'nĭm,
Tăp'pu-ah, and Ē'nam,
35 [d]Jär'mŭth, and [e]A-dŭl'lăm, [f]Sō'-
coh, and [g]A-zē'kah,
36 And [h]Shăr-ā'ĭm, and Ăd-i-thā'im,
and Gĕ-dē'rah, [7]and Gĕd-ĕ-rŏth-ā'im;
fourteen cities with their villages:
37 Zē'nan, and Hăd'a-shah, and
Mĭg'dal–găd,
38 And Dĭl'ĕ-an, and [i]Mĭz'peh, and
[j]Jŏk'the-el,
39 [k]Lā'chish, and [l]Bŏz'kăth, and
[m]Ĕg'lŏn,
40 And Căb'bon, and Läh'mam, and
Kĭth'lish,

41 And Gĕ-dē'rŏth, Bĕth–dā'gon,
and Nā'a-mah, and Măk-kē'dah; sixteen cities with their villages:
42 Lĭb'nah, and Ē'thĕr, and Ā'shan,
43 And Jĭph'tah, and Ăsh'nah, and
Nē'zib,
44 And Kē-ī'lah, and Ăch'zĭb, and
Ma-rē'shah; nine cities with their villages:
45 Ĕk'rŏn, with her towns and her
villages:
46 From Ĕk'rŏn even unto the sea,
all that *lay* [8]near [n]Ăsh'dŏd, with their
villages:
47 Ăsh'dŏd with her towns and her
villages, Gā'zȧ with her towns and her
villages, unto the [o]river of Ē'gypt, and
[p]the great sea, and the border *thereof:*
48 ¶ And in the mountains, Shā'mĭr,
and Jăt'tĭr, and Sō'coh,
49 And Dăn'nah, and Kĭr'jath–săn'-
nah, which *is* Dē'bĭr,
50 And Ā'nab, and Ĕsh'te-mōh, and
Ā'nĭm,
51 And [q]Gō'shen, and Hō'lŏn, and
Gī'loh; eleven cities with their villages:
52 Ă'rab, and Dụ'mah, and Ē'shĕ-
an,
53 And [9]Jā'num, and Bĕth–tăp'pu-
ah, and A-phē'kah,
54 And Hŭm'tah, and [r]Kĭr'jath–är'-
bȧ, which *is* Hē'bron, and Zī'or; nine
cities with their villages:
55 Mā'on, Cär'mel, and Zĭph, and
Jŭt'tah,
56 And Jĕz're-el, and Jŏk'de-ăm,
and Za-nō'ah,
57 Cāin, Gĭb'e-ah, and Tĭm'nah; ten
cities with their villages:
58 Hăl'hŭl, Bĕth'–zûr, and Gē'dôr,
59 And Mā'a-răth, and Bĕth–ā'nŏth,
and Ĕl'te-kon; six cities with their villages:
60 [s]Kĭr'jath–bā'al, which *is* Kĭr'-
jath–jē'a-rĭm, and Răb'bah; two cities
with their villages:
61 In the wilderness, Bĕth–ăr'ă-bah,
Mĭd'din, and Sĕc'a-cah,
62 And Nĭb'shăn, and the city of
Salt, and [t]Ĕn–gē'dī; six cities with
their villages.
63 ¶ As for the Jĕb'u-sītes the inhabitants of Je-rụ'sa-lĕm, [u]the children of
Jū'dah could not drive them out: [v]but
the Jĕb'u-sītes dwell with the children
of Jū'dah at Je-rụ'sa-lĕm unto this day.

16 And the lot of the children of Jō'-
seph [1]fell from Jôr'dan by Jĕr'ī-
chō, unto the water of Jĕr'ī-chō on
the east, to the wilderness that goeth
up from Jĕr'ī-chō throughout mount
Bĕth'–el,
2 And goeth out from Bĕth'–el to
[a]Lŭz, and passeth along unto the borders of Ăr'chī to Ăt'a-rŏth,
3 And goeth down westward to the
coast of Jăph-lē'tī, [b]unto the coast of
Bĕth–hō'rŏn the nether, and to [c]Gē'-
zĕr: and the goings out thereof are at
the sea.
4 [d]So the children of Jō'seph, Ma-
năs'seh and Ē'phră-ĭm, took their inheritance.
5 ¶ And the border of the children of
Ē'phră-ĭm according to their families
was *thus:* even the border of their inheritance on the east side was [e]Ăt'a-
rŏth–ăd'där, [f]unto Bĕth–hō'rŏn the upper;
6 And the border went out toward the
sea to [g]Mĭch'mĕ-thah on the north side;
and the border went about eastward
unto Tā'a-năth–shī'lōh, and passed by
it on the east to Ja-nō'hah;
7 And it went down from Ja-nō'hah
to Ăt'a-rŏth, [h]and to Nā'a-răth, and
came to Jĕr'ī-chō, and went out at Jôr'-
dan.
8 The border went out from Tăp'pu-
ah westward unto the [i]river Kā'nah;
and the goings out thereof were at the
sea. This *is* the inheritance of the tribe
of the children of Ē'phră-ĭm by their
families.
9 And the separate cities for the children of Ē'phră-ĭm *were* among the inheritance of the children of Ma-
năs'seh, all the cities with their villages.
10 [j]And they drave not out the Cā'-
năan-ītes that dwelt in Gē'zĕr: but the
Cā'năan-ītes dwell among the Ē'phră-
ĭm-ites unto this day, and serve [k]under
tribute.

17 There was also a lot for the tribe
of Ma-năs'seh; for he *was* the
[a]firstborn of Jō'seph; *to wit,* for [b]Mā'-
chĭr the firstborn of Ma-năs'seh, the
father of Gĭl'e-ăd: because he was a
man of war, therefore he had [c]Gĭl'e-ăd
and Bā'shăn.
2 There was also *a lot* for [d]the rest
of the children of Ma-năs'seh by their
families; for [e]the children of [1]Ā-bĭ-ē'-
zĕr, and for the children of Hē'lek, and
[f]for the children of Ăs'rĭ-el, and for the
children of Shē'chem, and for the children of Hē'phĕr, and for the children
of She-mī'dȧ: these *were* the male children of Ma-năs'seh the son of Jō'seph
by their families.
3 ¶ But [g]Ze-lō'phe-hăd, the son of
Hē'phĕr, the son of Gĭl'e-ăd, the son of
Mā'chĭr, the son of Ma-năs'seh, had no
sons, but daughters: and these *are* the
names of his daughters, Măh'lah, and
Nō'ah, Hŏg'lah, Mĭl'cah, and Tĭr'zah.
4 And they came near before [h]Ē-le-
ā'zar the priest, and before Jŏsh'u-ȧ
the son of Nŭn, and before the princes,
saying, [i]The LORD commanded Mō'ses
to give us an inheritance among our
brethren. Therefore according to the
[2]commandment of the LORD he gave
them an inheritance among the brethren of their father.
5 And there fell ten portions to Ma-
năs'seh, beside the land of Gĭl'e-ăd
and Bā'shăn, which *were* on the other
side Jôr'dan;
6 Because the daughters of Ma-năs'-
seh had an inheritance among his sons:
and [j]the rest of Ma-năs'seh's sons had
the land of Gĭl'e-ăd.
7 ¶ And the coast of Ma-năs'seh was
from Ăsh'ĕr to Mĭch'mĕ-thah, that *lieth*
before Shē'chem; and the border went
along on the right hand unto the inhabitants of Ĕn–tăp'pu-ah.

46 [8]by the place of
[n]ch. 13.3
47 [o]Gen. 15.18
[p]Num. 34.6
51 [q]ch. 10.41; ch. 11.16
53 [9]Or, Janus
54 [r]Gen. 23.2; ch. 14.15
60 [s]ch. 18.14; 1 Sam. 7.1-2; 1 Chr. 13.6
62 [t]1 Sam. 23.29
63 [u]Judg. 1.8-21
[v]Judg. 1.21; 2 Sam. 24.16-18; 2 Chr. 3.1; Zech. 9.7

CHAPTER 16
1 [1]went forth
2 [a]Gen. 28.19; ch. 18.13; Judg. 1.26
3 [b]ch. 18.13; 2 Chr. 8.5
[c]1 Chr. 7.28
4 [d]ch. 17.14
5 [e]ch. 18.13
[f]2 Chr. 8.5
6 [g]ch. 17.7
7 [h]1 Chr. 7.28
8 [i]ch. 17.9; ch. 19.28
10 [j]ch. 15.63; 1 Ki. 9.16
[k]Gen. 9.25; ch. 17.12-13; 1 Ki. 9.20-21

CHAPTER 17
1 [a]Gen. 41.51; Gen. 46.20; Gen. 48.18
[b]Gen. 50.23; 1 Chr. 7.14
[c]Deut. 3.13
2 [d]Num. 26.29-32
[e]1 Chr. 7.18
[1]Jeezer
[f]Num. 26.32
3 [g]Num. 26.33
4 [h]ch. 14.1
[i]Num. 27.6-7
[2]mouth
6 [j]Num. 26.29

8 *Now* Ma-năs'seh had the land of
[3][k]Tăp'pu-ah: but Tăp'pu-ah on the border of Ma-năs'seh *belonged* to the children of Ē'phră-ĭm;
9 And the coast descended [l]unto the
[4]river Kā'nah, southward of the river:
[m]these cities of Ē'phră-ĭm *are* among
the cities of Ma-năs'seh: the coast of
Ma-năs'seh also *was* on the north side
of the river, and the outgoings of it
were at the sea:
10 Southward *it was* Ē'phră-ĭm's,
and northward *it was* Ma-năs'seh's,
and the sea is his border; and they met
together in Ăsh'ēr on the north, and in
Ĭs'sa-char on the east.
11 [n]And Ma-năs'seh had in Ĭs'sa-
char and in Ăsh'ēr [o]Bĕth–shē'ăn and
her towns, and Ĭb'le-ăm and her towns,
and the inhabitants of Dôr and her
towns, and the inhabitants of Ĕn'–dôr
and her towns, and the inhabitants of
Tā'a-năch and her towns, and the inhabitants of Me-gĭd'do and her towns,
even three countries.
12 Yet [p]the children of Ma-năs'seh
could not drive out *the inhabitants of*
those cities; but the Cā'năan-ītes would
dwell in that land.
13 Yet it came to pass, when the children of Ĭs'ra-el were waxen strong,
that they put the Cā'năan-ītes to [q]trib-
ute; but [5]did not utterly drive them out.
14 And [r]the children of Jō'seph
spake unto Jŏsh'u-ȧ, saying, Why hast
thou given me *but* [s]one lot and one
portion to inherit, seeing I *am* [t]a great
people, forasmuch as the LORD hath
blessed me hitherto?
15 And Jŏsh'u-ȧ answered them, If
thou *be* a great people, *then* get thee
up to the wood *country,* and cut down
for thyself there in the land of the
Pĕr'ĭz-zītes and of the [6]giants, if mount
Ē'phră-ĭm be too narrow for thee.
16 And the children of Jō'seph said,
The hill is not enough for us: and all
the Cā'năan-ītes that dwell in the land
of the valley have [u]chariots of iron,
both they who *are* of Bĕth–shē'ăn and
her towns, and *they* who *are* [v]of the
valley of Jĕz're-el.
17 And Jŏsh'u-ȧ spake unto the
house of Jō'seph, *even* to Ē'phră-ĭm
and to Ma-năs'seh, saying, Thou *art* a
great people, and hast great power:
thou shalt not have one lot *only:*
18 But the mountain shall be thine;
for it *is* a wood, and thou shalt cut
it down: and the outgoings of it shall
be thine: for thou shalt drive out the
Cā'năan-ītes, [w]though they have iron
chariots, *and* though they *be* strong.

18 And the whole congregation of
the children of Ĭs'ra-el assembled
together [a]at Shī'lōh, and [b]set up the
tabernacle of the congregation [1]there.
And the land was subdued before them.
2 And there remained among the
children of Ĭs'ra-el seven tribes, which
had not yet received their inheritance.
3 And Jŏsh'u-ȧ said unto the children of Ĭs'ra-el, [c]How long *are* ye slack
to go to possess the land, which the
LORD God of your fathers hath given
you?
4 Give out from among you three
men for *each* tribe: and I will send them,
and they shall rise, and go through the
land, and describe it according to the
inheritance of them; and they shall
come *again* to me.
5 And they shall divide it into seven
parts: [d]Jū'dah shall abide in their coast
on the south, and [e]the house of Jō'seph
shall abide in their coasts on the north.
6 Ye shall therefore describe the
land *into* seven parts, and bring *the
description* hither to me, [f]that I may
cast lots for you here before the LORD
our God.
7 [g]But the Lē'vītes have no part
among you; for the [h]priesthood of the
LORD *is* their inheritance: [i]and Găd,
and Reu'ben, and half the tribe of
Ma-năs'seh, have received their inheritance beyond Jôr'dan on the east,
which Mō'ses the servant of the LORD
gave them.
8 ¶ And the men arose, and went
away: and Jŏsh'u-ȧ charged them that
went to describe the land, saying, Go
and walk through the land, and describe it, and come again to me, that I
may here cast lots for you before the
LORD in Shī'lōh.
9 And the men went and passed
through the land, and described it by
cities into seven parts in a book, and
came *again* to Jŏsh'u-ȧ to the host at
Shī'lōh.
10 ¶ And Jŏsh'u-ȧ [j]cast lots for them
in Shī'lōh before the LORD: and there
Jŏsh'u-ȧ divided the land unto the children of Ĭs'ra-el according to their divisions.
11 ¶ And the lot of the tribe of the
children of Bĕn'ja-min came up according to their families: and the coast of
their lot came forth between the children of Jū'dah and the children of Jō'-
seph.
12 And [k]their border on the north
side was from Jôr'dan; and the border
went up to the side of Jĕr'ĭ-chō on the
north side, and went up through the
mountains westward; and the goings
out thereof were at the wilderness of
Bĕth–ā'ven.
13 And the border went over from
thence toward Lŭz, to the side of Lŭz,
[l]which *is* Bĕth'–el, southward; and the
border descended to Ăt'a-rŏth–ā'där,
near the hill that *lieth* on the south side
[m]of the nether Bĕth–hō'rŏn.
14 And the border was drawn *thence,*
and compassed the corner of [2]the sea
southward, from the hill that *lieth* before Bĕth–hō'rŏn southward; and the
goings out thereof were at [n]Kĭr'jath–
bā'al, which *is* Kĭr'jath–jē'a-rĭm, a city
of the children of Jū'dah: this *was* the
west quarter.
15 And the south quarter *was* from
the end of Kĭr'jath–jē'a-rĭm, and the
border went out on the west, and went
out to [o]the well of waters of Nĕph'to-
ah:

8 [3]Or, City of apples [k]ch. 12.17; ch. 15.34; ch. 16.8
9 [l]ch. 16.8 [4]Or, brook of reeds [m]ch. 16.9
11 [n]ch. 16.9; 1 Chr. 7.29 [o]1 Sam. 31.10; 1 Ki. 4.12
12 [p]Ex. 23.29-33
13 [q]ch. 16.10 [5]driving they drove them not out
14 [r]ch. 16.4 [s]Gen. 48.22 [t]Gen. 48.19
15 [6]Rephaims
16 [u]Judg. 1.19 [v]ch. 19.18; Judg. 6.33; 1 Ki. 4.12; 1 Ki. 18.46
18 [w]ch. 11.4-6; ch. 13.6; Rom. 8.31; Heb. 13.6

CHAPTER 18
1 [a]ch. 19.51; ch. 21.2; ch. 22.9; Judg. 21.19; 1 Sam. 14.3; Ps. 78.58-59-60; Jer. 7.12 [b]Judg. 18.31; 1 Sam. 1.3-24; 1 Sam. 4.3-4 [1]Where it remained till taken by the Philistines at the death of Eli
3 [c]Prov. 2.2-6; Prov. 10.4; Zeph. 3.16; Matt. 20.6; Phil. 3.13-14
5 [d]ch. 15.1 [e]ch. 16.1-4
6 [f]ch. 14.2
7 [g]ch. 13.33 [h]Deut. 10.9; Ezek. 44.28 [i]ch. 13.8
10 [j]Prov. 16.33
12 [k]ch. 16.1
13 [l]Gen. 28.19 [m]ch. 16.3
14 [2]The pool of Gibeon [n]ch. 9.17; 1 Chr. 13.6
15 [o]ch. 15.9

16 And the border came down to the end of the mountain that *lieth* before [p]the valley of the son of Hĭn′nom, *and* which *is* in the [3]valley of the giants on the north, and descended to the valley of Hĭn′nom, to the side of Je-bū′si on the south, and descended to [4]Ĕn–rō′gel,

17 And was drawn from the north, and went forth to Ĕn–shē′mesh, and went forth toward Gĕl′ĭ-lŏth, which *is* over against the going up of A-dŭm′mĭm, and descended to the [q]stone of Bō′han the son of Reu′ben,

18 And passed along toward the side over against [5]Ăr′a-bah northward, and went down unto Ăr′a-bah:

19 And the border passed along to the side of Bĕth–hŏg′lah northward: and the outgoings of the border were at the north [6]bay of the salt sea at the south end of Jôr′dan: this *was* the south coast.

20 And Jôr′dan was the border of it on the east side. This *was* the inheritance of the children of Bĕn′ja-min, by the coasts thereof round about, according to their families.

21 Now the cities of the tribe of the children of Bĕn′ja-min according to their families were [r]Jĕr′ĭ-chō, and [s]Bĕth–hŏg′lah, and the valley of Kē′ziz,

22 And Bĕth–ăr′ă-bah, and Zĕm-a-rā′im, and Bĕth′–el,

23 And Ā′vĭm, and Pā′rah, and Ŏph′rah,

24 And Chē′phăr–ha-ăm′mo-nāi, and Ŏph′nī, and [t]Gā′bȧ; twelve cities with their villages:

25 Gĭb′e-on, and Rā′mah, and Be-ē′rŏth,

26 And Mĭz′peh, and Che-phī′rah, and Mō′zah,

27 And Rē′kem, and Ĭr′pĕ-el, and Tăr′a-lah,

28 And [u]Zē′lah, Ē′leph, and [7]Je-bū′si, which *is* Je-ru′sa-lĕm, Gĭb′e-ath, *and* Kĭr′jath; fourteen cities with their villages. This *is* the inheritance of the children of Bĕn′ja-min [v]according to their families.

19 And the second lot came forth to Sĭm′e-on, *even* for the tribe of the children of Sĭm′e-on according to their families: and their inheritance was [a]within the inheritance of the children of Jū′dah.

2 And [b]they had in their inheritance [c]Bē′er–shē′bȧ, and Shē′bȧ, and [d]Mŏl′a-dah,

3 And Hā′zar–shu′al, and Bā′lah, and Ā′zem,

4 And [e]Ĕl′to-lăd, and Bē′thŭl, and Hôr′mah,

5 And Zĭk′lag, and Bĕth–mär′că-bŏth, and Hā′zar–sū′sah,

6 And Bĕth–lĕb′a-ŏth, and Sha-ru′hen; thirteen cities and their villages:

7 Ā′in, Rĕm′mon, and Ē′thĕr, and Ā′shan; four cities and their villages:

8 And all the villages that *were* round about these cities to Bā′al-ath-bē′ĕr, Rā′math of the south. This *is* the inheritance of the tribe of the children of Sĭm′e-on according to their families.

9 Out of the portion of the children of Jū′dah *was* the inheritance of the children of Sĭm′e-on: for the part of the children of Jū′dah was too much for them: therefore the children of Sĭm′e-on had their inheritance within the inheritance of them.

10 ¶ And the third lot came up for the children of Zĕb′u-lun according to their families: and the border of their inheritance was unto Sā′rid:

11 [f]And their border went up toward the sea, and Măr′a-lah, and reached to Dăb′ba-shĕth, and reached to the river that *is* [g]before Jŏk′ne-ăm;

12 And turned from Sā′rid eastward toward the sunrising unto the border of Chĭs′lŏth–tā′bôr, and then goeth out to Dăb′e-răth, and goeth up to Ja-phī′ȧ,

13 And from thence passeth on along on the east to Gĭt′tah–hē′phĕr, to Ĭt′tah–kā′zin, and goeth out to Rĕm′mon–[1]mĕth′o-är to Nē′ah;

14 And the border compasseth it on the north side to Hăn′na-thon: and the outgoings thereof are in the valley of Jĭph′thah–el:

15 And [h]Kăt′tath, and Na-hăl′lal, and [i]Shĭm′ron, and I-dā′lah, and Bĕth′–lĕ-hĕm: twelve cities with their villages.

16 [j]This *is* the inheritance of the children of Zĕb′u-lun according to their families, these cities with their villages.

17 ¶ *And* the fourth lot came out to Ĭs′sa-char, for the children of Ĭs′sa-char according to their families.

18 And their border was toward [k]Jĕz′re-el, and Che-sŭl′lŏth, and [l]Shu′nem,

19 And Haph-rā′im, and Shī′hŏn, and Ă-nă-hā′rath,

20 And Răb′bĭth, and Kĭsh′ĭ-ŏn, and Ā′bĕz,

21 And [m]Rē′meth, and Ĕn–găn′nĭm, and Ĕn–hăd′dah, and Bĕth–păz′zez;

22 And the coast reacheth [n]to Tā′bôr, and Sha-hăz′i-mah, and Bĕth–shē′mĕsh; and the outgoings of their border were at Jôr′dan: sixteen cities with their villages.

23 This *is* the inheritance of the tribe of the children of Ĭs′sa-char according to their families, the cities and their villages.

24 ¶ And the fifth lot came out for the tribe of the children of Ăsh′ĕr according to their families.

25 And their border was [o]Hĕl′kăth, and Hā′lī, and Bē′ten, and Ăch′shăph,

26 And A-lăm′me-lech, and Ā′măd, and Mī′she-al; and reacheth to [p]Cär′mel westward, and to Shī′hôr–lĭb′nath;

27 And turneth toward the sunrising to Bĕth–dā′gon, and reacheth to Zĕb′u-lun, and to the valley of Jĭph′thah–el toward the north side of Bĕth–ē′mĕk, and Nē′ĭ-el, and goeth out to [q]Cā′bŭl on the left hand,

28 And Hē′bron, and Rē′hŏb, and Hăm′mŏn, and [r]Kā′nah, *even* unto great [s]Zī′dŏn;

16 [p]ch. 15.8; 2 Ki. 23.10; 2 Chr. 28.3; Jer. 19.2
[3]Or, Rephaim
[4]Fuller's fountain
17 [q]ch. 15.6
18 [5]Or, the plain, ch. 15.6
19 [6]tongue
21 [r]ch. 2.1; Luke 19.1
[s]ch. 15.6
24 [t]ch. 21.17; Isa. 10.29
28 [u]2 Sam. 21.14
[7]Which belonged partly to Benjamin, and partly to Judah, ch. 15.8
[v]Gen. 46.21; Acts 17.26

CHAPTER 19
1 [a]Gen 49.7
2 [b]1 Chr. 4.28
[c]Gen. 21.14-31; ch. 15.28
[d]Neh. 11.26
4 [e]1 Chr. 4.29-30
11 [f]Gen. 49.13; The Mediterranean
[g]ch. 12.22; 1 Chr. 6.68
13 [1]Or, which is drawn
15 [h]ch. 21.34
[i]ch. 11.1; ch. 12.20
16 [j]Acts 17.26
18 [k]ch. 17.16; Hos. 1.4-5
[l]1 Sam. 28.4; 2 Ki. 4.8
21 [m]ch. 21.29, Jarmuth
22 [n]Judg. 4.6; Ps. 89.12
25 [o]2 Sam. 2.16; 1 Chr. 6.75, Hukok
26 [p]1 Ki. 18.19; Mic. 7.14
27 [q]1 Ki. 9.13
28 [r]John 2.1-Cana
[s]Gen. 10.15-19; Acts 27.3

29 And *then* the coast turneth to Rā'-
mah, and to the strong city [2]Tȳre; and
the coast turneth to Hō'sah; and the
outgoings thereof are at the sea from
the coast to [t]Ăch'zĭb:
30 Ŭm'mah also, and Ā'phek, and
Rē'hŏb: twenty and two cities with
their villages.
31 This *is* the inheritance of the tribe
of the children of Ăsh'ẽr according to
their families, these cities with their villages.
32 ¶ The sixth lot came out to the
children of Năph'ta-lī *even* for the children of Năph'ta-lī according to their
families.
33 And their coast was from Hē'-
lĕph, from Ăl'lŏn to Zā-a-năn'nim, and
Ăd'a-mī, Nē'keb, and Jăb'nĕ-el, unto
Lā'kŭm; and the outgoings thereof
were at Jôr'dan:
34 And *then* [u]the coast turneth westward to Ăz'nŏth–tā'bôr, and goeth out
from thence to Hŭk'kŏk, and reacheth
to Zĕb'u-lun on the south side, and
reacheth to Ăsh'ẽr on the west side,
and to Jū'dah upon Jôr'dan toward the
sunrising.
35 And the fenced cities *are* Zĭd'-
dim, Zẽr, and [v]Hăm'măth, Răk'kăth,
and [w]Chĭn'ne-rĕth,
36 And Ăd'a-mah, and Rā'mah, and
Hā'zôr,
37 And Kē'desh, and Ĕd're-ī, and
Ĕn–hā'zôr,
38 And Ī'ron, and Mĭg'dal–ĕl, Hō'-
rem, and Bĕth–ā'năth, and Bĕth–shē'-
mĕsh; nineteen cities with their villages.
39 This *is* the inheritance of the tribe
of the children of Năph'ta-lī according
to their families, the cities and their villages.
40 ¶ *And* the seventh lot came out
for the tribe of the children of Dăn according to their families.
41 And the coast of their inheritance
was [x]Zō'rah, and Ĕsh'tă-ŏl, and Īr–
shē'mĕsh,
42 And [y]Sha-al-ăb'bin, and Ăj'a-
lŏn, and Jĕth'lah,
43 And Ē'lon, and Thĭm'na-thah, and
Ĕk'rŏn,
44 And Ĕl'te-keh, and Gĭb'be-thon,
and Bā'al-ath,
45 And Jē'hŭd, and Bĕn'e–bē'răk,
and Găth–rĭm'mon,
46 And Me–jăr'kŏn, and Răk'kŏn,
with the border [3]before [4]Jā'phō.
47 And [z]the coast of the children of
Dăn went out *too little* for them: therefore the children of Dăn went up to
fight against Lē'shem, and took it, and
[a]smote it with the edge of the sword,
and possessed it, and dwelt therein,
and called Lē'shem, [b]Dăn, after the
name of Dăn their father.
48 [c]This *is* the inheritance of the
tribe of the children of Dăn according
to their families, these cities with their
villages.
49 ¶ When they had made an end of
dividing the land for inheritance by
their coasts, the children of Ĭs'ra-el

29 [2]Tzor, that is, The rock
[t]Gen. 38.5; Mic. 1.14
34 [u]Deut. 33.23
35 [v]Gen. 10.18
[w]Deut. 3.17; ch. 11.2; ch. 12.3; Mark 6.53; Luke 5.1
41 [x]Judg. 13.2
42 [y]1 Ki. 4.9
46 [3]Or, over against
[4]Or, Joppa
47 [z]Judg. 18
[a]Gen. 49.17
[b]Judg. 18.29
48 [c]Num. 26.54; Acts 17.26
50 [d]ch. 24.30
[e]1 Chr. 7.24
51 [f]Num. 34.17; ch. 14.1
[g]ch. 18.1-10; Ps. 78.60; Jer. 7.12
CHAPTER 20
2 [a]Ex. 21.13; Deut. 4.41-43; Rom. 8.1-33-34; Heb. 6.18-19
4 [b]Ruth 4.1-2; Job 5.4; Jer. 38.7
[1]gather, Ps. 26.9
5 [c]Num. 35.12
6 [d]Num. 35.12-25
7 [2]sanctified
[e]ch. 21.32; 1 Chr. 6.76
[f]Gen. 33.18-19; ch. 21.21; 2 Chr. 10.1
[g]ch. 14.15; ch. 21.11-13
[h]Luke 1.39
8 [i]ch. 21.36; 1 Chr. 6.78
[j]ch. 21.38; 1 Ki. 22.3
[k]ch. 21.27
9 [l]Num. 35.15
CHAPTER 21
1 [a]ch. 14.1; ch. 17.4
2 [b]ch. 18.1

gave an inheritance to Jŏsh'u-ȧ the son
of Nŭn among them:
50 According to the word of the
LORD they gave him the city which
he asked, *even* [d]Tĭm'nath–[e]sĕ'rah in
mount Ē'phră-ĭm: and he built the city,
and dwelt therein.
51 [f]These *are* the inheritances, which
Ē-le-ā'zar the priest, and Jŏsh'u-ȧ the
son of Nŭn, and the heads of the fathers
of the tribes of the children of Ĭs'ra-el,
divided for an inheritance by lot [g]in
Shī'lōh before the LORD, at the door of
the tabernacle of the congregation. So
they made an end of dividing the country.

20 The LORD also spake unto Jŏsh'-
u-ȧ, saying,
2 Speak to the children of Ĭs'ra-el,
saying, [a]Appoint out for you cities of
refuge, whereof I spake unto you by
the hand of Mō'ses:
3 That the slayer that killeth *any* person unawares *and* unwittingly may flee
thither: and they shall be your refuge
from the avenger of blood.
4 And when he that doth flee unto
one of those cities shall stand at the
entering of [b]the gate of the city, and
shall declare his cause in the ears of
the elders of that city, they shall [1]take
him into the city unto them, and give
him a place, that he may dwell among
them.
5 And [c]if the avenger of blood pursue after him, then they shall not deliver the slayer up into his hand; because he smote his neighbour unwittingly, and hated him not beforetime.
6 And he shall dwell in that city, [d]un-
til he stand before the congregation for
judgment, *and* until the death of the
high priest that shall be in those days:
then shall the slayer return, and come
unto his own city, and unto his own
house, unto the city from whence he
fled.
7 ¶ And they [2]appointed [e]Kē'desh
in Găl'ĭ-lee in mount Năph'ta-lī, and
[f]Shē'chem in mount Ē'phră-ĭm, and
[g]Kĭr'jath–är'bȧ, which *is* Hē'bron, in
[h]the mountain of Jū'dah.
8 And on the other side Jôr'dan by
Jĕr'ĭ-chō eastward, they assigned [i]Bē'-
zẽr in the wilderness upon the plain
out of the tribe of Reu'ben, and [j]Rā'-
moth in Gĭl'e-ăd out of the tribe of Găd,
and [k]Gō'lan in Bā'shăn out of the tribe
of Ma-năs'seh.
9 [l]These were the cities appointed
for all the children of Ĭs'ra-el, and for
the stranger that sojourneth among
them, that whosoever killeth *any* person at unawares might flee thither, and
not die by the hand of the avenger of
blood, until he stood before the congregation.

21 Then came near the heads of the
fathers of the Lē'vītes unto [a]Ē-
le-ā'zar the priest, and unto Jŏsh'u-ȧ
the son of Nŭn, and unto the heads of
the fathers of the tribes of the children
of Ĭs'ra-el;
2 And they spake unto them at [b]Shī'-
lōh in the land of Cā'năan, saying,

[c]The LORD commanded by the hand of
Mō'ses to give us cities to dwell in, with
the suburbs thereof for our cattle.
3 And the children of Ĭs'ra-el gave
unto the Lē'vītes out of their inheritance, at the commandment of the
LORD, these cities and their suburbs.
4 And the lot came out for the families of the Kō'hath-ītes: and the children of Aâr'on the priest, *which were*
of the Lē'vītes, [d]had by lot out of the
tribe of Jū'dah, and out of the tribe of
Sĭm'e-on, and out of the tribe of Bĕn'-
ja-min, thirteen cities.
5 And the rest of the children of
Kō'hath *had* by lot out of the families
of the tribe of Ē'phră-ĭm, and out of the
tribe of Dăn, and out of the half tribe of
Ma-năs'seh, ten cities.
6 And the children of Gēr'shŏn *had*
by lot out of the families of the tribe
of Ĭs'sa-char, and out of the tribe of
Ăsh'ēr, and out of the tribe of Năph'ta-
lī, and out of the half tribe of Ma-
năs'seh in Bā'shăn, thirteen cities.
7 The children of Me-rā'rī by their
families *had* out of the tribe of Reu'-
ben, and out of the tribe of Găd, and
out of the tribe of Zĕb'u-lun, twelve cities.
8 And [e]the children of Ĭs'ra-el gave
by lot unto the Lē'vītes these cities
with their suburbs, [f]as the LORD commanded by the hand of Mō'ses.
9 ¶ And they gave out of the tribe of
the children of Jū'dah, and out of the
tribe of the children of Sĭm'e-on, these
cities which are *here* [1]mentioned by
name,
10 Which the children of Aâr'on, *being* of the families of the Kō'hath-ītes,
who were of the children of Lē'vī, had:
for theirs was the first lot.
11 And [g]they gave them [2]the city of
Ăr'bȧ the father of [h]Ā'năk, which *city
is* Hē'bron, [i]in the hill *country* of Jū'-
dah, with the suburbs thereof round
about it.
12 But [j]the fields of the city, and the
villages thereof, gave they to Cā'leb
the son of Je-phŭn'neh for his possession.
13 ¶ Thus [k]they gave to the children
of Aâr'on the priest [l]Hē'bron with her
suburbs, *to be* a city of refuge for the
slayer; and [m]Lĭb'nah with her suburbs,
14 And [n]Jăt'tĭr with her suburbs,
and [o]Ĕsh-te-mō'ȧ with her suburbs,
15 And [p]Hō'lŏn with her suburbs,
and [q]Dē'bĭr with her suburbs,
16 And [r]Ā'in with her suburbs, and
[s]Jŭt'tah with her suburbs, *and* [t]Bĕth-
shē'mĕsh with her suburbs; nine cities
out of those two tribes.
17 And out of the tribe of Bĕn'ja-
min, [u]Gĭb'e-on with her suburbs, [v]Gē'-
bȧ with her suburbs,
18 Ăn'a-thoth with her suburbs, and
[w]Ăl'mŏn with her suburbs; four cities.
19 All the cities of the children of
Aâr'on, the priests, *were* thirteen cities
with their suburbs.
20 ¶ [x]And the families of the children of Kō'hath, the Lē'vītes which
remained of the children of Kō'hath,
even they had the cities of their lot out
of the tribe of Ē'phră-ĭm.
21 For they gave them [y]Shē'chem
with her suburbs in mount Ē'phră-ĭm,
to be a city of refuge for the slayer; and
Gē'zēr with her suburbs,
22 And Kĭb'za-im with her suburbs,
and Bĕth–hō'rŏn with her suburbs;
four cities.
23 And out of the tribe of Dăn, Ĕl'-
te-keh with her suburbs, Gĭb'be-thon
with her suburbs,
24 Āi'ja-lŏn with her suburbs, Găth–
rĭm'mon with her suburbs; four cities.
25 And out of the half tribe of Ma-
năs'seh, Tā'năch with her suburbs, and
Găth–rĭm'mon with her suburbs; two
cities.
26 All the cities *were* ten with their
suburbs for the families of the children
of Kō'hath that remained.
27 ¶ [z]And unto the children of Gēr'-
shŏn, of the families of the Lē'vītes,
out of the *other* half tribe of Ma-năs'-
seh *they gave* [a]Gō'lan in Bā'shăn with
her suburbs, *to be* a city of refuge for
the slayer; and [3]Be-ĕsh'–te-rah with
her suburbs; two cities.
28 And out of the tribe of Ĭs'sa-char,
Kī'shon with her suburbs, Dăb'a-reh
with her suburbs,
29 Jär'mŭth with her suburbs, Ĕn–
găn'nĭm with her suburbs; four cities.
30 And out of the tribe of Ăsh'ēr,
Mī'shal with her suburbs, Ăb'dŏn with
her suburbs,
31 Hĕl'kăth with her suburbs, and
Rē'hŏb with her suburbs; four cities.
32 And out of the tribe of Năph'ta-lī,
[b]Kē'desh in Găl'ĭ-lee with her suburbs,
to be a city of refuge for the slayer; and
Hăm'moth–dôr with her suburbs, and
Kar'tan with her suburbs; three cities.
33 All the cities of the Gēr'shon-ītes
according to their families *were* thirteen cities with their suburbs.
34 ¶ [c]And unto the families of the
children of Me-rā'rī, the rest of the
Lē'vītes, out of the tribe of Zĕb'u-lun,
Jŏk''ne-ăm with her suburbs, and Kär'-
tah with her suburbs,
35 Dĭm'nah with her suburbs, Nā'-
ha-lăl with her suburbs; four cities.
36 And out of the tribe of Reu'ben,
[d]Bē'zēr with her suburbs, and Ja-hā'-
zah with her suburbs,
37 Kĕd'e-mŏth with her suburbs, and
Mĕph'a-ăth with her suburbs; four cities.
38 And out of the tribe of Găd, [e]Rā'-
moth in Gĭl'e-ăd with her suburbs, *to
be* a city of refuge for the slayer; and
[f]Mā-ha-nā'im with her suburbs,
39 Hĕsh'bŏn with her suburbs, Jā'-
zēr with her suburbs; four cities in all.
40 So all the cities for the children of
Me-rā'rī by their families, which were
remaining of the families of the Lē'-
vītes, were *by* their lot twelve cities.
41 [g]All the cities of the Lē'vītes
within the possession of the children
of Ĭs'ra-el *were* forty and eight cities
with their suburbs.

[c]Num. 35.2; Matt. 10.10; Gal. 6.6; 1 Tim. 5.17-18
4 [d]ch. 24.33
8 [e]Gen. 49.7; ch. 18.6; Prov. 16.33
[f]Num. 35.2
9 [1]called
11 [g]1 Chr. 6.55
[2]Or, Kirjath-arba
[h]ch. 14.15; ch. 15.13
[i]2 Sam. 2.1-3; 2 Sam. 5.1-5; Luke 1.39
12 [j]ch. 14.14
13 [k]ch. 20.7-9; 1 Chr. 6.57
[l]ch. 15.54
[m]ch. 10.29; ch. 15.42; Isa. 37.8
14 [n]ch. 15.48
[o]ch. 15.50
15 [p]1 Chr. 6.58-Hilen
[q]ch. 15.49
16 [r]1 Chr. 6.59-Ashan
[s]ch. 15.55
[t]ch. 15.10
17 [u]ch. 18.25
[v]ch. 18.24-Gaba
18 [w]1 Chr. 6.60-Alemeth
20 [x]1 Chr. 6.66
21 [y]Gen. 33.19; ch. 20.7; 1 Ki. 12.1
27 [z]1 Chr. 6.71
[a]Deut. 1.4; ch. 20.8; 1 Chr. 6.71
[3]Or, Ashtaroth
32 [b]ch. 20.7
34 [c]1 Chr. 6.77
36 [d]ch. 20.8
38 [e]Deut. 4.43; 1 Ki. 4.13
[f]Gen. 32.2; 2 Sam. 2.8
41 [g]Gen. 49.7

42 These cities were every one with [4]their suburbs round about them: thus *were* all these cities.

43 ¶ And the LORD gave unto Ĭs'ra-el [h]all the land which he sware to give unto their fathers; and they possessed it, and dwelt therein.

44 [i]And the LORD gave them rest round about, according to all that he sware unto their fathers: and there [j]stood not a man of all their enemies before them; the LORD delivered all their enemies into their hand.

45 [k]There failed not ought of any good thing which the LORD had spoken unto the house of Ĭs'ra-el; all came to pass.

CHAPTER 22

22 Then Jŏsh'u-ȧ called the Reu̯'ben-ītes, and the Găd'ītes, and the half tribe of Ma-năs'seh,

2 And said unto them, Ye have kept [a]all that Mō'ses the servant of the LORD commanded you, [b]and have obeyed my voice in all that I commanded you:

3 Ye have not left your brethren these many days unto this day, but have kept the charge of the commandment of the LORD your God.

4 And now the LORD your God hath given rest unto your brethren, as he promised them: therefore now return ye, and get you unto your tents, *and* unto the land of your possession, [c]which Mō'ses the servant of the LORD gave you on the other side Jôr'dan.

5 But [d]take diligent heed to do the commandment and the law, which Mō'ses the servant of the LORD charged you, [e]to love the LORD your God, and to walk in all his ways, and to keep his commandments, and to cleave unto him, and to serve him with all your heart and with all your soul.

6 So Jŏsh'u-ȧ [f]blessed them, and sent them away: and they went unto their tents.

7 ¶ Now to the *one* half of the tribe of Ma-năs'seh Mō'ses had given *possession* in Bā'shăn: [g]but unto the *other* half thereof gave Jŏsh'u-ȧ among their brethren on this side Jôr'dan westward. And when Jŏsh'u-ȧ sent them away also unto their tents, then he blessed them,

8 And he spake unto them, saying, Return with much riches unto your tents, and with very much cattle, with silver, and with gold, and with brass, and with iron, and with very much raiment: [h]divide the spoil of your enemies with your brethren.

9 ¶ And the children of Reu̯'ben and the children of Găd and the half tribe of Ma-năs'seh returned, and departed from the children of Ĭs'ra-el out of Shī'lōh, which *is* in the land of Cā'năan, to go unto the [i]country of Gĭl'e-ăd, to the land of their possession, whereof they were possessed, according to the word of the LORD by the hand of Mō'ses.

10 ¶ And when they came unto the borders of Jôr'dan, that *are* in the land of Cā'năan, the children of Reu̯'ben and the children of Găd and the half tribe of Ma-năs'seh built there an altar by Jôr'dan, a great altar to see to.

11 ¶ And the children of Ĭs'ra-el [j]heard say, Behold, the children of Reu̯'ben and the children of Găd and the half tribe of Ma-năs'seh have built an altar over against the land of Cā'năan, in the borders of Jôr'dan, at the passage of the children of Ĭs'ra-el.

12 And when the children of Ĭs'ra-el heard *of it,* [k]the whole congregation of the children of Ĭs'ra-el gathered themselves together at Shī'lōh, to go up to war against them.

13 And the children of Ĭs'ra-el [l]sent unto the children of Reu̯'ben, and to the children of Găd, and to the half tribe of Ma-năs'seh, into the land of Gĭl'e-ăd, [m]Phĭn'e-has the son of Ē-le-ā'zar the priest,

14 And with him ten princes, of each [1]chief house a prince throughout all the tribes of Ĭs'ra-el; and [n]each one *was* an head of the house of their fathers among the thousands of Ĭs'ra-el.

15 ¶ And they came unto the children of Reu̯'ben, and to the children of Găd, and to the half tribe of Ma-năs'seh, unto the land of Gĭl'e-ăd, and they spake with them, saying,

16 Thus saith the whole congregation of the LORD, What trespass *is* this that ye have committed against the God of Ĭs'ra-el, to turn away this day from following the LORD, in that ye have builded you an altar, [o]that ye might rebel this day against the LORD?

17 *Is* the iniquity [p]of Pē'or too little for us, from which we are not cleansed until this day, although there was a plague in the congregation of the LORD,

18 But that ye must turn away this day from following the LORD? and it will be, *seeing* ye rebel to day against the LORD, that to morrow [q]he will be wroth with the whole congregation of Ĭs'ra-el.

19 Notwithstanding, if the land of your possession *be* unclean, *then* pass ye over unto the land of the possession of the LORD, [r]wherein the LORD'S tabernacle dwelleth, and take possession among us: but rebel not against the LORD, nor rebel against us, in building you an altar beside the altar of the LORD our God.

20 [s]Did not Ā'chăn the son of Zē'rah commit a trespass in the accursed thing, and wrath fell on all the congregation of Ĭs'ra-el? and that man perished not alone in his iniquity.

21 ¶ [t]Then the children of Reu̯'ben and the children of Găd and the half tribe of Ma-năs'seh answered, and said unto the heads of the thousands of Ĭs'ra-el,

22 The LORD [u]God of gods, the LORD God of gods, he [v]knoweth, and Ĭs'ra-el he shall know; if *it be* in rebellion, or if in transgression against the LORD, (save us not this day,)

23 That we have built us an altar to turn from following the LORD, or if to offer thereon burnt offering or meat offering, or if to offer peace offerings

42 [4]That is, 608 yards broad for barns, gardens, etc., and 1216 more for fields and vineyards

43 [h]Gen. 13.15; Gen. 26.3

44 [i]ch. 11.23; ch. 22.4

[j]Deut. 7.24

45 [k]ch. 23.14; Luke 21.33

CHAPTER 22

2 [a]Num. 32.20

[b]ch. 1.16-17

4 [c]Deut. 29.8; ch. 13.8

5 [d]Deut. 6.6-17; 1 Tim. 1.5

[e]Deut. 10.12; Jude 21

6 [f]Gen. 47.7; Luke 24.50

7 [g]ch. 17.5

8 [h]1 Sam. 30.24

9 [i]Num. 32.1-26-29

11 [j]Lev. 17.8; Deut. 13.12

12 [k]Judg. 20.1-12

13 [l]Deut. 13.14

[m]Ex. 6.25

14 [1]house of the father

[n]Num. 1.4

16 [o]Lev. 17.8-9; 1 Sam. 15.23

17 [p]Deut. 4.3

18 [q]Gen. 18.23-25; 1 Chr. 21.1-14

19 [r]Lev. 17.8-9; ch. 18.1

20 [s]ch. 7.1-5; 1 Chr. 2.6-7

21 [t]Prov. 15.1;

22 [u]Ex. 15.11;

[v]1 Ki. 8.39

thereon, let the LORD himself [w]require
it;
24 And if we have not *rather* done it
for fear of *this* thing, saying, [2]In time to
come your children might speak unto
our children, saying, What have ye to
do with the LORD God of Ĭs'ra-el?
25 For the LORD hath made Jôr'dan
a border between us and you, ye children of Reṳ'ben and children of Găd;
ye have no part in the LORD: so shall
your children make our children cease
from fearing the LORD.
26 Therefore we said, Let us now
prepare to build us an altar, not for
burnt offering, nor for sacrifice:
27 But *that* it *may be* [x]a witness between us, and you, and our generations after us, that we might [y]do the
service of the LORD before him with
our burnt offerings, and with our sacrifices, and with our peace offerings;
that your children may not say to our
children in time to come, Ye have no
part in the LORD.
28 Therefore said we, that it shall
be, when they should *so* say to us or to
our generations in time to come, that
we may say *again,* Behold the pattern
of the altar of the LORD, which our fathers made, not for burnt offerings,
nor for sacrifices; but it *is* a witness
between us and you.
29 God forbid that we should rebel
against the LORD, and turn this day
from following the LORD, [z]to build an
altar for burnt offerings, for meat offerings, or for sacrifices, beside the altar
of the LORD our God that *is* before his
tabernacle.
30 ¶ And when Phĭn'e-has the priest,
and the princes of the congregation
and heads of the thousands of Ĭs'ra-el
which *were* with him, heard the words
that the children of Reṳ'ben and the
children of Găd and the children of Ma-
năs'seh spake, [3]it pleased them.
31 And Phĭn'e-has the son of Ē-le-
ā'zar the priest said unto the children
of Reṳ'ben, and to the children of Găd,
and to the children of Ma-năs'seh,
This day we perceive that the LORD *is*
[a]among us, because ye have not committed this trespass against the LORD:
[4]now ye have delivered the children of
Ĭs'ra-el out of the hand of the LORD.
32 ¶ And Phĭn'e-has the son of Ē-le-
ā'zar the priest, and the princes, returned from the children of Reṳ'ben,
and from the children of Găd, out of
the land of Gĭl'e-ăd, unto the land of
Cā'năan, to the children of Ĭs'ra-el,
and brought them word again.
33 And the thing pleased the children of Ĭs'ra-el; and the children of
Ĭs'ra-el [b]blessed God, and did not intend to go up against them in battle, to
destroy the land wherein the children
of Reṳ'ben and Găd dwelt.
34 And the children of Reṳ'ben and
the children of Găd called the altar
[5]*Ed:* for it *shall be* a witness between
us that the LORD *is* God.
23 And it came to pass a long time
after that the LORD [a]had given
rest unto Ĭs'ra-el from all their enemies
round about, that Jŏsh'u-ȧ [b]waxed old
and [1]stricken in age.
2 And Jŏsh'u-ȧ [c]called for all Ĭs'ra-
el, *and* for their elders, and for their
heads, and for their judges, and for
their officers, and said unto them, I am
old *and* stricken in age:
3 And ye have seen all that the LORD
your God hath done unto all these nations because of you; for the LORD
your God *is* he that hath fought for
you.
4 Behold, I have divided unto you by
lot these nations that remain, to be an
inheritance for your tribes, from Jôr'-
dan, with all the nations that I have cut
off, even unto the great sea [2]westward.
5 And the LORD your God, [d]he shall
expel them from before you, and drive
them from out of your sight; and ye
shall possess their land, [e]as the LORD
your God hath promised unto you.
6 Be ye therefore very courageous
to keep and to do all that is written in
the book of the law of Mō'ses, [f]that ye
turn not aside therefrom *to* the right
hand or *to* the left;
7 That ye [g]come not among these
nations, these that remain among you;
neither [h]make mention of the name
of their gods, nor cause to swear *by
them,* neither serve them, nor bow
yourselves unto them:
8 [3]But cleave unto the LORD your
God, as ye have done unto this day.
9 [4]For the LORD hath driven out from
before you great nations and strong:
but *as for* you, [i]no man hath been able
to stand before you unto this day.
10 One [j]man of you shall chase a
thousand: for the LORD your God, he *it
is* that fighteth for you, as he hath
promised you.
11 Take good heed therefore unto
[5]yourselves, that ye love the LORD your
God.
12 Else if ye do in any wise [k]go
back, and cleave unto the remnant of
these nations, *even* these that remain
among you, and shall make marriages
with them, and go in unto them, and
they to you:
13 Know for a certainty that [l]the
LORD your God will no more drive out
any of these nations from before you;
[m]but they shall be snares and traps
unto you, and scourges in your sides,
and thorns in your eyes, until ye perish
from off this good land which the LORD
your God hath given you.
14 And, behold, this day [n]I *am* going the way of all the earth: and ye
know in all your hearts and in all your
souls, that [o]not one thing hath failed of
all the good things which the LORD
your God spake concerning you; all
are come to pass unto you, *and* not one
thing hath failed thereof.
15 [p]Therefore it shall come to pass,
that as all good things are come upon
you, which the LORD your God promised you; so shall the LORD bring upon
you [q]all evil things, until he have destroyed you from off this good land

23 [w]Deut. 18.19; 1 Sam. 20.16; Ps. 7.3-5; Ps. 10.13-14
24 [2]To morrow
27 [x]Gen. 31.48; ch. 24.27; 1 Sam. 7.12
[y]Deut. 12.5-6-11-12-17-18-26-27
29 [z]Deut. 12.13-14
30 [3]it was good in their eyes
31 [a]Ex. 25.8; Lev. 26.11-12; 2 Chr. 15.2; Zech. 8.23; 1 Cor. 14.25; Rev. 21.3
[4]then
33 [b]1 Chr. 29.20; Dan. 2.19; Luke 2.28
34 [5]That is, A witness

CHAPTER 23
1 [a]ch. 21.44
[b]ch. 13.1
[1]come into days
2 [c]Deut. 31.28; ch. 24.1
4 [2]at the sunset
5 [d]Ex. 23.30; Ex. 33.2; Deut. 11.23
[e]Num. 33.53
6 [f]Deut. 5.32
7 [g]Ex. 23.33; Deut. 7.2-3; Eph. 5.11
[h]Ex. 23.13; Zeph. 1.5
8 [3]Or, For if ye will cleave
9 [4]Or, Then the LORD will drive
[i]ch. 1.5
10 [j]Judg. 3.31; 2 Sam. 23.8
11 [5]your souls
12 [k]Heb. 10.38; 2 Pet. 2.20
13 [l]Judg. 2.3
[m]1 Ki. 11.4
14 [n]Eccl. 12.3-7; Heb. 9.27
[o]Luke 21.33
15 [p]Deut. 28.63
[q]Lev. 26.16; Luke 21.22

which the LORD your God hath given
you.
16 When ye have transgressed the
covenant of the LORD your God, which
he commanded you, and have gone
and served other gods, and bowed
yourselves to them; then shall the anger of the LORD be kindled against
you, and ye shall perish quickly from
off the good land which he hath given
unto you.

24 And Jŏsh'u-ȧ gathered all the
tribes of Ĭs'ra-el to [a]Shē'chem,
and [b]called for the elders of Ĭs'ra-
el, and for their heads, and for their
judges, and for their officers; and they
[c]presented themselves before God.
2 And Jŏsh'u-ȧ said unto all the people, Thus saith the LORD God of Ĭs'ra-
el, [d]Your fathers dwelt on the other
side of the flood in old time, *even* Tē'-
rah, the father of Ā'bră-hăm, and the
father of Nā'chôr: and [e]they served
other gods.
3 And [f]I took your father Ā'bră-hăm
from the other side of the flood, and led
him throughout all the land of Cā'năan,
and multiplied his seed, and [g]gave him
Ī'saac.
4 And I gave unto Ī'saac Jā'cob and
Ē'sau: and I gave unto [h]Ē'sau mount
Sē'ĭr, to possess it; but Jā'cob and his
children went down into Ē'ġypt.
5 [i]I sent Mō'ṣeṣ also and Aâr'on,
and [j]I plagued Ē'ġypt, according to
that which I did among them: and afterward I brought you out.
6 And I [k]brought your fathers out of
Ē'ġypt: and ye came unto the sea; [l]and
the E-ġȳp''tians pursued after your fathers with chariots and horsemen unto
the Red sea.
7 And when they cried unto the
LORD, he put darkness between you
and the E-ġȳp''tians, and brought the
sea upon them, and covered them; and
your eyes have seen what I have done
in Ē'ġypt: and ye dwelt in the wilderness a long season.
8 And I brought you into the land
of the Ăm'ôr-ītes, which dwelt on the
other side Jôr'dan; [m]and they fought
with you: and I gave them into your
hand, that ye might possess their land;
and I destroyed them from before you.
9 Then [n]Bā'lăk the son of Zĭp'-
por, king of Mō'ab, arose and warred
against Ĭs'ra-el, and [o]sent and called
Bā'laam the son of Bē'or to curse you:
10 [p]But I would not hearken unto
Bā'laam; [q]therefore he blessed you
still: so I delivered you out of his hand.
11 And ye went over Jôr'dan, and
came unto Jĕr'ĭ-chō: and the men of
Jĕr'ĭ-chō fought against you, the Ăm'-
ôr-ītes, and the Pĕr'ĭz-zītes, and the
Cā'năan-ītes, and the Hĭt'tītes, and the
Gĭr'ga-shītes, the Hī'vītes, and the Jĕb'-
u-sītes; and I delivered them into your
hand.
12 And [r]I sent the hornet before you,
which drave them out from before you,
even the two kings of the Ăm'ôr-ītes;
but [s]not with thy sword, nor with thy
bow.
13 And I have given you a land for
which ye did not labour, and [t]cities
which ye built not, and ye dwell in
them; of the vineyards and oliveyards
which ye planted not do ye eat.
14 ¶ [u]Now therefore fear the LORD,
and serve him in [v]sincerity and in truth:
and [w]put away the gods which your
fathers served on the other side of the
flood, and [x]in Ē'ġypt; and serve ye the
LORD.
15 And if it seem evil unto you to
serve the LORD, choose you this day
whom ye will serve; whether the gods
which your fathers served that *were* on
the other side of the flood, or [y]the gods
of the Ăm'ôr-ītes, in whose land ye
dwell: [z]but as for me and my house,
we will serve the LORD.
16 And the people answered and
said, God forbid that we should forsake the LORD, to serve other gods;
17 For the LORD our God, he *it is*
that brought us up and our fathers out
of the land of Ē'ġypt, from the house of
bondage, and which did those great
signs in our sight, and preserved us
in all the way wherein we went, and
among all the people through whom
we passed:
18 And the LORD drave out from before us all the people, even the Ăm'ôr-
ītes which dwelt in the land: *therefore*
will we also serve the LORD; for he *is*
our God.
19 And Jŏsh'u-ȧ said unto the people, [a]Ye cannot serve the LORD: for he
is an [b]holy God; he *is* a jealous God;
[c]he will not forgive your transgressions nor your sins.
20 [d]If ye forsake the LORD, and serve
strange gods, [e]then he will turn and do
you hurt, and consume you, after that
he hath done you good.
21 And the people said unto Jŏsh'-
u-ȧ, Nay; but we will serve the LORD.
22 And Jŏsh'u-ȧ said unto the people, Ye *are* witnesses against yourselves that [f]ye have chosen you the
LORD, to serve him. And they said, *We
are* witnesses.
23 Now therefore [g]put away, *said
he,* the strange gods which *are* among
you, and incline your heart unto the
LORD God of Ĭs'ra-el.
24 And the people said unto Jŏsh'-
u-ȧ, The LORD our God will we serve,
and his voice will we obey.
25 So Jŏsh'u-ȧ [h]made a covenant
with the people that day, and set them
a statute and an ordinance in Shē'-
chem.
26 ¶ And Jŏsh'u-ȧ [i]wrote these words
in the book of the law of God, and took
[j]a great stone, and [k]set it up there under
an oak, that *was* by the sanctuary of the
LORD.
27 And Jŏsh'u-ȧ said unto all the
people, Behold, this stone shall be [l]a
witness unto us; for [m]it hath heard all
the words of the LORD which he spake
unto us: it shall be therefore a witness
unto you, lest ye deny your God.
28 So Jŏsh'u-ȧ let the people depart,
every man unto his inheritance.

CHAPTER 24
1 [a]Gen. 12.6; Judg. 9.1-3
[b]Ex. 18.25; ch. 23.2
[c]1 Sam. 10.19; Acts 10.33
2 [d]Gen. 11.26; Isa. 51.2
[e]Gen. 31.53
3 [f]Acts 7.2-3
[g]Ps. 127.3
4 [h]Gen. 36.8; Acts 17.26
5 [i]Ex. 3.10
[j]Ex. 7; Ex. 9
6 [k]Ex. 12.37-51; Mic. 6.4
[l]Ex. 14.9; Heb. 11.29
8 [m]Num. 21.21-33; Deut. 2.32
9 [n]Judg. 11.25
[o]Num. 22.5
10 [p]Deut. 23.5
[q]Num. 23.11
12 [r]Ex. 23.28; Deut. 7.20
[s]Ps. 44.3-6
13 [t]Deut. 6.10;
14 [u]Deut. 10.12;
[v]Gen. 17.1;
[w]Lev. 17.7
[x]Ezek. 20.7
15 [y]Ex. 23.24
[z]Gen. 18.19
19 [a]Ruth 1.15;
[b]Lev. 19.2;
[c]Ex. 23.21;
20 [d]ch. 23.12-15;
[e]Isa. 63.10;
22 [f]Ps. 119.173
23 [g]Gen. 35.2;
25 [h]Ex. 15.25
26 [i]Deut. 31.24
[j]Judg. 9.6
[k]Gen. 28.18;
27 [l]Gen. 31.48
[m]Deut. 32.1

29 ¶ And it came to pass after these things, that Jŏsh'u-ȧ the son of Nŭn, the servant of the LORD, died, *being* an hundred and ten years old.

30 And they buried him in the border of his inheritance in [n]Tĭm'nath–sē'rah, which *is* in mount Ē'phră-ĭm, on the north side of the hill of Gā'ăsh.

31 And [o]Ĭs'ra-el served the LORD all the days of Jŏsh'u-ȧ, and all the days of the elders that [1]overlived Jŏsh'u-ȧ, and which had known all the works of the LORD, that he had done for Ĭs'ra-el.

32 ¶ And [p]the bones of Jō'seph, which the children of Ĭs'ra-el brought up out of Ē'ġypt, buried they in Shē'chem, in a parcel of ground [q]which Jā'cob bought of the sons of Hā'mor the father of Shē'chem for an hundred [2]pieces of silver: and it became the inheritance of the children of Jō'seph.

33 And Ē-le-ā'zar the son of Aâr'on died; and they buried him in a hill *that pertained to* [r]Phĭn'e-has his son, which was given him in mount Ē'phră-ĭm.

30 [n]ch. 19.50
31 [o]Judg. 2.7 [1]prolonged their days after Joshua
32 [p]Gen. 50.25; Ex. 13.19; Acts 7.16
[q]Gen. 33.19 [2]Or, lambs
33 [r]Ex. 6.25

THE BOOK OF

JUDGES

Life's Questions

Where is God in life's treacherous transitions?
What responsibility does God place on leaders?
What happens when God's people lack leadership?

God's Answers

Judges shows what happens when God's people face the transition from wilderness nomads to landed citizens? In three unequal parts Judges shows: without leadership God's people disobey and create chaos (1:1—3:6); repentance and cries for help bring divinely chose leaders and deliverance (3:7—16:31); and ongoing disobedience without leadership brings moral and social chaos (17:1—21:25).

Judges contrasts God's faithfulness with Israel's unfaithfulness as the culture of a new land proves more enticing than the promises of God's covenant.

Partial obedience is disobedience, exposing the people to added temptation (1:1—2:5).

Leaders who neglect covenant and people who ignore God's leaders lead to punishment (2:6–23).

God tests His people (3:1–6).

God hears His people's agonized cries (3:7–31).

God provides leaders and deliverance in time of need (4:1—7:25).

God the King can rule without traditional institutions and self-seeking leaders but honors humble, obedient leaders (8:1—12:15).

God uses even selfish tricksters for His purposes (13:1—16:31).

Without godly leaders, people lose all moral values (17:1—21:25).

Judges pictures a series of men and women God called after a people rebelled against Him with substitutes for God. These God-called leaders display various degrees of obedience as God uses them to bring victory for His people. Without leaders morality becomes individual choice and total chaos.

1 Now after the death of Jŏsh'u-ȧ it came to pass, that the children of Ĭs'ra-el [a]asked the LORD, saying, Who shall go up for us against the Cā'năan-ītes first, to fight against them?

2 And the LORD said, [b]Jū'dah shall go up: behold, I have delivered the land into his hand.

3 And Jū'dah said unto Sĭm'e-on his brother, Come up with me into my lot, that we may fight against the Cā'năan-ītes; and I likewise will go with thee into thy lot. [c]So Sĭm'e-on went with him.

4 And Jū'dah went up; and [d]the LORD delivered the Cā'năan-ītes and the Pĕr'ĭz-zītes into their hand: and they slew of them in Bē'zek ten thousand men.

5 And they found A-dŏn'i–bē'zek in Bē'zek: and they fought against him, and they slew the Cā'năan-ītes and the Pĕr'ĭz-zītes.

6 But A-dŏn'i–bē'zek fled; and they pursued after him, and caught him, and cut off his thumbs and his great toes.

7 And A-dŏn'i–bē'zek said, Threescore and ten kings, having [1]their thumbs and their great toes cut off, [2]gathered *their meat* under my table: [e]as I have done, so God hath requited me. And they brought him to Je-ru'sa-lĕm, and there he died.

8 Now [f]the children of Jū'dah had fought against Je-ru'sa-lĕm, and had taken it, and smitten it with the edge of the sword, and set the city on fire.

9 ¶ [g]And afterward the children of Jū'dah went down to fight against the Cā'năan-ītes, that dwelt in the mountain, and in the south, and in the [3]valley.

10 And Jū'dah went against the Cā'năan-ītes that dwelt in Hē'bron: (now the name of Hē'bron before *was* [h]Kĭr'jath–är'bȧ:) and they slew Shē'shāi, and A-hī'măn, and Tăl'māi.

11 [i]And from thence he went against the inhabitants of Dē'bĭr: and the name of Dē'bĭr before *was* Kĭr'jath–sē'phĕr:

CHAPTER 1
1 [a]Ex. 28.30; ch. 20.18; 1 Sam. 23.9-10
2 [b]Gen. 49.8
3 [c]Eccl. 4.9; Mark 6.7; 1 Cor. 12.26; Gal. 6.2
4 [d]Deut. 9.1; Ps. 44.2
7 [1]the thumbs of their hands and of their feet [2]Or, gleaned [e]Lev. 24.19; Mark 4.24
8 [f]Josh. 15.63
9 [g]Josh. 10.12-36 [3]Or, low country
10 [h]Josh. 14.15
11 [i]Josh. 15.15

12 And Cā'leb said, He that smiteth
Kĭr'jath–sē'phēr, and taketh it, to him
will I give Ăch'sah my daughter to
wife.
13 And Ŏth'nĭ-el the son of Kē'năz,
[j]Cā'leb's younger brother, took it: and
he gave him Ăch'sah his daughter to
wife.
14 [k]And it came to pass, when she
came *to him,* that she moved him to ask
of her father a field; and she lighted
from off *her* ass; and Cā'leb said unto
her, What wilt thou?
15 And she said unto him, [l]Give me
a [4]blessing: for thou hast given me a
south land; give me also springs of water. And Cā'leb gave her the upper
springs and the nether springs.
16 ¶ And [m]the children of the Kĕn'-
īte, Mō'ses' father in law, went up
out [n]of the city of palm trees with the
children of Jū'dah into the wilderness
of Jū'dah, which *lieth* in the south
of [o]Ā'răd; [p]and they went and dwelt
among the people.
17 And Jū'dah went with Sĭm'e-on
his brother, and they slew the Cā'-
năan-ītes that inhabited Zē'phath, and
utterly destroyed it. And the name of
the city was called [q]Hôr'mah.
18 Also Jū'dah took [r]Gā'zȧ with the
coast thereof, and Ăs'ke-lŏn with the
coast thereof, and Ĕk'rŏn with the
coast thereof.
19 And [s]the LORD was with Jū'dah;
and [5]he drave out *the inhabitants of*
the mountain; but could not drive out
the inhabitants of the valley, because
they had [t]chariots of iron.
20 [u]And they gave Hē'bron unto
Cā'leb, as Mō'ses said: and he expelled
thence the three sons of Ā'năk.
21 [v]And the children of Bĕn'ja-min
did not drive out the Jĕb'u-sītes that
inhabited Je-ru'sa-lĕm; but the Jĕb'u-
sītes dwell with the children of Bĕn'ja-
min in Je-ru'sa-lĕm unto this day.
22 ¶ And the house of Jō'seph, they
also went up against Bĕth'–el: and the
LORD *was* with them.
23 And the house of Jō'seph [w]sent
to descry Bĕth'–el. (Now the name of
the city before *was* [x]Lŭz.)
24 And the spies saw a man come
forth out of the city, and they said unto
him, Shew us, we pray thee, the entrance into the city, and [y]we will shew
thee mercy.
25 And when he shewed them the
entrance into the city, they smote the
city with the edge of the sword; but
they let go the man and all his family.
26 And the man went into the land
of the Hĭt'tītes, and built a city, and
called the name thereof Lŭz: which *is*
the name thereof unto this day.
27 ¶ Neither did [z]Ma-năs'seh drive
out *the inhabitants of* Bĕth–shē'ăn and
her towns, nor [a]Tā'a-năch and her
towns, nor the inhabitants of Dôr and
her towns, nor the inhabitants of Ĭb'le-
ăm and her towns, nor the inhabitants
of Me-gĭd'do and her towns: but the
Cā'năan-ītes would dwell in that land.

13 [j]ch. 3.9
14 [k]Josh. 15.18
15 [l]Gen. 33.11; Heb. 6.7
[4]Or, present
16 [m]Num. 10.29-32; Jer. 35.2
[n]Deut. 34.3; 2 Chr. 28.15
[o]Num. 21.1
[p]Num. 10.32
17 [q]Num. 21.3
18 [r]Josh. 11.22; 1 Sam. 6.17
19 [s]Gen. 39.2-21; Rom. 8.31
[5]Or, he possessed the mountain
[t]Josh. 17.16
20 [u]Num. 14.24;
21 [v]Josh. 15.63;
23 [w]Josh. 2.1;
[x]Gen. 28.19
24 [y]1 Sam. 30.15
27 [z]Josh. 17.11
[a]Josh. 21.25
28 [6]driving he drove them not out
29 [b]1 Ki. 9.16
30 [c]Josh. 19.15
31 [d]Josh. 19.24-30
32 [e]Ps. 106.34-35
33 [f]Josh. 19.38
35 [g]ch. 12.12
[7]was heavy
36 [h]Num. 34.4
[8]Or, Maaleh-akrabbim

CHAPTER 2
1 [a]Gen. 16.7;
[1]Or, messenger
[b]Gen. 17.7
3 [c]Josh. 23.13
[d]Ex. 23.33
5 [2]That is, Weepers
7 [3]prolonged days after Joshua

28 And it came to pass, when Ĭs'ra-
el was strong, that they put the Cā'-
năan-ītes to tribute, and [6]did not utterly drive them out.
29 ¶ [b]Neither did Ē'phră-ĭm drive
out the Cā'năan-ītes that dwelt in Gē'-
zēr; but the Cā'năan-ītes dwelt in Gē'-
zēr among them.
30 ¶ Neither did Zĕb'u-lun drive out
the inhabitants of Kĭt'rŏn, nor the [c]in-
habitants of Nā'ha-lŏl; but the Cā'-
năan-ītes dwelt among them, and became tributaries.
31 ¶ [d]Neither did Ăsh'ēr drive out
the inhabitants of Ăc'chō, nor the inhabitants of Zī'dŏn, nor of Äh'lăb,
nor of Ăch'zĭb, nor of Hĕl'bah, nor of
Ā'phĭk, nor of Rē'hŏb:
32 But the Ăsh'ēr-ītes [e]dwelt among
the Cā'năan-ītes, the inhabitants of the
land: for they did not drive them out.
33 ¶ [f]Neither did Năph'ta-lī drive out
the inhabitants of Bĕth–shē'mĕsh, nor
the inhabitants of Bĕth–ā'năth; but he
dwelt among the Cā'năan-ītes, the inhabitants of the land: nevertheless the
inhabitants of Bĕth–shē'mĕsh and of
Bĕth–ā'năth became tributaries unto
them.
34 And the Ăm'ôr-ītes forced the
children of Dăn into the mountain: for
they would not suffer them to come
down to the valley:
35 But the Ăm'ôr-ītes would dwell
in mount Hē'rēs [g]in Āij'a-lŏn, and in
Sha-ăl'bim: yet the hand of the house
of Jō'seph [7]prevailed, so that they became tributaries.
36 And the coast of the Ăm'ôr-ītes
was [h]from [8]the going up to A-krăb'-
bim, from the rock, and upward.

2 And an [a][1]angel of the LORD came
up from Gĭl'găl to Bō'chim, and
said, I made you to go up out of Ē'gypt,
and have brought you unto the land
which I sware unto your fathers; and
[b]I said, I will never break my covenant
with you.
2 And ye shall make no league with
the inhabitants of this land; ye shall
throw down their altars: but ye have
not obeyed my voice: why have ye
done this?
3 Wherefore I also said, I will not
drive them out from before you; but
they shall be [c]*as thorns* in your sides,
and [d]their gods shall be a snare unto
you.
4 And it came to pass, when the angel of the LORD spake these words
unto all the children of Ĭs'ra-el, that the
people lifted up their voice, and wept.
5 And they called the name of that
place [2]Bō'chim: and they sacrificed
there unto the LORD.
6 ¶ And when Jŏsh'u-ȧ had let the
people go, the children of Ĭs'ra-el went
every man unto his inheritance to possess the land.
7 And the people served the LORD
all the days of Jŏsh'u-ȧ, and all the
days of the elders that [3]outlived Jŏsh'-
u-ȧ, who had seen all the great works
of the LORD, that he did for Ĭs'ra-el.

8 And Jŏsh'u-ȧ the son of Nŭn, the
servant of the LORD, died, *being* an hundred and ten years old.
9 And they buried him in the border
of his inheritance in Tĭm'nath–hē'res,
in the mount of Ē'phră-ĭm, on the north
side of the hill Gā'ăsh.
10 And also all that generation were
gathered unto their fathers: and there
arose another generation after them,
which [e]knew not the LORD, nor yet the
works which he had done for Ĭs'ra-el.
11 ¶ And the children of Ĭs'ra-el did
evil in the sight of the LORD, and served
Bā'al-ĭm:
12 And they [f]forsook the LORD God
of their fathers, which brought them
out of the land of Ē'gypt, and followed
[g]other gods, of the gods of the people that *were* round about them, and
[h]bowed themselves unto them, and
provoked the LORD to anger.
13 And they forsook the LORD, and
served Bā'al and Ăsh'ta-rŏth.
14 ¶ [i]And the anger of the LORD
was hot against Ĭs'ra-el, and [j]he delivered them into the hands of spoilers
that spoiled them, and [k]he sold them
into the hands of their enemies round
about, so that [l]they could not any
longer stand before their enemies.
15 Whithersoever they went out, the
hand of the LORD was against them for
evil, as the LORD had said, and [m]as the
LORD had sworn unto them: and they
were greatly distressed.
16 ¶ Nevertheless [n]the LORD raised
up judges, which [4]delivered them out
of the hand of those that spoiled them.
17 And yet they would not hearken
unto their judges, but they [o]went a
whoring after other gods, and bowed
themselves unto them: they turned
quickly out of the way which their fathers walked in, obeying the commandments of the LORD; *but* they did not so.
18 And when the LORD raised them
up judges, then [p]the LORD was with the
judge, and delivered them out of the
hand of their enemies all the days of the
judge: for [q]it repented the LORD because of their groanings by reason of
them that oppressed them and vexed
them.
19 And it came to pass, when the
judge was dead, *that* they returned,
and [5]corrupted *themselves* more than
their fathers, in following other gods to
serve them, and to bow down unto
them; [6]they ceased not from their own
doings, nor from their stubborn way.
20 ¶ And the anger of the LORD
was hot against Ĭs'ra-el; and he said,
Because that this people hath [r]trans-
gressed my covenant which I commanded their fathers, and have not
hearkened unto my voice;
21 I also will not henceforth drive
out any from before them of the nations which Jŏsh'u-ȧ left when he died:
22 That through them I [s]may prove
Ĭs'ra-el, whether they will keep the way
of the LORD to walk therein, as their
fathers did keep *it*, or not.

10 [e]Ex. 5.2; Tit. 1.16
12 [f]Deut. 13.5; 1 Chr. 28.9
[g]Deut. 6.14
[h]Ex. 20.5
14 [i]ch. 3.8; Isa. 1.28
[j]2 Ki. 17.20
[k]ch. 3.8; Isa. 50.1
[l]Lev. 26.37; Josh. 7.12
15 [m]Lev. 26.14-34; Deut. 28.15-68
16 [n]ch. 3.9; Acts 13.20
[4]saved
17 [o]Ex. 34.15-16; Rev. 17.1-5
18 [p]Josh. 1.5
[q]Gen. 6.6; Jer. 18.7-10
19 [5]Or, were corrupt
[6]they let nothing fall of their
20 [r]Josh. 23.16
22 [s]Deut. 8.2
23 [7]Or, suffered
CHAPTER 3
1 [a]Gen. 22.1; 1 Cor. 11.19
3 [b]Josh. 13.3
5 [c]Ps. 106.35
6 [d]Ex. 34.16; Ezra 9.12
7 [e]ch. 2.11
[f]Ex. 34.13;
8 [g]Hab. 3.7
[1]Aram-naharaim
9 [h]ch. 6.7;
[i]ch. 2.16
[2]saviour
[j]ch. 1.13
10 [k]Num. 11.17;
[3]was
[4]Aram
12 [l]ch. 2.19;
[m]1 Sam. 12.9
13 [n]ch. 5.14
[o]Deut. 34.3;
14 [p]Lev. 26.23-25;
15 [q]Ps. 50.15;
[5]Or, the son of Jemini
[6]shut of his right hand

23 Therefore the LORD [7]left those nations, without driving them out hastily;
neither delivered he them into the hand
of Jŏsh'u-ȧ.

3

Now these *are* the nations which
the LORD left, [a]to prove Ĭs'ra-el by
them, *even* as many *of Ĭs'ra-el* as had
not known all the wars of Cā'năan;
2 Only that the generations of the
children of Ĭs'ra-el might know, to
teach them war, at the least such as
before knew nothing thereof;
3 *Namely,* [b]five lords of the Phĭ-
lĭs'tĭnes, and all the Cā'năan-ītes, and
the Sī-dō'nĭ-ans, and the Hī'vītes that
dwelt in mount Lĕb'a-non, from mount
Bā'al–hĕr'mŏn unto the entering in of
Hā'math.
4 And they were to prove Ĭs'ra-el
by them, to know whether they would
hearken unto the commandments of
the LORD, which he commanded their
fathers by the hand of Mō'ses.
5 ¶ [c]And the children of Ĭs'ra-el
dwelt among the Cā'năan-ītes, Hĭt'-
tītes, and Ăm'ôr-ītes, and Pĕr'ĭz-zītes,
and Hī'vītes, and Jĕb'u-sītes:
6 And [d]they took their daughters to
be their wives, and gave their daughters to their sons, and served their gods.
7 [e]And the children of Ĭs'ra-el did
evil in the sight of the LORD, and forgat
the LORD their God, and served Bā'al-
ĭm and [f]the groves.
8 ¶ Therefore the anger of the LORD
was hot against Ĭs'ra-el, and he sold
them into the hand of [g]Chū'shan–
rĭsha-thā'im king of [1]Mĕs-o-po-tā'mĭ-ȧ:
and the children of Ĭs'ra-el served
Chū'shan–rĭsh-a-thā'im eight years.
9 And when the children of Ĭs'ra-el
[h]cried unto the LORD, the LORD [i]raised
up a [2]deliverer to the children of Ĭs'ra-
el, who delivered them, *even* [j]Ŏth'nĭ-el
the son of Kē'năz, Cā'leb's younger
brother.
10 And [k]the Spirit of the LORD [3]came
upon him, and he judged Ĭs'ra-el, and
went out to war: and the LORD delivered Chū'shan–rĭsh-a-thā'im king of
[4]Mĕs-o-po-tā'mĭ-ȧ into his hand; and
his hand prevailed against Chū'shan–
rĭsh-a-thā'im.
11 And the land had rest forty years.
And Ŏth'nĭ-el the son of Kē'năz died.
12 ¶ [l]And the children of Ĭs'ra-el did
evil again in the sight of the LORD:
and the LORD strengthened [m]Ĕg'lŏn
the king of Mō'ab against Ĭs'ra-el, because they had done evil in the sight of
the LORD.
13 And he gathered unto him the
children of Ăm'mŏn and [n]Ăm'a-lĕk,
and went and smote Ĭs'ra-el, and possessed [o]the city of palm trees.
14 So the children of Ĭs'ra-el [p]served
Ĕg'lŏn the king of Mō'ab eighteen
years.
15 But when the children of Ĭs'ra-el
[q]cried unto the LORD, the LORD raised
them up a deliverer, Ē'hŭd the son
of Gē'rȧ, [5]a Bĕn'ja-mīte, a man [6]left-
handed: and by him the children of
Ĭs'ra-el sent a present unto Ĕg'lŏn the
king of Mō'ab.

16 But Ē'hŭd made him a dagger which had two edges, of a cubit length; and he did gird it under his raiment upon his right thigh.

17 And he brought the present unto Ĕg'lŏn king of Mō'ab: and Ĕg'lŏn *was* a very fat man.

18 And when he had made an end to offer the present, he sent away the people that bare the present.

19 But he himself turned again [r]from the [7]quarries that *were* by Gĭl'găl, and said, I have a secret errand unto thee, O king: who said, Keep silence. And all that stood by him went out from him.

20 And Ē'hŭd came unto him; and he was sitting in [8]a summer parlour, which he had for himself alone. And Ē'hŭd said, I have a message from God unto thee. And he arose out of *his* seat.

21 And Ē'hŭd put forth his left hand, and took the dagger from his right thigh, and thrust it into his belly:

22 And the haft also went in after the blade; and the fat closed upon the blade, so that he could not draw the dagger out of his belly; and [9]the dirt came out.

23 Then Ē'hŭd went forth through the porch, and shut the doors of the parlour upon him, and locked them.

24 When he was gone out, his servants came; and when they saw that, behold, the doors of the parlour *were* locked, they said, Surely he [10]covereth his feet in his summer chamber.

25 And they tarried till they were ashamed: and, behold, he opened not the doors of the parlour; therefore they took a key, and opened *them:* and, behold, their lord *was* fallen down dead on the earth.

26 And Ē'hŭd escaped while they tarried, and passed beyond the quarries, and escaped unto Sē'ĭ-răth.

27 And it came to pass, when he was come, that [s]he blew a trumpet in the [t]mountain of Ē'phră-ĭm, and the children of Ĭs'ra-el went down with him from the mount, and he before them.

28 And he said unto them, Follow after me: for [u]the LORD hath delivered your enemies the Mō'ab-ītes into your hand. And they went down after him, and took [v]the fords of Jôr'dan toward Mō'ab, and suffered not a man to pass over.

29 And they slew of Mō'ab at that time about ten thousand men, all [11]lusty, and all men of valour; and there escaped not a man.

30 So Mō'ab was subdued that day under the hand of Ĭs'ra-el. And the land had rest fourscore years.

31 ¶ And after him was [12]Shăm'gär the son of Ā'năth, which slew of the Phĭ-lĭs'tĭnes six hundred men [w]with an ox goad: [x]and he also delivered [13]Ĭs'ra-el.

CHAPTER 4

4 And [a]the children of Ĭs'ra-el again did evil in the sight of the LORD, when Ē'hŭd was dead.

2 And the LORD sold them into the hand of Jā'bin king of Cā'năan, that reigned in [b]Hā'zôr; the captain of whose host *was* [c]Sĭs'e-rȧ, which dwelt in Ha-rō'sheth of the Gĕn'tīles.

3 And the children of Ĭs'ra-el cried unto the LORD: for he had nine hundred [d]chariots of iron; and twenty years [e]he mightily oppressed the children of Ĭs'ra-el.

4 ¶ [f]And Dĕb'o-rah, a prophetess, the wife of Lăp'ĭ-dŏth, she judged Ĭs'ra-el at that time.

5 [g]And she dwelt under the palm tree of Dĕb'o-rah between Rā'mah and Bĕth'–el in mount Ē'phră-ĭm: and the children of Ĭs'ra-el came up to her for judgment.

6 And she sent and called [h]Bā'rak the son of A-bĭn'ŏ-ăm out [i]of Kē'desh–năph'ta-lī, and said unto him, Hath not the LORD God of Ĭs'ra-el commanded, *saying,* Go and draw toward mount Tā'bôr, and take with thee ten thousand men of the children of Năph'ta-lī and of the children of Zĕb'u-lun?

7 And [j]I will draw unto thee to the [k]river Kī'shon Sĭs'e-rȧ, the captain of Jā'bin's army, with his chariots and his multitude; and I will deliver him into thine hand.

8 And Bā'rak said unto her, If thou wilt go with me, then I will go: but if thou wilt not go with me, *then* I will not go.

9 And she said, I will surely go with thee: notwithstanding the journey that thou takest shall not be for thine honour; for the LORD shall [l]sell Sĭs'e-rȧ into the hand of a woman. And Dĕb'o-rah arose, and went with Bā'rak to Kē'desh.

10 ¶ And Bā'rak called [m]Zĕb'u-lun and Năph'ta-lī to Kē'desh; and he went up with ten thousand men [n]at his feet: and Dĕb'o-rah went up with him.

11 Now Hē'bĕr [o]the Ken'ite, *which was* of the children of [p]Hō'băb the father in law of Mō'ses, had severed himself from [q]the Kĕn'ītes, and pitched his tent unto the plain of Zā-a-nā'im, which *is* by Kē'desh.

12 And they shewed Sĭs'e-rȧ that Bā'rak the son of A-bĭn'ŏ-ăm was gone up to mount Tā'bôr.

13 And Sĭs'e-rȧ [1]gathered together all his chariots, *even* nine hundred chariots of iron, and all the people that *were* with him, from Ha-rō'sheth of the Gĕn'tīles unto the river of Kī'shon.

14 And Dĕb'o-rah said unto Bā'rak, Up; for this *is* the day in which the LORD hath delivered Sĭs'e-rȧ into thine hand: [r]is not the LORD gone out before thee? So Bā'rak went down from mount Tā'bôr, and ten thousand men after him.

15 And [s]the LORD discomfited Sĭs'e-rȧ, and all *his* chariots, and all *his* host, with the edge of the sword before Bā'rak; so that Sĭs'e-rȧ lighted down off *his* chariot, and fled away on his feet.

16 But Bā'rak pursued after the chariots, and after the host, unto Ha-rō'sheth of the Gĕn'tīles: and all the host of Sĭs'e-rȧ fell upon the edge of the sword; *and* there was not [2]a man left.

19 [r]Josh. 4.20 [7]Or, graven images
20 [8]a parlour of cooling
22 [9]Or, it came out at the fundament
24 [10]Or, easeth nature
27 [s]ch. 5.14; ch. 6.34; 1 Sam. 13.3 [t]Josh. 17.15; ch. 7.24; ch. 17.1
28 [u]ch. 7.9-15; 1 Sam. 17.47 [v]Josh. 2.7; ch. 12.5
29 [11]fat
31 [12]This seems to concern only the country next to the Philistines [w]1 Sam. 17.47-50 [x]ch. 2.16 [13]So part is called Israel, ch. 4.1-and ch. 10.7

CHAPTER 4
1 [a]ch. 2.19
2 [b]Josh. 11.1 [c]1 Sam. 12.9; Ps. 83.9
3 [d]Josh. 17.18; ch. 1.19 [e]Deut. 28.29-33-47-48; ch. 5.8; Ps. 106.42
4 [f]2 Ki. 22.14; 1 Cor. 1.27
5 [g]Gen. 35.8
6 [h]Heb. 11.32 [i]Josh. 19.37
7 [j]Ex. 14.4; Ezek. 38.10-16; Joel 3.11-14 [k]ch. 5.21; Ps. 83.9
9 [l]ch. 2.14; Ps. 44.12; Isa. 50.1
10 [m]ch. 5.18 [n]Ex. 11.8
11 [o]ch. 1.16 [p]Ex. 3.1; Ex. 18.1 [q]Num. 24.21
13 [1]gathered by cry, or, proclamation
14 [r]Deut. 9.3; 2 Sam. 5.24; Ps. 68.7; Isa. 52.12; Mic. 2.13
15 [s]Ps. 83.9-10; Josh. 10.10
16 [2]unto one

17 Howbeit Sĭs'e-rȧ [t]fled away on
his feet to the tent of Jā'el the wife
of Hē'bẽr the Kĕn'īte: for *there was*
peace between Jā'bin the king of Hā'-
zôr and the house of Hē'bẽr the Kĕn'-
īte.
18 ¶ And Jā'el went out to meet Sĭs'-
e-rȧ, and said unto him, Turn in, my
lord, turn in to me; fear not. And when
he had turned in unto her into the tent,
she covered him with a [3]mantle.
19 And he said unto her, Give me, I
pray thee, a little water to drink; for I
am thirsty. And she opened [u]a bottle
of milk, and gave him drink, and covered him.
20 Again he said unto her, Stand in
the door of the tent, and it shall be,
when any man doth come and inquire
of thee, and say, Is there any man
here? that thou shalt say, No.
21 Then Jā'el Hē'bẽr's wife [v]took a
nail of the tent, and [4]took an hammer
in her hand, and went softly unto him,
and smote the nail into his temples,
and fastened it into the ground: for he
was fast asleep and weary. So he died.
22 And, behold, as Bā'rak pursued
Sĭs'e-rȧ, Jā'el came out to meet him,
and said unto him, Come, and I will
shew thee the man whom thou seekest.
And when he came into her *tent*, behold, Sĭs'e-rȧ lay dead, and the nail
was in his temples.
23 So [w]God subdued on that day
Jā'bin the king of Cā'năan before the
children of Ĭs'ra-el.
24 And the hand of the children
of Ĭs'ra-el [5]prospered, and prevailed
against Jā'bin the king of Cā'năan, until they had destroyed Jā'bin king of
Cā'năan.

5 Then sang Dĕb'o-rah and Bā'rak
the son of A-bĭn'ō-ăm on that day,
saying,
2 Praise ye the LORD for the avenging of Ĭs'ra-el, when the people willingly offered themselves.
3 Hear, O ye kings; give ear, O ye
princes; I, *even* I, will sing unto the
LORD; I will sing *praise* to the LORD
God of Ĭs'ra-el.
4 LORD, [a]when thou wentest out of
Sē'ĭr, when thou marchedst out of the
field of Ē'dom, [b]the earth trembled,
and the heavens dropped, the clouds
also dropped water.
5 [c]The mountains [1]melted from before the LORD, *even* that Sī'nāi from
before the LORD God of Ĭs'ra-el.
6 In the days of [d]Shăm'găr the son
of Ā'năth, in the days of Jā'el, [e]the
highways were unoccupied, and the
[2]travellers walked through [3]byways.
7 *The inhabitants of* the villages
ceased, they ceased in Ĭs'ra-el, until
that I Dĕb'o-rah arose, that I arose [f]a
mother in Ĭs'ra-el.
8 They [g]chose new gods; then *was*
war in the gates: [h]was there a shield or
spear seen among forty thousand in
Ĭs'ra-el?
9 My heart *is* toward the governors
of Ĭs'ra-el, that offered themselves willingly among the people. Bless ye the
LORD.
10 [4]Speak, ye [i]that ride on white
asses, ye that sit in judgment, and walk
by the way.
11 *They that are delivered* from the
noise of archers in the places of drawing water, there shall they rehearse the
[5]righteous acts of the LORD, *even* the
righteous acts *toward the inhabitants*
of his villages in Ĭs'ra-el: then shall the
people of the LORD go down to the
gates.
12 Awake, awake, Dĕb'o-rah: awake,
awake, utter a song: arise, Bā'rak, and
lead thy captivity captive, thou son of
A-bĭn'ō-ăm.
13 Then he made him that remaineth have dominion over the nobles
among the people: the LORD made me
have dominion over the mighty.
14 [j]Out of Ē'phră-ĭm *was there* a
root of them against Ăm'a-lĕk; after
thee, Bĕn'ja-min, among thy people;
out of [k]Mā'chĭr came down governors,
and out of Zĕb'u-lun they that [6]handle
the pen of the writer.
15 And the princes of Ĭs'sa-char *were*
with Dĕb'o-rah; even Ĭs'sa-char, and
also Bā'rak: he was sent on [7]foot into
the valley. [8]For the divisions of Reu'ben
there were great [9]thoughts of heart.
16 Why abodest thou [l]among the
sheepfolds, to hear the bleatings of the
flocks? [10]For the divisions of Reu'ben
there were great searchings of heart.
17 [m]Gĭl'e-ăd abode beyond Jôr'dan:
and why did Dăn remain in ships?
[n]Ăsh'ẽr continued on the sea [11]shore,
and abode in his [12]breaches.
18 [o]Zĕb'u-lun and Năph'ta-lī *were*
a people *that* [13]jeoparded their lives
unto the death in the high places of the
field.
19 The kings came *and* fought, then
fought the kings of Cā'năan in Tā'a-
năch by the waters of Me-gĭd'do; [p]they
took no gain of money.
20 [q]They fought from heaven; the
[r]stars in their [14]courses fought against
Sĭs'e-rȧ.
21 [s]The river of Kī'shon swept them
away, that ancient river, the river Kī'-
shon. O my soul, thou hast trodden
down strength.
22 Then were the horsehoofs broken by the means of the [15]pransings,
the pransings of their mighty ones.
23 Curse ye Mē'rŏz, said the angel
of the LORD, curse ye bitterly the inhabitants thereof; [t]because they came not
to the help [u]of the LORD, to the help of
the LORD against the mighty.
24 Blessed above women shall Jā'el
the wife of Hē'bẽr the Kĕn'īte be,
[v]blessed shall she be above women in
the tent.
25 He asked water, *and* she gave
him milk; she brought forth butter in a
lordly dish.
26 She put her hand to the nail, and
her right hand to the workmen's hammer; and [16]with the hammer she smote
Sĭs'e-rȧ, she smote off his head, when

17 [t]Job 12.21-24; Amos 5.19
18 [3]Or, rug, or, blanket
19 [u]ch. 5.25
21 [v]ch. 5.26 [4]put
23 [w]1 Chr. 22.18; Ps. 18.47
24 [5]going went and was hard

CHAPTER 5
4 [a]Deut. 33.2; Ps. 68.7-8 [b]Isa. 64.3; Hab. 3.3
5 [c]Deut. 4.11 [1]flowed
6 [d]ch. 3.31 [e]Lev. 26.22; Lam. 1.4 [2]walkers of paths [3]crooked ways
7 [f]ch. 4.4-6; Isa. 49.23
8 [g]Deut. 32.16; ch. 2.12 [h]1 Sam. 13.19-22;
10 [4]Or, Meditate [i]ch. 12.14
11 [5]righteousnesses of the LORD
14 [j]ch. 3.27 [k]Num. 32.39 [6]draw with the pen, etc
15 [7]his feet [8]Or, In the divisions, etc [9]impressions
16 [l]Num. 32.1 [10]Or, In
17 [m]Josh. 13.25 [n]Josh. 19.29 [11]Or, port [12]Or, creeks
18 [o]ch. 4.10 [13]exposed to reproach
19 [p]ch. 4.16;
20 [q]Josh. 10.11 [r]ch. 4.15 [14]paths
21 [s]ch. 4.7
22 [15]Or, tramplings, or, plungings
23 [t]ch. 21.9 [u]1 Sam. 17.47
24 [v]Prov. 31.31;
26 [16]she hammered

she had pierced and stricken through
his temples.
27 [17]At her feet he bowed, he fell, he
lay down: at her feet he bowed, he fell:
where he bowed, there he fell down
[18]dead.
28 The mother of Sĭs'e-rȧ looked out
at a window, and cried through the lattice, Why is his chariot *so* long in coming? why tarry the wheels of his chariots?
29 Her wise ladies answered her,
yea, she returned [19]answer to herself,
30 [w]Have they not sped? have they
not divided the prey; [20]to every man a
damsel *or* two; to Sĭs'e-rȧ a prey of divers colours, a prey of divers colours of
needlework, of divers colours of needlework on both sides, *meet* for the
necks of *them that take* the spoil?
31 [x]So let all thine enemies perish,
O LORD: but *let* them that love him *be*
[y]as the sun [z]when he goeth forth in
his might. And the land had rest forty
years.

6 And [a]the children of Ĭs'ra-el did
evil in the sight of the LORD: and
the LORD delivered them into the hand
[b]of Mĭd'ĭ-an seven years.
2 And the hand of Mĭd'ĭ-an [1]pre-
vailed against Ĭs'ra-el: *and* because of
the Mĭd'ĭ-an-ītes the children of Ĭs'ra-
el made them [c]the dens which *are* in
the mountains, and caves, and strong
holds.
3 And *so* it was, when Ĭs'ra-el had
sown, that the Mĭd'ĭ-an-ītes came up,
and the Ăm'a-lĕk-ītes, [d]and the children of the east, even they came up
against them;
4 And they encamped against them,
and [e]destroyed the increase of the
earth, till thou come unto Gā'zȧ, and
left no sustenance for Ĭs'ra-el, neither
[2]sheep, nor ox, nor ass.
5 For they came up with their cattle
and their tents, and they came as grasshoppers for multitude; *for* both they
and their camels were without number: and they entered into the land to
destroy it.
6 And Ĭs'ra-el was greatly impoverished because of the Mĭd'ĭ-an-ītes; and
the children of Ĭs'ra-el [f]cried unto the
LORD.
7 ¶ And it came to pass, when the
children of Ĭs'ra-el cried unto the LORD
because of the Mĭd'ĭ-an-ītes,
8 That the LORD sent [3]a prophet unto
the children of Ĭs'ra-el, which said unto
them, Thus saith the LORD God of Ĭs'ra-
el, I brought you up from Ē'ġypt, and
brought you forth out of the house of
bondage;
9 And I delivered you out of the hand
of the E-ġӯp''tians, and out of the hand
of all that oppressed you, and drave
them out from before you, and gave
you their land;
10 And I said unto you, I *am* the
LORD your God; [g]fear not the gods of
the Ăm'ôr-ītes, in whose land ye dwell:
but ye have not obeyed my voice.
11 ¶ And there came an angel of the
LORD, and sat under an oak which *was*
in Ŏph'rah, that *pertained* unto Jō'ăsh
[h]the Ā'bĭ–ĕz'rīte: and his son Gĭd'e-on
threshed wheat by the winepress, [4]to
hide *it* from the Mĭd'ĭ-an-ītes.
12 And the [i]angel of the LORD appeared unto him, and said unto him,
The LORD *is* with thee, thou mighty
man of valour.
13 And Gĭd'e-on said unto him, Oh
my Lord, if the LORD be with us, why
then is all this befallen us? and [j]where
be all his miracles which our fathers
told us of, saying, Did not the LORD
bring us up from Ē'ġypt? but now the
LORD hath [k]forsaken us, and delivered
us into the hands of the Mĭd'ĭ-an-ītes.
14 And the LORD looked upon him,
and said, [l]Go in this thy might, and
thou shalt save Ĭs'ra-el from the hand
of the Mĭd'ĭ-an-ītes: [m]have not I sent
thee?
15 And he said unto him, Oh my
Lord, wherewith shall I save Ĭs'ra-el?
behold, [5]my family *is* poor in Ma-năs'-
seh, and I *am* the least in my father's
house.
16 And the LORD said unto him,
[n]Surely I will be with thee, and thou
shalt smite the Mĭd'ĭ-an-ītes as one
man.
17 And he said unto him, If now I
have found grace in thy sight, then
[o]shew me a sign that thou talkest with
me.
18 [p]Depart not hence, I pray thee,
until I come unto thee, and bring forth
my [6]present, and set *it* before thee.
And he said, I will tarry until thou
come again.
19 ¶ And Gĭd'e-on went in, and made
ready [7]a kid, and unleavened cakes of
an ephah of flour: the flesh he put in a
basket, and he put the broth in a pot,
and brought *it* out unto him under the
oak, and presented *it*.
20 And the angel of God said unto
him, Take the flesh and the unleavened cakes, and [q]lay *them* upon this
rock, and [r]pour out the broth. And he
did so.
21 ¶ Then the angel of the LORD put
forth the end of the staff that *was* in his
hand, and touched the flesh and the
unleavened cakes; and [s]there rose up
fire out of the rock, and consumed the
flesh and the unleavened cakes. Then
the angel of the LORD departed out of
his sight.
22 And when Gĭd'e-on perceived
that he *was* an angel of the LORD,
Gĭd'e-on said, Alas, O Lord GOD! [t]for
because I have seen an angel of the
LORD face to face.
23 And the LORD said unto him,
[u]Peace *be* unto thee; fear not: thou
shalt not die.
24 Then Gĭd'e-on built an altar there
unto the LORD, and called it [8]Je-hō'-
vah–shā'lom: unto this day it *is* yet [v]in
Ŏph'rah of the Ā'bĭ-ĕz'rītes.
25 ¶ And it came to pass the same
night, that the LORD said unto him,
Take thy father's young bullock, [9]even
the second bullock of seven years old,
and throw down the altar of Bā'al that

27 [17]Between [18]destroyed
29 [19]her words
30 [w]Ex. 15.9 [20]to the head of a man
31 [x]Ps. 48.4-5; Ps. 58.11; Ps. 68.1-3; Ps. 83.9; Rev. 6.10; Rev. 18.20 [y]2 Sam. 23.4; Ps. 37.6; Matt. 13.43 [z]Ps. 19.5

CHAPTER 6
1 [a]Lev. 26.14; ch. 2.19 [b]Gen. 25.2; Hab. 3.7
2 [1]was strong [c]1 Sam. 13.6; Heb. 11.38
3 [d]Gen. 29.1; ch. 7.12; 1 Ki. 4.30; Job 1.3
4 [e]Lev. 26.16; Mic. 6.15 [2]Or, goat
6 [f]Ps. 50.15; Hos. 5.15
8 [3]a man a prophet
10 [g]2 Ki. 17.35
11 [h]Josh. 17.2; ch. 8.2 [4]to cause it to flee
12 [i]Gen. 16.7-13; Luke 1.11-28
13 [j]Ps. 89.49; Isa. 59.1 [k]2 Chr. 15.2
14 [l]1 Sam. 12.11; Heb. 11.32 [m]Josh. 1.9
15 [5]my thousand is the meanest
16 [n]Ex. 3.12
17 [o]Ex. 4.1-8
18 [p]Gen. 18.3 [6]Or, meat offering
19 [7]a kid of the goats
20 [q]ch. 13.19 [r]1 Ki. 18.33
21 [s]Lev. 9.24; 2 Chr. 7.1
22 [t]Gen. 16.13; ch. 13.22
23 [u]Dan. 10.19; Luke 24.36
24 [8]That is, The LORD send peace [v]ch. 8.32
25 [9]Or, and

thy father hath, and [w]cut down the
grove that *is* by it:
26 And build an altar unto the LORD
thy God upon the top of this [10]rock, [11]in
the ordered place, and take the second
bullock, and offer a burnt sacrifice with
the wood of the grove which thou shalt
cut down.
27 Then Ḡĭd′e-on took ten men of
his servants, and did as the LORD had
said unto him: and *so* it was, because
he feared his father's household, and
the men of the city, that he could not
do *it* by day, that he did *it* [x]by night.
28 ¶ And when the men of the city
arose early in the morning, behold, the
altar of Bā′al was cast down, and the
grove was cut down that *was* by it, and
the second bullock was offered upon
the altar *that was* built.
29 And they said one to another,
Who hath done this thing? And when
they inquired and asked, they said,
Ḡĭd′e-on the son of Jō′ăsh hath done
this thing.
30 Then the men of the city said
unto Jō′ăsh, [y]Bring out thy son, that
he may die: because he hath cast down
the altar of Bā′al, and because he hath
cut down the grove that *was* by it.
31 And Jō′ăsh said unto all that
stood against him, Will ye plead for
Bā′al? will ye save him? he that will
plead for him, let him be put to death
whilst *it is yet* morning: if he *be* a god,
let him plead for himself, because *one*
hath cast down his altar.
32 Therefore on that day he called
him [12][z]Je-rŭb′ba-ăl, saying, Let Bā′al
plead against him, because he hath
thrown down his altar.
33 ¶ Then all the Mĭd′ĭ-an-ītes and
the Ăm′a-lĕk-ītes and the children of
the east were gathered together, and
went over, and pitched in [a]the valley
of Jĕz′re-el.
34 But [b]the Spirit of the LORD [13]came
upon Ḡĭd′e-on, and he [c]blew a trumpet; and Ā′bĭ–ē′zēr [14]was gathered after him.
35 And he sent messengers throughout all Ma-năs′seh; who also was gathered after him: and he sent messengers
unto Āsh′ēr, and unto Zĕb′u-lun, and
unto Năph′ta-lī; and they came up to
meet them.
36 ¶ And Ḡĭd′e-on said unto God, If
thou wilt save Ĭs′ra-el by mine hand, as
thou hast said,
37 [d]Behold, I will put a fleece of
wool in the floor; *and* if the dew be on
the fleece only, and *it be* dry upon all
the earth *beside*, then shall I know that
thou wilt save Ĭs′ra-el by mine hand, as
thou hast said.
38 And it was so: for he rose up
early on the morrow, and thrust the
fleece together, and wringed the dew
out of the fleece, a bowl full of water.
39 And Ḡĭd′e-on said unto God, [e]Let
not thine anger be hot against me, and I
will speak but this once: let me prove, I
pray thee, but this once with the fleece;
let it now be dry only upon the fleece,
and upon all the ground let there be
dew.
40 And God did so that night: for
it was dry upon the fleece only, and
there was dew on all the ground.

7 Then [a]Je-rŭb′ba-ăl, who *is* Ḡĭd′e-
on, and all the people that *were* with
him, [b]rose up early, and pitched beside
the well of [1]Hā′rod: so that the host of
the Mĭd′ĭ-an-ītes were on the north side
of them, by the hill of [c]Mō′reh, in the
valley.
2 And the LORD said unto Ḡĭd′e-on,
The people that *are* with thee *are* too
many for me to give the Mĭd′ĭ-an-ītes
into their hands, lest Ĭs′ra-el [d]vaunt
themselves against me, saying, Mine
own hand hath saved me.
3 Now therefore go to, proclaim in
the ears of the people, saying, [e]Whoso-
ever *is* fearful and afraid, let him return and depart early from mount Ḡĭl′-
e-ăd. And there returned of the people
twenty and two thousand; and there
remained ten thousand.
4 And the LORD said unto Ḡĭd′e-on,
The people *are* yet *too* many; bring
them down unto the water, and I will
[2]try them for thee there: and it shall be,
that of whom I say unto thee, This
shall go with thee, the same shall go
with thee; and of whomsoever I say
unto thee, This shall not go with thee,
the same shall not go.
5 So he brought down the people
unto the water: and the LORD said unto
Ḡĭd′e-on, Every one that lappeth of the
water with his tongue, as a dog lappeth, him shalt thou set by himself;
likewise every one that boweth down
upon his knees to drink.
6 And the number of them that
lapped, *putting* their hand to their
mouth, were three hundred men: but
all the rest of the people bowed down
upon their knees to drink water.
7 And the LORD said unto Ḡĭd′e-on,
[f]By the three hundred men that lapped
will I save you, and deliver the Mĭd′ĭ-
an-ītes into thine hand: and let all the
other people go every man unto his
place.
8 So the people took victuals in their
hand, and their trumpets: and he sent
all *the rest of* Ĭs′ra-el every man unto
his tent, and retained those three hundred men: and the host of Mĭd′ĭ-an was
beneath him in the valley.
9 ¶ And it came to pass the same
[g]night, that the LORD said unto him,
Arise, get thee down unto the host; for
I have delivered it into thine hand.
10 But if thou fear to go down, go
thou with Phū′rah thy servant down to
the host:
11 And thou shalt [h]hear what they
say; and afterward shall thine hands be
strengthened to go down unto the host.
Then went he down with Phū′rah his
servant unto the outside of the [3]armed
men that *were* in the host.
12 And the Mĭd′ĭ-an-ītes and the
Ăm′a-lĕk-ītes and [i]all the children of
the east lay along in the valley like
grasshoppers for multitude; and their

[w]Ex. 34.13; Deut. 7.5; ch. 3.7
26 [10]strong place
[11]Or, in an orderly manner
27 [x]John 3.2
30 [y]John 16.2; Acts 26.9
32 [12]That is, Let Baal plead
[z]1 Sam. 12.11; Or, Jerubbesheth; that is, Let shame, or, confusion, plead, 2 Sam. 11.21; Jer. 11.13; Hos. 9.10
33 [a]Josh. 17.16; 1 Ki. 18.45
34 [b]ch. 3.10; ch. 11.29; ch. 13.25; 1 Chr. 12.18; 2 Chr. 24.20; 1 Cor. 12.8-11
[13]clothed
[c]ch. 3.27
[14]was called after him
37 [d]Ex. 4.3-4-6-7; Deut. 32.2; Ps. 72.6; Hos. 6.3-4
39 [e]Gen. 18.32
CHAPTER 7
1 [a]ch. 6.32; 1 Sam. 12.11
[b]Gen. 22.3; Josh. 3.1; Eccl. 9.10
[1]That is, Trembling
[c]Gen. 12.6
2 [d]Deut. 8.17; Deut. 9.4; Eph. 2.9
3 [e]Deut. 20.8
4 [2]separate, or, purify
7 [f]1 Sam. 14.6; Isa. 41.14-18
9 [g]Gen. 46.2-3; Acts 27.23
11 [h]Gen. 24.14; 1 Sam. 14.9-10
[3]Or, ranks by five
12 [i]ch. 6.5-33; ch. 8.10

camels *were* without number, as the
sand by the sea side for multitude.
13 And when Ḡĭd'e-on was come,
behold, *there was* a man that told a
dream unto his fellow, and said, Behold, I dreamed a dream, and, lo, [j]a
cake of barley bread tumbled into the
host of Mĭd'ĭ-an, and came unto a tent,
and smote it that it fell, and overturned
it, that the tent lay along.
14 And [k]his fellow answered and
said, This *is* nothing else save the sword
of Ḡĭd'e-on the son of Jō'ăsh, a man of
Ĭs'ra-el: *for* into his hand hath God delivered Mĭd'ĭ-an, and all the host.
15 ¶ And it was *so*, when Ḡĭd'e-on
heard the telling of the dream, and
[4]the interpretation thereof, that he worshipped, and returned into the host of
Ĭs'ra-el, and said, Arise; for the LORD
hath delivered into your hand the host
of Mĭd'ĭ-an.
16 And he divided the three hundred
men *into* three companies, and he put
[5]a trumpet in every man's hand, with
empty pitchers, and [6]lamps within the
pitchers.
17 And he said unto them, Look on
me, and do likewise: and, behold, when
I come to the outside of the camp, it
shall be *that*, as I do, so shall ye do.
18 When I blow with a trumpet, I
and all that *are* with me, then blow ye
the trumpets also on every side of all
the camp, and say, *The sword* of the
LORD, and of Ḡĭd'e-on.
19 ¶ So Ḡĭd'e-on, and the hundred
men that *were* with him, came unto the
outside of the camp in the beginning of
the [l]middle watch; and they had but
newly set the watch: and they blew the
trumpets, and brake the pitchers that
were in their hands.
20 And the three companies blew
the trumpets, and brake the pitchers,
and held the lamps in their left hands,
and the trumpets in their right hands
to blow *withal:* and they cried, The
sword of the LORD, and of Ḡĭd'e-on.
21 And they [m]stood every man in
his place round about the camp: [n]and
all the host ran, and cried, and fled.
22 And the three hundred [o]blew the
trumpets, and [p]the LORD set [q]every
man's sword against his fellow, even
throughout all the host: and the host
fled to Bĕth–shĭt'tah [7]in Zĕr'e-răth,
and to the [8]border of Ā'bel–me-hō'lah,
unto Tăb'bath.
23 And the men of Ĭs'ra-el gathered
themselves together out of Năph'ta-lī,
and out of Ăsh'ēr, and out of all Ma-
năs'seh, and pursued after the Mĭd'ĭ-
an-ītes.
24 ¶ And Ḡĭd'e-on sent messengers
throughout all [r]mount Ē'phră-ĭm, saying, Come down against the Mĭd'ĭ-an-
ītes, and take before them the waters unto Bĕth–bā'rah and Jôr'dan.
Then all the men of Ē'phră-ĭm gathered themselves together, and [s]took
the waters unto [t]Bĕth–bā'rah and Jôr'-
dan.
25 And they took [u]two princes of
the Mĭd'ĭ-an-ītes, Ō'reb and Zē'eb; and
they slew Ō'reb upon [v]the rock Ō'reb,
and Zē'eb they slew at the winepress
of Zē'eb, and pursued Mĭd'ĭ-an, and
brought the heads of Ō'reb and Zē'eb
to Ḡĭd'e-on on the [w]other side Jôr'dan.

8 And [a]the men of Ē'phră-ĭm said
unto him, [1]Why hast thou served us
thus, that thou calledst us not, when
thou wentest to fight with the Mĭd'ĭ-
an-ītes? And they did chide with him
[2]sharply.
2 And he said unto them, What have
I done now in comparison of you? *Is* not
the gleaning of the grapes of Ē'phră-ĭm
better than the vintage of Ā'bĭ–ē'zēr?
3 [b]God hath delivered into your
hands the princes of Mĭd'ĭ-an, Ō'reb
and Zē'eb: and what was I able to do in
comparison of you? Then their [3]anger
was abated toward him, when he had
said that.
4 ¶ And Ḡĭd'e-on came to Jôr'dan,
and passed over, he, and the three hundred men that *were* with him, faint, yet
pursuing *them*.
5 And he said unto the men [c]of Sŭc'-
coth, Give, I pray you, loaves of bread
unto the people that follow me; for
they *be* faint, and I am pursuing after
Zē'bah and Zal-mŭn'nȧ, kings of Mĭd'-
ĭ-an.
6 ¶ And the princes of Sŭc'coth said,
[d]*Are* the hands of Zē'bah and Zal-
mŭn'nȧ now in thine hand, that [e]we
should give bread unto thine army?
7 And Ḡĭd'e-on said, Therefore when
the LORD hath delivered Zē'bah and
Zal-mŭn'nȧ into mine hand, then I will
[4]tear your flesh with the thorns of the
wilderness and with briers.
8 ¶ And he went up thence [f]to Pe-
nū'el, and spake unto them likewise:
and the men of Pe-nū'el answered him
as the men of Sŭc'coth had answered
him.
9 And he spake also unto the men of
Pe-nū'el, saying, When I [g]come again
in peace, I will break down this tower.
10 ¶ Now Zē'bah and Zal-mŭn'nȧ
were in Kar'kôr, and their hosts with
them, about fifteen thousand *men*, all
that were left of all [h]the hosts of the
children of the east: for there fell [5]an
hundred and twenty thousand men
that drew sword.
11 ¶ And Ḡĭd'e-on went up by the
way of them that dwelt in tents on the
east [i]of Nō'bah and Jŏg'be-hah, and
smote the host: for the host was [j]se-
cure.
12 And when Zē'bah and Zal-mŭn'-
nȧ fled, he pursued after them, and
[k]took the two kings of Mĭd'ĭ-an, Zē'-
bah and Zal-mŭn'nȧ, and [6]discomfited
all the host.
13 ¶ And Ḡĭd'e-on the son of Jō'ăsh
returned from battle before the sun
was up,
14 And caught a young man of the
men of Sŭc'coth, and inquired of him:
and he [7]described unto him the princes
of Sŭc'coth, and the elders thereof,
even threescore and seventeen men.
15 And he came unto the men of
Sŭc'coth, and said, Behold Zē'bah and

13 [j]ch. 6.16; Isa. 41.14-15; 1 Cor. 1.27
14 [k]Gen. 40.8
15 [4]the breaking thereof
16 [5]trumpets in the hand of all of them [6]Or, firebrands, or, torches
19 [l]Ex. 14.24; Luke 12.38; Rev. 16.15
21 [m]Ex. 14.13-14; 2 Chr. 20.17; Isa. 30.7-15 [n]Ex. 14.25; 2 Ki. 7.7; Job 15.21-22; Prov. 28.1
22 [o]2 Cor. 4.7 [p]1 Sam. 14.16-20; Ps. 83.9; Isa. 9.4 [q]1 Sam. 14.20; 2 Chr. 20.23 [7]Or, toward [8]lip
24 [r]ch. 3.27; Rom. 15.30; Phil. 1.27 [s]ch. 3.28 [t]John 1.28
25 [u]ch. 8.3; Ps. 83.11 [v]Isa. 10.26 [w]ch. 8.4

CHAPTER 8
1 [a]ch. 12.1; 2 Sam. 19.41 [1]What thing is this thou hast done unto us? [2]strongly
3 [b]ch. 7.24; Rom. 12.3-6 [3]spirit
5 [c]Gen. 33.17; Ps. 60.6
6 [d]1 Ki. 20.11 [e]1 Sam. 25.11
7 [4]thresh
8 [f]Gen. 32.30
9 [g]1 Ki. 22.27; 1 Thess. 5.2-3
10 [h]ch. 7.12 [5]Or, an hundred and twenty thousand, every one drawing a sword
11 [i]Num. 32.35 [j]ch. 18.27; 1 Thess. 5.3
12 [k]Ps. 83.11 [6]terrified
14 [7]writ

Zal-mŭn'nȧ, with whom ye did upbraid me, saying, *Are* the hands of Zē'bah and Zal-mŭn'nȧ now in thine hand, that we should give bread unto thy men *that are* weary?

16 And he took the elders of the city, and thorns of the wilderness and briers, and with them he [8]taught the men of Sŭc'coth.

17 And he beat down the tower of [l]Pe-nū'el, and slew the men of the city.

18 ¶ Then said he unto Zē'bah and Zal-mŭn'nȧ, What manner of men *were they* whom ye slew [m]at Tā'bôr? And they answered, As thou *art*, so *were* they; each one [9]resembled the children of a king.

19 And he said, They *were* my brethren, *even* the sons of my mother: *as* the LORD liveth, if ye had saved them alive, I would not slay you.

20 And he said unto Jē'thẽr his firstborn, Up, *and* slay them. But the youth drew not his sword: for he feared, because he *was* yet a youth.

21 Then Zē'bah and Zal-mŭn'nȧ said, Rise thou, and fall upon us: for as the man *is, so is* his strength. And Ḡĭd'e-on arose, and [n]slew Zē'bah and Zal-mŭn'nȧ, and took away the [10]ornaments that *were* on their camels' necks.

22 ¶ Then the men of Ĭs'ra-el said unto Ḡĭd'e-on, Rule thou over us, both thou, and thy son, and thy son's son also: for thou hast delivered us from the hand of Mĭd'ĭ-an.

23 And Ḡĭd'e-on said unto them, I will not rule over you, neither shall my son rule over you: [o]the LORD shall rule over you.

24 ¶ And Ḡĭd'e-on said unto them, I would desire a request of you, that ye would give me every man the earrings of his prey. (For they had golden earrings, [p]because they *were* Ĭsh'ma-el-ītes.)

25 And they answered, We will willingly give *them*. And they spread a garment, and did cast therein every man the earrings of his prey.

26 And the weight of the golden earrings that he requested was a thousand and seven hundred *shekels* of gold; beside ornaments, and [11]collars, and purple raiment that *was* on the kings of Mĭd'ĭ-an, and beside the chains that *were* about their camels' necks.

27 And Ḡĭd'e-on [q]made an ephod thereof, and put it in his city, *even* [r]in Ŏph'rah: and all Ĭs'ra-el [s]went thither a whoring after it: which thing became [t]a snare unto Ḡĭd'e-on, and to his house.

28 ¶ Thus was Mĭd'ĭ-an subdued before the children of Ĭs'ra-el, so that they lifted up their heads no more. And the country was in quietness forty years in the days of Ḡĭd'e-on.

29 ¶ And Je-rŭb'ba-ăl the son of Jō'ăsh went and dwelt in his own house.

30 And Ḡĭd'e-on had [u]threescore and ten sons [12]of his body begotten: for he had many wives.

31 And his concubine that *was* in Shē'chem, she also bare him a son, whose name he [13]called [14]A-bĭm'ĕ-lech.

32 ¶ And Ḡĭd'e-on the son of Jō'ăsh died in a good old age, and was buried in the sepulchre of Jō'ăsh his father, [v]in Ŏph'rah of the Ā'bĭ–ĕz'rītes.

33 And it came to pass, [w]as soon as Ḡĭd'e-on was dead, that the children of Ĭs'ra-el turned again, and went a whoring after Bā'al-ĭm, and [x]made [15]Bā'al–bē'rith their god.

34 And the children of Ĭs'ra-el [y]remembered not the LORD their God, who had delivered them out of the hands of all their enemies on every side:

35 [z]Neither shewed they kindness to the house of Je-rŭb'ba-ăl, *namely*, Ḡĭd'e-on, according to all the goodness which he had shewed unto Ĭs'ra-el.

9 And A-bĭm'ĕ-lech the son of Je-rŭb'ba-ăl went to Shē'chem unto [a]his mother's brethren, and communed with them, and with all the family of the house of his mother's father, saying,

2 Speak, I pray you, in the ears of all the men of Shē'chem, [1]Whether *is* better for you, either that all the sons of Je-rŭb'ba-ăl, *which are* [b]threescore and ten persons, reign over you, or that one reign over you? remember also that I *am* [c]your bone and your flesh.

3 And his mother's brethren spake of him in the ears of all the men of Shē'chem all these words: and their hearts inclined [2]to follow A-bĭm'ĕ-lech; for they said, He *is* our [d]brother.

4 And they gave him threescore and ten *pieces* of silver out of the house of [e]Bā'al–bē'rith, wherewith A-bĭm'ĕ-lech hired [f]vain and light persons, which followed him.

5 And he went unto his father's house [g]at Ŏph'rah, and [h]slew his brethren the sons of Je-rŭb'ba-ăl, *being* threescore and ten persons, upon one stone: notwithstanding yet Jō'tham the youngest son of Je-rŭb'ba-ăl was left; for he hid himself.

6 And all the men of Shē'chem gathered together, and all the house of Mĭl'lo, and went, and made A-bĭm'ĕ-lech king, [3]by the plain of the pillar that *was* in Shē'chem.

7 ¶ And when they told *it* to Jō'tham, he went and stood in the top of [i]mount Ḡĕr'ĭ-zĭm, and lifted up his voice, and cried, and said unto them, Hearken unto me, ye men of Shē'chem, that God may hearken unto you.

8 [j]The trees went forth *on a time* to anoint a king over them; and they said unto the olive tree, [k]Reign thou over us.

9 But the olive tree said unto them, Should I leave my fatness, [l]wherewith by me they honour God and man, and [4]go to be promoted over the trees?

10 And the trees said to the fig tree, Come thou, *and* reign over us.

11 But the fig tree said unto them, Should I forsake my sweetness, and my good fruit, and go to be promoted over the trees?

16 [8]made to know
17 [l]1 Ki. 12.25
18 [m]ch. 4.6; Ps. 89.12
[9]according to the form, etc
21 [n]Ps. 83.11
[10]Or, ornaments like the moon
23 [o]1 Sam. 8.7; Hos. 13.10
24 [p]Gen. 16.10; Gen. 37.25
26 [11]Or, sweet jewels
27 [q]ch. 17.5; ch. 18.14-17
[r]ch. 6.24
[s]Ex. 23.33; Ps. 106.39
[t]Deut. 7.16
30 [u]ch. 9.2-5; ch. 10.4
[12]going out of his thigh
31 [13]set
[14]That is, My father the king
32 [v]ch. 6.24
33 [w]ch. 2.19
[x]ch. 9.4
[15]That is, Idol of the covenant
34 [y]Ps. 78.11-42; Eccl. 12.1
35 [z]ch. 9.16; Eccl. 9.14-15
CHAPTER 9
1 [a]ch. 8.31
2 [1]What is good? whether, etc
[b]ch. 8.30
[c]Gen. 29.14; Heb. 2.14
3 [2]after
[d]Gen. 29.15
4 [e]ch. 8.33
[f]ch. 11.3; Acts 17.5
5 [g]ch. 6.24
[h]2 Ki. 10.17
6 [3]Or, by the oak of the pillar
7 [i]Deut. 11.29;
8 [j]2 Ki. 14.9
[k]ch. 8.22
9 [l]Ps. 104.15
[4]go up and down for other trees

12 Then said the trees unto the vine, Come thou, *and* reign over us.

13 And the vine said unto them, Should I leave my wine, which cheereth God and man, and go to be promoted over the trees?

14 Then said all the trees unto the [5]bramble, Come thou, *and* reign over us.

15 And the bramble said unto the trees, If in truth ye anoint me king over you, *then* come *and* put your trust in my [m]shadow: and if not, [n]let fire come out of the bramble, and devour the [o]cedars of Lĕb′a-non.

16 Now therefore, if ye have done truly and sincerely, in that ye have made A-bĭm′ĕ-lech king, and if ye have dealt well with Je-rŭb′ba-ăl and his house, and have done unto him [p]according to the deserving of his hands;

17 (For my father fought for you, and [6]adventured his life far, and delivered you out of the hand of Mĭd′ĭ-an:

18 And ye are risen up against my father's house this day, and have slain his sons, threescore and ten persons, upon one stone, and have made A-bĭm′ĕ-lech, the son of his maidservant, king over the men of Shē′chem, because he *is* your brother;)

19 If ye then have dealt truly and sincerely with Je-rŭb′ba-ăl and with his house this day, *then* [q]rejoice ye in A-bĭm′ĕ-lech, and let him also rejoice in you:

20 But if not, let fire come out from A-bĭm′ĕ-lech, and devour the men of Shē′chem, and the house of Mĭl′lo; and let fire come out from the men of Shē′chem, and from the house of Mĭl′lo, and devour A-bĭm′ĕ-lech.

21 And Jō′tham ran away, and fled, and went to [r]Bē′er, and dwelt there, for fear of A-bĭm′ĕ-lech his brother.

22 ¶ When A-bĭm′ĕ-lech had reigned three years over Ĭs′ra-el,

23 Then [s]God sent an evil spirit between A-bĭm′ĕ-lech and the men of Shē′chem; and the men of Shē′chem [t]dealt treacherously with A-bĭm′ĕ-lech:

24 [u]That the cruelty *done* to the threescore and ten sons of Je-rŭb′ba-ăl might come, and their blood be laid upon A-bĭm′ĕ-lech their brother, which slew them; and upon the men of Shē′chem, which [7]aided him in the killing of his brethren.

25 And the men of Shē′chem set liers in wait for him in the top of the mountains, and they robbed all that came along that way by them: and it was told A-bĭm′ĕ-lech.

26 And Gā′al the son of E′bed came with his brethren, and went over to Shē′chem: and the men of Shē′chem put their confidence in him.

27 And they went out into the fields, and gathered their vineyards, and trode *the grapes,* and made [8]merry, and went into [v]the house of their god, and did eat and drink, and cursed A-bĭm′ĕ-lech.

28 And Gā′al the son of E′bed said, [w]Who *is* A-bĭm′ĕ-lech, and who *is* Shē′chem, that we should serve him? *is* not *he* the son of Je-rŭb′ba-ăl? and Zē′bul his officer? serve the men of [x]Hā′mor the father of Shē′chem: for why should we serve him?

29 And [y]would to God this people were under my hand! then would I remove A-bĭm′ĕ-lech. And he said to A-bĭm′ĕ-lech, Increase thine army, and come out.

30 ¶ And when Zē′bul the ruler of the city heard the words of Gā′al the son of E′bed, his anger was [9]kindled.

31 And he sent messengers unto A-bĭm′ĕ-lech [10]privily, saying, Behold, Gā′al the son of E′bed and his brethren be come to Shē′chem; and, behold, they fortify the city against thee.

32 Now therefore up by night, thou and the people that *is* with thee, and lie in wait in the field:

33 And it shall be, *that* in the morning, as soon as the sun is up, thou shalt rise early, and set upon the city: and, behold, *when* he and the people that *is* with him come out against thee, then mayest thou do to them [11]as thou shalt find occasion.

34 ¶ And A-bĭm′ĕ-lech rose up, and all the people that *were* with him, by night, and they laid wait against Shē′chem in four companies.

35 And Gā′al the son of E′bed went out, and stood in the entering of the gate of the city: and A-bĭm′ĕ-lech rose up, and the people that *were* with him, from lying in wait.

36 And when Gā′al saw the people, he said to Zē′bul, Behold, there come people down from the top of the mountains. And Zē′bul said unto him, [z]Thou seest the shadow of the mountains as *if they were* men.

37 And Gā′al spake again and said, See there come people down by the [12]middle of the land, and another company come along by the plain of [13]Me-ŏn′e-nīm.

38 Then said Zē′bul unto him, Where *is* now thy mouth, wherewith thou saidst, Who *is* A-bĭm′ĕ-lech, that we should serve him? *is* not this the people that thou hast despised? [a]go out, I pray now, and fight with them.

39 And Gā′al went out before the men of Shē′chem, and fought with A-bĭm′ĕ-lech.

40 And A-bĭm′ĕ-lech chased him, and he fled before him, and many were overthrown *and* wounded, *even* unto the entering of the gate.

41 And A-bĭm′ĕ-lech dwelt at A-rụ′mah: and Zē′bul thrust out Gā′al and his brethren, that they should not dwell in Shē′chem.

42 And it came to pass on the morrow, that the people went out into the field; and they told A-bĭm′ĕ-lech.

43 And he took the people, and divided them into three companies, and laid wait in the field, and looked, and, behold, the people *were* come forth out of the city; and he rose up against them, and smote them.

44 And A-bĭm′ĕ-lech, and the company that *was* with him, rushed

14 [5]Or, thistle

15 [m]Isa. 30.2; Dan. 4.12; Hos. 14.7

[n]Ezek. 19.14

[o]2 Ki. 14.9; Ps. 104.16; Isa. 2.13

16 [p]ch. 8.35

17 [6]cast his life

19 [q]Isa. 8.6; Phil. 3.3; Jas. 4.16

21 [r]Num. 21.16; Josh. 19.8; 2 Sam. 20.14

23 [s]1 Sam. 16.14; 1 Sam. 18.9-10; 1 Ki. 12.15; 1 Ki. 18.19; 2 Chr. 18.19-22; Isa. 19.2-14; 2 Thess. 2.1-11

[t]Isa. 33.1; Matt. 7.2

24 [u]1 Sam. 15.33; 1 Ki. 2.32; Esth. 9.25; Ps. 7.16; Ps. 58.10-11; Matt. 23.35
[7]strengthened his hands to kill

27 [8]Or, songs

[v]ch. 8.33

28 [w]Ex. 5.2; 1 Sam. 25.10

[x]Gen. 34.2

29 [y]2 Sam. 15.4; 1 Ki. 20.11; Ps. 10.3

30 [9]Or, hot

31 [10]craftily, or, to Tormah

33 [11]as thine hand shall find

36 [z]Mark 8.24

37 [12]navel
[13]Or, The regarders of the times, soothsayers

38 [a]2 Sam. 2.26-27; 2 Ki. 14.8; Jer. 2.28

forward, and stood in the entering of
the gate of the city: and the two *other*
companies ran upon all *the people* that
were in the fields, and slew them.
45 And A-bĭm'ĕ-lech fought against
the city all that day; and he took the
city, and slew the people that *was*
therein, and [b]beat down the city, and
[14]sowed it with salt.
46 ¶ And when all the men of the
tower of Shē'chem heard *that,* they entered into an hold of the house [c]of the
god Bē'rith.
47 And it was told A-bĭm'ĕ-lech, that
all the men of the tower of Shē'chem
were gathered together.
48 And A-bĭm'ĕ-lech gat him up to
mount [d]Zăl'mŏn, he and all the people
that *were* with him; and A-bĭm'ĕ-lech
took an ax in his hand, and cut down a
bough from the trees, and took it, and
laid *it* on his shoulder, and said unto
the people that *were* with him, What
ye have seen [15]me do, make haste, *and*
do as I *have done.*
49 And all the people likewise cut
down every man his bough, and followed A-bĭm'ĕ-lech, and put *them* to
the hold, and set the hold on fire upon
them; so that all the men of the tower
of Shē'chem died also, about a thousand men and women.
50 ¶ Then [e]went A-bĭm'ĕ-lech to
Thē'bez, and encamped against Thē'-
bez, and took it.
51 But there was a strong tower
within the city, and thither fled all the
men and women, and all they of the
city, and shut *it* to them, and gat them
up to the top of the tower.
52 And A-bĭm'ĕ-lech came unto the
tower, and fought against it, and went
hard unto the door of the tower to burn
it with fire.
53 And [f]a certain woman cast a
piece of a millstone upon A-bĭm'ĕ-
lech's head, and all to brake his skull.
54 Then [g]he called hastily unto the
young man his armourbearer, and said
unto him, Draw thy sword, and slay
me, that men say not of me, A woman
slew him. And his young man thrust
him through, and he died.
55 And when the men of Ĭs'ra-el saw
that A-bĭm'ĕ-lech was dead, they departed every man unto his place.
56 ¶ [h]Thus God rendered the wickedness of A-bĭm'ĕ-lech, which he did
unto his father, in slaying his seventy
brethren:
57 And all the evil of the men of
Shē'chem did God render upon their
heads: and upon them came the curse
of Jō'tham the son of Je-rŭb'ba-ăl.

10 And after A-bĭm'ĕ-lech there
arose to [a][1]defend Ĭs'ra-el Tō'là
the son of Pū'ah, the son of Dō'do,
a man of Ĭs'sa-char; and he dwelt in
Shā'mĭr in mount Ē'phră-ĭm.
2 And he judged Ĭs'ra-el twenty and
three years, and died, and was buried
in Shā'mĭr.
3 ¶ And after him arose Jā'ĭr, a Gĭl'e-
ăd-īte, and judged Ĭs'ra-el twenty and
two years.
4 And he had thirty sons that [b]rode
on thirty ass colts, and they had thirty
cities, [c]which are called [2]Hā'voth–jā'ĭr
unto this day, which *are* in the land of
Gĭl'e-ăd.
5 And Jā'ĭr died, and was buried in
Cā'mŏn.
6 ¶ And [d]the children of Ĭs'ra-el did
evil again in the sight of the LORD, and
[e]served Bā'al-ĭm, and Ăsh'ta-rŏth, and
[f]the gods of Sy̆r'ĭ-à, and the gods of
[g]Zī'dŏn, and the gods of Mō'ab, and
the gods of the children of Ăm'mŏn,
and the gods of the Phĭ-lĭs'tĭnes, and
forsook the LORD, and served not him.
7 And the anger of the LORD was hot
against Ĭs'ra-el, and he [h]sold them into
the hands of the Phĭ-lĭs'tĭnes, and into
the hands of the children of Ăm'mŏn.
8 And that year they vexed and [3]op-
pressed the children of Ĭs'ra-el: eighteen years, all the children of Ĭs'ra-el
that *were* on the other side Jôr'dan in
the land of the Ăm'ôr-ītes, which *is* in
Gĭl'e-ăd.
9 Moreover the children of Ăm'-
mŏn passed over Jôr'dan to fight also
against Jū'dah, and against Bĕn'ja-
min, and against the house of Ē'phră-
ĭm; so that Ĭs'ra-el was sore distressed.
10 ¶ [i]And the children of Ĭs'ra-el
cried unto the LORD, saying, We have
sinned against thee, both because we
have forsaken our God, and also served
Bā'al-ĭm.
11 And the LORD said unto the children of Ĭs'ra-el, *Did* not *I deliver you*
[j]from the E-ġy̆p'tians, and [k]from the
Ăm'ôr-ītes, [l]from the children of Ăm'-
mŏn, [m]and from the Phĭ-lĭs'tĭnes?
12 [n]The Zī-dō'nĭ-ans also, [o]and the
Ăm'a-lĕk-ītes, and the Mā'on-ītes, did
[p]oppress you; and ye cried to me, and I
delivered you out of their hand.
13 [q]Yet ye have forsaken me, and
served other gods: wherefore I will deliver you no more.
14 Go and [r]cry unto the gods which
ye have chosen; let them deliver you in
the time of your tribulation.
15 ¶ And the children of Ĭs'ra-el
said unto the LORD, We have sinned:
[s]do thou unto us whatsoever [4]seemeth
good unto thee; deliver us only, we
pray thee, this day.
16 [t]And they put away the [5]strange
gods from among them, and served the
LORD: and [u]his soul [6]was grieved for
the misery of Ĭs'ra-el.
17 Then the children of Ăm'mŏn
were [7]gathered together, and encamped
in Gĭl'e-ăd. And the children of Ĭs'ra-el
assembled themselves together, and encamped in [v]Mĭz'peh.
18 And the people *and* princes of
Gĭl'e-ăd said one to another, What man
is he that will begin to fight against the
children of Ăm'mŏn? he shall be head
over all the inhabitants of Gĭl'e-ăd.

11 Now Jĕph'thah the Gĭl'e-ăd-īte
was [a]a mighty man of valour,
and he *was* the son of [1]an harlot: and
Gĭl'e-ăd begat Jĕph'thah.
2 And Gĭl'e-ăd's wife bare him sons;
and his wife's sons grew up, and they

45 [b]Deut. 29.23; [14]Thus marking it out for perpetual desolation and barrenness
46 [c]ch. 8.33;
48 [d]Ps. 68.14 [15]I have done
50 [e]2 Sam. 11.21
53 [f]ch. 4.17;
54 [g]1 Sam. 31.4
56 [h]Gen. 9.5-6;

CHAPTER 10

1 [a]ch. 2.16; [1]save, or, deliver
4 [b]ch. 5.10 [c]Deut. 3.14 [2]Or, The villages of Jair
6 [d]ch. 2.11; [e]ch. 2.13; [f]ch. 2.12 [g]1 Ki. 11.33;
7 [h]1 Sam. 12.9
8 [3]crushed
10 [i]1 Sam. 12.10
11 [j]Ex. 14.30; [k]Num. 21.21-24 [l]ch. 3.12 [m]ch. 3.31
12 [n]ch. 5.19 [o]ch. 6.3 [p]Ps. 106.42
13 [q]Deut. 32.15;
14 [r]2 Ki. 3.13
15 [s]1 Sam. 3.18 [4]is good in thine eyes
16 [t]2 Chr. 7.14 [5]gods of strangers [u]Ps. 106.44 [6]was shortened
17 [7]cried together [v]Gen. 31.49

CHAPTER 11

1 [a]ch. 6.12 [1]a woman an harlot

thrust out Jĕph′thah, and said unto
him, Thou shalt not inherit in our father's house; for thou *art* the son of a
strange woman.
3 Then Jĕph′thah fled [2]from his
brethren, and dwelt in the land of Tŏb:
and there were gathered [b]vain men to
Jĕph′thah, and went out with him.
4 ¶ And it came to pass [3]in process
of time, that the children of Ăm′mŏn
made war against Ĭs′ra-el.
5 And it was so, that when the children of Ăm′mŏn made war against
Ĭs′ra-el, the elders of Gĭl′e-ăd went to
fetch Jĕph′thah out of the land of Tŏb:
6 And they said unto Jĕph′thah,
Come, and be our captain, that we may
fight with the children of Ăm′mŏn.
7 And Jĕph′thah said unto the elders of Gĭl′e-ăd, [c]Did not ye hate me,
and expel me out of my father's house?
and why are ye come unto me now
when ye are in distress?
8 And the elders of Gĭl′e-ăd said unto
Jĕph′thah, Therefore we [d]turn again to
thee now, that thou mayest go with us,
and fight against the children of Ăm′-
mŏn, and be our [e]head over all the inhabitants of Gĭl′e-ăd.
9 And Jĕph′thah said unto the elders of Gĭl′e-ăd, If ye bring me home
again to fight against the children of
Ăm′mŏn, and the LORD deliver them
before me, shall I be your head?
10 And the elders of Gĭl′e-ăd said
unto Jĕph′thah, [f]the LORD [4]be witness
between us, if we do not so according
to thy words.
11 Then Jĕph′thah went with the elders of Gĭl′e-ăd, and the people made
him head and captain over them: and
Jĕph′thah uttered all his words [g]be-
fore the LORD in Mĭz′peh.
12 ¶ And Jĕph′thah sent messengers
unto the king of the children of Ăm′-
mŏn, saying, What hast thou to do
with me, that thou art come against me
to fight in my land?
13 And the king of the children of
Ăm′mŏn answered unto the messengers of Jĕph′thah, [h]Because Ĭs′ra-el
took away my land, when they came up
out of Ē′gypt, from Ăr′nŏn even unto
[i]Jăb′bok, and unto Jôr′dan: now therefore restore those *lands* again peaceably.
14 And Jĕph′thah sent messengers
again unto the king of the children of
Ăm′mŏn:
15 And said unto him, Thus saith
Jĕph′thah, [j]Ĭs′ra-el took not away the
land of Mō′ab, nor the land of the children of Ăm′mŏn:
16 But when Ĭs′ra-el came up from
Ē′gypt, and [k]walked through the wilderness unto the Red sea, and [l]came to
Kā′desh;
17 Then [m]Ĭs′ra-el sent messengers
unto the king of Ē′dom, saying, Let me,
I pray thee, pass through thy land: but
the king of Ē′dom would not hearken
thereto. And in like manner they sent
unto the king of Mō′ab: but he would
not *consent*: and Ĭs′ra-el [n]abode in Kā′-
desh.
18 Then they went along through
the wilderness, and [o]compassed the
land of Ē′dom, and the land of Mō′ab,
and [p]came by the east side of the land
of Mō′ab, and pitched on the other side
of Ăr′nŏn, but came not within the border of Mō′ab: for Ăr′nŏn *was* the border of Mō′ab.
19 And [q]Ĭs′ra-el sent messengers
unto Sī′hŏn king of the Ăm′ôr-ītes,
the king of Hĕsh′bŏn; and Ĭs′ra-el said
unto him, Let us pass, we pray thee,
through thy land into my place.
20 But Sī′hŏn trusted not Ĭs′ra-el
to pass through his coast: but Sī′hŏn
gathered all his people together, and
pitched in Jā′hăz, and fought against
Ĭs′ra-el.
21 And the LORD God of Ĭs′ra-el delivered Sī′hŏn and all his people into
the hand of Ĭs′ra-el, and they [r]smote
them: so Ĭs′ra-el possessed all the land
of the Ăm′ôr-ītes, the inhabitants of
that country.
22 And they possessed all the coasts
of the Ăm′ôr-ītes, from Ăr′nŏn even
unto Jăb′bok, and from the wilderness
even unto Jôr′dan.
23 So now the LORD God of Ĭs′ra-el
hath dispossessed the Ăm′ôr-ītes from
before his people Ĭs′ra-el, and shouldest thou possess it?
24 Wilt not thou possess that which
[s]Chē′mŏsh thy god giveth thee to possess? So whomsoever [t]the LORD our
God shall drive out from before us,
them will we possess.
25 And now *art* thou any thing better than [u]Bā′lăk the son of Zĭp′por,
king of Mō′ab? did he ever strive
against Ĭs′ra-el, or did he ever fight
against them,
26 While Ĭs′ra-el dwelt in Hĕsh′bŏn
and her towns, and in [v]Ăr′ō-ĕr and her
towns, and in all the cities that *be*
along by the coasts of Ăr′nŏn, three
hundred years? why therefore did ye
not recover *them* within that time?
27 Wherefore I have not sinned
against thee, but thou doest me wrong
to war against me: the LORD [w]the
Judge be judge this day between the
children of Ĭs′ra-el and the children of
Ăm′mŏn.
28 Howbeit the king of the children
of Ăm′mŏn hearkened not unto the
words of Jĕph′thah which he sent him.
29 ¶ Then [x]the Spirit of the LORD
came upon Jĕph′thah, and he passed
over Gĭl′e-ăd, and Ma-năs′seh, and
passed over Mĭz′peh of Gĭl′e-ăd, and
from Mĭz′peh of Gĭl′e-ăd he passed
over *unto* the children of Ăm′mŏn.
30 And Jĕph′thah [y]vowed a vow
unto the LORD, and said, If thou shalt
without fail deliver the children of Ăm′-
mŏn into mine hands,
31 Then it shall be, that [5]whatsoever
cometh forth of the doors of my house
to meet me, when I return in peace
from the children of Ăm′mŏn, [z]shall
surely be the LORD'S, [6]and I will offer it
up for a burnt offering.
32 ¶ So Jĕph′thah passed over unto
the children of Ăm′mŏn to fight against

3 [2]from the face
[b]ch. 9.4; Acts 17.5
4 [3]after days
7 [c]Gen. 26.27
8 [d]Luke 17.4
[e]ch. 10.18
10 [f]Gen. 31.50; 1 Thess. 2.5
[4]be the hearer between us
11 [g]ch. 10.17; Prov. 16.3
13 [h]Num. 21.24
[i]Gen. 32.22
15 [j]Num. 22.13-15; 2 Chr. 20.10
16 [k]Num. 14.25; Josh. 5.6
[l]Num. 13.26; Deut. 1.46
17 [m]Num. 20.14
[n]Num. 20.1
18 [o]Num. 21.4
[p]Num. 21.11
19 [q]Num. 21.21-35; Josh. 13.8-12
21 [r]Num. 21.24; Deut. 2.33-34
24 [s]Num. 21.29; Jer. 48.7
[t]Ex. 23.28-31; Acts 13.19
25 [u]Num. 22.2; Mic. 6.5
26 [v]Deut. 2.36
27 [w]Gen. 18.25;
29 [x]ch. 3.10
30 [y]Gen. 28.20;
31 [5]that which cometh forth, which shall come forth
[z]Lev. 27.2;
[6]Or, or I will offer it, etc

them; and the LORD delivered them
into his hands.
33 And he smote them from Ăr'ŏ-ĕr,
even till thou come to [a]Mĭn'nith, *even*
twenty cities, and unto [7]the plain of the
vineyards, with a very great slaughter.
Thus the children of Ăm'mŏn were subdued before the children of Ĭs'ra-el.
34 ¶ And Jĕph'thah came to [b]Mĭz'-
peh unto his house, and, behold, [c]his
daughter came out to meet him with
timbrels and with dances: and she *was*
his only child; [8]beside her he had neither son nor daughter.
35 And it came to pass, when he saw
her, that he [d]rent his clothes, and said,
Alas, my daughter! thou hast brought
me very low, and thou art one of them
that trouble me: for I [e]have opened my
mouth unto the LORD, and [f]I cannot go
back.
36 And she said unto him, My father, *if* thou hast opened thy mouth
unto the LORD, [g]do to me according to
that which hath proceeded out of thy
mouth; forasmuch as [h]the LORD hath
taken vengeance for thee of thine enemies, *even* of the children of Ăm'mŏn.
37 And she said unto her father, Let
this thing be done for me: let me alone
two months, that I may [9]go up and
down upon the mountains, and bewail
[i]my virginity, I and my fellows.
38 And he said, Go. And he sent her
away *for* two months: and she went
with her companions, and bewailed
her virginity upon the mountains.
39 And it came to pass at the end of
two months, that she returned unto her
father, who [j]did with her *according* to
his vow which he had vowed: and she
knew no man. And it was a [10]custom in
Ĭs'ra-el,
40 *That* the daughters of Ĭs'ra-el
went [11]yearly to [12]lament the daughter
of Jĕph'thah the Gĭl'e-ăd-īte four days
in a year.

12 And [a]the men of Ē'phră-ĭm [1]gath-
ered themselves together, and
went northward, and said unto Jĕph'-
thah, Wherefore passedst thou over to
fight against the children of Ăm'mŏn,
and didst not call us to go with thee? we
will burn thine house upon thee with
fire.
2 And Jĕph'thah said unto them, I
and my people were at great strife with
the children of Ăm'mŏn; and when I
called you, ye delivered me not out of
their hands.
3 And when I saw that ye delivered
me not, I [b]put my life in my hands,
and passed over against the children
of Ăm'mŏn, and the LORD delivered
them into my hand: wherefore then
are ye come up unto me this day, to
fight against me?
4 Then Jĕph'thah gathered together
all the men of Gĭl'e-ăd, and fought with
Ē'phră-ĭm: and the men of Gĭl'e-ăd
smote Ē'phră-ĭm, because they said, Ye
Gĭl'e-ăd-ītes [c]*are* fugitives of Ē'phră-ĭm
among the Ē'phră-ĭm-ites, *and* among
the Ma-năs'sītes.
5 And the Gĭl'e-ăd-ītes took [d]the
passages of Jôr'dan before the Ē'phră-
ĭm-ites: and it was *so,* that when
those Ē'phră-ĭm-ites which were escaped said, Let me go over; that the
men of Gĭl'e-ăd said unto him, *Art*
thou an Ē'phră-ĭm-īte? If he said, Nay;
6 Then said they unto him, Say now
[2]Shib'bo-leth: and he said Sĭb'bo-lĕth:
for he could not frame to pronounce *it*
right. Then they took him, and slew
him at the passages of Jôr'dan: and
there fell at that time of the Ē'phră-ĭm-
ites forty and two thousand.
7 And Jĕph'thah judged Ĭs'ra-el six
years. Then died Jĕph'thah the Gĭl'e-
ăd-īte, and was buried in *one of* the
cities of Gĭl'e-ăd.
8 ¶ And after him [3]Ĭb'zăn of Bĕth'–
lĕ-hĕm judged Ĭs'ra-el.
9 And he had thirty sons, and thirty
daughters, *whom* he sent abroad, and
took in thirty daughters from abroad
for his sons. And he judged Ĭs'ra-el
seven years.
10 Then died Ĭb'zăn, and was buried
at Bĕth'–lĕ-hĕm.
11 ¶ And after him [4]Ē'lon, a Zĕb'u-
lon-īte, judged Ĭs'ra-el; and he judged
Ĭs'ra-el ten years.
12 And Ē'lon the Zĕb'u-lon-īte died,
and was buried in Āij'a-lŏn in the country of Zĕb'u-lun.
13 ¶ And after him [5]Ăb'dŏn the son
of Hĭl'lel, a Pĭr'a-thon-īte, judged Ĭs'ra-
el.
14 And he had forty sons and thirty
[6]nephews, that [e]rode on threescore
and ten ass colts: and he judged Ĭs'ra-el
eight years.
15 And Ăb'dŏn the son of Hĭl'lel the
Pĭr'a-thon-īte died, and was buried in
Pĭr'a-thon in the land of Ē'phră-ĭm, in
the mount of the Ăm'a-lĕk-ītes.

13 And the children of Ĭs'ra-el [1]did
evil again in the sight of the
LORD; [2]and the LORD delivered them
[a]into the hand of the Phĭ-lĭs'tĭnes forty
years.
2 ¶ And there was a certain man of
[b]Zō'rah, of the family of the Dăn'ītes,
whose name *was* Ma-nō'ah; and his
wife *was* barren, and bare not.
3 And the [c]angel of the LORD appeared unto the woman, and said unto
her, Behold now, thou *art* barren, and
bearest not: but thou shalt conceive,
and bear a son.
4 Now therefore beware, I pray thee,
and [d]drink not wine nor strong drink,
and eat not any unclean *thing:*
5 For, lo, thou shalt conceive, and
bear a son; and no [e]rasor shall come
on his head: for the child shall be a
Năz'a-rīte unto God from the womb:
and he shall [f]begin to deliver Ĭs'ra-el
out of the hand of the Phĭ-lĭs'tĭnes.
6 ¶ Then the woman came and told
her husband, saying, [g]A man of God
came unto me, and [h]his countenance
was like the countenance of an angel
of God, very terrible: but I asked him
not whence he *was,* neither told he me
his name:

33 [a]Ezek. 27.17
[7]Or, Abel
34 [b]ch. 10.17
[c]Ex. 15.20;
[8]of himself, or, he had not of his own either son or daughter
35 [d]Gen. 37.29;
[e]Eccl. 5.2
[f]Ps. 15.4;
36 [g]Num. 30.2
[h]2 Sam. 18.19
37 [9]go and go down
[i]Gen. 30.23;
39 [j]1 Sam. 1.22
[10]Or, ordinance
40 [11]from year to year
[12]Or, talk with

CHAPTER 12
1 [a]ch. 8.1
[1]were called
3 [b]1 Sam. 19.5;
4 [c]1 Sam. 25.10;
5 [d]Josh. 22.11;
6 [2]Which signifieth a burden, or, ear of corn, or, stream
8 [3]He seems to have been only a civil Judge to do justice in North east Israel
11 [4]A civil Judge in North east Israel
13 [5]A civil Judge also in North east Israel
14 [6]sons' sons
[e]ch. 5.10;

CHAPTER 13
1 [1]added to commit, etc
[2]This seems a partial captivity
[a]1 Sam. 12.9
2 [b]Josh. 15.33
3 [c]Gen. 16.7-13
4 [d]Num. 6.2-3
5 [e]Num. 6.5;
[f]1 Sam. 7.13
6 [g]Deut. 33.1;
[h]Matt. 28.3

7 But he said unto me, Behold, thou shalt conceive, and bear a son; and now drink no wine nor strong drink, neither eat any unclean *thing:* for the child shall be a Năz'a-rīte to God from the womb to the day of his death.

8 ¶ Then Ma-nō'ah intreated the LORD, and said, O my Lord, let the man of God which thou didst send come again unto us, and teach us what we shall do unto the child that shall be born.

9 And God hearkened to the voice of Ma-nō'ah; and the angel of God came again unto the woman as she sat in the field: but Ma-nō'ah her husband *was* not with her.

10 And the woman made haste, and ran, and shewed her husband, and said unto him, Behold, the man hath appeared unto me, that came unto me the *other* day.

11 And Ma-nō'ah arose, and went after his wife, and came to the man, and said unto him, *Art* thou the man that spakest unto the woman? And he said, I *am.*

12 And Ma-nō'ah said, Now let thy words come to pass. [3]How shall we order the child, and [4]*how* shall we do unto him?

13 And the angel of the LORD said unto Ma-nō'ah, Of all that I said unto the woman let her beware.

14 She may not eat of any *thing* that cometh of the vine, neither let her drink wine or strong drink, nor eat any unclean *thing:* all that I commanded her let her observe.

15 ¶ And Ma-nō'ah said unto the angel of the LORD, I pray thee, [i]let us detain thee, until we shall have made ready a kid [5]for thee.

16 And the angel of the LORD said unto Ma-nō'ah, Though thou detain me, I will not eat of thy bread: and if thou wilt offer a burnt offering, thou must offer it unto the LORD. For Ma-nō'ah knew not that he *was* an angel of the LORD.

17 And Ma-nō'ah said unto the angel of the LORD, What *is* thy name, that when thy sayings come to pass we may do thee honour?

18 And the angel of the LORD said unto him, [j]Why askest thou thus after my name, seeing it *is* [6]secret?

19 So Ma-nō'ah took a kid with a meat offering, [k]and offered *it* upon a rock unto the LORD: and *the angel* did wonderously; and Ma-nō'ah and his wife looked on.

20 For it came to pass, when the flame went up toward heaven from off the altar, that the angel of the LORD ascended in the flame of the altar. And Ma-nō'ah and his wife looked on *it,* and [l]fell on their faces to the ground.

21 But the angel of the LORD did no more appear to Ma-nō'ah and to his wife. [m]Then Ma-nō'ah knew that he *was* an angel of the LORD.

22 And Ma-nō'ah said unto his wife, [n]We shall surely die, because we have seen God.

23 But his wife said unto him, If the LORD were pleased to kill us, he would not have received a burnt offering and a meat offering at our hands, neither would he have [o]shewed us all these *things,* nor would as at this time have told us *such things* as these.

24 ¶ And the woman bare a son, and called his name [7]Săm'son: and the [p]child grew, and the LORD blessed him.

25 And [q]the Spirit of the LORD began to move him at times in [8]the camp of Dăn [r]between Zō'rah and Ĕsh'tă-ŏl.

14 And Săm'son went down [a]to Tĭm'nath, and [b]saw a woman in Tĭm'nath of the daughters of the Phĭ-lĭs'tĭnes.

2 And he came up, and told his father and his mother, and said, I have seen a woman in Tĭm'nath of the daughters of the Phĭ-lĭs'tĭnes: now therefore [c]get her for me to wife.

3 Then his father and his mother said unto him, *Is there* never a woman among the daughters of [d]thy brethren, or among all my people, that thou goest to take a wife of the [e]uncircumcised Phĭ-lĭs'tĭnes? And Săm'son said unto his father, Get her for me; for [1]she pleaseth me well.

4 But his father and his mother knew not that it *was* [f]of the LORD, that he sought an occasion against the Phĭ-lĭs'tĭnes: for at that time the Phĭ-lĭs'tĭnes had dominion over Ĭs'ra-el.

5 ¶ Then went Săm'son down, and his father and his mother, to Tĭm'nath, and came to the vineyards of Tĭm'nath: and, behold, a young lion roared [2]against him.

6 And [g]the Spirit of the LORD came mightily upon him, and he rent him as he would have rent a kid, and *he had* nothing in his hand: but he told not his father or his mother what he had done.

7 And he went down, and talked with the woman; and she pleased Săm'son well.

8 ¶ And after a time he returned to take her, and he turned aside to see the carcase of the lion: and, behold, *there was* a swarm of bees and honey in the carcase of the lion.

9 And he took thereof in his hands, and went on eating, and came to his father and mother, and he gave them, and they did eat: but he told not them that he had taken the honey out of the carcase of the lion.

10 ¶ So his father went down unto the woman: and Săm'son made there a feast; for so used the young men to do.

11 And it came to pass, when they saw him, that they brought thirty companions to be with him.

12 ¶ And Săm'son said unto them, I will now [h]put forth a riddle unto you: if ye can certainly declare it me [i]within the seven days of the feast, and find *it* out, then I will give you thirty [3]sheets and thirty [j]change of garments:

13 But if ye cannot declare *it* me, then shall ye give me thirty sheets and thirty change of garments. And they

---

12 [3]What shall be the manner of the, etc [4]what shall be his work? or, what shall he do?
15 [i]Gen. 18.5; ch. 6.18 [5]before thee
18 [j]Gen. 32.29 [6]Or, wonderful
19 [k]ch. 6.19-20; 1 Ki. 18.30-38
20 [l]Lev. 9.24; 1 Chr. 21.16; Ezek. 1.28; Dan. 10.9; Hos. 12.4-5; Matt. 17.6
21 [m]ch. 6.22
22 [n]Gen. 32.30; Ex. 33.20; Deut. 4.3; ch. 6.22; Isa. 6.5
23 [o]Ps. 25.14; Prov. 3.22; John 14.20-23
24 [7]That is, Serving like the sun [p]1 Sam. 3.19; Luke 1.80; Luke 2.52
25 [q]ch. 3.10; ch. 6.34; 1 Sam. 11.6; Matt. 4.1; John 3.34 [8]Mahaneh-dan [r]Josh. 15.33

CHAPTER 14

1 [a]Gen. 38.13; Josh. 15.10 [b]Gen. 34.2; Ps. 119.37
2 [c]Gen. 21.21; Gen. 24.2-13
3 [d]Gen. 24.3-4 [e]Ex. 34.16; Deut. 7.3 [1]she is right in mine eyes
4 [f]Josh. 11.20; 2 Chr. 10.15
5 [2]in meeting him
6 [g]ch. 3.10; ch. 13.25; 1 Sam. 11.6
12 [h]1 Ki. 10.1; Ezek. 17.2; Luke 14.7 [i]Gen. 29.27 [3]Or, shirts [j]Gen. 45.22

said unto him, Put forth thy riddle, that
we may hear it.
14 And he said unto them, Out of the
eater came forth meat, and out of the
strong came forth sweetness. And they
could not in three days expound the
riddle.
15 And it came to pass on the seventh day, that they said unto Săm'-
son's wife, [k]Entice thy husband, that
he may declare unto us the riddle, [l]lest
we burn thee and thy father's house
with fire: have ye called us [4]to take
that we have? *is it* not *so?*
16 And Săm'son's wife wept before
him, and said, [m]Thou dost but hate me,
and lovest me not: thou hast put forth a
riddle unto the children of my people,
and hast not told *it* me. And he said
unto her, Behold, I have not told *it* my
father nor my mother, and shall I tell *it*
thee?
17 And she wept before him [5]the
seven days, while their feast lasted:
and it came to pass on the seventh day,
that he told her, because she lay sore
upon him: and she told the riddle to the
children of her people.
18 And the men of the city said unto
him on the seventh day before the
sun went down, What *is* sweeter than
honey? and what *is* stronger than a
lion? And he said unto them, If ye had
not plowed with my heifer, ye had not
found out my riddle.
19 ¶ And [n]the Spirit of the LORD
came upon him, and he went down
to Ăsh'ke-lŏn, and slew thirty men of
them, and took their [6]spoil, and gave
change of garments unto them which
expounded the riddle. And his anger
was kindled, and he went up to his father's house.
20 But Săm'son's wife [o]was *given* to
his companion, whom he had used as
[p]his friend.

15 But it came to pass within a while
after, in the time of wheat harvest, that Săm'son visited his wife with
[a]a kid; and he said, I will go in to my
wife into the chamber. But her father
would not suffer him to go in.
2 And her father said, I verily thought
that thou hadst utterly [b]hated her; therefore I gave her to thy companion: *is* not
her younger sister fairer than she? [1]take
her, I pray thee, instead of her.
3 ¶ And Săm'son said concerning
them, [2]Now shall I be more blameless
than the Phĭ-lĭs'tĭnes, though I do them
a displeasure.
4 And Săm'son went and caught
three hundred [3]foxes, and took [4]fire-
brands, and turned tail to tail, and put
a firebrand in the midst between two
tails.
5 And when he had set the brands on
fire, he let *them* go into the standing
corn of the Phĭ-lĭs'tĭnes, and burnt up
both the shocks, and also the standing
corn, with the vineyards *and* olives.
6 ¶ Then the Phĭ-lĭs'tĭnes said, Who
hath done this? And they answered,
Săm'son, the son in law of the Tĭm'-
nīte, because he had taken his wife,
and given her to his companion. [c]And
the Phĭ-lĭs'tĭnes came up, and burnt
her and her father with fire.
7 ¶ And Săm'son said unto them,
Though ye have done this, yet will I be
avenged of you, and after that I will
cease.
8 And he smote them [5]hip and thigh
with a great slaughter: and he went
down and dwelt in the top of the rock
[d]Ē'tam.
9 ¶ Then the Phĭ-lĭs'tĭnes went up,
and pitched in Jū'dah, and spread
themselves in Lē'hī.
10 And the men of Jū'dah said, Why
are ye come up against us? And they
answered, To bind Săm'son are we
come up, to do to him as he hath done
to us.
11 Then three thousand men of Jū'-
dah [6]went to the top of the rock Ē'tam,
and said to Săm'son, Knowest thou not
that the Phĭ-lĭs'tĭnes *are* [e]rulers over
us? what *is* this *that* thou hast done
unto us? And he said unto them, As
they did unto me, so have I done unto
them.
12 And they said unto him, We are
come down to bind thee, that we may
deliver thee into the hand of the Phĭ-
lĭs'tĭnes. And Săm'son said unto them,
Swear unto me, that ye will not fall
upon me yourselves.
13 And they spake unto him, saying,
No; but we will bind thee fast, and deliver thee into their hand: but surely
we will not kill thee. And they bound
him with two new cords, and brought
him up from the rock.
14 ¶ *And* when he came unto Lē'hī,
the Phĭ-lĭs'tĭnes shouted against him:
and the Spirit of the LORD came mightily upon him, and the cords that *were*
upon his arms became as flax that was
burnt with fire, and his bands [7]loosed
from off his hands.
15 And he found a [8]new jawbone of
an ass, and put forth his hand, and took
it, and [f]slew a thousand men therewith.
16 And Săm'son said, With the jawbone of an ass, [9]heaps upon heaps,
with the jaw of an ass have I slain a
thousand men.
17 And it came to pass, when he had
made an end of speaking, that he cast
away the jawbone out of his hand, and
called that place [10]Rā'math–le'hī.
18 ¶ And he was sore athirst, and
called on the LORD, and said, [g]Thou
hast given this great deliverance into
the hand of thy servant: and now shall
I die for thirst, and fall into the hand of
the uncircumcised?
19 But God clave an hollow place
that *was* in [11]the jaw, and there came
water thereout; and when he had
drunk, [h]his spirit came again, and he
revived: wherefore he called the name
thereof [12]Ĕn–hăk'ko-rē, which *is* in
Lē'hī unto this day.
20 [13]And he judged Ĭs'ra-el [i]in the
days of the Phĭ-lĭs'tĭnes twenty years.

16 Then went Săm'son to Gā'zȧ, and
saw there [1]an harlot, and went in
unto her.

15 [k]Gen. 3.6; [l]ch. 15.6
[4]to possess us, or, to impoverish us?
16 [m]ch. 16.15
17 [5]Or, the rest of the seven days, etc
19 [n]Num. 11.17; [6]Or, apparel
20 [o]ch. 15.2 [p]John 3.29

CHAPTER 15
1 [a]Gen. 38.17;
2 [b]ch. 14.20 [1]let her be thine
3 [2]Or, Now shall I be blameless from the Philistines, though, etc
4 [3]Or, jackals, which were in great numbers in some parts of Palestine [4]Or, torches
6 [c]ch. 14.15
8 [5]That is, with great confusion [d]1 Chr. 4.3;
11 [6]went down [e]Lev. 26.25;
14 [7]were melted
15 [8]moist [f]Lev. 26.8;
16 [9]an heap, two heaps
17 [10]That is, The lifting up of the jawbone, or, casting away of the jawbone
18 [g]Ps. 3.7
19 [11]Lehi, the name of the place [h]Gen. 45.27; [12]That is, The well of him that called, or, cried
20 [13]He seems to have judged southwest Israel during twenty years of their servitude of the Philistines [i]ch. 13.1

CHAPTER 16
1 [1]a woman an harlot

2 *And it was told* the Gā'zītes, saying, Săm'son is come hither. And they [a]compassed *him* in, and laid wait for him all night in the gate of the city, and were [2]quiet all the night, saying, In the morning, when it is day, we shall kill him.

3 And Săm'son lay till midnight, and arose at midnight, and took the doors of the gate of the city, and the two posts, and went away with them, [3]bar and all, and put *them* upon his shoulders, and carried them up to the top of an hill that *is* before Hē'bron.

4 ¶ And it came to pass afterward, that he loved a woman [4]in the valley of Sō'rek, whose name *was* De-lī'lah.

5 And the lords of the Phĭ-lĭs'tĭnes came up unto her, and said unto her, [b]Entice him, and see wherein his great strength *lieth,* and by what *means* we may prevail against him, that we may bind him to [5]afflict him: and we will give thee every one of us eleven hundred *pieces* of silver.

6 ¶ And De-lī'lah said to Săm'son, Tell me, I pray thee, wherein thy great strength *lieth,* and wherewith thou mightest be bound to afflict thee.

7 And Săm'son said unto her, If they bind me with seven [6]green withs that were never dried, then shall I be weak, and be as [7]another man.

8 Then the lords of the Phĭ-lĭs'tĭnes brought up to her seven green withs which had not been dried, and she [c]bound him with them.

9 Now *there were* men lying in wait, abiding with her in the chamber. And she said unto him, The Phĭ-lĭs'tĭnes *be* upon thee, Săm'son. And he brake the withs, as a thread of tow is broken when it [8]toucheth the fire. [d]So his strength was not known.

10 And De-lī'lah said unto Săm'son, Behold, thou hast mocked me, and told me lies: now tell me, I pray thee, wherewith thou mightest be bound.

11 And he said unto her, If they bind me fast with new ropes [9]that never were occupied, then shall I be weak, and be as another man.

12 De-lī'lah therefore took new ropes, and [e]bound him therewith, and said unto him, The Phĭ-lĭs'tĭnes *be* upon thee, Săm'son. And *there were* liers in wait abiding in the chamber. And he brake them from off his arms like a thread.

13 And De-lī'lah said unto Săm'son, Hitherto thou hast mocked me, and told me lies: tell me wherewith thou mightest be bound. And he said unto her, If thou weavest the seven locks of my head with the web.

14 And she fastened *it* with the pin, and said unto him, The Phĭ-lĭs'tĭnes *be* upon thee, Săm'son. And he awaked out of his sleep, and went away with the pin of the beam, and with the web.

15 ¶ And she said unto him, [f]How canst thou say, I love thee, when thine heart *is* not with me? thou hast mocked me these three times, and hast not told me wherein thy great strength *lieth.*

16 And it came to pass, when she pressed him daily with her words, and urged him, *so* that his soul was [10]vexed unto death;

17 That he [g]told her all his heart, and said unto her, [h]There hath not come a rasor upon mine head; for I *have been* a Năz'a-rīte unto God from my mother's womb: if I be shaven, then my strength will go from me, and I shall become weak, and be like any *other* man.

18 And when De-lī'lah saw that he had told her all his heart, she sent and called for the lords of the Phĭ-lĭs'tĭnes, saying, Come up this once, for he hath shewed me all his heart. Then the lords of the Phĭ-lĭs'tĭnes came up unto her, and brought money in their hand.

19 And [i]she made him sleep upon her knees; and she called for a man, and she caused him to shave off the seven locks of his head; and she began to afflict him, and his strength went from him.

20 And she said, The Phĭ-lĭs'tĭnes *be* upon thee, Săm'son. And he awoke out of his sleep, and said, I will go out as at other times before, and shake myself. And he wist not that the LORD [j]was departed from him.

21 ¶ But the Phĭ-lĭs'tĭnes took him, and [11]put out his eyes, and brought him down to Gā'zȧ, and bound him with fetters of brass; and he did grind in the prison house.

22 Howbeit the hair of his head began to grow again [12]after he was shaven.

23 Then the lords of the Phĭ-lĭs'tĭnes gathered them together for to offer a great sacrifice unto [13]Dā'gŏn their god, and to rejoice: for they said, Our god hath delivered Săm'son our enemy into our hand.

24 And when the people saw him, they praised [k]their god: for they said, Our god hath delivered into our hands our enemy, and the destroyer of our country, [14]which slew many of us.

25 And it came to pass, when their hearts were [l]merry, that they said, Call for Săm'son, that he may make us sport. And they called for Săm'son out of the prison house; and he made [15]them sport: and they set him between the pillars.

26 And Săm'son said unto the lad that held him by the hand, Suffer me that I may feel the pillars whereupon the house standeth, that I may lean upon them.

27 Now the house was full of men and women; and all the lords of the Phĭ-lĭs'tĭnes *were* there; and *there were* upon the [m]roof about three thousand men and women, that beheld while Săm'son made sport.

28 And Săm'son called unto the LORD, and said, O Lord GOD, [n]remember me, I pray thee, and strengthen me, I pray thee, only this once, O God, that

2 [a]1 Sam. 19.11; 1 Sam. 23.26; Ps. 118.10-11-12; Acts 9.24; 2 Cor. 11.32-33
[2]silent
3 [3]with the bar
4 [4]Or, by the brook
5 [b]ch. 14.15; Prov. 2.16-19; Prov. 5.3-11; Prov. 7.21
[5]Or, humble
7 [6]moist
[7]one
8 [c]Prov. 6.26
9 [8]smelleth
[d]John 5.14
11 [9]wherewith work hath not been done
12 [e]Prov. 7.22
15 [f]ch. 14.16; Prov. 2.16
16 [10]shortened
17 [g]1 Chr. 28.9; 2 Chr. 15.2; Prov. 18.2; Mic. 7.5
[h]Num. 6.5; ch. 13.5; Acts 18.18
19 [i]Prov. 5.3-4; Prov. 7.21; Eccl. 7.25-26
20 [j]Num. 14.9-42-43; Josh. 7.12; 1 Sam. 16.14; 1 Sam. 18.12; 2 Chr. 15.2; Ps. 33.16; Prov. 22.14; Jer. 9.23-24; Hos. 9.12
21 [11]bored out
22 [12]Or, as when he was shaven
23 [13]Signifieth a fish
24 [k]1 Sam. 31.9; 1 Chr. 10.9; Ps. 97.7; Ps. 115.4-8; Ps. 135.15-18; Dan. 5.4-23; 1 Cor. 10.19-20
[14]and who multiplied our slain
25 [l]verses 6-9; Matt. 14.6-7
[15]before them
27 [m]Deut. 22.8
28 [n]Jer. 15.15

I may be at once avenged of the Phĭ-
lĭs'tĭnes for my two eyes.
29 And Săm'son took hold of the two
middle pillars upon which the house
stood, and [16]on which it was borne up,
of the one with his right hand, and of
the other with his left.
30 And Săm'son said, Let [17]me die
with the Phĭ-lĭs'tĭnes. And he bowed
himself with *all his* might; and the
house fell upon the lords, and upon all
the people that *were* therein. So the
dead which he slew at his death were
more than *they* which he slew in his
life.
31 Then his brethren and all the
house of his father came down, and
took him, and brought *him* up, and
[o]buried him between Zō'rah and Ĕsh'-
tă-ŏl in the buryingplace of Ma-nō'-
ah his father. And he judged Ĭs'ra-el
twenty years.

17 And there was a man of mount
Ē'phră-ĭm, whose name *was* Mī'-
cah.
2 And he said unto his mother, The
eleven hundred *shekels* of silver that
were taken from thee, about which
thou cursedst, and spakest of also in
mine ears, behold, the silver *is* with
me; I took it. And his mother said,
[a]Blessed *be thou* of the LORD, my son.
3 And when he had restored the
eleven hundred *shekels* of silver to his
mother, his mother said, I had wholly
dedicated the silver unto the LORD
from my hand for my son, to [b]make a
graven image and a molten image: now
therefore I will restore it unto thee.
4 Yet he restored the money unto
his mother; and his mother [c]took two
hundred *shekels* of silver, and gave
them to the founder, who made thereof
a graven image and a molten image:
and they were in the house of Mī'cah.
5 And the man Mī'cah had an house
of gods, and made an [d]ephod, and
[e]teraphim, and [1]consecrated one of his
sons, who became his priest.
6 [f]In those days *there was* no king
in Ĭs'ra-el, [g]*but* every man did *that
which was* right in his own eyes.
7 ¶ And there was a young man out
[h]of Bĕth'–lĕ-hĕm–jū'dah of the family
of Jū'dah, who *was* a Lē'vīte, and he
sojourned there.
8 And the man departed out of the
city from Bĕth'–lĕ-hĕm–jū'dah to sojourn where he could find *a place:* and
he came to mount Ē'phră-ĭm to the
house of Mī'cah, [2]as he journeyed.
9 And Mī'cah said unto him, Whence
comest thou? And he said unto him, I
am a Lē'vīte of Bĕth'–lĕ-hĕm–jū'dah,
and I go to sojourn where I may find *a
place.*
10 And Mī'cah said unto him, Dwell
with me, [i]and be unto me a [j]father and
a priest, and I will give thee ten *shekels*
of silver by the year, and [3]a suit of apparel, and thy victuals. So the Lē'vīte
went in.
11 And the Lē'vīte was content to
dwell with the man; and the young
man was unto him as one of his sons.
12 And Mī'cah consecrated the Lē'-
vīte; and the young man became his
priest, and was in the house of Mī'cah.
13 Then said Mī'cah, Now know I
that the LORD will do me good, seeing I
have a Lē'vīte to *my* priest.

18 In [a]those days *there was* no king
in Ĭs'ra-el: and in those days [b]the
tribe of the Dăn'ītes sought them an
inheritance to dwell in; for unto that
day *all their* inheritance had not fallen
unto them among the tribes of Ĭs'ra-el.
2 And the children of Dăn sent of
their family five men from their coasts,
[1]men of valour, from [c]Zō'rah, and from
Ĕsh'tă-ŏl, [d]to spy out the land, and to
search it; and they said unto them, Go,
search the land: who when they came
to mount Ē'phră-ĭm to the [e]house of
Mī'cah, they lodged there.
3 When they *were* by the house of
Mī'cah, they knew the voice of the
young man the Lē'vīte: and they turned
in thither, and said unto him, Who
brought thee hither? and what makest
thou in this *place?* and what hast thou
here?
4 And he said unto them, Thus and
thus dealeth Mī'cah with me, and hath
[f]hired me, and I am his priest.
5 And they said unto him, [g]Ask
counsel, we pray thee, [h]of God, that
we may know whether our way which
we go shall be prosperous.
6 And the priest said unto them, [i]Go
in peace: before the LORD *is* your way
wherein ye go.
7 ¶ Then the five men departed, and
came to [j]Lā'ish, and saw the people
that *were* therein, how they dwelt careless, after the manner of the Zī-dō'nĭ-
ans, quiet and secure; and *there was*
no [2]magistrate in the land, that might
put *them* to shame in *any* thing; and
they *were* far from the Zī-dō'nĭ-ans,
and had no business with *any* man.
8 And they came unto their brethren to Zō'rah and Ĕsh'tă-ŏl: and their
brethren said unto them, What *say* ye?
9 And they said, [k]Arise, that we may
go up against them: for we have seen
the land, and, behold, it *is* very good:
and *are* [l]ye still? be not slothful to go,
and to enter to possess the land.
10 When ye go, ye shall come unto a
people secure, and to a large land: for
God hath given it into your hands; [m]a
place where *there is* no want of any
thing that *is* in the earth.
11 ¶ And there went from thence of
the family of the Dăn'ītes, out of Zō'-
rah and out of Ĕsh'tă-ŏl, six hundred
men [3]appointed with weapons of war.
12 And they went up, and pitched in
[n]Kĭr'jath–jē'a-rĭm, in Jū'dah: wherefore they called that place [4]Mā'ha-neh–
dăn unto this day: behold, *it is* behind
Kĭr'jath–jē'a-rĭm.
13 And they passed thence unto
mount Ē'phră-ĭm, and came unto the
house of Mī'cah.
14 ¶ [o]Then answered the five men
that went to spy out the country of
Lā'ish, and said unto their brethren,
Do ye know that [p]there is in these

29 [16]Or, he leaned on them
30 [17]my soul
31 [o]ch. 13.25

CHAPTER 17
2 [a]Gen. 14.19; 2 Sam. 2.5
3 [b]Ex. 20.4-23; Ps. 115.4-8
4 [c]Isa. 46.6
5 [d]Ex. 28.4-15; 1 Sam. 23.6
[e]Gen. 31.19; Hos. 3.4
[1]filled the hand
6 [f]ch. 18.1; Deut. 33.5
[g]Deut. 12.8
7 [h]Josh. 19.15; Matt. 2.1-5-6
8 [2]in making his way
10 [i]Gen. 45.8; Isa. 22.21
[j]Gen. 45.8; Job 29.16
[3]an order of garments, or, a double suit, etc

CHAPTER 18
1 [a]ch. 17.6;
[b]Josh. 19.47
2 [1]sons
[c]ch. 13.25
[d]Num. 13.17
[e]ch. 17.1
4 [f]ch. 17.10;
5 [g]1 Ki. 22.5;
[h]ch. 17.5
6 [i]1 Ki. 22.6
7 [j]Josh. 19.47, called Leshem
[2]possessor, or, heir of restraint
9 [k]Num. 13.30;
[l]1 Ki. 22.3
10 [m]Deut. 8.9
11 [3]girded
12 [n]Josh. 15.60
[4]That is, Camp of Dan
14 [o]1 Sam. 14.28
[p]ch. 8.27

houses an ephod, and teraphim, and a
graven image, and a molten image?
now therefore consider what ye have
to do.
15 And they turned thitherward, and
came to the house of the young man the
Lē'vīte, *even* unto the house of Mī'cah,
and [5]saluted him.
16 And the six hundred men appointed with their weapons of war,
which *were* of the children of Dăn,
stood by the entering of the gate.
17 And the five men that went to spy
out the land went up, *and* came in
thither, *and* took [q]the graven image,
and the ephod, and the teraphim, and
the molten image: and the priest stood
in the entering of the gate with the
six hundred men *that were* appointed
with weapons of war.
18 And these went into Mī'cah's
house, and fetched the carved image,
the ephod, and the teraphim, and the
molten image. Then said the priest
unto them, What do ye?
19 And they said unto him, Hold thy
peace, [r]lay thine hand upon thy mouth,
and go with us, [s]and be to us a father
and a priest: *is it* better for thee to be a
priest unto the house of one man, or
that thou be a priest unto a tribe and a
family in Ĭs'ra-el?
20 And the priest's heart was glad,
and he took the ephod, and the teraphim, and the graven image, and went
in the midst of the people.
21 So they turned and departed, and
put the little ones and the cattle and
the carriage before them.
22 ¶ *And* when they were a good
way from the house of Mī'cah, the men
that *were* in the houses near to Mī'-
cah's house were gathered together,
and overtook the children of Dăn.
23 And they cried unto the children
of Dăn. And they turned their faces,
and said unto Mī'cah, What aileth thee,
[6]that thou comest with such a company?
24 And he said, Ye have taken away
my gods which I made, and the priest,
and ye are gone away: and what have I
more? and what *is* this *that* ye say unto
me, What aileth thee?
25 And the children of Dăn said unto
him, Let not thy voice be heard among
us, lest [7]angry fellows run upon thee,
and [8]thou lose thy life, with the lives of
thy household.
26 And the children of Dăn went
their way: and when Mī'cah saw that
they *were* too strong for him, he turned
and went back unto his house.
27 And they took *the things* which
Mī'cah had made, and the priest which
he had, and [t]came unto Lā'ish, unto a
people *that were* at quiet and secure:
[u]and they smote them with the edge of
the sword, and burnt the city with fire.
28 And *there was* no deliverer, because it *was* [v]far from Zī'dŏn, and
they had no business with *any* man;
and it was in the valley that *lieth* [w]by
Bĕth–rē'hŏb. And they built a city, and
dwelt therein.
29 And [x]they called the name of the
city [y]Dăn, after the name of Dăn their
father, who was born unto Ĭs'ra-el:
howbeit the name of the city *was* Lā'-
ish at the first.
30 ¶ And the children of Dăn set up
the graven image: and Jŏn'a-than, the
son of Gĕr'shŏm, the son of Ma-năs'-
seh, he and his sons were priests to the
tribe of Dăn [z]until the day of the captivity of the land.
31 And they set them up Mī'cah's
graven image, which he made, [a]all the
time that the house of God was in Shī'-
lōh.

19 And it came to pass in those days,
[a]when *there was* no king in Ĭs'ra-
el, that there was a certain Lē'vīte sojourning on the side of mount Ē'phră-
ĭm, who took to him [1]a concubine out of
[b]Bĕth'–lĕ-hĕm–jū'dah.
2 And his concubine played the
whore against him, and went away
from him unto her father's house to
Bĕth'–lĕ-hĕm–jū'dah, and was there
[2]four whole months.
3 And her husband arose, and went
after her, to speak [3]friendly unto her,
and to bring her again, having his servant with him, and a couple of asses:
and she brought him into her father's
house: and when the father of the damsel saw him, he rejoiced to meet him.
4 And his father in law, the damsel's
father, retained him; and he abode with
him three days: so they did eat and
drink, and lodged there.
5 ¶ And it came to pass on the fourth
day, when they arose early in the morning, that he rose up to depart: and the
damsel's father said unto his son in
law, [4]Comfort thine heart with a morsel of bread, and afterward go your
way.
6 And they sat down, and did eat
and drink both of them together: for
the damsel's father had said unto the
man, Be content, I pray thee, and tarry
all night, and let thine heart be merry.
7 And when the man rose up to depart, his father in law urged him: therefore he lodged there again.
8 And he arose early in the morning
on the fifth day to depart: and the damsel's father said, Comfort thine heart, I
pray thee. And they tarried [5]until after-
noon, and they did eat both of them.
9 And when the man rose up to depart, he, and his concubine, and his servant, his father in law, the damsel's father, said unto him, Behold, now the
day [6]draweth toward evening, I pray
you tarry all night: behold, [7]the day
groweth to an end, lodge here, that
thine heart may be merry; and to morrow get you early on your way, that
thou mayest go [8]home.
10 But the man would not tarry that
night, but he rose up and departed, and
came [9]over against [c]Jē'bus, which *is*
Je-ru'sa-lĕm; and *there were* with him
two asses saddled, his concubine also
was with him.
11 *And* when they *were* by Jē'bus,
the day was far spent; and the servant

15 [5]asked him of peace
17 [q]Gen. 31.19-30; ch. 6.31; 2 Ki. 19.18; Isa. 41.29; Mic. 5.13
19 [r]Job 21.5; Job 29.9; Prov. 30.32; Mic. 7.16
[s]Gen. 45.8; ch. 17.10; 2 Ki. 6.21; Job 29.16; Isa. 22.21; Matt. 23.9
23 [6]that thou art gathered together
25 [7]bitter of soul
[8]gather thy soul and the soul of thy household
27 [t]Deut. 33.22
[u]Josh. 19.47
28 [v]verse 7; Gen. 49.13; Josh. 11.8; ch. 10.12; Isa. 23.4-12; Ezek. 27.8
[w]Num. 13.21; 2 Sam. 10.6
29 [x]Josh. 19.47
[y]Gen. 14.14; ch. 20.1; 1 Ki. 12.29
30 [z]ch. 13.1; 1 Sam. 4.2; Ps. 78.60
31 [a]Josh. 18.1; 1 Sam. 4

CHAPTER 19
1 [a]ch. 17.6
[1]a woman a concubine, or, a wife a concubine
[b]ch. 17.7
2 [2]days four months, or, a year and four months
3 [3]to her heart
5 [4]Strengthen
8 [5]till the day declined
9 [6]is weak
[7]it is the pitching time of the day
[8]to thy tent
10 [9]to over against
[c]Josh. 18.28; 2 Sam. 5.6

said unto his master, Come, I pray
thee, and let us turn in into this city [d]of
the Jĕb'u-sītes, and lodge in it.
12 And his master said unto him,
We will not turn aside hither into the
city of a stranger, that *is* not of the children of Ĭs'ra-el; we will pass over [e]to
Gĭb'e-ah.
13 And he said unto his servant,
Come, and let us draw near to one of
these places to lodge all night, in Gĭb'-
e-ah, or in Rā'mah.
14 And they passed on and went
their way; and the sun went down
upon them *when they were* by Gĭb'e-
ah, which *belongeth* to Bĕn'ja-min.
15 And they turned aside thither, to
go in *and* to lodge in Gĭb'e-ah: and
when he went in, he sat him down in a
street of the city: for *there was* no man
that [10]took them into his house to lodging.
16 ¶ And, behold, there came an old
man from [f]his work out of the field at
even, which *was* also of mount Ē'phră-
ĭm; and he sojourned in Gĭb'e-ah: but
the men of the place *were* [11]Bĕn'ja-
mītes.
17 And when he had lifted up his
eyes, he saw a wayfaring man in the
street of the city: and the old man said,
Whither goest thou? and whence comest thou?
18 And he said unto him, We *are*
passing from Bĕth'–lĕ-hĕm–jū'dah toward the side of mount Ē'phră-ĭm;
from thence *am* I: and I went to Bĕth'–
lĕ-hĕm–jū'dah, but I *am now* going to
[g]the house of the LORD; and there *is* no
man that [12]receiveth me to house.
19 Yet there is both straw and provender for our asses; and there is bread
and wine also for me, and for thy handmaid, and for the young man *which is*
with thy servants: *there is* no want of
any thing.
20 And the old man said, [h]Peace *be*
with thee; howsoever *let* all thy wants
lie upon me; [i]only lodge not in the
street.
21 [j]So he brought him into his house,
and gave provender unto the asses:
[k]and they washed their feet, and did
eat and drink.
22 ¶ *Now* as they were making their
hearts merry, behold, [l]the men of the
city, certain [m]sons of Bē'lĭ-al, beset the
house round about, *and* beat at the
door, and spake to the master of the
house, the old man, saying, [n]Bring
forth the man that came into thine
house, that we may know him.
23 And [o]the man, the master of the
house, went out unto them, and said
unto them, Nay, my brethren, *nay,* I
pray you, do not *so* wickedly; seeing
that this man is come into mine house,
[p]do not this folly.
24 [q]Behold, *here is* my daughter a
maiden, and his concubine; them I will
bring out now, and [r]humble ye them,
and do with them what seemeth good
unto you: but unto this man do not [13]so
vile a thing.
25 But the men would not hearken
to him: so the man took his concubine,
and brought her forth unto them; and
they [s]knew her, and abused her all the
night until the morning: and when the
day began to spring, they let her go.
26 Then came the woman in the
dawning of the day, and fell down at
the door of the man's house where her
lord *was,* till it was light.
27 And her lord rose up in the morning, and opened the doors of the house,
and went out to go his way: and, behold, the woman his concubine was
fallen down *at* the door of the house,
and her hands *were* upon the threshold.
28 And he said unto her, Up, and
let us be going. But [t]none answered.
Then the man took her *up* upon an ass,
and the man rose up, and gat him unto
his place.
29 ¶ And when he was come into his
house, he took a knife, and laid hold
on his concubine, [u]and divided her,
together with her bones, into twelve
pieces, and sent her into all the coasts
of Ĭs'ra-el.
30 And it was so, that all that saw it
said, There was no such deed done nor
seen from the day that the children of
Ĭs'ra-el came up out of the land of
Ē'gypt unto this day: consider of it,
[v]take advice, and speak *your minds.*

20

Then [a]all the children of Ĭs'ra-el
went out, and the congregation
was gathered together as one man,
from [1]Dăn even to Bē'er–shē'bȧ, with
the land of Gĭl'e-ăd, unto the LORD [b]in
Mĭz'peh.
2 And the chief of all the people,
even of all the tribes of Ĭs'ra-el, presented themselves in the assembly of
the people of God, four hundred thousand footmen [c]that drew sword.
3 (Now the children of Bĕn'ja-min
heard that the children of Ĭs'ra-el were
gone up to Mĭz'peh.) Then said the children of Ĭs'ra-el, Tell *us,* how was this
wickedness?
4 And [2]the Lē'vīte, the husband of
the woman that was slain, answered
and said, [d]I came into Gĭb'e-ah that
belongeth to Bĕn'ja-min, I and my concubine, to lodge.
5 [e]And the men of Gĭb'e-ah rose
against me, and beset the house round
about upon me by night, *and* thought
to have slain me: [f]and my concubine
have they [3]forced, that she is dead.
6 And [g]I took my concubine, and
cut her in pieces, and sent her throughout all the country of the inheritance
of Ĭs'ra-el: for they [h]have committed
lewdness and folly in Ĭs'ra-el.
7 Behold, ye *are* all children of Ĭs'ra-
el; [i]give here your advice and counsel.
8 ¶ And all the people arose as one
man, saying, We will not any *of us* go
to his tent, neither will we any *of us*
turn into his house.
9 But now this *shall be* the thing
which we will do to Gĭb'e-ah; *we will
go up* by lot against it;

11 [d]Gen. 10.15-16; 1 Chr. 1.13-14
12 [e]Josh. 18.28; Hos. 5.8
15 [10]gathered
16 [f]Ps. 104.23
[11]sons of Jemini
18 [g]Josh. 18.1; 1 Sam. 1.3-7
[12]gathereth
20 [h]Gen. 43.23; ch. 6.23
[i]Gen. 19.2
21 [j]Gen. 24.32; Gen. 43.24
[k]Gen. 18.4; 1 Tim. 5.10
22 [l]Gen. 19.4; Hos. 10.9
[m]Deut. 13.13; 2 Cor. 6.15
[n]Gen. 19.5; Rom. 1.26-27
23 [o]Gen. 19.6
[p]2 Sam. 13.12
24 [q]Gen. 19.8
[r]Gen. 34.2; Deut. 21.14
[13]the matter of this folly
25 [s]Gen. 4.1
28 [t]ch. 20.5
29 [u]ch. 20.6; 1 Sam. 11.7
30 [v]ch. 20.7; Prov. 20.18

CHAPTER 20
1 [a]Deut. 13.12; 1 Sam. 11.7
[1]That is, The whole country
[b]Judg. 10.17; 2 Ki. 25.23
2 [c]ch. 8.10;
4 [2]the man the Levite
[d]ch. 19.15
5 [e]ch. 19.22
[f]ch. 19.25-26
[3]humbled
6 [g]ch. 19.29
[h]Gen. 34.7;
7 [i]Ex. 19.5-6

10 And we will take ten men of an
hundred throughout all the tribes of
Ĭs′ra-el, and an hundred of a thousand,
and a thousand out of ten thousand, to
fetch victual for the people, that they
may do, when they come to Gĭb′e-ah of
Bĕn′ja-min, according to all the folly
that they have wrought in Ĭs′ra-el.
11 So all the men of Ĭs′ra-el were
gathered against the city, [4]knit together
as one man.
12 ¶ [i]And the tribes of Ĭs′ra-el sent
men through all the tribe of Bĕn′ja-
min, saying, What wickedness *is* this
that is done among you?
13 Now therefore, deliver *us* the
men, [k]the children of Bē′lĭ-al, which
are in Gĭb′e-ah, that we may put them
to death, and [l]put away evil from Ĭs′-
ra-el. But the children of Bĕn′ja-min
would not [m]hearken to the voice of
their brethren the children of Ĭs′ra-el:
14 But the children of Bĕn′ja-min
gathered themselves together out of
the cities unto Gĭb′e-ah, to go out to
battle against the children of Ĭs′ra-el.
15 And the children of Bĕn′ja-min
were numbered at that time out of the
cities twenty and six thousand men
that drew sword, beside the inhabitants of Gĭb′e-ah, which were numbered seven hundred chosen men.
16 Among all this people *there were*
seven hundred chosen [n]men left-
handed; every one could sling stones
at an hair *breadth*, and not miss.
17 And the men of Ĭs′ra-el, beside
Bĕn′ja-min, were numbered four hundred thousand men that drew sword:
all these *were* men of war.
18 ¶ And the children of Ĭs′ra-el
arose, and went up to the house of God,
and [o]asked counsel of God, and said,
Which of us shall go up first to the battle against the children of Bĕn′ja-min?
And the LORD said, Jū′dah *shall go up*
first.
19 And the children of Ĭs′ra-el rose
up in the morning, and encamped
against Gĭb′e-ah.
20 And the men of Ĭs′ra-el went out
to battle against Bĕn′ja-min; and the
men of Ĭs′ra-el put themselves in array
to fight against them at Gĭb′e-ah.
21 And [p]the children of Bĕn′ja-min
came forth out of Gĭb′e-ah, and [q]de-
stroyed down to the ground of the Ĭs′-
ra-el-ītes that day twenty and two thousand men.
22 And the people the men of Ĭs′ra-el
encouraged themselves, and set their
battle again in array in the place where
they put themselves in array the first
day.
23 (And the children of Ĭs′ra-el went
up and [r]wept before the LORD until
even, and asked counsel of the LORD,
saying, Shall I go up again to battle
against the children of Bĕn′ja-min my
brother? And the LORD said, Go up
against him.)
24 And the children of Ĭs′ra-el came
near against the children of Bĕn′ja-
min the second day.
25 And Bĕn′ja-min went forth against
them out of Gĭb′e-ah the second day,
and [s]destroyed down to the ground
of the children of Ĭs′ra-el again eighteen thousand men; all these drew the
sword.
26 ¶ Then all the children of Ĭs′ra-el,
and all the people, went up, and came
unto the house of God, and wept, and
sat there before the LORD, and fasted
that day until even, and offered burnt
offerings and peace offerings before
the LORD.
27 And the children of Ĭs′ra-el [t]in-
quired of the LORD, (for [u]the ark of the
covenant of God *was* there in those
days,
28 [v]And Phĭn′e-has, the son of Ē-le-
ā′zar, the son of Aâr′on, [w]stood before
it in those days,) saying, Shall I yet
again go out to battle against the children of Bĕn′ja-min my brother, or shall
I cease? And the LORD said, Go up; for
to-morrow I will deliver them into thine
hand.
29 And Ĭs′ra-el [x]set liers in wait
round about Gĭb′e-ah.
30 And the children of Ĭs′ra-el went
up against the children of Bĕn′ja-min
on the third day, and put themselves
in array against Gĭb′e-ah, as at other
times.
31 And the children of Bĕn′ja-min
went out against the people, *and* were
drawn away from the city; and they
began [5]to smite of the people, *and* kill,
as at other times, in the highways, of
which one goeth up to [6]the house of
God, and the other to Gĭb′e-ah in the
field, about thirty men of Ĭs′ra-el.
32 And the children of Bĕn′ja-min
said, They *are* smitten down before us,
as at the first. But the children of Ĭs′ra-
el said, Let us flee, and draw them
from the city unto the highways.
33 And all the men of Ĭs′ra-el rose
up out of their place, and put themselves in array at Bā′al–tā′mär: and
the liers in wait of Ĭs′ra-el came forth
out of their places, *even* out of the
meadows of Gĭb′e-ah.
34 And there came against Gĭb′e-ah
ten thousand chosen men out of all
Ĭs′ra-el, and the battle was sore: [y]but
they knew not that evil *was* near them.
35 And the LORD smote Bĕn′ja-min
before Ĭs′ra-el: and the children of Ĭs′-
ra-el destroyed of the Bĕn′ja-mītes that
day twenty and five thousand and an
hundred men: all these drew the sword.
36 So the children of Bĕn′ja-min saw
that they were smitten: [z]for the men of
Ĭs′ra-el gave place to the Bĕn′ja-mītes,
because they trusted unto the liers in
wait which they had set beside Gĭb′e-
ah.
37 [a]And the liers in wait hasted, and
rushed upon Gĭb′e-ah; and the liers
in wait [7]drew *themselves* along, and
smote all the city with the edge of the
sword.
38 Now there was an appointed [8]sign
between the men of Ĭs′ra-el [9]and the
liers in wait, that they should make a

11 [4]fellows
12 [i]Deut. 13.14; Josh. 22.13-16; Matt. 18.15-18; Rom. 12.18
13 [k]Deut. 13.13; ch. 19.22; 1 Sam. 30.22; 2 Sam. 20.1; 1 Ki. 21.13; 2 Chr. 13.7; 2 Cor. 6.15
[l]Deut. 13.5; Deut. 17.12; 1 Cor. 5.13
[m]2 Chr. 25.16; Rom. 1.32
16 [n]ch. 3.15; 1 Chr. 12.2
18 [o]Ex. 28.30; Num. 27.21; Josh. 9.14; ch. 1.1; 1 Sam. 22.10-13-15; Ezra 8.21
21 [p]Gen. 49.27
[q]Deut. 23.9; Eccl. 9.1-11
23 [r]Ps. 78.34-36; Hos. 5.15
25 [s]Job 9.12; Ps. 66.18; Ps. 97.2; Hos. 10.9; Mic. 3.4; John 9.31
27 [t]Job 22.27; Ps. 50.15; Ps. 91.15; Prov. 3.6
[u]Josh. 18.1; 1 Sam. 4.3-4; Ps. 78.60-61; Jer. 7.12
28 [v]Ex. 6.25; Ps. 106.30-31
[w]Deut. 10.8
29 [x]Josh. 8.4; 2 Sam. 5.23
31 [5]to smite of the people wounded as at, etc
[6]Or, Beth-el
34 [y]Josh. 8.14; 1 Thess. 5.3
36 [z]Josh. 8.15
37 [a]Josh. 8.19
[7]Or, made a long sound with the trumpet
38 [8]Or, time
[9]with

great [10]flame with smoke rise up out of the city.

39 And when the men of Ĭs′ra-el retired in the battle, Bĕn′ja-min began [11]to smite *and* kill of the men of Ĭs′ra-el about thirty persons: for they said, Surely they are smitten down before us, as *in* the first battle.

40 But when the flame began to arise up out of the city with a pillar of smoke, the Bĕn′ja-mītes [b]looked behind them, and, behold, [12]the flame of the city ascended up to heaven.

41 And when the men of Ĭs′ra-el turned again, [c]the men of Bĕn′ja-min were amazed: for they saw that evil [13]was come upon them.

42 Therefore they turned *their backs* before the men of Ĭs′ra-el unto the way of the wilderness; but the battle overtook them; and them which *came* out of the cities they destroyed in the midst of them.

43 *Thus* they [d]inclosed the Bĕn′ja-mītes round about, *and* chased them, *and* trode them down [14]with ease [15]over against Ḡĭb′e-ah toward the sunrising.

44 And there fell of Bĕn′ja-min eighteen thousand men; all these *were* men of valour.

45 And they turned and fled toward the wilderness unto the rock of [e]Rĭm′mon: and they gleaned of them in the highways five thousand men; and pursued hard after them unto Ḡī′dom, and slew two thousand men of them.

46 So that all which fell that day of Bĕn′ja-min were twenty and five thousand men that drew the sword; all these *were* men of valour.

47 [f]But six hundred men turned and fled to the wilderness unto the rock Rĭm′mon, and abode in the rock Rĭm′mon four months.

48 And the men of Ĭs′ra-el turned again upon the children of Bĕn′ja-min, and smote them with the edge of the sword, as well the men of *every* city, as the beast, and all that [16]came to hand: also they set on fire all the cities that [17]they came to.

21 Now [a]the men of Ĭs′ra-el had sworn in Mĭz′peh, saying, There shall not any of us give his daughter unto Bĕn′ja-min to wife.

2 And the people came [b]to the house of God, and abode there till even before God, and lifted up their voices, and wept sore;

3 And said, O LORD God of Ĭs′ra-el, why is this come to pass in Ĭs′ra-el, that there should be to day one tribe lacking in Ĭs′ra-el?

4 And it came to pass on the morrow, that the people rose early, and [c]built there an altar, and offered burnt offerings and peace offerings.

5 And the children of Ĭs′ra-el said, Who *is there* among all the tribes of Ĭs′ra-el that came not up with the congregation unto the LORD? [d]For they had made a great oath concerning him that came not up to the LORD to Mĭz′peh, saying, He shall surely be put to death.

6 And the children of Ĭs′ra-el repented them for Bĕn′ja-min their brother, and said, There is one tribe cut off from Ĭs′ra-el this day.

7 How shall we do for wives for them that remain, seeing we have sworn by the LORD that we will not give them of our daughters to wives?

8 ¶ And they said, What one *is there* of the tribes of Ĭs′ra-el that came not up to Mĭz′peh to the LORD? And, behold, there came none to the camp from [e]Jā′besh–ḡĭl′e-ăd to the assembly.

9 For the people were numbered, and, behold, *there were* none of the inhabitants of Jā′besh–ḡĭl′e-ăd there.

10 And the congregation sent thither twelve thousand men of the valiantest, and commanded them, saying, [f]Go and smite the inhabitants of Jā′besh–ḡĭl′e-ăd with the edge of the sword, with the women and the children.

11 And this *is* the thing that ye shall do, [g]Ye shall utterly destroy every male, and every woman that [1]hath lain by man.

12 And they found among the inhabitants of Jā′besh–ḡĭl′e-ăd four hundred [2]young virgins, that had known no man by lying with any male: and they brought them unto the camp to [h]Shī′lōh, which *is* in the land of Cā′năan.

13 And the whole congregation sent *some* [3]to speak to the children of Bĕn′ja-min [i]that *were* in the rock Rĭm′mon, and to [4]call peaceably unto them.

14 And Bĕn′ja-min came again at that time; and they gave them wives which they had saved alive of the women of Jā′besh–ḡĭl′e-ăd: and yet so they sufficed them not.

15 And the people repented them for Bĕn′ja-min, because that the LORD had made a breach in the tribes of Ĭs′ra-el.

16 ¶ Then the elders of the congregation said, How shall we do for wives for them that remain, seeing the women are destroyed out of Bĕn′ja-min?

17 And they said, *There must be* an inheritance for them that be escaped of Bĕn′ja-min, that a tribe be not destroyed out of Ĭs′ra-el.

18 Howbeit we may not give them wives of our daughters: [j]for the children of Ĭs′ra-el have sworn, saying, Cursed *be* he that giveth a wife to Bĕn′ja-min.

19 Then they said, Behold, *there is* a feast of the LORD in Shī′lōh [5]yearly *in a place* which *is* on the north side of Bĕth′–el, [6]on the east side [7]of the highway that goeth up from Bĕth′–el to Shē′chem, and on the south of Le′bō-nah.

20 Therefore they commanded the children of Bĕn′ja-min, saying, Go and lie in wait in the vineyards;

21 And see, and, behold, if the daughters of Shī′lōh come out [k]to dance in dances, then come ye out of the vineyards, and catch you every man his wife

[10]elevation
39 [11]to smite the wounded
40 [b]Josh. 8.20
[12]the whole consumption
41 [c]Ex. 15.9-10; Prov. 5.22; Prov. 11.5-6; Isa. 33.14; Luke 17.27-28
[13]touched them
43 [d]Hos. 9.9
[14]Or, from Menuchah, etc
[15]unto over against
45 [e]Josh. 15.32
47 [f]ch. 21.13; Isa. 1.9; Jer. 14.9-10; Lam. 3.32; Hab. 3.2
48 [16]was found
[17]were found

CHAPTER 21
1 [a]ch. 20.1; 1 Sam. 7.5-6
2 [b]Josh. 18.1; ch. 20.18-26
4 [c]Gen. 8.20; Ex. 20.24-25; ch. 6.26; 1 Sam. 14.35; Heb. 13.10
5 [d]Lev. 27.28-29; Jer. 48.10
8 [e]1 Sam. 11.1; 2 Sam. 2.5-6
10 [f]Deut. 13.15; 1 Sam. 11.7
11 [g]Num. 31.17
[1]knoweth the lying with man
12 [2]young women virgins
[h]Josh. 18.1; Jer. 7.12-14
13 [3]and spake and called
[i]ch. 20.47
[4]Or, proclaim peace
18 [j]ch. 11.35
19 [5]from year to year
[6]Or, toward the sunrising
[7]Or, on
21 [k]Ex. 15.20; Jer. 31.4-13

of the daughters of Shī'lōh, and go to
the land of Běn'ja-min.
22 And it shall be, when their fathers
or their brethren come unto us to complain, that we will say unto them, [8]Be
favourable unto them for our sakes: because we reserved not to each man his
wife in the war: for ye did not give unto
them at this time, *that* ye should be
guilty.
23 And the children of Běn'ja-min
did so, and took *them* wives, according
to their number, of them that danced,
whom they caught: and they went and
returned unto their inheritance, and
[l]repaired the cities, and dwelt in them.
24 And the children of Ĭs'ra-el departed thence at that time, every man
to his tribe and to his family, and they
went out from thence every man to his
inheritance.
25 [m]In those days *there was* no king
in Ĭs'ra-el: [n]every man did *that which
was* right in his own eyes.

22 [8]Or, Gratify us in them
23 [l]ch. 20.48
25 [m]ch. 17.6; ch. 18.1
[n]Deut. 12.8; ch. 17.6; Lam. 5.14

THE BOOK OF

RUTH

Life's Questions

Do foreigners and aliens have a part in God's kingdom?
Where is God in crisis, pain, and poverty?
How did God provide a king for His people?

God's Answers

Ruth shows that God uses people from all backgrounds and social classes to accomplish His work. If God could use a young, Moabite woman like Ruth, He can use anyone. Ruth shows this in four parts: Trial and tragedy seem to rule out God's grace (1:1–22); God uses the extraordinary loyalty of a foreign widow to prepare for His blessing (2:1–23); God changes a potential scandal into His opportunity for grace (3:1–18) and God used the loyalty of a Hebrew landowner to show His grace to a family and a nation, preparing for the Messiah (4:1–22).

Joshua thus shows God's grace in including all people of faith in His kingdom and using them to carry out His plan for world redemption through His chosen anointed one.

CHAPTER 1

1 Now it came to pass in the days
when the [a]judges [1]ruled, that there
was [b]a famine in the land. And a
certain man of [c]Běth'–lĕ-hĕm–jū'dah
went to sojourn in the country of
Mō'ab, he, and his wife, and his two
sons.
2 And the name of the man *was* E-
lĭm'ĕ-lech, and the name of his wife
Na-ō'mī, and the name of his two
sons Mäh'lon and Chĭl'ĭ-on, [d]Ĕph'-
rath-ītes of Běth'–lĕ-hĕm–jū'dah. And
they came [e]into the country of Mō'ab,
and [2]continued there.
3 And E-lĭm'ĕ-lech Na-ō'mī's husband died; and she was left, and her
two sons.
4 And they took them wives of the
women of Mō'ab; the name of the one
was Ôr'pah, and the name of the other
Ruth: and they dwelled there about ten
years.
5 And Mäh'lon and Chĭl'ĭ-on died
also both of them; and the woman was
left of her two sons and her husband.
6 ¶ Then she arose with her daughters in law, that she might return from
the country of Mō'ab: for she had
heard in the country of Mō'ab how that
the LORD had [f]visited his people in
[g]giving them bread.
7 Wherefore she went forth out of
the place where she was, and her two
daughters in law with her; and they
went on the way to return unto the
land of Jū'dah.
8 And Na-ō'mī said unto her two
daughters in law, [h]Go, return each to
her mother's house: [i]the LORD deal
kindly with you, as ye have dealt with
the dead, and with me.
9 The LORD grant you that ye may
find [j]rest, each *of you* in the house of
her husband. Then she kissed them;
and they lifted up their voice, and wept.
10 And they said unto her, Surely
we will return with thee unto thy people.
11 And Na-ō'mī said, Turn again,
my daughters: why will ye go with me?
are there yet *any more* sons in my
womb, [k]that they may be your husbands?
12 Turn again, my daughters, go
your way; for I am too old to have an
husband. If I should say, I have hope,
[3]*if* I should have an husband also to
night, and should also bear sons;
13 Would ye [4]tarry for them till they
were grown? would ye stay for them
from having husbands? nay, my daughters; for [5]it grieveth me much for your
sakes that [l]the hand of the LORD is
gone out against me.
14 And they lifted up their voice,
and wept again: and Ôr'pah kissed her
mother in law; but Ruth [m]clave unto
her.
15 And she said, Behold, thy sister
in law is gone back unto her people,
and unto her [n]gods: return thou after
thy sister in law.
16 And Ruth said, [6]Intreat me not to
leave thee, *or* to return from following
after thee: for whither thou goest, I
will go; and where thou lodgest, I will
lodge: thy people *shall be* my people,
and thy God my God:

1 [a]Judg. 2.16 [1]judged [b]Gen. 12.10; [c]Judg. 17.8
2 [d]Gen. 35.19 [e]Judg. 3.30 [2]were
6 [f]Ex. 4.31 [g]Gen. 28.20
8 [h]Josh. 24.15 [i]2 Tim. 1.16
9 [j]ch. 3.1
11 [k]Gen. 38.11
12 [3]Or, if I were with an husband
13 [4]hope [5]I have much bitterness [l]Judg. 2.15
14 [m]Deut. 4.4;
15 [n]Josh. 24.15-19-21
16 [6]Or, Be not against me

17 Where thou diest, will I die, and there will I be buried: [o]the LORD do so to me, and more also, *if ought* but death part thee and me.

18 [p]When she saw that she [7]was stedfastly minded to go with her, then she left speaking unto her.

19 ¶ So they two went until they came to Bĕth'–lĕ-hĕm. And it came to pass, when they were come to Bĕth'–lĕ-hĕm, that [q]all the city was moved about them, and they said, [r]*Is* this Na-ō'mī?

20 And she said unto them, Call me not [8]Na-ō'mī, call me [9]Mā'rȧ: for the Almighty hath dealt very bitterly with me.

21 I went out full, [s]and the LORD hath brought me home again empty: why *then* call ye me Na-ō'mī, seeing the LORD hath testified against me, and the Almighty hath afflicted me?

22 So Na-ō'mī returned, and Rụth the Mō'ab-ĭt-ess, her daughter in law, with her, which returned out of the country of Mō'ab: and they came to Bĕth'–lĕ-hĕm [t]in the beginning of barley harvest.

2 And Na-ō'mī had a [a]kinsman of her husband's, a mighty man of wealth, of the family of E-lĭm'ĕ-lech; and his name *was* [1]Bō'ăz.

2 And Rụth the Mō'ab-ĭt-ess said unto Na-ō'mī, Let me now go to the field, and glean [b]ears of corn after *him* in whose sight I shall find grace. And she said unto her, Go, my daughter.

3 And she went, and came, and gleaned in the field after the reapers: and her [2]hap was to light on a part of the field *belonging* unto Bō'ăz, who *was* of the kindred of E-lĭm'ĕ-lech.

4 ¶ And, behold, Bō'ăz came from Bĕth'–lĕ-hĕm, and said unto the reapers, [c]The LORD *be* with you. And they answered him, [d]The LORD bless thee.

5 Then said Bō'ăz unto his servant that was set over the reapers, Whose damsel *is* this?

6 And the servant that was set over the reapers answered and said, It *is* the Mō'ab-ĭt-ish damsel that [e]came back with Na-ō'mī out of the country of Mō'ab:

7 And she said, I pray you, let me glean and gather after the reapers among the sheaves: so she came, and hath continued even from the morning until now, that she tarried a little in the house.

8 Then said Bō'ăz unto Rụth, Hearest thou not, my daughter? Go not to glean in another field, neither go from hence, but abide here fast by my maidens:

9 *Let* thine eyes *be* on the field that they do reap, and go thou after them: have I not charged the young men that they shall not touch thee? and when thou art athirst, go unto the vessels, and drink of *that* which the young men have drawn.

10 Then she [f]fell on her face, and bowed herself to the ground, and said unto him, Why have I found grace in thine eyes, that thou shouldest take knowledge of me, seeing I *am* a stranger?

11 And Bō'ăz answered and said unto her, [g]It hath fully been shewed me, [h]all that thou hast done unto thy mother in law since the death of thine husband: and *how* thou hast left thy father and thy mother, and the land of thy nativity, and art come unto a people which thou knewest not heretofore.

12 [i]The LORD recompense thy work, and a full reward be given thee of the LORD God of Ĭs'ra-el, [j]under whose wings thou art come to trust.

13 Then she said, [3]Let me find favour in thy sight, my lord; for that thou hast comforted me, and for that thou hast spoken [4]friendly unto thine handmaid, [k]though I be not like unto one of thine handmaidens.

14 And Bō'ăz said unto her, At mealtime come thou hither, and eat of the bread, and dip thy morsel in the vinegar. And she sat beside the reapers: and he reached her parched *corn*, and she did eat, and was sufficed, and left.

15 And when she was risen up to glean, Bō'ăz commanded his young men, saying, Let her glean even among the sheaves, and [5]reproach her not:

16 And let fall also *some* of the handfuls of purpose for her, and leave *them*, that she may glean *them*, and rebuke her not.

17 So she gleaned in the field until even, and beat out that she had gleaned: and it was about an ephah of barley.

18 ¶ And she took *it* up, and went into the city: and her mother in law saw what she had gleaned: and she brought forth, and gave to her that she had reserved after she was sufficed.

19 And her mother in law said unto her, Where hast thou gleaned to day? and where wroughtest thou? blessed be he that did [l]take knowledge of thee. And she shewed her mother in law with whom she had wrought, and said, The man's name with whom I wrought to day *is* Bō'ăz.

20 And Na-ō'mī said unto her daughter in law, [m]Blessed *be* he of the LORD, who [n]hath not left off his kindness to the living and to the dead. And Na-ō'mī said unto her, The man *is* near of kin unto us, [6]one of our next kinsmen.

21 And Rụth the Mō'ab-ĭt-ess said, He said unto me also, Thou shalt keep fast by my young men, until they have ended all my harvest.

22 And Na-ō'mī said unto Rụth her daughter in law, *It is* good, my daughter, that thou go out with his maidens, that they [7]meet thee not in any other field.

23 So she kept fast by the maidens of Bō'ăz to glean unto the end of barley harvest and of wheat harvest; and dwelt with her mother in law.

3 Then Na-ō'mī her mother in law said unto her, My daughter, [a]shall I

---

17 [o]1 Sam. 3.17; 2 Ki. 6.31
18 [p]Acts 21.14
[7]strengthened herself
19 [q]Matt. 21.10
[r]Isa. 23.7; Lam. 2.15
20 [8]That is, Pleasant
[9]That is, Bitter
21 [s]1 Sam. 2.7-8
22 [t]Ex. 9.31; 2 Sam. 21.9

CHAPTER 2
1 [a]ch. 3.2-12
[1]That is, Strength is in him
2 [b]Lev. 19.9; Deut. 24.19
3 [2]hap, happened
4 [c]Judg. 6.12; Ps. 118.26; Ps. 129.7-8; Luke 1.28; 2 Thess. 3.16; 2 Tim. 4.22
[d]Col. 4.6
6 [e]ch. 1.22
10 [f]Gen. 18.2; 1 Sam. 25.23
11 [g]Prov. 31.31
[h]ch. 1.14; Luke 5.11-28; Luke 14.33; Heb. 11.8-9-24-26
12 [i]1 Sam. 24.19; Ps. 19.11; Ps. 58.11; Prov. 11.18; Matt. 5.12; Matt. 6.1; Luke 6.35; 2 Tim. 1.18; Heb. 6.10
[j]Ps. 17.8; Ps. 36.7; Ps. 57.1; Ps. 63.7
13 [3]Or, I find favour
[4]to the heart
[k]1 Sam. 25.41; Phil. 2.3
15 [5]shame her not
19 [l]Ps. 41.1
20 [m]ch. 3.10; 2 Tim. 1.16
[n]Prov. 17.17
[6]Or, one that hath right to redeem
22 [7]Or, fall upon thee

CHAPTER 3
1 [a]1 Cor. 7.36; 1 Tim. 5.8

not seek [b]rest for thee, that it may be
well with thee?
2 And now *is* not Bō'ăz of our kindred, [c]with whose maidens thou wast?
Behold, he winnoweth barley to night
in the threshingfloor.
3 Wash thyself therefore, [d]and
anoint thee, and put thy raiment upon
thee, and get thee down to the floor:
but make not thyself known unto the
man, until he shall have done eating
and drinking.
4 And it shall be, when he lieth down,
that thou shalt mark the place where he
shall lie, and thou shalt go in, and [1]un-
cover his feet, and lay thee down; and
he will tell thee what thou shalt do.
5 And she said unto her, [e]All that
thou sayest unto me I will do.
6 ¶ And she went down unto the
floor, and did according to all that her
mother in law bade her.
7 And when Bō'ăz had eaten and
drunk, and [f]his heart was merry, he
went to lie down at the end of the heap
of corn: and she came softly, and uncovered his feet, and laid her down.
8 ¶ And it came to pass at midnight,
that the man was afraid, and [2]turned
himself: and, behold, a woman lay at
his feet.
9 And he said, Who *art* thou? And
she answered, I *am* Ruth thine handmaid: [g]spread therefore thy skirt over
thine handmaid; for thou *art* [3]a near
kinsman.
10 And he said, [h]Blessed *be* thou of
the LORD, my daughter: *for* thou hast
shewed more kindness in the latter
end than [i]at the beginning, inasmuch
as thou followedst not young men,
whether poor or rich.
11 And now, my daughter, fear not; I
will do to thee all that thou requirest:
for all the [4]city of my people doth know
that thou *art* [j]a virtuous woman.
12 And now it is true that I *am thy*
near kinsman: howbeit [k]there is a kinsman nearer than I.
13 Tarry this night, and it shall be in
the morning, *that* if he will [l]perform
unto thee the part of a kinsman, well;
let him do the kinsman's part: but if he
will not do the part of a kinsman to
thee, then will I do the part of a kinsman to thee, [m]*as* the LORD liveth: lie
down until the morning.
14 ¶ And she lay at his feet until the
morning: and she rose up before one
could know another. And he said, [n]Let
it not be known that a woman came
into the floor.
15 Also he said, Bring the vail that
thou hast upon thee, and hold it. And
when she held it, he measured six *measures* of barley, and laid *it* on her: and
she went into the city.
16 And when she came to her mother
in law, she said, Who *art* thou, my
daughter? And she told her all that the
man had done to her.
17 And she said, These six *measures*
of barley gave he me; for he said to me,
Go not empty unto thy mother in law.

[b]Deut. 4.40; ch. 1.9; Ps. 128.2; Jer. 22.15-16
2 [c]ch. 2.8
3 [d]2 Sam. 14.2
4 [1]Or, lift up the clothes that are on his feet
5 [e]Eph. 6.1; Col. 3.20
7 [f]Judg. 19.6; 2 Sam. 13.28; Esth. 1.10
8 [2]Or, took hold on
9 [g]Ezek. 16.8 [3]Or, one that hath right to redeem
10 [h]ch. 2.20 [i]ch. 1.8
11 [4]gate [j]Prov. 12.4
12 [k]ch. 4.1; 1 Thess. 4.6
13 [l]Deut. 25.5; ch. 4.5; Matt. 22.24 [m]Judg. 8.19; Jer. 4.2; Heb. 6.16
14 [n]Rom. 12.17; 1 Cor. 10.32; 2 Cor. 8.21; 1 Thess. 5.22; 1 Pet. 2.12
CHAPTER 4
1 [a]ch. 3.12
2 [b]Ex. 18.21-22; Deut. 16.18; Deut. 17.9; 1 Ki. 21.8; Ps. 82.2; Prov. 31.23
4 [1]I said I will reveal in thine ear [c]Jer. 32.7-8; Phil. 4.8 [d]Gen. 23.18 [e]Lev. 25.25
5 [f]Gen. 38.8; Matt. 22.24
6 [g]ch. 3.12-13
7 [h]Deut. 25.7-9
10 [i]Deut. 25.6
11 [j]Gen. 1.28; Ps. 128.3 [k]Deut. 25.9 [2]Or, get thee riches, or, power [l]Gen. 35.16; Mic. 5.2 [3]proclaim thy name
12 [m]Gen. 38.29; Matt. 1.3 [n]1 Sam. 2.20

18 Then said she, Sit still, my daughter, until thou know how the matter
will fall: for the man will not be in rest,
until he have finished the thing this
day.

4 Then went Bō'ăz up to the gate, and
sat him down there: and, behold,
[a]the kinsman of whom Bō'ăz spake
came by; unto whom he said, Ho, such
a one! turn aside, sit down here. And
he turned aside, and sat down.
2 And he took ten men of [b]the elders of the city, and said, Sit ye down
here. And they sat down.
3 And he said unto the kinsman, Na-
ō'mī, that is come again out of the country of Mō'ab, selleth a parcel of land,
which *was* our brother E-lĭm'ĕ-lech's:
4 And [1]I thought to advertise thee,
saying, [c]Buy *it* [d]before the inhabitants, and before the elders of my people. If thou wilt redeem *it*, redeem *it*:
but if thou wilt not redeem *it*, *then* tell
me, that I may know: [e]for *there is*
none to redeem *it* beside thee; and I
am after thee. And he said, I will redeem *it*.
5 Then said Bō'ăz, What day thou
buyest the field of the hand of Na-ō'mī,
thou must buy *it* also of Ruth the Mō'-
ab-īt-ess, the wife of the dead, [f]to raise
up the name of the dead upon his inheritance.
6 ¶ [g]And the kinsman said, I cannot
redeem *it* for myself, lest I mar mine
own inheritance: redeem thou my right
to thyself; for I cannot redeem *it*.
7 [h]Now this *was the manner* in
former time in Ĭs'ra-el concerning redeeming and concerning changing, for
to confirm all things; a man plucked off
his shoe, and gave *it* to his neighbour:
and this *was* a testimony in Ĭs'ra-el.
8 Therefore the kinsman said unto
Bō'ăz, Buy *it* for thee. So he drew off
his shoe.
9 ¶ And Bō'ăz said unto the elders,
and *unto* all the people, Ye *are* witnesses this day, that I have bought all
that *was* E-lĭm'ĕ-lech's, and all that
was Chĭl'ĭ-on's and Măh'lon's, of the
hand of Na-ō'mī.
10 Moreover Ruth the Mō'ab-īt-ess,
the wife of Măh'lon, have I purchased
to be my wife, to raise up the name of
the dead upon his inheritance, [i]that
the name of the dead be not cut off
from among his brethren, and from the
gate of his place: ye *are* witnesses this
day.
11 And all the people that *were* in the
gate, and the elders, said, *We are* witnesses. [j]The LORD make the woman
that is come into thine house like Rā'-
chel and like Lē'ah, which two did
[k]build the house of Ĭs'ra-el: and [2]do
thou worthily in [l]Ĕph'ra-tah, and [3]be
famous in Bĕth'–lĕ-hĕm:
12 And let thy house be like the
house of Phā'rĕz, [m]whom Tā'mar bare
unto Jū'dah, of [n]the seed which the
LORD shall give thee of this young
woman.
13 ¶ So Bō'ăz took Ruth, and she
was his wife: and when he went in

unto her, [o]the LORD gave her conception, and she bare a son.
14 And [p]the women said unto Na-
ō'mī, Blessed *be* the LORD, which hath
not [4]left thee this day without a [5]kins-
man, that his name may be famous in
Is'ra-el.
15 And he shall be unto thee a restorer of *thy* life, and [6]a nourisher of
[7]thine old age: for thy daughter in law,
which loveth thee, which is [q]better to
thee than seven sons, hath born him.
16 And Na-ō'mī took the child, and
laid it in her bosom, and became nurse
unto it.

13 [o]Gen. 29.31
14 [p]Luke 1.58; Rom. 12.15
[4]caused to cease unto thee
[5]Or, redeemer
15 [6]to nourish
[7]thy gray hairs
[q]1 Sam. 1.8
17 [r]Luke 1.58-59
18 [s]1 Chr. 2.4; Matt. 1.3
20 [t]Num. 1.7
[8]Or, Salmah

17 [r]And the women her neighbours
gave it a name, saying, There is a son
born to Na-ō'mī; and they called his
name Ō'bed: he *is* the father of Jĕs'se,
the father of Dā'vid.
18 ¶ Now these *are* the generations
of Phā'rĕz: [s]Phā'rĕz begat Hĕz'ron,
19 And Hĕz'ron begat Răm, and
Răm begat Ăm-mĭn'a-dab,
20 And Ăm-mĭn'a-dab begat [t]Näh'-
shon, and Näh'shon begat [8]Săl'mŏn,
21 And Săl'mŏn begat Bō'ăz, and
Bō'ăz begat Ō'bed,
22 And Ō'bed begat Jĕs'se, and
Jĕs'se begat Dā'vid.

THE FIRST BOOK OF

SAMUEL

Life's Questions

How do you recognize God's chosen leader?
How does God deal with disobedient leaders?
Does God have a long range plan?

God's Answers

The two books of Samuel show God's response to the immoral state of His leaderless people shown in Judges. God raised up a king and promised to use that king's family to bless His people forever. First and 2 Samuel show God's response in seven parts:

God reveals an example of righteous leadership in the prophet Samuel (1 Samuel 1—7);
God accepts the office of kingship but rejects the disobedient Saul (1 Samuel 8—15);
God prepares of His chosen leader David (1 Samuel 16—31);
God honors David's obedience rather than treachery (2 Samuel 1—6);
God establishes His purposes through His faithful but sinful servant (2 Samuel 7—12);
God brings trouble for a leader who ignores His family (2 Samuel 13—20);
God teaches His people through His faithful leader's example (2 Samuel 21—24).

The two books of Samuel thus show God at work choosing, guiding, chastising, and blessing His chosen leader David and setting His people up for the eventual coming of a new David to bring eternal salvation.

1 Now there was a certain man of
Rā-math-ā'im–zō'phim, of mount
Ē'phră-ĭm, and his name *was* [a]Ĕl'kă-
nah, the son of Jĕr'o-hăm, the son of E-
lī'hū, the son of Tō'hu, the son of
Zŭph, [b]an Ĕph'răth-īte:
2 And he had two wives; the name
of the one *was* Hăn'nah, and the name
of the other Pe-nĭn'nah: and Pe-nĭn'-
nah had children, but Hăn'nah had no
children.
3 And this man went up out of his
city [1]yearly [c]to worship and to sacrifice unto the LORD of hosts in [d]Shī'lōh.
And the two sons of Ē'lī, Hŏph'nī and
Phĭn'e-has, the priests of the LORD,
were there.
4 ¶ And when the time was that Ĕl'-
kă-nah offered, he gave to Pe-nĭn'nah
his wife, and to all her sons and her
daughters, portions:
5 But unto Hăn'nah he gave [2]a worthy portion; for he loved Hăn'nah: [e]but
the LORD had shut up her womb.
6 And her adversary also [3]provoked
her sore, for to make her fret, because
the LORD had shut up her womb.

CHAPTER 1
1 [a]1 Chr. 6.27
[b]Ruth 1.2
3 [1]from year to year
[c]Deut. 12.5
[d]Josh. 18.1; Judg. 18.31
5 [2]Or, a double portion
[e]Gen. 30.2
6 [3]angered her
7 [f]Ex. 23.14;
[4]from her going up, or, from the time that she, etc
8 [g]Ruth 4.15
9 [h]ch. 3.3
10 [i]Job 7.11
[5]bitter of soul
11 [j]Gen. 28.20;
[k]Gen. 29.32;
[l]Gen. 8.1;
[6]seed of men
[m]Num. 6.5

7 And *as* he did so [f]year by year,
[4]when she went up to the house of the
LORD, so she provoked her; therefore
she wept, and did not eat.
8 Then said Ĕl'kă-nah her husband
to her, Hăn'nah, why weepest thou?
and why eatest thou not? and why is
thy heart grieved? *am* not I [g]better to
thee than ten sons?
9 ¶ So Hăn'nah rose up after they
had eaten in Shī'lōh, and after they had
drunk. Now Ē'lī the priest sat upon a
seat by a post of the [h]temple of the
LORD.
10 And [i]she *was* [5]in bitterness of
soul, and prayed unto the LORD, and
wept sore.
11 And she [j]vowed a vow, and said,
O LORD of hosts, if thou wilt indeed
[k]look on the affliction of thine handmaid, and [l]remember me, and not forget thine handmaid, but wilt give unto
thine handmaid [6]a man child, then I
will give him unto the LORD all the
days of his life, and [m]there shall no
rasor come upon his head.

12 And it came to pass, as she [7]continued praying before the LORD, that Ē'lī marked her mouth.

13 Now Hăn'nah, she spake in her heart; only her lips moved, but her voice was not heard: therefore Ē'lī thought she had been drunken.

14 And Ē'lī said unto her, How long wilt thou be drunken? put away thy wine from thee.

15 And Hăn'nah answered and said, No, my lord, I *am* a woman [8]of a sorrowful spirit: I have drunk neither wine nor strong drink, but have [n]poured out my soul before the LORD.

16 Count not thine handmaid for a daughter of [o]Bē'lĭ-al: for out of the abundance of my [9]complaint and grief have I spoken hitherto.

17 Then Ē'lī answered and said, [p]Go in peace: and [q]the God of Ĭs'ra-el grant *thee* thy petition that thou hast asked of him.

18 And she said, [r]Let thine handmaid find grace in thy sight. So the woman [s]went her way, and did eat, and her countenance was no more *sad.*

19 ¶ And they rose up in the morning early, and worshipped before the LORD, and returned, and came to their house to Rā'mah: and Ĕl'kă-nah knew Hăn'nah his wife; and [t]the LORD remembered her.

20 Wherefore it came to pass, [10]when the time was come about after Hăn'nah had conceived, that she bare a son, and called his name [11]Săm'u-el, *saying,* Because I have asked him of the LORD.

21 And the man Ĕl'kă-nah, and all his house, went up to offer unto the LORD the yearly sacrifice, and his vow.

22 But Hăn'nah went not up; for she said unto her husband, *I will not go up* until the child be weaned, and *then* I will [u]bring him, that he may appear before the LORD, and there [v]abide for ever.

23 And [w]Ĕl'kă-nah her husband said unto her, Do what seemeth thee good; tarry until thou have weaned him; [x]only the LORD establish his word. So the woman abode, and gave her son suck until she weaned him.

24 ¶ And when she had weaned him, she [y]took him up with her, with three bullocks, and one ephah of flour, and a bottle of wine, and brought him unto the house of the LORD in Shī'lōh: and the child *was* young.

25 And they slew a bullock, and brought the child to Ē'lī.

26 And she said, Oh my lord, *as* thy soul liveth, my lord, I *am* the woman that stood by thee here, praying unto the LORD.

27 [z]For this child I prayed; and the LORD hath given me my petition which I asked of him:

28 Therefore also I have [12]lent him to the LORD; as long as he liveth [13]he shall be lent to the LORD. And he [a]worshipped the LORD there.

2 And Hăn'nah [a]prayed, and said, [b]My heart rejoiceth in the LORD, mine horn is exalted in the LORD: my mouth is enlarged over mine enemies; because I [c]rejoice in thy salvation.

2 [d]*There is* none holy as the LORD: for *there is* [e]none beside thee: neither *is there* any rock like our God.

3 Talk no more so exceeding proudly; [f]let *not* [1]arrogancy come out of your mouth: for the LORD *is* a God of knowledge, and by him actions are weighed.

4 The bows of the mighty men *are* broken, and they that stumbled are girded with strength.

5 [g]*They that were* full have hired out themselves for bread; and *they that were* hungry ceased: so that [h]the barren hath born seven; and [i]she that hath many children is waxed feeble.

6 [j]The LORD killeth, and maketh alive: he bringeth down to the grave, and bringeth up.

7 The LORD [k]maketh poor, and maketh rich: [l]he bringeth low, and lifteth up.

8 [m]He raiseth up the poor out of the dust, *and* lifteth up the beggar from the dunghill, [n]to set *them* among princes, and to make them inherit the throne of glory: for [o]the pillars of the earth *are* the LORD'S, and he hath set the world upon them.

9 [p]He will keep the feet of his saints, and the wicked shall be silent in darkness; [q]for by strength shall no man prevail.

10 The adversaries of the LORD shall be broken to pieces; out of heaven shall he thunder upon them: [r]the LORD shall judge the ends of the earth; and he shall give strength unto his king, and exalt the horn of his anointed.

11 And Ĕl'kă-nah went to Rā'mah to his house. [s]And the child did minister unto the LORD before Ē'lī the priest.

12 ¶ Now the sons of Ē'lī *were* [t]sons of Bē'lĭ-al; [u]they knew not the LORD.

13 And the priest's custom with the people *was, that,* when any man offered sacrifice, the priest's servant came, while the flesh was in seething, with a fleshhook of three teeth in his hand;

14 And he struck *it* into the pan, or kettle, or caldron, or pot; all that the fleshhook brought up the priest took for himself. So they did in Shī'lōh unto all the Ĭs'ra-el-ītes that came thither.

15 Also before they burnt the fat, the priest's servant came, and said to the man that sacrificed, Give flesh to roast for the priest; for he will not have sodden flesh of thee, but raw.

16 And *if* any man said unto him, Let them not fail to burn the fat [2]presently, and *then* take *as much* as thy soul desireth; then he would answer him, *Nay;* but thou shalt give *it me* now: and if not, I will take *it* by force.

17 Wherefore the sin of the young men was very great [v]before the LORD: for men [w]abhorred the offering of the LORD.

18 ¶ But Săm'u-el ministered before the LORD, *being* a child, [x]girded with a linen ephod.

12 [7]multiplied to pray
15 [8]hard of spirit
[n]Ps. 62.8
16 [o]2 Cor. 6.15
[9]Or, meditation
17 [p]Judg. 18.6; ch. 25.35
[q]Ps. 20.4-5
18 [r]Gen. 33.15
[s]Eccl. 9.7; John 16.24
19 [t]Gen. 30.22
20 [10]in revolution of days
[11]That is, Asked of God
22 [u]Luke 2.22
[v]ch. 2.11
23 [w]Num. 30.7
[x]2 Sam. 7.25
24 [y]Deut. 12.5
27 [z]Matt. 7.7
28 [12]Or, returned him, whom I have obtained by petition, to the LORD
[13]Or, he whom I have obtained by petition shall be returned
[a]Gen. 24.26-52

CHAPTER 2
1 [a]Phil. 4.6
[b]Luke 1.46
[c]Ps. 9.14; Ps. 13.5
2 [d]Ex. 15.11; Isa. 6.3
[e]Deut. 4.35; Ps. 73.25
3 [f]Mal. 3.13
[1]hard
5 [g]Luke 1.53
[h]Ps. 113.9
[i]Isa. 54.1;
6 [j]Deut. 32.39
7 [k]Job 1.21;
[l]Ps. 75.7
8 [m]Dan. 4.17
[n]Gen. 41.14;
[o]Heb. 1.3
9 [p]Ps. 91.11
[q]1 Sam. 14.6
10 [r]Ps. 96.13
11 [s]ch. 3.1
12 [t]Deut. 13.13
[u]Rom. 1.28
16 [2]as on the day
17 [v]Gen. 6.11
[w]Mal. 2.8;
18 [x]Ex. 28.4

19 Moreover his mother made him a
little coat, and brought *it* to him from
year to year, when she came up with
her husband to offer the yearly sacrifice.
20 ¶ And Ē'lī blessed Ĕl'kā-nah and
his wife, and said, The LORD give thee
seed of this woman for the [3]loan which
is lent to the LORD. And they went unto
their own home.
21 And the LORD [y]visited Hăn'nah,
so that she conceived, and bare three
sons and two daughters. And the child
Săm'u-el [z]grew before the LORD.
22 ¶ Now Ē'lī was very old, and
heard all that his sons did unto all
Ĭs'ra-el; and how they lay with the
women that [4]assembled *at* the door of
the tabernacle of the congregation.
23 And he said unto them, Why do
ye such things? for [5]I hear of your evil
dealings by all this people.
24 Nay, my sons; for *it is* no good
report that I hear: ye make the LORD'S
people [6]to transgress.
25 If one man sin against another,
the judge shall judge him: but if a man
[a]sin against the LORD, who shall intreat for him? Notwithstanding they
hearkened not unto the voice of their
father, [b]because the LORD would slay
them.
26 And the child Săm'u-el grew on,
and was [c]in favour both with the LORD,
and also with men.
27 ¶ [d]And there came a man of God
unto Ē'lī, and said unto him, Thus saith
the LORD, [e]Did I plainly appear unto
the house of thy father, when they
were in Ē'gypt in Phā'raōh's house?
28 And did I [f]choose him out of all
the tribes of Ĭs'ra-el *to be* my priest, to
offer upon mine altar, to burn incense,
to wear an ephod before me? and [g]did
I give unto the house of thy father all
the offerings made by fire of the children of Ĭs'ra-el?
29 Wherefore [h]kick ye at my sacrifice and at mine offering, which I
have commanded *in* [i]*my* habitation;
and honourest thy sons above me, to
make yourselves fat with the chiefest
of all the offerings of Ĭs'ra-el my people?
30 Wherefore the LORD God of Ĭs'ra-
el saith, I said indeed *that* thy house,
and the house of thy father, should
walk before me for ever: but now the
LORD saith, [j]Be it far from me; for them
that honour me [k]I will honour, and
[l]they that despise me shall be lightly
esteemed.
31 Behold, [m]the days come, that I
will cut off thine arm, and the arm of
thy father's house, that there shall not
be an old man in thine house.
32 And thou shalt see [7]an enemy *in
my* habitation, in all *the wealth* which
God shall give Ĭs'ra-el: and there shall
not be an [n]old man in thine house for
ever.
33 And the man of thine, *whom* I
shall not cut off from mine altar, *shall
be* to consume thine eyes, and to grieve
thine heart: and all the increase of

20 [3]Or, petition which she asked, etc
21 [y]Gen. 21.1 [z]Luke 2.40
22 [4]assembled by troops
23 [5]Or, I hear evil words of you
24 [6]Or, to cry out
25 [a]Num. 15.30 [b]Deut. 2.30; Prov. 15.10
26 [c]Prov. 3.4; Rom. 14.18
27 [d]1 Ki. 13.1 [e]Ex. 4.14
28 [f]Ex. 28.1 [g]Lev. 2.3
29 [h]Deut. 32.15; Mal. 1.12 [i]Deut. 12.5
30 [j]1 Chr. 15.2; Jer. 18.9 [k]Ps. 18.20; [l]Num. 11.20
31 [m]ch. 4.11
32 [7]Or, the affliction of the tabernacle, for all the wealth which God would have given Israel [n]Zech. 8.4
33 [8]men
34 [o]ch. 4.11
35 [p]1 Ki. 2.35; [q]2 Sam. 7.11 [r]Ps. 2.2
36 [s]1 Ki. 2.27 [9]Join [10]Or, somewhat about the priesthood

CHAPTER 3
1 [a]Ps. 74.9
3 [b]Ex. 27.21
7 [1]Or, Thus did Samuel before he knew the LORD, and before the word of the LORD was revealed unto him [c]Jer. 9.24
10 [d]Ps. 85.8
12 [e]ch. 2.30 [2]beginning and ending
13 [3]Or, And I will tell him [f]ch. 2.12 [4]Or, accursed [5]frowned not upon them

thine house shall die [8]in the flower of
their age.
34 And this *shall be* a sign unto thee,
that shall come upon thy two sons, on
Hŏph'nī and Phĭn'e-has; [o]in one day
they shall die both of them.
35 [p]And I will raise me up a faithful
priest, *that* shall do according to *that*
which *is* in mine heart and in my mind:
and [q]I will build him a sure house; and
he shall walk before [r]mine anointed
for ever.
36 [s]And it shall come to pass, *that*
every one that is left in thine house
shall come *and* crouch to him for a
piece of silver and a morsel of bread,
and shall say, [9]Put me, I pray thee, into
[10]one of the priests' offices, that I may
eat a piece of bread.

3 And [a]the child Săm'u-el ministered
unto the LORD before Ē'lī. And the
word of the LORD was precious in those
days; *there was* no open vision.
2 And it came to pass at that time,
when Ē'lī *was* laid down in his place,
and his eyes began to wax dim, *that* he
could not see;
3 And ere [b]the lamp of God went
out in the temple of the LORD, where
the ark of God *was*, and Săm'u-el was
laid down *to sleep;*
4 That the LORD called Săm'u-el:
and he answered, Here *am* I.
5 And he ran unto Ē'lī, and said,
Here *am* I; for thou calledst me. And he
said, I called not; lie down again. And
he went and lay down.
6 And the LORD called yet again,
Săm'u-el. And Săm'u-el arose and
went to Ē'lī, and said, Here *am* I; for
thou didst call me. And he answered, I
called not, my son; lie down again.
7 [1]Now Săm'u-el [c]did not yet know
the LORD, neither was the word of the
LORD yet revealed unto him.
8 And the LORD called Săm'u-el
again the third time. And he arose and
went to Ē'lī, and said, Here *am* I; for
thou didst call me. And Ē'lī perceived
that the LORD had called the child.
9 Therefore Ē'lī said unto Săm'u-el,
Go, lie down: and it shall be, if he call
thee, that thou shalt say, Speak, LORD;
for thy servant heareth. So Săm'u-el
went and lay down in his place.
10 And the LORD came, and stood,
and called as at other times, Săm'u-
el, Săm'u-el. Then Săm'u-el answered,
[d]Speak; for thy servant heareth.
11 ¶ And the LORD said to Săm'u-el,
Behold, I will do a thing in Ĭs'ra-el, at
which both the ears of every one that
heareth it shall tingle.
12 In that day I will perform against
Ē'lī all [e]*things* which I have spoken
concerning his house: [2]when I begin, I
will also make an end.
13 [3]For I have told him that I will
judge his house for ever for the iniquity which he knoweth; because [f]his
sons made themselves [4]vile, and he [5]re-
strained them not.
14 And therefore I have sworn unto
the house of Ē'lī, that the iniquity of

Ē'lī's house [g]shall not be purged with
sacrifice nor offering for ever.
15 ¶ And Săm'u-el lay until the morning, and opened the doors of the house
of the LORD. And Săm'u-el feared to
shew Ē'lī the vision.
16 Then Ē'lī called Săm'u-el, and
said, Săm'u-el, my son. And he answered, Here *am* I.
17 And he said, What *is* the thing
that *the LORD* hath said unto thee? I
pray thee hide *it* not from me: [h]God do
so to thee, and [6]more also, if thou hide
any [7]thing from me of all the things
that he said unto thee.
18 And Săm'u-el told him [8]every
whit, and hid nothing from him. And
he said, [i]It *is* the LORD: let him do what
seemeth him good.
19 ¶ And Săm'u-el grew, and [j]the
LORD was with him, [k]and did let none
of his words fall to the ground.
20 And all Ĭs'ra-el [l]from Dăn even
to Bē'er–shē'bȧ knew that Săm'u-el
was [9]established *to be* a prophet of the
LORD.
21 And [m]the LORD appeared again
in Shī'lōh: for the LORD revealed himself to Săm'u-el in Shī'lōh by the word
of the LORD.

4 And the word of Săm'u-el [1]came to
all Ĭs'ra-el. Now Ĭs'ra-el went out
against the Phĭ-lĭs'tĭnes to battle, and
pitched [a]beside Ĕb'en–ē'zẽr: and the
Phĭ-lĭs'tĭnes pitched in Ā'phek.
2 And the Phĭ-lĭs'tĭnes put themselves in array against Ĭs'ra-el: and
when [2]they joined battle, Ĭs'ra-el was
smitten before the Phĭ-lĭs'tĭnes: and
they slew of [3]the army in the field
about four thousand men.
3 ¶ And when the people were come
into the camp, the elders of Ĭs'ra-el
said, Wherefore hath the LORD smitten
us to day before the Phĭ-lĭs'tĭnes? Let
us [4]fetch the ark of the covenant of the
LORD out of Shī'lōh unto us, that, when
it cometh among us, it may save us out
of the hand of our enemies.
4 So the people sent to Shī'lōh, that
they might bring from thence the ark
of the covenant of the LORD of hosts,
[b]which dwelleth *between* [c]the cherubims: and the two sons of Ē'lī, Hŏph'nī
and Phĭn'e-has, *were* there with the
ark of the covenant of God.
5 And when the ark of the covenant
of the LORD came into the camp, all
Ĭs'ra-el shouted with a great shout, so
that the earth rang again.
6 And when the Phĭ-lĭs'tĭnes heard
the noise of the shout, they said, What
meaneth the noise of this great shout
in the camp of the Hē'brews? And they
understood that the ark of the LORD
was come into the camp.
7 And the Phĭ-lĭs'tĭnes were afraid,
for they said, God is come into the
camp. And they said, Woe unto us! for
there hath not been such a thing [5]here-
tofore.
8 Woe unto us! who shall deliver us
out of the hand of these mighty Gods?
these *are* the Gods that smote the Ē-
ġy̆p'tians with all the plagues in the
wilderness.
9 [d]Be strong, and quit yourselves
like men, O ye Phĭ-lĭs'tĭnes, that ye be
not servants unto the Hē'brews, [e]as
they have been to you: [6]quit yourselves
like men, and fight.
10 ¶ And the Phĭ-lĭs'tĭnes fought, and
[f]Ĭs'ra-el was smitten, and they fled every man into his tent: and there was a
very great slaughter; for there fell of
Ĭs'ra-el thirty thousand footmen.
11 And [g]the ark of God was taken;
[h]and the two sons of Ē'lī, Hŏph'nī and
Phĭn'e-has, [7]were slain.
12 ¶ And there ran a man of Bĕn'ja-
min out of the army, and came to Shī'-
lōh the same day with his clothes rent,
and [i]with earth upon his head.
13 And when he came, lo, Ē'lī sat
upon [j]a seat by the wayside watching:
for his heart trembled for the ark of
God. And when the man came into the
city, and told *it*, all the city cried out.
14 And when Ē'lī heard the noise
of the crying, he said, What *meaneth*
the noise of this tumult? And the man
came in hastily, and told Ē'lī.
15 Now Ē'lī was ninety and eight
years old; and his eyes [8]were dim, that
he could not see.
16 And the man said unto Ē'lī, I *am*
he that came out of the army, and I fled
to day out of the army. And he said,
[k]What [9]is there done, my son?
17 And the messenger answered and
said, Ĭs'ra-el is fled before the Phĭ-
lĭs'tĭnes, and there hath been also a
great slaughter among the people, and
thy two sons also, Hŏph'nī and Phĭn'e-
has, are dead, and the ark of God is
taken.
18 And it came to pass, when he
made mention of the ark of God, that he
fell from off the seat backward by the
side of the gate, and his neck brake,
and he died: for he was an old man, and
heavy. And he had judged Ĭs'ra-el forty
years.
19 ¶ And his daughter in law, Phĭn'-
e-has' wife, was with child, *near* [10]to be
delivered: and when she heard the tidings that the ark of God was taken, and
that her father in law and her husband
were dead, she bowed herself and travailed; for her pains [11]came upon her.
20 And about the time of her death
[l]the women that stood by her said
unto her, Fear not; for thou hast born a
son. But she answered not, [12]neither
did she regard *it*.
21 And she named the child [13]Ī'–cha-
bŏd, saying, [m]The glory is departed
from Ĭs'ra-el: because the ark of God
was taken, and because of her father in
law and her husband.
22 And she said, The glory is departed from Ĭs'ra-el: for the ark of God
is taken.

5 And the Phĭ-lĭs'tĭnes took the ark of
God, and brought it from Ĕb'en–
ē'zẽr unto Ăsh'dŏd.
2 When the Phĭ-lĭs'tĭnes took the ark
of God, they brought it into the house of
Dā'gŏn, and set it by Dā'gŏn.

14 [g]Num. 15.30; Isa. 22.14; Heb. 10.26-31
17 [h]Ruth 1.17; Matt. 26.63
[6]so add
[7]Or, word
18 [8]all the things, or, words
[i]Gen. 18.25; ch. 16.10-12; Job 1.21
19 [j]Gen. 39.2; ch. 18.14; 2 Tim. 4.22
[k]ch. 9.6
20 [l]Judg. 20.1
[9]Or, faithful
21 [m]Gen. 12.7; Num. 12.6

CHAPTER 4

1 [1]was, or, came to pass
[a]ch. 7.12
2 [2]the battle was spread
[3]the array
3 [4]take unto us
4 [b]2 Sam. 6.2; Ps. 80.1
[c]Ex. 25.18; Num. 7.89
7 [5]yesterday, or, the third day
9 [d]2 Sam. 10.12; 1 Chr. 19.13; 1 Cor. 16.13; Eph. 6.10-11
[e]Judg. 13.1; ch. 12.9
[6]be men
10 [f]Lev. 26.17; Deut. 28.25; Ps. 78.9-62
11 [g]ch. 2.32; Ps. 78.61
[h]Ps. 78.64
[7]died
12 [i]Josh. 7.6; Job 2.12
13 [j]ch. 1.9
15 [8]stood
16 [k]2 Sam. 1.4
[9]is the thing
19 [10]Or, to cry out
[11]were turned
20 [l]Gen. 35.17
[12]set not her heart
21 [13]That is, Where is the glory? or, There is no glory
[m]Ps. 26.8; Hos. 9.12

3 ¶ And when they of Ăsh'dŏd arose
early on the morrow, behold, [a]Dā'gŏn
was [b]fallen upon his face to the earth
before the ark of the LORD. And they
took Dā'gŏn, and [c]set him in his place
again.
4 And when they arose early on the
morrow morning, behold, Dā'gŏn *was*
fallen upon his face to the ground before the ark of [d]the LORD; and [e]the
head of Dā'gŏn and both the palms of
his hands *were* cut off upon the threshold; only [1]*the stump of* Dā'gŏn was left
to him.
5 Therefore neither the priests of
Dā'gŏn, nor any that come into Dā'-
gŏn's house, tread [f]on the threshold of
Dā'gŏn in Ăsh'dŏd unto this day.
6 But [g]the hand of the LORD was
heavy upon them of Ăsh'dŏd, and he
[h]destroyed them, and smote them with
[i]emerods, *even* Ăsh'dŏd and the coasts
thereof.
7 And when the men of Ăsh'dŏd saw
that *it was* so, they said, The ark of the
God of Ĭs'ra-el shall not abide with us:
for his hand is sore upon us, and upon
Dā'gŏn our god.
8 They sent therefore and gathered
all the lords of the Phĭ-lĭs'tĭnes unto
them, and said, What shall we do with
the ark of the God of Ĭs'ra-el? And they
answered, Let the ark of the God of
Ĭs'ra-el be carried about unto Găth.
And they carried the ark of the God of
Ĭs'ra-el about *thither*.
9 And it was *so*, that, after they had
carried it about, [j]the hand of the LORD
was against the city with a very great
destruction: and [k]he smote the men of
the city, both small and great, and they
had emerods in their secret parts.
10 ¶ Therefore they sent the ark of
God to Ĕk'rŏn. And it came to pass, as
the ark of God came to Ĕk'rŏn, that
the Ĕk'rŏn-ītes cried out, saying, They
have brought about the ark of the God
of Ĭs'ra-el to [2]us, to slay us and our
people.
11 So they sent and gathered together all the lords of the Phĭ-lĭs'tĭnes,
and said, Send away the ark of the God
of Ĭs'ra-el, and let it go again to his
own place, that it slay [3]us not, and our
people: for there was a deadly destruction throughout all the city; the hand
of God was very heavy there.
12 And [l]the men that died not were
smitten with the emerods: and the cry
of the city went up to heaven.

6 And the ark of the LORD was in the
country of the Phĭ-lĭs'tĭnes seven
months.
2 And the Phĭ-lĭs'tĭnes [a]called for
the priests and the diviners, saying,
What shall we do to the ark of the
LORD? tell us wherewith we shall send
it to his place.
3 And they said, If ye send away the
ark of the God of Ĭs'ra-el, send it not
[b]empty; but in any wise return him
[c]a trespass offering: then ye shall be
healed, and it shall be known to you
why his hand is not removed from you.
4 Then said they, What *shall be* the
trespass offering which we shall return
to him? They answered, Five golden
emerods, and five golden mice, [d]*according to* the number of the lords of
the Phĭ-lĭs'tĭnes: for one plague *was* on
[1]you all, and on your lords.
5 Wherefore ye shall make images
of your emerods, and images of your
mice that [e]mar the land; and ye shall
[f]give glory unto the God of Ĭs'ra-el: peradventure he will [g]lighten his hand
from off you, and from off your gods,
and from off your land.
6 Wherefore then do ye harden
your hearts, [h]as the E-ġўp''tians and
Phā'raōh hardened their hearts? when
he had wrought [2]wonderfully among
them, [i]did they not let [3]the people go,
and they departed?
7 Now therefore make [j]a new cart,
and take two milch kine, [k]on which
there hath come no yoke, and tie the
kine to the cart, and bring their calves
home from them:
8 And take the ark of the LORD, and
lay it upon the cart; and put the jewels
of gold, which ye return him *for* a trespass offering, in a coffer by the side
thereof; and send it away, that it may
go.
9 And see, if it goeth up by the way
of his own coast to [l]Bĕth–shē'mĕsh,
then [4]he hath done us this great evil:
but if not, then we shall know that *it is*
not his hand *that* smote us; it *was* a
chance *that* happened to us.
10 ¶ And the men did so; and took
two milch kine, and tied them to the
cart, and shut up their calves at home:
11 And they laid the ark of the LORD
upon the cart, and the coffer with the
mice of gold and the images of their
emerods.
12 And the kine took the straight
way to the way of Bĕth–shē'mĕsh, *and*
[5]went along the highway, lowing as
they went, and turned not aside *to* the
right hand or *to* the left; and the lords
of the Phĭ-lĭs'tĭnes went after them
unto the border of Bĕth–shē'mĕsh.
13 And *they of* Bĕth–shē'mĕsh *were*
reaping their wheat harvest in the valley: and they lifted up their eyes, and
saw the ark, and rejoiced to see *it*.
14 And the cart came into the field of
Jŏsh'u-ȧ, a Bĕth–shē'mīte, and stood
there, where *there was* a great stone:
and they clave the wood of the cart, and
offered the kine a burnt offering unto
the LORD.
15 And the Lē'vītes took down the
ark of the LORD, and the coffer that
was with it, wherein the jewels of gold
were, and put *them* on the great stone:
and the men of Bĕth–shē'mĕsh offered
burnt offerings and sacrificed sacrifices the same day unto the LORD.
16 And when [m]the five lords of the
Phĭ-lĭs'tĭnes had seen *it*, they returned
to Ĕk'rŏn the same day.
17 And these *are* the golden emerods which the Phĭ-lĭs'tĭnes returned *for*
a trespass offering unto the LORD; for

CHAPTER 5
3 [a]Ex. 12.12; Judg. 16.23
[b]Ex. 18.11; 1 Chr. 16.24-25-26; Ps. 95.3; Ps. 96.4-5; Isa. 19.1; Nah. 1.14
[c]Isa. 46.7
4 [d]Isa. 40.18
[e]Jer. 50.2; Ezek. 6.4-6; Mic. 1.7
[1]Or, the fishy part. The upper part of Dagon resembled a man, and the lower a fish
5 [f]Zeph. 1.9
6 [g]verses 7-11; Ex. 9.3; Ps. 9.17; Ps. 32.4; Acts 13.11
[h]ch. 6.5
[i]Deut. 28.27; Ps. 78.66
9 [j]Deut. 2.15; ch. 7.13
[k]Ps. 78.66
10 [2]me, to slay me and my
11 [3]me not, and my
12 [l]Ex. 11.6; Amos 5.17

CHAPTER 6
2 [a]Gen. 41.8; Matt. 2.4
3 [b]Ex. 23.15; Deut. 16.16
[c]Lev. 5.15; Lev. 6.6
4 [d]Josh. 13.3; Judg. 3.3
[1]them
5 [e]ch. 5.6
[f]Josh. 7.19; Rev. 14.7
[g]Ex. 9.3; Acts 13.11
6 [h]Ex. 7.13; Ex. 8.15
[2]Or, reproachfully
[i]Ex. 3.19-20; Ps. 105.38
[3]them
7 [j]2 Sam. 6.3
[k]Num. 19.2
9 [l]Josh. 15.10
[4]Or, it
12 [5]in a street they went
16 [m]Josh. 13.3; Zeph. 2.5

Ăsh′dŏd one, for Gā′zȧ one, for Ăs′ke-
lŏn one, for Găth one, for Ĕk′rŏn one;
18 And the golden mice, *according*
to the number of all the cities of the
Phĭ-lĭs′tĭnes *belonging* to the five lords,
both of fenced cities, and of country
villages, even unto the [6]great *stone of*
Ā′bĕl, whereon they set down the ark
of the LORD: *which stone remaineth*
unto this day in the field of Jŏsh′u-ȧ,
the Bĕth–shē′mīte.
19 ¶ And [n]he smote the men of Bĕth–
shē′mĕsh, because they had looked into
the ark of the LORD, even he smote of
the people fifty thousand and threescore and ten men: and the people lamented, because the LORD had smitten
many of the people with a great slaughter.
20 And the men of Bĕth–shē′mĕsh
said, [o]Who is able to stand before this
holy LORD God? and to whom shall he
go up from us?
21 ¶ And they sent messengers to
the inhabitants of [p]Kĭr′jath–jē′a-rĭm,
saying, The Phĭ-lĭs′tĭnes have brought
again the ark of the LORD; come ye
down, *and* fetch it up to you.

7 And the men of [a]Kĭr′jath–jē′a-rĭm
came, and fetched up the ark of the
LORD, and brought it into the house of
[b]A-bĭn′ă-dăb in the hill, and sanctified
Ē-le-ā′zar his son to keep the ark of the
LORD.
2 And it came to pass, while the
ark abode in Kĭr′jath–jē′a-rĭm, that
the time was long; for it was twenty
years: and all the house of Ĭs′ra-el lamented after the LORD.
3 ¶ And Săm′u-el spake unto all the
house of Ĭs′ra-el, saying, If ye do [c]re-
turn unto the LORD with all your hearts,
then [d]put away the strange gods and
[e]Ăsh′ta-rŏth from among you, and
[f]prepare your hearts unto the LORD,
and [g]serve him only: and he will deliver you out of the hand of the Phĭ-
lĭs′tĭnes.
4 Then the children of Ĭs′ra-el did
put away [h]Bā′al-ĭm and Ăsh′ta-rŏth,
and served the LORD only.
5 And Săm′u-el said, [i]Gather all Ĭs′-
ra-el to Mĭz′peh, and I will pray for you
unto the LORD.
6 And they gathered together to
Mĭz′peh, and [j]drew water, and poured
it out before the LORD, and [k]fasted on
that day, and said there, [l]We have
sinned against the LORD. And Săm′u-
el judged the children of Ĭs′ra-el in
Mĭz′peh.
7 And when the Phĭ-lĭs′tĭnes heard
that the children of Ĭs′ra-el were gathered together to Mĭz′peh, the lords of
the Phĭ-lĭs′tĭnes went up against Ĭs′ra-
el. And when the children of Ĭs′ra-el
heard *it*, they were afraid of the Phĭ-
lĭs′tĭnes.
8 And the children of Ĭs′ra-el said to
Săm′u-el, [1]Cease not to cry unto the
LORD our God for us, that he will save
us out of the hand of the Phĭ-lĭs′tĭnes.
9 ¶ And Săm′u-el took a sucking
lamb, and offered *it for* a burnt offering
wholly unto the LORD: and [m]Săm′u-el
cried unto the LORD for Ĭs′ra-el; and the
LORD [2]heard him.
10 And as Săm′u-el was offering
up the burnt offering, the Phĭ-lĭs′tĭnes
drew near to battle against Ĭs′ra-el:
[n]but the LORD thundered with a great
thunder on that day upon the Phĭ-lĭs′-
tĭnes, and discomfited them; and they
were smitten before Ĭs′ra-el.
11 And the men of Ĭs′ra-el went out
of Mĭz′peh, and pursued the Phĭ-lĭs′-
tĭnes, and smote them, until *they came*
under Bĕth′–căr.
12 Then Săm′u-el took a stone, and
set *it* between Mĭz′peh and Shĕn, and
called the name of it [3]Ĕb′en–ē′zēr, saying, Hitherto hath the LORD helped us.
13 ¶ [o]So the Phĭ-lĭs′tĭnes were subdued, and they [p]came no more into the
coast of Ĭs′ra-el: and the hand of the
LORD was against the Phĭ-lĭs′tĭnes all
the days of Săm′u-el.
14 And the cities which the Phĭ-lĭs′-
tĭnes had taken from Ĭs′ra-el were restored to Ĭs′ra-el, from Ĕk′rŏn even
unto Găth; and the coasts thereof did
Ĭs′ra-el deliver out of the hands of the
Phĭ-lĭs′tĭnes. And there was peace between Ĭs′ra-el and the Ăm′ôr-ītes.
15 And Săm′u-el [q]judged Ĭs′ra-el all
the days of his life.
16 And he went from year to year [4]in
circuit to Bĕth′–el, and Gĭl′găl, and
Mĭz′peh, and judged Ĭs′ra-el in all those
places.
17 And his return *was* to Rā′mah;
for there *was* his house; and there he
judged Ĭs′ra-el; and there he built [r]an
altar unto the LORD.

8 And it came to pass, when Săm′u-el
was old, that he [a]made his [b]sons
judges over Ĭs′ra-el.
2 Now the name of his firstborn was
[1]Jō′el; and the name of his second,
A-bī′ah: *they were* judges in Bē′er–
shē′bȧ.
3 And his sons [c]walked not in his
ways, but turned aside after [d]lucre,
and [e]took bribes, and perverted judgment.
4 Then all the elders of Ĭs′ra-el gathered themselves together, and came to
Săm′u-el unto Rā′mah,
5 And said unto him, Behold, thou
art old, and thy sons walk not in thy
ways: now [f]make us a king to judge us
like all the nations.
6 ¶ But the thing [2]displeased Săm′u-
el, when they said, Give us a king to
judge us. And Săm′u-el [g]prayed unto
the LORD.
7 And the LORD said unto Săm′u-el,
Hearken unto the voice of the people
in all that they say unto thee: for [h]they
have not rejected thee, but [i]they have
rejected me, that I should not reign
over them.
8 According to all the works which
they have done since the day that I
brought them up out of Ē′gypt even
unto this day, wherewith they have forsaken me, and served other gods, so do
they also unto thee.
9 Now therefore [3]hearken unto their
voice: [4]howbeit yet protest solemnly

18 [6]Or, great Abel, that is, mourning
19 [n]Ex. 19.21; 1 Pet. 4.17
20 [o]2 Sam. 6.9;
21 [p]Josh. 18.14

CHAPTER 7
1 [a]ch. 6.21;
[b]2 Sam. 6.3
3 [c]Deut. 30.2;
[d]Gen. 35.2
[e]Judg. 2.13
[f]Deut. 30.6;
[g]Deut. 6.13
4 [h]Judg. 2.11
5 [i]Judg. 10.17
6 [j]2 Sam. 14.14
[k]Neh. 9.1-2;
[l]Lev. 26.40
8 [1]Be not silent from us from crying
9 [m]Ps. 99.6
[2]Or, answered
10 [n]Josh. 10.10
12 [3]That is, The stone of help
13 [o]Judg. 13.1
[p]ch. 13.5
15 [q]ch. 12.11
16 [4]and he circuited
17 [r]Judg. 21.4

CHAPTER 8
1 [a]Deut. 16.18
[b]Judg. 10.4;
2 [1]Vashni
3 [c]Eccl. 2.19;
[d]Ex. 18.21;
[e]Deut. 16.19
5 [f]ch. 12.13
6 [2]was evil in the eyes of Samuel
[g]ch. 15.11;
7 [h]Ex. 16.8;
[i]ch. 10.19
9 [3]Or, obey
[4]Or, notwithstanding when thou hast solemnly protested against them, then thou shalt shew, etc

unto them, and shew them the manner
of the king that shall reign over them.
10 ¶ And Săm'u-el told all the words
of the LORD unto the people that asked
of him a king.
11 And he said, [j]This will be the
manner of the king that shall reign
over you: [k]He will take your sons, and
appoint *them* for himself, for his chariots, and *to be* his horsemen; and *some*
shall run before his chariots.
12 And he will appoint him captains
over thousands, and captains over fifties; and *will set them* to ear his
ground, and to reap his harvest, and to
make his instruments of war, and instruments of his chariots.
13 And he will take your daughters
to be confectionaries, and *to be* cooks,
and *to be* bakers.
14 And [l]he will take your fields, and
your vineyards, and your oliveyards,
even the best *of them*, and give *them* to
his servants.
15 And he will take the tenth of your
seed, and of your vineyards, and give
to his [5]officers, and to his servants.
16 And he will take your menservants, and your maidservants, and
your goodliest young men, and your
asses, and put *them* to his work.
17 He will take the tenth of your
sheep: and ye shall be his servants.
18 And ye shall cry out in that day
because of your king which ye shall
have chosen you; and the LORD [m]will
not hear you in that day.
19 ¶ Nevertheless the people [n]re-
fused to obey the voice of Săm'u-el;
and they said, Nay; but we will have a
king over us;
20 That we also may be like all the
nations; and that our king may judge
us, and go out before us, and fight our
battles.
21 And Săm'u-el heard all the words
of the people, and he rehearsed them in
the ears of the LORD.
22 And the LORD said to Săm'u-el,
[o]Hearken unto their voice, and make
them a king. And Săm'u-el said unto
the men of Ĭs'ra-el, Go ye every man
unto his city.

9 Now there was a man of Bĕn'ja-
min, whose name *was* [a]Kĭsh, the
son of A-bī'el, the son of Zē'rôr, the son
of Be-chō'răth, the son of A-phī'ah, [1]a
Bĕn'ja-mīte, a mighty man of [2]power.
2 And he had a son, whose name
was Sa̤ul, a choice young man, and a
goodly: and *there was* not among the
children of Ĭs'ra-el a goodlier person
than he: [b]from his shoulders and upward *he was* higher than any of the
people.
3 And the asses of Kĭsh Sa̤ul's father
were lost. And Kĭsh said to Sa̤ul his
son, Take now one of the servants with
thee, and arise, go seek the asses.
4 And he passed through mount
Ē'phră-ĭm, and passed through the
land of [c]Shăl'ĭ-shă, but they found
them not: then they passed through the
land of Shā'lim, and *there they were*
not: and he passed through the land of
the Bĕn'ja-mītes, but they found *them*
not.
5 *And* when they were come to the
land of [d]Zŭph, Sa̤ul said to his servant
that *was* with him, Come, and let us
return; lest my father leave *caring* for
the asses, and take thought for us.
6 And he said unto him, Behold now,
there is in this city [e]a man of God, and
he is an honourable man; all [f]that he
saith cometh surely to pass: now let us
go thither; peradventure he can shew
us our way that we should go.
7 Then said Sa̤ul to his servant, But,
behold, *if* we [g]go, what shall we bring
the man? for the bread [3]is spent in our
vessels, and *there is* not a present to
bring to the man of God: what [4]have
we?
8 And the servant answered Sa̤ul
again, and said, Behold, [5]I have here at
hand the fourth part of a shekel of silver: *that* will I give to the man of God,
to tell us our way.
9 (Beforetime in Ĭs'ra-el, when a man
[h]went to inquire of God, thus he spake,
Come, and let us go to the seer: for *he
that is* now *called* a Prophet was beforetime called [i]a Seer.)
10 Then said Sa̤ul to his servant,
[6]Well said; come, let us go. So they
went unto the city where the man of
God *was*.
11 ¶ *And* as they went up [7]the hill to
the city, [j]they found young maidens
going out to draw water, and said unto
them, Is the seer here?
12 And they answered them, and
said, He is; behold, *he is* before you:
make haste now, for he came to day to
the city; for [k]*there is* a [8]sacrifice of the
people to day in the [l]high place:
13 As soon as ye be come into the
city, ye shall straightway find him, before he go up to the high place to eat:
for the people will not eat until he
come, because he doth bless the sacrifice; *and* afterwards they eat that be
bidden. Now therefore get you up; for
about [9]this time ye shall find him.
14 And they went up into the city:
and when they were come into the
city, behold, Săm'u-el came out against
them, for to go up to the high place.
15 ¶ [m]Now the LORD had [10]told Săm'-
u-el in his ear a day before Sa̤ul came,
saying,
16 To morrow about this time I will
send thee a man out of the land of
Bĕn'ja-min, and [n]thou shalt anoint him
to be captain over my people Ĭs'ra-el,
that he may save my people out of the
hand of the Phĭ-lĭs'tīnes: for I have
[o]looked upon my people, because their
cry is come unto me.
17 And when Săm'u-el saw Sa̤ul, the
LORD said unto him, [p]Behold the man
whom I spake to thee of! this same shall
[11]reign over my people.
18 Then Sa̤ul drew near to Săm'u-el
in the gate, and said, Tell me, I pray
thee, where the seer's house *is*.
19 And Săm'u-el answered Sa̤ul, and
said, I *am* the seer: go up before me
unto the high place; for ye shall eat

11 [j]Deut. 17.16
[k]ch. 14.52; 2 Chr. 26.10-15
14 [l]1 Ki. 21.7
15 [5]eunuchs
18 [m]Job 27.9; Ps. 18.41; Prov. 1.25; Isa. 1.15; Mic. 3.4; Luke 13.25
19 [n]Isa. 66.4; Jer. 44.16
22 [o]Hos. 13.11
CHAPTER 9
1 [a]ch. 14.51; 1 Chr. 8.33; Acts 13.21
[1]Or, the son of a man of Jemini
[2]Or, substance
2 [b]ch. 10.23
4 [c]2 Ki. 4.42
5 [d]ch. 1.1
6 [e]Deut. 33.1; ch. 2.27; 1 Ki. 13.1; 2 Ki. 6.6; 1 Tim. 6.11
[f]ch. 3.19; Isa. 44.26; Matt. 24.35
7 [g]Judg. 6.18; 2 Ki. 4.42
[3]is gone out of, etc
[4]is with us
8 [5]there is found in my hand
9 [h]Gen. 25.22; Judg. 1.1
[i]2 Sam. 24.11; Amos 7.12
10 [6]Thy word is good
11 [7]in the ascent of the city
[j]Gen. 24.11; Ex. 2.16
12 [k]Gen. 31.54; ch. 16.2
[8]Or, feast
[l]1 Ki. 3.2
13 [9]today
15 [m]ch. 15.1; Acts 13.21
[10]revealed the ear of Samuel
16 [n]ch. 10.1; ch. 16.3
[o]Ex. 2.25; Ex. 3.7-9
17 [p]ch. 16.12; Hos. 13.11
[11]restrain in

with me to day, and to morrow I will let
thee go, and will tell thee all that *is* in
thine heart.
20 And as for thine asses that were
lost [12]three days ago, set not thy mind
on them; for they are found. And on
whom *is* all the desire of Ĭs′ra-el? *Is it*
not on thee, and on all thy father's
house?
21 And Saul answered and said, *Am*
not I a Bĕn′ja-mīte, of [q]the smallest of
the tribes of Ĭs′ra-el? and my [r]family
the least of all the families of the tribe
of Bĕn′ja-min? wherefore then speakest thou [13]so to me?
22 And Săm′u-el took Saul and his
servant, and brought them into the parlour, and made them sit in the chiefest
place among them that were bidden,
which *were* about thirty persons.
23 And Săm′u-el said unto the cook,
Bring the portion which I gave thee, of
which I said unto thee, Set it by thee.
24 And the cook took up [s]the shoulder, and *that* which *was* upon it, and
set *it* before Saul. And *Săm′u-el* said,
Behold that which is [14]left! set *it* before
thee, *and* eat: for unto this time hath it
been kept for thee since I said, I have
invited the people. So Saul did eat with
Săm′u-el that day.
25 ¶ And when they were come down
from the high place into the city, *Sam′-*
u-el communed with Saul upon [t]the
top of the house.
26 And they arose early: and it came
to pass about the spring of the day,
that Săm′u-el called Saul to the top of
the house, saying, Up, that I may send
thee away. And Saul arose, and they
went out both of them, he and Săm′u-
el, abroad.
27 *And* as they were going down to
the end of the city, Săm′u-el said to
Saul, Bid the servant pass on before us,
(and he passed on,) but stand thou still
[15]a while, that I may [16]shew thee the
word of God.

10 Then [a]Săm′u-el took a vial of oil,
and poured *it* upon his head, and
kissed him, and said, *Is it* not because
the LORD hath anointed thee *to be* captain over [b]his inheritance?
2 When thou art departed from me
to day, then thou shalt find two men by
[c]Rā′chel's sepulchre in the border of
Bĕn′ja-min [d]at Zĕl′zah; and they will
say unto thee, The asses which thou
wentest to seek are found: and, lo, thy
father hath left [1]the care of the asses,
and sorroweth for you, saying, What
shall I do for my son?
3 Then shalt thou go on forward
from thence, and thou shalt come to
the plain of [e]Tā′bôr, and there shall
meet thee three men going up to God
[f]to Bĕth′–el, one carrying three kids,
and another carrying three loaves of
bread, and another carrying a bottle of
wine:
4 And they will [2]salute thee, and give
thee two *loaves* of bread; which thou
shalt receive of their hands.
5 After that thou shalt come to the
hill of God, [g]where *is* the garrison of
the Phĭ-lĭs′tĭnes: and it shall come to
pass, when thou art come thither to the
city, that thou shalt meet a company of
prophets coming down [h]from the high
place with a psaltery, and a tabret, and
a pipe, and a harp, before them; [i]and
they shall prophesy:
6 And [j]the Spirit of the LORD will
come upon thee, and [k]thou shalt prophesy with them, and shalt be turned into
another man.
7 And [3]let it be, when [l]these signs
are come unto thee, [4]*that* thou do as
occasion serve thee; for [m]God *is* with
thee.
8 And thou shalt go down before me
[n]to Gĭl′găl; and, behold, I will come
down unto thee, to offer burnt offerings, *and* to sacrifice sacrifices of peace
offerings: [o]seven days shalt thou tarry,
till I come to thee, and shew thee what
thou shalt do.
9 ¶ And it was *so,* that when he had
turned his [5]back to go from Săm′u-el,
God [6]gave him another heart: and all
those signs came to pass that day.
10 And when they came thither to
the hill, behold, [p]a company of prophets met him; and the Spirit of God
came upon him, and [q]he prophesied
among them.
11 And it came to pass, when all
that knew him beforetime saw that, behold, he prophesied among the prophets, then the people said [7]one to another, What *is* this *that* is come unto
the son of Kĭsh? [r]*Is* Saul also among
the prophets?
12 And one [8]of the same place answered and said, But [s]who *is* their father? Therefore it became a proverb, *Is*
Saul also among the prophets?
13 And when he had made an end
of prophesying, he came to the high
place.
14 ¶ And Saul's [t]uncle said unto him
and to his servant, Whither went ye?
And he said, To seek the asses: and
when we saw that *they were* no where,
we came to Săm′u-el.
15 And Saul's uncle said, Tell me, I
pray thee, what Săm′u-el said unto
you.
16 And Saul said unto his uncle, He
told us plainly that the asses were
found. But of the matter of the kingdom, whereof Săm′u-el spake, he told
him not.
17 ¶ And Săm′u-el called the people
together [u]unto the LORD [v]to Mĭz′peh;
18 And said unto the children of Ĭs′-
ra-el, [w]Thus saith the LORD God of
Ĭs′ra-el, I brought up Ĭs′ra-el out of
Ē′gypt, and delivered you out of the
hand of the E-gyp′′tians, and out of the
hand of all kingdoms, *and* of them that
oppressed you:
19 And [x]ye have this day rejected
your God, who himself saved you out
of all your adversities and your tribulations; and ye have said unto him, *Nay,*
but set a king over us. Now therefore
present yourselves before the LORD by
your tribes, and by your thousands.

20 [12]today three days
21 [q]Judg. 20.46-48; Ps. 68.27
[r]Judg. 6.15
[13]according to this word?
24 [s]Lev. 7.32; Ezek. 24.4
[14]Or, reserved
25 [t]Deut. 22.8; Acts 10.9
27 [15]today
[16]Or, cause thee to hear

CHAPTER 10
1 [a]ch. 16.13; 2 Ki. 9.3
[b]Ex. 19.5-6; Jer. 10.16
2 [c]Gen. 35.19
[d]Josh. 18.28
[1]the business
3 [e]Josh. 19.22; Ps. 89.12
[f]Gen. 28.22; Gen. 35.1
4 [2]ask thee of peace
5 [g]ch. 13.3
[h]ch. 9.12
[i]Ex. 15.20; 1 Cor. 14.1
6 [j]Num. 11.25; Matt. 7.22
[k]ch. 19.23
7 [3]it shall come to pass, that when those signs, etc
[l]Ex. 4.8
[4]do for thee as thine hand shall find
[m]Gen. 21.20; Matt. 1.23
8 [n]ch. 11.14
[o]ch. 13.8
9 [5]shoulder
[6]turned
10 [p]ch. 19.20
[q]Matt. 7.21-23
11 [7]a man to his neighbour
[r]Matt. 13.54; Acts 4.13
12 [8]from thence
[s]Isa. 54.13
14 [t]ch. 14.50
17 [u]Judg. 11.11; ch. 11.15
[v]ch. 7.5
18 [w]Ex. 3.7-8;
19 [x]ch. 8.7

20 And when Săm'u-el had [y]caused
all the tribes of Ĭs'ra-el to come near,
the tribe of Bĕn'ja-min was taken.
21 When he had caused the tribe of
Bĕn'ja-min to come near by their families, the family of Mā'trī was taken,
and Sạul the son of Kĭsh was taken:
and when they sought him, he could
not be found.
22 Therefore they [z]inquired of the
LORD further, if the man should yet
come thither. And the LORD answered,
Behold, he hath hid himself among the
stuff.
23 And they ran and fetched him
thence: and when he stood among the
people, he was higher than any of the
people from his shoulders and upward.
24 And Săm'u-el said to all the people, See ye him whom the LORD hath
chosen, that *there is* none like him
among all the people? And all the people shouted, and said, [9]God save the
king.
25 Then Săm'u-el told the people the
[a]manner of the kingdom, and wrote *it*
in a book, and laid *it* up before the
LORD. And Săm'u-el sent all the people
away, every man to his house.
26 ¶ And Sạul also went home to
Gĭb'e-ah; and there went with him a
band of men, whose hearts God had
touched.
27 But [b]the children of Bē'lĭ-al said,
How shall this man save us? And they
despised him, [c]and brought him no
presents. But he [10]held his peace.

11 Then Nā'hăsh the Ăm'mŏn-īte
came up, and encamped against
[a]Jā'besh–gĭl'e-ăd: and all the men of
Jā'besh said unto Nā'hăsh, [b]Make a
covenant with us, and we will serve
thee.
2 And Nā'hăsh the Ăm'mŏn-īte answered them, On this *condition* will I
make *a covenant* with you, that I may
thrust out all your right eyes, and lay it
for [c]a reproach upon all Ĭs'ra-el.
3 And the elders of Jā'besh said unto
him, [1]Give us seven days' respite, that
we may send messengers unto all the
coasts of Ĭs'ra-el: and then, if *there be*
no man to save us, we will come out to
thee.
4 ¶ Then came the messengers [d]to
Gĭb'e-ah of Sạul, and told the tidings in
the ears of the people: and [e]all the people lifted up their voices, and wept.
5 And, behold, Sạul came after the
herd out of the field; and Sạul said,
What *aileth* the people that they weep?
And they told him the tidings of the
men of Jā'besh.
6 [f]And the Spirit of God came upon
Sạul when he heard those tidings, and
his anger was kindled greatly.
7 And he took a yoke of oxen, and
[g]hewed them in pieces, and sent *them*
throughout all the coasts of Ĭs'ra-el
by the hands of messengers, saying,
[h]Whosoever cometh not forth after
Sạul and after Săm'u-el, so shall it be
done unto his oxen. [i]And the fear of
the LORD fell on the people, and they
came out [2]with one consent.
8 And when he numbered them in
[j]Bē'zek, the children [k]of Ĭs'ra-el were
three hundred thousand, and the men
of Jū'dah thirty thousand.
9 And they said unto the messengers that came, Thus shall ye say unto
the men of Jā'besh–gĭl'e-ăd, To morrow, by *that time* the sun be hot, ye
shall have [3]help. And the messengers
came and shewed *it* to the men of
Jā'besh; and they were glad.
10 Therefore the men of Jā'besh
said, To morrow we will come out unto
you, and ye shall do with us all that
seemeth good unto you.
11 And it was *so* on the morrow, that
[l]Sạul put the people [m]in three companies; and they came into the midst of
the host in the morning watch, and
slew the Ăm'mŏn-ītes until the heat
of the day: and it came to pass, that
they which remained were scattered,
so [n]that two of them were not left together.
12 ¶ And the people said unto Săm'-
u-el, [o]Who *is* he that said, Shall Sạul
reign over us? [p]bring the men, that we
may put them to death.
13 And Sạul said, [q]There shall not a
man be put to death this day: for to day
[r]the LORD hath wrought salvation in
Ĭs'ra-el.
14 Then said Săm'u-el to the people,
Come, and let us go [s]to Gĭl'găl, and
renew the kingdom there.
15 And all the people went to Gĭl'-
găl; and there they made Sạul king before the LORD in Gĭl'găl; and there they
sacrificed sacrifices of peace offerings
before the LORD; and there Sạul and all
the men of Ĭs'ra-el rejoiced greatly.

12 And Săm'u-el said unto all Ĭs'ra-
el, Behold, I have hearkened unto
[a]your voice in all that ye said unto me,
and [b]have made a king over you.
2 And now, behold, the king [c]walk-
eth before you: and I am old and grayheaded; and, behold, my sons *are* with
you: and I have walked before you
from my childhood unto this day.
3 Behold, here I *am:* witness against
me before the LORD, and before his
anointed: [d]whose ox have I taken? or
whose ass have I taken? or whom have
I defrauded? whom have I oppressed?
or of whose hand have I received *any*
[1]bribe [2]to [e]blind mine eyes therewith?
and I will restore it you.
4 And they said, Thou hast not defrauded us, nor oppressed us, neither
hast thou taken ought of any man's
hand.
5 And he said unto them, The LORD
is witness against you, and his anointed
is witness this day, [f]that ye have not
found ought [g]in my hand. And they answered, *He is* witness.
6 ¶ And Săm'u-el said unto the people, [h]*It is* the LORD that [3]advanced Mō'-
ses and Aâr'on, and that brought your
fathers up out of the land of Ē'gypt.
7 Now therefore stand still, that I
may [i]reason with you before the LORD
of all the [4]righteous acts of the LORD,

20 [y]Josh. 7.14; Acts 1.22-24
22 [z]ch. 23.2
24 [9]Let the king live
25 [a]Deut. 17.14-20; ch. 8.11
27 [b]Deut. 13.13; Acts 7.35-51-52
[c]2 Sam. 8.2; Matt. 2.11
[10]Or, he was as though he had been deaf

CHAPTER 11

1 [a]Judg. 21.8; ch. 31.11-13
[b]Gen. 26.28; Ezek. 17.13
2 [c]Gen. 34.14; ch. 17.26
3 [1]Forbear us
4 [d]ch. 10.26; 2 Sam. 21.6
[e]Judg. 2.4; Rom. 12.15
6 [f]Judg. 3.10
7 [g]Judg. 19.29
[h]Judg. 21.5
[i]Gen. 35.5;
[2]as one man
8 [j]Judg. 1.5
[k]2 Sam. 24.9
9 [3]Or, deliverance
11 [l]ch. 31.11
[m]Judg. 7.16
[n]Jas. 2.13
12 [o]ch. 10.27;
[p]Luke 19.27
13 [q]2 Sam. 19.22
[r]Ex. 14.13-30
14 [s]ch. 10.8

CHAPTER 12

1 [a]ch. 8.5
[b]ch. 10.24
2 [c]Num. 27.17
3 [d]Num. 16.15;
[1]ransom
[2]Or, that I should hide mine eyes at him
[e]Deut. 16.19
5 [f]John 18.38;
[g]Ex. 22.4
6 [h]Ex. 6.26;
[3]Or, made
7 [i]Isa. 1.18;
[4]righteousnesses, or, benefits

which he did [5]to you and to your fathers.

8 When Jā'cob was come into Ē'gypt, and your fathers cried unto the LORD, then the LORD sent Mō'ses and Aâr'on, which brought forth your fathers out of Ē'gypt, and made them dwell in this place.

9 And when they forgat the LORD their God, he sold them into the hand of Sĭs'e-rȧ, captain of the host of Hā'zôr, and into the hand of the Phĭ-lĭs'tĭnes, and into the hand of the king of Mō'ab, and they fought against them.

10 And they cried unto the LORD, and said, We have sinned, because we have forsaken the LORD, and have served Bā'al-ĭm and Ăsh'ta-rŏth: but now deliver us out of the hand of our enemies, and we will serve thee.

11 And the LORD sent Je-rŭb'ba-ăl, and Bē'dăn, and Jĕph'thah, and Săm'u-el, and delivered you out of the hand of your enemies on every side, and ye dwelled safe.

12 And when ye saw that Nā'hăsh the king of the children of Ăm'mŏn came against you, ye said unto me, Nay; but a king shall reign over us: when [j]the LORD your God *was* your king.

13 Now therefore behold the king whom ye have chosen, *and* whom ye have desired! and, behold, [k]the LORD hath set a king over you.

14 If ye will [l]fear the LORD, and serve him, and obey his voice, and not rebel against the [6]commandment of the LORD, then shall both ye and also the king that reigneth over you [7]continue following the LORD your God:

15 But if ye will [m]not obey the voice of the LORD, but rebel against the commandment of the LORD, then shall the hand of the LORD be against you, as *it was* against your fathers.

16 ¶ Now therefore stand and see this great thing, which the LORD will do before your eyes.

17 *Is it* not [n]wheat harvest today? [o]I will call unto the LORD, and he shall send thunder and rain; that ye may perceive and see that [p]your wickedness *is* great, which ye have done in the sight of the LORD, in asking you a king.

18 So Săm'u-el called unto the LORD; and the LORD sent thunder and rain that day: [q]and all the people greatly feared the LORD and Săm'u-el.

19 And all the people said unto Săm'u-el, [r]Pray for thy servants unto the LORD thy God, that we die not: for we have added unto all our sins *this* evil, to ask us a king.

20 ¶ And Săm'u-el said unto the people, Fear not: ye have done all this wickedness: yet turn not aside from following the LORD, but serve the LORD with all your heart;

21 And turn ye not aside: [s]for *then should ye go* after vain *things,* which cannot profit nor deliver; for they *are* vain.

22 For the LORD will not forsake his people [t]for his great name's sake: because [u]it hath pleased the LORD to make you his people.

23 Moreover as for me, [v]God forbid that I should sin against the LORD [8]in ceasing to pray for you: but I will teach you the [w]good and the right way:

24 Only fear the LORD, and serve him in truth with all your [x]heart: for consider [9]how great *things* he hath done for you.

25 But if ye shall still do wickedly, [y]ye shall be consumed, [z]both ye and your king.

13

Saul [1]reigned one year; and when he had reigned two years over Ĭs'ra-el,

2 Saul chose him three thousand *men* of Ĭs'ra-el; *whereof* two thousand were with Saul in Mĭch'mash and in mount Bĕth'–el, and a thousand were with Jŏn'a-than in Gĭb'e-ah of Bĕn'ja-min: and the rest of the people he sent every man to his tent.

3 And Jŏn'a-than smote [a]the garrison of the Phĭ-lĭs'tĭnes that *was* in [2]Gē'bȧ, and the Phĭ-lĭs'tĭnes heard *of it.* And Saul blew the trumpet throughout all the land, saying, Let the Hē'brews hear.

4 And all Ĭs'ra-el heard say *that* Saul had smitten a garrison of the Phĭ-lĭs'tĭnes, and *that* Ĭs'ra-el also [3]was had in abomination with the Phĭ-lĭs'tĭnes. And the people were called together after Saul to Gĭl'găl.

5 ¶ And the Phĭ-lĭs'tĭnes gathered themselves together to fight with Ĭs'ra-el, thirty thousand chariots, and six thousand horsemen, and people as the sand which *is* on the sea shore in multitude: and they came up, and pitched in Mĭch'mash, eastward [b]from Bĕth–ā'-ven.

6 When the men of Ĭs'ra-el saw that they were in a strait, (for the people were distressed,) then the people [c]did hide themselves in caves, and in thickets, and in rocks, and in high places, and in pits.

7 And *some of* the Hē'brews went over Jôr'dan to the land of Găd and Gĭl'e-ăd. As for Saul, he *was* yet in Gĭl'găl, and all the people [4]followed him trembling.

8 ¶ [d]And he tarried seven days, according to the set time that Săm'u-el *had appointed:* but Săm'u-el came not to Gĭl'găl; and the people were scattered from him.

9 And Saul said, Bring hither a burnt offering to me, and peace offerings. And he [e]offered the burnt offering.

10 And it came to pass, that as soon as he had made an end of offering the burnt offering, behold, Săm'u-el came; and Saul went out to meet him, that he might [5]salute him.

11 ¶ And Săm'u-el said, What hast thou done? And Saul said, Because I saw that the people were scattered from me, and *that* thou camest not within the days appointed, and *that* the Phĭ-lĭs'tĭnes gathered themselves together at Mĭch'mash;

[5]with
12 [j]Gen. 17.7; Judg. 8.23; ch. 8.7
13 [k]Hos. 13.11
14 [l]Deut. 6.13; Deut. 10.12; Deut. 13.4; Deut. 14.23; Deut. 17.19; Josh. 24.14; Ps. 81.13; Eccl. 8.12; Isa. 3.10
[6]mouth
[7]be after
15 [m]Lev. 26.14; Deut. 28.15; Josh. 24.20
17 [n]Prov. 26.1
[o]Josh. 10.12; ch. 7.9; Jas. 5.16
[p]ch. 8.7; Hos. 13.10
18 [q]Ex. 14.31; Ezra 10.9
19 [r]Gen. 20.7; Ex. 9.28; Ps. 78.34-35; Acts 8.24; Jas. 5.15; 1 John 5.16
21 [s]Jer. 16.19; Hab. 2.18; 1 Cor. 8.4
22 [t]Ps. 106.8; Jer. 14.21
[u]Mal. 1.2; Matt. 11.26; John 15.16
23 [v]1 Cor. 9.16
[8]from ceasing
[w]1 Ki. 8.36; 2 Chr. 6.27; Jer. 6.16
24 [x]Ezra 9.13
[9]Or, what a great thing, etc
25 [y]Josh. 24.20
[z]Deut. 28.36

CHAPTER 13
1 [1]the son of one year in his reigning
3 [a]ch. 10.5
[2]Or, The hill
4 [3]did stink
5 [b]Josh. 18.12
6 [c]Judg. 6.2
7 [4]trembled after him
8 [d]ch. 10.8
9 [e]Deut. 12.5-14; ch. 15.22; 1 Ki. 3.4; Heb. 5.4
10 [5]bless him

12 Therefore said I, The Phĭ-lĭs'tĭnes
will come down now upon me to Gĭl'-
găl, and I have not [6]made supplication
unto the LORD: I forced myself therefore, and offered a burnt offering.
13 And Săm'u-el said to Saul, [f]Thou
hast done foolishly: [g]thou hast not
kept the commandment of the LORD
thy God, which he commanded thee:
for now would the LORD have established thy kingdom upon Ĭs'ra-el for
ever.
14 [h]But now thy kingdom shall not
continue: [i]the LORD hath sought him a
man after his own heart, and the LORD
hath commanded him *to be* captain
over his people, because thou hast not
kept *that* which the LORD commanded
thee.
15 And Săm'u-el arose, and gat him
up from Gĭl'găl unto Gĭb'e-ah of Bĕn'-
ja-min. And Saul numbered the people
that were [7]present with him, [j]about
six hundred men.
16 And Saul, and Jŏn'a-than his son,
and the people *that were* present with
them, abode in [8]Gĭb'e-ah of Bĕn'ja-
min: but the Phĭ-lĭs'tĭnes encamped in
Mĭch'mash.
17 ¶ And the spoilers came out of the
camp of the Phĭ-lĭs'tĭnes in three companies: one company turned unto the
way *that leadeth to* [k]Ŏph'rah, unto the
land of Shu'al:
18 And another company turned the
way *to* [l]Bĕth–hō'rŏn: and another
company turned *to* the way of the border that looketh to the valley of [9]Ze-
bō'im toward the wilderness.
19 ¶ Now [m]there was no smith found
throughout all the land of Ĭs'ra-el: for
the Phĭ-lĭs'tĭnes said, Lest the Hē'-
brews make *them* swords or spears:
20 But all the Ĭs'ra-el-ītes went down
to the Phĭ-lĭs'tĭnes, to sharpen every
man his share, and his coulter, and his
ax, and his mattock.
21 Yet they had [10]a file for the mat-
tocks, and for the coulters, and for
the forks, and for the axes, and [11]to
sharpen the goads.
22 So it came to pass in the day of
battle, that [n]there was neither sword
nor spear found in the hand of any of
the people that *were* with Saul and
Jŏn'a-than: but with Saul and with
Jŏn'a-than his son was there found.
23 And the [12]garrison of the Phĭ-lĭs'-
tĭnes went out to the passage of [o]Mĭch'-
mash.

14 Now [1]it came to pass upon a day,
that Jŏn'a-than the son of Saul
said unto the young man that bare his
armour, Come, and let us go over to
the Phĭ-lĭs'tĭnes' garrison, that *is* on
the other side. But he told not his father.
2 And Saul tarried in the uttermost
part of Gĭb'e-ah under a pomegranate
tree which *is* in Mĭg'rŏn: and the people that *were* with him *were* [a]about six
hundred men;
3 And [b]A-hī'ah, the son of A-hī'tub,
[c]Ī–cha-bŏd's brother, the son of Phĭn'-
e-has, the son of Ē'lī, [d]the LORD'S priest
in Shī'lōh, wearing an ephod. And the
people knew not that Jŏn'a-than was
gone.
4 ¶ And between the passages, by
which Jŏn'a-than sought to go over
[e]unto the Phĭ-lĭs'tĭnes' garrison, *there
was* a sharp rock on the one side, and a
sharp rock on the other side: and the
name of one *was* Bō'zĕz, and the name
of the other Sē'neh.
5 The [2]forefront of the one *was* situate northward over against Mĭch'-
mash, and the other southward over
against Gĭb'e-ah.
6 And Jŏn'a-than said to the young
man that bare his armour, Come, and
let us go over unto the garrison of
these [f]uncircumcised: it may be that
the LORD will work for us: for *there is*
no restraint to the LORD [g]to save by
many or by few.
7 And his armourbearer said unto
him, Do all that *is* in thine heart: turn
thee; behold, I *am* with thee according
to thy heart.
8 Then said Jŏn'a-than, Behold, we
will pass over unto *these* men, and we
will discover ourselves unto them.
9 If they say thus unto us, [3]Tarry until we come to you; then we will stand
still in our place, and will not go up
unto them.
10 But if they say thus, Come up
unto us; then we will go up: for the
LORD hath delivered them into our
hand: and [h]this *shall be* a sign unto us.
11 And both of them discovered
themselves unto the garrison of the
Phĭ-lĭs'tĭnes: and the Phĭ-lĭs'tĭnes said,
Behold, the Hē'brews come forth out
of the holes where they had hid themselves.
12 And the men of the garrison answered Jŏn'a-than and his armourbearer, and said, Come up to us, and we
will shew you a thing. And Jŏn'a-than
said unto his armourbearer, Come up
after me: for the LORD hath delivered
them into the hand of Ĭs'ra-el.
13 And Jŏn'a-than climbed up upon
his hands and upon his feet, and his
armourbearer after him: and they fell
before Jŏn'a-than; and his armourbearer slew after him.
14 And that first slaughter, which
Jŏn'a-than and his armourbearer made,
was about twenty men, within as it were
[4]an half acre of land, *which* a yoke *of
oxen might plow*.
15 And [i]there was trembling in the
host, in the field, and among all the
people: the garrison, and [j]the spoilers, they also trembled, and the earth
quaked: so it was [5]a very great trembling.
16 And the watchmen of Saul in
Gĭb'e-ah of Bĕn'ja-min looked; and, behold, the multitude melted away, and
they went on beating down *one another*.
17 Then said Saul unto the people
that *were* with him, Number now,
and see who is gone from us. And
when they had numbered, behold,

12 [6]intreated the face
13 [f]2 Sam. 12.7-9; 1 Ki. 18.18; 2 Chr. 16.9; Job 34.18; Prov. 19.3; Matt. 14.3-4
[g]ch. 15.11; Lev. 17; Num. 18.7
14 [h]ch. 2.30; ch. 15.28
[i]2 Sam. 7.15; Ps. 78.70; Ps. 89.20; Acts 13.22
15 [7]found
[j]ch. 14.2
16 [8]Geba
17 [k]Josh. 18.23
18 [l]Josh. 18.13-14; 1 Chr. 6.68; 2 Chr. 8.5
[9]Or, serpents
19 [m]2 Ki. 24.14; Jer. 24.1
21 [10]a file with mouths
[11]to set
22 [n]Judg. 3.31; ch. 17.47-50; Zech. 4.6; 1 Cor. 1.27-29
23 [12]Or, standing camp
[o]ch. 14.5

CHAPTER 14
1 [1]Or, there was a day
2 [a]ch. 13.15
3 [b]ch. 22.9-Ahimelech
[c]ch. 4.21
[d]Ex. 28.30; ch. 2.28; ch. 22.18
4 [e]ch. 13.23
5 [2]tooth
6 [f]Gen. 17.7-11; Judg. 14.3; ch. 17.36; 2 Sam. 1.20; 1 Chr. 10.4; Eph. 2.11-12; Phil. 3.3
[g]Deut. 32.30; Rom. 8.31
9 [3]Be still
10 [h]Gen. 24.14; Isa. 7.11-14
14 [4]Or, half a furrow of an acre of land
15 [i]Josh. 2.9; Ps. 14.5
[j]ch. 13.17
[5]a trembling of God

Jŏn'a-than and his armourbearer *were* not *there*.

18 And Sa̤ul said unto A-hī'ah, Bring hither the ark of God. For the ark of God was at that time with the children of Ĭs'ra-el.

19 ¶ And it came to pass, while Sa̤ul [k]talked unto the priest, that the [6]noise that *was* in the host of the Phĭ-lĭs'tĭnes went on and increased: and [l]Sa̤ul said unto the priest, Withdraw thine hand.

20 And Sa̤ul and all the people that *were* with him [7]assembled themselves, and they came to the battle: and, behold, [m]every man's sword was against his fellow, *and there was* a very great discomfiture.

21 Moreover the Hē'brews *that* were with the Phĭ-lĭs'tĭnes before that time, which went up with them into the camp *from the country* round about, even they also *turned* to be with the Ĭs'ra-el-ītes that *were* with Sa̤ul and Jŏn'a-than.

22 Likewise all the men of Ĭs'ra-el which [n]had hid themselves in mount Ē'phră-ĭm, *when* they heard that the Phĭ-lĭs'tĭnes fled, even they also followed hard after them in the battle.

23 So [o]the LORD saved Ĭs'ra-el that day: and the battle passed over [p]unto Bĕth–ā'ven.

24 ¶ And the men of Ĭs'ra-el were distressed that day: for Sa̤ul had [q]adjured the people, saying, Cursed *be* the man that eateth *any* food until evening, that I may be avenged on mine enemies. So none of the people tasted *any* food.

25 [r]And all *they of* the land came to a wood; and there was [s]honey upon the ground.

26 And when the people were come into the wood, behold, the honey dropped; but no man put his hand to his mouth: for the people feared the oath.

27 But Jŏn'a-than heard not when his father charged the people with the oath: wherefore he put forth the end of the rod that *was* in his hand, and dipped it in an [8]honeycomb, and put his hand to his mouth; and his eyes were enlightened.

28 Then answered one of the people, and said, Thy father [9]straitly charged the people with an oath, saying, Cursed *be* the man that eateth *any* food this day. And the people were [10]faint.

29 Then said Jŏn'a-than, My father hath troubled the land: see, I pray you, how mine eyes have been enlightened, because I tasted a little of this honey.

30 How much more, if haply the people had eaten freely to day of the spoil of their enemies which they found? for had there not been now a much greater slaughter among the Phĭ-lĭs'tĭnes?

31 And they smote the Phĭ-lĭs'tĭnes that day from Mĭch'mash to Ăi'ja-lŏn: and the people were very faint.

32 And the people flew upon the spoil, and took sheep, and oxen, and calves, and slew *them* on the ground: and the people did eat *them* [t]with the blood.

19 [k]Num. 27.21
[6]Or, tumult
[l]Josh. 9.14; Ps. 106.13
20 [7]were cried together
[m]Judg. 7.22; Isa. 9.19-21
22 [n]ch. 13.6
23 [o]Ex. 14.30; Hos. 1.7
[p]ch. 13.5
24 [q]Lev. 27.29; Prov. 11.9
25 [r]Deut. 9.28; Matt. 3.5
[s]Ex. 3.8; Matt. 3.4
27 [8]Or, woodhoney
28 [9]adjuring, adjured
[10]Or, weary
32 [t]Gen. 9.4; Acts 15.20-29
33 [11]Or, dealt treacherously
34 [12]in his hand
35 [u]Judg. 21.4; 2 Sam. 24.25
[13]that altar he began to build unto the LORD
36 [v]Mal. 2.7; Jas. 4.8
37 [w]Ex. 14.3-5; John 9.31
38 [x]Josh. 7.14; ch. 10.19
[14]corners
39 [y]ch. 19.6; Eccl. 9.2
41 [15]Or, Shew the innocent
[z]Josh. 7.16; John 1.7
[16]went forth
43 [a]Josh. 7.19
44 [b]ch. 25.22
45 [c]2 Sam. 14.11; Luke 21.18
[d]Isa. 13.3; 2 Cor. 6.1
47 [e]ch. 11.11

33 ¶ Then they told Sa̤ul, saying, Behold, the people sin against the LORD, in that they eat with the blood. And he said, Ye have [11]transgressed: roll a great stone unto me this day.

34 And Sa̤ul said, Disperse yourselves among the people, and say unto them, Bring me hither every man his ox, and every man his sheep, and slay *them* here, and eat; and sin not against the LORD in eating with the blood. And all the people brought every man his ox [12]with him that night, and slew *them* there.

35 And Sa̤ul [u]built an altar unto the LORD: [13]the same was the first altar that he built unto the LORD.

36 ¶ And Sa̤ul said, Let us go down after the Phĭ-lĭs'tĭnes by night, and spoil them until the morning light, and let us not leave a man of them. And they said, Do whatsoever seemeth good unto thee. Then said the priest, [v]Let us draw near hither unto God.

37 And Sa̤ul asked counsel of God, Shall I go down after the Phĭ-lĭs'tĭnes? wilt thou deliver them into the hand of Ĭs'ra-el? But [w]he answered him not that day.

38 And Sa̤ul said, [x]Draw ye near hither, all the [14]chief of the people: and know and see wherein this sin hath been this day.

39 For, [y]*as* the LORD liveth, which saveth Ĭs'ra-el, though it be in Jŏn'a-than my son, he shall surely die. But *there was* not a man among all the people *that* answered him.

40 Then said he unto all Ĭs'ra-el, Be ye on one side, and I and Jŏn'a-than my son will be on the other side. And the people said unto Sa̤ul, Do what seemeth good unto thee.

41 Therefore Sa̤ul said unto the LORD God of Ĭs'ra-el, [15]Give a perfect *lot*. [z]And Sa̤ul and Jŏn'a-than were taken: but the people [16]escaped.

42 And Sa̤ul said, Cast *lots* between me and Jŏn'a-than my son. And Jŏn'a-than was taken.

43 Then Sa̤ul said to Jŏn'a-than, [a]Tell me what thou hast done. And Jŏn'a-than told him, and said, I did but taste a little honey with the end of the rod that *was* in mine hand, *and*, lo, I must die.

44 And Sa̤ul answered, [b]God do so and more also: for thou shalt surely die, Jŏn'a-than.

45 And the people said unto Sa̤ul, Shall Jŏn'a-than die, who hath wrought this great salvation in Ĭs'ra-el? God forbid: [c]*as* the LORD liveth, there shall not one hair of his head fall to the ground; [d]for he hath wrought with God this day. So the people rescued Jŏn'a-than, that he died not.

46 Then Sa̤ul went up from following the Phĭ-lĭs'tĭnes: and the Phĭ-lĭs'tĭnes went to their own place.

47 ¶ So Sa̤ul took the kingdom over Ĭs'ra-el, and fought against all his enemies on every side, against Mō'ab, and against the children of [e]Ăm'mŏn, and against Ē'dom, and against the kings of

[f]Zō'bah, and against the Phĭ-lĭs'tĭnes: and whithersoever he turned himself, he [g]vexed *them*.

48 And he [17]gathered an host, and [h]smote the Ăm'a-lĕk-ītes, and delivered Ĭs'ra-el out of the hands of them that spoiled them.

49 Now [i]the sons of Saul were Jŏn'a-than, and Ĭsh'u-ī, and Mĕl'chī–shu'ȧ: and the names of his two daughters *were these;* the name of the firstborn Mē'rab, and the name of the younger Mī'chal:

50 And the name of Saul's wife *was* A-hĭn'o-am, the daughter of A-hĭm'a-ăz: and the name of the captain of his host *was* [18]Ăb'nēr, the son of Nēr, Saul's uncle.

51 [j]And Kĭsh *was* the father of Saul; and Nēr the father of Ăb'nēr *was* the son of A-bī'el.

52 And there was sore war against the Phĭ-lĭs'tĭnes all the days of Saul: and when Saul saw any strong man, or any valiant man, [k]he took him unto him.

15 Săm'u-el also said unto Saul, The [a]LORD sent me to anoint thee *to be* king over his people, over Ĭs'ra-el: now therefore hearken thou unto the voice of the words of the LORD.

2 Thus saith the LORD of hosts, I remember *that* which Ăm'a-lĕk did to Ĭs'ra-el, [b]how he laid *wait* for him in the way, when he came up from Ē'gypt.

3 Now go and smite Ăm'a-lĕk, and [c]utterly destroy all that they have, and spare them not; but slay both man and woman, [d]infant and suckling, [e]ox and sheep, camel and ass.

4 And Saul gathered the people together, and numbered them [f]in Tĕl'a-im, two hundred thousand footmen, and ten thousand men of Jū'dah.

5 And Saul came to a city of Ăm'a-lĕk, and [1]laid wait in the valley.

6 ¶ And Saul said unto [g]the Kĕn'ītes, [h]Go, depart, get you down from among the Ăm'a-lĕk-ītes, lest I destroy you with them: [i]for ye shewed kindness to all the children of Ĭs'ra-el, when they came up out of Ē'gypt. So the Kĕn'ītes departed from among the Ăm'a-lĕk-ītes.

7 And [j]Saul smote the Ăm'a-lĕk-ītes from [k]Hăv'ĭ-lah *until* thou comest to [l]Shûr, that *is* over against Ē'gypt.

8 And [m]he took Ā'găg the king of the Ăm'a-lĕk-ītes alive, and [n]utterly destroyed all the people with the edge of the sword.

9 But Saul and the people spared Ā'găg, and [o]the best of the sheep, and of the oxen, and [2]of the fatlings, and the lambs, and all *that was* good, and would not utterly destroy them: but every thing *that was* vile and refuse, that they destroyed utterly.

10 ¶ Then came the word of the LORD unto Săm'u-el, saying,

11 [p]It repenteth me that I have set up Saul *to be* king: for he is [q]turned back from following me, and [r]hath not performed my commandments. And it [s]grieved Săm'u-el; and he cried unto the LORD all night.

12 And when Săm'u-el rose early to meet Saul in the morning, it was told Săm'u-el, saying, Saul came to [t]Cär'mel, and, behold, he set him up a place, and is gone about, and passed on, and gone down to Gĭl'găl.

13 And Săm'u-el came to Saul: and Saul said unto [u]him, Blessed *be* thou of the LORD: [v]I have performed the commandment of the LORD.

14 And Săm'u-el said, What *meaneth* then this bleating of the sheep in mine ears, and the lowing of the oxen which I hear?

15 And Saul said, They have brought them from the Ăm'a-lĕk-ītes: [w]for the people spared the best of the sheep and of the oxen, to sacrifice unto the LORD thy God; and the rest we have utterly destroyed.

16 Then Săm'u-el said unto Saul, Stay, and I will tell thee what the LORD hath said to me this night. And he said unto him, Say on.

17 And Săm'u-el said, When thou *wast* little in thine own sight, *wast* thou not *made* the head of the tribes of Ĭs'ra-el, and the LORD anointed thee king over Ĭs'ra-el?

18 And the LORD sent thee on a journey, and said, Go and utterly destroy the sinners the Ăm'a-lĕk-ītes, and fight against them until [3]they be consumed.

19 Wherefore then didst thou not obey the voice of the LORD, but didst fly upon the spoil, and didst evil in the sight of the LORD?

20 And Saul said unto Săm'u-el, Yea, I have obeyed the voice of the LORD, and have gone the way which the LORD sent me, and have brought Ā'găg the king of Ăm'a-lĕk, and have utterly destroyed the Ăm'a-lĕk-ītes.

21 But the people took of the spoil, sheep and oxen, the chief of the things which should have been utterly destroyed, to sacrifice unto the LORD thy God in Gĭl'găl.

22 And Săm'u-el said, [x]Hath the LORD *as great* delight in burnt offerings and sacrifices, as in obeying the voice of the LORD? Behold, [y]to obey *is* better than sacrifice, *and* to hearken than the fat of rams.

23 For rebellion *is as* the sin of [4]witchcraft, and stubbornness *is as* iniquity and idolatry. Because thou hast rejected the word of the LORD, he hath also rejected thee from *being* king.

24 ¶ And [z]Saul said unto Săm'u-el, [a]I have sinned: for I have transgressed the commandment of the LORD, and thy words: because [b]I feared the people, and obeyed their voice.

25 Now therefore, I pray thee, pardon my sin, and turn again with me, that I may worship the LORD.

26 And Săm'u-el said unto Saul, I will not return with thee: [c]for thou hast rejected the word of the LORD, and the LORD hath rejected thee from being king over Ĭs'ra-el.

[f]2 Sam. 10.6
[g]Num. 25.17
48 [17]Or, wrought mightily
[h]ch. 15.3-7
49 [i]ch. 31.2; 1 Chr. 8.33
50 [18]Abiner
51 [j]ch. 9.1
52 [k]ch. 8.11
CHAPTER 15
1 [a]ch. 9.16
2 [b]Ex. 17.8; Deut. 25.17
3 [c]Lev. 27.28; Josh. 6.17
[d]Ex. 20.5; Isa. 14.21
[e]Gen. 3.17; Josh. 7.24
4 [f]Josh. 15.24
5 [1]Or, fought
6 [g]Num. 24.21; Judg. 1.16
[h]Gen. 18.25; Rev. 18.4
[i]Ex. 18.10; Num. 10.29
7 [j]ch. 14.48
[k]Gen. 2.11; Gen. 25.18
[l]Gen. 16.7; ch. 27.8
8 [m]1 Ki. 20.34; Esth. 3.1
[n]ch. 30.1
9 [o]Prov. 15.27; 1 Tim. 6.10
[2]Or, of the second sort
11 [p]Gen. 6.6; 2 Sam. 24.16
[q]Josh. 22.16; Matt. 24.13
[r]ch. 13.13
[s]ch. 16.1; Rom. 9.1-3
12 [t]Josh. 15.55
13 [u]Gen. 14.19; Ruth 3.2
[v]Luke 18.11
15 [w]Gen. 3.12; Prov. 28.13
18 [3]they consume them
22 [x]Ps. 50.8-9;
[y]Ex. 19.5;
23 [4]divination
24 [z]2 Sam. 12.13
[a]Ex. 9.27;
[b]Ex. 23.2;
26 [c]ch. 2.30

27 And as Săm'u-el turned about to go away, [d]he laid hold upon the skirt of his mantle, and it rent.

28 And Săm'u-el said unto him, [e]The LORD hath rent the kingdom of Ĭs'ra-el from thee this day, and hath given it to a neighbour of thine, *that is* better than thou.

29 And also the [5]Strength of Ĭs'ra-el [f]will not lie nor repent: for he *is* not a man, that he should repent.

30 Then he said, I have sinned: *yet* [g]honour me now, I pray thee, before the elders of my people, and before Ĭs'ra-el, and turn again with me, that I may worship the LORD thy God.

31 So Săm'u-el turned again after Sạul; and Sạul worshipped the LORD.

32 ¶ Then said Săm'u-el, Bring ye hither to me Ā'găg the king of the Ăm'a-lĕk-ītes. And Ā'găg came unto him delicately. And Ā'găg said, Surely the bitterness of death is past.

33 And Săm'u-el said, [h]As thy sword hath made women childless, so shall thy mother be childless among women. And [i]Săm'u-el hewed Ā'găg in pieces before the LORD in Gĭl'găl.

34 ¶ Then Săm'u-el went to Rā'mah; and Sạul went up to his house to [j]Gĭb'-e-ah of Sạul.

35 And Săm'u-el came no more to see Sạul until the day of his death: nevertheless Săm'u-el mourned for Sạul: and the LORD repented that he had made Sạul king over Ĭs'ra-el.

16 And the LORD said unto Săm'u-el, How long wilt thou mourn for Sạul, seeing I have rejected him from reigning over Ĭs'ra-el? [a]fill thine horn with oil, and go, I will send thee to Jĕs'se the Bĕth'–lĕ-hĕm-īte: for [b]I have provided me a king among his sons.

2 And Săm'u-el said, How can I go? if Sạul hear *it*, he will kill me. And the LORD said, Take an heifer [1]with thee, and say, [c]I am come to sacrifice to the LORD.

3 And call Jĕs'se to the [2]sacrifice, and [d]I will shew thee what thou shalt do: and [e]thou shalt anoint unto me *him* whom I name unto thee.

4 And Săm'u-el did that which the LORD spake, and came to Bĕth'–lĕ-hĕm. And the elders of the town [f]trembled at his [3]coming, and said, [g]Comest thou peaceably?

5 And he said, Peaceably: I am come to sacrifice unto the LORD: [h]sanctify yourselves, and come with me to the sacrifice. And he sanctified Jĕs'se and his sons, and called them to the sacrifice.

6 ¶ And it came to pass, when they were come, that he looked [i]on E-lī'ab, and [j]said, Surely the LORD'S anointed *is* before him.

7 But the LORD said unto Săm'u-el, Look not on [k]his countenance, or on the height of his stature; because I have refused him: [l]for *the LORD seeth* not as man seeth; for man [m]looketh on the [4]outward appearance, but the LORD looketh on the [n]heart.

27 [d]1 Ki. 11.30
28 [e]ch. 28.17
29 [5]Or, Eternity, or, Victory
[f]Num. 23.19; Ezek. 24.14; 2 Tim. 2.13; Tit. 1.2
30 [g]ch. 2.30; Ps. 49.20; Prov. 4.8; Prov. 26.1; Rom. 2.28-29
33 [h]Gen. 9.6; Ex. 17.11; Judg. 1.7; Matt. 7.2; Rev. 16.6
[i]1 Ki. 18.40
34 [j]ch. 11.4
CHAPTER 16
1 [a]2 Ki. 9.1
[b]Ps. 78.70; Acts 13.22
2 [1]in thine hand
[c]ch. 20.29
3 [2]Or, feast
[d]Ex. 4.15
[e]ch. 9.16
4 [f]ch. 21.1; 2 Sam. 6.9; Hos. 6.5; Hos. 11.10; Luke 5.8; Acts 24.25
[3]meeting
[g]1 Ki. 2.13
5 [h]Ex. 19.10
6 [i]Called Elihu, 1 Chr. 27.18
[j]1 Ki. 12.26
7 [k]Ps. 147.10
[l]Isa. 55.8
[m]2 Cor. 10.7
[4]eyes
[n]1 Chr. 28.9; 2 Chr. 16.9; Ps. 7.9; Jer. 11.20; Acts 1.24; Rev. 2.23
11 [o]ch. 17.12
[p]2 Sam. 7.8; Ps. 78.70
[5]round
12 [q]Song 5.10
[6]fair of eyes
[r]ch. 9.17
13 [s]Ps. 89.20
[t]Num. 27.18; Judg. 11.29
14 [u]ch. 18.12; Ps. 51.11
[v]ch. 19.9
[7]Or, terrified
18 [8]Or, speech
21 [w]Gen. 41.46; 1 Ki. 10.8; Prov. 22.29

8 Then Jĕs'se called A-bĭn'ă-dăb, and made him pass before Săm'u-el. And he said, Neither hath the LORD chosen this.

9 Then Jĕs'se made Shăm'mah to pass by. And he said, Neither hath the LORD chosen this.

10 Again, Jĕs'se made seven of his sons to pass before Săm'u-el. And Săm'u-el said unto Jĕs'se, The LORD hath not chosen these.

11 And Săm'u-el said unto Jĕs'se, Are here all *thy* children? And he said, [o]There remaineth yet the youngest, and, behold, he keepeth the sheep. And Săm'u-el said unto Jĕs'se, [p]Send and fetch him: for we will not sit [5]down till he come hither.

12 And he sent, and brought him in. Now he *was* [q]ruddy, *and* withal [6]of a beautiful countenance, and goodly to look to. [r]And the LORD said, Arise, anoint him: for this *is* he.

13 Then Săm'u-el took the horn of oil, and [s]anointed him in the midst of his brethren: and [t]the Spirit of the LORD came upon Dā'vid from that day forward. So Săm'u-el rose up, and went to Rā'mah.

14 ¶ [u]But the Spirit of the LORD departed from Sạul, and [v]an evil spirit from the LORD [7]troubled him.

15 And Sạul's servants said unto him, Behold now, an evil spirit from God troubleth thee.

16 Let our lord now command thy servants, *which are* before thee, to seek out a man, *who is* a cunning player on an harp: and it shall come to pass, when the evil spirit from God is upon thee, that he shall play with his hand, and thou shalt be well.

17 And Sạul said unto his servants, Provide me now a man that can play well, and bring *him* to me.

18 Then answered one of the servants, and said, Behold, I have seen a son of Jĕs'se the Bĕth'–lĕ-hĕm-īte, *that is* cunning in playing, and a mighty valiant man, and a man of war, and prudent in [8]matters, and a comely person, and the LORD *is* with him.

19 ¶ Wherefore Sạul sent messengers unto Jĕs'se, and said, Send me Dā'vid thy son, which *is* with the sheep.

20 And Jĕs'se took an ass *laden* with bread, and a bottle of wine, and a kid, and sent *them* by Dā'vid his son unto Sạul.

21 And Dā'vid came to Sạul, and [w]stood before him: and he loved him greatly; and he became his armourbearer.

22 And Sạul sent to Jĕs'se, saying, Let Dā'vid, I pray thee, stand before me; for he hath found favour in my sight.

23 And it came to pass, when the *evil* spirit from God was upon Sạul, that Dā'vid took an harp, and played with his hand: so Sạul was refreshed, and was well, and the evil spirit departed from him.

17 Now the Phĭ-lĭs'tĭnes gathered together their armies to battle,

and were gathered together at [a]Shō'choh, which *belongeth* to Jū'dah, and pitched between Shō'choh and A-zē'kah, in [1]Ē'phes–dăm'mim.

2 And Saul and the men of Ĭs'ra-el were gathered together, and pitched by the valley of Ē'lah, and [2]set the battle in array against the Phĭ-lĭs'tĭnes.

3 And the Phĭ-lĭs'tĭnes stood on a mountain on the one side, and Ĭs'ra-el stood on a mountain on the other side: and *there was* a valley between them.

4 ¶ And there went out [3]a champion out of the camp of the Phĭ-lĭs'tĭnes, named [b]Go-lī'ath, of [c]Găth, whose height *was* [4]six cubits and a span.

5 And *he had* an helmet of brass upon his head, and he *was* [5]armed with a coat of mail; and the weight of the coat *was* five thousand shekels of brass.

6 And *he had* greaves of brass upon his legs, and a [6]target of brass between his shoulders.

7 And the [d]staff of his spear *was* like a weaver's beam; and his spear's head *weighed* six hundred shekels of iron: and one bearing a shield went before him.

8 And he stood and cried unto the armies of Ĭs'ra-el, and said unto them, Why are ye come out to set *your* battle in array? *am* not I a Phĭ-lĭs'tĭne, and ye [e]servants to Saul? choose you a man for you, and let him come down to me.

9 If he be able to fight with me, and to kill me, then will we be your servants: but if I prevail against him, and kill him, then shall ye be our servants, and [f]serve us.

10 And the Phĭ-lĭs'tĭne said, I [g]defy the armies of Ĭs'ra-el this day; give me a man, that we may fight together.

11 When Saul and all Ĭs'ra-el heard those words of the Phĭ-lĭs'tĭne, they were dismayed, and greatly afraid.

12 ¶ Now Dā'vid *was* [h]the son of that [i]Ĕph'răth-īte of Bĕth'–lĕ-hĕm–jū'dah, whose name *was* Jĕs'se; and he had [j]eight sons: and the man went among men *for* an old man in the days of Saul.

13 And the three eldest sons of Jĕs'se went *and* followed Saul to the battle: and the [k]names of his three sons that went to the battle *were* E-lī'ab the firstborn, and next unto him A-bĭn'ā-dăb, and the third Shăm'mah.

14 And Dā'vid *was* the youngest: and the three eldest followed Saul.

15 But Dā'vid went and returned from Saul to feed his father's sheep at Bĕth'–lĕ-hĕm.

16 And the Phĭ-lĭs'tĭne drew near morning and evening, and presented himself forty days.

17 And Jĕs'se said unto Dā'vid his son, Take now for thy brethren an ephah of this parched *corn,* and these ten loaves, and run to the camp to thy brethren;

18 And carry these ten [7]cheeses unto the [8]captain of *their* thousand, and [l]look how thy brethren fare, and take their pledge.

19 Now Saul, and they, and all the men of Ĭs'ra-el, *were* in the valley of Ē'lah, fighting with the Phĭ-lĭs'tĭnes.

20 ¶ And Dā'vid rose up early in the morning, and left the sheep with a keeper, and took, and went, as Jĕs'se had commanded him; and he came to the [9]trench, as the host was going forth to the [10]fight, and shouted for the battle.

21 For Ĭs'ra-el and the Phĭ-lĭs'tĭnes had put the battle in array, army against army.

22 And Dā'vid left [11]his carriage in the hand of the keeper of the carriage, and ran into the army, and came and [12]saluted his brethren.

23 And as he talked with them, behold, there came up the champion, the Phĭ-lĭs'tĭne of Găth, Go-lī'ath by name, out of the armies of the Phĭ-lĭs'tĭnes, and spake according to the same words: and Dā'vid heard *them.*

24 And all the men of Ĭs'ra-el, when they saw the man, fled [13]from him, and were sore afraid.

25 And the men of Ĭs'ra-el said, Have ye seen this man that is come up? surely to defy Ĭs'ra-el is he come up: and it shall be, *that* the man who killeth him, the king will enrich him with great riches, and [m]will give him his daughter, and make his father's house free in Ĭs'ra-el.

26 And Dā'vid spake to the men that stood by him, saying, What shall be done to the man that killeth this Phĭ-lĭs'tĭne, and taketh away [n]the reproach from Ĭs'ra-el? for who *is* this [o]uncircumcised Phĭ-lĭs'tĭne, that he should defy the armies of [p]the living God?

27 And the people answered him after this manner, saying, So shall it be done to the man that killeth him.

28 ¶ And E-lī'ab his eldest brother heard when he spake unto the men; and E-lī'ab's [q]anger was kindled against Dā'vid, and he said, Why camest thou down hither? and with whom hast thou left those few sheep in the wilderness? I know thy pride, and the naughtiness of thine heart; for thou art come down that thou mightest see the battle.

29 And Dā'vid said, What have I now done? [r]*Is there* not a cause?

30 ¶ And he turned from him toward another, and spake after the same [14]manner: and the people answered him again after the former manner.

31 And when the words were heard which Dā'vid spake, they rehearsed *them* before Saul: and he [15]sent for him.

32 ¶ And Dā'vid said to Saul, [s]Let no man's heart fail because of him; [t]thy servant will go and fight with this Phĭ-lĭs'tĭne.

33 And Saul said to Dā'vid, [u]Thou art not able to go against this Phĭ-lĭs'tĭne to fight with him: for thou *art but* a youth, and he a man of war from his youth.

34 And Dā'vid said unto Saul, Thy servant kept his father's sheep, and

CHAPTER 17

1 [a]Josh. 15.35; 2 Chr. 28.18
[1]Or, The coast of bloods, called Pasdammim
2 [2]ranged the battle
4 [3]a treaderdown
[b]2 Sam. 21.19; 1 Chr. 20.5
[c]Josh. 11.22; Amos 6.2
[4]About eleven feet and a half
5 [5]clothed
6 [6]Or, gorget
7 [d]2 Sam. 21.19; 1 Chr. 11.23
8 [e]ch. 8.17; 1 Chr. 21.3
9 [f]ch. 11.1
10 [g]Num. 23.7-8; Neh. 2.19
12 [h]Ruth 4.22; ch. 16.1-18
[i]Gen. 35.19
[j]ch. 16.10-11; 1 Chr. 2.13
13 [k]ch. 16.6; 1 Chr. 2.13
18 [7]cheeses of milk
[8]captain of a thousand
[l]Gen. 37.14
20 [9]Or, place of the carriage
[10]battle array, or, place of fight
22 [11]the vessels from upon him
[12]asked his brethren of peace, as Gen. 43.27; Judg. 18.15
24 [13]from his face
25 [m]Josh. 15.16
26 [n]ch. 11.2
[o]ch. 14.6
[p]Deut. 5.26
28 [q]Gen. 37.4
29 [r]Prov. 15.1
30 [14]word
31 [15]took him
32 [s]Num. 13.30;
[t]ch. 16.18
33 [u]Num. 13.31

there came a lion, and a bear, and took
a [16]lamb out of the flock:
35 And I went out after him, and
smote him, and delivered *it* out of his
mouth: and when he arose against me,
I caught *him* by his beard, and smote
him, and slew him.
36 Thy servant slew both the lion
and the bear: and this uncircumcised
Phĭ-lĭs'tĭne shall be as one of them, seeing he hath defied the armies of the
living God.
37 Dā'vid said moreover, [v]The LORD
that delivered me out of the paw of the
lion, and out of the paw of the bear, he
will deliver me out of the hand of this
Phĭ-lĭs'tĭne. And Saul said unto Dā'vid,
Go, and [w]the LORD be with thee.
38 ¶ And Saul [17]armed Dā'vid with
his armour, and he put an helmet of
brass upon his head; also he armed
him with a coat of mail.
39 And Dā'vid girded his sword
upon his armour, and he assayed to go;
for he had not proved *it*. And Dā'vid
said unto Saul, I cannot go with these;
for I have not proved *them*. And Dā'-
vid put them off him.
40 And he took his staff in his hand,
and chose him five smooth stones out
of the [18]brook, and put them in a shepherd's [19]bag which he had, even in a
scrip; and his sling *was* in his hand:
and he drew near to the Phĭ-lĭs'tĭne.
41 And the Phĭ-lĭs'tĭne came on and
drew near unto Dā'vid; and the man
that bare the shield *went* before him.
42 And when the Phĭ-lĭs'tĭne looked
about, and saw Dā'vid, he [x]disdained
him: for he was *but* a youth, and
[y]ruddy, and of a fair countenance.
43 And the Phĭ-lĭs'tĭne said unto Dā'-
vid, [z]*Am* I a dog, that thou comest to
me with staves? And the Phĭ-lĭs'tĭne
cursed Dā'vid by his gods.
44 And the Phĭ-lĭs'tĭne [a]said to Dā'-
vid, Come to me, and I will give thy
flesh unto the fowls of the air, and to
the beasts of the field.
45 Then said Dā'vid to the Phĭ-lĭs'-
tĭne, Thou comest to me with a sword,
and with a spear, and with a shield:
[b]but I come to thee in the name of the
LORD of hosts, the God of the armies of
Ĭs'ra-el, whom thou hast defied.
46 This day will the LORD [20]deliver
thee into mine hand; and I will smite
thee, and take thine head from thee;
and I will give [c]the carcases of the host
of the Phĭ-lĭs'tĭnes this day unto the
fowls of the air, and to the wild beasts
of the earth; [d]that all the earth may
know that there is a God in Ĭs'ra-el.
47 And all this assembly shall know
that the LORD [e]saveth not with sword
and spear: for [f]the battle *is* the LORD'S,
and he will give you into our hands.
48 And it came to pass, when the
Phĭ-lĭs'tĭne arose, and came and drew
nigh to meet Dā'vid, that Dā'vid hasted,
and ran toward the army to meet the
Phĭ-lĭs'tĭne.
49 And Dā'vid put his hand in his
bag, and took thence a stone, and slang
it, and smote the Phĭ-lĭs'tĭne in his forehead, that the stone [21]sunk into his forehead; and he fell upon his face to the
earth.
50 So [g]Dā'vid prevailed over the
Phĭ-lĭs'tĭne with a sling and with a
stone, and smote the Phĭ-lĭs'tĭne, and
slew him; but *there was* no sword in
the hand of Dā'vid.
51 Therefore Dā'vid ran, and stood
upon the Phĭ-lĭs'tĭne, and took his
sword, and drew it out of the sheath
thereof, and slew him, and cut off his
head therewith. And when the Phĭ-
lĭs'tĭnes saw their champion was dead,
[h]they fled.
52 And the men of Ĭs'ra-el and of
Jū'dah arose, and shouted, and pursued the Phĭ-lĭs'tĭnes, until thou come
to the valley, and to the gates of Ĕk'rŏn.
And the wounded of the Phĭ-lĭs'tĭnes
fell down by the way to [i]Sha-a-rā'im,
even unto Găth, and unto Ĕk'rŏn.
53 And the children of Ĭs'ra-el returned from chasing after the Phĭ-lĭs'-
tĭnes, and they spoiled their tents.
54 And Dā'vid took the head of the
Phĭ-lĭs'tĭne, and brought it to Je-ru'sa-
lĕm; but he put his armour in his tent.
55 ¶ And when Saul saw Dā'vid go
forth against the Phĭ-lĭs'tĭne, he said
unto Ăb'nēr, the captain of the host,
Ăb'nēr, [j]whose son *is* this youth? And
Ăb'nēr said, *As* thy soul liveth, O king,
I cannot tell.
56 And the king said, Inquire thou
whose son the stripling *is*.
57 And as Dā'vid returned from the
slaughter of the Phĭ-lĭs'tĭne, Ăb'nēr
took him, and brought him before Saul
with the head of the Phĭ-lĭs'tĭne in his
hand.
58 And Saul said to him, Whose son
art thou, *thou* young man? And Dā'vid
answered, *I am* the son of thy servant
[k]Jĕs'se the Bĕth'-lĕ-hĕm-īte.

18 And it came to pass, when he
had made an end of speaking
unto Saul, that [a]the soul of Jŏn'a-than
was knit with the soul of Dā'vid, [b]and
Jŏn'a-than loved him as his own soul.
2 And Saul took him that day, and
[c]would let him go no more home to his
father's house.
3 Then Jŏn'a-than and Dā'vid made
a covenant, because he loved him as
his own soul.
4 And Jŏn'a-than stripped himself
of the robe that *was* upon him, and
gave it to Dā'vid, and his garments,
even to his sword, and to his bow, and
to his girdle.
5 ¶ And Dā'vid went out whithersoever Saul sent him, *and* [1]behaved himself wisely: and Saul set him over the
men of war, and he was accepted in the
sight of all the people, and also in the
sight of Saul's servants.
6 And it came to pass as they came,
when Dā'vid was returned from the
slaughter of the [2]Phĭ-lĭs'tĭne, that [d]the
women came out of all cities of Ĭs'ra-el,
singing and dancing, to meet king Saul,
with tabrets, with joy, and with [3]instru-
ments of musick.

34 [16]Or, kid
37 [v]ch. 7.12; 2 Tim. 4.17-18
[w]ch. 20.13; 1 Chr. 22.11-16
38 [17]clothed David with his clothes
40 [18]Or, valley
[19]vessel
42 [x]Ps. 123.4; 1 Cor. 1.27-28
[y]ch. 16.12
43 [z]ch. 24.14; 2 Sam. 3.8
44 [a]1 Ki. 20.10-11; Ezek. 28.2-9-10
45 [b]2 Sam. 22.33-35; Heb. 11.33-34
46 [20]shut thee up
[c]Deut. 28.26
[d]Josh. 4.24; Isa. 52.10
47 [e]Ps. 44.6-7; Zech. 4.6
[f]2 Chr. 20.15
49 [21]sunk as a stone in the water
50 [g]ch. 21.9; 2 Sam. 23.21
51 [h]Heb. 11.34
52 [i]Josh. 15.36
55 [j]ch. 16.21-22
58 [k]Ruth 4.22; Rom. 15.12
CHAPTER 18
1 [a]Gen. 44.30; Col. 2.2
[b]Deut. 13.6; 1 John 3.12-14
2 [c]ch. 8.11; ch. 14.52
5 [1]Or, prospered
6 [2]Or, Philistines
[d]Ex. 15.20; Jer. 31.4
[3]three-stringed instruments

7 And the women [e]answered *one an-
other as they played, and said, Sa̧ul
hath slain his thousands, and Dā′vid
his ten thousands.
8 And Sa̧ul was very wroth, and the
saying [4]displeased him; and he said,
They have ascribed unto Dā′vid ten
thousands, and to me they have ascribed *but* thousands: and *what* can he
have more but the kingdom?
9 And Sa̧ul [f]eyed Dā′vid from that
day and forward.
10 ¶ And it came to pass on the morrow, that [g]the evil spirit from God
came upon Sa̧ul, [h]and he prophesied
in the midst of the house: and Dā′vid
played with his hand, as at other times:
and *there was* a javelin in Sa̧ul's hand.
11 And Sa̧ul [i]cast the javelin; for he
said, I will smite Dā′vid even to the
wall *with it.* And Dā′vid avoided out of
his presence twice.
12 ¶ And Sa̧ul was afraid of Dā′vid,
because [j]the LORD was with him, and
was [k]departed from Sa̧ul.
13 Therefore Sa̧ul removed him from
him, and made him his captain over a
thousand; and [l]he went out and came in
before the people.
14 And Dā′vid [5]behaved himself
wisely in all his ways; and [m]the LORD
was with him.
15 Wherefore when Sa̧ul saw that
he behaved himself very wisely, he
was afraid of him.
16 But all Ĭs′ra-el and Jū′dah loved
Dā′vid, because he went out and came
in before them.
17 ¶ And Sa̧ul said to Dā′vid, Behold
my elder daughter Mē′rab, [n]her will I
give thee to wife: only be thou [6]valiant
for me, and fight [o]the LORD'S battles.
For Sa̧ul said, [p]Let not mine hand be
upon him, but let the hand of the Phĭ-
lĭs′tĭnes be upon him.
18 And Dā′vid said unto Sa̧ul, [q]Who
am I? and what *is* my life, *or* my father's family in Ĭs′ra-el, that I should
be son in law to the king?
19 But it came to pass at the time
when Mē′rab Sa̧ul's daughter should
have been given to Dā′vid, that she
was given [r]unto Ā′drĭ-el the [s]Me-hŏl′-
ath-īte to wife.
20 And Mī′chal Sa̧ul's daughter loved
Dā′vid: and they told Sa̧ul, and the thing
[7]pleased him.
21 And Sa̧ul said, I will give him her,
that she may be [t]a snare to him, and
that the hand of the Phĭ-lĭs′tĭnes may
be against him. Wherefore Sa̧ul said to
Dā′vid, Thou shalt this day be my son
in law in *the one of* the twain.
22 ¶ And Sa̧ul commanded his servants, *saying*, Commune with Dā′vid
secretly, and say, Behold, the king hath
delight in thee, and all his servants love
thee: now therefore be the king's son in
law.
23 And Sa̧ul's servants spake those
words in the ears of Dā′vid. And Dā′-
vid said, Seemeth it to you *a* light *thing*
to be a king's son in law, seeing that I
am a poor man, and lightly esteemed?
24 And the servants of Sa̧ul told him,
saying, [8]On this manner spake Dā′vid.
25 And Sa̧ul said, Thus shall ye say
to Dā′vid, The king desireth not any
[u]dowry, but an hundred foreskins of
the Phĭ-lĭs′tĭnes, to be [v]avenged of the
king's enemies. But Sa̧ul thought to
make Dā′vid fall by the hand of the
Phĭ-lĭs′tĭnes.
26 And when his servants told Dā′-
vid these words, it [9]pleased Dā′vid well
to be the king's son in law: and the days
were not [10]expired.
27 Wherefore Dā′vid arose and
went, he and his men, and slew of
the Phĭ-lĭs′tĭnes two hundred men; and
[w]Dā′vid brought their foreskins, and
they gave them in full tale to the king,
that he might be the king's son in law.
And Sa̧ul gave him Mī′chal his daughter to wife.
28 ¶ And Sa̧ul saw and knew that
the LORD *was* with Dā′vid, and *that*
Mī′chal Sa̧ul's daughter loved him.
29 And [x]Sa̧ul was yet the more
afraid of Dā′vid; and Sa̧ul became Dā′-
vid's enemy continually.
30 Then the princes of the Phĭ-lĭs′-
tĭnes [y]went forth: and it came to pass,
after they went forth, *that* Dā′vid behaved himself [z]more wisely than all
the servants of Sa̧ul; so that his name
was much [11]set by.

19 And Sa̧ul [a]spake to Jŏn′a-than
his son, and to all his servants,
that they should kill Dā′vid.
2 But Jŏn′a-than Sa̧ul's son delighted
much in Dā′vid: and Jŏn′a-than told
Dā′vid, [b]saying, Sa̧ul my father seeketh
to kill thee: now therefore, I pray thee,
take heed to thyself until the morning,
and abide in a secret *place,* and hide
thyself:
3 And I will go out and stand beside
my father in the field where thou *art,*
and I will commune with my father of
thee; and what I see, that I will tell
thee.
4 ¶ And Jŏn′a-than [c]spake good of
Dā′vid unto Sa̧ul his father, and said
unto him, Let not the king [d]sin against
his servant, against Dā′vid; because he
hath not sinned against thee, and because his works *have been* to thee-
ward very good:
5 For he did put his [e]life in his hand,
and [f]slew the Phĭ-lĭs′tĭne, and [g]the
LORD wrought a great salvation for all
Ĭs′ra-el: thou sawest *it,* and didst rejoice: [h]wherefore then wilt thou [i]sin
against innocent blood, to slay Dā′vid
without a cause?
6 And Sa̧ul hearkened unto the voice
of Jŏn′a-than: and Sa̧ul sware, *As* the
LORD liveth, he shall not be slain.
7 And Jŏn′a-than called Dā′vid, and
Jŏn′a-than shewed him all those
things. And Jŏn′a-than brought Dā′vid
to Sa̧ul, and he was in his presence, as
[1]in times past.
8 ¶ And there was war again: and
Dā′vid went out, and fought with the
Phĭ-lĭs′tĭnes, and slew them with a
great slaughter; and they fled from
[2]him.

7 [e]Ex. 15.21; Isa. 5.1
8 [4]was evil in his eyes
9 [f]Gen. 4.5; Luke 15.28
10 [g]ch. 16.14
[h]ch. 19.24; Acts 16.16
11 [i]ch. 19.10; Prov. 27.4
12 [j]ch. 16.13
[k]ch. 28.15
13 [l]Num. 27.17; 2 Sam. 5.2
14 [5]Or, prospered
[m]Gen. 39.2; Acts 7.9
17 [n]ch. 17.25
[6]a son of valour
[o]Num. 32.20; ch. 25.28
[p]2 Sam. 12.9
18 [q]Ruth 2.10; Prov. 15.33
19 [r]2 Sam. 21.8
[s]Judg. 7.22
20 [7]was right in his eyes
21 [t]Ex. 10.7; Jer. 5.26
24 [8]According to these words
25 [u]Gen. 34.12; Ex. 22.17
[v]ch. 14.24
26 [9]was right in the eyes of
[10]fulfilled
27 [w]2 Sam. 3.14
29 [x]ch. 12.15; Jas. 2.13
30 [y]2 Sam. 11.1
[z]Luke 21.15
[11]precious

CHAPTER 19
1 [a]Prov. 27.4
2 [b]Acts 23.16
4 [c]Prov. 31.8
[d]Gen. 42.22; 1 John 3.15
5 [e]Judg. 9.17; Ps. 119.109
[f]ch. 17.49
[g]1 Sam. 11.13; 1 Chr. 11.14
[h]ch. 20.32
[i]Matt. 27.4
7 [1]yesterday third day
8 [2]his face

9 And [j]the evil spirit from the LORD was upon Sa̤ul, as he sat in his house with his javelin in his hand: and Dā'vid played with *his* hand.

10 And Sa̤ul [k]sought to smite Dā'vid even to the wall with the javelin; but he slipped away out of Sa̤ul's presence, and he smote the javelin into the wall: and Dā'vid fled, and escaped that night.

11 [l]Sa̤ul also sent messengers unto Dā'vid's house, to watch him, and to slay him in the morning: and Mī'chal Dā'vid's wife told him, saying, If thou save not thy life to night, to morrow thou shalt be slain.

12 ¶ So Mī'chal [m]let Dā'vid down through a window: and he went, and fled, and escaped.

13 And Mī'chal took an [3]image, and laid *it* in the bed, and put a pillow of goats' *hair* for his bolster, and covered *it* with a cloth.

14 And when Sa̤ul sent messengers to take Dā'vid, she said, He *is* sick.

15 And Sa̤ul sent the messengers *again* to see Dā'vid, saying, Bring him up to me in the bed, that I may slay him.

16 And when the messengers were come in, behold, *there was* an image in the bed, with a pillow of goats' *hair* for his bolster.

17 And Sa̤ul said unto Mī'chal, Why hast thou deceived me so, and sent away mine enemy, that he is escaped? And Mī'chal answered Sa̤ul, He said unto me, Let me go; [n]why should I kill thee?

18 ¶ So Dā'vid fled, and escaped, and came to [o]Săm'u-el to Rā'mah, and told him all that Sa̤ul had done to him. And he and Săm'u-el went and dwelt in Nā'ioth.

19 And it was told Sa̤ul, saying, Behold, Dā'vid *is* at Nā'ioth in Rā'mah.

20 And [p]Sa̤ul sent messengers to take Dā'vid: [q]and when they saw the company of the prophets prophesying, and Săm'u-el standing *as* appointed over them, the Spirit of God was upon the messengers of Sa̤ul, and they also [r]prophesied.

21 And when it was told Sa̤ul, he sent other messengers, and they prophesied likewise. And Sa̤ul sent messengers again the third time, and they prophesied also.

22 Then went he also to Rā'mah, and came to a great well that *is* in Sē'chu: and he asked and said, Where *are* Săm'u-el and Dā'vid? And *one* said, Behold, *they be* at Nā'ioth in Rā'mah.

23 And he went thither to Nā'ioth in Rā'mah: and [s]the Spirit of God was upon him also, and he went on, and prophesied, until he came to Nā'ioth in Rā'mah.

24 [t]And he stripped off his clothes also, and prophesied before Săm'u-el in like manner, and [4]lay down [u]naked all that day and all that night. Wherefore they say, [v]*Is* Sa̤ul also among the prophets?

9 [j]ch. 16.14; ch. 18.10
10 [k]Job 5.2; Prov. 29.10
11 [l]Ps. 59-title
12 [m]Josh. 2.15; Acts 9.24-25
13 [3]teraphim
17 [n]2 Sam. 2.22
18 [o]Prov. 17.17; Mal. 2.7
20 [p]John 7.32-45
[q]ch. 10.5-6; 1 Cor. 14.3-24-25
[r]Num. 11.25; Joel 2.28
23 [s]Gen. 31.24; 1 Cor. 13.2
24 [t]Isa. 20.2 [4]fell
[u]2 Sam. 6.14-20; Mic. 1.8
[v]ch. 10.11; Acts 9.21
CHAPTER 20
2 [a]Gen. 44.7; Josh. 22.29 [1]uncover mine ear
4 [2]Or, say what is thy mind, and I will do, etc [3]speaketh, or, thinketh
5 [b]Num. 10.10;
[c]ch. 19.2
6 [d]ch. 16.4 [4]Or, feast
7 [e]Deut. 1.23
8 [f]Josh. 2.14
[g]ch. 18.3
[h]2 Sam. 14.32
12 [i]Josh. 22.22 [5]searched [6]uncover thine ear
13 [j]Ruth 1.17
[k]Josh. 1.5
15 [l]Gen. 21.23

20 And Dā'vid fled from Nā'ioth in Rā'mah, and came and said before Jŏn'a-than, What have I done? what *is* mine iniquity? and what *is* my sin before thy father, that he seeketh my life?

2 And he said unto him, [a]God forbid; thou shalt not die: behold, my father will do nothing either great or small, but that he will [1]shew it me: and why should my father hide this thing from me? it *is* not *so*.

3 And Dā'vid sware moreover, and said, Thy father certainly knoweth that I have found grace in thine eyes; and he saith, Let not Jŏn'a-than know this, lest he be grieved: but truly *as* the LORD liveth, and *as* thy soul liveth, *there is* but a step between me and death.

4 Then said Jŏn'a-than unto Dā'vid, [2]Whatsoever thy soul [3]desireth, I will even do *it* for thee.

5 And Dā'vid said unto Jŏn'a-than, Behold, to morrow *is* the [b]new moon, and I should not fail to sit with the king at meat: but let me go, that I may [c]hide myself in the field unto the third *day* at even.

6 If thy father at all miss me, then say, Dā'vid earnestly asked *leave* of me that he might run [d]to Bĕth'–lĕ-hĕm his city: for *there is* a yearly [4]sacrifice there for all the family.

7 [e]If he say thus, *It is* well; thy servant shall have peace: but if he be very wroth, *then* be sure that evil is determined by him.

8 Therefore thou shalt [f]deal kindly with thy servant; for [g]thou hast brought thy servant into a covenant of the LORD with thee: notwithstanding, [h]if there be in me iniquity, slay me thyself; for why shouldest thou bring me to thy father?

9 And Jŏn'a-than said, Far be it from thee: for if I knew certainly that evil were determined by my father to come upon thee, then would not I tell it thee?

10 Then said Dā'vid to Jŏn'a-than, Who shall tell me? or what *if* thy father answer thee roughly?

11 ¶ And Jŏn'a-than said unto Dā'vid, Come, and let us go out into the field. And they went out both of them into the field.

12 And Jŏn'a-than said unto Dā'vid, [i]O LORD God of Ĭs'ra-el, when I have [5]sounded my father about to morrow any time, *or* the third *day*, and, behold, *if there be* good toward Dā'vid, and I then send not unto thee, and [6]shew it thee;

13 [j]The LORD do so and much more to Jŏn'a-than: but if it please my father *to do* thee evil, then I will shew it thee, and send thee away, that thou mayest go in peace: and [k]the LORD be with thee, as he hath been with my father.

14 And thou shalt not only while yet I live shew me the kindness of the LORD, that I die not:

15 But *also* [l]thou shalt not cut off thy kindness from my house for ever: no, not when the LORD hath cut off the enemies of Dā'vid every one from the face of the earth.

16 So Jŏn'a-than [7]made *a covenant*
with the house of Dā'vid, *saying,* [m]Let
the LORD even require *it* at the hand of
Dā'vid's enemies.
17 And Jŏn'a-than caused Dā'vid to
swear again, [8]because he loved him:
for he loved him as he loved his own
soul.
18 Then Jŏn'a-than said to Dā'vid,
To morrow *is* the new moon: and thou
shalt be missed, because thy seat will
be [9]empty.
19 And *when* thou hast stayed three
days, *then* thou shalt go down [10]quickly,
and come to [n]the place where thou didst
hide thyself [11]when the business was *in
hand,* and shalt remain by the stone
[12]Ē'zel.
20 And I will shoot three arrows on
the side *thereof,* as though I shot at a
mark.
21 And, behold, I will send a lad,
saying, Go, find out the arrows. If I
expressly say unto the lad, Behold,
the arrows *are* on this side of thee,
take them; then come thou: for *there
is* peace to thee, and [13]no hurt; [o]*as* the
LORD liveth.
22 But if I say thus unto the young
man, Behold, the arrows *are* beyond
thee; go thy way: for the LORD hath
sent thee away.
23 And *as touching* the matter which
thou and I have spoken of, behold, the
LORD *be* between thee and me for ever.
24 ¶ So Dā'vid [p]hid himself in the
field: and when the new moon was
come, the king sat him down to eat
meat.
25 And the king sat upon his seat, as
at other times, *even* upon a seat by the
wall: and Jŏn'a-than arose, and [q]Ăb'-
nẽr sat by Sa̧ul's side, and Dā'vid's
place was empty.
26 Nevertheless Sa̧ul spake not any
thing that day: for he thought, Something hath befallen him, he *is* [r]not
clean; surely he *is* not clean.
27 And it came to pass on the morrow, *which was* the second *day* of the
month, that Dā'vid's place was empty:
and Sa̧ul said unto Jŏn'a-than his son,
Wherefore cometh not the son of Jĕs'se
to meat, neither yesterday, nor to day?
28 And Jŏn'a-than answered Sa̧ul,
Dā'vid earnestly asked *leave* of me *to
go* to Bĕth'–lĕ-hĕm:
29 And he said, Let me go, I pray
thee; for our family hath a sacrifice in
the city; and my brother, he hath commanded me *to be there:* and now, if I
have found favour in thine eyes, let me
get away, I pray thee, and see my brethren. Therefore he cometh not unto the
king's table.
30 Then Sa̧ul's anger was kindled
against Jŏn'a-than, and he said unto
him, [14]Thou son of the perverse rebellious *woman,* do not I know that thou
hast chosen the son of Jĕs'se to thine
own confusion, and unto the confusion
of thy mother's nakedness?
31 For as long as the son of Jĕs'se
liveth upon the ground, thou shalt
not be established, nor thy kingdom.

16 [7]cut
[m]ch. 25.22; 2 Sam. 21.8
17 [8]Or, by his love toward him
18 [9]missed
19 [10]greatly, or, diligently
[n]ch. 19.2
[11]in the day of the business
[12]Or, that sheweth the way
21 [13]not any thing
[o]Deut. 6.13; Jer. 4.2
24 [p]Prov. 27.12
25 [q]ch. 14.50
26 [r]Lev. 6.2-3; Eph. 5.11
30 [14]Son of perverse rebellion, or, Thou perverse rebel
31 [15]is the son of death
32 [s]Gen. 31.36; John 15.25
36 [16]to pass over him
40 [17]instruments
[18]that was his
42 [19]Or, the LORD be witness of that which, etc
CHAPTER 21
1 [a]ch. 22.19; Isa. 10.32
[b]ch. 14.3-called Ahiah; Called also Abiathar
2 [c]Gen. 27.20-24; Col. 3.9
3 [1]found
4 [d]Ex. 25.30; Matt. 12.4
[e]Ex. 19.15; Zech. 7.3

Wherefore now send and fetch him
unto me, for he [15]shall surely die.
32 And Jŏn'a-than answered Sa̧ul
his father, and said unto him, [s]Where-
fore shall he be slain? what hath he
done?
33 And Sa̧ul cast a javelin at him to
smite him: whereby Jŏn'a-than knew
that it was determined of his father to
slay Dā'vid.
34 So Jŏn'a-than arose from the table in fierce anger, and did eat no meat
the second day of the month: for he
was grieved for Dā'vid, because his father had done him shame.
35 ¶ And it came to pass in the morning, that Jŏn'a-than went out into the
field at the time appointed with Dā'vid,
and a little lad with him.
36 And he said unto his lad, Run,
find out now the arrows which I shoot.
And as the lad ran, he shot an arrow
[16]beyond him.
37 And when the lad was come to
the place of the arrow which Jŏn'a-
than had shot, Jŏn'a-than cried after
the lad, and said, *Is* not the arrow beyond thee?
38 And Jŏn'a-than cried after the
lad, Make speed, haste, stay not. And
Jŏn'a-than's lad gathered up the arrows, and came to his master.
39 But the lad knew not any thing:
only Jŏn'a-than and Dā'vid knew the
matter.
40 And Jŏn'a-than gave his [17]artil-
lery unto [18]his lad, and said unto him,
Go, carry *them* to the city.
41 ¶ *And* as soon as the lad was
gone, Dā'vid arose out of *a place* toward the south, and fell on his face to
the ground, and bowed himself three
times: and they kissed one another,
and wept one with another, until Dā'-
vid exceeded.
42 And Jŏn'a-than said to Dā'vid,
Go in peace, [19]forasmuch as we have
sworn both of us in the name of the
LORD, saying, The LORD be between
me and thee, and between my seed and
thy seed for ever. And he arose and
departed: and Jŏn'a-than went into the
city.

21 Then came Dā'vid to [a]Nŏb to
[b]A-hĭm'e-lech the priest: and A-
hĭm'e-lech was afraid at the meeting of
Dā'vid, and said unto him, Why *art*
thou alone, and no man with thee?
2 And Dā'vid said unto A-hĭm'e-lech
the priest, [c]The king hath commanded
me a business, and hath said unto me,
Let no man know any thing of the business whereabout I send thee, and what
I have commanded thee: and I have appointed *my* servants to such and such a
place.
3 Now therefore what is under thine
hand? give *me* five *loaves of* bread in
mine hand, or what there is [1]present.
4 And the priest answered Dā'vid,
and said, *There is* no common bread
under mine hand, but there is [d]hal-
lowed bread; [e]if the young men have
kept themselves at least from women.

5 And Dā′vid answered the priest, and said unto him, Of a truth women *have been* kept from us about these three days, since I came out, and the [f]vessels of the young men are holy, and *the bread is* in a manner common, [2]yea, though it were sanctified this day [g]in the vessel.

6 So the priest [h]gave him hallowed *bread:* for there was no bread there but the shewbread, [i]that was taken from before the LORD, to put hot bread in the day when it was taken away.

7 Now a certain man of the servants of Sa̧ul *was* there that day, detained before the LORD; and his name *was* [j]Dō′eg, an Ē′dom-īte, the chiefest of the herdmen that *belonged* to Sa̧ul.

8 ¶ And Dā′vid said unto A-hĭm′e-lech, And is there not here under thine hand spear or sword? for I have neither brought my sword nor my weapons with me, because the king's business required haste.

9 And the priest said, The sword of Go-lī′ath the Phĭ-lĭs′tīne, whom thou slewest in the valley of Ē′lah, [k]behold, it *is here* wrapped in a cloth behind the ephod: if thou wilt take that, take *it:* for *there is* no other save that here. And Dā′vid said, *There is* none like that; give it me.

10 ¶ And Dā′vid arose, and fled that day for fear of Sa̧ul, and went to [3]Ā′chĭsh the king of Găth.

11 And [l]the servants of Ā′chĭsh said unto him, *Is* not this Dā′vid the king of the land? did they not sing one to another of him in dances, saying, [m]Sa̧ul hath slain his thousands, and Dā′vid his ten thousands?

12 And Dā′vid laid up these words in his heart, and was sore afraid of Ā′chĭsh the king of Găth.

13 And [n]he changed his behaviour before them, and feigned himself mad in their hands, and [4]scrabbled on the doors of the gate, and let his spittle fall down upon his bea̧rd.

14 Then said Ā′chĭsh unto his servants, Lo, ye see the man [5]is mad: wherefore *then* have ye brought him to me?

15 Have I need of mad men, that ye have brought this *fellow* to play the mad man in my presence? shall this *fellow* come into my house?

22 Dā′vid therefore departed thence, and [a]escaped [b]to the cave A-dŭl′-lăm: and when his brethren and all his father's house heard *it,* they went down thither to him.

2 [c]And every one *that was* in distress, and every one that [1]*was* in debt, and every one *that was* [2]discontented, gathered themselves unto him; and he became a captain over them: and there were with him about four hundred men.

3 ¶ And Dā′vid went thence to Mĭz′-peh of Mō′ab: and he said unto the king of Mō′ab, [d]Let my father and my mother, I pray thee, come forth, *and be* with you, till I know what God will do for me.

4 And he brought them before the king of Mō′ab: and they dwelt with him all the while that Dā′vid was in the hold.

5 ¶ And the prophet [e]Găd said unto Dā′vid, Abide not in the hold; depart, and get thee into the land of Jū′dah. Then Dā′vid departed, and came into the forest of Hā′reth.

6 ¶ When Sa̧ul heard that Dā′vid was discovered, and the men that *were* with him, (now Sa̧ul abode in Gĭb′e-ah under a [3]tree in Rā′mah, having his spear in his hand, and all his servants *were* standing about him;)

7 Then Sa̧ul said unto his servants that stood about him, Hear now, ye Bĕn′ja-mītes; will the son of Jĕs′se [f]give every one of you fields and vineyards, *and* make you all captains of thousands, and captains of hundreds;

8 That all of you have conspired against me, and *there is* none that [4]sheweth me that [g]my son hath made a league with the son of Jĕs′se, and *there is* none of you that is sorry for me, or sheweth unto me that my son hath stirred up my servant against me, to lie in wait, as at this day?

9 ¶ Then answered [h]Dō′eg the Ē′dom-īte, which was set over the servants of Sa̧ul, and said, I saw the son of Jĕs′se coming to Nŏb, to [i]A-hĭm′e-lech the son of [j]A-hī′tub.

10 And [k]he inquired of the LORD for him, and [l]gave him victuals, and gave him the sword of Go-lī′ath the Phĭ-lĭs′tīne.

11 Then the king sent to call A-hĭm′e-lech the priest, the son of A-hī′tub, and all his father's house, the priests that *were* in Nŏb: and they came all of them to the king.

12 And Sa̧ul said, Hear now, thou son of A-hī′tub. And he answered, [5]Here I *am,* my lord.

13 And Sa̧ul said unto him, Why have ye conspired against me, thou and the son of Jĕs′se, in that thou hast given him bread, and a sword, and hast inquired of God for him, that he should rise against me, to lie in wait, as at this day?

14 Then A-hĭm′e-lech [m]answered the king, and said, And who *is so* faithful among all thy servants as Dā′vid, which is the king's son in law, and goeth at thy bidding, and is honourable in thine house?

15 Did I then begin to inquire of God for him? be it far from me: let not the king impute *any* thing unto his servant, *nor* to all the house of my father: for thy servant knew nothing of all this, [6]less or more.

16 And the king said, Thou shalt surely die, A-hĭm′e-lech, thou, and all thy father's house.

17 ¶ And the king said unto the [7]footmen that stood about him, Turn, and slay the priests of the LORD; because their hand also *is* with Dā′vid, and because they knew when he fled, and did not shew it to me. But the servants of the king [n]would not put forth their

5 [f]1 Thess. 4.4
[2]Or, especially when this day there is other sanctified in the vessel
[g]Lev. 8.26
6 [h]Matt. 12.3; Mark 2.25; Luke 6.3
[i]Lev. 24.8
7 [j]ch. 22.9; Ps. 52-title
9 [k]ch. 31.10
10 [3]Or, Abimelech
11 [l]Ps. 56-title
[m]ch. 18.7
13 [n]Ps. 34-title
[4]Or, made marks
14 [5]Or, playeth the mad man

CHAPTER 22

1 [a]Ps. 57-title; Ps. 142-title
[b]Josh. 12.15; Heb. 11.38
2 [c]Judg. 11.3
[1]had a creditor
[2]bitter of soul
3 [d]Gen. 47.11; 1 Tim. 5.4
5 [e]2 Sam. 24.11; 2 Chr. 29.25
6 [3]Or, grove in a high place
7 [f]ch. 8.14
8 [4]uncovereth mine ear
[g]ch. 18.3; ch. 20.30
9 [h]ch. 21.7; Ps. 52-title
[i]ch. 21.1
[j]ch. 14.3
10 [k]Num. 27.21
[l]ch. 21.6-9
12 [5]Behold me
14 [m]ch. 19.4-5; Prov. 31.9
15 [6]little, or, great
17 [7]runners, or, guard
[n]Ex. 1.17; Acts 4.19

hand to fall upon the priests of the
LORD.
18 And [o]the king said to Dō'eg, Turn
thou, and fall upon the priests. And
Dō'eg the Ē'dom-īte turned, and he fell
upon the priests, and [p]slew on that
day fourscore and five persons that did
wear a [q]linen ephod.
19 [r]And Nŏb, the city of the priests,
smote [s]he with the edge of the sword,
both men and women, children and
sucklings, and oxen, and asses, and
sheep, with the edge of the sword.
20 ¶ [t]And one of the sons of A-hĭm'-
e-lech the son of A-hī'tub, named A-
bī'a-thär, [u]escaped, and fled after Dā'-
vid.
21 And A-bī'a-thär shewed Dā'vid
that Sa̤ul had slain the LORD'S priests.
22 And Dā'vid said unto A-bī'a-thär,
I knew *it* that day, when Dō'eg the
Ē'dom-īte *was* there, that he would
surely tell Sa̤ul: I have occasioned *the
death* of all the persons of thy father's
house.
23 Abide thou with me, fear not: [v]for
he that seeketh my life seeketh thy life:
but with me thou *shalt be* in safeguard.
23 Then they told Dā'vid, saying,
Behold, the Phĭ-lĭs'tīnes fight
against [a]Kēi'lah, and they rob the
threshingfloors.
2 Therefore Dā'vid [b]inquired of the
LORD, saying, Shall I go and smite
these Phĭ-lĭs'tīnes? And the LORD said
unto Dā'vid, Go, and smite the Phĭ-
lĭs'tīnes, and save Kēi'lah.
3 And Dā'vid's men said unto him,
Behold, we be afraid here in Jū'dah:
how much more then if we come to
Kēi'lah against the armies of the Phĭ-
lĭs'tīnes?
4 Then Dā'vid inquired of the LORD
yet again. And the LORD answered him
and said, Arise, go down to Kēi'lah; for
I will deliver the Phĭ-lĭs'tīnes into thine
hand.
5 So Dā'vid and his men went to
Kēi'lah, and fought with the Phĭ-lĭs'-
tīnes, and brought away their cattle,
and smote them with a great slaughter.
So Dā'vid saved the inhabitants of Kēi'-
lah.
6 And it came to pass, when A-bī'a-
thär the son of A-hĭm'e-lech [c]fled to
Dā'vid to Kēi'lah, *that* he came down
with an ephod in his hand.
7 ¶ And it was told Sa̤ul that Dā'vid
was come to Kēi'lah. And Sa̤ul said,
God [d]hath delivered him into mine
hand; for he is shut in, by entering into
a town that hath gates and bars.
8 And Sa̤ul called all the people together to war, to go down to Kēi'lah, to
besiege Dā'vid and his men.
9 ¶ And Dā'vid knew that Sa̤ul secretly practised mischief against him;
and [e]he said to A-bī'a-thär the priest,
Bring hither the ephod.
10 Then said Dā'vid, O LORD God
of Ĭs'ra-el, thy servant hath certainly
heard that Sa̤ul seeketh to come to
Kēi'lah, [f]to destroy the city for my
sake.
11 Will the men of Kēi'lah deliver
me up into his hand? will Sa̤ul come
down, as thy servant hath heard? O
LORD God of Ĭs'ra-el, I beseech thee,
tell thy servant. And the LORD said, He
will come down.
12 Then said Dā'vid, Will the men of
Kēi'lah [1]deliver me and my men into
the hand of Sa̤ul? And the LORD said,
They will deliver *thee* up.
13 ¶ Then Dā'vid and his men,
[g]*which were* about six hundred, arose
and departed out of Kēi'lah, and went
whithersoever they could go. And it
was told Sa̤ul that Dā'vid was escaped
from Kēi'lah; and he forbare to go
forth.
14 And Dā'vid abode in the wilderness in strong holds, and remained in
[h]a mountain in the wilderness of [i]Zĭph.
And Sa̤ul [j]sought him every day, but
[k]God delivered him not into his hand.
15 And Dā'vid saw that Sa̤ul was
come out to seek his life: and Dā'vid
was in the wilderness of Zĭph in a
wood.
16 ¶ And Jŏn'a-than Sa̤ul's son arose,
and went to Dā'vid into the wood, and
strengthened his hand in God.
17 And he said unto him, Fear not:
for the hand of Sa̤ul my father shall not
find thee; and thou shalt be king over
Ĭs'ra-el, and I shall be next unto thee;
and [l]that also Sa̤ul my father knoweth.
18 And they two [m]made a covenant
before the LORD: and Dā'vid abode in
the wood, and Jŏn'a-than went to his
house.
19 ¶ Then [n]came up the Zĭph'ītes to
Sa̤ul to Gĭb'e-ah, saying, Doth not Dā'-
vid hide himself with us in strong holds
in the wood, in the hill of Hăch'ĭ-lah,
which *is* [2]on the south of [3]Jĕsh'i-mŏn?
20 Now therefore, O king, come
down according to all the desire of thy
soul to come down; and [4]our part *shall
be* to deliver him into the king's hand.
21 And Sa̤ul said, Blessed *be* ye of
the LORD; for ye have compassion on
me.
22 Go, I pray you, prepare yet, and
know and see his place where his
[5]haunt is, *and* who hath seen him there:
for it is told me *that* he dealeth very
subtilly.
23 See therefore, and take knowledge of all the lurking places where he
hideth himself, and come ye again to
me with the certainty, and I will go
with you: and it shall come to pass, if
he be in the land, that I will search him
out throughout all the thousands of
Jū'dah.
24 And they arose, and went to Zĭph
before Sa̤ul: but Dā'vid and his men
were in the wilderness [o]of Mā'on, in
the plain on the south of Jĕsh'i-mŏn.
25 Sa̤ul also and his men went to
seek *him*. And they told Dā'vid: wherefore he came down [6]into a rock, and
abode in the wilderness of Mā'on. And
when Sa̤ul heard *that*, he pursued after Dā'vid in the wilderness of Mā'on.

18 [o]Ps. 12.5; Prov. 28.15
[p]ch. 2.31
[q]Ex. 28.40
19 [r]Neh. 11.32; Isa. 10.32
[s]Ps. 10.2-8; Isa. 26.13
20 [t]ch. 23.6
[u]Judg. 9.5; ch. 2.33
23 [v]1 Ki. 2.26; Matt. 24.9; John 16.2; Heb. 12.1-3
CHAPTER 23
1 [a]Josh. 15.44
2 [b]Num. 27.21; ch. 28.6; ch. 30.8; 2 Sam. 5.19-23; 1 Chr. 10.14; Ps. 37.5; Prov. 3.5-6
6 [c]ch. 22.20
7 [d]Ex. 15.6; ch. 24.4-6; ch. 26.8-9; Ps. 71.11
9 [e]Num. 27.21; ch. 30.7
10 [f]ch. 22.19; 2 Sam. 20.20; Esth. 3.6; Ps. 44.22
12 [1]shut up
13 [g]ch. 22.2
14 [h]Ps. 11.1
[i]Josh. 15.55
[j]ch. 27.1; Ps. 54.3-4; Prov. 1.16
[k]Deut. 33.3; ch. 2.9; Ps. 32.7; Ps. 33.18; Ps. 121.3-8; Prov. 2.8; Prov. 21.30; Rom. 8.31; 2 Tim. 3.11
17 [l]ch. 24.20
18 [m]ch. 18.3; 2 Sam. 21.7
19 [n]ch. 26.1; Ps. 54-title
[2]on the right hand
[3]Or, the wilderness
20 [4]it becometh me
22 [5]foot shall be
24 [o]Josh. 15.55; ch. 25.2
25 [6]Or, from the rock

26 And Sa̧ul went on this side of the
mountain, and Dā'vid and his men on
that side of the mountain: [p]and Dā'vid
made haste to get away for fear of Sa̧ul;
for Sa̧ul and his men [q]compassed Dā'-
vid and his men round about to take
them.
27 ¶ [r]But there came a messenger
unto Sa̧ul, saying, Haste thee, and
come; for the Phĭ-lĭs'tĭnes have [7]in-
vaded the land.
28 Wherefore Sa̧ul returned from
pursuing after Dā'vid, and went against
the Phĭ-lĭs'tĭnes: therefore they called
that place [8]Sē'lȧ–hăm-mah-lē'koth.
29 ¶ And Dā'vid went up from thence,
and dwelt in strong holds at [s]En–ge'di.

24 And it came to pass, [a]when Sa̧ul
was returned from [1]following the
Phĭ-lĭs'tĭnes, that it was told him, saying, Behold, Dā'vid *is* in the wilderness
of Ēn–ḡē'dī.
2 Then Sa̧ul took three thousand
chosen men out of all Ĭs'ra-el, [b]and
went to seek Dā'vid and his men upon
the rocks of the wild goats.
3 And he came to the sheepcotes by
the way, where *was* a cave; and Sa̧ul
went in to [c]cover his feet: and [d]Dā'vid
and his men remained in the sides of
the cave.
4 [e]And the men of Dā'vid said unto
him, Behold the day of which the LORD
said unto thee, Behold, I will deliver
thine enemy into thine hand, that thou
mayest do to him as it shall seem good
unto thee. Then Dā'vid arose, and cut
off the skirt of [2]Sa̧ul's robe privily.
5 And it came to pass afterward, that
[f]Dā'vid's heart smote him, because he
had cut off Sa̧ul's skirt.
6 And he said unto his men, [g]The
LORD forbid that I should do this thing
unto my master, the LORD'S anointed,
to stretch forth mine hand against him,
seeing he *is* the anointed of the LORD.
7 So Dā'vid [3]stayed his servants with
these words, and suffered them not to
rise against Sa̧ul. But Sa̧ul rose up out
of the cave, and went on *his* way.
8 Dā'vid also arose afterward, and
went out of the cave, and cried after
Sa̧ul, saying, My lord the king. And
when Sa̧ul looked behind him, Dā'vid
stooped with his face to the earth, and
bowed himself.
9 ¶ And Dā'vid said to Sa̧ul, [h]Where-
fore hearest thou men's words, saying,
Behold, Dā'vid seeketh thy hurt?
10 Behold, this day thine eyes have
seen how that the LORD had delivered
thee to day into mine hand in the cave:
and *some* bade *me* kill thee: but *mine
eye* spared thee; and I said, I will not
put forth mine hand against my lord;
for he *is* the LORD'S anointed.
11 Moreover, my father, see, yea,
see the skirt of thy robe in my hand:
for in that I cut off the skirt of thy robe,
and killed thee not, know thou and see
that *there is* neither [i]evil nor transgression in mine hand, and I have not
sinned against thee; yet thou [j]huntest
my soul to take it.
12 [k]The LORD judge between me and
thee, and the LORD avenge me of thee:
but mine hand shall not be upon thee.
13 As saith the proverb of the ancients, Wickedness proceedeth from
the wicked: but mine hand shall not be
upon thee.
14 After whom is the [l]king of Ĭs'ra-
el come out? after whom dost thou pursue? [m]after a dead dog, after [n]a flea.
15 The LORD therefore be judge, and
judge between me and thee, and [o]see,
and [p]plead my cause, and [4]deliver me
out of thine hand.
16 ¶ And it came to pass, when Dā'-
vid had made an end of speaking these
words unto Sa̧ul, that Sa̧ul said, [q]*Is*
this thy voice, my son Dā'vid? And
Sa̧ul lifted up his voice, and wept.
17 And he said to Dā'vid, Thou *art*
[r]more righteous than I: for [s]thou hast
rewarded me good, whereas I have rewarded thee evil.
18 And thou hast shewed this day
how that thou hast dealt well with
me: forasmuch as when the LORD had
[5]delivered me into thine hand, thou
killedst me not.
19 For if a man find his enemy, will
he let him go well away? wherefore the
LORD reward thee good for that thou
hast done unto me this day.
20 And now, behold, [t]I know well
that thou shalt surely be king, and that
the kingdom of Ĭs'ra-el shall be established in thine hand.
21 Swear now therefore unto me by
the LORD, that thou wilt not cut off my
seed after me, and that thou wilt not
destroy my name out of my father's
house.
22 And Dā'vid sware unto Sa̧ul. And
Sa̧ul went home; but Dā'vid and his
men gat them up unto the hold.

25 And [a]Săm'u-el died; and all the
Ĭs'ra-el-ītes were gathered together, and [b]lamented him, and buried
him in his house at Rā'mah. And Dā'-
vid arose, and went down [c]to the wilderness of Pā'ran.
2 And *there was* a man [d]in Mā'on,
whose [1]possessions *were* in [e]Cär'mel;
and the man *was* very great, and he
had three thousand sheep, and a thousand goats: and he was [f]shearing his
sheep in Cär'mel.
3 Now the name of the man *was*
Nā'bal; and the name of his wife Ăb'ĭ-
gāil: and *she was* a [g]woman of good
understanding, and of a beautiful countenance: but the man *was* [h]churlish
and evil in his doings; and he *was* of
the house of Cā'leb.
4 ¶ And Dā'vid heard in the wilderness that Nā'bal did [i]shear his sheep.
5 And Dā'vid sent out ten young
men, and Dā'vid said unto the young
men, Get you up to Cär'mel, and go to
Nā'bal, and [2]greet him in my name:
6 And thus shall ye say to him that
liveth *in prosperity,* [j]Peace *be* both to
thee, and peace *be* to thine house, and
peace *be* unto all that thou hast.
7 And now I have heard that thou
hast shearers: now thy shepherds which

26 [p]ch. 19.12; Ps. 31.22
[q]2 Chr. 20.12; 2 Cor. 1.8
27 [r]Deut. 32.36; Isa. 37.6-9
[7]spread themselves upon, etc
28 [8]That is, The rock of divisions
29 [s]2 Chr. 20.2

CHAPTER 24
1 [a]ch. 23.28
[1]after
2 [b]Ps. 38.12
3 [c]Judg. 3.24
[d]Ps. 57-title
4 [e]ch. 26.8
[2]the robe which was Saul's
5 [f]2 Sam. 24.10
6 [g]ch. 26.11; Job 31.29-30
7 [3]cut off
9 [h]Ps. 141.6; Prov. 17.9
11 [i]Ps. 7.3; Ps. 35.7
[j]ch. 26.20
12 [k]Gen. 16.5; Judg. 11.27
14 [l]Prov. 5.23
[m]ch. 17.43; 2 Sam. 9.8
[n]ch. 26.20
15 [o]2 Chr. 24.22
[p]Ps. 35.1;
[4]judge
16 [q]ch. 26.17
17 [r]Gen. 38.26;
[s]Matt. 5.44
18 [5]shut up
20 [t]ch. 23.17

CHAPTER 25
1 [a]ch. 28.3;
[b]Gen. 50.11;
[c]Gen. 14.6
2 [d]ch. 23.24
[1]Or, business
[e]Josh. 15.55
[f]Gen. 38.13
3 [g]Ruth 4.11;
[h]Isa. 32.5-7
4 [i]Gen. 38.13
5 [2]ask him in my name of peace
6 [j]2 Sam. 18.28

were with us, we [3]hurt them not, neither
was there ought missing unto them, all
the while they were in Cär'mel.
8 Ask thy young men, and they will
shew thee. Wherefore let the young
men find favour in thine eyes: for we
come in [k]a good day: give, I pray thee,
whatsoever cometh to thine hand unto
thy servants, and to thy son Dā'vid.
9 And when Dā'vid's young men
came, they spake to Nā'bal according
to all those words in the name of Dā'-
vid, and [4]ceased.
10 ¶ And Nā'bal answered Dā'vid's
servants, and said, [l]Who *is* Dā'vid?
and who *is* the son of Jěs'se? there be
many servants now a days that break
away every man from his master.
11 [m]Shall I then take my bread, and
my water, and my [5]flesh that I have
killed for my shearers, and give *it* unto
men, whom I know not whence they
be?
12 So Dā'vid's young men turned
their way, and went again, and came
and told him all those sayings.
13 And Dā'vid said unto his men,
Gird ye on every man his sword. And
they girded on every man his sword;
and Dā'vid also girded on his sword:
and there went up after Dā'vid about
four hundred men; and two hundred
[n]abode by the stuff.
14 ¶ But one of the young men told
Ăb'ĭ-gāil, Nā'bal's wife, saying, Behold, Dā'vid sent messengers out of
the wilderness to salute our master;
and he [6]railed on them.
15 But the men *were* very good unto
us, and we were not [7]hurt, neither
missed we any thing, as long as we
were conversant with them, when we
were in the fields:
16 They were [o]a wall unto us both
by night and day, all the while we were
with them keeping the sheep.
17 Now therefore know and con-
sider what thou wilt do; for evil is determined against our master, and against
all his household: for he *is such* a son
of Bē'lĭ-al, that *a man* cannot speak to
him.
18 ¶ Then Ăb'ĭ-gāil made haste, and
[p]took two hundred loaves, and two
bottles of wine, and five sheep ready
dressed, and five measures of parched
corn, and an hundred [8]clusters of raisins, and two hundred cakes of figs,
and laid *them* on asses.
19 And she said unto her servants,
[q]Go on before me; behold, I come after
you. But she told not her husband Nā'-
bal.
20 And it was *so, as* she rode on the
ass, that she came down by the covert
of the hill, and, behold, Dā'vid and his
men came down against her; and she
met them.
21 Now Dā'vid had said, Surely in
vain have I kept all that this *fellow*
hath in the wilderness, so that nothing
was missed of all that *pertained* unto
him: and he hath [r]requited me evil for
good.

7 [3]shamed
8 [k]Neh. 8.10; Esth. 9.19
9 [4]rested
10 [l]Judg. 9.28; Ps. 73.7-8
11 [m]Judg. 8.6 [5]slaughter
13 [n]ch. 30.24
14 [6]flew upon them
15 [7]shamed
16 [o]Ex. 14.22; Job 1.10; Zech. 2.5
18 [p]Gen. 32.13; 2 Sam. 17.28-29; Prov. 18.16 [8]Or, lumps
19 [q]Gen. 32.16
21 [r]Gen. 44.4; Ps. 35.12; Prov. 17.13; 1 Pet. 2.20
22 [s]Ruth 1.17; ch. 3.17; ch. 20.13-16
23 [t]Josh. 15.18
24 [9]ears
25 [10]lay it to his heart [11]That is, Fool
26 [u]2 Ki. 2.2 [v]Gen. 20.6 [12]saving thyself [w]2 Sam. 18.32
27 [x]Gen. 33.11 [13]Or, present [14]walk at the feet of, etc
28 [y]2 Sam. 7.11; 1 Ki. 9.5; 1 Chr. 17.16 [z]ch. 24.11
29 [a]Deut. 33.29; Ps. 66.9; Matt. 10.29-30; Acts 17.28 [b]Jer. 10.18 [15]in the midst of the bought of a sling
31 [16]no staggering, or, stumbling
32 [c]Gen. 24.27; Ex. 18.10; Ezra 7.27; Ps. 41.12-13; Ps. 72.18; Luke 1.68
35 [d]ch. 20.42; 2 Sam. 15.9; Luke 7.50 [e]Gen. 19.21

22 [s]So and more also do God unto
the enemies of Dā'vid, if I leave of all
that *pertain* to him by the morning
light any that pisseth against the wall.
23 And when Ăb'ĭ-gāil saw Dā'vid,
she hasted, and [t]lighted off the ass,
and fell before Dā'vid on her face, and
bowed herself to the ground,
24 And fell at his feet, and said, Upon
me, my lord, *upon* me *let this* iniquity
be: and let thine handmaid, I pray thee,
speak in thine [9]audience, and hear the
words of thine handmaid.
25 Let not my lord, I pray thee, [10]re-
gard this man of Bē'lĭ-al, *even* Nā'bal:
for as his name *is,* so *is* he; [11]Nā'bal *is*
his name, and folly *is* with him: but
I thine handmaid saw not the young
men of my lord, whom thou didst send.
26 Now therefore, my lord, [u]*as* the
LORD liveth, and *as* thy soul liveth, seeing the LORD hath [v]withholden thee
from coming to *shed* blood, and from
[12]avenging thyself with thine own hand,
now [w]let thine enemies, and they that
seek evil to my lord, be as Nā'bal.
27 And now [x]this [13]blessing which
thine handmaid hath brought unto my
lord, let it even be given unto the young
men that [14]follow my lord.
28 I pray thee, forgive the trespass
of thine handmaid: for [y]the LORD will
certainly make my lord a sure house;
because my lord fighteth the battles
of the LORD, and [z]evil hath not been
found in thee *all* thy days.
29 Yet a man is risen to pursue thee,
and to seek thy soul: but the soul of my
lord shall be [a]bound in the bundle of
life with the LORD thy God; and the
souls of thine enemies, them shall he
[b]sling out, [15]*as out* of the middle of a
sling.
30 And it shall come to pass, when
the LORD shall have done to my lord
according to all the good that he hath
spoken concerning thee, and shall have
appointed thee ruler over Ĭs'ra-el;
31 That this shall be [16]no grief unto
thee, nor offence of heart unto my lord,
either that thou hast shed blood causeless, or that my lord hath avenged himself: but when the LORD shall have
dealt well with my lord, then remember thine handmaid.
32 ¶ And Dā'vid said to Ăb'ĭ-gāil,
[c]Blessed *be* the LORD God of Ĭs'ra-el,
which sent thee this day to meet me:
33 And blessed *be* thy advice, and
blessed *be* thou, which hast kept me
this day from coming to *shed* blood,
and from avenging myself with mine
own hand.
34 For in very deed, *as* the LORD God
of Ĭs'ra-el liveth, which hath kept me
back from hurting thee, except thou
hadst hasted and come to meet me,
surely there had not been left unto
Nā'bal by the morning light any that
pisseth against the wall.
35 So Dā'vid received of her hand
that which she had brought him, and
said unto her, [d]Go up in peace to thine
house; see, I have hearkened to thy
voice, and have accepted [e]thy person.

36 ¶ And Ăb'ĭ-gāil came to Nā'bal;
and, behold, [f]he held a feast in his
house, like the feast of a king; and
Nā'bal's heart *was* merry within him,
for he *was* [g]very drunken: wherefore
she told him nothing, less or more, until the morning light.
37 But it came to pass in the morning, when the wine was gone out of
Nā'bal, and his wife had told him these
things, that his [h]heart died within him,
and he became *as* a stone.
38 And it came to pass about ten
days *after,* that [i]the LORD smote Nā'-
bal, that he died.
39 ¶ And when Dā'vid heard that
Nā'bal was dead, he said, Blessed *be*
the LORD, that hath [j]pleaded the cause
of my reproach from the hand of Nā'-
bal, and hath kept his servant from
evil: for the LORD hath [k]returned the
wickedness of Nā'bal upon his own
head. And Dā'vid sent and communed
with Ăb'ĭ-gāil, to take her to him to
wife.
40 And when the servants of Dā'vid
were come to Ăb'ĭ-gāil to Cär'mel, they
spake unto her, saying, Dā'vid sent us
unto thee, to take thee to him to wife.
41 And she arose, and bowed herself on *her* face to the earth, and said,
Behold, *let* [l]thine handmaid *be* a servant to wash the feet of the servants of
my lord.
42 And Ăb'ĭ-gāil hasted, and arose,
and rode upon an ass, with five damsels of hers that went [17]after her; and
she went after the messengers of Dā'-
vid, and became his wife.
43 Dā'vid also took A-hĭn'o-am [m]of
Jĕz're-el; [n]and they were also both of
them his wives.
44 ¶ But Saul had given [o]Mī'chal his
daughter, Dā'vid's wife, to [18]Phăl'tī the
son of Lā'ish, which *was* of [p]Găl'lĭm.

26

And the Zĭph'ītes came unto Saul
to Gĭb'e-ah, saying, [a]Doth not
Dā'vid hide himself in the hill of Hăch'-
ĭ-lah, *which is* before Jĕsh'i-mŏn?
2 Then Saul arose, and went down
to the wilderness of Zĭph, having three
thousand chosen men of Ĭs'ra-el with
him, to seek Dā'vid in the wilderness
of Zĭph.
3 And Saul pitched in the hill of
Hăch'ĭ-lah, which *is* before Jĕsh'i-mŏn,
by the way. But Dā'vid abode in the
wilderness, and he saw that Saul came
after him into the wilderness.
4 Dā'vid therefore sent out spies,
and understood that Saul was come in
very deed.
5 ¶ And Dā'vid arose, and came to
the place where Saul had pitched: and
Dā'vid beheld the place where Saul
lay, and [b]Ăb'nēr the son of Nēr, the
captain of his host: and Saul lay in the
[1]trench, and the people pitched round
about him.
6 Then answered Dā'vid and said
to A-hĭm'e-lech the Hĭt'tīte, and to A-
bĭsh'ă-ī [c]the son of Zĕr-u-ī'ah, brother
to Jō'ab, saying, Who will [d]go down
with me to Saul to the camp? And A-
bĭsh'ă-ī said, I will go down with thee.
7 So Dā'vid and A-bĭsh'ă-ī came to
the people by night: and, behold, Saul
lay sleeping within the trench, and his
spear stuck in the ground at his bolster: but Ăb'nēr and the people lay
round about him.
8 Then said A-bĭsh'ă-ī to Dā'vid,
God hath [2]delivered thine enemy into
thine hand this day: now therefore let
me smite him, I pray thee, with the
spear even to the earth at once, and I
will not *smite* him the second time.
9 And Dā'vid said to A-bĭsh'ă-ī, Destroy him not: for who can stretch forth
his hand against the LORD'S anointed,
and be guiltless?
10 Dā'vid said furthermore, *As* the
LORD liveth, [e]the LORD shall smite him;
or [f]his day shall come to die; or he shall
[g]descend into battle, and perish.
11 [h]The LORD forbid that I should
stretch forth mine hand against the
LORD'S anointed: but, I pray thee, take
thou now the spear that *is* at his bolster, and the cruse of water, and let us
go.
12 So Dā'vid took the spear and the
cruse of water from Saul's bolster; and
they gat them away, and no man saw
it, nor knew *it,* neither awaked: for
they *were* all asleep; because [i]a deep
sleep from the LORD was fallen upon
them.
13 ¶ Then Dā'vid went over to the
other side, and stood on the top of an
hill afar off; a great space *being* between them:
14 And Dā'vid cried to the people,
and to Ăb'nēr the son of Nēr, saying,
Answerest thou not, Ăb'nēr? Then Ăb'-
nēr answered and said, Who *art* thou
that criest to the king?
15 And Dā'vid said to Ăb'nēr, *Art*
not thou a *valiant* man? and who *is* like
to thee in Ĭs'ra-el? wherefore then hast
thou not kept thy lord the king? for
there came one of the people in to destroy the king thy lord.
16 This thing *is* not good that thou
hast done. *As* the LORD liveth, ye *are*
[3]worthy to die, because ye have not
kept your master, the LORD'S anointed.
And now see where the king's spear *is,*
and the cruse of water that *was* at his
bolster.
17 And Saul knew Dā'vid's voice,
and said, [j]*Is* this thy voice, my son Dā'-
vid? And Dā'vid said, *It is* my voice,
my lord, O king.
18 And he said, [k]Wherefore doth
my lord thus pursue after his servant?
for what have I done? [l]or what evil *is*
in mine hand?
19 Now therefore, I pray thee, let
my lord the king hear the words of his
servant. If the LORD have [m]stirred thee
up against me, let him [4]accept an offering; but if *they be* the children of
men, cursed *be* they before the LORD;
[n]for they have driven me out this day
from [5]abiding in the [o]inheritance of the
LORD, saying, Go, serve other gods.
20 Now therefore, let not my blood
fall to the earth before the face of the
LORD: for the king of Ĭs'ra-el is come

36 [f]2 Sam. 13.23
[g]Prov. 20.1; Isa. 5.11; Hos. 4.11; Luke 21.34; Eph. 5.18
37 [h]Deut. 28.28; Job 15.21
38 [i]Ex. 12.29; 2 Sam. 6.7; Job 12.10; Ps. 104.29; Acts 12.23
39 [j]Prov. 22.23
[k]2 Sam. 3.28-29; Esth. 7.10; Ps. 7.16
41 [l]Ruth 2.10-13; Prov. 15.33
42 [17]at her feet
43 [m]Josh. 15.56; 2 Sam. 3.2
[n]Gen. 2.24; ch. 27.3; Matt. 19.5-8
44 [o]2 Sam. 3.14
[18]Phaltiel
[p]Isa. 10.30

CHAPTER 26
1 [a]ch. 23.19; Ps. 54-title
5 [b]ch. 14.50; ch. 17.55; 2 Sam. 2.8
[1]Or, midst of his carriages
6 [c]1 Chr. 2.16
[d]Judg. 7.10
8 [2]shut up
10 [e]ch. 24.15; Ps. 94.1-2-23; Prov. 20.22; Luke 18.7; Rom. 12.19; Rev. 18.8
[f]Gen. 47.29; Ps. 37.13
[g]ch. 31.6
11 [h]Lev. 19.18; 1 Pet. 3.9
12 [i]Gen. 2.21; Isa. 29.10
16 [3]the sons of death
17 [j]ch. 24.16
18 [k]ch. 24.9-11
[l]Ps. 7.3
19 [m]ch. 16.14-23; 2 Sam. 16.11
[4]smell
[n]Deut. 4.20; Ps. 120.5
[5]cleaving
[o]Ex. 15.17; Isa. 19.25

out to seek [p]a flea, as when one doth hunt a partridge in the mountains.

21 ¶ Then said Saul, [q]I have sinned: return, my son Dā'vid: for I will no more do thee harm, because my soul was [r]precious in thine eyes this day: behold, I have played the fool, and have erred exceedingly.

22 And Dā'vid answered and said, Behold the king's spear! and let one of the young men come over and fetch it.

23 [s]The LORD render to every man his righteousness and his faithfulness: for the LORD delivered thee into *my* hand to day, but I would not stretch forth mine hand against the LORD'S anointed.

24 And, behold, as thy life was much set by this day in mine eyes, so let my life be much set by in the eyes of the LORD, and let him deliver me out of all tribulation.

25 Then Saul said to Dā'vid, Blessed *be* thou, my son Dā'vid: thou shalt both do great *things*, and also shalt still [t]prevail. So Dā'vid went on his way, and Saul returned to his place.

27

And Dā'vid said in his heart, I shall now [1]perish one day by the hand of Saul: *there is* nothing better for me than that I should speedily escape into the land of the Phĭ-lĭs'tĭnes; and Saul shall despair of me, to seek me any more in any coast of Ĭs'ra-el: so shall I escape out of his hand.

2 And Dā'vid arose, [a]and he passed over with the six hundred men that *were* with him [b]unto Ā'chĭsh, the son of Mā'och, king of Găth.

3 And Dā'vid dwelt with Ā'chĭsh at Găth, he and his men, every man with his household, *even* Dā'vid with his two wives, A-hĭn'o-am the Jĕz're-el-ĭt-ess, and Ăb'ĭ-gāil the Cär'mel-ĭt-ess, Nā'bal's wife.

4 And it was told Saul that Dā'vid was fled to Găth: and he sought no more again for him.

5 ¶ And Dā'vid said unto Ā'chĭsh, If I have now found grace in thine eyes, let them give me a place in some town in the country, that I may dwell there: for why should thy servant dwell in the royal city with thee?

6 Then Ā'chĭsh gave him Zĭk'lag that day: wherefore [c]Zĭk'lag pertaineth unto the kings of Jū'dah unto this day.

7 And [2]the time that Dā'vid dwelt in the country of the Phĭ-lĭs'tĭnes was [3]a full year and four months.

8 ¶ And Dā'vid and his men went up, and invaded [d]the Gĕsh'u-rītes, [e]and the [4]Gĕz'rītes, and [f]the Ăm'a-lĕk-ītes: for those *nations were* of old the inhabitants of the land, [g]as thou goest to Shûr, even unto the land of Ē'gypt.

9 And Dā'vid smote the land, and left neither man nor woman alive, and took away the sheep, and the oxen, and the asses, and the camels, and the apparel, and returned, and came to Ā'chĭsh.

10 And Ā'chĭsh said, [5]Whither have ye made a road to day? And Dā'vid said, [h]Against the south of Jū'dah, and against the south of [i]the Je-răh'me-el-ītes, and against the south of the Kĕn'-ītes.

11 And Dā'vid saved neither man nor woman alive, to bring *tidings* to Găth, saying, Lest they should tell on us, saying, So did Dā'vid, and so *will be* his manner all the while he dwelleth in the country of the Phĭ-lĭs'tĭnes.

12 And Ā'chĭsh believed Dā'vid, saying, He hath [6]made his people Ĭs'ra-el utterly to abhor him; therefore he shall be my servant for ever.

28

And [a]it came to pass in those days, that the Phĭ-lĭs'tĭnes gathered their armies together for warfare, to fight with Ĭs'ra-el. And Ā'chĭsh said unto Dā'vid, [1]Know thou assuredly, that thou shalt go out with me to battle, thou and thy men.

2 And Dā'vid said to Ā'chĭsh, [b]Surely thou shalt know what thy servant can do. And Ā'chĭsh said to Dā'vid, Therefore will I make thee keeper of mine head for ever.

3 ¶ Now [c]Săm'u-el was dead, and all Ĭs'ra-el had lamented him, and buried him in Rā'mah, even in his own city. And Saul had put away [d]those that had familiar spirits, and the wizards, out of the land.

4 And the Phĭ-lĭs'tĭnes gathered themselves together, and came and pitched in [e]Shu'nem: and Saul gathered all Ĭs'ra-el together, and they pitched in [f]Gĭl-bō'a.

5 And when Saul saw the host of the Phĭ-lĭs'tĭnes, he was [g]afraid, and his heart greatly trembled.

6 And when Saul inquired of the LORD, [h]the LORD answered him not, neither by [i]dreams, nor [j]by Ū'rim, nor by prophets.

7 ¶ Then said Saul unto his servants, Seek me a woman that hath a familiar spirit, that I may go to her, and inquire of her. And his servants said to him, Behold, *there is* a woman that hath a familiar spirit at Ĕn'–dôr.

8 And Saul disguised himself, and put on other raiment, and he went, and two men with him, and they came to the woman by night: and [k]he said, I pray thee, divine unto me by the familiar spirit, and bring me *him* up, whom I shall name unto thee.

9 And the woman said unto him, Behold, thou knowest what Saul hath done, how he hath cut off those that have familiar spirits, and the wizards, out of the land: wherefore then layest thou a snare for my life, to cause me to die?

10 And Saul sware to her by the LORD, saying, *As* the LORD liveth, there shall no punishment happen to thee for this thing.

11 Then said the woman, Whom shall I bring up unto thee? And he said, Bring me up Săm'u-el.

12 And when the woman [l]saw Săm'-u-el, she cried with a loud voice: and the woman spake to Saul, saying, Why

20 [p]ch. 24.14
21 [q]Ex. 9.27; Num. 22.34; ch. 15.24; Matt. 27.4
[r]ch. 18.30
23 [s]Ps. 7.8; Ps. 18.20; Ps. 28.4; Eccl. 8.12; Isa. 3.10-11
25 [t]Gen. 32.28; Isa. 54.17

CHAPTER 27
1 [1]be consumed
2 [a]ch. 25.13
[b]ch. 21.10
6 [c]Josh. 15.31
7 [2]the number of days
[3]a year of days; ch. 29.3-till 1056
8 [d]Josh. 13.2
[e]Judg. 1.29
[4]Or, Gerzites
[f]Ex. 17.16; ch. 15.7-8
[g]Gen. 25.18
10 [5]Or, did you not make a road, etc
[h]Ps. 141.3
[i]1 Chr. 2.9
12 [6]made himself to stink to his people Israel

CHAPTER 28
1 [a]ch. 29.1
[1]Knowing, know
2 [b]Rom. 12.9
3 [c]ch. 25.1; Isa. 57.1-2; Acts 16.16-19
[d]Ex. 22.18; Lev. 19.31; Deut. 18.10
4 [e]Josh. 19.18
[f]ch. 31.1
5 [g]Job 15.21; Ps. 48.5-6; Isa. 57.20; Dan. 5.6
6 [h]Prov. 1.28; Lam. 2.9
[i]Num. 12.6
[j]Ex. 28.30; Num. 27.21
8 [k]Deut. 18.11; 1 Chr. 10.13; Isa. 8.19
12 [l]Isa. 57.2; Rev. 14.13

hast thou deceived me? for thou *art* Sa̯ul.

13 And the king said unto her, Be not afraid: for what sawest thou? And the woman said unto Sa̯ul, I saw [m]gods ascending out of the earth.

14 And he said unto her, [2]What form *is* he of? And she said, An old man cometh up; and he *is* covered with [n]a mantle. And Sa̯ul perceived that it *was* Săm'u-el, and he [o]stooped with *his* face to the ground, and bowed himself.

15 ¶ And Săm'u-el said to Sa̯ul, Why hast thou disquieted me, to bring me up? And Sa̯ul answered, [p]I am sore distressed; for the Phĭ-lĭs'tĭnes make war against me, and [q]God is departed from me, and answereth me no more, neither [3]by prophets, nor by dreams: therefore I have called thee, that thou mayest make known unto me what I shall do.

16 Then said Săm'u-el, Wherefore then dost thou ask of me, seeing the LORD is departed from thee, and is become thine enemy?

17 And the LORD hath done [4]to him, [r]as he spake by [5]me: for the LORD hath rent the kingdom out of thine hand, and given it to thy neighbour, *even* to Dā'vid:

18 [s]Because thou obeyedst not the voice of the LORD, nor executedst his fierce wrath upon Ăm'a-lĕk, therefore hath the LORD done this thing unto thee this day.

19 Moreover the LORD will also deliver Ĭs'ra-el with thee into the hand of the Phĭ-lĭs'tĭnes: and to morrow *shalt* thou and thy sons *be* with me: the LORD also shall deliver the host of Ĭs'ra-el into the hand of the Phĭ-lĭs'tĭnes.

20 Then Sa̯ul [6]fell straightway all along on the earth, and [t]was sore afraid, because of the words of Săm'u-el: and there was no strength in him; for he had eaten no bread all the day, nor all the night.

21 ¶ And the woman came unto Sa̯ul, and saw that he was sore troubled, and said unto him, Behold, thine handmaid hath obeyed thy voice, and I have [u]put my life in my hand, and have hearkened unto thy words which thou spakest unto me.

22 Now therefore, I pray thee, hearken thou also unto the voice of thine handmaid, and let me set a morsel of bread before thee; and eat, that thou mayest have strength, when thou goest on thy way.

23 But he refused, and said, [v]I will not eat. But his servants, together with the woman, compelled him; and he hearkened unto their voice. So he arose from the earth, and sat upon the bed.

24 And the woman had [w]a fat calf in the house; and she hasted, and killed it, and took flour, and kneaded *it*, and did bake unleavened bread thereof:

25 And she brought *it* before Sa̯ul, and before his servants; and they did eat. Then they rose up, and went away that night.

13 [m]Ex. 22.28; Ps. 138.1
14 [2]What is his form? [n]ch. 15.27 [o]2 Thess. 2.10-11
15 [p]Prov. 5.11; Prov. 14.14 [q]ch. 18.12 [3]by the hand of prophets
17 [4]Or, for himself [r]ch. 15.28 [5]mine hand
18 [s]ch. 15.9; 1 Chr. 10.13
20 [6]made haste, and fell with the fulness of his stature [t]ch. 25.37; Ps. 50.21
21 [u]Judg. 12.3; ch. 19.5
23 [v]Gen. 4.6; Prov. 25.20-21
24 [w]Gen. 18.7-8; Luke 15.23-27-30

CHAPTER 29
1 [a]ch. 28.1 [b]ch. 4.1; 1 Ki. 20.30
2 [c]ch. 28.1-2
3 [d]ch. 27.7 [e]Dan. 6.5; 1 Pet. 3.16
4 [f]1 Chr. 12.19 [g]ch. 14.21
5 [h]ch. 18.7; Prov. 27.14
6 [i]Num. 27.17; Isa. 37.28 [1]thou art not good in the eyes of the lords
7 [2]do not evil in the eyes of the lords
8 [3]before thee
9 [j]2 Sam. 14.17
11 [k]Ps. 37.23; [l]2 Sam. 4.4

CHAPTER 30
1 [a]Ex. 17.8-14-16;
2 [b]Job 38.11

29

Now [a]the Phĭ-lĭs'tĭnes gathered together all their armies [b]to Ā'phek: and the Ĭs'ra-el-ītes pitched by a fountain which *is* in Jĕz're-el.

2 And the lords of the Phĭ-lĭs'tĭnes passed on by hundreds, and by thousands: but Dā'vid and his men passed on in the rereward [c]with Ā'chĭsh.

3 Then said the princes of the Phĭ-lĭs'tĭnes, What *do* these Hē'brews *here?* And Ā'chĭsh said unto the princes of the Phĭ-lĭs'tĭnes, *Is* not this Dā'vid, the servant of Sa̯ul the king of Ĭs'ra-el, which hath been with me [d]these days, or these years, and I have [e]found no fault in him since he fell *unto me* unto this day?

4 And the princes of the Phĭ-lĭs'tĭnes were wroth with him; and the princes of the Phĭ-lĭs'tĭnes said unto him, [f]Make this fellow return, that he may go again to his place which thou hast appointed him, and let him not go down with us to battle, lest [g]in the battle he be an adversary to us: for wherewith should he reconcile himself unto his master? *should it* not *be* with the heads of these men?

5 *Is* not this Dā'vid, of whom they sang one to another in dances, saying, [h]Sa̯ul slew his thousands, and Dā'vid his ten thousands?

6 ¶ Then Ā'chĭsh called Dā'vid, and said unto him, Surely, *as* the LORD liveth, thou hast been upright, and [i]thy going out and thy coming in with me in the host *is* good in my sight: for I have not found evil in thee since the day of thy coming unto me unto this day: nevertheless [1]the lords favour thee not.

7 Wherefore now return, and go in peace, that thou [2]displease not the lords of the Phĭ-lĭs'tĭnes.

8 ¶ And Dā'vid said unto Ā'chĭsh, But what have I done? and what hast thou found in thy servant so long as I have been [3]with thee unto this day, that I may not go fight against the enemies of my lord the king?

9 And Ā'chĭsh answered and said to Dā'vid, I know that thou *art* good in my sight, [j]as an angel of God: notwithstanding the princes of the Phĭ-lĭs'tĭnes have said, He shall not go up with us to the battle.

10 Wherefore now rise up early in the morning with thy master's servants that are come with thee: and as soon as ye be up early in the morning, and have light, depart.

11 [k]So Dā'vid and his men rose up early to depart in the morning, to return into the land of the Phĭ-lĭs'tĭnes. [l]And the Phĭ-lĭs'tĭnes went up to Jĕz're-el.

30

And it came to pass, when Dā'vid and his men were come to Zĭk'lag on the third day, that the [a]Ăm'a-lĕk-ītes had invaded the south, and Zĭk'lag, and smitten Zĭk'lag, and burned it with fire;

2 And had taken the women captives, that *were* therein: [b]they slew not any, either great or small, but carried *them* away, and went on their way.

3 ¶ So Dā'vid and his men came to
the city, and, behold, *it was* burned
with fire; and their wives, and their
sons, and their daughters, were taken
captives.
4 Then Dā'vid and the people that
were with him [c]lifted up their voice and
wept, until they had no more power to
weep.
5 And Dā'vid's [d]two wives were
taken captives, A-hĭn'o-am the Jĕz're-
el-ī-tess, and Ăb'ĭ-gāil the wife of Nā'-
bal the Cär'mel-īte.
6 And Dā'vid was greatly distressed;
[e]for the people spake of stoning him,
because the soul of all the people was
[1]grieved, every man for his sons and
for his daughters: but [f]Dā'vid encouraged himself in the LORD his God.
7 [g]And Dā'vid said to A-bī'a-thär
the priest, A-hĭm'e-lech's son, I pray
thee, bring me hither the ephod. And
A-bī'a-thär brought thither the ephod
to Dā'vid.
8 [h]And Dā'vid inquired at the LORD,
saying, Shall I pursue after this troop?
shall I overtake them? And he [i]an-
swered him, Pursue: for thou shalt
surely overtake *them*, and without fail
recover *all*.
9 So Dā'vid went, he and the six
hundred men that *were* with him, and
came to the brook Bē'sôr, where those
that were left behind stayed.
10 But Dā'vid pursued, he and four
hundred men: for two hundred abode
behind, which were so faint that they
could not go over the brook Bē'sôr.
11 ¶ [j]And they found an E-gy̆p'tian
in the field, and brought him to Dā'vid,
and gave him bread, and he did eat;
and they made him drink water;
12 And they gave him a piece of a
cake of figs, and two clusters of raisins: and [k]when he had eaten, his
spirit came again to him: for he had
eaten no bread, nor drunk *any* water,
three days and three nights.
13 And Dā'vid said unto him, To
whom *belongest* thou? and whence *art*
thou? And he said, I *am* a young man
of Ē'gy̆pt, servant to an Ăm'a-lĕk-īte;
and my master left me, because three
days agone I fell sick.
14 We made an invasion *upon* the
south of [l]the Chĕr'eth-ītes, and upon
the coast which *belongeth* to Jū'dah,
and upon the south [m]of Cā'leb; and we
burned Zĭk'lag with fire.
15 And Dā'vid said to him, Canst
thou bring me down to this company?
And he said, Swear unto me by God,
that thou wilt neither kill me, nor deliver me into the hands of my master,
and I will bring thee down to this company.
16 ¶ And when he had brought him
down, behold, *they were* spread abroad
upon all the earth, [n]eating and drinking, and dancing, because of all the
great spoil that they had taken out of
the land of the Phĭ-lĭs'tĭnes, and out of
the land of Jū'dah.
17 And Dā'vid [o]smote them from
the twilight even unto the evening of

4 [c]Num. 14.1
5 [d]ch. 25.42-43
6 [e]Ex. 17.4
[1]bitter
[f]Ps. 31.24; Ps. 33.18; Ps. 39.7; Ps. 42.5; Ps. 43.5; Ps. 71.4-5; Ps. 119.81; Ps. 146.5; Lam. 3.24-25; Joel 3.16; Hab. 3.17-18; Rom. 4.20
7 [g]ch. 23.6-9
8 [h]ch. 23.2-4
[i]Ps. 22.4-5; Ps. 28.6; Ps. 50.15
11 [j]Ps. 111.2
12 [k]Judg. 15.19; ch. 14.27
14 [l]2 Sam. 8.18; Ezek. 25.16; Zeph. 2.5
[m]Josh. 14.13
16 [n]Ex. 32.6; ch. 25.36-38; 2 Sam. 13.28; Dan. 5.1-4; Luke 12.19-20; Luke 21.34; 1 Thess. 5.3; Rev. 11.10-13
17 [o]Job 20.5
[2]their morrow
18 [p]Gen. 14.16
21 [3]Or, asked them how they did
22 [q]Deut. 13.13; ch. 22.2; ch. 25.17-25
[4]men
24 [r]Num. 31.27; Ps. 68.12
25 [5]and forward
26 [6]blessing
27 [s]Gen. 12.8
[t]Josh. 19.8
[u]Josh. 15.48
28 [v]Josh. 13.16
[w]Josh. 15.50
29 [x]ch. 27.10
[y]Judg. 1.16
30 [z]Judg. 1.17
31 [a]2 Sam. 2.1
CHAPTER 31
1 [a]ch. 29.1; 1 Chr. 10.1

[2]the next day: and there escaped not a
man of them, save four hundred young
men, which rode upon camels, and
fled.
18 And Dā'vid [p]recovered all that
the Ăm'a-lĕk-ītes had carried away:
and Dā'vid rescued his two wives.
19 And there was nothing lacking to
them, neither small nor great, neither
sons nor daughters, neither spoil, nor
any *thing* that they had taken to them:
Dā'vid recovered all.
20 And Dā'vid took all the flocks
and the herds, *which* they drave before
those *other* cattle, and said, This *is*
Dā'vid's spoil.
21 ¶ And Dā'vid came to the two
hundred men, which were so faint that
they could not follow Dā'vid, whom
they had made also to abide at the
brook Bē'sôr: and they went forth to
meet Dā'vid, and to meet the people
that *were* with him: and when Dā'vid
came near to the people, he [3]saluted
them.
22 Then answered all the wicked
men and *men* [q]of Bē'lĭ-al, of [4]those
that went with Dā'vid, and said, Because they went not with us, we will
not give them *ought* of the spoil that
we have recovered, save to every man
his wife and his children, that they
may lead *them* away, and depart.
23 Then said Dā'vid, Ye shall not do
so, my brethren, with that which the
LORD hath given us, who hath preserved us, and delivered the company
that came against us into our hand.
24 For who will hearken unto you in
this matter? but [r]as his part *is* that
goeth down to the battle, so *shall* his
part *be* that tarrieth by the stuff: they
shall part alike.
25 And it was *so* from that day [5]for-
ward, that he made it a statute and an
ordinance for Ĭs'ra-el unto this day.
26 ¶ And when Dā'vid came to Zĭk'-
lag, he sent of the spoil unto the elders
of Jū'dah, *even* to his friends, saying,
Behold a [6]present for you of the spoil
of the enemies of the LORD;
27 To *them* which *were* in [s]Bĕth'-
el, and to *them* which *were* in [t]south
Rā'moth, and to *them* which *were* in
[u]Jăt'tĭr,
28 And to *them* which *were* in [v]Ăr'-
ō-ēr, and to *them* which *were* in Sĭph'-
moth, and to *them* which *were* in [w]Ĕsh-
te-mō'ā,
29 And to *them* which *were* in Rā'-
chăl, and to *them* which *were* in the
cities of [x]the Je-răh'me-el-ītes, and to
them which *were* in the cities of the
[y]Kĕn'ītes,
30 And to *them* which *were* in [z]Hôr'-
mah, and to *them* which *were* in Chōr-
ā'shan, and to *them* which *were* in
Ā'thăch,
31 And to *them* which *were* [a]in Hē'-
bron, and to all the places where Dā'-
vid himself and his men were wont to
haunt.

31 Now [a]the Phĭ-lĭs'tĭnes fought
against Ĭs'ra-el: and the men
of Ĭs'ra-el fled from before the

Phĭ-lĭs'tĭnes, and fell down [1]slain in mount [b]Gĭl-bō'ȧ.

2 And the Phĭ-lĭs'tĭnes followed hard upon Sa̤ul and upon his sons; and the Phĭ-lĭs'tĭnes slew [c]Jŏn'a-than, and A-bĭn'ă-dăb, and Mĕl'chĭ–shṳ'ȧ, Sa̤ul's sons.

3 And [d]the battle went sore against Sa̤ul, and the [2]archers [3]hit him; and he was sore wounded of the archers.

4 [e]Then said Sa̤ul unto his armourbearer, Draw thy sword, and thrust me through therewith; lest [f]these uncircumcised come and thrust me through, and [4]abuse me. But his armourbearer would not; for he was sore afraid. Therefore Sa̤ul took a sword, and [g]fell upon it.

5 And when his armourbearer saw that Sa̤ul was dead, he fell likewise upon his sword, and died with him.

6 So Sa̤ul [h]died, and his three sons, and his armourbearer, and all his men, that same day together.

7 ¶ And when the men of Ĭs'ra-el that *were* on the other side of the valley, and *they* that *were* on the other side Jôr'dan, saw that the men of Ĭs'ra-el fled, and that Sa̤ul and his sons were dead, they forsook the cities, and fled; and the Phĭ-lĭs'tĭnes came and dwelt in them.

8 And it came to pass on the morrow, when the Phĭ-lĭs'tĭnes came to strip the slain, that they found Sa̤ul and his three sons fallen in mount Gĭl-bō'ȧ.

9 And they cut off his head, and stripped off his armour, and sent into the land of the Phĭ-lĭs'tĭnes round about, to [i]publish *it in* the house of their idols, and among the people.

10 [j]And they put his armour in the house of [k]Ăsh'ta-rŏth: and they fastened his body to the wall of [l]Bĕth'–shăn.

11 ¶ And when the inhabitants of Jā'besh–gĭl'e-ăd heard [5]of that which the Phĭ-lĭs'tĭnes had done to Sa̤ul;

12 [m]All the valiant men arose, and went all night, and took the body of Sa̤ul and the bodies of his sons from the wall of Bĕth'–shăn, and came to Jā'besh, and [n]burnt them there.

13 And they took their bones, and [o]buried *them* under a tree at Jā'besh, [p]and fasted seven days.

[1]Or, wounded
[b]ch. 28.4
2 [c]1 Chr. 8.33
3 [d]2 Sam. 1.6
[2]shooters, men with bows
[3]found him
4 [e]Judg. 9.54
[f]ch. 14.6
[4]Or, mock me
[g]2 Sam. 1.10
6 [h]ch. 12.25; Rom. 6.23
9 [i]2 Sam. 1.20
10 [j]ch. 21.9
[k]Judg. 2.13
[l]Josh. 17.11
11 [5]Or, concerning him
12 [m]ch. 11.1-11; 2 Sam. 2.4-7
[n]2 Chr. 16.14; Amos 6.10
13 [o]2 Sam. 21.12-13-14
[p]Gen. 50.10

THE SECOND BOOK OF

SAMUEL

1 Now it came to pass after the death of Sa̤ul, when Dā'vid was returned from [a]the slaughter of the Ăm'a-lĕk-ītes, and Dā'vid had abode two days in Zĭk'lag;

2 It came even to pass on the third day, that, behold, [b]a man came out of the camp from Saul [c]with his clothes rent, and earth upon his head: and *so* it was, when he came to Dā'vid, that he fell to the earth, and did obeisance.

3 And Dā'vid said unto him, From whence comest thou? And he said unto him, Out of the camp of Ĭs'ra-el am I escaped.

4 And Dā'vid said unto him, [1]How went the matter? I pray thee, tell me. And he answered, That the people are fled from the battle, and many of the people also are fallen and dead; and Sa̤ul and Jŏn'a-than his son are dead also.

5 And Dā'vid said unto the young man that told him, How knowest thou that Sa̤ul and Jŏn'a-than his son be dead?

6 And the young man that told him said, [2]As I happened by chance upon [d]mount Gĭl-bō'ȧ, behold, [e]Sa̤ul leaned upon his spear; and, lo, the chariots and horsemen followed hard after him.

7 And when he looked behind him, he saw me, and called unto me. And I answered, [3]Here *am* I.

8 And he said unto me, Who *art* thou? And I answered him, I *am* an Ăm'a-lĕk-īte.

9 He said unto me again, Stand, I pray thee, upon me, and slay me: for [4]anguish is come upon me, because my life *is* yet whole in me.

10 So I stood upon him, and [f]slew him, because I was sure that he could not live after that he was fallen: and I took the crown that *was* upon his head, and the bracelet that *was* on his arm, and have brought them hither unto my lord.

11 Then Dā'vid took hold on his clothes, and [g]rent them; and likewise all the men that *were* with him:

12 And they mourned, and wept, and fasted until even, for Sa̤ul, and for Jŏn'a-than his son, and for the people of the LORD, and for the house of Ĭs'ra-el; because they were fallen by the sword.

13 ¶ And Dā'vid said unto the young man that told him, Whence *art* thou? And he answered, I *am* the son of a stranger, an Ăm'a-lĕk-īte.

14 And Dā'vid said unto him, [h]How wast thou not afraid to stretch forth thine hand to destroy the LORD'S anointed?

15 And [i]Dā'vid called one of the young men, and said, Go near, *and* fall upon him. And he smote him that he died.

16 And Dā'vid said unto him, [j]Thy blood *be* upon thy head; for [k]thy mouth hath testified against thee, saying, I have slain the LORD'S anointed.

17 ¶ And Dā'vid lamented with this lamentation over Sa̤ul and over Jŏn'a-than his son:

CHAPTER 1
1 [a]1 Sam. 11.11; 1 Ki. 20.29-30
2 [b]ch. 4.10
[c]Gen. 37.29; Num. 14.6; Josh. 7.6; 1 Sam. 4.12; Job 1.20; Acts 14.14
4 [1]What was, etc
6 [2]Meeting, I met
[d]1 Sam. 31.1
[e]1 Sam. 31.2-4
7 [3]Behold me
9 [4]Or, my coat of mail, or, my embroidered coat hindereth me, that my, etc
10 [f]Judg. 9.54
11 [g]ch. 3.31; 2 Chr. 34.27; Ezra 9.3
14 [h]Num. 12.8; 1 Sam. 24.6; Ps. 105.15
15 [i]1 Sam. 22.17-18; ch. 4.10
16 [j]1 Sam. 26.9
[k]Luke 19.22

18 (Also he bade them teach the children of Jū'dah [5]*the use of* the bow: behold, *it is* written [l]in the book [6]of Jā'shēr.)

19 The beauty of Ĭs'ra-el is slain upon thy high places: how are the mighty fallen!

20 [m]Tell *it* not in Găth, publish *it* not in the streets of Ăs'ke-lŏn; lest [n]the daughters of the Phĭ-lĭs'tĭnes rejoice, lest the daughters of [o]the uncircumcised triumph.

21 Ye mountains of Ḡĭl-bō'ȧ, [p]*let there be* no dew, neither *let there be* rain, upon you, nor fields of offerings: for there the shield of the mighty is vilely cast away, the shield of Saul, *as though he had* not *been* [q]anointed with oil.

22 From the blood of the slain, from the fat of the mighty, [r]the bow of Jŏn'a-than turned not back, and the sword of Saul returned not empty.

23 Saul and Jŏn'a-than *were* lovely and [7]pleasant in their lives, and in their death they were not divided: they were swifter than eagles, they were [s]stronger than lions.

24 Ye daughters of Ĭs'ra-el, weep over Saul, who clothed you in scarlet, with *other* delights, who put on ornaments of gold upon your apparel.

25 How are the mighty fallen in the midst of the battle! O Jŏn'a-than, *thou wast* slain in thine high places.

26 I am distressed for thee, my brother Jŏn'a-than: very pleasant hast thou been unto me: [t]thy love to me was wonderful, passing the love of women.

27 How are the mighty fallen, and the weapons of war perished!

2 And it came to pass after this, that Dā'vid [a]inquired of the LORD, saying, Shall I go up into any of the cities of Jū'dah? And the LORD said unto him, Go up. And Dā'vid said, Whither shall I go up? And he said, Unto [b]Hē'bron.

2 So Dā'vid went up thither, and his two wives also, A-hĭn'o-am the Jĕz're-el-ī-tess, and Ăb'ĭ-gāil Nā'bal's wife the Căr'mel-īte.

3 And [c]his men that *were* with him did Dā'vid bring up, every man with his household: and they dwelt in the [1]cities of Hē'bron.

4 [d]And the men of Jū'dah came, and there they anointed Dā'vid king over the house of Jū'dah. And they told Dā'vid, saying, *That* [e]the men of Jā'besh–ḡĭl'e-ăd *were they* that buried Saul.

5 ¶ And Dā'vid sent messengers unto the men of Jā'besh–ḡĭl'e-ăd, and said unto them, [f]Blessed *be* ye of the LORD, that ye have shewed this kindness unto your lord, *even* unto Saul, and have buried him.

6 And now [g]the LORD shew kindness and truth unto you: and [h]I also will requite you this kindness, because ye have done this thing.

7 Therefore now let your hands be strengthened, and [2]be ye valiant: for your master Saul is dead, and also the house of Jū'dah have anointed me king over them.

8 ¶ But [i]Ăb'nēr the son of Nēr, captain of [3]Saul's host, took [4]Ĭsh–bō'sheth the son of Saul, and brought him over to [j]Mā-ha-nā'im;

9 And made him king over Ḡĭl'e-ăd, and over the Ăsh'ŭr-ītes, and over Jĕz're-el, and over Ē'phră-ĭm, and over Bĕn'ja-min, and over all Ĭs'ra-el.

10 Ĭsh–bō'sheth Saul's son *was* forty years old when he began to reign over Ĭs'ra-el, and reigned two years. But the house of Jū'dah followed Dā'vid.

11 And the [5]time that Dā'vid was king in Hē'bron over the house of Jū'dah was seven years and six months.

12 ¶ And Ăb'nēr the son of Nēr, and the servants of Ĭsh–bō'sheth the son of Saul, went out from Mā-ha-nā'im to [k]Gĭb'e-on.

13 And Jō'ab the son of Zĕr-u-ī'ah, and the servants of Dā'vid, went out, and met [6]together by [l]the pool of Gĭb'e-on: and they sat down, the one on the one side of the pool, and the other on the other side of the pool.

14 And Ăb'nēr said to Jō'ab, [m]Let the young men now arise, and play before us. And Jō'ab said, Let them arise.

15 Then there arose and went over by number twelve of Bĕn'ja-min, which *pertained* to Ĭsh–bō'sheth the son of Saul, and twelve of the servants of Dā'vid.

16 And they caught every one his fellow by the head, and *thrust* his sword in his fellow's side; so they fell down together: wherefore that place was called [7]Hĕl'kăth–hăz'zu-rĭm, which *is* in Gĭb'e-on.

17 And there was a very sore battle that day; [n]and Ăb'nēr was beaten, and the men of Ĭs'ra-el, before the servants of Dā'vid.

18 ¶ And there were [o]three sons of Zĕr-u-ī'ah there, Jō'ab, and A-bĭsh'ă-ī, and Ā'sa-hĕl: and Ā'sa-hĕl *was* [p]*as* light [8]of foot [9]as a wild roe.

19 And Ā'sa-hĕl pursued after Ăb'nēr; and in going he turned not to the right hand nor to the left [10]from following Ăb'nēr.

20 Then Ăb'nēr looked behind him, and said, *Art* thou Ā'sa-hĕl? And he answered, I *am*.

21 And Ăb'nēr said to him, Turn thee aside to thy right hand or to thy left, and lay thee hold on one of the [q]young men, and take thee his [11]armour. But Ā'sa-hĕl would not turn aside from following of him.

22 And Ăb'nēr said again to Ā'sa-hĕl, Turn thee aside from following me: wherefore should I smite thee to the ground? how then should I hold up my face to Jō'ab thy brother?

23 Howbeit he refused to turn aside: wherefore Ăb'nēr with the hinder end of the spear smote him [r]under the fifth *rib*, that the spear came out behind him; and he fell down there, and died in the same place: and it came to pass, *that* as many as came to the place

18 [5]Or, the ode of the bow
[l]Josh. 10.13
[6]Or, of the upright
20 [m]1 Sam. 31.9; Mic. 1.10
[n]Ex. 15.20; 1 Sam. 18.6
[o]1 Sam. 31.4
21 [p]Job 3.3-4
[q]1 Sam. 10.1
22 [r]1 Sam. 18.4
23 [7]Or, sweet
[s]Judg. 14.18
26 [t]1 Sam. 18.1-3;

CHAPTER 2
1 [a]Num. 27.21;
[b]1 Sam. 30.31
3 [c]1 Sam. 27.2
[1]That is, Suburbs
4 [d]ch. 5.5
[e]1 Sam. 31.11
5 [f]Ps. 115.15
6 [g]2 Tim. 1.16
[h]Matt. 5.44
7 [2]be ye the sons of valour
8 [i]1 Sam. 14.50;
[3]the host which was Saul's
[4]Esh-baal
[j]Gen. 32.2;
11 [5]number of days
12 [k]Josh. 9.3;
13 [6]Them together
[l]Jer. 41.12
14 [m]Prov. 10.23;
16 [7]That is, The field of strong men, or, of rocks
17 [n]1 Ki. 20.11
18 [o]1 Chr. 2.16
[p]1 Chr. 12.8
[8]of his feet
[9]as one of the roes that is in the field
19 [10]from after Abner
21 [q]1 Sam. 17.42
[11]garment, or, spoil
23 [r]ch. 3.27;

where Ā'sa-hĕl fell down and died stood still.

24 Jō'ab also and A-bĭsh'ă-ī pursued after Ăb'nēr: and the sun went down when they were come to the hill of Ăm'mah, that *lieth* before Gī'ah by the way of the wilderness of [s]Gĭb'e-on.

25 ¶ And the children of Bĕn'ja-min gathered themselves together after Ăb'nēr, and became one troop, and stood on the top of an hill.

26 Then Ăb'nēr called to Jō'ab, and said, Shall the sword devour for ever? knowest thou not that it will be bitterness in the latter end? how long shall it be then, ere thou bid the people return from following their [t]brethren?

27 And Jō'ab said, *As* God liveth, unless [u]thou hadst spoken, surely then [12]in the morning the people had [13]gone up every one from following his brother.

28 So Jō'ab blew a trumpet, and all the people stood still, and pursued after Ĭs'ra-el no more, neither fought they any more.

29 And Ăb'nēr and his men walked all that night through the plain, and passed over Jôr'dan, and went through all [v]Bĭth'rŏn, and they came to [w]Mā-ha-nā'im.

30 And Jō'ab returned from following Ăb'nēr: and when he had gathered all the people together, there lacked of Dā'vid's servants nineteen men and Ā'sa-hĕl.

31 But the servants of Dā'vid had smitten of Bĕn'ja-min, and of Ăb'nēr's men, *so that* three hundred and threescore men died.

32 ¶ And they took up Ā'sa-hĕl, and buried him in the [x]sepulchre of his father, which *was in* Bĕth'–lĕ-hĕm. And Jō'ab and his men went all night, and they came to Hē'bron at break of day.

3 Now there was long [a]war between the house of Saul and the house of Dā'vid: but Dā'vid waxed stronger and stronger, and the house of Saul waxed weaker and weaker.

2 ¶ And [b]unto Dā'vid were sons born in Hē'bron: and his firstborn was Ăm'nŏn, [c]of A-hĭn'o-am the Jĕz're-el-ī-tess;

3 And his second, [1]Chĭl'e-ăb, of Ăb'ĭ-gāil the wife of Nā'bal the Cär'mel-īte; and the third, Ăb'sa-lŏm the son of Mā'a-cah the daughter of Tăl'māi king [d]of Gē'shŭr;

4 And the fourth, [e]Ăd-ŏ-nī'jah the son of Hăg'gĭth; and the fifth, Shĕph-a-tī'ah the son of Ăb'i-tal;

5 And the sixth, Ĭth're-ăm, by Ĕg'lah Dā'vid's wife. These were born to Dā'vid in Hē'bron.

6 ¶ And it came to pass, while there was war between the house of Saul and the house of Dā'vid, that Ăb'nēr [f]made himself strong for the house of Saul.

7 And Saul had a concubine, whose name *was* [g]Rĭz'pah, the daughter of A-ī'ah: and *Ĭsh–bō'sheth* said to Ăb'nēr, Wherefore hast thou [h]gone in unto my father's concubine?

8 Then was Ăb'nēr very wroth for the words of Ĭsh–bō'sheth, and said, *Am* I [i]a dog's head, which against Jū'dah do shew kindness this day unto the house of Saul thy father, to his brethren, and to his friends, and have not delivered thee into the hand of Dā'vid, that thou chargest me to day with a fault concerning this woman?

9 [j]So do God to Ăb'nēr, and more also, except, [k]as the LORD hath sworn to Dā'vid, even so I do to him;

10 To translate the kingdom from the house of Saul, and to set up the throne of Dā'vid over Ĭs'ra-el and over Jū'dah, [l]from Dăn even to Bē'er–shē'bȧ.

11 And he could not answer Ăb'nēr a word again, because he feared him.

12 ¶ And Ăb'nēr sent messengers to Dā'vid on his behalf, saying, Whose *is* the land? saying *also,* Make thy league with me, and, behold, my hand *shall be* with thee, to bring about all Ĭs'ra-el unto thee.

13 ¶ And he said, Well; I will make a league with thee: but one thing I require of thee, [2]that is, [m]Thou shalt not see my face, except thou first bring [n]Mī'chal Saul's daughter, when thou comest to see my face.

14 And Dā'vid sent messengers to Ĭsh–bō'sheth Saul's son, saying, Deliver *me* my wife Mī'chal, which I espoused to me [o]for an hundred foreskins of the Phĭ-lĭs'tĭnes.

15 And Ĭsh–bō'sheth sent, and took her from *her* husband, *even* from [p]Phăl'tĭ-el the son of Lā'ish.

16 And her husband went with her [3]along weeping behind her to [q]Ba-hū'rim. Then said Ăb'nēr unto him, Go, return. And he returned.

17 ¶ And Ăb'nēr had communication with the elders of Ĭs'ra-el, saying, Ye sought for Dā'vid [4]in times past *to be* king over you:

18 Now then do *it:* for the LORD hath spoken of Dā'vid, saying, By the hand of my servant Dā'vid I will save my people Ĭs'ra-el out of the hand of the Phĭ-lĭs'tĭnes, and out of the hand of all their enemies.

19 And Ăb'nēr also spake in the ears of [r]Bĕn'ja-min: and Ăb'nēr went also to speak in the ears of Dā'vid in Hē'bron all that seemed good to Ĭs'ra-el, and that seemed good to the whole house of Bĕn'ja-min.

20 So Ăb'nēr came to Dā'vid to Hē'bron, and twenty men with him. And Dā'vid made Ăb'nēr and the men that *were* with him a feast.

21 And Ăb'nēr said unto Dā'vid, I will arise and go, and will gather all Ĭs'ra-el unto my lord the king, that they may make a league with thee, and that thou mayest [s]reign over all that thine heart desireth. And Dā'vid sent Ăb'nēr away; and he went in peace.

22 ¶ And, behold, the servants of Dā'vid and Jō'ab came from *pursuing* a troop, and brought in a great spoil with them: but Ăb'nēr *was* not with

24 [s]Josh. 9.3
26 [t]Ps. 4.2; Acts 7.26
27 [u]Prov. 17.14; Prov. 20.18; Prov. 25.8; Luke 14.31-32
[12]from the morning
[13]Or, gone away
29 [v]Song 2.17
[w]Gen. 32.2; Josh. 21.38; ch. 17.24
32 [x]Gen. 47.29-30; Gen. 49.29; ch. 17.23; ch. 19.37

CHAPTER 3
1 [a]Ps. 46.9; Isa. 2.4; Mic. 4.3; Matt. 10.35-36; Gal. 5.17
2 [b]1 Chr. 3.1
[c]1 Sam. 25.43
3 [1]Or, Daniel
[d]ch. 13.37; 1 Sam. 27.8
4 [e]1 Ki. 1.5
6 [f]ch. 2.8-9; 2 Chr. 25.8
7 [g]ch. 21.8-10
[h]ch. 16.21
8 [i]Deut. 23.18; 1 Sam. 24.15; ch. 16.9
9 [j]Ruth 1.17
[k]1 Sam. 15.28; 1 Chr. 12.23; Ps. 78.70; Ps. 89.19-20; Acts 13.22
10 [l]Judg. 20.1; ch. 17.11
13 [2]saying
[m]Gen. 43.3; Gen. 44.23-26
[n]1 Sam. 18.20
14 [o]1 Sam. 18.25-27
15 [p]1 Sam. 25.44, Phalti
16 [3]going and weeping
[q]ch. 19.16
17 [4]both yesterday and the third day
19 [r]1 Chr. 12.29
21 [s]Deut. 14.26

Dā'vid in Hē'bron; for he had sent him
away, and he was gone in peace.
23 When Jō'ab and all the host that
was with him were come, they told
Jō'ab, saying, Ăb'nēr the son of Nēr
came to the king, and he hath sent him
away, and he is gone in peace.
24 Then Jō'ab came to the king, and
said, What hast thou done? behold,
Ăb'nēr came unto thee; why *is* it *that*
thou hast sent him away, and he is
[5]quite gone?
25 Thou knowest Ăb'nēr the son of
Nēr, that he came to deceive thee, and
to know [t]thy going out and thy coming
in, and to know all that thou doest.
26 And when Jō'ab was come out
from Dā'vid, he sent messengers after
Ăb'nēr, which brought him again from
the well of Sī'rah: but Dā'vid knew *it*
not.
27 And when Ăb'nēr was returned
to Hē'bron, Jō'ab [u]took him aside in
the gate to speak with him [6]quietly, and
smote him there [v]under the fifth *rib,*
that he died, for the blood of [w]Ă'sa-hĕl
his brother.
28 ¶ And afterward when Dā'vid
heard *it,* he said, I and my kingdom *are*
guiltless before the LORD for ever, from
the [7]blood of Ăb'nēr the son of Nēr:
29 [x]Let it rest on the head of Jō'ab,
and on all his father's house; and let
there not [8]fail from the house of Jō'ab
one [y]that hath an issue, or that is a
leper, or that leaneth on a staff, or that
falleth on the sword, or that lacketh
bread.
30 So Jō'ab and A-bĭsh'ă-ī his
brother slew Ăb'nēr, because he had
slain their brother [z]Ă'sa-hĕl at Gĭb'e-
on in the battle.
31 ¶ And Dā'vid said to Jō'ab, and
to all the people that *were* with him,
[a]Rend your clothes, and [b]gird you with
sackcloth, and mourn before Ăb'nēr.
And king Dā'vid *himself* followed the
[9]bier.
32 And they buried Ăb'nēr in Hē'-
bron: and the king lifted up his voice,
and [c]wept at the grave of Ăb'nēr; and
all the people wept.
33 And the king lamented over Ăb'-
nēr, and said, Died Ăb'nēr as a [d]fool
dieth?
34 Thy hands *were* not bound, nor
thy feet put into fetters: as a man falleth
before [10]wicked men, *so* fellest thou.
And all the people wept again over
him.
35 And when all the people came to
[e]cause Dā'vid to eat meat while it was
yet day, Dā'vid sware, saying, [f]So do
God to me, and more also, if I taste
bread, or ought else, [g]till the sun be
down.
36 And all the people took notice *of
it,* and it [11]pleased them: as whatsoever the king did pleased all the people.
37 For all the people and all Ĭs'ra-el
understood that day that it was not of
the king to slay Ăb'nēr the son of Nēr.
38 And the king said unto his servants, Know ye not that there is a

24 [5]going, gone
25 [t]Num. 27.17; 1 Sam. 29.6; Ps. 121.8; Isa. 37.28
27 [u]1 Ki. 2.5; ch. 20.9-10
[6]Or, peaceably
[v]Gen. 4.8; ch. 2.23; ch. 4.6
[w]ch. 2.23
28 [7]bloods
29 [x]Judg. 9.54-56-57; 1 Ki. 2.32-33; Ps. 7.11-16; Prov. 5.22
[8]be cut off
[y]Lev. 15.2
30 [z]ch. 2.23
31 [a]Josh. 7.6; 2 Ki. 19.1
[b]Gen. 37.34; Job 16.15
[9]bed
32 [c]1 Sam. 30.4; Prov. 24.17
33 [d]ch. 13.13; Eccl. 2.15-16
34 [10]children of iniquity
35 [e]ch. 12.17
[f]Ruth 1.17
[g]ch. 1.12
36 [11]was good in their eyes
39 [12]tender
[h]ch. 19.7
[i]ch. 19.13; 2 Tim. 4.14

CHAPTER 4
2 [1]second
[a]Josh. 9.17
3 [b]Neh. 11.33
4 [c]ch. 9.3
[d]1 Sam. 29.1
[2]Or, Merib-baal
6 [e]Judg. 5.25; Ps. 147.14
[f]ch. 2.23; ch. 3.27
7 [g]1 Sam. 17.54; Matt. 14.11
8 [h]1 Sam. 19.2; 1 Sam. 23.15
9 [i]Gen. 48.16; Ps. 103.4
10 [j]ch. 1.2
[3]he was in his own eyes as a bringer, etc
[4]Or, which was the reward I gave him for his tidings
11 [k]Gen. 9.5-6

prince and a great man fallen this day
in Ĭs'ra-el?
39 And I *am* this day [12]weak, though
anointed king; and these men the sons
of Zĕr-u-ī'ah [h]*be* too hard for me: [i]the
LORD shall reward the doer of evil according to his wickedness.
4 And when Saul's son heard that
Ăb'nēr was dead in Hē'bron, his
hands were feeble, and all the Ĭs'ra-el-
ītes were troubled.
2 And Saul's son had two men *that
were* captains of bands: the name of
the one *was* Bā'a-nah, and the name of
the [1]other Rē'chăb, the sons of Rĭm'-
mon a Be-ē'rŏth-īte, of the children of
Bĕn'ja-min: (for [a]Be-ē'rŏth also was
reckoned to Bĕn'ja-min.
3 And the Be-ē'rŏth-ītes [b]fled to Gĭt'-
ta-ĭm, and were sojourners there until
this day.)
4 And [c]Jŏn'a-than, Saul's son, had a
son *that was* lame of *his* feet. He was
five years old when the tidings came of
Saul and Jŏn'a-than [d]out of Jĕz're-el,
and his nurse took him up, and fled:
and it came to pass, as she made haste
to flee, that he fell, and became lame.
And his name *was* [2]Me-phĭb'o-sheth.
5 And the sons of Rĭm'mon the Be-
ē'rŏth-īte, Rē'chăb and Bā'a-nah, went,
and came about the heat of the day to
the house of Ĭsh–bō'sheth, who lay on a
bed at noon.
6 And they came thither into the
midst of the house, [e]*as though* they
would have fetched wheat; and they
smote him [f]under the fifth *rib:* and
Rē'chăb and Bā'a-nah his brother escaped.
7 For when they came into the house,
he lay on his bed in his bedchamber,
and they smote him, and slew him, and
beheaded him, and [g]took his head, and
gat them away through the plain all
night.
8 And they brought the head of Ĭsh–
bō'sheth unto Dā'vid to Hē'bron, and
said to the king, Behold the head of
Ĭsh–bō'sheth the son of Saul thine enemy, [h]which sought thy life; and the
LORD hath avenged my lord the king
this day of Saul, and of his seed.
9 ¶ And Dā'vid answered Rē'chăb
and Bā'a-nah his brother, the sons of
Rĭm'mon the Be-ē'rŏth-īte, and said
unto them, *As* the LORD liveth, [i]who
hath redeemed my soul out of all adversity,
10 When [j]one told me, saying, Behold, Saul is dead, [3]thinking to have
brought good tidings, I took hold of
him, and slew him in Zĭk'lag, [4]who
thought that I would have given him a
reward for his tidings:
11 How much more, when wicked
men have slain a righteous person in
his own house upon his bed? shall I not
therefore now [k]require his blood of
your hand, and take you away from
the earth?
12 And Dā'vid commanded his
young men, and they slew them, and
cut off their hands and their feet, and
hanged *them* up over the pool in

Hē'bron. But they took the head of
Ĭsh–bō'sheth, and buried *it* in the
sepulchre of Ăb'nēr in Hē'bron.

5

Then [a]came all the tribes of Ĭs'ra-el
to Dā'vid unto Hē'bron, and spake,
saying, Behold, [b]we *are* thy bone and
thy flesh.
2 Also in time past, when Saul was
king over us, [c]thou wast he that leddest out and broughtest in Ĭs'ra-el: and
the LORD said to thee, [d]Thou shalt feed
my people Ĭs'ra-el, and thou shalt be a
captain over Ĭs'ra-el.
3 [e]So all the elders of Ĭs'ra-el came
to the king to Hē'bron; [f]and king
Dā'vid made a league with them in
Hē'bron [g]before the LORD: and they
anointed Dā'vid king over Ĭs'ra-el.
4 ¶ Dā'vid *was* thirty years old when
he began to reign, [h]*and* he reigned
forty years.
5 In Hē'bron he reigned over Jū'dah
[i]seven years and six months: and in Je-
ru'sa-lĕm he reigned thirty and three
years over all Ĭs'ra-el and Jū'dah.
6 ¶ And the king and his men went
[j]to Je-ru'sa-lĕm unto [k]the Jĕb'u-sītes,
the inhabitants of the land: which
spake unto Dā'vid, saying, Except thou
take away the blind and the lame, thou
shalt not come in hither: [1]thinking, Dā'-
vid cannot come in hither.
7 Nevertheless Dā'vid took the
strong hold of Zī'ŏn: the same *is* the
city of Dā'vid.
8 And Dā'vid said on that day, Whosoever getteth up to the gutter, and
smiteth the Jĕb'u-sītes, and the lame
and the blind, *that are* hated of Dā'-
vid's soul, [l]*he shall be chief and captain.* [2]Wherefore they said, The blind
and the lame shall not come into the
house.
9 So Dā'vid dwelt in the fort, and
called it the city of Dā'vid. And Dā'vid
built round about [m]from Mĭl'lo and inward.
10 And Dā'vid [3]went on, and grew
great, and the LORD God of hosts *was*
with him.
11 ¶ And [n]Hī'ram king of Tȳre sent
messengers to Dā'vid, and cedar trees,
and carpenters, and [4]masons: and they
built Dā'vid an house.
12 And Dā'vid perceived that the
LORD had established him king over
Ĭs'ra-el, and that he had exalted his
kingdom [o]for his people Ĭs'ra-el's sake.
13 ¶ And [p]Dā'vid took *him* more
concubines and wives out of Je-ru'sa-
lĕm, after he was come from Hē'bron:
and there were yet sons and daughters
born to Dā'vid.
14 And these *be* the names of those
that were born unto him in Je-ru'sa-
lĕm; Shăm-mū'ah, and Shō'băb, and
Nā'than, and Sŏl'o-mon,
15 Ĭb'hăr also, and Ĕl-ĭ-shu'ȧ, and
Nē'pheg, and Ja-phī'ȧ,
16 And E-lĭsh'a-mȧ, and E-lī'a-dȧ,
and E-lĭph'a-lĕt.
17 ¶ [q]But when the Phĭ-lĭs'tĭnes
heard that they had anointed Dā'vid
king over Ĭs'ra-el, all the Phĭ-lĭs'tĭnes
came up to seek Dā'vid; and Dā'vid
heard *of it*, [r]and went down to the
hold.
18 The Phĭ-lĭs'tĭnes also came and
spread themselves in [s]the valley of
[5]Rĕph'a-ĭm.
19 And Dā'vid inquired of the LORD,
saying, Shall I go up to the Phĭ-
lĭs'tĭnes? wilt thou deliver them into
mine hand? And the LORD said unto
Dā'vid, Go up: for I will doubtless deliver the Phĭ-lĭs'tĭnes into thine hand.
20 And Dā'vid came to Bā'al–pĕr'a-
zĭm, and Dā'vid smote them there,
and said, The LORD hath broken forth
upon mine enemies before me, as the
breach of waters. Therefore he called
the name of that place [6]Bā'al–pĕr'a-
zĭm.
21 And there they left their images,
and Dā'vid and his men [7]burned them.
22 ¶ And the Phĭ-lĭs'tĭnes came up
yet again, and spread themselves in
the valley of Rĕph'a-ĭm.
23 And when Dā'vid inquired of the
LORD, he said, Thou shalt not go up;
but fetch a compass behind them, and
come upon them over against the mulberry trees.
24 And let it be, when thou hearest
the sound of a going in the tops of the
mulberry trees, that then thou shalt be-
stir thyself: for then shall the LORD go
out before thee, to smite the host of the
Phĭ-lĭs'tĭnes.
25 And Dā'vid did so, as the LORD
had commanded him; and smote the
Phĭ-lĭs'tĭnes from Gē'bȧ until thou come
to Gā'zēr.

6

Again, Dā'vid gathered together all
the chosen *men* of Ĭs'ra-el, thirty
thousand.
2 And [a]Dā'vid arose, and went with
all the people that *were* with him from
[1]Bā'ă-lē of Jū'dah, to bring up from
thence the ark of God, [2]whose name is
called by the name of the LORD of hosts
[b]that dwelleth *between* the cherubims.
3 And they [3]set the ark of God [c]upon
a new cart, and brought it out of the
house of A-bĭn'ă-dăb that *was* in [4]Gĭb'-
e-ah: and Ŭz'zah and A-hī'o, the sons
of A-bĭn'ă-dăb, drave the new cart.
4 And they brought it out of the
house of A-bĭn'ă-dăb which *was* at
Gĭb'e-ah, [5]accompanying the ark of
God: and A-hī'o went before the ark.
5 And Dā'vid and all the house of
Ĭs'ra-el played before the LORD on all
manner of *instruments made of* fir
wood, even on harps, and on psalteries, and on timbrels, and on cornets,
and on cymbals.
6 ¶ And when they came to [6]Nā'-
chŏn's threshingfloor, Ŭz'zah [d]put
forth *his hand* to the ark of God, and
took hold of it; for the oxen [7]shook *it*.
7 And the anger of the LORD was kindled against Ŭz'zah; and [e]God smote
him there for *his* [8]error; and there he
died by the ark of God.
8 And Dā'vid was displeased, because the LORD had [9]made a breach
upon Ŭz'zah: and he called the name of
the place [10]Pē'rez–ŭz'zah to this day.

CHAPTER 5
1 [a]1 Chr. 12.23-40
[b]Gen. 29.14
2 [c]1 Sam. 18.13
[d]1 Sam. 16.1; Ps. 78.71
3 [e]1 Chr. 11.3
[f]2 Ki. 11.17
[g]1 Sam. 23.18
4 [h]1 Chr. 26.31
5 [i]1 Chr. 3.4
6 [j]Judg. 1.21
[k]Josh. 15.63
[1]Or, saying, David shall not, etc
8 [l]1 Chr. 11.6
[2]Or, Because they had said
9 [m]1 Ki. 9.24; 2 Chr. 32.5
10 [3]went, going and growing
11 [n]1 Ki. 5.2
[4]hewers of the stone of the wall
12 [o]2 Chr. 2.11
13 [p]Gen. 25.5-6
17 [q]1 Chr. 11.16
[r]ch. 23.14
18 [s]Isa. 17.5
[5]Or, Giants
20 [6]That is, The plain of breaches
21 [7]Or, took them away

CHAPTER 6
2 [a]1 Chr. 13.5
[1]Or, Baalah, that is, Kirjath-jearim
[2]Or, at which the name, even the name of the LORD of hosts, was called upon
[b]1 Sam. 4.4;
3 [3]made to ride
[c]Num. 7.9
[4]Or, The hill
4 [5]with
6 [6]Or, Chidon, 1 Chr. 13.9, that is, Destroying stroke
[d]Num. 4.15
[7]Or, stumbled
7 [e]1 Sam. 6.19
[8]Or, rashness
8 [9]broken
[10]That is, The breach of Uzzah

9 And [f]Dā'vid was afraid of the
LORD that day, and said, How shall the
ark of the LORD come to me?
10 So Dā'vid would not remove the
ark of the LORD unto him into the city of
Dā'vid: but Dā'vid carried it aside into
the house of Ō'bed–ē'dom the Gĭt'tīte.
11 And the ark of the LORD continued in the house of Ō'bed–ē'dom the
Gĭt'tīte three months: and the LORD
[g]blessed Ō'bed–ē'dom, and all his
household.
b12 ¶ And it was told king Dā'vid, saying, The LORD hath blessed the house of
Ō'bed–ē'dom, and all that *pertaineth*
unto him, because of the ark of God. So
Dā'vid went and brought up the ark of
God from the house of Ō'bed–ē'dom
into the city of Dā'vid with gladness.
13 And it was *so,* that when [h]they
that bare the ark of the LORD had gone
six paces, he sacrificed [i]oxen and fatlings.
14 And Dā'vid [j]danced before the
LORD with all *his* might; and Dā'vid
was girded [k]with a linen ephod.
15 So Dā'vid and all the house of
Ĭs'ra-el brought up the ark of the LORD
with shouting, and with the sound of
the trumpet.
16 And as the ark of the LORD came
into the city of Dā'vid, Mī'chal Saul's
daughter looked through a window,
and saw king Dā'vid leaping and dancing before the LORD; and she despised
him in her heart.
17 ¶ And they brought in the ark of
the LORD, and set it in [l]his place, in the
midst of the tabernacle that Dā'vid had
[11]pitched for it: and Dā'vid [m]offered
burnt offerings and peace offerings before the LORD.
18 And as soon as Dā'vid had made
an end of offering burnt offerings and
peace offerings, he blessed the people
in the name of the LORD of hosts.
19 And he dealt among all the people, *even* among the whole multitude
of Ĭs'ra-el, as well to the women as
men, to every one a cake of bread, and
a good piece *of flesh,* and a flagon *of*
wine. So all the people departed every
one to his house.
20 ¶ [n]Then Dā'vid returned to bless
his household. And Mī'chal the daughter of Saul came out to meet Dā'vid,
and said, [o]How glorious was the king
of Ĭs'ra-el to day, who [p]uncovered himself to day in the eyes of the handmaids of his servants, as one of the
[q]vain fellows [12]shamelessly uncovereth himself!
21 And Dā'vid said unto Mī'chal, *It*
was before the LORD, [r]which chose me
before thy father, and before all his
house, to appoint me ruler over the people of the LORD, over Ĭs'ra-el: therefore
will I play before the LORD.
22 And I will yet be more vile than
thus, and will be base in mine own
sight: and [13]of the maidservants which
thou hast spoken of, of them shall I be
had in honour.
23 Therefore Mī'chal the daughter
of Saul had no child [s]unto the day of
her death.

7 And it came to pass, [a]when the
king sat in his house, and the LORD
had given him rest round about from
all his enemies;
2 That the king said unto Nā'than
the prophet, See now, I dwell in [b]an
house of cedar, but the ark of God
dwelleth within [c]curtains.
3 And Nā'than said to the king, Go,
do all that *is* [d]in thine heart; for the
LORD *is* with thee.
4 ¶ And it came to pass that night,
that the word of the LORD came unto
Nā'than, saying,
5 Go and tell [1]my servant Dā'vid,
Thus saith the LORD, Shalt thou build
me an house for me to dwell in?
6 Whereas I have not dwelt in *any*
house since [e]the time that I brought up
the children of Ĭs'ra-el out of Ē'gypt,
even to this day, but have walked in a
tent and in a tabernacle.
7 In all *the places* wherein I have
[f]walked with all the children of Ĭs'ra-el
spake I a word with [2]any of the tribes
of Ĭs'ra-el, whom I commanded [g]to
feed my people Ĭs'ra-el, saying, Why
build ye not me an house of cedar?
8 Now therefore so shalt thou say
unto my servant Dā'vid, Thus saith the
LORD of hosts, I took thee from the
sheepcote, [3]from following the sheep,
to be ruler over my people, over Ĭs'ra-
el:
9 And I was with thee whithersoever thou wentest, and have cut off all
thine enemies [4]out of thy sight, and
have made thee [h]a great name, like
unto the name of the great *men* that
are in the earth.
10 Moreover I will appoint a place
for my people Ĭs'ra-el, and [i]will plant
them, that they may dwell in a place of
their own, and move no more; neither
shall the children of wickedness afflict
them any more, as beforetime,
11 And as since the time that I commanded judges *to be* over my people
Ĭs'ra-el, and have caused thee to rest
from all thine enemies. Also the LORD
telleth thee that he will make thee an
house.
12 ¶ And [j]when thy days be fulfilled,
and thou [k]shalt sleep with thy fathers,
[l]I will set up thy seed after thee, which
shall proceed out of thy bowels, and I
will establish his kingdom.
13 [m]He shall build an house for my
name, and I will [n]stablish the throne of
his kingdom for ever.
14 [o]I will be his father, and he shall
be my son. If [p]he commit iniquity, I
will chasten him with the rod of men,
and with the stripes of the children of
men:
15 But my mercy shall not depart
away from him, [q]as I took *it* from Saul,
whom I put away before thee.
16 And [r]thine house and thy kingdom shall be established for ever before thee: thy throne shall be established for ever.

9 [f]Num. 17.12-13; Ps. 119.120; Luke 5.8
11 [g]Gen. 30.27; Prov. 3.9-10; Isa. 61.9
13 [h]Num. 4.15; 1 Chr. 15.2-15
[i]1 Ki. 8.5; 2 Chr. 5.6
14 [j]Ex. 15.20; Judg. 11.34; Ps. 30.11
[k]1 Sam. 2.18
17 [l]1 Chr. 15.1
[11]stretched
[m]1 Ki. 8.5
20 [n]Ps. 30, title
[o]Eccl. 7.16
[p]1 Sam. 19.24
[q]Judg. 9.4
[12]Or, openly
21 [r]1 Sam. 13.14
22 [13]Or, of the handmaids of my servants
23 [s]1 Sam. 15.35; Isa. 22.14

CHAPTER 7
1 [a]1 Chr. 17.1; Dan. 4.29-30
2 [b]ch. 5.11
[c]Ex. 26.1
3 [d]1 Ki. 8.17; 1 Chr. 22.7
5 [1]to my servant, to David
6 [e]1 Ki. 8.16
7 [f]Lev. 26.11
[2]1 Chr. 17.6, any of the judges
[g]ch. 5.2; Ps. 78.71-72; Ezek. 34.2-15-23; Matt. 2.6; Acts 20.28
8 [3]from after
9 [4]from thy face
[h]Gen. 12.2; Luke 1.52
10 [i]Ps. 44.2; Amos 9.15
12 [j]1 Ki. 2.1
[k]Deut. 31.16; Acts 13.36
[l]Ps. 132.11; Isa. 11.1-3-10
13 [m]1 Ki. 5.5
[n]Ps. 89.4
14 [o]Heb. 1.5
[p]Ps. 89.30
15 [q]1 Sam. 15.23
16 [r]Ps. 89.36-37; John 12.34

17 According to all these words, and
according to all this vision, so did Nā'-
than speak unto Dā'vid.
18 ¶ Then went king Dā'vid in, and
sat before the LORD, and he said, [s]Who
am I, O Lord GOD? and what *is* my
house, that thou hast brought me hitherto?
19 And this was yet a small thing in
thy sight, O Lord GOD; but thou hast
spoken also of thy servant's house for
a great while to come. And [t]*is* this the
[5]manner of man, O Lord GOD?
20 And what can Dā'vid say more
unto thee? for thou, Lord GOD, [u]know-
est thy servant.
21 For thy [v]word's sake, and according to thine own heart, hast thou done
all these great things, to make thy servant know *them*.
22 Wherefore [w]thou art great, O
LORD God: for [x]*there is* none like thee,
neither *is there any* God beside thee,
according to all that we have heard
with our ears.
23 And [y]what one nation in the earth
is like thy people, *even* like Ĭs'ra-el,
whom God went to redeem for a people
to himself, and to make him a name,
and to do for you great things and terrible, for thy land, before [z]thy people, which thou redeemedst to thee
from Ē'gypt, *from* the nations and their
gods?
24 For [a]thou hast confirmed to thyself thy people Ĭs'ra-el *to be* a people
unto thee for ever: and thou, LORD, art
become their God.
25 And now, O LORD God, the word
that thou hast spoken concerning thy
servant, and concerning his house, establish *it* for ever, and do as thou hast
said.
26 And let [b]thy name be magnified
for ever, saying, The LORD of hosts *is*
the God over Ĭs'ra-el: and let the house
of thy servant Dā'vid be established
before thee.
27 For thou, O LORD of hosts, God of
Ĭs'ra-el, hast [6]revealed to thy servant,
saying, I will build thee an house: therefore hath thy servant found in his heart
to pray this prayer unto thee.
28 And now, O Lord GOD, thou *art*
that God, and [c]thy words be true, and
thou hast promised this goodness unto
thy servant:
29 Therefore now [7]let it please thee
to bless the house of thy servant, that it
may continue for ever before thee: for
thou, O Lord GOD, hast spoken *it*: and
with thy blessing let the house of thy
servant be blessed for ever.

8 And [a]after this it came to pass, that
Dā'vid smote the Phĭ-lĭs'tĭnes, and
subdued them: and Dā'vid took [1]Mē'-
theg-ăm'mah out of the hand of the
Phĭ-lĭs'tĭnes.
2 And [b]he smote Mō'ab, and measured them with a line, casting them
down to the ground; even with two
lines measured he to put to death, and
with one full line to keep alive. And *so*
the Mō'ab-ītes became Dā'vid's servants, *and* [c]brought gifts.
3 ¶ Dā'vid smote also Hăd-ăd-ē'zĕr,
the son of Rē'hŏb, king of [d]Zō'bah, as
he went to recover [e]his border at the
river Eū-phrā'tēs.
4 And Dā'vid took [2]from him a
thousand *chariots*, and seven hundred
horsemen, and twenty thousand footmen: and Dā'vid houghed all the chariot *horses*, but reserved of them *for* an
hundred chariots.
5 And when the Sy̆r'ĭ-ans of Da-
măs'cus came to succour Hăd-ăd-ē'zĕr
king of Zō'bah, Dā'vid slew of the Sy̆r'-
ĭ-ans two and twenty thousand men.
6 Then Dā'vid put garrisons in
Sy̆r'ĭ-ȧ of Da-măs'cus: and the Sy̆r'ĭ-
ans became servants to Dā'vid, *and*
brought gifts. And the LORD preserved
Dā'vid whithersoever he went.
7 And Dā'vid took the shields of
gold that were on the servants of Hăd-
ăd-ē'zĕr, and brought them to Je-ru'sa-
lĕm.
8 And from [3]Bē'tah, and from [4]Bĕr'-
o-thāi, cities of Hăd-ăd-ē'zĕr, king Dā'-
vid took exceeding much brass.
9 ¶ When Tō'ī king of Hā'math heard
that Dā'vid had smitten all the host of
Hăd-ăd-ē'zĕr,
10 Then Tō'ī sent Jō'ram his son
unto king Dā'vid, to [5]salute him, and
to bless him, because he had fought
against Hăd-ăd-ē'zĕr, and smitten him:
for Hăd-ăd-ē'zĕr [6]had wars with Tō'ī.
And *Jō'ram* [7]brought with him vessels
of silver, and vessels of gold, and vessels of brass:
11 Which also king Dā'vid [f]did dedicate unto the LORD, with the silver and
gold that he had dedicated of all nations which he subdued;
12 Of Sy̆r'ĭ-ȧ, and of Mō'ab, and of
the children of Ăm'mŏn, and of the
Phĭ-lĭs'tĭnes, and of Ăm'a-lĕk, and of
the spoil of Hăd-ăd-ē'zĕr, son of Rē'-
hŏb, king of Zō'bah.
13 And Dā'vid gat *him* a name when
he returned from [8]smiting of the Sy̆r'ĭ-
ans in [g]the valley of salt, [9]*being* eighteen thousand *men*.
14 ¶ And he put garrisons in Ē'dom;
throughout all Ē'dom put he garrisons,
and [h]all they of Ē'dom became Dā'-
vid's servants. And the LORD [i]pre-
served Dā'vid whithersoever he went.
15 And Dā'vid reigned over all Ĭs'-
ra-el; and Dā'vid executed judgment
and justice unto all his people.
16 [j]And Jō'ab the son of Zĕr-u-ī'ah
was over the host; and [k]Je-hŏsh'a-phăt
the son of A-hī'lud *was* [10]recorder;
17 And [l]Zā'dŏk the son of A-hī'tub,
and A-hĭm'e-lech the son of A-bī'a-
thär, *were* the priests; and Sĕr-a-ī'ah
was the [11]scribe;
18 [m]And Be-nā'iah the son of Je-
hoi'a-dȧ *was over* both the [n]Chĕr'eth-
ītes and the Pē'leth-ītes; and Dā'vid's
sons were [12]chief rulers.

9 And Dā'vid said, Is there yet any
that is left of the house of Saul, that
I may [a]shew him kindness for Jŏn'a-
than's sake?
2 And *there was* of the house of Saul
a servant whose name *was* [b]Zī'bȧ. And

18 [s]Gen. 32.10
19 [t]Isa. 55.8 [5]law
20 [u]Gen. 18.19
21 [v]Eph. 4.32
22 [w]1 Chr. 16.25; Ps. 135.5 [x]Deut. 3.24; Isa. 45.5
23 [y]Deut. 4.7; Ps. 147.20 [z]Neh. 1.10
24 [a]Deut. 26.18
26 [b]Ps. 72.19; Matt. 6.9
27 [6]opened the ear
28 [c]John 17.17
29 [7]be thou pleased and bless

CHAPTER 8
1 [a]ch. 7.9; 1 Chr. 18.1 [1]Or, The bridle of Ammah
2 [b]1 Sam. 14.47; Ps. 60.8 [c]Ps. 72.10
3 [d]ch. 10.6; [e]Gen. 15.18
4 [2]Or, of his
8 [3]Or, Tibhath [4]Or, Chun
10 [5]ask him of peace [6]was a man of wars with [7]in his hand were
11 [f]1 Ki. 7.51;
13 [8]his smiting [g]2 Ki. 14.7 [9]Or, slaying
14 [h]Gen. 27.29 [i]Ps. 37.28;
16 [j]ch. 19.13 [k]1 Ki. 4.3 [10]Or, remembrancer, or, writer of chronicles
17 [l]1 Chr. 24.3 [11]Or, secretary
18 [m]1 Chr. 18.17 [n]1 Sam. 30.14 [12]Or, princes

CHAPTER 9
1 [a]1 Sam. 18.3;
2 [b]ch. 16.1

when they had called him unto Dā'vid,
the king said unto him, *Art* thou Zī'bȧ?
And he said, Thy servant *is he.*
3 And the king said, *Is* there not yet
any of the house of Saul, that I may
shew [c]the kindness of God unto him?
And Zī'bȧ said unto the king, Jŏn'a-
than hath yet a son, *which is* [d]lame on
his feet.
4 And the king said unto him, Where
is he? And Zī'bȧ said unto the king, Behold, he *is* in the house of [e]Mā'chĭr, the
son of Ăm'mĭ-el, in Lo–dē'bär.
5 ¶ Then king Dā'vid sent, and
fetched him out of the house of Mā'-
chĭr, the son of Ăm'mĭ-el, from Lo–
dē'bär.
6 Now when [1]Me-phĭb'o-sheth, the
son of Jŏn'a-than, the son of Saul, was
come unto Dā'vid, he fell on his face,
and did reverence. And Dā'vid said,
Me-phĭb'o-sheth. And he answered,
Behold thy servant!
7 ¶ And Dā'vid said unto him, [f]Fear
not: for I will surely shew thee kindness for Jŏn'a-than thy father's sake,
and will restore thee all the land of
Saul thy father; and thou shalt [g]eat
bread at my table continually.
8 And he bowed himself, and said,
What *is* thy servant, that thou shouldest look upon such [h]a dead dog as I
am?
9 ¶ Then the king called to Zī'bȧ,
Saul's servant, and said unto him, [i]I
have given unto thy master's son all
that pertained to Saul and to all his
house.
10 Thou therefore, and thy sons, and
thy servants, shall till the land for him,
and thou shalt bring in *the fruits,* that
thy master's son may have food to eat:
but Me-phĭb'o-sheth thy master's son
shall eat bread alway at my table. Now
Zī'bȧ had [j]fifteen sons and twenty servants.
11 Then said Zī'bȧ unto the king,
[k]According to all that my lord the king
hath commanded his servant, so shall
thy servant do. As for Me-phĭb'o-sheth,
said the king, he shall eat at my table,
as one of the king's sons.
12 And Me-phĭb'o-sheth had a young
son, [l]whose name *was* Mī'chȧ. And all
that dwelt in the house of Zī'bȧ *were*
servants unto Me-phĭb'o-sheth.
13 So Me-phĭb'o-sheth dwelt in Je-
ru'sa-lĕm: for he did [m]eat continually
at the king's table; and was lame on
both his feet.

10 And it came to pass after this,
that the [a]king of the children
of Ăm'mŏn died, and Hā'nŭn his son
reigned in his stead.
2 Then said Dā'vid, I will shew kindness unto Hā'nŭn the son of Nā'hăsh,
as his father shewed kindness unto
me. And Dā'vid sent to comfort him by
the hand of his servants for his father.
And Dā'vid's servants came into the
land of the children of Ăm'mŏn.
3 And the princes of the children
of Ăm'mŏn said unto Hā'nŭn their
lord, [1]Thinkest thou that Dā'vid doth
honour thy father, that he hath sent

3 [c]Deut. 10.15; 1 Sam. 20.14; Luke 6.36; Tit. 3.3-4
[d]ch. 4.4
4 [e]ch. 17.27
6 [1]Called Meribbaal
7 [f]Gen. 43.18-23; 1 Sam. 12.19-20-24
[g]Jer. 52.33
8 [h]1 Sam. 24.14; ch. 16.9
9 [i]ch. 16.4; ch. 19.29; Isa. 32.8
10 [j]ch. 19.17
11 [k]ch. 16.1-4; Prov. 12.17
12 [l]1 Chr. 8.34
13 [m]ch. 19.33-36; 2 Ki. 25.29
CHAPTER 10
1 [a]1 Sam. 11.1; ch. 17.27-29; 1 Chr. 19.1
3 [1]In thine eyes doth David
4 [b]Isa. 3.17; Isa. 20.4; Jer. 13.22-26; Ezek. 16.37; Mic. 1.11; Nah. 3.5
5 [2]Probably some village near to it; Compare Josh. 6.24 with 1 Ki. 16.34
6 [c]Gen. 34.30; Ex. 5.21; 1 Sam. 13.4
[d]ch. 8.3-5
[3]Or, The men of Tob
7 [e]ch. 23.8
12 [f]Deut. 31.6
[g]1 Sam. 4.9
[h]1 Sam. 3.18; ch. 15.26; Ps. 20.7; Ps. 37.3-5-40; Ps. 44.5-6; Ps. 118.8; Prov. 29.25
16 [4]That is, Euphrates
[5]Or, Shophach

comforters unto thee? hath not Dā'vid
rather sent his servants unto thee, to
search the city, and to spy it out, and
to overthrow it?
4 Wherefore Hā'nŭn took Dā'vid's
servants, and shaved off the one half
of their beards, and cut off their garments in the middle, [b]*even* to their buttocks, and sent them away.
5 When they told *it* unto Dā'vid, he
sent to meet them, because the men
were greatly ashamed: and the king
said, Tarry at [2]Jĕr'ĭ-chō until your
beards be grown, and *then* return.
6 ¶ And when the children of Ăm'-
mŏn saw that they [c]stank before Dā'-
vid, the children of Ăm'mŏn sent and
hired [d]the Sўr'ĭ-ans of Bĕth–rē'hŏb,
and the Sўr'ĭ-ans of Zō'bȧ, twenty
thousand footmen, and of king Mā'a-
cah a thousand men, and of [3]Ĭsh'–tŏb
twelve thousand men.
7 And when Dā'vid heard of *it,* he
sent Jō'ab, and all the host of [e]the
mighty men.
8 And the children of Ăm'mŏn came
out, and put the battle in array at the
entering in of the gate: and the Sўr'ĭ-
ans of Zō'bȧ, and of Rē'hŏb, and Ĭsh'–
tŏb, and Mā'a-cah, *were* by themselves
in the field.
9 When Jō'ab saw that the front
of the battle was against him before
and behind, he chose of all the choice
men of Ĭs'ra-el, and put *them* in array
against the Sўr'ĭ-ans:
10 And the rest of the people he delivered into the hand of A-bĭsh'-ă-ī his
brother, that he might put *them* in array against the children of Ăm'mŏn.
11 And he said, If the Sўr'ĭ-ans be
too strong for me, then thou shalt help
me: but if the children of Ăm'mŏn be
too strong for thee, then I will come
and help thee.
12 [f]Be of good courage, and let [g]us
play the men for our people, and for
the cities of our God: and [h]the LORD do
that which seemeth him good.
13 And Jō'ab drew nigh, and the
people that *were* with him, unto the battle against the Sўr'ĭ-ans: and they fled
before him.
14 And when the children of Ăm'-
mŏn saw that the Sўr'ĭ-ans were fled,
then fled they also before A-bĭsh'ă-ī,
and entered into the city. So Jō'ab returned from the children of Ăm'mŏn,
and came to Je-ru'sa-lĕm.
15 ¶ And when the Sўr'ĭ-ans saw
that they were smitten before Ĭs'ra-el,
they gathered themselves together.
16 And Hăd-är-ē'zĕr sent, and
brought out the Sўr'ĭ-ans that *were* beyond the [4]river: and they came to Hē'-
lam; and [5]Shō'băch the captain of the
host of Hăd-är-ē'zĕr *went* before them.
17 And when it was told Dā'vid,
he gathered all Ĭs'ra-el together, and
passed over Jôr'dan, and came to Hē'-
lam. And the Sўr'ĭ-ans set themselves
in array against Dā'vid, and fought
with him.
18 And the Sўr'ĭ-ans fled before Ĭs'-
ra-el; and Dā'vid slew *the men of* seven

hundred chariots of the Sȳr'ĭ-ans, and forty thousand [6]horsemen, and smote Shō'băch the captain of their host, who died there.

19 And when all the kings *that were* [i]servants to Hăd-är-ē'zĕr saw that they were smitten before Is'ra-el, they made peace with Is'ra-el, and served them. So the Sȳr'ĭ-ans feared to help the children of Am'mŏn any more.

11

11 And it came to pass, [1]after the year was expired, at the time when kings go forth *to battle,* that Dā'vid [a]sent Jō'ab, and his servants with him, and all Is'ra-el; and they destroyed the children of Am'mŏn, and besieged Răb'bah. But Dā'vid tarried still at Je-ru'sa-lĕm.

2 ¶ And it came to pass in an eveningtide, that Dā'vid arose from off his bed, [b]and walked upon the roof of the king's house: and from the roof he [c]saw a woman washing herself; and the woman *was* very beautiful to look upon.

3 And Dā'vid sent and inquired after the woman. And *one* said, *Is* not this [2]Băth'–shĕ-bȧ, the daughter of [3]E-lī'ăm, the wife [d]of U-rī'ah the Hĭt'tīte?

4 And Dā'vid sent messengers, and took her; and she came in unto him, and [e]he lay with her; [4]for she was [f]purified from her uncleanness: and she returned unto her house.

5 And the woman conceived, and sent and told Dā'vid, and said, [g]I *am* with child.

6 ¶ And Dā'vid sent to Jō'ab, *saying,* Send me U-rī'ah the Hĭt'tīte. And Jō'ab sent U-rī'ah to Dā'vid.

7 And when U-rī'ah was come unto him, Dā'vid demanded *of him* [5]how Jō'ab did, and how the people did, and how the war prospered.

8 And Dā'vid said to U-rī'ah, [h]Go down to thy house, and [i]wash thy feet. And U-rī'ah departed out of the king's house, and there [6]followed him a mess *of meat* from the king.

9 [j]But U-rī'ah slept at the door of the king's house, with all the servants of his lord, and went not down to his house.

10 And when they had told Dā'vid, saying, U-rī'ah went not down unto his house, Dā'vid said unto U-rī'ah, Camest thou not from *thy* journey? why *then* didst thou not go down unto thine house?

11 And U-rī'ah said unto Dā'vid, [k]The ark, and Is'ra-el, and Jū'dah, abide in tents; and [l]my lord Jō'ab, and the servants of my lord, [m]are encamped in the open fields; shall I then go into mine house, to eat and to drink, and to lie with my wife? *as* thou livest, and *as* thy soul liveth, I will not do this thing.

12 And Dā'vid said to U-rī'ah, [n]Tarry here to day also, and to morrow I will let thee depart. So U-rī'ah abode in Je-ru'sa-lĕm that day, and the morrow.

13 And when Dā'vid had called him, he did eat and drink before him; and he made him [o]drunk: and at even he went out to lie on his bed with the servants of his lord, but went not down to his house.

14 ¶ And it came to pass in the morning, that Dā'vid [p]wrote a letter to Jō'ab, and sent *it* by the hand of U-rī'ah.

15 And he wrote in the letter, saying, Set ye U-rī'ah in the forefront of the [7]hottest battle, and retire ye [8]from him, that he may [q]be smitten, and die.

16 And it came to pass, when Jō'ab observed the city, that he assigned U-rī'ah unto a place where he knew that valiant men *were.*

17 And the men of the city went out, and fought with Jō'ab: and there fell *some* of the people of the servants of Dā'vid; and U-rī'ah the Hĭt'tīte died also.

18 ¶ Then Jō'ab sent and told Dā'vid all the things concerning the war;

19 And charged the messenger, saying, When thou hast made an end of telling the matters of the war unto the king,

20 And if so be that the king's wrath arise, and he say unto thee, Wherefore approached ye so nigh unto the city when ye did fight? knew ye not that they would shoot from the wall?

21 Who smote [r]A-bĭm'ĕ-lech the son of [s]Je-rŭb'be-shĕth? did not a woman cast a piece of a millstone upon him from the wall, that he died in Thē'bez? why went ye nigh the wall? then say thou, Thy servant U-rī'ah the Hĭt'tīte is dead also.

22 ¶ So the messenger went, and came and shewed Dā'vid all that Jō'ab had sent him for.

23 And the messenger said unto Dā'vid, Surely the men prevailed against us, and came out unto us into the field, and we were upon them even unto the entering of the gate.

24 And the shooters shot from off the wall upon thy servants; and *some* of the king's servants be dead, and thy servant U-rī'ah the Hĭt'tīte is dead also.

25 Then Dā'vid said unto the messenger, Thus shalt thou say unto Jō'ab, Let not this thing [9]displease thee, for the sword devoureth [10]one as well as another: make thy battle more strong against the city, and overthrow it: and encourage thou him.

26 ¶ And when the wife of U-rī'ah heard that U-rī'ah her husband was dead, she mourned for her husband.

27 And when the mourning was past, Dā'vid sent and fetched her to his house, and she [t]became his wife, and bare him a son. But the thing that Dā'vid had done [11]displeased the LORD.

12

12 And the LORD sent Nā'than unto Dā'vid. And [a]he came unto him, and [b]said unto him, There were two men in one city; the one rich, and the other poor.

2 The rich *man* had exceeding many flocks and herds:

3 But the poor *man* had nothing, save one little ewe lamb, which he had bought and nourished up: and it grew

18 [6]1 Chr. 19.18, footmen
19 [i]Gen. 14.4

CHAPTER 11
1 [1]at the return of the year
[a]1 Chr. 20.1
2 [b]Deut. 22.8
[c]Gen. 34.2; Matt. 5.28
3 [2]Or, Bathshuah
[3]Or, Ammiel
[d]ch. 23.39
4 [e]Ex. 20.17; Jas. 1.14
[4]Or, and when she had purified herself, etc., she returned
[f]Lev. 15.19
5 [g]Lev. 20.10
7 [5]of the peace of, etc
8 [h]Ps. 44.21; Ps. 55.21
[i]Gen. 18.4
[6]went out after him
9 [j]Job 5.12-14
11 [k]ch. 7.2-6; 1 Sam. 4.4
[l]ch. 20.6; Matt. 10.25
[m]2 Tim. 2.3
12 [n]Job 20.12-14
13 [o]Gen. 9.21-22;
14 [p]1 Ki. 21.8
15 [7]strong
[8]from after him
[q]ch. 12.9
21 [r]Judg. 9.53;
[s]Judg. 6.32, Jerubbaal
25 [9]be evil in thine eyes
[10]so and such
27 [t]ch. 12.9
[11]was evil in the eyes of; Job 10.14; Ps. 5.4; Ps. 45.7; Ps. 139.1-5; Prov. 15.9; Hab. 1.13

CHAPTER 12
1 [a]Ps. 51, title
[b]ch. 14.5

up together with him, and with his children; it did eat of his own [1]meat, and
drank of his own cup, and lay in his
bosom, and was unto him as a daughter.
4 And there came a traveller unto
the rich man, and he spared to take
of his own flock and of his own herd,
to dress for the wayfaring man that
was come unto him; but took the poor
man's lamb, and dressed it for the man
that was come to him.
5 And Dā′vid's anger was greatly
kindled against the man; and he said to
Nā′than, *As* the LORD liveth, the man
that hath done this *thing* [2]shall surely
die:
6 And he shall restore the lamb
[c]fourfold, because he did this thing,
and because he had no pity.
7 ¶ And Nā′than said to Dā′vid, Thou
art the man. Thus saith the LORD God
of Ĭs′ra-el, [d]I anointed thee king over
Ĭs′ra-el, and I delivered thee out of the
hand of Saul;
8 And I gave thee thy master's house,
and thy master's wives into thy bosom,
and gave thee the house of Ĭs′ra-el and
of Jū′dah; and if *that had been* too little, I would moreover have given unto
thee such and such things.
9 [e]Wherefore hast thou [f]despised
the commandment of the LORD, to do
evil in his sight? [g]thou hast killed Ū-
rī′ah the Hĭt′tīte with the sword, and
hast taken his wife *to be* thy wife, and
hast slain him with the sword of the
children of Ăm′mŏn.
10 Now therefore [h]the sword shall
never depart from thine house; because thou hast despised me, and hast
taken the wife of Ū-rī′ah the Hĭt′tīte to
be thy wife.
11 Thus saith the LORD, Behold, I
will raise up evil against thee out of
thine own house, and I will [i]take thy
wives before thine eyes, and give *them*
unto thy neighbour, and he shall lie
with thy wives in the sight of this sun.
12 For thou didst *it* secretly: [j]but I
will do this thing before all Ĭs′ra-el,
and before the sun.
13 [k]And Dā′vid said unto Nā′than,
[l]I have sinned against the LORD. And
Nā′than said unto Dā′vid, The LORD
also hath [m]put away thy sin; thou shalt
not die.
14 Howbeit, because by this deed
thou hast given great occasion to the
enemies of the LORD [n]to blaspheme,
the child also *that is* born unto thee
shall surely die.
15 ¶ And Nā′than departed unto his
house. And the LORD [o]struck the child
that Ū-ri′ah's wife bare unto Dā′vid,
and it was very sick.
16 Dā′vid therefore [p]besought God
for the child; and Dā′vid [3]fasted, and
went in, and [q]lay all night upon the
earth.
17 And the elders of his house arose,
and went to him, to raise him up from
the earth: but he would not, neither did
he eat bread with them.
18 And it came to pass on the seventh day, that the child died. And the
servants of Dā′vid feared to tell him
that the child was dead: for they said,
Behold, while the child was yet alive,
we spake unto him, and he would not
hearken unto our voice: how will he
then [4]vex himself, if we tell him that
the child is dead?
19 But when Dā′vid saw that his servants whispered, Dā′vid perceived that
the child was dead: therefore Dā′vid
said unto his servants, Is the child
dead? And they said, He is dead.
20 Then Dā′vid arose from the earth,
and washed, and [r]anointed *himself,*
and changed his apparel, and came
into the house of the LORD, and [s]wor-
shipped: then he came to his own
house; and when he required, they set
bread before him, and he did eat.
21 Then said his servants unto him,
What thing *is* this that thou hast done?
thou didst fast and weep for the child,
while it was alive; but when the child
was dead, thou didst rise and eat bread.
22 And he said, While the child was
yet alive, I fasted and wept: [t]for I said,
Who can tell *whether* GOD will be gracious to me, that the child may live?
23 But now he is dead, wherefore
should I fast? can I bring him back
again? [u]I shall go to him, but [v]he shall
not return to me.
24 ¶ And Dā′vid comforted Băth′–
shĕ-bȧ his wife, and went in unto her,
and lay with her: and [w]she bare a son,
and [x]he called his name [5]Sŏl′o-mon:
and the LORD loved him.
25 And he sent by the hand of Nā′-
than the prophet; and he called his
name [6]Jĕd-ĭ-dī′ah, because of the LORD.
26 ¶ And [y]Jō′ab fought against
[z]Răb′bah of the children of Ăm′mŏn,
and took the royal city.
27 And Jō′ab sent messengers to
Dā′vid, and said, I have fought against
Răb′bah, and have taken [7]the city of
waters.
28 Now therefore gather the rest
of the people together, and encamp
against the city, and take it: lest I take
the city, and [8]it be called after my
name.
29 And Dā′vid gathered all the people together, and went to Răb′bah, and
fought against it, and took it.
30 [a]And he took their king's crown
from off his head, the weight whereof
was a talent of gold with the precious
stones: and it was *set* on Dā′vid's head.
And he brought forth the spoil of the
city [9]in great abundance.
31 And he brought forth the people
that *were* therein, and [10]put *them* under saws, and under harrows of iron,
and under axes of iron, and made them
pass through the brickkiln: and thus
did he unto all the cities of the children
of Ăm′mŏn. So Dā′vid and all the people returned unto Je-ru′sa-lĕm.

CHAPTER 13

13 And it came to pass after this,
that [a]Ăb′sa-lŏm the son of Dā′-
vid had a fair sister, whose name *was*

3 [1]morsel
5 [2]is a son of death, or, is worthy to die
6 [c]Ex. 22.1; Luke 19.8
7 [d]1 Sam. 16.13; ch. 7.8
9 [e]Gen. 9.5-6; 1 Sam. 15.19
[f]Lev. 26.15-16; Num. 15.31; Prov. 13.13; Isa. 5.24
[g]ch. 11.15
10 [h]Amos 7.9
11 [i]Deut. 28.30
12 [j]ch. 16.22
13 [k]1 Sam. 15.24
[l]ch. 24.10; Job 7.20; Ps. 32.5; Prov. 28.13
[m]Ps. 32.1; Zech. 3.4
14 [n]Isa. 52.5; Rom. 2.24
15 [o]Gen. 4.7; Amos 3.2
16 [p]Isa. 26.16; Jer. 18.8
[3]fasted a fast
[q]ch. 13.31
18 [4]do hurt
20 [r]Ruth 3.3
[s]Ps. 95.6-7-8; Prov. 16.6
22 [t]Isa. 38.1-5; Jon. 3.9
23 [u]2 Cor. 5.1-8; Heb. 11.10
[v]Job 7.8-9
24 [w]Matt. 1.6
[x]1 Chr. 22.9
[5]That is, Peaceable and perfect
25 [6]That is, Beloved of the LORD
26 [y]1 Chr. 20.1
[z]Deut. 3.11
27 [7]That part where the cisterns were
28 [8]my name be called upon it
30 [a]1 Chr. 20.2
[9]very great
31 [10]Or, made them saw wood and stones, dig iron, and labour about furnaces
CHAPTER 13
1 [a]ch. 3.2-3

[b]Tā'mar; and Ăm'nŏn the son of Dā'vid loved her.

2 And Ăm'nŏn was so vexed, that he fell sick for his sister Tā'mar; for she *was* a virgin; and [1]Ăm'nŏn thought it hard for him to do any thing to her.

3 But Ăm'nŏn had a friend, whose name *was* Jŏn'a-dăb, [c]the son of Shĭm'e-ah Dā'vid's brother: and Jŏn'a-dăb *was* a very subtil man.

4 And he said unto him, Why *art* thou, *being* the king's son, [2]lean [3]from day to day? wilt thou not tell me? And Ăm'nŏn said unto him, [d]I love Tā'mar, my brother Ăb'sa-lŏm's sister.

5 And Jŏn'a-dăb said unto him, Lay thee down on thy bed, and make thyself sick: and when thy father cometh to see thee, say unto him, I pray thee, Let my sister Tā'mar come, and give me meat, and dress the meat in my sight, that I may see *it*, and eat *it* at her hand.

6 ¶ So Ăm'nŏn lay down, and made himself sick: and when the king was come to see him, Ăm'nŏn said unto the king, I pray thee, let Tā'mar my sister come, and [e]make me a couple of cakes in my sight, that I may eat at her hand.

7 Then Dā'vid sent home to Tā'mar, saying, Go now to thy brother Ăm'nŏn's house, and dress him meat.

8 So Tā'mar went to her brother Ăm'nŏn's house; and he was laid down. And she took [4]flour, and kneaded *it*, and made cakes in his sight, and did bake the cakes.

9 And she took a pan, and poured *them* out before him; but he refused to eat. And Ăm'nŏn said, [f]Have out all men from me. And they went out every man from him.

10 And Ăm'nŏn said unto Tā'mar, Bring the meat into the chamber, that I may eat of thine hand. And Tā'mar took the cakes which she had made, and brought *them* into the chamber to Ăm'nŏn her brother.

11 And when she had brought *them* unto him to eat, he [g]took hold of her, and said unto her, Come lie with me, my sister.

12 And she answered him, Nay, my brother, do not [5]force me; for [6]no such thing ought to be done in Ĭs'ra-el: do not thou this [h]folly.

13 And I, whither shall I cause my shame to go? and as for thee, thou shalt be as one of the fools in Ĭs'ra-el. Now therefore, I pray thee, speak unto the king; [i]for he will not withhold me from thee.

14 Howbeit he would not hearken unto her voice: but, being stronger than she, [j]forced her, and lay with her.

15 ¶ Then Ăm'nŏn hated her [7]exceedingly; so that the hatred wherewith he hated her *was* greater than the love wherewith he had loved her. And Ăm'nŏn said unto her, Arise, be gone.

16 And she said unto him, *There is* no cause: this evil in sending me away *is* greater than the other that thou didst unto me. But he would not hearken unto her.

[b]1 Chr. 3.9
2 [1]It was marvellous, or, hidden in the eyes of Amnon
3 [c]1 Chr. 2.13
4 [2]thin [3]morning by morning [d]Isa. 3.9
6 [e]Gen. 18.6
8 [4]Or, paste
9 [f]Gen. 45.1; Judg. 3.19
11 [g]Gen. 39.12; Prov. 7.13; Eccl. 7.26
12 [5]humble me [6]it ought not so to be done [h]Gen. 34.7; Judg. 19.23; Prov. 7.7-23
13 [i]Gen. 19.8; Lev. 18.9-11; Judg. 19.24
14 [j]Lev. 18.9; Deut. 22.25; Judg. 20.5; ch. 12.11; Esth. 7.8
15 [7]with great hatred greatly
18 [k]Gen. 37.3; Judg. 5.30; Ps. 45.14
19 [l]Josh. 7.6; ch. 1.2; Job 2.12 [m]Jer. 2.37
20 [8]Aminon [9]set not thine heart [10]and desolate
22 [n]Lev. 19.17; Prov. 10.18; Eph. 4.26-31; 1 John 2.9-11
23 [o]Gen. 38.12; 1 Sam. 25.4; 2 Ki. 3.4 [p]Josh. 17.18
28 [q]Gen. 9.21; Ruth 3.7; 1 Sam. 25.36; Esth. 1.10; Ps. 104.15 [11]Or, will you not, since I have commanded you? [12]sons of valour
29 [13]rode
31 [r]Gen. 37.29-34; ch. 1.11 [s]ch. 12.16
32 [14]mouth

17 Then he called his servant that ministered unto him, and said, Put now this *woman* out from me, and bolt the door after her.

18 And *she had* [k]a garment of divers colours upon her: for with such robes were the king's daughters *that were* virgins apparelled. Then his servant brought her out, and bolted the door after her.

19 ¶ And Tā'mar put [l]ashes on her head, and rent her garment of divers colours that *was* on her, and [m]laid her hand on her head, and went on crying.

20 And Ăb'sa-lŏm her brother said unto her, Hath [8]Ăm'nŏn thy brother been with thee? but hold now thy peace, my sister: he *is* thy brother; [9]regard not this thing. So Tā'mar remained [10]desolate in her brother Ăb'sa-lŏm's house.

21 ¶ But when king Dā'vid heard of all these things, he was very wroth.

22 And Ăb'sa-lŏm spake unto his brother Ăm'nŏn neither good nor bad: for Ăb'sa-lŏm [n]hated Ăm'nŏn, because he had forced his sister Tā'mar.

23 ¶ And it came to pass after two full years, that Ăb'sa-lŏm [o]had sheepshearers in Bā'al–hā'zôr, which *is* beside [p]Ē'phră-ĭm: and Ăb'sa-lŏm invited all the king's sons.

24 And Ăb'sa-lŏm came to the king, and said, Behold now, thy servant hath sheepshearers; let the king, I beseech thee, and his servants go with thy servant.

25 And the king said to Ăb'sa-lŏm, Nay, my son, let us not all now go, lest we be chargeable unto thee. And he pressed him: howbeit he would not go, but blessed him.

26 Then said Ăb'sa-lŏm, If not, I pray thee, let my brother Ăm'nŏn go with us. And the king said unto him, Why should he go with thee?

27 But Ăb'sa-lŏm pressed him, that he let Ăm'nŏn and all the king's sons go with him.

28 ¶ Now Ăb'sa-lŏm had commanded his servants, saying, Mark ye now when Ăm'nŏn's [q]heart is merry with wine, and when I say unto you, Smite Ăm'nŏn; then kill him, fear not: [11]have not I commanded you? be courageous, and be [12]valiant.

29 And the servants of Ăb'sa-lŏm did unto Ăm'nŏn as Ăb'sa-lŏm had commanded. Then all the king's sons arose, and every man [13]gat him up upon his mule, and fled.

30 ¶ And it came to pass, while they were in the way, that tidings came to Dā'vid, saying, Ăb'sa-lŏm hath slain all the king's sons, and there is not one of them left.

31 Then the king arose, and [r]tare his garments, and [s]lay on the earth; and all his servants stood by with their clothes rent.

32 And Jŏn'a-dăb, the son of Shĭm'e-ah Dā'vid's brother, answered and said, Let not my lord suppose *that* they have slain all the young men the king's sons; for Ăm'nŏn only is dead: for by the [14]appointment of Ăb'sa-lŏm this

hath been [15]determined from the day
that he forced his sister Tā'mar.
33 Now therefore [t]let not my lord
the king take the thing to his heart, to
think that all the king's sons are dead:
for Ăm'nŏn only is dead.
34 But Ăb'sa-lŏm fled. And the
young man that kept the watch lifted
up his eyes, and looked, and, behold,
there came much people by the way of
the hill side behind him.
35 And Jŏn'a-dăb said unto the king,
Behold, the king's sons come: [16]as thy
servant said, so it is.
36 And it came to pass, as soon as he
had made an end of speaking, that, behold, the king's sons came, and lifted
up their voice and wept: and the king
also and all his servants wept [17]very
sore.
37 ¶ But Ăb'sa-lŏm fled, and went
to [u]Tăl'māi, the son of [18]Ăm-mī'hŭd,
king of Gē'shŭr. And *Dā'vid* mourned
for his son every day.
38 So Ăb'sa-lŏm fled, and went to
[v]Gē'shŭr, and was there three years.
39 And *the soul of* king Dā'vid
[19]longed to go forth unto Ăb'sa-lŏm: for
he was [w]comforted concerning Ăm'-
nŏn, seeing he was dead.

14

Now Jō'ab the son of Zĕr-u-ī'ah
perceived that the king's heart
was toward Ăb'sa-lŏm.
2 And Jō'ab sent to [a]Te-kō'ah, and
fetched thence a wise woman, and said
unto her, I pray thee, feign thyself to be
a mourner, [b]and put on now mourning
apparel, and anoint not thyself with
oil, but be as a woman that had a long
time mourned for the dead:
3 And come to the king, and speak
on this manner unto him. So Jō'ab
[c]put the words in her mouth.
4 ¶ And when the woman of Te-
kō'ah spake to the king, she [d]fell on
her face to the ground, and did obeisance, and said, [1]Help, O king.
5 And the king said unto her, What
aileth thee? And she answered, [e]I *am*
indeed a widow woman, and mine husband is dead.
6 And thy handmaid had two sons,
and they two strove together in the
field, and *there was* [2]none to part them,
but the one smote the other, and slew
him.
7 And, behold, [f]the whole family
is risen against thine handmaid, and
they said, Deliver him that smote his
brother, that we may kill him, for the
life of his brother whom he slew; and
we will destroy the heir also: and so
they shall quench my coal which is
left, and shall not leave to my husband
neither name nor remainder [3]upon the
earth.
8 And the king said unto the woman,
Go to thine house, and I will give
charge concerning thee.
9 And the woman of Te-kō'ah said
unto the king, My lord, O king, [g]the
iniquity *be* on me, and on my father's
house: [h]and the king and his throne *be*
guiltless.

[15]Or, settled
33 [t]ch. 19.19
35 [16]according to the word of thy servant
36 [17]with a great weeping greatly
37 [u]ch. 3.3
[18]Ammihur
38 [v]ch. 14.23
39 [19]Or, was consumed
[w]Gen. 38.12
CHAPTER 14
2 [a]2 Chr. 11.6; 2 Chr. 20.20; Neh. 3.5-27; Jer. 6.1; Amos 1.1
[b]Ruth 3.3
3 [c]Ex. 4.15
4 [d]1 Sam. 20.41; ch. 1.2
[1]Save; 2 Ki. 6.26
5 [e]ch. 12.1
6 [2]no deliverer between them
7 [f]Gen. 4.14; Num. 35.19; Deut. 19.12
[3]upon the face of the earth
9 [g]Gen. 27.13; 1 Sam. 25.24; Matt. 27.25
[h]Num. 35.33; ch. 3.28
11 [4]that the revenger of blood do not multiply to destroy
[i]Num. 35.19; Josh. 20.3-6
[j]1 Sam. 14.45; Acts 27.34
13 [k]Judg. 20.2
[l]ch. 13.37
14 [m]Job 30.23; Eccl. 3.19; Heb. 9.27
[5]Or, because God hath not taken away his life, he hath also devised means, etc
[n]Num. 35.15
17 [6]for rest
[o]1 Sam. 29.9
[7]to hear
20 [p]ch. 19.27
22 [8]blessed
[9]Or, thy

10 And the king said, Whosoever
saith *ought* unto thee, bring him to me,
and he shall not touch thee any more.
11 Then said she, I pray thee, let
the king remember the LORD thy God,
[4]that thou wouldest not suffer [i]the re-
vengers of blood to destroy any more,
lest they destroy my son. And he said,
[j]*As* the LORD liveth, there shall not one
hair of thy son fall to the earth.
12 Then the woman said, Let thine
handmaid, I pray thee, speak *one* word
unto my lord the king. And he said,
Say on.
13 And the woman said, Wherefore
then hast thou thought such a thing
against [k]the people of God? for the
king doth speak this thing as one which
is faulty, in that the king doth not fetch
home again [l]his banished.
14 For we [m]must needs die, and *are*
as water spilt on the ground, which
cannot be gathered up again; [5]neither
doth God respect *any* person: yet doth
he [n]devise means, that his banished be
not expelled from him.
15 Now therefore that I am come to
speak of this thing unto my lord the
king, *it is* because the people have
made me afraid: and thy handmaid
said, I will now speak unto the king; it
may be that the king will perform the
request of his handmaid.
16 For the king will hear, to deliver
his handmaid out of the hand of the
man *that would* destroy me and my
son together out of the inheritance of
God.
17 Then thine handmaid said, The
word of my lord the king shall now be
[6]comfortable: for [o]as an angel of God,
so *is* my lord the king [7]to discern good
and bad: therefore the LORD thy God
will be with thee.
18 Then the king answered and said
unto the woman, Hide not from me, I
pray thee, the thing that I shall ask
thee. And the woman said, Let my lord
the king now speak.
19 And the king said, *Is not* the hand
of Jō'ab with thee in all this? And
the woman answered and said, *As* thy
soul liveth, my lord the king, none can
turn to the right hand or to the left
from ought that my lord the king hath
spoken: for thy servant Jō'ab, he bade
me, and he put all these words in the
mouth of thine handmaid:
20 To fetch about this form of speech
hath thy servant Jō'ab done this thing:
and my lord *is* wise, [p]according to the
wisdom of an angel of God, to know all
things that *are* in the earth.
21 ¶ And the king said unto Jō'ab,
Behold now, I have done this thing: go
therefore, bring the young man Ăb'sa-
lŏm again.
22 And Jō'ab fell to the ground on his
face, and bowed himself, and [8]thanked
the king: and Jō'ab said, To day thy servant knoweth that I have found grace in
thy sight, my lord, O king, in that the
king hath fulfilled the request of [9]his
servant.

23 So Jō'ab arose [q]and went to Gē'-
shŭr, and brought Ăb'sa-lŏm to Je-ru'-
sa-lĕm.
24 And the king said, Let him turn to
his own house, and let him [r]not see my
face. So Ăb'sa-lŏm returned to his own
house, and saw not the king's face.
25 ¶ [10]But in all Is'ra-el there was
none to be so much praised as Ăb'sa-
lŏm for his beauty: [s]from the sole of
his foot even to the crown of his head
there was no blemish in him.
26 And when he polled his head, (for
it was at every year's end that he polled
it: because [t]*the hair* was heavy on him,
therefore he polled it:) he weighed the
hair of his head at [11]two hundred shekels after the king's weight.
27 And [u]unto Ăb'sa-lŏm there were
born three sons, and one daughter,
whose name was Tā'mar: she was a
woman of a fair countenance.
28 ¶ So Ăb'sa-lŏm dwelt two full
years in Je-ru'sa-lĕm, and saw not the
king's face.
29 Therefore Ăb'sa-lŏm sent for
Jō'ab, to have sent him to the king; but
he would not come to him: and when
he sent again the second time, he
would not come.
30 Therefore he said unto his servants, See, Jō'ăb's field is [12]near mine,
and he hath barley there; [v]go and set it
on fire. And Ăb'sa-lŏm's servants set
the field on fire.
31 Then Jō'ab arose, and came to
Ăb'sa-lŏm unto *his* house, and said
unto him, Wherefore have thy servants
set my field on fire?
32 And Ăb'sa-lŏm answered Jō'ab,
Behold, I sent unto thee, saying, Come
hither, that I may send thee to the king,
to say, Wherefore am I come from Gē'-
shŭr? *it had been* good for me *to have
been* there still: now therefore let me
see the king's face; and if [w]there be
any iniquity in me, let him kill me.
33 So Jō'ab came to the king, and
told him: and when he had called
for Ăb'sa-lŏm, he came to the king,
and bowed himself on his face to the
ground before the king: and the king
[x]kissed Ăb'sa-lŏm.

15 And [a]it came to pass after this,
that Ăb'sa-lŏm [b]prepared him
chariots and horses, and fifty men to
run before him.
2 And Ăb'sa-lŏm [c]rose up early, and
stood beside the way of the gate: and it
was *so,* that when any man that had a
controversy [1]came to the king for judgment, then Ăb'sa-lŏm called unto him,
and said, Of what city *art* thou? And he
said, Thy servant *is* of one of the tribes
of Is'ra-el.
3 And Ăb'sa-lŏm said unto him,
[d]See, thy matters *are* good and right;
but [2]*there is* no man *deputed* of the
king to hear thee.
4 Ăb'sa-lŏm said moreover, [e]Oh that
I were made judge in the land, that every man which hath any suit or cause
might come unto me, and I would do
him justice!
5 And it was *so,* that when any man
came nigh *to him* to do him obeisance,
he put forth his hand, and [f]took him,
and kissed him.
6 And on this manner did Ăb'sa-
lŏm to all Is'ra-el that came to the king
for judgment: [g]so Ăb'sa-lŏm stole the
hearts of the men of Is'ra-el.
7 ¶ And it came to pass after [3]forty
years, that Ăb'sa-lŏm said unto the
king, I pray thee, let me go and pay
my vow, which I have vowed unto the
LORD, in [h]Hē'bron.
8 [i]For thy servant [j]vowed a vow
[k]while I abode at Gē'shŭr in Sўr'ĭ-ȧ,
saying, If the LORD shall bring me
again indeed to Je-ru'sa-lĕm, then I
will serve the LORD.
9 And the king said unto him, Go in
peace. So he arose, and went to Hē'-
bron.
10 ¶ But Ăb'sa-lŏm sent spies
throughout all the tribes of Is'ra-el,
saying, As soon as ye hear the sound
of the trumpet, then ye shall say, Ăb'-
sa-lŏm reigneth in Hē'bron.
11 And with Ăb'sa-lŏm went two
hundred men out of Je-ru'sa-lĕm, *that
were* [l]called; and they went [m]in their
simplicity, and they knew not any
thing.
12 And Ăb'sa-lŏm sent for A-hĭth'o-
phel the Gī'lo-nīte, [n]Dā'vid's counsellor, from his city, *even* from [o]Gī'-
loh, while he offered sacrifices. And
the conspiracy was strong; for the people [p]increased continually with
Ăb'sa-lŏm.
13 ¶ And there came a messenger to
Dā'vid, saying, [q]The hearts of the men
of Is'ra-el are after Ăb'sa-lŏm.
14 And Dā'vid said unto all his servants that *were* with him at Je-ru'sa-
lĕm, Arise, and let us [r]flee; for we shall
not *else* escape from Ăb'sa-lŏm: make
speed to depart, lest he overtake us suddenly, and [4]bring evil upon us, and
smite the city with the edge of the
sword.
15 And the king's servants said unto
the king, Behold, thy servants *are ready
to do* whatsoever my lord the king shall
[5]appoint.
16 And [s]the king went forth, and all
his household [6]after him. And the king
left [t]ten women, *which were* concubines, to keep the house.
17 And the king went forth, and all
the people after him, and tarried in a
place that was far off.
18 And all his servants passed on beside him; [u]and all the Chĕr'eth-ītes,
and all the Pē'leth-ītes, and all the Gĭt'-
tītes, six hundred men which came after him from Găth, passed on before
the king.
19 ¶ Then said the king to [v]Ĭt'ta-ī
the Gĭt'tīte, Wherefore goest thou also
with us? return to thy place, and abide
with the king: for thou *art* a stranger,
and also an exile.
20 Whereas thou camest *but* yesterday, should I this day [7]make thee
go up and down with us? seeing I go
[w]whither I may, return thou, and take

23 [q]Deut. 3.14; ch. 3.3
24 [r]Gen. 43.3; Rev. 22.4
25 [10]And as Absalom there was not a beautiful man in all Israel to praise greatly
[s]Deut. 28.35; Isa. 1.6
26 [t]ch. 18.9
[11]Six pounds and a quarter
27 [u]ch. 18.18
30 [12]near my place
[v]ch. 13.28; Prov. 29.12
32 [w]Prov. 28.13
33 [x]Gen. 33.4; Luke 15.20

CHAPTER 15
1 [a]ch. 12.11
[b]1 Ki. 1.5; Prov. 11.2
2 [c]Prov. 1.16
[1]to come
3 [d]Prov. 12.2
[2]Or, none will hear thee from the king downward
4 [e]Judg. 9.29
5 [f]Ps. 12.2
6 [g]Rom. 16.18
7 [3]Forty years from David's anointing, as recorded in 1 Sam. 16.1; Or, four years from Absalom's return
[h]ch. 2.1
8 [i]1 Sam. 16.2
[j]Gen. 28.20; Ps. 56.12
[k]ch. 13.38
11 [l]1 Sam. 9.13
[m]Gen. 20.5;
12 [n]Ps. 41.9;
[o]Josh. 15.51
[p]Ps. 3.1
13 [q]Judg. 9.3
14 [r]ch. 19.9;
[4]thrust
15 [5]choose
16 [s]Ps. 3, title
[6]at his feet
[t]ch. 12.11;
18 [u]ch. 8.18
19 [v]ch. 18.2
20 [7]make thee wander in going
[w]1 Sam. 23.13

back thy brethren: mercy and truth *be* with thee.

21 And Ĭt'ta-ī answered the king, and said, [x]*As* the LORD liveth, and *as* my lord the king liveth, surely in what place my lord the king shall be, whether in death or life, even there also will thy servant be.

22 And Dā'vid said to Ĭt'ta-ī, Go and pass over. And Ĭt'ta-ī the Gĭt'tīte passed over, and all his men, and all the little ones that *were* with him.

23 And all the country wept with a loud voice, and all the people passed over: the king also himself passed over the [y]brook Kĭd'ron, and all the people passed over, toward the way of the [z]wilderness.

24 ¶ And lo Zā'dŏk also, and all the Lē'vītes *were* with him, [a]bearing the ark of the covenant of God: and they set down the ark of God; and A-bī'a-thär went up, until all the people had done passing out of the city.

25 And the king said unto Zā'dŏk, Carry back the ark of God into the city: if I shall find favour in the eyes of the LORD, he [b]will bring me again, and shew me *both* it, and his [c]habitation:

26 But if he thus say, I have no [d]delight in thee; behold, *here am* I, [e]let him do to me as seemeth good unto him.

27 The king said also unto Zā'dŏk the priest, *Art not* thou a [f]seer? return into [g]the city in peace, and your two sons with you, A-hĭm'a-ăz thy son, and Jŏn'a-than the son of A-bī'a-thär.

28 See, I will tarry in the plain of the wilderness, until there come word from you to certify me.

29 Zā'dŏk therefore and A-bī'a-thär carried the ark of God again to Je-ru'sa-lĕm: and they tarried there.

30 ¶ And Dā'vid went up by the ascent of *mount* [h]Ŏl'i-vĕt, [8]and wept as he went up, and [i]had his head covered, and he went [j]barefoot: and all the people that *was* with him [k]covered every man his head, and they went up, [l]weeping as they went up.

31 ¶ And *one* told Dā'vid, saying, [m]A-hĭth'o-phel *is* among the conspirators with Ăb'sa-lŏm. And Dā'vid said, O LORD, I pray thee, turn [n]the counsel of A-hĭth'o-phel into foolishness.

32 ¶ And it came to pass, that *when* Dā'vid was come to the top *of the mount,* where he worshipped God, behold, Hū'shāi the [o]Ăr'chīte came to meet him [p]with his coat rent, and earth upon his head:

33 Unto whom Dā'vid said, If thou passest on with me, then thou shalt be [q]a burden unto me:

34 But if thou return to the city, and say unto Ăb'sa-lŏm, I will be thy servant, O king; *as* I *have been* thy father's servant hitherto, so *will* I now also *be* thy servant: then mayest thou for me defeat the counsel of A-hĭth'o-phel.

35 And *hast thou* not there with thee Zā'dŏk and A-bī'a-thär the priests? therefore it shall be, *that* what thing soever thou shalt hear out of the king's house, thou shalt tell *it* to Zā'dŏk and A-bī'a-thär the priests.

36 Behold, *they have* there with them their two sons, A-hĭm'a-ăz Zā'dok's *son,* and Jŏn'a-than A-bī'a-thär's *son;* and by them ye shall send unto me every thing that ye can hear.

37 So Hū'shāi [r]Dā'vid's friend came into the city, [s]and Ăb'sa-lŏm came into Je-ru'sa-lĕm.

16 And [a]when Dā'vid was a little past the top *of the hill,* behold, [b]Zī'bȧ the servant of Me-phĭb'o-sheth met him, with a couple of asses saddled, and upon them two hundred *loaves* of bread, and an hundred bunches of raisins, and an hundred of summer fruits, and a bottle of wine.

2 And the king said unto Zī'bȧ, What meanest thou by these? And Zī'bȧ said, The asses *be* for the king's household [c]to ride on; and the bread and summer fruit for the [d]young men to eat; and the wine, [e]that such as be faint in the wilderness may drink.

3 And the king said, And where *is* thy master's son? [f]And Zī'bȧ said unto the king, Behold, he abideth at Je-ru'sa-lĕm: for he said, To day shall the house of Ĭs'ra-el restore me the kingdom of my father.

4 [g]Then said the king to Zī'bȧ, Behold, thine *are* all that *pertained* unto Me-phĭb'o-sheth. And Zī'bȧ said, [1]I humbly beseech thee *that* I may find grace in thy sight, my lord, O king.

5 ¶ And when king Dā'vid came to Ba-hū'rim, behold, thence came out a man of the family of the house of Saul, whose name [h]*was* Shĭm'e-ī, the son of Gē'rȧ: [2]he came forth, and cursed still as he came.

6 And he cast stones at Dā'vid, and at all the servants of king Dā'vid: and all the people and all the mighty men *were* on his right hand and on his left.

7 And thus said Shĭm'e-ī when he cursed, Come out, come out, thou [3]bloody man, and thou man of Bē'lĭ-al:

8 The LORD hath [i]returned upon thee all [j]the blood of the house of Saul, in whose stead thou hast reigned; and the LORD hath delivered the kingdom into the hand of Ăb'sa-lŏm thy son: and, [4]behold, thou *art taken* in thy mischief, because thou *art* a bloody man.

9 ¶ Then said A-bĭsh'ă-ī the son of Zĕr-u-ī'ah unto the king, Why should this dead dog [k]curse my lord the king? let me go over, I pray thee, and take off his head.

10 And the king said, [l]What have I to do with you, ye sons of Zĕr-u-ī'ah? so let him curse, because [m]the LORD hath said unto him, Curse Dā'vid. [n]Who shall then say, Wherefore hast thou done so?

11 And Dā'vid said to A-bĭsh'ă-ī, and to all his servants, Behold, my son, which came forth of my bowels, seeketh my life: how much more now *may this* Bĕn'ja-mīte *do it?* let him alone, and let him curse; for the LORD hath bidden him.

21 [x]Ruth 1.16; 1 Sam. 20.3; 2 Ki. 2.2-4-6
23 [y]1 Ki. 2.37; 2 Chr. 30.14
[z]ch. 16.2; Matt. 3.1-3
24 [a]Num. 4.15
25 [b]Ps. 43.3
[c]ch. 6.17
26 [d]Num. 14.8; 1 Ki. 10.9; 2 Chr. 9.8
[e]1 Sam. 3.18
27 [f]ch. 24.11
[g]ch. 17.17
30 [h]Zech. 14.4; Matt. 21.1; Luke 19.29; Acts 1.12
[8]going up, and weeping
[i]Esth. 6.12
[j]Isa. 20.2
[k]Jer. 14.3
[l]Ps. 126.6; Matt. 5.4; Rom. 12.15
31 [m]Ps. 3.1; Ps. 55.12
[n]ch. 16.23
32 [o]Josh. 16.2
[p]ch. 1.2
33 [q]ch. 19.35
37 [r]ch. 16.16; Prov. 17.17
[s]ch. 16.15

CHAPTER 16

1 [a]ch. 15.30
[b]ch. 9.2
2 [c]Judg. 5.10; ch. 15.1
[d]1 Sam. 25.27
[e]ch. 15.23; Ps. 104.15; Prov. 31.6; 1 Tim. 5.23
3 [f]ch. 19.27
4 [g]Prov. 18.13
[1]I do obeisance
5 [h]ch. 19.16
[2]Or, he still came forth and cursed
7 [3]man of blood
8 [i]Judg. 9.24; Rev. 16.6
[j]ch. 1.16; ch. 3.28-29
[4]behold thee in thy evil
9 [k]Ex. 22.28
10 [l]ch. 3.39; 1 Pet. 2.23
[m]2 Ki. 18.25; Lam. 3.38
[n]Rom. 9.20

12 It may be that the LORD will look
on mine [5]affliction, and that the LORD
will [o]requite me good for his cursing
this day.
13 And as Dā'vid and his men went
by the way, Shĭm'e-ī went along on the
hill's side over against him, and cursed
as he went, and threw stones at him,
and [6]cast dust.
14 And the king, and all the people
that *were* with him, came weary, and
refreshed themselves there.
15 ¶ And Ăb'sa-lŏm, and all the people the men of Ĭs'ra-el, came to Je-
ru'sa-lĕm, and A-hĭth'o-phel with him.
16 And it came to pass, when Hū'-
shāi the Ăr'chīte, Dā'vid's friend, was
come unto Ăb'sa-lŏm, that Hū'shāi
said unto Ăb'sa-lŏm, [7]God save the
king, God save the king.
17 And Ăb'sa-lŏm said to Hū'shāi, *Is*
this thy kindness to thy friend? [p]why
wentest thou not with thy friend?
18 And Hū'shāi said unto Ăb'sa-lŏm,
Nay; but whom the LORD, and this people, and all the men of Ĭs'ra-el, choose,
his will I be, and with him will I abide.
19 And again, [q]whom should I serve?
should I not *serve* in the presence of his
son? as I have served in thy father's
presence, so will I be in thy presence.
20 ¶ Then said Ăb'sa-lŏm to A-hĭth'-
o-phel, Give [r]counsel among you what
we shall do.
21 And A-hĭth'o-phel said unto Ăb'-
sa-lŏm, Go in unto thy father's [s]concu-
bines, which he hath left to keep the
house; and all Ĭs'ra-el shall hear that
thou [t]art abhorred of thy father: then
shall [u]the hands of all that *are* with
thee be strong.
22 So they spread Ăb'sa-lŏm a tent
upon the top of the house; and Ăb'sa-
lŏm went in unto his father's concubines [v]in the sight of all Ĭs'ra-el.
23 And the counsel of A-hĭth'o-phel,
which he counselled in those days, *was*
as if a man had inquired at the [8]oracle
of God: so *was* all the counsel of A-
hĭth'o-phel [w]both with Dā'vid and
with Ăb'sa-lŏm.

17 Moreover A-hĭth'o-phel said unto
Ăb'sa-lŏm, Let me now choose
out twelve thousand men, and I will
arise and pursue after Dā'vid this night:
2 And I will come upon him while he
is [a]weary and weak handed, and will
make him afraid: and all the people
that *are* with him shall flee; and I will
[b]smite the king only:
3 And I will bring back all the people unto thee: the man whom thou
seekest *is* as if all returned: *so* all the
people shall be in [c]peace.
4 And the saying [1]pleased Ăb'sa-
lŏm well, and all the elders of Ĭs'ra-el.
5 Then said Ăb'sa-lŏm, Call now
Hū'shāi the Ăr'chīte also, and let us
hear likewise [2]what he saith.
6 And when Hū'shāi was come to
Ăb'sa-lŏm, Ăb'sa-lŏm spake unto him,
saying, A-hĭth'o-phel hath spoken after this manner: shall we do *after* his
[3]saying? if not; speak thou.
7 And Hū'shāi said unto Ăb'sa-lŏm,
The counsel that A-hĭth'o-phel hath
[4]given *is* not good at this time.
8 For, said Hū'shāi, thou knowest
thy father and his men, that they *be*
mighty men, and they *be* [5]chafed in
their minds, as [d]a bear robbed of her
whelps in the field: and thy father *is* a
man of war, and will not lodge with the
people.
9 Behold, he is hid now in some pit,
or in some *other* place: and it will
come to pass, when some of them be
[6]overthrown at the first, that whosoever heareth it will say, There is a
slaughter among the people that follow Ăb'sa-lŏm.
10 And he also *that is* [7]valiant, whose
heart *is* as the heart of a lion, shall utterly melt: for all Ĭs'ra-el knoweth that
thy father *is* a mighty man, and *they*
which *be* with him *are* valiant men.
11 Therefore I counsel that all Ĭs'-
ra-el be generally gathered unto thee,
from Dăn even to Bē'er–shē'bȧ, [e]as
the sand that *is* by the sea for multitude; [8]and that thou go to battle in
thine own person.
12 So shall we come upon him in
some place where he shall be found,
and we will light upon him as the dew
falleth on the ground: and of him and
of all the men that *are* with him there
shall not be left so much as one.
13 Moreover, if he be gotten into a
city, then shall all Ĭs'ra-el bring ropes
to that city, and we will draw it into the
river, until there be not one small stone
found there.
14 And Ăb'sa-lŏm and all the men of
Ĭs'ra-el said, The counsel of Hū'shāi the
Ăr'chīte *is* better than the counsel of A-
hĭth'o-phel. For [f]the LORD had
[9]appointed to defeat the good counsel
of A-hĭth'o-phel, to the intent that the
LORD might bring evil upon Ăb'sa-lŏm.
15 ¶ Then said Hū'shāi unto Zā'dŏk
and to A-bī'a-thăr the priests, Thus and
thus did A-hĭth'o-phel counsel Ăb'sa-
lŏm and the elders of Ĭs'ra-el; and thus
and thus have I counselled.
16 Now therefore send quickly, and
tell Dā'vid, saying, Lodge not this night
in the plains of the wilderness, but
speedily pass over; lest the king be
swallowed up, and all the people that
are with him.
17 [g]Now Jŏn'a-than and A-hĭm'a-ăz
stayed [h]by [i]Ĕn–rō'gĕl; for they might
not be seen to come into the city: and a
wench went and told them; and they
went and told king Dā'vid.
18 Nevertheless a lad saw them, and
told Ăb'sa-lŏm: but they went both of
them away quickly, and came to a
man's house [j]in Ba-hū'rim, which had
a well in his court; whither they went
down.
19 And [k]the woman took and spread
a covering over the well's mouth, and
spread ground corn thereon; and the
thing was not known.
20 And when Ăb'sa-lŏm's servants
came to the woman to the house,
they said, Where *is* A-hĭm'a-ăz and

12 [5]eye, or, tears
[o]Ps. 37.7; Lam. 3.22-26; Matt. 5.11-12; Rom. 8.28; 2 Cor. 4.17
13 [6]dusted him with dust
16 [7]Let the king live
17 [p]ch. 15.32-37; Prov. 17.17
19 [q]1 Sam. 28.2
20 [r]Ex. 1.10; Ps. 2.2; Prov. 21.30; Matt. 27.1
21 [s]Gen. 35.22; ch. 12.11; ch. 15.16
[t]Gen. 34.30
[u]ch. 2.7; Zech. 8.13
22 [v]Lev. 18.8; Deut. 22.30; ch. 12.11; Prov. 28.7; Isa. 3.9; Mic. 7.3-6
23 [8]word
[w]ch. 15.12

CHAPTER 17
2 [a]Deut. 25.18; ch. 16.14; 1 Ki. 22.31; John 11.50
[b]Zech. 13.7; Matt. 21.38
3 [c]Jer. 6.14
4 [1]was right in the eyes of, etc
5 [2]what is in his mouth
6 [3]word?
7 [4]counselled
8 [5]bitter of soul
[d]Hos. 13.8
9 [6]fallen
10 [7]a son of valour
11 [e]Gen. 22.17
[8]that thy face, or, presence go, etc
14 [f]ch. 15.31-34; Ps. 9.15
[9]commanded
17 [g]ch. 15.27-36
[h]Josh. 2.4
[i]Josh. 15.7; 1 Ki. 1.9; That is, the fuller's well
18 [j]ch. 3.16; ch. 16.5; ch. 19.16
19 [k]Josh. 2.6

Jŏn'a-than? And [l]the woman said
unto them, They be gone over the
brook of water. And when they had
sought and could not find *them*, they
returned to Je-ru'sa-lĕm.
21 And it came to pass, after they
were departed, that they came up out of
the well, and went and told king Dā'-
vid, and said unto Dā'vid, Arise, and
pass quickly over the water: for thus
hath A-hĭth'o-phel counselled against
you.
22 Then Dā'vid arose, and all the
people that *were* with him, and they
passed over Jôr'dan: by the morning
light there lacked not one of them that
was not gone over Jôr'dan.
23 ¶ And when A-hĭth'o-phel saw
that his counsel was not [10]followed, he
saddled *his* ass, and arose, and gat
him home to his house, to [m]his city,
and [11]put his household in order, and
[n]hanged himself, and died, and was
buried in the sepulchre of his father.
24 Then Dā'vid came to [o]Mā-ha-nā'-
im. And Ăb'sa-lŏm passed over Jôr'-
dan, he and all the men of Ĭs'ra-el with
him.
25 ¶ And Ăb'sa-lŏm made Ā'm'a-sȧ
captain of the host instead of Jō'ab:
which Ăm'a-sȧ *was* a man's son, whose
name *was* [12]Ĭth'rȧ an Ĭs'ra-el-īte, that
went in to [13]Ăb'ĭ-gāil the daughter of
Nā'hăsh, sister to Zĕr-u-ī'ah Jō'ăb's
mother.
26 So Ĭs'ra-el and Ăb'sa-lŏm pitched
in the land of Gĭl'e-ăd.
27 ¶ And it came to pass, when Dā'-
vid was come to Mā-ha-nā'im, that
[p]Shō'bī the son of Nā'hăsh of Răb'bah
of the children of Ăm'mŏn, and [q]Mā'-
chĭr the son of Ăm'mĭ-el of Lo–dē'bär,
and [r]Bär-zĭl'la-ī the Gĭl'e-ăd-īte of Ro-
gē'lim,
28 Brought [s]beds, and [14]basons, and
earthen vessels, and wheat, and barley, and flour, and parched *corn*, and
beans, and lentiles, and parched *pulse*,
29 And honey, and butter, and sheep,
and cheese of kine, for Dā'vid, and for
the people that *were* with him, [t]to eat:
for they said, The people *is* hungry, and
weary, and thirsty, in the wilderness.

18 And Dā'vid numbered the people that *were* with him, and set
captains of thousands and captains of
hundreds over them.
2 And Dā'vid sent forth a third part
of the people under the hand of Jō'ab,
and a third part under the hand of A-
bĭsh'ă-ī the son of Zĕr-u-ī'ah, Jō'ăb's
brother, [a]and a third part under the
hand of Ĭt'ta-ī the Gĭt'tīte. And the king
said unto the people, I will surely go
forth with you myself also.
3 [b]But the people answered, Thou
shalt not go forth: for if we flee away,
they will not [1]care for us; neither if half
of us die, will they care for us: but now
thou art [2]worth ten thousand of us:
therefore now *it is* better that thou
[3]succour us out of the city.
4 And the king said unto them, What
seemeth you best I will do. And the
king stood by the gate side, and all the
people came out by hundreds and by
thousands.
5 And the king commanded Jō'ab
and A-bĭsh'ă-ī and Ĭt'ta-ī, saying, *Deal*
gently for my sake with the young
man, *even* with Ăb'sa-lŏm. And all the
people heard when the king gave all
the captains charge concerning Ăb'sa-
lŏm.
6 ¶ So the people went out into the
field against Ĭs'ra-el: and the battle
was in the [c]wood of Ē'phră-ĭm;
7 Where the people of Ĭs'ra-el were
slain before the servants of Dā'vid,
and there was there [d]a great slaughter
that day of twenty thousand *men*.
8 For the battle was there scattered
over the face of all the country: and the
wood [4]devoured more people that day
than the sword devoured.
9 ¶ And Ăb'sa-lŏm met the servants
of Dā'vid. And Ăb'sa-lŏm rode upon a
mule, and the mule went under the
thick boughs of a great oak, and [e]his
head caught hold of the oak, and he
was taken up between the heaven and
the earth; and the mule that *was* under
him went away.
10 And a certain man saw *it*, and
told Jō'ab, and said, Behold, I saw Ăb'-
sa-lŏm hanged in an oak.
11 And Jō'ab said unto the man that
told him, And, behold, thou sawest
him, and why didst thou not smite him
there to the ground? and I would have
given thee ten *shekels* of silver, and a
girdle.
12 And the man said unto Jō'ab,
Though I should [5]receive a thousand
shekels of silver in mine hand, *yet*
would I not put forth mine hand against
the king's son: for in our hearing the
king charged thee and A-bĭsh'ă-ī and
Ĭt'ta-ī, saying, [6]Beware that none *touch*
the young man Ăb'sa-lŏm.
13 Otherwise I should have wrought
falsehood against mine own life: for
there is no matter hid from the king,
and thou thyself wouldest have set thyself against *me*.
14 Then said Jō'ab, I may not tarry
thus [7]with thee. And he took three darts
in his hand, and thrust them through
the heart of Ăb'sa-lŏm, while he *was*
yet alive in the [8]midst of the oak.
15 And ten young men that bare
Jō'ăb's armour compassed about and
smote Ăb'sa-lŏm, and slew him.
16 And Jō'ab blew the trumpet, and
the people returned from pursuing after Ĭs'ra-el: for Jō'ab held back the people.
17 And they took Ăb'sa-lŏm, and
cast him into a great pit in the wood,
and [f]laid a very great heap of stones
upon him: and all Ĭs'ra-el fled every
one to his tent.
18 ¶ Now Ăb'sa-lŏm in his lifetime
had taken and reared up for himself a
pillar, which *is* in [g]the king's dale: for
he said, [h]I have no son to keep my
name in remembrance: and he [i]called
the pillar after his own name: and it is
called unto this day, Ăb'sa-lŏm's place.

20 [l]Ex. 1.19; 1 Sam. 27.11-12
23 [10]done
[m]ch. 15.12
[11]gave charge concerning his house
[n]1 Sam. 31.4-5; Matt. 27.5
24 [o]Gen. 32.2; ch. 2.8
25 [12]Or, Jether an Ishmaelite
[13]Abigal
27 [p]1 Sam. 11.1; ch. 10.1
[q]ch. 9.4
[r]ch. 19.31-32; Ezra 2.61
28 [s]1 Sam. 25.18; Matt. 5.7
[14]Or, cups
29 [t]Deut. 15.7; Rom. 12.13
CHAPTER 18
2 [a]ch. 15.19
3 [b]ch. 21.17
[1]set their heart on us
[2]as ten thousand of us
[3]be to succour
6 [c]Josh. 17.15-18; Judg. 12.6
7 [d]Prov. 11.21
8 [4]multiplied to devour
9 [e]ch. 14.26; 1 Cor. 11.14
12 [5]weigh upon mine hand
[6]Beware whosoever ye be of, etc
14 [7]before thee
[8]heart
17 [f]Josh. 7.26;
18 [g]Gen. 14.17
[h]ch. 14.27;
[i]Ps. 49.11

19 ¶ Then said [j]A-hĭm'a-ăz the son
of Zā'dŏk, Let me now run, and bear
the king tidings, how that the LORD
hath [9]avenged him of his enemies.
20 And Jō'ab said unto him, Thou
shalt not [10]bear tidings this day, but
thou shalt bear tidings another day:
but this day thou shalt bear no tidings,
because the king's son is dead.
21 Then said Jō'ab to [11]Cu̯'shī, Go
tell the king what thou hast seen. And
Cu̯'shī bowed himself unto Jō'ab, and
ran.
22 Then said A-hĭm'a-ăz the son of
Zā'dŏk yet again to Jō'ab, But [12]howso-
ever, let me, I pray thee, also run after
Cu̯'shī. And Jō'ab said, Wherefore wilt
thou run, my son, seeing that thou hast
no tidings [13]ready?
23 But howsoever, *said he,* let me
run. And he said unto him, Run. Then
A-hĭm'a-ăz ran by the way of the plain,
and overran Cu̯'shī.
24 And Dā'vid sat [k]between the two
gates: and [l]the watchman went up to
the roof over the gate unto the wall,
and lifted up his eyes, and looked, and
behold a man running alone.
25 And the watchman cried, and told
the king. And the king said, If he *be*
alone, *there is* tidings in his mouth.
And he came apace, and drew near.
26 And the watchman saw another
man running: and the watchman called
unto the porter, and said, Behold *another* man running alone. And the king
said, He also bringeth tidings.
27 And the watchman said, [14]Me
thinketh the running of the foremost is
like the running of A-hĭm'a-ăz the son
of Zā'dŏk. And the king said, [m]He *is* a
good man, and cometh with good tidings.
28 And A-hĭm'a-ăz called, and said
unto the king, [15]All is well. And he fell
down to the earth upon his face before
the king, and said, Blessed *be* the LORD
thy God, which hath [16]delivered up the
men that lifted up their hand against
my lord the king.
29 And the king said, [17]Is the young
man Ăb'sa-lŏm safe? And A-hĭm'a-ăz
answered, When Jō'ab sent the king's
servant, and *me* thy servant, I saw a
great tumult, but I knew not what *it
was.*
30 And the king said *unto him,* Turn
aside, *and* stand here. And he turned
aside, and stood still.
31 And, behold, Cu̯'shī came; and
Cu̯'shī said, [18]Tidings, my lord the king:
for the LORD [n]hath avenged thee this
day of all them that rose up against
thee.
32 And the king said unto Cu̯'shī, *Is*
the young man Ăb'sa-lŏm safe? And
Cu̯'shī answered, The enemies of my
lord the king, and all that rise against
thee to do *thee* hurt, be as *that* young
man *is.*
33 ¶ And the king was much moved,
and went up to the chamber over the
gate, and wept: and as he went, thus he
said, [o]O my son Ăb'sa-lŏm, my son,
my son Ăb'sa-lŏm! would God I had
died for thee, O Ăb'sa-lŏm, my son, my
son!

19 And it was told Jō'ab, Behold,
the king weepeth and mourneth
for Ăb'sa-lŏm.
2 And the [1]victory that day was
turned into mourning unto all the people: for the people heard say that day
how the king was grieved for his son.
3 And the people gat them by stealth
that day into the city, as people being
ashamed steal away when they flee in
battle.
4 But the king [a]covered his face,
and the king cried with a loud voice,
[b]O my son Ăb'sa-lŏm, O Ăb'sa-lŏm,
my son, my son!
5 And Jō'ab came into the house to
the king, and said, Thou hast shamed
this day the faces of all thy servants,
which this day have saved thy life, and
the lives of thy sons and of thy daughters, and the lives of thy wives, and the
lives of thy concubines;
6 [2]In that thou lovest thine enemies,
and hatest thy friends. For thou hast
declared this day, [3]that thou regardest
neither princes nor servants: for this
day I perceive, that if Ăb'sa-lŏm had
lived, and all we had died this day,
then it had pleased thee well.
7 Now therefore arise, go forth, and
speak [4]comfortably unto thy servants:
for I swear by the LORD, if thou go not
forth, [c]there will not tarry one with
thee this night: and that will be worse
unto thee than all the evil that befell
thee from thy youth until now.
8 Then the king arose, and sat [d]in
the gate. And they told unto all the people, saying, Behold, the king doth sit in
the gate. And all the people came before the king: [e]for Ĭs'ra-el had fled every man to his tent.
9 ¶ And all the people were at strife
throughout all the tribes of Ĭs'ra-el, saying, [f]The king saved us out of the hand
of our enemies, and he delivered us out
of the hand of the Phĭ-lĭs'tĭnes; and
now he is [g]fled out of the land for
Ăb'sa-lŏm.
10 And Ăb'sa-lŏm, whom we
anointed over us, is dead in battle.
Now therefore why [5]speak ye not a
word of bringing the king back?
11 ¶ And king Dā'vid sent to Zā'dŏk
and to A-bī'a-thär the priests, saying,
Speak unto the elders of Jū'dah, saying, Why are ye the last to bring the
king back to his house? seeing the
speech of all Ĭs'ra-el is come to the
king, *even* to his house.
12 Ye *are* my brethren, ye *are* [h]my
bones and my flesh: wherefore then
are ye the last to bring back the king?
13 [i]And say ye to Ăm'a-să, *Art* thou
not of my bone, and of my flesh? [j]God
do so to me, and more also, if thou be
not captain of the host before me continually [k]in the room of Jō'ab.
14 And he bowed the heart of all the
men of Jū'dah, [l]even as *the heart of*
one man; so that they sent *this word*
unto the king, Return thou, and all thy
servants.

19 [j]ch. 15.36; ch. 17.17 [9]judged him from the hand, etc
20 [10]be a man of tidings
21 [11]The Ethiopian
22 [12]be what may [13]Or, convenient
24 [k]1 Sam. 1.9; 1 Sam. 4.13 [l]ch. 13.34; 2 Ki. 9.17
27 [14]I see the running [m]1 Ki. 1.42
28 [15]Peace, or, Peace be to thee [16]shut up
29 [17]Is there peace?
31 [18]Tidings is brought [n]Ps. 27.2; Ps. 55.18
33 [o]ch. 19.4; Prov. 10.1; Prov. 19.13

CHAPTER 19
2 [1]salvation, or, deliverance
4 [a]ch. 15.30; 1 Sam. 4.12 [b]ch. 18.33
6 [2]By loving, etc [3]that princes or servants are not to thee
7 [4]to the heart of thy servants [c]Prov. 14.28
8 [d]Ruth 4.1; ch. 18.4-24 [e]1 Ki. 12.16; 2 Ki. 14.12
9 [f]ch. 5.18; 1 Sam. 17.1 [g]ch. 15.14
10 [5]are ye silent?
12 [h]Gen. 2.23; Judg. 9.2; ch. 5.1
13 [i]ch. 17.25; 1 Chr. 2.16-17; 1 Chr. 12.18 [j]Ruth 1.17; 1 Ki. 19.2 [k]ch. 3.29-30; ch. 8.16
14 [l]Judg. 20.1; Ps. 110.2-3; Acts 4.32

15 So the king returned, and came
to Jôr'dan. And Jū'dah came to [m]Gĭl'-
găl, to go to meet the king, to conduct
the king over Jôr'dan.
16 ¶ And [n]Shĭm'e-ī the son of Gē'rȧ,
a Bĕn'ja-mīte, which *was* of Ba-hū'-
rim, hasted and came down with the
men of Jū'dah to meet king Dā'vid.
17 And *there were* a thousand men
of Bĕn'ja-min with him, and [o]Zī'bȧ the
servant of the house of Saul, and his
fifteen sons and his twenty servants
with him; and they went over Jôr'dan
before the king.
18 And there went over a ferry boat
to carry over the king's household,
and to do [6]what he thought good. And
Shĭm'e-ī the son of Gē'rȧ fell down before the king, as he was come over
Jôr'dan;
19 And said unto the king, [p]Let not
my lord impute iniquity unto me, neither do thou remember [q]that which
thy servant did perversely the day that
my lord the king went out of Je-ru'sa-
lĕm, that the king should [r]take it to his
heart.
20 For thy servant doth know that I
have sinned: therefore, behold, I am
come the first this day of all [s]the house
of Jō'seph to go down to meet my lord
the king.
21 But A-bĭsh'ă-ī the son of Zĕr-
u-ī'ah answered and said, Shall not
Shĭm'e-ī be put to death for this, because he [t]cursed the LORD'S anointed?
22 And Dā'vid said, [u]What have I to
do with you, ye sons of Zĕr-u-ī'ah, that
ye should this day be adversaries unto
me? [v]shall there any man be put to
death this day in Ĭs'ra-el? for do not I
know that I *am* this day king over
Ĭs'ra-el?
23 Therefore [w]the king said unto
Shĭm'e-ī, Thou shalt not die. And the
king sware unto him.
24 ¶ And [x]Me-phĭb'o-sheth the son
of Saul came down to meet the king,
and had neither dressed his feet, nor
trimmed his beard, nor washed his
clothes, from the day the king departed
until the day he came *again* in peace.
25 And it came to pass, when he was
come to Je-ru'sa-lĕm to meet the king,
that the king said unto him, [y]Where-
fore wentest not thou with me, Me-
phĭb'o-sheth?
26 And he answered, My lord, O
king, my servant deceived me: for thy
servant said, I will saddle me an ass,
that I may ride thereon, and go to the
king; because thy servant *is* lame.
27 And [z]he hath slandered thy servant unto my lord the king; [a]but my
lord the king *is* as an angel of God: do
therefore *what is* good in thine eyes.
28 For all *of* my father's house were
but [7]dead men before my lord the king:
[b]yet didst thou set thy servant among
them that did eat at thine own table.
What right therefore have I yet to cry
any more unto the king?
29 And the king said unto him, Why
speakest thou any more of thy matters? I have said, [c]Thou and Zī'bȧ divide the land.
30 And Me-phĭb'o-sheth said unto
the king, Yea, let him take all, forasmuch as my lord the king is come
again in peace unto his own house.
31 ¶ And [d]Bär-zĭl'la-ī the Gĭl'e-ăd-
īte came down from Ro-gē'lim, and
went over Jôr'dan with the king, to conduct him over Jôr'dan.
32 Now Bär-zĭl'la-ī was a very aged
man, *even* fourscore years old: and
[e]he had provided the king of sustenance while he lay at Mā-ha-nā'im; for
he *was* a very great man.
33 And the king said unto Bär-zĭl'la-
ī, Come thou over with me, and I will
feed thee with me in Je-ru'sa-lĕm.
34 And Bär-zĭl'la-ī said unto the king,
[8]How long have I to live, that I should go
up with the king unto Je-ru'sa-lĕm?
35 I *am* this day [f]fourscore years
old: *and* can I discern between good
and evil? can thy servant taste what I
eat or what I drink? can I [g]hear any
more the voice of singing men and singing women? wherefore then should thy
servant be yet a burden unto my lord
the king?
36 Thy servant will go a little way
over Jôr'dan with the king: and why
should the king recompense it me with
such a reward?
37 Let thy servant, I pray thee, turn
back again, that I may die in mine own
city, *and be buried* by the grave of my
father and of my mother. But behold
thy servant [h]Chĭm'ham; let him go
over with my lord the king; and do to
him what shall seem good unto thee.
38 And the king answered, Chĭm'-
ham shall go over with me, and I will
do to him that which shall seem good
unto thee: and whatsoever thou shalt
[9]require of me, *that* will I do for thee.
39 And all the people went over Jôr'-
dan. And when the king was come
over, the king [i]kissed Bär-zĭl'la-ī, and
[j]blessed him; and he returned unto his
own place.
40 Then the king went on to Gĭl'găl,
and [10]Chĭm'ham went on with him:
and all the people of Jū'dah conducted
the king, and also half the people of
Ĭs'ra-el.
41 ¶ And, behold, all the men of Ĭs'-
ra-el came to the king, and said unto
the king, Why have our brethren the
men of Jū'dah stolen thee away, and
[k]have brought the king, and his household, and all Dā'vid's men with him,
over Jôr'dan?
42 And all the men of Jū'dah answered the men of Ĭs'ra-el, Because the
king *is* [l]near of kin to us: wherefore
then be ye angry for this matter? have
we eaten at all of the king's *cost?* or
hath he given us any gift?
43 And the men of Ĭs'ra-el answered
the men of Jū'dah, and said, We have
ten [m]parts in the king, and we have
also more *right* in Dā'vid than ye: why
then did ye [11]despise us, that our advice should not be first had in bringing
back our king? [n]And the words of the

15 [m]Josh. 5.9; 1 Sam. 11.14-15
16 [n]ch. 16.5
17 [o]ch. 9.2-10; ch. 16.1-2
18 [6]the good in his eyes
19 [p]Ps. 32.2; Rom. 4.6-8; 2 Cor. 5.19
[q]ch. 16.5-6; Prov. 28.13; Matt. 5.25
[r]ch. 13.33
20 [s]ch. 16.5
21 [t]Ex. 22.28; 1 Sam. 24.6; ch. 16.5-7-13; Eccl. 10.20; Acts 23.5; 2 Pet. 2.10-11
22 [u]1 Sam. 26.8; ch. 16.10; Matt. 8.29
[v]1 Sam. 11.13
23 [w]1 Ki. 2.8-9-37-46
24 [x]ch. 9.6
25 [y]ch. 16.17
27 [z]ch. 16.3; Ps. 15.3; Ps. 63.11; Ps. 101.7; Prov. 6.16-17; Prov. 21.6
[a]1 Sam. 29.9; ch. 14.17-20
28 [7]men of death
[b]ch. 9.7-10-13
29 [c]Deut. 19.16-21; Ps. 82.2; Ps. 101; Prov. 29.4
31 [d]1 Ki. 2.7; Ezra 2.61; Neh. 7.63
32 [e]ch. 17.27
34 [8]How many days are the years of my life?
35 [f]Ps. 90.10
[g]Eccl. 12.3-6
37 [h]1 Ki. 2.7; Jer. 41.17
38 [9]choose
39 [i]Gen. 31.55
[j]Gen. 14.19; 1 Sam. 2.20
40 [10]Chimhan
41 [k]verse 15
42 [l]verse 12; Matt. 1.1-6
43 [m]1 Ki. 11.30-31
[11]set us at light
[n]Judg. 8.1

men of Jū'dah were fiercer than the
words of the men of Ĭs'ra-el.
20 And there [a]happened to be there
a man of [b]Bē'lĭ-al, whose name
was Shē'bȧ, the son of Bĭch'rī, a Bĕn'-
ja-mīte: and he blew a trumpet, and
said, [c]We have no part in Dā'vid, neither have we inheritance in the son of
Jĕs'se: [d]every man to his tents, O Ĭs'ra-
el.
2 [e]So every man of Ĭs'ra-el went up
from after Dā'vid, *and* followed Shē'bȧ
the son of Bĭch'rī: but the men of Jū'-
dah clave unto their king, from Jôr'dan
even to Je-ru'sa-lĕm.
3 ¶ And Dā'vid came to his house at
Je-ru'sa-lĕm; and the king took the ten
women *his* [f]concubines, whom he had
left to keep the house, and put them in
[1]ward, and fed them, but went not in
unto them. So they were [2]shut up unto
the day of their death, [3]living in widowhood.
4 ¶ Then said the king to Ā'ma-sȧ,
[4]Assemble me the men of Jū'dah within
three days, and be thou here present.
5 So Ā'ma-sȧ went to assemble *the*
men of Jū'dah: but he tarried longer
than the set time which he had appointed him.
6 And Dā'vid said to [g]A-bĭsh'ă-ī,
Now shall Shē'bȧ the son of Bĭch'rī do
us more harm than *did* Ăb'sa-lŏm: take
thou [h]thy lord's servants, and pursue
after him, lest he get him fenced cities,
and [5]escape us.
7 And there went out after him Jō'-
ăb's men, and the [i]Chĕr'eth-ītes, and
the Pē'leth-ītes, and all the mighty men:
and they went out of Je-ru'sa-lĕm, to
pursue after Shē'bȧ the son of Bĭch'rī.
8 When they *were* at the great stone
which *is* in Gĭb'e-on, Ā'ma-sȧ went before them. And Jō'ăb's garment that he
had put on was girded unto him, and
upon it a girdle *with* a sword fastened
upon his loins in the sheath thereof;
and as he went forth it fell out.
9 And Jō'ab said to Ā'ma-sȧ, *Art*
thou in health, my brother? [j]And Jō'ab
took Ā'ma-sȧ by the beard with the
right hand to kiss him.
10 But Ā'ma-sȧ took no heed to the
sword that *was* in Jō'ăb's hand: so [k]he
smote him therewith [l]in the fifth *rib*,
and shed out his bowels to the ground,
and [6]struck him not again; and he died.
So Jō'ab and A-bĭsh'ă-ī his brother pursued after Shē'bȧ the son of Bĭch'rī.
11 And one of Jō'ăb's men stood by
him, and said, He that favoureth Jō'ab,
and he that *is* for Dā'vid, *let him go*
after Jō'ab.
12 And Ā'ma-sȧ wallowed in blood
in the midst of the highway. And when
the man saw that all the people stood
still, he removed Ā'ma-sȧ out of the
highway into the field, and cast a cloth
upon him, when he saw that every one
that came by him stood still.
13 When he was removed out of the
highway, all the people went on after
Jō'ab, to pursue after Shē'bȧ the son of
Bĭch'rī.
14 ¶ And he went through all the
tribes of Ĭs'ra-el unto [m]Ā'bĕl, and to
Bĕth–mā'a-chah, and all the Bē'rītes:
and they were gathered together, and
went also after him.
15 And they came and besieged him
in Ā'bĕl of Bĕth–mā'a-chah, and they
[n]cast up a bank against the city, and [7]it
stood in the trench: and all the people
that *were* with Jō'ab [8]battered the wall,
to throw it down.
16 ¶ Then cried a wise woman out of
the city, Hear, hear; say, I pray you,
unto Jō'ab, Come near hither, that I
may speak with thee.
17 And when he was come near unto
her, the woman said, *Art* thou Jō'ab?
And he answered, I *am he.* Then she
said unto him, Hear the words of thine
handmaid. And he answered, I do hear.
18 Then she spake, saying, [9]They
were wont to speak in old time, saying,
They shall surely ask *counsel* at Ā'bĕl:
and so they ended *the matter.*
19 I *am one of them that are* peaceable *and* faithful in Ĭs'ra-el: thou seekest to destroy a city and a [10]mother in
Ĭs'ra-el: why wilt thou swallow up [o]the
inheritance of the LORD?
20 And Jō'ab answered and said, Far
be it, far be it from me, that I should
swallow up or destroy.
21 The matter *is* not so: but a man of
mount Ē'phră-ĭm, Shē'bȧ the son of
Bĭch'rī [11]by name, hath lifted up his
hand against the king, *even* against
Dā'vid: deliver him only, and I will depart from the city. And the woman said
unto Jō'ab, Behold, his head shall be
thrown to thee over the wall.
22 Then the woman went unto all
the people [p]in her wisdom. And they
cut off the head of Shē'bȧ the son of
Bĭch'rī, and cast *it* out to Jō'ab. And he
blew a trumpet, and they [12]retired from
the city, every man to his tent. And
Jō'ab returned to Je-ru'sa-lĕm unto the
king.
23 ¶ Now [q]Jō'ab *was* over all the
host of Ĭs'ra-el: and Be-nā'iah the son
of Je-hoi'a-dȧ *was* over the Chĕr'eth-
ītes and over the Pē'leth-ītes:
24 And A-dō'răm *was* [r]over the tribute: and [s]Je-hŏsh'a-phăt the son of A-
hī'lud *was* [13]recorder:
25 And Shē'vȧ *was* scribe: and [t]Zā'-
dŏk and A-bī'a-thär *were* the priests:
26 [u]And Ī'rȧ also the Jā'ĭr-īte was
[14]a chief ruler about Dā'vid.
21 Then there was a famine in the
days of Dā'vid three years, year
after year; and Dā'vid [1]inquired of the
LORD. And the LORD answered, [a]*It is*
for Saul, and for *his* bloody house, because he slew the Gĭb'e-on-ītes.
2 And the king called the Gĭb'e-on-
ītes, and said unto them; (now the Gĭb'-
e-on-ītes *were* not of the children of
Ĭs'ra-el, but [b]of the remnant of the
Ăm'ôr-ītes; and the children of Ĭs'ra-el
had sworn unto them: and Saul sought
to slay them in his zeal to the children
of Ĭs'ra-el and Jū'dah.)
3 Wherefore Dā'vid said unto the
Gĭb'e-on-ītes, What shall I do for you?

CHAPTER 20
1 [a]ch. 12.10
[b]Deut. 13.13;
2 Chr. 13.7
[c]ch. 19.43
[d]1 Ki. 12.16;
2 Chr. 10.16
2 [e]Prov.
17.14
3 [f]ch. 15.16
[1]an house of
ward
[2]bound
[3]in widow-
hood of life
4 [4]Call
6 [g]1 Sam.
26.6;
ch. 2.18
[h]ch. 11.11;
1 Ki. 1.33
[5]deliver him-
self from our
eyes
7 [i]ch. 8.18;
1 Ki. 1.38
9 [j]Matt.
26.49;
Luke 22.47
10 [k]Gen. 4.8;
ch. 2.23
[l]ch. 2.23
[6]doubled not
his stroke
14 [m]1 Ki.
15.20;
2 Chr. 16.4
15 [n]2 Ki.
19.32;
Luke 19.43
[7]Or, it stood
against the
outmost wall
[8]marred to
throw down
18 [9]Or, They
plainly spake
in the begin-
ning, saying,
Surely they
will ask of
Abel, and so
make an end
19 [10]That is, a
chief city
[o]1 Sam.
26.19
21 [11]by his
name
22 [p]Eccl. 7.19
[12]were scat-
tered
23 [q]ch. 8.16
24 [r]1 Ki. 4.6
[s]1 Ki. 4.3
[13]Or, remem-
brancer
25 [t]ch. 8.17
26 [u]ch. 23.38
[14]Or, a prince

CHAPTER 21
1 [1]sought the
face, etc
[a]Lev. 18.25;
Isa. 26.21
2 [b]Josh. 9.3

and wherewith shall I make the atonement, that ye may bless [c]the inheritance of the LORD?
4 And the Gĭb'e-on-ītes said unto
him, [2]We will have no silver nor gold
of Saul, nor of his house; neither for us
shalt thou kill any man in Ĭs'ra-el. And
he said, What ye shall say, *that* will I
do for you.
5 And they answered the king, The
man that consumed us, and that [3]de-
vised against us *that* we should be destroyed from remaining in any of the
coasts of Ĭs'ra-el,
6 Let seven men of his sons be delivered unto us, and we will hang them up
unto the LORD [d]in Gĭb'e-ah of Saul,
[4]*whom* the LORD did choose. And the
king said, I will give *them*.
7 But the king spared Me-phĭb'o-
sheth, the son of Jŏn'a-than the son
of Saul, because of [e]the LORD'S oath
that *was* between them, between Dā'-
vid and Jŏn'a-than the son of Saul.
8 But the king took the two sons of
[f]Rĭz'pah the daughter of A-ī'ah, whom
she bare unto Saul, Ăr-mō'nī and Me-
phĭb'o-sheth; and the five sons of [5]Mī'-
chal the daughter of Saul, whom she
[6]brought up for Ā'drĭ-el the son of Bär-
zĭl'la-ī the Me-hŏl'ath-īte:
9 And he delivered them into the
hands of the Gĭb'e-on-ītes, and they
hanged them in the hill [g]before the
LORD: and they fell *all* seven together,
and were put to death in the days of
harvest, in the first *days*, in the beginning of barley harvest.
10 ¶ And [h]Rĭz'pah the daughter of
A-ī'ah took sackcloth, and spread it for
her upon the rock, [i]from the beginning
of harvest until water dropped upon
them out of heaven, and suffered neither the birds of the air to rest on them
by day, nor the beasts of the field by
night.
11 And it was told Dā'vid what Rĭz'-
pah the daughter of A-ī'ah, the concubine of Saul, had done.
12 ¶ And Dā'vid went and took the
bones of Saul and the bones of Jŏn'a-
than his son from the men of [j]Jā'besh–
gĭl'e-ăd, which had stolen them from
the street of Bĕth'–shăn, where the
Phĭ-lĭs'tĭnes had hanged them, when
the Phĭ-lĭs'tĭnes had slain Saul in Gĭl-
bō'a:
13 And he brought up from thence
the bones of Saul and the bones of
Jŏn'a-than his son; and they gathered
the bones of them that were hanged.
14 And the bones of Saul and Jŏn'a-
than his son buried they in the country
of Bĕn'ja-min in [k]Zē'lah, in the sepulchre of Kĭsh his father: and they performed all that the king commanded.
And after that [l]God was intreated for
the land.
15 ¶ Moreover the Phĭ-lĭs'tĭnes had
yet war again with Ĭs'ra-el; and Dā'vid
went down, and his servants with him,
and fought against the Phĭ-lĭs'tĭnes:
and Dā'vid waxed faint.
16 And Ĭsh'bi–bē'nŏb, which *was* of
the sons of [7]the giant, the weight of
whose [8]spear *weighed* [9]three hundred
shekels of brass in weight, he being
girded with a new *sword*, thought to
have slain Dā'vid.
17 But A-bĭsh'ă-ī the son of Zĕr-u-
ī'ah succoured him, and smote the Phĭ-
lĭs'tĭne, and killed him. Then the men
of Dā'vid sware unto him, saying, Thou
shalt go no more out with us to battle,
that thou quench not the [10]light of Ĭs'ra-
el.
18 And it came to pass after this,
that there was again a battle with the
Phĭ-lĭs'tĭnes at Gŏb: then [m]Sĭb'be-chāi
the Hū'shath-īte slew [11]Săph, which
was of the sons of [12]the giant.
19 And there was again a battle in
Gŏb with the Phĭ-lĭs'tĭnes, where Ĕl-
hā'nan the son of [13]Ja-är'ĕ–ŏr'e-gĭm, a
Bĕth'–lĕ-hĕm-īte, slew *the brother of*
Go-lī'ath the Gĭt'tīte, the staff of whose
spear *was* like a weaver's beam.
20 And [n]there was yet a battle in
Găth, where was a man of *great* stature, that had on every hand six fingers,
and on every foot six toes, four and
twenty in number; and he also was
born to [14]the giant.
21 And when he [15]defied Ĭs'ra-el,
Jŏn'a-than the son of Shĭm'e-ah the
brother of Dā'vid slew him.
22 These four were born to the giant
in Găth, and fell by the hand of Dā'vid,
and by the hand of his servants.

22 And Dā'vid [a]spake unto the LORD
the words of this song in the day
that the LORD had delivered him out of
the hand of all his enemies, and out of
the hand of Saul:
2 And he said, [b]The LORD *is* my
rock, and my fortress, and my deliverer;
3 The God of my rock; [c]in him will I
trust: *he is* my [d]shield, and the [e]horn
of my salvation, my high [f]tower, and
my [g]refuge, my saviour; thou savest
me from violence.
4 I will call on the LORD, *who is* worthy to be praised: so shall I be saved
from mine enemies.
5 When the [1]waves of death compassed me, the floods of [2]ungodly men
made me afraid;
6 The [3]sorrows of hell compassed me
about; the snares of death prevented
me;
7 In my distress [h]I called upon the
LORD, and cried to my God: and he did
[i]hear my voice out of his temple, and
my cry *did enter* into his ears.
8 Then [j]the earth shook and trembled; the foundations of heaven moved
and shook, because he was wroth.
9 There went up a smoke [4]out of his
nostrils, and [k]fire out of his mouth devoured: coals were kindled by it.
10 He [l]bowed the heavens also, and
came down; and darkness *was* under
his feet.
11 And he rode upon a cherub, and
did fly: and he was seen upon [m]the
wings of the wind.
12 And he made darkness pavilions
round about him, [5]dark waters, *and*
thick clouds of the skies.

3 [c]ch. 20.19
4 [2]Or, It is not silver nor gold that we have to do with Saul or his house, neither pertains it to us to kill, etc
5 [3]Or, cut us off
6 [d]Judg. 20.4
[4]Or, chosen of the LORD
7 [e]1 Sam. 18.3; 1 Sam. 23.18
8 [f]ch. 3.7
[5]Or, Michal's sister
[6]bare to Adriel
9 [g]ch. 6.17
10 [h]ch. 3.7
[i]Deut. 21.23
12 [j]1 Sam. 31.11-12-13
14 [k]Josh. 18.28
[l]Josh. 7.26
16 [7]Or, Rapha
[8]the staff, or, the head
[9]Nine pounds and a half
17 [10]candle, or, lamp
18 [m]1 Chr. 11.29
[11]Or, Sippai
[12]Or, Rapha
19 [13]Or, Jair
20 [n]1 Chr. 20.6
[14]Or, Rapha
21 [15]Or, reproached

CHAPTER 22

1 [a]Ex. 15.1
2 [b]Gen. 15.1; Deut. 32.4; 1 Sam. 2.2; Matt. 18.11
3 [c]Heb. 2.13
[d]Gen. 15.1; Ps. 3.3
[e]Luke 1.69
[f]Prov. 18.10
[g]Ps. 9.9; Isa. 32.2
5 [1]Or, pangs
[2]Belial
6 [3]Or, cords
7 [h]Ps. 116.4
[i]Ex. 3.7
8 [j]Judg. 5.4; Ps. 77.18
9 [4]by
[k]Ps. 97.3; Heb. 12.29
10 [l]Isa. 64.1
11 [m]Ps. 104.3
12 [5]binding of waters

13 Through the brightness before him were coals of fire kindled.

14 The LORD [n]thundered from heaven, and the most High uttered his voice.

15 And he sent out [o]arrows, and scattered them; lightning, and discomfited them.

16 And the channels of the sea appeared, the foundations of the world were discovered, at the rebuking of the LORD, at the blast of the breath of his [6]nostrils.

17 He sent from above, he took me; he drew me out of [7]many waters;

18 He delivered me from my strong enemy, *and* from them that hated me: for they were too strong for me.

19 They prevented me in the day of my calamity: but the LORD was my stay.

20 [p]He brought me forth also into a large place: he delivered me, because he [q]delighted in me.

21 The LORD rewarded me according to my righteousness: according to the cleanness of my hands hath he recompensed me.

22 For I have kept the ways of the LORD, and have not wickedly departed from my God.

23 For all his [r]judgments *were* before me: and *as for* his statutes, I did not depart from them.

24 I was also [s]upright [8]before him, and have kept myself from mine iniquity.

25 Therefore the LORD hath recompensed me according to my righteousness; according to my cleanness [9]in his eye sight.

26 With [t]the merciful thou wilt shew thyself merciful, *and* with the upright man thou wilt shew thyself upright.

27 With the pure thou wilt shew thyself pure; and [u]with the froward thou wilt [10]shew thyself unsavoury.

28 And the [v]afflicted people thou wilt save: but thine eyes *are* upon the haughty, *that* thou mayest bring *them* down.

29 For thou *art* my [11]lamp, O LORD: and the LORD will lighten my darkness.

30 For by thee I have [12]run through a troop: by my God have I leaped over a wall.

31 *As for* God, [w]his way *is* perfect; [x]the word of the LORD *is* [13]tried: he *is* a buckler to all them that trust in him.

32 For [y]who *is* God, save the LORD? and who *is* a rock, save our God?

33 God *is* my [z]strength *and* power: and he [14]maketh my way [a]perfect.

34 He [15]maketh my feet like hinds' *feet:* and setteth me upon my high places.

35 He teacheth my hands [16]to war; so that a bow of steel is broken by mine arms.

36 Thou hast also given me the shield of thy salvation: and thy gentleness hath [17]made me great.

37 Thou hast enlarged my steps under me; so that my [18]feet did not slip.

14 [n]Isa. 30.30
15 [o]Deut. 32.23; Ps. 7.13; Ps. 77.17; Ps. 144.6; Hab. 3.11
16 [6]Or, anger
17 [7]Or, great
20 [p]Ps. 31.8
[q]ch. 15.26
23 [r]Deut. 7.12
24 [s]Gen. 6.9; Job 1.1
[8]to him
25 [9]before his eyes
26 [t]Matt. 5.7
27 [u]Lev. 26.23
[10]Or, wrestle
28 [v]Ps. 12.5; Matt. 5.3
29 [11]Or, candle
30 [12]Or, broken a troop
31 [w]Dan. 4.37; Rev. 15.3
[x]Ps. 12.6; Prov. 30.5
[13]Or, refined
32 [y]Deut. 32.31; 1 Sam. 2.2; Isa. 45.5-6
33 [z]Ps. 27.1
[14]riddeth, or, looseth
[a]Deut. 18.13
34 [15]equalleth
35 [16]for the war
36 [17]multiplied me
37 [18]ankles
40 [19]caused to bow
42 [b]1 Sam. 28.6
[c]Prov. 1.28
44 [d]Deut. 28.13
[e]Isa. 55.5
45 [20]Sons of the stranger
[21]lie, or, yield feigned obedience
46 [f]Mic. 7.17
47 [g]Ps. 89.26
48 [22]giveth avengement for me
[h]Ps. 144.2
50 [i]Rom. 15.9

CHAPTER 23
2 [a]2 Pet. 1.21
3 [1]Or, Be thou ruler, etc
[b]Ex. 18.21
4 [c]Prov. 4.18
5 [d]1 Ki. 9.4-6

38 I have pursued mine enemies, and destroyed them; and turned not again until I had consumed them.

39 And I have consumed them, and wounded them, that they could not arise: yea, they are fallen under my feet.

40 For thou hast girded me with strength to battle: them that rose up against me hast thou [19]subdued under me.

41 Thou hast also given me the necks of mine enemies, that I might destroy them that hate me.

42 [b]They looked, but *there was* none to save; *even* [c]unto the LORD, but he answered them not.

43 Then did I beat them as small as the dust of the earth, I did stamp them as the mire of the street, *and* did spread them abroad.

44 Thou also hast delivered me from the strivings of my people, thou hast kept me *to be* [d]head of the heathen: [e]a people *which* I knew not shall serve me.

45 [20]Strangers shall [21]submit themselves unto me: as soon as they hear, they shall be obedient unto me.

46 Strangers shall fade away, and they shall be afraid [f]out of their close places.

47 The LORD liveth; and blessed *be* my rock; and exalted be the God of the [g]rock of my salvation.

48 It *is* God that [22]avengeth me, and that [h]bringeth down the people under me,

49 And that bringeth me forth from mine enemies: thou also hast lifted me up on high above them that rose up against me: thou hast delivered me from the violent man.

50 Therefore I will give thanks unto thee, O LORD, among [i]the heathen, and I will sing praises unto thy name.

51 *He is* the tower of salvation for his king: and sheweth mercy to his anointed, unto Dā'vid, and to his seed for evermore.

23 Now these *be* the last words of Dā'vid. Dā'vid the son of Jĕs'se said, and the man *who was* raised up on high, the anointed of the God of Jā'cob, and the sweet psalmist of Is'ra-el, said,

2 [a]The Spirit of the LORD spake by me, and his word *was* in my tongue.

3 The God of Is'ra-el said, the Rock of Is'ra-el spake to me, [1]He that ruleth over men *must be* just, ruling [b]in the fear of God.

4 And [c]*he shall be* as the light of the morning, *when* the sun riseth, *even* a morning without clouds; *as* the tender grass *springing* out of the earth by clear shining after rain.

5 [d]Although my house *be* not so with God; yet he hath made with me an everlasting covenant, ordered in all *things*, and sure: for *this is* all my salvation, and all *my* desire, although he make *it* not to grow.

6 ¶ But *the sons* of Bē'lĭ-al *shall be* all of them as thorns thrust away, because they cannot be taken with hands:

7 But the man *that* shall touch them must be [2]fenced with iron and the staff of a spear; and they shall be utterly burned with fire in the *same* place.

8 ¶ These *be* the names of the mighty men whom Dā'vid had: [3]The Tăch'mo-nīte that sat in the seat, chief among the captains; the same *was* Ăd'ĭ-nō the Ĕz'nīte: *he lift up his spear* against eight hundred, [4]whom he slew at one time.

9 And after him *was* [e]Ē-le-ā'zar the son of Dō'do the A-hō'hīte, *one* of the three mighty men with Dā'vid, when they defied the Phĭ-lĭs'tĭnes *that* were there gathered together to battle, and the men of Ĭs'ra-el were gone away:

10 He arose, and smote the Phĭ-lĭs'tĭnes until his hand was weary, and his hand clave unto the sword: and the LORD wrought a great victory that day; and the people returned after him only to spoil.

11 And after him *was* Shăm'mah the son of Ā'gē-ē the Hā'ra-rīte. [f]And the Phĭ-lĭs'tĭnes were gathered together [5]into a troop, where was a piece of ground full of lentiles: and the people fled from the Phĭ-lĭs'tĭnes.

12 But he stood in the midst of the ground, and defended it, and slew the Phĭ-lĭs'tĭnes: and the LORD wrought a great victory.[g]

13 And [6]three of the thirty chief went down, and came to Dā'vid in the harvest time unto the cave of A-dŭl'lăm: and the troop of the Phĭ-lĭs'tĭnes pitched in [h]the valley of Rĕph'a-ĭm.

14 And Dā'vid *was* then in [i]an hold, and the garrison of the Phĭ-lĭs'tĭnes *was* then *in* Bĕth'–lĕ-hĕm.

15 And Dā'vid longed, and said, Oh that one would give me drink of the water of the well of Bĕth'–lĕ-hĕm, which *is* by the gate!

16 And the three mighty men brake through the host of the Phĭ-lĭs'tĭnes, and drew water out of the well of Bĕth'–lĕ-hĕm, that *was* by the gate, and took *it*, and brought *it* to Dā'vid: nevertheless he would not drink thereof, but poured it out unto the LORD.

17 And he said, Be it far from me, O LORD, that I should do this: *is not this* [j]the blood of the men that went in jeopardy of their lives? therefore he would not drink it. These things did these three mighty men.

18 And [k]A-bĭsh'ă-ī, the brother of Jō'ab, the son of Zĕr-u-ī'ah, was chief among three. And he lifted up his spear against three hundred, [7]*and* slew *them*, and had the name among three.

19 Was he not most honourable of three? therefore he was their captain: howbeit he attained not unto the *first* three.

20 And Be-nā'iah the son of Je-hoi'a-dȧ, the son of a valiant man, of [l]Kăb'ze-el, [8]who had done many acts, [m]he slew two [9]lionlike men of Mō'ab: he went down also and slew a lion in the midst of a pit in time of snow:

21 And he slew an E-ġȳp'tian, [10]a goodly man: and the E-ġȳp'tian had a spear in his hand; but he went down to him with a staff, and plucked the spear out of the E-ġȳp'tian's hand, and slew him with his own spear.

22 These *things* did Be-nā'iah the son of Je-hoi'a-dȧ, and had the name among three mighty men.

23 He was [11]more honourable than the thirty, but he attained not to the *first* three. And Dā'vid set him [n]over his [12]guard.

24 [o]Ă'sa-hĕl the brother of Jō'ab *was* one of the thirty; Ĕl-hā'nan the son of Dō'do of Bĕth'–lĕ-hĕm,

25 [p]Shăm'mah the Hā'rod-īte, Ĕl'i-kȧ the Hā'rod-īte,

26 Hē'lez the Păl'tīte, Ī'rȧ the son of Ĭk'kĕsh the Te-kō'īte,

27 Ā-bĭ-ē'zĕr the Ăn'ĕ-thŏth-īte, Me-bun'nāi the Hū'shath-īte,

28 Zăl'mŏn the A-hō'hīte, Ma-hăr'a-ī the Ne-toph'a-thīte,

29 Hē'leb the son of Bā'a-nah, a Ne-toph'a-thīte, Ĭt'ta-ī the son of Rī'bāi out of Ġĭb'e-ah of the children of Bĕn'ja-min,

30 Be-nā'iah the [q]Pĭr'a-thon-īte, Hĭd'da-ī of the [13]brooks of [r]Gā'ăsh,

31 Ā'bĭ–ăl'bŏn the Ăr'bath-īte, Ăz'ma-veth the Bär-hū'mīte,

32 E-lī'ah-bȧ the Sha-ăl'bo-nīte, of the sons of Jā'shen, Jŏn'a-than,

33 Shăm'mah the Hā'ra-rīte, A-hī'am the son of Shā'rär the Hā'ra-rīte,

34 E-lĭph'e-lĕt the son of A-hăs'ba-ī, the son of the Ma-ăch'a-thīte, E-lī'ăm the son of A-hĭth'o-phel the Ġī'lo-nīte,

35 Hĕz'ra-ī the Cär'mel-īte, Pā'a-rāi the Ăr'bīte,

36 Ī'găl the son of Nā'than of Zō'bah, Bā'nī the Găd'īte,

37 Zē'lek the Ăm'mŏn-īte, Nā'ha-rī the Be-ē'rŏth-īte, armourbearer to Jō'ab the son of Zĕr-u-ī'ah,

38 [s]Ī'rȧ an [t]Ĭth'rīte, Gā'rĕb an Ĭth'rīte,

39 [u]U-rī'ah the Hĭt'tīte: thirty and seven in all.

24 And [a]again the anger of the LORD was kindled against Ĭs'ra-el, and [1]he moved Dā'vid against them to say, [b]Go, number Ĭs'ra-el and Jū'dah.

2 For the king said to Jō'ab the captain of the host, which *was* with him, [2]Go now through all the tribes of Ĭs'ra-el, from Dăn even to Bē'er–shē'bȧ, and number ye the people, that [c]I may know the number of the people.

3 And Jō'ab said unto the king, Now the LORD thy God add unto the people, how many soever they be, an hundredfold, and that the eyes of my lord the king may see *it*: but why doth my lord the king delight in this thing?

4 Notwithstanding [d]the king's word prevailed against Jō'ab, and against the captains of the host. And Jō'ab and the captains of the host went out from the presence of the king, to number the people of Ĭs'ra-el.

7 [2]filled
8 [3]Or, Josheb-bassebet, the Tachmonite, head of the three [4]slain
9 [e]1 Chr. 11.12
11 [f]1 Chr. 11.12 [5]Or, for foraging [g]Deut. 33.29; 1 Sam. 22.1; 1 Chr. 29.11; 2 Chr. 14.11-14; Ps. 3.8; Ps. 46.1; Ps. 98.1; Prov. 21.30-31; Rom. 8.31
13 [6]Or, the three captains over the thirty [h]Or, giants
14 [i]1 Sam. 22.4; 1 Chr. 12.16
17 [j]Lev. 17.10
18 [k]ch. 2.18 [7]slain
20 [l]Josh. 15.21 [8]great of acts [m]Ex. 15.15 [9]lions of God
21 [10]a man of countenance, or, sight; 1 Chr. 11.23-a man of great stature
23 [11]Or, honourable among the thirty [n]ch. 8.18 [12]at his command, or, council
24 [o]ch. 2.18
25 [p]1 Chr. 11.27
30 [q]Judg. 12.15 [13]Or, valleys [r]Judg. 2.9
38 [s]ch. 20.26 [t]1 Chr. 2.53
39 [u]ch. 11.3-6

CHAPTER 24
1 [a]ch. 16.10; 1 Ki. 22.22 [1]Satan [b]1 Chr. 27.23
2 [2]Or, Compass [c]Gen. 26.4; Deut. 8.13-14; 2 Chr. 32.25-26; Prov. 18.12
4 [d]1 Chr. 21.4; Eccl. 8.4; Acts 5.29

5 ¶ And they passed over Jôr'dan,
and pitched in [e]Ăr'ŏ-ēr, on the right
side of the city that *lieth* in the midst of
the [3]river of Găd, and toward [f]Jā'zēr:
6 Then they came to Gĭl'e-ăd, and to
the [4]land of Täh'tim–hŏd'shī; and they
came to [g]Dăn–jā'an, and about to [h]Zī'-
dŏn,
7 And came to the strong hold of
Tȳre, and to all the cities of the Hī'-
vītes, and of the Cā'năan-ītes: and they
went out to the south of Jū'dah, *even* to
Bē'er–shē'bȧ.
8 So when they had gone through
all the land, they came to Je-ru̧'sa-lĕm
at the end of nine months and twenty
days.
9 And Jō'ab gave up the sum of the
number of the people unto the king:
[i]and there were in Ĭs'ra-el eight hundred thousand valiant men that drew
the sword; and the men of Jū'dah *were*
five hundred thousand men.
10 ¶ And [j]Dā'vid's heart smote him
after that he had numbered the people.
And Dā'vid said unto the LORD, [k]I have
sinned greatly in that I have done:
and now, I beseech thee, O LORD, take
away the iniquity of thy servant; for I
have [l]done very foolishly.
11 For when Dā'vid was up in the
morning, the word of the LORD came
unto the prophet [m]Găd, Dā'vid's [n]seer,
saying,
12 Go and say unto Dā'vid, Thus
saith the LORD, I offer thee three *things;*
choose thee one of them, that I may *do*
it unto thee.
13 So Găd came to Dā'vid, and told
him, and said unto him, Shall [o]seven
years of famine come unto thee in thy
land? or wilt thou flee three months
before thine enemies, while they pursue thee? or that there be three days'
pestilence in thy land? now advise, and
see what answer I shall return to him
that sent me.
14 And Dā'vid said unto Găd, I am
in a great strait: let us fall now into the
hand of the LORD; [p]for his mercies *are*
[5]great: and [q]let me not fall into the
hand of man.
15 ¶ So [r]the LORD sent a pestilence
upon Ĭs'ra-el from the morning even to
the time appointed: and there died of
the people from Dăn even to Bē'er–
shē'bȧ seventy thousand men.

5 [e]Deut. 2.36
[3]Or, valley
[f]Num. 32.1-3
6 [4]Or, nether land newly inhabited
[g]Josh. 19.47
[h]Judg. 18.28
9 [i]1 Chr. 21.5
10 [j]1 Sam. 24.5; Prov. 18.4; 1 John. 3.20
[k]ch. 12.13; 1 Chr. 21.8
[l]1 Sam. 13.13
11 [m]1 Sam. 22.5
[n]1 Sam. 9.9
13 [o]1 Chr. 21.12; That is, three years and the present added to those mentioned, ch. 21.1
14 [p]Ps. 103.8; Ps. 119.156
[5]Or, many
[q]Isa. 47.6; Zech. 1.15
15 [r]1 Chr. 21.14; 1 Chr. 27.24
16 [s]Ex. 12.23; 1 Chr. 21.15; Ps. 104.4
[t]Gen. 6.6; 1 Sam. 15.11; Ps. 78.38; Joel 2.13; Jon. 3.10
[u]1 Chr. 21.15-Ornan
17 [v]1 Chr. 21.17
18 [w]1 Chr. 21.18
[6]Araniah
21 [x]Gen. 23.8
[y]Num. 16.48
22 [z]1 Ki. 19.21
23 [a]Ps. 20.3; Ezek. 20.40; 1 Pet. 2.5
24 [b]1 Chr. 21.24
25 [7]Which became the site of the Temple
[c]2 Chr. 33.13; Isa. 19.22

16 And when the [s]angel stretched
out his hand upon Je-ru̧'sa-lĕm to destroy it, [t]the LORD repented him of the
evil, and said to the angel that destroyed the people, It is enough: stay
now thine hand. And the angel of the
LORD was by the threshingplace of [u]A-
ra̧u'nah the Jĕb'u-site.
17 And Dā'vid spake unto the LORD
when he saw the angel that smote the
people, and said, Lo, [v]I have sinned,
and I have done wickedly: but these
sheep, what have they done? let thine
hand, I pray thee, be against me, and
against my father's house.
18 ¶ And Găd came that day to Dā'-
vid, and said unto him, [w]Go up, rear an
altar unto the LORD in the threshingfloor of [6]A-ra̧u'nah the Jĕb'u-site.
19 And Dā'vid, according to the saying of Găd, went up as the LORD commanded.
20 And A-ra̧u'nah looked, and saw
the king and his servants coming on
toward him: and A-ra̧u'nah went out,
and bowed himself before the king on
his face upon the ground.
21 And A-ra̧u'nah said, Wherefore
is my lord the king come to his servant? [x]And Dā'vid said, To buy the
threshingfloor of thee, to build an altar
unto the LORD, that [y]the plague may
be stayed from the people.
22 And A-ra̧u'nah said unto Dā'vid,
Let my lord the king take and offer up
what *seemeth* good unto him: [z]behold,
here be oxen for burnt sacrifice, and
threshing instruments and *other* instruments of the oxen for wood.
23 All these *things* did A-ra̧u'nah,
as a king, give unto the king. And A-
ra̧u'nah said unto the king, The LORD
thy God [a]accept thee.
24 And the king said unto A-ra̧u'-
nah, Nay; but I will surely buy *it* of
thee at a price: neither will I offer
burnt offerings unto the LORD my God
of that which doth cost me nothing. So
[b]Dā'vid bought the threshingfloor and
the oxen for fifty shekels of silver.
25 And Dā'vid built there [7]an altar
unto the LORD, and offered burnt offerings and peace offerings. So the LORD
was [c]intreated for the land, and the
plague was stayed from Ĭs'ra-el.

THE FIRST BOOK OF THE

KINGS

Life's Questions

Are God's promises totally independent of His people's response to Him?
How does God relate to international politics?
How do you explain the absolute defeat of God's people?

God's Answers

The two Books of Kings trace Israel's history and that of leading messengers of God to show how God's promise to David worked out as the nation and its leaders departed from God and His covenant. From Solomon's coronation about 965 B.C. through the division into Judah and Israel about 925, the destruction of the northern kingdom Israel by Assyria in 722, to the final destruction of Jerusalem and the temple in 586, Kings shows Israel's history as history controlled by God responding to His people as they obeyed and disobeyed Him. In eight parts Kings shows why the triumphs of David turned to the tragedies of Jeroboam II, Hoshea, Manasseh, and Zedekiah: God works His purposes through human revenge and treachery (1 Kings 1—2); God works through the wisdom He gives His humble leader Solomon (3—7); God responds to the worship and sin of His people (8—11); God punishes a disobedient people (12—16) ; God works through His chosen prophetic messengers Elijah and Micaiah (17—22); God guides history through His prophet Elisha (2 Kings 1—9); God shows the limits of His mercy as Israel falls (10—17), and God honors righteous rulers like Hezekiah and Josiah but punishes a sinful people as Judah falls (18—25).

First and 2 Kings paint history as God's story revealed through His prophets and determined by the covenant relationship with His people. Over it all stands the promise to David even after failure.

1 Now king Dā'vid was old *and*
[1]stricken in years; and they covered
him with clothes, but he gat no heat.
2 Wherefore his servants said unto
him, [2]Let there be sought for my lord
the king [3]a young virgin: and [a]let her
stand before the king, and let her [4]cherish him, and let her lie in thy bosom,
that my lord the king may get heat.
3 So they sought for a fair damsel
throughout all the coasts of Ĭs'ra-el,
and found Ăb'ĭ-shag a [b]Shụ'nam-mīte,
and brought her to the king.
4 And the damsel *was* very fair, and
cherished the king, and ministered to
him: but the king [c]knew her not.
5 ¶ Then [d]Ăd-ŏ-nī'jah the son of
Hăg'gith exalted himself, saying, I will
[5]be king: and [e]he prepared him chariots and horsemen, and fifty men to run
before him.
6 And his father had [f]not displeased
him [6]at any time in saying, Why hast
thou done so? and he also *was a* very
goodly *man;* [g]and *his mother* bare him
after Ăb'sa-lŏm.
7 And [7]he conferred with Jō'ab the
son of Zĕr-ụ-ī'ah, and with [h]A-bī'a-thär the priest: and [i]they [8]following
Ăd-ŏ-nī'jah helped *him.*
8 But Zā'dŏk the priest, and Be-nā'-iah the son of Je-hoi'a-dȧ, and Nā'than
the prophet, and [j]Shĭm'e-ī, and Rē'ī,
and [k]the mighty men which *belonged*
to Dā'vid, were not with Ăd-ŏ-nī'jah.
9 And Ăd-ŏ-nī'jah slew sheep and
oxen and fat cattle by the stone of
Zō'he-lĕth, which *is* by [9]Ĕn–rō'gel, and
called all his brethren the king's sons,
and all the men of Jū'dah the king's
servants:

10 But Nā'than the prophet, and Be-nā'iah, and the mighty men, and Sŏl'o-mon his brother, he called not.
11 ¶ Wherefore Nā'than spake unto
Băth'–shĕ-bȧ the mother of Sŏl'o-mon,
saying, Hast thou not heard that Ăd-ŏ-nī'jah the son of [l]Hăg'gith doth reign,
and Dā'vid our lord knoweth *it* not?
12 Now therefore come, let me, I
pray thee, give [m]thee counsel, that
thou mayest save thine own life, and
the life of thy son Sŏl'o-mon.
13 Go and get thee in unto king Dā'-vid, and say unto him, Didst not thou,
my lord, O king, swear unto thine
handmaid, saying, [n]Assuredly Sŏl'o-mon thy son shall reign after me, and
he shall sit upon my throne? why then
doth Ăd-ŏ-nī'jah reign?
14 Behold, while thou yet talkest
there with the king, I also will come in
after thee, and [10]confirm thy words.
15 ¶ And Băth'–shĕ-bȧ went in unto
the king into the chamber: and the king
was very old; and Ăb'ĭ-shag the Shụ'-nam-mīte ministered unto the king.
16 And Băth'–shĕ-bȧ bowed, and
did obeisance unto the king. And the
king said, [11]What wouldest thou?
17 And she said unto him, My lord,
[o]thou swarest by the LORD thy God
unto thine handmaid, *saying,* Assuredly Sŏl'o-mon thy son shall reign after
me, and he shall sit upon my throne.
18 And now, behold, Ăd-ŏ-nī'jah
reigneth; and now, my lord the king,
thou knowest *it* not:
19 And he hath slain oxen and fat
cattle and sheep in abundance, and
hath called all the sons of the king, and
A-bī'a-thär the priest, and Jō'ab the

CHAPTER 1
1 [1]entered into days
2 [2]Let them seek
[3]a damsel, a virgin
[a]1 Sam. 16.21
[4]be a cherisher unto him
3 [b]Josh. 19.18
4 [c]Gen. 4.1;
5 [d]2 Sam. 3.4;
[5]reign
[e]Deut. 17.16;
6 [f]1 Sam. 3.13;
[6]from his days
[g]2 Sam. 3.3
7 [7]his words were with Joab
[h]2 Sam. 20.25
[i]ch. 2.22
[8]helped after Adonijah
8 [j]ch. 4.18
[k]2 Sam. 23.8
9 [9]Or, the fuller's well
11 [l]2 Sam. 3.4
12 [m]Prov. 11.14
13 [n]1 Chr. 22.9
14 [10]fill up
16 [11]What to thee?
17 [o] Gen. 18.12;

captain of the host: but Sŏl′o-mon thy
servant hath he not called.
20 And thou, my lord, O king, the
eyes of all Ĭs′ra-el *are* upon thee, that
thou shouldest tell them who shall sit
on the throne of my lord the king after
him.
21 Otherwise it shall come to pass,
when my lord the king shall [12]sleep
with his fathers, that I and my son
Sŏl′o-mon shall be counted [13]offend-
ers.
22 ¶ And, lo, while she yet talked
with the king, Nā′than the prophet also
came in.
23 And they told the king, saying,
Behold Nā′than the prophet. And when
he was come in before the king, he
bowed himself before the king with his
face to the ground.
24 And Nā′than said, My lord, O
king, hast thou said, Ăd-ŏ-nī′jah shall
reign after me, and he shall sit upon
my throne?
25 For he is gone down this day, and
hath slain oxen and fat cattle and sheep
in abundance, and hath called all the
king's sons, and the captains of the
host, and A-bī′a-thär the priest; and,
behold, they eat and drink before him,
and say, [14]God save king Ăd-ŏ-nī′jah.
26 But me, *even* me thy servant, and
Zā′dŏk the priest, and Be-nā′iah the
son of Je-hoi′a-dȧ, and thy servant
Sŏl′o-mon, hath he not called.
27 Is this thing done by my lord the
king, and thou hast not shewed *it* unto
thy servant, who should sit on the
throne of my lord the king after him?
28 ¶ Then king Dā′vid answered and
said, Call me Băth′–shĕ-bȧ. And she
came [15]into the king's presence, and
stood before the king.
29 And the king sware, and said,
[p]*As* the LORD liveth, that [q]hath redeemed my soul out of all distress,
30 Even as I sware unto thee by the
LORD God of Ĭs′ra-el, saying, Assuredly Sŏl′o-mon thy son shall reign after me, and he shall sit upon my throne
in my stead; even so will I certainly do
this day.
31 Then Băth′–shĕ-bȧ bowed with
her face to the earth, and did reverence
to the king, and said, [r]Let my lord king
Dā′vid live for ever.
32 ¶ And king Dā′vid said, Call me
Zā′dŏk the priest, and Nā′than the
prophet, and Be-nā′iah the son of Je-
hoi′a-dȧ. And they came before the
king.
33 The king also said unto them,
[s]Take with you the servants of your
lord, and cause Sŏl′o-mon my son to
ride upon [16]mine own mule, and bring
him down to [t]Gī′hon:
34 And let Zā′dŏk the priest and Nā′-
than the prophet [u]anoint him there
king over Ĭs′ra-el: and [v]blow ye with
the trumpet, and say, God save king
Sŏl′o-mon.
35 Then ye shall come up after him,
that he may come and sit upon my
throne; for he shall be king in my stead:
and I have appointed him to be ruler
over Ĭs′ra-el and over Jū′dah.
36 And Be-nā′iah the son of Je-
hoi′a-dȧ answered the king, and said,
[w]Amen: the LORD God of my lord the
king say so *too*.
37 [x]As the LORD hath been with my
lord the king, even so be he with Sŏl′o-
mon, and make his throne greater than
the throne of my lord king Dā′vid.
38 So Zā′dŏk the priest, and Nā′-
than the prophet, [y]and Be-nā′iah the
son of Je-hoi′a-dȧ, and the Chĕr′eth-
ītes, and the Pē′leth-ītes, went down,
and caused Sŏl′o-mon to ride upon
king Dā′vid's mule, and brought him
to Gī′hon.
39 And Zā′dŏk the priest took an
horn of oil [z]out of the tabernacle, and
[a]anointed Sŏl′o-mon. And they blew
the trumpet; [b]and all the people said,
God save king Sŏl′o-mon.
40 And all the people came up after
him, and the people piped with [17]pipes,
and rejoiced with great joy, so that the
earth rent with the sound of them.
41 ¶ And Ăd-ŏ-nī′jah and all the
guests that *were* with him heard *it* as
they had made an end of eating. And
when Jō′ab heard the sound of the
trumpet, he said, Wherefore *is this*
noise of the city being in an uproar?
42 And while he yet spake, behold,
Jŏn′a-than the son of A-bī′a-thär the
priest came: and Ăd-ŏ-nī′jah said unto
him, Come in; for [c]thou *art* a valiant
man, and bringest good tidings.
43 And Jŏn′a-than answered and
said to Ăd-ŏ-nī′jah, Verily our lord king
Dā′vid hath made Sŏl′o-mon king.
44 And the king hath sent with him
Zā′dŏk the priest, and Nā′than the
prophet, and Be-nā′iah the son of Je-
hoi′a-dȧ, and the Chĕr′eth-ītes, and the
Pē′leth-ītes, and they have caused him
to ride upon the king's mule:
45 And Zā′dŏk the priest and Nā′-
than the prophet have anointed him
king in Gī′hon: and they are come up
from thence rejoicing, so that the city
rang again. This *is* the noise that ye
have heard.
46 And also Sŏl′o-mon [d]sitteth on
the throne of the kingdom.
47 And moreover the king's servants
came to bless our lord king Dā′vid, saying, God make the name of Sŏl′o-mon
better than thy name, and make his
throne greater than thy throne. [e]And
the king bowed himself upon the bed.
48 And also thus said the king,
Blessed *be* the LORD God of Ĭs′ra-el,
which hath [f]given *one* to sit on my
throne this day, mine eyes even seeing
it.
49 And all the guests that *were* with
Ăd-ŏ-nī′jah were afraid, and rose up,
and went every man his way.
50 ¶ And Ăd-ŏ-nī′jah feared because
of Sŏl′o-mon, and arose, and went, and
[g]caught hold on the horns of the altar.
51 And it was told Sŏl′o-mon, saying, Behold, Ăd-ŏ-nī′jah feareth king
Sŏl′o-mon: for, lo, he hath caught hold
on the horns of the altar, saying, Let

21 [12]lie down [13]sinners
25 [14]Let king Adonijah live
28 [15]before the king
29 [p]Judg. 8.19; 1 Sam. 14.39; 1 Sam. 25.34; 2 Sam. 4.9; ch. 17.1; 2 Ki. 4.30
[q]Gen. 48.16; 2 Sam. 4.9; Ps. 19.14; Ps. 31.5-7; Ps. 34.19-22; Ps. 71.23; Ps. 103.1-4; Lam. 3.58
31 [r]Neh. 2.3; Dan. 2.4
33 [s]2 Sam. 20.6; Esth. 6.8
[16]which belongeth to me
[t]2 Chr. 32.30
34 [u]1 Sam. 10.1; 1 Sam. 16.3-12; 2 Sam. 2.4; 2 Sam. 5.3; ch. 19.16; 2 Ki. 9.3
[v]2 Sam. 15.10; 2 Ki. 9.13; Mark. 11.9-10
36 [w]Deut. 27.15-26; Jer. 11.5; Matt. 6.13
37 [x]Deut. 2.7; Josh. 1.5-17; 1 Sam. 20.13; ch. 8.57; 2 Ki. 2.9; 1 Chr. 28.20
38 [y]2 Sam. 8.18
39 [z]Ex. 30.23-25-32; Ps. 89.20
[a]1 Sam. 10.1; 1 Chr. 29.22; Ps. 89.20
[b]1 Sam. 10.24
40 [17]Or, flutes
42 [c]2 Sam. 18.27
46 [d]1 Chr. 29.23
47 [e]Gen. 47.31
48 [f]ch. 3.6; Ps. 132.11-12
50 [g]Ex. 21.14

king Sŏl'o-mon swear unto me to day
that he will not slay his servant with
the sword.
52 And Sŏl'o-mon said, If he will
shew himself a worthy man, [h]there
shall not an hair of him fall to the earth:
[i]but if wickedness shall be found in
him, he shall die.
53 So king Sŏl'o-mon sent, and they
brought him down from the altar. And
he came and bowed himself to king
Sŏl'o-mon: and Sŏl'o-mon said unto
him, Go to thine house.
2 Now [a]the days of Dā'vid drew nigh
that he should die; and he charged
Sŏl'o-mon his son, saying,
2 [b]I go the way of all the earth: be
thou strong therefore, and shew thyself a man;
3 And keep the charge of the LORD
thy God, [c]to walk in his ways, to keep
his statutes, and his commandments,
and his judgments, and his testimonies,
as it is written in the law of Mō'ses, that
thou mayest [1]prosper in all that thou
doest, and whithersoever thou turnest
thyself:
4 That the LORD may [d]continue his
word which he spake concerning me,
saying, [e]If thy children take heed to
their way, to [f]walk before me in truth
with all their heart and with all their
soul, [g]there shall not [2]fail thee (said
he) a man on the throne of Is'ra-el.
5 Moreover thou knowest also what
Jō'ab the son of Zĕr-u-ī'ah [h]did to me,
and what he did to the two captains of
the hosts of Is'ra-el, unto [i]Ăb'nĕr the
son of Nĕr, and unto [j]Ăm'a-sȧ the son
of Jē'thĕr, whom he slew, and [3]shed
the blood of war in peace, and put the
blood of war upon his girdle that *was*
about his loins, and in his shoes that
were on his feet.
6 Do therefore [k]according to thy
wisdom, and let not his hoar head go
down to the grave in peace.
7 But shew kindness unto the sons
of [l]Bär-zĭl'la-ī the Gĭl'e-ăd-īte, and let
them be of those that [m]eat at thy table:
for so [n]they came to me when I fled
because of Ăb'sa-lŏm thy brother.
8 And, behold, *thou hast* with thee
[o]Shĭm'e-ī the son of Gē'rȧ, a Bĕn'ja-
mīte of Ba-hū'rim, which cursed me
with a [4]grievous curse in the day when
I went to Mā-ha-nā'im: but he came
down to meet me at Jôr'dan, and I
sware to him by the LORD, saying, I
will not put thee to death with the
sword.
9 Now therefore [p]hold him not guiltless: for thou *art* a wise man, and knowest what thou oughtest to do unto him;
but his hoar head bring thou down to
the grave with blood.
10 So [q]Dā'vid slept with his fathers,
and was buried in [r]the city of Dā'vid.
11 And the days that Dā'vid [s]reigned
over Is'ra-el *were* forty years: seven
years reigned he in Hē'bron, and thirty
and three years reigned he in Je-ru'sa-
lĕm.

12 ¶ [t]Then sat Sŏl'o-mon upon the
throne of Dā'vid his father; and his
kingdom was established greatly.
13 ¶ And Ăd-o-nī'jah the son of Hăg'-
gith came to Băth'–shĕ-bȧ the mother
of Sŏl'o-mon. And she said, [u]Comest
thou peaceably? And he said, Peaceably.
14 He said moreover, I have somewhat to say unto thee. And she said,
Say on.
15 And he said, Thou knowest that
the kingdom was mine, and *that* all
Is'ra-el set their faces on me, that I
should reign: howbeit the kingdom is
turned about, and is become my brother's: for [v]it was his from the LORD.
16 And now I ask one petition of
thee, [5]deny me not. And she said unto
him, Say on.
17 And he said, Speak, I pray thee,
unto Sŏl'o-mon the king, (for he will
not say thee nay,) that he give me
[w]Ăb'ĭ-shag the Shu'nam-mīte to wife.
18 And Băth'–shĕ-bȧ said, Well; I
will speak for thee unto the king.
19 ¶ Băth'–shĕ-bȧ therefore went
unto king Sŏl'o-mon, to speak unto
him for Ăd-ŏ-nī'jah. And the king rose
up to meet her, and [x]bowed himself
unto her, and sat down on his throne,
and caused a seat to be set for the
king's mother; [y]and she sat on his right
hand.
20 Then she said, I desire one small
petition of thee; *I pray thee,* say me not
nay. And the king said unto her, Ask
on, my mother: for I will not say thee
nay.
21 And she said, Let Ăb'ĭ-shag the
Shu'nam-mīte be given to Ăd-ŏ-nī'jah
thy brother to wife.
22 And king Sŏl'o-mon answered
and said unto his mother, And why
dost thou ask Ăb'ĭ-shag the Shu'nam-
mīte for Ăd-ŏ-nī'jah? ask for him the
kingdom also; for he *is* mine elder
brother; even for him, and for [z]A-bī'a-
thär the priest, and for Jō'ab the son of
Zĕr-u-ī'ah.
23 Then king Sŏl'o-mon sware by
the LORD, saying, [a]God do so to me,
and more also, if Ăd-ŏ-nī'jah have not
spoken this word against his own life.
24 Now therefore, *as* the LORD liveth, which hath established me, and
set me on the throne of Dā'vid my father, and who hath made me an house,
as he [b]promised, Ăd-ŏ-nī'jah shall be
put to death this day.
25 And king Sŏl'o-mon sent by the
hand of Be-nā'iah the son of Je-hoi'a-
dȧ; and he fell upon him that he died.
26 ¶ And unto A-bī'a-thär the priest
said the king, Get thee to [c]Ăn'a-thoth,
unto thine own fields; for thou *art*
[6]worthy of death: but I will not at this
time put thee to death, [d]because thou
barest the ark of the Lord GOD before
Dā'vid my father, and because [e]thou
hast been afflicted in all wherein my
father was afflicted.
27 So Sŏl'o-mon thrust out A-bī'a-
thär from being priest unto the LORD;
that he might [f]fulfil the word of the

52 [h]1 Sam. 14.45; [i]Deut. 1.17
CHAPTER 2
1 [a]Gen. 3.19;
2 [b]Josh. 23.14;
3 [c]Deut. 17.19; [1]Or, do wisely
4 [d]2 Sam. 7.25
[e]Ps. 132.12
[f]2 Ki. 20.3
[g]2 Sam. 7.12 [2]be cut off from thee from the throne
5 [h]2 Sam. 3.39;
[i]2 Sam. 3.27
[j]2 Sam. 20.10 [3]put
6 [k]Prov. 20.26
7 [l]2 Sam. 19.31
[m]2 Sam. 9.7
[n]2 Sam. 17.27
8 [o]2 Sam. 16.5 [4]strong
9 [p]Ex. 20.7
10 [q]ch. 1.21;
[r]2 Sam. 5.7
11 [s]2 Sam. 5.4;
12 [t]1 Chr. 29.23;
13 [u]1 Sam. 16.4
15 [v]1 Chr. 22.9;
16 [5]turn not away my face
17 [w]ch. 1.3-4
19 [x]Ex. 20.12;
[y]Ps. 45.9;
22 [z]ch. 1.7
23 [a]Ruth 1.17;
24 [b]2 Sam. 7.11-13
26 [c]Josh. 21.18 [6]a man of death
[d]1 Sam. 23.6;
[e]1 Sam. 22.20;
27 [f]1 Sam. 2.31

LORD, which he spake concerning the
house of Ē'lī in Shī'lōh.
28 ¶ Then tidings came to Jō'ab: for
Jō'ab [g]had turned after Ăd-ŏ-nī'jah,
though he turned not after Ăb'sa-lŏm.
And Jō'ab fled unto the tabernacle of
the LORD, and [h]caught hold on the
horns of the altar.
29 And it was told king Sŏl'o-mon
that Jō'ab was fled unto the tabernacle
of the LORD; and, behold, *he is* by the
altar. Then Sŏl'o-mon sent Be-nā'iah
the son of Je-hoi'a-dȧ, saying, Go, fall
upon him.
30 And Be-nā'iah came to the tabernacle of the LORD, and said unto
him, Thus saith the king, Come forth.
And he said, Nay: but I will die here.
And Be-nā'iah brought the king word
again, saying, Thus said Jō'ab, and
thus he answered me.
31 And the king said unto him, [i]Do
as he hath said, and fall upon him, and
bury him; [j]that thou mayest take away
the innocent blood, which Jō'ab shed,
from me, and from the house of my
father.
32 And the LORD [k]shall return his
blood upon his own head, who fell
upon two men more righteous [l]and better than he, and slew them with the
sword, my father Dā'vid not knowing
thereof, to wit, [m]Ăb'nẽr the son of
Nẽr, captain of the host of Ĭs'ra-el, and
[n]Ăm'a-sȧ the son of Jē'thẽr, captain of
the host of Jū'dah.
33 Their blood shall therefore return
upon the head of Jō'ab, and [o]upon the
head of his seed for ever: [p]but upon
Dā'vid, and upon his seed, and upon
his house, and upon his throne, shall
there be peace for ever from the LORD.
34 So Be-nā'iah the son of Je-hoi'a-
dȧ went up, and fell upon him, and
slew him: and he was buried in his
own house in [q]the wilderness.
35 ¶ And the king put Be-nā'iah the
son of Je-hoi'a-dȧ in his room over the
host: and [r]Zā'dŏk the priest did the
king put in the room of Ā-bī'a-thär.
36 ¶ And the king sent and called for
[s]Shĭm'e-ī, and said unto him, [t]Build
thee an house in Je-rṳ'sa-lĕm, and
dwell there, and go not forth thence
any whither.
37 For it shall be, *that* on the day
thou goest out, and passest over the
brook [u]Kĭd'ron, thou shalt know for
certain that thou shalt surely die: [v]thy
blood shall be upon thine own head.
38 And Shĭm'e-ī said unto the king,
The saying *is* good: as my lord the king
hath said, so will thy servant do. And
Shĭm'e-ī dwelt in Je-rṳ'sa-lĕm many
days.
39 And it came to pass at the end of
three years, that two of the servants of
Shĭm'e-ī ran away unto [w]Ā'chĭsh son
of Mā'a-chah king of Găth. And they
told Shĭm'e-ī, saying, Behold, thy servants *be* in Găth.
40 And Shĭm'e-ī [x]arose, and saddled
his ass, and went to Găth to Ā'chĭsh to
seek his servants: and Shĭm'e-ī went,
and brought his servants from Găth.
41 And it was told Sŏl'o-mon that
Shĭm'e-ī had gone from Je-rṳ'sa-lĕm
to Găth, and was come again.
42 And the king sent and called for
Shĭm'e-ī, and said unto him, Did I not
make thee to [y]swear by the LORD, and
protested unto thee, saying, Know for
a certain, on the day thou goest out,
and walkest abroad any whither, that
thou shalt surely die? and thou saidst
unto me, The word *that* I have heard *is*
good.
43 Why then hast thou not kept the
[z]oath of the LORD, and the commandment that I have charged thee with?
44 The king said moreover to Shĭm'-
e-ī, Thou knowest all the wickedness
which thine heart is privy to, that thou
didst to Dā'vid my father: therefore
the LORD shall [a]return thy wickedness
upon thine own head;
45 And king Sŏl'o-mon *shall be*
blessed, and [b]the throne of Dā'vid
shall be established before the LORD
for ever.
46 So the king commanded Be-nā'-
iah the son of Je-hoi'a-dȧ; which went
out, and fell upon him, that he died.
And the kingdom was established in
the hand of Sŏl'o-mon.

3 And Sŏl'o-mon made affinity with
Phā'raōh king of Ē'gypt, and took
Phā'raōh's daughter, and brought her
into the city of Dā'vid, until he had
made an end of building his own house,
and [a]the house of the LORD, and the
wall of Je-rṳ'sa-lĕm round about.
2 [b]Only the people sacrificed in high
places, because there was no house
built unto the name of the LORD, until
those days.
3 And Sŏl'o-mon [c]loved the LORD,
walking in the statutes of Dā'vid his
father: only he sacrificed and burnt incense in high places.
4 And the king went to Ḡĭb'e-on to
sacrifice there; [d]for that *was* the great
high place: a thousand burnt offerings
did Sŏl'o-mon offer upon that altar.
5 ¶ [e]In Ḡĭb'e-on the LORD appeared
to Sŏl'o-mon [f]in a dream by night: and
God said, [g]Ask what I shall give thee.
6 [h]And Sŏl'o-mon said, Thou hast
shewed unto thy servant Dā'vid my
father great [1]mercy, according as he
walked before thee in truth, and in
righteousness, and in uprightness of
heart with thee; and thou hast kept for
him this great kindness, that thou hast
given him a son to sit on his throne, as
it is this day.
7 And now, O LORD my God, thou
hast made thy servant king instead of
Dā'vid my father: [i]and I *am but* a little
child: I know not *how* [j]to go out or
come in.
8 And thy servant *is* in the midst of
thy people which thou [k]hast chosen,
a great people, [l]that cannot be numbered nor counted for multitude.
9 [m]Give therefore thy servant an
[2]understanding heart [n]to judge thy
people, that I may [o]discern between
good and bad: for who is able to judge
this thy so great a people?

28 [g]ch. 1.7
[h]ch. 1.50; Ex. 21.14
31 [i]Ex. 21.14
[j]Num. 35.33; Deut. 19.13
32 [k]Gen. 4.11; Judg. 9.24; Ps. 7.16; Ps. 9.15-16
[l]2 Sam. 3.27; 2 Chr. 21.13; Esth. 1.19
[m]2 Sam. 3.27
[n]2 Sam. 20.10
33 [o]2 Sam. 3.29
[p]2 Sam. 3.28; Acts 7.45-46
34 [q]Josh. 15.61; Matt. 3.1
35 [r]Num. 25.11-13; 1 Chr. 6.53
36 [s]2 Sam. 16.5
[t]Prov. 20.8-26
37 [u]2 Sam. 15.23; 2 Ki. 23.6
[v]Lev. 20.9; Ezek. 18.13
39 [w]1 Sam. 27.2
40 [x]Prov. 15.27
42 [y]Ps. 15.4
43 [z]Ezek. 17.19
44 [a]Ps. 7.16
45 [b]Prov. 25.5
CHAPTER 3
1 [a]ch. 9.15
2 [b]Lev. 17.3; ch. 22.43
3 [c]Deut. 6.5; 1 John 5.3
4 [d]1 Chr. 16.39
5 [e]ch. 9.2; 2 Chr. 1.3
[f]Num. 12.6; Matt. 1.20
[g]John 15.7
6 [h]2 Chr. 1.8
[1]Or, bounty
7 [i]1 Chr. 29.1; Jer. 1.6
[j]Num. 27.17
8 [k]Deut. 7.6
[l]Gen. 13.16
9 [m]2 Chr. 1.10; Jas. 1.5
[2]hearing
[n]Ps. 72.1
[o]Heb. 5.14

10 And the speech pleased the Lord, that Sŏl'o-mon had asked this thing.

11 And God said unto him, Because thou hast asked this thing, and hast [p]not asked for thyself [3]long life; neither hast asked riches for thyself, nor hast asked the life of thine enemies; but hast asked for thyself understanding [4]to discern judgment;

12 [q]Behold, I have done according to thy words: [r]lo, I have given thee a wise and an understanding heart; so that there was none like thee before thee, neither after thee shall any arise like unto thee.

13 And I have also [s]given thee that which thou hast not asked, both [t]riches, and honour: so that there [5]shall not be any among the kings like unto thee all thy days.

14 And if thou wilt walk in my ways, to keep my statutes and my commandments, as thy father Dā'vid did walk, then I will [u]lengthen thy days.

15 And Sŏl'o-mon [v]awoke; and, behold, *it was* a dream. And he came to Je-ru'sa-lĕm, and stood before the ark of the covenant of the LORD, and offered up burnt offerings, and offered peace offerings, and [w]made a feast to all his servants.

16 ¶ Then came there two women, *that were* [x]harlots, unto the king, and [y]stood before him.

17 And the one woman said, O my lord, I and this woman dwell in one house; and I was delivered of a child with her in the house.

18 And it came to pass the third day after that I was delivered, that this woman was delivered also: and we *were* together; *there was* no stranger with us in the house, save we two in the house.

19 And this woman's child died in the night; because she overlaid it.

20 And she arose at midnight, and took my son from beside me, while thine handmaid slept, and laid it in her bosom, and laid her dead child in my bosom.

21 And when I rose in the morning to give my child suck, behold, it was dead: but when I had considered it in the morning, behold, it was not my son, which I did bear.

22 And the other woman said, Nay; but the living *is* my son, and the dead *is* thy son. And this said, No; but the dead *is* thy son, and the living *is* my son. Thus they spake before the king.

23 Then said the king, The one saith, This *is* my son that liveth, and thy son *is* the dead: and the other saith, Nay; but thy son *is* the dead, and my son *is* the living.

24 And the king said, Bring me a sword. And they brought a sword before the king.

25 And the king said, Divide the living child in two, and give half to the one, and half to the other.

26 Then spake the woman whose the living child *was* unto the king, for [z]her bowels [6]yearned upon her son, and she said, O my lord, give her the living child, and in no wise slay it. But the other said, Let it be neither mine nor thine, *but* divide *it*.

27 Then the king answered and said, Give her the living child, and in no wise slay it: she *is* the mother thereof.

28 And all Ĭs'ra-el heard of the judgment which the king had judged; and they feared the king: for they saw that the [a]wisdom of God *was* [7]in him, to do judgment.

4 So king Sŏl'o-mon was king over all Ĭs'ra-el.

2 And these *were* the princes which he had; Ăz-a-rī'ah the son of Zā'dŏk [1]the priest,

3 Ĕl-i-hō'reph and A-hī'ah, the sons of Shī'shȧ, [2]scribes; [a]Je-hŏsh'a-phăt the son of A-hī'lud, the [3]recorder.

4 And [b]Be-nā'iah the son of Je-hoi'-a-dȧ *was* over the host: and Zā'dŏk and [c]A-bī'a-thär *were* the priests:

5 And Ăz-a-rī'ah the son of Nā'than *was* over the officers: and Zā'bud the son of Nā'than *was* [d]principal officer, *and* [e]the king's friend:

6 And A-hī'shär *was* over the household: and [f]Ăd-ŏ-nī'ram the son of Ăb'-dȧ *was* over the [4]tribute.

7 ¶ And Sŏl'o-mon had twelve officers over all Ĭs'ra-el, which provided victuals for the king and his household: each man his month in a year made provision.

8 And these *are* their names: [5]The son of Hûr, in mount Ē'phrā-ĭm:

9 [6]The son of Dē'kär, in Mā'kăz, and in Sha-ăl'bim, and Bĕth–shē'mĕsh, and Ē'lon–bĕth–hā'năn:

10 [7]The son of Hē'sed, in Ăr'u-bŏth; to him *pertained* Sō'choh, and all the land of Hē'phẽr:

11 [8]The son of A-bĭn'ă-dăb, in all the region of Dôr; which had Tā'phath the daughter of Sŏl'o-mon to wife:

12 Bā'a-nȧ the son of A-hī'lud; *to him pertained* Tā'a-năch and Me-gĭd'do, and all Bĕth–shē'ăn, which *is* by Zär'ta-nah beneath Jĕz're-el, from Bĕth–shē'ăn to Ā'bel–me-hō'lah, *even* unto *the place that is* beyond Jŏk''ne-ăm:

13 [9]The son of Gē'bẽr, in Rā'moth–gĭl'e-ăd; to him *pertained* [g]the towns of Jā'ĭr the son of Ma-năs'seh, which *are* in Gĭl'e-ăd; to him *also pertained* [h]the region of Ăr'gŏb, which *is* in Bā'-shăn, threescore great cities with walls and brasen bars:

14 A-hĭn'a-dăb the son of Ĭd'dō *had* [10]Mā-ha-nā'im:

15 A-hĭm'a-ăz *was* in Năph'ta-lī; he also took Băs'măth the daughter of Sŏl'o-mon to wife:

16 Bā'a-nah the son of Hū'shāi *was* in Ăsh'ẽr and in Ā'lŏth:

17 Je-hŏsh'a-phăt the son of Păr'u-ah, in Ĭs'sa-char:

18 Shĭm'e-ī the son of Ē'lah, in Bĕn'-ja-min:

19 Gē'bẽr the son of Ū'ri *was* in the country of Gĭl'e-ăd, *in* [i]the country of Sī'hŏn king of the Ăm'ôr-ītes, and of

11 [p]Jas. 4.3 [3]many days [4]to hear
12 [q]1 John 5.14 [r]ch. 4.29; ch. 5.12; Prov. 3.13-18; Eccl. 1.16
13 [s]Matt. 6.33; Eph. 3.20 [t]ch. 10.23; Prov. 3.16; 1 Cor. 3.21-23; 2 Cor. 6.10 [5]Or, hath not been
14 [u]Ps. 91.16; Prov. 3.2
15 [v]Gen. 41.7; Jer. 31.26 [w]Gen. 31.54; ch. 8.65; Esth. 1.3; Dan. 5.1; Mark 6.21
16 [x]Lev. 19.29; Deut. 23.17 [y]Num. 27.2
26 [z]Gen. 43.30; Isa. 49.15; Jer. 31.20; Hos. 11.8 [6]were hot
28 [a]Ezra 7.25; Isa. 11.3; Dan. 1.17; Col. 2.2-3 [7]in the midst of him

CHAPTER 4
2 [1]Or, the chief officer
3 [2]Or, secretaries [a]2 Sam. 8.16 [3]Or, remembrancer
4 [b]ch. 2.35 [c]ch. 2.27
5 [d]2 Sam. 8.18 [e]2 Sam. 15.37; 1 Chr. 27.33
6 [f]ch. 5.14 [4]Or, levy
8 [5]Or, Ben-hur
9 [6]Or, Ben-dekar
10 [7]Or, Ben-hesed
11 [8]Or, Ben-abinadab
13 [9]Or, Ben-geber [g]Num. 32.41 [h]Deut. 3.4
14 [10]Or, to Mahanaim
19 [i]Deut. 3.8

Ŏg king of Bā'shăn; and *he was* the
only officer which *was* in the land.
20 ¶ Jū'dah and Ĭs'ra-el *were* many,
[j]as the sand which *is* by the sea in multitude, [k]eating and drinking, and making merry.
21 And Sŏl'o-mon reigned over all
kingdoms from [l]the river unto the land
of the Phĭ-lĭs'tĭnes, and unto the border
of Ē'gypt: they brought presents, and
served Sŏl'o-mon all the days of his
life.
22 ¶ And Sŏl'o-mon's [11]provision for
one day was thirty [12]measures of fine
flour, and threescore measures of meal,
23 Ten fat oxen, and twenty oxen
out of the pastures, and an hundred
sheep, beside harts, and roebucks, and
fallowdeer, and fatted fowl.
24 For he had dominion over all *the*
region on this side the river, from Tĭph'-
sah even [m]to Ăz'zah, over all the kings
on this side the river: and he had peace
on all sides round about him.
25 And Jū'dah and Ĭs'ra-el [n]dwelt
[13]safely, every man under his vine and
under his fig tree, from Dăn even to Bē'-
er–shē'bȧ, all the days of Sŏl'o-mon.
26 ¶ And Sŏl'o-mon had forty thousand stalls [o]of horses for his chariots,
and twelve thousand horsemen.
27 And [p]those officers provided victual for king Sŏl'o-mon, and for all that
came unto king Sŏl'o-mon's table, every man in his month: they lacked nothing.
28 Barley also and straw for the
horses and [14]dromedaries brought they
unto the place where *the officers* were,
every man according to his charge.
29 ¶ And God gave Sŏl'o-mon wisdom and understanding exceeding
much, and largeness of heart, even as
the sand that *is* on the sea shore.
30 And Sŏl'o-mon's wisdom excelled
the wisdom of all the children [q]of the
east country, and all [r]the wisdom of
Ē'gypt.
31 For he was wiser than all men;
[s]than Ē'than the Ĕz'ra-hīte, [t]and Hē'-
man, and Chăl'cŏl, and Där'dȧ, the
sons of Mā'hol: and his fame was in all
nations round about.
32 And [u]he spake three thousand
proverbs: and his [v]songs were a thousand and five.
33 And he spake of trees, from the
cedar tree that *is* in Lĕb'a-non even
unto the hyssop that springeth out of
the wall: he spake also of beasts, and
of fowl, and of creeping things, and of
fishes.
34 And [w]there came of all people to
hear the wisdom of Sŏl'o-mon, from
all kings of the earth, which had heard
of his wisdom.

5

5 And Hī'ram king of Tȳre sent his
servants unto Sŏl'o-mon; for he had
heard that they had anointed him king
in the room of his father: [a]for Hī'ram
was ever a lover of Dā'vid.
2 And [b]Sŏl'o-mon sent to Hī'ram,
saying,
3 Thou knowest how that Dā'vid my
father [c]could not build an house unto
the name of the LORD his God [d]for the
wars which were about him on every
side, until the LORD put them under the
soles of his feet.
4 But now the LORD my God hath
given me [e]rest on every side, *so that*
there is neither adversary nor evil oc-
current.
5 [f]And, behold, I [1]purpose to build
an house unto the name of the LORD
my God, [g]as the LORD spake unto Dā'-
vid my father, saying, Thy son, whom I
will set upon thy throne in thy room,
he shall build an house unto my name.
6 Now therefore command thou that
they hew me [h]cedar trees out of Lĕb'a-
non; and my servants shall be with thy
servants: and unto thee will I give hire
for thy servants according to all that
thou shalt [2]appoint: for thou knowest
that *there is* not among us any that can
skill to hew timber like unto the [i]Sī-
dō'nĭ-ans.
7 ¶ And it came to pass, when Hī'ram
heard the words of Sŏl'o-mon, that he
rejoiced greatly, and said, Blessed *be*
the LORD this day, which hath given
unto Dā'vid a wise son over this great
people.
8 And Hī'ram sent to Sŏl'o-mon, saying, I have [3]considered the things which
thou sentest to me for: *and* I will do all
thy desire concerning timber of cedar,
and concerning timber of fir.
9 My [j]servants shall bring *them*
down from Lĕb'a-non unto the sea:
[k]and I will convey them by sea in floats
unto the place that thou shalt [4]appoint
me, and will cause them to be dis-
charged there, and thou shalt receive
them: and thou shalt accomplish my
desire, [l]in giving food for my household.
10 So Hī'ram gave Sŏl'o-mon cedar
trees and fir trees *according to* all his
desire.
11 [m]And Sŏl'o-mon gave Hī'ram
twenty thousand [5]measures of wheat
for food to his household, and [6]twenty
measures of pure oil: thus gave Sŏl'o-
mon to Hī'ram year by year.
12 And the LORD gave Sŏl'o-mon
wisdom, [n]as he promised him: and
there was peace between Hī'ram and
Sŏl'o-mon; and they two made a league
together.
13 ¶ And king Sŏl'o-mon raised a
[7]levy out of all Ĭs'ra-el; and the levy
was thirty thousand men.
14 And he sent them to Lĕb'a-non,
ten thousand a month by courses: a
month they were in Lĕb'a-non, *and*
two months at home: and [o]Ăd-ŏ-nī'-
ram *was* over the levy.
15 And Sŏl'o-mon had threescore
and ten thousand that bare burdens,
and fourscore thousand hewers in the
mountains;
16 Beside the chief of Sŏl'o-mon's officers which *were* over the work, three
thousand and three hundred, which
ruled over the people that wrought in
the work.
17 And the king commanded, and
they brought great stones, costly stones,

20 [j]Gen. 22.17; ch. 3.8
[k]1 Sam. 30.16; Acts 2.46
21 [l]Gen. 15.18; Ps. 72.8-10
22 [11]bread
[12]cors; A cor is about 75 gallons
24 [m]Gen. 10.19
25 [n]Deut. 33.28-29; Zech. 3.10
[13]confidently
26 [o]Deut. 17.16; Ps. 20.7
27 [p]verse 7
28 [14]Or, mules, or, swift beasts
30 [q]Gen. 25.6; Matt. 2.1
[r]Acts 7.22
31 [s]1 Chr. 15.19; Ps. 89-title
[t]1 Chr. 6.33; Ps. 88-title
32 [u]Prov. 1.1; Eccl. 12.9
[v]Song 1.1
34 [w]ch. 10.1
CHAPTER 5
1 [a]Amos 1.9
2 [b]2 Chr. 2.3
3 [c]2 Sam. 7.5-13;
[d]1 Chr. 22.8
4 [e]1 Chr. 22.9;
5 [f]2 Chr. 2.4
[1]say
[g]2 Sam. 7.13;
6 [h]ch. 6.9-10-16-20
[2]say
[i]Ezek. 27.5
8 [3]heard
9 [j]ch. 9.20-21
[k]2 Chr. 2.16
[4]send
[l]Ezra 3.7;
11 [m]2 Chr. 2.10
[5]cors; That is, about 42,500 boles
[6]About 1560 gallons, wine measure
12 [n]ch. 3.12;
13 [7]tribute of men
14 [o]ch. 12.18

and hewed stones to lay the foundation of the house.

18 And Sŏl'o-mon's builders and Hī'-ram's builders did hew *them*, and the [8]stonesquarers: so they prepared timber and stones to build the house.

6

And it came to pass in the four hundred and eightieth year after the children of Is'ra-el were come out of the land of E'gypt, in the fourth year of Sŏl'o-mon's reign over Is'ra-el, in the month Zif, which *is* the second [1]month, that he [2]began to build the house of the LORD.

2 And [a]the house which king Sŏl'-o-mon built for the LORD, the length thereof *was* threescore cubits, and the breadth thereof twenty *cubits*, and the height thereof thirty cubits.

3 And the porch before the temple of the house, twenty cubits *was* the length thereof, according to the breadth of the house; *and* ten cubits *was* the breadth thereof before the house.

4 And for the house he made [3]windows of narrow lights.

5 ¶ And [4]against the wall of the house he built [5]chambers round about, *against* the walls of the house round about, *both* of the temple and of the [6]oracle: and he made [7]chambers round about:

6 The nethermost chamber *was* five cubits broad, and the middle *was* six cubits broad, and the third *was* seven cubits broad: for without *in the wall* of the house he made [8]narrowed rests round about, that *the beams* should not be fastened in the walls of the house.

7 And the house, when it was in building, was built of stone made ready before it was brought thither: so that there was neither hammer nor ax *nor* any tool of iron heard in the house, while it was in building.

8 The door for the middle chamber *was* in the right [9]side of the house: and they went up with winding stairs into the middle *chamber*, and out of the middle into the third.

9 So he built the house, and finished it; and covered the house [10]with beams and boards of cedar.

10 And *then* he built chambers against all the house, five cubits high: and they rested on the house with timber of cedar.

11 ¶ And the word of the LORD came to Sŏl'o-mon, saying,

12 *Concerning* this house which thou art in building, if thou wilt walk in my statutes, and execute my judgments, and keep all my commandments to walk in them; then will I perform my word with thee, which I spake unto Dā'vid thy father:

13 And [b]I will dwell among the children of Is'ra-el, and will not [c]forsake my people Is'ra-el.

14 So Sŏl'o-mon built the house, and finished it.

15 And he built the walls of the house within with boards of cedar, [11]both the floor of the house, and the walls of the ceiling: *and* he covered *them* on the inside with wood, and covered the floor of the house with planks of fir.

16 And he built twenty cubits on the sides of the house, both the floor and the walls with boards of cedar: he even built *them* for it within, *even* for the oracle, *even* for the [d]most holy *place*.

17 And the house, that *is*, the temple before it, was forty cubits *long*.

18 And the cedar of the house within *was* carved with [12]knops and [13]open flowers: all *was* cedar; there was no stone seen.

19 And the oracle he prepared in the house within, to [e]set there the ark of the covenant of the LORD.

20 And the oracle in the forepart *was* twenty cubits in length, and twenty cubits in breadth, and twenty cubits in the height thereof: and he overlaid it with [14]pure gold; and *so* covered the altar *which was of* cedar.

21 So Sŏl'o-mon overlaid the house within with pure gold: and he made a partition by the chains of gold before the oracle; and he overlaid it with gold.

22 And the whole house he overlaid with gold, until he had finished all the house: also [f]the whole altar that *was* by the oracle he overlaid with gold.

23 ¶ And within the oracle [g]he made two cherubims *of* [15]olive tree, *each* ten cubits high.

24 And five cubits *was* the one wing of the cherub, and five cubits the other wing of the cherub: from the uttermost part of the one wing unto the uttermost part of the other *were* ten cubits.

25 And the other cherub *was* ten cubits: both the cherubims *were* of one measure and one size.

26 The height of the one cherub *was* ten cubits, and so *was it* of the other cherub.

27 And he set the cherubims within the inner house: and [16]they stretched forth the wings of the cherubims, so that the wing of the one touched the *one* wall, and the wing of the other cherub touched the other wall; and their wings touched one another in the midst of the house.

28 And he overlaid the cherubims with gold.

29 And he carved all the walls of the house round about with carved figures of cherubims and palm trees and [17]open flowers, within and without.

30 And the floor of the house he overlaid with gold, within and without.

31 ¶ And for [h]the entering of the oracle he made doors *of* olive tree: the lintel *and* side posts *were* [18]a fifth part *of the wall*.

32 The [19]two doors also *were of* olive tree; and he carved upon them carvings of cherubims and palm trees and [20]open flowers, and overlaid *them* with gold, and spread gold upon the cherubims, and upon the palm trees.

33 So also made he for the door of the temple posts *of* olive tree, [21]a fourth part *of the wall*.

18 [8]Or, Giblites

CHAPTER 6

1 [1]Of the sacred year: about the end of April [2]built

2 [a]Ezek. 41.1

4 [3]Or, windows broad within, and narrow without: or, skewed and closed

5 [4]Or, upon, or, joining to [5]floors [6]Or, holy of holies [7]ribs

6 [8]narrowings, or, rebatements

8 [9]shoulder

9 [10]Or, the vault-beams and the ceilings with cedar

13 [b]Ex. 25.8; Rev. 21.3 [c]Deut. 31.6; Heb. 13.5

15 [11]Or, from the floor of the house unto the walls, etc; and so verse 16

16 [d]Ex. 32.34; Heb. 9.3

18 [12]Or, gourds [13]openings of flowers

19 [e]Ex. 40.20; ch. 8.6-10

20 [14]shut up

22 [f]Ex. 30.1

23 [g]Ex. 25.20; 2 Chr. 5.8 [15]trees of oil, or, oily trees

27 [16]Or, the cherubims stretched forth their wings

29 [17]openings of flowers

31 [h]John 10.7 [18]Or, five-square

32 [19]Or, leaves of the doors [20]openings of flowers

33 [21]Or, four-square

34 And the two doors *were of* fir tree: the [i]two leaves of the one door *were* folding, and the two leaves of the other door *were* folding.

35 And he carved *thereon* cherubims and palm trees and open flowers: and covered *them* with gold fitted upon the carved work.

36 ¶ And he built the inner court with three rows of hewed stone, and a row of cedar beams.

37 ¶ In the fourth year was the foundation of the house of the LORD laid, in the month Zĭf:

38 And in the eleventh year, in [22]the month Bŭl, which *is* the eighth month, was the house finished [23]throughout all the parts thereof, and according to all the fashion of it. So was he seven years in building it.

7 But Sŏl'o-mon was building his own house [a]thirteen years, and he finished all his house.

2 ¶ He built also the house of the forest of Lĕb'a-non; the length thereof *was* an hundred cubits, and the breadth thereof fifty cubits, and the height thereof thirty cubits, upon four rows of cedar pillars, with cedar beams upon the pillars.

3 And *it was* covered with cedar above upon the [1]beams, that *lay* on forty five pillars, fifteen *in* a row.

4 And *there were* windows *in* three rows, and [2]light *was* against light *in* three ranks.

5 And all the [3]doors and posts *were* square, with the windows: and light *was* against light *in* three ranks.

6 ¶ And he made a porch of pillars; the length thereof *was* fifty cubits, and the breadth thereof thirty cubits: and the porch *was* [4]*before them: and the other* pillars and the thick beam *were* [5]before them.

7 ¶ Then he made a porch for [b]the throne where he might judge, *even* the porch of judgment: and *it was* covered with cedar [6]from one side of the floor to the other.

8 ¶ And his house where he dwelt *had* another court within the porch, *which* was of the like work. Sŏl'o-mon made also an house for Phā'raōh's daughter, [c]whom he had taken *to wife,* like unto this porch.

9 All these *were of* costly stones, according to the measures of hewed stones, sawed with saws, within and without, even from the foundation unto the coping, and *so* on the outside toward the great court.

10 And the foundation *was of* costly stones, even great stones, stones of ten cubits, and stones of eight cubits.

11 And above *were* costly stones, after the measures of hewed stones, and cedars.

12 And the great court round about *was* with three rows of hewed stones, and a row of cedar beams, both for the inner court of the house of the LORD, [d]and for the porch of the house.

13 ¶ And king Sŏl'o-mon sent and fetched [e]Hī'ram out of Tȳre.

14 [f]He *was* [7]a widow's son of the tribe of Năph'ta-lī, and [g]his father *was* a man of Tȳre, a worker in brass: and [h]he was filled with wisdom, and understanding, and cunning to work all works in brass. And he came to king Sŏl'o-mon, and wrought all his work.

15 For he [8]cast [i]two pillars of brass, of eighteen cubits high apiece: and a line of twelve cubits did compass either of them about.

16 And he made two chapiters *of* molten brass, to set upon the tops of the pillars: the height of the one chapiter *was* five cubits, and the height of the other chapiter *was* five cubits:

17 *And* nets of checker work, and wreaths of chain work, for the chapiters which *were* upon the top of the pillars; seven for the one chapiter, and seven for the other chapiter.

18 And he made the pillars, and two rows round about upon the one network, to cover the chapiters that *were* upon the top, with pomegranates: and so did he for the other chapiter.

19 And the chapiters that *were* upon the top of the pillars *were* of lily work in the porch, four cubits.

20 And the chapiters upon the two pillars *had pomegranates* also above, over against the belly which *was* by the network: and the pomegranates *were* [j]two hundred in rows round about upon the other chapiter.

21 [k]And he set up the pillars in [l]the porch of the temple: and he set up the right pillar, and called the name thereof [9]Jă'chin: and he set up the left pillar, and called the name thereof [10]Bō'ăz.

22 And upon the top of the pillars *was* lily work: so was the work of the pillars finished.

23 ¶ And he made [m]a molten sea, ten cubits [11]from the one brim to the other: *it was* round all about, and his height *was* five cubits: and a line of thirty cubits did compass it round about.

24 And under the brim of it round about *there were* knops compassing it, ten in a cubit, [n]compassing the sea round about: the knops *were* cast in two rows, when it was cast.

25 It stood upon [o]twelve oxen, three looking toward the north, and three looking toward the west, and three looking toward the south, and three looking toward the east: and the sea *was set* above upon them, and all their hinder parts *were* inward.

26 And it *was* an hand breadth thick, and the brim thereof was wrought like the brim of a cup, with flowers of lilies: it contained [12]two thousand baths.

27 ¶ And he made ten bases of brass; four cubits *was* the length of one base, and four cubits the breadth thereof, and three cubits the height of it.

28 And the work of the bases *was* on this *manner:* they had [13]borders, and the borders *were* between the ledges:

29 And on the borders that *were* between the ledges *were* [p]lions, oxen, and cherubims: and upon the ledges

34 [i]Ezek. 41.23
38 [22]About the end of October [23]Or, with all the appurtenances thereof, and with all the ordinances thereof

CHAPTER 7
1 [a]ch. 9.10
3 [1]ribs
4 [2]sight against sight
5 [3]Or, spaces and pillars were square in prospect
6 [4]Or, according to them [5]Or, according to them
7 [b]ch. 10.18; [6]from floor to floor
8 [c]ch. 3.1
12 [d]John 10.23
13 [e]2 Chr. 4.11-Huram
14 [f]2 Chr. 2.14 [7]the son of a widow woman [g]2 Chr. 4.16 [h]Ex. 28.3
15 [8]fashioned [i]2 Ki. 25.17
20 [j]2 Ki. 25.17
21 [k]2 Chr. 3.17; [l]ch. 6.3 [9]That is, He shall establish [10]That is, In it is strength
23 [m]2 Ki. 25.13; [11]from his brim to his brim
24 [n]2 Chr. 4.3
25 [o]2 Chr. 4.4-5
26 [12]There were but 2000 baths in it usually, but when quite filled it contained 3000, or 22,210 gallons, wine measure
28 [13]shootings
29 [p]Gen. 3.24

there was a base above: and beneath the lions and oxen *were* certain additions made of thin work.

30 And every base had four brasen wheels, and plates of brass: and the four corners thereof had undersetters: under the laver *were* undersetters molten, at the side of every addition.

31 And the mouth of it within the chapiter and above *was* a cubit: but the mouth thereof *was* round *after* the work of the base, a cubit and an half: and also upon the mouth of it *were* gravings with their borders, foursquare, not round.

32 And under the borders *were* four wheels; and the axletrees of the wheels *were* [14]*joined* to the base: and the height of a wheel *was* a cubit and half a cubit.

33 And the work of the wheels *was* like the work of a chariot wheel: their axletrees, and their naves, and their felloes, and their spokes, *were* all molten.

34 And *there were* four undersetters to the four corners of one base: *and* the undersetters *were* of the very base itself.

35 And in the top of the base *was there* a round compass of half a cubit high: and on the top of the base the ledges thereof and the borders thereof *were* of the same.

36 For on the plates of the [15]ledges thereof, and on the borders thereof, he graved cherubims, lions, and palm trees, according to the [16]proportion of every one, and additions round about.

37 After this *manner* he made the ten bases: all of them had one casting, one measure, *and* one size.

38 ¶ Then [q]made he ten lavers of brass: one laver contained forty baths: *and* every laver was four cubits: *and* upon every one of the ten bases one laver.

39 And he put five bases on the right [17]side of the house, and five on the left side of the house: and he set the sea on the right side of the house eastward over against the south.

40 ¶ And Hī'ram made the lavers, and the shovels, and the basons. So Hī'ram made an end of doing all the work that he made king Sŏl'o-mon for the house of the LORD:

41 The two pillars, and the *two* bowls of the chapiters that *were* on the top of the two pillars; and the two networks, to cover the two bowls of the chapiters which *were* upon the top of the pillars;

42 And four hundred pomegranates for the two networks, *even* two rows of pomegranates for one network, to cover the two bowls of the chapiters that *were* [18]*upon the pillars;*

43 And the ten bases, and ten lavers on the bases;

44 And one sea, and twelve oxen under the sea;

45 [r]And the pots, and the shovels, and the basons: and all these vessels, which Hī'ram made to king Sŏl'o-mon for the house of the LORD, *were of* [19]bright brass.

46 [s]In the plain of Jôr'dan did the king cast them, [20]in the clay ground between [t]Sŭc'coth and [u]Zär'than.

47 And Sŏl'o-mon left all the vessels *unweighed,* [21]because they were exceeding many: neither was the weight of the brass [22]found out.

48 And Sŏl'o-mon made all the vessels that *pertained* unto the house of the LORD: [v]the altar of gold, and [w]the table of gold, whereupon [x]the shewbread *was,*

49 And the candlesticks of pure gold, five on the right *side,* and five on the left, before the oracle, with the flowers, and the lamps, and the tongs *of* gold,

50 And the bowls, and the snuffers, and the basons, and the spoons, and the [23]censers *of* pure gold; and the hinges *of* gold, *both* for the doors of the inner house, the most holy *place, and* for the doors of the house, *to wit,* of the temple.

51 So was ended all the work that king Sŏl'o-mon made for the house of the LORD. And Sŏl'o-mon brought in the [24]things which Dā'vid his father had dedicated; *even* the silver, and the gold, and the vessels, did he put among the treasures of the house of the LORD.

8 Then Sŏl'o-mon assembled the elders of Ĭs'ra-el, and all the heads of the tribes, the [1]chief of the fathers of the children of Ĭs'ra-el, unto king Sŏl'o-mon in Je-rṳ'sa-lĕm, [a]that they might bring up the ark of the covenant of the LORD [b]out of the city of Dā'vid, which *is* Zī'ŏn.

2 And all the men of Ĭs'ra-el assembled themselves unto king Sŏl'o-mon at the feast [c]in the month Ĕth'a-nĭm, which *is* the seventh month.

3 And all the elders of Ĭs'ra-el came, [d]and the priests took up the ark.

4 And they brought up the ark of the LORD, [e]and the tabernacle of the congregation, and all the holy vessels that *were* in the tabernacle, even those did the priests and the Lē'vītes bring up.

5 And king Sŏl'o-mon, and all the congregation of Ĭs'ra-el, that were assembled unto him, *were* with him before the ark, sacrificing sheep and oxen, that could not be told nor numbered for multitude.

6 And the priests brought in the ark of the covenant of the LORD unto [f]his place, into the oracle of the house, to the most holy *place, even* [g]under the wings of the cherubims.

7 For the cherubims spread forth *their* two wings over the place of the ark, and the cherubims covered the ark and the staves thereof above.

8 And they [h]drew out the staves, that the [2]ends of the staves were seen out in the [3]holy *place* before the oracle, and they were not seen without: and there they are unto this day.

9 [i]*There was* nothing in the ark [j]save the two tables of stone, which Mō'ses [k]put there at Hō'reb, [4]when the LORD made *a covenant* with the

32 [14]in the base
36 [15]hands, or, handles [16]nakedness
38 [q]Ex. 30.18; 2 Chr. 4.6; Zech. 13.1; Tit. 3.5
39 [17]shoulder
42 [18]upon the face of the pillars
45 [r]Ex. 27.3; 2 Chr. 4.16; Zech. 14.20-21 [19]made bright, or, scoured
46 [s]2 Chr. 4.17 [20]in the thickness of the ground [t]Gen. 33.17; Josh. 3.16; 2 Chr. 4.17 [u]Josh. 3.16
47 [21]for the exceeding multitude [22]searched, 1 Chr. 22.14
48 [v]Ex. 37.25 [w]Ex. 37.10 [x]Ex. 25.30; Lev. 24.5-8
50 [23]ash pans
51 [24]holy things of David

CHAPTER 8
1 [1]princes [a]Num. 10.33; 2 Sam. 6.17; ch. 3.15; 1 Chr. 13.3 [b]2 Sam. 5.7
2 [c]Lev. 23.34; Deut. 16.13; 2 Chr. 7.8
3 [d]Num. 4.15; Deut. 31.9; Josh. 3.3-6; 1 Chr. 15.14
4 [e]ch. 3.4; 2 Chr. 1.3
6 [f]Ex. 26.33 [g]ch. 6.27
8 [h]Ex. 25.14 [2]heads [3]Or, ark
9 [i]Ex. 25.21; Deut. 10.2 [j]Deut. 10.5; Heb. 9.4 [k]Ex. 40.20 [4]Or, where

children of Ĭs′ra-el, when they came
out of the land of Ē′gypt.
10 And it came to pass, when the
priests were come out of the holy *place,*
that the cloud filled the house of the
LORD,
11 So that the priests could not stand
to minister because of the cloud: for the
glory of the LORD had filled the house
of the LORD.
12 ¶ Then spake Sŏl′o-mon, The
LORD said that he would dwell [l]in the
thick darkness.
13 I have surely built thee an house
to dwell in, [m]a settled place for thee to
abide in for ever.
14 And the king turned his face
about, and [n]blessed all the congregation of Ĭs′ra-el: (and all the congregation of Ĭs′ra-el stood;)
15 And he said, [o]Blessed *be* the
LORD God of Ĭs′ra-el, which spake with
his mouth unto Dā′vid my father, and
hath with his hand fulfilled *it,* saying,
16 [p]Since the day that I brought
forth my people Ĭs′ra-el out of Ē′gypt, I
chose no city out of all the tribes of
Ĭs′ra-el to build an house, that [q]my
name might be therein; but I chose
Dā′vid to be over my people Ĭs′ra-el.
17 And it was in the heart of Dā′vid
my father to build an house for the
name of the LORD God of Ĭs′ra-el.
18 And the LORD said unto Dā′vid
my father, Whereas it was in thine
heart to build an house unto my name,
thou didst well that it was in thine
heart.
19 Nevertheless thou shalt not build
the house; but thy son that shall come
forth out of thy loins, he shall build the
house unto my name.
20 And the LORD hath performed his
word that he spake, and I am risen up in
the room of Dā′vid my father, and sit
on the throne of Ĭs′ra-el, as the LORD
promised, and have built an house for
the name of the LORD God of Ĭs′ra-el.
21 And I have set there a place for
the ark, wherein *is* [r]the covenant of
the LORD, which he made with our fathers, when he brought them out of the
land of Ē′gypt.
22 ¶ And Sŏl′o-mon stood before
[s]the altar of the LORD in the presence
of all the congregation of Ĭs′ra-el, and
spread forth his hands toward heaven:
23 And he said, LORD God of Ĭs′ra-el,
[t]*there is* no God like thee, in heaven
above, or on earth beneath, [u]who keepest covenant and mercy with thy servants that [v]walk before thee with all
their heart:
24 Who hast kept with thy servant
Dā′vid my father that thou promisedst
him: thou spakest also with thy mouth,
and has fulfilled *it* with thine hand, as
it is this day.
25 Therefore now, LORD God of Ĭs′-
ra-el, keep with thy servant Dā′vid my
father that thou promisedst him, saying, [5]There shall not fail thee a man in
my sight to sit on the throne of Ĭs′ra-el;
[6]so that thy children take heed to their
way, that they walk before me as thou
hast walked before me.
26 [w]And now, O God of Ĭs′ra-el,
let thy word, I pray thee, be verified,
which thou spakest unto thy servant
Dā′vid my father.
27 But [x]will God indeed dwell on
the earth? behold, the heaven and
[y]heaven of heavens cannot contain
thee; how much less this house that I
have builded?
28 Yet have thou respect unto the
[z]prayer of thy servant, and to his supplication, O LORD my God, to hearken
unto the cry and to the prayer, which
thy servant prayeth before thee to day:
29 That thine eyes may be open toward this house night and day, *even*
toward the place of which thou hast
said, My name shall be there: that thou
mayest hearken unto the prayer which
thy servant shall make [a][7]toward this
place.
30 [b]And hearken thou to the supplication of thy servant, and of thy people
Ĭs′ra-el, when they shall pray [8]toward
this place: and hear thou in heaven thy
dwelling place: and when thou hearest, [c]forgive.
31 ¶ If any man trespass against his
neighbour, [9]and an oath be laid upon
him to cause him to swear, and the
oath come before thine altar in this
house:
32 Then hear thou in heaven, and
do, and judge thy servants, [d]condemn-
ing the wicked, to bring his way upon
his head; and justifying the righteous,
to give him according to his righteousness.
33 ¶ [e]When thy people Ĭs′ra-el be
smitten down before the enemy, because they have sinned against thee,
and [f]shall turn again to thee, and confess thy name, and pray, and make supplication unto thee [10]in this house:
34 Then hear thou in heaven, and
forgive the sin of thy people Ĭs′ra-el,
and bring them again unto the land
which thou gavest unto their fathers.
35 ¶ When heaven is shut up, and
there is no rain, because they have
sinned against thee; if they pray toward this place, and confess thy name,
and turn from their sin, when thou af-
flictest them:
36 Then hear thou in heaven, and
forgive the sin of thy servants, and of
thy people Ĭs′ra-el, that thou [g]teach
them [h]the good way wherein they
should walk, and give rain upon thy
land, which thou hast given to thy people for an inheritance.
37 ¶ [i]If there be in the land famine, if
there be pestilence, blasting, mildew,
locust, *or* if there be caterpiller; if their
enemy besiege them in the land of
their [11]cities; whatsoever plague, whatsoever sickness *there be;*
38 What prayer and supplication soever be *made* by any man, *or* by all thy
people Ĭs′ra-el, which shall know every man the plague of his own heart,
and spread forth his hands toward this
house:

12 [l]Lev. 16.2; Ps. 97.2
13 [m]Ps. 132.14; Acts 6.14
14 [n]Josh. 22.6; 2 Chr. 6.3
15 [o]Luke 1.68
16 [p]2 Chr. 6.5
[q]Deut. 12.11
21 [r]Deut. 31.26
22 [s]2 Ki. 23.3; 1 Tim. 2.8
23 [t]Ex. 15.11; Mic. 7.18
[u]Deut. 7.9; Dan. 9.4
[v]Gen. 17.1; 2 Ki. 20.3
25 [5]There shall not be cut off unto thee a man from my sight
[6]only if
26 [w]2 Sam. 7.25
27 [x]2 Chr. 2.6; Acts 7.49
[y]2 Cor. 12.2
28 [z]Phil. 4.6
29 [a]Dan. 6.10
[7]Or, in this place
30 [b]2 Chr. 20.9; Neh. 1.6
[8]Or, in this place
[c]Ex. 34.6-7;
31 [9]and he require an oath of him
32 [d]Deut. 25.1
33 [e]Deut. 28.25
[f]Lev. 26.40;
[10]Or, toward
36 [g]Ps. 5.8;
[h]1 Sam. 12.23
37 [i]Lev. 26.16;
[11]Or, jurisdiction

39 Then hear thou in heaven thy dwelling place, and forgive, and do, and give to every man according to his ways, whose heart thou knowest; (for thou, *even* thou only, [j]knowest the hearts of all the children of men;)

40 That they may fear thee all the days that they live in the land which thou gavest unto our fathers.

41 Moreover concerning a stranger, that *is* not of thy people Ĭs′ra-el, but cometh out of a far country for thy name's sake;

42 (For they shall hear of thy great name, and of thy [k]strong hand, and of thy stretched out arm:) when he shall come and pray toward this house;

43 Hear thou in heaven thy dwelling place, and do according to all that the stranger calleth to thee for: [l]that all people of the earth may know thy name, to [m]fear thee, as *do* thy people Ĭs′ra-el; and that they may know that [12]this house, which I have builded, is called by thy name.

44 ¶ If thy people go out to battle against their enemy, whithersoever thou shalt send them, and shall pray unto the LORD [13]toward the city which thou hast chosen, and *toward* the house that I have built for thy name:

45 Then hear thou in heaven their prayer and their supplication, and maintain their [14]cause.

46 If they sin against thee, ([n]for *there is* no man that sinneth not,) and thou be angry with them, and deliver them to the enemy, so that they carry them away captives unto the land of the enemy, far or near;

47 [o]*Yet* if they shall [15]bethink themselves in the land whither they were carried captives, and repent, and make supplication unto thee in the land of them that carried them captives, [p]saying, We have sinned, and have done perversely, we have committed wickedness;

48 And *so* [q]return unto thee with all their heart, and with all their soul, in the land of their enemies, which led them away captive, and [r]pray unto thee toward their land, which thou gavest unto their fathers, the city which thou hast chosen, and the house which I have built for thy name:

49 Then hear thou their prayer and their supplication in heaven thy dwelling place, and maintain their [16]cause,

50 And forgive thy people that have sinned against thee, and all their transgressions wherein they have transgressed against thee, and [s]give them compassion before them who carried them captive, that they may have compassion on them:

51 For they *be* thy people, and thine inheritance, which thou broughtest forth out of Ē′ġypt, from the midst of the furnace of iron:

52 That thine eyes may be open unto the supplication of thy servant, and unto the supplication of thy people Ĭs′ra-el, to hearken unto them in all that they call for unto thee.

53 For thou didst separate them from among all the people of the earth, *to be* thine inheritance, as thou spakest by the hand of Mō′ses thy servant, when thou broughtest our fathers out of Ē′ġypt, O Lord GOD.

54 And it was *so*, that when Sŏl′o-mon had made an end of praying all this prayer and supplication unto the LORD, he arose from before the altar of the LORD, from kneeling on his knees with his hands spread up to heaven.

55 And he stood, [t]and blessed all the congregation of Ĭs′ra-el with a loud voice, saying,

56 Blessed *be* the LORD, that hath given rest unto his people Ĭs′ra-el, according to all that he promised: [u]there hath not [17]failed one word of all his good promise, which he promised by the hand of Mō′ses his servant.

57 The LORD our God be with us, as he was with our fathers: [v]let him not leave us, nor forsake us:

58 That he may [w]incline our hearts unto him, to walk in all his ways, and to keep his commandments, and his statutes, and his judgments, which he commanded our fathers.

59 And let these my words, wherewith I have made supplication before the LORD, be nigh unto the LORD our God day and night, that he maintain the cause of his servant, and the cause of his people Ĭs′ra-el [18]at all times, as the matter shall require:

60 [x]That all the people of the earth may know that [y]the LORD *is* God, *and that there is* none else.

61 Let your [z]heart therefore be perfect with the LORD our God, to walk in his statutes, and to keep his commandments, as at this day.

62 ¶ And the king, and all Ĭs′ra-el with him, offered sacrifice before the LORD.

63 And Sŏl′o-mon offered a sacrifice of peace offerings, which he offered unto the LORD, two and twenty thousand oxen, and an hundred and twenty thousand sheep. So the king and all the children of Ĭs′ra-el dedicated the house of the LORD.

64 The same day did the king hallow the middle of the court that *was* before the house of the LORD: for there he offered burnt offerings, and meat offerings, and the fat of the peace offerings: because the brasen altar that *was* before the LORD *was* too little to receive the burnt offerings, and meat offerings, and the fat of the peace offerings.

65 And at that time Sŏl′o-mon held [a]a feast, and all Ĭs′ra-el with him, a great congregation, from [b]the entering in of Hā′math unto [c]the river of Ē′ġypt, before the LORD our God, seven days and seven days, *even* fourteen days.

66 On the eighth day he sent the people away: and they [19]blessed the king, and went unto their tents joyful and glad of heart for all the goodness that the LORD had done for Dā′vid his servant, and for Ĭs′ra-el his people.

---

39 [j]1 Chr. 28.9; Ps. 11.4; Jer. 17.10; Acts 1.24
42 [k]Deut. 3.24
43 [l]1 Sam. 17.46; Ps. 67.2
[m]Ps. 102.15
[12]thy name is called upon this house
44 [13]the way of the city
45 [14]Or, right
46 [n]2 Chr. 6.36; Job 9.2; Ps. 130.3; Ps. 143.2; Prov. 20.9; Eccl. 7.20; Jas. 3.2; 1 John 1.8
47 [o]Lev. 26.40
[15]bring back to their heart
[p]Neh. 1.6; Ps. 106.6; Dan. 9.5
48 [q]Deut. 4.29; Neh. 1.9; Prov. 23.26; Jer. 29.12; Dan. 6.10; Acts 8.37; Rom. 10.10
[r]2 Chr. 6.38; Ps. 5.7; Dan. 6.10
49 [16]Or, right
50 [s]Ezra 7.6; Ps. 106.46
55 [t]2 Sam. 6.18
56 [u]Deut. 12.10; Josh. 21.45
[17]fallen
57 [v]Deut. 31.6
58 [w]Ps. 119.36; Jer. 10.23; 2 Cor. 3.5
59 [18]the thing of a day in this day
60 [x]Josh. 4.24; 1 Sam. 17.46; 2 Ki. 19.19
[y]Deut. 4.35; ch. 18.39; Jer. 10.10-12
61 [z]ch. 11.4
65 [a]Lev. 23.34
[b]Num. 34.8; Josh. 13.5; Judg. 3.3
[c]Gen. 15.18; Ex. 23.31
66 [19]Or, thanked

9 And [a]it came to pass, when Sŏl'o-mon had finished the building of the house of the LORD, [b]and the king's house, and [c]all Sŏl'o-mon's desire which he was pleased to do,

2 That the LORD appeared to Sŏl'o-mon the second time, [d]as he had appeared unto him at Gĭb'e-on.

3 And the LORD said unto him, [e]I have heard thy prayer and thy supplication, that thou hast made before me: I have hallowed this house, which thou hast built, [f]to put my name there for ever; [g]and mine eyes and mine heart shall be there perpetually.

4 And if thou wilt [h]walk before me, as Dā'vid thy father walked, in integrity of heart, and in uprightness, to do according to all that I have commanded thee, *and* wilt keep my statutes and my judgments:

5 Then I will establish the throne of thy kingdom upon Ĭs'ra-el for ever, [i]as I promised to Dā'vid thy father, saying, There shall not fail thee a man upon the throne of Ĭs'ra-el.

6 [j]*But* if ye shall at all turn from following me, ye or your children, and will not keep my commandments *and* my statutes which I have set before you, but go and serve other gods, and worship them:

7 [k]Then will I cut off Ĭs'ra-el out of the land which I have given them; and this house, which I have hallowed [l]for my name, will I cast out of my sight; [m]and Ĭs'ra-el shall be a proverb and a byword among all people:

8 And [n]at this house, *which* is high, every one that passeth by it shall be astonished, and shall hiss; and they shall say, [o]Why hath the LORD done thus unto this land, and to this house?

9 And they shall answer, Because they forsook the LORD their God, who brought forth their fathers out of the land of Ē'ġypt, and have taken hold upon other gods, and have worshipped them, and served them: therefore hath the LORD brought upon them all this evil.

10 ¶ And it came to pass at the end of twenty years, when Sŏl'o-mon had built the two houses, the house of the LORD, and the king's house,

11 (*Now* Hī'ram the king of Tȳre had furnished Sŏl'o-mon with cedar trees and fir trees, and with gold, according to all his desire,) that then king Sŏl'o-mon gave Hī'ram twenty cities [1]in the land of Găl'ĭ-lee.

12 And Hī'ram came out from Tȳre to see the cities which Sŏl'o-mon had given him; and they [2]pleased him not.

13 And he said, What cities *are* these which thou hast given me, my brother? And he called them the land of [3]Cā'bŭl unto this day.

14 And Hī'ram sent to the king sixscore talents of gold.

15 ¶ And this *is* the reason of [p]the levy which king Sŏl'o-mon raised; for to build the house of the LORD, and his own house, and [q]Mĭl'lo, and the wall of Je-ru'sa-lĕm, and [r]Hā'zôr, and [s]Me-ġĭd'do, and [t]Ġē'zēr.

16 *For* Phā'raōh king of Ē'ġypt had gone up, and taken Ġē'zēr, and burnt it with fire, [u]and slain the Cā'năan-ītes that dwelt in the city, and given it *for* a present unto his daughter, Sŏl'o-mon's wife.

17 And Sŏl'o-mon built Ġē'zēr, and [v]Bĕth–hō'rŏn the nether,

18 And [w]Bā'al-ath, and Tăd'môr in the wilderness, in the land,

19 And all the cities of store that Sŏl'o-mon had, and cities for his chariots, and cities for his horsemen, and [4]that which Sŏl'o-mon desired to build in Je-ru'sa-lĕm, and in Lĕb'a-non, and in all the land of his dominion.

20 *And* all the people *that were* left of the Ăm'ôr-ītes, Hĭt'tītes, Pĕr'ĭz-zītes, Hī'vītes, and Jĕb'u-sītes, which *were* not of the children of Ĭs'ra-el,

21 Their children [x]that were left after them in the land, whom the children of Ĭs'ra-el also were not able utterly to destroy, upon those did Solomon levy a tribute of [y]bondservice unto this day.

22 But of the children of Ĭs'ra-el did Sŏl'o-mon [z]make no bondmen: but they *were* men of war, and his servants, and his princes, and his captains, and rulers of his chariots, and his horsemen.

23 These *were* the chief of the officers that *were* over Sŏl'o-mon's work, five hundred and fifty, which bare rule over the people that wrought in the work.

24 ¶ But Phā'raōh's daughter came up out of the city of Dā'vid unto [a]her house which *Sŏl'o-mon* had built for her: [b]then did he build Mĭl'lo.

25 ¶ And three times in a year did Sŏl'o-mon offer burnt offerings and peace offerings upon the altar which he built unto the LORD, and he burnt incense [5]upon the altar that *was* before the LORD. So he finished the house.

26 ¶ And king Sŏl'o-mon made a navy of ships in [c]Ē'zĭ-on–ġē'bēr, which *is* beside Ē'lŏth, on the [6]shore of the Red sea, in the land of Ē'dom.

27 [d]And Hī'ram sent in the navy his servants, shipmen that had knowledge of the sea, with the servants of Sŏl'o-mon.

28 And they came to [e]Ō'phĭr, and fetched from thence gold, four hundred and twenty talents, and brought *it* to king Sŏl'o-mon.

10 And when the [a]queen of Shē'bȧ heard of the fame of Sŏl'o-mon concerning the name of the LORD, she came [b]to prove him with hard questions.

2 And she came to Je-ru'sa-lĕm with a very great train, with camels that bare spices, and very much gold, and precious stones: and when she was come to Sŏl'o-mon, she communed with him of all that was in her heart.

3 And Sŏl'o-mon [c]told her all her [1]questions: there was not *any* thing hid from the king, which he told her not.

CHAPTER 9
1 [a]2 Chr. 7.11
[b]ch. 7.1; Eccl. 2.4
[c]2 Chr. 8.6
2 [d]ch. 3.5
3 [e]2 Ki. 20.5; Dan. 9.23
[f]ch. 8.29
[g]Deut. 11.12
4 [h]Gen. 5.22; Mal. 2.6
5 [i]2 Sam. 7.12; 1 Chr. 22.10
6 [j]2 Sam. 7.14; Ps. 89.30
7 [k]Deut. 4.26;
[l]Jer. 7.14
[m]Deut. 28.37;
8 [n]Deut. 29.24;
[o]Jer. 22.8
11 [1]Which were inhabited by Canaanites
12 [2]were not right in his eyes
13 [3]That is, Displeasing, or, Dirty
15 [p]ch. 5.13
[q]2 Sam. 5.9
[r]Josh. 19.36
[s]Josh. 17.11
[t]Judg. 1.29
16 [u]Josh. 16.10
17 [v]Josh. 16.3;
18 [w]Josh. 19.44
19 [4]the desire of Solomon which he desired
21 [x]Judg. 1.21
[y]Gen. 9.25
22 [z]Lev. 25.39
24 [a]ch. 3.1;
[b]ch. 11.27
25 [5]upon it
26 [c]Num. 33.35;
[6]lip
27 [d]ch. 5.6-7
28 [e]Gen. 10.29

CHAPTER 10
1 [a]2 Chr. 9.1;
[b]Judg. 14.12
3 [c]Prov. 1.5
[1]words

4 And when the queen of Shē'bȧ had seen all Sŏl'o-mon's wisdom, and the house that he had built,

5 And the meat of his table, and the sitting of his servants, and the [2]attendance of his ministers, and their apparel, and his [3]cupbearers, [d]and his ascent by which he went up unto the house of the LORD; there was no more spirit in her.

6 And she said to the king, It was a true [4]report that I heard in mine own land of thy [5]acts and of thy wisdom.

7 Howbeit I believed not the words, until I came, and mine eyes had seen *it:* and, behold, the half was not told me: [6]thy wisdom and prosperity exceedeth the fame which I heard.

8 [e]Happy *are* thy men, happy *are* these thy servants, which stand continually before thee, *and* that hear thy wisdom.

9 [f]Blessed be the LORD thy God, which delighted in thee, to set thee on the throne of Is'ra-el: because the LORD loved Is'ra-el for ever, therefore [g]made he thee king, [h]to do judgment and justice.

10 And she gave the king an hundred and twenty talents of gold, and of spices very great store, and precious stones: there came no more such abundance of spices as these which the queen of Shē'bȧ gave to king Sŏl'o-mon.

11 [i]And the navy also of Hī'ram, that brought gold from [j]Ō'phĭr, brought in from Ō'phĭr great plenty of [7]almug trees, and precious stones.

12 And [k]the king made of the almug trees [8]pillars for the house of the LORD, and for the king's house, harps also and psalteries for singers: there came no such almug trees, nor were seen unto this day.

13 And king Sŏl'o-mon gave unto the queen of Shē'bȧ all her desire, whatsoever she asked, beside *that* which Sŏl'o-mon gave her [9]of his royal bounty. So she turned and went to her own country, she and her servants.

14 ¶ Now the weight of gold that came to Sŏl'o-mon in one year was six hundred threescore and six talents of gold,

15 Beside *that he had* of the merchantmen, and of the traffick of the spice merchants, and [l]of all the kings of A-rā'bĭ-ȧ, and of the [10]governors of the country.

16 ¶ And king Sŏl'o-mon made two hundred targets *of* beaten gold: six hundred *shekels* of gold went to one target.

17 And *he made* [m]three hundred shields *of* beaten gold; three pound of gold went to one shield: and the king put them in [n]the house of the forest of Lĕb'a-non.

18 ¶ [o]Moreover the king made a great throne of ivory, and overlaid it with the best gold.

19 The throne had six steps, and the top of the throne *was* round [11]behind: and *there were* [12]stays on either side on the place of the seat, and two lions stood beside the stays.

20 And twelve lions stood there on the one side and on the other upon the six steps: there was not [13]the like made in any kingdom.

21 ¶ And all king Sŏl'o-mon's drinking vessels *were of* gold, and all the vessels of the house of the forest of Lĕb'a-non *were of* pure gold; [14]none *were of* silver: it was nothing accounted of in the days of Sŏl'o-mon.

22 For the king had at sea a navy of [p]Thär'shish with the navy of Hī'ram: once in three years came the navy of Thär'shish, bringing gold, and silver, [15]ivory, and apes, and peacocks.

23 So king Sŏl'o-mon exceeded all the kings of the earth for riches and for wisdom.

24 ¶ And all the earth [16]sought to Sŏl'o-mon, to hear his wisdom, which God had put in his heart.

25 And [q]they brought every man his present, vessels of silver, and vessels of gold, and garments, and armour, and spices, horses, and mules, a rate year by year.

26 ¶ [r]And Sŏl'o-mon gathered together chariots and horsemen: and he had a thousand and four hundred chariots, and twelve thousand horsemen, whom he bestowed in the cities for chariots, and with the king at Je-ru'sa-lĕm.

27 [s]And the king [17]made silver *to be* in Je-ru'sa-lĕm as stones, and cedars made he *to be* as the sycomore trees that *are* in the vale, for abundance.

28 ¶ [18]And Sŏl'o-mon had horses brought out of Ē'gypt, and [t]linen yarn: the king's merchants received the linen yarn at a price.

29 And a chariot came up and went out of Ē'gypt for six hundred *shekels* of silver, and an horse for an hundred and fifty: [u]and so for all the kings of the Hĭt'tītes, and for the kings of Sȳr'-ĭ-ȧ, did they bring *them* out [19]by their means.

11 But king Sŏl'o-mon loved [a]many strange women, [1]together with the daughter of Phā'raōh, women of the Mō'ab-ītes, Ăm'mŏn-ītes, Ē'dom-ītes, Zī-dō'nĭ-ans, *and* Hĭt'tītes;

2 Of the nations *concerning* which the LORD said unto the children of Is'-ra-el, [b]Ye shall not go in to them, neither shall they come in unto you: *for* surely they will turn away your heart after their gods: Sŏl'o-mon clave unto these in love.

3 And he had seven hundred wives, princesses, and three hundred concubines: and his wives turned away his heart.

4 For it came to pass, when Sŏl'o-mon was old, [c]*that* his wives turned away his heart after other gods: and his heart was not perfect with the LORD his God, as *was* the heart of Dā'vid his father.

5 For Sŏl'o-mon went after [d]Ăsh'tō-rĕth the goddess of the Zī-dō'nĭ-ans,

---

5 [2]standing [3]Or, butlers [d]1 Chr. 26.16
6 [4]word [5]Or, sayings
7 [6]thou hast added wisdom and goodness to the fame
8 [e]Prov. 8.34
9 [f]ch. 5.7 [g]Deut. 7.8; Dan. 2.21 [h]2 Sam. 8.15; Prov. 8.15
11 [i]ch. 9.27 [j]Job 22.24 [7]algum trees
12 [k]2 Chr. 9.11 [8]a prop, or, rails
13 [9]according to the hand of king Solomon
15 [l]Ps. 72.10; Gal. 4.25 [10]Or, captains
17 [m]ch. 14.26 [n]ch. 7.2
18 [o]2 Chr. 9.17; Rev. 20.11
19 [11]on the hinder part thereof [12]bands
20 [13]so
21 [14]Or, there was no silver in them
22 [p]Gen. 10.4; Isa. 2.16 [15]Or, elephants' teeth
24 [16]sought the face of
25 [q]Job 42.11; Matt. 2.11
26 [r]Deut. 17.16
27 [s]2 Chr. 1.15 [17]gave
28 [18]And the going forth of the horses which was Solomon's [t]Ezek. 27.7
29 [u]Josh. 1.4 [19]by their hand

CHAPTER 11
1 [a]Gen. 6.2 [1]Or, beside
2 [b]Ex. 34.16
4 [c]Deut. 17.17
5 [d]Judg. 2.13

and after Mĭl'com the abomination of
the Ăm'mŏn-ītes.
6 And Sŏl'o-mon did evil in the sight
of the LORD, and [2]went not fully after
the LORD, as *did* Dā'vid his father.
7 [e]Then did Sŏl'o-mon build an high
place for [f]Chē'mŏsh, the abomination
of Mō'ab, in [g]the hill that *is* before Je-
ru'sa-lĕm, and for Mō'lech, the abomination of the children of Ăm'mŏn.
8 And likewise did he for all his
strange wives, which burnt incense
and sacrificed unto their gods.
9 ¶ And the LORD was [h]angry with
Sŏl'o-mon, because his heart was
turned from the LORD God of Ĭs'ra-el,
[i]which had appeared unto him twice,
10 And [j]had commanded him concerning this thing, that he should not
go after other gods: but he kept not
that which the LORD commanded.
11 Wherefore the LORD said unto
Sŏl'o-mon, Forasmuch as this [3]is done
of thee, and thou hast not kept my covenant and my statutes, which I have
commanded thee, [k]I will surely rend
the kingdom from thee, and will give it
to thy servant.
12 Notwithstanding in thy days I will
not do it for Dā'vid thy father's sake:
but I will rend it out of the hand of thy
son.
13 [l]Howbeit I will not rend away
all the kingdom; *but* will give [m]one
tribe to thy son [n]for Dā'vid my servant's sake, and for Je-ru'sa-lĕm's
sake [o]which I have chosen.
14 ¶ And the LORD [p]stirred up an
adversary unto Sŏl'o-mon, Hā'dăd the
Ē'dom-īte: he *was* of the king's seed in
Ē'dom.
15 [q]For it came to pass, when Dā'-
vid was in Ē'dom, and Jō'ab the captain of the host was gone up to bury the
slain, [r]after he had smitten every male
in Ē'dom;
16 (For six months did Jō'ab remain
there with all Ĭs'ra-el, until he had cut
off every male in Ē'dom:)
17 That Hā'dăd fled, he and certain
Ē'dom-ītes of his father's servants with
him, to go into Ē'ġypt; Hā'dăd *being*
yet a little child.
18 And they arose out of Mĭd'ĭ-an,
and came to Pā'ran: and they took
men with them out of Pā'ran, and they
came to Ē'ġypt, unto Phā'raōh king of
Ē'ġypt; which gave him an house, and
appointed him victuals, and gave him
land.
19 And Hā'dăd found great favour in
the sight of Phā'raōh, so that he gave
him to wife the sister of his own wife,
the sister of Täh'pen-ēs the queen.
20 And the sister of Täh'pen-ēs bare
him Ge-nū'băth his son, whom Täh'-
pen-ēs weaned in Phā'raōh's house:
and Ge-nū'băth was in Phā'raōh's
household among the sons of Phā'-
raōh.
21 [s]And when Hā'dăd heard in
Ē'ġypt that Dā'vid slept with his fathers, and that Jō'ab the captain of the
host was dead, Hā'dăd said to Phā'-
raōh, [4]Let me depart, that I may go to
mine own country.
22 Then Phā'raōh said unto him, But
what hast thou lacked with me, that,
behold, thou seekest to go to thine own
country? And he answered, [5]Nothing:
howbeit let me go in any wise.
23 ¶ And God stirred him up *another*
adversary, Rē'zon the son of E-lī'a-
dah, which fled from his lord [t]Hăd-ăd-
ē'zēr king of Zō'bah:
24 And he gathered men unto him,
and became captain over a band, [u]when
Dā'vid slew them *of Zō'bah:* and they
went to Da-măs'cus, and dwelt therein,
and reigned in Da-măs'cus.
25 And he was an [v]adversary to
Ĭs'ra-el all the days of Sŏl'o-mon, beside the mischief that Hā'dăd *did:* and
he abhorred Ĭs'ra-el, and reigned over
Sy̆r'ĭ-ȧ.
26 ¶ And [w]Jĕr-o-bō'am the son of
Nē'băt, an Ĕph'răth-īte of Zĕr'e-dȧ,
Sŏl'o-mon's servant, whose mother's
name *was* Ze-ru'ah, a widow woman,
even he [x]lifted up *his* hand against the
king.
27 And this *was* the cause that he
lifted up *his* hand against the king:
[y]Sŏl'o-mon built Mĭl'lo, *and* [6]repaired
the breaches of the city of Dā'vid his
father.
28 And the man Jĕr-o-bō'am *was* a
mighty man of valour: and Sŏl'o-mon
seeing the young man that he [7]was in-
dustrious, he made him ruler over all
the [8]charge of the house of Jō'seph.
29 And it came to pass at that time
when Jĕr-o-bō'am went out of Je-ru'-
sa-lĕm, that the prophet [z]A-hī'jah the
Shī'lo-nīte found him in the way; and
he had clad himself with a new garment; and they two *were* alone in the
field:
30 And A-hī'jah caught the new garment that *was* on him, and [a]rent it *in*
twelve pieces:
31 And he said to Jĕr-o-bō'am, Take
thee ten pieces: for thus saith the LORD,
the God of Ĭs'ra-el, Behold, I [b]will rend
the kingdom out of the hand of Sŏl'o-
mon, and will give ten tribes to thee:
32 (But he shall have one tribe for
my servant Dā'vid's sake, and for Je-
ru'sa-lĕm's sake, the city which I have
chosen out of all the tribes of Ĭs'ra-el:)
33 Because that they have forsaken
me, and have worshipped [c]Ăsh'tŏ-rĕth
the goddess of the Zī-dō'nĭ-ans, [d]Chē'-
mŏsh the god of the Mō'ab-ītes, and
[e]Mĭl'com the god of the children of
Ăm'mŏn, and have not walked in my
ways, to do *that which is* right in mine
eyes, and *to keep* my statutes and my
judgments, as *did* Dā'vid his father.
34 Howbeit I will not take the whole
kingdom out of his hand: but I will
make him prince all the days of his life
for Dā'vid my servant's sake, whom I
chose, because he kept my commandments and my statutes:
35 But I will take the kingdom out of
his son's hand, and will give it unto
thee, *even* ten tribes.

6 [2]fulfilled not after
7 [e]Num. 33.52
[f]Num. 21.29
[g]2 Ki. 23.13
9 [h]Deut. 7.3; Ps. 90.7
[i]ch. 3.5
10 [j]ch. 6.12; 2 Chr. 7.17-22
11 [3]is with thee
[k]ch. 12.15; 2 Ki. 17.15-21
13 [l]2 Sam. 7.15; 1 Chr. 17.13-14; Ps. 89.33
[m]ch. 12.20
[n]Ex. 32.13; 2 Ki. 13.23
[o]Deut. 12.11; 2 Ki. 21.4; Ps. 132.13-14; Isa. 14.32
14 [p]Deut. 31.16-17; 1 Chr. 5.26; Isa. 10.5-26; Hos. 9.12; Nah. 1.2
15 [q]1 Chr. 18.12-13; Ps. 108.10
[r]Num. 24.19; Deut. 20.13; Ps. 60-title; Mal. 1.2-3-4
21 [s]ch. 2.10-34
[4]Send me away
22 [5]Not
23 [t]2 Sam. 8.3
24 [u]2 Sam. 10.8-18
25 [v]2 Chr. 15.2
26 [w]ch. 12.2; 2 Chr. 13.6
[x]2 Sam. 20.21
27 [y]ch. 9.24
[6]closed
28 [7]did work
[8]burden
29 [z]ch. 14.2; Josh. 18.1
30 [a]1 Sam. 15.27
31 [b]ch. 12.1-16-20
33 [c]Judg. 2.13
[d]Num. 21.29; Jer. 48.7-13
[e]Acts 7.43

36 And unto his son will I give one
tribe, that [f]Dā'vid my servant may
have a [9]light alway before me in Je-
rṳ'sa-lĕm, the city which I have chosen
me to put my name there.
37 And I will take thee, and thou
shalt reign according to all that thy
ṣoul desireth, and shalt be king over
Ĭs'ra-el.
38 And it shall be, if thou wilt hearken unto all that I command thee, and
wilt walk in my ways, and do *that is*
right in my sight, to keep my statutes
and my commandments, as Dā'vid my
servant did; that [g]I will be with thee,
and [h]build thee a sure house, as I built
for Dā'vid, and will give Ĭs'ra-el unto
thee.
39 And I will for this afflict the seed
of Dā'vid, but not for ever.
40 Sŏl'o-mon sought therefore to kill
Jĕr-o-bō'am. And Jĕr-o-bō'am arose,
and fled into Ē'ġypt, unto Shī'shăk
king of Ē'ġypt, and was in Ē'ġypt until
the death of Sŏl'o-mon.
41 ¶ And [i]the rest of the [10]acts of
Sŏl'o-mon, and all that he did, and his
wisdom, *are* they not written in the
book of the acts of Sŏl'o-mon?
42 [j]And the [11]time that Sŏl'o-mon
reigned in Je-rṳ'sa-lĕm over all Ĭs'ra-el
was forty years.
43 [k]And Sŏl'o-mon slept with his fathers, and was buried in the city of
Dā'vid his father: and [l]Rē-ho-bō'am
his son reigned in his stead.
12 And [a]Rē-ho-bō'am went to Shē'-
chem: for all Ĭs'ra-el were come
to Shē'chem to make him king.
2 And it came to pass, when [b]Jĕr-o-
bō'am the son of Nē'băt, who was yet
in [c]Ē'ġypt, heard *of it,* (for he was fled
from the presence of king Sŏl'o-mon,
and Jĕr-o-bō'am dwelt in Ē'ġypt;)
3 That they sent and called him. And
Jĕr-o-bō'am and all the congregation
of Ĭs'ra-el came, and spake unto Rē-ho-
bō'am, saying,
4 Thy father made our [d]yoke grievous: now therefore make thou the grievous service of thy father, and his heavy
yoke which he put upon us, lighter, and
we will serve thee.
5 And he said unto them, Depart yet
for three days, then come again to me.
And the people departed.
6 ¶ And king Rē-ho-bō'am [e]con-
sulted with the old men, that stood before Sŏl'o-mon his father while he yet
lived, and said, How do ye advise that I
may answer this people?
7 And they spake unto him, saying,
[f]If thou wilt be a servant unto this people this day, and wilt serve them, and
answer them, and speak good words to
them, then they will be thy servants for
ever.
8 But he forsook the counsel of the
old men, which they had given him,
and consulted with the young men that
were grown up with him, *and* which
stood before him:
9 And he said unto them, What counsel give ye that we may answer this
people, who have spoken to me, saying, Make the yoke which thy father
did put upon us lighter?
10 And the young men that were
grown up with him spake unto him,
saying, Thus shalt thou speak unto this
people that spake unto thee, saying,
Thy father made our yoke heavy, but
make thou *it* lighter unto us; thus shalt
thou say unto them, [g]My little *finger*
shall be thicker than my father's loins.
11 And now whereas my father did
lade you with a heavy yoke, I will add
to your yoke: my father hath chastised
you with whips, but I will chastise you
with scorpions.
12 ¶ So Jĕr-o-bō'am and all the people came to Rē-ho-bō'am the third day,
as the king had appointed, saying,
Come to me again the third day.
13 And the king answered the people [1]roughly, and forsook the old men's
counsel that they gave him;
14 And spake to them after the counsel of the young men, saying, My father made your yoke heavy, and I will
add to your yoke: my father *also* chastised you with whips, but I will chastise
you with scorpions.
15 Wherefore the king hearkened
not unto the people; for [h]the cause was
from the LORD, that he might perform
his saying, which the LORD [i]spake
by A-hī'jah the Shī'lo-nīte unto Jĕr-o-
bō'am the son of Nē'băt.
16 ¶ So when all Ĭs'ra-el saw that
the king hearkened not unto them,
the people answered the king, saying,
[j]What portion have we in Dā'vid? neither *have we* inheritance in the son of
Jĕs'se: to your tents, O Ĭs'ra-el: now
ṣee to thine own house, Dā'vid. So
Ĭs'ra-el departed unto their tents.
17 But [k]*as for* the children of Ĭs'ra-el
which dwelt in the cities of Jū'dah, Rē-
ho-bō'am reigned over them.
18 Then king Rē-ho-bō'am [l]sent A-
dō'răm, who *was* over the tribute; and
all Ĭs'ra-el stoned him with stones, that
he died. Therefore king Rē-ho-bō'am
[2]made speed to get him up to his chariot, to flee to Je-rṳ'sa-lĕm.
19 So [m]Ĭs'ra-el [3]rebelled against the
house of Dā'vid unto this day.
20 And it came to pass, when all Ĭs'-
ra-el heard that Jĕr-o-bō'am was come
again, that they sent and called him
unto the congregation, and made him
king over all Ĭs'ra-el: there was none
that followed the house of Dā'vid, but
the tribe of Jū'dah [n]only.
21 ¶ And when [o]Rē-ho-bō'am was
come to Je-rṳ'sa-lĕm, he assembled all
the house of Jū'dah, with the tribe of
Bĕn'ja-min, an hundred and fourscore
thousand chosen men, which were war-
riors, to fight against the house of Ĭs'ra-
el, to bring the kingdom again to Rē-
ho-bō'am the son of Sŏl'o-mon.
22 But [p]the word of God came unto
Shĕm-a-ī'ah the man of God, saying,
23 Speak unto Rē-ho-bō'am, the son
of Sŏl'o-mon, king of Jū'dah, and unto
all the house of Jū'dah and Bĕn'ja-min,
and to the remnant of the people, saying,

36 [f]2 Sam. 7.29; ch. 15.4; Ps. 132.17; Luke 1.69-70-78-79; Acts 15.16-17
[9]lamp, or, candle
38 [g]Deut. 31.8; Josh. 1.5
[h]1 Chr. 17.10-24-27
41 [i]2 Chr. 9.29
[10]Or, words, or, things
42 [j]2 Chr. 9.30
[11]days
43 [k]2 Chr. 9.31
[l]Matt. 1.7- called Roboam

CHAPTER 12
1 [a]2 Chr. 10.1
2 [b]ch. 11.26
[c]ch. 11.40
4 [d]1 Sam. 8.11-18; ch. 4.7-22; Job 20.19-20-22-23; Prov. 3.31; Eccl. 5.8; Isa. 58.6; Ezek. 45.8; Amos 4.1-2; Mic. 2.1-3; Mal. 3.5; 1 Thess. 4.6
6 [e]Job 12.12; Prov. 27.10; Jer. 42.2-5
7 [f]2 Chr. 10.7; Prov. 15.1
10 [g]ch. 3.7; Isa. 47.6
13 [1]hardly
15 [h]Judg. 14.4; Amos 3.6
[i]ch. 11.11
16 [j]2 Sam. 20.1
17 [k]ch. 11.13; 2 Chr. 11.13-17
18 [l]2 Sam. 20.24; 2 Chr. 10.13
[2]strengthened himself
19 [m]1 Sam. 10.19; 2 Chr. 10.19
[3]Or, fell away
20 [n]ch. 11.13
21 [o]2 Chr. 11.1
22 [p]2 Chr. 11.2

24 Thus saith the LORD, Ye shall not
go up, nor fight against your brethren
the children of Ĭs'ra-el: return every
man to his house; for this thing is
[q]from me. They hearkened therefore
to the word of the LORD, and returned
to depart, according to the word of the
LORD.
25 ¶ Then Jĕr-o-bō'am [r]built Shē'-
chem in mount Ē'phră-ĭm, and dwelt
therein; and went out from thence, and
built [s]Pe-nū'el.
26 And Jĕr-o-bō'am said in [t]his
heart, Now shall the kingdom return to
the house of Dā'vid:
27 If this people [u]go up to do sacrifice in the house of the LORD at Je-
ru'sa-lĕm, then shall the heart of this
people turn again unto their lord, *even*
unto Rē-ho-bō'am king of Jū'dah, and
they shall kill me, and go again to Rē-
ho-bō'am king of Jū'dah.
28 Whereupon the king took counsel, and [v]made two calves *of* gold, and
said unto them, It is too much for you
to go up to Je-ru'sa-lĕm: [w]behold thy
gods, O Ĭs'ra-el, which brought thee up
out of the land of Ē'gypt.
29 And he set the one in [x]Bĕth'–el,
and the other put he in [y]Dăn.
30 And this thing became [z]a sin: for
the people went *to worship* before the
one, *even* unto Dăn.
31 And he made an [a]house of high
places, [b]and made priests of the lowest of the people, which were not of the
sons of Lē'vī.
32 And Jĕr-o-bō'am ordained a feast
in the eighth month, on the fifteenth
day of the month, like unto [c]the feast
that *is* in Jū'dah, and he [4]offered upon
the altar. So did he in Bĕth'–el, [5]sacri-
ficing unto the calves that he had made:
[d]and he placed in Bĕth'–el the priests
of the high places which he had made.
33 So he [6]offered upon the altar
which he had made in Bĕth'–el the fifteenth day of the eighth month, *even* in
the month which he [e]had devised of
his own heart; and ordained a feast
unto the children of Ĭs'ra-el: and he offered upon the altar, [7]and [f]burnt incense.

13

And, behold, there [a]came a man
of God out of Jū'dah by the word
of the LORD unto Bĕth'–el: [b]and Jĕr-o-
bō'am stood by the altar to [1]burn incense.
2 And he cried against the altar in
the word of the LORD, and said, O altar,
altar, thus saith the LORD; Behold, a
child shall be born unto the house of
Dā'vid, [c]Jo-sī'ah by name; and upon
thee shall he offer the priests of the
high places that burn incense upon
thee, and men's bones shall be burnt
upon thee.
3 And he gave [d]a sign the same day,
saying, This *is* the sign which the LORD
hath spoken; Behold, the altar shall be
rent, and the ashes that *are* upon it
shall be poured out.
4 And it came to pass, when king
Jĕr-o-bō'am heard the saying of the
man of God, which had cried against

24 [q]Prov. 16.9
25 [r]Gen. 12.6; Judg. 9.45
[s]Gen. 32.30-31; Judg. 8.17
26 [t]Ps. 14.1; Rom. 8.7
27 [u]Deut. 12.5
28 [v]2 Ki. 10.29; Hos. 8.4-7
[w]Ex. 32.4
29 [x]Gen. 28.19; Hos. 4.15
[y]Judg. 18.29
30 [z]ch. 13.34
31 [a]ch. 13.32
[b]Num. 3.10; ch. 13.33
32 [c]Lev. 23.33; Num. 29.12
[4]Or, went up to the altar, etc
[5]Or, to sacrifice
[d]Amos 7.13
33 [6]Or, went up to the altar, etc
[e]Num. 15.39
[7]to burn incense
[f]ch. 13.1

CHAPTER 13
1 [a]2 Ki. 23.17
[b]ch. 12.32
[1]Or, to offer
2 [c]2 Ki. 23.15-16
3 [d]Ex. 4.8-9; 1 Cor. 1.22
4 [e]Jer. 20.2; Acts 12.1
[f]Prov. 21.30; 2 Cor. 10.6
6 [g]Ex. 8.8; Jas. 5.16
[h]Ex. 8.12; Rom. 12.20
[2]the face of the LORD
7 [i]1 Sam. 9.7; 1 Cor. 2.14
8 [j]Num. 22.18
9 [k]1 Cor. 5.11
11 [3]son
17 [4]a word was
[l]ch. 20.35; 1 Thess. 4.15
18 [m]Jer. 5.12;
[n]Gal. 1.8
[o]Ps. 63.11
20 [p]Num. 23.5

the altar in Bĕth'–el, that he [e]put forth
his hand from the altar, saying, Lay
hold on him. And his hand, which he
put forth against him, [f]dried up, so
that he could not pull it in again to him.
5 The altar also was rent, and the
ashes poured out from the altar, according to the sign which the man of
God had given by the word of the LORD.
6 And the king answered and said
unto the man of God, [g]Intreat now the
face of the LORD thy God, and pray for
me, that my hand may be restored me
again. And the man of God [h]besought
[2]the LORD, and the king's hand was restored him again, and became as *it
was* before.
7 And the king said unto the man of
God, Come home with me, and refresh
thyself, and [i]I will give thee a reward.
8 And the man of God said unto the
king, [j]If thou wilt give me half thine
house, I will not go in with thee, neither will I eat bread nor drink water in
this place:
9 For so was it charged me by the
word of the LORD, saying, [k]Eat no
bread, nor drink water, nor turn again
by the same way that thou camest.
10 So he went another way, and returned not by the way that he came to
Bĕth'–el.
11 ¶ Now there dwelt an old prophet
in Bĕth'–el; and his [3]sons came and
told him all the works that the man of
God had done that day in Bĕth'–el: the
words which he had spoken unto the
king, them they told also to their father.
12 And their father said unto them,
What way went he? For his sons had
seen what way the man of God went,
which came from Jū'dah.
13 And he said unto his sons, Saddle
me the ass. So they saddled him the
ass: and he rode thereon,
14 And went after the man of God,
and found him sitting under an oak:
and he said unto him, *Art* thou the man
of God that camest from Jū'dah? And
he said, I *am*.
15 Then he said unto him, Come
home with me, and eat bread.
16 And he said, I may not return
with thee, nor go in with thee: neither
will I eat bread nor drink water with
thee in this place:
17 For [4]it was said to [l]me by the
word of the LORD, Thou shalt eat no
bread nor drink water there, nor turn
again to go by the way that thou
camest.
18 He said unto him, [m]I *am* a prophet
also as thou *art:* and [n]an angel spake
unto me by the word of the LORD, saying, Bring him back with thee into thine
house, that he may eat bread and drink
water. *But* he [o]lied unto him.
19 So he went back with him, and
did eat bread in his house, and drank
water.
20 ¶ And it came to pass, as they sat
at the table, that the [p]word of the LORD
came unto the prophet that brought
him back:

21 And he cried unto the man of
God that came from Jū'dah, saying,
Thus saith the LORD, Forasmuch as
thou hast disobeyed the mouth of the
LORD, and hast not kept the commandment which the LORD thy God commanded thee,
22 But camest back, and hast eaten
bread and drunk water in the place, of
the which *the LORD* did say to thee, Eat
no bread, and drink no water; thy carcase shall not come unto the sepulchre
of thy fathers.
23 ¶ And it came to pass, after he had
eaten bread, and after he had drunk,
that he saddled for him the ass, *to wit,*
for the prophet whom he had brought
back.
24 And when he was gone, [q]a lion
met him by the way, and slew him: and
his carcase was cast in the way, and
the ass stood by it, the lion also stood
by the carcase.
25 And, behold, men passed by, and
saw the carcase cast in the way, and
the lion standing by the carcase: and
they came and told *it* in the city where
the old prophet dwelt.
26 And when the prophet that
brought him back from the way heard
thereof, he said, It *is* the man of God,
who was disobedient unto the word of
the LORD: therefore the LORD hath delivered him unto the lion, which hath
[5]torn him, and slain him, according to
the word of the LORD, which he spake
unto him.
27 And he spake to his sons, saying,
Saddle me the ass. And they saddled
him.
28 And he went and found his carcase cast in the way, and the ass and
the lion standing by the carcase: the
lion had [r]not eaten the carcase, nor
[6]torn the ass.
29 And the prophet took up the carcase of the man of God, and laid it
upon the ass, and brought it back: and
the old prophet came to the city, to
mourn and to bury him.
30 And he laid his carcase in his
own grave; and they mourned over
him, *saying,* [s]Alas, my brother!
31 And it came to pass, after he had
buried him, that he spake to his sons,
saying, When I am dead, then bury me
in the sepulchre wherein the man of
God *is* buried; [t]lay my bones beside
his bones:
32 [u]For the saying which he cried by
the word of the LORD against the altar
in Bĕth'-el, and against all the [v]houses
of the high places which *are* in the cities of [w]Sa-mā'rĭ-ȧ, shall surely come to
pass.
33 ¶ [x]After this thing Jĕr-o-bō'am
returned not from his evil way, but
[7]made again of the lowest of the people
priests of the high places: whosoever
would, he [8]consecrated him, and he became *one* of the priests of the high
places.
34 [y]And this thing became sin unto
the house of Jĕr-o-bō'am, even to [z]cut

24 [q]Deut. 4.24; ch. 20.36; 2 Sam. 6.7; 2 Ki. 2.24; Eccl. 12.13-14; Nah. 1.2; 1 Pet. 4.17
26 [5]broken
28 [r]Lev. 10.2-5; Job 5.22-23; Dan. 6.22 [6]broken
30 [s]ch. 14.13; Jer. 22.18; Acts 8.2
31 [t]Ruth 1.17; Ps. 26.9; Eccl. 8.10
32 [u]2 Ki. 23.16-19 [v]Lev. 26.30; Hos. 12.11 [w]ch. 16.24; John 4.5; Acts 8.1-14
33 [x]2 Chr. 13.9; Jer. 3.8 [7]returned and made [8]filled his hand
34 [y]ch. 12.30; 2 Ki. 10.31 [z]ch. 14.10; 2 Ki. 17.20-23

CHAPTER 14
2 [a]ch. 11.31
3 [b]1 Sam. 9.7 [1]in thine hand [2]Or, cakes [3]Or, bottle
4 [c]ch. 11.29 [4]stood for his hoariness
5 [d]Prov. 21.30
6 [5]hard
7 [e]2 Sam. 12.7; ch. 16.2
8 [f]ch. 11.31 [g]ch. 15.5
9 [h]2 Chr. 11.15 [i]Neh. 9.26; Ps. 50.17; Ezek. 23.35
10 [j]ch. 15.29 [k]ch. 21.21; 2 Ki. 9.8 [l]Deut. 32.36
11 [m]ch. 21.24
13 [n]2 Chr. 12.12; Philem. 6; 2 Pet. 2.8-9
14 [o]ch. 15.27

it off, and to destroy *it* from off the
face of the earth.
14 At that time A-bī'jah the son of
Jĕr-o-bō'am fell sick.
2 And Jĕr-o-bō'am said to his wife,
Arise, I pray thee, and disguise thyself,
that thou be not known to be the wife
of Jĕr-o-bō'am; and get thee to Shī'lōh:
behold, there *is* A-hī'jah the prophet,
which told me that [a]*I should be* king
over this people.
3 [b]And take [1]with thee ten loaves,
and [2]cracknels, and a [3]cruse of honey,
and go to him: he shall tell thee what
shall become of the child.
4 And Jĕr-o-bō'am's wife did so, and
arose, [c]and went to Shī'lōh, and came
to the house of A-hī'jah. But A-hī'jah
could not see; for his eyes [4]were set by
reason of his age.
5 ¶ [d]And the LORD said unto A-hī'-
jah, Behold, the wife of Jĕr-o-bō'am
cometh to ask a thing of thee for her
son; for he *is* sick: thus and thus shalt
thou say unto her: for it shall be, when
she cometh in, that she shall feign herself *to be* another *woman.*
6 And it was *so,* when A-hī'jah heard
the sound of her feet, as she came in at
the door, that he said, Come in, thou
wife of Jĕr-o-bō'am; why feignest thou
thyself *to be* another? for I *am* sent to
thee *with* [5]heavy *tidings.*
7 Go, tell Jĕr-o-bō'am, Thus saith
the LORD God of Is'ra-el, [e]Forasmuch
as I exalted thee from among the people, and made thee prince over my people Is'ra-el,
8 And [f]rent the kingdom away from
the house of Dā'vid, and gave it thee:
and *yet* thou hast not been as my servant Dā'vid, [g]who kept my commandments, and who followed me with all
his heart, to do *that* only *which was*
right in mine eyes;
9 But hast done evil above all that
were before thee: [h]for thou hast gone
and made thee other gods, and molten
images, to provoke me to anger, and
[i]hast cast me behind thy back:
10 Therefore, behold, [j]I will bring
evil upon the house of Jĕr-o-bō'am, and
[k]will cut off from Jĕr-o-bō'am him that
pisseth against the wall, [l]*and* him that
is shut up and left in Is'ra-el, and will
take away the remnant of the house of
Jĕr-o-bō'am, as a man taketh away
dung, till it be all gone.
11 [m]Him that dieth of Jĕr-o-bō'am
in the city shall the dogs eat; and him
that dieth in the field shall the fowls of
the air eat: for the LORD hath spoken
it.
12 Arise thou therefore, get thee to
thine own house: *and* when thy feet
enter into the city, the child shall die.
13 And all Is'ra-el shall mourn for
him, and bury him: for he only of Jĕr-o-
bō'am shall come to the grave, because
in him [n]there is found *some* good thing
toward the LORD God of Is'ra-el in the
house of Jĕr-o-bō'am.
14 [o]Moreover the LORD shall raise
him up a king over Is'ra-el, who shall

cut off the house of Jĕr-o-bō'am that
day: but what? even now.
15 For the LORD shall smite Ĭs'ra-el,
as a reed is shaken in the water, and
he shall [p]root up Ĭs'ra-el out of this
[q]good land, which he gave to their fathers, and shall scatter them [r]beyond
the river, [s]because they have made
their groves, provoking the LORD to
anger.
16 And [t]he shall give Ĭs'ra-el up because of the sins of Jĕr-o-bō'am, [u]who
did sin, and who made Ĭs'ra-el to sin.
17 ¶ And Jĕr-o-bō'am's wife arose,
and departed, and came to [v]Tĭr'zah:
and when she came to the threshold of
the door, the child died;
18 And they buried him; and all Ĭs'-
ra-el mourned for him, according to
the word of the LORD, which he spake
by the hand of his servant A-hī'jah the
prophet.
19 And the rest of the acts of Jĕr-o-
bō'am, how he [w]warred, and how he
reigned, behold, they *are* written in the
book of the chronicles of the kings of
Ĭs'ra-el.
20 And the days which Jĕr-o-bō'am
reigned *were* two and twenty years:
and he [6]slept with his fathers, and Nā'-
dăb his son reigned in his stead.
21 ¶ And Rē-ho-bō'am the son of
Sŏl'o-mon reigned in Jū'dah. Rē-ho-
bō'am *was* [x]forty and one years old
when he began to reign, and he reigned
seventeen years in Je-ru'sa-lĕm, the
city [y]which the LORD did choose out of
all the tribes of Ĭs'ra-el, to put his name
there. And his mother's name *was*
Nā'a-mah an Ăm'mŏn-īt-ess.
22 And [z]Jū'dah did evil in the sight
of the LORD, and they [a]provoked him
to jealousy with their sins which they
had committed, above all that their fathers had done.
23 For they also built them [b]high
places, and [7]images, [c]and groves, on
every high hill, and [d]under every green
tree.
24 [e]And there were also sodomites
in the land: *and* they did according
to all the abominations of the nations
which the LORD cast out before the children of Ĭs'ra-el.
25 ¶ [f]And it came to pass in the fifth
year of king Rē-ho-bō'am, *that* Shī'-
shăk king of Ē'gypt came up against
Je-ru'sa-lĕm:
26 And [g]he took away the treasures
of the house of the LORD, and the treasures of the king's house; he even took
away all: and he took away all the
shields of gold [h]which Sŏl'o-mon had
made.
27 And king Rē-ho-bō'am made in
their stead brasen shields, and committed *them* unto the hands of the chief of
the [8]guard, which kept the door of the
king's house.
28 And it was *so,* when the king went
into the house of the LORD, that the
guard bare them, and brought them
back into the guard chamber.
29 ¶ Now the rest of the acts of Rē-
ho-bō'am, and all that he did, *are* they

15 [p]Deut. 29.28; Matt. 15.13
[q]Josh. 23.15
[r]2 Ki. 15.29
[s]Ex. 34.13; Deut. 12.3
16 [t]Isa. 13.14
[u]ch. 12.30; Matt. 18.7
17 [v]ch. 16.6; Song 6.4
19 [w]2 Chr. 13.2-20
20 [6]lay down
21 [x]Job 32.9; Eccl. 4.13
[y]ch. 11.36
22 [z]2 Chr. 12.1
[a]Ps. 78.58; 1 Cor. 10.22
23 [b]Deut. 12.2
[7]Or, standing images, or, statues
[c]2 Ki. 17.9
[d]Isa. 57.5
24 [e]Gen. 19.5; ch. 15.12
25 [f]ch. 11.40
26 [g]ch. 7.51; 2 Chr. 12.9
[h]ch. 10.17; Prov. 23.5
27 [8]runners
30 [i]ch. 12.24
CHAPTER 15
2 [a]2 Chr. 13.2; Michaiah the daughter of Uriel
[b]2 Chr. 11.21- Absalom
3 [c]ch. 11.4; Ps. 119.80
4 [d]Gen. 12.2; Isa. 37.35
[1]Or, candle
5 [e]ch. 14.8; Luke 1.6
7 [f]2 Chr. 13.2-3-22
8 [g]2 Chr. 14.1
10 [2]That is, grandmother's
11 [h]2 Chr. 14.2;
12 [i]ch. 14.24;
13 [j]Deut. 13.6;
[3]cut off
[k]Ex. 32.20
14 [l]ch. 22.43
15 [4]holy

not written in the book of the chronicles of the kings of Jū'dah?
30 And there was [i]war between Rē-
ho-bō'am and Jĕr-o-bō'am all *their*
days.
31 And Rē-ho-bō'am slept with his
fathers, and was buried with his fathers
in the city of Dā'vid. And his mother's
name *was* Nā'a-mah an Ăm'mŏn-īt-ess.
And A-bī'jam his son reigned in his
stead.

15 Now in the eighteenth year of
king Jĕr-o-bō'am the son of Nē'-
băt reigned A-bī'jam over Jū'dah.
2 Three years reigned he in Je-ru'-
sa-lĕm. And his mother's name *was*
[a]Mā'a-chah, the daughter [b]of A-bĭsh'-
a-lŏm.
3 And he walked in all the sins of his
father, which he had done before him:
and [c]his heart was not perfect with the
LORD his God, as the heart of Dā'vid
his father.
4 Nevertheless [d]for Dā'vid's sake
did the LORD his God give him a [1]lamp
in Je-ru'sa-lĕm, to set up his son after
him, and to establish Je-ru'sa-lĕm:
5 Because Dā'vid [e]did *that which*
was right in the eyes of the LORD, and
turned not aside from any *thing* that he
commanded him all the days of his life,
save only in the matter of U-rī'ah the
Hĭt'tīte.
6 And there was war between Rē-
ho-bō'am and Jĕr-o-bō'am all the days
of his life.
7 [f]Now the rest of the acts of A-bī'-
jam, and all that he did, *are* they not
written in the book of the chronicles of
the kings of Jū'dah? And there was war
between A-bī'jam and Jĕr-o-bō'am.
8 [g]And A-bī'jam slept with his fathers; and they buried him in the city
of Dā'vid: and Ā'sȧ his son reigned in
his stead.
9 ¶ And in the twentieth year of Jĕr-
o-bō'am king of Ĭs'ra-el reigned Ā'sȧ
over Jū'dah.
10 And forty and one years reigned
he in Je-ru'sa-lĕm. And his [2]mother's
name *was* Mā'a-chah, the daughter of
A-bĭsh'a-lŏm.
11 [h]And Ā'sȧ did *that which was*
right in the eyes of the LORD, as *did*
Dā'vid his father.
12 [i]And he took away the sodomites
out of the land, and removed all the
idols that his fathers had made.
13 And also Mā'a-chah his mother,
even [j]her he removed from *being* queen,
because she had made an idol in a
grove; and Ā'sȧ [3]destroyed her idol, and
[k]burnt *it* by the brook Kĭd'ron.
14 [l]But the high places were not removed: nevertheless Ā'sȧ's heart was
perfect with the LORD all his days.
15 And he brought in the [4]things
which his father had dedicated, and the
things which himself had dedicated,
into the house of the LORD, silver, and
gold, and vessels.
16 ¶ And there was war between
Ā'sȧ and Bā'a-shȧ king of Ĭs'ra-el all
their days.

17 And [m]Bā'a-shȧ king of Ĭs'ra-el went up against Jū'dah, and built [n]Rā'mah, [o]that he might not suffer any to go out or come in to Ā'sȧ king of Jū'dah.

18 Then Ā'sȧ took all the silver and the gold *that were* left in the treasures of the house of the LORD, and the treasures of the king's house, and delivered them into the hand of his servants: and king Ā'sȧ sent them to [p]Bĕn–hā'dăd, the son of Tăb'rĭ-mŏn, the son of Hē'zĭ-on, king of Sy̆r'ĭ-ȧ, that dwelt at [q]Da-măs'cus, saying,

19 *There is* a league between me and thee, *and* between my father and thy father: behold, I have sent unto thee a present of silver and gold; come and break thy league with Bā'a-shȧ king of Ĭs'ra-el, that he may [5]depart from me.

20 So Bĕn–hā'dăd hearkened unto king Ā'sȧ, and sent the captains of the hosts which he had against the cities of Ĭs'ra-el, and smote [r]Ī'jon, and [s]Dăn, and [t]Ā'bĕl–bĕth–mā'a-chah, and all Cĭn'ne-rŏth, with all the land of Năph'ta-lī.

21 And it came to pass, when Bā'a-shȧ heard *thereof,* that he left off building of Rā'mah, and dwelt in Tĭr'zah.

22 [u]Then king Ā'sȧ made a proclamation throughout all Jū'dah; none *was* [6]exempted: and they took away the stones of Rā'mah, and the timber thereof, wherewith Bā'a-shȧ had builded; and king Ā'sȧ built with them [v]Gē'bȧ of Bĕn'ja-min, and [w]Mĭz'pah.

23 The rest of all the acts of Ā'sȧ, and all his might, and all that he did, and the cities which he built, *are* they not written in the book of the chronicles of the kings of Jū'dah? Nevertheless [x]in the time of his old age he was diseased in his feet.

24 And Ā'sȧ slept with his fathers, and was buried with his fathers in the city of Dā'vid his father: [y]and [z]Je-hŏsh'a-phăt his son reigned in his stead.

25 ¶ And Nā'dăb the son of Jĕr-o-bō'am [7]began to reign over Ĭs'ra-el in the second year of Ā'sȧ king of Jū'dah, and reigned over Ĭs'ra-el two years.

26 And he did evil in the sight of the LORD, and walked in the way of his father, and in [a]his sin wherewith he made Ĭs'ra-el to sin.

27 ¶ [b]And Bā'a-shȧ the son of A-hī'jah, of the house of Ĭs'sa-char, conspired against him; and Bā'a-shȧ smote him at [c]Gĭb'be-thon, which *belonged* to the Phĭ-lĭs'tĭnes; for Nā'dăb and all Ĭs'ra-el laid siege to Gĭb'be-thon.

28 Even in the third year of Ā'sȧ king of Jū'dah did Bā'a-shȧ [d]slay him, and reigned in his stead.

29 And it came to pass, when he reigned, *that* he smote all the house of Jĕr-o-bō'am; he left not to Jĕr-o-bō'am any that breathed, until he had [e]destroyed him, according unto the saying of the LORD, which he spake by his servant A-hī'jah the Shī'lo-nīte:

30 Because of the sins of Jĕr-o-bō'am which he sinned, and which he

17 [m]2 Chr. 16.1
[n]Josh. 18.25; 1 Sam. 15.34
[o]ch. 12.27
18 [p]ch. 20.1-5-33-34; 2 Ki. 8.7-15
[q]Gen. 14.15; ch. 11.23
19 [5]go up
20 [r]2 Ki. 15.29
[s]Judg. 18.29
[t]2 Sam. 20.14
22 [u]2 Chr. 16.6
[6]free
[v]Josh. 21.17
[w]1 Sam. 7.6; Jer. 40.6-10
23 [x]2 Chr. 16.12; Ps. 90.10; Eccl. 12.1
24 [y]ch. 22.41-43; Matt. 1.8
[z]Matt. 1.8- called Josaphat
25 [7]reigned
26 [a]ch. 12.30
27 [b]ch. 14.14
[c]Josh. 19.44; ch. 16.15
28 [d]Deut. 32.35
29 [e]ch. 14.10-14; Job 18.13-21; Ps. 21.10; Isa. 14.20
34 [f]ch. 12.28-29; ch. 13.33
CHAPTER 16
1 [a]ch. 21.20-24; 2 Chr. 19.2
2 [b]1 Sam. 2.8; ch. 14.7; Ps. 75.6-7; Dan. 2.21
[c]ch. 15.34
3 [d]ch. 14.10; Isa. 66.24
4 [e]ch. 14.11
5 [f]2 Chr. 16.1
6 [g]ch. 14.17
7 [h]Ps. 115.4; Isa. 2.8
[i]ch. 14.14; Hos. 1.4
9 [j]ch. 15.27; 2 Ki. 12.20
[k]1 Sam. 25.36-38; Isa. 1.28
[1]which was over
11 [l]1 Sam. 25.22
[2]Or, both his kinsmen and his friends
12 [3]by the hand of

made Ĭs'ra-el sin, by his provocation wherewith he provoked the LORD God of Ĭs'ra-el to anger.

31 ¶ Now the rest of the acts of Nā'dăb, and all that he did, *are* they not written in the book of the chronicles of the kings of Ĭs'ra-el?

32 And there was war between Ā'sȧ and Bā'a-shȧ king of Ĭs'ra-el all their days.

33 In the third year of Ā'sȧ king of Jū'dah began Bā'a-shȧ the son of A-hī'jah to reign over all Ĭs'ra-el in Tĭr'zah, twenty and four years.

34 And he did evil in the sight of the LORD, and walked in [f]the way of Jĕr-o-bō'am, and in his sin wherewith he made Ĭs'ra-el to sin.

16 Then the word of the LORD came to [a]Jē'hū the son of Ha-nā'nī against Bā'a-shȧ, saying,

2 [b]Forasmuch as I exalted thee out of the dust, and made thee prince over my people Ĭs'ra-el; and [c]thou hast walked in the way of Jĕr-o-bō'am, and hast made my people Ĭs'ra-el to sin, to provoke me to anger with their sins;

3 Behold, I will take away the posterity of Bā'a-shȧ, and the posterity of his house; and will make thy house like [d]the house of Jĕr-o-bō'am the son of Nē'băt.

4 [e]Him that dieth of Bā'a-shȧ in the city shall the dogs eat; and him that dieth of his in the fields shall the fowls of the air eat.

5 Now the rest of the acts of Bā'a-shȧ, and what he did, and his might, [f]*are* they not written in the book of the chronicles of the kings of Ĭs'ra-el?

6 So Bā'a-shȧ slept with his fathers, and was buried in [g]Tĭr'zah: and Ē'lah his son reigned in his stead.

7 And also by the hand of the prophet Jē'hū the son of Ha-nā'nī came the word of the LORD against Bā'a-shȧ, and against his house, even for all the evil that he did in the sight of the LORD, in provoking him to anger with the [h]work of his hands, in being like the house of Jĕr-o-bō'am; and because [i]he killed him.

8 ¶ In the twenty and sixth year of Ā'sȧ king of Jū'dah began Ē'lah the son of Bā'a-shȧ to reign over Ĭs'ra-el in Tĭr'zah, two years.

9 [j]And his servant Zĭm'rī, captain of half *his* chariots, conspired against him, as he was in Tĭr'zah, [k]drinking himself drunk in the house of Ar'zȧ [1]steward of *his* house in Tĭr'zah.

10 And Zĭm'rī went in and smote him, and killed him, in the twenty and seventh year of Ā'sȧ king of Jū'dah, and reigned in his stead.

11 ¶ And it came to pass, when he began to reign, as soon as he sat on his throne, *that* he slew all the house of Bā'a-shȧ, he left him [l]not one that pisseth against a wall, [2]neither of his kinsfolks, nor of his friends.

12 Thus did Zĭm'rī destroy all the house of Bā'a-shȧ, according to the word of the LORD, which he spake against Bā'a-shȧ [3]by Jē'hū the prophet,

13 [m]For all the sins of Bā'a-shȧ, and
the sins of Ē'lah his son, by which they
sinned, and by which they made Is'ra-
el to sin, in provoking the LORD God of
Is'ra-el to anger [n]with their vanities.
14 Now the rest of the acts of Ē'lah,
and all that he did, *are* they not written
in the book of the chronicles of the
kings of Is'ra-el?
15 ¶ In the twenty and seventh year
of Ā'sȧ king of Jū'dah did Zĭm'rī reign
[o]seven days in Tīr'zah. And the people
were encamped [p]against Gĭb'be-thon,
which *belonged* to the Phĭ-lĭs'tĭnes.
16 And the people *that were* encamped heard say, Zĭm'rī hath conspired, and hath also slain the king:
wherefore all Is'ra-el made Ŏm'rī, the
captain of the host, king over Is'ra-el
that day in the camp.
17 And Ŏm'rī went up from Gĭb'be-
thon, and all Is'ra-el with him, and
they besieged Tīr'zah.
18 And it came to pass, when Zĭm'rī
saw that the city was taken, that he
went into the palace of the king's
house, and burnt the king's house over
him with fire, and [q]died,
19 For his sins which he sinned in
[r]doing evil in the sight of the LORD, [s]in
walking in the way of Jĕr-o-bō'am,
and in his sin which he did, to make
Is'ra-el to sin.
20 Now the rest of the acts of Zĭm'rī,
and his treason that he wrought, *are*
they not written in the book of the
chronicles of the kings of Is'ra-el?
21 ¶ Then were the people of Is'ra-el
divided into [t]two parts: half of the people followed Tĭb'nī the son of Gī'nath,
to make him king; and half followed
Ŏm'rī.
22 But the people that followed Ŏm'rī
prevailed against the people that followed Tĭb'nī the son of Gī'nath: so
Tĭb'nī died, and Ŏm'rī reigned.
23 ¶ In the thirty and first year of
Ā'sȧ king of Jū'dah began Ŏm'rī to
reign over Is'ra-el, twelve years: six
years reigned he in Tīr'zah.
24 And he bought the hill Sa-mā'rĭ-ȧ
of Shē'mĕr for two talents of silver,
and built on the hill, and called the
name of the city which he built, after
the name of Shē'mĕr, owner of the hill,
[4]Sa-mā'rĭ-ȧ.
25 ¶ But [u]Ŏm'rī wrought evil in the
eyes of the LORD, and did worse than
all that *were* before him.
26 For he walked in all the way of
Jĕr-o-bō'am the son of Nē'băt, and in
his sin wherewith he made Is'ra-el to
sin, to provoke the LORD God of Is'ra-
el to anger with their [v]vanities.
27 Now the rest of the acts of Ŏm'rī
which he did, and his might that he
shewed, *are* they not written in the
book of the chronicles of the kings of
Is'ra-el?
28 So Ŏm'rī slept with his fathers,
and was buried in Sa-mā'rĭ-ȧ: and
Ā'hăb his son reigned in his stead.
29 ¶ And in the thirty and eighth year
of Ā'sȧ king of Jū'dah began Ā'hăb the
son of Ŏm'rī to reign over Is'ra-el: and

13 [m]Isa. 3.16
[n]Deut. 32.21; 1 Sam. 12.21; Isa. 41.29; Jer. 10.8-15; Jon. 2.8; 1 Cor. 8.4
15 [o]Job 20.5; Ps. 37.35
[p]ch. 15.27
18 [q]Judg. 9.54
19 [r]Ps. 9.16
[s]ch. 12.28
21 [t]Isa. 9.18
24 [4]Shomeron
25 [u]ch. 14.9; Mic. 6.16
26 [v]Jer. 16.19; Acts 14.15
31 [5]was it a light thing, etc
[w]Gen. 6.2; Josh. 23.12; ch. 18.4-19
[x]Judg. 18.7
[y]ch. 21.25; 2 Ki. 10.18
32 [z]2 Ki. 10.21-26-27
33 [a]Ex. 34.13; Jer. 17.2
[b]ch. 21.25
34 [c]Num. 15.30; Ps. 119.89-126; Prov. 13.13; Isa. 40.8; Matt. 24.35; Luke 21.33; 1 Pet. 1.25
CHAPTER 17
1 [1]Elijahu, Luke 1.17; Luke 4.25, Elias
[a]2 Ki. 3.14
[b]Deut. 10.8
[c]Jas. 5.17
[d]Luke 4.25
4 [e]Ps. 37.3
7 [2]at the end of days
9 [f]Obad. 20; Luke 4.26, Sarepta
10 [g]Gen. 24.17; Ps. 24.1; John 4.7; Heb. 11.37
12 [h]Gen. 18.6

Ā'hăb the son of Ŏm'rī reigned over
Is'ra-el in Sa-mā'rĭ-ȧ twenty and two
years.
30 And Ā'hăb the son of Ŏm'rī did
evil in the sight of the LORD above all
that *were* before him.
31 And it came to pass, [5]as if it had
been a light thing for him to walk in
the sins of Jĕr-o-bō'am the son of Nē'-
băt, [w]that he took to wife Jĕz'e-bĕl the
daughter of Ĕth'bā-al king of the [x]Zī-
dō'nĭ-ans, [y]and went and served Bā'al,
and worshipped him.
32 And he reared up an altar for
Bā'al in [z]the house of Bā'al, which he
had built in Sa-mā'rĭ-ȧ.
33 [a]And Ā'hăb made a grove; and
Ā'hăb [b]did more to provoke the LORD
God of Is'ra-el to anger than all the
kings of Is'ra-el that were before him.
34 ¶ In his days did Hī'el the Bĕth'–
el-īte build Jĕr'ĭ-chō: he laid the foundation thereof in A-bī'răm his firstborn, and set up the gates thereof in
his youngest *son* Sē'gub, [c]according
to the word of the LORD, which he
spake by Jŏsh'u-ȧ the son of Nŭn.

17 And [1]E-lī'jah the Tĭsh'bīte, *who*
was of the inhabitants of Gĭl'e-
ăd, said unto Ā'hăb, [a]*As* the LORD God
of Is'ra-el liveth, [b]before whom I stand,
[c]there shall not be dew nor rain [d]these
years, but according to my word.
2 And the word of the LORD came
unto him, saying,
3 Get thee hence, and turn thee eastward, and hide thyself by the brook
Chē'rĭth, that *is* before Jôr'dan.
4 And it shall be, *that* thou shalt
drink of the brook; and [e]I have commanded the ravens to feed thee there.
5 So he went and did according unto
the word of the LORD: for he went and
dwelt by the brook Chē'rĭth, that *is* before Jôr'dan.
6 And the ravens brought him bread
and flesh in the morning, and bread
and flesh in the evening; and he drank
of the brook.
7 And it came to pass, [2]after a while,
that the brook dried up, because there
had been no rain in the land.
8 ¶ And the word of the LORD came
unto him, saying,
9 Arise, get thee to [f]Zăr'e-phăth,
which *belongeth* to Zī'dŏn, and dwell
there: behold, I have commanded a
widow woman there to sustain thee.
10 So he arose and went to Zăr'e-
phăth. And when he came to the gate
of the city, behold, the widow woman
was there gathering of sticks: and he
called to her, and said, [g]Fetch me, I
pray thee, a little water in a vessel, that
I may drink.
11 And as she was going to fetch *it*,
he called to her, and said, Bring me, I
pray thee, a morsel of bread in thine
hand.
12 And she said, *As* the LORD thy
God liveth, I have not [h]a cake, but an
handful of meal in a barrel, and a little
oil in a cruse: and, behold, I *am* gathering two sticks, that I may go in and

dress it for me and my son, that we
may eat it, and [i]die.
13 And E-lī'jah said unto her, Fear
not; go *and* do as thou hast said: but
[j]make me thereof a little cake first,
and bring *it* unto me, and after make
for thee and for thy son.
14 For thus saith the LORD God of
Ĭs'ra-el, [k]The barrel of meal shall not
waste, neither shall the cruse of oil fail,
until the day *that* the LORD [3]sendeth
rain upon the earth.
15 And she went and [l]did according
to the saying of E-lī'jah: and she, and
he, and her house, did eat [4]*many* days.
16 *And* [m]the barrel of meal wasted
not, neither did the cruse of oil fail,
according to the word of the LORD,
which he spake [5]by E-lī'jah.
17 ¶ And it came to pass after these
things, *that* the son of the woman, the
mistress of the house, fell sick; and his
sickness was so sore, that there was no
breath left in him.
18 And she said unto E-lī'jah, [n]What
have I to do with thee, O thou man of
God? art thou come unto me to call my
sin to remembrance, and to slay my
son?
19 And he said unto her, Give me
thy son. And he took him out of her
bosom, and carried him up into a loft,
where he abode, and laid him upon his
own bed.
20 [o]And he cried unto the LORD,
and said, O LORD my God, hast thou
also brought evil upon the widow with
whom I sojourn, by slaying her son?
21 [p]And he [6]stretched himself upon
the child three times, and cried unto
the LORD, and said, O LORD my God, I
pray thee, let this child's soul come
[7]into him again.
22 And the LORD [q]heard the voice of
E-lī'jah; and the soul of the child came
into him again, and he [r]revived.
23 And E-lī'jah took the child, and
brought him down out of the chamber
into the house, and delivered him unto
his mother: and E-lī'jah said, See, thy
son liveth.
24 ¶ And the woman said to E-lī'jah,
Now by this [s]I know that thou *art* a
man of God, *and* that the word of the
LORD in thy mouth *is* truth.

18 And it came to pass *after* [a]many
days, that the word of the LORD
came to E-lī'jah in the third year, saying, Go, shew thyself unto Ā'hăb; and
[b]I will send rain upon the earth.
2 And E-lī'jah went to shew himself
unto Ā'hăb. And *there was* a sore famine in Sa-mā'rĭ-ȧ.
3 And Ā'hăb called [1]Ō-ba-dī'ah,
which *was* [2]the governor of *his* house.
(Now Ō-ba-dī'ah [c]feared the LORD
greatly:
4 For it was *so*, when [3]Jĕz'e-bĕl cut
off the prophets of the LORD, that Ō-ba-
dī'ah took an hundred prophets, and
hid them by fifty in a cave, and [d]fed
them with bread and water.)
5 And Ā'hăb said unto Ō-ba-dī'ah,
Go into the land, unto all fountains of
water, and unto all brooks: peradventure we may find grass to save the
horses and mules alive, [4]that we lose
not all the beasts.
6 So they divided the land between
them to pass throughout it: Ā'hăb went
one way by himself, and Ō-ba-dī'ah
went another way by himself.
7 ¶ And as Ō-ba-dī'ah was in the
way, behold, E-lī'jah met him: and he
knew him, and fell on his face, and
said, *Art* thou that my lord E-lī'jah?
8 And he answered him, I *am:* go,
tell thy lord, Behold, E-lī'jah *is here.*
9 And he said, What have I sinned,
that thou wouldest deliver thy servant
into the hand of Ā'hăb, to slay me?
10 *As* the LORD thy God liveth, there
is no nation or kingdom, whither my
lord hath not sent to seek thee: and
when they said, *He is* not *there;* he
took an oath of the kingdom and nation, that they found thee not.
11 And now thou sayest, Go, tell thy
lord, Behold, E-lī'jah *is here.*
12 And it shall come to pass, *as soon
as* I am gone from thee, that [e]the Spirit
of the LORD shall carry thee whither I
know not; and *so* when I come and tell
Ā'hăb, and he cannot find thee, he
shall slay me: but I thy servant fear the
LORD from my youth.
13 Was it not told my lord what I did
when Jĕz'e-bĕl slew the prophets of
the LORD, how I hid an hundred men of
the LORD'S prophets by fifty in a cave,
and fed them with bread and water?
14 And now thou sayest, Go, tell thy
lord, Behold, E-lī'jah *is here:* and he
shall slay me.
15 And E-lī'jah said, *As* the LORD of
hosts liveth, before whom I stand, I
will surely shew myself unto him to
day.
16 So Ō-ba-dī'ah went to meet Ā'hăb,
and told him: and Ā'hăb went to meet E-
lī'jah.
17 ¶ And it came to pass, when Ā'hăb
saw E-lī'jah, that Ā'hăb said unto him,
[f]*Art* thou he [g]that troubleth Ĭs'ra-el?
18 And he answered, I have not troubled Ĭs'ra-el; but thou, and thy father's
house, [h]in that ye have forsaken the
commandments of the LORD, and thou
hast followed Bā'al-ĭm.
19 Now therefore send, *and* gather
to me all Ĭs'ra-el unto mount [i]Căr'mel,
and the prophets of Bā'al four hundred and fifty, [j]and the prophets of
the groves four hundred, which eat at
Jĕz'e-bĕl's table.
20 So Ā'hăb sent unto all the children of Ĭs'ra-el, and [k]gathered the
prophets together unto mount Căr'mel.
21 And E-lī'jah came unto all the
people, and said, [l]How long halt ye between two [5]opinions? if the LORD *be*
God, follow him: but if Bā'al, [m]*then*
follow him. And the people answered
him not a word.
22 Then said E-lī'jah unto the people, [n]I, *even* I only, remain a prophet of
the LORD; but Bā'al's prophets *are* four
hundred and fifty men.
23 Let them therefore give us two
bullocks; and let them choose one

[i]Gen. 21.15-16
13 [j]Gen. 22.1-2; 1 Pet. 1.7
14 [k]Ps. 34.11; Phil. 4.19; 1 Tim. 4.8
[3]giveth
15 [l]2 Chr. 20.20; Matt. 20.28; Heb. 11.8
[4]Or, a full year
16 [m]Deut. 15.10; Prov. 11.24
[5]by the hand of
18 [n]2 Sam. 16.10; Luke 4.34; John 2.4
20 [o]Ex. 15.25; Num. 11.11; 1 Sam. 7.8; ch. 18.36-37; Phil. 4.6; Jas. 5.13-16
21 [p]2 Ki. 4.34-35
[6]measured
[7]into his inward parts
22 [q]Ps. 65.2; Prov. 15.8-29; 1 John 3.22
[r]Deut. 32.39; Heb. 11.35
24 [s]John 3.2; John 16.30

CHAPTER 18
1 [a]Luke 4.25
[b]Deut. 28.12
3 [1]Obadiahu
[2]over his house
[c]Neh. 7.2; Job 28.28
4 [3]Izebel
[d]Matt. 10.40-42
5 [4]that we cut not off ourselves from the beasts
12 [e]Ezek. 3.12-14; Acts 8.39
17 [f]ch. 21.20
[g]Josh. 7.25; Acts 16.20
18 [h]ch. 9.9; 2 Chr. 15.2
19 [i]Jer. 46.18
[j]ch. 16.33
20 [k]ch. 22.6
21 [l]Matt. 6.24; Rev. 3.15
[5]Or, thoughts
[m]Josh. 24.15; Ps. 100.3
22 [n]ch. 19.10-14

bullock for themselves, and cut it in
pieces, and lay *it* on wood, and put no
fire *under:* and I will dress the other
bullock, and lay *it* on wood, and put
no fire *under:*
24 And call ye on the name of your
gods, and I will call on the name of the
LORD: and the God that [o]answereth by
fire, let him be God. And all the people
answered and said, [6]It is well spoken.
25 And E-lī'jah said unto the prophets of Bā'al, Choose you one bullock
for yourselves, and dress *it* first; for ye
are many; and call on the name of your
gods, but put no fire *under.*
26 And they took the bullock which
was given them, and they dressed *it,*
and called on the name of Bā'al from
morning even until noon, saying, O
Bā'al, [7]hear us. But *there was* [p]no
voice, nor any that [8]answered. And
they [9]leaped upon the altar which was
made.
27 And it came to pass at noon, that
E-lī'jah mocked them, and said, Cry
[10]aloud: for he *is* a god; either [11]he is
talking, or he [12]is pursuing, or he is in a
journey, *or* peradventure he sleepeth,
and must be awaked.
28 And they cried aloud, and [q]cut
themselves after their manner with
knives and lancets, till [13]the blood
gushed out upon them.
29 And it came to pass, when midday was past, [r]and they prophesied until the *time* of the [14]offering of the *evening* sacrifice, that *there was* neither
voice, nor any to answer, nor any [15]that
regarded.
30 And E-lī'jah said unto all the people, Come near unto me. And all the
people came near unto him. And he
repaired the altar of the LORD *that was*
broken down.
31 And E-lī'jah took twelve stones,
according to the number of the tribes
of the sons of Jā'cob, unto whom the
word of the LORD came, saying, [s]Is'ra-
el shall be thy name:
32 And with the stones he built an
altar [t]in the name of the LORD: and he
made a trench about the altar, as great
as would contain two measures of seed.
33 And he [u]put the wood in order,
and cut the bullock in pieces, and laid
him on the wood, and said, Fill four
barrels with water, and [v]pour *it* on the
burnt sacrifice, and on the wood.
34 And he said, Do *it* the second
time. And they did *it* the second time.
And he said, Do *it* the third time. And
they did *it* the third time.
35 And the water [16]ran round about
the altar; and he filled the trench also
with water.
36 And it came to pass at [w]*the time
of* the offering of the *evening* sacrifice,
that E-lī'jah the prophet came near,
and said, LORD [x]God of Ā'bră-hăm,
Ī'saac, and of Ĭs'ra-el, [y]let it be known
this day that thou *art* God in Ĭs'ra-el,
and *that* I *am* thy servant, and *that* [z]I
have done all these things at thy word.
37 Hear me, O LORD, hear me, that
this people may know that thou *art* the
LORD God, and *that* thou hast [a]turned
their heart back again.
38 Then [b]the fire of the LORD fell,
and consumed the burnt sacrifice, and
the wood, and the stones, and the dust,
and licked up the water that *was* in the
trench.
39 And when all the people saw *it,*
they fell on their faces: and they said,
The LORD, he *is* the God; the LORD, he
is the God.
40 And E-lī'jah said unto them,
[17]Take the prophets of Bā'al; let not
one of them escape. And they took
them: and E-lī'jah brought them down
to the brook Kī'shon, and [c]slew them
there.
41 ¶ And E-lī'jah said unto Ā'hăb,
Get thee up, eat and drink; for *there is*
[18]a sound of abundance of rain.
42 So Ā'hăb went up to eat and to
drink. And E-lī'jah went up to the top
of Cär'mel; [d]and he cast himself down
upon the earth, and put his face between his knees,
43 And said to his servant, Go up
now, look toward the sea. And he went
up, and looked, and said, *There is* nothing. And he said, [e]Go again seven
times.
44 And it came to pass at the seventh time, that he said, Behold, there
ariseth a little cloud out of the sea, like
a man's hand. And he said, Go up, say
unto Ā'hăb, [19]Prepare *thy chariot,* and
get thee down, that the rain stop thee
not.
45 And it came to pass in the mean
while, that the heaven was black with
clouds and wind, and there was a great
rain. And Ā'hăb rode, and went to
Jĕz're-el.
46 And [f]the hand of the LORD was
on E-lī'jah; and he girded up his loins,
and ran before Ā'hăb [20]to the entrance
of Jĕz're-el.

19

And Ā'hăb told Jĕz'e-bĕl all that
E-lī'jah had done, and withal how
he had [a]slain all the prophets with the
sword.
2 Then Jĕz'e-bĕl sent a messenger
unto E-lī'jah, saying, [b]So let the gods
do *to me,* and more also, if I make not
thy life as the life of one of them by [c]to
morrow about this time.
3 And when he saw *that,* he arose,
and went for his life, and came to Bē'-
er–shē'bȧ, which *belongeth* to Jū'dah,
and left his servant there.
4 ¶ But he himself went a day's journey into the wilderness, and came and
sat down under a juniper tree: and he
[d]requested [1]for himself that he might
die; and said, It is enough; now, O
LORD, take away my life; for I *am* not
better than my fathers.
5 And as he lay and slept under a
juniper tree, behold, then [e]an angel
touched him, and said unto him, Arise
and eat.
6 And he looked, and, behold, *there
was* a cake baken on the coals, and
a cruse of water at his [2]head. And he
did eat and drink, and laid him down
again.

24 [o]Lev. 9.24; 1 Chr. 21.26; 2 Chr. 7.1 [6]The word is good
26 [7]Or, answer [p]Ps. 115.5; Jer. 10.5; 1 Cor. 8.4 [8]Or, heard [9]Or, leaped up and down at the altar
27 [10]with a great voice [11]Or, he meditateth [12]hath a pursuit
28 [q]Lev. 19.28 [13]poured out blood upon them
29 [r]1 Cor. 11.4-5 [14]ascending [15]attention
31 [s]Gen. 32.28
32 [t]Col. 3.17
33 [u]Lev. 1.6 [v]Judg. 6.20
35 [16]went
36 [w]Ex. 29.39 [x]Gen. 28.13; Ex. 3.6; Matt. 22.32; Heb. 11.16 [y]ch. 8.43; 2 Ki. 19.19; Ps. 83.18 [z]Num. 16.28
37 [a]Jer. 10.23
38 [b]Lev. 9.24; Judg. 6.21; 2 Chr. 7.1
40 [17]Or, Apprehend [c]Deut. 13.5; Rev. 19.20
41 [18]Or, a sound of a noise of rain
42 [d]Jas. 5.17
43 [e]Hab. 2.3
44 [19]Tie, or, Bind
46 [f]2 Ki. 3.15; Ezek. 1.3 [20]till thou come to Jezreel

CHAPTER 19
1 [a]ch. 18.40
2 [b]Ruth 1.17; ch. 2.23 [c]Prov. 27.1
4 [d]Num. 11.15; Jon. 4.3-8; Phil. 1.21-24 [1]for his life
5 [e]Ps. 34.7; Acts 12.7; Heb. 1.14
6 [2]bolster

7 And the angel of the LORD came
again the second time, and touched
him, and said, Arise *and* eat; because
the journey *is* too great for thee.
8 And he arose, and did eat and
drink, and went in the strength of that
meat [f]forty days and forty nights unto
[g]Hō'reb the mount of God.
9 ¶ And he came thither [h]unto a
cave, and lodged there; and, behold,
the word of the LORD *came* to him, and
he said unto him, What doest thou
here, E-lī'jah?
10 And he said, [i]I have been very
[j]jealous for the LORD God of hosts: for
the children of Ĭs'ra-el have forsaken
thy covenant, thrown down thine altars, and [k]slain thy prophets with the
sword; and [l]I, *even* I only, am left; and
they seek my life, to take it away.
11 And he said, Go forth, and stand
[m]upon the mount before the LORD.
And, behold, the LORD passed by, and
[n]a great and strong wind rent the
mountains, and brake in pieces the
rocks before the LORD; *but* the LORD
was not in the wind: and after the wind
an earthquake; *but* the LORD *was* not
in the earthquake:
12 And after the earthquake a fire;
but the LORD *was* not in the fire: and
after the fire a [o]still small voice.
13 And it was *so*, when E-lī'jah heard
it, that [p]he wrapped his face in his mantle, and went out, and stood in the entering in of the cave. And, behold, *there*
came a voice unto him, and said, What
doest thou here, E-lī'jah?
14 And he said, I have been very jealous for the LORD God of hosts: because
the children of Ĭs'ra-el have forsaken
thy covenant, thrown down thine altars, and slain thy prophets with the
sword; and I, *even* I only, am left; and
they seek my life, to take it away.
15 And the LORD said unto him, Go,
return on thy way to the wilderness of
Da-măs'cus: [q]and when thou comest,
anoint Hăz'a-el *to be* king over Sȳr'ĭ-ȧ:
16 And [r]Jē'hū the son of Nĭm'shī
shalt thou anoint *to be* king over Ĭs'ra-
el: and [s]E-lī'shȧ the son of Shā'phat of
Ā'bel-me-hō'lah shalt thou anoint *to*
be prophet in thy room.
17 And [t]it shall come to pass, *that*
him that escapeth the sword of Hăz'a-
el shall Jē'hū slay: and him that escapeth from the sword of Jē'hū [u]shall
E-lī'shȧ slay.
18 [3]Yet I [v]have left *me* seven thousand in Ĭs'ra-el, all the knees which
have not bowed unto Bā'al, [w]and every mouth which hath not kissed him.
19 ¶ So he departed thence, and
found E-lī'shȧ the son of Shā'phat, who
was plowing *with* twelve yoke *of oxen*
before him, and he with the twelfth:
and E-lī'jah passed by him, and cast his
mantle upon him.
20 And he left the oxen, and ran after E-lī'jah, and said, Let me, I pray
thee, kiss my father and my mother,
and *then* I will follow thee. And he said
unto him, [4]Go back again: for what
have I done to thee?

8 [f]Ex. 24.18; Deut. 9.9-18; Luke 4.2
[g]Ex. 3.1
9 [h]Ex. 33.21
10 [i]Rom. 11.3
[j]Ex. 20.5; Ps. 69.9
[k]ch. 18.4
[l]ch. 18.22; Rom. 11.3
11 [m]Ex. 24.12
[n]Ezek. 1.4
12 [o]Num. 14.18; Jas. 5.11
13 [p]Ex. 3.6; Isa. 6.2
15 [q]2 Ki. 8.12-13
16 [r]2 Ki. 9.1
[s]Luke 4.27, called Eliseus
17 [t]2 Ki. 8.12; Amos 2.14
[u]2 Ki. 2.23-24; Rev. 19.21
18 [3]Or, I will leave
[v]Isa. 1.9; Rom. 11.4
[w]Job 31.27; Hos. 13.2
20 [4]Go return
21 [x]2 Sam. 24.22
[y]Matt. 4.18-22; Luke 5.27-28
[z]Ex. 24.13
CHAPTER 20
1 [a]Gen. 14.1-2; 2 Ki. 8.7-15
4 [b]Deut. 28.48
6 [1]desirable
7 [c]Ex. 3.16; Lev. 4.15
[2]I kept not back from him
10 [d]ch. 19.2; Acts 23.12
[3]are at my feet
11 [e]Prov. 27.1; Eccl. 7.8
12 [4]word
[f]ch. 16.9; Eccl. 10.17
[5]Or, tents
[6]Or, Place the engines: And they placed engines
13 [7]approached
[g]Ex. 7.17; Ps. 9.16

21 And he returned back from him,
and took a yoke of oxen, and slew
them, and [x]boiled their flesh with the
instruments of the oxen, and gave unto
the people, and they did eat. [y]Then
he arose, and went after E-lī'jah, and
[z]ministered unto him.

20

And Bĕn–hā'dăd the king of Sȳr'-
ĭ-ȧ gathered all his host together:
[a]and *there were* thirty and two kings
with him, and horses, and chariots: and
he went up and besieged Sa-mā'rĭ-ȧ,
and warred against it.
2 And he sent messengers to Ā'hăb
king of Ĭs'ra-el into the city, and said
unto him, Thus saith Bĕn–hā'dăd,
3 Thy silver and thy gold *is* mine;
thy wives also and thy children, *even*
the goodliest, *are* mine.
4 And the king of Ĭs'ra-el answered
and said, My lord, O king, according to
thy saying, [b]I *am* thine, and all that I
have.
5 And the messengers came again,
and said, Thus speaketh Bĕn–hā'dăd,
saying, Although I have sent unto thee,
saying, Thou shalt deliver me thy silver, and thy gold, and thy wives, and
thy children;
6 Yet I will send my servants unto
thee to morrow about this time, and
they shall search thine house, and the
houses of thy servants; and it shall be,
that whatsoever is [1]pleasant in thine
eyes, they shall put *it* in their hand,
and take *it* away.
7 Then the king of Ĭs'ra-el called all
[c]the elders of the land, and said, Mark,
I pray you, and see how this *man* seeketh mischief: for he sent unto me for
my wives, and for my children, and for
my silver, and for my gold; and [2]I denied him not.
8 And all the elders and all the people said unto him, Hearken not *unto*
him, nor consent.
9 Wherefore he said unto the messengers of Bĕn–hā'dăd, Tell my lord
the king, All that thou didst send for to
thy servant at the first I will do: but this
thing I may not do. And the messengers departed, and brought him word
again.
10 And Bĕn–hā'dăd sent unto him,
and said, [d]The gods do so unto me,
and more also, if the dust of Sa-mā'rĭ-ȧ
shall suffice for handfuls for all the people that [3]follow me.
11 And the king of Ĭs'ra-el answered
and said, Tell *him*, [e]Let not him that
girdeth on *his harness* boast himself as
he that putteth it off.
12 And it came to pass, when *Bĕn–*
hā'dăd heard this [4]message, as he *was*
[f]drinking, he and the kings in the [5]pa-
vilions, that he said unto his servants,
[6]Set *yourselves in array*. And they set
themselves in array against the city.
13 ¶ And, behold, there [7]came a
prophet unto Ā'hăb king of Ĭs'ra-el,
saying, Thus saith the LORD, Hast thou
seen all this great multitude? behold, I
will deliver it into thine hand this day;
and [g]thou shalt know that I *am* the
LORD.

14 And Ā'hăb said, By whom? And he said, Thus saith the LORD, *Even* by the [8]young men of the princes of the provinces. Then he said, Who shall [9]order the battle? And he answered, Thou.

15 Then he numbered the young men of the princes of the provinces, and they were two hundred and thirty two: and after them he numbered all the people, *even* all the children of Ĭs'ra-el, *being* seven thousand.

16 And they went out at noon. But Bĕn–hā'dăd *was* [h]drinking himself drunk in the pavilions, he and the kings, the thirty and two kings that helped him.

17 And the young men of the princes of the provinces went out first; and Bĕn–hā'dăd sent out, and they told him, saying, There are men come out of Sa-mā'rĭ-ȧ.

18 And he said, [i]Whether they be come out for peace, take them alive; or whether they be come out for war, take them alive.

19 So these young men of the princes of the provinces came out of the city, and the army which followed them.

20 And they slew every one his man: and the Sy̆r'ĭ-ans [j]fled; and Ĭs'ra-el pursued them: and [k]Bĕn–hā'dăd the king of Sy̆r'ĭ-ȧ escaped on an horse with the horsemen.

21 And the king of Ĭs'ra-el went out, and smote the horses and chariots, and slew the Sy̆r'ĭ-ans with a great slaughter.

22 ¶ And the prophet came to the king of Ĭs'ra-el, and said unto him, Go, strengthen thyself, and mark, and see what thou doest: [l]for at the return of the year the king of Sy̆r'ĭ-ȧ will come up against thee.

23 And the servants of the king of Sy̆r'ĭ-ȧ said unto him, [m]Their gods *are* gods of the hills; therefore they were stronger than we; but let us fight against them in the plain, and surely we shall be stronger than they.

24 And do this thing, [n]Take the kings away, every man out of his place, and put captains in their rooms:

25 And number thee an army, like the army that [10]thou hast lost, horse for horse, and chariot for chariot: and we will fight against them in the plain, *and* surely we shall be stronger than they. And he hearkened unto their voice, and did so.

26 And it came to pass at the return of the year, that Bĕn–hā'dăd numbered the Sy̆r'ĭ-ans, and went up to [o]Ā'phek, [11]to fight against Ĭs'ra-el.

27 And the children of Ĭs'ra-el were numbered, and [12]were all present, and went against them: and the children of Ĭs'ra-el pitched before them like two little flocks of kids; but the Sy̆r'ĭ-ans [p]filled the country.

28 ¶ And there came a man of God, and spake unto the king of Ĭs'ra-el, and said, Thus saith the LORD, [q]Because the Sy̆r'ĭ-ans have said, The LORD *is* God of the hills, but he *is* not God of the valleys, therefore will I deliver all this great multitude into thine hand, and ye shall know that I *am* the LORD.

29 And they pitched one over against the other seven days. And *so* it was, that in the seventh day the battle was joined: and the children of Ĭs'ra-el slew of the Sy̆r'ĭ-ans an hundred thousand footmen in one day.

30 But the rest fled to Ā'phek, into the city; and *there* a wall fell upon twenty and seven thousand of the men *that were* left. And Bĕn–hā'dăd fled, and came into the city, [13]into an inner chamber.

31 ¶ And his servants said unto him, Behold now, we have heard that the kings of the house of Ĭs'ra-el *are* merciful kings: let us, I pray thee, [r]put sackcloth on our loins, and ropes upon our heads, and go out to the king of Ĭs'ra-el: peradventure he will save thy life.

32 So they girded sackcloth on their loins, and *put* ropes on their heads, and came to the king of Ĭs'ra-el, and said, Thy servant Bĕn–hā'dăd saith, I pray thee, let me live. And he said, *Is* he yet alive? he *is* my brother.

33 Now the men did diligently observe whether *any thing would come* from him, and did hastily catch *it:* and they said, Thy brother Bĕn–hā'dăd. Then he said, Go ye, bring him. Then Bĕn–hā'dăd came forth to him; and he caused him to come up into the chariot.

34 And *Bĕn–hā'dăd* said unto him, [s]The cities, which my father took from thy father, I will restore; and thou shalt make streets for thee in Da-măs'cus, as my father made in Sa-mā'rĭ-ȧ. Then *said Ā'hăb,* I will send thee away with this covenant. So [t]he made a covenant with him, and sent him away.

35 ¶ And a certain man of [u]the sons of the prophets said unto his neighbour [v]in the word of the LORD, Smite me, I pray thee. And the man refused to smite him.

36 Then said he unto him, Because thou hast not obeyed the voice of the LORD, behold, as soon as thou art departed from me, a lion shall slay thee. And as soon as he was departed from him, [w]a lion found him, and slew him.

37 Then he found another man, and said, Smite me, I pray thee. And the man smote him, [14]so that in smiting he wounded *him.*

38 So the prophet departed, and waited for the king by the way, and disguised himself with ashes upon his face.

39 And [x]as the king passed by, he cried unto the king: and [y]he said, Thy servant went out into the midst of the battle; and, behold, a man turned aside, and brought a man unto me, and said, Keep this man:if by any means he be missing, then [z]shall thy life be for his life, or else thou shalt [15]pay a talent of silver.

40 And as thy servant was busy here and there, [16]he was gone. And the king of Ĭs'ra-el said unto him, [a]So *shall* thy judgment *be:* thyself hast decided *it.*

14 [8]Or, servants [9]bind, or, tie
16 [h]ch. 16.9; Prov. 20.1; Dan. 5.2-30; Hos. 4.11; Eph. 5.18
18 [i]1 Sam. 2.3; 2 Ki. 14.8-12; Prov. 16.18; Luke 14.11
20 [j]Lev. 26.8; Ps. 33.16 [k]Job 40.11
22 [l]2 Sam. 11.1; 2 Chr. 36.10
23 [m]2 Chr. 32.13-19; Isa. 42.8; Rom. 1.21-23
24 [n]Job 5.12-13
25 [10]that was fallen
26 [o]Josh. 13.4 [11]to the war with Israel
27 [12]Or, were victualled [p]Judg. 6.5
28 [q]Ex. 20.5; Deut. 4.24; Josh. 24.19; Ps. 33.10; Ps. 47.8; Ps. 149.7; Isa. 30.27-28; Nah. 1.2
30 [13]into a chamber within a chamber, or, from chamber to chamber
31 [r]Gen. 37.34
34 [s]ch. 15.20 [t]Isa. 26.10; Isa. 28.15
35 [u]2 Ki. 2.3-5-7-15 [v]ch. 13.17-18
36 [w]ch. 13.24
37 [14]smiting and wounding
39 [x]2 Sam. 12.1 [y]Judg. 9.7-20; 2 Sam. 14.5-7 [z]2 Ki. 10.24 [15]weigh
40 [16]he was not [a]Job 15.6; Matt. 21.41; Luke 19.22

41 And he hasted, and took the ashes
away from his face; and the king of
Is'ra-el discerned him that he *was* of
the prophets.
42 And he said unto him, Thus saith
the LORD, [b]Because thou hast let go
out of *thy* hand a man [17]whom I appointed to utter destruction, therefore
thy life shall go for his life, and thy
people for his people.
43 And the king of Is'ra-el [c]went to
his house heavy and displeased, and
came to Sa-mā'rĭ-ȧ.
21 And it came to pass after these
things, *that* Nā'bŏth the Jĕz're-
el-īte had a vineyard, which *was* in
[a]Jĕz're-el, hard by the palace of Ā'hăb
king of Sa-mā'rĭ-ȧ.
2 And Ā'hăb spake unto Nā'bŏth,
saying, [b]Give me thy [c]vineyard, that I
may have it for a garden of herbs, because it *is* near unto my house: and I
will give thee for it a better vineyard
than it; *or,* if it [1]seem good to thee, I
will give thee the worth of it in money.
3 And Nā'bŏth said to Ā'hăb, The
LORD forbid it me, [d]that I should give
the inheritance of my fathers unto thee.
4 And Ā'hăb came into his house
heavy and displeased because of the
word which Nā'bŏth the Jĕz're-el-īte
had spoken to him: for he had said, I
will not give thee the inheritance of my
fathers. And he laid him down upon
his bed, and turned away his face, and
would eat no bread.
5 ¶ But Jĕz'e-bĕl his wife came to
him, and said unto him, Why is thy
spirit so sad, that thou eatest no bread?
6 And he said unto her, Because I
spake unto Nā'bŏth the Jĕz're-el-īte,
and said unto him, Give me thy vineyard for money; or else, if it please
thee, I will give thee *another* vineyard
for it: and he answered, I will not give
thee my vineyard.
7 And Jĕz'e-bĕl his wife said unto
him, Dost thou [e]now govern the kingdom of Is'ra-el? arise, *and* eat bread,
and let thine heart be merry: I [f]will
give thee the vineyard of Nā'bŏth the
Jĕz're-el-īte.
8 So she wrote letters in Ā'hăb's
name, and sealed *them* with his seal,
and sent the letters unto the elders and
to the nobles that *were* in his city,
dwelling with Nā'bŏth.
9 And she wrote in the letters, saying, [2]Proclaim a fast, and set Nā'bŏth
[3]on high among the people:
10 And set two men, [g]sons of Bē'lĭ-
al, before him, to bear witness against
him, saying, Thou [h]didst blaspheme
God and the king. And *then* carry him
out, and [i]stone him, that he may die.
11 And the men of his city, *even* the
elders and the nobles who were the inhabitants in his city, did as Jĕz'e-bĕl
had sent unto them, *and* as it *was* written in the letters which she had sent
unto them.
12 [j]They proclaimed a fast, and set
Nā'bŏth on high among the people.
13 And there came in two men, children of Bē'lĭ-al, and sat before him: and
the men of Bē'lĭ-al witnessed against
him, *even* against Nā'bŏth, in the presence of the people, saying, Nā'bŏth did
blaspheme God and the king. [k]Then
they carried him forth out of the city,
and stoned him with stones, that he
died.
14 Then they sent to Jĕz'e-bĕl, saying, Nā'bŏth is stoned, and is dead.
15 ¶ And it came to pass, when Jĕz'e-
bĕl heard that Nā'bŏth was stoned, and
was dead, that Jĕz'e-bĕl said to Ā'hăb,
Arise, take possession of the vineyard
of Nā'bŏth the Jĕz're-el-īte, which he
refused to give thee for money: for
Nā'bŏth is not alive, but dead.
16 And it came to pass, when Ā'hăb
heard that Nā'bŏth was dead, that
Ā'hăb rose up to go down to the vineyard of Nā'bŏth the Jĕz're-el-īte, to
take possession of it.
17 ¶ [l]And the word of the LORD came
to E-lī'jah the Tĭsh'bīte, saying,
18 Arise, go down to meet Ā'hăb
king of Is'ra-el, [m]which *is* in Sa-mā'rĭ-
ȧ: behold, *he is* in the vineyard of Nā'-
bŏth, whither he is gone down to possess it.
19 And thou shalt speak unto him,
saying, Thus saith the LORD, [n]Hast
thou killed, and also taken possession?
And thou shalt speak unto him, saying,
Thus saith the LORD, [o]In the place
where dogs licked the blood of Nā'-
bŏth shall dogs lick thy blood, even
thine.
20 And Ā'hăb said to E-lī'jah, Hast
thou found me, [p]O mine enemy? And
he answered, I have found *thee:* because [q]thou hast sold thyself to work
evil in the sight of the LORD.
21 Behold, [r]I will bring evil upon
thee, and will take away thy posterity,
and will cut off from Ā'hăb [s]him that
pisseth against the wall, and [t]him that
is shut up and left in Is'ra-el,
22 And will make thine house like
the house of [u]Jĕr-o-bō'am the son of
Nē'băt, and like the house of [v]Bā'a-
shȧ the son of A-hī'jah, for the provocation wherewith thou hast provoked *me*
to anger, and made Is'ra-el to sin.
23 And [w]of Jĕz'e-bĕl also spake the
LORD, saying, The dogs shall eat Jĕz'e-
bĕl by the [4]wall of Jĕz're-el.
24 [x]Him that dieth of Ā'hăb in the
city the dogs shall eat; and him that
dieth in the field shall the fowls of the
air eat.
25 ¶ But [y]there was none like unto
Ā'hăb, which did sell himself to work
wickedness in the sight of the LORD,
[z]whom Jĕz'e-bĕl his wife [5]stirred up.
26 And he did very abominably in
following idols, according to all *things*
[a]as did the Ăm'ôr-ītes, whom the LORD
cast out before the children of Is'ra-el.
27 And it came to pass, when Ā'hăb
heard those words, that he rent his
clothes, and [b]put sackcloth upon his
flesh, and fasted, and lay in sackcloth,
and went softly.
28 And the word of the LORD came
to E-lī'jah the Tĭsh'bīte, saying,

42 [b]1 Sam. 15.9; ch. 22.31-37
[17]of my curse
43 [c]ch. 21.4; Esth. 5.13; Job 5.2; Prov. 19.3

CHAPTER 21

1 [a]Judg. 6.33; 1 Sam. 29.1
2 [b]Gen. 3.6; Ex. 20.17; Deut. 5.21; Hab. 2.9; Luke 12.15; 1 Tim. 6.9-10; Jas. 1.14-15
[c]1 Sam. 8.14
[1]be good in thine eyes
3 [d]Lev. 25.23; Ezek. 46.18
7 [e]1 Sam. 8.14
[f]Jer. 6.7; Mic. 2.1
9 [2]Or, Call an assembly
[3]in the top of the people
10 [g]Deut. 13.13; 2 Cor. 6.15
[h]Ex. 22.28; Acts 6.11
[i]Lev. 24.14
12 [j]Job 15.34; 1 Tim. 4.2
13 [k]Num. 15.36; Heb. 11.37
17 [l]Ps. 9.12
18 [m]ch. 13.32
19 [n]Gen. 4.9-11
[o]ch. 22.38
20 [p]ch. 18.17; Amos 5.10
[q]2 Ki. 17.17; Rom. 7.14
21 [r]ch. 14.10; Ps. 94
[s]1 Sam. 25.22
[t]ch. 14.10
22 [u]ch. 15.29
[v]ch. 16.3-11
23 [w]2 Ki. 9.36; Ps. 7.16
[4]Or, ditch
24 [x]ch. 14.11
25 [y]ch. 16.30
[z]ch. 11.1-4; Gen. 6.2-5
[5]Or, incited
26 [a]2 Ki. 21.11; Gen. 15.16
27 [b]Gen. 37.34

29 Seest thou how Ā'hăb [c]humbleth
himself before me? because he humbleth himself before me, I will not bring
the evil in his days: *but* [d]in his son's
days will I bring the evil upon his
house.

22

22 And they continued three years
without war between Sy̆r'ĭ-ȧ and
Ĭs'ra-el.
2 And it came to pass in the third
year, that [a]Je-hosh'a-phat the king of
Jū'dah came down to the king of Ĭs'ra-
el.
3 And the king of Ĭs'ra-el said unto
his servants, Know ye that [b]Rā'moth
in Gĭl'e-ăd *is* ours, and we *be* [1]still, *and*
take it not out of the hand of the king of
Sy̆r'ĭ-ȧ?
4 And he said unto Je-hŏsh'a-phăt,
Wilt thou go with me to battle to
Rā'moth–gĭl'e-ăd? And Je-hŏsh'a-phăt
said to the king of Ĭs'ra-el, [c]I *am* as thou
art, my people as thy people, my horses
as thy horses.
5 And Je-hŏsh'a-phăt said unto the
king of Ĭs'ra-el, Inquire, I pray thee, at
the word of the LORD to day.
6 Then the king of Ĭs'ra-el [d]gathered
the prophets together, about [2]four hundred men, and said unto them, Shall I
go against Rā'moth–gĭl'e-ăd to battle,
or shall I forbear? And they said, Go
up; for the Lord shall deliver *it* into the
hand of the king.
7 And [e]Je-hŏsh'a-phăt said, *Is there*
not here a prophet of the LORD besides,
that we might inquire of him?
8 And the king of Ĭs'ra-el said unto
Je-hŏsh'a-phăt, [f]*There is* yet one man,
Mī-cā'iah the son of Ĭm'lah, by whom
we may inquire of the LORD: but [g]I
hate him; for he doth not prophesy
good concerning me, but evil. And Je-
hŏsh'a-phăt said, Let not the king say
so.
9 Then the king of Ĭs'ra-el called an
[3]officer, and said, Hasten *hither* Mī-
cā'iah the son of Ĭm'lah.
10 And the king of Ĭs'ra-el and Je-
hŏsh'a-phăt the king of Jū'dah sat each
on his throne, having put on their robes,
in a [4]void place in the entrance of the
gate of Sa-mā'rĭ-ȧ; and all the prophets
prophesied before them.
11 And Zĕd-e-kī'ah the son of Chĕ-
nā'ă-nah made him horns of iron: and
he said, Thus saith the LORD, With
these shalt thou push the Sy̆r'ĭ-ans, until thou have consumed them.
12 And all the prophets prophesied
so, saying, [h]Go up to Rā'moth–gĭl'e-
ăd, and prosper: for the LORD shall deliver *it* into the king's hand.
13 And the messenger that was gone
to call Mī-cā'iah spake unto him, saying, Behold now, the words of the
prophets *declare* good unto the king
with one mouth: let thy word, I pray
thee, be like the word of one of them,
and speak *that which is* good.
14 And Mī-cā'iah said, *As* the LORD
liveth, [i]what the LORD saith unto me,
that will I speak.
15 ¶ So he came to the king. And the
king said unto him, Mī-cā'iah, shall we

29 [c]Ps. 78.34-37
[d]2 Ki. 9.25
CHAPTER 22
2 [a]2 Chr. 18.2-34
3 [b]Deut. 4.43
[1]silent from taking it
4 [c]2 Ki. 3.7
6 [d]ch. 18.19
[2]They were prophets of the groves, hirelings of Jezebel
7 [e]2 Ki. 3.11
8 [f]ch. 19.10
[g]ch. 20.43
9 [3]Or, eunuch
10 [4]floor
12 [h]Jer. 23.25-32
14 [i]Num. 22.38; Ps. 27; Ps. 56.1-10; Prov. 28.1; Jer. 1.7-17-19; Ezek. 2.3-8; Acts 4.13-29-31; Acts 9.29; Rom. 8.31; 2 Cor. 3.12; Gal. 1.9-10; Eph. 6.19-20; Phil. 1.20; 1 Thess. 2.2-6; 1 Tim. 3.13; 2 Tim. 4.1-5; Tit. 1.9-10; Heb. 13.5-6
17 [j]Matt. 9.36
19 [k]Isa. 6.1; Dan. 7.9
[l]Job 1.6; Ps. 103.20; Dan. 7.10; Zech. 1.10; Matt. 18.10; Heb. 1.7-14
20 [5]Or, deceive
22 [m]Job 12.16; Ezek. 14.9; 2 Thess. 2.11
23 [n]Ezek. 14.9
24 [o]Jer. 28.16
[p]2 Chr. 18.23
25 [6]Or, from chamber to chamber
[7]a chamber in a chamber
28 [q]Num. 16.29; Deut. 18.20
30 [8]Or, when he was to disguise himself, and enter into the battle
[r]2 Chr. 35.22

go against Rā'moth–gĭl'e-ăd to battle,
or shall we forbear? And he answered
him, Go, and prosper: for the LORD
shall deliver *it* into the hand of the
king.
16 And the king said unto him, How
many times shall I adjure thee that
thou tell me nothing but *that which is*
true in the name of the LORD?
17 And he said, I saw all Ĭs'ra-el [j]scat-
tered upon the hills, as sheep that have
not a shepherd: and the LORD said,
These have no master: let them return
every man to his house in peace.
18 And the king of Ĭs'ra-el said unto
Je-hŏsh'a-phăt, Did I not tell thee that
he would prophesy no good concerning me, but evil?
19 And he said, Hear thou therefore
the word of the LORD: [k]I saw the LORD
sitting on his throne, [l]and all the host
of heaven standing by him on his right
hand and on his left.
20 And the LORD said, Who shall
[5]persuade Ā'hăb, that he may go up
and fall at Rā'moth–gĭl'e-ăd? And one
said on this manner, and another said
on that manner.
21 And there came forth a spirit,
and stood before the LORD, and said, I
will persuade him.
22 And the LORD said unto him,
Wherewith? And he said, I will go
forth, and I will be a lying spirit in the
mouth of all his prophets. And he said,
[m]Thou shalt persuade *him*, and prevail
also: go forth, and do so.
23 [n]Now therefore, behold, the LORD
hath put a lying spirit in the mouth of
all these thy prophets, and the LORD
hath spoken evil concerning thee.
24 But Zĕd-e-kī'ah the son of Chĕ-
nā'ă-nah went near, and [o]smote Mī-
cā'iah on the cheek, and said, [p]Which
way went the Spirit of the LORD from
me to speak unto thee?
25 And Mī-cā'iah said, Behold, thou
shalt see in that day, when thou shalt
go [6]into [7]an inner chamber to hide thyself.
26 And the king of Ĭs'ra-el said, Take
Mī-cā'iah, and carry him back unto
Ā'mon the governor of the city, and to
Jō'ăsh the king's son;
27 And say, Thus saith the king, Put
this *fellow* in the prison, and feed him
with bread of affliction and with water
of affliction, until I come in peace.
28 And Mī-cā'iah said, If thou return
at all in peace, [q]the LORD hath not
spoken by me. And he said, Hearken,
O people, every one of you.
29 So the king of Ĭs'ra-el and Je-
hŏsh'a-phăt the king of Jū'dah went
up to Rā'moth–gĭl'e-ăd.
30 And the king of Ĭs'ra-el said unto
Je-hŏsh'a-phăt, [8]I will disguise myself,
and enter into the battle; but put thou
on thy robes. And the king of Ĭs'ra-el
[r]disguised himself, and went into the
battle.
31 But the king of Sy̆r'ĭ-ȧ commanded his thirty and two captains
that had rule over his chariots, saying,

Fight neither with small nor great, save only with the king of Ĭs'ra-el.

32 And it came to pass, when the captains of the chariots saw Je-hŏsh'a-phăt, that they said, Surely it *is* the king of Ĭs'ra-el. And they turned aside to fight against him: and Je-hŏsh'a-phăt [s]cried out.

33 And it came to pass, when the captains of the chariots perceived that it *was* not the king of Ĭs'ra-el, that they turned back from pursuing him.

34 And a *certain* man drew a bow [9]at a venture, and smote the king of Ĭs'ra-el between the [10]joints of the harness: wherefore he said unto the driver of his chariot, Turn thine hand, and carry me out of the host; for I am [11]wounded.

35 And the battle [12]increased that day: and the king was stayed up in his chariot against the Sȳr'ĭ-ans, and died at even: and the blood ran out of the wound into the [13]midst of the chariot.

36 And there went a proclamation throughout the host about the going down of the sun, saying, Every man to his city, and every man to his own country.

37 ¶ So the king died, and [14]was brought to Sa-mā'rĭ-ȧ; and they buried the king in Sa-mā'rĭ-ȧ.

38 And *one* washed the chariot in the pool of Sa-mā'rĭ-ȧ; and the dogs licked up his blood; and they washed his armour; according [t]unto the word of the LORD which he spake.

39 Now the rest of the acts of Ā'hăb, and all that he did, and [u]the ivory house which he made, and all the cities that he built, *are* they not written in the book of the chronicles of the kings of Ĭs'ra-el?

40 So Ā'hăb slept with his fathers; and Ā-ha-zī'ah his son reigned in his stead.

41 ¶ And [v]Je-hŏsh'a-phăt the son of Ā'sȧ began to reign over Jū'dah in the fourth year of Ā'hăb king of Ĭs'ra-el.

42 Je-hŏsh'a-phăt *was* thirty and five years old when he began to reign; and he reigned twenty and five years in Je-ru'sa-lĕm. And his mother's name *was* A-zū'bah the daughter of Shĭl'hī.

43 And [w]he walked in all the ways of Ā'sȧ his father; he turned not aside from it, doing *that which was* right in the eyes of the LORD: nevertheless [x]the high places were not taken away; *for* the people offered and burnt incense yet in the high places.

44 And [y]Je-hŏsh'a-phăt made peace with the king of Ĭs'ra-el.

45 Now the rest of the acts of Je-hŏsh'a-phăt, and his might that he shewed, and how he warred, *are* they not written in the book of the chronicles of the kings of Jū'dah?

46 [z]And the remnant of the sodomites, which remained in the days of his father Ā'sȧ, he took out of the land.

47 [a]*There was* then no king in Ē'dom: a deputy *was* king.

48 Je-hŏsh'a-phăt [15b]made ships of Thär'shish to go to Ō'phĭr for gold: [c]but they went not; for the ships were broken at [d]Ē'zĭ-on–ğē'bĕr.

49 Then said Ā-ha-zī'ah the son of Ā'hăb unto Je-hŏsh'a-phăt, Let my servants go with thy servants in the ships. But Je-hŏsh'a-phăt would not.

50 ¶ And [e]Je-hŏsh'a-phăt slept with his fathers, and was buried with his fathers in the city of Dā'vid his father: and Je-hō'ram his son reigned in his stead.

51 ¶ Ā-ha-zī'ah the son of Ā'hăb began to reign over Ĭs'ra-el in Sa-mā'rĭ-ȧ the seventeenth year of Je-hŏsh'a-phăt king of Jū'dah, and reigned two years over Ĭs'ra-el.

52 And he did evil in the sight of the LORD, and [f]walked in the way of his father, and in the way of his mother, and in the way of Jĕr-o-bō'am the son of Nē'băt, who made Ĭs'ra-el to sin:

53 For [g]he served Bā'al, and worshipped him, and provoked to anger the LORD God of Ĭs'ra-el, according to all that his father had done.

32 [s]2 Chr. 18.31; Prov. 13.20
34 [9]in his simplicity [10]joints and the breastplate [11]made sick
35 [12]ascended [13]bosom
37 [14]came
38 [t]Deut. 32.35; ch. 21.19; Ps. 33.11; Ps. 119.89; Isa. 14.27; Nah. 1.2; Matt. 24.35; 1 Pet. 1.25
39 [u]Amos 3.15
41 [v]2 Chr. 20.31
43 [w]2 Chr. 17.3 [x]ch. 14.23; Deut. 12.5-14
44 [y]2 Chr. 19.2; 2 Cor. 6.14
46 [z]Gen. 13.13; ch. 14.24; Jude 7
47 [a]Gen. 25.23; 2 Sam. 8.14; 2 Ki. 3.9
48 [15]Or, had ten ships [b]2 Chr. 20.36 [c]2 Chr. 20.37 [d]ch. 9.26
50 [e]2 Chr. 21.1
52 [f]ch. 15.26
53 [g]Judg. 2.11; ch. 16.31

THE SECOND BOOK OF THE KINGS

1 Then Mō'ab [a]rebelled against Ĭs'ra-el [b]after the death of Ā'hăb.

2 And Ā-ha-zī'ah fell down through a lattice in his upper chamber that *was* in Sa-mā'rĭ-ȧ, and was sick: and he sent messengers, and said unto them, Go, inquire [1]of Bā'al–zē'bŭb the god of [c]Ĕk'rŏn whether I shall recover of this disease.

3 But the angel of the LORD said to E-lī'jah the Tĭsh'bīte, Arise, go up to meet the messengers of the king of Sa-mā'rĭ-ȧ, and say unto them, [d]*Is it* not because *there is* not a God in Ĭs'ra-el, *that* ye go to inquire of Bā'al–zē'bŭb the god of Ĕk'rŏn?

4 Now therefore thus saith the LORD, [2]Thou shalt not come down from that bed on which thou art gone up, [e]but shalt surely die. And E-lī'jah departed.

5 ¶ And when the messengers turned back unto him, he said unto them, Why are ye now turned back?

6 And they said unto him, There came a man up to meet us, and said unto us, Go, turn again unto the king that sent you, and say unto him, Thus saith the LORD, *Is it* not because *there is* not a God in Ĭs'ra-el, *that* thou sendest to inquire of Bā'al–zē'bŭb the god of Ĕk'rŏn? therefore thou shalt not

CHAPTER 1
1 [a]2 Sam. 8.2 [b]ch. 3.5
2 [1]The master of flies [c]1 Sam. 5.10
3 [d]Isa. 8.19; Jer. 2.10-13
4 [2]The bed whither thou art gone up, thou shalt not come down from it [e]Job 18.14-21

come down from that bed on which
thou art gone up, but shalt [f]surely die.
7 And he said unto them, [3]What
manner of man *was he* which came up
to meet you, and told you these words?
8 And they answered him, *He was*
[g]an hairy man, and girt with a girdle of
leather about his loins. And he said, It
is E-lī'jah the Tĭsh'bīte.
9 Then the king [h]sent unto him a
captain of fifty with his fifty. And he
went up to him: and, behold, he sat on
the top of an hill. And he spake unto
him, Thou [i]man of God, the king hath
said, Come down.
10 And E-lī'jah answered and said to
the captain of fifty, If I *be* a man of God,
then [j]let fire come down from heaven,
and consume thee and thy fifty. And
there came down fire from heaven, and
consumed him and his fifty.
11 [k]Again also he sent unto him another captain of fifty with his fifty. And
he answered and said unto him, O man
of God, thus hath the king said, Come
down quickly.
12 And E-lī'jah answered and said
unto them, If I *be* a man of God, let
fire come down from heaven, and consume thee and thy fifty. And the fire of
God came down from heaven, and consumed him and his fifty.
13 ¶ And he sent [l]again a captain of
the third fifty with his fifty. And the
third captain of fifty went up, and came
and [4]fell on his knees before E-lī'jah,
and besought him, and said unto him,
O man of God, I pray thee, let my life,
and the life of these fifty thy servants,
[m]be precious in thy sight.
14 Behold, there came fire down
from heaven, and burnt up the two captains of the former fifties with their fifties: therefore let my life now be precious in thy sight.
15 And the angel of the LORD said
unto E-lī'jah, Go down with him: be
not [n]afraid of him. And he arose, and
went down with him unto the king.
16 And he said unto him, Thus saith
the LORD, Forasmuch as thou hast sent
messengers to inquire of Bā'al-zē'bŭb
the god of Ĕk'rŏn, *is it* not because
there is no God in Ĭs'ra-el to inquire
of his word? therefore thou shalt not
come down off that bed on which thou
art gone up, but shalt surely die.
17 ¶ So he died according to the
word of the LORD which E-lī'jah had
spoken. And [5]Je-hō'ram reigned in his
stead in the second year of Je-hō'ram
the son of Je-hŏsh'a-phăt king of Jū'-
dah; because he had no son.
18 Now the rest of the acts of Ā-ha-
zī'ah which he did, *are* they not written
in the book of the chronicles of the
kings of Ĭs'ra-el?
2 And it came to pass, when the LORD
would [a]take up E-lī'jah into heaven
by a whirlwind, that E-lī'jah went with
[b]E-lī'shȧ from Gĭl'găl.
2 And E-lī'jah said unto E-lī'shȧ,
[c]Tarry here, I pray thee; for the LORD
hath sent me to Bĕth'-el. And E-lī'shȧ
said *unto him*, *As* the LORD liveth, and
[d]*as* thy soul liveth, I will not leave
thee. So they went down to Bĕth'-el.
3 And [e]the sons of the prophets that
were at Beth'-el came forth to E-lī'shȧ,
and said unto him, Knowest thou that
the LORD will take away thy master
from thy head to day? And he said,
Yea, I know *it;* hold ye your peace.
4 And E-lī'jah said unto him, E-lī'-
shȧ, tarry here, I pray thee; for the
LORD hath sent me to Jĕr'ĭ-chō. And he
said, *As* the LORD liveth, and *as* thy
soul liveth, I will not leave thee. So
they came to Jĕr'ĭ-chō.
5 And the sons of the prophets that
were at Jĕr'ĭ-chō came to E-lī'shȧ, and
said unto him, Knowest thou that the
LORD will take away thy master from
thy head to day? And he answered,
Yea, I know *it:* hold ye your peace.
6 And E-lī'jah said unto him, Tarry,
I pray thee, here; for the LORD hath
sent me to Jôr'dan. And he said, *As* the
LORD liveth, and *as* thy soul liveth, I
will not leave thee. And they two went
on.
7 And fifty men of the sons of the
prophets went, and stood [1]to view afar
off: and they two stood by Jôr'dan.
8 And E-lī'jah took his mantle, and
wrapped *it* together, and smote the waters, and [f]they were divided hither and
thither, so that they two went over on
dry ground.
9 ¶ And it came to pass, when they
were gone over, that E-lī'jah said unto
E-lī'shȧ, Ask what I shall do for thee,
before I be taken away from thee. And
E-lī'shȧ said, I pray thee, let a [g]double
portion of thy spirit be upon me.
10 And he said, [2]Thou hast asked a
hard thing: *nevertheless,* if thou [h]see
me *when I am* taken from thee, it shall
be so unto thee; but if not, it shall not
be *so.*
11 And it came to pass, as they still
went on, and talked, that, behold, *there
appeared* [i]a chariot of fire, and horses
of fire, and parted them both asunder;
and E-lī'jah went up by a whirlwind
into heaven.
12 ¶ And E-lī'shȧ saw *it,* and he cried,
[j]My father, my father, the chariot of
Ĭs'ra-el, and the horsemen thereof. And
he [k]saw him no more: and he took hold
of his own clothes, and [l]rent them in
two pieces.
13 He took up also the mantle of E-
lī'jah that fell from him, and went back
and stood by the [3]bank of Jôr'dan;
14 And he took the mantle of E-lī'-
jah that fell from him, and [m]smote the
waters, and said, Where *is* the LORD
God of E-lī'jah? and when he also had
smitten the waters, they parted hither
and thither: and E-lī'shȧ went over.
15 And when the sons of the prophets which *were* to view at Jĕr'ĭ-chō saw
him, they said, The spirit of E-lī'jah
doth rest on E-lī'shȧ. And they came to
meet him, and bowed themselves to
the ground before him.
16 ¶ And they said unto him, Behold
now, there be with thy servants fifty
[4]strong men; let them go, we pray thee,

6 [f]Prov. 14.32
7 [3]What was the manner of the man?
8 [g]Zech. 13.4; Matt. 3.4
9 [h]ch. 6.13-14; Ps. 105.15
[i]Amos 7.12; Matt. 27.29
10 [j]Num. 11.1; Luke 9.54
11 [k]Isa. 26.11
13 [l]Prov. 27.22; Eccl. 9.3; Isa. 1.5; Jer. 5.3
[4]bowed
[m]1 Sam. 26.21; Ps. 72.14
15 [n]Isa. 51.12; Jer. 1.17; Ezek. 2.6
17 [5]The second year that Jehoram was Prorex, and the eighteenth of Jehoshaphat
CHAPTER 2
1 [a]Gen. 5.24; Heb. 11.5
[b]1 Ki. 19.21
2 [c]Ruth 1.15-16
[d]1 Sam. 1.26; ch. 4.30
3 [e]1 Sam. 19.20; 1 Ki. 20.35; ch. 4.1-38
7 [1]in sight, or, over against
8 [f]Ex. 14.21; Josh. 3.16
9 [g]Num. 11.17-25
10 [2]Thou hast done hard in asking
[h]Acts 1.10
11 [i]ch. 6.17; Ps. 68.17; Heb. 1.7-14
12 [j]ch. 13.14
[k]Acts 1.9
[l]Gen. 37.29-34; Josh. 7.6
13 [3]lip
14 [m]John 14.12
16 [4]sons of strength

and seek thy master: [n]lest peradventure the Spirit of the LORD hath taken him up, and cast him upon [5]some mountain, or into some valley. And he said, Ye shall not send.

17 And when they urged him till he was ashamed, he said, Send. They sent therefore fifty men; and they sought three days, but found him not.

18 And when they came again to him, (for he tarried at Jĕr'ĭ-chō,) he said unto them, Did I not say unto you, Go not?

19 ¶ And the men of the city said unto E-lī'shȧ, Behold, I pray thee, the situation of this city *is* pleasant, as my lord seeth: but the [o]water *is* naught, and the ground [6]barren.

20 And he said, Bring me a new cruse, and put salt therein. And they brought *it* to him.

21 And he went forth unto the spring of the waters, and [p]cast the salt in there, and said, Thus saith the LORD, I have healed these waters; there shall not be from thence any more death or barren *land*.

22 So the waters were healed unto this day, according to the saying of E-lī'shȧ which he spake.

23 ¶ And he went up from thence unto Bĕth'–el: and as he was going up by the way, there came forth little children out of the city, and [q]mocked him, and said unto him, Go up, thou bald head; go up, thou bald head.

24 And he turned back, and looked on them, and cursed them in the name of the LORD. And there came forth two she bears out of the wood, [r]and tare forty and two children of them.

25 And he went from thence to mount Căr'mel, and from thence he returned to Sa-mā'rĭ-ȧ.

3 Now [a]Je-hō'ram the son of Ā'hăb began to reign over Ĭs'ra-el in Sa-mā'rĭ-ȧ the eighteenth year of Je-hŏsh'-a-phăt king of Jū'dah, and reigned twelve years.

2 And he wrought evil in the sight of the LORD; but not like his father, and like his mother: for he put away the [1]image of Bā'al [b]that his father had made.

3 Nevertheless he [c]cleaved unto [d]the sins of Jĕr-o-bō'am the son of Nē'băt, which made Ĭs'ra-el to sin; he departed not therefrom.

4 ¶ And Mē'shȧ king of Mō'ab was [e]a sheepmaster, and rendered unto the king of Ĭs'ra-el an hundred thousand [f]lambs, and an hundred thousand rams, with the wool.

5 But it came to pass, when [g]Ā'hăb was dead, that the king of Mō'ab rebelled against the king of Ĭs'ra-el.

6 ¶ And king Je-hō'ram went out of Sa-mā'rĭ-ȧ the same time, and numbered all Ĭs'ra-el.

7 And he went and sent to Je-hŏsh'a-phăt the king of Jū'dah, saying, The king of Mō'ab hath rebelled against me: wilt thou go with me against Mō'ab to battle? And he said, I will go up: [h]I *am* as thou *art*, my people as thy people, *and* my horses as thy horses.

8 And he said, Which way shall we go up? And he answered, The way through the wilderness of Ē'dom.

9 So the king of Ĭs'ra-el went, and the king of Jū'dah, and the king of Ē'dom: and they fetched a compass of seven days' journey: and there was no water for the host, and for the cattle [2]that followed them.

10 And the king of Ĭs'ra-el said, [i]Alas! that the LORD hath called these three kings together, to deliver them into the hand of Mō'ab!

11 But [j]Je-hŏsh'a-phăt said, *Is there* not here a [k]prophet of the LORD, that we may [l]inquire of the LORD by him? And one of the king of Ĭs'ra-el's servants answered and said, Here *is* E-lī'shȧ the son of Shā'phat, which poured water on the hands of E-lī'jah.

12 And Je-hŏsh'a-phăt said, The word of the LORD is with him. So the king of Ĭs'ra-el and Je-hŏsh'a-phăt and the king of Ē'dom [m]went down to him.

13 And E-lī'shȧ said unto the king of Ĭs'ra-el, [n]What have I to do with thee? [o]get thee to [p]the prophets of thy father, and to the prophets of thy mother. And the king of Ĭs'ra-el said unto him, Nay: for the LORD hath called these three kings together, to deliver them into the hand of Mō'ab.

14 And E-lī'shȧ said, [q]*As* the LORD of hosts liveth, before whom I stand, surely, were it not that I regard [r]the presence of Je-hŏsh'a-phăt the king of Jū'dah, I would not look toward thee, nor see thee.

15 But now bring me [s]a minstrel. And it came to pass, when the minstrel played, that [t]the hand of the LORD came upon him.

16 And he said, Thus saith the LORD, [u]Make this valley full of ditches.

17 For thus saith the LORD, Ye shall not see wind, neither shall ye see rain; yet that valley [v]shall be filled with water, that ye may drink, both ye, and your cattle, and your beasts.

18 And this is *but* a [w]light thing in the sight of the LORD: [x]he will deliver the Mō'ab-ītes also into your hand.

19 [y]And ye shall smite every fenced city, and every choice city, and shall fell every good tree, and stop all wells of water, and [3]mar every good piece of land with stones.

20 And it came to pass in the morning, when [z]the meat offering was offered, that, behold, there came water by the way of Ē'dom, and the country was filled with water.

21 ¶ And when all the Mō'ab-ītes heard that the kings were come up to fight against them, they [4]gathered all that were able to [5]put on armour, and upward, and stood in the border.

22 And they rose up early in the morning, and the sun shone upon the water, and the Mō'ab-ītes saw the water on the other side *as* red as blood:

23 And they said, This *is* blood: the kings are surely [6]slain, and they have

[n]1 Ki. 18.12; Acts 8.39
[5]one of the mountains
19 [o]Josh. 6.26
[6]causing to miscarry
21 [p]Ex. 15.25; John 9.6
23 [q]2 Chr. 36.16; Jude 14-15-18
24 [r]Deut. 32.35-41-43; Heb. 10.30-31

CHAPTER 3
1 [a]ch. 1.17
2 [1]statue
[b]1 Ki. 16.31-32
3 [c]ch. 10.28-31
[d]1 Ki. 12.28-31-32
4 [e]Gen. 13.2; Job 1.3
[f]Isa. 16.1
5 [g]ch. 1.1
7 [h]1 Ki. 22.4
9 [2]at their feet
10 [i]Ps. 78.34; Isa. 8.21
11 [j]1 Ki. 22.7
[k]Amos 3.7
[l]1 Chr. 28.9; Prov. 3.5-6
12 [m]ch. 2.25
13 [n]Ezek. 14.3
[o]Judg. 10.14; Ruth 1.15
[p]1 Ki. 18.19
14 [q]1 Ki. 17.1; ch. 5.16
[r]Ps. 15.4
15 [s]1 Sam. 10.5
[t]Ezek. 1.3; Ezek. 8.1
16 [u]ch. 4.3
17 [v]Ps. 107.35
18 [w]Jer. 32.17-27; Eph. 3.20
[x]1 Ki. 20.28
19 [y]1 Sam. 15.3
[3]grieve
20 [z]Ex. 29.39-40
21 [4]were cried together
[5]gird himself with a girdle
23 [6]destroyed

smitten one another: now therefore,
Mō'ab, to the spoil.
24 And when they came to the camp
of Ĭs'ra-el, the Ĭs'ra-el-ītes rose up and
smote the Mō'ab-ītes, so that they fled
before them: but [7]they went forward
smiting the Mō'ab-ītes, even in *their*
country.
25 And they beat down the cities,
and on every good piece of land cast
every man his stone, and filled it; and
they stopped all the wells of water, and
felled all the good trees: [8]only in [a]Kīr-
hăr'a-sĕth left they the stones thereof;
howbeit the slingers went about *it*, and
smote it.
26 ¶ And when the king of Mō'ab
saw that the battle was too sore for
him, he took with him seven hundred men that drew swords, to break
through *even* unto the king of Ē'dom:
but they could not.
27 Then he took [9]his eldest son that
should have reigned in his stead, and
[b]offered him *for* a burnt offering upon
the wall. And there was great indignation against Ĭs'ra-el: and they departed
[10]from him, and returned to *their own*
land.

4 Now there cried a certain woman of
the wives of [a]the sons of the prophets unto E-lī'shȧ, saying, Thy servant
my husband is dead; and thou knowest
that thy servant did fear the LORD: and
the creditor is come [b]to take unto him
my two sons to be bondmen.
2 And E-lī'shȧ said unto her, What
shall I do for thee? tell me, what hast
thou in the house? And she said, Thine
handmaid hath not any thing in the
house, save [c]a pot of oil.
3 Then he said, Go, borrow thee vessels abroad of all thy neighbours, *even*
empty vessels; [1]borrow not a few.
4 And when thou art come in, thou
shalt shut the door upon thee and upon
thy sons, and shalt pour out into all
those vessels, and thou shalt set aside
that which is full.
5 So she went from him, and shut
the door upon her and upon her sons,
who brought *the vessels* to her; and
she poured out.
6 And it came to pass, when [d]the
vessels were full, that she said unto her
son, Bring me yet a vessel. And he said
unto her, *There is* not a vessel more.
And the oil stayed.
7 Then she came and told the man of
God. And he said, Go, sell the oil, and
pay thy [2]debt, and live thou and thy
children of the rest.
8 ¶ And [3]it fell on a day, that E-lī'shȧ
passed to [e]Shụ'nem, where *was* a great
woman; and she [4]constrained him to
eat bread. And *so* it was, *that* as oft as
he passed by, he turned in thither to eat
bread.
9 And she said unto [f]her husband,
Behold now, I perceive that this *is* an
holy man of God, which passeth by us
continually.
10 [g]Let us make a little chamber, I
pray thee, on the wall; and let us set for
him there a bed, and a table, and a
stool, and a candlestick: and it shall
be, when he cometh to us, that he shall
turn in thither.
11 And it fell on a day, that he came
thither, and he turned into the chamber, and lay there.
12 And he said to Gē-hā'zī his servant, Call this Shụ'nam-mīte. And when
he had called her, she stood before him.
13 And he said unto him, Say now
unto her, Behold, thou hast been careful for us with all this care; what *is* to
be done for thee? wouldest thou be
spoken for to the king, or to the captain of the host? And she answered, I
dwell among mine own people.
14 And he said, What then *is* to be
done for her? And Gē-hā'zī answered,
Verily she hath no child, and her husband is old.
15 And he said, Call her. And when
he had called her, she stood in the
door.
16 And he said, [h]About this [5]season,
according to the time of life, thou shalt
embrace a son. And she said, Nay, my
lord, *thou* man of God, do not lie unto
thine handmaid.
17 And the woman conceived, and
bare a son at that season that E-lī'shȧ
had said unto her, according to the
time of life.
18 ¶ And when the child was grown,
it fell on a day, that he went out to his
father to the reapers.
19 And he said unto his father, My
head, my head. And he said to a lad,
Carry him to his mother.
20 And when he had taken him, and
brought him to his mother, he sat on
her knees till noon, and *then* died.
21 And she went up, and laid him on
the bed of the man of God, and shut *the*
door upon him, and went out.
22 And she called unto her husband,
and said, Send me, I pray thee, one of
the young men, and one of the asses,
that I may run to the man of God, and
come again.
23 And he said, Wherefore wilt thou
go to him to day? *it is* neither new
moon, nor sabbath. And she said, *It*
shall be [6]well.
24 Then she saddled an ass, and said
to her servant, Drive, and go forward;
[7]slack not *thy* riding for me, except I
bid thee.
25 So she went and came unto the
man of God [i]to mount Căr'mel. And it
came to pass, when the man of God
saw her afar off, that he said to Gē-
hā'zī his servant, Behold, *yonder is*
that Shụ'nam-mīte:
26 Run now, I pray thee, to meet
her, and say unto her, *Is it* well with
thee? *is it* well with thy husband? *is it*
well with the child? And she answered,
It is well.
27 And when she came to the man of
God to the hill, she caught [8]him by the
feet: but Gē-hā'zī [j]came near to thrust
her away. And the man of God said, Let
her alone; for her soul *is* [9]vexed within
her: and the LORD hath hid *it* from me,
and hath not told me.

24 [7]Or, they smote in it even smiting

25 [8]until he left the stones thereof in Kir-haraseth

[a]Isa. 16.7-11

27 [9]Perhaps the king of Edom's son

[b]Lev. 18.21; Deut. 12.31; ch. 17.17; 2 Chr. 28.3; Ps. 106.37-38; Jer. 7.31; Ezek. 16.20; Ezek. 20.26-31

[10]As they saw the Moabites so desperately resolute

CHAPTER 4

1 [a]1 Ki. 20.35; ch. 2.3-5-7

[b]Ex. 21.2; Lev. 25.39; Deut. 15.12-15-18; Neh. 5.1-13; Jer. 34.8-18; Matt. 18.25

2 [c]1 Ki. 17.12

3 [1]Or, scant not

6 [d]Matt. 14.20

7 [2]Or, creditor

8 [3]there was a day

[e]Josh. 19.18; 1 Sam. 28.4

[4]laid hold on him

9 [f]Prov. 31.10-11

10 [g]Matt. 10.41-42; Matt. 25.40; Rom. 12.13; Heb. 13.1-2

16 [h]Gen. 18.10-14

[5]set time

23 [6]peace

24 [7]restrain not for me to ride

25 [i]ch. 2.25

27 [8]by his feet

[j]Matt. 15.23

[9]bitter

28 Then she said, Did I desire a son of my lord? did I not say, Do not deceive me?

29 Then he said to Ḡe-hā'zī, [k]Gird up thy loins, and take my staff in thine hand, and go thy way: if thou meet any man, [l]salute him not; and if any salute thee, answer him not again: and [m]lay my staff upon the face of the child.

30 And the mother of the child said, [n]*As* the LORD liveth, and *as* thy soul liveth, I will not leave thee. And he arose, and followed her.

31 And Ḡe-hā'zī passed on before them, and laid the staff upon the face of the child; but *there was* neither voice, nor [10]hearing. Wherefore he went again to meet him, and told him, saying, The child is [o]not awaked.

32 And when E-lī'shȧ was come into the house, behold, the child was dead, *and* laid upon his bed.

33 He [p]went in therefore, and shut the door upon them twain, [q]and prayed unto the LORD.

34 And he went up, and lay upon the child, and put his mouth upon his mouth, and his eyes upon his eyes, and his hands upon his hands: and [r]he stretched himself upon the child; and the flesh of the child waxed warm.

35 Then he returned, and walked in the house [11]to and fro; and went up, [s]and stretched himself upon him: and [t]the child sneezed seven times, and the child opened his eyes.

36 And he called Ḡe-hā'zī, and said, Call this Shụ'nam-mīte. So he called her. And when she was come in unto him, he said, Take up thy son.

37 Then she went in, and fell at his feet, and bowed herself to the ground, and [u]took up her son, and went out.

38 ¶ And E-lī'shȧ came again to [v]Gĭl'găl: and *there was* a dearth in the land; and the sons of the prophets *were* [w]sitting before him: and he said unto his servant, Set on the great pot, and seethe pottage for the sons of the prophets.

39 And one went out into the field to gather herbs, and found a wild vine, and gathered thereof wild gourds his lap full, and came and shred *them* into the pot of pottage: for they [x]knew *them* not.

40 So they poured out for the men to eat. And it came to pass, as they were eating of the pottage that they cried out, and said, O *thou* man of God, *there is* [y]death in the pot. And they could not eat *thereof*.

41 But he said, Then bring meal. And [z]he cast *it* into the pot; and he said, Pour out for the people, that they may eat. And there was no [12]harm in the pot.

42 ¶ And there came a man from [a]Bā'al–shăl'ĭ-shȧ, [b]and brought the man of God bread of the firstfruits, twenty loaves of barley, and full ears of corn [13]in the husk thereof. And he said, Give unto the people, that they may eat.

43 And his servitor said, [c]What, should I set this before an hundred men? He said again, Give the people, that they may eat: for thus saith the LORD, They shall eat, and shall leave *thereof*.

44 So he set *it* before them, and they did eat, [d]and left *thereof*, according to the [e]word of the LORD.

5 Now [a]Nā'a-man, captain of the host of the king of Sȳr'ĭ-ȧ, was a [b]great man [1]with his master, and [2]honourable, because by him the LORD had given [3]deliverance unto Sȳr'ĭ-ȧ: he was also a mighty man in valour, *but he was* a leper.

2 And the Sȳr'ĭ-ans had gone out by companies, and had brought away captive out of the land of Ĭs'ra-el a little maid; and she [4]waited on Nā'a-man's wife.

3 And she said unto her mistress, Would God my lord *were* [5]with the prophet that *is* in Sa-mā'rĭ-ȧ! for he would [6]recover him of his leprosy.

4 And *one* went in, and told his lord, saying, Thus and thus said the maid that *is* of the land of Ĭs'ra-el.

5 And the king of Sȳr'ĭ-ȧ said, Go to, go, and I will send a letter unto the king of Ĭs'ra-el. And he departed, and [c]took [7]with him ten talents of silver, and six thousand *pieces* of gold, and ten changes of raiment.

6 And he brought the letter to the king of Ĭs'ra-el, saying, Now when this letter is come unto thee, behold, I have *therewith* sent Nā'a-man my servant to thee, that thou mayest recover him of his leprosy.

7 And it came to pass, when the king of Ĭs'ra-el had read the letter, that he [d]rent his clothes, and said, *Am* I [e]God, to kill and to make alive, that this man doth send unto me to recover a man of his leprosy? wherefore consider, I pray you, and see how he seeketh a quarrel against me.

8 ¶ And it was *so*, when E-lī'shȧ the man of God had heard that the king of Ĭs'ra-el had rent his clothes, that he sent to the king, saying, Wherefore hast thou rent thy clothes? let him come now to me, and [f]he shall know that there is a prophet in Ĭs'ra-el.

9 So Nā'a-man came with his horses and with his chariot, and stood at the door of the house of E-lī'shȧ.

10 And E-lī'shȧ sent a messenger unto him, saying, Go and [g]wash in Jôr'-dan seven times, and thy flesh shall come again to thee, and thou shalt be clean.

11 But Nā'a-man was [h]wroth, and went away, and said, Behold, [8]I thought, He will surely come out to me, and stand, and call on the name of the LORD his God, and [9]strike his hand over the place, and recover the leper.

12 *Are* not [10]Ăb'ă-nȧ and Phär'par, rivers of Da-măs'cus, better than all the waters of Ĭs'ra-el? may I not wash in them, and be clean? So he turned and [i]went away in a rage.

13 And his servants came near, and spake unto him, and said, My father, *if* the prophet had bid thee *do some* great

29 [k]1 Ki. 18.46; ch. 9.1 [l]Luke 10.4 [m]Ex. 7.19; Acts 19.12
30 [n]ch. 2.2
31 [10]attention [o]John 11.11
33 [p]Matt. 6.6 [q]1 Ki. 17.20; Jas. 5.16
34 [r]Acts 20.10
35 [11]once hither, and once thither [s]1 Ki. 17.21 [t]ch. 8.1
37 [u]Heb. 11.35
38 [v]ch. 2.1 [w]Luke 10.39; Acts 22.3
39 [x]Matt. 7.16
40 [y]Ex. 10.17
41 [z]Ex. 15.25; John 9.6 [12]evil thing
42 [a]1 Sam. 9.4 [b]1 Cor. 9.11; Gal. 6.6 [13]Or, in his scrip, or, garment
43 [c]Luke 9.13; John 6.9
44 [d]Matt. 14.20; John 6.13 [e]Gen. 18.14

CHAPTER 5
1 [a]Luke 4.27 [b]Ex. 11.3; [1]before [2]lifted up, or, accepted in countenance, or, gracious [3]Or, victory
2 [4]was before
3 [5]before [6]gather in
5 [c]1 Sam. 9.8 [7]in his hand
7 [d]Gen. 37.29 [e]Gen. 30.2;
8 [f]Ex. 4.30
10 [g]ch. 4.41
11 [h]1 Cor. 2.14 [8]I said, or, I said with myself, He will surely come out, etc [9]move up and down
12 [10]Or, Amana [i]Prov. 14.17

thing, wouldest thou not have done *it?*
how much rather then, when he saith
to thee, Wash, and be clean?
14 Then went he down, and dipped
himself seven times in Jôr'dan, according to the saying of the man of God:
and [j]his flesh came again like unto the
flesh of a little child, and [k]he was
clean.
15 ¶ [l]And he returned to the man
of God, he and all his company, and
came, and stood before him: and he
said, Behold, now [m]I know that *there
is* [n]no God in all the earth, but in Ĭs'ra-
el: now therefore, I pray thee, take [o]a
blessing of thy servant.
16 But he said, [p]*As* the LORD liveth,
before whom I stand, [q]I will receive
none. And he urged him to take *it;* but
he refused.
17 And Nā'a-man said, Shall there
not then, I pray thee, be given to thy
servant two mules' burden of earth? for
thy servant will henceforth offer neither burnt offering nor sacrifice unto
other gods, but unto the LORD.
18 In this thing the LORD pardon thy
servant, *that* when my master goeth
into the house of Rĭm'mon to worship
there, and [r]he leaneth on my hand,
and I bow myself in the house of Rĭm'-
mon: when I bow down myself in the
house of Rĭm'mon, the LORD pardon
thy servant in this thing.
19 And he said unto him, Go in
peace. So he departed from him [11]a little way.
20 ¶ But Gē-hā'zī, the servant of E-
lī'shȧ the man of God, said, Behold,
my master hath spared Nā'a-man this
Sy̆r'ĭ-an, in not receiving at his hands
that which he brought: but, *as* the LORD
liveth, I will [s]run after him, and take
somewhat of him.
21 So Gē-hā'zī followed after Nā'a-
man. And when Nā'a-man saw *him*
running after him, he lighted down
from the chariot to meet him, and said,
[12]*Is* all well?
22 And he said, All *is* well. My master hath sent me, saying, Behold, even
now there be come to me from mount
Ē'phrȧ-ĭm two young men of the sons
of the prophets: give them, I pray thee,
a talent of silver, and two changes of
garments.
23 And Nā'a-man said, Be content,
take two talents. And he urged him,
and bound two talents of silver in two
bags, with two changes of garments,
and laid *them* upon two of his servants; and they bare *them* before him.
24 And when he came to the [13]tower,
he took *them* from their hand, and bestowed *them* in the house: and he let
the men go, and they departed.
25 But he went in, and [t]stood before
his master. And E-lī'shȧ said unto him,
Whence *comest thou,* Gē-hā'zī? And
he said, Thy servant went [14]no whither.
26 And [u]he said unto him, Went not
mine heart *with thee,* when the man
turned again from his chariot to meet
thee? *Is it* a time to receive money, and
to receive garments, and oliveyards,

14 [j]Job 33.25 [k]Luke 4.27
15 [l]Luke 17.15 [m]Isa. 43.10-11; Rom. 10.10 [n]Dan. 2.47 [o]Gen. 33.11
16 [p]ch. 3.14 [q]Gen. 14.23; Matt. 10.8; Acts 8.18-20
18 [r]ch. 7.2-17
19 [11]a little piece of ground, as, Gen. 35.16
20 [s]Ex. 20.17; Josh. 6.18; 1 Sam. 8.3-5; Ps. 10.3; Prov. 1.19; Prov. 15.27; Luke 12.15; Col. 3.5; 1 Tim. 6.10
21 [12]Is there peace?
24 [13]Or, secret place
25 [t]Prov. 30.20; Ezek. 33.31 [14]not hither or thither
26 [u]Ps. 32.10; Ps. 63.11; Ps. 140.11; Prov. 13.21; Isa. 3.11; Isa. 57.21; Acts 13.9
27 [v]1 Tim. 6.10 [w]Ex. 4.6; Lev. 13.2-3; Lev. 14.3-35; Num. 12.10; ch. 15.5; 2 Chr. 26.19-20

CHAPTER 6
1 [a]1 Sam. 10.12; ch. 2.3; ch. 4.1-38; ch. 9.1 [1]sit before
5 [2]iron
6 [b]Ex. 15.25; ch. 4.41
8 [3]Or, encamping
9 [c]ch. 13.14; Matt. 5.13
12 [4]No
13 [d]Gen. 37.17
14 [5]heavy
15 [6]Or, minister
16 [e]2 Sam. 22.3-31; Rom. 8.31

and vineyards, and sheep, and oxen,
and menservants, and maidservants?
27 The leprosy therefore of Nā'a-
man [v]shall cleave unto thee, and unto
thy seed for ever. And he went out
from his presence [w]a leper *as white* as
snow.

6

And [a]the sons of the prophets said
unto E-lī'shȧ, Behold now, the place
where we [1]dwell with thee is too strait
for us.
2 Let us go, we pray thee, unto Jôr'-
dan, and take thence every man a
beam, and let us make us a place
there, where we may dwell. And he
answered, Go ye.
3 And one said, Be content, I pray
thee, and go with thy servants. And he
answered, I will go.
4 So he went with them. And when
they came to Jôr'dan, they cut down
wood.
5 But as one was felling a beam, the
[2]ax head fell into the water: and he
cried, and said, Alas, master! for it was
borrowed.
6 And the man of God said, Where
fell it? And he shewed him the place.
And [b]he cut down a stick, and cast *it* in
thither; and the iron did swim.
7 Therefore said he, Take *it* up to
thee. And he put out his hand, and took
it.
8 ¶ Then the king of Sy̆r'ĭ-ȧ warred
against Ĭs'ra-el, and took counsel with
his servants, saying, In such and such
a place *shall be* my [3]camp.
9 And the man of God sent unto the
king of Ĭs'ra-el, saying, [c]Beware that
thou pass not such a place; for thither
the Sy̆r'ĭ-ans are come down.
10 And the king of Ĭs'ra-el sent to
the place which the man of God told
him and warned him of, and saved himself there, not once nor twice.
11 Therefore the heart of the king
of Sy̆r'ĭ-ȧ was sore troubled for this
thing; and he called his servants, and
said unto them, Will ye not shew me
which of us *is* for the king of Ĭs'ra-el?
12 And one of his servants said,
[4]None, my lord, O king: but E-lī'shȧ,
the prophet that *is* in Ĭs'ra-el, telleth
the king of Ĭs'ra-el the words that thou
speakest in thy bedchamber.
13 ¶ And he said, Go and spy where
he *is,* that I may send and fetch him.
And it was told him, saying, Behold, *he
is* in [d]Dō'than.
14 Therefore sent he thither horses,
and chariots, and a [5]great host: and
they came by night, and compassed
the city about.
15 And when the [6]servant of the man
of God was risen early, and gone forth,
behold, an host compassed the city
both with horses and chariots. And his
servant said unto him, Alas, my master! how shall we do?
16 And he answered, Fear not: for
[e]they that *be* with us *are* more than
they that *be* with them.
17 And E-lī'shȧ prayed, and said,
LORD, I pray thee, open his eyes, that
he may see. And the LORD opened the

eyes of the young man; and he saw:
and, behold, the mountain *was* full
of [f]horses and chariots of fire round
about E-lī'shȧ.
18 And when they came down to
him, E-lī'shȧ prayed unto the LORD,
and said, Smite this people, I pray thee,
with blindness. And [g]he smote them
with blindness according to the word
of E-lī'shȧ.
19 ¶ And E-lī'shȧ said unto them,
This *is* not the way, neither *is* this the
city: [7]follow me, and I will bring you to
the man whom ye seek. But he led
them to Sa-mā'rĭ-ȧ.
20 And it came to pass, when they
were come into Sa-mā'rĭ-ȧ, that E-lī'-
shȧ said, LORD, open the eyes of these
men, that they may see. And the LORD
opened their eyes, and they saw; and,
behold, *they were* in the midst of Sa-
mā'rĭ-ȧ.
21 And the king of Ĭs'ra-el said unto
E-lī'shȧ, when he saw them, [h]My father, shall I smite *them?* shall I smite
them?
22 And he answered, Thou shalt not
smite *them:* wouldest thou smite those
whom thou hast taken captive with thy
sword and with thy bow? [i]set bread
and water before them, that they may
eat and drink, and go to their master.
23 And he prepared great provision
for them: and when they had eaten and
drunk, he sent them away, and they
went to their master. So [j]the bands of
Sȳr'ĭ-ȧ came no more into the land of
Ĭs'ra-el.
24 ¶ And it came to pass after this,
that Bĕn–hā'dăd king of Sȳr'ĭ-ȧ gathered all his host, and went up, and besieged Sa-mā'rĭ-ȧ.
25 And there was a great [k]famine in
Sa-mā'rĭ-ȧ: and, behold, they besieged
it, until an ass's head was *sold* for fourscore *pieces* of silver, and the [8]fourth
part of a cab of dove's dung for five
pieces of silver.
26 And as the king of Ĭs'ra-el was
passing by upon the wall, there cried a
woman unto him, saying, Help, my
lord, O king.
27 And he said, [9]If the LORD do not
help thee, whence shall I help thee? out
of the barnfloor, or out of the winepress?
28 And the king said unto her, [l]What
aileth thee? And she answered, This
woman said unto me, Give thy son, that
we may eat him to day, and we will eat
my son to morrow.
29 So [m]we boiled my son, and did
eat him: and I said unto her on the
[10]next day, Give thy son, that we may
eat him: and she hath hid her son.
30 ¶ And it came to pass, when the
king heard the words of the woman,
that he [n]rent his clothes; and he passed
by upon the wall, and the people looked,
and, behold, *he had* sackcloth within
upon his flesh.
31 Then he said, [o]God do so and
more also to me, if the head of E-lī'shȧ
the son of Shā'phat shall stand on him
this day.
32 But E-lī'shȧ [p]sat in his house,
and [q]the elders sat with him; and *the
king* sent a man from before him: but
ere the messenger came to him, he said
to the elders, [r]See ye how this son of
[s]a murderer hath sent to take away
mine head? look, when the messenger
cometh, shut the door, and hold him
fast at the door: *is* not the sound of his
master's feet behind him?
33 And while he yet talked with
them, behold, the messenger came
down unto him: and [11]he said, Behold,
this evil *is* of the LORD; [t]what should I
wait for the LORD any longer?
7 Then E-lī'shȧ said, Hear ye the word
of the LORD; Thus saith the LORD,
[a]To morrow about this time *shall* a
measure of fine flour *be sold* for a shekel, and two measures of barley for a
shekel, in the gate of Sa-mā'rĭ-ȧ.
2 Then [1]a lord on whose hand the
king leaned answered the man of God,
and said, Behold, [b]*if* the LORD would
make windows in heaven, might this
thing be? And he said, Behold, thou
shalt see *it* with thine eyes, but [c]shalt
not eat thereof.
3 ¶ And there were four leprous men
[d]at the entering in of the gate: and
they said one to another, Why sit we
here until we die?
4 If we say, We will enter into the
city, then the famine *is* in the city, and
we shall die there: and if we sit still
here, we die also. Now therefore come,
and let us fall unto the host of the Sȳr'ĭ-
ans: if they save us alive, we shall live;
and if [e]they kill us, we shall but die.
5 And they rose up in the twilight, to
go unto the camp of the Sȳr'ĭ-ans: and
when they were come to the uttermost
part of the camp of Sȳr'ĭ-ȧ, behold,
there was no man there.
6 For the Lord had made the host of
the Sȳr'ĭ-ans [f]to hear a noise of chariots, and a noise of horses, *even* the
noise of a great host: and they said one
to another, Lo, the king of Ĭs'ra-el hath
hired against us [g]the kings of the Hĭt'-
tītes, and the kings of the E-ġȳp''tians,
to come upon us.
7 Wherefore they [h]arose and fled in
the twilight, and left their tents, and
their horses, and their asses, even the
camp as it *was,* and fled for their life.
8 And when these lepers came to the
uttermost part of the camp, they went
into one tent, and did eat and drink,
and carried thence silver, and gold,
and raiment, and went and hid *it;* and
came again, and entered into another
tent, and carried thence *also,* and went
and hid *it.*
9 Then they said one to another, [i]We
do not well: this day *is* a day of [j]good
tidings, and we hold our peace: if we
tarry till the morning light, [2]some mischief will come upon us: now therefore
come, that we may go and tell the
king's household.
10 So they came and called unto the
porter of the city: and they told them,
saying, We came to the camp of the
Sȳr'ĭ-ans, and, behold, *there was* no

17 [f]ch. 2.11; Ps. 34.7; Zech. 1.8; Heb. 1.14
18 [g]Gen. 19.11; Acts 13.9
19 [7]come ye after me
21 [h]ch. 2.12
22 [i]Prov. 25.21; Rom. 12.20
23 [j]ch. 5.2
25 [k]Lev. 26.26
[8]That is, about three gills, a cab being about three pints
27 [9]Or, let not the LORD save thee
28 [l]Judg. 18.23; Isa. 22.1
29 [m]Lev. 26.29
[10]other
30 [n]Gen. 37.29-34; ch. 5.7
31 [o]Ruth 1.17; 2 Sam. 3.9-35; Acts 23.14
32 [p]Ps. 118.6-9
[q]Ezek. 8.1; Mal. 3.16
[r]Luke 13.32
[s]1 Ki. 18.4
33 [11]That is, Jehoram
[t]Job 21.15; Ps. 27.14; Rev. 16.9
CHAPTER 7
1 [a]Ex. 8.23; Ps. 46.1
2 [1]a lord which belonged to the king leaning upon his hand
[b]Gen. 7.11; Mal. 3.10
[c]Deut. 3.27; Heb. 3.17
3 [d]Lev. 13.46; Luke 17.12
4 [e]Esth. 4.16; Luke 15.17-19
6 [f]Lev. 26.36; Rev. 6.15-16
[g]1 Ki. 10.29
7 [h]Job 18.11; Jer. 48.8-9
9 [i]Phil. 2.14; 2 Pet. 1.19
[j]Esth. 9.17; Nah. 1.15
[2]we shall find punishment

man there, neither voice of man, but horses tied, and asses tied, and the tents as they *were*.

11 And he called the porters; and they told *it* to the king's house within.

12 ¶ And the king arose in the night, and said unto his servants, I will now shew you what the Sy̆r′ĭ-ans have done to us. They know that we *be* hungry; therefore are they gone out of the camp to hide themselves in the field, saying, When they come out of the city, we shall catch them alive, and get into the city.

13 And one of his servants answered and said, Let *some* take, I pray thee, five of the horses that remain, which are left [3]in the city, (behold, they *are* as all the multitude of Ĭs′ra-el that are left in it: behold, *I say*, they *are* even as all the multitude of the Ĭs′ra-el-ītes that are consumed:) and let us send and see.

14 They took therefore two chariot horses; and the king sent after the host of the Sy̆r′ĭ-ans, saying, Go and see.

15 And they went after them unto Jôr′dan: and, lo, all the way *was* full of garments and [4]vessels, which the Sy̆r′ĭ-ans had cast away in their haste. And the messengers returned, and told the king.

16 And the people went out, and spoiled the tents of the Sy̆r′ĭ-ans. So a measure of fine flour was *sold* for a shekel, and two measures of barley for a shekel, [k]according to the word of the LORD.

17 ¶ And the king appointed the lord on whose hand he leaned to have the charge of the gate: and the people trode upon him in the gate, and he died, [l]as the man of God had said, who spake when the king came down to him.

18 And it came to pass as the man of God had spoken to the king, saying, [m]Two measures of barley for a shekel, and a measure of fine flour for a shekel, shall be to morrow about this time in the gate of Sa-mā′rĭ-ȧ:

19 And that lord answered the man of God, and said, Now, behold, *if* the LORD should make windows in heaven, might such a thing be? And he said, Behold, thou shalt see it with thine eyes, but shalt not eat thereof.

20 And [n]so it fell out unto him: for the people trode upon him in the gate, and he died.

8 Then spake E-lī′shȧ unto the woman, [a]whose son he had restored to life, saying, Arise, and go thou and thine household, and sojourn wheresoever thou canst sojourn: for the LORD [b]hath called for a famine; and it shall also come upon the land seven years.

2 And the woman arose, and did after the saying of the man of God: and she went with her household, and sojourned in the land of the Phĭ-lĭs′tĭnes seven years.

3 And it came to pass at the seven years' end, that the woman returned out of the land of the Phĭ-lĭs′tĭnes: and she went forth to cry unto the king for her house and for her land.

4 And the king talked with [c]Ḡe-hā′zī the servant of the man of God, saying, Tell me, I pray thee, all the great things that E-lī′shȧ hath done.

5 And it came to pass, as he was telling the king how he had [d]restored a dead body to life, that, behold, the woman, whose son he had restored to life, cried to the king for her house and for her land. And Ḡe-hā′zī said, My lord, O king, this *is* the woman, and this *is* her son, whom E-lī′shȧ restored to life.

6 And when the king asked the woman, she told him. So the king appointed unto her a certain [1]officer, saying, Restore all that *was* hers, and all the fruits of the field since the day that she left the land, even until now.

7 ¶ And E-lī′shȧ came to Da-măs′cus; and Bĕn–hā′dăd the king of Sy̆r′ĭ-ȧ was sick; and it was told him, saying, The man of God is come hither.

8 And the king said unto [e]Hăz′a-el, [f]Take a present in thine hand, and go, meet the man of God, and [g]inquire of the LORD by him, saying, Shall I recover of this disease?

9 So Hăz′a-el went to meet him, and took a present [2]with him, even of every good thing of Da-măs′cus, forty camels' burden, and came and stood before him, and said, Thy son Bĕn–hā′dăd king of Sy̆r′ĭ-ȧ hath sent me to thee, saying, Shall I recover of this disease?

10 And E-lī′shȧ said unto him, Go, say unto him, Thou mayest certainly recover: howbeit the LORD hath shewed me that he shall surely die.

11 And he settled his countenance [3]stedfastly, until he was ashamed: [h]and the man of God wept.

12 And Hăz′a-el said, Why weepeth my lord? And he answered, Because I know [i]the evil that thou wilt do unto the children of Ĭs′ra-el: their strong holds wilt thou set on fire, and their young men wilt thou slay with the sword, and [j]wilt dash their children, and rip up their women with child.

13 And Hăz′a-el said, But what, [k]*is* thy servant a dog, that he should do this great thing? And E-lī′shȧ answered, [l]The LORD hath shewed me that thou *shalt be* king over Sy̆r′ĭ-ȧ.

14 So he departed from E-lī′shȧ, and came to his master; who said to him, What said E-lī′shȧ to thee? And he answered, He told me *that* thou shouldest surely recover.

15 And it came to pass on the morrow, that he took a thick cloth, and dipped *it* in water, and spread *it* on his face, so that he died: and Hăz′a-el reigned in his stead.

16 ¶ And in the fifth year of Jō′ram the son of Ā′hăb king of Ĭs′ra-el, Je-hŏsh′a-phăt *being* then king of Jū′dah, [m]Je-hō′ram the son of Je-hŏsh′a-phăt king of Jū′dah [4]began to reign.

17 [n]Thirty and two years old was he when he began to reign; and he reigned eight years in Je-ru̧′sa-lĕm.

18 And he walked in the way of the kings of Ĭs′ra-el, as did the house of

13 [3]in it
15 [4]Or, furniture
16 [k]Num. 23.19; Ps. 89.2; Isa. 40.8; Isa. 44.26; Matt. 24.35; Mark 13.31; 1 Cor. 1.9; 1 Thess. 5.24; 1 Pet. 1.25
17 [l]Deut. 32.35-39-40; ch. 6.32; 2 Chr. 36.16; Job 31.3; Ps. 94-4-21-23; Prov. 13.13; Isa. 5.24; Isa. 28.22; Jer. 5.11-14; Nah. 1.2; Luke 10.16; 1 Thess. 4.8; Heb. 10.30-31; Jude 14-15
18 [m]verse 1
20 [n]Num. 20.12; Job 20.23; Jer. 17.6; Heb. 3.18

CHAPTER 8
1 [a]ch. 4.35
[b]Lev. 26.19-20-26; 2 Sam. 24.13; 1 Ki. 17.1; Ps. 105.16; Hag. 1.11
4 [c]ch. 5.27
5 [d]ch. 4.35
6 [1]Or, eunuch
8 [e]1 Ki. 19.15
[f]1 Sam. 9.7; ch. 5.5
[g]Josh. 9.14; 1 Sam. 9.9; ch. 1.2
9 [2]in his hand
11 [3]and set it
[h]Gen. 45.2; Ps. 119.136; Jer. 9.1-18; Luke 19.41
12 [i]ch. 10.32; ch. 12.17; Amos 1.3
[j]ch. 15.16; Hos. 13.16; Amos 1.13
13 [k]1 Sam. 17.43
[l]1 Ki. 19.15
16 [m]2 Chr. 21.3-4
[4]reigned; Began to reign in consort with his father
17 [n]2 Chr. 21.5

Ā'hăb: for the daughter of Ā'hăb was
his wife: and he did evil in the sight of
the LORD.
19 Yet the LORD would not destroy
Jū'dah for Dā'vid his servant's sake,
[o]as he promised him to give him alway
a [5]light, *and* to his children.
20 ¶ In his days [p]Ē'dom revolted
from under the hand of Jū'dah, [q]and
made a king over themselves.
21 So Jō'ram went over to Zā'ir, and
all the chariots with him: and he rose
by night, and smote the Ē'dom-ītes
which compassed him about, and the
captains of the chariots: and the people fled into their tents.
22 [6]Yet Ē'dom revolted from under
the hand of Jū'dah unto this day. [r]Then
Lĭb'nah revolted at the same time.
23 And the rest of the acts of Jō'ram,
and all that he did, *are* they not written
in the book of the chronicles of the
kings of Jū'dah?
24 And Jō'ram slept with his fathers,
and was buried with his fathers in the
city of Dā'vid: and [7]Ā-ha-zī'ah his son
reigned in his stead.
25 ¶ In the twelfth year of Jō'ram
the son of Ā'hăb king of Īs'ra-el did Ā-
ha-zī'ah the son of Je-hō'ram king of
Jū'dah begin to reign.
26 [s]Two and twenty years old *was*
Ā-ha-zī'ah when he began to reign;
and he reigned one year in Je-ru'sa-
lĕm. And his mother's name *was* Ăth-
a-lī'ah, the [8]daughter of Ŏm'rī king of
Īs'ra-el.
27 [t]And he walked in the way of the
house of Ā'hăb, and did evil in the
sight of the LORD, as *did* the house of
Ā'hăb: for he *was* the son in law of the
house of Ā'hăb.
28 ¶ And he went with Jō'ram the
son of Ā'hăb to the war against Hăz'a-
el king of Sȳr'ĭ-ȧ in Rā'moth–gĭl'e-ăd;
and the Sȳr'ĭ-ans wounded Jō'ram.
29 And [u]king Jō'ram went back to
be healed in Jĕz're-el of the wounds
[9]which the Sȳr'ĭ-ans had given him
at [10]Rā'mah, when he fought against
Hăz'a-el king of Sȳr'ĭ-ȧ. [v]And Ā-ha-
zī'ah the son of Je-hō'ram king of Jū'-
dah went down to see Jō'ram the son
of Ā'hăb in Jĕz're-el, because he was
[11]sick.

9 And E-lī'shȧ the prophet called one
of [a]the children of the prophets,
and said unto him, [b]Gird up thy loins,
and take this box of oil in thine hand,
[c]and go to Rā'moth–gĭl'e-ăd:
2 And when thou comest thither,
look out there Jē'hū the son of Je-
hŏsh'a-phăt the son of Nĭm'shī, and go
in, and make him arise up from among
his brethren, and carry him to an [1]in-
ner chamber;
3 Then [d]take the box of oil, and
pour *it* on his head, and say, Thus saith
the LORD, I have anointed thee king
over Īs'ra-el. Then open the door, and
flee, and tarry not.
4 ¶ So the young man, *even* the
young man the prophet, went to Rā'-
moth–gĭl'e-ăd.

19 [o]2 Sam. 7.13; 2 Chr. 21.7
[5]candle, or, lamp
20 [p]Gen. 27.40; 2 Chr. 21.8-10
[q]1 Ki. 22.47
22 [6]And so fulfilled
[r]Josh. 21.13; 2 Chr. 21.10
24 [7]called, Azariah, 2 Chr. 22.6, and Jehoahaz, 2 Chr. 21.17; 2 Chr. 25.23
26 [s]2 Chr. 22.2
[8]Or, granddaughter
27 [t]2 Chr. 22.3-4
29 [u]ch. 9.15
[9]wherewith the Syrians had wounded
[10]Ramoth
[v]ch. 9.16; 2 Chr. 22.6
[11]wounded

CHAPTER 9
1 [a]1 Ki. 20.35; Jer. 1.9-10
[b]ch. 4.29; Jer. 1.17
[c]ch. 8.28
2 [1]chamber in a chamber
3 [d]1 Ki. 19.16
6 [e]1 Sam. 2.7-8; Dan. 2.21
7 [f]Ps. 58.10-11
[g]1 Ki. 18.4
8 [h]1 Ki. 14.10; Ps. 110.5
[i]1 Sam. 25.22
[j]Deut. 32.36
9 [k]1 Ki. 14.10
[l]1 Ki. 16.3
10 [m]verses 35-37;
11 [n]Jer. 29.26;
13 [o]Matt. 21.7-8;
[2]reigneth
15 [p]ch. 8.29;
[3]Jehoram
[4]smote
[5]let no escaper go, etc

5 And when he came, behold, the
captains of the host *were* sitting; and
he said, I have an errand to thee, O
captain. And Jē'hū said, Unto which of
all us? And he said, To thee, O captain.
6 And he arose, and went into the
house; and he poured the oil on his
head, and said unto him, [e]Thus saith the
LORD God of Īs'ra-el, I have anointed
thee king over the people of the LORD,
even over Īs'ra-el.
7 And thou shalt smite the house of
Ā'hăb thy master, [f]that I may avenge
the blood of my servants the prophets,
and the blood of all the servants of the
LORD, [g]at the hand of Jĕz'e-bĕl.
8 For the whole house of Ā'hăb shall
perish: and [h]I will cut off from Ā'hăb
[i]him that pisseth against the wall, and
[j]him that is shut up and left in Īs'ra-el:
9 And I will make the house of Ā'hăb
like the house of [k]Jĕr-o-bō'am the son
of Nē'băt, and like the house of [l]Bā'a-
shȧ the son of A-hī'jah:
10 [m]And the dogs shall eat Jĕz'e-bĕl
in the portion of Jĕz're-el, and *there
shall be* none to bury *her*. And he
opened the door, and fled.
11 ¶ Then Jē'hū came forth to the
servants of his lord: and *one* said unto
him, *Is* all well? wherefore came [n]this
mad *fellow* to thee? And he said unto
them, Ye know the man, and his communication.
12 And they said, *It is* false; tell us
now. And he said, Thus and thus spake
he to me, saying, Thus saith the LORD,
I have anointed thee king over Īs'ra-el.
13 Then they hasted, and [o]took every man his garment, and put *it* under
him on the top of the stairs, and blew
with trumpets, saying, Jē'hū [2]is king.
14 So Jē'hū the son of Je-hŏsh'-
a-phăt the son of Nĭm'shī conspired
against Jō'ram. (Now Jō'ram had kept
Rā'moth–gĭl'e-ăd, he and all Īs'ra-el,
because of Hăz'a-el king of Sȳr'ĭ-ȧ.
15 But [p]king [3]Jō'ram was returned
to be healed in Jĕz're-el of the wounds
which the Sȳr'ĭ-ans [4]had given him,
when he fought with Hăz'a-el king of
Sȳr'ĭ-ȧ.) And Jē'hū said, If it be your
minds, *then* [5]let none go forth *nor* escape out of the city to go to tell *it* in
Jĕz're-el.
16 So Jē'hū rode in a chariot, and
went to Jĕz're-el; for Jō'ram lay there.
And Ā-ha-zī'ah king of Jū'dah was
come down to see Jō'ram.
17 And there stood a watchman on
the tower in Jĕz're-el, and he spied the
company of Jē'hū as he came, and
said, I see a company. And Jō'ram
said, Take an horseman, and send to
meet them, and let him say, *Is it* peace?
18 So there went one on horseback
to meet him, and said, Thus saith the
king, *Is it* peace? And Jē'hū said, What
hast thou to do with peace? turn thee
behind me. And the watchman told,
saying, The messenger came to them,
but he cometh not again.
19 Then he sent out a second on
horseback, which came to them, and
said, Thus saith the king, *Is it* peace?

And Jē'hū answered, What hast thou
to do with peace? turn thee behind me.
20 And the watchman told, saying,
He came even unto them, and cometh
not again: and the [6]driving *is* like the
driving of Jē'hū the son of Nĭm'shī; for
he driveth [7]furiously.
21 And Jō'ram said, [8]Make ready.
And his chariot was made ready. And
[q]Jō'ram king of Ĭs'ra-el and Ā-ha-
zī'ah king of Jū'dah went out, each in
his chariot, and they went out against
Jē'hū, and [9]met him in the portion of
Nā'bŏth the Jĕz're-el-īte.
22 And it came to pass, when Jō'-
ram saw Jē'hū, that he said, *Is it* peace,
Jē'hū? And he answered, What peace,
[r]so long as the whoredoms of thy
mother Jĕz'e-bĕl and her witchcrafts
are so many?
23 And Jō'ram turned his hands, and
fled, and said to Ā-ha-zī'ah, *There is*
treachery, O Ā-ha-zī'ah.
24 And Jē'hū [10]drew a bow with his
full strength, and smote Je-hō'ram between his arms, and the arrow went
out at his heart, and he [11]sunk down in
his chariot.
25 Then said Jē'hū to Bĭd'kär his
captain, Take up, *and* cast him in the
portion of the field of Nā'bŏth the Jĕz'-
re-el-īte: for remember how that, when
I and thou rode together after Ā'hăb
his father, [s]the LORD laid this burden
upon him;
26 Surely I have seen yesterday the
[12]blood of Nā'bŏth, and the blood of his
sons, saith the LORD; and [t]I will requite
thee in this [13]plat, saith the LORD. Now
therefore take *and* cast him into the
plat *of ground,* according to the word of
the LORD.
27 ¶ But when Ā-ha-zī'ah the king of
Jū'dah saw *this,* he fled by the way of
the garden house. And Jē'hū followed
after him, and said, Smite him also in
the chariot. *And they did so* at the going up to Gûr, which *is* by Ĭb'le-ăm.
And he fled to [u]Me-gĭd'do, and died
there.
28 And his servants carried him in
a chariot to Je-ru'sa-lĕm, and buried
him in his sepulchre with his fathers in
the city of Dā'vid.
29 And in the eleventh year of Jō'-
ram the son of Ā'hăb began Ā-ha-zī'ah
to reign [14]over Jū'dah.
30 ¶ And when Jē'hū was come to
Jĕz're-el, Jĕz'e-bĕl heard *of it;* [v]and
she [15]painted her face, and tired her
head, and looked out at a window.
31 And as Jē'hū entered in at the
gate, she said, [w]*Had* Zĭm'rī peace, who
slew his master?
32 And he lifted up his face to the
window, and said, Who *is* on my side?
who? And there looked out to him two
or three [16]eunuchs.
33 And he said, Throw her down. So
they threw her down: and *some* of her
blood was sprinkled on the wall, and
on the horses: and he trode her under
foot.
34 And when he was come in, he did
eat and drink, and said, Go, see now

20 [6]Or, marching [7]in madness
21 [8]Bind
[q]ch. 8.29; 2 Chr. 22.7 [9]found
22 [r]1 Ki. 16.30-33; Rev. 17.1-5
24 [10]filled his hand with a bow [11]bowed
25 [s]1 Ki. 21.29; Matt. 11.30
26 [12]bloods
[t]1 Ki. 21.19; Esth. 7.10 [13]Or, portion
27 [u]Judg. 1.27; Zech. 12.11
29 [14]as viceroy to his father in his sickness, 2 Chr. 21.18; But in Joram's 12th year he began to reign alone, ch. 8.25
30 [v]Ezek. 23.40 [15]put her eyes in painting
31 [w]1 Ki. 16.9-20
32 [16]Or, chamberlains
34 [x]Prov. 10.7; Isa. 65.15
[y]1 Ki. 16.31
36 [17]by the hand of
[z]1 Ki. 21.23
37 [a]Ps. 83.10; Jer. 8.2
CHAPTER 10
1 [a]Deut. 16.18 [1]nourishers
2 [b]ch. 5.6
4 [c]ch. 9.24-27; Luke 14.31
5 [d]Josh. 9.11-24-25
6 [2]for me
[e]Ex. 20.5
7 [f]1 Ki. 21.21
9 [g]ch. 9.14-24
10 [h]1 Sam. 3.19; [3]by the hand of

[x]this cursed *woman,* and bury her: for
[y]she *is* a king's daughter.
35 And they went to bury her: but
they found no more of her than the
skull, and the feet, and the palms of *her*
hands.
36 Wherefore they came again, and
told him. And he said, This *is* the word
of the LORD, which he spake [17]by his
servant E-lī'jah the Tĭsh'bīte, saying,
[z]In the portion of Jĕz're-el shall dogs
eat the flesh of Jĕz'e-bĕl:
37 And the carcase of Jĕz'e-bĕl shall
be [a]as dung upon the face of the field
in the portion of Jĕz're-el; *so* that they
shall not say, This *is* Jĕz'e-bĕl.
10 And Ā'hăb had seventy sons in
Sa-mā'rĭ-ȧ. And Jē'hū wrote letters, and sent to Sa-mā'rĭ-ȧ, unto the
[a]rulers of Jĕz're-el, to the elders, and
to [1]them that brought up Ā'hăb's *chil-*
dren, saying,
2 [b]Now as soon as this letter cometh
to you, seeing your master's sons *are*
with you, and *there are* with you chariots and horses, a fenced city also, and
armour;
3 Look even out the best and meetest of your master's sons, and set *him*
on his father's throne, and fight for
your master's house.
4 But they were exceedingly afraid,
and said, Behold, [c]two kings stood not
before him: how then shall we stand?
5 And he that *was* over the house,
and he that *was* over the city, the elders also, and the bringers up *of the*
children, sent to Jē'hū, saying, [d]We
are thy servants, and will do all that
thou shalt bid us; we will not make any
king: do thou *that which is* good in
thine eyes.
6 Then he wrote a letter the second
time to them, saying, If ye *be* [2]mine,
and *if* ye will hearken unto my voice,
take ye the heads of the men your master's [e]sons, and come to me to Jĕz'-
re-el by to morrow this time. Now
the king's sons, *being* seventy persons, *were* with the great men of the
city, which brought them up.
7 And it came to pass, when the letter came to them, that they took the
king's sons, and [f]slew seventy persons, and put their heads in baskets,
and sent him *them* to Jĕz're-el.
8 ¶ And there came a messenger, and
told him, saying, They have brought
the heads of the king's sons. And he
said, Lay ye them in two heaps at
the entering in of the gate until the
morning.
9 And it came to pass in the morning, that he went out, and stood, and
said to all the people, Ye *be* righteous:
behold, [g]I conspired against my master, and slew him: but who slew all
these?
10 Know now that there shall [h]fall
unto the earth nothing of the word of
the LORD, which the LORD spake concerning the house of Ā'hăb: for the
LORD hath done *that* which he spake
[3]by his servant E-lī'jah.

11 So Jē'hū slew all that remained of the house of Ā'hăb in Jĕz're-el, and all his great men, and his [4]kinsfolks, and his [i]priests, until he left him none remaining.

12 ¶ And he arose and departed, and came to Sa-mā'rī-ȧ. *And* as he *was* at the [5]shearing house in the way,

13 [j]Jē'hū [6]met with the brethren of Ā-ha-zī'ah king of Jū'dah, and said, Who *are* ye? And they answered, We *are* the brethren of Ā-ha-zī'ah; and we go down [7]to salute the children of the king and the children of the queen.

14 And he said, Take them alive. And they took them alive, and slew them at the pit of the shearing house, *even* two and forty men; neither left he any of them.

15 ¶ And when he was departed thence, he [8]lighted on [k]Je-hŏn'a-dăb the son of [l]Rē'chăb *coming* to meet him: and he [9]saluted him, and said to him, Is thine heart right, as my heart *is* with thy heart? And Je-hŏn'a-dăb answered, It is. If it be, [m]give *me* thine hand. And he gave *him* his hand; and he took him up to him into the chariot.

16 And he said, Come with me, and see my [n]zeal for the LORD. So they made him ride in his chariot.

17 And when he came to Sa-mā'rī-ȧ, [o]he slew all that remained unto Ā'hăb in Sa-mā'rī-ȧ, till he had [p]destroyed him, according to the saying of the LORD, [q]which he spake to Ē-lī'jah.

18 ¶ And Jē'hū gathered all the people together, and said unto them, [r]Ā'hăb served Bā'al a little; *but* Jē'hū shall serve him much.

19 Now therefore call unto me all the [s]prophets of Bā'al, all his servants, and all his priests; let none be wanting: for I have a great sacrifice *to do* to Bā'al; whosoever shall be wanting, he shall not live. But Jē'hū did *it* in subtilty, to the intent that he might destroy the worshippers of Bā'al.

20 And Jē'hū said, [10]Proclaim a solemn assembly for Bā'al. And they proclaimed *it*.

21 And Jē'hū sent through all Ĭs'ra-el: and all the worshippers of Bā'al came, so that there was not a man left that came not. And they came into the [t]house of Bā'al; and the house of Bā'al was [11]full from one end to another.

22 And he said unto him that *was* over the vestry, Bring forth vestments for all the worshippers of Bā'al. And he brought them forth vestments.

23 And Jē'hū went, and Je-hŏn'a-dăb the son of Rē'chăb, into the house of Bā'al, and said unto the worshippers of Bā'al, Search, and look that there be here with you none of the servants of the LORD, but the worshippers of Bā'al only.

24 And when they went in to offer sacrifices and burnt offerings, Jē'hū appointed fourscore men without, and said, *If* any of the men whom I have brought into your hands escape, *he that letteth him go,* [u]his life *shall be* for the life of him.

25 And it came to pass, as soon as he had made an end of offering the burnt offering, that Jē'hū said to the guard and to the captains, Go in, *and* slay them; let none come forth. And they smote them with [12]the edge of the sword; and the guard and the captains cast *them* out, and went to the city of the house of Bā'al.

26 And they brought forth the [13]images out of the house of Bā'al, and burned them.

27 And they brake down the image of Bā'al, and brake down the house of Bā'al, [v]and made it a draught house unto this day.

28 Thus Jē'hū destroyed Bā'al out of Ĭs'ra-el.

29 ¶ Howbeit *from* the sins of Jĕr-o-bō'am the son of Nē'băt, who made Ĭs'ra-el to sin, Jē'hū departed not from after them, *to wit,* [w]the golden calves that *were* in Bĕth'–el, and that *were* in Dăn.

30 And the LORD said unto Jē'hū, Because thou hast done well in executing *that which is* right in mine eyes, *and* hast done unto the house of Ā'hăb according to all that *was* in mine heart, [x]thy children of the fourth *generation* shall sit on the throne of Ĭs'ra-el.

31 But Jē'hū [14]took no [y]heed to walk in the law of the LORD God of Ĭs'ra-el with all his heart: for he departed not from [z]the sins of Jĕr-o-bō'am, which made Ĭs'ra-el to sin.

32 ¶ In those days the LORD began [15]to cut Ĭs'ra-el short: and [a]Hăz'a-el smote them in all the coasts of Ĭs'ra-el;

33 From Jôr'dan [16]eastward, all the land of Gĭl'e-ăd, the Găd'ītes, and the Reu'ben-ītes, and the Ma-năs'sītes, from Ā'rō-ēr, which *is* by the river Ār'nŏn, [17]even [b]Gĭl'e-ăd and Bā'shăn.

34 Now the rest of the acts of Jē'hū, and all that he did, and all his might, *are* they not written in the book of the chronicles of the kings of Ĭs'ra-el?

35 And Jē'hū slept with his fathers: and they buried him in Sa-mā'rī-ȧ. And Je-hō'a-hăz his son reigned in his stead.

36 And [18]the time that Jē'hū reigned over Ĭs'ra-el in Sa-mā'rī-ȧ *was* twenty and eight years.

11 And when [a]Ăth-a-lī'ah [b]the mother of Ā-ha-zī'ah saw that her son was dead, she arose and destroyed all the [1]seed royal.

2 But [2]Je-hŏsh'e-bȧ, the daughter of king Jō'ram, sister of Ā-ha-zī'ah, took [3]Jō'ăsh the son of Ā-ha-zī'ah, and stole him from among the king's sons *which were* slain; and they hid him, *even* him and his nurse, in the bedchamber from Ăth-a-lī'ah, so that he was not slain.

3 And he was with her hid in the house of the LORD six years. And Ăth-a-lī'ah did [c]reign over the land.

4 ¶ And [d]the seventh year Je-hoi'a-dȧ sent and fetched the rulers over hundreds, with the captains and the guard, and brought them to him into the house of the LORD, and made a covenant with them, and took an oath of them in the

11 [4]Or, acquaintance [i]1 Ki. 18.19
12 [5]house of shepherds binding sheep
13 [j]ch. 8.29 [6]found [7]to the peace of, etc
15 [8]found [k]Jer. 35.6 [l]1 Chr. 2.55 [9]blessed [m]Ezra 10.19
16 [n]Prov. 27.2; Rom. 10.2
17 [o]ch. 9.8; [p]Job 18.5-21; [q]1 Ki. 21.21
18 [r]1 Ki. 16.31-32
19 [s]1 Ki. 22.6
20 [10]Sanctify
21 [t]1 Ki. 16.32 [11]Or, so full, that they stood mouth to mouth
24 [u]1 Ki. 20.39
25 [12]the mouth
26 [13]statues
27 [v]Ezra 6.11;
29 [w]Ex. 32.4;
30 [x]ch. 13.1
31 [14]observed not [y]Prov. 4.23 [z]Lev. 26.14-17;
32 [15]to cut off the ends [a]ch. 8.12;
33 [16]toward the rising of the sun [17]Or, even to Gilead and Bashan [b]Amos 1.3
36 [18]the days were

CHAPTER 11
1 [a]2 Chr. 22.10 [b]ch. 8.26 [1]seed of the kingdom
2 [2]2 Chr. 22.11, Jehoshabeath [3]Or, Jehoash
3 [c]2 Chr. 22.12
4 [d]2 Chr. 23.1

house of the LORD, and shewed them the king's son.

5 And he commanded them, saying, This *is* the thing that ye shall do; A third part of you that enter in [e]on the sabbath shall even be keepers of the watch of the king's house;

6 And a third part *shall be* at the gate of Sûr; and a third part at the gate behind the guard: so shall ye keep the watch of the house, [4]that it be not broken down.

7 And two [5]parts of all you that go forth on the sabbath, even they shall keep the watch of the house of the LORD about the king.

8 And ye shall compass the king round about, every man with his weapons in his hand: and he that cometh within the ranges, let him be slain: and be ye with the king as he goeth out and as he cometh in.

9 [f]And the captains over the hundreds did according to all *things* that Je-hoi'a-dȧ the priest commanded: and they took every man his men that were to come in on the sabbath, with them that should go out on the sabbath, and came to Je-hoi'a-dȧ the priest.

10 And to the captains over hundreds did the priest give king Dā'vid's [g]spears and shields, that *were* in the temple of the LORD.

11 And the guard stood, every man with his weapons in his hand, round about the king, from the right [6]corner of the temple to the left corner of the temple, *along* by the altar and the temple.

12 And he brought forth the king's son, and put the crown upon him, and *gave him* the [h]testimony; and they made him king, and anointed him; and they clapped their hands, and said, [7]God save the king.

13 ¶ [i]And when Ăth-a-lī'ah heard the noise of the guard *and* of the people, she came to the people into the temple of the LORD.

14 And when she looked, behold, the king stood by [j]a pillar, as the manner *was*, and the princes and the trumpeters by the king, and [k]all the people of the land rejoiced, and blew with trumpets: and Ăth-a-lī'ah rent her clothes, and cried, [l]Treason, Treason.

15 But Je-hoi'a-dȧ the priest commanded the captains of the hundreds, the officers of the host, and said unto them, Have her forth without the ranges: and him that followeth her kill with the sword. For the priest had said, Let her not be slain in the house of the LORD.

16 And they laid hands on her; and she went by the way by the which the horses came into the king's house: [m]and there was she slain.

17 ¶ And Je-hoi'a-dȧ made [n]a covenant between the LORD and the king and the people, that they should be the LORD'S people; [o]between the king also and the people.

18 And all the people of the land went into the [p]house of Bā'al, and brake it down; his altars and his images [q]brake they in pieces thoroughly, and slew Măt'tan the priest of Bā'al before the altars. And [r]the priest appointed [8]officers over the house of the LORD.

19 And he took the rulers over hundreds, and the captains, and the guard, and all the people of the land; and they brought down the king from the house of the LORD, and came by the way of the gate of the guard to the king's house. And he sat on the throne of the kings.

20 And all [s]the people of the land rejoiced, and the city was in quiet: and they slew Ăth-a-lī'ah with the sword *beside* the king's house.

21 Seven years old *was* Je-hō'ash when he began to reign.

12 In the seventh year of Jē'hū Je-hō'ash [a]began to reign; and forty years reigned he in Je-ru'sa-lĕm. And his mother's name *was* Zĭb'ĭ-ah of Bē'-er–shē'bȧ.

2 And Je-hō'ash did *that which was* right in the sight of the LORD all his days wherein Je-hoi'a-dȧ the priest instructed him.

3 But [b]the high places were not taken away: the people still sacrificed and burnt incense in the high places.

4 ¶ And Je-hō'ash said to the priests, [c]All the money of the [1]dedicated things that is brought into the house of the LORD, *even* the [d]money of every one that passeth *the account*, [2]the money that every man is set at, *and* all the money that [3]cometh into any man's heart to bring into the house of the LORD,

5 Let the priests take *it* to them, every man of his acquaintance: and let them repair the breaches of the house, wheresoever any breach shall be found.

6 But it was *so, that* [4]in the three and twentieth year of king Je-hō'ash [e]the priests had not repaired the breaches of the house.

7 Then king Je-hō'ash called for Je-hoi'a-dȧ the priest, and the *other* priests, and said unto them, Why repair ye not the breaches of the house? now therefore receive no *more* money of your acquaintance, but deliver it for the breaches of the house.

8 And the priests consented to receive no *more* money of the people, neither to repair the breaches of the house.

9 But Je-hoi'a-dȧ the priest took [f]a chest, and bored a hole in the lid of it, and set it beside the altar, on the right side as one cometh into the house of the LORD: and the priests that kept the [5]door put therein all the money *that was* brought into the house of the LORD.

10 And it was *so*, when they saw that *there was* much money in the chest, that the king's [6]scribe and the high priest came up, and they [7]put up in bags, and told the money that was found in the house of the LORD.

---

5 [e]1 Chr. 9.25
6 [4]Or, from breaking up
7 [5]bands, or, companies
9 [f]2 Chr. 23.8
10 [g]1 Sam. 21.9; 2 Sam. 8.7; 1 Chr. 26.26-27
11 [6]shoulder
12 [h]Ex. 25.16; Deut. 17.14; Ps. 19.7; Isa. 8.16
[7]Let the king live
13 [i]2 Chr. 23.12
14 [j]ch. 23.3
[k]Prov. 29.2; Matt. 21.9; Luke 19.37; Rev. 19.1-7
[l]1 Ki. 18.17-18; ch. 9.23
16 [m]Gen. 9.6; Ex. 21.12-14; Lev. 24.17; Rev. 13.10
17 [n]Deut. 5.2-3; Jer. 11.3-6
[o]1 Sam. 10.25
18 [p]ch. 10.26; 2 Chr. 23.17
[q]Ex. 32.20; 2 Chr. 23.17
[r]2 Chr. 23.18
[8]offices
20 [s]Prov. 11.10

CHAPTER 12

1 [a]2 Chr. 24.1
3 [b]1 Ki. 15.14; ch. 14.4
4 [c]ch. 22.4
[1]holinesses, or, holy things
[d]Ex. 30.13
[2]the money of the souls of his estimation
[3]ascendeth upon the heart of a man
6 [4]twentieth year and third year
[e]2 Chr. 24.5
9 [f]Luke 21.1
[5]threshold
10 [6]Or, secretary
[7]bound up

11 And they gave the money, being
told, into the hands of them that did
the work, that had the oversight of the
house of the LORD: and they [8]laid it out
to the carpenters and builders, that
wrought upon the house of the LORD,
12 And to masons, and hewers of
stone, and to buy timber and hewed
stone to repair the breaches of the
house of the LORD, and for all that [9]was
laid out for the house to repair *it*.
13 Howbeit there were not made for
the house of the LORD bowls of silver,
snuffers, basons, trumpets, any vessels of gold, or vessels of silver, of the
money *that was* brought into the house
of the LORD:
14 But they gave that to the workmen, and repaired therewith the house
of the LORD.
15 Moreover they reckoned not with
the men, into whose hand they delivered the money to be bestowed on
workmen: for they dealt [g]faithfully.
16 [h]The trespass money and sin
money was not brought into the house
of the LORD: [i]it was the priests'.
17 ¶ Then [j]Hăz'a-el king of Sy̆r'ĭ-ȧ
went up, and fought against Găth, and
took it: and Hăz'a-el set his face to go
up to Je-ru̧'sa-lĕm.
18 And Je-hō'ash king of Jū'dah
[k]took all the hallowed things that Je-
hŏsh'a-phăt, and Je-hō'ram, and Ā-ha-
zī'ah, his fathers, kings of Jū'dah,
had dedicated, and his own hallowed
things, and all the gold *that was* found
in the treasures of the house of the
LORD, and in the king's house, and sent
it to Hăz'a-el king of Sy̆r'ĭ-ȧ: and he
[10]went away from Je-ru̧'sa-lĕm.
19 ¶ And the rest of the acts of Jō'-
ăsh, and all that he did, *are* they not
written in the book of the chronicles of
the kings of Jū'dah?
20 And his servants arose, and made
a conspiracy, and slew Jō'ăsh in [11]the
house of Mĭl'lo, which goeth down to
Sĭl'lȧ.
21 For [l]Jŏz'a-chär the son of Shĭm'e-
ăth, and Je-hŏz'a-băd the son of [12]Shō'-
mer, his servants, smote him, and he
died; and they buried him with his fathers in the city of Dā'vid: and [m]Ăm-a-
zī'ah his son reigned in his stead.

13

In [1]the three and twentieth year
of Jō'ăsh the son of Ā-ha-zī'ah
king of Jū'dah Je-hō'a-hăz the son of
Jē'hū began to reign over Ĭs'ra-el in Sa-
mā'rĭ-ȧ, *and reigned* seventeen years.
2 And he did *that which was* evil in
the sight of the LORD, and [2]followed
the sins of Jĕr-o-bō'am the son of Nē'-
băt, which made Ĭs'ra-el to sin; he departed not therefrom.
3 ¶ And [a]the anger of the LORD was
kindled against Ĭs'ra-el, and he delivered them into the hand of [b]Hăz'a-el
king of Sy̆r'ĭ-ȧ, and into the hand of
Bĕn–hā'dăd the son of Hăz'a-el, all
their days.
4 And Je-hō'a-hăz [c]besought the
LORD, and the LORD hearkened unto
him: for [d] he saw the oppression of
Ĭs'ra-el, because the king of Sy̆r'ĭ-ȧ oppressed them.
5 ([e]And the LORD gave Ĭs'ra-el a saviour, so that they went out from under
the hand of the Sy̆r'ĭ-ans: and the children of Ĭs'ra-el dwelt in their tents, [3]as
beforetime.
6 Nevertheless they departed not
from the sins of the house of Jĕr-
o-bō'am, who made Ĭs'ra-el sin, *but*
[4]walked therein: [f]and there [5]remained
the grove also in Sa-mā'rĭ-ȧ.)
7 Neither did he leave of the people
to Je-hō'a-hăz but fifty horsemen, and
ten chariots, and ten thousand footmen; for the king of Sy̆r'ĭ-ȧ had destroyed them, [g]and had made them
like the dust by threshing.
8 ¶ Now the rest of the acts of Je-
hō'a-hăz, and all that he did, and his
might, *are* they not written in the book
of the chronicles of the kings of Ĭs'ra-
el?
9 And Je-hō'a-hăz slept with his fathers; and they buried him in Sa-mā'-
rĭ-ȧ: and Jō'ăsh his son reigned in his
stead.[6]
10 ¶ In the thirty and seventh year of
Jō'ăsh king of Jū'dah began [7]Je-hō'-
ash the son of Je-hō'a-hăz to reign
over Ĭs'ra-el in Sa-mā'rĭ-ȧ, *and reigned*
sixteen years.
11 And he did *that which was* evil in
the sight of the LORD; he departed not
from all the sins of Jĕr-o-bō'am the son
of Nē'băt, who made Ĭs'ra-el sin: *but*
he walked therein.
12 [h]And the rest of the acts of Jō'-
ash, and all that he did, and [i]his might
wherewith he fought against Ăm-a-
zī'ah king of Jū'dah, *are* they not written in the book of the chronicles of the
kings of Ĭs'ra-el?
13 And Jō'ăsh slept with his fathers;
and Jĕr-o-bō'am sat upon his throne:
and Jō'ăsh was buried in Sa-mā'rĭ-ȧ
with the kings of Ĭs'ra-el.
14 ¶ Now E-lī'shȧ was fallen sick of
his sickness whereof he died. And Jō'-
ash the king of Ĭs'ra-el came down unto
him, and wept over his face, and said, O
my father, my father, [j]the chariot of
Ĭs'ra-el, and the horsemen thereof.
15 And E-lī'shȧ said unto him, Take
bow and arrows. And he took unto him
bow and arrows.
16 And he said to the king of Ĭs'ra-
el, [8]Put thine hand upon the bow. And
he put his hand *upon it:* and E-lī'shȧ
put his [k]hands upon the king's hands.
17 And he said, Open the window
eastward. And he opened *it*. Then E-
lī'shȧ said, Shoot. And he shot. And he
said, The arrow of the LORD'S deliverance, and the arrow of deliverance
from Sy̆r'ĭ-ȧ: for thou shalt smite the
Sy̆r'ĭ-ans in [l]Ā'phek, till thou have consumed *them*.
18 And he said, Take the arrows. And
he took *them*. And he said unto the king
of Ĭs'ra-el, [m]Smite upon the ground.
And he smote thrice, and stayed.
19 And the man of God was wroth
with him, and said, Thou shouldest
have smitten five or six times; then

11 [8]brought it forth
12 [9]went forth
15 [g]2 Chr. 34.12; Matt. 24.45; 1 Cor. 4.2
16 [h]Lev. 5.15; Num. 5.8-10
[i]Lev. 7.7; Num. 18.9
17 [j]ch. 8.12
18 [k]1 Ki. 15.18; ch. 16.8; 2 Chr. 16.2
[10]went up
20 [11]Or, Beth-millo
21 [l]2 Chr. 24.26, Zabad
[12]Or, Shimrith
[m]2 Chr. 24.27

CHAPTER 13
1 [1]the twentieth year and third year
2 [2]walked after
3 [a]Lev. 26.17; Deut. 4.23-24; Deut. 6.13; Deut. 7.4; Judg. 2.14; Ps. 7.11; Isa. 10.5-6; Nah. 1.3-6
[b]ch. 8.12
4 [c]Num. 21.7; Judg. 6.6-8; Ps. 78.34; Jer. 2.27
[d]Ex. 3.7; ch. 14.26; Prov. 15.3
5 [e]ch. 14.25-27; Luke 2.11
[3]as yesterday, and third day
6 [4]he walked
[f]1 Ki. 16.33
[5]stood
7 [g]Amos 1.3
9 [6]Alone
10 [7]In consort with his father
12 [h]ch. 14.15
[i]ch. 14.9; 2 Chr. 25.17
14 [j]ch. 2.12
16 [8]Make thine hand to ride
[k]Gen. 49.24
17 [l]1 Ki. 20.26
18 [m]Ex. 17.11

hadst thou smitten Sy̆r'ĭ-ȧ till thou
hadst consumed *it:* whereas now thou
shalt smite Sy̆r'ĭ-ȧ *but* thrice.
20 ¶ And [9]E-lī'shȧ died, and they buried him. And [n]the bands of the Mō'ab-
ītes invaded the land at the coming in
of the year.
21 And it came to pass, as they were
burying a man, that, behold, they spied
a band *of men;* and they cast the man
into the sepulchre of E-lī'shȧ: and when
the man [10]was let down, and touched
the bones of E-lī'shȧ, he [o]revived, and
stood up on his feet.
22 ¶ But [p]Hăz'a-el king of Sy̆r'ĭ-ȧ oppressed Ĭs'ra-el all the days of Je-hō'a-
hăz.
23 [q]And the LORD was gracious unto
them, and had compassion on them,
and [r]had respect unto them, [s]because
of his covenant with Ā'bră-hăm, Ī'saac,
and Jā'cob, and would not destroy
them, neither cast he them from his
[11]presence as yet.
24 So Hăz'a-el king of Sy̆r'ĭ-ȧ died;
and Bĕn–hā'dăd his son reigned in his
stead.
25 And Je-hō'ash the son of Je-hō'-
a-hăz [12]took again out of the hand of
Bĕn–hā'dăd the son of Hăz'a-el the cities, which he had taken out of the
hand of Je-hō'a-hăz his father by war.
[t]Three times did Jō'ăsh beat him, and
recovered the cities of Ĭs'ra-el.

14 In [a]the second year of Jō'ăsh
son of Je-hō'a-hăz king of Ĭs'ra-
el reigned [b]Ăm-a-zī'ah the son of Jō'-
ash king of Jū'dah.
2 He was twenty and five years old
when he began to reign, and reigned
twenty and nine years in Je-rụ'sa-lĕm.
And his mother's name *was* Je-ho-ăd'-
dan of Je-rụ'sa-lĕm.
3 And he did *that which was* right in
the sight of the LORD, yet not like Dā'-
vid his father: he did according to all
things as Jō'ăsh his father did.
4 [c]Howbeit the high places were not
taken away: as yet the people did sacrifice and burnt incense on the high
places.
5 ¶ And it came to pass, as soon
as the kingdom was confirmed in his
hand, that he slew his servants [d]which
had slain the king his father.
6 But the children of the murderers
he slew not: according unto that which
is written in the book of the law of Mō'-
ses, wherein the LORD commanded,
saying, [e]The fathers shall not be put to
death for the children, nor the children
be put to death for the fathers; but every man shall be put to death for his
own sin.
7 [f]He slew of Ē'dom in [g]the valley
of salt ten thousand, and took [1]Sē'lah
by war, and called the name of it [h]Jŏk'-
the-el unto this day.
8 ¶ [i]Then Ăm-a-zī'ah sent messengers to Je-hō'ash, the son of Je-hō'a-
hăz son of Jē'hū, king of Ĭs'ra-el, saying, [j]Come, let us look one another in
the face.
9 And Je-hō'ash the king of Ĭs'ra-el
sent to Ăm-a-zī'ah king of Jū'dah, saying, [k]The thistle that *was* in Lĕb'a-non
sent to the [l]cedar that *was* in Lĕb'a-
non, saying, Give thy daughter to my
son to wife: and there passed by a wild
beast that *was* in Lĕb'a-non, and trode
down the thistle.
10 Thou hast indeed smitten Ē'dom,
and [m]thine heart hath lifted thee up:
glory *of this,* and tarry [2]at home: for
why shouldest thou [n]meddle to *thy*
hurt, that thou shouldest fall, *even* thou,
and Jū'dah with thee?
11 But Ăm-a-zī'ah would not hear.
Therefore Je-hō'ash king of Ĭs'ra-el
went up; and he and Ăm-a-zī'ah king of
Jū'dah looked one another in the face
at [o]Bĕth–shē'mĕsh, which *belongeth*
to Jū'dah.
12 And Jū'dah [3]was put to the worse
before Ĭs'ra-el; and they fled every man
to their tents.
13 And Je-hō'ash king of Ĭs'ra-el
took Ăm-a-zī'ah king of Jū'dah, the
son of Je-hō'ash the son of Ă-ha-zī'ah,
at Bĕth–shē'mĕsh, and came to Je-
rụ'sa-lĕm, and brake down the wall of
Je-rụ'sa-lĕm from [p]the gate of Ē'phră-
ĭm unto [q]the corner gate, four hundred
cubits.
14 And he took all [r]the gold and silver, and all the vessels that were found
in the house of the LORD, and in the
treasures of the king's house, and hostages, and returned to Sa-mā'rĭ-ȧ.
15 ¶ [s]Now the rest of the acts of Je-
hō'ash which he did, and his might,
and how he fought with Ăm-a-zī'ah
king of Jū'dah, *are* they not written in
the book of the chronicles of the kings
of Ĭs'ra-el?
16 And Je-hō'ash slept with his fathers, and was buried in Sa-mā'rĭ-ȧ
with the kings of Ĭs'ra-el; and Jĕr-o-
bō'am his son reigned in his stead.
17 ¶ [t]And Ăm-a-zī'ah the son of Jō'-
ăsh king of Jū'dah lived after the death
of Je-hō'ash son of Je-hō'a-hăz king of
Ĭs'ra-el fifteen years.
18 And the rest of the acts of Ăm-a-
zī'ah, *are* they not written in the book
of the chronicles of the kings of Jū'-
dah?
19 Now [u]they made a conspiracy
against him in Je-rụ'sa-lĕm: and he
fled to [v]Lā'chish; but they sent after
him to Lā'chish, and slew him there.
20 And they brought him on horses:
and he was buried at Je-rụ'sa-lĕm with
his fathers in the city of Dā'vid.
21 ¶ And all the people of Jū'dah
took [w]Ăz-a-rī'ah, which *was* sixteen
years old, and made him king instead
of his father Ăm-a-zī'ah.
22 He built [x]Ē'lăth, and restored it
to Jū'dah, after that the king slept with
his fathers.
23 ¶ In the [4]fifteenth year of Ăm-a-
zī'ah the son of Jō'ăsh king of Jū'dah
Jĕr-o-bō'am the son of Jō'ăsh king of
Ĭs'ra-el began to reign in Sa-mā'rĭ-ȧ,
and reigned forty and one years.
24 And he did *that which was* evil in
the sight of the LORD: he departed not
from all the sins of Jĕr-o-bō'am the son
of Nē'băt, who made Ĭs'ra-el to sin.

20 [9]He prophesied about sixty years
[n]ch. 24.2
21 [10]went down
[o]ch. 4.35; John 5.25-28-29
22 [p]ch. 8.12
23 [q]Ex. 33.19; Lam. 3.32
[r]Ex. 2.24-25
[s]Ex. 32.13; Luke 1.54-55-72-73
[11]face
25 [12]returned and took
[t]verses 18-19

CHAPTER 14
1 [a]ch. 13.10
[b]2 Chr. 25.1
4 [c]ch. 12.3; 1 Ki. 15.14
5 [d]ch. 12.20
6 [e]Deut. 24.16
7 [f]2 Chr. 25.11
[g]2 Sam. 8.13; Ps. 60, title
[1]Or, The rock
[h]Josh. 15.38
8 [i]2 Chr. 25.17-18
[j]Prov. 17.14
9 [k]Judg. 9.8
[l]1 Ki. 4.33
10 [m]2 Chr. 32.25; Hab. 2.4
[2]at thy house
[n]2 Chr. 35.21; Prov. 26.17
11 [o]Josh. 21.16
12 [3]was smitten
13 [p]2 Chr. 25.23; Neh. 8.16
[q]Jer. 31.38; Zech. 14.10
14 [r]ch. 24.13
15 [s]ch. 13.12
17 [t]2 Chr. 25.25
19 [u]ch. 12.20-21;
[v]Josh. 10.31
21 [w]ch. 15.13;
22 [x]Deut. 2.8;
23 [4]Now he begins to reign alone

25 He restored the coast of Ĭs'ra-el [y]from the entering of Hā'math unto [z]the sea of the plain, according to the word of the LORD God of Ĭs'ra-el, which he spake by the hand of his servant [a]Jō'nah, the son of A-mĭt'ta-ī, the prophet, which *was* of [b]Găth–hē'phĕr.

26 For the LORD [c]saw the affliction of Ĭs'ra-el, *that it was* very bitter: for [d]*there was* not any shut up, nor any left, nor any helper for Ĭs'ra-el.

27 [e]And the LORD said not that he would blot out the name of Ĭs'ra-el from under heaven: but he saved them by the hand of Jĕr-o-bō'am the son of Jō'ăsh.

28 ¶ Now the rest of the acts of Jĕr-o-bō'am, and all that he did, and his might, how he warred, and how he recovered Da-măs'cus, and Hā'math, [f]*which belonged* to Jū'dah, for Ĭs'ra-el, *are* they not written in the book of the chronicles of the kings of Ĭs'ra-el?

29 And Jĕr-o-bō'am slept with his fathers, *even* with the kings of Ĭs'ra-el; and [5]Zăch-a-rī'ah his son reigned in his stead.

15 In the [1]twenty and seventh year of Jĕr-o-bō'am king of Ĭs'ra-el began [a]Ăz-a-rī'ah son of Ăm-a-zī'ah king of Jū'dah to reign.

2 Sixteen years old was he when he began to reign, and he reigned two and fifty years in Je-ru'sa-lĕm. And his mother's name *was* Jĕch-o-lī'ah of Je-ru'sa-lĕm.

3 And he did *that which was* right in the sight of the LORD, according to all that his father Ăm-a-zī'ah had done;

4 [b]Save that the high places were not removed: the people sacrificed and burnt incense still on the high places.

5 ¶ And the LORD [c]smote the king, so that he was a leper unto the day of his death, and [d]dwelt in a several house. And Jō'tham the king's son *was* over the house, judging the people of the land.

6 And the rest of the acts of Ăz-a-rī'ah, and all that he did, *are* they not written in the book of the chronicles of the kings of Jū'dah?

7 So Ăz-a-rī'ah slept with his fathers; and [e]they buried him with his fathers in the city of Dā'vid: and Jō'tham his son reigned in his stead.

8 ¶ In the thirty and eighth year of Ăz-a-rī'ah king of Jū'dah did Zăch-a-rī'ah the son of Jĕr-o-bō'am reign over Ĭs'ra-el in Sa-mā'rĭ-ȧ six months.

9 And he did *that which was* evil in the sight of the LORD, as his fathers had done: he departed not from the sins of Jĕr-o-bō'am the son of Nē'băt, who made Ĭs'ra-el to sin.

10 And Shăl'lum the son of Jā'besh conspired against him, and [f]smote him before the people, and slew him, and reigned in his stead.

11 And the rest of the acts of Zăch-a-rī'ah, behold, they *are* written in the book of the chronicles of the kings of Ĭs'ra-el.

12 This *was* [g]the word of the LORD which he spake unto Jē'hū, saying, Thy sons shall sit on the throne of Ĭs'ra-el unto the fourth *generation*. And so it came to pass.

13 ¶ Shăl'lum the son of Jā'besh began to reign in the nine and thirtieth year of [h]Ūz-zī'ah king of Jū'dah; and he reigned [2]a full month in Sa-mā'rĭ-ȧ.

14 For Mĕn'a-hĕm the son of Gā'dī went up from [i]Tĭr'zah, and came to Sa-mā'rĭ-ȧ, and smote Shăl'lum the son of Jā'besh in Sa-mā'rĭ-ȧ, and slew him, and reigned in his stead.

15 And the rest of the acts of Shăl'lum, and his conspiracy which he made, behold, they *are* written in the book of the chronicles of the kings of Ĭs'ra-el.

16 ¶ Then Mĕn'a-hĕm smote [j]Tĭph'sah, and all that *were* therein, and the coasts thereof from Tĭr'zah: because they opened not *to him*, therefore he smote *it: and* all [k]the women therein that were with child he ripped up.

17 In the nine and thirtieth year of Ăz-a-rī'ah king of Jū'dah began Mĕn'a-hĕm the son of Gā'dī to reign over Ĭs'ra-el, *and reigned* ten years in Sa-mā'rĭ-ȧ.

18 And he did *that which was* evil in the sight of the LORD: he departed not all his days from the sins of Jĕr-o-bō'am the son of Nē'băt, who made Ĭs'ra-el to sin.

19 *And* [l]Pŭl the king of Ăs-sy̆r'ĭ-ȧ came against the land: and Mĕn'a-hĕm gave Pŭl a thousand talents of silver, that his hand might be with him to [m]confirm the kingdom in his hand.

20 And Mĕn'a-hĕm [3]exacted the money of Ĭs'ra-el, *even* of all the mighty men of wealth, of each man fifty shekels of silver, to give to the king of Ăs-sy̆r'ĭ-ȧ. So the king of Ăs-sy̆r'ĭ-ȧ turned back, and stayed not there in the land.

21 ¶ And the rest of the acts of Mĕn'a-hĕm, and all that he did, *are* they not written in the book of the chronicles of the kings of Ĭs'ra-el?

22 And Mĕn'a-hĕm slept with his fathers; and Pĕk-a-hī'ah his son reigned in his stead.

23 ¶ In the fiftieth year of Ăz-a-rī'ah king of Jū'dah Pĕk-a-hī'ah the son of Mĕn'a-hĕm began to reign over Ĭs'ra-el in Sa-mā'rĭ-ȧ, *and reigned* [n]two years.

24 And he did *that which was* evil in the sight of the LORD: he departed not from the sins of Jĕr-o-bō'am the son of Nē'băt, who made Ĭs'ra-el to sin.

25 But Pē'kah the son of Rĕm-a-lī'ah, a captain of his, conspired against him, and smote him in Sa-mā'rĭ-ȧ, in the palace of the king's house, with Ar'gŏb and A-rī'eh, and with him fifty men of the Gĭl'e-ăd-ītes: and he killed him, and reigned in his room.

26 And the rest of the acts of Pĕk-a-hī'ah, and all that he did, behold, they *are* written in the book of the chronicles of the kings of Ĭs'ra-el.

27 ¶ In the two and fiftieth year of Ăz-a-rī'ah king of Jū'dah [o]Pē'kah the son of Rĕm-a-lī'ah began to reign over Ĭs'ra-el in Sa-mā'rĭ-ȧ, *and reigned* twenty years.

25 [y]Num. 13.21; Ezek. 47.16-18; Amos 6.14
[z]Deut. 3.17
[a]Jon. 1.1; Matt. 12.39
[b]Josh. 19.13
26 [c]Ex. 3.7-9; ch. 13.4
[d]Deut. 32.36
27 [e]ch. 13.5
28 [f]2 Sam. 8.6
29 [5]After an interregnum of 11 years

CHAPTER 15
1 [1]This is the 27th year of Jeroboam's partnership in the kingdom with his father, who made him consort at his going to the Syrian wars. It is the 16th year of Jeroboam's monarchy
[a]ch. 14.21
4 [b]ch. 12.3
5 [c]2 Chr. 26.19
[d]Lev. 13.46
7 [e]2 Chr. 26.23
10 [f]As prophesied, Hos. 1.4; Amos 7.9; Job 20.4-29; Job 27.13-23; Job 31.2-3; Ps. 1.4; Ps. 37.37; Prov. 2.22
12 [g]ch. 10.30; 1 Pet. 1.25
13 [h]verse 1, Azariah; Matt. 1.8, Ozias
[2]a month of days
14 [i]Josh. 12.24; Song 6.4
16 [j]1 Ki. 4.24
[k]ch. 8.12; Isa. 13.16-18
19 [l]1 Chr. 5.26; Isa. 9.1
[m]ch. 14.5
20 [3]caused to come forth
23 [n]1 Ki. 15.25; Job 20.5
27 [o]2 Chr. 28.6; Isa. 7.1

28 And he did *that which was* evil in the sight of the LORD: he departed not from the sins of Jĕr-o-bō'am the son of Nē'băt, who made Ĭs'ra-el to sin.

29 In the days of Pē'kah king of Ĭs'ra-el [p]came Tĭg'lath–pĭ-lē'ser king of Ăs-sўr'ĭ-ȧ, and took [q]Ī'jon, and Ā'bĕl–bĕth–mā'a-chah, and Ja-nō'ah, and Kē'desh, and Hā'zôr, and Gĭl'e-ăd, and Găl'ĭ-lee, all the land of Năph'ta-lī, and carried them captive to Ăs-sўr'ĭ-ȧ.

30 And Ho-shē'ȧ the son of Ē'lah made a conspiracy against Pē'kah the son of Rĕm-a-lī'ah, and smote him, and slew him, and reigned [4]in his stead, [5]in the twentieth year of Jō'tham the son of Ŭz-zī'ah.

31 And the rest of the acts of Pē'kah, and all that he did, behold, they *are* written in the book of the chronicles of the kings of Ĭs'ra-el.

32 ¶ In the second year of Pē'kah the son of Rĕm-a-lī'ah king of Ĭs'ra-el began [r]Jō'tham the son of Ŭz-zī'ah king of Jū'dah to reign.

33 Five and twenty years old was he when he began to reign, and he reigned sixteen years in Je-ru'sa-lĕm. And his mother's name *was* Je-ru'shȧ, the daughter of Zā'dŏk.

34 And he did *that which was* right in the sight of the LORD: he did according to all that his father Ŭz-zī'ah had done.

35 ¶ [s]Howbeit the high places were not removed: the people sacrificed and burned incense still in the high places. [t]He built the higher gate of the house of the LORD.

36 ¶ Now the rest of the acts of Jō'tham, and all that he did, *are* they not written in the book of the chronicles of the kings of Jū'dah?

37 [u]In those days the LORD began to send against Jū'dah [v]Rē'zin the king of Sўr'ĭ-ȧ, and Pē'kah the son of Rĕm-a-lī'ah.

38 And Jō'tham slept with his fathers, and was buried with his fathers in the city of Dā'vid his father: and Ā'hăz his son reigned in his stead.

16 In the seventeenth year of Pē'kah the son of Rĕm-a-lī'ah [a]Ā'hăz the son of Jō'tham king of Jū'dah began to reign.

2 Twenty years old *was* Ā'hăz when he began to reign, and reigned sixteen years in Je-ru'sa-lĕm, and did not *that which was* right in the sight of the LORD his God, like Dā'vid his father.

3 But he walked in the way of the kings of Ĭs'ra-el, yea, [b]and made his son to pass through the fire, according to the [c]abominations of the heathen, whom the LORD cast out from before the children of Ĭs'ra-el.

4 And he sacrificed and burnt incense in the high places, and [d]on the hills, and under every green tree.

5 ¶ [e]Then Rē'zin king of Sўr'ĭ-ȧ and Pē'kah son of Rĕm-a-lī'ah king of Ĭs'ra-el came up to Je-ru'sa-lĕm to war: and they besieged Ā'hăz, but could not overcome *him*.

6 At that time Rē'zin king of Sўr'ĭ-ȧ [f]recovered Ē'lăth to Sўr'ĭ-ȧ, and drave the Jews from [1]Ē'lăth: and the Sўr'ĭ-ans came to Ē'lăth, and dwelt there unto this day.

7 So Ā'hăz sent messengers [g]to [2]Tĭg'-lath–pĭ-lē'ser king of Ăs-sўr'ĭ-ȧ, saying, I *am* thy servant and thy son: come up, and save me out of the hand of the king of Sўr'ĭ-ȧ, and out of the hand of the king of Ĭs'ra-el, which rise up against me.

8 And Ā'hăz [h]took the silver and gold that was found in the house of the LORD, and in the treasures of the king's house, and sent *it for* a present to the king of Ăs-sўr'ĭ-ȧ.

9 And the king of Ăs-sўr'ĭ-ȧ hearkened unto him: for the king of Ăs-sўr'ĭ-ȧ went up against [3]Da-măs'cus, and [i]took it, and carried *the people of* it captive to [4]Kīr, and slew Rē'zin.

10 ¶ And king Ā'hăz went to Da-măs'cus to meet Tĭg'lath–pĭ-lē'ser king of Ăs-sўr'ĭ-ȧ, and saw an altar that *was* at Da-măs'cus: and king Ā'hăz sent to U-rī'jah the priest the fashion of the altar, and the pattern of it, according to all the workmanship thereof.

11 And U-rī'jah the priest built an altar according to all that king Ā'hăz had sent from Da-măs'cus: so U-rī'jah the priest made *it* against king Ā'hăz came from Da-măs'cus.

12 And when the king was come from Da-măs'cus, the king saw the altar: and [j]the king approached to the altar, and offered thereon.

13 And he burnt his burnt offering and his meat offering, and poured his drink offering, and sprinkled the blood of [5]his peace offerings, upon the altar.

14 And he brought also [k]the brasen altar, which *was* before the LORD, from the forefront of the house, from between the altar and the house of the LORD, and put it on the north side of the altar.

15 And king Ā'hăz commanded U-rī'jah the priest, saying, Upon the great altar burn [l]the morning burnt offering, and the evening meat offering, and the king's burnt sacrifice, and his meat offering, with the burnt offering of all the people of the land, and their meat offering, and their drink offerings; and sprinkle upon it all the blood of the burnt offering, and all the blood of the sacrifice: and the brasen altar shall be for me [m]to inquire *by*.

16 Thus did U-rī'jah the priest, according to all that king Ā'hăz commanded.

17 ¶ [n]And king Ā'hăz cut off [o]the borders of the bases, and removed the laver from off them; and took down [p]the sea from off the brasen oxen that *were* under it, and put it upon a pavement of stones.

18 And the covert for the sabbath that they had built in the house, and the king's entry without, turned he from the house of the LORD for the king of Ăs-sўr'ĭ-ȧ.

---

29 [p]1 Chr. 5.26; Isa. 9.1
[q]1 Ki. 15.20
30 [4]After an anarchy for some years
[5]In the fourth year of Ahaz, in the 20th year after Jotham had begun to reign
32 [r]1 Chr. 3.12; Matt. 1.9
35 [s]verse 4
[t]2 Chr. 27.3
37 [u]ch. 10.32; 2 Chr. 28.6; At the end of Jotham's reign
[v]2 Chr. 28.5-6; Isa. 7.1

CHAPTER 16
1 [a]2 Chr. 28.1
3 [b]Lev. 18.21; Deut. 18.10; ch. 17.17; 2 Chr. 28.3; Ps. 106.37; Jer. 7.31; Ezek. 16.20
[c]Deut. 12.31; ch. 21.2-11; 2 Chr. 33.2
4 [d]Isa. 57.5-7; Jer. 17.2
5 [e]Isa. 7.1
6 [f]ch. 14.22
[1]Eloth
7 [g]ch. 15.29
[2]Tilgath-pileser, 1 Chr. 5.26; 2 Chr. 28.20, Tilgath-pileser
8 [h]ch. 12.18
9 [3]Dammesek
[i]Foretold, Amos 1.5
[4]That is, Media
12 [j]2 Chr. 26.16-19
13 [5]which were his
14 [k]Ex. 40.6-29; 2 Chr. 4.1
15 [l]Ex. 29.39-40-41
[m]Gen. 44.5; 2 Chr. 33.6; Isa. 2.6; Hos. 4.12
17 [n]2 Chr. 28.24
[o]1 Ki. 7.27
[p]ch. 25.13-16; 2 Chr. 4.15

19 ¶ Now the rest of the acts of Ā'hăz
which he did, *are* they not written in the
book of the chronicles of the kings of
Jū'dah?
20 And Ā'hăz slept with his fathers,
and [q]was buried with his fathers in the
city of Dā'vid: and Hĕz-e-kī'ah his son
reigned in his stead.

17 In the twelfth year of Ā'hăz king
of Jū'dah began [a]Ho-shē'ȧ the
son of Ē'lah to reign in Sa-mā'rĭ-ȧ over
Ĭs'ra-el nine years.
2 And he did *that which was* evil in
the sight of the LORD, but not as the
kings of Ĭs'ra-el that were before him.
3 ¶ Against him came up [b]Shăl-man-
ē'ser king of Ăs-sȳr'ĭ-ȧ; and Ho-shē'ȧ
became his servant, and [1]gave him
[2]presents.
4 And the king of Ăs-sȳr'ĭ-ȧ found
conspiracy in Ho-shē'ȧ: for he had sent
messengers to Sō king of Ē'gypt, and
brought no present to the king of Ăs-
sȳr'ĭ-ȧ, as *he had done* year by year:
therefore the king of Ăs-sȳr'ĭ-ȧ shut
him up, and bound him in prison.
5 ¶ Then [c]the king of Ăs-sȳr'ĭ-ȧ came
up throughout all the land, and went up
to Sa-mā'rĭ-ȧ, and besieged it three
years.
6 ¶ [d]In the ninth year of Ho-shē'ȧ the
king of Ăs-sȳr'ĭ-ȧ took Sa-mā'rĭ-ȧ, and
[e]carried Ĭs'ra-el away into Ăs-sȳr'ĭ-ȧ,
[f]and placed them in Hā'lah and in Hā'-
bôr *by* the river of Gō'zan, and in the
cities of the Mēdes.
7 For *so* it was, that the children of
Ĭs'ra-el had sinned against the LORD
their God, which had brought them up
out of the land of Ē'gypt, from under
the hand of Phā'raōh king of Ē'gypt,
and had feared other gods,
8 And [g]walked in the statutes of the
heathen, whom the LORD cast out from
before the children of Ĭs'ra-el, and of
the kings of Ĭs'ra-el, which they had
made.
9 And the children of Ĭs'ra-el did secretly [h]*those* things that *were* not right
against the LORD their God, and they
built them high places in all their cities, [i]from the tower of the watchmen
to the fenced city.
10 [j]And they set them up [3]images
and [k]groves [l]in every high hill, and
under every green tree:
11 And there they burnt incense in
all the high places, as *did* the heathen
whom the LORD carried away before
them; and wrought wicked things to
provoke the LORD to anger:
12 For they served idols, [m]whereof
the LORD had said unto them, [n]Ye shall
not do this thing.
13 Yet the LORD testified against Ĭs'-
ra-el, and against Jū'dah, [4]by all the
prophets, *and by* all [o]the seers, saying,
[p]Turn ye from your evil ways, and
keep my commandments *and* my statutes, according to all the law which I
commanded your fathers, and which I
sent to you by my servants the prophets.
14 Notwithstanding they would not
hear, but [q]hardened their necks, like

20 [q]ch. 21.18-26; 2 Chr. 28.27
CHAPTER 17
1 [a]After an interregnum; ch. 15.30
3 [b]ch. 18.9 [1]rendered [2]Or, tribute
5 [c]ch. 18.9
6 [d]ch. 18.10; Hos. 13.16, foretold [e]Lev. 26.32; Deut. 28.36-64 [f]1 Chr. 5.26
8 [g]Lev. 18.3; Deut. 18.9; ch. 16.3
9 [h]Deut. 13.6; Ezek. 8.12 [i]ch. 18.8
10 [j]Isa. 57.5 [3]statues [k]Ex. 34.13; Mic. 5.14 [l]Deut. 12.2; ch. 16.4
12 [m]Ex. 20.3; Deut. 5.7 [n]Deut. 4.19
13 [4]by the hand of all [o]1 Sam. 9.9 [p]Isa. 1.16-20; Jer. 18.11
14 [q]Deut. 31.27; Prov. 29.1
15 [r]Deut. 29.25 [s]Deut. 32.21; 1 Cor. 8.4 [t]Ps. 115.8; Rom. 1.21 [u]Deut. 12.30-31
16 [v]Ex. 32.8 [w]1 Ki. 14.15 [x]1 Ki. 16.31; ch. 11.18
17 [y]Lev. 18.21; Ezek. 16.20 [z]Deut. 18.10; Gal. 5.20 [a]Isa. 50.1
18 [b]1 Ki. 11.13-32
19 [c]Jer. 3.8
20 [d]ch. 13.3
21 [e]1 Ki. 11.11-31 [f]1 Ki. 12.20-28
23 [g]1 Ki. 14.16
24 [h]Ezra 4.2 [i]ch. 18.34
25 [j]Eph. 2.12
27 [k]Judg. 17.13

to the neck of their fathers, that did not
believe in the LORD their God.
15 And they rejected his statutes,
[r]and his covenant that he made with
their fathers, and his testimonies which
he testified against them; and they
followed [s]vanity, and [t]became vain,
and went after the heathen that *were*
round about them, *concerning* whom
the LORD had charged them, that they
should [u]not do like them.
16 And they left all the commandments of the LORD their God, and
[v]made them molten images, *even* two
calves, [w]and made a grove, and worshipped all the host of heaven, [x]and
served Bā'al.
17 [y]And they caused their sons and
their daughters to pass through the
fire, and [z]used divination and enchantments, and [a]sold themselves to do evil
in the sight of the LORD, to provoke
him to anger.
18 Therefore the LORD was very angry with Ĭs'ra-el, and removed them
out of his sight: there was none left
[b]but the tribe of Jū'dah only.
19 Also [c]Jū'dah kept not the commandments of the LORD their God, but
walked in the statutes of Ĭs'ra-el which
they made.
20 And the LORD rejected all the
seed of Ĭs'ra-el, and afflicted them, and
[d]delivered them into the hand of spoilers, until he had cast them out of his
sight.
21 For [e]he rent Ĭs'ra-el from the
house of Dā'vid; and [f]they made Jĕr-o-
bō'am the son of Nē'băt king: and Jĕr-
o-bō'am drave Ĭs'ra-el from following
the LORD, and made them sin a great
sin.
22 For the children of Ĭs'ra-el walked
in all the sins of Jĕr-o-bō'am which he
did; they departed not from them;
23 Until the LORD removed Ĭs'ra-el
out of his sight, [g]as he had said by all
his servants the prophets. So was Ĭs'-
ra-el carried away out of their own
land to Ăs-sȳr'ĭ-ȧ unto this day.
24 ¶ [h]And the king of Ăs-sȳr'ĭ-ȧ
brought *men* from Băb'ȳ-lon, and from
Cū'thah, and from [i]Ā'vȧ, and from
Hā'math, and from Sĕph-ar-vā'im, and
placed *them* in the cities of Sa-mā'rĭ-ȧ
instead of the children of Ĭs'ra-el: and
they possessed Sa-mā'rĭ-ȧ, and dwelt
in the cities thereof.
25 And *so* it was at the beginning of
their dwelling there, *that* [j]they feared
not the LORD: therefore the LORD sent
lions among them, which slew *some* of
them.
26 Wherefore they spake to the king
of Ăs-sȳr'ĭ-ȧ, saying, The nations which
thou hast removed, and placed in the
cities of Sa-mā'rĭ-ȧ, know not the manner of the God of the land: therefore
he hath sent lions among them, and,
behold, they slay them, because they
know not the manner of the God of the
land.
27 Then the king of Ăs-sȳr'ĭ-ȧ commanded, saying, Carry thither one of
[k]the priests whom ye brought from

thence; and let them go and dwell there, and let him teach them the manner of the God of the land.

28 Then one of the priests whom they had carried away from Sa-mā'rĭ-ȧ came and dwelt in Bĕth'–el, and taught them how they should fear the LORD.

29 Howbeit every nation made gods of their own, and put *them* in the houses of the high places which the Sa-măr'ĭ-tans had made, every nation in their cities wherein they dwelt.

30 And the men of Băb'ȳ-lon made Sŭc'coth–bē'noth, and the men of Cŭth made Nĕr'gal, and the men of Hā'math made Ăsh'ĭ-mȧ,

31 And the Ā'vītes made Nĭb'hăz and Tär'tak, and the Sĕph'ar-vītes [l]burnt their children in fire to A-drăm'me-lech and A-năm'me-lech, the gods of Sĕph-ar-vā'im.

32 So they feared the LORD, [m]and made unto themselves of the lowest of them priests of the high places, which sacrificed for them in the houses of the high places.

33 [n]They feared the LORD, and served their own gods, after the manner of the nations [5]whom they carried away from thence.

34 Unto this day they do after the former manners: they fear not the LORD, neither do they after their statutes, or after their ordinances, or after the law and commandment which the LORD commanded the children of Jā'cob, [o]whom he named Ĭs'ra-el;

35 With whom the LORD had made a covenant, and charged them, saying, [p]Ye shall not fear other gods, nor [q]bow yourselves to them, nor serve them, nor sacrifice to them:

36 But the LORD, who brought you up out of the land of Ē'gypt with great power and a [r]stretched out arm, [s]him shall ye fear, and him shall ye worship, and to him shall ye do sacrifice.

37 And the statutes, and the ordinances, and the law, and the commandment, which he wrote for you, [t]ye shall observe to do for evermore; and ye shall not fear other gods.

38 And the covenant that I have made with you [u]ye shall not forget; neither shall ye fear other gods.

39 But the LORD your God ye shall fear; and he shall deliver you out of the hand of all your enemies.

40 Howbeit they did not hearken, but they did after their former manner.

41 So these nations [v]feared the LORD, and served their graven images, both their children, and their children's children: as did their fathers, so do they unto this day.

18 Now it came to pass in the third year of Ho-shē'ȧ son of Ē'lah king of Ĭs'ra-el, *that* [a]Hĕz-e-kī'ah the son of Ā'hăz king of Jū'dah began to reign.

2 Twenty and five years old was he when he began to reign; and he reigned twenty and nine years in Je-ru'sa-lĕm. His mother's name also *was* [b]Ā'bī, the daughter of Zăch-a-rī'ah.

3 And he did *that which was* right in the sight of the LORD, according to all that Dā'vid his father did.

4 ¶ [c]He removed the high places, and brake the [1]images, and cut down the groves, and brake in pieces the [d]brasen serpent that Mō'ses had made: for unto those days the children of Ĭs'ra-el did burn incense to it: and he called it [2]Ne-hŭsh'tan.

5 He [e]trusted in the LORD God of Ĭs'ra-el; [f]so that after him was none like him among all the kings of Jū'dah, nor *any* that were before him.

6 For he [g]clave to the LORD, *and* departed not [3]from following him, but kept his commandments, which the LORD commanded Mō'ses.

7 And the LORD [h]was with him; *and* he prospered [i]whithersoever he went forth: and he [j]rebelled against the king of Ăs-sȳr'ĭ-ȧ, and served him not.

8 [k]He smote the Phĭ-lĭs'tīnes, *even* unto [4]Gā'zȧ, and the borders thereof, from the tower of the watchmen to the fenced city.

9 ¶ And [l]it came to pass in the fourth year of king Hĕz-e-kī'ah, which *was* the seventh year of Ho-shē'ȧ son of Ē'lah king of Ĭs'ra-el, *that* Shăl-man-ē'ser king of Ăs-sȳr'ĭ-ȧ came up against Sa-mā'rĭ-ȧ, and besieged it.

10 And at the end of three years they took it: *even* in the sixth year of Hĕz-e-kī'ah, that *is* [m]the ninth year of Ho-shē'ȧ king of Ĭs'ra-el, Sa-mā'rĭ-ȧ was taken.

11 And the king of Ăs-sȳr'ĭ-ȧ did carry away Ĭs'ra-el unto Ăs-sȳr'ĭ-ȧ, and put them [n]in Hā'lah and in Hā'bôr *by* the river of Gō'zan, and in the cities of the Mēdes:

12 [o]Because they obeyed not the voice of the LORD their God, but transgressed his covenant, *and* all that Mō'ses the servant of the LORD commanded, and would not hear *them*, nor do *them*.

13 ¶ Now [p]in the fourteenth year of king Hĕz-e-kī'ah did [5]Sĕn-năch'e-rĭb king of Ăs-sȳr'ĭ-ȧ come up against all the fenced cities of Jū'dah, and took them.

14 And Hĕz-e-kī'ah king of Jū'dah sent to the king of Ăs-sȳr'ĭ-ȧ to Lā'chish, saying, I have offended; return from me: that which thou puttest on me will I bear. And the king of Ăs-sȳr'ĭ-ȧ appointed unto Hĕz-e-kī'ah king of Jū'dah three hundred talents of silver and thirty talents of gold.

15 And Hĕz-e-kī'ah [q]gave *him* all the silver that was found in the house of the LORD, and in the treasures of the king's house.

16 At that time did Hĕz-e-kī'ah cut off *the gold from* the doors of the temple of the LORD, and *from* the pillars which Hĕz-e-kī'ah king of Jū'dah had overlaid, and gave [6]it to the king of Ăs-sȳr'ĭ-ȧ.

17 ¶ And the king of Ăs-sȳr'ĭ-ȧ sent Tär'tan and Răb'sa-rĭs and Răb''–sha-keh from Lā'chish to king Hĕz-e-kī'ah with a [7]great host against Je-ru'sa-lĕm.

31 [l]Lev. 18.21; Deut. 12.31
32 [m]1 Ki. 12.31
33 [n]Isa. 29.13; Hos. 10.2; Zeph. 1.5; Matt. 6.24; Luke 16.13 [5]Or, who carried them away from thence
34 [o]Gen. 32.28
35 [p]Judg. 6.10 [q]Ex. 20.5
36 [r]Ex. 6.6 [s]Deut. 10.20; Rev. 15.4
37 [t]Deut. 5.32
38 [u]Deut. 4.23
41 [v]Josh. 24.14; Zeph. 1.5; Luke 16.13; John 4.24; Rev. 3.15

CHAPTER 18
1 [a]2 Chr. 28.27
2 [b]2 Chr. 29.1-Abijah
4 [c]2 Chr. 31.1 [1]statues [d]Num. 21.9 [2]That is, A piece of brass
5 [e]ch. 19.10; 2 Chr. 32.7-8; Job 13.15; Ps. 13.5; Ps. 46.1-2; Matt. 27.43; Eph. 1.12 [f]ch. 23.25
6 [g]Deut. 10.20; Josh. 23.8 [3]from after him
7 [h]Gen. 39.2-3; 2 Chr. 15.2; Ps. 46.11; Matt. 1.23 [i]Ps. 60.12 [j]ch. 16.7
8 [k]1 Chr. 4.41; Isa. 14.29 [4]Azzah
9 [l]ch. 17.3
10 [m]ch. 17.6
11 [n]1 Chr. 5.26
12 [o]ch. 17.7; Dan. 9.6-10
13 [p]2 Chr. 32.1 [5]Sanherib
15 [q]ch. 12.18; 2 Chr. 12.9
16 [6]them
17 [7]heavy

And they went up and came to Je-
rṳ'sa-lĕm. And when they were come
up, they came and stood by the conduit
of the upper pool, [r]which *is* in the highway of the fuller's field.
18 And when they had called to the
king, there came out to them E-lī'a-
kĭm the son of Hĭl-kī'ah, which *was*
over the household, and Shĕb'na̤ the
[8]scribe, and Jō'ah the son of Ā'saph
the recorder.
19 And Răb''–sha-keh said unto
them, Speak ye now to Hĕz-e-kī'ah,
Thṳs saith the great king, the king
of Ăs-sy̆r'ĭ-a̤, [s]What confidence *is* this
wherein thou trustest?
20 Thou [9]sayest, (but *they are but*
[10]vain words,) [11]*I have* counsel and
strength for the war. Now on whom
dost thou trust, that thou [t]rebellest
against me?
21 [u]Now, behold, thou [12]trustest
upon the staff of this bruised reed,
even upon Ē'ġypt, on which if a man
lean, it will go into his hand, and pierce
it: so *is* Phā'raōh king of Ē'ġypt unto
all that trust on him.
22 But if ye say unto me, We trust
in the LORD our God: *is* not that he,
[v]whose high places and whose altars
Hĕz-e-kī'ah hath taken away, and hath
said to Jū'dah and Je-rṳ'sa-lĕm, Ye
shall worship before this altar in Je-
rṳ'sa-lĕm?
23 Now therefore, I pray thee, give
[13]pledges to my lord the king of Ăs-
sy̆r'ĭ-a̤, and I will deliver thee two thousand horses, if thou be able on thy part
to set riders upon them.
24 How then wilt thou turn away the
face of one captain of the least of my
master's servants, and put thy trust on
Ē'ġypt for chariots and for horsemen?
25 Am I now come up without the
LORD against this place to destroy it?
The LORD [w]said to me, Go up against
this land, and destroy it.
26 Then said E-lī'a-kĭm the son of
Hĭl-kī'ah, and Shĕb'na̤, and Jō'ah, unto
Răb''–sha-keh, Speak, I pray thee, to
thy servants in the Sy̆r'ĭ-an language;
for we understand *it:* and talk not with
us in the Jews' language in the ears of
the people that *are* on the wall.
27 But Răb''–sha-keh said unto
them, Hath my master sent me to thy
master, and to thee, to speak these
words? *hath he* not *sent me* to the men
which sit on the wall, that they may eat
their own dung, and drink [14]their own
piss with you?
28 Then Răb''–sha-keh stood and
cried with a loud voice in the Jews'
language, and spake, saying, Hear the
word of the great king, the king of Ăs-
sy̆r'ĭ-a̤:
29 Thus saith the king, [x]Let not Hĕz-
e-kī'ah deceive you: for he shall not be
able to deliver you out of his hand:
30 Neither let Hĕz-e-kī'ah make you
trust in the LORD, saying, The LORD
will surely deliver us, and this city
shall not be delivered into the hand of
the king of Ăs-sy̆r'ĭ-a̤.
31 Hearken not to Hĕz-e-kī'ah: for
thus saith the king of Ăs-sy̆r'ĭ-a̤, [15]Make
an agreement with me by a present,
and come out to me, and *then* eat ye
every man of his own vine, and every
one of his fig tree, and drink ye every
one the waters of his [16]cistern:
32 Until I come and take you away
to a land like your own land, [y]a land
of corn and wine, a land of bread
and vineyards, a land of oil olive and
of honey, that ye may live, and not
die: and hearken not unto Hĕz-e-kī'ah,
when he [17]persuadeth you, saying, The
LORD will deliver us.
33 [z]Hath any of the gods of the nations delivered at all his land out of the
hand of the king of Ăs-sy̆r'ĭ-a̤?
34 [a]Where *are* the gods of Hā'math,
and of Är'pad? where *are* the gods
of Sĕph-ar-vā'im, Hē'na̤, and [b]Ī'vah?
have they delivered Sa-mā'rĭ-a̤ out of
mine hand?
35 Who *are* they among all the gods
of the countries, that have delivered
their country out of mine hand, [c]that
the LORD should deliver Je-rṳ'sa-lĕm
out of mine hand?
36 But the people held their peace,
and answered him not a word: for the
king's commandment was, saying, Answer him not.
37 Then came E-lī'a-kĭm the son of
Hĭl-kī'ah, which *was* over the household, and Shĕb'na̤ the scribe, and Jō'ah
the son of Ā'saph the recorder, to Hĕz-
e-kī'ah [d]with *their* clothes rent, and
told him the words of Răb''–sha-keh.

19 And it came to pass, when king
Hĕz-e-kī'ah heard *it,* that he rent
his clothes, and covered himself with
sackcloth, and went into the house of
the [a]LORD.
2 And he sent E-lī'a-kĭm, which *was*
over the household, and Shĕb'na̤ the
scribe, and the elders of the priests,
covered with sackcloth, to I-sā'iah the
prophet the son of Ā'moz.
3 And they said unto him, Thus saith
Hĕz-e-kī'ah, This day *is* a day of trouble, and of rebuke, and [1]blasphemy: for
the children are come to the birth, and
there is not strength to bring forth.
4 [b]It may be the LORD thy God will
hear all the words of Răb''–sha-keh,
[c]whom the king of Ăs-sy̆r'ĭ-a̤ his master hath sent to reproach the living
God; and will [d]reprove the words
which the LORD thy God hath heard:
wherefore [e]lift up *thy* prayer for the
remnant that are [2]left.
5 So the servants of king Hĕz-e-kī'-
ah came to I-sā'iah.
6 ¶ [f]And I-sā'iah said unto them,
Thus shall ye say to your master, Thus
saith the LORD, [g]Be not afraid of the
words which thou hast heard, with
which the servants of the king of Ăs-
sy̆r'ĭ-a̤ have blasphemed me.
7 Behold, I will send [h]a blast upon
him, and he shall hear a rumour, and
shall return to his own land; and I will
cause him to fall by the sword in his
own land.

[r]Isa. 7.3
18 [8]Or, secretary
19 [s]2 Chr. 32.10
20 [9]Or, talkest [10]word of the lips [11]Or, But counsel and strength are for the war [t]Ezra 4.15
21 [u]Isa. 36.6; Ezek. 29.6-7 [12]trustest thee
22 [v]2 Chr. 31.1; Isa. 36.7
23 [13]Or, hostages
25 [w]ch. 19.6-22; 2 Chr. 35.21; Isa. 7.17
27 [14]the water of their feet
29 [x]2 Chr. 32.15; Job 5.19; Dan. 3.15-17
31 [15]Make with me a blessing, or, seek my favour [16]Or, pit
32 [y]Deut. 8.7-8 [17]Or, deceiveth
33 [z]ch. 19.12; 2 Chr. 32.14; Isa. 10.10-11
34 [a]ch. 19.13 [b]ch. 17.24- Ava?
35 [c]Ps. 2.2-4; Ps. 50.21; Ps. 59.7-8; Isa. 10.5-15; Dan. 3.15; Rom. 1.21-22-23
37 [d]Job 1.20; Isa. 33.7; Jer. 36.24

CHAPTER 19
1 [a]Ps. 3.4-8; 1 Pet. 5.6-7
3 [1]Or, provocation
4 [b]2 Sam. 16.12 [c]ch. 18.35 [d]Ps. 50.21 [e]Jas. 5.16 [2]found
6 [f]Isa. 37.6 [g]Ex. 14.13; ch. 6.16
7 [h]Job 4.9; Ps. 11.6

8 ¶ So Răb′′–sha-keh returned, and
found the king of Ăs-sy̆r′ĭ-ȧ warring
against Lĭb′nah: for he had heard that
he was departed [i]from Lā′chish.
9 And [j]when he heard say of Tĭr′-
ha-kah king of Ē-thĭ-ō′pĭ-a, Behold, he
is come out to fight against thee: he
sent messengers again unto Hĕz-e-kī′-
ah, saying,
10 Thus shall ye speak to Hĕz-e-kī′-
ah king of Jū′dah, saying, Let not thy
God [k]in whom thou trustest deceive
thee, saying, Je-ru′sa-lĕm shall not be
delivered into the hand of the king of
Ăs-sy̆r′ĭ-ȧ.
11 Behold, thou hast heard what the
kings of Ăs-sy̆r′ĭ-ȧ have done to all
lands, by destroying them utterly: and
shalt thou be delivered?
12 Have the gods of the nations delivered them which my fathers have destroyed; *as* Gō′zan, [l]and Hā′ran, and
Rē′zeph, and the children of [m]Ē′dĕn
which *were* in The-lā′sar?
13 [n]Where *is* the king of Hā′math,
and the king of Ăr′pad, and the king of
the city of Sĕph-ar-vā′im, of Hē′nȧ,
and [o]Ī′vah?
14 ¶ [p]And Hĕz-e-kī′ah received the
letter of the hand of the messengers,
and read it: and Hĕz-e-kī′ah went up
into the house of the LORD, and spread
it before the LORD.
15 And Hĕz-e-kī′ah prayed before
the LORD, and said, O LORD God of
Ĭs′ra-el, [q]which dwellest *between* the
cherubims, [r]thou art the God, *even*
thou alone, of all the kingdoms of
the earth; thou hast made heaven and
earth.
16 LORD, [s]bow down thine ear, and
hear: [t]open, LORD, thine eyes, and see:
and hear the words of Sĕn-năch′e-rĭb,
which hath sent him to reproach the
living God.
17 Of a truth, LORD, the kings of Ăs-
sy̆r′ĭ-ȧ have destroyed the nations and
their lands,
18 And have [3]cast their gods into
the fire: for they *were* no gods, but
the [u]work of men's hands, wood and
stone: therefore they have destroyed
them.
19 Now therefore, O LORD our God,
I beseech thee, save thou us out of his
hand, [v]that all the kingdoms of the
earth may know that thou *art* the LORD
God, *even* thou only.
20 ¶ Then I-sā′iah the son of Ā′moz
sent to Hĕz-e-kī′ah, saying, Thus saith
the LORD God of Ĭs′ra-el, *That* which
thou hast prayed to me against Sĕn-
năch′e-rĭb king of Ăs-sy̆r′ĭ-ȧ [w]I have
heard.
21 This *is* the word that the LORD
hath spoken concerning him; The virgin [x]the daughter of Zī′ŏn hath despised thee, *and* laughed thee to scorn;
the daughter of Je-ru′sa-lĕm [y]hath
shaken her head at thee.
22 Whom hast thou reproached and
blasphemed? and against whom hast
thou exalted *thy* voice, and lifted up
thine eyes on high? *even* against [z]the
Holy *One* of Ĭs′ra-el.

8 [i]ch. 18.14
9 [j]1 Sam. 23.27; Isa. 37.9
10 [k]ch. 18.5; Isa. 37.10-14
12 [l]Gen. 11.31 [m]Ezek. 27.23
13 [n]ch. 18.34 [o]ch. 17.24
14 [p]Isa. 37.14
15 [q]Ex. 25.22; Ps. 80.1 [r]Ps. 96.5; Isa. 44.6
16 [s]Ps. 31.2 [t]2 Chr. 6.40
18 [3]given [u]Ps. 115.4
19 [v]Ps. 83.18
20 [w]Ps. 65.2
21 [x]Lam. 2.13 [y]Job 16.4; Lam. 2.15
22 [z]Ps. 71.22; Jer. 51.5
23 [4]By the hand of [a]Ps. 20.7 [5]the tallness, etc [6]Or, the forest and his fruitful field
24 [7]Or, fenced
25 [8]Or, Hast thou not heard how I have made it long ago, and formed it of ancient times? should I now bring it to be laid waste, and fenced cities to be ruinous heaps? [b]Ps. 33.11; [c]Isa. 10.5
26 [9]short of hand [d]Ps. 129.6
27 [e]Ps. 139.1 [10]Or, sitting
28 [f]Job 41.2
29 [g]ch. 20.8-9
30 [11]the escaping of the house of Judah that remaineth
31 [12]the escaping [h]Isa. 9.7
34 [i]ch. 20.6 [j]1 Ki. 11.12-13
35 [k]2 Chr. 32.21
36 [l]Gen. 10.11

23 [4]By thy messengers thou hast
reproached the Lord, and hast said,
[a]With the multitude of my chariots
I am come up to the height of the
mountains, to the sides of Lĕb′a-non,
and will cut down [5]the tall cedar trees
thereof, *and* the choice fir trees thereof:
and I will enter into the lodgings of
his borders, *and into* [6]the forest of his
Cär′mel.
24 I have digged and drunk strange
waters, and with the sole of my feet
have I dried up all the rivers of [7]be-
sieged places.
25 [8]Hast thou not heard long ago
how [b]I have done it, *and* of ancient
times that I have formed it? now have I
brought it to pass, that [c]thou shouldest
be to lay waste fenced cities *into* ruinous heaps.
26 Therefore their inhabitants were
[9]of small power, they were dismayed
and confounded; they were *as* the grass
of the field, and *as* the green herb, *as*
[d]the grass on the house tops, and *as*
corn blasted before it be grown up.
27 But [e]I know thy [10]abode, and thy
going out, and thy coming in, and thy
rage against me.
28 Because thy rage against me and
thy tumult is come up into mine ears,
therefore [f]I will put my hook in thy
nose, and my bridle in thy lips, and
I will turn thee back by the way by
which thou camest.
29 And this *shall be* [g]a sign unto
thee, Ye shall eat this year such things
as grow of themselves, and in the second year that which springeth of the
same; and in the third year sow ye, and
reap, and plant vineyards, and eat the
fruits thereof.
30 And [11]the remnant that is escaped
of the house of Jū′dah shall yet again
take root downward, and bear fruit upward.
31 For out of Je-ru′sa-lĕm shall go
forth a remnant, and [12]they that escape
out of mount Zī′ŏn: [h]the zeal of the
LORD *of hosts* shall do this.
32 Therefore thus saith the LORD
concerning the king of Ăs-sy̆r′ĭ-ȧ, He
shall not come into this city, nor shoot
an arrow there, nor come before it with
shield, nor cast a bank against it.
33 By the way that he came, by the
same shall he return, and shall not
come into this city, saith the LORD.
34 For [i]I will defend this city, to
save it, for mine own sake, and [j]for my
servant Dā′vid's sake.
35 ¶ And [k]it came to pass that night,
that the angel of the LORD went out,
and smote in the camp of the Ăs-sy̆r′-
ĭ-ans an hundred fourscore and five
thousand: and when they arose early
in the morning, behold, they *were* all
dead corpses.
36 So Sĕn-năch′e-rĭb king of Ăs-sy̆r′-
ĭ-ȧ departed, and went and returned,
and dwelt at [l]Nĭn′e-veh.
37 And it came to pass, as he was
worshipping in the house of Nĭs′rŏch
his god, that A-drăm′me-lech and Sha-
rē′zer his sons smote him with the

sword: and they escaped into the land of [13]Ar-mē'nĭ-ȧ. And [m]Ē'sar–hăd'don his son reigned in his stead.

20 In [a]those days was Hĕz-e-kī'ah sick unto death. And the prophet I-sā'iah the son of Ā'moz came to him, and said unto him, Thus saith the LORD, [1]Set thine house in order; for thou shalt die, and not live.

2 Then he turned his face to the wall, and prayed unto the LORD, saying,

3 I beseech thee, O LORD, [b]remember now how I have [c]walked before thee in truth and with a perfect heart, and have done *that which is* good in thy sight. And Hĕz-e-kī'ah wept [2]sore.

4 And it came to pass, afore I-sā'iah was gone out into the middle [3]court, that the word of the LORD came to him, saying,

5 Turn again, and tell Hĕz-e-kī'ah the captain of my people, Thus saith the LORD, the God of Dā'vid thy father, [d]I have heard thy prayer, I have seen [e]thy tears: behold, I will heal thee: on the third day thou shalt go up unto the house of the LORD.

6 And I will add unto thy days fifteen years; and I will deliver thee and this city out of the hand of the king of Ȧs-sȳr'ĭ-ȧ; and [f]I will defend this city for mine own sake, and for my servant Dā'vid's sake.

7 And I-sā'iah said, Take a lump of figs. And they took and laid *it* on the boil, and he recovered.

8 ¶ And Hĕz-e-kī'ah said unto I-sā'iah, What *shall be* the sign that the LORD will heal me, and that I shall go up into the house of the LORD the third day?

9 And I-sā'iah said, [g]This sign shalt thou have of the LORD, that the LORD will do the thing that he hath spoken: shall the shadow go forward ten degrees, or go back ten degrees?

10 And Hĕz-e-kī'ah answered, It is a light thing for the shadow to go down ten degrees: nay, but let the shadow return backward ten degrees.

11 And I-sā'iah the prophet cried unto the LORD: and [h]he brought the shadow ten degrees backward, by which it had gone down in the [4]dial of Ā'hăz.

12 ¶ [i]At that time [5]Be-rō'dach–băl'-a-dăn, the son of Băl'a-dăn, king of Băb'ȳ-lon, sent letters and a present unto Hĕz-e-kī'ah: for he had heard that Hĕz-e-kī'ah had been sick.

13 And [j]Hĕz-e-kī'ah hearkened unto them, and shewed them all the house of his [6]precious things, the silver, and the gold, and the spices, and the precious ointment, and *all* the house of his [7]armour, and all that was found in his treasures: there was nothing in his house, nor in all his dominion, that Hĕz-e-kī'ah shewed them not.

14 ¶ Then came I-sā'iah the prophet unto king Hĕz-e-kī'ah, and said unto him, What said these men? and from whence came they unto thee? And Hĕz-e-kī'ah said, They are come from a far country, *even* from Băb'ȳ-lon.

15 And he said, What have they seen in thine house? And Hĕz-e-kī'ah answered, All *the things* that *are* in mine house have they seen: there is nothing among my treasures that I have not shewed them.

16 And I-sā'iah said unto Hĕz-e-kī'ah, Hear the word of the LORD.

17 Behold, the days come, that all that *is* in thine house, and that which thy fathers have laid up in store unto this day, [k]shall be carried into Băb'ȳ-lon: nothing shall be left, saith the LORD.

18 And of thy sons that shall issue from thee, which thou shalt beget, [l]shall they take away; [8]and they shall be eunuchs in the palace of the king of Băb'ȳ-lon.

19 Then said Hĕz-e-kī'ah unto I-sā'iah, [m]Good *is* the word of the LORD which thou hast spoken. And he said, [9]*Is it* not *good*, if peace and truth be in my days?

20 ¶ And the rest of the acts of Hĕz-e-kī'ah, and all his might, and how he [n]made a pool, and a conduit, and brought water into the city, *are* they not written in the book of the chronicles of the kings of Jū'dah?

21 And Hĕz-e-kī'ah slept with his fathers: and Ma-năs'seh his son reigned in his stead.

21 Ma-năs'seh *was* twelve years old when he began to reign, and reigned fifty and five years in Je-rụ'sa-lĕm. And his mother's name *was* Hĕph'zĭ–bah.

2 And he did *that which was* evil in the sight of the LORD, [a]after the abominations of the heathen, whom the LORD cast out before the children of Ĭs'ra-el.

3 For he built up again the high places [b]which Hĕz-e-kī'ah his father had destroyed; and he reared up altars for Bā'al, and made a grove, [c]as did Ā'hăb king of Ĭs'ra-el; and [d]worshipped all the host of heaven, and served them.

4 And [e]he built altars in the house of the LORD, of which the LORD said, [f]In Je-rụ'sa-lĕm will I put my name.

5 And he built altars for all the host of heaven in the two courts of the house of the LORD.

6 [g]And he made his son pass through the fire, and observed [h]times, and used enchantments, and dealt with familiar spirits and wizards: he wrought much wickedness in the sight of the LORD, to provoke *him* to anger.

7 And he set a graven image of the grove that he had made in the house, of which the LORD said to Dā'vid, and to Sŏl'o-mon his son, [i]In this house, and in Je-rụ'sa-lĕm, which I have chosen out of all tribes of Ĭs'ra-el, will I put my name for ever:

8 Neither will I make the feet of Ĭs'ra-el move any more out of the land which I gave their fathers; only if they will observe to do according to all that I have commanded them, and according to all the law that my servant Mō'ses commanded them.

37 [13]Ararat [m]Ezra 4.2

CHAPTER 20

1 [a]2 Chr. 32.24; Isa. 38.1 [1]Give charge concerning thine house
3 [b]Neh. 13.22; Ps. 132.1-5; Isa. 38.3 [c]Gen. 5.22-24 [2]with a great weeping
4 [3]Or, city
5 [d]1 Ki. 18.37; ch. 19.20; 2 Chr. 32.20-21; Ps. 65.2; Luke 11.9-10; Acts 10.31 [e]Job 16.20; Ps. 39.12; Rev. 7.17
6 [f]ch. 19.34; 2 Chr. 32.22
9 [g]Isa. 38.7
11 [h]Josh. 10.12-14; Isa. 38.8 [4]degrees
12 [i]Isa. 39.1 [5]Or, Merodach-baladan
13 [j]2 Chr. 32.27-31 [6]Or, spicery [7]Or, jewels
17 [k]Lev. 26.33; ch. 24.13; Jer. 27.21
18 [l]ch. 24.12 [8]Fulfilled, Dan. 1.3
19 [m]1 Sam. 3.18; Ps. 39.9; Lam. 3.22-39 [9]Or, Shall there not be peace and truth, etc
20 [n]Neh. 3.16

CHAPTER 21

2 [a]ch. 16.3
3 [b]ch. 18.4 [c]1 Ki. 16.32 [d]Deut. 4.19; ch. 17.16
4 [e]Jer. 32.34 [f]2 Sam. 7.13; 1 Ki. 8.29
6 [g]Lev. 18.21; ch. 16.3; 2 Chr. 28.3 [h]Lev. 19.26-31; Deut. 18.10; ch. 17.17
7 [i]1 Ki. 8.29; ch. 23.27; Ps. 132.13-14; Jer. 32.34

9 But they hearkened not: and Ma-
năs'seh [i]seduced them to do more evil
than did the nations whom the LORD
destroyed before the children of Is'ra-
el.
10 ¶ And the LORD spake by his servants the prophets, saying,
11 [k]Because Ma-năs'seh king of Jū'-
dah hath done these abominations,
[l]*and* hath done wickedly above all that
the Ăm'ôr-ītes did, which *were* before
him, and hath made Jū'dah also to sin
with his idols:
12 Therefore thus saith the LORD
God of Is'ra-el, Behold, I *am* bringing
such evil upon Je-rṳ'sa-lĕm and Jū'-
dah, that whosoever heareth of it, both
[m]his ears shall tingle.
13 And I will stretch over Je-rṳ'sa-
lĕm [n]the line of Sa-mā'rī-ȧ, and the
plummet of the house of A'hăb: and I
will wipe Je-rṳ'sa-lĕm as *a man* wipeth
a dish, [1]wiping *it*, and turning *it* upside
down.
14 And I will forsake [o]the remnant
of mine inheritance, and deliver them
into the hand of their enemies; and
they shall become a prey and a spoil to
all their enemies;
15 Because they have done *that*
which was evil in my sight, and have
provoked me to anger, since the day
their fathers came forth out of E'gypt,
even unto this day.
16 [p]Moreover Ma-năs'seh shed innocent blood very much, till he had
filled Je-rṳ'sa-lĕm [2]from one end to
another; beside his sin wherewith he
made Jū'dah to sin, in doing *that which*
was evil in the sight of the LORD.
17 ¶ Now [q]the rest of the acts of Ma-
năs'seh, and all that he did, and his sin
that he sinned, *are* they not written in
the book of the chronicles of the kings
of Jū'dah?
18 And [r]Ma-năs'seh slept with his
fathers, and was buried in the garden
of his own house, in the garden of
Ŭz'zȧ: and A'mon his son reigned in
his stead.
19 ¶ [s]A'mon *was* twenty and two
years old when he began to reign, and
he reigned two years in Je-rṳ'sa-lĕm.
And his mother's name *was* Me-shŭl'-
le-mĕth, the daughter of Hā'ruz of Jŏt'-
bah.
20 And he did *that which was* evil in
the sight of the LORD, as his father Ma-
năs'seh did.
21 And he walked in all the way that
his father walked in, and served the
idols that his father served, and worshipped them:
22 And he [t]forsook the LORD God of
his fathers, and walked not in the way
of the LORD.
23 ¶ [u]And the servants of A'mon
conspired against him, and slew the
king in his own house.
24 And the people of the land slew
all them that had conspired against
king A'mon; and the people of the land
made Jo-sī'ah his son king in his stead.
25 Now the rest of the acts of A'mon
which he did, *are* they not written in
the book of the chronicles of the kings
of Jū'dah?
26 And he was buried in his sepulchre in the garden of Ŭz'zȧ: and [v]Jo-
sī'ah his son reigned in his stead.

22 Jo-sī'ah [a]*was* eight years old
when he began to reign, and he
reigned thirty and one years in Je-
rṳ'sa-lĕm. And his mother's name *was*
Je-dī'dah, the daughter of Ăd-a-ī'ah of
[b]Bŏs'cath.
2 And he did *that which was* right in
the sight of the LORD, and walked in
all the way of Dā'vid his father, and
[c]turned not aside to the right hand or
to the left.
3 ¶ [d]And it came to pass in the eighteenth year of king Jo-sī'ah, *that* the
king sent Shā'phan the son of Ăz-
a-lī'ah, the son of Me-shŭl'lam, the
scribe, to the house of the LORD, saying,
4 Go up to Hĭl-kī'ah the high priest,
that he may sum the silver which is
[e]brought into the house of the LORD,
which [f]the keepers of the [1]door have
gathered of the people:
5 And let them [g]deliver it into the
hand of the doers of the work, that
have the oversight of the house of the
LORD: and let them give it to the doers
of the work which *is* in the house of the
LORD, to repair the breaches of the
house,
6 Unto carpenters, and builders, and
masons, and to buy timber and hewn
stone to repair the house.
7 Howbeit [h]there was no reckoning
made with them of the money that was
delivered into their hand, because they
dealt [i]faithfully.
8 ¶ And Hĭl-kī'ah the high priest said
unto Shā'phan the scribe, [j]I have found
the book of the law in the house of the
LORD. And Hĭl-kī'ah gave the book to
Shā'phan, and he read it.
9 And Shā'phan the scribe came to
the king, and brought the king word
again, and said, Thy servants have
[2]gathered the money that was found in
the house, and have delivered it into
the hand of them that do the work, that
have the oversight of the house of the
LORD.
10 And Shā'phan the scribe shewed
the king, saying, Hĭl-kī'ah the priest
hath delivered me a book. And Shā'-
phan [k]read it before the king.
11 And it came to pass, when the
king had heard the words of the book
of the law, that he rent his clothes.
12 And the king commanded Hĭl-
kī'ah the priest, and A-hī'kam the son
of Shā'phan, and [l]Ăch'bôr the son of
[3]Mī-chā'iah, and Shā'phan the scribe,
and A-sa-hī'ah a servant of the king's,
saying,
13 Go ye, [m]inquire of the LORD for
me, and for the people, and for all Jū'-
dah, concerning the words of this book
that is found: for great *is* [n]the wrath of
the LORD that is kindled against us, because our fathers have not hearkened
unto the words of this book, to do

9 [i]1 Ki. 14.16; 2 Chr. 33.9; Prov. 29.12
11 [k]ch. 23.26; Jer. 15.4
[l]1 Ki. 21.26; 1 Pet. 4.3; Rev. 21.8
12 [m]1 Sam. 3.11; Jer. 19.3
13 [n]Isa. 34.11; Lam. 2.8; Amos 7.7-8
[1]he wipeth and turneth it upon the face thereof
14 [o]ch. 19.30
16 [p]Gen. 9.6; ch. 24.4; Ps. 10.2-8; Ps. 106.38; Prov. 6.16-17; Isa. 59.3-7; Jer. 2.34; Lam. 4.13-14; Ezek. 9.9; Joel 3.19; Mic. 3.9-12
[2]from mouth to mouth
17 [q]2 Chr. 33.11-19
18 [r]2 Chr. 33.20; Jer. 22.19
19 [s]2 Chr. 33.21-23
22 [t]Deut. 32.15; Judg. 2.12
23 [u]ch. 12.20; 2 Chr. 33.24-25
26 [v]Matt. 1.10-called Josias

CHAPTER 22
1 [a]1 Chr. 3.14; 2 Chr. 34.1; Jer. 1.2; Matt. 1.10
[b]Josh. 15.39
2 [c]Deut. 5.32; Prov. 4.27
3 [d]2 Chr. 34.8
4 [e]ch. 12.4; Mark 12.41-42
[f]ch. 12.9; Ps. 84.10
[1]threshold
5 [g]ch. 12.11-12-14
7 [h]ch. 12.15
[i]Neh. 7.2; 1 Cor. 4.2
8 [j]Deut. 31.24
9 [2]melted
10 [k]Jer. 36.21
12 [l]Abdon, 2 Chr. 34.20
[3]Or, Micah
13 [m]Ps. 25.14; Prov. 3.6
[n]Deut. 29.27

according unto all that which is written concerning us.

14 So Hĭl-kī'ah the priest, and A-hī'kam, and Ăch'bôr, and Shā'phan, and Ă-sa-hī'ah, went unto Hŭl'dah the [o]prophetess, the wife of Shăl'lum the son of [p]Tĭk'vah, the son of [4]Här'has, keeper of the [5]wardrobe; (now she dwelt in Je-ru'sa-lĕm [6]in the college;) and they communed with her.

15 ¶ And she said to them, Thus saith the LORD God of Ĭs'ra-el, Tell the man that sent you to me,

16 Thus saith the LORD, Behold, [q]I will bring evil upon this place, and upon the inhabitants thereof, *even* all the words of the book which the king of Jū'dah hath read:

17 Because they have forsaken me, and have burned incense unto other gods, that they might provoke me to anger with all the [r]works of their hands; therefore my wrath shall be kindled against this place, and shall not be quenched.

18 But to [s]the king of Jū'dah which sent you to inquire of the LORD, [t]thus shall ye say to him, Thus saith the LORD God of Ĭs'ra-el, *As touching* the words which thou hast heard;

19 Because thine [u]heart was tender, and thou hast [v]humbled thyself before the LORD, when thou heardest what I spake against this place, and against the inhabitants thereof, that they should become [w]a desolation and [x]a curse, and hast rent thy clothes, and wept before me; I also have heard *thee,* saith the LORD.

20 Behold therefore, I will gather thee unto thy fathers, and thou [y]shalt be gathered into thy grave in peace; and thine eyes shall not see all the evil which I will bring upon this place. And they brought the king word again.

23 And [a]the king sent, and they gathered unto him all the elders of Jū'dah and of Je-ru'sa-lĕm.

2 And the king went up into the house of the LORD, and all the men of Jū'dah and all the inhabitants of Je-ru'sa-lĕm with him, and the priests, and the prophets, and all the people, [1]both small and great: and he read in their ears all the words of the book of the covenant [b]which was found in the house of the LORD.

3 ¶ And the king [c]stood by a pillar, and made a covenant before the LORD, to walk after the LORD, and to keep his commandments and his testimonies and his statutes with all *their* heart and all *their* soul, to perform the words of this covenant that were written in this book. And [d]all the people stood to the covenant.

4 And the king commanded Hĭl-kī'ah the high priest, and the priests of the second order, and the keepers of the door, to bring forth out of the temple of the LORD all the vessels that were made for Bā'al, and for [e]the grove, and for all the host of heaven: and he burned them without Je-ru'sa-lĕm in the fields of Kĭd'ron, and carried the ashes of them unto Bĕth'–el.

5 And he [2]put down [3]the idolatrous priests, whom the kings of Jū'dah had ordained to burn incense in the high places in the cities of Jū'dah, and in the places round about Je-ru'sa-lĕm; them also that burned incense unto Bā'al, to the sun, and to the moon, and to the [4]planets, and to [f]all the host of heaven.

6 And he brought out the grove from the house of the LORD, without Je-ru'sa-lĕm, unto the brook Kĭd'ron, and burned it at the brook Kĭd'ron, and stamped *it* small to powder, and cast the powder thereof upon the [g]graves of the children of the people.

7 And he brake down the houses [h]of the sodomites, that *were* by the house of the LORD, [i]where the women wove [5]hangings for the grove.

8 And he brought all the priests out of the cities of Jū'dah, and defiled the high places where the priests had burned incense, from [j]Gē'bȧ to Bē'er–shē'bȧ, and brake down the high places of the gates that *were* in the entering in of the gate of Jŏsh'u-ȧ the governor of the city, which *were* on a man's left hand at the gate of the city.

9 [k]Nevertheless the priests of the high places came not up to the altar of the LORD in Je-ru'sa-lĕm, [l]but they did eat of the unleavened bread among their brethren.

10 And he defiled [m]Tō'pheth, which *is* in [n]the valley of the children of Hĭn'nom, [o]that no man might make his son or his daughter to pass through the fire to Mō'lech.

11 And he took away the horses that the kings of Jū'dah had given to [p]the sun, at the entering in of the house of the LORD, by the chamber of Nā'than–mē'lech the [6]chamberlain, which *was* in the suburbs, and burned the chariots of the sun with fire.

12 And the altars that *were* [q]on the top of the upper chamber of Ā'hăz, which the kings of Jū'dah had made, and the altars which [r]Ma-năs'seh had made in the two courts of the house of the LORD, did the king beat down, and [7]brake *them* down from thence, and cast the dust of them into the brook Kĭd'ron.

13 And the high places that *were* before Je-ru'sa-lĕm, which *were* on the right hand of [8]the mount of corruption, which [s]Sŏl'o-mon the king of Ĭs'ra-el had builded for Ăsh'tō-rĕth the abomination of the Zī-dō'nĭ-ans, and for Chē'mŏsh the abomination of the Mō'ab-ītes, and for [9]Mĭl'com the abomination of the children of Ăm'mŏn, did the king defile.

14 And he [t]brake in pieces the [10]images, and cut down the groves, and filled their places with the bones of men.

15 ¶ Moreover the altar that *was* at Bĕth'–el, *and* the high place [u]which Jĕr-o-bō'am the son of Nē'băt, who made Ĭs'ra-el to sin, had made, both that altar and the high place he brake

14 [o]Ex. 15.20; 1 Cor. 11.5
[p]Tikvath, 2 Chr. 34.22
[4]Or, Hasrah
[5]garments
[6]Or, in the second part
16 [q]Dan. 9.11-14
17 [r]Ps. 115.4; Mic. 5.13
18 [s]2 Chr. 34.26
[t]Eccl. 8.12
19 [u]Ps. 51.17; Isa. 57.15
[v]Ex. 10.3; 1 Pet. 5.5-6
[w]Lev. 26.31-32
[x]Jer. 26.6
20 [y]Ps. 37.37; Isa. 57.1-2

CHAPTER 23
1 [a]2 Chr. 34.29-30
2 [1]from small even unto great
[b]ch. 22.8
3 [c]ch. 11.14
[d]Jer. 4.2
4 [e]ch. 21.3-7
5 [2]caused to cease
[3]Chemarim
[4]Or, twelve signs, or, constellations
[f]ch. 21.3
6 [g]2 Chr. 34.4
7 [h]1 Ki. 14.24
[i]Ezek. 16.16
[5]houses
8 [j]1 Ki. 15.22
9 [k]Ezek. 44.10; Mal. 2.8
[l]1 Sam. 2.36
10 [m]Isa. 30.33
[n]Josh. 15.8
[o]Lev. 18.21
11 [p]Deut. 4.19;
[6]Or, eunuch, or, officer
12 [q]Jer. 19.13
[r]ch. 21.5;
[7]Or, ran from thence
13 [8]That is, the mount of Olives
[s]Neh. 13.26
[9]Or, Molech
14 [t]Ex. 23.24;
[10]statues
15 [u]1 Ki. 12.28-33

down, and burned the high place, *and*
stamped *it* small to powder, and burned
the grove.
16 And as Jo-sī'ah turned himself,
he spied the sepulchres that *were* there
in the mount, and sent, and took the
bones out of the sepulchres, and burned
them upon the altar, and polluted it,
according to the [v]word of the LORD
which the man of God proclaimed, who
proclaimed these words.
17 Then he said, What title *is* that
that I see? And the men of the city told
him, *It is* the sepulchre of the man of
God, which came from Jū'dah, and proclaimed these things that thou hast
done against the altar of Bĕth'–el.
18 And he said, Let him alone; let no
man move his bones. So they let his
bones [11]alone, with the bones of the
prophet that came out of Sa-mā'rĭ-ȧ.
19 And all the houses also of the
high places that *were* [w]in the cities of
Sa-mā'rĭ-ȧ, which the kings of Is'ra-el
had made to provoke *the LORD* to anger, Jo-sī'ah took away, and did to
them according to all the acts that he
had done in Bĕth'–el.
20 And he [12]slew all the priests of
the high places that *were* there upon
the altars, and [x]burned men's bones
upon them, and returned to Je-ru'sa-
lĕm.
21 ¶ And the king commanded all
the people, saying, [y]Keep the passover
unto the LORD your God, [z]as *it is* written in the book of this covenant.
22 Surely there was not holden such
a passover from the days of the judges
that judged Is'ra-el, nor in all the days
of the kings of Is'ra-el, nor of the kings
of Jū'dah;
23 But in the eighteenth year of king
Jo-sī'ah, *wherein* this passover was
holden to the LORD in Je-ru'sa-lĕm.
24 ¶ Moreover, [a]the *workers with* familiar spirits, and the wizards, and the
[13]images, and the idols, and all the
abominations that were spied in the
land of Jū'dah and in Je-ru'sa-lĕm, did
Jo-sī'ah put away, that he might perform the words of [b]the law which were
written in the book that Hĭl-kī'ah the
priest found in the house of the LORD.
25 [c]And like unto him was there no
king before him, that turned to the
LORD with all his heart, and with all his
soul, and with all his might, according
to all the law of Mō'ses; neither after
him arose there *any* like him.
26 ¶ Notwithstanding the LORD
turned not from the fierceness of his
great wrath, wherewith his anger was
kindled against Jū'dah, because [d]of
all the [14]provocations that Ma-năs'seh
had provoked him withal.
27 And the LORD said, I will remove
Jū'dah also out of my sight, as [e]I have
removed Is'ra-el, and will cast off this
city Je-ru'sa-lĕm which I have chosen,
and the house of which I said, [f]My
name shall be there.
28 Now the rest of the acts of Jo-
sī'ah, and all that he did, *are* they not
written in the book of the chronicles of
the kings of Jū'dah?
29 ¶ In his days Phā'raōh–nē'choh
king of E'gypt went up against the king
of As-syr'ĭ-ȧ to the river Eū-phrā'tēs:
and king Jo-sī'ah went against him;
and he slew him at [g]Me-gĭd'do, when
he [h]had seen him.
30 And his servants carried him in
a chariot dead from Me-gĭd'do, and
brought him to Je-ru'sa-lĕm, and buried him in his own sepulchre. And the
people of the land took [i]Je-hō'a-hăz
the son of Jo-sī'ah, and anointed him,
and made him king in his father's stead.
31 ¶ Je-hō'a-hăz *was* twenty and
three years old when he began to reign;
and he reigned three months in Je-ru'-
sa-lĕm. And his mother's name *was*
[j]Ha-mū'tal, the daughter of Jĕr-e-mī'-
ah of Lĭb'nah.
32 And he did *that which was* evil in
the sight of the LORD, according to all
that his fathers had done.
33 And Phā'raōh–nē'choh put him
in bands [k]at Rĭb'lah in the land of
Hā'math, [15]that he might not reign in
Je-ru'sa-lĕm; and [16]put the land to a
tribute of an hundred talents of silver,
and a talent of gold.
34 And Phā'raōh–nē'choh made E-
lī'a-kĭm the son of Jo-sī'ah king in the
room of Jo-sī'ah his father, and [l]turned
his name to [m]Je-hoi'a-kim, and took
Je-hō'a-hăz away: [n]and he came to
E'gypt, and died there.
35 And Je-hoi'a-kim gave the silver
and the gold to Phā'raōh; but he taxed
the land to give the money according
to the commandment of Phā'raōh: he
[o]exacted the silver and the gold of the
people of the land, of every one according to his taxation, to give *it* unto Phā'-
raōh–nē'choh.
36 ¶ Je-hoi'a-kim *was* twenty and
five years old when he began to reign;
and he reigned eleven years in Je-ru'-
sa-lĕm. And his mother's name *was*
Ze-bū'dah, the daughter of Pe-dā'iah
of Ru'mah.
37 And he did *that which was* evil in
the sight of the LORD, according to all
that his fathers had done.

CHAPTER 24

24 In [a]his days Nĕb-u-chăd-nĕz'zar
king of Băb'y̆-lon came up, and
Je-hoi'a-kim became his servant three
years: then he turned and rebelled
against him.
2 [b]And the LORD sent against him
bands of the Chăl'dees, and bands of
the Sy̆r'ĭ-ans, and bands of the Mō'ab-
ītes, and bands of the children of Am'-
mŏn, and sent them against Jū'dah to
destroy it, [c]according to the word of
the LORD, which he spake [1]by his servants the prophets.
3 Surely at the commandment of the
LORD came *this* upon Jū'dah, to remove *them* out of his sight, [d]for the
sins of Ma-năs'seh, according to all
that he did;
4 [e]And also for the innocent blood
that he shed: for he filled Je-ru'sa-lĕm
with innocent blood; which [f]the LORD
would not pardon.

16 [v]1 Ki. 13.2
18 [11]to escape
19 [w]2 Chr. 34.6
20 [12]Or, sacrificed
[x]2 Chr. 34.5
21 [y]2 Chr. 35.1-17;
[z]Ex. 12.3; Lev. 23.5; Num. 9.2; Deut. 16.2
24 [a]ch. 21.6; 1 Chr. 10.13
[13]Or, teraphim
[b]Lev. 19.31; Lev. 20.27; Deut. 18.11; ch. 22.8-13; 2 Chr. 34.14-19
25 [c]ch. 18.5
26 [d]ch. 21.11; ch. 24.3; Jer. 15.4
[14]angers
27 [e]ch. 17.18
[f]1 Ki. 8.29
29 [g]Judg. 1.27; ch. 9.27; Zech. 12.11
[h]ch. 14.8
30 [i]ch. 14.21; 2 Chr. 36.1-2; Jer. 22.11
31 [j]ch. 24.18
33 [k]Num. 34.11; ch. 25.6
[15]Or, because he reigned
[16]set a mulet upon the land
34 [l]ch. 24.17; Dan. 1.7
[m]Matt. 1.11-Jakim
[n]Jer. 22.11
35 [o]Prov. 11.11
CHAPTER 24
1 [a]Lev. 26.25; ch. 17.5; 2 Chr. 36.6; Jer. 25.1-9; Dan. 1.1
2 [b]Deut. 28.49-50; Jer. 25.9; Ezek. 19.8
[c]ch. 20.17; ch. 21.12
[1]by the hand of
3 [d]ch. 21.2-11; ch. 23.26
4 [e]ch. 21.16
[f]Jer. 15.1; Lam. 3.42

5 ¶ Now the rest of the acts of Je-
hoi'a-kim, and all that he did, *are* they
not written in the book of the chronicles of the kings of Jū'dah?
6 [g]So Je-hoi'a-kim slept with his fathers: and Je-hoi'a-chin his son reigned
in his stead.
7 And [h]the king of Ē'gypt came not
again any more out of his land: for [i]the
king of Băb'y̆-lon had taken from the
river of Ē'gypt unto the river Eū-phrā'-
tēs all that pertained to the king of
Ē'gypt.
8 ¶[2]Je-hoi'a-chin *was* eighteen years
old when he began to reign, and he
reigned in Je-ru̇'sa-lĕm three months.
And his mother's name *was* Ne-hŭsh'-
tȧ, the daughter of Ĕl'na-than of Je-
ru̇'sa-lĕm.
9 And he did *that which was* evil in
the sight of the LORD, according to all
that his father had done.
10 ¶ [j]At that time the servants of
Nĕb-u-chăd-nĕz'zar king of Băb'y̆-lon
came up against Je-ru̇'sa-lĕm, and the
city [3]was besieged.
11 And Nĕb-u-chăd-nĕz'zar king of
Băb'y̆-lon came against the city, and
his servants did besiege it.
12 [k]And Je-hoi'a-chin the king of
Jū'dah went out to the king of Băb'y̆-
lon, he, and his mother, and his servants, and his princes, and his [4]offi-
cers: [l]and the king of Băb'y̆-lon [m]took
him [n]in the eighth year of his reign.
13 [o]And he carried out thence all
the treasures of the house of the LORD,
and the treasures of the king's house,
and [p]cut in pieces all the vessels of
gold which Sŏl'o-mon king of Is'ra-el
had made in the temple of the LORD,
[q]as the LORD had said.
14 And [r]he carried away all Je-ru̇'-
sa-lĕm, and all the princes, and all the
mighty men of valour, *even* ten thousand captives, and [s]all the craftsmen
and smiths: none remained, save [t]the
poorest sort of the people of the land.
15 And [u]he carried away Je-hoi'-
a-chin to Băb'y̆-lon, and the king's
mother, and the king's wives, and his
[5]officers, and the mighty of the land,
those carried he into captivity from Je-
ru̇'sa-lĕm to Băb'y̆-lon.
16 And [v]all the men of might, *even*
seven thousand, and craftsmen and
smiths a thousand, all *that were* strong
and apt for war, even them the king of
Băb'y̆-lon brought captive to Băb'y̆-
lon.
17 ¶ And [w]the king of Băb'y̆-lon
made Măt-ta-nī'ah [x]his father's brother
king in his stead, [y]and changed his
name to Zĕd-e-kī'ah.
18 [z]Zĕd-e-kī'ah *was* twenty and one
years old when he began to reign, and
he reigned eleven years in Je-ru̇'sa-
lĕm. And his mother's name *was* [a]Ha-
mū'tal, the daughter of Jĕr-e-mī'ah of
Lĭb'nah.
19 And he did *that which was* evil in
the sight of the LORD, according to all
that Je-hoi'a-kim had done.
20 For [b]through the anger of the
LORD it came to pass in Je-ru̇'sa-lĕm
and Jū'dah, until he had cast them out
from his presence, that Zĕd-e-kī'ah [c]re-
belled against the king of Băb'y̆-lon.

25

And it came to pass [a]in the ninth
year of his reign, in the tenth
month, in the tenth *day* of the month,
that Nĕb-u-chăd-nĕz'zar king of Băb'-
y̆-lon came, he, and all his host, against
Je-ru̇'sa-lĕm, and pitched against it;
and they built forts against it round
about.
2 And the city was besieged unto the
eleventh year of king Zĕd-e-kī'ah.
3 And on the ninth *day* of the *fourth*
month the famine prevailed in the city,
and there was no bread for the people
of the land.
4 ¶ And the city was broken up, and
all the men of war *fled* by night by the
way of the gate between two walls,
which *is* by the king's garden: (now the
Chăl'dees *were* against the city round
about:) and [b]*the king* went the way
toward the plain.
5 And the army of the Chăl'dees pursued after the king, and overtook him
in the plains of Jĕr'ĭ-chō: and all his
army was scattered from him.
6 So they took the king, and brought
him up to the king of Băb'y̆-lon [c]to
Rĭb'lah; and they [1]gave judgment upon
him.
7 And they slew the sons of Zĕd-e-
kī'ah before his eyes, and [2]put out the
eyes of Zĕd-e-kī'ah, and bound him
with fetters of brass, and carried him
to Băb'y̆-lon.
8 ¶ And in the fifth month, on the
seventh *day* of the month, which *is* [d]the
nineteenth year of king Nĕb-u-chăd-
nĕz'zar king of Băb'y̆-lon, came Nĕb'u-
zär–ā'dan, [3]captain of the guard, a servant of the king of Băb'y̆-lon, unto
Je-ru̇'sa-lĕm:
9 [e]And he burnt the house of the
LORD, [f]and the king's house, and all
the houses of Je-ru̇'sa-lĕm, and every
great *man's* house burnt he with fire.
10 And all the army of the Chăl'-
dees, that *were with* the captain of the
guard, [g]brake down the walls of Je-
ru̇'sa-lĕm round about.
11 [h]Now the rest of the people *that*
were left in the city, and the [4]fugitives
that fell away to the king of Băb'y̆-
lon, with the remnant of the multitude,
did Nĕb'u-zär–ā'dan the captain of the
guard carry away.
12 But the captain of the guard [i]left
of the poor of the land *to be* vinedressers and husbandmen.
13 And [j]the [k]pillars of brass that
were in the house of the LORD, and
[l]the bases, and the brasen sea that *was*
in the house of the LORD, did the Chăl'-
dees break in pieces, and carried the
brass of them to Băb'y̆-lon.
14 And the pots, and the shovels,
and the snuffers, and the spoons, and
all the vessels of brass wherewith they
ministered, took they away.
15 And the firepans, and the bowls,
and such [m]things as *were* of gold, *in*
gold, and of silver, *in* silver, the captain of the guard took away.

---

6 [g]2 Chr. 36.6
7 [h]Jer. 37.5
[i]Jer. 46.2
8 [2]Jeconiah, 1 Chr. 3.16; Jer. 24.1 and Coniah, Jer. 22.24
10 [j]Dan. 1.1
[3]came into siege
12 [k]Jer. 24.1; Ezek. 17.12
[4]Or, eunuchs
[l]Jer. 25.1
[m]ch. 25.27
[n]Jer. 52.28
13 [o]Isa. 39.6
[p]Dan. 5.2
[q]1 Ki. 14.15
14 [r]2 Chr. 36.9-10
[s]1 Sam. 13.19-22
[t]ch. 25.12; Jer. 39.10
15 [u]2 Chr. 36.10; Esth. 2.6
[5]Or, eunuchs
16 [v]Jer. 52.28
17 [w]Jer. 37.1
[x]1 Chr. 3.15; 2 Chr. 36.10-11
[y]ch. 23.34; 2 Chr. 36.4
18 [z]2 Chr. 36.11; Jer. 37.1
[a]ch. 23.31
20 [b]Deut. 4.24; ch. 23.26-27
[c]Ezek. 17.15; 2 Chr. 36.13

CHAPTER 25
1 [a]2 Chr. 36.17; Ezek. 24.1
4 [b]Jer. 39.4
6 [c]ch. 23.33
[1]spake judgment with him
7 [2]made blind
8 [d]ch. 24.12
[3]Or, chief marshal
9 [e]2 Chr. 36.19; Mic. 3.12
[f]Amos 2.5
10 [g]Neh. 1.3
11 [h]Jer. 39.9
[4]fallen away
12 [i]ch. 24.14
13 [j]ch. 20.17
[k]1 Ki. 7.15
[l]Ex. 27.3
15 [m]Ex. 37.23

16 The two pillars, [5]one sea, and the
bases which Sŏl'o-mon had made for
the house of the LORD; the brass of all
these vessels was without weight.
17 The height of the one pillar *was*
eighteen cubits, and the chapiter upon it
was brass: and the height of the chapiter three cubits; and the wreathen work,
and pomegranates upon the chapiter
round about, all of brass: and like
unto these had the second pillar with
wreathen work.
18 ¶ [n]And the captain of the guard
took [o]Sĕr-a-ī'ah the chief priest, and
[p]Zĕph-a-nī'ah the second priest, and
the three keepers of the [6]door:
19 And out of the city he took an [7]of-
ficer that was set over the men of war,
and [q]five men of them that [8]were in the
king's presence, which were found in
the city, and the [9]principal scribe of the
host, which mustered the people of the
land, and threescore men of the people
of the land *that were* found in the city:
20 And Nĕb'u-zär–ā'dan captain of
the guard took these, and brought them
to the king of Băb'y̆-lon to Rĭb'lah:
21 And the king of Băb'y̆-lon smote
them, and slew them at Rĭb'lah in the
land of Hā'math. [r]So Jū'dah was carried away out of their land.
22 ¶ [s]And *as for* the people that remained in the land of Jū'dah, whom
Nĕb-u-chăd-nĕz'zar king of Băb'y̆-lon
had left, even over them he made Gĕd-
a-lī'ah the son of A-hī'kam, the son of
Shā'phan, ruler.
23 And when all the captains of the
armies, they and their men, heard that
the king of Băb'y̆-lon had made Gĕd-a-
lī'ah governor, there came to Gĕd-a-
lī'ah to Mĭz'pah, even Ĭsh'ma-el the son
of Nĕth-a-nī'ah, and Jo-hā'nan the son
of Ca-rē'ah, and Sĕr-a-ī'ah the son of
Tăn'hu-mĕth the Ne-toph'a-thīte, and
Ja-ăz-a-nī'ah the son of a Ma-ăch'a-
thīte, they and their men.
24 And Gĕd-a-lī'ah sware to them,
and to their men, and said unto them,
[t]Fear not to be the servants of the
Chăl'dees: dwell in the land, and serve
the king of Băb'y̆-lon; and it shall be
well with you.
25 But [u]it came to pass in the seventh month, that Ĭsh'ma-el the son of
Nĕth-a-nī'ah, the son of E-lĭsh'a-mȧ, of
the seed [10]royal, came, and ten men
with him, and smote Gĕd-a-lī'ah, that
he died, and the Jews and the Chăl'-
dees that were with him at Mĭz'pah.
26 And all the people, both small
and great, and the captains of the armies, arose, [v]and came to Ē'gypt: for
they were afraid of the Chăl'dees.
27 ¶ [w]And it came to pass in the
seven and thirtieth year of the captivity of Je-hoi'a-chin king of Jū'dah, in
the twelfth month, on the seven and
twentieth *day* of the month, *that* Ē'vĭl–
me-rō'dach king of Băb'y̆-lon in the
year that he began to reign [x]did lift up
the head of Je-hoi'a-chin king of Jū'-
dah out of prison;
28 And he spake [11]kindly to him,
and set his throne above the throne of
[y]the kings that *were* with him in Băb'-
y̆-lon;
29 And [z]changed his prison garments: and he did [a]eat bread continually before him all the days of his life.
30 And his allowance *was* a continual allowance given him of the king, a
daily rate for every day, all the days of
his life.

16 [5]the one sea
18 [n]Jer. 52.24 [o]1 Chr. 6.14; Ezra 7.1 [p]Jer. 21.1 [6]threshold
19 [7]Or, eunuch [q]Jer. 52.25 [8]saw the king's face [9]Or, scribe of the captain of the host
21 [r]Lev. 26.33; Deut. 4.26; ch. 17.20; ch. 23.27; Jer. 24.9-10; Amos 5.27
22 [s]Jer. 40.5
24 [t]Jer. 27.12
25 [u]Jer. 41.1-2; Zech. 7.5 [10]of the kingdom
26 [v]Jer. 41.16-18
27 [w]Deut. 28.68; Jer. 41.17 [x]Gen. 40.13-20
28 [11]good things with him [y]Jer. 27.6-11; Dan. 2.37
29 [z]Gen. 41.14-42; Esth. 4.4 [a]2 Sam. 9.7

THE FIRST BOOK OF THE

CHRONICLES

Life's Questions

How are worship and life related?
Does God offer a punished people a second chance?
How do you start over again ?

God's Answers

First and 2 Chronicles takes the history of Samuel and Kings and applies its lessons to the generation returning from Babylonian exile and seeking to start life over again with God. Chronicles shows God's people they can start again if they renew their covenant commitment to God and worship Him as He expects. Ignoring the Israelites who have disappeared from history, Chronicles shows Judah that God is still at work in their history with His grace and deserves obedience more than foreign gods and more than the faded hopes and traditions of the past.

First and 2 Chronicles uses six parts to teach God's people how to live under foreign rule in a restored homeland: roll call of membership recalls God's faithfulness to His promises (1 Chronicles 1—9); review of David's faithfulness shows God's desire for unity and obedience (10—20); David's commitment to worship calls for similar commitment to new worship (21—29); past glory came from devotion to God's house (2 Chronicles 1—9); God works His plan even when His people are divided (10—36); God has plans for renewal through a foreign ruler (36:22–23).

Thus Chronicles shows that God's plan for redeeming and delivering His people still lives, and so should the hopes of the people as they begin anew.

1 Ad'am, [a]Shěth, Ē'nosh,
2 Kē'nan, Ma-hā'la-lē-el, Jē'rěd,
3 [b]Hē'noch, Me-thụ'se-lah, Lā'mech,
4 Nō'ah, Shěm, Hăm, and Jā'pheth.
5 ¶ [c]The sons of Jā'pheth; Gō'mer,
and Mā'gŏg, and Măd'a-ī, and Jā'văn,
and Tụ'bal, and Mē'shech, and Tī'ras.
6 And the sons of Gō'mer; Ăsh'chě-
naz, and [1]Rī'phath, and To-gär'mah.
7 And the sons of Jā'văn; E-lī'shah,
and Tär'shish, Kĭt'tĭm, and [2]Dŏd'a-nĭm.
8 ¶ [d]The sons of Hăm; Cŭsh, and
Mĭz'ra-ĭm, Pŭt, and Cā'năan.
9 And the sons of Cŭsh; Sē'bȧ, and
Hăv'ĭ-lah, and Săb'tȧ, and Rā'a-mah,
and Săb'te-chȧ. And the sons of Rā'a-
mah; Shē'bȧ, and Dē'dan.
10 And Cŭsh [e]begat Nĭm'rŏd: he began to be mighty upon the earth.
11 And Mĭz'ra-ĭm begat Lụ'dĭm, and
Ăn'a-mĭm, and Lē'ha-bĭm, and Năph'-
tu-hĭm,
12 And Păth-rụ'sĭm, and Căs'lụ-hĭm,
(of whom came the Phĭ-lĭs'tĭnes,) and
[f]Căph'tho-rĭm.
13 And Cā'năan begat Zī'dŏn his
firstborn, and Hĕth,
14 The Jĕb'u-site also, and the Ăm'-
ôr-īte, and the Gĭr'ga-shīte,
15 And the Hī'vīte, and the Ärk'īte,
and the Sĭn'īte,
16 And the Är'vad-īte, and the Zĕm'-
a-rīte, and the Hā'math-īte.
17 ¶ The sons of [g]Shĕm; Ē'lăm, and
Ăssh'ụr, and Är-'phăx'ăd, and Lŭd,
and Ā'ram, and Ŭz, and Hŭl, and Gē'-
thēr, and [3]Mē'shech.
18 And Är-'phăx'ăd begat Shē'lah,
and Shē'lah begat Ē'bēr.
19 And unto Ē'bēr were born two
sons: the name of the one *was* [4]Pē'-
leg; because in his days the earth was
divided: and his brother's name *was*
Jŏk'tan.
20 And Jŏk'tan begat Ăl-mō'dăd,
and Shē'leph, and Hā'zar-mā'veth,
and Jē'răh,
21 Ha-dō'ram also, and Ū'zal, and
Dĭk'lah,
22 And Ē'bal, and A-bĭm'ă-el, and
Shē'bȧ,
23 And Ō'phĭr, and Hăv'ĭ-lah, and
Jō'băb. All these *were* the sons of Jŏk'-
tan.
24 ¶ [h]Shĕm, Är-'phăx'ăd, Shē'lah,
25 [i]Ē'bēr, Pē'leg, Rē'u,
26 Sē'rug, Nā'hor, Tē'rah,
27 [j]Ā'brăm; the same *is* Ā'bră-hăm.
28 The sons of Ā'bră-hăm; [k]Ī'saac,
and [l]Ĭsh'ma-el.
29 ¶ These *are* their generations:
The [m]firstborn of Ĭsh'ma-el, Ne-bā'-
ioth; then Kē'där, and Ăd'be-el, and
Mĭb'sam,
30 Mĭsh'mȧ, and Dụ'mah, Măs'sȧ,
[5]Hā'dăd, and Tē'mȧ,
31 Je'tŭr, Nā'phish, and Kĕd'e-mah.
These are the sons of Ĭsh'ma-el.
32 ¶ Now [n]the sons of Ke-tū'rah,
Ā'bră-hăm's concubine: she bare Zĭm'-
răn, and Jŏk'shan, and Mē'dan, and
Mĭd'ĭ-an, and Ĭsh'băk, and Shụ'ah. And
the sons of Jŏk'shan; Shē'bȧ, and Dē'-
dan.
33 And the sons of Mĭd'ĭ-an; Ē'phah,
and Ē'phēr, and Hē'noch, and A-bī'dȧ,
and Ĕl'da-ah. All these *are* the sons of
Ke-tū'rah.
34 And [o]Ā'bră-hăm begat Ī'saac.
[p]The sons of Ī'saac; Ē'sạu and Ĭs'ra-el.
35 ¶ The son's of [q]Ē'sạu; Ĕl'ĭ-phăz,
Reụ'el, and Jē'ush, and Ja-ā'lam, and
Kō'rah.
36 The sons of Ĕl'ĭ-phăz; Tē'man,
and Ō'mar, [6]Zē'phī, and Gā'tam, Kē'-
năz, and Tĭm'nȧ, and Ăm'a-lĕk.
37 The sons of Reụ'el; Nā'hăth, Zē'-
rah, Shăm'mah, and Mĭz'zah.
38 And [r]the sons of Sē'ĭr; Lō'tan,
and Shō'bal, and Zĭb'e-on, and Ā'nah,
and Dī'shon, and Ē'zär, and Dī'shan.
39 And the sons of Lō'tan; Hō'rī,
and [7]Hō'mam: and Tĭm'nȧ *was* Lō'-
tan's sister.
40 The sons of Shō'bal; [8]A-lī'an, and
Măn'a-hăth, and Ē'bal, [9]Shē'phī, and
Ō'nam. And the sons of Zĭb'e-on; A-
ī'ah, and Ā'nah.
41 The sons of Ā'nah; [s]Dī'shon. And
the sons of Dī'shon; [10]Ăm'răm, and
Ĕsh'ban, and Ĭth'ran, and Chē'ran.
42 The sons of Ē'zēr; Bĭl'hăn, and
Zā'van, *and* [11]Jā'kan. The sons of Dī'-
shan; Ŭz, and Ā'răn.
43 ¶ Now these *are* the [t]kings that
reigned in the land of Ē'dom before
any king reigned over the children of
Ĭs'ra-el; Bē'lȧ the son of Bē'or: and the
name of his city *was* Dĭn'hā-bah.
44 And when Bē'lȧ was dead, Jō'băb
the son of Zē'rah of Bŏz'rah reigned in
his stead.
45 And when Jō'băb was dead, Hū'-
sham of the land of the Tē'man-ītes
reigned in his stead.
46 And when Hū'sham was dead,
[u]Hā'dăd the son of Bē'dăd, which
smote Mĭd'ĭ-an in the field of Mō'ab,
reigned in his stead: and the name of
his city *was* Ā'vĭth.
47 And when Hā'dăd was dead,
Săm'lah of Măs're-kah reigned in his
stead.
48 [v]And when Săm'lah was dead,
Shā'ul of Rē-hō'both by the river
reigned in his stead.
49 And when Shā'ul was dead, Bā'-
al–hā'nan the son of Ăch'bôr reigned
in his stead.
50 And when Bā'al–hā'nan was
dead, [12]Hā'dăd reigned in his stead:
and the name of his city *was* [13]Pā'ī;
and his wife's name *was* Me-hĕt'a-bel,
the daughter of Mā'tred, the daughter
of Mĕz'a-hab.
51 ¶ Hā'dăd died also. And the
[w]dukes of Ē'dom were; duke Tĭm'nah,
duke [14]A-lī'ah, duke Jē'theth,
52 Duke A-hō-lĭb'ă-mah, duke Ē'lah,
duke Pī'non,
53 Duke Kē'năz, duke Tē'man, duke
Mĭb'zar,
54 Duke Măg'dĭ-el, duke Ī'ram. These
are the dukes of Ē'dom.

CHAPTER 1
1 [a]Gen. 4.25
3 [b]Jude 14
5 [c]Gen. 10.2
6 [1]Or, Diphath, as it is in some copies
7 [2]Or, Rodanim, according to some copies
8 [d]Gen. 10.6
10 [e]Gen. 10.8-13
12 [f]Gen. 10.14;
17 [g]Gen. 9.23-26
[3]Or, Mash, Gen. 10.23
19 [4]That is, Division
24 [h]Gen. 11.10;
25 [i]Num. 24.24;
27 [j]2 Chr. 20.7;
28 [k]Gen. 21.2-3
[l]Gen. 16.11-15
29 [m]Gen. 25.13-16
30 [5]Or, Hadar, Gen. 25.15
32 [n]Gen. 25.1-2
34 [o]Gen. 21.2-3
[p]Gen. 25.25
35 [q]Deut. 2.22;
36 [6]Or, Zepho, Gen. 36.11
38 [r]Gen. 36.20
39 [7]Or, Hemam, Gen. 36.22
40 [8]Or, Alvan, Gen. 36.23
[9]Or, Shepho, Gen. 36.23
41 [s]Gen. 36.25
[10]Or, Hemdan, Gen. 36.26
42 [11]Or, Akan, Gen. 36.27
43 [t]Gen. 36.31
46 [u]1 Ki. 11.14
48 [v]Gen. 36.37
50 [12]Or, Hadar, Gen. 36.39
[13]Or, Pau, Gen. 36.39
51 [w]Ex. 15.15
[14]Or, Alvah

2 These *are* the sons of [1]Ĭs′ra-el;
[a]Re̤u′ben, Sĭm′e-on, Lē′vī, and Jū′-
dah, Ĭs′sa-char, and Zĕb′u-lun,
2 Dăn, Jō′seph, a̤nd Bĕn′ja-min,
Năph′ta-lī, Găd, and Ăsh′ēr.
3 ¶ The sons of [b]Jū′dah; Ēr, and
Ō′nan, and Shē′lah: *which* three were
born unto him of the daughter of
[c]Shu̧′ȧ the Cā′năan-īt-ess. And [d]Ēr,
the firstborn of Jū′dah, was evil in the
sight of the LORD; and he slew him.
4 And [e]Tā′mar his daughter in law
bare him Phā′rĕz and Zē′rah. All the
sons of Jū′dah *were* five.
5 The sons of [f]Phā′rĕz; Hĕz′ron, and
Hā′mŭl.
6 And the sons of Zē′rah; [2]Zĭm′rī,
and [g]Ē′than, and Hē′man, and Căl′cŏl,
and [3]Dā′rȧ: five of them in all.
7 And the sons of [h]Cär′mī; [4]Ā′chär,
the troubler of Ĭs′ra-el, who transgressed in the thing [i]accursed.
8 And the sons of Ē′than; Ăz-a-rī′ah.
9 The sons also of Hĕz′ron, that were
born unto him; Je-räh′me-el, and [5]Răm,
and [6]Che-lū′bāi.
10 And Răm [j]begat Ăm-mĭn′a-dab;
and Ăm-mĭn′a-dab begat Näh′shon,
[k]prince of the children of Jū′dah;
11 And Näh′shon begat [7]Săl′mȧ, and
Săl′mȧ begat Bō′ăz,
12 And Bō′ăz begat Ō′bed, and
Ō′bed begat Jĕs′se,
13 ¶ [l]And Jĕs′se begat his firstborn
E-lī′ab, and A-bĭn′ă-dăb the second,
and [8]Shĭm′mȧ the third,
14 Ne-thăn′e-el the fourth, Răd′da-ī
the fifth,
15 Ō′zem the sixth, Dā′vid the seventh:
16 Whose sisters *were* Zĕr-u̧-ī′ah,
and Ăb′ĭ-gāil. [m]And the sons of Zĕr-u̧-
ī′ah; A-bĭsh′ă-ī, and Jō′ab, and Ā′sa-
hĕl, three.
17 And [n]Ăb′ĭ-gāil bare Ām′a-sȧ: and
the father of Ām′a-sȧ *was* [9]Jē′thēr the
Ĭsh′me-el-īte.
18 ¶ And Cā′leb the son of Hĕz′ron
begat *children* of A-zū′bah *his* wife,
and of Jē′rī-ŏth: her sons *are* these;
Jē′shēr, and Shō′băb, and Är′dŏn.
19 And when A-zū′bah was dead,
Cā′leb took unto him Ĕph′răth, which
bare him Hûr.
20 And Hûr begat Ū′ri, and Ū′ri
begat [o]Be-zăl′ĕ-el.
21 ¶ And afterward Hĕz′ron went in
to the daughter of [p]Mā′chĭr the father
of Ḡĭl′e-ăd, whom he [10]married when
he *was* threescore years old; and she
bare him Sē′gu̧b.
22 And Sē′gu̧b begat Jā′īr, who had
three and twenty cities in the land of
Ḡĭl′e-ăd.
23 [q]And he took Ḡē′shŭr, and Ā′ram,
with the towns of Jā′īr, from them, with
Kē′nath, and the towns thereof, *even*
threescore cities. All these *belonged to*
the sons of Mā′chĭr the father of Ḡĭl′e-
ăd.
24 And after that Hĕz′ron was dead
in Cā′leb–ĕph′ra-tah, then A-bī′ah
Hĕz′rŏn's wife bare him [r]Ăsh′ŭr the
father of [s]Te-kō′ȧ.

CHAPTER 2
1 [1]Or, Jacob, Gen. 32.28; Ex. 32.13; Num. 13.3-15
[a]Gen. 29.32; Gen. 30.5; Ex. 1.2
3 [b]Gen. 29.35; Gen. 38.3; Deut. 33.7; Num. 26.19
[c]Gen. 38.2
[d]Gen. 38.7
4 [e]Gen. 38.29-30; Matt. 1.3
5 [f]Gen. 46.12; Ruth 4.18
6 [2]Or, Zabdi, Josh. 7.1
[g]1 Ki. 4.31
[3]Or, Darda
7 [h]ch. 4.1
[4]Or, Achan
[i]Josh. 6.18
9 [5]Or, Aram, Matt. 1.3-4
[6]Or, Caleb
10 [j]Ruth 4.19; Matt. 1.4
[k]Num. 1.7; Num. 2.3
11 [7]Or, Salmon, Ruth 4.21; Matt. 1.4
13 [l]1 Sam. 16.6
[8]Or, Shammah, 1 Sam. 16.9
16 [m]2 Sam. 2.18
17 [n]2 Sam. 17.25
[9]Ithra an Israelite, 2 Sam. 17.25
20 [o]Ex. 31.2; 2 Chr. 1.5
21 [p]Num. 27.1
[10]took
23 [q]Num. 32.41; Deut. 3.14
24 [r]ch. 4.5
[s]2 Sam. 14.2; ch. 4.5; 2 Chr. 11.6; 2 Chr. 20.20; Neh. 3.5; Jer. 6.1; Amos 1.1
36 [t]ch. 11.41
42 [11]Called father, because his descendants peopled that city
49 [u]Josh. 15.17

25 ¶ And the sons of Je-räh′me-el
the firstborn of Hĕz′ron were, Răm the
firstborn, and Bū′nah, and Ō′ren, and
Ō′zem, *and* A-hī′jah.
26 Je-räh′me-el had also another
wife, whose name *was* Ăt′a-rah; she
was the mother of Ō′nam.
27 And the sons of Răm the firstborn of Je-räh′me-el were, Mā′ăz, and
Jā′min, and Ē′kēr.
28 And the sons of Ō′nam were,
Shăm′ma-ī, and Jā′dȧ. And the sons of
Shăm′ma-ī; Nā′dăb and Ăb′ĭ-shu̧r.
29 And the name of the wife of Ăb′ĭ-
shu̧r *was* Ăb-i-hā′il, and she bare him
Ăh′băn, and Mō′lid.
30 And the sons of Nā′dăb; Sē′led,
and Ăp′pa-im: but Sē′led died without
children.
31 And the sons of Ăp′pa-im; Ĭsh′ī.
And the sons of Ĭsh′ī; Shē′shan. And
the children of Shē′shan; Ăh′lāi.
32 And the sons of Jā′dȧ the brother
of Shăm′ma-ī; Jē′thēr, and Jŏn′a-than:
and Jē′thēr died without children.
33 And the sons of Jŏn′a-than; Pē′-
leth, and Zā′zȧ. These were the sons of
Je-räh′me-el.
34 ¶ Now Shē′shan had no sons, but
daughters. And Shē′shan had a servant, an E-ġȳp′tian, whose name *was*
Jär′hȧ.
35 And Shē′shan gave his daughter
to Jär′hȧ his servant to wife; and she
bare him Ăt′tāi.
36 And Ăt′tāi begat Nā′than, and
Nā′than begat [t]Zā′băd,
37 And Zā′băd begat Ĕph′lăl, and
Ĕph′lăl begat Ō′bed.
38 And Ō′bed begat Jē′hū, and Jē′hū
begat Ăz-a-rī′ah,
39 And Ăz-a-rī′ah begat Hē′lez, and
Hē′lez begat E-lē′a-sah,
40 And E-lē′a-sah begat Sĭ-săm′a-ī,
and Sĭ-săm′a-ī begat Shăl′lum,
41 And Shăl′lum begat Jĕk-a-mī′ah,
and Jĕk-a-mī′ah begat E-lĭsh′a-mȧ.
42 ¶ Now the sons of Cā′leb the
brother of Je-räh′me-el *were*, Mē′shȧ
his firstborn, which *was* the [11]father of
Zĭph; and the sons of Ma-rē′shah the
father of Hē′bron.
43 And the sons of Hē′bron; Kō′-
rah, and Tăp′pu-ah, and Rē′kem, and
Shē′mȧ.
44 And Shē′mȧ begat Rā′hăm, the
father of Jôr′ko-ăm: and Rē′kem begat
Shăm′ma-ī.
45 And the son of Shăm′ma-ī *was*
Mā′on: and Mā′on *was* the father of
Bĕth′–zûr.
46 And Ē′phah, Cā′leb's concubine,
bare Hā′ran, and Mō′zȧ, and Gā′zĕz:
and Hā′ran begat Gā′zĕz.
47 And the sons of Jäh′da-ī; Rē′-
ḡem, and Jō′tham, and Ḡē′shăm, and
Pē′let, and Ē′phah, and Shā′aph.
48 Mā′a-chah, Cā′leb's concubine,
bare Shē′ber, and Tĭr′ha-nah.
49 She bare also Shā′aph the father of Măd-măn′nah, Shē′vȧ the father of Măch′be-nah, and the father of
Ḡĭb′e-a̤: and the daughter of Cā′leb
was [u]Ăch′sȧ.

50 ¶ These were the sons of Cā'leb
the son of Hûr, the firstborn of Ĕph'ra-
tah; Shō'bal the father of Kĭr'jath–jē'-
a-rĭm,
51 Săl'mȧ the father of Bĕth'–lĕ-
hĕm, Hā'reph the father of Bĕth–gā'-
dĕr.
52 And Shō'bal the father of Kĭr'-
jath–jē'a-rĭm had sons; [12]Hăr'ŏ-eh, *and*
[13]half of the Ma-nā'heth-ītes.
53 And the families of Kĭr'jath–jē'-
a-rĭm; the Ĭth'rītes, and the Pū'hītes,
and the Shu'math-ītes, and the Mĭsh'-
ra-ītes; of them came the Zā're-ath-
ītes, and the Ĕsh'tă-ul-ītes.
54 The sons of Săl'mȧ; Bĕth'–lĕ-
hĕm, and the Ne-tŏph'a-thītes, [14]Ăt'a-
rŏth, the house of Jō'ab, and half of the
Ma-nā'heth-ītes, the Zō'rītes.
55 And the families of the scribes
which dwelt at Jā'bĕz; the Tī'rath-ītes,
the Shĭm'e-ath-ītes, *and* Sū'chath-ītes.
These *are* the [v]Kĕn'ītes that came of
Hē'măth, the father of the house of
[w]Rē'chăb.

3 Now these were the sons of Dā'vid,
which were born unto him in Hē'-
bron; the firstborn [a]Ăm'nŏn, of A-hĭn'-
o-am the [b]Jĕz're-el-īt-ess; the second
[1]Dăn'iel, of Ăb'ĭ-gāil the Cär'mel-īt-
ess:
2 The third, Ăb'sa-lŏm the son of
Mā'a-chah the daughter of Tăl'māi
king of Gē'shûr: the fourth, Ăd-ŏ-nī'jah
the son of Hăg'gĭth:
3 The fifth, Shĕph-a-tī'ah, of Ăb'i-
tal: the sixth, Ĭth're-ăm by [c]Ĕg'lah his
wife.
4 *These* six were born unto him in
Hē'bron; and [d]there he reigned seven
years and six months: and [e]in Je-ru'sa-
lĕm he reigned thirty and three years.
5 [f]And these were born unto him in
Je-ru'sa-lĕm; [2]Shĭm'e-ȧ, and Shō'băb,
and Nā'than, and [g]Sŏl'o-mon, four, of
[3]Băth'–shu-ȧ the daughter of [4]Ăm'mĭ-
el:
6 Ĭb'hār also, and [5]E-lĭsh'a-mȧ, and
E-lĭph'e-lĕt,
7 And Nō'gah, and Nē'pheg, and Ja-
phī'ȧ,
8 And E-lĭsh'a-mȧ, and [6]E-lī'a-dȧ,
and E-lĭph'e-lĕt, [h]nine.
9 *These were* all the sons of Dā'vid,
beside the sons of the concubines, and
[i]Tā'mar their sister.
10 ¶ And Sŏl'o-mon's son *was* [j]Rē-
ho-bō'am, [7]A-bī'ȧ his son, Ā'sȧ his son,
Je-hŏsh'a-phăt his son,
11 Jō'ram his son, Ā-ha-zī'ah his
son, Jō'ăsh his son,
12 Ăm-a-zī'ah his son, Ăz-a-rī'ah his
son, Jō'tham his son,
13 Ā'hăz his son, Hĕz-e-kī'ah his
son, Ma-năs'seh his son,
14 Ā'mon his son, Jo-sī'ah his son.
15 And the sons of Jo-sī'ah *were,*
the firstborn Jo-hā'nan, the second Je-
hoi'a-kim, the third Zĕd-e-kī'ah, the
fourth Shăl'lum.
16 And the sons of [k]Je-hoi'a-kim:
Jĕc-o-nī'ah his son, Zĕd-e-kī'ah [l]his
son.
17 ¶ And the sons of Jĕc-o-nī'ah;
Ăs'sĭr, [8]Sa-lā'-thĭ-el [m]his son,
18 Măl-chī'ram also, and Pe-dā'iah,
and She-nā'zar, Jĕc-a-mī'ah, Hŏsh'a-
mȧ, and Nĕd-a-bī'ah.
19 And the sons of Pe-dā'iah *were,*
[n]Ze-rŭb'ba-bĕl, and Shĭm'e-ī: and the
sons of Ze-rŭb'ba-bĕl; Me-shŭl'lam,
and Hăn-a-nī'ah, and Shĕl'o-mĭth their
sister:
20 And Ha-shu'bah, and Ō'hel, and
Bĕr-e-chī'ah, and Hăs-a-dī'ah, Jū'shăb-
hē'sĕd, five.
21 And the sons of Hăn-a-nī'ah; Pĕl-
a-tī'ah, and Je'sā'iah: the sons of Rĕph-
a-ī'ah, the sons of Är'nan, the sons of
Ō-ba-dī'ah, the sons of Shĕch-a-nī'ah.
22 And the sons of Shĕch-a-nī'ah;
Shĕm-a-ī'ah: and the sons of Shĕm-a-
ī'ah; [o]Hăt'tŭsh, and Ĭg'e-ăl, and Ba-
rī'ah, and Nē-a-rī'ah, and Shā'phat,
six.
23 And the sons of Nē-a-rī'ah; Ĕl-i-
ō-ē'nā-ī, and [9]Hĕz-e-kī'ah, and Ăz'rī-
kam, three.
24 And the sons of Ĕl-i-ō-ē'nā-ī *were,*
Hŏd-a-ī'ah, and Ē-lī'a-shib, and Pĕl-a-
ī'ah, and Ăk'kŭb, and Jo-hā'nan, and
Dăl-a-ī'ah, and Ā-nā'nī, seven.

4 The sons of Jū'dah; [a]Phā'rĕz, Hĕz'-
ron, and [1]Cär'mī, and Hûr, and
Shō'bal.
2 And [2]Rē-a-ī'ah the son of Shō'bal
begat Jā'hăth; and Jā'hăth begat A-
hū'ma-ī, and Lā'hăd. These *are* the
families of the Zō'rath-ītes.
3 And these *were of* the father of
Ē'tam; Jĕz're-el, and Ĭsh'mȧ, and Ĭd'-
băsh: and the name of their sister *was*
Hăz-e-lĕl-pō'nī:
4 And Pe-nū'el the father of Gē'dôr,
and Ē'zĕr the father of Hū'shah. These
are the sons of Hûr, the firstborn of
Ĕph'ra-tah, the father of Bĕth'–lĕ-hĕm.
5 ¶ And Ăsh'ŭr the father of Te-kō'ȧ
had two wives, Hē'lah and Nā'a-rah.
6 And Nā'a-rah bare him A-hū'zam,
and Hē'phĕr, and Tĕm'e-nī, and Hā-a-
hăsh'ta-rī. These *were* the sons of Nā'-
a-rah.
7 And the sons of Hē'lah *were,* Zē'-
reth, and Jĕz'o-ar, and Ĕth-nan.
8 And Cŏz begat A'nub, and Zo-bē'-
bah, and the families of A-här'hel the
son of Hā'rum.
9 ¶ And Jā'bĕz was [b]more honourable than his brethren: and his mother
called his name [3]Jā'bĕz, saying, Because [c]I bare him with sorrow.
10 And Jā'bĕz [d]called on the God of
Ĭs'ra-el, saying, [4]Oh that thou wouldest
bless me indeed, and enlarge my coast,
and that thine hand might be with me,
and that thou wouldest [5]keep *me* from
evil, that it may not grieve me! And
God [e]granted him that which he requested.
11 ¶ And Chē'lŭb the brother of
Shu'ah begat Mē'hĭr, which *was* the
father of Ĕsh'ton.
12 And Ĕsh'ton begat Bĕth–rā'phȧ,
and Pa-sē'ah, and Te-hĭn'nah the father of [6]Ĭr–nā'hăsh. These *are* the men
of Rē'chah.
13 And the sons of Kē'năz; [f]Ŏth'nĭ-
el, and Sĕr-a-ī'ah: and the sons of Ŏth'-
nĭ-el; [7]Hā'thăth.

52 [12]Or, Reaiah, ch. 4.2 [13]Or, half of the Menuchites, or, Hatsihammenuchoth
54 [14]Or, Atarites, or, crowns of the house of Joab
55 [v]Gen. 15.19; [w]Jer. 35.2

CHAPTER 3
1 [a]1 Sam. 25.43; [b]Josh. 15.56 [1]Or, Chileab, 2 Sam. 3.3
3 [c]2 Sam. 3.5
4 [d]2 Sam. 2.11 [e]2 Sam. 5.5
5 [f]ch. 14.4 [2]Or, Shammua [g]2 Sam. 12.24 [3]Or, Bathsheba [4]Or, Eliam
6 [5]Or, Elishua
8 [6]Or, Beeliada, ch. 14.7 [h]2 Sam. 5.14
9 [i]2 Sam. 13.1
10 [j]1 Ki. 11.43 [7]Or, Abijam, 1 Ki. 15.1
16 [k]Matt. 1.11 [l]2 Ki. 24.17;
17 [8]Shealtiel [m]Matt. 1.12
19 [n]Ezra 3.2
22 [o]Ezra 8.2
23 [9]Hiskijah

CHAPTER 4
1 [a]Gen. 38.29; [1]Or, Chelubai, ch. 2.9, or, Caleb, ch. 2.18
2 [2]Or, Haroeh, ch. 2.52
9 [b]Gen. 34.19; [3]That is, Sorrowful [c]Gen. 3.16
10 [d]ch. 16.8; [4]If thou wilt, etc [5]Do me [e]Job 22.27-28;
12 [6]Or, the city of Nahash
13 [f]Josh. 15.17 [7]Or, Hathath, and Meonothai, who begat, etc

14 And Me-ŏn'o-thāi begat Ŏph'rah: and Sĕr-a-ī'ah begat Jō'ab, the father of [g]the [8]valley of [9]Chăr'a-shĭm; for they were craftsmen.

15 And the sons of Cā'leb the son of Je-phŭn'neh; Ī'rụ, Ē'lah, and Nā'am: and the sons of Ē'lah, [10]even Kē'năz.

16 And the sons of Jē-ha-lē'le-el; Zīph, and Zī'phah, Tĭr'ĭ-a, and A-sā'-re-el.

17 And the sons of Ĕz'rȧ *were,* Jē'-thĕr, and Mē'rĕd, and Ē'phĕr, and Jā'lon: and she bare Mĭr'ĭ-am, and Ṣhăm'ma-ī, and Ĭsh'bah the father of Ĕsh-te-mō'ȧ.

18 And his wife [11]Jē-hū-dī'jah bare Jē'rĕd the father of Gē'dôr, and Hē'bĕr the father of Sō'cho, and Je-ku'thĭ-el the father of Za-nō'ah. And these *are* the sons of Bĭth'ĭ-ah the daughter of Phā'raōh, which Mē'rĕd took.

19 And the sons of *his* wife [12]Ho-dī'ah the sister of Nā'ham, the father of Kēi'lah the Gär'mīte, and Ĕsh-te-mō'ȧ the Ma-ăch'a-thīte.

20 And the sons of Shī'mon *were,* Ăm'nŏn, and Rĭn'nah, Bĕn–hā'năn, and Tī'lon. And the sons of Ĭsh'ī *were,* Zō'heth, and Bĕn–zō'heth.

21 ¶ The sons of Shē'lah [h]the son of Jū'dah *were,* Ēr the father of Lē'cah, and Lā'a-dah the father of Ma-rē'shah, and the families of the house of them that wrought fine linen, of the house of Ăsh-bē'ȧ,

22 And Jō'kim, and the men of Chō'-ze-bȧ, and Jō'ăsh, and Sā'răph, who had the [i]dominion in Mō'ab, and Jăsh'-ụ-bī–lē'hĕm. And *these are* ancient things.

23 These *were* the potters, and those that dwelt among plants and hedges: there they dwelt with the king for his work.

24 ¶ The sons of Sĭm'e-on *were,* [13]Ne-mū'el, and Jā'min, [14]Jā'rib, Zē'-rah, *and* Shā'ul:

25 Shăl'lum his son, Mĭb'sam his son, Mĭsh'mȧ his son.

26 And the sons of Mĭsh'mȧ; Ha-mū'el his son, Zăc'chur his son, Shĭm'-e-ī his son.

27 And Shĭm'e-ī had sixteen sons and six daughters; but his brethren had not many children, neither did all their family multiply, [15]like to the children of Jū'dah.

28 And they dwelt at Bē'er–shē'bȧ, and Mŏl'a-dah, and Hā'zar–shụ'al,

29 And at [16]Bĭl'hah, and at Ē'zĕm, and at [17]Tō'lăd,

30 And at Bĕth–ụ'el, and at Hôr'-mah, and at Zĭk'lag,

31 And at Bĕth–mär'că-bŏth, and [18]Hā'zar–su'-sim, and at Bĕth–bĭr'e-ī, and at Shā-a-rā'im. These *were* their cities unto the reign of Dā'vid.

32 And their villages *were,* [19]Ē'tam, and Ā'in, Rĭm'mon, and Tō'chen, and Ā'shan, five cities:

33 And all their villages that *were* round about the same cities, unto [20]Bā'al. These *were* their habitations, and [21]their genealogy.

34 And Me-shō'băb, and Jăm'lech, and Jō'shah the son of Ăm-a-zī'ah,

35 And Jō'el, and Jē'hū the son of Jŏs-ĭ-bī'ah, the son of Sĕr-a-ī'ah, the son of Ā'sĭ-el,

36 And Ĕl-i-ō-ē'nă-ī, and Ja-ăk'o-bah, and Jĕsh-o-ha-ī'ah, and Ă-sa-ī'ah, and A-dī'el, and Jē-sĭm'i-el, and Be-nā'iah,

37 And Zī'zȧ the son of Shī'phī, the son of Ăl'lŏn, the son of Je-dā'iah, the son of Shĭm'rī, the son of Shĕm-a-ī'ah;

38 These [22]mentioned by *their* names *were* princes in their families: and the house of their fathers increased greatly.

39 ¶ And they went to the entrance of Gē'dôr, *even* unto the east side of the valley, to seek pasture for their flocks.

40 And they found fat pasture and good, and the land *was* wide, and quiet, and peaceable; for *they* of [j]Hăm had dwelt there of old.

41 And these written by name came in the days of Hĕz-e-kī'ah king of Jū'-dah, and [k]smote their tents, and the habitations that were found there, and destroyed them utterly unto this day, and dwelt in their rooms: because *there was* pasture there for their flocks.

42 And *some* of them, *even* of the sons of Sĭm'e-on, five hundred men, went to mount Sē'ĭr, having for their captains Pĕl-a-tī'ah, and Nē-a-rī'ah, and Rĕph-a-ī'ah, and Ŭz'zĭ-el, the sons of Ĭsh'ī.

43 And they smote [l]the rest of the Ăm'a-lĕk-ītes that were escaped, and dwelt there unto this day.

5 Now the sons of Reụ'ben the firstborn of Ĭs'ra-el, (for [a]he *was* the firstborn; but, forasmuch as he [b]defiled his father's bed, [c]his birthright was given unto the sons of Jō'seph the son of Ĭs'ra-el: and the genealogy is not to be reckoned after the birthright.

2 For [d]Jū'dah prevailed above his brethren, and of him *came* the [e]chief [1]ruler; but the birthright *was* Jō'seph's:)

3 The sons, *I say,* of [f]Reụ'ben the firstborn of Ĭs'ra-el *were,* Hā'noch, and Păl'lu, Hĕz'ron, and Cär'mī.

4 The sons of Jō'el; Shĕm-a-ī'ah his son, Gŏg his son, Shĭm'e-ī his son,

5 Mī'cah his son, Rē-a-ī'ȧ his son, Bā'al his son,

6 Be-ē'rah his son, whom [2]Tĭl'gath–pĭl-nē'ser king of Ăs-sỹr'ĭ-ȧ carried away *captive:* he *was* prince of the Reụ'ben-ītes.

7 And his brethren by their families, [g]when the genealogy of their generations was reckoned, *were* the chief, Je-ī'el, and Zĕch-a-rī'ah,

8 And Bē'lȧ the son of Ā'zaz, the son of [3]Shē'mȧ, the son of Jō'el, who dwelt in [h]Ăr'ō-ĕr, even unto Nē'bo and Bā'al–mē'on:

9 And eastward he inhabited unto the entering in of the wilderness from the river Eū-phrā'tēs: because their cattle were multiplied [i]in the land of Gĭl'-e-ăd.

10 And in the days of Sạul they made war [j]with the Hā'gar-ītes, who fell by

14 [g]Neh. 11.35
[8]Or, inhabitants of the valley
[9]That is, Craftsmen
15 [10]Or, Uknaz
18 [11]Or, the Jewess
19 [12]Or, Jehudijah, mentioned before
21 [h]Gen. 38.1
22 [i]2 Sam. 8.2
24 [13]Or, Jemuel, Gen. 46.10; Ex. 6.15; Num. 26.12
[14]Or, Jachin, Zohar
27 [15]unto
29 [16]Or, Balah, Josh. 19.3
[17]Or, Eltolad, Josh. 19.4
31 [18]Or, Hazarsusah, Josh. 19.5
32 [19]Or, Ether
33 [20]Or, Baalath-beer
[21]Or, as they divided themselves by nations among them
38 [22]coming
40 [j]Gen. 9.22; Ps. 78.51
41 [k]2 Ki. 18.8
43 [l]1 Sam. 15.8; 2 Sam. 8.12

CHAPTER 5

1 [a]Gen. 29.32
[b]Gen. 35.22
[c]Gen. 48.15
2 [d]Gen. 49.8; Num. 2.3; Ps. 60.7
[e]Ps. 78.68-71; Jer. 23.5-6; Mic. 5.2; Matt. 2.6
[1]Or, prince
3 [f]Ex. 6.14; Num. 26.5
6 [2]Or, Tiglath-pileser, 2 Ki. 15.29
7 [g]verse 17
8 [3]Or, Shemaiah, verse 4
[h]Josh. 13.15
9 [i]Josh. 22.9; Song 4.1; Mic. 7.14
10 [j]Gen. 25.12

their hand: and they dwelt in their tents [4]throughout all the east *land* of Gĭl'e-ăd.

11 ¶ And the children of Găd dwelt over against them, in the land of [k]Bā'shăn unto Săl'cah:

12 Jō'el the chief, and Shā'pham the next, and Ja-ā'nāi, and Shā'phat in Bā'shăn.

13 And their brethren of the house of their fathers *were,* Mī'chaēl, and Me-shŭl'lam, and Shē'bȧ, and Jō'ra-ī, and Jā'chan, and Zī'ȧ, and Hē'bẽr, seven.

14 These *are* the children of Ăb-i-hā'il the son of Hū'rī, the son of Ja-rō'ah, the son of Gĭl'e-ăd, the son of Mī'chaēl, the son of Je-shĭsh'a-ī, the son of Jăh'dō, the son of Bŭz;

15 Ā'hī the son of Ăb'dĭ-ĕl, the son of Gū'nī, chief of the house of their fathers.

16 And they dwelt in Gĭl'e-ăd in Bā'shăn, and in her towns, and in all the suburbs of [l]Shâr'on, upon [5]their borders.

17 All these were reckoned by genealogies in the days of [m]Jō'tham king of Jū'dah, and in the days of [n]Jĕr-o-bō'am king of Ĭs'ra-el.

18 ¶ The sons of Reu'ben, and the Găd'ītes, and half the tribe of Ma-năs'seh, [6]of valiant men, men able to bear buckler and sword, and to shoot with bow, and skilful in war, *were* four and forty thousand seven hundred and threescore, that went out to the war.

19 And they made war with the Hā'gar-ītes, with [o]Je'tŭr, and Nē'phish, and Nō'dăb.

20 And they were helped against them, and the Hā'gar-ītes were delivered into their hand, and all that *were* with them: for they cried to God in the battle, and he was intreated of them; because they [p]put their trust in him.

21 And they [7]took away their cattle; of their camels fifty thousand, and of sheep two hundred and fifty thousand, and of asses two thousand, and of [8]men an hundred thousand.

22 For there fell down many slain, because the war *was* [q]of God. And they dwelt in their steads until [r]the captivity.

23 ¶ And the children of the half tribe of Ma-năs'seh dwelt in the land: they increased from Bā'shăn unto Bā'al-hẽr'mŏn and Sē'nĭr, and unto mount Hẽr'mŏn.

24 And these *were* the heads of the house of their fathers, even Ē'phẽr, and Ĭsh'ī, and E-lī'el, and Ăz'rĭ-el, and Jĕr-e-mī'ah, and Hŏd-a-vī'ah, and Jăh'dĭ-el, mighty men of valour, [9]famous men, *and* heads of the house of their fathers.

25 ¶ And they [s]transgressed against the God of their fathers, and went a whoring after the gods of the people of the land, whom God destroyed before them.

26 And the God of Ĭs'ra-el stirred up the spirit of Pŭl king of Ăs-sy̆r'ĭ-ȧ, and the spirit of Tĭl'gath-pĭl-nē'ser king of Ăs-sy̆r'ĭ-ȧ, and he carried them away, even the Reu'ben-ītes, and the Găd'ītes, and the half tribe of Ma-năs'seh, and brought them unto Hā'lah, and Hā'bôr, and Hā'rȧ, and to the river Gō'zan, unto this day.

6 The sons of Lē'vī; [a]Gẽr'shŏn, Kō'hath, and Me-rā'rī.

2 And the sons of Kō'hath; Ăm'răm, Ĭz'har, and Hē'bron, and Ŭz'zĭ-el.

3 And the children of Ăm'răm; Aâr'on, and Mō'ses, and Mĭr'ĭ-am. The sons also of Aâr'on; [b]Nā'dăb, and A-bī'hū, Ē-le-ā'zar, and Ĭth'a-mär.

4 ¶ Ē-le-ā'zar begat Phĭn'e-has, Phĭn'e-has begat A-bĭsh'u-ȧ,

5 And A-bĭsh'u-ȧ begat Bŭk'kī, and Bŭk'kī begat Ŭz'zī,

6 And Ŭz'zī begat Zĕr-a-hī'ah, and Zĕr-a-hī'ah begat Me-rā'ioth,

7 Me-rā'ioth begat Ăm-a-rī'ah, and Ăm-a-rī'ah begat A-hī'tub,

8 And [c]A-hī'tub begat Zā'dŏk, and [d]Zā'dŏk begat A-hĭm'a-ăz,

9 And A-hĭm'a-ăz begat Ăz-a-rī'ah, and Ăz-a-rī'ah begat Jo-hā'nan,

10 And Jo-hā'nan begat Ăz-a-rī'ah, (he *it is* that [e]executed the priest's office [1]in the [f]temple that Sŏl'o-mon built in Je-ru'sa-lĕm:)

11 And [g]Ăz-a-rī'ah begat Ăm-a-rī'ah, and Ăm-a-rī'ah begat A-hī'tub,

12 And A-hī'tub begat Zā'dŏk, and Zā'dŏk begat [2]Shăl'lum,

13 And Shăl'lum begat Hĭl-kī'ah, and Hĭl-kī'ah begat Ăz-a-rī'ah,

14 And Ăz-a-rī'ah begat [h]Sĕr-a-ī'ah, and Sĕr-a-ī'ah begat Je-hŏz'a-dăk,

15 And Je-hŏz'a-dăk went *into captivity,* when [i]the LORD carried away Jū'dah and Je-ru'sa-lĕm by the hand of Nĕb-u-chăd-nĕz'zar.

16 ¶ The sons of Lē'vī; [j]Gẽr'shŏm, Kō'hath, and Me-rā'rī.

17 And these *be* the names of the sons of Gẽr'shŏm; Lĭb'nī, and Shĭm'e-ī.

18 And the sons of Kō'hath *were,* Ăm'răm, and Ĭz'har, and Hē'bron, and Ŭz'zĭ-el.

19 The sons of [k]Me-rā'rī; Măh'lī, and Mū'shī. And these *are* the families of the Lē'vītes according to their fathers.

20 Of Gẽr'shŏm; Lĭb'nī his son, Jā'hăth his son, Zĭm'mah his son,

21 [l]Jō'ah his son, [m]Ĭd'dō his son, Zē'rah his son, [n]Jē-ăt'e-rāi his son.

22 The sons of Kō'hath; [o]Ăm-mĭn'a-dab his son, Kō'rah his son, Ăs'sĭr his son,

23 Ĕl'kă-nah his son, and E-bī'a-săph his son, and Ăs'sĭr his son,

24 Tā'hăth his son, [p]Ū'rĭ-el his son, Ŭz-zī'ah his son, and Shā'ul his son.

25 And the sons of Ĕl'kă-nah; [q]A-măs'a-ī, and A-hī'mŏth.

26 *As for* Ĕl'kă-nah: the sons of Ĕl'kă-nah; [r]Zō'phāi his son, and [s]Nā'hăth his son,

27 [t]E-lī'ab his son, Jĕr'o-hăm his son, Ĕl'kă-nah his son.

28 And the sons of Săm'u-el; the firstborn [3]Văsh'nī, and A-bī'ah.

29 The sons of Me-rā'rī; Măh'lī, Lĭb'nī his son, Shĭm'e-ī his son, Ŭz'zȧ his son,

[4]upon all the face of the east
11 [k]Josh. 13.11-24-25
16 [l]ch. 27.29; Isa. 35.2
[5]their goings forth
17 [m]2 Ki. 15.5
[n]2 Ki. 14.16-28
18 [6]sons of valour
19 [o]Gen. 25.15
20 [p]Ps. 9.10; Ps. 22.4-5
21 [7]led captive
[8]souls of men
22 [q]Deut. 20.1-4; Rom. 8.31
[r]2 Ki. 15.29
24 [9]men of names
25 [s]Deut. 32.15; Isa. 1.4

CHAPTER 6
1 [a]Gen. 46.11
3 [b]Ex. 6.23; Lev. 10.1
8 [c]2 Sam. 8.17
[d]2 Sam. 15.27
10 [e]2 Chr. 26.17-18
[1]in the house
[f]2 Chr. 3
11 [g]Ezra 7.3
12 [2]Or, Meshullam, ch. 9.11
14 [h]Neh. 11.11
15 [i]2 Chr. 36.17-21
16 [j]Ex. 6.16
19 [k]Num. 3.33
21 [l]verse 42, Ethan
[m]verse 41, Adaiah
[n]verse 41, Ethni
22 [o]verses 2-18, Izhar
24 [p]verse 36, Zephaniah, Azariah, Joel
25 [q]verses 35-36
26 [r]verse 35, Zuph; 1 Sam. 1.1
[s]verse 34, Toah
27 [t]verse 34, Eliel
28 [3]Called also Joel, 1 Sam. 8.2

30 Shĭm'e-à his son, Hag-gī'ah his son, A-sa-ī'ah his son.

31 And these *are they* whom Dā'vid set over the service of song in the house of the LORD, after that the [u]ark had rest.

32 And they ministered before the dwelling place of the tabernacle of the congregation with singing, until Sŏl'o-mon had built the house of the LORD in Je-ru'sa-lĕm: and *then* they waited on their office according to their order.

33 And these *are* they that [4]waited with their children. Of the sons of the Kō'hath-ītes: Hē'man a singer, the son of Jō'el, the son of She-mū'el,

34 The son of Ĕl'kă-nah, the son of Jĕr'o-hăm, the son of E-lī'el, the son of [5]Tō'ah,

35 The son of [6]Zŭph, the son of Ĕl'kă-nah, the son of Mā'hath, the son of A-măs'a-ī,

36 The son of Ĕl'kă-nah, the son of [v]Jō'el, the son of Ăz-a-rī'ah, the son of Zĕph-a-nī'ah,

37 The son of Tā'hăth, the son of Ăs'sĭr, the son of [w]E-bī'a-săph, the son of Kō'rah,

38 The son of Ĭz'har, the son of Kō'hath, the son of Lē'vī, the son of Ĭs'ra-el.

39 And his brother Ā'saph, who stood on his right hand, *even* Ā'saph the son of Bĕr-a-chī'ah, the son of Shĭm'e-à,

40 The son of Mī'chaĕl, the son of Bā-a-sē'iah, the son of Măl-chī'ah,

41 The son of [x]Ĕth'nī, the son of Zē'rah, the son of Ăd-a-ī'ah,

42 The son of [y]Ē'than, the son of Zĭm'mah, the son of Shĭm'e-ī,

43 The son of Jā'hăth, the son of Gĕr'shŏm, the son of Lē'vī.

44 And their brethren the sons of Me-rā'rī *stood* on the left hand: [7]Ē'than the son of [8]Kĭsh'ī, the son of Ăb'dī, the son of Măl'luch,

45 The son of Hash-a-bī'ah, the son of Ăm-a-zī'ah, the son of Hĭl-kī'ah,

46 The son of Ăm'zī, the son of Bā'nī, the son of Shā'mer,

47 The son of Mäh'lī, the son of Mū'shī, the son of Me-rā'rī, the son of Lē'vī.

48 Their brethren also the Lē'vītes *were* appointed unto all manner of service of the tabernacle of the house of God.

49 ¶ But Aâr'on and his sons offered [z]upon the altar of the burnt offering, and [a]on the altar of incense, *and were appointed* for all the work of the *place* most holy, and to make an atonement for Ĭs'ra-el, according to all that Mō'ses the servant of God had commanded.

50 And these *are* [b]the sons of Aâr'on; Ē-le-ā'zar his son, Phĭn'e-has his son, A-bĭsh'u-à his son,

51 Bŭk'kī his son, Ŭz'zī his son, Zĕr-a-hī'ah his son,

52 Me-rā'ioth his son, Ăm-a-rī'ah his son, A-hī'tub his son,

53 Zā'dŏk his son, A-hĭm'a-ăz his son.

54 ¶ [c]Now these *are* their dwelling-places throughout their castles in their coasts, of the sons of Aâr'on, of the families of the Kō'hath-ītes: for theirs was the lot.

55 [d]And they gave them Hē'bron in the land of Jū'dah, and the suburbs thereof round about it.

56 [e]But the fields of the city, and the villages thereof, they gave to Cā'leb the son of Je-phŭn'neh.

57 And [f]to the sons of Aâr'on they gave the cities of Jū'dah, *namely,* Hē'bron, *the city* of refuge, and Lĭb'nah with her suburbs, and Jăt'tĭr, and Ĕsh-te-mō'à, with their suburbs,

58 And [g]Hī'len with her suburbs, Dē'bĭr with her suburbs,

59 And [h]Ā'shan with her suburbs, and Bĕth–shē'mĕsh with her suburbs:

60 And out of the tribe of Bĕn'ja-min; Gē'bà with her suburbs, and [i]Ăl'e-mĕth with her suburbs, and Ăn'a-thoth with her suburbs. All their cities throughout their families *were* thirteen cities.

61 And unto the sons of Kō'hath, [j]*which were* left of the family of that tribe, *were cities given* out of the half tribe, *namely, out of* the half *tribe* of Ma-năs'seh, [k]by lot, ten cities.

62 And to the sons of Gĕr'shŏm throughout their families out of the tribe of Ĭs'sa-char, and out of the tribe of Ăsh'ēr, and out of the tribe of Naph'-ta-li, and out of the tribe of Ma-nas'seh in Bā'shăn, thirteen cities.

63 Unto the sons of Me-rā'rī *were given* by lot, throughout their families, out of the tribe of Reu'ben, and out of the tribe of Găd, and out of the tribe of Zĕb'u-lun, [l]twelve cities.

64 And [m]the children of Ĭs'ra-el gave to the Lē'vītes *these* cities with their suburbs.

65 And they gave by lot out of the tribe of the children of Jū'dah, and out of the tribe of the children of Sĭm'e-on, and out of the tribe of the children of Bĕn'ja-min, these cities, which are called by *their* names.

66 And [n]*the residue* of the families of the sons of Kō'hath had cities of their coasts out of the tribe of Ē'phră-ĭm.

67 [o]And they gave unto them, *of* the cities of refuge, Shē'chem in mount Ē'phră-ĭm with her suburbs; *they gave* also Gē'zĕr with her suburbs,

68 And [9]Jŏk'me-ăm with her suburbs, and Bĕth–hō'rŏn with her suburbs.

69 And Ăij'a-lŏn with her suburbs, and Găth–rĭm'mon with her suburbs:

70 And out of the half tribe of Ma-năs'seh; Ā'nēr with her suburbs, and Bĭl'ĕ-ăm with her suburbs, for the family of the remnant of the sons of Kō'hath.

71 Unto the sons of Gĕr'shŏm *were given* out of the family of the half tribe of Ma-năs'seh, Gō'lan in Bā'shăn with her suburbs, and [p10]Ăsh'ta-rŏth with her suburbs:

31 [u]ch. 16.1; 2 Sam. 6.17
33 [4]stood
34 [5]verse 26, Nahath
35 [6]Or, Zaphai
36 [v]verse 24; Shaul, Uzziah, Uriel
37 [w]Ex. 6.24
41 [x]verse 21, Jeaterai
42 [y]verse 21, Joah
44 [7]Called Jeduthun, ch. 9.16; 2 Chr. 35.15; Ps. 62, title
[8]Or, Kushaiah, ch. 15.17
49 [z]Ex. 29.38; Lev. 9.12-13; Num. 3.10; Heb. 5.1
[a]Ex. 30.7; 1 Sam. 2.28; ch. 23.13; Luke 1.9
50 [b]Ex. 6.23; Lev. 10.1; Num. 3.2; ch. 24.1; Ezra 7.2-5
54 [c]Num. 35.1-8; Josh. 21.9-19; In this list Gibeon and Juttah are omitted
55 [d]Josh. 21.11-12
56 [e]Josh. 14.13
57 [f]Josh. 21.13
58 [g]Josh. 21.15, Holon
59 [h]Josh. 21.16, Ain
60 [i]Josh. 21.18, Almon
61 [j]verse 66
[k]Josh. 21.5
63 [l]Josh. 21.7-34
64 [m]Num. 35.1-8
66 [n]Josh. 21.4-5-20-26
67 [o]Gen. 33.19
68 [9]See Josh. 21.22-35, where many of these cities have other names. Perhaps some of the cities were exchanged for others
71 [p]Deut. 1.4
[10]Josh. 21.27, Beesh-terah

72 And out of the tribe of Ĭs'sa-char; [q]Kē'desh with her suburbs, Dăb'e-răth with her suburbs,
73 And Rā'moth with her suburbs, and Ā'nem with her suburbs:
74 And out of the tribe of Ăsh'ēr; Mā'shal with her suburbs, and Ăb'dŏn with her suburbs,
75 And Hū'kŏk with her suburbs, and Rē'hŏb with her suburbs:
76 And out of the tribe of Năph'ta-lī; Kē'desh in Găl'ĭ-lee with her suburbs, and Hăm'mŏn with her suburbs, and Kĭr-jath-ā'im with her suburbs.
77 Unto the rest of the children of Me-rā'rī *were given* out of the tribe of Zĕb'u-lun, Rĭm'mon with her suburbs, Tā'bôr with her suburbs:
78 And on the other side Jôr'dan by Jĕr'ĭ-chō, on the east side of Jôr'dan, *were given them* out of the tribe of Reu'ben, Bē'zēr in the wilderness with her suburbs, and Jäh'zah with her suburbs,
79 Kĕd'e-mŏth also with her suburbs, and Mĕph'a-ăth with her suburbs:
80 And out of the tribe of Găd; Rā'moth in Gĭl'e-ăd with her suburbs, and Mā-ha-nā'im with her suburbs,
81 And [r]Hĕsh'bŏn with her suburbs, and Jā'zēr with her suburbs.

7 Now the sons of [a]Ĭs'sa-char *were*, [b]Tō'lȧ, and [c]Pū'ah, Jăsh'ŭb, and Shĭm'rŏm, four.
2 And the sons of Tō'lȧ; Ŭz'zī, and Rĕph-a-ī'ah, and Jē'rĭ-el, and Jäh'ma-ī, and Jĭb'sam, and She-mū'el, heads of their father's house, *to wit*, of Tō'lȧ: *they were* valiant men of might in their generations; [d]whose number *was* in the days of Dā'vid two and twenty thousand and six hundred.
3 And the sons of Ŭz'zī; Ĭz-ra-hī'ah: and the sons of Ĭz-ra-hī'ah; Mī'chaĕl, and Ō-ba-dī'ah, and Jō'el, Ĭsh-ī'ah, five: all of them [e]chief men.
4 And with them, by their generations, after the house of their fathers, *were* bands of soldiers for war, six and thirty thousand *men*: for they had many wives and sons.
5 And their brethren among all the families of Ĭs'sa-char *were* valiant men of might, reckoned in all by their genealogies fourscore and seven thousand.
6 ¶ *The sons* of [f]Bĕn'ja-min; Bē'lȧ, and Bē'chēr, and Je-dī'a-el, three.
7 And the sons of Bē'lȧ; Ĕz'bŏn, and Ŭz'zī, and Ŭz'zĭ-el, and Jĕr'i-mŏth, and Ī'rī, five; heads of the house of *their* fathers, mighty men of valour; and were reckoned by their genealogies twenty and two thousand and thirty and four.
8 And the sons of Bē'chēr; Ze-mī'rȧ, and Jō'ăsh, and E-li-ē'zēr, and Ĕl-i-ō-ē'nā-ī, and Ŏm'rī, and Jĕr'i-mŏth, and A-bī'ah, and Ăn'a-thoth, and Ăl'a-mĕth. All these *are* the sons of Bē'chēr.
9 And the number of them, after their genealogy by their generations, heads of the house of their fathers, mighty men of valour, *was* twenty thousand and two hundred.

72 [q]Josh. 21.28, Kishon
81 [r]Num. 21.25; Deut. 2.24; Josh. 12.2-5; Neh. 9.22; Song 7.4; Isa. 15.4
CHAPTER 7
1 [a]Gen. 30.17-18; Num. 1.28-29
[b]Gen. 46.13; Num. 26.23
[c]Gen. 46.13, Phuvah, Job
2 [d]2 Sam. 24.1-2; ch. 21.1-5
3 [e]ch. 5.24
6 [f]Gen. 46.21; Num. 26.38
12 [g]Num. 26.39, Shupham, and Hupham
[h]verse 7, Iri
[i]Num. 26.38, Ahiram
13 [j]Gen. 46.24, Shillem
14 [k]Num. 27.1
15 [1]Herzon, a grandson of Judah, married Machir's daughter, and their child was reckoned to the tribe of Manasseh
[l]Num. 27.1-11
17 [m]1 Sam. 12.11
18 [n]Num. 26.30, Jezer
20 [o]Gen. 41.52; Num. 26.35-36; Deut. 33.13-17; Ps. 60.7
22 [p]Gen. 37.34-35; 2 Sam. 1.11-12; Job 2.11; Ps. 69.11
23 [2]That is, In evil
24 [q]Josh. 16.3; 1 Sam. 13.18; 2 Chr. 8.5
27 [r]Num. 13.8-16, Nun
28 [s]Josh. 16.7, Naarath
[3]daughters
29 [t]Josh. 17.7

10 The sons also of Je-dī'a-el; Bĭl'hăn: and the sons of Bĭl'hăn; Jē'ush, and Bĕn'ja-min, and Ē'hŭd, and Chē-nā'ă-nah, and Zē'than, and Thär'shish, and A-hĭsh'a-här.
11 All these the sons of Je-dī'a-el, by the heads of their fathers, mighty men of valour, *were* seventeen thousand and two hundred *soldiers*, fit to go out for war *and* battle.
12 [g]Shŭp'pim also, and Hŭp'pim, the children of [h]Ĭr, *and* Hū'shim, the sons of [i]Ā'hēr.
13 ¶ The sons of Năph'ta-lī; Jäh'zĭ-el, and Gū'nī, and Jē'zēr, and [j]Shăl'lum, the sons of Bĭl'hah.
14 ¶ [k]The sons of Ma-năs'seh; Ăsh'rĭ-el, whom she bare: (*but* his concubine the Ā'ram-ĭt-ess bare Mā'chĭr the father of Gĭl'e-ăd:
15 And [1]Mā'chĭr took to wife *the sister* of Hŭp'pim and Shŭp'pim, whose sister's name *was* Mā'a-chah;) and the name of the second *was* Ze-lō'phe-hăd: and [l]Ze-lō'phe-hăd had daughters.
16 And Mā'a-chah the wife of Mā'chĭr bare a son, and she called his name Pē'resh; and the name of his brother *was* Shē'resh; and his sons *were* Ū'lam and Rā'kem.
17 And the sons of Ū'lam; [m]Bē'dăn. These *were* the sons of Gĭl'e-ăd, the son of Mā'chĭr, the son of Ma-năs'seh.
18 And his sister Hăm-mŏl'e-kĕth bare Ī'shod, and [n]Ā-bĭ-ē'zēr, and Ma-hā'lah.
19 And the sons of She-mī'dah were, A-hī'an, and Shē'chem, and Lĭk'hī, and Ā'nĭ-am.
20 ¶ And [o]the sons of Ē'phră-ĭm; Shu'the-lah, and Bē'red his son, and Tā'hăth his son, and Ĕl'ă-dah his son, and Tā'hăth his son,
21 ¶ And Zā'băd his son, and Shu'the-lah his son, and Ē'zēr, and Ē'le-ăd, whom the men of Găth *that were* born in *that* land slew, because they came down to take away their cattle.
22 And Ē'phră-ĭm their father [p]mourned many days, and his brethren came to comfort him.
23 ¶ And when he went in to his wife, she conceived, and bare a son, and he called his name [2]Be-rī'ah, because it went evil with his house.
24 (And his daughter *was* Shē'rah, who built [q]Bĕth–hō'rŏn the nether, and the upper, and Ŭz'-zen–shē'rah.)
25 And Rē'phah *was* his son, also Rē'sheph, and Tē'lah his son, and Tā'hăn his son,
26 Lā'ă-dăn his son, Ăm-mī'hŭd his son, E-lĭsh'a-mȧ his son,
27 [r]Nŏn his son, Je-hŏsh'u-ah his son.
28 ¶ And their possessions and habitations *were*, Bĕth'–el and the towns thereof, and eastward [s]Nā'a-răn, and westward Gē'zēr, with the [3]towns thereof; Shē'chem also and the towns thereof, unto Gā'zȧ and the towns thereof:
29 And by the borders of the children of [t]Ma-năs'seh, Bĕth–shē'ăn and

her towns, Tā'a-năch and her towns,
[u]Me-ḡĭd'do and her towns, Dôr and
her towns. In these dwelt the [v]children
of Jō'seph the son of Ĭs'ra-el.
30 ¶ [w]The sons of Ăsh'ēr; Ĭm'nah,
and Ĭs'u-ah, and Ĭsh'u-āi, and Be-rī'ah,
and Sē'rah their sister.
31 And the sons of Be-rī'ah; Hē'bēr,
and Măl'chĭ-el, who *is* the father of
Bĭr'za-vĭth.
32 And Hē'bēr begat Jăph'let, and
[x]Shō'mer, and Hō'tham, and Shụ'ȧ
their sister.
33 And the sons of Jăph'let; Pā'sach,
and Bĭm'hăl, and Ăsh'vath. These *are*
the children of Jăph'let.
34 And the sons of [y]Shā'mer; Ā'hī,
and Rōh'gah, Je-hŭb'bah, and Ā'ram.
35 And the sons of his brother Hē'-
lem; Zō'phah, and Ĭm'nȧ, and Shē'-
lesh, and Ā'măl.
36 The sons of Zō'phah; Sū'ah, and
Här'ne-phĕr, and Shụ'al, and Bē'rī,
and Ĭm'rah,
37 Bē'zēr, and Hŏd, and Shăm'mȧ,
and Shĭl'shah, and Ĭth'ran, and Be-
ē'rȧ.
38 And the sons of Jē'thēr; Je-phŭn'-
neh, and Pĭs'pah, and Ā'rȧ.
39 And the sons of Ŭl'lȧ; Ā'rah, and
Hăn'ĭ-el, and Re-zī'ȧ.
40 All these *were* the children of
Ăsh'ēr, heads of *their* father's house,
choice *and* mighty men of valour,
chief of the princes. And the number
throughout the genealogy of them that
were [z]apt to the war *and* to battle *was*
twenty and six thousand men.
8 Now Bĕn'ja-min begat [a]Bē'lȧ his
firstborn, Ăsh'bel the second, and
A-hăr'ah the third,
2 Nō'hah the fourth, and Rā'phȧ the
fifth.
3 And the sons of Bē'lȧ were, [1]Ăd'-
där, and Ḡē'rȧ, and A-bī'hŭd,
4 And A-bĭsh'u-ȧ, and Nā'a-man,
and A-hō'ah,
5 And Ḡē'rȧ, and [2]She-phū'phan,
and Hū'ram.
6 And these *are* the sons of Ē'hŭd:
these are the heads of the fathers of
the inhabitants of Ḡē'bȧ, and they removed them to [b]Măn'a-hăth:
7 And Nā'a-man, and A-hī'ah, and
Ḡē'rȧ, he removed them, and begat
Ŭz'zȧ, and A-hī'hud.
8 And Shā-ha-rā'im begat *children*
in [c]the country of Mō'ab, after he had
sent them away; Hū'shim and Bā'a-rȧ
were his wives.
9 And he begat of Hŏ'desh his wife,
Jō'băb, and Zĭb'ĭ-ȧ, and Mē'shȧ, and
Măl'cham,
10 And Jē'ŭz, and Shăch-ī'ȧ and
Mĭr'mȧ. These *were* his sons, heads of
the fathers.
11 And of Hū'shim he begat Ăb'ĭ-
tŭb, and Ĕl'pă-al.
12 The sons of Ĕl'pă-al; Ē'bēr, and
Mĭ'sham, and Shā'med, who built
[d]Ō'no, and Lŏd, with the towns thereof:
13 Be-rī'ah also, and [e]Shē'mȧ, who
were heads of the fathers of the inhabitants of [f]Āij'a-lŏn, who drove away the
inhabitants of Găth:
14 And A-hī'o, Shā'shak, and Jĕr'e-
mŏth,
15 And Zĕb-a-dī'ah, and Ā'răd, and
Ā'der,
16 And Mī'chaĕl, and Ĭs'pah, and
Jō'hȧ, the sons of Be-rī'ah;
17 And Zĕb-a-dī'ah, and Me-shŭl'-
lam, and Hĕz'e-kī, and Hē'bēr,
18 Ĭsh'mĕ-rāi also, and Jĕz-lī'ah, and
Jō'băb, the sons of Ĕl'pă-al;
19 And Jā'kim, and Zĭch'rī, and
Zăb'dī,
20 And E-li-ē'na-ī, and Zĭl'thāi, and
E-lī'el,
21 And Ăd-a-ī'ah, and Bĕr-a-ī'ah,
and Shĭm'rath, the sons of [3]Shĭm'hī;
22 And Ĭsh'păn, and Hē'bēr, and E-
lī'el,
23 And Ăb'dŏn, and Zĭch'rī, and
Hā'nan,
24 And Hăn-a-nī'ah, and Ē'lăm, and
Ăn-to-thī'jah,
25 And Ĭph-e-dē'iah, and Pe-nū'el,
the sons of Shā'shak;
26 And Shăm-she-rā'ī, and Shē-ha-
rī'ah, and Ăth-a-lī'ah,
27 And Jăr'ĕ-sī'ah, and E-lī'ah, and
Zĭch'rī, the sons of Jĕr'o-hăm.
28 These *were* heads of the fathers,
by their generations, chief *men*. These
dwelt in Je-rụ'sa-lĕm.
29 And at Ḡĭb'e-on dwelt the [4]father
of Ḡĭb'e-on; whose [g]wife's name *was*
Mā'a-chah:
30 And his firstborn son Ăb'dŏn, and
Zûr, and Kĭsh, and Bā'al, and Nā'dăb,
31 And Ḡē'dôr, and A-hī'o, and [h]Zā'-
cher.
32 And Mĭk'loth begat [i]Shĭm'e-ah.
And these also dwelt with their brethren in Je-rụ'sa-lĕm, over against them.
33 ¶ And [j]Nēr begat Kĭsh, and Kĭsh
begat Saul, and Saul begat Jŏn'a-than,
and Măl-chĭ-shụ'ȧ, and [k]A-bĭn'ă-dăb,
and [l]Ĕsh-bā'al.
34 And the son of Jŏn'a-than *was*
[m]Mĕr'ib–bā'al: and Mĕr'ib–bā'al begat
[n]Mī'cah.
35 And the sons of Mī'cah *were*, Pī'-
thon, and Mē'lech, and [o]Tā're-ȧ, and
Ā'hăz.
36 And Ā'hăz begat [p]Je-hō'a-dah;
and Je-hō'a-dah begat Ăl'e-mĕth, and
Ăz'ma-veth, and Zĭm'rī; and Zĭm'rī
begat Mō'zȧ,
37 And Mō'zȧ begat Bĭn'e-ȧ: [q]Rā'-
phȧ *was* his son, E-lē'a-sah his son,
Ā'zel his son:
38 And Ā'zel had six sons, whose
names *are* these, Ăz'rĭ-kam, Bŏch'e-
rụ, and Ĭsh'ma-el, and Shē-a-rī'ah, and
Ō-ba-dī'ah, and Hā'nan. All these *were*
the sons of Ā'zel.
39 And the sons of Ē'shĕk his brother
were, Ū'lam his firstborn, Jē'hŭsh the
second, and E-lĭph'e-lĕt the third.
40 And the sons of Ū'lam were
mighty men of valour, [r]archers, and
had many sons, and sons' sons, an hundred and fifty. All these *are* of the sons
of Bĕn'ja-min.
9 So [a]all Ĭs'ra-el were reckoned by
genealogies; and, behold, they *were*
written in the book of the kings of
Ĭs'ra-el and Jū'dah, *who* were [b]carried

[u]Josh. 17.11
[v]Judg. 1.22-29
30 [w]Gen. 46.17; Num. 26.44-46; Deut. 33.24
32 [x]verse 34, Shamer
34 [y]verse 32
40 [z]Deut. 2.14
CHAPTER 8
1 [a]Gen. 46.21; Num. 26.38; ch. 7.6
3 [1]Or, Ard, Gen. 46.21
5 [2]Or, Shupham, Num. 26.39; ch. 7.12, Shuppim
6 [b]ch. 2.52
8 [c]Ruth 1.1
12 [d]Ezra 2.33; Neh. 6.2
13 [e]verse 21
[f]Josh. 19.42
21 [3]Or, Shema, verse 13
29 [4]Called, Jehiel, ch. 9.35
[g]ch. 9.35
31 [h]ch. 9.37, Zechariah
32 [i]ch. 9.38, Shimeam
33 [j]1 Sam. 9.1; ch. 9.36-39; Acts 13.21
[k]1 Sam. 14.49, Ishui
[l]2 Sam. 2.8, Ish-bosheth
34 [m]2 Sam. 9.6-10, Mephibosheth
[n]2 Sam. 9.12; ch. 9.40
35 [o]ch. 9.41, Tahrea
36 [p]ch. 9.42, Jarah
37 [q]ch. 9.43, Rephaiah
40 [r]ch. 12.2; 2 Chr. 11.1; 2 Chr. 13.3; 2 Chr. 14.8; 2 Chr. 17.14-19; Neh. 4.13; Song 3.7-8; Eph. 6.11-20
CHAPTER 9
1 [a]Ezra 2.59
[b]Lev. 26.33; 2 Chr. 33.11

away to Băb'y̆-lon for their transgression.
2 ¶ [c]Now the first inhabitants that
dwelt in their possessions in their cities *were,* the Is'ra-el-ītes, the priests,
Lē'vītes, and the [d]Nĕth'i-nĭms.
3 And in [e]Je-ru̧'sa-lĕm dwelt of the
children of Jū'dah, and of the children
of Bĕn'ja-min, and of the children of
Ē'phră-ĭm, and Ma-năs'seh;
4 Ū'tha-ī the son of Ăm-mī'hŭd, the
son of Ŏm'rī, the son of Ĭm'rī, the son
of Bā'nī, of the children of Phā'rĕz [f]the
son of Jū'dah.
5 And of the Shī'lo-nītes; Ā-sa-ī'ah
the firstborn, and his sons.
6 And of the sons of Zē'rah; Je-ū'el,
and their brethren, six hundred and
ninety.
7 And of the sons of Bĕn'ja-min;
Săl'lu the son of Me-shŭl'lam, the son
of Hŏd-a-vī'ah, the son of Hăs-e-nū'ah,
8 And Ĭb-nē'iah the son of Jĕr'o-
hăm, and Ē'lah the son of Ŭz'zī, the
son of Mĭch'rī, and Me-shŭl'lam the
son of Shĕph-a-thī'ah, the son of Re-
u̧'el, the son of Ĭb-nī'jah;
9 And their brethren, according to
their generations, nine hundred and
fifty and six. All these men *were* chief
of the fathers in the house of their fathers.
10 ¶ [g]And of the priests; Je-dā'iah,
and Je-hoi'a-rīb, and Jā'chin,
11 And [1]Ăz-a-rī'ah the son of Hĭl-
kī'ah, the son of Me-shŭl'lam, the son
of Zā'dŏk, the son of Me-rā'ioth, the
son of A-hī'tub, the ruler of the house
of God;
12 And Ăd-a-ī'ah the son of Jĕr'o-
hăm, the son of Păsh'ŭr, the son of
Măl-chī'jah, and Ma-ăs'ī-āi the son of
A-dī'el, the son of Jăh'zĕ-rah, the son
of Me-shŭl'lam, the son of Me-shĭl'le-
mĭth, the son of Ĭm'mĕr;
13 And their brethren, heads of the
house of their fathers, a thousand and
seven hundred and threescore; [2]very
able men for the work of the service of
the house of God.
14 And of [h]the Lē'vītes; Shĕm-a-ī'ah
the son of Hăs'shub, the son of Ăz'rī-
kam, the son of Hash-a-bī'ah, of the
sons of Me-rā'rī;
15 And Băk-băk'kar, Hē'resh, and
Gā'lăl, and Măt-ta-nī'ah, the son of
Mī'cah, the son of Zĭch'rī, the son of
Ā'saph;
16 And Ō-ba-dī'ah the son of Shĕm-
a-ī'ah, the son of Gā'lăl, the son of
Jĕd'u-thŭn, and Bĕr-e-chī'ah the son of
Ā'sȧ, the son of Ĕl'kă-nah, that dwelt
in the villages of [i]the Ne-tŏph'a-thītes.
17 And [j]the porters *were,* Shăl'lum,
and Ăk'kŭb, and Tăl'mon, and A-hī'-
măn, and their brethren: Shăl'lum *was*
the chief;
18 Who hitherto *waited* in [k]the
king's gate eastward: they *were* porters in the companies of the children of
Lē'vī.
19 And Shăl'lum the son of Kō're,
the son of E-bī'a-săph, the son of Kō'-
rah, and his brethren, of the house of
his father, [l]the Kō'rah-ītes, *were* over
the work of the service, keepers of the
[3]gates of the tabernacle: and their fathers, *being* over the host of the LORD,
were keepers of the entry.
20 And [m]Phĭn'e-has the son of Ē-le-
ā'zar was the ruler over them in time
past, *and* the LORD *was* with him.
21 *And* Zĕch-a-rī'ah the son of Me-
shĕl-e-mī'ah *was* porter of the door of
the tabernacle of the congregation.
22 All these *which were* chosen to
be porters in the gates *were* two hundred and twelve. These were reckoned
by their genealogy in their villages,
whom [n]Dā'vid and Săm'u-el [o]the seer
[4]did ordain in their [5]set office.
23 So they and their children *had*
the oversight of the gates of the house
of the LORD, *namely,* the house of the
tabernacle, by wards.
24 [p]In four quarters were the porters,
toward the east, west, north, and south.
25 And their brethren, *which were*
in their villages, *were* to come [q]after
seven days from time to time with
them.
26 For these Lē'vītes, the four chief
porters, were in *their* [6]set office, and
were over the [7]chambers and treasuries of the house of God.
27 ¶ And they lodged round about the
house of God, because the charge *was*
upon them, and the opening thereof every morning *pertained* to them.
28 And *certain* of them had the
charge of the ministering vessels, that
they should [8]bring them in and out by
tale.
29 *Some* of them also *were* appointed
to oversee the vessels, and all the [9]in-
struments of the sanctuary, and the fine
flour, and the wine, and the oil, and the
frankincense, and the spices.
30 And *some* of the sons of the priests
made [r]the ointment of the spices.
31 And Măt-ti-thī'ah, *one* of the Lē'-
vītes, who *was* the firstborn of Shăl'-
lum the Kō'rah-īte, had the [10]set office
[s]over the things that were made [11]in
the pans.
32 And *other* of their brethren, of
the sons of the Kō'hath-ītes, *were* over
the [12]shewbread, to prepare *it* every
sabbath.
33 And these *are* [t]the singers, chief
of the fathers of the Lē'vītes, *who remaining* in the chambers *were* free: for
[13]they were employed in *that* work
day and night.
34 These chief fathers of the Lē'-
vītes *were* chief throughout their generations; these dwelt at Je-ru̧'sa-lĕm.
35 ¶ And in Gĭb'e-on dwelt the father of Gĭb'e-on, Je-hī'el, whose wife's
name *was* [u]Mā'a-chah:
36 And his firstborn son Ăb'dŏn,
then Zûr, and Kĭsh, and Bā'al, and Nĕr,
and Nā'dăb,
37 And Gē'dôr, and A-hī'o, and
Zĕch-a-rī'ah, and Mĭk'loth.
38 And Mĭk'loth begat Shĭm'e-ăm.
And they also dwelt with their brethren at Je-ru̧'sa-lĕm, over against their
brethren.

2 [c]Ezra 2.70; Neh. 7.73
[d]Josh. 9.27; Ezra 2.43
3 [e]Neh. 11.1
4 [f]Gen. 46.12; Num. 26.20
10 [g]Neh. 11.10
11 [1]Neh. 11.11, Seraiah
13 [2]mighty men of valour
14 [h]ch. 6.19; Neh. 11.15-19
16 [i]ch. 2.54; Neh. 7.26
17 [j]ch. 23.5
18 [k]2 Ki. 11.19; Ezek. 44.2-3
19 [l]Num. 26.9-11; ch. 6.33-38; Ps. 42, title
[3]thresholds
20 [m]Ex. 6.25; Num. 3.32; Josh. 22.30-31; Ps. 106.30
22 [n]ch. 26.1-2
[o]1 Sam. 9.9
[4]founded
[5]Or, trust
24 [p]ch. 26.13-19
25 [q]2 Chr. 23.8
26 [6]Or, trust
[7]Or, storehouses
28 [8]bring them in by tale, and carry them out by tale
29 [9]Or, vessels
30 [r]Ex. 30.23; Song 1.3-13; Jer. 6.20; Ezek. 27.19-22; Mark 14.3
31 [10]Or, trust
[s]Lev. 6.21
[11]Or, on flat plates, or, slices
32 [12]bread of ordering
33 [t]ch. 6.31; ch. 13.8
[13]upon them
35 [u]ch. 8.29

39 [v]And Nēr begat Kĭsh; and Kĭsh begat Saul; and Saul begat Jŏn′a-than, and Măl-chĭ-shu′ȧ, and A-bĭn′ă-dăb, and Ĕsh–bā′al.

40 And the son of Jŏn′a-than *was* Mĕr′ib–bā′al: and Mĕr′ib–bā′al begat Mī′cah.

41 And the sons of [w]Mī′cah *were,* Pī′thon, and Mē′lech, and [14]Tăh-rē′ȧ, [x]*and Ā′hăz.*

42 And Ā′hăz begat [15]Jā′rah; and Jā′rah begat Ăl′e-mĕth, and Ăz′ma-veth, and Zĭm′rī; and Zĭm′rī begat Mō′zȧ;

43 And Mō′zȧ begat Bĭn′e-ȧ; and [16]Rĕph-a-ī′ah his son, E-lē′a-sah his son, Ā′zel his son.

44 And Ā′zel had six sons, whose names *are* these, Ăz′rĭ-kam, Bŏch′e-ru, and Ĭsh′ma-el, and Shē-a-rī′ah, and Ō-ba-dī′ah, and Hā′nan: these *were* the sons of Ā′zel.

10 Now [a]the Phĭ-lĭs′tĭnes fought against Ĭs′ra-el; and the men of Ĭs′ra-el fled from before the Phĭ-lĭs′tĭnes, and fell down [1]slain in mount Gĭl-bō′ȧ.

2 And the Phĭ-lĭs′tĭnes followed hard after Saul, and after his sons; and the Phĭ-lĭs′tĭnes slew Jŏn′a-than, and [2]A-bĭn′ă-dăb, and Măl-chĭ–shu′ȧ, the sons of Saul.

3 And the battle went sore against Saul, and the [3]archers [4]hit him, and he was wounded of the archers.

4 Then said Saul to his armourbearer, Draw thy sword, and thrust me through therewith; lest these uncircumcised come and [5]abuse me. But his armourbearer would not; for he was sore afraid. So Saul took a sword, and fell upon it.

5 And when his armourbearer saw that Saul was dead, he fell likewise on the sword, and died.

6 So Saul died, and his three sons, and all his house died together.

7 And when all the men of Ĭs′ra-el that *were* in the valley saw that they fled, and that Saul and his sons were dead, then they forsook their cities, and fled: and the Phĭ-lĭs′tĭnes came and dwelt in them.

8 ¶ And it came to pass on the morrow, when the Phĭ-lĭs′tĭnes came to strip the slain, that they found Saul and his sons fallen in mount Gĭl-bō′ȧ.

9 And when they had stripped him, they took his head, and his armour, and sent into the land of the Phĭ-lĭs′tĭnes round about, to carry tidings unto their idols, and to the people.

10 [b]And they put his armour in the house of their gods, and fastened his head in the temple of Dā′gŏn.

11 ¶ And when all Jā′besh–gĭl′e-ăd heard all that the Phĭ-lĭs′tĭnes had done to Saul,

12 They arose, all the valiant men, and took away the body of Saul, and the bodies of his sons, and brought them to Jā′besh, and buried their bones under the oak in Jā′besh, and fasted seven days.

39 [v]ch. 8.33
41 [w]2 Sam. 9.12
[14]Or, Tarea, ch. 8.35
[x]ch. 8.35
42 [15]Or, Jehoadah, ch. 8.36
43 [16]Or, Rapha, ch. 8.37

CHAPTER 10

1 [a]1 Sam. 7.7; 1 Sam. 13.5
[1]thrust through, or, wounded
2 [2]Or, Ishui, 1 Sam. 14.49
3 [3]shooters with bows
[4]found him
4 [5]Or, mock me
10 [b]1 Sam. 31.10; Isa. 48.5
13 [6]transgressed
[c]1 Sam. 13.13;
[d]Ex. 22.18;
[e]1 Sam. 28.7
14 [f]1 Sam. 13.14
[7]Isai

CHAPTER 11

1 [a]2 Sam. 5.1;
2 [1]both yesterday and the third day
[2]Or, rule, Ps. 78.70-71
3 [b]2 Sam. 5.3
[c]Rom. 8.31
[3]by the hand of
[d]1 Sam. 16.1
4 [e]2 Sam. 5.6
[f]Gen. 10.16;
6 [4]head
7 [5]That is, Zion
8 [6]revived
9 [7]went in going and increasing
10 [g]2 Sam. 23.8
[8]Or, held strongly with him
[h]1 Sam. 16.1-12
11 [9]Or, son of Hachmoni
13 [10]Or, Ephesdammim, 1 Sam. 17.1
14 [11]Or, stood
[12]Or, salvation

13 ¶ So Saul died for his transgression which he [6]committed against the LORD, [c]*even* against the word of the LORD, which he kept not, and also for asking *counsel* of *one that had* a [d]familiar spirit, [e]to inquire *of it;*

14 And inquired not of the LORD: therefore he slew him, and [f]turned the kingdom unto Dā′vid the son of [7]Jĕs′se.

11 Then [a]all Ĭs′ra-el gathered themselves to Dā′vid unto Hē′bron, saying, Behold, we *are* thy bone and thy flesh.

2 And moreover [1]in time past, even when Saul was king, thou *wast* he that leddest out and broughtest in Ĭs′ra-el: and the LORD thy God said unto thee, Thou shalt [2]feed my people Ĭs′ra-el, and thou shalt be ruler over my people Ĭs′ra-el.

3 Therefore came all the elders of Ĭs′ra-el to the king to Hē′bron; and Dā′vid made a covenant with them in Hē′bron before the LORD; and [b]they anointed Dā′vid king over Ĭs′ra-el, according to the word of the [c]LORD [3]by [d]Săm′u-el.

4 ¶ And Dā′vid and all Ĭs′ra-el [e]went to Je-ru′sa-lĕm, which *is* Jē′bus; [f]where the Jĕb′u-sītes *were,* the inhabitants of the land.

5 And the inhabitants of Jē′bus said to Dā′vid, Thou shalt not come hither. Nevertheless Dā′vid took the castle of Zī′ŏn, which *is* the city of Dā′vid.

6 And Dā′vid said, Whosoever smiteth the Jĕb′u-sītes first shall be [4]chief and captain. So Jō′ab the son of Zĕr-u-ī′ah went first up, and was chief.

7 And Dā′vid dwelt in the castle; therefore they called [5]it the city of Dā′vid.

8 And he built the city round about, even from Mĭl′lo round about: and Jō′ab [6]repaired the rest of the city.

9 So Dā′vid [7]waxed greater and greater: for the LORD of hosts *was* with him.

10 ¶ [g]These also *are* the chief of the mighty men whom Dā′vid had, who [8]strengthened themselves with him in his kingdom, *and* with all Ĭs′ra-el, to make him king, according to [h]the word of the LORD concerning Ĭs′ra-el.

11 And this *is* the number of the mighty men whom Dā′vid had; Ja-shō′be-ăm, [9]an Hăch′mo-nīte, the chief of the captains: he lifted up his spear against three hundred slain *by him* at one time.

12 And after him *was* Ē-le-ā′zar the son of Dō′do, the A-hō′hīte, who *was* *one* of the three mighties.

13 He was with Dā′vid at [10]Păs–dăm′mim, and there the Phĭ-lĭs′tĭnes were gathered together to battle, where was a parcel of ground full of barley; and the people fled from before the Phĭ-lĭs′tĭnes.

14 And they [11]set themselves in the midst of *that* parcel, and delivered it, and slew the Phĭ-lĭs′tĭnes; and the LORD saved *them* by a great [12]deliverance.

15 ¶ Now [13]three of the thirty captains [i]went down to the rock to Dā'vid, into the cave of A-dŭl'lăm; and the host of the Phĭ-lĭs'tĭnes encamped [j]in the valley of [14]Rĕph'a-ĭm.

16 And Dā'vid *was* then in the hold, and the Phĭ-lĭs'tĭnes' garrison *was* then at Bĕth'–lĕ-hĕm.

17 And Dā'vid longed, and said, Oh that one would give me drink of the water of the well of Bĕth'–lĕ-hĕm, that *is* at the gate!

18 And the three brake through the host of the Phĭ-lĭs'tĭnes, and drew water out of the well of Bĕth'–lĕ-hĕm, that *was* by the gate, and took *it*, and brought *it* to Dā'vid: but Dā'vid would not drink *of* it, but poured it out to the LORD,

19 And said, My God forbid it me, that I should do this thing: shall I drink the blood of these men [15]that have put their lives in jeopardy? for with *the jeopardy of* their lives they brought it. Therefore he would not drink it. These things did these three mightiest.

20 ¶ [k]And A-bĭsh'ā-ī the brother of Jō'ab, he was chief of the three: for lifting up his spear against three hundred, he slew *them*, and had a name among the three.

21 [l]Of the three, he was more honourable than the two; for he was their captain: howbeit he attained not to the *first* three.

22 Be-nā'iah the son of Je-hoi'a-dȧ, the son of a valiant man of Kăb'ze-el, [16]who had done many acts; [m]he slew two lionlike men of Mō'ab: also he went down and slew a lion in a pit in a snowy day.

23 And he slew an E-ġy̆p'tian, [17]a man of *great* stature, five cubits high; and in the E-ġy̆p'tian's hand *was* a spear like a weaver's beam; and he went down to him with a staff, and plucked the spear out of the E-ġy̆p'tian's hand, and slew him with his own spear.

24 These *things* did Be-nā'iah the son of Je-hoi'a-dȧ, and had the name among the three mighties.

25 Behold, he was honourable among the thirty, but attained not to the *first* three: and Dā'vid set him over his guard.

26 ¶ Also the valiant men of the armies *were*, [n]Ā'sa-hĕl the brother of Jō'ab, Ĕl-hā'nan the son of Dō'do of Bĕth'–lĕ-hĕm,

27 [18]Shăm'moth the [19]Hā'ro-rīte, Hē'lez the [20]Pĕl'o-nīte,

28 Ī'rȧ the son of Ĭk'kĕsh the Te-kō'īte, Ā-bĭ–ē'zĕr the Ăn'toth-īte,

29 [21]Sĭb'be-cāi the Hū'shath-īte, [22]Ī'lāi the A-hō'hīte,

30 Ma-hăr'a-ī the Ne-toph'a-thīte, [23]Hē'led the son of Bā'a-nah the Ne-toph'a-thīte,

31 Ĭth'a-ī the son of Rī'bāi of Ğĭb'e-ah, *that pertained* to the children of Bĕn'ja-min, Be-nā'iah the Pĭr'a-thon-īte,

32 [24]Hū'rāi of the brooks of Gā'ăsh, [25]A-bī'el the Ăr'bath-īte,

33 Ăz'ma-veth the Ba-hā'rŭm-īte, E-lī'ah-bȧ the Sha-ăl'bo-nīte,

34 The sons of [26]Hā'shem the Ğī'zo-nīte, Jŏn'a-than the son of Shā'ġē the Hā'ra-rīte,

35 A-hī'am the son of [27]Sā'car the Hā'ra-rīte, [28]Ĕl'ĭ-phal the son of [29]Ûr,

36 Hē'phĕr the Mĕch'e-rath-īte, A-hī'jah the Pĕl'o-nīte,

37 [30]Hĕz'rō the Cär'mel-īte, [31]Nā'a-rāi the son of Ĕz'bā-ī,

38 Jō'el the brother of Nā'than, Mĭb'har [32]the son of Hag-ğē'rī,

39 Zē'lek the Ăm'mŏn-īte, Nā-hăr'a-ī the Bē'rŏth-īte, the armourbearer of Jō'ab the son of Zĕr-u-ī'ah,

40 Ī'rȧ the [o]Ĭth'rīte, Gā'rĕb the Ĭth'rīte,

41 [p]U-rī'ah the Hĭt'tīte, Zā'băd the son of Ăh'lāi,

42 Ăd'ĭ-nȧ the son of Shī'zȧ the Reu'ben-īte, a captain of the Reu'ben-ītes, and thirty with him,

43 Hā'nan the son of Mā'a-chah, and Jŏsh'a-phăt the Mĭth'nīte,

44 Ŭz-zī'ȧ the Ăsh'tĕ-răth-īte, Shā'mȧ and Je-hī'el the sons of Hō'than the Ăr'ō-ĕr-īte,

45 Je-dī'a-el the son of Shĭm'rī, and Jō'hȧ his brother, the Tī'zīte,

46 E-lī'el the Mā'ha-vīte, and Jĕr'ĭ-bāi, and Jŏsh-a-vī'ah, the sons of Ĕl'na-ăm, and Ĭth'mah the Mō'ab-īte,

47 E-lī'el, and Ō'bed, and Jā'sĭ-el the Mĕs'o-ba-īte.

12 Now [a]these *are* they that came to Dā'vid to [b]Zĭk'lag, [1]while he yet kept himself close because of Saul the son of Kĭsh: and they *were* among the mighty men, helpers of the war.

2 *They were* armed with bows, and could use both the right hand and the [c]left in *hurling* stones and *shooting* arrows out of a bow, *even* of Saul's brethren of Bĕn'ja-min.

3 The chief *was* Ā-hi-ē'zĕr, then Jō'ăsh, the sons of [2]She-mā'ah the Ğĭb'e-ath-īte; and Jē'zĭ-el, and Pē'let, the sons of Ăz'ma-veth; and Bĕr'ā-chah, and Jē'hū [d]the Ăn'toth-īte,

4 And Ĭs-ma-ī'ah the [e]Ğĭb'e-on-īte, a mighty man among the thirty, and over the thirty; and Jĕr-e-mī'ah, and Ja-hā'zĭ-el, and Jo-hā'nan, and Jŏs'a-băd the Ğĕd'ē-răth-īte,

5 E-lū'za-ī, and Jĕr'ĭ-mŏth, and Bē-a-lī'ah, and Shĕm-a-rī'ah, and Shĕph-a-tī'ah the Hăr'u-phīte,

6 Ĕl'kā-nah, and Je-sī'ah, and A-zăr'e-el, and Jo-ē'zĕr, and Ja-shō'be-ăm, the Kôr'hītes,

7 And Jo-ē'lah, and Zĕb-a-dī'ah, the sons of Jĕr'o-hăm of Ğē'dôr.

8 And of the Găd'ītes there separated themselves unto Dā'vid into the [f]hold to the wilderness men of might, *and* men [3]of war *fit* for the battle, that could handle shield and buckler, whose [g]faces *were like* the faces of lions, and *were* [4]as swift as the roes upon the mountains;

9 Ē'zĕr the first, Ō-ba-dī'ah the second, E-lī'ab the third,

10 Mĭsh-măn'nah the fourth, Jĕr-e-mī'ah the fifth,

15 [13]Or, three captains over the thirty
[i]2 Sam. 23.13
[j]ch. 14.9
[14]Or, giants, Isa. 17.5
19 [15]with their lives?
20 [k]1 Sam. 26.6-8;
21 [l]2 Sam. 23.19;
22 [16]great of deeds
[m]2 Sam. 1.23;
23 [17]a man of measure
26 [n]2 Sam. 2.18-23;
27 [18]Or, Shammah
[19]Or, Harodite, 2 Sam. 23.25
[20]Or, Paltite, 2 Sam. 23.26
29 [21]Or, Mebunnai
[22]Or, Zalmon
30 [23]Or, Heleb
32 [24]Or, Hiddai
[25]Or, Abialbon
34 [26]Or, Jashen; See 2 Sam. 23.32
35 [27]Or, Sharar
[28]Or, Eliphelet
[29]Or, Ahasbai
37 [30]Or, Hezrai
[31]Or, Paarai the Arbite
38 [32]Or, the Haggerite
40 [o]ch. 2.50-53
41 [p]2 Sam. 11.3

CHAPTER 12
1 [a]1 Sam. 27.2
[b]1 Sam. 27.6
[1]being yet shut up
2 [c]Judg. 20.16
3 [2]Or, Hasmaah
[d]ch. 11.28
4 [e]Josh. 10.2;
8 [f]1 Sam. 23.14-29;
[3]of the host
[g]2 Sam. 17.10;
[4]as the roes upon the mountains to make haste

11 Ăt'tāi the sixth, E-lī'el the seventh,
12 Jo-hā'nan the eighth, Ĕl'za-băd
the ninth,
13 Jĕr-e-mī'ah the tenth, Măch'ba-
nāi the eleventh.
14 These *were* of the sons of Găd,
captains of the host: [5]one of the least
was over an hundred, and the greatest
over a thousand.
15 These *are* they that went over
Jôr'dan in the first month, when it had
[6]overflown all his [h]banks; and they
put to flight all *them* of the valleys,
both toward the east, and toward the
west.
16 And there came of the children of
Bĕn'ja-min and Jū'dah to the hold unto
Dā'vid.
17 And Dā'vid went out [7]to meet
them, and answered and said unto
them, If ye be come peaceably unto me
to help me, mine heart shall [8]be knit
unto you: but if *ye be come* to betray
me to mine enemies, seeing *there is* no
[9]wrong in mine hands, the God of our
fathers look *thereon,* and [i]rebuke *it.*
18 Then [10]the spirit came [j]upon A-
măs'a-ī, *who was* chief of the captains,
and he said, Thine *are we,* Dā'vid, and
on thy side, thou son of Jĕs'se: peace,
peace *be* unto thee, and peace *be* to
thine helpers; for thy God helpeth thee.
Then Dā'vid received them, and made
them captains of the band.
19 And there fell *some* of Ma-năs'-
seh to Dā'vid, [k]when he came with the
Phĭ-lĭs'tĭnes against Sa̤ul to battle: but
they helped them not: for the lords of
the Phĭ-lĭs'tĭnes upon advisement sent
him away, saying, He [l]will fall to his
master Sa̤ul [11]to *the jeopardy of* our
heads.
20 As he went to Zĭk'lag, there fell to
him of Ma-năs'seh, Ăd'nah, and Jŏz'a-
băd, and Je-dī'a-el, and Mī'chaĕl, and
Jŏz'a-băd, and E-lī'hū, and Zĭl'thāi,
captains of the thousands that *were* of
Ma-năs'seh.
21 And they helped Dā'vid [12]against
[m]the band *of the rovers:* for they *were*
all mighty men of valour, and were captains in the host.
22 For at *that* time day by day there
came to Dā'vid to help him, until *it was*
a great host, like the host of God.
23 ¶ And these *are* the numbers of
the [13]bands *that were* ready armed to
the war, *and* [n]came to Dā'vid to Hē'-
bron, to [o]turn the kingdom of Sa̤ul to
him, [p]according to the word of the
LORD.
24 The children of Jū'dah that bare
shield and spear *were* six thousand
and eight hundred, ready [14]armed to
the war.
25 Of the children of Sĭm'e-on,
mighty men of valour for the war,
seven thousand and one hundred.
26 Of the children of Lē'vī four thousand and six hundred.
27 And Je-hoi'a-dȧ *was* the leader
of the Aâr'on-ītes, and with him *were*
three thousand and seven hundred;
28 And [q]Zā'dŏk, a young man
mighty of valour, and of his father's
house twenty and two captains.
29 And of the children of Bĕn'ja-
min, the [15]kindred of Sa̤ul, three thousand: for hitherto [16]the greatest part of
them had kept the ward of the house of
Sa̤ul.
30 And of the children of Ē'phră-
ĭm twenty thousand and eight hundred, mighty men of valour, [17]famous
throughout the house of their fathers.
31 And of the half tribe of Ma-năs'-
seh eighteen thousand, which were expressed by name, to come and make
Dā'vid king.
32 And of the children of Ĭs'sa-char,
which were men [r]that had understanding of the times, to know what Ĭs'ra-el
ought to do; the heads of them *were*
two hundred; and all their brethren
were at their commandment.
33 Of Zĕb'u-lun, such as went forth
to battle, [18]expert in war, with all instruments of war, fifty thousand, which
could [19]keep rank: *they were* [20]not of
double heart.
34 And of Năph'ta-lī a thousand captains, and with them with shield and
spear thirty and seven thousand.
35 And of the Dăn'ītes expert in war
twenty and eight thousand and six hundred.
36 And of Ăsh'ēr, such as went forth
to battle, [21]expert in war, forty thousand.
37 And on the other side of Jôr'dan,
of the Reu̥'ben-ītes, and the Găd'ītes,
and of the half tribe of Ma-năs'seh,
with all manner of instruments of war
for the battle, an hundred and twenty
thousand.
38 All these men of war, that could
keep rank, came with a perfect heart to
Hē'bron, to make Dā'vid king over all
Ĭs'ra-el: and all the rest also of Ĭs'ra-el
were of one heart to make Dā'vid king.
39 And there they were with Dā'vid
three days, eating and drinking: for
their brethren had prepared for them.
40 Moreover they that were nigh
them, *even* unto Ĭs'sa-char and Zĕb'u-
lun and Năph'ta-lī, brought bread on
asses, and on camels, and on mules,
and on oxen, *and* [22]meat, meal, cakes
of figs, and bunches of raisins, and
wine, and oil, and oxen, and sheep
abundantly: for *there was* joy in Ĭs'ra-
el.

13 And Dā'vid [a]consulted with the
captains of thousands and hundreds, *and* with every leader.
2 And Dā'vid said unto all the congregation of Ĭs'ra-el, If *it seem* good
unto you, and *that it be* of the LORD
our God, [1]let us send abroad unto our
brethren every where, *that are* [b]left in
all the land of Ĭs'ra-el, and with them
also to the priests and Lē'vītes *which
are* [2]in their cities *and* suburbs, that
they may gather themselves unto us:
3 And let us [3]bring again the ark of
our God to us: [c]for we inquired not at
it in the days of Sa̤ul.

14 [5]Or, one that was least could resist an hundred, and the greatest a thousand
15 [6]filled over
[h]Jer. 12.5
17 [7]before them
[8]be one
[9]Or, violence
[i]Zech. 3.2
18 [10]the spirit clothed Amasai
[j]2 Sam. 17.25
19 [k]1 Sam. 29.2
[l]1 Sam. 29.4
[11]on our heads
21 [12]Or, with a band
[m]1 Sam. 30.1
23 [13]heads, or, captains, or, men
[n]2 Sam. 2.3
[o]ch. 10.14
[p]1 Sam. 16.1; ch. 11.10
24 [14]Or, prepared
28 [q]2 Sam. 8.17; 1 Ki. 1.8; ch. 6.8; Ezek. 44.15
29 [15]brethren, Gen. 31.23
[16]a multitude of them
30 [17]men of names
32 [r]Esth. 1.13
33 [18]Or, rangers of battle, or, ranged in battle
[19]Or, set the battle in array
[20]without a heart and a heart
36 [21]Or, keeping their rank
40 [22]Or, victual of meal
CHAPTER 13
1 [a]2 Sam. 5.1; ch. 12.14; Prov. 15.22
2 [1]let us break forth and send
[b]ch. 10.7; Isa. 37.4
[2]in the cities of their suburbs
3 [3]bring about
[c]1 Sam. 7.1; 1 Sam. 14.18

4 And all the congregation said that
they would do so: for the thing was
right in the eyes of all the people.
5 So [d]Dā'vid gathered all Ĭs'ra-el together, from [e]Shī'hôr of Ē'ġypt even
unto the entering of Hē'măth, to bring
the ark of God [f]from Kĭr'jath–jē'a-rĭm.
6 And Dā'vid went up, and all Ĭs'ra-
el, to Bā'al-ah, [g]*that is,* to Kĭr'jath–
jē'a-rĭm, which *belonged* to Jū'dah, to
bring up thence the ark of God the
LORD, [h]that dwelleth *between* the cherubims, whose name is called *on it.*
7 And they [4]carried the ark of God
[i]in a new cart out of the house of A-
bĭn'ă-dăb: and Ŭz'zȧ and A-hī'o drave
the cart.
8 And Dā'vid and all Ĭs'ra-el [j]played
before God with all *their* might, and
with [5]singing, and with harps, and with
psalteries, and with timbrels, and with
cymbals, and with trumpets.
9 ¶ And when they came unto the
threshingfloor of [k]Chī'don, Ŭz'zȧ put
forth his hand to hold the ark; for the
oxen [6]stumbled.
10 And the anger of the LORD was
kindled against Ŭz'zȧ, and he smote
him, [l]because he put his hand to the
ark: and there he [m]died before God.
11 And Dā'vid was displeased, because the LORD had made a breach
upon Ŭz'zȧ: wherefore that place is
called [7]Pē'rez–ŭz'zȧ to this day.
12 And Dā'vid was afraid of God
that day, saying, How shall I bring the
ark of God *home* to me?
13 So Dā'vid [8]brought not the ark
home to himself to the city of Dā'vid,
but carried it aside into the house of
Ō'bed–ē'dom the Ġĭt'tīte.
14 [n]And the ark of God remained
with the family of Ō'bed–ē'dom in his
house three months. And the LORD
blessed [o]the house of Ō'bed–ē'dom,
and all that he had.

14 Now [a]Hī'ram king of Tȳre sent
messengers to Dā'vid, and timber of cedars, with masons and carpenters, to build him an house.
2 And Dā'vid perceived that the
LORD had confirmed him king over
Ĭs'ra-el, for his kingdom was lifted up
on high, because of his people Ĭs'ra-el.
3 ¶ And Dā'vid took [1]more wives at
Je-ru'sa-lĕm: and Dā'vid begat more
sons and daughters.
4 Now [b]these *are* the names of *his*
children which he had in Je-ru'sa-lĕm;
Shăm-mū'ȧ, and Shō'băb, Nā'than,
and Sŏl'o-mon,
5 And Ĭb'hăr, and Ĕl-ĭ-shu'ȧ, and Ĕl'-
pa-let,
6 And Nō'gah, and Nē'pheg, and Ja-
phī'ȧ,
7 And E-lĭsh'a-mȧ, and [2]Bē-ĕl-ī'a-
dȧ, and E-lĭph'a-lĕt.
8 ¶ And when the Phĭ-lĭs'tīnes heard
that [c]Dā'vid was anointed king over
all Ĭs'ra-el, all the Phĭ-lĭs'tīnes went up
to seek Dā'vid. And Dā'vid heard *of it,*
and went out against them.
9 And the Phĭ-lĭs'tīnes came and
spread themselves in the valley of
[3]Rĕph'a-ĭm.

5 [d]2 Sam. 6.1
[e]Josh. 13.3
[f]1 Sam. 6.21
6 [g]Josh. 15.9-60
[h]Ex. 25.22; 1 Sam. 4.4
7 [4]made the ark to ride
[i]Num. 4.15
8 [j]2 Sam. 6.5
[5]songs
9 [k]2 Sam. 6.6
[6]shook it
10 [l]Num. 4.15; ch. 15.13-15
[m]Lev. 10.2
[7]That is, The breach of Uzza
13 [8]removed
14 [n]2 Sam. 6.11
[o]Gen. 30.27; ch. 26.5; Ps. 37.22; Prov. 3.9-10; Mal. 3.10

CHAPTER 14
1 [a]2 Sam. 5.11
3 [1]yet, Deut. 17.14-17
4 [b]2 Sam. 5.14; ch. 3.5
7 [2]Or, Eliada, 2 Sam. 5.16
8 [c]2 Sam. 5.17; ch. 11.3; Ps. 2.1-5
9 [3]Or, giants, ch. 11.15
11 [4]That is, A place of breaches, Isa. 28.21
13 [d]2 Sam. 5.22
14 [e]2 Sam. 5.23
16 [f]2 Sam. 5.25, Geba
17 [g]2 Chr. 26.8
[h]Deut. 2.25

CHAPTER 15
1 [a]ch. 16.1; Ps. 132.2-5; Acts 7.46
2 [1]It is not to carry the ark of God, but for the Levites
[b]Num. 4.2-15; Deut. 10.8
3 [c]1 Ki. 8.1; ch. 13.5
5 [d]Ex. 6.16-18
[2]Or, kinsmen
8 [e]Ex. 6.22
9 [f]Num. 26.58

10 And Dā'vid inquired of God, saying, Shall I go up against the Phĭ-lĭs'-
tīnes? And wilt thou deliver them into
mine hand? And the LORD said unto
him, Go up; for I will deliver them into
thine hand.
11 So they came up to Bā'al–pĕr'-
a-zĭm; and Dā'vid smote them there.
Then Dā'vid said, God hath broken in
upon mine enemies by mine hand like
the breaking forth of waters: therefore
they called the name of that place [4]Bā'-
al–pĕr'a-zĭm.
12 And when they had left their gods
there, Dā'vid gave a commandment,
and they were burned with fire.
13 [d]And the Phĭ-lĭs'tīnes yet again
spread themselves abroad in the valley.
14 Therefore Dā'vid inquired again
of God; and God said unto him, Go not
up after them; turn away from them,
[e]and come upon them over against the
mulberry trees.
15 And it shall be, when thou shalt
hear a sound of going in the tops of the
mulberry trees, *that* then thou shalt go
out to battle: for God is gone forth before thee to smite the host of the Phĭ-
lĭs'tīnes.
16 Dā'vid therefore did as God commanded him: and they smote the host
of the Phĭ-lĭs'tīnes from [f]Ġĭb'e-on even
to Gā'zĕr.
17 And [g]the fame of Dā'vid went out
into all lands; and the LORD [h]brought
the fear of him upon all nations.

15 And *Dā'vid* made him houses in
the city of Dā'vid, and prepared
[a]a place for the ark of God, and pitched
for it a tent.
2 Then Dā'vid said, [1]None ought to
carry the [b]ark of God but the Lē'-
vītes: for them hath the LORD chosen
to carry the ark of God, and to minister
unto him for ever.
3 And Dā'vid [c]gathered all Ĭs'ra-el
together to Je-ru'sa-lĕm, to bring up
the ark of the LORD unto his place,
which he had prepared for it.
4 And Dā'vid assembled the children of Aâr'on, and the Lē'vītes:
5 Of the sons of [d]Kō'hath; Ū'rĭ-el
the chief, and his [2]brethren an hundred
and twenty:
6 Of the sons of Me-rā'rī; Ā-sa-ī'ah
the chief, and his brethren two hundred and twenty:
7 Of the sons of Gĕr'shŏm; Jō'el the
chief, and his brethren an hundred and
thirty:
8 Of the sons of [e]E-lĭz'a-phan; Shĕm-
a-ī'ah the chief, and his brethren two
hundred:
9 Of the sons of [f]Hē'bron; E-lī'el the
chief, and his brethren fourscore:
10 Of the sons of Ŭz'zĭ-el; Ăm-mĭn'-
a-dab the chief, and his brethren an
hundred and twelve.
11 And Dā'vid called for Zā'dŏk and
A-bī'a-thär the priests, and for the Lē'-
vītes, for Ū'rĭ-el, Ā-sa-ī'ah, and Jō'el,
Shĕm-a-ī'ah, and E-lī'el, and Ăm-mĭn'-
a-dab,

12 And said unto them, Ye *are* the
chief of the fathers of the Lē′vītes:
[g]sanctify yourselves, *both* ye and your
brethren, that ye may bring up the ark
of the LORD God of Ĭs′ra-el unto *the*
place that I have prepared for it.
13 For [h]because ye *did it* not at the
first, [i]the LORD our God made a breach
upon us, for that we sought him not
after the due order.
14 So the priests and the Lē′vītes
sanctified themselves to bring up the
ark of the LORD God of Ĭs′ra-el.
15 And the children of the Lē′vītes
bare the ark of God upon their shoulders with the staves thereon, as [j]Mō′-
ses commanded according to the word
of the LORD.
16 And Dā′vid spake to the chief of
the Lē′vītes to appoint their brethren
to be the singers with [k]instruments of
musick, psalteries and harps and cymbals, sounding, by lifting up the voice
with joy.
17 So the Lē′vītes appointed [l]Hē′-
man the son of Jō′el; and of his brethren, [m]Ā′saph the son of Bĕr-e-chī′ah;
and of the sons of Me-rā′rī their brethren, [n]Ē′than the son of Kŭsh-ā′iah;
18 And with them their brethren of
the second *degree,* Zĕch-a-rī′ah, Bĕn,
and Ja-ā′zĭ-el, and She-mĭr′a-mŏth,
and Je-hī′el, and Ŭn′nī, E-lī′ab, and
Be-nā′iah, and Mā-a-sē′iah, and Măt-
ti-thī′ah, and E-lĭph′e-leh, and Mĭk-nē′-
iah, and Ō′bed–ē′dom, and Je-ī′el, the
porters.
19 So the singers, Hē′man, Ā′saph,
and Ē′than, *were appointed* to sound
with cymbals of brass;
20 And Zĕch-a-rī′ah, and [3]Ā′zĭ-el,
and She-mĭr′a-mŏth, and Je-hī′el, and
Ŭn′nī, and E-lī′ab, and Mā-a-sē′iah,
and Be-nā′iah, with psalteries on [4]Ăl′-
a-mŏth;
21 And Măt-ti-thī′ah, and E-lĭph′e-
leh, and Mĭk-nē′iah, and Ō′bed–ē′-
dom, and Je-ī′el, and Ăz-a-zī′ah, with
harps [5]on the Shĕm′i-nĭth to excel.
22 And Chĕn-a-nī′ah, chief of the
Lē′vītes, [6]*was* for [7]song: he instructed
about the song, because he *was* skilful.
23 And Bĕr-e-chī′ah and Ĕl′kă-nah
were doorkeepers for the ark.
24 And Shĕb-a-nī′ah, and Je-hŏsh′-
a-phăt, and Ne-thăn′e-el, and A-măs′-
a-ī, and Zĕch-a-rī′ah, and Be-nā′iah,
and E-li-ē′zĕr, the priests, [o]did blow
with the trumpets before the ark of
God: and Ō′bed–ē′dom and Je-hī′ah
were doorkeepers for the ark.
25 ¶ So [p]Dā′vid, and the elders of
Ĭs′ra-el, and the captains over thousands, went to bring up the ark of the
covenant of the LORD out of the house
of Ō′bed–ē′dom with [q]joy.
26 And it came to pass, when God
helped the Lē′vītes that bare the ark of
the covenant of the LORD, that they [r]of-
fered seven bullocks and seven rams.
27 And Dā′vid *was* clothed with a
robe of fine linen, and all the Lē′vītes
that bare the ark, and the singers, and
Chĕn-a-nī′ah the master of the [8]song
with the singers: Dā′vid also *had* upon
him an ephod of linen.
28 [s]Thus all Ĭs′ra-el brought up the
ark of the covenant of the LORD with
shouting, and with sound of the cornet,
and with trumpets, and with cymbals,
making a noise with psalteries and
harps.
29 ¶ And it came to pass, [t]*as* the ark
of the covenant of the LORD came to the
city of Dā′vid, that Mī′chal the daughter of Saul looking out at a window saw
king Dā′vid dancing and playing: and
she [u]despised him in her heart.

16 So [a]they brought the ark of God,
and set it in the midst of the tent
that Dā′vid had pitched for it: and they
offered burnt sacrifices and peace offerings before God.
2 And when Dā′vid had made an
end of offering the burnt offerings and
the peace offerings, he blessed the people in the name of the LORD.
3 And he dealt to every one of Ĭs′ra-
el, both man and woman, to every one
a loaf of bread, and a good piece of
flesh, and a flagon *of wine.*
4 ¶ And he appointed *certain* of the
Lē′vītes to minister before the ark of
the LORD, and to [b]record, and to thank
and praise the LORD God of Ĭs′ra-el:
5 Ā′saph the chief, and next to him
Zĕch-a-rī′ah, Je-ī′el, and She-mĭr′a-
mŏth, and Je-hī′el, and Măt-ti-thī′ah,
and E-lī′ab, and Be-nā′iah, and Ō′bed–
ē′dom: and Je-ī′el [1]with psalteries and
with harps; but Ā′saph made a sound
with cymbals;
6 Be-nā′iah also and Ja-hā′zĭ-el the
priests with trumpets continually before the ark of the covenant of God.
7 ¶ Then on that day Dā′vid delivered [c]first *this psalm* to thank the LORD
into the hand of Ā′saph and his brethren.
8 [d]Give thanks unto the LORD, call
upon his name, make known his deeds
among the people.
9 [e]Sing unto him, sing psalms unto
him, talk ye of all his wondrous works.
10 [f]Glory ye in his holy name: let
the heart of them rejoice that seek the
LORD.
11 [g]Seek the LORD and his strength,
seek his face continually.
12 Remember his [h]marvellous
works that he hath done, his wonders,
and the judgments of his mouth;
13 O ye seed of Ĭs′ra-el his servant,
ye children of Jā′cob, his chosen ones.
14 He *is* the LORD our God; his judgments *are* in all the earth.
15 Be ye mindful always of his covenant; the word *which* he commanded
to a thousand generations;
16 *Even of the* [i]*covenant* which he
made with Ā′brā-hăm, and of his oath
unto Ī′saac;
17 And hath confirmed the same to
Jā′cob for a law, *and* to Ĭs′ra-el *for* an
everlasting covenant,
18 Saying, Unto thee will I give the
land of Cā′năan, [2]the lot of your inheritance;

12 [g]Ex. 19.10-22; Lev. 10.3; 1 Sam. 7.1; 2 Chr. 5.11; Ezek. 48.11; John 17.17; Rom. 12.1-2
13 [h]2 Sam. 6.3; ch. 13.7 [i]ch. 13.10-11
15 [j]Ex. 25.14; Num. 4.15
16 [k]ch. 6.31; ch. 13.8; Ps. 33.2; Ps. 149.3
17 [l]ch. 6.33 [m]ch. 6.39 [n]ch. 6.44
20 [3]Jaaziel, verse 18 [4]That is, virginal, or, treble
21 [5]Or, on the eighth to oversee, Ps. 6, title
22 [6]Or, was for the carriage: he instructed about the carriage [7]lifting up
24 [o]Num. 10.8; Ps. 81.3
25 [p]2 Sam. 6.12-13 [q]Deut. 12.7-18
26 [r]Num. 23.1; Job 42.8
27 [8]Or, carriage
28 [s]ch. 13.8
29 [t]2 Sam. 6.16 [u]Acts 2.13

CHAPTER 16
1 [a]2 Sam. 6.17-19
4 [b]Ps. 38, Ps. 70, title
5 [1]with instruments of psalteries and harps
7 [c]2 Sam. 23.1
8 [d]Ps. 105.1
9 [e]Ps. 95.1-2
10 [f]Ps. 34.3; Isa. 45.25
11 [g]Amos 5.6-14
12 [h]Ps. 103.2; Ps. 111.2
16 [i]Gen. 15.18; Gen. 26.3; Gen. 28.13; Neh. 9.8; Heb. 6.13-18
18 [2]the cord

19 When ye were but [3]few, [j]even a
few, and strangers in it.
20 And *when* they went from nation
to nation, and from *one* kingdom to another people;
21 He suffered no man to do them
wrong: yea, he [k]reproved kings for
their sakes,
22 *Saying,* [l]Touch not mine anointed,
and do my prophets no harm.
23 [m]Sing unto the LORD, all the
earth; shew forth from day to day his
salvation.
24 [n]Declare his glory among the
heathen; his marvellous works among
all nations.
25 [o]For great *is* the LORD, and greatly
to be praised: he also *is* to be feared
above all gods.
26 For all the gods [p]of the people
are idols: but the LORD made the heavens.
27 [q]Glory and honour *are* in his
presence; strength and gladness *are* in
his place.
28 Give unto the LORD, ye kindreds
of the people, give unto the LORD glory
and strength.
29 Give unto the LORD the glory *due*
unto his name: bring an offering, and
come before him: worship the LORD in
the beauty of holiness.
30 Fear before him, all the earth: the
world also shall be stable, that it be not
moved.
31 Let the [r]heavens be glad, and
let the earth rejoice: and let *men* say
among the nations, The LORD reigneth.
32 Let [s]the sea roar, and the fulness
thereof: let the fields rejoice, and all
that *is* therein.
33 Then shall the trees of the wood
sing out at the presence of the LORD,
because he cometh to judge the earth.
34 [t]O give thanks unto the LORD;
for *he is* good; for his mercy *endureth*
for ever.
35 [u]And say ye, Save us, O God of
our salvation, and gather us together,
and deliver us from the heathen, that
we may give thanks to thy holy name,
and glory in thy praise.
36 [v]Blessed *be* the LORD God of Is'-
ra-el for ever and ever. And all [w]the
people said, Amen, and praised the
LORD.
37 ¶ So he left there before the ark of
the covenant of the LORD Ā'saph and
his brethren, to minister before the ark
continually, as every day's work required:
38 And Ō'bed–ē'dom with their
brethren, threescore and eight; Ō'bed–
ē'dom also the son of Jĕd'u-thŭn and
Hō'sah *to be* porters:
39 And Zā'dŏk the priest, and his
brethren the priests, [x]before the tabernacle of the LORD [y]in the high place
that *was* at Gĭb'e-on,
40 To offer burnt offerings unto the
LORD upon the altar of the burnt offering continually [4]morning and evening,
and *to do* according to all that is written in the law of the LORD, which he
commanded Is'ra-el;
41 And with them Hē'man and Jĕd'u-
thŭn, and the rest that were chosen,
who were expressed by name, to give
thanks to the LORD, [z]because his mercy
endureth for ever;
42 And with them Hē'man and Jĕd'-
u-thŭn with trumpets and cymbals for
those that should make a sound, and
with musical instruments of God. And
the sons of Jĕd'u-thŭn *were* [5]porters.
43 [a]And all the people departed every man to his house: and Dā'vid returned to [b]bless his house.

17 Now [a]it came to pass, as Dā'vid
sat in his house, that Dā'vid said
to Nā'than the prophet, Lo, I [b]dwell in
an house of cedars, but the ark of the
covenant of the LORD *remaineth* under
curtains.
2 Then Nā'than said unto Dā'vid,
Do all that *is* in thine heart; for God *is*
with thee.
3 ¶ And it came to pass the same
night, that the word of God came to
Nā'than, saying,
4 Go and tell Dā'vid my servant,
Thus saith the LORD, Thou shalt not
build me an house to dwell in:
5 For I have not dwelt in an house
since the day that I brought up Is'ra-el
unto this day; but [1]have gone from
[c]tent to tent, and from *one* tabernacle
to another.
6 Wheresoever I have walked with
all Is'ra-el, spake I a word to any of the
judges of Is'ra-el, whom I commanded
to feed my people, saying, Why have
ye not built me an house of cedars?
7 Now therefore thus shalt thou say
unto my servant Dā'vid, Thus saith the
LORD of hosts, I took thee from the
sheepcote, *even* [2]from following the
sheep, that thou shouldest be ruler over
my people Is'ra-el:
8 And I have been with thee whithersoever thou hast walked, and have cut
off all thine enemies from before thee,
and have made thee a name like the
name of the great men that *are* in the
earth.
9 Also I [d]will ordain a place for my
people Is'ra-el, and will plant them,
and they shall dwell in their place, and
shall be moved no more; neither shall
the children of wickedness waste them
[e]any more, as at the beginning,
10 And since the time that I commanded judges *to be* over my people Is'ra-el. Moreover I will subdue all
thine enemies. Furthermore I tell thee
that the LORD will build thee an house.
11 ¶ And it shall come to pass, when
thy days be expired that thou must go
to be with thy fathers, that I will raise
up thy seed after thee, which shall be
of thy sons; and I will establish his
kingdom.
12 He shall build me an house, and I
will stablish his throne for ever.
13 [f]I will be his father, and he shall
be my son: and I will not take my
mercy away from him, as I took *it* from
him that was before thee:
14 But [g]I will settle him in mine
house and in my kingdom for ever:

19 [3]men of number
[j]Gen. 34.30; Heb. 11.13
21 [k]Gen. 12.17; Ex. 7.15-18
22 [l]Ps. 105.15; 1 John 2.27
23 [m]Ps. 47.1; Ps. 96.1
24 [n]Isa. 12.4
25 [o]Ps. 24.8; Isa. 40.25-26
26 [p]Lev. 19.4; Ps. 115.4-8; Isa. 45.20; 1 Cor. 8.4
27 [q]Ps. 8.1
31 [r]Isa. 35.10; Luke 2.13; Rev. 14.2
32 [s]Ps. 96.11
34 [t]Ps. 106.1; Ps. 107.1; Ps. 118.1
35 [u]Ps. 106.47-48
36 [v]Ps. 72.18-19
[w]Deut. 27.15; Neh. 8.6
39 [x]ch. 21.29; 2 Chr. 1.3
[y]1 Ki. 3.4
40 [4]in the morning, and in the evening
41 [z]2 Chr. 5.13; 2 Chr. 7.3; Ezra 3.11; Neh. 9.17; Ps. 25.10; Ps. 33.5; Ps. 86.5-15; Ps. 100.5; Jas. 5.11
42 [5]for the gate
43 [a]2 Sam. 6.19-20
[b]Gen. 18.19
CHAPTER 17
1 [a]2 Sam. 7.1
[b]ch. 14.1; Acts 7.46
5 [1]have been
[c]Ex. 40.2; 2 Sam. 6.17
7 [2]from after
9 [d]Jer. 31.12
[e]2 Chr. 15.2; Isa. 49.17
13 [f]2 Sam. 7.14-15; Heb. 1.5
14 [g]Ps. 2.6; Heb. 1.8

and his throne shall be established for evermore.

15 According to all these words, and according to all this vision, so did Nā′than speak unto Dā′vid.

16 ¶ [h]And Dā′vid the king came and sat before the LORD, and said, [i]Who *am* I, O LORD God, and what *is* mine house, that thou hast brought me hitherto?

17 And *yet* this was a small thing in thine eyes, O God; for thou hast *also* spoken of thy servant's house for a great while to come, and hast regarded me according to the estate of a man of high degree, O LORD God.

18 What can Dā′vid *speak* more to thee for the honour of thy servant? for [j]thou knowest thy servant.

19 O LORD, for thy servant's sake, and according [k]to thine own heart, hast thou done all this greatness, in making known all *these* [3]great things.

20 O LORD, *there is* [l]none like thee, neither *is there any* God beside thee, according to all that we have heard with our ears.

21 And what one nation in the earth *is* like thy people Is′ra-el, whom God went to redeem *to be* his own people, to make thee a name of greatness and terribleness, by driving out nations from before thy people, whom thou hast redeemed out of E′gypt?

22 For thy people Is′ra-el didst thou make thine own people for ever; and thou, LORD, becamest their God.

23 Therefore now, LORD, let the thing that thou hast spoken concerning thy servant and concerning his house be established for ever, and do as thou hast said.

24 Let it even be established, that [m]thy name may be magnified for ever, saying, The LORD of hosts *is* the God of Is′ra-el, *even* a God to Is′ra-el: and *let* the house of Dā′vid thy servant *be* established before thee.

25 For thou, O my God, [4]hast told thy servant that thou wilt build him an house: therefore thy servant hath found *in his heart* to pray before thee.

26 And now, LORD, thou art God, and hast [n]promised this goodness unto thy servant:

27 Now therefore [5]let it please thee to bless the house of thy servant, that it may be before thee for ever: for [o]thou blessest, O LORD, and *it shall be* blessed for ever.

18 Now after this [a]it came to pass, that Dā′vid smote the Phĭ-lĭs′tĭnes, and subdued them, and took Găth and her towns out of the hand of the Phĭ-lĭs′tĭnes.

2 And he [b]smote Mō′ab; and the Mō′ab-ītes became Dā′vid's servants, *and* brought gifts.

3 ¶ And Dā′vid smote [1]Hăd-ār-ē′zĕr king of Zō′bah unto Hā′math, as he [c]went to stablish his dominion by the river Eū-phrā′tēs.

4 And Dā′vid took from him a thousand chariots, and [d]seven thousand horsemen, and twenty thousand footmen: Dā′vid also houghed all the chariot *horses*, but reserved of them an hundred chariots.

5 And when the Sȳr′ĭ-ans of [2]Da-măs′cus came to help Hăd-ār-ē′zĕr king of Zō′bah, Dā′vid slew of the Sȳr′ĭ-ans two and twenty thousand men.

6 Then Dā′vid put *garrisons* in Sȳr′ĭ-ȧ–da-măs′cus; and the Sȳr′ĭ-ans became Dā′vid's servants, *and* brought gifts. Thus the LORD [e]preserved Dā′vid whithersoever he went.

7 And Dā′vid took the shields of gold that were on the servants of Hăd-ār-ē′zĕr, and brought them to Je-ru′sa-lĕm.

8 Likewise from [3]Tĭb′hath, and from Chŭn, cities of Hăd-ār-ē′zĕr, brought Dā′vid very much brass, wherewith [f]Sŏl′o-mon made the brasen sea, and the pillars, and the vessels of brass.

9 ¶ Now when [g]Tō′u king of Hā′math heard how Dā′vid had smitten all the host of Hăd-ār-ē′zĕr king of Zō′bah;

10 He sent [h]Ha-dō′ram his son to king Dā′vid, [4]to inquire of his welfare, and [5]to congratulate him, because he had fought against Hăd-ār-ē′zĕr, and smitten him; (for Hăd-ār-ē′zĕr [6]had war with Tō′u;) and *with him* all manner of vessels of gold and silver and brass.

11 ¶ Them also king Dā′vid dedicated unto the LORD, with the silver and the gold that he brought from all *these* nations; from E′dom, and from Mō′ab, and from the children of Ăm′mŏn, and from the Phĭ-lĭs′tĭnes, and from Ăm′a-lĕk.

12 Moreover [7]A-bĭsh′ă-ī the son of Zĕr-u-ī′ah slew of the E′dom-ītes in the valley of salt [i]eighteen thousand.

13 ¶ [j]And he put garrisons in E′dom; and all the E′dom-ītes became Dā′vid's servants. Thus the LORD preserved Dā′vid whithersoever he went.

14 ¶ So Dā′vid reigned over all Is′ra-el, and executed judgment and justice among all his people.

15 And Jō′ab the son of Zĕr-u-ī′ah *was* over the host; and Je-hŏsh′a-phăt the son of A-hī′lud, [8]recorder.

16 And Zā′dŏk the son of A-hī′tub, and [9]A-bĭm′ĕ-lech the son of A-bī′a-thär, *were* the priests; and [10]Shăv′shȧ was scribe;

17 [k]And Be-nā′iah the son of Je-hoi′a-dȧ *was* over the Chĕr′eth-ītes and the Pē′leth-ītes; and the sons of Dā′vid *were* chief [11]about the king.

19 Now [a]it came to pass after this, that [b]Nā′hăsh the king of the children of Ăm′mŏn died, and his son reigned in his stead.

2 And Dā′vid said, I will shew kindness unto Hā′nŭn the son of Nā′hăsh, because his father shewed kindness to me. And Dā′vid sent messengers to comfort him concerning his father. So the servants of Dā′vid came into the land of the children of Ăm′mŏn to Hā′nŭn, to comfort him.

3 But the princes of the children of Ăm′mŏn said to Hā′nŭn, [1]Thinkest

---

16 [h]2 Sam. 7.18 [i]Gen. 32.10; Ps. 144.3
18 [j]Ps. 139.1; John 21.17
19 [k]Matt. 11.26; Eph. 1.11 [3]greatnesses
20 [l]Ex. 15.11; Ps. 86.8
24 [m]2 Chr. 6.33;
25 [4]hast revealed the ear of thy servant
26 [n]Ex. 34.6;
27 [5]Or, it hath pleased thee [o]Ps. 72.17;

CHAPTER 18
1 [a]2 Sam. 8.1
2 [b]Num. 24.17
3 [1]Or, Hadadezer, 2 Sam. 8.3 [c]Gen. 15.18;
4 [d]2 Sam. 8.4, seven hundred
5 [2]Darmesek
6 [e]ch. 17.8;
8 [3]Called in the book of Samuel, Betah, and Berothai [f]2 Chr. 4.12-15-16
9 [g]2 Sam. 8.9, Toi
10 [h]2 Sam. 8.10, Joram [4]Or, to salute [5]to bless [6]was the man of wars
12 [7]Abshai [i]2 Sam. 8.13
13 [j]Gen. 27.29;
15 [8]Or, remembrancer
16 [9]Called Ahimelech, 2 Sam. 8.17 [10]Called Seraiah, 2 Sam. 8.17, and Shisha, 1 Ki. 4.3
17 [k]2 Sam. 8.18 [11]at the hand of the king

CHAPTER 19
1 [a]2 Sam. 10.1 [b]1 Sam. 11.1
3 [1]In thine eyes doth David, etc

thou that Dā'vid doth honour thy father, that he hath sent comforters unto thee? are not his servants come unto thee for to search, and to overthrow, and to spy out the land?

4 Wherefore Hā'nŭn took Dā'vid's servants, and shaved them, and cut off their garments in the midst hard by their buttocks, and sent them away.

5 Then there went *certain*, and told Dā'vid how the men were served. And he sent to meet them: for the men were greatly ashamed. And the king said, Tarry at [c]Jĕr'ĭ-chō until your beards be grown, and *then* return.

6 ¶ And when the children of Ăm'mŏn saw that they had made themselves [2]odious to Dā'vid, Hā'nŭn and the children of Ăm'mŏn sent a thousand talents of silver to hire them chariots and horsemen out of Mĕs-o-po-tā'mĭ-ȧ, and out of Sȳr'ĭ-ȧ–mā'a-chah, [d]and out of Zō'bah.

7 So they hired thirty and two thousand chariots, and the king of Mā'a-chah and his people; who came and pitched before [e]Mĕd'e-bȧ. And the children of Ăm'mŏn gathered themselves together from their cities, and came to battle.

8 And when Dā'vid heard *of it*, he sent Jō'ab, and all the host of the mighty men.

9 And the children of Ăm'mŏn came out, and put the battle in array before the gate of [f]the city: and the kings that were come *were* by themselves in the field.

10 Now when Jō'ab saw that [3]the battle was set against him before and behind, he chose out of all the [4]choice of Ĭs'ra-el, and put *them* in array against the Sȳr'ĭ-ans.

11 And the rest of the people he delivered unto the hand of [5]A-bĭsh'ă-ī his brother, and they set *themselves* in array against the children of Ăm'mŏn.

12 And he said, If the Sȳr'ĭ-ans be too strong for me, then thou shalt help me: but if the children of Ăm'mŏn be too strong for thee, then I will help thee.

13 Be of good courage, and let us behave ourselves valiantly for our people, and for the cities of our God: [g]and let the LORD do *that which is* good in his sight.

14 So Jō'ab and the people that *were* with him drew nigh before the Sȳr'ĭ-ans unto the battle; and they [h]fled before him.

15 And when the children of Ăm'mŏn saw that the Sȳr'ĭ-ans were fled, they likewise fled before A-bĭsh'ă-ī his brother, and entered into the city. Then Jō'ab came to Je-rṳ'sa-lĕm.

16 ¶ And when the Sȳr'ĭ-ans saw that they were put to the worse before Ĭs'ra-el, they sent messengers, and drew forth the Sȳr'ĭ-ans that *were* beyond the [6]river: and [i]Shō'phăch the captain of the host of Hăd-är-ē'zĕr *went* before them.

17 And it was told Dā'vid; and he gathered all Ĭs'ra-el, and passed over Jôr'dan, and came upon them, and set *the battle* in array against them. So when Dā'vid had put the battle in array against the Sȳr'ĭ-ans, they fought with him.

18 But the Sȳr'ĭ-ans [j]fled before Ĭs'ra-el; and Dā'vid slew of the Sȳr'ĭ-ans seven thousand *men which fought in* chariots, and forty thousand footmen, and killed Shō'phăch the captain of the host.

19 And when the servants of Hăd-är-ē'zĕr saw that they were put to the worse before Ĭs'ra-el, they made peace with Dā'vid, and became his servants: neither would the Sȳr'ĭ-ans help the children of Ăm'mŏn any more.

20 And [a]it came to pass, that [1]after the year was expired, at the time that kings go out *to battle*, Jō'ab led forth the power of the army, and wasted the country of the children of Ăm'mŏn, and came and beseiged Răb'bah. But Dā'vid tarried at Je-rṳ'sa-lĕm. And [b]Jō'ab smote Răb'bah, and destroyed it.

2 And Dā'vid [c]took the crown of their king from off his head, and found it [2]to weigh a talent of gold, and *there were* precious stones in it; and it was set upon Dā'vid's head: and he brought also exceeding much spoil out of the city.

3 And he brought out the people that *were* in it, and [3]cut *them* with saws, and with harrows of iron, and with axes. Even so dealt Dā'vid with all the cities of the children of Ăm'mŏn. And Dā'vid and all the people returned to Je-rṳ'sa-lĕm.

4 ¶ And it came to pass after this, that there [4]arose war at [5]Gē'zĕr with the Phĭ-lĭs'tĭnes; at which time Sĭb'be-chāi the Hū'shath-īte slew [6]Sĭp'pāi, *that was* of the children of [7]the giant: and they were subdued.

5 And there was war again with the Phĭ-lĭs'tĭnes; and Ĕl-hā'nan the son of [8]Jā'ĭr slew Lăh'mī the brother of Go-lī'ath the Gĭt'tīte, whose spear staff *was* like a weaver's beam.

6 And yet again there was war at Găth, where was [9]a man of *great* stature, whose fingers and toes *were* four and twenty, six *on each hand*, and six *on each foot*: and he also was [10]the son of the giant.

7 But when he [11]defied Ĭs'ra-el, Jŏn'a-than the son of [12]Shĭm'e-ȧ Dā'vid's brother slew him.

8 These were born unto the giant in Găth; and they fell by the hand of Dā'vid, and by the hand of his servants.

21 And [a]Sā'tan stood up against Ĭs'ra-el, and provoked Dā'vid to number Ĭs'ra-el.

2 And Dā'vid said to Jō'ab and to the rulers of the people, Go, number Ĭs'ra-el from Bē'er–shē'bȧ even to Dăn; [b]and bring the number of them to me, that I may know *it*.

3 And Jō'ab answered, The LORD make his people an hundred times so many more as they *be*: but, my lord the

5 [c]Josh. 6.24-26
6 [2]to stink
[d]1 Sam. 14.47; ch. 18.5-9
7 [e]Num. 21.30; Isa. 15.2
9 [f]2 Sam. 11.1
10 [3]the face of the battle was
[4]Or, young men
11 [5]Abshai
13 [g]Ps. 20.7; Isa. 30.18
14 [h]Lev. 26.7-8; Deut. 28.7
16 [6]That is, Euphrates
[i]2 Sam. 10.16, Shobach
18 [j]Ps. 33.16; Prov. 21.31
CHAPTER 20
1 [a]2 Sam. 11.1;
[1]at the return of the year
[b]2 Sam. 12.26
2 [c]2 Sam. 12.30-31
[2]the weight of
3 [3]Or, made them sawers of stone, diggers of iron, and cutters of wood
4 [4]stood, or, continued
[5]Or, Gob
[6]Or, Saph
[7]Or, Rapha, 2 Sam. 21.18
5 [8]Jaare-oregim, 2 Sam. 21.19
6 [9]a man of measure
[10]born to the giant, or, Rapha
7 [11]Or, reproached
[12]Called Shammah, 1 Sam. 16.9
CHAPTER 21
1 [a]2 Sam. 24.1;
2 [b]ch. 27.23

king, *are* they not all my lord's servants? why then doth my lord require
this thing? why will he be a cause of
trespass to Ĭs'ra-el?
4 Nevertheless [c]the king's word prevailed against Jō'ab. Wherefore Jō'ab
departed, and went throughout all Ĭs'-
ra-el, and came to Je-ru'sa-lĕm.
5 ¶ And Jō'ab gave the sum of the
number of the people unto Dā'vid. And
all *they of* Ĭs'ra-el were a thousand
thousand and an hundred thousand
men that drew sword: and Jū'dah *was*
four hundred threescore and ten thousand men that drew sword.
6 [d]But Lē'vī and Bĕn'ja-min counted
he not among them: for the king's word
was abominable to Jō'ab.
7 [1]And God was displeased with this
thing; therefore he smote Ĭs'ra-el.
8 And Dā'vid said unto God, [e]I have
sinned greatly, because I have done
this thing: [f]but now, I beseech thee, do
away the iniquity of thy servant; for I
have done very foolishly.
9 ¶ And the LORD spake unto Găd,
Dā'vid's [g]seer, saying,
10 Go and tell Dā'vid, saying, Thus
saith the LORD, I [2]offer thee three
things: choose thee one of them, that I
may do *it* unto thee.
11 So Găd came to Dā'vid, and said
unto him, Thus saith the LORD, [3]Choose
thee
12 [h]Either three years' famine; or
three months to be destroyed before
thy foes, while that the sword of thine
enemies overtaketh *thee;* or else three
days the sword of the LORD, even the
pestilence, in the land, and the angel of
the LORD destroying throughout all the
coasts of Ĭs'ra-el. Now therefore advise thyself what word I shall bring
again to him that sent me.
13 And Dā'vid said unto Găd, I am
in a great strait: let me fall now into the
hand of the LORD; for very [4]great *are*
his mercies: but let me not fall into the
hand of man.
14 ¶ So the LORD sent pestilence
upon Ĭs'ra-el: and there fell of Ĭs'ra-el
seventy thousand men.
15 And God sent an [i]angel unto Je-
ru'sa-lĕm to destroy it: and as he was
destroying, the LORD beheld, and [j]he
repented him of the evil, and said to
the angel that destroyed, It is enough,
stay now thine hand. And the angel of
the LORD stood by the threshingfloor
of [5]Ôr'nan the Jĕb'u-site.
16 And Dā'vid lifted up his eyes, and
[k]saw the angel of the LORD stand between the earth and the heaven, having
a drawn sword in his hand stretched
out over Je-ru'sa-lĕm. Then Dā'vid and
the elders *of Ĭs'ra-el, who were* clothed
in sackcloth, fell upon their faces.
17 And Dā'vid said unto God, *Is it*
not I *that* commanded the people to be
numbered? even I it is that have sinned
and done evil indeed; but *as for* these
sheep, what have they done? let thine
hand, I pray thee, O LORD my God, be
on me, and on my father's house; but
not on thy people, that they should be
plagued.
18 ¶ Then the angel of the LORD commanded Găd to say to Dā'vid, that
Dā'vid should go up, and set up an altar unto the LORD in the threshingfloor
of Ôr'nan the Jĕb'u-site.
19 And Dā'vid went up at the saying
of Găd, which he spake in the name of
the LORD.
20 [6]And Ôr'nan turned back, and
saw the angel; and his four sons with
him hid themselves. Now Ôr'nan was
threshing wheat.
21 And as Dā'vid came to Ôr'nan,
Ôr'nan looked and saw Dā'vid, and
went out of the threshingfloor, and
bowed himself to Dā'vid with *his* face
to the ground.
22 Then Dā'vid said to Ôr'nan,
[7]Grant me the place of *this* threshingfloor, that I may build an altar
therein unto the LORD: thou shalt grant
it me for the full price: that the plague
may be [l]stayed from the people.
23 And Ôr'nan said unto Dā'vid,
Take *it* to thee, and let my lord the king
do *that which is* good in his eyes: lo, I
give *thee* the oxen *also* for burnt offerings, and the threshing instruments for
wood, and the wheat for the meat offering; I give it all.
24 And king Dā'vid said to Ôr'nan,
Nay; but I will verily buy it for the full
price: for I will not take *that* which *is*
thine for the LORD, nor offer burnt offerings without cost.
25 So [m]Dā'vid gave to Ôr'nan for
the place six hundred shekels of gold
by weight.
26 And Dā'vid built there an altar
unto the LORD, and offered burnt offerings and peace offerings, and called
upon the LORD; and [n]he answered him
from heaven by fire upon the altar of
burnt offering.
27 And the LORD commanded the angel; and he put up his sword again into
the sheath thereof.
28 ¶ At that time when Dā'vid saw
that the LORD had answered him in
the threshingfloor of Ôr'nan the Jĕb'u-
site, then he sacrificed there.
29 [o]For the tabernacle of the LORD,
which Mō'ses made in the wilderness,
and the altar of the burnt offering,
were at that season in the high place at
[p]Gĭb'e-on.
30 But Dā'vid could not go before it
to inquire of God: for he [q]was afraid
because of the sword of the angel of
the LORD.

22

22 Then Dā'vid said, [a]This *is* the
house of the LORD God, and this
is the altar of the burnt offering for
Ĭs'ra-el.
2 And Dā'vid commanded to gather
together [b]the strangers that *were* in
the land of Ĭs'ra-el; and he set masons
to hew wrought stones to build the
house of God.
3 And Dā'vid prepared iron in abundance for the nails for the doors of the
gates, and for the joinings; and brass
in abundance [c]without weight;

4 [c]Prov. 29.25; Eccl. 8.4; Acts 4.19
6 [d]Num. 1.47-49; ch. 27.24
7 [1]And it was evil in the eyes of the LORD concerning this thing
8 [e]2 Sam. 12.13; Ps. 25.11; Prov. 28.13-14; 2 Cor. 7.10
[f]2 Sam. 12.13; Ps. 51.1-3; Hos. 14.2
9 [g]1 Sam. 9.9
10 [2]stretch out
11 [3]Take to thee
12 [h]2 Sam. 24.13
13 [4]Or, many, Neh. 9.17; Ps. 100.5; Lam. 3.22
15 [i]2 Sam. 24.16; Jer. 26.18; Matt. 23.37-38
[j]Gen. 6.6
[5]Araunah, 2 Sam. 24.18
16 [k]2 Chr. 3.1
20 [6]Or, When Ornan turned back and saw the angel, then he and his four sons with him hid themselves
22 [7]Give
[l]Num. 16.48
25 [m]2 Sam. 24.24
26 [n]Lev. 9.24; 2 Chr. 3.1
29 [o]ch. 16.39
[p]1 Ki. 3.4; ch. 16.39
30 [q]2 Sam. 6.9; ch. 13.12; Job 13.21; Ps. 119.120
CHAPTER 22
1 [a]Deut. 12.5; 2 Sam. 24.18; ch. 21.18-19-26-28
2 [b]1 Ki. 9.21
3 [c]1 Ki. 7.47

4 Also cedar trees in abundance: for
the [d]Zī-dō'nĭ-ans and they of Tȳre
brought much cedar wood to Dā'vid.
5 And Dā'vid said, [e]Sŏl'o-mon my
son *is* young and tender, and the house
that is to be builded for the LORD *must*
be exceeding magnifical, of fame and
of glory throughout all countries: I will
therefore now make preparation for it.
So Dā'vid prepared abundantly before
his death.
6 ¶ Then he called for Sŏl'o-mon
his son, and charged him to build an
house for the LORD God of Ĭs'ra-el.
7 And Dā'vid said to Sŏl'o-mon, My
son, as for me, [f]it was in my mind to
build an house [g]unto the name of the
LORD my God:
8 But the word of the LORD came to
me, saying, [h]Thou hast shed blood
abundantly, and hast made great wars:
thou shalt not build an house unto my
name, because thou hast shed much
blood upon the earth in my sight.
9 [i]Behold, a son shall be born to
thee, who shall be a man of rest; and I
will give him [j]rest from all his enemies
round about: for his name shall be
[1]Sŏl'o-mon, and I will give peace and
quietness unto Ĭs'ra-el in his days.
10 [k]He shall build an house for my
name; and [l]he shall be my son, and I
will be his father; and I will establish
the throne of his kingdom over Ĭs'ra-el
for ever.
11 Now, my son, [m]the LORD be with
thee; and prosper thou, and build the
house of the LORD thy God, as he hath
said of thee.
12 Only the LORD [n]give thee wisdom and understanding, and give thee
charge concerning Ĭs'ra-el, that thou
mayest keep the law of the LORD thy
God.
13 [o]Then shalt thou prosper, if thou
takest heed to fulfil the statutes and
judgments which the LORD charged
Mō'ses with concerning Ĭs'ra-el: [p]be
strong, and of good courage; dread
not, nor be dismayed.
14 Now, behold, [2]in my trouble I
have prepared for the house of the
LORD an hundred thousand talents of
gold, and a thousand thousand talents
of silver; and of brass and iron without
weight; for it is in abundance: timber
also and stone have I prepared; and
thou mayest add thereto.
15 Moreover *there are* workmen with
thee in abundance, hewers and [3]work-
ers of stone and timber, and all manner
of cunning men for every manner of
work.
16 Of the gold, the silver, and the
brass, and the iron, *there is* no number. Arise *therefore,* and be doing, and
the LORD be with thee.
17 ¶ Dā'vid also commanded all the
princes of Ĭs'ra-el to help Sŏl'o-mon
his son, *saying,*
18 *Is* not the LORD your God with
you? [q]and hath he *not* given you rest
on every side? for he hath given the
inhabitants of the land into mine hand;

4 [d]1 Ki. 5.6
5 [e]ch. 29.1
7 [f]2 Sam. 7.2; ch. 17.1; Acts 7.46
[g]Deut. 12.5
8 [h]1 Ki. 5.3; ch. 28.3
9 [i]ch. 28.5
[j]1 Ki. 4.25
[1]That is, Peaceable and perfect
10 [k]2 Sam. 7.13; 1 Ki. 5.5; ch. 17.12
[l]Ps. 89.26-27; Heb. 1.5
11 [m]Rom. 8.31
12 [n]Deut. 4.6; 1 Ki. 3.9; Ps. 72.1
13 [o]Josh. 1.7; 1 Ki. 6.12-13; ch. 11.9-14; Isa. 3.10
[p]ch. 28.20
14 [2]Or, in my poverty
15 [3]That is, masons and carpenters
18 [q]Deut. 12.10; 2 Sam. 7.1; ch. 23.25
19 [r]2 Chr. 20.3
[s]1 Ki. 8.6; 2 Chr. 5.7

CHAPTER 23
1 [a]ch. 28.5; ch. 29.22-25
3 [b]Num. 4.3
4 [1]Or, to oversee
[c]Deut. 16.18; ch. 26.29
5 [d]2 Chr. 29.25-26; Amos 6.5
6 [e]Ex. 6.16; Num. 26.57; ch. 6.1; 2 Chr. 8.14
[2]divisions
11 [3]did not multiply sons
12 [f]Ex. 6.18; ch. 6.2
13 [g]Ex. 28.1; Num. 18.1-7; Heb. 5.4
[h]Ex. 30.7; Lev. 10.1-2; Num. 16.40; 1 Sam. 2.28
[i]Deut. 21.5
[j]Num. 6.23
15 [k]Ex. 2.22
17 [4]Or, the first
[5]were highly multiplied

and the land is subdued before the
LORD, and before his people.
19 Now [r]set your heart and your
soul to seek the LORD your God; arise
therefore, and build ye the sanctuary
of the LORD God, to [s]bring the ark of
the covenant of the LORD, and the holy
vessels of God, into the house that is to
be built to the name of the LORD.

23

So when Dā'vid was old and full
of days, he made [a]Sŏl'o-mon his
son king over Ĭs'ra-el.
2 ¶ And he gathered together all the
princes of Ĭs'ra-el, with the priests and
the Lē'vītes.
3 Now the Lē'vītes were numbered
from the age of [b]thirty years and upward: and their number by their polls,
man by man, was thirty and eight thousand.
4 Of which, twenty and four thousand *were* [1]to set forward the work of
the house of the LORD; and six thousand *were* [c]officers and judges:
5 Moreover four thousand *were* porters; and four thousand praised the
LORD with the instruments which [d]I
made, *said Dā'vid,* to praise *therewith.*
6 And [e]Dā'vid divided them into
[2]courses among the sons of Lē'vī,
namely, Gēr'shŏn, Kō'hath, and Me-
rā'rī.
7 ¶ Of the Gēr'shon-ītes *were,* Lā'ă-
dăn, and Shĭm'e-ī.
8 The sons of Lā'ă-dăn; the chief
was Je-hī'el, and Zē'tham, and Jō'el,
three.
9 The sons of Shĭm'e-ī; Shĕl'o-mĭth,
and Hā'zĭ-el, and Hā'ran, three. These
were the chief of the fathers of Lā'ă-
dăn.
10 And the sons of Shĭm'e-ī *were,*
Jā'hăth, Zī'nȧ, and Jē'ush, and Be-
rī'ah. These four *were* the sons of
Shĭm'e-ī.
11 And Jā'hăth was the chief, and
Zī'zah the second: but Jē'ush and Be-
rī'ah [3]had not many sons; therefore
they were in one reckoning, according
to *their* father's house.
12 ¶ [f]The sons of Kō'hath; Ăm'răm,
Ĭz'har, Hē'bron, and Ŭz'zĭ-el, four.
13 The sons of Ăm'răm; Aâr'on and
Mō'ses: and [g]Aâr'on was separated,
that he should sanctify the most holy
things, he and his sons for ever, [h]to
burn incense before the LORD, [i]to minister unto him, and [j]to bless in his
name for ever.
14 Now *concerning* Mō'ses the man
of God, his sons were named of the
tribe of Lē'vī.
15 [k]The sons of Mō'ses *were,* Gēr'-
shŏm, and E-li-ē'zēr.
16 Of the sons of Gēr'shŏm, Shĕb'u-
el *was* the chief.
17 And the sons of E-li-ē'zēr *were,*
Rē-ha-bī'ah [4]the chief. And E-li-ē'zēr
had none other sons; but the sons of
Rē-ha-bī'ah [5]were very many.
18 Of the sons of Ĭz'har; Shĕl'o-mĭth
the chief.
19 Of the sons of Hē'bron; Je-rī'-
ah the first, Ăm-a-rī'ah the second,

Ja-hā'zĭ-el the third, and Jĕk-a-mē'am
the fourth.
20 Of the sons of Ŭz'zĭ-el; Mī'cah
the first, and Je-sī'ah the second.
21 ¶ The sons of Me-rā'rī; Mäh'lī,
and Mū'shī. The sons of Mäh'lī; Ē-le-
ā'zar, and Kĭsh.
22 And Ē-le-ā'zar died, and had no
sons, but daughters: and their [6]breth-
ren the sons of Kĭsh [l]took them.
23 [m]The sons of Mū'shī; Mäh'lī, and
Ē'dĕr, and Jĕr'e-mŏth, three.
24 ¶ These *were* the sons of [n]Lē'vī
after the house of their fathers; *even*
the chief of the fathers, as they were
counted by number of names by their
polls, that did the work for the service
of the house of the LORD, from the age
of [o]twenty years and upward.
25 For Dā'vid said, The LORD God of
Ĭs'ra-el hath given rest unto his people,
[7]that they may dwell in Je-ru'sa-lĕm
for ever:
26 And also unto the Lē'vītes; they
shall no *more* [p]carry the tabernacle,
nor any vessels of it for the service
thereof.
27 For by the last words of Dā'-
vid the Lē'vītes *were* [8]numbered from
twenty years old and above:
28 Because [9]their office *was* to wait
on the sons of Âr'on for the service of
the house of the LORD, in the courts,
and in the chambers, and in the purifying of all holy things, and the work of
the service of the house of God;
29 Both for [q]the shewbread, and for
[r]the fine flour for meat offering, and
for [s]the unleavened cakes, and for *that
which is baked in* the [10]pan, and for that
which is fried, and for all manner of
[t]measure and size;
30 And [u]to stand every morning to
thank and praise the LORD, and likewise at even;
31 And to offer all burnt sacrifices
unto the LORD [v]in the sabbaths, in the
new moons, and on the [w]set feasts, by
number, according to the order commanded unto them, continually before
the LORD:
32 And that they should [x]keep the
charge of the tabernacle of the congregation, and the charge of the holy
place, and [y]the charge of the sons of
Âr'on their brethren, in the service of
the house of the LORD.

24 Now *these are* the divisions of
the sons of Âr'on. The sons of
Âr'on; [a]Nā'dăb, and A-bī'hū, Ē-le-
ā'zar, and Ĭth'a-mär.
2 But [b]Nā'dăb and A-bī'hū died before their father, and had no children:
therefore Ē-le-ā'zar and Ĭth'a-mär executed the priest's office.
3 And Dā'vid distributed them, both
Zā'dŏk of the sons of Ē-le-ā'zar, and
A-hĭm'e-lech of the sons of Ĭth'a-mär,
according to their offices in their service.
4 And there were more chief men
found of the sons of Ē-le-ā'zar than of
the sons of Ĭth'a-mär; and *thus* were
they divided. Among the sons of Ē-le-
ā'zar *there were* sixteen chief men of
the house of *their* fathers, and eight
among the sons of Ĭth'a-mär according
to the house of their fathers.
5 Thus were they divided [c]by lot,
one sort with another; for the governors of the sanctuary, and governors
of the house of God, were of the sons of
Ē-le-ā'zar, and of the sons of Ĭth'a-
mär.
6 And Shĕm-a-ī'ah the son of Ne-
thăn'e-el [d]the scribe, *one* of the Lē'-
vītes, wrote them before the king, and
the princes, and Zā'dŏk the priest, and
A-hĭm'e-lech the son of A-bī'a-thär,
and *before* the chief of the fathers of
the priests and Lē'vītes: one [1]principal
household being taken for Ē-le-ā'zar,
and *one* taken for Ĭth'a-mär.
7 Now the first lot came forth to Je-
hoi'a-rĭb, the second to [e]Je-dā'iah.
8 The third to [f]Hā'rim, the fourth to
Se-ō'rim,
9 The fifth to Măl-chī'jah, the sixth
to Mĭj'a-mĭn,
10 The seventh to Hăk'kŏz, the eighth
to [g]A-bī'jah,
11 The ninth to Jĕsh'u-ah, the tenth
to Shĕch-a-nī'ah,
12 The eleventh to Ē-lī'a-shib, the
twelfth to Jā'kim,
13 The thirteenth to Hŭp'pah, the
fourteenth to Je-shĕb'e-ăb,
14 The fifteenth to Bĭl'gah, the sixteenth to Ĭm'mĕr,
15 The seventeenth to Hē'zīr, the
eighteenth to Ăph'sēs,
16 The nineteenth to Pĕth-a-hī'ah,
the twentieth to Je-hĕz'e-kĕl,
17 The one and twentieth to Jā'chin,
the two and twentieth to Gā'mŭl,
18 The three and twentieth to Dĕl-a-
ī'ah, the four and twentieth to Mā-a-
zī'ah.
19 These *were* the [h]orderings of
them in their service to come into the
house of the LORD, according to [i]their
manner, under Âr'on their father, as
the LORD God of Ĭs'ra-el had commanded him.
20 ¶ And the rest of the sons of Lē'vī
were these: Of the sons of Ăm'răm;
[j]Shu'ba-el: of the sons of Shu'ba-el;
Jeh-dē'iah.
21 Concerning [k]Rē-ha-bī'ah: of the
sons of Rē-ha-bī'ah, the first *was* Ĭssh-
ī'ah.
22 Of the Ĭz'har-ītes; [l]Shĕl'o-mŏth:
of the sons of Shĕl'o-mŏth; Jā'hăth.
23 And the sons *of* [m]*Hē'bron;* Je-
rī'ah *the first*, Ăm-a-rī'ah the second,
Ja-hā'zĭ-el the third, Jĕk-a-mē'am the
fourth.
24 *Of* the sons of Ŭz'zĭ-el; Mī'chah:
of the sons of Mī'chah; Shā'mĭr.
25 The brother of Mī'chah *was* Ĭssh-
ī'ah: of the sons of Ĭssh-ī'ah; Zĕch-a-
rī'ah.
26 [n]The sons of Me-rā'rī *were* Mäh'-
lī and Mū'shī: the sons of Ja-a-zī'ah;
Bē'nō.
27 ¶ The sons of Me-rā'rī by Ja-a-
zī'ah; Bē'nō, and Shō'hăm, and Zăc'-
cur, and Ĭb'rī.
28 Of Mäh'lī *came* Ē-le-ā'zar, [o]who
had no sons.

22 [6]Or, kinsmen, Gen. 13.8
[l]Num. 36.6
23 [m]ch. 24.30
24 [n]Num. 10.17
[o]Num. 1.3
25 [7]Or, and he dwelleth in Jerusalem, etc
26 [p]Num. 4.5
27 [8]number
28 [9]their station was at the hand of the sons of Aaron
29 [q]Ex. 25.30; Lev. 24.5-9
[r]Lev. 6.20
[s]Lev. 2.4
[10]Or, flat plate
[t]Lev. 19.35
30 [u]ch. 6.31-33; ch. 9.33; 2 Chr. 31.2; Ps. 137.2-4; Rev. 5.8-14
31 [v]Num. 10.10; Ps. 81.3; Isa. 1.13-14
[w]Lev. 23.4
32 [x]Num. 1.53
[y]Num. 3.6-9

CHAPTER 24
1 [a]Ex. 6.23; Lev. 10.1; Num. 3.2
2 [b]Num. 3.4
5 [c]Josh. 18.10; Prov. 16.33; Acts 1.26
6 [d]Neh. 8.4
[1]house of the father
7 [e]Neh. 7.39
8 [f]Ezra 10.21
10 [g]Neh. 12.4-17; Luke 1.5
19 [h]Num. 4.49; ch. 9.25
[i]ch. 9.25; Luke 1.8-23
20 [j]ch. 23.16-Shebuel
21 [k]ch. 23.17
22 [l]ch. 23.18-Shelomith
23 [m]ch. 15.9
26 [n]Ex. 6.19; ch. 23.21
28 [o]ch. 23.22

29 Concerning Kĭsh: the son of Kĭsh
was Je-räh'me-el.
30 [p]The sons also of Mū'shī; Mäh'lī,
and Ē'dẽr, and Jĕr'i-mŏth. These *were*
the sons of the Lē'vītes after the house
of their fathers.
31 These likewise cast lots over
against their brethren the sons of
Aâr'on in the presence of Dā'vid the
king, and Zā'dŏk, and A-hĭm'e-lech,
and the chief of the fathers of the priests
and Lē'vītes, even the principal fathers
over against their younger brethren.
25 Moreover Dā'vid and the [a]cap-
tains of the host separated to the
service of the sons of [b]Ā'saph, and of
Hē'man, and of Jĕd'u-thŭn, who should
[c]prophesy with harps, with psalteries,
and with cymbals: and the number of
the workmen according to their service
was:
2 Of the sons of Ā'saph; Zăc'cur, and
Jō'seph, and Nĕth-a-nī'ah, and [1]Ăs-ă-
rē'lah, the sons of Ā'saph under the
hands of Ā'saph, which prophesied [2]ac-
cording to the order of the king.
3 Of Jĕd'u-thŭn: the sons of Jĕd'u-
thŭn; Gĕd-a-lī'ah, and [d]Zē'rī, and Je-
shā'iah, Hash-a-bī'ah, and Măt-ti-
thī'ah, [3]six, under the hands of their
father Jĕd'u-thŭn, who prophesied
with a harp, to give thanks and to
praise the LORD.
4 Of Hē'man: the sons of Hē'-
man; Bŭk-kī'ah, Măt-ta-nī'ah, [e]Ŭz'zī-
el, [f]Shĕb'u-el, and Jĕr'i-mŏth, Hăn-a-
nī'ah, Ha-nā'nī, E-lī'a-thah, Gĭd-dăl'tī,
and Ro-măm'tĭ–ē'zẽr, Jŏsh-bĕk'a-shah,
Măl'lo-thī, Hō'thĭr, *and* Ma-hā'zĭ-ŏth:
5 All these *were* the sons of Hē'man
the king's [g]seer in the [4]words of God,
to lift up the horn. And [h]God gave to
Hē'man fourteen sons and three daughters.
6 All these *were* under the hands of
their father for song *in* the house of the
LORD, with cymbals, psalteries, and
harps, for the service of the house of
God, [5]according to the king's order to
Ā'saph, Jĕd'u-thŭn, and Hē'man.
7 So the number of them, with their
brethren that were instructed in the
[i]songs of the LORD, *even* all that were
cunning, was two hundred fourscore
and eight.
8 ¶ And they cast lots, ward against
ward, as well the small as the great,
[j]the teacher as the scholar.
9 Now the first lot came forth for
Ā'saph to Jō'seph: the second to Gĕd-
a-lī'ah, who with his brethren and sons
were twelve:
10 The third to Zăc'cur, *he,* his sons,
and his brethren, *were* twelve:
11 The fourth to Ĭz'rī, *he,* his sons,
and his brethren, *were* twelve:
12 The fifth to Nĕth-a-nī'ah, *he,* his
sons, and his brethren, *were* twelve:
13 The sixth to Bŭk-kī'ah, *he,* his
sons, and his brethren, *were* twelve:
14 The seventh to Je-shăr'e-lah, *he,*
his sons, and his brethren, *were* twelve:
15 The eighth to Je-shā'iah, *he,* his
sons, and his brethren, *were* twelve:
16 The ninth to Măt-ta-nī'ah, *he,* his
sons, and his brethren, *were* twelve:
17 The tenth to Shĭm'e-ī, *he,* his sons,
and his brethren, *were* twelve:
18 The eleventh to A-zăr'e-el, *he,* his
sons, and his brethren, *were* twelve:
19 The twelfth to Hash-a-bī'ah, *he,*
his sons, and his brethren, *were* twelve:
20 The thirteenth to Shu'ba-el, *he,*
his sons, and his brethren, *were* twelve:
21 The fourteenth to Măt-ti-thī'ah,
he, his sons, and his brethren, *were*
twelve:
22 The fifteenth to Jĕr'e-mŏth, *he,*
his sons, and his brethren, *were* twelve:
23 The sixteenth to Hăn-a-nī'ah, *he,*
his sons, and his brethren, *were* twelve:
24 The seventeenth to Jŏsh-bĕk'a-
shah, *he,* his sons, and his brethren,
were twelve:
25 The eighteenth to Ha-nā'nī, *he,*
his sons, and his brethren, *were* twelve:
26 The nineteenth to Măl'lo-thī, *he,*
his sons, and his brethren, *were* twelve:
27 The twentieth to E-lī'a-thah, *he,*
his sons, and his brethren, *were* twelve:
28 The one and twentieth to Hō'thĭr,
he, his sons, and his brethren, *were*
twelve:
29 The two and twentieth to Gĭd-
dăl'tī, *he,* his sons, and his brethren,
were twelve:
30 The three and twentieth to Ma-
hā'zĭ-ŏth, *he,* his sons, and his brethren, *were* twelve:
31 [k]The four and twentieth to Ro-
măm'tĭ–ē'zẽr, *he,* his sons, and his
brethren, *were* twelve.
26 Concerning the divisions of the
[a]porters: Of the [b]Kôr'hītes *was*
[c]Me-shĕl-e-mī'ah the son of Kō're, of
the sons of [1][d]Ā'saph.
2 And the sons of Me-shĕl-e-mī'ah
were, Zĕch-a-rī'ah the firstborn, Je-dī'-
a-el the second, Zĕb-a-dī'ah the third,
Jăth'nī-el the fourth,
3 Ē'lăm the fifth, Je-ho-hā'nan the
sixth, Ĕl-i-ō-ē'nă-ī the seventh.
4 Moreover the sons of Ō'bed–ē'dom
were, Shĕm-a-ī'ah the firstborn, Je-
hŏz'a-băd the second, Jō'ah the third,
and Sā'car the fourth, and Ne-thăn'e-el
the fifth,
5 Ăm'mī-el the sixth, Ĭs'sa-char the
seventh, Pe-ŭl'thāi the eighth: for God
[e]blessed [2]him.
6 Also unto Shĕm-a-ī'ah his son were
sons born, that ruled throughout the
house of their father: for they *were*
mighty men of valour.
7 The sons of Shĕm-a-ī'ah; Ŏth'nī,
and Rē'pha-el, and Ō'bed, Ĕl'za-băd,
whose brethren *were* strong men, E-
lī'hū, and Sĕm-a-chī'ah.
8 All these of the sons of Ō'bed–
ē'dom: they and their sons and their
brethren, able men for strength for the
service, *were* threescore and two of
Ō'bed–ē'dom.
9 And Me-shĕl-e-mī'ah had sons and
brethren, strong men, eighteen.
10 Also [f]Hō'sah, of the children of
Me-rā'rī, had sons; Sĭm'rī the chief,
(for *though* he was not [g]the firstborn,
yet his father made him the chief;)

30 [p]ch. 23.23
CHAPTER 25
1 [a]ch. 12.28; ch. 23.2 [b]ch. 6.33; ch. 15.17 [c]Ex. 15.20; Num. 11.25; 1 Sam. 10.5; ch. 15.16; ch. 16.4; Ps. 150.3-5; 1 Cor. 14.1; Rev. 15.2-4
2 [1]Otherwise called Jesharelah, verse 14 [2]by the hands of the king
3 [d]verse 11-Izri [3]With Shimei mentioned, verse 17
4 [e]verse 18-Azareel [f]verse 20-Shubael
5 [g]1 Sam. 9.9; 2 Sam. 24.11; ch. 21.9; ch. 26.28; Amos 7.12 [4]Or, matters [h]Gen. 33.5; ch. 28.5; Ps. 127.3; Isa. 8.18
6 [5]by the hands of the king
7 [i]Ps. 150.1; Eph. 5.19; Col. 3.16
8 [j]2 Chr. 23.13
31 [k]Rev. 4.4; Rev. 5.8; Rev. 11.16
CHAPTER 26
1 [a]ch. 9.17; ch. 15.18; 2 Chr. 23.19 [b]Num. 16.1-2; Num. 26.9-11; Jude 11 [c]verse 14-Shelemiah [1]ch. 6.37; ch. 9.19-Ebiasaph [d]ch. 6.39; ch. 9.15; ch. 16.37
5 [e]Gen. 33.5; ch. 13.14; Ps. 127.3 [2]That is, Obed-edom
10 [f]ch. 16.38 [g]Gen. 4.7; Gen. 49.3; Deut. 21.17; ch. 5.1

11 Hĭl-kī'ah the second, Tĕb-a-lī'ah
the third, Zĕch-a-rī'ah the fourth: all
the sons and brethren of Hō'sah *were*
thirteen.
12 Among these *were* the divisions
of the porters, *even* among the chief
men, *having* wards one against another, to minister in the house of the
LORD.
13 ¶ And they cast lots, [3][h]as well the
small as the great, according to the
house of their fathers, for every gate.
14 And the lot eastward fell to [4]Shĕl-
e-mī'ah. Then for Zĕch-a-rī'ah his son,
a wise counseller, they cast lots; and
his lot came out northward.
15 To Ō'bed-ĕ'dom southward; and
to his sons the house of [5]A-sŭp'pim.
16 To Shŭp'pim and Hō'sah *the lot*
came forth westward, with the gate
Shăl'le-chĕth, by the causeway of the
[i]going up, [j]ward against ward.
17 Eastward *were* six Lē'vītes, northward four a day, southward four a day,
and toward A-sŭp'pim two *and* two.
18 At Pär'bar westward, four at the
causeway, *and* two at [6]Pär'bar.
19 These *are* the divisions of the
porters among the sons of Kō're, and
among the sons of Me-rā'rī.
20 ¶ And of the Lē'vītes, A-hī'jah
was [k]over the treasures of the house of
God, and over the treasures of the [7]ded-
icated things.
21 *As concerning* the sons of [l]Lā'ă-
dăn; the sons of the Gĕr'shon-īte Lā'ă-
dăn, chief fathers, *even* of Lā'ă-dăn the
Gĕr'shon-īte, *were* [m]Je-hī'e-lī.
22 The sons of Je-hī'e-lī; Zē'tham,
and Jō'el his brother, *which were* over
the treasures of the house of the LORD.
23 Of the [n]Ăm'răm-ītes, *and* the Ĭz'-
har-ītes, the Hē'bron-ītes, *and* the Ŭz'-
zĭ-el-ītes:
24 And [o]Shĕb'u-el the son of Gĕr'-
shŏm, the son of Mō'ses, *was* ruler of
the treasures.
25 And his brethren by E-li-ē'zĕr;
Rē-ha-bī'ah his son, and Je-shā'iah his
son, and Jō'ram his son, and Zĭch'rī
his son, and [p]Shĕl'o-mĭth his son.
26 Which Shĕl'o-mĭth and his brethren *were* over all the treasures of the
dedicated things, which Dā'vid the
king, and the chief fathers, the captains over thousands and hundreds,
and the captains of the host, had dedicated.
27 [8]Out of the spoils won in battles did they dedicate [q]to maintain the
house of the LORD.
28 And all that Săm'u-el [r]the seer,
and Saul the son of Kĭsh, and Ăb'nēr
the son of Nēr, and Jō'ab the son of
Zĕr-u-ī'ah, had dedicated; *and* whosoever had dedicated *any thing, it was*
under the hand of Shĕl'o-mĭth, and of
his brethren.
29 ¶ Of the Ĭz'har-ītes, Chĕn-a-nī'ah
and his sons *were* for the outward business over Ĭs'ra-el, for [s]officers and
judges.
30 *And* of the Hē'bron-ītes, Hash-a-
bī'ah and his brethren, men of valour,
a thousand and seven hundred, *were*
[9]officers among them of Ĭs'ra-el on this
side Jôr'dan westward in all the business of the LORD, and in the service of
the king.
31 Among the Hē'bron-ītes *was* [t]Je-
rī'jah the chief, *even* among the Hē'-
bron-ītes, according to the generations
of his fathers. In the [u]fortieth year of
the reign of Dā'vid they were sought
for, and there were found among them
mighty men of valour [v]at Jā'zēr of
Gĭl'e-ăd.
32 And his brethren, men of valour,
were two thousand and seven hundred
chief fathers, whom king Dā'vid made
rulers over the Reu'ben-ītes, the Găd'-
ītes, and the half tribe of Ma-năs'seh,
for every matter pertaining to God,
and [10][w]affairs of the king.

27 Now the children of Ĭs'ra-el after
their number, *to wit,* the chief fathers and captains of thousands and
hundreds, and their officers that served
the king in any matter of the courses,
which came in and went out month by
month throughout all the months of the
year, of every course *were* twenty and
four thousand.
2 Over the first course for the first
month *was* [a]Ja-shō'be-ăm the son
of Zăb'dĭ-el: and in his course *were*
twenty and four thousand.
3 Of the children of [b]Pē'rez *was* the
chief of all the captains of the host for
the first month.
4 And over the course of the second month *was* [c]Dŏd'a-ī an A-hō'hīte,
and of his course *was* Mĭk'loth also
the ruler: in his course likewise *were*
twenty and four thousand.
5 The third captain of the host for
the third month *was* Be-nā'iah the son
of Je-hoi'a-dȧ, a [1]chief priest: and in
his course *were* twenty and four thousand.
6 This *is that* Be-nā'iah, *who was*
[d]mighty *among* the thirty, and above
the thirty: and in his course *was* Ăm-
mĭz'a-bad his son.
7 The fourth *captain* for the fourth
month *was* [e]Ā'sa-hĕl the brother of
Jō'ab, and Zĕb-a-dī'ah his son after
him: and in his course *were* twenty
and four thousand.
8 The fifth captain for the fifth month
was Shăm'huth the Ĭz'ra-hīte: and in
his course *were* twenty and four thousand.
9 The sixth *captain* for the sixth
month *was* [f]Ī'rȧ the son of Ĭk'kĕsh
the Te-kō'īte: and in his course *were*
twenty and four thousand.
10 The seventh *captain* for the seventh month *was* [g]Hē'lez the Pĕl'o-nīte,
of the children of Ē'phră-ĭm: and in
his course *were* twenty and four thousand.
11 The eighth *captain* for the eighth
month *was* [h]Sĭb'be-cāi the Hū'shath-
īte, of the Zär'hītes: and in his course
were twenty and four thousand.
12 The ninth *captain* for the ninth
month *was* [i]Ā-bĭ-ē'zĕr the Ăn'ĕ-tŏth-
īte, of the Bĕn'ja-mītes: and in his
course *were* twenty and four thousand.

---

13 [3]Or, as well for the small as for the great
[h]Josh. 18.10; Col. 3.11
14 [4]Meshelemiah, verse 1
15 [5]gatherings
16 [i]1 Ki. 10.5; 2 Chr. 9.4
[j]ch. 24.31; Neh. 12.24
18 [6]Or, out part, 2 Ki. 23.11
20 [k]Deut. 12.6; Mal. 3.10
[7]holy things, 2 Chr. 31.11-12
21 [l]ch. 6.17-Libni
[m]ch. 29.8-Jehiel
23 [n]Ex. 6.18; ch. 23.12
24 [o]ch. 23.16
25 [p]ch. 23.18
27 [8]Out of the battles and spoils
[q]2 Ki. 12.14;
28 [r]1 Sam. 9.9
29 [s]Deut. 1.16;
30 [9]over the charge
31 [t]ch. 23.19
[u]2 Sam. 5.4;
[v]Num. 32.1-3-35;
32 [10]thing
[w]2 Chr. 19.11
CHAPTER 27
2 [a]2 Sam. 23.8;
3 [b]Gen. 38.29-Pharez
4 [c]2 Sam. 23.9-Dodo
5 [1]Or, principal officer
6 [d]2 Sam. 23.20-22-23
7 [e]2 Sam. 2.18-23;
9 [f]2 Sam. 23.26
10 [g]ch. 11.27
11 [h]2 Sam. 21.18;
12 [i]ch. 11.28

13 The tenth *captain* for the tenth month *was* [j]Ma-hăr'a-ī the Ne-toph'a-thīte, of the Zär'hītes: and in his course *were* twenty and four thousand.

14 The eleventh *captain* for the eleventh month *was* [k]Be-nā'iah the Pĭr'a-thon-īte, of the children of Ē'phră-ĭm: and in his course *were* twenty and four thousand.

15 The twelfth *captain* for the twelfth month *was* [l]Hĕl'da-ī the Ne-toph'a-thīte, [m]of Ŏth'nĭ-el: and in his course *were* twenty and four thousand.

16 ¶ Furthermore over the tribes of Ĭs'ra-el: the ruler of the Reu'ben-ītes *was* E-li-ē'zēr the son of Zĭch'rī: of the Sĭm'e-on-ītes, Shĕph-a-tī'ah the son of Mā'a-chah:

17 Of the Lē'vītes, [n]Hash-a-bī'ah the son of Ke-mŭ'el: of the Aâr'on-ītes, Zā'dŏk:

18 Of Jū'dah, [o]E-lī'hū, *one* of the brethren of Dā'vid: of Ĭs'sa-char, Ŏm'rī the son of Mī'chaĕl:

19 Of Zĕb'u-lun, Ĭsh-ma-ī'ah the son of Ō-ba-dī'ah: of Năph'ta-lī, Jĕr'i-mŏth the son of Ăz'rĭ-el:

20 Of the children of Ē'phră-ĭm, Ho-shē'à the son of Ăz-a-zī'ah: of the half tribe of Ma-năs'seh, Jō'el the son of Pe-dā'iah:

21 Of the half *tribe* of Ma-năs'seh in Gĭl'e-ăd, Ĭd'dō the son of Zĕch-a-rī'ah: of Bĕn'ja-min, Ja-ā'sĭ-el the son of Ăb'nēr:

22 Of Dăn, A-zăr'e-el the son of Jĕr'o-hăm. These *were* the princes of the tribes of Ĭs'ra-el.

23 ¶ But Dā'vid took not the number of them from twenty years old and under: because [p]the LORD had said he would increase Ĭs'ra-el like to the stars of the heavens.

24 Jō'ab the son of Zĕr-u-ī'ah began to number, but he finished not, because [q]there fell wrath for it against Ĭs'ra-el; neither [2]was the number put in the account of the chronicles of king Dā'vid.

25 ¶ And over the king's treasures *was* Ăz'ma-veth the son of A-dī'el: and over the storehouses in the fields, in the cities, and in the villages, and in the castles, *was* Je-hŏn'a-than the son of Ŭz-zī'ah:

26 And over them that did the work of the field for tillage of the ground *was* Ĕz'rī the son of Chē'lŭb:

27 And over [r]the vineyards *was* Shĭm'e-ī the Rā'math-īte: [3]over the increase of the vineyards for the wine cellars *was* Zăb'dī the Shĭph'mīte:

28 And over the olive trees and the sycomore trees that *were* in the low plains *was* Bā'al–hā'nan the Gĕd'ĕ-rīte: and over the cellars of oil *was* Jō'ăsh:

29 And over the herds that fed in Shâr'on *was* Shĭt'ra-ī the Shâr'on-īte: and over the herds *that were* in the valleys *was* Shā'phat the son of Ăd'la-ī:

30 Over the camels also *was* Ō'bil the Ĭsh'ma-el-īte: and over the asses *was* Jeh-dē'iah the Me-rŏn'o-thīte:

31 And over the flocks *was* Jā'zĭz the Hā'gēr-īte. All these *were* the rulers of the substance which *was* king Dā'vid's.

32 Also Jŏn'a-than Dā'vid's [4]uncle was a counseller, a wise man, and a [5]scribe: and Je-hī'el the [6]son of Hăch'mo-nī *was* with the king's sons:

33 And A-hĭth'o-phel *was* the king's counseller: and Hū'shāi the Ăr'chīte *was* the king's companion:

34 And after A-hĭth'o-phel *was* Je-hoi'a-dà the son of Be-nā'iah, and A-bī'a-thär: and the general of the king's army *was* Jō'ab.

28 And Dā'vid assembled all the princes of Ĭs'ra-el, [a]the princes of the tribes, and [b]the captains of the companies that ministered to the king by course, and the captains over the thousands, and captains over the hundreds, and [c]the stewards over all the substance and [1]possession of the king, [2]and of his sons, with the [3]officers, and with [d]the mighty men, and with all the valiant men, unto Je-ru'sa-lĕm.

2 Then Dā'vid the king stood up upon his feet, and said, Hear me, my [e]brethren, and my people: *As for me,* [f]I *had* in mine heart to build an house of rest for the ark of the covenant of the LORD, and for [g]the footstool of our God, and had made ready for the building:

3 But God said unto me, [h]Thou shalt not build an house for my name, because thou *hast been* a man of war, and hast shed [4]blood.

4 Howbeit the LORD God of Ĭs'ra-el [i]chose me before all the house of my father to be king over Ĭs'ra-el for ever: for he hath chosen [j]Jū'dah *to be* the ruler; and of the house of Jū'dah, [k]the house of my father; and [l]among the sons of my father he liked me to make *me* king over all Ĭs'ra-el:

5 [m]And of all my sons, (for the LORD hath given me many sons,) [n]he hath chosen Sŏl'o-mon my son to sit upon the throne of the kingdom of the LORD over Ĭs'ra-el.

6 And he said unto me, [o]Sŏl'o-mon thy son, he shall build my house and my courts: for I have chosen him *to be* my son, and I will be his father.

7 Moreover I will establish his kingdom for ever, [p]if he be [5]constant to do my commandments and my judgments, as at this day.

8 Now therefore in the sight of all Ĭs'ra-el the congregation of the LORD, and in the audience of our God, [q]keep and seek for all the commandments of the LORD your God: that ye may possess this good land, and leave *it* for an inheritance for your children after you for ever.

9 ¶ And thou, Sŏl'o-mon my son, [r]know thou the God of thy father, and serve him [s]with a perfect heart and with a willing mind: for [t]the LORD searcheth all hearts, and understandeth all the imaginations of the thoughts: [u]if thou seek him, he will be found of

13 [j]2 Sam. 23.28; ch. 11.30
14 [k]2 Sam. 23.30; ch. 11.31
15 [l]ch. 11.30, Heled
[m]Judg. 3.9
17 [n]ch. 26.30
18 [o]1 Sam. 16.6-Eliab
23 [p]Gen. 15.5; Ex. 32.13; Deut. 1.10; Deut. 10.22; Heb. 11.12
24 [q]2 Sam. 24.15; ch. 21.7
[2]ascended
27 [r]Song 8.11
[3]over that which was of the vineyards
32 [4]Or, nephew
[5]Or, secretary
[6]Or, Hachmonite

CHAPTER 28
1 [a]Josh. 23.2; ch. 23.2; ch. 27.16
[b]Ex. 18.25; ch. 27.1-15
[c]ch. 27.25
[1]Or, cattle
[2]Or, and his sons
[3]Or, eunuchs
[d]ch. 11.10
2 [e]Deut. 17.20; Heb. 2.11
[f]2 Sam. 7.2; Ps. 132.3
[g]Ps. 99.5
3 [h]2 Sam. 7.5; ch. 17.4
[4]bloods
4 [i]1 Sam. 16.7
[j]Gen. 49.8
[k]1 Sam. 16.1
[l]1 Sam. 16.12
5 [m]ch. 3.1; ch. 14.4-7
[n]ch. 22.9
6 [o]2 Chr. 1.9
7 [p]1 Ki. 9.4; ch. 22.13
[5]strong
8 [q]Deut. 4.1
9 [r]Ps. 9.10; Hos. 4.1
[s]2 Ki. 20.3; Ps. 101.2
[t]1 Sam. 16.7; Rev. 2.23
[u]2 Chr. 15.2; Matt. 7.7

thee; but if thou forsake him, he will
cast thee off for ever.
10 [v]Take heed now; for the LORD
hath chosen thee to build an house for
the sanctuary: be strong, and do *it*.
11 ¶ Then Dā'vid gave to Sŏl'o-mon
his son [w]the pattern of [x]the porch, and
of the houses thereof, and of the treasuries thereof, and of the upper chambers thereof, and of the inner parlours
thereof, and of the place of the mercy
seat,
12 And the pattern [6]of all that he
had by the spirit, of the courts of the
house of the LORD, and of all the chambers round about, [y]of the treasuries of
the house of God, and of the treasuries
of the dedicated things:
13 Also for the courses of the priests
and the Lē'vītes, and for all the work
of the service of the house of the LORD,
and for all the vessels of service in the
house of the LORD.
14 *He gave* of gold by weight for
things of gold, for all instruments of all
manner of service; *silver also* for all
instruments of silver by weight, for all
instruments of every kind of service:
15 Even the weight for the candlesticks of gold, and for their lamps of
gold, by weight for every candlestick,
and for the lamps thereof: and for the
candlesticks of silver by weight, *both*
for the candlestick, and *also* for the
lamps thereof, according to the use of
every candlestick.
16 And by weight *he gave* gold for
the tables of [z]shewbread, for every table; and *likewise* silver for the tables of
silver:
17 Also pure gold for the fleshhooks,
and the bowls, and the cups: and for the
golden basons *he gave gold* by weight
for every bason; and *likewise silver* by
weight for every bason of silver:
18 And for the altar of [a]incense refined gold by weight; and gold for the
pattern of the chariot of the [b]cheru-
bims, that spread out *their wings*, and
covered the ark of the covenant of the
LORD.
19 All *this, said Dā'vid,* [c]the LORD
made me understand in writing by *his*
hand upon me, *even* all the works of
this pattern.
20 And Dā'vid said to Sŏl'o-mon his
son, [d]Be strong and of good courage,
and do *it:* fear not, nor be dismayed: for
the LORD God, *even* my God, *will be*
with thee; [e]he will not fail thee, nor
forsake thee, until thou hast finished
all the work for the service of the house
of the LORD.
21 And, behold, [f]the courses of the
priests and the Lē'vītes, *even they shall*
be with thee for all the service of the
house of God: and *there shall be* with
thee for all manner of workmanship
[g]every willing skilful man, for any
manner of service: also the princes and
all the people *will be* wholly at thy commandment.
29 Furthermore Dā'vid the king said
unto all the congregation, Sŏl'o-
mon my son, whom alone God hath
chosen, *is yet* [a]young and tender, and
the work *is* great: for the palace *is* not
for man, but for the LORD God.
2 Now I have prepared with all my
might for the house of my God the gold
for *things to be made* of gold, and the
silver for *things* of silver, and the brass
for *things* of brass, the iron for *things*
of iron, and wood for *things* of wood;
[b]onyx stones, and *stones* to be set,
glistering stones, and of divers colours,
and all manner of precious stones, and
marble stones in abundance.
3 Moreover, because I have [c]set my
affection to the house of my God, I
have of mine [d]own proper good, of
gold and silver, *which* I have given to
the house of my God, over and above
all that I have prepared for the holy
house,
4 *Even* three thousand talents of
gold, of the gold of [e]Ō'phĭr, and seven
thousand talents of refined silver, to
overlay the walls of the houses *withal:*
5 The gold for *things* of gold, and
the silver for *things* of silver, and for
all manner of work *to be made* by the
hands of artificers. And who *then* is
willing [1]to consecrate his service this
day unto the LORD?
6 ¶ Then [f]the chief of the fathers and
princes of the tribes of Is'ra-el, and the
captains of thousands and of hundreds,
with [g]the rulers of the king's work, offered willingly,
7 And gave for the service of the
house of God of gold five thousand
talents and ten thousand drams, and
of silver ten thousand talents, and of
brass eighteen thousand talents, and
one hundred thousand talents of iron.
8 And they with whom *precious*
stones were found gave *them* to the
treasure of the house of the LORD, by
the hand of [h]Je-hī'el the Gĕr'shon-īte.
9 Then the people rejoiced, for that
they offered willingly, because with
perfect heart they [i]offered willingly to
the LORD: and Dā'vid the king also rejoiced with great joy.
10 ¶ Wherefore Dā'vid blessed the
LORD before all the congregation: and
Dā'vid said, [j]Blessed *be* thou, LORD
God of Is'ra-el our father, for ever and
ever.
11 [k]Thine, O LORD, *is* the greatness,
and the power, and the glory, and the
victory, and the majesty: for all *that is*
in the heaven and in the earth *is thine;*
thine *is* the kingdom, O LORD, and
thou art exalted as head above all.
12 [l]Both riches and honour *come* of
thee, and thou reignest over all; and in
thine hand *is* power and might; and in
thine hand *it is* to make great, and to
give strength unto all.
13 Now therefore, our God, we thank
thee, and praise thy glorious name.
14 But who *am* I, and what *is* my people, that we should [2]be able to offer so
willingly after this sort? for all things
come of thee, and [3]of thine own have
we given thee.
15 For [m]we *are* strangers before
thee, and sojourners, as *were* all our

10 [v]ch. 22.16; Prov. 4.23
11 [w]Ex. 25.40
[x]1 Ki. 6.2
12 [6]of all that was with him
[y]ch. 26.20
16 [z]Ex. 25.23; 1 Ki. 7.48; 2 Chr. 4.8
18 [a]Ex. 30.1
[b]Ex. 25.18; 1 Sam. 4.4; 1 Ki. 6.23; Ps. 18.10; Ps. 68.17; Ps. 80.1
19 [c]Ex. 25.40
20 [d]Deut. 31.7; Josh. 1.6-7; ch. 22.13
[e]Josh. 1.5; Heb. 13.5
21 [f]ch. 24; ch. 25
[g]Ex. 35.25
CHAPTER 29
1 [a]1 Ki. 3.7; ch. 22.5; Prov. 4.3
2 [b]Ex. 28.9; Isa. 54.11-12; Rev. 21.18
3 [c]Ps. 26.8; Ps. 27.4; Ps. 84.1
[d]Prov. 3.9
4 [e]1 Ki. 9.28; 2 Chr. 8.18
5 [1]to fill his hand
6 [f]ch. 27.1
[g]ch. 27.25
8 [h]ch. 26.21
9 [i]1 Ki. 8.61; 2 Cor. 9.7
10 [j]1 Ki. 8.15-16; 2 Chr. 6.4; Ps. 72.18
11 [k]Dan. 4.34-35; Matt. 6.13; 1 Tim. 1.17; Rev. 5.13
12 [l]Deut. 8.18; 1 Sam. 2.7-8; Ps. 75.6; Prov. 10.22; Rom. 11.36
14 [2]retain, or, obtain strength
[3]of thine hand
15 [m]Gen. 47.9; Ps. 39.12; Heb. 11.13; 1 Pet. 2.11

fathers: [n]our days on the earth *are* as a shadow, and *there is* none [4]abiding.

16 O LORD our God, all this store that we have prepared to build thee an house for thine holy name *cometh* of thine hand, and *is* all thine own.

17 I know also, my God, that thou [o]triest the heart, and [p]hast pleasure in uprightness. As for me, in the uprightness of mine heart I have willingly offered all these things: and now have I seen with joy thy people, which are [5]present here, to offer willingly unto thee.

18 O LORD God of Ā'bră-hăm, Ī'saac, and of Ĭs'ra-el, our fathers, keep this for ever in the imagination of the thoughts of the heart of thy people, and [6]prepare their heart unto thee:

19 And [q]give unto Sŏl'o-mon my son a perfect heart, to keep thy commandments, thy testimonies, and thy statutes, and to do all *these things*, and to build the palace, *for* the which [r]I have made provision.

20 ¶ And Dā'vid said to all the congregation, Now bless the LORD your God. And all the congregation blessed the LORD God of their fathers, and bowed down their heads, and worshipped the LORD, and the king.

21 And they sacrificed sacrifices unto the LORD, and offered burnt offerings unto the LORD, on the morrow after that day, *even* a thousand bullocks, a thousand rams, *and* a thousand lambs, with their drink offerings, and sacrifices in abundance for all Ĭs'ra-el:

[n]Job 14.2; Ps. 90.9; Ps. 102.11
[4]expectation
17 [o]Deut. 8.2; 1 Sam. 16.7; ch. 28.9; Ps. 7.9; Prov. 16.2; Jer. 17.10; Heb. 4.13
[p]Ps. 11.7; Prov. 11.20
[5]Or, found
18 [6]Or, stablish; Ps. 10.17; Jer. 10.23
19 [q]Ps. 72.1
[r]ch. 22.14
24 [7]gave the hand under Solomon; Gen. 24.2; Gen. 47.29; 2 Chr. 30.8; Ezek. 17.18
25 [s]2 Chr. 1.12; Eccl. 2.9; Dan. 5.18-19; Heb. 2.9
27 [t]2 Sam. 5.4; 1 Ki. 2.11
[u]2 Sam. 5.5
28 [v]Gen. 15.15; Num. 23.10
29 [8]words, or history
30 [w]Dan. 2.21

22 And did eat and drink before the LORD on that day with great gladness. And they made Sŏl'o-mon the son of Dā'vid king the second time, and anointed *him* unto the LORD *to be* the chief governor, and Zā'dŏk *to be* priest.

23 Then Sŏl'o-mon sat on the throne of the LORD as king instead of Dā'vid his father, and prospered; and all Ĭs'ra-el obeyed him.

24 And all the princes, and the mighty men, and all the sons likewise of king Dā'vid, [7]submitted themselves unto Sŏl'o-mon the king.

25 And the LORD magnified Sŏl'o-mon exceedingly in the sight of all Ĭs'ra-el, and [s]bestowed upon him *such* royal majesty as had not been on any king before him in Ĭs'ra-el.

26 ¶ Thus Dā'vid the son of Jĕs'se reigned over all Ĭs'ra-el.

27 [t]And the time that he reigned over Ĭs'ra-el *was* forty years; [u]seven years reigned he in Hē'bron, and thirty and three *years* reigned he in Je-ru̧'sa-lĕm.

28 And he [v]died in a good old age, full of days, riches, and honour: and Sŏl'o-mon his son reigned in his stead.

29 Now the acts of Dā'vid the king, first and last, behold, they *are* written in the [8]book of Săm'u-el the seer, and in the book of Nā'than the prophet, and in the book of Găd the seer,

30 With all his reign and his might, [w]and the times that went over him, and over Ĭs'ra-el, and over all the kingdoms of the countries.

THE SECOND BOOK OF THE

CHRONICLES

1 And [a]Sŏl'o-mon the son of Dā'vid was strengthened in his kingdom, and [b]the LORD his God *was* with him, and [c]magnified him exceedingly.

2 Then Sŏl'o-mon spake unto all Ĭs'ra-el, to [d]the captains of thousands and of hundreds, and to the judges, and to every governor in all Ĭs'ra-el, the chief of the fathers.

3 So Sŏl'o-mon, and all the congregation with him, went to the high place that *was* at [e]Gĭb'e-on; for there was the tabernacle of the congregation of God, which Mō'ses the servant of the LORD had made in the wilderness.

4 [f]But the ark of God had Dā'vid brought up from Kĭr'jath–jē'a-rĭm to *the place which* Dā'vid had prepared for it: for he had pitched a tent for it at Je-ru̧'sa-lĕm.

5 Moreover [g]the brasen altar, that [h]Be-zăl'ē-el the son of Ū'ri, the son of Hûr had made, [1]he put before the tabernacle of the LORD: and Sŏl'o-mon and the congregation sought unto it.

6 And Sŏl'o-mon went up thither to the brasen altar before the LORD,

CHAPTER 1
1 [a]1 Ki. 2.46
[b]Gen. 21.22; Matt. 28.20
[c]1 Chr. 29.25; Phil. 2.9-11
2 [d]1 Chr. 27.1; ch. 29.20
3 [e]1 Ki. 3.4
4 [f]2 Sam. 6.2; 1 Chr. 15.1
5 [g]Ex. 27.1
[h]Ex. 31.2
[1]Or, was there
6 [i]1 Ki. 3.4
7 [j]Prov. 3.5; Isa. 58.9
8 [k]1 Chr. 28.5
9 [l]1 Ki. 3.7
[2]much as the dust of the earth
10 [m]1 Ki. 3.9;
[n]Num. 27.17;
11 [o]1 Sam. 16.7;

which *was* at the tabernacle of the congregation, and offered a [i]thousand burnt offerings upon it.

7 ¶ [j]In that night did God appear unto Sŏl'o-mon, and said unto him, Ask what I shall give thee.

8 And Sŏl'o-mon said unto God, Thou hast shewed great mercy unto Dā'vid my father, and hast made me [k]to reign in his stead.

9 Now, O LORD God, let thy promise unto Dā'vid my father be established: [l]for thou hast made me king over a people [2]like the dust of the earth in multitude.

10 [m]Give me now wisdom and knowledge, that I may [n]go out and come in before this people: for who can judge this thy people, *that is so* great?

11 [o]And God said to Sŏl'o-mon, Because this was in thine heart, and thou hast not asked riches, wealth, or honour, nor the life of thine enemies, neither yet hast asked long life; but hast asked wisdom and knowledge for

thyself, that thou mayest judge my people, over whom I have made thee king:
12 Wisdom and knowledge [p]*is*
granted unto thee; and I will give thee
riches, and wealth, and honour, such
as [q]none of the kings have had that
have been before thee, neither shall
there any after thee have the like.
13 ¶ Then Sŏl'o-mon came *from his*
journey to the high place that *was* at
Gĭb'e-on to Je-rụ'sa-lĕm, from before
the tabernacle of the congregation, and
reigned over Ĭs'ra-el.
14 [r]And Sŏl'o-mon gathered chariots and horsemen: and he had a thousand and four hundred chariots, and
twelve thousand horsemen, which he
placed in the chariot cities, and with
the king at Je-rụ'sa-lĕm.
15 [s]And the king [3]made silver and
gold at Je-rụ'sa-lĕm *as plenteous* as
stones, and cedar trees made he as the
sycomore trees that *are* in the vale for
abundance.
16 [4]And Sŏl'o-mon had horses
brought out of Ē'ġypt, and linen yarn:
the king's merchants received the
linen yarn at a price.
17 And they fetched up, and brought
forth out of Ē'ġypt a chariot for six hundred *shekels* of siver, and an horse for
an hundred and fifty: and so brought
they out *horses* for all the kings of the
Hĭt'tītes, and for the kings of Sȳr'ĭ-ȧ,
[5]by their means.

2 And Sŏl'o-mon [a]determined to build
an house for the name of the LORD,
and an house for his kingdom.
2 And [b]Sŏl'o-mon told out threescore and ten thousand men to bear
burdens, and fourscore thousand to
hew in the mountain, and three thousand and six hundred to oversee them.
3 ¶ And Sŏl'o-mon sent to Hū'ram
the king of Tȳre, saying, [c]As thou
didst deal with Dā'vid my father, and
didst sent him cedars to build him an
house to dwell therein, *even so deal*
with me.
4 Behold, I build an house to the
name of the LORD my God, to dedicate
it to him, *and* [d]to burn before him
[1]sweet incense, and for [e]the continual
shewbread, and for [f]the burnt offerings morning and evening, on the sabbaths, and on the new moons, and on
the solemn feasts of the LORD our God.
This *is an ordinance* for ever to Ĭs'ra-el.
5 And the house which I build *is*
great: for [g]great *is* our God above all
gods.
6 [h]But who [2]is able to build him an
house, seeing the heaven and heaven
of heavens cannot contain him? who
am I then, that I should build him an
house, save only to burn sacrifice before him?
7 Send me now therefore a man cunning to work in gold, and in silver, and
in brass, and in iron, and in purple, and
crimson, and blue, and that can skill [3]to
grave with the cunning men that *are*
with me in Jū'dah and in Je-rụ'sa-lĕm,
[i]whom Dā'vid my father did provide.

8 [j]Send me also cedar trees, fir trees,
and [4]algum trees, out of Lĕb'a-non: for
I know that thy servants can skill to cut
timber in Lĕb'a-non; and, behold, my
servants *shall be* with thy servants,
9 Even to prepare me timber in abundance: for the house which I am about
to build *shall be* [5]wonderful great.
10 [k]And, behold, I will give to thy
servants, the hewers that cut timber,
twenty thousand measures of beaten
wheat, and twenty thousand measures
of barley, and twenty thousand baths
of wine, and twenty thousand baths of
oil.
11 ¶ Then Hū'ram the king of Tȳre
answered in writing, which he sent to
Sŏl'o-mon, [l]Because the LORD hath
loved his people, he hath made thee
king over them.
12 Hū'ram said moreover, [m]Blessed
be the LORD God of Ĭs'ra-el, [n]that made
heaven and earth, who hath given to
Dā'vid the king a wise son, [6]endued
with prudence and understanding, that
might build an house for the LORD, and
an house for his kingdom.
13 And now I have sent a cunning
man, endued with understanding, of
Hū'ram my father's,
14 [o]The son of a woman of the
daughters of Dăn, and his father *was* a
man of Tȳre, skilful to work in gold,
and in silver, in brass, in iron, in stone,
and in timber, in purple, in blue, and in
fine linen, and in crimson; also to
grave any manner of graving, and to
find out every device which shall be
put to him, with thy cunning men, and
with the cunning men of my lord Dā'-
vid thy father.
15 Now therefore the wheat, and the
barley, the oil, and the wine, which my
lord hath spoken of, let him send unto
his servants:
16 [p]And we will cut wood out of
Lĕb'a-non, [7]as much as thou shalt need:
and we will bring it to thee in floats by
sea to [8]Jŏp'pȧ; and thou shalt carry it
up to Je-rụ'sa-lĕm.
17 ¶ [q]And Sŏl'o-mon numbered all
[9]the strangers that *were* in the land of
Ĭs'ra-el, after the numbering wherewith [r]Dā'vid his father had numbered
them; and they were found an hundred
and fifty thousand and three thousand
and six hundred.
18 And he set threescore and ten
thousand of them *to be* bearers of burdens, and fourscore thousand *to be*
hewers in the mountain, and three
thousand and six hundred overseers to
set the people a work.

3 Then [a]Sŏl'o-mon began to build
the house of the LORD at [b]Je-rụ'sa-
lĕm in mount Mo-rī'ah, [1]where *the*
LORD appeared unto Dā'vid his father,
in the place that Dā'vid had prepared
in the threshingfloor of [2c]Ôr'nan the
Jĕb'u-site.
2 And he began to build in the second *day* of the second month, in the
fourth year of his reign.
3 ¶ Now these *are the things*
[d]*wherein* Sŏl'o-mon was [3]instructed

12 [p]Ps. 34.9-10; Eph. 3.20
[q]1 Chr. 29.25; Eccl. 2.9
14 [r]1 Ki. 4.26
15 [s]Job 22.24
[3]gave
16 [4]the going forth of the horses which was Solomon's
17 [5]by their hands

CHAPTER 2
1 [a]1 Ki. 5.5
2 [b]1 Ki. 5.15
3 [c]1 Chr. 14.1
4 [d]Ex. 30.7
[1]incense of spices
[e]Ex. 25.30; Matt. 12.4
[f]Ex. 29.38-42; Num. 28.3
5 [g]Ex. 15.11;
6 [h]ch. 6.18;
[2]hath retained, or, obtained strength
7 [3]to grave gravings
[i]1 Chr. 22.15
8 [j]1 Ki. 5.6
[4]Or, algummim, 1 Ki. 10.11
9 [5]great and wonderful
10 [k]1 Ki. 5.11
11 [l]Deut. 33.3
12 [m]1 Ki. 5.7
[n]Gen. 1;
[6]knowing prudence and understanding
14 [o]1 Ki. 7.13
16 [p]1 Ki. 5.8
[7]according to all thy need
[8]Japho, Josh. 19.46; Acts 9.36
17 [q]1 Ki. 5.13;
[9]the men the strangers
[r]1 Chr. 22.2

CHAPTER 3
1 [a]1 Ki. 6.1;
[b]Gen. 22.2
[1]Or, which was seen of David his father
[2]Or, Araunah
[c]1 Chr. 22.1
3 [d]1 Ki. 6.2
[3]founded

for the building of the house of God. The length by cubits after the first measure *was* threescore cubits, and the breadth twenty cubits.

4 And the [e]porch that *was* in the front *of the house,* the length *of it was* according to the breadth of the house, twenty cubits, and the height *was* an hundred and twenty: and he overlaid it within with pure gold.

5 And [f]the greater house he cieled with fir tree, which he overlaid with fine gold, and set thereon palm trees and chains.

6 And he [4]garnished the house with precious stones for beauty: and the gold *was* gold of Pär-vā'im.

7 He overlaid also the house, the beams, the posts, and the walls thereof, and the doors thereof, with gold; and graved cherubims on the walls.

8 And he made the [5]most holy house, the length whereof *was* according to the breadth of the house, twenty cubits, and the breadth thereof twenty cubits: and he overlaid it with fine gold, *amounting* to six hundred talents.

9 And the weight of the nails *was* fifty shekels of gold. And he overlaid the upper chambers with gold.

10 [g]And in the most holy house he made two cherubims [6]of image work, and overlaid them with gold.

11 ¶ And the wings of the cherubims *were* twenty cubits long: one wing *of the one cherub was* five cubits, reaching to the wall of the house: and the other wing *was likewise* five cubits, reaching to the wing of the other cherub.

12 And *one* wing of the other cherub *was* five cubits, reaching to the wall of the house: and the other wing *was* five cubits *also,* joining to the wing of the other cherub.

13 The wings of these cherubims spread themselves forth twenty cubits: and they stood on their feet, and their faces *were* [7]inward.

14 ¶ And he made the [h]vail *of* blue, and purple, and crimson, and fine linen, and [8]wrought cherubims thereon.

15 Also he made before the house [i]two pillars of thirty and five cubits [9]high, and the chapiter that *was* on the top of each of them *was* five cubits.

16 And he made chains, *as* in the oracle, and put *them* on the heads of the pillars; and made an hundred pomegranates, and put *them* on the chains.

17 And he reared up the pillars before the temple, one on the right hand, and the other on the left; and called the name of that on the right hand [10]Jă'chin, and the name of that on the left [11]Bō'ăz.

4 Moreover he made [a]an altar of brass, twenty cubits the length thereof, and twenty cubits the breadth thereof, and ten cubits the height thereof.

2 ¶ [b]Also he made a molten sea of ten cubits [1]from brim to brim, round in compass, and five cubits the height thereof; and a line of thirty cubits did compass it round about.

3 [c]And under it *was* the similitude of oxen, which did compass it round about: ten in a cubit, compassing the sea round about. Two rows of oxen *were* cast, when it was cast.

4 It stood upon twelve oxen, three looking toward the north, and three looking toward the west, and three looking toward the south, and three looking toward the east: and the sea *was set* above upon them, and all their hinder parts *were* inward.

5 And the thickness of it *was* an handbreadth, and the brim of it like the work of the brim of a cup, [2]with flowers of lilies; *and* it received and held [d]three thousand baths.

6 ¶ He made also [e]ten lavers, and put five on the right hand, and five on the left, to wash in them: [3]such things as they offered for the burnt offering they washed in them; [f]but the sea *was* for the priests to wash in.

7 And [g]he made ten candlesticks of gold according [h]to their form, and set *them* in the temple, five on the right hand, and five on the left.

8 He [i]made also ten tables, and placed *them* in the temple, five on the right side, and five on the left. And he made an hundred [4]basons of gold.

9 ¶ Furthermore [j]he made the court of the priests, and the great court, and doors for the court, and overlaid the doors of them with brass.

10 And [k]he set the sea on the right side of the east end, over against the south.

11 And [l]Hū'ram made the pots, and the shovels, and the [5]basons. And Hū'ram [6]finished the work that he was to make for king Sŏl'o-mon for the house of God;

12 *To wit,* the two pillars, and [m]the pommels, and the chapiters *which were* on the top of the two pillars, and the two wreaths to cover the two pommels of the chapiters which *were* on the top of the pillars;

13 And [n]four hundred pomegranates on the two wreaths; two rows of pomegranates on each wreath, to cover the two pommels of the chapiters which *were* [7]upon the pillars.

14 He made also [o]bases, and [8]lavers made he upon the bases;

15 One sea, and twelve oxen under it.

16 The pots also, and the shovels, and the fleshhooks, and all their instruments, did [p]Hū'ram his father make to king Sŏl'o-mon for the house of the LORD of [9]bright brass.

17 [q]In the plain of Jôr'dan did the king cast them, in the [10]clay ground between Sŭc'coth and Ze-rĕd'a-thah.

18 [r]Thus Sŏl'o-mon made all these vessels in great abundance: for the weight of the brass could not be found out.

19 ¶ And [s]Sŏl'o-mon made all the vessels that *were for* the house of God,

4 [e]1 Ki. 6.3
5 [f]1 Ki. 6.17
6 [4]covered
8 [5]house of holiness of holinesses, or, oracle
10 [g]1 Ki. 6.23 [6]Or, (as some think,) of moveable work
13 [7]Or, toward the house
14 [h]Ex. 26.31; Matt. 27.51; Heb. 9.3 [8]caused to ascend
15 [i]1 Ki. 7.15 [9]long
17 [10]That is, He shall establish [11]That is, In it is strength

CHAPTER 4
1 [a]Ex. 27.1; 1 Ki. 9.25; 2 Ki. 16.14
2 [b]Ex. 30.18 [1]from his brim to his brim
3 [c]1 Ki. 7.24
5 [2]Or, like a lily flower [d]1 Ki. 7.26
6 [e]1 Ki. 7.38 [3]the work of burnt offering [f]Heb. 9.9
7 [g]1 Ki. 7.49 [h]Ex. 25.31
8 [i]1 Ki. 7.48 [4]Or, bowls
9 [j]1 Ki. 6.36
10 [k]1 Ki. 7.39
11 [l]1 Ki. 7.40 [5]Or, bowls [6]finished to make
12 [m]1 Ki. 7.41
13 [n]Ex. 28.33-34; 1 Ki. 7.20; Song 4.13 [7]upon the face
14 [o]1 Ki. 7.27-43 [8]Or, caldrons
16 [p]1 Ki. 7.14-45 [9]made bright, or, scoured
17 [q]1 Ki. 7.46 [10]thicknesses of the ground
18 [r]1 Ki. 7.47
19 [s]1 Ki. 7.48-50; 2 Ki. 24.13; Jer. 28.3; Dan. 5.2-3

the golden altar also, and the tables whereon [t]the shewbread *was set;*

20 Moreover the candlesticks with their lamps, that they should burn [u]after the manner before the oracle, of pure gold;

21 And [v]the flowers, and the lamps, and the tongs, *made he of* gold, *and* that [11]perfect gold;

22 And the snuffers, and the [12]basons, and the spoons, and the censers, *of* pure gold: and the entry of the house, the inner doors thereof for the most holy *place*, and the doors of the house of the temple, *were of* [13]gold.

5 Thus [a]all the work that Sŏl′o-mon made for the house of the LORD was finished: and Sŏl′o-mon brought in *all* the things that Dā′vid his father had dedicated; and the silver, and the gold, and all the instruments, put he among the treasures of the house of God.

2 ¶ [b]Then Sŏl′o-mon assembled the elders of Ĭs′ra-el, and all the heads of the tribes, the chief of the fathers of the children of Ĭs′ra-el, unto Je-ru̦′sa-lĕm, to bring up the ark of the covenant of the LORD [c]out of the city of Dā′vid, which *is* Zī′ŏn.

3 [d]Wherefore all the men of Ĭs′ra-el assembled themselves unto the king [e]in the feast which *was* in the seventh month.

4 And all the elders of Ĭs′ra-el came; and the [f]Lē′vītes took up the ark.

5 And they brought up the ark, and the tabernacle of the congregation, and all the holy vessels that *were* in the tabernacle, these did the priests *and* the Lē′vītes bring up.

6 Also king Sŏl′o-mon, and all the congregation of Ĭs′ra-el that were assembled unto him before the ark, sacrificed sheep and oxen, which could not be told nor numbered for multitude.

7 And the priests brought in the ark of the covenant of the LORD unto his place, to the oracle of the house, into the most holy *place, even* under the wings of the cherubims:

8 For the cherubims spread forth *their* wings over the place of the ark, and the cherubims covered the ark and the staves thereof above.

9 And they drew out the staves *of the ark*, that the ends of the staves were seen from the ark before the oracle; but they were not seen without. And [1]there it is unto this day.

10 *There was* nothing in the ark save the two tables which Mō′ses [g]put *therein* at Hō′reb, [2]when the LORD made *a covenant* with the children of Ĭs′ra-el, when they came out of Ē′ġypt.

b11 ¶ And it came to pass, when the priests were come out of the holy *place:* (for all the priests *that were* [3]present were sanctified, *and* did not *then* wait by course:

12 [h]Also the Lē′vītes *which were* the singers, all of them of Ā′saph, of Hē′man, of Jĕd′u̦-thŭn, with their sons and their brethren, *being* arrayed in white linen, having cymbals and psalteries and harps, stood at the east end of the altar, and [i]with them an hundred and twenty priests sounding with trumpets:)

13 It came even to pass, as the trumpeters and singers *were* as one, to make one sound to be heard in praising and thanking the LORD; and when they lifted up *their* voice with the trumpets and cymbals and instruments of musick, and praised the LORD, *saying,* [j]For *he is* good; for his mercy *endureth* for ever: that *then* the house was filled with a cloud, *even* the house of the LORD;

14 So that the priests could not stand to minister by reason of the cloud: [k]for the glory of the LORD had filled the house of God.

6 Then [a]said Sŏl′o-mon, The LORD hath said that he would dwell in the [b]thick darkness.

2 But I have built an house of habitation for thee, and a place for thy dwelling for ever.

3 And the king turned his face, and blessed the whole congregation of Ĭs′ra-el: and all the congregation of Ĭs′ra-el stood.

4 And he said, Blessed *be* the LORD God of Ĭs′ra-el, who hath with his hands fulfilled *that* which he spake with his mouth to my father Dā′vid, saying,

5 Since the day that I brought forth my people out of the land of Ē′ġypt I chose no city among all the tribes of Ĭs′ra-el to build an house in, that my name might be there; neither chose I any man to be a ruler over my people Ĭs′ra-el:

6 [c]But I have chosen Je-ru̦′sa-lĕm, that my name might be there; and [d]have chosen Dā′vid to be over my people Ĭs′ra-el.

7 Now [e]it was in the heart of Dā′vid my father to build an house for the name of the LORD God of Ĭs′ra-el.

8 But the LORD said to Dā′vid my father, Forasmuch as it was in thine heart to build an house for my name, thou didst [f]well in that it was in thine heart:

9 Notwithstanding thou shalt not build the house; but thy son which shall come forth out of thy loins, he shall build the house for my name.

10 The LORD therefore hath performed his word that he hath spoken: for I am risen up in the room of Dā′vid my father, and am set on the throne of Ĭs′ra-el, as the LORD promised, and have built the house for the name of the LORD God of Ĭs′ra-el.

11 And in it have I put the ark, [g]wherein *is* the covenant of the LORD, that he made with the children of Ĭs′ra-el.

12 ¶ [h]And he stood before the altar of the LORD in the presence of all the congregation of Ĭs′ra-el, and [i]spread forth his hands:

13 For Sŏl′o-mon had made a brasen scaffold, of five cubits [1]long, and five cubits broad, and three cubits high, and had set it in the midst of the court:

[t]Ex. 25.30; 1 Chr. 28.16
20 [u]Ex. 27.20-21
21 [v]Ex. 25.31 [11]perfections of gold
22 [12]Or, bowls [13]That is, overlaid with gold

CHAPTER 5
1 [a]1 Ki. 7.51; 1 Chr. 22.14
2 [b]1 Ki. 8.1; 1 Chr. 29.1; ch. 1.2
[c]2 Sam. 6.12
3 [d]1 Ki. 8.2
[e]ch. 7.8-9-10
4 [f]Josh. 3.6
9 [1]Or, they are there, as 1 Ki. 8.8
10 [g]Deut. 10.2; ch. 6.11 [2]Or, where
11 [3]found
12 [h]1 Chr. 15.16-22; ch. 29.25
[i]1 Chr. 15.24
13 [j]1 Chr. 16.34-41; ch. 7.3; Ps. 136.1-26
14 [k]Ex. 40.35; ch. 7.2; Isa. 6.4; Hag. 2.7; 2 Cor. 3.11; Rev. 15.8

CHAPTER 6
1 [a]1 Ki. 8.12
[b]Ex. 20.21; Lev. 16.2; Ps. 18.8-11; Heb. 12.18
6 [c]ch. 12.13; Ps. 48.1
[d]1 Sam. 16.1; 1 Chr. 28.4; Ps. 89.19-20
7 [e]2 Sam. 7.2; 1 Ki. 5.3; 1 Chr. 17.1
8 [f]1 Ki. 8.18-21; 2 Cor. 8.12
11 [g]Ex. 40.20; ch. 5.10
12 [h]1 Ki. 8.22
[i]Ezra 9.5; 1 Tim. 2.8
13 [1]the length thereof, etc

and upon it he stood, and kneeled
down upon his knees before all the congregation of Ĭs′ra-el, and spread forth
his hands toward heaven,
14 And said, O LORD God of Ĭs′ra-el,
[j]*there is* no God like thee in the heaven,
nor in the earth; which [k]keepest covenant, and *shewest* mercy unto thy servants, that [l]walk before thee with all
their hearts:
15 [m]Thou which hast kept with thy
servant Dā′vid my father that which
thou hast promised him; and spakest
with thy mouth, and hast fulfilled *it*
with thine hand, as *it is* this day.
16 Now therefore, O LORD God of
Ĭs′ra-el, keep with thy servant Dā′vid
my father that which thou hast promised him, saying, [2]There shall not fail
thee a man in my sight to sit upon the
throne of Ĭs′ra-el; [n]yet so that thy children take heed to their way to walk in
my law, as thou hast walked before
me.
17 Now then, O LORD God of Ĭs′ra-
el, let thy word be verified, which thou
hast spoken unto thy servant Dā′vid.
18 But [o]will God in very deed dwell
with men on the earth? [p]behold,
heaven and the heaven of heavens cannot contain thee; how much less this
house which I have built!
19 Have respect therefore to the
prayer of thy servant, and to his supplication, O LORD my God, to hearken
unto the cry and the prayer which thy
servant prayeth before thee:
20 That thine [q]eyes may be open
upon this house day and night, upon
the place whereof thou hast said that
thou wouldest put thy name there; to
hearken unto the prayer which thy servant [r]prayeth [3]toward this place.
21 Hearken therefore unto the supplications of thy servant, and of thy
people Ĭs′ra-el, which they shall [4]make
toward this place: hear thou from thy
dwelling place, *even* from heaven; and
when thou hearest, [s]forgive.
22 ¶ If a man sin against his neighbour, [5]and an oath be laid upon him to
make him swear, and the oath come
before thine altar in this house;
23 Then hear thou from heaven, and
do, and judge thy servants, by [t]requit-
ing the wicked, by recompensing his
way upon his own head; and by justifying the righteous, by giving him according to his righteousness.
24 ¶ And if thy people Ĭs′ra-el [6]be
put to the worse before the enemy, because [u]they have sinned against thee;
and shall return and confess thy name,
and pray and make supplication before thee [7]in this house;
25 Then hear thou from the heavens, and forgive the sin of thy people
Ĭs′ra-el, and bring them again unto the
land which thou gavest to them and to
their fathers.
26 ¶ When the [v]heaven is shut up,
and there is no rain, because they have
sinned against thee; *yet* if they pray toward this place, and confess thy name,
and turn from their sin, when thou dost
afflict them;
27 Then hear thou from heaven, and
forgive the sin of thy servants, and of
thy people Ĭs′ra-el, [w]when thou hast
taught them the good way, wherein
they should walk; and [x]send rain upon
thy land, which thou hast given unto
thy people for an inheritance.
28 ¶ If there [y]be dearth in the land, if
there be pestilence, if there be blasting,
or mildew, locusts, or caterpillers; if
their enemies besiege them [8]in the cities of their land; whatsoever sore or
whatsoever sickness *there be:*
29 *Then* what prayer *or* what supplication soever shall be made of any
man, or of all thy people Ĭs′ra-el, when
every one shall know his own sore and
his own grief, and shall spread forth
his hands [9]in this house:
30 Then hear thou from heaven thy
dwelling place, and forgive, and render unto every man according unto all
his ways, whose heart thou knowest;
(for thou only [z]knowest the hearts of
the children of men:)
31 That they may fear thee, to walk
in thy ways, [10]so long as they live [11]in
the land which thou gavest unto our
fathers.
32 ¶ Moreover concerning the
stranger, [a]which is not of thy people
Ĭs′ra-el, but is come from a far country
for thy great name's sake, and thy
mighty hand, and thy stretched out
arm; if they come and pray in this
house;
33 Then hear thou from the heavens, *even* from thy dwelling place, and
do according to all that the stranger
calleth to thee for; that all people of the
earth may know thy name, and fear
thee, as *doth* thy people Ĭs′ra-el, and
may know that [12]this house which I
have built is called by thy name.
34 If thy people go out to war against
their enemies by the way that thou
shalt send them, and they pray unto
thee toward this city which thou hast
chosen, and the house which I have
built for thy name;
35 Then hear thou from the heavens
their prayer and their supplication,
and maintain their [13]cause.
36 If they sin against thee, (for *there
is* [b]no man which sinneth not,) and
thou be angry with them, and deliver
them over before *their* enemies, and
[14]they carry them away captives unto a
land far off or near;
37 Yet *if* they [15]bethink themselves
in the land whither they are carried
captive, and turn and pray unto thee in
the land of their captivity, saying, We
have sinned, we have done amiss, and
have dealt wickedly;
38 If they return to thee [c]with all
their heart and with all their soul in the
land of their captivity, whither they
have carried them captives, and pray
toward their land, which thou gavest
unto their fathers, and *toward* the city
which thou hast chosen, and toward

14 [j]Ex. 15.11; Deut. 4.39; Ps. 86.8
[k]Dan. 9.4
[l]Gen. 5.24
15 [m]1 Chr. 22.9-10
16 [2]There shall not a man be cut off
[n]Ps. 132.12
18 [o]Ps. 113.5-6
[p]ch. 2.6; Acts 7.49
20 [q]Ps. 33.18; Ps. 34.15
[r]Dan. 6.10
[3]Or, in this place
21 [4]pray
[s]Isa. 43.25; Isa. 44.22
22 [5]and he require an oath of him
23 [t]Prov. 1.31; Rom. 2.8
24 [6]Or, be smitten
[u]Deut. 32.15; Ps. 51.4
[7]Or, toward
26 [v]Lev. 26.19; Luke 4.25
27 [w]Ps. 94.12; John 6.45
[x]Zech. 10.1
28 [y]ch. 20.9
[8]in the land of their gates
29 [9]Or, toward this house
30 [z]1 Chr. 28.9; Ps. 11.4
31 [10]all the days which
[11]upon the face of the land
32 [a]Deut. 4.6-7-8; Acts 8.27
33 [12]thy name is called upon this house
35 [13]Or, right
36 [b]Job 15.14-16; Eccl. 7.20
[14]they that take them captives carry them away
37 [15]bring back to their heart
38 [c]Jer. 29.12-13

the house which I have built for thy
name:
39 Then hear thou from the heavens, *even* from thy dwelling place,
their prayer and their supplications,
and maintain their [16]cause, and forgive
thy people which have sinned against
thee.
40 Now, my God, let, I beseech thee,
thine eyes be open, and *let* thine ears
be attent [17]unto the prayer *that is*
made in this place.
41 Now [d]therefore arise, O LORD
God, into thy [e]resting place, thou, and
the ark of thy strength: let thy priests,
O LORD God, be [f]clothed with salvation, and let thy saints [g]rejoice in
goodness.
42 O LORD God, turn not away the
face of thine anointed: [h]remember the
mercies of Dā'vid thy servant.
7 Now [a]when Sŏl'o-mon had made
an end of praying, the [b]fire came
down from heaven, and consumed the
burnt offering and the sacrifices; and
[c]the glory of the LORD filled the house.
2 [d]And the priests could not enter
into the house of the LORD, because the
glory of the LORD had filled the LORD'S
house.
3 And when all the children of Ĭs'-
ra-el saw how the fire came down,
and the glory of the LORD upon the
house, they bowed themselves with
their faces to the ground upon the pavement, and worshipped, and praised the
LORD, [e]*saying*, For *he is* good; [f]for his
mercy *endureth* for ever.
4 ¶ [g]Then the king and all the people offered sacrifices before the LORD.
5 And king Sŏl'o-mon offered a sacrifice of twenty and two thousand oxen,
and an hundred and twenty thousand
sheep: so the king and all the people
dedicated the house of God.
6 [h]And the priests waited on their offices: the Lē'vītes also with instruments
of musick of the LORD, which Dā'vid
the king had made to praise the LORD,
because his mercy *endureth* for ever,
when Dā'vid praised [1]by their ministry;
and the [i]priests sounded trumpets before them, and all Ĭs'ra-el stood.
7 Moreover [j]Sŏl'o-mon hallowed the
middle of the court that *was* before the
house of the LORD: for there he offered burnt offerings, and the fat of the
peace offerings, because the brasen altar which Sŏl'o-mon had made was not
able to receive the burnt offerings, and
the meat offerings, and the fat.
8 ¶ [k]Also at the same time Sŏl'o-
mon kept the feast seven days, and all
Ĭs'ra-el with him, a very great congregation, from the entering in of Hā'-
math unto [l]the river of Ē'gypt.
9 And in the eighth day they made
[2]a solemn assembly: for they kept the
dedication of the altar seven days, and
the feast seven days.
10 And [m]on the three and twentieth
day of the seventh month he sent the
people away into their tents, glad and
merry in heart for the goodness that the
LORD had shewed unto Dā'vid, and to
Sŏl'o-mon, and to Ĭs'ra-el his people.
11 Thus [n]Sŏl'o-mon finished the
house of the LORD, and the king's
house: and all that came into Sŏl'o-
mon's heart to make in the house of
the LORD, and in his own house, he
prosperously effected.
12 ¶ And the LORD [o]appeared to
Sŏl'o-mon by night, and said unto him,
I have heard thy prayer, [p]and have
chosen this place to myself for an
house of sacrifice.
13 [q]If I shut up heaven that there be
no rain, or if I command the locusts to
devour the land, or if I send pestilence
among my people;
14 If my people, [3]which are called by
my name, shall [r]humble themselves,
and pray, and seek my face, and turn
from their wicked ways; [s]then will
I hear from heaven, and will forgive
their sin, and will heal their land.
15 Now [t]mine eyes shall be open,
and mine ears attent [4]unto the prayer
that is made in this place.
16 For now have [u]I chosen and sanctified this house, that my name may be
there for ever: and mine eyes and mine
heart shall be there perpetually.
17 [v]And as for thee, if thou wilt
walk before me, as Dā'vid thy father
walked, and do according to all that I
have commanded thee, and shalt observe my statutes and my judgments;
18 Then will I stablish the throne of
thy kingdom, according as I have covenanted with Dā'vid thy father, saying,
[5]There shall not fail thee a man *to be*
ruler in Ĭs'ra-el.
19 [w]But if ye turn away, and forsake
my statutes and my commandments,
which I have set before you, and shall
go and serve other gods, and worship
them;
20 Then will I [x]pluck them up by
the roots out of my land which I have
given them; and this house, which I
have sanctified for my name, will I
cast out of my sight, and will make it
to be a proverb and a byword among
all nations.
21 And [y]this house, which is high,
shall be an astonishment to every one
that passeth by it; so that he shall say,
[z]Why hath the LORD done thus unto
this land, and unto this house?
22 And it shall be answered, Because they [a]forsook the LORD God of
their fathers, which brought them forth
out of the land of Ē'gypt, and laid hold
on other gods, and worshipped them,
and served them: therefore [b]hath he
brought all this evil upon them.
8 And [a]it came to pass at the end of
twenty years, wherein Sŏl'o-mon
had built the house of the LORD, and
his own house,
2 That the cities which Hū'ram had
restored to Sŏl'o-mon, Sŏl'o-mon built
them, and caused the children of Ĭs'ra-
el to dwell there.
3 And Sŏl'o-mon went to [b]Hā'math–
zō'bah, and prevailed against it.

39 [16]Or, right
40 [17]to the prayer of this place
41 [d]Ps. 132.8-9-10-16
[e]1 Chr. 28.2
[f]Isa. 61.10
[g]Neh. 9.25
42 [h]Ps. 89.20-28; Isa. 55.3

CHAPTER 7
1 [a]1 Ki. 8.54; Isa. 65.24; Dan. 9.20; Acts 4.31
[b]Gen. 15.17; Lev. 9.24; Judg. 6.21; 1 Ki. 18.38; 1 Chr. 21.26
[c]Lev. 9.23; ch. 5.13; Ezek. 10.3; Rev. 21.23
2 [d]ch. 5.14
3 [e]ch. 5.13; Ps. 103.17; Ps. 136.1
[f]ch. 20.21
4 [g]1 Ki. 8.62
6 [h]1 Chr. 15.16
[1]by their hand
[i]ch. 5.12
7 [j]Num. 16.37; ch. 36.14; Heb. 13.10-12
8 [k]1 Ki. 8.65
[l]Gen. 15.18
9 [2]a restraint
10 [m]1 Ki. 8.66
11 [n]1 Ki. 9.1
12 [o]Gen. 12.7
[p]Deut. 12.5; Ps. 78.68-69
13 [q]ch. 6.26
14 [3]upon whom my name is called
[r]Jas. 4.10
[s]ch. 6.27
15 [t]ch. 6.40
[4]to the prayer of this place
16 [u]ch. 6.6
17 [v]1 Ki. 9.4
18 [5]There shall not be cut off to thee
19 [w]Lev. 26.14; Deut. 28.15
20 [x]Ps. 5.5
21 [y]Jer. 7.14; Lam. 2.15
[z]Deut. 29.24
22 [a]Judg. 2.13
[b]2 Ki. 17.18; Dan. 9.12

CHAPTER 8
1 [a]1 Ki. 9.10
3 [b]2 Sam. 8.3

4 [c]And he built Tăd'môr in the wilderness, and all the store cities, which
he built in Hā'math.
5 Also he built Bĕth–hō'rŏn the upper, and Bĕth–hō'rŏn the nether, fenced
cities, with walls, gates, and bars;
6 And [d]Bā'al-ath, and all the store
cities that Sŏl'o-mon had, and all the
chariot cities, and the cities of the
horsemen, and [1]all that Sŏl'o-mon desired to build in Je-ru'sa-lĕm, and in
Lĕb'a-non, and throughout all the land
of his dominion.
7 ¶ [e]*As for* all the people *that were*
left of the [f]Hĭt'tītes, and the Ăm'ôr-
ītes, and the Pĕr'ĭz-zītes, and the Hī'-
vītes, and the Jĕb'u-sītes, which *were*
not of Ĭs'ra-el,
8 *But* of their children, who were left
after them in the land, whom the children of Ĭs'ra-el consumed not, them did
Sŏl'o-mon make to pay tribute until
this day.
9 [g]But of the children of Ĭs'ra-el did
Sŏl'o-mon make no servants for his
work; but they *were* men of war, and
chief of his captains, and captains of
his chariots and horsemen.
10 And these *were* the chief of king
Sŏl'o-mon's officers, *even* [h]two hundred and fifty, that bare rule over the
people.
11 ¶ And Sŏl'o-mon [i]brought up the
daughter of Phā'raŏh out of the city of
Dā'vid unto the house that he had built
for her: for he said, My wife shall not
dwell in the house of Dā'vid king of
Ĭs'ra-el, because *the places are* [2]holy,
whereunto the ark of the LORD hath
come.
12 ¶ Then Sŏl'o-mon offered burnt
offerings unto the LORD on the altar of
the LORD, which he had built before
the porch,
13 Even after a certain rate [j]every
day, offering according to the commandment of Mō'ses, on the sabbaths,
and on the new moons, and on the solemn feasts, [k]three times in the year,
even in the feast of unleavened bread,
and in the feast of weeks, and in the
feast of tabernacles.
14 ¶ And he appointed, according to
the order of Dā'vid his father, the
[l]courses of the priests to their service,
and [m]the Lē'vītes to their charges, to
praise and minister before the priests,
as the duty of every day required: the
[n]porters also by their courses at every
gate: for [3]so had Dā'vid the man of
God commanded.
15 And they departed not from the
commandment of the king unto the
priests and Lē'vītes concerning any
matter, or concerning the treasures.
16 Now all the work of Sŏl'o-mon
was prepared unto the day of the foundation of the house of the LORD, and
until it was finished. *So* the house of
the LORD was perfected.
17 ¶ Then went Sŏl'o-mon to [o]Ē'zĭ-
on–gē'bĕr, and to [p]Ē'lŏth, at the sea
side in the land of Ē'dom.
18 [q]And Hū'ram sent him by the
hands of his servants ships, and servants that had knowledge of the sea;
and they went with the servants of
Sŏl'o-mon to [r]Ō'phĭr, and took thence
four hundred and fifty talents of gold,
and brought *them* to king Sŏl'o-mon.

9 And [a]when the queen of Shē'bȧ
heard of the fame of Sŏl'o-mon, she
came to [b]prove Sŏl'o-mon with hard
questions at Je-ru'sa-lĕm, with a very
great company, and camels that bare
spices, and gold in abundance, and precious stones: and when she was come
to Sŏl'o-mon, she communed with him
of all that was in her heart.
2 And Sŏl'o-mon told her all her
[1]questions: and there was nothing hid
from Sŏl'o-mon which he told her not.
3 And when the queen of Shē'bȧ
had seen the wisdom of Sŏl'o-mon,
and the house that he had built,
4 And the meat of his table, and the
sitting of his servants, and the attendance of his ministers, and their apparel; his [2]cupbearers also, and their
apparel; and his ascent by which he
went up into the house of the LORD;
there was no more spirit in her.
5 And she said to the king, *It was* a
true [3]report which I heard in mine own
land of thine [4]acts, and of thy wisdom:
6 Howbeit I believed not their words,
until I came, and mine eyes had seen *it*:
and, behold, the one half of the greatness of thy wisdom was not told me: *for*
thou [5]exceedest the fame that I heard.
7 Happy *are* thy men, and happy *are*
these thy servants, which stand continually before thee, and hear thy wisdom.
8 [c]Blessed be the LORD thy God,
which delighted in thee to set thee on
his throne, *to be* king for the LORD thy
God: because thy God loved Ĭs'ra-el, to
establish them for ever, therefore made
he thee king over them, to do judgment
and justice.
9 And she gave the king an hundred
and twenty talents of gold, and of
spices great abundance, and precious
stones: neither was there any such
spice as the queen of Shē'bȧ gave king
Sŏl'o-mon.
10 And the servants also of Hū'ram,
and the servants of Sŏl'o-mon, [d]which
brought gold from Ō'phĭr, brought [e]al-
gum trees and precious stones.
11 And the king made *of* the algum
trees [6]terraces to the house of the
LORD, and to the king's palace, and
harps and psalteries for singers: and
there were none such seen before in
the land of Jū'dah.
12 And king Sŏl'o-mon gave to the
queen of Shē'bȧ all her desire, whatsoever she asked, beside *that* which she
had brought unto the king. So she
turned, and went away to her own
land, she and her servants.
13 ¶ Now the weight of gold that
came to Sŏl'o-mon in one year was six
hundred and threescore and six talents
of gold;
14 Beside *that which* chapmen and
merchants brought. And all [f]the kings
of A-rā'bĭ-ȧ and [7]governors of the

4 [c]1 Ki. 9.17
6 [d]Josh. 15.11
[1]all the desire of Solomon which he desired to build
7 [e]1 Ki. 9.20
[f]Gen. 10.16; Deut. 7.1
9 [g]Ex. 19.5; Deut. 23.19; Lev. 25.39; Gal. 4.28-31
10 [h]1 Ki. 5.16; ch. 2.18
11 [i]1 Ki. 3.1
[2]holiness
13 [j]Ex. 29.38; Num. 28.3-9-11-26
[k]Ex. 23.14; Deut. 16.16
14 [l]1 Chr. 24.1; ch. 5.11; Luke 1.5-8
[m]1 Chr. 25.1
[n]1 Chr. 9.17
[3]so was the commandment of David the man of God
17 [o]1 Ki. 9.26
[p]Deut. 2.8; 2 Ki. 14.22-Elath
18 [q]1 Ki. 9.27; ch. 9.10-13
[r]Gen. 10.29; Job 22.24; Isa. 13.12

CHAPTER 9
1 [a]1 Ki. 10.1; Matt. 12.42; Luke 11.31
[b]Ps. 49.4; Ps. 78.2; Prov. 1.5; Ezek. 20.49; Matt. 13.11-35
2 [1]words
4 [2]Or, butlers
5 [3]word
[4]Or, sayings
6 [5]hast added to
8 [c]Ps. 72.18-19
10 [d]1 Ki. 5.2-6; 1 Ki. 9.27-28; ch. 8.18; Ps. 72.10
[e]1 Ki. 10.11-almug trees
11 [6]highways, or, stairs
14 [f]Ps. 68.29; Ps. 72.10; Isa. 45.14; Isa. 60.6; Jer. 25.24
[7]Or, captains

country brought gold and silver to Sŏl′o-mon.
15 ¶ And king Sŏl′o-mon made two hundred targets *of* beaten gold: six hundred *shekels* of beaten gold went to one target.
16 And three hundred shields *made he of* beaten gold: three hundred *shekels* of gold went to one shield. And the king put them in the house of the forest of Lĕb′a-non.
17 Moreover the king made a great throne of ivory, and overlaid it with pure gold.
18 And *there were* six steps to the throne, with a footstool of gold, *which were* fastened to the throne, and [8]stays on each side of the sitting place, and two lions standing by the stays:
19 And twelve lions stood there on the one side and on the other upon the six steps. There was not the like made in any kingdom.
20 ¶ And all the drinking vessels of king Sŏl′o-mon *were of* gold, and all the vessels of the house of the forest of Lĕb′a-non *were of* [9]pure gold: [10]none *were of* silver; it was *not* any thing accounted of in the days of Sŏl′o-mon.
21 For the king's ships went to [g]Tär′shish with the servants of Hū′ram: every three years once came the ships of Tär′shish bringing gold, and silver, [11]ivory, and apes, and peacocks.
22 And king Sŏl′o-mon [h]passed all the kings of the earth in riches and wisdom.
23 ¶ And all the kings of the earth sought the presence of Sŏl′o-mon, to hear his wisdom, that God had put in his heart.
24 [i]And they brought every man his present, vessels of silver, and vessels of gold, and raiment, harness, and spices, horses, and mules, a rate year by year.
25 ¶ And Sŏl′o-mon [j]had four thousand stalls for horses and chariots, and twelve thousand horsemen; whom he bestowed in the chariot cities, and with the king at Je-ru̱′sa-lĕm.
26 ¶ [k]And he reigned over all the kings [l]from the [12]river even unto the land of the Phĭ-lĭs′tīnes, and to the border of Ē′ġypt.
27 [m]And the king [13]made silver in Je-ru̱′sa-lĕm as stones, and cedar trees made he as the sycomore trees that *are* in the low plains in abundance.
28 [n]And they brought unto Sŏl′o-mon horses out of Ē′ġypt, and out of all lands.
29 ¶ [o]Now the rest of the acts of Sŏl′o-mon, first and last, *are* they not written in the [14]book of Nā′than the prophet, and in the prophecy of [p]A-hī′jah the Shī′lo-nīte, and in the visions of [q]Ĭd′dō the seer against Jĕr-o-bō′am the son of Nē′băt?
30 [r]And Sŏl′o-mon reigned in Je-ru̱′sa-lĕm over all Ĭs′ra-el forty years.
31 And Sŏl′o-mon slept with his fathers, and he was buried in the city of Dā′vid his father: and [15]Rē-ho-bō′am his son reigned in his stead.

18 [8]hands
20 [9]shut up
[10]Or, there was no silver in them
21 [g]1 Ki. 10.22; Ps. 48.7; Ps. 72.10; Isa. 2.16; Isa. 23.6-14; Jon. 1.3
[11]Or, elephants' teeth
22 [h]1 Ki. 3.12-13; Ps. 89.27; Matt. 12.42; Col. 2.2-3
24 [i]Ps. 72.10-15
25 [j]1 Ki. 4.26; ch. 1.14
26 [k]1 Ki. 4.21
[l]Gen. 15.18; Ps. 72.8
[12]That is, Euphrates
27 [m]1 Ki. 10.27; ch. 1.15
[13]gave
28 [n]Deut. 17.16; 1 Ki. 4.26; ch. 1.16; Isa. 2.7; Isa. 31.1
29 [o]1 Ki. 11.41
[14]words
[p]1 Ki. 11.29
[q]ch. 12.15
30 [r]1 Ki. 11.42-43
31 [15]That is, Enlarger of the people

CHAPTER 10

1 [a]1 Ki. 12.1
2 [b]1 Ki. 11.40
4 [c]1 Sam. 8.11-18; 1 Ki. 4.7; Matt. 23.4; 1 John 5.3
6 [d]Job 8.8-9; Job 32.7
7 [1]for good
[e]Prov. 15.1
8 [f]2 Sam. 17.14; ch. 25.16; Prov. 1.25; Prov. 13.20; Eccl. 10.2
11 [2]laded
13 [g]Prov. 12.13; Prov. 14.16
15 [h]1 Sam. 2.25; 1 Ki. 12.15
[i]1 Ki. 11.29

10 And [a]Rē-ho-bō′am went to Shē′chem: for to Shē′chem were all Ĭs′ra-el come to make him king.
2 And it came to pass, when Jĕr-o-bō′am the son of Nē′băt, who *was* in Ē′ġypt, [b]whither he had fled from the presence of Sŏl′o-mon the king, heard *it*, that Jĕr-o-bō′am returned out of Ē′ġypt.
3 And they sent and called him. So Jĕr-o-bō′am and all Ĭs′ra-el came and spake to Rē-ho-bō′am, saying,
4 Thy father made our yoke [c]grievous: now therefore ease thou somewhat the grievous servitude of thy father, and his heavy yoke that he put upon us, and we will serve thee.
5 And he said unto them, Come again unto me after three days. And the people departed.
6 ¶ And king Rē-ho-bō′am took counsel with the [d]old men that had stood before Sŏl′o-mon his father while he yet lived, saying, What counsel give ye *me* to return answer to this people?
7 And they spake unto him, saying, If thou be [1]kind to this people, and please them, [e]and speak good words to them, they will be thy servants for ever.
8 But he [f]forsook the counsel which the old men gave him, and took counsel with the young men that were brought up with him, that stood before him.
9 And he said unto them, What advice give ye that we may return answer to this people, which have spoken to me, saying, Ease somewhat the yoke that thy father did put upon us?
10 And the young men that were brought up with him spake unto him, saying, Thus shalt thou answer the people that spake unto thee, saying, Thy father made our yoke heavy, but make thou *it* somewhat lighter for us; thus shalt thou say unto them, My little *finger* shall be thicker than my father's loins.
11 For whereas my father [2]put a heavy yoke upon you, I will put more to your yoke: my father chastised you with whips, but I *will chastise you* with scorpions.
12 So Jĕr-o-bō′am and all the people came to Rē-ho-bō′am on the third day, as the king bade, saying, Come again to me on the third day.
13 And the king [g]answered them roughly; and king Rē-ho-bō′am forsook the counsel of the old men,
14 And answered them after the advice of the young men, saying, My father made your yoke heavy, but I will add thereto: my father chastised you with whips, but I *will chastise you* with scorpions.
15 So the king hearkened not unto the people: [h]for the cause was of God, that the LORD might perform his word, which he spake by the [i]hand of A-hī′jah the Shī′lo-nīte to Jĕr-o-bō′am the son of Nē′băt.
16 ¶ And when all Ĭs′ra-el *saw* that the king would not hearken unto them,

the people answered the king, saying,
What portion have we in Dā'vid? and
we have none inheritance in the son of
Jĕs'se: every man to your tents, O
Ĭs'ra-el: *and* now, Dā'vid, see to thine
own house. So all Ĭs'ra-el went to their
tents.
17 But *as for* the children of Ĭs'ra-el
that dwelt in the cities of Jū'dah, Rē-
ho-bō'am reigned over them.
18 Then king Rē-ho-bō'am sent Ha-
dō'ram that was over the tribute; and
the children of Ĭs'ra-el stoned him with
stones, that he died. But king Rē-ho-
bō'am [3]made speed to get him up to *his*
chariot, to flee to Je-ru'sa-lĕm.
19 [i]And Ĭs'ra-el rebelled against the
house of Dā'vid unto this day.

11 And [a]when Rē-ho-bō'am was
come to Je-ru'sa-lĕm, he gathered of the house of Jū'dah and Bĕn'ja-
min an hundred and fourscore thousand chosen *men*, which were war-
riors, to fight against Ĭs'ra-el, that
he might bring the kingdom again to
Rē-ho-bō'am.
2 But the word of the LORD came [b]to
Shĕm-a-ī'ah the man of God, saying,
3 Speak unto Rē-ho-bō'am the son of
Sŏl'o-mon, king of Jū'dah, and to all Ĭs'-
ra-el in Jū'dah and Bĕn'ja-min, saying,
4 Thus saith the LORD, Ye shall not
go up, nor fight against your brethren:
return every man to his house: for this
thing is done of me. And they obeyed
the words of the LORD, and returned
from going against Jĕr-o-bō'am.
5 ¶ And Rē-ho-bō'am dwelt in Je-
ru'sa-lĕm, and built cities for defence
in Jū'dah.
6 He built even [c]Bĕth'–lĕ-hĕm, and
[d]Ē'tam, and [e]Te-kō'ȧ,
7 And Bĕth'–zûr, and Shō'cō, and
A-dŭl'lăm,
8 And Găth, and Ma-rē'shah, and
Zĭph,
9 And Ăd-ŏ-rā'ĭm, and Lā'chish, and
A-zē'kah,
10 And Zō'rah, and Ăij'a-lŏn, and
Hē'bron, which *are* in Jū'dah and in
Bĕn'ja-min fenced cities.
11 And he fortified the strong holds,
and put captains in them, and store of
victual, and of oil and wine.
12 And in every several city *he put*
shields and spears, and made them
exceeding strong, having Jū'dah and
Bĕn'ja-min on his side.
13 ¶ And the priests and the Lē'vītes
that *were* in all Ĭs'ra-el [1]resorted to him
out of all their coasts.
14 For the Lē'vītes left [f]their suburbs and their possession, and came to
Jū'dah and Je-ru'sa-lĕm: for [g]Jĕr-o-
bō'am and his sons had cast them off
from executing the priest's office unto
the LORD:
15 [h]And he ordained him priests for
the high places, and for [i]the devils,
and [j]for the calves which he had made.
16 [k]And after them out of all the
tribes of Ĭs'ra-el such as set their hearts
to seek the LORD God of Ĭs'ra-el came
to Je-ru'sa-lĕm, to sacrifice unto the
LORD God of their fathers.
17 So they [l]strengthened the kingdom of Jū'dah, and made Rē-ho-bō'am
the son of Sŏl'o-mon strong, three
years: for [m]three years they walked in
the way of Dā'vid and Sŏl'o-mon.
18 ¶ And Rē-ho-bō'am took him Mā'-
ha-lath the daughter of Jĕr'i-mŏth the
son of Dā'vid to wife, *and* Ăb-i-hā'il the
daughter of E-lī'ab the son of Jĕs'se;
19 Which bare him children; Jē'ush,
and Shăm-a-rī'ah, and Zā'ham.
20 And after her he took [n]Mā'a-
chah the daughter of Ăb'sa-lŏm; which
bare him A-bī'jah, and Ăt'tāi, and
Zī'zȧ, and Shĕl'o-mĭth.
21 And Rē-ho-bō'am loved Mā'a-
chah the daughter of Ăb'sa-lŏm above
all his wives and his concubines: (for
he took eighteen wives, and threescore
concubines; and begat twenty and
eight sons, and threescore daughters.)
22 And Rē-ho-bō'am [o]made A-bī'-
jah the son of Mā'a-chah the chief, *to
be* ruler among his brethren: for *he
thought* to make him king.
23 And he dealt wisely, and dispersed of all his children throughout
all the countries of Jū'dah and Bĕn'ja-
min, unto every fenced city: and he
gave them victual in abundance. And
he desired [2]many wives.

12 And [a]it came to pass, when Rē-
ho-bō'am had established the
kingdom, and had strengthened himself, [b]he forsook the law of the LORD,
and all Ĭs'ra-el with him.
2 [c]And it came to pass, *that* in the
fifth year of king Rē-ho-bō'am Shī'-
shăk king of Ē'gypt came up against
Je-ru'sa-lĕm, because they had transgressed against the LORD,
3 With twelve hundred chariots, and
threescore thousand horsemen: and the
people *were* without number that came
with him out of Ē'gypt; [d]the Lu'bĭms,
the Sŭk'kĭ-ĭms, and the Ē-thĭ-ō'pĭ-ans.
4 And he took the fenced cities which
pertained to Jū'dah, and came to Je-
ru'sa-lĕm.
5 ¶ Then came [e]Shĕm-a-ī'ah the
prophet to Rē-ho-bō'am, and *to* the
princes of Jū'dah, that were gathered
together to Je-ru'sa-lĕm because of
Shī'shăk, and said unto them, Thus
saith the LORD, [f]Ye have forsaken me,
and therefore have I also left you in the
hand of Shī'shăk.
6 Whereupon the princes of Ĭs'ra-el
and the king [g]humbled themselves;
and they said, [h]The LORD *is* righteous.
7 And when the LORD saw that they
humbled themselves, [i]the word of the
LORD came to Shĕm-a-ī'ah, saying,
They have humbled themselves; *therefore* I will not destroy them, but I will
grant them [1]some deliverance; and my
wrath shall not be poured out upon Je-
ru'sa-lĕm by the hand of Shī'shăk.
8 Nevertheless [j]they shall be his servants; that they may know [k]my service, and the service of the kingdoms
of the countries.
9 [l]So Shī'shăk king of Ē'gypt came
up against Je-ru'sa-lĕm, and took away
the treasures of the house of the LORD,

18 [3]strengthened himself
19 [i]1 Ki. 12.19; Eccl. 2.19
CHAPTER 11
1 [a]1 Ki. 12.21
2 [b]Deut. 33.1; 1 Tim. 6.11
6 [c]Gen. 35.19; Matt. 2.1
[d]Judg. 15.8; 1 Chr. 4.32
[e]2 Sam. 14.2; Amos 1.1
13 [1]presented themselves to him
14 [f]Num. 35.2; Josh. 21.20-42
[g]1 Ki. 12.28-33; ch. 13.9
15 [h]1 Ki. 12.31; Hos. 13.2
[i]Lev. 17.7; Rev. 16.14
[j]1 Ki. 12.28
16 [k]ch. 15.9; Ps. 69.32
17 [l]ch. 12.1
[m]Hos. 6.4
20 [n]1 Ki. 15.2;
22 [o]Deut. 21.15-16-17
23 [2]a multitude of wives
CHAPTER 12
1 [a]ch. 11.17
[b]Deut. 8.14
2 [c]1 Ki. 14.24-25
3 [d]ch. 16.8
5 [e]ch. 11.2
[f]Deut. 28.25
6 [g]Ex. 10.3;
[h]Ex. 9.27
7 [i]1 Ki. 21.28-29
[1]Or, a little while
8 [j]Isa. 26.13
[k]Deut. 28.47-48
9 [l]1 Ki. 14.25-26

and the treasures of the king's house;
he took all: he carried away also the
shields of gold which Sŏl'o-mon had
[m]made.
10 Instead of which king Rē-ho-bō'-
am made shields of brass, and committed *them* [n]to the hands of the chief of
the guard, that kept the entrance of the
king's house.
11 And when the king entered into
the house of the LORD, the guard came
and fetched them, and brought them
again into the guard chamber.
12 And when he humbled himself,
the wrath of the LORD turned from
him, that he would not destroy *him* altogether: [2]and also in Jū'dah things
went well.
13 ¶ So king Rē-ho-bō'am strengthened himself in Je-ru̧'sa-lĕm, and
reigned: for [o]Rē-ho-bō'am *was* one
and forty years old when he began to
reign, and he reigned seventeen years
in Je-ru̧'sa-lĕm, [p]the city which the
LORD had chosen out of all the tribes
of Ĭs'ra-el, to put his name there. And
his mother's name *was* Nā'a-mah an
Ăm'mŏn-īt-ess.
14 And he did evil, because he [3]pre-
pared not his heart to seek the LORD.
15 Now the acts of Rē-ho-bō'am,
first and last, *are* they not written in
the [4]book of Shĕm-a-ī'ah the prophet,
[q]and of Ĭd'dō the seer concerning genealogies? [r]And *there were* wars between Rē-ho-bō'am and Jĕr-o-bō'am
continually.
16 And Rē-ho-bō'am slept with his
fathers, and was buried in the city of
Dā'vid: and A-bī'jah his son reigned in
his stead.

13 Now [a]in the eighteenth year of
king Jĕr-o-bō'am began A-bī'jah
to reign over Jū'dah.
2 He reigned three years in Je-ru̧'-
sa-lĕm. His mother's name also *was*
[b]Mī-chā'iah the daughter of Ū'rĭ-el of
Ḡĭb'e-ah. And there was war between
A-bī'jah and Jĕr-o-bō'am.
3 And A-bī'jah [1]set the battle in array with an army of valiant men of war,
even four hundred thousand chosen
men: Jĕr-o-bō'am also set the battle in
array against him with eight hundred
thousand chosen men, *being* mighty
men of valour.
4 ¶ And A-bī'jah stood up upon
mount Zĕm-a-rā'im, [c]which *is* in mount
Ē'phră-ĭm, and said, Hear me, thou Jĕr-
o-bō'am, and all Ĭs'ra-el;
5 Ought ye not to know that the
LORD God of Ĭs'ra-el [d]gave the kingdom over Ĭs'ra-el to Dā'vid for ever,
even to him and to his sons by a [2]cove-
nant of salt?
6 Yet Jĕr-o-bō'am the son of Nē'băt,
the servant of Sŏl'o-mon the son of
Dā'vid, is risen up, and hath [e]rebelled
against his lord.
7 And there are gathered unto him
[f]vain men, the children of Bē'lĭ-al, and
have strengthened themselves against
Rē-ho-bō'am the son of Sŏl'o-mon,
when Rē-ho-bō'am was young and ten-

[m]1 Ki. 10.16-17; ch. 9.15-16
10 [n]2 Sam. 8.18; 1 Chr. 11.25
12 [2]Or, and yet in Judah there were good things
13 [o]1 Ki. 14.21; ch. 13.7
[p]ch. 6.6; Ps. 48.1-3
14 [3]Or, fixed
15 [4]words
[q]ch. 9.29
[r]1 Ki. 14.30

CHAPTER 13
1 [a]1 Ki. 15.1
2 [b]ch. 11.20
3 [1]bound together
4 [c]Josh. 18.22
5 [d]Judg. 11.21-24; 1 Sam. 16.12-13; 2 Sam. 7.12-13-16; Ps. 89.20; Luke 1.31-33
[2]That is, a perpetual covenant of friendship
6 [e]1 Ki. 11.26; ch. 10.19
7 [f]Judg. 9.4; Ps. 26.4; Prov. 12.11; Acts 17.5
8 [g]Hos. 8.6
9 [h]ch. 11.14-15
[i]Ex. 29.35
[3]to fill his hand
11 [j]ch. 2.4
[k]Lev. 24.6
[l]Ex. 27.20-21; Lev. 24.2-3
12 [m]Deut. 20.4; Josh. 5.14; Ps. 20.7
[n]Num. 10.8
[o]Job 15.25-26; Acts 5.39
15 [p]Num. 32.4; ch. 14.12
18 [4]humbled
[q]1 Chr. 5.20; ch. 16.8-9; ch. 20.20; Ps. 22.5
19 [r]Josh. 15.9; John 11.54
20 [s]1 Sam. 25.38; Ezek. 24.16; Acts 12.23
[t]1 Ki. 14.20

derhearted, and could not withstand
them.
8 And now ye think to withstand the
kingdom of the LORD in the hand of the
sons of Dā'vid; and ye *be* a great multitude, and *there are* with you golden
calves, which Jĕr-o-bō'am [g]made you
for gods.
9 Have [h]ye not cast out the priests of
the LORD, the sons of Aâr'on, and the
Lē'vītes, and have made you priests after the manner of the nations of *other*
lands? [i]so that whosoever cometh [3]to
consecrate himself with a young bullock and seven rams, *the same* may be a
priest of *them that are* no gods.
10 But as for us, the LORD *is* our
God, and we have not forsaken him;
and the priests, which minister unto
the LORD, *are* the sons of Aâr'on, and
the Lē'vītes *wait* upon *their* business:
11 [j]And they burn unto the LORD every morning and every evening burnt
sacrifices and sweet incense: the [k]shew-
bread also *set they in order* upon the
pure table; and the candlestick of gold
with the lamps thereof, [l]to burn every
evening: for we keep the charge of the
LORD our God; but ye have forsaken
him.
12 And, behold, [m]God himself *is*
with us for *our* captain, [n]and his priests
with sounding trumpets to cry alarm
against you. O children of Ĭs'ra-el,
[o]fight ye not against the LORD God of
your fathers; for ye shall not prosper.
13 ¶ But Jĕr-o-bō'am caused an ambushment to come about behind them:
so they were before Jū'dah, and the
ambushment *was* behind them.
14 And when Jū'dah looked back,
behold, the battle *was* before and behind: and they cried unto the LORD, and
the priests sounded with the trumpets.
15 Then the men of Jū'dah gave
a shout: and as the men of Jū'dah
shouted, it came to pass, that God
[p]smote Jĕr-o-bō'am and all Ĭs'ra-el before A-bī'jah and Jū'dah.
16 And the children of Ĭs'ra-el fled
before Jū'dah: and God delivered them
into their hand.
17 And A-bī'jah and his people slew
them with a great slaughter: so there
fell down slain of Ĭs'ra-el five hundred
thousand chosen men.
18 Thus the children of Ĭs'ra-el were
[4]brought under at that time, and the
children of Jū'dah prevailed, [q]because
they relied upon the LORD God of their
fathers.
19 And A-bī'jah pursued after Jĕr-
o-bō'am, and took cities from him,
Bĕth'-el with the towns thereof, and
Jĕsh'a-nah with the towns thereof, and
[r]Ē'phră-ĭn with the towns thereof.
20 Neither did Jĕr-o-bō'am recover
strength again in the days of A-bī'jah:
and the LORD [s]struck him, and [t]he
died.
21 ¶ But A-bī'jah waxed mighty,
and married fourteen wives, and begat twenty and two sons, and sixteen
daughters.

22 And the rest of the acts of A-
bī'jah, and his ways, and his sayings,
are written in the [5]story of the prophet
[u]Ĭd'dō.

14 So A-bī'jah slept with his fathers, and they buried him in
the city of Dā'vid: and [a]Ā'sȧ his son
reigned in his stead. In his days the
land was quiet ten years.
2 And Ā'sȧ did *that which was* good
and right in the eyes of the LORD his
God:
3 For he took away the altars of the
strange *gods*, and [b]the high places,
and [c]brake down the [1]images, [d]and
cut down the groves:
4 And commanded Jū'dah to seek
the LORD God of their fathers, and to
do the law and the commandment.
5 Also he took away out of all the
cities of Jū'dah the high places and the
[2]images: and the kingdom was quiet
before him.
6 ¶ And he built fenced cities in
Jū'dah: for the land had rest, and he
had no war in those years; because the
LORD had given him rest.
7 Therefore he said unto Jū'dah, Let
us build these cities, and make about
them walls, and towers, gates, and
bars, *while* the land *is* yet before us;
because we have sought the LORD our
God, we have sought *him*, and he hath
given us rest on every side. So they
built and prospered.
8 And Ā'sȧ had an army *of men* that
bare targets and spears, out of Jū'dah
three hundred thousand; and out of
Bĕn'ja-min, that bare shields and drew
bows, two hundred and fourscore thousand: all these *were* mighty men of
valour.
9 ¶ [e]And there came out against
them Zē'rah the Ē-thĭ-ō'pĭ-an with
an host of a thousand thousand, and
three hundred chariots; and came unto
[f]Ma-rē'shah.
10 Then Ā'sȧ went out against him,
and they set the battle in array in the
valley of Zĕph'a-thah at Ma-rē'shah.
11 And Ā'sȧ [g]cried unto the LORD
his God, and said, LORD, *it is* [h]nothing
with thee to help, whether with many,
or with them that have no power: help
us, O LORD our God; for we rest on
thee, and [i]in thy name we go against
this multitude. O LORD, thou *art* our
God; let not [3]man prevail against thee.
12 So the LORD [j]smote the Ē-thĭ-ō'-
pĭ-ans before Ā'sȧ, and before Jū'dah;
and the Ē-thĭ-ō'pĭ-ans fled.
13 And Ā'sȧ and the people that
were with him pursued them unto [k]Gē'-
rär: and the Ē-thĭ-ō'pĭ-ans were overthrown, that they could not recover
themselves; for they were [4]destroyed
before the LORD, and before his host;
and they carried away very much spoil.
14 And they smote all the cities
round about Gē'rär; for [l]the fear of
the LORD came upon them: and they
spoiled all the cities; for there was exceeding much spoil in them.
15 They smote also the tents of cattle, and carried away sheep and cam-

22 [5]Or, commentary
[u]ch. 9.29

CHAPTER 14
1 [a]1 Ki. 15.8
3 [b]ch. 15.17
[c]Ex. 34.13
[1]statues
[d]1 Ki. 11.7
5 [2]sun images
9 [e]ch. 16.8
[f]Josh. 15.44; Mic. 1.15
11 [g]Ex. 14.10; 1 Chr. 5.20; ch. 13.14; Ps. 22.5; Acts 2.21
[h]Judg. 7.7; 1 Sam. 14.6; 2 Cor. 12.9-10
[i]1 Sam. 17.45; Nah. 1.7; Prov. 18.10
[3]Or, mortal man
12 [j]ch. 13.15
13 [k]Gen. 10.19
[4]broken; Ps. 46
14 [l]Gen. 35.5; Ex. 15.16; Deut. 11.25; ch. 17.10

CHAPTER 15
1 [a]Num. 24.2; Judg. 3.10; 2 Sam. 23.2; ch. 20.14; 2 Pet. 1.21
2 [1]before Asa
[b]Jas. 4.8
[c]1 Chr. 28.9; ch. 33.12-13; Matt. 7.7
[d]1 Chr. 28.9; Heb. 12.25
3 [e]Hos. 3.4
[f]Lev. 10.11
4 [g]Deut. 4.29
5 [h]Judg. 5.6
6 [i]Matt. 24.7
[2]beaten in pieces
7 [j]Gen. 15.1; Col. 3.24
8 [3]abominations
[k]ch. 13.19
9 [l]ch. 11.16
11 [m]ch. 14.15
[4]in that day
12 [n]ch. 34.31; Neh. 10.29
13 [o]Ex. 22.20
[p]Deut. 13.5-9-15
16 [5]That is, grandmother
[6]horror

els in abundance, and returned to Je-
ru'sa-lĕm.

15 And [a]the Spirit of God came
upon Ăz-a-rī'ah the son of Ō'ded:
2 And he went out to [1]meet Ā'sȧ,
and said unto him, Hear ye me, Ā'sȧ,
and all Jū'dah and Bĕn'ja-min; [b]The
LORD *is* with you, while ye be with
him; and [c]if ye seek him, he will be
found of you; but [d]if ye forsake him,
he will forsake you.
3 Now [e]for a long season Ĭs'ra-el
hath been without the true God, and
without [f]a teaching priest, and without
law.
4 But [g]when they in their trouble
did turn unto the LORD God of Ĭs'ra-el,
and sought him, he was found of them.
5 And [h]in those times *there was*
no peace to him that went out, nor to
him that came in, but great vexations
were upon all the inhabitants of the
countries.
6 [i]And nation was [2]destroyed of nation, and city of city: for God did vex
them with all adversity.
7 Be ye strong therefore, and let not
your hands be weak: for your work
shall be [j]rewarded.
8 And when Ā'sȧ heard these words,
and the prophecy of Ō'ded the prophet,
he took courage, and put away the
[3]abominable idols out of all the land of
Jū'dah and Bĕn'ja-min, and out of the
cities [k]which he had taken from mount
Ē'phră-ĭm, and renewed the altar of the
LORD, that *was* before the porch of the
LORD.
9 And he gathered all Jū'dah and
Bĕn'ja-min, and [l]the strangers with
them out of Ē'phră-ĭm and Ma-năs'-
seh, and out of Sĭm'e-on: for they fell
to him out of Ĭs'ra-el in abundance,
when they saw that the LORD his God
was with him.
10 So they gathered themselves together at Je-ru'sa-lĕm in the third
month, in the fifteenth year of the reign
of Ā'sȧ.
11 [m]And they offered unto the LORD
[4]the same time, of the spoil *which* they
had brought, seven hundred oxen and
seven thousand sheep.
12 And they [n]entered into a covenant to seek the LORD God of their fathers with all their heart and with all
their soul;
13 [o]That whosoever would not seek
the LORD God of Ĭs'ra-el [p]should be
put to death, whether small or great,
whether man or woman.
14 And they sware unto the LORD
with a loud voice, and with shouting,
and with trumpets, and with cornets.
15 And all Jū'dah rejoiced at the
oath: for they had sworn with all their
heart, and sought him with their whole
desire; and he was found of them: and
the LORD gave them rest round about.
16 ¶ And also *concerning* Mā'a-chah
the [5]mother of Ā'sȧ the king, he removed her from *being* queen, because
she had made an [6]idol in a grove: and
Ā'sȧ cut down her idol, and stamped *it*,
and burnt *it* at the brook Kĭd'ron.

17 But [a]the high places were not taken away out of Ĭs'ra-el: nevertheless the heart of Ā'sȧ was perfect all his days.

18 ¶ And he brought into the house of God the things that his father had dedicated, and that he himself had dedicated, silver, and gold, and vessels.

19 And there was no *more* war unto the five and thirtieth year of the reign of Ā'sȧ.

16 In the [1]six and thirtieth year of the reign of Ā'sȧ [a]Bā'a-shȧ king of Ĭs'ra-el came up against Jū'dah, and built Rā'mah, [b]to the intent that he might let none go out or come in to Ā'sȧ king of Jū'dah.

2 Then Ā'sȧ brought out silver and gold out of the treasures of the house of the LORD and of the king's house, and sent to Bĕn–hā'dăd king of Sỹr'ĭ-ȧ, that dwelt at [2]Da-măs'cus, saying,

3 *There is* a league between me and thee, as *there was* between my father and thy father: behold, I have sent thee silver and gold; go, break thy league with Bā'a-shȧ king of Ĭs'ra-el, that he may depart from me.

4 And Bĕn–hā'dăd hearkened unto king Ā'sȧ, and sent the captains of [3]his armies against the cities of Ĭs'ra-el; and they smote Ī'jon, and Dăn, and Ā'bĕl–mā'im, and all the store cities of Năph'ta-lī.

5 And it came to pass, when Bā'a-shȧ heard *it*, that he left off building of Rā'mah, and let his work cease.

6 Then Ā'sȧ the king took all Jū'dah; and they carried away the stones of Rā'mah, and the timber thereof, wherewith Bā'a-shȧ was building; and he built therewith Gē'bȧ and Mĭz'pah.

7 ¶ And at that time [c]Ha-nā'nī the seer came to Ā'sȧ king of Jū'dah, and said unto him, [d]Because thou hast relied on the king of Sỹr'ĭ-ȧ, and not relied on the LORD thy God, therefore is the host of the king of Sỹr'ĭ-ȧ escaped out of thine hand.

8 Were not [e]the Ē-thĭ-ō'pĭ-ans and [f]the Lu'bĭms [4]a huge host, with very many chariots and horsemen? yet, because thou didst rely on the LORD, he delivered them into thine hand.

9 [g]For the eyes of the LORD run to and fro throughout the whole earth, [5]to shew himself strong in the behalf of *them* whose heart *is* perfect toward him. Herein [h]thou hast done foolishly: therefore from henceforth [i]thou shalt have wars.

10 Then Ā'sȧ was wroth with the seer, and [j]put him in a prison house; for *he was* in a rage with him because of this *thing*. And Ā'sȧ [6]oppressed *some* of the people the same time.

11 ¶ And, behold, the acts of Ā'sȧ, first and last, lo, they *are* written in the book of the kings of Jū'dah and Ĭs'ra-el.

12 And Ā'sȧ in the thirty and ninth year of his reign was [k]diseased in his feet, until his disease *was* exceeding *great:* yet in his disease he [l]sought not to the LORD, but to the physicians.

17 [a]1 Ki. 3.2-4; 2 Ki. 12.3; ch. 14.3-5

CHAPTER 16

1 [1]That is, from the rending of the ten tribes from Judah, over which Asa was now king
[a]1 Ki. 15.17
[b]ch. 15.9

2 [2]Darmesek

4 [3]which were his

7 [c]1 Ki. 16.1; ch. 19.2
[d]Ps. 146.3-6; Isa. 31.1; Jer. 17.5; Eph. 1.12-13

8 [e]ch. 14.9
[f]ch. 12.3
[4]in abundance

9 [g]ch. 6.20; 1 Pet. 3.12
[5]Or, strongly to hold with them, etc
[h]1 Sam. 13.13; 1 Cor. 15.36
[i]1 Ki. 15.32

10 [j]ch. 18.26; Matt. 14.3
[6]crushed

12 [k]Deut. 28.22
[l]Jer. 17.5

14 [7]digged
[m]Gen. 50.2; Mark 16.1

CHAPTER 17

2 [a]ch. 11.11
[b]ch. 15.8

3 [c]Rom. 8.31
[1]Or, of his father, and of David

4 [d]Luke 1.6
[e]1 Ki. 12.28

5 [2]gave
[f]1 Ki. 10.27; ch. 18.1

6 [3]That is, was encouraged
[g]1 Ki. 22.43; ch. 20.33

7 [h]ch. 15.3

9 [i]ch. 35.3; Mal. 2.7

10 [j]Gen. 35.5; ch. 14.14
[4]was

12 [5]Or, palaces

13 ¶ And Ā'sȧ slept with his fathers, and died in the one and fortieth year of his reign.

14 And they buried him in his own sepulchres, which he had [7]made for himself in the city of Dā'vid, and laid him in the bed which was filled [m]with sweet odours and divers kinds *of spices* prepared by the apothecaries' art: and they made a very great burning for him.

17 And Je-hŏsh'a-phăt his son reigned in his stead, and strengthened himself against Ĭs'ra-el.

2 And he [a]placed forces in all the fenced cities of Jū'dah, and set garrisons in the land of Jū'dah, and in the cities of Ē'phrā-ĭm, [b]which Ā'sȧ his father had taken.

3 And the LORD was [c]with Je-hŏsh'a-phăt, because he walked in the first ways [1]of his father Dā'vid, and sought not unto Bā'al-ĭm;

4 But sought to the *LORD* God of his father, and [d]walked in his commandments, and not after [e]the doings of Ĭs'ra-el.

5 Therefore the LORD stablished the kingdom in his hand: and all Jū'dah [2]brought to Je-hŏsh'a-phăt presents; [f]and he had riches and honour in abundance.

6 And his heart [3]was lifted up in the ways of the LORD: moreover [g]he took away the high places and groves out of Jū'dah.

7 ¶ Also in the third year of his reign he sent to his princes, *even* to Bĕn–hā'il, and to Ō-ba-dī'ah, and to Zĕch-a-rī'ah, and to Ne-thăn'e-el, and to Mī-chā'iah, [h]to teach in the cities of Jū'dah.

8 And with them *he sent* Lē'vītes, *even* Shĕm-a-ī'ah, and Nĕth-a-nī'ah, and Zĕb-a-dī'ah, and Ā'sa-hĕl, and Shemĭr'a-mŏth, and Je-hŏn'a-than, and Ăd-ō-nī'jah, and To-bī'jah, and Tŏb–ăd-o-nī'jah, Lē'vītes; and with them E-lĭsh'a-mȧ and Je-hō'ram, priests.

9 [i]And they taught in Jū'dah, and *had* the book of the law of the LORD with them, and went about throughout all the cities of Jū'dah, and taught the people.

10 ¶ And [j]the fear of the LORD [4]fell upon all the kingdoms of the lands that *were* round about Jū'dah, so that they made no war against Je-hŏsh'a-phăt.

11 Also *some* of the Phĭ-lĭs'tĭnes [k]brought Je-hŏsh'a-phăt presents, and tribute silver; and the A-rā'bĭ-ans brought him flocks, seven thousand and seven hundred rams, and seven thousand and seven hundred he goats.

12 ¶ And Je-hŏsh'a-phăt waxed great exceedingly; and he built in Jū'dah [5]castles, and cities of store.

13 And he had much business in the cities of Jū'dah: and the men of war, mighty men of valour, *were* in Je-ru'sa-lĕm.

14 And these *are* the numbers of them according to the house of their fathers: Of Jū'dah, the captains of thousands; Ăd'nah the chief, and with him

mighty men of valour three hundred
thousand.
15 And [6]next to him *was* Je-ho-hā'-
nan the captain, and with him two hundred and fourscore thousand.
16 And next him *was* Ăm-a-sī'ah the
son of Zĭch'rī, [l]who willingly offered
himself unto the LORD; and with him
two hundred thousand mighty men of
valour.
17 And of Bĕn'ja-min; E-lī'a-dȧ a
mighty man of valour, and with him
armed men with bow and shield two
hundred thousand.
18 And next him *was* Je-hŏz'a-băd,
and with him an hundred and fourscore thousand ready prepared for the
war.
19 These waited on the king, beside
those whom the king put in the fenced
cities throughout all Jū'dah.

18 Now Je-hŏsh'a-phăt [a]had riches
and honour in abundance, and
[b]joined affinity with Ā'hăb.
2 And [1]after [c]*certain* years he went
down to Ā'hăb to Sa-mā'rĭ-ȧ. And
Ā'hăb killed sheep and oxen for him in
abundance, and for the people that *he
had* with him, and persuaded him to go
up *with him* to Rā'moth–gĭl'e-ăd.
3 And Ā'hăb king of Ĭs'ra-el said
unto Je-hŏsh'a-phăt king of Jū'dah,
Wilt thou go with me to Rā'moth–
gĭl'e-ăd? And he answered him, I *am*
as thou *art*, and my people as thy people; and *we will be* with thee in the
war.
4 ¶ And Je-hŏsh'a-phăt said unto the
king of Ĭs'ra-el, [d]Inquire, I pray thee,
at the word of the LORD to day.
5 Therefore the king of Ĭs'ra-el gathered together of prophets four hundred men, and said unto them, Shall
we go to Rā'moth–gĭl'e-ăd to battle, or
shall I forbear? And they said, [e]Go up;
for God will deliver *it* into the king's
hand.
6 But Je-hŏsh'a-phăt said, *Is there*
not here a prophet of the LORD [2]be-
sides, that we might inquire of him?
7 And the king of Ĭs'ra-el said unto
Je-hŏsh'a-phăt, *There is* yet one man,
by whom we may inquire of the LORD:
but I hate him; for he never prophesied
good unto me, but always evil: the
same *is* Mī-cā'iah the son of Ĭm'lȧ. And
Je-hŏsh'a-phăt said, Let not the king
say so.
8 And the king of Ĭs'ra-el called for
one *of his* [3]officers, and said, [4]Fetch
quickly Mī-cā'iah the son of Ĭm'lȧ.
9 And the king of Ĭs'ra-el and Je-
hŏsh'a-phăt king of Jū'dah sat either
of them on his throne, clothed in *their*
robes, and they sat in a [5]void place at
the entering in of the gate of Sa-mā'-
rĭ-ȧ; and all the prophets prophesied
before them.
10 And Zĕd-e-kī'ah the son of Chĕ-
nā'ă-nah had made him horns of iron,
and said, Thus saith the LORD, With
these thou shalt push Sy̆r'ĭ-ȧ until [6]they
be consumed.
11 And all the prophets prophesied
so, saying, Go up to Rā'moth–gĭl'e-ăd,

15 [6]at his hand
16 [l]Judg. 5.2-9; 1 Chr. 29.9-14-17; Ps. 110.3; 2 Cor. 8.12
CHAPTER 18
1 [a]Deut. 8.10-18; 1 Sam. 2.7-30; 1 Chr. 29.11-12; ch. 17.5; Ps. 112.2-3-9; Prov. 4.5-6-7-8; Prov. 10.22; Prov. 22.4; Eccl. 5.19; 1 Tim. 4.8
[b]Gen. 6.2; 2 Cor. 6.14
2 [1]at the end of years
[c]1 Ki. 22.2; ch. 19.2
4 [d]1 Sam. 23.2-4-9; 2 Sam. 2.1; ch. 34.26; Jer. 21.2
5 [e]Jer. 23.17; Ezek. 13.3; Matt. 23.16-19
6 [2]yet, or, more
8 [3]Or, eunuchs
[4]Hasten
9 [5]Or, floor
10 [6]thou consume them
12 [7]with one mouth
13 [f]Num. 22.18-20-35; Num. 24.13; 1 Ki. 22.14; Jer. 32.8; Ezek. 2.7; Mic. 2.6-7; Acts 20.27; 1 Cor. 11.23; 1 Thess. 2.4
17 [8]Or, but for evil?
18 [g]Ps. 103.20; Dan. 7.9
20 [h]Job 1.6; 2 Thess. 2.9
21 [i]Hos. 4.12; Zech. 13.2; John 8.44
22 [j]Job 12.16; Jas. 1.13
23 [k]Mark 14.65; Acts 23.2
24 [9]Or, from chamber to chamber
[10]a chamber in a chamber
26 [l]ch. 16.10; Luke 23.2

and prosper: for the LORD shall deliver
it into the hand of the king.
12 And the messenger that went to
call Mī-cā'iah spake to him, saying, Behold, the words of the prophets *declare*
good to the king [7]with one assent; let
thy word therefore, I pray thee, be like
one of theirs, and speak thou good.
13 And Mī-cā'iah said, *As* the LORD
liveth, [f]even what my God saith, that
will I speak.
14 And when he was come to the
king, the king said unto him, Mī-cā'-
iah, shall we go to Rā'moth–gĭl'e-ăd to
battle, or shall I forbear? And he said,
Go ye up, and prosper, and they shall
be delivered into your hand.
15 And the king said to him, How
many times shall I adjure thee that
thou say nothing but the truth to me in
the name of the LORD?
16 Then he said, I did see all Ĭs'ra-
el scattered upon the mountains, as
sheep that have no shepherd: and the
LORD said, These have no master; let
them return *therefore* every man to his
house in peace.
17 And the king of Ĭs'ra-el said to
Je-hŏsh'a-phăt, Did I not tell thee *that*
he would not prophesy good unto me,
[8]but evil?
18 Again he said, Therefore hear
the word of the LORD; [g]I saw the LORD
sitting upon his throne, and all the host
of heaven standing on his right hand
and *on* his left.
19 And the LORD said, Who shall
entice Ā'hăb king of Ĭs'ra-el, that he
may go up and fall at Rā'moth–gĭl'e-
ăd? And one spake saying after this
manner, and another saying after that
manner.
20 Then there came out a [h]spirit,
and stood before the LORD, and said, I
will entice him. And the LORD said
unto him, Wherewith?
21 And he said, I will go out, and be
[i]a lying spirit in the mouth of all his
prophets. And *the LORD* said, Thou
shalt entice *him*, and thou shalt also
prevail: go out, and do *even* so.
22 Now therefore, behold, [j]the LORD
hath put a lying spirit in the mouth of
these thy prophets, and the LORD hath
spoken evil against thee.
23 Then Zĕd-e-kī'ah the son of Chĕ-
nā'ă-nah came near, and [k]smote Mī-
cā'iah upon the cheek, and said, Which
way went the Spirit of the LORD from
me to speak unto thee?
24 And Mī-cā'iah said, Behold, thou
shalt see on that day when thou shalt
go [9]into [10]an inner chamber to hide
thyself.
25 Then the king of Ĭs'ra-el said,
Take ye Mī-cā'iah, and carry him back
to Ā'mon the governor of the city, and
to Jō'ăsh the king's son;
26 And say, Thus saith the king,
[l]Put this *fellow* in the prison, and feed
him with bread of affliction and with
water of affliction, until I return in
peace.
27 And Mī-cā'iah said, If thou certainly return in peace, *then* hath not

the LORD spoken by me. And he said,
Hearken, all ye people.
28 So the king of Ĭs'ra-el and Je-
hŏsh'a-phăt the king of Jū'dah went
up to Rā'moth–gĭl'e-ăd.
29 And the king of Ĭs'ra-el said unto
Je-hŏsh'a-phăt, [m]I will disguise myself, and will go to the battle; but put
thou on thy robes. So the king of Ĭs'ra-
el disguised himself; and they went to
the battle.
30 Now the king of Sy̆r'ĭ-ȧ had commanded the captains of the chariots
that *were* with him, saying, Fight ye
not with small or great, save only with
the king of Ĭs'ra-el.
31 And it came to pass, when the
captains of the chariots saw Je-hŏsh'a-
phăt, that they said, It *is* the king of
Ĭs'ra-el. Therefore they [n]compassed
about him to fight: but Je-hŏsh'a-phăt
cried out, and the LORD helped him;
and God [o]moved them *to depart* from
him.
32 For it came to pass, that, when
the captains of the chariots perceived
that it was not the king of Ĭs'ra-el,
they turned back again [11]from pursuing him.
33 And a *certain* man drew a bow
[12]at a venture, and smote the king of
Ĭs'ra-el [13]between the joints of the harness: therefore he said to his chariot
man, Turn thine hand, that thou mayest carry me out of the host; for I am
[14]wounded.
34 And the battle increased that day:
howbeit the king of Ĭs'ra-el stayed *himself* up in *his* chariot against the Sy̆r'ĭ-
ans until the even: and about the time
of the sun going down he died.

19 And Je-hŏsh'a-phăt the king of
Jū'dah returned to his house in
peace to Je-ru'sa-lĕm.
2 And Jē'hū the son of [a]Ha-nā'nī
the seer went out to meet him, and said
to king Je-hŏsh'a-phăt, Shouldest thou
help the ungodly, and [b]love them that
hate the LORD? therefore *is* [c]wrath
upon thee from before the LORD.
3 Nevertheless there are [d]good
things found in thee, in that thou hast
taken away the groves out of the land,
and hast [e]prepared thine heart to seek
God.
4 And Je-hŏsh'a-phăt dwelt at Je-ru'-
sa-lĕm: and [1]he went out again through
the people from Bē'er–shē'bȧ to mount
Ē'phră-ĭm, and brought them back unto
the LORD God of their fathers.
5 ¶ And he [f]set judges in the land
throughout all the fenced cities of Jū'-
dah, city by city,
6 And said to the judges, Take heed
what ye do: for [g]ye judge not for man,
but for the LORD, [h]who *is* with you [2]in
the judgment.
7 Wherefore now let the fear of the
LORD be upon you; take heed and do *it*:
for [i]*there is* no iniquity with the LORD
our God, nor [j]respect of persons, nor
taking of gifts.
8 ¶ Moreover in Je-ru'sa-lĕm did Je-
hŏsh'a-phăt [k]set of the Lē'vītes, and *of*
the priests, and of the chief of the fathers of Ĭs'ra-el, for the judgment of
the LORD, and for controversies, when
they returned to Je-ru'sa-lĕm.
9 And he charged them, saying, Thus
shall ye do [l]in the fear of the LORD, faithfully, and with a perfect heart.
10 [m]And what cause soever shall
come to you of your brethren that
dwell in their cities, between blood
and blood, between law and commandment, statutes and judgments, ye shall
even warn them that they trespass not
against the LORD, and *so* [n]wrath come
upon [o]you, and upon your brethren:
this do, and ye shall not trespass.
11 And, behold, Ăm-a-rī'ah the chief
priest *is* over you in all matters of the
LORD; and Zĕb-a-dī'ah the son of Ĭsh'-
ma-el, the ruler of the house of Jū'dah,
for all the king's matters: also the
Lē'vītes *shall be* officers before you.
[3]Deal courageously, and the LORD shall
be with the good.

20 It came to pass after this also,
that the children of Mō'ab, and
the children of Ăm'mŏn, and with them
other beside the Ăm'mŏn-ītes, came
against Je-hŏsh'a-phăt to battle.
2 Then there came some that told
Je-hŏsh'a-phăt, saying, There cometh
a great multitude against thee from beyond the sea on this side Sy̆r'ĭ-ȧ; and,
behold, they *be* [a]in Hăz'a-zŏn–tā'mar,
which *is* [b]Ĕn–gē'dī.
3 And Je-hŏsh'a-phăt feared, and
set [1]himself to seek the LORD, and [c]pro-
claimed a fast throughout all Jū'dah.
4 And [d]Jū'dah gathered themselves
together, to ask *help* of the LORD: even
out of all the cities of Jū'dah they came
to seek the LORD.
5 ¶ And Je-hŏsh'a-phăt stood in the
congregation of Jū'dah and Je-ru'sa-
lĕm, in the house of the LORD, before
the new court,
6 And said, O LORD God of our fathers, *art* not thou [e]God in heaven?
and [f]rulest *not* thou over all the kingdoms of the heathen? and [g]in thine
hand *is there not* power and might, so
that none is able to withstand thee?
7 *Art* not thou [h]our God, [2]*who* didst
drive out the inhabitants of this land
before thy people Ĭs'ra-el, and gavest it
to the seed of Ā'bră-hăm [i]thy friend
for ever?
8 And they dwelt therein, and have
built thee a sanctuary therein for thy
name, saying,
9 [j]If, *when* evil cometh upon us, *as*
the sword, judgment, or pestilence, or
famine, we stand before this house,
and in thy presence, (for thy name *is* in
this house,) and cry unto thee in our
affliction, then thou wilt hear and help.
10 And now, behold, the children of
Ăm'mŏn and Mō'ab and mount Sē'ĭr,
whom thou [k]wouldest not let Ĭs'ra-el
invade, when they came out of the land
of Ē'gypt, but [l]they turned from them,
and destroyed them not;
11 Behold, *I say, how* they reward
us, [m]to come to cast us out of thy possession, which thou hast given us to
inherit.

29 [m]1 Sam. 28.8; Prov. 10.24
31 [n]Prov. 13.20 [o]Ps. 46.1
32 [11]from after him
33 [12]in his simplicity [13]between the joints and between the breastplate [14]made sick

CHAPTER 19

2 [a]1 Sam. 9.9 [b]Ps. 15.4; Prov. 1.10 [c]ch. 32.25
3 [d]ch. 12.12 [e]Ezra 7.10
4 [1]he returned and went out
5 [f]Deut. 16.18
6 [g]Deut. 1.17 [h]Ps. 82.1; Eccl. 5.8 [2]in the matter of judgment
7 [i]Deut. 32.4; Rom. 9.14 [j]Deut. 10.17; Job 34.19; Acts 10.34; Rom. 2.11; Gal. 2.6; Eph. 6.9; Col. 3.25; 1 Pet. 1.17
8 [k]Deut. 16.18; 1 Chr. 23.4; ch. 17.8
9 [l]2 Sam. 23.3
10 [m]Deut. 17.8 [n]Num. 16.46 [o]Ezek. 3.18
11 [3]Take courage and do

CHAPTER 20

2 [a]Gen. 14.7 [b]Josh. 15.62; 1 Sam. 23.29; Song 1.14
3 [1]his face [c]Judg. 20.26; Esth. 4.16
4 [d]Joel 1.14
6 [e]Deut. 4.39; Matt. 6.9 [f]1 Chr. 29.11-12; Dan. 4.17 [g]Ps. 62.11; Matt. 6.13
7 [h]Gen. 17.7; Ex. 6.7 [2]thou [i]Isa. 41.8; Jas. 2.23
9 [j]ch. 6.28-29
10 [k]Deut. 2.4 [l]Num. 20.21
11 [m]Ps. 83.12

12 O our God, wilt thou not [n]judge
them? [o]for we have no might against
this great company that cometh against
us; neither know we what to do: but
[p]our eyes *are* upon thee.
13 And all Jū'dah stood before the
LORD, with their little ones, their wives,
and their children.
14 ¶ Then upon Ja-hā'zĭ-el the son of
Zĕch-a-rī'ah, the son of Be-nā'iah, the
son of Je-ī'el, the son of Măt-ta-nī'ah, a
Lē'vīte of the sons of Ā'saph, [q]came
the Spirit of the LORD in the midst of
the congregation;
15 And he said, Hearken ye, all Jū'-
dah, and ye inhabitants of Je-rṳ'sa-lĕm,
and thou king Je-hŏsh'a-phăt, Thus
saith the LORD unto you, [r]Be not afraid
nor dismayed by reason of this great
multitude; for the battle *is* not yours,
but God's.
16 To morrow go ye down against
them: behold, they come up by the
[3]cliff of Zĭz; and ye shall find them at
the end of the [4]brook, before the wilderness of Jĕr'u-el.
17 [s]Ye shall not *need* to fight in this
battle: set yourselves, stand ye *still,*
and see the salvation of the LORD with
you, O Jū'dah and Je-rṳ'sa-lĕm: fear
not, nor be dismayed; to morrow go
out against them: [t]for the LORD *will be*
with you.
18 And Je-hŏsh'a-phăt [u]bowed his
head with *his* face to the ground: and
all Jū'dah and the inhabitants of Je-
rṳ'sa-lĕm fell before the LORD, worshipping the LORD.
19 And the Lē'vītes, of the children
of the Kō'hath-ītes, and of the children
of the Kôr'hītes, stood up to praise the
LORD God of Ĭs'ra-el with a loud voice
on high.
20 ¶ And they rose early in the morning, and went forth into the wilderness
of Te-kō'ȧ: and as they went forth, Je-
hŏsh'a-phăt stood and said, Hear me,
O Jū'dah, and ye inhabitants of Je-
rṳ'sa-lĕm; [v]Believe in the LORD your
God, so shall ye be established; believe
his prophets, so shall ye prosper.
21 And when he had consulted with
the people, he appointed singers unto
the LORD, [w]and [5]that should praise the
beauty of holiness, as they went out
before the army, and to say, [x]Praise
the LORD; [y]for his mercy *endureth* for
ever.
22 ¶ [6]And when they began [7]to sing
and to praise, [z]the LORD set ambush-
ments against the children of Ăm'mŏn,
Mō'ab, and mount Sē'ïr, which were
come against Jū'dah; and [8]they were
smitten.
23 For the children of Ăm'mŏn and
Mō'ab stood up against the inhabitants
of mount Sē'ïr, utterly to slay and destroy *them:* and when they had made
an end of the inhabitants of Sē'ïr, every
one helped [9]to destroy another.
24 And when Jū'dah came toward
the watch tower in the wilderness,
they looked unto the multitude, and,
[a]behold, they *were* dead bodies fallen
to the earth, and [10]none escaped.

12 [n]1 Sam. 3.13; Rev. 19.11
[o]2 Cor. 3.5
[p]Ps. 25.15; Ps. 123.1
14 [q]Num. 11.25; ch. 15.1
15 [r]Ex. 14.13; ch. 32.7
16 [3]ascent
[4]Or, valley
17 [s]Ex. 14.13
[t]Num. 14.9; Amos 5.14
18 [u]Ex. 4.31
20 [v]Isa. 7.9; Rom. 8.31
21 [w]1 Chr. 16.29; Ps. 50.2
[5]praisers
[x]1 Chr. 16.34; Ps. 106.1
[y]ch. 5.13; ch. 7.3
22 [6]And in the time that they, etc
[7]in singing and praise
[z]Judg. 7.22; 1 Sam. 14.20
[8]Or, they smote one another
23 [9]for the destruction
24 [a]Ex. 14.13; Jer. 33.5
[10]there was not an escaping
25 [11]vessels of desire
26 [12]That is, Blessing
27 [13]head
[b]Neh. 12.43
29 [c]ch. 17.10
30 [d]ch. 15.15; Job 34.29
31 [e]1 Ki. 22.41
33 [f]ch. 12.14
34 [14]words
[g]1 Ki. 16.1
[15]was made to ascend
36 [16]At first Jehoshaphat was unwilling
37 [h]Gen. 10.4;
CHAPTER 21
1 [1]Alone

25 And when Je-hŏsh'a-phăt and his
people came to take away the spoil of
them, they found among them in abundance both riches with the dead bodies, and [11]precious jewels, which they
stripped off for themselves, more than
they could carry away: and they were
three days in gathering of the spoil, it
was so much.
26 ¶ And on the fourth day they assembled themselves in the valley of
[12]Bĕr'ă-chah; for there they blessed
the LORD: therefore the name of the
same place was called, The valley of
Bĕr'ă-chah, unto this day.
27 Then they returned, every man of
Jū'dah and Je-rṳ'sa-lĕm, and Je-hŏsh'-
a-phăt in the [13]forefront of them, to go
again to Je-rṳ'sa-lĕm with joy; for the
LORD had [b]made them to rejoice over
their enemies.
28 And they came to Je-rṳ'sa-lĕm
with psalteries and harps and trumpets unto the house of the LORD.
29 And [c]the fear of God was on all
the kingdoms of *those* countries, when
they had heard that the LORD fought
against the enemies of Ĭs'ra-el.
30 So the realm of Je-hŏsh'a-phăt
was quiet: for his [d]God gave him rest
round about.
31 ¶ [e]And Je-hŏsh'a-phăt reigned
over Jū'dah: *he was* thirty and five
years old when he began to reign, and
he reigned twenty and five years in Je-
rṳ'sa-lĕm. And his mother's name *was*
Ă-zū'bah the daughter of Shĭl'hī.
32 And he walked in the way of Ā'sȧ
his father, and departed not from it,
doing *that which was* right in the sight
of the LORD.
33 Howbeit the high places were not
taken away: for as yet the people had
not [f]prepared their hearts unto the
God of their fathers.
34 Now the rest of the acts of Je-
hŏsh'a-phăt, first and last, behold, they
are written in the [14]book of Jē'hū the
son of Ha-nā'nī, [g]who [15]*is* mentioned
in the book of the kings of Ĭs'ra-el.
35 ¶ And after this did Je-hŏsh'a-
phăt king of Jū'dah join himself with
Ă-ha-zī'ah king of Ĭs'ra-el, who did
very wickedly:
36 And [16]he joined himself with him
to make ships to go to Tär'shish: and
they made the ships in Ē'zĭ-on–gā'bĕr.
37 Then E-li-ē'zĕr the son of Dŏd'a-
vah of Ma-rē'shah prophesied against
Je-hŏsh'a-phăt, saying, Because thou
hast joined thyself with Ă-ha-zī'ah, the
LORD hath broken thy works. And the
ships were broken, that they were not
able to go [h]to Tär'shish.
21 Now Je-hŏsh'a-phăt slept with
his fathers, and was buried with
his fathers in the city of Dā'vid. And Je-
hō'ram his son reigned in his stead.[1]
2 And he had brethren the sons
of Je-hŏsh'a-phăt, Ăz-a-rī'ah, and Je-
hī'el, and Zĕch-a-rī'ah, and Ăz-a-rī'ah,
and Mī'chaĕl, and Shĕph-a-tī'ah: all
these *were* the sons of Je-hŏsh'a-phăt
king of Ĭs'ra-el.

3 And their father gave them great
gifts of silver, and of gold, and of precious things, with fenced cities in Jū′-
dah: but the kingdom gave he to [2]Je-
hō′ram; because he *was* the firstborn.
4 Now when Je-hō′ram was risen
up to the kingdom of his father, he
strengthened himself, and [a]slew all his
brethren with the sword, and *divers*
also of the princes of Ĭs′ra-el.
5 ¶ [b]Je-hō′ram *was* thirty and two
years old when he began to reign, and
he reigned eight years in Je-ru̮′sa-lĕm.
6 And he walked in the way of the
kings of Ĭs′ra-el, like as did the house
of Ā′hăb: for he had the daughter of
[c]Ā′hăb to wife: and he wrought *that
which was* evil in the eyes of the LORD.
7 Howbeit the LORD would not destroy the house of Dā′vid, because of
the covenant that he had made with
Dā′vid, and as he promised to give a
[3]light to him and to his [d]sons for ever.
8 ¶ [e]In his days the Ē′dom-ītes revolted from under the [4]dominion of
Jū′dah, and made themselves a king.
9 Then Je-hō′ram went forth with
his princes, and all his chariots with
him: and he rose up by night, and
smote the Ē′dom-ītes which compassed
him in, and the captains of the chariots.
10 So the [f]Ē′dom-ītes revolted from
under the hand of Jū′dah unto this day.
The same time *also* did Lĭb′nah revolt
from under his hand; because he had
forsaken the LORD God of his fathers.
11 Moreover he made high places in
the mountains of Jū′dah, and caused
the inhabitants of Je-ru̮′sa-lĕm to [g]com-
mit fornication, and compelled Jū′dah
thereto.
12 ¶ And there came a [5]writing to
him from E-lī′jah the prophet, saying,
Thus saith the LORD God of Dā′vid thy
father, Because thou hast not walked
in the ways of Je-hŏsh′a-phăt thy father, nor in the ways of Ā′sȧ king of
Jū′dah,
13 But hast walked in the way of the
kings of Ĭs′ra-el, and hast made Jū′dah
and the inhabitants of Je-ru̮′sa-lĕm to
[h]go a whoring, like to the [i]whoredoms
of the house of Ā′hăb, and also hast
slain thy brethren of thy father's house,
which were better than thyself:
14 Behold, with [6]a great plague will
the LORD smite thy people, and thy children, and thy wives, and all thy goods:
15 And thou *shalt have* great sickness by disease of thy bowels, until thy
bowels fall out by reason of the sickness day by day.
16 ¶ Moreover the LORD [j]stirred up
against Je-hō′ram the spirit of the Phĭ-
lĭs′tĭnes, and of the A-rā′bĭ-ans, that
were near the Ē-thĭ-ō′pĭ-ans:
17 And they came up into Jū′dah,
and brake into it, and [7]carried away all
the substance that was found in the
king's house, and [k]his sons also, and
his wives; so that there was never a
son left him, save [8]Je-hō′a-hăz, the
youngest of his sons.
18 ¶ And after all this the LORD
smote him in his bowels with an incurable disease.
19 And it came to pass, that in process of time, after the end of two years,
his bowels fell out by reason of his sickness: so he died of sore diseases. And
his people made no burning for him,
like the burning of his fathers.
20 Thirty and two years old was
he when he began to reign, and he
reigned in Je-ru̮′sa-lĕm eight years,
and departed [9]without being desired.
Howbeit they buried him in the city of
Dā′vid, but not in the sepulchres of the
kings.
22 And the inhabitants of Je-ru̮′sa-
lĕm made [a]Ā-ha-zī′ah his youngest son king in his stead: for the band
of men that came with the A-rā′bĭ-ans
to the camp had slain all the [b]eldest.
So Ā-ha-zī′ah the son of Je-hō′ram
king of Jū′dah reigned.
2 [c]Forty and two years old *was* Ā-
ha-zī′ah when he began to reign, and
he reigned one year in Je-ru̮′sa-lĕm.
His mother's name also *was* [d]Ăth-a-
lī′ah the daughter of Ŏm′rī.
3 He also walked in the ways of the
house of Ā′hăb: for his mother was his
counseller to do wickedly.
4 Wherefore he did evil in the sight
of the LORD like the house of Ā′hăb:
for they were his counsellers after the
death of his father to [e]his destruction.
5 ¶ He walked also after their counsel, and [f]went with Je-hō′ram the son of
Ā′hăb king of Ĭs′ra-el to war against
Hăz′a-el king of Sȳr′ĭ-ȧ at Rā′moth–gĭl′-
e-ăd: and the Sȳr′ĭ-ans smote Jō′ram.
6 [g]And he returned to be healed
in Jĕz′re-el because of the wounds
[1]which were given him at Rā′mah,
when he fought with Hăz′a-el king of
Sȳr′ĭ-ȧ. And [2]Ăz-a-rī′ah the son of Je-
hō′ram king of Jū′dah went down to
see Je-hō′ram the son of Ā′hăb at
Jĕz′re-el, because he was sick.
7 And the [3]destruction of Ā-ha-zī′ah
[h]was of God by coming to Jō′ram:
for when he was come, he [i]went
out with Je-hō′ram against Jē′hū the
son of Nĭm′shī, [j]whom the LORD had
anointed to cut off the house of Ā′hăb.
8 And it came to pass, that, when
Jē′hū was [k]executing judgment upon
the house of Ā′hăb, and found the
princes of Jū′dah, and the sons of the
brethren of Ā-ha-zī′ah, that ministered
to Ā-ha-zī′ah, he slew them.
9 [l]And he sought Ā-ha-zī′ah: and
they caught him, (for he was hid in Sa-
mā′rĭ-ȧ,) and brought him to Jē′hū:
and when they had slain him, they buried him: Because, said they, he *is* the
son of Je-hŏsh′a-phăt, who sought the
LORD with all his heart. So the house of
Ā-ha-zī′ah had no power to keep still
the kingdom.
10 ¶ But when Ăth-a-lī′ah the mother
of Ā-ha-zī′ah saw that her son was
dead, she arose and destroyed all the
seed royal of the house of Jū′dah.
11 But [4]Je-ho-shăb′e-ăth, the daughter of the king, took Jō′ăsh the son of

3 [2]Jehoram made partner of the kingdom with his father
4 [a]Gen. 4.8; 1 John 3.12
5 [b]In consort, 2 Ki. 8.17
6 [c]2 Ki. 8.18;
7 [3]lamp, or, candle
[d]2 Sam. 7.12-13;
8 [e]Gen. 27.40; [4]hand
10 [f]Gen. 27.40
11 [g]Lev. 17.7
12 [5]Which was writ before his death
13 [h]Ex. 34.15
[i]2 Ki. 9.22
14 [6]a great stroke
16 [j]2 Sam. 24.1;
17 [7]carried captive
[k]ch. 24.7 or, Azariah, ch. 22.6; [8]Or, Ahaziah, ch. 22.1
20 [9]without desire

CHAPTER 22
1 [a]2 Ki. 8.24
[b]ch. 21.17
2 [c]2 Ki. 8.26
[d]ch. 21.6
4 [e]ch. 24.17-18;
5 [f]2 Ki. 8.28
6 [g]2 Ki. 9.15 [1]wherewith they wounded him [2]Otherwise called Ahaziah, verse 1, and Jehoahaz, ch. 21.17
7 [3]treading down
[h]Judg. 14.4;
[i]2 Ki. 9.21
[j]1 Ki. 19.16
8 [k]2 Ki. 10.10-11
9 [l]2 Ki. 9.27, at Megiddo in the kingdom of Samaria
11 [4]Jehosheba, 2 Ki. 11.2

Ā-ha-zī'ah, and stole him from among
the king's sons that were slain, and put
him and his nurse in a bedchamber. So
Je-ho-shăb'e-ăth, the daughter of king
Je-hō'ram, the wife of Je-hoi'a-dȧ the
priest, (for she was the sister of Ā-ha-
zī'ah,) hid him from Ăth-a-lī'ah, so
that she slew him not.
12 And he was with them hid in the
house of God six years: and Ăth-a-lī'ah
reigned over the land.
23 And [a]in the seventh year Je-hoi'-
a-dȧ strengthened himself, and
took the captains of hundreds, Ăz-a-
rī'ah the son of Jĕr'o-hăm, and Ĭsh'ma-
el the son of Je-ho-hā'nan, and Ăz-a-
rī'ah the son of Ō'bed, and Mā-a-sē'iah
the son of Ăd-a-ī'ah, and E-lĭsh'a-phăt
the son of Zĭch'rī, into covenant with
him.
2 And they [b]went about in Jū'dah,
and gathered the Lē'vītes out of all the
cities of Jū'dah, and the chief of the
fathers of Ĭs'ra-el, and they came to
Je-ru'sa-lĕm.
3 And all the congregation made a
covenant with the king in the house of
God. And he said unto them, Behold,
the king's son shall reign, as the LORD
hath [c]said of the sons of Dā'vid.
4 This *is* the thing that ye shall do; A
third part of you [d]entering on the sabbath, of the priests and of the Lē'vītes,
shall be porters of the [1]doors;
5 And a third part *shall be* at the
king's house; and a third part at the
[e]gate of the foundation: and all the people *shall be* in the courts of the house
of the LORD.
6 But let none come into the house
of the LORD, save the priests, and [f]they
that minister of the Lē'vītes; they shall
go in, for they *are* [2]holy: but all the
people shall keep the watch of the
LORD.
7 And the Lē'vītes shall compass the
king round about, every man with his
weapons in his hand; and whosoever
else cometh into the house, he shall be
put to death: but be ye with the king
when he cometh in, and when he goeth
out.
8 So the Lē'vītes and all Jū'dah did
according to all things that Je-hoi'a-dȧ
the priest had commanded, and took
every man his men that were to come in
on the sabbath, with them that were to
go *out* on the sabbath: for Je-hoi'a-dȧ
the priest dismissed not [g]the courses.
9 Moreover Je-hoi'a-dȧ the priest delivered to the captains of hundreds
spears, and bucklers, and shields, that
had been king Dā'vid's, which *were* in
the house of God.
10 And he set all the people, every
man having his weapon in his hand,
from the right [3]side of the [4]temple to
the left side of the temple, along by the
altar and the temple, by the king round
about.
11 Then they brought out the king's
son, and put upon him the crown, and
[h]*gave him* the testimony, and made
him king. And Je-hoi'a-dȧ and his sons

CHAPTER 23
1 [a]2 Ki. 11.4
2 [b]Ps. 112.5
3 [c]2 Sam. 7.12; 1 Ki. 2.4; ch. 6.16; ch. 7.18; Ps. 89.29-36
4 [d]1 Chr. 9.25; Luke 1.8-9 [1]thresholds
5 [e]Acts 3.2
6 [f]1 Chr. 23.28-29 [2]holiness
8 [g]1 Chr. 24.
10 [3]shoulder [4]house
11 [h]Ex. 25.16; Deut. 17.18; Ps. 2.10-12; Isa. 8.16-20 [5]Let the king live
13 [i]1 Chr. 25.8 [6]Conspiracy
14 [j]Num. 5.2; Num. 19.14
15 [k]Neh. 3.28 [l]Gen. 9.5; ch. 22.10; Matt. 7.2
16 [m]Deut. 5.2-3; 2 Ki. 11.17; ch. 15.12; ch. 29.10; Ezra 10.3; Neh. 9.38
17 [n]2 Ki. 10.23; ch. 34.4-7 [o]Deut. 13.9; 2 Ki. 11.18-19
18 [p]1 Chr. 23.6-30-31; 1 Chr. 24.1 [q]Ex. 29.38; Num. 28.2 [7]by the hands of David
19 [r]1 Chr. 26.1
20 [s]2 Ki. 11.19
21 [t]1 Sam. 11.15; 1 Ki. 1.40; Ps. 58.10; Prov. 11.10

CHAPTER 24
1 [a]2 Ki. 11.21
2 [b]ch. 25.2; ch. 26.5
4 [1]to renew

anointed him, and said, [5]God save the
king.
12 ¶ Now when Ăth-a-lī'ah heard
the noise of the people running and
praising the king, she came to the people into the house of the LORD:
13 And she looked, and, behold, the
king stood at his pillar at the entering
in, and the princes and the trumpets by
the king: and all the people of the land
rejoiced, and sounded with trumpets,
also the singers with instruments of musick, and [i]such as taught to sing praise.
Then Ăth-a-lī'ah rent her clothes, and
said, [6]Treason, Treason.
14 Then Je-hoi'a-dȧ the priest
brought out the captains of hundreds
that were set over the host, and said
unto them, Have her forth of the
ranges: and whoso followeth her, let
him be slain with the sword. For the
priest said, [j]Slay her not in the house
of the LORD.
15 So they laid hands on her; and
when she was come to the entering [k]of
the horse gate by the king's house,
they [l]slew her there.
16 ¶ And Je-hoi'a-dȧ [m]made a covenant between him, and between all the
people, and between the king, that
they should be the LORD'S people.
17 Then all the people [n]went to the
house of Bā'al, and brake it down, and
brake his altars and his images in
pieces, and [o]slew Măt'tan the priest of
Bā'al before the altars.
18 Also Je-hoi'a-dȧ appointed the offices of the house of the LORD by the
hand of the priests the Lē'vītes, whom
Dā'vid had [p]distributed in the house of
the LORD, to offer the burnt offerings
of the LORD, as *it is* written in the [q]law
of Mō'ses, with rejoicing and with singing, *as it was ordained* [7]by Dā'vid.
19 And he set the [r]porters at the
gates of the house of the LORD, that
none *which was* unclean in any thing
should enter in.
20 [s]And he took the captains of hundreds, and the nobles, and the governors of the people, and all the people of
the land, and brought down the king
from the house of the LORD: and they
came through the high gate into the
king's house, and set the king upon the
throne of the kingdom.
21 [t]And all the people of the land
rejoiced: and the city was quiet, after
that they had slain Ăth-a-lī'ah with the
sword.
24 Jō'ăsh [a]*was* seven years old
when he began to reign, and he
reigned forty years in Je-ru'sa-lĕm.
His mother's name also *was* Zĭb'ī-ah of
Bē'er–shē'bȧ.
2 And Jō'ăsh [b]did *that which was*
right in the sight of the LORD all the
days of Je-hoi'a-dȧ the priest.
3 And Je-hoi'a-dȧ took for him two
wives; and he begat sons and daughters.
4 ¶ And it came to pass after this,
that Jō'ăsh was minded [1]to repair the
house of the LORD.
5 And he gathered together the
priests and the Lē'vītes, and said to

them, Go out unto the cities of Jū'dah,
and [c]gather of all Ĭs'ra-el money to repair the house of your God from year
to year, and see that ye hasten the matter. Howbeit the Lē'vītes hastened *it*
not.
6 [d]And the king called for Je-hoi'a-
dȧ the chief, and said unto him, Why
hast thou not required of the Lē'vītes
to bring in out of Jū'dah and out of Je-
rṳ'sa-lĕm the collection, *according to*
the commandment of [e]Mō'ses the servant of the LORD, and of the congregation of Ĭs'ra-el, for the [f]tabernacle of
witness?
7 For [g]the sons of Ăth-a-lī'ah, that
wicked woman, had broken up the
house of God; and also all the [h]dedi-
cated things of the house of the LORD
did they bestow upon Bā'al-ĭm.
8 And at the king's commandment
[i]they made a chest, and set it without
at the gate of the house of the LORD.
9 And they made [2]a proclamation
through Jū'dah and Je-rṳ'sa-lĕm, to
bring in to the LORD the collection *that*
Mō'ses the servant of God *laid* upon
Ĭs'ra-el in the wilderness.
10 And all the princes and all the
people rejoiced, and brought in, and
cast into the chest, until they had made
an end.
11 Now it came to pass, that at what
time the chest was brought unto the
king's office by the hand of the Lē'-
vītes, and [j]when they saw that *there*
was much money, the king's scribe
and the high priest's officer came and
emptied the chest, and took it, and carried it to his place again. Thus they did
day by day, and gathered money in
abundance.
12 And the king and Je-hoi'a-dȧ
gave it to such as did the work of the
service of the house of the LORD, and
hired masons and carpenters to repair
the house of the LORD, and also such as
wrought iron and brass to mend the
house of the LORD.
13 So the workmen wrought, and
the [3]work was perfected by them, and
they set the house of God in his state,
and strengthened it.
14 And when they had finished *it*,
they brought the rest of the money before the king and Je-hoi'a-dȧ, [k]whereof
were made vessels for the house of the
LORD, *even* vessels to minister, and [4]to
offer *withal*, and spoons, and vessels of
gold and silver. And they [l]offered burnt
offerings in the house of the LORD continually all the days of Je-hoi'a-dȧ.
15 ¶ But Je-hoi'a-dȧ waxed old, and
was [m]full of days when he died; an
hundred and thirty years old *was he*
when he died.
16 And they buried him in [n]the city
of Dā'vid among the kings, because he
had done good in Ĭs'ra-el, both toward
God, and toward his house.
17 Now after [o]the death of Je-hoi'a-
dȧ came the princes of Jū'dah, and
made obeisance to the king. Then the
king hearkened unto them.
18 And they left the house of the
LORD God of their fathers, and served
[p]groves and idols: and [q]wrath came
upon Jū'dah and Je-rṳ'sa-lĕm for this
their trespass.
19 Yet he [r]sent prophets to them, to
bring them again unto the LORD; and
they testified against them: but they
would not give ear.
20 And [s]the Spirit of God [5]came
upon Zĕch-a-rī'ah the son of Je-hoi'a-
dȧ the priest, which stood above the
people, and said unto them, Thus saith
God, [t]Why transgress ye the commandments of the LORD, that ye cannot prosper? [u]because ye have forsaken the LORD, he hath also forsaken
you.
21 And they conspired against him,
and [v]stoned him with stones at the
commandment of the king in the court
of the house of the LORD.
22 Thus Jō'ăsh the king remembered not the kindness which Je-hoi'a-
dȧ his father had done to him, but slew
his son. And when he died, he said,
The LORD look upon *it*, and require *it*.
23 ¶ And it came to pass [6]at the end
of the year, *that* [w]the host of Sy̆r'ĭ-ȧ
came up against him: and they came
to Jū'dah and Je-rṳ'sa-lĕm, and destroyed all the princes of the people from among the people, and sent
all the spoil of them unto the king of
[7]Da-măs'cus.
24 For the army of the Sy̆r'ĭ-ans
[x]came with a small company of men,
and the LORD [y]delivered a very great
host into their hand, because they had
forsaken the LORD God of their fathers.
So they [z]executed judgment against
Jō'ăsh.
25 And when they were departed
from him, (for they left him in great
diseases,) [a]his own servants conspired
against him for [b]the blood of the sons
of Je-hoi'a-dȧ the priest, and slew him
on his bed, and he died: and they buried him in the city of Dā'vid, but they
buried him not in the sepulchres of the
kings.
26 And these are they that conspired
against him; [8]Zā'băd the son of Shĭm'e-
ăth an Ăm'mŏn-īt-ess, and Je-hŏz'a-
băd the son of [9]Shĭm'rith a Mō'ab-īt-ess.
27 ¶ Now *concerning* his sons, and
the greatness of [c]the burdens *laid* upon
him, and the [10]repairing of the house of
God, behold, they *are* written in the
[11]story of the book of the kings. And
Ăm-a-zī'ah his son reigned in his stead.

25 Ăm-a-zī'ah [a]*was* twenty and five
years old *when* he began to reign,
and he reigned twenty and nine years
in Je-rṳ'sa-lĕm. And his mother's name
was Je-ho-ăd'dan of Je-rṳ'sa-lĕm.
2 And he did *that which was* right in
the sight of the LORD, [b]but not with a
perfect heart.
3 ¶ [c]Now it came to pass, when the
kingdom was [1]established to him, that
he slew his servants that had killed the
king his father.
4 But he slew not their children, but
did as *it is* written in the law in the

5 [c]ch. 29.3; ch. 34.8
6 [d]2 Ki. 12.7
[e]Ex. 30.12-13-14-16
[f]Num. 1.50; Num. 17.7-8; Acts 7.44
7 [g]ch. 21.17; Ps. 12.8
[h]2 Ki. 12.4
8 [i]2 Ki. 12.9
9 [2]a voice; Ex. 36.6
11 [j]2 Ki. 12.10
13 [3]the healing went up upon the work, or, by their hand
14 [k]1 Ki. 7.50
[4]Or, pestils
[l]Ex. 29.38; Rev. 5.9
15 [m]Job 5.26
16 [n]1 Ki. 2.10
17 [o]Acts 20.29
18 [p]1 Ki. 14.23
[q]Josh. 22.20; Hos. 5.10
19 [r]ch. 36.15; Luke 11.47-51
20 [s]ch. 15.1
[5]clothed
[t]Num. 14.41; 1 Sam. 13.13-14
[u]Deut. 29.25-26; Jer. 2.19
21 [v]Matt. 23.35; Acts 7.58
23 [6]in the revolution of the year
[w]2 Ki. 12.17
[7]Darmesek
24 [x]Lev. 26.8; Isa. 30.17
[y]Lev. 26.25; Deut. 28.25
[z]Isa. 10.5
25 [a]2 Ki. 12.20
[b]Ps. 10.14
26 [8]Or, Jozachar
[9]Or, Shomer
27 [c]2 Ki. 12.18
[10]founding
[11]Or, commentary

CHAPTER 25
1 [a]2 Ki. 14.1
2 [b]2 Ki. 14.4; Hos. 10.2
3 [c]2 Ki. 14.5
[1]confirmed upon him

book of Mō'ses, where the LORD commanded, saying, [d]The fathers shall not
die for the children, neither shall the
children die for the fathers, but every
man shall die for his own sin.
5 ¶ Moreover Ăm-a-zī'ah gathered
Jū'dah together, and made them captains over thousands, and captains over
hundreds, according to the houses of
their fathers, throughout all Jū'dah and
Bĕn'ja-min: and he numbered them
[e]from twenty years old and above, and
found them three hundred thousand
choice *men, able* to go forth to war, that
could handle spear and shield.
6 He hired also an hundred thousand mighty men of valour out of Ĭs'ra-
el for an hundred talents of silver.
7 But there came a man of God to
him, saying, O king, let not the army of
Ĭs'ra-el go with thee; for the [f]LORD *is*
not with Ĭs'ra-el, *to wit, with* all the
children of Ē'phră-ĭm.
8 But if thou wilt go, do *it,* be strong
for the battle: God shall make thee
fall before the enemy: for God hath
[g]power to help, and to cast down.
9 And Ăm-a-zī'ah said to the man of
God, But what shall we do for the hundred talents which I have given to the
[2]army of Ĭs'ra-el? And the man of God
answered, [h]The LORD is able to give
thee much more than this.
10 Then Ăm-a-zī'ah separated them,
to wit, the army that was come to him
out of Ē'phră-ĭm, to go [3]home again:
wherefore their anger was greatly kindled against Jū'dah, and they returned
home [4]in great anger.
11 ¶ And Ăm-a-zī'ah strengthened
himself, and led forth his people, and
went to [i]the valley of salt, and smote of
the children of Sē'ĭr ten thousand.
12 And *other* ten thousand *left* alive
did the children of Jū'dah carry away
captive, and brought them unto the top
of the rock, and cast them down from
the top of the rock, that they all were
broken in pieces.
13 ¶ But [5]the soldiers of the army
which Ăm-a-zī'ah sent back, that they
should not go with him to battle, fell
upon the cities of Jū'dah, from Sa-
mā'rĭ-ȧ even unto Bĕth–hō'rŏn, and
smote three thousand of them, and
took much spoil.
14 ¶ Now it came to pass, after that
Ăm-a-zī'ah was come from the slaughter of the Ē'dom-ītes, that [j]he brought
the gods of the children of Sē'ĭr, and set
them up *to be* [k]his gods, and bowed
down himself before them, and burned
incense unto them.
15 Wherefore the anger of the LORD
was kindled against Ăm-a-zī'ah, and
he sent unto him a prophet, which said
unto him, Why hast thou sought after
[l]the gods of the people, which could
not deliver their own people out of
thine hand?
16 And it came to pass, as he talked
with him, that *the king* said unto him,
Art thou made of [m]the king's counsel?
forbear; why shouldest thou be smitten? Then the prophet forbare, and

4 [d]Deut. 24.16; 2 Ki. 14.6; Jer. 31.30
5 [e]Num. 1.3
7 [f]ch. 15.2; 1 Ki. 12.28; Isa. 28.1-3; Hos. 4.6-15-19; Hos. 5.6-7-15
8 [g]Gen. 18.14; Judg. 7.7; 1 Sam. 14.6; 1 Chr. 29.11; ch. 14.11; ch. 20.6; Job 5.18; Ps. 20.7; Ps. 118.6; Jer. 32.17; Matt. 19.26; Rom. 8.31
9 [2]band [h]Deut. 8.18; ch. 1.12; Prov. 10.22; Hag. 2.8
10 [3]to their place [4]in heat of anger
11 [i]2 Ki. 14.7
13 [5]the sons of the band
14 [j]ch. 28.23 [k]Ex. 20.3-5
15 [l]Ps. 96.5; Ps. 115.3-8; Isa. 46.1-2; 1 Cor. 8.4
16 [m]ch. 16.10; 2 Tim. 4.3 [6]counselled
17 [n]2 Ki. 14.8-9
18 [7]Or, furze bush, or, thorn [8]a beast of the field
19 [o]ch. 35.21; Prov. 12.15
20 [p]1 Ki. 12.15; ch. 22.7
22 [9]smitten
23 [q]ch. 21.17; ch. 22.1-6 [10]the gate of it that looketh
24 [11]sons of pledge, or, power
25 [r]2 Ki. 14.17
27 [12]from after [13]conspired a conspiracy
28 [14]That is, The city of David, as it is

CHAPTER 26
1 [1]Or, Azariah

said, I know that God hath [6]deter-
mined to destroy thee, because thou
hast done this, and hast not hearkened
unto my counsel.
17 ¶ Then [n]Ăm-a-zī'ah king of Jū'-
dah took advice, and sent to Jō'ăsh, the
son of Je-hō'a-hăz, the son of Jē'hū,
king of Ĭs'ra-el, saying, Come, let us see
one another in the face.
18 And Jō'ăsh king of Ĭs'ra-el sent
to Ăm-a-zī'ah king of Jū'dah, saying,
The [7]thistle that *was* in Lĕb'a-non sent
to the cedar that *was* in Lĕb'a-non, saying, Give thy daughter to my son to
wife: and there passed by [8]a wild beast
that *was* in Lĕb'a-non, and trode down
the thistle.
19 Thou sayest, Lo, thou hast smitten the Ē'dom-ītes; and thine heart
lifteth thee up to boast: abide now at
home; why shouldest thou [o]meddle to
thine hurt, that thou shouldest fall,
even thou, and Jū'dah with thee?
20 But Ăm-a-zī'ah would not hear;
for [p]it *came* of God, that he might deliver them into the hand *of their enemies,* because they sought after the
gods of Ē'dom.
21 So Jō'ăsh the king of Ĭs'ra-el went
up; and they saw one another in the
face, *both* he and Ăm-a-zī'ah king of
Jū'dah, at Bĕth–shē'mĕsh, which *belongeth* to Jū'dah.
22 And Jū'dah was [9]put to the worse
before Ĭs'ra-el, and they fled every
man to his tent.
23 And Jō'ăsh the king of Ĭs'ra-el
took Ăm-a-zī'ah king of Jū'dah, the
son of Jō'ăsh, the son of [q]Je-hō'a-hăz,
at Bĕth–shē'mĕsh, and brought him
to Je-rụ'sa-lĕm, and brake down the
wall of Je-rụ'sa-lĕm from the gate of
Ē'phră-ĭm to [10]the corner gate, four
hundred cubits.
24 And *he took* all the gold and the
silver, and all the vessels that were
found in the house of God with Ō'bed–
ē'dom, and the treasures of the king's
house, the [11]hostages also, and returned to Sa-mā'rĭ-ȧ.
25 ¶ [r]And Ăm-a-zī'ah the son of
Jō'ăsh king of Jū'dah lived after the
death of Jō'ăsh son of Je-hō'a-hăz
king of Ĭs'ra-el fifteen years.
26 Now the rest of the acts of Ăm-a-
zī'ah, first and last, behold, *are* they
not written in the book of the kings of
Jū'dah and Ĭs'ra-el?
27 ¶ Now after the time that Ăm-a-
zī'ah did turn away [12]from following
the LORD they [13]made a conspiracy
against him in Je-rụ'sa-lĕm; and he
fled to Lā'chish: but they sent to Lā'-
chish after him, and slew him there.
28 And they brought him upon
horses, and buried him with his fathers
in the city of [14]Jū'dah.

26 Then all the people of Jū'dah
took [1]Ŭz-zī'ah, who *was* sixteen
years old, and made him king in the
room of his father Ăm-a-zī'ah.
2 He built Ē'lŏth, and restored it to
Jū'dah, after that the king slept with
his fathers.

3 Sixteen years old *was* Ŭz-zī'ah
when he began to reign, and he reigned
fifty and two years in Je-rṳ'sa-lĕm. His
mother's name also *was* Jĕc-o-lī'ah of
Je-rṳ'sa-lĕm.
4 And he did *that which was* right in
the sight of the LORD, according to all
that his father Ăm-a-zī'ah did.
5 And [a]he sought God in the days of
Zĕch-a-rī'ah, who [b]had understanding
[2]in the visions of God: and as long as
he sought the LORD, God made him to
prosper.
6 And he went forth and [c]warred
against the Phĭ-lĭs'tīnes, and brake
down the wall of Găth, and the wall of
Jăb'neh, and the wall of Ăsh'dŏd, and
built cities [3]about Ăsh'dŏd, and among
the Phĭ-lĭs'tīnes.
7 And God helped him against [d]the
Phĭ-lĭs'tīnes, and against the A-rā'bĭ-
ans that dwelt in Gûr-bā'al, and the
Me-hu'nims.
8 And the [e]Ăm'mŏn-ītes gave gifts
to Ŭz-zī'ah: and his name [4]spread
abroad *even* to the entering in of
Ē'gypt; for he strengthened *himself*
exceedingly.
9 Moreover Ŭz-zī'ah built towers in
Je-rṳ'sa-lĕm at the [f]corner gate, and at
the valley gate, and at the turning *of
the wall*, and [5]fortified them.
10 Also he built towers in the desert, and [6]digged many wells: for he
had much cattle, both in the low country, and in the plains: husbandmen
also, and vine dressers in the mountains, and in [7]Cär'mel: for he loved
[8]husbandry.
11 Moreover Ŭz-zī'ah had an host of
fighting men, that went out to war by
bands, according to the number of
their account by the hand of Je-ī'el the
scribe and Mā-a-sē'iah the ruler, under
the hand of Hăn-a-nī'ah, *one* of the
king's captains.
12 The whole number of the chief of
the fathers of the mighty men of valour
were two thousand and six hundred.
13 And under their hand *was* [9]an
army, three hundred thousand and
seven thousand and five hundred, that
made war with mighty power, to help
the king against the enemy.
14 And Ŭz-zī'ah prepared for them
throughout all the host shields, and
spears, and helmets, and habergeons,
and bows, and [10]slings *to cast* stones.
15 And he made in Je-rṳ'sa-lĕm engines, invented by cunning men, to be
on the towers and upon the bulwarks, to
shoot arrows and great stones withal.
And his name [11]spread far abroad; for
he was marvellously helped, till he was
strong.
16 ¶ But [g]when he was strong, his
heart was [h]lifted up to *his* destruction:
for he transgressed against the LORD
his God, and [i]went into the temple of
the LORD to burn incense upon the altar of incense.
17 And [j]Ăz-a-rī'ah the priest went
in after him, and with him fourscore
priests of the LORD, *that were* valiant
men:
18 And they [k]withstood Ŭz-zī'ah the
king, and said unto him, *It* [l]*appertaineth* not unto thee, Ŭz-zī'ah, to burn
incense unto the LORD, but to the
[m]priests the sons of Aâr'on, that are
consecrated to burn incense: go out
of the sanctuary; for thou hast trespassed; neither *shall it be* for thine honour from the LORD God.
19 Then Ŭz-zī'ah was wroth, and
had a censer in his hand to burn incense: and while he was wroth with
the priests, [n]the leprosy even rose up
in his forehead before the priests in the
house of the LORD, from beside the incense altar.
20 And Ăz-a-rī'ah the chief priest,
and all the priests, looked upon him,
and, behold, he *was* leprous in his forehead, and they thrust him out from
thence; yea, himself [o]hasted also to go
out, because the LORD had smitten
him.
21 [p]And Ŭz-zī'ah the king was a
leper unto the day of his death, and
dwelt in a [12]several house, *being* a
leper; for he was cut off from the house
of the LORD: and Jō'tham his son *was*
over the king's house, judging the people of the land.
22 ¶ Now the rest of the acts of Ŭz-
zī'ah, first and last, did [q]I-sā'iah the
prophet, the son of Ā'moz, write.
23 [r]So Ŭz-zī'ah slept with his fathers, and they buried him with his fathers in the field of the burial which
belonged to the kings; for they said, He
is a leper: and Jō'tham his son reigned
in his stead.

27

Jō'tham [a]*was* twenty and five
years old when he began to reign,
and he reigned sixteen years in Je-
rṳ'sa-lĕm. His mother's name also *was*
Je-rṳ-'shah, the daughter of Zā'dŏk.
2 And he did *that which was* right
in the sight of the LORD, according to
all that his father Ŭz-zī'ah did: howbeit [b]he entered not into the temple
of the LORD. And [c]the people did yet
corruptly.
3 He built the high gate of the house
of the LORD, and on the wall of [1]Ō'phel
he built much.
4 Moreover he built cities in the
mountains of Jū'dah, and in the forests
he built castles and towers.
5 ¶ He [d]fought also with the king of
the Ăm'mŏn-ītes, and prevailed against
them. And the children of Ăm'mŏn
gave him the same year an hundred talents of silver, and ten thousand measures of wheat, and ten thousand of
barley. [2]So much did the children of
Ăm'mŏn pay unto him, both the second
year, and the third.
6 So Jō'tham became mighty, because he [3][e]prepared his ways before
the LORD his God.
7 ¶ Now the rest of the acts of Jō'-
tham, and all his wars, and his ways,
lo, they *are* written in the book of the
kings of Ĭs'ra-el and Jū'dah.
8 He was five and twenty years old
when he began to reign, and reigned
sixteen years in Je-rṳ'sa-lĕm.

5 [a]ch. 24.2 [b]Gen. 41.15; Dan. 1.17; Dan. 2.19 [2]in the seeing of God
6 [c]ch. 21.16; Isa. 14.29 [3]Or, in the country of Ashdod
7 [d]1 Chr. 5.20; ch. 14.11; Acts 26.22
8 [e]Gen. 19.38; 1 Sam. 11.1; 2 Sam. 8.2; ch. 17.11 [4]went
9 [f]2 Ki. 14.13; Zech. 14.10 [5]Or, repaired
10 [6]Or, cut out many cisterns [7]Or, Fruitful fields [8]ground
13 [9]the power of an army
14 [10]stones of slings
15 [11]went forth
16 [g]Deut. 32.15; ch. 25.19; Hab. 2.4; Col. 2.18 [h]Deut. 8.14; ch. 25.19 [i]2 Ki. 16.12-13
17 [j]1 Chr. 6.10
18 [k]ch. 19.2; Matt. 14.4 [l]Num. 16.40 [m]Ex. 30.7
19 [n]Num. 12.10
20 [o]Esth. 6.12
21 [p]2 Ki. 15.5 [12]free
22 [q]Isa. 1.1
23 [r]Isa. 6.1

CHAPTER 27
1 [a]2 Ki. 15.32; Mic. 1.1
2 [b]ch. 26.16-21; Ps. 119.120 [c]2 Ki. 15.35
3 [1]Or, The tower, ch. 33.14
5 [d]ch. 20.1; Jer. 49.1-6 [2]This
6 [3]Or, established [e]1 Sam. 2.30; Ps. 84.5

9 ¶ And Jō'tham slept with his fathers, and they buried him in the city of Dā'vid: and Ā'hăz his son reigned in his stead.

28

A'hăz [a]*was* twenty years old when he began to reign, and he reigned sixteen years in Je-ru'sa-lĕm: but he did not *that which was* right in the sight of the LORD, like Dā'vid his father:

2 For he walked in the ways of the kings of Ĭs'ra-el, and made also [b]molten images for [c]Bā'al-ĭm.

3 Moreover he [1]burnt incense in [d]the valley of the son of Hĭn'nom, and burnt his [e]children in the fire, after the abominations of the heathen whom the LORD had cast out before the children of Ĭs'ra-el.

4 He sacrificed also and burnt incense in the high places, and on the hills, and under every green tree.

5 Wherefore [f]the LORD his God delivered him into the hand of the king of Sy̆r'ĭ-ȧ; and they [g]smote him, and carried away a great multitude of them captives, and brought *them* to [2]Da-măs'cus. And he was also delivered into the hand of the king of Ĭs'ra-el, who smote him with a great slaughter.

6 ¶ For [h]Pē'kah the son of Rĕm-a-lī'ah slew in Jū'dah an hundred and twenty thousand in one day, *which were* all [3]valiant men; because they had [i]forsaken the LORD God of their fathers.

7 And Zĭch'rī, a mighty man of Ē'phră-ĭm, slew Mā-a-sē'iah the king's son, and Ăz'rĭ-kam the governor of the house, and Ĕl'kă-nah *that was* [4]next to the king.

8 And the children of Ĭs'ra-el carried away captive of their [j]brethren two hundred thousand, women, sons, and daughters, and took also away much spoil from them, and brought the spoil to Sa-mā'rĭ-ȧ.

9 But a prophet of the LORD was there, whose name *was* O'ded: and he went out before the host that came to Sa-mā'rĭ-ȧ, and said unto them, Behold, [k]because the LORD God of your fathers was wroth with Jū'dah, he hath delivered them into your hand, and ye have slain them in a rage *that* [l]reacheth up unto heaven.

10 And now ye purpose to keep under the children of Jū'dah and Je-ru'sa-lĕm for [m]bondmen and bondwomen unto you: *but are there* not with [n]you, even with you, sins against the LORD your God?

11 Now hear me therefore, and deliver the captives again, which ye have taken captive of your brethren: [o]for the fierce wrath of the LORD *is* upon you.

12 Then certain of the heads of the children of Ē'phră-ĭm, Ăz-a-rī'ah the son of Jo-hā'nan, Bĕr-e-chī'ah the son of Me-shĭl'le-mŏth, and Je-hĭz-kī'ah the son of Shăl'lum, and Ăm'a-sȧ the son of Hăd'la-ī, stood up against them that came from the war,

13 And said unto them, Ye shall not bring in the captives hither: for whereas we have offended against the LORD *already,* ye intend to [p]add *more* to our sins and to our trespass: for our trespass is great, and *there is* fierce wrath against Ĭs'ra-el.

14 So the armed men left the captives and the spoil before the princes and all the congregation.

15 And the men which were expressed by name rose up, and took the captives, and with the spoil clothed all that were naked among them, and arrayed them, and shod them, and [q]gave them to eat and to drink, and anointed them, and carried all the feeble of them upon asses, and brought them to Jĕr'ĭ-chō, the [r]city of palm trees, to their brethren: then they returned to Sa-mā'rĭ-ȧ.

16 ¶ At [s]that time did king Ā'hăz send unto the kings of Ăs-sy̆r'ĭ-ȧ to help him.

17 For [t]again the Ē'dom-ītes had come and smitten Jū'dah, and carried away [5]captives.

18 [u]The Phĭ-lĭs'tĭnes also had invaded the cities of the low country, and of the south of Jū'dah, and had taken Bĕth–shē'mĕsh, and Ăj'a-lŏn, and Gĕ-dē'rŏth, and Shō'chō with the villages thereof, and Tĭm'nah with the villages thereof, Gĭm'zō also and the villages thereof: and they dwelt there.

19 For the LORD brought Jū'dah low because of Ā'hăz king of [v]Ĭs'ra-el; for he [w]made Jū'dah naked, and transgressed sore against the LORD.

20 And [x]Tĭl'gath–pĭl-nē'ser king of Ăs-sy̆r'ĭ-ȧ came unto him, and distressed him, but strengthened him not.

21 For Ā'hăz took away a portion *out* of the house of the LORD, and *out* of the house of the king, and of the princes, and gave *it* unto the king of Ăs-sy̆r'ĭ-ȧ: but he helped him not.

22 ¶ And in the time [y]of his distress did he trespass yet more against the LORD: this *is that* king Ā'hăz.

23 For [z]he sacrificed unto the gods of [6]Da-măs'cus, which smote him: and he said, Because the gods of the kings of Sy̆r'ĭ-ȧ help them, *therefore* will I sacrifice to them, that [a]they may help me. But they were the ruin of him, and of all Ĭs'ra-el.

24 And Ā'hăz gathered together the vessels of the house of God, and cut in pieces the vessels of the house of God, [b]and shut up the doors of the house of the LORD, and he made him altars in every corner of Je-ru'sa-lĕm.

25 And in every several city of Jū'dah he made high places [7]to burn incense unto other gods, and provoked to anger the LORD God of his fathers.

26 ¶ [c]Now the rest of his acts and of all his ways, first and last, behold, they *are* written in the book of the kings of Jū'dah and Ĭs'ra-el.

27 And Ā'hăz slept with his fathers, and they buried him in the city, *even* in Je-ru'sa-lĕm: but they brought him not into the sepulchres of the kings

CHAPTER 28
1 [a]2 Ki. 16.2
2 [b]Ex. 34.17; Lev. 19.4
[c]Judg. 2.11
3 [1]Or, offered sacrifice
[d]2 Ki. 23.10; Jer. 7.31
[e]Lev. 18.21; ch. 33.6; Mic. 6.7
5 [f]Isa. 7.1
[g]2 Ki. 16.5
[2]Darmesek
6 [h]2 Ki. 15.27; Isa. 9.21
[3]sons of valour
[i]Josh. 23.16
7 [4]the second to the king
8 [j]ch. 11.4
9 [k]Judg. 3.8; Ps. 69.26; Ezek. 26.2; Zech. 1.15
[l]Gen. 4.10; Ezra 9.6; Rev. 18.5
10 [m]Lev. 25.39
[n]Jer. 25.29; 1 Pet. 4.17
11 [o]Jas. 2.13
13 [p]Num. 32.14; Josh. 22.17
15 [q]2 Ki. 6.22; Rom. 12.20
[r]Deut. 34.3
16 [s]2 Ki. 16.7
17 [t]Lev. 26.18
[5]a captivity
18 [u]Josh. 15.22
19 [v]ch. 21.20
[w]Ex. 32.25; Rev. 16.15
20 [x]2 Ki. 15.29; Isa. 7.20
22 [y]ch. 33.12; Ps. 50.15; Rev. 16.11
23 [z]ch. 25.14
[6]Darmesek
[a]Jer. 44.17-18
24 [b]ch. 29.3-7
25 [7]Or, to offer
26 [c]2 Ki. 16.19-20; ch. 27.7-9

of Ĭs'ra-el: and Hĕz-e-kī'ah his son
reigned in his stead.

29 Hĕz-e-kī'ah [a]began to reign *when*
he was five and twenty years
old, and he reigned nine and twenty
years in Je-ru'sa-lĕm. And his mother's
name *was* Ā-bī'jah, the daughter [b]of
Zĕch-a-rī'ah.
2 And he did *that which was* right in
the sight of the LORD, according to all
that Dā'vid his father had done.
3 ¶ He in the first year of his reign, in
the [c]first month, [d]opened the doors of
the house of the LORD, and repaired
them.
4 And he brought in the priests and
the Lē'vītes, and gathered them together into the east street,
5 And said unto them, Hear me,
ye Lē'vītes, [e]sanctify now yourselves,
and sanctify the house of the LORD
God of your fathers, and carry forth
the [1]filthiness out of the holy *place*.
6 For our fathers have trespassed,
and done *that which was* evil in the
eyes of the LORD our God, and have
forsaken him, and have [f]turned away
their faces from the habitation of the
LORD, and [2]turned *their* backs.
7 Also [g]they have shut up the doors
of the porch, and put out the lamps,
and have not burned incense nor offered burnt offerings in the holy *place*
unto the God of Ĭs'ra-el.
8 Wherefore the [h]wrath of the LORD
was upon Jū'dah and Je-ru'sa-lĕm, and
he hath delivered them to [3]trouble, to
astonishment, and to [i]hissing, as ye see
with you eyes.
9 For, lo, [j]our fathers have fallen by
the sword, and our sons and our daughters and our wives *are* in captivity for
this.
10 Now *it is* in mine heart to make
[k]a covenant with the LORD God of
Ĭs'ra-el, that his fierce wrath may turn
away from us.
11 My sons, [4]be not now negligent:
for the LORD hath [l]chosen you to stand
before him, to serve him, and that ye
should minister unto him, and [5]burn
incense.
12 ¶ Then the Lē'vītes arose, Mā'-
hath the son of A-măs'a-ī, and Jō'el the
son of Ăz-a-rī'ah, of the sons of the
Kō'hath-ītes: and of the sons of Me-
rā'rī, Kĭsh the son of Ăb'dī, and Ăz-a-
rī'ah the son of Je-hăl'e-lĕl: and of the
Gēr'shon-ītes; Jō'ah the son of Zĭm'-
mah, and Ē'dĕn the son of Jō'ah:
13 And of the sons of Ĕl'za-phăn;
Shĭm'rī, and Je-ī'el: and of the sons of
Ā'saph; Zĕch-a-rī'ah, and Măt-ta-nī'ah:
14 And of the sons of Hē'man; Je-
hī'el, and Shĭm'e-ī: and of the sons of
Jĕd'u-thŭn; Shĕm-a-ī'ah, and Ŭz'zī-el.
15 And they gathered their brethren, and sanctified themselves, and
came, according to the commandment
of the king, [6]by the words of the LORD,
[m]to cleanse the house of the LORD.
16 And the priests went into [n]the inner part of the house of the LORD, to
cleanse *it*, and brought out all the uncleanness that they found in the temple of the LORD into the court of the
house of the LORD. And the Lē'vītes
took *it*, to carry *it* out abroad into the
brook Kĭd'ron.
17 Now they began on the first *day*
of the first month to sanctify, and on
the eighth day of the month came they
to the [o]porch of the LORD: so they sanctified the house of the LORD in eight
days; and in the sixteenth day of the
first month they made an end.
18 Then they went in to Hĕz-e-kī'ah
the king, and said, We have cleansed
all the house of the LORD, and the altar
of burnt offering, with all the vessels
thereof, and the shewbread table, with
all the vessels thereof.
19 Moreover all the vessels, which
king Ā'hăz in his reign did [p]cast away
in his transgression, have we prepared
and sanctified, and, behold, they *are*
before the altar of the LORD.
20 ¶ Then Hĕz-e-kī'ah the king rose
early, and gathered the rulers of the
city, and went up to the house of the
LORD.
21 And they brought seven bullocks,
and seven rams, and seven lambs, and
seven he goats, for a [q]sin offering for
the kingdom, and for the sanctuary,
and for Jū'dah. And he commanded the
priests the sons of Aâr'on to offer *them*
on the altar of the LORD.
22 So they killed the bullocks, and
the priests received the blood, and
[r]sprinkled *it* on the altar: likewise,
when they had killed the rams, they
sprinkled the blood upon the altar:
they killed also the lambs, and they
sprinkled the blood upon the altar.
23 And they brought [7]forth the he
goats *for* the sin offering before the
king and the congregation; and they
laid their [s]hands upon them:
24 And the priests killed them, and
they made reconciliation with their
blood upon the altar, [t]to make an
atonement for all Ĭs'ra-el: for the king
commanded *that* the burnt offering
and the sin offering *should be made* for
all Ĭs'ra-el.
25 [u]And he set the Lē'vītes in the
house of the LORD with cymbals, with
psalteries, and with harps, [v]according
to the commandment of Dā'vid, and of
[w]Găd the king's seer, and Nā'than the
prophet: [x]for *so was* the commandment [8]of the LORD [9]by his prophets.
26 And the Lē'vītes stood with the
instruments [y]of Dā'vid, and the priests
with [z]the trumpets.
27 And Hĕz-e-kī'ah commanded to
offer the burnt offering upon the altar.
And [10]when the burnt offering began,
[a]the song of the LORD began *also*
with the trumpets, and with the [11]in-
struments *ordained* by Dā'vid king of
Ĭs'ra-el.
28 And all the congregation worshipped, and the [12]singers sang, and
the trumpeters sounded: *and* all *this*
continued until the burnt offering was
finished.
29 And when they had made an end
of offering, [b]the king and all that were

CHAPTER 29
1 [a]2 Ki. 18.1; Hos. 1.1
[b]ch. 26.5
3 [c]Prov. 8.17
[d]ch. 28.24
5 [e]1 Chr. 15.12; 2 Cor. 6.16
[1]That is, idols, etc
6 [f]Jer. 2.27; Ezek. 8.16
[2]given the neck
7 [g]2 Ki. 16.17-18; ch. 28.24
8 [h]Deut. 28.15-20
[3]commotion, Deut. 28.25
[i]1 Ki. 9.8; Jer. 18.16
9 [j]Lev. 26.17;
10 [k]ch. 15.12;
11 [4]Or, be not now deceived, 1 Cor. 6.9
[l]Num. 3.6
[5]Or, offer sacrifice
15 [6]Or, in the business of the LORD, ch. 30.12
[m]1 Chr. 23.28
16 [n]1 Ki. 6.23;
17 [o]1 Ki. 6.3
19 [p]ch. 28.24
21 [q]Lev. 4.3-14
22 [r]Lev. 8.14-15-19-24
23 [7]near
[s]Lev. 4.15-24
24 [t]Lev. 14.20;
25 [u]1 Chr. 16.4
[v]1 Chr. 23.5;
[w]2 Sam. 24.11
[x]ch. 30.12
[8]by the hand of the LORD
[9]by the hand of
26 [y]Num. 10.10;
[z]Num. 10.8-10;
27 [10]in the time
[a]ch. 20.21
[11]hands of instruments
28 [12]song
29 [b]ch. 20.18;

[13]present with him bowed themselves,
and worshipped.
30 Moreover Hĕz-e-kī'ah the king
and the princes commanded the Lē'-
vītes to sing praise unto the LORD with
the words of Dā'vid, and of Ā'saph the
seer. And they sang [c]praises with gladness, and they bowed their heads and
worshipped.
31 Then Hĕz-e-kī'ah answered and
said, Now ye have [14]consecrated yourselves unto the LORD, come near and
bring sacrifices and [d]thank offerings
into the house of the LORD. And the
congregation brought in sacrifices and
thank offerings; and as many as were
of a free heart burnt offerings.
32 And the number of the burnt offerings, which the congregation brought,
was threescore and ten bullocks, an
hundred rams, *and* two hundred lambs:
all these *were* for a burnt offering to the
LORD.
33 And the consecrated things *were*
six hundred oxen and three thousand
sheep.
34 But the priests were too few, so
that they could not flay all the burnt
offerings: wherefore [e]their brethren
the Lē'vītes [15]did help them, till the
work was ended, and until the *other*
priests had sanctified themselves: [f]for
the Lē'vītes *were* more [g]upright in
heart to sanctify themselves than the
priests.
35 And also the burnt offerings *were*
in abundance, with [h]the fat of the
peace offerings, and [i]the drink offerings for *every* burnt offering. So the service of the house of the LORD was set in
order.
36 And Hĕz-e-kī'ah rejoiced, and all
the people, that God had prepared
the people: for [j]the thing was *done*
suddenly.

30 And Hĕz-e-kī'ah sent to all Ĭs'ra-
el and Jū'dah, and wrote letters
also to Ē'phră-ĭm and Ma-năs'seh, that
they should come to the house of the
LORD at Je-ru'sa-lĕm, to keep the passover unto the LORD God of Ĭs'ra-el.
2 For the king had taken counsel,
and his princes, and all the congregation in Je-ru'sa-lĕm, to keep the passover in the second [a]month.
3 For they could not keep it [b]at that
time, [c]because the priests had not sanctified themselves sufficiently, neither
had the people gathered themselves together to Je-ru'sa-lĕm.
4 And the thing [1]pleased the king
and all the congregation.
5 So they established a decree to
make proclamation throughout all Ĭs'-
ra-el, from Bē'er–shē'bȧ even to Dăn,
that they should come to keep the passover unto the LORD God of Ĭs'ra-el at
Je-ru'sa-lĕm: for they had not done *it*
of a long *time in such sort* as it was
written.
6 So the posts went with the letters
[2]from the king and his princes throughout all Ĭs'ra-el and Jū'dah, and according to the commandment of the king,
saying, Ye children of Ĭs'ra-el, [d]turn
again unto the LORD God of Ā'bră-
hăm, Ī'saac, and Ĭs'ra-el, and he will
return to the remnant of you, that are
escaped out of the hand of [e]the kings
of Ăs-sȳr'ĭ-ȧ.
7 And be not ye [f]like your fathers,
and like your brethren, which trespassed against the LORD God of their
fathers, *who* therefore [g]gave them up
to desolation, as ye see.
8 Now [3]be ye not [h]stiffnecked, as
your fathers *were, but* [4]yield yourselves unto the LORD, and enter into
his sanctuary, which he hath sanctified for ever: and serve the LORD your
God, [i]that the fierceness of his wrath
may turn away from you.
9 For if ye turn again unto the LORD,
your brethren and your children *shall
find* [j]compassion before them that lead
them captive, so that they shall come
again into this land: for the LORD your
God *is* [k]gracious and merciful, and will
not turn away *his* face from you, if ye
[l]return unto him.
10 So the posts passed from city to
city through the country of Ē'phră-ĭm
and Ma-năs'seh even unto Zĕb'u-lun:
but [m]they laughed them to scorn, and
mocked them.
11 Nevertheless [n]divers of Ăsh'ēr
and Ma-năs'seh and of Zĕb'u-lun humbled themselves, and came to Je-ru'sa-
lĕm.
12 Also in Jū'dah [o]the hand of God
was to give them one heart to do the
commandment of the king and of the
princes, [p]by the word of the LORD.
13 ¶ And there assembled at Je-ru'-
sa-lĕm much people to keep the feast
of unleavened bread in the second
month, a very great congregation.
14 And they arose and took away
the [q]altars that *were* in Je-ru'sa-lĕm,
and all the altars for incense took they
away, and cast *them* into the brook
Kĭd'ron.
15 Then they killed the passover
on the fourteenth *day* of the second
month: and the priests and the Lē'vītes
were [r]ashamed, and sanctified themselves, and brought in the burnt offerings into the house of the LORD.
16 And they stood in [5]their place after their manner, according to the law
of Mō'ses the man of God: the priests
sprinkled the blood, *which they received* of the hand of the Lē'vītes.
17 For *there were* many in the congregation that were not sanctified:
[s]therefore the Lē'vītes had the charge
of the killing of the passovers for every
one *that was* not clean, to sanctify
them unto the LORD.
18 For a multitude of the people,
even many of Ē'phră-ĭm, and Ma-năs'-
seh, Ĭs'sa-char, and Zĕb'u-lun, had not
cleansed themselves, [t]yet did they eat
the passover otherwise than it was
written. But Hĕz-e-kī'ah prayed for
them, saying, The good LORD pardon
every one
19 *That* [u]prepareth his heart to seek
God, the LORD God of his fathers,

[13]found
30 [c]Ps. 32.11; Phil. 4.4
31 [14]Or, filled your hand, ch. 13.9
[d]Lev. 7.12
34 [e]Num. 8.15; ch. 35.11
[15]strengthened them
[f]ch. 30.3
[g]1 Chr. 29.17; Ps. 7.10
35 [h]Ex. 29.13; Lev. 3.16
[i]Gen. 35.14
36 [j]Ps. 118.23; Acts 2.41
CHAPTER 30
2 [a]Num. 9.10
3 [b]Ex. 12.6
[c]ch. 29.34
4 [1]was right in the eyes of the king
6 [2]from the hand
[d]1 Sam. 7.3-4; Hos. 6.1; Joel 2.13; Mal. 3.7
[e]2 Ki. 15.19-29
7 [f]Ezek. 20.18
[g]ch. 29.8
8 [3]harden not your necks
[h]Deut. 10.16
[4]give the hand
[i]ch. 29.10
9 [j]Lev. 26.40
[k]Ex. 34.6; Mic. 7.18
[l]Isa. 55.7
10 [m]ch. 36.16; Neh. 2.19; Matt. 21.35; Acts 17.32
11 [n]ch. 11.16
12 [o]ch. 29.36; Ps. 110.3; 2 Cor. 3.5; Heb. 13.21
[p]ch. 29.25
14 [q]ch. 28.24; Isa. 2.17-21
15 [r]ch. 29.34
16 [5]their standing
17 [s]ch. 29.34
18 [t]Ex. 12.43
19 [u]1 Sam. 7.3; 1 Chr. 29.18; ch. 19.3; Job 11.13

though *he be* not *cleansed* according to
the purification of the sanctuary.
20 And the LORD hearkened to Hĕz-
e-kī'ah, and [v]healed the people.
21 And the children of Ĭs'ra-el that
were [6]present at Je-ru'sa-lĕm, kept [w]the
feast of unleavened bread seven days
with great gladness: and the Lē'vītes
and the priests praised the LORD day
by day, *singing* with [7]loud instruments
unto the LORD.
22 And Hĕz-e-kī'ah spake [8]comfort-
ably unto all the Lē'vītes [x]that taught
the good knowledge of the LORD: and
they did eat throughout the feast seven
days, offering peace offerings, and
[y]making confession to the LORD God
of their fathers.
23 And the whole assembly took
counsel to keep [z]other seven days:
and they kept *other* seven days with
gladness.
24 For Hĕz-e-kī'ah king of Jū'dah
[9][a]did give to the congregation a thousand bullocks and seven thousand
sheep; and the princes gave to the congregation a thousand bullocks and ten
thousand sheep: and a great number of
priests [b]sanctified themselves.
25 And all the congregation of Jū'-
dah, with the priests and the Lē'vītes,
and all the congregation [c]that came
out of Ĭs'ra-el, and the strangers that
came out of the land of Ĭs'ra-el, and
that dwelt in Jū'dah, rejoiced.
26 So there was great joy in Je-
ru'sa-lĕm: for since the time of Sŏl'o-
mon the son of Dā'vid king of Ĭs'ra-el
there was not the like in Je-ru'sa-lĕm.
27 ¶ Then the priests the Lē'vītes
arose and [d]blessed the people: and
their voice was heard, and their prayer
came *up* to [10]his holy dwelling place,
even unto heaven.
31 Now when all this was finished,
all Ĭs'ra-el that were [1]present
went out to the cities of Jū'dah, and
[a]brake the [2]images in pieces, and cut
down the groves, and threw down the
high places and the altars out of all
Jū'dah and Bĕn'ja-min, in Ē'phră-ĭm
also and Ma-năs'seh, [3]until they had
utterly destroyed them all. Then all the
children of Ĭs'ra-el returned, every man
to his possession, into their own cities.
2 ¶ And Hĕz-e-kī'ah appointed [b]the
courses of the priests and the Lē'vītes
after their courses, every man according to his service, the priests and
Lē'vītes [c]for burnt offerings and for
peace offerings, to minister, and to
give thanks, and to praise in the gates
of the tents of the LORD.
3 *He appointed* also the king's portion of his substance for the burnt offerings, *to wit,* for the morning and evening burnt offerings, and the burnt offerings for the sabbaths, and for the
new moons, and for the set feasts, as *it
is* written in the [d]law of the LORD.
4 Moreover he commanded the people that dwelt in Je-ru'sa-lĕm to give
the [e]portion of the priests and the
Lē'vītes, that they might be encouraged in [f]the law of the LORD.
5 ¶ And as soon as the commandment [4]came abroad, the children of Ĭs'-
ra-el brought in abundance [g]the firstfruits of corn, wine, and oil, and [5]honey,
and of all the increase of the field; and
the tithe of all *things* brought they in
abundantly.
6 And *concerning* the children of
Ĭs'ra-el and Jū'dah, that dwelt in the
cities of Jū'dah, they also brought in
the tithe of oxen and sheep, and the
[h]tithe of holy things which were consecrated unto the LORD their God, and
laid *them* [6]by heaps.
7 In the third month they began to
lay the foundation of the heaps, and
finished *them* in the seventh month.
8 And when Hĕz-e-kī'ah and the
princes came and saw the heaps, they
blessed the LORD, and [i]his people
Ĭs'ra-el.
9 Then Hĕz-e-kī'ah questioned with
the priests and the Lē'vītes concerning
the heaps.
10 And Ăz-a-rī'ah the chief priest of
the house of Zā'dŏk answered him,
and said, [j]Since *the people* began to
bring the offerings into the house of
the LORD, we have had enough to eat,
and have left plenty: for the LORD hath
blessed his people; and that which is
left *is* this great store.
11 ¶ Then Hĕz-e-kī'ah commanded
to prepare [7]chambers in the house of
the LORD; and they prepared *them,*
12 And brought in the offerings and
the tithes and the dedicated *things* faithfully: [k]over which Cŏn-ŏ-nī'ah the
Lē'vīte *was* ruler, and Shĭm'e-ī his
brother *was* the next.
13 And Je-hī'el, and Ăz-a-zī'ah, and
Nā'hăth, and Ā'sa-hĕl, and Jĕr'i-mŏth,
and Jŏz'a-băd, and E-lī'el, and Ĭs-ma-
chī'ah, and Mā'hath, and Be-nā'iah,
were overseers [8]under the hand of
Cŏn-ŏ-nī'ah and Shĭm'e-ī his brother,
at the commandment of Hĕz-e-kī'ah
the king, and Ăz-a-rī'ah the ruler of
the house of God.
14 And Kō're the son of Ĭm'nah the
Lē'vīte, the porter toward the east, *was*
over the freewill offerings of God, to
distribute the oblations of the LORD,
and the [9]most holy things.
15 And [10]next him *were* Ē'dĕn, and
Mĭ-nī'a-min, and Jĕsh'u-à, and Shĕm-
a-ī'ah, Ăm-a-rī'ah, and Shĕc-a-nī'ah,
in [l]the cities of the priests, in *their* [11]set
office, to give to their brethren by
courses, as well to the great as to the
small:
16 Beside their genealogy of males,
from three years old and upward, *even*
unto every one that entereth into the
house of the LORD, his [12]daily portion
for their service in their charges according to their courses;
17 Both to the genealogy of the
priests by the house of their fathers,
and the Lē'vītes [m]from twenty years
old and upward, in their charges by
their courses;
18 And to the genealogy of all their
little ones, their wives, and their sons,
and their daughters, through all the

20 [v]Ex. 15.26; Jas. 5.16
21 [6]found [w]Ex. 12.15; Luke 22.1-7; 1 Cor. 5.7-8 [7]instruments of strength
22 [8]to the heart of all; Isa. 40.2 [x]Deut. 33.10; ch. 17.9; 2 Tim. 4.2 [y]Ezra 10.11
23 [z]1 Ki. 8.65
24 [9]lifted up, or, offered [a]ch. 35.7-8 [b]ch. 29.34
25 [c]verses 11, 18
27 [d]Num. 6.23 [10]the habitation of his holiness, Ps. 68.5

CHAPTER 31
1 [1]found [a]2 Ki. 18.4 [2]statues, ch. 30.14 [3]until to make an end
2 [b]1 Chr. 23.6 [c]1 Chr. 23.30-31
3 [d]Num. 28
4 [e]Num. 18.8; 1 Cor. 9.13 [f]Mal. 2.7
5 [4]brake forth [g]Ex. 22.29; Num. 18.12; Prov. 3.9; Ezek. 20.40; Jas. 1.18 [5]Or, dates
6 [h]Lev. 27.30; Deut. 14.28 [6]heaps, heaps
8 [i]Gen. 14.19; Ps. 33.12
10 [j]Hag. 2.19; Mal. 3.10
11 [7]Or, storehouses
12 [k]Neh. 13.13
13 [8]at the hand
14 [9]holinesses of holinesses
15 [10]at his hand [l]Josh. 21.9 [11]Or, trust, 1 Chr. 9.22
16 [12]for the things of the day upon his day
17 [m]1 Chr. 23.24-27

congregation: for in their [13]set office
they sanctified themselves in holiness:
19 Also of the sons of Aâr'on the
priests, *which were* in [n]the fields of the
suburbs of their cities, in every several
city, the men that [o]were expressed by
name, to give portions to all the males
among the priests, and to all that were
reckoned by genealogies among the
Lē'vītes.
20 ¶ And thus did Hĕz-e-kī'ah
throughout all Jū'dah, and [p]wrought
that which was good and right and
truth before the LORD his God.
21 And in every work that he began
in the service of the house of God, and
in the law, and in the commandments,
to seek his God, he did *it* with all his
heart, and [q]prospered.

32

After [a]these things, and the establishment thereof, Sĕn-năch'e-rĭb
king of Ăs-sỹr'ĭ-ȧ came, and entered
into Jū'dah, and encamped against the
fenced cities, and thought [1]to win them
for himself.
2 And when Hĕz-e-kī'ah saw that
Sĕn-năch'e-rĭb was come, and that
[2]he was purposed to fight against
Je-rụ'sa-lĕm,
3 He took counsel with his princes
and his mighty men to stop the waters
of the fountains which *were* without
the city: and they did help him.
4 So there was gathered much people together, who stopped all the fountains, and the brook that [3]ran through
the midst of the land, saying, Why
should the kings of Ăs-sỹr'ĭ-ȧ come,
and find much water?
5 Also [b]he strengthened himself,
[c]and built up all the wall that was broken, and raised *it* up to the towers, and
another wall without, and repaired
[d]Mĭl'lo *in* the city of Dā'vid, and made
[4]darts and shields in abundance.
6 And he set captains of war over the
people, and gathered them together to
him in the street of the gate of the
city, and [5]spake comfortably to them,
saying,
7 [e]Be strong and courageous, [f]be
not afraid nor dismayed for the king of
Ăs-sỹr'ĭ-ȧ, nor for all the multitude
that *is* with him: for [g]*there be* more
with us than with him:
8 With him *is* an [h]arm of flesh; but
[i]with us *is* the LORD our God to help
us, and to fight our battles. And the
people [6]rested themselves upon the
words of Hĕz-e-kī'ah king of Jū'dah.
9 ¶ [j]After this did Sĕn-năch'e-rĭb
king of Ăs-sỹr'ĭ-ȧ send his servants to
Je-rụ'sa-lĕm, (but he *himself laid siege*
against Lā'chish, and all his [7]power
with him,) unto Hĕz-e-kī'ah king of
Jū'dah, and unto all Jū'dah that *were*
at Je-rụ'sa-lĕm, saying,
10 Thus saith Sĕn-năch'e-rĭb king of
Ăs-sỹr'ĭ-ȧ, Whereon do ye trust, that
ye abide [8]in the siege in Je-rụ'sa-lĕm?
11 Doth not Hĕz-e-kī'ah persuade
you to give over yourselves to die by
famine and by thirst, saying, The LORD
our God shall deliver us out of the
hand of the king of Ăs-sỹr'ĭ-ȧ?
12 Hath not the same Hĕz-e-kī'ah
taken away his high places and his altars, and commanded Jū'dah and Je-
rụ'sa-lĕm, saying, Ye shall worship before one altar, and burn incense upon
it?
13 Know ye not what I and my fathers have done unto all the people of
other lands? [k]were the gods of the nations of those lands any ways able to
deliver their lands out of mine hand?
14 Who *was there* among all the
gods of those nations that my fathers
utterly destroyed, that could deliver
his people out of mine hand, that your
God should be able to deliver you out
of mine hand?
15 Now therefore let not Hĕz-e-kī'-
ah deceive you, nor persuade you on
this manner, neither yet believe him:
for no god of any nation or kingdom
was able to deliver his people out of
mine hand, and out of the hand of my
fathers: [l]how much less shall your
God deliver you out of mine hand?
16 And his servants spake yet *more*
against the LORD God, and against his
servant Hĕz-e-kī'ah.
17 [m]He wrote also letters to rail on
the LORD God of Ĭs'ra-el, and to speak
against him, saying, As the gods of the
nations of *other* lands have not delivered their people out of mine hand, so
shall not the God of Hĕz-e-kī'ah deliver his people out of mine hand.
18 [n]Then they cried with a loud
voice in the Jews' speech unto the people of Je-rụ'sa-lĕm that *were* on the
wall, to affright them, and to trouble
them; that they might take the city.
19 And [o]they spake against the God
of Je-rụ'sa-lĕm, as against the gods of
the people of the earth, *which were*
[p]the work of the hands of man.
20 And for this *cause* Hĕz-e-kī'ah
the king, and the prophet I-sā'iah the
son of Ā'moz, prayed and cried to
heaven.
21 ¶ And the LORD sent an angel,
which cut off all the mighty men of
valour, and the leaders and captains in
the camp of the king of Ăs-sỹr'ĭ-ȧ. So
he returned with shame of face to his
own land. And when he was come into
the house of his god, they that came
forth of his own bowels [9]slew him
there with the sword.
22 Thus the LORD [q]saved Hĕz-e-kī'-
ah and the inhabitants of Je-rụ'sa-lĕm
from the hand of Sĕn-năch'e-rĭb the
king of Ăs-sỹr'ĭ-ȧ, and from the hand
of all *other*, and guided them on every
side.
23 And many brought gifts unto the
LORD to Je-rụ'sa-lĕm, and [10][r]presents
to Hĕz-e-kī'ah king of Jū'dah: so that
he was [s]magnified in the sight of all
nations from thenceforth.
24 ¶ [t]In those days Hĕz-e-kī'ah was
sick to the death, and prayed unto the
LORD: and he spake unto him, and he
[11]gave him a sign.
25 But Hĕz-e-kī'ah [u]rendered not
again according to the benefit *done*
unto him; for [v]his heart was lifted up:

18 [13]Or, trust
19 [n]Lev. 25.34; Num. 35.2
[o]verses 12-15
20 [p]1 Ki. 15.5; John 1.47
21 [q]Deut. 29.9; 1 Tim. 4.8
CHAPTER 32
1 [a]2 Ki. 18.13
[1]to break them up
2 [2]his face was to war
4 [3]overflowed
5 [b]Isa. 22.9-10
[c]ch. 25.23
[d]2 Sam. 5.9
[4]Or, swords, or, weapons
6 [5]spake to their heart, ch. 30.22; Isa. 40.2
7 [e]Deut. 31.6; Josh. 1.6-7
[f]ch. 20.15
[g]2 Ki. 6.16
8 [h]Jer. 17.5; 1 John 4.4
[i]Num. 14.9; Rom. 8.31
[6]leaned
9 [j]2 Ki. 18.17
[7]dominion
10 [8]Or, in the strong hold
13 [k]2 Ki. 18.33-35; Ps. 115.4-8
15 [l]Ex. 5.2; John 19.10-11
17 [m]2 Ki. 19.9
18 [n]2 Ki. 18.28
19 [o]Isa. 10.10
[p]Deut. 4.28; Hos. 8.5-6
21 [9]made him fall
22 [q]Ps. 18.48-50
23 [10]precious things
[r]ch. 17.5
[s]1 Chr. 29.25.-ch. 1.1
24 [t]Isa. 38.1
[11]Or, wrought a miracle for him
25 [u]Deut. 32.6; Luke 17.17
[v]Deut. 8.12-14-17;

[w]therefore there was wrath upon him, and upon Jū'dah and Je-ru̧'sa-lĕm.

26 [x]Notwithstanding Hĕz-e-kī'ah humbled himself for [12]the pride of his heart, *both* he and the inhabitants of Je-ru̧'sa-lĕm, so that the wrath of the LORD came not upon them [y]in the days of Hĕz-e-kī'ah.

27 ¶ And Hĕz-e-kī'ah had exceeding much riches and honour: and he made himself treasuries for silver, and for gold, and for precious stones, and for spices, and for shields, and for all manner of [13]pleasant jewels;

28 Storehouses also for the increase of corn, and wine, and oil; and stalls for all manner of beasts, and cotes for flocks.

29 Moreover he provided him cities, and possessions of flocks and herds in abundance: for God had given [z]him substance very much.

30 [a]This same Hĕz-e-kī'ah also stopped the upper watercourse of Gī'hon, and brought it straight down to the west side of the city of Dā'vid. And Hĕz-e-kī'ah prospered in all his works.

31 ¶ Howbeit in *the business of* the [14]ambassadors of the princes of Băb'y̆lon, who [b]sent unto him to inquire of the wonder that was *done* in the land, God left him, to [c]try him, that he might know all *that was* in his heart.

32 ¶ Now the rest of the acts of Hĕz-e-kī'ah, and his [15]goodness, behold, they *are* written in [d]the vision of I-sā'iah the prophet, the son of Ā'moz, *and* in the [e]book of the kings of Jū'dah and Ĭs'ra-el.

33 And Hĕz-e-kī'ah slept with his fathers, and they buried him in the [16]chiefest of the sepulchres of the sons of Dā'vid: and all Jū'dah and the inhabitants of Je-ru̧'sa-lĕm did him [f]honour at his death. And Ma-năs'seh his son reigned in his stead.

33 Ma-năs'seh [a]*was* twelve years old when he began to reign, and he reigned fifty and five years in Je-ru̧'sa-lĕm:

2 But did *that which was* evil in the sight of the LORD, like unto the [b]abominations of the heathen, whom the LORD had cast out before the children of Ĭs'ra-el.

3 ¶ For [1]he built again the high places which Hĕz-e-kī'ah his father had [c]broken down, and he reared up altars for Bā'al-ĭm, and [d]made groves, and worshipped [e]all the host of heaven, and served them.

4 Also he built altars in the house of the LORD, whereof the LORD had said, [f]In Je-ru̧'sa-lĕm shall my name be for ever.

5 And he built altars for all the host of heaven [g]in the two courts of the house of the LORD.

6 [h]And he caused his children to pass through the fire in the valley of the son of Hĭn'nom: [i]also he observed times, and used enchantments, and used witchcraft, and [j]dealt with a familiar spirit, and with wizards: he wrought much evil in the sight of the LORD, to provoke him to anger.

7 And [k]he set a carved image, the idol which he had made, in the house of God, of which God had said to Dā'vid and to Sŏl'o-mon his son, In [l]this house, and in Je-ru̧'sa-lĕm, which I have chosen before all the tribes of Ĭs'ra-el, will I put my name for ever:

8 [m]Neither will I any more remove the foot of Ĭs'ra-el from out of the land which I have appointed for your fathers; so that they will take heed to do all that I have commanded them, according to the whole law and the statutes and the ordinances by the hand of Mō'ses.

9 So Ma-năs'seh made Jū'dah and the inhabitants of Je-ru̧'sa-lĕm to err, *and* to do worse than the heathen, whom the LORD had destroyed before the children of Ĭs'ra-el.

10 And the [n]LORD spake to Ma-năs'seh, and to his people: but they would not hearken.

11 ¶ [o]Wherefore the LORD brought upon them the captains of the host [2]of the king of Ăs-sy̆r'ĭ-ȧ, which took Ma-năs'seh among the thorns, and [p]bound him with [3]fetters, and carried him to Băb'y̆-lon.

12 And when [q]he was in affliction, he besought the LORD his God, and [r]humbled himself greatly before the God of his fathers,

13 And prayed unto him: and he was [s]intreated of him, and heard his supplication, and brought him again to Je-ru̧'sa-lĕm into his kingdom. Then Ma-năs'seh [t]knew that the LORD he *was* God.

14 Now after this he built a wall without the city of Dā'vid, on the west side of [u]Gī'hon, in the valley, even to the entering in at the fish gate, and compassed [v]about [4]Ō'phel, and raised it up a very great height, and put captains of war in all the fenced cities of Jū'dah.

15 And he took away the strange gods, and the idol out of the house of the LORD, and all the altars that he had built in the mount of the house of the LORD, and in Je-ru̧'sa-lĕm, and cast *them* out of the city.

16 And he repaired the altar of the LORD, and sacrificed thereon peace offerings and [w]thank offerings, and commanded Jū'dah to serve the LORD God of Ĭs'ra-el.

17 [x]Nevertheless the people did sacrifice still in the high places, *yet* unto the LORD their God only.

18 ¶ Now the rest of the acts of Ma-năs'seh, and his prayer unto his God, and the words of the seers that spake to him in the name of the LORD God of Ĭs'ra-el, behold, they *are written* in the book of the kings of Ĭs'ra-el.

19 His prayer also, and *how God* was intreated of him, and all his sins, and his trespass, and the places wherein he built high places, and set up groves and graven images, before

[w]ch. 24.18
26 [x]Jer. 26.18
[12]the lifting up
[y]2 Ki. 20.19
27 [13]instruments of desire
29 [z]ch. 29.12
30 [a]Isa. 22.9
31 [14]interpreters
[b]Isa. 39.1
[c]Gen. 22.1; John 1.12
32 [15]kindnesses
[d]Isa. 36
[e]2 Ki. 18
33 [16]Or, highest
[f]1 Sam. 2.30
CHAPTER 33
1 [a]2 Ki. 21.1
2 [b]Lev. 18.24-30; ch. 28.3
3 [1]he returned and built
[c]2 Ki. 18.4; ch. 31.1
[d]Deut. 16.21
[e]Deut. 4.19; Zeph. 1.5
4 [f]Deut. 12.11; 1 Ki. 8.29
5 [g]ch. 4.9
6 [h]Lev. 18.21; ch. 28.3
[i]Deut. 18.10
[j]2 Ki. 21.6
7 [k]2 Ki. 21.7
[l]Ps. 132.14
8 [m]2 Sam. 7.10
10 [n]Neh. 9.29
11 [o]Deut. 28.36
[2]which were the king's
[p]Ps. 107.10-11; Job 36.8
[3]Or, chains
12 [q]Deut. 4.30-31; Luke 15.16-18
[r]Ex. 10.3; ch. 32.26; 1 Pet. 5.6
13 [s]1 Chr. 5.20; Ezra 8.23; Lam. 3.55-56
[t]Ps. 9.16; Dan. 4.25
14 [u]1 Ki. 1.33
[v]ch. 27.3
[4]Or, The tower
16 [w]Lev. 7.12
17 [x]1 Ki. 22.43; ch. 15.17; ch. 32.12

he was humbled: behold, they *are* written among the sayings of [5]the seers.
20 ¶ So Ma-năs'seh slept with his fathers, and they buried him in his own
house: and Ā'mon his son reigned in
his stead.
21 ¶ Ā'mon *was* two and twenty
years old when he began to reign, and
reigned two years in Je-rṳ'sa-lĕm.
22 But he did *that which was* evil in
the sight of the LORD, as did Ma-
năs'seh his father: for Ā'mon sacrificed unto all the carved images which
Ma-năs'seh his father had made, and
served them;
23 And humbled not himself before
the LORD, as Ma-năs'seh his father had
humbled himself; but Ā'mon [6y]tres-
passed more and more.
24 [z]And his servants conspired
against him, and slew him in his own
house.
25 ¶ But the people of the land slew
all them that had conspired against
king Ā'mon; and the people of the land
made Jo-sī'ah his son king in his stead.

34 Jo-sī'ah [a]*was* eight years old
when he began to reign, and he
reigned in Je-rṳ'sa-lĕm one and thirty
years.
2 And he did *that which was* right in
the sight of the LORD, and walked in
the ways of Dā'vid his father, and declined *neither* to the right hand, nor to
the left.
3 ¶ For in the eighth year of his
reign, while he was yet [b]young, he began to [c]seek after the God of Dā'vid
his father: and in the twelfth year he
began [d]to purge Jū'dah and Je-rṳ'sa-
lĕm [e]from the high places, and the
groves, and the carved images, and the
molten images.
4 [f]And they brake down the altars of
Bā'al-ĭm in his presence; and the [1]im-
ages, that *were* on high above them, he
cut down; and the groves, and the
carved images, and the molten images,
he brake in pieces, and made dust *of
them,* [g]and strowed *it* upon the [2]graves
of them that had sacrificed unto them.
5 And he [h]burnt the bones of the
priests upon their altars, and cleansed
Jū'dah and Je-rṳ'sa-lĕm.
6 And *so did he* in the cities of Ma-
năs'seh, and Ē'phră-ĭm, and Sĭm'e-on,
even unto Năph'ta-lī, with their [3]mat-
tocks round about.
7 And when he had broken down
the altars and the groves, and had
[i]beaten the graven images [4]into powder, and cut down all the idols throughout all the land of Ĭs'ra-el, he returned
to Je-rṳ'sa-lĕm.
8 ¶ Now [j]in the eighteenth year of
his reign, when he had purged the
land, and the house, he sent Shā'phan
the son of Ăz-a-lī'ah, and Mā-a-sē'iah
the governor of the city, and Jō'ah the
son of Jō'a-hăz the recorder, to repair
the house of the LORD his God.
9 And when they came to Hĭl-kī'ah
the high priest, they delivered [k]the
money that was brought into the house
of God, which the Lē'vītes that kept
the doors had gathered of the hand of
Ma-năs'seh and Ē'phră-ĭm, and of all
the remnant of Ĭs'ra-el, and of all Jū'-
dah and Bĕn'ja-min; and they returned
to Je-rṳ'sa-lĕm.
10 And they put *it* in the hand of the
workmen that had the oversight of the
house of the LORD, and they gave it to
the workmen that wrought in the house
of the LORD, to repair and amend the
house:
11 Even to the artificers and builders gave they *it,* to buy hewn stone,
and timber for couplings, and [5]to floor
the houses which the kings of Jū'dah
had destroyed.
12 And the men did the [l]work faithfully: and the overseers of them *were*
Jā'hăth and Ō-ba-dī'ah, the Lē'vītes,
of the sons of Me-rā'rī; and Zĕch-a-
rī'ah and Me-shŭl'lam, of the sons of
the Kō'hath-ītes, to set *it* forward; and
other of the Lē'vītes, all that could skill
of instruments of musick.
13 Also *they were* over the bearers
of burdens, and *were* overseers of all
that wrought the work in any manner
of service: [m]and of the Lē'vītes *there
were* scribes, and officers, and porters.
14 ¶ And when they brought out the
money that was brought into the house
of the LORD, Hĭl-kī'ah the priest [n]found
a book of the law of the LORD *given* [6]by
Mō'ses.
15 And Hĭl-kī'ah answered and said
to Shā'phan the scribe, I have found
the book of the law in the house of
the LORD. And Hĭl-kī'ah delivered the
book to Shā'phan.
16 And Shā'phan carried the book
to the king, and brought the king word
back again, saying, All that was committed [7]to thy servants, they do *it.*
17 And they have [8]gathered together
the money that was found in the house
of the LORD, and have delivered it into
the hand of the overseers, and to the
hand of the workmen.
18 Then Shā'phan the scribe told
the king, saying, Hĭl-kī'ah the priest
hath given me a book. And Shā'phan
read [9]it before the king.
19 And it came to pass, when the
king had heard the [o]words of the law,
that he [p]rent his clothes.
20 And the king commanded Hĭl-
kī'ah, and A-hī'kam the son of Shā'-
phan, and [10]Ăb'dŏn the son of Mī'cah,
and Shā'phan the scribe, and Ā-sa-ī'ah
a servant of the king's, saying,
21 Go, inquire of the LORD for me,
and for them that are [q]left in Ĭs'ra-el
and in Jū'dah, concerning the words of
the book that is found: for great *is* the
wrath of the LORD that is poured out
upon us, because our fathers have not
kept the word of the LORD, to do after
all that is written in this book.
22 And Hĭl-kī'ah, and *they* that the
king *had appointed,* went to Hŭl'dah
the [r]prophetess, the wife of Shăl'lum
the son of [s]Tĭk'vath, the son of [11]Hăs'-
rah, keeper of the [12]wardrobe; (now
she dwelt in Je-rṳ'sa-lĕm [13]in the

19 [5]Or, Hosai
23 [6]multiplied trespass
[y]2 Tim. 3.13
24 [z]2 Ki. 21.23-24; ch. 24.25-26; ch. 25.27-28; Ps. 55.23

CHAPTER 34
1 [a]1 Ki. 3.7-9; 1 Chr. 3.14-15; ch. 35.25
3 [b]1 Sam. 1.24; Ps. 119.9; Prov. 8.17; Eccl. 12.1; 2 Tim. 3.15
[c]ch. 15.2
[d]1 Ki. 13.2
[e]ch. 33.17-22
4 [f]Lev. 26.30
[1]Or, sun images
[g]Ex. 32.20
[2]face of the graves
5 [h]1 Ki. 13.2
6 [3]Or, mauls
7 [i]Deut. 9.21
[4]to make powder
8 [j]2 Ki. 22.3
9 [k]2 Ki. 12.4
11 [5]Or, to rafter
12 [l]2 Ki. 12.15; Neh. 7.2; Prov. 28.20; 1 Cor. 4.2
13 [m]1 Chr. 23.4-5; Jer. 8.8; Matt. 26.3
14 [n]Deut. 31.24-26
[6]by the hand of
16 [7]to the hand of
17 [8]poured out, or, melted
18 [9]in it; Deut. 17.19; Josh. 1.8
19 [o]Deut. 28; Rom. 7.7-14; Gal. 3.10-13
[p]Gen. 37.34; Hab. 3.16
20 [10]Or, Achbor, 2 Ki. 22.12
21 [q]2 Ki. 17.6
22 [r]Ex. 15.20; Acts 21.9
[s]2 Ki. 22.14
[11]Or, Harhas
[12]garments
[13]Or, in the school, or, in the second part

college:) and they spake to her to that
effect.
23 ¶ And she answered them, Thus
saith the LORD God of Ĭs'ra-el, Tell ye
the man that sent you to me,
24 Thus saith the LORD, Behold, I
[t]will bring evil upon this place, and
upon the inhabitants thereof, *even* all
the curses that are written in the book
which they have read before the king
of Jū'dah:
25 Because they have forsaken me,
and have burned incense unto other
gods, that they might provoke me
to anger with all the works of their
hands; therefore my wrath shall be
poured out upon this place, and shall
not be quenched.
26 And as for the king of Jū'dah,
who sent you to inquire of the LORD, so
shall ye say unto him, Thus saith the
LORD God of Ĭs'ra-el *concerning* the
words which thou hast heard;
27 Because thine heart was [u]tender,
and thou didst humble thyself before
God, when thou heardest his words
against this place, and against the inhabitants thereof, and humbledst thyself before me, and didst rend thy
clothes, and weep before me; I have
even [v]heard *thee* also, saith the LORD.
28 Behold, I will gather thee to thy
fathers, and thou shalt be gathered to
thy grave in peace, neither shall thine
eyes see all the evil that I will bring
upon this place, and upon the inhabitants of the same. So they brought the
king word again.
29 ¶ [w]Then the king sent and gathered together all the elders of Jū'dah
and Je-ru̯'sa-lĕm.
30 And the king went up into the
house of the LORD, and all the men of
Jū'dah, and the inhabitants of Je-ru̯'-
sa-lĕm, and the priests, and the Lē'-
vītes, and all the people, [14]great and
small: and he read in their ears all the
words of the book of the covenant that
was found in the house of the LORD.
31 And the king stood in [x]his place,
and made a covenant before the LORD,
to walk after the LORD, and to keep his
commandments, and his testimonies,
and his statutes, with all his heart, and
with all his soul, to perform the words
of the covenant which are written in
this book.
32 And he caused all that were
[15]present in Je-ru̯'sa-lĕm and Bĕn'ja-
min to stand *to it*. And the inhabitants
of Je-ru̯'sa-lĕm did according to the
covenant of God, the God of their
fathers.
33 And Jo-sī'ah took away all the
[y]abominations out of all the countries
that *pertained* to the children of Ĭs'ra-
el, and made all that were present in
Ĭs'ra-el to serve, *even* to serve the LORD
their God. [z]*And* all his days they departed not [16]from following the LORD,
the God of their fathers.

35 Moreover [a]Jo-sī'ah kept a passover unto the LORD in Je-ru̯'sa-
lĕm: and they killed the passover on
the [b]fourteenth *day* of the first month.

24 [t]Josh. 23.16; ch. 36.6-21; Jer. 25.9; Zech. 1.6
27 [u]Ps. 51.17
[v]Ps. 86.5
29 [w]2 Ki. 23.1
30 [14]from great even to small
31 [x]2 Ki. 11.14
32 [15]found
33 [y]1 Ki. 11.5
[z]Jer. 3.10
[16]from after
CHAPTER 35
1 [a]2 Ki. 23.21
[b]Ex. 12.6
2 [c]ch. 23.18; Ezra 6.18
[d]1 Chr. 22.19
3 [e]Deut. 33.10
[f]ch. 34.14
[g]ch. 5.7
[h]1 Chr. 23.26
4 [i]1 Chr. 9.10
[j]1 Chr. 23
[k]ch. 8.14
5 [l]Ps. 134.1
[1]the house of the fathers
[2]the sons of the people
6 [m]Ex. 19.10; ch. 29.5; Job 1.5; Ps. 51.7; Heb. 9.13-14
7 [3]offered
8 [4]offered; 2 Cor. 9.7
9 [5]offered
10 [n]Ezra 6.18
11 [o]Lev. 1.5-6; ch. 29.22
[p]ch. 29.34
12 [q]Lev. 3.3
13 [r]Ex. 12.8; Deut. 16.7
[s]1 Sam. 2.13-14-15
[6]made them run
15 [7]station

2 And he set the priests in their
[c]charges, and [d]encouraged them to
the service of the house of the LORD,
3 And said unto the Lē'vītes [e]that
taught all Ĭs'ra-el, which were holy
unto the LORD, [f]Put the holy ark [g]in
the house which Sŏl'o-mon the son of
Dā'vid king of Ĭs'ra-el did build; [h]*it*
shall not *be* a burden upon *your* shoulders: serve now the LORD your God,
and his people Ĭs'ra-el,
4 And prepare *yourselves* by the
[i]houses of your fathers, after your
courses, according to the [j]writing of
Dā'vid king of Ĭs'ra-el, and according
to the [k]writing of Sŏl'o-mon his son.
5 And [l]stand in the holy *place* according to the divisions of [1]the families
of the fathers of your brethren [2]the people, and *after* the division of the families of the Lē'vītes.
6 So kill the passover, and [m]sanctify
yourselves, and prepare your brethren,
that *they* may do according to the word
of the LORD by the hand of Mō'ses.
7 And Jo-sī'ah [3]gave to the people,
of the flock, lambs and kids, all for the
passover offerings, for all that were
present, to the number of thirty thousand, and three thousand bullocks:
these *were* of the king's substance.
8 And his princes [4]gave willingly
unto the people, to the priests, and to
the Lē'vītes: Hĭl-kī'ah and Zĕch-a-
rī'ah and Je-hī'el, rulers of the house
of God, gave unto the priests for the
passover offerings two thousand and
six hundred *small cattle*, and three
hundred oxen.
9 Cŏn-a-nī'ah also, and Shĕm-a-ī'ah
and Ne-thăn'e-el, his brethren, and
Hash-a-bī'ah and Je-ī'el and Jŏz'a-
băd, chief of the Lē'vītes, [5]gave unto
the Lē'vītes for passover offerings five
thousand *small cattle*, and five hundred oxen.
10 So the service was prepared, and
the priests [n]stood in their place, and
the Lē'vītes in their courses, according
to the king's commandment.
11 And they killed the passover, and
the priests [o]sprinkled *the blood* from
their hands, and the Lē'vītes [p]flayed
them.
12 And they removed the burnt offerings, that they might give according
to the divisions of the families of the
people, to offer unto the LORD, as *it is*
written [q]in the book of Mō'ses. And so
did they with the oxen.
13 And they [r]roasted the passover
with fire according to the ordinance:
but the *other* holy *offerings* [s]sod they
in pots, and in caldrons, and in pans,
and [6]divided *them* speedily among all
the people.
14 And afterward they made ready
for themselves, and for the priests: because the priests the sons of Aâr'on
were busied in offering of burnt offerings and the fat until night; therefore
the Lē'vītes prepared for themselves,
and for the priests the sons of Aâr'on.
15 And the singers the sons of Ā'saph
were in their [7]place, according to the

[t]commandment of Dā'vid, and Ā'saph, and Hē'man, and Jĕd'ṳ-thŭn the king's seer; and the porters [u]*waited* at every gate; they might not depart from their service; for their brethren the Lē'vītes prepared for them.

16 So all the service of the LORD was prepared the same day, to keep the passover, and to offer burnt offerings upon the altar of the LORD, according to the commandment of king Jo-sī'ah.

17 And the children of Ĭs'ra-el that were [8]present kept the passover at that time, and the feast of [v]unleavened bread seven days.

18 And [w]there was no passover like to that kept in Ĭs'ra-el from the days of Săm'u-el the prophet; neither did all the kings of Ĭs'ra-el keep such a passover as Jo-sī'ah kept, and the priests, and the Lē'vītes, and all Jū'dah and Ĭs'ra-el that were present, and the inhabitants of Je-rṳ'sa-lĕm.

19 In the eighteenth year of the reign of Jo-sī'ah was this passover kept.

20 ¶ [x]After all this, when Jo-sī'ah had prepared the [9]temple, Nē'cho king of Ē'ġypt came up to fight against Chär'chĕ-mĭsh by Eū-phrā'tēs: and Jo-sī'ah went out against him.

21 But he sent ambassadors to him, saying, What have I to do with thee, thou king of Jū'dah? *I come* not against thee this day, but against [10]the house wherewith I have war: for [y]God commanded me to make haste: forbear thee from *meddling with* God, who *is* with me, that he destroy thee not.

22 Nevertheless Jo-sī'ah would not turn his face from him, but [z]disguised himself, that he might fight with him, and hearkened not unto the words of Nē'cho from the mouth of God, and came to fight in the valley of Me-ġĭd'do.

23 And the archers shot at king Jo-sī'ah; and the king said to his servants, Have me away; for I am sore [11]wounded.

24 [a]His servants therefore took him out of that chariot, and put him in the second chariot that he had; and they brought him to Je-rṳ'sa-lĕm, and he died, and was buried [12]in *one of* the sepulchres of his fathers. And [b]all Jū'dah and Je-rṳ'sa-lĕm mourned for Jo-sī'ah.

25 ¶ And Jĕr-e-mī'ah [c]lamented for Jo-sī'ah: and [d]all the singing men and the singing women spake of Jo-sī'ah in their lamentations to this day, [e]and made them an ordinance in Ĭs'ra-el: and, behold, they *are* written in the lamentations.

26 Now the rest of the acts of Jo-sī'ah, and his [13f]goodness, according to *that which was* written in the law of the LORD,

27 And his deeds, first and last, behold, they *are* written in the book of the kings of Ĭs'ra-el and Jū'dah.

36 Then [a]the people of the land took Je-hō'a-hăz the son of Jo-sī'ah, and made him king in his father's stead in Je-rṳ'sa-lĕm.

2 Je-hō'a-hăz *was* twenty and three years old when he began to reign, and he reigned three months in Je-rṳ'sa-lĕm.

3 And the king of Ē'ġypt [1]put him down at Je-rṳ'sa-lĕm, and [2]condemned the land in an hundred talents of silver and a talent of gold.

4 And the king of Ē'ġypt made E-lī'a-kĭm his brother king over Jū'dah and Je-rṳ'sa-lĕm, and turned his name to Je-hoi'a-kim. And Nē'cho took [b]Je-hō'a-hăz his brother, and carried him to Ē'ġypt.

5 ¶ [c]Je-hoi'a-kim *was* twenty and five years old when he began to reign, and he reigned eleven years in Je-rṳ'sa-lĕm: and he did *that which was* evil in the sight of the LORD his God.

6 [d]Against him came up Nĕb-u-chăd-nĕz'zar king of Băb'ȳ-lon, and bound him in [3]fetters, to [e]carry him to Băb'ȳ-lon.

7 [f]Nĕb-u-chăd-nĕz'zar also carried of the vessels of the house of the LORD to Băb'ȳ-lon, and put them in his temple at Băb'ȳ-lon.

8 Now the rest of the acts of Je-hoi'a-kim, and his abominations which he did, and that which was found in him, behold, they *are* written in the book of the kings of Ĭs'ra-el and Jū'dah: and [4]Je-hoi'a-chin his son reigned in his stead.

9 ¶ [g]Je-hoi'a-chin *was* eight years old when he began to reign, and he reigned three months and ten days in Je-rṳ'sa-lĕm: and he did *that which was* evil in the sight of the LORD.

10 And [5]when the year was expired, king Nĕb-u-chăd-nĕz'zar sent, and brought him to Băb'ȳ-lon, [h]with the [6]goodly vessels of the house of the LORD, and made Zĕd-e-kī'ah his brother king over Jū'dah and Je-rṳ'sa-lĕm.

11 ¶ [i]Zĕd-e-kī'ah *was* one and twenty years old when he began to reign, and reigned eleven years in Je-rṳ'sa-lĕm.

12 And he did *that which was* evil in the sight of the LORD his God, *and* humbled not himself before Jĕr-e-mī'ah the prophet *speaking* from the mouth of the LORD.

13 And [j]he also rebelled against king Nĕb-u-chăd-nĕz'zar, who had made him swear by God: but he [k]stiffened his neck, and hardened his heart from turning unto the LORD God of Ĭs'ra-el.

14 ¶ Moreover all the chief of the priests, and the people, transgressed very much after all the abominations of the heathen; and polluted the house of the LORD which he had hallowed in Je-rṳ'sa-lĕm.

15 [l]And the LORD God of their fathers sent to them [7]by his messengers, rising up [8]betimes, and sending; because he had [m]compassion on his people, and on his dwelling place:

16 But [n]they mocked the messengers of God, and [o]despised his words, and [p]misused his prophets, until the [q]wrath of the LORD arose against his people, till *there was* no [9]remedy.

17 [r]Therefore he brought upon them the king of the Chăl'dees, who slew

[t]1 Chr. 25.1
[u]1 Chr. 9.17-18; 1 Chr. 26.14
17 [8]found
[v]Ex. 12.15; 1 Cor. 5.7-8
18 [w]2 Ki. 23.22-23
20 [x]2 Ki. 23.29; Jer. 46.2
[9]house
21 [10]the house of my war
[y]2 Ki. 18.25
22 [z]1 Ki. 14.2;
23 [11]made sick, 1 Ki. 22.34
24 [a]2 Ki. 23.30
[12]Or, among the sepulchres
[b]Zech. 12.11
25 [c]Jer. 22.10;
[d]Eccl. 12.5;
[e]Jer. 22.20
26 [13]kindnesses
[f]Ps. 112.6;

CHAPTER 36
1 [a]2 Ki. 23.30;
3 [1]removed him
[2]mulcted
4 [b]Ezek. 19.3
5 [c]2 Ki. 23.36-37
6 [d]2 Ki. 24.1;
[3]Or, chains; Foretold, Hab. 1.6-10
[e]2 Ki. 24.6
7 [f]Dan. 1.1
8 [4]Jeconiah, 1 Chr. 3.16
9 [g]2 Ki. 24.8
10 [5]at the return of the year
[h]Dan. 1.1
[6]vessels of desire
11 [i]2 Ki. 24.17;
13 [j]Ezek. 17.15
[k]2 Ki. 17.14
15 [l]Jer. 25.3
[7]by the hand of his messengers
[8]That is, continually and carefully
[m]Hos. 11.8
16 [n]ch. 30.10;
[o]Prov. 1.25;
[p]Jer. 32.3
[q]Ps. 74.1
[9]healing
17 [r]Deut. 28.49;

their young men with the sword in the house of their sanctuary, and had no compassion upon young man or maiden, old man, or him that stooped for age: he gave *them* all into his hand.

18 [s]And all the vessels of the house of God, great and small, and the treasures of the house of the LORD, and the treasures of the king, and of his princes; all *these* he brought to Băb'ȳ-lon.

19 [t]And they burnt the house of God, and brake down the wall of Je-rụ'sa-lĕm, and burnt all the palaces thereof with fire, and destroyed all the goodly vessels thereof.

20 And [10]them that had escaped from the sword carried he away to Băb'ȳ-lon; [u]where they were servants to him and his sons until the reign of the kingdom of Pĕr'siȧ:

21 To fulfil the word of the LORD by the mouth of [v]Jĕr-e-mī'ah, until the land [w]had enjoyed her sabbaths: *for* as long as she lay desolate [x]she kept sabbath, to fulfil threescore and ten years.

22 ¶ Now in the first year of Cȳ'rus king of Pĕr'siȧ, that the word of the LORD *spoken* by the mouth of [y]Jĕr-e-mī'ah might be accomplished, the LORD stirred up the spirit of [z]Cȳ'rus king of Pĕr'siȧ, that he made a proclamation throughout all his kingdom, and *put it* also in writing, saying,

23 Thus saith Cȳ'rus king of Pĕr'siȧ, All the kingdoms of the earth hath [a]the LORD God of heaven given me; and he hath charged me to build him an house in Je-rụ'sa-lĕm, which *is* in Jū'dah. Who *is there* among you of all his people? The LORD his God *be* with him, and let him go up.

18 [s]2 Ki. 25.13
19 [t]2 Ki. 25.9; Ps. 74.6-7
20 [10]the remainder from the sword
[u]Jer. 27.7
21 [v]Jer. 25.9
[w]Lev. 26.34
[x]Lev. 25.4-5
22 [y]Jer. 29.10
[z]Isa. 44.28
23 [a]Dan. 2.21

THE BOOK OF

EZRA

Life's Questions

Is religion always dull and meaningless?
Must the world always laugh at God's people?
Where do I learn how to please God?

God's Answers

Ezra is the first part of a two-part work: Ezra/Nehemiah. The work tells a brief bit of Judah's struggle after returning from exile in 538 B.C. Ezra a scribe and Bible scholar returned to Palestine in 458 B.C. Nehemiah , a court official for the Persian king, returned in 445 B.C. Ezra taught the law. Nehemiah rebuilt the city's defenses. Both showed God's hope for a disenchanted people.

In two parts Ezra shows that God's worship must be restored (1—6) and God's Word must be followed (7—10). Commitment to God's worship and Word give hope to a people mired in meaningless ritual and immoral lives.

1 Now in the first year of Cȳ'rus king of Pĕr'siȧ, that the word of the LORD [a]by the mouth of Jĕr-e-mī'ah might be fulfilled, the LORD [b]stirred up the spirit of Cȳ'rus king of Pĕr'siȧ, [c]that he [1]made a proclamation throughout all his kingdom, and *put it* also in writing, saying,

2 Thus saith Cȳ'rus king of Pĕr'siȧ, The LORD God of heaven hath given me all the kingdoms of the earth; and he hath [d]charged me to build him an house at Je-rụ'sa-lĕm, which *is* in Jū'dah.

3 Who *is there* among you of all his people? his God be with him, and let him go up to Je-rụ'sa-lĕm, which *is* in Jū'dah, and build the house of the LORD God of Is'ra-el, (he [e]*is* the God,) which *is* in Je-rụ'sa-lĕm.

4 And whosoever remaineth in any place where he sojourneth, let the men of his place [2]help him with silver, and with gold, and with goods, and with beasts, beside the freewill offering for the house of God that *is* in Je-rụ'sa-lĕm.

5 ¶ Then rose up the chief of the fathers of Jū'dah and Bĕn'ja-min, and the priests, and the Lē'vītes, with all *them* whose spirit [f]God had raised, to go up to build the house of the LORD which *is* in Je-rụ'sa-lĕm.

6 And all they that *were* about them [3]strengthened their hands with vessels of silver, with gold, with goods, and with beasts, and with precious things, beside all *that* was willingly offered.

7 ¶ [g]Also Cȳ'rus the king brought forth the vessels of the house of the LORD, [h]which Nĕb-u-chăd-nĕz'zar had brought forth out of Je-rụ'sa-lĕm, and had put them in the house of his gods;

8 Even those did Cȳ'rus king of Pĕr'siȧ bring forth by the hand of Mĭth're-dăth the treasurer, and numbered them unto [i]Shĕsh-băz'zar, the prince of Jū'dah.

9 And this *is* the number of them: thirty chargers of gold, a thousand chargers of silver, nine and twenty knives,

10 Thirty basons of gold, silver basons of a second *sort* four hundred and ten, *and* other vessels a thousand.

11 All the vessels of gold and of silver *were* five thousand and four hundred. All *these* did Shĕsh-băz'zar bring up with *them of* [4]the captivity that were brought up from Băb'ȳ-lon unto Je-rụ'sa-lĕm.

CHAPTER 1
1 [a]2 Chr. 36.22; Jer. 25.12
[b]Lev. 26.42
[c]ch. 5.13
[1]caused a voice to pass
2 [d]Isa. 44.28
3 [e]Deut. 3.24; 2 Sam. 22.32; Ps. 86.10; Isa. 37.16; Dan. 6.26; Mark 12.32; 1 Cor. 8.6
4 [2]lift him up
5 [f]Prov. 16.1; Phil. 2.13
6 [3]That is, helped them
7 [g]ch. 5.14; ch. 6.5
[h]2 Ki. 24.13; 2 Chr. 36.7
8 [i]ch. 5.14
11 [4]the transportation

2 Now [a]these *are* the children of the [b]province that went up out of the captivity, of those which had been carried away, [c]whom Nĕb-u-chăd-nĕz'-zar the king of Băb'ȳ-lon had carried away unto Băb'ȳ-lon, and came again unto Je-ru̧'sa-lĕm and Jū'dah, every one unto his city;

2 Which came with Ze-rŭb'ba-bĕl: Jĕsh'u-ȧ, Nē-he-mī'ah, [1]Sĕr-a-ī'ah, [2]Rē-el-ā'iah, Môr'de-cāi, Bĭl'shăn, [3]Mĭz'par, Bĭg'va-ī, [4]Rē'hŭm, Bā'a-nah. The number of the men of the people of Is'ra-el:

3 The children of Pā'rŏsh, two thousand an hundred seventy and two.

4 The children of Shĕph-a-tī'ah, three hundred seventy and two.

5 The children of Ā'rah, [d]seven hundred seventy and five.

6 The children of [e]Pā'hath–mō'ab, of the children of Jĕsh'u-ȧ *and* Jō'ab, two thousand eight hundred and twelve.

7 The children of Ē'lăm, a thousand two hundred fifty and four.

8 The children of Zăt'tu, nine hundred forty and five.

9 The children of Zăc'ca-ī, seven hundred and threescore.

10 The children of [5]Bā'nī, six hundred forty and two.

11 The children of Bĕb'ă-ī, six hundred twenty and three.

12 The children of Ăz'gad, a thousand two hundred twenty and two.

13 The children of [f]A-dŏn'ĭ-kăm, six hundred sixty and six.

14 The children of Bĭg'va-ī, two thousand fifty and six.

15 The children of Ā'dĭn, four hundred fifty and four.

16 The children of A'tēr of Hĕz-e-kī'ah, ninety and eight.

17 The children of Bē'zāi, three hundred twenty and three.

18 The children of [6]Jō'rah, an hundred and twelve.

19 The children of Hā'shum, two hundred twenty and three.

20 The children of [7]Gĭb'bar, ninety and five.

21 The children of [g]Bĕth'–lĕ-hĕm, an hundred twenty and three.

22 The men of Ne-tō'phah, fifty and six.

23 The men of Ăn'a-thoth, an hundred twenty and eight.

24 The children of [8]Ăz'ma-veth, forty and two.

25 The children of Kĭr'jath–ā'rim, Che-phī'rah, and Be-ē'rŏth, seven hundred and forty and three.

26 The children of [h]Rā'mah and Gā'bȧ, six hundred twenty and one.

27 The men of Mĭch'mas, an hundred twenty and two.

28 The men of Bĕth'–el and Ā'ī, two hundred twenty and three.

29 The children of Nē'bo, fifty and two.

30 The children of Măg'bish, an hundred fifty and six.

31 The children of the other [i]Ē'lăm, a thousand two hundred fifty and four.

32 The children of Hā'rim, three hundred and twenty.

33 The children of Lŏd, [9]Hā'did, and Ō'no, seven hundred twenty and five.

34 The children of [j]Jĕr'ĭ-chō, three hundred forty and five.

35 The children of Se-nā'ah, three thousand and six hundred and thirty.

36 ¶ The priests: the children of [k]Je-dā'iah, of the house of Jĕsh'u-ȧ, nine hundred seventy and three.

37 The children of [l]Ĭm'mēr, a thousand fifty and two.

38 The children of [m]Păsh'ŭr, a thousand two hundred forty and seven.

39 The children of [n]Hā'rim, a thousand and seventeen.

40 ¶ The Lē'vītes: the children of Jĕsh'u-ȧ and Kăd'mĭ-el, of the children of [10]Hŏd-a-vī'ah, seventy and four.

41 ¶ The singers: the children of Ā'saph, an hundred twenty and eight.

42 ¶ The children of the porters: the children of Shăl'lum, the children of A'tēr, the children of Tăl'mon, the children of Ăk'kŭb, the children of Hăt'ĭ-tȧ, the children of Shō'ba-ī, *in* all an hundred thirty and nine.

43 ¶ [o]The Nĕth'i-nĭms: the children of Zī'hȧ, the children of Ha-sū'phȧ, the children of Tăb'ba-ŏth,

44 The children of Kē'ros, the children of [11]Sī'a-hȧ, the children of Pā'don,

45 The children of Lĕb'a-nah, the children of Hăg'a-bah, the children of Ăk'kŭb,

46 The children of Hā'găb, the children of [12]Shăl'ma-ī, the children of Hā'nan,

47 The children of Gĭd'del, the children of Gā'hăr, the children of Rē-a-ī'ah,

48 The children of Rē'zin, the children of Ne-ko'dȧ, the children of Găz'-zam,

49 The children of Ŭz'zȧ, the children of Pa-sē'ah, the children of Bē'sāi,

50 The children of Ăs'nah, the children of Me-hū'nim, the children of [13]Ne-phū'sim,

51 The children of Băk'bŭk, the children of Ha-kū'phȧ, the children of Hăr'hûr,

52 The children of [14]Băz'lŭth, the children of Me-hī'dȧ, the children of Hăr'shȧ,

53 The children of Băr'kŏs, the children of Sĭs'e-rȧ, the children of Thā'-mah,

54 The children of Ne-zī'ah, the children of Hăt'ĭ-phȧ.

55 ¶ The children of [p]Sŏl'o-mon's servants: the children of Sō'ta-ī, the children of Sŏph'e-rĕth, the children of [15]Pe-ru̧'dȧ,

56 The children of Ja-ā'lah, the children of Dăr'kon, the children of Gĭd'del,

57 The children of Shĕph-a-tī'ah, the children of Hăt'til, the children of Pŏch'e-rĕth of Ze-bā'im, the children of [16]Ā'mī.

58 All the [q]Nĕth'i-nĭms, and the children of [r]Sŏl'o-mon's servants, *were* three hundred ninety and two.

59 And these *were* they which went up from Tĕl–mē'lah, Tĕl–hăr'sȧ,

CHAPTER 2
1 [a]Neh. 7.6 [b]ch. 5.8; Esth. 8.9 [c]2 Ki. 24.14-16; 2 Chr. 36.20
2 [1]Or, Azariah, Neh. 7.7 [2]Or, Raamiah [3]Or, Mispereth [4]Or, Nehum
5 [d]Neh. 6.18; Neh. 7.10
6 [e]Neh. 7.11
10 [5]Or, Binnui, Neh. 7.15
13 [f]ch. 8.13
18 [6]Or, Hariph, Neh. 7.24
20 [7]Or, Gibeon, Josh. 9.17; 2 Sam. 21.2; Neh. 7.25
21 [g]Gen. 35.19;
24 [8]Or, Beth-azmaveth, Neh. 7.28
26 [h]Josh. 18.25;
31 [i]verse 7;
33 [9]Or, Harid, as it is in some copies
34 [j]Deut. 34.3;
36 [k]1 Chr. 9.10;
37 [l]1 Chr. 24.14;
38 [m]1 Chr. 9.12;
39 [n]1 Chr. 24.8
40 [10]Or, Judah, ch. 3.9: called also Hodevah, Neh. 7.43
43 [o]1 Chr. 9.2;
44 [11]Or, Sia
46 [12]Or, Shamlai
50 [13]Or, Nephishesim
52 [14]Or, Bazlith, Neh. 7.54
55 [p]1 Ki. 9.21 [15]Or, Perida, Neh. 7.57
57 [16]Or, Amon, Neh. 7.59
58 [q]Josh. 9.21-27; [r]1 Ki. 9.21

Chē'rub, [17]Ă'dăn, *and* Ĭm'mēr: but
they could not shew their father's
house, and their [18]seed, whether they
were of Ĭs'ra-el:
60 The children of Del-a-ī'ah, the
children of To-bī'ah, the children of
Ne-ko'dȧ, six hundred fifty and two.
61 ¶ And of the children of the
priests: the children of Ha-bā'iah, the
children of Kŏz, the children of Bär-
zĭl'la-ī; which took a wife of the daughters of [s]Bär-zĭl'la-ī the Gĭl'e-ăd-īte, and
was called after their name:
62 These sought their register *among*
those that were reckoned by genealogy,
but they were not found: [t][19]therefore
were they, as polluted, put from the
priesthood.
63 And the [20]Tĭr'sha-thȧ said unto
them, that they [u]should not eat of the
most holy things, till there stood up a
priest with [v]Ū'rim and with Thŭm'mim.
64 ¶ [w]The whole congregation together *was* forty and two thousand
three hundred *and* threescore,
65 Beside their servants and their
maids, of whom *there were* seven thousand three hundred thirty and seven:
and *there were* among them two hundred singing men and singing women.
66 Their horses *were* seven hundred
thirty and six; their mules, two hundred forty and five;
67 Their camels, four hundred thirty
and five; *their* asses, six thousand
seven hundred and twenty.
68 ¶ [x]And *some* of the chief of the
fathers, when they came to the house
of the LORD which *is* at Je-ru'sa-lĕm,
offered freely for the house of God to
set it up in his place:
69 They gave after their ability unto
the treasure of the work threescore
and one thousand drams of gold, and
five thousand pound of silver, and one
hundred priests' garments.
70 So the priests, and the Lē'vītes,
and *some* of the people, and the singers, and the porters, and the Nĕth'i-
nĭms, dwelt in their cities, and all Ĭs'ra-
el in their cities.
3 And when the seventh month was
come, and the children of Ĭs'ra-el
were in the cities, the people gathered themselves together as one man
to Je-ru'sa-lĕm.
2 Then stood up [a]Jĕsh'u-ȧ the son of
Jŏz'a-dăk, and his brethren the priests,
and [b][1]Ze-rŭb'ba-bĕl the son of [c]She-
ăl'tĭ-el, and his brethren, and builded
the altar of the God of Ĭs'ra-el, to offer
burnt offerings thereon, as *it is* [d]writ-
ten in the law of Mō'ses the man of
God.
3 And they set the altar upon his
bases; for fear *was* upon them because
of the people of those countries: and
they offered burnt offerings thereon
unto the LORD, *even* [e]burnt offerings
morning and evening.
4 [f]They kept also the feast of tabernacles, [g]as *it is* written, and [h]*offered*
the daily burnt offerings by number,
according to the custom, [2]as the duty
of every day required;
5 And afterward *offered* the [i]contin-
ual burnt offering, both of the new
moons, and of all the set feasts of the
LORD that were consecrated, and of every one that willingly offered a freewill
offering unto the LORD.
6 From the first day of the seventh
month began they to offer burnt offerings unto the LORD. But [3]the foundation of the temple of the LORD was not
yet laid.
7 They gave money also unto the
masons, and to the [4]carpenters; and
[j]meat, and drink, and oil, unto them of
Zī'dŏn, and to them of Tȳre, to bring
cedar trees from Lĕb'a-non to the sea
of [k]Jŏp'pȧ, [l]according to the grant
that they had of Cȳ'rus king of Pĕr'siȧ.
8 ¶ Now in the second year of their
coming unto the house of God at Je-
ru'sa-lĕm, in the second month, began
Ze-rŭb'ba-bĕl the son of She-ăl'tĭ-el,
and Jĕsh'u-ȧ the son of Jŏz'a-dăk,
and the remnant of their brethren the
priests and the Lē'vītes, and all they
that were come out of the captivity
unto Je-ru'sa-lĕm; [m]and appointed the
Lē'vītes, from twenty years old and upward, to set forward the work of the
house of the LORD.
9 Then stood [n]Jĕsh'u-ȧ *with* his sons
and his brethren, Kăd'mĭ-el and his
sons, the sons of [o]Jū'dah, [5]together,
to set forward the workmen in the
house of God: the sons of Hĕn'a-dăd,
with their sons and their brethren the
Lē'vītes.
10 And when the builders laid the
foundation [p]of the temple of the LORD,
[q]they set the priests in their apparel
with trumpets, and the Lē'vītes the
sons of Ā'saph with cymbals, to praise
the LORD, after the [r]ordinance of Dā'-
vid king of Ĭs'ra-el.
11 [s]And they sang together by course
in praising and giving thanks unto the
LORD; [t]because *he is* good, [u]for his
mercy *endureth* for ever toward Ĭs'ra-
el. And all the people shouted with
a great shout, when they praised the
LORD, because the foundation of the
house of the LORD was laid.
12 But many of the priests and Lē'-
vītes and chief of the fathers, *who were*
ancient men, that had seen the first
house, when the foundation of this
house was laid before their eyes, wept
with a loud voice; and many shouted
aloud for joy;
13 So that the people could not discern the noise of the shout of joy from
the noise of the weeping of the people:
for the people shouted with a loud
shout, and the noise was heard afar
off.
4 Now when the adversaries of Jū'-
dah and Bĕn'ja-min heard that [1]the
children of the captivity builded the
temple unto the LORD God of Ĭs'ra-el;
2 Then they came to Ze-rŭb'ba-bĕl,
and to the chief of the fathers, and said
unto them, [a]Let us build with you: for
we seek your God, as ye [b]*do;* and we
do sacrifice unto him since the days of

59 [17]Or, Addon, Neh. 7.61
[18]Or, pedigree
61 [s]1 Ki. 2.7
62 [t]Num. 3.10
[19]they were polluted from the priesthood
63 [20]Or, governor, Neh. 8.9
[u]Lev. 22.2-10-15-16; Num. 18.9-11
[v]Ex. 28.30
64 [w]Isa. 10.22
68 [x]Ex. 25.2

CHAPTER 3
2 [a]Hag. 1.1; Zech. 3.1-Joshua
[b]ch. 2.2; Zech. 4.6-10
[1]Matt. 1.12-Zorobabel
[c]Luke 3.27-Salathiel
[d]Ex. 20.24; Deut. 12.5
3 [e]Ex. 29.38-42
4 [f]Neh. 8.14; Zech. 14.16
[g]Ex. 23.16
[h]Num. 29.12
[2]the matter of the day in his day
5 [i]Ex. 29.38; Num. 28.3
6 [3]the temple of the LORD was not yet founded
7 [4]Or, workmen
[j]2 Chr. 2.10; Acts 12.20
[k]Acts 9.36
[l]ch. 6.3
8 [m]1 Chr. 23.24-27
9 [n]ch. 2.40
[o]ch. 2.40-Hodaviah
[5]as one
10 [p]Zech. 4.6-10
[q]1 Chr. 15.27-28
[r]1 Chr. 6.31
11 [s]Ex. 15.21; 2 Chr. 7.3; Jer. 33.11
[t]Ps. 136.1
[u]Jer. 33.11; Luke 1.50

CHAPTER 4
1 [1]the sons of the transportation
2 [a]Esth. 8.17
[b]2 Ki. 17.24-32-33

Ē'sar–hăd'don king of Ăs'sur, which
brought us up hither.
3 But Ze-rŭb'ba-bĕl, and Jĕsh'u-ȧ,
and the rest of the chief of the fathers
of Iṡ'ra-el, said unto them, [c]Ye have
nothing to do with us to build an house
unto our God; but we ourselves together will build unto the LORD God of
Iṡ'ra-el, as [d]king Cȳ'rus the king of
Pĕr'siȧ hath commanded us.
4 Then [e]the people of the land weakened the hands of the people of Jū'dah,
and troubled them in building,
5 And hired counsellers against
them, to frustrate their purpose, all
the days of Cȳ'rus king of Pĕr'siȧ,
even until the reign of Da-rī'us king of
Pĕr'siȧ.
6 And in the reign of [2]A-hăs-ū-ē'rŭs,
in the beginning of his reign, wrote they
unto him an accusation against the inhabitants of Jū'dah and Je-ru'sa-lĕm.
7 ¶ And in the days of Ăr-tăx-ĕrx'ēs
wrote [3]Bĭsh'lăm, Mĭth're-dăth, Tā'be-
el, and the rest of their [4]companions,
unto Ăr-tăx-ĕrx'ēs king of Pĕr'siȧ; and
the writing of the letter *was* written in
the Sȳr'ĭ-an tongue, and interpreted in
the Sȳr'ĭ-an tongue.
8 Rē'hŭm the chancellor and Shĭm'-
shāi the [5]scribe wrote a letter against
[f]Je-ru'sa-lĕm to Ăr-tăx-ĕrx'ēs the king
in this sort:
9 Then *wrote* Rē'hŭm the chancellor,
and Shĭm'shāi the scribe, and the rest of
their [6]companions; [g]the Dī'na-ītes, the
A-phär'sath-chītes, the Tär'pel-ītes, the
A-phär'sītes, the Ăr'chĕ-vītes, the Băb-
ȳ-lō'nĭ-ans, the Su'san-chītes, the De-
hā'vītes, *and* the Ē'lăm-ītes,
10 And the rest of the nations whom
the great and noble Ăs-năp'pĕr brought
over, and set in the cities of Sa-mā'rĭ-ȧ,
and the rest *that are* on this side the
river, [h]and [7]at such a time.
11 ¶ This *is* the copy of the letter that
they sent unto him, *even* unto Ăr-tăx-
ĕrx'ēs the king; Thy servants the men
on this side the river, and at such a
time.
12 Be it known unto the king, that
the Jews which came up from thee to
us are come unto Je-ru'sa-lĕm, building [i]the rebellious and the bad city,
and have [8]set up the walls *thereof,* and
[9]joined the foundations.
13 Be it known now unto the king,
that, if this city be builded, and the
walls set up *again, then* will they not
[10]pay [j]toll, tribute, and custom, and so
thou shalt endamage the [11]revenue of
the kings.
14 Now because [12]we have mainte-
nance from *the king's* palace, and it
was not meet for us to see the king's
dishonour, therefore have we sent and
certified the king;
15 That search may be made in the
book of the records of thy fathers: so
shalt thou find in the book of the records, and know that this city *is* a rebellious city, and [k]hurtful unto kings
and provinces, and that they have
[13]moved sedition [14]within the same of

3 [c]John 4.9; Acts 8.21
[d]2 Chr. 36.22-23; ch. 6.3; Isa. 44.28
4 [e]ch. 3.3; Isa. 35.3-4; Jer. 38.4
6 [2]Ahash-verosh
7 [3]Or, in peace
[4]societies
8 [5]Or, secretary
[f]Ps. 112.6; Zech. 1.14; Rom. 8.28
9 [6]societies
[g]2 Ki. 17.30-31
10 [h]ch. 7.12
[7]Cheeneth
12 [i]Amos 7.10; Luke 23.2; Acts 24.5
[8]Or, finished
[9]sewed together
13 [10]give
[j]ch. 7.24; Matt. 9.9
[11]Or, strength
14 [12]we are salted with the salt of the palace
15 [k]Esth. 3.8; Acts 17.6-7
[13]made
[14]in the midst thereof
17 [15]societies
19 [16]by me a decree is set
[17]lifted up itself
20 [l]1 Chr. 18.3; Ps. 72.8
[m]Gen. 15.18
21 [18]Make a decree
23 [n]Prov. 4.16
[19]by arm and power
24 [o]Job 20.5

CHAPTER 5
1 [a]Hag. 1.1
[b]Zech. 1.1
2 [c]Hag. 1.12-15
[d]ch. 6.14; Eccl. 12.11; Hag. 2.4-9
3 [e]ch. 6.6
[1]Westward of Euphrates
4 [2]that build this building?
5 [f]2 Chr. 16.9; ch. 7.6-28; Ps. 33.18; 1 Pet. 3.12
[g]ch. 6.6
6 [h]ch. 4.9

old time: for which cause was this city
destroyed.
16 We certify the king that, if this
city be builded *again,* and the walls
thereof set up, by this means thou shalt
have no portion on this side the river.
17 ¶ *Then* sent the king an answer
unto Rē'hŭm the chancellor, and *to*
Shĭm'shāi the scribe, and *to* the rest of
their [15]companions that dwell in Sa-
mā'rĭ-ȧ, and *unto* the rest beyond the
river, Peace, and at such a time.
18 The letter which ye sent unto us
hath been plainly read before me.
19 And [16]I commanded, and search
hath been made, and it is found that
this city of old time hath [17]made insurrection against kings, and *that* rebellion and sedition have been made
therein.
20 There have been mighty kings
also over Je-ru'sa-lĕm, which have
[l]ruled over all *countries* [m]beyond the
river; and toll, tribute, and custom,
was paid unto them.
21 [18]Give ye now commandment to
cause these men to cease, and that this
city be not builded, until *another* commandment shall be given from me.
22 Take heed now that ye fail not to
do this: why should damage grow to
the hurt of the kings?
23 ¶ Now when the copy of king Ăr-
tăx-ĕrx'ēs' letter *was* read before Rē'-
hŭm, and Shĭm'shāi the scribe, and
their companions, they [n]went up in
haste to Je-ru'sa-lĕm unto the Jews,
and made them to cease [19]by force and
power.
24 Then ceased the work of the
house of God which *is* at Je-ru'sa-lĕm.
So it ceased unto [o]the second year of
the reign of Da-rī'us king of Pĕr'siȧ.
5 Then the prophets, [a]Hăg'ga-ī the
prophet, and [b]Zĕch-a-rī'ah the son
of Ĭd'dō, prophesied unto the Jews that
were in Jū'dah and Je-ru'sa-lĕm in the
name of the God of Iṡ'ra-el, *even* unto
them.
2 Then rose up [c]Ze-rŭb'ba-bĕl the
son of She-ăl'tĭ-el, and Jĕsh'u-ȧ the
son of Jŏz'a-dăk, and began to build
the house of God which *is* at Je-ru'sa-
lĕm: and with them *were* the prophets
of God [d]helping them.
3 ¶ At the same time came to them
[e]Tatnai, governor on [1]this side the
river, and Shē'thär–bŏz'na-ī, and their
companions, and said thus unto them,
Who hath commanded you to build
this house, and to make up this wall?
4 Then said we unto them after this
manner, What are the names of the
men [2]that make this building?
5 But [f]the eye of their God was upon
the elders of the Jews that they could
not cause them to cease, till the matter
came to Da-rī'us: and then they returned [g]answer by letter concerning
this *matter.*
6 ¶ The copy of the letter that Tăt'-
na-ī, governor on this side the river,
and Shē'thär–bŏz'na-ī, [h]and his companions the A-phär'săch-ītes, which

were on this side the river, sent unto
Da-rī'us the king:
7 They sent a letter unto him,
[3]wherein was written thus; Unto Da-
rī'us the king, all peace.
8 Be it known unto the king, that we
went into the province of Jū-dē'ȧ, to
the house of the great God, which is
builded with [4]great stones, and timber
is laid in the walls, and this work goeth
fast on, and prospereth in their hands.
9 Then asked we those elders, *and*
said unto them thus, Who commanded
you to build this house, and to make up
these walls?
10 We asked their names also, to
certify thee, that we might write the
names of the men that *were* the chief
of them.
11 And thus they returned us answer, saying, We are the [i]servants of
the God of heaven and earth, and build
the house that was builded these many
years ago, which a great king of Ĭs'ra-
el builded [j]and set up.
12 But [k]after that our fathers had
provoked the God of heaven unto
wrath, he gave them into the hand of
[l]Nĕb-u-chăd-nĕz'zar the king of Băb'-
ў-lon, the Chăl-dē'an, who destroyed
this house, and carried the people away
into Băb'ў-lon.
13 But in the first year of [m]Cȳ'rus
the king of Băb'ў-lon *the same* king
Cȳ'rus made a decree to build this
house of God.
14 And [n]the vessels also of gold and
silver of the house of God, which Nĕb-
u-chăd-nĕz'zar took out of the temple
that *was* in Je-rụ'sa-lĕm, and brought
them into the temple of Băb'ў-lon,
those did Cȳ'rus the king take out of
the temple of Băb'ў-lon, and they were
delivered unto *one,* [o]whose name *was*
Shĕsh-băz'zar, whom he had made
[5]governor;
15 And said unto him, Take these
vessels, go, carry them into the temple
that *is* in Je-rụ'sa-lĕm, and let the
house of God be builded in his place.
16 Then came the same Shĕsh-băz'-
zar, *and* [p]laid the foundation of the
house of God which *is* in Je-rụ'sa-lĕm:
and since that time even until now
hath it been in building, and [q]*yet* it is
not finished.
17 Now therefore, if *it seem* good to
the king, [r]let there be search made in
the king's treasure house, which *is*
there at Băb'ў-lon, whether it be *so,*
that a decree was made of Cȳ'rus the
king to build this house of God at Je-
rụ'sa-lĕm, and let the king send his
pleasure to us concerning this matter.
6 Then Da-rī'us the king made a decree, and [a]search was made in the
house of the [1]rolls, where the treasures
were [2]laid up in Băb'ў-lon.
2 And there was found at [3]Ăch'me-
thȧ, in the palace that *is* in the province
of the Mēdes, a roll, and therein *was* a
record thus written:
3 In the first year of Cȳ'rus the king
the same Cȳ'rus the king made a decree
concerning the house of God at Je-

7 [3]in the midst whereof
8 [4]stones of rolling
11 [i]Josh. 24.15; Ps. 119.46; Jon. 1.9; Matt. 10.32; Luke 12.8; Acts 27.23
[j]1 Ki. 6.1
12 [k]2 Chr. 34.24-25; 2 Chr. 36.16-17
[l]2 Ki. 24.2; Jer. 39.1
13 [m]ch. 1.1
14 [n]ch. 1.7-8
[o]Hag. 1.14
[5]Or, deputy
16 [p]ch. 3.8-10
[q]ch. 6.15
17 [r]ch. 6.1-2; Prov. 25.2
CHAPTER 6
1 [a]ch. 5.17
[1]books
[2]made to descend
2 [3]Or, Ecbatana, the chief city of Media, or, in a coffer
4 [b]1 Ki. 6.36
[c]Ps. 68.29; Isa. 60.6
5 [d]ch. 1.7-8; Jer. 27.16-18-22; Dan. 1.2
[4]go
6 [e]ch. 5.3
[5]their societies
8 [6]by me a decree is made
[7]made to cease
10 [f]ch. 7.23; Jer. 29.7
[8]of rest
[g]Gen. 8.21; Lev. 1.9
[h]1 Tim. 2.1-2
11 [9]let him be destroyed
[i]Dan. 2.5
12 [j]Deut. 12.11; 2 Chr. 7.16; Ps. 132.13
13 [k]Job 5.12; Ps. 9.16; 1 Cor. 3.19
14 [l]ch. 5.1-2
[10]decree
[m]ch. 1.1
[n]ch. 4.24
[o]ch. 7.1

rụ'sa-lĕm, Let the house be builded, the
place where they offered sacrifices, and
let the foundations thereof be strongly
laid; the height thereof threescore cubits, *and* the breadth thereof threescore
cubits;
4 [b]*With* three rows of great stones,
and a row of new timber: and [c]let the
expenses be given out of the king's
house:
5 And also let [d]the golden and silver
vessels of the house of God, which
Nĕb-u-chăd-nĕz'zar took forth out of
the temple which *is* at Je-rụ'sa-lĕm,
and brought unto Băb'ў-lon, be restored, and [4]brought again unto the
temple which *is* at Je-rụ'sa-lĕm, *every*
one to his place, and place *them* in the
house of God.
6 [e]Now *therefore,* Tăt'na-ī, governor beyond the river, Shē'thär–bŏz'-
na-ī, and [5]your companions the A-
phär'săch-ītes, which *are* beyond the
river, be ye far from thence:
7 Let the work of this house of God
alone; let the governor of the Jews and
the elders of the Jews build this house
of God in his place.
8 Moreover [6]I make a decree what
ye shall do to the elders of these Jews
for the building of this house of God:
that of the king's goods, *even* of the
tribute beyond the river, forthwith expenses be given unto these men, that
they be not [7]hindered.
9 And that which they have need of,
both young bullocks, and rams, and
lambs, for the burnt offerings of the
God of heaven, wheat, salt, wine, and
oil, according to the appointment of
the priests which *are* at Je-rụ'sa-lĕm,
let it be given them day by day without
fail:
10 [f]That they may offer sacrifices
[8][g]of sweet savours unto the God of
heaven, and [h]pray for the life of the
king, and of his sons.
11 Also I have made a decree, that
whosoever shall alter this word, let timber be pulled down from his house,
and being set up, [9]let him be hanged
thereon; [i]and let his house be made a
dunghill for this.
12 And the God that hath caused his
[j]name to dwell there destroy all kings
and people, that shall put to their hand
to alter *and* to destroy this house of
God which *is* at Je-rụ'sa-lĕm. I Da-rī'us
have made a decree; let it be done with
speed.
13 ¶ Then Tăt'na-ī, governor on this
side the river, Shē'thär–bŏz'na-ī, and
their companions, according to that
which Da-rī'us the king had sent, so
they [k]did speedily.
14 [l]And the elders of the Jews
builded, and they prospered through
the prophesying of Hăg'ga-ī the prophet
and Zĕch-a-rī'ah the son of Ĭd'dō. And
they builded, and finished *it,* according
to the commandment of the God of
Ĭs'ra-el, and according to the [10]com-
mandment of [m]Cȳ'rus, and [n]Da-rī'us,
and [o]Ar-tăx-ērx'ēs king of Pēr'siȧ.

15 And this house was finished on
the third day of the month Ā'dār, which
was in the sixth year of the reign of Da-
rī'us the king.
16 ¶ And the children of Ĭs'ra-el, the
priests, and the Lē'vītes, and the rest
of [11]the children of the captivity, kept
[p]the dedication of this house of God
with joy,
17 And [q]offered at the dedication of
this house of God an hundred bullocks, two hundred rams, four hundred
lambs; and for a sin offering for all
Ĭs'ra-el, twelve he goats, according to
the number of the tribes of Ĭs'ra-el.
18 And they set the priests in their
[r]divisions, and the Lē'vītes in their
[s]courses, for the service of God, which
is at Je-ru'sa-lĕm; [12]as it is written in
the book of Mō'ses.
19 And the children of the captivity kept the passover [t]upon the fourteenth *day* of the first month.
20 For the priests and the Lē'vītes
were [u]purified together, all of them
were pure, and [v]killed the passover
for all the children of the captivity,
and for their brethren the priests, and
for themselves.
21 And the children of Ĭs'ra-el, which
were come again out of captivity, and
all such as had separated [w]themselves
unto them from the filthiness of the heathen of the land, to seek the LORD God of
Ĭs'ra-el, did eat,
22 And kept the [x]feast of unleavened bread seven days with joy: for
the LORD had made them joyful, and
[y]turned the heart of the king of As-
sy̆r'ĭ-ȧ unto them, to strengthen their
hands in the work of the house of God,
the God of Ĭs'ra-el.
7 Now after these things, in the reign
of [1]Ăr-tăx-ĕrx'ēs king of Pĕr'siȧ,
Ez'rȧ [a]the son of Sĕr-a-ī'ah, the son of
Ăz-a-rī'ah, the son of Hĭl-kī'ah,
2 The son of Shăl'lum, the son of
Zā'dŏk, the son of A-hī'tub,
3 The son of Ăm-a-rī'ah, the son of
Ăz-a-rī'ah, the son of Me-rā'ioth,
4 The son of Zĕr-a-hī'ah, the son of
Ŭz'zī, the son of Bŭk'kī,
5 The son of A-bĭsh'u-ȧ, the son of
Phĭn'e-has, the son of Ē-le-ā'zar, the
son of Aâr'on the chief priest:
6 This Ez'rȧ went up from Băb'y̆-
lon; and he *was* a ready scribe in the
law of Mō'ses, which the LORD God
of Ĭs'ra-el had given: and the king
granted him all his request, [b]accord-
ing to the hand of the LORD his God
upon him.
7 [c]And there went up *some* of the
children of Ĭs'ra-el, and of the priests,
and the Lē'vītes, and the singers, and
the porters, and [d]the Nĕth'i-nĭms, unto
Je-ru'sa-lĕm, in the seventh year of Ăr-
tăx-ĕrx'ēs the king.
8 And he came to Je-ru'sa-lĕm in the
fifth month, which *was* in the seventh
year of the king.
9 For upon the first *day* of the first
month [2]began he to go up from Băb'y̆-
lon, and on the first *day* of the fifth
month came he to Je-ru'sa-lĕm, [e]ac-
cording to the good hand of his God
upon him.
10 For Ez'rȧ had prepared his heart
to [f]seek the law of the LORD, and to do
it, and to [g]teach in Ĭs'ra-el statutes and
judgments.
11 ¶ Now this *is* the copy of the letter
that the king Ăr-tăx-ĕrx'ēs gave unto
Ez'rȧ the priest, the scribe, *even* a
scribe of the words of the commandments of the LORD, and of his statutes
to Ĭs'ra-el.
12 Ăr-tăx-ĕrx'ēs, [h]king of kings,
[3]unto Ez'rȧ the priest, a scribe of the
law of the God of heaven, perfect *peace*,
[i]and at such a time.
13 I make a decree, that all they of
the people of Ĭs'ra-el, and *of* his priests
and Lē'vītes, in my realm, which are
minded of their own freewill to go up
to Je-ru'sa-lĕm, go with thee.
14 Forasmuch as thou art sent [4]of
the king, and of his [j]seven counsellers,
to inquire concerning Jū'dah and Je-
ru'sa-lĕm, according to the law of thy
God which *is* in thine hand;
15 And to carry the silver and gold,
which the king and his counsellers have
freely offered unto the God of Ĭs'ra-el,
[k]whose habitation *is* in Je-ru'sa-lĕm,
16 [l]And all the silver and gold that
thou canst find in all the province of
Băb'y̆-lon, with the freewill offering of
the people, and of the priests, [m]offer-
ing willingly for the house of their God
which *is* in Je-ru'sa-lĕm:
17 That thou mayest buy speedily
with this money bullocks, rams, lambs,
with their [n]meat offerings and their
drink offerings, and offer them [o]upon
the altar of the house of your God
which *is* in Je-ru'sa-lĕm.
18 And whatsoever shall seem good
to thee, and to thy brethren, to do with
the rest of the silver and the gold, that
do after the will of your God.
19 The vessels also that are given
thee for the service of the house of thy
God, *those* deliver thou before the God
of Je-ru'sa-lĕm.
20 And [p]whatsoever more shall be
needful for the house of thy God, which
thou shalt have occasion to bestow, bestow *it* out of the king's treasure house.
21 And I, *even* I Ăr-tăx-ĕrx'ēs the
king, do make a [q]decree to all the treasurers which *are* beyond the river, that
whatsoever Ez'rȧ the priest, the scribe
of the law of the God of heaven, shall
require of you, it be done speedily,
22 Unto an hundred talents of silver,
and to an hundred [5]measures of wheat,
and to an hundred baths of wine, and
to an hundred baths of oil, and salt
without prescribing *how much*.
23 [6]Whatsoever is commanded by
the God of heaven, let it be diligently
done for the house of the God of
heaven: [r]for why should there be wrath
against the realm of the king and his
sons?
24 Also we certify you, that touching any of the priests and Lē'vītes, singers, porters, Nĕth'i-nĭms, or ministers
of this house of God, it shall not be

16 [11]the sons of the transportation
[p]1 Ki. 8.63; John 10.22
17 [q]Num. 7.2-3; ch. 8.35
18 [r]1 Chr. 24.1
[s]1 Chr. 23.6
[12]according to writing
19 [t]Ex. 12.6
20 [u]2 Chr. 29.34
[v]Ex. 12.21; 2 Chr. 35.11
21 [w]Ex. 12.48; Ps. 93.5
22 [x]Ex. 12.15
[y]Prov. 21.1

CHAPTER 7

1 [1]Longimanus, Neh. 2.1
[a]1 Chr. 6.14
6 [b]Gen. 32.28; Neh. 1.10-11
7 [c]ch. 8.1
[d]ch. 2.43
9 [2]was the foundation of the going up
[e]Neh. 2.8
10 [f]1 Sam. 7.3; Ps. 119.45
[g]Deut. 33.10; 2 Tim. 4.2
12 [h]Ezek. 26.7; Dan. 2.37
[3]Or, to Ezra the priest, a perfect scribe of the law of the God of heaven, peace, etc
[i]ch. 4.10
14 [4]from before the king
[j]Esth. 1.14
15 [k]2 Chr. 6.2;
16 [l]ch. 8.26
[m]1 Chr. 29.6
17 [n]Num. 15.4-13
[o]Deut. 12.5
20 [p]1 Cor. 4.1-2
21 [q]ch. 4.16-20;
22 [5]cors
23 [6]Whatsoever is of the decree
[r]ch. 6.10;

lawful to impose toll, tribute, or custom, upon them.

25 And thou, Ĕz′rȧ, after the wisdom of thy God, that *is* in thine hand, [s]set magistrates and judges, which may judge all the people that *are* beyond the river, all such as know the laws of thy God; and [t]teach ye them that know *them* not.

26 And whosoever will not do the law of thy God, and the law of the king, let judgment be executed speedily upon him, whether *it be* unto death, or [7]to banishment, or to confiscation of goods, or to imprisonment.

27 ¶ [u]Blessed *be* the LORD God of our fathers, [v]which hath put *such a thing* as this in the king's heart, to beautify the house of the LORD which *is* in Je-ru̇′sa-lĕm:

28 And [w]hath extended mercy unto me before the king, and his counsellers, and before all the king's mighty princes. And I was strengthened as [x]the hand of the LORD my God *was* upon me, and I gathered together out of Ĭs′ra-el chief men to go up with me.

8 These *are* now the chief of their fathers, and *this is* the genealogy of them that went up with me from Băb′-y̆-lon, in the reign of Ar-tăx-ērx′ēs the king.

2 Of the sons of Phĭn′e-has; Gēr′-shŏm: of the sons of Ĭth′a-mär; Dăn′-iel: of the sons of Dā′vid; [a]Hăt′tŭsh.

3 Of the sons of Shĕch-a-nī′ah, of the sons of [b]Phā′rŏsh; Zĕch-a-rī′ah: and with him were reckoned by genealogy of the males an hundred and fifty.

4 Of the sons of Pā′hath–mō′ab; Ĕl-i-hō-ē′nā-ī the son of Zĕr-a-hī′ah, and with him two hundred males.

5 Of the sons of Shĕch-a-nī′ah; the son of Ja-hā′zĭ-el, and with him three hundred males.

6 Of the sons also of [c]Ā′dĭn; E′bed the son of Jŏn′a-than, and with him fifty males.

7 And of the sons of Ē′lăm; Je-shā′-iah the son of Ăth-a-lī′ah, and with him seventy males.

8 And of the sons of Shĕph-a-tī′ah; Zĕb-a-dī′ah the son of Mī′chaĕl, and with him fourscore males.

9 Of the sons of Jō′ab; Ō-ba-dī′ah the son of Je-hī′el, and with him two hundred and eighteen males.

10 And of the sons of Shĕl′o-mĭth; the son of Jŏs-ĭ-phī′ah, and with him an hundred and threescore males.

11 And of the sons of Bĕb′ă-ī; Zĕch-a-rī′ah the son of Bĕb′ă-ī, and with him twenty and eight males.

12 And of the sons of Ăz′gad; Jo-hā′nan [1]the son of Hăk′ka-tăn, and with him an hundred and ten males.

13 And of the last sons of A-dŏn′ĭ-kăm, whose names *are* these, E-lĭph′e-lĕt, Je-ī′el, and Shĕm-a-ī′ah, and with them threescore males.

14 Of the sons also of Bĭg′va-ī; Ū′tha-ī, and [2]Zăb′bud, and with them seventy males.

15 ¶ And I gathered them together to the river [d]that runneth to A-hā′vȧ; and there [3]abode we in tents three days: and I viewed the [e]people, and the priests, and found there none of the [f]sons of Lē′vī.

16 Then sent I for E-li-ē′zēr, for Ā′rĭ-el, for Shĕm-a-ī′ah, and for Ĕl′na-than, and for Jā′rib, and for Ĕl′na-than, and for Nā′than, and for Zĕch-a-rī′ah, and for Me-shŭl′lam, chief men; also for Joi′a-rĭb, and for Ĕl′na-than, men of understanding.

17 And I sent them with commandment unto Ĭd′dō the chief at the place Ca-sĭph′ĭ-ȧ, and [4]I told them what they should say unto Ĭd′dō, *and* to his brethren the Nĕth′i-nĭms, at the place Ca-sĭph′ĭ-ȧ, that they should bring unto us ministers for the house of our God.

18 And by the [g]good hand of our God upon us they [h]brought us a man of understanding, of the sons of Māh′lī, the son of Lē′vī, the son of Ĭs′ra-el; and Shĕr-e-bī′ah, with his sons and his brethren, eighteen;

19 And Hash-a-bī′ah, and with him Je-shā′iah of the sons of Me-rā′rī, his brethren and their sons, twenty;

20 [i]Also of the Nĕth′i-nĭms, whom Dā′vid and the princes had appointed for the service of the Lē′vītes, two hundred and twenty Nĕth′i-nĭms: all of them were expressed by name.

21 ¶ Then I [j]proclaimed a fast there, at the river of A-hā′vȧ, that we might [k]afflict ourselves before our God, to seek of him a [l]right way for us, and for our little ones, and for all our substance.

22 For [m]I was ashamed to require of the king a band of soldiers and horsemen to help us against the enemy in the way: because we had spoken unto the king, saying, [n]The hand of our God *is* upon all them for [o]good that seek him; but his power and his wrath *is* [p]against all them [q]that forsake him.

23 So we fasted and besought our God for this: and he was [r]intreated of us.

24 ¶ Then I separated twelve of the chief of the priests, Shĕr-e-bī′ah, Hash-a-bī′ah, and ten of their brethren with them,

25 And weighed unto them [s]the silver, and the gold, and the vessels, *even* the offering of the house of our God, which the king, and his counsellers, and his lords, and all Ĭs′ra-el *there* present, had offered:

26 I even weighed unto their hand six hundred and fifty talents of silver, and silver vessels an hundred talents, *and* of gold an hundred talents;

27 Also twenty basons of gold, of a thousand drams; and two vessels of [5]fine copper, [6]precious as gold.

28 And I said unto them, Ye *are* [t]holy unto the LORD; the vessels *are* [u]holy also; and the silver and the gold *are* a freewill offering unto the LORD God of your fathers.

29 [v]Watch ye, and keep *them*, until ye weigh *them* before the chief of the priests and the Lē′vītes, and chief of the fathers of Ĭs′ra-el, at Je-ru̇′sa-lĕm,

---

25 [s]Ex. 18.21; Deut. 16.18; 1 Ki. 3.28; Ps. 19.7 [t]2 Chr. 17.7; Col. 1.28
26 [7]to rooting out
27 [u]1 Chr. 29.10; Phil. 4.10 [v]ch. 6.22; 2 Cor. 8.16
28 [w]ch. 9.9; Neh. 1.11 [x]ch. 5.5

CHAPTER 8
2 [a]1 Chr. 3.22
3 [b]ch. 2.3
6 [c]ch. 2.15; Neh. 7.20
12 [1]Or, the youngest son
14 [2]Or, Zaccur, as some read
15 [d]Ps. 137.1; Acts 16.13 [3]Or, pitched [e]Prov. 27.23; Heb. 13.17 [f]ch. 7.7; Num. 8
17 [4]I put words in their mouth
18 [g]ch. 7.28; Rom. 8.28 [h]Lev. 10.10-11; Neh. 8.7
20 [i]ch. 2.43
21 [j]2 Chr. 20.3 [k]Lev. 16.29; Isa. 58.3-5 [l]Ps. 5.8
22 [m]1 Cor. 9.15 [n]1 Chr. 28.9; 1 Pet. 3.12 [o]Ps. 33.18 [p]Ps. 34.16 [q]2 Chr. 15.2
23 [r]Deut. 4.29; Jer. 29.12-13
25 [s]ch. 7.15-16
27 [5]yellow, or, shining brass [6]desirable
28 [t]Deut. 33.8; Isa. 52.11 [u]Lev. 22.2-3; 2 Chr. 24.14
29 [v]1 Chr. 26.20-26; Luke 12.37-38

in the chambers of the house of the
LORD.
30 So took the priests and the Lē'-
vītes the weight of the silver, and the
gold, and the vessels, to bring *them* to
Je-rụ'sa-lĕm unto the house of our God.
31 ¶ Then we departed from the
river of A-hā'vȧ on the twelfth *day* of
the first month, to go unto Je-rụ'sa-
lĕm: and [w]the hand of our God was
upon us, and he delivered us from the
hand of the enemy, and of such as lay
in wait by the way.
32 And we [x]came to Je-rụ'sa-lĕm,
and abode there three days.
33 ¶ Now on the fourth day was the
silver and the gold and the vessels
weighed in the house of our God by
the hand of Mĕr'e-mŏth the son of
U-rī'ah the priest; and with him *was*
E-le-a'zar the son of Phin'e-has; and
with them *was* Jŏz'a-băd the son of
Jĕsh'u-ȧ, and Nō-a-dī'ah the son of
Bĭn'nụ-ī, Lē'vītes;
34 By number *and* by weight of every one: and all the weight was written
at that time.
35 *Also* the children of those that
had been carried away, which were
come out of the captivity, [y]offered
burnt offerings unto the God of Ĭs'ra-el,
twelve bullocks for all Ĭs'ra-el, ninety
and six rams, seventy and seven lambs,
twelve he goats *for* a sin offering: all
this was a burnt offering unto the
LORD.
36 ¶ And they delivered the king's
[z]commissions unto the king's lieutenants, and to the governors on this side
the river: and they furthered [a]the people, and the house of God.

CHAPTER 9

9 Now when these things were done,
the princes came to me, saying, The
people of Ĭs'ra-el, and the priests, and
the Lē'vītes, have not [a]separated themselves from the people of the lands,
[b]*doing* according to their abominations, *even* of the Cā'năan-ītes, the
Hĭt'tītes, the Pĕr'ĭz-zītes, the Jĕb'u-
sītes, the Ăm'mŏn-ītes, the Mō'ab-ītes,
the E-gy̆p'tians, and the Ăm'ôr-ītes.
2 For they have [c]taken of their
daughters for themselves, and for their
sons: so that the [d]holy seed have
[e]mingled themselves with the people
of *those* lands: yea, the hand of the
princes and rulers hath been chief in
this trespass.
3 And when I heard this thing, [f]I
rent my garment and my mantle, and
plucked off the hair of my head and of
my beard, and sat down [g]astonied.
4 Then were assembled unto me every one that [h]trembled at the words of
the God of Ĭs'ra-el, because of the transgression of those that had been carried
away; and I sat astonied until the [i]eve-
ning sacrifice.
5 ¶ And at the evening sacrifice I
arose up from my [1]heaviness; and having rent my garment and my mantle, I
fell upon my knees, and [j]spread out
my hands unto the LORD my God,
6 And said, O my God, I am
[k]ashamed and blush to lift up my face
to thee, my God: for our iniquities are
increased over *our* head, and our [2]tres-
pass is grown up unto the heavens.
7 Since the days of our fathers *have*
[l]we *been* in a great trespass unto this
day; and for our iniquities [m]have we,
our kings, *and* our priests, been delivered into the hand of the kings of the
lands, to the sword, to captivity, and to
a spoil, and to confusion of face, as *it is*
this day.
8 And now for a [3]little space grace
hath been *shewed* from the LORD our
God, to leave us a remnant to escape,
and to give us [4]a nail in his holy place,
that our God may [n]lighten our eyes,
and give us a little reviving in our
bondage.
9 [o]For we *were* bondmen; [p]yet our
God hath not forsaken us in our bondage, but [q]hath extended mercy unto us
in the sight of the kings of Pĕr'siȧ, to
give us a reviving, to set up the house
of our God, and [5]to repair the desolations thereof, and to give us [r]a wall in
Jū'dah and in Je-rụ'sa-lĕm.
10 And now, O our God, what shall
we say after this? for we have forsaken
thy commandments,
11 Which thou hast commanded
[6]by thy servants the prophets, saying,
The land, unto which ye go to possess
it, is an unclean land with the filthiness of the people of the lands, with
their abominations, which have filled
it [7]from one end to another with their
uncleanness.
12 Now therefore [s]give not your
daughters unto their sons, neither take
their daughters unto your sons, [t]nor
seek their peace or their wealth for
ever: that ye may be strong, and eat
the good of the land, and [u]leave *it* for
an inheritance to your children for
ever.
13 And after all that is come upon us
for our evil deeds, and for our great
trespass, seeing that thou our God
[8]hast punished us less than our iniquities *deserve*, and hast given us *such* deliverance as this;
14 Should we [v]again break thy commandments, and [w]join in affinity with
the people of these abominations?
wouldest not thou be angry with us till
thou hadst consumed *us*, so that *there*
should be no remnant nor escaping?
15 O LORD God of Ĭs'ra-el, [x]thou *art*
righteous: for we remain yet escaped,
as *it is* this day: behold, we *are* [y]before
thee in our trespasses: for we cannot
[z]stand before thee because of this.

CHAPTER 10

10 Now [a]when Ĕz'rȧ had prayed,
and when he had confessed,
weeping and casting himself down [b]be-
fore the house of God, there assembled
unto him out of Ĭs'ra-el a very great
congregation of men and women and
children: for the people [1]wept very
sore.
2 And Shĕch-a-nī'ah the son of Je-
hī'el, *one* of the sons of Ē'lăm, answered and said unto Ĕz'rȧ, We have
[c]trespassed against our God, and have

31 [w]ch. 7.6-9-28; Job 5.19-24; Isa. 41.10-14
32 [x]Neh. 2.11
35 [y]ch. 6.17
36 [z]ch. 7.21
[a]Isa. 14.1; Isa. 56.6; Zech. 8.1-23

CHAPTER 9
1 [a]Neh. 9.2
[b]Deut. 12.30
2 [c]Deut. 7.3
[d]Ex. 22.31
[e]2 Cor. 6.14
3 [f]Isa. 15.2
[g]Ps. 143.4
4 [h]ch. 10.3; Isa. 66.2
[i]Ex. 29.39
5 [1]Or, affliction
[j]Ex. 9.29
6 [k]Dan. 9.7
[2]Or, guiltiness
7 [l]Ps. 106.6
[m]Deut. 28.36
8 [3]moment
[4]Or, a pin that is, a constant and sure abode
[n]Ps. 13.3
9 [o]Neh. 9.36
[p]Ps. 136.23
[q]ch. 7.28
[5]to set up
[r]Isa. 5.2
11 [6]by the hand of thy servants
[7]from mouth to mouth
12 [s]Ex. 23.32; Deut. 7.3; Josh. 23.12
[t]Deut. 23.6; 2 Chr. 19.2
[u]Gen. 18.19; Prov. 13.22
13 [8]hast withheld beneath our iniquities
14 [v]Ex. 23.32-33; Judg. 2.2; John 5.14; 2 Pet. 2.20
[w]2 Cor. 6.14
15 [x]Neh. 9.33; Dan. 9.14
[y]Rom. 3.19
[z]Ps. 130.3

CHAPTER 10
1 [a]Dan. 9.20
[b]2 Chr. 20.9
[1]wept a great weeping
2 [c]Ex. 34.13

taken strange wives of the people of
the land: yet now there is hope in Ĭs'ra-
el concerning this thing.
3 Now therefore let us make a covenant with our God [2]to put away all the
wives, and such as are born of them,
according to the counsel of my lord,
and of those that [d]tremble at [e]the commandment of our God; and let it be
done according to the law.
4 Arise; for *this* matter *belongeth*
unto thee: we also *will be* with thee:
[f]be of good courage, and do *it*.
5 Then arose Ēz'rȧ, and made the
chief priests, the Lē'vītes, and all Ĭs'ra-
el, [g]to swear that they should do according to this word. And they sware.
6 ¶ Then Ēz'rȧ rose up from before
the house of God, and went into the
chamber of Jo-hā'nan the son of Ē-lī'a-
shib: and *when* he came thither, he
[h]did eat no bread, nor drink water: for
he mourned because of the transgression of them that had been carried
away.
7 And they made proclamation
throughout Jū'dah and Je-ru'sa-lĕm
unto all the children of the captivity,
that they should gather themselves together unto Je-ru'sa-lĕm;
8 And that whosoever would not
come within three days, according to
the counsel of the princes and the elders, all his substance should be [3]for-
feited, and himself separated from the
congregation of those that had been
carried away.
9 ¶ Then all the men of Jū'dah and
Bĕn'ja-min gathered themselves together unto Je-ru'sa-lĕm within three
days. It *was* the ninth month, on the
twentieth *day* of the month; and [i]all
the people sat in the street of the house
of God, trembling because of *this* matter, and for [4]the great rain.
10 And Ēz'rȧ the priest stood up, and
said unto them, Ye have transgressed,
and [5]have taken strange wives, to increase the trespass of Ĭs'ra-el.
11 Now therefore [j]make confession
unto the LORD God of your fathers, and
[k]do his pleasure: and separate yourselves from the people of the land, and
from the strange wives.
12 Then all the congregation answered and said with a loud voice, As
thou hast said, so must we do.
13 But the people *are* many, and *it is*
a time of much rain, and we are not
able to stand without, neither *is this* a
work of one day or two: for [6]we are
many that have transgressed in this
thing.
14 Let now our rulers of all the congregation stand, and let all them which
have taken strange wives in our cities
come at appointed times, and with
them the elders of every city, and the
judges thereof, until [l]the fierce wrath
of our God [7]for this matter be turned
from us.
15 ¶ Only Jŏn'a-than the son of Ā'sa-
hĕl and Ja-ha-zī'ah the son of Tĭk'vah
[8]were employed about this *matter*: and

3 [2]to bring forth
[d]ch. 9.4; Ps. 119.53-120; Isa. 66.2
[e]Deut. 7.2-3
4 [f]1 Chr. 28.10; Isa. 35.3-4
5 [g]Neh. 5.12
6 [h]Deut. 9.18
8 [3]devoted, Lev. 27.28; Josh. 6.19
9 [i]1 Sam. 12.18
[4]the showers
10 [5]have caused to dwell, or, have brought back
11 [j]Prov. 28.13; Jer. 3.13
[k]Isa. 1.16-17; Rom. 12.2
13 [6]Or, we have greatly offended in this thing
14 [l]Num. 25.4; 2 Ki. 23.26; 2 Chr. 28.11-13; 2 Chr. 29.10; 2 Chr. 30.8; Ps. 78.38; Isa. 12.1
[7]Or, till this matter be dispatched
15 [8]stood
18 [m]ch. 5.2; Hag. 1.1-12; Zech. 3.1; Zech. 6.11
19 [n]2 Ki. 10.15; 1 Chr. 29.24; 2 Chr. 30.8; Prov. 6.1; Prov. 22.26; Gal. 2.9
[o]Lev. 5.15; Lev. 6.4-5-6
25 [p]ch. 2.3; ch. 8.3; Neh. 7.8
27 [q]ch. 2.8; Neh. 7.13
31 [r]Neh. 3.11-Malchijah

Me-shŭl'lam and Shab-bĕth'a-ī the Lē'-
vīte helped them.
16 And the children of the captivity
did so. And Ēz'rȧ the priest, *with* certain chief of the fathers, after the house
of their fathers, and all of them by
their names, were separated, and sat
down in the first day of the tenth
month to examine the matter.
17 And they made an end with all
the men that had taken strange wives
by the first day of the first month.
18 ¶ And among the sons of the
priests there were found that had taken
strange wives: *namely*, of the sons of
[m]Jēsh'u-ȧ the son of Jŏz'a-dăk, and his
brethren; Mā-a-sē'iah, and E-li-ē'zēr,
and Jā'rib, and Gĕd-a-lī'ah.
19 And they [n]gave their hands that
they would put away their wives; and
being [o]guilty, *they offered* a ram of the
flock for their trespass.
20 And of the sons of Ĭm'mēr; Ha-
nā'nī, and Zĕb-a-dī'ah.
21 And of the sons of Hā'rim; Mā-a-
sē'iah, and E-lī'jah, and Shĕm-a-ī'ah,
and Je-hī'el, and Ŭz-zī'ah.
22 And of the sons of Păsh'ŭr; Ĕl-i-
ō-ē'nă-ī, Mā-a-sē'iah, Ĭsh'ma-el, Ne-
thăn'e-el, Jŏz'a-băd, and Ĕl'-a-sah.
23 Also of the Lē'vītes; Jŏz'a-băd,
and Shĭm'e-ī, and Ke-lā'iah, (the same
is Kĕl'ĭ-tȧ,) Pĕth-a-hī'ah, Jū'dah, and
E-li-ē'zēr.
24 Of the singers also; Ē-lī'a-shib:
and of the porters; Shăl'lum, and Tē'-
lem, and Ū'ri.
25 Moreover of Ĭs'ra-el: of the sons of
[p]Pā'rŏsh; Ra-mī'ah, and Je-zī'ah, and
Măl-chī'ah, and Mī'a-mĭn, and Ē-le-ā'-
zar, and Măl-chī'jah, and Be-nā'iah.
26 And of the sons of Ē'lăm; Măt-ta-
nī'ah, Zĕch-a-rī'ah, and Je-hī'el, and
Ăb'dī, and Jĕr'e-mŏth, and E-lī'ah.
27 And of the sons of [q]Zăt'tu; Ĕl-i-
ō-ē'nă-ī, Ē-lī'a-shib, Măt-ta-nī'ah, and
Jĕr'e-mŏth, and Zā'băd, and A-zī'zȧ.
28 Of the sons also of Bĕb'ă-ī; Je-
ho-hā'nan, Hăn-a-nī'ah, Zăb'bāi, *and*
Ăth'lāi.
29 And of the sons of Bā'nī; Me-shŭl'-
lam, Măl'luch, and Ăd-a-ī'ah, Jăsh'ŭb,
and Shē'al, and Rā'moth.
30 And of the sons of Pā'hath–mō'-
ab; Ăd'nȧ, and Chē'lăl, Be-nā'iah, Mā-
a-sē'iah, Măt-ta-nī'ah, Be-zăl'ĕ-el, and
Bĭn'nu-ī, and Ma-năs'seh.
31 And *of* the sons of Hā'rim; E-li-
ē'zēr, Ĭsh-ī'jah, [r]Măl-chī'ah, Shĕm-a-
ī'ah, Shĭm'e-on,
32 Bĕn'ja-min, Măl'luch, *and* Shĕm-
a-rī'ah.
33 Of the sons of Hā'shum; Măt-te-
nā'ī, Măt'ta-thah, Zā'băd, E-lĭph'e-lĕt,
Jĕr'e-māi, Ma-năs'seh, *and* Shĭm'e-ī.
34 Of the sons of Bā'nī, Ma-ăd'āi,
Ăm'răm, and Ū'el,
35 Be-nā'iah, Be-dē'iah, Chĕl'luh,
36 Va-nī'ah, Mĕr'e-mŏth, Ē-lī'a-shib,
37 Măt-ta-nī'ah, Măt-te-nā'ī, and Jā'-
a-sau,
38 And Bā'nī, and Bĭn'nu-ī, Shĭm'e-ī,
39 And Shĕl-e-mī'ah, and Nā'than,
and Ăd-a-ī'ah,

40 [9]Măch-nă-dē'bai, Shăsh'ā-ī,
Shăr'a-ī,
41 A-zăr'e-el, and Shĕl-e-mī'ah,
Shĕm-a-rī'ah,
42 Shăl'lum, Ăm-a-rī'ah, *and* Jō'-
seph.

40 [9]Or, Mabnadebai, according to some copies
43 [s]Num. 32.38;
44 [t]Gen. 6.2-5;

43 Of the sons of [s]Nē'bo; Je-ī'el, Măt-
ti-thī'ah, Zā'băd, Ze-bī'nȧ, Ja-dā'u, and
Jō'el, Be-nā'iah.
44 [t]All these had taken strange
wives: and *some* of them had wives by
whom they had children.

THE BOOK OF

NEHEMIAH

Life's Questions

How do I respond when people ridicule me for serving God?
Can God's people impress the world?
What changes does God expect in my life?

God's Answers

Nehemiah is part two of Ezra/Nehemiah (see introduction to Ezra). Nehemiah the layman gave Judah administrative leadership at a crucial time when foreign opposition and internal confusion threatened God's people.

Nehemiah shows in two parts: God's work must be done despite opposition and ridicule (1—7) and God uses His Word to reform His people (8—13).

Nehemiah calls God's people to dedication to His task and His Word if they want to participate in His joy and hope.

1 The words of [a]Nē-he-mī'ah the son
of Hăch-a-lī'ah. And it came to pass
in the month Chĭs'leū, in the [b]twen-
tieth year, as I was in [c]Shu'shan the
palace,
2 That Ha-nā'nī, one of my brethren,
came, he and *certain* men of Jū'dah;
and I asked them concerning the Jews
that had escaped, which were left of the
captivity, and concerning Je-ru'sa-
lĕm.
3 And they said unto me, The remnant that are left of the captivity there
in the province *are* in great affliction
and reproach: [d]the wall of Je-ru'sa-
lĕm also [e]*is* broken down, and the
gates thereof are burned with fire.
4 ¶ And it came to pass, when I
heard these words, that I sat down and
wept, and mourned *certain* days, and
fasted, and prayed before the God of
heaven,
5 And said, I beseech thee, [f]O LORD
God of heaven, the great and terrible God, [g]that keepeth covenant and
mercy for them that love him and observe his commandments:
6 Let thine ear now be attentive, and
[h]thine eyes open, that thou mayest
hear the prayer of thy servant, which I
pray before thee now, day and night,
for the children of Ĭs'ra-el thy servants,
and confess [i]the sins of the children of
Ĭs'ra-el, which we have sinned against
thee: both I and my father's house
have sinned.
7 [j]We have dealt very corruptly
against thee, and have [k]not kept the
commandments, nor the statutes, nor
the judgments, which thou commandedst thy servant Mō'ses.
8 Remember, I beseech thee, the
word that thou commandedst thy servant Mō'ses, saying, [l]*If* ye transgress,

CHAPTER 1
1 [a]ch. 10.1
[b]ch. 2.1
[c]Esth. 1.2; Dan. 8.2
3 [d]ch. 2.17; Jer. 5.10
[e]2 Ki. 25.10
5 [f]Deut. 10.17; Job 37.22
[g]Ex. 20.6; Heb. 6.13-18
6 [h]1 Ki. 8.28-29; 2 Chr. 6.40
[i]Dan. 9.20
7 [j]Ps. 106.6
[k]Deut. 28.15
8 [l]Lev. 26.33; Deut. 4.25
9 [m]Lev. 26.39; Deut. 4.29
[n]Deut. 30.4
10 [o]Deut. 9.29; Dan. 9.15
11 [p]Ps. 119.4; Heb. 13.18
[q]Gen. 32.11; Prov. 16.3
[r]ch. 2.1
CHAPTER 2
1 [a]Ezra 7.1; That is, of Artaxerxes Longimanus
[b]ch. 1.11
2 [c]Prov. 15.13
3 [d]1 Ki. 1.31; Dan. 5.10
[e]ch. 1.3;
4 [f]1 Sam. 1.13;

I will scatter you abroad among the
nations:
9 [m]But *if* ye turn unto me, and
keep my commandments, and do them;
[n]though there were of you cast out
unto the uttermost part of the heaven,
yet will I gather them from thence, and
will bring them unto the place that I
have chosen to set my name there.
10 [o]Now these *are* thy servants and
thy people, whom thou hast redeemed
by thy great power, and by thy strong
hand.
11 O Lord, I beseech thee, let now
thine ear be attentive to the prayer of
thy servant, and to the prayer of thy
servants, who [p]desire to fear thy name:
and prosper, I pray thee, thy servant
this day, and [q]grant him mercy in the
sight of this man. For I was the king's
[r]cupbearer.
2 And it came to pass in the month
Nī'san, in the twentieth year of [a]Ăr-
tăx-ērx'ēs the king, *that* wine *was* before him: and [b]I took up the wine, and
gave *it* unto the king. Now I had not
been *beforetime* sad in his presence.
2 Wherefore the king said unto me,
Why *is* thy countenance sad, seeing
thou *art* not sick? this *is* nothing *else*
but [c]sorrow of heart. Then I was very
sore afraid,
3 And said unto the king, [d]Let the
king live for ever: why should not my
countenance be sad, when [e]the city,
the place of my fathers' sepulchres,
lieth waste, and the gates thereof are
consumed with fire?
4 Then the king said unto me, For
what dost thou make request? [f]So I
prayed to the God of heaven.
5 And I said unto the king, If it
please the king, and if thy servant have
found favour in thy sight, that thou
wouldest send me unto Jū'dah, unto

the city of my fathers' sepulchres, that
I may build it.
6 And the king said unto me, (the
[1]queen also sitting by him,) For how
long shall thy journey be? and when
wilt thou return? So it pleased the king
to send me; and I set him [g]a time.
7 Moreover I said unto the king, If it
please the king, let letters be given me
to the governors beyond the river, that
they may convey me over till I come
into Jū'dah;
8 And a letter unto Ā'saph the keeper
of the king's forest, that he may give me
timber to make beams for the gates of
the palace which *appertained* [h]to the
house, and for the wall of the city, and
for the house that I shall enter into. And
the king granted me, [i]according to the
good hand of my God upon me.
9 ¶ Then I came to the governors beyond the river, and gave them the
king's letters. Now the king had sent
captains of the army and horsemen
with me.
10 When Săn-băl'lat the [2]Hŏr'o-nīte,
and To-bī'ah the servant, the Am'mŏn-
īte, heard *of it,* it grieved them exceedingly that there was come a man to
seek the welfare of the children of
Is'ra-el.
11 So I [j]came to Je-ru̯'sa-lĕm, and
was there three days.
12 ¶ And I arose in the night, I and
some few men with me; neither told I
any man what my God had put in my
heart to do at Je-ru̯'sa-lĕm: neither
was there any beast with me, save the
beast that I rode upon.
13 And I went out by night [k]by the
gate of the valley, even before the
dragon well, and to the dung port,
and viewed the walls of Je-ru̯'sa-lĕm,
which were [l]broken down, and the
gates thereof were consumed with fire.
14 Then I went on to the [m]gate of
the fountain, and to the king's pool:
but *there was* no place for the beast
that was under me to pass.
15 Then went I up in the night by
the [n]brook, and viewed the wall, and
turned back, and entered by the gate of
the valley, and *so* returned.
16 And the rulers knew not whither
I went, or what I did; neither had I as
yet told *it* to the Jews, nor to the
priests, nor to the nobles, nor to the
rulers, nor to the rest that did the work.
17 ¶ Then said I unto them, Ye see
the distress that we *are* in, how Je-
ru̯'sa-lĕm *lieth* waste, and the gates
thereof are burned with fire: come,
and let us build up the wall of Je-ru̯'sa-
lĕm, that we be no more [o]a reproach.
18 Then I told them of the hand of
my God which was good upon me;
as also the king's words that he had
spoken unto me. And they said, Let us
rise up and build. So they [p]strength-
ened their hands for *this* good *work.*
19 But when Săn-băl'lat the Hŏr'o-
nīte, and To-bī'ah the servant, the Am'-
mŏn-īte, and Gē'shem the A-rā'bĭ-an,
heard *it,* they [q]laughed us to scorn,
and despised us, and said, What *is* this

6 [1]wife. Probably Esther
[g]ch. 5.14
8 [h]Ezra 10.6-9; ch. 3.7; That is, the temple
[i]Ezra 5.5; Prov. 21.1; Isa. 66.14; Dan. 1.9; Acts 7.10
10 [2]Or, Moabite
11 [j]Ezra 8.32
13 [k]2 Chr. 26.9; ch. 3.13
[l]ch. 1.3; Jer. 5.10
14 [m]2 Ki. 20.20; 2 Chr. 32.30; ch. 3.15
15 [n]2 Sam. 15.23; Jer. 31.40; John 18.1
17 [o]1 Sam. 11.2; ch. 1.3; Ezek. 5.14
18 [p]2 Sam. 2.7
19 [q]Ps. 44.13; Ps. 79.4
20 [r]Ps. 127.1; Rom. 8.31
[s]Ezra 4.3; Acts 8.21

CHAPTER 3
1 [a]ch. 12.10
[b]ch. 12.39; John 5.2
[c]ch. 12.39
[d]Jer. 31.38; Zech. 14.10
2 [1]at his hand
[e]Ezra 2.34; ch. 7.36
3 [f]2 Chr. 33.14; Zeph. 1.10
[g]ch. 6.1
5 [h]Judg. 5.23
6 [i]ch. 12.39
7 [j]Josh. 9.3
[k]ch. 2.8
8 [2]Or, left Jerusalem unto the broad wall
[l]ch. 12.38
11 [m]Ezra 2.32
[3]second measure
[n]ch. 12.38
12 [o]Ex. 35.25; Phil. 4.3
13 [p]ch. 2.13
[q]Josh. 15.34
[r]ch. 2.13
14 [s]Jer. 6.1; Mic. 1.11

thing that ye do? will ye rebel against
the king?
20 Then answered I them, and said
unto them, [r]The God of heaven, he
will prosper us; therefore we his servants will arise and build: but [s]ye
have no portion, nor right, nor memorial, in Je-ru̯'sa-lĕm.

3 Then [a]Ē-lī'a-shib the high priest
rose up with his brethren the priests,
[b]and they builded the sheep gate; they
sanctified it, and set up the doors of
it; [c]even unto the tower of Mē'ah
they sanctified it, unto the tower of
[d]Ha-năn'e-el.
2 And [1]next unto him builded [e]the
men of Jĕr'ĭ-chō. And next to them
builded Zăc'cur the son of Ĭm'rī.
3 [f]But the fish gate did the sons of
Hăs-sĕ-nā'ah build, who *also* laid the
beams thereof, and [g]set up the doors
thereof, the locks thereof, and the bars
thereof.
4 And next unto them repaired Mĕr'-
e-mŏth the son of U-rī'jah, the son
of Kŏz. And next unto them repaired
Me-shŭl'lam the son of Bĕr-e-chī'ah,
the son of Me-shĕz'a-be-el. And next
unto them repaired Zā'dŏk the son of
Bā'a-nȧ.
5 And next unto them the Te-kō'ītes
repaired; but their nobles put not their
necks to [h]the work of their Lord.
6 Moreover [i]the old gate repaired
Je-hoi'a-dȧ the son of Pa-sē'ah, and
Me-shŭl'lam the son of Bĕs-ŏ-dē'iah;
they laid the beams thereof, and set
up the doors thereof, and the locks
thereof, and the bars thereof.
7 And next unto them repaired Mĕl-
a-tī'ah the Gĭb'e-on-īte, and Jā'don the
Me-rŏn''o-thīte, the men of [j]Gĭb'e-on,
and of Mĭz'pah, unto the [k]throne of
the governor on this side the river.
8 Next unto him repaired Ŭz'zĭ-el
the son of Här-ha-ī'ah, of the goldsmiths. Next unto him also repaired
Hăn-a-nī'ah the son of *one of* the apothecaries, and they [2]fortified Je-ru̯'sa-
lĕm unto the [l]broad wall.
9 And next unto them repaired Rĕph-
a-ī'ah the son of Hûr, the ruler of the
half part of Je-ru̯'sa-lĕm.
10 And next unto them repaired Je-
dā'iah the son of Ha-ru̯'maph, even
over against his house. And next unto
him repaired Hăt'tŭsh the son of Hăsh-
ab-nī'ah.
11 Măl-chī'jah [m]the son of Hā'rim,
and Hā'shub the son of Pā'hath–mō'ab,
repaired the [3]other piece, [n]and the
tower of the furnaces.
12 And next unto him repaired Shăl'-
lum the son of Ha-lō'hesh, the ruler of
the half part of Je-ru̯'sa-lĕm, he and
[o]his daughters.
13 [p]The valley gate repaired Hā'-
nŭn, and the inhabitants [q]of Za-nō'ah;
they built it, and set up the doors
thereof, the locks thereof, and the bars
thereof, and a thousand cubits on the
wall unto [r]the dung gate.
14 But the dung gate repaired Măl-
chī'ah the son of Rē'chăb, the ruler of
part of [s]Bĕth–hăc'çĕ-rĕm; he built it,

and set up the doors thereof, the locks thereof, and the bars thereof.

15 But [t]the gate of the fountain repaired Shăl'lun the son of Cŏl–hō'zeh, the ruler of part of [u]Mĭz'pah; he built it, and covered it, and set up the doors thereof, the locks thereof, and the bars thereof, and the wall of the pool of [v]Sĭ-lō'ah by the king's garden, and unto the stairs that go down from the city of Dā'vid.

16 After him repaired Nē-he-mī'ah the son of Ăz'buk, the ruler of the half part of Bĕth'–zûr, unto *the place* over against the sepulchres of Dā'vid, and to the [w]pool that was made, and unto the [x]house of the mighty.

17 After him repaired the Lē'vītes, Rē'hŭm the son of Bā'nī. Next unto him repaired Hash-a-bī'ah, the ruler of the half part of Kēi'lah, in his part.

18 After him repaired their brethren, Băv'ā-ī the son of Hĕn'a-dăd, the ruler of the half part [y]of Kēi'lah.

19 And next to him repaired Ē'zēr the son of Jĕsh'u-ȧ, the ruler of Mĭz'-pah, another piece over against the going up to the armoury at the [z]turning *of the wall.*

20 After him Bā'rụch the son of [4]Zăb'bāi earnestly [a]repaired the other piece, from the turning *of the wall* unto the door of the house of Ē-lī'a-shib the high priest.

21 After him repaired Mĕr'e-mŏth the son of U-rī'jah the son of Kŏz another piece, from the door of the house of Ē-lī'a-shib even to the end of the house of Ē-lī'a-shib.

22 And after him repaired the priests, the men of the plain.

23 After him repaired Bĕn'ja-min and Hā'shub over against their house. After him repaired Ăz-a-rī'ah the son of Mā-a-sē'iah the son of Ăn-a-nī'ah by his house.

24 After him repaired Bĭn'nụ-ī the son of Hĕn'a-dăd another piece, from the house of Ăz-a-rī'ah unto the turning *of the wall,* even unto the corner.

25 Pā'lal the son of Ū'za-ī, over against the turning *of the wall,* and the tower which lieth out from the king's high house, that *was* by the [b]court of the prison. After him Pe-dā'iah the son of Pā'rŏsh.

26 Moreover [c]the Nĕth'i-nĭms [5]dwelt in [6]Ō'phel, unto *the place* over against [d]the water gate toward the east, and the tower that lieth out.

27 After them the Te-kō'ītes repaired another piece, over against the great tower that lieth out, even unto the wall of Ō'phel.

28 From above the [e]horse gate repaired the priests, every one over against his house.

29 After them repaired Zā'dŏk the son of Ĭm'mēr over against his house. After him repaired also Shĕm-a-ī'ah the son of Shĕch-a-nī'ah, the keeper of [7]the east gate.

30 After him repaired Hăn-a-nī'ah the son of Shĕl-e-mī'ah, and Hā'nŭn the sixth son of Zā'laph, another piece.

15 [t]ch. 2.14
[u]Josh. 18.26; Jer. 40.6
[v]Isa. 8.6; John 9.7
16 [w]2 Ki. 20.20; Isa. 22.11
[x]Song 3.7
18 [y]Josh. 15.44; 1 Sam. 23.1
19 [z]2 Chr. 26.9
20 [4]Or, Zaccai
[a]Eccl. 9.10; Rom. 12.11
25 [b]ch. 12.39; Jer. 32.2
26 [c]Ezra 2.43; ch. 7.46
[5]Or, which dwelt in Ophel, repaired unto
[6]Or, The tower
[d]ch. 8.1-3
28 [e]2 Ki. 11.16; Jer. 31.40
29 [7]the sun gate; Jer. 19.2
31 [8]Or, corner chamber
32 [f]ch. 12.39; John 5.2
CHAPTER 4
1 [a]Ezra 4.1-5; Acts 5.17
2 [1]leave to themselves
3 [b]ch. 2.10-19
4 [c]Ps. 123.3-4; Luke 16.14
[2]despite
[d]1 Sam. 17.26; Hos. 12.14
5 [e]Ps. 59.5-13; 2 Tim. 4.14
7 [3]ascended
8 [f]Ps. 2.1-3; Acts 23.12-13
[4]to make an error to it
9 [g]Job 22.27; Matt. 26.41
12 [5]Or, That from all places ye must return to us
13 [6]from the lower parts of the place, etc
14 [h]Num. 14.9;
[i]Deut. 10.17;
[j]2 Sam. 10.12

After him repaired Me-shŭl'lam the son of Bĕr-e-chī'ah over against his chamber.

31 After him repaired Măl-chī'ah the goldsmith's son unto the place of the Nĕth'i-nĭms, and of the merchants, over against the gate Mĭph'kăd, and to the [8]going up of the corner.

32 And between the going up of the corner unto [f]the sheep gate repaired the goldsmiths and the merchants.

4 But it came to pass, [a]that when Săn-băl'lat heard that we builded the wall, he was wroth, and took great indignation, and mocked the Jews.

2 And he spake before his brethren and the army of Sa-mā'rĭ-ȧ, and said, What do these feeble Jews? will they [1]fortify themselves? will they sacrifice? will they make an end in a day? will they revive the stones out of the heaps of the rubbish which are burned?

3 Now [b]To-bī'ah the Ăm'mŏn-īte *was* by him, and he said, Even that which they build, if a fox go up, he shall even break down their stone wall.

4 [c]Hear, O our God; for we are [2]despised: and [d]turn their reproach upon their own head, and give them for a prey in the land of captivity:

5 And [e]cover not their iniquity, and let not their sin be blotted out from before thee: for they have provoked *thee* to anger before the builders.

6 So built we the wall; and all the wall was joined together unto the half thereof: for the people had a mind to work.

7 ¶ But it came to pass, *that* when Săn-băl'lat, and To-bī'ah, and the A-rā'bĭ-ans, and the Ăm'mŏn-ītes, and the Ăsh'dŏd-ītes, heard that the walls of Je-rụ'sa-lĕm [3]were made up, *and* that the breaches began to be stopped, then they were very wroth,

8 And [f]conspired all of them together to come *and* to fight against Je-rụ'sa-lĕm, and [4]to hinder it.

9 Nevertheless [g]we made our prayer unto our God, and set a watch against them day and night, because of them.

10 And Jū'dah said, The strength of the bearers of burdens is decayed, and *there is* much rubbish; so that we are not able to build the wall.

11 And our adversaries said, They shall not know, neither see, till we come in the midst among them, and slay them, and cause the work to cease.

12 And it came to pass, that when the Jews which dwelt by them came, they said unto us ten times, [5]From all places whence ye shall return unto us *they will be upon you.*

13 ¶ Therefore set I [6]in the lower places behind the wall, *and* on the higher places, I even set the people after their families with their swords, their spears, and their bows.

14 And I looked, and rose up, and said unto the nobles, and to the rulers, and to the rest of the people, [h]Be not ye afraid of them: remember the Lord, *which* [i]*is* great and terrible, and [j]fight for your brethren, your sons,

and your daughters, your wives, and your houses.

15 And it came to pass, when our enemies heard that it was known unto us, [k]and God had brought their counsel to nought, that we returned all of us to the wall, every one unto his work.

16 And it came to pass from that time forth, *that* the half of my servants wrought in the work, and the other half of them held both the spears, the shields, and the bows, and the habergeons; and the rulers *were* behind all the house of Jū'dah.

17 They which builded on the wall, and they that bare burdens, with those that laded, *every one* with [l]one of his hands wrought in the work, and with the other *hand* held a weapon.

18 For the builders, every one had his sword girded [7]by his side, and *so* builded. And he that sounded the trumpet *was* by me.

19 ¶ And I said unto the nobles, and to the rulers, and to the rest of the people, The work *is* great and large, and we are separated upon the wall, one far from another.

20 In what place *therefore* ye hear the sound of the trumpet, resort ye thither unto us: [m]our God shall fight for us.

21 So we laboured in the work: and half of them held the spears from the rising of the morning till the stars appeared.

22 Likewise at the same time said I unto the people, Let every one with his servant lodge within Je-ru'sa-lĕm, that in the night they may be a guard to us, and labour on the day.

23 So neither I, nor my brethren, nor my servants, nor the men of the guard which followed me, none of us put off our clothes, [8]*saving that* every one put them off for washing.

5 And there was a great [a]cry of the people and of their wives against their [b]brethren the Jews.

2 For there were that said, We, our sons, and our daughters, *are* many: therefore we [c]take up corn *for them*, that we may eat, and live.

3 *Some* also there were that said, We have mortgaged our lands, vineyards, and houses, that we might buy corn, because of the dearth.

4 There were also that said, We have borrowed money for the king's tribute, *and that upon* our lands and vineyards.

5 Yet now [d]our flesh *is* as the flesh of our brethren, our children as their children: and, lo, we [e]bring into bondage our sons and our daughters to be servants, and *some* of our daughters are brought unto bondage *already:* neither *is it* in our power *to redeem them;* for other men have our lands and vineyards.

6 ¶ And I was very [f]angry when I heard their cry and these words.

7 Then [1]I consulted with myself, and [g]I rebuked the nobles, and the rulers, and said unto them, [h]Ye exact usury, every one of his brother. And I set [i]a great assembly against them.

8 And I said unto them, We after our ability have [j]redeemed our brethren the Jews, which were sold unto the heathen; and will ye even sell your brethren? or shall they be sold unto us? Then held they their peace, and found nothing *to answer*.

9 Also I said, It *is* not good that ye do: ought ye not to walk [k]in the fear of our God [l]because of the reproach of the heathen our enemies?

10 I likewise, *and* my brethren, and my servants, might exact of them money and corn: I pray you, let us leave off this usury.

11 Restore, I pray you, to them, even this day, their lands, their vineyards, their oliveyards, and their houses, also the hundredth *part* of the money, and of the corn, the wine, and the oil, that ye exact of them.

12 Then said they, We will restore *them*, and will require nothing of them; so will we do as thou sayest. Then I called the priests, [m]and took an oath of them, that they should do according to this promise.

13 Also [n]I shook my lap, and said, So God [o]shake out every man from his house, and from his labour, that performeth not this promise, even thus be he shaken out, and [2]emptied. And all the congregation said, Amen, and praised the LORD. [p]And the people did according to this promise.

14 ¶ Moreover from the time that I was appointed to be their governor in the land of Jū'dah, from the twentieth year [q]even unto the two and thirtieth year of Är-tăx-ērx'ēs the king, *that is*, twelve years, I and my brethren have not [r]eaten the bread of the governor.

15 But the former governors that *had been* before me were chargeable unto the people, and had taken of them bread and wine, beside forty shekels of silver; yea, even their servants bare rule over the people: but [s]so did not I, because of the [t]fear of God.

16 Yea, also I continued in the work of this wall, neither bought we any land: and all my servants *were* gathered thither unto the work.

17 Moreover *there were* [u]at my table an hundred and fifty of the Jews and rulers, beside those that came unto us from among the heathen that *are* about us.

18 Now *that* [v]which was prepared *for me* daily *was* one ox *and* six choice sheep; also fowls were prepared for me, and once in ten days store of all sorts of wine: yet for all this required not I the bread of the governor, because the bondage was heavy upon this people.

19 [w]Think upon me, my God, for good, *according* to all that I have done for this people.

6 Now it came to pass, [a]when Săn-băl'lat, and To-bī'ah, and [1]Gē'shem the A-rā'bĭ-an, and the rest of our enemies, heard that I had builded the wall,

15 [k]Job 5.12; Ps. 33.10
17 [l]1 Cor. 16.13; Eph. 6.10
18 [7]on his loins
20 [m]Ex. 14.14; Deut. 1.30; Deut. 3.22; Josh. 23.10
23 [8]Or, every one went with his weapon for water

CHAPTER 5
1 [a]Isa. 5.7; Jas. 5.4
[b]Lev. 25.35; Deut. 15.7
2 [c]Gen. 41.57; Hag. 1.6
5 [d]Gen. 37.27; Isa. 58.7; Acts 17.26
[e]Ex. 21.7; Matt. 18.25
6 [f]Ex. 11.8; ch. 13.8; Mark 3.5; Eph. 4.26
7 [1]my heart consulted in me
[g]Lev. 19.17; 1 Tim. 5.20
[h]Ex. 22.25; Deut. 23.19; Ps. 15.5
[i]Prov. 27.5; Matt. 18.17
8 [j]Lev. 25.48
9 [k]Gen. 20.11; Lev. 25.36; Acts 9.31
[l]Gen. 13.7-8; 1 Pet. 2.12
12 [m]Ezra 10.5; Jer. 34.8-9
13 [n]Matt. 10.14; Acts 13.51
[o]Zech. 5.4
[2]empty, or, void
[p]2 Ki. 23.3
14 [q]ch. 13.6
[r]1 Cor. 9.4
15 [s]2 Cor. 11.9
[t]Gen. 42.18; Luke 18.2-4
17 [u]2 Sam. 9.7
18 [v]1 Ki. 4.22
19 [w]ch. 13.22

CHAPTER 6
1 [a]ch. 2.10
[1]Or, Gashmu, verse 6

and *that* there was no breach left therein; ([b]though at that time I had not set up the doors upon the gates;)

2 That Săn-băl'lat and Gē'shem [c]sent unto me, saying, Come, let us meet together in *some one of* the villages in the plain of [d]Ō'no. But they [e]thought to do me mischief.

3 And I [f]sent messengers unto them, saying, I *am* doing a great work, so that I cannot come down: why should the work cease, whilst I leave it, and come down to you?

4 Yet they sent unto me [g]four times after this sort; and I answered them after the same manner.

5 Then sent Săn-băl'lat his servant unto me in like manner the fifth time with an open letter in his hand;

6 Wherein *was* written, [h]It is reported among the heathen, and [2]Găsh'mū saith *it*, [i]*that* thou and the Jews think to rebel: for which cause thou buildest the wall, that thou mayest be their king, according to these words.

7 And thou hast also appointed prophets to preach of thee at Je-ru'sa-lĕm, saying, *There is* a king in Jū'dah: and now shall it be reported to the king according to these words. Come now therefore, and let us take counsel together.

8 Then I sent unto him, saying, There are no such things done as thou sayest, but thou [j]feignest them out of thine own heart.

9 For they all made us afraid, saying, Their hands shall be weakened from the work, that it be not done. Now therefore, [k]*O God,* strengthen my hands.

10 Afterward I came unto the house of Shĕm-a-ī'ah the son of Del-a-ī'ah the son of Me-hĕt'a-beel, who *was* shut up; and he said, Let [l]us meet together in the house of God, within the temple, and let us shut the doors of the temple: for they will come to slay thee; yea, in the night will they come to slay thee.

11 And I said, [m]Should such a man as I flee? and who *is there,* that, *being* as I *am,* would go into the temple to save his life? I will not go in.

12 And, lo, I perceived that God had not sent him; but that [n]he pronounced this prophecy against me: for To-bī'ah and Săn-băl'lat had hired him.

13 Therefore *was* he hired, that I should be afraid, and do so, and sin, and *that* they might have *matter* for an evil report, that they might reproach me.

14 [o]My God, think thou upon To-bī'ah and Săn-băl'lat according to these their works, and on the [p]prophetess Nō-a-dī'ah, and the rest of the prophets, that would have put me in fear.

15 ¶ So the wall was finished in the twenty and fifth *day* of *the month* Ē'lŭl, in fifty and two days.

16 And it came to pass, that [q]when all our enemies heard *thereof,* and all the heathen that *were* about us saw *these things,* they were much cast down in their own eyes: for [r]they perceived that this work was wrought of our God.

17 ¶ Moreover in those days the nobles of Jū'dah [3]sent many letters unto To-bī'ah, and *the letters* of To-bī'ah came unto them.

18 For *there were* many in Jū'dah sworn unto him, because he *was* the son in law of Shĕch-a-nī'ah the son of Ā'rah; and his son Jo-hā'nan had taken the daughter of Me-shŭl'lam the son of Bĕr-e-chī'ah.

19 Also they reported his good deeds before me, and uttered my [4]words to him. *And* To-bī'ah sent letters to put me in fear.

7 Now it came to pass, when the wall [a]was built, and I had [b]set up the doors, and the porters and the singers and the Lē'vītes were appointed,

2 That I gave my brother Ha-nā'nī, and Hăn-a-nī'ah the ruler [c]of the palace, charge over Je-ru'sa-lĕm: for he *was* [d]a faithful man, and [e]feared God above many.

3 And I said unto them, Let not the gates of Je-ru'sa-lĕm be opened until the sun be hot; and while they stand by, let them shut the doors, and bar *them:* and appoint watches of the inhabitants of Je-ru'sa-lĕm, every one in his watch, and every one *to be* over against his house.

4 Now the city *was* [1]large and great: but the people *were* few therein, and the houses *were* not builded.

5 ¶ And my God [f]put into mine heart to gather together the nobles, and the rulers, and the people, that they might be reckoned by genealogy. And I found [2]a register of the genealogy of them which came up at the first, and found written therein,

6 These *are* the children of the province, that went up out of the captivity, of those that had been carried away, whom Nĕb-u-chăd-nĕz'zar the king of Băb'y̆-lon had carried away, and came again to Je-ru'sa-lĕm and to Jū'dah, every one unto his city;

7 Who came with Ze-rŭb'ba-bĕl, Jĕsh'u-ȧ, Nē-he-mī'ah, [3]Ăz-a-rī'ah, Rā-a-mī'ah, Na-hăm'a-nī, Môr'de-cāi, Bĭl'shăn, Mĭs'pe-rĕth, Bĭg'va-ī, Nē'hum, Bā'a-nah. The number, *I say,* of the men of the people of Ĭs'ra-el *was this;*

8 The children of Pā'rŏsh, two thousand an hundred seventy and two.

9 The children of Shĕph-a-tī'ah, three hundred seventy and two.

10 The children of Ā'rah, six hundred fifty and two.

11 The children of Pā'hath–mō'ab, of the chiildren of Jĕsh'u-ȧ and Jō'ab, two thousand and eight hundred *and* eighteen.

12 The children of Ē'lăm, a thousand two hundred fifty and four.

13 The children of Zăt'tu, eight hundred forty and five.

14 The children of Zăc'ca-ī, seven hundred and threescore.

15 The children of [4]Bĭn'nu-ī, six hundred forty and eight.

[b]ch. 3.1-3
2 [c]Prov. 26.24
[d]1 Chr. 8.12; ch. 11.35
[e]Ps. 12.2; Prov. 26.24; Eccl. 4.4; Mic. 7.4-5
3 [f]Prov. 14.15
4 [g]Prov. 1.10
6 [h]Jer. 9.3; Rom. 3.8; 2 Cor. 6.8; 1 Pet. 2.12
[2]Or, Geshem, verse 1
[i]Ezra 4.13; ch. 2.19; Luke 23.2
8 [j]Job 13.4; Ps. 36.3; Isa. 59.4; Dan. 11.27
9 [k]Deut. 33.25; Ps. 56.3; Isa. 41.10; 2 Cor. 12.9
10 [l]Prov. 26.24
11 [m]Prov. 28.1
12 [n]Ezek. 13.22
14 [o]ch. 13.29
[p]Ezek. 13.17
16 [q]ch. 2.10; ch. 6.1
[r]Ps. 126.2
17 [3]multiplied their letters passing to Tobiah
19 [4]Or, matters
CHAPTER 7
1 [a]ch. 3
[b]ch. 6.1
2 [c]ch. 2.8
[d]Num. 12.7; 1 Cor. 4.2
[e]Gen. 42.18; Prov. 16.6
4 [1]broad in spaces
5 [f]Prov. 2.6; Jas. 1.17
[2]Perhaps the one in Ezra 2.1- contained the number enrolled for the journey, and this only those who actually returned, as they are not exactly the same
7 [3]Or, Seraiah, Ezra 2.2
15 [4]Or, Bani- Ezra 2.10

16 The children of Bĕb'ā-ī, six hundred twenty and eight.
17 The children of Ăz'gad, two thousand three hundred twenty and two.
18 The children of A-dŏn'ī-kăm, six
hundred threescore and seven.
19 The children of Bĭg'va-ī, two thousand threescore and seven.
20 The children of Ā'dĭn, six hundred fifty and five.
21 The children of A'tēr of Hĕz-e-
kī'ah, ninety and eight.
22 The children of Hā'shum, three
hundred twenty and eight.
23 The children of Bē'zāi, three hundred twenty and four.
24 The children of [5]Hā'riph, an hundred and twelve.
25 The children of [6]Gĭb'e-on, ninety
and five.
26 The men of [g]Bĕth'–lĕ-hĕm and
Ne-tō'phah, an hundred fourscore and
eight.
27 The men of [h]Ăn'a-thoth, an hundred twenty and eight.
28 The men of [7]Bĕth–ăz'ma-veth,
forty and two.
29 The men of [8]Kĭr'jath–jē'a-rĭm,
Che-phī'rah, and Be-ē'rŏth, seven hundred forty and three.
30 The men of Rā'mah and Gā'bȧ,
six hundred twenty and one.
31 The men of [i]Mĭch'mas, an hundred and twenty and two.
32 The men of Bĕth'–el and Ā'ī, an
hundred twenty and three.
33 The men of the other Nē'bo, fifty
and two.
34 The children of the other Ē'lăm, a
thousand two hundred fifty and four.
35 The children of Hā'rim, three hundred and twenty.
36 The children of Jĕr'ĭ-chō, three
hundred forty and five.
37 The children of Lŏd, Hā'did, and
Ō'no, seven hundred twenty and one.
38 The children of Se-nā'ah, three
thousand nine hundred and thirty.
39 ¶ The priests: the children of [j]Je-
dā'iah, of the house of Jĕsh'u-ȧ, nine
hundred seventy and three.
40 The children of [k]Ĭm'mēr, a thousand fifty and two.
41 The children of [l]Păsh'ŭr, a thousand two hundred forty and seven.
42 The children of [m]Hā'rim, a thousand and seventeen.
43 ¶ The Lē'vītes: the children of
Jĕsh'u-ȧ, of Kăd'mĭ-el, *and* of the children of [9]Ho-dē'vah, seventy and four.
44 ¶ The singers: the children of
Ā'saph, an hundred forty and eight.
45 ¶ The porters: the children of
Shăl'lum, the children of A'tēr, the
children of Tăl'mon, the children of
Ăk'kŭb, the children of Hăt'ĭ-tȧ, the
children of Shō'ba-ī, an hundred thirty
and eight.
46 ¶ The Nĕth'i-nĭms: the children
of Zī'hȧ, the children of Ha-shū'phȧ,
the children of Tăb'ba-ŏth,
47 The children of Kē'ros, the children of [10]Sī'ȧ, the children of Pā'don,

48 The children of Lĕb'a-nȧ, the
children of Hăg'a-bȧ, the children of
[11]Shăl'ma-ī,
49 The children of Hā'nan, the children of Gĭd'del, the children of Gā'här,
50 The children of Rē-a-ī'ah, the children of Rē'zin, the children of Ne-ko'dȧ,
51 The children of Găz'zam, the children of Ŭz'zȧ, the children of Pha-sē'ah,
52 The children of Bē'sāi, the children of Me-ū'nim, the children of [12]Ne-
phĭsh'e-sĭm,
53 The children of Băk'bŭk, the children of Ha-kū'phȧ, the children of
Här'hûr,
54 The children of [13]Băz'lith, the
children of Me-hī'dȧ, the children of
Här'shȧ,
55 The children of Bär'kŏs, the children of Sĭs'e-rȧ, the children of Tā'mah,
56 The children of Ne-zī'ah, the children of Hăt'ĭ-phȧ.
57 ¶ The [n]children of Sŏl'o-mon's
servants: the children of Sō'ta-ī, the
children of Sŏph'e-rĕth, the children of
[14]Pe-rī'dȧ,
58 The children of Ja-ā'lȧ, the children of Där'kon, the children of Gĭd'del,
59 The children of Shĕph-a-tī'ah, the
children of Hăt'til, the children of
Pŏch'e-rĕth of Ze-bā'im, the children
of [15]Ā'mon.
60 All the Nĕth'i-nĭms, and the children of Sŏl'o-mon's servants, *were*
three hundred ninety and two.
61 [o]And these *were* they which went
up *also* from Tĕl–mē'lah, Tĕl–ha-rē'-
shȧ, Chē'rub, [16]Ăd'dŏn, and Ĭm'mēr:
but they could not shew their father's
house, nor their [17]seed, whether they
were of Ĭs'ra-el.
62 The children of Del-a-ī'ah, the
children of To-bī'ah, the children of
Ne-ko'dȧ, six hundred forty and two.
63 ¶ And of the priests: the children
of Ha-bā'iah, the children of Kŏz, the
children of [p]Bär-zĭl'la-ī, which took
one of the daughters of Bär-zĭl'la-ī the
Gĭl'e-ăd-īte to wife, and was called after their name.
64 These sought their register *among*
those that were reckoned by genealogy, but it was not found: therefore
were they, as polluted, put from the
priesthood.
65 And [18]the Tĭr'sha-thȧ said unto
them, that they should not eat of the
most holy things, till there stood *up* a
priest with [q]Ū'rim and Thŭm'mim.
66 ¶ The whole congregation together *was* forty and two thousand
three hundred and threescore,
67 Beside their manservants and
their maidservants, of whom *there
were* seven thousand three hundred
thirty and seven: and they had two hundred forty and five singing men and
singing women.
68 Their horses, seven hundred thirty
and six: their mules, two hundred forty
and five:
69 *Their* camels, four hundred thirty
and five: six thousand seven hundred
and twenty asses.

24 [5]Or, Jorah, Ezra 2.18
25 [6]Or, Gibbar, Ezra 2.20
26 [g]Gen. 35.6; Ruth 2.4; 1 Sam. 17.12; 2 Chr. 11.6; Ezra 2.21; Mic. 5.2; Matt. 2.1
27 [h]Josh. 21.18; 1 Chr. 6.54-60; Ezra 2.23; Jer. 1.1
28 [7]Or, Azmaveth, Ezra 2.24
29 [8]Or, Kirjatharim, Ezra 2.25
31 [i]1 Sam. 13.2; Ezra 2.27; Isa. 10.28
39 [j]1 Chr. 24.7; Ezra 2.36
40 [k]1 Chr. 24.14; Ezra 2.37
41 [l]1 Chr. 9.12; 1 Chr. 24.9
42 [m]1 Chr. 24.8; Ezra 2.39; Ezra 10.31
43 [9]Or, Hodaviah, Ezra 2.40: or, Judah, Ezra 3.9
47 [10]Or, Siaha, Ezra 2.44
48 [11]Or, Shamlai
52 [12]Or, Nephusim, Ezra 2.50
54 [13]Or, Bazluth, Ezra 2.52
57 [n]Gen. 9.25-26; 1 Ki. 5.13-14; 2 Chr. 2.17-18
[14]Or, Peruda
59 [15]Or, Ami
61 [o]Ezra 2.59
[16]Or, Addan
[17]Or, pedigree
63 [p]2 Sam. 17.27; 2 Sam. 19.31-34; 1 Ki. 2.7; Ezra 2.61
65 [18]Or, the governor
[q]Ex. 28.30; Lev. 8.8; Num. 7.89; Num. 27.18-21; Deut. 33.8; Judg. 1.1

70 ¶ And [19]some of the chief of the fathers gave unto the work. [r]The Tĭr'sha-thȧ gave to the treasure a thousand drams of gold, fifty basons, five hundred and thirty priests' garments.

71 And *some* of the chief of the fathers gave to the treasure of the work [s]twenty thousand drams of gold, and two thousand and two hundred pound of silver.

72 And *that* which [t]the rest of the people gave *was* twenty thousand drams of gold, and two thousand pound of silver, and threescore and seven priests' garments.

73 So the priests, and the Lē'vītes, and the porters, and the singers, and *some* of the people, and the Nĕth'i-nĭms, and all Ĭs'ra-el, dwelt in [u]their cities; [v]and when the seventh month came, the children of Ĭs'ra-el *were* in their cities.

8 And all [a]the people gathered themselves together as one man into the street that *was* [b]before the water gate; and they spake unto Ēz'rȧ the [c]scribe to bring the book [d]of the law of Mō'ses, which the LORD had commanded to Ĭs'ra-el.

2 And Ēz'rȧ the priest brought [e]the law before the congregation both [f]of men and women, and all [1]that could hear with understanding, [g]upon the first day of the seventh month.

3 And he read therein before the street that *was* before the water gate [2]from the morning until midday, before the men and the women, and those that could understand; and the ears of all the people *were attentive* unto the book of the law.

4 And Ēz'rȧ the scribe stood upon a [3]pulpit of wood, which they had made for the purpose; and beside him stood Măt-ti-thī'ah, and Shē'mȧ, and Ăn-a-ī'ah, and U-rī'jah, and Hĭl-kī'ah, and Mā-a-sē'iah, on his right hand; and on his left hand, Pe-dā'iah, and Mĭsh'a-el, and Măl-chī'ah, and Hā'shum, and Hăsh-băd'a-nȧ, Zĕch-a-rī'ah, *and* Me-shŭl'lam.

5 And Ēz'rȧ opened the book in the [4]sight of all the people; (for he was above all the people;) and when he opened it, all the people [h]stood up:

6 And Ēz'rȧ blessed the LORD, the great God. And all the people [i]answered, Amen, Amen, with [j]lifting up their hands: and [k]they bowed their heads, and worshipped the LORD with *their* faces to the ground.

7 Also Jĕsh'u-ȧ, and Bā'nī, and Shĕr-e-bī'ah, Jā'min, Ăk'kŭb, Shab-bĕth'a-ī, Ho-dī'jah, Mā-a-sē'iah, Kĕl'ĭ-tȧ, Ăz-a-rī'ah, Jŏz'a-băd, Hā'nan, Pĕl-a-ī'ah, and the Lē'vītes, [l]caused the people to understand the law: and the people *stood* in their place.

8 So they read in the book in the law of God [m]distinctly, and gave the sense, and caused *them* to understand the reading.

9 ¶ [n]And Nē-he-mī'ah, which *is* [5]the Tĭr'sha-thȧ, and Ēz'rȧ the priest the scribe, [o]and the Lē'vītes that taught the people, said unto all the people, [p]This day *is* holy unto the LORD your God; [q]mourn not, nor weep. For all the people wept, when they heard the words of the law.

10 Then he said unto them, Go your way, eat the fat, and drink the sweet, [r]and send portions unto them for whom nothing is prepared: for *this* day *is* holy unto our Lord: neither be ye sorry; for the joy of the LORD is your strength.

11 So the Lē'vītes stilled all the people, saying, Hold your peace, for the day *is* holy; neither be ye grieved.

12 And all the people went their way to eat, and to drink, and to send portions, and to make great mirth, because they had understood the words that were declared unto them.

13 ¶ And on the second day were gathered together the chief of the fathers of all the people, the priests, and the Lē'vītes, unto Ēz'rȧ the scribe, even [6]to understand the words of the law.

14 And they found written in the law which the LORD had commanded [7]by Mō'ses, that the children of Ĭs'ra-el should dwell in [s]booths in the feast of the seventh month:

15 And that they should publish and proclaim in all their cities, and in Je-ru'sa-lĕm, saying, Go forth unto the mount, and fetch olive branches, and pine branches, and myrtle branches, and palm branches, and branches of thick trees, to make booths, as *it is* written.

16 ¶ So the people went forth, and brought *them*, and made themselves booths, every one upon the [t]roof of his house, and in their courts, and in the courts of the house of God, and in the street of the [u]water gate, [v]and in the street of the gate of Ē'phră-ĭm.

17 And all the congregation of them that were come again out of the captivity made booths, and sat under the booths: for since the days of Jĕsh'u-ȧ the son of Nŭn unto that day had not the children of Ĭs'ra-el done so. And there was very great gladness.

18 Also [w]day by day, from the first day unto the last day, he read in the book of the law of God. And they kept the feast seven days; and on the eighth day *was* [8]a solemn assembly, [x]according unto the manner.

9 Now in the twenty and fourth day of [a]this month the children of Ĭs'ra-el were assembled with fasting, and with sackclothes, [b]and earth upon them.

2 And [c]the seed of Ĭs'ra-el separated themselves from all [1]strangers, and stood [d]and confessed their sins, and the iniquities of their fathers.

3 And they stood up in their place, and [e]read in the book of the law of the LORD their God *one* fourth part of the day; and *another* fourth part they confessed, and worshipped the LORD their God.

4 ¶ Then stood up upon the [2]stairs, of the Lē'vītes, Jĕsh'u-ȧ, and Bā'nī, Kăd'mī-el, Shĕb-a-nī'ah, Bŭn'nī, Shĕr-e-bī'ah, Bā'nī, *and* Chĕn'a-nī, and cried

70 [19]part
[r]ch. 8.9; ch. 10.1
71 [s]Ezra 2.69
72 [t]Job 34.19; Gal. 3.28
73 [u]ch. 11.20-36
[v]Ex. 23.14-17; Ezra 3.1

CHAPTER 8
1 [a]Ezra 3.1
[b]ch. 3.26; ch. 12.37
[c]Ezra 7.6; Jer. 8.8-9
[d]2 Chr. 34.15;
2 [e]Deut. 31.11-12
[f]1 Pet. 3.7
[1]that understood in hearing
[g]Lev. 23.24
3 [2]from the light
4 [3]tower of wood
5 [4]eyes
[h]Judg. 3.20
6 [i]Num. 5.22;
[j]Lam. 3.41
[k]Ex. 4.31
7 [l]Lev. 10.11
8 [m]Hab. 2.2;
9 [n]Ezra 2.63;
[5]Or, the governor
[o]2 Chr. 35.3;
[p]Lev. 23.24
[q]Deut. 16.14;
10 [r]Esth. 9.19;
13 [6]Or, that they might instruct in the words of the law
14 [7]by the hand of
[s]Gen. 33.17;
16 [t]Deut. 22.8
[u]ch. 3.26
[v]ch. 12.39
18 [w]Deut. 31.10
[8]a restraint
[x]Num. 29.35

CHAPTER 9
1 [a]ch. 8.2
[b]Josh. 7.6;
2 [c]Ezra 10.11;
[1]strange children
[d]Prov. 28.13;
3 [e]ch. 8.7
4 [2]Or, scaffold

with a loud voice unto the LORD their
God.
5 Then the Lē'vītes, Jĕsh'u-ȧ, and
Kăd'mĭ-el, Bā'nī, Hăsh-ab-nī'ah, Shĕr-
e-bī'ah, Ho-dī'jah, Shĕb-a-nī'ah, *and*
Pĕth-a-hī'ah, said, Stand up *and* bless
the LORD your God for ever and ever:
and blessed be [f]thy glorious name,
which is exalted above all blessing and
praise.
6 [g]Thou, *even* thou, *art* LORD alone;
[h]thou hast made heaven, [i]the heaven
of heavens, with all their host, the
earth, and all *things* that *are* therein,
the seas, and all that *is* therein, and
thou [j]preservest them all; and the host
of heaven worshippeth thee.
7 Thou *art* the LORD the God, who
didst choose [k]Ā'brăm, and broughtest him forth out of Ŭr of the Chăl'-
dees, and gavest him the name of
Ā'brȧ-hăm;
8 And foundest his heart faithful before thee, and madest a covenant with
him to give the land of the Cā'năan-
ītes, the Hĭt'tītes, the Ăm'ôr-ītes, and
the Pĕr'ĭz-zītes, and the Jĕb'u-sītes,
and the Gĭr'ga-shītes, to give *it, I say,*
to his seed, and [l]hast performed thy
words; for thou *art* righteous:
9 And didst see the affliction of our
fathers in Ē'ġypt, and heardest their
cry by the Red sea;
10 And shewedst signs and wonders
upon Phā'raōh, and on all his servants,
and on all the people of his land: for
thou knewest that they dealt proudly
against them. So didst thou [m]get thee a
name, as *it is* this day.
11 And thou didst divide the sea before them, so that they went through
the midst of the sea on the dry land;
and their persecutors thou threwest
into the deeps, as a stone into the
mighty waters.
12 Moreover thou [n]leddest them in
the day by a cloudy pillar; and in the
night by a pillar of fire, to give them
light in the way wherein they should go.
13 Thou camest down also upon
mount Sī'nāi, and spakest with them
from heaven, and gavest them [o]right
judgments, and [3]true laws, good statutes and commandments:
14 And madest known unto them
thy [p]holy sabbath, and commandedst
them precepts, statutes, and laws, by
the hand of Mō'ses thy servant:
15 And [q]gavest them bread from
heaven for their hunger, and broughtest forth water for them out of the rock
for their thirst, and promisedst them
that they should [r]go in to possess the
land [4]which thou hadst sworn to give
them.
16 But they and our fathers dealt
proudly, and [s]hardened their necks,
and hearkened not to thy commandments,
17 And refused to obey, [t]neither
were mindful of thy wonders that thou
didst among them; but hardened their
necks, and in their rebellion appointed
[u]a captain to return to their bondage:
but thou *art* [5]a God ready to pardon,
[v]gracious and merciful, slow to anger,
and of great kindness, and forsookest
them not.
18 Yea, when they had made them a
molten calf, and said, This *is* thy God
that brought thee up out of Ē'ġypt, and
had wrought great provocations;
19 Yet thou in thy [w]manifold mercies forsookest them not in the wilderness: the [x]pillar of the cloud departed
not from them by day, to lead them in
the way; neither the pillar of fire by
night, to shew them light, and the way
wherein they should go.
20 Thou gavest also thy [y]good spirit
to instruct them, and withheldest not
thy manna from their mouth, and gavest them water for their thirst.
21 Yea, forty years didst thou sustain
them in the wilderness, *so that* they
lacked nothing; their [z]clothes waxed
not old, and their feet swelled not.
22 Moreover thou gavest them kingdoms and nations, and didst divide
them into corners: so they possessed
the land of Sī'hŏn, and the land of the
king of Hĕsh'bŏn, and the land of Ŏg
king of Bā'shăn.
23 [a]Their children also multipliedst
thou as the stars of heaven, and
broughtest them into the land, concerning which thou hadst promised to their
fathers, that they should go in to possess *it*.
24 So the children went in and possessed the land, and thou subduedst before them the inhabitants of the land,
the Cā'năan-ītes, and gavest them into
their hands, with their kings, and the
people of the land, that they might do
with them [6]as they would.
25 And they took strong cities, and a
[b]fat land, and possessed [c]houses full
of all goods, [7]wells digged, vineyards,
and oliveyards, and [8]fruit trees in abundance: so they did eat, and were filled,
and became [d]fat, and delighted themselves in thy [e]great goodness.
26 Nevertheless they were disobedient, and rebelled against thee, and cast
thy law behind their backs, and slew
thy [f]prophets which testified against
them to turn them to thee, and they
wrought great provocations.
27 Therefore thou deliveredst them
into the hand of their enemies, who
vexed them: and in the time of their
trouble, when they cried unto thee,
thou heardest *them* from heaven; and
according to thy manifold mercies thou
gavest them saviours, who saved them
out of the hand of their enemies.
28 But after they had rest, [9]they did
evil again before thee: therefore leftest
thou them in the hand of their enemies, so that they had the dominion
over them: yet when they returned,
and cried unto thee, thou heardest
them from heaven; and many times
didst thou deliver them according to
thy mercies;
29 And [g]testifiedst against them,
that thou mightest bring them again
unto thy law: yet they dealt proudly,
and hearkened not unto thy command-

5 [f]Ex. 15.6-11; 1 Chr. 29.13; 2 Cor. 4.6
6 [g]Deut. 6.4; Isa. 37.16; Mark 12.29
[h]Rev. 14.7
[i]Deut. 10.14
[j]Ps. 36.6
7 [k]Gen. 11.31
8 [l]Josh. 23.14
10 [m]Ex. 9.16; Jer. 32.20; Dan. 9.15; Rom. 9.17
12 [n]Ex. 13.21
13 [o]Ps. 19.8-9; Rom. 7.12
[3]laws of truth
14 [p]Gen. 2.3; Heb. 4.9
15 [q]Ex. 16.14-15; John 6.31
[r]Deut. 1.8
[4]which thou hadst lift up thine hand to give them
16 [s]Deut. 31.27; Jer. 19.15
17 [t]Ps. 78.11
[u]Num. 14.4
[5]a God of pardons
[v]Ex. 34.6; Joel 2.13
19 [w]Ps. 106.45
[x]Ex. 13.21-22; Num. 14.14
20 [y]Num. 11.17; Isa. 63.11
21 [z]Deut. 8.4; Ps. 34.10
23 [a]Gen. 15.5; 1 Chr. 27.23
24 [6]according to their will
25 [b]Deut. 8.7-10; Ezek. 20.6
[c]Deut. 6.11
[7]Or, cisterns
[8]tree of food
[d]Deut. 32.15; Hos. 13.6
[e]1 Ki. 8.66; Rom. 2.4
26 [f]Matt. 21.35; Acts 7.52
28 [9]they returned to do evil
29 [g]Deut. 4.26; Hos. 6.5

ments, but sinned against thy judgments, ([h]which if a man do, he shall
live in them;) and [10]withdrew the shoulder, and hardened their neck, and
would not hear.
30 Yet many years didst thou [11]for-
bear them, and testifiedst [i]against them
by thy spirit [12]in thy prophets: yet would
they not give ear: therefore gavest thou
them into the hand of the people of the
lands.
31 Nevertheless for thy great mercies' sake [j]thou didst not utterly consume them, nor forsake them; for thou
art a gracious and merciful God.
32 Now therefore, our God, the great,
the mighty, and the terrible God, who
keepest covenant and mercy, let not all
the [13]trouble seem little before thee,
[14]that hath come upon us, on our kings,
on our princes, and on our priests, and
on our prophets, and on our fathers, and
on all thy people, [k]since the time of the
kings of Ȧs-sy̆r'ĭ-ȧ unto this day.
33 Howbeit [l]thou *art* just in all that
is brought upon us; for thou hast done
right, but we have done wickedly:
34 Neither have our kings, our
princes, our priests, nor our fathers,
kept thy law, nor hearkened unto thy
commandments and thy testimonies,
wherewith thou didst testify against
them.
35 For they have not served thee in
their kingdom, and in thy great goodness that thou gavest them, and in the
large and fat land which thou gavest
before them, neither turned they from
their wicked works.
36 Behold, [m]we *are* servants this
day, and *for* the land that thou gavest
unto our fathers to eat the fruit thereof
and the good thereof, behold, we *are*
servants in it:
37 And [n]it yieldeth much increase
unto the kings whom thou hast set
over us because of our sins: also they
have [o]dominion over our bodies, and
over our cattle, at their pleasure, and
we *are* in great distress.
38 And because of all this we make
a sure *covenant,* and write *it;* and our
princes, Lē'vītes, *and* priests, [15]seal
unto it.

10 Now [1]those that sealed *were,* [a]Nē-
he-mī'ah, [2]the Tĩr'sha-thȧ, [b]the
son of Hăch-a-lī'ah, and Zĭd-kī'jah,
2 Sĕr-a-ī'ah, Ăz-a-rī'ah, Jĕr-e-mī'ah,
3 Păsh'ŭr, Ăm-a-rī'ah, Măl-chī'jah,
4 Hăt'tŭsh, Shĕb-a-nī'ah, Măl'luch,
5 Hā'rim, Mĕr'e-mŏth, Ō-ba-dī'ah,
6 Dăn'iel, Ĝĭn'nĕ-thon, Bā'ruch,
7 Me-shŭl'lam, A-bī'jah, Mĭj'a-mĭn,
8 Mā-a-zī'ah, Bĭl'ga-ī, Shĕm-a-ī'ah:
these *were* the priests.
9 And the [c]Lē'vītes: both Jĕsh'u-ȧ
the son of Ăz-a-nī'ah, Bĭn'nu-ī of the
sons of Hĕn'a-dăd, Kăd'mĭ-el;
10 And their brethren, Shĕb-a-nī'ah,
Ho-dī'jah, Kĕl'ĭ-tȧ, Pĕl-a-ī'ah, Hā'nan,
11 Mī'chȧ, Rē'hŏb, Hash-a-bī'ah,
12 Zăc'cur, Shĕr-e-bī'ah, Shĕb-a-nī'-
ah,
13 Ho-dī'jah, Bā'nī, Bĕn'ĭ-nū.
14 The chief of the people; Pā'rŏsh,
Pā'hath-mō'ab, Ē'lăm, Zăt'thu, Bā'nī,
15 Bŭn'nī, Ăz'gad, Bĕb'ā-ī,
16 Ăd-ŏ-nī'jah, Bĭg'va-ī, Ā'dĭn,
17 A'tĕr, Hĭz-kī'jah, Ăz'zur,
18 Ho-dī'jah, Hā'shum, Bē'zāi,
19 Hā'riph, Ăn'a-thoth, Nĕb'a-ī,
20 Măg'pĭ-ăsh, Me-shŭl'lam, Hē'zĭr,
21 Me-shĕz'a-be-el, Zā'dŏk, Jad-
dū'ȧ,
22 Pĕl-a-tī'ah, Hā'nan, Ăn-a-ī'ah,
23 Ho-shē'ȧ, Hăn-a-nī'ah, Hā'shub,
24 Hăl-lō'hesh, Pĭl'e-hȧ, Shō'bek,
25 Rē'hŭm, Ha-shăb'nah, Mā-a-sē'i-
ah,
26 And A-hī'jah, Hā'nan, Ā'nan,
27 Măl'luch, Hā'rim, Bā'a-nah.
28 ¶ And [d]the rest of the people, the
priests, the Lē'vītes, the porters, the
singers, the Nĕth'i-nĭms, [e]and all they
that had separated themselves from
the people of the lands unto the law of
God, their wives, their sons, and their
daughters, every one having knowledge, and having understanding;
29 They clave to their brethren, their
nobles, [f]and entered into a curse, and
into an oath, [g]to walk in God's law,
which was given [3]by Mō'ses the servant of God, and to observe and do
all the commandments of the LORD
our Lord, and his judgments and his
statutes;
30 And that we would not give [h]our
daughters unto the people of the land,
nor take their daughters for our sons:
31 [i]And *if* the people of the land
bring ware or any victuals on the sabbath day to sell, *that* we would not buy
it of them on the sabbath, or on the
holy day: and *that* we would leave the
[j]seventh year, and the [k]exaction of [4]ev-
ery debt.
32 Also we made [l]ordinances for us,
to charge ourselves yearly with the
third part of a shekel for the service of
the house of our God;
33 For [m]the shewbread, and for the
continual meat offering, and for the
continual burnt offering, of the sabbaths, of the new moons, for the set
feasts, and for the holy *things,* and for
the sin offerings to make an atonement
for Ĭs'ra-el, and *for* all the work of the
house of our God.
34 And we cast the lots among the
priests, the Lē'vītes, and the people,
[n]for the wood offering, to bring *it* into
the house of our God, after the houses of
our fathers, at times appointed year by
year, to burn upon the altar of the LORD
our God, [o]as *it is* written in the law:
35 And [p]to bring the firstfruits of
our ground, and the firstfruits of all
fruit of all trees, year by year, unto the
house of the LORD:
36 Also the firstborn of our sons,
and of our cattle, as *it is* [q]written in the
law, and the firstlings of our herds and
of our flocks, to bring to the house of
our God, unto the priests that minister
in the house of our God:
37 [r]And *that* we should bring the
firstfruits of our dough, and our offerings, and the fruit of all manner of

[h]Lev. 18.5; Gal. 3.12
[10]they gave a withdrawing shoulder
30 [11]protract over them
[i]Ps. 78.8-40; Acts 7.51
[12]in the hand of thy prophets
31 [j]Jer. 5.10
32 [13]weariness
[14]that hath found us
[k]2 Ki. 17.3; Isa. 7.17-18
33 [l]Gen. 18.25; Dan. 9.14
36 [m]Deut. 28.48
37 [n]Deut. 28.33
[o]Deut. 28.48
38 [15]are at the sealing, or, sealed
CHAPTER 10
1 [1]at the sealings
[a]ch. 8.9
[2]Or, the governor
[b]ch. 1.1
9 [c]ch. 12.8
28 [d]Ezra 2.36
[e]Ezra 9.1; ch. 13.3
29 [f]Deut. 29.12; Rom. 12.9
[g]2 Ki. 23.3
[3]by the hand of
30 [h]Gen. 6.2; Deut. 7.3
31 [i]Ex. 20.10; Jer. 17.21
[j]Ex. 23.10; Lev. 25.4
[k]Deut. 15.1; Deut. 5.12
[4]every hand
32 [l]Gen. 28.22
33 [m]Lev. 24.5; 2 Chr. 2.4
34 [n]ch. 13.31
[o]Lev. 6.12
35 [p]Ex. 23.19; Deut. 26.2
36 [q]Ex. 13.2-12-13; Lev. 27.26-27
37 [r]Lev. 23.17; Deut. 18.4

trees, of wine and of oil, unto the
priests, to the chambers of the house of
our God; and [s]the tithes of our ground
unto the Lē'vītes, that the same Lē'-
vītes might have the tithes in all the
cities of our tillage.
38 And the priest the son of Aâr'on
shall be with the Lē'vītes, [t]when the
Lē'vītes take tithes: and the Lē'vītes
shall bring up the tithe of the tithes
unto the house of our God, to [u]the
chambers, into the treasure house.
39 For the children of Ĭs'ra-el and
the children of Lē'vī [v]shall bring the
offering of the corn, of the new wine,
and the oil, unto the chambers, where
are the vessels of the sanctuary, and
the priests that minister, and the porters, and the singers: [w]and we will not
forsake the house of our God.
11 And the rulers of the people dwelt
at Je-ru'sa-lĕm: the rest of the
people also cast lots, to bring one of ten
to dwell in Je-ru'sa-lĕm [a]the holy city,
and nine parts *to dwell* in *other* cities.
2 And the people blessed all the men,
that willingly [b]offered themselves to
dwell at Je-ru'sa-lĕm.
3 ¶ [c]Now these *are* the chief of the
province that dwelt in Je-ru'sa-lĕm:
but in the cities of Jū'dah dwelt every
one in his possession in their cities, *to
wit,* Ĭs'ra-el, the priests, and the Lē'-
vītes, and [d]the Nĕth'i-nĭms, and [e]the
children of Sŏl'o-mon's servants.
4 And [f]at Je-ru'sa-lĕm dwelt *certain*
of the children of Jū'dah, and of the
children of Bĕn'ja-min. Of the children
of Jū'dah; Ăth-a-ī'ah the son of Ŭz-
zī'ah, the son of Zĕch-a-rī'ah, the son
of Ăm-a-rī'ah, the son of Shĕph-a-
tī'ah, the son of Ma-hā'la-lē-el, of the
children of [g]Pē'rez;
5 And Mā-a-sē'iah the son of Bā'-
ruch, the son of Cŏl–hō'zeh, the son of
Ha-zā'iah, the son of Ăd-a-ī'ah, the son
of Joi'a-rĭb, the son of Zĕch-a-rī'ah,
the son of Shi-lō'nī.
6 All the sons of Pē'rez that dwelt at
Je-ru'sa-lĕm *were* four hundred threescore and eight [1]valiant men.
7 And these *are* the sons of Bĕn'ja-
min; Săl'lu the son of Me-shŭl'lam, the
son of Jō'ed, the son of Pe-dā'iah, the
son of Kŏl-a-ī'ah, the son of Mā-a-
sē'iah, the son of Ĭth'ĭ-el, the son of
Je-sā'iah.
8 And after him Găb'ba-ī, Sal'la-i,
nine hundred twenty and eight.
9 And Jō'el the son of Zĭch'rī *was*
their overseer: and Jū'dah the son of
Se-nū'ah *was* second over the city.
10 [h]Of the priests: Je-dā'iah the son
of Joi'a-rĭb, Jā'chin.
11 Sĕr-a-ī'ah the son of Hĭl-kī'ah,
the son of Me-shŭl'lam, the son of
Zā'dŏk, the son of Me-rā'ioth, the son
of A-hī'tub, *was* the ruler of the house
of God.
12 And their brethren that did the
work of the house *were* eight hundred
twenty and two: and Ăd-a-ī'ah the son
of Jĕr'o-hăm, the son of Pĕl-a-lī'ah,
the son of Ăm'zī, the son of Zĕch-a-

[s]Lev. 27.30-32; 2 Chr. 31.6
38 [t]Num. 18.26
[u]1 Chr. 9.26; 2 Chr. 31.11
39 [v]Num. 18.30; Deut. 12.6; ch. 13.12
[w]ch. 13.10; Ps. 122.9; Matt. 18.20
CHAPTER 11
1 [a]Isa. 48.2; Matt. 4.5
2 [b]Judg. 5.9
3 [c]1 Chr. 9.2; ch. 7.6
[d]Ezra 2.43
[e]Ezra 2.55
4 [f]1 Chr. 9.3
[g]Gen. 38.29
6 [1]Or, men of activity
10 [h]1 Chr. 9.10
14 [2]Or, the son of Haggedolim
16 [3]were over
[i]2 Ki. 12.15-16; 1 Chr. 26.29; 2 Chr. 34.13; 1 Cor. 4.2
17 [4]1 Chr. 9.15- Zichri
[j]ch. 7.44
18 [k]1 Ki. 11.13; Ezra 9.8; Matt. 24.15; Rev. 11.2; Rev. 21.2
19 [l]1 Chr. 9.17; ch. 7.45; ch. 12.25
[5]at the gates
21 [m]Ezra 2.43-58; ch. 3.26
[6]Or, The tower
[n]2 Chr. 27.3
23 [o]Ezra 6.8-9
[7]Or, a sure ordinance
24 [p]Gen. 38.30- Zarah
[q]1 Chr. 18.17; 1 Chr. 23.28
25 [r]Gen. 23.2; Josh. 14.15
[s]Josh. 15.21- Kabzeel
31 [8]Or, of Geba
[9]Or, to Michmash

rī'ah, the son of Păsh'ŭr, the son of
Măl-chī'ah,
13 And his brethren, chief of the fathers, two hundred forty and two: and
A-măsh'a-ī the son of A-zăr'e-el, the
son of A-hăs'ă-ī, the son of Me-shĭl'le-
mŏth, the son of Ĭm'mĕr,
14 And their brethren, mighty men
of valour, an hundred twenty and eight:
and their overseer *was* Zăb'dĭ-el, [2]the
son of *one of* the great men.
15 Also of the Lē'vītes: Shĕm-a-ī'ah
the son of Hā'shub, the son of Ăz'rĭ-
kam, the son of Hash-a-bī'ah, the son
of Bŭn'nī;
16 And Shab-bĕth'a-ī and Jŏz'a-băd,
of the chief of the Lē'vītes, [3]*had* the
oversight of [i]the outward business of
the house of God.
17 And Măt-ta-nī'ah the son of Mī'-
chȧ, the son of [4]Zăb'dī, the [j]son of
Ā'saph, *was* the principal to begin the
thanksgiving in prayer: and Băk-bŭk-
ī'ah the second among his brethren,
and Ăb'dȧ the son of Shăm-mū'ȧ, the
son of Gā'lăl, the son of Jĕd'u-thŭn.
18 All the Lē'vītes in [k]the holy city
were two hundred fourscore and four.
19 Moreover [l]the porters, Ăk'kŭb,
Tăl'mon, and their brethren that kept
[5]the gates, *were* an hundred seventy
and two.
20 ¶ And the residue of Ĭs'ra-el, of
the priests, *and* the Lē'vītes, *were* in all
the cities of Jū'dah, every one in his
inheritance.
21 [m]But the Nĕth'i-nĭms dwelt in
[6][n]Ō'phel: and Zī'hȧ and Gĭs'pȧ *were*
over the Nĕth'i-nĭms.
22 The overseer also of the Lē'vītes
at Je-ru'sa-lĕm *was* Ŭz'zī the son of
Bā'nī, the son of Hash-a-bī'ah, the son
of Măt-ta-nī'ah, the son of Mī'chȧ. Of
the sons of Ā'saph, the singers *were*
over the business of the house of God.
23 For [o]*it was* the king's commandment concerning them, that [7]a certain
portion should be for the singers, due
for every day.
24 And Pĕth-a-hī'ah the son of Me-
shĕz'a-be-el, of the children of [p]Zē'-
rah the son of Jū'dah, *was* [q]at the
king's hand in all matters concerning
the people.
25 And for the villages, with their
fields, *some* of the children of Jū'dah
dwelt at [r]Kĭr'jath–är'bȧ, and *in* the villages thereof, and at Dī'bŏn, and *in* the
villages thereof, and at [s]Je-kăb'ze-el,
and *in* the villages thereof,
26 And at Jĕsh'u-ȧ, and at Mŏl'a-
dah, and at Bĕth–phē'let,
27 And at Hā'zar–shu'al, and at Bē'-
er–shē'bȧ, and *in* the villages thereof,
28 And at Zĭk'lag, and at Mĕk'o-
nah, and in the villages thereof,
29 And at Ĕn–rĭm'mon, and at Zā'-
re-ah, and at Jär'mŭth,
30 Za-nō'ah, A-dŭl'lăm, and *in* their
villages, at Lā'chish, and the fields
thereof, at A-zē'kah, and *in* the villages
thereof. And they dwelt from Bē'er–
shē'bȧ unto the valley of Hĭn'nom.
31 The children also of Bĕn'ja-min
[8]from Gē'bȧ *dwelt* [9]at Mĭch'mash, and

A-ī'jȧ, and Bĕth'–el, and *in* their villages,
32 *And* at [t]Ăn'a-thoth, Nŏb, Ăn-a-
nī'ah,
33 Hā'zôr, Rā'mah, Ḡĭt'ta-ĭm,
34 Hā'did, Ze-bō'im, Ne-băl'lat,
35 Lŏd, and Ō'no, [u]the valley of
craftsmen.
36 And of the [v]Lē'vītes *were* divisions *in* Jū'dah, *and* in Bĕn'ja-min.

12 Now these *are* the [a]priests and
the Lē'vītes that went up with
Ze-rŭb'ba-bĕl the son of She-ăl'tī-el,
and Jĕsh'u-ȧ: [b]Sĕr-a-ī'ah, Jĕr-e-mī'ah,
Ĕz'rȧ,
2 Ăm-a-rī'ah, [1]Măl'luch, Hăt'tŭsh,
3 [2]Shĕch-a-nī'ah, [3]Rē'hŭm, [4]Mĕr'e-
mŏth,
4 Ĭd'dō, [5]Gĭn'nĕ-thō, [c]A-bī'jah,
5 [6]Mī'a-mĭn, [7]Ma-a-dī'ah, Bĭl'gah,
6 Shĕm-a-ī'ah, and Joi'a-rĭb, Je-dā'-
iah,
7 [8]Săl'lu, Ā'mok, Hĭl-kī'ah, Je-dā'-
iah. These *were* the chief of the priests
and of their brethren in the days of
[d]Jĕsh'u-ȧ.
8 Moreover the Lē'vītes: Jĕsh'u-ȧ,
Bĭn'nu-ī, Kăd'mī-el, Shĕr-e-bī'ah, Jū'-
dah, *and* Măt-ta-nī'ah, [e]*which was*
over [9]the thanksgiving, he and his
brethren.
9 Also Băk-bŭk-ī'ah and Ŭn'nī, their
brethren, *were* over against them in the
watches.
10 ¶ And Jĕsh'u-ȧ begat Joi'a-kĭm,
Joi'a-kĭm also begat Ē-lī'a-shib, and Ē-
lī'a-shib begat Joi'a-dȧ,
11 And Joi'a-dȧ begat Jŏn'a-than,
and Jŏn'a-than begat Jad-dū'ȧ.
12 And in the days of Joi'a-kĭm were
priests, the chief of the fathers: of
Sĕr-a-ī'ah, Mĕr-a-ī'ah; of Jĕr-e-mī'ah,
Hăn-a-nī'ah;
13 Of Ĕz'rȧ, Me-shŭl'lam; of Ăm-a-
rī'ah, Je-ho-hā'nan;
14 Of Mĕl'i-cū, Jŏn'a-than; of Shĕb-
a-nī'ah, Jō'seph;
15 Of Hā'rim, Ăd'nȧ; of Me-rā'ioth,
Hĕl'ka-ī;
16 Of Ĭd'dō, Zĕch-a-rī'ah; of Ḡĭn'nĕ-
thon, Me-shŭl'lam;
17 Of A-bī'jah, Zĭch'rī; of Mĭ-nī'a-
min, of Mō-a-dī'ah, Pĭl'tāi;
18 Of Bĭl'gah, Shăm-mū'ȧ; of Shĕm-
a-ī'ah, Je-hŏn'a-than;
19 And of Joi'a-rĭb, Măt-te-nā'ī; of
Je-dā'iah, Ŭz'zī;
20 Of Săl'la-ī, Kăl'la-ī; of Ā'mok,
Ē'bĕr;
21 Of Hĭl-kī'ah, Hash-a-bī'ah; of Je-
dā'iah, Ne-thăn'e-el.
22 ¶ The Lē'vītes in the days of Ē-
lī'a-shib, Joi'a-dȧ, and Jo-hā'nan, and
Jad-dū'ȧ, *were* recorded chief of the
fathers: also the priests, to the reign of
Da-rī'us the Pĕr'sian.
23 The sons of Lē'vī, the chief of the
fathers, *were* written in the book of the
[f]chronicles, even until the days of Jo-
hā'nan the son of Ē-lī'a-shib.
24 And the chief of the Lē'vītes:
Hash-a-bī'ah, Shĕr-e-bī'ah, and Jĕsh'-
u-ȧ the son of Kăd'mī-el, with their
brethren over against them, to praise
and to give thanks, [g]according to the
commandment of Dā'vid the man of
God, [h]ward over against ward.
25 Măt-ta-nī'ah, and Băk-bŭk-ī'ah,
Ō-ba-dī'ah, Me-shŭl'lam, Tăl'mon, Ăk'-
kŭb, *were* porters keeping the ward at
the [10]thresholds of the gates.
26 These *were* in the days of Joi'a-
kĭm the son of Jĕsh'u-ȧ, the son of
Jŏz'a-dăk, and in the days of Nē-he-
mī'ah [i]the governor, and of Ĕz'rȧ the
priest, [j]the scribe.
27 ¶ And at [k]the dedication of the
wall of Je-ru'sa-lĕm they sought the
Lē'vītes out of all their places, to bring
them to Je-ru'sa-lĕm, to keep the dedication with gladness, [l]both with thanksgivings, and with singing, *with* cymbals, psalteries, and with harps.
28 And the sons of the singers gathered themselves together, both out
of the plain country round about Je-
ru'sa-lĕm, and from the villages of
Ne-tŏph'a-thī;
29 Also from the house of Ḡĭl'găl,
and out of the fields of Ḡē'bȧ and Ăz'-
ma-veth: for the singers had builded
them villages round about Je-ru'sa-lĕm.
30 And the priests and the Lē'vītes
[m]purified themselves, and purified the
people, and the gates, and the wall.
31 Then I brought up the princes of
Jū'dah upon the wall, and appointed
two great *companies of them that gave*
thanks, *whereof one* went on the right
hand upon the wall toward [n]the dung
gate:
32 And after them went Hŏsh-a-ī'-
ah, and half of the princes of Jū'dah,
33 And Ăz-a-rī'ah, Ĕz'rȧ, and Me-
shŭl'lam,
34 Jū'dah, and Bĕn'ja-min, and
Shĕm-a-ī'ah, and Jĕr-e-mī'ah,
35 And *certain* of the priests' sons
[o]with trumpets; *namely*, Zĕch-a-rī'ah
the son of Jŏn'a-than, the son of Shĕm-
a-ī'ah, the son of Măt-ta-nī'ah, the son
of Mī-chā'iah, the son of Zăc'cur, the
son of Ā'saph:
36 And his brethren, Shĕm-a-ī'ah,
and A-zăr'a-el, Mĭl-a-lā'ī, Ḡĭl'a-lāi, Ma-
ā'ī, Ne-thăn'e-el, and Jū'dah, Ha-nā'nī,
with [p]the musical instruments of Dā'-
vid the man of God, and Ĕz'rȧ the
scribe before them.
37 [q]And at the fountain gate, which
was over against them, they went up
by [r]the stairs of the city of Dā'vid, at
the going up of the wall, above the
house of Dā'vid, even unto [s]the water
gate eastward.
38 And the other *company of them*
that gave thanks went over against
them, and I after them, and the half of
the people upon the wall, from beyond
[t]the tower of the furnaces even unto
[u]the broad wall;
39 [v]And from above the gate of
Ē'phrȧ-ĭm, and above [w]the old gate,
and above the fish gate, and the tower
of Ha-năn'e-el, and the tower of Mē'ah,
even unto the sheep gate: and they
stood still in [x]the prison gate.
40 So stood the two *companies of*
them that gave [y]thanks in the house

32 [t]Jer. 1.1
35 [u]1 Chr. 4.14
36 [v]Gen. 49.7
CHAPTER 12
1 [a]Ezra 2.1 [b]ch. 10.2-8
2 [1]Or, Melicu, verse 14
3 [2]Or, Shebaniah [3]Or, Harim [4]Or, Meraioth
4 [5]Or, Ginnethon [c]Luke 1.5
5 [6]Or, Miniamin [7]Or, Moadiah
7 [8]Or, Sallai, verse 20 [d]Hag. 1.1; Zech. 3.1
8 [e]1 Chr. 16.8-41; ch. 11.17 [9]That is, the psalms of thanksgiving
23 [f]1 Chr. 9.14
24 [g]1 Chr. 23; 1 Chr. 25 [h]Ezra 3.11
25 [10]Or, treasuries, or, assemblies
26 [i]ch. 8.9 [j]Ezra 7.6-11
27 [k]Deut. 20.5; Ps. 30- title [l]1 Chr. 25.6; 2 Chr. 5.13; Ps. 81.1-3; Rev. 5.8
30 [m]Ex. 19.10
31 [n]ch. 2.13
35 [o]Num. 10.2; Josh. 6.4; 2 Chr. 5.12
36 [p]1 Chr. 23.5; 2 Chr. 8.14; Amos 6.5
37 [q]ch. 2.14 [r]2 Sam. 5.7-9; ch. 3.15 [s]ch. 3.26
38 [t]ch. 3.11 [u]ch. 3.8
39 [v]2 Ki. 14.13 [w]ch. 3.6 [x]Jer. 32.2
40 [y]Ps. 42.4

of God, and I, and the half of the rulers with me:

41 And the priests; E-lī'a-kĭm, Mā-a-sē'iah, Mĭ-nī'a-min, Mī-chā'iah, Ĕl-i-ō-ē'nă-ī, Zĕch-a-rī'ah, *and* Hăn-a-nī'ah, with trumpets;

42 And Mā-a-sē'iah, and Shĕm-a-ī'-ah, and Ē-le-ā'zar, and Ŭz'zī, and Je-ho-hā'nan, and Măl-chī'jah, and Ē'lăm, and Ē'zĕr. And the singers [11]sang loud, with Jĕz-ra-hī'ah *their* overseer.

43 Also that day they offered great sacrifices, and rejoiced: [z]for God had made them rejoice with great joy: the wives also and the children rejoiced: so that the joy of Je-rṳ'sa-lĕm was heard even afar off.

44 ¶ [a]And at that time were some appointed over the chambers for the treasures, for the offerings, for the firstfruits, and for the tithes, to gather into them out of the fields of the cities the portions [12]of the law for the priests and Lē'vītes: [13]for Jū'dah rejoiced for the priests and for the Lē'vītes [14]that waited.

45 And both the singers and the porters kept the ward of their God, and the ward of the purification, [b]according to the commandment of Dā'vid, *and* of Sŏl'o-mon his son.

46 For in the days of Dā'vid and Ā'saph of old *there were* chief of the singers, and songs of praise and thanksgiving unto God.

47 And all Ĭs'ra-el in the days of Ze-rŭb'ba-bĕl, and in the days of Nē-he-mī'ah, gave the portions of the singers and the porters, every day his portion: and they [15]sanctified *holy things* unto the Lē'vītes; and the Lē'vītes sanctified *them* unto the children of Aâr'on.

13 On that day [1]they read in the book of Mō'ses in the [2]audience of the people; and therein was found written, [a]that the Ăm'mŏn-īte and the Mō'ab-īte should not come into the congregation of God for ever;

2 Because they met not the children of Ĭs'ra-el with bread and with water, but [b]hired Bā'laam against them, that he should curse them: [c]howbeit our God turned the curse into a blessing.

3 Now it came to pass, when they had heard the law, [d]that they separated from Ĭs'ra-el all the mixed multitude.

4 ¶ And before this, Ē-lī'a-shib the priest, [3]having the oversight of the chamber of the house of our God, *was* allied unto To-bī'ah:

5 And he had prepared for him a great chamber, where aforetime they laid the meat offerings, the frankincense, and the vessels, and the tithes of the corn, the new wine, and the oil, [4]which was commanded *to be given* to the Lē'vītes, and the singers, and the porters; and the offerings of the priests.

6 But in all this *time* was not I at Je-rṳ'sa-lĕm: [e]for in the two and thirtieth year of Ăr-tăx-ĕrx'ēs king of Băb'y̆-lon came I unto the king, and [5]after certain days [6]obtained I leave of the king:

42 [11]made their voice to be heard; 2 Chr. 29.30; Ps. 30.4; Ps. 81.1; Ps. 95.1; Ps. 96.1; Ps. 98.1; Eph. 5.19; Col. 3.16
43 [z]Ps. 9.2; Ps. 92.4
44 [a]2 Chr. 31.11; ch. 13.5
[12]That is, appointed by the law
[13]for the joy of Judah
[14]that stood
45 [b]1 Chr. 25
47 [15]That is, set apart

CHAPTER 13
1 [1]there was read
[2]ears
[a]Deut. 23.3; Amos 2.1-3
2 [b]Num. 22.5; Josh. 24.9
[c]Num. 23.8-11; Mic. 6.5
3 [d]ch. 9.2;
4 [3]being set over
5 [4]the commandment of the Levites
6 [e]ch. 5.14
[5]at the end of days
[6]Or, I earnestly requested
8 [f]Ps. 69.9;
9 [g]2 Chr. 29.5
10 [h]ch. 10.37;
[i]Num. 35.2
11 [j]Prov. 28.4
[k]1 Sam. 2.17
[7]standing
12 [l]ch. 12.44
[8]Or, storehouses
13 [9]at their hand
[m]1 Cor. 4.2
[10]it was upon them
14 [n]ch. 5.19
[11]kindnesses
[12]Or, observations
15 [o]Ex. 20.10
[p]Jer. 17.21
18 [13]add fierce wrath
19 [q]Lev. 23.32
[r]Ex. 31.14-17;
21 [14]before the wall?

7 And I came to Je-rṳ'sa-lĕm, and understood of the evil that Ē-lī'a-shib did for To-bī'ah, in preparing him a chamber in the courts of the house of God.

8 And it grieved me sore: therefore [f]I cast forth all the household stuff of To-bī'ah out of the chamber.

9 Then I commanded, and they [g]cleansed the chambers: and thither brought I again the vessels of the house of God, with the meat offering and the frankincense.

10 ¶ And I perceived that the portions of the Lē'vītes had [h]not been given *them*: for the Lē'vītes and the singers, that did the work, were fled every one to [i]his field.

11 Then [j]contended I with the rulers, and said, [k]Why is the house of God forsaken? And I gathered them together, and set them in their [7]place.

12 [l]Then brought all Jū'dah the tithe of the corn and the new wine and the oil unto the [8]treasuries.

13 And I made treasurers over the treasuries, Shĕl-e-mī'ah the priest, and Zā'dŏk the scribe, and of the Lē'vītes, Pe-dā'iah: and [9]next to them *was* Hā'-nan the son of Zăc'cur, the son of Măt-ta-nī'ah: for they were counted [m]faithful, and [10]their office *was* to distribute unto their brethren.

14 [n]Remember me, O my God, concerning this, and wipe not out my [11]good deeds that I have done for the house of my God, and for the [12]offices thereof.

15 ¶ In those days saw I in Jū'-dah *some* treading wine presses on [o]the sabbath, and bringing in sheaves, and lading asses; as also wine, grapes, and figs, and all *manner of* burdens, [p]which they brought into Je-rṳ'sa-lĕm on the sabbath day: and I testified *against them* in the day wherein they sold victuals.

16 There dwelt men of Tȳre also therein, which brought fish, and all manner of ware, and sold on the sabbath unto the children of Jū'dah, and in Je-rṳ'sa-lĕm.

17 Then I contended with the nobles of Jū'dah, and said unto them, What evil thing *is* this that ye do, and profane the sabbath day?

18 Did not your fathers thus, and did not our God bring all this evil upon us, and upon this city? yet ye [13]bring more wrath upon Ĭs'ra-el by profaning the sabbath.

19 And it came to pass, that when the gates of Je-rṳ'sa-lĕm [q]began to be dark before the sabbath, I commanded that the gates should be shut, and charged that they should not be opened till after the sabbath: [r]and *some* of my servants set I at the gates, *that* there should no burden be brought in on the sabbath day.

20 So the merchants and sellers of all kind of ware lodged without Je-rṳ'sa-lĕm once or twice.

21 Then I testified against them, and said unto them, Why lodge ye [14]about

the wall? if ye do *so* again, I will lay
hands on you. From that time forth
came they no *more* on the sabbath.
22 And I commanded the Lē'vītes
that [s]they should cleanse themselves,
and *that* they should come *and* keep
the gates, to sanctify the sabbath day.
Remember me, O my God, *concerning*
this also, and spare me according to
the [15]greatness of thy mercy.
23 ¶ In those days also saw I Jews
that [16]had married wives of Ăsh'dŏd,
of Ăm'mŏn, *and* of Mō'ab:
24 And their children spake half in
the speech of Ăsh'dŏd, and [17]could
not speak in the Jews' language, but
according to the language [18]of each
people.
25 And I [t]contended with them, and
[19]cursed them, and [u]smote certain of
them, and plucked off their hair, and
made them [v]swear by God, *saying*, Ye
shall not give your daughters unto
their sons, nor take their daughters
unto your sons, or for yourselves.

22 [s] ch. 12.30
[15] Or, multitude
23 [16] had made to dwell with them
24 [17] they discerned not to speak
[18] of people and people
25 [t] Prov. 28.4
[19] Or, reviled them
[u] Deut. 25.2;
[v] Ezra 10.5;
26 [w] 1 Ki. 11.1
[x] 2 Sam. 12.24-25
27 [y] Ezra 10.2
28 [z] ch. 12.10
29 [a] ch. 6.14
[20] for the defilings
[b] Mal. 2.4
30 [c] ch. 10.30
[d] ch. 12.1

26 [w]Did not Sŏl'o-mon king of Ĭs'ra-
el sin by these things? [x]yet among
many nations was there no king like
him, who was beloved of his God, and
God made him king over all Ĭs'ra-el:
nevertheless even him did outlandish
women cause to sin.
27 Shall we then hearken unto you
to do all this great evil, to [y]transgress
against our God in marrying strange
wives?
28 And *one* of the sons [z]of Joi'a-dȧ,
the son of Ē-lī'a-shib the high priest,
was son in law to Săn-băl'lat the Hŏr'-
o-nīte: therefore I chased him from me.
29 Remember [a]them, O my God,
[20]because they have defiled the priesthood, and [b]the covenant of the priesthood, and of the Lē'vītes.
30 [c]Thus cleansed I them from all
strangers, and [d]appointed the wards
of the priests and the Lē'vītes, every
one in his business;
31 And for the wood offering, at
times appointed, and for the firstfruits.
Remember me, O my God, for good.

THE BOOK OF

ESTHER

Life's Questions

How do I respond to hatred and prejudice?
Can God save His people against the most overwhelming odds?
What does a powerless people have to celebrate?

God's Answers

Esther shows how God can use an inexperienced young lady to change international history, save His people from destruction, and give His people reason to celebrate. About 482 B.C. King Xerxes of Persia, angered at his wife, married the Jew Esther, unwittingly agreed to a plot to eliminate the Jews by his peeved official Haman, and then helped his wife and her uncle Mordecai save the Jews. This gave Jews reason to celebrate the feast of Purim.

Esther shows: an humble girl from God's people can attain international importance (1:1—2:18); faithfulness to God can be expressed by serving a foreign government (2:19—3:15); responsible positions call for faithfulness to God (4:1–17); God works in history to honor responsible action (5:1—8:17); celebration helps God's people remember God's salvation (9:1–32); and God honors His people with increased chances for service (10:1–3).

1 Now it came to pass in the days of
A-hăs-ū-ē'rŭs, (this *is* A-hăs-ū-ē'-
rŭs which reigned, from Ĭnd'iȧ even
unto Ē-thĭ-ō'pĭ-a, [a]*over* an hundred
and seven and twenty provinces:)
2 *That* in those days, when the king
A-hăs-ū-ē'rŭs [b]sat on the throne of his
kingdom, which *was* in [c]Shu'shan the
palace,
3 In the third year of his reign, he
[d]made a feast unto all his princes and
his servants; the power of Pĕr'siȧ and
Mē'dĭ-ȧ, the nobles and princes of the
provinces, *being* before him:
4 When he shewed the riches of his
glorious kingdom and the honour of
his excellent majesty many days, *even*
an hundred and fourscore days.
5 And when these days were expired, the king made a feast unto all
the people that were [1]present in Shu'-
shan the palace, both unto great and
small, seven days, in the court of the
garden of the king's palace;

CHAPTER 1
1 [a] ch. 8.9;
2 [b] 2 Sam. 7.1;
[c] Neh. 1.1;
3 [d] Gen. 40.20;
5 [1] found
6 [2] Or, violet
[e] ch. 7.8;
[3] Or, of porphyre, and marble, and alabaster, and stone of blue colour
7 [4] wine of the kingdom
[5] according to the hand of the king
8 [6] Or, trouble
10 [7] Or, eunuchs

6 *Where were* white, green, and
[2]blue, *hangings*, fastened with cords of
fine linen and purple to silver rings and
pillars of marble: [e]the beds *were of* gold
and silver, upon a pavement [3]of red, and
blue, and white, and black, marble.
7 And they gave *them* drink in vessels of gold, (the vessels being diverse
one from another,) and [4]royal wine in
abundance, [5]according to the state of
the king.
8 And the drinking *was* according
to the law; none did [6]compel: for so the
king had appointed to all the officers
of his house, that they should do according to every man's pleasure.
9 Also Văsh'tī the queen made a
feast for the women *in* the royal house
which *belonged* to king A-hăs-ū-ē'rŭs.
10 ¶ On the seventh day, when the
heart of the king was merry with wine,
he commanded Me-hū'man, Bĭz'thȧ,
Här-bō'nȧ, Bĭg'thȧ, and A-băg'thȧ, Zē'-
thär, and Cär'cas, the seven [7]chamber-

lains that served in the presence of A-hăs-ū-ē′rŭs the king,

11 To [f]bring Văsh′tī the queen before the king with the crown royal, to shew the people and the princes her beauty: for she *was* [8]fair to look on.

12 But the queen Văsh′tī refused to come at the king's commandment [9]by *his* chamberlains: therefore was the king very wroth, and his anger burned in him.

13 ¶ Then the king said to the [g]wise men, [h]which knew the times, (for so *was* the king's manner toward all that knew law and judgment:

14 And the next unto him *was* Cär-shē′nȧ, Shē′thär, Ȧd′mă-thȧ, Tär′shish, Mē′rēs, Mär′se-nȧ, *and* Me-mū′can, the [i]seven princes of Pẽr′siȧ and Mē′dĭ-ȧ, which saw the king's face, *and* which sat the first in the kingdom;)

15 [10]What shall we do unto the queen Văsh′tī according to law, because she hath not performed the commandment of the king A-hăs-ū-ē′rŭs by the chamberlains?

16 And Me-mū′can answered before the king and the princes, Văsh′tī the queen hath not done wrong to the king only, but also to all the princes, and to all the people that *are* in all the provinces of the king A-hăs-ū-ē′rŭs.

17 For *this* deed of the queen shall come abroad unto all women, so that they shall despise their husbands in their eyes, when it shall be reported, The king A-hăs-ū-ē′rŭs commanded Văsh′tī the queen to be brought in before him, but she came not.

18 *Likewise* shall the ladies of Pẽr′siȧ and Mē′dĭ-ȧ say this day unto all the king's princes, which have heard of the deed of the queen. Thus *shall there arise* too much contempt and wrath.

19 [11]If it please the king, let there go a royal commandment [12]from him, and let it be written among the laws of the Pẽr′sians and the Mēdes, [13]that it be not altered, That Văsh′tī come no more before king A-hăs-ū-ē′rŭs; and let the king give her royal estate [14]unto another that is better than she.

20 And when the king's decree which he shall make shall be published throughout all his empire, (for it is great,) all the wives shall [j]give to their husbands honour, both to great and small.

21 And the saying [15]pleased the king and the princes; and the king did according to the word of Me-mū′can:

22 For he sent letters into all the king's provinces, [k]into every province according to the writing thereof, and to every people after their language, that every man should [l]bear rule in his own house, and [16][m]that *it* should be published according to the language of every people.

2

After these things, when the wrath of king A-hăs-ū-ē′rŭs was appeased, he remembered Văsh′tī, and what she had done, and [a]what was decreed against her.

2 Then said the king's servants that ministered unto him, [b]Let there be fair young virgins sought for the king:

3 And let the king appoint officers in all the provinces of his kingdom, that they may gather together all the fair young virgins unto Shu̥′shan the palace, to the house of the women, [1]unto the custody of Hē′gē the king's chamberlain, keeper of the women; and let their things for purification be given *them:*

4 And let the maiden which pleaseth the king be queen instead of Văsh′tī. And the thing pleased the king; and he did so.

5 ¶ *Now* in Shu̥′shan the palace there was a certain Jew, whose name *was* Môr′de-cāi, the son of Jā′ĭr, the son of Shĭm′e-ī, the son of Kĭsh, a Bĕn′ja-mīte;

6 [c]Who had been carried away from Je-ru̥′sa-lĕm with the captivity which had been carried away with [2]Jĕc-o-nī′ah king of Jū′dah, whom Nĕb-u-chăd-nĕz′zar the king of Băb′ȳ-lon had carried away.

7 And he [3]brought up Ha-dăs′sah, that *is,* Ĕs′thẽr, his uncle's daughter: for she had neither father nor mother, and the maid *was* [4]fair and beautiful; whom Môr′de-cāi, when her father and mother were dead, took for his own daughter.

8 ¶ So it came to pass, when the king's commandment and his decree was heard, and when many maidens were gathered together unto Shu̥′shan the palace, to the custody of Hĕg′a-ī, that Ĕs′thẽr was brought also unto the king's house, to the custody of Hĕg′a-ī, keeper of the women.

9 And the maiden pleased him, and she obtained kindness of him; and he speedily gave her her things for purification, with [5]such things as belonged to her, and seven maidens, *which were* meet to be given her, out of the king's house: and [6]he preferred her and her maids unto the best *place* of the house of the women.

10 Ĕs′thẽr had not shewed her people nor her kindred: for Môr′de-cāi had charged her that she should [d]not shew *it.*

11 And Môr′de-cāi walked every day before the court of the women's house, [7]to know how Ĕs′thẽr did, and what should become of her.

12 ¶ Now when every maid's turn was come to go in to king A-hăs-ū-ē′rŭs, after that she had been twelve months, according to the manner of the women, (for so were the days of their purifications accomplished, *to wit,* six months with oil of myrrh, and six months with sweet odours, and with *other* things for the purifying of the women;)

13 Then thus came *every* maiden unto the king; whatsoever she desired was given her to go with her out of the house of the women unto the king's house.

14 In the evening she went, and on the morrow she returned into the second house of the women, to the cus-

11 [f]Prov. 16.9 [8]good of countenance
12 [9]which was by the hand of his eunuchs
13 [g]Jer. 10.7; Dan. 2.12 [h]1 Chr. 12.32; Isa. 7.14; Dan. 9.24; Mal. 3.1; Matt. 16.3
14 [i]Ezra 7.14
15 [10]What to do
19 [11]If it be good with the king [12]from before him [13]that it pass not away [14]unto her companion
20 [j]Eph. 5.22-23; Col. 3.18; 1 Pet. 3.1
21 [15]was good in the eyes of the king
22 [k]ch. 8.9 [l]Eph. 5.22-23-24 [16]that one should publish it according to the language of his people [m]ch. 3.12; Dan. 6.25
CHAPTER 2
1 [a]ch. 1.19
2 [b]Gen. 12.14-15; 1 Ki. 1.2
3 [1]unto the hand
6 [c]2 Ki. 24.14-15; 2 Chr. 36.10-20; Jer. 22.24 [2]Or, Jehoiachin
7 [3]nourished [4]fair of form, and good of countenance
9 [5]her portions [6]he changed her
10 [d]Lev. 26.36; Deut. 28.65; ch. 3.8
11 [7]to know the peace

tody of Sha-ăsh'găz, the king's chamberlain, which kept the concubines:
she came in unto the king no more,
except the king delighted in her, and
that she were called by name.
15 ¶ Now when the turn of Ĕs'thēr,
the daughter of Ăb-i-hā'il the uncle of
Môr'de-cāi, who had taken her for his
daughter, was come to go in unto the
king, she required nothing but what
Hĕg'a-ī the king's chamberlain, the
keeper of the women, appointed. And
Ĕs'thēr [e]obtained favour in the sight of
all them that looked upon her.
16 So Ĕs'thēr was taken unto king
A-hăs-ū-ē'rŭs into his house royal in
the [f]tenth month, which *is* the month
Tē'beth, in the seventh year of his
reign.
17 And the king loved Ĕs'thēr above
all the women, and she obtained grace
and [8]favour [9]in his sight more than all
the virgins; so that he [g]set the royal
crown upon her head, and made her
queen instead of Văsh'tī.
18 Then the king [h]made a great feast
unto all his princes and his servants,
even Ĕs'thēr's feast; and he made a [10]re-
lease to the provinces, and gave gifts,
according to the state of the king.
19 And when the virgins were gathered together the second time, then
Môr'de-cāi sat [i]in the king's gate.
20 Es'ther had not *yet* shewed her
kindred nor her people; as Môr'de-cāi
had charged her: for Ĕs'thēr did the
commandment of Môr'de-cāi, like as
when she was brought up with him.
21 ¶ In those days, while Môr'de-cāi
sat in the king's gate, two of the king's
chamberlains, [11]Bĭg'thăn and Tē'resh,
of those which kept [12]the door, were
wroth, and sought to lay hand on the
king A-hăs-ū-ē'rŭs.
22 And the thing was known to Môr'-
de-cāi, [j]who told *it* unto Ĕs'thēr the
queen; and Ĕs'thēr certified the king
thereof in Môr'de-cāi's name.
23 And when inquisition was made
of the matter, it was found out; therefore they were [k]both hanged on a tree:
and it was written in [l]the book of the
chronicles before the king.

3 After these things did king A-hăs-
ū-ē'rŭs promote Hā'man the son of
Hăm-mĕd'a-thȧ the [a]Ā'găg-īte, and ad-
vanced him, and set his seat above all
the princes that *were* with him.
2 And all the king's servants, that
were [b]in the king's gate, bowed, [c]and
reverenced Hā'man: for the king had
so commanded concerning him. But
Môr'de-cāi [d]bowed not, nor did *him*
reverence.
3 Then the king's servants, which
were in the king's gate, said unto Môr'-
de-cāi, Why transgressest thou the
king's commandment?
4 Now it came to pass, when they
spake daily unto him, and he hearkened not unto them, that they told
Hā'man, to see whether Môr'de-cāi's
matters would stand: for he had told
them that he *was* a Jew.

15 [e]Song 6.9; 2 Tim. 4.18
16 [f]ch. 3.7
17 [8]Or, kindness [9]before him
[g]Gen. 41.40; Rev. 3.21
18 [h]Gen. 29.22; Luke 14.8 [10]rest
19 [i]ch. 3.2
21 [11]Or, Bigthana [12]the threshold
22 [j]ch. 6.2; Jas. 1.19-20
23 [k]Gen. 40.19; Deut. 21.22
[l]ch. 6.1

CHAPTER 3

1 [a]Num. 24.7; 1 Sam. 15.8
2 [b]ch. 2.19
[c]Gen. 41.42; Phil. 2.10
[d]Ex. 1.17; Ps. 15.4
5 [e]ch. 5.9
[f]ch. 1.12; Dan. 3.19
6 [g]Ps. 83.4
7 [h]ch. 9.24; Acts 1.26
8 [i]Ezra 4.13; Acts 16.20 [1]meet, or, equal
9 [2]to destroy them [3]weigh
10 [j]Gen. 41.42
[k]ch. 8.2-8 [4]Or, oppressor
12 [l]ch. 8.9 [5]Or, secretaries
[m]ch. 1.22; ch. 8.9
[n]1 Ki. 21.8;
13 [o]ch. 8.10;
[p]ch. 8.12
[q]ch. 8.11;
14 [r]ch. 8.13-14
15 [s]Gen. 37.24-25;
[t]ch. 8.15;

CHAPTER 4

1 [a]2 Sam. 1.11;
[b]Josh. 7.6;

5 And when Hā'man saw that Môr'-
de-cāi [e]bowed not, nor did him reverence, then was Hā'man [f]full of wrath.
6 And he thought scorn to lay hands
on Môr'de-cāi alone; for they had
shewed him the people of Môr'de-cāi:
wherefore Hā'man [g]sought to destroy
all the Jews that *were* throughout the
whole kingdom of A-hăs-ū-ē'rŭs, *even*
the people of Môr'de-cāi.
7 ¶ In the first month, that *is,* the
month Nī'san, in the twelfth year of
king A-hăs-ū-ē'rŭs, [h]they cast Pûr, that
is, the lot, before Hā'man from day
to day, and from month to month, *to*
the twelfth *month,* that *is,* the month
Ā'dăr.
8 ¶ And Hā'man said unto king A-
hăs-ū-ē'rŭs, There is a certain people
scattered abroad and dispersed among
the people in all the provinces of thy
kingdom; and [i]their laws *are* diverse
from all people; neither keep they the
king's laws: therefore it *is* not [1]for the
king's profit to suffer them.
9 If it please the king, let it be written [2]that they may be destroyed: and I
will [3]pay ten thousand talents of silver
to the hands of those that have the
charge of the business, to bring *it* into
the king's treasuries.
10 And the king [j]took [k]his ring from
his hand, and gave it unto Hā'man the
son of Hăm-mĕd'a-thȧ the Ā'găg-īte,
the Jews' [4]enemy.
11 And the king said unto Hā'man,
The silver *is* given to thee, the people
also, to do with them as it seemeth
good to thee.
12 Then [l]were the king's [5]scribes
called on the thirteenth day of the first
month, and there was written according to all that Hā'man had commanded
unto the king's lieutenants, and to the
governors that *were* over every province, and to the rulers of every people
of every province [m]according to the
writing thereof, and *to* every people
after their language; [n]in the name of
king A-hăs-ū-ē'rŭs was it written, and
sealed with the king's ring.
13 And the letters were [o]sent by
posts into all the king's provinces, to
destroy, to kill, and to cause to perish,
all Jews, both young and old, little children and women, in [p]one day, *even*
upon the thirteenth *day* of the twelfth
month, which *is* the month Ā'dăr, and
[q]*to take* the spoil of them for a prey.
14 [r]The copy of the writing for a
commandment to be given in every
province was published unto all people, that they should be ready against
that day.
15 The posts went out, being hastened by the king's commandment,
and the decree was given in Shu'shan
the palace. And the king and Hā'man
[s]sat down to drink; but [t]the city Shu'-
shan was perplexed.

4 When Môr'de-cāi perceived all that
was done, Môr'de-cāi [a]rent his
clothes, and put on sackcloth [b]with
ashes, and went out into the midst of

the city, and [c]cried with a loud and a
bitter cry;
2 And came even before the king's
gate: for none *might* enter into the
king's gate clothed with sackcloth.
3 And in every province, whithersoever the king's commandment and his
decree came, *there was* great mourning among the Jews, and fasting, and
weeping, and wailing; and [1]many lay
in sackcloth and ashes.
4 ¶ So Ĕs'thēr's maids and her [2]cham-
berlains came and told *it* her. Then was
the queen exceedingly grieved; and she
sent raiment to clothe Môr'de-cāi, and
to take away his sackcloth from him:
but he received *it* not.
5 Then called Ĕs'thēr for Hā'tăch,
one of the king's chamberlains, [3]whom
he had appointed to attend upon her,
and gave him a commandment to Môr'-
de-cāi, to know what it *was*, and why it
was.
6 So Hā'tăch went forth to Môr'de-
cāi unto the street of the city, which
was before the king's gate.
7 And Môr'de-cāi told him of all that
had happened unto him, and of [d]the
sum of the money that Hā'man had
promised to pay to the king's treasuries for the Jews, to destroy them.
8 Also he gave him [e]the copy of the
writing of the decree that was given at
Shụ'sẖan to destroy them, to shew *it*
unto Ĕs'thēr, and to declare *it* unto
her, and to charge her that she should
go in unto the king, to [f]make supplication unto him, and to make request before him for her people.
9 And Hā'tăch came and told Ĕs'-
thēr the words of Môr'de-cāi.
10 ¶ Again Ĕs'thēr spake unto Hā'-
tăch, and gave him commandment unto
Môr'de-cāi;
11 All the king's servants, and the
people of the king's provinces, do
know, that whosoever, whether man or
woman, shall come unto the king into
[g]the inner court, who is not called,
[h]*there is* one law of his to put *him* to
death, [i]except such to whom the king
shall hold out the golden sceptre, that
he may live: but I have not been called to
come in unto the king these thirty days.
12 And they told to Môr'de-cāi Ĕs'-
thēr's words.
13 Then Môr'de-cāi commanded to
answer Ĕs'thēr, Think [j]not with thyself that thou shalt escape in the king's
house, more than all the Jews.
14 For if thou altogether holdest thy
peace at this time, *then* shall there [4]en-
largement and [k]deliverance arise to
the Jews from another place; but thou
and thy father's house shall be destroyed: and who knoweth whether
[l]thou art come to the kingdom for *such*
a time as this?
15 ¶ Then Ĕs'thēr bade *them* return
Môr'de-cāi *this answer,*
16 Go, gather together all the Jews
that are [5]present in Shụ'sẖan, and
[m]fast ye for me, and neither eat nor
drink [n]three days, night or day: I also
and my maidens will fast likewise; and
so will I go in unto the king, which *is*
not according to the law: [o]and if I perish, I perish.
17 So Môr'de-cāi [6]went his way, and
did according to all that Ĕs'thēr had
commanded him.

5 Now it came to pass [a]on the third
day, that Ĕs'thēr put on *her* royal
apparel, and stood in [b]the inner court
of the king's house, over against the
king's house: and the king sat upon his
royal throne in the royal house, over
against the gate of the house.
2 And it was so, when the king saw
Ĕs'thēr the queen standing in the court,
that [c]she obtained favour in his sight:
and [d]the king held out to Ĕs'thēr the
golden sceptre that *was* in his hand. So
Ĕs'thēr drew near, and touched the top
of the sceptre.
3 Then said the king unto her, What
wilt thou, queen Ĕs'thēr? and what *is*
thy request? [e]it shall be even given
thee to the half of the kingdom.
4 And Ĕs'thēr answered, If *it seem*
good unto the king, let the king and
Hā'man come this day unto the banquet that I have prepared for him.
5 Then the king said, Cause Hā'man
to make haste, that he may do as
Ĕs'thēr hath said. So the king and
Hā'man came to the banquet that Ĕs'-
thēr had prepared.
6 ¶ [f]And the king said unto Ĕs'-
thēr at the banquet of wine, [g]What *is*
thy petition? and it shall be granted
thee: and what *is* thy request? even
to the half of the kingdom it shall be
performed.
7 Then answered Ĕs'thēr, and said,
My petition and my request *is;*
8 If I have found favour in the sight
of the king, and if it please the king to
grant my petition, and [1]to perform my
request, let the king and Hā'man come
to the banquet that I shall prepare for
them, and I will do to morrow as the
king hath said.
9 ¶ Then went Hā'man forth that
day [h]joyful and with a glad heart: but
when Hā'man saw Môr'de-cāi in the
king's gate, [i]that he stood not up, nor
moved for him, he was full of indignation against Môr'de-cāi.
10 Nevertheless Hā'man [j]refrained
himself: and when he came home, he
sent and [2]called for his friends, and
Zē'resh his wife.
11 And Hā'man told them of [k]the
glory of his riches, and [l]the multitude of his children, and all *the things*
wherein the king had promoted him,
and how he had [m]advanced him above
the princes and servants of the king.
12 Hā'man said moreover, Yea, Ĕs'-
thēr the queen did let no man come in
with the king unto the banquet that she
had prepared but myself; and [n]to morrow am I invited unto her also with the
king.
13 Yet [o]all this availeth me nothing,
so long as I see Môr'de-cāi the Jew sitting at the king's gate.
14 ¶ Then said Zē'resh his wife and
all his friends unto him, Let a [3]gal-

[c]Gen. 27.34
3 [1]sackcloth and ashes were laid under many
4 [2]eunuchs
5 [3]whom he had set before her
7 [d]ch. 3.9
8 [e]ch. 3.14-15
[f]Job 9.15; Prov. 15.1; Acts 12.20
11 [g]ch. 5.1
[h]Dan. 2.9
[i]ch. 5.2; ch. 8.4
13 [j]Prov. 29.25
14 [4]respiration; Job 9.18
[k]Lev. 26.42; Num. 23.22-24; Jer. 30.10; Amos 9.8
[l]Ps. 75.5-6; Eccl. 3.1; Isa. 14.27; Isa. 54.17; Jer. 30.10-24; Dan. 4.17-35; Matt. 16.18
16 [5]found
[m]Joel 1.14; Jon. 3.5
[n]ch. 5.1
[o]Ps. 34.15-22; Ps. 37.3-5-28-40; Ps. 55.22; Ps. 62.8; Ps. 115.9-10-11; Prov. 29.25
17 [6]passed

CHAPTER 5
1 [a]ch. 4.16
[b]ch. 6.4
2 [c]Prov. 21.1
[d]ch. 8.4
3 [e]Mark 6.23
6 [f]ch. 7.2
[g]ch. 9.12
8 [1]to do
9 [h]Job 20.5; John 16.20; Jas. 4.9
[i]ch. 3.5; Ps. 15.4; Matt. 10.28
10 [j]Gen. 43.30-31
[2]caused to come
11 [k]Gen. 31.1; Job 31.24-25; Dan. 4.30; Mark 10.24
[l]ch. 9.7
[m]ch. 3.1
12 [n]Prov. 27.1; 1 Thess. 5.3
13 [o]1 Ki. 21.4-6; Job 5.2
14 [3]tree

lows be made of fifty cubits high, and to morrow [p]speak thou unto the king that Môr'de-cāi may be hanged thereon: then go thou in merrily with the king unto the banquet. And the thing pleased Hā'man; and he caused [q]the gallows to be made.

6 On that night [1]could not the king sleep, and he commanded to bring [a]the book of records of the chronicles; and they were read before the king.

2 And it was found written, that Môr'de-cāi had told of [2]Bĭg'tha-nȧ and Tē'resh, two of the king's chamberlains, the keepers of the [3]door, who sought to lay hand on the king A-hăs-ū-ē'rŭs.

3 And the king said, [b]What honour and dignity hath been done to Môr'de-cāi for this? Then said the king's servants that ministered unto him, There is nothing done for him.

4 ¶ And the king said, Who *is* in the court? Now Hā'man was come into [c]the outward court of the king's house, [d]to speak unto the king to hang Môr'de-cāi on the gallows that he had prepared for him.

5 And the king's servants said unto him, Behold, Hā'man standeth in the court. And the king said, Let him come in.

6 So Hā'man came in. And the king said unto him, What shall be done unto the man [4]whom the king delighteth to honour? Now Hā'man thought in his heart, To whom would the king delight to do honour more than to myself?

7 And Hā'man answered the king, For the man [5]whom the king delighteth to honour,

8 [6]Let the royal apparel be brought [7]which the king *useth* to wear, and [e]the horse that the king rideth upon, and the crown royal which is set upon his head:

9 And let this apparel and horse be delivered to the hand of one of the king's most noble princes, that they may array the man *withal* whom the king delighteth to honour, and [8]bring him on horseback through the street of the city, [f]and proclaim before him, Thus shall it be done to the man whom the king delighteth to honour.

10 Then the king said to Hā'man, [g]Make haste, *and* take the apparel and the horse, as thou hast said, and do even so to Môr'de-cāi the Jew, that sitteth at the king's gate: [9]let nothing fail of all that thou hast spoken.

11 Then took Hā'man the apparel and the horse, and arrayed Môr'de-cāi, and brought him on horseback through the street of the city, and proclaimed before him, Thus shall it be done unto the man whom the king delighteth to honour.

12 ¶ And Môr'de-cāi [h]came again to the king's gate. But Hā'man hasted to his house mourning, [i]and having his head covered.

13 And Hā'man told Zē'resh his wife and all his friends every *thing* that had befallen him. Then said his wise men and Zē'resh his wife unto him, If Môr'de-cāi *be* of the seed of the Jews, before whom thou hast begun to fall, thou shalt not prevail against him, but shalt surely fall before him.

14 And while they *were* yet talking with him, came the king's chamberlains, and hasted to bring Hā'man unto the banquet that Ĕs'thēr had prepared.

7 So the king and Hā'man came [1]to banquet with Ĕs'thēr the queen.

2 And the king said again unto Ĕs'thēr on the second day [a]at the banquet of wine, What *is* thy petition, queen Ĕs'thēr? and it shall be granted thee: and what *is* thy request? and it shall be performed, *even* to the half of the kingdom.

3 Then Ĕs'thēr the queen answered and said, If I have found favour in thy sight, O king, and if it please the king, let my life be given me at my petition, and my people at my request:

4 For we are [b]sold, I and my people, [2]to be destroyed, to be slain, and to perish. But if we had been sold for bondmen and bondwomen, I had held my tongue, although the enemy could not countervail the king's damage.

5 ¶ Then the king A-hăs-ū-ē'rŭs answered and said unto Ĕs'thēr the queen, Who is he, and where is he, [3]that durst presume in his heart to do so?

6 And Ĕs'thēr said, [4]The adversary and enemy *is* this wicked Hā'man. Then Hā'man was afraid [5]before the king and the queen.

7 ¶ And the king arising from the banquet of wine in his wrath *went* into the palace garden: and Hā'man [c]stood up to make request for his life to Ĕs'thēr the queen; for he saw that there was evil determined against him by the king.

8 Then the king returned out of the palace garden into the place of the banquet of wine; and Hā'man was fallen upon [d]the bed whereon Ĕs'thēr *was*. Then said the king, Will he force the queen also [6]before me in the house? As the word went out of the king's mouth, they [e]covered Hā'man's face.

9 And [f]Här-bō'nah, one of the chamberlains, said before the king, Behold also, [g]the [7]gallows fifty cubits high, which Hā'man had made for Môr'de-cāi, who [h]had spoken good for the king, standeth in the house of Hā'man. Then the king said, Hang him thereon.

10 So [i]they hanged Hā'man on the gallows that he had prepared for Môr'de-cāi. Then was the king's wrath pacified.

8 On that day did the king A-hăs-ū-ē'rŭs give the house of Hā'man the Jews' enemy unto Ĕs'thēr the queen. And Môr'de-cāi came before the king; for Ĕs'thēr had told [a]what he *was* unto her.

2 And the king took off [b]his ring, which he had taken from Hā'man, and gave it unto Môr'de-cāi. And Ĕs'thēr set Môr'de-cāi over the house of Hā'man.

3 ¶ And Ĕs'thēr spake yet again before the king, and fell down at his

---

[p]ch. 6.4
[q]ch. 7.10; Prov. 1.16

CHAPTER 6
1 [1]the king's sleep fled away
[a]ch. 2.23
2 [2]Or, Bigthan [3]threshold
3 [b]Gal. 6.9
4 [c]ch. 5.1
[d]ch. 5.14; Job 5.13
6 [4]in whose honour the king delighteth
7 [5]in whose honour the king delighteth
8 [6]Let them bring the royal apparel [7]wherewith the king clotheth himself
[e]1 Ki. 1.33
9 [8]cause him to ride
[f]Gen. 41.43
10 [g]Job 5.11-13; Luke 14.11 [9]suffer not a whit to fall
12 [h]ch. 2.19;
[i]2 Sam. 15.30

CHAPTER 7
1 [1]to drink
2 [a]ch. 5.6
4 [b]1 Sam. 22.23; [2]that they should destroy, and kill, and cause to perish
5 [3]whose heart hath filled him
6 [4]The man adversary [5]Or, at the presence of
7 [c]Prov. 14.19
8 [d]ch. 1.6 [6]with me
[e]Job 9.24
9 [f]ch. 1.10;
[g]ch. 5.14; [7]tree
[h]ch. 2.21-23;
10 [i]ch. 9.25;

CHAPTER 8
1 [a]ch. 2.7
2 [b]Gen. 41.42;

feet, [1]and besought him with tears to put away the mischief of Hā'man the A'găg-īte, and his device that he had devised against the Jews.

4 Then [c]the king held out the golden sceptre toward Ĕs'thĕr. So Ĕs'thĕr arose, and stood before the king,

5 And said, If it please the king, and if I have found favour in his sight, and the thing *seem* right before the king, and I *be* pleasing in his eyes, let it be written to reverse [2]the letters devised by Hā'man the son of Hăm-mĕd'a-thȧ the A'găg-īte, [3]which he wrote to destroy the Jews which *are* in all the king's provinces:

6 For how can I [4]endure to see [d]the evil that shall come unto my people? or how can I endure to see the destruction of my kindred?

7 ¶ Then the king A-hăs-ū-ē'rŭs said unto Ĕs'thĕr the queen and to Môr'de-cāi the Jew, Behold, [e]I have given Ĕs'thĕr the house of Hā'man, and him they have hanged upon the gallows, because he laid his hand upon the Jews.

8 Write ye also for the Jews, as it liketh you, in the king's name, and seal *it* with the king's ring: for the writing which is written in the king's name, and sealed with the king's ring, [f]may no man reverse.

9 [g]Then were the king's scribes called at that time in the third month, that *is*, the month Sī'van, on the three and twentieth *day* thereof; and it was written according to all that Môr'de-cāi commanded unto the Jews, and to the lieutenants, and the deputies and rulers of the provinces which *are* [h]from Ĭnd'iȧ unto Ē-thĭ-ō'pĭ-a, an hundred twenty and seven provinces, unto every province [i]according to the writing thereof, and unto every people after their language, and to the Jews according to their writing, and according to their language.

10 [j]And he wrote in the king A-hăs-ū-ē'rŭs' name, and sealed *it* with the king's ring, and sent letters by posts on horseback, *and* riders on mules, camels, *and* young dromedaries:

11 Wherein the king granted the Jews which *were* in every city to gather themselves together, and to stand for their life, to destroy, to slay, and to cause to perish, all the power of the people and province that would assault them, *both* little ones and women, and [k]*to take* the spoil of them for a prey,

12 [l]Upon one day in all the provinces of king A-hăs-ū-ē'rŭs, *namely*, upon the thirteenth *day* of the twelfth month, which *is* the month Ā'där.

13 [m]The copy of the writing for a commandment to be given in every province *was* [5]published unto all people, and that the Jews should be ready against that day to avenge themselves on their enemies.

14 *So* the posts that rode upon mules *and* camels went out, being hastened and pressed on by the king's commandment. And the decree was given at Shṳ'shan the palace.

15 ¶ And Môr'de-cāi went out from the presence of the king in royal apparel of [6]blue and white, and with a great crown of gold, and with a garment of fine linen and purple: and [n]the city of Shṳ'shan rejoiced and was glad.

16 The Jews had [o]light, and gladness, and joy, and honour.

17 And in every province, and in every city, whithersoever the king's commandment and his decree came, the Jews had joy and gladness, a feast [p]and a good day. And many of the people of the land [q]became Jews; for [r]the fear of the Jews fell upon them.

9 Now [a]in the twelfth month, that *is*, the month Ā'där, on the thirteenth day of the same, [b]when the king's commandment and his decree drew near to be put in execution, in the day that the enemies of the Jews hoped to have power over them, (though it was turned to the contrary, that the Jews [c]had rule over them that hated them;)

2 The Jews [d]gathered themselves together in their cities throughout all the provinces of the king A-hăs-ū-ē'rŭs, to lay hand on such as [e]sought their hurt: and no man could withstand them; for [f]the fear of them fell upon all people.

3 And all the rulers of the provinces, and the lieutenants, and the deputies, and [1]officers of the king, [g]helped the Jews; because the fear of Môr'de-cāi fell upon them.

4 For Môr'de-cāi *was* great in the king's house, and his fame went out throughout all the provinces: for this man Môr'de-cāi [h]waxed greater and greater.

5 Thus the Jews smote all their enemies with the stroke of the sword, and slaughter, and destruction, and did [2]what they would unto those that hated them.

6 And in Shṳ'shan the palace the Jews slew and destroyed five hundred men.

7 And Pär-shăn'da-thȧ, and Dăl'-phon and Ăs'pă-thȧ,

8 And Pŏr'a-thȧ, and Ăd-a-lī'ȧ, and A-rĭd'a-thȧ,

9 And Pär-măsh'tȧ, and A-rĭs'a-ī, and A-rĭd'a-ī, and Va-jĕz'a-thȧ,

10 [i]The ten sons of Hā'man the son of Hăm-mĕd'a-thȧ, the enemy of the Jews, slew they; [j]but on the spoil laid they not their hand.

11 On that day the number of those that were slain in Shṳ'shan the palace [3]was brought before the king.

12 ¶ And the king said unto Ĕs'thĕr the queen, The Jews have slain and destroyed five hundred men in Shṳ'shan the palace, and the ten sons of Hā'man; what have they done in the rest of the king's provinces? now [k]what *is* thy petition? and it shall be granted thee: or what *is* thy request further? and it shall be done.

13 Then said Ĕs'thĕr, If it please the king, let it be granted to the Jews which *are* in Shṳ'shan to do to morrow also [l]according unto this day's decree, and

3 [1]and she wept, and besought him
4 [c]ch. 4.11
5 [2]the device [3]Or, who wrote
6 [4]be able that I may see [d]Neh. 2.3; Ps. 137.6
7 [e]Prov. 13.22
8 [f]Dan. 6.8-12-15; 2 Tim. 2.19
9 [g]ch. 3.12 [h]ch. 1.1 [i]ch. 1.22
10 [j]1 Ki. 21.8
11 [k]ch. 3.13; Isa. 10.6
12 [l]Ex. 15.9-10; ch. 3.13
13 [m]ch. 3.14-15 [5]revealed
15 [6]Or, violet [n]ch. 3.15; Prov. 28.12-28
16 [o]ch. 9.17; Job 11.17; Ps. 18.28; Prov. 4.18
17 [p]1 Sam. 25.8; Neh. 8.10; ch. 9.19-22 [q]Ps. 18.43 [r]Gen. 35.5; Ex. 15.16; Deut. 2.25; ch. 9.2

CHAPTER 9
1 [a]ch. 8.12 [b]ch. 3.13 [c]2 Sam. 22.41; Isa. 14.2
2 [d]ch. 8.11 [e]Ps. 71.13 [f]Ex. 23.27; ch. 8.17
3 [1]those which did the business that belonged to the king [g]Prov. 16.7
4 [h]2 Sam. 3.1; 1 Chr. 11.9; Ps. 1.3; Prov. 4.18; Isa. 9.7
5 [2]according to their will
10 [i]Ex. 20.5; ch. 5.11; Job 18.19; Ps. 21.10 [j]Gen. 14.23; ch. 8.11
11 [3]came
12 [k]ch. 5.6
13 [l]ch. 8.11

[4]let Hā'man's ten sons [m]be hanged
upon the gallows.
14 And the king commanded it so to
be done: and the decree was given at
Shu̥'shan; and they hanged Hā'man's
ten sons.
15 For the Jews that *were* in Shu̥'-
shan [n]gathered themselves together
on the fourteenth day also of the month
Ā'där, and slew three hundred men at
Shu̥'shan; but on the prey they laid not
their hand.
16 But the other Jews that *were* in
the king's provinces [o]gathered themselves together, and stood for their
lives, and had rest from their enemies,
and slew of their foes seventy and
five thousand, [p]but they laid not their
hands on the prey,
17 On the thirteenth day of the month
Ā'där; and on the fourteenth day [5]of the
same rested they, and made it a day of
feasting and gladness.
18 But the Jews that *were* at Shu̥'-
shan assembled together on the thirteenth *day* thereof, and on the fourteenth thereof; and on the fifteenth *day*
of the same they rested, and made it a
day of feasting and gladness.
19 Therefore the Jews of the villages, that dwelt in the unwalled towns,
made the fourteenth day of the month
Ā'där [q]*a day of* gladness and feasting,
[r]and a good day, and of [s]sending portions one to another.
20 ¶ And Môr'de-cāi wrote these
things, and sent letters unto all the Jews
that *were* in all the provinces of the king
A-hăs-ū-ē'rŭs, *both* nigh and far,
21 To stablish *this* among them, that
they should [t]keep the fourteenth day
of the month Ā'där, and the fifteenth
day of the same, yearly,
22 As the days wherein the Jews
rested from their enemies, and the
month which was [u]turned unto them
from sorrow to joy, and from mourning into a good day: that they should
make them days of feasting and joy,
and of [v]sending portions one to another, and gifts to the poor.
23 And the Jews undertook to do as
they had begun, and as Môr'de-cāi had
written unto them;
24 Because Hā'man the son of Hăm-
mĕd'a-thȧ, the Ā'găg-īte, the enemy of
all the Jews, [w]had devised against the
Jews to destroy them, and had cast
Pûr, that *is*, the lot, to [6]consume them,
and to destroy them;

[4]let men hang
[m]2 Sam. 21.6-9
15 [n]ch. 8.11
16 [o]Lev. 26.7-8; ch. 8.11
[p]1 Thess. 5.22
17 [5]in it
19 [q]Deut. 16.11-14; Neh. 8.10-12; ch. 8.17; Ps. 118.15; Rev. 11.10
[r]1 Sam. 25.8; Neh. 8.10-12; ch. 8.17
[s]Neh. 8.10-12; Rev. 11.10
21 [t]Ps. 145.4
22 [u]Ps. 30.11; Matt. 5.4; John 16.20-22
[v]Neh. 8.11; Acts 2.44-46
24 [w]ch. 3.6-7
[6]crush
25 [7]when she came
[x]1 Sam. 24.12-13; ch. 7.10; Ps. 7.16; Ps. 37.12-13
26 [8]That is, Lot
27 [y]ch. 8.17; Isa. 56.3-6; Zech. 2.11
[9]pass
28 [10]pass
[11]be ended
29 [z]ch. 2.15
[12]all strength
[a]ch. 8.10
30 [b]ch. 1.1
CHAPTER 10
1 [a]Gen. 10.5; Ps. 72.10; Isa. 24.15
2 [1]made him great
3 [b]Gen. 41.40; 2 Chr. 28.7
[c]Neh. 2.10; Ps. 122.8
[d]Ps. 125.5; Prov. 12.20; Isa. 26.12

25 But [7]when *Ĕs'thĕr* came before
the king, he commanded by letters that
his wicked device, which he devised
against the Jews, should [x]return upon
his own head, and that he and his sons
should be hanged on the gallows.
26 Wherefore they called these days
Pū'rim after the name of [8]Pûr. Therefore for all the words of this letter, and
of that which they had seen concerning this matter, and which had come
unto them,
27 The Jews ordained, and took upon
them, and upon their seed, and upon
all such as [y]joined themselves unto
them, so as it should not [9]fail, that they
would keep these two days according to
their writing, and according to their *appointed* time every year;
28 And *that* these days *should be* remembered and kept throughout every
generation, every family, every province, and every city; and *that* these
days of Pū'rim should not [10]fail from
among the Jews, nor the memorial of
them [11]perish from their seed.
29 Then Ĕs'thĕr the queen, [z]the
daughter of Ăb-i-hā'il, and Môr'de-cāi
the Jew, wrote with [12]all authority, to
confirm this [a]second letter of Pū'rim.
30 And he sent the letters unto all the
Jews, to [b]the hundred twenty and seven
provinces of the kingdom of A-hăs-ū-
ē'rŭs, *with* words of peace and truth,
31 To confirm these days of Pū'rim
in their times *appointed*, according as
Môr'de-cāi the Jew and Ĕs'thĕr the
queen had enjoined them, and as they
had decreed for themselves and for
their seed, the matters of the fastings
and their cry.
32 And the decree of Ĕs'thĕr confirmed these matters of Pū'rim; and it
was written in the book.
10 And the king A-hăs-ū-ē'rŭs laid
a tribute upon the land, and *upon*
[a]the isles of the sea.
2 And all the acts of his power and of
his might, and the declaration of the
greatness of Môr'de-cāi, whereunto the
king [1]advanced him, *are* they not written in the book of the chronicles of the
kings of Mē'dĭ-ȧ and Pĕr'siȧ?
3 For Môr'de-cāi the Jew *was* [b]next
unto king A-hăs-ū-ē'rŭs, and great
among the Jews, and accepted of the
multitude of his brethren, [c]seeking the
wealth of his people, and speaking
[d]peace to all his seed.

THE BOOK OF JOB

Life's Questions

When I suffer, can I be certain God is punishing me?
What does God think when I argue with Him?
Are religious experts always right?

God's Answers

Job walks uncharted paths to explore questions most people fear to ask. Job shows life is not as simple and easy to understand as some religious experts try to convince us. Job is a prose story (1—2; 42:7–17) sandwiched around an extended poetic argument of Job with three religious expert friends, with himself, with a young man who knows everything, and with God. Satan gives the problem by asking why Job is so religious and getting permission to make him suffer. Job and his friends know nothing of Satan's activity and so seek religious answers to the problem of undeserved suffering. Job shows the experts' answers are too simple and claims his punishment does not result from his sin. Finally God shows that Job has claimed too much knowledge himself and must repent before God, who alone understands everything.

Job shows: an unjust world can have just people suffer (1—2); human answers do not satisfy, so one must call on God (3—14); a Redeemer, not undeserved repentance, is the only hope (15—21); when God is silent, humans can only fear Him and wait (22—28); a just person expects an answer from God (29—31); humans must let God be sovereign and mysterious (32—37); in face of God's knowledge and power, a person can only repent of pride and lack of trust (38:1—42:6); prayer brings reconciliation, forgiveness, and restoration (42:7–17).

1 There was a man [a]in the land of Ŭz,
whose name *was* [b]Jōb: and that
man was [c]perfect and upright, and one
that [d]feared God, and eschewed evil.
2 And there were born unto him
seven sons and three daughters.
3 His [1]substance also was seven
thousand sheep, and three thousand
camels, and five hundred yoke of oxen,
and five hundred she asses, and a very
great [2]household; so that this man was
the greatest of all the [3]men of the east.
4 And his sons went and feasted *in*
their houses, every one his day; and
sent and called for their three sisters to
eat and to drink with them.
5 And it was so, when the days of
their feasting were gone about, that
Jōb sent and sanctified them, and rose
up early in the morning, [e]and offered
burnt offerings *according* to the number of them all: for Jōb said, [f]It may
be that my sons have sinned, and
[g]cursed God in their hearts. Thus did
Jōb [4]continually.
6 ¶ Now [h]there was a day [i]when the
sons of God came to present themselves before the LORD, and [5]Sā'tan
came also [6]among them.
7 And the LORD said unto Sā'tan,
Whence comest thou? Then Sā'tan answered the LORD, and said, From [j]go-
ing to and fro in the earth, and from
walking up and down in it.
8 And the LORD said unto Sā'tan,
[7]Hast thou considered my servant Jōb,
that *there is* none like him in the earth,
a perfect and an upright man, one that
feareth God, and escheweth evil?
9 Then Sā'tan answered the LORD,
and said, Doth Jōb fear God for nought?
10 [k]Hast not thou made an hedge
about him, and about his house, and
about all that he hath on every side?
[l]thou hast blessed the work of his
hands, and his [8]substance is increased
in the land.
11 But put forth thine hand now,
and touch all that he hath, [9]and he will
curse thee to thy face.
12 And the LORD said unto Sā'tan,
Behold, all that he hath *is* in thy
[10]power; only upon himself put not
forth thine hand. So Sā'tan went forth
from the presence of the LORD.
13 ¶ And there was a day [m]when his
sons and his daughters *were* eating and
drinking wine in their eldest brother's
house:
14 And there came a messenger unto
Jōb, and said, The oxen were plowing,
and the asses feeding beside them:
15 And the [n]Sa-bē'ans fell *upon*
them, and took them away; yea, they
have slain the servants with the edge
of the sword; and I only am escaped
alone to tell thee.
16 While he *was* yet speaking, there
came also another, and said, [11]The fire
of God is fallen from heaven, and hath
burned up the sheep, and the servants,
and consumed them; and I only am escaped alone to tell thee.
17 While he *was* yet speaking, there
came also another, and said, The Chăl-
dē'ans made out three bands, and [12]fell
upon the camels, and have carried
them away, yea, and slain the servants
with the edge of the sword; and I only
am escaped alone to tell thee.
18 While he *was* yet speaking, there
came also another, and said, Thy sons
and thy daughters *were* eating and
drinking wine in their eldest brother's
house:
19 And, behold, there came a great
wind [13]from the wilderness, and smote
the four corners of the house, and it
fell upon the young men, and they are
dead; and I only am escaped alone to
tell thee.
20 Then Jōb arose, and rent his
[14]mantle, and shaved his head, and
[o]fell down upon the ground, and worshipped,
21 And said, Naked came I out of
my mother's womb, and naked shall I
return thither: the LORD [p]gave, and the
LORD hath taken away; [q]blessed be
the name of the LORD.
22 In all this Jōb sinned not, nor
[15]charged God foolishly.

2 Again there was a day when the
sons of God came to present themselves before the LORD, and Sā'tan
came also among them to present himself before the LORD.
2 And the LORD said unto Sā'tan,
From whence comest thou? And Sā'tan
answered the LORD, and said, From going to and fro in the earth, and from
walking up and down in it.
3 And the LORD said unto Sā'tan,
Hast thou considered my servant Jōb,
that *there is* none like him in the earth,
a perfect and an upright man, one that
feareth God, and escheweth evil? and
still he [a]holdeth fast his integrity,

CHAPTER 1
1 [a]Gen. 22.20
[b]Jas. 5.11
[c]Gen. 6.9
[d]Prov. 8.13; 1 Pet. 3.11
3 [1]Or, cattle
[2]Or, husbandry
[3]sons of the east
5 [e]Gen. 8.20; ch. 42.8
[f]2 Cor. 11.2
[g]1 Ki. 21.10-13
[4]all the days
6 [h]ch. 2.1
[i]ch. 38.7; Dan. 7.10
[5]the Adversary
[6]in the midst of them
7 [j]Matt. 12.43; 1 Pet. 5.8
8 [7]Hast thou set thy heart on
10 [k]Gen. 15.1; Ps. 34.7; Isa. 5.2
[l]Ps. 128.1
[8]Or, cattle
11 [9]if he curse thee not to thy face
12 [10]hand
13 [m]Eccl. 9.12; Luke 12.19-20
15 [n]Gen. 10.7
16 [11]Or, A great fire
17 [12]rushed
19 [13]from aside
20 [14]Or, robe
[o]Deut. 9.18; Matt. 26.39; 1 Pet. 5.6
21 [p]Jas. 1.17
[q]Gen. 45.5; Amos 3.6; Eph. 5.20
22 [15]Or, attributed folly to God

CHAPTER 2
3 [a]ch. 27.5-6; 1 Pet. 1.7

although thou movedst me against
him, [1][b]to destroy him without cause.
4 And Sā'tan answered the LORD,
and said, Skin for skin, yea, all that a
man hath will he give for his life.
5 But put forth thine hand now, and
touch his [c]bone and his flesh, and he
will curse thee to thy face.
6 And the LORD said unto Sā'tan, Behold, he *is* in thine hand; [2]but save his
life.
7 ¶ So went Sā'tan forth from the
presence of the LORD, and smote Jōb
with sore boils from the sole of his foot
unto his crown.
8 And he took him a potsherd to
scrape himself withal; [d]and he sat
down among the ashes.
9 ¶ Then said [e]his wife unto him,
[f]Dost thou still retain thine integrity?
curse God, and die.
10 But he said unto her, Thou speakest as one of the foolish women speaketh. What? [g]shall we receive good at
the hand of God, and shall we not receive evil? In all this did not Jōb [h]sin
with his lips.
11 ¶ Now when Jōb's three friends
heard of all this evil that was come
upon him, they came every one from
his own place; Ĕl'ĭ-phăz [i]the Tē'man-
īte, and Bĭl'dăd [j]the Shu'hīte, and Zō'-
phar the Nā'a-math-īte: for they had
made an appointment together to come
[k]to mourn with him and to comfort
him.
12 And when they lifted up their
eyes afar off, and knew him not, they
lifted up their voice, and wept; and
they rent every one his mantle, and
[l]sprinkled dust upon their heads toward heaven.
13 So they sat down with him upon
the ground [m]seven days and seven
nights, and none spake a word unto
him: for they saw that *his* grief was
very great.
3 After this opened Jōb his mouth,
and cursed his day.
2 And Jōb [1]spake, and said,
3 [a]Let the day perish wherein I was
born, and the night *in which* it was
said, There is a man child conceived.
4 Let that day be darkness; let not
God regard it from above, neither let
the light shine upon it.
5 Let darkness and [b]the shadow of
death [2]stain it; let a cloud dwell upon
it; [3]let the blackness of the day terrify
it.
6 *As for* that night, let darkness seize
upon it; [4]let it not be joined unto the
days of the year, let it not come into the
number of the months.
7 Lo, let that night be solitary, let no
joyful voice come therein.
8 Let them curse it that curse the
day, [c]who are ready to raise up [5]their
mourning.
9 Let the stars of the twilight thereof
be dark; let it look for light, but *have*
none; neither let it see [6]the dawning of
the day:
10 Because it shut not up the doors
of my *mother's* womb, nor hid sorrow
from mine eyes.
11 Why died I not from the womb?
why did I *not* give up the ghost when I
came out of the belly?
12 Why did the knees prevent me?
or why the breasts that I should suck?
13 For now should I have lain still
and been quiet, I should have slept:
then had I been at rest,
14 With kings and counsellers of the
earth, which built desolate places for
themselves;
15 Or with princes that had gold,
who filled their houses with silver:
16 Or as an hidden untimely birth I
had not been; as infants *which* never
saw light.
17 There the wicked cease *from* troubling; and there the [7]weary be at rest.
18 *There* the prisoners rest together;
they hear not the voice of the oppressor.
19 The small and great are there;
and the servant *is* free from his master.
20 [d]Wherefore is light given to him
that is in misery, and life unto the bitter *in* soul;
21 Which [8]long for death, but it *cometh* not; and dig for it more than [e]for
hid treasures;
22 Which rejoice exceedingly, *and*
are glad, when they can find the grave?
23 *Why is light given* to a man
whose way is hid, [f]and whom God
hath hedged in?
24 For my sighing cometh [9]before I
eat, and my roarings are poured out
like the waters.
25 For [10]the thing which I greatly
feared is come upon me, and that which
I was afraid of is come unto me.
26 I was not in safety, neither had I
rest, neither was I quiet; yet trouble
came.
4 Then Ĕl'ĭ-phăz the Tē'man-īte answered and said,
2 *If* we assay [1]to commune with thee,
wilt thou be grieved? but [2]who can
withhold himself from speaking?
3 Behold, thou hast instructed
many, and thou hast strengthened the
weak hands.
4 Thy words have upholden him that
was falling, and thou hast strengthened [3]the feeble knees.
5 But now it is come upon thee, and
thou [a]faintest; it toucheth thee, and
thou art troubled.
6 *Is* not *this* [b]thy fear, [c]thy confidence, thy hope, and the uprightness
of thy ways?
7 Remember, I pray thee, who *ever*
perished, being innocent? or where
were the righteous cut off?
8 Even as I have seen, [d]they that
plow iniquity, and sow wickedness,
reap the same.
9 By the blast of God they perish,
and [4]by the breath of his nostrils are
they consumed.
10 The roaring of the lion, and the
voice of the fierce lion, and [e]the teeth
of the young lions, are broken.

[1]to swallow him up
[b]Gen. 22.1; John 9.2
5 [c]ch. 19.20; Ps. 32.3-4
6 [2]Or, only
8 [d]2 Sam. 13.19;
9 [e]Gen. 3.6
[f]2 Ki. 6.33;
10 [g]2 Sam. 19.28;
[h]Ps. 39.1;
11 [i]Gen. 36.11;
[j]Gen. 25.2
[k]ch. 42.11;
12 [l]Neh. 9.1;
13 [m]Gen. 50.10

CHAPTER 3
2 [1]answered
3 [a]ch. 10.18-19;
5 [b]ch. 16.16;
[2]Or, challenge it
[3]Or, let them terrify it, as those who have a bitter day
6 [4]Or, let it not rejoice among the days
8 [c]Jer. 9.17
[5]Or, a leviathan
9 [6]the eyelids of the morning
17 [7]wearied in strength
20 [d]Jer. 20.18
21 [8]wait
[e]Prov. 2.4
23 [f]Lam. 3.7
24 [9]before my meat
25 [10]I feared a fear, and it came upon me

CHAPTER 4
2 [1]a word
[2]who can refrain from words?
4 [3]the bowing knees
5 [a]Prov. 24.10;
6 [b]ch. 1.1
[c]Prov. 3.26
8 [d]Ps. 7.14
9 [4]That is, by his anger, Isa. 30.33
10 [e]ch. 29.17;

11 [f]The old lion perisheth for lack of
prey, and the stout lion's whelps are
scattered abroad.
12 Now a thing was [5]secretly brought
to me, and mine ear received a little
thereof.
13 [g]In thoughts from the visions of
the night, when deep sleep falleth on
men,
14 Fear [6]came upon me, and trembling, which made [7]all my bones to
shake.
15 Then [h]a spirit passed before my
face; the hair of my flesh stood up:
16 It stood still, but I could not discern the form thereof: an image *was*
before mine eyes, [8]*there was* silence,
and I heard a voice, *saying*,
17 Shall mortal man be more just
than God? shall a man be more pure
than his maker?
18 Behold, he [i]put no trust in his servants; [9]and his angels he charged with
folly:
19 How much less *in* them that dwell
in houses of clay, whose foundation *is*
in the dust, *which* are crushed before
the moth?
20 They are [10]destroyed from morning to evening: they perish for ever
without any regarding *it*.
21 Doth not their excellency *which*
is in them go away? they die, even without wisdom.

5 Call now, if there be any that will
answer thee; and to which of the
saints wilt thou [1]turn?
2 For wrath killeth the foolish man,
and [2]envy slayeth the silly one.
3 I have seen the foolish taking root:
but suddenly I cursed his habitation.
4 His children are far from safety,
and they are crushed in the gate, neither *is there* any to deliver *them*.
5 Whose harvest the hungry eateth
up, and taketh it even out of the thorns,
and the robber swalloweth up their
substance.
6 Although [3]affliction cometh not
forth of the dust, neither doth trouble
spring out of the ground;
7 Yet man is born unto [4]trouble, as
[5]the sparks fly upward.
8 I would [a]seek unto God, and unto
God would I commit my cause:
9 Which doeth great things [6]and unsearchable; marvellous things [7]with-
out number:
10 Who giveth rain upon the earth,
and sendeth waters upon the [8]fields:
11 To set up on high those that be
low; that those which mourn may be
exalted to safety.
12 He disappointeth the devices of
the crafty, so that their hands [9]cannot
perform *their* enterprise.
13 He taketh the wise in their own
craftiness: and the counsel of the froward is carried headlong.
14 They [10]meet with darkness in the
daytime, and grope in the noonday as
in the night.
15 But he saveth the poor from the
sword, from their mouth, and from the
hand of the mighty.
16 So the poor hath hope, and iniquity stoppeth her mouth.
17 [b]Behold, happy *is* the man whom
God correcteth: therefore despise not
thou the chastening of the Almighty:
18 For he maketh sore, and bindeth
up: he woundeth, and his hands make
whole.
19 [c]He shall deliver thee in six troubles: yea, in seven [d]there shall no evil
touch thee.
20 In famine he shall redeem thee
from death: and in war [11]from the
power of the sword.
21 [e]Thou shalt be hid [12]from the
scourge of the tongue: neither shalt
thou be afraid of destruction when it
cometh.
22 At destruction and famine thou
shalt laugh: neither shalt thou be afraid
of the beasts of the earth.
23 [f]For thou shalt be in league with
the stones of the field: and the beasts
of the field shall be at peace with thee.
24 And thou shalt know [13]that thy
tabernacle *shall be* in peace; and thou
shalt visit thy habitation, and shalt not
[14]sin.
25 Thou shalt know also that thy
seed *shall be* [15]great, and thine offspring as the grass of the earth.
26 Thou shalt come to *thy* grave in a
full age, like as a shock of corn [16]com-
eth in in his season.
27 Lo this, we have searched it, so it
is; hear it, and know thou *it* [17]for thy
good.

6 But Jōb answered and said,
2 Oh that my grief were throughly
weighed, and my calamity [1]laid in the
balances together!
3 For now it would be heavier than
the sand of the sea: therefore [2]my
words are swallowed up.
4 [a]For the arrows of the Almighty
are within me, the poison whereof
drinketh up my spirit: the terrors of
God do set themselves in array against
me.
5 Doth the wild ass bray [3]when he
hath grass? or loweth the ox over his
fodder?
6 Can that which is unsavoury be
eaten without salt? or is there *any* taste
in the white of an egg?
7 The things *that* my soul refused to
touch *are* as my sorrowful meat.
8 Oh that I might have my request;
and that God would grant *me* [4]the
thing that I long for!
9 Even that it would please God to
destroy me; that he would let loose his
hand, and cut me off!
10 Then should I yet have comfort;
yea, [5]I would harden myself in sorrow:
let him not spare; for I have not concealed the words of the Holy One.
11 What *is* my strength, that I should
hope? and what *is* mine end, that I
should prolong my life?
12 *Is* my strength the strength of
stones? or *is* my flesh [6]of brass?
13 *Is* not my help in me? and is wisdom driven quite from me?

11 [f]Ps. 34.10
12 [5]by stealth
13 [g]ch. 33.15
14 [6]met me [7]the multitude of my bones
15 [h]Ps. 104.4;
16 [8]Or, I heard a still voice
18 [i]2 Pet. 2.4 [9]Or, nor in his angels, in whom he put light
20 [10]beaten in pieces

CHAPTER 5
1 [1]Or, look
2 [2]Or, indignation
6 [3]Or, iniquity
7 [4]Or, labour [5]the sons of the burning coal lift up to fly
8 [a]Ps. 50.15
9 [6]and there is no search [7]till there be no number
10 [8]outplaces
12 [9]Or, cannot perform any thing
14 [10]Or, run into
17 [b]Ps. 94.12;
19 [c]Ex. 12.46; [d]Ps. 91.10;
20 [11]from the hands
21 [e]Ps. 31.15 [12]Or, when the tongue scourgeth
23 [f]Ps. 91.12
24 [13]Or, that peace is thy tabernacle [14]Or, err
25 [15]Or, much
26 [16]ascendeth
27 [17]for thyself

CHAPTER 6
2 [1]lifted up
3 [2]That is, I want words to express my grief
4 [a]Deut. 32.23-42;
5 [3]at grass
8 [4]my expectation
10 [5]Or, though I should be burned with pain
12 [6]brasen?

14 [7]To him that is afflicted pity *should*
be shewed from his friend; but he forsaketh the fear of the Almighty.
15 My brethren have dealt deceitfully as a brook, *and* as the stream of
brooks they pass away;
16 Which [8]are blackish by reason of
the ice, *and* wherein the snow is hid:
17 What time they wax warm, [9]they
vanish: [10]when it is hot, they are [11]con-
sumed out of their place.
18 The paths of their way are turned
aside; they go to nothing, and perish.
19 The troops of Tē'mȧ looked, the
companies of Shē'bȧ waited for them.
20 They were confounded because
they had hoped; they came thither, and
were ashamed.
21 [12]For now ye are [13]nothing; ye see
[b]*my* casting down, and are afraid.
22 Did I say, [c]Bring unto me? or,
Give a reward for me of your substance?
23 Or, Deliver me from the enemy's
hand? or, Redeem me from the hand of
the mighty?
24 Teach me, and I will [d]hold my
tongue: and cause me to understand
wherein I have erred.
25 How forcible are right words! but
what doth your arguing reprove?
26 Do ye imagine to reprove words,
and the speeches of one that is desperate, *which are* as wind?
27 Yea, [14]ye overwhelm the fatherless, and ye dig *a pit* for your friend.
28 Now therefore be content, look
upon me; for *it is* [15]evident unto you if I
lie.
29 Return, I pray you, let it not be
iniquity; yea, return again, my righteousness *is* [16]in it.
30 Is there [e]iniquity in my tongue?
cannot [17]my taste discern perverse
things?

7 *Is there* not [1][a]an appointed time to
man upon earth? *are not* his days
also like the days of an hireling?
2 As a servant [2]earnestly desireth
the shadow, and as an hireling looketh
for *the reward of* his work:
3 So am I made to possess [b]months
of vanity, and wearisome nights are appointed to me.
4 When I lie down, I say, When shall
I arise, and [3]the night be gone? and I
am full of tossings to and fro unto the
dawning of the day.
5 My flesh is clothed [c]with worms
and clods of dust; my skin is broken,
and become loathsome.
6 My days are swifter than a weaver's shuttle, and are spent without
hope.
7 O remember that [d]my life *is* wind:
mine eye [4]shall no more [5]see good.
8 [e]The eye of him that hath seen me
shall see me no *more*: thine eyes *are*
upon me, and [6]I *am* not.
9 *As* the cloud is consumed and van-
isheth away: so [f]he that goeth down to
the grave shall come up no *more*.
10 He shall return no more to his
house, neither shall his place know
him any more.
11 Therefore I will [g]not refrain my
mouth; I will speak in the anguish of
my spirit; I will complain in the bitterness of my soul.
12 *Am* I a sea, or a whale, that thou
settest a watch over me?
13 When I say, My bed shall comfort
me, my couch shall ease my complaint;
14 Then thou scarest me with dreams,
and terrifiest me through visions:
15 So that my soul chooseth stran-
gling, *and* death rather [7]than my life.
16 [h]I loathe *it*: I would not live alway: let me alone; for [i]my days *are*
vanity.
17 [j]What *is* man, that thou shouldest magnify him? and that thou shouldest set thine heart upon him?
18 And *that* thou shouldest visit
him every morning, *and* try him every
moment?
19 How long wilt thou not depart
from me, nor let me alone till I swallow
down my spittle?
20 I have sinned; what shall I do unto
thee, [k]O thou [8]preserver of men? why
hast thou set me as a mark against thee,
so that I am a burden to myself?
21 And why dost thou not pardon
my transgression, and take away mine
iniquity? for now shall I sleep in the
dust; and thou shalt seek me in the
morning, but I *shall* not *be*.

8 Then answered Bĭl'dăd the Shu̥'-
hīte, and said,
2 How long wilt thou speak these
things? and *how long shall* the words
of thy mouth *be like* a strong wind?
3 [a]Doth God pervert judgment? or
doth the Almighty pervert justice?
4 If thy children have sinned against
him, and he have cast them away [1]for
their transgression;
5 If thou wouldest seek unto God
betimes, and make thy supplication to
the Almighty;
6 If thou *wert* pure and upright;
surely now he would awake for thee,
and make the habitation of thy righteousness prosperous.
7 Though thy beginning was small,
yet thy latter end should greatly increase.
8 [b]For inquire, I pray thee, of the
former age, and prepare thyself to the
search of their fathers:
9 (For [c]we *are but of* yesterday, and
know [2]nothing, because our days upon
earth *are* a shadow:)
10 Shall not they teach thee, *and*
tell thee, and utter words out of their
heart?
11 Can the rush grow up without
mire? can the flag grow without water?
12 [d]Whilst it *is* yet in his greenness,
and not cut down, it withereth before
any *other* herb.
13 So *are* the paths of all that forget
God; and the [e]hypocrite's hope shall
perish:
14 Whose hope shall be cut off, and
whose trust *shall be* [3]a spider's web.
15 [f]He shall lean upon his house,
but it shall not stand: he shall hold it
fast, but it shall not endure.

14 [7]To him that melteth
16 [8]Or, mourn
17 [9]they are cut off [10]in the heat thereof [11]extinguished
21 [12]Or, For now ye are like to them [13]not
[b]Ps. 38.11
22 [c]Acts 20.33
24 [d]Ps. 39.1
27 [14]ye cause to fall upon
28 [15]before your face
29 [16]That is, in this matter
30 [e]ch. 33.8-12; [17]my palate

CHAPTER 7
1 [1]Or, a warfare
[a]ch. 14.5-13-14;
2 [2]gapeth after
3 [b]Ps. 39.5;
4 [3]the evening be measured?
5 [c]ch. 17.14;
7 [d]Ps. 78.39; [4]shall not return [5]to see, that is, to enjoy
8 [e]ch. 20.9 [6]That is, I can live no longer
9 [f]2 Sam. 12.23;
11 [g]Ps. 39.1-9
15 [7]than my bones
16 [h]Gen. 27.46; [i]Ps. 62.9;
17 [j]Ps. 8.4;
20 [k]Ps. 36.6 [8]Or, observer

CHAPTER 8
3 [a]Gen. 18.25;
4 [1]in the hand of their transgression
8 [b]Deut. 4.32
9 [c]Gen. 47.9; [2]not
12 [d]Ps. 129.6;
13 [e]ch. 11.20;
14 [3]a spider's house
15 [f]ch. 27.18;

16 He *is* green before the sun, and his branch shooteth forth in his garden.

17 His roots are wrapped about the heap, *and* seeth the place of stones.

18 [g]If he destroy him from his place, then *it* shall deny him, *saying*, I have not seen thee.

19 Behold, this *is* the joy of his way, and [h]out of the earth shall others grow.

20 Behold, God will not [i]cast away a perfect *man*, neither will he [4]help the evildoers:

21 Till he fill thy mouth with laughing, and thy lips with [5]rejoicing.

22 They that hate thee shall be clothed with shame; and the dwelling place of the wicked [6]shall come to nought.

9 Then Jōb answered and said,

2 I know *it is* so of a truth: but how should [a]man be just [1]with God?

3 If he will contend with him, he cannot answer him one of a thousand.

4 *He is* wise in heart, and mighty in strength: who hath hardened *himself* against him, and hath prospered?

5 Which removeth the mountains, and they know not: which overturneth them in his anger.

6 Which [b]shaketh the earth out of her place, and the pillars thereof tremble.

7 Which commandeth the sun, and it riseth not; and sealeth up the stars.

8 Which alone spreadeth out the heavens, and treadeth upon the [2]waves of the sea.

9 [c]Which maketh [3]Ärc-tū'rus, O-rī'-on, and Plē'ia-dēs, and the chambers of the south.

10 Which doeth great things past finding out; yea, and wonders without number.

11 [d]Lo, he goeth by me, and I see *him* not: he passeth on also, but I perceive him not.

12 [e]Behold, he taketh away, [4]who can hinder him? who will say unto him, What doest thou?

13 *If* God will not withdraw his anger, the [5]proud helpers do stoop under him.

14 How much less shall I answer him, *and* choose out my words *to reason* with him?

15 [f]Whom, though I were righteous, *yet* would I not answer, *but* I would make supplication to my judge.

16 If I had called, and he had answered me; *yet* would I not believe that he had hearkened unto my voice.

17 For he breaketh me with a tempest, and multiplieth my wounds [g]without cause.

18 He will not suffer me to take my breath, but filleth me with bitterness.

19 If *I speak* of strength, lo, *he is* strong: and if of judgment, who shall set me a time *to plead?*

20 If I justify myself, mine own mouth shall condemn me: *if I say*, I *am* perfect, it shall also prove me perverse.

21 *Though* I *were* perfect, *yet* would I not know my soul: I would despise my life.

22 This *is* one *thing*, therefore I said *it*, [h]He destroyeth the perfect and the wicked.

23 If the scourge slay suddenly, he will laugh at the trial of the innocent.

24 The earth is given into the hand of the wicked: [i]he covereth the faces of the judges thereof; if not, where, *and* who *is* he?

25 Now my days are swifter than a post: they flee away, they see no good.

26 They are passed away as the [6]swift ships: as the eagle *that* hasteth to the prey.

27 If I say, I will forget my complaint, I will leave off my heaviness, and [7]comfort *myself*:

28 I am afraid of all my sorrows, I know that thou [j]wilt not hold me innocent.

29 *If* I be wicked, why then labour I in vain?

30 If I wash myself with snow water, and make my hands never so clean;

31 Yet shalt thou plunge me in the ditch, and mine own clothes shall [8]abhor me.

32 For [k]*he is* not a man, as I *am*, *that* I should answer him, *and* we should come together in judgment.

33 [l]Neither is there [9]any [10]daysman betwixt us, *that* might lay his hand upon us both.

34 Let him take his rod away from me, and let not his fear terrify me:

35 *Then* would I speak, and not fear him; [11]but *it is* not so with me.

10 My soul is [1]weary of my life; I will leave my complaint upon myself; I will speak in the bitterness of my soul.

2 I will say unto God, Do not condemn me; shew me wherefore thou contendest with me.

3 *Is it* good unto thee that thou shouldest oppress, that thou shouldest despise [2]the work of thine hands, and shine upon the counsel of the wicked?

4 Hast thou eyes of flesh? or [a]seest thou as man seeth?

5 *Are* thy days as the days of man? *are* thy years as man's days,

6 That thou inquirest after mine iniquity, and searchest after my sin?

7 [3]Thou knowest that I am not wicked; and *there is* none that can deliver out of thine hand.

8 [b]Thine hands have [4]made me and fashioned me together round about; yet thou dost destroy me.

9 Remember, I beseech thee, that [c]thou hast made me as the clay; and wilt thou bring me into dust again?

10 [d]Hast thou not poured me out as milk, and curdled me like cheese?

11 Thou hast clothed me with skin and flesh, and hast [5]fenced me with bones and sinews.

12 Thou hast granted me life and favour, and thy visitation hath preserved my spirit.

13 And these *things* hast thou hid in thine heart: I know that this *is* with thee.

18 [g]ch. 7.10; Ps. 37.36
19 [h]Ps. 113.7
20 [i]Ps. 37.24; 1 Thess. 5.23-24 [4]take the ungodly by the hand
21 [5]shouting for joy
22 [6]shall not be

CHAPTER 9
2 [a]Ps. 143.2; Rom. 3.20 [1]Or, before God
6 [b]Isa. 2.19-21;
8 [2]heights
9 [c]Gen. 1.16; [3]Ash, Cesil, and Cimah
11 [d]ch. 23.8
12 [e]Isa. 45.9; [4]who can turn him away?
13 [5]helpers of pride, or, strength
15 [f]ch. 10.15
17 [g]ch. 2.3;
22 [h]Eccl. 9.1-2;
24 [i]2 Sam. 15.30;
26 [6]ships of desire, or, ships of Ebeh
27 [7]Or, strengthen
28 [j]Ex. 20.7;
31 [8]Or, make me to be abhorred
32 [k]Eccl. 6.10;
33 [l]1 Sam. 2.25 [9]one that should argue [10]Or, umpire
35 [11]but I am not so with myself

CHAPTER 10
1 [1]Or, cut off while I live
3 [2]the labour of thine hands
4 [a]1 Sam. 16.7;
7 [3]it is upon thy knowledge
8 [b]Ps. 119.73; [4]took pains about me
9 [c]Gen. 2.7;
10 [d]Ps. 139.14
11 [5]hedged

14 If I sin, then thou markest me,
and thou wilt not acquit me from mine
iniquity.
15 If I be wicked, [e]woe unto me;
[f]and *if* I be righteous, *yet* will I not lift
up my head. *I am* full of confusion;
therefore [g]see thou mine affliction;
16 For it increaseth. [h]Thou huntest
me as a fierce lion: and again thou
shewest thyself marvellous upon me.
17 Thou renewest [6]thy witnesses
against me, and increasest thine indignation upon me; changes and war *are*
against me.
18 Wherefore then hast thou brought
me forth out of the womb? Oh that I had
given up the ghost, and no eye had seen
me!
19 I should have been as though I
had not been; I should have been carried from the womb to the grave.
20 *Are* not my days few? [i]cease *then,*
and [j]let me alone, that I may take comfort a little,
21 Before I go *whence* I shall not return, [k]*even* to the land of darkness
[l]and the shadow of death;
22 A land of darkness, as darkness
itself; and of the shadow of death, without any order, and *where* the light *is* as
darkness.

11 Then answered Zō'phar the Nā'-
a-math-īte, and said,
2 Should not the multitude of words
be answered? and should [1]a man full of
talk be justified?
3 Should thy [2]lies make men hold
their peace? and when thou mockest,
shall no man make thee ashamed?
4 For [a]thou hast said, My doctrine *is*
pure, and I am clean in thine eyes.
5 But oh that God would speak, and
open his lips against thee;
6 And that he would shew thee the
secrets of wisdom, that *they are* double to that which is! Know therefore
that [b]God exacteth of thee *less* than
thine iniquity *deserveth.*
7 [c]Canst thou by searching find out
God? canst thou find out the Almighty
unto perfection?
8 *It is* [3]as high as heaven; what
canst thou do? deeper than hell; what
canst thou know?
9 The measure thereof *is* longer than
the earth, and broader than the sea.
10 If he [4]cut off, and shut up, or
gather together, then [5]who can hinder
him?
11 For [d]he knoweth vain men: he
seeth wickedness also; will he not then
consider *it?*
12 For [6]vain man would be wise,
though man be born *like* a wild ass's
colt.
13 [e]If thou prepare thine heart, and
[f]stretch out thine hands toward him;
14 If iniquity *be* in thine hand, put it
far away, and let not wickedness dwell
in thy tabernacles.
15 [g]For then shalt thou lift up thy
face without spot; yea, thou shalt be
stedfast, and shalt not fear:
16 Because thou shalt forget *thy* misery, *and* remember *it* as waters *that*
pass away:
17 And *thine* age [7]shall be clearer
than the noonday; thou shalt shine
forth, thou shalt be as the morning.
18 And thou shalt be secure, because there is hope; yea, thou shalt dig
about thee, and thou shalt take thy
rest in safety.
19 Also thou shalt lie down, and
none shall make *thee* afraid; yea, many
shall [8]make suit unto thee.
20 But the eyes of the wicked shall
fail, and [9]they shall not escape, and
their hope *shall be as* [10]the giving up of
the ghost.

12 And Jōb answered and said,
2 No doubt but ye *are* the people,
and wisdom shall die with you.
3 But I have [1]understanding as well
as you; [2]I *am* not inferior to you: yea,
[3]who knoweth not such things as these?
4 I am *as* one mocked of his neighbour, who [a]calleth upon God, and he
answereth him: the just upright *man is*
laughed to scorn.
5 [b]He that is ready to slip with *his*
feet *is as* a lamp despised in the thought
of him that is at ease.
6 The tabernacles of robbers prosper, and they that provoke God are secure; into whose hand God bringeth
abundantly.
7 But ask now the beasts, and they
shall teach thee; and the fowls of the
air, and they shall tell thee:
8 Or speak to the earth, and it shall
teach thee: and the fishes of the sea
shall declare unto thee.
9 Who knoweth not in all these that
the hand of the LORD hath wrought
this?
10 [c]In whose hand *is* the [4]soul of every living thing, and the breath of [5]all
mankind.
11 Doth not the ear try words? and
the [6]mouth taste his meat?
12 With the ancient *is* wisdom; and
in length of days understanding.
13 [7]With him *is* wisdom and strength,
he hath counsel and understanding.
14 Behold, he breaketh down, and it
cannot be built again: he [d]shutteth [8]up
a man, and there can be no opening.
15 Behold, he [e]withholdeth the waters, and they dry up: also he [f]sendeth
them out, and they overturn the earth.
16 With him *is* strength and wisdom: the deceived and the deceiver *are*
his.
17 He leadeth counsellors away
spoiled, and maketh the judges fools.
18 He looseth the bond of kings, and
girdeth their loins with a girdle.
19 He leadeth princes away spoiled,
and overthroweth the mighty.
20 He removeth away [9]the speech of
the trusty, and taketh away the understanding of the aged.
21 He poureth contempt upon
princes, and [10]weakeneth the strength
of the mighty.

15 [e]Ps. 9.17; [f]ch. 9.12 [g]Ex. 3.7;
16 [h]Isa. 38.13;
17 [6]That is, thy plagues
20 [i]Ps. 39.13 [j]ch. 7.16
21 [k]ch. 3.5; [l]Ps. 23.4

CHAPTER 11
2 [1]a man of lips
3 [2]Or, devices
4 [a]ch. 6.10;
6 [b]Lam. 3.22
7 [c]ch. 5.9;
8 [3]the heights of heaven
10 [4]Or, make a change [5]who can turn him away?
11 [d]Ps. 10.11
12 [6]empty
13 [e]1 Sam. 7.3; [f]Ps. 143.6
15 [g]Gen. 4.5;
17 [7]shall arise above the noonday
19 [8]intreat thy face
20 [9]flight shall perish from them [10]Or, a puff of breath

CHAPTER 12
3 [1]an heart [2]I fall not lower than you [3]with whom are not such as these?
4 [a]ch. 16.20;
5 [b]Prov. 14.2
10 [c]Num. 16.22; [4]Or, life [5]all flesh of man
11 [6]palate
13 [7]That is, With God
14 [d]Rev. 3.7 [8]upon
15 [e]1 Ki. 17.1 [f]Gen. 7.11
20 [9]the lip of the faithful
21 [10]Or, looseth the girdle of the strong

22 [g]He discovereth deep things out
of darkness,and bringeth out to light
the shadow of death.
23 He increaseth the nations, and destroyeth them: he enlargeth the nations, and [11]straiteneth them *again*.
24 He taketh away the heart of the
chief of the people of the earth, and
causeth them to wander in a wilderness *where there is* no way.
25 They grope in the dark without
light, and he maketh them to [12]stagger
like *a* drunken *man*.

13

Lo, mine eye hath seen all *this*,
mine ear hath heard and understood it.
2 What ye know, *the same* do I
know also: I *am* not inferior unto you.
3 Surely I would speak to the Almighty, and I desire to reason with
God.
4 But ye *are* forgers of lies, ye *are* all
physicians of no value.
5 O that ye would altogether hold
your peace! and [a]it should be your
wisdom.
6 Hear now my reasoning, and hearken to the pleadings of my lips.
7 [b]Will ye speak wickedly for God?
and talk deceitfully for him?
8 Will [c]ye accept his person? will ye
contend for God?
9 Is it good that he should search
you out? or as one man mocketh another, do ye *so* mock him?
10 He will surely reprove you, if ye
do secretly accept persons.
11 Shall not his [1]excellency make
you afraid? and his dread fall upon
you?
12 Your remembrances *are* like unto
ashes, your bodies to bodies of clay.
13 [2]Hold your peace, let me alone,
that I may speak, and let come on me
what *will*.
14 Wherefore do I take my flesh in
my teeth, and [d]put my life in mine
hand?
15 [e]Though he slay me, yet will I
trust in him: [f]but I will [3]maintain mine
own ways before him.
16 He also *shall be* my [g]salvation:
for an hypocrite shall not come before
him.
17 Hear diligently my speech, and
my declaration with your ears.
18 Behold now, I have ordered *my*
cause; I know that I shall be justified.
19 [h]Who *is* he *that* will plead with
me? for now, if I hold my tongue, I
shall give up the ghost.
20 Only do not two *things* unto me:
then will I not hide myself from thee.
21 Withdraw thine hand far from
me: and let not thy dread make me
afraid.
22 Then call thou, and I will answer:
or let me speak, and answer thou me.
23 How many *are* mine iniquities
and sins? make me to know my transgression and my sin.
24 [i]Wherefore hidest thou thy face,
and [j]holdest me for thine enemy?
25 [k]Wilt thou break a leaf driven to
and fro? and wilt thou pursue the dry
stubble?
26 For thou writest bitter things
against me, and [l]makest me to possess
the iniquities of my youth.
27 [m]Thou puttest my feet also in the
stocks, and [4]lookest narrowly unto all
my paths; thou settest a print upon the
[5]heels of my feet.
28 And he, as a rotten thing, consumeth, as a garment that is moth
eaten.

14

Man *that is* born of a woman *is*
[1]of few days, and [a]full of trouble.
2 [b]He cometh forth like a flower,
and is cut down: he fleeth also as a
shadow, and continueth not.
3 And [c]dost thou open thine eyes
upon such an one, and [d]bringest me
into judgment with thee?
4 [2]Who [e]can bring a clean *thing* out
of an unclean? not one.
5 Seeing his days *are* determined,
the number of his months *are* with
thee, thou hast appointed his bounds
that he cannot pass:
6 [f]Turn from him, that he may [3]rest,
till he shall accomplish, as an hireling,
his day.
7 For there is hope of a tree, if it be
cut down, that it will sprout again, and
that the tender branch thereof will not
cease.
8 Though the root thereof wax old
in the earth, and the stock thereof die
in the ground;
9 *Yet* through the scent of water it
will bud, and bring forth boughs like a
plant.
10 But man dieth, and [4]wasteth
away: yea, man giveth up the ghost,
and where *is* he?
11 *As* the waters fail from the sea,
and the flood decayeth and drieth up:
12 So man lieth down, and riseth
not: [g]till the heavens *be* no more, they
shall not awake, nor be raised out of
their sleep.
13 O that thou wouldest hide me in
the grave, that thou wouldest keep me
secret, until thy wrath be past, that
thou wouldest appoint me a set time,
and remember me!
14 If a man die, shall he live *again*?
all the days of my appointed time [h]will
I wait, till [i]my change come.
15 [j]Thou shalt call, and I will answer thee: thou wilt have a desire to
the work of thine hands.
16 [k]For now thou numberest my
steps: dost thou not watch over my
sin?
17 My transgression *is* sealed up in a
bag, and thou sewest up mine iniquity.
18 And surely the mountain falling
[5]cometh to nought, and the rock is removed out of his place.
19 The waters wear the stones: thou
[6]washest away the things which grow
out of the dust of the earth; and thou
destroyest the hope of man.
20 Thou prevailest for ever against
him, and he passeth: thou changest his
countenance, and sendest him away.

22 [g]Matt. 10.26; 1 Cor. 4.5
23 [11]leadeth in
25 [12]wander
CHAPTER 13
5 [a]Prov. 17.28; Jas. 1.19
7 [b]ch. 17.5; Rom. 3.5-8
8 [c]Prov. 24.23
11 [1]Or, height of greatness
13 [2]Be silent from me
14 [d]Ps. 119.109
15 [e]Ps. 23.4; Rom. 8.38-39
[f]ch. 27.5
[3]prove, or, argue
16 [g]Isa. 12.1-2
19 [h]ch. 33.6;
24 [i]Ps. 10.1;
[j]Lam. 2.5;
25 [k]Isa. 17.13;
26 [l]Ps. 25.7
27 [m]ch. 33.11
[4]observest
[5]roots
CHAPTER 14
1 [1]short of days
[a]ch. 15.14;
2 [b]Isa. 40.6;
3 [c]Ps. 144.3
[d]Ps. 143.2
4 [2]Who will give
[e]Gen. 5.3;
6 [f]Ps. 39.13
[3]cease
10 [4]is weakened, or, cut off
12 [g]Ps. 102.26;
14 [h]ch. 13.15
[i]Ps. 16.10;
15 [j]ch. 13.22;
16 [k]Deut. 32.34;
18 [5]fadeth
19 [6]overflowest

21 His sons come to honour, and [l]he
knoweth *it* not; and they are brought
low, but he perceiveth *it* not of them.
22 [m]But his flesh upon him shall
have pain, and [n]his soul within him
shall mourn.

15 Then answered Ĕl′ĭ-phăz the Tē′-
man-īte, and said,
2 Should a wise man utter [1]vain
knowledge, and fill his belly with the
east wind?
3 Should he reason with unprofitable talk? or with speeches wherewith
he can do no good?
4 Yea, [2]thou castest off fear, and re-
strainest [3]prayer before God.
5 For thy mouth [4]uttereth thine iniquity, and thou choosest the tongue of
the crafty.
6 Thine own mouth condemneth
thee, and not I; yea, thine own lips testify against thee.
7 *Art* thou the first man *that* was
born? [a]or wast thou made before the
hills?
8 [b]Hast thou heard the secret of
God? and dost thou restrain wisdom to
thyself?
9 [c]What knowest thou, that we know
not? *what* understandest thou, which *is*
not in us?
10 [d]With us *are* both the grayheaded
and very aged men, much elder than
thy father.
11 *Are* the consolations of God small
with thee? is there any secret thing
with thee?
12 Why doth thine heart carry thee
away? and what do thy eyes wink at,
13 That thou turnest thy spirit against
God, and lettest *such* words go out of
thy mouth?
14 [e]What *is* man, that he should
be clean? and *he which is* born of a
woman, that he should be righteous?
15 [f]Behold, he putteth no trust in his
saints; yea, the heavens are not clean
in his sight.
16 [g]How much more abominable
and filthy *is* man, [h]which drinketh iniquity like water?
17 I will shew thee, hear me; and
that *which* I have seen I will declare:
18 Which wise men have told [i]from
their fathers, and have not hid *it:*
19 Unto whom alone the earth was
given, and [j]no stranger passed among
them.
20 The wicked man travaileth with
pain all *his* days, [k]and the number of
years is hidden to the oppressor.
21 A [5]dreadful sound *is* in his ears:
[l]in prosperity the destroyer shall come
upon him.
22 He believeth not that he shall return out of darkness, and he is waited
for of the sword.
23 He [m]wandereth abroad for bread,
saying, Where *is it?* he knoweth that
[n]the day of darkness is ready at his
hand.
24 Trouble and anguish shall make
him afraid; they shall prevail against
him, as a king ready to the battle.

21 [l]1 Sam. 4.20; Ps. 39.6; Eccl. 9.5; Isa. 63.16
22 [m]Ps. 49.14 [n]Prov. 14.32; Matt. 8.12

CHAPTER 15

2 [1]knowledge of wind
4 [2]thou makest void [3]Or, speech
5 [4]teacheth
7 [a]Prov. 8.25
8 [b]Matt. 11.25; Rom. 11.34; 1 Cor. 2.11
9 [c]ch. 13.2
10 [d]Deut. 32.7; ch. 8.8-10; Prov. 16.31
14 [e]ch. 14.4; Ps. 14.3; Prov. 20.9; Eccl. 7.20; Rom. 7.18; Eph. 2.2-3
15 [f]ch. 25.5
16 [g]Ps. 14.3 [h]Prov. 19.28
18 [i]Gen. 18.19
19 [j]Joel 3.17
20 [k]Ps. 90.12
21 [5]a sound of fears [l]1 Thess. 5.3
23 [m]Ps. 59.15 [n]ch. 18.12
25 [o]Mal. 3.13
27 [p]Ps. 17.10
30 [q]ch. 4.9; Isa. 11.4; Rev. 19.15
31 [r]Ps. 62.10; Isa. 59.4
32 [6]Or, cut off [s]ch. 22.16; Ps. 55.23
34 [t]Isa. 33.14
35 [u]Ps. 7.14; Isa. 59.4 [7]Or, iniquity

CHAPTER 16

2 [1]Or, troublesome
3 [2]words of wind
4 [a]2 Ki. 19.21; Ps. 22.7; Jer. 18.16; Lam. 2.15
6 [3]what goeth from me?
10 [b]Ps. 22.13 [c]1 Ki. 22.24; Lam. 3.30; Acts 23.2 [d]Ps. 35.15
11 [4]hath shut me up

25 [o]For he stretcheth out his hand
against God, and strengtheneth himself against the Almighty.
26 He runneth upon him, *even* on
his neck, upon the thick bosses of his
bucklers:
27 [p]Because he covereth his face
with his fatness, and maketh collops of
fat on *his* flanks.
28 And he dwelleth in desolate cities, *and* in houses which no man inhabiteth, which are ready to become
heaps.
29 He shall not be rich, neither shall
his substance continue, neither shall
he prolong the perfection thereof upon
the earth.
30 He shall not depart out of darkness; the flame shall dry up his
branches, and [q]by the breath of his
mouth shall he go away.
31 Let not him that is deceived trust
[r]in vanity: for vanity shall be his
recompence.
32 It shall be [6]accomplished [s]before
his time, and his branch shall not be
green.
33 He shall shake off his unripe
grape as the vine, and shall cast off his
flower as the olive.
34 [t]For the congregation of hypocrites *shall be* desolate, and fire shall
consume the tabernacles of bribery.
35 [u]They conceive mischief, and
bring forth [7]vanity, and their belly prepareth deceit.

16 Then Jōb answered and said,
2 I have heard many such things:
[1]miserable comforters *are* ye all.
3 Shall [2]vain words have an end?
or what emboldeneth thee that thou
answerest?
4 I also could speak as ye *do*: if your
soul were in my soul's stead, I could
heap up words against you, and [a]shake
mine head at you.
5 *But* I would strengthen you with
my mouth, and the moving of my lips
should asswage *your grief*.
6 Though I speak, my grief is not
asswaged: and *though* I forbear, [3]what
am I eased?
7 But now he hath made me weary:
thou hast made desolate all my company.
8 And thou hast filled me with wrin-
kles, *which* is a witness *against me:*
and my leanness rising up in me beareth witness to my face.
9 He teareth *me* in his wrath, who
hateth me: he gnasheth upon me with
his teeth; mine enemy sharpeneth his
eyes upon me.
10 They have [b]gaped upon me with
their mouth; they [c]have smitten me
upon the cheek reproachfully; they
have [d]gathered themselves together
against me.
11 God [4]hath delivered me to the ungodly, and turned me over into the
hands of the wicked.
12 I was at ease, but he hath broken
me asunder: he hath also taken *me* by

my neck, and shaken me to pieces, and
set me up for his mark.
13 His archers compass me round
about, he cleaveth my reins asunder,
and doth not spare; he poureth out my
gall upon the ground.
14 He breaketh me with breach upon
breach, he runneth upon me like a
giant.
15 I have sewed sackcloth upon my
skin, and [e]defiled my horn in the dust.
16 My face is foul with weeping, and
on my eyelids *is* the shadow of death;
17 Not for *any* injustice in mine
hands: also my prayer *is* pure.
18 O earth, cover not thou my blood,
and [f]let my cry have no place.
19 Also now, behold, [g]my witness *is*
in heaven, and my record *is* [5]on high.
20 My friends [6]scorn me: *but* mine
eye poureth out *tears* unto God.
21 [h]O that one might plead for a
man with God, as a man *pleadeth* for
his [7]neighbour!
22 When [8]a few years are come,
then I shall [i]go the way *whence* I shall
not return.

17 My [1]breath is corrupt, my days
are extinct, [a]the graves *are ready*
for me.
2 *Are there* not mockers with me?
and doth not mine eye [2]continue in
their [b]provocation?
3 Lay down now, put me in a surety
with thee; who *is* he *that* [c]will strike
hands with me?
4 For thou hast hid their heart from
understanding: therefore shalt thou not
exalt *them*.
5 He that speaketh flattery to *his*
friends, even the eyes of his children
shall fail.
6 He hath made me also [d]a byword
of the people; and [3]aforetime I was as a
tabret.
7 Mine eye also is dim by reason of
sorrow, and all [4]my members *are* as a
shadow.
8 Upright *men* shall be astonied at
this, and the innocent shall stir up himself against the hypocrite.
9 [e]The righteous also shall hold on
his way, and he that hath [f]clean hands
[5]shall be stronger and stronger.
10 But as for you all, [g]do ye return,
and come now: for I cannot find *one*
wise *man* among you.
11 [h]My days are past, my purposes
are broken off, *even* [6]the thoughts of
my heart.
12 They change the night into day:
the light *is* [7]short because of darkness.
13 If I wait, the grave *is* mine house:
I have made my bed in the darkness.
14 I have [8]said to corruption, Thou
art my father: to the worm, *Thou art*
my mother, and my sister.
15 And where *is* now my hope? as
for my hope, who shall see it?
16 [i]They shall go down [j]to the bars
of the pit, when *our* [k]rest together *is* in
the dust.

18 Then answered Bĭl′dăd the Shụ′-
hīte, and said,

15 [e]Ps. 7.5
18 [f]ch. 27.9
19 [g]Rom. 1.9
[5]in the high places
20 [6]are my scorners
21 [h]ch. 31.35
[7]Or, friend
22 [8]years of number
[i]Eccl. 12.5

CHAPTER 17
1 [1]Or, spirit is spent
[a]Ps. 88.3-4
2 [2]lodge
[b]1 Sam. 1.6
3 [c]Prov. 6.1
6 [d]1 Ki. 9.7; ch. 30.9
[3]Or, before them
7 [4]Or, my thoughts
9 [e]Prov. 4.18
[f]Ps. 24.4
[5]shall add strength
10 [g]ch. 6.29
11 [h]ch. 7.6; Isa. 38.10
[6]the possessions
12 [7]near
14 [8]cried, or, called
16 [i]2 Cor. 1.9
[j]Ps. 88.4-8
[k]ch. 3.17

CHAPTER 18
3 [a]ch. 12.7;
4 [b]ch. 13.14
[1]his soul
5 [2]Nevertheless
[c]Prov. 13.9
6 [3]Or, lamp
10 [4]hidden
11 [d]ch. 6.4;
[5]scatter him
12 [e]ch. 15.23;
13 [6]bars
14 [f]ch. 8.14;
15 [g]Gen. 19.24
17 [h]Ps. 34.16;
18 [7]They shall drive him
19 [i]Isa. 14.22;
20 [8]Or, lived with him
[9]laid hold on horror
21 [j]Jer. 9.3;

CHAPTER 19
2 [a]1 Sam. 1.6;
3 [1]Or, harden yourselves against me
4 [b]Ps. 19.12;
5 [c]Ps. 38.16;
6 [d]Lam. 1.13

2 How long *will it be ere* ye make an
end of words? mark, and afterwards
we will speak.
3 Wherefore are we counted [a]as
beasts, *and* reputed vile in your sight?
4 [b]He teareth [1]himself in his anger:
shall the earth be forsaken for thee?
and shall the rock be removed out of
his place?
5 [2]Yea, [c]the light of the wicked shall
be put out, and the spark of his fire
shall not shine.
6 The light shall be dark in his tabernacle, and his [3]candle shall be put out
with him.
7 The steps of his strength shall be
straitened, and his own counsel shall
cast him down.
8 For he is cast into a net by his own
feet, and he walketh upon a snare.
9 The gin shall take *him* by the heel,
and the robber shall prevail against
him.
10 The snare *is* [4]laid for him in the
ground, and a trap for him in the way.
11 [d]Terrors shall make him afraid
on every side, and shall [5]drive him to
his feet.
12 His strength shall be hungerbit-
ten, and [e]destruction *shall be* ready at
his side.
13 It shall devour the [6]strength of
his skin: *even* the firstborn of death
shall devour his strength.
14 [f]His confidence shall be rooted
out of his tabernacle, and it shall bring
him to the king of terrors.
15 It shall dwell in his tabernacle,
because *it is* none of his: [g]brimstone
shall be scattered upon his habitation.
16 His roots shall be dried up beneath, and above shall his branch be
cut off.
17 [h]His remembrance shall perish
from the earth, and he shall have no
name in the street.
18 [7]He shall be driven from light
into darkness, and chased out of the
world.
19 [i]He shall neither have son nor
nephew among his people, nor any remaining in his dwellings.
20 They that come after *him* shall be
astonied at his day, as they that [8]went
before [9]were affrighted.
21 Surely such *are* the dwellings of
the wicked, and this *is* the place *of him
that* [j]knoweth not God.

19 Then Jōb answered and said,
2 How long will ye [a]vex my soul,
and break me in pieces with words?
3 These ten times have ye reproached
me: ye are not ashamed *that* ye [1]make
yourselves strange to me.
4 And be it indeed *that* I have erred,
[b]mine error remaineth with myself.
5 If indeed ye will [c]magnify *yourselves* against me, and plead against
me my reproach:
6 Know now that [d]God hath overthrown me, and hath compassed me
with his net.

7 Behold, I cry out of [2]wrong, but I
am not heard: I cry aloud, but *there is*
no judgment.
8 [e]He hath fenced up my way that I
cannot pass, and he hath set darkness
in my paths.
9 He hath stripped me of my glory,
and taken the crown *from* my head.
10 He hath destroyed me on every
side, and I am gone: and mine hope
hath he removed like a tree.
11 He hath also [f]kindled his wrath
against me, and he counteth me unto
him as *one of* his enemies.
12 [g]His troops come together, and
raise up their way against me, and encamp round about my tabernacle.
13 [h]He hath put my brethren far
from me, and mine acquaintance are
verily estranged from me.
14 My kinsfolk have failed, and my
familiar friends have forgotten me.
15 They that dwell in mine house,
and my maids, count me for a stranger:
I am an alien in their sight.
16 I called my servant, and he gave
me no answer; I intreated him with my
mouth.
17 My breath is strange to my wife,
though I intreated for the children's
sake of [3]mine own body.
18 Yea, [4]young children despised
me; I arose, and they spake against
me.
19 All [5]my inward friends abhorred
me: and they whom I loved are turned
against me.
20 My bone cleaveth to my skin
[6]and to my flesh, and I am escaped
with the skin of my teeth.
21 Have pity upon me, have pity
upon me, O ye my friends; for the hand
of God hath touched me.
22 Why do ye persecute me as God,
and are not satisfied with my flesh?
23 [7]Oh that my words were now written! oh that they were printed in a
book!
24 That they were graven with an
iron pen and lead in the rock for ever!
25 For I know *that* my redeemer
liveth, and *that* he shall stand at the
latter *day* upon the earth:
26 [8]And *though* after my skin *worms*
destroy this *body*, yet in my flesh shall I
see God:
27 Whom I shall see for myself, and
mine eyes shall behold, and not [9]an-
other; [10]*though* my reins be consumed
[11]within me.
28 But ye should say, Why persecute we him, [12]seeing the root of the
matter is found in me?
29 Be ye afraid of the sword: for
wrath *bringeth* the punishments of the
sword, that ye may know *there is* a
judgment.

20

Then answered Zō'phar the Nā'-
a-math-īte, and said,
2 Therefore do my thoughts cause
me to answer, and for *this* [1]I make
haste.
3 I have heard the check of my reproach, and the spirit of my understanding causeth me to answer.
4 Knowest thou *not* this of old, since
man was placed upon earth,
5 [a]That the triumphing of the wicked
is [2]short, and the joy of the hypocrite
but for a moment?
6 Though his excellency mount up
to the heavens, and his head reach
unto the [3]clouds;
7 *Yet* he shall perish for ever like
his own dung: they which have seen
him shall say, Where *is* he?
8 He shall fly away as a dream, and
shall not be found: yea, he shall be
chased away as a vision of the night.
9 The eye also *which* saw him shall
see him no more; neither shall his
place any more behold him.
10 [4]His children shall seek to please
the poor, and his hands shall restore
their goods.
11 His bones are full *of the sin* of his
youth, which shall lie down with him
in the dust.
12 Though wickedness be sweet in
his mouth, *though* he hide it under his
tongue;
13 *Though* he spare it, and forsake it
not; but keep it still [5]within his mouth:
14 *Yet* his [b]meat in his bowels is
turned, *it is* the gall of asps within him.
15 He hath [c]swallowed down riches,
and he shall vomit them up again: God
shall cast them out of his belly.
16 He shall suck the poison of asps:
the viper's tongue shall slay him.
17 He shall not see [d]the rivers, [6]the
floods, the brooks of honey and butter.
18 That which he laboured for shall
he restore, and shall not swallow *it*
down: [7]according to *his* substance *shall*
the restitution *be*, and he shall not rejoice *therein*.
19 Because he hath [8]oppressed *and*
hath forsaken the poor; *because* he
hath violently taken away an house
which he builded not;
20 [e]Surely he shall not [9]feel quietness in his belly, he shall not save of
that which he desired.
21 [10]There shall none of his meat be
left; therefore shall no man look for his
goods.
22 In the fulness of his sufficiency
he shall be in straits: every hand of the
[11]wicked shall come upon him.
23 *When* he is about to fill his belly,
God shall cast the fury of his wrath
upon him, and shall rain *it* upon him
[f]while he is eating.
24 [g]He shall flee from the iron
weapon, *and* the bow of steel shall
strike him through.
25 It is drawn, and cometh out of the
body; yea, the glittering sword cometh
out of his gall: [h]terrors *are* upon him.
26 All darkness *shall be* hid in his
secret places: [i]a fire not blown shall
consume him; it shall go ill with him
that is left in his tabernacle.
27 The heaven [j]shall reveal his iniquity; and the earth shall rise up against
him.
28 The increase of his house shall
depart, *and his goods* shall flow away
in the day of his wrath.

7 [2]Or, violence
8 [e]Lam. 3.7-8
11 [f]Deut. 32.22
12 [g]Ps. 34.19
13 [h]Ps. 31.11; 2 Tim. 4.16
17 [3]my belly
18 [4]Or, the wicked
19 [5]the men of my secret
20 [6]Or, as
23 [7]Who will give, etc
26 [8]Or, After I shall awake, though this body be destroyed, yet out of my flesh shall I see God
27 [9]a stranger [10]Or, my reins within me are consumed with earnest desire for that day. [11]in my bosom
28 [12]Or, and what root of matter is found in me.

CHAPTER 20

2 [1]my haste is in me
5 [a]Ps. 37.35 [2]from near
6 [3]cloud
10 [4]Or, The poor shall oppress his children
13 [5]in the midst of his palate
14 [b]Jer. 4.19
15 [c]Matt. 27.3-4
17 [d]Jer. 17.6 [6]Or, streaming brooks
18 [7]according to the substance of his exchange
19 [8]crushed
20 [e]Eccl. 5.13 [9]know
21 [10]Or, There shall be none left for his meat
22 [11]Or, troublesome
23 [f]Num. 11.33;
24 [g]Isa. 24.18;
25 [h]ch. 18.11;
26 [i]Ps. 21.9
27 [j]Isa. 26.21

29 [k]This *is* the portion of a wicked man from God, and the heritage [12]appointed unto him by God.

21

But Jōb answered and said,

2 Hear diligently my speech, and let this be your consolations.

3 Suffer me that I may speak; and after that I have spoken, mock on.

4 As for me, *is* my complaint to man? and if *it were so,* why should not my spirit be [1]troubled?

5 [2]Mark me, and be astonished, and lay *your* hand upon *your* mouth.

6 Even when I remember I am afraid, and trembling taketh hold on my flesh.

7 Wherefore do the wicked live, become old, yea, are mighty in power?

8 Their seed is established in their sight with them, and their offspring before their eyes.

9 Their houses [3]*are* safe from fear, neither *is* the rod of God upon them.

10 Their bull gendereth, and faileth not; their cow calveth, and casteth not her calf.

11 They send forth their little ones like a flock, and their children dance.

12 They take the timbrel and harp, and rejoice at the sound of the organ.

13 They spend their days [4]in wealth, and in a moment go down to the grave.

14 Therefore they say unto God, Depart from us; for we desire not the knowledge of thy ways.

15 What *is* the Almighty, that we should serve him? and what profit should we have, if we pray unto him?

16 Lo, their good *is* not in their hand: the counsel of the wicked is far from me.

17 How oft is the [5]candle of the wicked put out! and *how oft* cometh their destruction upon them! *God* distributeth sorrows in his anger.

18 They are as stubble before the wind, and as chaff that the storm [6]carrieth away.

19 God layeth up [7]his iniquity for his children: he rewardeth him, and he shall know *it.*

20 His eyes shall see his destruction, and he shall drink of the wrath of the Almighty.

21 For what pleasure *hath* he in his house after him, when the number of his months is cut off in the midst?

22 Shall *any* teach God knowledge? seeing he judgeth those that are high.

23 One dieth [8]in his full strength, being wholly at ease and quiet.

24 His [9]breasts are full of milk, and his bones are moistened with marrow.

25 And another dieth in the bitterness of his soul, and never eateth with pleasure.

26 They shall lie down alike in the dust, and the worms shall cover them.

27 Behold, I know your thoughts, and the devices *which* ye wrongfully imagine against me.

28 For ye say, Where *is* the house of the prince? and where *are* [10]the dwelling places of the wicked?

29 Have ye not asked them that go by the way? and do ye not know their tokens,

30 That the wicked is reserved to the day of destruction? they shall be brought forth to [11]the day of wrath.

31 Who shall declare his way to his face? and who shall repay him *what* he hath done?

32 Yet shall he be brought to the [12]grave, and shall [13]remain in the tomb.

33 The clods of the valley shall be sweet unto him, and every man shall draw after him, as *there are* innumerable before him.

34 How then comfort ye me in vain, seeing in your answers there remaineth [14]falsehood?

22

Then Ĕl'ĭ-phăz the Tē'man-īte answered and said,

2 [a]Can a man be profitable unto God, [1]as he that is wise may be profitable unto himself?

3 *Is it* any pleasure to the Almighty, that thou are righteous? or *is it* gain *to him,* that thou makest thy ways perfect?

4 Will he reprove thee for fear of thee? will he enter with thee into judgment?

5 *Is* not thy wickedness great? and thine iniquities infinite?

6 For thou hast taken a pledge from thy brother for nought, and [2]stripped the naked of their clothing.

7 Thou hast not given water to the weary to drink, and thou [b]hast withholden bread from the hungry.

8 But *as for* [3]the mighty man, he had the earth; and the [4]honourable man dwelt in it.

9 Thou hast sent widows away empty, and the arms of the fatherless have been broken.

10 Therefore snares *are* round about thee, and sudden fear troubleth thee;

11 Or darkness, *that* thou canst not see; and abundance of waters cover thee.

12 [c]*Is* not God in the height of heaven? and behold [5]the height of the stars, how high they are!

13 And thou sayest, [6]How doth God know? can he judge through the dark cloud?

14 [d]Thick clouds *are* a covering to him, that he seeth not; and he walketh in the circuit of heaven.

15 Hast thou marked [e]the old way which wicked men have trodden?

16 Which were cut down out of time, [7]whose foundation was overflown with a flood:

17 Which said unto God, Depart from us: and what can the Almighty do [8]for them?

18 Yet he filled [f]their houses with good *things:* but the counsel of the wicked is far from me.

19 [g]The righteous see *it,* and are glad: and the innocent laugh them to scorn.

20 Whereas our [9]substance is not cut down, but [10]the remnant of them the fire consumeth.

29 [k]Deut. 29.20-28; [12]of his decree from God

CHAPTER 21
[1]shortened?
5 [2]Look unto me
9 [3]are peace from fear
13 [4]Or, in mirth
17 [5]Or, lamp
18 [6]stealeth away
19 [7]That is, the punishment of his iniquity
23 [8]in his very perfection, or, in the strength of his perfection
24 [9]Or, milk pails
28 [10]the tent of the tabernacles of the wicked
[11]the day of wraths
32 [12]graves
[13]watch in the heap
34 [14]transgression?

CHAPTER 22
2 [a]Ps. 16.2
[1]Or, if he may be profitable, doth his good success depend thereon?
6 [2]stripped the clothes of the naked
7 [b]ch. 31.16-17
8 [3]the man of arm
[4]eminent, or, accepted for countenance
12 [c]Isa. 66.1
[5]the head of the stars
13 [6]Or, What
14 [d]Ps. 139.12
15 [e]Gen. 6.11-13
16 [7]a flood was poured upon their foundation
17 [8]Or, to them?
18 [f]Ps. 17.13-14
19 [g]Ps. 107.42
20 [9]Or, estate
[10]Or, their excellency

21 Acquaint now thyself [11]with him,
and [h]be at peace: thereby good shall
come unto thee.
22 Receive, I pray thee, the law from
his mouth, and [i]lay up his words in
thine heart.
23 If thou return to the Almighty,
thou shalt be built up, thou shalt put
away iniquity far from thy tabernacles.
24 Then shalt thou lay up gold [12]as
dust, and the *gold* of Ō'phĭr as the
stones of the brooks.
25 Yea, the Almighty shall be thy
[13]defence, and thou shalt have [14]plenty
of silver.
26 For then shalt thou have thy delight in the Almighty, and shalt lift up
thy face unto God.
27 Thou shalt make thy prayer unto
him, and he shall hear thee, and thou
shalt pay thy vows.
28 [j]Thou shalt also decree a thing,
and it shall be established unto thee:
and the light shall shine upon thy
ways.
29 When *men* are cast down, then
thou shalt say, *There is* lifting up; and
he shall save [15]the humble person.
30 [16]He shall deliver the island of
the innocent: and it is delivered by the
pureness of thine hands.

23

Then Jōb answered and said,
2 Even to day *is* my complaint bitter: [1]my stroke is heavier than my
groaning.
3 Oh that I knew where I might find
him! *that* I might come *even* to his
seat!
4 I would order *my* cause before him,
and fill my mouth with arguments.
5 I would know the words *which*
he would answer me, and understand
what he would say unto me.
6 [a]Will he plead against me with *his*
great power? No; but he would put
strength in me.
7 There the righteous might dispute
with him; so should I be delivered for
ever from my judge.
8 [b]Behold, I go forward, but he *is*
not *there:* and backward, but I cannot
perceive him:
9 On the left hand, where he doth
work, but I cannot behold *him*: he
hideth himself on the right hand, that I
cannot see *him:*
10 But he knoweth [2]the way that I
take: *when* [c]he hath tried me, I shall
come forth as gold.
11 [d]My foot hath held his steps, his
way have I kept, and not declined.
12 Neither have I gone back from
the commandment of his lips; [3]I have
esteemed the words of his mouth more
than [4]my necessary *food.*
13 But he *is* in one *mind,* and [e]who
can turn him? and *what* his soul desireth, even *that* he doeth.
14 For he performeth *the thing that*
is [f]appointed for me: and many such
things are with him.
15 Therefore am I [g]troubled at his
presence: when I consider, I am afraid
of him.

21 [11]That is, with God
[h]Isa. 27.5
22 [i]Ps. 119.11; Jer. 15.16
24 [12]Or, on the dust
25 [13]Or, gold [14]silver of strength
28 [j]Prov. 16.3
29 [15]him that hath low eyes
30 [16]Or, The innocent shall deliver the island

CHAPTER 23
2 [1]my hand
6 [a]ch. 9.19; Isa. 27.4
8 [b]Ps. 10.1; 1 Tim. 6.16
10 [2]the way that is with me
[c]Ps. 17.3; Jas. 1.12
11 [d]Ps. 44.18
12 [3]I have hid, or, laid up
[4]Or, my appointed portion
13 [e]ch. 34.29; Eccl. 3.14; Rom. 9.19; Jas. 1.17
14 [f]1 Thess. 3.3
15 [g]Ps. 119.120
17 [h]ch. 6.9

CHAPTER 24
1 [a]Acts 1.7
2 [b]Deut. 19.14
[1]Or, feed them
3 [c]Deut. 24.6-10-12-17
4 [d]Prov. 28.28
6 [2]mingled corn, or, dredge
[3]the wicked gather the vintage
7 [e]Ex. 22.26; Deut. 24.12; Isa. 58.7
8 [f]Lam. 4.5
12 [g]Eccl. 8.11
15 [4]setteth his face in secret
16 [h]John 3.20
19 [5]violently take
20 [i]Prov. 10.7

16 For God maketh my heart soft
and the Almighty troubleth me:
17 Because I was not [h]cut off before
the darkness, *neither* hath he covered
the darkness from my face.

24

Why, seeing [a]times are not hidden from the Almighty, do they
that know him not see his days?
2 *Some* remove the [b]landmarks; they
violently take away flocks, and [1]feed
thereof.
3 They drive away the ass of the fatherless, they [c]take the widow's ox for
a pledge.
4 They turn the needy out of the
way: [d]the poor of the earth hide themselves together.
5 Behold, *as* wild asses in the desert, go they forth to their work; rising betimes for a prey: the wilderness
yieldeth food for them *and* for *their*
children.
6 They reap *every one* his [2]corn in
the field: and [3]they gather the vintage
of the wicked.
7 They [e]cause the naked to lodge
without clothing, that *they have* no covering in the cold.
8 They are wet with the showers of
the mountains, and [f]embrace the rock
for want of a shelter.
9 They pluck the fatherless from the
breast, and take a pledge of the poor.
10 They cause *him* to go naked without clothing, and they take away the
sheaf *from* the hungry;
11 *Which* make oil within their walls,
and tread *their* winepresses, and suffer
thirst.
12 Men groan from out of the city,
and the soul of the wounded crieth out:
[g]yet God layeth not folly *to them.*
13 They are of those that rebel
against the light; they know not the
ways thereof, nor abide in the paths
thereof.
14 The murderer rising with the light
killeth the poor and needy, and in the
night is as a thief.
15 The eye also of the adulterer waiteth for the twilight, saying, No eye
shall see me: and [4]disguiseth *his* face.
16 In the dark they dig through
houses, *which* they had marked for
themselves in the daytime: [h]they know
not the light.
17 For the morning *is* to them even
as the shadow of death: if *one* know
them, they are in the terrors of the
shadow of death.
18 He *is* swift as the waters; their
portion is cursed in the earth: he beholdeth not the way of the vineyards.
19 Drought and heat [5]consume the
snow waters: *so doth* the grave *those*
which have sinned.
20 The womb shall forget him; the
worm shall feed sweetly on him; [i]he
shall be no more remembered; and
wickedness shall be broken as a tree.
21 He evil entreateth the barren *that*
beareth not: and doeth not good to the
widow.
22 He draweth also the mighty with

his power: he riseth up, [6]and no *man* is
sure of life.
23 *Though* it be given him *to be* in
safety, whereon he resteth; yet [7]his
eyes *are* upon their ways.
24 They are exalted [i]for a little while,
but [8]are gone and brought low, they are
[9]taken out of the way as all *other,* and
cut off as the tops of the ears of corn.
25 And if *it be* not *so* now, who will
make me a liar, and make my speech
nothing worth?

25 Then answered Bĭl'dăd the Shụ'-
hīte, and said,
2 Dominion and fear *are* with him,
he maketh peace in his high places.
3 Is there any number of his armies?
and upon whom doth not [a]his light
arise?
4 [b]How then can man be justified
with God? or how can he be clean *that*
is born of a woman?
5 Behold even to the moon, and it
shineth not; yea, the stars are not pure
in his sight.
6 How much less man, *that is* [c]a
worm? and the son of man, *which is* a
worm?

26 But Jōb answered and said,
2 How hast thou [a]helped *him that is*
without power? *how* savest thou the
arm *that hath* no strength?
3 How hast thou [b]counselled *him*
that hath no wisdom? and *how* hast
thou plentifully declared the thing as it
is?
4 To whom hast thou uttered words?
and whose spirit came from thee?
5 Dead *things* are formed from under the waters, [1]and the inhabitants
thereof.
6 [c]Hell *is* naked before him, and destruction hath no covering.
7 [d]He stretcheth out the north over
the empty place, *and* hangeth the earth
upon nothing.
8 [e]He bindeth up the waters in his
thick clouds; and the cloud is not rent
under them.
9 He holdeth back the face of his
throne, *and* spreadeth his cloud upon it.
10 [f]He hath compassed the waters
with bounds, [2]until the day and night
come to an end.
11 The pillars of heaven tremble and
are astonished at his reproof.
12 [g]He divideth the sea with his
power, and by his understanding he
smiteth through [3]the proud.
13 [h]By his spirit he hath garnished
the heavens; his hand hath formed the
crooked serpent.
14 Lo, these *are* parts of his ways:
but how little a portion is heard of
him? but the thunder of his power who
can understand?

27 Moreover Jōb [1]continued his parable, and said,
2 *As* God liveth, [a]*who* hath taken
away my judgment; and the Almighty,
who hath [2]vexed my soul;
3 All the while my breath *is* in me,
and [3]the spirit of God *is* in my nostrils;
4 My lips shall not speak wickedness, nor my tongue utter deceit.
5 God forbid that I should justify
you: till I die [b]I will not remove mine
integrity from me.
6 My righteousness I [c]hold fast, and
will not let it go: [d]my heart shall not
reproach *me* [4]so long as I live.
7 Let mine enemy be as the wicked,
and he that riseth up against me as the
unrighteous.
8 [e]For what *is* the hope of the hypocrite, though he hath gained, when
God taketh away his soul?
9 [f]Will God hear his cry when trouble cometh upon him?
10 [g]Will he delight himself in the Almighty? will he always call upon God?
11 I will teach you [5]by the hand of
God: *that* which *is* with the Almighty
will I not conceal.
12 Behold, all ye yourselves have
seen *it;* why then are ye thus altogether vain?
13 This *is* the portion of a wicked
man with God, and the heritage of oppressors, *which* they shall receive of
the Almighty.
14 [h]If his children be multiplied, *it is*
for the sword: and his offspring shall
not be satisfied with bread.
15 Those that remain of him shall be
buried in death: and [i]his widows shall
not weep.
16 Though he heap up silver as the
dust, and prepare raiment as the clay;
17 He may prepare *it,* but [j]the just
shall put *it* on, and the innocent shall
divide the silver.
18 He buildeth his house as a moth,
and [k]as a booth *that* the keeper maketh.
19 The rich man shall lie down, but
he shall not be [l]gathered: he openeth
his eyes, and he *is* not.
20 Terrors take hold on him as waters, a tempest stealeth him away in
the night.
21 The east wind carrieth him away,
and he departeth: and as a storm hurl-
eth him out of his place.
22 For *God* shall cast upon him, and
not spare: [6]he would fain flee out of his
hand.
23 *Men* shall clap their hands at
him, and shall hiss him out of his
place.

28 Surely there is [1]a vein for the silver, and a place for gold *where*
they fine *it.*
2 Iron is taken out of the [2]earth, and
brass *is* molten *out of* the stone.
3 He setteth an end to darkness,
and [a]searcheth out all perfection: the
stones of darkness, and the shadow of
death.
4 The flood breaketh out from the
inhabitant; *even the waters* forgotten
of the foot: they are dried up, they are
gone away from men.
5 *As for* the earth, out of it cometh
bread: and under it is turned up as it
were fire.
6 The stones of it *are* the place of
sapphires: and it hath [3]dust of gold.

22 [6]Or, he trusteth not his own life
23 [7]That is, God's
24 [i]Ps. 37.35-36
[8]are not
[9]closed up
CHAPTER 25
3 [a]Gen. 1.3-5.14-16;
4 [b]ch. 4.17;
6 [c]Ps. 22.6
CHAPTER 26
2 [a]Prov. 25.11
3 [b]1 Cor. 2.4
5 [1]Or, with the inhabitants
6 [c]Ps. 139.8;
7 [d]Ps. 24.1-2
8 [e]Prov. 30.4
10 [f]Jer. 5.22
[2]until the end of light with darkness
12 [g]Ex. 14.21;
[3]pride, or, Rahab
13 [h]Ps. 33.6
CHAPTER 27
1 [1]added to take up
2 [a]ch. 34.5
[2]made my soul bitter
3 [3]That is, the breath which God gave him
5 [b]ch. 13.15
6 [c]ch. 2.3
[d]Acts 24.16
[4]from my days
8 [e]Matt. 16.26
9 [f]Prov. 1.28;
10 [g]ch. 22.26
11 [5]Or, being in the hand, etc
14 [h]Deut. 28.32-41;
15 [i]Ps. 78.64
17 [j]Prov. 28.8;
18 [k]Lam. 2.6
19 [l]Num. 20.26
22 [6]in fleeing he would flee
CHAPTER 28
1 [1]Or, a mine
2 [2]Or, dust
3 [a]Prov. 2.4;
6 [3]Or, gold ore

7 *There is* a path which no fowl knoweth, and which the vulture's eye hath not seen:

8 The lion's whelps have not trodden it, nor the fierce lion passed by it.

9 He putteth forth his hand upon the [4]rock; he overturneth the mountains by the roots.

10 He cutteth out rivers among the rocks; and his eye seeth every precious thing.

11 He bindeth the floods [5]from overflowing; and *the thing that is* hid bringeth he forth to light.

12 [b]But where shall wisdom be found? and where *is* the place of understanding?

13 Man knoweth not the [c]price thereof; neither is it found in the land of the living.

14 [d]The depth saith, It *is* not in me: and the sea saith, *It is* not with me.

15 [6]It [e]cannot be gotten for gold, neither shall silver be weighed *for* the price thereof.

16 It cannot be valued with the gold of Ō'phĭr, with the precious onyx, or the sapphire.

17 The gold and the crystal cannot equal it: and the exchange of it *shall not be for* [7]jewels of fine gold.

18 No mention shall be made of [8]coral, or of pearls: for the price of wisdom *is* above rubies.

19 The topaz of Ē-thĭ-ō'pĭ-a shall not equal it, neither shall it be valued with pure gold.

20 Whence then cometh wisdom? and where *is* the place of understanding?

21 Seeing it is hid from the eyes of all living, and kept close from the fowls of the [9]air.

22 Destruction and death say, We have heard the fame thereof with our ears.

23 God [f]understandeth the way thereof, and he knoweth the place thereof.

24 For he looketh to the ends of the earth, *and* [g]seeth under the whole heaven;

25 [h]To make the weight for the winds; and he weigheth the waters by measure.

26 When he [i]made a decree for the rain, and a way for the lightning of the thunder:

27 Then did he see it, and [10]declare it; he prepared it, yea, and searched it out.

28 And [j]unto man he said, Behold, [k]the fear of the Lord, that *is* wisdom; and to depart from evil *is* understanding.

29 Moreover Jōb [1]continued his parable, and said,

2 Oh that I were as *in* months past, as *in* the days *when* God preserved me;

3 [a]When his [2]candle shined upon my head, *and when* by his light I walked *through* darkness;

4 As I was in the days of my youth, when [b]the secret of God *was* upon my tabernacle;

5 When the Almighty *was* yet with me, *when* my children *were* about me;

6 When [c]I washed my steps with butter, and [d]the rock poured [3]me out rivers of oil;

7 When I went out to the gate through the city, *when* I prepared my seat in the street!

8 The young men saw me, and hid themselves: and the aged arose, *and* stood up.

9 The princes refrained talking, and laid *their* hand on their mouth.

10 [4]The nobles held their peace, and their [e]tongue cleaved to the roof of their mouth.

11 When the ear heard *me,* then it blessed me; and when the eye saw *me,* it gave witness to me:

12 Because [f]I delivered the poor that cried, and the fatherless, and *him that had* none to help him.

13 The blessing of him that was ready to perish came upon me: and I caused the widow's heart to sing for joy.

14 [g]I put on righteousness, and it clothed me: my judgment *was* as a robe and a diadem.

15 I was [h]eyes to the blind, and feet *was* I to the lame.

16 I *was* a father to the poor: and [i]the cause *which* I knew not I searched out.

17 And I brake [5]the jaws of the wicked, and [6]plucked the spoil out of his teeth.

18 Then I said, [j]I shall die in my nest, and I shall multiply *my* days as the sand.

19 [k]My root *was* [7]spread out [l]by the waters, and the dew lay all night upon my branch.

20 My glory *was* [8]fresh in me, and [m]my bow was [9]renewed in my hand.

21 Unto me *men* gave ear, and waited, and kept silence at my counsel.

22 After my words they spake not again; and my speech dropped upon them.

23 And they waited for me as for the rain; and they opened their mouth wide *as* for the latter rain.

24 *If* I laughed on them, they believed *it* not; and the light of my countenance they cast not down.

25 I chose out their way, and sat chief, and dwelt as a king in the army, as one *that* comforteth the mourners.

30 But now *they that are* [1]younger than I have me in derision, whose fathers I would have disdained to have set with the dogs of my flock.

2 Yea, whereto *might* the strength of their hands *profit* me, in whom old age was perished?

3 For want and famine *they were* [2]solitary; fleeing into the wilderness [3]in former time desolate and waste.

4 Who cut up mallows by the bushes, and juniper roots *for* their meat.

5 They were driven forth from among *men,* (they cried after them as *after* a thief;)

---

9 [4]Or, flint
11 [5]from weeping
12 [b]ch. 11.7-8; Eccl. 7.24
13 [c]Prov. 3.15
14 [d]Rom. 11.33
15 [6]Fine gold shall not be given for it [e]Prov. 3.13-14
17 [7]Or, vessels of fine gold
18 [8]Or, Ramoth
21 [9]Or, heaven
23 [f]Acts 15.18; Heb. 4.13
24 [g]Prov. 15.3
25 [h]Ps. 135.7
26 [i]ch. 38.25; Jer. 14.22
27 [10]Or, number it
28 [j]Deut. 29.29 [k]Deut. 4.6; Prov. 1.7

CHAPTER 29
1 [1]added to take up
3 [a]ch. 18.6; Ps. 18.28 [2]Or, lamp
4 [b]Ps. 25.14; Prov. 3.32
6 [c]Gen. 49.11; Deut. 32.13 [d]Ps. 81.16 [3]with me
10 [4]The voice of the nobles was hid [e]Ps. 137.6
12 [f]Ps. 72.12; Prov. 21.13
14 [g]Ps. 132.9; Eph. 6.14
15 [h]Num. 10.31
16 [i]Prov. 29.7
17 [5]the jawteeth, or, the grinders [6]cast
18 [j]Ps. 30.6
19 [k]Ps. 1.3; [7]opened [l]Ps. 1.3
20 [8]new [m]Gen. 49.24 [9]changed

CHAPTER 30
1 [1]of fewer days than I
3 [2]Or, dark as the night [3]yesternight

6 To dwell in the cliffs of the valleys,
in [4]caves of the earth, and *in* the rocks.
7 Among the bushes they brayed;
under the nettles they were gathered
together.
8 *They were* children of fools, yea,
children of [5]base men: they were viler
than the earth.
9 [a]And now am I their song, yea, I
am their byword.
10 They abhor me, they flee far from
me, [6]and spare not to spit in my face.
11 Because he [b]hath loosed my cord,
and afflicted me, they have also let
loose the bridle before me.
12 Upon *my* right *hand* rise the
youth; they push away my feet, and
[c]they raise up against me the ways of
their destruction.
13 [d]They mar my path, they set forward
my calamity, they have no helper.
14 They came *upon me* [e]as a wide
breaking in *of waters:* in the desolation
they rolled themselves *upon me.*
15 Terrors are turned upon me: they
pursue [7]my soul as the wind: and my
welfare passeth away as a cloud.
16 And now my soul is [f]poured out
upon me; the days of affliction have
taken hold upon me.
17 [g]My bones are pierced in me in
the night season: and my sinews take
no rest.
18 By the great force *of my disease*
is my garment changed: it bindeth me
[h]about as the collar of my coat.
19 He hath cast me into the mire,
and I am become like dust and ashes.
20 I [i]cry unto thee, and thou dost
not hear me: I stand up, and thou regardest
me *not.*
21 Thou art [8]become cruel to me:
with [9]thy strong hand thou opposest
thyself against me.
22 Thou liftest me up to the wind;
thou causest me to ride *upon it,* and
dissolvest my [10]substance.
23 For I know *that* thou wilt bring
me *to* death, and *to* the house appointed
for all living.
24 Howbeit he will not stretch out
his hand to the [11]grave, though they
cry in his destruction.
25 [j]Did not I weep [12]for him that was
in trouble? was *not* my soul [13][k]grieved
for the poor?
26 [l]When I looked for good, then
evil came *unto me:* and when I waited
for light, there came darkness.
27 My bowels boiled, and rested not:
the days of affliction prevented me.
28 I went mourning [m]without the
sun: I stood up, *and* I cried in the
congregation.
29 [n]I am a brother to dragons, and a
companion to [14]owls.
30 My skin is black upon me, and
my bones are burned with heat.
31 My harp also is *turned* to mourning,
and my organ into the voice of
them that weep.

31

I [a]made a covenant with mine
eyes; why then should I think
upon a maid?
2 For what portion of God *is there*
from above? and *what* inheritance of
the Almighty from on high?
3 *Is* not destruction to the wicked?
and a strange *punishment* to the workers
of iniquity?
4 [b]Doth not he see my ways, and
count all my steps?
5 If I have walked with vanity, or if
my foot hath hasted to deceit;
6 [1]Let me be weighed in an even
balance, that God may know mine
integrity.
7 If my step hath turned out of the
way, and [c]mine heart walked after
mine eyes, and if any blot hath cleaved
to mine hands;
8 *Then* let me sow, and let another
eat; yea, let my offspring be rooted out.
9 If mine heart have been deceived
by a woman, or *if* I have laid wait at my
neighbour's door;
10 *Then* let my wife grind unto another,
and let others bow down upon
her.
11 For this *is* an heinous crime; yea,
it *is* an iniquity *to be punished by* the
judges.
12 For it *is* a fire *that* consumeth to
destruction, and would root out all
mine increase.
13 If I did despise the cause of my
manservant or of my maidservant,
when they contended with me;
14 What then shall I do when God
riseth up? and when he visiteth, what
shall I answer him?
15 [d]Did not he that made me in the
womb make him? and [2]did not one
fashion us in the womb?
16 If I have withheld the poor from
their desire, or have caused the eyes of
the widow to fail;
17 Or have eaten my morsel myself
alone, and the fatherless hath not eaten
thereof;
18 (For from my youth he was
brought up with me, as *with* a father,
and I have guided [3]her from my mother's
womb;)
19 If I have seen any perish for
want of clothing, or any poor without
covering;
20 If his loins have not blessed me,
and *if he* were *not* warmed with the
fleece of my sheep;
21 If I have lifted up my hand against
the fatherless, when I saw my help in
the gate:
22 *Then* let mine arm fall from my
shoulder blade, and mine arm be broken
from [4]the bone.
23 For destruction *from* God *was* a
terror to me, and by reason of his highness
I could not endure.
24 If I have made gold my hope, or
have said to the fine gold, *Thou art* my
confidence;
25 If I rejoiced because my wealth
was great, and because mine hand had
[5]gotten much;
26 [e]If I beheld [6]the sun when it
shined, or the moon walking [7]*in* brightness;

6 [4]holes
8 [5]men of no name
9 [a]ch. 17.6; Ps. 69.12
10 [6]and withhold not spittle from my face
11 [b]ch. 12.18
12 [c]ch. 19.12
13 [d]Ps. 69.26
14 [e]Ps. 18.4; Isa. 8.7-8
15 [7]my principal one
16 [f]1 Sam. 1.15; Isa. 53.12
17 [g]ch. 33.19-21; Ps. 6.2
18 [h]ch. 2.7
20 [i]Ps. 22.2; Matt. 15.23
21 [8]turned to be cruel [9]the strength of thy hand
22 [10]Or, wisdom
24 [11]heap
25 [j]Luke 19.41; [12]for him that was hard of day? [13]burned [k]2 Cor. 11.29
26 [l]Jer. 8.15
28 [m]Lam. 3.1-2
29 [n]Ps. 102.6 [14]Or, ostriches

CHAPTER 31
1 [a]Matt. 5.28
4 [b]2 Chr. 16.9;
6 [1]Let him weigh me in balances of justice
7 [c]Num. 15.39;
15 [d]ch. 34.19; [2]Or, did he not fashion us in one womb?
18 [3]That is, the widow
22 [4]Or, the chanelbone
25 [5]found much
26 [e]Deut. 4.19; [6]the light [7]bright

27 And my heart hath been secretly
enticed, or [8]my mouth hath kissed my
hand:
28 This also *were* an iniquity *to be*
punished by the judge: for [f]I should
have denied the God *that is* above.
29 If I rejoiced at the destruction of
him that hated me, or lifted up myself
when evil found him:
30 [g]Neither have I suffered [9]my
mouth to sin by wishing a curse to his
soul.
31 If the men of my tabernacle said
not, Oh that we had of his flesh! we
cannot be satisfied.
32 [h]The stranger did not lodge in
the street: *but* I opened my doors [10]to
the traveller.
33 If I covered my transgressions
[11]as Ăd'ăm, by hiding mine iniquity in
my bosom:
34 Did I fear a great [i]multitude, or
did the contempt of families terrify me,
that I kept silence, *and* went not out of
the door?
35 Oh that one would hear me! behold, my desire *is, that* the Almighty
would answer me, and *that* mine adversary had written a book.
36 Surely I would take it upon my
shoulder, *and* bind it *as* a crown to me.
37 I would declare unto him the
number of my steps; as a prince would
I go near unto him.
38 If my land cry against me, or
that the furrows likewise thereof complain;
39 If I have eaten the fruits thereof
without money, or have caused the
owners therof to lose their life:
40 Let thistles grow instead of wheat,
and cockle instead of barley. The words
of Jōb are ended.

32 So these three men ceased [1]to answer Jōb, because he *was* righteous in his own eyes.
2 Then was kindled the wrath of E-
lī'hū the son of Băr'ă-chel [a]the Bū'zīte,
of the kindred of Răm: against Jōb was
his wrath kindled, because he justified
[2]himself rather than God.
3 Also against his three friends was
his wrath kindled, because they had
found no answer, and *yet* had condemned Jōb.
4 Now E-lī'hū had [3]waited till Jōb
had spoken, because they *were* [4]elder
than he.
5 When E-lī'hū saw that *there was*
no answer in the mouth of *these* three
men, then his wrath was kindled.
6 And E-lī'hū the son of Băr'ă-chel
the Bū'zīte answered and said, I *am*
[5]young, and ye *are* very old; wherefore
I was afraid, and [6]durst not shew you
mine opinion.
7 I said, [b]Days should speak, and
multitude of years should teach wisdom.
8 But *there is* a spirit in man: and
[c]the inspiration of the Almighty giveth
them understanding.
9 [d]Great men are not *always* wise:
neither do the aged understand judgment.
10 Therefore I said, Hearken to me;
I also will shew mine opinion.
11 Behold, I waited for your words; I
gave ear to your [7]reasons, whilst ye
searched out [8]what to say.
12 Yea, I [e]attended unto you, and,
behold, *there was* none of you that
convinced Jōb, *or* that answered his
words:
13 [f]Lest ye should say, We have
found out wisdom: God thrusteth him
down, not man.
14 Now he hath not [9]directed *his*
words against me: neither will I answer him with your speeches.
15 They were amazed, they answered
no more: [10]they left off speaking.
16 When I had waited, (for they
spake not, but stood still, *and* answered
no more;)
17 *I said,* I will answer also my part,
I also will shew mine opinion.
18 For I am full of [11]matter, [12]the
spirit within me constraineth me.
19 Behold, my belly *is* as wine *which*
[13]hath no vent; it is ready to burst like
new bottles.
20 I will speak, [14]that I may be refreshed: I will open my lips and answer.
21 Let me not, I pray you, accept
any man's person, neither let me give
flattering titles unto man.
22 For I know not [g]to give flattering
titles; *in so doing* my maker would
soon [h]take me away.

33 Wherefore, Jōb, I pray thee, [a]hear
my speeches, and hearken to all
my words.
2 Behold, now I have opened my
mouth, my tongue hath spoken [1]in my
mouth.
3 My words *shall be of* the [b]upright-
ness of my heart: and my lips shall utter knowledge [2]clearly.
4 The spirit of God hath [c]made me,
and the breath of the Almighty hath
given me life.
5 If thou canst answer me, set *thy*
words in order before me, stand up.
6 [d]Behold, I *am* [3]according to thy
wish in God's stead: I also am [4]formed
out of the clay.
7 [e]Behold, my terror shall not make
thee afraid, neither shall my hand be
heavy upon thee.
8 Surely thou hast spoken [5]in mine
hearing, and I have heard the voice of
thy words, *saying,*
9 [f]I am clean without transgression,
I *am* innocent; neither *is there* iniquity
in me.
10 Behold, he [g]findeth occasions
against me, he counteth me for his
enemy.
11 [h]He putteth my feet in the stocks,
he marketh all my paths.
12 Behold, *in* this thou art [i]not just: I
will answer thee, that God *is* greater
than man.
13 Why dost thou [j]strive against
him? for [6]he giveth not account of any
of his matters.
14 For God speaketh once, yea twice,
yet man perceiveth it not.

27 [8]my hand hath kissed my mouth
28 [f]Josh. 24.23-27;
30 [g]Matt. 5.44;
[9]my palate
32 [h]Gen. 19.2;
[10]Or, to the way
33 [11]Or, after the manner of men
34 [i]Ex. 23.2;

CHAPTER 32
1 [1]from answering
2 [a]Gen. 22.21
[2]his soul
4 [3]expected Job in words
[4]elder for days
6 [5]few of days
[6]feared
7 [b]ch. 8.8-9
8 [c]1 Ki. 3.9
9 [d]1 Cor. 1.21
11 [7]understandings
[8]words
12 [e]Prov. 18.13
13 [f]Jer. 9.23
14 [9]Or, ordered his words
15 [10]they removed speeches from themselves
18 [11]words
[12]the spirit of my belly
19 [13]is not opened
20 [14]that I may breathe
22 [g]Acts 12.22
[h]Acts 12.23

CHAPTER 33
1 [a]ch. 13.6
2 [1]in my palate
3 [b]1 Thess. 1.3
[2]purely
4 [c]Gen. 2.7
6 [d]ch. 9.32
[3]according to thy mouth
[4]cut out of the clay
7 [e]ch. 13.21
8 [5]in mine ears
9 [f]ch. 10.7
10 [g]ch. 13.24
11 [h]ch. 13.27
12 [i]Eccl. 7.20
13 [j]Isa. 45.9
[6]he answereth not

15 In a dream, in a vision of the
night, when deep sleep falleth upon
men, in slumberings upon the bed;
16 Then [7]he openeth the ears of men,
and sealeth their instruction,
17 That he may withdraw man *from
his* [8]purpose, and hide pride from man.
18 He keepeth back his soul from
the pit, and his life [9]from perishing by
the sword.
19 He is [k]chastened also with pain
upon his bed, and the multitude of his
bones with strong *pain:*
20 So that his life abhorreth bread,
and his soul [10]dainty meat.
21 His flesh is consumed away, that
it cannnot be seen; and [l]his bones *that*
were not seen stick out.
22 Yea, his soul draweth near unto
the grave, and his life to the destroyers.
23 If there be a [m]messenger with
him, an interpreter, one among a thousand, to shew unto man his uprightness:
24 Then he is [n]gracious unto him,
and saith, Deliver him from going down
to the pit: I have found [11]a ransom.
25 His flesh shall be fresher [12]than a
child's: he shall return to the days of
his youth:
26 He shall [o]pray unto God, and he
will be favourable unto him: and he
shall see his face with joy: for he will
render unto man his righteousness.
27 [13]He looketh upon men, and *if
any* say, I have sinned, and perverted
that which was right, and it profited
me not:
28 [14]He will deliver his soul from going into the pit, and his life shall see
the light.
29 Lo, all these *things* worketh God
oftentimes with man,
30 [p]To bring back his soul from the
pit, to be enlightened with the light of
the living.
31 Mark well, O Jōb, hearken unto
me: hold thy peace, and I will speak.
32 If thou hast any thing to say, [q]an-
swer me: speak, for I desire to justify
thee.
33 If not, [r]hearken unto me: hold thy
peace, and I shall teach thee wisdom.

34 Furthermore E-lī'hū answered
and said,
2 Hear my words, O ye wise *men;*
and give ear unto me, ye that have
knowledge.
3 For the ear trieth words, as the
[1]mouth tasteth meat.
4 Let us choose to us judgment: let us
know among ourselves what *is* good.
5 For Jōb hath said, [a]I am righteous: and [b]God hath taken away my
judgment.
6 [c]Should I lie against my right?
[2]my wound *is* incurable without transgression.
7 What man *is* like Jōb, *who* drinketh up scorning like water?
8 Which goeth in company with the
workers of iniquity, and walketh with
wicked men.
9 For [d]he hath said, It profiteth a
man nothing that he should delight
himself with God.
10 Therefore hearken unto me, ye
[3]men of understanding: [e]far be it from
God, *that he should do* wickedness;
and *from* the Almighty, *that he should
commit* iniquity.
11 [f]For the work of a man shall he
render unto him, and cause every man
to find according to *his* ways.
12 Yea, surely God will not do wickedly, neither will the Almighty pervert
judgment.
13 Who hath given him a charge
over the earth? or who hath disposed
[4]the whole world?
14 If he set his heart [5]upon man, *if*
he [g]gather unto himself his spirit and
his breath;
15 All flesh shall perish together,
and man shall turn again unto dust.
16 If now *thou hast* understanding,
hear this: hearken to the voice of my
words.
17 [h]Shall even he that hateth right
[6]govern? and wilt thou condemn him
that is most just?
18 *Is it fit* to say to a king, *Thou
art* wicked? *and* to princes, *Ye are*
ungodly?
19 *How much less to him* that [i]ac-
cepteth not the persons of princes, nor
regardeth the rich more than the poor?
for they all *are* the work of his hands.
20 In a moment shall they die, and
the people shall be troubled at midnight, and pass away: and [7]the mighty
shall be taken away without hand.
21 For his eyes *are* upon the ways of
man, and he seeth all his goings.
22 *There is* no darkness, nor shadow
of death, where the workers of iniquity
may hide themselves.
23 [j]For he will not lay upon man
more *than right;* that he should [8]enter
into judgment with God.
24 He shall break in pieces mighty
men [9]without number, and set others
in their stead.
25 Therefore he knoweth their
works, and he overturneth *them* in the
night, so that they are [10]destroyed.
26 He striketh them as wicked men
[11]in the open sight of others;
27 Because they turned back [12]from
him, and would not consider any of his
ways:
28 So that they [k]cause the cry of the
poor to come unto him, and he [l]hear-
eth the cry of the afflicted.
29 When he giveth quietness, who
then can make trouble? and when he
hideth *his* face, who then can behold
him? whether *it be done* against a nation, or against a man only:
30 That the hypocrite [m]reign not,
lest [n]the people be ensnared.
31 Surely it is meet to be said unto
God, I have borne *chastisement,* I will
not offend *any more:*
32 *That which* I see not teach thou
me: if I have done iniquity, I will do no
more.

16 [7]he revealeth, or, uncovereth
17 [8]work
18 [9]from passing by the sword
19 [k]Deut. 8.5; Ps. 94.12-13
20 [10]meat of desire
21 [l]Ps. 102.5
23 [m]2 Chr. 36.15-16; Mal. 2.7
24 [n]Rom. 3.24
[11]Or, an atonement
25 [12]than childhood
26 [o]2 Ki. 20.2-5; Ps. 6.1-9
27 [13]Or, He shall look upon men, and say, I have sinned
28 [14]Or, He hath delivered my soul, etc., and my life
30 [p]Ps. 40.2;
32 [q]2 Cor. 1.24
33 [r]Ps. 34.11

CHAPTER 34
3 [1]palate
5 [a]ch. 33.9
[b]ch. 27.2
6 [c]ch. 9.17
[2]mine arrow
9 [d]ch. 9.22
10 [3]men of heart
[e]Gen. 18.25;
11 [f]Prov. 24.12;
13 [4]all of it?
14 [5]upon him
[g]Eccl. 12.7
17 [h]Gen. 18.25
[6]bind?
19 [i]Deut. 10.17
20 [7]they shall take away the mighty
23 [j]Ezra 9.13
[8]go
24 [9]without searching out
25 [10]crushed
26 [11]in the place of beholders
27 [12]from after him
28 [k]Eccl. 5.8;
[l]Ex. 22.23;
30 [m]Prov. 29.2-12
[n]1 Ki. 12.28-30

33 [13]*Should it be* according to thy mind? he will recompense it, whether thou refuse, or whether thou choose; and not I: therefore speak what thou knowest.

34 Let men [14]of understanding tell me, and let a wise man hearken unto me.

35 [o]Jōb hath spoken without knowledge, and his words *were* without wisdom.

36 [15]My desire *is that* Jōb may be tried unto the end because of *his* answers for wicked men.

37 For he addeth rebellion unto his sin, he clappeth *his hands* among us, and multiplieth his words against God.

35

Elī'hū spake moreover, and said,

2 Thinkest thou this to be right, *that* thou saidst, My righteousness *is* more than God's?

3 For thou saidst, What advantage will it be unto thee? *and,* What profit shall I have, [1]*if I be cleansed* from my sin?

4 [2]I will answer thee, and thy companions with thee.

5 Look unto the heavens, and see; and behold the clouds *which* are higher than thou.

6 If thou sinnest, what doest thou against him? or *if* thy transgressions be multiplied, what doest thou unto him?

7 [a]If thou be righteous, what givest thou him? or what receiveth he of thine hand?

8 Thy wickedness *may hurt* a man as thou *art;* and thy righteousness *may profit* the son of man.

9 [b]By reason of the multitude of oppressions they make *the oppressed* to cry: they cry out by reason of the arm of the mighty.

10 But none saith, [c]Where *is* God my maker, [d]who giveth songs in the night;

11 Who [e]teacheth us more than the beasts of the earth, and maketh us wiser than the fowls of heaven?

12 [f]There they cry, but none giveth answer, because of the pride of evil men.

13 Surely God will not hear vanity, neither will the Almighty regard it.

14 Although thou sayest thou shalt not see him, *yet* judgment *is* before him; therefore trust thou in him.

15 But now, because *it is* not *so,* [3]he hath visited in his anger; yet [4]he knoweth *it* not in great extremity:

16 [g]Therefore doth Jōb open his mouth in vain; he multiplieth words without knowledge.

36

Elī'hū also proceeded, and said,

2 Suffer me a little, and I will shew thee [1]that *I have* yet to speak on God's behalf.

3 I will fetch my knowledge from afar, and will ascribe righteousness to my Maker.

4 For truly my words *shall* not *be* false: he that is perfect in knowledge *is* with thee.

5 Behold, God *is* mighty, and despiseth not *any: he is* mighty in strength *and* [2]wisdom.

6 He preserveth not the life of the wicked: but giveth right to the [3]poor.

7 He withdraweth not his eyes from the righteous: but [a]with kings *are they* on the throne; yea, he doth establish them for ever, and they are exalted.

8 And [b]if *they be* bound in fetters, *and* be holden in cords of affliction;

9 Then he sheweth them their work, and their transgressions that they have exceeded.

10 He openeth also their ear to discipline, and commandeth that they return from iniquity.

11 If they obey and serve *him,* they shall [c]spend their days in prosperity, and their years in pleasures.

12 But if they obey not, [4]they shall perish by the sword, and they shall die without knowledge.

13 But the hypocrites in heart heap up wrath: they cry not when he bindeth them.

14 [5]They die in youth, and their life *is* among the [6]unclean.

15 He delivereth the [7]poor in his affliction, and openeth their ears in oppression.

16 Even so would he have removed thee out of the strait *into* a broad place, where *there is* no straitness; and [8]that which should be set on thy table *should be* full of fatness.

17 But thou hast fulfilled the judgment of the wicked: [9]judgment and justice take hold *on thee.*

18 Because *there is* wrath, *beware* lest he take thee away with *his* stroke: then a great ransom cannot [10]deliver thee.

19 Will he esteem thy riches? *no,* not gold, nor all the forces of strength.

20 Desire not the night, when people are cut off in their place.

21 Take heed, regard not iniquity: for [d]this hast thou chosen rather than affliction.

22 Behold, God exalteth by his power: [e]who teacheth like him?

23 Who hath enjoined him his way? or [f]who can say, Thou hast wrought iniquity?

24 Remember that thou [g]magnify his work, which men behold.

25 [h]Every man may see it; man may behold *it* afar off.

26 Behold, God *is* great, and we [i]know *him* not, [j]neither can the number of his years be searched out.

27 For he maketh small the drops of water: they pour down rain according to the vapour thereof:

28 Which the clouds do drop *and* distil upon man abundantly.

29 Also can *any* understand the spreadings of the clouds, *or* the noise of his tabernacle?

30 Behold, he spreadeth his light upon it, and covereth [11]the bottom of the sea.

33 [13]Should it be from with thee?
34 [14]of heart
35 [o]ch. 38.2
36 [15]Or, My father, let Job be tried

CHAPTER 35
3 [1]Or, by it more than by my sin
4 [2]I will return to thee words
7 [a]Prov. 9.12; Rom. 11.35
9 [b]Ex. 2.23;
10 [c]Eccl. 12.1; [d]Ps. 42.8;
11 [e]ch. 32.8;
12 [f]Prov. 1.28
15 [3]That is, God [4]That is, Job
16 [g]ch. 34.35-37

CHAPTER 36
2 [1]that there are yet words for God
5 [2]heart
6 [3]Or, afflicted
7 [a]Ps. 113.8
8 [b]Ps. 107.10
11 [c]ch. 11.13-19;
12 [4]they shall pass away by the sword
14 [5]Their soul dieth [6]Or, sodomites, Deut. 23.17
15 [7]Or, afflicted
16 [8]the rest of thy table
17 [9]Or, judgment and justice should uphold thee
18 [10]turn thee aside
21 [d]Heb. 11.25
22 [e]Isa. 40.13;
23 [f]Deut. 32.4
24 [g]Ps. 33.4;
25 [h]Rom. 1.19
26 [i]1 Cor. 13.12 [j]Ps. 90.2;
30 [11]the roots

31 For by them judgeth he the people; he giveth meat in abundance.
32 With clouds he covereth the light;
and commandeth it *not to shine* by *the*
cloud that cometh betwixt.
33 The noise thereof sheweth concerning it, the cattle also concerning
[12]the vapour.

37 At this also my heart trembleth,
and is moved out of his place.
2 [1]Hear attentively the noise of his
voice, and the sound *that* goeth out of
his mouth.
3 He directeth it under the whole
heaven, and his [2]lightning unto the
[3]ends of the earth.
4 After it a voice roareth: he thundereth with the voice of his excellency;
and he will not stay them when his
voice is heard.
5 God thundereth marvellously with
his voice; great things doeth he, which
we cannot comprehend.
6 For he saith to the snow, Be thou
on the earth; [4]likewise to the small rain,
and to the great rain of his strength.
7 He sealeth up the hand of every
man; [a]that all men may know his
work.
8 Then the beasts go into dens, and
remain in their places.
9 [5]Out of the south cometh the whirlwind: and cold out of the [6]north.
10 By the breath of God frost is
given: and the breadth of the waters is
straitened.
11 Also by watering he wearieth the
thick cloud: he scattereth [7]his bright
cloud:
12 And it is turned round about by
his counsels: that they may do whatsoever he commandeth them upon the
face of the world in the earth.
13 He causeth it to come, whether
for [8]correction, or for his land, or for
mercy.
14 Hearken unto this, O Jōb: stand
still, and consider the wondrous works
of God.
15 Dost thou know when God disposed them, and caused the light of his
cloud to shine?
16 Dost thou know the balancings
of the clouds, the wondrous works of
[b]him which is perfect in knowledge?
17 How thy garments *are* warm,
when he quieteth the earth by the
south *wind?*
18 Hast thou with him [c]spread out
the sky, *which is* strong, *and* as a
molten looking glass?
19 Teach us what we shall say unto
him; *for* we cannot order *our speech* by
reason of darkness.
20 Shall it be told him that I speak?
if a man speak, surely he shall be swallowed up.
21 And now *men* see not the bright
light which *is* in the clouds: but the
wind passeth, and cleanseth them.
22 [9]Fair weather cometh out of the
north: with God *is* terrible majesty.
23 *Touching* the Almighty, [d]we cannot find him out: [e]*he is* excellent in
power, and in judgment, and in plenty
of justice: he will [f]not afflict.
24 Men do therefore [g]fear him: he
respecteth not any *that are* [h]wise of
heart.

38 Then the LORD answered Jōb
[a]out of the whirlwind, and said,
2 Who *is* this that darkeneth counsel
by words without knowledge?
3 [b]Gird up now thy loins like a man;
for I will demand of thee, and [1]answer
thou me.
4 [c]Where wast thou when I laid the
foundations of the earth? declare, [2]if
thou hast understanding.
5 Who hath laid the measures
thereof, if thou knowest? or who hath
stretched the line upon it?
6 Whereupon are the [3]foundations
thereof [4]fastened? or who laid the corner stone thereof;
7 When the morning stars sang together, and all [d]the sons of God shouted
for joy?
8 [e]Or *who* shut up the sea with
doors, when it brake forth, *as if* it had
issued out of the womb?
9 When I made the cloud the garment thereof, and thick darkness a
swaddlingband for it,
10 And [5]brake up for it my decreed
place, and set bars and doors,
11 And said, Hitherto shalt thou
come, but no further: and here shall
[6]thy proud waves be stayed?
12 Hast thou commanded the morning since thy days; *and* caused the
dayspring to know his place;
13 That it might take hold of the
[7]ends of the earth, that the wicked
might be shaken out of it?
14 It is turned as clay *to* the seal;
and they stand as a garment.
15 And from the wicked their light
is withholden, and the high arm shall
be broken.
16 Hast thou entered into the springs
of the sea? or hast thou walked in the
search of the depth?
17 Have the gates of death been
opened unto thee? or hast thou seen
the doors of the shadow of death?
18 Hast thou perceived the breadth
of the earth? declare if thou knowest it
all.
19 Where *is* the way *where* light
dwelleth? and *as for* darkness, where
is the place thereof,
20 That thou shouldest take it [8]to the
bound thereof, and that thou shouldest
know the paths *to* the house thereof?
21 Knowest thou *it,* because thou
wast then born? or *because* the number of thy days *is* great?
22 Hast thou entered into the treasures of the snow? or hast thou seen
the treasures of the hail,
23 [f]Which I have reserved against
the time of trouble, against the day of
battle and war?
24 By what way is the light parted,
which scattereth the east wind upon
the earth?

33 [12]that which goeth up

CHAPTER 37

2 [1]Hear in hearing

3 [2]light [3]wings of the earth

6 [4]and to the shower of rain, and to the showers of rain of his strength

7 [a]Ps. 111.2

9 [5]Out of the chamber [6]scattering winds

11 [7]the cloud of his light

13 [8]a rod

16 [b]ch. 36.4

18 [c]Gen. 1.6; ch. 38.11-18

22 [9]Gold

23 [d]Ex. 33.20; Matt. 11.27; John 1.18

[e]ch. 36.5; Ps. 99.4; Jer. 10.12

[f]Lam. 3.33; Heb. 12.10

24 [g]Matt. 10.28

[h]Matt. 11.25

CHAPTER 38

1 [a]Ex. 19.16-18; 1 Ki. 19.11; 2 Ki. 2.1; Ezek. 1.4

3 [b]Ex. 12.11; 1 Ki. 18.46 [1]make me know

4 [c]Ps. 104.5 [2]if thou knowest understanding

6 [3]sockets [4]made to sink

7 [d]ch. 1.6

8 [e]Gen. 1.9; Ps. 33.7; Prov. 8.29

10 [5]Or, established my decree upon it

11 [6]the pride of thy waves

13 [7]wings

20 [8]Or, at

23 [f]Ex. 9.18; Josh. 10.11; Ps. 9.13; Isa. 30.30

25 Who hath divided a watercourse for the overflowing of waters, or a way for the lightning of thunder;

26 To cause it to rain on the earth, *where* no man *is; on* the wilderness, wherein *there is* no man;

27 [g]To satisfy the desolate and waste *ground;* and to cause the bud of the tender herb to spring forth?

28 [h]Hath the rain a father? or who hath begotten the drops of dew?

29 Out of whose womb came the ice? and the [i]hoary frost of heaven, who hath gendered it?

30 The waters are hid as *with* a stone, and the face of the deep [9]is frozen.

31 Canst thou bind the sweet influences of [10]Plē'ia-dēs, or loose the bands of [11]O-rī'on?

32 Canst thou bring forth [12]Măz'-za-rŏth in his season? or canst thou [13]guide Ärc-tū'rus with his sons?

33 Knowest thou [j]the ordinances of heaven? canst thou set the dominion thereof in the earth?

34 Canst thou lift up thy voice to the clouds, that abundance of waters may cover thee?

35 Canst thou send lightnings, that they may go, and say unto thee, [14]Here we *are?*

36 [k]Who hath put wisdom in the inward parts? or who hath given understanding to the heart?

37 Who can number the clouds in wisdom? or [15]who can stay the bottles of heaven,

38 [16]When the dust [17]groweth into hardness, and the clods cleave fast together?

39 Wilt thou hunt the prey for the lion? or fill [18]the appetite of the young lions,

40 When they couch in *their* dens, *and* abide in the covert to lie in wait?

41 [l]Who provideth for the raven his food? when his young ones cry unto God, they wander for lack of meat.

39 Knowest thou the time when the wild goats of the rock bring forth? *or* canst thou mark when the hinds do calve?

2 Canst thou number the months *that* they fulfil? or knowest thou the time when they bring forth?

3 They bow themselves, they bring forth their young ones, they cast out their sorrows.

4 Their young ones are in good liking, they grow up with corn; they go forth, and return not unto them.

5 Who hath sent out the wild ass free? or who hath loosed the bands of the wild ass?

6 [a]Whose house I have made the wilderness, and the [1]barren land his dwellings.

7 He scorneth the multitude of the city, neither regardeth he the crying [2]of the driver.

8 The range of the mountains *is* his pasture, and he searcheth after every green thing.

9 Will the [3]unicorn be willing to serve thee, or abide by thy crib?

10 Canst thou bind the unicorn with his band in the furrow? or will he harrow the valleys after thee?

11 Wilt thou trust him, because his strength *is* great? or wilt thou leave thy labour to him?

12 Wilt thou believe him, that he will bring home thy seed, and gather *it into* thy barn?

13 *Gavest thou* the goodly wings unto the peacocks? or [4]wings and feathers unto the ostrich?

14 Which leaveth her eggs in the earth, and warmeth them in dust,

15 And forgetteth that the foot may crush them, or that the wild beast may break them.

16 She is [b]hardened against her young ones, as though *they were* not hers: her labour is in vain without fear;

17 Because God hath deprived her of wisdom, neither hath he [c]imparted to her understanding.

18 What time she lifteth up herself on high, she scorneth the horse and his rider.

19 Hast thou given the horse strength? hast thou clothed his neck with thunder?

20 Canst thou make him afraid as a grasshopper? the glory of his nostrils [5]*is* terrible.

21 [6]He paweth in the valley, and rejoiceth in *his* strength: [d]he goeth on to meet [7]the armed men.

22 He mocketh at fear, and is not affrighted; neither turneth he back from the sword.

23 The quiver rattleth against him, the glittering spear and the shield.

24 He swalloweth the ground with fierceness and rage: neither believeth he that *it is* the sound of the trumpet.

25 He saith among the trumpets, Ha, ha; and he smelleth the battle afar off, the thunder of the captains, and the shouting.

26 Doth the hawk fly by thy wisdom, *and* stretch her wings toward the south?

27 Doth the eagle mount up [8]at thy command, and [e]make her nest on high?

28 She dwelleth and abideth on the rock, upon the [9]crag of the rock, and the strong place.

29 From thence she seeketh the prey, *and* her eyes behold afar off.

30 Her young ones also suck up blood: and [f]where the slain *are,* there *is* she.

40 Moreover the LORD answered Jōb, and said,

2 Shall he that [a]contendeth with the Almighty instruct *him?* he that reproveth God, let him answer it.

3 ¶ Then Jōb answered the LORD, and said,

4 [b]Behold, I am vile; what shall I answer thee? [c]I will lay mine hand upon my mouth.

5 Once have I spoken; but I will not answer: yea, twice; but I will proceed no further.

27 [g]Ps. 107.35
28 [h]1 Sam. 12.17-18; ch. 5.9-10; Ps. 147.8
29 [i]ch. 6.16; Ps. 147.16
30 [9]is taken
31 [10]Cimah, or, the seven stars [11]Cesil
32 [12]Or, The twelve signs [13]guide them
33 [j]Gen. 1.10; Ps. 119.90-91; Jer. 31.35
35 [14]Behold us
36 [k]ch. 32.8; Ps. 51.6; Eccl. 2.26
37 [15]who can cause to lie down
38 [16]Or, When the dust is turned into mire [17]is poured
39 [18]the life
41 [l]Ps. 147.9; Matt. 6.26; Luke 12.24

CHAPTER 39
6 [a]ch. 24.5; Jer. 2.24; Hos. 8.9 [1]salt places
7 [2]of the exactor
9 [3]Or, rhinoceros
13 [4]Or, the feathers of the stork and ostrich
16 [b]Lev. 26.29; Isa. 49.15; Jer. 19.9; Lam. 2.20; Ezek. 5.10
17 [c]ch. 35.11
20 [5]terror
21 [6]Or, His feet dig [d]Jer. 8.6 [7]the armour
27 [8]by thy mouth [e]Jer. 49.16
28 [9]tooth
30 [f]Matt. 24.28; Luke 17.37

CHAPTER 40
2 [a]ch. 9.3; Isa. 45.9
4 [b]Ezra 9.6; Ps. 51.4 [c]ch. 29.9; Ps. 39.9; Zech. 2.13

6 ¶ Then [d]answered the LORD unto
Jōb out of the whirlwind, and said,
7 [e]Gird up thy loins now like a man:
[f]I will demand of thee, and declare
thou unto me.
8 [g]Wilt thou also disannul my judgment? wilt thou condemn me, that thou
mayest be righteous?
9 Hast thou an arm like God? or
canst thou thunder with [h]a voice like
him?
10 [i]Deck thyself now *with* majesty
and excellency; and array thyself with
glory and beauty.
11 Cast abroad the rage of thy wrath:
and behold every one *that is* proud,
and abase him.
12 Look on every one *that is* [j]proud,
and bring him low; and tread down the
wicked in their place.
13 Hide them in the dust together;
and bind their faces in secret.
14 Then will I also confess unto thee
that thine own right hand can save
thee.
15 ¶ Behold now [1]behemoth, which I
made with thee; he eateth grass as an
ox.
16 Lo now, his strength *is* in his
loins, and his force *is* in the navel of his
belly.
17 [2]He moveth his tail like a cedar:
the sinews of his stones are wrapped
together.
18 His bones *are as* strong pieces of
brass; his bones *are* like bars of iron.
19 He *is* the chief of the ways of
God: he that made him can make his
sword to approach *unto him.*
20 Surely the mountains [k]bring him
forth food, where all the beasts of the
field play.
21 He lieth under the shady trees, in
the covert of the reed, and fens.
22 The shady trees cover him *with*
their shadow; the willows of the brook
compass him about.
23 Behold, [3]he drinketh up a river,
and hasteth not: he trusteth that he can
draw up [l]Jôr′dan into his mouth.
24 [4]He taketh it with his eyes: *his*
nose pierceth through snares.

41 Canst thou draw out [1]leviathan
with an hook? or his tongue with
a cord [2]*which* thou lettest down?
2 Canst thou [a]put an hook into his
nose? or bore his jaw through with a
thorn?
3 Will he make many supplications
unto thee? will he speak soft *words*
unto thee?
4 Will he make a covenant with thee?
wilt thou take him for a servant for
ever?
5 Wilt thou play with him as *with* a
bird? or wilt thou bind him for thy
maidens?
6 Shall the companions make a banquet of him? shall they part him among
the merchants?
7 Canst thou fill his skin with barbed
irons? or his head with fish spears?
8 Lay thine hand upon him, remember the battle, do no more.
9 Behold, the hope of him is in vain:
shall not *one* be cast down even at the
sight of him?
10 None *is so* fierce that dare stir
him up: [b]who then is able to stand before me?
11 [c]Who hath prevented me, that I
should repay *him?* [d]*whatsoever is* under the whole heaven is mine.
12 I will not conceal his parts, nor
his power, nor his comely proportion.
13 Who can discover the face of his
garment? *or* who can come *to him*
[3]with his double bridle?
14 Who can open the doors of his
face? his teeth *are* terrible round about.
15 *His* [4]scales *are his* pride, shut up
together *as with* a close seal.
16 One is so near to another, that no
air can come between them.
17 They are joined one to another,
they stick together, that they cannot be
sundered.
18 By his neesings a light doth shine,
and his eyes *are* like the eyelids of the
morning.
19 Out of his mouth go burning
lamps, *and* sparks of fire leap out.
20 Out of his nostrils goeth smoke,
as *out* of a seething pot or caldron.
21 His breath kindleth coals, and a
flame goeth out of his mouth.
22 In his neck remaineth strength,
and [5]sorrow is turned into joy before
him.
23 [6]The flakes of his flesh are joined
together: they are firm in themselves;
they cannot be moved.
24 His heart is as firm as a stone;
yea, as hard as a piece of the nether
millstone.
25 When he raiseth up himself, the
mighty are afraid: by reason of break-
ings they purify themselves.
26 The sword of him that layeth at
him cannot hold: the spear, the dart,
nor the [7]habergeon.
27 He esteemeth iron as straw, *and*
brass as rotten wood.
28 The arrow cannot make him flee:
slingstones are turned with him into
stubble.
29 Darts are counted as stubble: he
laugheth at the shaking of a spear.
30 [8]Sharp stones *are* under him: he
spreadeth sharp pointed things upon
the mire.
31 He maketh the deep to boil like a
pot: he maketh the sea like a pot of
ointment.
32 He maketh a path to shine after
him; *one* would think the deep *to be*
hoary.
33 Upon earth there is not his like,
[9]who is made without fear.
34 He beholdeth all high *things:* he
is a king over all the children of pride.

42 Then Jōb answered the LORD,
and said,
2 I know that thou [a]canst do every
thing, and *that* [1]no thought can be
withholden from thee.
3 [b]Who *is* he that hideth counsel
without knowledge? therefore have I
uttered that I understood not; [c]things

6 [d]ch. 38.1; Ps. 50.3
7 [e]ch. 38.3 [f]ch. 42.4
8 [g]Ps. 51.4
9 [h]ch. 37.4; Ps. 29.3
10 [i]Ps. 93.1
12 [j]Isa. 2.12; Dan. 4.37; Luke 18.14
15 [1]Supposed to be either the elephant or the hippopotamus
17 [2]Or, He setteth up
20 [k]Ps. 104.14
23 [3]he oppresseth [l]Gen. 13.10; Jer. 12.5
24 [4]Or, Will any take him in his sight, or, bore his nose with a gin?

CHAPTER 41
1 [1]That is, a whale, or, whirlpool [2]which thou drownest
2 [a]Ps. 32.9; Isa. 30.28; Isa. 37.29; Ezek. 29.4
10 [b]ch. 9.4; ch. 40.9-14; 1 Cor. 10.22
11 [c]ch. 35.7; Rom. 11.35 [d]Gen. 14.19; 1 Cor. 10.26
13 [3]Or, within
15 [4]strong pieces of shields
22 [5]sorrow rejoiceth
23 [6]The fallings
26 [7]Or, breastplate
30 [8]Sharp pieces of potsherd
33 [9]Or, who behave themselves without fear

CHAPTER 42
2 [a]Jer. 32.17; Eph. 3.20 [1]Or, no thought of thine can be hindered
3 [b]1 Tim. 1.7 [c]Ps. 40.5

too wonderful for me, which I knew
not.
4 Hear, I beseech thee, and I will
speak: [d]I will demand of thee, and declare thou unto me.
5 I have [e]heard of thee by the hearing of the ear: [f]but now mine eye seeth
thee.
6 Wherefore I abhor *myself*, and repent in dust and ashes.
7 ¶ And it was *so*, that after the LORD
had spoken these words unto Jōb, the
LORD said to Ĕl'ĭ-phăz the Tē'man-īte,
My wrath is kindled against thee, and
against thy two friends: for ye have not
spoken of me *the thing that is* right, as
my servant Jōb *hath*.
8 Therefore take unto you now
[g]seven bullocks and seven rams, and
[h]go to my servant Jōb, and offer up for
yourselves a burnt offering; and my
servant Jōb shall [i]pray for you: for
[2]him will I accept: lest I deal with you
after your folly, in that ye have not
spoken of me *the thing which is* right,
like my servant Jōb.
9 So Ĕl'ĭ-phăz the Tē'man-īte and
Bĭl'dăd the Shu'hīte *and* Zō'phar the
Nā'a-math-īte went, and did according
as the LORD commanded them: the
LORD also accepted [3]Jōb.
10 And the LORD turned the captivity of Jōb, when he prayed for his

4 [d]ch. 38.3
5 [e]Rom. 10.17
[f]Num. 12.8-9; Isa. 6.1
8 [g]Num. 23.1; Heb. 10.4
[h]Matt. 5.24
[i]Gen. 20.17; Heb. 7.25; Jas. 5.16
[2]his face, or, person
9 [3]the face of Job
10 [4]added all that had been to Job unto the double
[j]Isa. 40.2
11 [k]ch. 19.13
12 [l]ch. 8.7
[m]ch. 1.3
14 [5]That is, Handsome as the day
[6]That is, Cassia
[7]That is, The horn, or, Child of beauty
16 [n]ch. 5.26
17 [o]Gen. 25.8

friends: also the LORD [4]gave Jōb [j]twice
as much as he had before.
11 Then came there unto him all his
[k]brethren, and all his sisters, and all
they that had been of his acquaintance
before, and did eat bread with him in
his house: and they bemoaned him,
and comforted him over all the evil
that the LORD had brought upon him:
every man also gave him a piece of
money, and every one an earring of
gold.
12 So the LORD blessed [l]the latter
end of Jōb more than his beginning:
for he had [m]fourteen thousand sheep,
and six thousand camels, and a thousand yoke of oxen, and a thousand she
asses.
13 He had also seven sons and three
daughters.
14 And he called the name of the
first, [5]Je-mī'mȧ; and the name of the
second, [6]Ke-zī'ȧ; and the name of the
third, [7]Kĕr'en–hăp'puch.
15 And in all the land were no women
found *so* fair as the daughters of Jōb:
and their father gave them inheritance
among their brethren.
16 After this [n]lived Jōb an hundred
and forty years, and saw his sons, and
his sons' sons, *even* four generations.
17 So Jōb died, *being* old and [o]full
of days.

THE PSALMS

Life's Questions

How do I talk to God?
How do I mix life's situations and faith in God together?
Who is God, and how do I worship Him?

God's Answers

Psalms collects the prayers of God's people into a worship manual for individuals and congregations. Psalms lets God speak to me through the prayers of His people through the centuries. Their experience with God becomes my word from God. Their experience in prayer becomes my guide to how to speak to God. Their faith teaches me what to believe. No brief outline can show what all the 150 psalms teach. Most helpful may be seeing different kinds of prayers:

Cries for help or laments express personal feelings in the midst of trouble, guilt, sickness, and national calamity (3,4,5,6,7,12,13,17,22,25,26,28,35,38,39,40,41,42,43,44,51,54,55,56,57, 59,60,61,63,64,69,70,71,74,77,79,80,83,85,86,88,90,94,102,109,123,126,130,134,137,140,141, 142,143,144).

Thanksgiving psalms describe how God delivered from trouble and praise Him (9—10,18, 30,31,32,34,66,92,107,116,118,120,124,129,138,139).

Hymns praise God by describing His majesty and greatness and inviting others to join in worship (8,19,29,33,65,100,103,104,105,111, 113,114,117,135,136, 145,146,147,148,149,150).

Wisdom psalms teach by probing life's mysteries (1,14,36,37,49,53,73,78,112,119,127,128, 133).

Kingship psalms describe the work of God's king and point to His Messiah (2,18,20,21,28, 45,61,63,72,89,101,110,132).

Entrance ceremonies teach what God expects of those who worship Him (15,24). Enthronement psalms praise God as king of the universe (47,93,96,97,98,99).

Songs of Zion praise God by praising the city where He lives in His temple (46,48,76,84,87, 122,132).

Psalms of confidence show trust in God (4,11,16,23,27,62,125,131).

Prophetic psalms announce God's will (50,52,58,81,82,91,95).

Liturgical psalms describe the congregation in worship (67,68,75,106,108, 115,121).

Psalm 1

1 Blessed [a]*is* the man that walketh not in the counsel of the [1]ungodly, nor standeth in the way of sinners, nor sitteth in the seat of the scornful.

2 But his delight *is* in the law of the LORD; and in his law doth he meditate day and night.

3 And he shall be like a tree planted by the rivers of water, that bringeth forth his fruit in his season; his leaf also shall not [2]wither; and whatsoever he doeth shall [b]prosper.

4 The ungodly *are* not so: but *are* like the chaff which the wind driveth away.

5 Therefore the ungodly shall not stand in the judgment, nor sinners in the congregation of the righteous.

6 For [c]the LORD knoweth the way of the righteous: but the way of the ungodly shall perish.

Psalm 2

1 Why do the heathen [1]rage, and the people [2]imagine a vain thing?

2 The kings of the earth set themselves, and the rulers take counsel together, against the LORD, and against his [a]anointed, *saying*,

3 [b]Let us break their bands asunder, and cast away their cords from us.

4 [c]He that sitteth in the heavens shall laugh: the Lord shall have them in derision.

5 Then shall he speak unto them in his wrath, and [3]vex them in his sore displeasure.

6 Yet have I [4]set my king [5]upon my holy hill of Zī′ŏn.

7 I will declare [6]the decree: the LORD hath said unto me, [d]Thou *art* my Son; this day have I begotten thee.

8 [e]Ask of me, and I shall give *thee* the heathen *for* thine inheritance, and the uttermost parts of the earth *for* thy possession.

9 [f]Thou shalt break them with a rod of iron; thou shalt dash them in pieces like a potter's vessel.

10 Be wise now therefore, O ye kings: be instructed, ye judges of the earth.

11 Serve the LORD with fear, and rejoice with trembling.

12 [g]Kiss the Son, lest he be angry, and ye perish *from* the way, when his wrath is kindled but a little. [h]Blessed *are* all they that put their trust in him.

Psalm 3

A Psalm of David, when he fled from Absalom his son

1 Lord, [a]how are they increased that trouble me! many *are* they that rise up against me.

2 Many *there be* which say of my soul, [b]*There is* no help for him in God. Sē′lah.

3 But thou, O LORD, *art* a shield [1]for me; my glory, and [c]the lifter up of mine head.

4 I cried unto the LORD with my voice, and he heard me out of his holy hill. Sē′lah.

5 [d]I laid me down and slept; I awaked; for the LORD sustained me.

6 I will not be afraid of ten thousands of people, that have set *themselves* against me round about.

7 Arise, O LORD; save me, O my God: for thou hast smitten all mine enemies *upon* the cheek bone; thou hast broken the teeth of the ungodly.

8 [e]Salvation *belongeth* unto the LORD: thy blessing *is* upon thy people. Sē′lah.

Psalm 4

*To the *chief Musician on Neginoth. A Psalm of David*

1 Hear me when I call, O God of my righteousness: thou hast enlarged me *when I was* in distress; [1]have mercy upon me, and hear my prayer.

2 O ye sons of men, how long *will ye turn* my glory into shame? *how long* will ye love vanity, *and* seek after leasing? Sē′lah.

3 But know that [a]the LORD hath set apart him that is godly for himself: the LORD will hear when I call unto him.

4 Stand [b]in awe, and sin not: commune with your own heart upon your bed, and be still. Sē′lah.

5 Offer [c]the sacrifices of righteousness, and [d]put your trust in the LORD.

6 *There be* many that say, Who will shew us *any* good? [e]LORD, lift thou up the light of thy countenance upon us.

7 Thou hast put gladness in my heart, more than in the time *that* their corn and their wine increased.

8 I will both lay me down in peace, and sleep: [f]for thou, LORD, only makest me dwell in safety.

Psalm 5

To the chief Musician upon Nehiloth, A Psalm of David

1 Give ear to my words, O LORD, consider my meditation.

2 Hearken unto the voice of my cry, my King, and my God: for unto thee will I pray.

3 [a]My voice shalt thou hear in the morning, O LORD; in the morning will I direct *my prayer* unto thee, and will look up.

4 For thou *art* not a God that hath [b]pleasure in wickedness: neither shall evil dwell with thee.

5 [c]The foolish shall not stand [1]in thy sight: thou hatest all workers of iniquity.

6 Thou shalt destroy them that speak leasing: the LORD will abhor [2]the bloody and deceitful man.

7 But as for me, I will come *into* thy house in the multitude of thy mercy: *and* in thy fear will I worship [d]toward [3]thy holy temple.

8 Lead me, O LORD, in thy righteousness because of [4]mine enemies; make thy way straight before my face.

Psalm 1
1 [a]Gen. 5.24; Prov. 4.14
[1]Or, wicked
3 [2]fade
[b]Gen. 39.3; Ps. 128.2
6 [c]Nah. 1.7; John 10.14

Psalm 2
1 [1]Or, tumultuously assemble
[2]meditate
2 [a]Ps. 45.7; John 1.41
3 [b]Luke 19.14
4 [c]Ps. 11.4
5 [3]Or, trouble
6 [4]anointed
[5]upon Zion, the hill of my holiness
7 [6]Or, for a decree
[d]Matt. 8.29; Heb. 1.5
8 [e]Dan. 7.13-14; John 17.4-5
9 [f]Matt. 21.44
12 [g]John 5.22-23
[h]Jer. 17.7

Psalm 3
1 [a]2 Sam. 15.12
2 [b]2 Sam. 16.8; Ps. 22.7-8
3 [1]Or, about
[c]2 Ki. 25.27; Ps. 27.6
5 [d]Ps. 4.8; Acts 12.6
8 [e]Ps. 37.39-40; Hos. 13.4

Psalm 4
*Or, overseer
1 [1]Or, be gracious unto me
3 [a]Ex. 33.16; 2 Pet. 2.9
4 [b]Prov. 3.7;
5 [c]Deut. 33.19
[d]Ps. 37.3
6 [e]Ps. 80.3
8 [f]Lev. 26.5;

Psalm 5
3 [a]Ps. 30.5
4 [b]Mal. 2.17
5 [c]Ps. 14.1;
[1]before thine eyes
6 [2]the man of bloods and deceit
7 [d]1 Ki. 8.29
[3]the temple of thy holiness
8 [4]those which observe me

9 For *there is* no [5]faithfulness [6]in
their mouth; their inward part *is* [7]very
wickedness; their throat *is* an open sepulchre; they flatter with their tongue.
10 [8]Destroy thou them, O God; let
them fall [9]by their own counsels; cast
them out in the multitude of their
transgressions; for they have rebelled
against thee.
11 But let all those that put their
trust in thee rejoice: let them ever
shout for joy, because [10]thou defendest
them: let them also [e]that love thy
name be joyful in thee.
12 For thou, LORD, wilt bless the
righteous; with favour wilt thou [11]com-
pass him as *with* a shield.

Psalm 6

To the chief Musician on Neginoth
**upon Sheminith, A Psalm of David*
1 O lord, rebuke me not in thine anger, neither chasten me in thy hot displeasure.
2 Have mercy upon me, O LORD; for
I *am* weak: O LORD, [a]heal me; for my
bones are vexed.
3 My soul is also sore vexed: but
thou, O LORD, [b]how long?
4 Return, O LORD, deliver my soul:
oh save me for thy mercies' sake.
5 [c]For in death *there is* no remembrance of thee: in the grave who shall
give thee thanks?
6 I am weary with my groaning; [1]all
the night make I my bed to swim; I
water my couch with my tears.
7 Mine eye is consumed because of
grief; it waxeth old because of all mine
enemies.
8 Depart from me, all ye workers of
iniquity; for the LORD hath heard the
voice of my weeping.
9 The LORD [d]hath heard my supplication; the LORD will receive my
prayer.
10 Let all mine enemies be ashamed
and sore vexed: let them return *and* be
ashamed suddenly.

Psalm 7

**Shiggaion of David, which he sang*
unto the LORD, concerning the
‡words of Cush the Benjamite
1 O lord my God, in thee do I put my
trust: save me from all them that persecute me, and deliver me:
2 Lest he tear my soul like [a]a lion,
rending *it* in pieces, while *there is*
[1]none to deliver.
3 O LORD my God, [b]if I have done
this; if there be iniquity in my hands;
4 If I have rewarded evil unto him
that was at peace with me; (yea, [c]I
have delivered him that without cause
is mine enemy:)
5 Let the enemy persecute my soul,
and take *it;* yea, let him tread down my
life upon the earth, and lay mine honour in the dust. Sē'lah.
6 Arise, O LORD, in thine anger, [d]lift

9 [5]Or, stedfastness [6]in his mouth, that is, in the mouth of any of them [7]wickednesses
10 [8]Or, Make them guilty [9]Or, from their counsels
11 [10]thou coverest over, or, protectest them [e]1 Cor. 2.9
12 [11]crown him

Psalm 6
*Or, upon the eighth
2 [a]Hos. 6.1
3 [b]Prov. 18.14; Matt. 26.38
5 [c]Ps. 30.9
6 [1]Or, every night
9 [d]Ps. 3.4; Ps. 31.22; Ps. 40.1-2

Psalm 7
*Hab. 3.1
†Or, business
2 [a]1 Pet. 5.8 [1]not a deliverer
3 [b]2 Sam. 16.7
4 [c]1 Sam. 24.7
6 [d]Ps. 94.2
9 [e]1 Sam. 16.7
10 [2]My buckler is upon God
11 [3]Or, God is a righteous judge
15 [4]He hath digged a pit [f]Esth. 7.10; Prov. 5.22
16 [g]1 Ki. 2.32

Psalm 8
*Ps. 81- title
2 [a]Matt. 11.25; 1 Cor. 1.27 [1]founded [b]Ps. 44.16
3 [c]Job 22.12; Ps. 19.1; Rom. 1.20
4 [d]Job 7.17; Ps. 144.3; Heb. 2.6
6 [e]Gen. 1.26 [f]1 Cor. 15.27; Heb. 2.8
7 [2]Flocks and oxen all of them
9 [g]Job 11.7; Ps. 35.10

up thyself because of the rage of mine
enemies: and awake for me *to* the judgment *that* thou hast commanded.
7 So shall the congregation of the
people compass thee about: for their
sakes therefore return thou on high.
8 The LORD shall judge the people:
judge me, O LORD, according to my
righteousness, and according to mine
integrity *that is* in me.
9 Oh let the wickedness of the wicked
come to an end; but establish the just;
[e]for the righteous God trieth the hearts
and reins.
10 [2]My defence *is* of God, which
saveth the upright in heart.
11 [3]God judgeth the righteous, and
God is angry *with the wicked* every
day.
12 If he turn not, he will whet his
sword; he hath bent his bow, and made
it ready.
13 He hath also prepared for him
the instruments of death; he ordaineth
his arrows against the persecutors.
14 Behold, he travaileth with iniquity, and hath conceived mischief, and
brought forth falsehood.
15 [4]He made a pit, and digged it,
[f]and is fallen into the ditch *which* he
made.
16 [g]His mischief shall return upon
his own head, and his violent dealing
shall come down upon his own pate.
17 I will praise the LORD according to his righteousness: and will sing
praise to the name of the LORD most
high.

Psalm 8

*To the chief Musician *upon Gittith,*
A Psalm of David
1 O lord our Lord, how excellent *is*
thy name in all the earth! who hast set
thy glory above the heavens.
2 [a]Out of the mouth of babes and
sucklings hast thou [1]ordained strength
because of thine enemies that thou
mightest still [b]the enemy and the avenger.
3 When I [c]consider thy heavens, the
work of thy fingers, the moon and the
stars, which thou hast ordained;
4 [d]What is man, that thou art mindful of him? and the son of man, that
thou visitest him?
5 For thou hast made him a little lower than the angels, and hast
crowned him with glory and honour.
6 [e]Thou madest him to have dominion over the works of thy hands; [f]thou
hast put all *things* under his feet:
7 [2]All sheep and oxen, yea, and the
beasts of the field;
8 The fowl of the air, and the fish
of the sea, *and whatsoever* passeth
through the paths of the seas.
9 O LORD our Lord, how [g]excellent
is thy name in all the earth!

Psalm 9

To the chief Musician upon Muth-labben, A Psalm of David

1 I will praise *thee,* O LORD, with my whole heart; I will shew forth all thy marvellous works.

2 I will be glad and rejoice in thee: I will sing praise to thy name, O thou most High.

3 When mine enemies are turned back, they shall fall and perish at thy presence.

4 For [1]thou hast maintained my right and my cause; thou satest in the throne judging [2]right.

5 Thou hast rebuked the heathen, thou hast destroyed the wicked, thou hast [a]put out their name for ever and ever.

6 [3]O thou enemy, destructions are come to a perpetual end: and thou hast destroyed cities; their memorial is perished with them.

7 [b]But the LORD shall endure for ever: he hath prepared his throne for judgment.

8 And he shall judge the world in righteousness, he shall minister judgment to the people in uprightness.

9 The LORD also will be [4]a refuge for the oppressed, a refuge in times of trouble.

10 And they that [c]know thy name will put their trust in thee: for thou, LORD, hast not forsaken them that seek thee.

11 Sing praises to the LORD, which dwelleth in Zī'ŏn: declare among the people his doings.

12 When he maketh inquisition for blood, he remembereth them: he forgetteth not the cry of the [5]humble.

13 Have mercy upon me, O LORD; consider my trouble *which I suffer* of them that hate me, thou that liftest me up from the gates of death:

14 That I may shew forth all thy praise in the gates of the daughter of Zī'ŏn: I will [d]rejoice in thy salvation.

15 The heathen are sunk down in the pit *that* they made: in the net which they hid is their own foot taken.

16 The LORD is [e]known *by* the judgment *which* he executeth: the wicked is snared in the work of his own hands. [6]Hig-gā'ion. Sē'lah.

17 The wicked shall be turned into hell, *and* all the nations [f]that forget God.

18 [g]For the needy shall not alway be forgotten: the expectation of the poor shall *not* perish for ever.

19 Arise, O LORD; let not man prevail: let the heathen be judged in thy sight.

20 Put them in fear, O LORD: *that* the nations may know themselves *to be but* men. Sē'lah.

Psalm 10

1 Why standest thou afar off, O LORD? *why* hidest thou *thyself* in times of trouble?

2 [1]The wicked in *his* pride doth persecute the poor: [a]let them be taken in the devices that they have imagined.

3 For the wicked boasteth of his [2]heart's desire, and [3]blesseth the covetous, *whom* the LORD abhorreth.

4 The wicked, [b]through the pride of his countenance, will not seek *after* God: [4]God *is* not in all his thoughts.

5 His ways are always grievous; thy judgments *are* far above out of his sight: *as for* all his enemies, he puffeth at them.

6 He hath said in his heart, I shall not be moved: for *I shall* [5]never *be* in adversity.

7 His mouth is full of cursing and [6]deceit and fraud: under his tongue *is* mischief and [7]vanity.

8 He sitteth in the lurking places of the villages: in the secret places doth he murder the innocent: his eyes [8]are privily set against the poor.

9 He lieth in wait [9]secretly as a lion in his den: he lieth in wait to catch the poor: he doth catch the poor, when he draweth him into his net.

10 [10]He croucheth, *and* humbleth himself, that the poor may fall [11]by his strong ones.

11 He hath said in his heart, God hath forgotten: he hideth his face; he will never see *it.*

12 Arise, O LORD; O God, lift up thine hand: forget not the [12]humble.

13 Wherefore doth the wicked contemn God? he hath said in his heart, Thou wilt not require *it.*

14 Thou hast seen *it;* for thou beholdest mischief and spite, to requite *it* with thy hand: the poor [13]committeth himself unto thee; thou art the helper of the fatherless.

15 Break thou the arm of the wicked and the evil *man:* seek out his wickedness *till* thou find none.

16 The LORD *is* King for ever and ever: the heathen are perished out of his land.

17 LORD, thou hast heard the desire of the humble: thou wilt [14]prepare their heart, thou wilt cause thine ear to hear:

18 To judge the fatherless and the oppressed, that the man of the earth may no more [15]oppress.

Psalm 11

To the chief Musician, A Psalm of David

1 In the LORD put I my trust: how say ye to my soul, Flee *as* a bird to your mountain?

2 For, lo, the wicked bend *their* bow, they make ready their arrow upon the string, that they may [1]privily shoot at the upright in heart.

3 If the foundations be destroyed, what can the righteous do?

4 [a]The LORD *is* in his holy temple, the LORD'S throne *is* in heaven: [b]his eyes behold, his eyelids try, the children of men.

Psalm 9
4 [1]thou hast made my judgment [2]in righteousness
5 [a]Deut. 9.14
6 [3]Or, The destructions of the enemy are come to a perpetual end: and their cities hast thou destroyed, etc
7 [b]Ps. 90.2; Heb. 1.11
9 [4]an high place
10 [c]Ps. 91.14; 1 John 2.3-4
12 [5]Or, afflicted
14 [d]Ps. 13.5
16 [e]Ex. 7.5 [6]That is, Meditation
17 [f]Job 8.13; Hos. 2.13
18 [g]Ps. 12.5

Psalm 10
2 [1]In the pride of the wicked he doth persecute [a]Prov. 5.22
3 [2]soul's [3]Or, the covetous blesseth himself, he abhorreth the LORD
4 [b]2 Ki. 18.35; [4]Or, all his thoughts are, There is no God
6 [5]unto generation and generation
7 [6]deceits [7]Or, iniquity
8 [8]hide themselves
9 [9]in the secret places
10 [10]He breaketh himself [11]Or, into his strong parts
12 [12]Or, afflicted
14 [13]leaveth
17 [14]Or, establish
18 [15]Or, terrify

Psalm 11
2 [1]in darkness
4 [a]Hab. 2.20 [b]Eph. 5.13;

5 The LORD [c]trieth the righteous:
but the wicked and him that loveth violence his soul hateth.
6 Upon the wicked he shall rain
[2]snares, fire and brimstone, and [3]an
horrible tempest: *this shall be* the portion of their cup.
7 For the righteous LORD loveth righteousness; his countenance doth behold the upright.

Psalm 12

*To the chief Musician *upon Sheminith, A Psalm of David*

1 [1]Help, LORD; for [a]the godly man
ceaseth; for the faithful fail from
among the children of men.
2 They speak vanity every one with
his neighbour: *with* flattering lips *and*
with [2]a double heart do they speak.
3 The LORD shall cut off all flattering lips, *and* the tongue that speaketh
[3]proud things:
4 Who have said, With our tongue
will we prevail; our lips [4]*are* our own:
who *is* lord over us?
5 For the [b]oppression of the poor,
for the sighing of the needy, now will I
arise, saith the LORD; I will set *him* in
safety *from him that* [5]puffeth at him.
6 The words of the LORD *are* [c]pure
words: *as* silver tried in a furnace of
earth, purified seven times.
7 Thou shalt keep them, O LORD,
thou shalt preserve [6]them from this
generation for ever.
8 The wicked walk on every side,
when [7]the vilest men are exalted.

Psalm 13

*To the *chief Musician, A Psalm of David*

1 How long wilt thou forget me, O
LORD? for ever? [a]how long wilt thou
hide thy face from me?
2 How long shall I take counsel in
my soul, *having* sorrow in my heart
daily? how long shall mine enemy be
exalted over me?
3 Consider *and* hear me, O LORD my
God: [b]lighten mine eyes, [c]lest I sleep
the *sleep of* death;
4 Lest mine enemy say, I have prevailed against him; *and* those that trouble me rejoice when I am moved.
5 But I have [d]trusted in thy mercy;
my heart shall rejoice in thy salvation.
6 I will sing unto the LORD, because
he hath dealt bountifully with me.

Psalm 14

To the chief Musician, A Psalm of David

1 The [a]fool hath said in his heart,
There is no God. [b]They are corrupt,
they have done abominable works,
there is none that doeth good.
2 The LORD looked down from
heaven upon the children of men, to
see if there were any that did understand, *and* seek God.

5 [c]Job 5.17; Ps. 94.12
6 [2]Or, quick burning coals [3]Or, a burning tempest
Psalm 12
*Or, upon the eighth
1 [1]Or, Save [a]Isa. 57.1
2 [2]an heart and an heart
3 [3]great things
4 [4]are with us
5 [b]Ex. 3.7-8 [5]Or, would ensnare him
6 [c]2 Sam. 22.31; Prov. 30.5
7 [6]him: that is, every one of them
8 [7]of the sons of men
Psalm 13
*Or, overseer
1 [a]Deut. 31.17; Isa. 59.2
3 [b]Ezra 9.8; Rev. 21.23 [c]Ps. 76.5-6; Eph. 5.14
5 [d]2 Chr. 20.12
Psalm 14
1 [a]Ps. 10.4; Prov. 1.7-22 [b]Gen. 6.12; Rom. 3.10
3 [1]stinking
5 [2]they feared a fear
7 [3]Who will give
Psalm 15
1 [1]sojourn [a]Ps. 2.6
2 [b]Ps. 84.11; Isa. 33.15-16
3 [2]Or, receiveth, or, endureth
4 [c]Josh. 9.18-20
5 [d]Ezek. 18.8-9
Psalm 16
*Or, A golden Psalm of David
1 [a]Ps. 25.20
4 [1]Or, give gifts to another
5 [2]of my part
9 [3]dwell confidently
10 [b]Ps. 49.15; [c]Dan. 9.24;
11 [d]Acts 2.28

3 They are all gone aside, they are
all together become [1]filthy: *there is*
none that doeth good, no, not one.
4 Have all the workers of iniquity no
knowledge? who eat up my people *as*
they eat bread, and call not upon the
LORD.
5 There [2]were they in great fear:
for God *is* in the generation of the
righteous.
6 Ye have shamed the counsel of the
poor, because the LORD *is* his refuge.
7 [3]Oh that the salvation of Is'ra-el
were come out of Zī'ŏn! when the
LORD bringeth back the captivity of his
people, Jā'cob shall rejoice, *and* Is'ra-
el shall be glad.

Psalm 15

A Psalm of David

1 Lord, who shall [1]abide in thy tabernacle? who shall dwell in [a]thy holy
hill?
2 He [b]that walketh uprightly, and
worketh righteousness, and speaketh
the truth in his heart.
3 *He that* backbiteth not with his
tongue, nor doeth evil to his neighbour,
nor [2]taketh up a reproach against his
neighbour.
4 In whose eyes a vile person is
contemned; but he honoureth them
that fear the LORD. *He that* [c]sweareth
to *his own* hurt, and changeth not.
5 [d]*He that* putteth not out his money
to usury, nor taketh reward against the
innocent. He that doeth these *things*
shall never be moved.

Psalm 16

**Michtam of David*

1 Preserve me, O God: [a]for in thee
do I put my trust.
2 *O my soul,* thou hast said unto the
Lord, Thou *art* my LORD: my goodness
extendeth not to thee;
3 *But* to the saints that *are* in the
earth, and *to* the excellent, in whom *is*
all my delight.
4 Their sorrows shall be multiplied
that [1]hasten *after* another *god:* their
drink offerings of blood will I not offer,
nor take up their names into my lips.
5 The LORD *is* the portion [2]of mine
inheritance and of my cup: thou main-
tainest my lot.
6 The lines are fallen unto me in
pleasant *places;* yea, I have a goodly
heritage.
7 I will bless the LORD, who hath
given me counsel: my reins also instruct me in the night seasons.
8 I have set the LORD always before
me: because *he is* at my right hand, I
shall not be moved.
9 Therefore my heart is glad, and
my glory rejoiceth: my flesh also shall
[3]rest in hope.
10 [b]For thou wilt not leave my soul
in hell; neither wilt thou suffer thine
[c]Holy One to see corruption.
11 Thou wilt shew me [d]the path of
life: in thy presence *is* fulness of joy; at

thy right hand *there are* pleasures for
evermore.

Psalm 17

A Prayer of David

1 Hear [1]the right, O LORD, attend
unto my cry, give ear unto my prayer,
that goeth [2]not out of feigned lips.
2 Let my sentence come forth from
thy presence; let thine eyes behold the
things that are equal.
3 Thou hast [a]proved mine heart;
thou hast visited *me* in the night; thou
hast tried me, *and* shalt find nothing; I
am purposed *that* my [b]mouth shall not
transgress.
4 Concerning the works of men, by
[c]the word of thy lips I have kept *me*
from the paths of the destroyer.
5 Hold up my goings in thy paths,
that my footsteps [3]slip not.
6 I have called upon thee, for thou
wilt hear me, O God: incline thine ear
unto me, *and hear* my speech.
7 Shew thy marvellous lovingkindness, O thou [4]that savest by thy right
hand them which put their trust *in thee*
from those that rise up *against them*.
8 [d]Keep me as the apple of the eye,
hide me under the shadow of thy wings,
9 From the wicked [5]that oppress me,
from [6]my deadly enemies, *who* compass me about.
10 They are inclosed in their own fat:
with their mouth they speak proudly.
11 They have now [e]compassed us in
our steps: they have set their eyes bowing down to the earth;
12 [7]Like as a lion *that* is greedy of
his prey, and as it were a young lion
[8]lurking in secret places.
13 Arise, O LORD, [9]disappoint him,
cast him down: deliver my soul from
the wicked, [10]*which is* thy sword:
14 From men *which are* thy hand, O
LORD, from men of the world, *which*
have their portion in *this* life, and
whose belly thou fillest with thy hid
treasure: [11]they are full of children,
and leave the rest of their *substance* to
their babes.
15 As for me, [f]I will behold thy face
in righteousness: I shall be satisfied,
when I awake, with [g]thy likeness.

Psalm 18

*To the chief Musician, A Psalm of David, the servant of the LORD, who spake unto the LORD the words of *this song in the day that the LORD delivered him from the hand of all his enemies, and from the hand of Saul: And he said*

1 I [a]WILL love thee, O LORD, my
strength.
2 The LORD *is* my rock, and my fortress, and my deliverer; my God, [1]my
strength, [b]in whom I will trust; my
buckler, and the horn of my salvation,
and my high tower.
3 I will call upon the LORD, [c]*who is*
worthy to be praised: so shall I be
saved from mine enemies.
4 [d]The sorrows of death compassed
me, and the floods of [2]ungodly men
made me afraid.
5 The [3]sorrows of hell compassed
me about: the snares of death prevented me.
6 In my distress I called upon the
LORD, and cried unto my God: he heard
my voice out of his temple, and my cry
came before him, *even* into his ears.
7 [e]Then the earth shook and trembled; the foundations also of the hills
moved and were shaken, because he
was wroth.
8 There went up a smoke [4]out of his
nostrils, and fire out of his mouth devoured: coals were kindled by it.
9 [f]He bowed the heavens also, and
came down: and darkness *was* under
his feet.
10 [g]And he rode upon a cherub, and
did fly: yea, [h]he did fly upon the wings
of the wind.
11 He made darkness his secret
place; his [i]pavilion round about him
were dark waters *and* thick clouds of
the skies.
12 At the brightness *that was* before him his thick clouds passed, hail
stones and coals of fire.
13 The LORD also thundered in the
heavens, and the Highest gave [j]his
voice; hail *stones* and coals of fire.
14 [k]Yea, he sent out his arrows, and
scattered them; and he shot out lightnings, and discomfited them.
15 Then the channels of waters were
seen, and the foundations of the world
were discovered at thy rebuke, O LORD,
at the blast of the breath of thy nostrils.
16 [l]He sent from above, he took me,
he drew me out of [5]many waters.
17 He delivered me from my strong
enemy, and from them which hated
me: for they were too strong for me.
18 They prevented me in the day of
my calamity: but the LORD was my
stay.
19 [m]He brought me forth also into a
large place; he delivered me, because
he delighted in me.
20 [n]The LORD rewarded me according to my righteousness; according to
the cleanness of my hands hath he recompensed me.
21 For I have kept the ways of the
LORD, and have not wickedly departed
from my God.
22 For all his judgments *were* before
me, and I did not put away his statutes
from me.
23 I was also upright [6]before him,
and I kept myself from mine iniquity.
24 [o]Therefore hath the LORD recompensed me according to my righteousness, according to the cleanness of my
hands [7]in his eyesight.
25 [p]With the merciful thou wilt shew
thyself merciful; with an upright man
thou wilt shew thyself upright;
26 With the pure thou wilt shew thyself pure; and [q]with the froward thou
wilt [8]shew thyself froward.
27 For thou wilt save the afflicted

Psalm 17
1 [1]justice [2]without lips of deceit
3 [a]Job 23.10 [b]Jas. 3.2
4 [c]Rom. 12.2
5 [3]be not moved
7 [4]Or, that savest them which trust in thee from those that rise up against thy right hand
8 [d]Deut. 32.10
9 [5]that waste me [6]my enemies against the soul
11 [e]1 Sam. 23.26
12 [7]The likeness of him (that is, of every one of them) is as a lion that desireth to ravin [8]sitting
13 [9]prevent his face [10]Or, by thy sword
14 [11]Or, their children are full
15 [f]Job 19.26-27 [g]Col. 1.15

Psalm 18
*2 Sam. 22
1 [a]Deut. 32.4;
2 [1]my rock [b]Heb. 2.13
3 [c]Ps. 76.4
4 [d]Ps. 116.3 [2]Belial
5 [3]Or, cords
7 [e]Acts 4.31
8 [4]by his
9 [f]Isa. 64.1
10 [g]Ps. 99.1 [h]Ps. 104.3
11 [i]Ps. 97.2
13 [j]Ps. 29.3
14 [k]Num. 24.8;
16 [l]Ps. 144.7 [5]Or, great waters
19 [m]Ps. 118.5
20 [n]2 Sam. 22.21;
23 [6]with
24 [o]Ruth 2.12; [7]before his eyes
25 [p]Matt. 18.32-35
26 [q]Lev. 26.23 [8]Or, wrestle

people; but wilt bring down [r]high looks.

28 [s]For thou wilt light my [9]candle: the LORD my God will enlighten my darkness.

29 For by thee I have [10]run through a troop; and by my God have I leaped over a wall.

30 *As for* God, [t]his way *is* perfect: [u]the word of the LORD is [11]tried: he *is* a buckler to all those that trust in him.

31 For [v]who *is* God save the LORD? or who *is* a rock save our God?

32 *It is* God that girdeth me with strength, and maketh my way perfect.

33 He maketh my feet like hinds' *feet,* and setteth me upon my high places.

34 He teacheth my hands to war, so that a bow of steel is broken by mine arms.

35 Thou hast also given me the shield of thy salvation: and thy right hand hath holden me up, and [12]thy gentleness hath made me great.

36 Thou hast enlarged my steps under me, that [13]my feet did not slip.

37 I have pursued mine enemies, and overtaken them: neither did I turn again till they were consumed.

38 I have wounded them that they were not able to rise: they are fallen under my feet.

39 For thou hast girded me with strength unto the battle: thou hast [14]subdued under me those that rose up against me.

40 Thou hast also given me the necks of mine enemies; that I might destroy them that hate me.

41 They cried, but *there was* none to save *them: even* unto the LORD, but he answered them not.

42 Then did I beat them small as the dust before the wind: I did cast them out as the dirt in the streets.

43 Thou hast delivered me from the strivings of the people; *and* thou hast made me the head of the heathen: a people *whom* I have not known shall serve me.

44 [15]As soon as they hear of me, they shall obey me: [16]the strangers shall [17]submit themselves unto me.

45 The strangers shall fade away, and be afraid out of their close places.

46 The LORD liveth; and blessed *be* my rock; and let the God of my salvation be exalted.

47 *It is* God that [18]avengeth me, and [19]subdueth the people under me.

48 He delivereth me from mine enemies: yea, thou liftest me up above those that rise up against me: thou hast delivered me from the [20]violent man.

49 Therefore will I [21]give thanks unto thee, O LORD, among the heathen, and sing praises unto thy name.

50 Great deliverance giveth he to his king; and sheweth mercy to his anointed, to Dā'vid, and to his seed for evermore.

27 [r]Prov. 6.17
28 [s]Job 18.6 [9]Or, lamp
29 [10]Or, broken
30 [t]Deut. 32.4; [u]Ps. 12.6 [11]Or, refined
31 [v]Deut. 32.31;
35 [12]Or, with thy meekness thou hast multiplied me
36 [13]mine ancles
39 [14]caused to bow
44 [15]At the hearing of the ear [16]the sons of the stranger [17]lie, or, yield feigned obedience
47 [18]giveth avengements for me [19]Or, destroyeth [20]man of violence
49 [21]Or, confess

Psalm 19
3 [1]without their voice heard, or, without these their voice is heard
4 [2]Or, Their rule, or, direction
7 [3]Or, doctrine [4]Or, restoring
9 [5]truth
10 [6]the dropping of honeycombs
13 [7]Or, much
14 [8]my rock

Psalm 20
1 [a]Isa. 50.10 [1]set thee on an high place
2 [2]thy help [3]support thee
3 [4]turn to ashes: or, make fat
4 [b]1 John 5.14-15
5 [c]Isa. 12.1-2 [d]1 Sam. 17.45
6 [5]from the heaven of his holiness [6]by the strength of the salvation of his right hand
7 [e]Judg. 7.7

Psalm 19

To the chief Musician, A Psalm of David

1 The heavens declare the glory of God; and the firmament sheweth his handywork.

2 Day unto day uttereth speech, and night unto night sheweth knowledge.

3 *There is* no speech nor language, [1]*where* their voice is not heard.

4 [2]Their line is gone out through all the earth, and their words to the end of the world. In them hath he set a tabernacle for the sun,

5 Which *is* as a bridegroom coming out of his chamber, *and* rejoiceth as a strong man to run a race.

6 His going forth *is* from the end of the heaven, and his circuit unto the ends of it: and there is nothing hid from the heat thereof.

7 The [3]law of the LORD *is* perfect, [4]converting the soul: the testimony of the LORD *is* sure, making wise the simple.

8 The statutes of the LORD *are* right, rejoicing the heart: the commandment of the LORD *is* pure, enlightening the eyes.

9 The fear of the LORD *is* clean, enduring for ever: the judgments of the LORD *are* [5]true *and* righteous altogether.

10 More to be desired *are they* than gold, yea, than much fine gold: sweeter also than honey and [6]the honeycomb.

11 Moreover by them is thy servant warned: *and* in keeping of them *there is* great reward.

12 Who can understand *his* errors? cleanse thou me from secret *faults.*

13 Keep back thy servant also from presumptuous *sins;* let them not have dominion over me: then shall I be upright, and I shall be innocent from [7]the great transgression.

14 Let the words of my mouth, and the meditation of my heart, be acceptable in thy sight, O LORD, [8]my strength, and my redeemer.

Psalm 20

To the chief Musician, A Psalm of David

1 The LORD hear thee in the day of trouble; [a]the name of the God of Jā'cob [1]defend thee;

2 Send [2]thee help from the sanctuary, and [3]strengthen thee out of Zī'ŏn;

3 Remember all thy offerings, and [4]accept thy burnt sacrifice; Sē'lah.

4 [b]Grant thee according to thine own heart, and fulfil all thy counsel.

5 We will [c]rejoice in thy salvation, and in the name of our God we [d]will set up *our* banners: the LORD fulfil all thy petitions.

6 Now know I that the LORD saveth his anointed; he will hear him [5]from his holy heaven [6]with the saving strength of his right hand.

7 Some *trust* in chariots, and some in horses: but we will [e]remember the name of the LORD our God.

8 They are brought down and fallen: but we are risen, and stand upright.

9 Save, LORD: let the king hear us when we call.

Psalm 21

To the chief Musician, A Psalm of David

1 The king shall joy in thy strength, O LORD; and in thy salvation how greatly shall he rejoice!

2 Thou hast given him [a]his heart's desire, and hast not withholden the request of his lips. Sē'lah.

3 For thou preventest him with the blessings of goodness: thou settest a crown of pure gold on his head.

4 He asked life of thee, [b]*and* thou gavest *it* him, *even* length of days for ever and ever.

5 His glory *is* great in thy salvation: honour and majesty hast thou laid upon him.

6 For thou hast [1]made him most blessed for ever: thou hast [2]made him exceeding glad with thy countenance.

7 For the king [c]trusteth in the LORD, and through the mercy of the most High he shall not be moved.

8 Thine hand shall find out all thine enemies: thy right hand shall find out those that hate thee.

9 Thou shalt make them as [d]a fiery oven in the time of thine anger: the LORD shall swallow them up in his wrath, and the fire shall devour them.

10 Their fruit shalt thou destroy from the earth, and their seed from among the children of men.

11 For they intended evil against thee: they imagined a mischievous device, *which* they are not able *to perform*.

12 Therefore [3]shalt thou make them turn their [4]back, *when* thou shalt make ready *thine arrows* upon thy strings against the face of them.

13 Be thou exalted, LORD, in thine own strength: *so* will we [e]sing and praise thy power.

Psalm 22

*To the chief Musician upon *Aijeleth Shahar, A Psalm of David*

1 My [a]God, my God, why hast thou forsaken me? *why art thou so* far [1]from helping me, *and from* [b]the words of my roaring?

2 O my God, I cry in the daytime, but thou hearest not; and in the night season, and [2]am not silent.

3 But thou *art* [c]holy, *O thou* that inhabitest the praises of Is'ra-el.

4 Our fathers trusted in thee: they trusted, and thou didst deliver them.

5 They cried unto thee, and were delivered: they trusted in thee, and were not confounded.

6 But I *am* a worm, and no man; [d]a reproach of men, and despised of the people.

7 [e]All they that see me laugh me to

Psalm 21
2 [a]John 11.42
4 [b]2 Sam. 7.19
6 [1]set him to be blessings [2]gladded him with joy
7 [c]Ps. 91.2
9 [d]Deut. 32.22
12 [3]Or, thou shalt set them as a butt [4]shoulder
13 [e]Rev. 15.3-4

Psalm 22
*Or, the hind of the morning
1 [a]Matt. 27.46 [1]from my salvation [b]Heb. 5.7
2 [2]there is no silence to me
3 [c]Isa. 6.3; Rev. 4.8
6 [d]Isa. 53.3
7 [e]Matt. 9.24; Mark 15.20; Luke 16.14 [3]open
8 [4]He rolled himself on the LORD [5]Or, if he delight in him
9 [6]Or, keptest me in safety
11 [7]not a helper
13 [8]opened their mouths against me [f]Ps. 35.21; 1 Pet. 5.8
14 [9]Or, sundered
15 [g]Prov. 17.22
16 [h]Zech. 12.10; Luke 23.33; John 20.27
18 [i]Matt. 27.35; Mark 15.24; Luke 23.34
20 [10]my only one [11]from the hand
21 [j]2 Tim. 4.17
22 [k]John 20.17
26 [l]John 6.57 [m]John 6.51
27 [n]Ps. 2.8
28 [o]Ps. 47.7-9; Zech. 14.9; Matt. 6.13
29 [p]Isa. 26.19

scorn: they [3]shoot out the lip, they shake the head, *saying*,

8 [4]He trusted on the LORD *that* he would deliver him: let him deliver him, [5]seeing he delighted in him.

9 But thou *art* he that took me out of the womb: thou [6]didst make me hope *when I was* upon my mother's breasts.

10 I was cast upon thee from the womb: thou *art* my God from my mother's belly.

11 Be not far from me; for trouble *is* near; for *there is* [7]none to help.

12 Many bulls have compassed me: strong *bulls* of Bā'shăn have beset me round.

13 They [8][f]gaped upon me *with* their mouths, *as* a ravening and a roaring lion.

14 I am poured out like water, and all my bones are [9]out of joint: my heart is like wax; it is melted in the midst of my bowels.

15 [g]My strength is dried up like a potsherd; and my tongue cleaveth to my jaws; and thou hast brought me into the dust of death.

16 For dogs have compassed me: the assembly of the wicked have inclosed me: [h]they pierced my hands and my feet.

17 I may tell all my bones: they look *and* stare upon me.

18 [i]They part my garments among them, and cast lots upon my vesture.

19 But be not thou far from me, O LORD: O my strength, haste thee to help me.

20 Deliver my soul from the sword; [10]my darling [11]from the power of the dog.

21 [j]Save me from the lion's mouth: for thou hast heard me from the horns of the unicorns.

22 I will declare thy name unto my [k]brethren: in the midst of the congregation will I praise thee.

23 Ye that fear the LORD, praise him; all ye the seed of Jā'cob, glorify him; and fear him, all ye the seed of Is'ra-el.

24 For he hath not despised nor abhorred the affliction of the afflicted; neither hath he hid his face from him; but when he cried unto him, he heard.

25 My praise *shall be* of thee in the great congregation: I will pay my vows before them that fear him.

26 [l]The meek shall eat and be satisfied: they shall praise the LORD that seek him: your heart [m]shall live for ever.

27 [n]All the ends of the world shall remember and turn unto the LORD: and all the kindreds of the nations shall worship before thee.

28 [o]For the kingdom *is* the LORD'S: and he *is* the governor among the nations.

29 All *they that be* fat upon earth shall eat and worship: [p]all they that go down to the dust shall bow before him: and none can keep alive his own soul.

30 A seed shall serve him; it shall be accounted to the Lord for a generation.

31 They shall come, and shall declare his righteousness unto a people
that shall be born, that he hath done
this.

Psalm 23

A Psalm of David

1 The LORD *is* [a]my shepherd; I shall
not want.
2 He maketh me to lie down in [1]green
pastures: [b]he leadeth me beside the
[2]still waters.
3 He restoreth my soul: he leadeth
me in the paths of righteousness for
his name's sake.
4 Yea, though I walk through the valley of the shadow of death, I will fear
no evil: [c]for thou *art* with me; thy rod
and thy staff they comfort me.
5 Thou preparest a table before me
in the presence of mine enemies: thou
[3]anointest my head with oil; my cup
runneth over.
6 Surely goodness and mercy shall
follow me all the days of my life: and I
will [d]dwell in the house of the LORD
[4]for ever.

Psalm 24

A Psalm of David

1 The [a]earth *is* the LORD'S, and the
fulness thereof; the world, and they
that dwell therein.
2 For he hath founded it upon the
seas, and established it upon the floods.
3 Who shall ascend into the hill of
the LORD? or who shall stand in his
holy place?
4 [1]He that hath clean hands, and [b]a
pure heart; who hath not lifted up his
soul unto vanity, nor sworn deceitfully.
5 He shall receive the blessing from
the LORD, and righteousness from the
God of his salvation.
6 This *is* the generation of them that
seek him, that seek thy face, [2]O Jā'cob.
Sē'lah.
7 Lift up your heads, O ye gates; and
be ye lift up, ye everlasting doors;
[c]and the King of glory shall come in.
8 Who *is* this King of glory? The
LORD strong and mighty, the LORD
mighty in battle.
9 Lift up your heads, O ye gates;
even lift *them* up, ye everlasting doors;
and the King of glory shall come in.
10 Who is this King of glory? The
LORD of hosts, he *is* the King of glory.
Sē'lah.

Psalm 25

A Psalm of David

1 Unto [a]thee, O LORD, do I lift up my
soul.
2 O my God, I [b]trust in thee: let me
not be ashamed, let not mine enemies
triumph over me.
3 Yea, let none that wait on thee be
ashamed: let them be ashamed which
transgress without cause.
4 [c]Shew me thy ways, O LORD; teach
me thy paths.

Psalm 23
1 [a]John 10.11; 1 Pet. 2.25
2 [1]pastures of tender grass [b]Ezek. 34.14 [2]waters of quietness
4 [c]Ps. 46.11; Isa. 8.10; Zech. 8.23; Matt. 1.23; Acts 18.9-10
5 [3]makest fat
6 [d]2 Cor. 5.1 [4]to length of days

Psalm 24
1 [a]Ex. 9.29; Job 41.11
4 [1]The clean of hands [b]Matt. 5.8
6 [2]Or, O God of Jacob
7 [c]Hag. 2.7; Mal. 3.1; 1 Cor. 2.8

Psalm 25
1 [a]1 Sam. 1.15; Ps. 86.4; Lam. 3.41
2 [b]Ps. 7.1; Ps. 18.2; Rom. 10.11
4 [c]Ex. 33.13; Ps. 143.8; Prov. 8.20
6 [1]thy bowels
7 [d]Ps. 51.1
11 [e]Ps. 31.3; Ps. 79.9 [f]Rom. 5.20
12 [g]Ps. 37.23
13 [2]shall lodge in goodness [h]Ps. 37.11-22-29
14 [i]Prov. 3.32; John 7.17; 2 Cor. 4.2-6 [3]Or, and his covenant to make them know it
15 [j]Ps. 141.8 [4]bring forth
16 [k]Ps. 69.16
18 [l]2 Sam. 16.12
19 [5]hatred of violence
22 [m]Ps. 130.8

Psalm 26
1 [a]Ps. 7.8 [b]Ps. 28.7; Prov. 29.25
4 [c]Ps. 1.1; Jer. 15.17
5 [d]Ps. 1.1; Ps. 5.5; Ps. 15.4; Ps. 31.6
6 [e]Ex. 30.19; Ps. 73.13; 1 Tim. 2.8

5 Lead me in thy truth, and teach
me: for thou *art* the God of my salvation; on thee do I wait all the day.
6 Remember, O LORD, [1]thy tender
mercies and thy lovingkindnesses; for
they *have been* ever of old.
7 Remember not the sins of my
youth, nor my transgressions: [d]accord-
ing to thy mercy remember thou me
for thy goodness' sake, O LORD.
8 Good and upright *is* the LORD:
therefore will he teach sinners in the
way.
9 The meek will he guide in judgment: and the meek will he teach his
way.
10 All the paths of the LORD *are*
mercy and truth unto such as keep his
covenant and his testimonies.
11 [e]For thy name's sake, O LORD,
pardon mine iniquity; [f]for it *is* great.
12 What man *is* he that feareth the
LORD? [g]him shall he teach in the way
that he shall choose.
13 His soul [2]shall dwell at ease; and
[h]his seed shall inherit the earth.
14 [i]The secret of the LORD *is* with
them that fear him; [3]and he will shew
them his covenant.
15 [j]Mine eyes *are* ever toward the
LORD; for he shall [4]pluck my feet out of
the net.
16 [k]Turn thee unto me, and have
mercy upon me; for I *am* desolate and
afflicted.
17 The troubles of my heart are enlarged: O bring thou me out of my
distresses.
18 [l]Look upon mine affliction and
my pain; and forgive all my sins.
19 Consider mine enemies; for they
are many; and they hate me with [5]cruel
hatred.
20 O keep my soul, and deliver me:
let me not be ashamed; for I put my
trust in thee.
21 Let integrity and uprightness preserve me; for I wait on thee.
22 [m]Redeem Is'ra-el, O God, out of
all his troubles.

Psalm 26

A Psalm of David

1 Judge [a]me, O LORD; for I have
walked in mine integrity: [b]I have
trusted also in the LORD; *therefore* I
shall not slide.
2 Examine me, O LORD, and prove
me; try my reins and my heart.
3 For thy lovingkindness *is* before
mine eyes: and I have walked in thy
truth.
4 [c]I have not sat with vain persons,
neither will I go in with dissemblers.
5 I have [d]hated the congregation of
evildoers; and will not sit with the
wicked.
6 [e]I will wash mine hands in innocency: so will I compass thine altar, O
LORD:
7 That I may publish with the voice
of thanksgiving, and tell of all thy wondrous works.

8 LORD, I have loved the habitation
of thy house, and the place [1]where
thine honour dwelleth.
9 [2]Gather not my soul with sinners,
nor my life with [3]bloody men:
10 In whose hands *is* mischief, and
their right hand is [4]full of bribes.
11 But as for me, I will walk in mine
integrity: redeem me, and be merciful
unto me.
12 My foot standeth in an even place:
in the congregations will I bless the
LORD.

Psalm 27

A Psalm of David

1 The LORD *is* my light and my salvation; whom shall I fear? the LORD *is* the
strength of my life; of whom shall I be
afraid?
2 When the wicked, *even* mine enemies and my foes, [1]came upon me to
eat up my flesh, they stumbled and fell.
3 Though an host should encamp
against me, my heart shall not fear:
though war should rise against me, in
this *will* I *be* confident.
4 One *thing* have I desired of the
LORD, that will I seek after; that I may
dwell in the house of the LORD all the
days of my life, to behold [2]the beauty of
the LORD, and to inquire in his temple.
5 For [a]in the time of trouble he shall
hide me in his pavilion: in the secret of
his tabernacle shall he hide me; he
shall set me up upon a rock.
6 And now shall mine head be lifted
up above mine enemies round about
me: therefore will I offer in his tabernacle sacrifices [3]of joy; I will sing, yea, I
will sing praises unto the LORD.
7 Hear, O LORD, *when* I cry with my
voice: have mercy also upon me, and
answer me.
8 [4]*When thou saidst,* Seek ye my
face; my heart said unto thee, Thy
face, LORD, will I seek.
9 Hide not thy face *far* from me; put
not thy servant away in anger: thou
hast been my help; leave me not, neither forsake me, O God of my salvation.
10 [b]When my father and my mother
forsake me, then the LORD [5]will take
me up.
11 Teach me thy way, O LORD, and
lead me in [6]a plain path, because of
[7]mine enemies.
12 Deliver me not over unto the will
of mine enemies: for [c]false witnesses
are risen up against me, and such as
breathe out cruelty.
13 *I had fainted,* [d]unless I had believed to see the goodness of the LORD
in the land of the living.
14 [e]Wait on the LORD: be of good
courage, and he shall strengthen thine
heart: wait, I say, on the LORD.

Psalm 28

A Psalm of David

1 Unto thee will I cry, O LORD my
rock; be not silent [1]to me: lest, *if* thou
be silent to me, I become like them that
go down into the pit.
2 Hear the voice of my supplications, when I cry unto thee, when I lift
up my hands [2]toward thy holy oracle.
3 Draw me not away with the wicked,
and with the workers of iniquity, which
speak peace to their neighbours, but
mischief *is* in their hearts.
4 [a]Give them according to their
deeds, and according to the wickedness of their endeavours: give them after the work of their hands; render to
them their desert.
5 Because they regard not the works
of the LORD, nor the operation of his
hands, he shall destroy them, and not
build them up.
6 Blessed *be* the LORD, because he
hath heard the voice of my supplications.
7 The LORD *is* [b]my strength and my
shield; my heart trusted in him, and I
am helped: therefore my heart greatly
rejoiceth; and with my song will I
praise him.
8 The LORD *is* [3]their strength, and he
is the [4]saving strength of his anointed.
9 Save thy people, and bless thine
inheritance: [5]feed them also, and lift
them up for ever.

Psalm 29

A Psalm of David

1 [a]Give unto the LORD, O [1]ye
mighty, give unto the LORD glory and
strength.
2 Give unto the LORD [2]the glory due
unto his name; worship the LORD [3]in
the beauty of holiness.
3 The voice of the LORD *is* upon the
waters: the God of glory thundereth:
the LORD *is* upon [4]many waters.
4 The voice of the LORD *is* [5]power-
ful; the voice of the LORD *is* [6]full of
majesty.
5 The voice of the LORD breaketh
the cedars; yea, the LORD breaketh the
cedars of Lĕb'a-non.
6 [b]He maketh them also to skip like
a calf; Lĕb'a-non and [c]Sĭr'i-ŏn like a
young unicorn.
7 The voice of the LORD [7]divideth
the flames of fire.
8 The voice of the LORD shaketh the
wilderness; the LORD shaketh the wilderness of [d]Kā'desh.
9 The voice of the LORD maketh the
hinds [8]to calve, and discovereth the forests: and in his temple [9]doth every one
speak of *his* glory.
10 The LORD [e]sitteth upon the flood;
yea, the LORD sitteth King for ever.
11 The LORD will [f]give strength unto
his people; the LORD will bless his people with peace.

Psalm 30

A Psalm and Song at the dedication of the house of David

1 I will extol thee, O LORD; for thou
hast lifted me up, and hast not made
my foes to rejoice over me.

8 [1]of the tabernacle of thy honour
9 [2]Or, Take not away [3]men of blood
10 [4]filled with

Psalm 27
2 [1]approached against me
4 [2]Or, the delight
5 [a]Prov. 18.10;
6 [3]of shouting
8 [4]Or, My heart said unto thee, Let my face seek thy face
10 [b]Isa. 49.15; [5]will gather me
11 [6]a way of plainness [7]those which observe me
12 [c]1 Sam. 22.9;
13 [d]Ps. 112.7-8
14 [e]Ps. 62.1-5;

Psalm 28
1 [1]from me
2 [2]Or, toward the oracle of thy sanctuary
4 [a]2 Tim. 4.14
7 [b]Ps. 18.2
8 [3]Or, his strength [4]strength of salvations
9 [5]Or, rule

Psalm 29
1 [a]1 Chr. 16.28-29 [1]ye sons of the mighty
2 [2]the honour of his name [3]Or, in his glorious sanctuary
3 [4]Or, great waters
4 [5]in power [6]in majesty
6 [b]Ps. 114.4 [c]Deut. 3.9
7 [7]cutteth out
8 [d]Num. 13.26
9 [8]Or, to be in pain, and so bring forth [9]Or, every whit of it uttereth, etc
10 [e]Ps. 93.4
11 [f]Isa. 40.29

2 O LORD my God, I [a]cried unto
thee, and thou hast healed me.
3 O LORD, [b]thou hast brought up my
soul from the grave: thou hast kept me
alive, that I should not go down to the
pit.
4 Sing unto the LORD, O ye saints of
his, and give thanks [1]at the remembrance of his holiness.
5 For [2]his anger *endureth but* a moment; [c]in his favour *is* life: weeping
may endure [3]for a night, but [4]joy *cometh* in the morning.
6 And [d]in my prosperity I said, I
shall never be moved.
7 LORD, by thy favour thou hast
[5]made my mountain to stand strong:
[e]thou didst hide thy face, *and* I was
troubled.
8 I cried to thee, O LORD; and unto
the LORD I made supplication.
9 What profit *is there* in my blood,
when I go down to the pit? [f]Shall the
dust praise thee? shall it declare thy
truth?
10 Hear, O LORD, [g]and have mercy
upon me: LORD, be thou my helper.
11 [h]Thou hast turned for me my
mourning into dancing: thou hast put
off my sackcloth, and girded me with
gladness;
12 To the end that [6]*my* glory may
sing praise to thee, and not be silent. O
LORD my God, I will give thanks unto
thee for ever.

Psalm 31

To the chief Musician, A Psalm of David

1 In thee, O LORD, do I put my trust;
let me never be ashamed: deliver me in
thy righteousness.
2 [a]Bow down thine ear to me; deliver me speedily: be thou [1]my strong
rock, for an house of defence to save
me.
3 For thou *art* my rock and my fortress; therefore [b]for thy name's sake
lead me, and guide me.
4 Pull me out of the net that they
have laid privily for me: for thou *art*
my strength.
5 [c]Into thine hand I commit my
spirit: thou hast redeemed me, O LORD
[d]God of truth.
6 I have hated them that regard lying vanities: but I trust in the LORD.
7 I will be glad and rejoice in thy
mercy: for thou hast considered my
trouble; thou hast [e]known my soul in
adversities;
8 And hast not shut me up into the
hand of the enemy: [f]thou hast set my
feet in a large room.
9 Have mercy upon me, O LORD, for
I am in trouble: mine eye is consumed
with grief, *yea,* my soul and my belly.
10 For my life is spent with grief, and
my years with sighing: my strength
faileth because of mine iniquity, and
my bones are consumed.
11 I was a reproach among all mine
enemies, but [g]especially among my
neighbours, and a fear to mine ac-

Psalm 30
2 [a]Ps. 6.2-4
3 [b]Ps. 40.1-2
4 [1]Or, to the memorial
5 [2]there is but a moment in his anger
[c]Ps. 16.11; Rev. 22.17
[3]in the evening
[4]singing
6 [d]Job 29.18
7 [5]settled strength for my mountain
[e]Ps. 104.29
9 [f]Ps. 115.17
10 [g]Ps. 4.1
11 [h]2 Sam. 6.14
12 [6]That is, my tongue, or, my soul

Psalm 31
2 [a]Ps. 71.2; Prov. 22.17
[1]to me for a rock of strength
3 [b]Ps. 23.3; Jer. 14.7
5 [c]Luke 23.46; 2 Tim. 1.12
[d]Heb. 6.18
7 [e]John 10.27
8 [f]Ps. 18.19
11 [g]Ps. 88.8
12 [2]a vessel that perisheth
13 [h]Jer. 20.3; Lam. 2.22
[i]Matt. 27.1
16 [j]Num. 6.25; Dan. 9.17
17 [k]Ps. 25.2
[3]Or, let them be cut off for the grave
18 [l]Ps. 12.3
[4]a hard thing
19 [m]Isa. 64.4; 1 Cor. 2.9
20 [n]Ps. 27.5
[o]Job 5.21
21 [5]Or, fenced city
23 [p]1 Pet. 1.5

Psalm 32
*Or, giving instruction
1 [a]Ps. 85.2;
2 [b]Lev. 17.4;
[c]John 1.47;
5 [d]Prov. 28.13;
6 [e]1 Tim. 1.16
[f]Isa. 55.6;
[1]in a time of finding
7 [g]Ps. 9.9;

quaintance: they that did see me without fled from me.
12 I am forgotten as a dead man out
of mind: I am like [2]a broken vessel.
13 For I have heard the slander of
many: [h]fear *was* on every side: while
they [i]took counsel together against
me, they devised to take away my life.
14 But I trusted in thee, O LORD: I
said, Thou *art* my God.
15 My times *are* in thy hand: deliver
me from the hand of mine enemies,
and from them that persecute me.
16 [j]Make thy face to shine upon thy
servant: save me for thy mercies' sake.
17 [k]Let me not be ashamed, O LORD;
for I have called upon thee: let the
wicked be ashamed, *and* [3]let them be
silent in the grave.
18 [l]Let the lying lips be put to silence; which speak [4]grievous things
proudly and contemptuously against
the righteous.
19 [m]*Oh* how great *is* thy goodness,
which thou hast laid up for them that
fear thee; *which* thou hast wrought for
them that trust in thee before the sons
of men!
20 [n]Thou shalt hide them in the secret of thy presence from the pride of
man: [o]thou shalt keep them secretly in
a pavilion from the strife of tongues.
21 Blessed *be* the LORD: for he hath
shewed me his marvellous kindness in
a [5]strong city.
22 For I said in my haste, I am cut off
from before thine eyes: nevertheless
thou heardest the voice of my supplications when I cried unto thee.
23 O love the LORD, all ye his saints:
for the LORD [p]preserveth the faithful,
and plentifully rewardeth the proud
doer.
24 Be of good courage, and he shall
strengthen your heart, all ye that hope
in the LORD.

Psalm 32

*A Psalm of David, *Maschil*

1 Blessed *is he whose* [a]transgres-
sion *is* forgiven, *whose* sin *is* covered.
2 Blessed *is* the man unto whom the
LORD [b]imputeth not iniquity, and [c]in
whose spirit *there is* no guile.
3 When I kept silence, my bones
waxed old through my roaring all the
day long.
4 For day and night thy hand was
heavy upon me: my moisture is turned
into the drought of summer. Sē'lah.
5 I acknowledged my sin unto thee,
and mine iniquity have I not hid. [d]I
said, I will confess my transgressions
unto the LORD; and thou forgavest the
iniquity of my sin. Sē'lah.
6 For [e]this shall every one that is
godly [f]pray unto thee [1]in a time when
thou mayest be found: surely in the
floods of great waters they shall not
come nigh unto him.
7 [g]Thou *art* my hiding place; thou
shalt preserve me from trouble; thou
shalt compass me about with songs of
deliverance. Sē'lah.

8 I will [h]instruct thee and teach thee
in the way which thou shalt go: [2]I will
guide thee with mine eye.
9 Be ye not as the horse, *or* as the
mule, *which* have no understanding:
whose mouth must be held in with bit
and bridle, lest they come near unto
thee.
10 [i]Many sorrows *shall be* to the
wicked: but [j]he that trusteth in the
LORD, mercy shall compass him about.
11 Be glad in the LORD, and rejoice,
ye righteous: and shout for joy, all *ye*
that are upright in heart.

Psalm 33

1 Rejoice in the LORD, O ye righteous: *for* praise is comely for the upright.
2 Praise the LORD with harp: sing
unto him with the psaltery *and* an instrument of ten strings.
3 [a]Sing unto him a new song; play
skilfully with a loud noise.
4 For the word of the LORD *is* right;
and all his works *are done* in truth.
5 He loveth righteousness and judgment: the earth is full of the [1]goodness
of the LORD.
6 [b]By the word of the LORD were the
heavens made; and all the host of them
[c]by the breath of his mouth.
7 He gathereth the waters of the sea
together as an heap: he layeth up the
depth in storehouses.
8 Let all the earth fear the LORD: let
all the inhabitants of the world stand
in awe of him.
9 For [d]he spake, and it was *done;* he
commanded, and it stood fast.
10 The LORD [2]bringeth the counsel
of the heathen to nought: he maketh
the devices of the people of none effect.
11 [e]The counsel of the LORD standeth for ever, the thoughts of his heart
[3]to all generations.
12 Blessed *is* the nation whose God
is the LORD; *and* the people *whom* he
hath chosen for his own inheritance.
13 [f]The LORD looketh from heaven;
he beholdeth all the sons of men.
14 From the place of his habitation
he looketh upon all the inhabitants of
the earth.
15 [g]He fashioneth their hearts alike;
[h]he considereth all their works.
16 There is no king saved by the multitude of an host: a mighty man is not
delivered by much strength.
17 An horse *is* a vain thing for safety:
neither shall he deliver *any* by his great
strength.
18 [i]Behold, the eye of the LORD *is*
upon them that fear him, upon them
that hope in his mercy;
19 To deliver their soul from death,
and to keep them alive in famine.
20 Our soul waiteth for the LORD: he
is our help and our shield.
21 For our heart shall rejoice in him,
because we have trusted in his holy
name.
22 Let thy mercy, O LORD, be upon
us, according as we hope in thee.

8 [h]Isa. 48.17
[2]I will counsel thee, mine eye shall be upon thee
10 [i]Prov. 13.21
[j]Ps. 34.8; Prov. 16.20; Jer. 17.7

Psalm 33
3 [a]Isa. 42.10
5 [1]Or, mercy
6 [b]John 1.1-3; Heb. 11.3
[c]Job 26.13
9 [d]Gen. 1.3
10 [2]maketh frustrate
11 [e]Job 23.13; Prov. 19.21; Ezek. 38.10; Acts 4.27-28
[3]to generation and generation
13 [f]2 Chr. 16.9; Job 28.24; Ps. 11.4
15 [g]Isa. 64.8
[h]Job 11.11; Ps. 44.21; Prov. 24.12; Jer. 32.19; Hos. 7.2
18 [i]Job 36.7; Ps. 34.15

Psalm 34
*Or, Achish; 1 Sam. 21.13
2 [a]Jer. 9.24; 1 Cor. 1.31
4 [b]Ps. 18.6; Jon. 2.2; Matt. 7.7; Luke 11.9
5 [1]Or, They flowed unto him
6 [c]Ps. 3.4
[d]2 Sam. 22.1
7 [e]Dan. 6.22
[f]Gen. 32.1; 2 Ki. 6.17
9 [g]Phil. 4.19
12 [h]1 Pet. 3.10
13 [i]1 Pet. 2.22
15 [j]Job 36.7
16 [k]Lev. 17.10; Jer. 44.11
[l]Prov. 10.7
18 [2]to the broken of heart
[3]contrite of spirit
20 [m]John 19.36
21 [n]Ps. 94.23
[4]Or, shall be guilty
22 [o]2 Sam. 4.9; Ps. 103.4

Psalm 34

*A Psalm of David, when he changed his behaviour before *Abimelech, who drove him away, and he departed*

1 I will bless the LORD at all times:
his praise *shall* continually *be* in my
mouth.
2 My soul shall make her [a]boast
in the LORD: the humble shall hear
thereof, and be glad.
3 O magnify the LORD with me, and
let us exalt his name together.
4 I [b]sought the LORD, and he heard
me, and delivered me from all my
fears.
5 [1]They looked unto him, and were
lightened: and their faces were not
ashamed.
6 [c]This poor man cried, and the
LORD heard *him,* and [d]saved him out
of all his troubles.
7 [e]The angel of the LORD [f]encamp-
eth round about them that fear him,
and delivereth them.
8 O taste and see that the LORD *is*
good: blessed *is* the man *that* trusteth
in him.
9 O fear the LORD, ye his saints: for
there is [g]no want to them that fear
him.
10 The young lions do lack, and suffer hunger: but they that seek the LORD
shall not want any good *thing.*
11 Come, ye children, hearken unto
me: I will teach you the fear of the
LORD.
12 [h]What man *is he that* desireth
life, *and* loveth *many* days, that he may
see good?
13 Keep thy tongue from evil, and
thy lips from [i]speaking guile.
14 Depart from evil, and do good;
seek peace, and pursue it.
15 [j]The eyes of the LORD *are* upon
the righteous, and his ears *are open*
unto their cry.
16 [k]The face of the LORD *is* against
them that do evil, [l]to cut off the remembrance of them from the earth.
17 *The righteous* cry, and the LORD
heareth, and delivereth them out of all
their troubles.
18 The LORD *is* nigh [2]unto them that
are of a broken heart; and saveth [3]such
as be of a contrite spirit.
19 Many *are* the afflictions of the
righteous: but the LORD delivereth him
out of them all.
20 He keepeth all his bones: [m]not
one of them is broken.
21 [n]Evil shall slay the wicked: and
they that hate the righteous [4]shall be
desolate.
22 The LORD [o]redeemeth the soul of
his servants: and none of them that
trust in him shall be desolate.

Psalm 35

A Psalm of David

1 Plead *my cause,* O LORD, with
them that strive with me: fight against
them that fight against me.

2 Take hold of shield and buckler,
and stand up for mine help.
3 Draw out also the spear, and stop
the way against them that persecute
me: say unto my soul, I *am* thy salvation.
4 Let them be confounded and put to
shame that seek after my soul: let them
be turned back and brought to confusion that devise my hurt.
5 Let them be as chaff before the
wind: and let the angel of the LORD
chase *them*.
6 Let their way be [1]dark and slippery: and let the angel of the LORD persecute them.
7 For without cause have they hid
for me their net *in* a pit, *which* without
cause they have digged for my soul.
8 Let [a]destruction come upon him
[2]at unawares; and [b]let his net that he
hath hid catch himself: into that very
destruction let him fall.
9 And my soul shall be joyful in the
LORD: it [c]shall rejoice in his salvation.
10 All my bones shall say, LORD,
[d]who *is* like unto thee, which deliverest the poor from him that is too strong
for him, yea, the poor and the needy
from him that spoileth him?
11 [3]False witnesses did rise up; [4]they
laid to my charge *things* that I knew
not.
12 They rewarded me evil for good
to the [5]spoiling of my soul.
13 But as for me, when they were
sick, my clothing *was* sackcloth: I
[6]humbled my soul with fasting; and my
prayer returned into mine own bosom.
14 I [7]behaved myself [8]as though *he
had been* my friend *or* brother: I bowed
down heavily, as one that mourneth
for his mother.
15 But in mine [9]adversity they rejoiced, and gathered themselves together: *yea*, the abjects gathered themselves together against me, and I knew
it not; they did tear *me*, and ceased
not:
16 With hypocritical mockers in
feasts, they gnashed upon me with
their teeth.
17 Lord, how long wilt thou look
on? rescue my soul from their destructions, [10]my darling from the lions.
18 I will give thee thanks in the
great congregation: I will praise thee
among [11]much people.
19 Let not them that are mine enemies [12]wrongfully rejoice over me: *neither* let them wink with the eye that
hate me without a cause.
20 For they speak not peace: but
they devise deceitful matters against
them that are quiet in the land.
21 Yea, they opened their mouth
wide against me, *and* said, Aha, aha,
our eye hath seen *it*.
22 *This* thou hast [e]seen, O LORD:
keep not silence: O Lord, be not far
from me.
23 Stir up thyself, and awake to my
judgment, *even* unto my cause, my
God and my Lord.
24 Judge me, O LORD my God, [f]ac-
cording to thy righteousness; and let
them not rejoice over me.
25 Let them not say in their hearts,
[13]Ah, so would we have it: let them not
say, We have swallowed him up.
26 Let them be ashamed and brought
to confusion together that rejoice at
mine hurt: let them be clothed with
shame and dishonour that magnify
themselves against me.
27 Let them shout for joy, and be
glad, that favour [14]my righteous cause:
yea, let them say continually, Let the
LORD be magnified, which hath pleasure in the prosperity of his servant.
28 And my tongue shall speak of thy
righteousness *and* of thy praise all the
day long.

Psalm 36

To the chief Musician, A Psalm of David the servant of the LORD

1 The transgression of the wicked
saith within my heart, *that* [a]*there is* no
fear of God before his eyes.
2 For he flattereth himself in his
own eyes, [1]until his iniquity be found
to be hateful.
3 The words of his mouth *are* iniquity and deceit: [b]he hath left off to be
wise, *and* to do good.
4 [c]He deviseth [2]mischief upon his
bed; he setteth himself [d]in a way *that
is* not good; he abhorreth not evil.
5 [e]Thy mercy, O LORD, *is* in the
heavens; *and* thy faithfulness *reacheth*
unto the clouds.
6 Thy righteousness *is* like [3]the great
mountains; [f]thy judgments *are* a great
deep: O LORD, [g]thou preservest man
and beast.
7 How [4]excellent *is* thy lovingkindness, O God! therefore the children of
men [h]put their trust under the shadow
of thy wings.
8 They shall be [5]abundantly satisfied with the fatness of thy house; and
thou shalt make them drink of [i]the
river of thy pleasures.
9 [j]For with thee *is* the fountain of
life: [k]in thy light shall we see light.
10 O [6]continue thy lovingkindness
[l]unto them that know thee; and thy
righteousness to the upright in heart.
11 Let not the foot of pride come
against me, and let not the hand of the
wicked remove me.
12 There are the workers of iniquity
fallen: they are cast down, and shall
not be able to rise.

Psalm 37

A Psalm of David

1 Fret not thyself because of evildoers, neither be thou envious against
the workers of iniquity.
2 For they shall soon be cut down
like the grass, and wither as the green
herb.
3 Trust in the LORD, and do good; *so*
shalt thou dwell in the land, and [1]verily
thou shalt be fed.

Psalm 35
6 [1]darkness and slipperiness
8 [a]1 Thess. 5.3
[2]which he knoweth not of
[b]Ps. 7.15; Prov. 5.22
9 [c]1 Sam. 2.1; Ps. 13.5; Isa. 61.10; Hab. 3.18
10 [d]Ps. 71.19
11 [3]Witnesses of wrong
[4]they asked me
12 [5]depriving
13 [6]Or, afflicted
14 [7]walked
[8]as a friend, as a brother to me
15 [9]halting
17 [10]my only one
18 [11]strong
19 [12]falsely
22 [e]Ex. 3.7
24 [f]Ps. 7.8; Ps. 26.1; 2 Thess. 1.6
25 [13]Ah, ah, our soul
27 [14]my righteousness

Psalm 36
1 [a]Gen. 20.11; Prov. 8.13; Eccl. 12.3
2 [1]to find his iniquity to hate
3 [b]Jer. 4.22
4 [c]Mic. 2.1
[2]Or, vanity
[d]Isa. 65.2
5 [e]Ps. 57.10
6 [3]the mountains of God
[f]Job 11.8; Rom. 11.33
[g]Job 7.20; Ps. 145.9
7 [4]precious
[h]Ruth 2.12
8 [5]watered
[i]Job 20.17; Rev. 22.1
9 [j]Isa. 12.3; Jer. 2.13; Zech. 13.1; Rev. 21.6
[k]Acts 26.18; 1 Pet. 2.9
10 [6]draw out at length
[l]Jer. 22.16

Psalm 37
3 [1]in truth, or, stableness

4 [a]Delight thyself also in the LORD; and he shall give thee the desires of thine heart.

5 [2]Commit thy way unto the LORD; trust also in him; and he shall bring *it* to pass.

6 [b]And he shall bring forth thy righteousness as the light, and thy judgment as the noonday.

7 [3]Rest in the LORD, and wait patiently for him: fret not thyself because of him who prospereth in his way, because of the man who bringeth wicked devices to pass.

8 Cease from anger, and forsake wrath: [c]fret not thyself in any wise to do evil.

9 For evildoers shall be cut off: but those that wait upon the LORD, they shall inherit the earth.

10 For yet a little while, and the wicked *shall* not *be:* yea, thou shalt diligently consider his place, and it *shall* not *be.*

11 But the meek shall inherit the earth; and shall delight themselves in the abundance of peace.

12 The wicked [4]plotteth against the just, and gnasheth upon him with his teeth.

13 The Lord shall laugh at him: for he seeth that [d]his day is coming.

14 The wicked have drawn out the sword, and have bent their bow, to cast down the poor and needy, *and* to slay [5]such as be of upright conversation.

15 Their sword shall enter into their own heart, and their bows shall be broken.

16 [e]A little that a righteous man hath *is* better than the riches of many wicked.

17 For the arms of the wicked shall be broken: but the LORD upholdeth the righteous.

18 The LORD [f]knoweth the days of the upright: and their inheritance shall be [g]for ever.

19 They shall not be ashamed in the evil time: and [h]in the days of famine they shall be satisfied.

20 But the wicked shall perish, and the enemies of the LORD *shall be* as [6]the fat of lambs: they shall consume; into smoke shall they consume away.

21 The wicked borroweth, and payeth not again: but the righteous sheweth mercy, and giveth.

22 [i]For *such as be* blessed of him shall inherit the earth; and *they that be* cursed of him shall be cut off.

23 [j]The steps of a *good* man are [7]ordered by the LORD: and he delighteth in his way.

24 [k]Though he fall, he shall not be utterly cast down: for the LORD upholdeth *him with* his hand.

25 I have been young, and *now* am old; yet have I not seen the righteous forsaken, nor his seed begging bread.

26 *He is* [8]ever merciful, and lendeth; and his seed *is* blessed.

27 Depart from evil, and do good; and dwell for evermore.

28 For the LORD [l]loveth judgment, and forsaketh not his saints; they are preserved for ever: but the seed of the wicked shall be cut off.

29 The righteous shall inherit the land, and dwell therein for ever.

30 The mouth of the righteous speaketh wisdom, and his tongue talketh of judgment.

31 The law of his God *is* in his heart; none of his [9]steps shall slide.

32 The wicked watcheth the righteous, and seeketh to slay him.

33 The LORD will not leave him in his hand, nor [m]condemn him when he is judged.

34 Wait on the LORD, and keep his way, and he shall exalt thee to inherit the land: when the wicked are cut off, thou shalt see *it.*

35 I have seen the wicked in great power, and spreading himself like [10]a green bay tree.

36 Yet he passed away, and, lo, he *was* not: yea, I sought him, but he could not be found.

37 Mark the perfect *man,* and behold the upright: for [n]the end of *that* man *is* peace.

38 But the transgressors shall be destroyed together: the end of the wicked shall be cut off.

39 But [o]the salvation of the righteous *is* of the LORD: *he is* their strength in the time of trouble.

40 And the LORD shall help them, and deliver them: he shall deliver them from the wicked, and save them, [p]because they trust in him.

Psalm 38

A Psalm of David, to bring to remembrance

1 O lord, rebuke me not in thy wrath: neither chasten me in thy hot displeasure.

2 For thine arrows stick fast in me, and thy hand presseth me sore.

3 *There is* no soundness in my flesh because of thine anger; neither *is there any* [1]rest in my bones because of my sin.

4 For mine iniquities are gone over mine head: as an heavy burden they are too heavy for me.

5 My wounds stink *and* are corrupt because of my foolishness.

6 I am [2]troubled; I am bowed down greatly; I go mourning all the day long.

7 For my loins are filled with a [a]loathsome *disease:* and *there is* no soundness in my flesh.

8 I am feeble and sore broken: I have roared by reason of the disquietness of my heart.

9 Lord, all my desire *is* before thee; and my groaning is not hid from thee.

10 My heart panteth, my strength faileth me: as for the light of mine eyes, it also [3]is gone from me.

11 My lovers and my friends [b]stand aloof from my [4]sore; and [5]my kinsmen stand afar off.

4 [a]Job 27.10; Song 2.3; Isa. 58.14; 1 Pet. 1.8
5 [2]Roll thy way upon the LORD
6 [b]Mic. 7.9
7 [3]Be silent to the LORD
8 [c]Job 5.2; Ps. 73.3; Prov. 14.29; Eph. 4.26; Jas. 1.19
12 [4]Or, practiseth
13 [d]1 Sam. 26.10
14 [5]the upright of way
16 [e]Prov. 15.16; 1 Tim. 6.6
18 [f]Ps. 1.6 [g]Isa. 60.21
19 [h]Job 5.20
20 [6]the preciousness of lambs
22 [i]Prov. 3.33
23 [j]Ps. 121.3; Prov. 16.9 [7]Or, established
24 [k]Mic. 7.8; 2 Cor. 4.9
26 [8]all the day
28 [l]Ps. 11.7
31 [9]Or, goings
33 [m]Ps. 109.31
35 [10]Or, a green tree that groweth in his own soil
37 [n]Job 1.1; Isa. 32.17; Luke 2.25-30; Acts 7.59-60; 1 Thess. 4.17; 2 Tim. 4.6-8; 2 Pet. 1.14
39 [o]Ps. 3.8; Isa. 12.2; Jon. 2.9
40 [p]1 Chr. 5.20; Dan. 3.17

Psalm 38
3 [1]peace, or, health
6 [2]wried
7 [a]Job 7.5
10 [3]is not with me
11 [b]Luke 10.31 [4]stroke [5]Or, my neighbours

12 They also that seek after my life
lay snares *for me:* and they that seek
my hurt speak mischievous things, and
imagine deceits all the day long.
13 But I, as a deaf *man,* heard not;
and *I was* as a dumb man *that* openeth
not his mouth.
14 Thus I was as a man that heareth not, and in whose mouth *are* no
reproofs.
15 For [6]in thee, O LORD, [c]do I hope:
thou wilt [7]hear, O Lord my God.
16 For I said, *Hear me,* lest *other-*
wise they should rejoice over me: when
my foot slippeth, they magnify *them-*
selves against me.
17 For I *am* ready [8]to halt, and my
sorrow *is* continually before me.
18 For I will [d]declare mine iniquity;
I will be [e]sorry for my sin.
19 But mine enemies [9]*are* lively, *and*
they are strong: and they that hate me
wrongfully are multiplied.
20 They also that render evil for
good are mine adversaries; [f]because I
follow *the thing that* good *is.*
21 [g]Forsake me not, O LORD: O my
God, be not far from me.
22 Make haste [10]to help me, O Lord
[h]my salvation.

Psalm 39

To the chief Musician, even to
**Jeduthun, A Psalm of David*

1 I said, I will [a]take heed to my
ways, that I sin not with my tongue: I
will keep [1]my mouth with a bridle,
[b]while the wicked is before me.
2 I was dumb with silence, I held my
peace, *even* from good; and my sorrow
was [2]stirred.
3 My heart was hot within me; while
I was musing [c]the fire burned: *then*
spake I with my tongue,
4 LORD, make me to know mine end,
and the measure of my days, what it *is;*
that I may know [3]how frail I *am.*
5 Behold, thou hast made my days
as an handbreadth; and [d]mine age *is*
as nothing before thee: verily every
man [4]at his best state *is* altogether vanity. Sē'lah.
6 Surely every man walketh in [5]a
vain shew: surely they are disquieted
in vain: he heapeth up *riches,* and
knoweth not who shall gather them.
7 And now, Lord, what wait I for?
my hope *is* in thee.
8 Deliver me from all my transgressions: make me not the reproach of the
foolish.
9 I was dumb, I opened not my
mouth; because thou didst *it.*
10 Remove thy stroke away from
me: I am consumed by the [6]blow of
thine hand.
11 When thou with rebukes dost correct man for iniquity, thou makest [7]his
beauty to consume away like a moth:
surely every man *is* vanity. Sē'lah.
12 Hear my prayer, O LORD, and
give ear unto my cry; hold not thy
peace at my tears: for [e]I *am* a stranger
with thee, *and* a sojourner, as all my
fathers *were.*
13 [f]O spare me, that I may recover
strength, before I go hence, and be no
more.

Psalm 40

To the chief Musician, A Psalm of
David

1 I [1]waited patiently for the LORD;
and he inclined unto me, and heard my
cry.
2 He brought me up also out of [2]an
horrible pit, out of the miry clay, and
set my feet upon a rock, *and* established my goings.
3 And he hath put a new song in
my mouth, *even* praise unto our God:
many shall see *it,* and fear, and shall
trust in the LORD.
4 [a]Blessed *is* that man that maketh
the LORD his trust, and respecteth not
the proud, nor such as turn aside to
lies.
5 Many, O LORD my God, *are* thy
wonderful works *which* thou hast done,
[b]and thy thoughts *which are* to us-
ward: [3]they cannot be reckoned up in
order unto thee: *if* I would declare and
speak *of them,* they are more than can
be numbered.
6 [c]Sacrifice and offering thou didst
not desire; mine ears hast thou [4]opened:
burnt offering and sin offering hast
thou not required.
7 Then said I, Lo, I come: in the volume of the book *it is* [d]written of me,
8 [e]I delight to do thy will, O my God:
yea, thy law *is* [5]within my heart.
9 I have preached righteousness in
the great congregation: lo, I have not refrained my lips, O LORD, [f]thou knowest.
10 [g]I have not hid thy righteousness
within my heart; I have declared thy
faithfulness and thy salvation: I have
not concealed thy lovingkindness and
thy truth from the great congregation.
11 Withhold not thou thy tender
mercies from me, O LORD: [h]let thy lovingkindness and thy truth continually
preserve me.
12 For innumerable evils have compassed me about: [i]mine iniquities have
taken hold upon me, so that I am not
able to look up; they are more than the
hairs of mine head: therefore my heart
[6]faileth me.
13 Be pleased, O LORD, to deliver
me: O LORD, make haste to help me.
14 Let them be ashamed and confounded together that seek after my
soul to destroy it; let them be driven
backward and put to shame that wish
me evil.
15 Let them be desolate for a reward
of their shame that say unto me, Aha,
aha.
16 Let all those that seek thee rejoice and be glad in thee: let such as
love thy salvation say continually, The
LORD be magnified.
17 But I *am* poor and needy; *yet* [j]the
Lord thinketh upon me: thou *art* my

15 [6]Or, thee do I wait for
[c]Jer. 14.8
[7]Or, answer
17 [8]for halting
18 [d]Job 31.33; Prov. 28.13
[e]2 Cor. 7.9
19 [9]being living, are strong
20 [f]1 Pet. 3.13; 1 John 3.12
21 [g]Ps. 22.1-11
22 [10]for my help
[h]Ex. 15.2; Isa. 12.2

Psalm 39
*1 Chr. 16.41
1 [a]1 Ki. 2.4; Heb. 2.1
[1]a bridle, or, muzzle for my mouth
[b]Col. 4.5
2 [2]troubled
3 [c]Jer. 20.9
4 [3]Or, what time I have here
5 [d]Ps. 90.4
[4]settled
6 [5]an image
10 [6]conflict
11 [7]that which is to be desired in him to melt away
12 [e]Lev. 25.23; 1 Chr. 29.15
13 [f]Job 10.20-21

Psalm 40
1 [1]In waiting I waited
2 [2]a pit of noise
4 [a]Ps. 2.12
5 [b]Isa. 55.8
[3]Or, none can order them unto thee
6 [c]Hos. 6.6; Matt. 9.13
[4]digged
7 [d]Luke 24.44; Heb. 10.7
8 [e]Job 23.12;
[5]in the midst of my bowels
9 [f]Ps. 139.2
10 [g]Acts 20.20;
11 [h]Ps. 43.3
12 [i]Ps. 38.4
[6]forsaketh
17 [j]Neh. 5.19;

help and my deliverer; make no tarrying, O my God.

Psalm 41

To the chief Musician, A Psalm of David

1 Blessed [a]*is* he that considereth [1]the poor: the LORD will deliver him [2]in time of trouble.

2 The LORD will preserve him, and keep him alive; *and* he shall be blessed upon the earth: and [3]thou wilt not deliver him unto the will of his enemies.

3 The LORD will strengthen him upon the bed of languishing: thou wilt [4]make all his bed in his sickness.

4 I said, LORD, be merciful unto me: [b]heal my soul; for I have sinned against thee.

5 Mine enemies speak evil of me, When shall he die, and his name perish?

6 And if he come to see *me*, he [c]speaketh vanity: his heart gathereth iniquity to itself; *when* he goeth abroad, he telleth *it*.

7 All that hate me whisper together against me: against me do they devise [5]my hurt.

8 [6]An evil disease, *say they*, cleaveth fast unto him: and *now* that he lieth he shall rise up no more.

9 Yea, [7]mine own familiar friend, in whom I trusted, [d]which did eat of my bread, hath [8]lifted up *his* heel against me.

10 But thou, O LORD, be merciful unto me, and raise me up, that I may requite them.

11 By this I know that thou favourest me, because mine enemy doth not triumph over me.

12 And as for me, thou upholdest me in mine integrity, and [e]settest me before thy face for ever.

13 Blessed *be* the LORD God of Ĭs'ra-el from everlasting, and to everlasting. Amen, and Amen.

Psalm 42

*To the chief Musician, *Maschil, for the sons of Korah*

1 As the hart [1]panteth after the water brooks, so panteth my soul after thee, O God.

2 [a]My soul thirsteth for God, for [b]the living God: when shall I come and appear before God?

3 My tears have been my meat day and night, while they continually say unto me, Where *is* thy God?

4 When I remember these *things*, I pour out my soul in me: for I had gone with the multitude, [c]I went with them to the house of God, with the voice of joy and praise, with a multitude that kept holyday.

5 Why art thou [2]cast down, O my soul? and *why* art thou disquieted in me? [d]hope thou in God: for I shall yet [3]praise him [4]*for* the help of his countenance.

6 O my God, my soul is cast down within me: therefore will I remember thee from the land of Jôr'dan, and of the Hẽr'mon-ītes, from [5]the hill Mī'zar.

7 [e]Deep calleth unto deep at the noise of thy waterspouts: all thy waves and thy billows are gone over me.

8 *Yet* the LORD will [f]command his lovingkindness in the daytime, and in the night his song *shall be* with me, *and* my prayer unto the God of my life.

9 I will say unto God my rock, Why hast thou forgotten me? why go I mourning because of the oppression of the enemy?

10 *As* with a [6]sword in my bones, mine enemies reproach me; while they say daily unto me, Where *is* thy God?

11 Why art thou cast down, O my soul? and why art thou disquieted within me? hope thou in God: for I shall yet praise him, *who is* the health of my countenance, and my God.

Psalm 43

1 [a]Judge me, O God, and plead my cause against an [1]ungodly nation: O deliver me [2]from the deceitful and unjust man.

2 For thou *art* the God of [b]my strength: why dost thou cast me off? why go I mourning because of the oppression of the enemy?

3 O send out thy light and thy truth: let them lead me; let them bring me unto [c]thy holy hill, and to thy tabernacles.

4 Then will I go unto the altar of God, unto God [3]my exceeding joy: yea, upon the harp will I praise thee, O God my God.

5 [d]Why art thou cast down, O my soul? and why art thou disquieted within me? hope in God: for I shall yet praise him, *who is* the health of my countenance, and my God.

Psalm 44

To the chief Musician for the sons of Korah, Maschil

1 We have heard with our ears, O God, our fathers have told us, *what* work thou didst in their days, in the times of old.

2 *How* [a]thou didst drive out the heathen with thy hand, and plantedst them; *how* thou didst afflict the people, and cast them out.

3 For [b]they got not the land in possession by their own sword, neither did their own arm save them: but thy right hand, and thine arm, and the light of thy countenance, [c]because thou hadst a favour unto them.

4 [d]Thou art my King, O God: command deliverances for Jā'cob.

5 Through thee [e]will we push down our enemies: through thy name will we tread them under that rise up against us.

6 For [f]I will not trust in my bow, neither shall my sword save me.

7 But thou hast saved us from our enemies, and hast put them to shame that hated us.

Psalm 41
1 [a]Prov. 14.21; Mark 10.21
[1]Or, the weak, or, sick
[2]in the day of evil
2 [3]Or, do not thou deliver
3 [4]turn
4 [b]Ps. 6.2
6 [c]Ps. 12.2
7 [5]evil to me
8 [6]A thing of Belial
9 [7]the man of my peace
[d]Obad. 7; John 13.18
[8]magnified
12 [e]Ps. 34.15; Acts 2.28

Psalm 42
*Or, A Psalm giving instruction of the sons
1 [1]brayeth
2 [a]John 7.37
[b]1 Thess. 1.9
4 [c]Isa. 30.29
5 [2]bowed down
[d]Ps. 56.3-11; Isa. 50.10; Lam. 3.24
[3]Or, give thanks
[4]Or, his presence is salvation
6 [5]Or, the little hill
7 [e]Ezek. 7.26
8 [f]Deut. 28.8
10 [6]Or, killing

Psalm 43
1 [a]Ps. 7.8
[1]Or, unmerciful
[2]from a man of deceit and iniquity
2 [b]Ps. 28.7; Isa. 26.4
3 [c]Ps. 2.6; Ps. 3.4
4 [3]the gladness of my joy
5 [d]Ps. 42.5-11

Psalm 44
2 [a]Ex. 15.17; Deut. 7.1; Josh. 10.42
3 [b]Josh. 24.12
[c]Deut. 4.37
4 [d]Ps. 74.12
5 [e]Dan. 8.4
6 [f]Ps. 33.16

8 [g]In God we boast all the day long,
and praise thy name for ever. Sē'lah.
9 But thou hast cast off, and put us
to shame; and goest not forth with our
armies.
10 Thou makest us to [h]turn back
from the enemy: and they which hate
us spoil for themselves.
11 Thou hast given us [1]like sheep *appointed* for meat; and hast [i]scattered
us among the heathen.
12 [j]Thou sellest thy people [2]for
nought, and dost not increase *thy
wealth* by their price.
13 Thou makest us a reproach to our
neighbours, a scorn and a derision to
them that are round about us.
14 Thou makest us a byword among
the heathen, a shaking of the head
among the people.
15 My confusion *is* continually before me, and the shame of my face
hath covered me,
16 For the voice of him that reproacheth and blasphemeth; [k]by reason of the enemy and avenger.
17 [l]All this is come upon us; yet
have we not forgotten thee, neither
have we dealt falsely in thy covenant.
18 Our heart is not turned back, neither have our [3]steps declined from thy
way;
19 Though thou hast sore broken us
in [m]the place of dragons, and covered
us with the shadow of death.
20 If we have forgotten the name of
our God, or stretched out our hands to
a strange god;
21 [n]Shall not God search this out?
for [o]he knoweth the secrets of the
heart.
22 Yea, for thy sake are we killed all
the day long; we are counted as sheep
for the slaughter.
23 Awake, why sleepest thou, O
Lord? arise, cast *us* not off for ever.
24 Wherefore hidest thou thy face,
and forgettest our affliction and our
oppression?
25 For our soul is bowed down to the
dust: our belly cleaveth unto the earth.
26 Arise [4]for our help, and redeem
us for thy mercies' sake.

Psalm 45

*To the chief Musician upon
Shoshannim, for the sons of Korah,
Maschil, A Song of loves

1 My heart [1]is inditing a good matter: I speak of the things which I have
made touching the king: my tongue *is*
the pen of a ready writer.
2 Thou art fairer than the children
of men: grace is poured into thy lips:
therefore God hath blessed thee for
ever.
3 Gird thy sword upon *thy* thigh, O
most mighty, with thy glory and thy
majesty.
4 And in thy majesty [2]ride prosperously because of truth and meekness
and righteousness; and thy right hand
shall teach thee terrible things.

8 [g]Ps. 34.2; Rom. 2.17; 1 Cor. 1.31
10 [h]Lev. 26.17; Deut. 28.25
11 [1]as sheep of meat
[i]Deut. 4.27; 2 Ki. 17.6; Ps. 60.1; Jer. 32.37; Luke 21.24
12 [j]Isa. 52.3-4
[2]without riches
16 [k]Ps. 8.2
17 [l]Dan. 9.13
18 [3]Or, goings
19 [m]Isa. 34.13
21 [n]Job 31.14; Ps. 139.1
[o]1 Sam. 16.7; Eccl. 12.14; John 2.25; Acts 1.24; Rev. 2.23
26 [4]a help for us
Psalm 45
*Or, of instruction
1 [1]boileth, or, bubbleth up
4 [2]prosper thou, ride thou
6 [a]Ps. 93.2; Heb. 1.8
7 [b]Ps. 33.5; Heb. 1.9
[3]Or, O God
[c]Isa. 61.1; John 20.17
10 [d]Deut. 21.13
11 [e]Ps. 95.6; Isa. 54.5
12 [4]thy face
13 [f]Rev. 19.7-8
16 [g]1 Pet. 2.9; Rev. 1.6
17 [h]Isa. 11.10; Mal. 1.11
Psalm 46
*Or, of
†1 Chr. 15.20
1 [1]the heart of the seas
4 [a]Isa. 8.7; Rev. 22.1
[b]2 Chr. 6.6; Heb. 12.22
5 [c]Deut. 23.14; Ezek. 43.7
[2]when the morning appeareth
7 [3]an high place for us

5 Thine arrows *are* sharp in the heart
of the king's enemies; *whereby* the people fall under thee.
6 [a]Thy throne, O God, *is* for ever
and ever: the sceptre of thy kingdom *is*
a right sceptre.
7 [b]Thou lovest righteousness, and
hatest wickedness: therefore [3]God, [c]thy
God, hath anointed thee with the oil of
gladness above thy fellows.
8 All thy garments *smell* of myrrh,
and aloes, *and* cassia, out of the ivory
palaces, whereby they have made thee
glad.
9 Kings' daughters *were* among thy
honourable women: upon thy right
hand did stand the queen in gold of
Ō'phĭr.
10 Hearken, O daughter, and consider, and incline thine ear; [d]forget
also thine own people, and thy father's
house;
11 So shall the king greatly desire
thy beauty: [e]for he *is* thy Lord; and
worship thou him.
12 And the daughter of Tȳre *shall be
there* with a gift; *even* the rich among
the people shall intreat [4]thy favour.
13 [f]The king's daughter *is* all glorious within: her clothing *is* of wrought
gold.
14 She shall be brought unto the
king in raiment of needlework: the virgins her companions that follow her
shall be brought unto thee.
15 With gladness and rejoicing shall
they be brought: they shall enter into
the king's palace.
16 Instead of thy fathers shall be thy
children, [g]whom thou mayest make
princes in all the earth.
17 [h]I will make thy name to be remembered in all generations: therefore shall the people praise thee for
ever and ever.

Psalm 46

*To the chief Musician *for the sons of
Korah, A Song upon † Alamoth*

1 God *is* our refuge and strength, a
very present help in trouble.
2 Therefore will not we fear, though
the earth be removed, and though the
mountains be carried into [1]the midst of
the sea;
3 *Though* the waters thereof roar
and be troubled, *though* the mountains shake with the swelling thereof.
Sē'lah.
4 *There is* [a]a river, the streams
whereof shall make glad [b]the city of
God, the holy *place* of the tabernacles
of the most High.
5 God *is* [c]in the midst of her; she
shall not be moved: God shall help her,
[2]*and that* right early.
6 The heathen raged, the kingdoms
were moved: he uttered his voice, the
earth melted.
7 The LORD of hosts *is* with us; the
God of Jā'cob *is* [3]our refuge. Sē'lah.
8 Come, behold the works of the
LORD, what desolations he hath made
in the earth.

9 He maketh wars to cease unto the
end of the earth; he breaketh the bow,
and cutteth the spear in sunder; he
burneth the chariot in the fire.
10 Be still, and know that I *am* God:
I will be exalted among the heathen, I
will be exalted in the earth.
11 The LORD of hosts *is* with us; the
God of Jā'cob *is* our refuge. Sē'lah.

Psalm 47

*To the chief Musician, A Psalm *for*
the sons of Korah
1 O clap your hands, all ye people;
shout unto God with the voice of triumph.
2 For the LORD most high *is* [a]terri-
ble; [b]*he is* a great King over all the
earth.
3 [c]He shall subdue the people under
us, and the nations under our feet.
4 He shall choose our [d]inheritance
for us, the excellency of Jā'cob whom
he loved. Sē'lah.
5 [e]God is gone up with a shout, the
LORD with the sound of a trumpet.
6 Sing praises to God, sing praises:
sing praises unto our King, sing praises.
7 [f]For God *is* the King of all the earth:
sing [g]ye praises [1]with understanding.
8 God reigneth over the heathen:
God sitteth upon the throne of his
holiness.
9 [2]The princes of the people are gathered together, *even* the people of the
God of Ā'brā-hăm: for the shields of
the earth *belong* unto God: he is greatly
exalted.

Psalm 48

*A Song and Psalm *for the sons of*
Korah
1 Great *is* the LORD, and greatly to
be praised in the city of our God, *in* the
[a]mountain of his holiness.
2 [b]Beautiful for situation, [c]the joy
of the whole earth, *is* mount Zī'ŏn, [d]*on*
the sides of the north, the [e]city of the
great King.
3 God is known in her palaces for a
refuge.
4 For, lo, [f]the kings were assembled, they passed by together.
5 They saw *it, and* so they marvelled; they were troubled, *and* hasted
away.
6 Fear took hold upon them there,
and pain, as of a woman in travail.
7 Thou [g]breakest the ships of Tär'-
shish with an east wind.
8 As we have heard, so have we
seen in the city of the LORD of hosts, in
the city of our God: God will [h]establish
it for ever. Sē'lah.
9 We have thought of thy lovingkindness, O God, in the midst of thy
temple.
10 According to [i]thy name, O God, so
is thy praise unto the ends of the earth:
thy right hand is full of righteousness.
11 Let mount Zī'ŏn rejoice, let the
daughters of Jū'dah be glad, because
of thy judgments.

Psalm 47
*Or, of
2 [a]Deut. 7.21; Neh. 1.5
[b]Mal. 1.14
3 [c]Ps. 18.47
4 [d]1 Pet. 1.4
5 [e]Ps. 24.7-10; Acts 1.9; 1 Tim. 3.16
7 [f]Zech. 14.9
[g]1 Cor. 14.15
[1]Or, every one that hath understanding
9 [2]Or, The voluntary of the people are gathered unto the people of the God of Abraham

Psalm 48
*Or, of
1 [a]Isa. 2.2; Mic. 4.1
2 [b]Jer. 3.19; Lam. 2.15
[c]Ezek. 20.6
[d]Isa. 14.13
[e]Matt. 5.35
4 [f]2 Sam. 10.6
7 [g]Ezek. 27.26
8 [h]Isa. 2.2; Mic. 4.1
10 [i]Mal. 1.11
13 [1]Set your heart to her bulwarks
[2]Or, raise up
14 [j]Isa. 25.9

Psalm 49
*Or, of
4 [a]Ps. 78.2
7 [b]Matt. 16.26
8 [c]Job 36.18
9 [d]Heb. 9.27
[e]Ps. 89.48
11 [1]to generation and generation
13 [2]delight in their mouth
14 [f]Dan. 7.22; Rev. 2.26
[3]Or, strength
[4]Or, the grave being an habitation to every one of them
15 [g]Hos. 13.14
[5]from the hand of the grave
[6]Or, hell
18 [7]in his life
19 [8]The soul shall go
20 [h]Eccl. 3.19-20-21

12 Walk about Zī'ŏn, and go round
about her: tell the towers thereof.
13 [1]Mark ye well her bulwarks, [2]con-
sider her palaces; that ye may tell *it* to
the generation following.
14 [j]For this God *is* our God for ever
and ever: he will be our guide *even*
unto death.

Psalm 49

*To the chief Musician, A Psalm *for*
the sons of Korah
1 Hear this, all *ye* people; give ear,
all *ye* inhabitants of the world:
2 Both low and high, rich and poor,
together.
3 My mouth shall speak of wisdom;
and the meditation of my heart *shall be*
of understanding.
4 [a]I will incline mine ear to a parable: I will open my dark saying upon
the harp.
5 Wherefore should I fear in the
days of evil, *when* the iniquity of my
heels shall compass me about?
6 They that trust in their wealth, and
boast themselves in the multitude of
their riches;
7 None *of them* can by any means
redeem his brother, nor [b]give to God a
ransom for him:
8 (For [c]the redemption of their soul
is precious, and it ceaseth for ever:)
9 That he should still [d]live for ever,
and not [e]see corruption.
10 For he seeth *that* wise men die,
likewise the fool and the brutish person perish, and leave their wealth to
others.
11 Their inward thought *is, that*
their houses *shall continue* for ever,
and their dwelling places [1]to all generations; they call *their* lands after their
own names.
12 Nevertheless man *being* in honour abideth not: he is like the beasts
that perish.
13 This their way *is* their folly: yet
their posterity [2]approve their sayings.
Sē'lah.
14 Like sheep they are laid in the
grave; death shall feed on them; and
[f]the upright shall have dominion over
them in the morning; and their [3]beauty
shall consume [4]in the grave from their
dwelling.
15 But God [g]will redeem my soul
[5]from the power of [6]the grave: for he
shall receive me. Sē'lah.
16 Be not thou afraid when one is
made rich, when the glory of his house
is increased;
17 For when he dieth he shall carry
nothing away: his glory shall not descend after him.
18 Though [7]while he lived he blessed
his soul: and *men* will praise thee,
when thou doest well to thyself.
19 [8]He shall go to the generation of
his fathers; they shall never see light.
20 Man *that is* in honour, and understandeth not, [h]is like the beasts *that*
perish.

Psalm 50

*A Psalm *of Asaph*

1 The mighty God, *even* the LORD, hath spoken, and called the earth from the rising of the sun unto the going down thereof.

2 Out of Zī′ŏn, the perfection of beauty, God hath shined.

3 Our God shall come, and shall not keep silence: a fire shall devour before him, and it shall be very tempestuous round about him.

4 [a]He shall call to the heavens from above, and to the earth, that he may judge his people.

5 Gather [b]my saints together unto me; [c]those that have made a covenant with me by sacrifice.

6 And the heavens shall declare his righteousness: for God *is* judge himself. Sē′lah.

7 Hear, O my people, and I will speak; O Ĭs′ra-el, and I will testify against thee: I *am* God, *even* thy God.

8 I will not reprove thee for thy sacrifices or thy burnt offerings, *to have been* continually before me.

9 [d]I will take no bullock out of thy house, *nor* he goats out of thy folds.

10 For every beast of the forest *is* mine, *and* the cattle upon a thousand hills.

11 I know all the fowls of the mountains: and the wild beasts of the field *are* [1]mine.

12 If I were hungry, I would not tell thee: for the world *is* mine, and the fulness thereof.

13 Will I eat the flesh of bulls, or drink the blood of goats?

14 [e]Offer unto God thanksgiving; and pay thy vows unto the most High:

15 And [f]call upon me in the day of trouble: I will deliver thee, and thou shalt [g]glorify me.

16 But unto the wicked God saith, What hast thou to do to declare my statutes, or *that* thou shouldest take my covenant in thy mouth?

17 [h]Seeing thou hatest instruction, and castest my words behind thee.

18 When thou sawest a thief, then thou [i]consentedst with him, and [2]hast been partaker with adulterers.

19 [3]Thou givest thy mouth to evil, and thy tongue frameth deceit.

20 Thou sittest *and* speakest against thy brother; thou slanderest thine own mother's son.

21 These *things* hast thou done, [j]and I kept silence; [k]thou thoughtest that I was altogether *such an one* as thyself: *but* I will reprove thee, and set *them* in order before thine eyes.

22 Now consider this, ye that forget God, lest I tear *you* in pieces, and *there be* none to deliver.

23 Whoso offereth praise glorifieth me: and to him [4]that ordereth *his* conversation *aright* will I shew the salvation of God.

Psalm 51

*To the chief Musician, *A Psalm of David, when Nathan the prophet came unto him, after he had gone in to Bath-sheba*

1 Have mercy upon me, O God, according to thy lovingkindness: according unto the multitude of thy tender mercies [a]blot out my transgressions.

2 [b]Wash me throughly from mine iniquity, and cleanse me from my sin.

3 For [c]I acknowledge my transgressions: and my sin *is* ever before me.

4 [d]Against thee, thee only, have I sinned, and done *this* evil [e]in thy sight: [f]that thou mightest be justified when thou speakest, *and* be clear when thou judgest.

5 [g]Behold, I was shapen in iniquity; and in sin did my mother [1]conceive me.

6 Behold, thou desirest truth in the inward parts: and in the hidden *part* thou shalt make me to know wisdom.

7 Purge me with hyssop, and I shall be clean: wash me, and I shall be whiter than snow.

8 Make me to hear joy and gladness; *that* the bones *which* thou hast broken may rejoice.

9 Hide thy face from my sins, and blot out all mine iniquities.

10 [h]Create in me a clean heart, O God; and renew [2]a right spirit within me.

11 Cast me not away [i]from thy presence; and take not thy [j]holy spirit from me.

12 Restore unto me the joy of thy salvation; and uphold me *with thy* [k]free spirit.

13 *Then* will I teach transgressors thy ways; and sinners shall be converted unto thee.

14 Deliver me from [3]bloodguiltiness, O God, thou God of my salvation: *and* my tongue shall sing aloud of thy righteousness.

15 O Lord, open thou my lips; and my mouth shall shew forth thy praise.

16 For thou desirest not sacrifice; [4]else would I give *it*: thou delightest not in burnt offering.

17 The sacrifices of God *are* a broken spirit: a broken and a contrite heart, O God, thou wilt not despise.

18 Do good in thy good pleasure unto Zī′ŏn: build thou the walls of Je-ru′sa-lĕm.

19 Then shalt thou be pleased with [l]the sacrifices of righteousness, with burnt offering and whole burnt offering: then shall they offer bullocks upon thine altar.

Psalm 52

*To the chief Musician, Maschil, A Psalm of David, *when Doeg the Edomite came and told Saul, and said unto him, David is come to the house of Ahimelech*

1 Why boastest thou thyself in mischief, O [a]mighty man? the goodness of God *endureth* continually.

Psalm 50
*Or, for
4 [a]Mic. 6.1-2
5 [b]Isa. 13.3; 1 Cor. 6.2; 1 Thess. 3.13; Jude 14
[c]Ex. 24.7; Isa. 59.20-21; Heb. 8.6
9 [d]Isa. 43.23; Mic. 6.6; Acts 17.25
11 [1]with me
14 [e]Hos. 14.2
15 [f]Job 22.27
[g]Ps. 22.23; Matt. 5.16; John 15.8
17 [h]Prov. 1.7-28-29; Prov. 5.12-13; Rom. 2.21; 2 Thess. 2.10-12
18 [i]Rom. 1.32
[2]thy portion was with adulterers
19 [3]thou sendest
21 [j]Eccl. 8.11
[k]Rom. 2.4
23 [4]that disposeth his way

Psalm 51
*2 Sam. 12.1
1 [a]Col. 2.14
2 [b]Ezek. 36.25; Zech. 13.1; 1 Cor. 6.11; Heb. 9.14; 1 John 1.7; Rev. 1.5
3 [c]Ps. 32.5
4 [d]Gen. 39.9
[e]Luke 15.21
[f]Rom. 3.4
5 [g]Job 14.4; John 3.6; Rom. 5.12
[1]warm me
10 [h]Prov. 20.9; Jer. 13.27; Ezek. 11.19; Acts 15.9; Eph. 2.10
[2]Or, a constant spirit
11 [i]Gen. 4.14
[j]Ezek. 36.27; Rom. 8.9
12 [k]Rom. 8.15; 2 Cor. 3.17
14 [3]bloods
16 [4]Or, that I should give it
19 [l]Mal. 3.3

Psalm 52
*1 Sam. 22.9
1 [a]1 Sam. 21.7

2 [b]Thy tongue deviseth mischiefs; like [c]a sharp razor, working deceitfully.

3 Thou lovest evil more than good; *and* [d]lying rather than to speak righteousness. Sē'lah.

4 Thou lovest all devouring words, [1]O *thou* deceitful tongue.

5 God shall likewise [2]destroy thee for ever, he shall take thee away, and pluck thee out of *thy* dwelling place, and [e]root thee out of the land of the living. Sē'lah.

6 [f]The righteous also shall see, and fear, [g]and shall laugh at him:

7 Lo, *this is* the man *that* made not God his strength; but [h]trusted in the abundance of his riches, *and* strengthened himself in his [3]wickedness.

8 But I *am* [i]like a green olive tree in the house of God: I trust in the mercy of God for ever and ever.

9 I will praise thee for ever, because thou hast done *it:* and I will wait on thy name; [j]for *it is* good before thy saints.

Psalm 53

To the chief Musician, upon Mahalath, Maschil, A Psalm of David

1 The [a]fool hath said in his heart, *There is* no God. Corrupt are they, and have done abominable iniquity: [b]*there is* none that doeth good.

2 God [c]looked down from heaven upon the children of men, to see if there were *any* that did understand, that did [d]seek God.

3 [e]Every one of them is gone back: they are altogether become filthy; *there is* none that doeth good, no, not one.

4 Have the workers of iniquity [f]no knowledge? who eat up my people *as* they eat bread: they have not called upon God.

5 There [1]were they in great fear, *where* no fear was: for God hath scattered the bones of him that encampeth *against* thee: thou hast put *them* to shame, because God hath despised them.

6 [2]Oh that the salvation of Ĭs'ra-el *were come* out of Zī'ŏn! When God bringeth back the captivity of his people, Jā'cob shall rejoice *and* Ĭs'ra-el shall be glad.

Psalm 54

*To the chief Musician on Neginoth, Maschil, A Psalm of David, *when the Ziphims came and said to Saul, Doth not David hide himself with us?*

1 Save me, O God, by thy name, and judge me by thy strength.

2 Hear my prayer, O God; give ear to the words of my mouth.

3 For strangers are risen up against me, and oppressors seek after my soul: they have not set God before them. Sē'lah.

4 Behold, God *is* mine helper: [a]the Lord *is* with them that uphold my soul.

5 He shall reward evil unto [1]mine enemies: cut them off [b]in thy truth.

2 [b]Ps. 50.19; Prov. 12.18
[c]Ps. 59.7
3 [d]Jer. 9.4
4 [1]Or, and the deceitful tongue
5 [2]beat thee down
[e]Prov. 2.22
6 [f]Job 22.19
[g]Ps. 58.10
7 [h]Job 31.24-25; Ps. 49.6
[3]Or, substance
8 [i]Ps. 92.13
9 [j]Ps. 54.6

Psalm 53
1 [a]Ps. 10.4
[b]Rom. 3.10
2 [c]Ps. 33.13
[d]2 Chr. 15.2
3 [e]Eccl. 7.29
4 [f]Jer. 4.22
5 [1]they feared a fear
6 [2]Who will give salvations, etc

Psalm 54
*1 Sam. 23.19; 1 Sam. 26.1
4 [a]Ps. 118.7; Isa. 41.10; Rom. 8.31-32; Heb. 13.6
5 [1]those that observe me
[b]Ps. 89.49

Psalm 55
4 [a]Ps. 102.3-5; Matt. 26.37-38; 2 Cor. 1.8-10
5 [1]covered me
9 [2]Swallow up
13 [3]a man according to my rank
[b]2 Sam. 15.12
14 [4]Who sweetened counsel
15 [c]Num. 16.30
[5]Or, the grave
17 [d]Dan. 6.10; Acts 3.1
18 [e]2 Chr. 32.7
19 [f]Deut. 33.27
[6]Or, With whom also there be no changes, yet they fear not God
20 [7]he hath profaned

6 I will freely sacrifice unto thee: I will praise thy name, O LORD; for *it is* good.

7 For he hath delivered me out of all trouble: and mine eye hath seen *his desire* upon mine enemies.

Psalm 55

To the chief Musician on Neginoth, Maschil, A Psalm of David

1 Give ear to my prayer, O God; and hide not thyself from my supplication.

2 Attend unto me, and hear me: I mourn in my complaint, and make a noise;

3 Because of the voice of the enemy, because of the oppression of the wicked: for they cast iniquity upon me, and in wrath they hate me.

4 My [a]heart is sore pained within me: and the terrors of death are fallen upon me.

5 Fearfulness and trembling are come upon me, and horror hath [1]overwhelmed me.

6 And I said, Oh that I had wings like a dove! *for then* would I fly away, and be at rest.

7 Lo, *then* would I wander far off, *and* remain in the wilderness. Sē'lah.

8 I would hasten my escape from the windy storm *and* tempest.

9 [2]Destroy, O Lord, *and* divide their tongues: for I have seen violence and strife in the city.

10 Day and night they go about it upon the walls thereof: mischief also and sorrow *are* in the midst of it.

11 Wickedness *is* in the midst thereof: deceit and guile depart not from her streets.

12 For *it was* not an enemy *that* reproached me; then I could have borne *it:* neither *was it* he that hated me *that* did magnify *himself* against me; then I would have hid myself from him:

13 But *it was* thou, [3]a man mine equal, [b]my guide, and mine acquaintance.

14 [4]We took sweet counsel together, *and* walked unto the house of God in company.

15 Let death seize upon them, *and* let them [c]go down quick into [5]hell: for wickedness *is* in their dwellings, *and* among them.

16 As for me, I will call upon God; and the LORD shall save me.

17 [d]Evening, and morning, and at noon, will I pray, and cry aloud: and he shall hear my voice.

18 He hath delivered my soul in peace from the battle *that was* against me: for [e]there were many with me.

19 God shall hear, and afflict them, [f]even he that abideth of old. Sē'lah. [6]Because they have no changes, therefore they fear not God.

20 He hath put forth his hands against such as be at peace with him: [7]he hath broken his covenant.

21 *The words* of his mouth were
smoother than butter, but war *was* in
his heart: his words were softer than
oil, yet *were* they drawn swords.
22 Cast thy [8][g]burden upon the LORD,
and he shall sustain thee: [h]he shall
never suffer the righteous to be moved.
23 But thou, O God, shalt bring
them down into the pit of destruction:
[9]bloody and deceitful men [10]shall not
live out half their days; but I will trust
in thee.

Psalm 56

*To the chief Musician upon Jonath-elem-rechokim, *Michtam of David, when the † Philistines took him in Gath*

1 Be [a]merciful unto me, O God: for
man would swallow me up; he fighting
daily oppresseth me.
2 [1]Mine enemies would daily [b]swal-
low *me* up: for *they be* many that fight
against me, O thou most High.
3 [c]What time I am afraid, I will trust
in thee.
4 In God I will praise his word, in
God I have put my trust; [d]I will not
fear what flesh can do unto me.
5 Every day they wrest my words:
all their thoughts *are* against me for
evil.
6 [e]They gather themselves together,
they hide themselves, they mark my
steps, when they wait for my soul.
7 Shall they escape by iniquity? in
thine anger cast down the people, O
God.
8 Thou tellest my wanderings: put
thou my tears into thy bottle: [f]*are they*
not in thy book?
9 When I cry *unto thee,* then shall
mine enemies turn back: this I know;
for [g]God *is* for me.
10 In God will I praise *his* word: in
the LORD will I praise *his* word.
11 In God have I put my trust: I will
not be afraid what man can do unto
me.
12 [h]Thy vows *are* upon me, O God: I
will render praises unto thee.
13 For thou hast delivered my soul
from death: *wilt* not *thou deliver* my
feet from falling, that I may walk before God in [i]the light of the living?

Psalm 57

*To the chief Musician, *Al-taschith, Michtam of David, † when he fled from Saul in the cave*

1 Be merciful unto me, O God, be
merciful unto me: for my soul trusteth
in thee: yea, in the shadow of thy
wings will I make my refuge, [a]until
these calamities be overpast.
2 I will cry unto God most high; unto
God [b]that performeth *all things* for
me.
3 [c]He shall send from heaven, and
save me [1]*from* the reproach of him that
would swallow me up. Sē′lah. God
[d]shall send forth his mercy and his
truth.
4 My soul *is* among lions: *and* I lie
even among them that are set on fire,
even the sons of men, [e]whose teeth *are*
spears and arrows, and [f]their tongue a
sharp sword.
5 [g]Be thou exalted, O God, above
the heavens; *let* thy glory *be* above all
the earth.
6 They have prepared a net for my
steps; my soul is bowed down: they
have digged a pit before me, into the
midst whereof they are fallen *themselves.* Sē′lah.
7 My heart is [2]fixed, O God, my
heart is fixed: I will sing and give
praise.
8 Awake up, my glory; awake, psaltery and harp: I *myself* will awake
early.
9 I will praise thee, O Lord, among
the people: I will sing unto thee among
the nations.
10 For thy mercy *is* great unto the
heavens, and thy truth unto the clouds.
11 Be thou exalted, O God, above
the heavens: *let* thy glory *be* above all
the earth.

Psalm 58

*To the chief Musician, *Al-taschith, Michtam of David*

1 Do ye indeed speak righteousness,
O congregation? do ye judge uprightly,
O ye sons of men?
2 Yea, in heart ye work wickedness;
[a]ye weigh the violence of your hands
in the earth.
3 [b]The wicked are estranged from
the womb: they go astray [1]as soon as
they be born, speaking lies.
4 [c]Their poison *is* [2]like the poison of
a serpent: *they are* like the deaf [3]adder
that stoppeth her ear;
5 Which will not hearken to the
voice of charmers, [4]charming never so
wisely.
6 [d]Break their teeth, O God, in their
mouth: break out the great teeth of the
young lions, O LORD.
7 Let them melt away as waters
which run continually: *when* he bendeth *his bow to shoot* his arrows, let
them be as cut in pieces.
8 As a snail *which* melteth, let *every
one of them* pass away: *like* the untimely birth of a woman, *that* they
may not see the sun.
9 Before your pots can feel the
thorns, he shall take them away [e]as
with a whirlwind, [5]both living, and in
his wrath.
10 [f]The righteous shall rejoice when
he seeth the vengeance: he shall wash
his feet in the blood of the wicked.
11 So that a man shall say, Verily
[g]*there is* [6]a reward for the righteous:
verily he is a God that judgeth [h]in the
earth.

22 [8]Or, gift [g]Matt. 6.25; [h]Ps. 37.24
23 [9]men of bloods and deceit [10]shall not half their days

Psalm 56
*Or, A golden Psalm of David
†1 Sam. 21.10-11
1 [a]Ps. 31.9
2 [1]Mine observers [b]Ps. 57.3
3 [c]1 Sam. 30.6;
4 [d]Heb. 13.5-6
6 [e]Acts 4.27-28
8 [f]Mal. 3.16
9 [g]Isa. 8.9-10
12 [h]Ps. 116.14-19
13 [i]Job 33.30

Psalm 57
*Or, Destroy not, A golden Psalm
†1 Sam. 22.1
1 [a]Isa. 26.20
2 [b]Ps. 138.8
3 [c]Ps. 144.5 [1]Or, he reproacheth him that would swallow me up [d]Ps. 40.11
4 [e]Prov. 30.14 [f]Ps. 64.3
5 [g]Ps. 108.5 [2]Or, prepared

Psalm 58
*Or, Destroy not, A golden Psalm of David
2 [a]Ps. 94.20
3 [b]Ps. 51.5 [1]from the belly
4 [c]Ps. 140.3 [2]according to the likeness [3]Or, asp
5 [4]Or, be the charmer never so cunning
6 [d]Job 4.10
9 [e]Prov. 10.25 [5]as living as wrath
10 [f]Deut. 32.43
11 [g]Rom. 2.6-11 [6]a fruit of the, etc [h]Job 34.11;

Psalm 59

*To the chief Musician, *Al-taschith,
Michtam of David, † when Saul sent,
and they watched the house to kill
him*

1 Deliver me from mine enemies, O
my God: [1]defend me from them that
rise up against me.
2 Deliver me from the workers of iniquity, and save me from bloody men.
3 For, lo, they lie in wait for my soul:
the mighty are gathered against me;
[a]not *for* my transgression, nor *for* my
sin, O LORD.
4 They run and prepare themselves
without *my* fault: awake [2]to help me,
and behold.
5 Thou therefore, O LORD God of
hosts, the God of Ĭs'ra-el, [b]awake to
visit all the heathen: be not merciful to
any wicked transgressors. Sē'lah.
6 They return at evening: they make
a noise like a dog, and go round about
the city.
7 Behold, they belch out with their
mouth: swords *are* in their lips: for
who, *say they,* doth hear?
8 But thou, O LORD, [c]shalt laugh at
them; thou shalt have all the heathen
in derision.
9 *Because of* his strength will I wait
upon thee: for God *is* [3]my defence.
10 The God of my mercy shall prevent me: God shall let me see *my desire*
upon [4]mine enemies.
11 [d]Slay them not, lest my people
forget: scatter them by thy power; and
bring them down, O Lord our shield.
12 *For* the sin of their mouth *and* the
words of their lips let them even be
taken in their pride: and for cursing
and lying *which* they speak.
13 Consume *them* in wrath, consume *them,* that they *may* not *be:* and
let them know that God ruleth in Jā'-
cob unto the ends of the earth. Sē'lah.
14 And at evening let them return;
and let them make a noise like a dog,
and go round about the city.
15 Let them wander up and down
[5]for meat, [6]and grudge if they be not
satisfied.
16 But I will sing of thy power; yea,
I will sing aloud of thy mercy in the
morning: for thou hast been my defence and refuge in the day of my
trouble.
17 Unto thee, O my strength, will I
sing: for God *is* my defence, *and* the
God of my mercy.

Psalm 60

*To the chief Musician upon Shushan-
eduth, *Michtam of David, to teach; †
when he strove with Aram-naharaim,
and with Aram-zobah, when Joab
returned, and smote of Edom in the
valley of Salt twelve thousand*

1 O God, thou hast cast us off, thou
hast [1]scattered us, thou hast been displeased; O turn thyself to us again.
2 Thou hast made the earth to tremble; thou hast broken it: heal the
breaches thereof; for it shaketh.
3 Thou hast shewed thy people hard
things: thou hast made us to drink the
wine of astonishment.
4 [a]Thou hast given a banner to them
that fear thee, that it may be displayed
because of the truth. Sē'lah.
5 [b]That thy beloved may be delivered; save *with* thy right hand, and
hear me.
6 God hath [c]spoken in his holiness;
I will rejoice, I will [d]divide Shē'chem,
and mete out [e]the valley of Sŭc'coth.
7 Gĭl'e-ăd *is* mine, and Ma-năs'seh
is mine; [f]Ē'phră-ĭm also *is* the strength
of mine head; [g]Jū'dah *is* my lawgiver;
8 Mō'ab *is* my washpot: over Ē'dom
will I cast out my shoe: Phĭ-lĭs'tĭ-ȧ, [2]tri-
umph thou because of me.
9 Who will bring me *into* the [3]strong
city? who will lead me into Ē'dom?
10 *Wilt* not thou, O God, *which*
[h]hadst cast us off? and *thou,* O God,
which didst not go out with our armies?
11 Give us help from trouble: for
vain *is* the [4]help of man.
12 Through God [i]we shall do valiantly: for he *it is that* shall tread down
our enemies.

Psalm 61

*To the chief Musician upon Neginah,
A Psalm of David*

1 Hear my cry, O God; attend unto
my prayer.
2 From the [a]end of the earth will I
cry unto thee, when my heart is overwhelmed: lead me to the rock *that* is
higher than I.
3 For thou hast been a shelter for me,
and [b]a strong tower from the enemy.
4 I will abide in [c]thy tabernacle for
ever: I will [1]trust in the covert of thy
wings. Sē'lah.
5 For thou, O God, hast heard my
vows: thou hast given *me* [d]the heritage of those that fear thy name.
6 [2]Thou wilt prolong the king's life:
and his years [3]as many generations.
7 He shall abide [e]before God for
ever: O prepare mercy and truth, *which*
may preserve him.
8 So will I [f]sing praise unto thy
name for ever, that I may daily perform my vows.

Psalm 62

*To the chief Musician, to Jeduthun, A
Psalm of David*

1 [1]Truly my soul [2]waiteth upon God:
from him *cometh* my salvation.
2 He only *is* my rock and my salvation; *he is* my [3]defence; I shall not be
greatly moved.
3 How long will ye imagine mischief
against a man? ye shall be slain all of
you: [a]as a bowing wall *shall ye be, and
as* a tottering fence.
4 They only consult to cast *him* down
from his excellency: they delight in

Psalm 59
*Or, Destroy not, A golden Psalm of David
†1 Sam. 19.11
1 [1]set me on high
3 [a]1 Sam. 26.18
4 [2]to meet me
5 [b]Dan. 4.35
8 [c]Ps. 2.4; Prov. 1.26
9 [3]my high place
10 [4]mine observers
11 [d]Gen. 4.12-15
15 [5]to eat
[6]Or, if they be not satisfied, then they will stay all night

Psalm 60
*Or, A golden Psalm
†2 Sam. 8.3
1 [1]broken
4 [a]Isa. 11.10
5 [b]Ps. 108.6
6 [c]Ps. 89.35
[d]Gen. 12.6
[e]Josh. 13.27
7 [f]Deut. 33.17
[g]Gen. 49.10
8 [2]Or, triumph thou over me (ironically)
9 [3]city of strength
10 [h]Ps. 44.9
11 [4]salvation
12 [i]1 Chr. 19.13

Psalm 61
2 [a]1 Tim. 2.8
3 [b]Prov. 18.10
4 [c]Ps. 15.1; Ps. 23.6; Rev. 3.12
[1]Or, make my refuge
5 [d]1 Cor. 3.21-23
6 [2]Thou shalt add days to the days of the king
[3]as generation and generation
7 [e]Ps. 41.12; Luke 1.32
8 [f]Ps. 56.12

Psalm 62
1 [1]Or, Only
[2]is silent
2 [3]high place
3 [a]Isa. 30.13

lies: [b]they bless with their mouth, but
they curse [4]inwardly. Sē'lah.
5 My soul, [c]wait thou only upon
God; for my expectation *is* from him.
6 He only *is* my rock and my salvation: *he is* my defence; I shall not be
moved.
7 [d]In God *is* my salvation and my
glory: the rock of my strength, *and* my
refuge, *is* in God.
8 Trust in him at all times; ye people, pour [e]out your heart before him:
God *is* a refuge for us. Sē'lah.
9 Surely men of low degree *are* vanity, *and* men of high degree *are* a lie: to
be laid in the balance, they *are* [5]alto-
gether *lighter* than vanity.
10 [f]Trust not in oppression, and become not vain in robbery: [g]if riches increase, set not your heart *upon them.*
11 God hath spoken once; twice have
I heard this; that [6]power *belongeth* unto
God.
12 Also unto thee, O Lord, *belongeth* mercy: for [h]thou renderest to every man according to his work.

Psalm 63

*A Psalm of David, *when he was in the wilderness of Judah*

1 O God, thou *art* my God; early will
I seek thee: my soul thirsteth for thee,
my flesh longeth for thee in a dry and
[1]thirsty land, where no water is;
2 To see [a]thy power and thy glory,
so *as* I have seen thee in the sanctuary.
3 [b]Because thy lovingkindness *is*
better than life, my lips shall praise
thee.
4 Thus will I bless thee while I live: I
will lift up my hands in thy name.
5 My soul shall be [c]satisfied as *with*
[2d]marrow and fatness; and my mouth
shall praise *thee* with joyful lips:
6 When I remember thee [e]upon my
bed, *and* meditate on thee in the *night*
watches.
7 Because thou hast been [f]my help,
therefore in the shadow of thy wings
will I rejoice.
8 My soul followeth hard after thee:
thy right hand upholdeth me.
9 But those *that* seek my soul, to destroy *it,* shall go into the lower parts of
the earth.
10 [3]They shall fall by the sword:
they shall be a portion for foxes.
11 But the king shall rejoice in God;
every one that sweareth by him shall
glory: but the mouth of them that speak
lies shall be stopped.

Psalm 64

To the chief Musician, A Psalm of David

1 Hear my voice, O God, in my
prayer: preserve my life from fear of
the enemy.
2 Hide me from the secret counsel of
the wicked; from the insurrection of
the workers of iniquity:
3 Who whet their tongue like a
sword, *and* bend *their bows to shoot*
their arrows, *even* bitter words:
4 That they may shoot in secret at
the perfect: suddenly do they shoot at
him, and fear not.
5 They encourage themselves *in* an
evil [1]matter: they commune [2]of laying
snares privily; they say, Who shall see
them?
6 They search out iniquities; [3]they
accomplish [4]a diligent search: both the
inward *thought* of every one *of them,*
and the heart, *is* deep.
7 But God shall shoot at them *with*
an arrow; suddenly [5]shall they be
wounded.
8 So they shall make their own
tongue to fall upon themselves: all that
see them shall flee away.
9 And all men shall fear, and shall
declare the work of God; for they shall
wisely consider of his doing.
10 The righteous shall be glad in the
LORD, and shall trust in him; and all
the upright in heart shall glory.

Psalm 65

To the chief Musician, A Psalm and Song of David

1 Praise [1]waiteth for thee, O God, in
Sī'ŏn: and unto thee shall the vow be
performed:
2 O thou that [a]hearest prayer, [b]unto
thee shall all flesh come.
3 [2]Iniquities prevail against me: *as
for* our transgressions, thou shalt
[c]purge them away.
4 [d]Blessed *is the man whom* thou
choosest, and causest to approach *unto
thee, that* he may dwell in thy courts:
we shall be satisfied with the goodness
of thy house, *even* of thy holy temple.
5 *By* terrible things in righteousness
wilt thou answer us, O God of our salvation; *who art* the confidence of all
the ends of the earth, and of them that
are afar off *upon* the sea:
6 Which by his strength setteth
fast the mountains; *being* girded with
power:
7 [e]Which stilleth the noise of the
seas, the noise of their waves, and the
tumult of the people.
8 They also that dwell in the uttermost parts [f]are afraid at thy tokens:
thou makest the outgoings of the morning and evening [3]to rejoice.
9 Thou visitest the earth, and [4]wa-
terest it: thou greatly enrichest it with
the river of God, *which* is full of water:
thou preparest them corn, when thou
hast so provided for it.
10 Thou waterest the ridges thereof
abundantly: [5]thou settlest the furrows
thereof: [6]thou makest it soft with showers: thou blessest the springing thereof.
11 Thou crownest [7]the year with thy
goodness; and thy [g]paths drop fatness.
12 They drop *upon* the pastures of
the wilderness: and the little hills [8]re-
joice on every side.
13 The pastures are clothed with
flocks; the valleys also are covered

---

4 [b]Ps. 28.3
[4]in their inward parts
5 [c]Mic. 7.7-10
7 [d]Jer. 3.23
8 [e]1 Sam. 1.15;
9 [5]Or, alike
10 [f]Isa. 26.4
[g]Mark 10.23;
11 [6]Or, strength
12 [h]1 Pet. 1.17

Psalm 63
*1 Sam. 23.14
1 [1]weary land without water
2 [a]1 Chr. 16.11
3 [b]John 3.16
5 [c]Ps. 17.15
[2]fatness
[d]Isa. 25.6
6 [e]Ps. 149.5
7 [f]2 Cor. 1.10
10 [3]They shall make him run out like water by the hands of the sword

Psalm 64
5 [1]Or, speech
[2]to hide snares
6 [3]Or, we are consumed by that which they have throughly searched
[4]a search searched
7 [5]their wound shall be

Psalm 65
1 [1]is silent
2 [a]Luke 11.9-10
[b]Isa. 66.23
3 [2]Words, or, Matters of iniquities
[c]Heb. 9.14
4 [d]Ps. 33.12
7 [e]Matt. 8.26
8 [f]Job 37.5
[3]Or, to sing
9 [4]Or, after thou hadst made it to desire rain
10 [5]Or, thou causest rain to descend into the furrows thereof
[6]thou dissolvest it
11 [7]the year of thy goodness
[g]Ps. 104.3
12 [8]are girded with joy

over with corn; they shout for joy, they also sing.

Psalm 66

To the chief Musician, A Song or Psalm

1 Make a joyful noise unto God, [1]all ye lands:

2 Sing forth the honour of his name: make his praise glorious.

3 Say unto God, How terrible *art thou in* thy works! [a]through the greatness of thy power shall thine enemies [2]submit themselves unto thee.

4 [b]All the earth shall worship thee, and shall sing unto thee; they shall sing *to* thy name. Sē'lah.

5 [c]Come and see the works of God: *he is* terrible *in his* doing toward the children of men.

6 [d]He turned the sea into dry *land:* [e]they went through the flood on foot: there did we rejoice in him.

7 He ruleth by his power for ever; [f]his eyes behold the nations: let not the rebellious exalt themselves. Sē'lah.

8 O bless our God, ye people, and make the voice of his praise to be heard:

9 Which [3]holdeth our soul in life, and suffereth not our feet to be moved.

10 For thou, O God, hast proved us: [g]thou hast tried us, as silver is tried.

11 Thou broughtest us into the net; thou laidst affliction upon our loins.

12 Thou hast caused men to ride over our heads; we went through fire and through water: but thou broughtest us out into a [4]wealthy *place.*

13 I will go into thy house with burnt offerings: [h]I will pay thee my vows,

14 Which my lips have [5]uttered, and my mouth hath spoken, when I was in trouble.

15 I will offer unto thee burnt sacrifices of [6]fatlings, with the incense of rams; I will offer bullocks with goats. Sē'lah.

16 Come *and* hear, all ye that fear God, and I will declare what he hath done for my soul.

17 I cried unto him with my mouth, and he was extolled with my tongue.

18 [i]If I regard iniquity in my heart, the Lord will not hear *me:*

19 *But* verily God hath heard *me;* he hath attended to the voice of my prayer.

20 Blessed *be* God, which hath not turned away my prayer, nor his mercy from me.

Psalm 67

To the chief Musician on Neginoth, A Psalm or Song

1 God be merciful unto us, and bless us; *and* [a]cause his face to shine [1]upon us; Sē'lah.

2 That [b]thy way may be known upon earth, [c]thy saving health among all nations.

3 [d]Let the people praise thee, O God; let all the people praise thee.

4 O let the nations be glad and sing for joy: for [e]thou shalt judge the people righteously, and [2]govern the nations upon earth. Sē'lah.

5 Let the people praise thee, O God; let all the people praise thee.

6 [f]*Then* shall the earth yield her increase; *and* God, *even* our own God, shall bless us.

7 God shall bless us; and [g]all the ends of the earth shall fear him.

Psalm 68

To the chief Musician, A Psalm or Song of David

1 Let God arise, let his enemies be scattered: let them also that hate him flee [1]before him.

2 As smoke is driven away, *so* drive *them* away: as wax melteth before the fire, *so* let the wicked perish at the presence of God.

3 But let the righteous be glad; let them rejoice before God: yea, let them [2]exceedingly rejoice.

4 Sing unto God, sing praises to his name: extol him that rideth [3]upon the heavens by his name JAH, and rejoice before him.

5 A father of the fatherless, and a judge of the widows, *is* God in his holy habitation.

6 [a]God setteth the solitary [4]in families: he bringeth out those which are bound with chains: but the rebellious dwell in a dry *land.*

7 O God, [b]when thou wentest forth before thy people, when thou didst march through the wilderness; Sē'lah:

8 The earth shook, the heavens also dropped at the presence of God: *even* Sī'nāi itself *was moved* at the presence of God, the God of Is'ra-el.

9 Thou, O God, didst [5]send a plentiful rain, whereby thou didst [6]confirm thine inheritance, when it was weary.

10 Thy congregation hath dwelt therein: [c]thou, O God, hast prepared of thy goodness for the poor.

11 The Lord gave the word: great *was* the [7]company of those that published *it.*

12 Kings of armies [8]did flee apace: and she that tarried at home divided the spoil.

13 [d]Though ye have lien among the pots, [e]*yet shall ye be as* the wings of a dove covered with silver, and her feathers with yellow gold.

14 When the Almighty scattered kings [9]in it, it was *white* as snow in Săl'mŏn.

15 The hill of God *is as* the hill of Bā'shăn; an high hill *as* the hill of Bā'shăn.

16 Why leap ye, ye high hills? *this is* the hill *which* God desireth to dwell in; yea, the LORD will dwell *in it* for ever.

17 [f]The chariots of God *are* twenty thousand, [10]*even* thousands of angels: the Lord *is* among them, *as in* Sī'nāi, in the holy *place.*

Psalm 66
1 [1]all the earth
3 [a]Ps. 18.44 [2]lie, or, yield feigned obedience
4 [b]Ps. 67.3
5 [c]Ps. 46.8
6 [d]Ex. 14.21; Ps. 78.13; Isa. 63.13-14 [e]Josh. 3.14
7 [f]Ps. 11.4
9 [3]putteth
10 [g]Zech. 13.9
12 [4]moist
13 [h]Ps. 116.14-18; Eccl. 5.4; Jon. 2.9
14 [5]opened
15 [6]marrow
18 [i]Job 11.14-15; Prov. 15.29; Isa. 1.15

Psalm 67
1 [a]Num. 6.25-26; Ps. 4.6; Ps. 31.16; Ps. 119.135; 2 Cor. 4.6 [1]with us
2 [b]Acts 13.10 [c]Luke 2.30-32; Tit. 2.11
3 [d]Isa. 24.15-16
4 [e]Ps. 96.10 [2]lead
6 [f]Lev. 26.4; Ps. 85.9-12; Isa. 1.19
7 [g]Ps. 22.27

Psalm 68
1 [1]from his face
3 [2]rejoice with gladness
4 [3]Or, through the deserts; in JAH is his name
6 [a]1 Sam. 2.5 [4]in a house
7 [b]Hab. 3.13
9 [5]shake out [6]confirm it
10 [c]Ps. 74.19
11 [7]army
12 [8]did flee, did flee
13 [d]Ps. 81.6 [e]Ps. 74.19; Eph. 5.26-27
14 [9]Or, for her, she was
17 [f]Deut. 33.2; 2 Ki. 6.17; Dan. 7.10 [10]Or, even many thousands

18 [g]Thou hast ascended on high, [h]thou hast led captivity captive: [i]thou hast received gifts [11]for men; yea, *for* [j]the rebellious also, [k]that the LORD God might dwell *among them.*

19 Blessed *be* the Lord, *who* daily loadeth us *with benefits, even* the God of our salvation. Sē'lah.

20 *He that is* our God *is* the God of salvation; and [l]unto GOD the Lord *belong* the issues from death.

21 But God shall wound the head of his enemies, *and* the hairy scalp of such an one as goeth on still in his trespasses.

22 The Lord said, I will bring again from Bā'shăn, I will bring *my people* again from the depths of the sea:

23 That thy foot may be [12]dipped in the blood of *thine* enemies, *and* the tongue of thy dogs in the same.

24 They have seen thy goings, O God; *even* the goings of my God, my King, in the sanctuary.

25 The singers went before, the players on instruments *followed* after; among *them were* the damsels playing with timbrels.

26 Bless ye God in the congregations, *even* the Lord, [13]from the fountain of Ĭs'ra-el.

27 There *is* little Bĕn'ja-min *with* their ruler, the princes of Jū'dah [14]*and* their council, the princes of Zĕb'u-lun, *and* the princes of Năph'ta-lī.

28 Thy God hath commanded thy strength: strengthen, O God, that which thou hast wrought for us.

29 Because of thy temple at Je-ru'sa-lĕm [m]shall kings bring presents unto thee.

30 Rebuke [15]the company of spearmen, the multitude of the bulls, with the calves of the people, *till every one* submit himself with pieces of silver: [16]scatter thou the people *that* delight in war.

31 [n]Princes shall come out of Ē'gypt; [o]Ē-thĭ-ō'pĭ-a shall soon stretch out her hands unto God.

32 Sing unto God, ye kingdoms of the earth; O sing praises unto the Lord; Sē'lah:

33 To him that rideth upon the heavens of heavens, *which were* of old; lo, he doth [17]send out his voice, *and that* a mighty voice.

34 Ascribe ye strength unto God: his excellency *is* over Ĭs'ra-el, and his strength *is* in the [18]clouds.

35 O God, *thou art* terrible out of thy holy places: the God of Ĭs'ra-el *is* he [p]that giveth strength and power unto *his* people. Blessed *be* God.

Psalm 69

To the chief Musician upon Shoshannim, A Psalm of David

1 Save me, O God; for the waters are come in unto *my* soul.

2 I sink in [1]deep mire, where *there is* no standing: I am come into [2]deep waters, where the floods overflow me.

18 [g]Acts 1.9; Eph. 4.8
[h]Judg. 5.12
[i]Acts 2.4
[11]in the man
[j]1 Tim. 1.13
[k]Ps. 78.60
20 [l]Deut. 32.39
23 [12]Or, red
26 [13]Or, ye that are of the fountain of Israel
27 [14]Or, with their company
29 [m]2 Chr. 32.23; Isa. 60.16
30 [15]Or, the beasts of the reeds
[16]Or, he scattereth
31 [n]Isa. 19.19
[o]Isa. 45.14; Zeph. 3.10; Acts 8.27-28
33 [17]give
34 [18]Or, heavens
35 [p]Isa. 41.10; Zech. 10.12; John 15.5; Eph. 6.10; Phil. 4.13
Psalm 69
2 [1]the mire of depth
[2]depth of waters
4 [a]John 15.25
5 [3]guiltiness
8 [b]Isa. 53.3; John 1.11
9 [c]1 Ki. 19.10; Ps. 119.139; John 2.17
[d]Rom. 15.3
11 [e]1 Ki. 9.7; Ps. 44.13-14; Jer. 24.9
12 [f]Job 17.6; Lam. 3.14
[4]drinkers of strong drink
13 [g]Isa. 49.8; 2 Cor. 6.2
17 [5]make haste to hear me
19 [h]Ps. 22.6; Isa. 53.3; Heb. 12.2
20 [6]to lament with me
[i]Ps. 142.4-5
21 [j]Matt. 27.34; Mark 15.36; John 19.29
23 [k]2 Cor. 3.14

3 I am weary of my crying: my throat is dried: mine eyes fail while I wait for my God.

4 They that [a]hate me without a cause are more than the hairs of mine head: they that would destroy me, *being* mine enemies wrongfully, are mighty: then I restored *that* which I took not away.

5 O God, thou knowest my foolishness; and my [3]sins are not hid from thee.

6 Let not them that wait on thee, O Lord GOD of hosts, be ashamed for my sake: let not those that seek thee be confounded for my sake, O God of Ĭs'ra-el.

7 Because for thy sake I have borne reproach; shame hath covered my face.

8 [b]I am become a stranger unto my brethren, and an alien unto my mother's children.

9 [c]For the zeal of thine house hath eaten me up; [d]and the reproaches of them that reproached thee are fallen upon me.

10 When I wept, *and chastened* my soul with fasting, that was to my reproach.

11 I made sackcloth also my garment; [e]and I became a proverb to them.

12 They that sit in the gate speak against me; and [f]I *was* the song of the [4]drunkards.

13 But as for me, my prayer *is* unto thee, O LORD, [g]*in* an acceptable time: O God, in the multitude of thy mercy hear me, in the truth of thy salvation.

14 Deliver me out of the mire, and let me not sink: let me be delivered from them that hate me, and out of the deep waters.

15 Let not the waterflood overflow me, neither let the deep swallow me up, and let not the pit shut her mouth upon me.

16 Hear me, O LORD; for thy lovingkindness *is* good: turn unto me according to the multitude of thy tender mercies.

17 And hide not thy face from thy servant; for I am in trouble: [5]hear me speedily.

18 Draw nigh unto my soul, *and* redeem it: deliver me because of mine enemies.

19 Thou hast known [h]my reproach, and my shame, and my dishonour: mine adversaries *are* all before thee.

20 Reproach hath broken my heart; and I am full of heaviness: and I looked *for some* [6][i]to take pity, but *there was* none; and for comforters, but I found none.

21 They gave me also gall for my meat; and [j]in my thirst they gave me vinegar to drink.

22 Let their table become a snare before them: and *that which should have been* for *their* welfare, *let it become* a trap.

23 [k]Let their eyes be darkened, that they see not; and make their loins continually to shake.

24 Pour out thine indignation upon them, and let thy wrathful anger take hold of them.

25 Let [7]their habitation be desolate; *and* [8]let none dwell in their tents.

26 For they persecute [l]*him* whom thou hast smitten; and they talk to the grief of [9]those whom thou hast wounded.

27 Add [10]iniquity unto their iniquity: [m]and let them not come into thy righteousness.

28 Let them [n]be blotted out of the book of the living, [o]and not be written with the righteous.

29 But I *am* poor and sorrowful: let thy salvation, O God, set me up on high.

30 I will praise the name of God with a song, and will magnify him with thanksgiving.

31 *This* also shall please the LORD better than an ox *or* bullock that hath horns and hoofs.

32 The [11]humble shall see *this, and* be glad: and your heart shall live that seek God.

33 For the LORD heareth the poor, and despiseth not his prisoners.

34 Let the heaven and earth praise him, the seas, and every thing that [12]moveth therein.

35 [p]For God will save Zī'ŏn, and will build the cities of Jū'dah: that they may dwell there, and have it in possession.

36 The seed also of his servants shall inherit it: and they that love his name shall dwell therein.

Psalm 70

To the chief Musician, A Psalm of David, to bring to remembrance

1 *Make haste,* O God, to deliver me; make haste [1]to help me, O LORD.

2 Let them be [a]ashamed and confounded that seek after my soul: let them be turned backward, and put to confusion, that desire my hurt.

3 Let them be turned back for a reward of their shame that say, Aha, aha.

4 [b]Let all those that seek thee rejoice and be glad in thee: and let such as love thy salvation say continually, Let God be magnified.

5 [c]But I *am* poor and needy: make haste unto me, O God, thou *art* my help and my deliverer; O LORD, make no [d]tarrying.

Psalm 71

1 In thee, O LORD, do I put my trust: let me never be put to confusion.

2 Deliver me in thy righteousness, and cause me to escape: incline thine ear unto me, and save me.

3 [1]Be thou my strong habitation, whereunto I may continually resort: thou hast given [a]commandment to save me; for thou *art* my rock and my fortress.

4 Deliver me, O my God, out of the hand of the wicked, out of the hand of the unrighteous and cruel man.

5 For thou *art* [b]my hope, O Lord GOD: *thou art* my trust from my youth.

6 By [c]thee have I been holden up from the womb: thou art he that took me out of my mother's bowels: my praise *shall be* continually of thee.

7 [d]I am as a wonder unto many; but thou *art* my strong refuge.

8 Let my mouth be filled *with* thy praise *and with* thy honour all the day.

9 Cast me not off in the time of old age; forsake me not when my strength faileth.

10 For mine enemies speak against me; and they that [2]lay wait for my soul [e]take counsel together,

11 Saying, God hath forsaken him: persecute and take him; for *there is* none to deliver *him.*

12 [f]O God, be not far from me: O my God, [g]make haste for my help.

13 [h]Let them be confounded *and* consumed that are adversaries to my soul; let them be covered *with* reproach and dishonour that seek my hurt.

14 But I will hope continually, and will yet praise thee more and more.

15 [i]My mouth shall shew forth thy righteousness *and* thy salvation all the day; for [j]I know not the numbers *thereof.*

16 I will go in [k]the strength of the Lord GOD: I will make mention of thy righteousness, *even* of thine only.

17 O God, thou hast taught me from my youth: and hitherto have I declared thy wondrous works.

18 Now also [3]when I am old and grayheaded, O God, forsake me not; until I have shewed [4]thy strength unto *this* generation, *and* thy power to every one *that* is to come.

19 [l]Thy righteousness also, O God, *is* very high, who hast done great things: [m]O God, who *is* like unto thee!

20 [n]*Thou,* which hast shewed me great and sore troubles, [o]shalt quicken me again, and shalt bring me up again from the depths of the earth.

21 Thou shalt increase my greatness, and comfort me on every side.

22 I will also praise thee [5]with the psaltery, *even* thy truth, O my God: unto thee will I sing with the harp, O thou [p]Holy One of Is'ra-el.

23 My lips shall greatly rejoice when I sing unto thee; and [q]my soul, which thou hast redeemed.

24 My tongue also shall talk of thy righteousness all the day long: for they are confounded, for they are brought unto shame, that seek my hurt.

Psalm 72

*A Psalm *for Solomon*

1 Give the king thy judgments, O God, and thy righteousness unto the king's son.

25 [7]their palace [8]let there not be a dweller
26 [l]Isa. 53.4 [9]thy wounded
27 [10]Or, punishment of iniquity [m]Rom. 9.31
28 [n]Ex. 32.32; Phil. 4.3; Rev. 3.5 [o]Ezek. 13.9; Luke 10.20; Heb. 12.23
32 [11]Or, meek, or afflicted
34 [12]creepeth
35 [p]Ps. 51.18; Ps. 102.13-16; Isa. 14.32; Isa. 44.26

Psalm 70
1 [1]to my help
2 [a]Ps. 109.29
4 [b]Isa. 61.10; 1 Pet. 1.2-9
5 [c]Ps. 40.17 [d]Judg. 5.28; Rev. 22.20

Psalm 71
3 [1]Be thou to me for a rock of habitation [a]Ps. 44.4
5 [b]Jer. 17.7; Rom. 15.13
6 [c]Ps. 22.9; Jer. 3.4
7 [d]Isa. 8.18; 1 Cor. 4.9
10 [2]watch, or, observe [e]2 Sam. 17.1; Matt. 27.1
12 [f]Ps. 22.11; Ps. 35.22 [g]Ps. 70.1
13 [h]Ps. 35.4; Ps. 40.14
15 [i]Ps. 35.28 [j]Ps. 40.5
16 [k]Zech. 10.12; 2 Tim. 2.1
18 [3]unto old age and gray hairs [4]thine arm
19 [l]Ps. 57.10; Isa. 5.16 [m]Ex. 15.11; Isa. 40.18-25
20 [n]Ps. 60.3 [o]Hos. 6.1
22 [5]with the instrument of psaltery [p]2 Ki. 19.22; Isa. 60.9
23 [q]Ps. 103.4

Psalm 72
*Or, of

2 [a]He shall judge thy people with righteousness, and thy poor with judgment.
3 The mountains shall bring peace to the people, and the little hills, by righteousness.
4 He shall judge the poor of the people, he shall save the children of the needy, and shall break in pieces the oppressor.
5 They shall fear thee as long as the sun and moon endure, throughout all generations.
6 [b]He shall come down like rain upon the mown grass: as showers *that* water the earth.
7 In his days shall the righteous flourish; [c]and abundance of peace [1]so long as the moon endureth.
8 [d]He shall have dominion also from sea to sea, and from the river unto the ends of the earth.
9 They that dwell in the wilderness shall bow before him; and his enemies shall lick the dust.
10 [e]The kings of Tär'shish and of the isles shall bring presents: the kings of Shē'bȧ and Sē'bȧ shall offer gifts.
11 Yea, all kings shall fall down before him: all nations shall serve him.
12 For he shall deliver the needy when he crieth; the poor also, and *him* that hath no helper.
13 He shall spare the poor and needy, and shall save the souls of the needy.
14 He shall redeem their soul from deceit and violence: and precious shall their blood be in his sight.
15 And he shall live, and to him [2]shall be given of the gold of Shē'bȧ: [f]prayer also shall be made for him continually; *and* daily shall he be praised.
16 There shall be an handful of corn in the earth upon the top of the mountains; the fruit thereof shall shake like Lĕb'a-non: [g]and *they* of the city shall flourish like grass of the earth.
17 His name [3]shall endure for ever: [4]his name shall be continued as long as the sun: and [h]*men* shall be blessed in him: [i]all nations shall call him blessed.
18 Blessed *be* the LORD God, the God of Ĭs'ra-el, who only doeth wondrous things.
19 And blessed *be* his glorious name for ever: and let the whole earth be filled *with* his glory; Amen, and Amen.
20 The prayers of Dā'vid the son of Jĕs'se are ended.

Psalm 73

A Psalm [*]*of Asaph*

1 [1]Truly God *is* good to Ĭs'ra-el, *even* to such as are [2]of a clean heart.
2 But as for me, my feet were almost gone; my steps had well nigh slipped.
3 For I was envious at the foolish, *when* I saw the prosperity of the wicked.
4 For *there are* no bands in their death: but their strength *is* [3]firm.
5 They *are* not [4]in trouble *as other* men; neither are they plagued [5]like *other* men.
6 Therefore [a]pride compasseth them about as a chain; violence covereth them *as* a garment.
7 Their eyes stand out with fatness: [6]they have more than heart could wish.
8 They are corrupt, and speak wickedly *concerning* oppression: they [b]speak loftily.
9 They set their mouth [c]against the heavens, and their tongue walketh through the earth.
10 Therefore his people return hither: and waters of a full *cup* are wrung out to them.
11 And they say, [d]How doth God know? and is there knowledge in the most High?
12 Behold, these *are* the ungodly, who prosper in the world; they increase *in* riches.
13 Verily I have cleansed my heart *in* vain, and [e]washed my hands in innocency.
14 For all the day long have I been plagued, and [7]chastened every morning.
15 If I say, I will speak thus; behold, I should offend *against* the generation of thy children.
16 [f]When I thought to know this, [8]it *was* too painful for me;
17 Until [g]I went into the sanctuary of God; *then* understood I their end.
18 Surely thou didst set them in slippery places: thou castedst them down into destruction.
19 How are they *brought* into desolation, as in a moment! they are utterly consumed with terrors.
20 As a dream when *one* awaketh; *so,* O Lord, when thou awakest, thou shalt despise their image.
21 Thus my heart was grieved, and I was pricked in my reins.
22 So foolish *was* I, and [9]ignorant: I was *as* a beast [10]before thee.
23 Nevertheless I *am* continually with thee: thou hast holden *me* by my right hand.
24 [h]Thou shalt guide me with thy counsel, and [i]afterward receive me *to* glory.
25 [j]Whom have I in heaven *but thee?* and *there is* none upon earth *that* I desire beside thee.
26 [k]My flesh and my heart faileth: *but* God *is* the [11]strength of my heart, and my portion for ever.
27 For, lo, they that are far from thee shall perish: thou hast destroyed all them that go a whoring from thee.
28 But *it is* good for me to [l]draw near to God: I have put my trust in the Lord GOD, that I may declare all thy works.

Psalm 74

[*]*Maschil of Asaph*

1 O god, why hast thou cast *us* off for ever? *why* doth thine anger smoke against [a]the sheep of thy pasture?

2 [a]Isa. 11.2
6 [b]2 Sam. 23.4; Hos. 6.3
7 [c]Isa. 2.4; Luke 1.33
[1]till there be no moon
8 [d]Ex. 23.31; Zech. 9.10
10 [e]Isa. 49.7
15 [2]one shall give
[f]Matt. 6.10; 1 Cor. 1.2-3
16 [g]1 Ki. 4.20
17 [3]shall be
[4]shall be as a son to continue his father's name for ever
[h]Gen. 12.3; Jer. 4.2
[i]Isa. 45.23-24; Phil. 2.9-11

Psalm 73
*Or, for
1 [1]Or, Yet
[2]clean of heart
4 [3]fat
5 [4]in the trouble of other men
[5]with
6 [a]Eccl. 8.11
7 [6]they pass the thoughts of the heart
8 [b]2 Pet. 2.18; Jude 16
9 [c]Rev. 13.6
11 [d]Job 22.13; Ps. 94.7
13 [e]Job 21.15; Heb. 10.19-22
14 [7]my chastisement was
16 [f]Eccl. 8.17
[8]it was labour in mine eyes
17 [g]Ps. 77.13
22 [9]I knew not
[10]with thee
24 [h]Isa. 58.8
[i]John 14.3; 2 Cor. 5.1
25 [j]Isa. 26.8-9; Hab. 3.17-18
26 [k]Ps. 84.2
[11]rock
28 [l]Heb. 10.22

Psalm 74
*Or, A Psalm for Asaph to give instruction
1 [a]Ps. 95.7;

2 Remember thy congregation, *which* thou hast purchased of old; the [1]rod of thine inheritance, *which* thou hast redeemed; this mount Zī'ŏn, wherein thou hast dwelt.

3 Lift up thy feet unto the perpetual desolations; *even* all *that* the enemy hath done wickedly in the sanctuary.

4 Thine enemies roar in the midst of thy congregations; [b]they set up their ensigns *for* signs.

5 *A man* was famous according as he had lifted up axes upon the thick trees.

6 But now they break down the carved work thereof at once with axes and hammers.

7 [2]They have cast fire into thy sanctuary, they have defiled *by casting down* the dwelling place of thy name to the ground.

8 [c]They said in their hearts, Let us [3]destroy them together: they have burned up all the synagogues of God in the land.

9 We see not our signs: [d]*there is* no more any prophet: neither *is there* among us any that knoweth how long.

10 O God, how long shall the adversary reproach? shall the enemy blaspheme thy name for ever?

11 Why withdrawest thou thy hand, even thy right hand? pluck *it* out of thy bosom.

12 For [e]God *is* my King of old, working salvation in the midst of the earth.

13 Thou didst [4]divide the sea by thy strength: [f]thou brakest the heads of the [5]dragons in the waters.

14 Thou brakest the heads of leviathan in pieces, *and* gavest him *to* [g]*be* meat [h]to the people inhabiting the wilderness.

15 [i]Thou didst cleave the fountain and the flood: thou driedst up [6]mighty rivers.

16 The day *is* thine, the night also *is* thine: thou hast prepared the light and the sun.

17 Thou hast [j]set all the borders of the earth: thou hast [7]made summer and winter.

18 [k]Remember this, *that* the enemy hath reproached, O LORD, and *that* the foolish people have blasphemed thy name.

19 O deliver not the soul [l]of thy turtledove unto the multitude *of the wicked:* forget not the congregation of thy poor for ever.

20 [m]Have respect unto the covenant: for the dark places of the earth are full of the habitations of cruelty.

21 O let not the [n]oppressed return ashamed: let the poor and needy praise thy name.

22 Arise, O God, plead thine own cause: remember how the foolish man reproacheth [o]thee daily.

23 Forget not the voice of thine enemies: the tumult of those that rise up against thee [8]increaseth continually.

Psalm 75

*To the chief Musician, *Al-taschith, A Psalm or Song †of Asaph*

1 Unto thee, O God, do we give thanks, *unto thee* do we give thanks: for *that* thy name is near thy wondrous works declare.

2 [1]When I shall receive the congregation I will judge uprightly.

3 The earth and all the inhabitants thereof are dissolved: I [a]bear up the pillars of it. Sē'lah.

4 I said unto the fools, Deal not foolishly: and to the wicked, Lift not up the horn:

5 Lift not up your horn on high: speak *not with* a stiff neck.

6 For promotion *cometh* neither from the east, nor from the west, nor from the [2]south.

7 But God *is* the judge: [b]he putteth down one, and setteth up another.

8 For [c]in the hand of the LORD *there is* a cup, and the wine is red; it is full of mixture; and he poureth out of the same: but the dregs thereof, all the wicked of the earth shall wring *them* out, *and* drink *them*.

9 But I will declare for ever; I will sing praises to the God of Jā'cob.

10 All the horns of the wicked also will I cut off; *but* the horns of the righteous shall be exalted.

Psalm 76

*To the chief Musician on Neginoth, A Psalm or Song *of Asaph*

1 In Jū'dah *is* God known: his name *is* great in Īs'ra-el.

2 In Sā'lem also is his tabernacle, and his dwelling place in Zī'ŏn.

3 [a]There brake he the arrows of the bow, the shield, and the sword, and the battle. Sē'lah.

4 Thou *art* more glorious *and* excellent [b]than the mountains of prey.

5 [c]The stouthearted are spoiled, [d]they have slept their sleep: and none of the men of might have found their hands.

6 [e]At thy rebuke, O God of Jā'cob, both the chariot and horse are cast into a dead sleep.

7 Thou, *even* thou, *art* to be feared: and [f]who may stand in thy sight when once thou art angry?

8 Thou didst cause judgment to be heard from heaven; the earth feared, and was still,

9 When God arose to judgment, to save all the meek of the earth. Sē'lah.

10 [g]Surely the wrath of man shall praise thee: the remainder of wrath shalt thou restrain.

11 [h]Vow, and pay unto the LORD your God: [i]let all that be round about him bring presents [1]unto him that ought to be feared.

12 He shall cut off the spirit of princes: [j]*he is* terrible to the kings of the earth.

2 [1]Or, tribe
4 [b]Dan. 6.27
7 [2]They have sent thy sanctuary into the fire
8 [c]Ps. 83.4 [3]break
9 [d]1 Sam. 3.1; Mic. 3.6; Matt. 16.4
12 [e]Ps. 44.4
13 [4]break [f]Isa. 51.9 [5]Or, whales
14 [g]Num. 14.9 [h]Ps. 72.9
15 [i]Ex. 17.5-6; Num. 20.11; Josh. 3.13; Ps. 105.41; Isa. 11.16; Hab. 3.9; Rev. 16.12 [6]rivers of strength
17 [j]Acts 17.26 [7]made them
18 [k]Rev. 16.19
19 [l]Song 2.14; Song 4.1
20 [m]Gen. 17.7; Lev. 26.44; Jer. 33.21
21 [n]Ps. 9.18
22 [o]Isa. 37.23
23 [8]ascendeth

Psalm 75
*Or, Destroy not
†Or, for
2 [1]Or, when I shall take a set time
3 [a]Heb. 1.3
6 [2]desert
7 [b]1 Sam. 2.7; 2 Sam. 5.2; Dan. 2.21; Luke 1.52
8 [c]Job 21.20; Jer. 25.15; Rev. 14.10

Psalm 76
*Or, for
3 [a]Ps. 46.9; Ezek. 39.9
4 [b]Ezek. 38.12
5 [c]Isa. 46.12 [d]Ps. 13.3; Jer. 51.39
6 [e]Ex. 15.1; Zech. 12.4
7 [f]Job 41.10; Nah. 1.6
10 [g]Ex. 9.16
11 [h]Eccl. 5.4 [i]Ps. 68.29 [1]to fear
12 [j]Ps. 68.35

Psalm 77

*To the chief Musician, to Jeduthun, A Psalm *of Asaph*

1 I cried unto God with my voice,
even unto God with my voice; and he
gave ear unto me.
2 [a]In the day of my trouble I [b]sought
the Lord: [1]my sore ran in the night,
and ceased not: my soul refused to be
comforted.
3 I remembered God, and was troubled: I complained, and my spirit was
overwhelmed. Sē'lah.
4 Thou holdest mine eyes waking: I
am so troubled that I cannot speak.
5 [c]I have considered the days of old,
the years of ancient times.
6 I call to remembrance my song
in the night: I commune with mine
own heart: and my spirit made diligent search.
7 Will the Lord cast off for ever? and
will he be favourable no more?
8 [d]Is his mercy clean gone for ever?
doth [e]*his* promise fail [2]for evermore?
9 Hath God [f]forgotten to be gracious? hath he in anger shut up his tender mercies? Sē'lah.
10 And I said, This *is* [g]my infirmity:
but I will remember the years of the
right hand of the most High.
11 [h]I will remember the works of
the LORD: surely I will remember thy
wonders of old.
12 I will meditate also of all thy
work, and talk of thy doings.
13 [i]Thy way, O God, *is* in the sanctuary: who *is so* great a God as *our* God?
14 Thou *art* the God that doest wonders: thou hast declared thy strength
among the people.
15 Thou hast with *thine* arm redeemed thy people, the sons of Jā'cob
and Jō'seph. Sē'lah.
16 [j]The waters saw thee, O God, the
waters saw thee; they were afraid: the
depths also were troubled.
17 [3]The clouds poured out water:
the skies sent out a sound: thine arrows also went abroad.
18 The voice of thy thunder *was*
in the heaven: the lightnings lightened the world: the earth trembled
and shook.
19 [k]Thy way *is* in the sea, and thy
path in the great waters, [l]and thy footsteps are not known.
20 [m]Thou leddest thy people like
a flock by the hand of Mō'ses and
Aâr'on.

Psalm 78

**Maschil of Asaph*

1 [a]Give ear, O my people, *to* my
law: incline your ears to the words of
my mouth.
2 [b]I will open my mouth in a parable: I will utter dark sayings of old:
3 [c]Which we have heard and known,
and our fathers have told us.
4 [d]We will not hide *them* from their
children, [e]shewing to the generation
to come the praises of the LORD, and
his strength, and his wonderful works
that he hath done.
5 For he established a testimony in
Jā'cob, and appointed a law in Ĭs'ra-el,
which he commanded our fathers, that
they should make them known to their
children:
6 [f]That the generation to come might
know *them, even* the children *which*
should be born; *who* should arise and
declare *them* to their children:
7 That they might set their hope in
God, and not forget the works of God,
but keep his commandments:
8 And might not be as their fathers,
a stubborn and rebellious generation;
a generation [1]*that* set not their heart
aright, and whose spirit was not stedfast with God.
9 The children of Ē'phră-ĭm, *being*
armed, *and* [2]carrying bows, turned
back in the day of battle.
10 They kept not the covenant of
God, and refused to walk in his law;
11 And [g]forgat his works, and his
wonders that he had shewed them.
12 Marvellous things did he in the
sight of their fathers, in the land of
Ē'gypt, [h]*in* the field of Zō'an.
13 He divided the sea, and caused
them to pass through; and he made the
waters to stand as an heap.
14 In the daytime also he led them
with a cloud, and all the night with a
light of fire.
15 [i]He clave the rocks in the wilderness, and gave *them* drink as *out of* the
great depths.
16 He brought [j]streams also out of
the rock, and caused waters to run
down like rivers.
17 And they sinned yet more against
him by [k]provoking the most High in
the wilderness.
18 And they tempted God in their
heart by asking meat for their lust.
19 [l]Yea, they spake against God;
they said, Can God [3]furnish a table in
the wilderness?
20 [m]Behold, he smote the rock, that
the waters gushed out, and the streams
overflowed; can he give bread also?
can he provide flesh for his people?
21 Therefore the LORD heard *this,*
and was wroth: so a fire was kindled
against Jā'cob, and anger also came
up against Ĭs'ra-el;
22 Because they [n]believed not in
God, and trusted not in his salvation:
23 Though he had commanded the
clouds from above, [o]and opened the
doors of heaven,
24 [p]And had rained down manna
upon them to eat, and had given them
of the corn of heaven.
25 [4]Man did eat angels' food: he sent
them meat to the full.
26 He caused an east wind [5]to blow
in the heaven: and by his power he
brought in the south wind.
27 He rained flesh also upon them
as dust, and [6]feathered fowls like as
the sand of the sea:

Psalm 77
*Or, for
2 [a]Ps. 50.15
[b]Isa. 26.9
[1]my hand.
5 [c]Deut. 32.7; Isa. 51.9
8 [d]Isa. 27.11; Jon. 2.4
[e]Num. 23.19; Rom. 9.6
[2]to generation and generation
9 [f]Isa. 49.15
10 [g]Job 42.3; Jer. 10.19
11 [h]1 Chr. 16.12; Isa. 5.12
13 [i]Ps. 73.17
16 [j]Ex. 14.21; Josh. 3.15-16
17 [3]The clouds were poured forth with water
19 [k]Hab. 3.15
[l]Ex. 14.28; Job 37.23
20 [m]Isa. 63.11

Psalm 78
*Or, A Psalm for Asaph to give instruction
1 [a]Ex. 19.5; Deut. 32.29
2 [b]Ps. 49.4; Matt. 13.35
3 [c]Ps. 44.1
4 [d]Deut. 4.9
[e]Ex. 12.26; Josh. 4.6-7
6 [f]Ps. 102.18
8 [1]that prepared not their heart
9 [2]throwing forth
11 [g]Isa. 17.10; Jer. 2.32
12 [h]Gen. 32.3; Isa. 19.11
15 [i]Ex. 17.6; Isa. 41.18
16 [j]Deut. 9.21
17 [k]Heb. 3.16
19 [l]Num. 11.4
[3]order
20 [m]Ex. 17.6; Num. 20.11
22 [n]Heb. 3.10
23 [o]Gen. 7.11;
24 [p]Neh. 9.15-20;
25 [4]Or, Every one did eat the bread of the mighty
26 [5]to go
27 [6]fowl of wing

28 And he let *it* fall in the midst of their camp, round about their habitations.
29 So they did eat, and were well filled: for he gave them their own desire;
30 They were not estranged from their lust. But while their meat *was* yet in their mouths,
31 The wrath of God came upon them, and slew the fattest of them, and [7]smote down the [8]chosen *men* of Is′ra-el.
32 For all this they sinned still, and believed not for his wondrous works.
33 Therefore their days did he consume in vanity, and their years in trouble.
34 [q]When he slew them, then they sought him: and they returned and inquired early after God.
35 And they remembered that God *was* their rock, and the high God their redeemer.
36 Nevertheless they did [r]flatter him with their mouth, and they lied unto him with their tongues.
37 For their heart was not right with him, neither were they stedfast in his covenant.
38 But he, *being* [s]full of compassion, forgave *their* iniquity, and destroyed *them* not: yea, many a time [t]turned he his anger away, and did not stir up all his wrath.
39 For he remembered [u]that they *were but* flesh; [v]a wind that passeth away, and cometh not again.
40 How oft did they [9]provoke him in the wilderness, *and* grieve him in the desert!
41 Yea, they turned back and tempted God, and limited the Holy One of Is′ra-el.
42 They remembered not his hand, *nor* the day when he delivered them [10]from the enemy.
43 How he had [11]wrought his signs in Ē′gypt, and his wonders in the field of Zō′an:
44 And had turned their rivers into blood; and their floods, that they could not drink.
45 He sent divers sorts of flies among them, which devoured them; and frogs, which destroyed them.
46 He gave also their increase unto the caterpiller, and their labour unto the locust.
47 He [12]destroyed their vines with hail, and their sycomore trees with [13]frost.
48 [14]He gave up their cattle also to the hail, and their flocks to [15]hot thunderbolts.
49 He cast upon them the [w]fierceness of his anger, wrath, and indignation, and trouble, by sending evil angels *among them*.
50 [16]He made a way to his anger; he spared not their soul from death, but gave their [17]life over to the pestilence;
51 And smote all the firstborn in Ē′gypt; the chief of *their* strength in the tabernacles of [x]Hăm:
52 But made his own people to go forth like sheep, and guided them in the wilderness like a flock.
53 And he led them on safely, so that they feared not: but the sea [18]overwhelmed their enemies.
54 And he brought them to the border of his [y]sanctuary, *even to* this mountain, *which* his right hand had purchased.
55 He cast out the heathen also before them, and divided them an inheritance by line, and made the tribes of Is′ra-el to dwell in their tents.
56 Yet they tempted and provoked the most high God, and kept not his testimonies:
57 But [z]turned back, and dealt unfaithfully like their fathers: they were turned aside [a]like a deceitful bow.
58 For they provoked him to anger with their [b]high places, and moved him to jealousy with their graven images.
59 When God [c]heard *this*, he was wroth, and greatly abhorred Is′ra-el:
60 [d]So that he forsook the tabernacle of Shī′lōh, the tent *which* he placed among men;
61 [e]And delivered his [f]strength into captivity, and his glory into the enemy's hand.
62 He gave his people over also unto the sword; and was wroth with his inheritance.
63 The fire consumed their young men; and their maidens were not [19]given to marriage.
64 Their priests fell by the sword; and [g]their widows made no lamentation.
65 Then the Lord awaked as one out of sleep, *and* [h]like a mighty man that shouteth by reason of wine.
66 And he smote his enemies in the hinder parts: he put them to a perpetual reproach.
67 Moreover he refused the tabernacle of Jō′seph, and chose not the tribe of Ē′phră-ĭm:
68 But chose the tribe of Jū′dah, the mount Zī′ŏn which he loved.
69 And he [i]built his sanctuary like high *palaces*, like the earth which he hath [20]established for ever.
70 He chose Dā′vid also his servant, and took him from the sheepfolds:
71 [21]From following the ewes great with young he brought him [j]to feed Jā′cob his people, and Is′ra-el his inheritance.
72 So he fed them according to the [k]integrity of his heart; and guided them by the skilfulness of his hands.

Psalm 79

*A Psalm *of Asaph*

1 O God, the heathen are come into thine inheritance; thy holy temple have they defiled; [a]they have laid Je-ru′sa-lĕm on heaps.
2 [b]The dead bodies of thy servants have they given *to be* meat unto the fowls of the heaven, the flesh of thy saints unto the beasts of the earth.

31 [7]made to bow [8]Or, young men
34 [q]Hos. 5.15
36 [r]Ezek. 33.31
38 [s]Ex. 34.6; Neh. 9.17; Ps. 86.15
[t]1 Ki. 21.29; Isa. 48.9; Mic. 7.18; Rom. 2.4
39 [u]Gen. 6.3; John 3.6; Jas. 4.14
[v]Job 7.7-16
40 [9]Or, rebel against him
42 [10]Or, from affliction
43 [11]set
47 [12]killed [13]Or, great hailstones
48 [14]He shut up [15]Or, lightnings
49 [w]Rom. 2.8
50 [16]He weighed a path [17]Or, their beasts to the murrain
51 [x]Gen. 9.22
53 [18]covered
54 [y]Ex. 15.17
57 [z]Ezek. 20.27
[a]Hos. 7.16
58 [b]Lev. 26.30; Num. 33.52; Deut. 12.2
59 [c]Heb. 4.13
60 [d]1 Sam. 4.11; Jer. 7.12
61 [e]Judg. 18.30
[f]1 Sam. 4.12
63 [19]praised
64 [g]Job 27.15
65 [h]Isa. 42.13
69 [i]1 Ki. 6 [20]founded
71 [21]From after
[j]2 Sam. 5.2; 1 Chr. 11.2; Mic. 5.2-4; Zech. 11.4
72 [k]1 Ki. 9.4
Psalm 79 *Or, for
1 [a]2 Ki. 25.9; Jer. 26.18
2 [b]Jer. 7.33

3 Their blood have they shed like
water round about Je-rụ′sa-lĕm; [c]and
there was none to bury *them*.
4 We are become a reproach to our
neighbours, a scorn and derision to
them that are round about us.
5 How long, LORD? wilt thou be angry for ever? shall thy [d]jealousy burn
like fire?
6 Pour out thy wrath upon the heathen that have [e]not known thee, and
upon the kingdoms that have [f]not
called upon thy name.
7 For they have devoured Jā′cob,
and laid waste his dwelling place.
8 [g]O remember not against us
[1]former iniquities: let thy tender mercies speedily prevent us: for we are
brought very low.
9 Help us, O God of our salvation,
for the glory of thy name: and deliver
us, and purge away our sins, [h]for thy
name's sake.
10 Wherefore should the heathen
say, Where *is* their God? let him be
known among the heathen in our sight
by the [2]revenging of the blood of thy
servants *which is* shed.
11 Let the sighing of the prisoner
come before thee; [i]according to the
greatness of [3]thy power [4]preserve thou
those that are appointed to die;
12 And render unto our neighbours
sevenfold into their bosom their reproach, wherewith they have reproached thee, O Lord.
13 So we thy people and sheep of
thy pasture will give thee thanks for
ever: [j]we will shew forth thy praise [5]to
all generations.

Psalm 80

*To the chief Musician upon Shoshannim-eduth, A Psalm *of Asaph*

1 Give ear, O Shepherd of Ĭs′ra-el,
thou that leadest Jō′seph like a flock;
[a]thou that dwellest *between* the cherubims, [b]shine forth.
2 Before Ē′phrā-ĭm and Bĕn′ja-min
and Ma-năs′seh stir up thy strength,
and [1]come *and* save us.
3 Turn [c]us again, O God, and cause
thy face to shine; and we shall be
saved.
4 O LORD God of hosts, how long
[2]wilt thou be angry against the prayer
of thy people?
5 Thou feedest them with the bread
of tears; and givest them tears to drink
in great measure.
6 Thou makest us a strife unto our
neighbours: and our enemies laugh
among themselves.
7 [d]Turn us again, O God of hosts,
and cause thy face to shine; and we
shall be saved.
8 Thou hast brought [e]a vine out of
Ē′gypt: thou hast cast out the heathen,
and planted it.
9 Thou preparedst *room* before it,
and didst cause it to take deep root,
and it filled the land.
10 The hills were covered with the
shadow of it, and the boughs thereof
were like [3]the goodly cedars.
11 She sent out her boughs unto the
sea, and her branches [f]unto the river.
12 Why hast thou *then* [g]broken
down her hedges, so that all they
which pass by the way do pluck her?
13 The boar out of the wood doth
waste it, and the wild beast of the field
doth devour it.
14 Return, [h]we beseech thee, O God
of hosts: [i]look down from heaven, and
behold, and visit this vine;
15 And the vineyard which thy right
hand hath planted, and the branch
that thou madest strong for [j]thyself.
16 *It is* burned with fire, *it is* cut
down: they perish at the rebuke of thy
countenance.
17 [k]Let thy hand be upon the [l]man
of thy right hand, upon the son of man
whom thou madest strong for thyself.
18 So will not we go back from thee:
quicken us, and we will call upon thy
name.
19 Turn us again, O LORD God of
hosts, cause [m]thy face to shine; and we
shall be saved.

Psalm 81

*To the chief Musician upon Gittith, A Psalm *of Asaph*

1 Sing aloud unto God our strength:
make a joyful noise unto the God of
Jā′cob.
2 Take a psalm, and bring hither the
timbrel, the pleasant harp with the
psaltery.
3 Blow up the trumpet in the new
moon, in the time appointed, on our
solemn feast day.
4 For [a]this *was* a statute for Ĭs′ra-el,
and a law of the God of Jā′cob.
5 This he ordained in Jō′seph *for* a
testimony, when he went out [1]through
the land of Ē′gypt: *where* I heard a language *that* I understood not.
6 I removed his shoulder from the
burden: his hands [2]were delivered from
the [3]pots.
7 Thou calledst in trouble, and I delivered thee; I answered thee in the secret place of thunder: I proved thee at
the waters of [4]Meribah. Sē′lah.
8 Hear, O my people, and I will testify unto thee: O Ĭs′ra-el, if thou wilt
hearken unto me;
9 There shall no strange god be in
thee; neither shalt thou worship any
strange god.
10 I *am* the LORD thy God, which
brought thee out of the land of Ē′gypt:
[b]open thy mouth wide, and I will fill it.
11 But my people would not hear-
ken to my voice; and Ĭs′ra-el would
none of me.
12 [c]So I gave them up [5]unto their
own hearts' lust: *and* they walked in
their own counsels.
13 [d]Oh that my people had hearkened unto me, *and* Ĭs′ra-el had walked
in my ways!

3 [c]Rev. 11.9
5 [d]Deut. 29.20; Ezek. 36.5
6 [e]Isa. 45.4
[f]Ps. 53.4
8 [g]Isa. 43.25
[1]Or, the iniquities of them that were before us
9 [h]Josh. 7.9; Jer. 14.7
10 [2]vengeance
11 [i]Num. 14.17
[3]thine arm
[4]reserve the children of death
13 [j]Isa. 43.21
[5]to generation and generation

Psalm 80
*Or, for
1 [a]1 Sam. 4.4; Ps. 99.1
[b]Deut. 33.2
2 [1]come for salvation to us
3 [c]1 Ki. 18.37
4 [2]wilt thou smoke
7 [d]1 Ki. 18.37
8 [e]Isa. 5.1-7; Ezek. 15.6
10 [3]the cedars of God
11 [f]Ex. 23.31; Ps. 72.8
12 [g]Isa. 5.5
14 [h]Zech. 1.12-16-17
[i]Isa. 63.15
15 [j]Isa. 49.5
17 [k]Ps. 89.21
[l]Ex. 4.22; John 5.21-27
19 [m]Num. 6.25; Ps. 27.4-9

Psalm 81
*Or, for
4 [a]Lev. 23.24; Num. 10.10
5 [1]Or, against
6 [2]passed away
[3]Or, baskets
7 [4]Or, Strife
10 [b]Ps. 37.3;
12 [c]Acts 7.42;
[5]Or, to the hardness of their hearts, or, imaginations
13 [d]Deut. 5.29;

14 I should soon have subdued their enemies, and turned my hand against their adversaries.

15 The haters of the LORD should have [6]submitted themselves unto him: but their time should have endured for ever.

16 He should have fed them also [7]with the finest of the wheat: and with honey out of the rock should I have satisfied thee.

Psalm 82

*A Psalm *of Asaph*

1 God [a]standeth in the congregation of the mighty; he judgeth among [b]the gods.

2 How long will ye judge unjustly, and [c]accept the persons of the wicked? Sē'lah.

3 [1]Defend the poor and fatherless: do justice to the afflicted and needy.

4 Deliver the poor and needy: rid *them* out of the hand of the wicked.

5 They know not, neither will they understand; they walk on in darkness: [d]all the foundations of the earth are [2]out of course.

6 [e]I have said, Ye *are* gods; and all of you *are* children of the most High.

7 But [f]ye shall die like men, and fall like one of the princes.

8 Arise, O God, judge the earth: [g]for thou shalt inherit all nations.

Psalm 83

*A Song or Psalm *of Asaph*

1 Keep not thou silence, O God: hold not thy peace, and be not still, O God.

2 For, lo, [a]thine enemies make a tumult: and they that hate thee have lifted up the head.

3 They have taken crafty counsel against thy people, and consulted [b]against thy hidden ones.

4 They have said, Come, and [c]let us cut them off from *being* a nation; that the name of Ĭs'ra-el may be no more in remembrance.

5 For they have consulted together with one [1]consent: they are confederate against thee:

6 The tabernacles of Ē'dom, and the Ĭsh'ma-el-ītes; of Mō'ab, and the Hā'gar-ēnes;

7 Gē'bal, and Ăm'mŏn, and Ăm'a-lĕk; the Phĭ-lĭs'tĭnes with the inhabitants of Tȳre;

8 Ăs'sur also is joined with them: [2]they have holpen the children of Lŏt. Sē'lah.

9 Do unto them as *unto* the [d]Mĭd'ĭ-an-ītes; as *to* [e]Sĭs'e-rȧ, as *to* Jā'bin, at the brook of Kī'son:

10 *Which* perished at Ĕn'-dôr: they became *as* dung for the earth.

11 Make their nobles like Ō'reb, and like Zē'eb: yea, all their princes as Zē'bah, and as Zal-mŭn'nȧ:

12 Who said, Let us take to ourselves the houses of God in possession.

13 O my God, make them like a wheel; as the stubble before the wind.

14 As the fire burneth a wood, and as the flame setteth the mountains on fire;

15 So persecute them with thy tempest, and make them afraid with thy storm.

16 Fill their faces with shame; that they may seek thy name, O LORD.

17 Let them be confounded and troubled for ever; yea, let them be put to shame, and perish:

18 That *men* may know that thou, whose name alone *is* JE-HŌ'VAH, *art* the most high over all the earth.

Psalm 84

*To the chief Musician upon Gittith, A Psalm *for the sons of Korah*

1 How [a]amiable *are* thy tabernacles, O LORD of hosts!

2 My soul longeth, yea, even fainteth for the courts of the LORD: my heart and my flesh crieth out for the living God.

3 [1]Yea, the sparrow hath found an house, and the swallow a nest for herself, where she may lay her young, *even* thine altars, O LORD of hosts, my King, and my God.

4 Blessed *are* they that dwell in thy house: they will be still praising thee. Sē'lah.

5 Blessed *is* the man whose strength *is* in thee; in whose heart *are* the ways *of them*.

6 *Who* passing through the valley [2]of Bā'cȧ make it a well; the rain also [3]filleth the pools.

7 They go [4]from strength to strength, *every one of them* in Zī'ŏn [b]appeareth before God.

8 O LORD God of hosts, hear my prayer: give ear, O God of Jā'cob. Sē'lah.

9 Behold, [c]O God our shield, and look upon the face of thine anointed.

10 For a day in thy courts *is* better than a thousand. [5]I had rather be a doorkeeper in the house of my God, than to dwell in the tents of wickedness.

11 For the LORD God *is* a sun and shield: the LORD will give grace and glory: no good *thing* will he withhold from them that walk uprightly.

12 O LORD of hosts, blessed *is* the man that trusteth in thee.

Psalm 85

*To the chief Musician, A Psalm *for the sons of Korah*

1 Lord, thou hast been [1]favourable unto thy land: thou hast [a]brought back the captivity of Jā'cob.

2 Thou hast forgiven the iniquity of thy people, thou hast covered all their sin. Sē'lah.

3 Thou hast taken away all thy wrath: [2]thou hast turned *thyself* from the fierceness of thine anger.

4 Turn us, O God of our salvation, and cause thine anger toward us to cease.

---

15 [6]lied, or, yielded feigned obedience
16 [7]with the fat of wheat

Psalm 82
*Or, for
1 [a]Eccl. 5.8 [b]Ex. 21.6
2 [c]Deut. 1.17; Ps. 58.1-2
3 [1]Judge
5 [d]Ps. 11.3 [2]moved
6 [e]Ex. 22.9; John 10.34
7 [f]Job 21.32; Ezek. 31.14
8 [g]Ps. 2.8; Rev. 11.15

Psalm 83
*Or, for
2 [a]Ps. 2.1
3 [b]Ps. 27.5; Col. 3.3
4 [c]2 Sam. 10.6; 2 Chr. 20.1
5 [1]heart
8 [2]they have been an arm to the children of Lot
9 [d]Num. 31.7-8; Judg. 7.22; Isa. 9.4 [e]Judg. 4.15

Psalm 84
*Or, of
1 [a]Ps. 26.8; Rev. 21.2-3
3 [1]Or, As the sparrow findeth a house, and the swallow a nest for herself, so findeth my soul thine altars
6 [2]Or, of mulberry trees make him a well, etc [3]covereth
7 [4]Or, from company to company [b]Deut. 16.16
9 [c]Gen. 15.1
10 [5]I would choose rather to sit at the threshold

Psalm 85
*Or, of
1 [1]Or, well pleased [a]Jer. 30.18; Ezek. 39.25
3 [2]Or, thou hast turned thine anger from waxing hot

5 Wilt thou be angry with us for
ever? wilt thou draw out thine anger to
all generations?
6 Wilt thou not [b]revive us again:
that thy people may rejoice in thee?
7 Shew us thy mercy, O LORD, and
grant us thy salvation.
8 [c]I will hear what God the LORD
will speak: for [d]he will speak peace
unto his people, and to his saints: but
let them not turn [e]again to folly.
9 Surely his salvation *is* nigh them
that fear him; that glory may dwell in
our land.
10 [f]Mercy and truth are met together; [g]righteousness and peace have
kissed *each other*.
11 [h]Truth shall spring out of the
earth; and righteousness shall look
down from heaven.
12 [i]Yea, the LORD shall give *that
which is* good; and our land shall yield
her increase.
13 Righteousness shall go before
him; and shall set *us* in the way of his
steps.

Psalm 86

**A Prayer of David*

1 Bow down thine ear, O LORD, hear
me: for I *am* poor and needy.
2 Preserve my soul; for I *am* [1]holy: O
thou my God, save thy servant that
trusteth in thee.
3 Be merciful unto me, O Lord: for I
cry unto thee [2]daily.
4 Rejoice the soul of thy servant: for
unto thee, O Lord, do I lift up my soul.
5 [a]For thou, Lord, *art* good, and
ready to forgive; and plenteous in
mercy unto all them that call upon thee.
6 Give ear, O LORD, unto my prayer;
and attend to the voice of my supplications.
7 In the day of my trouble I will call
upon thee: for thou wilt answer me.
8 [b]Among the gods *there is* none
like unto thee, O Lord; neither *are
there any works* like unto thy works.
9 [c]All nations whom thou hast made
shall come and worship before thee, O
Lord; and shall glorify thy name.
10 For thou *art* great, and doest wondrous things: [d]thou *art* God alone.
11 Teach me thy way, O LORD; I will
walk in thy truth: unite my heart to
fear thy name.
12 I will praise thee, O Lord my God,
with all my heart: and I will glorify thy
name for evermore.
13 For great *is* thy mercy toward
me: and thou hast [e]delivered my soul
from the lowest [3]hell.
14 O God, the proud are risen against
me, and the assemblies of [4]violent *men*
have sought after my soul; and have
not set thee before them.
15 [f]But thou, O Lord, *art* a God full
of compassion, and gracious, longsuffering, and plenteous in mercy and
truth.
16 O turn unto me, and have mercy
upon me; give thy strength unto thy
servant, and save the son of thine
handmaid.
17 Shew me a token for good; that
they which hate me may see *it*, and be
ashamed: because thou, LORD, hast
holpen me, and comforted me.

Psalm 87

*A Psalm or Song *for the sons of
Korah*

1 His foundation *is* in the holy mountains.
2 The LORD loveth the gates of Zī'ŏn
more than all the dwellings of Jā'cob.
3 [a]Glorious things are spoken of
thee, O city of God. Sē'lah.
4 I will make mention of [1]Rā'hăb
and Băb'ȳ-lon to them that know me:
behold Phĭ-lĭs'tiȧ, and Tȳre, with Ē-thĭ-
ō'pĭ-a; this *man* was born there.
5 And of Zī'ŏn it shall be said, This
and that man was born in her: and
[b]the highest himself shall establish
her.
6 [c]The LORD shall count, when he
[d]writeth up the people, *that* this *man*
was born there. Sē'lah.
7 As well the singers as the players
on instruments *shall be there*: all my
springs *are* in thee.

Psalm 88

*A Song or Psalm *for the sons of
Korah, to the chief Musician upon
Mahalath Leannoth, †Maschil of
Heman the Ezrahite*

1 O lord God of my salvation, I have
cried day *and* night before thee:
2 Let my prayer come before thee:
incline thine ear unto my cry;
3 For my soul is full of troubles: and
my life [a]draweth nigh unto the grave.
4 I am counted with them that go
down into the pit: I am as a man *that
hath* no strength:
5 Free among the dead, like the slain
that lie in the grave, whom thou rememberest no more: and they are cut
off [1]from thy hand.
6 Thou hast laid me in the lowest pit,
in darkness, in the deeps.
7 Thy wrath lieth hard upon me, and
thou hast afflicted *me* with all thy
waves. Sē'lah.
8 Thou hast put away mine acquaintance far from me; thou hast made me
an abomination unto them: *I am* shut
up, and I cannot come forth.
9 Mine eye mourneth by reason of
affliction: LORD, I have called daily
upon thee, I have stretched out my
hands unto thee.
10 Wilt thou shew wonders to the
dead? shall the dead arise *and* praise
thee? Sē'lah.
11 Shall thy lovingkindness be declared in the grave? *or* thy faithfulness
in destruction?
12 [b]Shall thy wonders be known in
the dark? [c]and thy righteousness in
the land of forgetfulness?

6 [b]Hab. 3.2
8 [c]Hab. 2.1
[d]Zech. 9.10
[e]2 Pet. 2.20
10 [f]Mic. 7.20; John 1.17
[g]Ps. 72.2-3; Isa. 32.17; Luke 2.14; John 14.27
11 [h]Isa. 45.8; 2 Cor. 5.14-21
12 [i]Jas. 1.17

Psalm 86
*Or, A Prayer, being a Psalm of David
2 [1]Or, one whom thou favourest
3 [2]Or, all the day
5 [a]verse 15; Ps. 130.7-8; Joel 2.13
8 [b]Ex. 15.11; Deut. 3.24; 1 Sam. 2.2; 2 Sam. 7.22; 1 Ki. 8.23
9 [c]Ps. 95.6-7; Isa. 43.7; Rev. 15.4
10 [d]Deut. 6.4; Isa. 37.16; Mark 12.29; 1 Cor. 8.4; Eph. 4.6
13 [e]Ps. 56.13
[3]Or, grave
14 [4]terrible
15 [f]verse 5; Ex. 34.6; Num. 14.18; Neh. 9.17; Ps. 103.8; Ps. 111.4; Joel 2.13

Psalm 87
*Or, of
3 [a]Isa. 60
4 [1]Or, Egypt
5 [b]Ezek. 48.35; Matt. 16.18
6 [c]Ps. 22.30
[d]Isa. 4.3; Jer. 3.19; Ezek. 13.9

Psalm 88
*Or, of
†Or, A Psalm of Heman the Ezrahite, giving instruction
3 [a]Job 33.22; Ps. 107.18; Isa. 38.10
5 [1]Or, by thy hand
12 [b]Job 10.21
[c]Ps. 31.12; Eccl. 8.10

13 But unto thee have I cried, O
LORD; and in the morning shall my
prayer prevent thee.
14 LORD, why castest thou off my
soul? *why* hidest thou thy face from
me?
15 I *am* afflicted and ready to die
from *my* youth up: *while* I [d]suffer thy
terrors I am distracted.
16 Thy [2]fierce wrath goeth over me;
thy terrors have cut me off.
17 They came round about me [3]daily
like water; they compassed me about
together.
18 [e]Lover and friend hast thou put
far from me, *and* mine acquaintance
into darkness.

Psalm 89

**Maschil of †Ethan the Ezrahite*
1 I will sing of the mercies of the
LORD for ever: with my mouth will I
make known thy faithfulness [1]to all
generations.
2 For I have said, Mercy shall be
built up for ever; thy faithfulness shalt
thou establish in the very heavens.
3 I have made a covenant with my
chosen, I have [a]sworn unto Dā'vid my
servant,
4 Thy seed will I establish for ever,
and build up thy throne [b]to all generations. Sē'lah.
5 And the heavens shall praise thy
wonders, O LORD: thy faithfulness also
in the congregation of the saints.
6 For who in the heaven can be compared unto the LORD? *who* among the
sons of the mighty can be likened unto
the LORD?
7 God is greatly to be feared in the
assembly of the saints, and to be had in
reverence of all *them that are* about
him.
8 O LORD God of hosts, who *is* a
strong LORD like unto thee? or to thy
faithfulness round about thee?
9 [c]Thou rulest the raging of the sea:
when the waves thereof arise, thou still-
est them.
10 [d]Thou hast broken [2]Rā'hăb in
pieces, as one that is slain; thou hast
scattered thine enemies [3]with thy strong
arm.
11 The heavens *are* thine, the earth
also *is* thine: *as for* the world and
the fulness thereof, thou hast founded
them.
12 The north and the south thou
hast created them: [e]Tā'bôr and [f]Hēr'-
mŏn shall rejoice in thy name.
13 Thou hast [4]a mighty arm: strong
is thy hand, *and* high is thy right hand.
14 Justice and judgment *are* the [5]hab-
itation of thy throne: mercy and truth
shall go before thy face.
15 Blessed *is* the people that know
the [g]joyful sound: they shall walk, O
LORD, in the light of thy countenance.
16 In thy name shall they rejoice all
the day: and in thy righteousness shall
they be exalted.
17 For thou *art* the glory of their
strength: and in thy favour our horn
shall be exalted.
18 For [6]the LORD *is* our defence; and
the [h]Holy One of Is'ra-el *is* our king.
19 Then thou spakest in vision to
thy holy one, and saidst, I have laid
help upon *one that is* mighty; I have
exalted *one* chosen out of the people.
20 I have found Dā'vid my servant;
with my holy oil have I anointed him:
21 With whom my hand shall be
established: mine arm also shall
strengthen him.
22 The enemy shall not exact upon
him; nor the son of wickedness afflict
him.
23 And I will beat down his foes before his face, and plague them that
hate him.
24 But [i]my faithfulness and my
mercy *shall be* with him: and in my
name shall his horn be exalted.
25 I will set his hand also in the sea,
and his right hand in the rivers.
26 He shall cry unto me, Thou *art*
[j]my father, my God, and the rock of
my salvation.
27 Also I will make him [k]*my* firstborn, higher than the kings of the
earth.
28 [l]My mercy will I keep for him
for evermore, and my covenant shall
stand fast with him.
29 His seed also will I make *to endure* for ever, [m]and his throne [n]as the
days of heaven.
30 [o]If his children [p]forsake my law,
and walk not in my judgments;
31 If they [7]break my statutes, and
keep not my commandments;
32 Then will I visit their transgression with the rod, and their iniquity
with stripes.
33 Nevertheless my lovingkindness
[8]will I not utterly take from him, nor
suffer my faithfulness [9]to fail.
34 My covenant will I not break, nor
alter the thing that is gone out of my
lips.
35 Once have I sworn [q]by my holiness [10]that I will not lie unto Dā'vid.
36 [r]His seed shall endure for ever,
and his throne as the sun before me.
37 [s]It shall be established for ever
as the moon, and *as* a faithful witness
in heaven. Sē'lah.
38 But thou hast cast off and abhorred, thou hast been wroth with
thine anointed.
39 Thou hast made void the covenant of thy servant: [t]thou hast profaned his crown *by casting it* to the
ground.
40 Thou hast broken down all his
hedges; thou hast brought his strong
holds to ruin.
41 All that pass by the way spoil
him: he is a reproach to his neighbours.
42 Thou hast set up the right hand of
his adversaries; thou hast made all his
enemies to rejoice.
43 Thou hast also turned the edge of
his sword, and hast not made him to
stand in the battle.

15 [d]Job 6.4; Isa. 53.8; Dan. 9.26
16 [2]burnings
17 [3]Or, all the day
18 [e]Job 19.13
Psalm 89
*Or, A Psalm for Ethan the Ezrahite, to give instruction
†1 Ki. 4.31
1 [1]to generation and generation
3 [a]Ezek. 34.23; Hos. 3.5; Acts 2.30; Heb. 7.21
4 [b]2 Sam. 7.16; 1 Ki. 9.5; Isa. 9.6-7; Luke 1.32; Rom. 1.3
9 [c]Job 38.11; Nah. 1.4; Matt. 8.26
10 [d]Isa. 30.7
[2]Or, Egypt
[3]with the arm of thy strength
12 [e]Josh. 19.22; Judg. 4.6
[f]Josh. 12.1
13 [4]an arm with might
14 [5]Or, establishment
15 [g]Num. 10.10
18 [6]Or, our shield is of the LORD, and our king is of the Holy One of Israel
[h]Hos. 13.10
24 [i]Ps. 61.7
26 [j]2 Sam. 7.14; 1 Chr. 22.10; John 5.17
27 [k]Ps. 2.7
28 [l]Isa. 55.3
29 [m]Isa. 9.7; Jer. 33.17; Dan. 7.14
[n]Deut. 11.21
30 [o]2 Sam. 7.14
[p]Jer. 9.13
31 [7]profane my statutes
33 [8]I will not make void from him
[9]to lie
35 [q]Ps. 110.4; Heb. 6.13-17
[10]if I lie
36 [r]2 Sam. 7.16; John 12.34
37 [s]Jer. 31.35
39 [t]Lam. 5.16

44 Thou hast made his [11]glory to
cease, and cast his throne down to the
ground.
45 The days of his youth hast thou
shortened: thou hast covered him with
shame. Sē'lah.
46 How long, LORD? wilt thou hide
thyself for ever? shall thy wrath burn
like fire?
47 [u]Remember how short my time
is: wherefore hast thou made all men
in vain?
48 What man *is he that* liveth, and
shall not [v]see death? shall he deliver
his soul from the hand of the grave?
Sē'lah.
49 Lord, where *are* thy former lovingkindnesses, *which* thou [w]swarest
unto Dā'vid in thy truth?
50 Remember, Lord, the reproach of
thy servants; *how* I do bear in my
bosom *the reproach of* all the mighty
people;
51 Wherewith thine enemies have
reproached, O LORD; wherewith they
have reproached the footsteps of thine
anointed.
52 Blessed *be* the LORD for evermore. Amen, and Amen.

Psalm 90

**A Prayer of Moses the man of God*
1 Lord, thou hast been our dwelling
place [1]in all generations.
2 [a]Before the mountains were
brought forth, or ever thou hadst
formed the earth and the world, even
from everlasting to everlasting, thou
art God.
3 Thou turnest man to destruction;
and sayest, [b]Return, ye children of
men.
4 [c]For a thousand years in thy sight
are but as yesterday [2]when it is past,
and *as* a watch in the night.
5 Thou carriest them away as with a
flood; they are *as* a sleep: in the morning [d]*they are* like grass *which* [3]grow-
eth up.
6 [e]In the morning it flourisheth, and
groweth up; in the evening it is cut
down, and withereth.
7 For we are consumed by thine anger, and by thy wrath are we troubled.
8 [f]Thou hast set our iniquities before thee, our [g]secret *sins* in the light
of thy countenance.
9 For all our days are [4]passed away
in thy wrath: we spend our years [5]as a
tale *that is told*.
10 [6]The days of our years *are* threescore years and ten; and if by reason of
strength *they be* fourscore years, yet *is*
their strength labour and sorrow; for it
is soon cut off, and we fly away.
11 Who knoweth the power of thine
anger? even according to thy fear, *so is*
thy wrath.
12 [h]So teach *us* to number our days,
that we may [7]apply *our* hearts unto
wisdom.
13 Return, O LORD, how long? and let
it [i]repent thee concerning thy servants.

44 [11]bright-ness
47 [u]Job 7.7
48 [v]Heb. 11.5
49 [w]2 Sam. 7.15; Isa. 55.3

Psalm 90
*Or, A Prayer, being a Psalm of Moses
1 [1]in generation and generation
2 [a]Job 38.4-6; Prov. 8.25
3 [b]Gen. 3.19; Eccl. 12.7
4 [c]Heb. 13.8; 2 Pet. 3.8
[2]Or, when he hath passed them
5 [d]Isa. 40.6
[3]Or, is changed
6 [e]Job 14.2; Ps. 92.7
8 [f]Ps. 50.21; Jer. 16.17
[g]Ps. 19.12; Heb. 4.12-13
9 [4]turned away
[5]Or, as a meditation
10 [6]As for the days of our years, in them are seventy years
12 [h]Ps. 39.4
[7]cause to come
13 [i]Deut. 32.36
16 [j]Ps. 44.1; Hab. 3.2
17 [k]Isa. 26.12; 2 Thess. 2.16-17

Psalm 91
1 [1]lodge
4 [a]Ps. 61.4
5 [b]Job 5.19; Isa. 43.2
8 [c]Mal. 1.5
10 [d]Prov. 1.33; 2 Pet. 2.9
11 [e]Ps. 34.7; Heb. 1.14
12 [f]Job 5.23;
13 [2]Or, asp
15 [g]Job 22.27;
[h]Ps. 43.2
[i]1 Sam. 2.30
16 [3]length of days

Psalm 92
2 [1]in the nights

14 O satisfy us early with thy mercy;
that we may rejoice and be glad all our
days.
15 Make us glad according to the
days *wherein* thou hast afflicted us, *and*
the years *wherein* we have seen evil.
16 Let [j]thy work appear unto thy servants, and thy glory unto their children.
17 And let the beauty of the LORD
our God be upon us: and [k]establish
thou the work of our hands upon us;
yea, the work of our hands establish
thou it.

Psalm 91

1 He that dwelleth in the secret place
of the most High shall [1]abide under the
shadow of the Almighty.
2 I will say of the LORD, *He is* my
refuge and my fortress: my God; in
him will I trust.
3 Surely he shall deliver thee from
the snare of the fowler, *and* from the
noisome pestilence.
4 [a]He shall cover thee with his feathers, and under his wings shalt thou
trust: his truth *shall be thy* shield and
buckler.
5 [b]Thou shalt not be afraid for the
terror by night; *nor* for the arrow *that*
flieth by day;
6 *Nor* for the pestilence *that* walketh in darkness; *nor* for the destruction
that wasteth at noonday.
7 A thousand shall fall at thy side,
and ten thousand at thy right hand;
but it shall not come nigh thee.
8 Only [c]with thine eyes shalt thou
behold and see the reward of the
wicked.
9 Because thou hast made the LORD,
which is my refuge, *even* the most
High, thy habitation;
10 [d]There shall no evil befall thee,
neither shall any plague come nigh thy
dwelling.
11 [e]For he shall give his angels
charge over thee, to keep thee in all thy
ways.
12 They shall bear thee up in *their*
hands, [f]lest thou dash thy foot against
a stone.
13 Thou shalt tread upon the lion
and [2]adder: the young lion and the
dragon shalt thou trample under feet.
14 Because he hath set his love upon
me, therefore will I deliver him: I will
set him on high, because he hath known
my name.
15 [g]He shall call upon me, and I will
answer him: [h]I *will be* with him in trouble; I will deliver him, and [i]honour him.
16 With [3]long life will I satisfy him,
and shew him my salvation.

Psalm 92

A Psalm or Song for the sabbath day
1 *It is a* good *thing* to give thanks
unto the LORD, and to sing praises unto
thy name, O most High:
2 To shew forth thy lovingkindness
in the morning, and thy faithfulness
[1]every night,

3 Upon an instrument of ten strings,
and upon the psaltery; [2]upon the harp
with [3]a solemn sound.
4 For thou, Lord, hast made me glad
through thy work: I will triumph in the
works of thy hands.
5 O LORD, how great are thy works!
and thy [a]thoughts are very deep.
6 [b]A brutish man knoweth not; neither doth a fool understand this.
7 When [c]the wicked spring as the
grass, and when all the workers of iniquity do flourish; *it is* that they shall be
destroyed for ever:
8 But thou, LORD, *art most* high for
evermore.
9 For, lo, thine enemies, O LORD, for,
lo, thine enemies shall perish; all the
workers of iniquity shall be scattered.
10 But my horn shalt thou exalt like
the horn of an unicorn: I shall be
anointed with fresh oil.
11 Mine eye also shall see *my desire*
on mine enemies, *and* mine ears shall
hear *my desire* of the wicked that rise
up against me.
12 [d]The righteous shall flourish like
the palm tree: he shall grow like a cedar in Lĕb'a-non.
13 Those that be [e]planted in the
house of the LORD shall flourish in the
courts of our God.
14 They shall still bring forth fruit in
old age; they shall be fat and [4]flourishing;
15 To shew that the LORD *is* upright:
[f]*he is* my rock, and [g]*there is* no unrighteousness in him.

Psalm 93

1 The [a]LORD reigneth, [b]he is clothed
with majesty; the LORD is clothed with
strength, *wherewith* he hath girded
himself: the world also is stablished,
that it cannot be moved.
2 [c]Thy throne *is* established [1]of old:
thou *art* from everlasting.
3 The floods have lifted up, O LORD,
the floods have lifted up their voice;
the floods lift up their waves.
4 [d]The LORD on high *is* mightier
than the noise of many waters, *yea,*
than the mighty waves of the sea.
5 Thy testimonies are very sure: holiness becometh thine house, O LORD,
[2]for ever.

Psalm 94

1 O lord [1]God, to whom vengeance
belongeth; O God, to whom vengeance
belongeth, [2]shew thyself.
2 Lift up thyself, thou [a]judge of the
earth: render a reward to the proud.
3 LORD, [b]how long shall the wicked,
how long shall the wicked triumph?
4 *How long* shall they [c]utter *and*
speak hard things? *and* all the workers
of iniquity boast themselves?
5 They break in pieces thy people, O
LORD, and afflict thine heritage.
6 They slay the widow and the
stranger, and murder the fatherless.

3 [2]Or, upon the solemn sound with the harp [3]Higgaion
5 [a]Isa. 28.29; Rom. 11.33
6 [b]Ps. 73.22
7 [c]Job 21.7; Mal. 3.15
12 [d]Ps. 52.8; Song 7.7
13 [e]Isa. 60.21; John 15.2-5
14 [4]green
15 [f]Deut. 32.4 [g]Rom. 9.14
Psalm 93
1 [a]Isa. 52.7; Rev. 19.6 [b]Job 40.10; Isa. 59.17
2 [c]Prov. 8.22 [1]from then
4 [d]Ps. 29.10
5 [2]to length of days
Psalm 94
1 [1]God of revenges [2]shine forth
2 [a]Gen. 18.25
3 [b]Job 20.5
4 [c]Jude 15
9 [d]Ex. 4.11; Prov. 20.12
10 [e]Job 35.11;
11 [f]1 Cor. 1.21
12 [g]Job 5.17;
14 [h]Deut. 31.6;
15 [3]shall be after it
17 [4]Or, quickly
20 [i]Amos 6.3; [j]Ps. 58.2;
21 [k]Matt. 27.1 [l]Ex. 23.7;
23 [m]Prov. 2.22
Psalm 95
2 [1]prevent his face
4 [2]In whose [3]Or, the heights of the hills are his
5 [4]Whose the sea is
6 [a]1 Ki. 8.54; [b]Job 35.10;
7 [c]Heb. 3.7
8 [d]Num. 14.22 [5]contention

7 Yet they say, The LORD shall not
see, neither shall the God of Jā'cob regard *it*.
8 Understand, ye brutish among the
people: and *ye* fools, when will ye be
wise?
9 [d]He that planted the ear, shall he
not hear? he that formed the eye, shall
he not see?
10 He that chastiseth the heathen,
shall not he correct? he that [e]teacheth
man knowledge, *shall not he know?*
11 [f]The LORD knoweth the thoughts
of man, that they *are* vanity.
12 [g]Blessed *is* the man whom thou
chastenest, O LORD, and teachest him
out of thy law;
13 That thou mayest give him rest
from the days of adversity, until the pit
be digged for the wicked.
14 For [h]the LORD will not cast off
his people, neither will he forsake his
inheritance.
15 But judgment shall return unto
righteousness: and all the upright in
heart [3]shall follow it.
16 Who will rise up for me against
the evildoers? *or* who will stand up for
me against the workers of iniquity?
17 Unless the LORD *had been* my
help, my soul had [4]almost dwelt in
silence.
18 When I said, My foot slippeth;
thy mercy, O LORD, held me up.
19 In the multitude of my thoughts
within me thy comforts delight my
soul.
20 Shall [i]the throne of iniquity have
fellowship with thee, which [j]frameth
mischief by a law?
21 [k]They gather themselves together
against the soul of the righteous, and
[l]condemn the innocent blood.
22 But the LORD is my defence; and
my God *is* the rock of my refuge.
23 And [m]he shall bring upon them
their own iniquity, and shall cut them
off in their own wickedness; *yea,* the
LORD our God shall cut them off.

Psalm 95

1 O come, let us sing unto the LORD:
let us make a joyful noise to the rock of
our salvation.
2 Let us [1]come before his presence
with thanksgiving, and make a joyful
noise unto him with psalms.
3 For the LORD *is* a great God, and a
great King above all gods.
4 [2]In his hand *are* the deep places of
the earth: [3]the strength of the hills *is*
his also.
5 [4]The sea *is* his, and he made it: and
his hands formed the dry *land.*
6 O come, let us worship and bow
down: let [a]us kneel before the LORD
our [b]maker.
7 For he *is* our God; and we *are* the
people of his pasture, and the sheep of
his hand. [c]To day if ye will hear his
voice,
8 Harden not your heart, [d]as in the
[5]provocation, *and* as *in* the day of temptation in the wilderness:

9 When your fathers tempted me,
proved me, and saw my work.
10 [e]Forty years long was I grieved
with *this* generation, and said, It *is* a
people that do err in their heart, and
they have not known my ways:
11 Unto whom [f]I sware in my wrath
[6]that they should not enter into my
rest.

Psalm 96

1 O sing unto the LORD a new song:
sing unto the LORD, all the earth.
2 Sing unto the LORD, bless his name;
shew forth his salvation from day to
day.
3 Declare his glory among the heathen, his wonders among all people.
4 For the LORD *is* great, and greatly
to be praised: he *is* to be feared above
all gods.
5 For [a]all the gods of the nations *are*
idols: [b]but the LORD made the heavens.
6 Honour and majesty *are* before
him: strength and beauty *are* in his
sanctuary.
7 [c]Give unto the LORD, O ye kindreds of the people, give unto the LORD
glory and strength.
8 Give unto the LORD the glory [1]*due
unto* his name: bring an offering, and
come into his courts.
9 O worship the LORD [2]in the beauty
of holiness: fear before him, all the
earth.
10 Say among the heathen *that* [d]the
LORD reigneth: the world also shall be
established that it shall not be moved:
[e]he shall judge the people righteously.
11 Let the heavens rejoice, and let
the earth be glad; let the sea roar, and
the fulness thereof.
12 Let the field be joyful, and all that
is therein: then shall all the trees of the
wood rejoice
13 Before the LORD: for he cometh,
for he cometh to judge the earth: [f]he
shall judge the world with righteousness, and the people with his truth.

Psalm 97

1 The LORD reigneth; let the earth
rejoice; let the [1a]multitude of isles be
glad *thereof*.
2 Clouds and darkness *are* round
about him: righteousness and judgment *are* the [2]habitation of his throne.
3 [b]A fire goeth before him, and burneth up his enemies round about.
4 His lightnings enlightened the
world: the earth saw, and trembled.
5 The hills melted like wax at the
presence of the LORD, at the presence
of the Lord of the whole earth.
6 The heavens declare his righteousness, and all the people see his glory.
7 [c]Confounded be all they that serve
graven images, that boast themselves
of idols: [d]worship him, all *ye* gods.
8 Zī'ŏn heard, and was glad; and the
daughters of Jū'dah rejoiced because
of thy judgments, O LORD.

10 [e]Heb. 3.10
11 [f]Num. 14.23; Heb. 4.3
[6]if they enter
Psalm 96
5 [a]Isa. 41.23-24; 1 Cor. 8.4-5
[b]Gen. 1.1; Jer. 10.11
7 [c]Ps. 29.1
8 [1]of his name
9 [2]Or, in the glorious sanctuary
10 [d]Rev. 11.15
[e]John 5.22
13 [f]Rev. 19.11
Psalm 97
1 [1]many, or, great isles
[a]Isa. 60.9
2 [2]Or, establishment
3 [b]Dan. 7.10; Hab. 3.5
7 [c]Ex. 20.4; Jer. 10.14
[d]Heb. 1.6
9 [e]Eph. 1.21
10 [f]Ps. 101.3; Rom. 7.15
[g]1 Sam. 2.9; Prov. 2.8
[h]Dan. 3.28
12 [3]Or, to the memorial
Psalm 98
1 [a]Isa. 59.16
2 [b]Isa. 52.10; Luke 2.30
[c]Isa. 62.2; Rom. 3.25
[1]Or, revealed
3 [d]Lev. 26.42; Luke 1.54
[e]Isa. 49.6; Acts 13.47
6 [f]Num. 10.10; 2 Chr. 29.27
Psalm 99
1 [1]stagger
3 [a]Deut. 28.58; Rev. 4.8
4 [b]Deut. 32.3-4;
[c]Gen. 18.25;
5 [d]1 Chr. 28.2;
[2]Or, it is holy
[e]Lev. 19.2
7 [f]Ex. 19.9;
8 [g]Num. 14.20;
[h]Deut. 9.20

9 For thou, LORD, *art* [e]high above
all the earth: thou art exalted far above
all gods.
10 Ye that love the LORD, [f]hate evil:
[g]he preserveth the souls of his saints;
[h]he delivereth them out of the hand of
the wicked.
11 Light is sown for the righteous,
and gladness for the upright in heart.
12 Rejoice in the LORD, ye righteous;
and give thanks [3]at the remembrance
of his holiness.

Psalm 98

A Psalm

1 O sing unto the LORD a new song;
for he hath done marvellous things:
[a]his right hand, and his holy arm, hath
gotten him the victory.
2 [b]The LORD hath made known his
salvation: [c]his righteousness hath he
[1]openly shewed in the sight of the
heathen.
3 He hath [d]remembered his mercy
and his truth toward the house of Is'ra-
el: [e]all the ends of the earth have seen
the salvation of our God.
4 Make a joyful noise unto the LORD,
all the earth: make a loud noise, and
rejoice, and sing praise.
5 Sing unto the LORD with the harp;
with the harp, and the voice of a psalm.
6 [f]With trumpets and sound of cornet make a joyful noise before the
LORD, the King.
7 Let the sea roar, and the fulness
thereof; the world, and they that dwell
therein.
8 Let the floods clap *their* hands: let
the hills be joyful together
9 Before the LORD; for he cometh to
judge the earth: with righteousness
shall he judge the world, and the people with equity.

Psalm 99

1 The LORD reigneth; let the people
tremble: he sitteth *between* the cherubims; let the earth [1]be moved.
2 The LORD *is* great in Zī'ŏn; and he
is high above all the people.
3 Let them praise [a]thy great and terrible name; *for* it *is* holy.
4 [b]The king's strength also loveth
judgment; thou dost [c]establish equity,
thou executest judgment and righteousness in Jā'cob.
5 Exalt ye the LORD our God, and
worship at [d]his footstool; *for* [2e]he *is*
holy.
6 Mō'ses and Aâr'on among his
priests, and Săm'u-el among them that
call upon his name; they called upon
the LORD, and he answered them.
7 [f]He spake unto them in the cloudy
pillar: they kept his testimonies, and
the ordinance *that* he gave them.
8 Thou answeredst them, O LORD
our God: [g]thou wast a God that forgavest them, though [h]thou tookest vengeance of their inventions.
9 Exalt the LORD our God, and

worship at his holy hill; for the LORD
our God *is* holy.

Psalm 100

*A Psalm of *praise*

1 Make a joyful noise unto the
LORD, [1]all ye lands.
2 Serve the LORD with gladness:
come before his presence with singing.
3 Know ye that the LORD he *is* God:
[a]*it is* he *that* hath made us, [2]and not
we ourselves; [b]*we are* his people, and
the sheep of his pasture.
4 Enter into his gates with thanksgiving, *and* into his courts with praise: be
thankful unto him, *and* bless his name.
5 For the LORD *is* good; his mercy *is*
everlasting; and his truth *endureth* [3]to
all generations.

Psalm 101

A Psalm of David

1 I will sing of mercy and judgment:
unto thee, O LORD, will I sing.
2 I will [a]behave myself wisely in a
perfect way. O when wilt thou come
unto me? I will [b]walk within my house
with a perfect heart.
3 I will set no [1]wicked thing before
mine eyes: I hate the work of them
[c]that turn aside; *it* shall not cleave to
me.
4 A froward heart shall depart from
me: I will not [d]know a wicked *person*.
5 Whoso privily slandereth his neighbour, him will I cut off: [e]him that hath
an high look and a proud heart will not I
suffer.
6 [f]Mine eyes *shall be* upon the faithful of the land, that they may dwell
with me: he that walketh [2]in a perfect
way, he shall serve me.
7 He that worketh deceit shall not
dwell within my house: he that telleth
lies [3]shall not tarry in my sight.
8 I will [g]early destroy all the wicked
of the land; that I may cut off all wicked
[h]doers from the city of the LORD.

Psalm 102

A Prayer of the afflicted, when he is overwhelmed, and poureth out his complaint before the LORD

1 Hear my prayer, O LORD, and let
my cry come unto thee.
2 Hide not thy face from me in the
day *when* I am in trouble; incline thine
ear unto me: in the day *when* I call
answer me speedily.
3 [a]For my days are consumed [1]like
smoke, and [b]my bones are burned as
an hearth.
4 My heart is smitten, and withered
like grass; so that I forget to eat my
bread.
5 By reason of the voice of my groaning my bones cleave to my [2]skin.
6 I am like [c]a pelican of the wilderness: I am like an owl of the desert.
7 I watch, and am as a sparrow
alone upon the house top.
8 Mine enemies reproach me all the
day; *and* they that are mad against me
are [d]sworn against me.
9 For I have eaten ashes like bread,
and mingled my drink with weeping,
10 Because of thine indignation and
thy wrath: for [e]thou hast lifted me up,
and cast me down.
11 My days *are* like a shadow that
declineth; and [f]I am withered like
grass.
12 But thou, O LORD, shalt [g]endure
for ever; and thy remembrance unto
all generations.
13 Thou shalt arise, *and* have mercy
upon Zī'ŏn: for the time to favour her,
yea, the [h]set time, is come.
14 For thy [i]servants take pleasure
in her stones, and favour the dust
thereof.
15 So the heathen shall [j]fear the
name of the LORD, and all the kings of
the earth thy glory.
16 When the LORD shall build up
Zī'ŏn, [k]he shall appear in his glory.
17 [l]He will regard the prayer of the
destitute, and not despise their prayer.
18 This shall be [m]written for the
generation to come: and [n]the people
which shall be created shall praise the
LORD.
19 For he hath [o]looked down from
the height of his sanctuary; from heaven
did the LORD behold the earth;
20 To hear the groaning of the prisoner; to loose [3]those that are appointed
to death;
21 To declare the name of the LORD
in Zī'ŏn, and his praise in Je-ru'sa-lĕm;
22 [p]When the people are gathered
together, and the kingdoms, to serve
the LORD.
23 He [4]weakened my strength in the
way; he shortened my days.
24 I said, O my God, take me not
away in the midst of my days: [q]thy
years *are* throughout all generations.
25 [r]Of old hast thou laid the foundation of the earth: and the heavens *are*
the work of thy hands.
26 [s]They shall perish, but thou shalt
[5]endure: yea, all of them shall wax
old like a garment; as a vesture shalt
thou change them, and they shall be
changed:
27 But [t]thou *art* the same, and thy
years shall have no end.
28 The children of thy servants shall
continue, and their seed shall be established before thee.

Psalm 103

A Psalm of David

1 Bless the LORD, O my soul: and all
that is within me, *bless* his holy name.
2 Bless the LORD, O my soul, and forget not all his benefits:
3 [a]Who forgiveth all thine iniquities; who [b]healeth all thy diseases;
4 Who redeemeth thy life from destruction; who crowneth thee with lovingkindness and tender mercies;

Psalm 100
*Or, thanksgiving
1 [1]all the earth
3 [a]Job 10.8-9; Eph. 2.10
[2]Or, and his we are
[b]Ezek. 34.30
5 [3]to generation and generation

Psalm 101
2 [a]1 Sam. 18.14
[b]Gen. 18.19; 1 Ki. 9.4
3 [1]thing of Belial
[c]Josh. 23.6; 1 Sam. 12.20
4 [d]Matt. 7.23; 2 Tim. 2.19
5 [e]Prov. 6.17; Luke 18.14
6 [f]Rom. 13.4
[2]Or, perfect in the way
7 [3]shall not be established
8 [g]Jer. 21.12
[h]Hos. 9.3

Psalm 102
3 [a]Jas. 4.14
[1]Or, (as some read,) into smoke
[b]Lam. 1.13
5 [2]Or, flesh
6 [c]Isa. 34.11; Zeph. 2.14
8 [d]Acts 23.12
10 [e]Ps. 30.7
11 [f]Jas. 1.10
12 [g]1 Tim. 6.16
13 [h]Isa. 40.2
14 [i]Dan. 9.2
15 [j]1 Ki. 8.43
16 [k]Isa. 60.1
17 [l]Neh. 2.8
18 [m]Rom. 15.4; 1 Cor. 10.11
[n]Ps. 22.31; Isa. 43.21
19 [o]Deut. 26.15; Ps. 14.2
20 [3]the children of death
22 [p]Hos. 1.11
23 [4]afflicted
24 [q]Ps. 90.2; Rev. 1.4-8
25 [r]Gen. 1.1; Heb. 1.10
26 [s]Isa. 66.22; 2 Pet. 3.7
[5]stand
27 [t]Mal. 3.6

Psalm 103
3 [a]Isa. 33.24;
[b]Ex. 15.26;

5 Who satisfieth thy mouth with good *things; so that* thy youth is renewed like the eagle's.

6 The LORD executeth righteousness and judgment for all that are oppressed.

7 He made known his ways unto Mō'ses, his acts unto the children of Is'ra-el.

8 [c]The LORD *is* merciful and gracious, slow to anger, and [1]plenteous in mercy.

9 [d]He will not always chide: neither will he keep *his anger* for ever.

10 [e]He hath not dealt with us after our sins; nor rewarded us according to our iniquities.

11 For [2]as the heaven is high above the earth, *so* great is his mercy toward them that fear him.

12 As far as the east is from the west, *so* far hath he [f]removed our transgressions from us.

13 [g]Like as a father pitieth *his* children, *so* the LORD pitieth them that fear him.

14 For he knoweth our frame; he remembereth that we *are* dust.

15 *As for* man, his days *are* as grass: as a flower of the field, so he flourisheth.

16 For the wind passeth over it, and [3]it is gone; and the place thereof shall know it no more.

17 But the mercy of the LORD *is* from everlasting to everlasting upon them that fear him, and his righteousness [h]unto children's children;

18 [i]To such as keep his covenant, and to those that remember his commandments to do them.

19 The LORD hath prepared his throne in the heavens; and [j]his kingdom ruleth over all.

20 Bless the LORD, ye his angels, [4]that excel in strength, that [k]do his commandments, hearkening unto the voice of his word.

21 Bless ye the LORD, all *ye* [l]his hosts; [m]*ye* ministers of his, that do his pleasure.

22 Bless the LORD, all his works in all places of his dominion: bless the LORD, O my soul.

Psalm 104

1 Bless the LORD, O my soul. O LORD my God, thou art very great; thou art clothed with honour and majesty.

2 Who coverest *thyself* with light as *with* a garment: who stretchest out the heavens like a curtain:

3 [a]Who layeth the beams of his chambers in the waters: [b]who maketh the clouds his chariot: who walketh upon the wings of the wind:

4 [c]Who maketh his angels spirits; his ministers a flaming fire:

5 [1]*Who* laid the foundations of the earth, *that* it should not be removed for ever.

6 Thou coveredst it with the deep as *with* a garment: the waters stood above the mountains.

7 At thy rebuke they fled; at the voice of thy thunder they hasted away.

8 [2]They go up by the mountains; they go down by the valleys [d]unto the place which thou hast founded for them.

9 [e]Thou hast set a bound that they may not pass over; [f]that they turn not again to cover the earth.

10 [3]He sendeth the springs into the valleys, *which* [4]run among the hills.

11 They give drink to every beast of the field: the wild asses [5]quench their thirst.

12 By them shall the fowls of the heaven have their habitation, *which* [6]sing among the branches.

13 He watereth the hills from his chambers: the earth is satisfied with the fruit of thy works.

14 [g]He causeth the grass to grow for the cattle, and herb for the service of man: that he may bring forth [h]food out of the earth;

15 And [i]wine *that* maketh glad the heart of man, *and* [7]oil to make *his* face to shine, and bread *which* strengtheneth man's heart.

16 The [8]trees of the LORD are full *of sap;* the cedars of Lĕb'a-non, [j]which he hath planted;

17 Where the birds make their nests: *as for* the stork, the fir trees *are* her house.

18 The high hills *are* a refuge for the wild goats; *and* the rocks for [k]the conies.

19 [l]He appointed the moon for seasons: the sun [m]knoweth his going down.

20 [n]Thou makest darkness, and it is night: wherein [9]all the beasts of the forest do creep *forth.*

21 [o]The young lions roar after their prey, and seek their meat from God.

22 The sun ariseth, they gather themselves together, and lay them down in their dens.

23 Man goeth forth unto [p]his work and to his labour until the evening.

24 [q]O LORD, how manifold are thy works! in wisdom hast thou made them all: the earth is full of thy riches.

25 *So is* this great and wide sea, wherein *are* things creeping innumerable, both small and great beasts.

26 There go the ships: *there is* that [r]leviathan, *whom* thou hast [10]made to play therein.

27 [s]These wait all upon thee; that thou mayest give *them* their meat in due season.

28 *That* thou givest them they gather: thou openest thine hand, they are filled with good.

29 Thou hidest thy face, they are troubled: [t]thou takest away their breath, they die, and return to their dust.

30 [u]Thou sendest forth thy spirit, they are created: and thou renewest the face of the earth.

31 The glory of the LORD [11]shall endure for ever: the LORD shall rejoice in his works.

32 He looketh on the earth, and it [v]trembleth: he toucheth the hills, and they smoke.

---

8 [c]Ex. 34.6; Deut. 5.10 [1]great of mercy
9 [d]Isa. 57.16;
10 [e]Ezra 9.13
11 [2]according to the height of the heaven
12 [f]Isa. 43.25;
13 [g]Deut. 8.5;
16 [3]it is not
17 [h]Ex. 20.6
18 [i]Deut. 7.9
19 [j]Ps. 47.2
20 [4]mighty in strength [k]Matt. 6.10
21 [l]Gen. 32.2 [m]Dan. 7.9

Psalm 104
3 [a]Amos 9.6 [b]Isa. 19.1
4 [c]Heb. 1.7
5 [1]He hath founded the earth upon her bases
8 [2]Or, The mountains ascend, the valleys descend [d]Job 38.10
9 [e]Job 26.10; [f]Gen. 9.11
10 [3]Who sendeth [4]walk
11 [5]break
12 [6]give a voice
14 [g]Gen. 1.29-30; [h]Job 28.5;
15 [i]Judg. 9.13; [7]to make his face shine with oil, or, more than oil
16 [8]That is, large trees [j]Num. 24.6;
18 [k]Prov. 30.26
19 [l]Gen. 1.14 [m]Job 38.12
20 [n]Isa. 45.7 [9]all the beasts thereof do trample on the forest
21 [o]Job 38.39
23 [p]Gen. 3.19
24 [q]Gen. 1.20-22
26 [r]Job 41.1 [10]formed
27 [s]Rom. 11.36
29 [t]Eccl. 12.7
30 [u]Isa. 32.15
31 [11]shall be
32 [v]Hab. 3.10

33 I will sing unto the LORD as long as I live: I will sing praise to my God while I have my being.

34 My meditation of him shall be sweet: I will be glad in the LORD.

35 Let [w]the sinners be consumed out of the earth, and let the wicked be no more. Bless thou the LORD, O my soul. [12]Praise ye the LORD.

Psalm 105

1 O [a]give thanks unto the LORD; call upon his name: make known his deeds among the people.

2 Sing unto him, sing psalms unto him: talk ye of all his wondrous works.

3 Glory ye in his holy name: let the heart of them rejoice that seek the LORD.

4 Seek the LORD, and his strength: [b]seek his face evermore.

5 [c]Remember his marvellous works that he hath done; his wonders, and the judgments of his mouth;

6 O ye seed of Ā′brā-hăm his servant, ye children of Jā′cob his chosen.

7 He *is* the LORD our God: [d]his judgments *are* in all the earth.

8 He hath [e]remembered his covenant for ever, the word *which* he commanded to a thousand generations.

9 [f]Which *covenant* he made with Ā′brā-hăm, and his oath unto Ī′saac;

10 And confirmed the same unto Jā′cob for a law, *and* to Ĭs′ra-el *for* an everlasting covenant:

11 Saying, [g]Unto thee will I give the land of Cā′năan [1]the lot of your inheritance:

12 [h]When they were *but* a few men in number; yea, very few, [i]and strangers in it.

13 When they went from one nation to another, from *one* kingdom to another people;

14 [j]He suffered no man to do them wrong: yea, [k]he reproved kings for their sakes;

15 *Saying,* Touch not mine anointed, and do my prophets no harm.

16 Moreover [l]he called for a famine upon the land: he brake the whole [m]staff of bread.

17 [n]He sent a man before them, *even* Jō′seph, *who* [o]was sold for a servant:

18 [p]Whose feet they hurt with fetters: [2]he was laid in iron:

19 Until the time that his word came: the word of the LORD tried him.

20 The king sent and loosed him; *even* the ruler of the people, and let him go free.

21 He made him lord of his house, and ruler of all his [3]substance:

22 To bind his princes at his pleasure; and teach his senators wisdom.

23 [q]Ĭs′ra-el also came into Ē′gypt; and Jā′cob sojourned in the land of Hăm.

24 And [r]he increased his people greatly; and made them stronger than their enemies.

25 He turned their heart to hate his people, to deal subtilly with his servants.

26 He sent Mō′ses his servant; *and* Aâr′on [s]whom he had chosen.

27 They shewed [4]his signs among them, and wonders in the land of Hăm.

28 He sent darkness, and made it dark; and [t]they rebelled not against his word.

29 He turned their waters into blood, and slew their fish.

30 Their land brought forth frogs in abundance, in the chambers of their kings.

31 He spake, and there came divers sorts of flies, *and* lice in all their coasts.

32 [5]He gave them hail for rain, *and* flaming fire in their land.

33 He smote their vines also and their fig trees; and brake the trees of their coasts.

34 He spake, and the locusts came, and caterpillers, and that without number,

35 And did eat up all the herbs in their land, and devoured the fruit of their ground.

36 He smote also all the firstborn in their land, [u]the chief of all their strength.

37 He brought them forth also with silver and gold: and *there was* not one feeble *person* among their tribes.

38 Ē′gypt was glad when they departed: for the fear of them fell upon them.

39 [v]He spread a cloud for a covering; and fire to give light in the night.

40 [w]*The people* asked, and he brought quails, and satisfied them with the bread of heaven.

41 [x]He opened the rock, and the waters gushed out; they ran in the dry places *like* a river.

42 For he remembered [y]his holy promise, *and* Ā′brā-hăm his servant.

43 And he brought forth his people with joy, *and* his chosen with [6]gladness:

44 [z]And gave them the lands of the heathen: and they inherited the labour of the people;

45 [a]That they might observe his statutes, and keep his laws. [7]Praise ye the LORD.

Psalm 106

1 [1]Praise ye the LORD. O give thanks unto the LORD; for *he is* [a]good: for his mercy *endureth* for ever.

2 [b]Who can utter the mighty acts of the LORD? *who* can shew forth all his praise?

3 Blessed *are* they that [c]keep judgment, *and* he that [d]doeth righteousness at [e]all times.

4 Remember me, O LORD, with the favour *that thou bearest unto* thy people: O visit me with thy salvation;

5 That I may see the good of thy chosen, that I may rejoice in the gladness of thy nation, that I may glory with thine inheritance.

35 [w]Prov. 2.22 [12]Hallelujah

Psalm 105
1 [a]Isa. 12.4
4 [b]Ps. 27.8
5 [c]Deut. 8.2
7 [d]Isa. 26.9
8 [e]Luke 1.72
9 [f]Gen. 17.2; Gen. 22.16; Gen. 26.3; Ps. 111.5-9; Dan. 9.4; Luke 1.73; Heb. 6.17
11 [g]Gen. 15.18 [1]the cord
12 [h]Gen. 34.30; Deut. 7.7 [i]Gen. 17.8; Heb. 11.9
14 [j]Gen. 35.5 [k]Gen. 12.17
16 [l]Gen. 41.54; 2 Ki. 8.1 [m]Lev. 26.26
17 [n]Gen. 45.5 [o]Gen. 37.28
18 [p]Gen. 40.15 [2]his soul came into iron
21 [3]possession
23 [q]Gen. 46.6
24 [r]Ex. 1.7; Deut. 26.5; Acts 7.17
26 [s]Ex. 3.10; Num. 16.5
27 [4]words of his signs
28 [t]Ps. 99.7
32 [5]He gave their rain hail
36 [u]Gen. 49.3
39 [v]Ex. 13.21; Neh. 9.12
40 [w]Ex. 16.12
41 [x]Ex. 17.6; Neh. 9.15; Isa. 48.21; 1 Cor. 10.4
42 [y]Gen. 15.4
43 [6]singing
44 [z]Deut. 6.10; Josh. 13.7
45 [a]Deut. 4.1 [7]Hallelujah

Psalm 106
1 [1]Hallelujah [a]Isa. 63.7; Matt. 19.17
2 [b]Ps. 40.5
3 [c]Jer. 22.15-16; Matt. 22.37 [d]Ps. 15.2 [e]Acts 24.16; Gal. 6.9

6 [f]We have sinned with our fathers,
we have committed iniquity, we have
done wickedly.
7 Our fathers understood not thy
wonders in Ē'ġypt; they remembered
not the multitude of thy mercies; but
provoked *him* at the sea, *even* at the
Red sea.
8 Nevertheless he saved them [g]for
his name's sake, that he might make
his mighty power to be known.
9 [h]He rebuked the Red sea also, and
it was dried up: so [i]he led them through
the depths, as through the wilderness.
10 And he saved them from the hand
of him that hated *them*, and redeemed
them from the hand of the enemy.
11 And the waters covered their enemies: there was not one of them left.
12 Then believed they his words;
they sang his praise.
13 [2]They soon forgat his works; they
waited not for his counsel:
14 But [3]lusted exceedingly in the wilderness, and tempted God in the desert.
15 And he gave them their request;
but [j]sent leanness into their soul.
16 [k]They envied Mō'ses also in the
camp, *and* Aâr'on the saint of the
LORD.
17 The earth opened and swallowed
up Dā'than, and covered the company
of A-bī'răm.
18 And a fire was kindled in their
company; the flame burned up the
wicked.
19 [l]They made a calf in Hō'reb, and
worshipped the molten image.
20 Thus [m]they changed their glory
into the similitude of an ox that eateth
grass.
21 They forgat God their saviour,
which had done great things in Ē'ġypt;
22 Wondrous works in the land of
Hăm, *and* terrible things by the Red
sea.
23 [n]Therefore he said that he would
destroy them, had not Mō'ses his chosen
[o]stood before him in the breach, to turn
away his wrath, lest he should destroy
them.
24 Yea, they despised [4]the pleasant
land, they [p]believed not his word:
25 But murmured in their tents, *and*
hearkened not unto the voice of the
LORD.
26 Therefore he lifted up his hand
against them, to overthrow them in the
wilderness:
27 [5]To overthrow their seed also
among the nations, and to scatter them
in the lands.
28 [q]They joined themselves also unto
Bā'al–pē'or, and ate the sacrifices of the
dead.
29 Thus they provoked *him* to anger
with their inventions: and the plague
brake in upon them.
30 Then stood up Phĭn'e-has, and
executed judgment: and *so* the plague
was stayed.
31 And that was counted unto him
for righteousness unto all generations
for evermore.

6 [f]Lev. 26.40; Dan. 9.5
8 [g]Josh. 7.9; Jer. 14.7-21
9 [h]Ex. 14.21; Nah. 1.4
[i]Isa. 63.11
13 [2]They made haste, they forgat
14 [3]lusted a lust
15 [j]Isa. 10.16
16 [k]Num. 16.1-3
19 [l]Ex. 32.4
20 [m]Jer. 2.11; Rom. 1.23
23 [n]Ex. 32.10; Ezek. 20.13
[o]Ezek. 13.5
24 [4]a land of desire.
[p]Heb. 3.18
27 [5]To make them fall
28 [q]Num. 25.2-3; Rev. 2.14
32 [r]Deut. 1.37
33 [s]Num. 20.10; Jas. 3.2
34 [t]Judg. 1.21
[u]Deut. 7.2; Judg. 2.2
35 [v]Judg. 3.5; Isa. 2.6
36 [w]Ex. 23.33; 2 Chr. 33.2-7
37 [x]Deut. 12.30-31; Ezek. 16.20
38 [y]Num. 35.33
41 [z]Judg. 2.14; Neh. 9.27
43 [6]Or, impoverished, or, weakened
44 [a]Judg. 10.10
45 [b]Lev. 26.41
[c]Lam. 3.32
46 [d]Ezra 9.9; Jer. 42.12
47 [e]Luke 1.74
[f]2 Cor. 5.15
Psalm 107
1 [a]Matt. 19.17
3 [b]Ps. 106.47; Ezek. 39.27
[1]from the sea
6 [c]Ps. 50.15;

32 They angered *him* also at the waters of strife, [r]so that it went ill with
Mō'ses for their sakes:
33 Because they provoked his spirit,
so that he [s]spake unadvisedly with his
lips.
34 [t]They did not destroy the nations, [u]concerning whom the LORD
commanded them:
35 [v]But were mingled among the
heathen, and learned their works.
36 And [w]they served their idols:
which were a snare unto them.
37 Yea, [x]they sacrificed their sons
and their daughters unto devils,
38 And shed innocent blood, *even*
the blood of their sons and of their
daughters, whom they sacrificed unto
the idols of Cā'năan: and [y]the land
was polluted with blood.
39 Thus were they defiled with their
own works, and went a whoring with
their own inventions.
40 Therefore was the wrath of the
LORD kindled against his people, insomuch that he abhorred his own
inheritance.
41 And [z]he gave them into the hand
of the heathen; and they that hated
them ruled over them.
42 Their enemies also oppressed
them, and they were brought into subjection under their hand.
43 Many times did he deliver them;
but they provoked *him* with their counsel, and were [6]brought low for their
iniquity.
44 Nevertheless he regarded their affliction, when [a]he heard their cry:
45 [b]And he remembered for them
his covenant, and [c]repented according
to the multitude of his mercies.
46 [d]He made them also to be pitied
of all those that carried them captives.
47 Save us, O LORD our God, and
gather us [e]from among the heathen, to
give thanks [f]unto thy holy name, *and*
to triumph in thy praise.
48 Blessed *be* the LORD God of Ĭs'ra-
el from everlasting to everlasting: and
let all the people say, Amen. Praise ye
the LORD.

Psalm 107

1 O give thanks unto the LORD, for
[a]*he is* good: for his mercy *endureth* for
ever.
2 Let the redeemed of the LORD say
so, whom he hath redeemed from the
hand of the enemy;
3 And [b]gathered them out of the
lands, from the east, and from the
west, from the north, and [1]from the
south.
4 They wandered in the wilderness
in a solitary way; they found no city to
dwell in.
5 Hungry and thirsty, their soul
fainted in them.
6 [c]Then they cried unto the LORD in
their trouble, *and* he delivered them
out of their distresses.

7 And he led them forth by the [d]right
way, that they might go to a city of
habitation.
8 Oh that *men* would praise the LORD
for his goodness, and *for* his wonderful
works to the children of men!
9 For [e]he satisfieth the longing soul,
and filleth the hungry soul with goodness.
10 Such as sit in darkness and in the
shadow of death, *being* [f]bound in affliction and iron;
11 Because they [g]rebelled against
the words of God, and contemned [h]the
counsel of the most High:
12 Therefore he brought down their
heart with labour; they fell down, and
there was [i]none to help.
13 Then they cried unto the LORD in
their trouble, *and* he saved them out of
their distresses.
14 [j]He brought them out of darkness and the shadow of death, and
brake their bands in sunder.
15 Oh that *men* would praise the
LORD *for* his goodness, and *for* his wonderful works to the children of men!
16 For he hath [k]broken the gates of
brass, and cut the bars of iron in sunder.
17 Fools [l]because of their transgression, and because of their iniquities,
are afflicted.
18 Their soul abhorreth all manner
of meat; and they draw near unto the
gates of death.
19 Then they cry unto the LORD in
their trouble, *and* he saveth them out
of their distresses.
20 [m]He sent his word, and healed
them, and delivered *them* from their
destructions.
21 Oh that *men* would praise the
LORD *for* his goodness, and *for* his wonderful works to the children of men!
22 And [n]let them sacrifice the sacrifices of thanksgiving, and declare his
works with [2]rejoicing.
23 They that go down to the sea in
ships, that do business in great waters;
24 These see the works of the LORD,
and his wonders in the deep.
25 For he commandeth, and [3]raiseth
the stormy wind, which lifteth up the
waves thereof.
26 They mount up to the heaven,
they go down again to the depths:
[o]their soul is melted because of trouble.
27 They reel to and fro, and stagger
like a drunken man, and [4]are at their
wit's end.
28 Then they cry unto the LORD in
their trouble, and he bringeth them out
of their distresses.
29 [p]He maketh the storm a calm, so
that the waves thereof are still.
30 Then are they glad because they
be quiet; so he bringeth them unto
their desired haven.
31 Oh that *men* would praise the
LORD *for* his goodness, and *for* his wonderful works to the children of men!
32 Let them exalt him also in the congregation of the people, and praise him
in the assembly of the elders.

7 [d]Ezra 8.21; Isa. 63.12
9 [e]Ps. 34.10; Isa. 55.1; Matt. 5.6; Luke 1.53
10 [f]Job 36.8
11 [g]Lam. 3.42
[h]Ps. 73.24; Luke 7.30; Acts 20.27
12 [i]Isa. 63.5
14 [j]Ps. 146.7; Acts 12.7
16 [k]Isa. 45.2
17 [l]Ps. 14.1; Prov. 1.22; Lam. 3.39
20 [m]Num. 21.8; 2 Ki. 20.4; Matt. 8.8
22 [n]Lev. 7.12; Ps. 50.14; Heb. 13.15
[2]singing
25 [3]maketh to stand
26 [o]Ps. 22.14; Isa. 13.7; Nah. 2.10
27 [4]all their wisdom is swallowed up
29 [p]Ps. 65.7; Isa. 50.2; Mark 4.39-41
33 [q]1 Ki. 17.1; Nah. 1.4
34 [r]Gen. 13.10
[5]saltness
35 [s]Isa. 41.18
36 [t]Acts 17.26
38 [u]Gen. 12.2
39 [v]2 Ki. 10.32
40 [w]Josh. 10.24-26; Job 12.21
[6]Or, void place
41 [x]1 Sam. 2.8; Job 8.7
[7]Or, after
42 [y]Job 22.19
[z]Job 5.16; Prov. 10.11
43 [a]Jer. 9.12; Dan. 12.10
Psalm 108
4 [a]Num. 14.18; Mic. 7.18-20
[1]Or, skies
5 [b]Ps. 57.5
8 [c]Gen. 49.10
10 [d]Ps. 60.9
12 [e]Isa. 30.3
13 [f]Isa. 25.10; Rev. 14.19-20

33 He [q]turneth rivers into a wilderness, and the watersprings into dry
ground;
34 A [r]fruitful land into [5]barrenness,
for the wickedness of them that dwell
therein.
35 [s]He turneth the wilderness into a
standing water, and dry ground into
watersprings.
36 And there he maketh the hungry
[t]to dwell, that they may prepare a city
for habitation;
37 And sow the fields, and plant
vineyards, which may yield fruits of
increase.
38 [u]He blesseth them also, so that
they are multiplied greatly; and suffereth not their cattle to decrease.
39 Again, they are [v]minished and
brought low through oppression, affliction, and sorrow.
40 [w]He poureth contempt upon
princes, and causeth them to wander
in the [6]wilderness, *where there is* no
way.
41 [x]Yet setteth he the poor on high
[7]from affliction, and maketh *him* families like a flock.
42 [y]The righteous shall see *it*, and
rejoice: and all [z]iniquity shall stop her
mouth.
43 [a]Whoso *is* wise, and will observe
these *things*, even they shall understand the lovingkindness of the LORD.

Psalm 108

A Song or Psalm of David

1 O God, my heart is fixed; I will sing
and give praise, even with my glory.
2 Awake, psaltery and harp: I *myself* will awake early.
3 I will praise thee, O LORD, among
the people: and I will sing praises unto
thee among the nations.
4 For thy [a]mercy *is* great above the
heavens: and thy truth *reacheth* unto
the [1]clouds.
5 [b]Be thou exalted, O God, above
the heavens: and thy glory above all
the earth;
6 That thy beloved may be delivered: save *with* thy right hand, and answer me.
7 God hath spoken in his holiness; I
will rejoice, I will divide Shē'chem,
and mete out the valley of Sŭc'coth.
8 Gĭl'e-ăd *is* mine; Ma-năs'seh *is*
mine; Ē'phră-ĭm also *is* the strength of
mine head; [c]Jū'dah *is* my lawgiver;
9 Mō'ab *is* my washpot: over Ē'dom
will I cast out my shoe; over Phĭ-lĭs'tiȧ
will I triumph.
10 [d]Who will bring me into the
strong city? who will lead me into
Ē'dom?
11 *Wilt* not *thou*, O God, *who* hast
cast us off? and wilt not thou, O God,
go forth with our hosts?
12 Give us help from trouble: for
[e]vain *is* the help of man.
13 Through God we shall do valiantly: for he [f]*it is that* shall tread
down our enemies.

Psalm 109

To the chief Musician, A Psalm of David

1 Hold [a]not thy peace, O God of my
praise;
2 For the mouth of the wicked and
the [1]mouth of the deceitful [2]are opened
against me: they have spoken against
me with a lying tongue.
3 They compassed me about also
with words of hatred; and fought
against me [b]without a cause.
4 For my love they are my adversaries: but I *give myself unto* prayer.
5 And [c]they have rewarded me evil
for good, and hatred for my love.
6 Set thou a wicked man over him:
and let [3]Sā'tan stand at his right hand.
7 When he shall be judged, let him
[4]be condemned: and [d]let his prayer become sin.
8 Let his days be few; *and* [e]let another take his [5]office.
9 [f]Let his children be fatherless, and
his wife a widow.
10 Let his children be continually
[g]vagabonds, and beg: let them seek
their bread also out of their desolate
places.
11 [h]Let the extortioner catch all that
he hath; and let the strangers spoil his
labour.
12 Let there be none to extend mercy
unto him: neither let there be any to
favour his fatherless children.
13 [i]Let his posterity be cut off; *and*
in the generation following let their
[j]name be blotted out.
14 [k]Let the iniquity of his fathers be
remembered with the LORD; and let
not the sin of his mother [l]be blotted
out.
15 Let them be before the LORD continually, that he may [m]cut off the memory of them from the earth.
16 Because that he remembered not
to shew mercy, but persecuted the
poor and needy man, that he might
even slay the broken in heart.
17 As he loved cursing, so let it
come unto him: as he delighted not in
blessing, so let it be far from him.
18 As he clothed himself with cursing like as with his garment, so let it
come [6]into his bowels like water, and
like oil into his bones.
19 Let it be unto him as the garment
which covereth him, and for a girdle
wherewith he is girded continually.
20 *Let* this *be* the reward of mine
adversaries from the LORD, and of
them that speak evil against my soul.
21 But do thou for me, O GOD the
Lord, for thy name's sake: because thy
mercy *is* good, deliver thou me.
22 For I *am* poor and needy, and my
heart is wounded within me.
23 I am gone like the shadow when
it declineth: I am tossed up and down
as the locust.
24 My [n]knees are weak through fasting; and my flesh faileth of fatness.
25 I became also a reproach unto
them: *when* they looked upon me [o]they
shaked their heads.
26 Help me, O LORD my God: O save
me according to thy mercy:
27 [p]That they may know that this *is*
thy hand; *that* thou, LORD, hast done it.
28 Let them curse, but bless thou:
when they arise, let them be ashamed;
but let thy [q]servant rejoice.
29 Let mine adversaries be clothed
with shame, and let them cover themselves with their own confusion, as
with a mantle.
30 I will greatly praise the LORD
with my mouth; yea, I will praise him
among the multitude.
31 For he shall stand at the right
hand of the poor, to save *him* [7]from
those that condemn his soul.

Psalm 110

A Psalm of David

1 The [a]LORD said unto my Lord, Sit
thou at my right hand, until I make
thine enemies thy footstool.
2 The LORD shall send the rod of thy
strength out of Zī'ŏn: rule thou in the
midst of thine enemies.
3 [b]Thy people *shall be* willing in the
day of thy power, [c]in the beauties of
holiness [1]from the womb of the morning: thou hast the dew of thy youth.
4 The LORD hath sworn, and [d]will
not repent, [e]Thou *art* a priest for ever
after the order of Měl-chĭz'e-děk.
5 The Lord [f]at thy right hand shall
strike through kings [g]in the day of his
wrath.
6 He shall judge among the heathen,
he shall fill *the places* with the dead
bodies; [h]he shall wound the heads
over [2]many countries.
7 [i]He shall drink of the brook in the
way: [j]therefore shall he lift up the
head.

Psalm 111

1 [1]Praise ye the LORD. I will praise
the LORD with *my* whole heart, in the
assembly of the upright, and *in* the congregation.
2 [a]The works of the LORD *are* great,
sought out of all them that have pleasure therein.
3 His work *is* honourable and glorious: and his righteousness endureth
for ever.
4 He hath made his wonderful works
to be remembered: the LORD *is* gracious and full of compassion.
5 He hath given [2]meat unto them
that fear him: he will ever be mindful
of his covenant.
6 He hath shewed his people the
power of his works, that he may give
them the heritage of the heathen.
7 The works of his hands *are* verity
and judgment; [b]all his commandments
are sure.
8 They [3]stand fast for ever and ever,
and are [c]done in truth and uprightness.

Psalm 109
1 [a]Ps. 83.1
2 [1]mouth of deceit [2]have opened themselves
3 [b]1 Sam. 19.4-5; Ps. 35.7-20; John 15.25
5 [c]Ps. 38.20
6 [3]Or, an adversary
7 [4]go out guilty, or, wicked [d]Prov. 28.9
8 [e]Acts 1.20 [5]Or, charge
9 [f]Ex. 22.24; Jer. 18.21
10 [g]Gen. 4.12
11 [h]Job 18.9
13 [i]Ps. 37.28 [j]Prov. 10.7
14 [k]Ex. 20.5 [l]Neh. 4.5
15 [m]Job 18.17
18 [6]within him
24 [n]Heb. 12.12
25 [o]Isa. 37.22; Matt. 27.39
27 [p]Job 37.7
28 [q]Num. 22.12; Isa. 65.14
31 [7]from the judges of his soul

Psalm 110
1 [a]Ps. 45.6; Matt. 22.44; Mark 12.36; Luke 20.42; 1 Cor. 15.25; Heb. 1.13
3 [b]Judg. 5.2 [c]Ps. 96.9; Acts 2.41 [1]Or, more than the womb of the morning: thou shalt have, etc
4 [d]Num. 23.19 [e]Zech. 6.13; Heb. 5.6
5 [f]Ps. 16.8 [g]Rom. 2.5; Rev. 11.18
6 [h]Hab. 3.13 [2]Or, great
7 [i]Isa. 61.1; John 3.34 [j]Isa. 53.12

Psalm 111
1 [1]Hallelujah
2 [a]Job 38, 39
5 [2]prey
7 [b]Ps. 19.7
8 [3]are established [c]Rev. 15.3

9 He sent redemption unto his people: he hath commanded his covenant for ever: holy and reverend *is* his name.

10 [d]The fear of the LORD *is* the beginning of wisdom: [4]a good understanding have all they [5]that do *his commandments:* his praise endureth for ever.

Psalm 112

1 [1]Praise ye the LORD. Blessed *is* the man *that* feareth the LORD, *that* delighteth greatly in his commandments.

2 His seed shall be mighty upon earth: the generation of the upright shall be blessed.

3 [a]Wealth and riches *shall be* in his house: and his righteousness endureth for ever.

4 Unto the upright there ariseth light in the darkness: *he is* gracious, and full of compassion, and righteous.

5 [b]A good man sheweth favour, and lendeth: he will guide his affairs with [2]discretion.

6 Surely he shall not be moved for ever: the righteous shall be in everlasting remembrance.

7 He shall not be afraid of evil tidings: his heart is fixed, trusting in the LORD.

8 His heart *is* established, he shall not be afraid, until he see *his desire* upon his enemies.

9 [c]He hath dispersed, he hath given to the poor; his righteousness endureth for ever; his horn shall be exalted with honour.

10 [d]The wicked shall see *it*, and be grieved; he shall gnash with his teeth, and melt away: the desire of the wicked shall perish.

Psalm 113

1 [1]Praise ye the LORD. Praise, O ye servants of the LORD, praise the name of the LORD.

2 [a]Blessed be the name of the LORD from this time forth and for evermore.

3 [b]From the rising of the sun unto the going down of the same the LORD'S name *is* to be praised.

4 The LORD *is* high above all nations, *and* his glory above the heavens.

5 Who *is* like unto the LORD our God, who [2]dwelleth on high,

6 [c]Who humbleth *himself* to behold *the things that are* in heaven, and in the earth!

7 [d]He raiseth up the poor out of the dust, *and* lifteth the needy out of the dunghill;

8 That he may [e]set *him* with princes, *even* with the princes of his people.

9 [f]He maketh the barren woman [3]to keep house, *and to be* a joyful mother of children. Praise ye the LORD.

Psalm 114

1 When Ĭs'ra-el went out of Ē'ġypt, the house of Jā'cob from a people of strange language;

2 Jū'dah was his sanctuary, *and* Ĭs'ra-el his dominion.

3 The sea saw *it*, and fled: Jôr'dan was driven back.

4 [a]The mountains skipped like rams, *and* the little hills like lambs.

5 What *ailed* thee, O thou sea, that thou fleddest? thou Jôr'dan, *that* thou wast driven back?

6 Ye mountains, *that* ye skipped like rams; *and* ye little hills, like lambs?

7 Tremble, thou earth, at the presence of the Lord, at the presence of the God of Jā'cob;

8 [b]Which turned the rock *into* a standing water, the flint into a fountain of waters.

Psalm 115

1 Not [a]unto us, O LORD, not unto us, but unto thy name give glory, for thy mercy, *and* for thy truth's sake.

2 Wherefore should the heathen say, [b]Where *is* now their God?

3 [c]But our God *is* in the heavens: he hath done whatsoever he hath pleased.

4 [d]Their idols *are* silver and gold, the work of men's hands.

5 They have mouths, but they speak not: eyes have they, but they see not:

6 They have ears, but they hear not: noses have they, but they smell not:

7 They have hands, but they handle not: feet have they, but they walk not: neither speak they through their throat.

8 [e]They that make them are like unto them; *so is* every one that trusteth in them.

9 O Ĭs'ra-el, trust thou in the LORD: [f]he *is* their help and their shield.

10 [g]O house of Aâr'on, trust in the LORD: he *is* their help and their shield.

11 Ye that fear the LORD, trust in the LORD: he *is* their help and their shield.

12 The LORD hath been mindful of us: he will [h]bless *us;* he will bless the house of Ĭs'ra-el; he will bless the house of Aâr'on.

13 [i]He will bless them that fear the LORD, *both* small [1]and great.

14 The LORD shall increase you more and more, you and your children.

15 Ye *are* [j]blessed of the LORD [k]which made heaven and earth.

16 The heaven, *even* the heavens, *are* the LORD'S: but the earth hath he given to the children of men.

17 The dead praise not the LORD, neither any that go down into silence.

18 [l]But we will bless the LORD from this time forth and for evermore. Praise the LORD.

Psalm 116

1 I love the LORD, because he hath heard my voice *and* my supplications.

2 Because he hath inclined his ear unto me, therefore will I call upon *him* [1]as long as I live.

3 The sorrows of death compassed me, and the pains of hell [2]gat hold upon me: I found trouble and sorrow.

---

10 [d]Deut. 4.6; Job 28.28; Eccl. 12.13 [4]Or, good success [5]that do them

Psalm 112
1 [1]Hallelujah
3 [a]Prov. 3.16; 2 Cor. 6.10
5 [b]Luke 6.35 [2]judgment
9 [c]Luke 11.41; 1 Tim. 6.18
10 [d]Luke 13.28

Psalm 113
1 [1]Hallelujah
2 [a]Dan. 2.20
3 [b]Isa. 59.19; Rev. 11.15
5 [2]exalteth himself to dwell
6 [c]Isa. 57.15
7 [d]1 Sam. 2.8; Dan. 12.2
8 [e]Job 36.7
9 [f]1 Sam. 2.5; Gal. 4.27 [3]to dwell in an house

Psalm 114
4 [a]Ps. 29.6; Hab. 3.6
8 [b]Ex. 17.6; Ps. 107.35

Psalm 115
1 [a]Isa. 48.11; Ezek. 36.32
2 [b]Ps. 42.3-10; Joel 2.17
3 [c]1 Chr. 16.26; Dan. 4.35
4 [d]Deut. 4.28; 1 Cor. 10.19-20
8 [e]Ps. 135.18; Hab. 2.18
9 [f]Ps. 33.20; Prov. 30.5
10 [g]Mal. 2.7
12 [h]Eph. 1.3
13 [i]Lev. 26.3; Prov. 10.6 [1]with
15 [j]Gen. 14.19 [k]Gen. 1.1; Ps. 96.5
18 [l]Ps. 145.2; Dan. 2.20

Psalm 116
2 [1]in my days
3 [2]found me

4 Then called I upon the name of the LORD; O LORD, I beseech thee, deliver my soul.

5 Gracious *is* the LORD, [a]and righteous; yea, our God *is* merciful.

6 The LORD preserveth the simple: I was brought low, and he helped me.

7 Return unto thy [b]rest, O my soul; for the LORD hath dealt bountifully with thee.

8 For thou hast delivered my soul from death, mine eyes from tears, *and* my feet from falling.

9 I will walk before the LORD in the land of the living.

10 [c]I believed, therefore have I spoken: I was greatly afflicted:

11 I said in my haste, [d]All men *are* liars.

12 What shall I render unto the LORD *for* all his benefits toward me?

13 I will take the cup of salvation, and call upon the name of the LORD.

14 [e]I will pay my vows unto the LORD now in the presence of all his people.

15 [f]Precious in the sight of the LORD *is* the death of his saints.

16 O LORD, truly I *am* thy servant; I *am* thy servant, *and* the son of thine handmaid: thou hast loosed my bonds.

17 I will offer to thee the sacrifice of thanksgiving, and will call upon the name of the LORD.

18 I will pay my vows unto the LORD now in the presence of all his people,

19 In the courts of the LORD'S house, in the midst of thee, O Je-rụ'sa-lĕm. Praise ye the LORD.

Psalm 117

1 O praise the LORD, all ye nations: praise him, all ye people.

2 For his merciful kindness is great toward us: and the truth of the LORD *endureth* for ever. Praise ye the LORD.

Psalm 118

1 O [a]give thanks unto the LORD; for *he is* good: because his mercy *endureth* for ever.

2 [b]Let Ĭs'ra-el now say, that his mercy *endureth* for ever.

3 Let the house of Aâr'on now say, that his mercy *endureth* for ever.

4 Let them now that fear the LORD say, that his mercy *endureth* for ever.

5 I called upon the LORD [1]in distress: the LORD answered me, *and* [c]*set me* in a large place.

6 The LORD *is* [2]on my side; I will not fear: what can man do unto me?

7 [d]The LORD taketh my part with them that help me: therefore shall I see *my desire* upon them that hate me.

8 [e]*It is* better to trust in the LORD than to put confidence in man.

9 [f]*It is* better to trust in the LORD than to put confidence in princes.

10 All nations compassed me about: but in the name of the LORD will I [3]destroy them.

11 They [g]compassed me about; yea, they compassed me about: but in the name of the LORD I will destroy them.

12 They compassed me about [h]like bees; they are quenched [i]as the fire of thorns: for in the name of the LORD I will [4]destroy them.

13 Thou hast thrust sore at me that I might fall: but the LORD helped me.

14 [j]The LORD *is* my strength and song, and is become my salvation.

15 The voice of rejoicing and salvation *is* in the tabernacles of the righteous: the right hand of the LORD doeth valiantly.

16 [k]The right hand of the LORD is exalted: the right hand of the LORD doeth valiantly.

17 [l]I shall not die, but live, and [m]declare the works of the LORD.

18 The LORD hath [n]chastened me sore: but he hath not given me over unto death.

19 [o]Open to me the gates of righteousness: I will go into them, *and* I will praise the LORD:

20 [p]This gate of the LORD, [q]into which the righteous shall enter.

21 I will praise thee: for thou hast heard me, and art become my salvation.

22 [r]The stone *which* the builders refused is become the head *stone* of the corner.

23 [5]This is the LORD'S doing; [s]it *is* marvellous in our eyes.

24 This *is* [t]the day *which* the LORD hath made; we will rejoice and be glad in it.

25 Save now, I beseech thee, O LORD: O LORD, I beseech thee, send now prosperity.

26 [u]Blessed *be* he that cometh in the name of the LORD: we have blessed you out of the house of the LORD.

27 God *is* the LORD, which hath shewed us [v]light: bind the sacrifice with cords, *even* unto the horns of the altar.

28 Thou *art* my God, and I will praise thee: [w]*thou art* my God, I will exalt thee.

29 O give thanks unto the LORD; for *he is* good: for his mercy *endureth* for ever.

Psalm 119

aleph

1 Blessed *are* the [1]undefiled in the way, [a]who walk in the law of the LORD.

2 Blessed *are* they that keep his testimonies, *and that* [b]seek him with the whole heart.

3 [c]They also do no iniquity: they walk in his ways.

4 Thou hast commanded *us* to keep thy precepts diligently.

5 [d]O that my ways were directed to keep thy statutes!

6 [e]Then shall I not be ashamed, when I have respect unto all thy commandments.

7 I will praise thee with uprightness of heart, when I shall have learned [2]thy righteous judgments.

5 [a]Ezra 9.15; Rev. 16.5
7 [b]Jer. 6.16; Matt. 11.29
10 [c]2 Cor. 4.13
11 [d]2 Ki. 4.16; Rom. 3.4
14 [e]Ps. 22.25; Jon. 2.9
15 [f]Job 5.26; Rev. 14.13

Psalm 118
1 [a]1 Chr. 16.8
2 [b]Ps. 115.9
5 [1]out of distress
[c]Ps. 18.19
6 [2]for me
7 [d]Ps. 54.4
8 [e]Ps. 62.8; Jer. 17.5-7
9 [f]Ps. 146.3; Isa. 30.2-3
10 [3]cut them off
11 [g]Ps. 88.17
12 [h]Deut. 1.44
[i]Eccl. 7.6
[4]cut down
14 [j]Ex. 15.2
16 [k]Ex. 15.6
17 [l]Ps. 6.5
[m]Ps. 73.28
18 [n]Prov. 3.11-12; 1 Cor. 11.32
19 [o]Isa. 26.2
20 [p]Ps. 24.7
[q]Isa. 35.8
22 [r]Matt. 21.42; 1 Pet. 2.4-7
23 [5]This is from the LORD
[s]Job 5.9
24 [t]2 Cor. 6.2
26 [u]Zech. 4.7; Luke 19.38
27 [v]Esth. 8.16; Mal. 4.2
28 [w]Ex. 15.2; Isa. 25.1

Psalm 119
1 [1]Or, perfect, or, sincere
[a]Ps. 128.1
2 [b]Deut. 4.29
3 [c]Rom. 7.16-17;
5 [d]Jer. 31.33;
6 [e]Job 22.26;
7 [2]judgments of thy righteousness

8 I will keep thy statutes: O forsake me not utterly.

beth

9 Wherewithal shall [f]a young man cleanse his way? by taking heed *thereto* according to thy word.

10 With my whole heart have I [g]sought thee: O let me not wander from thy commandments.

11 [h]Thy word have I hid in mine heart, that I might not sin against thee.

12 Blessed *art* thou, O LORD: [i]teach me thy statutes.

13 With my lips have I declared all the judgments of thy mouth.

14 I have rejoiced in the way of thy testimonies, as *much as* in all riches.

15 I will [j]meditate in thy precepts, and have respect unto thy ways.

16 I will delight myself in thy statutes: I will not forget thy word.

gimel

17 Deal bountifully with thy servant, *that* I may live, and keep thy word.

18 [3k]Open thou mine eyes, that I may behold wondrous things out of thy law.

19 [l]I *am* a stranger in the earth: hide not thy commandments from me.

20 My soul breaketh for the longing *that it hath* unto thy judgments at all times.

21 Thou hast rebuked the proud *that are* cursed, which do err from thy commandments.

22 Remove from me reproach and contempt; for I have kept thy testimonies.

23 Princes also did sit *and* speak against me: *but* thy servant did meditate in thy statutes.

24 Thy testimonies also *are* my delight *and* [4]my counsellers.

daleth

25 My soul cleaveth unto the dust: [m]quicken thou me according to thy word.

26 I have declared my ways, and thou heardest me: [n]teach me thy statutes.

27 Make me to understand the way of thy precepts: so shall I talk of thy wondrous works.

28 My soul [5]melteth for heaviness: strengthen thou me according unto thy word.

29 [o]Remove from me the way of lying: and [p]grant me thy law graciously.

30 I have chosen the way of truth: thy judgments have I laid *before me.*

31 I have stuck unto thy testimonies: O LORD, put me not to shame.

32 I will run the way of thy commandments, when thou shalt [q]enlarge my heart.

he

33 Teach me, O LORD, the way of thy statutes; and I shall keep it [r]*unto* the end.

34 [s]Give me understanding, and I shall keep thy law; yea, I shall observe it with *my* whole heart.

35 Make me to go in the path of thy commandments; for therein do I delight.

36 Incline my heart unto thy testimonies, and not to [t]covetousness.

37 [6u]Turn away mine eyes from [v]beholding vanity; *and* quicken thou me in thy way.

38 [w]Stablish thy word unto thy servant, who *is devoted* to thy fear.

39 Turn away my reproach which I fear: for thy judgments *are* good.

40 Behold, I have longed after thy precepts: quicken me in thy righteousness.

vau

41 Let thy mercies come also unto me, O LORD, *even* thy salvation, according to thy word.

42 [7]So shall I have wherewith to answer him that reproacheth me: for I trust in thy word.

43 And take not the word of truth utterly out of my mouth; for I have hoped in thy judgments.

44 So shall I keep thy law continually for ever and ever.

45 And I will walk [8x]at liberty: for I seek thy precepts.

46 [y]I will speak of thy testimonies also before kings, and will not be ashamed.

47 And I will delight myself in thy commandments, which I have loved.

48 My hands also will I lift up unto thy commandments, which I have loved; and I will meditate in thy statutes.

zain

49 Remember the word unto thy servant, upon which thou hast caused me to hope.

50 This *is* my [z]comfort in my affliction: for thy word hath quickened me.

51 The proud have had me greatly [a]in derision: *yet* have I not [b]declined from thy law.

52 I remembered thy judgments of old, O LORD; and have comforted myself.

53 [c]Horror hath taken hold upon me because of the wicked that forsake thy law.

54 Thy statutes have been my songs in the house of my pilgrimage.

55 [d]I have remembered thy name, O LORD, in the night, and have kept thy law.

56 This I had, because I kept thy precepts.

cheth

57 [e]*Thou art* my portion, O LORD: I have said that I would keep thy words.

58 I intreated thy [9f]favour with *my* whole heart: be merciful unto me according to thy word.

59 I [g]thought on my ways, and turned my feet unto thy testimonies.

60 I made haste, and delayed not to keep thy commandments.

9 [f]Prov. 1.4-10
10 [g]2 Chr. 15.15
11 [h]Luke 2.19
12 [i]Ps. 25.4
15 [j]Ps. 1.2
18 [3]Reveal [k]Eph. 1.17
19 [l]Gen. 47.9; Heb. 11.13
24 [4]men of my counsel
25 [m]Ps. 143.11
26 [n]1 Ki. 8.36; Ps. 27.11
28 [5]droppeth
29 [o]Prov. 30.8 [p]Heb. 8.10
32 [q]1 Ki. 4.29; Isa. 60.5; 2 Cor. 6.11
33 [r]Matt. 10.22; Rev. 2.26
34 [s]Prov. 2.6; Jas. 1.5
36 [t]Ezek. 33.31; Mark 7.21; Luke 12.15; 1 Tim. 6.10; Heb. 13.5
37 [6]Make to pass [u]Isa. 33.15 [v]Job 31.1
38 [w]2 Sam. 7.25
42 [7]Or, So shall I answer him that reproacheth me in a thing
45 [8]at large [x]John 8.32-36; Rom. 8.2; 1 Cor. 7.22-23; Gal. 5.1-13; Jas. 1.25; 1 Pet. 2.16
46 [y]Matt. 10.18; Acts 26.1-2
50 [z]Ps. 27.13; Jer. 15.16; Rom. 5.3-5; Heb. 6.17-19
51 [a]Jer. 20.7 [b]Job 23.11
53 [c]Ezra 9.3
55 [d]Ps. 63.6
57 [e]Ps. 16.5; Jer. 10.16; Lam. 3.24
58 [9]face [f]Job 11.19
59 [g]Lam. 3.40; Joel 2.13; Luke 15.17

61 The [10]bands of the wicked have
robbed me: *but* I have not forgotten
thy law.
62 [h]At midnight I will rise to give
thanks unto thee because of thy righteous judgments.
63 I *am* a companion of all *them* that
fear thee, and of them that keep thy
precepts.
64 [i]The earth, O LORD, is full of thy
mercy: teach me thy statutes.

teth

65 Thou hast dealt well with thy servant, O LORD, according unto thy word.
66 Teach me good judgment and
knowledge: for I have believed thy
commandments.
67 [j]Before I was afflicted I went astray: but now have I kept thy word.
68 Thou *art* [k]good, and doest good;
teach me thy statutes.
69 The proud have [l]forged a lie
against me: *but* I will keep thy precepts with *my* whole heart.
70 [m]Their heart is as fat as grease;
but I delight in thy law.
71 [n]*It is* good for me that I have
been afflicted; that I might learn thy
statutes.
72 [o]The law of thy mouth *is* better
unto me than thousands of gold and
silver.

jod

73 [p]Thy hands have made me and
fashioned me: give me understanding,
that I may learn thy commandments.
74 [q]They that fear thee will be glad
when they see me; because I have
hoped in thy word.
75 I know, O LORD, that thy judgments *are* [11]right, and [r]*that* thou in
faithfulness hast afflicted me.
76 Let, I pray thee, thy merciful kindness be [12]for my comfort, according to
thy word unto thy servant.
77 Let thy tender mercies come unto
me, that I may live: for thy law *is* my
delight.
78 Let the proud [s]be ashamed; for
they dealt perversely with me without
a cause: *but* I will meditate in thy
precepts.
79 Let those that fear thee turn unto
me, and those that have known thy
testimonies.
80 Let my heart be [t]sound in thy
statutes; that I be not ashamed.

caph

81 [u]My soul fainteth for thy salvation: *but* I hope in thy word.
82 [v]Mine eyes fail for thy word, saying, When wilt thou comfort me?
83 For [w]I am become like a bottle
in the smoke; *yet* do I not forget thy
statutes.
84 [x]How many *are* the days of thy
servant? [y]when wilt thou execute judgment on them that persecute me?
85 [z]The proud have digged pits for
me, which *are* not after thy law.
86 All thy commandments *are* [13]faith-
ful: they persecute me [a]wrongfully;
help thou me.
87 They had almost consumed me
upon earth; but I forsook not thy
precepts.
88 Quicken me after thy lovingkindness; so shall I keep the testimony of
thy mouth.

lamed

89 [b]For ever, O LORD, thy word is
settled in heaven.
90 Thy faithfulness *is* [14]unto all generations: thou hast established the
earth, and it [15]abideth.
91 They continue this day according to [c]thine ordinances: for all *are*
thy servants.
92 Unless [d]thy law *had been* my delights, I should then have perished in
mine affliction.
93 I will never forget thy precepts:
for with them thou hast quickened me.
94 I *am* [e]thine, save me; for I have
sought thy precepts.
95 The wicked have waited for me
to destroy me: *but* I will consider thy
testimonies.
96 [f]I have seen an end of all perfection: *but* thy commandment *is* exceeding broad.

mem

97 O how love I thy law! [g]it *is* my
meditation all the day.
98 Thou through thy commandments
hast made me [h]wiser than mine enemies: for [16]they *are* ever with me.
99 I have more understanding than
all my teachers: [i]for thy testimonies
are my meditation.
100 [j]I understand more than the ancients, because I keep thy precepts.
101 I have [k]refrained my feet from
every evil way, that I might keep thy
word.
102 I have not departed from thy
judgments: for thou hast taught me.
103 [l]How sweet are thy words unto
my [17]taste! *yea, sweeter* than honey to
my mouth!
104 Through thy precepts I get understanding: therefore I hate every
false way.

nun

105 Thy word *is* a [18]lamp unto my
feet, and a light unto my path.
106 [m]I have sworn, and I will perform *it*, that I will keep thy righteous
judgments.
107 I am afflicted very much: quicken
me, O LORD, according unto thy word.
108 Accept, I beseech thee, [n]the freewill offerings of my mouth, O LORD,
and teach me thy judgments.
109 [o]My soul *is* continually in my
hand: yet do I not forget thy law.
110 The wicked have laid a snare for
me: yet I erred not from thy precepts.
111 [p]Thy testimonies have I taken
as an heritage for ever: for they *are* the
rejoicing of my heart.
112 I have inclined mine heart [19]to

61 [10]Or, companies
62 [h]Acts 16.25
64 [i]Ps. 33.5
67 [j]Deut. 32.15; Rev. 3.19
68 [k]Ex. 34.6; Matt. 19.17
69 [l]Job 13.4
70 [m]Acts 28.27
71 [n]Heb. 12.10
72 [o]Ps. 19.10;
73 [p]Job 10.8;
74 [q]Ps. 34.2
75 [11]righteousness [r]Ps. 89.30-33;
76 [12]to comfort me
78 [s]Ps. 25.3
80 [t]2 Chr. 15.7;
81 [u]Ps. 42.1-2;
82 [v]Ps. 69.3
83 [w]Job 30.30
84 [x]Ps. 39.4 [y]Ps. 7.6;
85 [z]Ps. 35.7
86 [13]faithfulness [a]Ps. 7.1-5;
89 [b]Matt. 5.18;
90 [14]to generation and generation [15]standeth
91 [c]Gen. 8.22;
92 [d]Rom. 15.4
94 [e]Hos. 2.7-16
96 [f]Isa. 40.8;
97 [g]Ps. 1.2
98 [h]Deut. 4.6-8; [16]it is ever with me
99 [i]2 Tim. 3.15
100 [j]Job 12.12;
101 [k]2 Cor. 7.1;
103 [l]Ps. 19.10; [17]palate
105 [18]Or, candle
106 [m]Neh. 10.29
108 [n]Hos. 14.2;
109 [o]Judg. 12.3;
111 [p]Deut. 33.4
112 [19]to do

perform thy statutes alway, *even unto* the end.

samech

113 I hate *vain* thoughts: but thy law do I love.

114 [q]Thou *art* my hiding place and my shield: I hope in thy word.

115 [r]Depart from me, ye evildoers: for I will keep the commandments of my God.

116 Uphold me according unto thy word, that I may live: and let me not [s]be ashamed of my hope.

117 [t]Hold thou me up, and I shall be safe: and I will have respect unto thy statutes continually.

118 Thou hast trodden down all them that err from thy statutes: for their deceit *is* falsehood.

119 Thou [20]puttest away all the wicked of the earth [u]*like* dross: therefore I love thy testimonies.

120 [v]My flesh trembleth for fear of thee; and I am afraid of thy judgments.

ain

121 I have done judgment and justice: leave me not to mine oppressors.

122 Be [w]surety for thy servant for good: let not the proud oppress me.

123 Mine eyes fail for thy salvation, and for the word of thy righteousness.

124 Deal with thy servant according unto thy mercy, and teach me thy statutes.

125 I *am* thy servant; give me understanding, that I may know thy testimonies.

126 *It is* time for *thee,* LORD, to work: *for* they have made void thy law.

127 [x]Therefore I love thy commandments above gold; yea, above fine gold.

128 Therefore I esteem all *thy* precepts *concerning* all *things to be* right; *and* I hate every false way.

pe

129 Thy testimonies *are* wonderful: therefore doth my soul keep them.

130 The entrance of thy words giveth light; [y]it giveth understanding unto the simple.

131 I opened my mouth, and panted: for I longed for thy commandments.

132 [z]Look thou upon me, and be merciful unto me, [21]as thou usest to do unto those that love thy name.

133 Order my steps in thy word: and [a]let not any iniquity have dominion over me.

134 [b]Deliver me from the oppression of man: so will I keep thy precepts.

135 [c]Make thy face to shine upon thy servant; and teach me thy statutes.

136 [d]Rivers of waters run down mine eyes, because they keep not thy law.

tzaddi

137 [e]Righteous *art* thou, O LORD, and upright *are* thy judgments.

138 Thy testimonies *that* thou hast commanded *are* [22]righteous and very [23]faithful.

139 My zeal hath [24]consumed me, because mine enemies have forgotten thy words.

140 Thy word *is* very [25]pure: therefore thy servant loveth it.

141 I *am* [f]small and despised: *yet* do not I forget thy precepts.

142 Thy righteousness *is* an everlasting righteousness, and thy law *is* [g]the truth.

143 Trouble and anguish have [26]taken hold on me: *yet* thy commandments *are* my delights.

144 The righteousness of thy testimonies *is* everlasting: give me understanding, and I shall live.

koph

145 I cried with *my* whole heart; hear me, O LORD: I will keep thy statutes.

146 I cried unto thee; save me, [27]and I shall keep thy testimonies.

147 I prevented the dawning of the morning, and cried: I hoped in thy word.

148 [h]Mine eyes prevent the *night* watches, that I might meditate in thy word.

149 Hear my voice according unto thy lovingkindness: O LORD, quicken me according to thy judgment.

150 They draw nigh that follow after mischief: they are far from thy law.

151 Thou *art* [i]near, O LORD; and all thy commandments *are* truth.

152 Concerning thy testimonies, I have known of old that thou hast founded them [j]for ever.

resh

153 [k]Consider mine affliction, and deliver me: for I do not forget thy law.

154 [l]Plead my cause, and deliver me: quicken me according to thy word.

155 [m]Salvation *is* far from the wicked: for they seek not thy statutes.

156 [28]Great *are* thy tender mercies, O LORD: quicken me according to thy judgments.

157 Many *are* my persecutors and mine enemies; *yet* do I not decline from thy testimonies.

158 I beheld the transgressors, and was grieved; because they kept not thy word.

159 Consider how I love thy precepts: quicken me, O LORD, according to thy lovingkindness.

160 [29]Thy word *is* true *from* the beginning: and every one of thy righteous judgments *endureth* for ever.

schin

161 [n]Princes have persecuted me without a cause: but my heart standeth in awe of thy word.

162 I rejoice at thy word, as one that findeth great spoil.

163 I hate and abhor lying: *but* thy law do I love.

164 Seven times a day do I praise thee because of thy righteous judgments.

165 [o]Great peace have they which

114 [q]Ps. 32.7
115 [r]Ps. 6.8; Matt. 7.23
116 [s]Ps. 25.2; Rom. 9.33
117 [t]Ps. 71.6; Rom. 14.4
119 [20]causest to cease
[u]Ezek. 22.18
120 [v]Hab. 3.16
122 [w]Heb. 7.22
127 [x]Ps. 19.10; Eph. 3.8
130 [y]Ps. 19.7; 2 Pet. 1.19
132 [z]Ex. 4.31; Ps. 106.4
[21]according to the custom toward those, etc
133 [a]Rom. 6.12
134 [b]Luke 1.74
135 [c]Ps. 4.6
136 [d]Jer. 9.1
137 [e]Neh. 9.33; Dan. 9.7
138 [22]righteousness
[23]faithfulness
139 [24]cut me off
140 [25]tried, or, refined
141 [f]Prov. 15.16; Jas. 2.5
142 [g]Ps. 19.9;
143 [26]found me
146 [27]Or, that I may keep
148 [h]Ps. 63.1-6
151 [i]Ps. 145.18
152 [j]Luke 21.33
153 [k]Lam. 5.1
154 [l]1 Sam. 24.15;
155 [m]Job 5.4
156 [28]Or, Many
160 [29]The beginning of thy word is true
161 [n]1 Sam. 24.11
165 [o]Prov. 3.2;

love thy law: and [30]nothing shall offend them.
166 LORD, I have hoped for thy salvation, and done thy commandments.
167 My soul hath kept thy testimonies; and I love them exceedingly.
168 I have kept thy precepts and thy
testimonies: [p]for all my ways *are* before thee.

tau

169 Let my cry come near before
thee, O LORD: give me understanding
according to thy word.
170 Let my supplication come before thee: deliver me according to thy
word.
171 My lips shall utter praise, when
thou hast taught me thy statutes.
172 My tongue shall speak of thy
word: for all thy commandments *are*
righteousness.
173 Let thine hand help me; for [q]I
have chosen thy precepts.
174 I have longed for thy salvation,
O LORD; and thy law *is* my delight.
175 Let my soul live, and it shall
praise thee; and let thy judgments help
me.
176 [r]I have gone astray like a lost
sheep; [s]seek thy servant; for I do not
forget thy commandments.

Psalm 120

A Song of degrees

1 In my distress I cried unto the
LORD, and he heard me.
2 Deliver my soul, O LORD, from lying lips, *and* from a deceitful tongue.
3 [1]What shall be given unto thee? or
what shall be [2]done unto thee, thou
false tongue?
4 [3]Sharp arrows of the mighty, with
coals of juniper.
5 Woe is me, that I sojourn in [a]Mē'-
sech, *that* [b]I dwell in the tents of
Kē'där!
6 My soul hath long dwelt with him
that hateth peace.
7 I *am* [4]*for* peace: but when I speak,
they *are* for war.

Psalm 121

A Song of degrees

1 [1]I will lift up mine eyes unto the
hills, from whence cometh my help.
2 My help *cometh* from the LORD,
which made heaven and earth.
3 [a]He will not suffer thy foot to be
moved: [b]he that keepeth thee will not
slumber.
4 Behold, he that keepeth Ĭs'ra-el
shall neither slumber nor sleep.
5 The LORD *is* thy keeper: the LORD
is thy shade upon thy right hand.
6 [c]The sun shall not smite thee by
day, nor the moon by night.
7 The LORD shall preserve thee from
all evil: he shall [d]preserve thy soul.
8 The LORD shall [e]preserve thy going out and thy coming in from this
time forth, and even for evermore.

[30]they shall have no stumblingblock
168 [p]Job 34.21; Prov. 5.21
173 [q]Josh. 24.22; Prov. 1.29; Luke 10.42
176 [r]Isa. 53.6; Matt. 10.6; Luke 15.4; 1 Pet. 2.25 [s]Ezek. 34.6; Matt. 18.11

Psalm 120
3 [1]Or, What shall the deceitful tongue give unto thee? or, What shall it profit thee? [2]added
4 [3]Or, It is as the sharp arrows of the mighty man, with coals of juniper
5 [a]Gen. 10.2 [b]1 Sam. 25.1; Jer. 49.28
7 [4]Or, a man of peace

Psalm 121
1 [1]Or, Shall I lift up mine eyes to the hills? whence should my help come?
3 [a]1 Sam. 2.9 [b]Isa. 27.3
6 [c]Isa. 49.10
7 [d]Job 5.19; Ps. 91.9-10; Prov. 12.21
8 [e]Deut. 28.6; Prov. 2.8

Psalm 122
1 [a]Isa. 2.3; Jer. 31.6; Zech. 8.21
3 [b]2 Sam. 5.9; Eph. 2.21
4 [c]Deut. 16.16 [d]Ex. 16.34
5 [1]do sit
6 [e]Isa. 62.6; Jer. 51.50

Psalm 124
1 [a]Gen. 15.1; Num. 14.9; Josh. 1.5; Rom. 8.31; Heb. 13.5
3 [b]Ps. 35.25; Prov. 1.12; Jer. 51.34
8 [c]Ex. 18.4; Ps. 121.2; Prov. 18.10; Heb. 13.6

Psalm 122

A Song of degrees of David

1 I was glad when they said unto
me, [a]Let us go into the house of the
LORD.
2 Our feet shall stand within thy
gates, O Je-rų'sa-lĕm.
3 Je-rų'sa-lĕm is builded as a city
that is [b]compact together:
4 [c]Whither the tribes go up, the
tribes of the LORD, unto [d]the testimony
of Ĭs'ra-el, to give thanks unto the
name of the LORD.
5 For there [1]are set thrones of judgment, the thrones of the house of
Dā'vid.
6 [e]Pray for the peace of Je-rų'sa-
lĕm: they shall prosper that love thee.
7 Peace be within thy walls, *and*
prosperity within thy palaces.
8 For my brethren and companions'
sakes, I will now say, Peace *be* within
thee.
9 Because of the house of the LORD
our God I will seek thy good.

Psalm 123

A Song of degrees

1 Unto thee lift I up mine eyes, O
thou that dwellest in the heavens.
2 Behold, as the eyes of servants
look unto the hand of their masters,
and as the eyes of a maiden unto the
hand of her mistress; so our eyes *wait*
upon the LORD our God, until that he
have mercy upon us.
3 Have mercy upon us, O LORD,
have mercy upon us: for we are exceedingly filled with contempt.
4 Our soul is exceedingly filled with
the scorning of those that are at ease,
and with the contempt of the proud.

Psalm 124

A Song of degrees of David

1 If *it had not been* the LORD who
was [a]on our side, now may Ĭs'ra-el
say;
2 If *it had not been* the LORD who
was on our side, when men rose up
against us:
3 Then they had [b]swallowed us up
quick, when their wrath was kindled
against us:
4 Then the waters had overwhelmed
us, the stream had gone over our soul:
5 Then the proud waters had gone
over our soul.
6 Blessed *be* the LORD, who hath not
given us *as* a prey to their teeth.
7 Our soul is escaped as a bird out of
the snare of the fowlers: the snare is
broken, and we are escaped.
8 [c]Our help *is* in the name of the
LORD, who made heaven and earth.

Psalm 125

A Song of degrees

1 They that trust in the LORD *shall*
be as mount Zī'ŏn, *which* cannot be
removed, *but* abideth for ever.

2 *As* the mountains *are* round about Je-ru'sa-lĕm, so the LORD *is* round about his people from henceforth even for ever.

3 For the rod of [1][a]the wicked shall not rest upon the lot of the righteous; lest the righteous put forth their hands unto iniquity.

4 Do good, O LORD, unto *those that be* good, and to *them that are* upright in their hearts.

5 As for such as turn aside unto their [b]crooked ways, the LORD shall lead them forth with the workers of iniquity: *but* [c]peace *shall be* upon Ĭs'ra-el.

Psalm 126

A Song of degrees

1 When the LORD [1]turned again the captivity of Zī'ŏn, [a]we were like them that dream.

2 Then [b]was our mouth filled with laughter, and our tongue with singing: then said they among the heathen, The LORD [2]hath done great things for them.

3 The LORD hath done great things for us; *whereof* we are glad.

4 Turn again our captivity, O LORD, as the streams in the south.

5 [c]They that sow in tears shall reap in [3]joy.

6 He that goeth forth and weepeth, bearing [4]precious seed, shall doubtless come again with rejoicing, bringing his sheaves *with him.*

Psalm 127

*A Song of degrees *for Solomon*

1 Except the LORD build the house, they labour in vain [1]that build it: except the LORD keep the city, the watchman waketh *but* in vain.

2 *It is* vain for you to rise up early, to sit up late, to [a]eat the bread of sorrows: *for* so he giveth his beloved sleep.

3 Lo, [b]children *are* an heritage of the LORD: *and* [c]the fruit of the womb *is his* reward.

4 As arrows *are* in the hand of a mighty man; so *are* children of the youth.

5 Happy *is* the man that [2]hath his quiver full of them: they shall not be ashamed, but they [3]shall speak with the enemies in the gate.

Psalm 128

A Song of degrees

1 Blessed *is* every one that feareth the LORD; that walketh in his ways.

2 [a]For thou shalt eat the labour of thine hands: happy *shalt* thou *be*, and *it shall be* well with thee.

3 [b]Thy wife *shall be* [c]as a fruitful vine by the sides of thine house: thy children [d]like olive plants round about thy table.

4 Behold, that thus shall the man be blessed that feareth the LORD.

Psalm 125
3 [1]wickedness
[a]Prov. 22.8; Isa. 14.5
5 [b]Prov. 2.15; Phil. 2.15
[c]Gal. 6.16

Psalm 126
1 [1]returned the returning of Zion
[a]Acts 12.9
2 [b]Job 8.21
[2]hath magnified to do with them
5 [c]Isa. 12.1-3; 2 Cor. 7.8-11
[3]Or, singing
6 [4]Or, seed basket

Psalm 127
*Or, of
1 [1]that are builders of it in it
2 [a]Gen. 3.17
3 [b]Gen. 33.5
[c]Deut. 28.4
5 [2]hath filled his quiver with them
[3]Or, shall subdue, or, destroy

Psalm 128
2 [a]Isa. 3.10
3 [b]Prov. 5.15
[c]Ezek. 19.10
[d]Ps. 52.8
5 [e]Ps. 134.3
6 [f]Gen. 50.23

Psalm 129
1 [1]Or, Much
[a]Ezek. 23.3; Hos. 2.15
3 [b]Heb. 11.36
4 [c]2 Thess. 1.6
6 [d]Ps. 37.2; Jer. 17.5-6
8 [e]Ruth 2.4; Ps. 118.26

Psalm 130
1 [a]Lam. 3.55; Jon. 2.2
3 [b]Ps. 143.2; Rom. 3.20
4 [c]Ex. 34.7;
[d]1 Ki. 8.40;
5 [e]Isa. 26.8
6 [1]Or, which watch unto the morning
7 [f]Isa. 55.7
8 [g]Matt. 1.21

Psalm 131
1 [a]Rom. 12.16
[1]walk
[2]wonderful
2 [3]my soul
[b]Matt. 18.3
3 [4]from now

5 [e]The LORD shall bless thee out of Zī'ŏn: and thou shalt see the good of Je-ru'sa-lĕm all the days of thy life.

6 Yea, thou shalt [f]see thy children's children, *and* peace upon Ĭs'ra-el.

Psalm 129

A Song of degrees

1 [1]Many a time have they afflicted me from [a]my youth, may Ĭs'ra-el now say:

2 Many a time have they afflicted me from my youth: yet they have not prevailed against me.

3 [b]The plowers plowed upon my back: they made long their furrows.

4 The LORD *is* [c]righteous: he hath cut asunder the cords of the wicked.

5 Let them all be confounded and turned back that hate Zī'ŏn.

6 Let them be as [d]the grass *upon* the house tops, which withereth afore it groweth up:

7 Wherewith the mower filleth not his hand; nor he that bindeth sheaves his bosom.

8 Neither do they which go by say, [e]The blessing of the LORD *be* upon you: we bless you in the name of the LORD.

Psalm 130

A Song of degrees

1 Out [a]of the depths have I cried unto thee, O LORD.

2 Lord, hear my voice: let thine ears be attentive to the voice of my supplications.

3 [b]If thou, LORD, shouldest mark iniquities, O Lord, who shall stand?

4 But *there is* [c]forgiveness with thee, that thou mayest [d]be feared.

5 [e]I wait for the LORD, my soul doth wait, and in his word do I hope.

6 My soul *waiteth* for the Lord more than they that watch for the morning: [1]*I say, more than* they that watch for the morning.

7 Let Ĭs'ra-el hope in the LORD: for [f]with the LORD *there is* mercy, and with him *is* plenteous redemption.

8 And [g]he shall redeem Ĭs'ra-el from all his iniquities.

Psalm 131

A Song of degrees of David

1 Lord, my heart is not haughty, nor mine eyes lofty: [a]neither do I [1]exercise myself in great matters, or in things too [2]high for me.

2 Surely I have behaved and quieted [3]myself, [b]as a child that is weaned of his mother: my soul *is* even as a weaned child.

3 Let Ĭs'ra-el hope in the LORD [4]from henceforth and for ever.

Psalm 132

A Song of degrees

1 Lord, remember Dā'vid, *and* all his afflictions:

2 How he sware unto the LORD, *and*
vowed unto the mighty *God* of Jā'cob;
3 Surely I will not come into the tabernacle of my house, nor go up into my
bed;
4 I will [a]not give sleep to mine eyes,
or slumber to mine eyelids,
5 Until I find out a place for the
LORD, [1]an habitation for the mighty
God of Jā'cob.
6 Lo, we heard of it [b]at Ĕph'ra-tah:
[c]we found it [d]in the fields of the wood.
7 We will go into his tabernacles: we
will worship at his footstool.
8 [e]Arise, O LORD, into thy rest; thou,
and the ark of thy strength.
9 Let thy priests [f]be clothed with
righteousness; and let thy saints shout
for joy.
10 For thy servant Dā'vid's sake turn
not away the face of thine anointed.
11 The LORD hath sworn *in* truth
unto Dā'vid; he will not turn from it;
[g]Of the fruit of [2]thy body will I set
upon thy throne.
12 If thy children will keep my covenant and my testimony that I shall
teach them, their children shall also sit
upon thy throne for evermore.
13 For the LORD hath chosen Zī'ŏn;
he hath desired *it* for his habitation.
14 This *is* my rest for ever: here will
I dwell; for I have desired it.
15 I will [3]abundantly bless her provision: I will satisfy her poor with bread.
16 [h]I will also clothe her priests
with salvation: [i]and her saints shall
shout aloud for joy.
17 [j]There will I make the horn of
Dā'vid to bud: I have ordained a [4]lamp
for mine anointed.
18 His enemies will I clothe with
shame: but upon himself shall his
crown flourish.

Psalm 133

A Song of degrees of David

1 Behold, how good and how pleasant *it is* for [a]brethren to dwell [1]to-
gether in unity!
2 *It is* like [b]the precious ointment
upon the head, that ran down upon the
beard, *even* Aâr'on's beard: that went
down to the skirts of his garments;
3 As the dew of [c]Hĕr'mŏn, *and as
the dew* that descended upon the mountains of Zī'ŏn: for [d]there the LORD commanded the blessing, *even* [e]life for
evermore.

Psalm 134

A Song of degrees

1 Behold, bless ye the LORD, all *ye*
servants of the LORD, [a]which by night
stand in the house of the LORD.
2 [b]Lift up your hands [1]*in* the sanctuary, and bless the LORD.
3 [c]The LORD that made heaven and
earth bless [d]thee out of Zī'ŏn.

Psalm 132
4 [a]Ruth 3.18
5 [1]habitations
6 [b]Josh. 18.1; 1 Sam. 17.12
[c]1 Sam. 7.1
[d]1 Chr. 13.5
8 [e]Num. 10.35
9 [f]Job 29.14; Isa. 61.10
11 [g]1 Ki. 8.25; 2 Chr. 6.16; Luke 1.69
[2]thy belly
15 [3]Or, surely
16 [h]2 Chr. 6.41
[i]Hos. 11.12
17 [j]Ps. 92.10; Ezek. 29.21; Luke 1.69
[4]Or, candle

Psalm 133
1 [a]Gen. 13.8; 1 Cor. 1.10
[1]even together
2 [b]Ex. 30.25
3 [c]Deut. 4.48
[d]Lev. 25.21; Deut. 28.8
[e]Dan. 12.2-3; Matt. 25.34-46; John 4.14; John 17.3; Heb. 7.25; 1 John 5.20

Psalm 134
1 [a]Lev. 8.35; 1 Chr. 9.33; Luke 2.37
2 [b]Ps. 28.2; 1 Tim. 2.8
[1]Or, in holiness
3 [c]Ps. 124.8
[d]Ps. 128.5

Psalm 135
2 [a]Luke 2.37
4 [b]Ex. 19.5; Deut. 7.6-7
7 [c]Gen. 2.6; Jer. 10.13
[d]Job 28.25; Zech. 10.1
[e]Job 38.22
8 [1]from man unto beast
10 [f]Num. 21.24
11 [g]Josh. 12.7
12 [h]Gen. 17.8
13 [i]Ex. 3.15
[2]to generation and generation
14 [j]Deut. 32.36

Psalm 136
2 [a]Ex. 18.11; Deut. 10.17
3 [b]1 Tim. 6.15; Rev. 17.14
5 [c]Prov. 3.19

Psalm 135

1 Praise ye the LORD. Praise ye the
name of the LORD; praise *him*, O ye
servants of the LORD.
2 [a]Ye that stand in the house of the
LORD, in the courts of the house of our
God,
3 Praise the LORD; for the LORD *is*
good: sing praises unto his name; for *it
is* pleasant.
4 For [b]the LORD hath chosen Jā'cob
unto himself, *and* Ĭs'ra-el for his peculiar treasure.
5 For I know that the LORD *is* great,
and *that* our Lord *is* above all gods.
6 Whatsoever the LORD pleased, *that*
did he in heaven, and in earth, in the
seas, and all deep places.
7 [c]He causeth the vapours to ascend
from the ends of the earth; [d]he maketh
lightnings for the rain; he bringeth the
wind out of his [e]treasuries.
8 Who smote the firstborn of Ē'ġypt,
[1]both of man and beast.
9 *Who* sent tokens and wonders into
the midst of thee, O Ē'ġypt, upon Phā'-
raōh, and upon all his servants.
10 [f]Who smote great nations, and
slew mighty kings;
11 Sī'hŏn king of the Ăm'ôr-ītes,
and Ŏg king of Bā'shăn, and [g]all the
kingdoms of Cā'năan:
12 And gave their land *for* an heritage, an [h]heritage unto Ĭs'ra-el his
people.
13 [i]Thy name, O LORD, *endureth*
for ever; *and* thy memorial, O LORD,
[2]throughout all generations.
14 [j]For the LORD will judge his people, and he will repent himself concerning his servants.
15 The idols of the heathen *are* silver and gold, the work of men's hands.
16 They have mouths, but they speak
not; eyes have they, but they see not;
17 They have ears, but they hear
not; neither is there *any* breath in their
mouths.
18 They that make them are like
unto them: *so is* every one that trusteth
in them.
19 Bless the LORD, O house of Ĭs'ra-
el: bless the LORD, O house of Aâr'on:
20 Bless the LORD, O house of Lē'vī:
ye that fear the LORD, bless the LORD.
21 Blessed be the LORD out of Zī'ŏn,
which dwelleth at Je-ru̇'sa-lĕm. Praise
ye the LORD.

Psalm 136

1 O give thanks unto the LORD; for
he is good: for his mercy *endureth* for
ever.
2 O give thanks unto [a]the God of
gods: for his mercy *endureth* for ever.
3 O give thanks to the [b]Lord of
lords: for his mercy *endureth* for ever.
4 To him who alone doeth great wonders: for his mercy *endureth* for ever.
5 [c]To him that by wisdom made the
heavens: for his mercy *endureth* for
ever.

6 [d]To him that stretched out the earth above the waters: for his mercy *endureth* for ever.

7 [e]To him that made great lights: for his mercy *endureth* for ever:

8 The sun [1]to rule by day: for his mercy *endureth* for ever:

9 The moon and stars to rule by night: for his mercy *endureth* for ever.

10 To him that smote E'gypt in their firstborn: for his mercy *endureth* for ever:

11 [f]And brought out Is'ra-el from among them: for his mercy *endureth* for ever:

12 With a strong hand, and with a stretched out arm: for his mercy *endureth* for ever.

13 [g]To him which divided the Red sea into parts: for his mercy *endureth* for ever:

14 And made Is'ra-el to pass through the midst of it: for his mercy *endureth* for ever:

15 But [2]overthrew Phā'raōh and his host in the Red sea: for his mercy *endureth* for ever.

16 [h]To him which led his people through the wilderness: for his mercy *endureth* for ever.

17 To him which smote great kings: for his mercy *endureth* for ever:

18 [i]And slew famous kings: for his mercy *endureth* for ever:

19 [j]Sī'hŏn king of the Ăm'ôr-ītes: for his mercy *endureth* for ever:

20 And Ŏg the king of Bā'shăn: for his mercy *endureth* for ever:

21 [k]And gave their land for an heritage: for his mercy *endureth* for ever:

22 *Even* an heritage unto Ĭs'ra-el his servant: for his mercy *endureth* for ever.

23 Who [l]remembered us in our low estate: for his mercy *endureth* for ever.

24 And hath redeemed us from our enemies: for his mercy *endureth* for ever.

25 [m]Who giveth food to all flesh: for his mercy *endureth* for ever.

26 O give thanks unto the God of heaven: for his mercy *endureth* for ever.

Psalm 137

1 By [a]the rivers of Băb'ȳ-lon, there we sat down, yea, we wept, when we remembered Zī'ŏn.

2 We hanged our [b]harps upon the willows in the midst thereof.

3 For there they that carried us away captive required of us [1]a song; and they that [2]wasted us *required of us* mirth, *saying,* Sing us *one* of the songs of Zī'ŏn.

4 How shall we sing the LORD'S song in a [3]strange land?

5 If I forget thee, O Je-ru'sa-lĕm, let my right hand forget *her cunning.*

6 If I do not remember thee, let my [c]tongue cleave to the roof of my mouth; if I prefer not Je-ru'sa-lĕm above [4]my chief joy.

6 [d]Jer. 10.12
7 [e]Deut. 4.19
8 [1]for the rulings by day
11 [f]Ex. 12.51
13 [g]Ps. 78.13
15 [2]shaked off
16 [h]Deut. 8.15
18 [i]Deut. 29.7
19 [j]Num. 21.21
21 [k]Josh. 12.1
23 [l]Gen. 8.1; Deut. 32.36; Ps. 102.17; Isa. 63.9; Luke 1.48
25 [m]Ps. 104.27

Psalm 137
1 [a]Ezek. 1.1; Dan. 8.2
2 [b]Isa. 2.8; Lam. 5.15; Amos 8.10; Rev. 18.22
3 [1]the words of a song
[2]laid us on heaps
4 [3]land of a stranger
6 [c]Ezek. 3.26
[4]the head of my joy
7 [d]Lam. 4.22; Obad. 10
[5]Make bare
8 [e]Isa. 13.1-14
[6]wasted
[7]that recompenseth unto thee thy deed which thou didst to us
9 [8]the rock

Psalm 138
1 [a]Ps. 119.46
2 [b]1 Ki. 8.29; Ps. 5.7; Dan. 6.10; Jon. 2.7
[c]Isa. 42.21
3 [d]Zech. 10.12; 2 Cor. 12.9
6 [e]Prov. 3.34; Jas. 4.6
7 [f]Ps. 23.3
8 [g]Ps. 57.2; Phil. 1.6

Psalm 139
1 [a]Jer. 12.3; Rev. 2.23
2 [b]2 Ki. 19.27
[c]Matt. 9.4; John 2.24
3 [1]Or, winnowest.
4 [d]Heb. 4.13
8 [e]Prov. 15.11

7 Remember, O LORD, the [d]children of E'dom in the day of Je-ru'sa-lĕm; who said, [5]Rase *it,* rase *it, even* to the foundation thereof.

8 O daughter of Băb'ȳ-lon, [e]who art to be [6]destroyed; happy *shall he be,* [7]that rewardeth thee as thou hast served us.

9 Happy *shall he be,* that taketh and dasheth thy little ones against [8]the stones.

Psalm 138

A Psalm of David

1 I will praise thee with my whole heart: [a]before the gods will I sing praise unto thee.

2 I will worship [b]toward thy holy temple, and praise thy name for thy lovingkindness and for thy truth: for thou hast magnified thy [c]word above all thy name.

3 In the day when I cried thou answeredst me, *and* [d]strengthenedst me *with* strength in my soul.

4 All the kings of the earth shall praise thee, O LORD, when they hear the words of thy mouth.

5 Yea, they shall sing in the ways of the LORD: for great *is* the glory of the LORD.

6 Though the LORD *be* high, yet [e]hath he respect unto the lowly: but the proud he knoweth afar off.

7 [f]Though I walk in the midst of trouble, thou wilt revive me: thou shalt stretch forth thine hand against the wrath of mine enemies, and thy right hand shall save me.

8 [g]The LORD will perfect *that which* concerneth me: thy mercy, O LORD, *endureth* for ever: forsake not the works of thine own hands.

Psalm 139

To the chief Musician, A Psalm of David

1 O lord, [a]thou hast searched me, and known *me.*

2 [b]Thou knowest my downsitting and mine uprising, thou understandest [c]my thought afar off.

3 Thou [1]compassest my path and my lying down, and art acquainted *with* all my ways.

4 For *there is* not a word in my tongue, *but,* lo, O LORD, [d]thou knowest it altogether.

5 Thou hast beset me behind and before, and laid thine hand upon me.

6 *Such* knowledge *is* too wonderful for me; it is high, I cannot *attain* unto it.

7 Whither shall I go from thy spirit? or whither shall I flee from thy presence?

8 If I ascend up into heaven, thou *art* there: [e]if I make my bed in hell, behold, thou *art there.*

9 *If* I take the wings of the morning, *and* dwell in the uttermost parts of the sea;

10 Even there shall thy hand lead me, and thy right hand shall hold me.

11 If I say, Surely the darkness shall cover me; even the night shall be light about me.

12 Yea, the darkness [2]hideth not from thee; but the night shineth as the day: [3]the darkness and the light *are* both alike *to thee.*

13 For thou hast possessed my reins: thou hast covered me in my mother's womb.

14 I will praise thee; for I am fearfully *and* wonderfully made: marvellous *are* thy works; and *that* my soul knoweth [4]right well.

15 My [5]substance was not hid from thee, when I was made in secret, *and* curiously wrought in the lowest parts of the earth.

16 Thine eyes did see my substance, yet being unperfect; and in thy book [6]all *my members* were written, [7]*which* in continuance were fashioned, when *as yet there was* none of them.

17 How precious also are thy thoughts unto me, O God! how great is the sum of them!

18 *If* I should count them, they are more in number than the sand: when I awake, I am still with thee.

19 Surely thou wilt [f]slay the wicked, O God: depart from me therefore, ye bloody men.

20 For they [g]speak against thee wickedly, *and* thine enemies take *thy name* in vain.

21 Do not I hate them, O LORD, that hate thee? and am not I grieved with those that rise up against thee?

22 I hate them with perfect hatred: I count them mine enemies.

23 [h]Search me, O God, and know my heart: try me, and know my thoughts:

24 And see if *there be any* [8]wicked way in me, and [i]lead me in the way everlasting.

Psalm 140

To the chief Musician, A Psalm of David

1 Deliver me, O LORD from the evil man: preserve me from the [1]violent man;

2 Which imagine mischiefs in *their* heart; continually are they gathered together *for* war.

3 They have sharpened their tongues like a serpent; adders' poison *is* under their lips. Sē'lah.

4 Keep me, O LORD, from the hands of the wicked; preserve me from the violent man; who have purposed to overthrow my goings.

5 [a]The proud have hid a snare for me, and cords; they have spread a net by the wayside; they have set gins for me. Sē'lah.

6 I said unto the LORD, [b]Thou *art* my God: hear the voice of my supplications, O LORD.

7 O GOD the Lord, [c]the strength of my salvation, thou hast covered my head in the day of battle.

8 Grant not, O LORD, [d]the desires of the wicked: further not his wicked device; [2]*lest* they exalt themselves. Sē'lah.

9 *As for* the [e]head of those that compass me about, let the mischief of their own lips cover them.

10 [f]Let burning coals fall upon them: let them be cast into the fire; into deep pits, that they rise not up again.

11 Let not [3]an evil speaker be established in the earth: evil shall hunt the violent man to overthrow *him.*

12 I know that the LORD will [g]maintain the cause of the afflicted, *and* the right of the poor.

13 Surely the righteous shall give thanks unto thy name: the upright shall dwell in thy presence.

Psalm 141

A Psalm of David

1 Lord, I cry unto thee: make haste unto me; give ear unto my voice, when I cry unto thee.

2 Let my prayer be [1]set forth before thee [a]*as* incense; *and* the lifting up of my hands *as* the evening sacrifice.

3 Set a watch, O LORD, before my mouth; keep the door of my lips.

4 Incline not my heart to *any* evil thing, to practise wicked works with men that work iniquity: and let me not eat of their dainties.

5 [2]Let the righteous smite me; *it shall be* a kindness: and let him reprove me; *it shall be* an excellent oil, *which* shall not break my head: for yet my prayer also *shall be* in their calamities.

6 When their judges are overthrown in stony places, they shall hear my words; for they are sweet.

7 Our bones are scattered at the grave's mouth, as when one cutteth and cleaveth *wood* upon the earth.

8 But mine eyes *are* unto thee, O GOD the Lord: in thee is my trust; [3]leave not my soul destitute.

9 Keep me from the snares *which* they have laid for me, and the gins of the workers of iniquity.

10 Let the wicked fall into their own nets, whilst that I withal [4]escape.

Psalm 142

**Maschil of David; A Prayer †when he was in the cave*

1 I cried unto the LORD with my voice; with my voice unto the LORD did I make my supplication.

2 I poured out my complaint before him; I shewed before him my trouble.

3 When my spirit was overwhelmed within me, then thou knewest my path. In the way wherein I walked have they privily laid a snare for me.

4 [1]I looked on *my* right hand, and beheld, but *there was* no man that would know me: refuge [2]failed me; [3]no man cared for my soul.

12 [2]darkeneth not [3]as is the darkness, so is the light
14 [4]greatly
15 [5]Or, strength, or, body
16 [6]all of them [7]Or, what days they should be fashioned
19 [f]Isa. 11.4
20 [g]Job 21.14-15;
23 [h]Job 31.6
24 [8]way of pain, or, grief [i]Matt. 7.14;

Psalm 140
1 [1]man of violences
5 [a]Ps. 10.9;
6 [b]Ps. 16.2
7 [c]Deut. 33.27-29;
8 [d]Job 5.12-13 [2]Or, let them not be exalted
9 [e]Ps. 7.16
10 [f]Ps. 11.6
11 [3]a man of tongue, or, an evil speaker, a wicked man of violence, be established in the earth: let him be hunted to his overthrow
12 [g]Ps. 109.31

Psalm 141
2 [1]directed [a]Eph. 5.2
5 [2]Or, Let the righteous smite me kindly, and reprove me; let not their precious oil break my head, etc [3]make not my soul bare [4]pass over

Psalm 142
*Or, A Psalm of David, giving instruction †1 Sam. 22.1
4 [1]Or, Look on the right hand, and see [2]perished from me [3]no man sought after my soul

5 I cried unto thee, O LORD: I said,
Thou *art* my refuge *and* [a]my portion in
the land of the living.
6 Attend unto my cry; for I am
[b]brought very low: [c]deliver me from
my persecutors; for they are stronger
than I.
7 Bring my soul out of prison, that I
may praise thy name: [d]the righteous
shall compass me about; [e]for thou
shalt deal bountifully with me.

Psalm 143

A Psalm of David

1 Hear my prayer, O LORD, give ear
to my supplications: in thy faithfulness
answer me, *and* in thy righteousness.
2 And [a]enter not into judgment with
thy servant: for [b]in thy sight shall no
man living be justified.
3 For the [c]enemy hath persecuted
my soul; he hath smitten my life down
to the ground; he hath made me to
dwell in darkness, as those that have
been long dead.
4 [d]Therefore is my spirit overwhelmed within me; my heart within
me is desolate.
5 [e]I remember the days of old; I
meditate on all thy works; I muse on
the work of thy hands.
6 [f]I stretch forth my hands unto
thee: my soul *thirsteth* after thee, as a
thirsty land. Sē'lah.
7 Hear me speedily, O LORD: my
spirit faileth: hide not thy face from
me, [1]lest I be like unto them that go
down into the pit.
8 Cause me to hear thy lovingkindness in the morning; for in thee do
I trust: cause me to know the way
wherein I should walk; for I lift up my
soul unto thee.
9 Deliver me, O LORD, from mine
enemies: I [2]flee unto thee to hide me.
10 [g]Teach me to do thy will; for
thou *art* my God: [h]thy spirit *is* good;
lead me into the land of uprightness.
11 Quicken me, O LORD, for thy
name's sake: for thy righteousness'
sake bring my soul out of trouble.
12 And of thy mercy cut off mine
enemies, and destroy all them that afflict my soul: for I *am* thy servant.

Psalm 144

A Psalm of David

1 Blessed *be* the LORD [1]my strength,
[a]which teacheth my hands [2]to war,
and my fingers to fight:
2 [3]My goodness, and my fortress;
my high tower, and my deliverer; my
shield, and *he* in whom I trust; who
subdueth my people under me.
3 [b]LORD, what *is* man, that thou
takest knowledge of him! *or* the son of
man, that thou makest account of him!
4 Man is like to vanity: his days *are*
as a shadow that passeth away.
5 [c]Bow thy heavens, O LORD, and
come down: touch the mountains, and
they shall smoke.
6 Cast forth lightning, and scatter
them: shoot out thine arrows, and destroy them.
7 Send thine [4]hand from above; [d]rid
me, and deliver me out of great waters,
from the hand of [e]strange children;
8 Whose mouth speaketh vanity,
and their right hand *is* a right hand of
falsehood.
9 I will [f]sing a new song unto thee,
O God: upon a psaltery *and* an instrument of ten strings will I sing praises
unto thee.
10 *It is he* that giveth [5]salvation unto
kings: who delivereth Dā'vid his servant from the hurtful sword.
11 Rid me, and deliver me from the
hand of strange children, whose mouth
speaketh vanity, and their right hand *is*
a right hand of falsehood:
12 That our sons *may be* as plants
grown up in their youth; *that* our daughters *may be* as corner stones, [6]polished
after the similitude of a palace:
13 *That* our garners *may be* full, af-
fording [7]all manner of store: *that* our
sheep may bring forth thousands and
ten thousands in our streets:
14 *That* our oxen *may be* [8]strong to
labour; *that there be* [g]no breaking in,
nor going out; that *there be* no complaining in our streets.
15 [h]Happy *is that* people, that is in
such a case: *yea*, happy *is that* people,
whose God *is* the LORD.

Psalm 145

David's Psalm of praise

1 I will extol thee, my God, O king;
and I will bless thy name for ever and
ever.
2 Every day will I bless thee; and I
will praise thy name for ever and ever.
3 Great *is* the LORD, and greatly
to be praised; [1]and his greatness *is*
unsearchable.
4 One generation shall praise thy
works to another, and shall declare thy
mighty acts.
5 I will speak of the glorious honour
of thy majesty, and of thy wondrous
[2]works.
6 And *men* shall speak of the might
of thy terrible acts: and I will [3]declare
thy greatness.
7 They shall abundantly [4a]utter the
memory of thy great goodness, and
shall sing of thy righteousness.
8 [b]The LORD *is* gracious, and full of
compassion; slow to anger, and [5]of
great mercy.
9 [c]The LORD *is* good to all: and his
tender mercies *are* over all his works.
10 [d]All thy works shall praise thee,
O LORD; and thy saints shall bless
thee.
11 They shall speak of the glory of
thy kingdom, and talk of thy power;
12 To make known to the sons of
men his mighty acts, and the glorious
majesty of his kingdom.
13 Thy kingdom *is* [6e]an everlasting
kingdom, and thy dominion *endureth*
throughout all generations.

5 [a]Lam. 3.24
6 [b]Ps. 116.6
[c]Ps. 7.1
7 [d]Ps. 34.2
[e]Ps. 119.17

Psalm 143
2 [a]Job 14.3
[b]Job 4.17; Eccl. 7.20; Gal. 2.16
3 [c]Ps. 7.1-2
4 [d]Ps. 61.2
5 [e]Ps. 77.5-11
6 [f]Ps. 28.2
7 [1]Or, for I am become like, etc
9 [2]hide me with thee
10 [g]Ps. 25.4
[h]John 14.26; Rom. 5.5; Gal. 5.22-23; Eph. 4.30

Psalm 144
1 [1]my rock
[a]2 Sam. 22.35
[2]to the war, etc
2 [3]Or, My mercy
3 [b]Heb. 2.6
5 [c]Isa. 64.1
7 [4]hands
[d]Ps. 69.1
[e]Mal. 2.11
9 [f]Ps. 33.2
10 [5]Or, victory
12 [6]cut
13 [7]from kind to kind
14 [8]able to bear burdens, or, loaden with flesh
[g]Lev. 26.17
15 [h]Deut. 33.29

Psalm 145
3 [1]and of his greatness there is no search
5 [2]things, or, words
6 [3]declare it
7 [4]boil up
[a]Ps. 45.1
8 [b]Ex. 34.6; Num. 14.18; Ps. 57.10; Ps. 86.5-15; Lam. 3.22-23; John 1.17
[5]great in mercy
9 [c]Ps. 100.5; Nah. 1.7; Matt. 5.45; Acts 14.17
10 [d]Ps. 19.1
13 [6]a kingdom of all ages
[e]Isa. 9.7; Dan. 2.44; Rev. 11.15-17

14 The LORD upholdeth all that fall, and raiseth up all *those that be* bowed down.

15 The eyes of all [7]wait upon thee; and thou givest them their meat in due season.

16 Thou openest thine hand, and satisfiest the desire of every living thing.

17 The LORD *is* righteous in all his ways, and [8]holy in all his works.

18 [f]The LORD *is* nigh unto all them that call upon him, to all that call upon him [g]in truth.

19 [h]He will fulfil the desire of them that fear him: he also will hear their cry, and will save them.

20 [i]The LORD preserveth all them that love him: but all the wicked will he destroy.

21 My mouth shall speak the praise of the LORD: and let all flesh bless his holy name for ever and ever.

Psalm 146

1 [1]Praise ye the LORD. Praise the LORD, O my soul.

2 While I live will I praise the LORD: I will sing praises unto my God while I have any being.

3 [a]Put not your trust in princes, *nor* in the son of man, in whom *there is* no [2]help.

4 [b]His breath goeth forth, he returneth to his earth; in that very day [c]his thoughts perish.

5 [d]Happy *is he* that *hath* the God of Jā'cob for his help, whose hope *is* in the LORD his God:

6 [e]Which made heaven, and earth, the sea, and all that therein *is*: which [f]keepeth truth for ever:

7 Which executeth judgment for the oppressed: which giveth food to the hungry. The LORD looseth the prisoners:

8 The LORD openeth *the eyes of* the blind: the LORD raiseth them that are bowed down: the LORD loveth the righteous.

9 The LORD preserveth the strangers; he relieveth the fatherless and widow: but the way of the wicked he turneth upside down.

10 The LORD shall reign for ever, *even* thy God, O Zī'ŏn, unto all generations. Praise ye the LORD.

Psalm 147

1 Praise ye the LORD: for *it is* good to sing praises unto our God; for *it is* pleasant; *and* praise is comely.

2 The LORD doth build up Je-rụ'sa-lĕm: [a]he gathereth together the outcasts of Ĭs'ra-el.

3 [b]He healeth the broken in heart, and bindeth up their [1]wounds.

4 [c]He telleth the number of the stars; he calleth them all by *their* names.

5 [d]Great *is* our Lord, and of [e]great power: [2]his understanding *is* infinite.

6 [f]The LORD lifteth up the meek: he casteth the wicked down to the ground.

15 [7]Or, look unto thee
17 [8]Or, merciful, or, bountiful
18 [f]Ps. 91.1; Isa. 61.10; John 14.23; Jas. 4.8; Rev. 3.20
[g]John 4.24
19 [h]1 John 5.14
20 [i]1 Pet. 1.5

Psalm 146
1 [1]Hallelujah
3 [a]Isa. 2.22
[2]Or, salvation
4 [b]Eccl. 12.7
[c]1 Cor. 2.6
5 [d]Jer. 17.7
6 [e]Rev. 14.7
[f]Mic. 7.20

Psalm 147
2 [a]Deut. 30.3; Ezek. 36.24
3 [b]Isa. 61.1; Luke 4.18
[1]griefs
4 [c]Gen. 15.5; Isa. 40.26
5 [d]1 Chr. 16.25
[e]Nah. 1.3
[2]of his understanding there is no number
6 [f]Ps. 146.8
7 [g]Eph. 5.20
[3]answer
[h]Ex. 15.21
8 [i]Job 38.26
9 [j]Job 38.41; Luke 12.24
[k]Matt. 6.26
10 [l]Hos. 1.7
14 [4]Who maketh thy border peace
[5]fat of wheat
15 [m]Job 37.12
19 [6]his words
[n]Deut. 33.4; Rom. 3.2
20 [o]Deut. 4.32; Rom. 3.1-2

Psalm 148
1 [1]Hallelujah
2 [a]Dan. 7.10; Heb. 1.7
4 [b]1 Ki. 8.27
5 [c]Heb. 11.3
6 [d]Jer. 33.25
7 [e]Isa. 43.20
9 [f]Isa. 49.13
10 [2]birds of wing
11 [g]Acts 17.28
13 [h]Isa. 6.3; Phil. 2.9

7 Sing unto the LORD [g]with thanksgiving; [3][h]sing praise upon the harp unto our God:

8 [i]Who covereth the heaven with clouds, who prepareth rain for the earth, who maketh grass to grow upon the mountains.

9 [j]He giveth to the beast his food, *and* to [k]the young ravens which cry.

10 [l]He delighteth not in the strength of the horse: he taketh not pleasure in the legs of a man.

11 The LORD taketh pleasure in them that fear him, in those that hope in his mercy.

12 Praise the LORD, O Je-rụ'sa-lĕm; praise thy God, O Zī'ŏn.

13 For he hath strengthened the bars of thy gates; he hath blessed thy children within thee.

14 [4]He maketh peace *in* thy borders, *and* filleth thee with the [5]finest of the wheat.

15 [m]He sendeth forth his commandment *upon* earth: his word runneth very swiftly.

16 He giveth snow like wool: he scattereth the hoarfrost like ashes.

17 He casteth forth his ice like morsels: who can stand before his cold?

18 He sendeth out his word, and melteth them: he causeth his wind to blow, *and* the waters flow.

19 He sheweth [6]his word unto Jā'cob, [n]his statutes and his judgments unto Ĭs'ra-el.

20 [o]He hath not dealt so with any nation: and *as for his* judgments, they have not known them. Praise ye the LORD.

Psalm 148

1 [1]Praise ye the LORD. Praise ye the LORD from the heavens: praise him in the heights.

2 Praise ye him, all his [a]angels: praise ye him, all his hosts.

3 Praise ye him, sun and moon: praise him, all ye stars of light.

4 Praise him, [b]ye heavens of heavens, and ye waters that *be* above the heavens.

5 Let them praise the name of the LORD: for [c]he commanded, and they were created.

6 [d]He hath also stablished them for ever and ever: he hath made a decree which shall not pass.

7 Praise the LORD from the earth, [e]ye dragons, and all deeps:

8 Fire, and hail; snow, and vapours; stormy wind fulfilling his word:

9 [f]Mountains, and all hills; fruitful trees, and all cedars:

10 Beasts, and all cattle; creeping things, and [2]flying fowl:

11 Kings of the earth, and all people; princes, and [g]all judges of the earth:

12 Both young men, and maidens; old men, and children:

13 Let them praise the name of the LORD: for [h]his name alone is

[3]excellent; his glory *is* above the earth
and heaven.
14 He also exalteth the horn of his
people, the praise of all his saints; *even*
of the children of Ĭs′ra-el, [i]a people
near unto him. Praise ye the LORD.

Psalm 149

1 [1]Praise ye the LORD. [a]Sing unto
the LORD a new song, *and* his praise in
the congregation of saints.
2 Let Ĭs′ra-el rejoice in [b]him that
made him: let the children of Zī′ŏn be
joyful in their [c]King.
3 Let them praise his name [2]in the
dance: let them sing praises unto him
with the timbrel and harp.
4 For the LORD taketh [d]pleasure in
his people: he will beautify the meek
with salvation.
5 Let the saints be joyful in glory: let
them sing aloud upon their beds.
6 *Let* the high *praises* of God *be* [3]in
their mouth, and [e]a twoedged sword
in their hand;

[3]exalted
14 [i]Eph. 2.17; 1 Pet. 2.9
Psalm 149
1 [1]Hallelujah [a]Isa. 42.10
2 [b]Job 35.10 [c]Zech. 9.9
3 [2]Or, with the pipe
4 [d]Prov. 11.20
6 [3]in their throat [e]Deut. 7.1-2; Heb. 4.12; Rev. 1.16
9 [f]Deut. 7.1-2; Rom. 16.20 [g]Rom. 16.20; 1 John 5.4
Psalm 150
1 [1]Hallelujah
3 [2]Or, cornet
4 [a]Ex. 15.20 [3]Or, pipe [b]Isa. 38.20
6 [c]Rev. 5.13

7 To execute vengeance upon the
heathen, *and* punishments upon the
people;
8 To bind their kings with chains,
and their nobles with fetters of iron;
9 [f]To execute upon them the judgment written: [g]this honour have all his
saints. Praise ye the LORD.

Psalm 150

1 [1]Praise ye the LORD. Praise God in
his sanctuary: praise him in the firmament of his power.
2 Praise him for his mighty acts:
praise him according to his excellent
greatness.
3 Praise him with the sound of the
[2]trumpet: praise him with the psaltery
and harp.
4 Praise him [a]with the timbrel and
[3]dance: praise him [b]with stringed instruments and organs.
5 Praise him upon the loud cymbals:
praise him upon the high sounding
cymbals.
6 Let [c]every thing that hath breath
praise the LORD. Praise ye the LORD.

THE PROVERBS

Life's Questions

Can the experiences of daily life teach me about God?
What has the experience of God's people taught about the problems all people face?
What is the central experience of life?

God's Answers

Proverbs preserves what God taught Israel about the moral and spiritual order of life. What can we expect to happen when we live according to certain guidelines? The wise of Israel collected Israel's experiences with God and showed what kind of orderly world God had created. They did not teach laws that worked every time but guidelines that proved true in most cases.

Proverbs deals with government, economics, family life, religion, and personal morality among other topics. No outline can show its variety of lessons. Its central theme is clear: live in fear and awe of the Creator God. Fearing God promises life. Anything else guarantees death.

1 The [a]proverbs of Sŏl′o-mon the
son of Dā′vid, king of Ĭs′ra-el;
2 To know wisdom and instruction;
to perceive the words of understanding;
3 To [b]receive the instruction of wisdom, justice, and judgment, and [1]eq-
uity;
4 To give subtilty to the simple, to the
young man knowledge and [2]discretion.
5 A wise *man* will hear, and will increase learning; and a man of understanding shall attain unto wise counsels:
6 To understand a proverb, and [3]the
interpretation; the words of the wise,
and their dark sayings.
7 ¶ The fear of the LORD *is* [4]the beginning of knowledge: *but* fools despise
wisdom and instruction.
8 My son, hear the instruction of thy
father, and forsake not the law of thy
mother:
9 For they *shall be* [5]an ornament of
grace unto thy head, and chains about
thy neck.

CHAPTER 1
1 [a]1 Ki. 4.32
3 [b]ch. 2.1 [1]equities
4 [2]Or, advisement
6 [3]Or, an eloquent speech
7 [4]Or, the principal part
9 [5]an adding
10 [c]Gen. 39.7; Judg. 16.16-21; Eph. 5.11
11 [d]ch. 12.6; Mic. 7.2
12 [e]Ps. 28.1
15 [f]ch. 4.14
16 [g]Isa. 59.7
17 [6]in the eyes of every thing that hath a wing
19 [h]2 Ki. 5.20-27; 1 Tim. 6.10

10 ¶ My son, if sinners entice thee,
[c]consent thou not.
11 If they say, Come with us, let [d]us
lay wait for blood, let us lurk privily
for the innocent without cause:
12 Let us swallow them up alive as
the grave; and whole, [e]as those that go
down into the pit:
13 We shall find all precious substance, we shall fill our houses with
spoil:
14 Cast in thy lot among us; let us all
have one purse:
15 My son, [f]walk not thou in the
way with them; refrain thy foot from
their path:
16 [g]For their feet run to evil, and
make haste to shed blood.
17 Surely in vain the net is spread
[6]in the sight of any bird.
18 And they lay wait for their *own*
blood; they lurk privily for their *own*
lives.
19 [h]So *are* the ways of every one
that is greedy of gain; *which* taketh
away the life of the owners thereof.

20 ¶ [7]Wisdom crieth without; she uttereth her voice in the streets:

21 She crieth in the chief place of concourse, in the openings of the gates: in the city she uttereth her words, *saying*,

22 How long, ye simple ones, will ye love simplicity? and the scorners delight in their scorning, and fools hate knowledge?

23 Turn you at my reproof: behold, [i]I will pour out my spirit unto you, I will make known my words unto you.

24 ¶ Because [j]I have called, and ye refused; I have stretched out my hand, and no man regarded;

25 But ye [k]have set at nought all my counsel, and would none of my reproof:

26 I also will laugh at your calamity; I will mock when your fear cometh;

27 When your fear cometh as desolation, and your destruction cometh as a whirlwind; when distress and anguish cometh upon you.

28 [l]Then shall they call upon me, but I will not answer; they shall seek me early, but they shall not find me:

29 For that they [m]hated knowledge, and did not choose the fear of the LORD:

30 They would none of my counsel: they despised all my reproof.

31 Therefore [n]shall they eat of the fruit of their own way, and be filled with their own devices.

32 For the [8]turning away of the simple shall slay them, and the prosperity of fools shall destroy them.

33 But whoso hearkeneth unto me shall dwell safely, and shall be quiet from fear of evil.

2 My son, if thou wilt receive my words, and hide my commandments with thee;

2 So that thou incline thine ear unto wisdom, *and* apply thine heart to understanding;

3 Yea, if thou criest after knowledge, *and* [1]liftest up thy voice for understanding;

4 [a]If thou seekest her as silver, and searchest for her as *for* hid treasures;

5 Then shalt thou understand the fear of the LORD, and find the knowledge of God.

6 [b]For the LORD giveth wisdom: out of his mouth *cometh* knowledge and understanding.

7 He layeth up sound wisdom for the righteous: [c]*he is* a buckler to them that walk uprightly.

8 He keepeth the paths of judgment, and preserveth [d]the way of his saints.

9 Then shalt thou understand righteousness, and judgment, and equity; *yea*, every good path.

10 ¶ When wisdom entereth into thine heart, and knowledge is pleasant unto thy soul;

11 Discretion shall preserve thee, [e]understanding shall keep thee:

12 To deliver thee from the way of the evil *man*, from the man that speaketh froward things;

13 Who leave the paths of uprightness, to [f]walk in the ways of darkness;

14 Who rejoice to do evil, *and* delight in the frowardness of the wicked;

15 Whose ways *are* crooked, and *they* froward in their paths:

16 To deliver thee from the strange woman, *even* from the stranger *which* flattereth with her words;

17 [g]Which forsaketh the guide of her youth, and forgetteth [h]the covenant of her God.

18 For her house inclineth unto death, and her paths unto the dead.

19 [i]None that go unto her return again, neither take they hold of the paths of life.

20 That thou mayest [j]walk in the way of good *men*, and keep the paths of the righteous.

21 For the upright shall dwell in the land, and the perfect shall remain in it.

22 But the wicked shall be cut off from the earth, and the transgressors shall be [2]rooted out of it.

3 My son, forget not my law; [a]but let thine heart keep my commandments:

2 For length of days, and [1]long life, and peace, shall they add to thee.

3 Let not mercy and truth forsake thee: [b]bind them about thy neck; [c]write them upon the table of thine heart:

4 [d]So shalt thou find favour and [2]good understanding in the sight of God and man.

5 ¶ Trust in the LORD with all thine heart; [e]and lean not unto thine own understanding.

6 [f]In all thy ways acknowledge him, and he shall [g]direct thy paths.

7 ¶ [h]Be not wise in thine own eyes: fear the LORD, and depart from evil.

8 It shall be [3]health to thy navel, and [4]marrow to thy bones.

9 [i]Honour the LORD with thy substance, and with the firstfruits of all thine increase:

10 [j]So shall thy barns be filled with plenty, and thy presses shall burst out with new wine.

11 ¶ [k]My son, despise not the chastening of the LORD; neither be weary of his correction:

12 For whom the LORD loveth he correcteth; [l]even as a father the son *in whom* he delighteth.

13 ¶ Happy *is* the man *that* findeth wisdom, and [5]the man *that* getteth understanding.

14 [m]For the merchandise of it *is* better than the merchandise of silver, and the gain thereof than fine gold.

15 She *is* more precious than rubies: and [n]all the things thou canst desire are not to be compared unto her.

16 [o]Length of days *is* in her right hand; *and* in her left hand riches and honour.

17 [p]Her ways *are* ways of pleasantness, and all her paths *are* peace.

18 She *is* [q]a tree of life to them that lay hold upon her: and happy *is every one* that retaineth her.

---

20 [7]Wisdoms, that is, Excellent wisdom
23 [i]Joel 2.28; John 7.37
24 [j]Isa. 66.4; Zech. 7.11
25 [k]Luke 7.30
28 [l]Isa. 1.15; Jas. 4.3
29 [m]Job 21.14; Acts 7.51
31 [n]Isa. 3.11
32 [8]Or, ease of the simple

CHAPTER 2
3 [1]givest thy voice
4 [a]Ps. 19.10; Matt. 6.19-21
6 [b]Luke 21.15;
7 [c]Ps. 84.11
8 [d]1 Sam. 2.9;
11 [e]ch. 6.22
13 [f]John 3.19;
17 [g]Mal. 2.14 [h]Gen. 2.24
19 [i]Eccl. 7.26
20 [j]Heb. 6.12
22 [2]Or, plucked up

CHAPTER 3
1 [a]Deut. 30.16
2 [1]years of life
3 [b]Deut. 6.8 [c]Jer. 17.1
4 [d]1 Sam. 2.26; [2]Or, good success
5 [e]Jer. 9.23
6 [f]1 Chr. 28.9; [g]Jer. 10.23
7 [h]Rom. 12.16
8 [3]medicine [4]watering, or, moistening
9 [i]Ex. 23.19
10 [j]Deut. 28.8
11 [k]Job 5.17
12 [l]Deut. 8.5
13 [5]the man that draweth out understanding
14 [m]Job 28.13;
15 [n]Matt. 13.44
16 [o]1 Tim. 4.8
17 [p]Matt. 11.29
18 [q]Gen. 2.9

19 [r]The LORD by wisdom hath
founded the earth; by understanding
hath he [6]established the heavens.
20 By his knowledge the depths are
broken up, and [s]the clouds drop down
the dew.
21 ¶ My son, let not them depart
from thine eyes: keep sound wisdom
and discretion:
22 So shall they be life unto thy soul,
and grace to thy neck.
23 Then shalt thou walk in thy way
safely, and thy foot shall not stumble.
24 [t]When thou liest down, thou shalt
not be afraid: yea, thou shalt lie down,
and thy sleep shall be sweet.
25 Be not afraid of sudden fear, neither of the desolation of the wicked,
when it cometh.
26 For the LORD shall be thy confidence, and shall keep thy foot from being taken.
27 ¶ [u]Withhold not good from [7]them
to whom it is due, when it is in the
power of thine hand to do *it*.
28 [v]Say not unto thy neighbour, Go,
and come again, and to morrow I will
give; when thou hast it by thee.
29 [8]Devise not evil against thy neighbour, seeing he dwelleth securely by
thee.
30 ¶ [w]Strive not with a man without
cause, if he have done thee no harm.
31 ¶ Envy thou not [9]the oppressor,
and choose none of his ways.
32 For the froward *is* abomination
to the LORD: but his secret *is* with the
righteous.
33 ¶ [x]The curse of the LORD *is* in the
house of the wicked: but [y]he blesseth
the habitation of the just.
34 [z]Surely he scorneth the scorners: but he giveth grace unto the lowly.
35 The [a]wise shall inherit glory: but
shame [10]shall be the promotion of fools.

4 Hear, [a]ye children, the instruction
of a father, and attend to know
understanding.
2 For I give you good doctrine, forsake ye not my law.
3 For I was my father's son, [b]tender
and only *beloved* in the sight of my
mother.
4 [c]He taught me also, and said unto
me, Let thine heart retain my words:
keep my commandments, and live.
5 Get wisdom, get understanding:
forget *it* not; neither decline from the
words of my mouth.
6 Forsake her not, and she shall preserve thee: [d]love her, and she shall
keep thee.
7 [e]Wisdom *is* the principal thing;
therefore get wisdom: and with all thy
getting get understanding.
8 [f]Exalt her, and she shall promote
thee: she shall bring thee to honour,
when thou dost embrace her.
9 She shall give to thine head an ornament of grace: [1]a crown of glory
shall she deliver to thee.
10 Hear, O my son, and receive my
sayings; and the years of thy life shall
be many.

19 [r]ch. 8.27; Heb. 1.2
[6]Or, prepared
20 [s]Deut. 33.28; Job 36.28
24 [t]Lev. 26.6
27 [u]Rom. 13.7; Gal. 6.10
[7]the owners thereof
28 [v]Lev. 19.13; Deut. 24.15
29 [8]Or, Practise no evil
30 [w]Rom. 12.18
31 [9]a man of violence
33 [x]Zech. 5.4; Mal. 2.2
[y]Ps. 1.3
34 [z]Ps. 138.6
35 [a]Dan. 12.2
[10]exalteth the fools

CHAPTER 4
1 [a]Ps. 34.11
3 [b]2 Sam. 12.24;
4 [c]1 Chr. 28.9;
6 [d]2 Thess. 2.10
7 [e]Matt. 13.44
8 [f]1 Sam. 2.30
9 [1]Or, she shall compass thee with a crown of glory
12 [g]Ps. 18.36
[h]verse 19
18 [i]Matt. 5.14;
[j]2 Sam. 23.4
19 [k]1 Sam. 2.9
22 [2]medicine
23 [3]above all keeping
24 [4]frowardness of mouth, and perverseness of lips
26 [5]Or, all thy ways shall be ordered aright
27 [l]Isa. 1.16

CHAPTER 5
2 [a]Mal. 2.7
3 [1]palate
4 [b]Eccl. 7.26
[c]Heb. 4.12
5 [d]Heb. 13.4
10 [2]thy strength

11 I have taught thee in the way of
wisdom; I have led thee in right paths.
12 When thou goest, [g]thy steps shall
not be straitened; [h]and when thou run-
nest, thou shalt not stumble.
13 Take fast hold of instruction; let
her not go: keep her; for she *is* thy life.
14 ¶ Enter not into the path of the
wicked, and go not in the way of evil
men.
15 Avoid it, pass not by it, turn from
it, and pass away.
16 For they sleep not, except they
have done mischief; and their sleep is
taken away, unless they cause *some* to
fall.
17 For they eat the bread of wickedness, and drink the wine of violence.
18 [i]But the path of the just [j]*is* as the
shining light, that shineth more and
more unto the perfect day.
19 [k]The way of the wicked *is* as
darkness: they know not at what they
stumble.
20 ¶ My son, attend to my words;
incline thine ear unto my sayings.
21 Let them not depart from thine
eyes; keep them in the midst of thine
heart.
22 For they *are* life unto those that
find them, and [2]health to all their flesh.
23 ¶ Keep thy heart [3]with all diligence; for out of it *are* the issues of life.
24 Put away from thee [4]a froward
mouth, and perverse lips put far from
thee.
25 Let thine eyes look right on, and
let thine eyelids look straight before
thee.
26 Ponder the path of thy feet, and
[5]let all thy ways be established.
27 Turn not to the right hand nor to
the left: [l]remove thy foot from evil.

5 My son, attend unto my wisdom, *and*
bow thine ear to my understanding:
2 That thou mayest regard discretion, and *that* thy lips may [a]keep
knowledge.
3 ¶ For the lips of a strange woman
drop *as* an honeycomb, and her [1]mouth
is smoother than oil:
4 But her end is [b]bitter as wormwood, sharp [c]as a twoedged sword.
5 Her feet go down [d]to death; her
steps take hold on hell.
6 Lest thou shouldest ponder the
path of life, her ways are moveable,
that thou canst not know *them*.
7 Hear me now therefore, O ye children, and depart not from the words of
my mouth.
8 Remove thy way far from her, and
come not nigh the door of her house:
9 Lest thou give thine honour unto
others, and thy years unto the cruel:
10 Lest strangers be filled with [2]thy
wealth; and thy labours *be* in the house
of a stranger;
11 And thou mourn at the last, when
thy flesh and thy body are consumed,
12 And say, How have I hated instruction, and my heart despised reproof;

13 And have not obeyed the voice of
my teachers, nor inclined mine ear to
them that instructed me!
14 I was almost in all evil in the midst
of the congregation and assembly.
15 ¶ Drink waters out of thine own
cistern, and running waters out of thine
own well.
16 Let thy fountains be dispersed
abroad, *and* rivers of waters in the
streets.
17 Let them be only thine own, and
not strangers' with thee.
18 Let thy fountain be blessed: and
rejoice [e]with the wife of thy youth.
19 [f]*Let her be as* the loving hind and
pleasant roe; let her breasts [3]satisfy
thee at all times; and [4]be thou ravished
always with her love.
20 And why wilt thou, my son, be
ravished with a strange woman, and
embrace the bosom of a stranger?
21 For [g]the ways of man *are* before
the eyes of the LORD, and he pondereth
all his goings.
22 ¶ His [h]own iniquities shall take
the wicked himself, and he shall be
holden with the cords of his [5]sins.
23 He [i]shall die without instruction;
and in the greatness of his folly he
shall go astray.

6 My son, [a]if thou be surety for thy
friend, *if* thou [b]hast stricken thy
hand with a stranger,
2 Thou art snared with the words of
thy mouth, thou art taken with the
words of thy mouth.
3 Do this now, my son, and deliver
thyself, when thou art come into the
hand of thy friend; go, humble thyself,
[1]and make sure thy friend.
4 [c]Give not sleep to thine eyes, nor
slumber to thine eyelids.
5 Deliver thyself as a roe from the
hand *of the hunter,* and as a bird from
the hand of the fowler.
6 ¶ [d]Go to the ant, thou sluggard;
consider her ways, and be wise:
7 Which having no guide, overseer,
or ruler,
8 Provideth her meat in the summer,
and gathereth her food in the harvest.
9 How long wilt thou sleep, O sluggard? when wilt thou arise out of thy
sleep?
10 *Yet* a little sleep, a little slumber,
a little folding of the hands to sleep:
11 So shall thy poverty come as one
that travelleth, and thy want as an
armed man.
12 ¶ A naughty person, a wicked
man, walketh with a froward mouth.
13 [e]He winketh with his eyes, he
speaketh with his feet, he teacheth
with his fingers;
14 Frowardness *is* in his heart, [f]he
deviseth mischief continually; he [2]sow-
eth discord.
15 Therefore shall his calamity come
suddenly; suddenly shall he [g]be broken without remedy.
16 ¶ These six *things* doth the LORD
hate: yea, seven *are* an abomination
[3]unto him:

18 [e]Eccl. 9.9; Mal. 2.14
19 [f]Song 2.9 [3]water thee [4]err thou always in her love
21 [g]2 Chr. 16.9; Job 31.4; Jer. 16.17; Hos. 7.2; Heb. 4.13
22 [h]Ps. 9.15 [5]sin
23 [i]Job 4.21; ch. 10.21

CHAPTER 6
1 [a]Gen. 43.9; Heb. 7.22 [b]Ezra 10.19
3 [1]Or, so shalt thou prevail with thy friend
4 [c]Ruth 3.18
6 [d]Job 12.7
13 [e]Ps. 35.19; ch. 10.10
14 [f]Ps. 36.4; Matt. 26.4 [2]casteth forth
15 [g]Jer. 19.11
16 [3]of his soul
17 [4]Haughty eyes [h]Ps. 5.6; John 8.44 [i]ch. 1.11; Isa. 1.15
18 [j]Gen. 6.5 [k]Isa. 59.7; Rom. 3.15
19 [l]Ps. 27.12
20 [m]Eph. 6.1
23 [n]Ps. 19.8 [5]Or, candle
24 [6]Or, of the strange tongue
25 [o]2 Sam. 11.2-5; Matt. 5.28
26 [p]ch. 29.3 [7]the woman of a man, or, a man's wife [q]Ezek. 13.18
31 [r]Ex. 22.1-4
32 [8]heart [s]Job 31.12; Heb. 13.4
35 [9]He will not accept the face of any ransom

CHAPTER 7
2 [a]Lev. 18.5; Isa. 55.3 [b]Deut. 32.10
3 [c]Deut. 6.8; 2 Cor. 3.3
7 [1]the sons [d]ch. 6.32

17 [4]A proud look, [h]a lying tongue,
and [i]hands that shed innocent blood,
18 [j]An heart that deviseth wicked
imaginations, [k]feet that be swift in running to mischief,
19 [l]A false witness *that* speaketh
lies, and he that soweth discord among
brethren.
20 ¶ [m]My son, keep thy father's commandment, and forsake not the law of
thy mother:
21 Bind them continually upon thine
heart, *and* tie them about thy neck.
22 When thou goest, it shall lead
thee; when thou sleepest, it shall keep
thee; and *when* thou awakest, it shall
talk with thee.
23 [n]For the commandment *is* a [5]lamp;
and the law *is* light; and reproofs of instruction *are* the way of life:
24 To keep thee from the evil woman,
from the flattery [6]of the tongue of a
strange woman.
25 [o]Lust not after her beauty in thine
heart; neither let her take thee with her
eyelids.
26 For [p]by means of a whorish
woman *a man is brought* to a piece of
bread: and [7]the adulteress will [q]hunt
for the precious life.
27 Can a man take fire in his bosom,
and his clothes not be burned?
28 Can one go upon hot coals, and
his feet not be burned?
29 So he that goeth in to his neighbour's wife; whosoever toucheth her
shall not be innocent.
30 *Men* do not despise a thief, if he
steal to satisfy his soul when he is
hungry;
31 But *if* he be found, [r]he shall restore sevenfold; he shall give all the
substance of his house.
32 *But* whoso committeth adultery
with a woman lacketh [8]understanding:
he *that* doeth it [s]destroyeth his own
soul.
33 A wound and dishonour shall he
get; and his reproach shall not be
wiped away.
34 For jealousy *is* the rage of a man:
therefore he will not spare in the day
of vengeance.
35 [9]He will not regard any ransom;
neither will he rest content, though
thou givest many gifts.

7 My son, keep my words, and lay up
my commandments with thee.
2 [a]Keep my commandments, and
live; and [b]my law as the apple of thine
eye.
3 [c]Bind them upon thy fingers, write
them upon the table of thine heart.
4 Say unto wisdom, Thou *art* my sister; and call understanding *thy* kinswoman:
5 That they may keep thee from
the strange woman, from the stranger
which flattereth with her words.
6 ¶ For at the window of my house I
looked through my casement,
7 And beheld among the simple ones,
I discerned among [1]the youths, a young
man [d]void of understanding,

8 Passing through the street near
her corner; and he went the way to her
house,
9 In [e]the twilight, [2]in the evening, in
the black and dark night:
10 And, behold, there met him a
woman *with* the [f]attire of an harlot,
and subtil of heart.
11 (She *is* loud and stubborn; [g]her
feet abide not in her house:
12 Now *is she* without, now in the
streets, and lieth in wait at every
corner.)
13 So she caught him, and kissed
him, *and* [3]with an impudent face said
unto him,
14 [4]*I have* peace offerings with me;
this day have I payed my vows.
15 Therefore came I forth to meet
thee, diligently to seek thy face, and I
have found thee.
16 I have decked my bed with coverings of tapestry, with carved *works*,
with [h]fine linen of E'gypt.
17 I have perfumed my bed with
myrrh, aloes, and cinnamon.
18 Come, let us take our fill of love
until the morning: let us solace ourselves with loves.
19 For the goodman *is* not at home,
he is gone a long journey:
20 He hath taken a bag of money
[5]with him, *and* will come home at [6]the
day appointed.
21 With her much fair speech she
caused him to yield, with the flattering
of her lips she forced him.
22 He goeth after her [7]straightway,
as an ox goeth to the slaughter, or as a
fool to the correction of the stocks;
23 Till a dart strike through his liver;
as a bird hasteth to the snare, and
knoweth not that it *is* for his life.
24 ¶ Hearken unto me now therefore, O ye children, and attend to the
words of my mouth.
25 Let not thine heart decline to her
ways, go not astray in her paths.
26 For she hath cast down many
wounded: yea, [i]many strong *men* have
been slain by her.
27 Her house *is* the way to [j]hell, going down to the chambers of death.

8 Doth not [a]wisdom cry? and understanding put forth her voice?
2 She standeth in the top of high
places, by the way in the places of the
paths.
3 She crieth at the gates, at the entry
of the city, at the coming in at the
doors.
4 Unto you, O men, I call; and my
voice *is* to the sons of man.
5 O ye simple, understand wisdom:
and, ye fools, be ye of an understanding heart.
6 Hear; for I will speak of [b]excellent
things; and the opening of my lips *shall
be* right things.
7 For my mouth shall [c]speak truth;
and wickedness *is* [1]an abomination to
my lips.
8 All the words of my mouth *are* in
righteousness; *there is* nothing [2]frow-
ard or perverse in them.
9 They *are* all plain to him that understandeth, and right to them that
find knowledge.
10 Receive my instruction, and not
silver; and knowledge rather than
choice gold.
11 [d]For wisdom *is* better than rubies; and all the things that may be desired are not to be compared to it.
12 I wisdom dwell with [3]prudence,
and find out knowledge of witty inventions.
13 [e]The fear of the LORD *is* to hate
evil: [f]pride, and arrogancy, and the
evil way, and [g]the froward mouth, do I
hate.
14 Counsel *is* mine, and sound wisdom: I *am* understanding; [h]I have
strength.
15 [i]By me kings reign, and princes
decree justice.
16 By me princes rule, and nobles,
even all the judges of the earth.
17 [j]I love them that love me; and
[k]those that seek me early shall find
me.
18 [l]Riches and honour *are* with me;
yea, durable riches and righteousness.
19 [m]My fruit *is* better than gold,
yea, than fine gold; and my revenue
than choice silver.
20 I [4]lead in the way of righteousness, in the midst of the paths of
judgment:
21 That I may cause those that love
me to inherit substance; and I will fill
their treasures.
22 [n]The LORD possessed me in the
beginning of his way, before his works
of old.
23 [o]I was set up from everlasting,
from the beginning, or ever the earth
was.
24 When *there were* no depths, I
was brought forth; when *there were* no
fountains abounding with water.
25 [p]Before the mountains were settled, before the hills was I brought
forth:
26 While as yet he had not made the
earth, nor the [5]fields, nor [6]the highest
part of the dust of the world.
27 When he prepared the heavens, I
was there: when he set [7]a compass
upon the face of the depth:
28 When he established the clouds
above: when he strengthened the fountains of the deep:
29 [q]When he gave to the sea his decree, that the waters should not pass his
commandment: when [r]he appointed
the foundations of the earth:
30 [s]Then I was by him, *as* one
brought up *with him*: [t]and I was daily
his delight, rejoicing always before
him;
31 Rejoicing [u]in the habitable part
of his earth; and [v]my delights *were*
with the sons of men.
32 Now therefore hearken unto me,
O ye children: for [w]blessed *are they
that* keep my ways.
33 Hear instruction, and be wise,
and refuse it not.

9 [e]Job 24.15
[2]in the evening of the day
10 [f]1 Tim. 2.9
11 [g]1 Tim. 5.13; Tit. 2.5
13 [3]she strengthened her face and said
14 [4]Peace offerings are upon me
16 [h]Isa. 19.9
20 [5]in his hand
[6]Or, the new moon
22 [7]suddenly
26 [i]Neh. 13.26
27 [j]ch. 2.18; 1 Cor. 6.9-10; Heb. 13.4; Rev. 22.15

CHAPTER 8
1 [a]ch. 9.3; 1 Cor. 1.24
6 [b]Ps. 49.3; Col. 1.26
7 [c]John 8.14; Rom. 15.8
[1]the abomination of my lips
8 [2]wreathed
11 [d]Job 28.15; Ps. 19.10
12 [3]Or, subtilty
13 [e]ch. 16.6
[f]Zech. 8.17; 1 Pet. 5.5
[g]ch. 4.24
14 [h]Eccl. 7.19
15 [i]Dan. 2.21; Rom. 13.1
17 [j]1 Sam. 2.30
[k]Jas. 1.5
18 [l]Matt. 6.33
19 [m]Job 28.15; ch. 3.14
20 [4]Or, walk
22 [n]ch. 3.19; John 1.1
23 [o]Gen. 1.26; John 17.24
25 [p]Job 15.7
26 [5]Or, open places
[6]Or, the chief part
27 [7]Or, a circle
29 [q]Job 38.10
[r]Job 38.4
30 [s]John 1.1-2-18
[t]Matt. 3.17; Col. 1.13
31 [u]Isa. 4.2
[v]Ps. 16.3
32 [w]Luke 11.28

34 Blessed *is* the man that heareth me, watching daily at my gates, waiting at the posts of my doors.

35 [x]For whoso findeth me findeth life, and shall [8]obtain favour of the LORD.

36 But he that sinneth against me [y]wrongeth his own soul: all they that hate me love death.

9 Wisdom hath [a]builded her house, she hath hewn out her seven pillars:

2 She hath killed [1]her beasts; she hath mingled her wine; she hath also furnished her table.

3 She hath [b]sent forth her maidens: she crieth upon the highest places of the city,

4 [c]Whoso *is* simple, let him turn in hither: *as for* him that wanteth understanding, she saith to him,

5 [d]Come, eat of my bread, and drink of the wine *which* I have mingled.

6 Forsake the foolish, and live; and go in the way of understanding.

7 He that reproveth a scorner getteth to himself shame: and he that rebuketh a wicked *man getteth* himself a blot.

8 [e]Reprove not a scorner, lest he hate thee: [f]rebuke a wise man, and he will love thee.

9 Give *instruction* to a wise *man,* and he will be yet wiser: teach a just *man,* [g]and he will increase in learning.

10 [h]The fear of the LORD *is* the beginning of wisdom: and the knowledge of the holy *is* understanding.

11 [i]For by me thy days shall be multiplied, and the years of thy life shall be increased.

12 [j]If thou be wise, thou shalt be wise for thyself: but *if* thou scornest, thou alone shalt bear *it.*

13 ¶ A foolish woman *is* clamorous: *she is* simple, and knoweth nothing.

14 For she sitteth at the door of her house, on a seat in the high places of the city,

15 To call passengers who go right on their ways:

16 Whoso *is* simple, let him turn in hither: and *as for* him that wanteth understanding, she saith to him,

17 [k]Stolen waters are sweet, and bread [2]*eaten* in secret is pleasant.

18 But he knoweth not that the dead *are* there; *and that* her guests *are* in the depths of hell.

10 The proverbs of Sŏl'o-mon. A wise son maketh a glad father: but a foolish son *is* the heaviness of his mother.

2 [a]Treasures of wickedness profit nothing: [b]but righteousness delivereth from death.

3 [c]The LORD will not suffer the soul of the righteous to famish: but he casteth away [1]the substance of the wicked.

4 He becometh poor that dealeth *with* a slack hand: but [d]the hand of the diligent maketh rich.

5 He that gathereth in summer *is* a wise son: *but* he that sleepeth in harvest *is* a son that causeth shame.

6 Blessings *are* upon the head of the just: but [e]violence covereth the mouth of the wicked.

7 [f]The memory of the just *is* blessed: but the name of the wicked shall rot.

8 The wise in heart will receive commandments: but [2]a prating fool [3]shall fall.

9 [g]He that walketh uprightly walketh surely: but he that perverteth his ways shall be known.

10 He that winketh with the eye causeth sorrow: but a prating fool [4]shall fall.

11 [h]The mouth of a righteous *man is* a well of life: but [i]violence covereth the mouth of the wicked.

12 Hatred stirreth up strifes: but [j]love covereth all sins.

13 In the [k]lips of him that hath understanding wisdom is found: but a rod *is* for the back of him that is void of [5]understanding.

14 Wise *men* lay up knowledge: but the mouth of the foolish *is* near destruction.

15 [l]The rich man's wealth *is* his strong city: the destruction of the poor *is* their poverty.

16 The labour of the righteous *tendeth* to life: the fruit of the wicked to sin.

17 He *is in* the way of life that keepeth instruction: but he that refuseth reproof [6]erreth.

18 He that hideth hatred *with* lying lips, and he that uttereth a slander, *is* a fool.

19 [m]In the multitude of words there wanteth not sin: but [n]he that refraineth his lips *is* wise.

20 The tongue of the just *is as* choice silver: the heart of the wicked *is* little worth.

21 The lips of the righteous feed many: but fools die for want [7]of wisdom.

22 [o]The blessing of the LORD, it maketh rich, and he addeth no sorrow with it.

23 *It is* as sport to a fool to do mischief: but a man of understanding hath wisdom.

24 [p]The fear of the wicked, it shall come upon him: but [q]the desire of the righteous shall be granted.

25 As the whirlwind passeth, so *is* the wicked no *more:* but [r]the righteous *is* an everlasting foundation.

26 As vinegar to the teeth, and as smoke to the eyes, so *is* the sluggard to them that send him.

27 The fear of the LORD [8]prolongeth days: but [s]the years of the wicked shall be shortened.

28 [t]The hope of the righteous *shall be* gladness: but the [u]expectation of the wicked shall perish.

29 The way of the LORD [v]*is* strength to the upright: [w]but destruction *shall be* to the workers of iniquity.

30 The righteous shall never be removed: but the wicked shall not inhabit the earth.

31 The mouth of the just bringeth forth wisdom: but the froward tongue shall be cut out.

35 [x]John 3.16-36; Phil. 3.8-9
[8]bring forth
36 [y]Heb. 2.3

CHAPTER 9

1 [a]Matt. 16.18; Heb. 3.3-6
2 [1]her killing
3 [b]Matt. 22.3-4-9; Rom. 10.15
4 [c]ch. 6.32; Matt. 11.25
5 [d]Song 5.1; Matt. 26.26-28
8 [e]Matt. 7.6
[f]Ps. 141.5
9 [g]Matt. 13.12
10 [h]Job 28.28
11 [i]ch. 10.27
12 [j]Job 35.6-7
17 [k]ch. 20.17
[2]of secrecies

CHAPTER 10

2 [a]Ps. 49.6; Luke 12.19
[b]Dan. 4.27
3 [c]Ps. 10.14
[1]Or, the wicked for their wickedness
4 [d]ch. 13.4
6 [e]Esth. 7.8
7 [f]Ps. 9.5-6; Eccl. 8.10
8 [2]a fool of lips
[3]Or, shall be beaten
9 [g]Ps. 23.4; Isa. 33.15-16
10 [4]Or, shall be beaten
11 [h]Ps. 37.30
[i]Ps. 107.42
12 [j]1 Cor. 13.4
13 [k]Luke 4.22
[5]heart
15 [l]Job 31.24; 1 Tim. 6.17
17 [6]Or, causeth to err
19 [m]Eccl. 5.3
[n]Ps. 39.1
21 [7]of heart
22 [o]Gen. 12.2
24 [p]Job 15.21
[q]Matt. 5.6
25 [r]Ps. 15.5
27 [8]addeth
[s]Eccl. 7.17
28 [t]Ps. 16.9;
[u]Job 8.13
29 [v]Isa. 40.31;
[w]Ps. 1.6

32 The lips of the righteous know
what is acceptable: but the mouth of
the wicked *speaketh* [9]frowardness.

11 A [1]false balance *is* abomination
to the LORD: but [2]a just weight *is*
his delight.
2 [a]*When* pride cometh, then cometh
shame: but with the lowly *is* wisdom.
3 The integrity of the upright shall
guide them: but the perverseness of
transgressors shall destroy them.
4 [b]Riches profit not in the day of
wrath: but [c]righteousness delivereth
from death.
5 The righteousness of the perfect
shall [3]direct his way: but the wicked
shall fall by his own wickedness.
6 [d]The righteousness of the upright
shall deliver them: but [e]transgressors
shall be taken in *their own* naughtiness.
7 When a wicked man dieth, *his* expectation shall perish: and the hope of
unjust *men* perisheth.
8 The righteous is delivered out of
trouble, and the wicked cometh in his
stead.
9 An [f]hypocrite with *his* mouth destroyeth his neighbour: but through
knowledge shall the just be delivered.
10 [g]When it goeth well with the righteous, the city rejoiceth: and when the
wicked perish, *there is* shouting.
11 By the blessing of the upright the
city is exalted: but it is overthrown by
the mouth of the wicked.
12 He that is [4]void of wisdom despiseth his neighbour: but a man of understanding holdeth his peace.
13 [5]A talebearer revealeth secrets:
but he that is of a faithful spirit concealeth the matter.
14 Where [h]no counsel *is*, the people
fall: but in the multitude of counsellers
there is safety.
15 He that is surety for a stranger
[6]shall smart *for it*: and he that hateth
[7]suretiship is sure.
16 A gracious woman retaineth honour: and strong *men* retain riches.
17 [i]The merciful man doeth good to
his own soul: but *he that is* cruel troubleth his own flesh.
18 The wicked worketh a deceitful
work: but [j]to him that soweth righteousness *shall be* a sure reward.
19 As righteousness *tendeth* to life:
so he that pursueth evil *pursueth it* to
his own death.
20 They that are of a froward heart
are abomination to the LORD: but *such
as are* upright in *their* way *are* his
delight.
21 *Though* hand *join* in hand, the
wicked shall not be unpunished: but the
seed of the righteous shall be delivered.
22 *As* a jewel of gold in a swine's
snout, *so is* a fair woman which [8]is
without discretion.
23 The desire of the righteous *is*
only good: *but* the expectation of the
wicked [k]*is* wrath.
24 There is that scattereth, and yet
increaseth; and *there is* that withholdeth more than is meet, but *it tendeth* to
poverty.
25 [9]The liberal soul shall be made
fat: [l]and he that watereth shall be watered also himself.
26 [m]He that withholdeth corn, the
people shall curse him: [n]but blessing
shall be upon the head of him that
selleth *it*.
27 He that diligently seeketh good
procureth favour: [o]but he that seeketh
mischief, it shall come unto him.
28 [p]He that trusteth in his riches
shall fall: but [q]the righteous shall flourish as a branch.
29 He that troubleth his own house
[r]shall inherit the wind: and the fool
shall be servant to the wise of heart.
30 The fruit of the righteous *is* a tree
of life; and he that [10]winneth souls *is*
wise.
31 [s]Behold, the righteous shall be recompensed in the earth: much more
the wicked and the sinner.

12 Whoso loveth instruction loveth
knowledge: but he that hateth reproof *is* brutish.
2 A good *man* obtaineth favour of
the LORD: but a man of wicked devices
will he condemn.
3 A man shall not be established by
wickedness: but the root of the righteous shall not be moved.
4 [a]A virtuous woman *is* a crown
to her husband: but she that maketh
ashamed *is* [b]as rottenness in his bones.
5 The thoughts of the righteous *are*
right: *but* the counsels of the wicked
are deceit.
6 The words of the wicked *are* to lie
in wait for blood: but the mouth of the
upright shall deliver them.
7 [c]The wicked are overthrown, and
are not: but the house of the righteous
shall stand.
8 A man shall be commended according to his wisdom: [d]but he that is
[1]of a perverse heart shall be despised.
9 *He that is* despised, and hath a servant, *is* better than he that honoureth
himself, and lacketh bread.
10 [e]A righteous *man* regardeth the
life of his beast: but the [2]tender mercies of the wicked *are* cruel.
11 [f]He that tilleth his land shall be
satisfied with bread: but he that followeth vain *persons is* void of understanding.
12 The wicked desireth [3]the net of
evil *men*: but the [g]root of the righteous
yieldeth *fruit*.
13 [4]The wicked is snared by the
transgression of *his* lips: [h]but the just
shall come out of trouble.
14 A man shall be satisfied with
good by the fruit of *his* mouth: [i]and the
recompence of a man's hands shall be
rendered unto him.
15 [j]The way of a fool *is* right in his
own eyes: but he that hearkeneth unto
counsel *is* wise.
16 A fool's wrath is [5]presently
known: but a prudent *man* covereth
shame.
17 *He that* speaketh truth sheweth
forth righteousness: but a false witness deceit.

32 [9]frowardnesses
CHAPTER 11
1 [1]Balances of deceit [2]a perfect stone
2 [a]Dan. 4.30
4 [b]Ezek. 7.19; [c]Gen. 7.1
5 [3]rectify
6 [d]1 Tim. 4.8 [e]Eccl. 10.8
9 [f]Job 8.13
10 [g]Esth. 8.15
12 [4]destitute of heart
13 [5]He that walketh, being a talebearer
14 [h]1 Ki. 12.1
15 [6]shall be sore broken [7]those that strike hands
17 [i]Matt. 25.34
18 [j]Hos. 10.12;
22 [8]departeth from
23 [k]Rom. 2.8
25 [9]The soul of blessing [l]Matt. 5.7
26 [m]Amos 8.5 [n]Job 29.13
27 [o]Esth. 7.10
28 [p]Mark 10.24; [q]Jer. 17.8
29 [r]Eccl. 5.16
30 [10]taketh
31 [s]Jer. 25.29
CHAPTER 12
4 [a]ch. 31.23; [b]ch. 14.30
7 [c]Matt. 7.24
8 [d]1 Sam. 13.13; [1]perverse of heart
10 [e]Deut. 25.4 [2]Or, bowels
11 [f]Gen. 3.19
12 [3]Or, the fortress [g]Ps. 1.3
13 [4]The snare of the wicked is in the transgression of lips [h]2 Pet. 2.9
14 [i]Isa. 3.10
15 [j]Luke 18.11
16 [5]in that day

18 There is that speaketh like the
piercings of a sword: but the tongue of
the wise *is* health.
19 [k]The lip of truth shall be established for ever: but a lying tongue *is*
but for a moment.
20 Deceit *is* in the heart of them that
imagine evil: but to the counsellers of
peace *is* joy.
21 [l]There shall no evil happen to the
just: but the wicked shall be filled with
mischief.
22 [m]Lying lips *are* abomination to
the LORD: but they that deal truly *are*
his delight.
23 A prudent man concealeth knowledge: but the heart of fools proclaim-
eth foolishness.
24 [n]The hand of the diligent shall
bear rule: but the [6]slothful shall be under tribute.
25 Heaviness in the heart of man
maketh it stoop: but [o]a good word
maketh it glad.
26 The righteous *is* more [7]excellent
than his neighbour: but the way of the
wicked seduceth them.
27 The slothful *man* roasteth not
that which he took in hunting: but the
substance of a diligent man *is* precious.
28 In the way of [p]righteousness *is*
life; and *in* the pathway *thereof there*
is no death.

13 A wise son *heareth* his father's
instruction: [a]but a scorner heareth not rebuke.
2 A man shall eat good by the fruit
of *his* mouth: but the soul of the transgressors *shall eat* violence.
3 [b]He that keepeth his mouth keepeth his life: *but* he that openeth wide
his lips shall have destruction.
4 The soul of the sluggard desireth,
and *hath* nothing: but the soul of the
diligent shall be made fat.
5 A righteous *man* hateth [c]lying:
but a wicked *man* is loathsome, and
cometh to shame.
6 [d]Righteousness keepeth *him that*
is upright in the way: but wickedness
overthroweth [1]the sinner.
7 There is that maketh himself rich,
yet *hath* nothing: *there is* that maketh
himself poor, yet *hath* great riches.
8 The ransom of a man's life *are*
his riches: but the poor heareth not
rebuke.
9 The light of the righteous rejoiceth: but the [2]lamp of the wicked shall
be put out.
10 Only by pride cometh contention:
but with the well advised *is* wisdom.
11 [e]Wealth *gotten* by vanity shall
be diminished: but he that gathereth
[3]by labour shall increase.
12 Hope deferred maketh the heart
sick: but *when* the desire cometh, *it is*
a tree of life.
13 Whoso [f]despiseth the word shall
be destroyed: but he that feareth the
commandment [4]shall be rewarded.
14 [g]The law of the wise *is* a fountain
of life, to depart from [h]the snares of
death.
15 Good understanding giveth favour: but the way of transgressors *is*
hard.
16 [i]Every prudent *man* dealeth with
knowledge: but a fool [5]layeth open *his*
folly.
17 A wicked messenger falleth into
mischief: but [6]a faithful ambassador *is*
health.
18 Poverty and shame *shall be to* him
that refuseth instruction: but [j]he that regardeth reproof shall be honoured.
19 The desire accomplished is sweet
to the soul: but *it is* abomination to
fools to depart from evil.
20 He that walketh with wise *men*
shall be wise: but a companion of fools
[7]shall be destroyed.
21 [k]Evil pursueth sinners: but to the
righteous good shall be repayed.
22 A good *man* leaveth an inheritance to his children's children: and
[l]the wealth of the sinner *is* laid up for
the just.
23 [m]Much food *is in* the tillage of the
poor: but there is *that is* destroyed for
want of judgment.
24 [n]He that spareth his rod hateth
his son: but he that loveth him chasteneth him betimes.
25 The righteous eateth to the satisfying of his soul: but the belly of the
wicked shall want.

14 Every [a]wise woman buildeth her
house: but the foolish plucketh it
down with her hands.
2 He that walketh in his uprightness
feareth the LORD: [b]but *he that is* perverse in his ways despiseth him.
3 In the mouth of the foolish *is* a rod
of pride: [c]but the lips of the wise shall
preserve them.
4 Where no oxen *are*, the crib *is*
clean: but much increase *is* by the
strength of the ox.
5 [d]A faithful witness will not lie: but
a false witness will utter lies.
6 A scorner seeketh wisdom, and
findeth it not: but [e]knowledge *is* easy
unto him that understandeth.
7 Go from the presence of a foolish
man, when thou perceivest not *in him*
the lips of knowledge.
8 The wisdom of the prudent *is* to
understand his way: but [f]the folly of
fools *is* deceit.
9 [g]Fools make a mock at sin: but
among the righteous *there is* favour.
10 The heart knoweth [1]his own bitterness; and a stranger doth not in-
termeddle with his joy.
11 [h]The house of the wicked shall
be overthrown: but the tabernacle of
the upright shall flourish.
12 [i]There is a way which seemeth
right unto a man, but [j]the end thereof
are the ways of death.
13 Even in laughter the heart is sorrowful; and [k]the end of that mirth *is*
heaviness.
14 The backslider in heart shall be
[l]filled with his own ways: and a [m]good
man *shall be satisfied* from himself.

19 [k]Zech. 1.5-6
21 [l]Rom. 8.28; 2 Thess. 1.6; 2 Pet. 2.9
22 [m]Rev. 22.15
24 [n]1 Ki. 11.28; ch. 10.4
[6]Or, deceitful
25 [o]Isa. 50.4
26 [7]Or, abundant
28 [p]Deut. 30.15; Matt. 19.17; Rom. 5.21; 2 Cor. 4.17; Rev. 2.7

CHAPTER 13

1 [a]1 Sam. 2.25; ch. 9.7-8
3 [b]Ps. 39.1
5 [c]Rom. 12.9; Col. 3.9
6 [d]ch. 11.3
[1]sin
9 [2]Or, candle
11 [e]ch. 20.21
[3]with the hand
13 [f]2 Chr. 36.16
[4]Or, shall be in peace
14 [g]ch. 16.22
[h]2 Sam. 22.6; ch. 15.24; Ps. 116.3
16 [i]ch. 12.23
[5]spreadeth
17 [6]an ambassador of faithfulness
18 [j]ch. 15.5
20 [7]shall be broken
21 [k]Ps. 32.10
22 [l]Eccl. 2.26
23 [m]ch. 12.11
24 [n]ch. 19.18; ch. 22.15

CHAPTER 14

1 [a]Ruth 4.11; ch. 24.3-4
2 [b]Job 12.4
3 [c]ch. 12.6
5 [d]Ex. 20.16
6 [e]ch. 17.24
8 [f]Luke 12.20; 1 Cor. 3.19
9 [g]ch. 1.22
10 [1]the bitterness of his soul
11 [h]Job 8.15; ch. 3.33
12 [i]ch. 16.25
[j]Rom. 6.21
13 [k]Eccl. 2.2
14 [l]ch. 12.14
[m]2 Cor. 1.12; Phil. 4.7

15 The simple believeth every word:
but the prudent *man* looketh well to
his going.
16 [n]A wise *man* feareth, and departeth from evil: but the fool rageth,
and is confident.
17 *He that is* soon angry dealeth
foolishly: and a man of wicked devices
is hated.
18 The simple inherit folly: but the
prudent are crowned with knowledge.
19 The evil bow before the good;
and the wicked at the gates of the
righteous.
20 [o]The poor is hated even of his
own neighbour: but [2]the rich *hath*
many friends.
21 He that despiseth his neighbour
sinneth: [p]but he that hath mercy on
the poor, happy *is* he.
22 Do they not err that devise evil?
but mercy and truth *shall be* to them
that devise good.
23 In all labour there is profit: but
the talk of the lips *tendeth* only to
penury.
24 The crown of the wise *is* their
riches: *but* the foolishness of fools *is*
folly.
25 A true witness delivereth souls:
but a deceitful *witness* speaketh lies.
26 In the fear of the LORD *is* strong
confidence: and his children shall have
a place of refuge.
27 [q]The fear of the LORD *is* a fountain of life, to depart from the snares of
death.
28 In the multitude of people *is* the
king's honour: but in the want of people *is* the destruction of the prince.
29 [r]*He that is* slow to wrath *is* of
great understanding: but *he that is*
[3]hasty of spirit exalteth folly.
30 A sound heart *is* the life of the
flesh: but [s]envy the rottenness of the
bones.
31 [t]He that oppresseth the poor reproacheth [u]his Maker: but he that honoureth him hath mercy on the poor.
32 The wicked is driven away in his
wickedness: but [v]the righteous hath
hope in his death.
33 Wisdom resteth in the heart of
him that hath understanding: but *that
which is* in the midst of fools is made
known.
34 Righteousness exalteth a nation:
but sin *is* a reproach [4]to any people.
35 [w]The king's favour *is* toward a
wise servant: but his wrath *is against*
him that causeth shame.

15 A soft answer turneth away
wrath: but grievous words stir
up anger.
2 The tongue of the wise useth knowledge aright: but the mouth of fools
[1]poureth out foolishness.
3 [a]The eyes of the LORD *are* in every
place, beholding the evil and the good.
4 [2]A wholesome tongue *is* a tree
of life: but perverseness therein *is* a
breach in the spirit.
5 A fool despiseth his father's instruction: but he that regardeth reproof is prudent.
6 In the house of the righteous *is*
much treasure: but in the revenues of
the wicked is trouble.
7 The lips of the wise disperse knowledge: but the heart of the foolish *doeth*
not so.
8 [b]The sacrifice of the wicked *is* an
abomination to the LORD: [c]but the
prayer of the upright *is* his delight.
9 The way of the wicked *is* an abomination unto the LORD: but he loveth him
that [d]followeth after righteousness.
10 [3]Correction *is* grievous unto him
that forsaketh the way: *and* he that
hateth reproof shall die.
11 Hell and destruction *are* before
the LORD: how much more then [e]the
hearts of the children of men?
12 A scorner loveth not one that reproveth him: neither will he go unto
the wise.
13 A merry heart maketh a cheerful
countenance: but by sorrow of the
heart the spirit is broken.
14 The heart of him that hath understanding seeketh knowledge: but the
mouth of fools feedeth on foolishness.
15 All the days of the afflicted *are*
evil: but he that is of a merry heart
hath a continual feast.
16 [f]Better *is* little with the fear of the
LORD than great treasure and trouble
therewith.
17 Better *is* a dinner of herbs where
love is, than a stalled ox and hatred
therewith.
18 A wrathful man stirreth up strife:
but *he that is* slow to anger appeaseth
strife.
19 The way of the slothful *man is* as
an hedge of thorns: but the way of the
righteous [4g]*is* made plain.
20 A wise son maketh a glad father: but a foolish man despiseth his
mother.
21 Folly *is* joy to *him that is* [5]desti-
tute of wisdom: [h]but a man of understanding walketh uprightly.
22 Without counsel purposes are disappointed: but in the multitude of counsellers they are established.
23 A man hath joy by the answer of
his mouth: and a word *spoken* [6]*in due
season, how good is it!*
24 [i]The way of life *is* above to the
wise, that he may depart from hell
beneath.
25 The LORD will destroy the house
of the proud: but he will establish the
border of the widow.
26 The thoughts of the wicked *are*
an abomination to the LORD: but *the
words* of the pure *are* [7]*pleasant words.*
27 [j]He that is greedy of gain troubleth his own house; but he that hateth
gifts shall live.
28 The heart of the righteous [k]stud-
ieth to answer: but the mouth of the
wicked poureth out evil things.
29 [l]The LORD *is* far from the wicked:
but he [m]heareth the prayer of the
righteous.
30 The light of the eyes rejoiceth the
heart: *and* a good report maketh the
bones fat.

16 [n]ch. 22.3
20 [o]ch. 19.7 [2]many are the lovers of the rich
21 [p]Ps. 41.1
27 [q]ch. 13.14
29 [r]ch. 15.18; Matt. 11.29; 1 Cor. 13.4-7; Jas. 1.19 [3]short of spirit
30 [s]Job 5.2; Ps. 112.10; Jas. 4.5
31 [t]Job 31.15-16; 1 John 3.17 [u]Job 31.15; ch. 22.2
32 [v]Job 13.15; 2 Tim. 4.18
34 [4]to nations
35 [w]Matt. 24.45-47
CHAPTER 15
2 [1]belcheth, or, bubbleth
3 [a]2 Chr. 16.9; Heb. 4.13
4 [2]The healing of the tongue
8 [b]Isa. 61.8; Amos 5.22 [c]Luke 18.11
9 [d]ch. 21.21; 1 Tim. 6.11
10 [3]Or, Instruction
11 [e]John 2.24; Acts 1.24
16 [f]ch. 16.8; 1 Tim. 6.6
19 [4]is raised up as a causey [g]Isa. 35.8
21 [5]void of heart [h]Eph. 5.15
23 [6]in his season
24 [i]Phil. 3.20
26 [7]words of pleasantness
27 [j]Josh. 6.18; Zech. 5.3
28 [k]1 Pet. 3.15
29 [l]Eph. 2.12 [m]Ps. 34.15-16; Rom. 8.26

31 The ear that heareth the reproof of life abideth among the wise.

32 He that refuseth [8]instruction despiseth his own soul: but he that [9]heareth reproof [10]getteth understanding.

33 The fear of the LORD *is* the instruction of wisdom; and before honour *is* humility.

16 The [1a]preparations of the heart in man, [b]and the answer of the tongue, *is* from the LORD.

2 All the ways of a man *are* clean in his own eyes; but [c]the LORD weigheth the spirits.

3 [2]Commit thy works unto the LORD, and thy thoughts shall be established.

4 [d]The LORD hath made all *things* for himself: [e]yea, even the wicked for the day of evil.

5 Every one *that is* proud in heart *is* an abomination to the LORD: *though* hand *join* in hand, he shall not be [3]unpunished.

6 [f]By mercy and truth iniquity is purged: and by the fear of the LORD *men* depart from evil.

7 When a man's ways [g]please the LORD, he maketh even his enemies to be at peace with him.

8 Better *is* a little with righteousness than great revenues without right.

9 A man's heart deviseth his way: [h]but the LORD directeth his steps.

10 [4]A divine sentence *is* in the lips of the king: his mouth transgresseth not in judgment.

11 [i]A just weight and balance *are* the LORD'S: [5]all the weights of the bag *are* his work.

12 *It is* an abomination to kings to commit wickedness: for the throne is established by righteousness.

13 Righteous lips *are* the delight of kings; and they love him that speaketh right.

14 The wrath of a king *is as* messengers of death: but a wise man will pacify it.

15 In the light of the king's countenance *is* life; and his favour *is* as a cloud of the latter rain.

16 How much better *is it* to get wisdom than gold! and to get understanding rather to be chosen than silver!

17 [j]The highway of the upright *is* to depart from evil: he that keepeth his way preserveth his soul.

18 Pride *goeth* before destruction, and an haughty spirit before a fall.

19 Better *it is to be* of an humble spirit with the lowly, than to divide the spoil with the proud.

20 [6]He that handleth a matter wisely shall find good: and whoso [k]trusteth in the LORD, happy *is* he.

21 The wise in heart shall be called prudent: and the sweetness of the lips increaseth learning.

22 Understanding *is* a wellspring of life unto him that hath it: but the instruction of fools *is* folly.

23 [l]The heart of the wise [7]teacheth his mouth, and addeth learning to his lips.

24 Pleasant words *are as* an honeycomb, sweet to the soul, and health to the bones.

25 There is a way that seemeth right unto a man, but the end thereof *are* the ways of death.

26 [8]He that laboureth laboureth for himself; for his mouth [9]craveth it of him.

27 [10]An ungodly man diggeth up evil: and in his lips *there is* as a burning fire.

28 A froward man [11]soweth strife: and a whisperer separateth chief friends.

29 A violent man enticeth his neighbour, and leadeth him into the way *that is* not good.

30 He shutteth his eyes to devise froward things: moving his lips he bringeth evil to pass.

31 The hoary head *is* a crown of glory, *if* it be found in the way of righteousness.

32 *He that is* slow to anger *is* better than the mighty; and he that ruleth his spirit than he that taketh a city.

33 The lot is cast into the lap; but the whole disposing thereof *is* of the LORD.

17 Better *is* a dry morsel, and quietness therewith, than an house full of [1]sacrifices *with* strife.

2 A wise servant shall have rule over a son that causeth shame, and shall have part of the inheritance among the brethren.

3 [a]The fining pot *is* for silver, and the furnace for gold: but the LORD trieth the hearts.

4 A wicked doer giveth heed to false lips; *and* a liar giveth ear to a naughty tongue.

5 Whoso mocketh the poor reproacheth his Maker: *and* [b]he that is glad at calamities shall not be [2]unpunished.

6 Children's children *are* the crown of old men; and the glory of children *are* their fathers.

7 [3]Excellent speech becometh not a fool: much less do [4]lying lips a prince.

8 A gift *is as* [5c]a precious stone in the eyes of him that hath it: whithersoever it turneth, it [d]prospereth.

9 He that covereth a transgression [6]seeketh love; but he that repeateth a matter separateth *very* friends.

10 [7]A reproof entereth more into a wise man than an hundred stripes into a fool.

11 An evil *man* seeketh only rebellion: therefore a cruel messenger shall be sent against him.

12 Let a bear robbed of her whelps meet a man, rather than a fool in his folly.

13 Whoso [e]rewardeth evil for good, evil shall not depart from his house.

14 The beginning of strife *is as* when one letteth out water: therefore [f]leave off contention, before it be meddled with.

15 [g]He that justifieth the wicked, and he that condemneth the just, even they both *are* abomination to the LORD.

32 [8]Or, correction [9]Or, obeyeth [10]possesseth an heart

CHAPTER 16
1 [1]Or, disposings [a]Jer. 10.23 [b]Matt. 10.19
2 [c]1 Sam. 16.7; Dan. 5.27
3 [2]Roll
4 [d]Isa. 43.7; Rom. 11.36 [e]Job 21.30; Rom. 9.22
5 [3]held innocent
6 [f]Dan. 4.27; Luke 11.41
7 [g]Col. 1.10
9 [h]Jer. 10.23
10 [4]Divination
11 [i]Lev. 19.36 [5]all the stones
17 [j]ch. 4.24-27;
20 [6]Or, He that understandeth a matter [k]Isa. 30.18
23 [l]Matt. 12.34 [7]maketh wise
26 [8]The soul of him that laboureth [9]boweth unto him
27 [10]A man of Belial
28 [11]sendeth forth

CHAPTER 17
1 [1]Or, good cheer
3 [a]Ps. 26.2;
5 [b]Job 31.29; [2]held innocent
7 [3]a lip of excellency [4]a lip of lying
8 [5]a stone of grace [c]ch. 18.16 [d]Gen. 39.21;
9 [6]Or, procureth
10 [7]Or, A reproof aweth more a wise man, than to strike a fool an hundred times
13 [e]Jer. 18.20;
14 [f]ch. 20.3;
15 [g]Ex. 23.7

16 Wherefore *is there* a price in the
hand of a fool to get wisdom, seeing *he
hath* no heart *to it?*
17 A friend loveth at all times, and a
brother is born for adversity.
18 A man void of [8]understanding
striketh hands, *and* becometh surety in
the presence of his friend.
19 He loveth transgression that loveth strife: *and* he that exalteth his gate
seeketh destruction.
20 [9]He that hath a froward heart
findeth no good: and he that hath a
perverse tongue falleth into mischief.
21 He that begetteth a fool *doeth it*
to his sorrow: and the father of a fool
hath no joy.
22 A merry heart doeth good [10]*like* a
medicine: but a broken spirit drieth the
bones.
23 A wicked *man* taketh a gift out
of the bosom [h]to pervert the ways of
judgment.
24 [i]Wisdom *is* before him that hath
understanding; but the eyes of a fool
are in the ends of the earth.
25 A foolish son *is* a grief to his father, and bitterness to her that bare
him.
26 Also to punish the just *is* not
good, *nor* to strike princes for equity.
27 [j]He that hath knowledge spareth
his words: *and* a man of understanding
is of [11]an excellent spirit.
28 Even a fool, when he holdeth his
peace, is counted wise: *and* he that
shutteth his lips *is esteemed* a man of
understanding.

18 Through [1]desire a man, having
separated himself, seeketh *and*
intermeddleth with all wisdom.
2 A fool hath no delight in understanding, but that his heart may discover itself.
3 When the wicked cometh, *then*
cometh also contempt, and with igno-
miny reproach.
4 The words of a man's mouth *are*
as deep waters, [a]*and* the wellspring of
wisdom *as* a flowing brook.
5 [b]*It is* not good to accept the person of the wicked, to overthrow the
righteous in judgment.
6 A fool's lips enter into contention,
and his mouth calleth for strokes.
7 A fool's mouth *is* his destruction,
and his lips *are* the snare of his soul.
8 The words of a [2]talebearer *are* [3]as
wounds, and they go down into the [4]in-
nermost parts of the belly.
9 He also that is slothful in his work
is brother to him that is a great waster.
10 [c]The name of the LORD *is* a strong
tower: the righteous runneth into it,
and [5]is safe.
11 The rich man's wealth *is* his strong
city, and as an high wall in his own
conceit.
12 Before destruction the heart of
man is haughty, and before honour *is*
humility.
13 He that [6]answereth a matter before he heareth *it*, it *is* folly and shame
unto him.
14 The spirit of a man will sustain
his infirmity; but a wounded spirit who
can bear?
15 [d]The heart of the prudent getteth
knowledge; and the ear of the wise
seeketh knowledge.
16 [e]A man's gift maketh room for
him, and bringeth him before great
men.
17 *He that is* first in his own cause
seemeth just; but his neighbour cometh and searcheth him.
18 The lot causeth contentions to
cease, and parteth between the mighty.
19 A brother offended *is harder to be*
won than a strong city: and *their* contentions *are* like the bars of a castle.
20 A man's belly shall be satisfied
with the fruit of his mouth; *and* with the
increase of his lips shall he be filled.
21 [f]Death and life *are* in the power
of the tongue: and they that love it
shall eat the fruit thereof.
22 *Whoso* findeth a wife findeth a
good *thing*, and obtaineth favour of
the LORD.
23 The poor useth intreaties; but the
rich answereth [g]roughly.
24 A man [h]*that hath* friends must
shew himself friendly: and there is
a friend *that* sticketh closer than a
brother.

19 Better [a]*is* the poor that walketh
in his integrity, than *he that is*
perverse in his lips, and is a fool.
2 Also, *that* the [b]soul *be* without
knowledge, *it is* not good; and he that
hasteth with *his* feet sinneth.
3 The foolishness of man perverteth
his way: [c]and his heart fretteth against
the LORD.
4 Wealth maketh many friends; but
the poor is separated from his neighbour.
5 [d]A false witness shall not be [1]un-
punished, and *he that* speaketh lies
shall not escape.
6 Many will intreat the favour of the
prince: and every man *is* a friend to
[2]him that giveth gifts.
7 All the brethren of the poor do hate
him: how much more do his friends go
far from him? he pursueth *them with*
words, *yet* they *are* wanting *to him.*
8 He that getteth [3]wisdom loveth his
own soul: he that keepeth understanding shall find good.
9 [e]A false witness shall not be unpunished, and *he that* speaketh lies
shall perish.
10 Delight is not seemly for a fool;
much less [f]for a servant to have rule
over princes.
11 [g]The [4]discretion of a man de-
ferreth his anger; [h]and *it is* his glory to
pass over a transgression.
12 The king's wrath *is* as the roaring
of a lion; but his favour *is* as dew upon
the grass.
13 A foolish son *is* the calamity of
his father: and the contentions of a
wife *are* a continual dropping.
14 [i]House and riches *are* the inheritance of fathers: and [j]a prudent wife *is*
from the LORD.

18 [8]heart
20 [9]The froward of heart
22 [10]Or, to a medicine
23 [h]Ex. 23.8
24 [i]Eccl. 2.14
27 [j]Jas. 1.19
[11]Or, a cool spirit

CHAPTER 18
1 [1]Or, He that separateth himself seeketh according to his desire, and intermeddleth in every business: see Jude 19
4 [a]Ps. 78.2
5 [b]Lev. 19.15; Deut. 1.17; Job 13.7-8; ch. 24.23
8 [2]Or, whisperer
[3]Or, like as when men are wounded
[4]chambers
10 [c]2 Sam. 22.3-51; Ps. 18.2
[5]is set aloft
13 [6]returneth a word
15 [d]Eph. 1.17
16 [e]Gen. 39.2-6; Gen. 41.14-38-44; Dan. 1.17-19-20; Dan. 6.3
21 [f]Matt. 12.37
23 [g]Gen. 42.14-16; Jas. 2.3
24 [h]John 15.14-15

CHAPTER 19
1 [a]ch. 28.6
2 [b]Hos. 4.6; John 16.3; Rom. 10.2
3 [c]Ps. 37.7
5 [d]Ex. 23.1
[1]held innocent
6 [2]a man of gifts
8 [3]an heart
9 [e]Dan. 6.24
10 [f]Eccl. 10.6
11 [g]Jas. 1.19
[4]Or, prudence
[h]ch. 25.21; Matt. 5.44; Eph. 4.32
14 [i]2 Cor. 12.14
[j]ch. 18.22

15 Slothfulness casteth into a deep sleep; and an idle soul shall suffer hunger.

16 [k]He that keepeth the commandment keepeth his own soul; *but* he that despiseth his ways shall die.

17 [l]He that hath pity upon the poor lendeth unto the LORD; and [5]that which he hath given will he pay him again.

18 Chasten thy son while there is hope, and let not thy soul spare [6]for his crying.

19 A man of great wrath shall suffer punishment: for if thou deliver *him*, yet thou must [7]do it again.

20 Hear counsel, and receive instruction, that thou mayest be wise in thy latter end.

21 [m]*There are* many devices in a man's heart; nevertheless the counsel of the LORD, that shall stand.

22 The desire of a man *is* his kindness: and a poor man *is* better than a liar.

23 [n]The fear of the LORD *tendeth* to life: and *he that hath it* shall abide satisfied; he shall not be visited with evil.

24 A slothful *man* hideth his hand in *his* bosom, and will not so much as bring it to his mouth again.

25 Smite a scorner, and the simple [8][o]will beware: and reprove one that hath understanding, *and* he will understand knowledge.

26 He that wasteth *his* father, *and* chaseth away *his* mother, *is* a son that causeth shame, and bringeth reproach.

27 Cease, my son, to [p]hear the instruction *that causeth* to err from the words of knowledge.

28 [9]An ungodly witness scorneth judgment: and the mouth of the wicked devoureth iniquity.

29 Judgments are prepared for scorners, and stripes for the back of fools.

20 Wine [a]*is* a mocker, strong drink *is* raging: and whosoever is deceived thereby is not wise.

2 The fear of a king *is* as the roaring of a lion: *whoso* provoketh him to anger sinneth *against* his own soul.

3 [b]*It is* an honour for a man to cease from strife: but every fool will be meddling.

4 The sluggard will not plow by reason of the [1]cold; *therefore* shall he beg in harvest, and *have* nothing.

5 Counsel in the heart of man *is like* deep water; but a man of understanding will draw it out.

6 [c]Most men will proclaim every one his own [2]goodness: but [d]a faithful man who can find?

7 The just *man* walketh in his integrity: his children *are* blessed after him.

8 A king that sitteth in the throne of judgment scattereth away all evil with his eyes.

9 [e]Who can say, I have made my heart clean, I am pure from my sin?

10 [3]Divers weights, *and* [4]divers measures, both of them *are* alike abomination to the LORD.

11 Even a child is [f]known by his doings, whether his work *be* pure, and whether *it be* right.

12 [g]The hearing ear, and the seeing eye, the LORD hath made even both of them.

13 [h]Love not sleep, lest thou come to poverty; open thine eyes, *and* thou shalt be satisfied with bread.

14 *It is* naught, *it is* naught, saith the buyer: but when he is gone his way, then he boasteth.

15 There is gold, and a multitude of rubies: but the lips of knowledge *are* a precious jewel.

16 Take his garment that is surety *for* a stranger: and take a pledge of him for a strange woman.

17 [5]Bread of deceit *is* sweet to a man; but afterwards his mouth shall be filled with gravel.

18 *Every* purpose is established by counsel: and with good advice make war.

19 He that goeth about *as* a talebearer revealeth secrets: therefore meddle not with him that [6]flattereth with his lips.

20 [i]Whoso curseth his father or his mother, his [7]lamp shall be put out in obscure darkness.

21 An inheritance *may be* gotten hastily at the beginning; [j]but the end thereof shall not be blessed.

22 [k]Say not thou, I will recompense evil; *but* wait on the LORD, and he shall save thee.

23 Divers weights *are* an abomination unto the LORD; and [8]a false balance *is* not good.

24 [l]Man's goings *are* of the LORD; how can a man then understand his own way?

25 *It is* a snare to the man *who* devoureth *that which is* holy, and after vows to make enquiry.

26 A wise king scattereth the wicked, and bringeth the wheel over them.

27 The spirit of man *is* the [9]candle of the LORD, searching all the inward parts of the belly.

28 Mercy and truth preserve the king: and his throne is upholden by mercy.

29 The glory of young men *is* their strength: and the beauty of old men *is* the gray head.

30 The blueness of a wound [10]cleanseth away evil: so *do* stripes the inward parts of the belly.

21 The king's heart *is* in the hand of the LORD, *as* the rivers of water: he turneth it whithersoever he will.

2 Every way of a man *is* right in his own eyes: [a]but the LORD pondereth the hearts.

3 [b]To do justice and judgment *is* more acceptable to the LORD than sacrifice.

4 [1]An high look, and a proud heart, *and* [2]the plowing of the wicked, *is* sin.

5 The thoughts of the diligent *tend* only to plenteousness; but of every one *that is* hasty only to want.

6 The getting of treasures by a lying

---

16 [k]Luke 10.28; Rom. 2.7
17 [l]ch. 14.21; 2 Cor. 9.6 [5]Or, his deed
18 [6]Or, to his destruction: or, to cause him to die
19 [7]add
21 [m]Gen. 37.19-20; Heb. 6.17
23 [n]1 Tim. 4.8
25 [8]will be cunning [o]Deut. 13.11
27 [p]Matt. 7.15; 1 Tim. 4.6
28 [9]A witness of Belial

CHAPTER 20

1 [a]Gen. 9.21; Isa. 28.7
3 [b]Gen. 13.7
4 [1]Or, winter
6 [c]Matt. 6.2 [2]Or, bounty [d]Ps. 12.1; Luke 18.8
9 [e]Job 14.4; 1 John 1.8
10 [3]A stone and a stone [4]an ephah and an ephah
11 [f]Matt. 7.16
12 [g]Ex. 4.11; Rom. 11.36
13 [h]Rom. 12.11
17 [5]Bread of lying or, falsehood
19 [6]Or, enticeth
20 [i]Ex. 21.17; Rom. 3.23 [7]Or, candle
21 [j]ch. 28.8;
22 [k]Deut. 32.35;
23 [8]balances of deceit
24 [l]Jer. 10.23;
27 [9]Or, lamp
30 [10]is a purging medicine against evil

CHAPTER 21

2 [a]1 Sam. 16.7;
3 [b]Hos. 6.6
4 [1]Haughtiness of eyes [2]Or, the light of the wicked

tongue *is* a vanity tossed to and fro of them that seek death.

7 The robbery of the wicked shall [3]destroy them; because they refuse to do judgment.

8 The way of man *is* froward and strange: but *as for* the pure, his work *is* right.

9 *It is* better to dwell in a corner of the house top, than with [4]a brawling woman in [5]a wide house.

10 [c]The soul of the wicked desireth evil: his neighbour [6]findeth no favour in his eyes.

11 When the scorner is punished, the simple is made wise: and when the wise is instructed, he receiveth knowledge.

12 [d]The righteous *man* wisely considereth the house of the wicked: *but God* [e]overthroweth the wicked for *their* wickedness.

13 [f]Whoso stoppeth his ears at the cry of the poor, he also shall cry himself, but shall not be heard.

14 A gift in secret pacifieth anger: and a reward in the bosom strong wrath.

15 *It is* joy to the just to do judgment: but destruction *shall be* to the workers of iniquity.

16 The man that wandereth out of the way of understanding shall remain in the congregation of the dead.

17 He that loveth [7]pleasure *shall be* a poor man: he that loveth wine and oil shall not be rich.

18 [g]The wicked *shall be* a ransom for the righteous, and the transgressor for the upright.

19 *It is* better to dwell [8]in the wilderness, than with a contentious and an angry woman.

20 [h]*There is* treasure to be desired and oil in the dwelling of the wise; but a foolish man spendeth it up.

21 [i]He that followeth after righteousness and mercy findeth life, righteousness, and honour.

22 A wise *man* scaleth the city of the mighty, and casteth down the strength of the confidence thereof.

23 Whoso keepeth his mouth and his tongue keepeth his soul from troubles.

24 Proud *and* haughty scorner *is* his name, who dealeth [9]in proud wrath.

25 The desire of the slothful killeth him; for his hands refuse to labour.

26 He coveteth greedily all the day long: but the righteous giveth and spareth not.

27 The sacrifice of the wicked *is* abomination: how much more, *when* he bringeth it [10]with a wicked mind?

28 [11]A false witness shall perish: but the man that heareth speaketh constantly.

29 A wicked man hardeneth his face: but *as for* the upright, he [12]directeth his way.

30 *There is* no wisdom nor understanding nor counsel against the LORD.

31 The horse *is* prepared against the day of battle: but [13]safety *is* of the LORD.

22

A *good* name *is* rather to be chosen than great riches, *and* [1]loving favour rather than silver and gold.

2 [a]The rich and poor meet together: the LORD *is* the maker of them all.

3 [b]A prudent *man* forseeth the evil, and hideth himself: but the simple pass on, and are punished.

4 [2]By humility *and* the fear of the LORD *are* riches, and honour, and life.

5 Thorns *and* snares *are* in the way of the froward: [c]he that doth keep his soul shall be far from them.

6 [3]Train up a child [4]in the way he should go: and when he is old, he will not depart from it.

7 The rich ruleth over the poor, and the borrower *is* servant [5]to the lender.

8 [d]He that soweth iniquity shall reap vanity: [6]and the rod of his anger shall fail.

9 [7]He that hath a bountiful eye shall be blessed; for he giveth of his bread to the poor.

10 Cast out the scorner, and contention shall go out; yea, strife and reproach shall cease.

11 He that loveth pureness of heart, [8]*for* the grace of his lips the king *shall be* his friend.

12 The eyes of the LORD preserve knowledge, and he overthroweth [9]the words of the transgressor.

13 The slothful *man* saith, *There is* a lion without, I shall be slain in the streets.

14 [e]The mouth of strange women *is* a deep pit: he that is abhorred of the LORD shall fall therein.

15 Foolishness *is* bound in the heart of a child; *but* the rod of correction shall drive it far from him.

16 [f]He that oppresseth the poor to increase his *riches, and* he that giveth to the rich, *shall* surely *come* to want.

17 Bow down thine ear, and hear the words of the wise, and apply thine heart unto my knowledge.

18 For *it is* a pleasant thing if thou keep them [10]within thee; they shall withal be fitted in thy lips.

19 That thy trust may be in the LORD, I have made known to thee this day, [11]even to thee.

20 Have not I written to thee excellent things in counsels and knowledge,

21 That I might make thee know the certainty of the words of truth; [g]that thou mightest answer the words of truth [12]to them that send unto thee?

22 Rob not the poor, because he *is* poor: [h]neither oppress the afflicted in the gate:

23 For the LORD will plead their cause, and spoil the soul of those that spoiled them.

24 Make no friendship with an angry man; and with a furious man thou shalt not go:

25 Lest thou learn his ways, and get a snare to thy soul.

---

7 [3]saw them, or, dwell with them
9 [4]a woman of contentions [5]an house of society
10 [c]Jas. 4.5 [6]is not favoured
12 [d]1 Cor. 10.10 [e]Rom. 2.8
13 [f]Ps. 58.4;
17 [7]Or, sport
18 [g]Isa. 43.3-4
19 [8]in the land of the desert
20 [h]Ps. 112.3;
21 [i]1 Cor. 15.58
24 [9]in the wrath of pride
27 [10]in wickedness
28 [11]A witness of lies
29 [12]Or, considereth
31 [13]Or, victory

CHAPTER 22
1 [1]Or, favour is better than, etc
2 [a]Ps. 49.1-2
3 [b]Isa. 26.20
4 [2]Or, The reward of humility, etc
5 [c]1 John 5.18
6 [3]Or, Catechise [4]in his way
7 [5]to the man that lendeth
8 [d]Job 4.8; [6]Or, and with the rod of his anger he shall be consumed
9 [7]Good of eye
11 [8]Or, and hath grace in his lips
12 [9]Or, the matters
14 [e]ch. 2.16;
16 [f]Job 20.19-20-23;
18 [10]in thy belly
19 [11]Or, trust thou also
21 [g]1 Pet. 3.15 [12]Or, to those that send thee
22 [h]Mal. 3.5

26 Be not thou *one* of them that strike hands, *or* of them that are sureties for debts.

27 If thou hast nothing to pay, why should he take away thy bed from under thee?

28 [l]Remove not the ancient [13]landmark, which thy fathers have set.

29 Seest thou a man [j]diligent in his business? he shall stand before kings; he shall not stand before [14]mean *men.*

23 When thou sittest to eat with a ruler, consider diligently what *is* before thee:

2 And put a knife to thy throat, if thou *be* a man given to appetite.

3 Be not desirous of his dainties: for they *are* deceitful meat.

4 [a]Labour not to be rich: [b]cease from thine own wisdom.

5 [1]Wilt thou set thine eyes upon that which is not? for *riches* certainly make themselves wings; they fly away as an eagle toward heaven.

6 [c]Eat thou not the bread of *him that hath* [d]an evil eye, neither desire thou his dainty meats:

7 For as he thinketh in his heart, so *is* he: Eat and drink, saith he to thee; but his heart *is* not with thee.

8 The morsel *which* thou hast eaten shalt thou vomit up, and lose thy sweet words.

9 [e]Speak not in the ears of a fool: for he will despise the wisdom of thy words.

10 Remove not the old [2]landmark; and enter not into the fields of the fatherless:

11 [f]For their redeemer *is* mighty; he shall plead their cause with thee.

12 Apply thine heart unto instruction, and thine ears to the words of knowledge.

13 Withhold not correction from the child: for *if* thou beatest him with the rod, he shall not die.

14 Thou shalt beat him with the rod, and [g]shalt deliver his soul from hell.

15 My son, if thine heart be wise, my heart shall rejoice, [3]even mine.

16 Yea, my reins shall rejoice, when thy lips speak right things.

17 Let not thine heart envy sinners: but *be thou* in the fear of the LORD all the day long.

18 [h]For surely there is an [4]end; and thine expectation shall not be cut off.

19 Hear thou, my son, and be wise, and guide thine heart in the way.

20 [i]Be not among winebibbers; among riotous eaters [5]of flesh:

21 For the drunkard and the glutton shall come to poverty: and drowsiness shall clothe *a man* with rags.

22 [j]Hearken unto thy father that begat thee, and despise not thy mother when she is old.

23 [k]Buy the truth, and sell *it* not; *also* wisdom, and instruction, and understanding.

24 The father of the righteous shall greatly rejoice: and he that begetteth a wise *child* shall have joy of him.

25 Thy father and thy mother shall be glad, and she that bare thee shall rejoice.

26 My son, give me thine heart, and let thine eyes observe my ways.

27 For a whore *is* a deep ditch; and a strange woman *is* a narrow pit.

28 She also lieth in wait [6]as *for* a prey, and increaseth the transgressors among men.

29 [l]Who hath woe? who hath sorrow? who hath contentions? who hath babbling? who hath wounds without cause? who hath redness of eyes?

30 They that tarry long at the wine; they that go to seek mixed wine.

31 Look not thou upon the wine when it is red, when it giveth his colour in the cup, *when* it moveth itself aright.

32 At the last it biteth like a serpent, and stingeth like [7]an adder.

33 Thine eyes shall behold strange women, and thine heart shall utter perverse things.

34 Yea, thou shalt be as he that lieth down [8]in the midst of the sea, or as he that lieth upon the top of a mast.

35 [m]They have stricken me, *shalt thou say, and* I was not sick; they have beaten me, *and* [9]I felt *it* not: [n]when shall I awake? I will seek it yet again.

24 Be not thou envious against evil men, neither desire to be with them.

2 For their heart studieth destruction, and their lips talk of mischief.

3 Through wisdom is an house builded; and by understanding it is established:

4 And by knowledge shall the chambers be filled with all precious and pleasant riches.

5 A wise man [1]*is* strong; yea, a man of knowledge [2]increaseth strength.

6 For by wise counsel thou shalt make thy war: and in multitude of counsellers *there is* safety.

7 Wisdom *is* too high for a fool: he openeth not his mouth in the gate.

8 He that deviseth to do evil shall be called a mischievous person.

9 [a]The thought of foolishness *is* sin: and the scorner *is* an abomination to men.

10 *If* thou faint in the day of adversity, thy strength *is* [3]small.

11 [b]If thou forbear to deliver *them that are* drawn unto death, and *those that are* ready to be slain;

12 If thou sayest, Behold, we knew it not; doth not he that pondereth the heart consider *it?* and he that keepeth thy soul, doth *not* he know *it?* and shall *not* he render to *every* man [c]according to his works?

13 My son, eat thou honey, because *it is* good; and the honeycomb, *which is* sweet [4]to thy taste:

14 So *shall* the knowledge of wisdom *be* unto thy soul: when thou hast found *it,* then there shall be a reward, and thy expectation shall not be cut off.

---

28 [l]Deut. 19.14 [13]Or, bound
29 [j]1 Ki. 11.28; ch. 10.4; Eccl. 9.10; Matt. 25.21; Rom. 12.11 [14]obscure men

CHAPTER 23
4 [a]ch. 28.20; 1 Tim. 6.9 [b]ch. 3.5; Rom. 12.16
5 [1]Wilt thou cause thine eyes to fly upon
6 [c]Ps. 141.4 [d]Deut. 15.9; Mark 7.22
9 [e]Matt. 7.6
10 [2]Or, bound
11 [f]Job 31.21; Jer. 50.34
14 [g]1 Cor. 5.5
15 [3]Or, even I will rejoice
18 [h]Luke 16.25 [4]Or, reward
20 [i]Isa. 5.22; Eph. 5.18 [5]of their flesh
22 [j]Eph. 6.1
23 [k]Matt. 13.44
28 [6]Or, as a robber
29 [l]1 Ki. 20.16; Eph. 5.18
32 [7]Or, a cockatrice
34 [8]in the heart of the sea
35 [m]ch. 27.22; Jer. 5.3 [9]I knew it not [n]Deut. 29.19; 2 Pet. 2.22

CHAPTER 24
5 [1]is in strength [2]strengtheneth might
9 [a]Gen. 6.5; 2 Cor. 10.5
10 [3]narrow
11 [b]Isa. 58.6-7; 1 John 3.16
12 [c]Job 34.11; Rev. 2.23
13 [4]upon thy palate

15 Lay not wait, O wicked *man,* against the dwelling of the righteous; spoil not his resting place:

16 [d]For a just *man* falleth seven times, and riseth up again: but the wicked shall fall into mischief.

17 Rejoice not when thine enemy falleth, and let not thine heart be glad when he stumbleth:

18 Lest the LORD see *it,* and [5]it displease him, and he turn away his wrath from him.

19 [6]Fret not thyself because of evil *men,* neither be thou envious at the wicked;

20 For [e]there shall be no reward to the evil *man;* the [7]candle of the wicked shall be put out.

21 My son, [f]fear thou the LORD and the king: *and* meddle not with [8]them that are given to change:

22 For their calamity shall rise suddenly; and who knoweth the ruin of them both?

23 These *things* also *belong* to the wise. [g]*It is* not good to have respect of persons in judgment.

24 [h]He that saith unto the wicked, Thou *art* righteous; him shall the people curse, nations shall abhor him:

25 But to them that rebuke *him* shall be delight, and [9]a good blessing shall come upon them.

26 *Every man* shall kiss *his* lips [10]that giveth a right answer.

27 Prepare thy work without, and make it fit for thyself in the field; and afterwards build thine house.

28 [i]Be not a witness against thy neighbour without cause; and deceive *not* with thy lips.

29 [j]Say not, I will do so to him as he hath done to me: I will render to the man according to his work.

30 I went by the field of the slothful, and by the vineyard of the man void of understanding;

31 And, lo, [k]it was all grown over with thorns, *and* nettles had covered the face thereof, and the stone wall thereof was broken down.

32 Then I saw, *and* [11]considered *it* well: I looked upon *it, and* received instruction.

33 *Yet* a little sleep, a little slumber, a little folding of the hands to sleep:

34 So shall thy poverty come *as* one that travelleth; and thy want as [12]an armed man.

25 These *are* also proverbs of Sŏl'o-mon, which the men of Hĕz-e-kī'ah king of Jū'dah copied out.

2 [a]*It is* the glory of God to conceal a thing: but the honour of kings *is* [b]to search out a matter.

3 The heaven for height, and the earth for depth, and the heart of kings [1]*is* unsearchable.

4 Take away the dross from the silver, and there shall come forth a vessel for the finer.

5 Take away the wicked *from* before the king, and his throne shall be established in righteousness.

6 [2]Put not forth thyself in the presence of the king, and stand not in the place of great *men:*

7 For better *it is* that it be said unto thee, Come up hither; than that thou shouldest be put lower in the presence of the prince whom thine eyes have seen.

8 [c]Go not forth hastily to strive, lest *thou know not* what to do in the end thereof, when thy neighbour hath put thee to shame.

9 [d]Debate thy cause with thy neighbour *himself;* and [3]discover not a secret to another:

10 Lest he that heareth *it* put thee to shame, and thine infamy turn not away.

11 A word [4]fitly spoken *is like* apples of gold in pictures of silver.

12 *As* an earring of gold, and an ornament of fine gold, *so is* a wise reprover upon an obedient ear.

13 As the cold of snow in the time of harvest, *so is* a faithful messenger to them that send him: for he refresheth the soul of his masters.

14 Whoso boasteth himself [5]of a false gift *is like* [e]clouds and wind without rain.

15 By long forbearing is a prince persuaded, and a soft tongue breaketh the bone.

16 Hast thou found honey? eat so much as is sufficient for thee, lest thou be filled therewith, and vomit it.

17 [6]Withdraw thy foot from thy neighbour's house; lest he be [7]weary of thee, and *so* hate thee.

18 A man that beareth false witness against his neighbour [f]*is* a maul, and a sword, and a sharp arrow.

19 Confidence in an [g]unfaithful man in time of trouble *is like* a broken tooth, and a foot out of joint.

20 *As* he that taketh away a garment in cold weather, *and as* vinegar upon nitre, [h]so *is* he that singeth songs to an heavy heart.

21 [i]If thine enemy be hungry, give him bread to eat; and if he be thirsty, give him water to drink:

22 For thou shalt heap coals of fire upon his head, [j]and the LORD shall reward thee.

23 [8]The north wind driveth away rain: so *doth* an angry countenance a backbiting tongue.

24 *It is* better to dwell in the corner of the house top, than with a brawling woman and in a wide house.

25 *As* cold waters to a thirsty soul, so *is* good news from a far country.

26 [k]A righteous man falling down before the wicked *is as* a troubled fountain, and a corrupt spring.

27 *It is* not good to eat much honey: [l]so *for men* to search their own glory *is not* glory.

28 He that *hath* no rule over his own spirit *is like* a city *that is* broken down, *and* without walls.

26 As snow in summer, and as rain in harvest, [a]so honour is not seemly for a fool.

16 [d]Ps. 34.19; Mic. 7.8
18 [5]it be evil in his eyes
19 [6]Or, Keep not company with the wicked
20 [e]Ps. 11.6; Isa. 3.11
[7]Or, lamp
21 [f]Rom. 13.7; 1 Pet. 2.17
[8]changers
23 [g]Deut. 1.17;
24 [h]Isa. 5.23
25 [9]a blessing of good
26 [10]that answereth right words
28 [i]Eph. 4.25
29 [j]Matt. 5.39
31 [k]Jer. 4.3;
32 [11]set my heart
34 [12]a man of shield

CHAPTER 25
2 [a]Rom. 11.33
[b]Job 29.16
3 [1]there is no searching
6 [2]Set not out thy glory
8 [c]Matt. 5.25
9 [d]Matt. 18.15
[3]Or, discover not the secret of another
11 [4]spoken upon his wheels
14 [5]in a gift of falsehood
[e]Jude 12
17 [6]Or, Let thy foot be seldom in thy neighbour's house
[7]full of thee
18 [f]Ps. 140.3
19 [g]Job 6.14-20;
20 [h]Dan. 6.18
21 [i]Matt. 5.44
22 [j]2 Sam. 16.12
23 [8]Or, The north wind bringeth forth rain: so doth a backbiting tongue an angry countenance
26 [k]Mic. 7.8
27 [l]Luke 14.11

CHAPTER 26
1 [a]Ps. 12.8

2 As the bird by wandering, as the swallow by flying, so the curse causeless shall not come.

3 A whip for the horse, a bridle for the ass, and a rod for the fool's back.

4 Answer not a fool according to his folly, lest thou also be like unto him.

5 Answer a fool according to his folly, lest he be wise in [1]his own conceit.

6 He that sendeth a message by the hand of a fool cutteth off the feet, *and* drinketh [2]damage.

7 The legs of the lame [3]are not equal: so *is* a parable in the mouth of fools.

8 [4]As he that bindeth a stone in a sling, so *is* he that giveth honour to a fool.

9 *As* a thorn goeth up into the hand of a drunkard, so *is* a parable in the mouth of fools.

10 [5]The great *God* that formed all *things* both rewardeth the fool, and rewardeth transgressors.

11 As a dog returneth to his vomit, *so* a fool [6]returneth to his folly.

12 Seest thou a man wise in his own conceit? *there is* more hope of a fool than of him.

13 The slothful *man* saith, *There is* a lion in the way; a lion *is* in the streets.

14 *As* the door turneth upon his hinges, so *doth* the slothful upon his bed.

15 The slothful hideth his hand in *his* bosom; [7]it grieveth him to bring it again to his mouth.

16 The sluggard *is* wiser in his own conceit than seven men that can render a reason.

17 He that passeth by, *and* [8]meddleth with strife *belonging* not to him, *is like* one that taketh a dog by the ears.

18 As a mad *man* who casteth [9]firebrands, arrows, and death,

19 So *is* the man *that* deceiveth his neighbour, and saith, Am not I in sport?

20 [10]Where no wood is, *there* the fire goeth out: so where *there is* no [11]talebearer, the strife [12]ceaseth.

21 *As* coals *are* to burning coals, and wood to fire; so *is* a contentious man to kindle strife.

22 The words of a talebearer *are* as wounds, and they go down into the [13]innermost parts of the belly.

23 Burning lips and a wicked heart *are like* a potsherd covered with silver dross.

24 He that hateth [14]dissembleth with his lips, and layeth up deceit within him;

25 When he [15]speaketh fair, believe him not: for *there are* seven abominations in his heart.

26 [16]*Whose* hatred is covered by deceit, his wickedness shall be shewed before the *whole* congregation.

27 Whoso diggeth a pit shall fall therein: and he that rolleth a stone, it will return upon him.

28 A lying tongue hateth *those that are* afflicted by it; and a flattering mouth worketh ruin.

27 Boast [a]not thyself of [1]to morrow; for thou knowest not what a day may bring forth.

2 Let another man praise thee, and not thine own mouth; a stranger, and not thine own lips.

3 A stone *is* [2]heavy, and the sand weighty; but a [b]fool's wrath *is* heavier than them both.

4 [3]Wrath *is* cruel, and anger *is* outrageous; but [c]who *is* able to stand before [4]envy?

5 [d]Open rebuke *is* better than secret love.

6 Faithful *are* the wounds of a friend; but the kisses of an enemy *are* [5]deceitful.

7 The full soul [6]loatheth an honeycomb; but to the hungry soul every bitter thing is sweet.

8 As a bird that [e]wandereth from her nest, so *is* a man that wandereth from his place.

9 Ointment and perfume rejoice the heart: so *doth* the sweetness of a man's friend [7]by hearty counsel.

10 Thine own friend, and thy father's friend, forsake not; neither go into thy brother's house in the day of thy calamity: *for* better *is* a neighbour *that is* near than a brother far off.

11 My son, be wise, and make my heart glad, [f]that I may answer him that reproacheth me.

12 A prudent *man* [g]foreseeth the evil, *and* hideth himself; *but* the simple pass on, *and* are punished.

13 Take his garment that is surety for a stranger, and take a pledge of him for a strange woman.

14 He that [h]blesseth his friend with a loud voice, rising early in the morning, it shall be counted a curse to him.

15 A continual dropping in a very rainy day and a contentious woman are alike.

16 Whosoever hideth her hideth the wind, and the ointment of his right hand, *which* bewrayeth *itself*.

17 Iron sharpeneth iron; so a man sharpeneth the countenance of his friend.

18 Whoso keepeth the fig tree shall eat the fruit thereof: [i]so he that waiteth on his master shall be honoured.

19 As in water face *answereth* to face, so the heart of man to man.

20 [j]Hell and destruction are [8]never full; so the eyes of man are never satisfied.

21 *As* the fining pot for silver, and the furnace for gold; so *is* a man to his praise.

22 Though thou shouldest bray a fool in a mortar among wheat with a pestle, *yet* will not his foolishness depart from him.

23 Be thou diligent to know the state of thy flocks, *and* [9]look well to thy herds.

24 For [10]riches *are* not for ever: and doth the crown *endure* [11]to every generation?

5 [1]his own eyes
6 [2]Or, violence
7 [3]are lifted up
8 [4]Or, As he that putteth a precious stone in an heap of stones
10 [5]Or, A great man grieveth all, and he hireth the fool, he hireth also transgressors
11 [6]iterateth his folly
15 [7]Or, he is weary
17 [8]Or, is enraged
18 [9]flames, or, sparks
20 [10]Without wood
[11]Or, whisperer
[12]is silent
[13]chambers
24 [14]Or, is known
25 [15]maketh his voice gracious
26 [16]Or, hatred is covered in secret

CHAPTER 27
1 [a]Luke 12.19
[1]to morrow day
3 [2]heaviness
[b]Esth. 1.12
4 [3]Wrath is cruelty, and anger an overflowing
[c]1 John 3.12
[4]Or, jealousy
5 [d]Gal. 2.14
6 [5]Or, earnest, or, frequent
7 [6]treadeth under foot
8 [e]Job 39.14
9 [7]from the counsel of the soul
11 [f]Ps. 119.42
12 [g]Isa. 32.2
14 [h]Ps. 12.2
18 [i]Deut. 20.6;
20 [j]ch. 30.15-16;
[8]not
23 [9]set thy heart
24 [10]strength
[11]to generation and generation

25 The hay appeareth, and the tender grass sheweth itself, and herbs of
the mountains are gathered.
26 The lambs *are* for thy clothing,
and the goats *are* the price of the field.
27 And *thou shalt have* goats' milk
enough for thy food, for the food of thy
household, and *for* the [12]maintenance
for thy maidens.

28 The wicked flee when no man
pursueth: but the righteous are
bold as a lion.
2 For the transgression of a land
many *are* the princes thereof: but [1]by a
man of understanding *and* knowledge
the state *thereof* shall be prolonged.
3 [a]A poor man that oppresseth the
poor *is like* a sweeping rain [2]which
leaveth no food.
4 They that forsake the law praise
the wicked: [b]but such as keep the law
contend with them.
5 Evil men understand not judgment: but [c]they that seek the LORD understand all *things*.
6 Better *is* the poor that walketh in
his uprightness, than *he that is* perverse *in his* ways, though he *be* rich.
7 Whoso keepeth the law *is* a wise
son: but he that [3]is a companion of riotous *men* shameth his father.
8 He that by usury and [4]unjust gain
increaseth his substance, he shall
gather it for him that will pity the poor.
9 [d]He that turneth away his ear from
hearing the law, [e]even his prayer *shall
be* abomination.
10 Whoso causeth the righteous to
go astray in an evil way, he shall
fall himself into his own pit: [f]but
the upright shall have good *things* in
possession.
11 The rich man *is* wise [5]in his own
conceit; but the poor that hath understanding searcheth him out.
12 When righteous *men* do rejoice,
there is great glory: but when the
wicked rise, a man is [6]hidden.
13 He that covereth his sins shall
not prosper: but whoso confesseth and
forsaketh *them* shall have mercy.
14 Happy *is* the man that feareth
alway: but he that hardeneth his heart
shall fall into mischief.
15 *As* a roaring lion, and a ranging
bear; [g]*so is* a wicked ruler over the
poor people.
16 The prince that wanteth understanding *is* also a great oppressor: *but*
he that hateth covetousness shall prolong *his* days.
17 A man that doeth violence to the
blood of *any* person shall flee to the
pit; let no man stay him.
18 Whoso walketh uprightly shall
be saved: but *he that is* perverse *in his*
ways shall fall at once.
19 He that tilleth his land shall have
plenty of bread: but he that followeth
after vain *persons* shall have poverty
enough.
20 A faithful man shall abound with
blessings: but he that maketh haste to
be rich shall not be [7]innocent.
21 To have respect of persons *is* not
good: for for [h]a piece of bread *that*
man will transgress.
22 [8]He that hasteth to be rich *hath*
an evil eye, and considereth not that
poverty shall come upon him.
23 He that rebuketh a man afterwards shall find more favour than he
that flattereth with the tongue.
24 Whoso robbeth his father or his
mother, and saith, *It is* no transgression: the same *is* the companion of [9]a
destroyer.
25 He that is of a proud heart stirreth up strife: [i]but he that putteth his
trust in the LORD shall be made fat.
26 He that trusteth in his own heart
is a fool: but whoso walketh wisely, he
shall be delivered.
27 He that giveth unto the poor shall
not lack: but he that hideth his eyes
shall have many a curse.
28 When the wicked rise, men hide
themselves: but when they perish, the
righteous increase.

29 He, [1]that being often reproved
hardeneth *his* neck, shall suddenly be destroyed, and that without
remedy.
2 When the righteous are [2]in authority, the people rejoice: but when the
wicked beareth rule, the people mourn.
3 [a]Whoso loveth wisdom rejoiceth
his father: but he that keepeth company
with harlots spendeth *his* substance.
4 The king by judgment establisheth the land: but [3]he that receiveth
gifts overthroweth it.
5 A man that flattereth his neighbour spreadeth a net for his feet.
6 In the transgression of an evil man
there is a snare: but the righteous doth
sing and rejoice.
7 [b]The righteous considereth the
cause of the poor: *but* the wicked regardeth not to know *it*.
8 Scornful men [4]bring a city into a
snare: but wise *men* turn away wrath.
9 *If* a wise man contendeth with a
foolish man, whether he rage or laugh,
there is no rest.
10 [5]The bloodthirsty hate the upright: but the just seek his soul.
11 A fool uttereth all his mind: but a
wise *man* keepeth it in till afterwards.
12 If a ruler hearken to lies, all his
servants *are* wicked.
13 The poor and [6]the deceitful man
meet together: [c]the LORD lighteneth
both their eyes.
14 The king that [d]faithfully judgeth
the poor, his throne shall be established for ever.
15 The rod and reproof give wisdom: but a child left *to himself* bringeth his mother to shame.
16 When the wicked are multiplied,
transgression increaseth: but [e]the righteous shall see their fall.
17 [f]Correct thy son, and he shall
give thee rest; yea, he shall give delight
unto thy soul.
18 [g]Where *there is* no vision, the
people [7]perish: but [h]he that keepeth
the law, happy *is* he.

27 [12]life

CHAPTER 28

2 [1]Or, by men of understanding and wisdom shall they likewise be prolonged
3 [a]Matt. 18.28
[2]without food
4 [b]1 Ki. 18.18; 1 Tim. 5.20
5 [c]John 7.17
7 [3]Or, feedeth gluttons
8 [4]by increase
9 [d]2 Tim. 4.3
[e]Ps. 66.18; Luke 13.25-27
10 [f]Ps. 34.9-10; 1 Cor. 3.22-23
11 [5]in his eyes
12 [6]Or, sought for
15 [g]Matt. 2.16
20 [7]Or, unpunished
21 [h]Ezek. 13.19
22 [8]Or, He that hath an evil eye hasteth to be rich
24 [9]a man destroying
25 [i]1 Tim. 6.6

CHAPTER 29

1 [1]A man of reproofs
2 [2]Or, increased
3 [a]1 Ki. 1.48; Phil. 2.22
4 [3]a man of oblations
7 [b]Job 29.16
8 [4]Or, set a city on fire
10 [5]Men of blood
13 [6]Or, the usurer
[c]Matt. 5.45
14 [d]Ps. 72.2
16 [e]Ps. 37.36
17 [f]ch. 13.24
18 [g]1 Sam. 3.1;
[7]Or, is made naked
[h]John 13.17

19 A servant will not be corrected by words: for though he understand he will not answer.

20 Seest thou a man *that is* hasty [8]in his words? *there is* more hope of a fool than of him.

21 He that delicately bringeth up his servant from a child shall have him become *his* son at the length.

22 An angry man stirreth up strife, and a furious man aboundeth in transgression.

23 [i]A man's pride shall bring him low: but honour shall uphold the humble in spirit.

24 Whoso is partner with a thief hateth his own soul: [j]he heareth cursing, and bewrayeth *it* not.

25 [k]The fear of man bringeth a snare: but whoso putteth his trust in the LORD [9]shall be safe.

26 Many seek [10]the ruler's favour; but *every* man's judgment *cometh* from the LORD.

27 An unjust man *is* an abomination to the just: and *he that is* upright in the way *is* abomination to the wicked.

30 The words of Ā'gûr the son of Jā'keh, *even* the prophecy: the man spake unto Ĭth'ĭ-el, even unto Ĭth'ĭ-el and Ū'cal,

2 [a]Surely I *am* more brutish than *any* man, and have not the understanding of a man.

3 I neither learned wisdom, nor [1]have the knowledge of the holy.

4 [b]Who hath ascended up into heaven, or descended? [c]who hath gathered the wind in his fists? who hath bound the waters in a garment? who hath established all the ends of the earth? what *is* his name, and what *is* his son's name, if thou canst tell?

5 [d]Every word of God *is* [2]*pure:* [e]*he is* a shield unto them that put their trust in him.

6 [f]Add thou not unto his words, lest he reprove thee, and thou be found a liar.

7 Two *things* have I required of thee; [3]deny me *them* not before I die:

8 Remove far from me vanity and lies: give me neither poverty nor riches; [g]feed me with food [4]convenient for me:

9 [h]Lest I be full, and [5]deny *thee,* and say, Who *is* the LORD? or lest I be poor, and steal, and take the name of my God *in vain.*

10 [6]Accuse not a servant unto his master, lest he curse thee, and thou be found guilty.

11 *There is* a generation *that* curseth their father, and doth not bless their mother.

12 *There is* a generation [i]*that are* pure in their own eyes, and *yet* is not washed from their filthiness.

13 *There is* a generation, O how lofty are their eyes! and their eyelids are lifted up.

14 [j]*There is* a generation, whose teeth *are as* swords, and their jaw teeth *as* knives, [k]to devour the poor from off the earth, and the needy from *among* men.

15 The horseleach hath two daughters, *crying,* Give, give. There are three *things that* are never satisfied, *yea,* four *things* say not, [7]*It is* enough:

16 [l]The grave; and the barren womb; the earth *that* is not filled with water; and the fire *that* saith not, *It is* enough.

17 [m]The eye *that* mocketh at *his* father, and despiseth to obey *his* mother, the ravens of [8]the valley shall pick it out, and the young eagles shall eat it.

18 There be three *things which* are too wonderful for me, yea, four which I know not:

19 The way of an eagle in the air; the way of a serpent upon a rock; the way of a ship in the [9]midst of the sea; and the way of a man with a maid.

20 Such *is* the way of an adulterous woman; she eateth, and wipeth her mouth, and saith, I have done no wickedness.

21 For three *things* the earth is disquieted, and for four *which* it cannot bear:

22 For [n]a servant when he reigneth; and a fool when he is filled with meat;

23 For an odious *woman* when she is married; and an handmaid that is heir to her mistress.

24 There be four *things which are* little upon the earth, but they *are* [10]*exceeding wise:*

25 [o]The ants *are* a people not strong, yet they prepare their meat in the summer;

26 [p]The conies *are but* a feeble folk, yet make they their houses in the rocks;

27 The locusts have no king, yet go they forth all of them [11]by bands;

28 The spider taketh hold with her hands, and is in kings' palaces.

29 There be three *things* which go well, yea, four are comely in going:

30 A [12]lion *which is* strongest among beasts, and turneth not away for any;

31 A [13] [14]greyhound; an he goat also; and a king, against whom *there is* no rising up.

32 If thou hast done foolishly in lifting up thyself, or if thou hast thought evil, [q]*lay* thine hand upon thy mouth.

33 Surely the churning of milk bringeth forth butter, and the wringing of the nose bringeth forth blood: so the forcing of wrath bringeth forth strife.

31 The words of king Lĕm'u-el, the [1]prophecy that his mother taught him.

2 What, my son? and what, the son of my womb? and what, the son of my vows?

3 Give not thy strength unto women, nor thy ways [a]to that which destroyeth kings.

4 [b]*It is* not for kings, O Lĕm'u-el, *it is* not for kings to drink wine; nor for princes strong drink:

5 [c]Lest they drink, and forget the law, and [2]pervert the judgment [3]of any of the afflicted.

6 [d]Give strong drink unto him that is ready to perish, and wine unto those that be [4]of heavy hearts.

---

20 [8]Or, in his matters
23 [i]Isa. 2.11-12; Luke 14.11
24 [j]Lev. 5.1
25 [k]Gen. 12.12 [9]shall be set on high
26 [10]the face of a ruler

CHAPTER 30
2 [a]Ps. 73.22
3 [1]know
4 [b]John 3.13 [c]Job 38.4
5 [d]Ps. 12.6 [2]purified [e]Ps. 18.30; Ps. 84.11
6 [f]Deut. 4.2; Rev. 22.18
7 [3]withhold not from me
8 [g]Matt. 6.11 [4]of my allowance
9 [h]Deut. 8.12; Hos. 13.6 [5]belie thee
10 [6]Hurt not with thy tongue
12 [i]Isa. 65.5; Tit. 1.15-16
14 [j]Job 29.17 [k]Ps. 14.4; Amos 8.4
15 [7]Wealth
16 [l]ch. 27.20; Hab. 2.5
17 [m]Gen. 9.22; [8]Or, the brook
19 [9]heart
22 [n]ch. 19.10
24 [10]wise, made wise
25 [o]ch. 6.6
26 [p]Lev. 11.5
27 [11]gathered together
30 [12]mighty old lion
31 [13]Or, horse [14]girt in the loins
32 [q]Eccl. 8.3

CHAPTER 31
1 [1]burden
3 [a]Deut. 17.17;
4 [b]Eccl. 10.17
5 [c]Hos. 4.11 [2]alter [3]of all the sons of affliction
6 [d]Ps. 104.15 [4]bitter of soul

7 Let him drink, and forget his poverty, and remember his misery no more.
8 Open thy mouth for the dumb in
the cause of all [5]such as are appointed
to destruction.
9 Open thy mouth, [e]judge righteously, and [f]plead the cause of the
poor and needy.
10 ¶ Who can find a virtuous woman?
for her price *is* far above rubies.
11 The heart of her husband doth
safely trust in her, so that he shall have
no need of spoil.
12 She will do him good and not evil
all the days of her life.
13 She seeketh wool, and flax, and
worketh willingly with her hands.
14 She is like the merchants' ships;
she bringeth her food from afar.
15 [g]She riseth also while it is yet
night, and [h]giveth meat to her household, and a portion to her maidens.
16 She considereth a field, and [6]buy-
eth it: with the fruit of her hands she
planteth a vineyard.
17 She girdeth her loins with
strength, and strengtheneth her arms.
18 [7]She perceiveth that her merchandise *is* good: her candle goeth not out
by night.
19 She layeth her hands to the spin-
dle, and her hands hold the distaff.
20 [8]She stretcheth out her hand to
the poor; yea, she reacheth forth her
hands to the needy.
21 She is not afraid of the snow for
her household: for all her household
are clothed with [9]scarlet.
22 She maketh herself coverings of
tapestry; her clothing *is* silk and purple.
23 [i]Her husband is known in the
gates, when he sitteth among the elders of the land.
24 She maketh fine linen, and selleth *it;* and delivereth girdles unto the
merchant.
25 Strength and [j]honour *are* her
clothing; and she shall rejoice in time
to come.
26 She openeth her mouth with wisdom: and in her tongue *is* the law of
kindness.
27 [k]She looketh well to the ways
of her household, and eateth not the
bread of idleness.
28 [l]Her children arise up, and call
her blessed; her husband *also,* and he
praiseth her.
29 Many daughters [10]have done vir-
tuously, but thou excellest them all.
30 Favour *is* deceitful, and beauty *is*
vain: *but* a woman *that* [m]*feareth the*
LORD, she shall be praised.
31 Give her of the fruit of her hands;
and let her own works praise her in the
gates.

8 [5]the sons of destruction
9 [e]Lev. 19.15; Deut. 1.16; 2 Sam. 8.15; Isa. 1.17-23; Zech. 7.9; John 7.24; Heb. 1.9
[f]ch. 21.13; Isa. 1.17; Jer. 22.16
15 [g]Rom. 12.11
[h]Matt. 24.45; Luke 12.42
16 [6]taketh
18 [7]She tasteth
20 [8]She spreadeth
21 [9]Or, double garments
23 [i]Deut. 16.18; ch. 12.4
25 [j]1 Tim. 2.9-10
27 [k]ch. 14.1; 1 Tim. 5.14; 2 Tim. 3.15
28 [l]1 Ki. 2.19
29 [10]Or, have gotten riches
30 [m]Ps. 112.1

ECCLESIASTES

OR, THE PREACHER

Life's Questions

Does life with all its repetition and sorrow have meaning?
Does God really have any plan for this world?
How can I find joy in such a life as this?

God's Answers

Ecclesiastes shows us how honestly God's Word faces the world we live in. King Solomon or the Preacher, as the book calls him, reviews a life anyone would call successful and asks what it means when all he can hope for is death. He examines the large aspects of life: religion, time, work, friendship, wealth, pleasure, the relations of the sexes, morality. Each appears to be a vapor or meaningless. Ecclesiastes thus shows: repetition shows lack of meaning (1:1–11); wisdom brings no meaning (1:12–18); pleasure, wealth, wisdom, and work give no lasting meaning (2:1–26); God's plan cannot be known, so present joy is the only path (3:1–22); illustrations from politics, wealth, friendship, and religion caution one to fear God and hope for no more (4:1—5:11); wealth gives no advantage (5:8—6:12); proverbial wisdom offers no hope (7:1–14); personal morality leads nowhere (7:15–25); women lead the wrong way (7:26–29); obeying the king is necessary (8:1–9); righteousness goes unrewarded (8:10–17); death comes to all (9:1–12); wisdom cannot bring meaning in face of death (9:13—10:20); diversified action is the best plan (11:1–8); appreciation of youth is the only time of meaning (11:9—12:7); and so know all is meaningless and obey God (12:9–14).

Ecclesiastes uses the negative path to show the need for resurrection and life beyond. Jesus showed that life can be meaningful as His servant waiting for His promised resurrection.

1 The words of the Preacher, the son
of Dā'vid, king in Je-ru'sa-lĕm.
2 [a]Vanity of vanities, saith the
Preacher, vanity of vanities; [b]all *is*
vanity.
3 [c]What profit hath a man of all his
labour which he taketh under the sun?
4 *One* generation passeth away, and
another generation cometh: [d]but the
earth abideth for ever.
5 [e]The sun also ariseth, and the sun
goeth down, and [1]hasteth to his place
where he arose.
6 [f]The wind goeth toward the south,
and turneth about unto the north; it
whirleth about continually, and the
wind returneth again according to his
circuits.
7 [g]All the rivers run into the sea; yet
the sea *is* not full; unto the place from

CHAPTER 1
2 [a]Ps. 39.5
[b]Ps. 39.5-6; Rom. 8.20
3 [c]ch. 3.9
4 [d]Ps. 104.5; 2 Pet. 3.10
5 [e]Ps. 19.5
[1]panteth
6 [f]John 3.8
7 [g]Job 38.10

whence the rivers come, thither they [2]return again.

8 [h]All things *are* full of labour; man cannot utter *it*: [i]the eye is not satisfied with seeing, nor the ear filled with hearing.

9 [j]The thing that hath been, it *is* *that* which shall be; and that which is done *is* that which shall be done: and *there is* no new *thing* under the sun.

10 Is there *any* thing whereof it may be said, See, this *is* new? it hath been already of old time, which was before us.

11 *There is* no remembrance of former *things;* neither shall there be *any* remembrance of *things* that are to come with *those* that shall come after.

12 ¶ I the Preacher was king over Ĭs′ra-el in Je-ru̧′sa-lĕm.

13 And I gave my heart to seek and search out by wisdom concerning all *things* that are done under heaven: [k]this sore travail hath God given to the sons of man [3]to be exercised therewith.

14 I have seen all the works that are done under the sun; and, behold, all *is* vanity and vexation of spirit.

15 [l]*That which is* crooked cannot be made straight: and [4]that which is wanting cannot be numbered.

16 I communed with mine own heart, saying, Lo, I am come to great estate, and have gotten [m]more wisdom than all *they* that have been before me in Je-ru̧′sa-lĕm: yea, my heart [5]had great experience of wisdom and knowledge.

17 [n]And I gave my heart to know wisdom, and to know madness and folly: I perceived that this also is vexation of spirit.

18 For [o]in much wisdom *is* much grief: and he that increaseth knowledge increaseth sorrow.

2 [a]I said in mine heart, Go to now, I will prove thee with mirth, therefore enjoy pleasure: and, behold, [b]this also *is* vanity.

2 [c]I said of laughter, *It is* mad: and of mirth, What doeth it?

3 [d]I sought in mine heart [1]to give myself unto wine, yet acquainting mine heart with wisdom; and to lay hold on folly, till I might see what *was* that good for the sons of men, which they should do under the heaven [2]all the days of their life.

4 I made me great works; I builded me houses; I planted me vineyards:

5 I made me gardens and orchards, and I planted trees in them of all *kind of* fruits:

6 I made me pools of water, to water therewith the wood that bringeth forth trees:

7 I got *me* servants and maidens, and had [3]servants born in my house; also I had great possessions of great and small cattle above all that were in Je-ru̧′sa-lĕm before me:

8 [e]I gathered me also silver and gold, and the peculiar treasure of kings and of the provinces: I gat me men singers and women singers, and the delights of the sons of men, *as* [4]musical instruments, and that of all sorts.

9 So [f]I was great, and increased more than all that were before me in Je-ru̧′sa-lĕm: also my wisdom remained with me.

10 And whatsoever mine eyes desired I kept not from them, I withheld not my heart from any joy; for my heart rejoiced in all my labour: and [g]this was my portion of all my labour.

11 Then I looked on all the works that my hands had wrought, and on the labour that I had laboured to do: and, behold, all *was* vanity and vexation of spirit, and *there was* no profit under the sun.

12 ¶ And I turned myself to behold wisdom, [h]and madness, and folly: for what *can* the man *do* that cometh after the king? [5]*even* that which hath been already done.

13 Then I saw [6]that wisdom excelleth folly, as far as light excelleth darkness.

14 [i]The wise man's eyes *are* in his head; but the fool walketh in darkness: and I myself perceived also that [j]one event happeneth to them all.

15 Then said I in my heart, As it happeneth to the fool, so it [7]happeneth even to me; and why was I then more wise? Then I said in my heart, that this also *is* vanity.

16 For *there is* no remembrance of the wise more than of the fool for ever; seeing that which now *is* in the days to come shall all be forgotten. And how dieth the wise *man?* as the fool.

17 Therefore I hated life; because the work that is wrought under the sun *is* grievous unto me: for all *is* vanity and vexation of spirit.

18 ¶ Yea, I hated all my labour which I had [8]taken under the sun: because [k]I should leave it unto the man that shall be after me.

19 And who knoweth whether he shall be a wise *man* or [l]a fool? yet shall he have rule over all my labour wherein I have laboured, and wherein I have shewed myself wise under the sun. [m]This *is* also vanity.

20 Therefore I went about to cause my heart to despair of all the labour which I took under the sun.

21 For there is a man whose labour *is* in wisdom, and in knowledge, and in equity; yet to a man that hath not laboured therein shall he [9]leave it *for* his portion. This also *is* vanity and a great evil.

22 [n]For what hath man of all his labour, and of the vexation of his heart, wherein he hath laboured under the sun?

23 For all his days *are* [o]sorrows, and his travail grief; yea, his heart taketh not rest in the night. This is also vanity.

24 ¶ *There is* nothing better for a man, *than* that he should eat and drink, and *that* he [10]should make his soul enjoy good in his labour. This also I saw, that it *was* from the hand of God.

[2]return to go
8 [h]ch. 3.1
[i]Prov. 27.20
9 [j]Gen. 8.22; ch. 3.15
13 [k]Gen. 3.19; ch. 3.10
[3]Or, to afflict them
15 [l]ch. 7.13
[4]defect
16 [m]1 Ki. 3.12; ch. 2.9
[5]had seen much
17 [n]ch. 2.3; 1 Thess. 5.21
18 [o]Job 28.28; ch. 7.16; 1 Cor. 1.20

CHAPTER 2
1 [a]Ps. 10.6-11; Luke 12.19
[b]Isa. 50.11
2 [c]Prov. 14.13; ch. 7.6; Isa. 22.12-13; Amos 6.5-6
3 [d]ch. 1.17; Isa. 22.13; Amos 6.3-6; 1 Pet. 4.3
[1]to draw my flesh with wine
[2]the number of the days of their life
7 [3]sons of my house
8 [e]1 Ki. 9.28
[4]musical instrument and instruments
9 [f]ch. 1.16
10 [g]ch. 3.22
12 [h]ch. 1.17
[5]Or, in those things which have been already done
13 [6]that there is an excellency in wisdom more than in folly
14 [i]ch. 8.1
[j]ch. 9.2
15 [7]happeneth to me, even to me
18 [8]laboured
[k]Ps. 49.10
19 [l]1 Ki. 12.13
[m]1 Tim. 6.10
21 [9]give
22 [n]ch. 1.3
23 [o]Job 5.7
24 [10]Or, delight his senses

25 For who can eat, or who else can hasten *hereunto*, more than I?

26 For *God* giveth to a man that *is* good [11]in his sight wisdom, and knowledge, and joy: but to the sinner he giveth travail, to gather and to heap up, that he may give to *him that is* good before God. This also *is* vanity and vexation of spirit.

3

To every *thing there is* a season, and a [a]time to every purpose under the heaven:

2 A time [1]to be born, and [b]a time to die; a time to plant, and a time to pluck up *that which is* planted;

3 [c]A time to kill, and a time to heal; a time to break down, and a time to build up;

4 A time to weep, and a time to laugh; a time to mourn, and [d]a time to dance;

5 A time to cast away stones, and a time to gather stones together; a time to embrace, and a time [2]to refrain from embracing;

6 A time to [3]get, and a time to lose; a time to keep, and a time to cast away;

7 A time to rend, and a time to sew; [e]a time to keep silence, and a time to speak;

8 A time to love, and a time to [f]hate; a time of war, and a time of peace.

9 [g]What profit hath he that worketh in that wherein he laboureth?

10 [h]I have seen the travail, which God hath given to the sons of men to be exercised in it.

11 He [i]hath made every *thing* beautiful in his time: also he hath set the world in their heart, so that [j]no man can find out the work that God maketh from the beginning to the end.

12 I know that *there is* no good in them, but for *a man* to rejoice, and to do good in his life.

13 And also [k]that every man should eat and drink, and enjoy the good of all his labour, it *is* the gift of God.

14 I know that, whatsoever God doeth, it shall be for ever: [l]nothing can be put to it, nor any thing taken from it: and God doeth *it*, that *men* should fear before him.

15 [m]That which hath been is now; and that which is to be hath already been; and God requireth [4]that which is past.

16 ¶ And moreover [n]I saw under the sun the place of judgment, *that* wickedness *was* there; and the place of righteousness, *that* iniquity *was* there.

17 I said in mine heart, [o]God shall judge the righteous and the wicked: for *there is* a time there for every purpose and for every work.

18 I said in mine heart concerning the estate of the sons of men, [5]that God might manifest them, and that they might see that they themselves are beasts.

19 [p]For that which befalleth the sons of men befalleth beasts; even one thing befalleth them: as the one dieth, so dieth the other; yea, they have all one breath; so that a man hath no preeminence above a beast: for all *is* vanity.

20 All go unto one place; [q]all are of the dust, and all turn to dust again.

21 Who knoweth the spirit [6]of man that [7]goeth upward, and the spirit of the beast that goeth downward to the earth?

22 Wherefore I perceive that *there is* nothing better, than that a man should rejoice in his own works; for [r]that *is* his portion: for who shall bring him to see what shall be after him?

4

So I returned, and considered all the oppressions that are done under the sun: and behold the tears of *such as were* oppressed, and they had no comforter; and on the [1]side of their oppressors *there was* power; but they had no comforter.

2 [a]Wherefore I praised the dead which are already dead more than the living which are yet alive.

3 [b]Yea, better *is he* than both they, which hath not yet been, who hath not seen the evil work that is done under the sun.

4 ¶ Again, I considered all travail, and [2]every right work, that [3]for this a man is envied of his neighbour. This *is* also vanity and vexation of spirit.

5 [c]The fool foldeth his hands together, and eateth his own flesh.

6 Better *is* an handful *with* quietness, than both the hands full *with* travail and vexation of spirit.

7 ¶ Then I returned, and I saw vanity under the sun.

8 There is one *alone*, and *there is* not a second; yea, he hath neither child nor brother: yet *is there* no end of all his labour; neither is his [d]eye satisfied with riches; [e]neither *saith he*, For whom do I labour, and bereave my soul of good? This *is* also vanity, yea, it *is* a sore travail.

9 ¶ Two *are* better than one; because they have a good reward for their labour.

10 For if they fall, the one will lift up his fellow: but woe to him *that is* alone when he falleth; for *he hath* not another to help him up.

11 Again, if two lie together, then they have heat: but how can one be warm *alone?*

12 And if one prevail against him, two shall withstand him; and a threefold cord is not quickly broken.

13 ¶ Better *is* a poor and a wise child than an old and foolish king, [4]who will no more be admonished.

14 For out of prison he cometh to reign; whereas also *he that is* born in his kingdom becometh poor.

15 I considered all the living which walk under the sun, with the second child that shall stand up in his stead.

16 *There is* no end of all the people, *even* of all that have been before them: they also that come after shall not rejoice in him. Surely this also *is* vanity and vexation of spirit.

5

Keep [a]thy foot when thou goest to the house of God, and be more

---

26 [11]before him

CHAPTER 3
1 [a]ch. 8.6
2 [1]to bear [b]Gen. 47.29; Job 7.1; Isa. 38.1; John 11.14; Heb. 9.27
3 [c]Gen. 9.6; 1 Sam. 2.6; Hos. 6.1-2
4 [d]Ex. 15.20; 2 Sam. 6.16; Ps. 149.3
5 [2]to be far from
6 [3]Or, seek
7 [e]Amos 5.13
8 [f]Luke 14.26
9 [g]ch. 1.3
10 [h]ch. 1.13
11 [i]Deut. 32.4 [j]ch. 8.17; Rom. 11.33
13 [k]ch. 2.24
14 [l]Jas. 1.17
15 [m]ch. 1.9 [4]that which is driven away
16 [n]ch. 5.8
17 [o]Job 34.11; Matt. 16.27; Rom. 2.6; 2 Cor. 5.10; 2 Thess. 1.6
18 [5]Or, that they might clear God, and see, etc
19 [p]Ps. 49.12
20 [q]Gen. 3.19
21 [6]of the sons of man [7]is ascending
22 [r]ch. 2.10

CHAPTER 4
1 [1]hand
2 [a]Job 3.17; ch. 2.17
3 [b]Job 3.11; ch. 6.3; Matt. 24.19; Luke 23.29
4 [2]all the rightness of work [3]this is the envy of a man from his neighbour
5 [c]Prov. 6.10
8 [d]Prov. 27.20; ch. 1.8; Hab. 2.5-6; 1 John 2.16 [e]Ps. 39.6; Luke 12.20
13 [4]who knoweth not to be admonished

CHAPTER 5
1 [a]Ex. 3.5; Josh. 5.15; Ps. 89.7; Isa. 1.12

ready to hear, [b]than to give the sacrifice of fools: for they consider not that
they do evil.
2 Be not rash with thy mouth, and let
not thine heart be hasty to utter *any*
[1]thing before God: for God *is* in heaven,
and thou upon earth: therefore let thy
words [c]be few.
3 For a dream cometh through the
multitude of business; and a fool's voice
is known by multitude of words.
4 [d]When thou vowest a vow unto
God, defer not to pay it; for *he hath* no
pleasure in fools: [e]pay that which thou
hast vowed.
5 [f]Better *is it* that thou shouldest not
vow, than that thou shouldest vow and
not pay.
6 Suffer not thy mouth to cause thy
flesh to sin; [g]neither say thou before
the angel, that it *was* an error: wherefore should God be angry at thy voice,
and destroy the work of thine hands?
7 For in the multitude of dreams and
many words *there are* also *divers* vanities: but [h]fear thou God.
8 ¶ If thou [i]seest the oppression of
the poor, and violent perverting of
judgment and justice in a province,
marvel not [2]at the matter: for [j]*he that*
is higher than the highest regardeth;
and *there be* higher than they.
9 ¶ Moreover the profit of the earth
is for all: the king *himself* is served by
the field.
10 He that loveth silver shall not be
satisfied with silver; nor he that loveth
abundance with increase: this *is* also
vanity.
11 When goods increase, they are increased that eat them: and what good
is there to the owners thereof, saving
the beholding *of them* with their eyes?
12 The sleep of a labouring man *is*
sweet, whether he eat little or much:
but the abundance of the rich will not
suffer him to sleep.
13 [k]There is a sore evil *which* I have
seen under the sun, *namely,* riches
kept for the owners thereof to their
hurt.
14 But those riches perish by evil travail: and he begetteth a son, and *there*
is nothing in his hand.
15 [l]As he came forth of his mother's
womb, naked shall he return to go as
he came, and shall take nothing of his
labour, which he may carry away in
his hand.
16 And this also *is* a sore evil, *that*
in all points as he came, so shall he go:
and [m]what profit hath he [n]that hath
laboured for the wind?
17 All his days also [o]he eateth in
darkness, and *he hath* much sorrow
and wrath with his sickness.
18 ¶ Behold *that* which I have seen:
[3]*it is* good and comely *for one* to eat
and to drink, and to enjoy the good of
all his labour that he taketh under the
sun [4]all the days of his life, which God
giveth him: for it *is* his portion.
19 Every man also to whom God
hath given riches and wealth, and hath
given him power to eat thereof, and to

[b]1 Sam. 15.22; Hos. 6.6
2 [1]Or, word
[c]Ps. 39.1; Matt. 6.7
4 [d]Gen. 28.20; Isa. 19.21
[e]Ps. 66.13-14; Jon. 2.9
5 [f]Prov. 20.25; Acts 5.4
6 [g]1 Cor. 11.10; 1 Tim. 5.21
7 [h]Deut. 10.12; Heb. 12.28
8 [i]ch. 3.16
[2]at the will, or, purpose
[j]Ps. 12.5;
13 [k]ch. 6.1
15 [l]Job 1.21
16 [m]ch. 1.3
[n]Prov. 11.29
17 [o]Ps. 127.2
18 [3]there is a good which is comely, etc
[4]the number of the days
20 [5]Or, Though he give not much, yet he remembereth, etc
[p]Ex. 23.25
CHAPTER 6
2 [a]Deut. 8.7-10;
[b]Luke 12.20
3 [c]2 Ki. 9.35;
[d]Job 3.16
7 [e]Prov. 16.26;
[1]soul
9 [2]than the walking of the soul
10 [f]Job 9.32
12 [3]the number of the days of the life of his vanity
[g]Jas. 4.14
[h]Ps. 39.6
CHAPTER 7
1 [a]Phil. 1.23
2 [b]Matt. 5.4
3 [1]Or, Anger
[c]2 Cor. 7.10
6 [2]sound
7 [d]Ex. 23.8
8 [e]Prov. 14.29

take his portion, and to rejoice in his
labour; this *is* the gift of God.
20 [5]For he shall not much remember
the days of his life; because [p]God answereth *him* in the joy of his heart.
6 There is an evil which I have seen
under the sun, and it *is* common
among men:
2 A man to whom God hath given
riches, wealth, and honour, [a]so that he
wanteth nothing for his soul of all that
he desireth, [b]yet God giveth him not
power to eat thereof, but a stranger
eateth it: this *is* vanity, and it *is* an evil
disease.
3 ¶ If a man beget an hundred *chil-*
dren, and live many years, so that the
days of his years be many, and his soul
be not filled with good, and [c]also *that*
he have no burial; I say, *that* [d]an untimely birth *is* better than he.
4 For he cometh in with vanity, and
departeth in darkness, and his name
shall be covered with darkness.
5 Moreover he hath not seen the
sun, nor known *any thing:* this hath
more rest than the other.
6 ¶ Yea, though he live a thousand
years twice *told,* yet hath he seen no
good: do not all go to one place?
7 [e]All the labour of man *is* for his
mouth, and yet the [1]appetite is not filled.
8 For what hath the wise more than
the fool? what hath the poor, that
knoweth to walk before the living?
9 ¶ Better *is* the sight of the eyes
[2]than the wandering of the desire: this
is also vanity and vexation of spirit.
10 That which hath been is named
already, and it is known that it *is* man:
[f]neither may he contend with him that
is mightier than he.
11 ¶ Seeing there be many things
that increase vanity, what *is* man the
better?
12 For who knoweth what *is* good
for man in *this* life, [3]all the days of
his vain life which he spendeth as [g]a
shadow? for [h]who can tell a man what
shall be after him under the sun?
7 A good name *is* better than precious ointment; and [a]the day of
death than the day of one's birth.
2 ¶ *It is* better to go to the [b]house of
mourning, than to go to the house of
feasting: for that *is* the end of all men;
and the living will lay *it* to his heart.
3 [1]Sorrow *is* better than laughter:
[c]for by the sadness of the countenance
the heart is made better.
4 The heart of the wise *is* in the
house of mourning; but the heart of
fools *is* in the house of mirth.
5 *It is* better to hear the rebuke of
the wise, than for a man to hear the
song of fools.
6 For as the [2]crackling of thorns under a pot, so *is* the laughter of the fool:
this also *is* vanity.
7 ¶ Surely oppression maketh a wise
man mad; [d]and a gift destroyeth the
heart.
8 Better *is* the end of a thing than the
beginning thereof: *and* [e]the patient in
spirit *is* better than the proud in spirit.

9 [f]Be not hasty in thy spirit to be
angry: for anger resteth in the bosom
of fools.
10 Say not thou, What is *the cause*
that the former days were better than
these? for thou dost not inquire [3]wisely
concerning this.
11 ¶ Wisdom [4]*is* good with an inheritance: and *by it there is* profit to them
that see the sun.
12 For wisdom *is* a [5]defence, *and*
money *is* a defence: but the excellency
of knowledge *is, that* wisdom giveth
life to them that have it.
13 Consider the work of God: for
[g]who can make *that* straight, which
he hath made crooked?
14 In the day of prosperity be joyful,
but in the day of adversity consider:
God also hath [6]set the one over against
the other, to the end that man should
find nothing after him.
15 All *things* have I seen in the days
of my vanity: [h]there is a just *man*
that perisheth in his righteousness,
and there is a wicked *man* that pro-
longeth *his life* in his wickedness.
16 [i]Be not righteous over much; neither [j]make thyself over wise: why
shouldest thou [7]destroy thyself?
17 Be not over much wicked, neither
be thou foolish: [k]why shouldest thou
die [8]before thy time?
18 *It is* good that thou shouldest
take hold of this; yea, also from this
withdraw not thine hand: for he that
feareth God shall come forth of them
all.
19 Wisdom strengtheneth the wise
more than ten mighty *men* which are
in the city.
20 [l]For *there is* not a just man upon
earth, that doeth good, and sinneth
not.
21 Also [9]take no heed unto all words
that are spoken; lest thou hear thy servant curse thee:
22 For oftentimes also thine own
heart knoweth that thou thyself likewise hast cursed others.
23 ¶ All this have I proved by wisdom: I said, I will be wise; but it *was*
far from me.
24 That which is far off, and [m]ex-
ceeding deep, who can find it out?
25 [10]I applied mine heart to know,
and to search, and to seek out wisdom,
and the reason *of things,* and to know
the wickedness of folly, even of foolishness *and* madness:
26 And I find more bitter than death
the woman, whose heart *is* snares and
nets, *and* her hands *as* bands: [11]whoso
pleaseth God shall escape from her;
but the sinner shall be taken by her.
27 Behold, this have I found, saith
the preacher, [12]*counting* one by one, to
find out the account:
28 Which yet my soul seeketh, but I
find not: one man among a thousand
have I found; but a woman among all
those have I not found.

9 [f]Prov. 16.32
10 [3]out of wisdom
11 [4]Or, as good as an inheritance, yea, better too
12 [5]shadow
13 [g]Isa. 14.27
14 [6]made
15 [h]ch. 8.14
16 [i]Prov. 25.16; Phil. 3.6
[j]Rom. 12.3
[7]be desolate
17 [k]Job 15.32
[8]not in thy time
20 [l]1 Ki. 8.46; 2 Chr. 6.36; Prov. 20.9; Rom. 3.23; Gal. 3.22; 1 John 1.8
21 [9]give not thine heart
24 [m]Deut. 30.11-14; Job 11.12; Ps. 36.6; Isa. 55.8-9; Rom. 11.33; 1 Tim. 6.16
25 [10]I and my heart compassed
26 [11]he that is good before God
27 [12]Or, weighing one thing after another, to find out the reason
29 [n]Gen. 1.27

CHAPTER 8
1 [1]the strength
2 [a]Rom. 13.5
4 [b]Job 34.18
5 [2]shall know
6 [c]ch. 3.1
7 [d]Prov. 24.22; ch. 6.12
[3]Or, how it shall be
8 [e]Ps. 49.6
[f]Job 14.5
[4]Or, casting off weapons
9 [g]1 Sam. 18.12
11 [h]Job 21.14-15; Ps. 10.6; Isa. 26.10; Rom. 2.4-5; 2 Pet. 3.4-10
12 [i]Isa. 65.20; Rom. 2.5
[j]Prov. 1.32; Matt. 25.34
14 [k]Ps. 73.14; ch. 2.14
15 [l]ch. 3.12
[m]Lev. 26.5

29 Lo, this only have I found, [n]that
God hath made man upright; but they
have sought out many inventions.
8 Who *is* as the wise *man?* and who
knoweth the interpretation of a
thing? a man's wisdom maketh his face
to shine, and [1]the boldness of his face
shall be changed.
2 I *counsel thee* to keep the king's
commandment, [a]and *that* in regard of
the oath of God.
3 Be not hasty to go out of his sight:
stand not in an evil thing; for he doeth
whatsoever pleaseth him.
4 Where the word of a king *is, there*
is power: and [b]who may say unto him,
What doest thou?
5 Whoso keepeth the commandment
[2]shall feel no evil thing: and a wise
man's heart discerneth both time and
judgment.
6 ¶ Because [c]to every purpose there
is time and judgment, therefore the
misery of man *is* great upon him.
7 [d]For he knoweth not that which
shall be: for who can tell him [3]when it
shall be?
8 [e]*There is* no man that hath power
[f]over the spirit to retain the spirit; neither *hath he* power in the day of death:
and *there is* no [4]discharge in *that* war;
neither shall wickedness deliver those
that are given to it.
9 All this have I seen, and applied
my heart unto every work that is done
under the sun: *there is* a time wherein
[g]one man ruleth over another to his
own hurt.
10 And so I saw the wicked buried,
who had come and gone from the
place of the holy, and they were forgotten in the city where they had so done:
this *is* also vanity.
11 [h]Because sentence against an evil
work is not executed speedily, therefore the heart of the sons of men is fully
set in them to do evil.
12 ¶ [i]Though a sinner do evil an hundred times, and his *days* be prolonged,
yet surely I know that [j]it shall be well
with them that fear God, which fear
before him:
13 But it shall not be well with the
wicked, neither shall he prolong *his*
days, *which are* as a shadow; because
he feareth not before God.
14 There is a vanity which is done
upon the earth; that there be just *men,*
unto whom it [k]happeneth according to
the work of the wicked; again, there be
wicked *men,* to whom it happeneth according to the work of the righteous: I
said that this also *is* vanity.
15 [l]Then I commended mirth, because a man hath no better thing under
the sun, than to eat, and to drink, and
to be merry: for that shall abide with
him of his labour the days of his life,
[m]which God giveth him under the sun.
16 ¶ When I applied mine heart to
know wisdom, and to see the business
that is done upon the earth: (for also
there is that neither day nor night
seeth sleep with his eyes:)

17 Then I beheld all the work of God, that [n]a man cannot find out the work that is done under the sun: because though a man labour to seek *it* out, yet he shall not find *it:* yea farther; though a wise *man* think to know *it,* [o]yet shall he not be able to find *it.*

9 For all this [1]I considered in my heart even to declare all this, [a]that the righteous, and the wise, and their works, *are* in the hand of God: no man knoweth either love or hatred *by* all *that is* before them.

2 [b]All *things come* alike to all: *there is* one event to the righteous, and to the wicked; to the good and to the clean, and to the unclean; to him that sacrificeth, and to him that sacrificeth not: as *is* the good, so *is* the sinner; *and* he that sweareth, as *he* that feareth an oath.

3 This *is* an evil among all *things* that are done under the sun, that *there is* one event unto all: yea, also the heart of the sons of men is full of evil, and madness *is* in their heart while they live, and after that *they go* to the dead.

4 ¶ For to him that is joined to all the living there is hope: for a living dog is better than a dead lion.

5 For the living know that they shall die: but [c]the dead know not any thing, neither have they any more a reward; for [d]the memory of them is forgotten.

6 Also their love, and their hatred, and their envy, is now perished; neither have they any more a portion for ever in any *thing* that is done under the sun.

7 ¶ Go thy way, [e]eat thy bread with joy, and drink thy wine with a merry heart; for God now accepteth thy works.

8 Let thy garments be always white; and let thy head lack no ointment.

9 [2]Live joyfully with the wife whom thou lovest all the days of the life of thy vanity, which he hath given thee under the sun, all the days of thy vanity: [f]for that *is* thy portion in *this* life, and in thy labour which thou takest under the sun.

10 Whatsoever thy hand findeth to do, do *it* with thy might; for *there is* no work, nor device, nor knowledge, nor wisdom, in the grave, whither thou goest.

11 ¶ I returned, [g]and saw under the sun, that the race *is* not to the swift, nor the battle to the strong, neither yet bread to the wise, nor yet riches to men of understanding, nor yet favour to men of skill; but time and chance happeneth to them all.

12 For [h]man also knoweth not his time: as the fishes that are taken in an evil net, and as the birds that are caught in the snare; so *are* the sons of men [i]snared in an evil time, when it falleth suddenly upon them.

13 ¶ This wisdom have I seen also under the sun, and it *seemed* great unto me:

17 [n]Job 5.9; ch. 3.11; Isa. 40.28; Rom. 11.33
[o]Ps. 73.16
CHAPTER 9
1 [1]I gave, or, set to my heart
[a]1 Sam. 2.9; Job 5.8; Prov. 16.3; ch. 8.14; Isa. 26.12; 2 Cor. 3.5; 1 Pet. 1.5
2 [b]Ps. 73.3-12-13-17; Mal. 3.15
5 [c]Job 14.21; Ps. 6.5; Isa. 63.16
[d]Job 7.8; Isa. 26.14
7 [e]ch. 8.15
9 [2]See, or, Enjoy life
[f]ch. 2.10-24
11 [g]Amos 2.14; Jer. 9.23
12 [h]ch. 8.7
[i]Prov. 29.6; Luke 12.20; 1 Thess. 5.3
14 [j]2 Sam. 20.16-22
16 [k]Prov. 21.22; ch. 7.19
[l]Mark 6.2
17 [m]Gen. 41.14; 2 Sam. 20.17; Dan. 5.11
18 [n]Josh. 7.1; 2 Ki. 17.21; Rom. 6.12-16-23
CHAPTER 10
1 [1]Flies of death
2 [a]Matt. 6.33; Col. 3.1
3 [2]his heart
[b]Prov. 13.16
4 [c]ch. 8.3
[d]1 Sam. 25.24; Prov. 25.15
5 [3]from before
6 [4]in great heights
7 [e]Prov. 19.10
11 [f]Jer. 8.17
[5]the master of the tongue
12 [6]grace
13 [7]his mouth
14 [8]multiplieth words
[g]Jas. 4.14
16 [h]Isa. 3.4
17 [i]Prov. 31.4

14 [j]*There was* a little city, and few men within it; and there came a great king against it, and besieged it, and built great bulwarks against it:

15 Now there was found in it a poor wise man, and he by his wisdom delivered the city; yet no man remembered that same poor man.

16 [k]Then said I, Wisdom *is* better than strength: nevertheless [l]the poor man's wisdom *is* despised, and his words are not heard.

17 [m]The words of wise *men are* heard in quiet more than the cry of him that ruleth among fools.

18 Wisdom *is* better than weapons of war: but [n]one sinner destroyeth much good.

10 Dead [1]flies cause the ointment of the apothecary to send forth a stinking savour: *so doth* a little folly him that is in reputation for wisdom *and* honour.

2 [a]A wise man's heart *is* at his right hand; but a fool's heart at his left.

3 Yea also, when he that is a fool walketh by the way, [2]his wisdom faileth *him,* [b]and he saith to every one *that* he *is* a fool.

4 If the spirit of the ruler rise up against thee, [c]leave not thy place; for [d]yielding pacifieth great offences.

5 There is an evil *which* I have seen under the sun, as an error *which* proceedeth [3]from the ruler:

6 Folly is set [4]in great dignity, and the rich sit in low place.

7 I have seen servants [e]upon horses, and princes walking as servants upon the earth.

8 He that diggeth a pit shall fall into it; and whoso breaketh an hedge, a serpent shall bite him.

9 Whoso removeth stones shall be hurt therewith; *and* he that cleaveth wood shall be endangered thereby.

10 If the iron be blunt, and he do not whet the edge, then must he put to more strength: but wisdom *is* profitable to direct.

11 Surely the serpent will bite [f]without enchantment; and [5]a babbler is no better.

12 The words of a wise man's mouth *are* [6]gracious; but the lips of a fool will swallow up himself.

13 The beginning of the words of his mouth *is* foolishness: and the end of [7]his talk *is* mischievous madness.

14 A fool also [8]is full of words: a man cannot tell what shall be; and [g]what shall be after him, who can tell him?

15 The labour of the foolish wearieth every one of them, because he knoweth not how to go to the city.

16 ¶ [h]Woe to thee, O land, when thy king *is* a child, and thy princes eat in the morning!

17 Blessed *art* thou, O land, when thy king *is* the son of nobles, and [i]thy princes eat in due season, for strength, and not for drunkenness!

18 ¶ By much slothfulness the building decayeth; and through idleness of
the hands the house droppeth through.
19 ¶ A feast is made for laughter,
and wine [9]maketh merry: but money
answereth all *things*.
20 ¶ [i]Curse not the king, no not in
thy [10]thought; and curse not the rich in
thy bedchamber: for a bird of the air
shall carry the voice, and that which
hath wings shall tell the matter.

11 Cast thy bread [1]upon the waters:
[a]for thou shalt find it after many
days.
2 [b]Give a portion [c]to seven, and
also to eight; [d]for thou knowest not
what evil shall be upon the earth.
3 If the clouds be full of rain, they
empty *themselves* upon the earth: and
if the tree fall toward the south, or toward the north, in the place where the
tree falleth, there it shall be.
4 He that observeth the wind shall
not sow; and he that regardeth the
clouds shall not reap.
5 As [e]thou knowest not what *is* the
way of the spirit, *nor* how the bones *do*
grow in the womb of her that is with
child: even so thou knowest not the
works of God who maketh all.
6 In the morning sow thy seed, and
in the evening withhold not thine hand:
for thou knowest not whether [2]shall
prosper, either this or that, or whether
they both *shall be* alike good.
7 ¶ Truly the light *is* sweet, and a
pleasant *thing it is* for the eyes to behold the sun:
8 But if a man live many years, *and*
rejoice in them all; yet let him remember the days of darkness; for they shall
be many. All that cometh *is* vanity.
9 ¶ Rejoice, O young man, in thy
youth; and let thy heart cheer thee in
the days of thy youth, [f]and walk in the
ways of thine heart, and in the sight of
thine eyes: but know thou, that for all
these *things* [g]God will bring thee into
judgment.
10 Therefore remove [3]sorrow from
thy heart, [h]and put away evil from
thy flesh: for childhood and youth *are*
vanity.

12 Remember now thy Creator in
the days of thy youth, while the
evil days come not, nor the years draw
nigh, when thou shalt say, I have no
pleasure in them;
2 While the sun, or the light, or the
moon, or the stars, be not darkened,
nor the clouds return after the rain:
3 In the day when the keepers of the
[a]house shall tremble, and the strong
men shall bow themselves, and [1]the
grinders cease because they are few,
and [b]those that look out of the windows be darkened,
4 And the [c]doors shall be shut in the
streets, when the sound of the grinding
is low, and he shall rise up at the voice
of the bird, and all [d]the daughters of
musick shall be brought low;
5 Also *when* they shall be afraid of
that which is high, and fears *shall be* in
the way, and the [e]almond tree shall
flourish, and the grasshopper shall be
a burden, and desire shall fail: because
man goeth to his long home, and the
mourners go about the streets:
6 Or ever the silver cord be loosed,
or the golden bowl be broken, or the
pitcher be broken at the fountain, or
the wheel broken at the cistern.
7 Then [f]shall the dust return to the
earth as it was: [g]and the spirit shall
return unto God [h]who gave it.
8 ¶ Vanity of vanities, saith the
preacher; all *is* vanity.
9 And [2]moreover, because the
preacher was wise, he still taught the
people knowledge; yea, he gave good
heed, and sought out, *and* set in order
many proverbs.
10 The preacher sought to find out
[3]acceptable words: and *that which was*
written *was* upright, *even* words of
truth.
11 The words of the wise *are* as
goads, and as nails fastened *by* the
masters of assemblies, *which* are given
from one shepherd.
12 And further, by these, my son, be
admonished: of making many books
there is no end; and much [4]study *is* a
weariness of the flesh.
13 ¶ [5]Let us hear the conclusion
of the whole matter: Fear God, and
keep his commandments: for this *is*
the whole *duty* of man.
14 For [i]God shall bring every work
into judgment, with every secret thing,
whether *it be* good, or whether *it be*
evil.

19 [9]maketh glad the life
20 [i]Ex. 22.28 [10]Or, conscience, figure like, Luke 19.40

CHAPTER 11
1 [1]upon the face of the waters [a]Deut. 15.10; Prov. 11.18; Matt. 10.42; 2 Cor. 9.6
2 [b]Ps. 112.9; Luke 6.30 [c]Mic. 5.5 [d]Eph. 5.16
5 [e]John 3.8
6 [2]shall be right
9 [f]Deut. 29.19; Ps. 81.12; Acts 14.16; Eph. 2.2-3 [g]ch. 12.14; Rom. 2.6
10 [3]Or, anger [h]2 Cor. 7.1

CHAPTER 12
3 [a]Ps. 71.9; Zech. 8.4; 2 Cor. 5.1 [1]Or, the grinders fail, because they grind little [b]Gen. 27.1
4 [c]Mic. 7.1 [d]2 Sam. 19.35
5 [e]Lev. 19.32
7 [f]Gen. 3.19 [g]ch. 3.21 [h]Gen. 2.7; Num. 16.22
9 [2]Or, the more wise the preacher was, etc
10 [3]words of delight
12 [4]Or, reading
13 [5]Or, The end of the matter, even all that hath been heard, is
14 [i]Matt. 12.36

THE SONG OF SOLOMON

Life's Questions

How does God look at relationships between a man and a woman?
Am I free to express my love for my mate?
How does sex relate worship?

God's Answers

Song of Solomon preserves a few of Israel's cherished love songs. They say nothing about God explicitly. They concentrate on a groom and his wife expressing feelings and desires for one another. By becoming part of God's Word they show God's approval of such expressions of love within marriage. Such a love relationship as Song of Solomon pictures is possible only because in love God created the world and placed a man and a woman together in it. Such love can only reflect the love relationship God has with us.

Song of Solomon shows: Longing is a part of love (1:1–8); love will not be silent (1:9—2:7); spring and love go together (2:8–17); love is exclusive (3:1–5); love is enhanced by friendship (3:6–11); love sees only the beautiful (4:1–7); love involves giving and receiving (4:8—5:1); love risks the possibility of pain (5:2—6:3); words cannot express love (6:4—7:9); love must be given freely (7:10–13); and true love is priceless (8:1–14).

1 The [a]song of songs, which *is* Sŏl'o-mon's.

2 Let him kiss me with the kisses of his mouth: for [1]thy love *is* better than wine.

3 Because of the savour of thy good ointments thy name *is as* ointment poured forth, therefore do the [b]virgins love thee.

4 [c]Draw me, we [d]will run after thee: the king [e]hath brought me into his chambers: we will be glad and rejoice in thee, we will remember thy love more than wine: [2]the upright love thee.

5 I *am* black, but comely, O ye daughters of Je-ru̦'sa-lĕm, as the tents of Kē'-där, as the curtains of Sŏl'o-mon.

6 Look not upon me, because I *am* black, because the sun hath looked upon me: my mother's children were angry with me; they made me the keeper of the vineyards; *but* mine own vineyard have I not kept.

7 Tell me, O thou whom my soul loveth, where thou feedest, where thou [f]makest *thy flock* to rest at noon: for why should I be [3]as one that turneth aside by the flocks of thy companions?

8 ¶ If thou know not, O thou fairest among women, go thy way forth by the footsteps of the flock, and feed thy kids beside the shepherds' tents.

9 I have compared thee, [g]O my love, [h]to a company of horses in Phā'raōh's chariots.

10 [i]Thy cheeks are comely with rows *of jewels,* thy neck with chains *of gold.*

11 We will make thee borders of gold with studs of silver.

12 ¶ While the king *sitteth* at his table, my spikenard sendeth forth the smell thereof.

13 A bundle of myrrh *is* my wellbeloved unto me; he shall lie all night betwixt my breasts.

14 My beloved *is* unto me *as* a cluster of [4]camphire in the vineyards of En–ge'di.

15 [j]Behold, thou *art* fair, [5]my love; behold, thou *art* fair; thou *hast* doves' eyes.

16 Behold, thou *art* fair, my beloved, yea, pleasant: also our bed *is* green.

17 The beams of our house *are* cedar, *and* our [6]rafters of fir.

2 I *am* the rose of Shâr'on, *and* the lily of the valleys.

2 As the lily among thorns, so *is* my love among the daughters.

3 As the apple tree among the trees of the wood, so *is* my beloved among the sons. [1]I sat down under his shadow with great delight, [a]and his fruit *was* sweet to my [2]taste.

4 He brought me to the [3]banqueting house, and his banner over me *was* love.

5 Stay me with flagons, [4]comfort me with apples: for I *am* sick of love.

6 [b]His left hand *is* under my head, and his right hand doth embrace me.

7 [5]I charge you, O ye daughters of Je-ru̦'sa-lĕm, by the roes, and by the hinds of the field, that ye stir not up, nor awake *my* love, till he please.

8 ¶ [c]The voice of my beloved! behold, he cometh leaping upon the mountains, skipping upon the hills.

9 My beloved is like a roe or a young hart: behold, he standeth behind our wall, he looketh forth at the windows, [6]shewing himself through the lattice.

10 My beloved spake, and said unto me, Rise up, my love, my fair one, and come away.

11 For, lo, the winter is past, the rain is over *and* gone;

12 The flowers appear on the earth; the time of the singing *of birds* is come, and the voice of the turtle is heard in our land;

13 The fig tree putteth forth her green figs, and the vines *with* the tender grape give a *good* smell. Arise, my love, my fair one, and come away.

14 ¶ O my dove, *that art* in the clefts of the rock, in the secret *places* of the stairs, let me see thy countenance, [d]let me hear thy voice; for sweet *is* thy voice, and thy countenance *is* comely.

15 Take us [e]the foxes, the little foxes, that spoil the vines: for our vines *have* tender grapes.

16 ¶ [f]My beloved *is* mine, and I *am* his: he feedeth among the lilies.

17 [g]Until the day break, and the shadows flee away, turn, my beloved, and be thou like [h]a roe or a young hart upon the mountains [7]of Bē'thēr.

3 By [a]night on my bed I sought him whom my soul loveth: I sought him, but I found him not.

2 I will rise now, and go about the city in the streets, and in the broad ways I will seek him whom my soul loveth: I sought him, but I found him not.

3 [b]The watchmen that go about the city found me: *to whom I said,* Saw ye him whom my soul loveth?

4 *It was* but [c]a little that I passed from them, but I found him whom my soul loveth: [d]I held him, and would not let him go, until I had brought him into my mother's house, and into the chamber of her that conceived me.

5 [e]I charge you, O ye daughters of Je-ru̦'sa-lĕm, by the roes, and by the hinds of the field, that ye stir not up, nor awake *my* love, till he please.

6 ¶ [f]Who *is* this that cometh out of the wilderness like pillars of smoke, perfumed with myrrh and

CHAPTER 1
1 [a]1 Ki. 4.32
2 [1]thy loves
3 [b]ch. 6.8; Matt. 25.1; 2 Cor. 11.2
4 [c]Jer. 31.3; Hos. 11.4; John 6.44
[d]Phil. 3.12
[e]Ps. 45.14; John 14.2; Eph. 2.6
[2]Or, they love thee uprightly
7 [f]John 10.27
[3]Or, as one that is veiled
9 [g]ch. 2.2
[h]2 Chr. 1.16
10 [i]Ezek. 16.11
14 [4]Or, cypress
15 [j]ch. 4.1
[5]Or, my companion
17 [6]Or, galleries

CHAPTER 2
3 [1]I delighted and sat down, etc
[a]Gen. 3.6; Rev. 22.1
[2]palate
4 [3]house of wine
5 [4]straw me with apples
6 [b]ch. 8.3
7 [5]I adjure you
8 [c]John 10.4
9 [6]flourishing
14 [d]ch. 8.13
15 [e]Ps. 80.13; Ezek. 13.4; Luke 13.32
16 [f]ch. 6.3
17 [g]ch. 4.6; Luke 1.78; 2 Pet. 1.19
[h]ch. 8.14
[7]Or, of division

CHAPTER 3
1 [a]Ps. 4.4; Isa. 26.9
3 [b]ch. 5.7; Isa. 21.6-8-11-12
4 [c]Prov. 8.17
[d]Prov. 4.13; Rom. 8.35-39
5 [e]ch. 2.7
6 [f]ch. 8.5; Jer. 2.2

frankincense, with all powders of the
merchant?
7 Behold his bed, which *is* Sŏl'-
o-mon's; threescore valiant men *are*
about it, of the valiant of Ĭs'ra-el.
8 They all hold swords, *being* expert
in war: every man *hath* his sword upon
his thigh because of fear in the night.
9 King Sŏl'o-mon made himself [1]a
chariot of the wood of Lĕb'a-non.
10 He made the pillars thereof *of* silver, the bottom thereof *of* gold, the covering of it *of* purple, the midst thereof
being paved [g]*with* love, for the daughters of Je-ru'sa-lĕm.
11 Go forth, O ye daughters of Zī'ŏn,
and behold king Sŏl'o-mon with the
crown wherewith his mother crowned
him in the [h]day of his espousals, and in
the day of the gladness of his heart.
4 Behold, [a]thou *art* fair, my love; behold, thou *art* fair; thou *hast* doves'
eyes within thy locks: thy hair *is* as
a [b]flock of goats, [1]that appear from
mount Gĭl'e-ăd.
2 [c]Thy teeth *are* like a flock *of sheep*
that are even shorn, which came up
from the washing; whereof every one
bear twins, and none *is* barren among
them.
3 Thy lips *are* like a thread of scarlet, and thy speech *is* comely: thy temples *are* like a piece of a pomegranate
within thy locks.
4 [d]Thy neck *is* like the tower of Dā'-
vid builded [e]for an armoury, whereon
there hang a thousand bucklers, all
shields of mighty men.
5 [f]Thy two breasts *are* like two
young roes that are twins, which feed
among the lilies.
6 Until the day [2]break, and the shadows flee away, I will get me to the
mountain of myrrh, and to the hill of
frankincense.
7 [g]Thou *art* all fair, my love; *there is*
no spot in thee.
8 ¶ Come with me from Lĕb'a-non,
my spouse, with me from Lĕb'a-non:
look from the top of Ā'ma-nȧ, from the
top of Shē'nir [h]and Hĕr'mŏn, from the
lions' dens, from the mountains of the
leopards.
9 Thou hast [3]ravished my heart, my
sister, *my* [i]spouse; thou hast ravished
my heart with one of thine eyes, with
one chain of thy neck.
10 How fair is thy love, my sister,
my spouse! how much better is thy
love than wine! and the smell of thine
ointments than all spices!
11 Thy lips, O *my* spouse, drop *as* the
honeycomb: [j]honey and milk *are* under thy tongue; and the smell of thy garments *is* [k]like the smell of Lĕb'a-non.
12 [l]A garden [4]inclosed *is* my sister,
my spouse; a spring shut up, a fountain
sealed.
13 Thy plants *are* an orchard of pomegranates, with pleasant fruits; [5]cam-
phire, with spikenard,
14 Spikenard and saffron; calamus
and cinnamon, with all trees of frankincense; myrrh and aloes, with all the
chief spices:
15 A fountain of gardens, a well
of [m]living waters, and streams from
Lĕb'a-non.
16 ¶ Awake, O north wind; and come,
thou south; blow upon my garden, *that*
the [n]spices thereof may flow out. [o]Let
my beloved come into his garden, and
eat his pleasant fruits.
5 I [a]am come into my garden, my sister, *my* spouse: I have gathered my
myrrh with my spice; I have eaten my
honeycomb with my honey; I have
drunk my wine with my milk: eat,
O [b]friends; drink, [1]yea, drink abundantly, O beloved.
2 ¶ I sleep, but my heart waketh: *it is*
the voice of my beloved [c]that knocketh, *saying*, Open to me, my sister, my
love, my dove, my undefiled: for my
head is filled with dew, *and* my locks
with the drops of the night.
3 I have put off my coat; how shall I
put it on? I have washed my feet; how
shall I defile them?
4 My beloved put in his hand by the
hole *of the door*, and my bowels were
moved [2]for him.
5 I rose up to open to my beloved;
and my hands dropped *with* myrrh,
and my fingers *with* [3]sweet smelling
myrrh, upon the handles of the lock.
6 I opened to my beloved; but my
beloved had [d]withdrawn himself, *and*
was gone: my soul failed when he
spake: I sought him, but I could not
find him; [e]I called him, but he gave me
no answer.
7 [f]The watchmen that went about
the city found me, they smote me, they
wounded me; the keepers of the walls
took away my veil from me.
8 I charge you, O daughters of Je-
ru'sa-lĕm, if ye find my beloved, [4]that
ye tell him, that I *am* sick of love.
9 ¶ What *is* thy beloved more than
another beloved, O thou fairest among
women? what *is* thy beloved more than
another beloved, that thou dost so
charge us?
10 My beloved *is* white and ruddy,
[5]the chiefest among ten thousand.
11 His head *is as* the most fine gold,
his locks *are* [6]bushy, *and* black as a
raven.
12 [g]His eyes *are* as *the eyes* of doves
by the rivers of waters, washed with
milk, *and* [7]*fitly set*.
13 His cheeks *are* as a bed of spices,
as [8]sweet flowers: his lips *like* lilies,
dropping sweet smelling myrrh.
14 His hands *are as* gold rings set
with the beryl: his belly *is as* bright
ivory overlaid *with* sapphires.
15 His legs *are as* pillars of marble,
set upon sockets of fine gold: his countenance *is* as Lĕb'a-non, excellent as
the cedars.
16 [9]His mouth *is* most sweet: yea,
[h]he *is* altogether lovely. This *is* my beloved, and this *is* my friend, O daughters of Je-ru'sa-lĕm.
6 Whither is thy beloved gone, [a]O
thou fairest among women? whither
is thy beloved turned aside? that we
may seek him with thee.

9 [1]Or, a bed, or, throne
10 [g]Matt. 22.37; 1 Pet. 1.7-8
11 [h]Ps. 110.3; Rev. 11.15

CHAPTER 4
1 [a]ch. 1.15
[b]ch. 6.5
[1]Or, that eat of, etc
2 [c]ch. 6.6
4 [d]2 Sam. 22.51; ch. 1.10
[e]Neh. 3.19
5 [f]Prov. 5.19; 1 Pet. 2.2
6 [2]breathe
7 [g]Eph. 5.27
8 [h]Deut. 3.9
9 [3]Or, taken away my heart
[i]Isa. 54.5; Rev. 19.7-8
11 [j]Prov. 24.13-14
[k]Gen. 27.27;
12 [l]Isa. 58.11;
[4]barred
13 [5]Or, cypress
15 [m]John 4.10
16 [n]Gal. 5.22
[o]ch. 5.1

CHAPTER 5
1 [a]ch. 4.16
[b]Luke 15.7;
[1]Or, and be drunken with loves
2 [c]Prov. 8.4;
4 [2]Or, (as some read,) in me
5 [3]passing, or, running about
6 [d]Hos. 5.15
[e]Lam. 3.8
7 [f]ch. 3.3;
8 [4]what
10 [5]a standardbearer
11 [6]Or, curled
12 [g]ch. 1.15
[7]sitting in fulness, that is, fitly placed, and set as a precious stone in the foil of a ring
13 [8]Or, towers of perfumes
16 [9]His palate
[h]Ps. 45.2;

CHAPTER 6
1 [a]ch. 1.8

2 My beloved is gone down into his
garden, to the beds of spices, to [b]feed
in the gardens, and to [c]gather lilies.
3 [d]I *am* my beloved's, and my beloved *is* mine: he feedeth among the
lilies.
4 ¶ Thou *art* beautiful, O my love, as
Tī r'zah, comely as Je-rų'sa-lĕm, [e]terri-
ble as *an army* with banners.
5 Turn away thine eyes from me, for
[1]they have overcome me: thy hair *is*
[f]as a flock of goats that appear from
Gĭl'e-ăd.
6 Thy teeth *are* as a flock of sheep
which go up from the washing, whereof
every one beareth twins, and *there is*
not one barren among them.
7 As a piece of a pomegranate *are*
thy temples within thy locks.
8 There are threescore queens, and
fourscore concubines, and virgins without number.
9 My dove, my undefiled is *but* one;
she *is* the *only* one of her mother, she *is*
the choice *one* of her that bare her. The
daughters saw her, and blessed her;
yea, the queens and the concubines,
and they praised her.
10 ¶ Who *is* she *that* looketh forth as
the morning, fair as the moon, clear as
the sun, *and* terrible as *an army* with
banners?
11 I went down into the garden of
nuts to see the fruits of the valley, *and*
[g]to see whether the vine flourished,
and the pomegranates budded.
12 [2]Or ever I was aware, my soul
[3]made me *like* the chariots of Ăm-mi'–
na-dĭb.
13 Return, return, O Shų'lam-īte; return, return, that we may look upon
thee. What will ye see in the Shų'lam-
īte? As it were the company [4]of two
armies.

7

How beautiful are thy feet with
shoes, [a]O prince's daughter! the
joints of thy thighs *are* like jewels,
the work of the hands of a cunning
workman.
2 Thy navel *is like* a round goblet,
which wanteth not [1]liquor: thy belly *is*
like an heap of wheat set about with
lilies.
3 [b]Thy two breasts *are* like two
young roes *that are* twins.
4 Thy neck *is* as a tower of ivory;
thine eyes *like* the fishpools in Hĕsh'-
bŏn, by the gate of Băth–răb'bim: thy
nose *is* as the tower of Lĕb'a-non which
looketh toward Da-măs'cus.
5 Thine head upon thee *is* like [2]Cär'-
mel, and the hair of thine head like purple; the king *is* [3]held in the galleries.
6 How fair and how pleasant art
thou, O love, for delights!
7 This thy stature is like to a palm
tree, and thy breasts to clusters *of*
grapes.
8 I said, I will go up to the palm tree,
I will take hold of the boughs thereof:
now also thy breasts shall be as clusters of the vine, and the smell of thy
nose like apples;
9 And the roof of thy mouth like the
best wine for my beloved, that goeth

2 [b]Isa. 40.11; Zeph. 3.17; Rev. 7.17
[c]Isa. 56.8; John 10.16
3 [d]ch. 2.16; Rev. 21.2
4 [e]2 Cor. 10.4
5 [1]Or, they have puffed me up
[f]ch. 4.1
11 [g]ch. 7.12
12 [2]I knew not
[3]Or, set me on the chariots of my willing people
13 [4]Or, of Mahanaim
CHAPTER 7
1 [a]Ps. 45.13
2 [1]mixture
3 [b]ch. 4.5
5 [2]Or, crimson
[3]bound
9 [4]straightly
[5]Or, of the ancient
10 [c]ch. 2.16; Gal. 2.20
[d]Ps. 45.11
12 [e]ch. 6.11
[6]open
[f]Ps. 63.3-8; Ps. 73.25; ch. 4.16
13 [g]Gen. 30.14
[h]ch. 5.1; Matt. 13.52; John 15.8
CHAPTER 8
1 [1]they should not despise me
2 [a]Prov. 9.2
3 [b]ch. 2.6; Isa. 62.4-5; 2 Cor. 12.9
4 [2]why should ye stir up, or, why, etc
5 [c]John 17.14
6 [d]Isa. 49.16; Jer. 22.24; Hag. 2.23
[e]Phil. 3.8
[3]hard
7 [f]Prov. 6.35
8 [g]Ps. 22.27
9 [h]Rev. 3.20
10 [i]Col. 2.7
[j]Ezek. 16.7
[4]peace
11 [k]Matt. 21.33
13 [l]ch. 2.14
14 [5]Flee away
[m]ch. 2.17

down [4]sweetly, causing the lips [5]of
those that are asleep to speak.
10 ¶ [c]I *am* my beloved's, and [d]his
desire *is* toward me.
11 Come, my beloved, let us go forth
into the field; let us lodge in the villages.
12 Let us get up early to the vineyards; let us [e]see if the vine flourish,
whether the tender grape [6]appear, *and*
the pomegranates bud forth: there will
[f]I give thee my loves.
13 The [g]mandrakes give a smell,
and at our gates [h]*are* all manner of
pleasant *fruits,* new and old, *which* I
have laid up for thee, O my beloved.

8

O that thou *wert* as my brother, that
sucked the breasts of my mother!
when I should find thee without, I
would kiss thee; yea, [1]I should not be
despised.
2 I would lead thee, *and* bring thee
into my mother's house, *who* would instruct me: I would cause thee to drink
of [a]spiced wine of the juice of my
pomegranate.
3 [b]His left hand *should be* under my
head, and his right hand should embrace me.
4 I charge you, O daughters of Je-
rų'sa-lĕm, [2]that ye stir not up, nor
awake *my* love, until he please.
5 Who *is* this that cometh up from
[c]the wilderness, leaning upon her beloved? I raised thee up under the apple
tree: there thy mother brought thee
forth: there she brought thee forth *that*
bare thee.
6 ¶ [d]Set me as a seal upon thine
heart, as a seal upon thine arm: for
[e]love *is* strong as death; jealousy *is*
[3]cruel as the grave: the coals thereof
are coals of fire, *which hath* a most
vehement flame.
7 Many waters cannot quench love,
neither can the floods drown it: [f]if a
man would give all the substance of
his house for love, it would utterly be
contemned.
8 ¶ [g]We have a little sister, and she
hath no breasts: what shall we do for
our sister in the day when she shall be
spoken for?
9 If she *be* a wall, we will build upon
her a palace of silver: and if she *be* [h]a
door, we will inclose her with boards
of cedar.
10 [i]I *am* a wall, and [j]my breasts like
towers: then was I in his eyes as one
that found [4]favour.
11 Sŏl'o-mon had a vineyard at Bā'-
al–hā'mon; [k]he let out the vineyard
unto keepers; every one for the fruit
thereof was to bring a thousand *pieces*
of silver.
12 My vineyard, which *is* mine, *is* before me: thou, O Sŏl'o-mon, *must have*
a thousand, and those that keep the
fruit thereof two hundred.
13 Thou that dwellest in the gardens, the companions hearken to thy
voice: [l]cause me to hear *it.*
14 ¶ [5]Make haste, my beloved, and
[m]be thou like to a roe or to a young
hart upon the mountains of spices.

THE BOOK OF

ISAIAH

Life's Questions

Why does God punish me?
How can I respond to God's punishment?
What is the path to hope after punishment?

God's Answers

Isaiah led Israel through the long stretch of history from the good times of king Uzziah who died about 740 B.C. to Babylon's decimation of the nation under Hezekiah in 701. Isaiah pointed beyond that to the destruction of Jerusalem in 586, the return of the exiles in 538 and the rebuilding of the temple in 515. Isaiah's call vision in the temple in 740 gave direction to all this. He saw the holy God seeking a messenger to an obstinate people and calling for repentance, faith, righteousness, justice, and the willingness to become God's suffering servant. Through it all Isaiah showed God was justified in punishing a disobedient people with substitutes for God.

Isaiah shows: God knows His people's sins and need for faith but still calls them back to Himself and His promise of Messiah (1—12); God's sovereign plan includes judgment for all nations' with their injustice (13—23); God's promised triumph over evil means deliverance for His people (24—27); God's people must be different (28—39); God comforts His people with a call to return home and be the suffering servant (40—55); and salvation is available for a repentant people (56—66).

1 The [a]vision of I-sā'iah the son of
Ā'moz, which he saw concerning
Jū'dah and Je-ru'sa-lĕm in the [b]days
of Ŭz-zī'ah, Jō'tham, Ā'hăz, *and* Hĕz-
e-kī'ah, kings of Jū'dah.
2 Hear, O heavens, and give ear, O
earth: for the LORD hath spoken, I have
nourished and brought up children,
and they have rebelled against me.
3 The ox knoweth his owner, and
the ass his master's crib: *but* Is'ra-el
[c]doth not know, my people doth not
consider.
4 Ah sinful nation, a people [1]laden
with iniquity, [d]a seed of evildoers, children that are corrupters: they have forsaken the LORD, they have provoked
the Holy One of Is'ra-el unto anger,
they are [2]gone away backward.
5 ¶ [e]Why should ye be stricken any
more? ye will [3]revolt more and more:
the whole head is sick, and the whole
heart faint.
6 From the sole of the foot even unto
the head *there is* no soundness in it; *but*
wounds, and bruises, and putrifying
sores: [f]they have not been closed, neither bound up, neither mollified with
[4]ointment.
7 [g]Your country *is* desolate, your cities *are* burned with fire: your land,
strangers devour it in your presence,
and *it is* desolate, [5]as overthrown by
strangers.
8 And the daugher of Zī'ŏn is left as
a cottage in a vineyard, as a lodge in a
garden of cucumbers, as a besieged
city.
9 [h]Except the LORD of hosts had left
unto us a very small remnant, we should
have been as Sŏd'om, *and* we should
have been like unto Go-mŏr'rah.
10 ¶ Hear the word of the LORD, ye
rulers [i]of Sŏd'om; give ear unto the law
of our God, ye people of Go-mŏr'rah.

CHAPTER 1
1 [a]Num. 12.6
[b]2 Ki. 15.1
3 [c]Jer. 9.3-6
4 [1]of heaviness
[d]ch. 57.3-4
[2]alienated, or, separated
5 [e]ch. 9.13; Jer. 2.30
[3]increase revolt
6 [f]Jer. 8.22
[4]Or, oil
7 [g]Deut. 28.51
[5]as the overthrow of strangers
9 [h]Rom. 9.29
10 [i]Ezek. 16.46
11 [j]Ps. 50.8
[6]great he goats
12 [7]to be seen
13 [8]Or, grief
15 [k]Job 27.9
[l]1 Tim. 2.8
[9]multiply prayer
[10]bloods
16 [m]Jer. 4.14
[n]Rom. 12.9
17 [o]Mic. 6.8
[11]Or, righten
18 [p]1 Sam. 12.7; ch. 41.21; Mic. 6.2
[q]Ps. 51.7; ch. 44.22; Mic. 7.18; Eph. 1.6-8
19 [r]Deut. 28.1
20 [s]Tit. 1.2

11 To what purpose *is* the multitude
of your [j]sacrifices unto me? saith the
LORD: I am full of the burnt offerings
of rams, and the fat of fed beasts; and I
delight not in the blood of bullocks, or
of lambs, or of [6]he goats.
12 When ye come [7]to appear before
me, who hath required this at your
hand, to tread my courts?
13 Bring no more vain oblations; incense is an abomination unto me; the
new moons and sabbaths, the calling
of assemblies, I cannot away with; *it is*
[8]iniquity, even the solemn meeting.
14 Your new moons and your appointed feasts my soul hateth: they are
a trouble unto me; I am weary to bear
them.
15 And [k]when ye spread forth your
hands, I will hide mine eyes from you:
[l]yea, when ye [9]make many prayers, I
will not hear: your hands are full of
[10]blood.
16 ¶ [m]Wash you, make you clean;
put away the evil of your doings from
before mine eyes; [n]cease to do evil;
17 Learn to do well; [o]seek judgment, [11]relieve the oppressed, judge
the fatherless, plead for the widow.
18 Come now, and [p]let us reason together, saith the LORD: though your
sins be as scarlet, [q]they shall be as
white as snow; though they be red like
crimson, they shall be as wool.
19 [r]If ye be willing and obedient, ye
shall eat the good of the land:
20 But if ye refuse and rebel, ye
shall be devoured with the sword: [s]for
the mouth of the LORD hath spoken *it*.
21 ¶ How is the faithful city become
an harlot! it was full of judgment;
righteousness lodged in it; but now
murderers.
22 Thy silver is become dross, thy
wine mixed with water:

23 [t]Thy princes *are* rebellious, and companions of thieves: every one loveth gifts, and followeth after rewards: they judge not the fatherless, neither doth the cause of the widow come unto them.

24 Therefore saith the Lord, the LORD of hosts, the mighty One of Ĭs'ra-el, Ah, [u]I will ease me of mine adversaries, and avenge me of mine enemies:

25 ¶ [v]And I will turn my hand upon thee, and [12]purely purge away thy dross, and take away all thy tin:

26 And I will restore thy judges as at the first, and thy counsellers as at the beginning: afterward thou shalt be called, The city of righteousness, the faithful city.

27 Zī'ŏn shall be redeemed with judgment, and [13]her converts with righteousness.

28 ¶ And the [14]destruction of the transgressors and of the sinners *shall be* together, and they that forsake the LORD shall be consumed.

29 For they shall be ashamed of [w]the oaks which ye have desired, [x]and ye shall be confounded for the gardens that ye have chosen.

30 For ye shall be as an oak whose leaf fadeth, and as a garden that hath no water.

31 And the strong shall be as tow, [15]and the maker of it as a spark, and they shall both burn together, and none shall quench *them*.

2 The word that I-sā'iah the son of Ā'moz saw concerning Jū'dah and Je-rṳ'sa-lĕm.

2 And [a]it shall come to pass in the last days, [b]*that* the mountain of the LORD'S house shall [1]be established in the top of the mountains, and shall be exalted above the hills; and all nations shall flow unto it.

3 And many people shall go and say, [c]Come ye, and let us go up to the mountain of the LORD, to the house of the God of Jā'cob; and he will teach us of his ways, and we will walk in his paths: [d]for out of Zī'ŏn shall go forth the law, and the word of the LORD from Je-rṳ'sa-lĕm.

4 And he [e]shall judge among the nations, and shall rebuke many people: and [f]they shall beat their swords into plowshares, and their spears into [2]pruninghooks: nation shall not lift up sword against nation, neither shall they learn war any more.

5 O house of Jā'cob, come ye, and let us [g]walk in the light of the LORD.

6 ¶ Therefore thou hast forsaken thy people the house of Jā'cob, because they be replenished [3]from the east, and [h]*are* soothsayers like the Phĭ-lĭs'tĭnes, and they [4]please themselves in the children of strangers.

7 Their land also is full of silver and gold, neither *is there any* end of their treasures; their land is also full of horses, neither *is there any* end of their chariots:

8 Their land also is full of [5]idols; they worship the work of their own hands, that which their own fingers have made:

9 And the mean man boweth down, and the great man humbleth himself: therefore forgive them not.

10 ¶ Enter into the rock, and hide thee in the dust, for fear of the LORD, and for the glory of his majesty.

11 The lofty looks of man shall be humbled, and the haughtiness of men shall be bowed down, and the LORD alone shall be exalted [i]in that day.

12 For the day of the LORD of hosts *shall be* upon every *one that is* proud and lofty, and upon every *one that is* lifted up; and he shall be brought low:

13 And upon all the cedars of Lĕb'a-non, *that are* high and lifted up, and upon all the oaks of Bā'shăn,

14 And upon all the high mountains, and upon all the hills *that are* lifted up,

15 And upon every high tower, and upon every fenced wall,

16 And upon all the ships of Tär'-shish, and upon all [6]pleasant pictures.

17 And the loftiness of man shall be bowed down, and the haughtiness of men shall be made low: and the LORD alone shall be exalted in that day.

18 And [7]the idols he shall utterly abolish.

19 And they shall go into the [j]holes of the rocks, and into the caves of [8]the earth, [k]for fear of the LORD, and for the glory of his majesty, when he ariseth [l]to shake terribly the earth.

20 In that day a man shall cast [9]his idols of silver, and his idols of gold, [10]which they made *each one* for himself to worship, to the moles and to the bats;

21 To go into the clefts of the rocks, and into the tops of the ragged rocks, for fear of the LORD, and for the glory of his majesty, when he ariseth to shake terribly the earth.

22 [m]Cease ye from man, whose breath *is* in his nostrils: for wherein is he to be accounted of?

3 For, behold, the Lord, the LORD of hosts, doth take away from Je-rṳ'sa-lĕm and from Jū'dah [a]the stay and the staff, the whole stay of bread, and the whole stay of water,

2 The mighty man, and the man of war, the judge, and the prophet, and the prudent, and the ancient,

3 The captain of fifty, and [1]the honourable man, and the counseller, and the cunning artificer, and the [2]eloquent orator.

4 And I will give [b]children *to be* their princes, and babes shall rule over them.

5 And the [c]people shall be oppressed, every one by another, and every one by his neighbour: the child shall behave himself proudly against [d]the ancient, and the base against the honourable.

6 When a man shall take hold of his brother of the house of his father, *saying*, Thou hast clothing, be thou our ruler, and *let* this ruin *be* under thy hand:

23 [t]2 Chr. 36.14; Hos. 9.15
24 [u]Deut. 28.63
25 [v]Rev. 3.19 [12]according to pureness
27 [13]Or, they that return of her
28 [14]breaking
29 [w]ch. 57.5 [x]ch. 65.3
31 [15]Or, and his work

CHAPTER 2
2 [a]Mic. 4.1; Acts 2.17 [b]Dan. 2.35; Rev. 14.1 [1]Or, be prepared
3 [c]Zech. 8.21 [d]Luke 24.47
4 [e]John 5.22 [f]Hos. 2.18 [2]Or, scythes
5 [g]Acts 26.23
6 [3]Or, more than the east [h]Deut. 18.14 [4]Or, abound with the children
8 [5]Or, nonentities
11 [i]ch. 12.1-4; Mic. 5.10
16 [6]pictures of desire
18 [7]Or, the whole shall pass away
19 [j]Hos. 10.8; Rev. 6.16 [8]the dust [k]2 Thess. 1.9 [l]Ps. 7.6; Heb. 12.26
20 [9]the idols of his silver, etc [10]Or, which they made for him
22 [m]Prov. 23.4

CHAPTER 3
1 [a]Lev. 26.26; Ezek. 14.13
3 [1]a man eminent in countenance [2]Or, skilful of speech
4 [b]Eccl. 10.16
5 [c]Mic. 3 [d]Deut. 28.50

7 In that day shall he [3]swear, saying,
I will not be an [4]healer; for in my house
is neither bread nor clothing: make me
not a ruler of the people.
8 For Je-rụ'sa-lĕm is ruined, and Jū'-
dah is fallen: because their tongue and
their doings *are* against the LORD, to
provoke the eyes of his glory.
9 ¶ The shew of their countenance
doth witness against them; and they
declare their sin as Sŏd'om, they hide
it not. Woe unto their soul! for they
have rewarded evil unto themselves.
10 Say ye to the righteous, that *it*
shall be well *with him:* for they shall
eat the fruit of their doings.
11 Woe unto the wicked! *it shall be*
ill *with him:* for the reward of his
hands shall be [5]given him.
12 ¶ *As for* my people, children *are*
their oppressors, and women rule over
them. O my people, [6]they which lead
thee cause *thee* to err, and [7]destroy the
way of thy paths.
13 The LORD standeth up to plead,
and standeth to judge the people.
14 The LORD will enter into judgment with the ancients of his people,
and the princes thereof: for ye have
[8]eaten up [e]the vineyard; the spoil of
the poor *is* in your houses.
15 What mean ye *that* ye beat my
people to pieces, and grind the faces of
the poor? saith the Lord GOD of hosts.
16 ¶ Moreover the LORD saith, Because the daughters of Zī'ŏn are
haughty, and walk with stretched forth
necks and [9]wanton eyes, walking and
[10]mincing *as* they go, and making a tinkling with their feet:
17 Therefore the Lord will smite
with a scab the crown of the head of
the daughters of Zī'ŏn, and the LORD
will [11]discover their secret parts.
18 In that day the Lord will take
away the bravery of *their* tinkling ornaments *about their feet,* and *their*
[12]*cauls, and their* round tires like the
moon,
19 The [13]chains, and the bracelets,
and the [14]mufflers,
20 The bonnets, and the ornaments
of the legs, and the headbands, and the
[15]tablets, and the earrings,
21 The rings, and nose jewels,
22 The changeable suits of apparel,
and the mantles, and the wimples, and
the crisping pins,
23 The glasses, and the fine linen,
and the hoods, and the veils.
24 And it shall come to pass, *that*
instead of sweet smell there shall be
stink; and instead of a girdle a rent;
and instead of well set hair baldness;
and instead of a stomacher a girding
of sackcloth; *and* burning instead of
beauty.
25 Thy men shall fall by the sword,
and thy [16]mighty in the war.
26 And [f]her gates shall lament and
mourn; and she *being* [17]desolate shall
sit upon the ground.
4 And in that day seven women shall
take hold of one man, saying, We
will eat our own bread, and wear our
own apparel: only [1]let us be called by
thy name, [2]to take away [a]our reproach.
2 In that day shall [b]the branch of
the LORD be [3]beautiful and glorious,
and [c]the fruit of the earth *shall be* excellent and comely [4]for them that are
escaped of Ĭs'ra-el.
3 And it shall come to pass, *that he*
that is left in Zī'ŏn, and *he that* remaineth in Je-rụ'sa-lĕm, shall be called holy,
even every one that is written [5]among
the living in Je-rụ'sa-lĕm:
4 When the Lord shall have washed
away the filth of the daughters of Zī'ŏn,
and shall have purged the blood of Je-
rụ'sa-lĕm from the midst thereof by the
spirit of judgment, and by the spirit of
burning.
5 And the LORD will create upon every dwelling place of mount Zī'ŏn, and
upon her assemblies, [d]a cloud and
smoke by day, and the shining of a
flaming fire by night: for [6]upon all the
glory *shall be* [7]a defence.
6 And there shall be a tabernacle for
a shadow in the daytime from the heat,
and for a place of refuge, and for a
covert from storm and from rain.
5 Now will I sing to my wellbeloved a
song of my beloved touching [a]his
vineyard. My wellbeloved hath a vineyard in [1]a very fruitful hill:
2 And he [2]fenced it, and gathered
out the stones thereof, and planted it
with the choicest vine, and built a
tower in the midst of it, and also [3]made
a winepress therein: [b]and he looked
that it should bring forth grapes, and it
brought forth wild grapes.
3 And now, O inhabitants of Je-rụ'-
sa-lĕm, and men of Jū'dah, [c]judge, I
pray you, betwixt me and my vineyard.
4 What could have been done more
to my vineyard, that I have not done in
it? wherefore, when I looked that it
should bring forth grapes, brought it
forth wild grapes?
5 And now go to; I will tell you what
I will do to my vineyard: I will take
away the hedge thereof, and it shall be
eaten up; *and* break down the wall
thereof, and it shall be [4]trodden down:
6 And I will lay it waste: it shall not
be pruned, nor digged; but there shall
come up briers and thorns: I will also
command the clouds that they rain no
rain upon it.
7 For the vineyard of the LORD of
hosts *is* the house of Ĭs'ra-el, and the
men of Jū'dah [5]his pleasant plant: and
he looked for judgment, but behold [6]op-
pression; for righteousness, but behold
a cry.
8 ¶ Woe unto them that join [d]house
to house, *that* lay field to field, till
there be no place, that [7]they may be
placed alone in the midst of the earth!
9 [8]In mine ears *said* the LORD of
hosts, [9]Of a truth many houses shall be
desolate, *even* great and fair, without
inhabitant.
10 Yea, ten acres of vineyard shall
yield one [e]bath, and the seed of an homer shall yield an ephah.

7 [3]lift up the hand, Gen. 14.22-or, protest [4]binder up
11 [5]done to him
12 [6]Or, they which call thee blessed [7]swallow up
14 [8]Or, burnt [e]Matt. 21.33
16 [9]deceiving with their eyes [10]Or, tripping nicely
17 [11]make naked
18 [12]Or, networks
19 [13]Or, sweet balls [14]Or, spangled ornaments
20 [15]houses of the soul
25 [16]might
26 [f]Jer. 14.2; Lam. 1.4 [17]Or, cleansed, or, emptied

CHAPTER 4
1 [1]let thy name be called upon us [2]Or, take thou away [a]Luke 1.25
2 [b]ch. 11.1; Jer. 23.5 [3]beauty and glory [c]Rom. 1.3-4 [4]for the escaping of Israel
3 [5]Or, to life
5 [d]Ex. 13.21-22; [6]Or, above [7]a covering

CHAPTER 5
1 [a]Ps. 80.8 [1]the horn of the son of oil
2 [2]Or, made a wall about it [3]hewed [b]Deut. 32.6
3 [c]Rom. 3.4
5 [4]for a treading
7 [5]plant of his pleasures [6]a scab
8 [d]Mic. 2.2 [7]ye
9 [8]Or. This is in mine ears, saith the LORD, etc [9]If not, etc
10 [e]Lev. 27.16

11 ¶ [f]Woe unto them that rise up early in the morning, *that* they may follow strong drink; that continue until night, *till* wine [10]inflame them!

12 And [g]the harp, and the viol, the tabret, and pipe, and wine, are in their feasts: but [h]they regard not the work of the LORD, neither consider the operation of his hands.

13 ¶ [i]Therefore my people are gone into captivity, [j]because *they have* no knowledge: and [11]their honourable men *are* famished, and their multitude dried up with thirst.

14 Therefore hell hath enlarged herself, and opened her mouth without measure: and their glory, and their multitude, and their pomp, and he that rejoiceth, shall descend into it.

15 And the mean man shall be brought down, and the mighty man shall be humbled, and the eyes of the lofty shall be humbled:

16 But the LORD of hosts shall be exalted in judgment, and [12]God that is holy shall be sanctified in righteousness.

17 Then shall the lambs feed after their manner, and the waste places of the fat ones shall strangers eat.

18 Woe unto them that draw iniquity with cords of vanity, and sin as it were with a cart rope:

19 [k]That say, Let him make speed, *and* hasten his work, that we may see *it:* and let the counsel of the Holy One of Is'ra-el draw nigh and come, that we may know *it!*

20 ¶ Woe unto them [13]that call evil good, and good evil; that put darkness for light, and light for darkness; that put bitter for sweet, and sweet for bitter!

21 Woe unto *them that are* wise in their own eyes, and prudent [14]in their own sight!

22 Woe unto *them that are* mighty to drink wine, and men of strength to mingle strong drink:

23 Which justify the wicked for reward, and take away the righteousness of the righteous from him!

24 Therefore as [15]the fire devoureth the stubble, and the flame consumeth the chaff, *so* their root shall be as rottenness, and their blossom shall go up as dust: because they have cast away [l]the law of the LORD of hosts, and despised the word of the Holy One of Is'ra-el.

25 Therefore is the anger of the LORD kindled against his people, and he hath stretched forth his hand against them, and hath smitten them: and the hills did tremble, and their carcases *were* [16]torn in the midst of the streets. For all this his anger is not turned away, but his hand *is* stretched out still.

26 ¶ And he will lift up an ensign to the nations from far, and will hiss unto them from the end of the earth: and, behold, they shall come with speed swiftly:

27 None shall be weary nor stumble among them; none shall slumber nor sleep; neither shall the girdle of their loins be loosed, nor the latchet of their shoes be broken:

28 Whose arrows *are* sharp, and all their bows bent, their horses' hoofs shall be counted like flint, and their wheels like a whirlwind:

29 Their roaring *shall be* like a lion, they shall roar like young lions: yea, they shall roar, and lay hold of the prey, and shall carry *it* away safe, and none shall deliver *it*.

30 And in that day they shall roar against them like the roaring of the sea: and if *one* look unto the land, behold darkness *and* [17]sorrow, [18]and the light is darkened in the heavens thereof.

6 In the year that [a]king Ŭz-zī'ah died I [b]saw also the Lord sitting upon a throne, high and lifted up, and [1]his train filled the temple.

2 Above it stood the seraphims: each one had six wings; with twain he covered his face, and with twain he covered his feet, and with twain he did fly.

3 And [2]one cried unto another, and said, Holy, holy, holy, *is* the LORD of hosts: [3]the whole earth *is* full of his glory.

4 And the posts of the [4]door moved at the voice of him that cried, and the house was filled with smoke.

5 ¶ Then said I, Woe *is* me! for I am [5]undone; because I *am* a man of unclean lips, and I dwell in the midst of a people of unclean lips: for mine eyes have seen the King, the LORD of hosts.

6 Then flew one of the seraphims unto me, [6]having a live coal in his hand, *which* he had taken with the tongs from off [c]the altar:

7 And he [7]laid *it* upon my mouth, and said, Lo, this hath touched thy lips; and thine iniquity is taken away, and thy sin purged.

8 Also I heard the voice of the Lord, saying, Whom shall I send, and who will go for [d]us? Then said I, [8]Here *am* I; send me.

9 ¶ And he said, Go, and tell this people, [9]Hear ye indeed, but understand not; and see ye [10]indeed, but perceive not.

10 Make the heart of this people fat, and make their ears heavy, and shut their eyes; lest they see with their eyes, and hear with their ears, and understand with their heart, and convert, and be healed.

11 Then said I, Lord, how long? And he answered, Until the cities be wasted without inhabitant, and the houses without man, and the land [11]be utterly desolate,

12 And the LORD have [e]removed men far away, and *there be* a great forsaking in the midst of the land.

13 ¶ But yet in it *shall be* a tenth, [12]and *it* shall return, and shall be eaten: as a teil tree, and as an oak, whose [13]substance *is* in them, when they cast *their leaves: so* [f] *the holy seed shall be* the substance thereof.

7 And it came to pass in the days of [a]Ā'hăz the son of Jō'tham, the son

11 [f]Prov. 23.29-30 [10]Or, pursue them
12 [g]Amos 6.5 [h]Job 34.27; Hos. 4.11
13 [i]ch. 1.7; Hos. 4.6 [j]ch. 1.3; 2 Pet. 3.5 [11]their glory are men of famine
16 [12]the God the holy, or, the holy God
19 [k]ch. 66.5
20 [13]that say concerning evil, It is good, etc
21 [14]before their face
24 [15]the tongue of fire [l]2 Ki. 17.14
25 [16]Or, as dung
30 [17]Or, distress [18]Or, when it is light, it shall be dark in the destructions thereof

CHAPTER 6

1 [a]2 Ki. 15.7 [b]1 Ki. 22.19; [1]Or, the skirts thereof
3 [2]this cried to this [3]his glory is the fulness of the whole earth
4 [4]thresholds
5 [5]cut off
6 [6]and in his hand a live coal [c]Lev. 16.12
7 [7]caused it to touch
8 [d]Gen. 1.26 [8]Behold me
9 [9]Hear ye in hearing, or, without ceasing, etc [10]in seeing
11 [11]desolate with desolation
12 [e]Deut. 28.64
13 [12]Or, when it is returned, and hath been broused [13]Or, stock, or, stem [f]Rom. 11.5

CHAPTER 7

1 [a]2 Ki. 16.5

of Ŭz-zī'ah, king of Jū'dah, *that* Rē'zin
the king of Sӯr'ĭ-ȧ, and Pē'kah the son
of Rĕm-a-lī'ah, king of Ĭs'ra-el, went
up toward Je-ru'sa-lĕm to war against
it, but could not prevail against it.
2 And it was told the house of Dā'-
vid, saying, Sӯr'ĭ-ȧ [1]is confederate with
Ē'phră-ĭm. And his heart was moved,
and the heart of his people, as the trees
of the wood are moved with the wind.
3 Then said the LORD unto I-sā'iah,
Go forth now to meet Ā'hăz, thou, and
[2]Shē'ăr–jā'shŭb thy son, at the end of
the [b]conduit of the upper pool in the
[3]highway of the fuller's field;
4 And say unto him, Take heed, and
be quiet; fear not, [4]neither be fainthearted for the two tails of these smoking firebrands, for the fierce anger of
Rē'zin with Sӯr'ĭ-ȧ, and of the son of
Rĕm-a-lī'ah.
5 Because Sӯr'ĭ-ȧ, Ē'phră-ĭm, and
the son of Rĕm-a-lī'ah, have taken evil
counsel against thee, saying,
6 Let us go up against Jū'dah, and
[5]vex it, and let us make a breach therein
for us, and set a king in the midst of it,
even the son of Tā'be-al:
7 Thus saith the Lord GOD, It shall
not stand, neither shall it come to pass.
8 [c]For the head of Sӯr'ĭ-ȧ *is* Da-
măs'cus, and the head of Da-măs'cus
is Rē'zin; and within threescore and
five years shall Ē'phră-ĭm be broken,
[6]that it be not a people.
9 And the head of Ē'phră-ĭm *is* Sa-
mā'rĭ-ȧ, and the head of Sa-mā'rĭ-ȧ *is*
Rĕm-a-lī'ah's son. [7]If ye will not believe, surely ye shall not be established.
10 ¶ [8]Moreover the LORD spake again
unto Ā'hăz, saying,
11 Ask thee a sign of the LORD thy
God; [9]ask it either in the depth, or in
the height above.
12 But Ā'hăz said, I will not ask, neither will I tempt the LORD.
13 And he said, Hear ye now, O
house of Dā'vid; *Is it* a small thing for
you to weary men, but will ye weary
my God also?
14 Therefore the Lord himself shall
give you a sign; [d]Behold, a virgin shall
conceive, and bear [e]a son, and [10]shall
call his name [f]Im-man'u-el.
15 Butter and honey shall he eat,
that he may know to refuse the evil,
and choose the good.
16 For before the child shall know to
refuse the evil, and choose the good,
the land that thou abhorrest shall be
forsaken of [g]both her kings.
17 ¶ [h]The LORD shall bring upon
thee, and upon thy people, and upon
thy father's house, days that have not
come, from the day that [i]Ē'phră-ĭm departed from Jū'dah; *even* the king of
Ȧs-sӯr'ĭ-ȧ.
18 And it shall come to pass in that
day, *that* the LORD shall hiss for the fly
that *is* in the uttermost part of the rivers of Ē'gypt, and for the bee that *is* in
the land of Ȧs-sӯr'ĭ-ȧ.
19 And they shall come, and shall
rest all of them in the desolate valleys,
and in the holes of the rocks, and upon
all thorns, and upon all [11]bushes.
20 In the same day shall the Lord
shave with a [j]razor that is hired,
namely, by them beyond the river, by
the king of Ȧs-sӯr'ĭ-ȧ, the head, and
the hair of the feet: and it shall also
consume the beard.
21 And it shall come to pass in that
day, *that* a man shall nourish a young
cow, and two sheep;
22 And it shall come to pass, for the
abundance of milk *that* they shall give
he shall eat butter: for butter and honey
shall every one eat that is left [12]in the
land.
23 And it shall come to pass in that
day, *that* every place shall be, where
there were a thousand vines at a thousand silverlings, it shall *even* be for briers and thorns.
24 With arrows and with bows shall
men come thither; because all the land
shall become briers and thorns.
25 And *on* all hills that shall be
digged with the mattock, there shall
not come thither the fear of briers and
thorns: but it shall be for the sending
forth of oxen, and for the treading of
lesser cattle.
8 Moreover the LORD said unto me,
Take thee a great roll, and write in
it with a man's pen concerning [1]Mā'-
hĕr–shăl'al–hăsh'–băz.
2 And I took unto me faithful witnesses to record, [a]U-rī'ah the priest, and
Zĕch-a-rī'ah the son of Je-bĕr-e-chī'ah.
3 And I [2]went unto the prophetess;
and she conceived, and bare a son.
Then said the LORD to me, Call his
name Mā'hĕr–shăl'al–hăsh'–băz.
4 [b]For before the child shall have
knowledge to cry, My father, and my
mother, [3]the riches of Da-măs'cus and
the spoil of Sa-mā'rĭ-ȧ shall be taken
away before the king of Ȧs-sӯr'ĭ-ȧ.
5 ¶ The LORD spake also unto me
again, saying,
6 Forasmuch as this people refuseth
the waters of [c]Shi-lō'ah that go softly,
and rejoice in Rē'zin and Rĕm-a-lī'ah's
son;
7 Now therefore, behold, the Lord
bringeth up upon them the waters of
the river, strong and many, *even* the
king of Ȧs-sӯr'ĭ-ȧ, and all his glory:
and he shall come up over all his channels, and go over all his banks:
8 And he shall pass through Jū'dah;
he shall overflow and go over, he shall
reach *even* to the neck; and [4]the stretching out of his wings shall fill the breadth
of thy land, O [d]Ĭm-măn'ū-el.
9 ¶ Associate yourselves, O ye people, [5]and ye shall be broken in pieces;
and give ear, all ye of far countries:
gird yourselves, and ye shall be broken in pieces; gird yourselves, and ye
shall be broken in pieces.
10 [e]Take counsel together, and it
shall come to nought; speak the word,
and it shall not stand: [f]for God *is* with
us.
11 ¶ For the LORD spake thus to me
[6]with a strong hand, and instructed me

2 [1]resteth on Ephraim
3 [2]That is, The remnant shall return [b]2 Ki. 18.17; [3]Or, causeway
4 [4]let not thy heart be tender
6 [5]Or, waken
8 [c]2 Sam. 8.6 [6]from a people
9 [7]Or, Do ye not believe? it is because ye are not stable
10 [8]And the LORD added to speak
11 [9]Or, make thy petition deep
14 [d]Matt. 1.23; [e]ch. 9.6 [10]Or, thou, O virgin, shall call [f]1 Tim. 3.16
16 [g]2 Ki. 15.30
17 [h]2 Chr. 28.19; [i]1 Ki. 12.16
19 [11]Or, commendable trees
20 [j]2 Ki. 16.7
22 [12]in the midst of the land

CHAPTER 8
1 [1]In making speed to the spoil he hasteneth the prey, or, Make speed, etc
2 [a]2 Ki. 16.10
3 [2]approached unto
4 [b]ch. 7.16 [3]Or, he that is before the king of Assyria shall take away the riches
6 [c]Neh. 3.15
8 [4]the fulness of the breadth of thy land shall be the stretchings out of his wings [d]ch. 7.14
9 [5]Or, yet
10 [e]Job 5.12 [f]Deut. 20.1
11 [6]in strength of hand

that I should not walk in the way of this people, saying,

12 Say ye not, A confederacy, to all *them to* whom this people shall say, A confederacy; [g]neither fear ye their fear, nor be afraid.

13 [h]Sanctify the LORD of hosts himself; and [i]*let* him *be* your fear, and *let* him *be* your dread.

14 And [j]he shall be for a sanctuary; but for [k]a stone of stumbling and for a rock of offence to both the houses of Ĭs'ra-el, for a gin and for a snare to the inhabitants of Je-ru'sa-lĕm.

15 And many among them shall [l]stumble, and fall, and be broken, and be snared, and be taken.

16 [m]Bind up the testimony, seal the law among my disciples.

17 And I will wait upon the LORD, that hideth his face from the house of Jā'cob, and I [n]will look for him.

18 [o]Behold, I and the children whom the LORD hath given me [p]*are* for signs and for wonders in Ĭs'ra-el from the LORD of hosts, which dwelleth in mount Zī'ŏn.

19 ¶ And when they shall say unto you, Seek unto them that have familiar spirits, and unto wizards that peep, and that mutter: should not a people seek unto their God? for the living [q]to the dead?

20 To the law and to the testimony: if they speak not according to this word, *it is* because *there is* [7]no light in them.

21 And they shall pass through it, hardly bestead and hungry: and it shall come to pass, that when they shall be hungry, they shall fret themselves, and curse their king and their God, and look upward.

22 And they shall look unto the earth; and behold trouble and darkness, dimness of anguish; and *they shall be* driven to darkness.

9 Nevertheless the dimness *shall* not *be* such as *was* in her vexation, when at the [a]first he lightly afflicted the land of Zĕb'u-lun and the land of Năph'ta-lī, and [b]afterward did more grievously afflict *her by* the way of the sea, beyond Jôr'dan, in Găl'ĭ-lee [1]of the nations.

2 [c]The people that walked in darkness have seen a great light: they that dwell in the land of the shadow of death, upon them hath the light shined.

3 Thou hast multiplied the nation, *and* [2]not increased the joy: they joy before thee according to the joy in harvest, *and* as *men* rejoice when they divide the spoil.

4 [3]For thou hast broken the yoke of his burden, and the staff of his shoulder, the rod of his oppressor, as in the day of [d]Mĭd'ĭ-an.

5 [4]For every battle of the warrior *is* with confused noise, and garments rolled in blood; [5]but *this* shall be with burning *and* [6]fuel of fire.

6 [e]For unto us a child is born, unto us a [f]son is given: and [g]the government shall be upon his shoulder: and his name shall be called [h]Wonderful, Counseller, [i]The mighty God, The everlasting Father, [j]The Prince of Peace.

7 Of the increase of *his* government and peace [k]*there shall be* no end, upon the throne of Dā'vid, and upon his kingdom, to order it, and to establish it with judgment and with justice from henceforth even for ever. The zeal of the LORD of hosts will perform this.

8 ¶ The Lord sent a word into Jā'cob, and it hath lighted upon Ĭs'ra-el.

9 And all the people shall know, *even* Ē'phră-ĭm and the inhabitant of Sa-mā'rĭ-ȧ, that say in the pride and stoutness of heart,

10 The bricks are fallen down, but we will build with hewn stones: the sycomores are cut down, but we will change *them into* cedars.

11 Therefore the LORD shall set up the adversaries of Rē'zin against him, and [7]join his enemies together;

12 The Sўr'ĭ-ans before, and the Phĭ-lĭs'tĭnes behind; and they shall devour Ĭs'ra-el [8]with open mouth. For all this his anger is not turned away, but his hand *is* stretched out still.

13 ¶ For [l]the people turneth not unto him that smiteth them, neither do they seek the LORD of hosts.

14 Therefore the LORD will cut off from Ĭs'ra-el head and tail, branch and rush, in one day.

15 The ancient and honourable, he *is* the head; and the prophet that teacheth lies, he *is* the tail.

16 For [9]the leaders of this people cause *them* to err; and [10]*they that are* led of them *are* [11]*destroyed.*

17 Therefore the Lord shall have no joy in their young men, neither shall have mercy on their fatherless and widows: for every one *is* an hypocrite and an evildoer, and every mouth speaketh [12]folly. For all this his anger is not turned away, but his hand *is* stretched out still.

18 ¶ For wickedness burneth as the fire: it shall devour the briers and thorns, and shall kindle in the thickets of the forest, and they shall mount up *like* the lifting up of smoke.

19 Through the wrath of the LORD of hosts is the land darkened, and the people shall be as the [13]fuel of the fire: no man shall spare his brother.

20 And he shall [14]snatch on the right hand, and be hungry; and he shall eat on the left hand, [m]and they shall not be satisfied: they shall eat every man the flesh of his own arm:

21 Ma-năs'seh, Ē'phră-ĭm; and Ē'phră-ĭm, Ma-năs'seh: *and* they together *shall be* against Jū'dah. For all this his anger is not turned away, but his hand *is* stretched out still.

10 Woe unto them that decree unrighteous decrees, and [1]that write grievousness *which* they have prescribed;

2 To turn aside the needy from judgment, and to take away the right from the poor of my people, that widows

12 [g]1 Pet. 3.14
13 [h]Num. 20.12
[i]Luke 12.5
14 [j]Ezek. 11.16
[k]Luke 2.34; 1 Pet. 2.8
15 [l]Luke 20.18
16 [m]Dan. 12.4
17 [n]Hab. 2.3; Luke 2.25
18 [o]Heb. 2.13
[p]Zech. 3.8
19 [q]Ps. 106.28
20 [7]no morning

CHAPTER 9
1 [a]2 Ki. 15.29; 2 Chr. 16.4
[b]Lev. 26.24; Matt. 4.15
[1]Or, populous
2 [c]ch. 50.10; Eph. 5.8
3 [2]Or, to him
4 [3]Or, When thou brakest
[d]Judg. 7.22; ch. 10.26
5 [4]Or, When the whole battle of the warrior was, etc
[5]Or, and it was, etc
[6]meat
6 [e]Luke 2.11
[f]John 3.16
[g]Matt. 28.18; 1 Cor. 15.25
[h]Judg. 13.18
[i]Ps. 45.3-6; Tit. 2.13
[j]Eph. 2.14; Heb. 13.20
7 [k]Dan. 2.44; Luke 1.32
11 [7]mingle
12 [8]with whole mouth
13 [l]Jer. 5.3
16 [9]Or, they that call them blessed
[10]Or, they that are called blessed of them
[11]swallowed up
17 [12]Or, villany
19 [13]meat
20 [14]cut
[m]Lev. 26.26

CHAPTER 10
1 [1]Or, to the writers that write grievousness

may be their prey, and *that* they may rob the fatherless!

3 And what will ye do in [a]the day of visitation, and in the desolation *which* shall come from far? to whom will ye flee for help? and where will ye leave your glory?

4 Without me they shall bow down under the prisoners, and they shall fall under the slain. For all this his anger is not turned away, but his hand *is* stretched out still.

5 ¶ [2]O [3]Ăs-sȳr'ĭ-an, the rod of mine anger, [4]and the staff in their hand is mine indignation.

6 I will send him against an hypocritical nation, and against the people of my wrath will I give him a charge, to take the spoil, and to take the prey, and [5]to tread them down like the mire of the streets.

7 [b]Howbeit he meaneth not so, neither doth his heart think so; but *it is* in his heart to destroy and cut off nations not a few.

8 [c]For he saith, *Are* not my princes altogether kings?

9 *Is* not [d]Căl'nō as [e]Cär'chĕ-mĭsh? *is* not [f]Hā'math as Är'pad? *is* not Sa-mā'rĭ-ȧ [g]as Da-măs'cus?

10 As my hand hath found the kingdoms of the idols, and whose graven images did excel them of Je-ru'sa-lĕm and of Sa-mā'rĭ-ȧ;

11 Shall I not, as I have done unto Sa-mā'rĭ-ȧ and her idols, so do to Je-ru'sa-lĕm and her idols?

12 Wherefore it shall come to pass, *that* when the Lord hath performed his whole work upon mount Zī'ŏn and on Je-ru'sa-lĕm, I will [6]punish the fruit [7]of the stout heart of the king of Ăs-sȳr'ĭ-ȧ, and the glory of his high looks.

13 [h]For he saith, By the strength of my hand I have done *it,* and by my wisdom; for I am prudent: and I have removed the bounds of the people, and have robbed their treasures, and I have put down the inhabitants [8]like a valiant *man:*

14 And my hand hath found as a nest the riches of the people: and as one gathereth eggs *that are* left, have I gathered all the earth; and there was none that moved the wing, or opened the mouth, or peeped.

15 Shall [i]the ax boast itself against him that heweth therewith? *or* shall the saw magnify itself against him that shaketh it? [9]as if the rod should shake *itself* against them that lift it up, *or* as if the staff should lift up [10]*itself, as if it were* no wood.

16 Therefore shall the Lord, the Lord of hosts, send among his fat ones leanness; and under his glory he shall kindle a burning like the burning of a fire.

17 And the light of Ĭs'ra-el shall be for a fire, and his Holy One for a flame: and it shall burn and devour his thorns and his briers in one day;

18 And shall consume the glory of his forest, and of his fruitful field, [11]both soul and body: and they shall be as when a standardbearer fainteth.

19 And the rest of the trees of his forest shall be [12]few, that a child may write them.

20 ¶ And it shall come to pass in that day, *that* the remnant of Ĭs'ra-el, and such as are escaped of the house of Jā'cob, shall no more again stay upon him that smote them; but shall stay upon the LORD, the Holy One of Ĭs'ra-el, in truth.

21 The remnant shall return, *even* the remnant of Jā'cob, unto the mighty God.

22 [j]For though thy people Ĭs'ra-el be as the sand of the sea, *yet* a remnant [13]of them shall return: the consumption decreed shall overflow [14]with righteousness.

23 [k]For the Lord GOD of hosts shall make a consumption, even determined, in the midst of all the land.

24 ¶ Therefore thus saith the Lord GOD of hosts, O my people that dwellest in Zī'ŏn, be not afraid of the Ăs-sȳr'ĭ-an: he shall smite thee with a rod, [15]and shall lift up his staff against thee, after the manner of Ē'ġypt.

25 For yet a very little while, [l]and the indignation shall cease, and mine anger in their destruction.

26 And the LORD of hosts shall stir up a scourge for him according to the slaughter of Mĭd'ĭ-an at the rock of Ō'reb: and *as* his rod *was* upon the sea, so shall he lift it up after the manner of Ē'ġypt.

27 And it shall come to pass in that day, *that* his burden [16]shall be taken away from off thy shoulder, and his yoke from off thy neck, and the yoke shall be destroyed because of [m]the anointing.

28 He is come to [n]A-ī'ath, he is passed to Mĭg'rŏn; at Mĭch'mash he hath laid up his carriages:

29 They are gone over [o]the passage: they have taken up their lodging at Gē'bȧ; Rā'mah is afraid; Gĭb'e-ah of Saul is fled.

30 [17]Lift up thy voice, O daughter [p]of Găl'lĭm: cause it to be heard unto Lā'ish, O poor Ăn'a-thoth.

31 [q]Măd-mē'nah is removed; the inhabitants of Gē'bim gather themselves to flee.

32 As yet shall he remain [r]at Nŏb that day: he shall shake his hand *against* the mount of the daughter of Zī'ŏn, the hill of Je-ru'sa-lĕm.

33 Behold, the Lord, the LORD of hosts, shall lop the bough with terror: and the high ones of stature *shall be* hewn down, and the haughty shall be humbled.

34 And he shall cut down the thickets of the forest with iron, and Lĕb'a-non shall fall [18]by a mighty one.

11 And [a]there shall come forth a rod out of the [1]stem of [b]Jĕs'se, and [c]a Branch shall grow out of his roots:

2 [d]And the spirit of the LORD shall rest upon him, the spirit of wisdom and understanding, the spirit of counsel

3 [a]Hos. 9.7; Luke 19.44
5 [2]Or, Woe to the Assyrian [3]Asshur [4]Or, though
6 [5]to lay them a treading
7 [b]Mic. 4.12
8 [c]2 Ki. 18.24
9 [d]Amos 6.2 [e]2 Chr. 35.20; Jer. 46.2 [f]Num. 13.21; 2 Ki. 23.33 [g]2 Ki. 16.9
12 [6]visit upon [7]of the greatness of the heart
13 [h]Ex. 15.9; ch. 37.24 [8]Or, like many people
15 [i]Jer. 51.20; Rom. 9.20-21 [9]Or, as if a rod should shake them that lift it up [10]Or, that which is not wood
18 [11]from the soul, and even to the flesh
19 [12]number
22 [j]Mic. 5.3; Rom. 9.27 [13]in, or, among [14]Or, in
23 [k]ch. 28.22; Dan. 9.27
24 [15]Or, but he shall lift up his staff for thee
25 [l]Dan. 11.36
27 [16]shall remove [m]Ps. 105.15
28 [n]Neh. 11.31
29 [o]1 Sam. 13.23
30 [17]Cry shrill with thy voice [p]1 Sam. 25.44
31 [q]Josh. 15.31
32 [r]1 Sam. 21.1
34 [18]Or, mightily

CHAPTER 11
1 [a]ch. 53.2; Rev. 22.16 [1]Or, stump [b]Acts 13.23 [c]Jer. 23.5; Zech. 3.8
2 [d]ch. 42.1; Acts 10.38

and might, the spirit of knowledge and
of the fear of the LORD;
3 And shall make him of [2]quick understanding in the fear of the LORD:
and he shall not judge after the sight of
his eyes, neither reprove after the hearing of his ears:
4 But [e]with righteousness shall he
judge the poor, and [3]reprove with equity for the meek of the earth: and he
shall [f]smite the earth with the rod of
his mouth, and with the breath of his
lips shall he slay the wicked.
5 And [g]righteousness shall be the
girdle of his loins, and faithfulness the
girdle of his reins.
6 [h]The wolf also shall dwell with the
lamb, and the leopard shall lie down
with the kid; and the calf and the
young lion and the fatling together;
and a little child shall lead them.
7 And the cow and the bear shall
feed; their young ones shall lie down
together: and the lion shall eat straw
like the ox.
8 And the sucking child shall play
on the hole of the asp, and the weaned
child shall put his hand on the [4]cockatrice' den.
9 They shall not hurt nor destroy in
all my holy mountain: for [i]the earth
shall be full of the knowledge of the
LORD, as the waters cover the sea.
10 ¶ And in that day there shall be a
root of Jĕs'se, which shall stand for an
ensign of the people; to it shall the
[j]Gĕn-tīles seek: and [k]his rest shall be
[5]glorious.
11 And it shall come to pass in that
day, *that* the Lord shall set his hand
again the second time to recover the
remnant of his people, which shall be
left, [l]from Ăs-sȳr'ĭ-ȧ, and from Ē'ġypt,
and from Păth'ros, and from Cŭsh, and
from Ē'lăm, and from Shī'när, and
from Hā'math, and from the islands of
the sea.
12 And he shall set up an ensign for
the nations, and shall assemble the outcasts of Ĭs'ra-el, and gather together
[m]the dispersed of Jū'dah from the four
[6]corners of the earth.
13 [n]The envy also of Ē'phră-ĭm shall
depart, and the adversaries of Jū'dah
shall be cut off: Ē'phră-ĭm shall not
envy Jū'dah, and Jū'dah shall not vex
Ē'phră-ĭm.
14 But they shall fly upon the shoulders of the Phĭ-lĭs'tĭnes toward the
west; they shall spoil [7]them of the east
together: [8]they shall lay their hand
upon Ē'dom and Mō'ab; [9]and the children of Ăm'mŏn shall obey them.
15 And the LORD shall utterly destroy the tongue of the E-ġȳp'tian sea;
and with his mighty wind shall he
shake his hand over the river, and
shall smite it in the seven streams,
[o]and make *men* go over [10]dryshod.
16 And there shall be an highway
for the remnant of his people, which
shall be left, from Ăs-sȳr'ĭ-ȧ; [p]like as it
was to Ĭs'ra-el in the day that he came
up out of the land of Ē'ġypt.

3 [2]scent, or, smell
4 [e]Ps. 72.2-4; Rev. 19.11
[3]Or, argue
[f]Mal. 4.6; Rev. 2.16
5 [g]Eph. 6.14
6 [h]Hos. 2.18
8 [4]Or, adder's
9 [i]Hab. 2.14
10 [j]Rom. 15.10
[k]Heb. 4.1
[5]glory
11 [l]Zech. 10.10
12 [m]John 7.35
[6]wings
13 [n]Gal. 3.28
14 [7]the children of the east
[8]Edom and Moab shall be the laying on of their hand
[9]the children of Ammon their obedience
15 [o]Rev. 16.12
[10]in shoes
16 [p]Ex. 14.29; ch. 51.10

CHAPTER 12
1 [a]ch. 2.11; Zech. 14.20-21
3 [b]Jer. 2.13; John 4.10-14
4 [1]Or, proclaim his name
6 [c]ch. 54.1; Luke 19.37-40
[2]inhabitress

CHAPTER 13
2 [a]Jer. 50.2
[b]Jer. 51.25
3 [c]Joel 3.11
4 [1]the likeness of
6 [d]Amos 5.18;
7 [2]Or, fall down
8 [3]wonder
[4]every man at his neighbour
[5]faces of the flames
9 [e]Mal. 4.1
10 [f]Matt. 24.29
11 [6]That is, the Babylonian empire
13 [g]Joel 3.16;
[h]Lam. 1.12

12 And [a]in that day thou shalt say,
O LORD, I will praise thee: though
thou wast angry with me, thine anger is
turned away, and thou comfortedst me.
2 Behold, God *is* my salvation; I will
trust, and not be afraid: for the LORD
JE-HŌ'VAH *is* my strength and *my*
song; he also is become my salvation.
3 Therefore with joy shall ye draw
[b]water out of the wells of salvation.
4 And in that day shall ye say, Praise
the LORD, [1]call upon his name, declare
his doings among the people, make
mention that his name is exalted.
5 Sing unto the LORD; for he hath
done excellent things: this *is* known in
all the earth.
6 [c]Cry out and shout, thou [2]inhabitant of Zī'ŏn: for great *is* the Holy One
of Ĭs'ra-el in the midst of thee.
13 The burden of Băb'ȳ-lon, which
I-sā'iah the son of Ā'moz did see.
2 [a]Lift ye up a banner [b]upon the
high mountain, exalt the voice unto
them, shake the hand, that they may
go into the gates of the nobles.
3 I have commanded my sanctified
ones, I have also called [c]my mighty
ones for mine anger, *even* them that
rejoice in my highness.
4 The noise of a multitude in the
mountains, [1]like as of a great people; a
tumultuous noise of the kingdoms of
nations gathered together: the LORD of
hosts mustereth the host of the battle.
5 They come from a far country,
from the end of heaven, *even* the LORD,
and the weapons of his indignation, to
destroy the whole land.
6 ¶ Howl ye; [d]for the day of the
LORD *is* at hand; it shall come as a destruction from the Almighty.
7 Therefore shall all hands [2]be faint,
and every man's heart shall melt:
8 And they shall be afraid: pangs
and sorrows shall take hold of them;
they shall be in pain as a woman
that travaileth: they shall [3]be amazed
[4]one at another; their faces *shall be as*
[5]flames.
9 Behold, [e]the day of the LORD cometh, cruel both with wrath and fierce
anger, to lay the land desolate: and he
shall destroy the sinners thereof out of
it.
10 For the stars of heaven and the
constellations thereof shall not give
their light: the sun shall be [f]darkened
in his going forth, and the moon shall
not cause her light to shine.
11 And I will punish [6]the world for
their evil, and the wicked for their iniquity; and I will cause the arrogancy of
the proud to cease, and will lay low the
haughtiness of the terrible.
12 I will make a man more precious
than fine gold; even a man than the
golden wedge of Ō'phĭr.
13 [g]Therefore I will shake the heavens, and the earth shall remove out of
her place, in the wrath of the LORD of
hosts, and in [h]the day of his fierce
anger.
14 And it shall be as the chased roe,
and as a sheep that no man taketh up:

they shall every man turn to his own
people, and flee every one into his own
land.
15 Every one that is found shall be
thrust through; and every one that
is joined *unto them* shall fall by the
sword.
16 Their children also shall be
[i]dashed to pieces before their eyes;
their houses shall be spoiled, and their
wives ravished.
17 [j]Behold, I will stir up the Mēdes
against them, which shall not regard
silver; and *as for* gold, they shall not
delight in it.
18 *Their* bows also shall dash the
young men to pieces; and they shall
have no pity on the fruit of the womb;
their eye shall not spare children.
19 ¶ And Băb'ȳ-lon, the glory of
kingdoms, the beauty of the Chăl'dees'
excellency, shall be [7]as when God overthrew Sŏd'om and Go-mŏr'rah.
20 [k]It shall never be inhabited, neither shall it be dwelt in from generation to generation: neither shall the A-
rā'bĭ-an pitch tent there; neither shall
the shepherds make their fold there.
21 But [8]wild beasts of the desert
shall lie there; and their houses shall be
full of [9]doleful creatures; and [10][11]owls
shall dwell there, and [12]satyrs shall
dance there.
22 And [13]the wild beasts of the islands shall cry in their [14]desolate
houses, and [15]dragons in *their* pleasant
palaces: and her time *is* near to come,
and her days shall not be prolonged.

14 For the LORD will have mercy on
Jā'cob, and [a]will yet choose Ĭs'-
ra-el, and set them in their own land:
[b]and the strangers shall be joined with
them, and they shall cleave to the
house of Jā'cob.
2 And the people shall take them,
and bring them to their place: and the
house of Ĭs'ra-el shall possess them
in the land of the LORD for servants
and handmaids: and they shall take
them captives, [1]whose captives they
were; and they shall rule over their
oppressors.
3 And it shall come to pass in the
day that the LORD shall give thee rest
from thy sorrow, and from thy fear,
and from the hard bondage wherein
thou wast made to serve,
4 ¶ That thou [c]shalt take up this
[2]proverb against the king of Băb'ȳ-
lon, and say, How hath the oppressor
ceased! the [3]golden city ceased!
5 The LORD hath broken the staff
of the wicked, *and* the sceptre of the
rulers.
6 He who smote the people in wrath
with [4]a continual stroke, he that ruled
the nations in anger, is persecuted, *and*
none hindereth.
7 The whole earth is at rest, *and* is
quiet: they break forth into singing.
8 [d]Yea, the fir trees rejoice at thee,
and the cedars of Lĕb'a-non, *saying*,
Since thou art laid down, no feller is
come up against us.
9 [5]Hell from beneath is moved for
thee to meet *thee* at thy coming: it
stirreth up the dead for thee, *even* all
the [6]chief ones of the earth; it hath
raised up from their thrones all the
kings of the nations.
10 All they shall speak and say unto
thee, Art thou also become weak as
we? art thou become like unto us?
11 Thy pomp is brought down to the
grave, *and* the noise of thy viols: the
worm is spread under thee, and the
worms cover thee.
12 How art thou fallen from heaven,
[7]O Lu'çĭ-fēr, son of the morning! *how*
art thou cut down to the ground, which
didst weaken the nations!
13 For thou hast said in thine heart,
[e]I will ascend into heaven, [f]I will exalt
my throne above the stars of God: I
will sit also upon the mount of the congregation, [g]in the sides of the north:
14 I will ascend above the heights of
the clouds; [h]I will be like the most
High.
15 Yet thou [i]shalt be brought down
to hell, to the sides of the pit.
16 They that see thee shall narrowly
look upon thee, *and* consider thee, *saying, Is* this the man that made the earth
to tremble, that did shake kingdoms;
17 *That* made the world as a wilderness, and destroyed the cities thereof;
that [8]opened not the house of his
prisoners?
18 All the kings of the nations, *even*
all of them, lie in glory, every one in his
own house.
19 But thou art cast out of thy grave
like an abominable branch, *and as* the
raiment of those that are slain, thrust
through with a sword, that go down to
the stones of the pit; as a carcase trodden under feet.
20 Thou shalt not be joined with
them in burial, because thou hast destroyed thy land, *and* slain thy people:
the seed of evildoers shall never be renowned.
21 Prepare slaughter for his children [j]for the iniquity of their fathers;
that they do not rise, nor possess the
land, nor fill the face of the world with
cities.
22 For I will rise up against them,
saith the LORD of hosts, and cut off
from Băb'ȳ-lon the name, and remnant, [k]and son, and nephew, saith the
LORD.
23 I will also make it a possession
for the bittern, and pools of water: and
I will sweep it with the besom of destruction, saith the LORD of hosts.
24 ¶ The LORD of hosts hath sworn,
saying, Surely as I have thought, so
shall it come to pass; and as I have
purposed, *so* shall it stand:
25 That I will break the Ăs-sȳr'ĭ-an
in my land, and upon my mountains
tread him under foot: then shall his
yoke depart from off them, and his burden depart from off their shoulders.
26 This *is* the purpose that is purposed upon the whole earth: and this *is*

16 [i]Nah. 3.10
17 [j]Jer. 51.11
19 [7]as the overthrowing
20 [k]ch. 14.23
21 [8]Ziim [9]Ochim [10]Or, ostriches [11]daughters of the owl [12]shaggy beasts, or, wild goats
22 [13]Iim [14]Or, palaces [15]Or, jackals

CHAPTER 14
1 [a]Ps. 102.13-16; ch. 54.7-8; Jer. 31.3-4-10-11; Zech. 1.17 [b]ch. 60.4-5-10
2 [1]that had taken them captives
4 [c]ch. 13.19; Hab. 2.6 [2]Or, taunting speech [3]Or, exactress of gold
6 [4]a stroke without removing
8 [d]ch. 55.12; Ezek. 31.16
9 [5]Or, The grave [6]leaders, or, great goats
12 [7]Or, O day star
13 [e]Lam. 2.1; Matt. 11.23 [f]Dan. 8.10; Rev. 12.4 [g]Ps. 48.2
14 [h]Zeph. 2.15; 2 Thess. 2.4
15 [i]ch. 47.8; Ezek. 28.8-9; Matt. 11.23; Acts 12.23
17 [8]Or, did not let his prisoners loose homewards
21 [j]Ex. 20.5; Job 18.19; Matt. 23.35
22 [k]1 Ki. 14.10; Job 18.19; Prov. 10.7

the hand that is stretched out upon all
the nations.
27 For the LORD of hosts hath [l]pur-
posed, and who shall disannul *it?* and
his hand *is* stretched out, and who
shall turn it back?
28 In the year that [m]king Ā'hăz died
was this burden.
29 ¶ Rejoice not thou, whole Păl-es-
tī'nȧ, because the rod of him that smote
thee is broken: for out of the serpent's
root shall come forth a [9]cockatrice, and
his fruit *shall be* a fiery flying serpent.
30 And the firstborn of the poor shall
feed, and the needy shall lie down in
safety: and I will kill thy root with famine, and he shall slay thy remnant.
31 Howl, O gate; cry, O city; thou,
whole Păl-es-tī'nȧ, *art* dissolved: for
there shall come from the north a
smoke, and [10]none *shall be* alone in his
[11]appointed times.
32 What shall *one* then answer the
messengers of the nation? That the
LORD hath founded Zī'ŏn, and the poor
of his people shall [12]trust in it.
15 The [a]burden of Mō'ab. Because
in the night [b]Ar of Mō'ab is laid
waste, *and* [1]brought to silence; because in the night Kĭr of Mō'ab is laid
waste, *and* brought to silence;
2 He is gone up to Bā'jith, and to Dī'-
bŏn, the high places, to weep: Mō'ab
shall howl over Nē'bo, and over Mĕd'-
e-bȧ: on all their heads *shall be* baldness, *and* every beard cut off.
3 In their streets they shall gird themselves with sackcloth: on the tops of
their houses, and in their streets, every
one shall howl, [2]weeping abundantly.
4 And [c]Hĕsh'bŏn shall cry, and Ē-
le-ā'leh: their voice shall be heard *even*
unto Jā'hăz: therefore the armed soldiers of Mō'ab shall cry out; his life
shall be grievous unto him.
5 My heart shall cry out for Mō'ab;
[3]his fugitives *shall flee* unto Zō'ar, an
heifer of three years old: for [d]by the
mounting up of Lụ'hith with weeping
shall they go it up; for in the way of
Hŏr-o-nā'im they shall raise up a cry of
[4]destruction.
6 For the waters of Nĭm'rim shall
be [5]desolate: for the hay is withered
away, the grass faileth, there is no
green thing.
7 Therefore the abundance they have
gotten, and that which they have laid
up, shall they carry away to the [6]brook
of the willows.
8 For the cry is gone round about the
borders of Mō'ab; the howling thereof
unto Ĕg'la-ĭm, and the howling thereof
unto Bē'er–ē'lim.
9 For the waters of Dī'mon shall be
full of blood: for I will bring [7]more
upon Dī'mon, lions upon him that escapeth of Mō'ab, and upon the remnant of the land.
16 Send [a]ye the lamb to the ruler of
the land from [1]Sē'lȧ to the wilderness, unto the mount of the daughter of
Zī'ŏn.
2 For it shall be, *that,* as a wandering bird [2]cast out of the nest, *so* the
daughters of Mō'ab shall be at the
fords of [b]Ăr'nŏn.
3 [3]Take counsel, execute judgment;
make thy shadow as the night in the
midst of the noonday; hide the outcasts; bewray not him that wandereth.
4 Let mine outcasts dwell with thee,
Mō'ab; be thou a covert to them from
the face of the spoiler: for the [4]extor-
tioner is at an end, the spoiler ceaseth,
[5]the oppressors are consumed out of
the land.
5 And in mercy [c]shall the throne be
[6]established: and he shall sit upon it in
truth in the tabernacle of Dā'vid, judging, and seeking judgment, and hasting righteousness.
6 ¶ We have heard of the [d]pride of
Mō'ab; *he is* very proud: *even* of his
haughtiness, and his pride, and his
wrath: [7]*but* his lies *shall* not *be* so.
7 Therefore shall Mō'ab howl for
Mō'ab, every one shall howl: for the
foundations [e]of Kĭr–hăr'e-sĕth shall
ye [8]mourn; surely *they are* stricken.
8 For the fields of Hĕsh'bŏn languish, *and* the vine of Sĭb'mah: the
lords of the heathen have broken down
the principal plants thereof, they are
come *even* unto Jā'zēr, they wandered
through the wilderness: her branches
are [9]stretched out, they are gone over
the sea.
9 ¶ Therefore I will bewail with the
weeping of Jā'zēr the vine of Sĭb'mah: I
will water thee with my tears, O Hĕsh'-
bŏn, and Ē-le-ā'leh: for [10]the shouting
for thy summer fruits and for thy harvest is fallen.
10 And gladness is taken away, and
joy out of the plentiful field; and in the
vineyards there shall be no singing,
neither shall there be shouting: the
treaders shall tread out no wine in
their presses; I have made *their vintage* shouting to cease.
11 Wherefore my bowels shall sound
like an harp for Mō'ab, and mine inward parts for Kĭr–hā'resh.
12 ¶ And it shall come to pass, when
it is seen that Mō'ab is weary on [f]the
high place, that he shall come to his
sanctuary to pray; but he shall not
prevail.
13 This *is* the word that the LORD
hath spoken concerning Mō'ab since
that time.
14 But now the LORD hath spoken,
saying, Within three years, [g]as the
years of an hireling, and the glory of
Mō'ab shall be contemned, with all
that great multitude; and the remnant
shall be very small *and* [11]feeble.
17 The [a]burden of Da-măs'cus. Behold, Da-măs'cus is taken away
from *being* a city, and it shall be a ruinous heap.
2 The cities of Ăr'ō-ēr *are* forsaken:
they shall be for flocks, which shall lie
down, and [b]none shall make *them*
afraid.
3 [c]The fortress also shall cease from
Ē'phrā-ĭm, and the kingdom from Da-
măs'cus, and the remnant of Sŷr'ĭ-ȧ:

---

27 [l]2 Chr. 20.6; Jer. 4.28
28 [m]2 Ki. 16.20;
29 [9]Or, adder
31 [10]Or, he shall not be alone
[11]Or, assemblies
32 [12]Or, betake themselves unto it

CHAPTER 15
1 [a]ch. 11.14; [b]Num. 21.28
[1]Or, cut off
3 [2]descending into weeping, or, coming down with weeping
4 [c]Num. 32.3
5 [3]Or, to the borders thereof, even to Zoar, as an heifer
[d]Jer. 48.5
[4]breaking
6 [5]desolations
7 [6]Or, valley of the Arabians
9 [7]additions

CHAPTER 16
1 [a]2 Ki. 3.4
[1]a rock, or, Petra
2 [2]Or, a nest forsaken
[b]Num. 21.13
3 [3]Bring
4 [4]wringer
[5]the treaders down
5 [c]Ps. 89.14;
[6]Or, prepared
6 [d]Jer. 48.29
[7]Or, the falsehood of his pretensions
7 [e]2 Ki. 3.25
[8]Or, mutter
8 [9]Or, plucked up
9 [10]Or, the alarm is fallen upon, etc
12 [f]Num. 23.3;
14 [g]Deut. 15.18;
[11]Or, not many

CHAPTER 17
1 [a]Jer. 49.23
2 [b]Jer. 7.33
3 [c]ch. 7.16

they shall be as the glory of the children of Is'ra-el, saith the LORD of hosts.
4 And in that day it shall come to
pass, *that* the glory of Jā'cob shall be
made thin, and [d]the fatness of his flesh
shall wax lean.
5 [e]And it shall be as when the harvestman gathereth the corn, and reapeth the ears with his arm; and it shall
be as he that gathereth ears in the valley of Rĕph'a-ĭm.
6 ¶ Yet gleaning grapes shall be
left in it, as the shaking of an olive
tree, two *or* three berries in the top of
the uppermost bough, four *or* five in
the outmost fruitful branches thereof,
saith the LORD God of Is'ra-el.
7 At that day shall a man [f]look to
his Maker, and his eyes shall have respect to the Holy One of Is'ra-el.
8 And he shall not look to the altars,
the work of his hands, neither shall
respect *that* which his fingers have
made, either the groves, or the [1]images.
9 ¶ In that day shall his strong cities
be as a forsaken bough, and an uppermost branch, which they left because
of the children of Is'ra-el: and there
shall be desolation.
10 Because [g]thou hast forgotten the
God of thy salvation, and hast not been
mindful of the rock of thy strength,
therefore shalt thou plant pleasant
plants, and shalt set it with strange
slips:
11 In the day shalt thou make thy
plant to grow, and in the morning shalt
thou make thy seed to flourish: *but* the
harvest *shall be* [2]a heap in the day of
grief and of desperate sorrow.
12 ¶ Woe to the [3]multitude of many
people, *which* make a noise like the
noise of the seas; and to the rushing of
nations, *that* make a rushing like the
rushing of [4]mighty waters!
13 The nations shall rush like the
rushing of many waters: but *God* shall
rebuke them, and they shall flee far off,
and shall be chased as the chaff of the
mountains before the wind, and like [5]a
rolling thing before the whirlwind.
14 And behold at eveningtide trouble; *and* before the morning he *is* not.
[h]This *is* the portion of them that spoil
us, and the lot of them that rob us.

18 Woe to the land shadowing with
wings, which *is* beyond the rivers of Ē-thĭ-ō'pĭ-a:
2 That sendeth ambassadors by the
sea, even in vessels of bulrushes upon
the waters, *saying*, Go, ye swift messengers, to a nation [1]scattered and peeled,
to a people terrible from their beginning hitherto; [2]a nation meted out and
trodden down, [3]whose land the rivers
have spoiled!
3 All ye inhabitants of the world,
and dwellers on the earth, see ye,
when he lifteth up an ensign on the
mountains; and when he bloweth a
trumpet, hear ye.
4 For so the LORD said unto me, I
will take my rest, and I will [4]consider
in my dwelling place like a clear heat
[5]upon herbs, *and* like a cloud of dew in
the heat of harvest.
5 For afore the harvest, when the
bud is perfect, and the sour grape is
ripening in the flower, he shall both cut
off the sprigs with pruning hooks, and
take away *and* cut down the branches.
6 They shall be left together unto
the fowls of the mountains, and to the
beasts of the earth: and the fowls shall
summer upon them, and all the beasts
of the earth shall winter upon them.
7 ¶ In that time [a]shall the present be
brought unto the LORD of hosts of a
people [6]scattered and peeled, and from
a people terrible from their beginning
hitherto; a nation meted out and trodden under foot, whose land the rivers
have spoiled, to the place of the name
of the LORD of hosts, the mount Zī'ŏn.

19 The burden of Ē'gypt. Behold,
the LORD rideth upon a swift
cloud, and shall come into Ē'gypt: and
the idols of Ē'gypt shall be moved at
his presence, and the heart of Ē'gypt
shall melt in the midst of it.
2 And I will [1][a]set the E-gȳp'tians
against the E-gȳp'tians: and they shall
fight every one against his brother,
and every one against his neighbour;
city against city, *and* kingdom against
kingdom.
3 And the spirit of Ē'gypt [2]shall fail
in the midst thereof; and I will [3]destroy
the counsel thereof: and they shall
seek to the idols, and to the charmers,
and to them that have familiar spirits,
and to the wizards.
4 And the E-gȳp'tians will I [4]give
over into the hand of a cruel lord; and
a fierce king shall rule over them, saith
the Lord, the LORD of hosts.
5 And [b]the waters shall fail from the
sea, and the river shall be wasted and
dried up.
6 And they shall turn the rivers far
away; *and* the brooks [c]of defence shall
be emptied and dried up: the reeds and
flags shall wither.
7 The paper reeds by the brooks, by
the mouth of the brooks, and every
thing sown by the brooks, shall wither,
be driven away, [5]and be no *more*.
8 The fishers also shall mourn, and
all they that cast angle into the brooks
shall lament, and they that spread nets
upon the waters shall languish.
9 Moreover they that work in fine
flax, and they that weave [6]networks,
shall be confounded.
10 And they shall be broken in the
[7]purposes thereof, all that make sluices
and ponds [8]for fish.
11 ¶ Surely the princes of Zō'an *are*
fools, the counsel of the wise counsellors of Phā'raōh is become brutish:
how say ye unto Phā'raōh, I *am* the
son of the wise, the son of ancient
kings?
12 [d]Where *are* they? where *are* thy
wise *men?* and let them tell thee now,
and let them know what the LORD of
hosts hath purposed upon Ē'gypt.
13 The princes of Zō'an are become fools, [e]the princes of Nŏph

4 [d]ch. 10.16
5 [e]Jer. 51.33; Rev. 14.15-19
7 [f]2 Chr. 30.11; Ps. 34.5; Hos. 5.15; Mic. 7.7; Zech. 12.10
8 [1]Or, sun images
10 [g]Ps. 106.13-21
11 [2]Or, removed in the day of inheritance, and there shall be deadly sorrow
12 [3]Or, noise [4]Or, many
13 [5]Or, thistledown
14 [h]Judg. 5.31; Ps. 8.3-9-18; Prov. 22.23

CHAPTER 18
2 [1]Or, outspread and polished [2]a nation of line, line, and treading under foot: or, a nation that meteth out, and treadeth down [3]Or, whose land the rivers despise
4 [4]Or, regard my set dwelling [5]Or, after rain
7 [a]Ps. 68.31; Zeph. 3.10; Mal. 1.11 [6]Or, outspread and polished

CHAPTER 19
2 [1]mingle [a]Judg. 7.22; 2 Chr. 20.23
3 [2]shall be emptied [3]swallow up
4 [4]Or, shut up
5 [b]Jer. 51.36; Ezek. 30.12
6 [c]2 Ki. 19.24
7 [5]and shall not be
9 [6]Or, white works
10 [7]foundations [8]of living things
12 [d]ch. 41.22-23; 1 Cor. 1.20
13 [e]Jer. 2.16; Hos. 9.6

are deceived; they have also seduced
Ē'ġypt, *even* [9]*they that are* the stay
of the tribes thereof.
14 The LORD hath mingled [10]a perverse spirit in the midst thereof: and
they have caused Ē'ġypt to err in every
work thereof, as a drunken *man* stag-
gereth in his vomit.
15 Neither shall there be *any* work
for Ē'ġypt, which the head or tail,
branch or rush, may do.
16 In that day shall Ē'ġypt [f]be like
unto women: and it shall be afraid and
fear because of the shaking of the
hand of the LORD of hosts, which he
shaketh over it.
17 And the land of Jū'dah shall be
a terror unto Ē'ġypt, every one that
maketh mention thereof shall be afraid
in himself, because of the counsel of
the LORD of hosts, which he hath determined against it.
18 ¶ In that day shall five cities in
the land of Ē'ġypt speak [11]the language of Cā'năan, and swear to the
LORD of hosts; one shall be called, The
city [12]of destruction.
19 In that day [g]shall there be an altar to the LORD in the midst of the land
of Ē'ġypt, and a pillar at the border
thereof to the LORD.
20 And [h]it shall be for a sign and for
a witness unto the LORD of hosts in the
land of Ē'ġypt: for they shall cry unto
the LORD because of the oppressors,
and he shall send them a saviour, and
a great one, and he shall deliver them.
21 And the LORD shall be known to
Ē'ġypt, and the E-ġȳp'tians shall know
the LORD in that day, and [i]shall do sacrifice and oblation; yea, they shall vow
a vow unto the LORD, and perform *it.*
22 And the LORD shall smite Ē'ġypt:
he shall smite and heal *it:* and they
shall return *even* to the LORD, and he
shall be intreated of them, and shall
heal them.
23 ¶ In that day [j]shall there be a
highway out of Ē'ġypt to Ăs-sȳr'ĭ-ȧ,
and the Ăs-sȳr'ĭ-an shall come into
Ē'ġypt, and the E-ġȳp'tian into Ăs-
sȳr'ĭ-ȧ, and the E-ġȳp'tians shall serve
with the Ăs-sȳr'ĭ-ans.
24 In that day shall Ĭs'ra-el be the
third with Ē'ġypt and with Ăs-sȳr'ĭ-ȧ,
even a blessing in the midst of the
land:
25 Whom the LORD of hosts shall
bless, saying, Blessed *be* Ē'ġypt my
people, and Ăs-sȳr'ĭ-ȧ [k]the work of my
hands, and Ĭs'ra-el mine inheritance.

20 In the year that [a]Tär'tan came
unto Ăsh'dŏd, (when Sär'gon the
king of Ăs-sȳr'ĭ-ȧ sent him,) and fought
against Ăsh'dŏd, and took it;
2 At the same time spake the LORD
[1]by I-sā'iah the son of Ā'moz, saying,
Go and loose [b]the sackcloth from off
thy loins, and put off thy shoe from thy
foot. And he did so, [c]walking naked
and barefoot.
3 And the LORD said, Like as my servant I-sā'iah hath walked naked and
barefoot three years [d]*for* a sign and
wonder upon Ē'ġypt and upon
Ē-thĭ-ō'pĭ-a;
4 So shall the king of Ăs-sȳr'ĭ-ȧ
lead away [2]the E-ġȳp'tians prisoners,
and the Ē-thĭ-ō'pĭ-ans captives, young
and old, naked and barefoot, [e]even
with *their* buttocks uncovered, to the
[3]shame of Ē'ġypt.
5 [f]And they shall be afraid and
ashamed of Ē-thĭ-ō'pĭ-a their expectation, and of Ē'ġypt their glory.
6 And the inhabitant of this [4]isle
shall say in that day, Behold, such *is*
our expectation, whither we flee for
help to be delivered from the king of
Ăs-sȳr'ĭ-ȧ: and how shall we escape?

21 The burden of the desert of the
sea. As [a]whirlwinds in the south
pass through; *so* it cometh from the
desert, from a terrible land.
2 A [1]grievous vision is declared unto
me; [b]the treacherous dealer dealeth
treacherously, and the spoiler spoileth.
[c]Go up, O Ē'lăm: besiege, O Mē'dĭ-ȧ;
all the sighing thereof have I made to
cease.
3 Therefore are my loins filled with
pain: pangs have taken hold upon me,
as the pangs of a woman that travaileth: I was bowed down at the hearing *of it;* I was dismayed at the seeing
of it.
4 [2]My heart panted, fearfulness affrighted me: [d]the night of my pleasure
hath he [3]turned into fear unto me.
5 [e]Prepare the table, watch in the
watchtower, eat, drink: arise, ye
princes, *and* anoint the shield.
6 For thus hath the Lord said unto
me, Go, set a watchman, let him declare what he seeth.
7 And he saw a chariot *with* a couple of horsemen, a chariot of asses,
and a chariot of camels; and he hearkened diligently with much heed:
8 And [4]he cried, A lion: My lord, I
stand continually upon the [f]watch-
tower in the daytime, and I am set in
my ward [5]whole nights:
9 And, behold, here cometh a chariot of men, *with* a couple of horsemen.
And he answered and said, [g]Băb'ȳ-lon
is fallen, is fallen; and all the graven
images of her gods he hath broken
unto the ground.
10 [h]O my threshing, and the [6]corn
of my floor: that which I have heard of
the LORD of hosts, the God of Ĭs'ra-el,
have I declared unto you.
11 ¶ [i]The burden of Dū'mah. He
calleth to me out of Sē'ĭr, Watchman,
what of the night? Watchman, what of
the night?
12 The watchman said, The morning cometh, and also the night: if ye
will inquire, inquire ye: return, come.
13 ¶ The burden upon A-rā'bĭ-ȧ. In
the forest in A-rā'bĭ-ȧ shall ye lodge, O
ye travelling companies [j]of Dĕd'a-nĭm.
14 The inhabitants of the land of
[k]Tema [7]brought water to him that was
thirsty, they prevented with their bread
him that fled.
15 For they fled [8]from the swords,
from the drawn sword, and from the

---

[9]corners, or, governors
14 [10]a spirit of perverseness
16 [f]Ps. 48.6; Nah. 3.13
18 [11]the lip
[12]Or, of Heres, or, of the sun
19 [g]Gen. 12.7; Heb. 13.10
20 [h]Josh. 4.20; ch. 55.13
21 [i]Mal. 1.11
23 [j]ch. 11.15
25 [k]Ps. 100.3; Phil. 1.6

CHAPTER 20
1 [a]2 Ki. 18.17
2 [1]by the hand of Isaiah
[b]Zech. 13.4
[c]1 Sam. 19.24
3 [d]ch. 8.18
4 [2]the captivity of Egypt
[e]2 Sam. 10.4; Mic. 1.11
[3]nakedness
5 [f]2 Ki. 18.21; ch. 31.1-3
6 [4]Or, country

CHAPTER 21
1 [a]Zech. 9.14
2 [1]hard
[b]1 Sam. 24.13; ch. 24.16
[c]ch. 13.17; Jer. 49.34
4 [2]Or, My mind wandered
[d]Deut. 28.67
[3]put
5 [e]Dan. 5.5
8 [4]Or, cried as a lion
[f]Hab. 2.1
[5]Or, every night
9 [g]ch. 13.19; Rev. 14.8
10 [h]Jer. 51.33; Hab. 3.12
[6]son
11 [i]1 Chr. 1.30; Obad. 1
13 [j]1 Chr. 1.9
14 [k]Job 6.19
[7]Or, bring ye
15 [8]from the face, or, for fear

bent bow, and from the grievousness
of war.
16 For thus hath the Lord said unto
me, Within a year, according to the
years of an hireling, and all the glory
of [l]Kē'där shall fail:
17 And the residue of the number of
[9]archers, the mighty men of the children of Kē'där, shall be diminished:
for the LORD [m]God of Ĭs'ra-el hath
spoken *it*.

22

The burden of the valley of vision. What aileth thee now, that
thou art wholly gone up to the house
tops?
2 Thou that art full of stirs, a tumultuous city, a joyous city: thy slain *men*
are not slain with the sword, nor dead
in battle.
3 All thy rulers are fled together,
they are bound [1]by the archers: all that
are found in thee are bound together,
which have fled from far.
4 Therefore said I, Look away from
me; [2]I will weep bitterly, labour not to
comfort me, because of the spoiling of
the daughter of my people.
5 For *it is* a day of trouble, and of
treading down, and of perplexity [a]by
the Lord GOD of hosts in the valley of
vision, breaking down the walls, and
of crying to the mountains.
6 [b]And Ē'lăm bare the quiver with
chariots of men *and* horsemen, and Kīr
[3]uncovered the shield.
7 And it shall come to pass, *that*
[4]thy choicest valleys shall be full of
chariots, and the horsemen shall set
themselves in array [5]at the gate.
8 ¶ And he discovered the covering
of Jū'dah, and thou didst look in that
day to the armour [c]of the house of the
forest.
9 [d]Ye have seen also the breaches
of the city of Dā'vid, that they are
many: and ye gathered together the waters of the lower pool.
10 And ye have numbered the houses
of Je-ru'sa-lĕm, and the houses have ye
broken down to fortify the wall.
11 [e]Ye made also a ditch between
the two walls for the water of the
old pool: but ye have not looked unto
the maker thereof, neither had respect
unto him that fashioned it long ago.
12 And in that day did the Lord GOD
of hosts call to weeping, and to mourning, and to baldness, and to girding
with sackcloth:
13 [f]And behold joy and gladness,
slaying oxen, and killing sheep, eating
flesh, and drinking wine: let [g]us eat
and drink; for to morrow we shall die.
14 And it was revealed in mine ears
by the LORD of hosts, Surely this iniquity [h]shall not be purged from you till
ye die, saith the Lord GOD of hosts.
15 ¶ Thus saith the Lord GOD of
hosts, Go, get thee unto this treasurer,
even unto [i]Shĕb'na, [j]which *is* over the
house, *and say*,
16 What hast thou here? and whom
hast thou here, that thou hast hewed
thee out a sepulchre here, [6]*as* he that
heweth him out a sepulchre on high,
and that graveth an habitation for himself in a rock?
17 Behold, [7]the LORD will carry thee
away with [8]a mighty captivity, and will
surely cover thee.
18 He will surely violently turn and
toss thee *like* a ball into a [9]large country: there shalt thou die, and there the
chariots of thy glory *shall be* the shame
of thy lord's house.
19 And I will drive thee from thy station, and from thy state shall he pull
thee down.
20 ¶ And it shall come to pass in that
day, that I will call my servant [k]E-lī'a-
kĭm the son of Hĭl-kī'ah:
21 And I will clothe him with thy
robe, and strengthen him with thy girdle, and I will commit thy government
into his hand: and he shall be [l]a father
to the inhabitants of Je-ru'sa-lĕm, and
to the house of Jū'dah.
22 And the key of the house of Dā'-
vid will I lay upon his shoulder; so he
shall open, and none shall shut; and he
shall shut, and none shall open.
23 And I will fasten him *as* [m]a nail
in a sure place; and he shall be for a
glorious throne to his father's house.
24 And they shall hang upon him all
the glory of his father's house, the offspring and the issue, all vessels of small
quantity, from the vessels of cups, even
to all the [10]vessels of flagons.
25 In that day, saith the LORD of
hosts, shall the nail that is fastened in
the sure place be removed, and be cut
down, and fall; and the burden that
was upon it shall be cut off: for the
LORD hath spoken *it*.

23

The [a]burden of Tȳre. Howl, ye
ships of Tär'shish; for it is laid
waste, so that there is no house, no entering in: from the land of Chĭt'tim it is
revealed to them.
2 Be [1]still, ye inhabitants of the isle;
thou whom the merchants of Zī'dŏn,
that pass over the sea, have replenished.
3 And by great waters the seed of
Sī'hôr, the harvest of the river, *is* her
revenue; and [b]she is a mart of nations.
4 Be thou ashamed, O Zī'dŏn: for the
sea hath spoken, *even* the strength of
the sea, saying, I travail not, nor bring
forth children, neither do I nourish up
young men, *nor* bring up virgins.
5 [c]As at the report concerning
Ē'gypt, *so* shall they be sorely pained
at the report of Tȳre.
6 Pass ye over to Tär'shish; howl, ye
inhabitants of the isle.
7 *Is* this your [d]joyous *city*, whose an-
tiquity *is* of ancient days? her own feet
shall carry her [2]afar off to sojourn.
8 Who hath taken this counsel
against Tȳre, [e]the crowning *city*,
whose merchants *are* princes, whose
traffickers *are* the honourable of the
earth?
9 The LORD of hosts hath purposed
it, [3f]to stain the pride of all glory, *and*
to bring into contempt all the honourable of the earth.

16 [l]Gen. 25.13; ch. 60.7
17 [9]bows
[m]Num. 23.19; 1 Pet. 1.25

CHAPTER 22
3 [1]of the bow
4 [2]I will be bitter in weeping
5 [a]Esth. 3.15; Lam. 1.5
6 [b]ch. 21.2; Jer. 49.35
[3]made naked
7 [4]the choice of thy valleys
[5]Or, toward
8 [c]1 Ki. 7.2
9 [d]2 Ki. 20.20; Song 4.4
11 [e]Neh. 3.16
13 [f]ch. 5.12; Luke 17.26-29
[g]ch. 56.12; 1 Cor. 15.32
14 [h]1 Sam. 3.14; Ezek. 24.13
15 [i]2 Ki. 18.37; ch. 36.3
[j]1 Ki. 4.6
16 [6]Or, O he
17 [7]Or, the LORD who covered thee with an excellent covering, and clothed thee gorgeously, shall surely, etc
[8]the captivity of a man
18 [9]large of spaces
20 [k]2 Ki. 18.18
21 [l]Job 29.16
23 [m]Ezra 9.8
24 [10]Or, instruments of viols

CHAPTER 23
1 [a]Jer. 25.22; Zech. 9.2-4
2 [1]silent
3 [b]Ezek. 27.3
5 [c]ch. 19.16
7 [d]ch. 22.2
[2]from afar off
8 [e]ch. 2.12;
9 [3]to pollute
[f]ch. 2.11-17;

10 Pass through thy land as a river,
O daughter of Tär′shish: *there is* no
more [4]strength.
11 He stretched out his hand over
the sea, he shook the kingdoms: the
LORD hath given a commandment
[5]against [6]the merchant *city*, to destroy
the [7]strong holds thereof.
12 And he said, [g]Thou shalt no more
rejoice, O thou oppressed virgin, daughter of Zī′dŏn: arise, pass over to Chĭt′-
tim; there also shalt thou have no rest.
13 Behold the land of the Chăl-dē′-
ans; this people was not, *till* the Ăs-
sȳr′ĭ-an founded it for [h]them that dwell
in the wilderness: they set up the towers thereof, they raised up the palaces
thereof; *and* he brought it to ruin.
14 [i]Howl, ye ships of Tär′shish: for
your strength is laid waste.
15 And it shall come to pass in that
day, that Tȳre shall be forgotten seventy years, according to the days of
one king: after the end of seventy
years [8]shall Tȳre sing as an harlot.
16 Take an harp, go about the city,
thou harlot that hast been forgotten;
make sweet melody, sing many songs,
that thou mayest be remembered.
17 ¶ And it shall come to pass after
the end of seventy years, that the LORD
will visit Tȳre, and she shall turn to her
hire, and [j]shall commit fornication
with all the kingdoms of the world
upon the face of the earth.
18 And her merchandise and her
hire [k]shall be holiness to the LORD: it
shall not be treasured nor laid up; for
her merchandise shall be for them that
dwell before the LORD, to eat sufficiently, and for [9]durable clothing.

24 Behold, the LORD maketh the
earth empty, and maketh it waste,
and [1]turneth it upside down, and scattereth abroad the inhabitants thereof.
2 And it shall be, as with the people,
so with the [2]priest; as with the servant,
so with his master; as with the maid, so
with her mistress; [a]as with the buyer,
so with the seller; as with the lender, so
with the borrower; as with the taker of
usury, so with the giver of usury to
him.
3 The land shall be utterly emptied,
and utterly spoiled: for the LORD hath
spoken this word.
4 The earth mourneth *and* fadeth
away, the world languisheth *and* fadeth away, [3]the haughty people of the
earth do languish.
5 [b]The earth also is defiled under
the inhabitants thereof; because they
have transgressed the laws, changed
the ordinance, broken the everlasting
covenant.
6 Therefore hath [c]the curse devoured the earth, and they that dwell
therein are desolate: therefore the inhabitants of the earth are burned, and
few men left.
7 The new wine mourneth, the vine
languisheth, all the merryhearted do
sigh.
8 The mirth of tabrets ceaseth, the
noise of them that rejoice endeth, the
joy of the harp ceaseth.
9 They shall not drink wine with a
song; strong drink shall be bitter to
them that drink it.
10 The city of confusion is broken
down: every house is shut up, that no
man may come in.
11 *There is* a crying for wine in the
streets; all joy is darkened, the mirth of
the land is gone.
12 In the city is left desolation, and
the gate is smitten with destruction.
13 ¶ When thus it shall be in the
midst of the land among the people,
there shall be as the shaking of an olive tree, *and* as the gleaning grapes
when the vintage is done.
14 They shall lift up their voice, they
shall sing for the majesty of the LORD,
they shall cry aloud from the sea.
15 Wherefore glorify ye the LORD in
the [4]fires, *even* [d]the name of the LORD
God of Ĭs′ra-el in the isles of the sea.
16 ¶ From the [5]uttermost part of the
earth have we heard songs, *even* glory
to the righteous. But I said, [6]My leanness, my leanness, woe unto me! [e]the
treacherous dealers have dealt treacherously; yea, the treacherous dealers
have dealt very treacherously.
17 [f]Fear, and the pit, and the snare,
are upon thee, O inhabitant of the
earth.
18 And it shall come to pass, *that* he
who fleeth from the noise of the fear
shall fall into the pit; and he that cometh up out of the midst of the pit shall
be taken in the snare: for [g]the windows from on high are open, and [h]the
foundations of the earth do shake.
19 [i]The earth is utterly broken down,
the earth is clean dissolved, the earth is
moved exceedingly.
20 The earth shall reel to and fro
like a drunkard, and shall be removed
like a cottage; and the transgression
thereof shall be heavy upon it; and it
shall fall, and not rise again.
21 And it shall come to pass in that
day, *that* the LORD shall [7]punish the
host of the high ones *that are* on high,
[j]and the kings of the earth upon the
earth.
22 And they shall be gathered together, [8]*as* prisoners are gathered in
the [9]pit, and shall be shut up in the
prison, and after many days shall they
be [10]visited.
23 Then the moon shall be confounded, and the sun ashamed, when
the LORD of hosts shall [k]reign in mount
Zī′ŏn, and in Je-rṳ′sa-lĕm, and [11]before
his ancients gloriously.

25 O lord, thou *art* my God; [a]I will
exalt thee, I will praise thy name;
for thou hast done wonderful *things;*
[b]*thy* counsels of old *are* faithfulness
and truth.
2 For thou hast made [c]of a city an
heap; *of* a defenced city a ruin: a palace of strangers to be no city; it shall
never be built.

10 [4]girdle
11 [5]Or, concerning a merchantman [6]Canaan [7]Or, strengths
12 [g]Lam. 1.6; Hag. 2.22; Rev. 18.22
13 [h]Ps. 71.3
14 [i]ch. 2.16; Ezek. 27.25; Rev. 18.22
15 [8]it shall be unto Tyre as the song of an harlot
17 [j]Gen. 10.15-19; Rev. 17.2
18 [k]Deut. 28.65-66; Zech. 14.20-21 [9]old

CHAPTER 24
1 [1]perverteth the face thereof
2 [2]Or, prince [a]Ezek. 7.12
4 [3]the height of the people
5 [b]Gen. 3.17; Num. 35.33
6 [c]Lev. 26.15-16; Mal. 2.2
15 [4]Or, valleys [d]Mal. 1.11; ch. 66.19
16 [5]wing [6]Leanness to me, or, My secret to me [e]Jer. 3.20
17 [f]Jer. 48.43-44; Amos 5.19
18 [g]Gen. 7.11 [h]Ps. 18.7
19 [i]Jer. 4.23
21 [7]visit upon [j]Ps. 76.12
22 [8]with the gathering of prisoners [9]Or, dungeon [10]Or, found wanting
23 [k]Heb. 12.22; Rev. 19.4 [11]Or, there shall be glory before his ancients

CHAPTER 25
1 [a]Ex. 15.2 [b]Num. 23.19
2 [c]Jer. 51.37

3 Therefore shall the strong people [d]glorify thee, the city of the terrible nations shall fear thee.

4 For thou hast been a strength to the poor, a strength to the needy in his distress, [e]a refuge from the storm, a shadow from the heat, when the blast of the terrible ones *is* as a storm *against* the wall.

5 Thou shalt bring down the noise of strangers, as the heat in a dry place; *even* the heat with the shadow of a cloud: the branch of the terrible ones shall be brought low.

6 ¶ And in this mountain shall [f]the LORD of hosts make unto [g]all people a feast of fat things, a feast of wines on the lees, of fat things full of marrow, of wines on the lees well refined.

7 And he will [1]destroy in this mountain the face of the covering [2]cast over all people, and [h]the veil that is spread over all nations.

8 He will [i]swallow up death in victory; and the Lord GOD will [j]wipe away tears from off all faces; and the rebuke of his people shall he take away from off all the earth: for the LORD hath spoken *it*.

9 ¶ And it shall be said in that day, Lo, this *is* our God; [k]we have waited for him, and he will save us: this *is* the LORD; we have waited for him, we will be glad and rejoice in his salvation.

10 For in this mountain shall the hand of the LORD rest, and Mō'ab shall be [3]trodden down under him, even as straw is [4]trodden down for the dunghill.

11 And he shall spread forth his hands in the midst of them, as he that swimmeth spreadeth forth *his hands* to swim: and he shall [l]bring down their pride together with the spoils of their hands.

12 And the [m]fortress of the high fort of thy walls shall he bring down, lay low, *and* bring to the ground, *even* to the dust.

26

In that day shall this song be sung in the land of Jū'dah; We have a strong city; salvation will *God* appoint *for* walls and bulwarks.

2 [a]Open ye the gates, that the righteous nation which keepeth the [1]truth may enter in.

3 Thou wilt keep *him* in [2]perfect peace, *whose* [3]*mind is* stayed *on thee:* because he trusteth in thee.

4 Trust ye in the LORD for ever: for in the LORD JE-HŌ'VAH *is* [4]everlasting strength:

5 ¶ For he bringeth down them that dwell on high; the lofty city, he layeth it low; he layeth it low, *even* to the ground; he bringeth it *even* to the dust.

6 The foot shall tread it down, *even* the feet of the poor, *and* the steps of the needy.

7 The way of the just *is* uprightness: [b]thou, most upright, dost weigh the path of the just.

8 Yea, [c]in the way of thy judgments, O LORD, have we waited for thee; the desire of *our* soul *is* to thy name, and to the remembrance of thee.

9 [d]With my soul have I desired thee in the night; yea, with my spirit within me will I seek thee early: for [e]when thy judgments *are* in the earth, the inhabitants of the world will learn righteousness.

10 [f]Let favour be shewed to the wicked, *yet* will he not learn righteousness; in [g]the land of uprightness will he deal unjustly, and will not behold the majesty of the LORD.

11 LORD, *when* thy hand is lifted up, [h]they will not see: *but* they shall see, and be ashamed for *their* envy [5]at the people; yea, the fire of thine enemies shall devour them.

12 ¶ LORD, thou wilt ordain peace for us: for thou also hast wrought all our works [6]in us.

13 O LORD our God, [i]*other* lords beside thee have had dominion over us: *but* by thee only will we make mention of thy name.

14 *They are* dead, they shall not live; *they are* deceased, they shall not rise: therefore hast thou visited and destroyed them, and made all their memory to perish.

15 Thou hast increased the nation, O LORD, thou hast increased the nation: thou art glorified: thou hadst removed *it* far *unto* all the ends of the earth.

16 LORD, [j]in trouble have they visited thee, they poured out a [7]prayer *when* thy chastening *was* upon them.

17 Like as a woman with child, *that* draweth near the time of her delivery, is in pain, *and* crieth out in her pangs; so have we been in thy sight, O LORD.

18 We have been with child, we have been in pain, we have as it were brought forth wind; we have not wrought any deliverance in the earth; neither have [k]the inhabitants of the world fallen.

19 [l]Thy dead *men* shall live, *together with* my dead body shall they arise. [m]Awake and sing, ye that dwell in dust: for thy dew *is as* the dew of herbs, and the earth shall cast out the dead.

20 ¶ Come, my people, [n]enter thou into thy chambers, and shut thy doors about thee: hide thyself as it were [o]for a little moment, until the indignation be overpast.

21 For, behold, the LORD [p]cometh out of his place to punish the inhabitants of the earth for their iniquity: the earth also shall disclose her [8]blood, and shall no more cover her slain.

27

In that day the LORD with his sore and great and strong sword shall punish leviathan the [1]piercing serpent, [a]even leviathan that crooked serpent; and he shall slay [b]the dragon that *is* in the sea.

2 In that day sing ye unto her, A vineyard of red wine.

3 I the LORD do keep it; I will water it every moment: lest *any* hurt it, I will keep it night and day.

4 Fury *is* not in me: who would set [c]the briers *and* thorns against me in

---

3 [d]Rev. 11.13
4 [e]Ps. 46; Nah. 1.7
6 [f]Prov. 9.2; Matt. 22.4 [g]Dan. 7.14; Matt. 8.11
7 [1]swallow up [2]covered [h]2 Cor. 3.15; Eph. 1.17
8 [i]ch. 26.19; Heb. 2.14 [j]Rev. 7.17
9 [k]Gen. 49.18; Tit. 2.13
10 [3]Or, threshed [4]Or, threshed in Madmenah
11 [l]Job 40.11-12; ch. 2.10-12-15-17
12 [m]ch. 26.5

CHAPTER 26
2 [a]Ps. 118.19; Rev. 21.13-24-27 [1]truths
3 [2]peace, peace [3]Or, thought, or, imagination
4 [4]the rock of ages
7 [b]Deut. 32.4
8 [c]Ps. 18.22; Luke 1.6
9 [d]Ps. 63.6; Luke 6.12 [e]Ps. 83.16
10 [f]Eccl. 8.12; Rom. 2.4 [g]Ps. 143.10
11 [h]Job 34.27 [5]Or, toward thy people
12 [6]Or, for us
13 [i]Ps. 66.12
16 [j]2 Chr. 33.12; [7]secret speech
18 [k]Ps. 17.14
19 [l]ch. 25.8; [m]Dan. 12.2
20 [n]Gen. 7.1 [o]Ps. 30.5;
21 [p]Mic. 1.3; [8]bloods

CHAPTER 27
1 [1]Or, stiff, or, crossing like a bar [a]Ps. 74.13 [b]Ezek. 29.3
4 [c]2 Sam. 23.6

battle? I would [2]go through them, I would burn them together.

5 Or let him take hold of my strength, *that* he may [d]make peace with me; *and* he shall make peace with me.

6 He shall cause them that come of Jā′cob [e]to take root: Ĭs′ra-el shall blossom and bud, and fill the face of the world with fruit.

7 ¶ Hath he smitten him, [3]as he smote those that smote him? *or* is he slain according to the slaughter of them that are slain by him?

8 In [f]measure, [4]when it shooteth forth, thou wilt debate with it: [5]he stayeth his rough wind in the day of the east wind.

9 By this therefore shall the iniquity of Jā′cob be purged; and this *is* all the fruit to take away his sin; when he maketh all the stones of the altar as chalkstones that are beaten in sunder, the groves and [6]images shall not stand up.

10 Yet the defenced city *shall be* desolate, *and* the habitation forsaken, and left like a wilderness: [g]there shall the calf feed, and there shall he lie down, and consume the branches thereof.

11 When the boughs thereof are withered, they shall be broken off: the women come, *and* set them on fire: for [h]it *is* a people of no understanding: therefore he that made them will not have mercy on them, and he [i]that formed them will shew them no favour.

12 ¶ And it shall come to pass in that day, *that* the LORD shall beat off from the channel of the river unto the stream of Ē′gypt, and ye shall be gathered one by one, O ye children of Ĭs′ra-el.

13 [j]And it shall come to pass in that day, [k]*that* the great trumpet shall be blown, and they shall come which were ready to perish in the land of Ăs-sȳr′ĭ-ȧ, and the outcasts in the land of Ē′gypt, and shall worship the LORD in the holy mount at Je-rṳ′sa-lĕm.

28 Woe to the crown of pride, to the drunkards of Ē′phrā-ĭm, whose glorious beauty *is* a fading flower, which *are* on the head of the fat valleys of them that are [1]overcome with wine!

2 Behold, the Lord hath a mighty and strong one, [a]*which* as a tempest of hail *and* a destroying storm, as a flood of mighty waters overflowing, shall cast down to the earth with the hand.

3 The crown of pride, the drunkards of Ē′phrā-ĭm, shall be trodden [2]under feet:

4 And the glorious beauty, which *is* on the head of the fat valley, shall be a fading flower, *and* as the hasty fruit before the summer; which *when* he that looketh upon it seeth, while it is yet in his hand he [3]eateth it up.

5 ¶ In that day shall the LORD of hosts be for a crown of glory, and for a diadem of beauty, unto the residue of his people,

6 And for a spirit of judgment to him that sitteth in judgment, and for strength to them that turn the battle to the gate.

7 ¶ But they also [b]have erred through wine, and through strong drink are out of the way; [c]the priest and the prophet have erred through strong drink, they are swallowed up of wine, they are out of the way through strong drink; they err in vision, they stumble *in* judgment.

8 For all tables are full of vomit *and* filthiness, *so that there is* no place *clean.*

9 ¶ [d]Whom shall he teach knowledge? and whom shall he make to understand [4]doctrine? *them that are* weaned from the milk, *and* drawn from the breasts.

10 For precept [5]*must be* upon precept, precept upon precept; line upon line, line upon line; here a little *and* there a little:

11 For with [6]stammering lips and another tongue [7]will he speak to this people.

12 To whom he said, [e]This *is* the rest *wherewith* ye may cause the weary to rest; and this *is* the refreshing: yet they would not hear.

13 But the word of the LORD was unto them precept upon precept, precept upon precept; line upon line, line upon line; here a little, *and* there a little; that they might go, and fall backward, and be broken, and snared, and taken.

14 ¶ Wherefore hear the word of the LORD, ye scornful men, that rule this people which *is* in Je-rṳ′sa-lĕm.

15 Because ye have said, We have made a covenant with death, and with hell are we at agreement; when the overflowing scourge shall pass through, it shall not come unto us: for we have made lies our refuge, and under falsehood have we hid ourselves:

16 ¶ Therefore thus saith the Lord GOD, Behold, I lay in Zī′ŏn for a foundation [f]a stone, a tried stone, a precious corner *stone,* a sure foundation: he that believeth shall not make haste.

17 Judgment also will I lay to the line, and righteousness to the plummet: and the hail shall sweep away the refuge of lies, and the waters shall overflow the hiding place.

18 ¶ And your covenant with death shall be disannulled, and your agreement with hell shall not stand; when the overflowing scourge shall pass through, then ye shall be [8]trodden down by it.

19 From the time that it goeth forth it shall take you: for morning by morning shall it pass over, by day and by night: and it shall be a vexation only [9]*to* understand the report.

20 For the bed is shorter than that *a man* can stretch himself *on it:* and the covering narrower than that he can wrap himself *in it.*

21 For the LORD shall rise up as *in* mount [g]Pĕr′a-zĭm, he shall be wroth as *in* the valley of [h]Gĭb′e-on, that he may do his work, [i]his strange work; and bring to pass his act, his strange act.

[2]Or, march against
5 [d]Job 22.21; ch. 53.4-5; Eph. 2.12-13-14
6 [e]ch. 37.31; Hos. 14.5-6
7 [3]according to the stroke of those
8 [f]Job 23.6; Ps. 6.1; Jer. 10.24; 1 Cor. 10.13
[4]Or, when thou sendest it forth
[5]Or, when he removeth it
9 [6]Or, sun images
10 [g]ch. 17.2
11 [h]Deut. 32.28; Ps. 28.5; ch. 1.3; Jer. 4.22; 2 Thess. 1.8
[i]Deut. 32.18; ch. 44.2-21-24
13 [j]ch. 2.11
[k]Num. 10.2; Ps. 81.3; Hos. 8.1; Matt. 24.31; Rev. 11.15

CHAPTER 28

1 [1]broken
2 [a]ch. 30.30; Ezek. 13.11
3 [2]with feet
4 [3]swalloweth
7 [b]Lev. 10.9; Deut. 29.6; Prov. 20.1; Hos. 4.11
[c]ch. 56.10-12
9 [d]Jer. 6.10
[4]the hearing
10 [5]Or, hath been
11 [6]stammerings of lips
[7]Or, he hath spoken
12 [e]2 Chr. 14.7
16 [f]Gen. 49.24; Ps. 118.22; Matt. 21.42; Acts 4.11; Rom. 9.33; Eph. 2.20
18 [8]a treading down to it
19 [9]Or, when he shall make you to understand doctrine
21 [g]2 Sam. 5.20
[h]Josh. 10.10
[i]1 Sam. 3.11; Jer. 30.14; Lam. 3.33; Rom. 11.8

22 Now therefore be ye not mockers, lest your bands be made strong: for I have heard from the Lord GOD of hosts a consumption, even determined upon the whole earth.

23 ¶ Give ye ear, and hear my voice; hearken, and hear my speech.

24 Doth the plowman plow all day to sow? doth he open and break the clods of his ground?

25 When he hath made plain the face thereof, doth he not cast abroad the fitches, and scatter the cummin, and cast in [10]the principal wheat and the appointed barley and the [11]rie in their [12]place?

26 [13]For his God doth instruct him to discretion, *and* doth teach him.

27 For the fitches are not threshed with a threshing instrument, neither is a cart wheel turned about upon the cummin; but the fitches are beaten out with a staff, and the cummin with a rod.

28 Bread *corn* is bruised; because he will not ever be threshing it, nor break *it with* the wheel of his cart, nor bruise it *with* his horsemen.

29 This also cometh forth from the LORD of hosts, [j]*which* is wonderful in counsel, *and* excellent in working.

29

Woe [1]to Ā'rĭ-el, to Ā'rĭ-el, [2]the city *where* Dā'vid dwelt! add ye year to year; let them [3]kill sacrifices.

2 Yet I will distress Ā'rĭ-el, and there shall be heaviness and sorrow: and it shall be unto me as Ā'rĭ-el.

3 And I will camp against thee round about, and will lay siege against thee with a mount, and I will raise forts against thee.

4 And thou shalt be brought down, *and* shalt speak out of the ground, and thy speech shall be low out of the dust, and thy voice shall be, as of one that hath a familiar spirit, [a]out of the ground, and thy speech shall [4]whisper out of the dust.

5 Moreover the multitude of thy strangers shall be like small dust, and the multitude of the terrible ones *shall be* as chaff that passeth away: yea, it shall be at an instant suddenly.

6 Thou shalt be visited of the LORD of hosts with thunder, and with earthquake, and great noise, with storm and tempest, and the flame of devouring fire.

7 ¶ And the multitude of all the nations that fight against Ā'rĭ-el, even all that fight against her and her munition, and that distress her, shall be as a dream of a night vision.

8 It shall even be as when an hungry *man* dreameth, and, behold, he eateth; but he awaketh, and his soul is empty: or as when a thirsty man dreameth, and, behold, he drinketh; but he awaketh, and, behold, *he is* faint, and his soul hath appetite: so shall the multitude of all the nations be, that fight against mount Zī'ŏn.

9 ¶ Stay yourselves, and wonder; [5]cry ye out, and cry: they are drunken, but not with wine; they stagger, but not with strong drink.

10 For [b]the LORD hath poured out upon you the spirit of deep sleep, and hath [c]closed your eyes: the prophets and your [6]rulers, the seers hath he covered.

11 And the vision of all is become unto you as the words of a [7]book that is sealed, which *men* deliver to one that is learned, saying, Read this, I pray thee: [d]and he saith, I cannot; for it *is* sealed:

12 And the book is delivered to him that is not learned, saying, Read this, I pray thee: and he saith, I am not learned.

13 ¶ Wherefore the Lord said, [e]Forasmuch as this people draw near *me* with their mouth, and with their lips do honour me, but have removed their heart far from me, and their fear toward me is taught by the [f]precept of men:

14 Therefore, behold, [8]I will proceed to do a marvellous work among this people, *even* a marvellous work and a wonder: [g]for the wisdom of their wise *men* shall perish, and the understanding of their prudent *men* shall be hid.

15 Woe unto them that seek deep to hide their counsel from the LORD, and their works are in the dark, and [h]they say, Who seeth us? and who knoweth us?

16 Surely your turning of things upside down shall be esteemed as the potter's clay: for shall the work [i]say of him that made it, He made me not? or shall the thing framed say of him that framed it, He had no understanding?

17 *Is* it not yet a very little while, and Lĕb'a-non shall be turned into a fruitful field, and the fruitful field shall be esteemed as a forest?

18 ¶ And in that day shall the deaf hear the words of the book, and the eyes of the blind shall see out of obscurity, and out of darkness.

19 [j]The meek also [9]shall increase *their* joy in the LORD, and [k]the poor among men shall rejoice in the Holy One of Ĭs'ra-el.

20 For the terrible one is brought to nought, and the scorner is consumed, and all that [l]watch for iniquity are cut off:

21 That make a man an offender for a word, and [m]lay a snare for him that reproveth in the gate, and turn aside the just [n]for a thing of nought.

22 Therefore thus saith the LORD, [o]who redeemed Ā'bră-hăm, concerning the house of Jā'cob, Jā'cob shall not now be ashamed, neither shall his face now wax pale.

23 But when he seeth his children, [p]the work of mine hands, in the midst of him, they shall [q]sanctify my name, and sanctify the Holy One of Jā'cob, and shall [r]fear the God of Ĭs'ra-el.

24 They also [s]that erred in spirit [10]shall come to understanding, and they that murmured shall learn doctrine.

25 [10]Or, the wheat in the principal place, and barley in the appointed place
[11]Or, spelt
[12]border
26 [13]Or, And he bindeth it in such sort as his God doth teach him
29 [j]Ps. 40.5; Jer. 32.19; Rom. 11.33

CHAPTER 29
1 [1]Or, O Ariel, that is, the lion of God, or, hearth, or, fireplace of God
[2]Or, of the city
[3]cut off the heads
4 [a]ch. 8.19
[4]peep, or, chirp
9 [5]Or, take your pleasure, and riot
10 [b]Mic. 3.6; Rom. 11.8; 2 Thess. 2.10
[c]Ps. 69.23; ch. 6.10
[6]heads
11 [7]Or, letter
[d]Dan. 12.4; Matt. 11.25; Rev. 5.1
13 [e]Ps. 17.1; ch. 48.1-2; Jer. 12.2; Ezek. 33.31; Matt. 6.5; Mark 7.6
[f]Col. 2.22
14 [8]I will add
[g]Jer. 49.7; 1 Cor. 1.19
15 [h]Job 22.13-14; Ps. 10.11-13
16 [i]Ps. 94.9; Rom. 9.20
19 [j]John 15.11
[9]shall add
[k]Jas. 2.5
20 [l]Mic. 2.1
21 [m]Amos 5.10
[n]Prov. 28.21
22 [o]Josh. 24.3
23 [p]ch. 19.25; Eph. 2.10
[q]1 Pet. 4.11
[r]Hos. 3.5
24 [s]ch. 28.7
[10]shall know understanding

30 Woe to the rebellious children,
saith the LORD, that take counsel, but not of me; and that cover with a
covering, but not of my spirit, [a]that
they may add sin to sin:
2 That walk to go down into Ē'ġypt,
and [b]have not asked at my mouth; to
strengthen themselves in the strength
of Phā'raōh, and to trust in the shadow
of Ē'ġypt!
3 [c]Therefore shall the strength of
Phā'raōh be your shame, and the trust
in the shadow of Ē'ġypt *your* confusion.
4 For his princes were at Zō'an, and
his ambassadors came to Hā'nēs.
5 [d]They were all ashamed of a people *that* could not profit them, nor be
an help nor profit, but a shame, and
also a reproach.
6 [e]The burden of the beasts of the
south: into the land of trouble and anguish, from whence *come* the young
and old lion, the viper and fiery flying
serpent, they will carry their riches
upon the shoulders of young asses,
and their treasures upon the bunches
of camels, to a people *that* shall not
profit *them*.
7 [f]For the E-ġўp'tians shall help in
vain, and to no purpose: therefore have
I cried [1]concerning this, Their strength
is to sit still.
8 ¶ Now go, write it before them in a
table, and note it in a book, that it may
be for [2]the time to come for ever and
ever:
9 That [g]this *is* a rebellious people,
lying children, children *that* will not
hear the law of the LORD:
10 [h]Which say to the seers, See not;
and to the prophets, Prophesy not unto
us right things, [i]speak unto us smooth
things, prophesy deceits:
11 [j]Get you out of the way, turn
aside out of the path, cause the Holy
One of Ĭs'ra-el to cease from before us.
12 Wherefore thus saith the Holy
One of Ĭs'ra-el, Because ye despise this
word, and trust in [3]oppression and perverseness, and stay thereon:
13 Therefore this iniquity shall be to
you as a breach ready to fall, swelling
out in a high wall, whose breaking
cometh suddenly at an instant.
14 And [k]he shall break it as the
breaking of [4]the potters' vessel that is
broken in pieces; he shall not spare: so
that there shall not be found in the
bursting of it a sherd to take fire from
the hearth, or to take water *withal* out
of the pit.
15 For thus saith the Lord GOD, the
Holy One of Ĭs'ra-el; [l]In returning and
rest shall ye be saved; in quietness and
in confidence shall be your strength:
[m]and ye would not.
16 But ye said, No; for we will flee
upon horses; therefore shall ye flee:
and, We will ride upon the swift; therefore shall they that pursue you be
swift.
17 [n]One thousand *shall flee* at the
rebuke of one; at the rebuke of five
shall ye flee: till ye be left as [5]a beacon
upon the top of a mountain, and as an
ensign on an hill.
18 ¶ And therefore will the [o]LORD
wait, that he may be gracious unto you,
and therefore will he be exalted, that he
may have mercy upon you: for the
LORD *is* a God of judgment: [p]blessed
are all they that wait for him.
19 For the people shall dwell in Zī'ŏn
at Je-ru'sa-lĕm: thou shalt weep no
more: he will be very gracious unto
thee at the voice of thy cry; when he
shall hear it, he will answer thee.
20 And *though* the Lord give you
the bread of adversity, and the water
of [6]affliction, yet shall not thy teachers
be removed into a corner any more,
but thine eyes shall see thy teachers:
21 And thine ears shall hear a word
behind thee, saying, This *is* the way,
walk ye in it, when ye [q]turn to the right
hand, and when ye turn to the left.
22 [r]Ye shall defile also the covering
of [7]thy graven images of silver, and the
ornament of thy molten images of gold:
thou shalt [8]cast them away as a menstruous cloth; thou shalt say unto it,
Get thee hence.
23 [s]Then shall he give the rain of thy
seed, that thou shalt sow the ground
withal; and bread of the increase of the
earth, and it shall be fat and plenteous:
in that day shall thy cattle feed in large
pastures.
24 The oxen likewise and the young
asses that ear the ground shall eat
[9]clean provender, which hath been win-
nowed with the shovel and with the
fan.
25 And there shall be upon every
high mountain, and upon every [10]high
hill, rivers *and* streams of waters in the
day of the great slaughter, when the
towers fall.
26 Moreover [t]the light of the moon
shall be as the light of the sun, and the
light of the sun shall be sevenfold, as
the light of seven days, in the day that
the LORD bindeth up the breach of his
people, and healeth the stroke of their
wound.
27 ¶ Behold, the name of the LORD
cometh from far, burning *with* his
anger, [11]and the burden *thereof is*
[12]heavy: his lips are full of indignation,
and his tongue as a devouring fire:
28 And [u]his breath, as an overflowing stream, shall reach to the midst of
the neck, to sift the nations with the
sieve of vanity: and *there shall be* a
bridle in the jaws of the people, causing *them* to err.
29 Ye shall have a song, as in the
night *when* a holy solemnity is kept;
and gladness of heart, as when one
goeth with a pipe to come into the
mountain of the LORD, to the [13]mighty
One of Ĭs'ra-el.
30 And the LORD shall cause [14]his
glorious voice to be heard, and shall
shew the lighting down of his arm, with
the indignation of *his* anger, and *with*
the flame of a devouring fire, *with* scat-
tering, and tempest, and hailstones.

CHAPTER 30
1 [a]Deut. 29.19; Rom. 2.5; 2 Tim. 3.13
2 [b]Num. 27.21; 1 Ki. 22.7; Jer. 21.2
3 [c]Jer. 37.5-7
5 [d]Jer. 2.36
6 [e]Hos. 8.9
7 [f]Jer. 37.7 [1]Or, to her
8 [2]the latter day
9 [g]Deut. 32.20
10 [h]Jer. 11.21 [i]1 Ki. 22.13
11 [j]Acts 13.8
12 [3]Or, fraud
14 [k]Ps. 2.9; 2 Pet. 2.4-5 [4]the bottle of potters
15 [l]ch. 7.4 [m]Ps. 81.11; Prov. 1.24; Jer. 44.16; Matt. 23.37
17 [n]Lev. 26.8; Deut. 28.25; Josh. 23.10 [5]Or, a tree bereft of branches, or, boughs: or, a mast
18 [o]2 Pet. 3.9 [p]Ps. 2.12; Prov. 16.20; Jer. 17.7
20 [6]Or, oppression
21 [q]Deut. 5.32; Josh. 1.7; 2 Ki. 22.2; Prov. 4.27
22 [r]2 Chr. 31.1; ch. 2.20 [7]the graven images of thy silver [8]scatter
23 [s]Matt. 6.33; 1 Tim. 4.8
24 [9]leavened, or, savoury
25 [10]lifted up
26 [t]ch. 60.19; Zech. 2.5; Rev. 21.23
27 [11]Or, and the grievousness of flame [12]heaviness
28 [u]2 Thess. 2.8
29 [13]Rock
30 [14]the glory of his voice

31 For through the voice of the LORD
shalt the Ȧs-sȳr'ĭ-an be beaten down,
which smote with a rod.
32 And [15]*in* every place where the
grounded staff shall pass, which the
LORD shall [16]lay upon him, *it* shall be
with tabrets and harps: and in battles
of shaking will he fight [17]with it.
33 [v]For Tō'phet *is* ordained [18]of old;
yea, for the king it is prepared; he hath
made *it* deep *and* large: the pile thereof
is fire and much wood; the breath of
the LORD, like a stream of brimstone,
doth kindle it.

31 Woe to them [a]that go down to
Ē'ġypt for help; and [b]stay on
horses, and trust in chariots, because
they are many; and in horsemen, because they are very strong; but they
look not unto the Holy One of Ĭs'ra-el,
[c]neither seek the LORD!
2 Yet he also *is* wise, and will bring
evil, and will not [1]call back his words:
but will arise against the house of the
evildoers, and against the help of them
that work iniquity.
3 Now the E-ġȳp'tians *are* [d]men,
and not God; and their horses flesh,
and not spirit. When the LORD shall
stretch out his hand, both he that helpeth shall fall, and he that is holpen
shall fall down, and they all shall fail
together.
4 For thus hath the LORD spoken
unto me, Like as the lion and the
young lion roaring on his prey, when a
multitude of shepherds is called forth
against him, *he* will not be afraid of
their voice, nor abase himself for the
[2]noise of them: so shall the LORD of
hosts come down to fight for mount
Zī'ŏn, and for the hill thereof.
5 [e]As birds flying, so will the LORD
of hosts defend Je-ru̦'sa-lĕm; defend-
ing also he will deliver *it; and* passing
over he will preserve *it*.
6 ¶ Turn ye unto *him from* whom
the children of Ĭs'ra-el have [f]deeply
revolted.
7 For in that day every man shall
cast away his idols of silver, and [3]his
idols of gold, which your own hands
have made unto you *for* [g]a sin.
8 ¶ Then shall the Ȧs-sȳr'ĭ-an [h]fall
with the sword, not of a mighty man;
and the sword, not of a mean man,
shall devour him: but he shall flee
[4]from the sword, and his young men
shall be [5]discomfited.
9 And [6]he shall pass over to [7]his
strong hold for fear, and his princes
shall be afraid of the ensign, saith the
LORD, whose [i]fire *is* in Zī'ŏn, and his
furnace in Je-ru̦'sa-lĕm.

32 Behold, [a]a king shall reign in
righteousness, and princes shall
rule in judgment.
2 And a man shall be as an hiding
place from the wind, and a covert from
the tempest; as rivers of water in a dry
place, as the shadow of a [1]great rock in
a weary land.
3 And [b]the eyes of them that see
shall not be dim, and the ears of them
that hear shall hearken.

32 [15]every passing of the rod founded [16]cause to rest upon him [17]Or, against them
33 [v]Jer. 7.31 [18]from yesterday

CHAPTER 31
1 [a]Deut. 28.68; [b]Ps. 20.7 [c]Dan. 9.13;
2 [1]remove
3 [d]Ps. 9.20;
4 [2]Or, multitude
5 [e]Deut. 32.11;
6 [f]Hos. 9.9
7 [3]the idols of his gold [g]1 Ki. 12.30
8 [h]2 Ki. 19.35 [4]Or, for fear of the sword [5]for melting, or, tribute, or, tributary
9 [6]his rock shall pass away for fear [7]Or, his strength [i]Lev. 6.13

CHAPTER 32
1 [a]2 Chr. 31.20;
2 [1]heavy
3 [b]ch. 29.18
4 [2]hasty [3]Or, elegantly
7 [4]Or, when he speaketh against the poor in judgment
8 [5]Or, be established
9 [c]Amos 6.1
10 [6]Days above a year
12 [7]the fields of desire
13 [d]Hos. 9.6 [8]Or, burning upon
14 [9]Or, clifts and watchtowers
15 [e]Ps. 104.30
16 [f]Zech. 8.3
17 [g]Ps. 72.2-3;
[10]Or, and the city shall be utterly abased

CHAPTER 33
1 [a]Hab. 2.8 [b]Rev. 13.10

4 The heart also of the [2]rash shall
understand knowledge, and the tongue
of the stammerers shall be ready to
speak [3]plainly.
5 The vile person shall be no more
called liberal, nor the churl said *to be*
bountiful.
6 For the vile person will speak villany, and his heart will work iniquity,
to practise hypocrisy, and to utter error against the LORD, to make empty
the soul of the hungry, and he will
cause the drink of the thirsty to fail.
7 The instruments also of the churl
are evil: he deviseth wicked devices to
destroy the poor with lying words,
even [4]when the needy speaketh right.
8 But the liberal deviseth liberal
things; and by liberal things shall he
[5]stand.
9 ¶ Rise up, ye women [c]that are at
ease; hear my voice, ye careless daughters; give ear unto my speech.
10 [6]Many days and years shall ye be
troubled, ye careless women: for the
vintage shall fail, the gathering shall
not come.
11 Tremble, ye women that are at
ease; be troubled, ye careless ones:
strip you, and make you bare, and gird
sackcloth upon *your* loins.
12 They shall lament for the teats,
for [7]the pleasant fields, for the fruitful
vine.
13 [d]Upon the land of my people
shall come up thorns *and* briers; [8]yea,
upon all the houses of joy *in* the joyous
city:
14 Because the palaces shall be forsaken; the multitude of the city shall
be left; the [9]forts and towers shall be
for dens for ever, a joy of wild asses, a
pasture of flocks;
15 Until [e]the spirit be poured upon
us from on high, and the wilderness be
a fruitful field, and the fruitful field be
counted for a forest.
16 [f]Then judgment shall dwell in
the wilderness, and righteousness remain in the fruitful field.
17 [g]And the work of righteousness
shall be peace; and the effect of righteousness quietness and assurance for
ever.
18 And my people shall dwell in
a peaceable habitation, and in sure
dwellings, and in quiet resting places;
19 When it shall hail, coming down
on the forest; [10]and the city shall be
low in a low place.
20 Blessed *are* ye that sow beside all
waters, that send forth *thither* the feet
of the ox and the ass.

33 Woe to thee [a]that spoilest, and
thou *wast* not spoiled; and dealest treacherously, and they dealt not
treacherously with thee! [b]when thou
shalt cease to spoil, thou shalt be
spoiled; *and* when thou shalt make an
end to deal treacherously, they shall
deal treacherously with thee.
2 O LORD, be gracious unto us; we
have waited for thee: be thou their arm
every morning, our salvation also in
the time of trouble.

3 At the noise of the tumult the people fled; at the lifting up of thyself the nations were scattered.

4 And your spoil shall be gathered *like* the gathering of the caterpiller: as the running to and fro of locusts shall he run upon them.

5 [c]The LORD is exalted; for he dwelleth on high: he hath filled Zī'ŏn with judgment and righteousness.

6 [d]And wisdom and knowledge shall be the stability of thy times, *and* strength of [1]salvation: the fear of the LORD *is* his treasure.

7 Behold, their [2]valiant ones shall cry without: [e]the ambassadors of peace shall weep bitterly.

8 [f]The highways lie waste, the wayfaring man ceaseth: [g]he hath broken the covenant, he hath despised the cities, he regardeth no man.

9 The earth mourneth *and* languisheth: Lĕb'a-non is ashamed *and* [3]hewn down: Shâr'on is like a wilderness; and Bā'shăn and Cär'mel shake off *their fruits*.

10 [h]Now will I rise, saith the LORD; now will I be exalted; now will I lift up myself.

11 Ye shall conceive chaff, ye shall bring forth stubble: your breath, *as* fire, shall devour you.

12 And the people shall be *as* the burnings of lime: *as* thorns cut up shall they be burned in the fire.

13 ¶ Hear, ye *that are* far off, what I have done; and, ye *that are* near, acknowledge my might.

14 The sinners in Zī'ŏn are afraid; fearfulness hath surprised the hypocrites. Who among us shall dwell with the devouring fire? who among us shall dwell with everlasting burnings?

15 He that walketh [4]righteously, and speaketh [5]uprightly; he that despiseth the gain of [6]oppressions, that shaketh his hands from holding of bribes, that stoppeth his ears from hearing of [7]blood, and shutteth his eyes from seeing evil;

16 He shall dwell on [8]high: his place of defence *shall be* the munitions of rocks: bread shall be given him; his waters *shall be* sure.

17 Thine eyes shall see the king in his beauty: they shall behold [9]the land that is very far off.

18 Thine heart shall meditate terror. [i]Where *is* the scribe? where *is* the [10]receiver? where *is* he that counted the towers?

19 Thou shalt not see a fierce people, [j]a people of a deeper speech than thou canst perceive; of [11]a stammering tongue, *that thou canst* not understand.

20 Look upon Zī'ŏn, the city of our solemnities: thine eyes shall see Je-rụ'sa-lĕm a quiet habitation, a tabernacle *that* shall not be taken down; not one of the stakes thereof shall ever be removed, neither shall any of the cords thereof be broken.

21 But [k]there the glorious LORD *will be* unto us a place [12]of broad rivers *and* streams; wherein shall go no galley with oars, neither shall gallant ship pass thereby.

22 For the LORD *is* our judge, the LORD *is* our [13]lawgiver, [l]the LORD *is* our king; he will save us.

23 [14]Thy tacklings are loosed; they could not well strengthen their mast, they could not spread the sail: then is the prey of a great spoil divided; the lame take the prey.

24 And the inhabitant shall not say, I am sick: [m]the people that dwell therein *shall be* forgiven *their* iniquity.

34 Come near, ye nations, to hear; and hearken, ye people: let the earth hear, and all [1]that is therein; the world, and all things that come forth of it.

2 For the indignation of the LORD *is* upon all nations, and *his* fury upon all their armies: he hath utterly destroyed them, he hath delivered them to the slaughter.

3 Their slain also shall be cast out, and their stink shall come up out of their carcases, and the mountains shall be melted with their blood.

4 And [a]all the host of heaven shall be dissolved, and the heavens shall be rolled together as a scroll: and all their host shall fall down, as the leaf falleth off from the vine, and as a falling *fig* from the fig tree.

5 For [b]my sword shall be bathed in heaven: behold, it [c]shall come down upon I-dụ-mē'ȧ, and upon the people of my curse, to judgment.

6 The sword of the LORD is filled with blood, it is made fat with fatness, *and* with the blood of lambs and goats, with the fat of the kidneys of rams: for [d]the LORD hath a sacrifice in Bŏz'rah, and a great slaughter in the land of I-dụ-mē'ȧ.

7 And the [2]unicorns shall come down with them, and the bullocks with the bulls; and their land shall be [3]soaked with blood, and their dust made fat with fatness.

8 For *it is* the day of the LORD'S vengeance, *and* the year of recompences for the controversy of Zī'ŏn.

9 And the streams thereof shall be turned into pitch, and the dust thereof into brimstone, and the land thereof shall become burning pitch.

10 It shall not be quenched night nor day; the smoke thereof shall go up for ever: [e]from generation to generation it shall lie waste; none shall pass through it for ever and ever.

11 ¶ But the [4]cormorant and the bittern shall possess it; the owl also and the raven shall dwell in it: and he shall stretch out upon it the line of confusion, and the stones of emptiness.

12 They shall call the nobles thereof to the kingdom, but none *shall be* there, and all her princes shall be nothing.

13 And [f]thorns shall come up in her palaces, nettles and brambles in the fortresses thereof: and it shall be an habitation of dragons, *and* a court for [5,6]owls.

5 [c]Ps. 97.9
6 [d]Prov. 1.7; Matt. 6.33
[1]salvations
7 [2]Or, messengers
[e]2 Ki. 18.18
8 [f]Judg. 5.6
[g]2 Ki. 18.14
9 [3]Or, withered away
10 [h]Deut. 32.36-43; Ps. 12.5; ch. 42.13-14; Zeph. 3.8
15 [4]in righteousnesses
[5]uprightnesses
[6]Or, deceits
[7]bloods
16 [8]heights, or, high places
17 [9]the land of far distances
18 [i]1 Cor. 1.20
[10]weigher
19 [j]Jer. 5.15
[11]Or, ridiculous
21 [k]Zech. 2.5
[12]broad of spaces, or, hands
22 [13]statute maker
[l]Ps. 44.4; Matt. 21.5; Rev. 19.16
23 [14]Or, They have forsaken thy tacklings
24 [m]ch. 12.2; Rom. 11.27

CHAPTER 34
1 [1]the fulness thereof
4 [a]Ps. 102.26; Ezek. 32.7; Joel 2.31; Matt. 24.29; 2 Pet. 3.10
5 [b]Jer. 46.10
[c]Jer. 49.7; Mal. 1.4
6 [d]ch. 63.1; Zeph. 1.7
7 [2]Or, rhinoceros
[3]Or, drunken
10 [e]Mal. 1.4; Rev. 14.11; Rev. 18.18
11 [4]Or, pelican
13 [f]ch. 32.13; Hos. 9.6
[5]Or, ostriches
[6]daughters of the owl

14 [7]The wild beasts of the desert
shall also meet with [8]the wild beasts of
the island, and the satyr shall cry to his
fellow; the [9]screech owl also shall rest
there, and find for herself a place of
rest.
15 There shall the great owl make
her nest, and lay, and hatch, and gather
under her shadow: there shall the vul-
tures also be gathered, every one with
her mate.
16 ¶ Seek ye out of [g]the book of the
LORD, and read: no one of these shall
fail, none shall want her mate: for my
mouth it hath commanded, and his
spirit it hath gathered them.
17 And he hath cast the [h]lot for
them, and his hand hath divided it unto
them by line: they shall possess it for
ever, from generation to generation
shall they dwell therein.

35 The wilderness and the solitary
place shall be glad for them; and
the desert shall rejoice, and blossom as
the rose.
2 It shall blossom abundantly, and
rejoice even with joy and singing: the
glory of Lĕb′a-non shall be given unto
it, the excellency of Cär′mel and Shâr′-
on, they shall see the glory of the
LORD, *and* the excellency of our God.
3 ¶ [a]Strengthen ye the weak hands,
and confirm the feeble knees.
4 Say to them *that are* of a [1]fearful
heart, Be strong, fear not: behold, your
God will come *with* vengeance, *even*
God *with* a recompence; he will come
and save you.
5 Then the [b]eyes of the blind shall
be opened, and [c]the ears of the deaf
shall be unstopped.
6 Then shall the [d]lame *man* leap as
an hart, and the [e]tongue of the dumb
sing: for in the wilderness shall [f]waters
break out, and streams in the desert.
7 And the parched ground shall become a pool, and the thirsty land
springs of water: in the habitation
of dragons, where each lay, *shall be*
[2]grass with reeds and rushes.
8 And an highway shall be there,
and a way, and it shall be called The
way of holiness; [g]the unclean shall not
pass over it; [3]but it *shall be* for those:
the wayfaring men, though fools, shall
not err *therein.*
9 [h]No lion shall be there, nor *any*
ravenous beast shall go up thereon, it
shall not be found there; but the redeemed shall walk *there:*
10 And the [i]ransomed of the LORD
shall return, and come to Zī′ŏn with
songs and everlasting joy upon their
heads: they shall obtain joy and gladness, and [j]sorrow and sighing shall
flee away.

36 Now [a]it came to pass in the fourteenth year of king Hĕz-e-kī′ah,
that Sĕn-năch′e-rĭb king of Ăs-sȳr′ĭ-ȧ
came up against all the defenced cities
of Jū′dah, and took them.
2 And the king of Ăs-sȳr′ĭ-ȧ sent
Răb′sha-keh from [b]Lā′chish to Je-ru′-
sa-lĕm unto king Hĕz-e-kī′ah with a
great army. And he stood by the conduit of the upper pool in the highway
of the fuller's field.
3 Then came forth unto him E-lī′a-
kĭm, Hĭl-kī′ah's son, which was over
the house, and Shĕb′nȧ the [1]scribe,
and Jō′ah, Ā′saph's son, the recorder.
4 ¶ And Răb′sha-keh said unto them,
Say ye now to Hĕz-e-kī′ah, Thus saith
the great king, the king of Ăs-sȳr′ĭ-ȧ,
What confidence *is* this wherein thou
trustest?
5 I say, *sayest thou,* (but *they are*
but [2]vain words) [3]*I have* counsel and
strength for war: now on whom dost
thou trust, that thou rebellest against
me?
6 Lo, thou trustest in the [4]staff of
this broken reed, on Ē′gypt; whereon
if a man lean, it will go into his hand,
and pierce it: so *is* Phā′raōh king of
Ē′gypt to all that trust in him.
7 But if thou say to me, We trust in
the LORD our God: *is it* not he, whose
high places and [c]whose altars Hĕz-e-
kī′ah hath taken away, and said to
Jū′dah and to Je-ru′sa-lĕm, Ye shall
worship before this altar?
8 Now therefore [5]give pledges, I pray
thee, to my master the king of Ăs-sȳr′-
ĭ-ȧ, and I will give thee two thousand
horses, if thou be able on thy part to
set riders upon them.
9 How then wilt thou turn away the
face of one [6]captain of the least of my
master's servants, and put thy trust on
Ē′gypt for chariots and for horsemen?
10 And am I now come up without
the LORD against this land to destroy
it? the LORD said unto me, Go up
against this land, and destroy it.
11 ¶ Then said E-lī′a-ki′m and Shĕb′-
nȧ and Jō′ah unto Răb′sha-keh, Speak,
I pray thee, unto thy servants in the
[7]Sȳr′ĭ-an language; for we understand
it: and speak not to us in the Jews' language, in the ears of the people that *are*
on the wall.
12 ¶ But Răb′sha-keh said, Hath my
master sent me to thy master and to
thee to speak these words? *hath he* not
sent me to the men that sit upon the
wall, that they may eat their own dung,
and drink their own piss with you?
13 Then Răb′sha-keh stood, and
cried with a loud voice in the Jews' language, and said, Hear ye the words of
the great king, the king of Ăs-sȳr′ĭ-ȧ.
14 Thus saith the king, Let not Hĕz-
e-kī′ah deceive you: for he shall not be
able to deliver you.
15 Neither let Hĕz-e-kī′ah make you
trust in the LORD, saying, The LORD
will surely deliver us: this city shall not
be delivered into the hand of the king
of Ăs-sȳr′ĭ-ȧ.
16 Hearken not to Hĕz-e-kī′ah: for
thus saith the king of Ăs-sȳr′ĭ-ȧ, [8]Make
an agreement with me *by* a present,
and come out to me: [d]and eat ye every
one of his vine, and every one of his fig
tree, and drink ye every one the waters
of his own cistern;
17 Until I come and take you away
to a land like your own land, a land of

14 [7]Ziim
[8]Ijim
[9]Or, night monster
16 [g]Ps. 56.8; Dan. 7.10; Mal. 3.16
17 [h]Ps. 78.55; Prov. 16.33

CHAPTER 35
3 [a]Job 4.3-4; Heb. 12.12
4 [1]hasty
5 [b]ch. 29.18; Matt. 9.27-30; John 9.6
[c]ch. 29.18; Matt. 11.5; Mark 7.32
6 [d]Matt. 11.5; Luke 7.22; John 5.8; Acts 3.2
[e]Matt. 9.32
[f]John 7.38
7 [2]Or, a court for reeds, etc
8 [g]Joel 3.17; Rev. 21.27
[3]Or, for he shall be with them
9 [h]Lev. 26.6; ch. 11.9
10 [i]ch. 51.11; Eph. 1.7; Rev. 7.17
[j]ch. 25.8; Rev. 7.17

CHAPTER 36
1 [a]2 Chr. 32.1
2 [b]Josh. 10.3-5; Mic. 1.13
3 [1]Or, secretary
5 [2]a word of lips
[3]Or, but counsel and strength are for the war
6 [4]Or, support
7 [c]2 Ki. 18.4
8 [5]Or, engage, I pray thee, with
9 [6]governor (or, satrap) of the least of my master's servants. So thou hast reposed thyself on Egypt, etc
11 [7]Or, Aramean
16 [8]Make with me a blessing, or, Seek my favour by a present
[d]Mic. 4.4; Zech. 3.10

corn and wine, a land of bread and
vineyards.
18 *Beware* lest Hĕz-e-kī'ah persuade
you, saying, The LORD will deliver us.
Hath any of the gods of the nations delivered his land out of the hand of the
king of Ăs-sȳr'ĭ-ȧ?
19 Where *are* the gods of [e]Hā'math
and Är'phad? where *are* the gods of
Sĕph-ar-vā'im? and have they delivered Sa-mā'rĭ-ȧ out of my hand?
20 Who *are they* among all the gods
of these lands, that have delivered
their land out of my hand, that [f]the
LORD should deliver Je-ru'sa-lĕm out
of my hand?
21 But they held their peace, and
[g]answered him not a word: for the
king's commandment was, saying, Answer him not.
22 ¶ Then came E-lī'a-kĭm, the son of
Hĭl-kī'ah, that *was* over the household,
and Shĕb'nȧ the scribe, and Jō'ah, the
son of Ā'saph, the recorder, to Hĕz-e-
kī'ah with [h]*their* clothes rent, and told
him the words of Răb'sha-keh.

37

And [a]it came to pass, when king
Hĕz-e-kī'ah heard *it*, that he rent
his clothes, and covered himself with
sackcloth, and [b]went into the house of
the LORD.
2 And he sent E-lī'a-kĭm, who *was*
over the household, and Shĕb'nȧ the
scribe, and the elders of the priests covered with sackcloth, [c]unto I-sā'iah the
prophet the son of Ā'moz.
3 And they said unto him, Thus saith
Hĕz-e-kī'ah, This day *is* a day of trouble, and of [d]rebuke, and of [1]blasphemy:
for the children are come to the birth,
and *there is* not strength to bring forth.
4 It may be the LORD thy God will
hear the words of Răb'sha-keh, whom
the king of Ăs-sȳr'ĭ-ȧ his master hath
sent to reproach the living God, and
will reprove the words which the LORD
thy God hath heard: wherefore [e]lift up
thy prayer for the remnant that is [2]left.
5 So the servants of king Hĕz-e-
kī'ah came to I-sā'iah.
6 ¶ And I-sā'iah said unto them,
Thus shall ye say unto your master,
Thus saith the LORD, Be not afraid of
the words that thou hast heard, wherewith the servants of the king of Ăs-
sȳr'ĭ-ȧ have blasphemed me.
7 Behold, I will [3]send a blast upon
him, and he shall hear a rumour, and
return to his own land; and I will cause
him to fall by the sword in his own
land.
8 ¶ So Răb'sha-keh returned, and
found the king of Ăs-sȳr'ĭ-ȧ warring
against Lĭb'nah: for he had heard that
he was departed from [f]Lā'chish.
9 And he heard say concerning Tĭr'-
ha-kah king of Ē-thĭ-ō'pĭ-a, He is come
forth to make war with thee. And
when he heard *it*, he sent messengers
to Hĕz-e-kī'ah, saying,
10 Thus shall ye speak to Hĕz-e-
kī'ah king of Jū'dah, saying, Let not
thy God, in whom thou trustest, deceive thee, saying, Je-ru'sa-lĕm shall

19 [e]Num. 34.8; Josh. 13.5
20 [f]2 Chr. 32.15; Ps. 50.21; ch. 37.23; Dan. 3.15
21 [g]Ps. 38.13; Prov. 9.7; Amos 5.13; Matt. 7.6
22 [h]Gen. 37.34; 1 Sam. 4.12; 2 Sam. 1.11; 2 Ki. 18.18-37; Job 1.20; ch. 33.7

CHAPTER 37

1 [a]2 Ki. 19.1 [b]2 Chr. 6.24; Ps. 50.15; 1 Thess. 5.17
2 [c]2 Ki. 22.14
3 [d]2 Ki. 19.3; Hos. 5.9 [1]Or, provocation
4 [e]1 Sam. 7.8; Jas. 5.14-18 [2]found
7 [3]Or, put a spirit into him
8 [f]Josh. 15.39; Jer. 34.7
12 [g]Gen. 11.31
13 [h]Jer. 49.23
16 [i]Ex. 25.22
17 [j]Dan. 9.18
18 [4]lands
19 [5]given
24 [6]By the hand of thy servants [7]the tallness of the cedars thereof, and the choice of the fir trees thereof [8]Or, the forest and his fruitful field
25 [9]Or, fenced and closed
26 [10]Or, Hast thou not heard how I have made it long ago, and formed it of ancient times? should I now bring it to be laid waste, and defenced cities to be ruinous heaps? as 2 Ki. 19.25

not be given into the hand of the king
of Ăs-sȳr'ĭ-ȧ.
11 Behold, thou hast heard what the
kings of Ăs-sȳr'ĭ-ȧ have done to all
lands by destroying them utterly; and
shalt thou be delivered?
12 Have the gods of the nations delivered them which my fathers have destroyed, *as* Gō'zan, and [g]Hā'ran, and
Rē'zeph, and the children of Ē'dĕn
which *were* in Te-lăs'sar?
13 Where *is* the king of [h]Hā'math,
and the king of Är'phad, and the king
of the city of Sĕph-ar-vā'im, Hē'nȧ,
and Ī'vah?
14 ¶ And Hĕz-e-kī'ah received the
letter from the hand of the messengers, and read it: and Hĕz-e-kī'ah went
up unto the house of the LORD, and
spread it before the LORD.
15 And Hĕz-e-kī'ah prayed unto the
LORD, saying,
16 O LORD of hosts, God of Ĭs'ra-el,
that dwellest [i]*between* the cherubims,
thou *art* the God, *even* thou alone, of
all the kingdoms of the earth: thou
hast made heaven and earth.
17 [j]Incline thine ear, O LORD, and
hear; open thine eyes, O LORD, and see:
and hear all the words of Sĕn-năch'e-
rĭb, which hath sent to reproach the living God.
18 Of a truth, LORD, the kings of Ăs-
sȳr'ĭ-ȧ have laid waste all the [4]nations,
and their countries,
19 And have [5]cast their gods into the
fire: for they *were* no gods, but the
work of men's hands, wood and stone:
therefore they have destroyed them.
20 Now therefore, O LORD our God,
save us from his hand, that all the kingdoms of the earth may know that thou
art the LORD, *even* thou only.
21 ¶ Then I-sā'iah the son of Ā'moz
sent unto Hĕz-e-kī'ah, saying, Thus
saith the LORD God of Ĭs'ra-el, Whereas
thou hast prayed to me against Sĕn-
năch'e-rĭb king of Ăs-sȳr'ĭ-ȧ:
22 This *is* the word which the LORD
hath spoken concerning him; The virgin, the daughter of Zī'ŏn, hath despised
thee, *and* laughed thee to scorn; the
daughter of Je-ru'sa-lĕm hath shaken
her head at thee.
23 Whom hast thou reproached and
blasphemed? and against whom hast
thou exalted *thy* voice, and lifted up
thine eyes on high? *even* against the
Holy One of Ĭs'ra-el.
24 [6]By thy servants hast thou reproached the Lord, and hast said, By
the multitude of my chariots am I come
up to the height of the mountains, to
the sides of Lĕb'a-non; and I will cut
down the [7]tall cedars thereof, *and* the
choice fir trees thereof: and I will enter
into the height of his border, *and* [8]the
forest of his Cär'mel.
25 I have digged, and drunk water;
and with the sole of my feet have I
dried up all the rivers of the [9]besieged
places.
26 [10]Hast thou not heard long ago,
how I have done it; *and* of ancient
times, that I have formed it? now have

I brought it to pass, that thou shouldest
be to lay waste defenced cities *into* ruinous heaps.
27 Therefore their inhabitants *were*
[11]of small power, they were dismayed
and confounded: they were *as* the grass
of the field, and *as* the green herb, *as*
the grass on the housetops, and *as corn*
blasted before it be grown up.
28 But I know thy [12]abode, and thy
going out, and thy coming in, and thy
rage against me.
29 Because thy rage against me, and
thy tumult, is come up into mine ears,
therefore [k]will I put my hook in thy
nose, and my bridle in thy lips, and I
will turn thee back by the way by
which thou camest.
30 And this *shall be* a sign unto thee,
Ye shall eat *this* year such as groweth
of itself; and the second year that
which springeth of the same: and in the
third year sow ye, and reap, and plant
vineyards, and eat the fruit thereof.
31 And [13]the remnant that is escaped of the house of Jū'dah shall
again take root downward, and bear
fruit upward:
32 For out of Je-ru̦'sa-lĕm shall go
forth a remnant, and [14]they that escape
out of mount Zī'ŏn: the [l]zeal of the
LORD of hosts shall do this.
33 Therefore thus saith the LORD
concerning the king of Ăs-sy̆r'ĭ-ȧ, He
shall not come into this city, nor shoot
an arrow there, nor come before it with
[15]shields, nor cast a bank against it.
34 By the way that he came, by the
same shall he return, and shall not
come into this city, saith the LORD.
35 For I will [m]defend this city to
save it for mine own sake, and for my
servant Dā'vid's sake.
36 Then the [n]angel of the LORD went
forth, and smote in the camp of the Ăs-
sy̆r'ĭ-ans a hundred and fourscore and
five thousand: and when they arose
early in the morning, behold, they *were*
all dead corpses.
37 ¶ So Sĕn-năch'e-rĭb king of Ăs-
sy̆r'ĭ-ȧ departed, and went and returned, and dwelt at Nĭn'e-veh.
38 And it came to pass, as he was
worshipping in the house of Nĭs'rŏch
his god, that A-drăm'me-lech and Sha-
rē'zer his sons smote him with the
sword; and they escaped into the land
of [16]Ăr-mē'nĭ-ȧ: and Ē'sar–hăd'don his
son reigned in his stead.

38 In [a]those days was Hĕz-e-kī'ah
sick unto death. And I-sā'iah the
prophet the son of Ā'moz came unto
him, and said unto him, Thus saith the
LORD, [1]Set thine house in order: for
thou shalt die, and not live.
2 Then Hĕz-e-kī'ah turned his face
toward the wall, and prayed unto the
LORD,
3 And said, [b]Remember now, O
LORD, I beseech thee, how I have
walked before thee in truth and with
a perfect heart, and have done *that
which is* good in thy sight. And Hĕz-e-
kī'ah wept [2]sore.
4 ¶ Then came the word of the LORD
to I-sā'iah, saying,
5 Go, and say to Hĕz-e-kī'ah, Thus
saith the LORD, the God of Dā'vid thy
father, I have heard thy prayer, I have
seen thy tears: behold, I will add unto
thy days fifteen years.
6 And I will deliver thee and this city
out of the hand of the king of Ăs-sy̆r'ĭ-
ȧ: and [c]I will defend this city.
7 And this *shall be* [d]a sign unto thee
from the LORD, that the LORD will do
this thing that he hath spoken;
8 Behold, I will bring again the
shadow of the degrees, which is gone
down in the [3]sun dial of Ā'hăz, ten degrees backward. So the sun returned
ten degrees, by which degrees it was
gone down.
9 ¶ The writing of Hĕz-e-kī'ah king
of Jū'dah, when he had been sick, and
was recovered of his sickness:
10 I said in the cutting off of my
days, I shall go to the gates of the
grave: [e]I am deprived of the residue of
my years.
11 I said, I shall not see the LORD,
even the LORD, [f]in the land of the living: I shall behold man no more with
the inhabitants of the world.
12 [g]Mine age is departed, and is removed from me as a shepherd's tent: I
have cut off like a weaver my life: he
will cut me off [4]with pining sickness:
from day *even* to night wilt thou make
an end of me.
13 I reckoned till morning, *that*, as a
lion, so will he break all my bones:
from day *even* to night wilt thou make
an end of me.
14 Like a crane *or* a swallow, so did
I chatter: [h]I did mourn as a dove: mine
eyes fail *with looking* upward: O LORD,
I am oppressed; [5]undertake for me.
15 What shall I say? he hath both
spoken unto me, and himself hath done
it; I shall go softly all my years [i]in the
bitterness of my soul.
16 O Lord, by these *things men* live,
and in all these *things is* the life of my
spirit: so wilt thou recover me, and
make me to live.
17 Behold, [6]for peace I had great bitterness: but [7]thou hast in love to my
soul *delivered it* from the pit of corruption: for thou hast cast all my sins behind thy back.
18 For [j]the grave cannot praise thee,
death can *not* celebrate thee: they that
go down into the pit cannot hope for
thy truth.
19 The living, the living, he shall
praise thee, as I *do* this day: [k]the father to the children shall make known
thy truth.
20 The LORD *was ready* to [l]save me:
therefore we will sing my songs to the
stringed instruments all the days of
our life in the house of the LORD.
21 For [m]I-sā'iah had said, Let them
take a lump of figs, and lay *it* for a
plaister upon the boil, and he shall recover.

27 [11]short of hand
28 [12]Or, sitting
29 [k]Job 41.2; Ps. 32.9; ch. 30.28; Ezek. 29.4; Amos 4.2; Jas. 3.3
31 [13]the escaping of the house of Judah that remaineth
32 [14]the escaping
[l]2 Ki. 19.31
33 [15]shield
35 [m]2 Ki. 20.6; ch. 27.3
36 [n]2 Ki. 19.35
38 [16]Ararat

CHAPTER 38
1 [a]2 Ki. 20.1; 2 Chr. 32.24
[1]Give charge concerning thy house
3 [b]Neh. 5.19
[2]with great weeping
6 [c]ch. 37.35
7 [d]2 Ki. 20.8; ch. 37.30
8 [3]degrees by, or, with the sun
10 [e]Ps. 102.24
11 [f]Job 35.14; Ps. 27.13; Ps. 31.22; Ps. 116.9
12 [g]Job 7.6; Ps. 102.11-23-24; 2 Cor. 5.4
[4]Or, from the thrum
14 [h]ch. 59.11
[5]Or, ease me
15 [i]Job 7.11
17 [6]Or, on my peace came great bitterness
[7]thou hast loved my soul from the pit
18 [j]Ps. 6.5; Ps. 30.9; Eccl. 9.10
19 [k]Deut. 4.9; Ps. 78.3
20 [l]Ps. 9.13-14; Ps. 46.1; Ps. 66.12
21 [m]2 Ki. 20.7

22 Hĕz-e-kī'ah also had said, What *is* the sign that I shall go up to the house of the LORD?

39

At [a]that time Me-rō'dăch–băl'a-dăn, the son of Băl'a-dăn, king of Băb'y̆-lon, sent letters and a present to Hĕz-e-kī'ah: for he had heard that he had been sick, and was recovered.

2 [b]And Hĕz-e-kī'ah was glad of them, and shewed them the house of his [1]precious things, the silver, and the gold, and the spices, and the precious ointment, and all the house of his [2]armour, and all that was found in his treasures: there was nothing in his house, nor in all his dominion, that Hĕz-e-kī'ah shewed them not.

3 ¶ Then came I-sā'iah the prophet unto king Hĕz-e-kī'ah, and said unto him, What said these men? and from whence came they unto thee? And Hĕz-e-kī'ah said, They are come from a far country unto me, *even* from Băb'y̆-lon.

4 Then said he, What have they seen in thine house? And Hĕz-e-kī'ah answered, All that *is* in mine house have they seen: there is nothing among my treasures that I have not shewed them.

5 Then said I-sā'iah to Hĕz-e-kī'ah, Hear the word of the LORD of hosts:

6 Behold, the days come, [c]that all that *is* in thine house, and *that* which thy fathers have laid up in store until this day, shall be carried to Băb'y̆-lon: nothing shall be left, saith the LORD.

7 And of thy sons that shall issue from thee, which thou shalt beget, shall they take away; and [d]they shall be eunuchs in the palace of the king of Băb'y̆-lon.

8 Then said Hĕz-e-kī'ah to I-sā'iah, [e]Good *is* the word of the LORD which thou hast spoken. He said moreover, For there shall be peace and truth in my days.

40

Comfort ye, comfort ye my people, saith your God.

2 Speak ye [1]comfortably to Je-ru̧'sa-lĕm, and cry unto her, that her [2]warfare is accomplished, that her iniquity is pardoned: for she hath received of the LORD'S hand double for all her sins.

3 ¶ [a]The voice of him that crieth in the wilderness, [b]Prepare ye the way of the LORD, make straight in the desert a highway for our God.

4 Every valley shall be exalted, and every mountain and hill shall be made low: and the crooked shall be made [3]straight, and the rough places [4]plain:

5 [c]And the glory of the LORD shall be revealed, and all flesh shall see *it* together: for the mouth of the LORD hath spoken *it*.

6 The voice said, Cry. And he said, What shall I cry? All flesh *is* grass, and all the goodliness thereof *is* as the flower of the field:

7 The grass withereth, the flower fadeth: because the spirit of the LORD bloweth upon it: surely the people *is* grass.

8 The grass withereth, the flower fadeth: but [d]the word of our God shall stand for ever.

9 ¶ [5]O Zī'ŏn, that bringest good tidings, get thee up into the high mountain; [6]O Je-ru̧'sa-lĕm, that bringest good tidings, lift up thy voice with strength; lift *it* up, be not afraid; say unto the cities of Jū'dah, Behold your God!

10 Behold, the Lord GOD will come [7]with strong *hand*, and his arm shall rule for him: behold, his reward *is* with him, and [8]his work before him.

11 He shall [e]feed his flock like a shepherd: he shall gather the lambs with his arm, and carry *them* in his bosom, *and* shall gently lead those [9]that are with young.

12 ¶ Who hath measured the waters in the hollow of his hand, and meted out heaven with the span, and comprehended the dust of the earth in [10]a measure, and weighed the mountains in scales, and the hills in a balance?

13 Who hath directed the Spirit of the LORD, or *being* [11]his counseller hath taught him?

14 With whom took he counsel, and *who* [12]instructed him, and taught him in the path of judgment, and taught him knowledge, and shewed to him the way of [13]understanding?

15 Behold, the nations *are* as a drop of a bucket, and are counted as the small dust of the balance: behold, he taketh up the isles as a very little thing.

16 And Lĕb'a-non *is* not sufficient to burn, nor the beasts thereof sufficient for a burnt offering.

17 All nations before him *are* as nothing; and they are counted to him less than nothing, and vanity.

18 ¶ To whom then will ye [f]liken God? or what likeness will ye compare unto him?

19 The workman melteth a graven image, and the goldsmith spreadeth it over with gold, and casteth silver chains.

20 He that [14]*is* so impoverished that he hath no oblation chooseth a tree *that* will not rot; he seeketh unto him a cunning workman [g]to prepare a graven image, *that* shall not be moved.

21 [h]Have ye not known? have ye not heard? hath it not been told you from the beginning? have ye not understood from the foundations of the earth?

22 [15]*It is* he that sitteth upon the circle of the earth, and the inhabitants thereof *are* as grasshoppers; that [i]stretcheth out the heavens as a curtain, and spreadeth them out as a tent to dwell in:

23 That bringeth the [j]princes to nothing; he maketh the judges of the earth as vanity.

24 Yea, they shall not be planted; yea, they shall not be sown: yea, their stock shall not take root in the earth: and he shall also blow upon them, and they shall wither, and the whirlwind shall take them away as stubble.

25 [k]To whom then will ye liken me, or shall I be equal? saith the Holy One.

CHAPTER 39
1 [a]2 Ki. 20.12
2 [b]2 Chr. 32.31
[1]Or, spicery
[2]vessels, or, instruments, or, jewels
6 [c]Lev. 26.33; Deut. 28.64; 1 Ki. 14.15; 2 Chr. 36.18; Amos 5.27
7 [d]2 Ki. 24.12; Dan. 1.2
8 [e]1 Sam. 3.18

CHAPTER 40
2 [1]to the heart
[2]Or, appointed time
3 [a]Matt. 3.3
[b]Mal. 3.1; John 1.23
4 [3]Or, a straight place
[4]Or, a plain place
5 [c]Ex. 16.7; Luke 2.10
8 [d]1 Pet. 1.25
9 [5]Or, O thou that tellest good tidings to Zion
[6]Or, O thou that tellest good tidings to Jerusalem
10 [7]Or, against the strong
[8]Or, recompence for his work
11 [e]ch. 49.10; Rev. 7.17
[9]Or, that give suck
12 [10]a tierce
13 [11]man of his counsel
14 [12]made him understand
[13]understandings
18 [f]Acts 17.29
20 [14]is poor of oblation
[g]Jer. 10.4
21 [h]Ps. 19.1; Rom. 1.19
22 [15]Or, Him that sitteth, etc
[i]Gen. 1.1-6; Jer. 10.12
23 [j]Job 12.21
25 [k]Deut. 4.15; Acts 17.24-29

26 Lift up your eyes on high, and behold who hath created these *things*, that bringeth out their host by number: [l]he calleth them all by names by the greatness of his might, for that *he is* strong in power; not one faileth.

27 Why sayest thou, O Jā'cob, and speakest, O Is'ra-el, My way is hid from the LORD, and my judgment is passed over from my God?

28 ¶ Hast thou not known? hast thou not heard, *that* the everlasting God, the LORD, the Creator of the ends of the earth, fainteth not, neither is weary? [m]*there is* no searching of his understanding.

29 He giveth power to the faint; and to *them that have* no might he increaseth strength.

30 Even the youths shall faint and be weary, and the young men shall utterly fall:

31 But they that [n]wait upon the LORD shall [16]renew *their* strength; they shall mount up with wings as eagles; they shall run, and not be weary; *and* they shall walk, and not faint.

CHAPTER 41

41 Keep silence before me, O islands; and let the people renew *their* strength: let them come near; then let them speak: let us come near together to judgment.

2 Who raised up [1]the righteous *man* [a]from the east, called him to his foot, [b]gave the nations before him, and made *him* rule over kings? he gave *them* as the dust to his sword, *and* as driven stubble to his bow.

3 He pursued them, *and* passed [2]safely; *even* by the way *that* he had not gone with his feet.

4 [c]Who hath wrought and done *it*, calling the generations from the beginning? I the LORD, the [d]first, and with the last; I *am* he.

5 The isles saw *it*, and feared; the ends of the earth were afraid, drew near, and came.

6 They helped every one his neighbour; and *every one* said to his brother, [3]Be of good courage.

7 So the carpenter encouraged the [4]goldsmith, *and* he that smootheth *with* the hammer [5]him that smote the anvil, [6]saying, It *is* ready for the sodering: and he fastened it with nails, *that* it should not be moved.

8 But thou, Is'ra-el, *art* my servant, Jā'cob whom I have chosen, the seed of Ā'brā-hăm my [e]friend.

9 *Thou* whom I have taken from the ends of the earth, and called thee from the chief men thereof, and said unto thee, Thou *art* my servant; I have chosen thee, and not cast thee away.

10 ¶ Fear thou not; [f]for I *am* with thee: be not dismayed; for I *am* thy God: I will strengthen thee; yea, I will help thee; yea, I will uphold thee with the right hand of my righteousness.

11 Behold, all they that were incensed against thee shall be [g]ashamed and confounded: they shall be as nothing; and [7]they that strive with thee shall perish.

12 Thou shalt seek them, and shalt not find them, *even* [8]them that contended with thee: [9]they that war against thee shall be as nothing, and as a thing of nought.

13 For I the LORD thy God will hold thy right hand, saying unto thee, Fear not; I will help thee.

14 Fear not, thou worm Jā'cob, *and* ye [10]men of Is'ra-el; I will help thee, saith the LORD, [h]and thy redeemer, the Holy One of Is'ra-el.

15 Behold, [i]I will make thee a new sharp threshing instrument having [11]teeth: thou shalt thresh the mountains, and beat *them* small, and shalt make the hills as chaff.

16 Thou shalt [j]fan them, and the wind shall carry them away, and the whirlwind shall scatter them: and thou shalt rejoice in the LORD, *and* shalt glory in the Holy One of Is'ra-el.

17 *When* the poor and needy seek water, and *there is* none, *and* their tongue faileth for thirst, I the LORD will hear them, *I* the God of Is'ra-el will not forsake them.

18 I will open [k]rivers in high places, and fountains in the midst of the valleys: I will make the [l]wilderness a pool of water, and the dry land springs of water.

19 I will plant in the wilderness the cedar, the shittah tree, and the myrtle, and the oil tree; I will set in the desert the fir tree, *and* the pine, and the box tree together:

20 [m]That they may see, and know, and consider, and understand together, that the hand of the LORD hath done this, and the Holy One of Is'ra-el hath created it.

21 [12]Produce your cause, saith the LORD; bring forth your strong *reasons*, saith the King of Jā'cob.

22 Let them bring *them* forth, and shew us what shall happen: let them shew the former things, what they *be*, that we may [13]consider them, and know the latter end of them; or declare us things for to come.

23 [n]Shew the things that are to come hereafter, that we may know that ye *are* gods; yea, [o]do good, or do evil, that we may be dismayed, and behold *it* together.

24 Behold, ye *are* [14]of nothing, and your work [15]of nought: an abomination *is he that* chooseth you.

25 I have raised up *one* from the north, and he shall come: from the rising of the sun [p]shall he call upon my name: and he shall come upon princes as *upon* morter, and as the potter treadeth clay.

26 Who hath declared from the beginning, that we may know? and beforetime, that we may say, *He is* righteous? yea, *there is* none that sheweth, yea, *there is* none that declareth, yea, *there is* none that heareth your words.

27 [16]The first *shall say* to Zī'ŏn, Behold, behold them: and I will give to Je-ru'sa-lĕm one that bringeth good tidings.

---

26 [l]Ps. 147.4
28 [m]Ps. 147.5; Rom. 11.33
31 [n]Job 17.9; Ps. 25.3; ch. 8.17; Lam. 3.25; 2 Cor. 4.8-10, 16
[16]change

CHAPTER 41
2 [1]righteousness
[a]ch. 46.11
[b]ch. 45.1
3 [2]in peace
4 [c]ch. 44.7; Acts 15.18
[d]ch. 43.10; ch. 48.12; Rev. 1.11-17
6 [3]Be strong
7 [4]Or, founder
[5]Or, the smiting
[6]Or, saying of the soder, It is good
8 [e]Gen. 18.19; 2 Chr. 20.7; Neh. 9.7
10 [f]Deut. 31.6; Rom. 8.31
11 [g]Ex. 23.22; Zech. 12.3
[7]the men of thy strife
12 [8]the men of thy contention
[9]the men of thy war
14 [10]Or, few men
[h]Job 19.25
15 [i]Mic. 4.13; 2 Cor. 10.4-5
[11]mouths
16 [j]Jer. 51.2
18 [k]ch. 35.6-7
[l]Ps. 107.35
20 [m]Job 12.9
21 [12]Cause to come near
22 [13]set our heart upon them
23 [n]Deut. 18.22
[o]Jer. 10.5
24 [14]Or, worse than nothing
[15]Or, worse than of a viper
25 [p]Ezra 1.2
27 [16]Or, I the first say

28 [q]For I beheld, and *there was* no man; even among them, and *there was* no counseller, that, when I asked of them, could [17]answer a word.

29 Behold, they *are* all vanity; their works *are* nothing: their molten images *are* wind and confusion.

42 Behold [a]my servant, whom I uphold; mine elect, *in whom* my soul [b]delighteth; [c]I have put my spirit upon him: he shall bring forth judgment to the Gĕn'tīles.

2 He shall not cry, nor lift up, nor cause his voice to be heard in the street.

3 A bruised reed shall he not break, and the [1]smoking flax shall he not [2]quench: he shall bring forth judgment unto truth.

4 [d]He shall not fail nor be [3]discouraged, till he have set judgment in the earth: [e]and the isles shall wait for his law.

5 ¶ Thus saith God the LORD, [f]he that created the heavens, and stretched them out; he that spread forth the earth, and that which cometh out of it; [g]he that giveth breath unto the people upon it, and spirit to them that walk therein:

6 I the LORD have called thee in righteousness, and will hold thine hand, and will keep thee, and give thee for a covenant of the people, for [h]a light of the Gĕn'tīles;

7 To open the blind eyes, to [i]bring out the prisoners from the prison, *and* them that sit in [j]darkness out of the prison house.

8 [k]I *am* the LORD: that *is* my name: and my [l]glory will I not give to another, neither my praise to graven images.

9 Behold, the former things are come to pass, and new things do I declare: before they spring forth I tell you of them.

10 [m]Sing unto the LORD a new song, *and* his praise from the end of the earth, [n]ye that go down to the sea, and [4]all that is therein; the isles, and the inhabitants thereof.

11 Let the wilderness and the cities thereof lift up *their voice,* the villages *that* Kē'där doth inhabit: let the inhabitants of the rock sing, let them shout from the top of the mountains.

12 Let them give glory unto the LORD, and declare his praise in the islands.

13 The LORD shall go forth as a mighty man, he shall stir up jealousy like a man of war: he shall cry, yea, roar; he shall [5]prevail against his enemies.

14 I have long time holden my peace; I have been still, *and* refrained myself: *now* will I cry like a travailing woman; I will destroy and [6]devour at once.

15 I will make waste mountains and hills, and dry up all their herbs; and I will make the rivers islands, and I will dry up the pools.

16 And I will bring the blind by a way *that* they knew not; I will lead them in paths *that* they have not known: I will make darkness light before them, and crooked things [7]straight. These things will I do unto them, and not forsake them.

17 ¶ They shall be turned back, they shall be greatly ashamed, that trust in graven images, that say to the molten images, Ye *are* our gods.

18 Hear, ye deaf; and look, ye blind, that ye may see.

19 [o]Who *is* blind, but my servant? or deaf, as my messenger *that* I sent? who *is* blind as *he that is* perfect, and blind as the LORD'S servant?

20 Seeing many things, [p]but thou observest not; opening the ears, but he heareth not.

21 The LORD is well pleased for his righteousness' sake; he will magnify the law, and make [8]*it* honourable.

22 But this *is* a people robbed and spoiled; [9]*they are* all of them snared in holes, and they are hid in prison houses: they are for a prey, and none delivereth; for [10]a spoil, and none saith, Restore.

23 Who among you will give ear to this? *who* will hearken and hear [11]for the time to come?

24 Who gave Jā'cob for a spoil, and Ĭs'ra-el to the robbers? did not the LORD, he against whom we have sinned? for they would not walk in his ways, neither were they obedient unto his law.

25 Therefore he hath poured upon him the fury of his anger, and the strength of battle: [q]and it hath set him on fire round about, [r]yet he knew not; and it burned him, yet he laid *it* not to heart.

43 But now thus saith the LORD that created thee, O Jā'cob, and he that formed thee, O Ĭs'ra-el, Fear not: [a]for I have redeemed thee, [b]I have called *thee* by thy name; thou *art* mine.

2 [c]When thou passest through the waters, [d]I *will be* with thee; and through the rivers, they shall not overflow thee: when [e]thou walkest through the fire, thou shalt not be burned; neither shall the flame kindle upon thee.

3 For I *am* the LORD thy God, the Holy One of Ĭs'ra-el, thy Saviour: [f]I gave Ē'gypt *for* thy ransom, Ē-thĭ-ō'pĭ-a and Sē'bȧ for thee.

4 Since thou wast [g]precious in my sight, thou hast been honourable, and I have loved thee: therefore will I give men for thee, and people for thy [1]life.

5 [h]Fear not: for I *am* with thee: I will bring thy seed from the east, and gather thee from the west;

6 I will say to the north, Give up; and to the south, Keep not back: bring my sons from far, and my daughters from the ends of the earth;

7 *Even* every one that is [i]called by my name: for [j]I have created him for my glory, I have formed him; yea, I have made him.

8 ¶ [k]Bring forth the blind people that have eyes, and the deaf that have ears.

---

28 [q]ch. 63.5; Dan. 2.10 [17]return

CHAPTER 42

1 [a]ch. 49.3-6; ch. 52.13; Matt. 12.18; Phil. 2.7 [b]Matt. 3.17; John 3.35; Eph. 1.6; Col. 1.12-14 [c]ch. 11.2

3 [1]Or, dimly burning [2]quench it

4 [d]Heb. 12.2 [3]broken [e]Gen. 49.10

5 [f]ch. 44.24; Zech. 12.1 [g]Acts 17.25

6 [h]Luke 2.32; Acts 13.47

7 [i]Luke 4.18; 2 Tim. 2.26; Heb. 2.14 [j]ch. 9.2

8 [k]Ex. 3.14 [l]ch. 48.11

10 [m]Ps. 33.3; Ps. 40.3 [n]Ps. 107.23 [4]the fulness thereof

13 [5]Or, behave himself mightily

14 [6]swallow, or, sup up

16 [7]into straightness

19 [o]ch. 43.8; John 7.49

20 [p]Deut. 4.3; Rom. 2.21

21 [8]Or, him

22 [9]Or, in snaring all the young men of them [10]a treading

23 [11]for the after time

25 [q]2 Ki. 25.9 [r]Hos. 7.9

CHAPTER 43

1 [a]ch. 44.6 [b]ch. 42.6; 2 Tim. 1.9

2 [c]Ps. 66.12 [d]Deut. 31.6-8 [e]Dan. 3.25

3 [f]Prov. 21.18

4 [g]Ex. 19.5-6 [1]Or, person

5 [h]ch. 41.10-14; ch. 44.2

7 [i]ch. 63.19 [j]Ps. 100.3; Eph. 2.10

8 [k]ch. 6.9; ch. 42.19

9 Let all the nations be gathered together, and let the people be assembled: who among them can declare this, and shew us former things? let them bring forth their witnesses, that they may be justified: or let them hear, and say, *It is* truth.

10 [l]Ye *are* my witnesses, saith the LORD, [m]and my servant whom I have chosen: that ye may know and believe me, and understand that I *am* he: before me there was [2]no God formed, neither shall there be after me.

11 I, *even* I, *am* the LORD; and beside me *there is* no saviour.

12 I have declared, and have saved, and I have shewed, when *there was* no [n]strange *god* among you: therefore ye *are* my witnesses, saith the LORD, that I *am* God.

13 [o]Yea, before the day *was* I *am* he; and *there is* none that can deliver out of my hand: I will work, and who shall [3]let it?

14 ¶ Thus saith the LORD, your redeemer, the Holy One of Ĭs'ra-el; For your sake I have sent to Băb'ȳ-lon, and have brought down all their [4]nobles, and the Chăl-dē'ans, whose cry *is* in the ships.

15 I *am* the LORD, your Holy One, the creator of Ĭs'ra-el, your [p]King.

16 Thus saith the LORD, [q]which maketh a way in the sea, and a path in the mighty waters;

17 Which [r]bringeth forth the chariot and horse, the army and the power; they shall lie down together, they shall not rise: they are extinct, they are quenched as tow.

18 ¶ Remember ye not the former things, neither consider the things of old.

19 Behold, I will do a [s]new thing; now it shall spring forth; shall ye not know it? I will even make a way in the wilderness, *and* rivers in the desert.

20 The beast of the field shall honour me, the dragons and the [5][6]owls: because [t]I give waters in the wilderness, *and* rivers in the desert, to give drink to my people, my chosen.

21 [u]This people have I formed for myself; they shall shew forth my praise.

22 ¶ But thou hast not called upon me, O Jā'cob; but thou [v]hast been weary of me, O Ĭs'ra-el.

23 Thou hast not brought me the [7]small cattle of thy burnt offerings; neither hast thou honoured me with thy sacrifices. I have not caused thee to serve with an offering, nor wearied thee with incense.

24 Thou hast bought me no sweet cane with money, neither hast thou [8]filled me with the fat of thy sacrifices: but thou hast made me to serve with thy sins, thou hast [w]wearied me with thine iniquities.

25 I, *even* I, *am* he that [x]blotteth out thy transgressions [y]for mine own sake, and will not remember thy sins.

26 Put me in remembrance: let us plead together: declare thou, that thou mayest be justified.

10 [l]ch. 44.8; Rev. 1.5
[m]ch. 41.8
[2]Or, nothing formed of God
12 [n]Deut. 32.16
13 [o]Ps. 90.2; Matt. 19.26
[3]turn it back
14 [4]bars
15 [p]Hos. 13.10
16 [q]Ps. 77.19
17 [r]Ex. 14.4
19 [s]2 Cor. 5.17; Rev. 21.5
20 [5]Or, ostriches
[6]daughters of the owl
[t]ch. 48.21
21 [u]Luke 1.74; Eph. 1.5
22 [v]Mal. 1.13
23 [7]lambs, or, kids
24 [8]made me drunk, or, abundantly moistened
[w]ch. 1.14; Jude 4
25 [x]ch. 44.22; Mic. 7.18-19
[y]Ezek. 36.22
27 [z]Rom. 5.12
[9]interpreters, Mal. 2.7
28 [a]ch. 47.6; Lam. 2.2
[10]Or, holy princes
[b]Ps. 79.4; Zech. 8.13

CHAPTER 44

1 [a]ch. 41.8; Jer. 30.10
2 [b]Deut. 32.15
3 [c]Mal. 3.10; John 7.38
5 [d]Ex. 13.9; Neh. 9.38
6 [e]ch. 43.1
[f]ch. 41.4; Rev. 1.8
8 [g]Deut. 4.35; 2 Sam. 22.32
[1]rock
9 [h]ch. 41.24
[2]desirable
[i]Deut. 4.28; ch. 42.17-20
10 [j]Jer. 10.5;
11 [k]Ps. 97.7;
12 [l]ch. 40.19
[3]Or, with an ax
14 [4]Or, taketh courage

27 [z]Thy first father hath sinned, and thy [9]teachers have transgressed against me.

28 Therefore [a]I have profaned the [10]princes of the sanctuary, [b]and have given Jā'cob to the curse, and Ĭs'ra-el to reproaches.

44 Yet now hear, [a]O Jā'cob my servant; and Ĭs'ra-el, whom I have chosen:

2 Thus saith the LORD that made thee, and formed thee from the womb, *which* will help thee; Fear not, O Jā'cob, my servant; and thou, [b]Jĕs'u-rŭn, whom I have chosen.

3 For I will [c]pour water upon him that is thirsty, and floods upon the dry ground: I will pour my spirit upon thy seed, and my blessing upon thine offspring:

4 And they shall spring up *as* among the grass, as willows by the water courses.

5 One shall say, I *am* the LORD'S; and another shall call *himself* by the name of Jā'cob; and another shall [d]subscribe *with* his hand unto the LORD, and surname *himself* by the name of Ĭs'ra-el.

6 Thus saith the LORD the King of Ĭs'ra-el, [e]and his redeemer the LORD of hosts; [f]I *am* the first, and I *am* the last; and beside me *there is* no God.

7 And who, as I, shall call, and shall declare it, and set it in order for me, since I appointed the ancient people? and the things that are coming, and shall come, let them shew unto them.

8 Fear ye not, neither be afraid: have not I told thee from that time, and have delcared *it?* ye *are* even my witnesses. Is there a God beside me? yea, [g]*there is* no [1]God; I know not *any.*

9 ¶ [h]They that make a graven image *are* all of them vanity; and their [2]delectable things shall not profit; and they *are* their own witnesses; [i]they see not, nor know; that they may be ashamed.

10 Who hath formed a god, or molten a graven image [j]*that* is profitable for nothing?

11 Behold, all his fellows shall be [k]ashamed: and the workmen, they *are* of men: let them all be gathered together, let them stand up; *yet* they shall fear, *and* they shall be ashamed together.

12 [l]The smith [3]with the tongs both worketh in the coals, and fashioneth it with hammers, and worketh it with the strength of his arms: yea, he is hungry, and his strength faileth: he drinketh no water, and is faint.

13 The carpenter stretcheth out *his* rule; he marketh it out with a line; he fitteth it with planes, and he marketh it out with the compass, and maketh it after the figure of a man, according to the beauty of a man; that it may remain in the house.

14 He heweth him down cedars, and taketh the cypress and the oak, which he [4]strengtheneth for himself among the trees of the forest: he planteth an ash, and the rain doth nourish *it.*

15 Then shall it be for a man to
burn: for he will take thereof, and
warm himself; yea, he kindleth *it,* and
baketh bread; yea, he maketh a god,
and worshippeth *it;* he maketh it a graven image, and falleth down thereto.
16 He burneth part thereof in the
fire; with part thereof he eateth flesh;
he roasteth roast, and is satisfied: yea,
he warmeth *himself,* and saith, Aha, I
am warm, I have seen the fire:
17 And the residue thereof he maketh a god, *even* his graven image: he
falleth down unto it, and worshippeth
it, and prayeth unto it, and saith, Deliver me; for thou *art* my god.
18 [m]They have not known nor understood: for [n]he hath [5]shut their eyes,
that they cannot see; *and* their hearts,
that they cannot understand.
19 And none [6]considereth in his
heart, neither *is there* knowledge nor
understanding to say, I have burned
part of it in the fire; yea, also I have
baked bread upon the coals thereof; I
have roasted flesh, and eaten *it:* and
shall I make the residue thereof an
abomination? shall I fall down to [7]the
stock of a tree?
20 He feedeth on ashes: [o]a deceived
heart hath turned him aside, that he
cannot deliver his soul, nor say, *Is
there* not a lie in my right hand?
21 ¶ Remember these, O Jā′cob and
Ĭs′ra-el; for thou *art* my servant: I have
formed thee; thou *art* my servant: O
Ĭs′ra-el, thou shalt not be forgotten of
me.
22 [p]I have blotted out, as a thick
cloud, thy transgressions, and, as a
cloud, thy sins: return unto me; for [q]I
have redeemed thee.
23 [r]Sing, O ye heavens; for the LORD
hath done *it:* shout, ye lower parts of
the earth: break forth into singing, ye
mountains, O forest, and every tree
therein: for the LORD hath redeemed
Jā′cob, and glorified himself in Ĭs′ra-el.
24 Thus saith the LORD, [s]thy redeemer, and [t]he that formed thee from
the womb, I *am* the LORD that maketh
all *things;* [u]that stretcheth forth the
heavens alone; that spreadeth abroad
the earth by myself;
25 That frustrateth the tokens [v]of
the liars, and maketh diviners mad;
that turneth wise *men* backward, [w]and
maketh their knowledge foolish;
26 [x]That confirmeth the word of his
servant, and performeth the counsel of
his messengers; that saith to Je-ru′sa-
lĕm, Thou shalt be inhabited; and to
the cities of Jū′dah, Ye shall be built,
and I will raise up the [8]decayed places
thereof:
27 [y]That saith to the deep, Be dry,
and I will dry up thy rivers:
28 That saith of Cȳ′rus, *He is* my
shepherd, and shall perform all my
pleasure: even saying to Je-ru′sa-lĕm,
[z]Thou shalt be built; and to the temple,
Thy foundation shall be laid.
45 Thus saith the LORD to his
anointed, to Cȳ′rus, whose [a]right
hand I [1]have holden, to subdue nations
before him; and I will loose the loins of
kings, to open before him the two
leaved gates; and the gates shall not be
shut;
2 I will go before thee, and make the
crooked places straight: I will break in
pieces the gates of brass, and cut in
sunder the bars of iron:
3 And I will give thee the treasures
of darkness, and hidden riches of secret places, that thou mayest know
that I, the LORD which [b]call *thee* by
thy name, *am* the God of Ĭs′ra-el.
4 For [c]Jā′cob my servant's sake,
and Ĭs′ra-el mine elect, I have even
called thee by thy name: I have surnamed thee, though thou hast [d]not
known me.
5 ¶ I [e]*am* the LORD, and *there is*
none else, *there is* no God beside me:
[f]I girded thee, though thou hast not
known me:
6 [g]That they may know from the rising of the sun, and from the west, that
there is none beside me. I *am* the
LORD, and *there is* none else.
7 I form the light, and create darkness: I make peace, and [h]create evil: I
the LORD do all these *things.*
8 [i]Drop down, ye heavens, from
above, and let the skies pour down
righteousness: let the earth open, and
let them bring forth salvation, and let
righteousness spring up together; I the
LORD have created it.
9 Woe unto him that striveth with
[j]his Maker! *Let* the potsherd *strive*
with the potsherds of the earth. [k]Shall
the clay say to him that fashioneth it,
What makest thou? or thy work, He
hath no hands?
10 Woe unto him that saith unto *his*
father, What begettest thou? or to the
woman, What hast thou brought forth?
11 Thus saith the LORD, the Holy
One of Ĭs′ra-el, and his Maker, Ask
me of things to come concerning [l]my
sons, and concerning [m]the work of
my hands command ye me.
12 [n]I have made the earth, and created man upon it: I, *even* my hands,
have stretched out the heavens, and all
their host have I commanded.
13 I have raised him up in righteousness, and I will [2]direct all his ways: he
shall [o]build my city, and he shall let go
my captives, [p]not for price nor reward,
saith the LORD of hosts.
14 Thus saith the LORD, [q]The labour
of Ē′gypt, and merchandise of Ē-thĭ-
ō′pĭ-a and of the Sa-bē′ans, men of stature, shall come over unto thee, and
they shall be thine: they shall come after thee; in chains they shall come over,
and they shall fall down unto thee, they
shall make supplication unto thee, *saying,* [r]Surely God *is* in thee; and *there is*
none else, *there is* no God.
15 Verily thou *art* a God [s]that hidest
thyself, O God of Ĭs′ra-el, the Saviour.
16 They shall be ashamed, and also
confounded, all of them: they shall go
to confusion together *that are* makers
of idols.

18 [m]Ps. 81.12; ch. 45.20
[n]Rom. 11.8-10; 2 Thess. 2.11
[5]daubed
19 [6]setteth to his heart
[7]that which comes of a tree
20 [o]Hos. 4.12; Rom. 1.21; 2 Thess. 2.11
22 [p]ch. 1.18; ch. 43.25; ch. 53.11-12; Jer. 33.8; Mic. 7.18-19; Col. 1.14
[q]ch. 43.1; 1 Cor. 6.20; 1 Pet. 1.18-19
23 [r]Ps. 69.34; ch. 42.10; Rev. 18.20
24 [s]Job 19.25; ch. 43.14
[t]ch. 43.1
[u]Job 9.8; Ps. 104.2; ch. 40.22
25 [v]Jer. 50.36
[w]1 Cor. 1.20
26 [x]Zech. 1.6; Matt. 5.18
[8]wastes
27 [y]Jer. 50.38
28 [z]2 Chr. 36.22-23

CHAPTER 45
1 [a]Ps. 73.23; ch. 41.13
[1]Or, strengthened
3 [b]Ex. 33.12
4 [c]ch. 44.1
[d]Acts 17.23; Gal. 4.8-9; Eph. 2.12; 1 Thess. 4.5
5 [e]Deut. 4.35
[f]Ps. 18.32
6 [g]Ps. 102.15; Mal. 1.11
7 [h]Amos 3.6
8 [i]Ps. 85.11
9 [j]ch. 64.8
[k]Jer. 18.6; Rom. 9.20
11 [l]Jer. 31.9
[m]Isa. 29.23
12 [n]Jer. 27.5
13 [2]Or, make straight
[o]Ezra 1.1
[p]Rom. 3.24
14 [q]Ps. 68.31; Zech. 8.22
[r]1 Cor. 14.25
15 [s]Deut. 29.29; Rom. 11.33-34

17 [t]*But* Ĭs′ra-el shall be saved in the
LORD with an everlasting salvation: ye
shall not be ashamed nor confounded
world without end.
18 For thus saith the LORD that created the heavens; God himself that
formed the earth and made it; he hath
established it, he created it not in vain,
he formed it to be inhabited: I *am* the
LORD; and *there is* none else.
19 I have not spoken in [u]secret, in a
dark place of the earth: I said not unto
the seed of Jā′cob, Seek ye me in vain:
[v]I the LORD speak righteousness, I declare things that are right.
20 ¶ Assemble yourselves and come;
draw near together, ye *that are* [w]es-
caped of the nations: [x]they have no
knowledge that set up the wood of their
graven image, and pray unto a god *that*
cannot save.
21 Tell ye, and bring *them* near;
yea, let them take counsel together:
who hath declared this from ancient
time? *who* hath told it from that time?
have not I the LORD? and *there is* no
God else beside me; a just God and a
Saviour; *there is* none beside me.
22 [3]Look unto me, and be ye saved,
all the ends of the earth: for I *am* God,
and *there is* none else.
23 [y]I have sworn by myself, the
word is gone out of my mouth *in* righteousness, and shall not return, That
unto me every [z]knee shall bow, [a]every
tongue shall swear.
24 [4]Surely, shall *one* say, in the LORD
have I [5]righteousness and strength:
even to him shall *men* come; and all
that are incensed against him shall be
ashamed.
25 In the LORD shall all the seed of
Ĭs′ra-el be justified, and shall glory.

46 Bĕl [a]boweth down, Nē′bo stoop-
eth, their idols were upon the
beasts, and upon the cattle: your carriages *were* heavy loaden; [b]*they are* a
burden to the weary *beast*.
2 They stoop, they bow down together; they could not deliver the burden, but [1]themselves are gone into
captivity.
3 ¶ Hearken unto me, O house of
Jā′cob, and all the remnant of the
house of Ĭs′ra-el, [c]which are borne *by*
me from the belly, which are carried
from the womb:
4 And *even* to *your* old age [d]I *am* he;
and *even* to hoar hairs [e]will I carry
you: I have made, and I will bear; even
I will carry, and will deliver *you*.
5 ¶ To whom will ye liken me, and
make *me* equal, and compare me, that
we may be like?
6 They lavish gold out of the bag,
and weigh silver in the balance, *and*
hire a goldsmith; and he maketh it a
god: they fall down, yea, they worship.
7 [f]They bear him upon the shoulder,
they carry him, and set him in his
place, and he standeth; from his place
shall he not remove: yea, *one* shall cry
unto him, yet can he not answer, nor
save him out of his trouble.

17 [t]2 Sam. 23.5; Rom. 11.26
19 [u]Deut. 30.11
[v]Neh. 9.13; Rom. 7.12
20 [w]Jer. 44.28
[x]Rom. 1.22
22 [3]Or, turn
23 [y]Gen. 22.16; Heb. 6.13
[z]Rom. 14.11; Phil. 2.10
[a]Gen. 31.53; Ps. 63.11
24 [4]Or, Surely he shall say of me, In the LORD is all righteousness and strength
[5]righteousnesses

CHAPTER 46
1 [a]Jer. 51.44
[b]Jer. 10.5
2 [1]their soul
3 [c]Ex. 19.4; Deut. 1.31
4 [d]Ps. 102.27; Mal. 3.6
[e]Ps. 48.14
7 [f]Jer. 10.5
9 [g]Deut. 32.7
10 [h]Ps. 33.11; Heb. 6.17
11 [2]the man of my counsel
[i]Num. 23.19; Tit. 1.2
12 [j]Rom. 10.3
13 [k]Rom. 1.17
[l]ch. 56.1; 1 Tim. 1.15
[m]ch. 62.11; Zech. 9.9

CHAPTER 47
1 [a]Jer. 48.18;
2 [b]Ex. 11.5
3 [c]Nah. 3.5
[d]Matt. 7.2
5 [e]1 Sam. 2.9
[f]Dan. 2.37
6 [g]2 Chr. 28.9;
[h]Deut. 28.50
7 [i]verse 5
8 [j]Zeph. 2.15
[k]Rev. 18.7
9 [l]1 Thess. 5.3
[m]Dan. 2.2
10 [n]Ps. 52.7
[o]Ezek. 8.12
[1]Or, caused thee to turn away

8 Remember this, and shew yourselves men: bring *it* again to mind, O
ye transgressors.
9 [g]Remember the former things of
old: for I *am* God, and *there is* none
else; *I am* God, and *there is* none like
me,
10 Declaring the end from the beginning, and from ancient times *the*
things that are not *yet* done, saying,
[h]My counsel shall stand, and I will do
all my pleasure:
11 Calling a ravenous bird from the
east, [2]the man that executeth my counsel from a far country: yea, [i]I have
spoken *it*, I will also bring it to pass; I
have purposed *it*, I will also do it.
12 ¶ Hearken unto me, ye stouthearted, [j]that *are* far from righteousness:
13 [k]I bring near my righteousness;
it shall not be far off, and my salvation
[l]shall not tarry: and I will place [m]salva-
tion in Zī′ŏn for Ĭs′ra-el my glory.

47 Come [a]down, and sit in the dust,
O virgin daughter of Băb′ȳ-lon,
sit on the ground: *there is* no throne, O
daughter of the Chăl-dē′ans: for thou
shalt no more be called tender and
delicate.
2 [b]Take the millstones, and grind
meal; uncover thy locks, make bare
the leg, uncover the thigh, pass over
the rivers.
3 [c]Thy nakedness shall be uncovered, yea, thy shame shall be seen: [d]I
will take vengeance, and I will not
meet *thee as* a man.
4 *As for* our redeemer, the LORD of
hosts *is* his name, the Holy One of
Ĭs′ra-el.
5 Sit thou [e]silent, and get thee into
darkness, O daughter of the Chăl-dē′-
ans: [f]for thou shalt no more be called,
The lady of kingdoms.
6 ¶ [g]I was wroth with my people, I
have polluted mine inheritance, and
given them into thine hand: thou didst
shew them no mercy; [h]upon the ancient hast thou very heavily laid thy
yoke.
7 ¶ And thou saidst, I shall be [i]a lady
for ever: *so* that thou didst not lay
these *things* to thy heart, neither didst
remember the latter end of it.
8 Therefore hear now this, *thou that*
art given to pleasures, that dwellest
carelessly, that sayest in thine heart, [j]I
am, and none else beside me; [k]I shall
not sit *as* a widow, neither shall I know
the loss of children:
9 But these two *things* shall come to
thee [l]in a moment in one day, the loss
of children, and widowhood: they shall
come upon thee in their perfection
[m]for the multitude of thy sorceries,
and for the great abundance of thine
enchantments.
10 ¶ For thou [n]hast trusted in thy
wickedness: [o]thou hast said, None
seeth me. Thy wisdom and thy knowledge, it hath [1]perverted thee; and thou
hast said in thine heart, I *am*, and none
else beside me.

11 ¶ Therefore shall evil come upon
thee; thou shalt not know [2]from whence
it riseth: and mischief shall fall upon
thee; thou shalt not be able to [3]put it off:
and [p]desolation shall come upon thee
suddenly, *which* thou shalt not know.
12 Stand now with thine enchantments, and with the multitude of thy
sorceries, wherein thou hast laboured
from thy youth; if so be thou shalt
be able to profit, if so be thou mayest
prevail.
13 Thou art wearied in the multitude
of thy counsels. Let now the [4][q]astrolo-
gers, the stargazers, [5]the monthly prog-
nosticators, stand up, and save thee
from *these things* that shall come upon
thee.
14 Behold, they shall be [r]as stubble;
the fire shall burn them; they shall not
deliver [6]themselves from the power of
the flame: *there shall* not *be* a coal to
warm at, *nor* fire to sit before it.
15 Thus shall they be unto thee with
whom thou hast laboured, *even* [s]thy
merchants, from thy youth: they shall
wander every one to his quarter; none
shall save thee.

48 Hear ye this, O house of Jā'cob,
which are called by the name of
Ĭs'ra-el, and are come forth out of the
waters of Jū'dah, [a]which swear by the
name of the LORD, and make mention
of the God of Ĭs'ra-el, *but* not in truth,
nor in righteousness.
2 For they call themselves of the
holy city, and [b]stay themselves upon
the God of Ĭs'ra-el; The LORD of hosts
is his name.
3 I have declared the former things
from the beginning; and they went
forth out of my mouth, and I shewed
them; I did *them* suddenly, [c]and they
came to pass.
4 Because I knew that thou *art* [1]ob-
stinate, and [d]thy neck *is* an iron sinew,
and thy brow brass;
5 I have even from the beginning declared *it* to thee; before it came to pass
I shewed *it* thee: lest thou shouldest
say, Mine idol hath done them, and my
graven image, and my molten image,
hath commanded them.
6 Thou hast heard, see all this; and
will not ye declare *it?* I have shewed
thee new things from this time, even
hidden things, and thou didst not know
them.
7 They are created now, and not
from the beginning; even before the
day when thou heardest them not; lest
thou shouldest say, Behold, I knew
them.
8 Yea, thou heardest not; yea, thou
knewest not; yea, from that time *that*
thine ear was not opened: for I knew
that thou wouldest deal very treacherously, and wast called a [e]transgressor
from the womb.
9 ¶ [f]For my name's sake will I defer
mine anger, and for my praise will I
refrain for thee, that I cut thee not off.
10 Behold, [g]I have refined thee, but
not [2]with silver; I have chosen thee in
the furnace of affliction.

11 [2]the morn-
ing thereof
[3]expiate
[p]ch. 13.6;
Luke 17.27
13 [4]viewers
of the heav-
ens
[q]Dan. 2.2
[5]that give
knowledge
concerning
the months
14 [r]Nah.
1.10;
Mal. 4.1
[6]their souls
15 [s]Rev.
18.11

CHAPTER
48
1 [a]Deut.
6.13;
Zeph. 1.5
2 [b]Mic. 3.11;
Rom. 2.17
3 [c]Josh.
21.45
4 [1]hard
[d]Ex. 32.9;
Deut. 31.27
8 [e]Ps. 58.3
9 [f]Josh. 7.9;
Ps. 106.8
10 [g]Ps. 66.10;
Mal. 3.3
[2]Or, for silver
11 [h]Deut.
32.26
[i]ch. 42.8
12 [j]Deut.
32.39
[k]Rev. 1.17;
Rev. 22.13
13 [l]Ps. 102.25
[3]Or, the palm
of my right
hand hath
spread out
16 [m]Zech.
2.8-9
17 [n]Ps. 32.8
18 [o]Deut.
5.29;
Ps. 81.13
19 [p]Gen.
22.17;
Hos. 1.10
20 [q]Zech.
2.6-7;
[r]Ex. 19.4
21 [s]Num.
20.11;

CHAPTER
49
1 [a]Jer. 1.5;
2 [b]Hos. 6.5
3 [c]Zech. 3.8
[d]Matt. 17.17;
4 [e]Ezek. 3.19
[1]Or, my re-
ward
5 [2]Or, That Is-
rael may be
gathered to
him, and I
may, etc

11 For mine own sake, *even* for mine
own sake, will I do *it:* for [h]how should
my name be polluted? and [i]I will not
give my glory unto another.
12 ¶ Hearken unto me, O Jā'cob and
Ĭs'ra-el, my called; [j]I *am* he; I *am* [k]the
first, I also *am* the last.
13 [l]Mine hand also hath laid the
foundation of the earth, and [3]my right
hand hath spanned the heavens: *when*
I call unto them, they stand up together.
14 All ye, assemble yourselves, and
hear; which among them hath declared
these *things?* The LORD hath loved
him: he will do his pleasure on Băb'-
ȳ-lon, and his arm *shall be on* the
Chăl-dē'ans.
15 I, *even* I, have spoken; yea, I have
called him: I have brought him, and he
shall make his way prosperous.
16 ¶ Come ye near unto me, hear ye
this; I have not spoken in secret from
the beginning; from the time that it
was, there *am* I: and now [m]the Lord
GOD, and his Spirit, hath sent me.
17 Thus saith the LORD, thy Redeemer, the Holy One of Ĭs'ra-el; I *am*
the LORD thy God which teacheth thee
to profit, [n]which leadeth thee by the
way *that* thou shouldest go.
18 [o]O that thou hadst hearkened
to my commandments! then had thy
peace been as a river, and thy righteousness as the waves of the sea:
19 [p]Thy seed also had been as the
sand, and the offspring of thy bowels
like the gravel thereof; his name should
not have been cut off nor destroyed
from before me.
20 ¶ [q]Go ye forth of Băb'ȳ-lon, flee
ye from the Chăl-dē'ans, with a voice
of singing declare ye, tell this, utter it
even to the end of the earth; say ye,
The LORD hath [r]redeemed his servant
Jā'cob.
21 And they thirsted not *when* he led
them through the deserts: he [s]caused
the waters to flow out of the rock for
them: he clave the rock also, and the
waters gushed out.
22 *There is* no peace, saith the LORD,
unto the wicked.

49 Listen O isles, unto me; and hearken, ye people, from far; [a]The
LORD hath called me from the womb;
from the bowels of my mother hath he
made mention of my name.
2 And he hath made [b]my mouth like
a sharp sword; in the shadow of his
hand hath he hid me, and made me a
polished shaft; in his quiver hath he
hid me;
3 And said unto me, [c]Thou *art* my
servant, O Ĭs'ra-el, [d]in whom I will be
glorified.
4 [e]Then I said, I have laboured in
vain, I have spent my strength for
nought, and in vain: *yet* surely my judgment *is* with the LORD, and [1]my work
with my God.
5 ¶ And now, saith the LORD that
formed me from the womb *to be* his
servant, to bring Jā'cob again to him,
[2]Though Ĭs'ra-el be not gathered, yet
shall I be glorious in the eyes of

the LORD, and my God shall be my
strength.
6 And he said, [3]It is a light thing that
thou shouldest be my servant to raise
up the tribes of Jā'cob, and to restore
the [4]preserved of Is'ra-el: I will also
give thee for a [f]light to the Gĕn'tīles,
that thou mayest be my salvation unto
the end of the earth.
7 Thus saith the LORD, the Redeemer
of Is'ra-el, *and* his Holy One, [5]to him
whom man despiseth, to him whom the
nation abhorreth, to a servant of rulers,
Kings shall see and arise, princes also
shall worship, because of the LORD that
is faithful, *and* the Holy One of Is'ra-el,
and he shall choose thee.
8 Thus saith the LORD, [g]In an acceptable time have I heard thee, and in a
day of salvation have I helped thee:
and I will preserve thee, and give thee
for a covenant of the people, to [6]estab-
lish the earth, to cause to inherit the
desolate heritages;
9 That thou mayest say [h]to the prisoners, Go forth; to them that *are* in
darkness, Shew yourselves. They shall
feed in the ways, and their pastures
shall be in all high places.
10 They shall not [i]hunger nor thirst;
[j]neither shall the heat nor sun smite
them: for he that hath mercy on them
[k]shall lead them, even by the springs
of water shall he guide them.
11 And I will make all my mountains a way, and my highways shall be
exalted.
12 Behold, these shall come from
far: and, lo, these from the north and
from the west; and these from the land
of Sī'nim.
13 ¶ Sing, O heavens; and be joyful,
O earth; and break forth into singing,
O mountains: for the LORD hath comforted his people, and will have mercy
upon his afflicted.
14 But Zī'ŏn said, The LORD hath forsaken me, and my Lord hath forgotten
me.
15 [l]Can a woman forget her sucking child, [7]that she should not have
compassion on the son of her womb?
yea, they may forget, [m]yet will I not
forget thee.
16 Behold, [n]I have graven thee upon
the palms of *my* hands; thy walls *are*
continually before me.
17 Thy children shall make haste;
thy destroyers and they that made thee
waste shall go forth of thee.
18 ¶ Lift up thine eyes round about,
and behold: all these gather themselves together, *and* come to thee. *As* I
live, saith the LORD, thou shalt surely
clothe thee with them all, [o]as with an
ornament, and bind them *on thee,* as a
bride *doeth.*
19 For thy waste and thy desolate
places, and the land of thy destruction,
[p]shall even now be too narrow by reason of the inhabitants, and they that
swallowed thee up shall be far away.
20 The children which thou shalt
have, [q]after thou hast lost the other,
shall say again in thine ears, The place

6 [3]Or, Art thou lighter than that thou shouldest, etc
[4]Or, desolations
[f]Isa. 9.2; Luke 2.32
7 [5]Or, to him that is despised in soul
8 [g]Ps. 69.13
[6]Or, raise up
9 [h]ch. 42.7; Zech. 9.12
10 [i]Ps. 22.26; Rev. 7.16
[j]Ps. 121.6
[k]Ps. 23.2
15 [l]Ps. 103.13; Matt. 7.11
[7]from having compassion
[m]Rom. 11.29
16 [n]Ex. 13.9; Zech. 2.8
18 [o]Prov. 17.6
19 [p]ch. 54.1-2; Zech. 2.4
20 [q]Matt. 3.9; Rom. 11.11
21 [r]Gen. 42.13; Jer. 31.15
22 [8]bosom
23 [9]nourishers
[10]princesses
[s]Ps. 72.9; Mic. 7.17
[t]Ps. 34.22; Rom. 5.5
24 [u]Matt. 12.29; Luke 11.21
[11]the captivity of the just
25 [12]captivity
26 [v]Rev. 14.20
[13]Or, new wine
[w]Ps. 9.16; ch. 43.3
CHAPTER 50
1 [a]Deut. 24.1; Hos. 2.2
[b]2 Ki. 4.1; Matt. 18.25
2 [c]Prov. 1.24; Jer. 7.13
[d]Gen. 18.14; ch. 59.1
4 [e]Ex. 4.11; Luke 4.22-32
[f]Matt. 11.28
5 [g]Matt. 26.39;
6 [h]Matt. 26.67
[i]Lam. 3.30;
7 [j]Rom. 8.31
[k]Ezek. 3.8-9

is too strait for me: give place to me
that I may dwell.
21 Then shalt thou say in thine heart,
Who hath begotten me these, seeing [r]I
have lost my children, and am desolate,
a captive, and removing to and fro? and
who hath brought up these? Behold, I
was left alone; these, where *had* they
been?
22 Thus saith the Lord GOD, Behold,
I will lift up mine hand to the Gĕn'tīles,
and set up my standard to the people:
and they shall bring thy sons in *their*
[8]arms, and thy daughters shall be carried upon *their* shoulders.
23 And kings shall be thy [9]nursing
fathers, and their [10]queens thy nursing
mothers: they shall bow down to thee
with *their* face toward the earth, and
[s]lick up the dust of thy feet; and thou
shalt know that I *am* the LORD: for
[t]they shall not be ashamed that wait
for me.
24 ¶ [u]Shall the prey be taken from
the mighty, or [11]the lawful captive
delivered?
25 But thus saith the LORD, Even the
[12]captives of the mighty shall be taken
away, and the prey of the terrible shall
be delivered: for I will contend with
him that contendeth with thee, and I
will save thy children.
26 And I will feed them that oppress thee with their own flesh; and
they shall be drunken with their own
[v]blood, as with [13]sweet wine: and all
flesh [w]shall know that I the LORD *am*
thy Saviour and thy Redeemer, the
mighty One of Jā'cob.

50

Thus saith the LORD, Where *is*
[a]the bill of your mother's divorcement, whom I have put away? or
which of my [b]creditors *is it* to whom I
have sold you? Behold, for your iniquities have ye sold yourselves, and for
your transgressions is your mother put
away.
2 Wherefore, when I came, *was there*
no man? [c]when I called, *was there* none
to answer? [d]Is my hand shortened at all,
that it cannot redeem? or have I no
power to deliver? behold, at my rebuke I
dry up the sea, I make the rivers a wilderness: their fish stinketh, because
there is no water, and dieth for thirst.
3 I clothe the heavens with blackness, and I make sackcloth their covering.
4 [e]The Lord GOD hath given me the
tongue of the learned, that I should
know how to speak a word in season to
him that is [f]weary: he wakeneth morning by morning, he wakeneth mine ear
to hear as the learned.
5 ¶ The Lord GOD hath opened mine
ear, and I was not [g]rebellious, neither
turned away back.
6 [h]I gave my back to the smiters,
and [i]my cheeks to them that plucked
off the hair: I hid not my face from
shame and spitting.
7 ¶ For the Lord GOD will [j]help me;
therefore shall I not be confounded:
therefore have [k]I set my face like a

flint, and I know that I shall not be
ashamed.
8 *He is* near that justifieth me; who
will contend with me? [l]let us stand together: who *is* [1]mine adversary? let
him come near to me.
9 Behold, the Lord GOD will help
me; who *is* he *that* shall condemn me?
[m]lo, they all shall wax old as a garment; the moth shall eat them up.
10 ¶ Who *is* among you that feareth
the LORD, that obeyeth the voice of his
servant, that walketh *in* darkness, and
hath no light? [n]let him trust in the
name of the LORD, and stay upon his
God.
11 Behold, all ye that kindle a fire,
that compass *yourselves* about with
sparks: [o]walk in the light of your fire,
and in the sparks *that* ye have kindled.
[p]This shall ye have of mine hand; ye
shall lie down in sorrow.

51 Hearken to me, [a]ye that follow
after righteousness, ye that seek
the LORD: look unto the rock *whence*
ye are hewn, and to the hole of the pit
whence ye are digged.
2 [b]Look unto A'brā-hăm your father, and unto Sā'rah *that* bare you:
for I called him alone, and blessed him,
and increased him.
3 For the LORD [c]shall comfort Zī'ŏn:
he will comfort all her waste places;
and he will make her wilderness like
Ē'dĕn, and her desert [d]like the garden
of the LORD; joy and gladness shall be
found therein, thanksgiving, and the
voice of melody.
4 ¶ Hearken unto me, my people;
and give ear unto me, O my nation: for
a law shall proceed from me, and I will
make my judgment to rest for a light of
the people.
5 [e]My righteousness *is* near; my salvation is gone forth, and mine arms
shall judge the people; the isles shall
wait upon me, and [f]on mine arm shall
they trust.
6 Lift up your eyes to the heavens,
and look upon the earth beneath: for
[g]the heavens shall vanish away like
smoke, and the earth shall wax old like
a garment, and they that dwell therein
shall die in like manner: but my salvation shall be for ever, and my righteousness shall not be abolished.
7 ¶ Hearken unto me, ye that know
righteousness, the people [h]in whose
heart *is* my law; [i]fear ye not the reproach of men, neither be ye afraid of
their revilings.
8 For the moth shall eat them up like
a garment, and the worm shall eat
them like wool: but my righteousness
shall be for ever, and my salvation
from generation to generation.
9 ¶ Awake, awake, [j]put on strength,
O arm of the LORD; awake, as in the
ancient days, in the generations of old.
[k]*Art* thou not it that hath cut [l]Rā'hăb,
and wounded the [m]dragon?
10 *Art* thou not it which hath [n]dried
the sea, the waters of the great deep;
that hath made the depths of the sea a
way for the ransomed to pass over?

8 [l]1 Cor. 4.4
[1]the master of my cause
9 [m]Job 13.28; Ps. 39.11; Heb. 1.11-12
10 [n]2 Chr. 20.20
11 [o]Rom. 10.3
[p]John 9.39

CHAPTER 51
1 [a]Prov. 15.9; Matt. 6.33; Rom. 9.30
2 [b]Rom. 4.1; Heb. 11.11
3 [c]Ps. 102.13; ch. 40.1
[d]Gen. 13.10; Joel 2.3
5 [e]ch. 46.13
[f]Rom. 1.16
6 [g]Matt. 24.35; 2 Pet. 3.10
7 [h]Ps. 37.31
[i]Matt. 10.28; Luke 12.4; Acts 5.41
9 [j]Rev. 11.17
[k]Job 26.12
[l]Ps. 87.4
[m]Ezek. 29.3
10 [n]Ex. 14.21
12 [o]2 Cor. 1.3
[p]Ps. 118.6
[q]1 Pet. 1.24
13 [r]Job 9.8
[1]Or, made himself ready
[s]Job 20.7
14 [t]Zech. 9.11
15 [u]Ex. 14.21; Ps. 74.13; Ps. 93.3-4; ch. 17.12; ch. 43.16
16 [v]Deut. 18.18; ch. 59.21; John 3.34
[w]ch. 65.17; 2 Pet. 3.13
17 [x]Deut. 28.28-34; Ps. 60.3; Rev. 14.10
19 [2]happened
[3]breaking
[y]Amos 7.2
20 [z]Lam. 2.11-12
22 [a]Jer. 50.34
23 [b]Zech. 12.2
[c]Ps. 66.11-12

CHAPTER 52
1 [a]Rev. 21.2
[b]Nah. 1.15
[c]ch. 26.2; Rev. 21.27
2 [d]Zech. 2.7

11 Therefore the redeemed of the
LORD shall return, and come with singing unto Zī'ŏn; and everlasting joy
shall be upon their head: they shall obtain gladness and joy; *and* sorrow and
mourning shall flee away.
12 I, *even* I, *am* he [o]that comforteth
you: who *art* thou, that thou shouldest
be afraid of [p]a man *that* shall die, and
of the son of man *which* shall be made
[q]*as* grass;
13 And forgettest the LORD thy
maker, [r]that hath stretched forth the
heavens, and laid the foundations of
the earth; and hast feared continually
every day because of the fury of the
oppressor, as if he [1]were ready to destroy? [s]and where *is* the fury of the
oppressor?
14 The captive exile hasteneth that
he may be loosed, [t]and that he should
not die in the pit, nor that his bread
should fail.
15 But I *am* the LORD thy God, that
[u]divided the sea, whose waves roared:
The LORD of hosts *is* his name.
16 And [v]I have put my words in thy
mouth, and I have covered thee in the
shadow of mine hand, [w]that I may
plant the heavens, and lay the foundations of the earth, and say unto Zī'ŏn,
Thou *art* my people.
17 ¶ Awake, awake, stand up, O Je-
ru̦'sa-lĕm, which hast drunk at the
hand of the LORD the cup of his fury;
[x]thou hast drunken the dregs of the
cup of trembling, *and* wrung *them* out.
18 *There is* none to guide her among
all the sons *whom* she hath brought
forth; neither *is there any* that taketh
her by the hand of all the sons *that* she
hath brought up.
19 These two *things* [2]are come unto
thee; who shall be sorry for thee? desolation, and [3]destruction, and the famine, and the sword: [y]by whom shall I
comfort thee?
20 [z]Thy sons have fainted, they lie
at the head of all the streets, as a wild
bull in a net: they are full of the fury of
the LORD, the rebuke of thy God.
21 ¶ Therefore hear now this, thou
afflicted, and drunken, but not with
wine:
22 Thus saith thy Lord the LORD,
and thy God *that* [a]pleadeth the cause
of his people, Behold, I have taken out
of thine hand the cup of trembling,
even the dregs of the cup of my fury;
thou shalt no more drink it again:
23 But [b]I will put it into the hand of
them that afflict thee; [c]which have
said to thy soul, Bow down, that we
may go over: and thou hast laid thy
body as the ground, and as the street,
to them that went over.

52 Awake, awake; put on thy
strength, O Zī'ŏn; put on thy
beautiful garments, O Je-ru̦'sa-lĕm,
[a]the holy city: for [b]henceforth there
shall no more come into thee the uncircumcised [c]and the unclean.
2 Shake thyself from the dust; arise,
and sit down, O Je-ru̦'sa-lĕm: [d]loose

thyself from the bands of thy neck, O captive daughter of Zī'ŏn.

3 For thus saith the LORD, [e]Ye have sold yourselves for nought; and ye shall be redeemed without money.

4 For thus saith the Lord GOD, My people went down aforetime into Ē'ġypt to sojourn there; and the Ăs-sy̆r'ĭ-an oppressed them without cause.

5 Now therefore, what have I here, saith the LORD, that my people is taken away for nought? they that rule over them make them to howl, saith the LORD; and my name continually every day *is* [f]blasphemed.

6 Therefore my people shall know my name: therefore *they shall know* in that day that I *am* he that doth speak: behold, *it is* I.

7 ¶ [g]How beautiful upon the mountains are the feet of him that bringeth good tidings, that publisheth peace; that bringeth good tidings of good, that publisheth salvation; that saith unto Zī'ŏn, Thy God reigneth!

8 Thy watchmen shall lift up the voice; with the voice together shall they sing: for they shall [h]see eye to eye, when the LORD shall bring again Zī'ŏn.

9 ¶ Break forth into joy, sing together, ye waste places of Je-ru̥'sa-lĕm: for the LORD hath comforted his people, he hath redeemed Je-ru̥'sa-lĕm.

10 The LORD hath made bare his holy arm in the eyes of all the nations; and [i]all the ends of the earth shall see the salvation of our God.

11 ¶ [j]Depart ye, depart ye, go ye out from thence, touch no unclean *thing;* go ye out of the midst of her; be ye clean, that bear the vessels of the LORD.

12 For [k]ye shall not go out with haste, nor go by flight: [l]for the LORD will go before you; [m]and the God of Is'ra-el *will* [1]*be* your rereward.

13 ¶ Behold, [n]my servant shall [2]deal prudently, [o]he shall be exalted and extolled, and be very high.

14 As many were astonied at thee; his [p]visage was so marred more than any man, and his form more than the sons of men:

15 [q]So shall he sprinkle many nations; the kings shall shut their mouths at him: for *that* [r]which had not been told them shall they see; and *that* which they had not heard shall they consider.

53 Who [a]hath believed our [1]report? and to whom is [b]the arm of the LORD revealed?

2 For he shall grow up before him as a tender plant, and as a root out of a dry ground: [c]he hath no form nor comeliness; and when we shall see him, *there is* no beauty that we should desire him.

3 [d]He is despised and rejected of men; a man of sorrows, and [e]acquainted with grief: and [2]we hid as it were *our* faces from him; he was despised, and [f]we esteemed him not.

4 ¶ Surely [g]he hath borne our griefs, and carried our sorrows: yet we [h]did esteem him stricken, smitten of God, and afflicted.

5 But he *was* [3]wounded for our transgressions, *he was* bruised for our iniquities: the chastisement of our peace *was* upon him; and with his [4]stripes we are healed.

6 All we like sheep have gone astray; we have turned every one to his own way; and the LORD [5]hath laid on him the iniquity of us all.

7 He was oppressed, and he was afflicted, yet he opened not his mouth: [i]he is brought as a [j]lamb to the slaughter, and as a sheep before her shearers is dumb, so he openeth not his mouth.

8 [6]He was taken from prison and from judgment: and who shall declare his generation? for [k]he was cut off out of the land of the living: for the transgression of my people [7]was he stricken.

9 [l]And he made his grave with the wicked, and with the rich in his [8]death; because he had done no violence, neither *was any* [m]deceit in his mouth.

10 ¶ Yet it pleased the LORD to bruise him; he hath put *him* to grief: [9]when thou shalt make his soul [n]an offering for sin, he shall see *his* seed, [o]he shall prolong *his* days, and [p]the pleasure of the LORD shall prosper in his hand.

11 He shall see of the travail of his soul, *and* shall be satisfied: [q]by his knowledge shall [r]my righteous servant [s]justify many; for he shall bear their iniquities.

12 [t]Therefore will I divide him *a portion* with the great, [u]and he shall divide the spoil with the strong; because he hath poured out his soul unto death: and he was [v]numbered with the transgressors; and he bare the sin of many, and [w]made intercession for the transgressors.

54 Sing, [a]O barren, thou *that* didst not bear; break forth into singing, and cry aloud, thou *that* didst not travail with child: for more *are* the children of the desolate than the children of the married wife, saith the LORD.

2 Enlarge the place of thy tent, and let them stretch forth the curtains of thine habitations: spare not, lengthen thy cords, and strengthen thy stakes;

3 For thou shalt break forth on the right hand and on the left; and thy seed shall inherit the Gĕn'tīles, and make the desolate cities to be inhabited.

4 Fear not; for thou shalt not be ashamed: neither be thou confounded; for thou shalt not be put to shame: for thou shalt forget the shame of thy youth, and shalt not remember the reproach of thy widowhood any more.

5 For thy Maker *is* thine husband; the LORD of hosts *is* his name; and thy Redeemer the Holy One of Is'ra-el; [b]The God of the whole earth shall he be called.

6 For the LORD hath called thee as a woman forsaken and grieved in spirit, and a wife of youth, when thou wast refused, saith thy God.

3 [e]Ps. 45.12
5 [f]Rom. 2.24
7 [g]Rom. 10.15
8 [h]Zeph. 3.9
10 [i]Luke 3.6
11 [j]Jer. 50.8
12 [k]Ex. 12.33
[l]Mic. 2.13
[m]Num. 10.25;
[1]gather you up
13 [n]ch. 42.1
[2]Or, prosper
[o]Phil. 2.9
14 [p]Ps. 22.6
15 [q]Ezek. 36.25;
[r]Rom. 15.21

CHAPTER 53

1 [a]John 12.38
[1]hearing, or, doctrine
[b]1 Cor. 1.18
2 [c]Mark 9.12
3 [d]Ps. 22.6
[e]Heb. 4.15
[2]as an hiding of faces from him, or, from us. Or, he hid as it were his face from us
[f]John 1.10
4 [g]Matt. 8.17
[h]Matt. 26.66
5 [3]Or, tormented
[4]bruise
6 [5]hath made the iniquity of us all to meet on him
7 [i]Acts 8.32
[j]1 Pet. 1.19
8 [6]Or, He was taken away by distress and judgment: but, etc
[k]Dan. 9.26
[7]was the stroke upon him
9 [l]Matt. 27.57
[8]deaths
[m]1 Pet. 2.22
10 [9]Or, when his soul shall make an offering
[n]2 Cor. 5.21;
[o]Rom. 6.9
[p]Eph. 1.5
11 [q]John 17.3
[r]1 John 2.1
[s]Rom. 5.18
12 [t]Phil. 2.9
[u]Col. 2.15
[v]Mark 15.28
[w]Luke 23.34

CHAPTER 54

1 [a]Gal. 4.27
5 [b]Job 19.25

7 For [c]a small moment have I forsaken thee; but with great mercies will
I gather thee.
8 In a little wrath I hid my face from
thee for a moment; [d]but with everlasting kindness will I have mercy on thee,
saith the LORD thy Redeemer.
9 For this *is as* the waters of [e]Nō'ah
unto me: for *as* I have sworn that the
waters of Nō'ah should no more go
over the earth; so have I sworn that I
would not be wroth with thee, nor rebuke thee.
10 For [f]the mountains shall depart,
and the hills be removed; [g]but my kindness shall not depart from thee, neither shall the covenant of my peace
be removed, saith the LORD that hath
mercy on thee.
11 ¶ O thou afflicted, tossed with
tempest, *and* not comforted, behold, I
will lay thy stones with fair colours,
and lay thy foundations with sapphires.
12 And I will make thy windows of
agates, and thy gates of carbuncles,
and all thy borders of pleasant stones.
13 And all thy children *shall be*
[h]taught of the LORD; and great *shall be*
[i]the peace of thy children.
14 In righteousness shalt thou be established: thou shalt be far from oppression; for thou shalt not fear: and
from terror; for it shall not come near
thee.
15 Behold, they shall surely gather
together, *but* not by me: whosoever
shall gather together against thee shall
fall for thy sake.
16 Behold, I have created the smith
that bloweth the coals in the fire, and
that bringeth forth an instrument for
his work; and I have created the waster
to destroy.
17 ¶ [j]No weapon that is formed
against thee shall prosper; and every
tongue *that* shall rise against thee in
judgment thou shalt condemn. This *is*
the heritage of the servants of the
LORD, [k]and their righteousness *is* of
me, saith the LORD.

55 Ho, [a]every one that thirsteth,
come ye to the waters, and he
that hath no money; [b]come ye, buy,
and eat; yea, come, buy wine and milk
without money and without price.
2 Wherefore do ye [1]spend money
for *that which is* not bread? and your
labour for *that which* satisfieth not?
hearken diligently unto me, and eat ye
that which is good, and let your soul
delight itself in fatness.
3 Incline your ear, and [c]come unto
me: hear, and your soul shall live;
[d]and I will make an everlasting covenant with you, *even* the [e]sure mercies
of Dā'vid.
4 Behold, I have given him *for* [f]a witness to the people, [g]a leader and com-
mander to the people.
5 [h]Behold, thou shalt call a nation
that thou knowest not, and nations
that knew not thee shall run unto thee
because of the LORD thy God, and for
the Holy One of Is'ra-el; [i]for he hath
glorified thee.
6 ¶ [j]Seek ye the LORD while he may
be found, call ye upon him while he is
near:
7 Let the wicked forsake his way, and
[2]the unrighteous man [k]his thoughts:
and let him return unto the LORD, [l]and
he will have mercy upon him; and to our
God, for [3]he will abundantly pardon.
8 ¶ For my thoughts *are* not your
thoughts, neither *are* your ways my
ways, saith the LORD.
9 For *as* the heavens are higher than
the earth, so are my ways higher than
your ways, and my thoughts than your
thoughts.
10 For as the rain cometh down, and
the snow from heaven, and returneth
not thither, but watereth the earth, and
maketh it bring forth and bud, that it
may give seed to the sower, and bread
to the eater:
11 So shall my word be that goeth
forth out of my mouth: it shall not return unto me void, but it shall accomplish that which I please, and it shall
prosper *in the thing* whereto I sent it.
12 For ye shall go out with joy, and
be led forth with peace: the mountains
and the hills shall break forth before
you into singing, and all the trees of
the field shall clap *their* hands.
13 Instead of the thorn shall come
up the fir tree, and instead of the brier
shall come up the myrtle tree: and it
shall be to the LORD for a name, for an
everlasting sign *that* shall not be cut
off.

56 Thus saith the LORD, Keep ye
[1]judgment, and do justice: [a]for
my salvation *is* near to come, and my
righteousness to be revealed.
2 Blessed *is* the man *that* doeth this,
and the son of man *that* layeth hold on
it; [b]that keepeth the sabbath from polluting it, and keepeth his hand from
doing any evil.
3 ¶ Neither let [c]the son of the
stranger, that hath joined himself to
the LORD, speak, saying, The LORD
hath utterly separated me from his people: neither let the eunuch say, Behold,
I *am* a dry tree.
4 For thus saith the LORD unto the
eunuchs that keep my sabbaths, and
choose *the things* that please me, and
take hold of my covenant;
5 Even unto them will I give in [d]mine
house and within my walls a place
[e]and a name better than of sons and of
daughters: I will give them an everlasting name, that shall not be cut off.
6 Also the sons of the stranger, that
join themselves to the LORD, to serve
him, and to love the name of the LORD,
to be his servants, every one that keepeth the sabbath from polluting it, and
taketh hold of my covenant;
7 Even them will I [f]bring to my holy
mountain, and make them joyful in my
house of prayer: [g]their burnt offerings
and their sacrifices *shall be* accepted
upon mine altar; for [h]mine house shall
be called an house of prayer [i]for all
people.

7 [c]2 Cor. 4.17
8 [d]Jer. 31.3
9 [e]Jer. 31.35
10 [f]Ps. 46.2
[g]Ps. 89.33
13 [h]ch. 11.9; 1 Cor. 2.10; 1 Thess. 4.9
[i]John 14.27; Phil. 4.7
17 [j]ch. 50.8-9; Acts 6.10; 2 Cor. 2.14; Rev. 12.10
[k]ch. 45.24

CHAPTER 55
1 [a]John 4.14; Rev. 21.6
[b]Matt. 13.44; John 7.37; Rev. 3.18
2 [1]weigh
3 [c]Matt. 11.28
[d]ch. 54.8
[e]2 Sam. 7.8; Ps. 89.28; Acts 13.34
4 [f]Mal. 3.5; 1 Tim. 6.13; Rev. 1.5
[g]Ezek. 34.23; Dan. 9.25; Heb. 2.10
5 [h]ch. 52.15; Eph. 2.11-12
[i]Acts 3.13
6 [j]Ps. 32.6; Amos 5.4-14; Matt. 5.25; John 7.34; 2 Cor. 6.2; Heb. 3.13
7 [2]the man of iniquity
[k]Zech. 8.17
[l]Jer. 3.12
[3]he will multiply to pardon

CHAPTER 56
1 [1]Or, equity
[a]Matt. 3.2; Rom. 13.11
2 [b]Ex. 20.11; ch. 58.13
3 [c]Deut. 23.1; Acts 8.27; 1 Pet. 1.1
5 [d]Eph. 2.22; 1 Tim. 3.15; Heb. 3.6
[e]John 1.12; Rev. 3.12
7 [f]1 Pet. 1.1
[g]Ps. 4.5; Mal. 1.11; Rom. 12.1; Heb. 13.15; 1 Pet. 2.5
[h]Matt. 21.13; Mark 11.17; Luke 19.46
[i]Mal. 1.11

8 The Lord GOD which gathereth
the outcasts of Is'ra-el saith, [j]Yet will I
gather *others* to him, [2]beside those
that are gathered unto him.
9 ¶ All ye beasts of the field, come to
devour, *yea,* all ye beasts in the forest.
10 His watchmen *are* [k]blind: they
are all ignorant, [l]they *are* all dumb
dogs, they cannot bark; [3]sleeping, lying down, loving to slumber.
11 Yea, *they are* [4]greedy dogs *which*
[5]can never have enough, and they *are*
shepherds *that* cannot understand:
they all look to their own way, every
one for his gain, from his quarter.
12 Come ye, *say they,* I will fetch
wine, and we will fill ourselves with
strong drink; and to morrow shall be
as this day, *and* much more abundant.

57

57 The righteous perisheth, and no
man layeth *it* to heart: and [1]mer-
ciful men *are* taken away, none considering that the righteous is taken away
[2]from the evil *to come.*
2 He shall [3]enter into peace: they
shall rest in their beds, *each one* walking [4]*in* his uprightness.
3 ¶ But draw near hither, [a]ye sons of
the sorceress, the seed of the adulterer
and the whore.
4 Against whom do ye sport yourselves? against whom make ye a wide
mouth, *and* draw out the tongue? *are*
ye not children of transgression, a seed
of falsehood,
5 Enflaming yourselves [5]with idols
under every green tree, slaying the children in the valleys under the clifts of
the rocks?
6 Among the smooth *stones* of the
stream *is* thy portion; they, they *are*
thy lot: even to them hast thou poured
a drink offering, thou hast offered a
meat offering. Should I receive comfort in these?
7 Upon a lofty and high mountain
hast thou set [b]thy bed: even thither
wentest thou up to offer sacrifice.
8 Behind the doors also and the posts
hast thou set up thy remembrance: for
thou hast discovered *thyself to another*
than me, and art gone up; thou hast
enlarged thy bed, and [6]made thee *a cov-*
enant with them; [c]thou lovedst their
bed [7]where thou sawest *it.*
9 And [8]thou wentest to the king with
ointment, and didst increase thy perfumes, and didst send thy messengers
far off, and didst debase *thyself even*
unto hell.
10 Thou art wearied in the greatness
of thy way; *yet* saidst thou not, There
is no hope: thou hast found the [9]life of
thine hand; therefore thou wast not
grieved.
11 And of whom hast thou been
afraid or feared, that thou hast lied,
and hast not remembered me, nor laid
it to thy heart? [d]have not I held my
peace even of old, and thou fearest me
not?
12 I will declare thy righteousness,
and thy works; for they shall not profit
thee.
13 ¶ When thou criest, let thy companies deliver thee; but the wind shall
carry them all away; vanity shall take
them: but he that putteth his trust in
me shall [e]possess the land, and shall
inherit my holy mountain;
14 And shall say, Cast ye up, cast ye
up, prepare the way, take up the stumblingblock out of the way of my people.
15 For thus saith the high and lofty
One that inhabiteth eternity, [f]whose
name *is* Holy; [g]I dwell in the high and
holy *place,* [h]with him also *that is* of a
contrite and humble spirit, to revive
the spirit of the humble, and to revive
the heart of the contrite ones.
16 [i]For I will not contend for ever,
neither will I be always wroth: for the
spirit should fail before me, and the
souls [j]*which* I have made.
17 For the iniquity of his [k]covetous-
ness was I wroth, and smote him: I hid
me, and was wroth, and he went on
[10]frowardly in the way of his heart.
18 I have seen his ways, and will
heal him: [l]I will lead him also, and restore comforts unto him and to his
mourners.
19 I create the fruit of the lips;
Peace, peace to *him that is* far off, and
to *him that is* near, saith the LORD; and
I will heal him.
20 But the wicked *are* like the troubled sea, when it cannot rest, whose
waters cast up mire and dirt.
21 *There is* no peace, saith my God,
to the wicked.

58

58 Cry [1]aloud, spare not, lift up thy
voice like a trumpet, and shew
my people their transgression, and the
house of Jā'cob their sins.
2 Yet they seek me daily, and delight to know my ways, as a nation that
did righteousness, and forsook not the
ordinance of their God: they ask of me
the ordinances of justice; they take delight in approaching to God.
3 ¶ [a]Wherefore have we fasted, *say*
they, and thou seest not? *wherefore*
have we afflicted our soul, and thou
takest no knowledge? Behold, in the
day of your fast ye find pleasure, and
exact all your [2]labours.
4 Behold, ye fast for strife and debate, and to smite with the fist of wickedness: [3]ye shall not fast as *ye do this*
day, to make your voice to be heard on
high.
5 Is it [b]such a fast that I have chosen?
[4]a day for a man to afflict his soul? *is it*
to bow down his head as a bulrush, and
to spread sackcloth and ashes *under*
him? wilt thou call this a fast, and an
acceptable day to the LORD?
6 *Is* not this the fast that I have
chosen? to loose the bands of wickedness, to undo [5]the heavy burdens, and
to let the [6]oppressed go free, and that
ye break every yoke?
7 *Is it* not [c]to deal thy bread to the
hungry, and that thou bring the poor
that are [7]cast out to thy house? when
thou seest the naked, that thou cover
him; and that thou hide not thyself
from [d]thine own flesh?

8 [j]Gen. 49.10; [2]to his gathered
10 [k]Matt. 15.14 [l]Phil. 3.2 [3]Or, dreaming, or, talking in their sleep
11 [4]strong of appetite [5]know not to be satisfied

CHAPTER 57
1 [1]men of kindness, or, godliness [2]Or, from that which is evil
2 [3]Or, go in peace [4]Or, before him
3 [a]Mal. 3.5
5 [5]Or, among the oaks
7 [b]Ezek. 23.41
8 [6]Or, hewed it for thyself larger than theirs [c]Ezek. 16.26 [7]Or, thou providest room
9 [8]Or, thou respectedst the king
10 [9]Or, living
11 [d]Ps. 50.21
13 [e]Ps. 37.3-9;
15 [f]Job 6.10; [g]Ps. 68.4; [h]Ps. 34.18
16 [i]Ps. 78.38-39; [j]Heb. 12.9
17 [k]Ezek. 33.31 [10]turning away
18 [l]Ps. 73.24

CHAPTER 58
1 [1]with the throat
3 [a]Mal. 3.14 [2]griefs, or, things wherewith ye grieve others
4 [3]Or, ye fast not as this day
5 [b]Zech. 7.5 [4]Or, to afflict his soul for a day
6 [5]the bundles of the yoke [6]broken
7 [c]Ps. 112.9; [7]Or, afflicted [d]Gen. 29.14;

8 ¶ Then shall thy light break forth as the morning, and thine health shall spring forth speedily: and thy righteousness shall go before thee: the glory of the LORD [8]shall be thy rereward.

9 Then shalt thou call, and the LORD shall answer; thou shalt cry, and he shall say, Here I *am*. If thou take away from the midst of thee the yoke, the putting forth of the finger, and speaking vanity;

10 And *if* thou draw out thy soul to the hungry, and satisfy the afflicted soul; then shall [e]thy light rise in obscurity, and thy darkness *be* as the noon day:

11 And the LORD shall guide thee continually, and satisfy thy soul in [9]drought, and make fat thy bones: and thou shalt be like a watered garden, and like a spring of water, whose waters [10]fail not.

12 And *they that shall be* of thee shall build the old waste places: thou shalt raise up the foundations of many generations; and thou shalt be called, The repairer of the breach, The restorer of paths to dwell in.

13 ¶ If [f]thou turn away thy foot from the sabbath, *from* doing thy pleasure on my holy day; and call the sabbath a delight, the holy of the LORD, honourable; and shalt honour him, not doing thine own ways, nor finding thine own pleasure, nor [g]speaking *thine own* words:

14 [h]Then shalt thou delight thyself in the LORD; and I will cause thee to [i]ride upon the high places of the earth, and feed thee with the heritage of Jā'cob thy father: [j]for the mouth of the LORD hath spoken *it*.

59 Behold, the LORD'S hand is not [a]shortened, that it cannot save; neither his ear heavy, that it cannot hear:

2 But your iniquities have separated between you and your God, and your sins [1]have hid *his* face from you, that he will not hear.

3 For [b]your hands are defiled with blood, and your fingers with iniquity; your lips have spoken lies, your tongue hath muttered perverseness.

4 None calleth for justice, nor *any* pleadeth for truth: they trust in vanity, and speak lies; [c]they conceive mischief, and bring forth iniquity.

5 They hatch [2]cockatrice' eggs, and [d]weave the spider's web: he that eateth of their eggs dieth, and [3]that which is crushed breaketh out into a viper.

6 Their webs shall not become garments, neither shall they cover themselves with their works: their works *are* works of iniquity, and the act of violence *is* in their hands.

7 [e]Their feet run to evil, and they make haste to shed innocent blood: their thoughts *are* thoughts of iniquity; wasting and [4]destruction *are* in their paths.

8 The way of peace they know not; and *there is* no [5]judgment in their goings: [f]they have made them crooked paths: whosoever goeth therein shall not know peace.

9 ¶ Therefore is judgment far from us, neither doth justice overtake us: [g]we wait for light, but behold obscurity; for brightness, *but* we walk in darkness.

10 [h]We grope for the wall like the blind, and we grope as if *we had* no eyes: we stumble at noon day as in the night; *we are* in desolate places as dead *men*.

11 We roar all like bears, and mourn sore like doves: we look for judgment, but *there is* none; for salvation, *but* it is far off from us.

12 For our transgressions are multiplied before thee, and our sins testify against us: for our transgressions *are* with us; and *as for* our iniquities, we know them;

13 In transgressing and lying against the LORD, and departing away from our God, speaking oppression and revolt, conceiving and uttering [i]from the heart words of falsehood.

14 And judgment is turned away backward, and justice standeth afar off: for truth is fallen in [j]the street, and equity cannot enter.

15 Yea, truth faileth; and he *that* departeth from evil [6]maketh himself a prey: and the LORD saw *it*, and [7]it displeased him that *there was* no judgment.

16 ¶ [k]And he saw that *there was* no man, and [l]wondered that *there was* no intercessor: therefore his arm brought salvation unto him; and his righteousness, it sustained him.

17 [m]For he put on righteousness as a breastplate, and an helmet of salvation upon his head; and he put on the garments of vengeance *for* clothing, and was clad with zeal as a cloke.

18 According to *their* [8]deeds, accordingly he will repay, fury to his adversaries, recompence to his enemies; to the islands he will repay recompence.

19 [n]So shall they fear the name of the LORD from the west, and his glory from the rising of the sun. When the enemy shall come in [o]like a flood, the Spirit of the LORD shall [9]lift up a standard against him.

20 ¶ And [p]the Redeemer shall come to Zī'ŏn, and unto them that turn from transgression in Jā'cob, saith the LORD.

21 [q]As for me, this *is* my covenant with them, saith the LORD; [r]My spirit that *is* upon thee, and my words which I have put in thy mouth, shall not depart out of thy mouth, nor out of the mouth of thy seed, nor out of the mouth of thy seed's seed, saith the LORD, from henceforth and for ever.

60 Arise, [1]shine; for thy light is come, and [a]the glory of the LORD is risen upon thee.

2 For, behold, the darkness shall cover the earth, and gross darkness the people: but the LORD shall arise upon thee, and his glory shall be seen upon thee.

---

8 [8]shall gather thee up
10 [e]Job 11.17
11 [9]droughts [10]lie, or, deceive
13 [f]Lev. 19.30; ch. 56.2 [g]Matt. 12.36
14 [h]Job 22.26 [i]Deut. 32.13 [j]ch. 1.20; Mic. 4.4; Matt. 24.3-5

CHAPTER 59
1 [a]Num. 11.23; ch. 50.2
2 [1]Or, have made him hide
3 [b]ch. 1.15-21; Hos. 4.2; Mic. 3.10; Rom. 3.15
4 [c]Job 15.35; Ps. 7.14
5 [2]Or, adders' [d]Job 8.14 [3]Or, that which is sprinkled is as if there brake out a viper
7 [e]Prov. 1.16 [4]breaking
8 [5]Or, right [f]Ps. 125.5; Prov. 2.15
9 [g]Jer. 8.15
10 [h]Deut. 28.29; Amos 8.9; Zeph. 1.17
13 [i]Matt. 12.34
14 [j]Neh. 8.1
15 [6]Or, is accounted mad [7]it was evil in his eyes
16 [k]ch. 63.5; Ezek. 22.30 [l]Mark 6.6
17 [m]Ps. 35.2; Rev. 19.11
18 [8]recompences
19 [n]Ps. 113.3; Mal. 1.11 [o]Rev. 12.15 [9]Or, put him to flight
20 [p]Rom. 11.26
21 [q]Heb. 8.10 [r]ch. 61.1; Ezek. 36.37

CHAPTER 60
1 [1]Or, be enlightened: for thy light cometh [a]Mal. 4.2

3 And the [b]Gĕn'tīles shall come to
thy light, and kings to the brightness of
thy rising.
4 Lift up thine eyes round about,
and see: all they gather themselves together, they come to thee: thy sons
shall come from far, and thy daughters
shall be nursed at *thy* side.
5 Then thou shalt see, and flow together, and thine heart shall fear, and
be enlarged; because the [2]abundance
of the sea shall be converted unto thee,
the [3]forces of the Gĕn'tīles shall come
unto thee.
6 The multitude of camels shall cover
thee, the dromedaries of Mĭd'ĭ-an and
[c]Ē'phah; all they from [d]Shē'bȧ shall
come: they shall bring [e]gold and incense; and they shall shew forth the
praises of the LORD.
7 All the flocks of [f]Kē'dăr shall be
gathered together unto thee, the rams
of Ne-bā'ioth shall minister unto thee:
they shall come up with acceptance
on mine altar, and [g]I will glorify the
house of my glory.
8 Who *are* these *that* fly as a cloud,
and as the doves to their windows?
9 [h]Surely the isles shall wait for me,
and the ships of Tär'shish first, [i]to
bring thy sons from far, [j]their silver
and their gold with them, [k]unto the
name of the LORD thy God, and to the
Holy One of Ĭs'ra-el, [l]because he hath
glorified thee.
10 And [m]the sons of strangers shall
build up thy walls, [n]and their kings
shall minister unto thee: for in my
wrath I smote thee, but in my favour
have I had mercy on thee.
11 Therefore thy gates shall be open
continually; they shall not be shut day
nor night; that *men* may bring unto
thee the [4]forces of the Gĕn'tīles, and
that their kings *may be* brought.
12 For [o]the nation and kingdom that
will not serve thee shall perish; yea,
those nations shall be utterly wasted.
13 [p]The glory of Lĕb'a-non shall
come unto thee, the fir tree, the pine
tree, and the box together, to beautify
the place of my sanctuary; and I will
make [q]the place of my feet glorious.
14 The sons also of them that afflicted thee shall come bending unto
thee; and all they that despised thee
shall [r]bow themselves down at the
soles of thy feet; and they shall call
thee, The city of the LORD, [s]The Zī'ŏn
of the Holy One of Ĭs'ra-el.
15 Whereas thou hast been forsaken
and hated, so that no man went through
thee, I will make thee an eternal excellency, a joy of many generations.
16 Thou shalt also suck the milk of
the Gĕn'tīles, and shalt suck the breast
of kings: and thou shalt know that [t]I
the LORD *am* thy Saviour and thy Redeemer, the mighty One of Jā'cob.
17 For brass I will bring gold, and
for iron I will bring silver, and for
wood brass, and for stones iron: I will
also make thy officers peace, and thine
exactors righteousness.

3 [b]Rev. 21.24
5 [2]Or, noise of the sea shall be turned toward thee
[3]Or, wealth
6 [c]Gen. 25.4
[d]Ps. 72.10
[e]Matt. 2.11
7 [f]Gen. 25.13
[g]Hag. 2.7-9
9 [h]Ps. 72.10
[i]Gal. 4.26
[j]Zech. 14.14
[k]Jer. 3.17
[l]ch. 55.5
10 [m]Zech. 6.15
[n]Rev. 21.24
11 [4]Or, wealth
12 [o]Ps. 2.12; Zech. 14.17; Matt. 21.44; Luke 19.27; Rev. 2.26-27
13 [p]ch. 35.2
[q]1 Chr. 28.2; Heb. 12.22
14 [r]Rev. 3.9
[s]Heb. 12.22; Rev. 14.1
16 [t]Ps. 98.2; ch. 43.3; Ezek. 34.30; Rev. 5.9
18 [u]ch. 26.1
19 [v]Rev. 21.23
[w]Zech. 2.5
20 [x]Amos 8.9
21 [y]Ps. 37.11; Matt. 5.5
[z]Matt. 15.13
[a]Eph. 2.10
22 [b]Matt. 13.31; Hos. 1.10
CHAPTER 61
1 [a]ch. 11.2; Luke 4.18; John 1.32
[b]Ps. 34.18; Hos. 6.1
[c]Zech. 9.12; John 8.32-36
2 [d]Lev. 25.9
[e]Mal. 4.1-3
[f]Matt. 5.4
3 [g]Ps. 30.11
[h]ch. 60.21
[i]John 15.8
4 [j]Ezek. 36.33
5 [k]Eph. 2.12
6 [l]Ex. 19.6
7 [m]2 Ki. 2.9; ch. 40.2; Zech. 9.12
8 [n]ch. 55.3

18 Violence shall no more be heard
in thy land, wasting nor destruction
within thy borders; but thou shalt call
[u]thy walls Salvation, and thy gates
Praise.
19 The [v]sun shall be no more thy
light by day; neither for brightness
shall the moon give light unto thee: but
the LORD shall be unto thee an everlasting light, and [w]thy God thy glory.
20 [x]Thy sun shall no more go down;
neither shall thy moon withdraw itself:
for the LORD shall be thine everlasting
light, and the days of thy mourning
shall be ended.
21 Thy people also *shall be* all righteous: [y]they shall inherit the land for
ever, [z]the branch of my planting, [a]the
work of my hands, that I may be
glorified.
22 [b]A little one shall become a thousand, and a small one a strong nation: I
the LORD will hasten it in his time.

61

The [a]Spirit of the Lord GOD *is*
upon me; because the LORD hath
anointed me to preach good tidings
unto the meek; he hath sent me [b]to
bind up the brokenhearted, to proclaim [c]liberty to the captives, and the
opening of the prison to *them that are*
bound;
2 [d]To proclaim the acceptable year
of the LORD, and [e]the day of vengeance of our God; [f]to comfort all that
mourn;
3 To appoint unto them that mourn
in Zī'ŏn, [g]to give unto them beauty for
ashes, the oil of joy for mourning, the
garment of praise for the spirit of heaviness; that they might be called trees
of righteousness, [h]the planting of the
LORD, [i]that he might be glorified.
4 ¶ And they shall [j]build the old
wastes, they shall raise up the former
desolations, and they shall repair the
waste cities, the desolations of many
generations.
5 And [k]strangers shall stand and
feed your flocks, and the sons of the
alien *shall be* your plowmen and your
vinedressers.
6 But [l]ye shall be named the Priests
of the LORD: *men* shall call you the Ministers of our God: ye shall eat the
riches of the Gĕn'tīles, and in their
glory shall ye boast yourselves.
7 ¶ For [m]your shame *ye shall have*
double; and *for* confusion they shall rejoice in their portion: therefore in their
land they shall possess the double:
everlasting joy shall be unto them.
8 For I the LORD love judgment, I
hate robbery for burnt offering; and I
will direct their work in truth, [n]and I
will make an everlasting covenant with
them.
9 And their seed shall be known
among the Gĕn'tīles, and their offspring among the people: all that see
them shall acknowledge them, that
they *are* the seed *which* the LORD hath
blessed.
10 I will greatly rejoice in the LORD,
my soul shall be joyful in my God; for
he hath clothed me with the garments

of salvation, he hath covered me with the robe of righteousness, [o]as a bridegroom [1]decketh *himself* with ornaments, and as a bride adorneth *herself* with her jewels.

11 For as the earth bringeth forth her bud, and as the garden causeth the things that are sown in it to spring forth; so the Lord GOD will cause [p]righteousness and [q]praise to spring forth before all the nations.

62

62 For Zī'on's sake will I not hold my peace, and for Je-rụ'sa-lĕm's sake I will not rest, until the righteousness thereof go forth as brightness, and the salvation thereof as a lamp *that* burneth.

2 And the Gĕn'tīles shall see thy righteousness, and all kings thy glory: [a]and thou shalt be called by a new name, which the mouth of the LORD shall name.

3 Thou shalt also be [b]a crown of glory in the hand of the LORD, and a royal diadem in the hand of thy God.

4 [c]Thou shalt no more be termed Forsaken; neither shall thy land any more be termed [1]Desolate: but thou shalt be called [2]Hĕph'zi–bah, and thy land [3]Bēu'lah: for the LORD delighteth in thee, and thy land shall be married.

5 ¶ For *as* a young man marrieth a virgin, *so* shall thy sons marry thee: and [4]*as* the bridegroom rejoiceth over the bride, *so* shall thy God rejoice over thee.

6 [d]I have set watchmen upon thy walls, O Je-rụ'sa-lĕm, *which* shall never hold their peace day nor night: [5]ye that make mention of the LORD, keep not silence,

7 And give him no [6]rest, till he establish, and till he make Je-rụ'sa-lĕm [e]a praise in the earth.

8 The LORD hath sworn by his right hand, and by the arm of his strength, [7]Surely I will no more [f]give thy corn *to be* meat for thine enemies; and the sons of the stranger shall not drink thy wine, for the which thou hast laboured:

9 But they that have gathered it shall eat it, and praise the LORD; and they that have brought it together shall drink it [g]in the courts of my holiness.

10 ¶ Go through, go through the gates; prepare ye the way of the people; cast up, cast up the highway; gather out the stones; lift up a standard for the people.

11 Behold, the LORD hath proclaimed unto the end of the world, [h]Say ye to the daughter of Zī'ŏn, Behold, thy salvation cometh; behold, his [i]reward *is* with him, and his [8]work before him.

12 And they shall call them, The holy people, The redeemed of the LORD: and thou shalt be called, Sought out, A city not forsaken.

63

63 Who *is* this that cometh from Ē'dom, with dyed garments from Bŏz'rah? this *that is* [1]glorious in his apparel, travelling in the greatness of his strength? I that speak in righteousness, mighty to save.

2 Wherefore [a]*art thou* red in thine apparel, and thy garments like him that treadeth in the winefat?

3 I have [b]trodden the winepress alone; and of the people *there was* none with me: for I will tread them in mine anger, and trample them in my fury; and their blood shall be sprinkled upon my garments, and I will stain all my raiment.

4 For the day of vengeance *is* in mine heart, and the year of my redeemed is come.

5 And I looked, and [c]*there was* none to help; and I wondered that *there was* none to uphold: therefore mine own [d]arm brought salvation unto me; and my fury, it upheld me.

6 And I will tread down the people in mine anger, and [e]make them drunk in my fury, and I will bring down their strength to the earth.

7 ¶ I will mention the lovingkindnesses of the LORD, *and* the praises of the LORD, according to all that the LORD hath bestowed on us, and the great goodness toward the house of Is'ra-el, which he hath bestowed on them according to his mercies, and according to the multitude of his lovingkindnesses.

8 For he said, Surely they *are* my people, children *that* will not lie: [2]so he was their Saviour.

9 [f]In all their affliction he was afflicted, and [g]the angel of his presence saved them: [h]in his love and in his pity he redeemed them; and [i]he bare them, and carried them all the days of old.

10 ¶ But they rebelled, and [j]vexed his holy Spirit: therefore he was turned to be their enemy, *and* he fought against them.

11 Then he remembered the days of old, Mō'ses, *and* his people, *saying*, Where *is* he that brought them up out of the sea with the [3]shepherd of his flock? where *is* he that put his holy Spirit within him?

12 That led *them* by the right hand of Mō'ses with his glorious arm, dividing the water before them, to make himself an everlasting name?

13 That led them through the deep, as an horse in the wilderness, *that* they should not stumble?

14 As a beast goeth down into the valley, the Spirit of the LORD caused him to rest: so didst thou lead thy people, to make thyself a glorious name.

15 ¶ Look down from heaven, and behold from the habitation of thy holiness and of thy glory: where *is* thy zeal and thy strength, [4]the sounding of thy bowels and of thy mercies toward me? are they restrained?

16 Doubtless thou *art* our father, though Ā'brā-hăm [k]be ignorant of us, and Is'ra-el acknowledge us not: thou, O LORD, *art* our father, [5]our redeemer; thy name *is* from everlasting.

17 ¶ O LORD, why hast thou [l]made us to err from thy ways, *and* [m]hardened our hearts from thy fear? Return for thy servants' sake, the tribes of thine inheritance.

---

10 [o]Rev. 21.2 [1]decketh as a priest
11 [p]Ps. 72.3 [q]ch. 60.18

CHAPTER 62
2 [a]ch. 65.15; Rev. 3.12
3 [b]Zech. 9.16
4 [c]Hos. 1.10; 1 Pet. 2.10 [1]Azubah [2]That is, My delight is in her [3]That is, Married
5 [4]with the joy of the bridegroom
6 [d]Song 3.3; Heb. 13.17 [5]Or, ye that are the LORD'S remembrancers
7 [6]silence [e]ch. 61.11; Zeph. 3.20
8 [7]If I give, etc [f]Deut. 28.31; Jer. 5.17
9 [g]Deut. 12.12
11 [h]Zech. 9.9; John 12.15 [i]ch. 40.10; Rev. 22.12 [8]Or, recompence

CHAPTER 63
1 [1]decked
2 [a]Rev. 19.13
3 [b]Lam. 1.15; Rev. 14.19-20
5 [c]John 16.32 [d]Ps. 44.3; ch. 51.9
6 [e]Rev. 16.6
8 [2]Or, and he became a Saviour for them
9 [f]Acts 9.4 [g]Ex. 14.19; Acts 12.11 [h]Deut. 7.7 [i]Ex. 19.4
10 [j]Ps. 78.8-40; Heb. 10.29
11 [3]Or, shepherds
15 [4]Or, the multitude
16 [k]Gal. 3.28 [5]Or, our redeemer from everlasting is thy name
17 [l]Ps. 119.10 [m]ch. 6.10

18 [n]The people of thy holiness have possessed *it* but a little while: our adversaries have trodden down thy sanctuary.

19 We are *thine:* thou never barest rule over them; [6]they were not called by thy name.

64 Oh that thou wouldest rend the heavens, that thou wouldest come down, that the mountains might flow down at thy presence,

2 As *when* [1]the melting fire burneth, the fire causeth the waters to boil, to make thy name known to thine adversaries, *that* the nations may tremble at thy presence!

3 When thou didst terrible things *which* we looked not for, thou camest down, the mountains flowed down at thy presence.

4 For since the beginning of the world [a]*men* have not heard, nor perceived by the ear, neither hath the eye [2]seen, O God, beside thee, *what* he hath prepared for him that waiteth for him.

5 Thou meetest him that rejoiceth [b]and worketh righteousness, *those that* remember thee in thy ways: behold, thou art wroth; for we have sinned: [c]in those is continuance, and we shall be saved.

6 But we are all as an unclean *thing,* and all [d]our righteousnesses *are* as filthy rags; and we all do fade as a leaf; and our iniquities, like the wind, have taken us away.

7 And [e]*there is* none that calleth upon thy name, that stirreth up himself to take hold of thee: for thou hast hid thy face from us, and hast [3]consumed us, [4]because of our iniquities.

8 But now, O LORD, thou *art* our father; we *are* the clay, [f]and thou our potter; and we all *are* [g]the work of thy hand.

9 ¶ Be not wroth very sore, O LORD, neither remember iniquity for ever: behold, see, we beseech thee, we *are* all thy people.

10 Thy holy cities are a wilderness, Zī'ŏn is a wilderness, Je-ru̦'sa-lĕm a desolation.

11 [h]Our holy and our beautiful house, where our fathers praised thee, is burned up with fire: and all our [i]pleasant things are laid waste.

12 Wilt thou refrain thyself for these *things,* O LORD? wilt thou hold thy peace, and afflict us very sore?

65 I [a]am sought of *them that* asked not *for me;* I am found of *them that* sought me not: I said, Behold me, behold me, unto a nation *that* [b]was not called by my name.

2 [c]I have spread out my hands all the day unto a rebellious people, which [d]walketh in a way *that was* not good, after their own thoughts;

3 A people that provoketh me to anger continually to my face; [e]that sacrificeth in gardens, and burneth incense [1]upon altars of brick;

4 [f]Which remain among the graves, and lodge in the monuments, [g]which eat swine's flesh, and [2]broth of abominable *things is in* their vessels;

5 [h]Which say, Stand by thyself, come not near to me; for I am holier than thou. These *are* a smoke in my [3]nose, a fire that burneth all the day.

6 Behold, [i]*it is* written before me: I will not keep silence, but will recompense, even recompense into their bosom,

7 Your iniquities, and [j]the iniquities of your fathers together, saith the LORD, which have burned incense upon the mountains, and blasphemed me upon the hills: therefore will I measure their former work into their bosom.

8 ¶ Thus saith the LORD, As the new wine is found in the cluster, and *one* saith, Destroy it not; [k]for a blessing *is* in it: so will I do for my servants' sakes, that I may not destroy them all.

9 And I will bring forth a seed out of Jā'cob, and out of Jū'dah an inheritor of my mountains: and mine [l]elect shall inherit it, and my servants shall dwell there.

10 And Shâr'on shall be a fold of flocks, and [m]the valley of A'chôr a place for the herds to lie down in, for my people that have sought me.

11 ¶ But ye *are* they that forsake the LORD, that forget my holy mountain, that prepare [n]a table for [4]that troop, and that furnish the drink offering unto [5]that number.

12 Therefore will I number you to the sword, and ye shall all bow down to the slaughter: [o]because when I called, ye did not answer; when I spake, ye did not hear; but did evil before mine eyes, and did choose *that* wherein I delighted not.

13 Therefore thus saith the Lord GOD, Behold, my servants shall eat, but ye shall be hungry: behold, my servants shall drink, but ye shall be thirsty: behold, my servants shall rejoice, but ye shall be ashamed:

14 Behold, my servants shall sing for joy of heart, but ye shall cry for sorrow of heart, and shall howl for [6]vexation of spirit.

15 And ye shall leave your name [p]for a curse unto my chosen: for the Lord GOD shall slay thee, and [q]call his servants by another name:

16 That he who blesseth himself in the earth shall bless himself in the God of truth; and he that sweareth in the earth shall swear by the God of truth; because the former troubles are forgotten, and because they are hid from mine eyes.

17 ¶ For, behold, I create [r]new heavens and a new earth: and the former shall not be remembered, nor [7]come into mind.

18 But be ye glad and rejoice for ever *in that* which I create: for, behold, I create Je-ru̦'sa-lĕm a rejoicing, and her people a joy.

19 And I will rejoice in Je-ru̦'sa-lĕm, and joy in my people: and the [s]voice of weeping shall be no more heard in her, nor the voice of crying.

20 There shall be no more thence an infant of days, nor an old man that

18 [n]Dan. 8.24
19 [6]Or, thy name was not called upon them

CHAPTER 64
2 [1]the fire of meltings
4 [a]Ps. 31.19; 1 Cor. 2.9-10; Col. 1.26-27; 1 Tim. 3.16; Rev. 21.1-4
[2]Or, seen a God beside thee, which doeth so for him, etc
5 [b]Acts 10.35
[c]Mal. 3.6
6 [d]Phil. 3.9
7 [e]Hos. 7.7
[3]melted
[4]by the hand
8 [f]Jer. 18.6
[g]Eph. 2.10
11 [h]2 Ki. 25.9; Ps. 74.7
[i]Ezek. 24.21

CHAPTER 65
1 [a]Ps. 22.27; ch. 2.2-3; Rom. 10.20; Eph. 2.12-13
[b]ch. 63.19
2 [c]Rom. 10.21
[d]Deut. 32.5; Ps. 36.4
3 [e]Lev. 17.5; ch. 1.29
[1]upon bricks
4 [f]Deut. 18.11
[g]Lev. 11.7
[2]Or, pieces
5 [h]Matt. 9.11; Luke 5.30; Jude 19
[3]Or, anger
6 [i]Deut. 32.34; Mal. 3.16
7 [j]Lev. 26.39; Ps. 106.6; Matt. 23.32
8 [k]Joel 2.14
9 [l]Matt. 24.22
10 [m]Hos. 2.15
11 [n]Ezek. 23.41; 1 Cor. 10.21
[4]Or, Gad
[5]Or, Meni
12 [o]Prov. 1.24; Zech. 7.7
14 [6]breaking
15 [p]Prov. 10.7
[q]Acts 11.26
17 [r]2 Pet. 3.13
[7]come upon the heart
19 [s]Rev. 7.17

hath not filled his days: for the child shall die an hundred years old; [t]but the sinner *being* an hundred years old shall be accursed.

21 And [u]they shall build houses, and inhabit *them;* and they shall plant vineyards, and eat the fruit of them.

22 They shall not build, and another inhabit; they shall not plant, and another eat: for as the days of a tree *are* the days of my people, and mine elect [8]shall long enjoy the work of their hands.

23 They shall not labour in vain, [v]nor bring forth for trouble; for they *are* the seed of the blessed of the LORD, and their offspring with them.

24 And it shall come to pass, that [w]before they call, I will answer; and while they are yet speaking, I will hear.

25 The wolf and the lamb shall feed together, and the lion shall eat straw like the bullock: [x]and dust *shall be* the serpent's meat. They shall not hurt nor destroy in all my holy [y]mountain, saith the LORD.

66

Thus saith the LORD, [a]The heaven *is* my throne, and the earth *is* my footstool: where *is* the house that ye build unto me? and where *is* the place of my rest?

2 For all those *things* hath mine hand made, and all those *things* have been, saith the LORD: but to this *man* will I look, [b]*even* to *him that is* poor and of a contrite spirit, and [c]trembleth at my word.

3 He that killeth an ox *is as if* he slew a man; he that sacrificeth a [1]lamb, *as if* he cut off a dog's neck; he that offereth an oblation, *as if he offered* swine's blood; he that [2]burneth incense, *as if* he blessed an idol. Yea, they have chosen their own ways, and their soul delighteth in their abominations.

4 I also will choose their [3]delusions, and will bring their fears upon them; [d]because when I called, none did answer; when I spake, they did not hear: but they did evil before mine eyes, and chose *that* in which I delighted not.

5 ¶ Hear the word of the LORD, ye that tremble at his word; Your brethren that [e]hated you, that cast you out for [f]my name's sake, said, [g]Let the LORD be glorified: but [h]he shall appear to your joy, and they shall be ashamed.

6 A voice of noise from the city, a voice from the temple, a voice of the LORD that rendereth recompence to his enemies.

7 Before she travailed, she brought forth; before her pain came, she was delivered of a man child.

8 Who hath heard such a thing? who hath seen such things? Shall the earth be made to bring forth in one day? *or* shall a nation be born at once? for as soon as Zī'ŏn travailed, she brought forth her children.

9 Shall I bring to the birth, and not [4]cause to bring forth? saith the LORD: shall I cause to bring forth, and shut *the womb?* saith thy God.

10 Rejoice ye with Je-ru̧'sa-lĕm, and be glad with her, all ye that love her: rejoice for joy with her, all ye that mourn for her:

11 That ye may suck, and be satisfied with the breasts of her consolations; that ye may milk out, and be delighted with the [5]abundance of her glory.

12 For thus saith the LORD, Behold [i]I will extend peace to her like a river, and the glory of the Gĕn'tīles like a flowing stream: then shall ye [j]suck, ye shall be [k]borne upon *her* sides, and be dandled upon *her* knees.

13 As one whom his mother comforteth, so will I comfort you; and ye shall be comforted in Je-ru̧'sa-lĕm.

14 And when ye see *this,* your heart shall rejoice, and [l]your bones shall flourish like an herb: and the hand of the LORD shall be known toward his servants, and *his* indignation toward his enemies.

15 [m]For, behold, the LORD will come with fire, and with his chariots like a whirlwind, to render his anger with fury, and his rebuke with flames of fire.

16 For by fire and by [n]his sword will the LORD plead with all flesh: and the slain of the LORD shall be many.

17 [o]They that sanctify themselves, and purify themselves in the gardens, [6]behind one *tree* in the midst, eating swine's flesh, and the abomination, and the mouse, shall be consumed together, saith the LORD.

18 [p]For I *know* their works and their thoughts: it shall come, that I will gather all nations and tongues; and they shall come, and see my glory.

19 [q]And I will set a sign among them, and I will send those that escape of them unto the nations, *to* Tär'shish, Pŭl, and Lŭd, that draw the bow, *to* Tu̧'bal, and Jā'văn, *to* the isles afar off, that have not heard my fame, neither have seen my glory; [r]and they shall declare my glory among the Gĕn'tīles.

20 And they shall bring all your brethren [s]*for* an offering unto the LORD out of all nations upon horses, and in chariots, and in [7]litters, and upon mules, and upon swift beasts, to my holy mountain Je-ru̧'sa-lĕm, saith the LORD, as the children of Ĭs'ra-el bring an offering in a clean vessel into the house of the LORD.

21 And I will also take of them for [t]priests *and* for Lē'vītes, saith the LORD.

22 For as [u]the new heavens and the new earth, which I will make, shall remain before me, saith the LORD, so shall your seed and your name remain.

23 And [v]it shall come to pass, *that* [8]from one new moon to another, and from one sabbath to another, [w]shall all flesh come to worship before me, saith the LORD.

24 And they shall go forth, and look upon the carcases of the men that have transgressed against me: for their worm shall not die, neither shall their fire be quenched; and they shall be an abhorring unto all flesh.

20 [t]Eccl. 8.12
21 [u]Lev. 26.16
22 [8]shall make them continue long, or, shall wear out
23 [v]Deut. 28.41; Hos. 9.12
24 [w]Ps. 32.5; Acts 4.31
25 [x]Gen. 3.14; Rom. 16.20 [y]ch. 2.2; Rev. 14.1

CHAPTER 66
1 [a]1 Chr. 28.2; Acts 7.48-49
2 [b]Ps. 34.18 [c]Ezra 9.4; Prov. 28.14
3 [1]Or, kid [2]maketh a memorial of
4 [3]Or, devices [d]Prov. 1.24
5 [e]John 15.18 [f]Matt. 24.9 [g]ch. 5.19 [h]2 Thess. 1.10; Tit. 2.13
9 [4]Or, beget
11 [5]Or, brightness
12 [i]ch. 48.18; ch. 60.5 [j]ch. 60.16 [k]ch. 49.22; ch. 60.4
14 [l]Ezek. 37.1-10
15 [m]ch. 9.5; 2 Thess. 1.8
16 [n]ch. 27.1
17 [o]ch. 65.3-4 [6]Or, one after another
18 [p]Heb. 4.13; Rev. 2.2
19 [q]Luke 2.34 [r]Mal. 1.11
20 [s]Rom. 12.1; Rom. 15.16 [7]Or, coaches
21 [t]Ex. 19.6; ch. 61.6
22 [u]2 Pet. 3.13; Rev. 21.1
23 [v]Zech. 14.16 [8]from new moon to his new moon, and from sabbath to his sabbath [w]Ps. 65.2

THE BOOK OF

JEREMIAH

Life's Questions

How are faith and patriotism related?
What happens when God's call seems too hard for God's minister?
How does God want me to react while He disciplines me?

God's Answers

Jeremiah shows God leading a prophet to preach treason to a weak, unfaithful people. God was using Babylon to punish Judah for their devotion to substitutes for Him. Judah was deciding whether to remain independent and hope for victory, complete a defense treaty with Egypt, or surrender to Babylon and endure their punishment. Jeremiah recommended the latter option, but constantly argued with God as he did. Called under King Josiah in 626 B.C., Jeremiah watched Judah switch politics, kings, and gods until Babylon destroyed his country in 586, and his own countrymen forced him to go to Egypt about 584.

Jeremiah centers attention on Judah's forsaking of the love relationship covenant with God and on God's promise of a new covenant: God calls a prophet (ch. 1); God accuses His people of covenant unfaithfulness (2—6); God opposes the nation's traditional theology and security (7:1—11:17); God listens to His prophet's complaints (11:18—20:18); God warns unfaithful leaders (21:1—29:32); God promises restoration and a new covenant after exile (30—33); God protects and vindicates His persecuted prophet (34:1—40:6); God warns the unfaithful again (40:7—45:5); God judges unjust nations (46—51); Unfaithfulness brings destruction to God's people (52).

1 The words of Jĕr-e-mī'ah the son of
Hĭl-kī'ah, of the priests that *were* [a]in
Ăn'a-thoth in the land of Bĕn'ja-min:
2 To whom the [b]word of the LORD
came in the days of Jo-sī'ah the son of
Ā'mon king of Jū'dah, in [c]the thirteenth year of his reign.
3 It came also in the days of Je-
hoi'a-kim the son of Jo-sī'ah king of
Jū'dah, [d]unto the end of the eleventh
year of Zĕd-e-kī'ah the son of Jo-sī'ah
king of Jū'dah, [e]unto the carrying
away of Je-ru̥'sa-lĕm captive [f]in the
fifth month.
4 Then the word of the LORD came
unto me, saying,
5 Before I formed thee in the belly I
knew thee; and before thou camest
forth out of the womb I [g]sanctified
thee, *and* I [1]ordained thee a prophet
unto the nations.
6 Then said I, [h]Ah, Lord GOD! behold, I cannot speak: for I *am* a child.
7 ¶ But the LORD said unto me, Say
not, I *am* a child: [i]for thou shalt go to
all that I shall send thee, and [j]whatso-
ever I command thee thou shalt speak.
8 Be not afraid of their faces: for [k]I
am with thee to deliver thee, saith the
LORD.
9 Then the LORD put forth his hand,
and touched [l]my mouth. And the LORD
said unto me, Behold, I have [m]put my
words in thy mouth.
10 [n]See, I have this day set thee
over the nations and over the kingdoms, to [o]root out, and to pull down,
and to destroy, and to throw down, to
build, and to plant.
11 ¶ Moreover the word of the LORD
came unto me, saying, Jĕr-e-mī'ah,
what seest thou? And I said, I see a rod
of an almond tree.

CHAPTER 1
1 [a]Josh. 21.18
2 [b]2 Pet. 1.21
[c]ch. 25.3
3 [d]ch. 39.2
[e]ch. 52.12
[f]2 Ki. 25.8
5 [g]Luke 1.15
[1]gave
6 [h]Ex. 4.10
7 [i]Ex. 7.1-2; Ezek. 2.3-4; Matt. 28.20; Mark 16.15-16
[j]Num. 22.20; 1 Ki. 22.14
8 [k]Ex. 3.12; Acts 26.17
9 [l]Isa. 6.7
[m]Isa. 51.16
10 [n]1 Ki. 17.1; Rev. 11.3-6
[o]2 Cor. 10.4
12 [p]Deut. 32.35
13 [2]from the face of the north
14 [3]shall be opened
15 [q]ch. 39.3
16 [r]Lev. 26.15; ch. 4.12
[s]Deut. 28.20
17 [t]1 Ki. 18.46
[u]Ex. 3.12
[4]Or, break to pieces
19 [v]Num. 14.9; Rom. 8.31

12 Then said the LORD unto me,
Thou hast well seen: for I will hasten
[p]my word to perform it.
13 And the word of the LORD came
unto me the second time, saying, What
seest thou? And I said, I see a seething
pot; and the face thereof *is* [2]toward the
north.
14 Then the LORD said unto me, Out
of the north an evil [3]shall break forth
upon all the inhabitants of the land.
15 For, lo, I will call all the families
of the kingdoms of the north, saith the
LORD; and they shall come, and they
shall [q]set every one his throne at the
entering of the gates of Je-ru̥'sa-lĕm,
and against all the walls thereof round
about, and against all the cities of
Jū'dah.
16 And I will [r]utter my judgments
against them touching all their wickedness, [s]who have forsaken me, and
have burned incense unto other gods,
and worshipped the works of their
own hands.
17 ¶ Thou therefore [t]gird up thy
loins, and arise, and speak unto them
all that I command [u]thee: be not dismayed at their faces, lest I [4]confound
thee before them.
18 For, behold, I have made thee
this day a defenced city, and an iron
pillar, and brasen walls against the
whole land, against the kings of Jū'dah,
against the princes thereof, against the
priests thereof, and against the people
of the land.
19 And they shall fight against thee;
but they shall not prevail against thee;
[v]for I *am* with thee, saith the LORD, to
deliver thee.
2 Moreover the word of the LORD
came to me, saying,

2 Go and cry in the ears of Je-ru̦′-sa-lĕm, saying, Thus saith the LORD; I remember [1]thee, the kindness of thy [a]youth, the love of thine espousals, when thou wentest after me in the wilderness, in a land *that was* not sown.

3 Ĭs′ra-el *was* holiness unto the LORD, *and* [b]the firstfruits of his increase: all that devour him shall offend; evil shall come upon them, saith the LORD.

4 Hear ye the word of the LORD, O house of Jā′cob, and all the families of the house of Ĭs′ra-el:

5 ¶ Thus saith the LORD, [c]What iniquity have your fathers found in me, that they are gone far from me, [d]and have walked after vanity, and are become vain?

6 Neither said they, Where *is* the LORD that brought us up out of the land of Ē′gypt, that led us through the wilderness, through a land of deserts and of pits, through a land of drought, and of the shadow of death, through a land that no man passed through, and where no man dwelt?

7 And I brought you into [2]a plentiful country, to eat the fruit thereof and the goodness thereof; but when ye entered, ye defiled my land, and made mine heritage an abomination.

8 The priests said not, Where *is* the LORD? and they that handle the [e]law knew me not: the pastors also transgressed against me, and the prophets prophesied by Bā′al, and walked after *things that* do not profit.

9 ¶ Wherefore [f]I will yet plead with you, saith the LORD, and with your children's children will I plead.

10 For pass [3]over the isles of Chĭt′-tim, and see; and send unto Kē′där, and consider diligently, and see if there be such a thing.

11 [g]Hath a nation changed *their* gods, which *are* yet no gods? [h]but my people have changed their glory for *that which* doth not profit.

12 Be astonished, O ye heavens, at this, and be horribly afraid, be ye very desolate, saith the LORD.

13 For my people have committed two evils; they have forsaken me the [i]fountain of living waters, *and* hewed them out cisterns, broken cisterns, that can hold no water.

14 ¶ *Is* Ĭs′ra-el a servant? *is* he a homeborn *slave?* why is he [4]spoiled?

15 The young lions roared upon him, *and* [5]yelled, and they made his land waste: his cities are burned without inhabitant.

16 Also the children of Nŏph and Ta′hăp′a-nēs [6]have broken the crown of thy head.

17 Hast thou not procured this unto thyself, in that thou hast forsaken the LORD thy God, when he led thee by the way?

18 And now what hast thou to do [j]in the way of Ē′gypt, to drink the waters of [k]Sī′hôr? or what hast thou to do in the way of Ȧs-sўr′ĭ-ȧ, to drink the waters of the river?

19 Thine own [l]wickedness shall correct thee, and thy backslidings shall reprove thee: know therefore and see that *it is* an evil *thing* and bitter, that thou hast forsaken the LORD thy God, and that my fear *is* not in thee, saith the Lord GOD of hosts.

20 ¶ For of old time I have broken thy yoke, *and* burst thy bands; and [m]thou saidst, I will not [7]transgress; when upon every high hill and under every green tree thou wanderest, playing the harlot.

21 Yet I had [n]planted thee a noble vine, wholly a right seed: how then art thou turned into the degenerate plant of a strange vine unto me?

22 For though thou wash thee with nitre, and take thee much sope, *yet* [o]thine iniquity is marked before me, saith the Lord GOD.

23 [p]How canst thou say, I am not polluted, I have not gone after Bā′al-ĭm? see thy way [q]in the valley, know what thou hast done: [8]*thou art* a swift dromedary traversing her ways;

24 [9]A wild ass [10]used to the wilderness, *that* snuffeth up the wind at [11]her pleasure; in her occasion who can [12]turn her away? all they that seek her will not weary themselves; in her month they shall find her.

25 Withhold thy foot from being unshod, and thy throat from thirst: but thou saidst, [13]There is no hope: no; for I have loved strangers, and after them will I go.

26 As the thief is ashamed when he is found, so is the house of Ĭs′ra el ashamed; they, their kings, their princes, and their priests, and their prophets,

27 Saying to a stock, Thou *art* my father; and to a stone, Thou hast [14]brought me forth: for they have turned [15]*their* back unto me, and not *their* face: but in the time of their [r]trouble they will say, Arise, and save us.

28 But [s]where *are* thy gods that thou hast made thee? let them arise, if they [t]can save thee in the time of thy [16]trouble: for *according to* the number of thy cities are thy gods, O Jū′dah.

29 Wherefore will ye plead with me? ye all have transgressed against me, saith the LORD.

30 In vain have I smitten your children; they received no correction: your own sword hath [u]devoured your prophets, like a destroying lion.

31 ¶ O generation, see ye the word of the LORD. Have I been a wilderness unto Ĭs′ra-el? a land of darkness? wherefore say my people, [17]We are lords; we will come no more unto thee?

32 Can a maid forget her ornaments, *or* a bride her attire? yet my people [v]have forgotten me days without number.

33 Why trimmest thou thy way to seek love? therefore hast thou also taught the wicked ones thy ways.

34 Also in thy skirts is found [w]the blood of the souls of the poor innocents:

CHAPTER 2
2 [1]Or, for thy sake
[a]Ezek. 16.8; Hos. 2.15
3 [b]Jas. 1.18; Rev. 14.4
5 [c]Isa. 5.4; Mic. 6.3
[d]Isa. 44.9; Rom. 1.21
7 [2]Or, the land of Carmel
8 [e]Mal. 2.6; Rom. 2.20
9 [f]Isa. 3.13; Mic. 6.2
10 [3]Or, over to
11 [g]Mic. 4.5
[h]Ps. 106.20; Rom. 1.23
13 [i]Ps. 36.9; Rev. 21.6
14 [4]become a spoil
15 [5]gave out their voice
16 [6]Or, feed on thy crown
18 [j]Isa. 30.1-2
[k]Josh. 13.3
19 [l]Isa. 3.9; Hos. 5.5
20 [m]Ex. 19.8
[7]Or, serve
21 [n]Ps. 80.8; Mark 12.1
22 [o]Deut. 32.34;
23 [p]Gen. 3.12-13;
[q]ch. 7.31
[8]Or, O swift dromedary
24 [9]Or, O wild ass
[10]taught
[11]the desire of her heart
[12]Or, reverse it
25 [13]Or, Is the case desperate?
27 [14]Or, begotten me
[15]the hinder part of the neck
[r]Judg. 10.10
28 [s]Deut. 32.37
[t]Isa. 45.20
[16]evil
30 [u]2 Chr. 36.16;
31 [17]We have dominion
32 [v]Ps. 106.21;
34 [w]Ps. 106.38;

I have not found it by [18]secret search,
but upon all these.
35 Yet thou sayest, Because I am
innocent, surely his anger shall turn
from me. Behold, I will plead with
thee, [x]because thou sayest, I have not
sinned.
36 [y]Why gaddest thou about so
much to change thy way? [z]thou also
shalt be ashamed of Ē′ġypt, [a]as thou
wast ashamed of Ȧs-sȳr′ĭ-ȧ.
37 Yea, thou shalt go forth from him,
and thine [b]hands upon thine head:
for the LORD hath rejected thy confi-
dences, and thou shalt not prosper in
them.
3 [1]They say, If a man put away his
wife, and she go from him, and become another man's, [a]shall he return
unto her again? shall not that land be
greatly polluted? but thou hast [b]played
the harlot with many lovers; [c]yet return again to me, saith the LORD.
2 Lift up thine eyes unto [d]the high
places, and see where thou hast not
been lien with. [e]In the ways hast thou
sat for them, as the A-rā′bĭ-an in the
wilderness; and thou hast polluted the
land with thy whoredoms and with thy
wickedness.
3 Therefore the [f]showers have been
withholden, and there hath been no latter rain; and thou hadst a [g]whore's forehead, thou refusedst to be ashamed.
4 Wilt thou not from this time cry
unto me, My father, thou *art* the [h]guide
of [i]my youth?
5 Will he reserve *his anger* for ever?
will he keep *it* to the end? Behold, thou
hast spoken and done evil things as
thou couldest.
6 ¶ The LORD said also unto me in
the days of Jo-sī′ah the king, Hast thou
seen *that* which backsliding Ĭs′ra-el
hath done? she is gone up upon every
high mountain and under every green
tree, and there hath played the harlot.
7 [j]And I said after she had done all
these *things,* Turn thou unto me. But
she returned not. And her treacherous
sister Jū′dah saw *it.*
8 And I saw, when for all the causes
whereby backsliding Ĭs′ra-el committed adultery I had put her away, and
given her a bill of divorce; [k]yet her
treacherous sister Jū′dah feared not,
but went and played the harlot also.
9 And it came to pass through the
[2]lightness of her whoredom, that she
defiled the land, and committed adultery with stones and with stocks.
10 And yet for all this her treacherous sister Jū′dah hath not turned unto
me [l]with her whole heart, but [3]feign-
edly, saith the LORD.
11 And the LORD said unto me, The
backsliding Ĭs′ra-el hath justified herself more than treacherous Jū′dah.
12 ¶ Go and proclaim these words
toward the north, and say, Return,
thou [m]backsliding Ĭs′ra-el, saith the
LORD; *and* I will not cause mine anger
to fall upon you: for I *am* merciful,
saith the LORD, *and* I will not keep *anger* for ever.
13 [n]Only acknowledge thine iniquity, that thou hast transgressed against
the LORD thy God, and hast scattered
thy ways to the strangers under every
green tree, and ye have not obeyed my
voice, saith the LORD.
14 Turn, O backsliding children,
saith the LORD; for I am married unto
you: and I will take you [o]one of a city,
and two of a family, and I will bring
you to Zī′ŏn:
15 And I will give you [p]pastors according to mine heart, which shall
[q]feed you with knowledge and understanding.
16 And it shall come to pass, when
ye be multiplied and increased in the
land, in those days, saith the LORD,
they [r]shall say no more, The ark of the
covenant of the LORD: neither shall it
[4]come to mind: neither shall they remember it; neither shall they visit *it;*
neither shall [5]*that* be done any more.
17 At that time they shall call Je-
ru′sa-lĕm the throne of the LORD; and
all the nations shall be gathered unto
it, to the name of the LORD, to Je-
ru′sa-lĕm: neither shall they walk any
more after the [6]imagination of their
evil heart.
18 In those days [s]the house of Jū′-
dah shall walk [7]with the house of Ĭs′ra-
el, and they shall come together out of
the land of the north to [t]the land that I
have [8]given for an inheritance unto
your fathers.
19 But I said, How shall I put thee
among the children, and give thee a
[9]pleasant land, [10]a goodly heritage of
the hosts of nations? and I said, Thou
shalt call me, [u]My father; and shalt not
turn away [11]from me.
20 ¶ Surely *as* a wife treacherously
departeth from her [12]husband, so have
ye dealt treacherously with me, O
house of Ĭs′ra-el, saith the LORD.
21 A voice was heard upon [v]the high
places, weeping *and* supplications of
the children of Ĭs′ra-el: for they have
perverted their way, *and* they have forgotten the LORD their God.
22 [w]Return, ye backsliding children,
and I [x]will heal your backslidings. Behold, we come unto thee; for thou *art*
the LORD our God.
23 [y]Truly in vain *is salvation hoped
for* from the hills, *and from* the multitude of mountains: [z]truly in the LORD
our God *is* the salvation of Ĭs′ra-el.
24 [a]For shame hath devoured the labour of our fathers from our youth;
their flocks and their herds, their sons
and their daughters.
25 We lie down in our shame, and our
confusion covereth us: for [b]we have
sinned against the LORD our God, we
and our fathers, from our youth even
unto this day, and have not obeyed the
voice of the LORD our God.
4 If thou wilt return, O Ĭs′ra-el, saith
the LORD, [a]return unto me: and if
thou wilt put away thine abominations
out of my sight, then shalt thou not
remove.

[18]digging
35 [x]Prov. 28.13
36 [y]ch. 31.22; Hos. 5.13
[z]Isa. 30.3; ch. 37.7
[a]2 Chr. 28.16-21
37 [b]2 Sam. 13.19

CHAPTER 3
1 [1]Saying
[a]Deut. 24.4
[b]ch. 2.20
[c]ch. 4.1; Luke 15.16-24
2 [d]Deut. 12.2
[e]Gen. 38.14; Prov. 23.28
3 [f]Lev. 26.19
[g]Zeph. 3.5
4 [h]Prov. 2.17; Mal. 2.14
[i]ch. 2.2; Hos. 2.15
7 [j]2 Ki. 17.13
8 [k]Ezek. 23.11
9 [2]Or, fame
10 [l]Hos. 7.14
[3]in falsehood
12 [m]Isa. 44.22; ch. 4.1
13 [n]Lev. 26.40-42; Luke 15.18-21
14 [o]Rom. 11.5
15 [p]ch. 23.4;
[q]Acts 20.28
16 [r]John 4.21-24
[4]come upon the heart
[5]Or, it be magnified
17 [6]Or, stubbornness
18 [s]Isa. 11.13;
[7]Or, to
[t]Amos 9.15
[8]Or, caused your fathers to possess
19 [9]land of desire
[10]an heritage of glory, or, beauty
[u]Isa. 63.16
[11]from after me
20 [12]friend
21 [v]Isa. 15.2
22 [w]Hos. 14.1
[x]Hos. 6.1
23 [y]Ps. 121.1
[z]Ps. 3.8;
24 [a]Hos. 9.10
25 [b]Ezra 9.7

CHAPTER 4
1 [a]Joel 2.12

2 [b]And thou shalt swear, The LORD
liveth, [c]in truth, in judgment, and in
righteousness; [d]and the nations shall
bless themselves in him, and in him
shall they [e]glory.
3 ¶ For thus saith the LORD to the
men of Jū'dah and Je-rṳ'sa-lĕm, [f]Break
up your fallow ground, and [g]sow not
among thorns.
4 [h]Circumcise yourselves to the
LORD, and take away the foreskins of
your heart, ye men of Jū'dah and inhabitants of Je-rṳ'sa-lĕm: lest my [i]fury
come forth like fire, and burn that
none can quench *it*, because of the evil
of your doings.
5 Declare ye in Jū'dah, and publish
in Je-rṳ'sa-lĕm; and say, Blow ye the
trumpet in the land: cry, gather together, and say, Assemble yourselves,
and let us go into the defenced cities.
6 Set up the standard toward Zī'ŏn:
[1]retire, stay not: for I will bring evil from
the [j]north, and a great [2]destruction.
7 [k]The lion is come up from his
thicket, and the destroyer of the Gĕn-
tīles is on his way; he is gone forth
from his place to make thy land desolate; *and* thy cities shall be laid waste,
without an inhabitant.
8 For this [l]gird you with sackcloth,
lament and howl: for the fierce anger
of the LORD is not turned back from us.
9 And it shall come to pass at that
day, saith the LORD, *that* the heart of
the king shall perish, and the heart
of the princes; and the priests shall
be astonished, and the prophets shall
wonder.
10 Then said I, Ah, Lord GOD! [m]surely
thou hast greatly deceived this people
and Je-rṳ'sa-lĕm, saying, Ye shall have
peace; whereas the sword reacheth unto
the soul.
11 At that time shall it be said to this
people and to Je-rṳ'sa-lĕm, [n]A dry
wind of the high places in the wilderness toward the daughter of my people, not to fan, nor to cleanse,
12 *Even* [3]a full wind from those
places shall come unto me: now also
will I [4]give sentence against them.
13 Behold, he shall come up as
clouds, and his [o]chariots *shall be* as
a whirlwind: [p]his horses are swifter
than eagles. Woe unto us! for we are
spoiled.
14 O Je-rṳ'sa-lĕm, [q]wash thine heart
from wickedness, that thou mayest
be saved. How long shall thy vain
thoughts lodge within thee?
15 For a voice declareth [r]from Dăn,
and publisheth affliction from mount
Ē'phră-ĭm.
16 Make ye mention to the nations;
behold, publish against Je-rṳ'sa-lĕm,
that watchers come [s]from a far country, and give out their voice against the
cities of Jū'dah.
17 [t]As keepers of a field, are they
against her round about; because she
hath been rebellious against me, saith
the LORD.
18 Thy [u]way and thy doings have
procured these *things* unto thee; this *is*
thy wickedness, because it is bitter, because it reacheth unto thine heart.
19 ¶ My [v]bowels, my bowels! I am
pained at [5]my very heart; my heart
maketh a noise in me; I cannot hold
my peace, because thou hast heard, O
my soul, the sound of the trumpet, the
alarm of war.
20 [w]Destruction upon destruction is
cried; for the whole land is spoiled: suddenly are [x]my tents spoiled, *and* my
curtains in a moment.
21 How long shall I see the standard,
and hear the sound of the trumpet?
22 For my people *is* [y]foolish, they
have not known me; they *are* sottish
children, and they have none understanding: [z]they *are* wise to do evil, but
to do good they have no knowledge.
23 [a]I beheld the earth, and, lo, *it*
was [b]without form, and void; and the
heavens, and they *had* no light.
24 [c]I beheld the mountains, and, lo,
they trembled, and all the hills moved
lightly.
25 I beheld, and, lo, *there was* no
man, and [d]all the birds of the heavens
were fled.
26 I beheld, and, lo, the fruitful place
was a wilderness, and all the cities
thereof were broken down at the presence of the LORD, *and* by his fierce
anger.
27 For thus hath the LORD said, The
whole land shall be desolate; [e]yet will
I not make a full end.
28 For this [f]shall the earth mourn,
and [g]the heavens above be black: because I have spoken *it*, I have purposed *it*, and [h]will not repent, neither
will I turn back from it.
29 [i]The whole city shall flee for the
noise of the horsemen and bowmen;
they shall go into thickets, and climb
up upon the rocks: every city *shall be*
forsaken, and not a man dwell therein.
30 And *when* thou *art* spoiled, what
wilt thou do? Though thou clothest thyself with crimson, though thou deckest
thee with ornaments of gold, [j]though
thou rentest thy [6]face with painting, in
vain shalt thou make thyself fair; [k]*thy*
lovers will despise thee, they will seek
thy life.
31 For I have heard a voice as of a
woman in travail, *and* the anguish as of
her that bringeth forth her first child,
the voice of the daughter of Zī'ŏn, *that*
bewaileth herself, *that* [l]spreadeth her
hands, *saying*, Woe *is* me now! for my
soul is wearied because of murderers.

5 Run ye to and fro through the streets
of Je-rṳ'sa-lĕm, and see now, and
know, and seek in the broad places
thereof, [a]if ye can find a man, [b]if there
be *any* that executeth judgment, that
seeketh the truth; and I will pardon it.
2 And [c]though they say, The LORD
liveth; surely they swear falsely.
3 O LORD, *are* not [d]thine eyes upon
the truth? thou hast [e]stricken them,
but they have not grieved; thou hast
consumed them, [f]*but* they have refused to receive correction: they have

2 [b]Deut. 10.20; Isa. 45.23
[c]Isa. 48.1
[d]Gal. 3.8
[e]Isa. 45.25; 1 Cor. 1.31
3 [f]Hos. 10.12
[g]Matt. 13.7
4 [h]Deut. 10.16; Col. 2.11
[i]Zeph. 2.2
6 [1]Or, strengthen
[j]ch. 1.13
[2]breaking
7 [k]Dan. 7.4
8 [l]Isa. 22.12
10 [m]Isa. 63.17; 2 Thess. 2.11
11 [n]Isa. 27.8; Hos. 13.5
12 [3]Or, a fuller wind than those
[4]utter judgments
13 [o]Isa. 5.28
[p]Deut. 28.49; Hab. 1.8
14 [q]Isa. 1.16; Jas. 4.8
15 [r]ch. 8.16
16 [s]ch. 5.15
17 [t]2 Ki. 25.1
18 [u]Job 20.6-11; ch. 2.17
19 [v]Isa. 16.11; Luke 19.41-42
[5]the walls of my heart
20 [w]Ps. 42.7
[x]ch. 10.20
22 [y]Rom. 1.22
[z]Rom. 16.19; 1 Cor. 14.20
23 [a]Isa. 24.19
[b]Gen. 1.2
24 [c]Ezek. 38.20
25 [d]Zeph. 1.3
27 [e]ch. 5.10
28 [f]Isa. 33.9; Hos. 4.3
[g]Isa. 50.3
[h]Num. 23.19
29 [i]2 Ki. 25.4
30 [j]2 Ki. 9.30
[6]eyes
[k]Lam. 1.2-19
31 [l]Isa. 1.15
CHAPTER 5
1 [a]Ezek. 22.30;
[b]Ps. 12.1
2 [c]Tit. 1.16
3 [d]2 Chr. 16.9
[e]Isa. 1.5
[f]ch. 7.28

made their faces harder than a rock; they have refused to return.

4 Therefore I said, Surely these *are* poor; they are foolish: for [g]they know not the way of the LORD, *nor* the judgment of their God.

5 I will get me unto the great men, and will speak unto them; for [h]they have known the way of the LORD, *and* the judgment of their God: but these have altogether [i]broken the yoke, *and* burst the bonds.

6 Wherefore [j]a lion out of the forest shall slay them, [k]*and* a wolf of the [1]evenings shall spoil them, [l]a leopard shall watch over their cities: every one that goeth out thence shall be torn in pieces: because their transgressions are many, *and* their backslidings [2]are increased.

7 ¶ How shall I pardon thee for this? thy children have forsaken me, and [m]sworn by *them* [n]*that are* no gods: [o]when I had fed them to the full, they then committed adultery, and assembled themselves by troops in the harlots' houses.

8 [p]They were *as* fed horses in the morning: every one [q]neighed after his neighbour's wife.

9 Shall I not visit for these *things?* saith the LORD: [r]and shall not my soul be avenged on such a nation as this?

10 ¶ [s]Go ye up upon her walls, and destroy; but make not a full end: take away her battlements; for they *are* not the LORD'S.

11 For [t]the house of Ĭs'ra-el and the house of Jū'dah have dealt very treacherously against me, saith the LORD.

12 [u]They have belied the LORD, and said, [v]*It is* not he; neither shall evil come upon us; [w]neither shall we see sword nor famine:

13 And the prophets shall become wind, and the word *is* not in them: thus shall it be done unto them.

14 Wherefore thus saith the LORD God of hosts, Because ye speak this word, [x]behold, I will make my words in thy mouth fire, and this people wood, and it shall devour them.

15 Lo, I will bring a [y]nation upon you [z]from far, O house of Ĭs'ra-el, saith the LORD: it *is* a mighty nation, it *is* an ancient nation, a nation whose language thou knowest not, neither understandest what they say.

16 Their quiver *is* as an open sepulchre, they *are* all mighty men.

17 And they shall eat up thine [a]harvest, and thy bread, *which* thy sons and thy daughters should eat: they shall eat up thy flocks and thine herds: they shall eat up thy vines and thy fig trees: they shall impoverish thy fenced cities, wherein thou trustedst, with the sword.

18 Nevertheless in those days, saith the LORD, I will not make a full end with you.

19 ¶ And it shall come to pass, when ye shall say, [b]Wherefore doeth the LORD our God all these *things* unto us? then shalt thou answer them, Like as ye have forsaken me, and served strange gods in your land, so [c]shall ye serve strangers in a land *that is* not yours.

20 Declare this in the house of Jā'cob, and publish it in Jū'dah, saying,

21 Hear now this, O [d]foolish people, and without [3]understanding; which have eyes, and see not; which have ears, and hear not:

22 [e]Fear ye not me? saith the LORD: will ye not tremble at my presence, which have placed the sand *for* the [f]bound of the sea by a perpetual decree, that it cannot pass it: and though the waves thereof toss themselves, yet can they not prevail; though they roar, yet can they not pass over it?

23 But this people hath a revolting and a rebellious heart; they are revolted and gone.

24 Neither say they in their heart, Let us now fear the LORD our God, [g]that giveth rain, both the [h]former and the latter, in his season: [i]he reserveth unto us the appointed weeks of the harvest.

25 ¶ Your iniquities have turned away these *things*, and your sins have withholden good *things* from you.

26 For among my people are found wicked *men:* [4]they lay wait, as he that setteth snares; they set a trap, they catch men.

27 As a [5]cage is full of birds, so *are* their houses full of deceit: therefore they are become great, and waxen rich.

28 They are waxen fat, they shine: yea, they overpass the deeds of the wicked: they judge not the cause, the cause of the fatherless, [j]yet they prosper; and the right of the needy do they not judge.

29 [k]Shall I not visit for these *things?* saith the LORD: shall not my soul be avenged on such a nation as this?

30 ¶ [6]A wonderful and horrible thing is committed in the land;

31 The prophets prophesy [l]falsely, and the priests [7]bear rule by their means; and my people [m]love *to have it* so: and what will ye do in the end thereof?

6 O ye children of [a]Bĕn'ja-min, gather yourselves to flee out of the midst of Je-ru̧'sa-lĕm, and blow the trumpet in Te-kō'á, and set up a sign of fire in [b]Bĕth–hăc'çē-rĕm: for evil appeareth out of the north, and great destruction.

2 I have likened the daughter of Zī'ŏn to a [1]comely and delicate *woman.*

3 The shepherds with their flocks shall come unto her; [c]they shall pitch *their* tents against her round about; they shall feed every one in his place.

4 Prepare ye war against her; arise, and let us go up at noon. Woe unto us! for the day goeth away, for the shadows of the evening are stretched out.

5 Arise, and let us go by night, and let us destroy her palaces.

6 ¶ For thus hath the LORD of hosts said, Hew ye down trees, and [2]cast a mount against Je-ru̧'sa-lĕm: this *is* the city to be visited; she *is* wholly [d]oppression in the midst of her.

4 [g]ch. 8.7
5 [h]Mic. 3.1
[i]Ps. 2.3
6 [j]ch. 4.7
[k]Hab. 1.8
[1]Or, deserts
[l]Hos. 13.7
[2]are strong
7 [m]Josh. 23.7; Amos 8.14
[n]Gal. 4.8
[o]Deut. 32.15
8 [p]Ezek. 22.11
[q]2 Sam. 11.2-4; ch. 13.27
9 [r]Isa. 1.24; Ezek. 7.9
10 [s]ch. 39.8
11 [t]ch. 3.20
12 [u]2 Chr. 36.16
[v]Isa. 28.15
[w]ch. 14.13
14 [x]ch. 1.9; Rev. 11.5
15 [y]Deut. 28.49; ch. 1.15
[z]Isa. 39.3
17 [a]Lev. 26.16; Judg. 6.3-4
19 [b]Deut. 29.24; ch. 13.22
[c]Deut. 28.48
21 [d]Matt. 13.14;
[3]heart
22 [e]Rev. 15.4
[f]Job 26.10;
24 [g]Matt. 5.45
[h]Joel 2.23
[i]Gen. 8.22
26 [4]Or, they pry as fowlers lie in wait
27 [5]Or, coop
28 [j]Ps. 73.12
29 [k]Mal. 3.5
30 [6]Or, Astonishment and filthiness
31 [l]Ezek. 13.6
[7]Or, take into their hands
[m]Isa. 30.10

CHAPTER 6
1 [a]Josh. 18.28;
[b]Neh. 3.14
2 [1]Or, dwelling at home, or, pasture
3 [c]2 Ki. 25.1
6 [2]Or, pour out the engine of shot
[d]2 Ki. 21.16

7 As a fountain casteth out her waters, so she casteth out her wickedness: [e]violence and spoil is heard in
her; before me continually *is* grief and
wounds.
8 Be thou instructed, O Je-ru'sa-
lĕm, lest [f]my soul [3]depart from thee;
lest I make thee desolate, a land not
inhabited.
9 ¶ Thus saith the LORD of hosts,
They shall throughly glean the remnant of Is'ra-el as a vine: turn back
thine hand as a grapegatherer into the
baskets.
10 To whom shall I speak, and give
warning, that they may hear? behold,
their [g]ear *is* uncircumcised, and they
cannot hearken: behold, [h]the word of
the LORD is unto them a reproach; they
have no delight in it.
11 Therefore I am full of the fury
of the LORD; I am weary with holding
in: I will pour it out upon the children abroad, and upon the assembly
of young men together: for even the
husband with the wife shall be taken,
the aged with *him that is* full of days.
12 And [i]their houses shall be turned
unto others, *with their* fields and wives
together: for I will stretch out my hand
upon the inhabitants of the land, saith
the LORD.
13 For from the least of them even
unto the greatest of them every one *is*
given to [j]covetousness; and from the
prophet even unto the priest every one
dealeth falsely.
14 They have [k]healed also the [4]hurt
of the daughter of my people slightly,
saying, Peace, peace; when *there is* no
peace.
15 Were they [l]ashamed when they
had committed abomination? nay, they
were not at all ashamed, neither could
they blush: therefore they shall fall
among them that fall: at the time *that* I
visit them they shall be cast down, saith
the LORD.
16 Thus saith the LORD, Stand ye in
the ways, and see, and ask for the [m]old
paths, where *is* the good way, and
walk therein, and ye shall find [n]rest
for your souls. But they said, We will
not walk *therein*.
17 Also I set [o]watchmen over you,
saying, Hearken to the sound of the
trumpet. But they said, We will not
hearken.
18 ¶ Therefore hear, ye nations, and
know, O congregation, what *is* among
them.
19 Hear, O earth: behold, I will bring
evil upon this people, *even* [p]the fruit of
their thoughts, because they have not
hearkened unto my words, nor to my
law, but rejected it.
20 [q]To what purpose cometh there
to me incense [r]from Shē'bȧ, and the
sweet cane from a far country? your
burnt offerings *are* not acceptable, nor
your sacrifices sweet unto me.
21 Therefore thus saith the LORD,
Behold, [s]I will lay stumblingblocks before this people, and the fathers and the
sons together shall fall upon them; the
neighbour and his friend shall perish.
22 Thus saith the LORD, Behold, a
people cometh from the north country,
and a great nation shall be raised from
the sides of the earth.
23 They shall lay hold on bow and
spear; they *are* cruel, and have no
mercy; their voice [t]roareth like the
sea; and they ride upon horses, set in
array as men for war against thee, O
daughter of Zī'ŏn.
24 We have heard the fame thereof:
our hands wax feeble: [u]anguish hath
taken hold of us, *and* pain, as of a
woman in travail.
25 Go not forth into the field, nor
[v]walk by the way; for the sword of the
enemy *and* fear *is* on every side.
26 ¶ O daughter of my people, gird
thee with sackcloth, [w]and wallow thyself in ashes: [x]make thee mourning, *as*
for an only son, most bitter lamentation: for the spoiler shall suddenly
come upon us.
27 I have set thee [5]*for* a tower *and* a
fortress among my people, that thou
mayest know and try their way.
28 They *are* all grievous revolters,
walking with slanders: *they are* [y]brass
and iron; they *are* all corrupters.
29 The bellows are burned, the lead
is consumed of the fire; the founder
melteth in vain: for the wicked are not
plucked away.
30 [6]Reprobate silver shall *men* call
them, because the LORD hath [z]rejected
them.

7 The word that came to Jĕr-e-mī'ah
from the LORD, saying,
2 [a]Stand in the gate of the LORD'S
house, and proclaim there this word,
and say, Hear the word of the LORD, all
ye of Jū'dah, that enter in at these
gates to worship the LORD.
3 Thus saith the LORD of hosts, the
God of Is'ra-el, Amend your ways and
your doings, and I will cause you to
dwell in this place.
4 [b]Trust ye not in lying words, saying, The temple of the LORD, The temple of the LORD, The temple of the
LORD, *are* these.
5 For if ye throughly amend your
ways and your doings; if ye throughly
execute judgment between a man and
his neighbour;
6 *If* ye oppress not the stranger, the
fatherless, and the widow, and shed
not innocent blood in this place, [c]nei-
ther walk after other gods to your hurt:
7 [d]Then will I cause you to dwell in
this place, in the land that I gave to
your fathers, for ever and ever.
8 ¶ Behold, ye trust in lying words,
that cannot profit.
9 [e]Will ye steal, murder, and commit adultery, and swear falsely, and
burn incense unto Bā'al, and [f]walk after other gods whom ye know not;
10 [g]And come and stand before me
in this house, [1]which is called by my
name, and say, We are delivered to do
all these abominations?

7 [e]Ps. 55.9-11; ch. 20.8; Ezek. 7.11; Mic. 7.2-3
8 [f]Ezek. 23.18; Hos. 9.12
[3]be loosed, or, disjointed
10 [g]Ex. 6.12; ch. 7.26; Acts 7.51
[h]ch. 20.8; Luke 11.45; 2 Tim. 4.3-4
12 [i]ch. 8.10; Zeph. 1.13
13 [j]Isa. 56.11; Mic. 3.5
14 [k]Ezek. 13.10
[4]bruise, or, breach
15 [l]ch. 3.3
16 [m]ch. 18.15; Mal. 4.4; Luke 16.29
[n]Isa. 28.12; Matt. 11.29
17 [o]Isa. 21.11; ch. 25.4; Hab. 2.1
19 [p]Prov. 1.31
20 [q]Isa. 66.3; Mic. 6.6
[r]Isa. 60.6
21 [s]Job 5.12; Isa. 8.14; ch. 13.16
23 [t]Isa. 5.30
24 [u]Ps. 48.6; Isa. 21.3; ch. 4.31; ch. 13.21; ch. 30.6; ch. 49.24
25 [v]Judg. 5.6
26 [w]Isa. 32.11; ch. 4.8; Mic. 1.10
[x]Zech. 12.10
27 [5]Or, in
28 [y]Ezek. 22.18
30 [6]Or, Refuse silver
[z]Hos. 9.17; Zech. 11.8

CHAPTER 7
2 [a]ch. 19.2-3; ch. 26.2
4 [b]1 Sam. 4.4; Mic. 3.11
6 [c]Deut. 6.14; Deut. 8.19; ch. 13.10
7 [d]Deut. 4.40
9 [e]1 Ki. 18.21; Hos. 4.1
[f]Ex. 20.3
10 [g]Ezek. 23.39
[1]whereupon my name is called

11 Is [h]this house, which is called by
my name, become a [i]den of robbers in
your eyes? Behold, even [j]I have seen
it, saith the LORD.
12 But go ye now unto [k]my place
which *was* in Shī'lōh, [l]where I set my
name at the first, and see [m]what I did
to it for the wickedness of my people
Is'ra-el.
13 And now, because ye have done
all these works, saith the LORD, and
I spake unto you, [n]rising up early
and speaking, but ye heard not; and I
[o]called you, but ye answered not;
14 Therefore will I do unto *this*
house, which is called by my name,
wherein ye trust, and unto the place
which I gave to you and to your fathers, as I have done to [p]Shī'lōh.
15 And I will cast you out of my
sight, [q]as I have cast out all your brethren, *even* the whole seed of Ē'phră-ĭm.
16 Therefore [r]pray not thou for this
people, neither lift up cry nor prayer
for them, neither make intercession to
me: [s]for I will not hear thee.
17 ¶ Seest thou not what they do in
the cities of Jū'dah and in the streets of
Je-rụ'sa-lĕm?
18 The children gather wood, and
the fathers kindle the fire, and the
women knead *their* dough, to make
cakes to the [2]queen of heaven, and to
pour out drink offerings unto other
gods, that they may provoke me to
anger.
19 [t]Do they provoke me to anger?
saith the LORD: *do they* not *provoke*
themselves to the confusion of their
own faces?
20 Therefore thus saith the Lord
GOD; Behold, mine anger and my fury
shall be poured out upon this place,
upon man, and upon beast, and upon
the trees of the field, and upon the fruit
of the ground; and it shall burn, and
shall not be quenched.
21 ¶ Thus saith the LORD of hosts,
the God of Is'ra-el; [u]Put your burnt offerings unto your sacrifices, and eat
flesh.
22 [v]For I spake not unto your fathers, nor commanded them in the day
that I brought them out of the land of
Ē'gypt, [3]concerning burnt offerings or
sacrifices:
23 But this thing commanded I them,
saying, [w]Obey my voice, and [x]I will be
your God, and ye shall be my people:
and walk ye in all the ways that I have
commanded you, that it may be well
unto you.
24 But they hearkened not, nor inclined their ear, but [y]walked in the
counsels *and* in the [4]imagination of
their evil heart, and [5]went backward,
and not forward.
25 Since the day that your fathers
came forth out of the land of Ē'gypt
unto this day I have even [z]sent unto
you all my servants the prophets, daily
rising up early and sending *them*:
26 Yet they hearkened not unto me,
nor inclined their ear, but [a]hardened
their neck: they did worse than their
fathers.
27 Therefore [b]thou shalt speak all
these words unto them; but they will
not hearken to thee: thou shalt also
call unto them; but they will not answer thee.
28 But thou shalt say unto them,
This *is* a nation that obeyeth not the
voice of the LORD their God, nor receiveth [6]correction: truth is perished,
and is cut off from their mouth.
29 ¶ [c]Cut off thine hair, *O Je-rụ'sa-
lĕm,* and cast *it* away, and take up a
lamentation on high places; for the
LORD hath rejected and forsaken the
[d]generation of his wrath.
30 For the children of Jū'dah have
done evil in my sight, saith the LORD:
[e]they have set their abominations in
the house which is called by my name,
to pollute it.
31 And they have built the [f]high
places of Tō'phet, which *is* in the valley of the son of Hĭn'nom, to burn their
sons and their daughters in the fire;
[g]which I commanded *them* not, neither [7]came it into my heart.
32 ¶ Therefore, behold, the days
come, saith the LORD, that it shall no
more be called Tō'phet, nor the valley
of the son of Hĭn'nom, but the valley of
slaughter: [h]for they shall bury in Tō'-
phet, till there be no place.
33 And the carcases of this people
shall be meat for the fowls of the
heaven, and for the beasts of the earth;
and none shall fray *them* away.
34 Then will I cause to [i]cease from
the cities of Jū'dah, and from the streets
of Je-rụ'sa-lĕm, the voice of mirth, and
the voice of gladness, the voice of the
bridegroom, and the voice of the bride:
for [j]the land shall be desolate.
8 At that time, saith the LORD, they
shall bring out the bones of the
kings of Jū'dah, and the bones of his
princes, and the bones of the priests,
and the bones of the prophets, and the
bones of the inhabitants of Je-rụ'sa-
lĕm, out of their graves:
2 And they shall spread them before
the sun, and the moon, and all the
host of heaven, whom they have loved,
and whom they have served, and after
whom they have walked, and whom
they have sought, and [a]whom they
have worshipped: they shall not be
gathered, nor be buried; they shall be
for [b]dung upon the face of the earth.
3 And [c]death shall be chosen rather
than life by all the residue of them that
remain of this evil family, which remain in all the places whither I have
driven them, saith the LORD of hosts.
4 ¶ Moreover thou shalt say unto
them, Thus saith the LORD; Shall they
fall, and not arise? shall he turn away,
and not return?
5 Why *then* is this people of Je-
rụ'sa-lĕm slidden back by a perpetual backsliding? they hold fast deceit,
[d]they refuse to return.
6 [e]I hearkened and heard, *but* they
spake not aright: no man repented him

11 [h]Isa. 56.7 [i]Matt. 21.13; Mark 11.17 [j]John 2.24
12 [k]Josh. 18.1 [l]Deut. 12.11 [m]1 Sam. 4.10
13 [n]2 Chr. 36.15 [o]Prov. 1.24; Isa. 65.12
14 [p]Ps. 78.60
15 [q]2 Ki. 17.23
16 [r]Ex. 32.10 [s]ch. 15.1
18 [2]Or, frame, or, workmanship of heaven
19 [t]ch. 17.27; 1 Cor. 10.22
21 [u]Isa. 1.11; ch. 6.20; Amos 5.21
22 [v]1 Sam. 15.22; Ps. 51.16 [3]concerning the matter of
23 [w]Ex. 15.26; Lev. 26.3-12; Deut. 6.3; ch. 11.4-7 [x]Ex. 19.5; Lev. 26.12
24 [y]Deut. 29.19 [4]Or, stubbornness [5]were
25 [z]Neh. 9.30; ch. 25.4
26 [a]Neh. 9.17
27 [b]Ezek. 2.7
28 [6]Or, instruction
29 [c]Job 1.20; Isa. 15.2; ch. 16.6 [d]Eph. 2.3
30 [e]2 Ki. 21.4; 2 Chr. 33.4
31 [f]2 Ki. 23.10 [g]Deut. 17.3 [7]came it upon my heart
32 [h]2 Ki. 23.10
34 [i]Hos. 2.11 [j]Lev. 26.33

CHAPTER 8
2 [a]Deut. 4.19; 2 Ki. 23.5; ch. 44.19 [b]2 Ki. 9.36; Ps. 83.10
3 [c]Job 3.21; Rev. 9.6
5 [d]Isa. 1.20; ch. 5.3; Zech. 7.11
6 [e]2 Pet. 3.9

of his wickedness, saying, What have I
done? every one turned to his course,
as the horse rusheth into the battle.
7 Yea, [f]the stork in the heaven knoweth her appointed times; and [g]the turtle
and the crane and the swallow observe
the time of their coming; but my people
know not the judgment of the LORD.
8 How do ye say, We *are* wise, [h]and
the law of the LORD *is* with us? Lo, certainly [1]in vain made he *it;* the pen of
the scribes *is* in vain.
9 [2]The wise *men* are ashamed, they
are dismayed and taken: lo, they have
rejected the word of the LORD; and
[3]what wisdom *is* in them?
10 Therefore [i]will I give their wives
unto others, *and* their fields to them
that shall inherit *them:* for every one
from the least even unto the greatest
is given to covetousness, [j]from the
prophet even unto the priest every one
dealeth falsely.
11 For they have [k]healed the hurt of
the daughter of my people slightly, saying, [l]Peace, peace; when *there is* no
peace.
12 Were they [m]ashamed when they
had committed abomination? nay, they
were not at all ashamed, neither could
they blush: therefore shall they fall
among them that fall: in the time of
their visitation they shall be cast down,
saith the LORD.
13 ¶ [4]I will surely consume them,
saith the LORD: *there shall be* no grapes
[n]on the vine, nor figs on the [o]fig tree,
and the leaf shall fade; and *the things
that* I have given them shall pass away
from them.
14 Why do we sit still? assemble
yourselves, and let us enter into the defenced cities, and let us be silent there:
for the LORD our God hath put us to
silence, and given us [p]water of [5]gall to
drink, because we have sinned against
the LORD.
15 We [q]looked for peace, but no
good *came; and* for a time of health,
and behold trouble!
16 The snorting of his horses was
heard from Dăn: the whole land trembled at the sound of the neighing of his
strong ones; for they are come, and
have devoured the land, and [6]all that is
in it; the city, and those that dwell
therein.
17 For, behold, I will send serpents,
cockatrices, among you, which *will* not
be charmed, and they shall bite you,
saith the LORD.
18 ¶ *When* I would comfort myself
against sorrow, my heart *is* faint [7]in me.
19 Behold the voice of the cry of the
daughter of my people [8]because of
them that dwell in a far country: *Is* not
the LORD in Zī'ŏn? *is* not her king in
her? Why have they provoked me to
anger with their graven images, *and*
with strange vanities?
20 The harvest is past, the summer
is ended, and we are not saved.
21 For the hurt of the daughter of
my people am I hurt; I am [r]black; astonishment hath taken hold on me.
22 *Is there* no [s]balm in Gĭl'e-ăd; *is
there* no physician there? why then is
not the health of the daughter of my
people [9]recovered?

9 Oh [1]that my head were waters, and
mine eyes a fountain of tears, that I
might weep day and night for the slain
of the daughter of my people!
2 Oh that I had in the wilderness a
lodging place of wayfaring men; that I
might leave my people, and go from
them! for they *be* all adulterers, an assembly of treacherous men.
3 And they bend their tongues *like*
their bow *for* lies: but they are not valiant for the truth upon the earth; for
they proceed from evil to evil, and they
[a]know not me, saith the LORD.
4 [b]Take ye heed every one of his
[2]neighbour, and trust ye not in any
brother: for every brother will utterly
supplant, and every neighbour will
walk with slanders.
5 And they will [3]deceive every one
his neighbour, and will not speak the
truth: they have taught their tongue to
speak lies, *and* weary themselves to
commit iniquity.
6 Thine habitation *is* in the midst of
deceit; through deceit [c]they refuse to
know me, saith the LORD.
7 Therefore thus saith the LORD of
hosts, Behold, [d]I will melt them, and
try them; [e]for how shall I do for the
daughter of my people?
8 Their tongue *is as* an arrow shot
out; it speaketh deceit: *one* speaketh
peaceably to his neighbour with his
mouth, but [4]in heart he layeth [5]his
wait.
9 ¶ Shall I not visit them for these
things? saith the LORD: shall not my
soul be avenged on such a nation as
this?
10 For the mountains will I take up a
weeping and wailing, and for the [6]habi-
tations of the wilderness a lamentation, because they are [7]burned up, so
that none can pass through *them;* neither can *men* hear the voice of the cattle; [8]both the fowl of the heavens and
the beast are fled; they are gone.
11 And I will make Je-ru'sa-lĕm
heaps, *and* a den of dragons; and I will
make the cities of Jū'dah [9]desolate,
without an inhabitant.
12 ¶ [f]Who *is* the wise man, that may
understand this? and *who is he* to
whom the mouth of the LORD hath
spoken, that he may declare it, for
what the land perisheth *and* is burned
up like a wilderness, that none passeth
through?
13 And the LORD saith, Because they
have forsaken my law which I set before them, and have not obeyed my
voice, neither walked therein;
14 But have walked after the [10]imagi-
nation of their own heart, and after
Bā'al-ĭm, which [g]their fathers taught
them:
15 Therefore thus saith the LORD of
hosts, the God of Is'ra-el; Behold, I will
[h]feed them, *even* this people, [i]with

7 [f]Isa. 1.3 [g]Song 2.12
8 [h]Ps. 147.19-20; Hos. 8.12 [1]Or, the false pen of the scribes worketh for falsehood
9 [2]Or, Have they been ashamed, etc [3]the wisdom of what thing
10 [i]Deut. 28.30; Amos 5.11 [j]Isa. 28.7; Lam. 4.13
11 [k]ch. 6.14 [l]Ezek. 13.10
12 [m]Isa. 3.9; ch. 3.3
13 [4]Or, In gathering I will consume [n]Isa. 5.1 [o]Matt. 21.19; Luke 13.6
14 [p]ch. 23.15 [5]Or, poison
15 [q]ch. 14.19
16 [6]the fulness thereof
18 [7]upon
19 [8]because of the country of them that are far off
21 [r]Nah. 2.10
22 [s]Gen. 37.25 [9]gone up

CHAPTER 9
1 [1]Who will give my head, etc
3 [a]Judg. 2.10 1 Cor. 15.34
4 [b]Mic. 7.5-6 [2]Or, friend
5 [3]Or, mock
6 [c]Prov. 1.24
7 [d]Isa. 1.25 [e]Hos. 11.8
8 [4]in the midst of him [5]Or, wait for him
10 [6]Or, pastures [7]Or, desolate [8]from the fowl even to, etc
11 [9]desolation
12 [f]Ps. 107.43
14 [10]Or, stubbornness [g]Gal. 1.14
15 [h]Ps. 80.5 [i]Lam. 3.15

wormwood, and give them water of [11]gall to drink.

16 I will [j]scatter them also among the heathen, whom neither they nor their fathers have known: [k]and I will send a sword after them, till I have consumed them.

17 ¶ Thus saith the LORD of hosts, Consider ye, and call for [l]the mourning women, that they may come; and send for cunning *women,* that they may come:

18 And let them make haste, and take up a wailing for us, that [m]our eyes may run down with tears, and our eyelids gush out with waters.

19 For a voice of wailing is heard out of Zī'ŏn, How are we spoiled! we are greatly confounded, because we have forsaken the land, because our [n]dwellings have cast *us* out.

20 Yet hear the word of the LORD, O ye women, and let your ear receive the word of his mouth, and teach your daughters wailing, and every one her neighbour lamentation.

21 For death is come up into our windows, *and* is entered into our palaces, to cut off the children from without, *and* the young men from the streets.

22 Speak, Thus saith the LORD, Even the carcases of men shall fall as dung upon the open field, and as the handful after the harvestman, and none shall gather *them.*

23 ¶ Thus saith the LORD, [o]Let not the wise *man* glory in his wisdom, neither let the mighty *man* glory in his might, let not the rich *man* glory in his riches:

24 But [p]let him that glorieth glory in this, that he understandeth and knoweth me, that I *am* the LORD which exercise lovingkindness, judgment, and righteousness, in the earth: [q]for in these *things* I delight, saith the LORD.

25 ¶ Behold, the days come, saith the LORD, that [r]I will [12]punish all *them which are* circumcised with the uncircumcised;

26 Ē'ġypt, and Jū'dah, and Ē'dom, and the children of Ăm'mŏn, and Mō'ab, and all *that are* [13]in the utmost corners, that dwell in the wilderness: for all *these* nations *are* uncircumcised, and all the house of Ĭs'ra-el *are* [s]uncircumcised in the heart.

10 Hear ye the word which the LORD speaketh unto you, O house of Ĭs'ra-el:

2 Thus saith the LORD, [a]Learn not the way of the heathen, and be not dismayed at the signs of heaven, for the heathen are dismayed at them.

3 For the [1]customs of the people *are* vain: for *one* cutteth a tree out of the forest, the work of the hands of the workman, with the ax.

4 They deck it with silver and with gold; they fasten it with nails and with hammers, that it move not.

5 They *are* upright as the palm tree, [b]but speak not: they must needs be [c]borne, because they cannot go. Be not afraid of them; for they cannot do evil, neither also *is it* in them to do good.

6 Forasmuch as *there is* none [d]like unto thee, O LORD; thou *art* great, and thy name *is* great in might.

7 [e]Who would not fear thee, O King of nations? for [2]to thee doth it appertain: forasmuch as among all the wise *men* of the nations, and in all their kingdoms, *there is* none like unto thee.

8 But they are [3]altogether brutish and foolish: the stock *is* a doctrine of vanities.

9 Silver spread into plates is brought from Tär'shish, and [f]gold from Ū'phăz, the work of the workman, and of the hands of the founder: blue and purple *is* their clothing: they *are* all the work of cunning *men.*

10 But the LORD *is* the [4]true God, he *is* [g]the living God, and an [5][h]everlasting king: at his wrath the earth shall tremble, and the nations shall not be able to abide his indignation.

11 [6]Thus shall ye say unto them, The gods that have not made the heavens and the earth, *even* they shall perish from the earth, and from under these heavens.

12 He [i]hath made the earth by his power, he hath established the world by his wisdom, and hath stretched out the heavens by his discretion.

13 When he uttereth his voice, *there is* a [7]multitude of waters in the heavens, and he causeth the vapours to ascend from the ends of the earth; he maketh lightnings [8]with rain, and bringeth forth the wind out of his treasures.

14 Every man [9]is brutish in *his* knowledge: every founder is confounded by the graven image: for his molten image *is* falsehood, and *there is* no breath in them.

15 They *are* vanity, *and* the work of errors: in the time of their visitation they shall perish.

16 [j]The portion of Jā'cob *is* not like them: for he *is* the former of all *things;* and [k]Ĭs'ra-el *is* the rod of his inheritance: The LORD of hosts *is* his name.

17 ¶ Gather up thy wares out of the land, O [10]inhabitant of the fortress.

18 For thus saith the LORD, Behold, I will sling out the inhabitants of the land at this once, and will distress them, [l]that they may find *it so.*

19 ¶ Woe is me for my hurt! my wound is grievous: but I said, Truly this *is* a grief, and [m]I must bear it.

20 My tabernacle is spoiled, and all my cords are broken: my children are gone forth of me, and they *are* not: *there is* none to stretch forth my tent any more, and to set up my curtains.

21 For the pastors are become brutish, and have not sought the LORD: therefore they shall not prosper, and all their flocks shall be scattered.

22 Behold, the noise of the bruit is come, and a great commotion out of the north country, to make the cities of Jū'dah desolate, *and* a den of dragons.

[11]Or, hemlock
16 [j]Lev. 26.33; Deut. 28.64
[k]Ezek. 5.2
17 [l]Eccl. 12.5; Amos 5.16; Matt. 9.23
18 [m]ch. 14.17; Lam. 1.16
19 [n]Lev. 18.28
23 [o]Ps. 33.16; Eccl. 9.11; Isa. 5.21; Rom. 1.22
24 [p]Ps. 20.7; 1 Cor. 1.31
[q]Mic. 6.8
25 [r]Amos 3.2
[12]visit upon
26 [13]cut off into corners, or, having the corners of their hair polled
[s]Lev. 26.41; Rom. 2.28

CHAPTER 10
2 [a]Lev. 20.23
3 [1]statutes, or, ordinances are vanity
5 [b]Ps. 115.5; Hab. 2.19
[c]Ps. 115.7
6 [d]Ex. 8.9; Ps. 86.8-10
7 [e]Rev. 15.4
[2]Or, it liketh thee
8 [3]in one, or, at once
9 [f]Dan. 10.5
10 [4]God of truth
[g]1 Tim. 6.17
[5]king of eternity
[h]Isa. 57.15
11 [6]In the Chaldean language
12 [i]Gen. 1.1-6; Acts 14.15
13 [7]Or, noise
[8]Or, for rain
14 [9]Or, is more brutish than to know
16 [j]Ps. 16.5; Lam. 3.24
[k]Deut. 32.9; Ps. 74.2
17 [10]inhabitress
18 [l]Ezek. 6.10
19 [m]Mic. 7.9

23 ¶ O LORD, I know that the [n]way of man *is* not in himself: *it is* not in man that walketh to direct his steps.

24 O LORD, [o]correct me, but with judgment; not in thine anger, lest thou [11]bring me to nothing.

25 Pour out thy fury upon the heathen [p]that know thee not, and upon the families that call not on thy name: for they have eaten up Jā'cob, and devoured him, and consumed him, and have made his habitation desolate.

11 The word that came to Jĕr-e-mī'ah from the LORD, saying,

2 Hear ye the words of this covenant, and speak unto the men of Jū'dah, and to the inhabitants of Je-ru̥'sa-lĕm;

3 And say thou unto them, Thus saith the LORD God of Īs'ra-el; [a]Cursed *be* the man that obeyeth not the words of this covenant,

4 Which I commanded your fathers in the day *that* I brought them forth out of the land of Ē'ġypt, from the iron furnace, saying, [b]Obey my voice, and do them, according to all which I command you: so shall ye be my people, and I will be your God:

5 That I may perform the [c]oath which I have sworn unto your fathers, to give them a land flowing with milk and honey, as *it is* this day. Then answered I, and said, [1]So be it, O LORD.

6 Then the LORD said unto me, Proclaim all these words in the cities of Jū'dah, and in the streets of Je-ru̥'sa-lĕm, saying, Hear ye the words of this covenant, [d]and do them.

7 For I earnestly protested unto your fathers in the day *that* I brought them up out of the land of Ē'ġypt, *even* unto this day, rising early and protesting, saying, Obey my voice.

8 Yet they obeyed not, nor inclined their ear, but walked every one in the [2]imagination of their evil heart: therefore I will bring upon them all the words of this covenant, which I commanded *them* to do; but they did *them* not.

9 And the LORD said unto me, [e]A conspiracy is found among the men of Jū'dah, and among the inhabitants of Je-ru̥'sa-lĕm.

10 They are turned back to [f]the iniquities of their forefathers, which refused to hear my words; and they went after other gods to serve them: the house of Īs'ra-el and the house of Jū'dah have broken my covenant which I made with their fathers.

11 ¶ Therefore thus saith the LORD, Behold, I will bring evil upon them, which they shall not be able [3]to escape; and [g]though they shall cry unto me, I will not hearken unto them.

12 Then shall the cities of Jū'dah and inhabitants of Je-ru̥'sa-lĕm go, and [h]cry unto the gods unto whom they offer incense: but they shall not save them at all in the time of their [4]trouble.

13 For *according to* the number of thy cities were thy gods, O Jū'dah; and *according to* the number of the streets of Je-ru̥'sa-lĕm have ye set up altars to *that* [5]shameful thing, *even* altars to burn incense unto Bā'al.

14 Therefore [i]pray not thou for this people, neither lift up a cry or prayer for them: for I will not hear *them* in the time that they cry unto me for their [6]trouble.

15 [7]What hath my beloved to do in mine house, *seeing* she hath [j]wrought lewdness with many, and [k]the holy flesh is passed from thee? [8]when thou doest evil, then thou rejoicest.

16 The LORD called thy name, [l]A green olive tree, fair, *and* of goodly fruit: with the noise of a great tumult he hath kindled fire upon it, and the branches of it are broken.

17 For the LORD of hosts, [m]that planted thee, hath pronounced evil against thee, for the evil of the house of Īs'ra-el and of the house of Jū'dah, which they have done against themselves to provoke me to anger in offering incense unto Bā'al.

18 ¶ And the LORD hath given me knowledge *of it,* and I know *it:* then thou shewedst me their doings.

19 But I *was* like a lamb *or* an ox *that* is brought to the slaughter; and I knew not that they had devised devices against me, *saying,* Let us destroy [9]the tree with the fruit thereof, [n]and let us cut him off from the land of the living, that his name may be no more remembered.

20 But, O LORD of hosts, that [o]judgest righteously, that [p]triest the reins and the heart, let me see thy vengeance on them: for unto thee have I revealed my cause.

21 Therefore thus saith the LORD of the men of [q]Ăn'a-thoth, that seek thy life, saying, [r]Prophesy not in the name of the LORD, that thou die not by our hand:

22 Therefore thus saith the LORD of hosts, Behold, I will [10]punish them: the young men shall die by the sword; their sons and their daughters shall die by famine:

23 And there shall be no remnant of them: for I will bring evil upon the men of Ăn'a-thoth, *even* [s]the year of their visitation.

12 Righteous [a]*art* thou, O LORD, when I plead with thee: yet [1]let me talk with thee of *thy* judgments: [b]Wherefore doth the way of the wicked prosper? *wherefore* are all they happy that deal very treacherously?

2 Thou hast planted them, yea, they have taken root: [2]they grow, yea, they bring forth fruit: [c]thou *art* near in their mouth, and far from their reins.

3 But thou, O LORD, knowest me: thou hast seen me, and tried mine heart [3]toward thee: pull them out like sheep for the slaughter, and prepare them for [d]the day of slaughter.

4 How long shall the land mourn, and the herbs of every field wither, [e]for the wickedness of them that dwell therein? [f]the beasts are consumed, and the birds; because they said, He shall not see our last end.

---

23 [n]Ps. 17.5; Prov. 16.1
24 [o]Ps. 6.1; Hab. 3.2
[11]diminish me
25 [p]Job 18.21; 2 Thess. 1.8

CHAPTER 11
3 [a]Deut. 27.26; Gal. 3.10
4 [b]Lev. 26.3
5 [c]Deut. 7.12; Ps. 105.9
[1]Amen, Deut. 27.15
6 [d]John 13.17; Rom. 2.13
8 [2]Or, stubbornness
9 [e]Ezek. 22.25; Hos. 6.9
10 [f]Judg. 2.11
11 [3]to go forth of
[g]Ps. 18.41
12 [h]Deut. 32.37;
[4]evil
13 [5]shame
14 [i]Ex. 32.10;
[6]evil
15 [7]What is to my beloved in my house
[j]Ezek. 16.25
[k]Hag. 2.12;
[8]Or, when thy evil is
16 [l]Ps. 52.8
17 [m]Ps. 44.2
19 [9]the stalk with his bread
[n]Ps. 83.4
20 [o]Ps. 7.8;
[p]1 Sam. 16.7
21 [q]ch. 1.1
[r]Amos 2.12
22 [10]visit upon
23 [s]Luke 19.44

CHAPTER 12
1 [a]Gen. 18.25
[1]Or, let me reason the case with thee
[b]Job 12.6
2 [2]they go on
[c]Isa. 29.13
3 [3]with thee
[d]Jas. 5.5
4 [e]Ps. 107.34
[f]ch. 4.25

5 ¶ If thou hast run with the footmen, and they have wearied thee, then how canst thou contend with horses? and *if* in the land of peace, *wherein* thou trustedst, *they wearied thee,* then how wilt thou do in [g]the swelling of Jôr′dan?

6 For even thy brethren, and the house of thy father, even they have dealt treacherously with thee; yea, [4]they have called a multitude after thee: believe them not, though they speak [5]fair words unto thee.

7 ¶ I have forsaken mine house, I have left mine heritage; I have given [6]the dearly beloved of my soul into the hand of her enemies.

8 Mine heritage is unto me as a lion in the forest; it [7]crieth out against me: therefore [h]have I hated it.

9 Mine heritage *is* unto me *as* a [8]speckled bird, the birds round about *are* against her; come ye, assemble all the beasts of the field, [9]come to devour.

10 Many [i]pastors have destroyed [j]my vineyard, they have [k]trodden my portion under foot, they have made my [10]pleasant portion a desolate wilderness.

11 They have made it desolate, *and being* desolate it mourneth unto me; the whole land is made desolate, because [l]no man layeth *it* to heart.

12 The spoilers are come upon all high places through the wilderness: for the sword of the LORD shall devour from the *one* end of the land even to the *other* end of the land: no flesh shall have peace.

13 [m]They have sown wheat, but shall reap thorns: they have put themselves to pain, *but* shall not profit: and [11]they shall be ashamed of your revenues because of the fierce anger of the LORD.

14 ¶ Thus saith the LORD against all mine evil neighbours, that [n]touch the inheritance which I have caused my people Is′ra-el to inherit; Behold, I will [o]pluck them out of their land, and pluck out the house of Jū′dah from among them.

15 [p]And it shall come to pass, after that I have plucked them out I will return, and have compassion on them, [q]and will bring them again, every man to his heritage, and every man to his land.

16 And it shall come to pass, if they will diligently learn the ways of my people, [r]to swear by my name, The LORD liveth; as they taught my people to [s]swear by Bā′al; then shall they be [t]built in the midst of my people.

17 But if they will not [u]obey, I will utterly pluck up and destroy that nation, saith the LORD.

13 Thus saith the LORD unto me, Go and get thee a linen girdle, and put it upon thy loins, and put it not in water.

2 So I got a girdle according to the word of the LORD, and put *it* on my loins.

3 And the word of the LORD came unto me the second time, saying,

4 Take the girdle that thou hast got, which *is* upon thy loins, and arise, go to [a]Eū-phrā′tēs, and hide it there in a hole of the rock.

5 So I went, and hid it by Eū-phrā′tēs, as the LORD commanded me.

6 And it came to pass after many days, that the LORD said unto me, Arise, go to Eū-phrā′tēs, and take the girdle from thence, which I commanded thee to hide there.

7 Then I went to Eū-phrā′tēs, and digged, and took the girdle from the place where I had hid it: and, behold, the girdle was marred, it was [b]profitable for nothing.

8 Then the word of the LORD came unto me, saying,

9 Thus saith the LORD, After this manner [c]will I mar the pride of Jū′dah, and the great pride of Je-ru′sa-lĕm.

10 This evil people, which [d]refuse to hear my words, which [e]walk in the [1]imagination of their heart, and walk after other gods, to serve them, and to worship them, shall even be as this girdle, which is good for nothing.

11 For as the girdle cleaveth to the loins of a man, so have I caused to cleave unto me the whole house of Is′ra-el and the whole house of Jū′dah, saith the LORD; that [f]they might be unto me for a people, and [g]for a name, and for a praise, and for a glory: but they would not hear.

12 ¶ Therefore thou shalt speak unto them this word; Thus saith the LORD God of Is′ra-el, Every bottle shall be filled with wine: and they shall say unto thee, Do we not certainly know that every bottle shall be filled with wine?

13 Then shalt thou say unto them, Thus saith the LORD, Behold, I will fill all the inhabitants of this land, even the kings that sit upon Dā′vid's throne, and the priests, and the prophets, and all the inhabitants of Je-ru′sa-lĕm, [h]with drunkenness.

14 And I will dash them [2]one against another, even the fathers and the sons together, saith the LORD: I will not pity, nor spare, nor have mercy, [3]but destroy them.

15 ¶ Hear [i]ye, and give ear; be not proud: for the LORD hath spoken.

16 [j]Give glory to the LORD your God, before he cause [k]darkness, and before your feet stumble upon the dark mountains, and, while ye [l]look for light, he turn it into [m]the shadow of death, *and* make *it* gross darkness.

17 But if ye will not hear it, my soul shall weep in secret places for *your* pride; and mine eye shall weep sore, and run down with tears, because the LORD'S flock is carried away captive.

18 Say unto [n]the king and to the queen, Humble yourselves, sit down: for your [4]principalities shall come down, *even* the crown of your glory.

19 The cities of the south shall be shut up, and none shall open *them:*

5 [g] 1 Chr. 12.15; ch. 49.19
6 [4] Or, they cried after thee fully [5] good things
7 [6] the love
8 [7] giveth out his voice, or, yelleth [h] 2 Chr. 36.16
9 [8] Or, taloned [9] Or, cause them to come
10 [i] ch. 6.3 [j] Isa. 5.1-5 [k] Isa. 63.18 [10] portion of desire
11 [l] Isa. 42.25; Mal. 2.2
13 [m] Lev. 26.16 [11] Or, ye
14 [n] Zeph. 2.8-10 [o] Deut. 30.3; ch. 32.37
15 [p] Ezek. 28.25 [q] Amos 9.14
16 [r] ch. 4.2 [s] Josh. 23.7; Zeph. 1.5 [t] 1 Cor. 3.9-10; Eph. 2.20; 1 Pet. 2.5
17 [u] Ps. 2.8-9; 1 Pet. 2.8

CHAPTER 13

4 [a] Ps. 137.1; Mic. 4.10
7 [b] Isa. 64.6; Lam. 3.45
9 [c] Lev. 26.19
10 [d] 2 Chr. 36.15-16 [e] ch. 9.14; ch. 11.8 [1] Or, stubbornness
11 [f] Gen. 17.7; Ex. 19.5 [g] ch. 33.9
13 [h] Ps. 60.3; Rev. 14.10
14 [2] a man against his brother [3] from destroying them
15 [i] Deut. 32.29
16 [j] Josh. 7.19; Joel 2.12 [k] Isa. 5.30; Amos 8.9 [l] Isa. 59.9 [m] Ps. 44.19
18 [n] 2 Ki. 24.12 [4] Or, head tires

Jū'dah shall be carried away [o]captive all of it, it shall be wholly carried away captive.
20 Lift up your eyes, and behold them [p]that come from the north: where *is* the flock *that* was given thee, thy beautiful flock?
21 What wilt thou say when he shall [5]punish thee? for thou hast taught them *to be* captains, *and* as chief over thee: shall not sorrows take thee, as a woman in travail?
22 ¶ And if thou say in thine heart, [q]Wherefore come these things upon me? For the greatness of thine iniquity are [r]thy skirts discovered, *and* thy heels [6]made bare.
23 Can the Ē-thĭ-ō'pĭ-an change his skin, or the leopard his spots? *then* may ye also do good, that are [7]accustomed to do evil.
24 Therefore will I scatter them as the stubble that passeth away by the wind of the wilderness.
25 [s]This *is* thy lot, the portion of thy measures from me, saith the LORD; because thou hast forgotten me, and trusted in [t]falsehood.
26 Therefore [u]will I discover thy skirts upon thy face, that thy shame may appear.
27 I have seen thine adulteries, and thy [v]neighings, the lewdness of thy whoredom, *and* thine abominations [w]on the hills in the fields. Woe unto thee, O Je-rụ'sa-lĕm! wilt thou not be made clean? [8]when *shall it* once *be?*

14 The word of the LORD that came to Jĕr-e-mī'ah concerning [1]the dearth.
2 Jū'dah mourneth, and [a]the gates thereof languish; they are black unto the ground; and [b]the cry of Je-rụ'sa-lĕm is gone up.
3 And their nobles have sent their little ones to the waters: they came to the [2]pits, *and* found no water; they returned with their vessels empty; they were [c]ashamed and confounded, [d]and covered their heads.
4 Because the ground is chapt, for there was no rain in the earth, the plowmen were ashamed, they covered their heads.
5 Yea, the hind also calved in the field, and forsook *it,* because there was no grass.
6 And [e]the wild asses did stand in the high places, they snuffed up the wind like dragons; their eyes did fail, because *there was* no grass.
7 ¶ O LORD, though our iniquities testify against us, do thou *it* [f]for thy name's sake: for our backslidings are many; we have sinned against thee.
8 [g]O the hope of Is'ra-el, [h]the saviour thereof in time of trouble, why shouldest thou be as a stranger in the land, and as a wayfaring man *that* turneth aside to tarry for a night?
9 Why shouldest thou be as a man astonied, as a mighty man [i]*that* cannot save? yet thou, O LORD, [j]*art* in the midst of us, and [3]we are called by thy name; leave us not.
10 ¶ Thus saith the LORD unto this people, Thus have they loved to wander, they have not refrained their feet, therefore the LORD doth not accept them; [k]he will now remember their iniquity, and visit their sins.
11 Then said the LORD unto me, [l]Pray not for this people for *their* good.
12 [m]When they fast, I will not hear their cry; and when they offer burnt offering and an oblation, I will not accept them: but I will consume them by the sword, and by the famine, and by the pestilence.
13 ¶ Then said I, Ah, Lord GOD! behold, the prophets say unto them, Ye shall not see the sword, neither shall ye have famine; but I will give you [4]assured peace in this place.
14 Then the LORD said unto me, The prophets prophesy lies in my name: [n]I sent them not, neither have I commanded them, neither spake unto them: they prophesy unto you a false vision and divination, and a thing of nought, and the deceit of their heart.
15 Therefore thus saith the LORD concerning the prophets that prophesy in my name, and I sent them not, yet they say, Sword and famine shall not be in this land; By sword and famine shall [o]those prophets be consumed.
16 And the people to whom they prophesy shall be [p]cast out in the streets of Je-rụ'sa-lĕm because of the famine and the sword; [q]and they shall have none to bury them, them, their wives, nor their sons, nor their daughters: for I will pour their wickedness upon them.
17 ¶ Therefore thou shalt say this word unto them; [r]Let mine eyes run down with tears night and day, and let them not cease: [s]for the virgin daughter of my people is broken with a great breach, with a very grievous blow.
18 If I go forth into [t]the field, then behold the slain with the sword! and if I enter into the city, then behold them that are sick with famine! yea, both the prophet and the priest [5]go about into a land that they know not.
19 [u]Hast thou utterly rejected Jū'dah? hath thy soul loathed Zī'ŏn? why hast thou smitten us, and *there is* no healing for us? we looked for peace, and *there is* no good; and for the time of healing, and behold trouble!
20 [v]We acknowledge, O LORD, our wickedness, *and* the iniquity of our fathers: for [w]we have sinned against thee.
21 Do not abhor *us,* for thy name's sake, do not disgrace the [x]throne of thy glory: remember, break not thy covenant with us.
22 Are there *any* among the vanities of the Gĕn'tīles that can cause rain? or can the heavens give showers? [y]*art* not thou he, O LORD our God? therefore we will wait upon thee: for thou hast made all these *things.*

15 Then said the LORD unto me, [a]Though Mō'ses and [b]Săm'u-el

---

19 [o]Lev. 26.31
20 [p]ch. 6.22
21 [5]visit upon
22 [q]ch. 16.10
[r]Isa. 47.2; [6]Or, shall be violently taken away
23 [7]taught
25 [s]Job 20.29
[t]ch. 10.14;
26 [u]Lam. 1.8
27 [v]ch. 5.8
[w]Isa. 65.7; [8]after when yet

CHAPTER 14

1 [1]the words of the dearths, or, restraints
2 [a]Isa. 3.26
[b]Ex. 11.6
3 [2]Or, cisterns
[c]Ps. 40.14
[d]2 Sam. 15.30
6 [e]ch. 2.24
7 [f]Ps. 25.11
8 [g]ch. 17.13;
[h]Ps. 46.1
9 [i]Isa. 59.1
[j]Ex. 29.45
[3]thy name is called upon us
10 [k]1 Ki. 17.18
11 [l]Ex. 32.10
12 [m]Prov. 1.28
13 [4]peace of truth
14 [n]Isa. 30.10;
15 [o]ch. 23.15
16 [p]Matt. 15.14
[q]Ps. 79.3
17 [r]Lam. 1.16
[s]ch. 8.21
18 [t]Ezek. 7.15
[5]Or, make merchandise against a land, and men acknowledge it not
19 [u]2 Ki. 17.20;
20 [v]Ezra 9.5;
[w]Dan. 9.8
21 [x]ch. 17.12
22 [y]Isa. 30.23

CHAPTER 15

1 [a]Ex. 32.11
[b]1 Sam. 7.9

stood before me, *yet* my mind *could*
not *be* toward this people: cast *them*
out of my sight, and let them go forth.
2 And it shall come to pass, if they
say unto thee, Whither shall we go
forth? then thou shalt tell them, Thus
saith the LORD; [c]Such as *are* for death,
to death; and such as *are* for the sword,
to the sword; and such as *are* for the
famine, to the famine; and such as *are*
for the captivity, to the captivity.
3 And I will [d]appoint over them four
[1]kinds, saith the LORD: the sword to
slay, and the dogs to tear, and [e]the
fowls of the heaven, and the beasts of
the earth, to devour and destroy.
4 And [2]I will cause them to be [f]re-
moved into all kingdoms of the earth,
because of [g]Ma-năs'seh the son of
Hĕz-e-kī'ah king of Jū'dah, for *that*
which he did in Je-ru'sa-lĕm.
5 For [h]who shall have pity upon
thee, O Je-ru'sa-lĕm? or who shall bemoan thee? or who shall go aside [3]to
ask how thou doest?
6 Thou hast forsaken me, saith the
LORD, thou art gone backward: therefore will I stretch out my hand against
thee, and destroy thee; [i]I am weary
with repenting.
7 And I will fan them with a fan in
the gates of the land; I will bereave
them of [4]children, I will destroy my
people, *since* [j]they return not from
their ways.
8 Their widows are increased to me
above the sand of the seas: I have
brought upon them [5]against the mother
of the young men a spoiler at noonday:
I have caused *him* to fall upon it suddenly, and terrors upon the city.
9 [k]She that hath borne seven languisheth: she hath given up the ghost;
[l]her sun is gone down while *it was* yet
day: she hath been ashamed and confounded: and the residue of them will I
deliver to the sword before their enemies, saith the LORD.
10 ¶ [m]Woe is me, my mother, that
thou hast borne me a man of strife
and a man of contention to the whole
earth! I have neither lent on usury, nor
men have lent to me on usury; *yet* every one of them doth curse me.
11 The LORD said, Verily it shall be
well with thy remnant; verily [6]I will
cause the enemy to entreat thee *well*
in the time of evil and in the time of
affliction.
12 Shall iron break the northern iron
and the steel?
13 Thy substance and thy treasures
will I give to the [n]spoil without price,
and *that* for all thy sins, even in all thy
borders.
14 And I will make *thee* to pass with
thine enemies into a land *which* thou
knowest not: for [o]a fire is kindled in
mine anger, *which* shall burn upon
you.
15 ¶ O LORD, [p]thou knowest: remember me, and visit me, and [q]revenge me
of my persecutors; take me not away
in thy longsuffering: know that [r]for
thy sake I have suffered rebuke.

2 [c]Zech. 11.9
3 [d]Lev. 26.16
[1]families
[e]Deut. 28.26
4 [2]I will give them for a removing
[f]Ezek. 23.46
[g]2 Ki. 21.11
5 [h]Isa. 51.19
[3]to ask of thy peace
6 [i]Hos. 13.14
7 [4]Or, whatsoever is dear
[j]Isa. 9.13; ch. 5.3
8 [5]Or, against the mother city a young man spoiling, etc., or, against the mother and the young men
9 [k]1 Sam. 2.5; Isa. 47.9
[l]Amos 8.9
10 [m]Job 3.1
11 [6]Or, I will intreat the enemy for thee
13 [n]Ps. 44.12; Isa. 52.3; ch. 17.3
14 [o]Deut. 32.22
15 [p]Job 10.7; Ps. 17.3; ch. 12.3; John 21.15-17
[q]ch. 11.20
[r]Ps. 69.7
16 [s]Matt. 5.10-12; 1 Pet. 4.14-16; Ezek. 3.1
[t]Job 23.12
[7]thy name is called upon me
17 [u]Ps. 1.1
18 [v]ch. 30.15
[w]Job 6.15
[8]be not sure
19 [x]Zech. 3.7
[y]Ezek. 22.26
21 [z]Isa. 49.25
CHAPTER 16
2 [a]Gen. 19.14
5 [b]Ps. 78.64; Ezek. 24.17
[1]Or, mourning feast
6 [c]Deut. 14.1
[d]Isa. 22.12
7 [2]Or, break bread for them
[e]Prov. 31.6
9 [f]Isa. 24.7; ch. 7.34; Hos. 2.11; Rev. 18.23

16 Thy words were found, and I did
[s]eat them; and [t]thy word was unto me
the joy and rejoicing of mine heart: for
[7]I am called by thy name, O LORD God
of hosts.
17 [u]I sat not in the assembly of the
mockers, nor rejoiced; I sat alone because of thy hand: for thou hast filled
me with indignation.
18 Why is my [v]pain perpetual, and
my wound incurable, *which* refuseth
to be healed? wilt thou be altogether
unto me as a liar, *and* [w]*as* waters *that*
[8]fail?
19 ¶ Therefore thus saith the LORD,
[x]If thou return, then will I bring thee
again, *and* thou shalt stand before me:
and if thou [y]take forth the precious
from the vile, thou shalt be as my
mouth: let them return unto thee; but
return not thou unto them.
20 And I will make thee unto this
people a fenced brasen wall: and they
shall fight against thee, but they shall
not prevail against thee: for I *am* with
thee to save thee and to deliver thee,
saith the LORD.
21 And I will [z]deliver thee out of the
hand of the wicked, and I will redeem
thee out of the hand of the terrible.

16

The word of the LORD came also
unto me, saying,
2 [a]Thou shalt not take thee a wife,
neither shalt thou have sons or daughters in this place.
3 For thus saith the LORD concerning the sons and concerning the daughters that are born in this place, and concerning their mothers that bare them,
and concerning their fathers that begat
them in this land;
4 They shall die of grievous deaths;
they shall not be lamented; neither
shall they be buried; *but* they shall be
as dung upon the face of the earth: and
they shall be consumed by the sword,
and by famine; and their carcases shall
be meat for the fowls of heaven, and
for the beasts of the earth.
5 For thus saith the LORD, [b]Enter
not into the house of [1]mourning, neither go to lament nor bemoan them:
for I have taken away my peace from
this people, saith the LORD, *even* lovingkindness and mercies.
6 Both the great and the small shall
die in this land: they shall not be buried, neither shall *men* lament for them,
nor [c]cut themselves, nor [d]make themselves bald for them:
7 Neither shall *men* [2]tear *themselves*
for them in mourning, to comfort them
for the dead; neither shall *men* give
them the cup of consolation to [e]drink
for their father or for their mother.
8 Thou shalt not also go into the
house of feasting, to sit with them to
eat and to drink.
9 For thus saith the LORD of hosts,
the God of Is'ra-el; Behold, [f]I will
cause to cease out of this place in your
eyes, and in your days, the voice of
mirth, and the voice of gladness, the
voice of the bridegroom, and the voice
of the bride.

10 ¶ And it shall come to pass, when thou shalt shew this people all these words, and they shall say unto thee, [g]Wherefore hath the LORD pronounced all this great evil against us? or what *is* our iniquity? or what *is* our sin that we have committed against the LORD our God?

11 Then shalt thou say unto them, [h]Because your fathers have forsaken me, saith the LORD, and have walked after other gods, and have served them, and have worshipped them, and have forsaken me, and have not kept my law;

12 And ye have done [i]worse than your fathers; for, behold, ye walk every one after the [3]imagination of his evil heart, that they may not hearken unto me:

13 [j]Therefore will I cast you out of this [k]land into a land that ye know not, *neither* ye nor your fathers; and there shall ye serve other gods day and night; where I will not shew you favour.

14 ¶ [4]Therefore, behold, the days come, saith the LORD, that it shall no more be said, The LORD liveth, that brought up the children of Is'ra-el out of the land of E'gypt;

15 But, The LORD liveth, that brought up the children of Is'ra-el from the land of the north, and from all the lands whither he had driven them: and I will bring them again into their land that I gave unto their fathers.

16 ¶ Behold, I will send for many [l]fishers, saith the LORD, and they shall fish them; and after will I send for many hunters, and they shall hunt them from every mountain, and from every hill, and out of the holes of the rocks.

17 For mine [m]eyes *are* upon all their ways: they are not hid from my face, neither is their iniquity hid from mine eyes.

18 And [n]first I will recompense their iniquity and their sin double; because [o]they have defiled my land, they have filled mine inheritance with the carcases of their detestable and abominable things.

19 O LORD, [p]my strength, and my fortress, and my refuge in the day of affliction, the [q]Gĕn'tīles shall come unto thee from the ends of the earth, and shall say, Surely our fathers have inherited lies, vanity, and *things* [r]wherein *there is* no profit.

20 Shall a man make gods unto himself, and [s]they *are* no gods?

21 Therefore, behold, I will this once cause them to know, I will cause them to know mine hand and my might; and they shall know that my name *is* [5][t]The LORD.

17

The sin of Jū'dah *is* written with a [a]pen of iron, *and* with the [1]point of a diamond: *it is* [b]graven upon the table of their heart, and upon the horns of your altars;

2 Whilst their children remember their altars and their [c]groves by the green trees upon the high hills.

3 O my mountain in the field, [d]I will give thy substance *and* all thy treasures to the spoil, *and* thy high places for sin, throughout all thy borders.

4 And thou, even [2]thyself, shalt discontinue from thine heritage that I gave thee; and I will cause thee to serve thine enemies in [e]the land which thou knowest not: for ye have kindled a fire in mine anger, *which* shall burn for ever.

5 ¶ Thus saith the LORD; [f]Cursed *be* the man that trusteth in man, and maketh flesh his arm, and whose heart departeth from the LORD.

6 For he shall be like the heath in the desert, and [g]shall not see when good cometh; but shall inhabit the parched places in the wilderness, *in* a salt land and not inhabited.

7 [h]Blessed *is* the man that trusteth in the LORD, and whose hope the LORD is.

8 For he shall be as a tree planted by the waters, and *that* spreadeth out her roots by the river, and shall not see when heat cometh, but her leaf shall be green; and shall not be careful in the year of [3]drought, neither shall cease from yielding fruit.

9 ¶ [i]The heart *is* deceitful above all *things*, and desperately wicked: who can know it?

10 I the LORD [j]search the heart, *I* try the reins, [k]even to give every man according to his ways, *and* according to the fruit of his doings.

11 *As* the partridge [4]sitteth *on eggs*, and hatcheth *them* not; *so* he that getteth riches, and not by right, shall leave them in the midst of his days, and at his end shall be [l]a fool.

12 ¶ A glorious high throne from the beginning *is* the place of our sanctuary.

13 O LORD, the hope of Is'ra-el, [m]all that forsake thee shall be ashamed, *and* they that depart from me shall be [n]written in the earth, because they have forsaken the LORD, the fountain of living waters.

14 Heal me, O LORD, and I shall be healed; save me, and I shall be saved: for thou *art* my praise.

15 ¶ Behold, they say unto me, [o]Where *is* the word of the LORD? let it come now.

16 As for me, I have not hastened from *being* a pastor [5]to follow thee: neither have I desired the woeful day; thou knowest: that which came out of my lips was *right* before thee.

17 Be not a terror unto me: thou *art* my hope in the day of evil.

18 Let them be confounded that persecute me, but let not me be confounded: let them be dismayed, but let not me be dismayed: bring upon them the day of evil, and [6]destroy them with double destruction.

19 ¶ Thus said the LORD unto me; Go and stand in the gate of the children of the people, whereby the kings of Jū'dah come in, and by the which they go out, and in all the gates of Je-ru'sa-lĕm;

10 [g]Deut. 29.24; ch. 13.22
11 [h]Judg. 2.12-13; Dan. 9.10-12
12 [i]ch. 7.26; 2 Tim. 3.13 [3]Or, stubbornness
13 [j]Lev. 18.27-28; 2 Chr. 7.20 [k]ch. 15.14
14 [4]Or, Nevertheless
16 [l]Amos 4.2; Hab. 1.15
17 [m]Job 34.21; ch. 32.19
18 [n]Mic. 4.10 [o]Ezek. 43.7
19 [p]Ps. 18.2 [q]Ps. 22.27; Isa. 2.2 [r]Isa. 44.10
20 [s]Isa. 37.19
21 [5]Or, JEHOVAH, Ps. 83.18 [t]Ex. 15.3
CHAPTER 17
1 [a]Job 19.24 [1]nail [b]Prov. 3.3
2 [c]2 Ki. 16.4
3 [d]ch. 15.13
4 [2]in thyself [e]ch. 16.13
5 [f]Isa. 30.1
6 [g]Job 20.17
7 [h]Ps. 2.12
8 [3]Or, restraint
9 [i]Gen. 6.5
10 [j]1 Sam. 16.7; [k]Ps. 62.12
11 [4]Or, gathereth young which she hath not brought forth [l]Luke 12.20
13 [m]Ps. 73.27; [n]Luke 10.20
15 [o]Isa. 5.19
16 [5]after thee
18 [6]break them with a double breach

20 And say unto them, [p]Hear ye the word of the LORD, ye kings of Jū'dah, and all Jū'dah, and all the inhabitants of Je-ru̧'sa-lĕm, that enter in by these gates:

21 Thus saith the LORD; [q]Take heed to yourselves, and bear no burden on the sabbath day, nor bring *it* in by the gates of Je-ru̧'sa-lĕm;

22 Neither carry forth a burden out of your houses on the sabbath day, neither do ye any work, but hallow ye the sabbath day, as I [r]commanded your fathers.

23 But they obeyed not, neither inclined their ear, but made their neck stiff, that they might not hear, nor receive instruction.

24 And it shall come to pass, if ye diligently hearken unto me, saith the LORD, to bring in no burden through the gates of this city on the sabbath day, but hallow the sabbath day, to do no work therein;

25 Then [s]shall there enter into the gates of this city kings and princes sitting upon the throne of Dā'vid, riding in chariots and on horses, they, and their princes, the men of Jū'dah, and the inhabitants of Je-ru̧'sa-lĕm: and this city shall remain for ever.

26 And they shall come from the cities of Jū'dah, and from the places about Je-ru̧'sa-lĕm, and from the land of Bĕn'ja-min, and from [t]the plain, and from the mountains, and from the south, bringing burnt offerings, and sacrifices, and meat offerings, and incense, and bringing [u]sacrifices of praise, unto the house of the LORD.

27 But if ye will not hearken unto me to hallow the sabbath day, and not to bear a burden, even entering in at the gates of Je-ru̧'sa-lĕm on the sabbath day; then [v]will I kindle a fire in the gates thereof, [w]and it shall devour the palaces of Je-ru̧'sa-lĕm, and it shall not be quenched.

18 The word which came to Jĕr-e-mī'ah from the LORD, saying,

2 Arise, and go down to the potter's house, and there I will cause thee to hear my words.

3 Then I went down to the potter's house, and, behold, he wrought a work on the [1]wheels.

4 And the vessel [2]that he made of clay was [a]marred in the hand of the potter: so he [3]made it again another vessel, as seemed good to the potter to make *it*.

5 Then the word of the LORD came to me, saying,

6 O house of Ĭs'ra-el, [b]cannot I do with you as this potter? saith the LORD. Behold, [c]as the clay *is* in the potter's hand, so *are* ye in mine hand, O house of Ĭs'ra-el.

7 *At what* instant I shall speak concerning a nation, and concerning a kingdom, to [d]pluck up, and to pull down, and to destroy *it;*

8 [e]If that nation, against whom I have pronounced, turn from their evil, [f]I will repent of the evil that I thought to do unto them.

9 And *at what* instant I shall speak concerning a nation, and concerning a kingdom, to build and to plant *it;*

10 If it do evil in my sight, that it obey not my voice, then I will repent of the good, wherewith I said I would benefit them.

11 ¶ Now therefore go to, speak to the men of Jū'dah, and to the inhabitants of Je-ru̧'sa-lĕm, saying, Thus saith the LORD; Behold, I frame evil against you, and devise a device against you: [g]return ye now every one from his evil way, and make your ways and your doings good.

12 And they said, There is no hope: but we will walk after our own devices, and we will every one do the imagination of his evil heart.

13 Therefore thus saith the LORD; [h]Ask ye now among the heathen, who hath heard such things: the virgin of Ĭs'ra-el hath done a very horrible thing.

14 Will *a man* leave [4]the snow of Lĕb'a-non *which cometh* from the rock of the field? *or* shall the cold flowing waters that come from another place be forsaken?

15 Because my people hath forgotten [i]me, they have burned incense to [j]vanity, and they have caused them to stumble in their ways *from* the [k]ancient paths, to walk in [l]paths, *in* a way not cast up;

16 To make their land [m]desolate, *and* a perpetual [n]hissing; every one that passeth thereby shall be astonished, and wag his head.

17 [o]I will scatter them [p]as with an east wind before the enemy; I will shew them the back, and not the face, in the day of their calamity.

18 ¶ Then said they, [q]Come, and let us devise devices against Jĕr-e-mī'ah; [r]for the law shall not perish from the priest, nor counsel from the wise, nor the word from the prophet. Come, and let us smite him [5]with the tongue, and let us not give heed to any of his words.

19 Give heed to me, O LORD, and hearken to the voice of them that contend with me.

20 [s]Shall evil be recompensed for good? for [t]they have digged a pit for my soul. Remember that I stood before thee to speak good for them, *and* to turn away thy wrath from them.

21 Therefore deliver up their children to the famine, and [6]pour out their *blood* by the force of the sword; and let their wives be bereaved of their children, and *be* widows; and let their men be put to death; *let* their young men *be* slain by the sword in battle.

22 Let a cry be heard from their houses, when thou shalt bring a troop suddenly upon them: for they have digged a pit to take me, and hid snares for my feet.

23 Yet, LORD, thou knowest all their counsel against me [7]to slay *me:* [u]forgive not their iniquity, neither blot out their sin from thy sight, but let them be

20 [p]Ps. 49.1; ch. 19.3; ch. 22.2; Ezek. 2.7; Ezek. 3.17; Hos. 5.1; Mic. 3.1
21 [q]Num. 15.32; Neh. 13.19
22 [r]Ex. 20.8; Ex. 23.12; Ex. 31.13; Ezek. 20.12
25 [s]Deut. 4.40
26 [t]Zech. 7.7 [u]Ps. 107.22
27 [v]Lam. 4.11; Amos 1.4 [w]2 Ki. 25.9

CHAPTER 18
3 [1]Or, frames, or, seats
4 [2]Or, that he made was marred, as clay in the hand of the potter [a]Rom. 11.15 [3]returned and made
6 [b]Isa. 45.9 [c]Isa. 64.8
7 [d]ch. 1.10
8 [e]Judg. 10.15-16; Luke 13.3-5 [f]Jon. 3.10
11 [g]2 Ki. 17.13; Isa. 1.16-19
13 [h]ch. 2.10; 1 Cor. 5.1
14 [4]Or, my fields for a rock, or for the snow of Lebanon? shall the running waters be forsaken for the strange cold waters?
15 [i]ch. 2.13 [j]Deut. 32.21; ch. 10.15 [k]ch. 6.16 [l]Isa. 53.6
16 [m]ch. 49.13 [n]Deut. 29.24; Mic. 6.16
17 [o]ch. 13.24 [p]Ps. 48.7
18 [q]ch. 11.19; 2 Tim. 4.3 [r]Lev. 10.11; Mal. 2.7 [5]Or, for the tongue
20 [s]Ps. 109.4 [t]Ps. 35.7
21 [6]pour them out
23 [7]for death [u]Neh. 4.5

overthrown before thee; deal *thus* with them in the time of thine anger.

19 Thus saith the LORD, Go and get a potter's earthen bottle, and *take* of the ancients of the people, and of [a]the ancients of the priests;

2 And go forth unto [b]the valley of the son of Hĭn'nom, which *is* by the entry of [1]the east gate, [c]and proclaim there the words that I shall tell thee,

3 And say, Hear ye the word of the LORD, O kings of Jū'dah, and inhabitants of Je-ru̦'sa-lĕm; Thus saith the LORD of hosts, the God of Ĭs'ra-el; Behold, I will bring evil upon this place, the which whosoever heareth, his ears shall tingle.

4 Because they [d]have forsaken me, and have estranged this place, and have burned incense in it unto other gods, whom neither they nor their fathers have known, nor the kings of Jū'dah, and have filled this place with [e]the blood of innocents;

5 They have built also the high places of Bā'al, to burn their sons with fire *for* burnt offerings unto Bā'al, [f]which I commanded not, nor spake *it,* neither came *it* into my mind:

6 Therefore, behold, the days come, saith the LORD, that this place shall no more be called Tō'phet, nor [g]The valley of the son of Hĭn'nom, but The valley of slaughter.

7 And I will make void the counsel of Jū'dah and Je-ru̦'sa-lĕm in this place; [h]and I will cause them to fall by the sword before their enemies, and by the hands of them that seek their lives: and their [i]carcases will I give to be meat for the fowls of the heaven, and for the beasts of the earth.

8 And I will make this city [j]desolate, and an hissing; every one that passeth thereby shall be astonished and hiss because of all the plagues thereof.

9 And I will cause them to eat the [k]flesh of their sons and the flesh of their daughters, and they shall eat every one the flesh of his friend in the siege and straitness, wherewith their enemies, and they that seek their lives, shall straiten them.

10 [l]Then shalt thou break the bottle in the sight of the men that go with thee,

11 And shalt say unto them, Thus saith the LORD of hosts; [m]Even so will I break this people and this city as *one* breaketh a potter's vessel, that cannot [2]be made whole again: and they shall [n]bury *them* in Tō'phet, till *there be* no place to bury.

12 Thus will I do unto this place, saith the LORD, and to the inhabitants thereof, and *even* make this city as Tō'phet:

13 And the houses of Je-ru̦'sa-lĕm, and the houses of the kings of Jū'dah, shall be defiled [o]as the place of Tō'phet, because of all the houses upon whose [p]roofs they have burned incense unto all the host of heaven, and [q]have poured out drink offerings unto other gods.

CHAPTER 19
1 [a]Ezek. 8.11
2 [b]Josh. 15.8; 2 Ki. 23.10; 2 Chr. 28.3
[1]the sun gate
[c]Prov. 1.20
4 [d]Deut. 28.20; Isa. 65.11; ch. 17.13
[e]2 Ki. 21.16
5 [f]Lev. 18.21
6 [g]Josh. 15.8
7 [h]Lev. 26.17; Deut. 28.25; ch. 9.21
[i]Deut. 28.26; Ps. 79.2; ch. 7.33; Rev. 19.18
8 [j]Lev. 26.22; 1 Ki. 9.8; ch. 18.16; Lam. 2.15-16; Zeph. 2.15
9 [k]Lev. 26.29; Deut. 28.53; Lam. 4.10
10 [l]ch. 51.63
11 [m]Ps. 2.9; Lam. 4.2
[2]be healed
[n]ch. 7.32
13 [o]2 Ki. 23.10
[p]ch. 32.29; Zeph. 1.5
[q]ch. 7.18
14 [r]2 Chr. 20.5
15 [s]2 Chr. 36.16-17; Acts 7.51-52

CHAPTER 20
1 [a]1 Chr. 24.14
3 [1]That is, Fear round about
4 [b]Job 18.11; ch. 46.5
5 [c]2 Ki. 20.17; ch. 3.24
[2]Or, wealth
6 [d]ch. 14.13-14; ch. 28.15
7 [3]Or, enticed
[e]ch. 1.6-7
[f]Job 12.4; Lam. 3.14
8 [g]ch. 6.7
9 [h]1 Ki. 19.10; Ps. 39.3
[i]Job 32.18-19-20; Acts 18.5
10 [j]Ps. 31.13
[4]Every man of my peace
11 [k]Isa. 41.13; Rom. 8.31

14 Then came Jĕr-e-mī'ah from Tō'phet, whither the LORD had sent him to prophesy; and he stood in [r]the court of the LORD'S house; and said to all the people,

15 Thus saith the LORD of hosts, the God of Ĭs'ra-el; Behold, I will bring upon this city and upon all her towns all the evil that I have pronounced against it, because they [s]have hardened their necks, that they might not hear my words.

20 Now Păsh'ŭr the son of [a]Ĭm'mēr the priest, who *was* also chief governor in the house of the LORD, heard that Jĕr-e-mī'ah prophesied these things.

2 Then Păsh'ŭr smote Jĕr-e-mī'ah the prophet, and put him in the stocks that *were* in the high gate of Bĕn'ja-min, which *was* by the house of the LORD.

3 And it came to pass on the morrow, that Păsh'ŭr brought forth Jĕr-e-mī'ah out of the stocks. Then said Jĕr-e-mī'ah unto him, The LORD hath not called thy name Păsh'ŭr, but [1]Mā'gôr–mĭs'sa-bĭb.

4 For thus saith the LORD, Behold, I will make thee [b]a terror to thyself, and to all thy friends: and they shall fall by the sword of their enemies, and thine eyes shall behold *it:* and I will give all Jū'dah into the hand of the king of Băb'ȳ-lon, and he shall carry them captive into Băb'ȳ-lon, and shall slay them with the sword.

5 Moreover I [c]will deliver all the [2]strength of this city, and all the labours thereof, and all the precious things thereof, and all the treasures of the kings of Jū'dah will I give into the hand of their enemies, which shall spoil them, and take them, and carry them to Băb'ȳ-lon.

6 And thou, Păsh'ŭr, and all that dwell in thine house shall go into captivity: and thou shalt come to Băb'ȳ-lon, and there thou shalt die, and shalt be buried there, thou, and all thy friends, to whom thou hast [d]prophesied lies.

7 ¶ O LORD, thou hast deceived me, and I was [3]deceived: [e]thou art stronger than I, and hast prevailed: [f]I am in derision daily, every one mocketh me.

8 For since I spake, I cried out, [g]I cried violence and spoil; because the word of the LORD was made a reproach unto me, and a derision, daily.

9 Then I said, I will not make mention of him, nor speak any more in his name. But *his word* was in mine heart as a [h]burning fire shut up in my bones, and I was weary with forbearing, and [i]I could not *stay.*

10 ¶ [j]For I heard the defaming of many, fear on every side. Report, *say they,* and we will report it. [4]All my familiars watched for my halting, *saying,* Peradventure he will be enticed, and we shall prevail against him, and we shall take our revenge on him.

11 But [k]the LORD *is* with me as a mighty terrible one: therefore my

persecutors shall stumble, and they
shall not [l]prevail: they shall be
greatly ashamed; for they shall not
prosper: *their* everlasting confusion
shall never be forgotten.
12 But, O LORD of hosts, that [m]triest
the righteous, *and* seest the reins and
the heart, [n]let me see thy vengeance
on them: for unto thee have I opened
my cause.
13 Sing unto the LORD, praise ye the
LORD: for [o]he hath delivered the soul
of the poor from the hand of evildoers.
14 ¶ [p]Cursed *be* the day wherein I
was born: let not the day wherein my
mother bare me be blessed.
15 Cursed *be* the man who brought
tidings to my father, saying, A man
child is born unto thee; making him
very glad.
16 And let that man be as the cities
which the LORD [q]overthrew, and repented not: and let him [r]hear the cry
in the morning, and the shouting at
noontide;
17 [s]Because he slew me not from
the womb; or that my mother might
have been my grave, and her womb *to
be* always great *with me*.
18 [t]Wherefore came I forth out of
the womb to [u]see labour and sorrow,
that my days should be consumed with
shame?

21 The word which came unto Jĕr-
e-mī'ah from the LORD, when
king Zĕd-e-kī'ah sent unto him [a]Păsh'-
ŭr the son of Mĕl-chī'ah, and [b]Zĕph-a-
nī'ah the son of Mā-a-sē'iah the priest,
saying,
2 [c]Inquire, I pray thee, of the LORD
for us; for Neb-u-chad-rez'zar king of
Băb'ȳ-lon maketh war against us; if so
be that the LORD will deal with us according to all his wondrous works,
that he may go up from us.
3 ¶ Then said Jĕr-e-mī'ah unto them,
Thus shall ye say to Zĕd-e-kī'ah:
4 Thus saith the LORD God of Ĭs'ra-
el; Behold, I will turn back the weapons of war that *are* in your hands,
wherewith ye fight against the king of
Băb'ȳ-lon, and *against* the Chăl-dē'-
ans, which besiege you without the
walls, and [d]I will assemble them into
the midst of this city.
5 And I myself will fight against you
with an [e]outstretched hand and with a
strong arm, even in anger, and in fury,
and in great wrath.
6 And I will smite the inhabitants of
this city, both man and beast: they
shall die of a great pestilence.
7 And afterward, saith the LORD, [f]I
will deliver Zĕd-e-kī'ah king of Jū'dah,
and his servants, and the people, and
such as are left in this city from the
pestilence, from the sword, and from
the famine, into the hand of Nĕb-u-
chăd-rĕz'zar king of Băb'ȳ-lon, and
into the hand of their enemies, and into
the hand of those that seek their life:
and he shall smite them with the edge
of the sword; [g]he shall not spare them,
neither have pity, nor have mercy.
8 ¶ And unto this people thou shalt
say, Thus saith the LORD; Behold, [h]I
set before you the way of life, and the
way of death.
9 He that [i]abideth in this city shall
die by the sword, and by the famine,
and by the pestilence: but he that goeth
out, and falleth to the Chăl-dē'ans that
besiege you, he shall live, and [j]his life
shall be unto him for a prey.
10 For I have [k]set my face against
this city for evil, and not for good, saith
the LORD: [l]it shall be given into the
hand of the king of Băb'ȳ-lon, and he
shall [m]burn it with fire.
11 ¶ And touching the house of the
king of Jū'dah, *say*, Hear ye the word
of the LORD;
12 O house of Dā'vid, thus saith the
LORD; [1]Execute judgment [n]in the morning, and deliver *him that is* spoiled out
of the hand of the oppressor, lest my
fury go out like fire, and burn that
none can quench *it*, because of the evil
of your doings.
13 Behold, [o]I *am* against thee, O [2]in-
habitant of the valley, *and* rock of the
plain, saith the LORD; which say, [p]Who
shall come down against us? or who
shall enter into our habitations?
14 But I will [3]punish you according
to the [q]fruit of your doings, saith the
LORD: and I will kindle a fire in the
forest thereof, and [r]it shall devour all
things round about it.

22 Thus saith the LORD; Go down to
the house of the king of Jū'dah,
and speak there this word,
2 And say, Hear the word of the
LORD, O king of Jū'dah, that sittest
upon the throne of Dā'vid, thou, and
thy servants, and thy people that enter
in by these gates:
3 Thus saith the LORD; [a]Execute ye
judgment and righteousness, and deliver the spoiled out of the hand of the
oppressor: and do no wrong, do no violence to the stranger, the fatherless,
nor the widow, neither shed innocent
blood in this place.
4 For if ye do this thing indeed,
[b]then shall there enter in by the gates
of this house kings sitting [1]upon the
throne of Dā'vid, riding in chariots and
on horses, he, and his servants, and his
people.
5 But if ye will not hear these words,
[c]I swear by myself, saith the LORD, that
this house shall become a desolation.
6 For thus saith the LORD unto the
king's house of Jū'dah; Thou *art* Gĭl'e-
ăd unto me, *and* the head of Lĕb'a-
non: *yet* surely I will make thee [d]a
wilderness, *and* cities *which* are not
inhabited.
7 And I will prepare destroyers
against thee, every one with his weapons: and they shall cut down [e]thy
choice cedars, [f]and cast *them* into the
fire.
8 And many nations shall pass by
this city, and they shall say every man
to his neighbour, [g]Wherefore hath the
LORD done thus unto this great city?

[l]ch. 15.20; ch. 17.18
12 [m]ch. 11.20; ch. 17.10
[n]Ps. 54.7; Ps. 59.10; Ps. 109.6-20; ch. 11.20; ch. 12.3; ch. 17.18
13 [o]Ps. 35.9; Jas. 2.5-6
14 [p]Job 3.3; ch. 15.10
16 [q]Gen. 19.25
[r]ch. 18.22
17 [s]Job 3.10
18 [t]Job 3.20
[u]Lam. 3.1

CHAPTER 21
1 [a]ch. 38.1
[b]2 Ki. 25.18; ch. 29.25
2 [c]Ex. 9.28
4 [d]Isa. 13.4
5 [e]Ex. 6.6
7 [f]ch. 37.17; ch. 39.5
[g]Deut. 28.50; 2 Chr. 36.17
8 [h]Deut. 30.19; Isa. 1.19
9 [i]ch. 38.2
[j]ch. 39.18
10 [k]Lev. 17.10; ch. 44.11-27; Amos 9.4
[l]ch. 38.3
[m]ch. 34.2; ch. 37.10
12 [1]Judge
[n]Ps. 101.8
13 [o]Ezek. 13.8
[2]inhabitress
[p]ch. 49.4; Lam. 4.12; Obad. 3-4
14 [3]visit upon
[q]Prov. 1.31; Isa. 3.10
[r]2 Chr. 36.19; ch. 52.13

CHAPTER 22
3 [a]Isa. 58.6-7; ch. 7.23; Matt. 23.23
4 [b]ch. 17.25
[1]for David upon his throne
5 [c]Num. 23.19; Heb. 3.18
6 [d]Mic. 3.12
7 [e]Isa. 37.24
[f]ch. 21.14
8 [g]Deut. 29.24; 1 Ki. 9.8

9 Then they shall answer, [h]Because they have forsaken the covenant of the LORD their God, and worshipped other gods, and served them.

10 ¶ Weep ye not for [i]the dead, neither bemoan him: *but* weep sore for him that goeth away: for he shall return no more, nor see his native country.

11 For thus saith the LORD touching [j]Shăl'lum the son of Jo-sī'ah king of Jū'dah, which reigned instead of Jo-sī'ah his father, which went forth out of this place; He shall not return thither any more:

12 But he shall die in the place whither they have led him captive, and shall see this land no more.

13 ¶ Woe unto him that buildeth his house by unrighteousness, and his chambers by wrong; [k]*that* useth his neighbour's service without wages, and giveth him not for his work;

14 That saith, I will build me a wide house and [2]large chambers, and cutteth him out [3]windows; and *it is* cieled with cedar, and painted with vermilion.

15 Shalt thou reign, because thou closest *thyself* in cedar? did not thy father eat and drink, and do judgment and justice, *and* then [l]*it was* well with him?

16 He judged the cause of the poor and needy; then *it was* well *with him:* [m]*was* not this to know me? saith the LORD.

17 [n]But thine eyes and thine heart *are* not but for thy covetousness, and for to shed innocent blood, and for oppression, and for [4]violence, to do *it*.

18 Therefore thus saith the LORD concerning Je-hoi'a-kim the son of Jo-sī'ah king of Jū'dah; They shall not lament for him, *saying*, [o]Ah my brother! or, Ah sister! they shall not lament for him, *saying*, Ah lord! or, Ah his glory!

19 [p]He shall be buried with the burial of an ass, drawn and cast forth beyond the gates of Je-ru'sa-lĕm.

20 ¶ Go up to Lĕb'a-non, and cry; and lift up thy voice in Bā'shăn, and cry from the passages: for all thy lovers are destroyed.

21 I spake unto thee in thy [5]prosperity; *but* thou saidst, I will not hear. [q]This *hath been* thy manner from thy youth, that thou obeyedst not my voice.

22 The wind shall eat up all [r]thy pastors, and thy lovers shall go into captivity: surely then shalt thou be ashamed and confounded for all thy wickedness.

23 O [6]inhabitant of Lĕb'a-non, that makest thy nest in the cedars, how gracious shalt thou be when pangs come upon thee, [s]the pain as of a woman in travail!

24 *As* I live, saith the LORD, [t]though Co-nī'ah the son of Je-hoi'a-kim king of Jū'dah [u]were the signet upon my right hand, yet would I pluck thee thence;

25 [v]And I will give thee into the hand of them that seek thy life, and into the hand *of them* whose face thou fearest, even into the hand of Nĕb-u-chăd-rĕz'zar king of Băb'ȳ-lon, and into the hand of the Chăl-dē'ans.

26 [w]And I will cast thee out, and thy mother that bare thee, into another country, where ye were not born; and there shall ye die.

27 But to the land whereunto they [7]desire to return, thither shall they not return.

28 *Is* this man Co-nī'ah a despised broken idol? *is he* [x]a vessel wherein *is* no pleasure? wherefore are they cast out, he and his seed, and are cast into a land which they know not?

29 O earth, earth, earth, hear the word of the LORD.

30 Thus saith the LORD, Write ye this man [y]childless, a man *that* shall not prosper in his days: for no man of his seed shall prosper, sitting upon the throne of Dā'vid, and ruling any more in Jū'dah.

23 Woe [a]be unto the pastors that destroy and scatter the sheep of my pasture! saith the LORD.

2 Therefore thus saith the LORD God of Ĭs'ra-el against the pastors that feed my people; Ye have scattered my flock, and driven them away, and have not visited them: [b]behold, I will visit upon you the evil of your doings, saith the LORD.

3 And [c]I will gather the remnant of my flock out of all countries whither I have driven them, and will bring them again to their folds; and they shall be fruitful and increase.

4 And I will set up shepherds over them which shall feed them: and they shall fear no more, nor be dismayed, neither shall they be lacking, saith the LORD.

5 ¶ Behold, [d]the days come, saith the LORD, that I will raise unto Dā'vid a righteous Branch, and a King shall reign and prosper, [e]and shall execute judgment and justice in the earth.

6 [f]In his days Jū'dah shall be saved, and Ĭs'ra-el shall dwell safely: and [g]this *is* his name whereby he shall be called, [1]THE LORD OUR RIGHTEOUSNESS.

7 Therefore, behold, the days come, saith the LORD, that they shall no more say, The LORD liveth, which brought up the children of Ĭs'ra-el out of the land of Ē'gypt;

8 But, The LORD liveth, which brought up and which led the seed of the house of Ĭs'ra-el out of the north country, [h]and from all countries whither I had driven them; and they shall dwell in their own land.

9 ¶ Mine heart within me is broken because of the prophets; all [i]my bones shake; I am like a drunken man, and like a man whom wine hath overcome, because of the LORD, and because of the words of his holiness.

10 For the land is full of adulterers; for [j]because of [2]swearing the land mourneth; the pleasant places of the wilderness are dried up, and their [3]course is evil, and their force *is* not right.

9 [h]2 Ki. 22.17; 2 Chr. 34.25
10 [i]2 Ki. 22.20; Isa. 57.1-21
11 [j]1 Chr. 3.15; 2 Ki. 23.30
13 [k]Lev. 19.13; Mic. 3.10; Hab. 2.9; Jas. 5.4
14 [2]throughaired [3]Or, my windows
15 [l]Ps. 128.2; Isa. 3.10
16 [m]1 Chr. 28.9; Ps. 9.10; John 8.19; Tit. 1.16; Jas. 1.22; 1 John 2.3
17 [n]Ezek. 19.6 [4]Or, incursion
18 [o]1 Ki. 13.30
19 [p]2 Chr. 36.6
21 [5]prosperities [q]ch. 3.25
22 [r]ch. 23.1
23 [6]inhabitress [s]ch. 6.24
24 [t]2 Ki. 24.6; 1 Chr. 3.16 [u]Song 8.6; Hag. 2.23
25 [v]ch. 34.20
26 [w]2 Ki. 24.15
27 [7]lift up their mind
28 [x]Ps. 31.12; ch. 48.38
30 [y]1 Chr. 3.16; Matt. 1.12

CHAPTER 23

1 [a]Ezek. 34.2; Zech. 11.5-7-15-17; John 10.10-12
2 [b]Ex. 32.34
3 [c]ch. 32.37
5 [d]Isa. 4.2; Dan. 9.24 [e]Ps. 72.2; Isa. 32.1
6 [f]Deut. 33.28; Zech. 14.11 [g]ch. 33.16; 1 Cor. 1.30 [1]Jehovah-tsidkenu
8 [h]Isa. 43.5
9 [i]Hab. 3.16
10 [j]Hos. 4.2 [2]Or, cursing [3]Or, violence

11 For [k]both prophet and priest are profane; yea, [l]in my house have I found their wickedness, saith the LORD.

12 [m]Wherefore their way shall be unto them as slippery *ways* in the darkness: they shall be driven on, and fall therein: for I will bring evil upon them, *even* the year of their visitation, saith the LORD.

13 And I have seen [4]folly in the prophets of Sa-mā'rĭ-ȧ; [n]they prophesied in Bā'al, and [o]caused my people Is'ra-el to err.

14 I have seen also in the prophets of Je-ru̦'sa-lĕm [5]an horrible thing: they commit adultery, and walk in lies: they [p]strengthen also the hands of evildoers, that none doth return from his wickedness: they are all of them unto me as [q]Sŏd'om, and the inhabitants thereof as Go-mŏr'rah.

15 Therefore thus saith the LORD of hosts concerning the prophets; Behold, I will feed them with wormwood, and make them drink the water of gall: for from the prophets of Je-ru̦'sa-lĕm is [6]profaneness gone forth into all the land.

16 Thus saith the LORD of hosts, [r]Hearken not unto the words of the prophets that prophesy unto you: they make you vain: they speak a vision of their own heart, *and* not out of the mouth of the LORD.

17 They say still unto them that despise me, The LORD hath said, [s]Ye shall have peace; and they say unto every one that walketh after the [7]imagination of his own heart, [t]No evil shall come upon you.

18 For [u]who hath stood in the [8]counsel of the LORD, and hath perceived and heard his word? who hath marked his word, and heard *it?*

19 Behold, a [v]whirlwind of the LORD is gone forth in fury, even a grievous whirlwind: it shall fall grievously upon the head of the wicked.

20 The [w]anger of the LORD shall not return, until he have executed, and till he have performed the thoughts of his heart: [x]in the latter days ye shall consider it perfectly.

21 I have not sent these prophets, yet they ran: I have not spoken to them, yet they prophesied.

22 But if they had stood in my counsel, and had caused my people to hear my words, then they should have turned them from their evil way, and from the evil of their doings.

23 [y]*Am* I a God at hand, saith the LORD, and not a God afar off?

24 Can any [z]hide himself in secret places that I shall not see him? saith the LORD. [a]Do not I fill heaven and earth? saith the LORD.

25 I have [b]heard what the prophets said, that prophesy lies in my name, saying, I have dreamed, I have dreamed.

26 How long shall *this* be in the heart of the prophets that prophesy lies? yea, *they are* prophets of the deceit of their own heart;

27 Which think to [c]cause my people to forget my name by their dreams which they tell every man to his neighbour, [d]as their fathers have forgotten my name for Bā'al.

28 The prophet [9]that hath a dream, let him tell a dream; and he that hath my word, let him speak my [e]word faithfully. What *is* the chaff to the wheat? saith the LORD.

29 *Is* not my word like as a fire? saith the LORD; and like a hammer *that* breaketh the rock in pieces?

30 Therefore, behold, [f]I *am* against the prophets, saith the LORD, that steal my words every one from his neighbour.

31 Behold, I *am* against the prophets, saith the LORD, [10]that use their tongues, and say, He saith.

32 Behold, I *am* against them that prophesy false dreams, saith the LORD, and do tell them, and cause my people to err by their lies, and by [g]their lightness; yet I sent them not, nor commanded them: therefore they shall not profit this people at all, saith the LORD.

33 ¶ And when this people, or the prophet, or a priest, shall ask thee, saying, What *is* [h]the burden of the LORD? thou shalt then say unto them, What burden? I will even forsake you, saith the LORD.

34 And *as for* the prophet, and the priest, and the people, that shall say, The burden of the LORD, I will even [11]punish that man and his house.

35 Thus shall ye say every one to his neighbour, and every one to his brother, What hath the LORD answered? and, What hath the LORD spoken?

36 And the burden of the LORD shall ye mention no more: for every [i]man's word shall be his burden; for ye [j]have perverted the words of the living God, of the LORD of hosts our God.

37 Thus shalt thou say to the prophet, What hath the LORD answered thee? and, What hath the LORD spoken?

38 But since ye say, The burden of the LORD; therefore thus saith the LORD; Because ye say this word, The burden of the LORD, and I have sent unto you, saying, Ye shall not say, The burden of the LORD;

39 Therefore, behold, I, even I, [k]will utterly forget you, and I will forsake you, and the city that I gave you and your fathers, *and cast you* out of my presence:

40 And I will bring [l]an everlasting reproach upon you, and a perpetual shame, which shall not be forgotten.

24 The [a]LORD shewed me, and, behold, two baskets of figs *were* set before the temple of the LORD, after that Nĕb-u-chăd-rĕz'zar [b]king of Băb'ȳ-lon had carried away captive [c]Jĕc-o-nī'ah the son of Je-hoi'a-kim king of Jū'dah, and the princes of Jū'dah, with the carpenters and smiths, from Je-ru̦'sa-lĕm, and had brought them to Băb'ȳ-lon.

2 One basket *had* very good figs, *even* like the figs *that are* first ripe:

11 [k]Zeph. 3.4 [l]Ezek. 8.11
12 [m]Prov. 4.19
13 [4]unsavoury, or, an absurd thing [n]1 Ki. 18.18 [o]Isa. 9.16
14 [5]Or, filthiness [p]Ezek. 13.22 [q]Isa. 1.9
15 [6]Or, hypocrisy
16 [r]Prov. 19.27; Matt. 7.15
17 [s]Zech. 10.2 [7]Or, stubbornness [t]Mic. 3.11
18 [u]Job 15.8; 1 Cor. 2.16 [8]Or, secret
19 [v]ch. 25.32
20 [w]2 Ki. 23.26-27 [x]Gen. 49.1
23 [y]1 Ki. 20.23-28; Ps. 113.6
24 [z]Ps. 139.7; Prov. 15.11; Amos 9.2; Heb. 4.13 [a]1 Ki. 8.27; 2 Chr. 2.6; Ps. 11.4; Isa. 66.1
25 [b]Heb. 4.13
27 [c]Deut. 13.1; Acts 13.8; 2 Tim. 3.6-8 [d]Judg. 3.7
28 [9]with whom is [e]2 Cor. 2.17; 1 Pet. 4.10
30 [f]Deut. 18.20; ch. 14.14-15
31 [10]Or, that smooth their tongues
32 [g]Zeph. 3.4
33 [h]Isa. 13.1; ch. 17.15; Mal. 1.1
34 [11]visit upon
36 [i]Matt. 12.36 [j]Acts 13.10-11; Gal. 1.7-8
39 [k]Deut. 31.17-18; Hos. 4.6
40 [l]ch. 20.11; Dan. 9.16

CHAPTER 24
1 [a]Amos 7.1 [b]2 Ki. 24.12; 2 Chr. 36.10 [c]ch. 22.24

and the other basket *had* very naughty figs, which could not be eaten, [1]they were so bad.

3 Then said the LORD unto me, What seest thou, Jĕr-e-mī'ah? And I said, Figs; the good figs, very good; and the evil, very evil, that cannot be eaten, they are so evil.

4 ¶ Again the word of the LORD came unto me, saying,

5 Thus saith the LORD, the God of Ĭs'ra-el; Like these good figs, so [d]will I acknowledge [2]them that are carried away captive of Jū'dah, whom I have sent out of this place into the land of the Chăl-dē'ans for *their* good.

6 For I will set mine eyes upon them for good, and [e]I will bring them again to this land: and [f]I will build them, and not pull *them* down; and I will plant them, and not pluck *them* up.

7 And I will give them [g]an heart to know me, that I *am* the LORD: and they shall be [h]my people, and I will be their God: for they shall return unto me [i]with their whole heart.

8 ¶ And as the evil [j]figs, which cannot be eaten, they are so evil; surely thus saith the LORD, So will I give Zĕd-e-kī'ah the king of Jū'dah, and his princes, and the residue of Je-ru̯'sa-lĕm, that remain in this land, and [k]them that dwell in the land of Ē'gypt:

9 And I will deliver them [3]to be removed into all the kingdoms of the earth for *their* hurt, [l]*to be* a reproach and a proverb, a taunt and a curse, in all places whither I shall drive them.

10 And I will send the sword, the famine, and the pestilence, among them, till they be consumed from off the land that I gave unto them and to their fathers.

25 The word that came to Jĕr-e-mī'ah concerning all the people of Jū'dah [a]in the fourth year of Je-hoi'a-kim the son of Jo-sī'ah king of Jū'dah, that *was* the first year of Nĕb-u-chăd-rĕz'zar king of Băb'y̆-lon;

2 The which Jĕr-e-mī'ah the prophet spake unto all the people of Jū'dah, and to all the inhabitants of Je-ru̯'sa-lĕm, saying,

3 [b]From the thirteenth year of Jo-sī'ah the son of Ā'mon king of Jū'dah, even unto this day, that *is* the three and twentieth year, the word of the LORD hath come unto me, and I have spoken unto you, rising early and speaking; but ye have not hearkened.

4 And the LORD hath sent unto you all his [c]servants the prophets, rising early and sending *them;* but ye have not hearkened, nor inclined your ear to hear.

5 They said, [d]Turn ye again now every one from his evil way, and from the evil of your doings, and dwell in the land that the LORD hath given unto you and to your fathers for ever and ever:

6 And go not after other gods to serve them, and to worship them, and provoke me not to anger with the works of your hands; and I will do you no hurt.

2 [1]for badness
5 [d]Zech. 13.9; Heb. 2.11
[2]the captivity
6 [e]ch. 12.15; ch. 23.3; Ezek. 36.24
[f]ch. 32.41; ch. 33.7
7 [g]Deut. 30.6; Ezek. 11.19
[h]Isa. 51.16; ch. 7.23; ch. 30.22; Ezek. 14.11; Zech. 8.8
[i]ch. 29.13; Ps. 119.2
8 [j]ch. 29.17
[k]ch. 43
9 [3]for removing, or, vexation
[l]Ps. 44.13

CHAPTER 25

1 [a]2 Ki. 24.1-2; ch. 36.1; ch. 46.2; Dan. 1.1
3 [b]ch. 1.2
4 [c]2 Chr. 36.15; ch. 7.13-25; ch. 11.7; ch. 26.5; ch. 29.19
5 [d]2 Ki. 17.13; Ezek. 18.30; Luke 13.3-5
7 [e]ch. 7.19; ch. 32.30
9 [f]ch. 1.15
[g]ch. 40.2
[h]ch. 18.16
10 [1]I will cause to perish from them
[i]Rev. 18.23
12 [j]ch. 29.10; Dan. 9.2
[2]Beginning cir. 606, 2 Ki. 24.1; ending cir. 536, Ezra 1.1
[3]visit upon
[k]Isa. 13.19
14 [l]ch. 50.41
[m]ch. 27.7
[n]ch. 50.29; ch. 51.6-24
15 [o]Job 21.20; Ps. 11.6; Ps. 75.8; Isa. 51.17-22; Rev. 14.10
16 [p]Nah. 3.11
18 [q]Ps. 60.3; Ezek. 9.8; Amos 2.5
19 [r]ch. 46.2
20 [s]Job 1.1
[t]Isa. 20.1
22 [4]Or, region by the sea side

7 Yet ye have not hearkened unto me, saith the LORD; that ye might [e]provoke me to anger with the works of your hands to your own hurt.

8 ¶ Therefore thus saith the LORD of hosts; Because ye have not heard my words,

9 Behold, I will send and take [f]all the families of the north, saith the LORD, and Nĕb-u-chăd-rĕz'zar the king of Băb'y̆-lon, [g]my servant, and will bring them against this land, and against the inhabitants thereof, and against all these nations round about, and will utterly destroy them, and [h]make them an astonishment, and an hissing, and perpetual desolations.

10 Moreover [1]I will take from them the [i]voice of mirth, and the voice of gladness, the voice of the bridegroom, and the voice of the bride, the sound of the millstones, and the light of the candle.

11 And this whole land shall be a desolation, *and* an astonishment; and these nations shall serve the king of Băb'y̆-lon seventy years.

12 ¶ And [j]it shall come to pass, when [2]seventy years are accomplished, *that* I will [3]punish the king of Băb'y̆-lon, and that nation, saith the LORD, for their iniquity, and the land of the Chăl-dē'ans, [k]and will make it perpetual desolations.

13 And I will bring upon that land all my words which I have pronounced against it, *even* all that is written in this book, which Jĕr-e-mī'ah hath prophesied against all the nations.

14 For many nations [l]and great kings shall [m]serve themselves of them also: [n]and I will recompense them according to their deeds, and according to the works of their own hands.

15 ¶ For thus saith the LORD God of Ĭs'ra-el unto me; Take the [o]wine cup of this fury at my hand, and cause all the nations, to whom I send thee, to drink it.

16 And [p]they shall drink, and be moved, and be mad, because of the sword that I will send among them.

17 Then took I the cup at the LORD'S hand, and made all the nations to drink, unto whom the LORD had sent me:

18 *To wit,* [q]Je-ru̯'sa-lĕm, and the cities of Jū'dah, and the kings thereof, and the princes thereof, to make them a desolation, an astonishment, an hissing, and a curse; as *it is* this day;

19 [r]Phā'raōh king of Ē'gypt, and his servants, and his princes, and all his people;

20 And all the mingled people, and all the kings of [s]the land of Ŭz, and all the kings of the land of the Phĭ-lĭs'tĭnes, and Ăsh'ke-lŏn, and Ăz'zah, and Ĕk'rŏn, and [t]the remnant of Ăsh'dŏd,

21 Ē'dom, and Mō'ab, and the children of Ăm'mŏn,

22 And all the kings of Ty̆'rus, and all the kings of Zī'dŏn, and the kings of the [4]isles which *are* beyond the sea,

23 Dē'dan, and Tē'mȧ, and Bŭz, and
all [5]*that are* in the utmost corners,
24 And [u]all the kings of A-rā'bĭ-ȧ,
and all the kings of the [v]mingled people that dwell in the desert,
25 And all the kings of Zĭm'rī, and
all the kings of Ē'lăm, and all the kings
of the Mēdes,
26 And all the kings of the north, far
and near, one with another, and all the
kingdoms of the world, which *are* upon
the face of the earth: [w]and the king of
Shē'shăch shall drink after them.
27 Therefore thou shalt say unto
them, Thus saith the LORD of hosts, the
God of Ĭs'ra-el; [x]Drink ye, and be
drunken, and spue, and fall, and rise
no more, because of the sword which I
will send among you.
28 And it shall be, if they refuse to
take the cup at thine hand to drink,
then shalt thou say unto them, Thus
saith the LORD of hosts; Ye shall certainly drink.
29 For, lo, [y]I begin to bring evil on
the city [6]which is called by my name,
and should ye be utterly unpunished?
Ye shall not be unpunished: for [z]I will
call for a sword upon all the inhabitants of the earth, saith the LORD of
hosts.
30 Therefore prophesy thou against
them all these words, and say unto
them, The LORD shall [a]roar from on
high, and utter his voice from his holy
habitation; he shall mightily roar upon
[b]his habitation; he shall give a shout,
as they that tread *the grapes*, against
all the inhabitants of the earth.
31 A noise shall come *even* to the
ends of the earth; for the LORD hath [c]a
controversy with the nations, [d]he will
plead with all flesh; he will give them
that are wicked to the sword, saith the
LORD.
32 Thus saith the LORD of hosts, Behold, evil shall go forth from nation to
nation, and a great whirlwind shall be
raised up from the coasts of the earth.
33 [e]And the slain of the LORD shall
be at that day from *one* end of the earth
even unto the *other* end of the earth:
they shall not be lamented, neither
gathered, nor buried; they shall be
dung upon the ground.
34 ¶ Howl, ye shepherds, and cry;
and wallow yourselves *in the ashes*, ye
principal of the flock: for [7]the days of
your slaughter and of your dispersions
are accomplished; and ye shall fall like
[8]a pleasant vessel.
35 And [9]the shepherds shall have no
way to flee, nor the principal of the
flock to escape.
36 A voice of the cry of the shepherds, and an howling of the principal
of the flock, *shall be heard:* for the
LORD hath spoiled their pasture.
37 And the peaceable habitations
are cut down because of the fierce [f]an-
ger of the LORD.
38 He hath forsaken his covert, as
the lion: for their land is [10]desolate because of the fierceness of the oppressor, and because of his fierce anger.

26
In the beginning of the reign of
Je-hoi'a-kim the son of Jo-sī'ah
king of Jū'dah came this word from
the LORD, saying,
2 Thus saith the LORD; Stand in [a]the
court of the LORD'S house, and speak
unto all the cities of Jū'dah, which
[b]come to worship in the LORD'S house,
[c]all the words that I command thee
to speak unto them; [d]diminish not a
word:
3 [e]If so be they will hearken, and
turn every man from his evil way, that
I may [f]repent me of the evil, which I
purpose to do unto them because of the
evil of their doings.
4 And thou shalt say unto them,
Thus saith the LORD; [g]If ye will not
hearken to me, to walk in my law,
which I have set before you,
5 To hearken to the words of my servants the prophets, [h]whom I sent unto
you, both rising up early, and sending
them, but ye have not hearkened;
6 Then will I make this house like
[i]Shī'lōh, and will make this city [j]a
curse to all the nations of the earth.
7 So the priests and the prophets
and all the people heard Jĕr-e-mī'ah
speaking these words in the house of
the LORD.
8 ¶ Now it came to pass, when Jĕr-e-
mī'ah had made an end of speaking all
that the LORD had commanded *him* to
speak unto all the people, that [k]the
priests and the prophets and all the
people took him, saying, Thou shalt
surely die.
9 Why hast thou prophesied in the
name of the LORD, saying, This house
shall be like Shī'lōh, and this city shall
be desolate without an inhabitant? And
all the people were gathered against
Jĕr-e-mī'ah in the house of the LORD.
10 ¶ When the princes of Jū'dah
heard these things, then they came up
from the king's house unto the house
of the LORD, and sat down [1]in the entry
of the [l]new gate of the LORD'S *house*.
11 Then spake the priests and the
prophets unto the princes and to all the
people, saying, [2]This man *is* worthy to
die; [m]for he hath prophesied against
this city, as ye have heard with your
ears.
12 ¶ Then spake Jĕr-e-mī'ah unto all
the princes and to all the people, saying, The LORD sent me to prophesy
against this house and against this city
all the words that ye have heard.
13 Therefore now [n]amend your ways
and your doings, and obey the voice of
the LORD your God; and the LORD will
repent him of the evil that he hath pronounced against you.
14 As for me, behold, [o]I *am* in your
hand: do with me [3]as seemeth good
and meet unto you.
15 But know ye for certain, that if ye
put me to death, ye shall surely bring
innocent blood upon yourselves, and
upon this city, and upon the inhabitants thereof: for of a truth the LORD
hath sent me unto you to speak all
these words in your ears.

23 [5]cut off into corners, or, having the corners of the hair polled
24 [u]2 Chr. 9.14
[v]ch. 50.37
26 [w]ch. 51.41
27 [x]Hab. 2.16
29 [y]Prov. 11.31; 1 Pet. 4.17
[6]upon which my name is called
[z]Ezek. 38.21
30 [a]Isa. 42.13; Amos 1.2
[b]Ps. 68.16
31 [c]Hos. 4.1; Mic. 6.2
[d]Joel 3.2
33 [e]Isa. 34.2-8; Rev. 19.17-21
34 [7]your days for slaughter
[8]a vessel of desire
35 [9]flight shall perish from the shepherds, and escaping from, etc
37 [f]Ps. 97.1-3; Heb. 12.29
38 [10]a desolation

CHAPTER 26
2 [a]ch. 7.2; John 8.2
[b]Ex. 23.14; Deut. 12.5
[c]Matt. 28.20
[d]Acts 20.27
3 [e]ch. 36.3
[f]ch. 18.8
4 [g]Lev. 26.14
5 [h]ch. 7.13
6 [i]1 Sam. 4.10;
[j]Isa. 65.15
8 [k]Amos 5.10;
10 [1]Or, at the door
[l]2 Ki. 15.35
11 [2]the judgment of death is for this man
[m]ch. 38.4
13 [n]Isa. 1.19
14 [o]ch. 38.5
[3]as it is good and right in your eyes

16 ¶ Then said the princes and all
the people unto the priests and to the
prophets; This man *is* not worthy to
die: for he hath spoken to us in the
name of the LORD our God.
17 [p]Then rose up certain of the elders of the land, and spake to all the
assembly of the people, saying,
18 [q]Mī'cah the Mō'ras-thīte prophesied in the days of Hĕz-e-kī'ah king of
Jū'dah, and spake to all the people of
Ju'dah, saying, Thus saith the LORD of
hosts; [r]Zī'ŏn shall be plowed *like* a
field, and Je-ru̧'sa-lĕm shall become
heaps, and the mountain of the house
as the high places of a forest.
19 Did Hĕz-e-kī'ah king of Jū'dah
and all Jū'dah put him at all to death?
[s]did he not fear the LORD, and besought
[4]the LORD, and the LORD [t]repented him
of the evil which he had pronounced
against them? [u]Thus might we procure
great evil against our souls.
20 And there was also a man that
prophesied in the name of the LORD, U-
rī'jah the son of Shĕm-a-ī'ah of Kĭr'-
jath–jē'a-rĭm, who prophesied against
this city and against this land according to all the words of Jĕr-e-mī'ah:
21 And when Je-hoi'a-kim the king,
with all his mighty men, and all the
princes, heard his words, the [v]king
sought to put him to death: but when
U-rī'jah heard it, he was afraid, and
[w]fled, and went into Ē'ġypt;
22 And Je-hoi'a-kim the [x]king sent
men into Ē'ġypt, *namely*, Ĕl'na-than
the son of Ăch'bôr, and *certain* men
with him into Ē'ġypt.
23 And they fetched forth U-rī'jah
out of Ē'ġypt, and brought him unto
Je-hoi'a-kim the king; [y]who slew him
with the sword, and cast his dead body
into the graves of the [5]common people.
24 Nevertheless [z]the hand of A-hī'-
kam the son of Shā'phan was with Jĕr-
e-mī'ah, that they should not give him
into the hand of the people to put him
to death.

27 In the beginning of the reign of
Je-hoi'a-kim the son of Jo-sī'ah
[a]king of Jū'dah came this word unto
Jĕr-e-mī'ah from the LORD, saying,
2 Thus [1]saith the LORD to me; Make
thee bonds and yokes, [b]and put them
upon thy neck,
3 And send them to the king of
Ē'dom, and to the king of Mō'ab, and
to the king of the Ăm'mŏn-ītes, and to
the king of Tȳ'rus, and to the king of
Zī'dŏn, by the hand of the messengers
which come to Je-ru̧'sa-lĕm unto Zĕd-
e-kī'ah king of Jū'dah;
4 And command them [2]to say unto
their masters, Thus saith the LORD of
hosts, the God of Ĭs'ra-el; Thus shall ye
say unto your masters;
5 [c]I have made the earth, the man
and the beast that *are* upon the ground,
by my great power and by my outstretched arm, and [d]have given it unto
whom it seemed meet unto me.
6 [e]And now have I given all these
lands into the hand of Nĕb-u-chăd-
nĕz'zar the king of Băb'ȳ-lon, [f]my servant; and [g]the beasts of the field have I
given him also to serve him.
7 [h]And all nations shall serve him,
and his son, and his son's son, [i]until
the very time of his land come: and
then many nations and great kings
shall serve themselves of him.
8 And it shall come to pass, *that* the
nation and kingdom which will not
serve the same Nĕb-u-chăd-nĕz'zar the
king of Băb'ȳ-lon, and that will not put
their neck under the yoke of the king of
Băb'ȳ-lon, that nation will I [3]punish,
saith the LORD, with the sword, and
with the famine, and with the pestilence, until I have consumed them by
his hand.
9 Therefore [j]hearken not ye to your
prophets, nor to your diviners, nor to
your [4]dreamers, nor to your enchant-
ers, nor to your sorcerers, which speak
unto you, saying, Ye shall not serve
the king of Băb'ȳ-lon:
10 For they prophesy a lie unto you,
to remove you far from your land; and
that I should drive you out, and ye
should perish.
11 But the nations that bring their
neck under the yoke of the king of
Băb'ȳ-lon, and serve him, those will I
let remain still in their own land, saith
the LORD; and they shall till it, and
dwell therein.
12 ¶ I spake also to [k]Zĕd-e-kī'ah
king of Jū'dah according to all these
words, saying, Bring your necks under
the yoke of the king of Băb'ȳ-lon, and
serve him and his people, and live.
13 [l]Why will ye die, thou and thy
people, by the sword, by the famine,
and by the pestilence, as the LORD hath
spoken against the nation that will not
serve the king of Băb'ȳ-lon?
14 Therefore hearken not unto the
words of the prophets that speak unto
you, saying, Ye shall not serve the king
of Băb'ȳ-lon: for they prophesy [m]a lie
unto you.
15 For I have not sent them, saith
the LORD, yet they prophesy [5]a lie in
my name; that I might drive you out,
and that ye might perish, ye, and the
prophets that prophesy unto you.
16 Also I spake to the priests and to
all this people, saying, Thus saith the
LORD; Hearken not to the words of
your prophets that prophesy unto you,
saying, Behold, the [n]vessels of the
LORD'S house shall now shortly be
brought again from Băb'ȳ-lon: for they
prophesy a lie unto you.
17 Hearken not unto them; serve the
king of Băb'ȳ-lon, and live: [o]where-
fore should this city be laid waste?
18 But if they *be* prophets, and if the
word of the LORD be with them, let
them now [p]make intercession to the
LORD of hosts, that the vessels which
are left in the house of the LORD, and *in*
the house of the king of Jū'dah, and at
Je-ru̧'sa-lĕm, go not to Băb'ȳ-lon.
19 ¶ For thus saith the LORD of hosts
[q]concerning the pillars, and concerning the sea, and concerning the bases,

17 [p]Acts 5.34
18 [q]Mic. 1.1
[r]Mic. 3.12
19 [s]2 Chr. 32.26
[4]the face of the LORD
[t]Ex. 32.14; 2 Sam. 24.16
[u]Acts 5.39
21 [v]2 Chr. 16.10; 2 Chr. 24.21
[w]1 Ki. 19.3
22 [x]Ps. 12.8; Prov. 29.12
23 [y]Matt. 23.31
[5]sons of the people
24 [z]2 Ki. 22.12-14; ch. 39.14

CHAPTER 27
1 [a]ch. 28.1
2 [1]Or, hath the LORD said:
[b]ch. 28.10; Ezek. 4.1
4 [2]Or, concerning their masters, saying
5 [c]Ps. 96.5; Isa. 45.12
[d]Gen. 1.29-30; Dan. 4.17
6 [e]ch. 28.14; Dan. 2.37-38
[f]ch. 25.9; ch. 43.10
[g]Ps. 50.10-12; Dan. 2.38
7 [h]2 Chr. 36.20
[i]ch. 25.12; Dan. 5.26
8 [3]visit upon
9 [j]Prov. 19.27; Eph. 5.6
[4]dreams
12 [k]ch. 28.1; ch. 38.17
13 [l]Prov. 8.36; Ezek. 18.31
14 [m]ch. 14.14; ch. 23.21
15 [5]in a lie, or, lyingly
16 [n]2 Ki. 24.13
17 [o]Ezek. 18.31
18 [p]Gen. 20.7
19 [q]2 Ki. 25.13

and concerning the residue of the vessels that remain in this city,
20 Which Nĕb-u-chăd-nĕz'zar king
of Băb'ȳ-lon took not, when he carried
away [r]captive Jĕc-o-nī'ah the son of
Je-hoi'a-kim king of Jū'dah from Je-
ru̧'sa-lĕm to Băb'ȳ-lon, and all the [6]no-
bles of Jū'dah and Je-ru̧'sa-lĕm;
21 [s]Yea, thus saith the LORD of
hosts, the God of Ĭs'ra-el, concerning
the vessels that remain *in* the house of
the LORD, and *in* the house of the king
of Jū'dah and of Je-ru̧'sa-lĕm;
22 They shall be carried to Băb'ȳ-
lon, and there shall they be until the
day that I [t]visit them, saith the LORD;
then [u]will I bring them up, and restore
them to this place.

28

28 And [a]it came to pass the same
year, in the beginning of the
reign of Zĕd-e-kī'ah king of Jū'dah, in
the fourth year, *and* in the fifth month,
that [b]Hăn-a-nī'ah the son of Ā'zur the
prophet, which *was* of Gĭb'e-on, spake
unto me in the house of the LORD, in
the presence of the priests and of all
the people, saying,
2 Thus speaketh the LORD of hosts,
the God of Ĭs'ra-el, saying, I have broken [c]the yoke of the king of Băb'ȳ-lon.
3 Within [1]two full years will I bring
again into this place [d]all the vessels of
the LORD'S house, that Nĕb-u-chăd-
nĕz'zar king of Băb'ȳ-lon took away
from this place, and carried them to
Băb'ȳ-lon:
4 And I will bring again to this place
Jĕc-o-nī'ah the son of [2]Je-hoi'a-kim
king of Jū'dah, with all the [3]captives of
Jū'dah, that went into Băb'ȳ-lon, saith
the LORD: for I will break the yoke of
the king of Băb'ȳ-lon.
5 ¶ Then the prophet Jĕr-e-mī'ah
said unto the prophet Hăn-a-nī'ah in
the presence of the priests, and in the
presence of all the people that stood in
the house of the LORD,
6 Even the prophet Jĕr-e-mī'ah said,
[e]Amen: the LORD do so: the LORD perform thy words which thou hast prophesied, to bring again the vessels of the
LORD'S house, and all that is carried
away captive, from Băb'ȳ-lon into this
place.
7 Nevertheless hear thou now this
word that I speak in thine ears, and in
the ears of all the people;
8 The prophets that have been before me and before thee of old prophesied both against many countries, and
against great kingdoms, of war, and of
evil, and of pestilence.
9 [f]The prophet which prophesieth
of peace, when the word of the prophet
shall come to pass, *then* shall the
prophet be known, that the LORD hath
truly sent him.
10 ¶ Then Hăn-a-nī'ah the prophet
took the [g]yoke from off the prophet
Jĕr-e-mī'ah's neck, and brake it.
11 And Hăn-a-nī'ah spake in the
presence of all the people, saying, Thus
saith the LORD; Even so will I break the
yoke of Nĕb-u-chăd-nĕz'zar king of
Băb'ȳ-lon [h]from the neck of all nations
within the space of two full years. And
the prophet Jĕr-e-mī'ah [i]went his way.
12 ¶ Then the word of the LORD
came unto Jĕr-e-mī'ah *the prophet*, after that Hăn-a-nī'ah the prophet had
broken the yoke from off the neck of
the prophet Jĕr-e-mī'ah, saying,
13 Go and tell Hăn-a-nī'ah, saying,
Thus saith the LORD; Thou hast broken
the yokes of wood; but thou shalt make
for them yokes of iron.
14 For thus saith the LORD of hosts,
the God of Ĭs'ra-el; [j]I have put a yoke
of iron upon the neck of all these nations, that they may serve Nĕb-u-chăd-
nĕz'zar king of Băb'ȳ-lon; and they
shall serve him: and [k]I have given him
the beasts of the field also.
15 ¶ Then said the prophet Jĕr-e-
mī'ah unto Hăn-a-nī'ah the prophet,
Hear now, Hăn-a-nī'ah; The LORD hath
not sent thee; but [l]thou makest this
people to trust in a lie.
16 Therefore thus saith the LORD;
Behold, I will cast thee from off the
face of the earth: this year thou shalt
die, because thou hast taught [4]rebel-
lion against the LORD.
17 So Hăn-a-nī'ah the prophet died
the [m]same year in the seventh month.

29

29 Now these *are* the words of the
letter that Jĕr-e-mī'ah the prophet
sent from Je-ru̧'sa-lĕm unto the residue
of the elders which were carried away
captives, and to the priests, and to the
prophets, and to all the people whom
Nĕb-u-chăd-nĕz'zar had carried away
captive from Je-ru̧'sa-lĕm to Băb'ȳ-lon;
2 (After that [1]Jĕc-o-nī'ah the king,
and the queen, and the [2]eunuchs, the
princes of Jū'dah and Je-ru̧'sa-lĕm,
and the carpenters, and the smiths,
were departed from Je-ru̧'sa-lĕm;)
3 By the hand of Ĕl'-a-sah the son of
Shā'phan, and Gĕm-a-rī'ah the son of
Hĭl-kī'ah, (whom Zĕd-e-kī'ah king of
Jū'dah sent unto Băb'ȳ-lon to Nĕb-u-
chăd-nĕz'zar king of Băb'ȳ-lon) saying,
4 Thus saith the LORD of hosts, the
God of Ĭs'ra-el, unto all that are carried
away captives, whom I have caused
to be carried away from Je-ru̧'sa-lĕm
unto Băb'ȳ-lon;
5 Build ye houses, and dwell *in them;*
and plant gardens, and eat the fruit of
them;
6 Take ye wives, and beget sons and
daughters; and take wives for your
sons, and give your daughters to husbands, that they may bear sons and
daughters; that ye may be increased
there, and not diminished.
7 [a]And seek the peace of the city
whither I have caused you to be carried away captives, [b]and pray unto the
LORD for it: for in the peace thereof
shall ye have peace.
8 ¶ For thus saith the LORD of hosts,
the God of Ĭs'ra-el; Let not your prophets and your diviners, that *be* in the
midst of you, [c]deceive you, neither
hearken to your dreams which ye cause
to be dreamed.

20 [r]2 Ki. 24.14-15; ch. 24.1 [6]white ones
21 [s]Lev. 26.24; Isa. 5.25
22 [t]2 Chr. 36.21; ch. 29.10; ch. 32.5; Dan. 9.2 [u]Ezra 1.7

CHAPTER 28
1 [a]ch. 27.1 [b]ch. 36.12; 2 Tim. 3.8; 2 Pet. 2.1
2 [c]ch. 27.12
3 [1]two years of days [d]2 Ki. 24.13; 2 Chr. 36.10; ch. 27.16-22
4 [2]Or, Jehoiachin, 2 Ki. 24.12 [3]captivity
6 [e]1 Ki. 1.36; 1 Chr. 16.36; Ps. 41.13; Ps. 72.19; Ps. 89.52; Matt. 6.13; 1 Cor. 14.16; 2 Cor. 1.20; Rev. 1.18
9 [f]Deut. 18.22; Isa. 8.20
10 [g]1 Ki. 22.24; Ps. 10.13
11 [h]ch. 27.7 [i]Prov. 26.4
14 [j]Deut. 28.48; ch. 27.4-7 [k]ch. 27.6
15 [l]ch. 20.6; ch. 29.31
16 [4]revolt
17 [m]Deut. 32.35; 1 Sam. 2.9; Job 21.30; Ps. 9.16; Ps. 34.21; Prov. 11.21; Nah. 1.2-3; Rom. 2.2-3; Heb. 9.27; Heb. 12.29

CHAPTER 29
2 [1]Or, Jehoiachin, 2 Ki. 24.12; 2 Chr. 36.9 [2]Or, chamberlains
7 [a]Dan. 6.4; Rom. 13.1-5; 1 Tim. 2.1 [b]1 Tim. 2.2
8 [c]ch. 14.14; ch. 23.21; Eph. 5.6

9 For they prophesy [3]falsely unto you in my name: I have not sent them, saith the LORD.

10 ¶ For thus saith the LORD, That after [d]seventy years be accomplished at Băb'y̆-lon I will visit you, and perform my good word toward you, in causing you to return to this place.

11 For I know the thoughts that I think toward you, saith the LORD, thoughts of peace, and not of evil, to give you an [4]expected end.

12 Then shall ye [e]call upon me, and ye shall go and pray unto me, and I will hearken unto you.

13 And [f]ye shall seek me, and find *me*, when ye shall search for me [g]with all your heart.

14 And [h]I will be found of you, saith the LORD: and I will turn away your captivity, and [i]I will gather you from all the nations, and from all the places whither I have driven you, saith the LORD; and I will bring you again into the place whence I caused you to be carried away captive.

15 ¶ Because ye have said, The LORD hath raised us up prophets in Băb'y̆-lon;

16 *Know* that thus saith the LORD of the king that sitteth upon the throne of Dā'vid, and of all the people that dwelleth in this city, *and* of your brethren that are not gone forth with you into captivity;

17 Thus saith the LORD of hosts; Behold, I will send upon them the [j]sword, the famine, and the pestilence, and will make them [k]like vile figs, that cannot be eaten, they are so evil.

18 And I will persecute them with the sword, with the famine, and with the pestilence, and [l]will deliver them to be removed to all the kingdoms of the earth, [5]to be a curse, and an astonishment, and an hissing, and a reproach, among all the nations whither I have driven them:

19 Because they have not hearkened to my words, saith the LORD, which [m]I sent unto them by my servants the prophets, rising up early and sending *them;* but ye would not hear, saith the LORD.

20 ¶ Hear ye therefore the word of the LORD, all ye of the captivity, whom [n]I have sent from Je-ru̯'sa-lĕm to Băb'y̆-lon:

21 Thus saith the LORD of hosts, the God of Is'ra-el, of A'hăb the son of Kŏl-a-ī'ah, and of Zĕd-e-kī'ah the son of Mā-a-sē'iah, which [o]prophesy a lie unto you in my name; Behold, I will deliver them into the hand of Nĕb-u-chăd-rĕz'zar king of Băb'y̆-lon; and he shall slay them before your eyes;

22 [p]And of them shall be taken up a curse by all the captivity of Jū'dah which *are* in Băb'y̆-lon, saying, The LORD make thee like Zĕd-e-kī'ah and like A'hăb, [q]whom the king of Băb'y̆-lon roasted in the fire;

23 Because [r]they have committed villany in Is'ra-el, and have committed adultery with their neighbours' wives, and have spoken lying words in my name, which I have not commanded them; even I know, and *am* [s]a witness, saith the LORD.

24 ¶ *Thus* shalt thou also speak to Shĕm-a-ī'ah the [6]Ne-hĕl'a-mīte, saying,

25 Thus speaketh the LORD of hosts, the God of Is'ra-el, saying, Because thou hast sent letters in thy name unto all the people that *are* at Je-ru̯'sa-lĕm, [t]and to Zĕph-a-nī'ah the son of Mā-a-sē'iah the priest, and to all the priests, saying,

26 The LORD hath made thee priest in the stead of Je-hoi'a-dȧ the priest, that ye should be [u]officers in the house of the LORD, for every man *that is* [v]mad, and maketh himself a prophet, that thou shouldest [w]put him in prison, and in the stocks.

27 Now therefore why hast thou not [x]reproved Jĕr-e-mī'ah of An'a-thoth, which maketh himself a prophet to you?

28 For therefore he sent unto us *in* Băb'y̆-lon, saying, This *captivity is* long: build ye houses, and dwell *in them;* and plant gardens, and eat the fruit of them.

29 And Zĕph-a-nī'ah the priest read this letter in the ears of Jĕr-e-mī'ah the prophet.

30 ¶ Then came the word of the LORD unto Jĕr-e-mī'ah, saying,

31 Send to all them of the captivity, saying, Thus saith the LORD concerning Shĕm-a-ī'ah the Ne-hĕl'a-mīte; Because that Shĕm-a-ī'ah hath prophesied unto you, [y]and I sent him not, and he caused you to trust in a lie:

32 Therefore thus saith the LORD; Behold, I will punish [z]Shĕm-a-ī'ah the Ne-hĕl'a-mīte, and his seed: he shall not have a man to dwell among this people; neither shall he behold the good that I will do for my people, saith the LORD; [a]because he hath taught [7]rebellion against the LORD.

30 The word that came to Jĕr-e-mī'ah from the LORD, saying,

2 Thus speaketh the LORD God of Is'ra-el, saying, [a]Write thee all the words that I have spoken unto thee in a book.

3 For, lo, the days come, saith the LORD, that [b]I will bring again the captivity of my people Is'ra-el and Jū'dah, saith the LORD: and [c]I will cause them to return to the land that I gave to their fathers, and they shall possess it.

4 ¶ And these *are* the words that the LORD spake concerning Is'ra-el and concerning Jū'dah.

5 For thus saith the LORD; We have heard a voice of trembling, [1]of fear, and not of peace.

6 Ask ye now, and see whether [2]a man doth travail with child? wherefore do I see every man with his hands on his loins, as a woman in travail, and all faces are turned into paleness?

7 Alas! [d]for that day *is* great, [e]so that none *is* like it: it *is* even the time of Jā'cob's trouble; but he shall be saved out of it.

9 [3]in a lie
10 [d]2 Chr. 36.21-22; ch. 25.12; Dan. 9.2
11 [4]end and expectation
12 [e]Dan. 9.3
13 [f]Lev. 26.39-40; Deut. 30.1; Ps. 32.6; Matt. 7.7
[g]ch. 24.7
14 [h]Deut. 4.7; Ps. 32.6; Isa. 55.6; Rom. 10.20
[i]ch. 23.3-8; ch. 30.3
17 [j]ch. 24.10
[k]ch. 24.8
18 [l]Deut. 29.21-28; 1 Ki. 9.7-8; 2 Chr. 29.8; ch. 15.4; Lam. 2.15-16
[5]for a curse
19 [m]ch. 25.4; ch. 32.33
20 [n]Amos 3.6; Mic. 4.10
21 [o]2 Pet. 2.1
22 [p]Gen. 48.20; Isa. 65.15
[q]Dan. 3.6
23 [r]Zeph. 3.4
[s]Prov. 5.21; Heb. 4.13
24 [6]Or, dreamer
25 [t]2 Ki. 25.18; ch. 21.1
26 [u]ch. 20.1; Acts 4.1
[v]Deut. 13.1-5; Zech. 13.3-6
[w]2 Chr. 16.10; Acts 16.24
27 [x]Num. 16.3; Acts 4.17
31 [y]ch. 28.15
32 [z]Ex. 20.5; Rom. 2.8-9
[a]ch. 28.16
[7]revolt

CHAPTER 30
2 [a]Isa. 30.8
3 [b]Deut. 30.3; Amos 9.14
[c]ch. 16.15
5 [1]Or, there is fear, and not peace
6 [2]a male
7 [d]Isa. 22.4-5; 1 Thess. 4.16
[e]Dan. 12.1

8 For it shall come to pass in that
day, saith the LORD of hosts, *that* I will
break his yoke from off thy neck, and
will burst thy bonds, and strangers
shall no more serve themselves of him:
9 But they shall serve the LORD their
God, and [f]Dā′vid their king, whom I
will [g]raise up unto them.
10 ¶ Therefore [h]fear thou not, O my
servant Jā′cob, saith the LORD; neither
be dismayed, O Is′ra-el: for, lo, I will
save thee from afar, and thy seed from
the land of their captivity; and Jā′cob
shall return, and shall be in rest, and
be quiet, and none shall make *him*
afraid.
11 For I *am* with thee, saith the
LORD, to save thee: [i]though I make a
full end of all nations whither I have
scattered thee, [j]yet will I not make a
full end of thee: but I will correct thee
[k]in measure, and will not leave thee
altogether unpunished.
12 For thus saith the LORD, [l]Thy
bruise *is* incurable, *and* thy wound *is*
grievous.
13 *There is* none to plead thy cause,
[3]that thou mayest be bound up: thou
hast no healing medicines.
14 [m]All thy lovers have forgotten
thee; they seek thee not; for I have
wounded thee with the wound [n]of an
enemy, with the chastisement [o]of a
cruel one, for the multitude of thine iniquity; [p]*because* thy sins were increased.
15 Why criest thou for thine affliction? thy sorrow *is* incurable for the
multitude of thine iniquity: *because*
thy sins were increased, I have done
these things unto thee.
16 [4]Therefore all they that devour
thee [q]shall be devoured; and all thine
adversaries, every one of them, shall
go into captivity; and they that spoil
thee shall be a spoil, and all that prey
upon thee will I give for a prey.
17 [r]For I will restore health unto
thee, and I will heal thee of thy wounds,
saith the LORD; because they called
thee an Outcast, *saying*, This *is* Zī′ŏn,
whom no man seeketh after.
18 ¶ Thus saith the LORD; Behold, I
will bring again the captivity of Jā′-
cob's tents, and [s]have mercy on his
dwellingplaces; and the city shall be
builded upon her own [5]heap, and the
palace shall remain after the manner
thereof.
19 And [t]out of them shall proceed
thanksgiving and the voice of them
that make merry: [u]and I will multiply
them, and they shall not be few; I will
also glorify them, and they shall not be
small.
20 Their children also shall [v]be as
aforetime, and their congregation shall
be established before me, and I will
punish all that oppress them.
21 And [6]their nobles shall be of
themselves, [w]and their governor shall
proceed from the midst of them; and I
will [x]cause him to draw near, and he
shall approach unto me: for who *is* this
that engaged his heart to approach
unto me? saith the LORD.
22 And ye shall be [y]my people, and I
will be your God.
23 Behold, the [z]whirlwind of the
LORD goeth forth with fury, a [7]continu-
ing whirlwind: it shall [8]fall with pain
upon the head of the wicked.
24 The fierce anger of the LORD shall
not return, until he have done *it*, and
until he have performed the intents of
his heart: in the latter days ye shall consider it.

31 At the same time, saith the LORD,
will I be the God of all the families of Is′ra-el, and they shall be my
people.
2 Thus saith the LORD, The people
which were left of the sword found
grace in the wilderness; *even* Is′ra-el,
when [a]I went to cause him to rest.
3 The LORD hath appeared [1]of old
unto me, *saying*, Yea, [b]I have loved
thee with [c]an everlasting love: therefore [2]with lovingkindness have I drawn
thee.
4 Again I will build thee, and thou
shalt be built, O virgin of Is′ra-el: thou
shalt again be adorned with thy [3]tab-
rets, and shalt go forth in the dances of
them that make merry.
5 [d]Thou shalt yet plant vines upon
the mountains of Sa-mā′rĭ-ȧ: the plant-
ers shall plant, and shall [4]eat *them* as
common things.
6 For there shall be a day, *that* the
watchmen upon the mount Ē′phră-ĭm
shall cry, [e]Arise ye, and let us go up to
Zī′ŏn unto the LORD our God.
7 For thus saith the LORD; [f]Sing
with gladness for Jā′cob, and shout
among the chief of the nations: publish
ye, praise ye, and say, O LORD, save
thy people, the remnant of Is′ra-el.
8 Behold, I will bring them from the
north country, and [g]gather them from
the coasts of the earth, *and* with them
the blind and the lame, the woman
with child and her that travaileth with
child together: a great company shall
return thither.
9 [h]They shall come with weeping,
and with [5]supplications will I lead
them: I will cause them to walk [i]by the
rivers of waters in a straight way,
wherein they shall not stumble: for I
am a father to Is′ra-el, and Ē′phră-ĭm
is my [j]firstborn.
10 ¶ Hear the word of the LORD, O ye
nations, and declare *it* in the isles afar
off, and say, He that scattered Is′ra-el
[k]will gather him, and keep him, as a
shepherd *doth* his flock.
11 For [l]the LORD hath redeemed
Jā′cob, and ransomed him [m]from the
hand of *him that was* stronger than he.
12 Therefore they shall come and
sing in the height of Zī′ŏn, and shall
flow together to [n]the goodness of the
LORD, for wheat, and for wine, and for
oil, and for the young of the flock and
of the herd: and their soul shall be as a
[o]watered garden; [p]and they shall not
sorrow any more at all.
13 Then shall the virgin rejoice in
the dance, both young men and old together: for I will turn their mourning

9 [f]Isa. 55.3-4; Hos. 3.5 [g]Luke 1.69; Acts 2.30
10 [h]Isa. 41.13
11 [i]Amos 9.8 [j]ch. 4.27 [k]Ps. 6.1; Isa. 27.8
12 [l]2 Chr. 36.16; ch. 15.18
13 [3]for binding up, or, pressing
14 [m]Lam. 1.2 [n]Job 13.24 [o]Job 30.21 [p]ch. 5.6
16 [4]Or, Nevertheless [q]Ex. 23.22; Isa. 41.11
17 [r]Ex. 15.26; 1 Pet. 2.24
18 [s]Ps. 102.13 [5]Or, little hill
19 [t]Ezra 3.10-11; Isa. 35.10 [u]Zech. 10.8
20 [v]Isa. 1.26
21 [6]his glorious ones [w]Gen. 49.10 [x]Num. 16.5
22 [y]Ezek. 36.28
23 [z]ch. 25.32 [7]cutting [8]Or, remain

CHAPTER 31

2 [a]Num. 10.33
3 [1]from afar [b]Mal. 1.2 [c]Rom. 11.28 [2]Or, have I extended lovingkindness unto thee
4 [3]Or, timbrels
5 [d]Isa. 65.21; Amos 9.14 [4]profane them
6 [e]Isa. 2.3; Mic. 4.2
7 [f]Isa. 12.5
8 [g]Ezek. 34.13
9 [h]Ps. 126.5; ch. 50.4 [5]Or, favours [i]Isa. 49.10 [j]Ex. 4.22; ch. 3.4-19
10 [k]Isa. 40.11
11 [l]Isa. 44.23 [m]Isa. 49.24
12 [n]Hos. 3.5; Rev. 7.17 [o]Isa. 58.11 [p]Isa. 35.10; Rev. 21.4

into joy, and will comfort them, and make them rejoice from their sorrow.

14 And I will satiate the soul of the priests with fatness, and my people shall be satisfied with my goodness, saith the LORD.

15 ¶ Thus saith the LORD; [q]A voice was heard in [r]Rā'mah, lamentation, *and* bitter weeping; Rā'hel weeping for her children refused to be comforted for her children, because [s]they *were* not.

16 Thus saith the LORD; Refrain thy voice from weeping, and thine eyes from tears: for thy work shall be rewarded, saith the LORD; and [t]they shall come again from the land of the enemy.

17 And there is hope in thine end, saith the LORD, that thy children shall come again to their own border.

18 ¶ I have surely heard Ē'phră-ĭm bemoaning himself *thus;* Thou hast chastised me, and I was chastised, as a bullock unaccustomed *to the yoke:* [u]turn thou me, and I shall be turned; for thou *art* the LORD my God.

19 Surely [v]after that I was turned, I repented; and after that I was instructed, I smote upon *my* thigh: I was ashamed, yea, even confounded, because I did bear the reproach of my youth.

20 *Is* Ē'phră-ĭm my dear son? *is he* a pleasant child? for since I spake against him, I do earnestly remember him still: [w]therefore my bowels [6]are troubled for him; [x]I will surely have mercy upon him, saith the LORD.

21 Set thee up waymarks, make thee high heaps: [y]set thine heart toward the highway, *even* the way *which* thou wentest: turn again, O virgin of Ĭs'ra-el, turn again to these thy cities.

22 ¶ How long wilt thou [z]go about, O thou [a]backsliding daughter? for the LORD hath created a new thing in the earth, A woman shall compass a man.

23 Thus saith the LORD of hosts, the God of Ĭs'ra-el; As yet they shall use this speech in the land of Jū'dah and in the cities thereof, when I shall bring again their captivity; [b]The LORD bless thee, O habitation of justice, *and* [c]mountain of holiness.

24 And there shall dwell in Jū'dah itself, and [d]in all the cities thereof together, husbandmen, and they *that* go forth with flocks.

25 For I have satiated the weary soul, and I have replenished every sorrowful soul.

26 Upon this I awaked, and beheld; and my sleep was sweet unto me.

27 ¶ Behold, the days come, saith the LORD, that [e]I will sow the house of Ĭs'ra-el and the house of Jū'dah with the seed of man, and with the seed of beast.

28 And it shall come to pass, *that* like as I have [f]watched over them, [g]to pluck up, and to break down, and to throw down, and to destroy, and to afflict; so will I watch over them, [h]to build, and to plant, saith the LORD.

15 [q]Matt. 2.17
[r]Josh. 18.25
[s]Gen. 42.13; Job 7.21; Lam. 5.7; Matt. 2.18
16 [t]Ezek. 11.17-18; Hos. 1.11
18 [u]Ps. 85.4; ch. 17.14; Lam. 5.21
19 [v]Deut. 30.2
20 [w]Isa. 63.15; Hos. 11.8
[6]sound
[x]Isa. 57.18; Hos. 14.4; Mic. 7.18
21 [y]ch. 50.5
22 [z]ch. 2.18
[a]ch. 3.6; Hos. 4.16
23 [b]Ps. 122.5; Isa. 1.26
[c]Zech. 8.3
24 [d]ch. 33.12
27 [e]Hos. 2.23
28 [f]ch. 44.27; Dan. 9.14
[g]ch. 1.10
[h]ch. 24.6
29 [i]Ezek. 18.2
30 [j]Gal. 6.5
31 [k]ch. 32.40; ch. 33.14; Heb. 8.8
32 [l]John 1.17
[m]Deut. 1.31
[7]Or, should I have continued an husband unto them
33 [n]ch. 32.40
[o]Ps. 40.8; 2 Cor. 3.3
[p]ch. 24.7; ch. 30.22
34 [q]Isa. 54.13; John 6.45; 1 Cor. 2.10
[r]ch. 33.8; Rom. 11.27
35 [s]Gen. 1.16
[t]Isa. 51.15
[u]ch. 10.16
36 [v]Ps. 148.6
37 [w]ch. 33.22
38 [x]Neh. 3.1; Ps. 69.35; ch. 24.6; Dan. 9.25
39 [y]Zech. 2.1
40 [z]2 Chr. 23.15; Neh. 3.28
[a]Joel 3.17

CHAPTER 32
1 [a]2 Ki. 25.1; ch. 39.1
2 [b]Neh. 3.25; Matt. 5.12

29 [i]In those days they shall say no more, The fathers have eaten a sour grape, and the children's teeth are set on edge.

30 [j]But every one shall die for his own iniquity: every man that eateth the sour grape, his teeth shall be set on edge.

31 ¶ Behold, the [k]days come, saith the LORD, that I will make a new covenant with the house of Ĭs'ra-el, and with the house of Jū'dah:

32 Not [l]according to the covenant that I made with their fathers in the day *that* [m]I took them by the hand to bring them out of the land of Ē'gypt; which my covenant they brake, [7]although I was an husband unto them, saith the LORD:

33 [n]But this *shall be* the covenant that I will make with the house of Ĭs'ra-el; After those days, saith the LORD, [o]I will put my law in their inward parts, and write it in their hearts; [p]and will be their God, and they shall be my people.

34 And they shall teach no more every man his neighbour, and every man his brother, saying, Know the LORD: for [q]they shall all know me, from the least of them unto the greatest of them, saith the LORD: for [r]I will forgive their iniquity, and I will remember their sin no more.

35 ¶ Thus saith the LORD, [s]which giveth the sun for a light by day, *and* the ordinances of the moon and of the stars for a light by night, which divideth [t]the sea when the waves thereof roar; [u]The LORD of hosts *is* his name:

36 [v]If those ordinances depart from before me, saith the LORD, *then* the seed of Ĭs'ra-el also shall cease from being a nation before me for ever.

37 Thus saith the LORD; [w]If heaven above can be measured, and the foundations of the earth searched out beneath, I will also cast off all the seed of Ĭs'ra-el for all that they have done, saith the LORD.

38 ¶ Behold, the days come, saith the LORD, that the city shall be built to the LORD [x]from the tower of Ha-năn'e-el unto the gate of the corner.

39 And [y]the measuring line shall yet go forth over against it upon the hill Gā'rĕb, and shall compass about to Gō'ath.

40 And the whole valley of the dead bodies, and of the ashes, and all the fields unto the brook of Kĭd'ron, [z]unto the corner of the horse gate toward the east, [a]*shall be* holy unto the LORD; it shall not be plucked up, nor thrown down any more for ever.

32

The word that came to Jĕr-e-mī'ah from the LORD [a]in the tenth year of Zĕd-e-kī'ah king of Jū'dah, which *was* the eighteenth year of Nĕb-u-chăd-rĕz'zar.

2 For then the king of Băb'y̆-lon's army besieged Je-ru̧'sa-lĕm: and Jĕr-e-mī'ah the prophet was shut up in [b]the court of the prison, which *was* in the king of Jū'dah's house.

3 For Zĕd-e-kī'ah king of Jū'dah had shut him up, saying, Wherefore dost thou prophesy, and say, Thus saith the LORD, [c]Behold, I will give this city into the hand of the king of Băb'ȳ-lon, and he shall take it;

4 And Zĕd-e-kī'ah king of Jū'dah [d]shall not escape out of the hand of the Chăl-dē'ans, but shall surely be delivered into the hand of the king of Băb'ȳ-lon, and shall speak with him mouth to mouth, and his eyes shall behold his eyes;

5 And he shall lead Zĕd-e-kī'ah to Băb'ȳ-lon, and there shall he be [e]until I visit him, saith the LORD: [f]though ye fight with the Chăl-dē'ans, ye shall not prosper.

6 ¶ And Jĕr-e-mī'ah said, The word of the LORD came unto me, saying,

7 Behold, Ha-năm'e-el the son of Shăl'lum thine uncle shall come unto thee, saying, Buy thee my field that *is* in Ăn'a-thoth: for the [g]right of redemption *is* thine to buy *it*.

8 So Ha-năm'e-el mine uncle's son came to me in the court of the prison according to the word of the LORD, and said unto me, Buy my field, I pray thee, that *is* [h]in Ăn'a-thoth, which *is* in the country of Bĕn'ja-min: for the right of inheritance *is* thine, and [i]the redemption *is* thine; buy *it* for thyself. Then I knew that this *was* the word of the LORD.

9 And I bought the field of Ha-năm'e-el my uncle's son, that *was* in Ăn'a-thoth, and [j]weighed him the money, *even* [1]seventeen shekels of silver.

10 And I [2]subscribed the evidence, and sealed *it*, and [k]took witnesses, and weighed *him* the money in the balances.

11 So I took the evidence of the purchase, *both* that which was sealed *according* to the law and custom, and that which was open:

12 And I gave the evidence of the purchase unto [l]Bā'ruch the son of Ne-rī'ah, the son of Mā-a-sē'iah, in the sight of Ha-năm'e-el mine uncle's *son*, and in the presence of the [m]witnesses that subscribed the book of the purchase, before all the Jews that sat in the court of the prison.

13 ¶ And I charged Bā'ruch before them, saying,

14 Thus saith the LORD of hosts, the God of Ĭs'ra-el; Take these evidences, this evidence of the purchase, both which is sealed, and this evidence which is open; and put them in an earthen vessel, that they may continue many days.

15 For thus saith the LORD of hosts, the God of Ĭs'ra-el; Houses and fields and vineyards shall be possessed again in this land.

16 ¶ Now when I had delivered the evidence of the purchase unto Bā'ruch the son of Ne-rī'ah, [n]I prayed unto the LORD, saying,

17 Ah Lord GOD! behold, [o]thou hast made the heaven and the earth by thy great power and stretched out arm, *and* [p]there is nothing [3]too hard for thee:

18 Thou shewest [q]lovingkindness unto thousands, and recompensest the iniquity of the fathers into the bosom of their children after them: the Great, [r]the Mighty God, [s]the LORD of hosts, *is* his name,

19 [t]Great in counsel, and mighty in [4]work: for thine [u]eyes *are* open upon all the ways of the sons of men: [v]to give every one according to his ways, and according to the fruit of his doings:

20 Which hast set signs and wonders in the land of Ē'gypt, *even* unto this day, and in Ĭs'ra-el, and among *other* men; and hast made thee [w]a name, as at this day;

21 And [x]hast brought forth thy people Ĭs'ra-el out of the land of Ē'gypt with signs, and with wonders, and with a strong hand, and with a stretched out arm, and with great terror;

22 And hast given them this land, which thou didst swear to their fathers to give them, [y]a land flowing with milk and honey;

23 And they came in, and possessed it; but [z]they obeyed not thy voice, neither walked in thy law; they have done nothing of all that thou commandedst them to do: therefore thou hast caused all this evil to come upon them:

24 Behold the [5]mounts, they are come unto the city to take it; and the city is given into the hand of the Chăl-dē'ans, that fight against it, because of [a]the sword, and of the famine, and of the pestilence: and what thou hast spoken [b]is come to pass; and, behold, thou seest *it*.

25 And thou hast said unto me, O Lord GOD, Buy thee the field for money, and take witnesses; [6]for the city is given into the hand of the Chăl-dē'ans.

26 ¶ Then came the word of the LORD unto Jĕr-e-mī'ah, saying,

27 Behold, I *am* the LORD, the [c]God of all flesh: [d]is there any thing too hard for me?

28 Therefore thus saith the LORD; Behold, I will give this city into the hand of the Chăl-dē'ans, and into the hand of Nĕb-u-chăd-rĕz'zar king of Băb'ȳ-lon, and he shall take it:

29 And the Chăl-dē'ans, that fight against this city, shall come and [e]set fire on this city, and burn it with the houses, [f]upon whose roofs they have offered incense unto Bā'al, and poured out drink offerings unto other gods, to provoke me to anger.

30 For the children of Ĭs'ra-el and the children of Jū'dah [g]have only done evil before me from their youth: for the children of Ĭs'ra-el have only provoked me to anger with the work of their hands, saith the LORD.

31 For [h]this city hath been to me *as* [7]a provocation of mine anger and of my fury from the day that they built it even unto this day; [i]that I should remove it from before my face,

32 Because of all the evil of the children of Ĭs'ra-el and of the children of Jū'dah, which they have done

3 [c]ch. 21.4-7
4 [d]2 Ki. 25.4-7; ch. 39.5; ch. 52.9
5 [e]ch. 27.22
[f]Prov. 21.30; ch. 21.4
7 [g]Lev. 25.24-25-32; Ruth 4.4
8 [h]ch. 1.1
[i]Lev. 25.24
9 [j]Gen. 23.16
[1]Or, seven shekels and ten pieces of silver
10 [2]wrote in the book
[k]Isa. 8.2
12 [l]ch. 36.4
[m]Isa. 8.2
16 [n]Gen. 32.9-12; Dan. 9; Phil. 4.6-7
17 [o]2 Ki. 19.15
[p]Gen. 18.14; Zech. 8.6; Matt. 19.26; Mark 10.27; Luke 1.37; Rom. 4.21
[3]Or, hid from thee
18 [q]Ex. 20.6; Deut. 5.9-10
[r]Ps. 45.3-6; Isa. 9.6; Tit. 2.13
[s]ch. 10.16
19 [t]Isa. 28.29
[4]doing
[u]Job 34.21; Ps. 33.13-15; Prov. 5.21; ch. 16.17
[v]Ps. 62.12; Eccl. 12.14; ch. 17.10; Matt. 16.27; John 5.29
20 [w]Ex. 9.16; 1 Chr. 17.21; Isa. 63.12
21 [x]Ex. 6.6; 2 Sam. 7.23; 1 Chr. 17.21
22 [y]Ex. 3.8; ch. 11.5
23 [z]Neh. 9.26; Dan. 9.10
24 [5]Or, engines of shot
[a]ch. 14.12
[b]Josh. 23.15
25 [6]Or, though
27 [c]Isa. 64.8
[d]Ps. 115.3
29 [e]ch. 21.10
[f]ch. 19.13
30 [g]Ezek. 20.28
31 [h]Zeph. 3.1
[7]for my anger
[i]2 Ki. 23.27

to provoke me to anger, [j]they, their kings, their princes, their priests, and their prophets, and the men of Jū'dah, and the inhabitants of Je-ru̧'sa-lĕm.

33 And they have turned unto me the [8]back, and not the face: though I taught them, [k]rising up early and teaching *them,* yet they have not hearkened to receive instruction.

34 But they [l]set their abominations in the house, which is called by my name, to defile it.

35 And they built the high places of Bā'al, which *are* in the valley of the son of Hĭn'nom, to [m]cause their sons and their daughters to pass through *the fire* unto [n]Mō'lech; which I commanded them not, neither came it into my mind, that they should do this abomination, to cause Jū'dah to sin.

36 ¶ And now therefore thus saith the LORD, the God of Is'ra-el, concerning this city, whereof ye say, It shall be delivered into the hand of the king of Băb'ȳ-lon by the sword, and by the famine, and by the pestilence;

37 Behold, I will [o]gather them out of all countries, whither I have driven them in mine anger, and in my fury, and in great wrath; and I will bring them again unto this place, and I will cause them [p]to dwell safely:

38 And they shall be [q]my people, and I will be their God:

39 And I will [r]give them one heart, and one way, that they may fear me [9]for ever, for the good of them, and of their children after them:

40 And [s]I will make an everlasting covenant with them, that I will not turn away [10]from them, to do them good; but [t]I will put my fear in their hearts, that they shall not depart from me.

41 Yea, [u]I will rejoice over them to do them good, and [v]I will plant them in this land [11]assuredly with my whole heart and with my whole soul.

42 For thus saith the LORD; [w]Like as I have brought all this great evil upon this people, so will I bring upon them all the good that I have promised them.

43 And fields shall be bought in this land, [x]whereof ye say, *It is* desolate without man or beast; it is given into the hand of the Chăl-dē'ans.

44 Men shall buy fields for money, and subscribe evidences, and seal *them,* and take witnesses in [y]the land of Bĕn'-ja-min, and in the places about Je-ru̧'sa-lĕm, and in the cities of Jū'dah, and in the cities of the mountains, and in the cities of the valley, and in the cities of the south: for [z]I will cause their captivity to return, saith the LORD.

33 Moreover the word of the LORD came unto Jĕr-e-mī'ah the second time, while he was yet [a]shut up in the court of the prison, saying,

2 Thus saith the LORD the [b]maker thereof, the LORD that formed it, to establish it; [1][c]the LORD *is* his name;

3 [d]Call unto me, and I will answer thee, and shew thee great and [2]mighty things, which thou knowest not.

4 For thus saith the LORD, the God of Is'ra-el, concerning the houses of this city, and concerning the houses of the kings of Jū'dah, which are thrown down by [e]the mounts, and by the sword;

5 They come to fight with the Chăl-dē'ans, but *it is* to fill them with the dead bodies of men, whom I have slain in mine anger and in my fury, and for all whose wickedness I have hid my face from this city.

6 Behold, [f]I will bring it health and cure, and I will cure them, and will reveal unto them the abundance of peace and truth.

7 And [g]I will cause the captivity of Jū'dah and the captivity of Is'ra-el to return, and will build them, [h]as at the first.

8 And I will [i]cleanse them from all their iniquity, whereby they have sinned against me; and I will [j]pardon all their iniquities, whereby they have sinned, and whereby they have transgressed against me.

9 ¶ [k]And it shall be to me a name of joy, a praise and an honour before all the nations of the earth, which shall hear all the good that I do unto them: and they shall [l]fear and tremble for all the goodness and for all the prosperity that I procure unto it.

10 Thus saith the LORD; Again there shall be heard in this place, which ye say *shall be* desolate without man and without beast, *even* in the cities of Jū'dah, and in the streets of Je-ru̧'sa-lĕm, that are desolate, without man, and without inhabitant, and without beast,

11 The [m]voice of joy, and the voice of gladness, the voice of the bridegroom, and the voice of the bride, the voice of them that shall say, [n]Praise the LORD of hosts: for the LORD *is* good; for his mercy *endureth* for ever: *and* of them that shall bring [o]the sacrifice of praise into the house of the LORD. For I will cause to return the captivity of the land, as at the first, saith the LORD.

12 Thus saith the LORD of hosts; [p]Again in this place, which is desolate without man and without beast, and in all the cities thereof, shall be an habitation of shepherds causing *their* flocks to lie down.

13 [q]In the cities of the mountains, in the cities of the vale, and in the cities of the south, and in the land of Bĕn'ja-min, and in the places about Je-ru̧'sa-lĕm, and in the cities of Jū'dah, shall the flocks [r]pass again under the hands of him that telleth *them,* saith the LORD.

14 [s]Behold, the days come, saith the LORD, that [t]I will perform that good thing which I have promised unto the house of Is'ra-el and to the house of Jū'dah.

15 ¶ In those days, and at that time, will I cause the [u]Branch of righteousness to grow up unto Dā'vid; and he

32 [j]Isa. 1.4-6; Dan. 9.8
33 [8]neck
[k]ch. 7.13
34 [l]2 Chr. 33.4-5; ch. 7.30; Ezek. 8.5
35 [m]2 Ki. 23.10; ch. 19.5
[n]Lev. 18.21
37 [o]Deut. 30.3
[p]ch. 23.6
38 [q]ch. 24.7
39 [r]Ezek. 11.19
[9]all days
40 [s]Isa. 55.3
[10]from after them
[t]ch. 31.33
41 [u]Deut. 30.9
[v]ch. 24.6
[11]in truth, or, stability
42 [w]ch. 31.28
43 [x]ch. 33.10
44 [y]ch. 17.26
[z]ch. 33.7

CHAPTER 33
1 [a]ch. 32.2.ch. 37.21
2 [b]Isa. 37.26
[1]Or, JEHOVAH
[c]Ex. 15.3; Amos 5.8
3 [d]Gen. 18.17; Deut. 4.7-29; Ps. 50.15; Isa. 55.6-7; ch. 29.12; Acts 2.21
[2]Or, hidden
4 [e]ch. 32.24
6 [f]ch. 30.17
7 [g]ch. 32.44
[h]Isa. 1.26
8 [i]Ps. 85.2-3; Isa. 40.2; ch. 31.34; Zech. 13.1; Heb. 9.13
[j]Mic. 7.18; 1 John 1.7-9
9 [k]Ezra 1.2; Isa. 62.7
[l]Isa. 60.5
11 [m]Rev. 18.23
[n]1 Chr. 16.8; 2 Chr. 5.13
[o]Lev. 7.12; 2 Chr. 29.31; Ps. 107.22; Jon. 2.9; Heb. 13.15
12 [p]Isa. 65.10
13 [q]ch. 17.26
[r]Lev. 27.32
14 [s]ch. 23.5
[t]ch. 29.10
15 [u]Isa. 4.2

shall execute judgment and righteousness in the land.

16 [v]In those days shall Jū'dah be saved, and Je-rụ'sa-lĕm shall dwell safely: and [3]this *is the name* wherewith she shall be called, The LORD our righteousness.

17 ¶ For thus saith the LORD; [4]Dā'vid shall never want a man to sit upon the throne of the house of Ĭs'ra-el;

18 Neither shall the priests the Lē'vītes want a man before me to offer [w]burnt offerings, and to kindle meat offerings, and to do sacrifice continually.

19 ¶ And the word of the LORD came unto Jĕr-e-mī'ah, saying,

20 Thus saith the LORD; [x]If ye can break my covenant of the day, and my covenant of the night, and that there should not be day and night in their season;

21 *Then* may also my covenant be broken with Dā'vid my servant, that he should not have a son to reign upon his throne; and with the Lē'vītes the priests, my ministers.

22 As [y]the host of heaven cannot be numbered, neither the sand of the sea measured: so will I multiply the seed of Dā'vid my servant, and the Lē'vītes that minister unto me.

23 Moreover the word of the LORD came to Jĕr-e-mī'ah, saying,

24 Considerest thou not what this people have spoken, saying, The two families which the LORD hath chosen, he hath even cast them off? thus they have despised my people, that they should be no more a nation before them.

25 Thus saith the LORD; If [z]my covenant *be* not with day and night, *and if* I have not [a]appointed the ordinances of heaven and earth;

26 Then will I cast away the seed of Jā'cob, and Dā'vid my servant, *so* that I will not take *any* of his seed *to be* rulers over the seed of Ā'brā-hăm, Ī'saac, and Jā'cob: for [b]I will cause their captivity to return, and have mercy on them.

34 The word which came unto Jĕr-e-mī'ah from the LORD, [a]when Nĕb-u-chăd-nĕz'zar king of Băb'ȳ-lon, and all his army, and [b]all the kingdoms of the earth [1]of his dominion, and all the people, fought against Je-rụ'sa-lĕm, and against all the cities thereof, saying,

2 Thus saith the LORD, the God of Ĭs'ra-el; Go and speak to Zĕd-e-kī'ah king of Jū'dah, and tell him, Thus saith the LORD; Behold, [c]I will give this city into the hand of the king of Băb'ȳ-lon, and [d]he shall burn it with fire:

3 And [e]thou shalt not escape out of his hand, but shalt surely be taken, and delivered into his hand; and thine eyes shall behold the eyes of the king of Băb'ȳ-lon, and [2]he shall speak with thee mouth to mouth, and thou shalt go to Băb'ȳ-lon.

4 Yet hear the word of the LORD, O Zĕd-e-kī'ah king of Jū'dah; Thus saith the LORD of thee, Thou shalt not die by the sword:

5 *But* thou shalt die in peace: and with [f]the burnings of thy fathers, the former kings which were before thee, [g]so shall they burn *odours* for thee; and [h]they will lament thee, *saying*, Ah lord! for I have pronounced the word, saith the LORD.

6 Then Jĕr-e-mī'ah the prophet [i]spake all these words unto Zĕd-e-kī'ah king of Jū'dah in Je-rụ'sa-lĕm,

7 When the king of Băb'ȳ-lon's army fought against Je-rụ'sa-lĕm, and against all the cities of Jū'dah that were left, against Lā'chish, and against A-zē'kah: for [j]these defenced cities remained of the cities of Jū'dah.

8 ¶ *This is* the word that came unto Jĕr-e-mī'ah from the LORD, after that the king Zĕd-e-kī'ah had made a covenant with all the people which *were* at Je-rụ'sa-lĕm, to proclaim [k]liberty unto them;

9 [l]That every man should let his manservant, and every man his maidservant, *being* an Hē'brew or an Hē'brew-ess, go free; [m]that none should serve himself of them, *to wit*, of a Jew his brother.

10 Now when all the princes, and all the people, which had entered into the covenant, heard that every one should let his manservant, and every one his maidservant, go free, that none should serve themselves of them any more, then they obeyed, and let *them* go.

11 But [n]afterward they turned, and caused the servants and the handmaids, whom they had let go free, to return, and brought them into subjection for servants and for handmaids.

12 ¶ Therefore the word of the LORD came to Jĕr-e-mī'ah from the LORD, saying,

13 Thus saith the LORD, the God of Ĭs'ra-el; I made a covenant with your fathers in the day that I brought them forth out of the land of Ē'gypt, out of the house of bondmen, saying,

14 At the end of [o]seven years let ye go every man his brother an Hē'brew, which [3]hath been sold unto thee; and when he hath served thee six years, thou shalt let him go free from thee: but your fathers hearkened not unto me, neither inclined their ear.

15 And ye were [4]now turned, and had done right in my sight, in proclaiming liberty every man to his neighbour; and ye had [p]made a covenant before me [q]in the house [5]which is called by my name:

16 But ye turned and [r]polluted my name, and caused every man his servant, and every man his handmaid, whom he had set at liberty at their pleasure, to return, and brought them into subjection, to be unto you for servants and for handmaids.

17 Therefore thus saith the LORD; Ye have not [s]hearkened unto me, in proclaiming liberty, every one to his brother, and every man to his neighbour: [t]behold, I proclaim a liberty for you, saith the LORD, [u]to the sword, to the pestilence, and to the famine; and I

16 [v]Deut. 33.28; Isa. 45.17 [3]he who shall call her is Jehovah-tsidkenu
17 [4]There shall not be cut off from David
18 [w]Mal. 1.11; Rom. 12.1; 1 Pet. 2.5-9; Rev. 1.6
20 [x]Gen. 8.22; Ps. 89.37; Isa. 54.9; ch. 31.36
22 [y]Gen. 13.16; Gen. 15.5; ch. 31.37
25 [z]Gen. 8.22 [a]Ps. 74.16; Ps. 104.19; ch. 31.35
26 [b]Isa. 14.1; ch. 31.20; Zech. 10.6

CHAPTER 34
1 [a]2 Ki. 25.1; ch. 32.2 [b]ch. 1.15; Dan. 2.37 [1]the dominion of his hand
2 [c]ch. 21.10 [d]ch. 32.29
3 [e]ch. 32.4 [2]his mouth shall speak to thy mouth
5 [f]2 Chr. 16.14 [g]Dan. 2.46 [h]ch. 22.18
6 [i]1 Ki. 21.19; Ezek. 2.7; Matt. 14.4
7 [j]2 Ki. 18.13; 2 Chr. 11.5-9
8 [k]Ex. 21.2; Mic. 2.1-3-7-13
9 [l]Neh. 5.11 [m]Lev. 25.39
11 [n]ch. 37.5; Hos. 6.4
14 [o]Ex. 21.2; Deut. 15.12 [3]Or, hath sold himself
15 [4]to day [p]2 Ki. 23.3; Neh. 10.29 [q]ch. 7.10 [5]whereupon my name is called
16 [r]Ex. 20.7; Lev. 19.12
17 [s]Neh. 9.30 [t]Matt. 7.2; 1 Thess. 4.6 [u]ch. 32.24-36

will make you [6]to be removed into all the kingdoms of the earth.

18 And I will give the men that have [v]transgressed my covenant, which have not performed the words of the covenant which they had made before me, when [w]they cut the calf in twain, and passed between the parts thereof,

19 The princes of Jū'dah, and the princes of Je-ru̦'sa-lĕm, the eunuchs, and the priests, and all the people of the land, which passed between the parts of the calf;

20 I will even give them into the hand of their enemies, and into the hand of them that seek their life: and their [x]dead bodies shall be for meat unto the fowls of the heaven, and to the beasts of the earth.

21 And Zĕd-e-kī'ah king of Jū'dah and his princes will I give into the hand of their enemies, and into the hand of them that seek their life, and into the hand of the king of Băb'ȳ-lon's army, [y]which are gone up from you.

22 [z]Behold, I will command, saith the LORD, and cause them to return to this city; and they shall fight against it, [a]and take it, and burn it with fire: and [b]I will make the cities of Jū'dah a desolation without an inhabitant.

35 The word which came unto Jĕr-e-mī'ah from the LORD in the days of [a]Je-hoi'a-kim the son of Jo-sī'ah king of Jū'dah, saying,

2 Go unto the house of the [b]Re'-chab-ites, and speak unto them, and bring them into the house of the LORD, into one of [c]the chambers, and give them wine to drink.

3 Then I took Ja-ăz-a-nī'ah the son of Jĕr-e-mī'ah, the son of Hăb-a-zĭ-nī'ah, and his brethren, and all his sons, and the whole house of the Rē'chab-ītes;

4 And I brought them into the house of the LORD, into the chamber of the sons of Hā'nan, the son of Ĭg-da-lī'ah, a man of God, which *was* by the chamber of the princes, which *was* above the chamber of Mā-a-sē'iah the son of Shăl'lum, [d]the keeper of the [1]door:

5 And I set before the sons of the house of the Rē'chab-ītes pots full of wine, and cups, and I said unto them, Drink ye wine.

6 But they said, We will drink no wine: for [e]Jŏn'a-dăb the son of Rē'-chăb our father commanded us, saying, Ye shall drink no wine, *neither* ye, nor your sons for ever:

7 Neither shall ye build house, nor sow seed, nor plant vineyard, nor have *any*: but all your days ye shall dwell in tents; [f]that ye may live many days in the land where ye *be* strangers.

8 Thus have we [g]obeyed the voice of Jŏn'a-dăb the son of Rē'chăb our father in all that he hath charged us, to drink no wine all our days, we, our wives, our sons, nor our daughters;

9 Nor to build houses for us to dwell in: neither have we vineyard, nor field, nor seed:

10 But we have dwelt in tents, and have obeyed, and done according to all that Jŏn'a-dăb our father commanded us.

11 But it came to pass, [h]when Nĕb-u-chăd-rĕz'zar king of Băb'ȳ-lon came up into the land, that we said, Come, and let us go to Je-ru̦'sa-lĕm for fear of the army of the Chăl-dē'ans, and for fear of the army of the Sȳr'ĭ-ans: so we dwell at Je-ru̦'sa-lĕm.

12 ¶ Then came the word of the LORD unto Jĕr-e-mī'ah, saying,

13 Thus saith the LORD of hosts, the God of Ĭs'ra-el; Go and tell the men of Jū'dah and the inhabitants of Je-ru̦'sa-lĕm, Will ye not [i]receive instruction to hearken to my words? saith the LORD.

14 The words of Jŏn'a-dăb the son of Rē'chăb, that he commanded his sons not to drink wine, are performed; for unto this day they drink none, but obey their father's commandment: [j]notwithstanding I have spoken unto you, [k]rising early and speaking; [l]but ye hearkened not unto me.

15 [m]I have sent also unto you all my servants the prophets, rising up early and sending *them*, saying, [n]Return ye now every man from his evil way, and amend your doings, and go not after other gods to serve them, and ye shall dwell in the land which I have given to you and to your fathers: but ye have not inclined your ear, nor hearkened unto me.

16 Because the sons of Jŏn'a-dăb the son of Rē'chăb have performed the commandment of their father, which he commanded them; but this people hath not hearkened unto me:

17 Therefore thus saith the LORD God of hosts, the God of Ĭs'ra-el; Behold, I [o]will bring upon Jū'dah and upon all the inhabitants of Je-ru̦'sa-lĕm all the evil that I have pronounced against them: [p]because I have spoken unto them, but they have not heard; and I have called unto them, but they have not answered.

18 ¶ And Jĕr-e-mī'ah said unto the house of the Rē'chab-ītes, Thus saith the LORD of hosts, the God of Ĭs'ra-el; [q]Because ye have obeyed the commandment of Jŏn'a-dăb your father, and kept all his precepts, and done according unto all that he hath commanded you:

19 Therefore thus saith the LORD of hosts, the God of Ĭs'ra-el; [2]Jŏn'a-dăb the son of Rē'chăb shall not want a man to [r]stand before me for ever.

36 And it came to pass in the fourth year of Je-hoi'a-kim the son of Jo-sī'ah king of Jū'dah, *that* this word came unto Jĕr-e-mī'ah from the LORD, saying,

2 Take thee a [a]roll of a book, and write [b]therein all the words that I have spoken unto thee against Ĭs'ra-el, and against Jū'dah, and against [c]all the nations, from the day I spake unto thee, from the days of [d]Jo-sī'ah, even unto this day.

3 [e]It may be that the house of Jū'-dah will hear all the evil which I purpose to do unto them; that they may

[6]for a removing
18 [v]Rom. 2.8-9
[w]Gen. 15.10; Ps. 50.5
20 [x]Deut. 28.26; Ps. 79.2; ch. 7.33; ch. 16.4; Rev. 19.17-21
21 [y]ch. 37.5
22 [z]ch. 37.8; Amos 3.6
[a]ch. 38.3; ch. 39.1-2-8
[b]ch. 9.11; ch. 33.10; Mic. 7.13; Zech. 1.12

CHAPTER 35
1 [a]2 Ki. 23.34-35; ch. 22.18; Dan. 1.1
2 [b]2 Ki. 10.15; 1 Chr. 2.55
[c]1 Ki. 6.5
4 [d]2 Ki. 12.9; 1 Chr. 9.18-19
[1]threshold, or, vessel
6 [e]2 Ki. 10.15; 1 Chr. 2.55
7 [f]Ex. 20.12; Deut. 4.40; Eph. 6.2-3
8 [g]Prov. 1.8; Col. 3.20
11 [h]2 Ki. 24.1
13 [i]ch. 32.33
14 [j]2 Chr. 36.15
[k]ch. 7.13
[l]Isa. 30.9
15 [m]ch. 7.25
[n]Isa. 1.16-19; Acts 26.20
17 [o]Lev. 26.14; Mic. 3.12
[p]Prov. 1.24; ch. 7.13
18 [q]Ex. 20.12
19 [2]There shall not a man be cut off from Jonadab the son of Rechab to stand, etc
[r]ch. 15.19

CHAPTER 36
2 [a]Isa. 8.1
[b]ch. 30.2; Hab. 2.2
[c]ch. 25.15
[d]ch. 25.3
3 [e]ch. 18.8; Zeph. 2.3

[f]return every man from his evil way;
that I may forgive their iniquity and
their sin.
4 Then Jĕr-e-mī'ah [g]called Bā'rụch
the son of Ne-rī'ah: and [h]Bā'rụch
wrote from the mouth of Jĕr-e-mī'ah
all the words of the LORD, which he
had spoken unto him, upon a roll of a
book.
5 And Jĕr-e-mī'ah commanded Bā'-
rụch, saying, I *am* shut up; I cannot go
into the house of the LORD:
6 Therefore go thou, and read in the
roll, which thou hast written from my
mouth, the words of the LORD in the
ears of the people in the LORD'S house
upon [i]the fasting day: and also thou
shalt [j]read them in the ears of all
Jū'dah that come out of their cities.
7 It may be [1]they will present their
supplication before the LORD, and will
return every one from his evil way: for
[k]great *is* the anger and the fury that
the LORD hath pronounced against this
people.
8 And Bā'rụch the son of Ne-rī'ah
did according to all that Jĕr-e-mī'ah
the prophet commanded him, reading
in the book the words of the LORD in
the LORD'S house.
9 And it came to pass in the fifth
year of Je-hoi'a-kim the son of Jo-sī'ah
king of Jū'dah, in the ninth month,
that they [l]proclaimed a fast before the
LORD to all the people in Je-rụ'sa-lĕm,
and to all the people that came from
the cities of Jū'dah unto Je-rụ'sa-lĕm.
10 Then read Bā'rụch in the book
the words of Jĕr-e-mī'ah in the house
of the LORD, in the chamber of Gĕm-a-
rī'ah the son of Shā'phan the [2]scribe,
in the higher court, at the [3]entry of the
new gate of the LORD'S house, in the
ears of all the people.
11 ¶ When Mī-chā'iah the son of
Gĕm-a-rī'ah, the son of Shā'phan, had
heard out of the book all the words of
the LORD,
12 Then he went down into the king's
house, into the scribe's chamber: and,
lo, all the princes sat there, *even* E-
lĭsh'a-mȧ the scribe, and Del-a-ī'ah the
son of Shĕm-a-ī'ah, and Ĕl'na-than the
son of Ăch'bôr, and Gĕm-a-rī'ah the son
of Shā'phan, and Zĕd-e-kī'ah the son of
Hăn-a-nī'ah, and all the princes.
13 Then Mī-chā'iah declared unto
them all the words that he had heard,
when Bā'rụch read the book in the
ears of the people.
14 Therefore all the princes sent Je-
hū'dī the son of Nĕth-a-nī'ah, the son
of Shĕl-e-mī'ah, the son of Cụ'shī, unto
Bā'rụch, saying, Take in thine hand
the roll wherein thou hast read in the
ears of the people, and come. So Bā'-
rụch the son of Ne-rī'ah took the roll in
his hand, and [m]came unto them.
15 And they said unto him, Sit down
now, and read it in our ears. So Bā'-
rụch read *it* in their ears.
16 Now it came to pass, when they
had heard all the words, they were
[n]afraid both one and other, and said
unto Bā'rụch, We will surely tell the
king of all these words.
17 And they asked Bā'rụch, saying,
Tell us now, How didst thou write all
these words at his mouth?
18 Then Bā'rụch answered them,
[o]He pronounced all these words unto
me with his mouth, and I wrote *them*
with ink in the book.
19 Then said the princes unto Bā'-
rụch, Go, hide thee, thou and Jĕr-e-
mī'ah; and let no man know where ye
be.
20 ¶ And they went in to the king into
the court, but they laid up the roll in the
chamber of E-lĭsh'a-mȧ the scribe, and
told all the words in the ears of the
king.
21 So the king sent Je-hū'dī to fetch
the roll: and he took it out of E-lĭsh'a-
mȧ the scribe's chamber. And Je-hū'dī
read it in the ears of the king, and in
the ears of all the princes which stood
beside the king.
22 Now the king sat in [p]the win-
terhouse in the ninth month: and *there
was a fire* on the hearth burning before
him.
23 And it came to pass, *that* when
Je-hū'dī had read three or four leaves,
[q]he cut it with the penknife, and cast *it*
into the fire that *was* on the hearth,
until all the roll was consumed in the
fire that *was* on the hearth.
24 Yet they were not afraid, nor
[r]rent their garments, *neither* the king,
nor any of his servants that heard all
these words.
25 Nevertheless Ĕl'na-than and Del-
a-ī'ah and Gĕm-a-rī'ah [s]had made intercession to the king that he would
not burn the roll: but he would not
hear them.
26 But the king commanded Je-răh'-
me-el the son [4]of Hăm'me-lĕch, and
Sĕr-a-ī'ah the son of Ăz'rĭ-el, and Shĕl-
e-mī'ah the son of Ăb'de-el, to take
[t]Bā'rụch the scribe and Jĕr-e-mī'ah
the prophet: but [u]the LORD hid them.
27 ¶ Then the word of the LORD came
to Jĕr-e-mī'ah, [v]after that the king had
burned the roll, and the words which
Bā'rụch wrote at the mouth of Jĕr-e-
mī'ah, saying,
28 Take thee again another roll, and
write in it all the former words that
were in the first roll, which Je-hoi'a-
kim the king of Jū'dah hath burned.
29 And thou shalt say to Je-hoi'a-
kim king of Jū'dah, Thus saith the
LORD; Thou hast burned this roll, [w]say-
ing, Why hast thou written therein, saying, The king of Băb'y̆-lon shall certainly come and destroy this land, and
shall cause to cease from thence man
and beast?
30 Therefore thus saith the LORD of
Je-hoi'a-kim king of Jū'dah; [x]He shall
have none to sit upon the throne of
Dā'vid: and his dead body shall be
[y]cast out in the day to the heat, and in
the night to the frost.
31 And I will [5][z]punish him and his
seed and his servants for their iniquity;
and I will bring upon them, and upon

[f]Isa. 55.7; ch. 18.8; Jon. 3.8; Acts 26.20
4 [g]ch. 32.12
[h]ch. 45.1
6 [i]Lev. 16.29
[j]Lev. 23.4; Neh. 8.14-15
7 [1]their supplication shall fall
[k]Deut. 28.15; Deut. 29.18
9 [l]Judg. 20.26; 1 Sam. 7.6; 2 Chr. 20.3
10 [2]Or, secretary of state
[3]Or, door
14 [m]Ezek. 2.6
16 [n]1 Sam. 3.11; Acts 24.25
18 [o]Isa. 8.12; ch. 1.8; Matt. 10.16-32; Rom. 1.16; 1 Pet. 3.14-15
22 [p]Judg. 3.20; Amos 3.15
23 [q]1 Ki. 22.8; Isa. 29.21; 2 Tim. 4.3
24 [r]Gen. 37.29-34; 2 Sam. 1.11; 2 Ki. 22.11; Isa. 36.22
25 [s]Gen. 37.26; Isa. 53.12; Matt. 27.24; Rom. 8.34; Eph. 5.7-11; Heb. 7.25
26 [4]Or, of the king
[t]1 Ki. 19.14; Matt. 23.34-37
[u]Ps. 34.19-20; Ps. 46.1; ch. 1.19; 2 Pet. 2.9
27 [v]Prov. 21.30
29 [w]Amos 5.10
30 [x]2 Ki. 24.8-12; ch. 22.30
[y]ch. 22.19
31 [5]visit upon
[z]Isa. 3.11; ch. 21.7

the inhabitants of Je-ru̦'sa-lĕm, and upon the men of Jū'dah, all the evil that I have pronounced against them; but they hearkened not.

32 ¶ Then took Jĕr-e-mī'ah another roll, and gave it to Bā'ru̦ch the scribe, the son of Ne-rī'ah; [a]who wrote therein from the mouth of Jĕr-e-mī'ah all the words of the book which Je-hoi'a-kim king of Jū'dah had burned in the fire: and there were added besides unto them many [6]like words.

37

And king [a]Zĕd-e-kī'ah the son of Jo-sī'ah reigned instead of Co-nī'ah the son of Je-hoi'a-kim, whom Nĕb-u-chăd-rĕz'zar king of Băb'ȳ-lon made king in the land of Jū'dah.

2 But [b]neither he, nor his servants, nor the people of the land, did hearken unto the words of the LORD, which he spake [1]by the prophet Jĕr-e-mī'ah.

3 And Zĕd-e-kī'ah the king sent Jē'-hū-cal the son of Shĕl-e-mī'ah and [c]Zĕph-a-nī'ah the son of Mā-a-sē'iah the priest to the prophet Jĕr-e-mī'ah, saying, Pray now unto the LORD our God for us.

4 Now Jĕr-e-mī'ah came in and went out among the people: for they had not put him into prison.

5 Then [d]Phā'raōh's army was come forth out of Ē'gypt: [e]and when the Chăl-dē'ans that besieged Je-ru̦'sa-lĕm heard tidings of them, they departed from Je-ru̦'sa-lĕm.

6 ¶ Then came the word of the LORD unto the prophet Jĕr-e-mī'ah, saying,

7 Thus saith the LORD, the God of Ĭs'ra-el; Thus shall ye say to the king of Jū'dah, [f]that sent you unto me to inquire of me; Behold, Phā'raōh's army, which is come forth to help you, shall return to Ē'gypt into their own land.

8 [g]And the Chăl-dē'ans shall come again, and fight against this city, and take it, and burn it with fire.

9 Thus saith the LORD; Deceive not [2]yourselves, saying, The Chăl-dē'ans shall surely depart from us: for they shall not depart.

10 [h]For though ye had smitten the whole army of the Chăl-dē'ans that fight against you, and there remained *but* [3]wounded men among them, *yet* should they rise up every man in his tent, and burn this city with fire.

11 ¶ And it came to pass, that when the army of the Chăl-dē'ans was [4]broken up from Je-ru̦'sa-lĕm for fear of Phā'raōh's army,

12 Then Jĕr-e-mī'ah went forth out of Je-ru̦'sa-lĕm to go into the land of Bĕn'ja-min, [5]to separate himself thence in the midst of the people.

13 And when he was in the gate of Bĕn'ja-min, a captain of the ward *was* there, whose name *was* Ī-rī'jah, the son of Shĕl-e-mī'ah, the son of Hăn-a-nī'ah; and he took Jĕr-e-mī'ah the prophet, saying, Thou fallest away to the Chăl-dē'ans.

14 Then said Jĕr-e-mī'ah, *It is* [6]false; I fall not away to the Chăl-dē'ans. But he hearkened not to him: so Ī-rī'jah took Jĕr-e-mī'ah, and brought him to the princes.

15 Wherefore the princes [i]were wroth with Jĕr-e-mī'ah, and smote him, [j]and put him in prison in the house of Jŏn'a-than the scribe: for they had made that the prison.

16 ¶ When Jĕr-e-mī'ah was entered into [k]the dungeon, and into the [7]cabins, and Jĕr-e-mī'ah had remained there many days;

17 Then Zĕd-e-kī'ah the king sent, and took him out: and the king asked him secretly in his house, and said, [l]Is there *any* word from the LORD? And Jĕr-e-mī'ah said, There is: for, said he, thou shalt be delivered into the hand of the king of Băb'ȳ-lon.

18 Moreover Jĕr-e-mī'ah said unto king Zĕd-e-kī'ah, What have I offended against thee, or against thy servants, or against this people, that ye have put me in prison?

19 Where *are* now your prophets which prophesied unto you, saying, The king of Băb'ȳ-lon shall not come against you, nor against this land?

20 Therefore hear now, I pray thee, O my lord the king: [8]let my supplication, I pray thee, be accepted before thee; that thou cause me not to return to the house of Jŏn'a-than the scribe, lest I die there.

21 Then Zĕd-e-kī'ah the king commanded that they should commit Jĕr-e-mī'ah [m]into the court of the prison, and [n]that they should give him daily a piece of bread out of the bakers' street, [o]until all the bread in the city were spent. Thus Jĕr-e-mī'ah [p]remained in the court of the prison.

38

Then Shĕph-a̦-tī'ah the son of Măt'tan, and Ḡĕd-a-lī'ah the son of Păsh'ŭr, and [a]Jū'cal the son of Shĕl-e-mī'ah, and [b]Păsh'ŭr the son of Măl-chī'ah, [c]heard the words that Jĕr-e-mī'ah had spoken unto all the people, saying,

2 Thus saith the LORD, [d]He that remaineth in this city shall die by the sword, by the famine, and by the pestilence: but he that goeth forth to the Chăl-dē'ans shall live; for he shall have his life for a prey, and shall live.

3 Thus saith the LORD, [e]This city shall surely be given into the hand of the king of Băb'ȳ-lon's army, which shall take it.

4 Therefore the princes said unto the king, We beseech thee, [f]let this man be put to death: for thus he weakeneth the hands of the men of war that remain in this city, and the hands of all the people, in speaking such words unto them: for this man seeketh not the [1]welfare of this people, but the hurt.

5 Then Zĕd-e-kī'ah the king said, [g]Behold, he *is* in your hand: for the king *is* not *he that* can do *any* thing against you.

6 [h]Then took they Jĕr-e-mī'ah, and cast him into [i]the dungeon of Măl-chī'ah the son [2]of Hăm'me-lĕch, that *was* in the court of the prison: and they

---

32 [a]Ex. 4.15; Rom. 16.22
[6]as they

CHAPTER 37
1 [a]1 Chr. 3.16; 2 Chr. 36.10; Dan. 1.1
2 [b]2 Ki. 24.19-20; Prov. 29.12
[1]by the hand of the prophet
3 [c]ch. 21.1-2
5 [d]2 Ki. 24.7
[e]ch. 34.21
7 [f]ch. 21.2
8 [g]Ps. 33.10; Prov. 21.30; Isa. 30.1-7; ch. 34.22
9 [2]your souls
10 [h]Lev. 26.36-38; Isa. 30.17; ch. 21.4-5
[3]thrust through
11 [4]made to ascend
12 [5]Or, to slip away thence in the midst of the people
14 [6]falsehood, or, a lie
15 [i]ch. 20.1-3; Acts 5.40
[j]Gen. 39.20; Rev. 2.10
16 [k]ch. 38.6
[7]Or, cells
17 [l]Mark 6.20
20 [8]let my supplication fall
21 [m]ch. 32.2
[n]1 Ki. 17.6-9
[o]2 Ki. 25.3; ch. 38.9
[p]2 Cor. 6.4

CHAPTER 38
1 [a]ch. 37.3
[b]ch. 21.1
[c]ch. 21.8; Acts 4.2
2 [d]ch. 21.9; Matt. 24.7-8
3 [e]ch. 21.10
4 [f]Ps. 37.12-20; 1 John 3.12-13
[1]peace
5 [g]Eccl. 10.16
6 [h]ch. 37.21
[i]ch. 37.16; Mark 9.42
[2]Or, of the king

let down Jĕr-e-mī'ah with cords. And
in the dungeon *there was* no water, but
mire: so Jĕr-e-mī'ah sunk in the mire.
7 ¶ Now [j]when Ē'bĕd–mē'lĕch the
Ē-thĭ-ō'pĭ-an, one of the eunuchs which
was in the king's house, heard that they
had put Jĕr-e-mī'ah in the dungeon;
the king then sitting [k]in the gate of
Bĕn'ja-min;
8 Ē'bĕd–mē'lĕch went forth out of
the king's house, and [l]spake to the
king, saying,
9 My lord the king, these men have
done evil in all that they have done to
Jĕr-e-mī'ah the prophet, whom they
have cast into the dungeon; and [3]he is
like to die for hunger in the place
where he is: for *there is* no more bread
in the city.
10 Then the king commanded
Ē'bĕd–mē'lĕch the Ē-thĭ-ō'pĭ-an, saying, Take from hence thirty men [4]with
thee, and take up Jĕr-e-mī'ah the
prophet out of the dungeon, before he
die.
11 So Ē'bĕd–mē'lĕch took the men
with him, and went into the house of
the king under the treasury, and took
thence old cast clouts and old rotten
rags, and let them down by cords into
the dungeon to Jĕr-e-mī'ah.
12 [m]And Ē'bĕd–mē'lĕch the Ē-thĭ-
ō'pĭ-an said unto Jĕr-e-mī'ah, Put now
these old cast clouts and rotten rags
under thine armholes under the cords.
And Jĕr-e-mī'ah did so.
13 So they drew up Jĕr-e-mī'ah with
cords, and took him up out of the dungeon: and Jĕr-e-mī'ah remained [n]in
the court of the prison.
14 ¶ Then Zĕd-e-kī'ah the king sent,
and took Jĕr-e-mī'ah the prophet unto
him into the [5]third entry that *is* in the
house of the LORD: and the king said
unto Jĕr-e-mī'ah, I will ask thee a
thing; hide nothing from me.
15 Then Jĕr-e-mī'ah said unto Zĕd-
e-kī'ah, If I declare *it* unto thee, wilt
thou not surely put me to death? and if
I give thee counsel, wilt thou not hearken unto me?
16 So Zĕd-e-kī'ah the king sware secretly unto Jĕr-e-mī'ah, saying, *As* the
LORD liveth, [o]that made us this soul, I
will not put thee to death, neither will I
give thee into the hand of these men
that seek thy life.
17 Then said Jĕr-e-mī'ah unto Zĕd-
e-kī'ah, Thus saith the LORD, the God
of hosts, the God of Is'ra-el; If thou wilt
assuredly [p]go forth unto the king of
Băb'y̆-lon's princes, then thy soul shall
live, and this city shall not be burned
with fire; and thou shalt live, and thine
house:
18 But if thou wilt not go forth to the
king of Băb'y̆-lon's princes, then shall
this city be given into the hand of the
Chăl-dē'ans, and they shall burn it
with fire, and [q]thou shalt not escape
out of their hand.
19 And Zĕd-e-kī'ah the king said
unto Jĕr-e-mī'ah, [r]I am afraid of the
Jews that are fallen to the Chăl-dē'ans,
lest they deliver me into their hand,
and they [s]mock me.
20 But Jĕr-e-mī'ah said, They shall
not deliver *thee*. Obey, [t]I beseech thee,
the voice of the LORD, which I speak
unto thee: so it shall be well unto thee,
and thy soul shall live.
21 But if thou refuse to go forth, this
is the word that the LORD hath shewed
me:
22 And, behold, all the women that
are left in the king of Jū'dah's house
shall be brought forth to the king of
Băb'y̆-lon's princes, and those *women*
shall say, [6]Thy friends have set thee
on, and have prevailed against thee:
thy feet are sunk in the mire, *and* they
are turned away back.
23 So they shall bring out all thy
wives and [u]thy children to the Chăl-
dē'ans: and thou shalt not escape out
of their hand, but shalt be taken by the
hand of the king of Băb'y̆-lon: and
[7]thou shalt cause this city to be burned
with fire.
24 ¶ Then said Zĕd-e-kī'ah unto Jĕr-
e-mī'ah, Let no man know of these
words, and thou shalt not die.
25 But if the princes hear that I have
talked with thee, and they come unto
thee, and say unto thee, Declare unto
us now what thou hast said unto the
king, hide it not from us, and we will
not put thee to death; also what the
king said unto thee:
26 Then thou shalt say unto them, [v]I
presented my supplication before the
king, that he would not cause me to
return [w]to Jŏn'a-than's house, to die
there.
27 Then came all the princes unto
Jĕr-e-mī'ah, and asked him: and he
told them according to all these words
that the king had commanded. So [8]they
left off speaking with him; for the matter was not perceived.
28 So [x]Jĕr-e-mī'ah abode in the court
of the prison until the day that Je-ru'sa-
lĕm was taken: and he was *there* when
Je-ru'sa-lĕm was taken.

39 In the [a]ninth year of Zĕd-e-kī'-
ah king of Jū'dah, in the tenth
month, came Nĕb-u-chăd-rĕz'zar king
of Băb'y̆-lon and all his army against
Je-ru'sa-lĕm, and they besieged it.
2 *And* in the eleventh year of Zĕd-e-
kī'ah, in the fourth month, the ninth
day of the month, the city was broken
up.
3 [b]And all the princes of the king
of Băb'y̆-lon came in, and sat in the
middle gate, *even* Nēr'gal-sha-rē'zer,
Săm'găr–nē'bo, Săr-sē'chim, Răb'–sa-
rĭs, Nēr'gal-sha-rē'zer, Răb'–măg, with
all the residue of the princes of the king
of Băb'y̆-lon.
4 ¶ [c]And it came to pass, *that* when
Zĕd-e-kī'ah the king of Jū'dah saw
them, and all the men of war, then they
fled, and went forth out of the city by
night, by the way of the king's garden,
by the gate betwixt the two walls: and
he went out the way of the plain.
5 But the Chăl-dē'ans' army pursued
after them, and [d]overtook Zĕd-e-kī'ah

7 [j]Ps. 68.31; ch. 39.16
[k]Deut. 21.19
8 [l]Ps. 82.4; Prov. 14.25; Isa. 58.6
9 [3]he will die
10 [4]in thine hand
12 [m]Matt. 10.41; Mark 9.41; 1 Cor. 1.27; Eph. 4.32
13 [n]ch. 37.21; 2 Cor. 6.4-5
14 [5]Or, principal
16 [o]Num. 16.22; Isa. 42.5; Zech. 12.1; Acts 17.25-28; Heb. 12.9
17 [p]ch. 7.6-7.ch. 21.8-10
18 [q]ch. 32.4
19 [r]Prov. 29.25
[s]1 Sam. 31.4
20 [t]Dan. 9.16; 2 Cor. 5.20
22 [6]Men of thy peace
23 [u]ch. 39.6 [7]thou shalt burn, etc
26 [v]ch. 37.20
[w]ch. 37.15
27 [8]they were silent from him
28 [x]ch. 15.20-21; 2 Tim. 3.11
CHAPTER 39
1 [a]2 Ki. 25.1-4; ch. 52.4-7
3 [b]ch. 1.15.ch. 21.4
4 [c]2 Ki. 25.4; ch. 52.7
5 [d]Josh. 5.10; ch. 32.4; ch. 38.18

in the plains of Jĕr'ĭ-chō: and when they had taken him, they brought him up to Nĕb-u-chăd-nĕz'zar king of Băb'ȳ-lon to [e]Rĭb'lah in the land of Hā'math, where he [1]gave judgment upon him.

6 Then the king of Băb'ȳ-lon slew the sons of Zĕd-e-kī'ah in Rĭb'lah before his eyes: also the king of Băb'ȳ-lon slew all the nobles of Jū'dah.

7 Moreover [f]he put out Zĕd-e-kī'ah's eyes, and bound him [2]with chains, to carry him to Băb'ȳ-lon.

8 ¶ [g]And the Chăl-dē'ans burned the king's house, and the houses of the people, with fire, and brake down the walls of Je-ru'sa-lĕm.

9 [h]Then Nĕb'u-zär–ā'dan the [3]captain of the guard carried away captive into Băb'ȳ-lon the remnant of the people that remained in the city, and those that fell away, that fell to him, with the rest of the people that remained.

10 But Nĕb'u-zär–ā'dan the captain of the guard [i]left of the poor of the people, which had nothing, in the land of Jū'dah, and gave them vineyards and fields [4]at the same time.

11 ¶ Now Nĕb-u-chăd-rĕz'zar king of Băb'ȳ-lon gave charge concerning Jĕr-e-mī'ah [5]to Nĕb'u-zär–ā'dan the captain of the guard, saying,

12 Take him, and [6]look well to him, and do him no harm; but do unto him even as he shall say unto thee.

13 So Nĕb'u-zär–ā'dan the captain of the guard sent, and Nĕb-u-shăs'ban, Răb'–sa-rĭs, and Nĕr'gal–sha-rē'zer, Răb'–măg, and all the king of Băb'ȳ-lon's princes;

14 Even they sent, [j]and took Jĕr-e-mī'ah out of the court of the prison, and committed him [k]unto Gĕd-a-lī'ah the son of [l]A-hī'kam the son of Shā'phan, that he should carry him home: so he dwelt among the people.

15 ¶ Now the word of the LORD came unto Jĕr-e-mī'ah, while he was shut up in the court of the prison, saying,

16 Go and speak to [m]Ē'bĕd–mē'lĕch the Ē-thĭ-ō'pĭ-an, saying, Thus saith the LORD of hosts, the God of Īs'ra-el; Behold, [n]I will bring my words upon this city for evil, and not for good; and they shall be *accomplished* in that day before thee.

17 But I will deliver thee in that day, saith the LORD: and thou shalt not be given into the hand of the men of whom thou *art* afraid.

18 For I will surely deliver thee, and thou shalt not fall by the sword, but [o]thy life shall be for a prey unto thee: [p]because thou hast put thy trust in me, saith the LORD.

40 The word that came to Jĕr-e-mī'ah from the LORD, [a]after that Nĕb'u-zär–ā'dan the captain of the guard had let him go from Rā'mah, when he had taken him being bound in [1]chains among all that were carried away captive of Je-ru'sa-lĕm and Jū'dah, which were carried away captive unto Băb'ȳ-lon.

2 And the captain of the guard took Jĕr-e-mī'ah, and said unto him, [b]The LORD thy God hath pronounced this evil upon this place.

3 Now the LORD hath brought *it*, and done according as he hath said: [c]because ye have sinned against the LORD, and have not obeyed his voice, therefore this thing is come upon you.

4 And now, behold, I loose thee this day from the chains which [2]*were* upon thine hand. [d]If it seem good unto thee to come with me into Băb'ȳ-lon, come; and [3]I will look well unto thee: but if it seem ill unto thee to come with me into Băb'ȳ-lon, forbear: behold, [e]all the land *is* before thee: whither it seemeth good and convenient for thee to go, thither go.

5 Now while he was not yet gone back, *he said,* Go back also to Gĕd-a-lī'ah the son of A-hī'kam the son of Shā'phan, [f]whom the king of Băb'ȳ-lon hath made governor over the cities of Jū'dah, and dwell with him among the people: or go wheresoever it seemeth convenient unto thee to go. So the captain of the guard [g]gave him victuals and a reward, and let him go.

6 [h]Then went Jĕr-e-mī'ah unto Gĕd-a-lī'ah the son of A-hī'kam to [i]Mĭz'pah; and dwelt with him among the people that were left in the land.

7 ¶ [j]Now when all the captains of the forces which *were* in the fields, *even* they and their men, heard that the king of Băb'ȳ-lon had made Gĕd-a-lī'ah the son of A-hī'kam governor in the land, and had committed unto him men, and women, and children, and of [k]the poor of the land, of them that were not carried away captive to Băb'ȳ-lon;

8 Then they came to Gĕd-a-lī'ah to Mĭz'pah, [l]even Ĭsh'ma-el the son of Nĕth-a-nī'ah, and Jo-hā'nan and Jŏn'a-than the sons of Ka-rē'ah, and Sĕr-a-ī'ah the son of Tăn'hu-mĕth, and the sons of Ē'phāi the Ne-toph'a-thīte, and Jĕz-a-nī'ah the son of a Ma-ăch'a-thīte, they and their men.

9 And Gĕd-a-lī'ah the son of A-hī'kam the son of Shā'phan sware unto them and to their men, saying, Fear not [4]to serve the Chăl-dē'ans: dwell in the land, and serve the king of Băb'ȳ-lon, and it shall be well with you.

10 As for me, behold, I will dwell at Mĭz'pah, to serve the Chăl-dē'ans, which will come unto us: but ye, [m]gather ye wine, and summer fruits, and oil, and put *them* in your vessels, and dwell in your cities that ye have taken.

11 Likewise when all [n]the Jews that *were* in Mō'ab, and among the Ăm'mŏn-ītes, and in Ē'dom, and that *were* in all the countries, heard that the king of Băb'ȳ-lon had left a remnant of Jū'dah, and that he had set over them Gĕd-a-lī'ah the son of A-hī'kam the son of Shā'phan;

12 Even all the Jews returned out of all places whither they were driven, and came to the land of Jū'dah, to

[e]2 Ki. 23.33; ch. 52.9-26-27
[1]spake with him judgments
7 [f]2 Ki. 25.7; Ezek. 12.13- compared with ch. 32.4
[2]with two brasen chains, or, fetters
8 [g]2 Ki. 25.9; ch. 38.18
9 [h]2 Ki. 25.11; ch. 52.15
[3]chief of the executioners, or, slaughtermen, or, chief marshal
10 [i]2 Ki. 25.11
[4]in that day
11 [5]by the hand of
12 [6]set thine eyes upon him
14 [j]ch. 38.28
[k]ch. 40.5
[l]ch. 26.24
16 [m]Matt. 10.42
[n]Dan. 9.12
18 [o]ch. 21.9
[p]Ruth 2.12; Ps. 32.7

CHAPTER 40

1 [a]ch. 39.14
[1]Or, manicles
2 [b]Lev. 26.14-38; Lam. 2.17
3 [c]Deut. 29.24-25
4 [2]Or, are upon thine hand
[d]ch. 39.12
[3]I will set mine eye upon thee
[e]Gen. 13.9; Gen. 20.15
5 [f]2 Ki. 25.22
[g]Gen. 39.1; Acts 22.24-27-28
6 [h]ch. 39.14
[i]Judg. 20.1; 1 Sam. 7.5-6
7 [j]2 Ki. 25.23
[k]ch. 39.10
8 [l]2 Ki. 25.23; ch. 41.1
9 [4]to stand before: and so verse 10; Deut. 1.38
10 [m]Deut. 16.13; ch. 39.10
11 [n]Isa. 16.4;

Gĕd-a-lī'ah, unto Mĭz'pah, and gathered wine and summer fruits very
much.
13 ¶ Moreover Jo-hā'nan the son of
Ka-rē'ah, and all the captains of the
forces that *were* in the fields, came to
Gĕd-a-lī'ah to Mĭz'pah,
14 And said unto him, Dost thou certainly know that [o]Bā'a-lĭs the king of
the Ăm'mŏn-ītes hath sent Ĭsh'ma-el
the son of Nĕth-a-nī'ah [5]to slay thee?
But Gĕd-a-lī'ah the son of A-hī'kam believed them not.
15 Then Jo-hā'nan the son of Ka-
rē'ah spake to Gĕd-a-lī'ah in Mĭz'pah
secretly, saying, Let me go, I pray thee,
and I will slay Ĭsh'ma-el the son of
Nĕth-a-nī'ah, and no man shall know
it: wherefore should he slay thee, that
all the Jews which are gathered unto
thee should be scattered, and the remnant in Jū'dah perish?
16 But Gĕd-a-lī'ah the son of A-hī'-
kam said unto Jo-hā'nan the son of Ka-
rē'ah, Thou shalt [p]not do this thing:
for thou speakest falsely of Ĭsh'ma-el.
41 Now it came to pass in the seventh month, [a]*that* Ĭsh'ma-el the
son of Nĕth-a-nī'ah the son of E-lĭsh'a-
mȧ, of the seed royal, and the princes
of the king, even ten men with him,
came unto Gĕd-a-lī'ah the son of A-
hī'kam to Mĭz'pah; and there they
[b]did eat bread together in Mĭz'pah.
2 Then arose Ĭsh'ma-el the son of
Nĕth-a-nī'ah, and the ten men that
were with him, and [c]smote Gĕd-a-lī'ah
the son of A-hī'kam the son of Shā'-
phan with the sword, and slew him,
whom the king of Băb'y̆-lon had made
governor over the land.
3 Ĭsh'ma-el also [d]slew all the Jews
that were with him, *even* with Gĕd-a-lī'-
ah, at Mĭz'pah, and the Chăl-dē'ans that
were found there, *and* the men of war.
4 And it came to pass the second
day after he had slain Gĕd-a-lī'ah, and
no man knew *it,*
5 That there came certain [e]from
Shē'chem, from [f]Shī'lōh, and from Sa-
mā'rĭ-ȧ, *even* fourscore men, [g]having
their beards shaven, and their clothes
rent, and having cut themselves, with
offerings and incense in their hand, to
bring *them* to [h]the house of the LORD.
6 And Ĭsh'ma-el the son of Nĕth-a-
nī'ah went forth from Mĭz'pah to meet
them, [1]weeping all along as he went:
and it came to pass, as he met them, he
said unto them, Come to Gĕd-a-lī'ah
the son of A-hī'kam.
7 And it was *so,* when they came
into the midst of the city, that Ĭsh'ma-
el the son of Nĕth-a-nī'ah slew them,
and cast them into the midst of the pit,
he, and the men that *were* with him.
8 But ten men were found among
them that said unto Ĭsh'ma-el, Slay us
not: for we have treasures in the field,
of wheat, and of barley, and of oil, and
of honey. So he forbare, and slew them
not among their brethren.
9 Now the pit wherein Ĭsh'ma-el had
cast all the dead bodies of the men,
whom he had slain [2]because of Gĕd-a-
lī'ah, *was* it [i]which Ā'sȧ the king had
made for fear of Bā'a-shȧ king of Ĭs'ra-
el: *and* Ĭsh'ma-el the son of Nĕth-a-
nī'ah filled it with *them that were*
slain.
10 Then Ĭsh'ma-el carried away captive all the residue of the people that
were in Mĭz'pah, [j]*even* the king's
daughters, and all the people that remained in Mĭz'pah, [k]whom Nĕb'u-
zär–ā'dan the captain of the guard
had committed to Gĕd-a-lī'ah the son
of A-hī'kam: and Ĭsh'ma-el the son of
Nĕth-a-nī'ah carried them away captive, and departed to go over to [l]the
Ăm'mŏn-ītes.
11 ¶ But when Jo-hā'nan the son of
Ka-rē'ah, and all [m]the captains of the
forces that *were* with him, heard of all
the evil that Ĭsh'ma-el the son of Nĕth-
a-nī'ah had done,
12 Then they took all the men, and
went to fight with Ĭsh'ma-el the son of
Nĕth-a-nī'ah, and found him by [n]the
great waters that *are* in Gĭb'e-on.
13 Now it came to pass, *that* when
all the people which *were* with Ĭsh'ma-
el saw Jo-hā'nan the son of Ka-rē'ah,
and all the captains of the forces that
were with him, then they were glad.
14 So all the people that Ĭsh'ma-el
had carried away captive from Mĭz'-
pah cast about and returned, and went
unto Jo-hā'nan the son of Ka-rē'ah.
15 But Ĭsh'ma-el the son of Nĕth-a-
nī'ah [o]escaped from Jo-hā'nan with
eight men, and went to the Ăm'mŏn-
ītes.
16 Then took Jo-hā'nan the son of
Ka-rē'ah, and all the captains of the
forces that *were* with him, all the remnant of the people whom he had recovered from Ĭsh'ma-el the son of Nĕth-
a-nī'ah, from Mĭz'pah, after *that* he
had slain Gĕd-a-lī'ah the son of A-hī'-
kam, *even* mighty men of war, and the
women, and the children, and the eunuchs, whom he had brought again
from Gĭb'e-on:
17 And they departed, and dwelt in
the habitation of [p]Chĭm'ham, which is
by Bĕth'–lĕ-hĕm, to go to enter into
Ē'gypt,
18 [3]Because of the Chăl-dē'ans: for
they were afraid of them, because
Ĭsh'ma-el the son of Nĕth-a-nī'ah had
slain Gĕd-a-lī'ah the son of A-hī'kam,
[q]whom the king of Băb'y̆-lon made
governor in the land.
42 Then all the captains of the forces,
[a]and Jo-hā'nan the son of Ka-
rē'ah, and Jĕz-a-nī'ah the son of Hŏsh-
a-ī'ah, and all the people from the least
even unto the greatest, came near,
2 And said unto Jĕr-e-mī'ah the
prophet, [1]Let, we beseech thee, our supplication be accepted before thee, and
[b]pray for us unto the LORD thy God,
even for all this remnant; (for we are
left *but* [c]a few of many, as thine eyes
do behold us:)
3 That the LORD thy God may shew
us [d]the way wherein we may walk,
and the thing that we may do.

14 [o]ch. 25.21.ch. 41.10; Amos 1.13; Zech. 1.15 [5]to strike thee in soul
16 [p]1 Cor. 13.5

CHAPTER 41
1 [a]2 Ki. 25.25; ch. 40.6-8 [b]Ps. 41.9; Luke 22.21
2 [c]2 Sam. 3.27; 2 Ki. 25.25; Ps. 41.9
3 [d]Ps. 52; Prov. 1.16; Rom. 3.15
5 [e]Gen. 33.18; Josh. 24.32 [f]Josh. 18.1; ch. 7.12-14 [g]Lev. 19.27-28; Deut. 14.1; Isa. 15.2 [h]1 Sam. 1.7; 2 Ki. 25.9; Probably an altar built by Gedaliah
6 [1]in going and weeping
9 [2]by the hand, or, by the side of Gedaliah, or, near Gedaliah [i]Josh. 10.16-18
10 [j]ch. 43.6 [k]ch. 40.7 [l]Neh. 2.10-19
11 [m]ch. 40.7-8-13
12 [n]2 Sam. 2.13
15 [o]1 Sam. 30.17; 1 Ki. 20.20
17 [p]2 Sam. 19.37-38
18 [3]From the face of [q]ch. 40.5

CHAPTER 42
1 [a]ch. 40.8-13.ch. 41.11
2 [1]Or, Let our supplication fall before thee [b]Ex. 8.28; 1 Sam. 7.8; 1 Ki. 13.6; Isa. 37.4; ch. 21.2; Acts 8.24; Jas. 5.16 [c]Lev. 26.22
3 [d]Ezra 8.21; Prov. 3.5-6

4 Then Jĕr-e-mī'ah the prophet said unto them, I have heard *you;* behold, I will pray unto the LORD your God according to your words; and it shall come to pass, *that* [e]whatsoever thing the LORD shall answer you, I will declare *it* unto you; I will [f]keep nothing back from you.

5 Then they said to Jĕr-e-mī'ah, [g]The LORD be a true and faithful witness between us, if we do not even according to all things for the which the LORD thy God shall send thee to us.

6 Whether *it be* good, or whether *it be* evil, we will obey the voice of the LORD our God, to whom we send thee; [h]that it may be well with us, when we obey the voice of the LORD our God.

7 ¶ And it came to pass after ten days, that the word of the LORD came unto Jĕr-e-mī'ah.

8 Then called he Jo-hā'nan the son of Ka-rē'ah, and all the captains of the forces which *were* with him, and all the people from the least even to the greatest,

9 And said unto them, Thus saith the LORD, the God of Is'ra-el, unto whom ye sent me to present your supplication before him;

10 If ye will still abide in this land, then [i]will I build you, and not pull *you* down, and I will plant you, and not pluck *you* up: for I [j]repent me of the evil that I have done unto you.

11 Be not afraid of the king of Băb'ȳ-lon, of whom ye are afraid; be not afraid of him, saith the LORD: [k]for I *am* with you to save you, and to deliver you from his hand.

12 And [l]I will shew mercies unto you, that he may have mercy upon you, and cause you to return to your own land.

13 ¶ But if [m]ye say, We will not dwell in this land, neither obey the voice of the LORD your God,

14 Saying, No; but we will go into the land of Ē'ġypt, where we shall see no war, nor hear the sound of the trumpet, nor have hunger of bread; and there will we dwell:

15 And now therefore hear the word of the LORD, ye remnant of Jū'dah; Thus saith the LORD of hosts, the God of Is'ra-el; If ye [n]wholly set your faces to enter into Ē'ġypt, and go to sojourn there;

16 Then it shall come to pass, *that* the sword, [o]which ye feared, shall overtake you there in the land of Ē'ġypt, and the famine, whereof ye were afraid, [2]shall follow close after you there in Ē'ġypt; and there ye shall die.

17 [3]So shall it be with all the men that set their faces to go into Ē'ġypt to sojourn there; they shall die [p]by the sword, by the famine, and by the pestilence: and [q]none of them shall remain or escape from the evil that I will bring upon them.

18 For thus saith the LORD of hosts, the God of Is'ra-el; As mine anger and my fury hath been [r]poured forth upon the inhabitants of Je-ru'sa-lĕm; so shall my fury be poured forth upon you, when ye shall enter into Ē'ġypt: and [s]ye shall be an execration, and an astonishment, and a curse, and a reproach; and ye shall see this place no more.

19 ¶ The LORD hath said concerning you, O ye remnant of Jū'dah; [t]Go ye not into Ē'ġypt: know certainly that I have [4]admonished you this day.

20 For [5]ye dissembled in your hearts, when ye sent me unto the LORD your God, saying, Pray for us unto the LORD our God; and according unto all that the LORD our God shall say, so declare unto us, and we will do *it.*

21 And *now* I have this day declared *it* to you; but [u]ye have not obeyed the voice of the LORD your God, nor any *thing* for the which he hath sent me unto you.

22 Now therefore know certainly that [v]ye shall die by the sword, by the famine, and by the pestilence, in the place whither ye desire [6]to go *and* to sojourn.

43 And it came to pass, *that* when Jĕr-e-mī'ah had made an end of speaking unto all the people all the words of the LORD their God, for which the LORD their God had sent him to them, *even* all these words,

2 [a]Then spake Ăz-a-rī'ah the son of Hŏsh-a-ī'ah, and Jo-hā'nan the son of Ka-rē'ah, and all [b]the proud men, saying unto Jĕr-e-mī'ah, Thou speakest falsely: the LORD our God hath not sent thee to say, Go not into Ē'ġypt to sojourn there:

3 But Bā'ruch the son of Ne-rī'ah setteth thee on against us, for to deliver us into the hand of the Chăl-dē'ans, that they might put us to death, and carry us away captives into Băb'ȳ-lon.

4 So Jo-hā'nan the son of Ka-rē'ah, and all the captains of the forces, and all the people, obeyed not the voice of the LORD, to dwell in the land of Jū'dah.

5 But Jo-hā'nan the son of Ka-rē'ah, and all the captains of the forces, took [c]all the remnant of Jū'dah, that were returned from all nations, whither they had been driven, to dwell in the land of Jū'dah;

6 *Even* men, and women, and children, and the king's daughters, [d]and every person that Nĕb'u-zär–ā'dan the captain of the guard had left with Ġĕd-a-lī'ah the son of A-hī'kam the son of Shā'phan, and Jĕr-e-mī'ah the prophet, and Bā'ruch the son of Ne-rī'ah.

7 So they came into the land of Ē'ġypt: for they obeyed not the voice of the LORD: thus came they *even* to [e]Täh'pan-hēs.

8 ¶ Then came the word of the LORD unto Jĕr-e-mī'ah in Täh'pan-hēs, saying,

9 Take great stones in thine hand, and hide them in the clay in the brickkiln, which *is* at the entry of Phā'raōh's house in Täh'pan-hēs, in the sight of the men of Jū'dah;

4 [e]1 Ki. 22.14
[f]1 Sam. 3.18; Acts 20.20
5 [g]Gen. 31.50
6 [h]Deut. 6.3; ch. 7.23
10 [i]ch. 24.6; ch. 31.28
[j]Deut. 32.36; ch. 18.8
11 [k]Num. 14.9; Deut. 20.4; Ps. 46.7; Isa. 43.5; Rom. 8.31
12 [l]Ps. 106.45-46
13 [m]ch. 44.16
15 [n]Deut. 17.16; Luke 9.51
16 [o]Ezek. 11.8
[2]shall cleave after you
17 [3]So shall all the men be
[p]ch. 24.10
[q]ch. 44.14-28
18 [r]2 Chr. 34.25; ch. 6.11; Ezek. 22.22
[s]ch. 18.16; ch. 24.9; ch. 26.6
19 [t]Deut. 17.16
[4]testified against you
20 [5]Or, ye have used deceit against your souls
21 [u]Zech. 7.11
22 [v]Ezek. 6.11
[6]Or, to go to sojourn
CHAPTER 43
2 [a]ch. 42.1
[b]Ps. 12.4; ch. 42.1-2; Mal. 3.13; 2 Thess. 2.10-11-12
5 [c]ch. 40.11-12
6 [d]ch. 39.10
7 [e]ch. 2.16; ch. 44.1; called Hanes, Isa. 30.4

10 And say unto them, Thus saith
the LORD of hosts, the God of Ĭs'ra-el;
Behold, I [f]will send and take Nĕb-
u-chăd-rĕz'zar the king of Băb'y̆-lon,
[g]my servant, and will set his throne
upon these stones that I have hid; and
he shall spread his royal pavilion over
them.
11 [h]And when he cometh, he shall
smite the land of Ē'ġypt, *and deliver*
[i]such *as are* for death to death; and
such *as are* for captivity to captivity;
and such *as are* for the sword to the
sword.
12 And I will kindle a fire in the
houses of [j]the gods of Ē'ġypt; and he
shall burn them, and carry them away
captives: and he shall array himself
with the land of Ē'ġypt, as a shepherd
putteth on his garment; and he shall go
forth from thence in peace.
13 He shall break also the [1]images
of [2]Bĕth–shē'mĕsh, that *is* in the land
of Ē'ġypt; and the houses of the gods
of the Ē-ġy̆p''tians shall he burn with
fire.

44

44 The word that came to Jĕr-e-
mī'ah concerning all the Jews
which dwell in the land of Ē'ġypt,
which dwell at [a]Mĭg'dol, and at [b]Tăh'-
pan-hēs, and at [c]Nŏph, and in the country of [d]Păth'ros, saying,
2 Thus saith the LORD of hosts, the
God of Ĭs'ra-el; Ye have seen all the
evil that I have brought upon Je-ru'sa-
lĕm, and upon all the cities of Jū'dah;
and, behold, this day they *are* [e]a desolation, and no man dwelleth therein,
3 Because of their wickedness
which they have committed to provoke
me to anger, in that they went [f]to burn
incense, *and* to [g]serve other gods,
whom they knew not, *neither* they, ye,
nor your fathers.
4 Howbeit [h]I sent unto you all my
servants the prophets, rising early and
sending *them*, saying, Oh, do not this
abominable thing that I hate.
5 But they hearkened not, nor inclined their ear to turn from their wickedness, to burn no incense unto other
gods.
6 Wherefore [i]my fury and mine anger was poured forth, and was kindled
in the cities of Jū'dah and in the streets
of Je-ru'sa-lĕm; and they are wasted
and desolate, as at this day.
7 Therefore now thus saith the LORD,
the God of hosts, the God of Ĭs'ra-el;
Wherefore commit ye *this* great evil
[j]against your souls, to cut off from you
man and woman, child and suckling,
[1]out of Jū'dah, to leave you none to
remain;
8 In that ye [k]provoke me unto wrath
with the works of your hands, burning
incense unto other gods in the land of
Ē'ġypt, whither ye be gone to dwell,
that ye might cut yourselves off, and
that ye might be [l]a curse and a reproach among all the nations of the
earth?
9 Have ye forgotten the [2]wickedness
of your fathers, and the wickedness of
the kings of Jū'dah, and the wickedness of their wives, and your own wickedness, and the wickedness of your
wives, which they have committed in
the land of Jū'dah, and in the streets of
Je-ru'sa-lĕm?
10 They are not [3]humbled *even* unto
this day, neither have they [m]feared,
nor walked in my law, nor in my statutes, that I set before you and before
your fathers.
11 ¶ Therefore thus saith the LORD
of hosts, the God of Ĭs'ra-el; Behold, [n]I
will set my face against you for evil,
and to cut off all Jū'dah.
12 And I will take the remnant of
Jū'dah, that have set their faces to go
into the land of Ē'ġypt to sojourn there,
and [o]they shall all be consumed, *and*
fall in the land of Ē'ġypt; they shall
even be consumed by the sword *and* by
the famine: they shall die, from the
least even unto the greatest, by the
sword and by the famine: and [p]they
shall be an execration, *and* an astonishment, and a curse, and a reproach.
13 For I will [4]punish them that dwell
in the land of Ē'ġypt, as I have punished Je-ru'sa-lĕm, by the sword, by
the famine, and by the pestilence:
14 So that none of the remnant of
Jū'dah, which are gone into the land of
Ē'ġypt to sojourn there, shall escape or
remain, that they should return into
the land of Jū'dah, to the which they
[5]have a desire to return to dwell there:
for none shall return but such as shall
escape.
15 ¶ Then all the men which knew
that their wives had burned incense
unto other gods, and all the women
that stood by, a great multitude, even
all the people that dwelt in the land of
Ē'ġypt, in Păth'ros, answered Jĕr-e-
mī'ah, saying,
16 *As for* the word that thou hast
spoken unto us in the name of the
LORD, [q]we will not hearken unto thee.
17 But we will certainly do [r]whatso-
ever thing goeth forth out of our own
mouth, to burn incense unto the [6]queen
of heaven, and to pour out drink offerings unto her, as we have done, we and
our fathers, our kings, and our princes,
in the cities of Jū'dah, and in the streets
of Je-ru'sa-lĕm: for *then* had we plenty
of [7]victuals, and were well, and saw no
evil.
18 But since we left off to burn incense to the queen of heaven, and to
pour out drink offerings unto her, we
have wanted all *things*, and have been
consumed by the sword and by the
famine.
19 [s]And when we burned incense to
the queen of heaven, and poured out
drink offerings unto her, did we make
her cakes to worship her, and pour out
drink offerings unto her, without our
[8]men?
20 ¶ Then Jĕr-e-mī'ah said unto all
the people, to the men, and to the
women, and to all the people which
had given him *that* answer, saying,
21 The incense that ye burned in the
cities of Jū'dah, and in the streets of Je-

10 [f]Dan. 2.21 [g]ch. 25.9; Ezek. 29.18-20
11 [h]ch. 44.13 [i]ch. 15.2; Zech. 11.9
12 [j]Ex. 12.12; ch. 46.25
13 [1]statues, or, standing images [2]Or, The house of the sun
CHAPTER 44
1 [a]Ex. 14.2; ch. 46.14 [b]ch. 43.7 [c]Isa. 19.13; Hos. 9.6 [d]Isa. 11.11
2 [e]Lev. 26.32-34; Luke 13.35
3 [f]ch. 19.4 [g]Deut. 13.6
4 [h]2 Chr. 36.15; ch. 7.25
6 [i]ch. 42.18; 1 Cor. 10.11
7 [j]Num. 16.38; ch. 7.19 [1]out of the midst of Judah
8 [k]ch. 25.6-7 [l]ch. 42.18
9 [2]wickednesses, or, punishments, etc
10 [3]contrite, Ps. 34.18; Isa. 57.15 [m]Prov. 28.14
11 [n]Lev. 17.10; Amos 9.4
12 [o]Deut. 17.16; Matt. 2.13-14 [p]ch. 18.16; ch. 24.9; Zech. 8.13
13 [4]visit
14 [5]lift up their soul
16 [q]Ex. 5.2; Rom. 2.3-9
17 [r]Num. 30.12; [6]Or, frame of heaven [7]bread, Hos. 2.5
19 [s]ch. 7.18 [8]Or, husbands

rụ'sa-lĕm, ye, and your fathers, your
kings, and your princes, and the people
of the land, did not the LORD remember
them, and came it *not* into his mind?
22 So that the LORD could [t]no longer
bear, because of the evil of your doings, *and* because of the abominations
which ye have committed; therefore is
your land [u]a desolation, and an astonishment, and a curse, without an inhabitant, as at this day.
23 Because ye have burned incense,
and because ye have sinned against
the LORD, and have not obeyed the
voice of the LORD, nor walked in his
law, nor in his statutes, nor in his testimonies; [v]therefore this evil is happened unto you, as at this day.
24 Moreover Jĕr-e-mī'ah said unto
all the people, and to all the women,
Hear the word of the LORD, all Jū'dah
[w]that *are* in the land of Ē'ġypt:
25 Thus saith the LORD of hosts, the
God of Ĭs'ra-el, saying; Ye and your
wives have both spoken with your
mouths, and fulfilled with your hand,
saying, We will surely perform our
vows that we have vowed, to burn incense to the queen of heaven, and to
pour out drink offerings unto her: ye
will surely accomplish your vows, and
surely perform your vows.
26 Therefore hear ye the word of the
LORD, all Jū'dah that dwell in the land
of Ē'ġypt; Behold, [x]I have sworn by
my great name, saith the LORD, that
[y]my name shall no more be named in
the mouth of any man of Jū'dah in all
the land of Ē'ġypt, saying, The Lord
GOD liveth.
27 Behold, [z]I will watch over them
for evil, and not for good: and all the
men of Jū'dah that *are* in the land of
Ē'ġypt shall be consumed by the sword
and by the famine, until there be an end
of them.
28 Yet [a]a small number that escape
the sword shall return out of the land
of Ē'ġypt into the land of Jū'dah, and
all the remnant of Jū'dah, that are
gone into the land of Ē'ġypt to sojourn
there, shall know whose words shall
stand, [9]mine, or theirs.
29 ¶ And this *shall be* a sign unto
you, saith the LORD, that I will punish
you in this place, that ye may know that
my words shall [b]surely stand against
you for evil:
30 Thus saith the LORD; Behold, [c]I
will give Phā'raōh–hŏph'rȧ king of
Ē'ġypt into the hand of his enemies,
and into the hand of them that seek his
life; as I gave [d]Zĕd-e-kī'ah king of
Jū'dah into the hand of Nĕb-u-chăd-
rez'zar king of Băb'ȳ-lon, his enemy,
and that sought his life.

45 The [a]word that Jĕr-e-mī'ah the
prophet spake unto Bā'rụch the
son of Ne-rī'ah, when he had written
these words in a book at the mouth of
Jĕr-e-mī'ah, in the fourth year of Je-
hoi'a-kim the son of Jo-sī'ah king of
Jū'dah, saying,
2 Thus saith the LORD, the God of
Ĭs'ra-el, unto thee, O Bā'rụch;

22 [t]Gen. 6.3; Isa. 7.13; Isa. 43.24; Amos 2.13
[u]Gen. 19.13-24-25; Ps. 107.33-34; ch. 25.11-18-38
23 [v]Dan. 9.11-12
24 [w]ch. 43.7; ch. 46.14
26 [x]Gen. 22.16
[y]Ps. 50.16; Ezek. 20.39
27 [z]ch. 1.10; ch. 2.17-19; ch. 4.18; ch. 5.19-29; ch. 11.17; ch. 31.28; Ezek. 7.6
28 [a]Lev. 26.44; Isa. 27.13; Hab. 3.2
[9]from me, or, them
29 [b]Ps. 33.11
30 [c]ch. 46.25-26; Ezek. 29.3; Dan. 4.35
[d]ch. 39.5

CHAPTER 45

1 [a]Isa. 50.4; ch. 36.1-4-32
4 [b]Isa. 5.5
5 [c]Ps. 4.6; Matt. 6.34
[d]Gen. 6.12; Isa. 66.16
[e]ch. 21.9; ch. 38.2

CHAPTER 46

1 [a]ch. 25.15
2 [b]2 Ki. 23.29; 2 Chr. 35.20; ch. 25.9-19; Fulfilled presently
3 [c]Isa. 8.9-10; ch. 51.11-12; Joel 3.9-10; Nah. 2.1
5 [1]broken in pieces
[2]fled a flight
[d]ch. 6.25; ch. 20.4; Rev. 6.15-17
6 [e]Dan. 11.19
7 [f]Dan. 11.22
9 [3]Cush
[4]Put
10 [g]Joel 1.15
[h]Deut. 32.42
[i]Isa. 34.6
11 [j]ch. 8.22
[k]Isa. 47.1
[5]no cure shall be unto thee

3 Thou didst say, Woe is me now!
for the LORD hath added grief to my
sorrow; I fainted in my sighing, and I
find no rest.
4 ¶ Thus shalt thou say unto him,
The LORD saith thus; Behold, [b]*that*
which I have built will I break down,
and that which I have planted I will
pluck up, even this whole land.
5 And [c]seekest thou great things for
thyself? seek *them* not: for, behold, [d]I
will bring evil upon all flesh, saith the
LORD: but thy life will I give unto thee
[e]for a prey in all places whither thou
goest.

46 The word of the LORD which
came to Jĕr-e-mī'ah the prophet
against [a]the Gĕn'tīles;
2 Against Ē'ġypt, [b]against the army
of Phā'raōh–nē'cho king of Ē'ġypt,
which was by the river Eū-phrā'tēs in
Cär'chĕ-mĭsh, which Nĕb'u-chăd-rez'-
zar king of Băb'ȳ-lon smote in the
fourth year of Je-hoi'a-kim the son of
Jo-sī'ah king of Jū'dah.
3 [c]Order ye the buckler and shield,
and draw near to battle.
4 Harness the horses; and get up, ye
horsemen, and stand forth with *your*
helmets; furbish the spears, *and* put on
the brigandines.
5 Wherefore have I seen them dismayed *and* turned away back? and their
mighty ones are [1]beaten down, and are
[2]fled apace, and look not back: *for* [d]fear
was round about, saith the LORD.
6 Let not the swift flee away, nor the
mighty man escape; they shall [e]stum-
ble, and fall toward the north by the
river Eū-phrā'tēs.
7 Who *is* this *that* cometh up [f]as a
flood, whose waters are moved as the
rivers?
8 Ē'ġypt riseth up like a flood, and
his waters are moved like the rivers;
and he saith, I will go up, *and* will
cover the earth; I will destroy the city
and the inhabitants thereof.
9 Come up, ye horses; and rage, ye
chariots; and let the mighty men come
forth; [3]the Ē-thĭ-ō'pĭ-ans and [4]the Lĭb'-
ȳ-ans, that handle the shield; and the
Lȳd'ĭ-ans, that handle *and* bend the
bow.
10 For this *is* [g]the day of the Lord
GOD of hosts, a day of vengeance, that
he may avenge him of his adversaries:
and [h]the sword shall devour, and it
shall be satiate and made drunk with
their blood: for the Lord GOD of hosts
[i]hath a sacrifice in the north country
by the river Eū-phrā'tēs.
11 [j]Go up into Ġĭl'e-ăd, and take
balm, [k]O virgin, the daughter of Ē'ġypt:
in vain shalt thou use many medicines;
for [5]thou shalt not be cured.
12 The nations have heard of thy
shame, and thy cry hath filled the land:
for the mighty man hath stumbled
against the mighty, *and* they are fallen
both together.
13 ¶ The word that the LORD
spake to Jĕr-e-mī'ah the prophet, how
Nĕb-u-chăd-rez'zar king of Băb'ȳ-lon

should come *and* [l]smite the land of Ē'ġypt.

14 Declare ye in Ē'ġypt, and publish in Mĭg'dol, and publish in Nŏph and in Tăh'pan-hēs: say ye, Stand fast, and prepare thee; for the sword shall devour round about thee.

15 Why are thy valiant *men* swept away? they stood not, because the LORD did drive them.

16 He [6]made many to fall, yea, [m]one fell upon another: and they said, Arise, and let us go again to our own people, and to the land of our nativity, from the oppressing sword.

17 They did cry there, Phā'raōh king of Ē'ġypt *is but* a noise; he hath passed the time appointed.

18 *As* I live, saith the King, [n]whose name *is* the LORD of hosts, Surely as Tā'bôr *is* among the mountains, and as Cär'mel by the sea, [o]*so* shall he come.

19 O [p]thou daughter dwelling in Ē'ġypt, [7]furnish thyself to go into captivity: for Nŏph shall be waste and desolate without an inhabitant.

20 Ē'ġypt *is like* a very fair [q]heifer, *but* destruction cometh; it cometh [r]out of the north.

21 Also her hired men *are* in the midst of her like [8]fatted bullocks; for they also are turned back, *and* are fled away together: they did not stand, because the day of their calamity was come upon them, *and* the time of their visitation.

22 [s]The voice thereof shall go like a serpent; for they shall march with an army, and come against her with axes, as hewers of wood.

23 They shall cut down her forest, saith the LORD, though it cannot be searched; because they are more than the grasshoppers, and *are* innumerable.

24 The daughter of Ē'ġypt shall be confounded; she shall be delivered into the hand of the people of the north.

25 The LORD of hosts, the God of Ĭs'ra-el, saith; Behold, I will punish the [9]multitude of Nō, and Phā'raōh, and Ē'ġypt, [t]with their gods, and their kings; even Phā'raōh, and *all* them that trust in him:

26 [u]And I will deliver them into the hand of those that seek their lives, and into the hand of Nĕb-u-chăd-rez'zar king of Băb'ȳ-lon, and into the hand of his servants: and [v]afterward it shall be inhabited, as in the days of old, saith the LORD.

27 ¶ [w]But fear not thou, O my servant Jā'cob, and be not dismayed, O Ĭs'ra-el: for, behold, I will save thee from afar off, and thy seed from the land of their captivity; and Jā'cob shall return, and be in rest and at ease, and none shall make *him* afraid.

28 Fear thou not, O Jā'cob my servant, saith the LORD: for I *am* with thee; for I will make a full end of all the nations whither I have driven thee: but I will not make a full end of thee, but correct thee in measure; yet will I [10]not leave thee wholly unpunished.

47 The word of the LORD that came to Jĕr-e-mī'ah the prophet [a]against the Phĭ-lĭs'tĭnes, [b]before that Phā'raōh smote [1]Gā'zȧ.

2 Thus saith the LORD; Behold, [c]waters rise up [d]out of the north, and shall be an overflowing flood, and shall overflow the land, and [2]all that is therein; the city, and them that dwell therein: then the men shall cry, and all the inhabitants of the land shall howl.

3 At the [e]noise of the stamping of the hoofs of his strong *horses*, at the rushing of his chariots, *and at* the rumbling of his wheels, the fathers shall not look back to *their* children for feebleness of hands;

4 Because of the day that cometh to spoil all the Phĭ-lĭs'tĭnes, *and* to cut off from [f]Tȳ'rus and Zī'dŏn every helper that remaineth: for the LORD will spoil the Phĭ-lĭs'tĭnes, [g]the remnant of [3]the country of [h]Căph'tôr.

5 [i]Baldness is come upon Gā'zȧ; Ăsh'ke-lŏn is cut off *with* the remnant of their valley: how long wilt thou cut thyself?

6 O thou [j]sword of the LORD, how long *will it be* ere thou be quiet? [4]put up thyself into thy scabbard, rest, and be still.

7 [5]How can it be quiet, seeing the LORD hath [k]given it a charge against Ăsh'ke-lŏn, and against the sea shore? there hath he [l]appointed it.

48 Against [a]Mō'ab thus saith the LORD of hosts, the God of Ĭs'ra-el; Woe unto [b]Nē'bo! for it is spoiled: Kĭr-ī-a-thā'im is confounded *and* taken: [1]Mĭs'gab is confounded and dismayed.

2 *There shall be* no more praise of Mō'ab: in Hĕsh'bŏn they have devised evil against it; come, and let us cut it off from *being* a nation. Also thou shalt [2]be cut down, O Măd'men; the sword shall [3]pursue thee.

3 A voice of crying *shall be* from Hŏr-o-nā'im, spoiling and great destruction.

4 Mō'ab is destroyed; her little ones have caused a cry to be heard.

5 For in the going up of Lụ'hith [4]continual weeping shall go up; for in the going down of Hŏr-o-nā'im the enemies have heard a cry of destruction.

6 Flee, save your lives, and be like [5]the heath in the wilderness.

7 ¶ [c]For because thou hast trusted in thy works and in thy treasures, thou shalt also be taken: and [d]Chē'mŏsh shall go forth into captivity *with* his priests and his princes together.

8 And the spoiler shall come upon every city, and no city shall escape: the valley also shall perish, and the plain shall be destroyed, as the LORD hath spoken.

9 Give wings unto Mō'ab, that it may flee and get away: for the cities thereof shall be desolate, without any to dwell therein.

10 [e]Cursed *be* he that doeth the work of the LORD [6]deceitfully, and cursed *be* he that keepeth back his sword from blood.

13 [l]Isa. 19.1; Ezek. 29; Fulfilled B.C. 571
16 [6]multiplied the fallen
[m]Lev. 26.37
18 [n]Isa. 48.2; 1 Tim. 1.17
[o]Num. 23.19
19 [p]ch. 48.18
[7]make thee instruments of captivity
20 [q]Hos. 10.11
[r]ch. 1.14
21 [8]bullocks of the stall
22 [s]Isa. 29.4
25 [9]Amon, or, nourisher
[t]Ezek. 30.13
26 [u]ch. 44.30
[v]ch. 48.47; ch. 49.39
27 [w]Isa. 44.2
28 [10]Or, not utterly cut thee off

CHAPTER 47
1 [a]ch. 25.20; Zeph. 2.4-5
[b]Amos 1.6; Zech. 9.5-6
[1]Azzah
2 [c]Isa. 8.7
[d]ch. 1.14
[2]the fulness thereof
3 [e]Nah. 3.2
4 [f]ch. 25.22;
[g]Amos 9.7
[3]the isle
[h]Gen. 10.14
5 [i]Zeph. 2.4
6 [j]Ezek. 21.3
[4]gather thyself
7 [5]How canst thou
[k]1 Sam. 3.12
[l]Mic. 6.9

CHAPTER 48
1 [a]Isa. 15
[b]Num. 32.38
[1]Or, The high place
2 [2]Or, be brought to silence
[3]go after thee
5 [4]weeping with weeping
6 [5]Or, a naked tree, or, destitute
7 [c]Ps. 49.6-7;
[d]Num. 21.29
10 [e]1 Sam. 15.3
[6]Or, negligently

11 ¶ Mō'ab hath been at ease from
his youth, and [f]he hath settled on his
lees, and hath not been emptied from
vessel to vessel, neither hath he gone
into captivity: therefore his taste [7]re-
mained in him, and his scent is not
changed.
12 Therefore, behold, the days come,
saith the LORD, that I will send unto
him wanderers, that shall cause him to
wander, and shall empty his vessels
and break their bottles.
13 And Mō'ab shall be ashamed
of [g]Chē'mŏsh, as the house of Ĭs'ra-
el [h]was ashamed of [i]Bĕth'–el their
confidence.
14 ¶ How say ye, [j]We *are* mighty
and strong men for the war?
15 Mō'ab is spoiled, and gone up
out of her cities, and [8]his chosen young
men are [k]gone down to the slaughter,
saith [l]the King, whose name *is* the
LORD of hosts.
16 The calamity of Mō'ab *is* near to
come, and his affliction hasteth fast.
17 All ye that are about him, bemoan him; and all ye that know his
name, say, [m]How is the strong staff
broken, *and* the beautiful rod!
18 [n]Thou daughter that dost inhabit
[o]Dī'bŏn, come down from *thy* glory,
and sit in thirst; for the spoiler of
Mō'ab shall come upon thee, *and* he
shall destroy thy strong holds.
19 O [9]inhabitant of [p]Ăr'ō-ēr, [q]stand
by the way, and espy; ask him that
fleeth, and her that escapeth, *and* say,
What is done?
20 Mō'ab is confounded; for it is broken down: howl and cry; tell ye it in
[r]Ăr'nŏn, that Mō'ab is spoiled,
21 And judgment is come upon the
plain country; upon Hō'lŏn, and upon
Ja-hā'zah, and upon Mĕph'a-āth,
22 And upon Dī'bŏn, and upon
Nē'bo, and upon Bĕth–dĭb-la-thā'im,
23 And upon Kĭr-ī-a-thā'im, and upon
Bĕth–gā'mŭl, and upon Bĕth–mē'on,
24 And upon [s]Kē'rĭ-ŏth, and upon
Bŏz'rah, and upon all the cities of the
land of Mō'ab, far or near.
25 The horn of Mō'ab is cut off, and
his arm is broken, saith the LORD.
26 ¶ [t]Make ye him drunken: for he
magnified *himself* against the LORD:
Mō'ab also shall wallow in his vomit,
and he also shall be in derision.
27 For [u]was not Ĭs'ra-el a derision
unto thee? [v]was he found among
thieves? for since thou spakest of him,
thou [10]skippedst for joy.
28 O ye that dwell in Mō'ab, leave
the cities, and [w]dwell in the rock, and
be like [x]the dove *that* maketh her nest
in the sides of the hole's mouth.
29 We have heard the [y]pride of
Mō'ab, (he is exceeding proud) his loftiness, and his arrogancy, and his pride,
and the haughtiness of his heart.
30 I know his wrath, saith the LORD;
but *it shall* not *be* so; [11]his lies shall not
so effect *it*.
31 Therefore [z]will I howl for Mō'ab,
and I will cry out for all Mō'ab; *mine*

11 [f]Zeph. 1.12
[7]stood
13 [g]Judg. 11.24
[h]Hos. 10.6
[i]1 Ki. 12.29;
14 [j]Ps. 33.6
15 [8]the choice of
[k]ch. 50.27
[l]ch. 51.57
17 [m]Isa. 9.4
18 [n]Isa. 47.1;
[o]Num. 21.30
19 [9]inhabitress
[p]Deut. 2.36
[q]1 Sam. 4.13-16
20 [r]Num. 21.13
24 [s]Amos 2.2
26 [t]ch. 25.15
27 [u]Prov. 24.17;
[v]ch. 2.26
[10]Or, movedst thyself
28 [w]Ps. 55.6-7
[x]Song 2.14
29 [y]Isa. 16.6
30 [11]his bars, or, those on whom he stayeth, do not right
31 [z]Isa. 15.5
32 [a]Num. 21.32
33 [b]Isa. 16.9-10
34 [c]Isa. 15.4-5-6
[d]Isa. 15.5-6
[12]desolations
35 [e]Isa. 15.2
36 [f]Isa. 15.5
[g]Prov. 11.4
37 [h]Isa. 15.2-3;
[13]diminished
[i]Gen. 37.34
38 [j]ch. 22.28
39 [14]neck
40 [k]ch. 49.22;
[l]Isa. 8.8
41 [15]Or, The cities
[m]Isa. 13.8
42 [n]Ps. 83.4;
[o]Prov. 16.18
43 [p]Isa. 24.17-18
44 [q]ch. 11.23
45 [r]Num. 21.28
[s]Num. 24.17
[16]children of noise
46 [t]Num. 21.29;
[17]in captivity
47 [u]ch. 49.6-39

heart shall mourn for the men of
Kĭr–hĕ'rĕs.
32 O vine of Sĭb'mah, I will weep for
thee with the weeping of Jā'zēr: thy
plants are gone over the sea, they reach
even to [a]the sea of Jā'zēr: the spoiler
is fallen upon thy summer fruits and
upon thy vintage.
33 And [b]joy and gladness is taken
from the plentiful field, and from the
land of Mō'ab; and I have caused wine
to fail from the winepresses: none
shall tread with shouting; *their* shouting *shall be* no shouting.
34 [c]From the cry of Hĕsh'bŏn *even*
unto Ē-le-ā'leh, *and even* unto Jā'hăz,
have they uttered their voice, [d]from
Zō'ar *even* unto Hŏr-o-nā'im, *as* an
heifer of three years old: for the waters
also of Nĭm'rim shall be [12]desolate.
35 Moreover I will cause to cease in
Mō'ab, saith the LORD, [e]him that offereth in the high places, and him that
burneth incense to his gods.
36 Therefore [f]mine heart shall sound
for Mō'ab like pipes, and mine heart
shall sound like pipes for the men of
Kĭr–hē'res: because [g]the riches *that* he
hath gotten are perished.
37 For [h]every head *shall be* bald,
and every beard [13]clipped: upon all the
hands *shall be* cuttings, and [i]upon the
loins sackcloth.
38 *There shall be* lamentation generally upon all the house tops of Mō'ab
and in the streets thereof: for I have
broken Mō'ab like [j]a vessel wherein *is*
no pleasure, saith the LORD.
39 They shall howl, *saying,* How is it
broken down! how hath Mō'ab turned
the [14]back with shame! so shall Mō'ab
be a derision and a dismaying to all
them about him.
40 For thus saith the LORD; Behold,
[k]he shall fly as an eagle, and shall
[l]spread his wings over Mō'ab.
41 [15]Kē'rĭ-ŏth is taken, and the strong
holds are surprised, and [m]the mighty
men's hearts in Mō'ab at that day shall
be as the heart of a woman in her pangs.
42 And Mō'ab shall be destroyed
[n]from *being* a people, because he hath
[o]magnified *himself* against the LORD.
43 [p]Fear, and the pit, and the snare,
shall be upon thee, O inhabitant of
Mō'ab, saith the LORD.
44 He that fleeth from the fear shall
fall into the pit; and he that getteth up
out of the pit shall be taken in the
snare: for [q]I will bring upon it, *even*
upon Mō'ab, the year of their visitation, saith the LORD.
45 They that fled stood under the
shadow of Hĕsh'bŏn because of the
force: but [r]a fire shall come forth out
of Hĕsh'bŏn, and a flame from the
midst of Sī'hŏn, and [s]shall devour the
corner of Mō'ab, and the crown of the
head of the [16]tumultuous ones.
46 [t]Woe be unto thee, O Mō'ab!
the people of Chē'mŏsh perisheth: for
thy sons are taken [17]captives, and thy
daughters captives.
47 ¶ Yet will I bring again the captivity of Mō'ab [u]in the latter days, saith

the LORD. Thus far *is* the judgment of Mō'ab.

49 [1]Concerning the Ăm'mŏn-ītes, thus saith the LORD; Hath Ĭs'ra-el no sons? hath he no heir? why *then* doth [2]their king inherit [a]Găd, and his people dwell in his cities?

2 Therefore, behold, the days come, saith the LORD, that I will cause an alarm of war to be heard in [b]Răb'bah of the Ăm'mŏn-ītes; and it shall be a desolate heap, and her daughters shall be burned with fire: then shall Ĭs'ra-el be heir unto them that were his heirs, saith the LORD.

3 Howl, O Hĕsh'bŏn, for Ā'ī is spoiled: cry, ye daughters of Răb'bah, [c]gird you with sackcloth; lament, and run to and fro by the hedges; for [3]their king shall go into captivity, *and* his [d]priests and his princes together.

4 Wherefore gloriest thou in the valleys, [4]thy flowing valley, O backsliding daughter? that trusted in her treasures, [e]*saying,* Who shall come unto me?

5 Behold, I will bring a fear upon thee, saith the Lord GOD of hosts, from all those that be about thee; and ye shall be driven out every man right forth; and none shall gather up him that wandereth.

6 And [f]afterward I will bring again the captivity of the children of Ăm'mŏn, saith the LORD.

7 ¶ [g]Concerning Ē'dom, thus saith the LORD of hosts; [h]*Is* wisdom no more in Tē'man? [i]is counsel perished from the prudent? is their wisdom vanished?

8 Flee ye, [5]turn back, [j]dwell deep, O inhabitants of [k]Dē'dan; for I will [l]bring the calamity of Ē'sau upon him, the time *that* I will visit him.

9 If [m]grapegatherers come to thee, would they not leave *some* gleaning grapes? if thieves by night, they will destroy [6]till they have enough.

10 But I have made Ē'sau bare, I have uncovered his secret places, and he shall not be able to hide himself: his seed is spoiled, and his brethren, and his neighbours, and [n]he *is* not.

11 Leave thy [o]fatherless children, I will preserve *them* alive; and let thy widows trust in me.

12 For thus saith the LORD; Behold, [p]they whose judgment *was* not to drink of the cup have assuredly drunken; and *art* thou he *that* shall altogether go unpunished? thou shalt not go unpunished, but thou shalt surely drink *of it.*

13 For [q]I have sworn by myself, saith the LORD, that [r]Bŏz'rah shall become a desolation, a reproach, a waste, and a curse; and all the cities thereof shall be perpetual wastes.

14 I have heard a [s]rumour from the LORD, and an ambassador is sent unto the heathen, *saying,* Gather ye together, and come against her, and rise up to the battle.

15 For, lo, I will make thee small among the heathen, *and* depised among men.

16 Thy terribleness hath deceived thee, *and* the pride of thine heart, O thou that dwellest in the clefts of the rock, that holdest the height of the hill: though thou shouldest make thy [t]nest as high as the eagle, [u]I will bring thee down from thence, saith the LORD.

17 Also Ē'dom shall be a desolation: [v]every one that goeth by it shall be astonished, and shall hiss at all the plagues thereof.

18 [w]As in the overthrow of Sŏd'om and Go-mŏr'rah and the neighbour *cities* thereof, saith the LORD, no man shall abide there, neither shall a son of man dwell in it.

19 [x]Behold, he shall come up like a lion from [y]the swelling of Jôr'dan against the habitation of the strong: but I will suddenly make him run away from her: and who *is* a chosen *man, that* I may appoint over her? for [z]who *is* like me? and who will [7]appoint me the time? and [a]who *is* that shepherd that will stand before me?

20 [b]Therefore hear the counsel of the LORD, that he hath taken against Ē'dom; and his purposes, that he hath purposed against the inhabitants of Tē'man: Surely the least of the flock shall draw them out: surely he shall make their habitations desolate with them.

21 The earth is moved at the noise of their fall, at the cry the noise thereof was heard in the [8]Red sea.

22 Behold, [c]he shall come up and fly as the eagle, and spread his wings over Bŏz'rah: and at that day shall the heart of the mighty men of Ē'dom be as the heart of a woman in her pangs.

23 ¶ [d]Concerning Da-măs'cus. Hā'math is confounded, and Ar'pad: for they have heard evil tidings: they are [9]fainthearted; [e]*there is* sorrow [10]on the sea; it cannot be quiet.

24 Da-măs'cus is waxed feeble, *and* turneth herself to flee, and fear hath seized on *her:* [f]anguish and sorrows have taken her, as a woman in travail.

25 How is [g]the city of praise not left, the city of my joy!

26 Therefore her young men shall fall in her streets, and all the men of war shall be cut off in that day, saith the LORD of hosts.

27 And I will kindle a [h]fire in the wall of Da-măs'cus, and it shall consume the palaces of [i]Bĕn–hā'dăd.

28 ¶ [j]Concerning Kē'där, and concerning the kingdoms of Hā'zôr, which Nĕb-u-chăd-rĕz'zar king of Băb'ȳ-lon shall smite, thus saith the LORD; Arise ye, go up to Kē'där, and spoil [k]the men of the east.

29 Their [l]tents and their flocks shall they take away: they shall take to themselves their curtains, and all their vessels, and their camels; and they shall cry unto them, Fear *is* on every side.

30 ¶ Flee, [11]get you far off, dwell deep, O ye inhabitants of Hā'zôr, saith the LORD; for Nĕb-u-chăd-rĕz'zar king of Băb'ȳ-lon hath taken counsel against you, and hath conceived a purpose against you.

CHAPTER 49
1 [1]Or, Against
[2]Or, Melcom
[a]Amos 1.13
2 [b]Amos 1.14
3 [c]Isa. 32.11
[3]Or, Melcom
[d]ch. 48.7
4 [4]Or, thy valley floweth away
[e]ch. 21.13
6 [f]ch. 48.47
7 [g]Amos 1.11
[h]Job 5.12-14. Obad. 8
[i]Isa. 19.11
8 [5]Or, they are turned back
[j]Isa. 2.19
[k]ch. 25.23
[l]Mal. 1.3-4
9 [m]Isa. 17.6
[6]their sufficiency
10 [n]Isa. 17.14
11 [o]Deut. 10.18; Ps. 10.14-18; Jas. 1.27
12 [p]ch. 25.29; Obad. 16
13 [q]Gen. 22.16; Amos 6.8
[r]Isa. 34.6; Amos 1.12
14 [s]Obad. 1-2
16 [t]Job 39.27
[u]Prov. 15.25; Amos 9.2
17 [v]ch. 18.16; ch. 50.13
18 [w]Deut. 29.23; Amos 4.11
19 [x]ch. 4.7; Zech. 11.3
[y]ch. 12.5
[z]Ex. 15.11; Ps. 89.6-8
[7]Or, convent me in judgment
[a]Job 41.10
20 [b]ch. 50.45
21 [8]Weedy sea
22 [c]ch. 4.13
23 [d]Isa. 17.1; Amos 1.3
[9]melted
[e]Isa. 57.20
[10]Or, as on the sea
24 [f]Isa. 13.8
25 [g]ch. 51.41
27 [h]Amos 1.4
[i]2 Ki. 13.3
28 [j]Isa. 21.13
[k]Job 1.3
29 [l]Ps. 120.5
30 [11]flit greatly

31 Arise, get you up unto the wealthy
nation, [12]that dwelleth without care,
saith the LORD, which have neither
gates nor bars, *which* [m]dwell alone.
32 And their camels shall be a booty,
and the multitude of their cattle a spoil:
and I will [n]scatter into all winds [o]them
that are [13]in the utmost corners; and I
will bring their calamity from all sides
thereof, saith the LORD.
33 And Hā'zôr [p]shall be a dwelling
for dragons, *and* a desolation for ever:
there shall no man abide there, nor *any*
son of man dwell in it.
34 ¶ The word of the LORD that came
to Jĕr-e-mī'ah the prophet against
[q]Ē'lăm in the beginning of the reign of
Zĕd-e-kī'ah king of Jū'dah, saying,
35 Thus saith the LORD of hosts; Behold, I will break [r]the bow of Ē'lăm,
the chief of their might.
36 And upon Ē'lăm will I bring the
four winds from the four quarters of
heaven, and will scatter them toward
all those winds; and there shall be no
nation whither the outcasts of Ē'lăm
shall not come.
37 For I will cause Ē'lăm to be dismayed before their enemies, and before them that seek their life: and I will
bring evil upon them, *even* my fierce
anger, saith the LORD; [s]and I will send
the sword after them, till I have consumed them:
38 And I will [t]set my throne in Ē'lăm,
and will destroy from thence the king
and the princes, saith the LORD.
39 ¶ But it shall come to pass in the
latter days, *that* I will bring again the
captivity of Ē'lăm, saith the LORD.

50 The word that the LORD spake
[a]against Băb'y̆-lon *and* against
the land of the Chăl-dē'ans [1]by Jĕr-e-
mī'ah the prophet.
2 Declare ye among the nations, and
publish, and [2]set up a standard; publish, *and* conceal not: say, Băb'y̆-lon is
taken, [b]Bĕl is confounded, Me-rō'dach
is broken in pieces; [c]her idols are confounded, her images are broken in
pieces.
3 For out of the north there cometh
up [d]a nation against her, which shall
make her land desolate, and none shall
dwell therein: they shall remove, they
shall depart, both man and beast.
4 ¶ In those days, and in that time,
saith the LORD, the children of Ĭs'ra-el
shall come, [e]they and the children of
Jū'dah together, [f]going and weeping:
they shall go, [g]and seek the LORD their
God.
5 They shall ask the way to Zī'ŏn
with their faces thitherward, *saying*,
Come, and let us join ourselves to the
LORD in [h]a perpetual covenant *that*
shall not be forgotten.
6 My people hath been lost sheep:
their shepherds have caused them to
go astray, they have turned them away
on the mountains: they have gone from
mountain to hill, they have forgotten
their [3]restingplace.
7 All that found them have devoured
them: and [i]their adversaries said, [j]We
offend not, because they have sinned
against the LORD, [k]the habitation of
justice, even the LORD, the hope of their
fathers.
8 [l]Remove out of the midst of Băb'-
y̆-lon, and go forth out of the land of
the Chăl-dē'ans, and be as the he goats
before the flocks.
9 ¶ For, lo, I will raise and cause to
come up against Băb'y̆-lon an assembly of great nations from the north
country: and they shall set themselves
in array against her; from thence she
shall be taken: their arrows *shall be* as
of a mighty [4]expert man; none shall
return in vain.
10 And Chăl-dē'ȧ shall be a spoil:
[m]all that spoil her shall be satisfied,
saith the LORD.
11 [n]Because ye were glad, because
ye rejoiced, O ye destroyers of mine
heritage, because ye are grown [5]fat as
the heifer at grass, and [6]bellow as
bulls;
12 Your mother shall be sore confounded; she that bare you shall be
ashamed: behold, the hindermost of
the nations *shall be* a wilderness, a dry
land, and a desert.
13 Because of the wrath of the LORD
it shall not be inhabited, but it shall be
wholly desolate: every one that goeth
by Băb'y̆-lon shall be astonished, and
hiss at all her plagues.
14 Put yourselves in array against
Băb'y̆-lon round about: all ye that bend
the bow, shoot at her, spare no arrows:
for she hath sinned against the LORD.
15 Shout against her round about:
she hath [o]given her hand: her foundations are fallen, [p]her walls are thrown
down: for it *is* the vengeance of the
LORD: take vengeance upon her; [q]as
she hath done, do unto her.
16 Cut off the sower from Băb'y̆-lon,
and him that handleth the [7]sickle in
the time of harvest: for fear of the oppressing sword [r]they shall turn every
one to his people, and they shall flee
every one to his own land.
17 ¶ Israel *is* [s]a scattered sheep;
[t]the lions have driven *him* away: first
[u]the king of Ăs-sy̆r'ĭ-ȧ hath devoured
him; and last this [v]Nĕb-u-chăd-rĕz'-
zar king of Băb'y̆-lon hath broken his
bones.
18 Therefore thus saith the LORD of
hosts, the God of Ĭs'ra-el; Behold, I will
punish the king of Băb'y̆-lon and his
land, as I have punished the king of
Ăs-sy̆r'ĭ-ȧ.
19 [w]And I will bring Ĭs'ra-el again
to his habitation, and he shall feed on
Cär'mel and Bā'shăn, and his soul
shall be satisfied upon mount Ē'phră-
ĭm and Gĭl'e-ăd.
20 In those days, and in that time,
saith the LORD, [x]the iniquity of Ĭs'ra-el
shall be sought for, and *there shall be*
none; and the sins of Jū'dah, and they
shall not be found: for I will pardon
them [y]whom I reserve.
21 ¶ Go up against the land [8]of Mĕr-
a-thā'im, *even* against it, and against
the inhabitants of [9]Pē'kŏd: waste and

31 [12]Or, that is at ease
[m]Num. 23.9; Mic. 7.14
32 [n]Deut. 28.64; Ezek. 5.10
[o]ch. 25.23
[13]cut off into corners, or, that have the corners of their hair polled
33 [p]ch. 9.11; Mal. 1.3
34 [q]Gen. 10.22; ch. 25.25
35 [r]Gen. 14.1; Dan. 8.2
37 [s]ch. 48.2
38 [t]ch. 43.10; Dan. 7.9

CHAPTER 50
1 [a]Isa. 13.1; Isa. 21.1
[1]by the hand of Jeremiah
2 [2]lift up
[b]Isa. 46.1
[c]ch. 43.12
3 [d]Isa. 13.17
4 [e]Hos. 1.11
[f]Ps. 126.5; Zech. 12.10
[g]Ps. 105.4; Zech. 8.21-22
5 [h]ch. 31.31
6 [3]place to lie down in
7 [i]Zech. 11.5
[j]ch. 2.3;
[k]Ps. 22.4
8 [l]Isa. 48.20
9 [4]Or, destroyer
10 [m]Rev. 17.16
11 [n]Isa. 47.6
[5]big, or, corpulent
[6]Or, neigh as steeds
15 [o]1 Chr. 29.24;
[p]ch. 51.58
[q]Ps. 137.8
16 [7]Or, scythe
[r]Isa. 13.14
17 [s]ch. 23.2;
[t]ch. 2.15
[u]2 Ki. 17.6;
[v]2 Ki. 24.10-14
19 [w]Isa. 65.10
20 [x]ch. 31.34
[y]Isa. 1.9
21 [8]Or, of the rebels
[9]Or, Visitation

utterly destroy after them, saith the LORD, and do [z]according to all that I have commanded thee.

22 A sound of battle *is* in the land, and of great destruction.

23 How is [a]the hammer of the whole earth cut asunder and broken! how is Băb'y̆-lon become a desolation among the nations!

24 I have laid a snare for thee, and thou art also taken, O Băb'y̆-lon, [b]and thou wast not aware: thou art found, and also caught, because thou hast striven against the LORD.

25 The LORD hath opened his armoury, and hath brought forth [c]the weapons of his indignation: for this *is* the work of the Lord GOD of hosts in the land of the Chăl-dē'ans.

26 Come against her [10]from the utmost border, open her storehouses: [11]cast her up as heaps, and destroy her utterly: let nothing of her be left.

27 Slay all her [d]bullocks; let them go down to the slaughter: woe unto them! for their day is come, the time of [e]their visitation.

28 The voice of them that flee and escape out of the land of Băb'y̆-lon, [f]to declare in Zī'ŏn the vengeance of the LORD our God, the vengeance of his temple.

29 Call together the archers against Băb'y̆-lon: all ye that bend the bow, camp against it round about; let none thereof escape: [g]recompense her according to her work; according to all that she hath done, do unto her: [h]for she hath been proud against the LORD, against the Holy One of Ĭs'ra-el.

30 [i]Therefore shall her young men fall in the streets, and all her men of war shall be cut off in that day, saith the LORD.

31 Behold, I *am* against thee, *O thou* [12]most proud, saith the Lord GOD of hosts: for thy day is come, the time *that* I will visit thee.

32 And [13][j]the most proud shall stumble and fall, and none shall raise him up: and [k]I will kindle a fire in his cities, and it shall devour all round about him.

33 ¶ Thus saith the LORD of hosts; The children of Ĭs'ra-el and the children of Jū'dah *were* oppressed together: and all that took them captives held them fast; they refused to let them go.

34 [l]Their Redeemer *is* strong; [m]the LORD of hosts *is* his name: he shall throughly plead their cause, that he may give rest to the land, and disquiet the inhabitants of Băb'y̆-lon.

35 ¶ A sword *is* upon the Chăl-dē'ans, saith the LORD, and upon the inhabitants of Băb'y̆-lon, and [n]upon her princes, and upon [o]her wise *men*.

36 A sword *is* upon the [14]liars; and they shall dote: a sword *is* upon her mighty men; and they shall be dismayed.

37 A sword *is* upon their horses, and upon their chariots, and upon all [p]the mingled people that *are* in the midst of her; and [q]they shall become as women: a sword *is* upon her treasures; and they shall be robbed.

38 [r]A drought *is* upon her waters; and they shall be dried up: for it *is* the land of graven images, and they are mad upon *their* idols.

39 [s]Therefore the wild beasts of the desert with the wild beasts of the islands shall dwell *there*, and the owls shall dwell therein: [t]and it shall be no more inhabited for ever; neither shall it be dwelt in from generation to generation.

40 [u]As God overthrew Sŏd'om and Go-mŏr'rah and the neighbour *cities* thereof, saith the LORD; *so* shall no man abide there, neither shall any son of man dwell therein.

41 [v]Behold, a people shall come from the north, and a great nation, and many kings shall be raised up from the coasts of the earth.

42 [w]They shall hold the bow and the lance: [x]they *are* cruel, and will not shew mercy: [y]their voice shall roar like the sea, and they shall ride upon horses, *every one* put in array, like a man to the battle, against thee, O daughter of Băb'y̆-lon.

43 The king of Băb'y̆-lon hath heard the report of them, and his hands waxed feeble: [z]anguish took hold of him, *and* pangs as of a woman in travail.

44 Behold, he shall come up like a lion from the swelling of Jôr'dan unto the habitation of the strong: but I will make them suddenly run away from her: and who *is* a chosen *man, that* I may appoint over her? for who *is* like me? and who will [15]appoint me the time? and [a]who *is* that shepherd that will stand before me?

45 Therefore hear ye [b]the counsel of the LORD, that he hath taken against Băb'y̆-lon; and his purposes, that he hath purposed against the land of the Chăl-dē'ans: Surely [c]the least of the flock shall draw them out: surely he shall make *their* habitation desolate with them.

46 [d]At the noise of the taking of Băb'y̆-lon the earth is moved, and the cry is heard among the nations.

51 Thus saith the LORD; Behold, I will raise up against Băb'y̆-lon, and against them that dwell in the [1]midst of them that rise up against me, [a]a destroying wind;

2 And will send unto Băb'y̆-lon [b]fanners, that shall fan her, and shall empty her land: [c]for in the day of trouble they shall be against her round about.

3 Against *him that* bendeth let the archer bend his bow, and against *him that* lifteth himself up in his brigandine: and spare ye not her young men; destroy ye utterly all her host.

4 Thus the slain shall fall in the land of the Chăl-dē'ans, [d]and *they that are* thrust through in her streets.

5 [e]For Ĭs'ra-el *hath* not *been* forsaken, nor Jū'dah of his God, of the LORD of hosts; though their land was filled with sin against the Holy One of Ĭs'ra-el.

[z]Isa. 10.6
23 [a]Isa. 14.6; ch. 51.20
24 [b]Dan. 5.30
25 [c]Isa. 13.5
26 [10]from the end
[11]Or, tread her
27 [d]Ps. 22.12; Isa. 34.7
[e]ch. 48.44
28 [f]ch. 51.10
29 [g]Lam. 3.64; 2 Thess. 1.6
[h]Isa. 47.10
30 [i]ch. 49.26; ch. 51.4
31 [12]pride
32 [13]pride
[j]Hab. 2.5
[k]ch. 21.14
34 [l]Rev. 18.8
[m]Prov. 23.11; Isa. 47.4
35 [n]Dan. 5.30
[o]Isa. 34.13
36 [14]bars, or, chief stays
37 [p]ch. 25.20
[q]ch. 51.30; Nah. 3.13
38 [r]Isa. 44.27; ch. 51.32-36; Rev. 16.12
39 [s]Isa. 13.21; ch. 51.37; Rev. 18.2
[t]Isa. 13.20; ch. 25.12
40 [u]Gen. 19.24; Deut. 29.23; Isa. 1.9; ch. 49.18; Amos 4.11; Zeph. 2.9; 2 Pet. 2.6; Jude 7
41 [v]ch. 6.22; Rev. 17.16
42 [w]ch. 6.22
[x]Isa. 13.18
[y]Isa. 5.30
43 [z]ch. 49.24
44 [15]Or, convent me to plead
[a]Job 41.10; Dan. 5.2-20
45 [b]Ps. 33.11; Isa. 14.24; ch. 51.11; Acts 4.28; Eph. 1.11
[c]1 Cor. 1.27
46 [d]Rev. 18.9

CHAPTER 51
1 [1]heart
[a]2 Ki. 19.7; ch. 4.11
2 [b]ch. 15.7
[c]ch. 50.14
4 [d]ch. 49.26
5 [e]Ps. 94.14; Zech. 1.15

6 [f]Flee out of the midst of Băb'ӯ-lon,
and deliver every man his soul: be not
cut off in her iniquity; for this *is* the
time of the LORD'S vengeance; [g]he will
render unto her a recompence.
7 [h]Băb'ӯ-lon *hath been* a golden
cup in the LORD'S hand, that made all
the earth drunken: the [i]nations have
drunken of her wine; therefore the nations [j]are mad.
8 Băb'ӯ-lon is suddenly [k]fallen and
destroyed: [l]howl for her; [m]take balm
for her pain, if so be she may be healed.
9 We would have healed Băb'ӯ-lon,
but she is not healed: forsake her, and
[n]let us go every one into his own country: for her judgment reacheth unto
heaven, and is lifted up *even* to the
skies.
10 The LORD hath [o]brought forth
our righteousness: come, and let us declare in Zī'ŏn the work of the LORD our
God.
11 Make [2]bright the arrows; gather
the shields: [p]the LORD hath raised up
the spirit of the kings of the Mēdes: for
his device *is* against Băb'ӯ-lon, to destroy it; because it *is* the vengeance of
the LORD, the vengeance of his temple.
12 [q]Set up the standard upon the
walls of Băb'ӯ-lon, make the watch
strong, set up the watchmen, prepare
the [3]ambushes: for the LORD hath both
devised and done that which he spake
against the inhabitants of Băb'ӯ-lon.
13 [r]O thou that dwellest upon many
waters, abundant in treasures, thine
end is come, *and* the measure of thy
covetousness.
14 [s]The LORD of hosts hath sworn
[4]by himself, *saying,* Surely I will fill
thee with men, [t]as with caterpillers;
and they shall [5]lift up a shout against
thee.
15 [u]He hath made the earth by his
power, he hath established the world
by his wisdom, and [v]hath stretched
out the heaven by his understanding.
16 When he uttereth *his* voice, *there*
is a [6]multitude of waters in the heavens; and [w]he causeth the vapours to
ascend from the ends of the earth: he
maketh lightnings with rain, and bringeth forth the wind out of his treasures.
17 Every man [7]is brutish by *his*
knowledge; every founder is confounded by the graven image: [x]for his
molten image *is* falsehood, and *there is*
no breath in them.
18 [y]They *are* vanity, the work of errors: in the time of their visitation they
shall perish.
19 [z]The portion of Jā'cob *is* not like
them; for he *is* the former of all things:
and *Is'ra-el is* the rod of his inheritance: the LORD of hosts *is* his name.
20 [a]Thou *art* my battle ax *and* weapons of war: for [8]with thee will I break
in pieces the nations, and with thee
will I destroy kingdoms;
21 And with thee will I break in
pieces the horse and his rider; and
with thee will I break in pieces the chariot and his rider;

22 With thee also will I break in
pieces man and woman; and with thee
will I break in pieces [b]old and young;
and with thee will I break in pieces the
young man and the maid;
23 I will also break in pieces with
thee the shepherd and his flock; and
with thee will I break in pieces the husbandman and his yoke of oxen; and
with thee will I break in pieces captains and rulers.
24 [c]And I will render unto Băb'ӯ-
lon and to all the inhabitants of Chăl-
dē'ȧ all their evil that they have done
in Zī'ŏn in your sight, saith the LORD.
25 Behold, I *am* against thee, [d]O
destroying mountain, saith the LORD,
which destroyest all the earth: and I
will stretch out mine hand upon thee,
and roll thee down from the rocks,
[e]and will make thee a burnt mountain.
26 And they shall not take of thee a
stone for a corner, nor a stone for foundations; but thou shalt be [9]desolate for
ever, saith the LORD.
27 [f]Set ye up a standard in the land,
blow the trumpet among the nations,
[g]prepare the nations against her, call
together against her [h]the kingdoms
of Ar'ă-rat, Mĭn'nī, and Ăsh'chĕ-naz;
appoint a captain against her; cause
the horses to come up as the rough
caterpillers.
28 Prepare against her the nations
with the kings of the Mēdes, the captains thereof, and all the rulers thereof,
and all the land of his dominion.
29 And the land shall tremble and
sorrow: for every purpose of the LORD
shall be performed against Băb'ӯ-lon,
[i]to make the land of Băb'ӯ-lon a desolation without an inhabitant.
30 The mighty men of Băb'ӯ-lon
have forborn to fight, they have remained in *their* holds: their might hath
failed; [j]they became as women: they
have burned her dwellingplaces; [k]her
bars are broken.
31 [l]One post shall run to meet another, and one messenger to meet another, to shew the king of Băb'ӯ-lon
that his city is taken at *one* end,
32 And that the passages are stopped,
and the reeds they have burned with
fire, and the men of war are affrighted.
33 For thus saith the LORD of hosts,
the God of Is'ra-el; The daughter of
Băb'ӯ-lon *is* [m]like a threshingfloor, [10]*it*
is time to thresh her: yet a little while,
[n]and the time of her harvest shall come.
34 Nĕb-u-chăd-rĕz'zar the king of
Băb'ӯ-lon hath [o]devoured me, he hath
crushed me, he hath made me an empty
vessel, he hath swallowed me up like a
dragon, he hath filled his belly with my
delicates, he hath cast me out.
35 [11]The violence done to me and to
my [12]flesh *be* upon Băb'ӯ-lon, shall the
[13]inhabitant of Zī'ŏn say; and my blood
upon the inhabitants of Chăl-dē'ȧ, shall
Je-ru'sa-lĕm say.
36 Therefore thus saith the LORD; Behold, [p]I will plead thy cause, and take
vengeance for thee; [q]and I will dry up
her sea, and make her springs dry.

6 [f]Rev. 18.4
[g]ch. 25.14
7 [h]Rev. 17.4
[i]Rev. 14.8
[j]ch. 25.16
8 [k]Isa. 21.9; 1 Thess. 5.2; Rev. 14.8
[l]Rev. 18.9
[m]ch. 46.11
9 [n]Isa. 13.14; ch. 46.16
10 [o]Ps. 37.6
11 [2]pure
[p]Isa. 13.17
12 [q]Nah. 2.1
[3]liers in wait
13 [r]Rev. 17.1
14 [s]ch. 49.13
[4]by his soul
[t]Nah. 3.15
[5]utter
15 [u]Gen. 1.1; Ps. 146.5-6; Isa. 40.26; Acts 14.15; Col. 1.16-17; Heb. 1.2-3
[v]Job 9.8
16 [6]Or, noise
[w]Ps. 135.7
17 [7]Or, is more brutish than to know
[x]ch. 50.2
18 [y]Jon. 2.8
19 [z]Ps. 16.5; Ps. 73.26; ch. 10.16; Lam. 3.24
20 [a]Isa. 10.5; ch. 50.23
[8]Or, in thee, or, by thee
22 [b]2 Chr. 36.17
24 [c]ch. 50.15-16
25 [d]Isa. 13.2; Zech. 4.7
[e]Rev. 8.8
26 [9]everlasting desolations
27 [f]Isa. 13.2
[g]ch. 25.14
[h]ch. 50.41
29 [i]ch. 50.13
30 [j]Isa. 19.16
[k]Lam. 2.9; Amos 1.5
31 [l]ch. 50.24
33 [m]Isa. 21.10
[10]Or, in the time that he thresheth her
[n]Joel 3.13; Matt. 13.30
34 [o]2 Chr. 36.9-10; ch. 24
35 [11]My violence
[12]Or, remainder
[13]inhabitress
36 [p]Zech. 1.15
[q]ch. 50.38

37 [r]And Băb'ȳ-lon shall become
heaps, a dwellingplace for dragons,
[s]an astonishment, and an hissing, without an inhabitant.
38 They shall roar together like lions: they shall [14]yell as lions' whelps.
39 [t]In their heat I will make their
feasts, and I will make them drunken,
that they may rejoice, and sleep a perpetual sleep, and not wake, saith the
LORD.
40 I will bring them down like lambs
to the slaughter, like rams with he
goats.
41 How is [u]Shē'shăch taken! and
how is [v]the praise of the whole earth
surprised! how is Băb'ȳ-lon become an
astonishment among the nations!
42 [w]The sea is come up upon Băb'ȳ-
lon: she is covered with the multitude
of the waves thereof.
43 Her cities are a desolation, a dry
land, and a wilderness, a land wherein
no man dwelleth, neither doth *any* son
of man pass thereby.
44 [x]And I will punish Bĕl in Băb'ȳ-
lon, and I will bring forth out of his
mouth that which he hath swallowed
up: and the nations shall not flow together any more unto him: yea, the
wall of Băb'ȳ-lon shall fall.
45 [y]My people, go ye out of the midst
of her, and deliver ye every man his
soul from the fierce anger of the LORD.
46 And [15]lest your heart faint, and ye
fear [z]for the rumour that shall be heard
in the land; a rumour shall both come
one year, and after that in *another* year
shall come a rumour, and violence in
the land, ruler against ruler.
47 Therefore, behold, the days come,
that I will [16]do judgment upon the graven images of Băb'ȳ-lon: and her whole
land shall be confounded, and all her
slain shall fall in the midst of her.
48 Then [a]the heaven and the earth,
and all that *is* therein, shall sing for
Băb'ȳ-lon: [b]for the spoilers shall come
unto her from the north, saith the
LORD.
49 [17]As Băb'ȳ-lon *hath caused* the
slain of Is'ra-el to fall, so at Băb'ȳ-lon
shall fall the slain of all [18]the earth.
50 [c]Ye that have escaped the sword,
go away, stand not still: remember the
LORD afar off, and let Je-ru̦'sa-lĕm
come into your mind.
51 [d]We are confounded, because we
have heard reproach: shame hath covered our faces: for strangers are come
into the sanctuaries of the LORD'S house.
52 Wherefore, behold, the days come,
saith the LORD, that I will do judgment
upon her graven images: and through
all her land the wounded shall groan.
53 [e]Though Băb'ȳ-lon should mount
up to heaven, and though she should
fortify the height of her strength, *yet*
from me shall spoilers come unto her,
saith the LORD.
54 [f]A sound of a cry *cometh* from
Băb'ȳ-lon, and great destruction from
the land of the Chăl-dē'ans:
55 Because the LORD hath spoiled
Băb'ȳ-lon, and destroyed out of her the
great voice; when her waves do roar
like great waters, a noise of their voice
is uttered:
56 Because the spoiler is come upon
her, *even* upon Băb'ȳ-lon, and her
mighty men are taken, every one of
their bows is broken: [g]for the LORD God
of recompences shall surely requite.
57 And I will make drunk her princes,
and her wise *men*, her captains, and her
rulers, and her mighty men: and they
shall sleep a perpetual sleep, and not
wake, saith [h]the King, whose name *is*
the LORD of hosts.
58 Thus saith the LORD of hosts;
[19]The broad walls of Băb'ȳ-lon shall be
utterly [20]broken, and her high gates
shall be burned with fire; and [i]the people shall labour in vain, and the folk in
the fire, and they shall be weary.
59 ¶ The word which Jĕr-e-mī'ah
the prophet commanded Sĕr-a-ī'ah the
son of Ne-rī'ah, the son of Mā-a-sē'iah,
when he went [21]with Zĕd-e-kī'ah the
king of Jū'dah into Băb'ȳ-lon in the
fourth year of his reign. And *this* Sĕr-
a-ī'ah *was* a [22]quiet prince.
60 So Jĕr-e-mī'ah wrote in a book
all the evil that should come upon
Băb'ȳ-lon, *even* all these words that
are written against Băb'ȳ-lon.
61 And Jĕr-e-mī'ah said to Sĕr-a-
ī'ah, When thou comest to Băb'ȳ-lon,
and shalt see, and shalt read all these
words;
62 Then shalt thou say, O LORD,
thou hast spoken against this place, to
cut it off, that [j]none shall remain in it,
neither man nor beast, but that it shall
be [23]desolate for ever.
63 And it shall be, when thou hast
made an end of reading this book,
[k]*that* thou shalt bind a stone to it, and
cast it into the midst of Eū-phrā'tēs:
64 And thou shalt say, Thus shall
Băb'ȳ-lon sink, and shall not rise from
the evil that I will bring upon her: and
they shall be weary. Thus far *are* the
words of Jĕr-e-mī'ah.

52 Zĕd-e-kī'ah *was* [a]one and twenty
years old when he [1]began to
reign, and he reigned eleven years in
Je-ru̦'sa-lĕm. And his mother's name
was Ha-mū'tal the daughter of Jĕr-e-
mī'ah of Lĭb'nah.
2 And he did *that which was* evil in
the eyes of the LORD, according to all
that Je-hoi'a-kim had done.
3 For through the anger of the LORD
it came to pass in Je-ru̦'sa-lĕm and Jū'-
dah, till he had cast them out from his
presence, that Zĕd-e-kī'ah [b]rebelled
against the king of Băb'ȳ-lon.
4 ¶ And it came to pass in the [c]ninth
year of his reign, in the tenth month, in
the tenth *day* of the month, *that* Nĕb-u-
chăd-rĕz'zar king of Băb'ȳ-lon came,
he and all his army, against Je-ru̦'sa-
lĕm, and pitched [d]against it, and built
forts against it round about.
5 So the city was besieged unto the
eleventh year of king Zĕd-e-kī'ah.
6 And in the fourth month, in the
ninth *day* of the month, [e]the famine

37 [r]Isa. 13.22 [s]2 Chr. 29.8; ch. 18.16
38 [14]Or, shake themselves
39 [t]Dan. 5.1-30
41 [u]ch. 25.26 [v]Isa. 13.19; ch. 49.25; Dan. 4.30
42 [w]Isa. 8.7-8
44 [x]ch. 50.2
45 [y]Rev. 18.4
46 [15]Or, let not [z]2 Ki. 19.7
47 [16]visit upon
48 [a]Isa. 44.23 [b]ch. 50.3
49 [17]Or, Both Babylon is to fall, O ye slain of Israel, and with Babylon, etc [18]Or, the country
50 [c]ch. 44.28
51 [d]Ps. 44.15
53 [e]ch. 49.16; Amos 9.2
54 [f]Isa. 13.6-9; Isa. 15.5; ch. 50.22; Zeph. 1.10
56 [g]Deut. 32.35; Ps. 94.1; Isa. 34.8
57 [h]ch. 46.18; ch. 48.15
58 [19]Or, The walls of broad Babylon [20]Or, made naked [i]Hab. 2.13
59 [21]Or, on the behalf of [22]Or, prince of Menucha, or, chief chamberlain
62 [j]ch. 50.3-39 [23]desolations
63 [k]Rev. 18.21

CHAPTER 52
1 [a]2 Ki. 24.18; 2 Chr. 36.11 [1]reigned
3 [b]Ezek. 17.12-16
4 [c]2 Ki. 25.1; ch. 39.1; Zech. 8.19 [d]Deut. 28.52-57; Isa. 42.24-25; ch. 6.3-6
6 [e]Lev. 26.14-26; Isa. 3.1; Ezek. 4.16

was sore in the city, so that there was
no bread for the people of the land.
7 Then the city was broken up, and
all the men of war fled, and went forth
out of the city by night by the way of
the gate between the two walls, which
was by the king's garden; (now the
Chăl-dē'ans *were* by the city round
about:) and they went by the way of
the plain.
8 ¶ But the army of the Chăl-dē'ans
pursued after the king, and overtook
Zĕd-e-kī'ah in the plains of Jĕr'ĭ-chō;
and all his army was scattered from
him.
9 [f]Then they took the king, and carried him up unto the king of Băb'ȳ-lon
to Rĭb'lah in the land of Hā'math;
where he gave judgment upon him.
10 [g]And the king of Băb'ȳ-lon slew
the sons of Zĕd-e-kī'ah before his eyes:
he slew also all the princes of Jū'dah in
Rĭb'lah.
11 Then he [2h]put out the eyes of
Zĕd-e-kī'ah; and the king of Băb'ȳ-lon
bound him in [3]chains, and carried him
to Băb'ȳ-lon, and put him in [4]prison till
the day of his death.
12 ¶ [i]Now in the fifth month, in the
tenth *day* of the month, which *was* the
nineteenth year of Nĕb-u-chăd-rĕz'zar
king of Băb'ȳ-lon, [j]came Nĕb'u-zär–
ā'dan, [5]captain of the guard, *which*
[6]served the king of Băb'ȳ-lon, into
Je-ru̦'sa-lĕm,
13 And [k]burned the house of the
LORD, and the king's house; and all the
houses of Je-ru̦'sa-lĕm, and all the
houses of the great *men*, burned he
with fire:
14 And all the army of the Chăl-
dē'ans, that *were* with the captain of
the guard, brake down all the walls of
Je-ru̦'sa-lĕm round about.
15 Then Nĕb'u-zär–ā'dan the captain of the guard carried away captive
certain of the poor of the people, and
the residue of the people that remained
in the city, and those that fell away,
that fell to the king of Băb'ȳ-lon, and
the rest of the multitude.
16 But Nĕb'u-zär–ā'dan the captain
of the guard left *certain* of the poor
of the land for vinedressers and for
husbandmen.
17 [l]Also the pillars of brass that
were in the house of the LORD, and the
bases, and the brasen sea that *was* in
the house of the LORD, the Chăl-dē'ans
brake, and carried all the brass of
them to Băb'ȳ-lon.
18 [m]The caldrons also, and the [7]shov-
els, and the snuffers, and the [8]bowls,
and the spoons, and all the vessels of
brass wherewith they ministered, took
they away.
19 And the basons, and the
[9]firepans, and the bowls, and the caldrons, and the candlesticks, and the
spoons, and the cups; *that* which *was*
of gold *in* gold, and *that* which *was* of
silver *in* silver, took the captain of the
guard away.
20 The two pillars, one sea, and
twelve brasen bulls that *were* under
the bases, which king Sŏl'o-mon had
made in the house of the LORD: [10]the
brass of all these vessels was without
weight.
21 And *concerning* the [n]pillars, the
height of one pillar *was* eighteen cubits; and a [11]fillet of twelve cubits did
compass it; and the thickness thereof
was four fingers: *it was* hollow.
22 And a chapiter of brass *was* upon
it; and the height of one chapiter *was*
five cubits, with network and pomegranates upon the chapiters round
about, all *of* brass. The second pillar
also and the pomegranates *were* like
unto these.
23 And there were ninety and six
pomegranates on a side; *and* [o]all the
pomegranates upon the network *were*
an hundred round about.
24 ¶ And the captain of the guard
took [p]Sĕr-a-ī'ah the chief priest, [q]and
Zĕph-a-nī'ah the second priest, and
the three keepers of the [12]door:
25 He took also out of the city an
eunuch, which had the charge of the
men of war; and seven men of them
that [13]were near the king's person,
which were found in the city; and the
[14]principal scribe of the host, who mustered the people of the land; and threescore men of the people of the land,
that were found in the midst of the city.
26 So Nĕb'u-zär–ā'dan the captain of
the guard took them, and brought them
to the king of Băb'ȳ-lon to Rĭb'lah.
27 And the king of Băb'ȳ-lon smote
them, and put them to death in Rĭb'lah
in the land of Hā'math. Thus [r]Jū'dah
was carried away captive out of his
own land.
28 [s]This *is* the people whom Nĕb-u-
chăd-rĕz'zar carried away captive: in
the [t]seventh year three thousand Jews
and three and twenty:
29 [u]In the eighteenth year of Nĕb-u-
chăd-rĕz'zar he carried away captive
from Je-ru̦'sa-lĕm eight hundred thirty
and two [15]persons:
30 In the three and twentieth year of
Nĕb-u-chăd-rĕz'zar Nĕb'u-zär–ā'dan
the captain of the guard carried away
captive of the Jews seven hundred
forty and five persons: all the persons
were four thousand and six hundred.
31 ¶ [v]And it came to pass in the
seven and thirtieth year of the captivity of Je-hoi'a-chin king of Jū'dah, in
the twelfth month, in the five and twentieth *day* of the month, *that* Ē'vĭl–me-
rō'dach king of Băb'ȳ-lon in the *first*
year of his reign [w]lifted up the head
of Je-hoi'a-chin king of Jū'dah, and
brought him forth out of prison,
32 And spake [16]kindly unto him, and
set his throne above the throne of the
kings that *were* with him in Băb'ȳ-lon,
33 And changed his prison garments:
[x]and he did continually eat bread before him all the days of his life.
34 And *for* his diet, there was a continual diet given him of the king of Băb'-
ȳ-lon, [17]every day a portion until the
day of his death, all the days of his life.

9 [f]ch. 32.4
10 [g]ch. 39.6-7
11 [2]blinded
[h]Judg. 16.21
[3]Or, fetters
[4]house of the wards
12 [i]2 Ki. 25.8; Zech. 7.5
[j]ch. 39.9
[5]chief of the executioners, or, slaughtermen, or, chief marshal. And so verse 14
[6]stood before
13 [k]2 Ki. 25.9; Ps. 74.6-8; Isa. 64.10-11; ch. 26.18; Matt. 24.1-2
17 [l]ch. 27.19
18 [m]Ex. 27.3
[7]Or, instruments to remove the ashes
[8]Or, basons
19 [9]Or, censers
20 [10]their brass
21 [n]1 Ki. 7.15-21-22; 2 Chr. 3.15
[11]thread
23 [o]1 Ki. 7.20; 2 Chr. 3.16
24 [p]1 Chr. 6.14
[q]2 Ki. 25.18; ch. 21.1
[12]threshold
25 [13]saw the face of the king
[14]Or, scribe of the captain of the host
27 [r]Lev. 26.33
28 [s]2 Ki. 24.2
[t]2 Chr. 36.20
29 [u]ch. 39.9
[15]souls
31 [v]2 Ki. 25.27-30
[w]Gen. 40.13-20
32 [16]good things with him
33 [x]2 Sam. 9.13
34 [17]the matter of the day in his day

THE LAMENTATIONS

JEREMIAH

Life's Questions

How do God's people express grief?
What do I do when God is silent and seems to be defeated?
How do I express my anger to God?

God's Answers

Lamentations shows the worship of Judah in the ruins of the Jerusalem temple immediately after Babylon destroyed the city in 586 B.C. The people used poetic acrostics to confess their sin, plead for help, express their anger, seek for hope, and demonstrate their faith in life's darkest moment.

Lamentations cries out that hope is all we have by showing: the appalling price of sin (ch. 1), God is the One who punishes (ch. 2); an individual hope for help in the midst of suffering (ch. 3); a portrayal of suffering caused by sin (ch. 4), and a plea for God to act (ch. 5).

1 How doth the city sit solitary, *that was* full of people! [a]*how* is she become as a widow! she *that was* great among the nations, *and* [b]princess among the provinces, *how* is she become tributary!

2 She [c]weepeth sore in the [d]night, and her tears *are* on her cheeks: [e]among all her lovers she hath none to comfort *her:* all her friends have dealt treacherously with her, they are become her enemies.

3 [f]Jū'dah is gone into captivity because of affliction, and [1]because of great servitude: [g]she dwelleth among the heathen, she findeth no rest: all her persecutors overtook her between the straits.

4 The ways of Zī'ŏn do mourn, because none come to the solemn feasts: all her gates are desolate: her priests sigh, her virgins are afflicted, and she *is* in bitterness.

5 Her adversaries are the chief, her enemies prosper; for the LORD hath afflicted her [h]for the multitude of her transgressions: her children are gone into captivity before the enemy.

6 And from the daughter of Zī'ŏn all her beauty is departed: her princes are become like harts *that* find no pasture, and they are gone without strength before the pursuer.

7 Je-ru'sa-lĕm remembered in the days of her affliction and of her miseries all her [2]pleasant things that she had in the days of old, when her people fell into the hand of the enemy, and none did help her: the [i]adversaries saw her, *and* did mock at her sabbaths.

8 Je-ru'sa-lĕm hath grievously sinned; therefore she [3]is removed: all that honoured her despise her, because [j]they have seen her nakedness: yea, she sigheth, and turneth backward.

9 Her filthiness *is* in her skirts; she [k]remembereth not her last end; therefore she came down wonderfully: she had no comforter. O LORD, behold my affliction: for the enemy hath magnified *himself.*

10 The adversary hath spread out his hand upon all her [4]pleasant things: for she hath seen *that* the heathen entered into her sanctuary, whom thou didst command *that* [l]they should not enter into thy congregation.

11 All her people sigh, [m]they seek bread; they have given their pleasant things for meat [5]to relieve the soul: see, O LORD, and consider; for I am become vile.

12 ¶ [6]*Is it* nothing to you, all ye that [7]pass by? behold, and [n]see if there be any sorrow like unto my sorrow, which is done unto me, wherewith the LORD hath afflicted *me* in the day of his fierce anger.

13 From above hath he sent fire into my bones, and it prevaileth against them: he hath [o]spread a net for my feet, he hath turned me back: he hath made me desolate *and* faint all the day.

14 [p]The yoke of my transgressions is bound by his hand: they are wreathed, *and* come up upon my neck: he hath made my strength to fall, the Lord hath delivered me into *their* hands, *from whom* I am not able to rise up.

15 The Lord hath trodden under foot all my mighty *men* in the midst of me: he hath called an assembly against me to crush my young men: [q]the Lord hath trodden [8]the virgin, the daughter of Jū'dah, *as* in a winepress.

16 For these *things* I weep; mine eye, mine eye runneth down with water, because the comforter that should [9]relieve my soul is far from me: my children are desolate, because the enemy prevailed.

17 Zī'ŏn spreadeth forth her hands, *and there is* none to comfort her: the LORD hath commanded concerning Jā'cob, *that* his adversaries *should be* round about him: Je-ru'sa-lĕm is as a menstruous woman among them.

18 ¶ The LORD is [r]righteous; for I have [s]rebelled against his [10]commandment: hear, I pray you, all people, and behold my sorrow: my virgins and my young men are gone into captivity.

CHAPTER 1
1 [a]verse 9; Isa. 47.7
[b]Ezra 4.20
2 [c]verse 16; Jer. 13.17
[d]Job 7.3; Ps. 6.6
[e]Jer. 4.30
3 [f]Lev. 26.14-32-33
[1]for the greatness of servitude
[g]Deut. 28.64
5 [h]Jer. 30.14; ch. 3.39
7 [2]Or, desirable
[i]Mic. 4.11
8 [3]is become a removing, or, wandering
[j]Jer. 13.22
9 [k]Deut. 32.29
10 [4]Or, desirable
[l]Deut. 23.3;
11 [m]Jer. 38.9
[5]Or, to make the soul to come again
12 [6]Or, It is nothing
[7]pass by the way
[n]Dan. 9.12;
13 [o]Job 18.8;
14 [p]Deut. 28.48;
15 [q]Isa. 63.3;
[8]Or, the winepress of the virgin, etc
16 [9]bring back
18 [r]Neh. 9.33;
[s]1 Sam. 12.14
[10]mouth

19 I called for my lovers, *but* they deceived me: my priests and mine elders gave up the ghost in the city, while they sought their meat to relieve their souls.

20 Behold, O LORD; for I *am* in distress: my [t]bowels are troubled; mine heart is turned within me; for I have grievously rebelled: [u]abroad the sword bereaveth, at home *there is* as death.

21 They have heard that I sigh: *there is* none to comfort me: all mine enemies have heard of my trouble; they are glad that thou hast done *it:* thou wilt bring [v]the day *that* thou hast [11]called, and they shall be like unto me.

22 Let all their wickedness come before thee; and do unto them, as thou hast done unto me for all my transgressions: for my sighs *are* many, and my heart *is* faint.

2 How hath the Lord covered the daughter of Zī'ŏn with a cloud in his anger, [a]*and* cast down from heaven unto the earth [b]the beauty of Ĭs'ra-el, and remembered not [c]his footstool in the day of his anger!

2 The Lord hath swallowed up all the habitations of Jā'cob, and hath not pitied: he hath thrown down in his wrath the strong holds of the daughter of Jū'dah; he hath [1]brought *them* down to the ground: he [d]hath polluted the kingdom and the princes thereof.

3 He hath cut off in *his* fierce anger all the [e]horn of Ĭs'ra-el: [f]he hath drawn back his right hand from before the enemy, and he burned against Jā'cob like a flaming fire, *which* devoureth round about.

4 He [g]hath bent his bow like an enemy: he stood with his right hand as an adversary, and slew [2]all *that were* pleasant to the eye in the tabernacle of the daughter of Zī'ŏn: he poured out his fury like fire.

5 The Lord was as an enemy: he hath swallowed up Ĭs'ra-el, [h]he hath swallowed up all her palaces: he hath destroyed his strong holds, and hath increased in the daughter of Jū'dah mourning and lamentation.

6 And he hath violently [i]taken away his [3]tabernacle, [j]as *if it were of* a garden: he hath destroyed his places of the assembly: [k]the LORD hath caused the solemn feasts and sabbaths to be forgotten in Zī'ŏn, and hath despised in the indignation of his anger the king and the priest.

7 The Lord hath [l]cast off his altar, he hath abhorred his sanctuary, he hath [4]given up into the hand of the enemy the walls of her palaces; [m]they have made a noise in the house of the LORD, as in the day of a solemn feast.

8 The LORD hath purposed to destroy the wall of the daughter of Zī'ŏn: [n]he hath stretched out a line, he hath not withdrawn his hand from [5]destroying: therefore he made the rampart and the wall to lament; they languished together.

9 Her gates are sunk into the ground; he hath destroyed and broken her bars:

20 [t]Isa. 16.11; Hos. 11.8
[u]Deut. 32.25
21 [v]Jer. 46
[11]Or, proclaimed

CHAPTER 2
1 [a]Matt. 11.23
[b]2 Sam. 1.19
[c]1 Chr. 28.2
2 [1]made to touch
[d]Ps. 89.39
3 [e]Job 16.15
[f]Ps. 74.11
4 [g]Isa. 63.10
[2]all the desirable of the eye
5 [h]Jer. 52.13
6 [i]Ps. 80.12; Isa. 5.5
[3]Or, hedge
[j]Isa. 1.8
[k]Zeph. 3.18
7 [l]Ps. 78.59-61; Matt. 24.2
[4]shut up
[m]Ps. 74.4
8 [n]Isa. 34.11; Amos 7.7
[5]swallowing up
9 [o]Deut. 28.36; 2 Ki. 25.7
[p]2 Chr. 15.3
[q]Ps. 74.9; Mic. 3.6-7
10 [r]Job 2.13; ch. 4.5
11 [s]Ps. 6.7
[t]Job 16.13
[6]Or, faint
13 [u]Job 5.1; Dan. 9.12
14 [v]Isa. 58.1
15 [w]1 Ki. 9.8
[7]by the way
[x]Ps. 48.2
16 [y]Ps. 56.2
[z]Ps. 35.21
17 [a]Lev. 26.16;
[b]Deut. 28.43-44
18 [c]Jer. 14.17
19 [d]Mark 13.35
[e]Ps. 62.8
[f]Isa. 51.20; ch. 4.1
20 [g]Ex. 32.11
[h]Lev. 26.29;
[8]Or, swaddled with their hands
[i]ch. 4.13
21 [j]2 Chr. 36.17

[o]her king and her princes *are* among the Gĕn'tīles: [p]the law *is* no *more;* her [q]prophets also find no vision from the LORD.

10 The elders of the daughter of Zī'ŏn [r]sit upon the ground, *and* keep silence: they have cast up dust upon their heads; they have girded themselves with sackcloth: the virgins of Je-rų'sa-lĕm hang down their heads to the ground.

11 [s]Mine eyes do fail with tears, my bowels are troubled, [t]my liver is poured upon the earth, for the destruction of the daughter of my people; because the children and the sucklings [6]swoon in the streets of the city.

12 They say to their mothers, Where *is* corn and wine? when they swooned as the wounded in the streets of the city, when their soul was poured out into their mothers' bosom.

13 What thing shall I take to witness for thee? [u]what thing shall I liken to thee, O daughter of Je-rų'sa-lĕm? what shall I equal to thee, that I may comfort thee, O virgin daughter of Zī'ŏn? for thy breach *is* great like the sea: who can heal thee?

14 Thy prophets have seen vain and foolish things for thee: and they have not [v]discovered thine iniquity, to turn away thy captivity; but have seen for thee false burdens and causes of banishment.

15 [w]All that pass [7]by clap *their* hands at thee; they hiss and wag their head at the daughter of Je-rų'sa-lĕm, *saying, Is* this the city that *men* call [x]The perfection of beauty, The joy of the whole earth?

16 All thine enemies have opened their mouth against thee: they hiss and gnash the teeth: they say, [y]We have swallowed *her* up: certainly this *is* the day that we looked for; we have found, [z]we have seen *it.*

17 The LORD hath done *that* which he had [a]devised; he hath fulfilled his word that he had commanded in the days of old: he hath thrown down, and hath not pitied: and he hath caused *thine* enemy to [b]rejoice over thee, he hath set up the horn of thine adversaries.

18 Their heart cried unto the Lord, O wall of the daughter of Zī'ŏn, [c]let tears run down like a river day and night: give thyself no rest; let not the apple of thine eye cease.

19 Arise, cry out in the night: in the beginning of the watches [d]pour [e]out thine heart like water before the face of the Lord: lift up thy hands toward him for the life of thy young children, that faint for hunger [f]in the top of every street.

20 ¶ Behold, O LORD, and [g]consider to whom thou hast done this. [h]Shall the women eat their fruit, *and* children [8]of a span long? shall [i]the priest and the prophet be slain in the sanctuary of the Lord?

21 The [j]young and the old lie on the ground in the streets: my virgins and

my young men are fallen by the sword; thou hast slain *them* in the day of thine anger; thou hast killed, *and* not pitied.

22 Thou hast called as in a solemn day [k]my terrors round about, so that in the day of the LORD'S anger none escaped nor remained: [l]those that I have swaddled and brought up hath mine enemy consumed.

CHAPTER 3

3 I *am* the man *that* hath seen affliction by the rod of his wrath.

2 He hath led me, and brought *me into* darkness, but not *into* light.

3 Surely against me is he turned; he turneth his hand *against me* all the day.

4 My flesh and my skin hath he made old; he hath broken my bones.

5 He hath builded against me, and compassed *me* with gall and travail.

6 [a]He hath set me in dark places, as *they that be* dead of old.

7 He hath hedged me about, that I cannot get out: he hath made my chain heavy.

8 Also [b]when I cry and shout, he shutteth out my prayer.

9 He hath inclosed my ways with hewn stone, he hath made my paths crooked.

10 [c]He *was* unto me *as* a bear lying in wait, *and as* a lion in secret places.

11 He hath turned aside my ways, and [d]pulled me in pieces: he hath made me desolate.

12 He hath bent his bow, and [e]set me as a mark for the arrow.

13 He hath caused the [1]arrows of his quiver to enter into my reins.

14 I was a derision [f]to all my people; *and* their song all the day.

15 [g]He hath filled me with [2]bitterness, he hath made me drunken with wormwood.

16 He hath also broken my teeth [h]with gravel stones, he hath [3]covered me with ashes.

17 And thou hast removed my soul far off from peace: I forgat [4]prosperity.

18 [i]And I said, My strength and my hope is perished from the LORD:

19 [5]Remembering mine affliction and my misery, the wormwood and the gall.

20 My soul hath *them* still in remembrance, and is [6]humbled in me.

21 This I [7]recall to my mind, therefore have I hope.

22 ¶ [j]*It is of* the LORD'S mercies that we are not consumed, because his compassions fail not.

23 *They are* new [k]every morning: great *is* thy [l]faithfulness.

24 The LORD *is* my [m]portion, saith my soul; therefore will I hope in him.

25 The LORD *is* good unto them that [n]wait for him, to the soul *that* seeketh him.

26 *It is* good that *a man* should both hope [o]and quietly wait for the salvation of the LORD.

27 [p]*It is* good for a man that he bear the yoke in his youth.

28 [q]He sitteth alone and keepeth silence, because he hath borne *it* upon him.

29 [r]He putteth his mouth in the dust; if so be there may be hope.

30 [s]He giveth *his* cheek to him that smiteth him: he is filled full with reproach.

31 [t]For the Lord will not cast off for ever:

32 But though he cause grief, yet will he have compassion according to the multitude of his mercies.

33 For [u]he doth not afflict [8]willingly nor grieve the children of men.

34 To crush under his feet all the prisoners of the earth,

35 To turn aside the right of a man before the face of [9]the most High,

36 To subvert a man in his cause, [v]the Lord [10]approveth not.

37 ¶ Who *is* he [w]*that* saith, and it cometh to pass, *when* the Lord commandeth *it* not?

38 Out of the mouth of the most High proceedeth not [x]evil and good?

39 Wherefore doth a living man [11]complain, [y]a man for the punishment of his sins?

40 [z]Let us search and try our ways, and turn again to the LORD.

41 [a]Let us lift up our heart with *our* hands unto God in the heavens.

42 [b]We have transgressed and have rebelled: thou hast not pardoned.

43 Thou hast covered with anger, and persecuted us: thou hast slain, thou hast not pitied.

44 Thou hast covered thyself with a cloud, that *our* prayer should not pass through.

45 Thou hast made us *as* [c]the offscouring and refuse in the midst of the people.

46 All our enemies have opened their mouths against us.

47 Fear and a snare is come upon us, desolation and destruction.

48 Mine eye runneth down with rivers of water for the destruction of the daughter of my people.

49 Mine eye trickleth down, and ceaseth not, without any intermission,

50 Till the LORD [d]look down, and behold from heaven.

51 Mine eye affecteth [12]mine heart [13]because of all the daughters of my city.

52 Mine enemies chased me sore, like a bird, [e]without cause.

53 They have cut off my life [f]in the dungeon, and [g]cast a stone upon me.

54 [h]Waters flowed over mine head; *then* I said, I am cut off.

55 ¶ [i]I called upon thy name, O LORD, out of the low dungeon.

56 Thou [j]hast heard my voice: hide not thine ear at my breathing, at my cry.

57 Thou [k]drewest near in the day *that* I called upon thee: thou saidst, Fear not.

58 O Lord, thou hast [l]pleaded the causes of my soul; [m]thou hast redeemed my life.

---

22 [k]Ps. 31.13; Jer. 46.5 [l]Hos. 9.12

CHAPTER 3

6 [a]Ps. 88.5
8 [b]Job 30.20; Ps. 22.2
10 [c]Hos. 5.14
11 [d]Hos. 6.1
12 [e]Job 6.4; Ps. 38.2
13 [1]sons
14 [f]Neh. 4.2-4; Matt. 27.29-31
15 [g]Jer. 9.15 [2]bitternesses
16 [h]Prov. 20.17 [3]Or, rolled me in the ashes
17 [4]good
18 [i]Ps. 31.22
19 [5]Or, Remember
20 [6]bowed
21 [7]make to return to my heart
22 [j]Neh. 9.31; Mal. 3.6
23 [k]Isa. 33.2 [l]Heb. 10.23
24 [m]Ps. 16.5
25 [n]Ps. 130.6
26 [o]Ps. 37.7
27 [p]Ps. 94.12
28 [q]Jer. 15.17
29 [r]Job 42.6
30 [s]Mic. 5.1;
31 [t]Ps. 94.14
33 [u]Heb. 12.10 [8]from his heart
35 [9]Or, a superior
36 [v]Hab. 1.13 [10]Or, seeth not
37 [w]Ps. 33.9
38 [x]Job 2.10
39 [11]Or, murmur [y]Mic. 7.9
40 [z]Ps. 119.59
41 [a]Ps. 86.4
42 [b]Dan. 9.5
45 [c]1 Cor. 4.13
50 [d]Isa. 63.15
51 [12]my soul [13]Or, more than all
52 [e]Ps. 35.7;
53 [f]Jer. 37.16 [g]Dan. 6.17
54 [h]Ps. 69.2
55 [i]2 Chr. 33.12;
56 [j]Ps. 6.8;
57 [k]Ps. 69.18;
58 [l]1 Sam. 25.39; [m]Ps. 71.23

59 O LORD, thou hast seen my wrong:
judge thou my cause.
60 Thou hast seen all their vengeance *and* all their [n]imaginations
against me.
61 Thou hast heard their reproach,
O LORD, *and* all their imaginations
against me;
62 The lips of those that rose up
against me, and their device against
me all the day.
63 Behold their [o]sitting down, and
their rising up; I *am* their musick.
64 ¶ [p]Render unto them a recompence, O LORD, according to the work
of their hands.
65 Give them [14]sorrow of heart, thy
curse unto them.
66 Persecute and destroy them in anger from under the [q]heavens of the
LORD.
4 How is the gold become dim! *how* is
the most fine gold changed! the
stones of the sanctuary are poured out
in the top of every street.
2 The precious sons of Zī'ŏn, compa-
rable to fine gold, how are they esteemed [a]as earthen pitchers, the work
of the hands of the potter!
3 Even the [1]sea monsters draw out
the breast, they give suck to their young
ones: the daughter of my people *is become* cruel, [b]like the ostriches in the
wilderness.
4 The [c]tongue of the sucking child
cleaveth to the roof of his mouth for
thirst: the young children ask bread,
and no man breaketh *it* unto them.
5 They that did feed delicately are
desolate in the streets: they that were
brought up in scarlet [d]embrace dung-
hills.
6 For the [2]punishment of the iniquity of the daughter of my people is
greater than the punishment of the sin
of Sŏd'om, that was [e]overthrown as in
a moment, and no hands stayed on
her.
7 Her [3]Năz'a-rītes were purer than
snow, they were whiter than milk, they
were more ruddy in body than rubies,
their polishing *was* of sapphire:
8 Their visage is [4]blacker than a
coal; they are not known in the streets:
[f]their skin cleaveth to their bones; it is
withered, it is become like a stick.
9 *They that be* slain with the sword
are better than *they that be* slain with
hunger: for these [5]pine away, stricken
through for *want of* the fruits of the
field.
10 [g]The hands of the pitiful women
have sodden their own children: they
were their meat in the destruction of
the daughter of my people.
11 The LORD hath accomplished his
fury; he hath poured out his fierce anger, and [h]hath kindled a fire in Zī'ŏn,
and it hath devoured the foundations
thereof.
12 The kings of the earth, and all
[i]the inhabitants of the world, would
not have believed that the adversary
and the enemy should have entered
into the gates of Je-ru̥'sa-lĕm.
13 ¶ [j]For the sins of her prophets,
and the iniquities of her priests, [k]that
have shed the blood of the just in the
midst of her,
14 They have wandered *as* blind
men in the streets, [l]they have polluted
themselves with blood, [6]so that men
could not touch their garments.
15 They cried unto them, Depart ye;
[7]*it is* unclean; depart, depart, touch
not: when they fled away and wandered, they said among the heathen,
They shall no more sojourn *there.*
16 The [8]anger of the LORD hath divided them; he will no more regard
them: [m]they respected not the persons
of the priests, they favoured not the
elders.
17 As for us, [n]our eyes as yet failed
for our vain help: in our watching we
have watched for a nation *that* could
not save *us.*
18 [o]They hunt our steps, that we
cannot go in our streets: our end is
near, our days are fulfilled; for [p]our
end is come.
19 Our persecutors are swifter than
the eagles of the heaven: they pursued
us upon the mountains, they laid wait
for us in [9]the wilderness.
20 The [q]breath of our nostrils, the
anointed of the LORD, [r]was taken in
their pits, of whom we said, Under his
shadow we shall live among the heathen.
21 ¶ Rejoice and be glad, O daughter
of Ē'dom, that dwellest in the land of
Ūz; the cup also shall pass through
unto thee: thou shalt be drunken, and
shalt make thyself naked.
22 ¶ [10]The punishment of thine iniquity is accomplished, O daughter of
Zī'ŏn; he will no more carry thee away
into captivity: he will visit thine iniquity, O daughter of Ē'dom; he will [11]dis-
cover thy sins.
5 Remember, O LORD, what is come
upon us: consider, and behold our
reproach.
2 Our inheritance is turned to strangers, our houses to aliens.
3 We are orphans and fatherless,
our mothers *are* as widows.
4 We have drunken our water for
money; our wood [1]is sold unto us.
5 [2]Our necks *are* under persecution:
we labour, *and* have no rest.
6 [a]We have given the hand [b]*to* the
E-gy̆p''tians, *and to* the Ās-sy̆r'ĭ-ans,
to be satisfied with bread.
7 [c]Our fathers have sinned, *and are*
not; and we have borne their iniquities.
8 Servants have ruled over us: *there
is* none that doth deliver *us* out of their
hand.
9 We gat our bread with *the peril of*
our lives because of the sword of the
wilderness.
10 Our skin was black like an oven
because of the [3]terrible famine.
11 [d]They ravished the women in
Zī'ŏn, *and* the maids in the cities of
Jū'dah.

60 [n]Jer. 11.19
63 [o]Ps. 139.2
64 [p]Ps. 28.4; Jer. 11.20; 2 Tim. 4.14; Rev. 6.10
65 [14]Or, obstinacy of heart
66 [q]Ps. 8.3

CHAPTER 4
2 [a]2 Cor. 4.7
3 [1]Or, sea calves
[b]Job 39.14
4 [c]Ps. 22.15
5 [d]Job 24.8; Luke 15.16
6 [2]Or, iniquity
[e]Gen. 19.25
7 [3]Or, distinguished ones
8 [4]darker than blackness
[f]Ps. 102.5
9 [5]flow out
10 [g]ch. 2.20
11 [h]Deut. 32.22
12 [i]Deut. 29.24
13 [j]Jer. 5.31
[k]Matt. 23.31
14 [l]Jer. 2.34
[6]Or, in that they could not but touch
15 [7]Or, ye polluted
16 [8]Or, face
[m]ch. 5.12
17 [n]2 Ki. 24.7; Isa. 20.5-6
18 [o]2 Ki. 25.4
[p]Jer. 51.33
[9]Or, the lower grounds
20 [q]Gen. 2.7
[r]Jer. 52.9
22 [10]Or, Thine iniquity
[11]Or, carry thee captive for thy sins

CHAPTER 5
4 [1]cometh for price
5 [2]On our necks are we persecuted
6 [a]Gen. 24.2; Jer. 50.15
[b]Hos. 12.1
7 [c]Jer. 16.12; Ezek. 18.2; Matt. 23.32
10 [3]Or, terrors, or, storms
11 [d]Isa. 13.16

12 Princes are hanged up by their
hand: the faces of elders were not
honoured.
13 They took the young men [e]to
grind, and the children fell under the
wood.
14 [f]The elders have ceased from the
gate, the young men from their musick.
15 The joy of our heart is ceased;
our dance is turned into mourning.
16 [4]The crown is fallen *from* our
head: woe unto us, that we have sinned!
17 For this our heart is faint; [g]for
these *things* our eyes are dim.

13 [e]Judg. 16.21
14 [f]2 Ki. 25.18
16 [4]The crown of our head is fallen
17 [g]Job 17.7; Ps. 6.7
20 [5]for length of days
22 [6]Or, For wilt thou utterly reject us?

18 Because of the mountain of Zī'ŏn,
which is desolate, the foxes walk upon
it.
19 Thou, O LORD, remainest for
ever; thy throne from generation to
generation.
20 Wherefore dost thou forget us for
ever, *and* forsake us [5]so long time?
21 Turn thou us unto thee, O LORD,
and we shall be turned; renew our
days as of old.
22 [6]But thou hast utterly rejected us;
thou art very wroth against us.

THE BOOK OF

EZEKIEL

Life's Questions

How do I reform traditional religion when it proves wrong?
How do I know God is present where I am?
Where do I place my hope when life is horrible?

God's Answers

Ezekiel shows exiles in Babylon after 597 (see 2 Kings 24:14). trying to put life's pieces back together. In 593 God called Ezekiel, the exiled priest, to minister to his fellow exiles. Until about 571 Ezekiel showed them how to live as persecuted people in enemy territory with faith in the God of their fathers. They had to endure their punishment, not expect immediate return to their homeland, and believe that God was present among them not just in the Jerusalem temple.

Ezekiel taught: God's glory watches over the exiles (ch. 1), the glory continues to bring punishment to unfaithful Israel with hope only in the distance (2—24); the glory will punish the unjust nations (25—32); the glory will restore a dead people with a new covenant (33—39); the glory will restore His temple for pure worship (40—48).

1 Now it came to pass in [a]the thirtieth year, in the fourth *month*, in the
fifth *day* of the month, as I *was* among
the [1]captives by the river of Chē'bär,
that [b]the heavens were opened, and I
saw visions of God.
2 In the fifth *day* of the month, which
was the fifth year of king Je-hoi'a-
chin's captivity,
3 [c]The word of the LORD came expressly unto [2]E-zē'kĭ-ĕl the priest, the
son of Bū'zī, in the land of the Chăl-
dē'ans by the river Chē'bär; and [d]the
hand of the LORD was there upon him.
4 ¶ And I looked, and, behold, [e]a
whirlwind came [f]out of the north, a
great cloud, and a fire [3]infolding itself,
and a brightness *was* about it, and out
of the midst thereof as the colour of
amber, out of the midst of the fire.
5 [g]Also out of the midst thereof
came the likeness of four living creatures. And this [h]*was* their appearance;
they had the likeness of a man.
6 And every one had four faces, and
every one had four wings.
7 And their feet *were* [4]straight feet;
and the sole of their feet *was* like the
sole of a calf's foot: and they sparkled
[i]like the colour of burnished brass.
8 [j]And *they had* the hands of a man
under their wings on their four sides;
and they four had their faces and their
wings.

CHAPTER 1
1 [a]2 Ki. 23.3
[1]captivity
[b]Matt. 3.16
3 [c]2 Pet. 1.21
[2]Jehezkel
[d]2 Ki. 3.15
4 [e]Isa. 21.1; Jer. 23.19
[f]Jer. 1.14; Jer. 4.6
[3]catching itself
5 [g]Rev. 4.6
[h]ch. 10.8
7 [4]a straight foot
[i]Dan. 10.6; Rev. 1.15
8 [j]Isa. 6.6;
10 [k]Rev. 4.7
[l]Num. 2.10
11 [5]Or, divided above
[m]Isa. 6.2
13 [n]Dan. 10.5-6;
14 [o]Zech. 4.10
[p]Ex. 3.2;
15 [q]ch. 10.9
16 [r]ch. 10.9-10
[s]Dan. 10.6

9 Their wings *were* joined one to another; they turned not when they went;
they went every one straight forward.
10 As for [k]the likeness of their faces,
they four [l]had the face of a man, and
the face of a lion, on the right side: and
they four had the face of an ox on the
left side; they four also had the face of
an eagle.
11 Thus *were* their faces: and their
wings *were* [5]stretched upward; two
wings of every one *were* joined one
to another, and [m]two covered their
bodies.
12 And they went every one straight
forward: whither the spirit was to go,
they went; *and* they turned not when
they went.
13 As for the likeness of the living
creatures, their appearance *was* like
burning coals of fire, [n]*and* like the appearance of lamps: it went up and
down among the living creatures; and
the fire was bright, and out of the fire
went forth lightning.
14 And the living creatures [o]ran and
returned [p]as the appearance of a flash
of lightning.
15 ¶ Now as I beheld the living creatures, behold [q]one wheel upon the
earth by the living creatures, with his
four faces.
16 [r]The appearance of the wheels
and their work *was* [s]like unto the colour of a beryl: and they four had one
likeness: and their appearance and

their work *was* as it were a wheel in
the middle of a wheel.
17 When they went, they went upon
their four sides: *and* they turned not
when they went.
18 As for their rings, they were so
high that they were dreadful; and their
[6]rings *were* [t]full of eyes round about
them four.
19 And [u]when the living creatures
went, the wheels went by them: and
when the living creatures were lifted
up from the earth, the wheels were
lifted up.
20 Whithersoever the spirit was to
go, they went, thither *was their* spirit
to go; and the wheels were lifted up
over against them: for the spirit [7]of the
living creature *was* in the wheels.
21 When those went, *these* went;
and when those stood, *these* stood;
and when those were lifted up from the
earth, the wheels were lifted up over
against them: for the spirit [8]of the living creature *was* in the wheels.
22 [v]And the likeness of the firmament upon the heads of the living creature *was* as the colour of the terrible
crystal, stretched forth over their heads
above.
23 And under the firmament *were*
their wings straight, the one toward
the other: every one had two, which
covered on this side, and every one
had two, which covered on that side,
their bodies.
24 [w]And when they went, I heard
the noise of their wings, like [x]the noise
of great waters, as the [y]voice of the
Almighty, the voice of speech, as the
noise of an host: when they stood, they
let down their wings.
25 And there was a voice from the
firmament that *was* over their heads,
when they stood, *and* had let down
their wings.
26 ¶ [z]And above the firmament that
was over their heads *was* the likeness
of a throne, [a]as the appearance of a
sapphire stone: and upon the likeness
of the throne *was* the likeness [b]as the
appearance of a man above upon it.
27 [c]And I saw as the colour of amber, as the appearance of fire round
about within it, from the appearance of
his loins even upward, and from the
appearance of his loins even downward, I saw as it were the appearance
of fire, and it had brightness round
about.
28 [d]As the appearance of the bow
that is in the cloud in the day of rain, so
was the appearance of the brightness
round about. [e]This *was* the appearance of the likeness of the glory of the
LORD. And when I saw *it*, [f]I fell upon
my face, and I heard a voice of one that
spake.

2

2 And he said unto me, Son of man,
[a]stand upon thy feet, and I will
speak unto thee.
2 And [b]the spirit entered into me
when he spake unto me, and set me
upon my feet, that I heard him that
spake unto me.
3 And he said unto me, Son of man, I
send thee to the children of Is'ra-el, to
a rebellious [1]nation that hath rebelled
against me: [c]they and their fathers
have transgressed against me, *even*
unto this very day.
4 [d]For *they are* [2]impudent children
and stiffhearted. I do send thee unto
them; and thou shalt say unto them,
Thus saith the Lord GOD.
5 [e]And they, whether they will hear,
or whether they will forbear, (for they
are a rebellious house,) yet [f]shall know
that there hath been a prophet among
them.
6 ¶ And thou, son of man, [g]be not
afraid of them, neither be afraid of
their words, though [3]briers and thorns
be with thee, and thou dost dwell
among scorpions: [h]be not afraid of
their words, nor be dismayed at their
looks, [i]though they *be* a rebellious
house.
7 [j]And thou shalt speak my words
unto them, whether they will hear, or
whether they will forbear: for they *are*
[4]most rebellious.
8 But thou, son of man, hear what I
say unto thee; Be not thou rebellious
like that rebellious house: open thy
mouth, and [k]eat that I give thee.
9 ¶ And when I looked, behold, [l]an
hand *was* sent unto me; and, lo, [m]a roll
of a book *was* therein;
10 And he spread it before me; and
it *was* written within and without:
and *there was* written therein lamentations, and mourning, and [n]woe.

3

3 Moreover he said unto me, Son of
man, eat that thou findest; [a]eat this
roll, and go speak unto the house of
Is'ra-el.
2 So I opened my mouth, and he
caused me to eat that roll.
3 And he said unto me, Son of man,
cause thy belly to eat, and fill thy bowels with this roll that I give thee. Then
did I [b]eat *it*; and it was in my mouth as
honey for sweetness.
4 ¶ And he said unto me, Son of
man, go, get thee unto the house of
Is'ra-el, and speak with my words unto
them.
5 For thou *art* not sent to a people
[1]of a strange speech and of an hard
language, *but* to the house of Is'ra-el;
6 Not to many people [2]of a strange
speech and of an hard language,
whose words thou canst not understand. [3]Surely, had I sent thee to them,
they would have hearkened unto thee.
7 But the house of Is'ra-el will not
hearken unto thee; [c]for they will not
hearken unto me: for all the house of Is'-
ra-el *are* [4]impudent and hardhearted.
8 Behold, I have made thy face strong
against their faces, and thy forehead
strong against their foreheads.
9 [d]As an adamant harder than flint
have I made thy forehead: fear them
not, neither be dismayed at their looks,
though they *be* a rebellious house.
10 Moreover he said unto me, Son of
man, all my words that I shall speak

18 [6]Or, strakes
[t]Prov. 15.3; ch. 10.12; Rev. 5.6
19 [u]ch. 10.16-17
20 [7]Or, of life
21 [8]Or, of life
22 [v]ch. 10.1
24 [w]ch. 10.5
[x]Dan. 10.6; Rev. 1.15
[y]Job 37.4-5; Ps. 18.13; ch. 10.5
26 [z]ch. 10.1
[a]Ex. 24.10
[b]Isa. 6.1
27 [c]ch. 8.2
28 [d]Rev. 4.3
[e]Ex. 33.20; Num. 12.8; ch. 8.4
[f]ch. 43.3; Dan. 8.17; Acts 9.4; Rev. 1.17

CHAPTER 2
1 [a]Dan. 10.11
2 [b]Num. 11.25; Judg. 13.25; Neh. 9.30; ch. 3.24; Joel 2.28-29
3 [1]nations
[c]Jer. 3.25
4 [d]ch. 3.7
[2]hard of face
5 [e]ch. 3.11
[f]ch. 33.33
6 [g]Matt. 10.28
[3]Or, rebels
[h]Heb. 11.27; 1 Pet. 3.14
[i]ch. 3.26-27
7 [j]Jer. 1.7-17; Matt. 28.20
[4]rebellion
8 [k]Rev. 10.9
9 [l]Jer. 1.9
[m]ch. 3.1
10 [n]Isa. 3.11

CHAPTER 3
1 [a]ch. 2.8-9
3 [b]Rev. 10.9
5 [1]deep of lip, and heavy of tongue
6 [2]deep of lip, and heavy of language
[3]Or, If I had sent thee, etc., would they not have hearkened unto thee?
7 [c]John 15.20
[4]stiff of forehead, and hard of heart
9 [d]Jer. 1.18

unto thee receive in thine heart, and
hear with thine ears.
11 And go, get thee to them of the
captivity, unto the children of thy people, and speak unto them, and tell them,
Thus saith the Lord GOD; whether they
will hear, or whether they will forbear.
12 Then [e]the spirit took me up, and I
heard behind me a voice of a great
rushing, *saying,* Blessed *be* the glory
of the LORD from his place.
13 *I heard* also the noise of the
wings of the living creatures that [5]tou-
ched one another, and the noise of the
wheels over against them, and a noise
of a great rushing.
14 So the spirit lifted me up, and
took me away, and I went [6]in bitterness, in the [7]heat of my spirit; but [f]the
hand of the LORD was strong upon me.
15 ¶ Then I came to them of the captivity at Tĕl–ā'bib, that dwelt by the
river of Chē'bär, and [g]I sat where they
sat, and remained there astonished
among them seven days.
16 And it came to pass at the end of
seven days, that the word of the LORD
came unto me, saying,
17 Son of man, I have made thee [h]a
watchman unto the house of Is'ra-el:
therefore hear the word at my mouth,
and give them warning from me.
18 When I say unto the wicked, Thou
shalt surely die; and thou givest him
not warning, nor speakest to warn the
wicked from his wicked way, [i]to save
his life; the same wicked *man* [j]shall die
in his iniquity; but his blood will I require at thine hand.
19 Yet if thou warn the wicked, and
he turn not from his wickedness, nor
from his wicked way, he shall die in
his iniquity; [k]but thou hast delivered
thy soul.
20 Again, When a [l]righteous *man*
doth turn from his [8]righteousness, and
commit iniquity, and I lay a stumblingblock before him, he shall die: because thou hast not given him warning, he shall die in his sin, and his righteousness which he hath done shall
not be remembered; but his blood will
I require at thine hand.
21 Nevertheless if thou warn the
righteous *man,* that the righteous sin
not, and he doth not sin, he shall surely
[m]live, because he is warned; also [n]thou
hast delivered thy soul.
22 ¶ And the hand of the LORD was
there upon me; and he said unto me,
Arise, go forth into [o]the plain, and I
will there talk with thee.
23 Then I arose, and went forth into
the plain: and, behold, [p]the glory of
the LORD stood there, as the glory
which I [q]saw by the river of Chē'bär:
and I fell on my face.
24 Then [r]the spirit entered into me,
and set me upon my feet, and spake
with me, and said unto me, Go, shut
thyself within thine house.
25 But thou, O son of man, behold,
[s]they shall put bands upon thee, and
shall bind thee with them, and thou
shalt not go out among them:

12 [e]ch. 8.3; Acts 8.39
13 [5]kissed
14 [6]bitter [7]hot anger
[f]2 Ki. 3.15
15 [g]Job 2.13; Ps. 137.1
17 [h]Song 3.3; Song 5.7; Isa. 21.6-8-11-12; Isa. 52.8; Isa. 56.10; Jer. 6.17
18 [i]Rom. 1.16; 1 Tim. 4.16
[j]ch. 33.6
19 [k]Acts 20.26
20 [l]ch. 18.24; 2 Pet. 2.20 [8]righteousnesses
21 [m]Rom. 2.7
[n]Acts 18.6
22 [o]ch. 8.4
23 [p]ch. 1.28
[q]ch. 1.1
24 [r]ch. 2.2
25 [s]ch. 4.8
26 [t]ch. 24.27; Luke 1.20-22 [9]a man reproving
[u]ch. 2.5-6
27 [v]ch. 24.27; ch. 33.22
[w]ch. 12.2-3

CHAPTER 4

2 [1]Or, chief leaders
3 [2]Or, a flat plate, or, slice
[a]Isa. 8.18; ch. 12.6-11; Mark 14.22; Luke 2.34; John 4.48
5 [3]From the establishment of idolatry by Jeroboam, 1 Ki. 12.26-till B. C. 585
[b]Num. 14.34
6 [4]a day for a year, a day for a year
8 [c]ch. 3.25 [5]from thy side to thy side
9 [6]Or, spelt
13 [d]Dan. 1.8; Hos. 9.3
14 [e]ch. 9.8; Acts 10.14
[f]Ex. 22.31; Lev. 11.40

26 And [t]I will make thy tongue
cleave to the roof of thy mouth, that
thou shalt be dumb, and shalt not be to
them [9]a reprover: [u]for they *are* a rebellious house.
27 [v]But when I speak with thee, I
will open thy mouth, and thou shalt
say unto them, Thus saith the Lord
GOD; He that heareth, let him hear;
and he that forbeareth, let him forbear:
[w]for they *are* a rebellious house.

4

Thou also, son of man, take thee a
tile, and lay it before thee, and pour-
tray upon it the city, *even* Je-ru'sa-lĕm:
2 And lay siege against it, and build
a fort against it, and cast a mount
against it; set the camp also against it,
and set [1]*battering* rams against it round
about.
3 Moreover take thou unto thee [2]an
iron pan, and set it *for* a wall of iron
between thee and the city: and set thy
face against it, and it shall be besieged,
and thou shalt lay siege against it.
[a]This *shall be* a sign to the house of
Is'ra-el.
4 Lie thou also upon thy left side,
and lay the iniquity of the house of
Is'ra-el upon it: *according* to the number of the days that thou shalt lie upon
it thou shalt bear their iniquity.
5 For I have laid upon thee the years
of their iniquity, according to the number of the days, [3]three hundred and
ninety days: [b]so shalt thou bear the
iniquity of the house of Is'ra-el.
6 And when thou hast accomplished
them, lie again on thy right side, and
thou shalt bear the iniquity of the
house of Jū'dah forty days: I have appointed thee [4]each day for a year.
7 Therefore thou shalt set thy face
toward the siege of Je-ru'sa-lĕm, and
thine arm *shall be* uncovered, and thou
shalt prophesy against it.
8 [c]And, behold, I will lay bands
upon thee, and thou shalt not turn thee
[5]from one side to another, till thou hast
ended the days of thy siege.
9 ¶ Take thou also unto thee wheat,
and barley, and beans, and lentiles,
and millet, and [6]fitches, and put them
in one vessel, and make thee bread
thereof, *according* to the number of the
days that thou shalt lie upon thy side,
three hundred and ninety days shalt
thou eat thereof.
10 And thy meat which thou shalt
eat *shall be* by weight, twenty shekels
a day: from time to time shalt thou eat
it.
11 Thou shalt drink also water by
measure, the sixth part of an hin: from
time to time shalt thou drink.
12 And thou shalt eat it *as* barley
cakes, and thou shalt bake it with dung
that cometh out of man, in their sight.
13 And the LORD said, Even thus
[d]shall the children of Is'ra-el eat their
defiled bread among the Gĕn'tīles,
whither I will drive them.
14 Then said I, [e]Ah Lord GOD! behold, my soul hath not been polluted:
for from my youth up even till now
have I not eaten of [f]that which dieth

of itself, or is torn in pieces; neither came there [g]abominable flesh into my mouth.

15 Then he said unto me, Lo, I have given thee cow's dung for man's dung, and thou shalt prepare thy bread therewith.

16 Moreover he said unto me, Son of man, behold, I will break the [h]staff of bread in Je-rṳ'sa-lĕm: and they shall [i]eat bread by weight, and with care; and they shall drink water by measure, and with astonishment:

17 That they may want bread and water, and be astonied one with another, and consume [j]away for their iniquity.

5 And thou, son of man, take thee a sharp knife, take thee a barber's rasor, [a]and cause *it* to pass upon thine head and upon thy beard: then take thee balances to weigh, and divide the *hair*.

2 Thou shalt burn with fire a third part in the midst of [b]the city, when the days of the siege are fulfilled: and thou shalt take a third part, *and* smite about it with a knife: and a third part thou shalt scatter in the wind; and I will draw out a sword after them.

3 [c]Thou shalt also take thereof a few in number, and bind them in thy [1]skirts.

4 Then take of them again, and [d]cast them into the midst of the fire, and burn them in the fire; *for* thereof shall a fire come forth into all the house of Ĭs'ra-el.

5 ¶ Thus saith the Lord GOD; This *is* Je-rṳ'sa-lĕm: I have set it in the midst of the nations and countries *that are* round about her.

6 And she hath [e]changed my judgments into wickedness more than the nations, and my statutes more than the countries that *are* round about her: for they have refused my judgments and my statutes, they have not walked in them.

7 Therefore thus saith the Lord GOD; Because ye multiplied more than the nations that *are* round about you, *and* have not walked in my statutes, neither have kept my judgments, [f]neither have done according to the judgments of the nations that *are* round about you;

8 Therefore thus saith the Lord GOD; Behold, I, even I, *am* against thee, and will execute judgments in the midst of thee in the sight of the nations.

9 [g]And I will do in thee that which I have not done, and whereunto I will not do any more the like, because of all thine abominations.

10 Therefore the fathers [h]shall eat the sons in the midst of thee, and the sons shall eat their fathers; and I will execute judgments in thee, and the whole remnant of thee will I [i]scatter into all the winds.

11 Wherefore, *as* I live, saith the Lord GOD; Surely, because thou hast [j]defiled my sanctuary with all thy [k]detestable things, and with all thine abominations, therefore will I also diminish *thee;* neither shall mine eye spare, neither will I have any pity.

12 ¶ [l]A third part of thee shall die with the pestilence, and with famine shall they be consumed in the midst of thee: and a third part shall fall by the sword round about thee; and [m]I will scatter a third part into all the winds, and [n]I will draw out a sword after them.

13 Thus shall mine anger [o]be accomplished, and I will cause my fury to rest upon them, [p]and I will be comforted: and they shall know that I the LORD have spoken *it* in my zeal, when I have accomplished my fury in them.

14 Moreover [q]I will make thee waste, and a reproach among the nations that *are* round about thee, in the sight of all that pass by.

15 So it shall be a [r]reproach and a taunt, an [s]instruction and an astonishment unto the nations that *are* round about thee, when I shall execute judgments in thee in anger and in fury and in [t]furious rebukes. I the LORD have spoken *it*.

16 When I shall [u]send upon them the evil arrows of famine, which shall be for *their* destruction, *and* which I will send to destroy you: and I will increase the famine upon you, and will break your staff of bread:

17 So will I send upon you famine and [v]evil beasts, and they shall bereave thee; and [w]pestilence and blood shall pass through thee; and I will bring the sword upon thee. I the LORD have spoken *it*.

6 And the word of the LORD came unto me, saying,

2 Son of man, set thy face toward the [a]mountains of Ĭs'ra-el, and prophesy against them,

3 And say, Ye mountains of Ĭs'ra-el, hear the word of the Lord GOD; Thus saith the Lord GOD to the mountains, and to the hills, to the rivers, and to the valleys; Behold, I, *even* I, will bring a sword upon you, and [b]I will destroy your high places.

4 And your altars shall be desolate, and your [1]images shall be broken: and [c]I will cast down your slain *men* before your [2]idols.

5 And I will [3]lay the dead carcases of the children of Ĭs'ra-el before their idols; and I will scatter your bones round about your altars.

6 In all your dwellingplaces the cities shall be laid waste, and the high places shall be desolate; that your altars may be laid waste and made desolate, and your idols may be broken and cease, and your images may be cut down, and your works may be abolished.

7 And the slain shall fall in the midst of you, and ye shall know that I *am* the LORD.

8 ¶ [d]Yet will I leave a remnant, that ye may have *some* that shall escape the sword among the nations, when ye shall be scattered through the countries.

[g]Lev. 19.7; Deut. 14.3; Isa. 65.4
16 [h]Lev. 26.26; Ps. 105.16; Isa. 3.1; ch. 5.16
[i]Lev. 26.26; Deut. 28.48; Ps. 68.3; Lam. 1.11; ch. 12.18-19
17 [j]Lev. 26.39; ch. 24.23

CHAPTER 5
1 [a]Lev. 21.5; Isa. 7.20; ch. 44.20
2 [b]ch. 4.1
3 [c]Jer. 40.6
[1]wings
4 [d]Jer. 41.1-2
6 [e]Rom. 1.25; Jude 4
7 [f]Jer. 2.10; ch. 11.12
9 [g]Lam. 4.6; Dan. 9.12; Amos 3.2; Matt. 24.21
10 [h]Deut. 28.53; Jer. 19.9; Lam. 2.20
[i]Lev. 26.33; ch. 12.14
11 [j]2 Chr. 36.14; ch. 7.20
[k]ch. 11.21
12 [l]Jer. 15.2; ch. 6.12
[m]Jer. 9.16; ch. 6.8
[n]Lev. 26.33; ch. 12.14
13 [o]Lam. 4.11; Dan. 9.2
[p]Deut. 32.36; Isa. 1.24
14 [q]Lev. 26.31; Neh. 2.17
15 [r]Deut. 28.37; Ps. 79.4; Jer. 24.9; Lam. 2.15
[s]1 Cor. 10.11
[t]ch. 25.17
16 [u]Deut. 32.23-24; ch. 14.21
17 [v]Lev. 26.22
[w]ch. 38.22

CHAPTER 6
2 [a]ch. 36.1
3 [b]Lev. 26.30
4 [1]Or, sun images
[c]Lev. 26.30
[2]dungy gods
5 [3]give
8 [d]Jer. 44.28; ch. 5.2-12

9 And they that escape of you shall remember me among the nations whither they shall be carried captives, because [e]I am broken with their whorish heart, which hath departed from me, and [f]with their eyes, which go a whoring after their idols: and [g]they shall loathe themselves for the evils which they have committed in all their abominations.

10 And they shall know that I *am* the LORD, *and that* I have not said in vain that I would do this evil unto them.

11 ¶ Thus saith the Lord GOD; Smite [h]with thine hand, and stamp with thy foot, and say, Alas for all the evil abominations of the house of Is′ra-el! [i]for they shall fall by the sword, by the famine, and by the pestilence.

12 He that is far off shall die of the pestilence; and he that is near shall fall by the sword; and he that remaineth and is besieged shall die by the famine: thus will I accomplish my fury upon them.

13 Then shall ye know that I *am* the LORD, when their slain *men* shall be among their idols round about their altars, [j]upon every high hill, [k]in all the tops of the mountains, and [l]under every green tree, and under every thick oak, the place where they did offer sweet savour to all their idols.

14 So will I [m]stretch out my hand upon them, and make the land desolate, yea, [4]more desolate than the wilderness toward [n]Dĭb′lăth, in all their habitations: and they shall know that I *am* the LORD.

7

Moreover the word of the LORD came unto me, saying,

2 Also, thou son of man, thus saith the Lord GOD unto the land of Is′ra-el; [a]An end, the end is come upon the four corners of the land.

3 Now *is* the end *come* upon thee, and I will send mine anger upon thee, and will judge thee according to thy ways, and will [1]recompense upon thee all thine abominations.

4 And [b]mine eye shall not spare thee, neither will I have pity: but I will recompense thy ways upon thee, and thine abominations shall be in the midst of thee: [c]and ye shall know that I *am* the LORD.

5 Thus saith the Lord GOD; An evil, an only evil, behold, is come.

6 An end is come, the end is come: it [2]watcheth for thee; behold, it is come.

7 The morning is come unto thee, O thou that dwellest in the land: [d]the time is come, the day of trouble *is* near, and not the [3]sounding again of the mountains.

8 Now will I shortly [e]pour out my fury upon thee, and accomplish mine anger upon thee: and I will judge thee according to thy ways, and will recompense thee for all thine abominations.

9 And mine eye shall not spare, neither will I have pity: I will recompense [4]thee according to thy ways and thine abominations *that* are in the midst of thee; and ye shall know that I *am* the LORD that smiteth.

10 Behold the day, behold, it is come: the morning is gone forth; the rod hath blossomed, pride hath budded.

11 [f]Violence is risen up into a rod of wickedness: none of them *shall remain*, nor of their [5]multitude, nor of any of [6]theirs: [g]neither *shall there be* wailing for them.

12 The time is come, the day draweth near: let not the buyer rejoice, nor the seller mourn: for wrath *is* upon all the multitude thereof.

13 For the seller shall not return to that which is sold, [7]although they were yet alive: for the vision *is* touching the whole multitude thereof, *which* shall not return; neither shall any strengthen himself [8]in [9]the iniquity of his life.

14 They have blown the trumpet, even to make all ready; but none goeth to the battle: for my wrath *is* upon all the multitude thereof.

15 [h]The sword *is* without, and the pestilence and the famine within: he that *is* in the field shall die with the sword; and he that *is* in the city, famine and pestilence shall devour him.

16 ¶ But [i]they that escape of them shall escape, and shall be on the mountains like doves of the valleys, all of them mourning, every one for his iniquity.

17 All [j]hands shall be feeble, and all knees shall [10]be weak *as* water.

18 They shall also [k]gird *themselves* with sackcloth, and [l]horror shall cover them; and shame *shall be* upon all faces, and baldness upon all their heads.

19 They shall cast their silver in the streets, and their gold shall be [11]removed: their [m]silver and their gold shall not be able to deliver them in the day of the wrath of the LORD: they shall not satisfy their souls, neither fill their bowels: [12]because it is [n]the stumblingblock of their iniquity.

20 ¶ As for the beauty of his ornament, he set it in majesty: [o]but they made the images of their abominations *and* of their detestable things therein: therefore have I [13]set it far from them.

21 And I will give it into the hands of the strangers for a prey, and to the wicked of the earth for a spoil; and they shall pollute it.

22 My face will I turn also from them, and they shall pollute my secret *place*: for the [14]robbers shall enter into it, and defile it.

23 ¶ Make a chain: for [p]the land is full of bloody crimes, and the city is full of violence.

24 Wherefore I will bring [q]the worst of the heathen, and they shall possess their houses: I will also make the pomp of the strong to cease; and [15]their holy places shall be defiled.

25 [16]Destruction cometh; and they shall seek peace, and *there shall be* none.

26 [r]Mischief shall come upon mischief, and rumour shall be upon ru-

9 [e]Ps. 78.40; Isa. 7.13 [f]Num. 15.39; ch. 20.7 [g]Lev. 26.39; ch. 20.43 **11** [h]Lev. 26.36; [i]ch. 5.12 **13** [j]Jer. 2.20; [k]Hos. 4.13 [l]Isa. 57.5 **14** [m]Isa. 5.25 [4]Or, desolate from the wilderness [n]Num. 33.46

CHAPTER 7
2 [a]Deut. 32.20; **3** [1]give **4** [b]ch. 5.11 [c]ch. 6.7 **6** [2]awaketh against thee **7** [d]Isa. 13.22; [3]Or, echo **8** [e]Ps. 79.6; **9** [4]upon thee **11** [f]Jer. 6.7 [5]Or, tumult [6]Or, their tumultuous persons [g]Jer. 16.5 **13** [7]though their life were yet among the living [8]Or, whose life is in his iniquity [9]his iniquity **15** [h]Deut. 32.25 **16** [i]ch. 6.8 **17** [j]Isa. 13.7 [10]go into water **18** [k]Jer. 6.26 [l]Ps. 55.5 **19** [11]for a separation, or, uncleanness [m]Prov. 11.4; [12]Or, because their iniquity is their stumblingblock [n]ch. 44.12 **20** [o]Jer. 7.30 [13]Or, made it unto them an unclean thing **22** [14]Or, burglers **23** [p]Gen. 9.6; **24** [q]Hab. 1.6 [15]Or, they shall inherit their holy places **25** [16]Cutting off **26** [r]Deut. 32.23

mour; [s]then shall they seek a vision of
the prophet; but the law shall perish
from [t]the priest, and counsel from the
ancients.
27 The king shall mourn, and the
prince shall be clothed with desolation, and the hands of the people of the
land shall be troubled: I will do unto
them after their way, and [17]according
to their deserts will I judge them; and
they shall know that I *am* the LORD.

8

And it came to pass in the sixth
year, in the sixth *month*, in the fifth
day of the month, *as* I sat in mine
house, and the elders of Jū'dah sat before me, that the hand of the Lord GOD
fell there upon me.
2 [a]Then I beheld, and lo a likeness
as the appearance of fire: from the appearance of his loins even downward,
fire; and from his loins even upward,
as the appearance of brightness, as the
colour of amber.
3 And he [b]put forth the form of an
hand, and took me by a lock of mine
head; and the spirit lifted me up between the earth and the heaven, and
[c]brought me in the visions of God to Je-
ru'sa-lĕm, to the door [d]of the inner gate
that looketh toward the north; [e]where
was the seat of the image of jealousy,
which [f]provoketh to jealousy.
4 And, behold, the glory of the God
of Ĭs'ra-el *was* there, according to the
vision that I [g]saw in the plain.
5 ¶ Then said he unto me, Son of
man, lift up thine eyes now the way
toward the north. So I lifted up mine
eyes the way toward the north, and behold northward at the gate of the altar
this image of jealousy in the entry.
6 He said furthermore unto me, Son
of man, seest thou what they do?
even the great [h]abominations that the
house of Ĭs'ra-el committeth here, that
I should go far off from my sanctuary?
but turn thee yet again, *and* thou shalt
see greater abominations.
7 ¶ And he brought me to the door of
the court; and when I looked, behold a
hole in the wall.
8 Then said he unto me, Son of man,
dig now in the wall: and when I had
digged in the wall, behold a door.
9 And he said unto me, Go in, and
behold the wicked abominations that
they do here.
10 So I went in and saw; and behold
every form of creeping things, and
abominable beasts, and all the idols of
the house of Ĭs'ra-el, pourtrayed upon
the wall round about.
11 And there stood before them seventy men of the ancients of the house
of Ĭs'ra-el, and in the midst of them
stood Ja-ăz-a-nī'ah the son of [i]Shā'-
phan, with [j]every man his censer in
his hand; and a thick cloud of incense
went up.
12 Then said he unto me, Son of
man, hast thou seen what the ancients
of the house of Ĭs'ra-el do in the dark,
every man in the chambers of his imag-
ery? for they say, [k]The LORD seeth us
not; the LORD hath [l]forsaken the earth.

[s]Ps. 74.9; Lam. 2.9
[t]Mal. 2.7-8-9
27 [17]with their judg-ments
CHAPTER 8
2 [a]ch. 1.26; Dan. 7.9
3 [b]ch. 2.9; Dan. 5.5
[c]ch. 11.1
[d]2 Ki. 16.14
[e]Jer. 7.30
[f]Deut. 32.16; Ex. 20.4
4 [g]ch. 1.28
6 [h]Deut. 31.16; 2 Chr. 36.14
11 [i]2 Ki. 22.8; Jer. 26.24
[j]Num. 16.17
12 [k]Ps. 14.1; Isa. 29.15
[l]Ps. 10.11
14 [1]In a lewd and idola-trous man-ner, lament-ing the death of Tammuz, or, Adonis, supposed also to be Baal-peor, Num. 25.3
16 [m]Joel 2.17
[n]ch. 11.1
[o]Jer. 2.27
[p]Deut. 4.19; Jer. 44.17
17 [2]Or, Is there any-thing lighter than to com-mit, etc
[q]ch. 9.9
18 [r]ch. 5.13
[s]ch. 5.11
[t]Prov. 1.28
CHAPTER 9
1 [a]Ps. 103.20
2 [1]which is turned
[2]a weapon of his breaking in pieces
[b]Lev. 16.4
[3]upon his loins
4 [4]mark a mark
[c]Ps. 119.53
5 [5]mine ears
6 [6]to destruc-tion
[d]Rev. 9.4
[e]Jer. 25.29; Luke 12.47

13 ¶ He said also unto me, Turn thee
yet again, *and* thou shalt see greater
abominations that they do.
14 Then he brought me to the door of
the gate of the LORD'S house which *was*
toward the north; and, behold, there sat
[1]women weeping for Tăm'mŭz.
15 ¶ Then said he unto me, Hast
thou seen *this*, O son of man? turn thee
yet again, *and* thou shalt see greater
abominations than these.
16 And he brought me into the inner court of the LORD'S house, and behold, at the door of the temple of the
LORD, [m]between the porch and the altar, [n]*were* about five and twenty men,
[o]with their backs toward the temple
of the LORD, and their faces toward
the east; and they worshipped [p]the
sun toward the east.
17 ¶ Then he said unto me, Hast thou
seen *this*, O son of man? [2]Is it a light
thing to the house of Jū'dah that they
commit the abominations which they
commit here? for they have [q]filled the
land with violence, and have returned
to provoke me to anger: and, lo, they
put the branch to their nose.
18 [r]Therefore will I also deal in fury:
mine [s]eye shall not spare, neither will I
have pity: and though they [t]cry in mine
ears with a loud voice, *yet* will I not
hear them.

9

He cried also in mine ears with a
loud voice, saying, [a]Cause them
that have charge over the city to draw
near, even every man *with* his destroying weapon in his hand.
2 And, behold, six men came from
the way of the higher gate, [1]which lieth
toward the north, and every man [2]a
slaughter weapon in his hand; [b]and
one man among them *was* clothed
with linen, with a writer's inkhorn [3]by
his side: and they went in, and stood
beside the brasen altar.
3 And the glory of the God of Ĭs'ra-el
was gone up from the cherub, whereupon he was, to the threshold of the
house. And he called to the man clothed
with linen, which *had* the writer's inkhorn by his side;
4 And the LORD said unto him, Go
through the midst of the city, through
the midst of Je-ru'sa-lĕm, and [4]set a
mark upon the foreheads of the men
[c]that sigh and that cry for all the
abominations that be done in the midst
thereof.
5 ¶ And to the others he said in [5]mine
hearing, Go ye after him through the
city, and smite: let not your eye spare,
neither have ye pity:
6 Slay [6]utterly old *and* young, both
maids, and little children, and women:
but [d]come not near any man upon
whom *is* the mark; and [e]begin at my
sanctuary. Then they began at the ancient men which *were* before the house.
7 And he said unto them, Defile the
house, and fill the courts with the
slain: go ye forth. And they went forth,
and slew in the city.
8 ¶ And it came to pass, while they
were slaying them, and I was left, that I

[f]fell upon my face, and cried, and said, Ah Lord GOD! wilt thou destroy all the residue of Ĭs′ra-el in thy pouring out of thy fury upon Je-ru′sa-lĕm?

9 Then said he unto me, The iniquity of the house of Ĭs′ra-el and Jū′dah *is* exceeding great, and the land [g]is [7]full of blood, and the city full of [8]perverseness: for they say, The LORD hath forsaken the earth, and [h]the LORD seeth not.

10 And as for me also, mine eye shall not spare, neither will I have pity, *but* [i]I will recompense their way upon their head.

11 And, behold, the man clothed with linen, which *had* the inkhorn by his side, [9]reported the matter, saying, I have done as thou hast commanded me.

10

10 Then I looked, and, behold, in the [a]firmament that was above the head of the cherubims there appeared over them as it were a sapphire stone, as the appearance of the likeness of a throne.

2 [b]And he spake unto the man clothed with linen, and said, Go in between the wheels, *even* under the cherub, and fill [1]thine hand with [c]coals of fire from between the cherubims, and [d]scatter *them* over the city. And he went in in my sight.

3 Now the cherubims stood on the right side of the house, when the man went in; and the cloud filled the inner court.

4 [e]Then the glory of the LORD [2]went up from the cherub, *and stood* over the threshold of the house; and [f]the house was filled with the cloud, and the court was full of the brightness of the LORD'S glory.

5 And the [g]sound of the cherubims' wings was heard *even* to the outer court, as [h]the voice of the Almighty God when he speaketh.

6 And it came to pass, *that* when he had commanded the man clothed with linen, saying, Take fire from between the wheels, from between the cherubims; then he went in, and stood beside the wheels.

7 And *one* cherub [3]stretched forth his hand from between the cherubims unto the fire that *was* between the cherubims, and took *thereof,* and put *it* into the hands of *him that was* clothed with linen: who took *it,* and went out.

8 ¶ [i]And there appeared in the cherubims the form of a man's hand under their wings.

9 [j]And when I looked, behold the four wheels by the cherubims, one wheel by one cherub, and another wheel by another cherub: and the appearance of the wheels *was* as the colour of a beryl stone.

10 And *as for* their appearances, they four had one likeness, as if a wheel had been in the midst of a wheel.

11 When they went, they went upon their four sides; they turned not as they went, but to the place whither the head looked they followed it; they turned not as they went.

12 And their whole [4]body, and their backs, and their hands, and their wings, and [k]the wheels, *were* [l]full of eyes round about, *even* the wheels that they four had.

13 As for the wheels, [5]it was cried unto them in my hearing, O wheel.

14 [m]And every one had four faces: the first face *was* the face of a cherub, and the second [n]face *was* the face of a man, and the third the face of [o]a lion, and the fourth the face of an [p]eagle.

15 And the cherubims were lifted up. This *is* [q]the living creature that I saw by the river of Chē′bär.

16 [r]And when the cherubims went, the wheels went by them: and when the cherubims lifted up their wings to mount up from the earth, the same wheels also turned not from beside them.

17 [s]When they stood, *these* stood; and when they were lifted up, *these* lifted up themselves *also:* for the spirit [6]of the living creature *was* in them.

18 Then the glory of the LORD [t]departed from off the threshold of the house, and stood over the cherubims.

19 And [u]the cherubims lifted up their wings, and mounted up from the earth in my sight: when they went out, the wheels also *were* beside them, and *every one* stood at the door of the east gate of the LORD'S house; and the glory of the God of Ĭs′ra-el *was* over them above.

20 [v]This *is* the living creature that I saw under the God of Ĭs′ra-el by [w]the river of Chē′bär; and I knew that they *were* the cherubims.

21 [x]Every one had four faces apiece, and every one four wings; [y]and the likeness of the hands of a man *was* under their wings.

22 And [z]the likeness of their faces *was* the same faces which I saw by the river of Chē′bär, their appearances and themselves: [a]they went every one straight forward.

11

11 Moreover [a]the spirit lifted me up, and brought me unto the [b]east gate of the LORD'S house, which looketh eastward: and behold [c]at the door of the gate five and twenty men; among whom I saw Ja-ăz-a-nī′ah the son of Ā′zur, and Pĕl-a-tī′ah the son of Be-nā′iah, princes of the people.

2 Then said he unto me, Son of man, these *are* the men that devise mischief, and give wicked counsel in this city:

3 Which say, [1]*It is* not near; let us build houses: [d]this *city is* the caldron, and we *be* the flesh.

4 ¶Therefore prophesy against them, prophesy, O son of man.

5 And the Spirit of the LORD fell upon me, and said unto me, Speak; Thus saith the LORD; Thus have ye said, O house of Ĭs′ra-el: for [e]I know the things that come into your mind, *every one of* them.

---

8 [f]Num. 14.5; Deut. 9.18; Josh. 7.6
9 [g]2 Ki. 21.16
[7]filled with
[8]Or, wresting of judgment
[h]Ps. 10.11; Isa. 29.15
10 [i]Deut. 32.41
11 [9]returned the word

CHAPTER 10
1 [a]ch. 1.22; Rev. 4.3
2 [b]ch. 9.2-3
[1]the hollow of thine hand
[c]ch. 1.13
[d]Rev. 8.5
4 [e]ch. 1.28
[2]was lifted up
[f]Ex. 40.35; ch. 43.5
5 [g]ch. 1.24
[h]Ps. 29.3
7 [3]sent forth
8 [i]ch. 1.8
9 [j]ch. 1.15
12 [4]flesh
[k]ch. 1.18
[l]Rev. 4.8
13 [5]Or, they were called in my hearing, wheel, or, galgal, that is, move round
14 [m]ch. 1.6-10
[n]2 Sam. 14.17
[o]2 Sam. 24.16
[p]Dan. 9.21
15 [q]ch. 1.5
16 [r]ch. 1.19
17 [s]ch. 1.12
[6]Or, of life
18 [t]Ps. 78.60; Hos. 9.12
19 [u]ch. 9.2-3; ch. 11.22
20 [v]ch. 1.22
[w]ch. 1.1
21 [x]ch. 1.6; Rev. 4.7
[y]ch. 1.8
22 [z]ch. 1.10
[a]ch. 1.12; Ps. 103.20

CHAPTER 11
1 [a]1 Ki. 18.12; ch. 8.3
[b]ch. 10.19
[c]ch. 8.16
3 [1]Or, It is not for us to build houses near
[d]Jer. 1.13
5 [e]1 Chr. 28.9; Heb. 4.11

6 Ye have multiplied your slain in this city, and ye have filled the streets thereof with the slain.

7 Therefore thus saith the Lord GOD; [f]Your slain whom ye have laid in the midst of it, they *are* the flesh, and this *city is* the caldron: but I will bring you forth out of the midst of it.

8 Ye have [g]feared the sword; and I will bring a sword upon you, saith the Lord GOD.

9 And I will bring you out of the midst thereof, and deliver you into the hands of strangers, and [h]will execute judgments among you.

10 [i]Ye shall fall by the sword; I will judge you in [j]the border of Ĭs′ra-el; [k]and ye shall know that I *am* the LORD.

11 This *city* shall not be your caldron, neither shall ye be the flesh in the midst thereof; *but* I will judge you in [l]the border of Ĭs′ra-el:

12 And ye shall know that I *am* the LORD: [2]for ye have not walked in my statutes, neither executed my judgments, but [m]have done after the manners of the heathen that *are* round about you.

13 ¶ And it came to pass, when I prophesied, that [n]Pĕl-a-tī′ah the son of Be-nā′iah died. Then [o]fell I down upon my face, and cried with a loud voice, and said, Ah Lord GOD! wilt thou make a full end of the remnant of Ĭs′ra-el?

14 Again the word of the LORD came unto me, saying,

15 Son of man, thy brethren, *even* thy brethren, the men of thy kindred, and all the house of Ĭs′ra-el wholly, *are* they unto whom the inhabitants of Je-ru̧′sa-lĕm have said, Get you far from the LORD: unto us is this land given in possession.

16 Therefore say, Thus saith the Lord GOD; Although I have cast them far off among the heathen, and although I have scattered them among the countries, [p]yet will I be to them as a little sanctuary in the countries where they shall come.

17 Therefore say, Thus saith the Lord GOD; [q]I will even gather you from the people, and assemble you out of the countries where ye have been scattered, and I will give you the land of Ĭs′ra-el.

18 And they shall come thither, and [r]they shall take away all the detestable things thereof and all the abominations thereof from thence.

19 And [s]I will give them one heart, and I will put [t]a new spirit within you; and I will take [u]the stony heart out of their flesh, and will give them an heart of flesh:

20 That they may walk in my statutes, and keep mine ordinances, and do them: [v]and they shall be my people, and I will be their God.

21 But *as for them* whose [w]heart walketh after the heart of their detestable things and their abominations, I will recompense their way upon their own heads, saith the Lord GOD.

22 ¶ Then did the cherubims [x]lift up their wings, and the wheels beside them; and the glory of the God of Ĭs′ra-el *was* over them above.

23 And [y]the glory of the LORD went up from the midst of the city, and stood [z]upon the mountain [a]which *is* on the east side of the city.

24 ¶ Afterwards [b]the spirit took me up, and brought me in a vision by the Spirit of God into Chăl-dē′ȧ, to them of the captivity. So the vision that I had seen went up from me.

25 Then I [c]spake unto them of the captivity all the things that the LORD had shewed me.

12

The word of the LORD also came unto me, saying,

2 Son of man, thou dwellest in the midst of a rebellious house, which [a]have eyes to see, and see not; they have ears to hear, and hear not: for they *are* a rebellious house.

3 Therefore, thou son of man, prepare thee [1]stuff for removing, and remove by day in their sight; and thou shalt remove from thy place to another place in their sight: it may be they will consider, though they *be* a rebellious house.

4 Then shalt thou bring forth thy stuff by day in their sight, as stuff for removing: and thou shalt go forth at even in their sight, [2]as they that go forth into captivity.

5 [3]Dig thou through the wall in their sight, and carry out thereby.

6 In their sight shalt thou bear *it* upon *thy* shoulders, *and* carry *it* forth in the twilight: thou shalt cover thy face, that thou see not the ground: [b]for I have set thee *for* a sign unto the house of Ĭs′ra-el.

7 And I did so as I was commanded: I brought forth my stuff by day, as stuff for captivity, and in the even I [4]digged through the wall with mine hand; I brought *it* forth in the twilight, *and* I bare *it* upon *my* shoulder in their sight.

8 ¶ And in the morning came the word of the LORD unto me, saying,

9 Son of man, hath not the house of Ĭs′ra-el, the rebellious house, said unto thee, [c]What doest thou?

10 Say thou unto them, Thus saith the Lord GOD; This [d]burden *concerneth* the prince in Je-ru̧′sa-lĕm, and all the house of Ĭs′ra-el that *are* among them.

11 Say, I *am* your sign: like as I have done, so shall it be done unto them: [5]they shall remove *and* go into captivity.

12 And [e]the prince that *is* among them shall bear upon *his* shoulder in the twilight, and shall go forth: they shall dig through the wall to carry out thereby: he shall cover his face, that he see not the ground with *his* eyes.

13 My [f]net also will I spread upon him, and he shall be taken in my snare: and [g]I will bring him to Băb′y̆-lon *to* the land of the Chăl-dē′ans; yet shall he not see it, though he shall die there.

7 [f]Mic. 3.3
8 [g]Prov. 10.24
9 [h]Ps. 106.30
10 [i]Jer. 39.6
[j]2 Ki. 14.25
[k]Ps. 9.16
11 [l]Jer. 39.5
12 [2]Or, which have not walked
[m]Deut. 12.30; ch. 8.10
13 [n]Acts 5.5
[o]ch. 9.8
16 [p]Ps. 31.20; Isa. 8.14
17 [q]Jer. 24.5
18 [r]ch. 37.23
19 [s]Deut. 30.6; 2 Chr. 30.12; Jer. 24.7; Zeph. 3.9
[t]Ps. 51.10; Jer. 31.33
[u]Zech. 7.12
20 [v]Jer. 11.4; ch. 14.11; ch. 36.28; Heb. 8.10
21 [w]Heb. 3.12
22 [x]ch. 1.19
23 [y]ch. 8.4
[z]Zech. 14.4
[a]ch. 43.2
24 [b]ch. 8.3; 2 Cor. 12.2
25 [c]Acts 20.20

CHAPTER 12
2 [a]Isa. 6.9; Jer. 5.21; Matt. 13.13
3 [1]Or, instruments
4 [2]as the goings forth of captivity
5 [3]Dig for thee
6 [b]Isa. 8.18; ch. 4.3
7 [4]digged for me
9 [c]ch. 24.19
10 [d]Mal. 1.1
11 [5]by removing go into captivity
12 [e]Jer. 39.4
13 [f]Job 19.6; Jer. 52.9; Lam. 1.13
[g]Jer. 52.11; ch. 17.16

14 And [h]I will scatter toward every wind all that *are* about him to help him, and all his bands; and I will draw out the sword after them.

15 [i]And they shall know that I *am* the LORD, when I shall scatter them among the nations, and disperse them in the countries.

16 [j]But I will leave [6]a few men of them from the sword, from the famine, and from the pestilence; that they may declare all their abominations among the heathen whither they come; and they shall know that I *am* the LORD.

17 ¶ Moreover the word of the LORD came to me, saying,

18 Son of man, [k]eat thy bread with quaking, and drink thy water with trembling and with carefulness;

19 And say unto the people of the land, Thus saith the Lord GOD of the inhabitants of Je-ru'sa-lĕm, *and* of the land of Ĭs'ra-el; They shall eat their bread with carefulness, and drink their water with astonishment, that her land may [l]be desolate from [7]all that is therein, [m]because of the violence of all them that dwell therein.

20 And the cities that are inhabited shall be laid waste, and the land shall be desolate; and ye shall know that I *am* the LORD.

21 ¶ And the word of the LORD came unto me, saying,

22 Son of man, what *is* that proverb *that* ye have in the land of Ĭs'ra-el, saying, [n]The days are prolonged, and every vision faileth?

23 Tell them therefore, Thus saith the Lord GOD; I will make this proverb to cease, and they shall no more use it as a proverb in Ĭs'ra-el; but say unto them, [o]The days are at hand, and the effect of every vision.

24 For [p]there shall be no more any [q]vain vision nor flattering divination within the house of Ĭs'ra-el.

25 For I *am* the LORD: I will speak, and [r]the word that I shall speak shall come to pass; it shall be no more prolonged: for in your days, O rebellious house, will I say the word, and will perform it, saith the Lord GOD.

26 ¶ Again the word of the LORD came to me, saying,

27 Son of man, behold, *they of* the house of Ĭs'ra-el say, The vision that he seeth *is* [s]for many days *to come,* and he prophesieth of the times *that are* far off.

28 Therefore say unto them, Thus saith the Lord GOD; [t]There shall none of my words be prolonged any more, but the word which I have spoken shall be done, saith the Lord GOD.

13 And the word of the LORD came unto me, saying,

2 Son of man, prophesy against the prophets of Ĭs'ra-el that prophesy, and say thou unto [1]them that prophesy out of their own [a]hearts, Hear ye the word of the LORD:

3 Thus saith the Lord GOD; Woe unto the foolish prophets, that [2]follow their own spirit, [3]and have seen nothing!

14 [h]ch. 5.10
15 [i]Ps. 9.16; Isa. 26.9
16 [j]Isa. 1.8; Jer. 4.27; ch. 6.8
[6]men of number
18 [k]ch. 4.16; Lam. 5.9
19 [l]Zech. 7.14
[7]the fulness thereof
[m]Gen. 13.10; Ps. 107.34
22 [n]Isa. 5.19; ch. 11.3; 2 Pet. 3.4
23 [o]Joel 2.1; Obad. 15
24 [p]ch. 13.23
[q]Lam. 2.14
25 [r]Isa. 55.11; Dan. 9.12; Zech. 1.6
27 [s]Isa. 5.19; 2 Pet. 3.4
28 [t]Jer. 4.7; Rev. 3.3

CHAPTER 13

2 [1]them that are prophets out of their own hearts
[a]Jer. 14.14
3 [2]walk after
[3]Or, and things which they have not seen
4 [b]Song 2.15; 2 Cor. 11.13
5 [c]Ps. 106.23-30; ch. 22.30
[4]Or, breaches
[5]hedged the hedge
6 [d]ch. 12.24
[e]Prov. 14.15; 2 Thess. 2.11
9 [6]Or, secret, or, council
[f]Neh. 7.5; Rev. 13.8
[g]ch. 20.38
[h]Ps. 9.16; ch. 11.10-12
10 [i]2 Tim. 3.13
[j]Jer. 6.14
[7]Or, a slight wall
[k]ch. 22.28
11 [l]ch. 38.22
14 [m]ch. 14.8
16 [n]Jer. 6.14; Jer. 8.11
17 [o]ch. 4.3; ch. 20.46
[p]Ex. 15.20; Isa. 3.16
18 [8]Or, elbows
[q]ch. 22.25; 2 Pet. 2.14

4 O Ĭs'ra-el, thy prophets are [b]like the foxes in the deserts.

5 Ye [c]have not gone up into the [4]gaps, neither [5]made up the hedge for the house of Ĭs'ra-el to stand in the battle in the day of the LORD.

6 [d]They have seen vanity and lying divination, saying, The LORD saith: and the LORD hath not sent them: and they have made *others* to [e]hope that they would confirm the word.

7 Have ye not seen a vain vision, and have ye not spoken a lying divination, whereas ye say, The LORD saith *it;* albeit I have not spoken?

8 Therefore thus saith the Lord GOD; Because ye have spoken vanity, and seen lies, therefore, behold, I *am* against you, saith the Lord GOD.

9 And mine hand shall be upon the prophets that see vanity, and that divine lies: they shall not be in the [6]assembly of my people, [f]neither shall they be written in the writing of the house of Ĭs'ra-el, [g]neither shall they enter into the land of Ĭs'ra-el; [h]and ye shall know that I *am* the Lord GOD.

10 ¶ Because, even because they have [i]seduced my people, saying, [j]Peace; and *there was* no peace; and one built up [7]a wall, and, lo, others [k]daubed it with untempered *morter:*

11 Say unto them which daub *it* with untempered *morter,* that it shall fall: [l]there shall be an overflowing shower; and ye, O great hailstones, shall fall; and a stormy wind shall rend *it.*

12 Lo, when the wall is fallen, shall it not be said unto you, Where *is* the daubing wherewith ye have daubed *it?*

13 Therefore thus saith the Lord GOD; I will even rend *it* with a stormy wind in my fury; and there shall be an overflowing shower in mine anger, and great hailstones in *my* fury to consume *it.*

14 So will I break down the wall that ye have daubed with untempered *morter,* and bring it down to the ground, so that the foundation thereof shall be discovered, and it shall fall, and ye shall be consumed in the midst thereof: [m]and ye shall know that I *am* the LORD.

15 Thus will I accomplish my wrath upon the wall, and upon them that have daubed it with untempered *morter,* and will say unto you, The wall *is no more,* neither they that daubed it;

16 *To wit,* the prophets of Ĭs'ra-el which prophesy concerning Je-ru'sa-lĕm, and which [n]see visions of peace for her, and *there is* no peace, saith the Lord GOD.

17 ¶ Likewise, thou son of man, [o]set thy face against [p]the daughters of thy people, which prophesy out of their own heart; and prophesy thou against them,

18 And say, Thus saith the Lord GOD; Woe to the *women* that sew pillows to all [8]armholes, and make kerchiefs upon the head of every stature to hunt souls! Will ye [q]hunt the souls

of my people, and will ye save the
souls alive *that come* unto you?
19 And will ye pollute me among my
people [r]for handfuls of barley and for
pieces of bread, to slay the souls that
should not die, and to save the souls
alive that should not live, by your lying
to my people that hear *your* lies?
20 Wherefore thus saith the Lord
GOD; Behold, I *am* against your pillows, wherewith ye there hunt the souls
[9]to make *them* fly, and I will tear them
from your arms, and will let the souls
go, *even* the souls that ye hunt to make
them fly.
21 Your kerchiefs also will I tear,
and deliver my people out of your
hand, and they shall be no more in
your hand to be hunted; and ye shall
know that I *am* the LORD.
22 Because [s]with lies ye have made
the heart of the righteous sad, whom I
have not made sad; and [t]strengthened
the hands of the wicked, that he should
not return from his wicked way, [10]by
promising him life:
23 Therefore [u]ye shall see no more
vanity, nor divine divinations: for I will
deliver my people out of your hand:
[v]and ye shall know that I *am* the LORD.

14 Then [a]came certain of the elders
of Ĭs′ra-el unto me, and sat before me.
2 And the word of the LORD came
unto me, saying,
3 Son of man, these men have set up
their idols in their heart, and put [b]the
stumblingblock of their iniquity before
their face: [c]should I be inquired of at
all by them?
4 Therefore speak unto them, and
say unto them, Thus saith the Lord
GOD; Every man of the house of Ĭs′ra-
el that setteth up his idols in his heart,
and putteth the stumblingblock of his
iniquity before his face, and cometh to
the prophet; I the LORD will answer
him that cometh according to the multitude of his idols;
5 That I may take the house of Ĭs′ra-
el in their own [d]heart, because they
are all estranged from me through
their idols.
6 ¶ Therefore say unto the house of
Ĭs′ra-el, Thus saith the Lord GOD; Repent, and turn [1]*yourselves* from your
idols; and turn away your faces from
all your abominations.
7 For every one of the house of Ĭs′ra-
el, or of the stranger that sojourneth
in Ĭs′ra-el, which [e]separateth himself
from me, and setteth up his idols in his
heart, and putteth the stumblingblock
of his iniquity before his face, and cometh to a prophet to inquire of him concerning me; I the LORD will answer
him by myself:
8 And [f]I will set my face against that
man, and will make him a [g]sign and a
proverb, and I will cut him off from the
midst of my people; and ye shall know
that I *am* the LORD.
9 And if the prophet be deceived
when he hath spoken a thing, I the
LORD [h]have deceived that prophet,

19 [r]Prov. 28.21; Mic. 3.5; Rom. 14.15
20 [9]Or, into gardens
22 [s]Prov. 19.27
[t]Jer. 23.14
[10]by quickening him, or, that I should save his life
23 [u]ch. 12.24; Mic. 3.6
[v]ch. 14.8

CHAPTER 14

1 [a]ch. 8.1; ch. 20.1
3 [b]ch. 3.20; ch. 7.19; 1 Pet. 2.8; Rev. 2.14
[c]Prov. 15.8
5 [d]Heb. 3.12-19
6 [1]Or, others
7 [e]Jer. 2.13; Matt. 6.24; Jude 19
8 [f]Lev. 17.10; Jer. 44.11; ch. 15.7
[g]Num. 26.10; Deut. 28.37; ch. 5.15
9 [h]Job 12.16; Jer. 4.10; 2 Thess. 2.11
11 [i]Ps. 119.67-71; Jer. 31.18-19; 2 Pet. 2.15
[j]Jer. 24.7; ch. 36.28
13 [k]Lev. 26.26; ch. 4.16
14 [l]Jer. 15.1; Jer. 7.16
[m]Prov. 11.4; 2 Pet. 2.9
15 [n]Num. 21.6; Lev. 26.22
[2]Or, bereave
16 [3]in the midst of it
17 [o]Lev. 26.25; ch. 5.12
[p]Jer. 33.12; Hos. 4.3
19 [q]2 Sam. 24.15
[r]ch. 7.8; Rev. 16.3-6
21 [4]Or, also when
[s]Jer. 15.2-3; Rev. 6.4-8
22 [t]ch. 6.8
[u]ch. 20.43
23 [v]Jer. 22.8-9

and I will stretch out my hand upon
him, and will destroy him from the
midst of my people Ĭs′ra-el.
10 And they shall bear the punishment of their iniquity: the punishment
of the prophet shall be even as the punishment of him that seeketh *unto him;*
11 That the house of Ĭs′ra-el may
[i]go no more astray from me, neither be
polluted any more with all their transgressions; [j]but that they may be my
people, and I may be their God, saith
the Lord GOD.
12 ¶ The word of the LORD came
again to me, saying,
13 Son of man, when the land sinneth against me by trespassing grievously, then will I stretch out mine hand
upon it, and will break the [k]staff of the
bread thereof, and will send famine
upon it, and will cut off man and beast
from it:
14 [l]Though these three men, Nō′ah,
Dăn′iel, and Jōb, were in it, they should
deliver *but* their own souls [m]by their
righteousness, saith the Lord GOD.
15 ¶ If I cause [n]noisome beasts to
pass through the land, and they [2]spoil it,
so that it be desolate, that no man may
pass through because of the beasts:
16 *Though* these three men *were* [3]in
it, *as* I live, saith the Lord GOD, they
shall deliver neither sons nor daughters; they only shall be delivered, but
the land shall be desolate.
17 ¶ Or *if* [o]I bring a sword upon that
land, and say, Sword, go through the
land; so that I [p]cut off man and beast
from it:
18 Though these three men *were* in
it, *as* I live, saith the Lord GOD, they
shall deliver neither sons nor daughters, but they only shall be delivered
themselves.
19 ¶ Or *if* I send [q]a pestilence into
that land, and [r]pour out my fury upon
it in blood, to cut off from it man and
beast:
20 Though Nō′ah, Dăn′iel, and Jōb,
were in it, *as* I live, saith the Lord
GOD, they shall deliver neither son nor
daughter; they shall *but* deliver their
own souls by their righteousness.
21 For thus saith the Lord GOD;
[4]How much more when [s]I send my
four sore judgments upon Je-ru̥′sa-
lĕm, the sword, and the famine, and
the noisome beast, and the pestilence,
to cut off from it man and beast?
22 ¶ [t]Yet, behold, therein shall be
left a remnant that shall be brought
forth, *both* sons and daughters: behold, they shall come forth unto you,
and [u]ye shall see their way and their
doings: and ye shall be comforted concerning the evil that I have brought
upon Je-ru̥′sa-lĕm, *even* concerning all
that I have brought upon it.
23 And they shall comfort you, when
ye see their ways and their doings: and
ye shall know that I have not done
[v]without cause all that I have done in it,
saith the Lord GOD.

15 And the word of the LORD came
unto me, saying,

2 Son of man, What is the [a]vine tree more than any tree, *or than* a branch which is among the trees of the forest?

3 Shall wood be taken thereof to do any work? or will *men* take a pin of it to hang any vessel thereon?

4 Behold, [b]it is cast into the fire for fuel; the fire devoureth both the ends of it, and the midst of it is burned. [1]Is it meet for *any* work?

5 Behold, when it was whole, it was [2]meet for no work: how much less shall it be meet yet for *any* work, when the fire hath devoured it, and it is burned?

6 ¶ Therefore thus saith the Lord GOD; As the vine tree among the trees of the forest, which I have given to the fire for fuel, so will I give the inhabitants of Je-ru'sa-lĕm.

7 And [c]I will set my face against them; [d]they shall go out from *one* fire, and *another* fire shall devour them; [e]and ye shall know that I *am* the LORD, when I set my face against them.

8 And I will make the land desolate, because they have [3]committed a trespass, saith the Lord GOD.

16 Again the word of the LORD came unto me, saying,

2 Son of man, [a]cause Je-ru'sa-lĕm to know her abominations,

3 And say, Thus saith the Lord GOD unto Je-ru'sa-lĕm; Thy [1]birth and thy nativity *is* of the land of Că'năan; thy father *was* an Ăm'ôr-īte, and thy mother an Hĭt'tīte.

4 And *as for* thy nativity, [b]in the day thou wast born thy navel was not cut, neither wast thou washed in water [2]to supple *thee;* thou wast not salted at all, nor swaddled at all.

5 None eye pitied thee, to do any of these unto thee, to have compassion upon thee; but thou wast cast out in the open field, to the loathing of thy person, in the day that thou wast born.

6 ¶ And when I passed by thee, and saw thee [3]polluted in thine own blood, I said unto thee *when thou wast* in thy blood, Live; yea, I said unto thee *when thou wast* in thy blood, Live.

7 I have [4]caused thee to multiply as the bud of the field, and thou hast increased and waxen great, and thou art come to [5]excellent ornaments: *thy* breasts are fashioned, and thine hair is grown, whereas thou *wast* naked and bare.

8 Now when I passed by thee, and looked upon thee, behold, thy time *was* the time of love; [c]and I spread my skirt over thee, and covered thy nakedness: yea, I sware unto thee, and entered into a covenant with thee, saith the Lord GOD, and [d]thou becamest mine.

9 Then washed I thee with water; yea, I throughly washed away thy [6]blood from thee, and I anointed thee with oil.

10 I clothed thee also with broidered work, and shod thee with badgers' skin, and I girded thee about with fine linen, and I covered thee with silk.

CHAPTER 15
2 [a]Ps. 80.8; Hos. 10.1
4 [b]John 15.6
[1]Will it prosper?
5 [2]made fit
7 [c]Lev. 17.10; Jer. 21.10
[d]Isa. 24.18; Amos 5.19
[e]ch. 6.7; ch. 7.4
8 [3]trespassed a trespass

CHAPTER 16
2 [a]ch. 20.4
3 [1]cutting out, or, habitation
4 [b]Hos. 2.3
[2]Or, when I looked upon thee
6 [3]Or, trodden under foot
7 [4]made thee a million
[5]ornament of ornaments
8 [c]Ruth 3.9
[d]Ex. 19.5
9 [6]bloods
11 [e]Gen. 24.22
[f]Gen. 41.42; Dan. 5.7-16-29
12 [7]nose
13 [g]Deut. 32.13
[h]Ps. 48.2
14 [i]Lam. 2.15
15 [j]Deut. 32.15; Mic. 3.11
[k]Isa. 1.21; Hos. 1.2
16 [l]2 Ki. 23.7; Hos. 2.8
17 [8]of a male
19 [m]Deut. 32.13; Hos. 2.8
[9]a savour of rest
20 [n]2 Ki. 16.3; ch. 20.26
[10]to devour
21 [o]Gen. 17.7-11; Ex. 13.2
22 [p]Jer. 2.2; Hos. 2.3
24 [11]Or, brothel house
[q]Lev. 26.30; Jer. 2.20
25 [r]Prov. 9.14;
26 [s]ch. 8.10

11 I decked thee also with ornaments, and I [e]put bracelets upon thy hands, [f]and a chain on thy neck.

12 And I put a jewel on thy [7]forehead, and earrings in thine ears, and a beautiful crown upon thine head.

13 Thus wast thou decked with gold and silver; and thy raiment *was of* fine linen, and silk, and broidered work; [g]thou didst eat fine flour, and honey, and oil: and thou wast exceeding [h]beautiful, and thou didst prosper into a kingdom.

14 And [i]thy renown went forth among the heathen for thy beauty: for it *was* perfect through my comeliness, which I had put upon thee, saith the Lord GOD.

15 ¶ [j]But thou didst trust in thine own beauty, [k]and playedst the harlot because of thy renown, and pouredst out thy fornications on every one that passed by; his it was.

16 [l]And of thy garments thou didst take, and deckedst thy high places with divers colours, and playedst the harlot thereupon: *the like things* shall not come, neither shall it be *so.*

17 Thou hast also taken thy fair jewels of my gold and of my silver, which I had given thee, and madest to thyself images [8]of men, and didst commit whoredom with them,

18 And tookest thy broidered garments, and coveredst them: and thou hast set mine oil and mine incense before them.

19 [m]My meat also which I gave thee, fine flour, and oil, and honey, *wherewith* I fed thee, thou hast even set it before them for [9]a sweet savour: and *thus* it was, saith the Lord GOD.

20 [n]Moreover thou hast taken thy sons and thy daughters, whom thou hast borne unto me, and these hast thou sacrificed unto them [10]to be devoured. *Is this* of thy whoredoms a small matter,

21 That thou hast slain [o]my children, and delivered them to cause them to pass through *the fire* for them?

22 And in all thine abominations and thy whoredoms thou hast not remembered the days of thy [p]youth, when thou wast naked and bare, *and* wast polluted in thy blood.

23 And it came to pass after all thy wickedness, (woe, woe unto thee! saith the Lord GOD;)

24 *That* thou hast also built unto thee an [11]eminent place, [q]and hast made thee an high place in every street.

25 Thou hast built thy high place [r]at every head of the way, and hast made thy beauty to be abhorred, and hast opened thy feet to every one that passed by, and multiplied thy whoredoms.

26 Thou hast also committed fornication with [s]the E-ġy̆p''tians thy neighbours, great of flesh; and hast increased thy whoredoms, to provoke me to anger.

27 Behold, therefore I have stretched

out my hand over thee, and have diminished thine ordinary *food,* and delivered thee unto the will of them that hate thee, the [12]daughters of the Phĭ-lĭs′tĭnes, which are ashamed of thy lewd way.

28 [t]Thou hast played the whore also with the Ȧs-sỹr′ĭ-ans, because thou wast unsatiable; yea, thou hast played the harlot with them, and yet couldest not be satisfied.

29 Thou hast moreover multiplied thy fornication in the land of Cā′năan [u]unto Chăl-dē′ȧ; and yet thou wast not satisfied herewith.

30 How weak is thine heart, saith the Lord GOD, seeing thou doest all these *things,* the work of [v]an imperious whorish woman;

31 [13]In that thou buildest thine eminent place in the head of every way, and makest thine high place in every street; and hast not been as an harlot, in that thou scornest hire;

32 *But as* a wife that committeth adultery, *which* taketh strangers instead of her husband!

33 They give gifts to all whores: but [w]thou givest thy gifts to all thy lovers, and [14]hirest them, that they may come unto thee on every side for thy whoredom.

34 And the contrary is in thee from *other* women in thy whoredoms, whereas none followeth thee to commit whoredoms: and in that thou givest a reward, and no reward is given unto thee, therefore thou art contrary.

35 ¶ Wherefore, O harlot, hear the word of the LORD:

36 Thus saith the Lord GOD; Because thy filthiness was poured out, and thy nakedness discovered through thy whoredoms with thy lovers, and with all the idols of thy abominations, and by [x]the blood of thy children, which thou didst give unto them;

37 Behold, therefore [y]I will gather all thy lovers, with whom thou hast taken pleasure, and all *them* that thou hast loved, with all *them* that thou hast hated; I will even gather them round about against thee, and will discover thy nakedness unto them, that they may see all thy nakedness.

38 And I will judge thee, as [15]women that break wedlock and [z]shed blood are judged; and I will give thee blood in fury and jealousy.

39 And I will also give thee into their hand, and they shall throw down thine eminent place, and shall break down thy high places; [a]they shall strip thee also of thy clothes, and shall take [16]thy fair jewels, and leave thee naked and bare.

40 [b]They shall also bring up a company against thee, [c]and they shall stone thee with stones, and thrust thee through with their swords.

41 And they shall [d]burn thine houses with fire, and [e]execute judgments upon thee in the sight of many women: and I will cause thee to [f]cease from playing the harlot, and thou also shalt give no hire any more.

42 So [g]will I make my fury toward thee to rest, and my jealousy shall depart from thee, and I will be quiet, and will be no more angry.

43 Because [h]thou hast not remembered the days of thy youth, but hast fretted me in all these *things;* behold, therefore [i]I also will recompense thy way upon *thine* head, saith the Lord GOD: and thou shalt not commit this lewdness above all thine abominations.

44 ¶ Behold, every one that useth proverbs shall use *this* proverb against thee, saying, As *is* the mother, *so is* her daughter.

45 Thou *art* thy mother's daughter, that loatheth her husband and her children; and thou *art* the sister of thy sisters, which loathed their husbands and their children: your mother *was* an Hĭt′tīte, and your father an Ȧm′ôr-īte.

46 And thine elder sister *is* Sa-mā′rĭ-ȧ, she and her daughters that dwell at thy left hand: and [17]thy younger sister, that dwelleth at thy right hand, *is* Sŏd′om and her daughters.

47 Yet hast thou not walked after their ways, nor done after their abominations: but, [18]as *if that were* a very little *thing,* [j]thou wast corrupted more than they in all thy ways.

48 *As* I live, saith the Lord GOD, [k]Sŏd′om thy sister hath not done, she nor her daughters, as thou hast done, thou and thy daughters.

49 Behold, this was the iniquity of thy sister Sŏd′om, pride, [l]fulness of bread, and abundance of idleness was in her and in her daughters, [m]neither did she strengthen the hand of the poor and needy.

50 And they were haughty, and [n]committed abomination before me: therefore [o]I took them away as I saw *good.*

51 Neither hath Sa-mā′rĭ-ȧ committed half of thy sins; but thou hast multiplied thine abominations more than they, and [p]hast justified thy sisters in all thine abominations which thou hast done.

52 Thou also, which hast judged thy sisters, bear thine own shame for thy sins that thou hast committed more abominable than they: they are more righteous than thou: yea, be thou confounded also, and bear thy shame, in that thou hast justified thy sisters.

53 [q]When I shall bring again their captivity, [r]the captivity of Sŏd′om and her daughters, and the captivity of Sa-mā′rĭ-ȧ and her daughters, then *will I bring again* the captivity of thy captives in the midst of them:

54 That thou mayest bear thine own shame, and mayest be confounded in all that thou hast done, in that thou art [s]a comfort unto them.

55 When thy sisters, Sŏd′om and her daughters, shall return to their former estate, and Sa-mā′rĭ-ȧ and her daughters shall return to their former estate, then thou and thy daughters shall return to your former estate.

27 [12]Or, cities
28 [t]Judg. 10.6; 2 Ki. 16.7; Jer. 2.18
29 [u]ch. 23.14
30 [v]Prov. 30.20
31 [13]Or, In thy daughters is thine, etc
33 [w]Isa. 30.3 [14]bribest
36 [x]Ps. 106.38; Jer. 2.34
37 [y]Isa. 47.2-3; Jer. 13.22; Lam. 1.8; ch. 23.9; Hos. 2.10; Nah. 3.5
38 [15]with judgments of [z]Gen. 9.6; Ex. 21.12; Lev. 24.17; Matt. 26.52; Rev. 13.10
39 [a]ch. 23.26 [16]instruments of thine ornament
40 [b]ch. 23.46-47 [c]John 8.5
41 [d]Deut. 13.16; 2 Ki. 25.9; Jer. 39.8 [e]ch. 5.8; ch. 23.10; Rom. 2.8 [f]ch. 23.27
42 [g]ch. 5.13
43 [h]Ps. 78.42 [i]ch. 9.10; ch. 11.21
46 [17]lesser than thou
47 [18]Or, that was loathed as a small thing [j]2 Ki. 21.9; ch. 5.6-7
48 [k]Matt. 10.15; Mark 6.11; Luke 10.12
49 [l]Gen. 13.10 [m]Luke 16.20
50 [n]Gen. 13.13; Gen. 18.20 [o]Job 18.18
51 [p]Matt. 12.41
53 [q]Isa. 1.9; Rom. 9.29 [r]Jer. 20.16
54 [s]ch. 14.22-23

56 For thy sister Sŏd′om was not
[19]mentioned by thy mouth in the day of
thy [20]pride,
57 Before thy wickedness was discovered, as at the time of *thy* [t]re-
proach of the daughters of [21]Sy̆r′ĭ-ȧ,
and all *that are* round about her, the
daughters of the Phĭ-lĭs′tĭnes, which
[22]despise thee round about.
58 Thou hast [23]borne thy lewdness
and thine abominations, saith the LORD.
59 For thus saith the Lord GOD; I
will even deal with thee as thou hast
done, which hast [u]despised the oath in
breaking the covenant.
60 ¶ Nevertheless I will [v]remember
my covenant with thee in the days of
thy youth, and I will establish unto
thee [w]an everlasting covenant.
61 Then [x]thou shalt remember thy
ways, and be ashamed, when thou
shalt receive thy [y]sisters, thine elder
and thy younger: and I will give them
unto thee for [z]daughters, [a]but not by
thy covenant.
62 [b]And I will establish my covenant with thee; and thou shalt know
that I *am* the LORD:
63 That thou mayest remember, and
be confounded, [c]and never open thy
mouth any more because of thy shame,
when I am pacified toward thee for all
that thou hast done, saith the Lord
GOD.

17 And the word of the LORD came
unto me, saying,
2 Son of man, put forth a riddle, and
speak a parable unto the house of
Ĭs′ra-el;
3 And say, Thus saith the Lord GOD;
A great eagle with great wings, long-
winged, full of feathers, which had [1]div-
ers colours, came unto Lĕb′a-non, and
[a]took the highest branch of the cedar:
4 He cropped off the top of his young
twigs, and carried it into a land of traffick; he set it in a city of merchants.
5 He took also of the seed of the
land, and [2]planted it in [b]a fruitful field;
he placed *it* by great waters, *and* set it
[c]*as* a willow tree.
6 And it grew, and became a spreading vine of low stature, whose branches
turned toward him, and the roots
thereof were under him: so it became a
vine, and brought forth branches, and
shot forth sprigs.
7 There was also another great eagle
with great wings and many feathers:
and, behold, this vine did bend her
roots toward him, and shot forth her
branches toward him, that he might water it by the furrows of her plantation.
8 It was planted in a good [3]soil by
great waters, that it might bring forth
branches, and that it might bear fruit,
that it might be a goodly vine.
9 Say thou, Thus saith the Lord GOD;
Shall it prosper? [d]shall he not pull up
the roots thereof, and cut off the fruit
thereof, that it wither? it shall wither in
all the leaves of her spring, even without great power or many people to
pluck it up by the roots thereof.

56 [19]for a report, or, hearing [20]prides, or, excellences
57 [t]2 Ki. 16.5; Isa. 7.1 [21]Aram [22]Or, spoil
58 [23]borne them
59 [u]Deut. 29.12-14; ch. 17.13-16
60 [v]Ex. 2.24; Hos. 2.15 [w]Jer. 32.40
61 [x]ch. 20.43 [y]Song 8.8; Isa. 2.2 [z]Isa. 54.1; Gal. 4.26 [a]Jer. 31.31
62 [b]Hos. 2.19-20; Heb. 8.6-10, 13
63 [c]Rom. 3.19

CHAPTER 17
3 [1]embroidering [a]2 Ki. 24.12
5 [2]put it in a field of seed [b]Deut. 8.7-8-9 [c]Isa. 15.7
8 [3]field
9 [d]2 Ki. 25.7
10 [e]ch. 19.12; Jude 12
12 [f]ch. 2.5 [g]2 Ki. 24.11-16
13 [h]2 Ki. 24.17 [i]2 Chr. 36.13 [4]brought him to an oath
14 [j]ch. 29.14 [5]to keep his covenant, to stand to it
15 [k]2 Ki. 24.20; Jer. 52.3 [l]Deut. 17.16; Jer. 37.5-7
16 [m]Jer. 32.5; ch. 12.13
17 [n]Jer. 37.7; ch. 29.6-7 [o]Jer. 52.4
18 [p]1 Chr. 29.24
20 [q]Josh. 10.16-18; ch. 12.13 [r]ch. 20.36
21 [s]ch. 12.14
22 [t]Isa. 11.1; Jer. 23.5 [u]Isa. 53.2 [v]Ps. 2.6
23 [w]Isa. 2.2-3

10 Yea, behold, *being* planted, shall
it prosper? [e]shall it not utterly wither,
when the east wind toucheth it? it shall
wither in the furrows where it grew.
11 ¶ Moreover the word of the LORD
came unto me, saying,
12 Say now to [f]the rebellious house,
Know ye not what these *things mean?*
tell *them,* Behold, [g]the king of Băb′y̆-
lon is come to Je-ru̧′sa-lĕm, and hath
taken the king thereof, and the princes
thereof, and led them with him to
Băb′y̆-lon;
13 [h]And hath taken of the king's
seed, and made a covenant with him,
[i]and hath [4]taken an oath of him: he
hath also taken the mighty of the land:
14 That the kingdom might be [j]base,
that it might not lift itself up, [5]*but* that
by keeping of his covenant it might
stand.
15 But [k]he rebelled against him in
sending his ambassadors into Ē′ġypt,
[l]that they might give him horses and
much people. Shall he prosper? shall
he escape that doeth such *things?* or
shall he break the covenant, and be
delivered?
16 *As* I live, saith the Lord GOD,
surely in [m]the place *where* the king
dwelleth that made him king, whose
oath he despised, and whose covenant
he brake, *even* with him in the midst of
Băb′y̆-lon he shall die.
17 [n]Neither shall Phā′raōh with *his*
mighty army and great company make
for him in the war, [o]by casting up
mounts, and building forts, to cut off
many persons:
18 Seeing he despised the oath by
breaking the covenant, when, lo, he
had [p]given his hand, and hath done all
these *things,* he shall not escape.
19 Therefore thus saith the Lord
GOD; *As* I live, surely mine oath that he
hath despised, and my covenant that
he hath broken, even it will I recompense upon his own head.
20 And I will [q]spread my net upon
him, and he shall be taken in my snare,
and I will bring him to Băb′y̆-lon, and
[r]will plead with him there for his trespass that he hath trespassed against
me.
21 And [s]all his fugitives with all his
bands shall fall by the sword, and they
that remain shall be scattered toward
all winds: and ye shall know that I the
LORD have spoken *it.*
22 ¶ Thus saith the Lord GOD; I will
also take of the highest [t]branch of the
high cedar, and will set *it:* I will crop
off from the top of his young twigs [u]a
tender one, and will [v]plant *it* upon an
high mountain and eminent:
23 [w]In the mountain of the height of
Ĭs′ra-el will I plant it; and it shall bring
forth boughs, and bear fruit, and be a
goodly cedar: and under it shall dwell
all fowl of every wing; in the shadow of
the branches thereof shall they dwell.
24 And all the trees of the field shall
know that I the LORD have brought
down the high tree, have exalted the
low tree, have dried up the green tree,

and have made the dry tree to flourish: I the LORD have spoken and have done *it*.

18 The word of the LORD came unto me again, saying,

2 What mean ye, that ye use this proverb concerning the land of Is'ra-el, saying, The [a]fathers have eaten sour grapes, and the children's teeth are set on edge?

3 *As* I live, saith the Lord GOD, ye shall not have *occasion* any more to use this proverb in Is'ra-el.

4 Behold, [b]all souls are mine; as the soul of the father, so also the soul of the son is mine: [c]the soul that sinneth, it shall die.

5 ¶ But if a man be just, and do [1]that which is lawful and right,

6 [d]*And* hath not eaten upon the mountains, neither hath lifted up his eyes to the idols of the house of Is'ra-el, neither hath [e]defiled his neighbour's wife, neither hath come near to [f]a menstruous woman,

7 And hath not [g]oppressed any, *but* hath restored to the debtor his [h]pledge, hath spoiled none by violence, hath [i]given his bread to the hungry, and hath covered the naked with a garment;

8 He *that* hath not given forth upon [j]usury, neither hath taken any increase, *that* hath withdrawn his hand from iniquity, [k]hath executed true judgment between man and man,

9 Hath walked in my statutes, and hath kept my judgments, to deal truly; he *is* [l]just, he shall surely [m]live, saith the Lord GOD.

10 ¶ If he beget a son *that is* a [2]robber, [n]a shedder of blood, and [3]*that* doeth the like to *any* one of these *things*,

11 And that doeth not any of those *duties*, but even hath eaten upon the mountains, and [o]defiled his neighbour's wife,

12 Hath oppressed the poor and needy, hath spoiled by violence, hath not restored the pledge, and hath lifted up his eyes to the idols, hath [p]committed abomination,

13 [q]Hath given forth upon usury, and hath taken increase: shall he then live? he shall not live: he hath done all these abominations; he shall surely die; his [4]blood shall be upon him.

14 ¶ Now, lo, *if* he beget a son, that seeth all his father's sins which he hath done, and considereth, and doeth not such like,

15 *That* hath not eaten upon the mountains, neither hath lifted up his eyes to the idols of the house of Is'ra-el, hath not defiled his neighbour's wife,

16 Neither hath oppressed any, [5]hath not withholden the pledge, neither hath spoiled by violence, *but* hath given [r]his bread to the hungry, and hath covered the naked with a garment,

17 *That* hath taken off his hand from the poor, *that* hath not received usury nor increase, hath executed my judgments, hath walked in my statutes; [s]he shall not die for the iniquity of his father, he shall surely live.

18 *As for* his father, because he cruelly oppressed, spoiled his brother by violence, and did *that* which *is* not good among his people, lo, even [t]he shall die in his iniquity.

19 ¶ Yet say ye, Why? [u]doth not the son bear the iniquity of the father? When the son hath done that which is lawful and right, *and* hath kept all my statutes, and hath done them, he shall surely live.

20 The soul that sinneth, it shall die. [v]The son shall not bear the iniquity of the father, neither shall the father bear the iniquity of the son: [w]the righteousness of the righteous shall be upon him, [x]and the wickedness of the wicked shall be upon him.

21 But [y]if the wicked will turn from all his sins that he hath committed, and keep all my statutes, and do that which is lawful and right, he shall surely live, he shall not die.

22 [z]All his transgressions that he hath committed, they shall not be mentioned unto him: [a]in his righteousness that he hath done he shall live.

23 [b]Have I any pleasure at all that the wicked should die? saith the Lord GOD: *and* not that he should return from his ways, and live?

24 ¶ But [c]when the righteous turneth away from his righteousness, and committeth iniquity, *and* doeth according to all the abominations that the wicked *man* doeth, shall he live? [d]All his righteousness that he hath done shall not be mentioned: in his trespass that he hath trespassed, and in his sin that he hath sinned, in them shall he die.

25 ¶ Yet ye say, [e]The way of the Lord is not equal. Hear now, O house of Is'ra-el; Is not [f]my way equal? are not your ways unequal?

26 When a righteous *man* turneth away from his righteousness, and committeth iniquity, and dieth in them; for his iniquity that he hath done shall he die.

27 Again, [g]when the wicked *man* turneth away from his wickedness that he hath committed, and doeth that which is lawful and right, he shall save his soul alive.

28 Because he considereth, and turneth away from all his transgressions that he hath committed, he shall surely live, he shall not die.

29 Yet saith the house of Is'ra-el, The way of the Lord is not equal. O house of Is'ra-el, are not my ways equal? are not your ways unequal?

30 [h]Therefore I will judge you, O house of Is'ra-el, every one according to his ways, saith the Lord GOD. [i]Repent, and turn [6]*yourselves* from all your transgressions; so iniquity shall not be your ruin.

31 ¶ [j]Cast away from you all your transgressions, whereby ye have transgressed; and make you a [k]new heart

CHAPTER 18
2 [a]Lam. 5.7
4 [b]Zech. 12.1; Heb. 12.9 [c]Rom. 6.23
5 [1]judgment and justice
6 [d]ch. 22.9 [e]Heb. 13.4 [f]Lev. 18.19
7 [g]Lev. 25.14 [h]Deut. 24.12 [i]Isa. 58.7; Matt. 25.35
8 [j]Lev. 25.36 [k]Zech. 8.16
9 [l]Hab. 2.4; Rom. 8.1 [m]Amos 5.4
10 [2]Or, breaker up of an house [n]Ex. 21.12 [3]Or, that doeth to his brother besides any of these
11 [o]1 Cor. 6.9
12 [p]2 Ki. 21.11
13 [q]Ex. 22.25 [4]bloods
16 [5]hath not pledged the pledge, or, taken to pledge [r]Job 22.7; Prov. 22.9; Eccl. 11.1-2; Isa. 58.7-10; Matt. 25.35; Luke 11.41
17 [s]ch. 20.18; Matt. 23.29-32; Rom. 2.7
18 [t]ch. 3.18
19 [u]Ex. 20.5; Deut. 5.9
20 [v]Deut. 24.16; 2 Chr. 25.4 [w]Isa. 3.10 [x]Rom. 2.9
21 [y]ch. 33.12
22 [z]ch. 33.16 [a]Rom. 8.13
23 [b]2 Pet. 3.9
24 [c]ch. 33.12 [d]Heb. 10.38; 2 John 8
25 [e]Mal. 3.14 [f]Gen. 18.25; Deut. 32.4; Ps. 145.17
27 [g]Isa. 1.18
30 [h]Eccl. 12.14; ch. 7.3 [i]Matt. 3.2; Rev. 2.5 [6]Or, others
31 [j]Eph. 4.22 [k]Jer. 32.39; ch. 11.19

and a new spirit: for why will ye die, O
house of Ĭs'ra-el?
32 For [l]I have no pleasure in the
death of him that dieth, saith the Lord
GOD: wherefore turn [7]*yourselves,* and
live ye.
19 Moreover [a]take thou up a lamentation for the princes of Ĭs'ra-el,
2 And say, What *is* thy mother? A
lioness: she lay down among lions, she
nourished her whelps among young
lions.
3 And she brought up one of her
whelps: [b]it became a young lion, and it
learned to catch the prey; it devoured
men.
4 The nations also heard of him;
he was taken in their pit, and they
brought him with chains unto the land
of [c]Ē'ġypt.
5 Now when she saw that she had
waited, *and* her hope was lost, then she
took [d]another of her whelps, *and* made
him a young lion.
6 [e]And he went up and down among
the lions, he became a young lion, and
learned to catch the prey, *and* devoured men.
7 And he knew [1]their desolate palaces, and he laid waste their cities; and
the land was desolate, and the fulness
thereof, by the noise of his roaring.
8 [f]Then the nations set against him
on every side from the provinces, and
spread their net over him: he was
taken in their pit.
9 [g]And they put him in ward [2]in
chains, and brought him to the king of
Băb'ȳ-lon: they brought him into holes,
that his voice should no more be heard
upon [h]the mountains of Ĭs'ra-el.
10 ¶ Thy mother *is* [i]like a vine [3]in
thy blood, planted by the waters: she
was [j]fruitful and full of branches by
reason of many waters.
11 And she had strong rods for the
sceptres of them that bare rule, and
her [k]stature was exalted among the
thick branches, and she appeared in
her height with the multitude of her
branches.
12 But she was plucked up in fury,
she was cast down to the ground, and
the [l]east wind dried up her fruit: her
strong rods were broken and withered;
the fire consumed them.
13 And now she *is* [m]planted in the
wilderness, in a dry and thirsty ground.
14 [n]And fire is gone out of a rod of
her branches, *which* hath devoured
her fruit, so that she hath no strong rod
to be a sceptre to rule. This *is* a lamentation, and shall be for a lamentation.
20 And it came to pass in the seventh year, in the fifth *month,* the
tenth *day* of the month, *that* [a]certain
of the elders of Ĭs'ra-el came to inquire
of the LORD, and sat before me.
2 Then came the word of the LORD
unto me, saying,
3 Son of man, speak unto the elders
of Ĭs'ra-el, and say unto them, Thus
saith the Lord GOD; Are ye come to
inquire of me? *As* I live, saith the Lord
GOD, [b]I will not be inquired of by you.
4 Wilt thou [1]judge them, son of man,
wilt thou judge *them?* [c]cause them
to know the abominations of their
fathers:
5 ¶ And say unto them, Thus saith
the Lord GOD; In the day when [d]I
chose Ĭs'ra-el, and [2]lifted up mine hand
unto the seed of the house of Jā'cob,
and made myself [e]known unto them in
the land of Ē'ġypt, when I lifted up
mine hand unto them, saying, [f]I *am*
the LORD your God;
6 In the day *that* I lifted up mine
hand unto them, [g]to bring them forth
of the land of Ē'ġypt into a land that I
had espied for them, flowing with milk
and honey, [h]which *is* the glory of all
lands:
7 Then said I unto them, Cast ye
away every man [i]the abominations of
his eyes, and defile not yourselves with
[j]the idols of Ē'ġypt: I *am* the LORD
your God.
8 But they rebelled against me, and
would not hearken unto me: they did
not every man cast away the abominations of their eyes, neither did they forsake the idols of Ē'ġypt: then I said, I
will pour out my fury upon them, to
accomplish my anger against them in
the midst of the land of Ē'ġypt.
9 [k]But I wrought for my name's
sake, that it should not be polluted before the heathen, among whom they
were, in whose sight I made myself
known unto them, in bringing them
forth out of the land of Ē'ġypt.
10 ¶ Wherefore I caused them to go
forth out of the land of Ē'ġypt, and
brought them into the wilderness.
11 [l]And I gave them my statutes, and
[3]shewed them my judgments, [m]which
if a man do, he shall even live in them.
12 Moreover also I gave them my
[n]sabbaths, to be a sign between me
and them, that they might know that I
am the LORD that sanctify them.
13 But the house of Ĭs'ra-el rebelled
against me in the wilderness: they
walked not in my statutes, and they
[o]despised my judgments, which *if* a
man do, he shall even live in them; and
my sabbaths they greatly polluted:
then I said, I would pour out my fury
upon them in the wilderness, to consume them.
14 But I wrought for my name's sake,
that it should not be polluted before the
heathen, in whose sight I brought them
out.
15 Yet also [p]I lifted up my hand
unto them in the wilderness, that I
would not bring them into the land
which I had given *them,* flowing with
milk and honey, which *is* the glory of
all lands;
16 Because they despised my judgments, and walked not in my statutes,
but polluted my sabbaths: for [q]their
heart went after their idols.
17 [r]Nevertheless mine eye spared
them from destroying them, neither
did I make an end of them in the
wilderness.

32 [l]Lam. 3.33; 2 Pet. 3.9
[7]Or, others

CHAPTER 19
1 [a]ch. 26.17
3 [b]2 Ki. 23.31
4 [c]2 Ki. 23.33; Jer. 22.11
5 [d]2 Ki. 23.34
6 [e]Jer. 22.13
7 [1]Or, their widows
8 [f]2 Ki. 24.2
9 [g]2 Chr. 36.6; Jer. 22.18-19
[2]Or, in hooks
[h]ch. 6.2
10 [i]ch. 15.2; Ps. 80.8
[3]Or, in thy quietness, or, in thy likeness
[j]Deut. 8.7
11 [k]Dan. 4.11
12 [l]Hos. 13.15
13 [m]Deut. 28.48
14 [n]Judg. 9.15

CHAPTER 20
1 [a]ch. 8.1
3 [b]1 Sam. 28.6; Matt. 15.8
4 [1]Or, plead for them
[c]ch. 16.2; Matt. 23.32
5 [d]Ex. 6.7
[2]Or, sware
[e]Ex. 3.8; Deut. 4.34
[f]Gen. 17.7; Ex. 20.2
6 [g]Ex. 3.8-17; Jer. 32.22
[h]Ps. 48.2
7 [i]2 Chr. 15.8
[j]Deut. 29.16; Josh. 24.14
9 [k]Ex. 32.12; Num. 14.13
11 [l]Deut. 4.8; Neh. 9.13
[3]made them to know
[m]Rom. 10.5
12 [n]Ex. 20.8
13 [o]Prov. 1.25
15 [p]Num. 14.28
16 [q]Num. 15.39
17 [r]1 Sam. 24.10

18 But I said unto their children in the wilderness, Walk ye not in the statutes of your fathers, neither observe their judgments, nor defile yourselves with their idols:

19 I *am* the LORD your God; [s]walk in my statutes, and keep my judgments, and do them;

20 [t]And hallow my sabbaths; and they shall be a sign between me and you, that ye may know that I *am* the LORD your God.

21 Notwithstanding [u]the children rebelled against me: they walked not in my statutes, neither kept my judgments to do them, which *if* a man do, he shall even live in them; they polluted my sabbaths: then I said, I would pour out my fury upon them, to accomplish my anger against them in the wilderness.

22 [v]Nevertheless I withdrew mine hand, and wrought for my name's sake, that it should not be polluted in the sight of the heathen, in whose sight I brought them forth.

23 I lifted up mine hand unto them also in the wilderness, that [w]I would scatter them among the heathen, and disperse them through the countries;

24 Because they had not executed my judgments, but had despised my statutes, and had polluted my sabbaths, and [x]their eyes were after their fathers' idols.

25 Wherefore [y]I gave them also statutes *that were* not good, and judgments whereby they should not live;

26 And I polluted them in their own gifts, in that they caused to pass [z]through *the fire* all that openeth the womb, that I might make them desolate, to the end that they [a]might know that I *am* the LORD.

27 ¶ Therefore, son of man, speak unto the house of Ĭs'ra-el, and say unto them, Thus saith the Lord GOD; Yet in this your fathers have [b]blasphemed me, in that they have [4]committed a trespass against me.

28 *For* when I had brought them into the land, *for* the which I lifted up mine hand to give it to them, then [c]they saw every high hill, and all the thick trees, and they offered there their sacrifices, and there they presented the provocation of their offering: there also they made their [d]sweet savour, and poured out there their drink offerings.

29 Then [5]I said unto them, What *is* the high place whereunto ye go? And the name thereof is called Bā'mah unto this day.

30 Wherefore say unto the house of Ĭs'ra-el, Thus saith the Lord GOD; Are ye polluted after the manner of your fathers? and commit ye whoredom after their abominations?

31 For when ye offer your gifts, when ye make your sons to pass through the fire, ye pollute yourselves with all your idols, even unto this day: and [e]shall I be inquired of by you, O house of Ĭs'ra-el? *As* I live, saith the Lord GOD, I will not be inquired of by you.

32 And that [f]which cometh into your mind shall not be at all, that ye say, We will be as the heathen, as the families of the countries, to serve wood and stone.

33 ¶ *As* I live, saith the Lord GOD, surely with a mighty hand, and [g]with a stretched out arm, and with fury poured out, will I rule over you:

34 And I will bring you out from the people, and will gather you out of the countries wherein ye are scattered, with a mighty hand, and with a stretched out arm, and with fury poured out.

35 And I will bring you into the wilderness of the people, and there [h]will I plead with you face to face.

36 [i]Like as I pleaded with your fathers in the wilderness of the land of Ē'gypt, so will I plead with you, saith the Lord GOD.

37 And I will cause you to [j]pass under the rod, and I will bring you into [6]the bond of the covenant:

38 And [k]I will purge out from among you the rebels, and them that transgress against me: I will bring them forth out of the country where they sojourn, and [l]they shall not enter into the land of Ĭs'ra-el: and ye shall know that I *am* the LORD.

39 As for you, O house of Ĭs'ra-el, thus saith the Lord GOD; [m]Go ye, serve ye every one his idols, and hereafter *also*, if ye will not hearken unto me: [n]but pollute ye my holy name no more with your gifts, and with your idols.

40 For [o]in mine holy mountain, in the mountain of the height of Ĭs'ra-el, saith the Lord GOD, there shall all the house of Ĭs'ra-el, all of them in the land, serve me: there [p]will I accept them, and there will I require your offerings, and the [7]firstfruits of your oblations, with all your holy things.

41 I will accept you with your [8]sweet savour, when I bring you out from the people, and gather you out of the countries wherein ye have been scattered; and I will be sanctified in you before the heathen.

42 [q]And ye shall know that I *am* the LORD, [r]when I shall bring you into the land of Ĭs'ra-el, into the country *for* the which I lifted up mine hand to give it to your fathers.

43 And [s]there shall ye remember your ways, and all your doings, wherein ye have been defiled; and [t]ye shall loathe yourselves in your own sight for all your evils that ye have committed.

44 [u]And ye shall know that I *am* the LORD, when I have wrought with you [v]for my name's sake, not according to your wicked ways, nor according to your corrupt doings, O ye house of Ĭs'ra-el, saith the Lord GOD.

45 ¶ Moreover the word of the LORD came unto me, saying,

46 Son of man, set thy face toward the south, and drop *thy word* toward the south, and prophesy against the forest of the south field;

47 And say to the forest of the south, Hear the word of the LORD; Thus saith the Lord GOD; Behold, [w]I will kindle

19 [s]Deut. 5.32-33; Deut. 12
20 [t]Ex. 20.11; Jer. 17.22
21 [u]Num. 25.1-2; Deut. 9.23-24
22 [v]Ps. 78.38
23 [w]Lev. 26.33; Ps. 106.27
24 [x]ch. 6.9; Mark 7.22
25 [y]Ps. 81.12; Rom. 1.24
26 [z]2 Ki. 17.17; ch. 16.20-21
[a]ch. 6.7
27 [b]Rom. 1.23
[4]trespassed a trespass
28 [c]Isa. 57.5
[d]ch. 16.19
29 [5]Or, I told them what the high place was, or, Bamah
31 [e]Prov. 1.27-28; Matt. 25.11-12
32 [f]ch. 11.5
33 [g]Jer. 21.5
35 [h]ch. 17.20
36 [i]Num. 14.21
37 [j]Lev. 27.32; Jer. 33.13
[6]Or, a delivering
38 [k]ch. 34.17; Matt. 3.12
[l]Ps. 95.11; Heb. 4.6
39 [m]Ps. 81.12; Amos 4.4
[n]Prov. 21.27; ch. 23.38
40 [o]Isa. 2.2; ch. 17.23
[p]Isa. 56.7; Rom. 12.1
[7]Or, chief
41 [8]savour of rest
42 [q]Jer. 24.7; John 17.3
[r]ch. 11.17
43 [s]ch. 16.61
[t]Lev. 26.39;
44 [u]ch. 24.24
[v]ch. 36.22
47 [w]Jer. 21.14

a fire in thee, and it shall devour [x]ev-
ery green tree in thee, and every dry
tree: the flaming flame shall not
be quenched, and all faces [y]from the
south to the north shall be burned
therein.
48 And all flesh shall see that I the
LORD have kindled it: it shall not be
quenched.
49 Then said I, Ah Lord GOD! they
say of me, Doth he not speak parables?

21

And the word of the LORD came
unto me, saying,
2 [a]Son of man, set thy face toward
Je-ru'sa-lĕm, and [b]drop *thy word* toward the [c]holy places, and prophesy
against the land of Ĭs'ra-el,
3 And say to the land of Ĭs'ra-el,
Thus saith the LORD; Behold, I *am*
against thee, and will draw forth my
sword out of his sheath, and will cut
off from thee [d]the righteous and the
wicked.
4 Seeing then that I will cut off from
thee the righteous and the wicked,
therefore shall my sword go forth out
of his sheath against all flesh [e]from
the south to the north:
5 That all flesh may know that I the
LORD have drawn forth my sword out
of his sheath: it [f]shall not return any
more.
6 [g]Sigh therefore, thou son of man,
with the breaking of *thy* loins; and
with bitterness sigh before their eyes.
7 And it shall be, when they say
unto thee, Wherefore sighest thou?
that thou shalt answer, For the tidings;
because it cometh: and every heart
shall melt, and all hands shall be feeble, and every spirit shall faint, and all
knees [1]shall be weak *as* water: behold,
it cometh, and shall be brought to pass,
saith the Lord GOD.
8 ¶ Again the word of the LORD
came unto me, saying,
9 Son of man, prophesy, and say,
Thus saith the LORD; Say, [h]A sword, a
sword is sharpened, and also furbished:
10 It is sharpened to make a sore
slaughter; it is furbished that it may
glitter: should we then make mirth? [2]it
contemneth the rod of my son, *as* every tree.
11 And he hath given it to be furbished, that it may be handled: this
sword is sharpened, and it is furbished,
to give it into the hand of the slayer.
12 Cry and howl, son of man: for it
shall be upon my people, it *shall be*
upon all the princes of Ĭs'ra-el: [3]terrors
by reason of the sword shall be upon
my people: [i]smite therefore upon *thy*
thigh.
13 [4]Because *it is* [j]a trial, and what if
the sword contemn even the rod? it
shall be no *more,* saith the Lord GOD.
14 Thou therefore, son of man,
prophesy, and smite *thine* [5]hands together, and let the sword be doubled
the third time, the sword of the slain: it
is the sword of the great *men that are*
slain, which entereth into their [k]privy
chambers.

[x]Luke 23.31
[y]ch. 21.4
CHAPTER 21
2 [a]ch. 20.46
[b]Deut. 32.2; Amos 7.16
[c]1 Pet. 4.17
3 [d]Job 9.22
4 [e]ch. 20.47
5 [f]Isa. 45.23
6 [g]Isa. 22.4
7 [1]shall go into water
9 [h]Deut. 32.41
10 [2]Or, it is the rod of my son, it despiseth every tree
12 [3]Or, they are thrust down to the sword with my people
[i]Jer. 31.19
13 [4]Or, When the trial hath been, what then? shall they not also belong to the despising rod?
[j]Job 9.23
14 [5]hand to hand
[k]1 Ki. 20.30; ch. 8.12
15 [6]Or, glittering, or, fear
[7]Or, sharpened
16 [l]ch. 14.17
[8]set thyself, take the left hand
17 [m]ch. 22.13
[n]Deut. 28.63; ch. 16.42
20 [o]Deut. 3.11;
21 [9]mother of the way
[10]Or, knives
[11]teraphim
22 [12]rams, or, battering rams
[p]Jer. 51.14
[q]ch. 4.2
23 [13]Or, for the oaths made unto them
[r]ch. 17.13
25 [s]Gen. 13.13
26 [t]Luke 1.52
27 [14]Perverted, perverted, perverted, will I make it
[u]Gen. 49.10
30 [15]Or, Cause it to return

15 I have set the [6]point of the sword
against all their gates, that *their* heart
may faint, and *their* ruins be multiplied: ah! *it is* made bright, *it is*
[7]wrapped up for the slaughter.
16 [l]Go thee one way or other, *either*
on the right hand, [8]*or* on the left, whithersoever thy face *is* set.
17 I will also [m]smite mine hands together, and [n]I will cause my fury to
rest: I the LORD have said *it.*
18 ¶ The word of the LORD came
unto me again, saying,
19 Also, thou son of man, appoint
thee two ways, that the sword of the
king of Băb'y̆-lon may come: both
twain shall come forth out of one land:
and choose thou a place, choose *it* at
the head of the way to the city.
20 Appoint a way, that the sword
may come to [o]Răb'bath of the Ăm'-
mŏn-ītes, and to Jū'dah in Je-ru'sa-lĕm
the defenced.
21 For the king of Băb'y̆-lon stood at
the [9]parting of the way, at the head of
the two ways, to use divination: he
made *his* [10]arrows bright, he consulted
with [11]images, he looked in the liver.
22 At his right hand was the divination for Je-ru'sa-lĕm, to appoint [12]cap-
tains, to open the mouth in the slaughter, to [p]lift up the voice with shouting,
[q]to appoint *battering* rams against the
gates, to cast a mount, *and* to build a
fort.
23 And it shall be unto them as a
false divination in their sight, [13]to them
that [r]have sworn oaths: but he will call
to remembrance the iniquity, that they
may be taken.
24 Therefore thus saith the Lord
GOD; Because ye have made your iniquity to be remembered, in that your
transgressions are discovered, so that
in all your doings your sins do appear;
because, *I say,* that ye are come to remembrance, ye shall be taken with the
hand.
25 ¶ And thou, [s]profane wicked
prince of Ĭs'ra-el, whose day is come,
when iniquity *shall have* an end,
26 Thus saith the Lord GOD; Remove the diadem, and take off the
crown: this *shall* not *be* the same: [t]ex-
alt *him that is* low, and abase *him that*
is high.
27 [14]I will overturn, overturn, overturn, it: [u]and it shall be no *more,* until
he come whose right it is; and I will
give it *him.*
28 ¶ And thou, son of man, prophesy
and say, Thus saith the Lord GOD concerning the Ăm'mŏn-ītes, and concerning their reproach; even say thou, The
sword, the sword *is* drawn: for the
slaughter *it is* furbished, to consume
because of the glittering:
29 Whiles they see vanity unto thee,
whiles they divine a lie unto thee, to
bring thee upon the necks of *them that*
are slain, of the wicked, whose day is
come, when their iniquity *shall have*
an end.
30 [15]Shall I cause *it* to return into his
sheath? I will judge thee in the place

where thou wast created, in the land of
thy nativity.
31 And I will pour out mine indignation upon thee, I will blow against thee
in the fire of my wrath, and deliver
thee into the hand of [16]brutish men,
and skilful to destroy.
32 Thou shalt be for fuel to the fire;
thy blood shall be in the midst of the
land; thou shalt be no *more* remembered: for I the LORD have spoken *it*.

22

Moreover the word of the LORD
came unto me, saying,
2 Now, thou son of man, wilt thou
[1]judge, wilt thou judge the [2]bloody
city? yea, thou shalt [3]shew her all her
abominations.
3 Then say thou, Thus saith the Lord
GOD, The city sheddeth blood in the
midst of it, that her time may come, and
maketh [a]idols against herself to defile
herself.
4 Thou art become guilty in thy
blood that thou hast [b]shed; and hast
defiled thyself in thine idols which
thou hast made; and thou hast caused
thy days to draw near, and art come
even unto thy years: [c]therefore have I
made thee a reproach unto the heathen, and a mocking to all countries.
5 *Those that be* near, and *those that
be* far from thee, shall mock thee,
which art [4]infamous *and* much vexed.
6 Behold, [d]the princes of Is'ra-el, every one were in thee to their [5]power to
shed blood.
7 In thee have they [e]set light by father and mother: in the midst of thee
have they dealt by [6]oppression with
the stranger: in thee have they vexed
the fatherless and the widow.
8 Thou hast despised mine holy
things, and hast [f]profaned my sabbaths.
9 In thee are [7]men that carry tales to
shed blood: and in thee they eat upon
the mountains: in the midst of thee
they commit lewdness.
10 In thee have they [g]discovered
their fathers' nakedness: in thee have
they humbled her that was [h]set apart
for pollution.
11 And [8]one hath committed abomination [i]with his neighbour's wife;
and [9]another hath lewdly defiled his
daughter in law; and another in thee
hath humbled his sister, his father's
daughter.
12 In thee [j]have they taken gifts to
shed blood; [k]thou hast taken usury
and increase, and thou hast greedily
gained of thy neighbours by extortion,
and [l]hast forgotten me, saith the Lord
GOD.
13 ¶ Behold, therefore I have [m]smit-
ten mine hand at thy dishonest gain
which thou hast made, and at thy
blood which hath been in the midst of
thee.
14 [n]Can thine heart endure, or can
thine hands be strong, in the days that
I shall deal with thee? [o]I the LORD
have spoken *it*, and will do *it*.
15 And [p]I will scatter thee among
the heathen, and disperse thee in the

31 [16]Or, burning

CHAPTER 22
2 [1]Or, plead for
[2]city of bloods
[3]make her know
3 [a]Mic. 6.16
4 [b]Gen. 9.6; Ps. 106.38
[c]Deut. 28.37; Dan. 9.16
5 [4]polluted of name, much in vexation
6 [d]Isa. 1.23; Zeph. 3.3
[5]arm
7 [e]Deut. 27.16
[6]Or, deceit
8 [f]Lev. 19.30
9 [7]men of slanders
10 [g]Lev. 20.11; 1 Cor. 5.1
[h]Lev. 18.19
11 [8]Or, every one
[i]Jer. 5.8
[9]Or, every one hath by lewdness
12 [j]Deut. 16.19
[k]Ex. 22.25; Deut. 23.19
[l]Deut. 32.18; ch. 23.35
13 [m]ch. 21.17
14 [n]ch. 21.7; 1 Cor. 10.22
[o]ch. 17.24
15 [p]Deut. 4.27
16 [10]Or, shalt be profaned
[q]Ex. 8.22; Ps. 9.16
18 [r]Isa. 1.22
[11]drosses
20 [12]According to the gathering
25 [s]Jer. 6.13; Hos. 6.9
[t]Matt. 23.14; Acts 20.29
[u]Mic. 3.11;
26 [v]Mal. 2.8
[13]offered violence to
[w]1 Sam. 2.29
[x]Lev. 10.10
27 [y]Isa. 1.23
28 [z]ch. 13.10
29 [a]Jer. 5.26
[14]Or, deceit
[15]without right
30 [b]Jer. 5.1
[c]Gen. 18.23

countries, and will consume thy filthiness out of thee.
16 And thou [10]shalt take thine inheritance in thyself in the sight of the heathen, and [q]thou shalt know that I *am*
the LORD.
17 And the word of the LORD came
unto me, saying,
18 Son of man, [r]the house of Is'ra-el
is to me become dross: all they *are*
brass, and tin, and iron, and lead, in
the midst of the furnace; they are *even*
the [11]dross of silver.
19 Therefore thus saith the Lord
GOD; Because ye are all become dross,
behold, therefore I will gather you into
the midst of Je-ru'sa-lĕm.
20 [12]*As* they gather silver, and brass,
and iron, and lead, and tin, into the
midst of the furnace, to blow the fire
upon it, to melt *it*; so will I gather *you* in
mine anger and in my fury, and I will
leave *you there*, and melt you.
21 Yea, I will gather you, and blow
upon you in the fire of my wrath, and
ye shall be melted in the midst thereof.
22 As silver is melted in the midst of
the furnace, so shall ye be melted in
the midst thereof; and ye shall know
that I the LORD have poured out my
fury upon you.
23 ¶ And the word of the LORD came
unto me, saying,
24 Son of man, say unto her, Thou
art the land that is not cleansed, nor
rained upon in the day of indignation.
25 [s]*There is* a conspiracy of her
prophets in the midst thereof, like a
roaring lion ravening the prey; they
[t]have devoured souls; [u]they have
taken the treasure and precious things;
they have made her many widows in
the midst thereof.
26 Her [v]priests have [13]violated my
law, and have [w]profaned mine holy
things: they have put no [x]difference
between the holy and profane, neither
have they shewed *difference* between
the unclean and the clean, and have
hid their eyes from my sabbaths, and I
am profaned among them.
27 Her [y]princes in the midst thereof
are like wolves ravening the prey, to
shed blood, *and* to destroy souls, to get
dishonest gain.
28 And [z]her prophets have daubed
them with untempered *morter*, seeing
vanity, and divining lies unto them,
saying, Thus saith the Lord GOD, when
the LORD hath not spoken.
29 [a]The people of the land have
used [14]oppression, and exercised robbery, and have vexed the poor and
needy: yea, they have oppressed the
stranger [15]wrongfully.
30 [b]And I sought for a man among
them, that should make up the hedge,
and [c]stand in the gap before me for the
land, that I should not destroy it: but I
found none.
31 Therefore have I poured out mine
indignation upon them; I have consumed them with the fire of my wrath:
their own way have I recompensed
upon their heads, saith the Lord GOD.

23 The word of the LORD came again
unto me, saying,
2 Son of man, there were [a]two
women, the daughters of one mother:
3 And [b]they committed whoredoms
in Ē'ġypt; they committed whoredoms
in their youth: there were their breasts
pressed, and there they bruised the
teats of their virginity.
4 And the names of them *were* A-
hŏ'lah the elder, and A-hŏl'ĭ-bah her
sister: and they were mine, and they
bare sons and daughters. Thus *were*
their names; Sa-mā'rĭ-ȧ *is* [1]A-hŏ'lah,
and Je-ru̥'sa-lĕm [2]A-hŏl'ĭ-bah.
5 And A-hŏ'lah played the harlot
when she was mine; and she doted on
her lovers, on [c]the Ăs-sy̆r'ĭ-ans *her*
neighbours,
6 *Which were* clothed with blue,
captains and rulers, all of them desirable young men, horsemen riding
upon horses.
7 Thus she [3]committed her whoredoms with them, with all them *that*
were [4]the chosen men of Ăs-sy̆r'ĭ-ȧ,
and with all on whom she doted: with
all their idols she defiled herself.
8 Neither left she her whoredoms
brought from Ē'ġypt: for in her youth
they lay with her, and they bruised the
breasts of her virginity, and poured
their whoredom upon her.
9 Wherefore I have delivered her
into the hand of her lovers, into the
hand of the [d]Ăs-sy̆r'ĭ-ans, upon whom
she doted.
10 These [e]discovered her nakedness: they took her sons and her daughters, and slew her with the sword: and
she became [5]famous among women;
for they had executed judgment upon
her.
11 And when her sister A-hŏl'ĭ-bah
saw *this,* [6]she was more corrupt in her
inordinate love than she, and in her
whoredoms [7]more than her sister in
her whoredoms.
12 She doted upon the [f]Ăs-sy̆r'ĭ-ans
her neighbours, captains and rulers
clothed most gorgeously, horsemen
riding upon horses, all of them desirable young men.
13 Then I saw that she was defiled,
that they *took* both one way,
14 And *that* she increased her whoredoms: for when she saw men pourtrayed upon the wall, [g]the images of the
Chăl-dē'ans pourtrayed with vermilion,
15 Girded with girdles upon their
loins, exceeding in dyed attire upon
their heads, all of them princes to look
to, after the manner of the Băb-y̆-lō'-
nĭ-ans of Chăl-dē'ȧ, the land of their
nativity:
16 And [8]as soon as she saw them
with her eyes, she doted upon them,
and sent messengers unto them into
Chăl-dē'ȧ.
17 And the [9]Băb-y̆-lō'nĭ-ans came to
her into the bed of love, and they defiled her with their whoredom, and she
was polluted with them, and her mind
was [10]alienated from them.
18 So she discovered her whoredoms, and discovered her nakedness:
then [h]my mind was alienated from
her, like as my mind was alienated
from her sister.
19 Yet she multiplied her whoredoms, in calling to remembrance the
days of her youth, wherein she had
played the harlot in the land of Ē'ġypt.
20 For she doted upon their par-
amours, [i]whose flesh *is as* the flesh of
asses, and whose issue *is like* the issue
of horses.
21 Thus thou calledst to remembrance the lewdness of thy youth, in
bruising thy teats by the Ē-ġy̆p''tians
for the paps of thy youth.
22 ¶ Therefore, O A-hŏl'ĭ-bah, thus
saith the Lord GOD; [j]Behold, I will
raise up thy lovers against thee, from
whom thy mind is alienated, and I will
bring them against thee on every side;
23 The Băb-y̆-lō'nĭ-ans, and all the
Chăl-dē'ans, Pē'kŏd, and Shō'ȧ, and
Kō'ȧ, *and* all the Ăs-sy̆r'ĭ-ans with
them: all of them desirable young men,
captains and rulers, great lords and renowned, all of them riding upon horses.
24 And they shall come against thee
[k]with chariots, wagons, and wheels,
and with an assembly of people, *which*
shall set against thee buckler and
shield and helmet round about: and I
will set judgment before them, and
they shall [l]judge thee according to
their judgments.
25 And I will set my jealousy against
thee, and they shall deal furiously with
thee: they shall take away thy nose and
thine ears; and thy remnant shall fall
by the sword: they shall take thy sons
and thy daughters; and thy residue
shall be devoured by the fire.
26 [m]They shall also strip thee out of
thy clothes, and take away thy [11]fair
jewels.
27 Thus [n]will I make thy lewdness
to cease from thee, and thy whoredom
brought from the land of Ē'ġypt: so
that thou shalt not lift up thine eyes
unto them, nor remember Ē'ġypt any
more.
28 For thus saith the Lord GOD; Behold, I will deliver thee into the hand
of them [o]whom thou hatest, into the
hand *of them* from whom thy mind is
alienated:
29 And they shall deal with thee
hatefully, and shall take away all thy
labour, and [p]shall leave thee naked
and bare: and the nakedness of thy
whoredoms shall be discovered, both
thy lewdness and thy whoredoms.
30 I will do these *things* unto thee,
because thou hast [q]gone a whoring after the heathen, *and* because thou art
polluted with their idols.
31 Thou hast walked in the way of
thy sister; therefore will I give her [r]cup
into thine hand.
32 Thus saith the Lord GOD; Thou
shalt drink of thy sister's cup deep and
large: [s]thou shalt be laughed to scorn
and had in derision; it containeth much.

CHAPTER 23
2 [a]Jer. 3.7; ch. 16.46
3 [b]Lev. 17.7; ch. 20.8
4 [1]That is, His tent, or, tabernacle [2]That is, My tabernacle in her
5 [c]2 Ki. 15.19; Hos. 10.6
7 [3]bestowed her whoredoms upon them [4]the choice of the children of Asshur
9 [d]2 Ki. 17.3-4-5-6-23
10 [e]ch. 16.37-41 [5]a name
11 [6]she corrupted her inordinate love more than, etc [7]more than the whoredoms of her sister
12 [f]2 Ki. 16.7
14 [g]Jer. 50.2
16 [8]at the sight of her eyes
17 [9]children of Babel [10]loosed, or, disjointed
18 [h]Deut. 32.19; Zech. 11.8
20 [i]ch. 16.26
22 [j]Isa. 10.5-6; ch. 16.37
24 [k]Jer. 47.3; Nah. 3.2 [l]2 Sam. 24.14; ch. 16.38
26 [m]Jer. 13.22; Rev. 17.16 [11]instruments of thy decking
27 [n]ch. 16.41; Mic. 5.10
28 [o]Jer. 21.7; ch. 16.37
29 [p]ch. 16.39
30 [q]ch. 6.9
31 [r]Ps. 11.6; Dan. 9.12
32 [s]Deut. 28.37; ch. 22.4-5

33 Thou shalt be filled with drunkenness and sorrow, with the cup of astonishment and desolation, with the cup of thy sister Sa-mā'rĭ-ȧ.

34 Thou shalt [t]even drink it and suck *it* out, and thou shalt break the sherds thereof, and pluck off thine own breasts: for I have spoken *it,* saith the Lord GOD.

35 Therefore thus saith the Lord GOD; Because thou [u]hast forgotten me, and [v]cast me behind thy back, therefore bear thou also thy lewdness and thy whoredoms.

36 ¶ The LORD said moreover unto me; Son of man, wilt thou [12]judge A-hŏ'lah and A-hŏl'ĭ-bah? yea, [w]declare unto them their abominations;

37 That they have committed adultery, and [x]blood *is* in their hands, and with their idols have they committed adultery, and have also caused their sons, [y]whom they bare unto me, to pass for them through *the fire,* to devour *them.*

38 Moreover this they have done unto me: they have defiled my sanctuary in the same day, and [z]have profaned my sabbaths.

39 For when they had slain their children to their idols, then they came the same day into my sanctuary to profane it; and, lo, [a]thus have they done in the midst of mine house.

40 And furthermore, that ye have sent for men [13]to come from far, [b]unto whom a messenger *was* sent; and, lo, they came: for whom thou didst [c]wash thyself, [d]paintedst thy eyes, and deckedst thyself with ornaments,

41 And satest upon a [14]stately bed, and a table prepared before it, [e]whereupon thou hast set mine incense and mine oil.

42 And a voice of a multitude being at ease *was* with her: and with the men [15]of the common sort *were* brought [16]Sa-bē'ans from the wilderness, which put bracelets upon their hands, and beautiful crowns upon their heads.

43 Then said I unto *her that was* old in adulteries, Will they now commit [17]whoredoms with her, and she *with them?*

44 Yet they went in unto her, as they go in unto a woman that playeth the harlot: so went they in unto A-hŏ'lah and unto A-hŏl'ĭ-bah, the lewd women.

45 ¶ And the righteous men, they shall [f]judge them after the manner of adulteresses, and after the manner of women that shed blood; because they *are* adulteresses, and blood *is* in their hands.

46 For thus saith the Lord GOD; I will bring up a company upon them, and will give them [18]to be removed and spoiled.

47 [g]And the company shall stone them with stones, and [19]dispatch them with their swords; [h]they shall slay their sons and their daughters, and burn up their houses with fire.

48 Thus will I cause lewdness to cease out of the land, [i]that all women may be taught not to do after your lewdness.

49 And they shall recompense your lewdness upon you, and ye shall bear the sins of your idols: and ye shall know that I *am* the Lord GOD.

24

Again in the ninth year, in the tenth month, in the tenth *day* of the month, the word of the LORD came unto me, saying,

2 Son of man, write thee the name of the day, *even* of this same day: the king of Băb'ȳ-lon set himself against Je-ru̥'sa-lĕm this [a]same day.

3 [b]And utter a parable unto the rebellious house, and say unto them, Thus saith the Lord GOD; [c]Set on a pot, set *it* on, and also pour water into it:

4 Gather the pieces thereof into it, *even* every good piece, the thigh, and the shoulder; fill *it* with the choice bones.

5 Take the choice of the flock, and [1]burn also the bones under it, *and* make it boil well, and let them seethe the bones of it therein.

6 ¶ Wherefore thus saith the Lord GOD; Woe to [d]the bloody city, to the pot whose scum *is* therein, and whose scum is not gone out of it! bring it out piece by piece; let no [e]lot fall upon it.

7 For her blood is in the midst of her; she set it upon the top of a rock; [f]she poured it not upon the ground, to cover it with dust;

8 That it might cause fury to come up to take vengeance; [g]I have set her blood upon the top of a rock, that it should not be covered.

9 Therefore thus saith the Lord GOD; [h]Woe to the bloody city! I will even make the pile for fire great.

10 Heap on wood, kindle the fire, consume the flesh, and spice it well, and let the bones be burned.

11 Then set it empty upon the coals thereof, that the brass of it may be hot, and may burn, and *that* [i]the filthiness of it may be molten in it, *that* the scum of it may be consumed.

12 She hath wearied [2]*herself* with lies, and her great scum went not forth out of her: her scum *shall be* in the fire.

13 In thy filthiness *is* lewdness: because [j]I have purged thee, and thou wast not purged, thou shalt not be purged from thy filthiness any more, [k]till I have caused my fury to rest upon thee.

14 [l]I the LORD have spoken *it:* it shall come to pass, and I will do *it;* I will not go back, [m]neither will I spare, neither will I repent; according to thy ways, and according to thy doings, shall they judge thee, saith the Lord GOD.

15 ¶ Also the word of the LORD came unto me, saying,

16 Son of man, behold, I take away from thee the desire of thine eyes with a stroke: yet neither shalt thou mourn nor weep, neither shall thy tears [3]run down.

34 [t]Ps. 75.8; Isa. 51.17
35 [u]Jer. 2.32; Jer. 3.21
[v]1 Ki. 14.9; Neh. 9.26
36 [12]Or, plead for
[w]Isa. 58.1
37 [x]ch. 16.38
[y]ch. 16.20
38 [z]ch. 22.8
39 [a]2 Ki. 21.4; Jer. 23.11; ch. 44.7
40 [13]coming
[b]Isa. 57.9
[c]Ruth 3.3
[d]2 Ki. 9.30; Jer. 4.30
41 [14]honourable
[e]Prov. 7.17; Hos. 2.8
42 [15]of the multitude of men
[16]Or, drunkards
43 [17]her whoredoms
45 [f]ch. 16.38; John 8.4-7
46 [18]for a removing and spoil
47 [g]ch. 16.41
[19]Or, single them out
[h]2 Chr. 36.17; ch. 24.21
48 [i]Deut. 13.11; 2 Pet. 2.6

CHAPTER 24
2 [a]2 Ki. 25.1; Jer. 39.1
3 [b]Ps. 78.2; Luke 8.10
[c]Jer. 1.13; ch. 11.3
5 [1]Or, heap
6 [d]2 Ki. 21.16; Nah. 3.1
[e]Joel 3.3; Nah. 3.10
7 [f]Lev. 17.13; Deut. 12.16
8 [g]Jer. 16.17; Matt. 7.2
9 [h]Nah. 3.1; Hab. 2.12
11 [i]ch. 22.15
12 [2]Or, the Lord
13 [j]Amos 4.6
[k]ch. 5.13; ch. 8.18
14 [l]Num. 23.19; Ps. 33.9
[m]ch. 5.11
16 [3]go

17 [4]Forbear to cry, [n]make no mourning for the dead, [o]bind the tire of thine
head upon thee, and [p]put on thy shoes
upon thy feet, and [q]cover not *thy* [5]lips,
and eat not the bread of men.
18 So I spake unto the people in the
morning: and at even my wife died;
and I did in the morning as I was
commanded.
19 ¶ And the people said unto me,
[r]Wilt thou not tell us what these *things*
are to us, that thou doest *so?*
20 Then I answered them, The word
of the LORD came unto me, saying,
21 Speak unto the house of Is'ra-el,
Thus saith the Lord GOD; Behold, [s]I
will profane my sanctuary, the excellency of your strength, [t]the desire of
your eyes, and [6]that which your soul
pitieth; and your sons and your daughters whom ye have left shall fall by the
sword.
22 And ye shall do as I have done:
[u]ye shall not cover *your* lips, nor eat
the bread of men.
23 And your tires *shall be* upon your
heads, and your shoes upon your feet:
[v]ye shall not mourn nor weep; but [w]ye
shall pine away for your iniquities, and
mourn one toward another.
24 Thus [x]E-zē'kĭ-ĕl is unto you a
sign: according to all that he hath done
shall ye do: [y]and when this cometh,
[z]ye shall know that I *am* the Lord GOD.
25 Also, thou son of man, *shall it* not
be in the day when I take from them
their strength, the joy of their glory, the
desire of their eyes, and [7]that whereupon they set their minds, their sons
and their daughters,
26 *That* he that escapeth in that day
shall come unto thee, to cause *thee* to
hear *it* with *thine* ears?
27 [a]In that day shall thy mouth be
opened to him which is escaped, and
thou shalt speak, and be no more
dumb: and thou shalt be a sign unto
them; and they shall know that I *am*
the LORD.

25

25 The word of the LORD came again
unto me, saying,
2 Son of man, set thy face [a]against
the Ăm'mŏn-ītes, and prophesy against
them;
3 And say unto the Ăm'mŏn-ītes,
Hear the word of the Lord GOD; Thus
saith the Lord GOD; [b]Because thou
saidst, Aha, against my sanctuary,
when it was profaned; and against the
land of Is'ra-el, when it was desolate;
and against the house of Jū'dah, when
they went into captivity;
4 Behold, therefore I will deliver thee
to the [1]men of the east for a possession,
and they shall set their palaces in thee,
and make their dwellings in thee: [c]they
shall eat thy fruit, and they shall drink
thy milk.
5 And I will make [d]Răb'bah a stable
for camels, and the Ăm'mŏn-ītes a
couchingplace for flocks: and ye shall
know that I *am* the LORD.
6 For thus saith the Lord GOD; Because thou hast clapped *thine* [2]hands,
and stamped with the [3]feet, and re-

17 [4]Be silent [n]Num. 20.29; Jer. 16.5 [o]Lev. 10.6 [p]2 Sam. 15.30 [q]Mic. 3.7 [5]upper lip
19 [r]ch. 12.9
21 [s]Jer. 7.14; [t]Ps. 27.4 [6]the pity of your soul
22 [u]Jer. 16.6
23 [v]Job 27.15; [w]Lev. 26.39;
24 [x]Isa. 20.3; [y]Jer. 17.15; [z]ch. 25.5
25 [7]the lifting up of their soul
27 [a]ch. 3.26

CHAPTER 25
2 [a]Jer. 49.1;
3 [b]Prov. 17.5
4 [1]children [c]Gen. 45.18
5 [d]2 Sam. 12.26;
6 [2]hand [3]foot [4]soul
7 [5]Or, meat
8 [e]Deut. 2.4-5;
9 [6]shoulder of Moab
10 [7]Or, against the children of Ammon
12 [f]2 Chr. 28.17; [8]by revenging revengement
13 [9]Or, they shall fall by the sword unto Dedan
14 [g]Isa. 11.14
15 [h]Jer. 25.20; [10]Or, with perpetual hatred
16 [i]Zeph. 2.4 [j]1 Sam. 30.14 [11]Or, haven of the sea
17 [12]vengeances [k]Ps. 9.16;

CHAPTER 26
2 [a]Isa. 23; [b]ch. 25.3 [c]Ps. 40.15; [d]Joel 3.4-6

joiced in [4]heart with all thy despite
against the land of Is'ra-el;
7 Behold, therefore I will stretch out
mine hand upon thee, and will deliver
thee for a [5]spoil to the heathen; and I
will cut thee off from the people, and I
will cause thee to perish out of the
countries: I will destroy thee; and thou
shalt know that I *am* the LORD.
8 ¶ Thus saith the Lord GOD; Because that [e]Mō'ab and Sē'ïr do say,
Behold, the house of Jū'dah *is* like
unto all the heathen;
9 Therefore, behold, I will open the
[6]side of Mō'ab from the cities, from his
cities *which are* on his frontiers, the
glory of the country, Bĕth-jĕsh'ĭ-mŏth,
Bā'al-mē'on, and Kĭr-ī-a-thā'im,
10 Unto the men of the east [7]with the
Ăm'mŏn-ītes, and will give them in possession, that the Ăm'mŏn-ītes may not
be remembered among the nations.
11 And I will execute judgments
upon Mō'ab; and they shall know that
I *am* the LORD.
12 ¶ Thus saith the Lord GOD; [f]Be-
cause that Ē'dom hath dealt against
the house of Jū'dah [8]by taking vengeance, and hath greatly offended, and
revenged himself upon them;
13 Therefore thus saith the Lord
GOD; I will also stretch out mine hand
upon Ē'dom, and will cut off man and
beast from it; and I will make it desolate from Tē'man; and [9]they of Dē'dan
shall fall by the sword.
14 And [g]I will lay my vengeance
upon Ē'dom by the hand of my people
Is'ra-el: and they shall do in Ē'dom according to mine anger and according
to my fury; and they shall know my
vengeance, saith the Lord GOD.
15 ¶ Thus saith the Lord GOD; [h]Be-
cause the Phĭ-lĭs'tĭnes have dealt by revenge, and have taken vengeance with
a despiteful heart, to destroy *it* [10]for
the old hatred;
16 Therefore thus saith the Lord
GOD; Behold, [i]I will stretch out mine
hand upon the Phĭ-lĭs'tĭnes, and I will
cut off the [j]Chĕr'ĕth-ĭms, and destroy
the remnant of the [11]sea coast.
17 And I will execute great [12]ven-
geance upon them with furious rebukes; [k]and they shall know that I *am*
the LORD, when I shall lay my vengeance upon them.

26

26 And it came to pass in the eleventh year, in the first *day* of the
month, *that* the word of the LORD
came unto me, saying,
2 Son of man, [a]because that Tȳ'rus
hath said against Je-ru'sa-lĕm, [b]Aha,
she is broken *that was* [c]the gates of
the people: she is [d]turned unto me: I
shall be replenished, *now* she is laid
waste:
3 Therefore thus saith the Lord GOD;
Behold, I *am* against thee, O Tȳ'rus,
and will cause many nations to come
up against thee, as the sea causeth his
waves to come up.
4 And they shall destroy the walls of
Tȳ'rus, and break down her towers: I

will also scrape her dust from her, and
make her like the top of a rock.
5 It shall be *a place for* the spreading
of nets [e]in the midst of the sea: for I
have spoken *it*, saith the Lord GOD: and
it shall become a spoil to the nations.
6 And her daughters which *are* in
the field shall be slain by the sword;
[f]and they shall know that I *am* the
LORD.
7 ¶ For thus saith the Lord GOD; Behold, I will bring upon Tȳ'rus Nĕb-u-
chăd-rĕz'zar king of Băb'ȳ-lon, [g]a king
of kings, from the north, with horses,
and with chariots, and with horsemen,
and companies, and much people.
8 He shall slay with the sword thy
daughters in the field: and he shall
[h]make a fort against thee, and [1]cast a
mount against thee, and lift up the
buckler against thee.
9 And he shall set engines of war
against thy walls, and with his axes he
shall break down thy towers.
10 By reason of the abundance of
his horses their dust shall cover thee:
thy walls shall shake at the noise of the
horsemen, and of the wheels, and of
the chariots, when he shall enter into
thy gates, [2]as men enter into a city
wherein is made a breach.
11 With the hoofs of his horses shall
he tread down all thy streets: he shall
slay thy people by the sword, and thy
strong garrisons shall go down to the
ground.
12 And they shall make a spoil of
thy riches, and make a prey of thy merchandise: and they shall break down
thy walls, and destroy [3]thy pleasant
houses: and they shall lay thy stones
and thy timber and thy dust in the
midst of the water.
13 [i]And I will cause the noise of [j]thy
songs to cease; and the sound of thy
harps shall be no more heard.
14 And I will make thee like the top
of a rock: thou shalt be *a place* to
spread nets upon; thou shalt be built
no more: for I the LORD have spoken *it*,
saith the Lord GOD.
15 ¶ Thus saith the Lord GOD to
Tȳ'rus; Shall not the isles [k]shake at the
sound of thy fall, when the wounded
cry, when the slaughter is made in the
midst of thee?
16 Then all the [l]princes of the sea
shall [m]come down from their thrones,
and lay away their robes, and put off
their broidered garments: they shall
clothe themselves with [4]trembling;
[n]they shall sit upon the ground, and
[o]shall tremble at *every* moment, and
[p]be astonished at thee.
17 And they shall take up a [q]lamentation for thee, and say to thee, How
art thou destroyed, *that wast* inhabited [5]of seafaring men, the renowned
city, which wast strong [r]in the sea, she
and her inhabitants, which cause their
terror *to be* on all that haunt it!
18 Now shall the isles tremble in the
day of thy fall; yea, the isles that *are* in
the sea shall be troubled at thy departure.

19 For thus saith the Lord GOD;
When I shall make thee a desolate city,
like the cities that are not inhabited;
when I shall bring up the deep upon
thee, and great waters shall cover thee;
20 When I shall bring thee down
[s]with them that descend into the pit,
with the people of old time, and shall
set thee in the low parts of the earth, in
places desolate of old, with them that
go down to the pit, that thou be not
inhabited; and I shall set [t]glory in the
land of the living;
21 [u]I will make thee [6]a terror, and
thou *shalt be* no *more*: [v]though thou
be sought for, [w]yet shalt thou never be
found again, saith the Lord GOD.

27 The word of the LORD came again
unto me, saying,
2 Now, thou son of man, [a]take up a
lamentation for Tȳ'rus;
3 And say unto Tȳ'rus, [b]O thou that
art situate at the entry of the sea,
which art [c]a merchant of the people
for many isles, Thus saith the Lord
GOD; O Tȳ'rus, thou hast said, I *am* [1]of
perfect beauty.
4 Thy borders *are* in the [2]midst of
the seas, thy builders have perfected
thy beauty.
5 They have [3]made all thy *ship* boards
of fir trees of [d]Sē'nĭr: they have taken
cedars from Lĕb'a-non to make masts
for thee.
6 *Of* the oaks of Bā'shăn have they
made thine oars; [4]the company of the
Ăsh'ŭr-ītes have made thy benches
of ivory, *brought* out of [e]the isles of
Chĭt'tim.
7 Fine linen with broidered work
from Ē'ġypt was that which thou
spreadest forth to be thy sail; [5]blue and
purple from the isles of [f]E-lī'shah was
that which covered thee.
8 The inhabitants of Zī'dŏn and Är'-
văd were thy mariners: thy wise *men*,
O Tȳ'rus, *that* were in thee, were thy
pilots.
9 The ancients of [g]Gē'bal and the
wise *men* thereof were in thee thy
[6]calkers: all the ships of the sea with
their mariners were in thee to occupy
thy merchandise.
10 They of Pĕr'siȧ and of Lŭd and of
[h]Phŭt were in thine army, thy men of
war: they hanged the shield and helmet
in thee; they set forth thy comeliness.
11 The men of Är'văd with thine
army *were* upon thy walls round about,
and the Găm'ma-dĭms were in thy towers: they hanged their shields upon thy
walls round about; they have made thy
beauty perfect.
12 [i]Tär'shish *was* thy merchant by
reason of the multitude of all *kind of*
riches; with silver, iron, tin, and lead,
they traded in thy fairs.
13 [j]Jā'văn, Tu'bal, and Mē'shech,
they *were* thy merchants: they traded
[k]the persons of men and vessels of
brass in thy [7]market.
14 They of the house of [l]To-gär'-
mah traded in thy fairs with horses
and horsemen and mules.

5 [e]ch. 27.32; Matt. 4.19-21
6 [f]Ps. 83.18; Isa. 37.20; ch. 25.5
7 [g]Ezra 7.12; Dan. 2.37
8 [h]2 Sam. 20.15; Jer. 52.4; ch. 21.22
[1]Or, pour out the engine of shot
10 [2]according to the enterings of a city broken up
12 [3]houses of thy desire
13 [i]Isa. 14.11; Isa. 23.7-16; Rev. 18.22
[j]Isa. 23.16
15 [k]Jer. 49.21
16 [l]Isa. 23.8
[m]Jon. 3.6
[4]tremblings
[n]Job 2.13; Isa. 3.26
[o]ch. 32.10
[p]ch. 27.35
17 [q]Rev. 18.9
[5]of the seas
[r]Isa. 23.4
20 [s]ch. 32.18; Luke 10.15
[t]Isa. 4.5
21 [u]ch. 27.36
[6]terrors
[v]Ps. 37.36
[w]Jer. 51.64

CHAPTER 27
2 [a]ch. 26.17
3 [b]ch. 28.2
[c]Isa. 23.3
[1]perfect of beauty
4 [2]heart
5 [3]built
[d]Deut. 3.9
6 [4]the daughter, or, they have made thy hatches of ivory well trodden
[e]Jer. 2.10
7 [5]Or, purple and scarlet
[f]Gen. 10.4
9 [g]Josh. 13.5
[6]strengtheners, or, stoppers of chinks
10 [h]Jer. 46.9; ch. 30.5
12 [i]2 Chr. 20.36
13 [j]1 Chr. 1.5
[k]Joel 3.6
[7]Or, merchandise
14 [l]Gen. 10.3; 1 Chr. 1.6

15 The men of [m]Dē'dan *were* thy merchants; many isles *were* the merchandise of thine hand: they brought thee *for* a present horns of ivory and ebony.

16 Sȳr'ĭ-ȧ *was* thy merchant by reason of the multitude of [8]the wares of thy making: they occupied in thy fairs with emeralds, purple, and broidered work, and fine linen, and coral, and [9]agate.

17 Jū'dah, and the land of Ĭs'ra-el, they *were* thy merchants: they traded in thy market [n]wheat of Mĭn'nith, and Păn'năg, and honey, and oil, and [10]balm.

18 Da-măs'cus *was* thy merchant in the multitude of the wares of thy making, for the multitude of all riches; in the wine of Hĕl'bon, and white wool.

19 Dăn also and Jā'văn [11]going to and fro occupied in thy fairs: bright iron, cassia, and calamus, were in thy market.

20 [o]Dē'dan *was* thy merchant in [12]precious clothes for chariots.

21 A-rā'bĭ-ȧ, and all the princes of [p]Kē'där, [13]they occupied with thee in lambs, and rams, and goats: in these *were they* thy merchants.

22 The merchants of [q]Shē'bȧ and Rā'a-mah, they *were* thy merchants: they occupied in thy fairs with chief of all spices, and with all precious stones, and gold.

23 [r]Hā'ran, and Căn'neh, and Ē'dĕn, the merchants of [s]Shē'bȧ, Ăssh'ur, *and* Chĭl'măd, *were* thy merchants.

24 These *were* thy merchants in [14]all sorts *of things*, in blue [15]clothes, and broidered work, and in chests of rich apparel, bound with cords, and made of cedar, among thy merchandise.

25 [t]The ships of Tär'shish did sing of thee in thy market: and thou wast replenished, and made very glorious in the midst of the seas.

26 ¶ Thy rowers have brought thee into great waters: [u]the east wind hath broken thee in the [16]midst of the seas.

27 Thy [v]riches, and thy fairs, thy merchandise, thy mariners, and thy pilots, thy calkers, and the occupiers of thy merchandise, and all thy men of war, that *are* in thee, [17]and in all thy company which *is* in the midst of thee, shall fall into the [18]midst of the seas in the day of thy ruin.

28 The [19]suburbs shall shake at the sound of the cry of thy pilots.

29 And [w]all that handle the oar, the mariners, *and* all the pilots of the sea, shall come down from their ships, they shall stand upon the land;

30 And shall cause their voice to be heard against thee, and shall cry bitterly, and shall [x]cast up dust upon their heads, they [y]shall wallow themselves in the ashes:

31 And they shall make themselves utterly bald for thee, and gird them with sackcloth, and they shall weep for thee with bitterness of heart *and* bitter wailing.

15 [m]Gen. 10.7; 1 Chr. 1.9
16 [8]thy works [9]chrysoprase
17 [n]1 Ki. 5.9; Acts 12.20 [10]Or, rosin
19 [11]Or, Meuzal
20 [o]Gen. 25.3 [12]clothes of freedom
21 [p]Gen. 25.13; 1 Chr. 1.29 [13]they were the merchants of thy hand
22 [q]Gen. 10.7; Isa. 60.6
23 [r]Gen. 11.31; 2 Ki. 19.12 [s]Gen. 25.3
24 [14]Or, excellent things [15]foldings
25 [t]Isa. 2.16
26 [u]Ps. 48.7 [16]heart
27 [v]Prov. 11.4 [17]Or, even with all [18]heart
28 [19]Or, waves
29 [w]Rev. 18.17
30 [x]Neh. 9.1; [y]Esth. 4.1
35 [z]ch. 26.15
36 [a]Jer. 18.16 [20]terrors [21]shall not be for ever

CHAPTER 28
2 [a]Deut. 8.14; [1]heart [b]Ps. 9.20;
3 [c]Dan. 2.48;
5 [2]By the greatness of thy wisdom [d]Deut. 8.12-13-14
6 [e]Dan. 7.25-26;
7 [f]ch. 30.11
9 [3]Or, woundeth
10 [g]ch. 31.18
12 [h]ch. 27.3
13 [i]Gen. 2.8; [4]Or, ruby [5]Or, chrysolite [6]Or, chrysoprase

32 And in their wailing they shall take up a lamentation for thee, and lament over thee, *saying*, What *city is* like Tȳ'rus, like the destroyed in the midst of the sea?

33 When thy wares went forth out of the seas, thou filledst many people; thou didst enrich the kings of the earth with the multitude of thy riches and of thy merchandise.

34 In the time *when* thou shalt be broken by the seas in the depths of the waters thy merchandise and all thy company in the midst of thee shall fall.

35 [z]All the inhabitants of the isles shall be astonished at thee, and their kings shall be sore afraid, they shall be troubled in *their* countenance.

36 The merchants among the people [a]shall hiss at thee; thou shalt be [20]a terror, and [21]never *shalt be* any more.

28

The word of the LORD came again unto me, saying,

2 Son of man, say unto the prince of Tȳ'rus, Thus saith the Lord GOD; Because [a]thine heart *is* lifted up, and thou hast said, I *am* a God, I sit *in* the seat of God, in the [1]midst of the seas; [b]yet thou *art* a man, and not God, though thou set thine heart as the heart of God:

3 Behold, [c]thou *art* wiser than Dăn'iel; there is no secret that they can hide from thee:

4 With thy wisdom and with thine understanding thou hast gotten thee riches, and hast gotten gold and silver into thy treasures:

5 [2]By thy great wisdom *and* by thy traffick hast thou increased thy riches, and thine heart is lifted up [d]because of thy riches:

6 Therefore thus saith the Lord GOD; Because thou hast [e]set thine heart as the heart of God;

7 Behold, therefore I will bring strangers upon thee, [f]the terrible of the nations: and they shall draw their swords against the beauty of thy wisdom, and they shall defile thy brightness.

8 They shall bring thee down to the pit, and thou shalt die the deaths of *them that are* slain in the midst of the seas.

9 Wilt thou yet say before him that slayeth thee, I *am* God? but thou *shalt be* a man, and no God, in the hand of him that [3]slayeth thee.

10 Thou shalt die the deaths of [g]the uncircumcised by the hand of strangers: for I have spoken *it*, saith the Lord GOD.

11 ¶ Moreover the word of the LORD came unto me, saying,

12 Son of man, take up a lamentation upon the king of Tȳ'rus, and say unto him, Thus saith the Lord GOD; [h]Thou sealest up the sum, full of wisdom, and perfect in beauty.

13 Thou hast been in [i]Ē'dĕn the garden of God; every precious stone *was* thy covering, the [4]sardius, topaz, and the diamond, the [5]beryl, the onyx, and the jasper, the sapphire, the [6]emerald,

and the carbuncle, and gold: the workmanship of [j]thy tabrets and of thy
pipes was prepared in thee in the day
that thou wast created.
14 Thou *art* the anointed [k]cherub
that covereth; and I have set thee *so:*
thou wast upon [l]the holy mountain of
God; thou hast walked up and down in
the midst of the stones of fire.
15 Thou *wast* perfect in thy ways
from the day that thou wast created,
till iniquity was found in thee.
16 By the multitude of thy merchandise they have filled the midst of thee
with violence, and thou hast sinned:
therefore I will cast thee as profane out
of the mountain of God: and I will destroy thee, O covering cherub, from
the midst of the stones of fire.
17 Thine heart was lifted up because
of thy beauty, thou hast corrupted thy
wisdom by reason of thy brightness: I
will cast thee to the ground, [m]I will lay
thee before kings, that they may behold thee.
18 Thou hast defiled thy [7]sanctuar-
ies by the multitude of thine iniquities,
by the iniquity of thy traffick; therefore will I bring forth a [n]fire from the
midst of thee, it shall devour thee, and
I will bring thee to ashes upon the
earth in the sight of all them that behold thee.
19 All they that know thee among
the people shall be astonished at thee:
thou shalt be [8]a terror, and never *shalt*
thou *be* any more.
20 ¶ Again the word of the LORD
came unto me, saying,
21 Son of man, set thy face [o]against
Zī'dŏn, and prophesy against it,
22 And say, Thus saith the Lord
GOD; [p]Behold, I *am* against thee, O
Zī'dŏn; and I will be glorified in the
midst of thee: and [q]they shall know
that I *am* the LORD, when I shall have
executed judgments in her, and shall
be [r]sanctified in her.
23 [s]For I will send into her pestilence, and blood into her streets; and
the wounded shall be judged in the
midst of her by the sword upon her on
every side; and they shall know that I
am the LORD.
24 ¶ And there shall be no more [t]a
pricking brier unto the house of Ĭs'ra-
el, nor *any* grieving thorn of all *that
are* round about them, that despised
them; and they shall know that I *am*
the Lord GOD.
25 Thus saith the Lord GOD; When I
shall have [u]gathered the house of Ĭs'-
ra-el from the people among whom
they are scattered, and shall be sanctified in them in the sight of the heathen,
then shall they dwell in their land that
I have given to my servant Jā'cob.
26 And they shall dwell [9]safely
therein, and shall [v]build houses, and
[w]plant vineyards; yea, they shall dwell
with confidence, when I have executed
judgments upon all those that [10]de-
spise them round about them; and they
shall know that I *am* the LORD their
God.

29 In the tenth year, in the tenth
month, in the twelfth *day* of the
month, the word of the LORD came
unto me, saying,
2 Son of man, set thy face against
Phā'raōh king of Ē'ġypt, and prophesy
against him, and [a]against all Ē'ġypt:
3 Speak, and say, Thus saith the
Lord GOD; [b]Behold, I *am* against thee,
Phā'raōh king of Ē'ġypt, the great
[c]dragon that lieth in the midst of his
rivers, [d]which hath said, My river *is*
mine own, and I have made *it* for
myself.
4 But [e]I will put hooks in thy jaws,
and I will cause the fish of thy rivers to
stick unto thy scales, and I will bring
thee up out of the midst of thy rivers,
and all the fish of thy rivers shall stick
unto thy scales.
5 And I will leave thee *thrown* into
the wilderness, thee and all the fish of
thy rivers: thou shalt fall upon the
[1]open fields; [f]thou shalt not be brought
together, nor gathered: [g]I have given
thee for meat to the beasts of the field
and to the fowls of the heaven.
6 And all the inhabitants of Ē'ġypt
shall know that I *am* the LORD, because they have been a [h]staff of reed
to the house of Ĭs'ra-el.
7 [i]When they took hold of thee by
thy hand, thou didst break, and rend all
their shoulder: and when they leaned
upon thee, thou brakest, and madest all
their loins to be at a stand.
8 ¶ Therefore thus saith the Lord
GOD; Behold, I will bring a sword upon
thee, and cut off man and beast out of
thee.
9 And the land of Ē'ġypt shall be
desolate and waste; and they shall
know that I *am* the LORD: [j]because he
hath said, The river *is* mine, and I have
made *it.*
10 Behold, therefore I *am* against
thee, and against thy rivers, [k]and I
will make the land of Ē'ġypt [2]utterly
waste *and* desolate, [3]from the tower
of [4]Sȳ-ē'ne even unto the border of
Ē-thĭ-ō'pĭ-a.
11 [l]No foot of man shall pass through
it, nor foot of beast shall pass through it,
neither shall it be inhabited forty years.
12 [m]And I will make the land of
Ē'ġypt desolate in the midst of the
countries *that are* desolate, and her cities among the cities *that are* laid waste
shall be desolate forty years: and I will
scatter the E-ġȳp''tians among the nations, and will disperse them through
the countries.
13 ¶ Yet thus saith the Lord GOD; At
the [n]end of forty years will I gather the
E-ġȳp''tians from the people whither
they were scattered:
14 And I will bring again the captivity of Ē'ġypt, and will cause them to
return *into* the land of Păth'ros, into
the land of their [5]habitation; and they
shall be there a [6]base kingdom.
15 It shall be the basest of the kingdoms; neither shall it exalt itself any
more above the nations: for I will

[j]ch. 26.13
14 [k]Ex. 25.20
[l]ch. 20.40
17 [m]2 Pet. 2.6; Jude 7
18 [7]palaces
[n]Amos 1.10
19 [8]terrors
21 [o]Isa. 23.4-12; Jer. 25.22; ch. 32.30
22 [p]Ex. 14.4; ch. 39.13
[q]Ps. 9.16
[r]ch. 20.41
23 [s]ch. 38.22
24 [t]Num. 33.55; Josh. 23.13
25 [u]Isa. 11.12; Hos. 1.1; ch. 20.41
26 [9]Or, with confidence
[v]Isa. 65.21; Amos 9.14
[w]Jer. 31.5
[10]Or, spoil

CHAPTER 29
2 [a]Isa. 19.1; Jer. 25.19
3 [b]Jer. 44.30; ch. 28.22
[c]Ps. 74.13-14; Isa. 27.1; ch. 32.2
[d]ch. 28.2
4 [e]2 Ki. 19.28; Isa. 37.29; ch. 38.4
5 [1]face of the field
[f]Jer. 8.2
[g]Jer. 7.33
6 [h]2 Ki. 18.21; Isa. 36.6
7 [i]Jer. 37.5
9 [j]Prov. 16.18
10 [k]ch. 30.12
[2]wastes of waste
[3]Or, from Migdol to Syene
[4]Seveneh
11 [l]Jer. 43.11-12; ch. 30.10-13
12 [m]Jer. 25.17-18; ch. 30.7
13 [n]Isa. 19.23; Jer. 46.25-26
14 [5]Or, birth
[6]low, that is, tributary

diminish them, that they shall no more rule over the nations.

16 And it shall be no more [o]the confidence of the house of Is'ra-el, which bringeth *their* iniquity to remembrance, when they shall look after them: but they shall know that I *am* the Lord GOD.

17 ¶ And it came to pass in the seven and twentieth year, in the first *month,* in the first *day* of the month, the word of the LORD came unto me, saying,

18 Son of man, [p]Nĕb-u-chăd-rĕz'-zar king of Băb'ȳ-lon caused his army to serve a great service against Tȳ'rus: every head *was* made bald, and every shoulder *was* peeled: yet had he no wages, nor his army, for Tȳ'rus, for the service that he had served against it:

19 Therefore thus saith the Lord GOD; Behold, I will give the land of Ē'ġypt unto Nĕb-u-chăd-rĕz'zar king of Băb'ȳ-lon; and he shall take her multitude, and [7]take her spoil, and take her prey; and it shall be the wages for his army.

20 I have given him the land of Ē'ġypt [8]*for* his labour wherewith he [q]served against it, because they wrought for me, saith the Lord GOD.

21 ¶ In that day [r]will I cause the horn of the house of Is'ra-el to bud forth, and I will give thee [s]the opening of the mouth in the midst of them; and they shall know that I *am* the LORD.

30

The word of the LORD came again unto me, saying,

2 Son of man, prophesy and say, Thus saith the Lord GOD; [a]Howl ye, Woe worth the day!

3 For [b]the day *is* near, even the day of the LORD *is* near, a cloudy day; it shall be the time of the heathen.

4 And the sword shall come upon Ē'ġypt, and great [1]pain shall be in Ē-thĭ-ō'pĭ-a, when the slain shall fall in Ē'ġypt, and they shall [c]take away her multitude, and [d]her foundations shall be broken down.

5 Ē-thĭ-ō'pĭ-a, and [2]Lĭb'ȳ-ȧ, and Lȳd'ĭ-ȧ, and [e]all the mingled people, and Chŭb, and the [3]men of the land that is in league, shall fall with them by the sword.

6 Thus saith the LORD; They also that uphold Ē'ġypt shall fall; and the pride of her power shall come down: [4]from the tower of Sȳ-ē'ne shall they fall in it by the sword, saith the Lord GOD.

7 [f]And they shall be desolate in the midst of the countries *that are* desolate, and her cities shall be in the midst of the cities *that are* wasted.

8 And they shall know that I *am* the LORD, when I have set a fire in Ē'ġypt, and *when* all her helpers shall be [5]destroyed.

9 In that day [g]shall messengers go forth from me in ships to make the careless Ē-thĭ-ō'pĭ-ans afraid, and [h]great pain shall come upon them, as in the day of Ē'ġypt: for, lo, it cometh.

10 Thus saith the Lord GOD; [i]I will also make the multitude of Ē'ġypt to cease by the hand of Nĕb-u-chăd-rĕz'-zar king of Băb'ȳ-lon.

11 He and his people with him, [j]the terrible of the nations, shall be brought to destroy the land: and they shall draw their swords against Ē'ġypt, and fill the land with the slain.

12 And I will make the rivers [6]dry, and [k]sell the land into the hand of the wicked: and I will make the land waste, and [7]all that is therein, by the hand of strangers: I the LORD have spoken *it.*

13 Thus saith the Lord GOD; I will also [l]destroy the idols, and I will cause *their* [8]images to cease out of [9]Nŏph; [m]and there shall be no more a prince of the land of Ē'ġypt: [n]and I will put a fear in the land of Ē'ġypt.

14 And I will make [o]Păth'ros desolate, and will set fire in [10]Zō'an, and will execute judgments in [11]Nō.

15 And I will pour my fury upon [12]Sĭn, the strength of Ē'ġypt; and I will cut off the multitude of Nō.

16 And I will set fire in Ē'ġypt: Sĭn shall have great pain, and Nō shall be rent asunder, and Nŏph *shall have* distresses daily.

17 The young men of [13]Ā'ven and of [14]Pī-bē'seth shall fall by the sword: and these *cities* shall go into captivity.

18 [p]At Te-haph'ne-hēs also the day shall be [15]darkened, when I shall break there the yokes of Ē'ġypt: and the pomp of her strength shall cease in her: as for her, a cloud shall cover her, and her daughters shall go into captivity.

19 Thus will I execute judgments in Ē'ġypt: and they shall know that I *am* the LORD.

20 ¶ And it came to pass in the eleventh year, in the first *month,* in the seventh *day* of the month, *that* the word of the LORD came unto me, saying,

21 Son of man, I have [q]broken the arm of Phā'raōh king of Ē'ġypt; and, lo, [r]it shall not be bound up to be healed, to put a roller to bind it, to make it strong to hold the sword.

22 Therefore thus saith the Lord GOD; Behold, I *am* against Phā'raōh king of Ē'ġypt, and will [s]break his arms, the strong, and [t]that which was broken; and I will cause the sword to fall out of his hand.

23 [u]And I will scatter the Ē-ġȳp'tians among the nations, and will disperse them through the countries.

24 And I will strengthen the arms of the king of Băb'ȳ-lon, and put my sword in his hand: but I will break Phā'raōh's arms, and he shall groan before him with the groanings of a deadly wounded *man.*

25 But I will strengthen the arms of the king of Băb'ȳ-lon, and the arms of Phā'raōh shall fall down; and [v]they shall know that I *am* the LORD, when I shall put my sword into the hand of the king of Băb'ȳ-lon, and he shall stretch it out [w]upon the land of Ē'ġypt.

26 And I will scatter the Ē-ġȳp'tians among the nations, and disperse them among the countries; and they shall know that I *am* the LORD.

---

16 [o]Isa. 30.2; Jer. 2.18-19; Lam. 4.17
18 [p]Jer. 27.6; ch. 26.7
19 [7]spoil her spoil, and prey her prey
20 [8]Or, for his hire
[q]Jer. 25.9
21 [r]1 Sam. 2.10; Ps. 132.17
[s]Gen. 18.17; ch. 3.26; Dan. 9.22-27; Amos 3.7

CHAPTER 30
2 [a]Isa. 13.6
3 [b]ch. 7.7; Joel 2.1
4 [1]Or, fear
[c]ch. 29.19
[d]Jer. 50.15
5 [2]Phut
[e]Jer. 25.20
[3]children
6 [4]Or, from Migdol to Syene
7 [f]ch. 29.12
8 [5]broken
9 [g]Isa. 18.1-2; Zeph. 2.12
[h]Ps. 48.6; Isa. 19.17; ch. 26.16
10 [i]ch. 29.19
11 [j]ch. 28.7
12 [6]drought
[k]Isa. 19.4
[7]the fulness thereof
13 [l]Ex. 23.13; Zech. 13.2
[8]Or, nonentities
[9]Or, Memphis
[m]Zech. 10.11
[n]Isa. 19.16
14 [o]ch. 29.14
[10]Or, Tanis
[11]Or, Thebes
15 [12]Or, Pelusium
17 [13]Or, Heliopolis, or, On
[14]Or, Pubastum
18 [p]Jer. 2.16
[15]Or, restrained
21 [q]Jer. 48.25
[r]Jer. 46.11
22 [s]Ps. 37.17
[t]2 Ki. 24.7
23 [u]ch. 29.12
25 [v]Ex. 7.5; Ps. 9.16; Ps. 59.13
[w]Jer. 44.30

31

31 And it came to pass in the eleventh year, in the third *month,*
in the first *day* of the month, *that*
the word of the LORD came unto me,
saying,
2 Son of man, speak unto Phā′raōh
king of Ē′gypt, and to his multitude;
Whom art thou like in thy greatness?
3 ¶ [a]Behold, the Ăs-sўr′ĭ-an *was* a
cedar in Lĕb′a-non [1]with fair branches,
and with a shadowing shroud, and of
an high stature; and his top was among
the thick boughs.
4 The waters [2]made him great, the
deep [3]set him up on high with her rivers running round about his plants,
and sent out her [4]little rivers unto all
the trees of the field.
5 Therefore [b]his height was exalted
above all the trees of the field, and
his boughs were multiplied, and his
branches became long because of the
multitude of waters, [5]when he shot
forth.
6 All the [c]fowls of heaven made
their nests in his boughs, and under his
branches did all the beasts of the field
bring forth their young, and under his
shadow dwelt all great nations.
7 Thus was he fair in his greatness,
in the length of his branches: for his
root was by great waters.
8 The cedars in the [d]garden of God
could not hide him: the fir trees were
not like his boughs, and the chesnut
trees were not like his branches; nor
any tree in the garden of God was like
unto him in his beauty.
9 [e]I have made him fair by the multitude of his branches: so that all the
trees of Ē′dĕn, that *were* in the garden
of God, envied him.
10 ¶ Therefore thus saith the Lord
GOD; Because thou hast lifted up thyself in height, and he hath shot up his
top among the thick boughs, and [f]his
heart is lifted up in his height;
11 I have therefore delivered him
into the hand of the mighty one of the
heathen; [6]he shall surely deal with
him: I have driven him out for his
wickedness.
12 And strangers, [g]the terrible of
the nations, have cut him off, and have
left him: [h]upon the mountains and in
all the valleys his branches are fallen,
and his boughs are broken by all the
rivers of the land; and all the people of
the earth are gone down from his
shadow, and have left him.
13 [i]Upon his ruin shall all the fowls
of the heaven remain, and all the beasts
of the field shall be upon his branches:
14 To the end that none of all the
trees by the waters exalt themselves
for their height, neither shoot up their
top among the thick boughs, neither
their trees [7]stand up in their height, all
that drink water: for [j]they are all delivered unto death, [k]to the nether parts of
the earth, in the midst of the children
of men, with them that go down to the
pit.
15 Thus saith the Lord GOD; In the
day when he went down to the grave I
caused a mourning: I covered the deep
for him, and I restrained the floods
thereof, and the great waters were
stayed: and I caused Lĕb′a-non [8]to
mourn for him, and all the trees of the
field fainted for him.
16 I made the nations to [l]shake at
the sound of his fall, when [m]I cast him
down to hell with them that descend
into the pit: and [n]all the trees of Ē′dĕn,
the choice and best of Lĕb′a-non, all
that drink water, [o]shall be comforted
in the nether parts of the earth.
17 They also went down into hell
with him unto *them that be* slain with
the sword; and *they that were* his arm,
that [p]dwelt under his shadow in the
midst of the heathen.
18 ¶ [q]To whom art thou thus like in
glory and in greatness among the trees
of Ē′dĕn? yet shalt thou be brought
down with the trees of Ē′dĕn unto the
nether parts of the earth: [r]thou shalt
lie in the midst of the uncircumcised
with *them that be* slain by the sword.
[9]This is Phā′raōh and all his multitude,
saith the Lord GOD.

32

32 And it came to pass in the twelfth
year, in the twelfth month, in the
first *day* of the month, *that* the word of
the LORD came unto me, saying,
2 Son of man, [a]take up a lamentation for Phā′raōh king of Ē′gypt, and
say unto him, [b]Thou art like a young
lion of the nations, [c]and thou *art* as a
[1]whale in the seas: and thou camest
forth with thy rivers, and troubledst
the waters with thy feet, and [d]fouledst
their rivers.
3 Thus saith the Lord GOD; I will
therefore [e]spread out my net over thee
with a company of many people; and
they shall bring thee up in my net.
4 Then [f]will I leave thee upon the
land, I will cast thee forth upon the
open field, and [g]will cause all the
fowls of the heaven to remain upon
thee, and I will fill the beasts of the
whole earth with thee.
5 And I will lay thy flesh [h]upon the
mountains, and fill the valleys with thy
height.
6 I will also water with thy blood [2]the
land wherein thou swimmest, *even* to
the mountains; and the rivers shall be
full of thee.
7 And when I shall [3]put thee out, [i]I
will cover the heaven, and make the
stars thereof dark; I will cover the sun
with a cloud, and the moon shall not
give her light.
8 All the [4]bright lights of heaven
will I make [5]dark over thee, and set
darkness upon thy land, saith the Lord
GOD.
9 I will also [6]vex the hearts of many
people, when I shall bring thy destruction among the nations, into the countries which thou hast not known.
10 Yea, I will make many people
[j]amazed at thee, and their kings shall
be horribly afraid for thee, when I shall
brandish my sword before them; and
[k]they shall tremble at *every* moment,

CHAPTER 31
3 [a]Nah. 3.18; Zeph. 2.13 [1]fair of branches
4 [2]Or, nourished [3]Or, brought him up [4]Or, conduits
5 [b]Ps. 37.35-36; Dan. 4.11 [5]Or, when it sent them forth
6 [c]ch. 17.23; Dan. 4.12
8 [d]Gen. 2.8
9 [e]Ex. 9.16;
10 [f]2 Chr. 25.19;
11 [6]in doing he shall do unto him
12 [g]ch. 28.7 [h]ch. 32.5
13 [i]Isa. 18.6
14 [7]Or, stand upon themselves for their height [j]Ps. 82.7 [k]ch. 32.18
15 [8]to be black
16 [l]ch. 26.15 [m]Isa. 14.15 [n]Isa. 14.8 [o]ch. 32.31
17 [p]Lam. 4.20
18 [q]ch. 32.19 [r]ch. 28.10 [9]That is, an emblem of Pharaoh

CHAPTER 32
2 [a]ch. 27.2 [b]ch. 19.3-6 [c]ch. 29.3 [1]Or, dragon [d]ch. 34.18
3 [e]ch. 12.13
4 [f]1 Sam. 17.44-46; [g]1 Sam. 17.44
5 [h]ch. 31.12
6 [2]Or, the land of thy swimming
7 [3]Or, extinguish [i]Isa. 13.10;
8 [4]lights of the light in heaven [5]them dark
9 [6]provoke to anger, or, grief
10 [j]ch. 27.35 [k]ch. 26.16

every man for his own life, in the day of
thy fall.
11 ¶ [l]For thus saith the Lord GOD;
The sword of the king of Băb′y̆-lon
shall come upon thee.
12 By the swords of the mighty will I
cause thy multitude to fall, [m]the terrible of the nations, all of them: and
[n]they shall spoil the pomp of Ē′ġypt,
and all the multitude thereof shall be
destroyed.
13 I will destroy also all the beasts
thereof from beside the great waters;
[o]neither shall the foot of man trouble
them any more, nor the hoofs of beasts
trouble them.
14 Then will I make their waters
deep, and cause their rivers to run like
oil, saith the Lord GOD.
15 When I shall make the land of
Ē′ġypt desolate, and the country shall
be [7]destitute of that whereof it was full,
when I shall smite all them that dwell
therein, [p]then shall they know that I
am the LORD.
16 This *is* the [q]lamentation wherewith they shall lament her: the daughters of the nations shall lament her:
they shall lament for her, *even* for
Ē′ġypt, and for all her multitude, saith
the Lord GOD.
17 ¶ It came to pass also in the
twelfth year, in the fifteenth *day* of the
month, *that* the word of the LORD
came unto me, saying,
18 Son of man, wail for the multitude of Ē′ġypt, and [r]cast them down,
even her, and the daughters of the famous nations, unto the nether parts of
the earth, with them that go down into
the pit.
19 [s]Whom dost thou pass in beauty?
[t]go down, and be thou laid with the
uncircumcised.
20 They shall fall in the midst of
them that are slain by the sword: [8]she
is delivered to the sword: draw her and
all her multitudes.
21 [u]The strong among the mighty
shall speak to him out of the midst of
hell with them that help him: they are
gone down, they lie uncircumcised,
slain by the sword.
22 Ăssh′ụr *is* there and all her company: his graves *are* about him: all of
them slain, fallen by the sword:
23 [v]Whose graves are set in the sides
of the pit, and her company is round
about her grave: all of them slain, fallen
by the sword, which caused [9]terror in
the land of the living.
24 There *is* [w]Ē′lăm and all her multitude round about her grave, all of
them slain, fallen by the sword, which
are gone down uncircumcised into the
nether parts of the earth, which caused
their terror in the land of the living;
yet have they borne their shame with
them that go down to the pit.
25 They have set her a [10]bed in the
midst of the slain with all her multitude: her graves *are* round about him:
all of them uncircumcised, slain by the
sword: though their terror was caused
in the land of the living, yet have they

11 [l]Jer. 46.26
12 [m]ch. 28.7
[n]ch. 29.19
13 [o]ch. 29.11
15 [7]desolate from the fulness thereof
[p]Ex. 7.5; Ps. 9.16; ch. 6.6-7
16 [q]2 Sam. 1.17; 2 Chr. 35.25; ch. 26.17
18 [r]Jer. 1.10; ch. 26.20
19 [s]ch. 31.2
[t]ch. 28.10
20 [8]Or, the sword is laid
21 [u]Isa. 1.31
23 [v]Isa. 14.15
[9]Or, a dismaying
24 [w]Jer. 49.34
25 [10]Or, bier
26 [x]Gen. 10.2; ch. 27.13
27 [y]Isa. 14.18
[11]with weapons of their war
29 [z]ch. 25.12
[12]given, or, put
30 [a]ch. 38.6-15
[b]ch. 28.21
31 [c]ch. 14.22
CHAPTER 33
2 [a]ch. 3.11
[1]A land when I bring a sword upon her
[b]2 Sam. 18.24; Isa. 21.8; Hos. 9.8
4 [2]he that hearing heareth
[c]Lev. 20.9-11; 2 Sam. 1.16; ch. 18.13; Acts 18.6
6 [d]Isa. 56.10
7 [e]ch. 3.17; Hab. 2.1

borne their shame with them that go
down to the pit: he is put in the midst of
them that be slain.
26 There *is* [x]Mē′shech, Tụ′bal, and
all her multitude: her graves *are* round
about him: all of them uncircumcised,
slain by the sword, though they caused
their terror in the land of the living.
27 [y]And they shall not lie with the
mighty *that are* fallen of the uncircumcised, which are gone down to hell
[11]with their weapons of war: and they
have laid their swords under their
heads, but their iniquities shall be
upon their bones, though *they were*
the terror of the mighty in the land of
the living.
28 Yea, thou shalt be broken in the
midst of the uncircumcised, and shalt
lie with *them that are* slain with the
sword.
29 There *is* [z]Ē′dom, her kings, and
all her princes, which with their might
are [12]laid by *them that were* slain by
the sword: they shall lie with the uncircumcised, and with them that go down
to the pit.
30 [a]There *be* the princes of the north,
all of them, and all [b]the Zī-dō′nĭ-ans,
which are gone down with the slain;
with their terror they are ashamed of
their might; and they lie uncircumcised
with *them that be* slain by the sword,
and bear their shame with them that go
down to the pit.
31 Phā′raōh shall see them, and shall
be [c]comforted over all his multitude,
even Phā′raōh and all his army slain by
the sword, saith the Lord GOD.
32 For I have caused my terror in the
land of the living: and he shall be laid in
the midst of the uncircumcised with
them that are slain with the sword,
even Phā′raōh and all his multitude,
saith the Lord GOD.

33

Again the word of the LORD came
unto me, saying,
2 Son of man, speak to [a]the children of thy people, and say unto them,
[1]When I bring the sword upon a land,
if the people of the land take a man
of their coasts, and set him for their
[b]watchman:
3 If when he seeth the sword come
upon the land, he blow the trumpet,
and warn the people;
4 Then [2]whosoever heareth the
sound of the trumpet, and taketh not
warning; if the sword come, and take
him away, [c]his blood shall be upon his
own head.
5 He heard the sound of the trumpet, and took not warning; his blood
shall be upon him. But he that taketh
warning shall deliver his soul.
6 But if the watchman see the sword
come, and [d]blow not the trumpet, and
the people be not warned; if the sword
come, and take *any* person from among
them, he is taken away in his iniquity;
but his blood will I require at the watchman's hand.
7 ¶ [e]So thou, O son of man, I have
set thee a watchman unto the house of
Ĭs′ra-el; therefore thou shalt hear the

word at my mouth, and warn them from me.

8 When I say unto the wicked, [f]O wicked *man,* thou shalt surely die; if thou dost not speak to warn the wicked from his way, that wicked *man* shall die in his iniquity; but his blood will I require at thine hand.

9 Nevertheless, if thou warn the wicked of his way to turn from it; if [g]he do not turn from his way, he shall die in his iniquity; but thou hast delivered thy soul.

10 Therefore, O thou son of man, speak unto the house of Is'ra-el; Thus ye speak, saying, If our transgressions and our sins *be* upon us, and we [h]pine away in them, [i]how should we then live?

11 Say unto them, *As* I live, saith the Lord GOD, [j]I have no pleasure in the death of the wicked; but that the wicked turn from his way and live: turn ye, turn ye from your evil ways; for [k]why will ye die, O house of Is'ra-el?

12 Therefore, thou son of man, say unto the children of thy people, The [l]righteousness of the righteous shall not deliver him in the day of his transgression: as for the wickedness of the wicked, [m]he shall not fall thereby in the day that he turneth from his wickedness; neither shall the righteous be able to live for his *righteousness* in the day that he sinneth.

13 When I shall say to the righteous, *that* he shall surely live; [n]if he trust to his own righteousness, and commit iniquity, all his righteousnesses shall not be remembered; but for his iniquity that he hath committed, he shall die for it.

14 Again, when I say unto the wicked, Thou shalt surely die; if he turn from his sin, and do [3]that which is lawful and right;

15 *If* the wicked [o]restore the pledge, [p]give again that he had robbed, walk in [q]the statutes of life, without committing iniquity; he shall surely live, he shall not die.

16 None [r]of his sins that he hath committed shall be mentioned unto him: he hath done that which is lawful and right; he shall surely live.

17 ¶ Yet the children of thy people say, The way of the Lord is not equal: but as for them, their way is not equal.

18 When the righteous turneth from his righteousness, and committeth iniquity, he shall even die thereby.

19 But if the wicked turn from his wickedness, and do that which is lawful and right, he shall live thereby.

20 ¶ Yet ye say, [s]The way of the Lord is not equal. O ye house of Is'ra-el, I will judge you every one after his ways.

21 ¶ And it came to pass in the twelfth year [t]of our captivity, in the tenth *month,* in the fifth *day* of the month, [u]*that* one that had escaped out of Je-ru'sa-lĕm came unto me, saying, [v]The city is smitten.

22 Now [w]the hand of the LORD was upon me in the evening, afore he that was escaped came; and had opened my mouth, until he came to me in the morning; and my mouth was opened, and I was no more dumb.

23 Then the word of the LORD came unto me, saying,

24 Son of man, [x]they that inhabit those [y]wastes of the land of Is'ra-el speak, saying, [z]A'brā-hăm was one, and he inherited the land: [a]but we *are* many; the land is given us for inheritance.

25 Wherefore say unto them, Thus saith the Lord GOD; [b]Ye eat with the blood, and [c]lift up your eyes toward your idols, and [d]shed blood: and shall ye possess the land?

26 Ye stand upon your sword, ye work abomination, and ye defile every one his neighbour's wife: and shall ye possess the land?

27 Say thou thus unto them, Thus saith the Lord GOD; *As* I live, surely they that *are* in the wastes shall fall by the sword, and him that *is* in the open field [e]will I give to the beasts [4]to be devoured, and they that *be* in the forts and [f]in the caves shall die of the pestilence.

28 [g]For I will lay the land [5]most desolate, and the [h]pomp of her strength shall cease; and [i]the mountains of Is'ra-el shall be desolate, that none shall pass through.

29 Then shall they know that I *am* the LORD, when I have laid the land most desolate because of all their abominations which they have committed.

30 ¶ Also, thou son of man, the children of thy people still are talking [6]against thee by the walls and in the doors of the houses, and [j]speak one to another, every one to his brother, saying, Come, I pray you, and hear what is the word that cometh forth from the LORD.

31 And [k]they come unto thee [7]as the people cometh, and [8]they sit before thee *as* my people, and they hear thy words, but they will not do them: for with their mouth [9]they shew much love, *but* their heart goeth after their covetousness.

32 And, lo, thou *art* unto them as [10]a very lovely song of one that hath a pleasant voice, and can play well on an instrument: [l]for they hear thy words, but they do them not.

33 And when this cometh to pass, (lo, it will come,) then shall they know that a prophet hath been among them.

34 And the word of the LORD came unto me, saying,

2 Son of man, prophesy against the [a]shepherds of Is'ra-el, prophesy, and say unto them, Thus saith the Lord GOD unto the shepherds; [b]Woe *be* to the shepherds of Is'ra-el that do feed themselves! should not the shepherds feed the flocks?

3 [c]Ye eat the fat, and ye clothe you with the wool, [d]ye kill them that are fed: *but* ye feed not the flock.

8 [f]Prov. 8.36; Isa. 3.11
9 [g]Prov. 29.1; Luke 12.47; Acts 13.46; Heb. 2.2-3
10 [h]ch. 24.23
[i]Isa. 49.14
11 [j]2 Sam. 14.14; Lam. 3.33; Hos. 11.9; 1 Tim. 2.4
[k]Isa. 55.6-7; ch. 18.31
12 [l]ch. 3.20
[m]2 Chr. 7.14
13 [n]ch. 3.20; Luke 18.9
14 [3]judgment and justice
15 [o]ch. 18.7
[p]Ex. 22.1; Num. 5.6-7; Luke 19.8
[q]Lev. 18.5; ch. 20.11; Matt. 19.17
16 [r]ch. 18.22
20 [s]ch. 18.25
21 [t]ch. 1.2
[u]ch. 24.26
[v]2 Ki. 25.4
22 [w]ch. 1.3; ch. 3.22
24 [x]ch. 34.2
[y]ch. 36.4
[z]Isa. 51.2; Acts 7.5
[a]Mic. 3.11; John 8.39
25 [b]Gen. 9.4
[c]ch. 18.6
[d]ch. 22.6
27 [e]ch. 39.4
[4]to devour him
[f]Judg. 6.2
28 [g]2 Chr. 36.21; ch. 36.34
[5]desolation and desolation
[h]ch. 24.21
[i]ch. 6.2-3
30 [6]Or, of thee
[j]Isa. 29.13
31 [k]ch. 20.1
[7]according to the coming of the people
[8]Or, my people sit before thee
[9]they make loves, or, jests
32 [10]a song of loves
[l]Jas. 1.22

CHAPTER 34
2 [a]ch. 33.24
[b]Jer. 23.1
3 [c]Isa. 56.11
[d]Mic. 3.3

4 [e]The diseased have ye not strengthened, neither have ye healed that which
was sick, neither have ye bound up *that
which was* broken, neither have ye
brought again that which was driven
away, neither have ye [f]sought that
which was lost; but with [g]force and
with cruelty have ye ruled them.
5 And they were [h]scattered, [1]be-
cause *there is* no shepherd: [i]and they
became meat to all the beasts of the
field, when they were scattered.
6 My sheep wandered through all
the mountains, and upon every high
hill: yea, my flock was scattered upon
all the face of the earth, and none did
search or seek *after them.*
7 ¶ Therefore, ye shepherds, hear
the word of the LORD;
8 *As* I live, saith the Lord GOD, surely
because my flock became a prey, and
my flock became meat to every beast of
the field, because *there was* no shepherd, neither did my shepherds search
for my flock, but the shepherds fed
themselves, and fed not my flock;
9 Therefore, O ye shepherds, hear
the word of the LORD;
10 Thus saith the Lord GOD; Behold,
I *am* against the shepherds; and [j]I will
require my flock at their hand, and
cause them to cease from feeding the
flock; neither shall the shepherds feed
themselves any more; for I will deliver
my flock from their mouth, that they
may not be meat for them.
11 ¶ For thus saith the Lord GOD;
Behold, I, *even* I, will both search my
sheep, and seek them out.
12 [2]As a shepherd seeketh out his
flock in the day that he is among his
sheep *that are* scattered; so will I seek
out my sheep, and will deliver them
out of all places where they have been
scattered in [k]the cloudy and dark day.
13 And [l]I will bring them out from
the people, and gather them from the
countries, and will bring them to their
own land, and feed them upon the
mountains of Is'ra-el by the rivers,
and in all the inhabited places of the
country.
14 [m]I will feed them in a good pasture, and upon the high mountains of
Is'ra-el shall their fold be: [n]there shall
they lie in a good fold, and *in* a fat pasture shall they feed upon the mountains of Is'ra-el.
15 I will feed my flock, and I will
cause them to lie down, saith the Lord
GOD.
16 [o]I will seek that which was lost,
and bring again that which was driven
away, and will bind up *that which
was* broken, and will strengthen that
which was sick: but I will destroy the
fat and the strong; I will feed them
with judgment.
17 And *as for* you, O my flock, thus
saith the Lord GOD; [p]Behold, I judge
between [3]cattle and cattle, between the
rams and the [4]he goats.
18 *Seemeth it* a small thing unto
you to have eaten up the good pasture,
[q]but ye must tread down with your

4 [e]Zech. 11.16; 2 Tim. 2.24
[f]Luke 15.4
[g]1 Pet. 5.3
5 [h]Matt. 9.36
[1]Or, without a shepherd
[i]Isa. 56.9
10 [j]ch. 3.18; ch. 33.6-8; Heb. 13.17
12 [2]According to the seeking
[k]Jer. 13.16; ch. 30.3; Joel 2.2; Zeph. 1.15; Acts 2.19-21
13 [l]Isa. 65.9-10; Jer. 23.3; Jer. 36.24
14 [m]Ps. 23.2; Ps. 34.8-10; John 10.9
[n]Jer. 33.12
16 [o]Isa. 40.11; Mark 2.17
17 [p]ch. 20.37; Matt. 25.32
[3]small cattle of lambs and kids
[4]great he goats
18 [q]Matt. 23.13
23 [r]Isa. 40.11; Heb. 13.20
[s]Jer. 30.9; ch. 37.24
24 [t]Gen. 17.7; Ex. 29.45
[u]Luke 1.32
25 [v]Lev. 26.6; Isa. 11.6
[w]Jer. 23.6
26 [x]Isa. 56.7
[y]Gen. 12.2
[z]Lev. 26.4
[a]Ps. 68.9; Mal. 3.10
27 [b]Ps. 85.12
[c]Jer. 2.20
[d]Jer. 25.14
28 [e]ch. 36.4
29 [5]Or, for renown
[6]taken away
30 [f]2 Tim. 1.12
31 [g]Ps. 100.3
CHAPTER 35
2 [a]Amos 1.11; Obad. 10
3 [1]desolation and desolation

feet the residue of your pastures? and
to have drunk of the deep waters, but
ye must foul the residue with your
feet?
19 And *as for* my flock, they eat that
which ye have trodden with your feet;
and they drink that which ye have
fouled with your feet.
20 ¶ Therefore thus saith the Lord
GOD unto them; Behold, I, *even* I, will
judge between the fat cattle and between the lean cattle.
21 Because ye have thrust with side
and with shoulder, and pushed all the
diseased with your horns, till ye have
scattered them abroad;
22 Therefore will I save my flock,
and they shall no more be a prey; and I
will judge between cattle and cattle.
23 And I will set up one [r]shepherd
over them, and he shall feed them,
[s]*even* my servant Dā'vid; he shall feed
them, and he shall be their shepherd.
24 And [t]I the LORD will be their
God, and my servant Dā'vid [u]a prince
among them; I the LORD have spoken
it.
25 And I will make with them a covenant of peace, and [v]will cause the evil
beasts to cease out of the land: and
they [w]shall dwell safely in the wilderness, and sleep in the woods.
26 And I will make them and the
places round about [x]my hill [y]a blessing; and I will [z]cause the shower to
come down in his season; there shall
be [a]showers of blessing.
27 And [b]the tree of the field shall
yield her fruit, and the earth shall yield
her increase, and they shall be safe in
their land, and shall know that I *am* the
LORD, when I have [c]broken the bands
of their yoke, and delivered them out
of the hand of those that [d]served themselves of them.
28 And they shall no more [e]be a prey
to the heathen, neither shall the beast
of the land devour them; but they shall
dwell safely, and none shall make
them afraid.
29 And I will raise up for them a
plant [5]of renown, and they shall be no
more [6]consumed with hunger in the
land, neither bear the shame of the heathen any more.
30 Thus shall they [f]know that I the
LORD their God *am* with them, and
that they, *even* the house of Is'ra-el,
are my people, saith the Lord GOD.
31 And ye my [g]flock, the flock of
my pasture, *are* men, *and* I *am* your
God, saith the Lord GOD.

35 Moreover the word of the LORD
came unto me, saying,
2 Son of man, set thy face against
mount Sē'ĭr, and [a]prophesy against it,
3 And say unto it, Thus saith the
Lord GOD; Behold, O mount Sē'ĭr, I *am*
against thee, and I will stretch out
mine hand against thee, and I will
make thee [1]most desolate.
4 I will lay thy cities waste, and thou
shalt be desolate, and thou shalt know
that I *am* the LORD.

5 Because thou hast had a [2]perpetual hatred, and hast [3]shed *the blood of* the children of Ĭs′ra-el by the [4]force of the sword in the time of their calamity, [b]in the time *that their* iniquity *had* an end:

6 Therefore, *as* I live, saith the Lord GOD, I will prepare thee unto blood, and blood shall pursue thee: [c]sith thou hast not hated blood, even blood shall pursue thee.

7 Thus will I make mount Sē′ĭr [5]most desolate, and cut off from it him that passeth out and him that returneth.

8 And I will fill his mountains with his slain *men:* in thy hills, and in thy valleys, and in all thy rivers, shall they fall that are slain with the sword.

9 [d]I will make thee perpetual desolations, and thy cities shall not return: and ye shall know that I *am* the LORD.

10 Because thou hast said, [e]These two nations and these two countries shall be mine, and we will possess it; [6]whereas the LORD was there:

11 Therefore, *as* I live, saith the Lord GOD, I will even do [f]according to thine anger, and according to thine envy which thou hast used out of thy hatred against them; and I will make myself [g]known among them, when I have judged thee.

12 [h]And thou shalt know that I *am* the LORD, *and that* I have heard all thy blasphemies which thou hast spoken against the mountains of Ĭs′ra-el, saying, They are laid desolate, they are given us [7]to consume.

13 Thus with your mouth ye have [8]boasted against me, and have multiplied your words against me: I have heard *them.*

14 Thus saith the Lord GOD; When [i]the whole earth rejoiceth, I will make thee desolate.

15 [j]As thou didst rejoice at the inheritance of the house of Ĭs′ra-el, because it was desolate, so will I do unto thee: thou shalt be desolate, O mount Sē′ĭr, and all I-dụ-mē′ȧ, *even* all of it: and they shall know that I *am* the LORD.

36 Also, thou son of man, prophesy unto the mountains of Ĭs′ra-el, and say, Ye mountains of Ĭs′ra-el, hear the word of the LORD:

2 Thus saith the Lord GOD; Because the enemy hath said against you, Aha, [a]even the ancient high places are ours in possession:

3 Therefore prophesy and say, Thus saith the Lord GOD; [1]Because they have made *you* desolate, and swallowed you up on every side, that ye might be a possession unto the residue of the heathen, and [2]ye are taken up in the lips of talkers, and *are* an infamy of the people:

4 Therefore, ye mountains of Ĭs′ra-el, hear the word of the Lord GOD; Thus saith the Lord GOD to the mountains, and to the hills, to the [3]rivers, and to the valleys, to the desolate wastes, and to the cities that are forsaken, which became a prey and [b]derision to the residue of the heathen that *are* round about;

5 Therefore thus saith the Lord GOD; [c]Surely in the fire of my jealousy have I spoken against the residue of the heathen, and against all I-dụ-mē′ȧ, [d]which have appointed my land into their possession with the joy of all *their* heart, with despiteful minds, to cast it out for a prey.

6 Prophesy therefore concerning the land of Ĭs′ra-el, and say unto the mountains, and to the hills, to the rivers, and to the valleys, Thus saith the Lord GOD; Behold, I have spoken in my jealousy and in my fury, because ye have [e]borne the shame of the heathen:

7 Therefore thus saith the Lord GOD; I have [f]lifted up mine hand, Surely the heathen that *are* about you, they shall bear their shame.

8 ¶ But ye, O mountains of Ĭs′ra-el, ye shall shoot forth your branches, and yield your fruit to my people of Ĭs′ra-el: for they are at hand to come.

9 For, behold, I *am* for you, [g]and I will turn unto you, and ye shall be tilled and sown:

10 And I will multiply men upon you, all the house of Ĭs′ra-el, *even* all of it: and the cities shall be inhabited, and [h]the wastes shall be builded:

11 And [i]I will multiply upon you man and beast; and they shall increase and bring fruit: and I will settle you after your old estates, and will do better *unto you* than at your beginnings: [j]and ye shall know that I *am* the LORD.

12 Yea, I will cause men to walk upon you, *even* my people Ĭs′ra-el; [k]and they shall possess thee, and thou shalt be their inheritance, and thou shalt no more henceforth [l]bereave them *of men.*

13 Thus saith the Lord GOD; Because they say unto you, [m]Thou *land* devourest up men, and hast bereaved thy nations;

14 Therefore thou shalt devour men no more, neither [4]bereave thy nations any more, saith the Lord GOD.

15 [n]Neither will I cause *men* to hear in thee the shame of the heathen any more, neither shalt thou bear the reproach of the people any more, neither shalt thou cause thy nations to fall any more, saith the Lord GOD.

16 ¶ Moreover the word of the LORD came unto me, saying,

17 Son of man, when the house of Ĭs′ra-el dwelt in their own land, [o]they defiled it by their own way and by their doings: their way was before me as [p]the uncleanness of a removed woman.

18 Wherefore I poured my fury upon them [q]for the blood that they had shed upon the land, and for their [5]idols *wherewith* they had polluted it:

19 And I [r]scattered them among the heathen, and they were dispersed through the countries: [s]according to their way and according to their doings I judged them.

5 [2]Or, hatred of old [3]poured out the children [4]hands [b]Ps. 137.7
6 [c]Ps. 109.17
7 [5]desolation and desolation
9 [d]Jer. 49.17; Mal. 1.3-4
10 [e]Ps. 83.4 [6]Or, though the LORD was there
11 [f]Ps. 137.7; Matt. 7.2 [g]Isa. 26.9
12 [h]Ps. 9.16 [7]to devour
13 [8]magnified
14 [i]Isa. 14.7-8
15 [j]Prov. 17.5; Obad. 12

CHAPTER 36

2 [a]Deut. 32.13; Ps. 78.69; Isa. 58.14; Hab. 3.19
3 [1]Because for because [2]Or, ye are made to come upon the lip of the tongue
4 [3]Or, bottoms, or, dales [b]Ps. 79.4
5 [c]Deut. 4.24; Zech. 1.15 [d]ch. 35.10
6 [e]Ps. 123.3-4; ch. 34.29
7 [f]ch. 20.5
9 [g]Hos. 2.21-22-23; Hag. 2.19
10 [h]Isa. 58.12; Amos 9.14
11 [i]Jer. 31.27; Jer. 33.12 [j]ch. 35.9; 1 John 5.20
12 [k]Obad. 17 [l]Jer. 15.7
13 [m]Num. 13.32
14 [4]Or, cause to fall
15 [n]Isa. 60.14; Zeph. 3.19-20
17 [o]Jer. 2.7 [p]Lev. 15.19
18 [q]ch. 16.36 [5]dung gods
19 [r]ch. 22.15 [s]ch. 7.3

20 And when they entered unto the
heathen, whither they went, they [t]pro-
faned my holy name, when they said
to them, These *are* the people of the
LORD, and are gone forth out of his
land.
21 ¶ But I had pity [u]for mine holy
name, which the house of Ĭs′ra-el had
profaned among the heathen, whither
they went.
22 Therefore say unto the house of
Ĭs′ra-el, Thus saith the Lord GOD; I do
not *this* for your sakes, O house of
Ĭs′ra-el, [v]but for mine holy name's
sake, which ye have profaned among
the heathen, whither ye went.
23 And I will sanctify my great name,
which was profaned among the heathen, which ye have profaned in the
midst of them; and the heathen shall
know that I *am* the LORD, saith the Lord
GOD, when I shall be [w]sanctified in you
before [6]their eyes.
24 For [x]I will take you from among
the heathen, and gather you out of all
countries, and will bring you into your
own land.
25 ¶ [y]Then will I sprinkle clean water upon you, and ye shall be clean:
[z]from all your filthiness, and from all
your idols, will I cleanse you.
26 A [a]new heart also will I give you,
and a new spirit will I put within you:
and I will take away the stony heart
out of your flesh, and I will give you an
heart of flesh.
27 And I will put my [b]spirit within
you, and cause you to walk in my statutes, and ye shall keep my judgments,
and do *them*.
28 [c]And ye shall dwell in the land
that I gave to your fathers; [d]and ye
shall be my people, and I will be your
God.
29 I will also [e]save you from all
your uncleannesses: and [f]I will call for
the corn, and will increase it, and [g]lay
no famine upon you.
30 And I will multiply the fruit of the
tree, and the increase of the field, that
ye shall receive no more reproach of
famine among the heathen.
31 Then [h]shall ye remember your
own evil ways, and your doings that
were not good, and [i]shall loathe yourselves in your own sight for your iniquities and for your abominations.
32 [j]Not for your sakes do I *this*,
saith the Lord GOD, be it known unto
you: be ashamed and confounded for
your own ways, O house of Ĭs′ra-el.
33 Thus saith the Lord GOD; In the
day that I shall have cleansed you from
all your iniquities I [k]will also cause
you to dwell in the cities, and the
wastes shall be builded.
34 [l]And the desolate land shall be
tilled, whereas it lay desolate in the
sight of all that passed by.
35 And they shall say, This land that
was desolate is become like the garden
of [m]Ē′dĕn; and the waste and desolate
and ruined cities *are become* fenced,
and are inhabited.

20 [t]Isa. 52.5; Rom. 2.24
21 [u]ch. 20.9
22 [v]Deut. 9.5; Ps. 106.8
23 [w]ch. 20.41 [6]Or, your
24 [x]ch. 34.13
25 [y]Num. 19.13; Isa. 52.15 [z]Jer. 33.8; 1 John 1.7
26 [a]Ps. 51.10; John 3.3-5; 2 Cor. 3.18
27 [b]ch. 37.14; Isa. 44.3; Rom. 8.4-9; Gal. 5.5; Eph. 1.13
28 [c]ch. 28.25 [d]Jer. 30.22
29 [e]Matt. 1.21 [f]Ps. 105.16 [g]ch. 34.27
31 [h]ch. 6.9 [i]Lev. 26.39; ch. 6.9
32 [j]Deut. 9.5; Dan. 9.19
33 [k]Rom. 8.30-31-32
34 [l]Jer. 25.9
35 [m]Isa. 51.3
36 [n]Ps. 58.11; ch. 17.24 [o]ch. 17.24; ch. 22.14
37 [p]Ps. 102.17; Isa. 45.11-19; Jer. 29.11-13; ch. 14.3; Zech. 13.9; Matt. 7.7-8; Phil. 4.6; Jas. 4.3
38 [7]flock of holy things

CHAPTER 37
1 [a]ch. 3.14; Luke 4.1
2 [1]Or, champaign
3 [b]1 Sam. 2.6; Rom. 4.17; 2 Cor. 1.9
4 [c]Isa. 55.11; Rom. 10.17
5 [d]Ps. 104.30
6 [e]ch. 6.7; Joel 2.27
9 [2]Or, breath [f]Ps. 104.30
10 [g]Rev. 11.11
11 [h]Ps. 141.7; Isa. 49.14
12 [i]Isa. 26.19; Hos. 1.11 [j]ch. 36.24; Ezra 1.1; Amos 9.14
14 [k]ch. 36.27

36 Then the heathen that are left
round about you shall [n]know that I the
LORD build the ruined *places, and* plant
that that was desolate: [o]I the LORD
have spoken *it*, and I will do *it*.
37 Thus saith the Lord GOD; [p]I will
yet *for* this be inquired of by the house
of Ĭs′ra-el, to do *it* for them; I will increase them with men like a flock.
38 As the [7]holy flock, as the flock of
Je-ru′sa-lĕm in her solemn feasts; so
shall the waste cities be filled with
flocks of men: and they shall know
that I *am* the LORD.

37 The hand of the LORD was upon
me, and carried me out [a]in the
spirit of the LORD, and set me down in
the midst of the valley which *was* full
of bones,
2 And caused me to pass by them
round about: and, behold, *there were*
very many in the open [1]valley; and, lo,
they were very dry.
3 And he said unto me, Son of man,
can these bones live? And I answered,
O Lord GOD, [b]thou knowest.
4 Again he said unto me, [c]Prophesy
upon these bones, and say unto them,
O ye dry bones, hear the word of the
LORD.
5 Thus saith the Lord GOD unto these
bones; Behold, I will [d]cause breath to
enter into you, and ye shall live:
6 And I will lay sinews upon you,
and will bring up flesh upon you, and
cover you with skin, and put breath in
you, and ye shall live; [e]and ye shall
know that I *am* the LORD.
7 So I prophesied as I was commanded: and as I prophesied, there
was a noise, and behold a shaking, and
the bones came together, bone to his
bone.
8 And when I beheld, lo, the sinews
and the flesh came up upon them, and
the skin covered them above: but *there*
was no breath in them.
9 Then said he unto me, Prophesy
unto the [2]wind, prophesy, son of man,
and say to the wind, Thus saith the
Lord GOD; [f]Come from the four winds,
O breath, and breathe upon these slain,
that they may live.
10 So I prophesied as he commanded
me, [g]and the breath came into them,
and they lived, and stood up upon their
feet, an exceeding great army.
11 ¶ Then he said unto me, Son
of man, these bones are the whole
house of Ĭs′ra-el: behold, they say,
[h]Our bones are dried, and our hope is
lost: we are cut off for our parts.
12 Therefore prophesy and say unto
them, Thus saith the Lord GOD; Behold, [i]O my people, I will open your
graves, and cause you to come up out
of your graves, and [j]bring you into the
land of Ĭs′ra-el.
13 And ye shall know that I *am*
the LORD, when I have opened your
graves, O my people, and brought you
up out of your graves,
14 And [k]shall put my spirit in you,
and ye shall live, and I shall place you
in your own land: then shall ye know

that I the LORD have spoken *it,* and
performed *it,* saith the LORD.
15 ¶ The word of the LORD came
again unto me, saying,
16 Moreover, thou son of man, [l]take
thee one stick, and write upon it, For
Jū'dah, and for [m]the children of Ĭs'ra-
el his companions: then take another
stick, and write upon it, For Jō'seph,
the stick of Ē'phră-ĭm, and *for* all the
house of Ĭs'ra-el his companions:
17 And join them one to another
into one stick; and they shall become
one in thine hand.
18 ¶ And when the children of thy
people shall speak unto thee, saying,
[n]Wilt thou not shew us what thou
meanest by these?
19 [o]Say unto them, Thus saith the
Lord GOD; Behold, I will take the stick
of Jō'seph, which *is* in the hand of
Ē'phră-ĭm, and the tribes of Ĭs'ra-el his
fellows, and will put them with him,
even with the stick of Jū'dah, and
make them one stick, and they shall be
one in mine hand.
20 ¶ And the sticks whereon thou
writest shall be in thine hand [p]before
their eyes.
21 And say unto them, Thus saith
the Lord GOD; Behold, [q]I will take the
children of Ĭs'ra-el from among the
heathen, whither they be gone, and
will gather them on every side, and
bring them into their own land:
22 And [r]I will make them one nation in the land upon the mountains of
Ĭs'ra-el; and [s]one king shall be king to
them all: and they shall be no more
two nations, neither shall they be divided into two kingdoms any more at
all:
23 [t]Neither shall they defile themselves any more with their idols, nor
with their detestable things, nor with
any of their transgressions: but [u]I will
save them out of all their dwellingplaces, wherein they have sinned, and
will cleanse them: so shall they be my
people, and I will be their God.
24 And [v]Dā'vid my servant *shall be*
king over them; and [w]they all shall
have one shepherd: they shall also
walk in my judgments, and observe
my statutes, and do them.
25 And they shall dwell in the land
that I have given unto Jā'cob my servant, wherein your fathers have dwelt;
and they shall dwell therein, *even* they,
and their children, and their children's
children [x]for ever: and [y]my servant
Dā'vid *shall be* their prince for ever.
26 Moreover I will make a [z]cove-
nant of peace with them; it shall be an
everlasting covenant with them: and I
will place them, and multiply them, and
will set my [a]sanctuary in the midst of
them for evermore.
27 [b]My tabernacle also shall be with
them: yea, I will be their God, and they
shall be my people.
28 And the heathen shall know that
I the LORD do sanctify Ĭs'ra-el, when
my sanctuary shall be in the midst of
them for evermore.

38 And the word of the LORD came
unto me, saying,
2 Son of man, set thy face against
[a]Gŏg, the land of Mā'gŏg, [1]the chief
prince of [b]Mē'shech and Tu̦'bal, and
prophesy against him,
3 And say, Thus saith the Lord GOD;
Behold, I *am* against thee, O Gŏg, the
chief prince of Mē'shech and Tu̦'bal:
4 And [c]I will turn thee back, and put
hooks into thy jaws, and I will bring
thee forth, and all thine army, horses
and horsemen, [d]all of them clothed
with all sorts *of armour, even* a great
company *with* bucklers and shields,
all of them handling swords:
5 Pĕr'siȧ, Ē-thĭ-ō'pĭ-a, and [2]Lĭb'ȳ-ȧ
with them; all of them with shield and
helmet:
6 [e]Gō'mer, and all his bands; the
house of [f]To-gär'mah of the north
quarters, and all his bands: *and* many
people with thee.
7 [g]Be thou prepared, and prepare
for thyself, thou, and all thy company
that are assembled unto thee, and be
thou a guard unto them.
8 ¶ [h]After many days [i]thou shalt be
visited: in the latter years thou shalt
come into the land *that is* brought
back from the sword, [j]*and is* gathered
out of many people, against [k]the mountains of Ĭs'ra-el, which have been always waste: but it is brought forth out
of the nations, and they shall [l]dwell
safely all of them.
9 Thou shalt ascend and come [m]like
a storm, thou shalt be [n]like a cloud to
cover the land, thou, and all thy bands,
and many people with thee.
10 Thus saith the Lord GOD; It shall
also come to pass, *that* at the same
time shall things come into thy mind,
and thou shalt [3]think an evil thought:
11 And thou shalt say, I will go up to
the land of unwalled villages; I will [o]go
to them that are at rest, that dwell
[4]safely, all of them dwelling without
walls, and having neither bars nor
gates,
12 [5]To take a spoil, and to take a
prey; to turn thine hand upon the desolate places *that are now* inhabited, and
upon the people *that are* gathered out
of the nations, which have gotten cattle and goods, that dwell in the [6]midst
of the land.
13 [p]Shē'bȧ, and Dē'dan, and the
merchants of Tär'shish, with all [q]the
young lions thereof, shall say unto
thee, Art thou come to take a spoil?
hast thou gathered thy company to
take a prey? to carry away silver and
gold, to take away cattle and goods, to
take a great spoil?
14 ¶ Therefore, son of man, prophesy and say unto Gŏg, Thus saith the
Lord GOD; [r]In that day when my people of Ĭs'ra-el dwelleth safely, shalt
thou not know *it?*
15 [s]And thou shalt come from thy
place out of the north parts, thou, and
many people with thee, all of them riding upon horses, a great company, and
a mighty army:

16 [l]Num. 17.2
[m]2 Chr. 11.12-13-16
18 [n]ch. 12.9
19 [o]Zech. 10.6
20 [p]ch. 12.3
21 [q]ch. 36.24
22 [r]Isa. 11.13; Jer. 3.18; Hos. 1.11
[s]Gen. 49.10; Jer. 23.5-6; ch. 34.23; John 10.16
23 [t]Isa. 2.18; Zech. 13.1-2
[u]ch. 36.28-29
24 [v]Isa. 40.11; Luke 1.32
[w]Ps. 78.71-72; 1 Pet. 5.4
25 [x]Isa. 60.21; Amos 9.15
[y]John 12.34
26 [z]Ps. 89.3; ch. 34.25
[a]2 Cor. 6.16
27 [b]Lev. 26.11; John 1.14
CHAPTER 38
2 [a]Rev. 20.8
[1]Or, prince of the chief
[b]ch. 32.26
4 [c]ch. 29.4
[d]ch. 23.12
5 [2]Or, Phut
6 [e]Gen. 10.2
[f]ch. 27.14
7 [g]Isa. 8.9
8 [h]Deut. 4.30
[i]Isa. 29.6
[j]ch. 34.13
[k]ch. 36.1
[l]Jer. 23.6
9 [m]Isa. 28.2
[n]Jer. 4.13
10 [3]Or, conceive a mischievous purpose
11 [o]Judg. 18.7-27
[4]Or, confidently
12 [5]To spoil the spoil, and to prey the prey
[6]navel
13 [p]ch. 27.22
[q]ch. 19.3-5
14 [r]Isa. 4.1
15 [s]ch. 39.2

16 And thou shalt come up against
my people of Ĭs′ra-el, as a cloud to
cover the land; [t]it shall be in the latter
days, and I will bring thee against my
land, that the heathen may know me,
when I shall be sanctified in thee, O
Gŏg, before their eyes.
17 Thus saith the Lord GOD; *Art*
thou he of whom I have spoken in
old time [7]by my servants the prophets
of Ĭs′ra-el, which prophesied in those
days *many* years that I would bring
thee against them?
18 And it shall come to pass at the
same time when Gŏg shall come against
the land of Ĭs′ra-el, saith the Lord GOD,
that my fury shall come up in my face.
19 For [u]in my jealousy [v]*and* in the
fire of my wrath have I spoken, [w]Surely
in that day there shall be a great shaking in the land of Ĭs′ra-el;
20 So that [x]the fishes of the sea, and
the fowls of the heaven, and the beasts
of the field, and all creeping things that
creep upon the earth, and all the men
that *are* upon the face of the earth,
shall shake at my presence, [y]and the
mountains shall be thrown down, and
the [8]steep places shall fall, and every
wall shall fall to the ground.
21 And I will [z]call for a sword against
him throughout all my mountains, saith
the Lord GOD: every man's sword shall
be against his brother.
22 And I will plead against him with
pestilence and with blood; and I will
rain upon him, and upon his bands,
and upon the many people that *are*
with him, an overflowing rain, and
great hailstones, fire, and brimstone.
23 Thus will I magnify myself, and
sanctify myself; and I will be known in
the eyes of many nations, and they
shall know that I *am* the LORD.

39 Therefore, [a]thou son of man,
prophesy against Gŏg, and say,
Thus saith the Lord GOD; Behold, I *am*
against thee, O Gŏg, the chief prince of
Mē′shech and Tŭ′bal:
2 And I will turn thee back, and
[1]leave but the sixth part of thee, [2]and
will cause thee to come up from [3]the
north parts, and will bring thee upon
the mountains of Ĭs′ra-el:
3 And I will smite thy bow out of thy
left hand, and will cause thine arrows
to fall out of thy right hand.
4 Thou shalt fall upon the mountains
of Ĭs′ra-el, thou, and all thy bands, and
the people that *is* with thee: [b]I will give
thee unto the ravenous birds of every
[4]sort, and *to* the beasts of the field [5]to
be devoured.
5 Thou shalt fall upon [6]the open
field: for I have spoken *it,* saith the
Lord GOD.
6 [c]And I will send a fire on Mā′gŏg,
and among them that dwell [7]carelessly
in [d]the isles: and they shall know that I
am the LORD.
7 So will I make my holy name
known in the midst of my people Ĭs′ra-
el; and I will not *let them* [e]pollute my
holy name any more: [f]and the heathen
shall know that I *am* the LORD, the
Holy One in Ĭs′ra-el.
8 ¶ [g]Behold, it is come, and it is
done, saith the Lord GOD; this *is* the
day [h]whereof I have spoken.
9 And they that dwell in the cities of
Ĭs′ra-el shall go forth, and shall set on
fire and burn the weapons, both the
shields and the bucklers, the bows and
the arrows, and the [8]handstaves, and
the spears, and they shall [9]burn them
with fire seven years:
10 So that they shall take no wood
out of the field, neither cut down *any*
out of the forests; for they shall burn
the weapons with fire: [i]and they shall
spoil those that spoiled them, and rob
those that robbed them, saith the Lord
GOD.
11 ¶ And it shall come to pass in that
day, *that* I will give unto Gŏg a place
there of graves in Ĭs′ra-el, the valley of
the passengers on the east of the sea:
and it shall stop the [10]*noses* of the passengers: and there shall they bury Gŏg
and all his multitude: and they shall
call *it* The valley of [11]Hā′mon–gŏg.
12 And seven months shall the house
of Ĭs′ra-el be burying of them, [j]that
they may cleanse the land.
13 Yea, all the people of the land
shall bury *them;* and it shall be to them
[12]a renown the day that [k]I shall be glorified, saith the Lord GOD.
14 And they shall sever out [13]men
of continual employment, passing
through the land to bury with the passengers those that remain upon the
face of the earth, to cleanse it: after the
end of seven months shall they search.
15 And the passengers *that* pass
through the land, when *any* seeth a
man's bone, then shall he [14]set up a
sign by it, till the buriers have buried it
in the valley of Hā′mon–gŏg.
16 And also the name of the city
shall be [15]Ha-mō′nah. Thus shall they
cleanse the land.
17 ¶ And, thou son of man, thus
saith the Lord GOD; Speak [16]unto every feathered fowl, and to every beast
of the field, [l]Assemble yourselves, and
come; gather yourselves on every side
to my [17]sacrifice that I do sacrifice for
you, *even* a great sacrifice upon the
mountains of Ĭs′ra-el, that ye may eat
flesh, and drink blood.
18 Ye [m]shall eat the flesh of the
mighty, and drink the blood of the
princes of the earth, of rams, of lambs,
and of [18]goats, of bullocks, all of them
[n]fatlings of Bā′shăn.
19 And ye shall eat fat till ye be full,
and drink blood till ye be drunken, of
my sacrifice which I have sacrificed
for you.
20 [o]Thus ye shall be filled at my table with horses and chariots, [p]with
mighty men, and with all [19]men of war,
saith the Lord GOD.
21 [q]And I will set my glory among
the heathen, and all the heathen shall
see my judgment that I have executed,
and [r]my hand that I have laid upon
them.

16 [t]Ex. 14.4
17 [7]by the hands
19 [u]Deut. 29.20; [v]Ps. 89.46 [w]Hag. 2.6-7
20 [x]Hos. 4.3 [y]Jer. 4.24 [8]Or, towers, or, stairs
21 [z]Ps. 105.16

CHAPTER 39
1 [a]ch. 38.2
2 [1]Or, strike thee with six plagues; or, draw thee back with an hook of six teeth [2]Or, after I have caused and have brought [3]the sides of the north
4 [b]Isa. 34.2-8; [4]wing [5]to devour
5 [6]the face of the field
6 [c]Amos 1.4 [7]Or, confidently [d]Ps. 72.10
7 [e]Lev. 18.21 [f]ch. 38.16
8 [g]ch. 7.3-8 [h]ch. 38.17
9 [8]Or, javelins [9]Or, make a fire of them, or, use them for fuel
10 [i]Isa. 14.2
11 [10]Or, mouths [11]That is, The multitude of Gog
12 [j]Deut. 21.23
13 [12]Or, a day of renown [k]Ps. 126.2
14 [13]men of continuance
15 [14]build
16 [15]That is, The multitude
17 [16]to the fowl of every wing [l]Isa. 18.6 [17]Or, slaughter
18 [m]ch. 29.4 [18]great goats [n]Deut. 32.14;
20 [o]Ps. 76.6; [p]Rev. 19.18 [19]champions of war
21 [q]Ex. 9.16; [r]Ex. 7.4

22 So the house of Ĭs′ra-el shall know
that I *am* the LORD their God from that
day and forward.
23 ¶ And the heathen shall know
that the house of Ĭs′ra-el went into captivity for their iniquity: because they
trespassed against me, therefore [s]hid I
my face from them, and [t]gave them
into the hand of their enemies: so fell
they all by the sword.
24 [u]According to their uncleanness
and according to their transgressions
have I done unto them, and hid my
face from them.
25 Therefore thus saith the Lord
GOD; [v]Now will I bring again the captivity of Jā′cob, and have mercy upon
the [w]whole house of Ĭs′ra-el, and will
be jealous for my holy name;
26 [x]After that they have borne their
shame, and all their trespasses whereby
they have trespassed against me, when
they [y]dwelt safely in their land, and
none made *them* afraid.
27 [z]When I have brought them again
from the people, and gathered them out
of their enemies' lands, and [a]am sanctified in them in the sight of many
nations;
28 [b]Then shall they know that I *am*
the LORD their God, [20]which caused
them to be led into captivity among the
heathen: but I have gathered them
unto their own land, and have left none
of them any more there.
29 [c]Neither will I hide my face any
more from them: for I have [d]poured
out my spirit upon the house of Ĭs′ra-
el, saith the Lord GOD.
40 In the five and twentieth year of
our captivity, in the beginning of
the year, in the tenth *day* of the month,
in the fourteenth year after that [a]the
city was smitten, in the selfsame day
[b]the hand of the LORD was upon me,
and brought me thither.
2 [c]In the visions of God brought he
me into the land of Ĭs′ra-el, [d]and set
me upon a very high mountain, [1]by
which *was* as the frame of a city on the
south.
3 And he brought me thither, and,
behold, *there was* a man, whose appearance *was* [e]like the appearance of
brass, [f]with a line of flax in his hand,
[g]and a measuring reed; and he stood
in the gate.
4 And the man said unto me, [h]Son
of man, behold with thine eyes, and
hear with thine ears, and set thine
heart upon all that I shall shew thee;
for to the intent that I might shew *them*
unto thee *art* thou brought hither: [i]de-
clare all that thou seest to the house of
Ĭs′ra-el.
5 And behold [j]a wall on the outside
of the house round about, and in the
man's hand a measuring reed of six cubits *long* by the cubit and an hand
breadth: so he measured the breadth of
the building, one reed; and the height,
one reed.
6 ¶ Then came he unto the gate
[2]which looketh toward the east, and
went up the stairs thereof, and measured the threshold of the gate, *which*
was one reed broad; and the other
threshold *of the gate, which was* one
reed broad.
7 And *every* [k]little chamber *was*
one reed long, and one reed broad; and
between the little chambers *were* five
cubits; and the threshold of the gate by
the porch of the gate within *was* one
reed.
8 He measured also the porch of the
gate within, one reed.
9 Then measured he the porch of
the gate, eight cubits; and the posts
thereof, two cubits; and the porch of
the gate *was* inward.
10 [l]And the little chambers of the
gate eastward *were* three on this side,
and three on that side; they three *were*
of one measure: and the posts had one
measure on this side and on that side.
11 And he measured the breadth of
the entry of the gate, ten cubits; *and*
the [3]length of the gate, thirteen cubits.
12 The [4]space also before the little
chambers *was* one cubit *on this side,*
and the space *was* one cubit on that
side: and the little chambers *were* six
cubits on this side, and six cubits on
that side.
13 He measured then the gate from
the roof of *one* little chamber to the
roof of another: the breadth *was* five
and twenty cubits, door against door.
14 He made also [5]posts of threescore cubits, even unto the post of the
[m]court round about the gate.
15 And from the face of the gate of
the entrance unto the face of the porch
of the inner gate *were* fifty cubits.
16 And *there were* [6]narrow windows
to the little chambers, and to their posts
within the gate round about, and likewise to the [7]arches: and windows *were*
round about [8]inward: and upon *each*
post *were* palm trees.
17 Then brought he me into [n]the outward court, and, lo, *there were* [9]cham-
bers, and a pavement made for the
court round about: [o]thirty chambers
were upon the pavement.
18 And the pavement by the side of
the gates over against the length of the
gates *was* the lower pavement.
19 Then he measured the breadth
from the forefront of the lower gate
unto the forefront of the inner court
[10]without, an hundred cubits eastward
and northward.
20 ¶ And the gate of the outward
court [11]that looked toward the north,
he measured the length thereof, and
the breadth thereof.
21 And the little chambers thereof
were three on this side and three on
that side; and the posts thereof and the
[12]arches thereof were after the measure of the first gate: the length thereof
was fifty cubits, and the breadth five
and twenty cubits.
22 And their windows, and their
arches, and their palm trees, *were* after
the measure of the gate that looketh
toward the east; and they went up unto

23 [s]Deut. 31.17
[t]Lev. 26.25
24 [u]ch. 36.19
25 [v]Jer. 30.3
[w]Hos. 1.11
26 [x]Dan. 9.16
[y]Lev. 26.5
27 [z]ch. 28.25
[a]ch. 36.23
28 [b]ch. 34.30; Hos. 2.20
[20]by my causing of them, etc
29 [c]Isa. 54.8
[d]Joel 2.28

CHAPTER 40
1 [a]ch. 33.21
[b]ch. 1.3
2 [c]ch. 8.3
[d]Rev. 21.10
[1]Or, upon which
3 [e]Dan. 10.6
[f]ch. 47.3
[g]Rev. 11.1
4 [h]ch. 2.7-8; ch. 3.17
[i]ch. 43.10
5 [j]Isa. 26.1
6 [2]whose face was the way toward the east
7 [k]1 Chr. 9.18
10 [l]1 Chr. 26.12-13; Neh. 13.5-9-12-13; Song 1.4; Isa. 26.20; Jer. 35.2
11 [3]Or, height
12 [4]limit, or, bound
14 [5]Or, pillars, Prov. 9.1; Rev. 3.12
[m]Ex. 27.9; Lev. 6.16; Ps. 65.4; Ps. 84.2; Ps. 100.4; Isa. 54.2; Isa. 60.8-9; Isa. 62.9; ch. 8.7; ch. 42.1
16 [6]closed
[7]Or, galleries, or, porches
[8]Or, within
17 [n]Rev. 11.2
[9]Or, storehouses
[o]ch. 45.5
19 [10]Or, from without
20 [11]whose face was
21 [12]Or, galleries, or, porches

it by seven steps; and the arches thereof
were before them.
23 And the gate of the inner court
was over against the gate toward the
north, and toward the east; and he
measured from gate to gate an hundred cubits.
24 ¶ After that he brought me toward the south, and behold a gate toward the south: and he measured the
posts thereof and the arches thereof
according to these measures.
25 And *there were* [p]windows in it
and in the arches thereof round about,
like those windows: the length *was*
fifty cubits, and the breadth five and
twenty cubits.
26 And *there were* seven steps to go
up to it, and the arches thereof *were*
before them: and it had palm trees, one
on this side, and another on that side,
upon the posts thereof.
27 And *there was* a gate in the inner
court toward the south: and he measured from gate to gate toward the
south an hundred cubits.
28 And he brought me to the inner
court by the south gate: and he measured the south gate according to these
measures;
29 [q]And the little chambers thereof,
and the posts thereof, and the arches
thereof, according to these measures:
and *there were* windows in it and in
the arches thereof round about: *it was*
fifty cubits long, and five and twenty
cubits broad.
30 And the arches round about *were*
five and twenty cubits long, and five
cubits [13]broad.
31 And the arches thereof *were* toward the utter court; and [r]palm trees
were upon the posts thereof: and the
going up to it *had* eight steps.
32 ¶ And he brought me into the
inner court toward the east: and he
measured the gate according to these
measures.
33 And the little chambers thereof,
and the posts thereof, and the arches
thereof, *were* according to these measures: and *there were* windows therein
and in the arches thereof round about:
it was fifty cubits long, and five and
twenty cubits broad.
34 And the arches thereof *were* toward the outward court; and palm
trees *were* upon the posts thereof, on
this side, and on that side: and the going up to it *had* eight steps.
35 ¶ And he brought me to the north
gate, and measured *it* according to
these measures;
36 The little chambers thereof, the
posts thereof, and the arches thereof,
and the windows to it round about: the
length *was* fifty cubits, and the breadth
five and twenty cubits.
37 And the posts thereof *were* toward the utter court; and palm trees
were upon the posts thereof, on this
side, and on that side: and the going up
to it *had* eight steps.
38 And the chambers and the en-
tries thereof *were* by the posts of the
gates, where they [s]washed the burnt
offering.
39 ¶ And in the porch of the gate
were two tables on this side, and two
tables on that side, to slay thereon the
burnt offering and [t]the sin offering
and [u]the trespass offering.
40 And at the side without, [14]as one
goeth up to the entry of the north gate,
were two tables; and on the other side,
which *was* at the porch of the gate,
were two tables.
41 Four tables *were* on this side, and
four tables on that side, by the side of
the gate; eight tables, whereupon they
slew *their sacrifices*.
42 And the four tables *were* of hewn
stone for the burnt offering, of a cubit
and an half long, and a cubit and an
half broad, and one cubit high: whereupon also they laid the instruments
wherewith they slew the burnt offering and the sacrifice.
43 And within *were* [15]hooks, an hand
broad, fastened round about: and upon
the tables *was* the flesh of the offering.
44 ¶ And without the inner gate *were*
the chambers of [v]the singers in the inner court, which *was* at the side of the
north gate; and their prospect *was* toward the south: one at the side of the
east gate *having* the prospect toward
the north.
45 And he said unto me, This chamber, whose prospect *is* toward the
south, *is* for the priests, [w]the keepers
of the [16]charge of the house.
46 And the chamber whose prospect
is toward the north *is* for the priests,
[x]the keepers of the charge of the altar:
these *are* the sons of [y]Zā'dŏk among
the sons of Lē'vī, which [z]come near to
the LORD to minister unto him.
47 So he measured the court, an hundred cubits long, and an hundred cubits broad, foursquare; and the altar
that was before the house.
48 ¶ And he brought me to the porch
of the house, and measured *each* post
of the porch, five cubits on this side,
and five cubits on that side: and the
breadth of the gate *was* three cubits on
this side, and three cubits on that side.
49 [a]The length of the porch *was*
twenty cubits, and the breadth eleven
cubits; and *he brought me* by the steps
whereby they went up to it: and *there*
were [b]pillars by the posts, one on this
side, and another on that side.

41

Afterward he brought me to the
[a]temple, and measured the posts,
six cubits broad on the one side, and six
cubits broad on the other side, *which*
was the breadth of the tabernacle.
2 And the breadth of the [1]door *was*
ten cubits; and the sides of the door
were five cubits on the one side, and
five cubits on the other side: and he
measured the length thereof, forty cubits: and the breadth, twenty cubits.
3 Then went he inward, and measured the post of the door, two cubits; and the door, six cubits; and the
breadth of the door, seven cubits.

25 [p]1 Ki. 6.4; Isa. 54.12
29 [q]1 Ki. 6.5-6-10; 1 Chr. 28.11-12; 2 Chr. 3.9; 2 Chr. 31.11; Neh. 10.38-39; Neh. 12.44; Neh. 13.5-9-12-13; Jer. 35.2; Jer. 36.10
30 [13]breadth
31 [r]Ps. 92.12; Song 7.7; Jer. 10.5
38 [s]Lev. 1.9; Lev. 3.11; Heb. 9.14
39 [t]Lev. 4.2-3; Isa. 53.5; 2 Cor. 5.21; Tit. 2.14; Heb. 10.12-14; 1 Pet. 1.18-19; Rev. 5.9
[u]Lev. 5.6; Lev. 6.6; Lev. 7.1; Lev. 14.12-13; Lev. 19.21-22; Num. 6.12; ch. 42.13; ch. 44.29
40 [14]Or, at the step
43 [15]Or, endirons, or, the two hearthstones
44 [v]1 Chr. 6.31; Eph. 5.19; Col. 3.16
45 [w]Lev. 8.35; Num. 3.7; Deut. 11.1; 1 Ki. 2.3; Rev. 1.6
[16]Or, ward, or, ordinance
46 [x]Num. 18.5; ch. 44.15
[y]1 Ki. 2.35; ch. 43.19
[z]Eph. 2.17; Col. 4.12
49 [a]1 Ki. 6.3
[b]1 Ki. 7.21
CHAPTER 41
1 [a]Zech. 6.12; Matt. 16.18; 1 Cor. 3.16; 2 Cor. 6.16; Eph. 2.21; Rev. 3.12
2 [1]Or, entrance

4 So [b]he measured the length thereof, twenty cubits; and the breadth, twenty cubits, before the temple: and he said unto me, This *is* the most holy *place.*

5 After he measured the wall of the house, six cubits; and the breadth of *every* side chamber, four cubits, round about the house on every side.

6 [c]And the side chambers *were* three, [2]one over another, and [3]thirty in order; and they entered into the wall which *was* of the house for the side chambers round about, that they might [4]have hold, but they had not hold in the wall of the house.

7 And [5]*there was* an enlarging, and a winding about still upward to the side chambers: for the winding about of the house went still upward round about the house: therefore the breadth of the house *was still* upward, and so increased *from* the lowest *chamber* to the highest by the midst.

8 I saw also the height of the house round about: [d]the foundations of the side chambers *were* a full reed of six great cubits.

9 The thickness of the wall, which *was* for the side chamber without, *was* five cubits: and *that* which *was* left *was* the place of the side chambers that *were* within.

10 And between the chambers *was* the wideness of twenty cubits round about the house on every side.

11 And the doors of the side chambers *were* toward *the place that was* left, one door toward the north, and another door toward the south: and the breadth of the place that was left *was* five cubits round about.

12 Now the building that *was* before the separate place at the end toward the west *was* seventy cubits broad; and the wall of the building *was* five cubits thick round about, and the length thereof ninety cubits.

13 So he measured the house, an hundred cubits long; and the separate place, and the building, with the walls thereof, an hundred cubits long;

14 Also the breadth of the face of the house, and of the separate place toward the east, an hundred cubits.

15 And he measured the length of the building over against the separate place which *was* behind it, and the [6]galleries thereof on the one side and on the other side, an hundred cubits, with the inner temple, and the porches of the court;

16 The door posts, and [e]the narrow windows, and the galleries round about on their three stories, over against the door, [7]cieled with wood round about, [8]and from the ground up to the windows, and the windows *were* covered;

17 To that above the door, even unto the inner house, and without, and by all the wall round about within and without, by [9]measure.

18 And *it was* made [f]with cherubims and palm trees, so that a palm tree *was* between a cherub and a cherub; and *every* cherub had [g]two faces;

19 [h]So that the face of a man *was* toward the palm tree on the one side, and the face of a young lion toward the palm tree on the other side: *it was* made through all the house round about.

20 From the ground unto above the door *were* cherubims and palm trees made, and *on* the wall of the temple.

21 The [10]posts of the temple *were* squared, *and* the face of the sanctuary; the appearance *of the one* as the appearance *of the other.*

22 [i]The altar of wood *was* three cubits high, and the length thereof two cubits; and the corners thereof, and the length thereof, and the walls thereof, *were* of wood: and he said unto me, This *is* [j]the table that *is* [k]before the LORD.

23 [l]And the temple and the sanctuary had two doors.

24 And the doors had two leaves *apiece,* two turning leaves; two *leaves* for the one door, and two leaves for the other *door.*

25 And *there were* made on them, on the doors of the temple, cherubims and palm trees, like as *were* made upon the walls; and *there were* thick planks upon the face of the porch without.

26 And *there were* [m]narrow windows and palm trees on the one side and on the other side, on the sides of the porch, and *upon* the side chambers of the house, and thick planks.

42 Then [a]he brought me forth into the utter court, the way toward the north: and he brought me into [b]the chamber that *was* over against the separate place, and which *was* before the building toward the north.

2 Before the length of an hundred cubits *was* the north door, and the breadth *was* fifty cubits.

3 Over against the twenty *cubits* which *were* for the inner court, and over against the pavement which *was* for the utter court, *was* gallery against gallery in three *stories.*

4 And before the chambers *was* a walk of ten cubits breadth inward, a way of one cubit; and their doors toward the north.

5 Now the upper chambers *were* shorter: for the galleries [1]were higher than these, [2]than the lower, and than the middlemost of the building.

6 For they *were* in three *stories,* but had not pillars as the pillars of the courts: therefore *the building* was straitened more than the lowest and the middlemost from the ground.

7 And the wall that *was* without over against the chambers, toward the utter court on the forepart of the chambers, the length thereof *was* fifty cubits.

8 For the length of the chambers that *were* in the utter court *was* fifty cubits: and, lo, before the temple *were* an hundred cubits.

9 And [3]from under these chambers *was* [4]the entry on the east side, [5]as one goeth into them from the utter court.

4 [b]1 Ki. 6.20; 2 Chr. 3.8; Rev. 21.2-3-16-17
6 [c]1 Ki. 6.5-6 [2]side chamber over side chamber [3]Or, three and thirty times, or, foot [4]be holden
7 [5]it was made broader, and went round
8 [d]Isa. 28.16; ch. 40.5
15 [6]Or, several walks, or, walks with pillars
16 [e]ver. 26; 1 Ki. 7.4; Isa. 54.12; ch. 40.16; 1 Cor. 13.12 [7]cieling of wood [8]Or, and the ground unto the windows
17 [9]measures
18 [f]Gen 3.24; Ex. 25.22; 1 Sam. 4.4; 2 Sam. 22.11; 1 Ki. 6.29; 2 Chr. 3.10; Ps. 80.1; Ps. 99.1; ch. 10.2 [g]ch. 1.10; ch. 10-14; Rev. 4.7-9
19 [h]ch. 1.10
21 [10]post
22 [i]Ex. 30.1; 1 Ki. 7.48; 2 Chr. 4.19; Rev. 8.3 [j]Prov. 9.2; Mal. 1.7-12 [k]Ex. 30.8
23 [l]1 Ki. 6.31-35
26 [m]ver. 16; ch. 40.16

CHAPTER 42
1 [a]ch. 40.1; 2 Cor. 3.5 [b]ch. 40.17-20; Rev. 11.2
5 [1]Or, did eat of these [2]Or, and the building consisted of the lower and the middlemost
9 [3]Or, from the place [4]Or, he that brought me [5]Or, as he came

10 The chambers *were* in the thickness of the wall of the court toward the east, over against the separate place, and over against the building.

11 And the way before them *was* like the appearance of the chambers which *were* toward the north, as long as they, *and* as broad as they: and all their goings out *were* both according to their fashions, and according to their doors.

12 And according to the doors of the chambers that *were* toward the south *was* a door in the head of the way, *even* the way directly before the wall toward the east, as one entereth into them.

13 ¶ Then said he unto me, The north chambers *and* the south chambers, which *are* before the separate place, they *be* holy chambers, where the priests [c]that approach unto the LORD [d]shall eat the most holy things: there shall they lay the most holy things, and [e]the meat offering, and the sin offering, and the trespass offering; for the place *is* holy.

14 [f]When the priests enter therein, then shall they not go out of the holy *place* into the utter court, but there they shall lay their garments wherein they minister; for they *are* holy; and shall put on other garments, and shall approach to *those things* which *are* for the people.

15 Now when he had made an end of measuring the inner house, he brought me forth toward the gate whose prospect *is* toward the east, and measured it round about.

16 He measured the east [6]side with the measuring reed, five hundred reeds, with the measuring reed round about.

17 He measured the north side, five hundred reeds, with the measuring reed round about.

18 He measured the south side, five hundred reeds, with the measuring reed.

19 ¶ He turned about to the west side, *and* measured five hundred reeds with the measuring reed.

20 He measured it by the four sides: [g]it had a wall round about, [h]five hundred *reeds* long, and five hundred broad, to make [i]a separation between the sanctuary and the profane place.

43 Afterward he brought me to the gate, *even* the gate [a]that looketh toward the east:

2 [b]And, behold, the glory of the God of Is'ra-el came from the way of the east: and [c]his voice *was* like a noise of many waters: [d]and the earth shined with his glory.

3 And *it was* [e]according to the appearance of the vision which I saw, *even* according to the vision that I saw [1]when I came [f]to destroy the city: and the visions *were* like the vision that I saw [g]by the river Chē'bär; and I fell upon my face.

4 [h]And the glory of the LORD came into the house by the way of the gate whose prospect *is* toward the east.

5 [i]So the spirit took me up, and brought me into the inner court; and, behold, [j]the glory of the LORD filled the house.

6 And I heard *him* speaking unto me out of the house; and [k]the man stood by me.

7 ¶ And he said unto me, Son of man, [l]the place of my throne, and [m]the place of the soles of my feet, [n]where I will dwell in the midst of the children of Is'ra-el for ever, and my holy name, shall the house of Is'ra-el [o]no more defile, *neither* they, nor their kings, by their whoredom, nor by [p]the carcases of their kings in their high places.

8 [q]In their setting of their threshold by my thresholds, and their post by my posts, [2]and the wall between me and them, they have even defiled my holy name by their abominations that they have committed: wherefore I have consumed them in mine anger.

9 Now let them put away their whoredom, and the carcases of their kings, far from me, and I will dwell in the midst of them for ever.

10 ¶ Thou son of man, [r]shew the house to the house of Is'ra-el, that they may be ashamed of their iniquities: and let them measure the [3]pattern.

11 And if they be ashamed of all that they have done, [s]shew them the form of the house, and the fashion thereof, and the goings out thereof, and the comings in thereof, and all the forms thereof, and all the ordinances thereof, and all the forms thereof, and all the laws thereof: and write *it* in their sight, that they may keep the whole form thereof, and all the ordinances thereof, and do them.

12 This *is* the law of the house; Upon [t]the top of the mountain the whole limit thereof round about *shall be* most holy. Behold, this *is* the law of the house.

13 ¶ And these *are* the measures of the altar after the cubits: [u]The cubit *is* a cubit and an hand breadth; even the [4]bottom *shall be* a cubit, and the breadth a cubit, and the border thereof by the [5]edge thereof round about *shall be* a span: and this *shall be* the higher place of the altar.

14 And from the bottom *upon* the ground *even* to the lower settle *shall be* two cubits, and the breadth one cubit; and from the lesser settle *even* to the greater settle *shall be* four cubits, and the breadth *one* cubit.

15 So [6]the altar *shall be* four cubits; and from [7]the altar and upward *shall be* four horns.

16 And the altar *shall be* twelve *cubits* long, twelve broad, square in the four squares thereof.

17 And the settle *shall be* fourteen *cubits* long and fourteen broad in the four squares thereof; and the border about it *shall be* half a cubit; and the bottom thereof *shall be* a cubit about; and [v]his stairs shall look toward the east.

13 [c]Ex. 30.20; Lev. 10.3; Num. 16.5-40; Deut. 21.5; ch. 40.46
[d]Lev. 6.16; Lev. 24.9
[e]Lev. 2.3; Num. 18.9
14 [f]Ex. 28.40-43; Ex. 29.4-9; Lev. 8.7-13; ch. 44.19
16 [6]wind
20 [g]Isa. 5.2; ch. 40.5
[h]ch. 45.2
[i]2 Cor. 6.17

CHAPTER 43
1 [a]ch. 10.19
2 [b]Isa. 6.3; ch. 3.23; ch. 9.3; ch. 10.18-19
[c]Rev. 1.15
[d]Rev. 18.1
3 [e]ch. 1.4
[1]Or, when I came to prophesy that the city should be destroyed
[f]Jer. 1.10
[g]ch. 3.23
4 [h]ch. 10.19
5 [i]ch. 3.12
[j]1 Ki. 8.10
6 [k]ch. 40.3
7 [l]Ps. 99.1
[m]1 Chr. 28.2; Ps. 99.5
[n]Ex. 25.8; Lev. 26.12; Ps. 68.16
[o]ch. 39.7
[p]Lev. 26.30; Jer. 16.18
8 [q]2 Ki. 16.14
[2]Or, for there was but a wall between me and them
10 [r]ch. 40.4
[3]Or, sum, or, number
11 [s]ch. 44.5-6; Matt. 28.20
12 [t]Ps. 93.5; ch. 40.2; Rev. 21.27
13 [u]ch. 40.5
[4]bosom
[5]lip
15 [6]Harel, that is, the mountain of God
[7]Ariel, that is, the lion of God
17 [v]Ex. 20.26

18 ¶ And he said unto me, Son of
man, thus saith the Lord GOD; These
are the ordinances of the altar in the
day when they shall make it, to offer
burnt offerings thereon, and to [w]sprin-
kle blood thereon.
19 And thou shalt give to [x]the priests
the Lē′vītes that be of the seed of Zā′-
dŏk, which approach unto me, to minister unto me, saith the Lord GOD, [y]a
young bullock for a sin offering.
20 And thou shalt take of the blood
thereof, and put *it* on the four horns of
it, and on the four corners of the settle,
and upon the border round about: thus
shalt thou cleanse and purge it.
21 Thou shalt take the bullock also
of the sin offering, and he [z]shall burn
it in the appointed place of the house,
[a]without the sanctuary.
22 And on the second day thou shalt
offer a kid of the goats without blemish for a sin offering; and they shall
cleanse the altar, as they did cleanse *it*
with the bullock.
23 When thou hast made an end of
cleansing *it*, thou shalt offer a young
bullock without blemish, and a ram
out of the flock without blemish.
24 And thou shalt offer them before
the LORD, [b]and the priests shall cast
salt upon them, and they shall offer
them up *for* a burnt offering unto the
LORD.
25 [c]Seven days shalt thou prepare
every day a goat *for* a sin offering: they
shall also prepare a young bullock,
and a ram out of the flock, without
blemish.
26 Seven days shall they purge the
altar and purify it; and they shall [8]con-
secrate themselves.
27 [d]And when these days are expired, it shall be, *that* upon the eighth
day, and *so* forward, the priests shall
make your burnt offerings upon the altar, and your [9]peace offerings; and I
will [e]accept you, saith the Lord GOD.

44 Then he brought me back the
way of the gate of the outward
sanctuary which [a]looketh toward the
east; and it *was* shut.
2 Then said the LORD unto me; This
gate shall be shut, it shall not be
opened, and no man shall enter in by
it; because the LORD, the God of Ĭs′ra-
el, hath entered in by it, therefore it
shall be shut.
3 *It is* for [b]the prince; the prince, he
shall sit in it to [c]eat bread before the
LORD; [d]he shall enter by the way of the
porch of *that* gate, and shall go out by
the way of the same.
4 ¶ Then brought he me the way of
the north gate before the house: and I
looked, and, [e]behold, the glory of the
LORD filled the house of the LORD:
[f]and I fell upon my face.
5 And the LORD said unto me, [g]Son
of man, [1]mark well, and behold with
thine eyes, and hear with thine ears all
that I say unto thee concerning all the
ordinances of the house of the LORD,
and all the laws thereof; and mark well
the entering in of the house, with every
going forth of the sanctuary.
6 And thou shalt say to the [h]rebel-
lious, *even* to the house of Ĭs′ra-el,
Thus saith the Lord GOD; O ye house of
Ĭs′ra-el, [i]let it suffice you of all your
abominations,
7 [j]In that ye have brought *into my*
sanctuary [2]strangers, [k]uncircumcised
in heart, and uncircumcised in flesh, to
be in my sanctuary, to pollute it, *even*
my house, when ye offer [l]my bread,
[m]the fat and the blood, and they have
broken my covenant because of all
your abominations.
8 And ye have not [n]kept the charge
of mine holy things: but ye have set
keepers of my [3]charge in my sanctuary
for yourselves.
9 ¶ Thus saith the Lord GOD; [o]No
stranger, uncircumcised in heart, nor
uncircumcised in flesh, shall enter into
my sanctuary, of any stranger that *is*
among the children of Ĭs′ra-el.
10 [p]And the Lē′vītes that are gone
away far from me, when Ĭs′ra-el went
astray, which went astray away from
me after their idols; they shall even
bear their iniquity.
11 Yet they shall be ministers in my
sanctuary, [q]*having* charge at the gates
of the house, and ministering to the
house: they shall slay the burnt offering and the sacrifice for the people,
and [r]they shall stand before them to
minister unto them.
12 Because they ministered unto
them before their idols, and [4]caused
the house of Ĭs′ra-el to fall into iniquity; therefore have I [s]lifted up mine
hand against them, saith the Lord
GOD, and they shall bear their iniquity.
13 [t]And they shall not come near
unto me, to do the office of a priest
unto me, nor to come near to any of my
[5]holy things, in the most holy *place*:
but they shall [u]bear their shame, and
their abominations which they have
committed.
14 But I will make them [v]keepers of
the charge of the house, for all the service thereof, and for all that shall be
done therein.
15 ¶ [w]But the priests the Lē′vītes,
[x]the sons of Zā′dŏk, that kept the
charge of my sanctuary when the children of Ĭs′ra-el went astray from me,
they shall come near to me to minister
unto me, and they [y]shall stand before
me to offer unto me the fat and the
blood, saith the Lord GOD:
16 They shall enter into my sanctuary, and they shall come near to [z]my
table, to minister unto me, and they
shall [a]keep my charge.
17 ¶ And it shall come to pass, *that*
when they enter in at the gates of the
inner court, [b]they shall be clothed
with linen garments; and no wool shall
come upon them, whiles they minister
in the gates of the inner court, and
within.
18 They shall have linen bonnets
upon their heads, and shall have linen
breeches upon their loins; they shall

18 [w]Lev. 1.5; Heb. 9.18-22
19 [x]1Ki. 2.27-35; Isa. 61.5; Jer. 33.18; ch. 40.46
[y]Ex. 29.10; Lev. 8.14-15
21 [z]Ex. 29.14
[a]Heb. 13.11
24 [b]Lev. 2.13
25 [c]Ex. 29.35
26 [8]fill their hands
27 [d]Lev. 9.1
[9]Or, thank offerings
[e]Job 42.8

CHAPTER 44
1 [a]ch. 43.1
3 [b]Zech. 6.12; Phil. 2.8
[c]Gen. 31.54
[d]ch. 46.2-8
4 [e]ch. 3.23
[f]ch. 1.28
5 [g]ch. 40.4
[1]set thine heart
6 [h]ch. 2.5
[i]1 Pet. 4.3
7 [j]Acts 21.28
[2]children of a stranger
[k]Lev. 26.41; ch. 7.20
[l]Lev. 21.6
[m]Lev. 3.16
8 [n]Lev. 22.2; Num. 18.3; 2 Tim. 4.1
[3]Or, ward, or, ordinance
9 [o]Ps. 50.16
10 [p]2 Ki. 23.8; Neh. 9.34; Jer. 23.11; ch. 22.26
11 [q]1 Chr. 26.1
[r]Num. 16.9
12 [4]were for a stumblingblock of iniquity unto, etc
[s]Ps. 106.26
13 [t]Num. 18.3
[5]holinesses in the holinesses of holinesses
[u]ch. 32.30
14 [v]1 Chr. 23.28-32
15 [w]ch. 40.46
[x]1 Sam. 2.35
[y]Deut. 10.8
16 [z]ch. 41.22
[a]Mal. 2.7
17 [b]Ex. 28.39

not gird *themselves* [6]with any thing that causeth sweat.

19 And when they go forth into the utter court, *even* into the utter court to the people, [c]they shall put off their garments wherein they ministered, and lay them in the holy chambers, and they shall put on other garments; and they shall not [d]sanctify the people with their garments.

20 Neither shall they shave their heads, nor suffer their locks to grow long; they shall only poll their heads.

21 [e]Neither shall any priest drink wine, when they enter into the inner court.

22 Neither shall they take for their wives a widow, nor her that is [7]put away: but they shall take maidens of the seed of the house of Is'ra-el, or a widow [8]that had a priest before.

23 And [f]they shall teach my people *the difference* between the holy and profane, and cause them to discern between the unclean and the clean.

24 And [g]in controversy they shall stand in judgment; *and* they shall judge it according to my judgments: and they shall keep my [h]laws and my statutes in all mine assemblies; [i]and they shall hallow my sabbaths.

25 And they shall come at no dead person to defile themselves: but for father, or for mother, or for son, or for daughter, for brother, or for sister that hath had no husband, they may defile themselves.

26 And [j]after he is cleansed, they shall reckon unto him seven days.

27 And in the day that he goeth into the sanctuary, unto the inner court, to minister in the sanctuary, [k]he shall offer his sin offering, saith the Lord GOD.

28 And it shall be unto them for an inheritance: I [l]*am* their inheritance: and ye shall give them no possession in Is'ra-el: I *am* their possession.

29 They [m]shall eat the meat offering, and the sin offering, and the trespass offering; and [9][n]every dedicated thing in Is'ra-el shall be theirs.

30 And the [10]first of all the firstfruits of all *things*, and every oblation of all, of every *sort* of your oblations, shall be the priest's: ye [o]shall also give unto the priest the first of your dough, [p]that he may cause the blessing to rest in thine house.

31 The priests shall not eat of any thing that is [q]dead of itself, or torn, whether it be fowl or beast.

45 Moreover, [1]when ye shall divide by lot the land for inheritance, ye shall [a]offer an oblation unto the LORD, [2]an holy portion of the land: the length *shall be* the length of five and twenty thousand *reeds*, and the breadth *shall be* ten thousand. This *shall be* holy in all the borders thereof round about.

2 Of this there shall be for the sanctuary [b]five hundred *in length*, with five hundred *in breadth*, square round about; and fifty cubits round about for the [3]suburbs thereof.

3 And of this measure shalt thou measure the length of five and twenty thousand, and the breadth of ten thousand: and in it shall be the sanctuary *and* the most holy *place*.

4 The holy *portion* of the land shall be for the [c]priests the ministers of the sanctuary, which shall come near to minister unto the LORD: and it shall be a place for their houses, and an holy place for the sanctuary.

5 [d]And the five and twenty thousand of length, and the ten thousand of breadth, shall also the Lē'vītes, the ministers of the house, have for themselves, for a possession for [e]twenty chambers.

6 ¶ And ye shall appoint the possession of the city five thousand broad, and five and twenty thousand long, over against the oblation of the holy *portion*: it shall be for the whole house of Is'ra-el.

7 ¶ [f]And a *portion shall be* for the prince on the one side and on the other side of the oblation of the holy *portion*, and of the possession of the city, before the oblation of the holy *portion*, and before the possession of the city, from the west side westward, and from the east side eastward: and the length *shall be* over against one of the portions, from the west border unto the east border.

8 In the land shall be his possession in Is'ra-el: and [g]my princes shall no more oppress my people; and *the rest of* the land shall they give to the house of Is'ra-el according to their tribes.

9 ¶ Thus saith the Lord GOD; [h]Let it suffice you, O princes of Is'ra-el: [i]remove violence and spoil, and execute judgment and justice, take away your [4]exactions from my people, saith the Lord GOD.

10 Ye shall have just [j]balances, and a just ephah, and a just bath.

11 The ephah and the bath shall be of one measure, that the bath may contain the tenth part of an homer, and the ephah the tenth part of an homer: the measure thereof shall be after the homer.

12 And the [k]shekel *shall be* twenty gerahs: twenty shekels, five and twenty shekels, fifteen shekels, shall be your maneh.

13 This *is* the oblation that ye shall offer; the sixth part of an ephah of an homer of wheat, and ye shall give the sixth part of an ephah of an homer of barley:

14 Concerning the ordinance of oil, the bath of oil, *ye shall offer* the tenth part of a bath out of the cor, *which is* an homer of ten baths; for ten baths *are* an homer:

15 And one [5]lamb out of the flock, out of two hundred, out of the fat pastures of Is'ra-el; for a meat offering, and for a burnt offering, and for [6]peace offerings, [l]to make reconciliation for them, saith the Lord GOD.

16 All the people of the land [7]shall

18 [6]in, or, with sweat, or, in sweating places
19 [c]ch. 42.14
[d]Ex. 29.37
21 [e]Lev. 10.9; Luke 1.15; 1 Tim. 3.3
22 [7]thrust forth
[8]from a priest
23 [f]Mal. 2.7
24 [g]Deut. 17.8
[h]1 Tim. 4.12
[i]ch. 22.26
26 [j]Num. 6.10
27 [k]Lev. 4.3
28 [l]Num. 18.20; Deut. 10.9; Josh. 13.14-33; ch. 45.4
29 [m]Lev. 6.18
[9]Or, devoted
[n]Lev. 27.21-compared with Num. 18.14
30 [10]Or, chief
[o]Num. 15.20
[p]Prov. 3.9
31 [q]Ex. 22.31

CHAPTER 45
1 [1]when ye cause the land to fall
[a]Prov. 3.9-10; ch. 48.8
[2]holiness
2 [b]ch. 42.20
[3]Or, void places
4 [c]ch. 44.15
5 [d]ch. 48.13
[e]ch. 40.17
7 [f]Ps. 2.8; ch. 34.24; ch. 46.16-18; ch. 48.21
8 [g]Jer. 22.17; ch. 22.27; ch. 46.18
9 [h]ch. 44.6
[i]Jer. 22.3
[4]expulsions
10 [j]Lev. 19.35; Prov. 11.1
12 [k]Ex. 30.13; Lev. 27.25
15 [5]Or, kid
[6]Or, thank offerings
[l]Lev. 1.4; Rom. 5.10; 2 Cor. 5.18-19; Eph. 2.16; Col. 1.21; Tit. 2.14
16 [7]shall be for

give this oblation [8]for the prince in Is'ra-el.

17 And it shall be the prince's part *to give* burnt offerings, and meat offerings, and drink offerings, in the feasts, and in the new moons, and in the sabbaths, in all solemnities of the house of Is'ra-el: he [m]shall prepare the sin offering, and the meat offering, and the burnt offering, and the [9]peace offerings, to make reconciliation for the house of Is'ra-el.

18 Thus saith the Lord GOD; In the first *month,* in the first *day* of the month, thou shalt take a young bullock without blemish, and [n]cleanse the sanctuary:

19 [o]And the priest shall take of the blood of the sin offering, and put *it* upon the posts of the house, and upon the four corners of the settle of the altar, and upon the posts of the gate of the inner court.

20 And so thou shalt do the seventh *day* of the month [p]for every one that erreth, and for *him that is* simple: so shall ye reconcile the house.

21 [q]In the first *month,* in the fourteenth day of the month, ye shall have the passover, a feast of seven days; unleavened bread shall be eaten.

22 And upon that day shall [r]the prince prepare for himself and for all the people of the land [s]a bullock *for* a sin offering.

23 And [t]seven days of the feast he shall prepare a burnt offering to the LORD, seven bullocks and seven rams without blemish daily the seven days; [u]and a kid of the goats daily *for* a sin offering.

24 [v]And he shall prepare a meat offering of an ephah for a bullock, and an ephah for a ram, and an hin of oil for an ephah.

25 In the seventh *month,* in the fifteenth day of the month, shall he do the like in the [w]feast of the seven days, according to the sin offering, according to the burnt offering, and according to the meat offering, and according to the oil.

46

Thus saith the Lord GOD; The gate of the inner court that looketh toward the east shall be shut the six working days; but on the [a]sabbath it shall be opened, and in the day of the new moon it shall be opened.

2 [b]And the prince shall enter by the way of the porch of *that* gate without, and shall stand by the post of the gate, and the priests shall prepare his burnt offering and his peace offerings, and he shall worship at the threshold of the gate: then he shall go forth; [c]but the gate shall not be shut until the evening.

3 [d]Likewise the people of the land shall worship at the door of this gate before the LORD in the sabbaths and in the new moons.

4 [e]And the burnt offering that the prince shall offer unto the LORD in the sabbath day *shall be* six lambs without blemish, and a ram without blemish.

5 [f]And the meat offering *shall be* an ephah for a ram, and the meat offering for the lambs [1]as he shall be able to give, and an hin of oil to an ephah.

6 And in the day of the new moon *it shall be* a young bullock without blemish, and six lambs, and a ram: they shall be without blemish.

7 And he shall prepare a meat offering, an ephah for a bullock, and an ephah for a ram, and for the lambs according as his hand shall attain unto, and an hin of oil to an ephah.

8 And when the prince shall enter, he shall go in by the way of the porch of *that* gate, and he shall go forth by the way thereof.

9 ¶ But when the people of the land [g]shall come before the LORD in the solemn feasts, he that entereth in by the way of the north gate to worship shall go out by the way of the south gate; and he that entereth by the way of the south gate shall go forth by the way of the north gate: he shall not return by the way of the gate whereby he came in, but shall go forth over against it.

10 And the prince in the midst of them, when they go in, shall go in; and when they go forth, shall go forth.

11 And in the feasts and in the solemnities the meat offering shall be an ephah to a bullock, and an ephah to a ram, and to the lambs as he is able to give, and an hin of oil to an ephah.

12 Now when the prince shall prepare a voluntary [h]burnt offering or peace offerings voluntarily unto the LORD, [i]*one* shall then open him the gate that looketh toward the east, and he shall prepare his burnt offering and his peace offerings, as he did on the sabbath day: then he shall go forth; and after his going forth *one* shall shut the gate.

13 [j]Thou shalt daily prepare a burnt offering unto the LORD *of* a lamb [2]of the first year without blemish: thou shalt prepare it [3]every morning.

14 And thou shalt prepare a meat offering for it every morning, the sixth part of an ephah, and the third part of an hin of oil, to temper with the fine flour; a meat offering continually by a perpetual ordinance unto the LORD.

15 Thus shall they prepare the lamb, and the meat offering, and the oil, every morning *for* a continual burnt offering.

16 ¶ Thus saith the Lord GOD; If the prince give a gift unto any of his sons, the inheritance thereof shall be his sons'; it *shall be* their possession by inheritance.

17 But if he give a gift of his inheritance to one of his servants, then it shall be his to [k]the year of liberty; after it shall return to the prince: but his inheritance shall be his sons' for them.

18 Moreover [l]the prince shall not take of the people's inheritance by oppression, to thrust them out of their possession; *but* he shall give his sons inheritance out of his own possession: that my people be not scattered every man from his possession.

---

[8]Or, with
17 [m]John 6.51; 2 Cor. 5.21; Gal. 3.13; Col. 1.20; 1 Pet. 2.24
[9]Or, thank offerings
18 [n]Lev. 16.16; ch. 43.22-26; Heb. 9.22
19 [o]ch. 43.20
20 [p]Ps. 19.12; Lev. 4.27; Rom. 16.18; Heb. 5.2
21 [q]Ex. 12.18; Lev. 23.5-6; Num. 9.2-3; Deut. 16.1
22 [r]Matt. 20.28; 1 Pet. 2.24
[s]Lev. 4.14
23 [t]Lev. 23.8
[u]Num. 28.15
24 [v]ch. 46.5-7
25 [w]Lev. 23.33; Num. 29.12; Deut. 16.13

CHAPTER 46

1 [a]Isa. 66.23; ch. 45.17; Heb. 4.9-10
2 [b]ch. 44.3
[c]Matt. 25.10
3 [d]Ps. 100.4; Luke 1.10
4 [e]Num. 28.5-9-11-12; ch. 45.17; There was no such oblation appointed by Moses
5 [f]verse 14; Num. 28.12; ch. 45.24
[1]the gift of his hand
9 [g]Ex. 23.14-17; Deut. 16.16; Ps. 84.7
12 [h]Lev. 1.3; Lev. 23.37; Num. 29.39; Matt. 20.28; John 10.18; Gal. 2.20; Tit. 2.14
[i]ch. 44.3
13 [j]Ex. 29.38; Num. 28.3
[2]a son of his year
[3]morning by morning
17 [k]Lev. 25.9-10; Isa. 61.2
18 [l]Ps. 78.72; Jer. 23.5-6; ch. 45.8

19 ¶ After he brought me through the
entry, which *was* at the side of the gate,
into the holy chambers of the priests,
which looked toward the north: and,
behold, there *was* a place on the two
sides westward.
20 Then said he unto me, This *is* the
place where the priests shall [m]boil the
trespass offering and the sin offering,
where they shall [n]bake the meat offering; that they bear *them* not out into
the utter court, [o]to sanctify the people.
21 Then he brought me forth into
the utter court, and caused me to pass
by the four corners of the court; and,
behold, [4]in every corner of the court
there was a court.
22 In the four corners of the court
there were courts [5]joined of forty *cubits* long and thirty broad: these four
[6]corners *were* of one measure.
23 And *there was* a row *of building*
round about in them, round about them
four, and *it was* made with boiling
places under the rows round about.
24 Then said he unto me, These *are*
the places of them that boil, where the
ministers of the house shall [p]boil the
sacrifice of the people.
47 Afterward he brought me again
unto the door of the house; and,
behold, [a]waters issued out from under
the threshold of the house eastward:
for the forefront of the house *stood toward* the east, and the waters came
down from under from the right side of
the house, at the south *side* of the altar.
2 Then brought he me out of the way
of the gate northward, and led me
about the way without unto the utter
gate by the way that looketh eastward;
and, behold, there ran out waters on
the right side.
3 And when [b]the man that had the
line in his hand went forth eastward,
he measured a thousand cubits, and he
brought me through the waters; the
[1]waters *were* to the ancles.
4 Again he measured a thousand,
and brought me through the waters;
the waters *were* to the knees. Again he
measured a thousand, and brought me
through; the waters *were* to the loins.
5 Afterward he measured a thou-
sand; *and it was* a river that I could not
pass over: for the waters were risen,
[2]waters to swim in, a river that could
not be passed over.
6 ¶ And he said unto me, Son of
man, hast thou seen *this*? Then he
brought me, and caused me to return
to the brink of the river.
7 Now when I had returned, behold,
at the [3]bank of the river *were* very
many [c]trees on the one side and on the
other.
8 Then said he unto me, These waters issue out toward the east country,
and go down into the [4]desert, and
go into the sea: *which being* brought
forth into the sea, the [d]waters shall be
healed.
9 And it shall come to pass, *that* every thing that liveth, which moveth,
whithersoever the [5]rivers shall come,
[e]shall live: and there shall be a very
great multitude of fish, because these
waters shall come thither: for they
shall be healed; and every thing shall
live whither the river cometh.
10 And it shall come to pass, *that*
the [f]fishers shall stand upon it from
Ĕn–gē′dī even unto Ĕn–ĕg′la-ĭm; they
shall be a *place* to spread forth nets;
their fish shall be according to their
kinds, as the fish [g]of the great sea, exceeding many.
11 But the miry places thereof and
the marishes thereof [6]shall not be
healed; they shall be given to salt.
12 And by the river upon the bank
thereof, on this side and on that side,
[7]shall grow all trees for meat, [h]whose
leaf shall not fade, neither shall the
fruit thereof be consumed: it shall
bring forth [8]new fruit according to his
months, because their waters they issued out of the sanctuary: and the fruit
thereof shall be for meat, and the leaf
thereof [9]for medicine.
13 ¶ Thus saith the Lord GOD; This
shall be the border, whereby ye shall
inherit the land according to the twelve
tribes of Ĭs′ra-el: [i]Jō′seph *shall have
two* portions.
14 And ye shall inherit it, one as
well as another: *concerning* the which
I [10]lifted up mine hand to give it unto
your fathers: and this land shall [j]fall
unto you for inheritance.
15 And this *shall be* the border of
the land toward the north side, from
the great sea, [k]the way of Hĕth′lŏn, as
men go to [l]Zē′dăd;
16 [m]Hā′math, [n]Be-rō′thah, Sĭb′ra-
ĭm, which *is* between the border of Da-
măs′cus and the border of Hā′math;
[11]Hā′zar–hăt′tĭ-cŏn, which *is* by the
coast of Hau′ran.
17 And the border from the sea shall
be [o]Hā′zar–ē′nan, the border of Da-
măs′cus, and the north northward, and
the border of Hā′math. And *this is* the
north side.
18 And the east side ye shall measure [12]from Hau′ran, and from Da-
măs′cus, and from Gĭl′e-ăd, and from
the land of Ĭs′ra-el *by* Jôr′dan, from the
border unto the east sea. And *this is*
the east side.
19 And the south side southward,
from Tā′mar *even* to the waters of
[13]strife *in* Kā′desh, the [14]river to the
great sea. And *this is* the south side
[15]southward.
20 The west side also *shall be* the
great sea from the border, till a man
come over against Hā′math. This *is* the
west side.
21 So shall ye divide this land unto
you according to the tribes of Ĭs′ra-el.
22 ¶ And it shall come to pass, *that*
ye shall divide it by lot for an inheritance unto you, [p]and to the strangers
that sojourn among you, which shall
beget children among you: [q]and they
shall be unto you as born in the country among the children of Ĭs′ra-el; they
shall have inheritance with you among
the tribes of Ĭs′ra-el.

20 [m]2 Chr. 35.13; ch. 44.29
[n]Lev. 2.4-5-7; ch. 43.23-24
[o]Ex. 19.10; Heb. 10.22
21 [4]a court in a corner of a court, and a court in a corner of a court
22 [5]Or, made with chimneys
[6]cornered
24 [p]Rom. 12.1; Heb. 13.16

CHAPTER 47

1 [a]Ps. 46.4; Rev. 22.1
3 [b]ch. 40.3; Rev. 11.1
[1]waters of the ancles
5 [2]waters of swimming
7 [3]lip
[c]Ps. 1.3; Rev. 22.2
8 [4]Or, plain
[d]Zech. 2.11; Rev. 17.15
9 [5]two rivers
[e]John 5.25; 1 Cor. 15.45
10 [f]Matt. 4.19
[g]verse 15; Josh. 23.4
11 [6]Or, and that which shall not be healed
12 [7]shall come up
[h]Job 8.16; Isa. 61.3
[8]Or, principal
[9]Or, for bruises and sores
13 [i]Gen. 48.5
14 [10]Or, swore
[j]Num. 34.2
15 [k]ch. 48.1
[l]Num. 34.8
16 [m]Num. 34.8;
[n]2 Sam. 8.8
[11]Or, the middle village
17 [o]Num. 34.9
18 [12]from between
19 [13]Or, Meribah
[14]Or, valley
[15]Or, toward Teman
22 [p]Acts 2.5;
[q]Rom. 10.12

23 And it shall come to pass, *that* in what tribe the stranger sojourneth, there shall ye give *him* his inheritance, saith the Lord GOD.

48

48 Now these *are* the names of the tribes. [a]From the north end to the coast of the way of Hĕth'lŏn, as one goeth to Hā'math, Hā'zar–ē'nan, the border of Da-măs'cus northward, to the coast of Hā'math; for these are his sides east *and* west; [1]a *portion for* Dăn.

2 And by the border of Dăn, from the east side unto the west side, a *portion for* Ăsh'ēr.

3 And by the border of Ăsh'ēr, from the east side even unto the west side, a *portion for* Năph'ta-lī.

4 And by the border of Năph'ta-lī, from the east side unto the west side, a *portion for* Ma-năs'seh.

5 And by the border of Ma-năs'seh, from the east side unto the west side, a *portion for* Ē'phră-ĭm.

6 And by the border of Ē'phră-ĭm, from the east side even unto the west side, a *portion for* Reu̯'ben.

7 And by the border of Reu̯'ben, from the east side unto the west side, a *portion for* Jū'dah.

8 ¶ And by the border of Jū'dah, from the east side unto the west side, shall be [b]the offering which ye shall offer of five and twenty thousand *reeds in* breadth, and *in* length as one of the *other* parts, from the east side unto the west side: and the sanctuary shall be in the midst of it.

9 The oblation that ye shall offer unto the LORD *shall be* of five and twenty thousand in length, and of ten thousand in breadth.

10 And for them, *even* for the priests, shall be *this* holy oblation; toward the north five and twenty thousand *in length,* and toward the west ten thousand in breadth, and toward the east ten thousand in breadth, and toward the south five and twenty thousand in length: and the sanctuary of the LORD shall be in the midst thereof.

11 [2]*It shall be* for the priests that are sanctified of the sons of Zā'dŏk; which have kept my [3]charge, which went not astray when the children of Ĭs'ra-el went astray, as the [c]Lē'vītes went astray.

12 And *this* oblation of the land that is offered shall be unto them [4]a thing most holy by the border of the Lē'vītes.

13 And over against the border of the priests the Lē'vītes *shall have* five and twenty thousand in length, and ten thousand in breadth: all the length *shall be* five and twenty thousand, and the breadth ten thousand.

14 [d]And they shall not sell of it, neither exchange, nor alienate the firstfruits of the land: for *it is* holy unto the LORD.

15 ¶ [e]And the five thousand, that are left in the breadth over against the five and twenty thousand, shall be [f]a profane *place* for the city, for dwelling, and for suburbs: and the city shall be in the midst thereof.

16 And these *shall be* the measures thereof; the north side four thousand and five hundred, and the south side four thousand and five hundred, and on the east side four thousand and five hundred, and the west side four thousand and five hundred.

17 And the suburbs of the city shall be toward the north two hundred and fifty, and toward the south two hundred and fifty, and toward the east two hundred and fifty, and toward the west two hundred and fifty.

18 And the residue in length over against the oblation of the holy *portion shall be* ten thousand eastward, and ten thousand westward: and it shall be over against the oblation of the holy *portion;* and the increase thereof shall be for food unto them that serve the city.

19 [g]And they that serve the city shall serve it out of all the tribes of Ĭs'ra-el.

20 All the oblation *shall be* five and twenty thousand by five and twenty thousand: ye shall offer the holy [h]oblation foursquare, with the possession of the city.

21 ¶ And the residue *shall be* for the prince, on the one side and on the other of the holy oblation, and of the possession of the city, over against the five and twenty thousand of the oblation toward the east border, and westward over against the five and twenty thousand toward the west border, over against the portions for the prince: and it shall be the holy oblation; [i]and the sanctuary of the house *shall be* in the midst thereof.

22 Moreover from the possession of the Lē'vītes, and from the possession of the city, *being* in the midst *of that* which is the prince's, between the border of Jū'dah and the border of Bĕn'jamin, shall be for the prince.

23 As for the rest of the tribes, from the east side unto the west side, Bĕn'jamin *shall have* [5]a *portion.*

24 And by the border of Bĕn'ja-min, from the east side unto the west side, Sĭm'e-on *shall have* a *portion.*

25 And by the border of Sĭm'e-on, from the east side unto the west side, Ĭs'sa-char a *portion.*

26 And by the border of Ĭs'sa-char, from the east side unto the west side, Zĕb'u-lun a *portion.*

27 And by the border of Zĕb'u-lun, from the east side unto the west side, Găd a *portion.*

28 And by the border of Găd at the south side southward, the border shall be even from [j]Tā'mar *unto* the waters of [6k]strife *in* Kā'desh, *and* to [l]the river toward the great sea.

29 [m]This *is* the land which ye shall divide by lot unto the tribes of Ĭs'ra-el for inheritance, and these *are* their portions, saith the Lord GOD.

30 ¶ And these *are* the goings out of the city on the north side, four thousand and five hundred measures.

CHAPTER 48
1 [a]Num. 34.7-9; ch. 47.15
[1]one portion
8 [b]ch. 45.1-6
11 [2]Or, The sanctified portion shall be for the priests
[3]Or, ward, or, ordinance
[c]2 Chr. 29.4-5; Neh. 9.34; Jer. 23.11; ch. 22.26; ch. 44.10; Zeph. 3.4; Mal. 2.7-8
12 [4]holiness of holinesses
14 [d]Ex. 22.29; Lev. 27.10-28-33
15 [e]ch. 45.6
[f]Deut. 20.5; ch. 42.20; ch. 44.23; ch. 45.6
19 [g]Rev. 7.5
20 [h]Num. 24.5; Isa. 33.20; Rev. 21.16
21 [i]Josh. 18.1; Isa. 2.2; Isa. 11.10; Hos. 1.11; Hag. 2.7-9; Matt. 11.28; Matt. 13.16-17; John 12.32; Rom. 15.9-12; Rev. 2.1; Rev. 21.3
23 [5]one portion
28 [j]2 Chr. 20.2; ch. 47.19
[6]Meribah-kadesh
[k]Num. 20.1-13; Ps. 106.32; ch. 47.19
[l]Gen. 15.18; Num. 34.15; Josh. 15.47; Isa. 27.12
29 [m]ch. 47.14-21-22

31 [n]And the gates of the city *shall be*
after the names of the tribes of Ĭs'ra-el:
three gates northward; one gate of
Reu'ben, one gate of Jū'dah, one gate
of Lē'vī.
32 And at the east side four thousand and five hundred: and three gates;
and one gate of Jō'seph, one gate of
Bĕn'ja-min, one gate of Dăn.
33 And at the south side four thousand and five hundred measures: and
three gates; one gate of Sĭm'e-on, one
gate of Ĭs'sa-char, one gate of Zĕb'u-lun.
34 At the west side four thousand
and five hundred, *with* their three
gates; one gate of Găd, one gate of
Ăsh'ēr, one gate of Năph'ta-lī.
35 *It was* round about eighteen thousand *measures:* and the name of the
city from *that* day *shall be,* [7][o]The
LORD *is* there.

31 [n]Isa. 60.18; Rev. 21.12
35 [7]Jehovah-shammah
[o]Ex. 17.15; Judg. 6.24; Ps. 132.14; Joel 3.21; Zech. 2.10

THE BOOK OF

DANIEL

Life's Questions

When culture changes, how do I know God's way of life?
When history shows God is gone, how do I know where He is at work?
When substitutes for God hold power, what encourages me to faith in the God of my fathers?

God's Answers

Daniel uses a complex literary form called apocalyptic to reveal God's coming actions in history and encourage God's persecuted people to faith. Six stories about Israelite captives in Babylon after 597 B.C. join with a complex set of historical, apocalyptic visions to teach Israel: history teaches fidelity and perseverance in the face of radical change and new temptations (1—6); God's plan for history calls for fidelity and perseverance in life's most difficult times (7—12).

Daniel shows how and why to maintain faith and purity amidst cultural change and historical hopelessness.

1 In the third year of the reign of Je-
hoi'a-kim king of Jū'dah [a]came
Nĕb-u-chăd-nĕz'zar king of Băb'y̆-lon
unto Je-ru'sa-lĕm, and besieged it.
2 And the Lord gave Je-hoi'a-kim
king of Jū'dah into his hand, with part
[b]of the vessels of the house of God:
which he carried [c]into the land of
Shī'när to the house of his god; and he
brought the vessels into the treasure
house of his god.
3 ¶ And the king spake unto Ăsh'pe-
naz the master of his eunuchs, that he
should bring [1]*certain* of the children of
Ĭs'ra-el, and of the king's seed, and of
the princes;
4 Children [d]in whom *was* no blemish, but well favoured, and skilful in all
wisdom, and cunning in knowledge,
and understanding science, and such
as *had* ability in them to stand in the
king's palace, and [e]whom they might
teach the learning and the tongue of
the Chăl-dē'ans.
5 And the king appointed them a
daily provision of the king's meat, and
of [2]the wine which he drank: so nourishing them three years, that at the end
thereof they might stand before the
king.
6 Now among these were of the children of Jū'dah, Dăn'iel, Hăn-a-nī'ah,
Mĭsh'a-el, and Ăz-a-rī'ah:
7 [f]Unto whom the prince of the eunuchs gave names: [g]for he gave unto
Dăn'iel *the name* of Bĕl-te-shăz'zar;
and to Hăn-a-nī'ah, of Shā'drach; and
to Mĭsh'a-el, of Mē'shach; and to Ăz-a-
rī'ah, of A-bĕd'–nĕ-gō.
8 ¶ But Dăn'iel purposed in his heart
that he would not defile himself [h]with
the portion of the king's meat, nor with
the wine which he drank: therefore he
requested of the prince of the eunuchs
that he might not defile himself.
9 Now [i]God had brought Dăn'iel
into favour and tender love with the
prince of the eunuchs.
10 And the prince of the eunuchs
said unto Dăn'iel, I fear my lord the
king, who hath appointed your meat
and your drink: for why should he see
your faces [3]worse liking than the children which *are* of your [4]sort? then
shall ye make *me* endanger my head to
the king.
11 Then said Dăn'iel to [5]Mĕl'zar,
whom the prince of the eunuchs had
set over Dăn'iel, Hăn-a-nī'ah, Mĭsh'a-
el, and Ăz-a-rī'ah,
12 Prove thy servants, I beseech
thee, ten days; and let them give us
[6]pulse [7]to eat, and water to drink.
13 Then let our countenances be
looked upon before thee, and the countenance of the children that eat of the
portion of the king's meat: and as thou
seest, deal with thy servants.
14 So he consented to them in this
matter, and proved them ten days.
15 And at the end of ten days their
countenances appeared fairer and fat-
ter in flesh than all the children which
did eat the portion of the king's meat.
16 Thus Mĕl'zar took away the portion of their meat, and the wine that
they should drink; and gave them
pulse.

CHAPTER 1
1 [a]2 Ki. 24.1; 2 Chr. 36.6
2 [b]Jer. 27.19
[c]Gen. 10.10; Isa. 11.11; Zech. 5.11
3 [1]Foretold, 2 Ki. 20.17; Isa. 39.7
4 [d]Lev. 21.18; Judg. 8.18; Acts 7.20
[e]Acts 7.22
5 [2]the wine of his drink
7 [f]Gen. 41.45
[g]ch. 5.12
8 [h]Deut. 32.38; Ps. 141.4; Ezek. 4.13; Hos. 9.3-4
9 [i]Gen. 39.21; 1 Ki. 8.50
10 [3]sadder [4]Or, term, or, continuance
11 [5]Or, the steward
12 [6]of pulse [7]that we may eat, etc

17 ¶ As for these four children, [j]God
gave them [k]knowledge and skill in
all learning and wisdom: and [8]Dăn'iel
had understanding in all visions and
dreams.
18 Now at the end of the days that the
king had said he should bring them in,
then the prince of the eunuchs brought
them in before Nĕb-u-chăd-nĕz'zar.
19 And the king communed with
them; and among them all was found
none like Dăn'iel, Hăn-a-nī'ah, Mĭsh'-
a-el, and Ăz-a-rī'ah: therefore stood
they before the king.
20 And in all matters of [9]wisdom
and understanding, that the king inquired of them, he found them ten
times better than all the magicians *and*
astrologers that *were* in all his realm.
21 [l]And Dăn'iel continued *even* unto
the first year of king Cȳ'rus.

2

And in the second year of the reign
of Nĕb-u-chăd-nĕz'zar Nĕb-u-chăd-
nĕz'zar dreamed dreams, [a]wherewith
his spirit was troubled, and [b]his sleep
brake from him.
2 [c]Then the king commanded to call
the magicians, and the astrologers, and
the sorcerers, and the Chăl-dē'ans, for
to shew the king his dreams. So they
came and stood before the king.
3 And the king said unto them, I
have dreamed a dream, and my spirit
was troubled to know the dream.
4 Then spake the Chăl-dē'ans to the
king in Sȳr'ĭ-ack, O king, live for ever:
tell thy servants the dream, and we
will shew the interpretation.
5 The king answered and said to the
Chăl-dē'ans, The thing is gone from
me: if ye will not make known unto
me the dream, with the interpretation
thereof, ye shall be [1]cut in pieces, and
your houses shall be made a dunghill.
6 But if ye shew the dream, and the
interpretation thereof, ye shall receive
of me gifts and [2]rewards and great honour: therefore shew me the dream, and
the interpretation thereof.
7 They answered again and said, Let
the king tell his servants the dream,
and we will shew the interpretation of
it.
8 The king answered and said, I
know of certainty that ye would [3]gain
the time, because ye see the thing is
gone from me.
9 But if ye will not make known
unto me the dream, [d]*there is but* one
decree for you: for ye have prepared
lying and corrupt words to speak before me, till the time be changed: therefore tell me the dream, and I shall
know that ye can shew me the interpretation thereof.
10 ¶ The Chăl-dē'ans answered before the king, and said, There is not a
man upon the earth that can shew the
king's matter: therefore *there is* no
king, lord, nor ruler, *that* asked such
things at any magician, or astrologer,
or Chăl-dē'an.
11 And *it is* a rare thing that the
king requireth, and there is none other
that can shew it before the king, [e]ex-
cept the gods, whose dwelling is not
with flesh.
12 For this cause the [f]king was angry
and very furious, and commanded to
destroy all the wise *men* of Băb'ȳ-lon.
13 And the decree went forth that
the wise *men* should be slain; and they
sought Dăn'iel and his fellows to be
slain.
14 ¶ Then Dăn'iel [4]answered with
counsel and wisdom to Ā'rĭ-ŏch the
[5]captain of the king's guard, which
was gone forth to slay the wise *men* of
Băb'ȳ-lon:
15 He answered and said to Ā'rĭ-
ŏch the king's captain, Why *is* the decree *so* hasty from the king? Then
Ā'rĭ-ŏch made the thing known to
Dăn'iel.
16 Then Dăn'iel went in, and desired of the king that he would give
him time, and that he would shew the
king the interpretation.
17 Then Dăn'iel went to his house,
and made the thing known to Hăn-a-
nī'ah, Mĭsh'a-el, and Ăz-a-rī'ah, his
companions:
18 That they would desire mercies
[6]of the God of heaven concerning this
secret; [7]that Dăn'iel and his fellows
should not perish with the rest of the
wise *men* of Băb'ȳ-lon.
19 ¶ Then was the secret revealed
unto Dăn'iel [g]in a night vision. Then
Dăn'iel blessed the God of heaven.
20 Dăn'iel answered and said,
[h]Blessed be the name of God for ever
and ever: [i]for wisdom and might are
his:
21 And he changeth [j]the times and
the seasons: [k]he removeth kings, and
setteth up kings: [l]he giveth wisdom
unto the wise, and knowledge to them
that know understanding:
22 [m]He revealeth the deep and secret things: [n]he knoweth what *is* in the
darkness, and [o]the light dwelleth with
him.
23 I thank thee, and praise thee, O
thou God of my fathers, who hast
given me wisdom and might, and hast
[p]made known unto me now what we
desired of thee: for thou hast *now*
made known unto us the king's matter.
24 ¶ Therefore Dăn'iel went in unto
Ā'rĭ-ŏch, whom the king had ordained
to destroy the wise *men* of Băb'ȳ-lon:
he went and said thus unto him; Destroy not the wise *men* of Băb'ȳ-lon:
bring me in before the king, and I will
shew unto the king the interpretation.
25 Then Ā'rĭ-ŏch brought in Dăn'iel
before the king in haste, and said thus
unto him, [8]I have found a man of the
[9]captives of Jū'dah, that will make
known unto the king the interpretation.
26 The king answered and said to
Dăn'iel, whose name *was* Bĕl-te-shăz'-
zar, Art thou able to make known unto
me the dream which I have seen, and
the interpretation thereof?
27 Dăn'iel answered in the presence
of the king, and said, The secret which
the king hath demanded cannot the

17 [j] 1 Ki. 3.12; Ps. 119.98-100; Prov. 2.6; Eccl. 2.26; Isa. 28.29
[k] Acts. 7.22
[8] Or, he made Daniel understand
20 [9] wisdom of understanding
21 [l] ch. 6.28. ch. 10.1; He lived to see that glorious time of the return of his people from the Babylonian captivity, though he did not die then. So till is used; Ps. 112.8

CHAPTER 2
1 [a] Gen. 41.8
[b] Esth. 6.1
2 [c] Gen. 41.8; Ex. 7.11
5 [1] made pieces
6 [2] Or, fee
8 [3] buy
9 [d] Esth. 4.11
11 [e] Ex. 8.10; Matt. 19.26
12 [f] Ps. 76.10; Matt. 2.16
14 [4] returned
[5] chief of the executioners, or, slaughtermen, or, chief marshal
18 [6] from before God
[7] Or, that they should not destroy Daniel, etc
19 [g] Num. 12.6; Job 33.15-16
20 [h] Ps. 113.2
[i] Job 12.13; Matt. 6.13
21 [j] 1 Chr. 29.30; ch. 7.25
[k] Job 12.18; ch. 4.17
[l] Jas. 1.5
22 [m] Job 12.22; Ps. 25.14
[n] Ps. 139.11.12; Heb. 4.13
[o] ch. 5.11
23 [p] Amos 3.7
25 [8] That I have found
[9] children of the captivity of Judah

wise *men,* the astrologers, the magicians, the soothsayers, shew unto the
king;
28 [q]But there is a God in heaven
that revealeth secrets, [10]and maketh
known to the king Nĕb-u-chăd-nĕz'zar
what shall be in the latter days. Thy
dream, and the visions of thy head
upon thy bed, are these;
29 As for thee, O king, thy thoughts
[11]came *into thy mind* upon thy bed,
what should come to pass hereafter:
and he that revealeth secrets maketh
known to thee what shall come to pass.
30 [r]But as for me, this secret is not
revealed to me for *any* wisdom that I
have more than any living, [12]but for
their sakes that shall make known the
interpretation to the king, and that
thou mightest know the thoughts of
thy heart.
31 ¶ Thou, O king, [13]sawest, and behold a great image. This great image,
whose brightness *was* excellent, stood
before thee; and the form thereof *was*
terrible.
32 This image's head *was* of fine
gold, his breast and his arms of silver,
his belly and his [14]thighs of brass,
33 His legs of iron, his feet part of
iron and part of clay.
34 Thou sawest till that a stone was
cut out [15]without hands, which smote
the image upon his feet *that were*
of iron and clay, and brake them to
pieces.
35 Then was the iron, the clay, the
brass, the silver, and the gold, broken
to pieces together, and became like the
chaff of the summer threshingfloors;
and the wind carried them away, that
no place was found for them: and the
stone that smote the image [s]became a
great mountain, [t]and filled the whole
earth.
36 ¶ This *is* the dream; and we will
tell the interpretation thereof before
the king.
37 [u]Thou, O king, *art* a king of kings:
for [v]the God of heaven hath given thee
a kingdom, power, and strength, and
glory.
38 [w]And wheresoever the children
of men dwell, the beasts of the field
and the fowls of the heaven hath he
given into thine hand, and hath made
thee ruler over them all. Thou *art* this
head of gold.
39 And after thee shall arise [x]an-
other kingdom inferior to thee, and another third kingdom of brass, which
shall bear rule over all the earth.
40 And [y]the fourth kingdom shall be
strong as iron: forasmuch as iron breaketh in pieces and subdueth all *things:*
and as iron that breaketh all these, shall
it break in pieces and bruise.
41 And whereas thou sawest the feet
and toes, part of potters' clay, and part
of iron, the kingdom shall be divided;
but there shall be in it of the strength of
the iron, forasmuch as thou sawest the
iron mixed with miry clay.
42 And *as* the toes of the feet *were*
part of iron, and part of clay, *so* the
kingdom shall be partly strong, and
partly [16]broken.
43 And whereas thou sawest iron
mixed with miry clay, they shall mingle themselves with the seed of men:
but they shall not cleave [17]one to another, even as iron is not mixed with
clay.
44 And in [18]the days of these kings
shall the God of heaven set up a kingdom, [z]which shall never be destroyed:
and the [19]kingdom shall not be left to
other people, [a]*but* it shall break in
pieces and consume all these kingdoms, and it shall stand for ever.
45 [b]Forasmuch as thou sawest that
the stone was cut out of the mountain
[20]without hands, and that it brake in
pieces the iron, the brass, the clay, the
silver, and the gold; the great God
hath made known to the king what
shall come to pass [21]hereafter: and the
dream *is* certain, and the interpretation thereof sure.
46 ¶ [c]Then the king Nĕb-u-chăd-
nĕz'zar fell upon his face, and worshipped Dăn'iel, and commanded that
they should offer an oblation [d]and
sweet odours unto him.
47 The king answered unto Dăn'iel,
and said, Of a truth *it is,* that your God
is a God of gods, and a Lord of kings,
and a revealer of secrets, seeing thou
couldest reveal this secret.
48 Then the king made Dăn'iel a
great man, and gave him many great
gifts, and made him ruler over the
whole province of Băb'ȳ-lon, and [e]chief
of the governors over all the wise *men*
of Băb'ȳ-lon.
49 Then Dăn'iel requested of the
king, [f]and he set Shā'drach, Mē'shach,
and A-bĕd'–nĕ-gō, over the affairs of
the province of Băb'ȳ-lon: but Dăn'iel
[g]*sat* in the gate of the king.

3 Nĕb-u-chad-nĕz'zar the king made
[a]an image of gold, whose height
was threescore cubits, *and* the breadth
thereof six cubits: he set it up in the
plain of Dụ'râ, in the province of
Băb'ȳ-lon.
2 Then Nĕb-u-chăd-nĕz'zar the king
sent to gather together the princes,
the governors, and the captains, the
judges, the treasurers, the counsellers,
the sheriffs, and all the rulers of the
provinces, to come to the dedication of
the image which Nĕb-u-chăd-nĕz'zar
the king had set up.
3 Then the [b]princes, the governors,
and captains, the judges, the treasurers, the counsellers, the sheriffs, and
all the rulers of the provinces, were
gathered together unto the dedication
of the image that Nĕb-u-chăd-nĕz'zar
the king had set up; and they stood before the image that Neb-u-chad-nez'-
zar had set up.
4 Then an herald cried [1]aloud, To
you [2]it is commanded, [c]O people, nations, and languages,
5 *That* at what time ye hear the
sound of the cornet, flute, harp, sackbut, psaltery, [3]dulcimer, and all kinds
of musick, ye fall down and worship

28 [q]Gen. 40.8; Amos 4.13 [10]and hath made known
29 [11]came up
30 [r]Gen. 41.16; Acts. 3.12 [12]Or, but for the intent that the interpretation may be made known to the king
31 [13]wast seeing
32 [14]Or, sides
34 [15]Or, which was not in hands
35 [s]Isa. 2.2-3; Mic. 4.1.2
[t]Ps. 22.27; Rev. 11.15
37 [u]Ezra 7.12; Isa. 47.5
[v]Ezra 1.2
38 [w]ch. 4.21
39 [x]ch. 5.28
40 [y]ch. 7.7-23;
42 [16]Or, brittle
43 [17]this with this
44 [18]their days
[z]Gen. 49.10; [19]kingdom thereof
[a]Ps. 2.9
45 [b]Isa. 28.16 [20]Or, which was not in hand [21]after this
46 [c]Acts 10.25;
[d]Ezra 6.10
48 [e]Gen. 41.40
49 [f]Prov. 28.12;
[g]Esth. 2.19
CHAPTER 3
1 [a]1 Ki. 12.28
3 [b]Matt. 7.13
4 [1]with might [2]they command
[c]ch. 4.1
5 [3]symphony, or, singing

the golden image that Něb-u-chăd-
nĕz'zar the king hath set up:
6 And whoso falleth not down and
worshippeth shall the same hour [d]be
cast into the midst of a burning fiery
furnace.
7 Therefore at that time, when all
the people heard the sound of the cornet, flute, harp, sackbut, psaltery, and
all kinds of musick, all the people, the
nations, and the languages, fell down
and worshipped the golden image that
Něb-u-chăd-nĕz'zar the king had set
up.
8 ¶ Wherefore at that time certain
Chăl-dē'ans [e]came near, [f]and accused
the Jews.
9 They spake and said to the king
Něb-u-chăd-nĕz'zar, [g]O king, live for
ever.
10 Thou, O king, hast made a decree, that every man that shall hear the
sound of the cornet, flute, harp, sackbut, psaltery, and dulcimer, and all
kinds of musick, shall fall down and
worship the golden image:
11 And whoso falleth not down and
worshippeth, *that* he should be cast into
the midst of a burning fiery furnace.
12 [h]There are certain Jews whom
thou hast set over the affairs of the
province of Băb'y̆-lon, Shā'drach, Mē'-
shach, and A-bĕd'–nĕ-gō; these men,
O king, [4]have not regarded thee: they
serve not thy gods, nor worship the
golden image which thou hast set up.
13 ¶ Then Něb-u-chăd-nĕz'zar in *his*
rage and fury commanded to bring
Shā'drach, Mē'shach, and A-bĕd'–nĕ-
gō. [i]Then they brought these men before the king.
14 Neb-u-chad-nez'zar spake and
said unto them, *Is it* [5]true, O Shā'-
drach, Mē'shach, and A-bĕd'–ne-gō,
do not ye serve my [j]gods, nor worship
the golden image which I have set up?
15 Now if ye be ready that at what
time ye hear the sound of the cornet,
flute, harp, sackbut, psaltery, and dulcimer, and all kinds of musick, ye fall
down and worship the image which I
have made; [k]*well:* but if ye worship
not, ye shall be cast the same hour into
the midst of a burning fiery furnace;
[l]and who *is* that God that shall deliver
you out of my hands?
16 Shā'drach, Mē'shach, and A-
bĕd'–nĕ-gō, answered and said to the
king, O Něb-u-chăd-nĕz'zar, [m]we *are*
not careful to answer thee in this
matter.
17 If it be *so,* our God whom we
serve is able to deliver us from the
burning fiery furnace, and [n]he will deliver *us* out of thine hand, O king.
18 But if not, [o]be it known unto
thee, O king, that we will not serve thy
gods, nor worship the golden image
which thou hast set up.
19 ¶ Then was Něb-u-chăd-nĕz'zar
[6]full of fury, and the form of his visage was changed against Shā'drach,
Mē'shach, and A-bĕd'–nĕ-gō: *therefore* he spake, and commanded that
they should heat the furnace one seven
times more than it was wont to be
heated.
20 And he commanded the [7]most
mighty men that *were* in his army
to bind Shā'drach, Mē'shach, and A-
bĕd'–nĕ-gō, *and* to cast *them* into the
burning fiery furnace.
21 Then these men were bound in
their [8]coats, their hosen, and their
[9]hats, and their *other* garments, and
were cast into the midst of the burning
fiery furnace.
22 Therefore because the king's
[10]commandment was urgent, and the
furnace exceeding hot, the [11]flame of the
fire slew those men that took up Shā'-
drach, Mē'shach, and A-bĕd'–ne-gō.
23 And these three men, Shā'drach,
Mē'shach, and A-bĕd'–ne-gō, fell down
[p]bound into the midst of the burning
fiery furnace.
24 Then Něb-u-chăd-nĕz'zar the king
was astonied, and rose up in haste, *and*
spake, and said unto [12]his counsellers,
Did not we cast three men bound into
the midst of the fire? They answered
and said unto the king, True, O king.
25 He answered and said, Lo, I see
four men loose, [q]walking in the midst
of the fire, and [13]they have no hurt; and
the form of the fourth is like [r]the Son
of God.
26 ¶ Then Něb-u-chăd-nĕz'zar came
near to the [14]mouth of the burning fiery furnace, *and* spake, and said, Shā'-
drach, Mē'shach, and A-bĕd'–nĕ-gō,
ye servants of the most high God,
come forth, and come *hither.* Then
Shā'drach, Mē'shach, and A-bĕd'–nĕ-
gō, came forth of the midst of the fire.
27 And the princes, governors, and
captains, and the king's counsellers,
being gathered together saw these
men, [s]upon whose bodies the fire had
no power, nor was an hair of their
head singed, neither were their coats
changed, nor the smell of fire had
passed on them.
28 *Then* Něb-u-chăd-nĕz'zar spake,
and said, Blessed *be* the God of Shā'-
drach, Mē'shach, and A-bĕd'–nĕ-gō,
who hath sent his angel, and delivered
his servants that [t]trusted in him, and
have changed the king's word, and
yielded their bodies, that they might
not serve nor worship any god, except
their own God.
29 [u]Therefore [15]I make a decree,
That every people, nation, and language, which speak [16]any thing amiss
against the God of Shā'drach, Mē'-
shach, and A-bĕd'–nĕ-gō, shall be [17]cut
in pieces, and their houses shall be
made a dunghill: [v]because there is no
other God that can deliver after this
sort.
30 Then the king [18]promoted Shā'-
drach, Mē'shach, and A-bĕd'–nĕ-gō,
in the province of Băb'y̆-lon.

4

Něb-u-chad-nĕz'zar the king, [a]unto
all people, nations, and languages,
that dwell in all the earth; Peace be multiplied unto you.
2 [1]I thought it good to shew the

6 [d]Jer. 29.22; Rev. 13.15
8 [e]ch. 6.12
[f]Ezra 4.12-16; Esth. 3.6
9 [g]Neh. 2.3; Hos. 7.3
12 [h]Esth. 3.8; ch. 2.49
[4]have set no regard upon thee
13 [i]Matt. 10.18; Acts 5.25-27
14 [5]Or, of purpose, as Ex. 21.13
[j]Isa. 46.1
15 [k]Ex. 32.32; Luke 13.9
[l]Ex. 5.2; 2 Ki. 18.35
16 [m]Matt. 10.19; Acts 26.24
17 [n]1 Sam. 17.37; 2 Cor. 1.10
18 [o]Matt. 10.32; Heb. 11.25
19 [6]filled
20 [7]mighty of strength
21 [8]Or, mantles
[9]Or, turbans
22 [10]word
[11]Or, spark
23 [p]Ps. 33.18; 1 Pet. 4.12
24 [12]Or, his governors
25 [q]Isa. 43.2
[13]there is no hurt in them
[r]Job 1.6; Heb. 1.14
26 [14]door
27 [s]Mark 16.18; Heb. 11.34
28 [t]1 Chr. 5.20;
29 [u]ch. 6.26
[15]a decree is made by me
[16]error
[17]made pieces
[v]Deut. 32.31;
30 [18]made to prosper
CHAPTER 4
1 [a]ch. 3.4
2 [1]It was seemly before me

signs and wonders [b]that the high God
hath wrought toward me.
3 [c]How great *are* his signs! and
how mighty *are* his wonders! his kingdom *is* [d]an everlasting kingdom, and
his dominion *is* from generation to
generation.
4 ¶ I Nĕb-u-chăd-nĕz'zar was at rest
in mine house, and flourishing in my
palace:
5 I saw a dream which made me
afraid, [e]and the thoughts upon my bed
and the visions of my head [f]troubled
me.
6 Therefore made I a decree to bring
in all the wise *men* of Băb'ȳ-lon before
me, that they might make known unto
me the interpretation of the dream.
7 [g]Then came in the magicians, the
astrologers, the Chăl-dē'ans, and the
soothsayers: and I told the dream before them; but they did not make known
unto me the interpretation thereof.
8 ¶ But at the last Dăn'iel came in
before me, [h]whose name *was* Bĕl-te-
shăz'zar, according to the name of my
god, [i]and in whom *is* the spirit of the
holy gods: and before him I told the
dream, *saying,*
9 O Bĕl-te-shăz'zar, [j]master of the
magicians, because I know that the
spirit of the holy gods *is* in thee, and no
secret troubleth thee, tell me the visions of my dream that I have seen,
and the interpretation thereof.
10 Thus *were* the visions of mine
head in my bed; [2]I saw, and behold [k]a
tree in the midst of the earth, and the
height thereof *was* great.
11 The tree grew, and was strong,
and the height thereof reached unto
heaven, and the sight thereof to the
end of all the earth:
12 The leaves thereof *were* fair, and
the fruit thereof much, and in it *was*
meat for all: [l]the beasts of the field had
shadow under it, and the fowls of the
heaven dwelt in the boughs thereof,
and all flesh was fed of it.
13 I saw in the visions of my head
upon my bed, and, behold, [m]a watcher
and [n]an holy one came down from
heaven;
14 He cried [3]aloud, and said thus,
[o]Hew down the tree, and cut off his
branches, shake off his leaves, and
scatter his fruit: [p]let the beasts get
away from under it, and the fowls from
his branches:
15 Nevertheless leave the stump of
his roots in the earth, even with a band
of iron and brass, in the tender grass of
the field; and let it be wet with the dew
of heaven, and *let* his portion *be* with
the beasts in the grass of the earth:
16 Let his heart be changed from
man's, and let a beast's heart be given
unto him; and let seven [q]times pass
over him.
17 This matter *is* by the decree of
the watchers, and the demand by the
word of the holy ones: to the intent
[r]that the living may know [s]that the

[b]Ps. 66.16; ch. 3.26
3 [c]ch. 6.27
[d]ch. 2.44
5 [e]ch. 2.28
[f]ch. 2.1
7 [g]Gen. 41.8; Isa. 8.19
8 [h]ch. 1.7
[i]Ps. 25.14; Isa. 63.11; ch. 5.11-14
9 [j]ch. 1.20; ch. 2.48
10 [2]I was seeing
[k]Ps. 37.35-36; Isa. 10.33-34; Ezek. 31.3
12 [l]Ezek. 17.23; Lam. 4.20
13 [m]Ps. 103.20
[n]Isa. 6.3-8; ch. 8.13; Matt. 18.10; Mark 1.24; Luke 4.34; Jude 14
14 [3]with might
[o]ch. 5.20; Amos 3.6; Luke 3.9; Matt. 3.10
[p]Ezek. 31.12
16 [q]ch. 7.25; ch. 11.13; ch. 12.7
17 [r]Ps. 9.16; Ps. 83.18; Jer. 16.21
[s]ch. 2.21; ch. 5.21
18 [t]Gen. 41.8-15; Isa. 47.12-14; ch. 5.8-15
19 [u]2 Sam. 18.32; Jer. 29.7
22 [v]Job 20.5; ch. 2.38
[w]Jer. 27.6-7-8
23 [x]ch. 5.21
24 [y]Job 34.19; Ps. 107.40; Isa. 46.10-11
25 [z]Ps. 106.20
[a]Ps. 9.16; Ps. 58.11; Ps. 64.9; Ps. 83.18
[b]Jer. 27.5
26 [c]Matt. 21.25; Luke 15.18
27 [d]Isa. 58.7; Ezek. 18.7; Acts 8.22; 1 Pet. 4.8
[e]Ps. 41.1
[4]Or, an healing of thine error

most High ruleth in the kingdom of
men, and giveth it to whomsoever he
will, and setteth up over it the basest of
men.
18 This dream I king Nĕb-u-chăd-
nĕz'zar have seen. Now thou, O Bĕl-
te-shăz'zar, declare the interpretation
thereof, [t]forasmuch as all the wise
men of my kingdom are not able to
make known unto me the interpretation: but thou *art* able; for the spirit of
the holy gods *is* in thee.
19 ¶ Then Dăn'iel, whose name *was*
Bĕl-te-shăz'zar, was astonied for one
hour, and his thoughts troubled him.
The king spake, and said, Bĕl-te-shăz'-
zar, let not the dream, or the interpretation thereof, trouble thee. Bĕl-te-
shăz'zar answered and said, My lord,
[u]the dream *be* to them that hate thee,
and the interpretation thereof to thine
enemies.
20 The tree that thou sawest, which
grew, and was strong, whose height
reached unto the heaven, and the sight
thereof to all the earth;
21 Whose leaves *were* fair, and the
fruit thereof much, and in it *was* meat
for all; under which the beasts of the
field dwelt, and upon whose branches
the fowls of the heaven had their habitation:
22 [v]It *is* thou, O king, that art grown
and become strong: for thy greatness
is grown, and reacheth unto heaven,
[w]and thy dominion to the end of the
earth.
23 And whereas the king saw a
watcher and an holy one coming down
from heaven, and saying, Hew the tree
down, and destroy it; yet leave the
stump of the roots thereof in the earth,
even with a band of iron and brass, in
the tender grass of the field; and let it
be wet with the dew of heaven, [x]and
let his portion *be* with the beasts of the
field, till seven times pass over him;
24 This *is* the interpretation, O king,
and this *is* the decree of the most High,
which is come upon my lord [y]the king:
25 That they shall drive thee from
men, and thy dwelling shall be with
the beasts of the field, and they shall
make thee [z]to eat grass as oxen, and
they shall wet thee with the dew of
heaven, and seven times shall pass
over thee, [a]till thou know that the
most High ruleth in the kingdom of
men, and [b]giveth it to whomsoever he
will.
26 And whereas they commanded
to leave the stump of the tree roots; thy
kingdom shall be sure unto thee, after
that thou shalt have known that the
[c]heavens do rule.
27 Wherefore, O king, let my counsel be acceptable unto thee, and [d]break
off thy sins by righteousness, and thine
iniquities by shewing mercy to the
poor; [e]if it may be [4]a lengthening of thy
tranquillity.
28 ¶ All this came upon the king
Nĕb-u-chăd-nĕz'zar.
29 At the end of twelve months he

walked [5]in the palace of the kingdom of Băb'y̆-lon.

30 The king [f]spake, and said, Is not this great Băb'y̆-lon, that I have built for the house of the kingdom by the might of my power, and for the honour of my majesty?

31 [g]While the word *was* in the king's mouth, there fell a voice from heaven, *saying*, O king Nĕb-u-chăd-nĕz'zar, to thee it is spoken; The kingdom is departed from thee.

32 And they shall drive thee from men, and thy dwelling *shall be* with the beasts of the field: they shall make thee to eat grass as oxen, and seven times shall pass over thee, until thou know that the most High ruleth in the kingdom of men, and giveth it to whomsoever he will.

33 [h]The same hour was the thing fulfilled upon Nĕb-u-chăd-nĕz'zar: and he was driven from men, and did eat grass as oxen, and his body was wet with the dew of heaven, till his hairs were grown like eagles' *feathers*, and his nails like birds' *claws*.

34 And at the end of the days I Nĕb-u-chăd-nĕz'zar lifted up mine eyes unto heaven, and mine understanding returned unto me, and I blessed the most High, and I praised and honoured him [i]that liveth for ever, whose dominion *is* [j]an everlasting dominion, and his kingdom *is* from generation to generation:

35 And [k]all the inhabitants of the earth *are* reputed as nothing: and [l]he doeth according to his will in the army of heaven, and *among* the inhabitants of the earth: and [m]none can stay his hand, or say unto him, [n]What doest thou?

36 At the same time my reason returned unto me; and for the glory of my kingdom, mine honour and brightness returned unto me; and my counsellers and my lords sought unto me; and I was established in my kingdom, and excellent majesty was [o]added unto me.

37 Now I Nĕb-u-chăd-nĕz'zar praise and extol and honour the King of heaven, all whose works *are* truth, and his ways judgment: and those that walk in pride he is able to abase.

5 Bĕl-shăz'zar the king [a]made a great feast to a thousand of his lords, and drank wine before the thousand.

2 Bĕl-shăz'zar, whiles he tasted the wine, commanded to bring the golden and silver vessels which his [1]father Nĕb-u-chăd-nĕz'zar had [2]taken out of the temple which *was* in Je-ru'sa-lĕm; that the king, and his princes, his wives, and his concubines, might [b]drink therein.

3 Then they brought the golden vessels that were taken out of the temple of the house of God which *was* at Je-ru'sa-lĕm; and the king, and his princes, his wives, and his concubines, drank in them.

4 They drank wine, [c]and praised the gods of gold, and of silver, of brass, of iron, of wood, and of stone.

29 [5]Or, upon
30 [f]Prov. 16.18; Isa. 26.10
31 [g]ch. 5.5; Acts. 12.23
33 [h]Job 20.5; Ps. 37.35-36
34 [i]ch. 12.7; Rev. 4.10
[j]Ps. 10.16; Jer. 10.10; Mic. 4.7; Luke 1.33; Rev. 11.15
35 [k]Ps. 39.5; Isa. 40.15
[l]1 Sam. 3.18; Ps. 33.11; Isa. 46.10-11
[m]Job 34.29
[n]Job 9.12; Isa. 45.9
36 [o]Job 42.12
CHAPTER 5
1 [a]Esth. 1.3; Isa. 21.5; Jer. 51.39-57; Nah. 1.10; Mark 6.21
2 [1]Or, grandfather
[2]brought forth
[b]Prov. 20.1
4 [c]Ps. 115.4-8; Rev. 9.20
5 [d]ch. 4.31
6 [3]brightnesses
[4]changed it
[e]Job 18.11
[5]bindings, or, knots, or, girdles
[f]Nah. 2.10
7 [6]with might
[g]Isa. 47.13
[7]Or, purple
[h]ch. 6.2
8 [i]Gen. 41.8; Isa. 47.13
9 [8]brightnesses
10 [j]ch. 3.9
11 [9]Or, grandfather
[10]Or, grandfather
[k]ch. 4.9
12 [l]ch. 6.3
[11]Or, of an interpreter, etc
[12]Or, of a dissolver
[13]knots
13 [14]Or, grandfather
16 [15]interpret

5 ¶ [d]In the same hour came forth fingers of a man's hand, and wrote over against the candlestick upon the plaister of the wall of the king's palace: and the king saw the part of the hand that wrote.

6 Then the king's [3]countenance [4]was changed, and his [e]thoughts troubled him, so that the [5]joints of his loins were loosed, and his [f]knees smote one against another.

7 The king cried [6]aloud to bring in [g]the astrologers, the Chăl-dē'ans, and the soothsayers. *And* the king spake, and said to the wise *men* of Băb'y̆-lon, Whosoever shall read this writing, and shew me the interpretation thereof, shall be clothed with [7]scarlet, and *have* a chain of gold about his neck, [h]and shall be the third ruler in the kingdom.

8 Then came in all the king's wise *men*: [i]but they could not read the writing, nor make known to the king the interpretation thereof.

9 Then was king Bĕl-shăz'zar greatly troubled, and his [8]countenance was changed in him, and his lords were astonied.

10 ¶ *Now* the queen by reason of the words of the king and his lords came into the banquet house: *and* the queen spake and said, [j]O king, live for ever: let not thy thoughts trouble thee, nor let thy countenance be changed:

11 There is a man in thy kingdom, in whom *is* the spirit of the holy gods; and in the days of thy [9]father light and understanding and wisdom, like the wisdom of the gods, was found in him; whom the king Nĕb-u-chăd-nĕz'zar thy [10]father, the king, *I say*, thy father, made [k]master of the magicians, astrologers, Chăl-dē'ans, *and* soothsayers;

12 [l]Forasmuch as an excellent spirit, and knowledge, and understanding, [11]interpreting of dreams, and shewing of hard sentences, and [12]dissolving of [13]doubts, were found in the same Dăn'iel, whom the king named Bĕl-te-shăz'zar: now let Dăn'iel be called, and he will shew the interpretation.

13 Then was Dăn'iel brought in before the king. *And* the king spake and said unto Dăn'iel, *Art* thou that Dăn'iel, which *art* of the children of the captivity of Jū'dah, whom the king my [14]father brought out of Jew'ry̆?

14 I have even heard of thee, that the spirit of the gods *is* in thee, and *that* light and understanding and excellent wisdom is found in thee.

15 And now the wise *men*, the astrologers, have been brought in before me, that they should read this writing, and make known unto me the interpretation thereof: but they could not shew the interpretation of the thing:

16 And I have heard of thee, that thou canst [15]make interpretations, and dissolve doubts: now if thou canst read the writing, and make known to me the interpretation thereof, thou shalt be clothed with scarlet, and *have* a chain of gold about thy neck, and shalt be the third ruler in the kingdom.

17 ¶ Then Dăn'iel answered and said
before the king, Let thy gifts be to thyself, and give thy [16]rewards to another; yet I will read the writing unto
the king, and make known to him the
interpretation.
18 O thou king, [m]the most high God
gave Nĕb-u-chăd-nĕz'zar thy father a
kingdom, and majesty, and glory, and
honour:
19 And for the majesty that he gave
him, [n]all people, nations, and languages, trembled and feared before
him: whom he would he slew; and
whom he would he kept alive; and
whom he would he set up; and whom
he would he put down.
20 [o]But when his heart was lifted up,
and his mind hardened [17]in pride, he
was [18]deposed from his kingly throne,
and they took his glory from him:
21 And he was [p]driven from the
sons of men; and [19]his heart was made
like the beasts, and his dwelling *was*
with the wild asses: they fed him with
grass like oxen, and his body was wet
with the dew of heaven; [q]till he knew
that the most high God ruled in the
kingdom of men, and *that* he appoint-
eth over it whomsoever he will.
22 And thou his son, O Bĕl-shăz'zar,
[r]hast not humbled thine heart, though
thou knewest all this;
23 [s]But hast lifted up thyself against
the Lord of heaven; and they have
brought the vessels of his house before thee, and thou, and thy lords, thy
wives, and thy concubines, have drunk
wine in them; and thou hast praised the
gods of silver, and gold, of brass, iron,
wood, and stone, [t]which see not, nor
hear, nor know: and the God in whose
hand thy breath *is*, [u]and whose *are* all
thy ways, hast thou not glorified:
24 Then was the part of the hand
sent from him; and this writing was
written.
25 ¶ And this *is* the writing that
was written, MĒ'NE, MĒ'NE, TĒ'KEL,
U-PHÄR'SIN.
26 This *is* the interpretation of the
thing: MĒ'NE; God hath [v]numbered
thy kingdom, and finished it.
27 TĒ'KEL; [w]Thou art weighed in
the balances, and art found wanting.
28 PĒ'RĔS; Thy kingdom is divided,
and given to the [x]Mēdes and
[y]Pĕr'sians.
29 Then commanded Bĕl-shăz'zar,
and they clothed Dăn'iel with scarlet,
and *put* a chain of gold about his neck,
and made a proclamation concerning
him, that he should be the third ruler in
the kingdom.
30 ¶ [z]In that night was Bĕl-shăz'zar
the king of the Chăl-dē'ans slain.
31 [a]And Da-rī'us the Mē'dĭ-an took
the kingdom, [20]*being* [21]about threescore and two years old.

6

It pleased Da-rī'us to set [a]over the
kingdom an hundred and twenty
princes, which should be over the
whole kingdom;
2 And over these three presidents;
of whom [b]Dăn'iel *was* first: that the
princes might give accounts unto them,
and the king should have no damage.
3 Then this Dăn'iel was preferred
above the presidents and princes, [c]be-
cause an excellent spirit *was* in him;
and the king thought to set him over
the whole realm.
4 ¶ [d]Then the presidents and princes
sought to find occasion against Dăn'iel
concerning the kingdom; but [e]they
could find none occasion nor fault;
forasmuch as he *was* faithful, neither
was there any error or fault found in
him.
5 Then said these men, We shall not
find any occasion against this Dăn'iel,
except we find *it* against him concerning the law of his God.
6 Then these presidents and princes
[1]assembled together to the king, and
said thus unto him, [f]King Da-rī'us, live
for ever.
7 All the presidents of the kingdom,
the governors, and the princes, the
counsellers, and the captains, have
consulted together to establish a royal
statute, and to make a firm [2]decree,
that whosoever shall ask a petition of
any God or man for thirty days, save of
thee, O king, he shall be cast into the
den of lions.
8 Now, O king, establish the decree,
and sign the writing, that it be not
changed, according to the [g]law of the
Mēdes and Pĕr'sians, which [3]altereth
not.
9 [h]Wherefore king Da-rī'us signed
the writing and the decree.
10 ¶ Now when Dăn'iel knew that
the writing was signed, he went into his
house; and [i]his windows being open in
his chamber [j]toward Je-ru'sa-lĕm, he
kneeled upon his knees [k]three times a
day, and prayed, and gave thanks before his God, as he did aforetime.
11 Then these men assembled, and
found Dăn'iel praying and making supplication before his God.
12 [l]Then they came near, and spake
before the king concerning the king's
decree; Hast thou not signed a decree,
that every man that shall ask *a petition* of any God or man within thirty
days, save of thee, O king, shall be cast
into the den of lions? The king answered and said, The thing *is* true, according to the law of the Mēdes and
Pĕr'sians, which altereth not.
13 Then answered they and said before the king, That Dăn'iel, [m]which *is*
of the children of the captivity of Jū'-
dah, [n]regardeth not thee, O king, nor
the decree that thou hast signed, but
maketh his petition three times a day.
14 Then the king, when he heard
these words, [o]was sore displeased with
himself, and set *his* heart on Dăn'iel to
deliver him: and he laboured till the going down of the sun to deliver him.
15 Then these men assembled unto
the king, and said unto the king, Know,
O king, that the law of the Mēdes and
Pĕr'sians *is*, That no decree nor statute
which the king establisheth may be
changed.

17 [16]Or, fee
18 [m]ch. 2.37
19 [n]Jer. 25.9; ch. 3.4
20 [o]Ex. 9.17; Prov. 16.5; ch. 4.30
[17]Or, to deal proudly
[18]made to come down
21 [p]ch. 4.32
[19]Or, he made his heart equal, etc
[q]Ex. 9.14-16; ch. 4.17
22 [r]2 Chr. 33.23; Ps. 119.46
23 [s]Isa. 37.23; Rev. 13.6
[t]Ps. 115.5; Hab. 2.18
[u]Job 31.4; Prov. 20.24
26 [v]Jer. 25.12
27 [w]Ps. 62.9; Jer. 6.30
28 [x]Foretold, Isa. 21.2; ch. 9.1
[y]ch. 6.28
30 [z]Jer. 51.31-39-57
31 [a]ch. 9.1
[20]he as the son of, etc
[21]Or, now
CHAPTER 6
1 [a]Esth. 1.1
2 [b]1 Sam. 2.30
3 [c]Prov. 3.35; ch. 5.12
4 [d]Eccl. 4.4
[e]Phil. 2.15; 1 Pet. 2.12
6 [1]Or, came tumultuously
[f]Neh. 2.3; ch. 2.4
7 [2]Or, interdict
8 [g]Esth. 1.19
[3]passeth not
9 [h]Ps. 118.9
10 [i]Matt. 10.32
[j]Ps. 5.7; Jon. 2.4
[k]1 Ki. 18.36; 1 Thess. 5.17-18
12 [l]ch. 3.8
13 [m]ch. 1.6
[n]Esth. 3.8; Acts 17.7
14 [o]ch. 3.13; Mark 6.26

16 Then the king commanded, and they brought Dăn'iel, and cast *him* into the den of lions. *Now* the king spake and said unto Dăn'iel, [p]Thy God whom thou servest continually, he will deliver thee.

17 [q]And a stone was brought, and laid upon the mouth of the den; [r]and the king sealed it with his own signet, and with the signet of his lords; that the purpose might not be changed concerning Dăn'iel.

18 ¶ Then the king went to his palace, and passed the night fasting: neither were [4]instruments of musick brought before him: [s]and his sleep went from him.

19 Then the king arose very early in the morning, and went in haste unto the den of lions.

20 And when he came to the den, he cried with a lamentable voice unto Dăn'iel: *and* the king spake and said to Dăn'iel, O Dăn'iel, servant of the living God, [t]is thy God, whom thou servest continually, able to deliver thee from the lions?

21 Then said Dăn'iel unto the king, [u]O king, live for ever.

22 [v]My God hath sent [w]his angel, and hath [x]shut the lions' mouths, that they have not hurt me: forasmuch as before him innocency was found in me; and also before thee, O king, have I done no hurt.

23 Then was the king exceeding glad for him, and commanded that they should take Dăn'iel up out of the den. So Dăn'iel was taken up out of the den, [y]and no manner of hurt was found upon him, because he believed in his God.

24 ¶ And the king commanded, [z]and they brought those men which had accused Dăn'iel, and they cast *them* into the den of lions, them, [a]their children, and their wives; and the lions had the mastery of them, and brake all their bones in pieces or ever they came at the bottom of the den.

25 ¶ [b]Then king Da-rī'us wrote unto all people, nations, and languages, that dwell in all the earth; Peace be multiplied unto you.

26 [c]I make a decree, That in every dominion of my kingdom men [d]tremble and fear before the God of Dăn'iel: [e]for he *is* the living God, and stedfast for ever, and his kingdom *that* which shall not be [f]destroyed, and his dominion *shall be even* unto the end.

27 He delivereth and rescueth, [g]and he worketh signs and wonders in heaven and in earth, who hath delivered Dăn'iel from the [5]power of the lions.

28 So this Dăn'iel prospered in the reign of Da-rī'us, [h]and in the reign of [i]Cȳ'rus the Pēr'sian.

7 In the first year of Bĕl-shăz'zar king of Băb'ȳ-lon Dăn'iel [1]had a dream and [a]visions of his head upon his bed: then he wrote the dream, *and* told the sum of the [2]matters.

2 Dăn'iel spake and said, I saw in my vision by night, and, behold, the four winds of the heaven strove upon the great sea.

3 And four great beasts [b]came up from the sea, diverse one from another.

4 The first *was* [c]like a lion, and had eagle's wings: I beheld till the wings thereof were plucked, [3]and it was lifted up from the earth, and made stand upon the feet as a man, and a man's heart was given to it.

5 [d]And behold another beast, a second, like to a bear, and [4]it raised up itself on one side, and *it had* three ribs in the mouth of it between the teeth of it: and they said thus unto it, Arise, devour much flesh.

6 After this I beheld, and lo another, like a leopard, which had upon the back of it four wings of a fowl; the beast had also [e]four heads; and dominion was given to it.

7 After this I saw in the night visions, and behold a fourth beast, dreadful and terrible, and strong exceedingly; and it had great iron teeth: it devoured and brake in pieces, and stamped the residue with the feet of it: and it *was* diverse from all the beasts that *were* before it; [f]and it had ten horns.

8 I considered the horns, and, behold, [g]there came up among them another little horn, before whom there were three of the first horns plucked up by the roots: and, behold, in this horn *were* eyes like the eyes of man, and a mouth speaking great things.

9 ¶ [h]I beheld till the thrones were cast down, and [i]the Ancient of days did sit, [j]whose garment *was* white as snow, and the hair of his head like the pure wool: his throne *was like* the fiery flame, [k]*and* his wheels *as* burning fire.

10 A fiery stream issued and came forth from before him: [l]thousand thousands ministered unto him, and ten thousand times ten thousand stood before him: the judgment was set, and the books were opened.

11 I beheld then because of the voice of the great words which the horn spake: [m]I beheld *even* till the beast was slain, and his body destroyed, and given to the burning flame.

12 As concerning the rest of the beasts, they had their dominion taken away: yet [5]their lives were prolonged for a season and time.

13 I saw in the night visions, and, behold, [n]*one* like the Son of man came with the clouds of heaven, and came to the Ancient of days, and they brought him near before him.

14 [o]And there was given him dominion, and glory, and a kingdom, that all people, nations, and languages, should serve him: his dominion *is* [p]an everlasting dominion, which shall not pass away, and his kingdom *that* which shall not be destroyed.

15 ¶ I Dăn'iel was grieved in my spirit in the midst of *my* [6]body, and the visions of my head troubled me.

16 [p]Isa. 41.10; 2 Cor. 1.10
17 [q]Lam. 3.53; Mark 15.46
[r]Matt. 27.66
18 [4]Or, table
[s]Esth. 6.1; ch. 2.1
20 [t]Gen. 18.14; Luke 1.37
21 [u]ch. 2.4
22 [v]ch. 3.28
[w]Heb. 1.14
[x]1 Sam. 17.37; 2 Tim. 4.17
23 [y]Mark 16.18
24 [z]Deut. 19.19
[a]Deut. 24.16; Esth. 9.10
25 [b]ch. 4.1
26 [c]ch. 3.29
[d]Ps. 99.1
[e]ch. 4.34
[f]ch. 2.44; ch. 4.3-34; Luke 1.33
27 [g]ch. 4.3
[5]hand
28 [h]ch. 1.21
[i]Ezra 1.1
CHAPTER 7
1 [1]saw
[a]ch. 2.28
[2]Or, words
3 [b]Zech. 6.1-4; Rev. 13.1
4 [c]Deut. 28.49; Jer. 4.7-13
[3]Or, wherewith
5 [d]ch. 2.39
[4]Or, it raised up one dominion
6 [e]ch. 8.8-22
7 [f]Rev. 12.3
8 [g]ch. 8.9
9 [h]1 Cor. 15.24; Rev. 20.4
[i]Ps. 90.2
[j]Ps. 104.2;
[k]Ps. 104.3-4
10 [l]Deut. 33.2;
11 [m]Rev. 19.20
12 [5]a prolonging in life was given them
13 [n]Isa. 9.6-7
14 [o]Ps. 2.6;
[p]Isa. 9.7
15 [6]sheath

16 I came near unto one of them that stood by, and asked him the truth of all this. So he told me, and made me know the interpretation of the things.

17 These great beasts, which are four, *are* four kings, *which* shall arise out of the earth.

18 But [q]the saints of the [7]most High shall take the kingdom, and possess the kingdom for ever, even for ever and ever.

19 Then I would know the truth of the fourth beast, which was diverse [8]from all the others, exceeding dreadful, whose teeth *were of* iron, and his nails *of* brass; *which* devoured, brake in pieces, and stamped the residue with his feet;

20 And of the ten horns that *were* in his head, and *of* the other which came up, and before whom three fell; even *of* that horn that had eyes, and a mouth that spake very great things, whose look *was* more stout than his fellows.

21 I beheld, [r]and the same horn made war with the saints, and prevailed against them;

22 [s]Until the Ancient of days came, [t]and judgment was given to the saints of the most High; and the time came that the saints possessed the kingdom.

23 Thus he said, The fourth beast shall be the fourth kingdom upon earth, which shall be diverse from all kingdoms, and shall devour the whole earth, and shall tread it down, and break it in pieces.

24 [u]And the ten horns out of this kingdom *are* ten kings *that* shall arise: and another shall rise after them; and he shall be diverse from the first, and he shall subdue three kings.

25 [v]And he shall speak *great* words against the most High, and shall [w]wear out the saints of the most High, and [x]think to change times and laws: and [y]they shall be given into his hand [z]until a time and times and the dividing of time.

26 But the judgment shall sit, and they shall take away his dominion, to consume and to destroy *it* unto the end.

27 And the kingdom and dominion, and the greatness of the kingdom under the whole heaven, shall be given to the people of the saints of the most High, [a]whose kingdom *is* an everlasting kingdom, and all [9]dominions shall serve and obey him.

28 Hitherto *is* the end of the matter. As for me Dăn′iel, my cogitations much troubled me, and my countenance changed in me: but I [b]kept the matter in my heart.

8 In the third year of the reign of king Bĕl-shăz′zar a vision appeared unto me, *even unto* me Dăn′iel, after that which appeared unto me at the first.

2 And I saw in a vision; and it came to pass, when I saw, that I *was* at [a]Shụ′shan *in* the palace, which *is* in the province [b]of Ē′lăm; and I saw in a vision, and I was by the river of Ū′la-ī.

3 Then I lifted up mine eyes, and saw, and behold, there stood before the river a ram which had *two* horns: and the *two* horns *were* high; but one *was* higher than [1]the other, and the higher came up last.

4 I saw the ram pushing westward, and northward, and southward; so that no beasts might stand before him, neither *was there any* that could deliver out of his hand; [c]but he did according to his will, and became great.

5 And as I was considering, behold, an he goat came from the west on the face of the whole earth, and [2]touched not the ground: and the goat *had* [3]a notable horn between his eyes.

6 And he came to the ram that had *two* horns, which I had seen standing before the river, and ran unto him in the fury of his power.

7 And I saw him come close unto the ram, and he was moved with choler against him, and smote the ram, and brake his two horns: and there was no power in the ram to stand before him, but he cast him down to the ground, and stamped upon him: and there was none that could deliver the ram out of his hand.

8 Therefore the he goat waxed very great: and when he was strong, the great horn was broken; and for it came up [d]four notable ones toward the four winds of heaven.

9 And out of one of them came forth a little horn, which waxed exceeding great, [e]toward the south, and toward the east, and toward the [f]pleasant *land*.

10 [g]And it waxed great, *even* [4]to the host of heaven; and [h]it cast down *some* of the host and of the stars to the ground, and stamped upon them.

11 Yea, [i]he magnified *himself* even [5]to the prince of the host, and [6]by him the daily *sacrifice* was taken away, and the place of his sanctuary was cast down.

12 And [7]an host was given *him* against the daily *sacrifice* by reason of transgression, and it cast down the truth to the ground; and it practised, and prospered.

13 ¶ Then I heard [j]one saint speaking, and another saint said unto [8]that certain *saint* which spake, How long *shall be* the vision *concerning* the daily *sacrifice*, and the transgression [9]of desolation, to give both the sanctuary and the host to be trodden under foot?

14 And he said unto me, Unto two thousand and three hundred [10]days; then shall the sanctuary be [11]cleansed.

15 ¶ And it came to pass, when I, *even* I Dăn′iel, had seen the vision, and sought for the meaning, then, behold, there stood before me as the appearance of a man.

16 And I heard a man's voice between *the banks of* Ū′la-ī, which called, and said, [k]Gā′brĭ-el, make this *man* to understand the vision.

17 So he came near where I stood: and when he came, I was afraid, and [l]fell upon my face: but he said unto

18 [q]Isa. 60.12 [7]high ones, that is, things, or, places
19 [8]from all those
21 [r]Rev. 11.7
22 [s]2 Thess. 2.8 [t]1 Cor. 6.2; Rev. 1.6; Rev. 20.4
24 [u]Rev. 17.12
25 [v]Isa. 37.23 [w]Rev. 17.6; Rev. 18.24 [x]ch. 2.21 [y]Rev. 13.7 [z]ch. 12.7; Rev. 12.14
27 [a]Ps. 146.10; Luke 1.33; Rev. 11.15 [9]Or, rulers, Isa. 60.12
28 [b]Luke 2.19

CHAPTER 8
2 [a]Neh. 1.1; Esth. 2.8; Esth. 3.15; Esth. 4.16; Esth. 8.15; Esth. 9.11-15 [b]Gen. 10.22
3 [1]the second
4 [c]ch. 11.3
5 [2]Or, none touched him in the earth [3]a horn of sight
8 [d]ch. 7.6
9 [e]ch. 11.25 [f]Ps. 48.2
10 [g]Isa. 14.13; ch. 11.28 [4]Or, against the host [h]Rev. 12.4
11 [i]Jer. 48.26; 2 Thess. 2.4 [5]Or, against [6]Or, from him
12 [7]Or, the host was given over for the transgression against the daily sacrifice.
13 [j]1 Pet. 1.12 [8]Palmoni, or, the numberer of secrets, or the wonderful numberer [9]Or, making desolate
14 [10]evening, morning [11]justified
16 [k]ch. 9.21
17 [l]Rev. 1.17

me, Understand, O son of man: for at
the time of the end *shall be* the vision.
18 Now as he was speaking with
me, I was in a deep sleep on my face
toward the ground: but he touched me,
and [12]set me upright.
19 And he said, Behold, I will make
thee know what shall be in the last end
of the indignation: for at the time appointed the end *shall be*.
20 The ram which thou sawest having *two* horns *are* the kings of Mē'dĭ-ȧ
and Pēr'siȧ.
21 And the rough goat *is* the king of
Grē'çiȧ: and the great horn that *is* between his eyes *is* the first king.
22 Now that being broken, whereas
four stood up for it, four kingdoms
shall stand up out of the nation, but not
in his power.
23 And in the latter time of their
kingdom, when the transgressors [13]are
come to the full, a king [m]of fierce countenance, and understanding dark sentences, shall stand up.
24 And his power shall be mighty,
but [n]not by his own power: and he
shall destroy wonderfully, and shall
prosper, and practise, and shall destroy the mighty and the [14]holy people.
25 And through his policy also he
shall cause craft to prosper in his hand;
and he shall magnify *himself* in his
heart, and by [15]peace shall destroy
many: he shall also stand up against
the Prince of princes; but he shall be
[o]broken without hand.
26 And the vision of the evening and
the morning which was told *is* true:
[p]wherefore shut thou up the vision; for
it *shall be* for many days.
27 And I Dăn'iel fainted, and was
sick *certain* days; afterward I rose up,
[q]and did the king's business; and I was
astonished at the vision, but none understood *it*.

9

In the first year [a]of Da-rī'us the son
of A-hăs-ū-ē'rŭs, of the seed of the
Mēdes, [1]which was made king over the
realm of the Chăl-dē'ans;
2 In the first year of his reign I Dăn'-
iel understood by books the number of
the years, whereof the word of the LORD
came to [b]Jĕr-e-mī'ah the prophet, that
he would accomplish seventy years in
the desolations of Je-ru̥'sa-lĕm.
3 ¶ And I set my face unto the Lord
God, to seek by prayer and supplications, with fasting, and sackcloth, and
ashes:
4 And I prayed unto the LORD my
God, and made my confession, and
said, O Lord, the great and dreadful
God, keeping the covenant and mercy
to them that love him, and to them that
keep his commandments;
5 [c]We have sinned, and have committed iniquity, and have done wickedly, and have rebelled, even by departing from thy precepts and from thy
judgments:
6 [d]Neither have we hearkened unto
thy servants the prophets, which spake
in thy name to our kings, our princes,

18 [12]made me stand upon my standing
23 [13]are accomplished
[m]Deut. 28.50
24 [n]Rev. 13.7
[14]people of the holy ones
25 [15]Or, prosperity
[o]Job 34.20; Lam. 4.6
26 [p]Ezek. 12.27; ch. 10.14; Rev. 22.10
27 [q]ch. 2.48-49
CHAPTER 9
1 [a]ch. 1.21; ch. 5.31
[1]Or, in which he, etc
2 [b]2 Chr. 36.21; Ezra 1.1; Jer. 25.11-12
5 [c]1 Ki. 8.47; Ezra 9.6; Neh. 1.6; Neh. 9.33-34; Ps. 106.6; Isa. 64.5-6-7; Jer. 3.25; Jer. 14.7
6 [d]2 Chr. 36.15-16
7 [e]Ezra 9.15; Neh. 9.33; Ps. 51.4; Ps. 119.137; Jer. 12.1
[2]Or, thou hast, etc
9 [f]Ex. 34.6; Num. 14.18; Neh. 9.17; Joel 2.13
11 [g]Isa. 1.5-6; Jer. 8.10
[h]Deut. 27.15-26
12 [i]Lam. 2.17; Matt. 5.18
13 [3]intreated we not the face of the, etc
15 [4]made thee a name
18 [5]whereupon thy name is called
[6]cause to fall

and our fathers, and to all the people of
the land.
7 O Lord, [e]righteousness [2]*belong-*
eth unto thee, but unto us confusion of
faces, as at this day; to the men of
Jū'dah, and to the inhabitants of Je-
ru̥'sa-lĕm, and unto all Ĭs'ra-el, *that*
are near, and *that are* far off, through
all the countries whither thou hast
driven them, because of their trespass
that they have trespassed against thee.
8 O Lord, to us *belongeth* confusion
of face, to our kings, to our princes,
and to our fathers, because we have
sinned against thee.
9 To [f]the Lord our God *belong* mercies and forgivenesses, though we have
rebelled against him;
10 Neither have we obeyed the voice
of the LORD our God, to walk in his
laws, which he set before us by his servants the prophets.
11 Yea, [g]all Ĭs'ra-el have transgressed thy law, even by departing,
that they might not obey thy voice;
therefore the curse is [h]poured upon us,
and the oath that *is* written in the law
of Mō'ses the servant of God, because
we have sinned against him.
12 And he [i]hath confirmed his words,
which he spake against us, and against
our judges that judged us, by bringing
upon us a great evil: for under the whole
heaven hath not been done as hath been
done upon Je-ru̥'sa-lĕm.
13 As *it is* written in the law of
Mō'ses, all this evil is come upon us:
yet [3]made we not our prayer before the
LORD our God, that we might turn
from our iniquities, and understand
thy truth.
14 Therefore hath the LORD watched
upon the evil, and brought it upon us:
for the LORD our God *is* righteous in
all his works which he doeth: for we
obeyed not his voice.
15 And now, O Lord our God, that
hast brought thy people forth out of
the land of Ē'gypt with a mighty hand,
and hast [4]gotten thee renown, as at
this day; we have sinned, we have
done wickedly.
16 ¶ O Lord, according to all thy
righteousness, I beseech thee, let thine
anger and thy fury be turned away
from thy city Je-ru̥'sa-lĕm, thy holy
mountain: because for our sins, and
for the iniquities of our fathers, Je-
ru̥'sa-lĕm and thy people *are become* a
reproach to all *that are* about us.
17 Now therefore, O our God, hear
the prayer of thy servant, and his supplications, and cause thy face to shine
upon thy sanctuary that is desolate, for
the Lord's sake.
18 O my God, incline thine ear, and
hear; open thine eyes, and behold our
desolations, and the city [5]which is
called by thy name: for we do not [6]pres-
ent our supplications before thee for
our righteousnesses, but for thy great
mercies.
19 O Lord, hear; O Lord, forgive; O
Lord, hearken and do; defer not, for

thine own sake, O my God: for thy city and thy people are called by thy name.

20 ¶ And whiles I *was* speaking, and praying, and confessing my sin and the sin of my people Is'ra-el, and presenting my supplication before the LORD my God for the holy mountain of my God;

21 Yea, whiles I *was* speaking in prayer, even the man Gā'brĭ-el, whom I had seen in the vision at the beginning, being caused to fly [7]swiftly, touched me about the time of the evening oblation.

22 And he informed *me,* and talked with me, and said, O Dăn'iel, I am now come forth [8]to give thee skill and understanding.

23 At the beginning of thy supplications the [9]commandment came forth, and I am come to shew *thee;* for thou *art* [10]greatly beloved: therefore understand the matter, and consider the vision.

24 [11]Seventy weeks are determined upon thy people and upon thy holy city, [12]to finish the transgression, and [13]to make an end of sins, and to make reconciliation for iniquity, and to bring in everlasting righteousness, and to seal up the vision and [14]prophecy, and to anoint the most Holy.

25 Know therefore and understand, *that* from the going forth of the commandment [15]to restore and to build Je-ru'sa-lĕm unto the Mĕs-sī'ah the Prince *shall be* seven weeks, and threescore and two weeks: the street [16]shall be built again, and the [17]wall, even [18]in troublous times.

26 And after threescore and two weeks shall Mĕs-sī'ah be cut off, [19]but not for himself: [20]and the people of the prince that shall come shall destroy the city and the sanctuary; and the end thereof *shall be* with a flood, and unto the end of the war [21]desolations are determined.

27 And he shall confirm [22]the covenant with many for one week: and in the midst of the week he shall cause the sacrifice and the oblation to cease, [23]and for the overspreading of abominations he shall make *it* desolate, even until the consummation, and that determined shall be poured [24]upon the desolate.

10 In the third year of Cȳ'rus king of Pĕr'siȧ a thing was revealed unto Dăn'iel, whose name was called Bĕl-te-shăz'zar; and the thing *was* true, but the time appointed *was* [1]long: and he understood the thing, and had understanding of the vision.

2 In those days I Dăn'iel was mourning three [2]full weeks.

3 I ate no [3]pleasant bread, neither came flesh nor wine in my mouth, neither did I anoint myself at all, till three whole weeks were fulfilled.

4 And in the four and twentieth day of the first month, as I was by the side of the great river, which *is* [4]Hĭd'de-kel;

5 Then I lifted up mine eyes, and looked, and behold [5]a certain man clothed in linen, whose loins *were* girded with fine gold of Ū'phăz:

6 His body also *was* like the beryl, and his face [a]as the appearance of lightning, and his eyes as lamps of fire, and his arms and his feet like in colour to polished brass, and the voice of his words like the voice of a multitude.

7 And I Dăn'iel alone saw the vision: for the men that were with me saw not the vision; but a great quaking fell upon them, so that they fled to hide themselves.

8 Therefore I was left alone, and [b]saw this great vision, and there remained no strength in me: for my [6]comeliness was turned in me into corruption, and I retained no strength.

9 Yet heard I the voice of his words: and when I heard the voice of his words, then was I in a deep sleep on my face, and my face toward the [c]ground.

10 ¶ [d]And, behold, an hand touched me, which [7]set me upon my knees and *upon* the palms of my hands.

11 And he said unto me, O Dăn'iel, [8]a man greatly beloved, understand the words that I speak unto thee, and [9]stand upright: for unto thee am I now sent. And when he had spoken this word unto me, I stood trembling.

12 Then said he unto me, [e]Fear not, Dăn'iel: for from the first day that thou didst set thine heart to understand, and to chasten thyself before thy God, thy words were heard, and I am come for thy words.

13 But the prince of the kingdom of Pĕr'siȧ withstood me one and twenty days: but, lo, [f]Mī'chaĕl, [10]one of the chief princes, came to help me; and I remained there with the kings of Pĕr'siȧ.

14 Now I am come to make thee understand what shall befall thy people in the latter days: for yet the vision *is* for *many* days.

15 And when he had spoken such words unto me, [g]I set my face toward the ground, and I became dumb.

16 And, behold, *one* like the similitude of the sons of men [h]touched my lips: then I opened my mouth, and spake, and said unto him that stood before me, O my lord, by the vision my sorrows are turned upon me, and I have retained no strength.

17 For how can [11]the servant of this my lord talk with this my lord? for as for me, straightway there remained no strength in me, neither is there breath left in me.

18 Then there came again and touched me *one* like the appearance of a man, and he strengthened me,

19 And said, O man greatly beloved, fear not: peace *be* unto thee, be strong, yea, be strong. And when he had spoken unto me, I was strengthened, and said, Let my lord speak; for thou hast strengthened me.

20 Then said he, Knowest thou wherefore I come unto thee? and now will I return to fight with the prince of

21 [7]with weariness, or, flight
22 [8]to make thee skilful of understanding
23 [9]word [10]a man of desires
24 [11]They begin from the 20th of Artaxerxes [12]Or, to restrain [13]Or, to seal up [14]prophet
25 [15]Or, to build again Jerusalem [16]shall return and be built [17]Or, breach, or, ditch [18]in strait of times
26 [19]Or, and shall have nothing [20]Or, and the Jews they shall be no more his people: or, and the prince's Messiah's future people [21]Or, it shall be cut off by desolations
27 [22]Or, a [23]Or, and upon the battlements shall be the idols of the desolator [24]Or, upon the desolator

CHAPTER 10
1 [1]great
2 [2]weeks of days
3 [3]bread of desires
4 [4]Or, Tigris
5 [5]one man
6 [a]Ezek. 1.7
8 [b]Matt. 17.1-2 [6]Or, vigour
9 [c]Song 5.2
10 [d]Rev. 1.17 [7]moved
11 [8]a man of desires [9]stand upon thy standing
12 [e]Luke 2.10 [f]ch. 12.1;
13 [10]Or, the first
15 [g]ch. 8.18
16 [h]Isa. 6.7
17 [11]Or, this servant of my lord

Pēr'siȧ: and when I am gone forth, lo,
the prince of Grē'çiȧ shall come.
21 But I will shew thee that which is
noted in the scripture of truth: and
there is none that holdeth with me in
these things, but Mī'chaĕl your prince.

11 Also I [a]in the first year of [b]Da-
rī'us the Mēde, *even* I, stood to
confirm and to strengthen him.
2 And now will I shew thee the
truth. Behold, there shall stand up yet
three kings in Pēr'siȧ; and the fourth
shall be far richer than *they* all: and by
his strength through his riches he shall
stir up all against the realm of Grē'çiȧ.
3 And [c]a mighty king shall stand
up, that shall rule with great dominion,
and [d]do according to his will.
4 And when he shall stand up, [e]his
kingdom shall be broken, and shall
be divided toward the four winds of
heaven; and not to his posterity, [f]nor
according to his dominion which he
ruled: for his kingdom shall be plucked
up, even for others beside those.
5 ¶ And the king of the south shall
be strong, and *one* of his princes; and
he shall be strong above him, and
have dominion; his dominion *shall be*
a great dominion.
6 And in the end of years they [1]shall
join themselves together; for the king's
daughter of the south shall come to the
king of the north to make [2]an agreement: but she shall not retain the power
of the arm; neither shall he stand, nor
his arm: but she shall be given up, and
they that brought her, and [3]he that
begat her, and he that strengthened her
in *these* times.
7 But out of a branch of her roots
shall *one* stand up [4]in his estate, which
shall come with an army, and shall enter into the fortress of the king of the
north, and shall deal against them, and
shall prevail:
8 And shall also carry captives into
Ē'gypt their gods, with their princes,
and with [5]their precious vessels of silver and of gold; and he shall continue
more years than the king of the north.
9 So the king of the south shall come
into *his* kingdom, and shall return into
his own land.
10 But his sons [6]shall be stirred up,
and shall assemble a multitude of great
forces: and *one* shall certainly come,
[g]and overflow, and pass through: [7]then
shall he return, and be stirred up, *even*
to his fortress.
11 And the king of the south shall be
moved with choler, and shall come
forth and fight with him, *even* with the
king of the north: and he shall set forth
a great multitude; but the multitude
shall be given into his hand.
12 *And* when he hath taken away
the multitude, his [h]heart shall be lifted
up; and he shall cast down *many* ten
thousands: but he shall not be strengthened *by it*.
13 For the king of the north shall return, and shall set forth a multitude
greater than the former, and shall certainly come [8]after certain years with a
great army and with much riches.
14 And in those times there shall
many stand up against the king of the
south: also [9]the robbers of thy people
shall exalt themselves to establish the
vision; but they shall fall.
15 So the king of the north shall
come, [i]and cast up a mount, and take
[10]the most fenced cities: and the [j]arms
of the south shall not withstand, neither [11]his chosen people, neither *shall*
there be any strength to withstand.
16 But he that cometh against him
shall do according to his own will, and
[k]none shall stand before him: and he
shall stand in the [12]glorious land,
which by his hand shall be consumed.
17 He shall also [l]set his face to enter
with the strength of his whole kingdom, and [13]upright ones with him; thus
shall he do: and he shall give him the
daughter of women, [14]corrupting her:
but she shall not stand *on his side*,
[m]neither be for him.
18 After this shall he turn his face
unto the isles, and shall take many: but
a prince [15]for his own behalf shall
cause [16]the reproach offered by him to
cease; without his own reproach he
shall cause *it* to turn upon him.
19 Then he shall turn his face toward the fort of his own land: but he
shall stumble and fall, [n]and not be
found.
20 Then shall stand up [17]in his estate
[18]a raiser of taxes *in* the glory of the
kingdom: but within few days he shall
be destroyed, neither in [19]anger, nor in
battle.
21 And [20]in his estate [o]shall stand
up a vile person, to whom they shall
not give the honour of the kingdom:
but he shall come in peaceably, and
[p]obtain the kingdom by flatteries.
22 And with the arms of a flood
shall [q]they be overflown from before
him, and shall be broken; [r]yea, also
the prince of the covenant.
23 And after the league *made* with
him he shall work deceitfully: for he
shall come up, and shall become strong
with a small people.
24 He shall enter [21]peaceably even
upon the fattest places of the province;
and he shall do *that* which his fathers
have not done, nor his fathers' fathers; he shall scatter among them the
prey, and spoil, and riches: *yea*, and he
shall [22]forecast his devices against the
strong holds, even for a time.
25 And [23]he shall stir up his power
and his courage against the king of the
south with a great army; and the king
of the south shall be stirred up to battle
with a very great and mighty army; but
he shall not stand: for they shall fore-
cast devices against him.
26 Yea, they that [s]feed of the portion of his meat shall destroy him, and
his army shall overflow: and many
shall fall down slain.
27 And both these kings' [24]hearts
shall be to do mischief, and they shall
[t]speak lies at one table; but it shall not

CHAPTER 11
1 [a]ch. 9.1
[b]ch. 5.31
3 [c]ch. 7.6;
[d]ch. 8.4
4 [e]ch. 7.8;
[f]ch. 8.22
6 [1]shall associate themselves
[2]rights
[3]Or, whom she brought forth
7 [4]Or, in his place, or, office
8 [5]vessels of their desire
10 [6]Or, shall war
[g]Isa. 8.8;
[7]Or, then shall he be stirred up again
12 [h]2 Chr. 25.19
13 [8]at the end of times, even years
14 [9]the children of robbers
15 [i]Jer. 6.6
[10]the city of munitions
[j]Ps. 33.16
[11]the people of his choices
16 [k]Josh. 1.5
[12]the land of ornament, or, goodly land
17 [l]2 Chr. 20.3
[13]Or, much uprightness, or, equal conditions
[14]to corrupt
[m]ch. 9.26
18 [15]for him
[16]his reproach
19 [n]Ps. 37.36
[17]Or, in his place
[18]one that causeth an exactor to pass over
[19]angers
21 [20]Or, in his place
[o]1 Sam. 3.13
[p]2 Sam. 15.6
22 [q]ch. 8.24
[r]ch. 8.10
24 [21]Or, into the peaceable and fat, etc
[22]think his thoughts
25 [23]Fulfilled, B. C. 170
26 [s]Mic. 7.5
27 [24]their hearts
[t]Ps. 12.2

prosper: for yet the end *shall be* at the time appointed.

28 Then shall he return into his land with great riches; and his heart *shall be* against the holy covenant; and he shall do *exploits*, and return to his own land.

29 At the [25]time appointed he shall return, and come toward the south; but it shall not be as the former, or as the latter.

30 ¶ [26][u]For the ships of Chĭt'tim shall come against him: therefore he shall be grieved, and return, and have indignation against the holy covenant: so shall he do; he shall even return, and have intelligence with them that forsake the holy covenant.

31 And arms shall stand on his part, [v]and they shall pollute the sanctuary of strength, and shall take away the daily *sacrifice*, and they shall place the abomination that [27]maketh desolate.

32 And such as do wickedly against the covenant shall he [28]corrupt by flatteries: but the people that do [w]know their God shall be strong, and do *exploits*.

33 [x]And they that understand among the people shall instruct many:[y] yet they shall fall by the sword, and by flame, by captivity, and by spoil, *many* days.

34 Now when they shall fall, they shall be holpen with a little help: but many shall cleave to them with flatteries.

35 And *some* of them of understanding shall fall, to try [29]them, and to purge, and to make *them* white, *even* to the time of the end: because *it is* yet for a time appointed.

36 And the king shall do according to his will; and he shall [z]exalt himself, and magnify himself above every god, and shall speak marvellous things against the God of gods, and shall prosper till the indignation be accomplished: for that that is determined shall be done.

37 Neither shall he regard the God of his fathers, nor the desire of women, [a]nor regard any god: for he shall magnify himself above all.

38 [30]But [31]in his estate shall he honour the God of [32]forces: and a god whom his fathers knew not shall he honour with gold, and silver, and with precious stones, and [33]pleasant things.

39 Thus shall he do in the [34]most strong holds with a strange god, whom he shall acknowledge *and* increase with glory: and he shall cause them to rule over many, and shall divide the land for [35]gain.

40 And at the time of the end shall the king of the south push at him: and the king of the north shall come against him like a whirlwind, with chariots, and with horsemen, and with many ships; and he shall enter into the countries, and shall overflow and pass over.

41 He shall enter also into the [36]glorious land, and many *countries* shall be overthrown: but these shall escape out of his hand, *even* Ē'dom, and Mō'ab, and the chief of the children of Ăm'mŏn.

42 He shall [37]stretch forth his hand also upon the countries: and the land of Ē'gypt shall not escape.

43 But he shall have power over the treasures of gold and of silver, and over all the precious things of Ē'gypt: and the Lĭb'y̆-ans and the Ē-thĭ-ō'pĭ-ans *shall be* at his steps.

44 But tidings out of the east and out of the north shall trouble him: therefore he shall go forth with great fury to destroy, and utterly to make away many.

45 And he shall plant the tabernacles of his palace [b]between the seas in the [38]glorious holy mountain; yet he shall come to his end, and none shall help him.

12 And at that time shall Mī'chaĕl stand up, the great prince which standeth for the children of thy people: [a]and there shall be a time of trouble, such as never was since there was a nation *even* to that same time: and at that time thy people [b]shall be delivered, every one that shall be found [c]written in the book.

2 And many of them that sleep in the dust of the earth shall awake, [d]some to everlasting life, and some to shame *and* everlasting contempt.

3 And they that be [1]wise shall shine as the brightness of the firmament; and they that turn many to righteousness [e]as the stars for ever and ever.

4 But thou, O Dăn'iel, shut up the words, and seal the book, *even* to the time of the end: many shall run to and fro, and knowledge shall be increased.

5 ¶ Then I Dăn'iel looked, and, behold, there stood other two, the one on this side of the [2]bank of the river, and the other on that side of the bank of the river.

6 And *one* said to the man clothed in linen, which *was* [3]upon the waters of the river, [f]How long *shall it be to* the end of these wonders?

7 And I heard the man clothed in linen, which *was* upon the waters of the river, when he held up his right hand and his left hand unto heaven, and sware by him that liveth for ever [g]that *it shall be* for a time, times, and [4]an half; [h]and when he shall have accomplished to scatter the power of the holy people, all these *things* shall be finished.

8 And I heard, but I understood not: then said I, O my Lord, what *shall be* the end of these *things*?

9 And he said, Go thy way, Dăn'iel: for the words *are* closed up and sealed till the time of the end.

10 [i]Many shall be purified, and made white, and tried; but the wicked shall do wickedly: and none of the wicked shall understand; but [j]the wise shall understand.

11 And from the time *that* the daily *sacrifice* shall be taken away, and [5]the

---

29 [25]Fulfilled, B.C. 169
30 [26]Fulfilled, B.C. 168
[u]Num. 24.24; Jer. 2.10
31 [v]ch. 8.11
[27]Or, astonisheth
32 [28]Or, cause to dissemble
[w]1 Chr. 28.9
33 [x]Mal. 2.7
[y]Heb. 11.35
35 [29]Or, by them
36 [z]2 Thess. 2.4
37 [a]Isa. 14.13
38 [30]Or, But in his stead
[31]as for the Almighty God, in his seat he shall honour, yea, he shall honour a god, whom, etc
[32]Mauzzim, or, God's protectors, or, munitions
[33]things desired
39 [34]fortresses of munitions
[35]a price
41 [36]land of delight, or, ornament, or, goodly land
42 [37]send forth
45 [b]Ps. 48.2
[38]mountain of delight of holiness, or, goodly

CHAPTER 12
1 [a]Matt. 24.21; Rev. 16.18
[b]Isa. 11.11; Rom. 11.26
[c]Ex. 32.32; Luke 10.20
2 [d]Matt. 25.46
3 [1]Or, teachers
[e]1 Cor. 15.41
5 [2]lip
6 [3]Or, from above
[f]Ps. 74.9; Rev. 6.10
7 [g]ch. 7.25
[4]Or, part
[h]Luke 21.24
10 [i]Zech. 13.9
[j]John 7.17
11 [5]to set up the abomination, etc

abomination that [6]maketh desolate set
up, *there shall be* a thousand two hundred and ninety days.
12 Blessed *is* he that waiteth, and
cometh to the thousand three hundred
and five and thirty days.
13 But go thou thy way till the end
be: [7]for thou shalt rest, [k]and stand [l]in
thy lot at the end of the days.

[6]Or, astonisheth
13 [7]Or, and thou, etc
[k]Isa. 57.2
[l]Ps. 1.5

THE BOOK OF

HOSEA

Life's Questions

How do I know God loves me?
Has my sin separated me from God without another chance?
How can I be faithful to God during prosperous times?

God's Answers

About 750 B.C. God showed a prophet the depth of His love for His people by leading the prophet through the struggles of a marriage relationship with an unfaithful wife. Hosea had to lure Gomer back from the sexual worship practices of Baal worship just as God lured Israel back from the allures of Baal worship. Symbolic names for three children helped preach Israel's total unfaithfulness and God's unending love.

Hosea showed: God's love sets out future hope, but His forgiveness has limits (1—3); God judges His people for unfaithfulness to His covenant (4:1—9:9); God's love maintains the covenant love relationship even with an unfaithful people (9:10—14:9).

Hosea called Israel to loyal love and a personal relationship with God based on God's undeserved love, not on Israel's faithfulness.

1 The [a]word of the LORD that came
unto Ho-sē'ȧ, the son of Be-ē'rī, in
the days of Ŭz-zī'ah, Jō'tham, Ā'hăz,
and Hĕz-e-kī'ah, kings of Jū'dah, and
in the days of Jĕr-o-bō'am the son of
Jō'ăsh, king of Ĭs'ra-el.
2 The beginning of the word of the
LORD by Ho-sē'ȧ. And the LORD said to
Ho-sē'ȧ, Go, take unto thee a wife of
whoredoms and children of whoredoms: for [b]the land hath committed
great whoredom, *departing* from the
LORD.
3 So he went and took Gō'mer the
daughter of Dĭb'la-ĭm; which conceived,
and bare him a son.
4 And the LORD said unto him, Call
his name Jĕz're-el; for yet a little *while,*
and I will [1]avenge the blood of Jĕz're-
el upon the house of Jē'hū, and will
cause to cease the kingdom of the
house of Ĭs'ra-el.
5 And it shall come to pass at that
day, that I will break the bow of Ĭs'ra-
el in the valley of Jĕz're-el.
6 ¶ And she conceived again, and
bare a daughter. And *God* said unto
him, Call her name [2]Lo–rụ'ha-mah:
for [3]I will no more have mercy upon
the house of Ĭs'ra-el; [4]but I will utterly
take them away.
7 But I will have mercy upon the
house of Jū'dah, and will save them by
the LORD their God, and will not save
them by bow, nor by sword, nor by
battle, by horses, nor by horsemen.
8 ¶ Now when she had weaned Lo–
rụ'ha-mah, she conceived, and bare a
son.
9 Then said *God,* Call his name [5]Lo–
ăm'mī: for ye *are* not my people, and I
will not be your *God.*
10 ¶ Yet [c]the number of the children
of Ĭs'ra-el shall be as the sand of the
sea, which cannot be measured nor
numbered; and it shall come to pass,
that [6]in the place where it was said
unto them, Ye *are* not my people, *there*
it shall be said unto them, *Ye are* [d]the
sons of the living God.
11 Then shall the children of Jū'dah
and the children of Ĭs'ra-el be gathered
together, and appoint themselves one
head, and they shall come up out of the
land: for great *shall be* the day of
Jĕz're-el.
2 Say ye unto your brethren, [1]Ăm'mī;
and to your sisters, [2]Rụ'ha-mah.
2 Plead with your mother, plead: for
[a]she *is* not my wife, neither *am* I her
husband: let her therefore put away
her [b]whoredoms out of her sight, and
her adulteries from between her breasts;
3 Lest [c]I strip her naked, and set her
as in the day that she was born, and
make her [d]as a wilderness, and set her
like a dry land, and slay her with
[e]thirst.
4 And I will not have mercy upon
her children; for they *be* the children
of whoredoms.
5 For their mother hath played the
harlot: she that conceived them hath
done shamefully: for she said, I will go
after my lovers, [f]that give *me* my bread
and my water, my wool and my flax,
mine oil and my [3]drink.
6 ¶ Therefore, behold, [g]I will hedge
up thy way with thorns, and [4]make a
wall, that she shall not find her paths.
7 And she shall follow after her lovers, but she shall not overtake them;
and she shall seek them, but shall not
find *them:* then shall she say, [h]I will go
and return to my [i]first husband; for
then *was it* better with me than now.
8 For she did not know that I gave
her corn, and [5]wine, and oil, and

CHAPTER 1
1 [a]2 Pet. 1.21
2 [b]Deut. 31.16;
4 [1]visit
6 [2]That is, Not having obtained mercy
[3]I will not add any more to
[4]Or, that I should altogether pardon them
9 [5]That is, Not my people
10 [c]Gen. 26.4;
[6]Or, instead of that
[d]John 1.12

CHAPTER 2
1 [1]That is, My people
[2]That is, Having obtained mercy
2 [a]Isa. 50.1
[b]Jer. 3.1-9-13;
3 [c]Jer. 13.22
[d]Ezek. 19.13
[e]Amos 8.11
5 [f]Jer. 44.17
[3]drinks
6 [g]Job 19.8
[4]wall a wall
7 [h]Luke 15.18
[i]Ezek. 16.8
8 [5]new wine

multiplied her silver and gold, [6]*which*
they prepared for Bā'al.
9 Therefore will I return, and take
away my corn in the time thereof, and
my wine in the season thereof, and will
[7]recover my wool and my flax *given* to
cover her nakedness.
10 And now will I discover her [8]lewd-
ness in the sight of her lovers, and none
shall deliver her out of mine hand.
11 I [j]will also cause all her mirth to
cease, her feast days, her new moons,
and her sabbaths, and all her solemn
feasts.
12 And I will [9]destroy her vines and
her fig trees, whereof she hath said,
These *are* my rewards that my lovers
have given me: and [k]I will make them
a forest, and the beasts of the field
shall eat them.
13 And I will visit upon her [l]the
days of Bā'al-ĭm, wherein she burned
incense to them, and she [m]decked herself with her earrings and her jewels,
and she went after her lovers, and
forgat me, saith the LORD.
14 ¶ Therefore, behold, I will allure
her, and [n]bring her into the wilderness, and speak [10]comfortably unto
her.
15 And I will give her her vineyards
from thence, and [o]the valley of Ā'chôr
for a door of hope: and she shall sing
there, as in the days of her youth, and
as in the day when she came up out of
the land of Ē'gypt.
16 And it shall be at that day, saith
the LORD, *that* thou shalt call me [11]Ĭsh'ī;
and shalt call me no more [12]Bā'al-ī.
17 For [p]I will take away the names
of Bā'al-ĭm out of her mouth, and they
shall no more be remembered by their
name.
18 And in that day will I make a
[q]covenant for them with the beasts of
the field, and with the fowls of heaven,
and *with* the creeping things of the
ground: and [r]I will break the bow and
the sword and the battle out of the
earth, and will make them to [s]lie down
safely.
19 And I will betroth thee unto me
for ever; yea, I will betroth thee unto
me in righteousness, and in judgment,
and in lovingkindness, and in mercies.
20 I will even betroth thee unto me
in faithfulness: and [t]thou shalt know
the LORD.
21 And it shall come to pass in that
day, [u]I will hear, saith the LORD, I will
hear the heavens, and they shall hear
the earth;
22 And the earth shall hear the corn,
and the wine, and the oil; and they
shall hear Jĕz're-el.
23 And [v]I will sow her unto me in
the earth; and I will have mercy upon
her that had not obtained mercy; and I
[w]will say to *them which were* not my
people, Thou *art* my people; and they
shall say, *Thou art* my God.
3 Then said the LORD unto me, Go
yet, love a woman beloved of *her*
friend, yet an adulteress, according to
the love of the LORD toward the children of Ĭs'ra-el, who look to other
gods, and love flagons [1]of wine.
2 So I bought her to me for fifteen
pieces of silver, and *for* an homer of
barley, and an [2]half homer of barley:
3 And I said unto her, Thou shalt
[a]abide for me many days; thou shalt
not play the harlot, and thou shalt not
be for *another* man: so *will* I also *be* for
thee.
4 For the children of Ĭs'ra-el shall
abide many days without a king, and
without a prince, and without a sacrifice, and without [3]an image, and without an [b]ephod, and *without* teraphim:
5 Afterward shall the children of
Ĭs'ra-el return, and [c]seek the LORD
their God, and [d]Dā'vid their king; and
shall fear the LORD and his goodness
in the [e]latter days.
4 Hear the word of the LORD, ye children of Ĭs'ra-el: for the LORD hath a
[a]controversy with the inhabitants of
the land, because *there is* no truth, nor
mercy, nor [b]knowledge of God in the
land.
2 By swearing, and lying, and killing, and stealing, and committing
adultery, they break out, and [1]blood
toucheth blood.
3 Therefore [c]shall the land mourn,
and [d]every one that dwelleth therein
shall languish, with the beasts of the
field, and with the fowls of heaven;
yea, the fishes of the sea also shall be
taken away.
4 Yet let no man strive, nor reprove
another: for thy people *are* as they
[e]that strive with the priest.
5 Therefore shalt thou fall [f]in the
day, and the prophet also shall fall
with thee in the night, and I will [2]de-
stroy thy mother.
6 ¶ [g]My people are [3]destroyed for
lack of knowledge: because thou hast
rejected knowledge, I will also reject
thee, that thou shalt be no priest to me:
seeing thou hast forgotten the law of
thy God, I will also forget thy children.
7 As they were increased, so they
sinned against me: *therefore* will I
change their glory into shame.
8 They eat up the sin of my people,
and they [4]set their heart on their iniquity.
9 And there shall be, like people, like
priest: and I will [5]punish them for their
ways, and [6]reward them their doings.
10 For [h]they shall eat, and not have
enough: they shall commit whoredom,
and shall not increase: because they
have left off to take heed to the LORD.
11 Whoredom and wine and new
wine [i]take away the heart.
12 ¶ My people ask counsel at their
[j]stocks, and their staff declareth unto
them: for [k]the spirit of whoredoms
hath caused *them* to err, and they have
gone a whoring from under their God.
13 They sacrifice upon the tops of
the mountains, and burn incense upon
the hills, under oaks and poplars and
elms, because the shadow thereof *is*
good: [l]therefore your daughters shall

[6]Or, wherewith they made Baal
9 [7]Or, take away
10 [8]folly, or, villany
11 [j]Isa. 24.7; Amos 8.10
12 [9]make desolate
[k]Isa. 5.5
13 [l]Judg. 3.7
[m]Ezek. 23.40
14 [n]Ezek. 20.35
[10]to her heart, or, friendly
15 [o]Josh. 7.26; 1 Cor. 13.13
16 [11]That is, My husband
[12]That is, My lord
17 [p]Ex. 23.13
18 [q]Job 5.23; Isa. 11.6
[r]Isa. 2.4;
[s]Lev. 26.5
20 [t]Isa. 54.13;
21 [u]Zech. 8.12
23 [v]Zech. 10.9
[w]Zech. 13.9

CHAPTER 3
1 [1]of grapes
2 [2]lethech
3 [a]Deut. 21.13
4 [3]a standing, or, statue, or, pillar
[b]Ex. 28.6
5 [c]Isa. 27.12-13;
[d]1 Ki. 12.16;
[e]Mic. 4.1

CHAPTER 4
1 [a]Mic. 6.2
[b]Jer. 4.22
2 [1]bloods
3 [c]Amos 8.8
[d]Zeph. 1.3
4 [e]Deut. 17.12
[f]Jer. 6.4
[2]cut off
6 [g]Isa. 5.13
[3]cut off
8 [4]lift up their soul to their iniquity
9 [5]visit upon
[6]cause to return
10 [h]Mic. 6.14
11 [i]Isa. 28.7
12 [j]Jer. 2.27
[k]Isa. 44.20
13 [l]Job 31.9-10

commit whoredom, and your spouses shall commit adultery.

14 [7]I will not punish your daughters when they commit whoredom, nor your spouses when they commit adultery: for themselves are separated with whores, and they sacrifice with harlots: therefore the people *that* doth not understand shall [8]fall.

15 ¶ Though thou, Ĭs'ra-el, play the harlot, *yet* let not Jū'dah offend; [m]and come not ye unto Gĭl'găl, neither go ye up to [9]Bĕth–ā'ven, [n]nor swear, The LORD liveth.

16 For Ĭs'ra-el slideth back as a backsliding heifer: now the LORD will feed them as a lamb in a large place.

17 Ē'phră-ĭm *is* joined to idols: [o]let him alone.

18 Their drink [10]is sour: they have committed whoredom continually: her [11]rulers *with* shame do love, Give ye.

19 The wind hath bound her up in her wings, and they shall be ashamed because of their sacrifices.

5 Hear ye this, O priests; and hearken, ye house of Ĭs'ra-el; and give ye ear, O house of the king; for judgment *is* toward you, because ye have been a snare on Mĭz'pah, and a net spread upon Tā'bôr.

2 And the revolters are profound to make slaughter, [1]though I *have been* a rebuker of them all.

3 [a]I know Ē'phră-ĭm, and Ĭs'ra-el is not hid from me: for now, O Ē'phră-ĭm, thou committest whoredom, *and* Ĭs'ra-el is defiled.

4 [2]They will not frame their doings to turn unto their God: for the spirit of whoredoms *is* in the midst of them, and they have not known the LORD.

5 And the pride of Ĭs'ra-el doth testify to his face: therefore shall Ĭs'ra-el and Ē'phră-ĭm fall in their iniquity; Jū'dah also shall fall with them.

6 They shall go with their flocks and with their herds to seek the LORD; but they shall not find *him;* he hath withdrawn himself from them.

7 They have dealt treacherously against the LORD: for they have begotten strange children: now shall [b]a month devour them with their portions.

8 Blow ye the cornet in Gĭb'e-ah, *and* the trumpet in Rā'mah: cry aloud *at* [c]Bĕth–ā'ven, after thee, O Bĕn'ja-min.

9 Ē'phră-ĭm shall be desolate in the day of rebuke: among the tribes of Ĭs'ra-el have I made known that which shall surely be.

10 The princes of Jū'dah were like them that [d]remove the bound: *therefore* I will pour out my wrath upon them like water.

11 Ē'phră-ĭm *is* oppressed *and* broken in judgment, because he willingly walked after [e]the commandment.

12 Therefore *will* I *be* unto Ē'phră-ĭm as a moth, and to the house of Jū'dah as [3]rottenness.

13 When Ē'phră-ĭm saw his sickness, and Jū'dah *saw* his wound, then went Ē'phră-ĭm to the Ăs-sўr'ĭ-an, and sent [4]to king Jā'reb: yet could he not heal you, nor cure you of your wound.

14 For I *will be* unto Ē'phră-ĭm as a lion, and as a young lion to the house of Jū'dah: I, *even* I, will tear and go away; I will take away, and none shall rescue *him*.

15 ¶ I will go *and* return to my place, [5]till they acknowledge their offence, and seek my face: in their affliction they will seek me early.

6 Come, and let us return unto the LORD: for [a]he hath torn, and [b]he will heal us; he hath smitten, and he will bind us up.

2 After two days will he revive us: in the third day he will raise us up, and we shall live in his sight.

3 [c]Then shall we know, *if* we follow on to know the LORD: his going forth is prepared as the morning; and he shall come unto us [d]as the rain, as the latter *and* former rain unto the earth.

4 ¶ O Ē'phră-ĭm, what shall I do unto thee? O Jū'dah, what shall I do unto thee? for your [1]goodness *is* as a morning cloud, and as the early dew it goeth away.

5 Therefore have I hewed *them* [e]by the prophets; I have slain them by [f]the words of my mouth: [2]and thy judgments *are as* the light *that* goeth forth.

6 For I desired [g]mercy, and [h]not sacrifice; and the [i]knowledge of God more than burnt offerings.

7 But they [3]like men have transgressed the covenant: there have they dealt treacherously against me.

8 Gĭl'e-ăd *is* a city of them that work iniquity, *and is* [4]polluted with blood.

9 And as troops of robbers wait for a man, *so* the company of priests murder in the way [5]by consent: for they commit [6]lewdness.

10 I have seen an horrible thing in the house of Ĭs'ra-el: there *is* the whoredom of Ē'phră-ĭm, Ĭs'ra-el is defiled.

11 Also, O Jū'dah, he hath set an harvest for thee, [j]when I returned the captivity of my people.

7 When I would have healed Ĭs'ra-el, then the iniquity of Ē'phră-ĭm was discovered, and the [1]wickedness of Samā'rĭ-ȧ: for they commit falsehood; and the thief cometh in, *and* the troop of robbers [2]spoileth without.

2 And they [3]consider not in their hearts *that* I remember all their wickedness: now [a]their own doings have beset them about; they are [b]before my face.

3 They make the king glad with their wickedness, and the princes [c]with their lies.

4 They *are* all adulterers, as an oven heated by the baker, [4]*who* ceaseth [5]from raising after he hath kneaded the dough, until it be leavened.

5 In the day of our king the princes have made *him* sick [6]with bottles of wine; he stretched out his hand with scorners.

6 For they have [7]made ready their heart like an oven, whiles they lie in wait: their baker sleepeth all the night;

14 [7]Or, Shall I not, etc [8]Or, be punished
15 [m]ch. 9.15; [9]That is, House of idols [n]Amos 8.14
17 [o]Matt. 15.14
18 [10]is gone [11]shields

CHAPTER 5
2 [1]Or, and I have been a correction
3 [a]Ps. 90.8
4 [2]They will not give, or, Their doings will not suffer them
7 [b]Ezek. 12.28
8 [c]Josh. 7.2
10 [d]Deut. 19.14
11 [e]1 Ki. 12.28
12 [3]Or, a worm
13 [4]Or, to the kin of Jareb, or, to the king that should plead
15 [5]till they be guilty

CHAPTER 6
1 [a]Job 5.18 [b]Ex. 15.26
3 [c]Prov. 2.1-9; [d]Job 29.23
4 [1]Or, mercy, or, kindness
5 [e]Jer. 1.10 [f]Heb. 4.12 [2]Or, that thy judgments might be, etc
6 [g]Prov. 21.3; [h]Ps. 50.8 [i]John 17.3
7 [3]Or, like Adam
8 [4]Or, cunning for blood
9 [5]with one shoulder, or, to Shechem [6]Or, enormity
11 [j]Ps. 126.1

CHAPTER 7
1 [1]evils [2]strippeth
2 [3]say not to [a]Prov. 5.22 [b]Ps. 90.8
3 [c]Rom. 1.32
4 [4]Or, the raiser will cease [5]Or, from waking
5 [6]Or, with heat through wine
6 [7]Or, applied

in the morning it burneth as a flaming fire.

7 They are all hot as an oven, and have devoured their judges; all their kings [d]are fallen: [e]*there is* none among them that calleth unto me.

8 Ē'phră-ĭm, he [f]hath mixed himself among the people; Ē'phră-ĭm is a cake not turned.

9 Strangers have devoured his strength, and he knoweth *it* not: yea, gray hairs are [8]here and there upon him, yet he knoweth not.

10 And the pride of Ĭs'ra-el testifieth to his face: and they do not return to the LORD their God, nor seek him for all this.

11 ¶ Ē'phră-ĭm also is like a silly dove without heart: they call to Ē'gypt, they go to Ăs-sȳr'ĭ-ȧ.

12 When they shall go, I will spread my net upon them; I will bring them down as the fowls of the heaven; I will chastise them, as [g]their congregation hath heard.

13 Woe unto them! for they have fled from me: [9]destruction unto them! because they have transgressed against me: though I have redeemed them, yet they have spoken lies against me.

14 [h]And they have not cried unto me with their heart, when they howled upon their beds: they assemble themselves for corn and wine, *and* they rebel against me.

15 Though I [10]have bound *and* strengthened their arms, yet do they imagine mischief against me.

16 They return, *but* not to the most High: they are like a deceitful bow: their princes shall fall by the sword for the [i]rage of their tongue: this *shall be* their derision in the land of Ē'gypt.

8 *Set* the trumpet to [1]thy mouth. *He shall come* [a]as an eagle against the house of the LORD, because they have transgressed my covenant, and trespassed against my law.

2 [b]Ĭs'ra-el shall cry unto me, My God, we know thee.

3 Ĭs'ra-el hath cast off *the thing that is* good: the enemy shall pursue him.

4 [c]They have set up kings, but not by me: they have made princes, and I knew *it* not: of their silver and their gold have they made them idols, that they may be cut off.

5 ¶ Thy calf, O Sa-mā'rĭ-ȧ, hath cast *thee* off; mine anger is kindled against them: [d]how long *will it be* ere they attain to innocency?

6 For from Ĭs'ra-el *was* it also: the workman made it; therefore it *is* not God: but the calf of Sa-mā'rĭ-ȧ shall be broken in pieces.

7 For they have sown the wind, and they shall reap the whirlwind: it hath no [2]stalk: the bud shall yield no meal: if so be it yield, the strangers shall swallow it up.

8 Ĭs'ra-el is swallowed up: now shall they be among the Gĕn'tīles as a vessel wherein *is* no pleasure.

7 [d]2 Ki. 15.10 [e]Isa. 9.13
8 [f]Ps. 106.35
9 [8]sprinkled
12 [g]Lev. 26.14
13 [9]spoil
14 [h]Job 35.9; Ps. 78.34-37; Isa. 29.13; Jer. 3.10
15 [10]Or, chastened
16 [i]Ps. 73.9

CHAPTER 8
1 [1]the roof of thy mouth [a]Jer. 4.13; Hab. 1.8
2 [b]Ps. 78.34; Matt. 7.21
4 [c]1 Ki. 12.16-20; 2 Ki. 15.13-17-25; Shallum, Menahem, Pekahiah
5 [d]Jer. 13.27
7 [2]Or, standing corn
9 [e]2 Ki. 15.19 [3]loves
10 [4]Or, begin [5]Or, in a little while [f]Isa. 10.8; Ezek. 26.7; Dan. 2.37
12 [g]Deut. 4.6; Neh. 9.13-14; Prov. 22.20; Rom. 3.1-2 [h]Job 21.14
13 [6]Or, In the sacrifices of mine offerings they, etc
14 [i]1 Ki. 12.31

CHAPTER 9
1 [1]Or, in, etc
2 [2]Or, winefat
3 [a]Lev. 18.25; Deut. 4.26-27 [b]ch. 11.5; Not into Egypt itself, but into another bondage as bad as that [c]Ezek. 4.13
4 [d]Deut. 26.14
6 [3]spoil [4]the desire, or, their silver shall be desired, the nettle, etc
7 [5]man of the spirit
8 [6]Or, against
9 [e]Judg. 19.22
10 [f]Deut. 32.10 [g]Num. 25.3

9 For [e]they are gone up to Ăs-sȳr'ĭ-ȧ, a wild ass alone by himself: Ē'phră-ĭm hath hired [3]lovers.

10 Yea, though they have hired among the nations, now will I gather them, and they shall [4]sorrow [5]a little for the burden of [f]the king of princes.

11 Because Ē'phră-ĭm hath made many altars to sin, altars shall be unto him to sin.

12 I have written to him [g]the great things of my law, *but* they were counted as [h]a strange thing.

13 [6]They sacrifice flesh *for* the sacrifices of mine offerings, and eat *it; but* the LORD accepteth them not; now will he remember their iniquity, and visit their sins: they shall return to Ē'gypt.

14 For Ĭs'ra-el hath forgotten his Maker, and [i]buildeth temples; and Jū'dah hath multiplied fenced cities: but I will send a fire upon his cities, and it shall devour the palaces thereof.

9 Rejoice not, O Ĭs'ra-el, for joy, as *other* people: for thou hast gone a whoring from thy God, thou hast loved a reward [1]upon every cornfloor.

2 The floor and the [2]winepress shall not feed them, and the new wine shall fail in her.

3 They shall not dwell in [a]the LORD'S land; [b]but Ē'phră-ĭm shall return to Ē'gypt, and [c]they shall eat unclean *things* in Ăs-sȳr'ĭ-ȧ.

4 They shall not offer wine *offerings* to the LORD, neither shall they be pleasing unto him: their sacrifices *shall be* unto them as [d]the bread of mourners; all that eat thereof shall be polluted: for their bread for their soul shall not come into the house of the LORD.

5 What will ye do in the solemn day, and in the day of the feast of the LORD?

6 For, lo, they are gone because of [3]destruction: Ē'gypt shall gather them up, Mĕm'phis shall bury them: [4]the pleasant *places* for their silver, nettles shall possess them: thorns *shall be* in their tabernacles.

7 The days of visitation are come, the days of recompence are come; Ĭs'ra-el shall know *it:* the prophet *is* a fool, the [5]spiritual man *is* mad, for the multitude of thine iniquity, and the great hatred.

8 The watchman of Ē'phră-ĭm *was* with my God: *but* the prophet *is* a snare of a fowler in all his ways, *and* hatred [6]in the house of his God.

9 They have deeply corrupted *themselves,* as in the days of [e]Gĭb'e-ah: *therefore* he will remember their iniquity, he will visit their sins.

10 I [f]found Ĭs'ra-el like grapes in the wilderness; I saw your fathers as the firstripe in the fig tree at her first time: *but* they went to [g]Bā'al–pē'or, and separated themselves unto *that* shame; and *their* abominations were according as they loved.

11 *As for* Ē'phră-ĭm, their glory shall fly away like a bird, from the birth, and from the womb, and from the conception.

12 Though they bring up their chil-

dren, yet will I bereave them, *that there shall* not *be* a man *left:* yea, woe also to them when I [h]depart from them!

13 Ē'phră-ĭm, as I saw Tȳ'rus, *is* planted in a pleasant place: but Ē'phră-ĭm shall bring forth his children to the murderer.

14 [i]Give them, O LORD: what wilt thou give? give them a [7]miscarrying womb and dry breasts.

15 All their wickedness *is* in Gĭl'găl: for there I hated them: for the wickedness of their doings I will drive them out of mine house, I will love them no more: all their princes *are* revolters.

16 Ē'phră-ĭm is smitten, their root is dried up, they shall bear no fruit: yea, though they bring forth, yet will I slay *even* [8]the beloved *fruit* of their womb.

17 My God will [j]cast them away, because they did not hearken unto him: and they shall be wanderers among the nations.

10 Is'ra-el *is* [1]an empty vine, he bringeth forth fruit unto himself: according to the multitude of his fruit he hath increased the altars; according to the goodness of his land they have made goodly [2]images.

2 [3]Their heart is divided; now shall they be found faulty: he shall [4]break down their altars, he shall spoil their images.

3 For now they shall say, We have no king, because we feared not the LORD; what then should a king do to us?

4 They have spoken words, swearing falsely in making a covenant: thus judgment springeth up as hemlock in the furrows of the field.

5 The inhabitants of Sa-mā'rĭ-ȧ shall fear because of [a]the calves of Beth–a'ven: for the people thereof shall mourn over it, and [5]the priests thereof *that* rejoiced on it, for the glory thereof, because it is departed from it.

6 It shall be also carried unto Ȧs-sȳr'ĭ-ȧ *for* a present to [b]king Jā'reb: Ē'phră-ĭm shall receive shame, and Is'ra-el shall be ashamed of his own counsel.

7 *As for* Sa-mā'rĭ-ȧ, her king is cut off as the foam upon [6]the water.

8 The high places also of Ā'ven, [c]the sin of Is'ra-el, shall be destroyed: the thorn and the thistle shall come up on their altars; and they [d]shall say to the mountains, Cover us; and to the hills, Fall on us.

9 O Is'ra-el, thou hast sinned from the days of Gĭb'e-ah: there they stood: the battle in Gĭb'e-ah against the children of iniquity did not overtake them.

10 [e]*It is* in my desire that I should chastise them; and the people shall be gathered against them, [7]when they shall bind themselves in their two furrows.

11 And Ē'phră-ĭm *is as* an heifer *that is* taught, *and* loveth to tread out *the corn;* but I passed over upon [8]her fair neck: I will make Ē'phră-ĭm to ride; Jū'dah shall plow, *and* Jā'cob shall break his clods.

12 [f]Sow to yourselves in righteousness, reap in mercy; break up your fallow ground: for *it is* time to seek the LORD, till he come and rain righteousness upon you.

13 [g]Ye have plowed wickedness, ye have reaped iniquity; ye have eaten the fruit of lies: because thou didst trust in thy way, in the multitude of thy mighty men.

14 Therefore shall a tumult arise among thy people, and all thy fortresses shall be spoiled, as Shăl'man spoiled [h]Bĕth–är'bel in the day of battle: the mother was dashed in pieces upon *her* children.

15 So shall Bĕth'–el do unto you because of [9]your great wickedness: in a morning shall the king of Is'ra-el utterly be cut off.

11 When Is'ra-el *was* a child, then I loved him, and [a]called my [b]son out of Ē'ġypt.

2 *As* they called them, so they went from them: [c]they sacrificed unto Bā'-al-ĭm, and burned incense to graven images.

3 [d]I taught Ē'phră-ĭm also to go, taking them by their arms; but they knew not that [e]I healed them.

4 I drew them with cords of a man, with bands of love: and I was to them as they that [1]take off the yoke on their jaws, and [f]I laid meat unto them.

5 ¶ He shall not return into the land of Ē'ġypt, but the Ȧs-sȳr'ĭ-an shall be his king, because [g]they refused to return.[2]

6 And the sword shall abide on his cities, and shall consume his branches, and devour *them,* because of their own counsels.

7 And my people are bent to backsliding from me: though they called them to the most High, [3]none at all would exalt *him*.

8 [h]How shall I give thee up, Ē'phră-ĭm? *how* shall I deliver thee, Is'ra-el? how shall I make thee as [i]Ād'-mah? *how* shall I set thee as Ze-bō'im? [j]mine heart is turned within me, my repentings are kindled together.

9 I will not execute the fierceness of mine anger, I will not return to destroy Ē'phră-ĭm: [k]for I *am* God, and not man; the Holy One in the midst of thee: and I will not enter into the city.

10 They shall walk after the LORD: he shall roar like a lion: when he shall roar, then the children shall tremble from the west.

11 They shall tremble as a bird out of Ē'ġypt, and as a dove out of the land of Ȧs-sȳr'ĭ-ȧ: and I will place them in their houses, saith the LORD.

12 Ē'phră-ĭm compasseth me about with lies, and the house of Is'ra-el with deceit: but Jū'dah yet ruleth with God, and is faithful [4]with the saints.

12 Ē'phră-ĭm feedeth on wind, and followeth after the east wind: he daily increaseth lies and desolation; [a]and they do make a covenant with the Ȧs-sȳr'ĭ-ans, and [b]oil is carried into Ē'ġypt.

12 [h]Deut. 31.17
14 [i]Luke 23.29
[7]that casteth the fruit
16 [8]the desires
17 [j]2 Ki. 17.18

CHAPTER 10

1 [1]Or, a vine emptying the fruit which it giveth
[2]statues, or, standing images
2 [3]Or, He hath divided their heart
[4]behead
5 [a]1 Ki. 12.28;
[5]Or, Chemarim
6 [b]ch. 5.13
7 [6]the face of the water
8 [c]Deut. 9.21
[d]Rev. 6.16
10 [e]Deut. 28.63;
[7]Or, when I shall bind them for their two transgressions, or, in their two habitations
11 [8]the beauty of her neck
12 [f]Prov. 11.18
13 [g]Job 4.8
14 [h]2 Ki. 18.34
15 [9]the evil of your evil

CHAPTER 11

1 [a]Matt. 2.15
[b]Ex. 4.22
2 [c]2 Ki. 17.16
3 [d]Isa. 46.3
[e]Ex. 15.26
4 [1]lift up
[f]Ps. 78.25
5 [g]2 Ki. 17.13;
[2]B.C. 728, they became tributaries to Salmanasser
7 [3]together they exalted not
8 [h]Jer. 9.7
[i]Gen. 19.25
[j]Jer. 31.20
9 [k]Num. 23.19
12 [4]Or, with the most holy

CHAPTER 12

1 [a]2 Ki. 17.4
[b]Isa. 30.6

2 The LORD hath also a controversy
with Jū'dah, and will [1]punish Jā'cob
according to his ways; according to his
doings will he recompense him.
3 ¶ He took his brother by the heel in
the womb, and by his strength he [2]had
power with God:
4 Yea, he had power over the angel,
and prevailed: he wept, and made supplication unto him: he found him *in*
[c]Bĕth'–el, and there he spake with us;
5 Even the LORD God of hosts; the
LORD *is* his memorial.
6 Therefore turn thou to thy God:
keep mercy and judgment, and wait on
thy God continually.
7 ¶ *He is* [3]a merchant, the balances
of deceit *are* in his hand: he loveth to
[4]oppress.
8 And Ē'phră-ĭm said, Yet I am become rich, I have found me out substance: [5]*in* all my labours they shall
find none iniquity in me [6]that *were* sin.
9 And I *that am* the LORD thy God
from the land of Ē'ġypt will yet make
thee to dwell in tabernacles, as in the
days of the solemn feast.
10 I have also spoken by the prophets, and I have multiplied visions, and
used similitudes, [7]by the ministry of
the prophets.
11 *Is there* iniquity *in* Ġĭl'e-ăd? surely they are vanity: they sacrifice bullocks in [d]Ġĭl'găl; yea, their altars *are* as
heaps in the furrows of the fields.
12 And Jā'cob fled into the country
of Sỹr'ĭ-ȧ, and Ĭs'ra-el served for a
wife, and for a wife he kept *sheep*.
13 And by a prophet the LORD brought
Ĭs'ra-el out of Ē'ġypt, and by a prophet
was he preserved.
14 Ē'phră-ĭm provoked *him* to anger
[8]most bitterly: therefore shall he leave
his [9]blood upon him, and his [e]reproach
shall his LORD return unto him.

13 When Ē'phră-ĭm spake [a]trem-
bling, he exalted himself in Ĭs'ra-
el; but [b]when he offended in Bā'al, he
died.
2 And now [1]they sin more and more,
and have made them molten images of
their silver, *and* idols according to their
own understanding, all of it the work of
the craftsmen: they say of them, Let
[2]the men that sacrifice kiss the calves.
3 Therefore they shall be as the
morning cloud, and as the early dew
that passeth away, as the chaff *that* is
driven with the whirlwind out of the
floor, and as the smoke out of the
chimney.
4 Yet I *am* the LORD thy God from
the land of Ē'ġypt, and thou shalt
know no god but me: for *there is* no
saviour beside me.
5 ¶ I did know thee in the wilderness, in the land of [3]great drought.
6 According to their pasture, so were
they filled; they were filled, and their
heart was exalted; therefore have they
forgotten me.
7 Therefore I will be unto them as a
lion: as a leopard by the way will I observe *them*:
8 I will meet them as a bear *that is*
bereaved *of her whelps*, and will rend
the caul of their heart, and there will I
devour them like a lion: [4]the wild beast
shall tear them.
9 ¶ O Ĭs'ra-el, thou hast destroyed
thyself; but in me [5]*is* thine help.
10 [6]I will be thy king: where *is any*
other that may save thee in all thy cities? and thy judges of whom thou
saidst, Give me a king and princes?
11 [c]I gave thee a king in mine anger,
and took *him* away in my wrath.
12 [d]The iniquity of Ē'phră-ĭm *is*
bound up; his sin *is* hid.
13 The sorrows of a travailing woman shall come upon him: he *is* an unwise son; for he should not stay [7]long
in *the place of* the breaking forth of
children.
14 [e]I will ransom them from [8]the
power of the grave; I will redeem them
from death: [f]O death, I will be thy
plagues; O grave, I will be thy destruction: [g]repentance shall be hid from
mine eyes.
15 ¶ Though he be fruitful among
his brethren, an east wind shall come,
the wind of the LORD shall come up
from the wilderness, and his spring
shall become dry, and his fountain
shall be dried up: he shall spoil the treasure of all [9]pleasant vessels.
16 [10]Sa-mā'rĭ-ȧ shall become desolate; [h]for she hath rebelled against her
God: they shall fall by the sword: their
infants shall be dashed in pieces, and
their women with child shall be ripped
up.

14 O Ĭs'ra-el, [a]return unto the LORD
thy God; for thou hast fallen by
thine iniquity.
2 Take with you [b]words, and turn to
the LORD: say unto him, Take away all
iniquity, and [1]receive *us* graciously: so
will we render the [c]calves of our lips.
3 Ăssh'ụr shall not save us; we will
not ride upon horses: neither will we
say any more to the work of our hands,
Ye are our gods: for in thee the fatherless findeth mercy.
4 ¶ I will heal their backsliding, I
will love them freely: for mine anger is
turned away from him.
5 I will be as the dew unto Ĭs'ra-el:
he shall [2]grow as the lily, and [3]cast
forth his roots as Lĕb'a-non.
6 His branches [4]shall spread, and
his beauty shall be as the olive tree,
and his smell as Lĕb'a-non.
7 They that dwell under his shadow
shall return; they shall revive *as* the
corn, and [5]grow as the vine: the [6]scent
thereof *shall be* as the wine of Lĕb'a-non.
8 Ē'phră-ĭm *shall say*, What have I
to do any more with idols? [d]I have
heard *him*, and observed him: I *am* like
a green fir tree. [e]From me is thy fruit
found.
9 [f]Who *is* wise, and he shall understand these *things*? prudent, and he
shall know them? for [g]the ways of the
LORD *are* right, and the just shall walk
in them: but the transgressors shall fall
therein.

2 [1]visit upon
3 [2]was a prince, or, behaved himself princely
4 [c]Gen. 28.12
7 [3]Or, Canaan
[4]Or, deceive
8 [5]Or, all my labours suffice me not: he shall have punishment of iniquity in whom is sin
[6]which
10 [7]by the hand
11 [d]Amos 4.4
14 [8]with bitternesses
[9]bloods
[e]Deut. 28.37; Dan. 11.18

CHAPTER 13
1 [a]Prov. 18.12
[b]2 Ki. 17.16
2 [1]they add to sin
[2]Or, the sacrificers of men
5 [3]droughts
8 [4]the beast of the field
9 [5]in thy help
10 [6]Rather, Where is thy king? King Hoshea being then in prison
11 [c]1 Sam. 8.7
12 [d]Deut. 32.34
13 [7]a time
14 [e]Isa. 25.8
[8]the hand
[f]Isa. 26.19;
[g]Rom. 11.29
15 [9]vessels of desire
16 [10]Fulfilled, 2 Ki. 17.6
[h]2 Ki. 18.12

CHAPTER 14
1 [a]1 Sam. 7.3-4;
2 [b]Joel 2.17;
[1]Or, give good
[c]Heb. 13.15
5 [2]Or, blossom
[3]strike
6 [4]shall go
7 [5]Or, blossom
[6]Or, memorial
8 [d]Jer. 31.18
[e]Jas. 1.17
9 [f]John 18.37
[g]Matt. 11.19

THE BOOK OF

JOEL

Life's Questions

How do I explain natural calamity?
What response does God expect from me when all goes bad?
Why should I still have hope in God?

God's Answers

Joel shows God speaks through natural disasters and can be trusted even when the world seems about to end. Judah had experienced severe drought and the devastation of a locust plague. God told Joel this just reminded Judah that the day of the Lord was coming and the people needed to respond.

Joel shows: God's day calls for God's congregation to repent and witness to Him (1:1—2:17); God in pity will provide for the needs of His people and lead them to true worship (2:18–27); God is preparing a day of salvation for His people (2:28—3:21).

1 The [a]word of the LORD that came to
Jō'el the son of Pe-thū'el.
2 Hear this, ye old men, and give
ear, all ye inhabitants of the land.
[b]Hath this been in your days, or even
in the days of your fathers?
3 [c]Tell ye your children of it, and *let*
your children *tell* their children, and
their children another generation.
4 [1]That which the palmerworm hath
left hath the locust eaten; and that
which the locust hath left hath the cankerworm eaten; and that which the
cankerworm hath left hath the caterpiller eaten.
5 Awake, ye drunkards, and weep;
and howl, all ye drinkers of wine, because of the new wine; [d]for it is cut off
from your mouth.
6 For [e]a nation is come up upon my
land, strong, and without number,
[f]whose teeth *are* the teeth of a lion,
and he hath the cheek teeth of a great
lion.
7 He hath [g]laid my vine waste, and
[2]barked my fig tree: he hath made
it clean bare, and cast *it* away; the
branches thereof are made white.
8 ¶ [h]Lament like a virgin girded
with sackcloth for [i]the husband of her
youth.
9 [j]The meat offering and the drink
offering is cut off from the house of the
LORD; the priests, the LORD'S ministers, mourn.
10 The field is wasted, [k]the land
mourneth; for the corn is wasted: [l]the
new wine is [3]dried up, the oil languisheth.
11 [m]Be ye ashamed, O ye husbandmen; howl, O ye vinedressers, for the
wheat and for the barley; because the
harvest of the field is perished.
12 The vine is dried up, and the fig
tree languisheth; the pomegranate tree,
the palm tree also, and the apple tree,
even all the trees of the field, are withered: because [n]joy is withered away
from the sons of men.
13 [o]Gird yourselves, and lament, ye
priests: howl, ye ministers of the altar:
come, lie all night in sackcloth, ye ministers of my God: for the meat offering
and the drink offering is withholden
from the house of your God.
14 ¶ [p]Sanctify ye a fast, call a [4]sol-
emn assembly, gather the elders *and*
[q]all the inhabitants of the land *into* the
house of the LORD your God, and cry
unto the LORD,
15 [r]Alas for the day! for the day of
the LORD *is* at hand, and as a destruction from the Almighty shall it come.
16 Is not the meat cut off before our
eyes, *yea,* [s]joy and gladness from the
house of our God?
17 The [5]seed is rotten under their
clods, the garners are laid desolate, the
barns are broken down; for the corn is
withered.
18 How do [t]the beasts groan! the
herds of cattle are perplexed, because
they have no pasture; yea, the flocks of
sheep are made desolate.
19 O LORD, to thee will I cry: for the
fire hath devoured the [6]pastures of the
wilderness, and the flame hath burned
all the trees of the field.
20 The beasts of the field [u]cry also
unto thee: for [v]the rivers of waters are
dried up, and the fire hath devoured
the pastures of the wilderness.

2 Blow ye the [1]trumpet in Zī'ŏn, and
[a]sound an alarm in my holy mountain: let all the inhabitants of the land
tremble: for [b]the day of the LORD cometh, for *it is* nigh at hand;
2 [c]A day of darkness and of gloominess, a day of clouds and of thick
darkness, as the morning spread upon
the mountains: [d]a great people and a
strong; [e]there hath not been ever the
like, neither shall be any more after it,
even to the years [2]of many generations.
3 A fire devoureth before them; [f]and
behind them a flame burneth: the land
is as the garden of Ē'dĕn before them,
and behind them a desolate wilderness; yea, and nothing shall escape
them.
4 The appearance of them *is* as the
appearance of horses; and as horsemen, so shall they run.

CHAPTER 1
1 [a]Heb. 1.1; 2 Pet. 1.21
2 [b]Deut. 4.32; Matt. 24.21
3 [c]Ps. 78.4
4 [1]The residue of the palmerworm
5 [d]Isa. 32.10
6 [e]Prov. 30.25
[f]Rev. 9.8
7 [g]Isa. 5.6
[2]laid my fig tree for a barking
8 [h]Isa. 22.12
[i]Prov. 2.17
9 [j]ch. 2.14
10 [k]Jer. 12.11
[l]Isa. 24.7
[3]Or, ashamed
11 [m]Jer. 14.3
12 [n]Isa. 9.3; Hos. 9.1-2
13 [o]Jer. 4.8
14 [p]2 Chr. 20.3
[4]Or, day of restraint
[q]2 Chr. 20.13
15 [r]Jer. 30.7; Amos 5.16-18
16 [s]Deut. 12.7-12;
17 [5]grains
18 [t]1 Ki. 18.5
19 [6]Or, habitations
20 [u]Job 38.41;
[v]1 Ki. 17.7

CHAPTER 2
1 [1]Or, cornet
[a]Num. 10.5;
[b]Obad. 15
2 [c]Amos 5.18
[d]ch. 1.6
[e]Ex. 10.14
[2]of generation and generation
3 [f]Zech. 7.14

5 Like the noise of chariots on the tops of mountains shall they leap, like the noise of a flame of fire that devoureth the stubble, as a strong people set in battle array.

6 Before their face the people shall be much pained: [g]all faces shall gather [3]blackness.

7 They shall run like mighty men; they shall climb the wall like men of war; and they shall march every one on his ways, and they shall not break their ranks:

8 Neither shall one thrust another; they shall walk every one in his path: and *when* they fall upon the [4]sword, they shall not be wounded.

9 They shall run to and fro in the city; they shall run upon the wall, they shall climb up upon the houses; they shall enter in at the windows like a thief.

10 The earth shall quake before them; the heavens shall tremble: the sun and the moon shall be dark, and the stars shall withdraw their shining:

11 And the LORD shall utter his voice before his army: for his camp *is* very great: [h]for *he is* strong that executeth his word: for the day of the LORD *is* great and very terrible; and [i]who can abide it?

12 ¶ Therefore also now, saith the LORD, [j]turn ye *even* to me with all your heart, and with fasting, and with weeping, and with mourning:

13 And [k]rend your heart, and not your garments, and turn unto the LORD your God: for he *is* [l]gracious and merciful, slow to anger, and of great kindness, and repenteth him of the evil.

14 [m]Who knoweth *if* he will return and repent, and leave [n]a blessing behind him; *even* a meat offering and a drink offering unto the LORD your God?

15 ¶ Blow the trumpet in Zī'ŏn, sanctify a fast, call a solemn assembly:

16 Gather the people, [o]sanctify the congregation, assemble the elders, [p]gather the children, and those that suck the breasts: [q]let the bridegroom go forth of his chamber, and the bride out of her closet.

17 Let the priests, the ministers of the LORD, weep [r]between the porch and the altar, and let them say, [s]Spare thy people, O LORD, and give not thine heritage to reproach, that the heathen should [5]rule over them: wherefore should they say among the people, Where *is* their God?

18 ¶ Then will the LORD [t]be jealous for his land, [u]and pity his people.

19 Yea, the LORD will answer and say unto his people, Behold, I will send you [v]corn, and wine, and oil, and ye shall be satisfied therewith: and I will no more make you a reproach among the heathen:

20 But [w]I will remove far off from you the northern *army*, and will drive him into a land barren and desolate, with his face [x]toward the east sea, and his hinder part toward the utmost sea, and his stink shall come up, and his ill savour shall come up, because [6]he hath done great things.

21 ¶ [y]Fear not, O land; be glad and rejoice: for the LORD will do great things.

22 Be not afraid, ye beasts of the field: for [z]the pastures of the wilderness do spring, for the tree beareth her fruit, the fig tree and the vine do yield their strength.

23 Be glad then, ye children of Zī'ŏn, and [a]rejoice in the LORD your God: for he hath given you [7]the former rain [8]moderately, and he [b]will cause to come down for you [c]the rain, the former rain, and the latter rain in the first *month*.

24 And the floors shall be full of wheat, and the fats shall overflow with wine and oil.

25 And I will restore to you the years that the locust hath eaten, the cankerworm, and the caterpiller, and the palmerworm, my great army which I sent among you.

26 And ye shall [d]eat in plenty, and be satisfied, and praise the name of the LORD your God, that hath dealt wondrously with you: and my people shall never be ashamed.

27 And ye shall know that I *am* in [e]the midst of Ĭs'ra-el, and *that* [f]I *am* the LORD your God, and none else: and my people shall never be ashamed.

28 ¶ [g]And it shall come to pass afterward, *that* I [h]will pour out my spirit upon all flesh; [i]and your sons and [j]your daughters shall prophesy, your old men shall dream dreams, your young men shall see visions:

29 And also upon [k]the servants and upon the handmaids in those days will I pour out my spirit.

30 And [l]I will shew wonders in the heavens and in the earth, blood, and fire, and pillars of smoke.

31 The sun shall be turned into darkness, and the moon into blood, before the great and the terrible day of the LORD come.

32 And it shall come to pass, *that* [m]whosoever shall call on the name of the LORD shall be delivered: for [n]in mount Zī'ŏn and in Je-ru̧'sa-lĕm shall be deliverance, as the LORD hath said, and in [o]the remnant whom the LORD shall call.

3 For, behold, in those days, and in that time, when I shall bring again the captivity of Jū'dah and Je-ru̧'sa-lĕm,

2 [a]I will also gather all nations, and will bring them down into [b]the valley of Je-hŏsh'a-phăt, and [c]will plead with them there for my people and *for* my heritage Ĭs'ra-el, whom they have scattered among the nations, and parted my land.

3 And they have [d]cast lots for my people; and have given a boy for an harlot, and sold a girl for wine, that they might drink.

4 Yea, and what have ye to do with me, [e]O Tȳre, and Zī'dŏn, and all the coasts of Păl'es-tīne? [f]will ye render

6 [g]Jer. 8.21
[3]pot
8 [4]Or, dart
11 [h]Jer. 50.34
[i]Num. 24.23; Mal. 3.2
12 [j]Jer. 4.1; Hos. 12.6
13 [k]2 Ki. 22.19; Matt. 5.3-4
[l]Ex. 34.6; Jon. 4.2
14 [m]Josh. 14.12; Zeph. 2.3
[n]Isa. 65.8; Hag. 2.19
16 [o]Ex. 19.10
[p]2 Chr. 20.13
[q]1 Cor. 7.5
17 [r]Matt. 23.35
[s]Ex. 32.11; Isa. 37.20
[5]Or, use a byword against them
18 [t]Isa. 42.13; Zech. 1.14
[u]Deut. 32.36; Ps. 103.13
19 [v]Mal. 3.10
20 [w]Ex. 10.19
[x]Deut. 11.24
[6]he hath magnified to do
21 [y]1 John 4.18
22 [z]Zech. 8.12
23 [a]Ps. 28.7; Zech. 10.7
[7]Or, a teacher of righteousness
[8]according to righteousness
[b]Lev. 26.4
[c]Jas. 5.7
26 [d]Mic. 6.14
27 [e]Lev. 26.11
[f]Isa. 45.5
28 [g]Isa. 44.3
[h]John 7.39
[i]Isa. 54.13
[j]Acts 21.9
29 [k]1 Cor. 12.13
30 [l]Mark 13.24
32 [m]Ps. 50.15;
[n]Isa. 46.13;
[o]Isa. 11.11

CHAPTER 3
2 [a]Zech. 14.2
[b]2 Chr. 20.26
[c]Isa. 66.16
3 [d]Obad. 11
4 [e]Amos 1.6-9
[f]Ezek. 25.15

me a recompence? and if ye recompense me, [g]swiftly *and* speedily will I
return your recompence upon your
own head;
5 Because ye have taken my silver
and my gold, and have carried into
your temples my goodly [1]pleasant
things:
6 The children also of Jū'dah and
the children of Je-ru'sa-lĕm have ye
sold unto [2]the Grē'çians, that ye might
remove them far from their border.
7 Behold, I will raise them out of the
place whither ye have sold them, and
will return your recompence upon your
own head:
8 And I will sell your sons and your
daughters into the hand of the children
of Jū'dah, and they shall sell them to
the [h]Sa-bē'ans, to a people far off: for
the LORD hath spoken *it*.
9 ¶ Proclaim ye this among the Gĕn'-
tīles; [3]Prepare war, wake up the mighty
men, let all the men of war draw near;
let them come up:
10 [i]Beat your plowshares into
swords, and your [4]pruninghooks into
spears: [j]let the weak say, I *am* strong.
11 Assemble yourselves, and come,
all ye heathen, and gather yourselves
together round about: thither [5]cause
thy mighty ones to come down, O
LORD.
12 Let the heathen be wakened, and
come up to [k]the valley of Je-hŏsh'a-
phăt: for there will I sit to [l]judge all the
heathen round about.
13 [m]Put ye in the sickle, for the harvest is ripe: come, get you down; for
[n]the press is full, the fats overflow; for
their wickedness *is* great.
14 Multitudes, multitudes in the valley of [6]decision: for the day of the
LORD *is* near in the valley of decision.
15 The sun and the moon shall be
darkened, and the stars shall withdraw their shining.
16 The LORD also shall roar out of
Zī'ŏn, and utter his voice from Je-
ru'sa-lĕm; and the heavens and the
earth shall shake: but the LORD *will
be* the [7]hope of his people, and the
strength of the children of Ĭs'ra-el.
17 So shall ye know that I *am* the
LORD your God dwelling in Zī'ŏn, my
holy mountain: then shall Je-ru'sa-lĕm
be [8]holy, and there shall no [o]strangers
pass through her any more.
18 ¶ And it shall come to pass in that
day, *that* the mountains shall drop
down new wine, and the hills shall
flow with milk, and all the rivers of
Jū'dah shall [9]flow with waters, and [p]a
fountain shall come forth of the house
of the LORD, and shall water the valley
of Shĭt'tim.
19 Ē'gypt shall be a desolation, and
Ē'dom shall be a desolate wilderness,
for the violence *against* the children of
Jū'dah, because they have shed innocent blood in their land.
20 But Jū'dah shall [10]dwell for ever,
and Je-ru'sa-lĕm from generation to
generation.
21 For I will cleanse their blood *that*
I have not cleansed: [11]for the LORD
dwelleth in Zī'ŏn.

[g]Deut. 32.35; Luke 18.7; Jas. 2.13
5 [1]desirable
6 [2]the sons of the Grecians
8 [h]Ezek. 23.42
9 [3]Sanctify
10 [i]Isa. 2.4
[4]Or, scythes
[j]Zech. 12.8
11 [5]Or, the LORD shall bring down
12 [k]2 Chr. 20.26
[l]Ps. 96.13
13 [m]Rev. 14.15
[n]Jer. 51.33
14 [6]Or, concision, or, threshing
16 [7]place of repair, or, harbour
17 [8]holiness
[o]Isa. 35.8; Nah. 1.15; Rev. 21.27
18 [9]go
[p]Ezek. 47.1; Zech. 13.1; Rev. 22.1
20 [10]Or, abide
21 [11]Or, even I the LORD that dwelleth in Zion

THE BOOK OF AMOS

Life's Questions

Why would God punish me when I worship Him faithfully?
Does God expect changes in my business and personal life?
Can I depend on God's love without worrying about His judgment?

God's Answers

About 760 B.C. God sent a southern shepherd to warn the northern kingdom He was going to judge them because they had established prosperity through injustice rather than through faithfulness to Him. God announced God's certain judgment on a people certain He would not judge.

Amos shows: the loving God condemns the religious and ethical sins of His people and demands righteousness 1—6), and only a true vision and knowledge of God offers hope in the face of certain judgment (7—9).

Amos called a people to recognize their sins, know that God had freedom to judge them, and renew a love relationship so they could experience His mercy.

1 The words of Ā'mos, who was
among the herdmen of [a]Te-kō'ȧ,
which he saw concerning Ĭs'ra-el in
[b]the days of Ŭz-zī'ah king of Jū'dah,
and in the days of Jĕr-o-bō'am the son
of Jō'ăsh king of Ĭs'ra-el, two years before the [c]earthquake.
2 And he said, The LORD will roar
from Zī'ŏn, and utter his voice from Je-
ru'sa-lĕm; and the habitations of the
shepherds shall mourn, and the top of
Căr'mel shall wither.
3 Thus saith the LORD; For three
transgressions of [d]Da-măs'cus, [1]and
for four, I will not [2]turn away *the punishment* thereof; [e]because they have
threshed Gĭl'e-ăd with threshing instruments of iron:
4 But I will send a fire into the house
of Hăz'a-el, which shall devour the palaces of Bĕn–hā'dăd.
5 I will break also the bar of Da-
măs'cus, and cut off the inhabitant
from [3]the plain of Ā'ven, and him that

CHAPTER 1
1 [a]2 Sam. 14.2;
[b]Hos. 1.1
[c]Zech. 14.5
3 [d]Isa. 8.4
[1]Or, yea
[2]Or, convert it, or, let it be quiet
[e]2 Ki. 10.33
5 [3]Or, Bikath-aven

holdeth the sceptre from [4]the house of
Ē'dĕn: and [f]the people of Sȳr'ĭ-ȧ shall
go into captivity unto Kĭr, saith the
LORD.
6 ¶ Thus saith the LORD; For three
transgressions of [g]Gā'zȧ, and for four,
I will not turn away *the punishment*
thereof; because they [5]carried away
captive the whole captivity, to deliver
them up to Ē'dom:
7 But I will send a fire on the wall of
[h]Gā'zȧ, which shall devour the palaces thereof:
8 And I will cut off the inhabitant
from Ȧsh'dŏd, and him that holdeth
the sceptre from Ȧsh'ke-lŏn, and I will
turn mine hand against Ĕk'rŏn: and
the remnant of the Phĭ-lĭs'tĭnes shall
perish, saith the Lord GOD.
9 ¶ Thus saith the LORD; For three
transgressions of Tȳ'rus, and for four,
I will not turn away *the punishment*
thereof; because they delivered up the
whole captivity to Ē'dom, and remembered not [6]the brotherly covenant:
10 But I will send a fire on the wall
of Tȳ'rus, which shall devour the palaces thereof.
11 ¶ Thus saith the LORD; For three
transgressions of [i]Ē'dom, and for four,
I will not turn away *the punishment*
thereof; because he did pursue his
brother [j]with the sword, and [7]did cast
off all pity, and his anger did tear perpetually, and he kept his wrath for
ever:
12 But I will send a fire upon Tē'-
man, which shall devour the palaces of
Bŏz'rah.
13 ¶ Thus saith the LORD; For three
transgressions of the children of Ȧm'-
mŏn, and for four, I will not turn away
the punishment thereof; because they
have [8]ripped up the women with child
of Gĭl'e-ăd, that they might enlarge
their border:
14 But I will kindle a fire in the wall
of [k]Răb'bah, and it shall devour the
palaces thereof, with shouting in the
day of battle, with a tempest in the day
of the whirlwind:
15 And [l]their king shall go into captivity, he and his princes together, saith
the LORD.

2 Thus saith the LORD; For three transgressions of [a]Mō'ab, and for four, I
will not turn away *the punishment*
thereof; because he [b]burned the bones
of the king of Ē'dom into lime:
2 But I will send a fire upon Mō'ab,
and it shall devour the palaces of [c]Kĭr'-
ĭ-ŏth: and Mō'ab shall die with tumult,
with shouting, *and* with the sound of
the trumpet:
3 And I will cut off [d]the judge from
the midst thereof, and will slay all the
princes thereof with him, saith the
LORD.
4 ¶ Thus saith the LORD; For three
transgressions of Jū'dah, and for four,
I will not turn away *the punishment*
thereof; [e]because they have despised
the law of the LORD, and have not
kept his commandments, and [f]their
lies caused them to err, [g]after the which
their fathers have walked:
5 [h]But I will send a fire upon Jū'-
dah, and it shall devour the palaces of
Je-ru'sa-lĕm.
6 ¶ Thus saith the LORD; For three
transgressions of Ĭs'ra-el, and for four,
I will not turn away *the punishment*
thereof; because [i]they sold the righteous for silver, and the poor for a pair
of shoes;
7 That pant after the dust of the
earth on the head of the poor, and [j]turn
aside the way of the meek: [k]and a man
and his father will go in unto the *same*
[1]maid, [l]to profane my holy name:
8 And they lay *themselves* down
upon clothes [m]laid to pledge [n]by every
altar, and they drink the wine of [2]the
condemned *in* the house of their god.
9 ¶ Yet destroyed I the [o]Ȧm'ôr-īte
before them, whose height *was* like the
height of the cedars, and he *was* strong
as the oaks; yet I destroyed his fruit
from above, and his roots from beneath.
10 Also I brought you up from the
land of Ē'ġypt, and led you forty years
through the wilderness, to possess the
land of the Ȧm'ôr-īte.
11 And I raised up of your sons for
prophets, and of your young men for
[p]Năz'a-rītes. *Is it* not even thus, O ye
children of Ĭs'ra-el? saith the LORD.
12 But ye gave the Năz'a-rītes wine
to drink; and commanded the prophets, [q]saying, Prophesy not.
13 Behold, [3]I am pressed under you,
as a cart is pressed *that is* full of
sheaves.
14 Therefore the flight shall perish
from the swift, and the strong shall not
strengthen his force, neither shall the
mighty deliver [4]himself:
15 Neither shall he stand that handleth the bow; and *he that is* swift of
foot shall not deliver *himself*: neither
shall he that rideth the horse deliver
himself.
16 And *he that is* [5]courageous among
the mighty shall flee away naked in
that day, saith the LORD.

3 Hear this word that the LORD hath
spoken against you, O children of
Ĭs'ra-el, against the whole family which
I brought up from the land of Ē'ġypt,
saying,
2 You only have I known of all the
families of the earth: [a]therefore I will
[1]punish you for all your iniquities.
3 Can two walk together, except they
be agreed?
4 Will a lion roar in the forest, when
he hath no prey? will a young lion [2]cry
out of his den, if he have taken nothing?
5 Can a bird fall in a snare upon the
earth, where no gin *is* for him? shall
one take up a snare from the earth, and
have taken nothing at all?
6 Shall a [b]trumpet be blown in the
city, and the people [3]not be afraid?
shall there be evil in a city, [4]and the
LORD hath not done *it*?
7 Surely the Lord GOD will do nothing, but [c]he revealeth his secret unto
his servants the prophets.

[4]Or, Beth-eden
[f]Isa. 7.1
6 [g]2 Chr. 28.18
[5]Or, carried them away with an entire captivity
7 [h]2 Ki. 18.8
9 [6]the covenant of brethren
11 [i]Mal. 1.4
[j]2 Chr. 28.17
[7]corrupted his compassions
13 [8]Or, divided the mountains
14 [k]Deut. 3.11; Ezek. 25.5
15 [l]Jer. 49.3

CHAPTER 2
1 [a]Ezek. 25.8;
[b]2 Ki. 3.27
2 [c]Jer. 48.41
3 [d]Num. 24.17
4 [e]Lev. 26.14;
[f]Isa. 28.15;
[g]Ezek. 20.13
5 [h]Hos. 8.14
6 [i]Isa. 29.21
7 [j]Isa. 10.2
[k]Ezek. 22.11
[1]Or, young woman
[l]Lev. 20.3
8 [m]Ex. 22.26
[n]1 Cor. 10.21
[2]Or, such as have fined, or, mulcted
9 [o]Num. 21.24
11 [p]Judg. 13.5
12 [q]Isa. 30.10
13 [3]Or, I will press your place, as a cart full of sheaves presseth
14 [4]his soul, or, life
16 [5]strong of his heart

CHAPTER 3
2 [a]Ezek. 9.6;
[1]visit upon
4 [2]give forth his voice
6 [b]Ezek. 33.3
[3]Or, not run together
[4]Or, and shall not the LORD do somewhat?
7 [c]Gen. 6.13

8 The lion hath roared, who will not
fear? the Lord GOD hath spoken, [d]who
can but prophesy?
9 ¶ Publish in the palaces of Ăsh'-
dŏd, and in the palaces in the land of
Ē'ġypt, and say, Assemble yourselves
upon the mountains of Sa-mā'rĭ-ȧ, and
behold the great tumults in the midst
thereof, and the [5]oppressed in the midst
thereof.
10 For they know not to do right,
saith the LORD, who store up violence
and [6]robbery in their palaces.
11 Therefore thus saith the Lord
GOD; [e]An adversary *there shall be*
even round about the land; and he shall
bring down thy strength from thee, and
thy palaces shall be spoiled.
12 Thus saith the LORD; As the shepherd [7]taketh out of the mouth of the
lion two legs, or a piece of an ear; so
shall the children of Ĭs'ra-el be taken
out that dwell in Sa-mā'rĭ-ȧ in the corner of a bed, and [8]in Da-măs'cus *in* a
couch.
13 Hear ye, and testify in the house
of Jā'cob, saith the Lord GOD, the God
of hosts,
14 That in the day that I shall [9]visit
the transgressions of Ĭs'ra-el upon him
I will also visit the altars of Bĕth'–el:
and the horns of the altar shall be cut
off, and fall to the ground.
15 And I will smite the winter house
with the summer house; and the houses of ivory shall perish, and the great
houses shall have an end, saith the
LORD.
4 Hear this word, ye kine of Bā'shăn,
that *are* in the mountain of Sa-
mā'rĭ-ȧ, which oppress the poor, which
crush the needy, which say to their masters, Bring, and let us drink.
2 The Lord GOD hath sworn by his
holiness, that, lo, the days shall come
upon you, that he will take you away
with hooks, and your posterity with
fishhooks.
3 And ye shall go out at the breaches, every *cow at that which is* before
her; and [1]ye shall cast *them* into the
palace, saith the LORD.
4 ¶ [a]Come to Bĕth'–el, and transgress; at [b]Ğĭl'găl multiply transgression; and [c]bring your sacrifices every
morning, *and* your tithes after [2]three
years:
5 And [3]offer a sacrifice of thanksgiving with leaven, and proclaim *and* publish [d]the free offerings: for [4]this liketh
you, O ye children of Ĭs'ra-el, saith the
Lord GOD.
6 ¶ And I also have [e]given you cleanness of teeth in all your cities, and
want of bread in all your places: [f]yet
have ye not returned unto me, saith the
LORD.
7 And also I have withholden the
rain from you, when *there were* yet
three months to the harvest: and I
caused it to rain upon one city, and
caused it not to rain upon another
city: one piece was rained upon, and
the piece whereupon it rained not
withered.

8 [d]1 Cor. 9.16
9 [5]Or, oppressions
10 [6]Or, spoil
11 [e]2 Ki. 17.6
12 [7]delivereth
[8]Or, on the bed's feet
14 [9]Or, punish Israel for
CHAPTER 4
3 [1]Or, ye shall cast away the things of the palace
4 [a]Ezek. 20.39
[b]Hos. 4.15
[c]Num. 28.3-4
[2]three years of days
5 [3]offer by burning
[d]Deut. 12.6
[4]so ye love
6 [e]1 Ki. 17.1
[f]Isa. 9.13; Jer. 5.3; Hos. 5.15; Hag. 2.17
9 [g]Deut. 28.22
[5]Or, the multitude of your gardens, etc., did the palmerworm, etc
10 [6]Or, in the way
[7]with the captivity of your horses
11 [h]Isa. 13.19
[i]Zech. 3.2
12 [j]Ezek. 13.5; Matt. 5.25-26; 1 Thess. 5.2; Rev. 3.3
13 [8]Or, spirit
[k]Ps. 139.2; Dan. 2.28; Matt. 9.4; John 2.25
[l]Deut. 32.13
[m]Isa. 47.4
CHAPTER 5
1 [a]Jer. 7.29
4 [b]2 Chr. 15.2
[c]Isa. 55.3
5 [d]ch. 4.4
[e]ch. 8.14
8 [f]Job 38.31
[g]Job 38.34
[h]ch. 4.13
9 [1]spoil
10 [i]Isa. 29.21
[j]1 Ki. 22.8

8 So two *or* three cities wandered
unto one city, to drink water; but they
were not satisfied: yet have ye not returned unto me, saith the LORD.
9 [g]I have smitten you with blasting
and mildew: [5]when your gardens and
your vineyards and your fig trees and
your olive trees increased, the palmerworm devoured *them:* yet have ye not
returned unto me, saith the LORD.
10 I have sent among you the pestilence [6]after the manner of Ē'ġypt: your
young men have I slain with the sword,
[7]and have taken away your horses; and
I have made the stink of your camps to
come up unto your nostrils: yet have ye
not returned unto me, saith the LORD.
11 I have overthrown *some* of you,
as God overthrew [h]Sŏd'om and Go-
mŏr'rah, [i]and ye were as a firebrand
plucked out of the burning: yet have ye
not returned unto me, saith the LORD.
12 Therefore thus will I do unto thee,
O Ĭs'ra-el: *and* because I will do this
unto thee, [j]prepare to meet thy God, O
Ĭs'ra-el.
13 For, lo, he that formeth the mountains, and createth the [8]wind, [k]and declareth unto man what *is* his thought,
that maketh the morning darkness,
[l]and treadeth upon the high places of
the earth, [m]The LORD, The God of
hosts, *is* his name.
5 Hear ye this word which [a]I take up
against you, *even* a lamentation, O
house of Ĭs'ra-el.
2 The virgin of Ĭs'ra-el is fallen; she
shall no more rise: she is forsaken
upon her land; *there is* none to raise
her up.
3 For thus saith the Lord GOD; The
city that went out *by* a thousand shall
leave an hundred, and that which went
forth *by* an hundred shall leave ten, to
the house of Ĭs'ra-el.
4 ¶ For thus saith the LORD unto the
house of Ĭs'ra-el, [b]Seek ye me, [c]and ye
shall live:
5 But seek not [d]Bĕth'–el, nor enter
into Ğĭl'găl, and pass not to [e]Bē'er–
shē'bȧ: for Ğĭl'găl shall surely go into
captivity, and Bĕth'–el shall come to
nought.
6 Seek the LORD, and ye shall live;
lest he break out like fire in the house
of Jō'seph, and devour *it*, and *there be*
none to quench *it* in Bĕth'–el.
7 Ye who turn judgment to wormwood, and leave off righteousness in
the earth,
8 *Seek him* that maketh the [f]seven
stars and O-rī'on, and turneth the shadow of death into the morning, and
maketh the day dark with night: that
[g]calleth for the waters of the sea, and
poureth them out upon the face of the
earth: [h]The LORD *is* his name:
9 That strengtheneth the [1]spoiled
against the strong, so that the spoiled
shall come against the fortress.
10 [i]They hate him that rebuketh in
the gate, and they [j]abhor him that
speaketh uprightly.
11 Forasmuch therefore as your
treading *is* upon the poor, and ye take

from him burdens of wheat: [k]ye have
built houses of hewn stone, but ye shall
not dwell in them; ye have planted
[2]pleasant vineyards, but ye shall not
drink wine of them.
12 For I know your manifold transgressions and your mighty sins: they
afflict the just, they take [3]a bribe, and
they [l]turn aside the poor in the gate
from their right.
13 Therefore the prudent shall keep
silence in that time; for it *is* an evil
time.
14 [m]Seek good, and not evil, that ye
may live: and so the LORD, the God of
hosts, shall be with you, [n]as ye have
spoken.
15 [o]Hate the evil, and love the good,
and establish judgment in the gate: [p]it
may be that the LORD God of hosts
will be gracious unto the remnant of
Jō′seph.
16 Therefore the LORD, the God of
hosts, the Lord, saith thus; Wailing
shall be in all streets; and they shall
say in all the highways, Alas! alas!
and they shall call the husbandman to
mourning, and [q]such as are skilful of
lamentation to wailing.
17 And in all vineyards *shall be* wailing: for [r]I will pass through thee, saith
the LORD.
18 [s]Woe unto you that desire the
day of the LORD! to what end *is* it for
you? the day of the LORD *is* darkness,
and not light.
19 As if a man did flee from a lion,
and a bear met him; or went into the
house, and leaned his hand on the
wall, and a serpent bit him.
20 *Shall* not the day of the LORD *be*
darkness, and not light? even very
dark, and no brightness in it?
21 ¶ [t]I hate, I despise your feast
days, and I will not [4]smell in your solemn assemblies.
22 Though ye offer me burnt offerings and your meat offerings, I will not
accept *them:* neither will I regard the
[5]peace offerings of your fat beasts.
23 Take thou away from me the
noise of thy songs; for I will not hear
the melody of thy viols.
24 But let judgment [6]run down as
waters, and righteousness as a mighty
stream.
25 [u]Have ye offered unto me sacrifices and offerings in the wilderness
forty years, O house of Is′ra-el?
26 But ye have borne [7]the tabernacle of your Mō′loch and Chī′ŭn your
images, the star of your god, which ye
made to yourselves.
27 Therefore will I cause you to
go into captivity beyond Da-măs′cus,
saith the LORD, whose name *is* The
God of hosts.

6 Woe to them *that* [1]*are* at ease in
Zī′ŏn, and trust in the mountain of
Sa-mā′rĭ-ȧ, *which are* named [2]chief of
the nations, to whom the house of
Is′ra-el came!
2 Pass ye unto [a]Căl′neh, and see;
and from thence go ye to [b]Hā′math the
great: then go down to Găth of the Phĭ-
lĭs′tĭnes: *be they* better than these kingdoms? or their border greater than
your border?
3 Ye that [c]put far away the evil day,
and cause the [3]seat of violence to come
near;
4 That lie upon beds of ivory, and
[4]stretch themselves upon their couches, and eat the lambs out of the flock,
and the calves out of the midst of the
stall;
5 That [5]chant to the sound of the
viol, *and* invent to themselves instruments of musick like Dā′vid;
6 That drink [6]wine in bowls, and
anoint themselves with the chief ointments: but they are not grieved for the
[7]affliction of Jō′seph.
7 ¶ Therefore now shall they go captive with the first that go captive, and
the banquet of them that stretched
themselves shall be removed.
8 The Lord GOD hath sworn by himself, saith the LORD the God of hosts, I
abhor the excellency of Jā′cob, and
hate his palaces: therefore will I deliver
up the city with all [8]that is therein.
9 And it shall come to pass, if there
remain ten men in one house, that they
shall die.
10 And a man's uncle shall take him
up, and he that burneth him, to bring
out the bones out of the house, and
shall say unto him that *is* by the sides
of the house, *Is there* yet *any* with
thee? and he shall say, No. Then shall
he say, Hold thy tongue: for [9]we may
not make mention of the name of the
LORD.
11 For, behold, the LORD commandeth, and he will smite the great house
with [10]breaches, and the little house
with clefts.
12 ¶ Shall horses run upon the rock?
will *one* plow *there* with oxen? for ye
have turned judgment into gall, and the
fruit of righteousness into hemlock:
13 Ye which rejoice in a thing of
nought, which say, Have we not taken
to us horns by our own strength?
14 But, behold, I will raise up against
you a nation, O house of Is′ra-el, saith
the LORD the God of hosts; and they
shall afflict you from [d]the entering
in of Hē′măth unto the [11]river of the
wilderness.

7 Thus hath the Lord GOD shewed
unto me; and, behold, he formed
[1]grasshoppers in the beginning of the
shooting up of the latter growth; and,
lo, *it was* the latter growth after the
king's mowings.
2 And it came to pass, *that* when
they had made an end of eating the
grass of the land, then I said, O Lord
GOD, forgive, I beseech thee: [2]by whom
shall Jā′cob arise? for he *is* small.
3 [a]The LORD repented for this: It
shall not be, saith the LORD.
4 ¶ Thus hath the Lord GOD shewed
unto me: and, behold, the Lord GOD
called to contend by fire, and it devoured the great deep, and did eat up a
part.

11 [k]Mic. 6.15; Zeph. 1.13 [2]vineyards of desire
12 [3]Or, a ransom [l]Isa. 29.21
14 [m]Ps. 34.12-16; Rom. 2.7-9 [n]Mic. 3.11
15 [o]Rom. 12.9 [p]Ex. 32.30
16 [q]Jer. 9.17
17 [r]Ex. 12.12
18 [s]Isa. 5.19; 2 Pet. 3.4
21 [t]Isa. 1.11 [4]Or, smell your holy days
22 [5]Or, thank offerings
24 [6]roll
25 [u]Acts 7.42
26 [7]Or, Siccuth your king

CHAPTER 6
1 [1]Or, are secure, or, insolent [2]Or, firstfruits
2 [a]Gen. 10.10; Isa. 10.9; Taken, B.C. 794 [b]Num. 34.8; 2 Ki. 14.25
3 [c]Eccl. 8.11 [3]Or, habitation
4 [4]Or, abound with superfluities
5 [5]Or, quaver
6 [6]Or, in bowls of wine [7]breach
8 [8]the fulness thereof
10 [9]Or, they will not, or, have not
11 [10]Or, droppings
14 [d]1 Ki. 8.65 [11]Or, valley

CHAPTER 7
1 [1]Or, green worms
2 [2]Or, who of (or, for) Jacob shall stand?
3 [a]Deut. 32.36;

5 Then said I, O Lord GOD, cease, I
beseech thee: by whom shall Jā'cob
arise? for he *is* small.
6 The LORD [b]repented for this: This
also shall not be, saith the Lord GOD.
7 ¶ Thus he shewed me: and, behold,
the Lord stood upon a wall *made* by a
plumbline, with a plumbline in his
hand.
8 And the LORD said unto me, Ā'-
mos, what seest thou? And I said, A
plumbline. Then said the Lord, Behold,
[c]I will set a plumbline in the midst of
my people Ĭs'ra-el: [d]I will not again
pass by them any more:
9 [e]And the high places of Ī'saac
shall be desolate, and the sanctuaries
of Ĭs'ra-el shall be laid waste; and [f]I
will rise against the house of Jĕr-o-
bō'am with the sword.
10 ¶ Then Ăm-a-zī'ah [g]the priest of
Bĕth'–el sent to [h]Jĕr-o-bō'am king of
Ĭs'ra-el, saying, Ā'mos hath conspired
against thee in the midst of the house
of Ĭs'ra-el: the land is not able to bear
all his words.
11 For thus Ā'mos saith, Jĕr-o-bō'-
am shall die by the sword, and Ĭs'ra-el
shall surely be led away captive out of
their own land.
12 Also Ăm-a-zī'ah said unto Ā'mos,
O thou seer, go, flee thee away into the
land of Jū'dah, and there eat bread,
and prophesy there:
13 But [i]prophesy not again any more
at Bĕth'–el: [j]for it *is* the king's [3]cha-
pel, and it *is* the [4]king's court.
14 ¶ Then answered Ā'mos, and said
to Ăm-a-zī'ah, I *was* no prophet, neither *was* I [k]a prophet's son; [l]but I *was*
an herdman, and a gatherer of [5]syco-
more fruit:
15 And the LORD took me [6]as I followed the flock, and the LORD said
unto me, Go, prophesy unto my people
Ĭs'ra-el.
16 ¶ Now therefore hear thou the
word of the LORD: Thou sayest, Prophesy not against Ĭs'ra-el, and [m]drop not
thy word against the house of Ī'saac.
17 [n]Therefore thus saith the LORD;
[o]Thy wife shall be an harlot in the city,
and thy sons and thy daughters shall
fall by the sword, and thy land shall be
divided by line; and thou shalt die in a
polluted land: and Ĭs'ra-el shall surely
go into captivity forth of his land.

8 Thus hath the Lord GOD shewed
unto me: and behold a basket of
summer fruit.
2 And he said, Ā'mos, what seest
thou? And I said, A basket of summer
fruit. Then said the LORD unto me,
[a]The end is come upon my people of
Ĭs'ra-el; I will not again pass by them
any more.
3 And the songs of the temple [1]shall
be howlings in that day, saith the Lord
GOD: *there shall be* many dead bodies
in every place; they shall cast *them*
forth [2]with silence.
4 ¶ Hear this, O ye that swallow up
the needy, even to make the poor of
the land to fail,
5 Saying, When will the [3]new moon
be gone, that we may sell corn? and
[b]the sabbath, that we may [4]set forth
wheat, [c]making the ephah small, and
the shekel great, and [5]falsifying the balances by deceit?
6 That we may buy the poor for silver, and the needy for a pair of shoes;
yea, and sell the refuse of the wheat?
7 The LORD hath sworn by [d]the excellency of Jā'cob, Surely [e]I will never
forget any of their works.
8 [f]Shall not the land tremble for
this, and every one mourn that dwelleth therein? and it shall rise up wholly
as a flood; and it shall be cast out and
drowned, [g]as *by* the flood of Ē'ġypt.
9 And it shall come to pass in that
day, saith the Lord GOD, [h]that I will
cause the sun to go down at noon, and I
will darken the earth in the clear day:
10 And I will turn your feasts into
mourning, and all your songs into lamentation; and I will bring up sackcloth
upon all loins, and baldness upon every head; [i]and I will make it as the
mourning of an only *son,* and the end
thereof as a bitter day.
11 ¶ Behold, the days come, saith
the Lord GOD, that I will send a famine
in the land, not a famine of bread, nor a
thirst for water, but [j]of hearing the
words of the LORD:
12 And they shall wander from sea
to sea, and from the north even to the
east, they shall run to and fro to seek
the word of the LORD, and shall not
find *it.*
13 In that day shall the fair virgins
and young men faint for thirst.
14 They that swear by [k]the sin of
Sa-mā'rĭ-ȧ, and say, Thy god, O Dăn,
liveth; and, The [6]manner of Bē'er–
shē'bȧ liveth; even they shall fall, and
never rise up again.

9 I saw the Lord standing upon the
altar: and he said, Smite the [1]lintel
of the door, that the posts may shake:
and [2]cut them in the head, all of them;
and I will slay the last of them with the
sword: he that fleeth of them shall not
flee away, and he that escapeth of
them shall not be delivered.
2 [a]Though they dig into hell, thence
shall mine hand take them; [b]though
they climb up to heaven, thence will I
bring them down:
3 And though they [c]hide themselves
in the top of Cär'mel, I will search and
take them out thence; and though they
be hid from my sight in the bottom of
the sea, thence will I command the serpent, and he shall bite them:
4 And though they go into captivity
before their enemies, [d]thence will I
command the sword, and it shall slay
them: and [e]I will set mine eyes upon
them for evil, and not for good.
5 And the Lord GOD of hosts *is* he
that toucheth the land, and it shall
[f]melt, and all that dwell therein shall
mourn: and it shall rise up wholly like
a flood; and shall be drowned, as *by*
the flood of Ē'ġypt.

6 [b]Ps. 102.17
8 [c]2 Ki. 21.13; Isa. 28.17
[d]Mic. 7.18
9 [e]Beer-sheba, Gen. 26.23
[f]Fulfilled, 2 Ki. 15.10
10 [g]1 Ki. 12.32
[h]2 Ki. 14.23
13 [i]ch. 2.12
[j]1 Ki. 12.32
[3]Or, sanctuary
[4]house of the kingdom
14 [k]2 Ki. 2.5
[l]Zech. 13.5
[5]Or, wild figs
15 [6]from behind
16 [m]Isa. 30.10; Mic. 2.6
17 [n]Jer. 28.12; Jer. 29.21-25-31-32
[o]Lam. 5.11

CHAPTER 8
2 [a]Jer. 1.12; Lam. 4.18; Ezek. 7.2
3 [1]shall howl
[2]be silent
5 [3]Or, month
[b]Neh. 13.15
[4]open
[c]Mic. 6.10
[5]perverting the balances of deceit
7 [d]Ps. 68.34
[e]Hos. 8.13
8 [f]Hos. 4.3
[g]ch. 9.5
9 [h]Job 5.14; Isa. 13.10; Jer. 15.9; ch. 4.13; Mic. 3.6; 1 Thess. 5-2-3
10 [i]Jer. 6.26; Luke 7.12-13
11 [j]1 Sam. 3.1; Mic. 3.6
14 [k]Deut. 9.21; Mic. 1.5
[6]way

CHAPTER 9
1 [1]Or, chapiter, or, knop
[2]Or, wound them
2 [a]Ps. 139.8
[b]Job 20.6; Obad. 4
3 [c]Jer. 23.24
4 [d]Deut. 28.65
[e]Lev. 17.10
5 [f]Mic. 1.4

6 *It is* he that buildeth his [3]stories in the heaven, and hath founded his [4]troop in the earth; he that calleth for the waters of the sea, and poureth them out upon the face of the earth: The LORD *is* his name.

7 *Are* ye not as children of the Ē-thĭ-ō'pĭ-ans unto me, O children of Ĭs'ra-el? saith the LORD. Have not I brought up Ĭs'ra-el out of the land of Ē'ġypt? and the Phĭ-lĭs'tĭnes from [g]Căph'tôr, and the Sy̆r'ĭ-ans from [h]Kīr?

8 Behold, [i]the eyes of the Lord GOD *are* upon the sinful kingdom, and I [j]will destroy it from off the face of the earth; saving that I will not utterly destroy the house of Jā'cob, saith the LORD.

9 For, lo, I will command, and I will [5]sift the house of Ĭs'ra-el among all nations, like as *corn* is sifted in a sieve, yet shall not the least [6]grain fall upon the earth.

10 All the sinners of my people shall die by the sword, which say, The evil shall not overtake nor prevent us.

6 [3]ascensions, or, spheres
[4]Or, bundle
7 [g]Deut. 2.23; Jer. 47.4
[h]ch. 1.5
8 [i]Ps. 11.4
[j]Jer. 30.11
9 [5]cause to move
[6]stone
11 [k]Acts 15.16
[7]hedge, or, wall
12 [l]Obad. 19
[m]Num. 24.18
[8]upon whom my name is called
13 [n]Lev. 26.5
[9]draweth forth
[10]Or, new
14 [o]Isa. 61.4
15 [p]Isa. 60.21

11 ¶ [k]In that day will I raise up the tabernacle of Dā'vid that is fallen, and [7]close up the breaches thereof; and I will raise up his ruins, and I will build it as in the days of old:

12 [l]That they may possess the remnant of [m]Ē'dom, and of all the heathen, [8]which are called by my name, saith the LORD that doeth this.

13 Behold, [n]the days come, saith the LORD, that the plowman shall overtake the reaper, and the treader of grapes him that [9]soweth seed; [10]and the mountains shall drop sweet wine, and all the hills shall melt.

14 And I will bring again the captivity of my people of Ĭs'ra-el, and [o]they shall build the waste cities, and inhabit *them;* and they shall plant vineyards, and drink the wine thereof; they shall also make gardens, and eat the fruit of them.

15 And I will plant them upon their land, and [p]they shall no more be pulled up out of their land which I have given them, saith the LORD thy God.

THE BOOK OF

OBADIAH

Life's Questions

How do I respond to betrayal?
Where is God when all is lost?
How does hope appear in dispair?

God's Answers

About 586 as Babylon took Judah into exile and as neighbor Edom helped Babylon and took away Judah's southern territory, God sent His servant Obadiah to explain the situation to His people. Obadiah had two messages: God knows and will judge the sins of His people's enemies (1:1–14), and the day of the Lord will bring deliverance for God's people (1:15–21).

Obadiah shows God's justice, sovereignty, and grace amid disaster.

1 The vision of Ō-ba-dī'ah. Thus saith the Lord GOD [a]concerning Ē'dom; We have heard a rumour from the LORD, and an ambassador is sent among the heathen, Arise ye, and let us rise up against her in battle.

2 Behold, I have made thee small among the heathen: thou art greatly despised.

3 ¶ The pride of thine heart hath deceived thee, thou that dwellest in the clefts [b]of the rock, whose habitation *is* high; [c]that saith in his heart, Who shall bring me down to the ground?

4 [d]Though thou exalt *thyself* as the eagle, and though thou set thy nest among the stars, thence will I bring thee down, saith the LORD.

5 If thieves came to thee, if robbers by night, (how art thou cut off!) would they not have stolen till they had enough? if the grapegatherers came to thee, would they not leave [1]*some* grapes?

6 How are *the things* of Ē'sa̤u searched out! *how* are his hidden things sought up!

7 All the men of thy confederacy have brought thee *even* to the border: [2]the men that were at peace with thee have deceived thee, *and* prevailed against thee; [3]*they that eat* thy bread have laid a wound under thee: *there is* none understanding [4]in him.

CHAPTER 1
1 [a]Isa. 21.11; Mal. 1.3
3 [b]2 Ki. 14.7; 2 Chr. 25.12
[c]Isa. 14.13; Rev. 18.7
4 [d]Job 20.6
5 [1]Or, gleanings
7 [2]the men of thy peace
[3]the men of thy bread
[4]Or, of it
9 [e]Ps. 76.5
10 [f]Gen. 27.41
[g]Mal. 1.4
11 [5]Or, carried away his substance
[h]Nah. 3.10
12 [6]Or, do not behold, etc
[i]Mic. 4.11
[j]Prov. 24.17

8 Shall I not in that day, saith the LORD, even destroy the wise *men* out of Ē'dom, and understanding out of the mount of Ē'sa̤u?

9 And thy [e]mighty *men,* O Tē'man, shall be dismayed, to the end that every one of the mount of Ē'sa̤u may be cut off by slaughter.

10 ¶ For *thy* [f]violence against thy brother Jā'cob shame shall cover thee, and [g]thou shalt be cut off for ever.

11 In the day that thou stoodest on the other side, in the day that the strangers [5]carried away captive his forces, and foreigners entered into his gates, and [h]cast lots upon Je-ru̧'sa-lĕm, even thou *wast* as one of them.

12 But [6]thou shouldest not have looked [i]on the day of thy brother in the day that he became a stranger; neither shouldest thou have [j]rejoiced over the children of Jū'dah in the day of their destruction; neither shouldest thou

have [7]spoken proudly in the day of distress.

13 Thou shouldest not have entered into the gate of my people in the day of their calamity; yea, thou shouldest not have looked on their affliction in the day of their calamity, nor have laid *hands* on their [8]substance in the day of their calamity;

14 Neither shouldest thou have stood in the crossway, to cut off those of his that did escape; neither shouldest thou have [9]delivered up those of his that did remain in the day of distress.

15 For the day of the LORD *is* near upon all the heathen: [k]as thou hast done, it shall be done unto thee: thy reward shall return upon thine own head.

16 For as ye have drunk upon my holy mountain, *so* shall all the heathen drink continually, yea, they shall drink, and they shall [10]swallow down, and they shall be as though they had not been.

17 ¶ But upon mount Zī'ŏn shall be [11]deliverance, and [12]there shall be holiness; and the house of Jā'cob shall possess their possessions.

18 And the house of Jā'cob shall be a fire, and the house of Jō'seph a flame, and the house of Ē'sa̤u for stubble, and they shall kindle in them, and devour them; and there shall not be *any* remaining of the house of Ē'sa̤u; for the LORD hath spoken *it*.

19 And *they of* the south shall possess the mount of Ē'sa̤u; [l]and *they of* the plain the Phĭ-lĭs'tĭnes: and they shall possess the fields of Ē'phrā-ĭm, and the fields of Sa-ma̤'rĭ-ȧ: and Bĕn'-ja-min *shall possess* Gĭl'e-ăd.

20 And the captivity of this host of the children of Is'ra-el *shall possess* that of the Cā'năan-ītes, *even* [m]unto Zăr'e-phăth; and the captivity of Je-ru̥'sa-lĕm, [13]which *is* in Sĕph'a-răd, shall possess the cities of the south.

21 And [n]saviours shall come up on mount Zī'ŏn to judge the mount of Ē'sa̤u; and the [o]kingdom shall be the LORD'S.

[7]magnified thy mouth
13 [8]Or, forces
14 [9]Or, shut up
15 [k]Judg. 1.7; Ps. 137.8; Ezek. 35.15; Joel 3.7-8
16 [10]Or, sup up
17 [11]Or, they that escape [12]Or, it shall be holy
19 [l]Zeph. 2.7
20 [m]1 Ki. 17.9 [13]Or, shall possess that which is in Sepharad
21 [n]Isa. 19.20 [o]Dan. 2.44; Zech. 14.9; Rev. 11.15

THE BOOK OF

JONAH

Life's Questions

Who can I hate since God does not love them?
Where does God work in this world?
How does God expect me to relate to my enemies?

God's Answers

About 780 B.C. Jonah became a national hero by helping King Jeroboam II extend Israel's territory (2 Kings 14:24). Then God gave Him a hard mission: preach to the enemy in the enemy's territory. Almost comically, Jonah fled from God. God used pious pagan sailors and a monstrous fish to set Jonah back on course. He preached five words leading to the world's greatest revival. Jonah pouted. He wanted the enemy destroyed.

Through Jonah God shows: people with a bad reputation can be pious and come to know God (1:1–16); God hears the distress calls of His people (1:17—2:10); the loving God does not judge a people who repents (3:1–10); God's people should mirror God's compassion (4:1–11).

Jonah preaches love your enemies and lead them to God long before Jesus came.

1 Now the word of the LORD came unto [a]Jō'nah the son of A-mĭt'ta-ī, saying,

2 Arise, go to Nĭn'e-veh, that [b]great city, and cry against it; for [c]their wickedness is come up before me.

3 But Jō'nah rose up to flee unto [d]Tär'shish from the presence of the LORD, and went down to [e]Jŏp'pȧ; and he found a ship going to Tär'shish: so he paid the fare thereof, and went down into it, to go with them unto Tär'shish [f]from the presence of the LORD.

4 ¶ But the LORD [1]sent out a great wind into the sea, and there was a mighty tempest in the sea, so that the ship was [2]like to be broken.

5 Then the mariners were afraid, and cried every man unto his god, and cast forth the wares that *were* in the ship into the sea, to lighten *it* of them. But Jō'nah was gone down into the sides of the ship; and he lay, and was fast asleep.

6 So the shipmaster came to him, and said unto him, What meanest thou, O sleeper? arise, [g]call upon thy God, if so be that God will think upon us, that we perish not.

7 And they said every one to his fellow, Come, and let us [h]cast lots, that we may know for whose cause this evil *is* upon us. So they cast lots, and the lot fell upon Jō'nah.

8 Then said they unto him, [i]Tell us, we pray thee, for whose cause this evil *is* upon us; What *is* thine occupation? and whence comest thou? what *is* thy country? and of what people *art* thou?

9 And he said unto them, I *am* an Hē'brew; and I fear [3]the LORD, the God of heaven, which hath made the sea and the dry *land*.

10 Then were the men [4]exceedingly afraid, and said unto him, Why hast thou done this? For the men knew that

CHAPTER 1
1 [a]2 Ki. 14.25
2 [b]Gen. 10.11; ch. 3.3; Nah. 2.8; Matt. 12.41 [c]Gen. 18.20; Jas. 5.4
3 [d]Isa. 23.1 [e]Josh. 19.46; Acts 9.36 [f]Gen. 4.16
4 [1]cast forth [2]thought to be broken
6 [g]Ps. 78.34; Matt. 8.25
7 [h]Josh. 7.14; Acts 1.26
8 [i]Josh. 7.19
9 [3]Or, JEHOVAH
10 [4]with great fear

he fled from the presence of the LORD,
because he had told them.
11 ¶ Then said they unto him, What
shall we do unto thee, that the sea
[5]may be calm unto us? for the sea
[6]wrought, and was tempestuous.
12 And he said unto them, Take me
up, and cast me forth into the sea; so
shall the sea be calm unto you: for I
know that [j]for my sake this great tempest *is* upon you.
13 Nevertheless the men [7]rowed
hard to bring *it* to the land; [k]but they
could not: for the sea wrought, and was
tempestuous against them.
14 Wherefore they cried unto the
LORD, and said, We beseech thee, O
LORD, we beseech thee, let us not perish for this man's life, and [l]lay not
upon us innocent blood: for thou, O
LORD, hast done as it pleased thee.
15 So they took up Jō'nah, and cast
him forth into the sea: and the sea
[8]ceased from her raging.
16 Then the men feared the LORD exceedingly, and [9]offered a sacrifice unto
the LORD, and made vows.
17 ¶ Now the LORD had prepared a
great fish to swallow up Jō'nah. And
[m]Jō'nah was in the [10]belly of the fish
three days and three nights.

2 Then Jō'nah prayed unto the LORD
his God out of the fish's belly,
2 And said, I cried [1]by reason of
mine affliction unto the LORD, and he
heard me; out of the belly of [2]hell cried
I, *and* thou heardest my voice.
3 [a]For thou hadst cast me into the
deep, in the [3]midst of the seas; and the
floods compassed me about: all thy billows and thy waves passed over me.
4 [b]Then I said, I am cast out of thy
sight; yet I will look again [c]toward thy
holy temple.
5 The waters compassed me about,
even to the soul: the depth closed me
round about, the weeds were wrapped
about my head.
6 I went down to the [4]bottoms of the
mountains; the earth with her bars
was about me for ever: yet hast thou
brought up my life from [5]corruption, O
LORD my God.
7 When my soul fainted within me I
remembered the LORD: [d]and my prayer came in unto thee, into thine holy
temple.
8 They that observe [e]lying vanities
forsake their own mercy.
9 But I will [f]sacrifice unto thee with
the voice of thanksgiving; I will pay
that that I have vowed. Salvation *is* of
the LORD.
10 ¶ And the LORD [g]spake unto the
fish, and it vomited out Jō'nah upon
the dry *land*.

3 And the word of the LORD came
unto Jō'nah the second time, saying,
2 Arise, go unto Nĭn'e-veh, that great
city, and preach unto it the preaching
that I bid thee.
3 So Jō'nah arose, and went unto
Nĭn'e-veh, according to the word of
the LORD. Now Nĭn'e-veh was an [1]ex-
ceeding great city of three days' journey.
4 And Jō'nah began to enter into the
city a day's journey, and [a]he cried, and
said, Yet forty days, and Nĭn'e-veh
shall be overthrown.
5 ¶ So the people of Nĭn'e-veh [b]be-
lieved God, and proclaimed a fast, and
put on sackcloth, from the greatest of
them even to the least of them.
6 For word came unto the king of
Nĭn'e-veh, and he arose from his throne,
and he laid his robe from him, and covered *him* with sackcloth, [c]and sat in
ashes.
7 [d]And he caused *it* to be proclaimed and [2]published through Nĭn'e-veh
by the decree of the king and his [3]no-
bles, saying, Let neither man nor beast,
herd nor flock, taste any thing: let them
not feed, nor drink water:
8 But let man and beast be covered
with sackcloth, and cry mightily unto
God: yea, [e]let them turn every one
from his evil way, and from the violence that *is* in their hands.
9 Who can tell *if* God will turn and
repent, and turn away from his fierce
anger, that we perish not?
10 ¶ And God saw their works, that
they turned from their evil way; and
God repented of the evil, that he had
said that he would do unto them; and
he did *it* not.

4 But [a]it displeased Jō'nah exceedingly, and he was very angry.
2 And he prayed unto the LORD,
and said, I pray thee, O LORD, *was* not
this my saying, when I was yet in my
country? Therefore I fled before unto
Tär'shish: for I knew that thou *art* a
[b]gracious God, and merciful, slow to
anger, and of great kindness, and re-
pentest thee of the evil.
3 [c]Therefore now, O LORD, take, I
beseech thee, my life from me; for *it is*
better for me to die than to live.
4 ¶ Then said the LORD, [1]Doest thou
well to be angry?
5 So Jō'nah went out of the city, and
sat on the east side of the city, and
there made him a booth, and sat under
it in the shadow, till he might see what
would become of the city.
6 And the LORD God prepared a
[2]gourd, and made *it* to come up over
Jō'nah, that it might be a shadow over
his head, to deliver him from his grief.
So Jō'nah [3]was exceeding glad of the
gourd.
7 But God prepared a worm when
the morning rose the next day, and it
smote the gourd that it withered.
8 And it came to pass, when the sun
did arise, that God prepared a [4]vehe-
ment east wind; and [d]the sun beat upon
the head of Jō'nah, that he fainted, and
wished in himself to die, and said, *It is*
better for me to die than to live.
9 And God said to Jō'nah, [5]Doest
thou well to be angry for the gourd?
And he said, [6]I do well to be angry,
even unto death.
10 Then said the LORD, Thou hast
[7]had pity on the gourd, for the which

11 [5]may be silent from us
[6]went, or, grew more and more tempestuous
12 [j]Eccl. 9.18
13 [7]digged
[k]Prov. 21.30
14 [l]Deut. 21.8
15 [8]stood
16 [9]sacrificed a sacrifice unto the LORD, and vowed vows
17 [m]Matt. 12.40
[10]bowels

CHAPTER 2
2 [1]Or, out of mine affliction
[2]Or, the grave
3 [a]Ps. 88.6
[3]heart
4 [b]Ps. 31.22; Isa. 49.14
[c]1 Ki. 8.38
6 [4]cuttings off
[5]Or, the pit
7 [d]Ps. 18.6; Jer. 2.13
8 [e]2 Ki. 17.15; Jer. 10.8
9 [f]Ps. 50.14; Heb. 13.15
10 [g]ch. 1.17; Matt. 8.9

CHAPTER 3
3 [1]of God
4 [a]Deut. 18.22
5 [b]Matt. 12.41; Luke 11.32
6 [c]Job 2.8; Mic. 1.10
7 [d]2 Chr. 20.3;
[2]said
[3]great men
8 [e]Isa. 1.16;

CHAPTER 4
1 [a]Matt. 20.15
2 [b]Ex. 34.6
3 [c]1 Ki. 19.4
4 [1]Or, Art thou greatly angry?
6 [2]Kikajon, or, palmcrist
[3]rejoiced with great joy
8 [4]Or, silent
[d]Ps. 121.6
9 [5]Or, Art thou greatly angry?
[6]Or, I am greatly angry
10 [7]Or, spared

thou hast not laboured, neither madest
it grow; which [8]came up in a night, and
perished in a night:
11 And should not I [e]spare Nĭn'e-
veh, that great city, wherein are more
than sixscore thousand persons [f]that
cannot discern between their right
hand and their left hand; and *also*
much [g]cattle?

[8]was the son of the night
11 [e]Ezek. 33.11
[f]Deut. 1.39
[g]Ps. 36.6

THE BOOK OF

MICAH

Life's Questions

Does prosperity prove God is blessing me?
What do I do about the plight of the poor?
Do I need forgiveness?

God's Answers

About 735 B.C. God called a young man from the country to go to the capital city and announce His judgment upon a prosperous people. Micah continued preaching through the defeat and fall of Israel (733–721), and the decline and decimation of the southern kingdom (715–701). He begged Judah's leaders to answer God's call to justice before it was too late.

Micah shows: God judges all sin, religious, economic, political (1—3); God promises a day of peace and worship for all (4—5); God judges a people for whom He has done all possible in redemption and in showing His expectations (6:1—7:6); after judgment God will in love forgive and renew His people (7:7–20).

Micah seeks to convince God's people that His love demands our justice.

1 The [a]word of the LORD that came
to [b]Mī'cah the Mō'ras-thīte in the
days of Jō'tham, Ā'hăz, *and* Hĕz-e-
kī'ah, kings of Jū'dah, which he saw
concerning Sa-mā'rĭ-ȧ and Je-rụ'sa-
lĕm.
2 [1]Hear, all ye people; hearken, O
earth, and [2]all that therein is: and let
the Lord GOD be witness against you,
the Lord from his holy temple.
3 For, behold, [c]the LORD cometh
forth out of his place, and will come
down, and tread upon the high places
of the earth.
4 And the mountains shall be molten
under him, and the valleys shall be
cleft, as wax before the fire, *and* as the
waters *that are* poured down [3]a steep
place.
5 For the [d]transgression of Jā'cob *is*
all this, and for the sins of the house of
Ĭs'ra-el. What *is* the transgression of
Jā'cob? *is it* not Sa-mā'rĭ-ȧ? and what
are the high places of Jū'dah? *are they*
not Je-rụ'sa-lĕm?
6 Therefore I will make Sa-mā'rĭ-ȧ
[e]as an heap of the field, *and* as plant-
ings of a vineyard: and I will pour
down the stones thereof into the valley, and I will discover the foundations
thereof.
7 And all the graven images thereof
shall be beaten to pieces, and all the
hires thereof shall be burned with the
fire, and all the idols thereof will I lay
desolate: for she gathered *it* of the hire
of an harlot, and they shall return to
the hire of an harlot.
8 Therefore I will wail and howl, I
will go stripped and naked: I will make
a wailing like the dragons, and mourning as the [4]owls.
9 For [5]her wound *is* incurable; for [f]it
is come unto Jū'dah; he is come unto
the gate of my people, *even* to Je-rụ'sa-
lĕm.
10 ¶ Declare ye *it* not at Găth, weep
ye not at all: in the house of [6]Ăph'rah
roll thyself in the dust.
11 Pass ye away, [7]thou inhabitant of
Săph'ĭr, having thy shame naked: the
inhabitant of [8]Zā'a-năn came not forth
in the mourning of [9]Bĕth–ē'zel; he
shall receive of you his standing.
12 For the inhabitant of Mā'roth
[10]waited carefully for good: but evil
came down from the LORD unto the
gate of Je-rụ'sa-lĕm.
13 O thou inhabitant of Lā'chish,
bind the chariot to the swift beast: she
is the beginning of the sin to the daughter of Zī'ŏn: for the transgressions of
Ĭs'ra-el were found in thee.
14 Therefore shalt thou give presents [11]to Mŏr'esh-eth–găth: the houses
of [12]Ăch'zĭb *shall be* a lie to the kings
of Ĭs'ra-el.
15 Yet will I bring an heir unto thee,
O inhabitant of Ma-rē'shah: [13]he shall
come unto A-dŭl'lăm the glory of Ĭs'ra-
el.
16 Make thee bald, and poll thee for
thy delicate children; enlarge thy baldness as the eagle; [g]for they are gone
into captivity from thee.

2 Woe to them [a]that devise iniquity,
and [b]work evil upon their beds!
when the morning is light, they practise it, because [c]it is in the power of
their hand.
2 And they covet fields, and take
them by violence; and houses, and
take *them* away: so they [1]oppress a
man and his house, even a man and his
heritage.
3 Therefore thus saith the LORD; Behold, against [d]this family do I devise
an evil, from which ye shall not re-

CHAPTER 1
1 [a]2 Pet. 1.21
[b]Jer. 26.18
2 [1]Hear, ye people, all of them
[2]the fulness thereof
3 [c]Isa. 26.21
4 [3]a descent
5 [d]Jer. 2.18-19
6 [e]2 Ki. 19.25
8 [4]daughters of the owl
9 [5]Or, she is grievously sick of her wounds
[f]2 Ki. 18.13
10 [6]That is, Dust
11 [7]thou inhabitress, or, thou that dwellest fairly
[8]Or, the country of flocks
[9]Or, a place near
12 [10]Or, was grieved
14 [11]Or, for
[12]That is, A lie
15 [13]Or, the glory of Israel shall come, etc
16 [g]2 Ki. 17.6
CHAPTER 2
1 [a]Esth. 3.8-9;
[b]Ps. 36.4
[c]Gen. 31.29
2 [1]Or, defraud
3 [d]Jer. 8.3

move your necks; neither shall ye go haughtily: for this time *is* evil.

4 ¶ In that day shall *one* take up a parable against you, and lament [2]with a doleful lamentation, *and* say, We be utterly spoiled: he hath changed the portion of my people: how hath he removed *it* from me! [3]turning away he hath divided our fields.

5 Therefore thou shalt have none that shall [e]cast a cord by lot in the congregation of the LORD.

6 [4]Prophesy ye not, *say they to them that* prophesy: they shall not prophesy to them, *that* they shall not take shame.

7 ¶ O *thou that art* named the house of Jā'cob, is the spirit of the LORD [5]straitened? *are* these his doings? do not my words do good to him that walketh [6]uprightly?

8 Even [7]of late my people is risen up as an enemy: ye pull off the robe [8]with the garment from them that pass by securely as men averse from war.

9 The [9]women of my people have ye cast out from their pleasant houses; from their children have ye taken away my glory for ever.

10 Arise ye, and depart; for this *is* not *your* [f]rest: because it is polluted, it shall destroy *you*, even with a sore destruction.

11 If a man [10]walking in the spirit and falsehood do lie, *saying*, I will prophesy unto thee of wine and of strong drink; he shall even be the prophet of this people.

12 ¶ I will surely assemble, O Jā'cob, all of thee; I will surely gather the [g]remnant of Ĭs'ra-el; I will put them together as the sheep of Bŏz'rah, as the flock in the midst of their fold: they shall make great noise by reason of *the multitude of* men.

13 The breaker is come up before them: they have broken up, and have passed through the gate, and are gone out by it: and their king shall pass before them, and the LORD on the head of them.

3 And I said, Hear, I pray you, O heads of Jā'cob, and ye princes of the house of Ĭs'ra-el; [a]*Is it* not for you to know judgment?

2 Who hate the good, and love the evil; who pluck off their skin from off them, and their flesh from off their bones;

3 Who also [b]eat the flesh of my people, and flay their skin from off them; and they break their bones, and chop them in pieces, as for the pot, and as flesh within the caldron.

4 Then [c]shall they cry unto the LORD, but he will not hear them: he will even hide his face from them at that time, as they have behaved themselves ill in their doings.

5 ¶ Thus saith the LORD [d]concerning the prophets that make my people err, that [e]bite with their teeth, and cry, Peace; and he that putteth not into their mouths, they even prepare war against him.

4 [2]with a lamentation of lamentations [3]Or, instead of restoring
5 [e]Deut. 32.8-9
6 [4]Drop, etc., or, Prophesy not as they prophesy
7 [5]Or, shortened [6]upright
8 [7]yesterday [8]over against a garment
9 [9]Or, wives
10 [f]Deut. 12.9
11 [10]Or, walk with the wind, and lie falsely
12 [g]Isa. 11.11; ch. 4.6-7; Zeph. 3.19

CHAPTER 3
1 [a]Jer. 5.4-5
3 [b]Ps. 14.4
4 [c]Prov. 1.28
5 [d]Isa. 56.10 [e]Matt. 7.15
6 [f]Ezek. 13.23 [1]from a vision [2]from divining
7 [3]upper lip [g]Ps. 74.9; Amos 8.11
8 [h]1 Cor. 2.1-4 [i]Isa. 58.1
10 [4]bloods
11 [j]Isa. 1.23; Ezek. 22.12; Hos. 4.18; ch. 7.3 [k]Jer. 6.13; Tit. 1.11 [l]1 Sam. 4.5-6; Isa. 48.2 [5]saying
12 [m]ch. 1.6 [n]Ps. 79.1

CHAPTER 4
1 [a]Isa. 2.2; Ezek. 17.22; Dan. 2.44
2 [b]John 6.45
3 [c]Isa. 2.4; Joel 3.10 [1]Or, scythes [d]Ps. 72.7; Luke 1.33
4 [e]1 Ki. 4.25; Zech. 3.10
5 [f]Jer. 2.11 [g]Ex. 3.14-15
6 [h]Isa. 56.8; Zeph. 3.19 [i]Ps. 147.2; Ezek. 34.13
7 [j]Isa. 9.6; Rev. 11.15
8 [2]Or, Edar

6 [f]Therefore night *shall be* unto you, [1]that ye shall not have a vision; and it shall be dark unto you, [2]that ye shall not divine; and the sun shall go down over the prophets, and the day shall be dark over them.

7 Then shall the seers be ashamed, and the diviners confounded: yea, they shall all cover their [3]lips; [g]for *there is* no answer of God.

8 ¶ But truly I am full of power by the [h]spirit of the LORD, and of judgment, and of might, [i]to declare unto Jā'cob his transgression, and to Ĭs'ra-el his sin.

9 Hear this, I pray you, ye heads of the house of Jā'cob, and princes of the house of Ĭs'ra-el, that abhor judgment, and pervert all equity.

10 They build up Zī'ŏn with [4]blood, and Je-rṳ'sa-lĕm with iniquity.

11 [j]The heads thereof judge for reward, and [k]the priests thereof teach for hire, and the prophets thereof divine for money: [l]yet will they lean upon the LORD, [5]and say, *Is* not the LORD among us? none evil can come upon us.

12 Therefore shall Zī'ŏn for your sake be [m]plowed *as* a field, [n]and Je-rṳ'sa-lĕm shall become heaps, and the mountain of the house as the high places of the forest.

4 But [a]in the last days it shall come to pass, *that* the mountain of the house of the LORD shall be established in the top of the mountains, and it shall be exalted above the hills; and people shall flow unto it.

2 And many nations shall come, and say, Come, and let us go up to the mountain of the LORD, and to the house of the God of Jā'cob; and he [b]will teach us of his ways, and we will walk in his paths: for the law shall go forth of Zī'ŏn, and the word of the LORD from Je-rṳ'sa-lĕm.

3 ¶ And he shall judge among many people, and rebuke strong nations afar off; and they shall beat their swords into [c]plowshares, and their spears into [1]pruninghooks: nation shall not lift up a sword against nation, [d]neither shall they learn war any more.

4 [e]But they shall sit every man under his vine and under his fig tree; and none shall make *them* afraid: for the mouth of the LORD of hosts hath spoken *it*.

5 For [f]all people will walk every one in the name of his god, and [g]we will walk in the name of the LORD our God for ever and ever.

6 In that day, saith the LORD, [h]will I assemble her that halteth, [i]and I will gather her that is driven out, and her that I have afflicted;

7 And I will make her that halted a remnant, and her that was cast far off a strong nation: and the LORD [j]shall reign over them in mount Zī'ŏn from henceforth, even for ever.

8 ¶ And thou, O tower of [2]the flock, the strong hold of the daughter of Zī'ŏn, unto thee shall it come, even the

first dominion; the kingdom shall come
to the daughter of Je-rụ'sa-lĕm.
9 Now why dost thou cry out aloud?
is there no king in thee? is thy counseller perished? for pangs have taken
thee as a woman in travail.
10 Be in pain, and labour to bring
forth, O daughter of Zī'ŏn, like a woman in travail: for now shalt thou go
forth out of the city, and thou shalt
dwell in the field, and thou shalt go
even to Băb'ȳ-lon; there shalt thou be
delivered; there the LORD shall redeem
thee from the hand of thine enemies.
11 ¶ Now also many nations are
gathered against thee, that say, Let her
be defiled, and let our eye look upon
Zī'ŏn.
12 But they know not the thoughts
of the LORD, neither understand they
his counsel: for he shall gather them as
the sheaves into the floor.
13 Arise and thresh, O daughter of
Zī'ŏn: for I will make thine horn iron,
and I will make thy hoofs brass: and
thou shalt beat in pieces many people:
[k]and I will consecrate their gain unto
the LORD, and their substance unto the
Lord of the whole earth.
5 Now gather thyself in troops, O
daughter of troops: he hath laid
siege against us: they shall [a]smite the
judge of Ĭs'ra-el with a rod upon the
cheek.
2 But thou, [b]Bĕth'–lĕ-hĕm Ĕph'ra-
tah, *though* thou be little among the
thousands of Jū'dah, *yet* out of thee
shall he come forth unto me *that is* to
be [c]ruler in Ĭs'ra-el; [d]whose goings
forth *have been* from of old, from [1]ever-
lasting.
3 Therefore will he give them up, until the time *that* she which travaileth
hath brought forth: then the remnant
of his brethren shall return unto the
children of Ĭs'ra-el.
4 ¶ And he shall stand and [2]feed in
the strength of the LORD, in the majesty of the name of the LORD his God;
and they shall abide: for now [e]shall he
be great unto the ends of the earth.
5 And this *man* [f]shall be the peace,
when the Ăs-sȳr'ĭ-an shall come into
our land: and when he shall tread in
our palaces, then shall we raise against
him seven shepherds, and eight [3]princi-
pal men.
6 And they shall [4]waste the land of
Ăs-sȳr'ĭ-ȧ with the sword, and the land
of [g]Nĭm'rŏd [5]in the entrances thereof:
thus shall he [h]deliver *us* from the Ăs-
sȳr'ĭ-an, when he cometh into our land,
and when he treadeth within our borders.
7 And the remnant of Jā'cob shall
be in the midst of many people [i]as a
dew from the LORD, as the showers
upon the grass, that tarrieth not for
man, nor waiteth for the sons of men.
8 ¶ And the remnant of Jā'cob shall
be among the Gĕn'tīles in the midst of
many people as a lion among the
beasts of the forest, as a young lion
among the flocks of [6]sheep: who, if he
go through, both treadeth down, and
teareth in pieces, and none can deliver.
9 Thine hand shall be lifted up upon
thine adversaries, and all thine enemies shall be cut off.
10 [j]And it shall come to pass in that
day, saith the LORD, that I will cut off
thy horses out of the midst of thee, and
I will destroy thy chariots:
11 And I will cut off the cities of thy
land, and throw down all thy strong
holds:
12 And I will cut off witchcrafts out
of thine hand; and thou shalt have no
more soothsayers:
13 [k]Thy graven images also will I
cut off, and thy [7]standing images out of
the midst of thee; and thou shalt [l]no
more worship the work of thine hands.
14 And I will pluck up thy groves
out of the midst of thee: so will I destroy thy [8]cities.
15 And I will execute vengeance in
anger and fury upon the heathen, such
as they have not heard.
6 Hear ye now what the LORD saith;
Arise, contend thou [1]before the
mountains, and let the hills hear thy
voice.
2 Hear ye, O mountains, [a]the LORD'S
controversy, and ye strong foundations of the earth: for the LORD hath a
controversy with his people, and he
will plead with Ĭs'ra-el.
3 O my people, [b]what have I done
unto thee? and wherein have I wearied
thee? testify against me.
4 For I brought thee up out of the
land of Ē'ġypt, and redeemed thee out
of the house of servants; and I sent before thee Mō'ses, Aâr'on, and Mĭr'ĭ-
am.
5 O my people, remember now what
Bā'lăk [c]king of Mō'ab consulted, and
what Bā'laam the son of Bē'or answered him from [d]Shĭt'tim unto Ġĭl'-
găl; that ye may know the [e]righteous-
ness of the LORD.
6 ¶ Wherewith [f]shall I come before
the LORD, *and* bow myself before the
high God? shall I come before him
with burnt offerings, with calves [2]of a
year old?
7 [g]Will the LORD be pleased with
thousands of rams, *or* with ten thousands of rivers of oil? [h]shall I give my
firstborn *for* my transgression, the fruit
of my [3]body *for* the sin of my soul?
8 He hath shewed thee, O man, what
is good; and what doth the LORD require of thee, but to do justly, and to
love mercy, and to [4]walk humbly with
thy God?
9 The LORD'S voice crieth unto the
city, and [5]*the man of* wisdom shall see
thy name: hear ye the rod, and who
hath appointed it.
10 ¶ [6]Are there yet the treasures of
wickedness in the house of the wicked,
and the [7]scant measure *that is* abominable?
11 [8]Shall I count *them* pure with
[i]the wicked balances, and with the bag
of deceitful weights?

13 [k]Rev. 21.24

CHAPTER 5

1 [a]Job 16.10; Lam. 3.30; Matt. 27.30
2 [b]Gen. 35.19; Ps. 132.6; Matt. 2.6; John 7.42
[c]Gen. 49.10; Isa. 9.6
[d]Ps. 90.2; Prov. 8.22; John 1.1
[1]the days of eternity
4 [2]Or, rule
[e]Ps. 72.8; Isa. 52.13; Zech. 9.10; Luke 1.32
5 [f]Isa. 9.6; Col. 1.20
[3]princes of men
6 [4]eat up
[g]Gen. 10.8
[5]Or, with her own naked swords
[h]Luke 1.71
7 [i]Ps. 110.3
8 [6]Or, goats
10 [j]Zech. 9.10
13 [k]Zech. 13.2
[7]Or, statues
[l]Isa. 2.8
14 [8]Or, enemies

CHAPTER 6

1 [1]Or, with
2 [a]Hos. 12.2
3 [b]Ps. 50.7; Jer. 2.5-31
5 [c]Num. 22.5; Rev. 2.14
[d]Num. 25.1
[e]Judg. 5.11
6 [f]Ps. 15.1; John 6.28
[2]sons of a year
7 [g]Ps. 50.9; Isa. 1.11
[h]2 Ki. 16.3
[3]belly
8 [4]humble thyself to walk
9 [5]Or, thy name shall see that which is
10 [6]Or, Is there yet unto every man an house of the wicked, etc
[7]measure of leanness
11 [8]Or, Shall I be pure with, etc
[i]Hos. 12.7; Amos 3.10

12 For the rich men thereof are full of violence, and the inhabitants thereof have spoken lies, and their tongue *is* deceitful in their mouth.

13 Therefore also will I make *thee* sick in smiting thee, in making *thee* desolate because of thy sins.

14 Thou shalt eat, but not be satisfied; and thy casting down *shall be* in the midst of thee; and thou shalt take hold, but shalt not deliver; and *that* which thou deliverest will I give up to the sword.

15 Thou shalt sow, but thou shalt not reap; thou shalt tread the olives, but thou shalt not anoint thee with oil; and sweet wine, but shalt not drink wine.

16 ¶ For [9]the statutes of [i]Ŏm'rī are ķept, and all the works of the house of Ā'hăb, and ye walk in their counsels; that I should make thee a [10]desolation, and the inhabitants thereof an hissing: therefore ye shall bear the reproach of my people.

7 Woe is me! for I am as [1]when they have gathered the summer fruits, as the grapegleanings of the vintage: *there is* no cluster to eat: [a]my soul desired the firstripe fruit.

2 The [2]good *man* is perished out of the earth: and *there is* none upright among men: they all lie in wait for blood; [b]they hunt every man his brother with a net.

3 ¶ That they may do evil with both hands earnestly, [c]the prince asketh, [d]and the judge *asketh* for a reward; and the great *man,* he uttereth [3]his mischievous desire: so they wrap it up.

4 The best of them *is* as a brier: the most upright *is sharper* than a thorn hedge: the day of thy watchmen *and* thy visitation cometh; now shall be their perplexity.

5 ¶ Trust ye not in a friend, put ye not confidence in a guide: keep the doors of thy mouth from her that lieth in thy bosom.

6 For [e]the son dishonoureth the father, the daughter riseth up against her mother, the daughter in law against her mother in law; a man's enemies *are* the men of his own house.

7 Therefore I will look unto the LORD; I will wait for the God of my salvation: my God will hear me.

8 ¶ [f]Rejoice not against me, O mine enemy: when I fall, I shall arise; when I sit in darkness, the LORD *shall be* a light unto me.

9 I will bear the indignation of the LORD, because I have sinned against him, until he plead my cause, and execute judgment for me: he will bring me forth to the light, *and* I shall behold his righteousness.

10 [4]Then *she that is* mine enemy shall see *it,* and shame shall cover her which said unto me, Where is the LORD thy God? mine eyes shall behold her: now [5]shall she be trodden down as the mire of the streets.

11 *In* the day that thy walls are to be built, *in* that day shall the decree be far removed.

12 *In* that day *also* he shall come even to thee from Ȧs-sȳr'ĭ-ȧ, [6]and *from* the fortified cities, and from the fortress even to the river, and from sea to sea, and *from* mountain to mountain.

13 [7]Notwithstanding the land shall be desolate because of them that dwell therein, for the fruit of their doings.

14 ¶ [8]Feed thy people with thy rod, the flock of thine heritage, which dwell solitarily *in* [g]the wood, in the midst of Çär'mel: let them feed *in* Bā'shăn and Ğĭl'e-ăd, as in the days of old.

15 According to the days of thy coming out of the land of Ē'ġypt will I shew unto him marvellous *things.*

16 ¶ The nations [h]shall see and be confounded at all their might: they shall lay *their* hand upon *their* mouth, their ears shall be deaf.

17 They shall lick the dust like a serpent, they shall move out of their holes like [9]worms of the earth: they shall be afraid of the LORD our God, and shall fear because of thee.

18 [i]Who *is* a God like unto thee, that [j]pardoneth iniquity, and passeth by the transgression of the remnant of his heritage? [k]he retaineth not his anger for ever, because he delighteth *in* mercy.

19 He will turn again, he will have compassion upon us; he will [l]subdue our iniquities; and thou wilt cast all their sins into the depths of the sea.

20 [m]Thou wilt perform the truth to Jā'cob, *and* the mercy to Ā'brā-hăm, which thou hast sworn unto our fathers from the days of old.

16 [9]Or, he doth much keep the, etc
[i]1 Ki. 16.25
[10]Or, astonishment

CHAPTER 7
1 [1]the gatherings of summer
[a]Jer. 2.3; Hos. 9.10
2 [2]Or, godly, or, merciful
[b]1 Sam. 24.11; Ps. 57.6; Hab. 1.15
3 [c]Hos. 4.18
[d]Isa. 1.23
[3]the mischief of his soul
6 [e]Gen. 9.22-24; Matt. 10.21
8 [f]Ps. 37.5-6; Prov. 24.17; Lam. 4.21
10 [4]Or, and thou wilt see her that is mine enemy, and cover her with shame
[5]she shall be for a treading down
12 [6]Or, even to
13 [7]Or, after that it hath been
14 [8]Or, Rule
[g]Num. 23.9; Deut. 33.28
16 [h]Isa. 26.11
17 [9]Or, creeping things
18 [i]Ex. 15.11; Ps. 89.6-8
[j]Ex. 34.6-7
[k]Ps. 103.9; Isa. 57.16
19 [l]Rom. 6.6
20 [m]Rom. 11.29

THE BOOK OF

NAHUM

Life's Questions

Why do I suffer so?
Has God forgotten me?
How can I know where He is at work?

God's Answers

About 625 God send Nahum to a despondent people suffering affliction under Assyria's cruel rule of the world. Nahum proclaimed an eloquent vision of hope for a people in despair.

Nahum shows: the sovereign God does reveal Himself to His people (1:1–11); God defeats the enemy and offers His people hope (1:12–15); the enemy cannot prevent God's judgment on them (2—3).

Nahum lets us know God will win in the end, and wickedness faces destruction.

1 The burden of Nĭn'e-veh. The book
of the vision of Nā'hum the Ĕl'-
kosh-īte.
2 [1]God *is* jealous, and the LORD revengeth; the LORD revengeth, and [2]*is*
furious; the LORD will take vengeance
on his adversaries, and he reserveth
wrath for his enemies.
3 The LORD *is* [a]slow to anger, and
great in power, and will not at all acquit *the wicked:* [b]the LORD *hath* his
way in the whirlwind and in the storm,
and the clouds *are* the dust of his feet.
4 [c]He rebuketh the sea, and maketh
it dry, and drieth up all the rivers:
Bā'shăn languisheth, and Cär'mel, and
the flower of Lĕb'a-non languisheth.
5 [d]The mountains quake at him,
and the hills melt, and the earth is
burned at his presence, yea, the world,
and all that dwell therein.
6 Who can stand before his indignation? and who can [3]abide in the fierceness of his anger? his fury is poured
out like fire, and the rocks are thrown
down by him.
7 The LORD *is* good, a [4]strong hold
in the day of trouble; and he knoweth
them that trust in him.
8 But with an overrunning flood he
will make an utter end of the place
thereof, and darkness shall pursue his
enemies.
9 What do ye imagine against the
LORD? he will make an utter end: affliction shall not rise up the second time.
10 For while *they be* folden together
as thorns, and while they are drunken
as drunkards, they shall be devoured
as stubble fully dry.
11 There is *one* come out of thee,
that imagineth evil against the LORD, a
wicked counseller.
12 Thus saith the LORD; [5]Though
they be quiet, and likewise many, yet
thus shall they be [6]cut down, when he
shall pass through. Though I have afflicted thee, I will afflict thee no more.
13 For now will I break his yoke
from off thee and will burst thy bonds
in sunder.
14 And the LORD hath given a commandment concerning thee, *that* no
more of thy name be sown: out of the
house of thy gods will I cut off the graven image and the molten image: I will
make thy grave; for thou art vile.
15 Behold upon the mountains the
feet of him that bringeth good tidings,
that publisheth peace! O Jū'dah, [7]keep
thy solemn feasts, perform thy vows:
for [8]the wicked shall no more pass
through thee; he is utterly cut off.
2 He [1]that dasheth in pieces is come
up before thy face: keep the munition, watch the way, make *thy* loins
strong, fortify *thy* power mightily.
2 For the LORD hath turned away
[2]the excellency of Jā'cob, as the excellency of Ĭs'ra-el: for the emptiers have
emptied them out, and marred their
vine branches.
3 The shield of his mighty men is
made red, the valiant men *are* [3]in scarlet: the chariots *shall be* with [4]flaming
torches in the day of his preparation,
and the fir trees shall be terribly
shaken.
4 The chariots shall rage in the
streets, they shall justle one against
another in the broad ways: [5]they shall
seem like torches, they shall run like
the lightnings.
5 He shall recount his [6]worthies:
they shall stumble in their walk; they
shall make haste to the wall thereof,
and the [7]defence shall be prepared.
6 The gates of the rivers shall be
opened, and the palace shall be [8]dis-
solved.
7 And [9]Hŭz'zăb shall be [10]led away
captive, she shall be brought up, and
her maids shall lead *her* as with the
voice of doves, tabering upon their
breasts.
8 But Nĭn'e-veh *is* [11]of old like a pool
of water: yet they shall flee away.
Stand, stand, *shall they cry;* but none
shall [12]look back.
9 Take ye the spoil of silver, take the
spoil of gold: [13]for *there is* none end of
the store *and* glory out of all the [14]pleas-
ant furniture.
10 She is empty, and void, and waste:
and the heart melteth, and the knees
smite together, and much pain *is* in all
loins, and the faces of them all gather
blackness.
11 Where *is* the dwelling of the lions, and the feedingplace of the young
lions, where the lion, *even* the old lion,
walked, *and* the lion's whelp, and none
made *them* afraid?
12 The lion did tear in pieces enough
for his whelps, and strangled for his
lionesses, and filled his holes with
prey, and his dens with ravin.
13 Behold, I *am* against thee, saith
the LORD of hosts, and I will burn her
chariots in the smoke, and the sword
shall devour thy young lions: and I will
cut off thy prey from the earth, and the
voice of thy messengers shall no more
be heard.
3 Woe to the [1]bloody city! it *is* all full
of lies *and* robbery; the prey departeth not;
2 The noise of a whip, and the noise
of the rattling of the wheels, and of the
pransing horses, and of the jumping
chariots.
3 The horseman lifteth up both [2]the
bright sword and the glittering spear:
and *there is* a multitude of slain, and a
great number of carcases; and *there is*
none end of *their* corpses; they stumble upon their corpses:
4 Because of the multitude of the
whoredoms of the wellfavoured harlot, [a]the mistress of witchcrafts, that
selleth nations through her whore-

CHAPTER 1
2 [1]Or, The LORD is a jealous God, and a revenger [2]that hath fury
3 [a]Ex. 34.6-7; [b]Ex. 19.16
4 [c]Josh. 3.15-16
5 [d]2 Sam. 22.8
6 [3]stand up
7 [4]Or, strength
12 [5]Or, if they would have been at peace, so should they have been many, and so should they have been shorn, and he should have passed away [6]shorn
15 [7]feast [8]Belial

CHAPTER 2
1 [1]Or, The disperser, or, hammer
2 [2]Or, the pride of Jacob as the pride of Israel
3 [3]Or, dyed scarlet [4]Or, fiery torches
4 [5]their shew
5 [6]Or, gallants [7]covering, or, coverer
6 [8]Or, molten
7 [9]Or, that which was established, or, there was a stand made [10]Or, discovered
8 [11]Or, from the days that she hath been [12]Or, cause them to turn
9 [13]Or, and their infinite store [14]vessels of desire

CHAPTER 3
1 [1]city of bloods
3 [2]the flame of the sword, and the lightning of the spear
4 [a]Isa. 47.9

doms, and families through her witchcrafts.
5 Behold, I *am* against thee, saith
the LORD of hosts; and I will discover
thy skirts upon thy face, and [b]I will
shew the nations thy nakedness, and
the kingdoms thy shame.
6 And I will cast abominable filth
upon thee, and make thee vile, and will
set thee as a gazingstock.
7 And it shall come to pass, *that* all
they that look upon thee shall flee
from thee, and say, Nĭn'e-veh is laid
waste: who will bemoan her? whence
shall I seek comforters for thee?
8 Art thou better than [3]populous Nō,
that was situate among the rivers, *that*
had the waters round about it, whose
rampart *was* the sea, *and* her wall *was*
from the sea?
9 [c]Ē-thĭ-ō'pĭ-a and Ē'gypt *were* her
strength, and *it was* infinite; Pŭt and
Lu̥'bĭm were [4]thy helpers.
10 Yet *was* she carried away, she
went into captivity: her young children
also were dashed in pieces at the top of
all the streets: and they [d]cast lots for
her honourable men, and all her great
men were bound in chains.
11 Thou also shalt be drunken: thou
shalt be hid, thou also shalt seek strength
because of the enemy.
12 All thy strong holds *shall be like*
[e]fig trees with the firstripe figs: if they
be shaken, they shall even fall into the
mouth of the eater.
13 Behold, [f]thy people in the midst
of thee *are* women: the gates of thy
land shall be set wide open unto thine
enemies: the fire shall devour thy bars.
14 Draw thee waters for the siege,
fortify thy strong holds: go into clay,
and tread the morter, make strong the
brickkiln.
15 There shall the fire devour thee;
the sword shall cut thee off, it shall eat
thee up like [g]the cankerworm: make
thyself many as the cankerworm, make
thyself many as the locusts.
16 Thou hast multiplied [5]thy merchants above the stars of heaven: the
cankerworm [6]spoileth, and fleeth
away.
17 [h]Thy crowned *are* as the locusts,
and thy captains as the great grasshoppers, which camp in the hedges in the
cold day, *but* when the sun ariseth
they flee away, and their place is not
known where they *are*.
18 Thy shepherds slumber, O [i]king
of Ăs-sўr'ĭ-ȧ: thy [7]nobles shall dwell *in*
the dust: thy people is [j]scattered upon
the mountains, and no man gathereth
them.
19 *There is* no [8]healing of thy bruise;
thy wound is grievous: [k]all that hear
the bruit of thee shall clap the hands
over thee: for upon whom hath not thy
wickedness passed continually?

5 [b]Isa. 47.2-3
8 [3]No Amon, or, nourishing
9 [c]Ezek. 30.5 [4]in thy help
10 [d]Joel 3.3; Obad. 11
12 [e]Rev. 6.13
13 [f]Isa. 19.16; Jer. 50.37
15 [g]Joel 1.4
16 [5]Or, thy hired soldiers [6]Or, spreadeth himself
17 [h]Rev. 9.7
18 [i]Jer. 50.18; Ezek. 31.3 [7]Or, valiant ones [j]1 Ki. 22.17
19 [8]wrinkling [k]Isa. 14.8; Lam. 2.15; Zeph. 2.15

THE BOOK OF

HABAKKUK

Life's Questions

What is faith?
Why does a loving God allow people to suffer?
Why does God not punish the wicked immediately?

God's Answers

About 605 B.C. God called a sensitive man to show His people God's purposes as the wicked Babylonians gained control of the world and made demands on Judah. Habakkuk used dialog with God and a hymn from the temple to show what faith is, why God would use such a wicked people as Babylon, and why God would let His people suffer.

Habakkuk shows: a prophet can be perplexed at God's rule of history (ch. 1); God wants persistent commitment to and trust in Him (ch. 2); and a psalm of confidence expresses faith in tumultuous times (ch. 3).

Habakkuk is a call to faith for people who see no hope.

1 The burden which Ha-băk'kŭk the
prophet did see.
2 O LORD, how long [a]shall I cry, and
thou wilt not hear! *even* cry out unto
thee *of* violence, and thou wilt not
save!
3 Why dost thou shew me iniquity,
and cause *me* to behold grievance? for
spoiling and violence *are* before me:
and there are *that* raise up strife and
contention.
4 [b]Therefore the law is slacked, and
judgment doth never go forth: for the
wicked doth compass about the righteous; therefore [1]wrong judgment proceedeth.
5 ¶ Behold ye among the heathen,
and regard, and wonder marvellously:
for *I* will work a work in your days,
which ye will not believe, though it be
told *you*.
6 For, lo, [2]I raise up the Chăl-dē'ans,
that bitter and hasty nation, which
shall march through the [3]breadth of
the land, to possess the dwellingplaces
that are not theirs.
7 They *are* terrible and dreadful:
[4]their judgment and their dignity shall
proceed of themselves.
8 [c]Their horses also are swifter than
the leopards, and are more [5]fierce than
the evening wolves: and their horsemen shall spread themselves, and their

CHAPTER 1
2 [a]Ps. 27.7; 2 Pet. 2.8
4 [b]Job 12.6; [1]Or, wrested
6 [2]Fulfilled, 2 Chr. 36.6 [3]breadths
7 [4]Or, from them shall proceed the judgment of these, and the captivity of these
8 [c]Deut. 28.49-50 [5]sharp

horsemen shall come from far; they
shall fly as the eagle *that* hasteth to eat.
9 They shall come all for violence:
[6]their faces shall sup up *as* the east
wind, and they shall gather the captivity as the sand.
10 And they shall scoff at the kings,
and the princes shall be a scorn unto
them: they shall deride every strong
hold; for they shall heap dust, and take
it.
11 Then shall *his* mind change, and
he shall pass over, and offend, *imputing* this his power unto his god.
12 ¶ *Art* thou not from everlasting,
O LORD my God, mine Holy One? we
shall not die. O LORD, thou hast ordained them for judgment; and, O
[7]mighty God, thou hast [8]established
them for correction.
13 *Thou art* of purer eyes than to
behold evil, and canst not look on [9]in-
iquity: wherefore lookest thou upon
them that deal treacherously, *and* holdest thy tongue when the wicked devoureth *the man that is* more righteous than he?
14 And makest men as the fishes of
the sea, as the creeping things, *that
have* no ruler over them?
15 They take up all of them with the
angle, they catch them in their net, and
gather them in their [10]drag: therefore
they rejoice and are glad.
16 Therefore they sacrifice unto their
net, and burn incense unto their drag;
because by them their portion *is* fat, and
their meat [11]plenteous.
17 Shall they therefore [12]empty their
net, and not spare continually to slay
the nations?

2 I WILL [a]stand upon my watch, and
set me upon the [1]tower, and will
watch to see what he will say [2]unto me,
and what I shall answer [3]when I am
reproved.
2 And the LORD answered me, and
said, [b]Write the vision, and make *it*
plain upon tables, that he may run that
readeth it.
3 For [c]the vision *is* yet for an appointed time, but at the end it shall
speak, and not lie: though it tarry, wait
for it; because it will surely come, it
will not tarry.
4 Behold, his soul *which* is lifted up
is not upright in him: but the [d]just
shall live by his faith.
5 ¶ [4]Yea also, because he transgresseth by wine, *he is* a proud man, neither keepeth at home, who enlargeth
his desire as hell, and *is* as death, and
cannot be satisfied, but gathereth unto
him all nations, and heapeth unto him
all people:
6 Shall not all these take up a parable against him, and a taunting proverb against him, and say, [5]Woe to him
that increaseth *that which is* not his!
how long? and to him that ladeth himself with thick clay!
7 Shall they not rise up suddenly
that shall bite thee, and awake that
shall vex thee, and thou shalt be for
booties unto them?
8 Because thou hast spoiled many nations, all the remnant of the people shall
spoil thee; because of men's [6]blood, and
for the violence of the land, of the city,
and of all that dwell therein.
9 ¶ Woe to him that [7]coveteth an evil
covetousness to his house, that he may
set his nest on high, that he may be
delivered from the [8]power of evil!
10 Thou hast consulted shame to
thy house by cutting off many people,
and hast sinned *against* thy soul.
11 For the stone shall cry out of the
wall, and the [9]beam out of the timber
shall [10]answer it.
12 ¶ Woe to him that buildeth a
town with [11]blood, and stablisheth a
city by iniquity!
13 Behold, *is it* not of the LORD of
hosts that the people shall labour in
the very fire, and the people shall
weary themselves [12]for very vanity?
14 For the earth shall be filled [13]with
the knowledge of the glory of the LORD,
as the waters cover the sea.
15 ¶ Woe unto him that giveth his
neighbour drink, that puttest thy bottle
to *him*, and makest *him* drunken also,
that thou mayest look on their nakedness!
16 Thou art filled [14]with shame for
glory: drink thou also, and let thy foreskin be uncovered: the cup of the
LORD'S right hand shall be turned unto
thee, and shameful spewing *shall be*
on thy glory.
17 For the violence of Lĕb'a-non
shall cover thee, and the spoil of beasts,
which made them afraid, because of
men's blood, and for the violence of the
land, of the city, and of all that dwell
therein.
18 ¶ What profiteth the graven image that the maker thereof hath graven
it; the molten image, and a teacher of
lies, that [15]the maker of his work trusteth therein, to make dumb idols?
19 Woe unto him that saith to the
wood, Awake; to the dumb stone, Arise,
it shall teach! Behold, it *is* laid over with
gold and silver, and *there is* no breath at
all in the midst of it.
20 But the LORD *is* in his holy temple: [16]let all the earth keep silence before him.

3 A PRAYER of Ha-băk'kŭk the prophet upon [1]Shĭ-gī'o-noth.
2 O LORD, I have heard [2]thy speech,
and was afraid: O LORD, [3]revive thy
work in the midst of the years, in the
midst of the years make known; in
wrath remember mercy.
3 God came from [4]Tē'man, and the
Holy One from mount Pā'ran. Sē'lah.
His glory covered the heavens, and the
earth was full of his praise.
4 And *his* brightness was as the
light; he had [5]horns *coming* out of his
hand: and there *was* the hiding of his
power.
5 Before him went the pestilence,
and [6]burning coals went forth at his
feet.
6 He stood, and [a]measured the earth:
he beheld, and [b]drove asunder the na-

9 [6]the opposition of their faces toward the east: or, the supping up of their faces, etc., or, their faces shall look toward the east
12 [7]rock [8]founded
13 [9]Or, grievance
15 [10]Or, flue net
16 [11]fat, or, dainty
17 [12]Or, spread

CHAPTER 2
1 [a]Ps. 73.16-17; [1]fenced place [2]Or, in me [3]upon my reproof, or, arguing, or, when I am argued with
2 [b]Deut. 27.8
3 [c]Dan. 10.14
4 [d]John 3.36
5 [4]Or, How much more
6 [5]Or, Ho, he
8 [6]bloods
9 [7]Or, gaineth an evil gain [8]palm of the hand
11 [9]Or, piece, or, fastening [10]Or, witness against it
12 [11]bloods
13 [12]Or, in vain
14 [13]Or, by knowing the glory
16 [14]Or, more with shame than with glory
18 [15]the fashioner of his fashion
20 [16]be silent all the earth before him

CHAPTER 3
1 [1]Or, according to variable songs, or, tunes
2 [2]thy report, or, thy hearing [3]Or, preserve alive
3 [4]Or, the south
4 [5]Or, bright beams out of his side
5 [6]Or, burning diseases
6 [a]Ex. 23.31; [b]Num. 21.24-34

tions; and the everlasting mountains
were scattered, the perpetual hills did
bow: his ways *are* everlasting.
7 I saw the tents of [7]Cu̦'shan [8]in affliction: *and* the curtains of the land of
Mĭd'ĭ-an did tremble.
8 [c]Was the LORD displeased against
the rivers? *was* thine anger against the
rivers? *was* thy wrath against the sea,
that thou didst ride upon thine horses
and thy chariots [9]of salvation?
9 Thy bow was made quite naked,
according to the oaths of the tribes,
even thy word. Sē'lah. Thou didst
cleave the [10]earth with rivers.
10 The mountains saw thee, *and*
they trembled: the overflowing of the
water passed by: the deep uttered his
voice, *and* lifted up his hands on high.
11 The sun *and* moon stood still in
their habitation: [11]at the light of thine
arrows they went, *and* at the shining of
thy glittering spear.
12 Thou didst march through the
land in indignation, [d]thou didst thresh
the heathen in anger.
13 Thou wentest forth [e]for the salvation of thy people, *even* for salvation
with thine anointed; thou woundedst
the head out of the house of the wicked, [12]by discovering the foundation
unto the neck. Sē'lah.
14 Thou didst strike through with
his staves the head of his villages: they
[13]came out as a whirlwind to scatter
me: their rejoicing *was* as to devour
the poor secretly.
15 Thou didst walk through the sea
with thine horses, *through* the [14]heap
of great waters.
16 When I heard, my belly trembled; my lips quivered at the voice: rottenness entered into my bones, and I
trembled in myself, that I might rest in
the day of trouble: when he cometh up
unto the people, he will [15]invade them
with his troops.
17 ¶ [f]Although the fig tree shall not
blossom, neither *shall* fruit *be* in the
vines; the labour of the olive shall
[16]fail, and the fields shall yield no
meat; the flock shall be cut off from the
fold, and *there shall be* no herd in the
stalls:
18 [g]Yet I will rejoice in the LORD, I
will joy in the God of my salvation.
19 The LORD God *is* [h]my strength,
and he will make my feet like hinds'
feet, and he will make me to walk upon
mine high places. To the chief singer
on my [17]stringed instruments.

7 [7]Ethiopia [8]Or, under affliction, or, vanity
8 [c]Ex. 14.21-22 [9]Or, were salvation
9 [10]Or, rivers of the earth
11 [11]Or, thine arrows walked in the light
12 [d]Ps. 44.2-3; Mic. 4.13
13 [e]2 Sam. 5.20 [12]making naked
14 [13]were tempestuous
15 [14]Or, mud
16 [15]Or, cut them in pieces
17 [f]2 Cor. 4.8-9 [16]lie
18 [g]Ps. 42.5; Isa. 61.10; 2 Cor. 4.8-9
19 [h]Ps. 27.1 [17]Neginoth

THE BOOK OF

ZEPHANIAH

Life's Questions

Will God's patience with His people run out?
What can protect me from God's wrath and judgment?
Who will God use in His kingdom on earth after judgment ?

God's Answers

About 654 B.C. God raised a prophet besides Jeremiah to warn Judah of God's impending day of judgment. Zephaniah wove a message around the theme of the Day of the Lord. as he called His people to repent.

Zephaniah shows: God's coming day of judgment includes all sinners, and humans have no resources to prevent it (1:1—3:8); God promises to form and rule a new remnant people including the nations (3:9–20).

Zephaniah shows us not to have confidence in His day when we have substitutes for God.

1 The [a]word of the LORD which came
unto Zĕph-a-nī'ah the son of Cu̦'-
shī, the son of Gĕd-a-lī'ah, the son of
Ăm-a-rī'ah, the son of Hĭz-kī'ah, in the
days of Jo-sī'ah the son of Ā'mon, king
of Jū'dah.
2 [1]I will utterly consume all *things*
from off [2]the land, saith the LORD.
3 I will consume man and beast; I
will consume the fowls of the heaven,
and the fishes of the sea, and the [3]stum-
blingblocks with the wicked; and I will
cut off man from off the land, saith the
LORD.
4 I will also stretch out mine hand
upon Jū'dah, and upon all the inhabitants of Je-ru̦'sa-lĕm; and [4]I will cut off
the remnant of Bā'al from this place,
and the name of [b]the Chĕm'a-rĭms
with the priests;
5 And them that worship the host of
heaven upon the house tops; and them
that worship *and* that swear [5]by the
LORD, and that swear [c]by Măl'cham;
6 And them that are turned back
from the LORD; and *those* that have
not sought the LORD, nor inquired for
him.
7 Hold thy peace at the presence of
the Lord GOD: for the day of the LORD
is at hand: for the LORD hath prepared
a sacrifice, he hath [6]bid his guests.
8 And it shall come to pass in the
day of the LORD'S sacrifice, that I will
[7]punish [d]the princes, and the king's
children, and all such as are clothed
with strange apparel.
9 In the same day also will I punish
all those that leap on the threshold,

CHAPTER 1
1 [a]2 Tim. 3.16; 2 Pet. 1.21
2 [1]By taking away I will make an end [2]the face of the land
3 [3]Or, idols
4 [4]Fulfilled, B.C. 624 [b]Hos. 10.5
5 [5]Or, to the LORD [c]1 Ki. 11.33
7 [6]sanctified, or, prepared
8 [7]visit upon [d]Jer. 39.6

which fill their masters' houses with violence and deceit.

10 And it shall come to pass in that day, saith the LORD, *that there shall be* the noise of a cry from [e]the fish gate, and an howling from the second, and a great crashing from the hills.

11 [f]Howl, ye inhabitants of [8]Măk'-tesh, for all the merchant people are cut down; all they that bear silver are cut off.

12 And it shall come to pass at that time, *that* I will search Je-ru'sa-lĕm with candles, and punish the men that are [9]settled on their lees: [g]that say in their heart, The LORD will not do good, neither will he do evil.

13 Therefore their goods shall become a booty, and their houses a desolation: they shall also build houses, but [h]not inhabit *them;* and they shall plant vineyards, but [i]not drink the wine thereof.

14 [j]The great day of the LORD *is* near, *it is* near, and hasteth greatly, *even* the voice of the day of the LORD: the mighty man shall cry there bitterly.

15 That day *is* a day of wrath, a day of trouble and distress, a day of wasteness and desolation, a day of darkness and gloominess, a day of clouds and thick darkness,

16 A day of [k]the trumpet and alarm against the fenced cities, and against the high towers.

17 And I will bring distress upon men, that they shall walk like blind men, because they have sinned against the LORD: and their blood shall be poured out as dust, and their flesh as the dung.

18 [l]Neither their silver nor their gold shall be able to deliver them in the day of the LORD'S wrath; but the whole land shall be [m]devoured by the fire of his jealousy: for he shall make even a speedy riddance of all them that dwell in the land.

2 [a]Gather yourselves together, yea, gather together, O nation [1]not desired;

2 Before the decree bring forth, *before* the day pass as the chaff, before [b]the fierce anger of the LORD come upon you, before the day of the LORD'S anger come upon you.

3 [c]Seek ye the LORD, [d]all ye meek of the earth, which have wrought his judgment; seek righteousness, seek meekness: [e]it may be ye shall be hid in the day of the LORD'S anger.

4 ¶ For Gā'zȧ shall be forsaken, and Ăsh'ke-lŏn a desolation: they shall drive out Ăsh'dŏd [f]at the noon day, and Ĕk'rŏn shall be rooted up.

5 Woe unto the inhabitants of [g]the sea coast, the nation of the Chĕr'eth-ītes! the word of the LORD *is* against you; O [h]Cā'năan, the land of the Phĭ-lĭs'tĭnes, I will even destroy thee, that there shall be no inhabitant.

6 And the sea coast shall be dwellings *and* cottages for shepherds, [i]and folds for flocks.

7 And the coast shall be for [j]the remnant of the house of Jū'dah; they shall feed thereupon: in the houses of Ăsh'ke-lŏn shall they lie down in the evening: [2]for the LORD their God shall [k]visit them, and [l]turn away their captivity.

8 ¶ [m]I have heard the reproach of Mō'ab, and the revilings of the children of Ăm'mŏn, whereby they have reproached my people, and [n]magnified *themselves* against their border.

9 Therefore *as* I live, saith the LORD of hosts, the God of Ĭs'ra-el, Surely [o]Mō'ab shall be as Sŏd'om, and [p]the children of Ăm'mŏn as Go-mŏr'rah, *even* the breeding of nettles, and saltpits, and a perpetual desolation: the residue of my people shall spoil them, and the remnant of my people shall possess them.

10 This shall they have for their pride, because they have reproached and magnified *themselves* against the people of the LORD of hosts.

11 The LORD *will be* terrible unto them: for he will [3]famish all the gods of the earth; and [q]*men* shall worship him, every one from his place, *even* all [r]the isles of the heathen.

12 ¶ [s]Ye Ē-thĭ-ō'pĭ-ans also, ye *shall be* slain by my sword.

13 And he will stretch out his hand against the north, and destroy Ăs-sÿr'ĭ-ȧ; and will make Nĭn'e-veh a desolation, *and* dry like a wilderness.

14 And flocks shall lie down in the midst of her, all [t]the beasts of the nations: both the [4]cormorant and the bittern shall lodge in the [5]upper lintels of it; *their* voice shall sing in the windows; desolation *shall be* in the thresholds: [6]for he shall uncover the cedar work.

15 This *is* the rejoicing city [u]that dwelt carelessly, [v]that said in her heart, I *am*, and *there is* none beside me: how is she become a desolation, a place for beasts to lie down in! every one that passeth by her shall hiss, *and* wag his hand.

3 Woe to [1]her that is filthy and polluted, to the oppressing city!

2 She [a]obeyed not the voice; she [b]received not [2]correction; she trusted not in the LORD; she drew not near to her God.

3 Her princes within her *are* roaring lions; her judges *are* evening wolves; they gnaw not the bones till the morrow.

4 Her [c]prophets *are* light *and* treacherous persons: her priests have polluted the sanctuary, they have done [d]violence to the law.

5 The just LORD [e]*is* in the midst thereof; he will not do iniquity: [3]every morning doth he bring his judgment to light, he faileth not; but the unjust knoweth no shame.

6 I have cut off the nations: their [4]towers are desolate; I made their streets waste, that none passeth by: their cities are destroyed, so that there is no man, that there is none inhabitant.

10 [e]2 Chr. 33.14; Neh. 3.13
11 [f]Jas. 5.1; Rev. 18.11-12 [8]the merchant street
12 [9]curded, or, thickened [g]Job 21.15; Ps. 10.11-13
13 [h]Deut. 28.30; Amos 5.11 [i]Mic. 6.15
14 [j]Jer. 30.7; Rev. 6.17
16 [k]Jer. 4.19; Amos 3.6
18 [l]Ezek. 7.19 [m]ch. 3.8

CHAPTER 2
1 [a]Joel 2.16 [1]Or, not desirous
2 [b]2 Ki. 23.26
3 [c]Amos 5.6 [d]Ps. 76.9 [e]Joel 2.14
4 [f]Jer. 6.4
5 [g]Ezek. 25.16 [h]Josh. 13.3
6 [i]Isa. 17.2
7 [j]Isa. 11.11; [2]Or, when, etc [k]Ex. 4.31; [l]Ps. 126.4;
8 [m]Jer. 48.27; [n]Jer. 49.1
9 [o]Isa. 15.1; [p]Amos 1.13
11 [3]make lean [q]Gen. 49.10; [r]Gen. 10.5
12 [s]Isa. 18.1
14 [t]Isa. 13.21 [4]Or, pelican [5]Or, knops, or, chapiters [6]Or, when he hath uncovered
15 [u]Isa. 47.8 [v]Rev. 18.7

CHAPTER 3
1 [1]craw, or, gluttonous
2 [a]Jer. 22.21 [b]Jer. 5.3 [2]Or, instruction
4 [c]Jer. 23.11 [d]Ezek. 22.26
5 [e]Deut. 32.4; [3]morning by morning
6 [4]Or, corners

7 I said, Surely thou wilt fear me, thou wilt receive instruction; so their dwelling should not be cut off, howsoever I punished them: but they rose early, *and* [f]corrupted all their doings.

8 ¶ Therefore [g]wait ye upon me, saith the LORD, until the day that I rise up to the prey: for my determination *is* to [h]gather the nations, that I may assemble the kingdoms, to pour upon them mine indignation, *even* all my fierce anger: for all the earth shall be devoured with the fire of my jealousy.

9 For then will I turn to the people a pure [5]language, that they may all call upon the name of the LORD, to serve him with one [6]consent.

10 [i]From beyond the rivers of Ē-thĭ-ō'pĭ-a my suppliants, *even* the daughter of my dispersed, shall bring mine offering.

11 In that day shalt thou not be ashamed for all thy doings, wherein thou hast transgressed against me: for then I will take away out of the midst of thee them that [j]rejoice in thy pride, and thou shalt no more be haughty [7]because of my holy mountain.

12 I will also leave in the midst of thee [k]an afflicted and poor people, and they shall trust in the name of the LORD.

13 The remnant of Ĭs'ra-el shall not do iniquity, nor speak lies; neither shall a deceitful tongue be found in their mouth: for they shall feed and lie down, and none shall make *them* afraid.

14 ¶ Sing, O daughter of Zī'ŏn; shout, O Ĭs'ra-el; [l]be glad and rejoice with all the heart, O daughter of Je-ru̦'sa-lĕm.

15 The LORD hath taken away thy judgments, he hath cast out thine enemy: [m]the king of Ĭs'ra-el, *even* the LORD, [n]*is* in the midst of thee: thou shalt not see evil any more.

16 In that day it shall be said to Je-ru̦'sa-lĕm, Fear thou not: *and to* Zī'ŏn, [o]Let not thine hands be [8]slack.

17 The LORD thy God in the midst of thee *is* mighty; he will save, he will rejoice over thee with joy; [9]he will rest in his love, he will joy over thee with singing.

18 I will gather *them that* [p]*are* sorrowful for the solemn assembly, *who* are of thee, *to whom* [10]the reproach of it *was* a burden.

19 Behold, at that time I will undo all that afflict thee: and I will save her that halteth, and gather her that was driven out; and [11]I will get them praise and fame in every land [12]where they have been put to shame.

20 At that time [q]will I bring you *again*, even in the time that I gather you: for I will make you a name and a praise among all people of the earth, when I turn back your captivity before your eyes, saith the LORD.

7 [f]Gen. 6.12
8 [g]Prov. 20.22
[h]Joel 3.2
9 [5]lip
[6]shoulder
10 [i]Ps. 68.31; Mal. 1.11; Acts 8.27
11 [j]Matt. 3.9
[7]in my holy
12 [k]Isa. 14.32; Isa. 57.15; Matt. 5.3; Luke 6.20
14 [l]Ps. 14.7
15 [m]John 1.49
[n]Ezek. 48.35; Rev. 21.3
16 [o]Isa. 35.3
[8]Or, faint
17 [9]he will be silent
18 [p]Lam. 2.6
[10]the burden upon it was reproach
19 [11]I will set them for a praise
[12]of their shame
20 [q]Ps. 22.27

THE BOOK OF

HAGGAI

Life's Questions

How do I determine priority number 1 for me?
Why should I act when all God gives is a promise?
What does God expect from me in the midst of darkness?

God's Answers

Cyrus of Persia let Israel return from exile in 538 B.C. Gradually some returned. Under Zerubbabel they began building the temple, but soon quit. In 520 God raised an elderly Haggai to rouse His people to action in building the temple. He had to inspire a disheartened people to make God's work first priority.

Haggai shows: God's call takes precedence over materialistic needs (ch. 1); God's promise and power, not human achievement, gives encouragement (2:1–9); God expects an impure people to repent (2:10–19); God's power ensures He will overcome opposition (2:20–23).

Haggai calls us to make God's work the center of life and destroy our excuses.

1 In the second year of Da-rī'us the king, in the sixth month, in the first day of the month, came the word of the LORD [1]by Hăg'ga-ī the prophet unto [a]Ze-rŭb'ba-bĕl the son of She-ăl'tĭ-el, [2]governor of Jū'dah, and to Jŏsh'u-ȧ the son of [b]Jŏs'e-dĕch, the high priest, saying,

2 Thus speaketh the LORD of hosts, saying, This people say, The time is not come, the time that the LORD'S house should be built.

3 Then came the word of the LORD [c]by Hăg'ga-ī the prophet, saying,

4 *Is it* time for you, O ye, to dwell in your cieled houses, and this house *lie* waste?

5 Now therefore thus saith the LORD of hosts; [3]Consider your ways.

6 Ye have sown much, and bring in little; ye eat, but ye have not enough; ye drink, but ye are not filled with drink; ye clothe you, but there is none warm; and he that earneth wages earneth wages *to put it* into a bag [4]with holes.

7 ¶ Thus saith the LORD of hosts; Consider your ways.

8 Go up to the mountain, and bring wood, and build the house; and I will take pleasure in it, and I will be glorified, saith the LORD.

9 Ye looked for much, and, lo, *it came* to little; and when ye brought *it*

CHAPTER 1
1 [1]by the hand of Haggai
[a]1 Chr. 3.17
[2]Or, captain
[b]1 Chr. 6.15
3 [c]Ezra 5.1
5 [3]Set your heart on your ways
6 [4]pierced through

home, I did [5]blow upon it. Why? saith
the LORD of hosts. Because of mine
house that *is* waste, and ye run every
man unto his own house.
10 Therefore [d]the heaven over you
is stayed from dew, and the earth is
stayed *from* her fruit.
11 And I [e]called for a drought upon
the land, and upon the mountains, and
upon the corn, and upon the new wine,
and upon the oil, and upon *that* which
the ground bringeth forth, and upon
men, and upon cattle, and [f]upon all the
labour of the hands.
12 ¶ [g]Then Ze-rŭb'ba-bĕl the son of
She-ăl'tī-el, and Jŏsh'u-ȧ the son of
Jŏs'e-dĕch, the high priest, with all the
remnant of the people, obeyed the voice
of the LORD their God, and the words of
Hăg'ga-ī the prophet, as the LORD their
God had sent him, and the people did
[h]fear before the LORD.
13 Then spake Hăg'ga-ī the LORD'S
messenger in the LORD'S message unto
the people, saying, [i]I *am* with you,
saith the LORD.
14 And [j]the LORD stirred up the
spirit of Ze-rŭb'ba-bĕl the son of She-
ăl'tī-el, [k]governor of Jū'dah, and the
spirit of Jŏsh'u-ȧ the son of Jŏs'e-dĕch,
the high priest, and the spirit of all the
remnant of the people; [l]and they came
and did work in the house of the LORD
of hosts, their God,
15 In the four and twentieth day of
the sixth month, in the second year of
Da-rī'us the king.

2 In the seventh *month*, in the one
and twentieth *day* of the month,
came the word of the LORD [1]by the
prophet Hăg'ga-ī, saying,
2 Speak now to Ze-rŭb'ba-bĕl the
son of She-ăl'tī-el, governor of Jū'dah,
and to Jŏsh'u-ȧ the son of Jŏs'e-dĕch,
the high priest, and to the residue of
the people, saying,
3 [a]Who *is* left among you that saw
this house in her first glory? and how
do ye see it now? [b]*is it* not in your eyes
in comparison of it as nothing?
4 Yet now [c]be strong, O Ze-rŭb'ba-
bĕl, saith the LORD; and be strong, O
Jŏsh'u-ȧ, son of Jŏs'e-dĕch, the high
priest; and be strong, all ye people of
the land, saith the LORD, and work:
[d]for I *am* with you, saith the LORD of
hosts:
5 [e]*According to* the word that I covenanted with you when ye came out of
Ē'gypt, so [f]my spirit remaineth among
you: fear ye not.
6 For thus saith the LORD of hosts;
[g]Yet once, it *is* a little while, and [h]I will
shake the heavens, and the earth, and
the sea, and the dry *land;*
7 And I will shake all nations, [i]and
the desire of all nations shall come:
and I will fill [j]this house with glory,
saith the LORD of hosts.
8 The silver *is* mine, and the gold *is*
mine, saith the LORD of hosts.
9 [k]The glory of this latter house
shall be greater than of the former,
saith the LORD of hosts: and in this
place will I give [l]peace, saith the LORD
of hosts.
10 ¶ In the four and twentieth *day* of
the ninth *month*, in the second year of
Da-rī'us, came the word of the LORD
by Hăg'ga-ī the prophet, saying,
11 Thus saith the LORD of hosts;
[m]Ask now the priests *concerning* the
law, saying,
12 If one bear holy flesh in the skirt
of his garment, and with his skirt do
touch bread, or pottage, or wine, or oil,
or any meat, shall it be holy? And the
priests answered and said, No.
13 Then said Hăg'ga-ī, If *one that is*
[n]unclean by a dead body touch any of
these, shall it be unclean? And the
priests answered and said, It shall be
unclean.
14 Then answered Hăg'ga-ī, and
said, [o]So *is* this people, and so *is* this
nation before me, saith the LORD; and
so *is* every work of their hands; and
that which they offer there *is* unclean.
15 And now, I pray you, [p]consider
from this day and upward, from before
a stone was laid upon a stone in the
temple of the LORD:
16 Since those *days* were, when *one*
came to an heap of twenty *measures*,
there were *but* ten: when *one* came to
the pressfat for to draw out fifty *vessels* out of the press, there were *but*
twenty.
17 [q]I smote you with blasting and
with mildew and with hail in all the
labours of your hands; [r]yet ye *turned*
not to me, saith the LORD.
18 Consider now from this day and
upward, from the four and twentieth
day of the ninth *month*, *even* from [s]the
day that the foundation of the LORD'S
temple was laid, consider *it*.
19 Is the seed yet in the barn? yea,
as yet the vine, and the fig tree, and the
pomegranate, and the olive tree, hath
not brought forth: from this day will I
bless *you*.
20 ¶ And again the word of the LORD
came unto Hăg'ga-ī in the four and
twentieth *day* of the month, saying,
21 Speak to Ze-rŭb'ba-bĕl, governor
of Jū'dah, saying, [t]I will shake the
heavens and the earth;
22 And [u]I will overthrow the throne
of kingdoms, and I will destroy the
strength of the kingdoms of the heathen; and [v]I will overthrow the chariots, and those that ride in them; and
the horses and their riders shall come
down, every one by the sword of his
brother.
23 In that day, saith the LORD of
hosts, will I take thee, O Ze-rŭb'ba-bĕl,
my servant, the son of She-ăl'tī-el,
saith the LORD, [w]and will make thee as
a signet: for [x]I have chosen thee, saith
the LORD of hosts.

9 [5]Or, blow it away
10 [d]Deut. 28.23; 2 Chr. 6.26; Jer. 3.3; Joel 1.18-19
11 [e]1 Ki. 17.1
[f]ch. 2.17
12 [g]Ezra 5.2; Isa. 55.11
[h]Ps. 111.10; Prov. 1.7; Eccl. 12.13
13 [i]2 Chr. 15.2; Isa. 41.10; Matt. 28.20; Rom. 8.31
14 [j]2 Chr. 36.22; Ps. 110.3
[k]ch. 2.21
[l]1 Cor. 15.58

CHAPTER 2
1 [1]by the hand of
3 [a]Ezra. 3.12
[b]Zech. 4.10
4 [c]Zech. 8.9
[d]Ex. 3.12; 1 Sam. 16.18; ch. 1.13; Mark 16.20; Rom. 8.31
5 [e]Ex. 29.45-46
[f]Neh. 9.20; Isa. 63.11; Zech. 4.6
6 [g]Heb. 12.26
[h]Isa. 34.4; Jer. 4.26
7 [i]Gen. 3.16; Deut. 18.15; Mal. 3.1
[j]Ps. 24.7
9 [k]John 1.14; Luke 11.31
[l]Ps. 85.8-9; Isa. 9.6; Luke 2.14
11 [m]Lev. 10.10; Deut. 33.10
13 [n]Num. 19.11
14 [o]Tit. 1.15
15 [p]ch. 1.5
17 [q]Deut. 28.22; 1 Ki. 8.37
[r]Jer. 5.3; Amos 4.6-8-11
18 [s]Zech. 8.9
21 [t]Ezek. 21.27; Heb. 12.26
22 [u]Dan. 2.44; Matt. 24.7
[v]Mic. 5.10
23 [w]Song 8.6; Jer. 22.24
[x]Isa. 42.1

THE BOOK OF

ZECHARIAH

Life's Questions

Why does God not give me prosperity?
What more does God expect me to do?
Why is God punishing us?

God's Answers

Besides Haggai, God also called Zechariah about 520 B.C. for a two-year ministry seeking to get the returned exiles to build the temple and make God their priority. As with few of the prophets, their message was heard and obeyed. In 515 the temple was completed. Zechariah had stirred to action if not to obedience.

Zechariah shows: God's ways are just (1:1–6); God promises prosperity to a purified people (1:7—6:15); a jealous God seeks a righteous remnant, not more ritual (7:1—8:23); God controls His people's future (9—11); God will purge and deliver His people on His day (12—14).

Zechariah provides hope and a call to action for God's people.

1 In the eighth month, [a]in the second
year of Da-rī'us, came the word of
the LORD [b]unto Zĕch-a-rī'ah, the son
of Bĕr-e-chī'ah, the son of Ĭd'dō the
prophet, saying,
2 The LORD hath been [1]sore displeased with your fathers.
3 Therefore say thou unto them, Thus
saith the LORD of hosts; Turn [c]ye unto
me, saith the LORD of hosts, and I will
turn unto you, saith the LORD of hosts.
4 Be ye not as your fathers, unto
whom the former prophets have cried,
saying, Thus saith the LORD of hosts;
[d]Turn ye now from your evil ways,
and *from* your evil doings: but they did
not hear, nor hearken unto me, saith
the LORD.
5 Your fathers, where *are* they? and
the prophets, do they live for ever?
6 But [e]my words and my statutes,
which I commanded my servants the
prophets, did they not [2]take hold of your
fathers? and they returned and said,
[f]Like as the LORD of hosts thought to do
unto us, according to our ways, and according to our doings, so hath he dealt
with us.
7 ¶ Upon the four and twentieth day
of the eleventh month, which *is* the
month Sē'băt, in the second year of Da-
rī'us, came the word of the LORD unto
Zĕch-a-rī'ah, the son of Bĕr-e-chī'ah,
the son of Ĭd'dō the prophet, saying,
8 I saw by night, and behold [g]a man
riding upon a red horse, and he stood
among the myrtle trees that *were* in
the bottom; and behind him *were there*
[h]red horses, [3]speckled, and white.
9 Then said I, O my lord, what *are*
these? And the angel that talked with
me said unto me, I will shew thee what
these *be*.
10 And the man that stood among
the myrtle trees answered and said,
[i]These *are they* whom the LORD hath
sent to walk to and fro through the
earth.
11 [j]And they answered the angel of
the LORD that stood among the myrtle
trees, and said, We have walked to and
fro through the earth, and, behold, all
the earth sitteth still, and is at rest.
12 ¶ Then the angel of the LORD answered and said, [k]O LORD of hosts,
how long wilt thou not have mercy on
Je-rṳ'sa-lĕm and on the cities of Jū'-
dah, against which thou hast had indignation [l]these threescore and ten
years?
13 And the LORD answered the angel that talked with me *with* [m]good
words *and* comfortable words.
14 So the angel that communed with
me said unto me, Cry thou, saying,
Thus saith the LORD of hosts; I am
[n]jealous for Je-rṳ'sa-lĕm and for Zī'ŏn
with a great jealousy.
15 And I am very sore displeased
with the heathen *that are* at ease: for
[o]I was but a little displeased, and they
helped forward the affliction.
16 Therefore thus saith the LORD; [p]I
am returned to Je-rṳ'sa-lĕm with mercies: my house shall be built in it, saith
the LORD of hosts, and [q]a line shall be
stretched forth upon Je-rṳ'sa-lĕm.
17 Cry yet, saying, Thus saith the
LORD of hosts; My cities through [4]pros-
perity shall yet be spread abroad; [r]and
the LORD shall yet comfort Zī'ŏn, and
[s]shall yet choose Je-rṳ'sa-lĕm.
18 ¶ Then lifted I up mine eyes, and
saw, and behold four horns.
19 And I said unto the angel that
talked with me, What *be* these? And he
answered me, [t]These *are* the horns
which have scattered Jū'dah, Ĭs'ra-el,
and Je-rṳ'sa-lĕm.
20 And the LORD shewed me four
carpenters.
21 Then said I, What come these to
do? And he spake, saying, These *are*
the horns which have scattered Jū'-
dah, so that no man did lift up his head:
but these are come to fray them, to cast
out the horns of the Gĕn'tīles, which
[u]lifted up *their* horn over the land of
Jū'dah to scatter it.

2 I LIFTED up mine eyes again, and
looked, and behold [a]a man with a
measuring line in his hand.

CHAPTER 1
1 [a]Ezra 4.24; Hag. 1.1
[b]Ezra 5.1
2 [1]with displeasure
3 [c]Jer. 25.5; Mic. 7.19; Mal. 3.7; Luke 15.20
4 [d]Isa. 1.16-17; Jer. 3.12; Ezek. 33.11; Hos. 14.1; Matt. 3.8-9; Acts 3.19
6 [e]Isa. 55.1
[2]Or, overtake
[f]Lam. 1.18
8 [g]Josh. 5.13; Rev. 6.4
[h]ch. 6.2
[3]Or, bay
10 [i]Ps. 91.11; Heb. 1.14
11 [j]Ps. 103.20
12 [k]Ps. 102.13; Rev. 6.10
[l]Dan. 9.2; ch. 7.5
13 [m]Isa. 40.1-2; Jer. 29.10
14 [n]Joel 2.18; ch. 8.2
15 [o]Isa. 47.6
16 [p]Isa. 12.1
[q]ch. 2.1-2
17 [4]good
[r]Isa. 51.3
[s]ch. 3.2
19 [t]Ezra 4.1; Hab. 3.14
21 [u]Ps. 75.4-5

CHAPTER 2
1 [a]Ezek. 40.3; ch. 1.16

2 Then said I, Whither goest thou? And he said unto me, [b]To measure Je-rụ'sa-lĕm, to see what *is* the breadth thereof, and what *is* the length thereof.

3 And, behold, the angel that talked with me went forth, and another angel went out to meet him,

4 And said unto him, Run, speak to this young man, saying, [c]Je-rụ'sa-lĕm shall be inhabited *as* towns without walls for the multitude of men and cattle therein:

5 For I, saith the LORD, will be unto her [d]a wall of fire round about, [e]and will be the glory in the midst of her.

6 ¶ Ho, ho, *come forth,* and flee from the land of the north, saith the LORD: for I have [f]spread you abroad as the four winds of the heaven, saith the LORD.

7 Deliver thyself, O Zī'ŏn, that dwellest *with* the daughter of Băb'y̆-lon.

8 For thus saith the LORD of hosts; After the glory hath he sent me unto the nations which spoiled you: for he that [g]toucheth you toucheth the apple of his eye.

9 For, behold, I will shake mine hand upon them, and they shall be a spoil to their servants: and ye shall know that the LORD of hosts hath sent me.

10 ¶ Sing and rejoice, O daughter of Zī'ŏn: for, lo, I come, and I [h]will dwell in the midst of thee, saith the LORD.

11 [i]And many nations shall be joined to the LORD in that day, and shall be [j]my people: and I will dwell in the midst of thee, and [k]thou shalt know that the LORD of hosts hath sent me unto thee.

12 And the LORD shall [l]inherit Jū'dah his portion in the holy land, and shall choose Je-rụ'sa-lĕm again.

13 [m]Be silent, O all flesh, before the LORD: for he is raised up out of [1]his holy habitation.

3 And he shewed me [a]Jŏsh'u-ȧ the high priest standing before the angel of the LORD, and [1]Sā'tan standing at his right hand [2]to resist him.

2 [b]And the LORD said unto Sā'tan, [c]The LORD rebuke thee, O Sā'tan; even the LORD that [d]hath chosen Je-rụ'sa-lĕm rebuke thee: [e]*is* not this a brand plucked out of the fire?

3 Now Jŏsh'u-ȧ was clothed with [f]filthy garments, and stood before the angel.

4 And he answered and spake unto those that stood before him, saying, Take away the filthy garments from him. And unto him he said, Behold, I have caused thine iniquity to pass from thee, [g]and I will clothe thee with change of raiment.

5 And I said, Let them set a fair [h]mitre upon his head. So they set a fair mitre upon his head, and clothed him with garments. And the angel of the LORD stood by.

6 And the angel of the LORD protested unto Jŏsh'u-ȧ, saying,

2 [b]Rev. 11.1
4 [c]Ezek. 36.10
5 [d]Ps. 46.11; Isa. 4.5
[e]Rev. 21.23
6 [f]Deut. 28.64
8 [g]2 Thess. 1.6
10 [h]Lev. 26.12; 2 Cor. 6.16
11 [i]Isa. 2.2-3
[j]Ex. 12.49
[k]Ezek. 33.33
12 [l]Deut. 32.9
13 [m]Ps. 46.10;
[1]the habitation of his holiness

CHAPTER 3
1 [a]Hag. 1.1
[1]That is, an adversary
[2]to be his adversary
2 [b]Ps. 109.31;
[c]Jude 9
[d]Rom. 8.33
[e]Rom. 11.5
3 [f]Isa. 64.6
4 [g]Rev. 19.8
5 [h]Ex. 29.6
7 [3]Or, ordinance
[i]Deut. 17.9
[4]walks
8 [5]men of wonder, or, sign
[j]Isa. 42.1
[k]Isa. 4.2
9 [l]Isa. 28.16
[m]Rev. 5.6
[n]Isa. 53.4
10 [o]1 Ki. 4.25

CHAPTER 4
1 [a]Dan. 8.18
2 [b]Ex. 25.31
[1]with her bowl
[c]Ex. 25.37;
[2]Or, seven several pipes to the lamps, etc
3 [d]Rev. 11.4
6 [3]Or, army
7 [e]Isa. 40.3-4;
[f]Ps. 118.22
[g]Ezra 3.11
9 [h]Ezra 6.15
[i]1 Cor. 2.4
10 [j]Hag. 2.3
[4]Or, since the seven eyes of the LORD shall rejoice
[5]stone of tin
[k]2 Chr. 16.9
12 [6]by the hand
[7]Or, empty out of themselves oil into the gold
[8]the gold

7 Thus saith the LORD of hosts; If thou wilt walk in my ways, and if thou wilt keep my [3]charge, then thou shalt also [i]judge my house, and shalt also keep my courts, and I will give thee [4]places to walk among these that stand by.

8 Hear now, O Jŏsh'u-ȧ the high priest, thou, and thy fellows that sit before thee: for they *are* men [5]wondered at: for, behold, I will bring forth [j]my servant the [k]BRANCH.

9 For behold the stone that I have laid before Jŏsh'u-ȧ; [l]upon one stone *shall be* [m]seven eyes: behold, I will engrave the graving thereof, saith the LORD of hosts, and [n]I will remove the iniquity of that land in one day.

10 In that day, saith the LORD of hosts, shall ye call every man his neighbour [o]under the vine and under the fig tree.

4 And the angel that talked with me came again, and waked me, [a]as a man that is wakened out of his sleep,

2 And said unto me, What seest thou? And I said, I have looked, and behold [b]a candlestick all *of* gold, [1]with a bowl upon the top of it, [c]and his seven lamps thereon, and [2]seven pipes to the seven lamps, which *are* upon the top thereof:

3 [d]And two olive trees by it, one upon the right *side* of the bowl, and the other upon the left *side* thereof.

4 So I answered and spake to the angel that talked with me, saying, What *are* these, my lord?

5 Then the angel that talked with me answered and said unto me, Knowest thou not what these be? And I said, No, my lord.

6 Then he answered and spake unto me, saying, This *is* the word of the LORD unto Ze-rŭb'ba-bĕl, saying, Not by [3]might, nor by power, but by my spirit, saith the LORD of hosts.

7 Who *art* thou, [e]O great mountain? before Ze-rŭb'ba-bĕl *thou shalt become* a plain: and he shall bring forth [f]the headstone *thereof* [g]*with* shoutings, *crying,* Grace, grace unto it.

8 Moreover the word of the LORD came unto me, saying,

9 The hands of Ze-rŭb'ba-bĕl have laid the foundation of this house; his hands [h]shall also finish it; and [i]thou shalt know that the LORD of hosts hath sent me unto you.

10 For who hath despised the day of [j]small things? [4]for they shall rejoice, and shall see the [5]plummet in the hand of Ze-rŭb'ba-bĕl *with* those seven; [k]they *are* the eyes of the LORD, which run to and fro through the whole earth.

11 ¶ Then answered I, and said unto him, What *are* these two olive trees upon the right *side* of the candlestick and upon the left *side* thereof?

12 And I answered again, and said unto him, What *be these* two olive branches which [6]through the two golden pipes [7]empty [8]the golden *oil* out of themselves?

13 And he answered me and said,
Knowest thou not what these *be?* And I
said, No, my lord.
14 Then said he, These *are* the two
[9]anointed ones, that stand by the Lord
of the whole earth.
5 Then I turned, and lifted up mine
eyes, and looked, and behold a flying roll.
2 And he said unto me, What seest
thou? And I answered, I see a flying
roll; the length thereof *is* twenty cubits, and the breadth thereof ten cubits.
3 Then said he unto me, This *is* the
[a]curse that goeth forth over the face of
the whole earth: for [1]every one that
stealeth shall be cut off *as* on this side
according to it; and every one that
sweareth shall be cut off *as* on that
side according to it.
4 I will bring it forth, saith the LORD
of hosts, and it shall enter into the
house of the thief, and into the house
of [b]him that sweareth falsely by my
name, and it shall remain in the midst
of his house, and [c]shall consume it
with the timber thereof and the stones
thereof.
5 ¶ Then the angel that talked with
me went forth, and said unto me, Lift
up now thine eyes, and see what *is* this
that goeth forth.
6 And I said, What *is* it? And he said,
This *is* an ephah that goeth forth. He
said moreover, This *is* their resem-
blance through all the earth.
7 And, behold, there was lifted up a
[2]talent of lead: and this *is* a woman
that sitteth in the midst of the ephah.
8 And he said, This *is* wickedness.
And he cast it into the midst of the
ephah; and he cast the weight of lead
upon the mouth thereof.
9 Then lifted I up mine eyes, and
looked, and, behold, there came out two
women, and the wind *was* in their
wings; for they had wings like the wings
of a stork: and they lifted up the ephah
between the earth and the heaven.
10 Then said I to the angel that
talked with me, Whither do these bear
the ephah?
11 And he said unto me, To [d]build it
an house in the land of Shī'när: and it
shall be established, and set there
upon her own base.
6 And I turned, and lifted up mine
eyes, and looked, and, behold, there
came four chariots out from between
two mountains; and the mountains
were mountains of brass.
2 In the first chariot *were* [a]red horses; and in the second chariot black
horses;
3 And in the third chariot [b]white
horses; and in the fourth chariot grisled and [1]bay horses.
4 Then I answered [c]and said unto
the angel that talked with me, What
are these, my lord?
5 And the angel answered and said
unto me, [d]These *are* the four [2]spirits of
the heavens, which go forth from [e]stan-
ding before the Lord of all the earth.

14 [9]sons of oil

CHAPTER 5

3 [a]Prov. 3.33; Isa. 24.6; Mal. 4.6; Gal. 3.10-13; Heb. 6.8
[1]Or, every one of this people that stealeth holdeth himself guiltless, as it doth

4 [b]Lev. 19.12; Matt. 5.33-36; Jas. 5.12
[c]Lev. 14.45

7 [2]Or, weighty piece

11 [d]Jer. 29.5

CHAPTER 6

2 [a]ch. 1.8; Rev. 6.4

3 [b]Rev. 6.2
[1]Or, strong

4 [c]ch. 5.10

5 [d]Ps. 68.17; Heb. 1.7-14
[2]Or, winds
[e]1 Ki. 22.19; Job 1.6; Dan. 7.10; Luke 1.19

6 [f]Jer. 1.14

7 [g]Gen. 13.17

8 [h]Eccl. 10.4

10 [i]Ezra 1.11

11 [j]Ex. 28.36

12 [k]Isa. 9.6; Mic. 5.5; ch. 13.7; Mal. 3.1; Mark 15.39; Luke 1.78; John 1.45
[l]Ps. 80.15-17; Isa. 4.2; ch. 3.8
[3]Or, branch up from under him
[m]Matt. 16.18; Eph. 2.20; Phil. 2.9; Heb. 2.9

13 [n]Ps. 21.5; Isa. 22.24
[o]Ps. 110.4; Heb. 3.1

14 [p]Mark 14.9

15 [q]Eph. 2.13

CHAPTER 7

2 [1]to entreat the face of the LORD

3 [a]Deut. 17.9; Mal. 2.7

5 [b]ch. 1.12
[c]Isa. 58.4; Matt. 6.16; Rom. 14.6

6 The black horses which *are*
therein go forth into [f]the north country; and the white go forth after them;
and the grisled go forth toward the
south country.
7 And the bay went forth, and
sought to go that they might [g]walk to
and fro through the earth: and he said,
Get you hence, walk to and fro through
the earth. So they walked to and fro
through the earth.
8 Then cried he upon me, and spake
unto me, saying, Behold, these that go
toward the north country have quieted
my [h]spirit in the north country.
9 ¶ And the word of the LORD came
unto me, saying,
10 Take of *them of* the captivity,
even of Hĕl'da-ī, of To-bī'jah, and of
Je-dā'iah, which are [i]come from Băb'-
ȳ-lon, and come thou the same day,
and go into the house of Jo-sī'ah the
son of Zĕph-a-nī'ah;
11 Then take silver and gold, and
make [j]crowns, and set *them* upon the
head of Jŏsh'u-ȧ the son of Jŏs'e-dĕch,
the high priest;
12 And speak unto him, saying,
Thus speaketh the LORD of hosts, saying, Behold [k]the man whose name *is*
The [l]BRANCH; and he shall [3]grow up
out of his place, [m]and he shall build the
temple of the LORD:
13 Even he shall build the temple of
the LORD; and he [n]shall bear the glory,
and shall sit and rule upon his throne;
and [o]he shall be a priest upon his
throne: and the counsel of peace shall
be between them both.
14 And the crowns shall be to Hē'-
lem, and to To-bī'jah, and to Je-dā'iah,
and to Hĕn the son of Zĕph-a-nī'ah,
[p]for a memorial in the temple of the
LORD.
15 And [q]they *that are* far off shall
come and build in the temple of the
LORD, and ye shall know that the LORD
of hosts hath sent me unto you. And
this shall come to pass, if ye will diligently obey the voice of the LORD your
God.
7 And it came to pass in the fourth
year of king Da-rī'us, *that* the word
of the LORD came unto Zĕch-a-rī'ah in
the fourth *day* of the ninth month, *even*
in Chĭs'leū;
2 When they had sent unto the house
of God She-rē'zer and Rē'ḡem-mē'-
lech, and their men, [1]to pray before the
LORD,
3 *And* to [a]speak unto the priests
which *were* in the house of the LORD of
hosts, and to the prophets, saying,
Should I weep in the fifth month, sepa-
rating myself, as I have done these so
many years?
4 ¶ Then came the word of the LORD
of hosts unto me, saying,
5 Speak unto all the people of the
land, and to the priests, saying, When
ye fasted and mourned in the fifth and
seventh *month*, [b]even those seventy
years, did ye at all fast [c]unto me, *even*
to me?

6 And when ye did eat, and when ye
did drink, [2]did not ye eat *for yourselves,* and drink *for yourselves?*
7 [3]*Should ye* not *hear* the words
which the LORD hath cried [4]by the
former prophets, when Je-rṳ'sa-lĕm
was inhabited and in prosperity, and
the cities thereof round about her,
when *men* inhabited [d]the south and
the plain?
8 ¶ And the word of the LORD came
unto Zĕch-a-rī'ah, saying,
9 Thus speaketh the LORD of hosts,
saying, [5]Execute true judgment, and
shew mercy and compassions every
man to his brother:
10 And oppress not the widow, nor
the fatherless, the stranger, nor the
poor; and let none of you imagine evil
against his brother in your heart.
11 But they refused to hearken, and
[6]pulled away the shoulder, and [7]stop-
ped their ears, that they should not
hear.
12 Yea, they made their hearts *as* an
adamant stone, lest they should hear
the law, and the words which the LORD
of hosts hath sent in his spirit [8]by the
former prophets: therefore came a great
wrath from the LORD of hosts.
13 Therefore it is come to pass, *that*
as he cried, and they would not hear;
so they cried, and I would not hear,
saith the LORD of hosts:
14 But I scattered them with a whirlwind among all the nations whom they
knew not. Thus the land was desolate
after them, that no man passed through
nor returned: for they laid the [9]pleasant
land desolate.

8 Again the word of the LORD of
hosts came *to me,* saying,
2 Thus saith the LORD of hosts; [a]I
was jealous for Zī'ŏn with great jealousy, and I was jealous for her with
great fury.
3 Thus saith the LORD; I am returned unto Zī'ŏn, and will dwell in the
midst of Je-rṳ'sa-lĕm: and Je-rṳ'sa-
lĕm [b]shall be called a city of truth; and
[c]the mountain of the LORD of hosts
[d]the holy mountain.
4 Thus saith the LORD of hosts;
[e]There shall yet old men and old
women dwell in the streets of Je-rṳ'sa-
lĕm, and every man with his staff in his
hand [1]for very age.
5 And the streets of the city shall be
full of boys and girls playing in the
streets thereof.
6 Thus saith the LORD of hosts; If it be
[2]marvellous in the eyes of the remnant
of this people in these days, [f]should it
also be marvellous in mine eyes? saith
the LORD of hosts.
7 Thus saith the LORD of hosts; Behold, I will save my people from the
east country, and from [3]the west country;
8 And I will bring them, and they
shall dwell in the midst of Je-rṳ'sa-
lĕm: [g]and they shall be my people, and
I will be their God, in truth and in righteousness.

9 ¶ Thus saith the LORD of hosts;
[h]Let your hands be strong, ye that
hear in these days these words by the
mouth of [i]the prophets, which *were* in
[j]the day *that* the foundation of the
house of the LORD of hosts was laid,
that the temple might be built.
10 For before these days [4]there was
no hire for man, nor any hire for beast;
neither *was there any* peace to him
that went out or came in because of the
affliction: for I set all men every one
against his neighbour.
11 But now I *will* not *be* unto the residue of this people as in the former
days, saith the LORD of hosts.
12 For the seed *shall be* [5]prosper-
ous; the vine shall give her fruit, and
the ground shall give her increase, and
the heavens shall give their dew; and I
will cause the remnant of this people to
[k]possess all these *things.*
13 And it shall come to pass, *that* as
ye were [l]a curse among the heathen, O
house of Jū'dah, and house of Ĭs'ra-el;
so will I save you, and [m]ye shall be a
blessing: [n]fear not, *but* let your hands
be strong.
14 For thus saith the LORD of hosts;
[o]As I thought to punish you, when
your fathers provoked me to wrath,
saith the LORD of hosts, [p]and I repented not:
15 So again have I thought in these
days to do well unto Je-rṳ'sa-lĕm and
to the house of Jū'dah: fear ye not.
16 ¶ These *are* the things that ye
shall do; [q]Speak ye every man the
truth to his neighbour; [6]execute the
judgment of truth and peace in your
gates:
17 [r]And let none of you imagine evil
in your hearts against his neighbour;
and love no false oath: for all these *are*
things that I [s]hate, saith the LORD.
18 ¶ And the word of the LORD of
hosts came unto me, saying,
19 Thus saith the LORD of hosts;
[t]The fast of the fourth *month,* and the
fast of the fifth, [u]and the fast of the
seventh, and the fast of the tenth, shall
be to the house of Jū'dah [v]joy and gladness, and cheerful [7]feasts; therefore
love the truth and peace.
20 Thus saith the LORD of hosts; *It
shall* yet *come to pass,* that there shall
come people, and the inhabitants of
many cities:
21 And the inhabitants of one *city*
shall go to another, saying, Let us go
[8]speedily [9]to pray before the LORD, and
to seek the LORD of hosts: I will go
also.
22 Yea, many people and strong nations shall come to seek the LORD of
hosts in Je-rṳ'sa-lĕm, and to pray before the LORD.
23 Thus saith the LORD of hosts; In
those days *it shall come to pass,* that
ten men shall take hold out of all languages of the nations, even shall take
hold of the skirt of him that is a Jew,
saying, We will go with you: for we
have heard *that* God *is* with you.

6 [2]Or, be not ye they that, etc
7 [3]Or, Are not these the words? [4]by the hand of, etc [d]Jer. 17.26
9 [5]Judge judgment of truth
11 [6]they gave a backsliding shoulder [7]made heavy
12 [8]by the hand of
14 [9]land of desire

CHAPTER 8
2 [a]Nah. 1.2
3 [b]Isa. 1.21 [c]Isa. 2.2-3 [d]Ps. 48.1-2; Jer. 31.23
4 [e]1 Sam. 2.31; Isa. 65.20 [1]for multitude of days
6 [2]Or, hard, or, difficult [f]Num. 11.23; Job 42.2; Luke 1.37; Rom. 4.21
7 [3]the country of the going down of the sun
8 [g]Lev. 25.17; Jer. 4.2; Ezek. 11.20; ch. 13.9; Rev. 21.3
9 [h]Hag. 2.4 [i]Ezra 5.1-2 [j]Hag. 2.18
10 [4]Or, the hire of man became nothing, etc
12 [5]of peace [k]Isa. 61.7; 1 Tim. 4.8
13 [l]Jer. 42.18 [m]Gen. 12.2 [n]Deut. 20.3-4; Eph. 6.10
14 [o]Jer. 31.28 [p]2 Chr. 36.16
16 [q]Prov. 12.19 [6]judge truth, and the judgment of peace
17 [r]Prov. 3.29 [s]Prov. 6.16
19 [t]Jer. 52.6 [u]Jer. 41.1 [v]Isa. 35.10 [7]Or, solemn, or, set times
21 [8]going, or, continually [9]to intreat the face of the LORD

9 The burden of the word of the LORD
in the land of Hā'drăch, and [a]Da-
măs'cus *shall be* the rest thereof: when
[b]the eyes of man, as of all the tribes of
Ĭs'ra-el, *shall be* toward the LORD.
2 And [c]Hā'math also shall border
thereby; [d]Tȳ'rus, and [e]Zī'dŏn, though
it be very [f]wise.
3 And Tȳ'rus did build herself a
strong hold, and heaped up silver as
the dust, and fine gold as the mire of
the streets.
4 Behold, the Lord will cast her out,
and he will smite [g]her power in the
sea; and she shall be devoured with
fire.
5 [h]Ăsh'ke-lŏn shall see *it*, and fear;
[i]Gā'zȧ also *shall see it*, and be very
sorrowful, and Ĕk'rŏn; for her expectation shall be ashamed; and the king
shall perish from Gā'zȧ, and Ăsh'ke-
lŏn shall not be inhabited.
6 And a bastard shall dwell in Ăsh'-
dŏd, and I will cut off the pride of the
Phĭ-lĭs'tĭnes.
7 And I will take away his [1]blood out
of his mouth, and his abominations
from between his teeth: but he that remaineth, even he, *shall be* for our God,
and he shall be as a governor in Jū'-
dah, and Ĕk'rŏn as a Jĕb'u-site.
8 And [j]I will encamp about mine
house because of the army, because of
him that passeth by, and because of
him that returneth: and no oppressor
shall pass through them any more: for
now [k]have I seen with mine eyes.
9 ¶ [l]Rejoice greatly, O daughter of
Zī'ŏn; shout, O daughter of Je-ru'sa-
lĕm: behold, [m]thy King cometh unto
thee: he *is* [n]just, and [2]having salvation;
lowly, and riding upon an ass, and
upon a colt the foal of an ass.
10 And I will cut off the chariot from
Ē'phrā-ĭm, and the horse from Je-
ru'sa-lĕm, and the battle bow shall be
cut off: and he shall speak [o]peace unto
the heathen: and his dominion *shall be*
[p]from sea *even* to sea, and from the
river *even* to the ends of the earth.
11 As for thee also, [3]by the blood of
thy covenant I have sent forth thy
[q]prisoners out of the pit wherein *is* no
water.
12 ¶ Turn you to the strong hold, ye
prisoners of hope: even to day do I declare *that* I will render double unto
thee;
13 When I have bent Jū'dah for me,
filled the bow with Ē'phrā-ĭm, and
raised up thy sons, O Zī'ŏn, against thy
sons, O Grēece, and made thee as the
sword of a mighty man.
14 And the LORD shall be seen over
them, and his arrow shall go forth as
the lightning: and the Lord GOD shall
blow the trumpet, and shall go with
whirlwinds of the south.
15 The LORD of hosts shall defend
them; and they shall devour, and [4]sub-
due with sling stones; and they shall
drink, *and* make a noise as through
wine; and they [5]shall be filled like
bowls, *and* as [r]the corners of the altar.

CHAPTER 9
1 [a]Amos 1.3
[b]Ps. 145.15
2 [c]Jer. 49.23
[d]Amos 1.9
[e]Obad. 20
[f]Ezek. 28.3
4 [g]Ezek. 26.17
5 [h]Zeph. 2.4
[i]Acts 8.26
7 [1]bloods
8 [j]Deut. 33.27; Ps. 34.7
[k]Ex. 3.7
9 [l]Matt. 21.5; John 12.15
[m]Ps. 2.6; Matt. 21.5; John 1.49
[n]Isa. 45.21; 1 Pet. 3.18
[2]Or, saving himself
10 [o]Ps. 72.3-7; Col. 1.20-21
[p]Ps. 2.8; Rev. 11.15
11 [3]Or, whose covenant is by blood
[q]Isa. 61.1
15 [4]Or, subdue the stones of the sling
[5]Or, shall fill both the bowls, etc
[r]Lev. 4.25
16 [s]Ezek. 37.23
[t]Mal. 3.17
[u]Isa. 11.12
17 [6]Or, grow, or, speak
CHAPTER 10
1 [a]Jer. 14.22
[b]Joel 2.23
[1]Or, lightnings
2 [2]teraphims
[3]Or, answered that, etc
3 [c]Ezek. 34.17
[4]visited upon
[d]Ex. 4.31; 1 Pet. 2.12
4 [e]Isa. 22.23
5 [5]Or, they shall make the riders on horses ashamed
8 [f]Isa. 5.26
10 [g]Rom. 11.25
[h]Ex. 14.26-27; Isa. 49.20
11 [i]Ezek. 30.13

16 And [s]the LORD their God shall
save them in that day as the flock of his
people: for [t]*they shall be as* the stones
of a crown, [u]lifted up as an ensign
upon his land.
17 For how great *is* his goodness,
and how great *is* his beauty! corn shall
make the young men [6]cheerful, and
new wine the maids.
10 Ask ye [a]of the LORD rain [b]in the
time of the latter rain; *so* the
LORD shall make [1]bright clouds, and
give them showers of rain, to every
one grass in the field.
2 For the [2]idols have spoken vanity,
and the diviners have seen a lie, and
have told false dreams; they comfort in
vain: therefore they went their way as
a flock, they [3]were troubled, because
there was no shepherd.
3 Mine anger was kindled against
the shepherds, [c]and I [4]punished the
goats: for the LORD of hosts [d]hath visited his flock the house of Jū'dah, and
hath made them as his goodly horse in
the battle.
4 Out of him came forth the corner,
out of him [e]the nail, out of him the
battle bow, out of him every oppressor
together.
5 ¶ And they shall be as mighty *men*,
which tread down *their enemies* in the
mire of the streets in the battle: and
they shall fight, because the LORD *is*
with them, and [5]the riders on horses
shall be confounded.
6 And I will strengthen the house of
Jū'dah, and I will save the house of
Jō'seph, and I will bring them again to
place them; for I have mercy upon
them: and they shall be as though I had
not cast them off: for I *am* the LORD
their God, and will hear them.
7 And *they of* Ē'phrā-ĭm shall be
like a mighty *man*, and their heart
shall rejoice as through wine: yea,
their children shall see *it*, and be glad;
their heart shall rejoice in the LORD.
8 I will [f]hiss for them, and gather
them; for I have redeemed them: and
they shall increase as they have increased.
9 And I will sow them among the
people: and they shall remember me in
far countries; and they shall live with
their children, and turn again.
10 [g]I will bring them again also out
of the land of Ē'gypt, and gather them
out of Ăs-sȳr'ĭ-ȧ; and I will bring them
into the land of Gĭl'e-ăd and Lĕb'a-
non; and [h]*place* shall not be found for
them.
11 And he shall pass through the
sea with affliction, and shall smite the
waves in the sea, and all the deeps of
the river shall dry up: and the pride of
Ăs-sȳr'ĭ-ȧ shall be brought down, and
[i]the sceptre of Ē'gypt shall depart
away.
12 And I will strengthen them in the
LORD; and they shall walk up and
down in his name, saith the LORD.
11 Open thy doors, O Lĕb'a-non,
that the fire may devour thy cedars.

2 Howl, fir tree; for the cedar is fallen; because the [1]mighty are spoiled: howl, O ye oaks of Bā'shăn; for [2]the forest of the vintage is come down.

3 ¶ *There is* a voice of the howling of the shepherds; for their glory is spoiled: a voice of the roaring of young lions; for the pride of Jôr'dan is spoiled.

4 Thus saith the LORD my God; Feed the flock of the slaughter;

5 Whose possessors slay them, and [a]hold themselves not guilty: and they that sell them [b]say, Blessed *be* the LORD; for I am rich: and their own shepherds pity them not.

6 For I will no more pity the inhabitants of the land, saith the LORD: but, lo, I will [3]deliver the men every one into his neighbour's hand, and into the hand of his king: and they shall smite the land, and out of their hand I will not deliver *them*.

7 And I will feed the flock of slaughter, [4]*even* you, [c]O poor of the flock. And I took unto me two staves; the one I called Beauty, and the other I called [5]Bands; and I fed the flock.

8 Three shepherds also I cut off [d]in one month; and my soul [6]loathed them, and their soul also abhorred me.

9 Then said I, I will not feed you: [e]that that dieth, let it die; and that that is to be cut off, let it be cut off; and let the rest eat every one the flesh [7]of another.

10 ¶ And I took my staff, *even* Beauty, and cut it asunder, that I might break my covenant which I had made with all the people.

11 And it was broken in that day: and [8]so the poor of the flock that waited upon me knew that it *was* the word of the LORD.

12 And I said unto them, [9]If ye think good, give *me* my price; and if not, forbear. So they [f]weighed for my price thirty *pieces* of silver.

13 And the LORD said unto me, Cast it unto the [g]potter: a goodly price that I was prised at of them. And I took the thirty *pieces* of silver, and cast them to the potter in the house of the LORD.

14 Then I cut asunder mine other staff, *even* [10]Bands, that I might break the brotherhood between Jū'dah and Is'ra-el.

15 ¶ And the LORD said unto me, [h]Take unto thee yet the instruments of a foolish shepherd.

16 For, lo, I will raise up a shepherd in the land, *which* shall not visit those that be [11]cut off, neither shall seek the young one, nor heal that that is broken, nor [12]feed that that standeth still: but he shall eat the flesh of the fat, and tear their claws in pieces.

17 [i]Woe to the idol shepherd that leaveth the flock! the sword *shall be* upon his arm, and upon his right eye: his arm shall be clean dried up, and his right eye shall be utterly [j]darkened.

12 The burden of the word of the LORD for Is'ra-el, saith the LORD, which stretcheth forth the heavens, and layeth the foundation of the earth, and [a]formeth the spirit of man within him.

2 Behold, I will make Je-rṳ'sa-lĕm a cup of [1]trembling unto all the people round about, [2]when they shall be in the siege both against Jū'dah *and* against Je-rṳ'sa-lĕm.

3 ¶ And in that day will I make Je-rṳ'sa-lĕm [b]a burdensome stone for all people: all that burden themselves with it shall be cut in pieces, though all the people of the earth be gathered together against it.

4 In that day, saith the LORD, [c]I will smite every horse with astonishment, and his rider with madness: and I will open mine eyes upon the house of Jū'dah, and will smite every horse of the people with blindness.

5 And the governors of Jū'dah shall say in their heart, [3]The inhabitants of Je-rṳ'sa-lĕm *shall be* my strength in the LORD of hosts their God.

6 ¶ In that day will I make the governors of Jū'dah like an hearth of fire among the wood, and like a torch of fire in a sheaf; and they shall devour all the people round about, on the right hand and on the left: and Je-rṳ'sa-lĕm shall be inhabited again in her own place, *even* in Je-rṳ'sa-lĕm.

7 The LORD also shall [d]save the tents of Jū'dah first, that the glory of the house of Dā'vid and the glory of the inhabitants of Je-rṳ'sa-lĕm do not magnify *themselves* against Jū'dah.

8 In that day shall the LORD defend the inhabitants of Je-rṳ'sa-lĕm; and [e]he that is [4]feeble among them at that day shall be as Dā'vid; and the house of Dā'vid *shall be* as God, as the angel of the LORD before them.

9 ¶ And it shall come to pass in that day, *that* I will seek to destroy all the nations that come against Je-rṳ'sa-lĕm.

10 [f]And I will pour upon the house of Dā'vid, and upon the inhabitants of Je-rṳ'sa-lĕm, the spirit of grace and of supplications: and they shall [g]look upon me whom they have pierced, and they shall mourn for him, as one mourneth for *his* only *son*, and shall be in bitterness for him, as one that is in bitterness for *his* firstborn.

11 In that day shall there be a great [h]mourning in Je-rṳ'sa-lĕm, as the mourning of Hā-dăd-rĭm'mon in the valley of Me-gĭd'don.

12 And the land shall mourn, [5]every family apart; the family of the house of Dā'vid apart, and their wives apart; the family of the house of Nā'than apart, and their wives apart;

13 The family of the house of Lē'vī apart, and their wives apart; the family [6]of Shĭm'e-ī apart, and their wives apart;

14 All the families that remain, every family apart, and their wives apart.

13 In that day there shall be [a]a fountain opened to the house of Dā'vid and to the inhabitants of Je-rṳ'salĕm for sin and for [1]uncleanness.

CHAPTER 11
2 [1]Or, gallants
[2]Or, the defenced forest
5 [a]Deut. 29.19; [b]Deut. 29.19;
6 [3]make to be found
7 [4]Or, verily the poor
[c]Zeph. 3.12;
[5]Or, Binders
8 [d]Hos. 5.7
[6]was straitened for them
9 [e]Jer. 15.2
[7]of his fellow, or, neighbour
11 [8]Or, the poor of the flock, etc., certainly knew
12 [9]If it be good in your eyes
[f]Ex. 21.32;
13 [g]Matt. 27.9
14 [10]Or, Binders
15 [h]Ezek. 34.2
16 [11]Or, hidden
[12]Or, bear
17 [i]Jer. 23.1;
[j]Mic. 3.6

CHAPTER 12
1 [a]Heb. 12.9
2 [1]Or, slumber, or, poison
[2]Or, and also against Judah shall he be which shall be in siege against Jerusalem
3 [b]Matt. 21.44
4 [c]Ps. 76.6
5 [3]Or, There is strength to me and to the inhabitants, etc
7 [d]1 Cor. 1.27-29-31
8 [e]Joel 3.10
[4]fallen, or, abject
10 [f]Joel 2.28
[g]Ps. 22.16;
11 [h]Acts 2.37
12 [5]families, families
13 [6]Or, of Simeon, as LXX

CHAPTER 13
1 [a]Isa. 1.16-17;
[1]separation for uncleanness

2 ¶ And it shall come to pass in that
day, saith the LORD of hosts, *that* I will
[b]cut off the names of the idols out of
the land, and they shall no more be
remembered: and also I will cause [c]the
prophets and the unclean spirit to pass
out of the land.
3 And it shall come to pass, *that*
when any shall yet prophesy, then his
[d]father and his mother that begat him
shall say unto him, Thou shalt not live;
for thou speakest lies in the name of the
LORD: and his father and his mother
that begat him shall thrust him through
when he prophesieth.
4 And it shall come to pass in that
day, *that* the prophets shall be ashamed every one of his vision, when he
hath prophesied; neither shall they
wear [2]a rough garment [3]to deceive:
5 But he shall say, I *am* no prophet, I
am an husbandman; for man taught
me to keep cattle from my youth.
6 And *one* shall say unto him, What
are these wounds in thine hands? Then
he shall answer, *Those* with which I was
wounded *in* the house of my friends.
7 ¶ Awake, O sword, against [e]my
shepherd, and against the man [f]*that is*
my fellow, saith the LORD of hosts:
[g]smite the shepherd, and the sheep
shall be scattered: and I will turn mine
hand upon [h]the little ones.
8 And it shall come to pass, *that* in
all the land, saith the LORD, two parts
therein shall be cut off *and* die; [i]but the
third shall be left therein.
9 And I will bring the third part
[j]through the fire, and will [k]refine them
as silver is refined, and will try them as
gold is tried: they shall call on my
name, and I will hear them: I will say, It
is my people: and they shall say, The
LORD *is* my God.

14

Behold, the day of the LORD cometh, and thy spoil shall be divided in the midst of thee.
2 For [a]I will gather all nations against Je-ru͏̮'sa-lĕm to battle; and the city
shall be taken, and the houses rifled,
and the women ravished; and half of
the city shall go forth into captivity,
and the residue of the people shall not
be cut off from the city.
3 Then shall the LORD go forth, and
fight against those nations, as when he
fought in the day of battle.
4 ¶ And his feet shall stand in that
day [b]upon the mount of Ŏl'īves, which
is before Je-ru͏̮'sa-lĕm on the east, and
the mount of Ŏl'īves shall cleave in the
midst thereof toward the east and toward the west, [c]*and there shall be* a
very great valley; and half of the mountain shall remove toward the north,
and half of it toward the south.
5 And ye shall flee *to* the valley of
[1]the mountains; [2]for the valley of the
mountains shall reach unto Ā'zăl: yea,
ye shall flee, like as ye fled from before
the [d]earthquake in the days of Ŭz-
zī'ah king of Jū'dah: [e]and the LORD
my God shall come, *and* [f]all the saints
with thee.
6 And it shall come to pass in that
day, [3]*that* the light shall not be [4]clear,
nor [5]dark:
7 But [6]it shall be one day which shall
be known to the LORD, not day, nor
night: but it shall come to pass, *that* at
[g]evening time it shall be light.
8 And it shall be in that day, *that*
living [h]waters shall go out from Je-
ru͏̮'sa-lĕm; half of them toward the
[7]former sea, and half of them toward
the hinder sea: in summer and in winter shall it be.
9 And the LORD shall be [i]king over
all the earth: in that day shall there be
[j]one LORD, and his name one.
10 All the land shall be [8]turned as a
plain from Gē'bȧ to Rĭm'mon south of
Je-ru͏̮'sa-lĕm: and it shall be lifted up,
and [9]inhabited in her place, from Bĕn'-
ja-min's gate unto the place of the first
gate, unto the corner gate, [k]and *from*
the tower of Ha-năn'e-el unto the king's
winepresses.
11 And *men* shall dwell in it, and
there shall be [l]no more utter destruction; but Je-ru͏̮'sa-lĕm [10]shall be safely
inhabited.
12 ¶ And this shall be the plague
wherewith the LORD will smite all the
people that have fought against Je-
ru͏̮'sa-lĕm; Their flesh shall consume
away while they stand upon their feet,
and their eyes shall consume away in
their holes, and their tongue shall consume away in their mouth.
13 And it shall come to pass in that
day, *that* [m]a great tumult from the
LORD shall be among them; and they
shall lay hold every one on the hand of
his neighbour, and his hand shall rise
up against the hand of his neighbour.
14 And [11]Jū'dah also shall fight [12]at
Je-ru͏̮'sa-lĕm; and the wealth of all the
heathen round about shall be gathered
together, gold, and silver, and apparel,
in great abundance.
15 And so shall be the plague of the
horse, of the mule, of the camel, and of
the ass, and of all the beasts that shall
be in these tents, as this plague.
16 ¶ And it shall come to pass, *that*
every one that is left of all the nations
which came against Je-ru͏̮'sa-lĕm shall
even [n]go up from year to year to worship [o]the King, the LORD of hosts, and
to keep [p]the feast of tabernacles.
17 [q]And it shall be, *that* whoso will
not come up of *all* the families of the
earth unto Je-ru͏̮'sa-lĕm to worship the
King, the LORD of hosts, even upon
them shall be no rain.
18 And if the family of Ē'ġypt go not
up, and come not, [13]that *have* no *rain;*
there shall be the plague, wherewith
the LORD will smite the heathen that
come not up to keep the feast of tabernacles.
19 This shall be the [14]punishment of
Ē'ġypt, and the punishment of all nations that come not up to keep the feast
of tabernacles.
20 ¶ In that day shall there be upon
the [15]bells of the horses, HOLINESS
UNTO THE LORD; and the pots in the

2 [b]Ex. 23.13
[c]2 Pet. 2.1
3 [d]Deut. 13.6
4 [2]a garment of hair
[3]to lie
7 [e]Isa. 40.11; Heb. 13.20
[f]John 10.30
[g]Isa. 53.4-6; Mark 14.27; John 1.29
[h]Luke 12.32
8 [i]Rom. 11.5
9 [j]Isa. 48.10
[k]Ps. 66.10; Isa. 48.10; Mal. 3.3; 1 Pet. 1.6-7; Rev. 2.10

CHAPTER 14
2 [a]Joel 3.2
4 [b]Ezek. 11.23; Acts 1.11-12
[c]Joel 3.12
5 [1]Or, my mountains
[2]Or, when he shall touch the valley of the mountains to the place he separated
[d]Amos 1.1
[e]Matt. 24.30
[f]Joel 3.11
6 [3]That is, it shall not be clear in some places, and dark in other places, of the world
[4]precious
[5]thickness
7 [6]Or, the day shall be one
[g]Rev. 21.23
8 [h]Ezek. 47.1
[7]Or, eastern
9 [i]Ps. 2.8
[j]Eph. 4.5-6
10 [8]Or, compassed
[9]Or, shall abide
[k]Neh. 3.1
11 [l]Jer. 31.40
[10]Or, shall abide
13 [m]1 Sam. 14.15
14 [11]Or, thou also, O Judah, shalt
[12]Or, against
16 [n]Isa. 66.23
[o]1 Tim. 6.15
[p]Lev. 23.34; Hos. 12.9
17 [q]Isa. 60.12
18 [13]upon whom there is not
19 [14]Or, sin
20 [15]Or, bridles

LORD'S house shall be like the bowls
before the altar.
21 [r]Yea, every pot in Je-rṳ'sa-lĕm
and in Jū'dah shall be holiness unto
the LORD of hosts: and all they that
sacrifice shall come and take of them,
and seethe therein: and in that day
there shall be no more the [s]Cā'-
năan-īte in the [t]house of the LORD of
hosts.

21 [r]Col. 3.17
[s]Isa. 35.8; Rev. 21.27
[t]Eph. 2.19

THE BOOK OF

MALACHI

Life's Questions

What interest does God have in my marriage?
Can I be sure God loves me?
Does God really expect a tithe?

God's Answers

God called the last of the prophets about 440 B.C. shortly after the ministry of Ezra and Nehemiah. The new temple was 75 years old. Political, religious, and economic conditions seemed to show no improvement. What more could God want from His people? Malachi showed what faithfulness means in a boring moment in history.

Malachi shows: God does not want you to doubt His love (1:1–5); God does not want you to profane His worship (1:6—2:9); God says to dishonor marriage agreements is to dishonor Him (2:10–16); God does not want you to doubt His justice (2:17—3:5); God does not want you to rob Him of His tithe (3:6–12); God wants you to know that honoring Him is worth the wait (3:13—4:6).

Malachi shows God is interested in every area of your life and is still at work to complete His plan of salvation .

1 The burden of the word of the LORD
to Is'ra-el [1]by Măl'a-chī.
2 I have loved you, saith the LORD.
Yet ye say, Wherein hast thou loved
us? *Was* not Ē'sạu Jā'cob's brother?
saith the LORD: yet [a]I loved Jā'cob,
3 And I hated Ē'sạu, and [b]laid his
mountains and his heritage waste for
the dragons of the wilderness.
4 Whereas Ē'dom saith, We are impoverished, but we will return and
build the desolate places; thus saith
the LORD of hosts, They shall build, but
I will throw down; and they shall call
them, The border of wickedness, and,
The people against whom the LORD
hath indignation for ever.
5 And your eyes shall see, and ye
shall say, [c]The LORD will be magnified
[2]from the border of Is'ra-el.
6 ¶ A son [d]honoureth *his* father, and
a servant his master: [e]if then I *be* a
father, where *is* mine honour? and if I
be a master, where *is* my fear? saith
the LORD of hosts unto you, O priests,
that despise my name. And ye say,
Wherein have we despised thy name?
7 [3]Ye offer polluted bread upon mine
altar; and ye say, Wherein have we polluted thee? In that ye say, [f]The table of
the LORD *is* contemptible.
8 And if ye offer the blind [4]for sacrifice, *is it* not evil? and if ye offer the
lame and sick, *is it* not evil? offer it
now unto thy governor; will he be
pleased with thee, or [g]accept thy person? saith the LORD of hosts.
9 And now, I pray you, beseech [5]God
that he will be gracious unto us: [h]this
hath been [6]by your means: will he regard your persons? saith the LORD of
hosts.
10 Who *is there* even among you
that would shut the doors *for nought?*
[i]neither do ye kindle *fire* on mine altar
for nought. I have no pleasure in you,
saith the LORD of hosts, [j]neither will I
accept an offering at your hand.
11 For [k]from the rising of the sun
even unto the going down of the same
my name *shall be* great among the
Gĕn'tīles; [l]and in every place [m]incense
shall be offered unto my name, and a
pure offering: [n]for my name *shall be*
great among the heathen, saith the
LORD of hosts.
12 ¶ But ye have profaned it, in that
ye say, The table of the LORD *is* polluted; and the fruit thereof, *even* his
meat, *is* contemptible.
13 Ye said also, Behold, what a weariness *is it!* [7]and ye have snuffed at it,
saith the LORD of hosts; and ye brought
that which was torn, and the lame, and
the sick; thus ye brought an offering:
[o]should I accept this of your hand?
saith the LORD.
14 [p]But cursed *be* the deceiver,
[8]which hath in his flock a male, and
voweth, and sacrificeth unto the Lord
a corrupt thing: for I *am* a great King,
saith the LORD of hosts, and my name
is dreadful among the heathen.

2 And now, O ye priests, this commandment *is* for you.
2 [a]If ye will not hear, and if ye will
not lay *it* to heart, to give glory unto
my name, saith the LORD of hosts, I
will even send a curse upon you, and I
will curse your blessings: yea, I have
cursed them already, because ye do
not lay *it* to heart.
3 Behold, I will [1]corrupt your seed,
and [2]spread dung upon your faces,
even the dung of your solemn feasts;
and [3]*one* shall take you away with it.
4 And ye shall know that I have sent
this commandment unto you, that my

CHAPTER 1
1 [1]by the hand of Malachi
2 [a]Gen. 25.23
3 [b]Ezek. 35.3
5 [c]Ps. 35.27; [2]from upon, or, upon
6 [d]Ex. 20.12; [e]Luke 6.46
7 [3]Or, Bring unto, etc [f]Ezek. 41.22
8 [4]to sacrifice [g]Job 42.8
9 [5]the face of God [h]Hos. 13.9 [6]from your hand
10 [i]1 Cor. 9.13; [j]Isa. 1.11
11 [k]Isa. 59.19 [l]John 4.21; [m]Rev. 8.3 [n]Isa. 66.19
13 [7]Or, whereas ye might have blown it away [o]Lev. 22.20
14 [p]Acts 5.1 [8]Or, in whose flock is

CHAPTER 2
2 [a]Deut. 28.15
3 [1]Or, reprove [2]scatter [3]Or, it shall take you away to it

covenant might be with Lē′vī, saith the
LORD of hosts.
5 [b]My covenant was with him of life
and peace; and I gave them to him [c]*for*
the fear wherewith he feared me, and
was afraid before my name.
6 The law of truth was in his mouth,
and iniquity was not found in his lips:
he walked with me in peace and equity, and did [d]turn many away from
iniquity.
7 [e]For the priest's lips should keep
knowledge, and they should seek the
law at his mouth: [f]for he *is* the messenger of the LORD of hosts.
8 But ye are departed out of the
way; ye have [g]caused many to [4]stum-
ble at the law; ye have corrupted the
covenant of Lē′vī, saith the LORD of
hosts.
9 Therefore have I also made you
contemptible and base before all the
people, according as ye have not kept
my ways, but [5]have been partial in the
law.
10 [h]Have we not all one father? [i]hath
not one God created us? why do we deal
treacherously every man against his
brother, by profaning the covenant of
our fathers?
11 ¶ Jū′dah hath dealt treacherously, and an abomination is committed in Ĭs′ra-el and in Je-rụ′sa-lĕm; for
Jū′dah hath profaned the holiness of
the LORD which he [6]loved, and [j]hath
married the daughter of a strange god.
12 The LORD will cut off the man
that doeth this, [7]the master and the
scholar, out of the tabernacles of Jā′-
cob, and him that offereth an offering
unto the LORD of hosts.
13 And this have ye done again, covering the altar of the LORD with tears,
with weeping, and with crying out, insomuch that he regardeth not the offering any more, or receiveth *it* with good
will at your hand.
14 ¶ Yet ye say, Wherefore? Because the LORD hath been witness between thee and the wife of thy youth,
against whom thou hast dealt treacherously: yet *is* she thy companion, and
the wife of thy covenant.
15 And [k]did not he make one? Yet
had he the [8]residue of the spirit. And
wherefore one? That he might seek [9]a
godly seed. Therefore take heed to
your spirit, and let none deal [10]treach-
erously against the wife of his youth.
16 For [l]the LORD, the God of Ĭs′ra-el,
saith [11]that he hateth [12]putting away:
for *one* covereth violence with his garment, saith the LORD of hosts: therefore
take heed to your spirit, that ye deal not
treacherously.
17 ¶ Ye have wearied the LORD with
your words. Yet ye say, Wherein have
we wearied *him?* When ye say, Every
one that doeth evil *is* good in the sight
of the LORD, and he delighteth in them;
or, Where *is* the God of judgment?
3 Behold, [a]I will send my messenger,
and he shall [b]prepare the way before me: [c]and the Lord, whom ye seek,
shall suddenly come to his temple,

5 [b]Num. 25.12
[c]Deut. 33.8
6 [d]Dan. 12.3
7 [e]Deut. 17.9
[f]Isa. 42.19
8 [g]1 Sam. 2.17
[4]Or, fall in the law
9 [5]accepted faces, or, lifted up the face against
10 [h]Isa. 51.2;
[i]Ps. 100.3
11 [6]Or, ought to love
[j]Neh. 13.23
12 [7]Or, him that waketh and him that answereth
15 [k]Matt. 19.4-5
[8]Or, excellency
[9]a seed of God
[10]Or, unfaithfully
16 [l]Deut. 24.1
[11]Or, if he hate her, put her away
[12]to put away
CHAPTER 3
1 [a]Mark 1.2
[b]Isa. 40.3
[c]Acts 7.38
[d]Isa. 63.9
[e]Hag. 2.7
2 [f]Rev. 6.17
[g]Isa. 4.4
3 [h]Isa. 1.25;
[i]Rom. 15.16
4 [1]Or, ancient
5 [j]1 Thess. 1.7;
[k]Jas. 5.4
[2]Or, defraud
6 [l]Num. 23.19;
[m]1 Sam. 15.29
7 [n]Acts 7.51
[o]Deut. 30.1-4
8 [p]Neh. 13.10
10 [q]Prov. 3.9
[r]1 Chr. 26.20
[s]Gen. 7.11
[3]empty out
11 [t]Amos 4.9
[4]corrupt
12 [u]Dan. 8.9
14 [v]Job 21.14;
[5]his observation
[6]in black
15 [w]Ps. 73.12
[7]are built
[x]Ps. 95.9
16 [y]Gen. 22.12;
[z]Heb. 3.13

[d]even the messenger of the covenant,
whom ye delight in: behold, [e]he shall
come, saith the LORD of hosts.
2 But who may abide the day of his
coming? and [f]who shall stand when he
appeareth? for [g]he *is* like a refiner's
fire, and like fullers' sope:
3 And [h]he shall sit *as* a refiner and
purifier of silver: and he shall purify
the sons of Lē′vī, and purge them as
gold and silver, that they may [i]offer
unto the LORD an offering in righteousness.
4 Then shall the offering of Jū′dah
and Je-rụ′sa-lĕm be pleasant unto the
LORD, as in the days of old, and as in
[1]former years.
5 [j]And I will come near to you to
judgment; and I will be a swift witness
against the sorcerers, and against the
adulterers, [k]and against false swear-
ers, and against those that [2]oppress the
hireling in *his* wages, the widow, and
the fatherless, and that turn aside the
stranger *from his right,* and fear not
me, saith the LORD of hosts.
6 For I *am* the LORD, [l]I change not;
[m]therefore ye sons of Jā′cob are not
consumed.
7 ¶ Even from the days of [n]your fathers ye are gone away from mine ordinances, and have not kept *them.* [o]Re-
turn unto me, and I will return unto
you, saith the LORD of hosts. But ye
said, Wherein shall we return?
8 ¶ Will a man rob God? Yet ye have
robbed me. But ye say, Wherein have
we robbed thee? [p]In tithes and offerings.
9 Ye *are* cursed with a curse: for ye
have robbed me, *even* this whole nation.
10 [q]Bring ye all the tithes into [r]the
storehouse, that there may be meat in
mine house, and prove me now herewith, saith the LORD of hosts, if I will
not open you the [s]windows of heaven,
and [3]pour you out a blessing, that
there shall not *be room* enough *to receive it.*
11 And I will rebuke [t]the devourer
for your sakes, and he shall not [4]de-
stroy the fruits of your ground; neither
shall your vine cast her fruit before the
time in the field, saith the LORD of
hosts.
12 And all nations shall call you
blessed: for ye shall be [u]a delightsome
land, saith the LORD of hosts.
13 ¶ Your words have been stout
against me, saith the LORD. Yet ye say,
What have we spoken *so much* against
thee?
14 [v]Ye have said, It *is* vain to serve
God: and what profit *is it* that we have
kept [5]his ordinance, and that we have
walked [6]mournfully before the LORD
of hosts?
15 And now [w]we call the proud
happy; yea, they that work wickedness [7]are set up; yea, *they that* [x]tempt
God are even delivered.
16 ¶ Then they [y]that feared the LORD
[z]spake often one to another: and the
LORD hearkened, and heard *it,* and a

book of remembrance was written before him for them that feared the LORD,
and that thought upon his name.
17 And they shall be mine, saith the
LORD of hosts, in that day when I make
up my [8]jewels; and I will spare them,
as a man spareth his own son that
serveth him.
18 Then shall ye return, and discern
between the righteous and the wicked,
between him that serveth God and him
that serveth him not.

4

For, behold, the day cometh, that
shall burn as an oven; and all the
proud, yea, and all that do wickedly,
shall be stubble: and the day that cometh shall burn them up, saith the LORD
of hosts, that it shall leave them neither root nor branch.
2 ¶ But unto you that fear my name
shall the [a]Sun of righteousness arise
with healing in his wings; and ye shall
go forth, and grow up as calves of the
stall.
3 [b]And ye shall tread down the
wicked; for they shall be ashes under
the soles of your feet in the day that I
shall do *this,* saith the LORD of hosts.
4 ¶ Remember ye the law of Mō'ses
my servant, which I commanded unto
him [c]in Hō'reb for all Is'ra-el, *with* the
statutes and judgments.
5 ¶ Behold, I will send you [d]E-lī'jah
the prophet [e]before the coming of the
great and dreadful day of the LORD:
6 And he shall [f]turn the heart of the
fathers to the children, and the heart of
the children to their fathers, lest I come
and smite the earth with [g]a curse.

17 [8]Or, special treasure

CHAPTER 4

2 [a]Luke 1.78; Eph. 5.14; 2 Pet. 1.19

3 [b]Mic. 7.10

4 [c]Deut. 4.10

5 [d]Matt. 11.14

[e]Joel 2.31

6 [f]Luke 1.17

[g]Dan. 9.26; Luke 19.27-43; Luke 21.20; Mark 13.14

The NEW TESTAMENT

THE GOSPEL ACCORDING TO

MATTHEW

Life's Questions

Is God King , or is He dead?
What does Jesus expect of citizens of His kingdom?
What does Jesus as King relate to Judaism as God's revealed religion?

God's Answers

About A.D. 65 God led a former Roman tax collector to collect and write down the teachings of Jesus, especially as those teachings related to faith in Him as compared to the Jewish religion. Matthew thus wrote a Gospel to the Jews showing how Jesus was the promised Messiah and King, fulfilling God's promises to the Jews and extending God's salvation to the nations.

Matthew shows: Jesus' birth fulfilled Jewish prophecy (1—2); obedient to the Father, Jesus invites people to kingdom service (3—4); Jesus taught God's way to live (5—7); Jesus' power and call reveal His authority (8—10); Jesus' call for faith, mercy, repentance, and obedience led to controversy (11—12); Jesus' kingdom teachings involve new and old understandings (ch. 13); knowingly facing rejection and death, Jesus calls for compassion, personal sacrifice, faith, and confession of Him as Messiah (14—17); Jesus described kingdom life as radical, childlike faith, forgiveness, and obedience (18—20); unbelieving authorities unable to interpret Scripture reject Jesus (21:1—23:36); Jesus reveals the future judgment (23:37—25:46); obeying God and Scripture, Jesus prepared to die (ch. 26); Jesus conquered death and sent His disciples on mission (26—28).

Matthew invites you to join Jesus, the Jewish Messiah, in kingdom living and in kingdom mission.

1 The book of the [a]generation of
Jē'sus Chrīst, [b]the son of Dā'vid,
[c]the son of Ā'brā-hăm.
2 Ā'brā-hăm begat Ī'saac; and Ī'-
saac begat Jā'cob; and Jā'cob begat
Jū'das and his brethren;
3 And Jū'das begat Phā'rēs and Zā'-
ră of Thā'mar; and [d]Phā'rēs begat
Ēs'rom; and Ēs'rom begat Ā'ram;
4 And Ā'ram begat A-mĭn'a-dăb; and
A-mĭn'a-dăb begat [e]Na-ăs'son; and Na-
ăs'son begat Săl'mŏn;
5 And Săl'mŏn begat Bō'ŏz [f]of Rā'-
chăb; and Bō'ŏz begat Ō'bed of Ruth;
and Ō'bed begat Jĕs'se;
6 And [g]Jĕs'se begat Dā'vid the king;
and [h]Dā'vid the king begat Sŏl'o-mon
of her *that had been the wife* of U-rī'as;
7 And [i]Sŏl'o-mon begat Ro-bō'am;
and Ro-bō'am begat A-bī'ȧ; and A-bī'ȧ
begat Ā'sȧ;
8 And Ā'sȧ begat Jŏs'a-phăt; and
Jŏs'a-phăt begat Jō'ram; and Jō'ram
begat O-zī'as;
9 And O-zī'as begat Jō'a-thăm; and
Jō'a-thăm begat Ā'chăz; and Ā'chăz
begat Ēz-e-kī'as;
10 And [j]Ēz-e-kī'as begat Ma-
năs'sēs; and Ma-năs'sēs begat Ā'mon;
and Ā'mon begat Jo-sī'as;
11 And [1]Jo-sī'as begat Jĕch-o-nī'as
and his brethren, about the time they
were [k]carried away to Băb'y̆-lon:
12 And after they were brought to
Băb'y̆-lon, Jĕch-o-nī'as begat Sa-lā'thi-
el; and Sa-lā'thi-el begat [l]Zo-rŏb'a-bĕl;
13 And Zo-rŏb'a-bĕl begat A-bī'ud;
and A-bī'ud begat E-lī'a-kĭm; and E-
lī'a-kĭm begat Ā'zôr;
14 And Ā'zôr begat Sā'dŏc; and Sā'-
dŏc begat Ā'chim; and Ā'chim begat
E-lī'ud;
15 And E-lī'ud begat Ē-le-ā'zar; and
Ē-le-ā'zar begat Măt'than; and Măt'-
than begat Jā'cob;
16 And Jā'cob begat Jō'seph the husband of Mā'ry̆, of whom was born
[m]Jē'sus, who is called Chrīst.
17 So all the generations from Ā'brā-
hăm to Dā'vid *are* fourteen generations;
and from Dā'vid until the carrying
away into Băb'y̆-lon *are* fourteen generations; and from the carrying away
into Băb'y̆-lon unto Chrīst *are* fourteen
generations.
18 ¶ Now the [n]birth of Jē'sus Chrīst
was on this wise: When as his mother
Mā'ry̆ was espoused to Jō'seph, before
they came together, she was found
with child of the Hō'ly̆ Ghōst.
19 Then Jō'seph her husband, being
a just *man,* and not willing [o]to make
her a publick example, was minded to
put her away privily.
20 But while he thought on these
things, behold, the angel of the Lord
appeared unto him in a dream, saying,
Jō'seph, thou son of Dā'vid, fear not to
take unto thee Mā'ry̆ thy wife: [p]for
that which is [2]conceived in her is of the
Hō'ly̆ Ghōst.
21 And she shall bring forth a son,
and thou shalt call his name [3]JĒ'SUS:
for [q]he shall save his people from their
sins.
22 Now all this was done, that it
might be fulfilled which was spoken of
the Lord by the prophet, saying,
23 [r]Behold, a virgin shall be with
child, and shall bring forth a son, and
[4]they shall call his name Ēm-măn'u-el,
which being interpreted is, [s]God with
us.

CHAPTER 1
1 [a]Luke 3.23 [b]Ps. 132.11; Rom. 1.3 [c]Gal. 3.16
3 [d]Ruth 4.18; 1 Chr. 2.5-9
4 [e]Num. 1.7
5 [f]Josh. 6.22; Heb. 11.31
6 [g]1 Sam. 16.1 [h]2 Sam. 12.24
7 [i]1 Ki. 11.43; 2 Chr. 13.7
10 [j]2 Ki. 20.21
11 [1]Some read, Josias begat Jakim, and Jakim begat Jechonias; 1 Chr. 3.15 [k]2 Ki. 25.11; Dan. 1.2
12 [l]Ezra 3.2
16 [m]Gen. 3.15
18 [n]Gal. 4.4
19 [o]Deut. 24.1
20 [p]Luke 1.35 [2]begotten
21 [3]That is, Saviour [q]Gen. 49.10
23 [r]Isa. 7.14 [4]Or, his name shall be called [s]Isa. 9.6

24 Then Jō'seph being raised from
sleep did as the angel of the Lord had
bidden him, and took unto him his
wife:
25 And knew her not till she had
brought forth her firstborn son: and he
called his name JĒ'SUS.

2 Now when [a]Jē'sus was born in
Bĕth'lĕ-hĕm of Jū-dæ'à in the days
of Hĕr'od the king, behold, there came
wise men [b]from the east to Je-rụ'sa-
lĕm,
2 Saying, [c]Where is he that is born
King of the Jews? for we have seen his
[d]star in the east, and are come to worship him.
3 When Hĕr'od the king had heard
these things, he was troubled, and all
Je-rụ'sa-lĕm with him.
4 And when he had gathered all the
[e]chief priests and [f]scribes of the people together, [g]he demanded of them
where Chrīst should be born.
5 And they said unto him, In Bĕth'-
lĕ-hĕm of Jū-dæ'à: for thus it is written
by the prophet,
6 And [h]thou Bĕth'lĕ-hĕm, *in* the land
of Jū'dà, art not the least among the
princes of Jū'dà: for out of thee shall
come a Governor, that [i]shall [1]rule my
people Is'ra-el.
7 Then Hĕr'od, when he had privily
called the wise men, inquired of them
diligently what time the star appeared.
8 And he sent them to Bĕth'lĕ-hĕm,
and said, Go and search diligently for
the young child; and when ye have
found *him*, bring me word again, that I
may come and worship him also.
9 When they had heard the king,
they departed; and, lo, the star, which
they saw in the east, went before them,
till it came and stood over where the
young child was.
10 When they saw the star, they rejoiced with exceeding great joy.
11 ¶ And when they were come into
the house, they saw the young child
with Mā'rȳ his mother, and fell down,
and [j]worshipped him: and when they
had opened their treasures, they [2]pre-
sented unto him gifts; gold, and frankincense, and myrrh.
12 And being warned of God [k]in a
dream that they should not return to
Hĕr'od, they departed into their own
country another way.
13 And when they were departed,
behold, the angel of the Lord appeareth to Jō'seph in a dream, saying,
Arise, and take the young child and his
mother, and flee into Ē'ġȳpt; and be
thou there until I bring thee word: for
Hĕr'od will seek the young child to destroy him.
14 When he arose, he took the young
child and his mother by night, and departed into Ē'ġȳpt:
15 And was there until the death of
Hĕr'od: that it might be fulfilled which
was spoken of the Lord by the prophet,
saying, [l]Out of Ē'ġȳpt have I called my
son.
16 ¶ Then Hĕr'od, when he saw that
he was mocked of the wise men, was
exceeding wroth, and sent forth, and
slew all the children that were in Bĕth'-
lĕ-hĕm, and in all the coasts thereof,
from two years old and under, according to the time which he had diligently
inquired of the wise men.
17 Then was fulfilled that which was
spoken by [m]Jĕr'e-mȳ the prophet, saying,
18 In Rā'mà was there a voice
heard, lamentation, and weeping, and
great mourning, Rā'chel weeping *for*
her children, and would not be comforted, because they are not.
19 ¶ But when Hĕr'od was dead, behold, an angel of the Lord appeareth in
a dream to Jō'seph in Ē'ġȳpt,
20 Saying, Arise, and take the young
child and his mother, and go into the
land of Is'ra-el: for they are dead which
sought the young child's life.
21 And he arose, and took the young
child and his mother, and came into the
land of Is'ra-el.
22 But when he heard that Är-chĕ-
lā'us did reign in Jū-dæ'à in the room of
his father Hĕr'od, he was afraid to go
thither: notwithstanding, being warned
of God in a dream, he turned aside [n]into
the parts of Găl'ĭ-lee:
23 And he came and dwelt in a city
called [o]Nāz'a-rĕth: that it might be fulfilled [p]which was spoken by the prophets, He shall be called a [3]Năz'a-rēne.

3 In those days came [a]Jŏhn the Băp'-
tĭst, preaching [b]in the wilderness of
Jū-dæ'à,
2 And saying, Repent ye: [c]for the
kingdom of heaven is at hand.
3 For this is he that was spoken of
by the prophet E-sā'ias, saying, The
[d]voice of one crying in the wilderness,
[e]Prepare ye the way of the Lord, make
his paths straight.
4 And [f]the same Jŏhn [g]had his raiment of camel's hair, and a leathern
girdle about his loins; and his meat
was [h]locusts and wild [i]honey.
5 Then went out to him Je-rụ'sa-
lĕm, and all Jū-dæ'à, and all the region
round about Jôr'dan,
6 And [j]were baptized of him in Jôr'-
dan, confessing their sins.
7 ¶ But when he saw many of the
Phăr'ĭ-sees and Săd'dū-çees come to
his baptism, he said unto them, O generation of vipers, who hath warned
you to flee from [k]the wrath to come?
8 Bring forth therefore fruits [1]meet
for repentance:
9 And think not to say within yourselves, [l]We have Ā'brā-hăm to *our* father: for I say unto you, that God is
able of these stones to raise up children unto Ā'brā-hăm.
10 And now also the ax is laid unto
the root of the trees: [m]therefore every
tree which bringeth not forth good
fruit is hewn down, and cast into the
fire.
11 [n]I indeed baptize you with water
unto repentance: but he that cometh
after me is mightier than I, whose
shoes I am not worthy to bear: [o]he

CHAPTER 2
1 [a]Dan. 9.24; Luke 2.4
[b]1 Ki. 4.30; Isa. 11.10
2 [c]Ps. 2.6; Luke 2.11
[d]Num. 24.17; Rev. 22.16
4 [e]Ps. 2.1
[f]2 Chr. 34.13; Luke 20.19
[g]Mal. 2.7
6 [h]Mic. 5.2; John 7.42
[i]Gen. 49.10; Ps. 2.1-6
[1]Or, feed; Isa. 40.11
11 [j]Ps. 2.12; John 5.23
[2]Or, offered; Ps. 22.29; Ps. 72.10; Isa. 49.7; Isa. 60.6
12 [k]Job 33.15; ch. 1.20
15 [l]Num. 24.8; Hos. 11.1
17 [m]Jer. 31.15
22 [n]ch. 3.13
23 [o]John 1.45;
[p]Judg. 13.5;
[3]That is, Branch, or, Separated one; Num. 6.2; Zech. 6.12

CHAPTER 3
1 [a]Mal. 3.1;
[b]Josh. 14.10
2 [c]Dan. 2.44
3 [d]Isa. 40.3;
[e]Luke 1.76
4 [f]Mark 1.6
[g]2 Ki. 1.8;
[h]Lev. 11.22
[i]Deut. 8.8
6 [j]Acts 19.4
7 [k]Rom. 5.9
8 [1]Or, answerable to amendment of life; 2 Cor. 7.1-11
9 [l]John 8.33
10 [m]Ps. 80.15-16;
11 [n]Mark 1.8;
[o]Isa. 4.4

shall baptize you with the Hō'lȳ Ghōst, and *with* fire:

12 [p]Whose fan *is* in his hand, and he will throughly purge his floor, and gather his wheat into the garner; but he will [q]burn up the chaff with unquenchable fire.

13 ¶ Then cometh Jē'sus [r]from Găl'ĭ-lee to Jôr'dan unto Jŏhn, to be baptized of him.

14 But Jŏhn forbad him, saying, I have need to be baptized of thee, and comest thou to me?

15 And Jē'sus answering said unto him, Suffer *it to be so* now: for thus it becometh us to [s]fulfil all righteousness. Then he suffered him.

16 And [t]Jē'sus, when he was baptized, went up straightway out of the water: and, lo, the heavens were opened unto him, and he saw [u]the Spirit of God descending like a dove, and lighting upon him:

17 And [v]lo a voice from heaven, saying, [w]This is my beloved Son, in whom I am well pleased.

4 Then was [a]Jē'sus led up of [b]the spirit into the wilderness to be [c]tempted of the devil.

2 And when he had [d]fasted forty days and forty nights, he was afterward an hungred.

3 And when the tempter came to him, he said, If thou be the Son of God, command that these stones be made bread.

4 But he answered and said, [e]It is written, [f]Man shall not live by bread alone, but by every word that proceedeth out of the mouth of God.

5 Then the devil taketh him up into [g]the holy city, and setteth him on a pinnacle of the temple,

6 And saith unto him, If thou be the Son of God, cast thyself down: for it is written, [h]He shall give his angels charge concerning thee: and in *their* hands they shall bear thee up, lest at any time thou dash thy foot against a stone.

7 Jē'sus said unto him, It is written again, [i]Thou shalt not tempt the Lord thy God.

8 Again, the devil taketh him up into an exceeding high mountain, and sheweth him all the kingdoms of the world, and the glory of them;

9 And saith unto him, All these things will I give thee, if thou wilt fall down and worship me.

10 Then saith Jē'sus unto him, Get thee hence, Sā'tan: for it is written, [j]Thou shalt worship the Lord thy God, and him only shalt thou serve.

11 Then the devil [k]leaveth him, and, behold, [l]angels came and ministered unto him.

12 ¶ Now [m]when Jē'sus had heard that Jŏhn was [1]cast into prison, he departed into Găl'ĭ-lee;

13 And leaving Nāz'a-rĕth, he came and dwelt in Ca-pêr'na-ŭm, which is upon the sea coast, in the borders of Zăb'u-lon and Nĕph'tha-lĭm:

12 [p]Mal. 3.3
[q]Mal. 4.1; ch. 13.30
13 [r]ch. 2.22
15 [s]Dan. 9.24
16 [t]Mark 1.10
[u]Isa. 11.2; John 1.32
17 [v]John 12.28
[w]Ps. 2.7; Col. 1.13

CHAPTER 4
1 [a]Mark 1.12; Luke 4.1
[b]1 Ki. 18.12; Acts 8.39
[c]Heb. 4.15
2 [d]Ex. 34.28
4 [e]Eph. 6.17
[f]Deut. 8.3
5 [g]Neh. 11.1
6 [h]Ps. 91.11
7 [i]Deut. 6.16
10 [j]Deut. 6.13
11 [k]Jas. 4.7
[l]Heb. 1.14
12 [m]Luke 3.20
[1]Or, delivered up
15 [n]Isa. 9.1-2
16 [o]Isa. 42.7; Luke 2.32
17 [p]Mark 1.14
[q]ch. 10.7
18 [r]Mark 1.16
[s]Matt. 16.18; John 1.42
19 [t]Ezek. 47.10; Luke 5.10
20 [u]Mark 10.28; Luke 18.28
21 [v]Mark 1.19; Luke 5.10
23 [w]ch. 9.35; Luke 4.15
24 [x]Isa. 52.13

CHAPTER 5
1 [a]Mark 3.13
3 [b]Ps. 51.17; 1 Cor. 1.26
4 [c]Isa. 61.2-3; Rev. 21.4
5 [d]Num. 12.3; Gal. 5.23
[e]Rom. 4.13
6 [f]Isa. 65.13
7 [g]Ps. 41.1
8 [h]Ps. 15.1-2;
[i]1 Cor. 13.12
9 [j]Heb. 12.14
10 [k]Mark 10.30

14 That it might be fulfilled which was spoken by E-sā'ias the prophet, saying,

15 The [n]land of Zăb'u-lon, and the land of Nĕph'tha-lĭm, *by* the way of the sea, beyond Jôr'dan, Găl'ĭ-lee of the Gĕn'tīles;

16 The [o]people which sat in darkness saw great light; and to them which sat in the region and shadow of death light is sprung up.

17 ¶ From [p]that time Jē'sus began to preach, and to say, [q]Repent: for the kingdom of heaven is at hand.

18 ¶ And [r]Jē'sus, walking by the sea of Găl'ĭ-lee, saw two brethren, Sī'mon [s]called Pē'tĕr, and Ăn'drew his brother, casting a net into the sea: for they were fishers.

19 And he saith unto them, Follow me, and I [t]will make you fishers of men.

20 And [u]they straightway left *their* nets, and followed him.

21 And [v]going on from thence, he saw other two brethren, Jāmes *the son* of Zēb'e-dee, and Jŏhn his brother, in a ship with Zēb'e-dee their father, mending their nets; and he called them.

22 And they immediately left the ship and their father, and followed him.

23 ¶ And Jē'sus went about all Găl'ĭ-lee, teaching [w]in their synagogues, and preaching the gospel of the kingdom, and healing all manner of sickness and all manner of disease among the people.

24 And his [x]fame went throughout all Sȳr'ĭ-ȧ: and they brought unto him all sick people that were taken with divers diseases and torments, and those which were possessed with devils, and those which were lunatick, and those that had the palsy; and he healed them.

25 And there followed him great multitudes of people from Găl'ĭ-lee, and *from* De-căp'ŏ-lis, and *from* Je-ru̦'sa-lĕm, and *from* Jū-dæ'ȧ, and *from* beyond Jôr'dan.

5 And seeing the multitudes, [a]he went up into a mountain: and when he was set, his disciples came unto him:

2 And he opened his mouth, and taught them, saying,

3 Blessed [b]*are* the poor in spirit: for theirs is the kingdom of heaven.

4 Blessed [c]*are* they that mourn: for they shall be comforted.

5 Blessed [d]*are* the meek: for [e]they shall inherit the earth.

6 Blessed *are* they which do hunger and thirst after righteousness: [f]for they shall be filled.

7 Blessed *are* the merciful: [g]for they shall obtain mercy.

8 Blessed [h]*are* the pure in heart: for [i]they shall see God.

9 Blessed *are* [j]the peacemakers: for they shall be called the children of God.

10 Blessed [k]*are* they which are persecuted for righteousness' sake: for theirs is the kingdom of heaven.

11 Blessed are ye, when *men* shall revile you, and persecute *you*, and shall say all manner of evil against you [1]falsely, for my sake.

12 Rejoice, and be exceeding glad: for great *is* your reward in heaven: for so persecuted they the prophets which were before you.

13 ¶ Ye are the salt of the earth: but if the salt have lost his savour, wherewith shall it be salted? it is thenceforth good for nothing, but to be cast out, and to be trodden under foot of men.

14 Ye [l]are the light of the world. A city that is set on an hill cannot be hid.

15 Neither do men light a candle, and put it under a [2]bushel, but on a candlestick; and it giveth light unto all that are in the house.

16 Let your light so shine before men, that [m]they may see your good works, and glorify [n]your Father which is in heaven.

17 ¶ Think [o]not that I am come to destroy the law, or the prophets: I am not come to destroy, but to fulfil.

18 For verily I say unto you, [p]Till heaven and earth pass, one jot or one tittle shall in no wise pass from the law, till all be fulfilled.

19 Whosoever [q]therefore shall break one of these least commandments, and shall teach men so, he shall be called the least in the kingdom of heaven: but whosoever shall do and teach *them*, the same shall be called great in the kingdom of heaven.

20 For I say unto you, That except your righteousness shall exceed [r]*the righteousness* of the scribes and Phăr′ĭ-sees, ye shall in no case enter into the kingdom of heaven.

21 ¶ Ye have heard that it was said [3]by them of old time, [s]Thou shalt not kill; and whosoever shall kill shall be in danger of the judgment:

22 But I say unto you, That whosoever [t]is angry with his brother without a cause shall be in danger of the judgment: and whosoever shall say to his brother, [4]Rācȧ, shall be in danger of the council: but whosoever shall say, Thou [5]fool, shall be in danger of hell fire.

23 Therefore if thou bring thy gift to the altar, and there rememberest that thy brother hath ought against thee;

24 Leave [u]there thy gift before the altar, and go thy way; first be reconciled to thy brother, and then come and offer thy gift.

25 Agree [v]with thine adversary quickly, whiles [w]thou art in the way with him; lest at any time the adversary deliver thee to the judge, and the judge deliver thee to the officer, and thou be cast into prison.

26 Verily I say unto thee, [x]Thou shalt by no means come out thence, till thou hast paid the uttermost farthing.

27 ¶ Ye have heard that it was said by them of old time, Thou shalt not commit adultery:

28 But I say unto you, That whosoever looketh [y]on a woman to lust after her hath committed adultery with her already in his heart.

29 And [z]if thy right eye [6]offend thee, pluck it out, and cast *it* from thee: for it is profitable for thee that one of thy members should perish, and not *that* thy whole body should be cast into hell.

30 And if thy right hand offend thee, cut it off, and cast *it* from thee: for it is profitable for thee that one of thy members should perish, and not *that* thy whole body should be cast into hell.

31 It hath been said, [a]Whosoever shall put away his wife, let him give her a writing of divorcement:

32 But I say unto you, That [b]whosoever shall put away his wife, saving for the cause of fornication, causeth her to commit adultery: and whosoever shall marry her that is divorced committeth adultery.

33 ¶ Again, ye have heard that it hath been said [7]by them of old time, [c]Thou shalt not forswear thyself, but [d]shalt perform unto the Lord thine oaths:

34 But I say unto you, [e]Swear not at all; neither by heaven; for it is [f]God's throne:

35 Nor by the earth; for it is his footstool: neither by Je-rụ′sa-lĕm; for it is the city of the great King.

36 Neither shalt thou swear by thy head, because thou canst not make one hair white or black.

37 But [g]let your communication be, Yea, yea; Nay, nay: for whatsoever is more than these cometh of evil.

38 ¶ Ye have heard that it hath been said, [h]An eye for an eye, and a tooth for a tooth:

39 But I say unto you, [i]That ye resist not evil: [j]but whosoever shall smite thee on thy right cheek, turn to him the other also.

40 And if any man will sue thee at the law, and take away thy coat, let him have *thy* cloke also.

41 And whosoever [k]shall compel thee to go a mile, go with him twain.

42 Give to him that asketh thee, and from [l]him that would borrow of thee turn not thou away.

43 ¶ Ye have heard that it hath been said, [m]Thou shalt love thy neighbour, [n]and hate thine enemy.

44 But I say unto you, [o]Love your enemies, bless them that curse you, do good to them that hate you, and pray [p]for them which despitefully use you, and persecute you;

45 That ye may be the children of your Father which is in heaven: for he maketh his sun to rise on the evil and on the good, and sendeth rain on the just and on the unjust.

46 For [q]if ye love them which love you, what reward have ye? do not even the publicans the same?

47 And if ye salute your brethren only, what do ye more *than others?* do not even the publicans so?

48 Be [r]ye therefore perfect, even as [s]your Father which is in heaven is perfect.

11 [1]lying
14 [l]Prov. 4.18; Phil. 2.15
15 [2]modius. It contained nearly a peck
16 [m]1 Pet. 2.12
[n]John 15.8; 1 Cor. 14.25
17 [o]Dan. 9.24; Gal. 3.24
18 [p]Luke 16.17
19 [q]Jas. 2.10
20 [r]Rom. 10.3
21 [3]Or, to them
[s]Ex. 20.13
22 [t]1 John 3.15
[4]That is, vain fellow
[5]Or, graceless wretch; John 8.44; Acts 13.10
24 [u]Job 42.8 1 Pet. 3.7
25 [v]Job 22.21;
[w]Job 22.21
26 [x]2 Thess. 1.9
28 [y]Gen. 34.2
29 [z]Mark 9.43
[6]Or, do cause thee to offend
31 [a]Deut. 24.1
32 [b]Rom. 7.3
33 [7]to the ancients
[c]Ex. 20.7;
[d]Deut. 23.23
34 [e]Jas. 5.12
[f]Isa. 66.1
37 [g]Col. 4.6
38 [h]Lev. 24.20
39 [i]Prov. 20.22;
[j]Isa. 50.6
41 [k]Mark 15.21
42 [l]Deut. 15.8
43 [m]Lev. 19.18
[n]Deut. 23.6
44 [o]Prov. 25.21;
[p]Luke 23.34
46 [q]Luke 6.32
48 [r]Gen. 17.1;
[s]Eph. 5.1

6 Take heed that ye do not your [1]alms
before men, to be seen of them: otherwise ye have no reward [2]of your Father which is in heaven.
2 Therefore [a]when thou doest *thine*
alms, [3]do not sound a trumpet before
thee, as the hypocrites do in the synagogues and in the streets, that they
may have glory of men. Verily I say
unto you, They have their reward.
3 But when thou doest alms, let not
thy left hand know what thy right
hand doeth:
4 That thine alms may be in secret:
and thy Father which seeth in secret
himself shall reward thee openly.
5 ¶ And when thou prayest, thou
shalt not be as the hypocrites *are:* for
they love to pray standing in the synagogues and in the corners of the streets,
that they may be seen of men. Verily I
say unto you, They have their reward.
6 But thou, when thou prayest, enter
[b]into thy closet, and when thou hast
shut thy door, pray to thy Father which
is in secret; and thy Father [c]which seeth
in secret shall reward thee openly.
7 But when ye pray, [d]use not vain
repetitions, as the heathen *do:* [e]for
they think that they shall be heard for
their much speaking.
8 Be not ye therefore like unto them:
for your [f]Father knoweth what things
ye have need of, before ye ask him.
9 After this manner therefore pray
ye: [g]Our Father which art in heaven,
[h]Hallowed be thy name.
10 Thy kingdom come. Thy will be
done in earth, [i]as *it is* in heaven.
11 Give us this day our [j]daily bread.
12 And forgive us our debts, as we
forgive our debtors.
13 And [k]lead us not into temptation,
but [l]deliver us from evil: For thine is
the kingdom, and the power, and the
glory, for ever. Amen.
14 For [m]if ye forgive men their trespasses, your heavenly Father will also
forgive you:
15 But [n]if ye forgive not men their
trespasses, neither will your Father forgive your trespasses.
16 ¶ Moreover [o]when ye fast, be
not, as the hypocrites, of a sad countenance: for they disfigure their faces,
that they may appear unto men to fast.
Verily I say unto you, They have their
reward.
17 But thou, when thou fastest,
anoint thine head, and wash thy face;
18 That thou appear not unto men to
fast, but unto thy Father which is in
secret: and thy Father, which seeth in
secret, shall reward thee openly.
19 ¶Lay [p]not up for yourselves treasures upon earth, where moth and rust
doth corrupt, and where thieves break
through and steal:
20 But [q]lay up for yourselves treasures in heaven, where neither moth
nor rust doth corrupt, and where
thieves do not break through nor steal:
21 For where your treasure is, there
will your heart be also.
22 The [r]light of the body is the eye:
if therefore thine eye be single, thy
whole body shall be full of light.
23 But if thine eye be evil, thy whole
body shall be full of darkness. If therefore the light that is in thee be darkness, [s]how great *is* that darkness!
24 ¶ No [t]man can serve two masters: for either he will hate the one, and
love the other; or else he will hold to
the one, and despise the other. [u]Ye cannot serve God and mammon.
25 Therefore I say unto you, [4]Take
no thought for your life, what ye shall
eat, or what ye shall drink; nor yet for
your body, what ye shall put on. Is not
the life more than meat, and the body
than raiment?
26 Behold [v]the fowls of the air: for
they sow not, neither do they reap, nor
gather into barns; yet your heavenly
Father feedeth them. Are ye not much
better than they?
27 Which of you by taking thought
can add one cubit unto his stature?
28 And why take ye thought for raiment? Consider the lilies of the field,
how they grow; they toil not, neither
do they spin:
29 And yet I say unto you, That even
Sŏl′o-mon in all his glory was not arrayed like one of these.
30 Wherefore, if God so clothe the
grass of the field, which to day is, and
to morrow is cast into the oven, *shall
he* not much more *clothe* you, O ye of
little faith?
31 Therefore take no thought, saying, What shall we eat? or, What shall
we drink? or, Wherewithal shall we be
clothed?
32 (For after all these things do the
Gĕn′tīles seek:) for [w]your heavenly Father knoweth that ye have need of all
these things.
33 But [x]seek ye first the kingdom of
God, and his righteousness; and all
these things shall be added unto you.
34 Take therefore no [5]thought for
the morrow: for the morrow shall take
thought for the things of itself. Sufficient unto the day *is* the evil thereof.
7 Judge [a]not, that ye be not judged.
2 For with what judgment ye judge,
ye shall be judged: [b]and with what
measure ye mete, it shall be measured
to you again.
3 And [c]why beholdest thou the mote
that is in thy brother's eye, but considerest not the beam that is in thine
own eye?
4 Or how wilt thou say to thy brother,
Let me pull out the mote out of thine
eye; and, behold, a beam *is* in thine own
eye?
5 Thou hypocrite, first cast out the
beam out of thine own eye; and then
shalt thou see clearly to cast out the
mote out of thy brother's eye.
6 ¶Give [d]not that which is holy unto
the dogs, neither cast ye your pearls
before swine, lest they trample them
under their feet, and turn again and
rend you.

CHAPTER 6
1 [1]Or, righteousness; 2 Cor. 9.9
[2]Or, with
2 [a]Rom. 12.8
[3]Or, cause not a trumpet to be sounded; 1 Cor. 10.31
6 [b]2 Ki. 4.33
[c]Jer. 17.10
7 [d]Eccl. 5.2
[e]1 Ki. 18.26
8 [f]Ps. 139.2
9 [g]Deut. 32.6; Heb. 12.9
[h]Lev. 10.3; Rev. 4.11
10 [i]Ps. 103.20
11 [j]Job 23.12; Prov. 30.8
13 [k]ch. 26.41; Rev. 3.10
[l]John 17.15; Gal. 1.4
14 [m]Mark 11.25; Col. 3.13
15 [n]ch. 18.35; Jas. 2.13
16 [o]Isa. 58.5
19 [p]Prov. 23.4; Jas. 5.1
20 [q]ch. 19.21; 1 Pet. 1.4
22 [r]Ps. 119.18
23 [s]Rom. 1.21
24 [t]Luke 16.13
[u]Gal. 1.10
25 [4]Be not anxiously careful; Ps. 55.22; Luke 12.22-23
26 [v]Job 38.41
32 [w]Ps. 23.1
33 [x]1 Ki. 3.13
34 [5]anxious thought
CHAPTER 7
1 [a]Ezek. 16.52
2 [b]Mark 4.24
3 [c]Luke 6.41
6 [d]Prov. 9.7-8

7 ¶ Ask, [e]and it shall be given you;
seek, and ye shall find; knock, and it
shall be opened unto you:
8 For [f]every one that asketh receiveth; and he that seeketh findeth; and to
him that knocketh it shall be opened.
9 Or what man is there of you, whom
if his son ask bread, will he give him a
stone?
10 Or if he ask a fish, will he give
him a serpent?
11 If ye then, being evil, know how
to give good gifts unto your children,
how much [g]more shall your Father
which is in heaven give good things to
them that ask him?
12 Therefore all things [h]whatsoever
ye would that men should do to you, do
ye even so to them: for this [i]is the law
and the prophets.
13 ¶ Enter [j]ye in at the strait gate:
[k]for wide *is* the gate, and broad *is* the
way, that leadeth to destruction, and
many there be which go in thereat:
14 [1]Because strait *is* the gate, and
narrow *is* the way, which leadeth unto
life, and few there be that find it.
15 ¶ Beware [l]of false prophets, which
[m]come to you in sheep's clothing, but
inwardly they [n]are ravening wolves.
16 Ye shall know them by their fruits.
[o]Do men gather grapes of thorns, or figs
of thistles?
17 Even so [p]every good tree bringeth forth good fruit; but a corrupt tree
bringeth forth evil fruit.
18 A good tree cannot bring forth
evil fruit, neither *can* a corrupt tree
bring forth good fruit.
19 Every tree that bringeth not forth
good fruit is hewn down, and cast into
the fire.
20 Wherefore by their fruits ye shall
know them.
21 ¶ Not every one that saith unto me,
[q]Lord, Lord, shall enter into the kingdom of heaven; but he that doeth the
will of my Father which is in heaven.
22 Many will say to me in that day,
Lord, Lord, have we [r]not prophesied
in thy name? and in thy name have
cast out devils? and in thy name done
many wonderful works?
23 And then will I profess unto them,
I never knew you: [s]depart from me, ye
that work iniquity.
24 ¶ Therefore [t]whosoever heareth
these sayings of mine, and doeth them,
I will liken him unto a wise man, which
built his house upon a rock:
25 And [u]the rain descended, and the
floods came, and the winds blew, and
beat upon that house; and [v]it fell not:
for it was founded upon a rock.
26 And every one that heareth these
sayings of mine, and doeth them not,
shall be likened unto a foolish man,
which built his house upon the sand:
27 And the rain descended, and the
floods came, and the winds blew, and
beat upon that house; and it fell: [w]and
great was the fall of it.
28 And it came to pass, when Jē′sus
had ended these sayings, [x]the people
were astonished at his doctrine:
29 For [y]he taught them as *one* having authority, and not as the scribes.

8 When he was come down from
the mountain, great multitudes followed him.
2 And, [a]behold, there came a leper
and worshipped him, saying, Lord, if
thou wilt, thou canst make me clean.
3 And Jē′sus put forth *his* hand, and
touched him, saying, I will; be thou
clean. And immediately his leprosy
was cleansed.
4 And Jē′sus saith unto him, [b]See
thou tell no man; but go thy way, shew
thyself to the priest, and offer the gift
that [c]Mō′ses commanded, for a testimony unto them.
5 ¶ And [d]when Jē′sus was entered
into Ca-pêr′na-ŭm, there came unto
him a centurion, beseeching him,
6 And saying, Lord, my servant lieth
at home sick of the palsy, grievously
tormented.
7 And Jē′sus saith unto him, I will
come and heal him.
8 The centurion answered and said,
Lord, I [e]am not worthy that thou
shouldest come under my roof: but
[f]speak the word only, and my servant
shall be healed.
9 For I am a man under authority,
having soldiers under me; and I say to
this *man*, Go, and he goeth; and to another, Come, and he cometh; and to
my servant, Do this, and he doeth *it*.
10 When Jē′sus heard *it*, he marvelled, and said to them that followed,
Verily I say unto you, I have not found
so great faith, no, not in Is′ra-el.
11 And I say unto you, [g]That many
shall come from the east and west, and
shall sit down with Ā′bră-hăm, and
Ī′saac, and Jā′cob, in the kingdom of
heaven.
12 But [h]the children of the kingdom
[i]shall be cast out into outer darkness:
there shall be weeping and gnashing
of teeth.
13 And Jē′sus said unto the centurion, Go thy way; and as thou hast believed, *so* be it done unto thee. And his
servant was healed in the selfsame
hour.
14 ¶ And [j]when Jē′sus was come
into Pē′têr's house, he saw [k]his wife's
mother laid, and sick of a fever.
15 And he touched her hand, and
the fever left her: and she arose, and
ministered unto them.
16 ¶ When [l]the even was come, they
brought unto him many that were possessed with devils: and he cast out the
spirits with *his* word, and healed all
that were sick:
17 That it might be fulfilled which
was spoken by E-sā′ias the prophet,
saying, Himself [m]took our infirmities,
and bare *our* sicknesses.
18 ¶ Now when Jē′sus saw great multitudes about him, he gave commandment to depart unto the other side.
19 And [n]a certain scribe came, and
said unto him, Master, I will follow
thee whithersoever thou goest.

7 [e]ch. 21.22; John 16.23
8 [f]Prov. 8.17; Acts 9.11
11 [g]Isa. 49.15; Rom. 8.32
12 [h]Luke 6.31
[i]Lev. 19.18; 1 Tim. 1.5
13 [j]Ezek. 18.30-32; Luke 14.33
[k]1 John 5.19
14 [1]Or, How
15 [l]Deut. 13.3; Col. 2.8
[m]Mic. 3.5; 2 Tim. 3.5
[n]Acts 20.29
16 [o]Luke 6.43
17 [p]Jer. 11.19
21 [q]Hos. 8.2; Jas. 1.22
22 [r]Num. 24.4; John 11.51
23 [s]Ps. 5.5; ch. 25.41
24 [t]Luke 6.47
25 [u]Acts 14.22; 2 Tim. 3.12
[v]2 Tim. 2.19; 1 Pet. 1.5
27 [w]Heb. 10.31; 2 Pet. 2.20
28 [x]ch. 13.54; Luke 4.32
29 [y]Isa. 50.4
CHAPTER 8
1 [a]Mark 1.40
4 [b]ch. 9.30;
[c]Lev. 14.3
5 [d]Luke 7.1
8 [e]Luke 15.19
[f]Ex. 15.26
11 [g]Gen. 12.3
12 [h]ch. 21.43
[i]ch. 13.42
14 [j]Mark 1.29;
[k]1 Cor. 9.5
16 [l]Mark 1.32
17 [m]Isa. 53.4
19 [n]Luke 9.57

20 And Jē′sus saith unto him, The
foxes have holes, and the birds of the
air *have* nests; but [o]the Son of man
hath not where to lay *his* head.
21 And [p]another of his disciples said
unto him, Lord, [q]suffer me first to go
and bury my father.
22 But Jē′sus said unto him, Follow
me; and let [r]the dead bury their dead.
23 ¶ And when he was entered into a
ship, his disciples followed him.
24 And, [s]behold, there arose a great
tempest in the sea, insomuch that the
ship was covered with the waves: but
he was asleep.
25 And his disciples came to *him*,
and awoke him, saying, Lord, save us:
we perish.
26 And he saith unto them, Why
[t]are ye fearful, O ye of little faith? Then
[u]he arose, and rebuked the winds and
the sea; and there was a great calm.
27 But the men marvelled, saying,
What manner of man is this, that even
the winds and the sea obey him!
28 ¶ And [v]when he was come to the
other side into the country of the Gĕr′-
gĕ-sēnes, there met him two possessed
with devils, coming out of the tombs,
exceeding fierce, so that no man might
pass by that way.
29 And, behold, they cried out, saying, What [w]have we to do with thee,
Jē′sus, thou Son of God? art thou come
hither to torment us before the time?
30 And there was a good way off
from them an herd of many [x]swine
feeding.
31 So the devils [y]besought him, saying, If thou cast us out, suffer us to go
away into the herd of swine.
32 And he said unto them, Go. And
when they were come out, they went
into the herd of swine: and, behold,
the whole herd of swine ran violently
down a steep place into the sea, and
perished in the waters.
33 And they that kept them fled, and
went their ways into the city, and told
every thing, and what was befallen to
the possessed of the devils.
34 And, behold, the whole city came
out to meet Jē′sus: and when they saw
him, they [z]besought *him* that he would
depart out of their coasts.
9 And he entered into a ship, and
passed over, [a]and came into his
own city.
2 And, [b]behold, they brought to him
a man sick of the palsy, lying on a bed:
[c]and Jē′sus seeing their faith said unto
the sick of the palsy; Son, be of good
cheer; [d]thy sins be forgiven thee.
3 And, behold, certain of the scribes
said within themselves, This *man* blasphemeth.
4 And Jē′sus [e]knowing their
thoughts said, Wherefore think ye evil
in your hearts?
5 For whether is easier, to say, *Thy*
sins be forgiven thee; or to say, Arise,
and walk?
6 But that ye may know that the
[f]Son of man hath power on earth to
forgive sins, (then saith he to the sick

20 [o]Ps. 22.6; Phil. 2.7-8
21 [p]Luke 9.59
[q]1 Ki. 19.20
22 [r]Eph. 2.1
24 [s]Mark 4.37; Luke 8.23
26 [t]Phil. 4.6
[u]Job 38.8-11; Nah. 1.4
28 [v]Mark 5.1
29 [w]2 Sam. 16.10; 2 Pet. 2.4
30 [x]Deut. 14.8
31 [y]Phil. 2.10
34 [z]Deut. 5.25; Acts 16.39
CHAPTER 9
1 [a]ch. 4.13
2 [b]Mark 2.3; Luke 5.8
[c]ch. 8.10
[d]Ps. 32.1-2; Eph. 1.7
4 [e]Ps. 139.2; Luke 11.17
6 [f]Mark 2.7-10; Eph. 1.7
9 [g]Mark 2.14; Luke 5.27
10 [h]Mark 2.15; Luke 5.29
11 [i]Isa. 64.5;
[j]Gal. 2.15
13 [k]Prov. 21.3;
[l]Isa. 55.6-7
14 [m]Mark 2.18
15 [n]John 3.29
[o]Acts 13.2
16 [1]Or, raw, or, unwrought cloth
18 [p]Mark 5.22
20 [q]Mark 5.25
22 [r]Mark 10.52
23 [s]Mark 5.38;
[t]2 Chr. 35.25
24 [u]Acts 20.10

of the palsy,) Arise, take up thy bed,
and go unto thine house.
7 And he arose, and departed to his
house.
8 But when the multitudes saw *it*,
they marvelled, and glorified God,
which had given such power unto men.
9 ¶ And [g]as Jē′sus passed forth from
thence, he saw a man, named Măt′-
thew, sitting at the receipt of custom:
and he saith unto him, Follow me. And
he arose, and followed him.
10 ¶ And [h]it came to pass, as Jē′sus
sat at meat in the house, behold, many
publicans and sinners came and sat
down with him and his disciples.
11 And when the Phăr′ĭ-sees saw *it*,
they said unto his disciples, Why eateth your Master [i]with publicans and
[j]sinners?
12 But when Jē′sus heard *that*, he
said unto them, They that be whole
need not a physician, but they that are
sick.
13 But go ye and learn what *that*
meaneth, I [k]will have mercy, and not
sacrifice: for I am not come to call the
righteous, [l]but sinners to repentance.
14 ¶ Then came to him the disciples
of Jŏhn, saying, [m]Why do we and the
Phăr′ĭ-sees fast oft, but thy disciples
fast not?
15 And Jē′sus said unto them, Can
[n]the children of the bridechamber
mourn, as long as the bridegroom is
with them? but the days will come,
when the bridegroom shall be taken
from them, and [o]then shall they fast.
16 No man putteth a piece of [1]new
cloth unto an old garment, for that
which is put in to fill it up taketh from
the garment, and the rent is made
worse.
17 Neither do men put new wine
into old bottles: else the bottles break,
and the wine runneth out, and the bottles perish: but they put new wine into
new bottles, and both are preserved.
18 ¶ While [p]he spake these things
unto them, behold, there came a certain ruler, and worshipped him, saying, My daughter is even now dead:
but come and lay thy hand upon her,
and she shall live.
19 And Jē′sus arose, and followed
him, and *so did* his disciples.
20 ¶ And, [q]behold, a woman, which
was diseased with an issue of blood
twelve years, came behind *him*, and
touched the hem of his garment:
21 For she said within herself, If I
may but touch his garment, I shall be
whole.
22 But Jē′sus turned him about, and
when he saw her, he said, Daughter,
be of good comfort; [r]thy faith hath
made thee whole. And the woman was
made whole from that hour.
23 And [s]when Jē′sus came into the
ruler's house, and saw [t]the minstrels
and the people making a noise,
24 He said unto them, [u]Give place:
for the maid is not dead, but sleepeth.
And they laughed him to scorn.

25 But when the people were put forth, he went in, and took her by the hand, and the maid arose.

26 And [2]the fame hereof went abroad into all that land.

27 ¶ And when Jē'sus departed thence, two blind men followed him, crying, and saying, [v]*Thou* son of Dā'-vid, have mercy on us.

28 And when he was come into the house, the blind men came to him: and Jē'sus saith unto them, Believe ye that I am able to do this? They said unto him, Yea, Lord.

29 Then touched he their eyes, saying, According to your faith be it unto you.

30 And [w]their eyes were opened; and Jē'sus straitly charged them, saying, See [x]*that* no man know *it.*

31 But [y]they, when they were departed, spread abroad his fame in all that country.

32 ¶ As [z]they went out, behold, they brought to him a dumb man possessed with a devil.

33 And when the devil was cast out, the dumb spake: and the multitudes marvelled, saying, It was never so seen in Is'ra-el.

34 But the Phăr'ĭ-sees said, He casteth out devils through the prince of the devils.

35 And [a]Jē'sus went about all the cities and villages, teaching in their synagogues, and preaching the gospel of the kingdom, and healing every sickness and every disease among the people.

36 ¶ But when he saw the multitudes, he was moved with compassion on them, because they [3]fainted, and were scattered abroad, as sheep having no shepherd.

37 Then saith he unto his disciples, [b]The harvest truly *is* plenteous, but the labourers *are* few;

38 Pray [c]ye therefore the Lord of the harvest, that he will send forth labourers into his harvest.

10

And [a]when he had called unto *him* his twelve disciples, he gave them power [1]*against* unclean spirits, to cast them out, and to heal all manner of sickness and all manner of disease.

2 Now the names of the twelve apostles are these; The first, Șī'mon, who [b]is called Pē'tēr, and Ăn'drew his brother; Jāmes *the son* of Zēb'e-dee, and Jŏhn his brother;

3 Phĭl'ĭp, and Bär-thŏl'ŏ-mew; Thŏm'as, and Măț'thew the publican; Jāmes *the son* of Ăl-phæ'us, and Lĕbbæ'us, whose surname was [2]Thăd-dæ'us;

4 Șī'mon [c]the Cā'năan-īte, and Jū'-das [d]Ĭs-căr'ĭ-ot, who also betrayed him.

5 These twelve Jē'sus sent forth, and commanded them, saying, Go not into the way of the Gĕn'tīles, and into *any* city of [e]the Sa-măr'ĭ-tans enter ye not:

6 But [f]go rather to the [g]lost sheep of the house of Is'ra-el.

7 And [h]as ye go, preach, saying, The kingdom of heaven is at hand.

8 Heal the sick, cleanse the lepers, raise the dead, cast out devils: freely ye have received, freely give.

9 [3]Provide neither gold, nor silver, nor brass in your purses,

10 Nor scrip for *your* journey, neither two coats, neither shoes, nor yet [4]staves: [i]for the workman is worthy of his meat.

11 And into whatsoever city or town ye shall enter, inquire who in it is worthy; and there abide till ye go thence.

12 And when ye come into an house, salute it.

13 And if the house be worthy, let your peace come upon it: but if it be not worthy, let your peace return to you.

14 And whosoever shall not receive you, nor hear your words, when ye depart out of that house or city, [j]shake off the dust of your feet.

15 Verily I say unto you, It shall be more tolerable for the land of Sŏd'om and Go-mŏr'rhȧ in the day of judgment, than for that city.

16 ¶ Behold, I send you forth as sheep in the midst of wolves: [k]be ye therefore wise as serpents, and [5]harmless as doves.

17 But beware of men: for they will deliver you up to the councils, and [l]they will scourge you in their synagogues;

18 And [m]ye shall be brought before governors and kings for my sake, for a testimony against them and the Gĕn'tīles.

19 But when they deliver you up, take no thought how or what ye shall speak: for [n]it shall be given you in that same hour what ye shall speak.

20 For [o]it is not ye that speak, but the Spirit of your Father which speaketh in you.

21 And [p]the brother shall deliver up the brother to death, and the father the child: and the children shall rise up against *their* parents, and cause them to be put to death.

22 And ye shall be hated of all *men* for my name's sake: [q]but he that endureth to the end shall be saved.

23 But [r]when they persecute you in this city, flee ye into another: for verily I say unto you, Ye shall not [6]have gone over the cities of Is'ra-el, till [s]the Son of man be come.

24 The disciple is not above *his* master, nor the servant above his lord.

25 It is enough for the disciple that he be as his master, and the servant as his lord. If they have called the master of the house [7]Be-ĕl'ze-bŭb, how much more *shall they call* them of his household?

26 Fear them not therefore: for there is nothing covered, that shall not be revealed; and hid, that shall not be known.

27 What I tell you in darkness, *that* speak ye in light: and what ye hear in the ear, *that* preach ye upon the house tops.

28 And [t]fear not them which kill the body, but are not able to kill the soul:

26 [2]Or, this fame; Isa. 52.13
27 [v]ch. 15.22; Luke 18.38
30 [w]Ps. 146.8; John 9.7-14-26
[x]Luke 5.14
31 [y]Mark 7.36
32 [z]Luke 11.14
35 [a]Mark 6.6; Luke 13.22
36 [3]Or, were tired and lay down
37 [b]Luke 10.2; 1 Thess. 5.12-13
38 [c]Acts 13.2; 2 Thess. 3.1

CHAPTER 10
1 [a]Mark 3.13; Luke 9.1
[1]Or, over
2 [b]ch. 4.18; John 1.42
3 [2]Or, Judas
4 [c]Acts 1.13
[d]John 13.26
5 [e]2 Ki. 17.24; John 4.9-20
6 [f]ch. 15.24; Acts 13.46
[g]Isa. 53.6; 1 Pet. 2.25
7 [h]Mark 6.12; Luke 10.1-2
9 [3]Or, get; 1 Sam. 9.7; Luke 22.35
10 [4]a staff
[i]Luke 10.7; 1 Tim. 5.18
14 [j]Acts 13.51; Acts 18.6
16 [k]Rom. 16.19;
[5]Or, simple; 1 Cor. 14.20
17 [l]Acts 5.40
18 [m]Acts 12.1
19 [n]Ex. 4.12;
20 [o]2 Sam. 23.2
21 [p]Mic. 7.6
22 [q]Dan. 12.12
23 [r]John 7.1;
[6]Or, end, or, finish
[s]ch. 16.28
25 [7]Beelzebul
28 [t]Isa. 8.12

but rather fear him which is able to destroy both soul and body in hell.

29 Are not two sparrows sold for a [8]farthing? and one of them shall not fall on the ground without your Father.

30 But [u]the very hairs of your head are all numbered.

31 Fear ye not therefore, ye are of more value than many sparrows.

32 Whosoever [v]therefore shall confess me before men, [w]him will I confess also before my Father which is in heaven.

33 But [x]whosoever shall deny me before men, him will I also deny before my Father which is in heaven.

34 Think not that I am come to send peace on earth: I came not to send peace, but a sword.

35 For I am come to set a man at variance [y]against his father, and the daughter against her mother, and the daughter in law against her mother in law.

36 And a man's foes *shall be* they of his own household.

37 He that loveth father or mother more than me is not worthy of me: and he that loveth son or daughter more than me is not worthy of me.

38 And he that taketh not his cross, and followeth after me, is not worthy of me.

39 He [z]that findeth his life shall lose it: and he that loseth his life for my sake shall find it.

40 ¶ He that receiveth you receiveth me, and he that receiveth me receiveth him that sent me.

41 He [a]that receiveth a prophet in the name of a prophet shall receive a prophet's reward; and he that receiveth a righteous man in the name of a righteous man shall receive a righteous man's reward.

42 And [b]whosoever shall give to drink unto one of these little ones a cup of cold *water* only in the name of a disciple, verily I say unto you, he shall in no wise lose his reward.

11 And it came to pass, when Jē'sus had made an end of commanding his twelve disciples, he departed thence to teach and to preach in their cities.

2 Now [a]when Jŏhn had heard in [b]the prison the works of Chrīst, he sent two of his disciples,

3 And said unto him, Art thou he [c]that should come, or do we look for another?

4 Jē'sus answered and said unto them, Go and shew Jŏhn again those things which ye do hear and see:

5 The [d]blind receive their sight, and the lame walk, the lepers are cleansed, and the deaf hear, the dead are raised up, and the [e]poor have the gospel preached to them.

6 And blessed is *he*, whosoever shall not be [f]offended in me.

7 ¶ And [g]as they departed, Jē'sus began to say unto the multitudes concerning Jŏhn, What went ye out into the wilderness to see? A reed shaken with the wind?

8 But what went ye out for to see? A man clothed in soft raiment? behold, they that wear soft *clothing* are in kings' houses.

9 But what went ye out for to see? A prophet? yea, I say unto you, [h]and more than a prophet.

10 For this is *he*, of whom it is written, [i]Behold, I send my messenger before thy face, which shall prepare thy way before thee.

11 Verily I say unto you, Among them that are born of women there hath not risen a greater than Jŏhn the Băp'tīst: notwithstanding he that is least in the kingdom of heaven is greater than he.

12 And [j]from the days of Jŏhn the Băp'tīst until now the kingdom of heaven [1]suffereth violence, and the violent take it by force.

13 For [k]all the prophets and the law prophesied until Jŏhn.

14 And if ye will receive *it*, this is [l]E-lī'ăs, which was for to come.

15 He [m]that hath ears to hear, let him hear.

16 ¶ But [n]whereunto shall I liken this generation? It is like unto children sitting in the markets, and calling unto their fellows,

17 And saying, We have piped unto you, and ye have not danced; we have mourned unto you, and ye have not lamented.

18 For Jŏhn came neither eating nor drinking, and they say, He hath a devil.

19 The Son of man came eating and drinking, and they say, Behold a man gluttonous, and a winebibber, [o]a friend of publicans and sinners. [p]But wisdom is justified of her children.

20 ¶ Then [q]began he to upbraid the cities wherein most of his mighty works were done, because they repented not:

21 Woe unto thee, Cho-rā'zin! woe unto thee, Bĕth-sā'ĭ-dȧ! for if the mighty works, which were done in you, had been done in Tȳre and Sī'dŏn, they would have repented long ago [r]in sackcloth and ashes.

22 But I say unto you, It shall be more tolerable for Tȳre and Sī'dŏn at the day of judgment, than for you.

23 And thou, Ca-pêr'na-ŭm, [s]which art exalted unto heaven, shalt be brought down to hell: for if the mighty works, which have been done in thee, had been done in Sŏd'om, it would have remained until this day.

24 But I say unto you, That it shall be more tolerable for the land of Sŏd'om in the day of judgment, than for thee.

25 ¶ At that time Jē'sus answered and said, I thank thee, O Father, Lord of heaven and earth, because thou [t]hast hid these things from the wise and prudent, and hast revealed them unto babes.

26 Even so, Father: for so it seemed good in thy sight.

29 [8]It is in value halfpenny farthing in the original, as being the tenth part of the Roman penny; ch. 18.28
30 [u]Acts 27.34
32 [v]Ps. 119.46; Rev. 2.13
[w]1 Sam. 2.30; Rev. 3.5
33 [x]ch. 26.70-75; 2 Tim. 2.12
35 [y]Mic. 7.6; Mark 13.12
39 [z]ch. 16.25; Rev. 2.10
41 [a]1 Ki. 17.10;
42 [b]ch. 25.40;
CHAPTER 11
2 [a]Luke 7.18
[b]ch. 14.3;
3 [c]Gen. 49.10
5 [d]Isa. 29.18;
[e]Ps. 22.26
6 [f]Isa. 8.14
7 [g]Luke 7.24
9 [h]Luke 1.76
10 [i]Mal. 3.1
12 [j]Luke 16.16
[1]Or, is gotten by force, and they that thrust men
13 [k]Mal. 4.6
14 [l]Mal. 4.5
15 [m]ch. 13.9-43
16 [n]Luke 7.31
19 [o]ch. 9.10;
[p]Luke 7.29-35
20 [q]Luke 10.13
21 [r]Jon. 3.8
23 [s]Isa. 14.13
25 [t]Ps. 8.2

27 All [u]things are delivered unto me
of my Father: and no man knoweth the
Son, but the Father; neither [v]knoweth
any man the Father, save the Son, and
he to whomsoever the Son will reveal
him.
28 ¶ Come unto me, all *ye* that labour and are heavy laden, and I will
give you rest.
29 Take my yoke upon you, [w]and
learn of me; for I am meek and lowly
[x]in heart: and [y]ye shall find rest unto
your souls.
30 For [z]my yoke *is* easy, and my burden is light.

12 At that time [a]Jē′sus went on the
sabbath day through the corn;
and his disciples were an hungred, and
began to pluck the ears of corn, and to
eat.
2 But when the Phăr′ĭ-sees saw *it*,
they said unto him, Behold, thy disciples do that which is not lawful to do
upon the sabbath day.
3 But he said unto them, Have ye not
read [b]what Dā′vid did, when he was
an hungred, and they that were with
him;
4 How he entered into the house
of God, and did eat [c]the shewbread,
which was not lawful for him to eat,
neither for them which were with him,
[d]but only for the priests?
5 Or have ye not read in the [e]law,
how that on the sabbath days the
priests in the temple profane the sabbath, and are blameless?
6 But I say unto you, That in this
place is *one* [f]greater than the temple.
7 But if ye had known what *this*
meaneth, I [g]will have mercy, and not
sacrifice, ye would not have condemned
the guiltless.
8 For the [h]Son of man is Lord even
of the sabbath day.
9 And [i]when he was departed thence,
he went into their synagogue:
10 ¶ And, behold, there was a man
which had *his* hand withered. And
they asked him, saying, [j]Is it lawful to
heal on the sabbath days? that they
might accuse him.
11 And he said unto them, What
man shall there be among you, that
shall have one sheep, and [k]if it fall into
a pit on the sabbath day, will he not lay
hold on it, and lift *it* out?
12 How much then is a man better
than a sheep? Wherefore it is lawful to
do well on the sabbath days.
13 Then saith he to the man, Stretch
forth thine hand. And he stretched *it*
forth; and it was restored whole, like
as the other.
14 ¶ Then [l]the Phăr′ĭ-sees went out,
and [1]held a council against him, how
they might destroy him.
15 But when Jē′sus [m]knew *it*, [n]he
withdrew himself from thence: and
great multitudes followed him, and he
healed them all;
16 And charged them that they
should not make him known:
17 That it might be fulfilled which
was spoken by E-sā′ias the prophet,
saying,
18 Behold [o]my servant, whom I have
chosen; my beloved, in whom my soul
is well pleased: I will put my [p]spirit
upon him, and he shall shew judgment
to the Gĕn′tīles.
19 He shall not strive, nor cry; neither shall any man hear his voice in the
streets.
20 A [q]bruised reed shall he not
break, and smoking flax shall he not
quench, till he send forth judgment
unto victory.
21 And in his name shall the Gĕn′-
tīles trust.
22 ¶ Then [r]was brought unto him
one possessed with a devil, blind, and
dumb: and he healed him, insomuch
that the blind and dumb both spake
and saw.
23 And all the people were amazed,
and said, Is not this [s]the son of Dā′vid?
24 But [t]when the Phăr′ĭ-sees heard
it, they said, This *fellow* doth not cast
out devils, but by [2]Be-ĕl′ze-bŭb the
prince of the devils.
25 And Jē′sus [u]knew their thoughts,
and said unto them, Every [v]kingdom
divided against itself is brought to desolation; and every city or house divided
against itself shall not stand:
26 And if Sā′tan cast out Sā′tan, he
is divided against himself; how shall
then his kingdom stand?
27 And if I by Be-ĕl′ze-bŭb cast out
devils, by whom do your children cast
them out? therefore they shall be your
judges.
28 But if I cast out devils by the
Spirit of God, then [w]the kingdom of
God is come unto you.
29 Or [x]else how can one enter into
a strong man's house, and spoil his
goods, except he first bind the strong
man? and then he will spoil his house.
30 He that is not with me is against
me; and he that gathereth not with me
scattereth abroad.
31 ¶ Wherefore I say unto you, [y]All
manner of sin and blasphemy shall
be forgiven unto men: [z]but the blasphemy *against* the Hō′lȳ Ghōst shall
not be forgiven unto men.
32 And whosoever [a]speaketh a word
against the Son of man, [b]it shall be
forgiven him: but whosoever speaketh
against the Hō′lȳ Ghōst, it shall not be
forgiven him, neither in this world, neither in the *world* to come.
33 Either make the tree good, and
his [c]fruit good; or else make the tree
corrupt, and his fruit corrupt: for the
tree is known by *his* fruit.
34 O [d]generation of vipers, how can
ye, being evil, speak good things? [e]for
out of the abundance of the heart the
mouth speaketh.
35 A good man out of the good treasure of the heart bringeth forth good
things: and an evil man out of the evil
treasure bringeth forth evil things.
36 But I say unto you, That every
[f]idle word that men shall speak, they

27 [u]ch. 28.18; Eph. 1.21
[v]John 1.18; John 10.15
29 [w]Phil. 2.5; 1 John 2.6
[x]Zech. 9.9; Phil. 2.7-8
[y]Jer. 6.16
30 [z]1 John 5.3

CHAPTER 12
1 [a]Deut. 23.25; Mark 2.23
3 [b]1 Sam. 21.6
4 [c]Ex. 25.30; Lev. 24.5
[d]Ex. 29.32; Lev. 24.9
5 [e]Num. 28.9; John 7.22
6 [f]1 Chr. 6.18; Mal. 3.1
7 [g]Hos. 6.6; Mic. 6.6
8 [h]Dan. 7.13; Luke 6.5
9 [i]Mark 3.1; Luke 6.6
10 [j]Luke 13.14; John 9.16
11 [k]Ex. 23.4; Deut. 22.4
14 [l]Mark 3.6; John 11.53
[1]Or, took counsel
15 [m]Heb. 4.13; Ps. 139.2
[n]Mark 3.7
18 [o]Isa. 42.1;
[p]Isa. 11.2
20 [q]Isa. 40.11
22 [r]Mark 3.11
23 [s]Rom. 9.5
24 [t]Mark 3.22
[2]Beelzebul
25 [u]ch. 9.4;
[v]Gal. 5.15
28 [w]Dan. 2.44
29 [x]Isa. 49.24
31 [y]Mark 3.28;
[z]Acts 7.51
32 [a]ch. 11.19;
[b]1 Tim. 1.13
33 [c]ch. 7.17
34 [d]ch. 3.7;
[e]Luke 6.45
36 [f]Eph. 5.4

shall give account thereof in the day of
judgment.
37 For by thy words thou shalt be
justified, and by thy words thou shalt
be condemned.
38 ¶ Then [g]certain of the scribes and
of the Phăr'ĭ-sees answered, saying,
Master, we would see a sign from thee.
39 But he answered and said unto
them, An evil and [h]adulterous generation seeketh after a sign; and there
shall no sign be given to it, but the sign
of the prophet Jō'nas:
40 For [i]as Jō'nas was three days
and three nights in the whale's belly;
so shall the Son of man be three days
and three nights in the heart of the
earth.
41 The [j]men of Nĭn'e-veh shall rise
in judgment with this generation, and
[k]shall condemn it: [l]because they repented at the preaching of Jō'nas; and,
behold, [m]a greater than Jō'nas *is* here.
42 The [n]queen of the south shall
rise up in the judgment with this generation, and shall condemn it: for she
came from the uttermost parts of the
earth to hear the wisdom of Sŏl'o-mon;
and, behold, a [o]greater than Sŏl'o-
mon *is* here.
43 When [p]the unclean spirit is gone
out of a man, [q]he walketh through dry
places, seeking rest, and findeth none.
44 Then he saith, I will return into
my house from whence I came out; and
when he is come, he findeth *it* empty,
swept, and garnished.
45 Then goeth he, and taketh with
himself seven other spirits more wicked
than himself, and they enter in and
dwell there: and [r]the last *state* of
that man is worse than the first. Even
so shall it be also unto this wicked
generation.
46 ¶ While he yet talked to the people, behold, [s]*his* mother and his [t]breth-
ren stood without, desiring to speak
with him.
47 Then one said unto him, Behold,
thy mother and thy brethren stand
without, desiring to speak with thee.
48 But he answered and said unto
him that told him, Who is my mother?
and who are my brethren?
49 And he stretched forth his hand
toward his disciples, and said, Behold
my mother and my brethren!
50 For [u]whosoever shall do the will
of my Father which is in heaven, the
same is my brother, and sister, and
mother.

13 The same day went Jē'sus out of
the house, [a]and sat by the sea
side.
2 And [b]great multitudes were gathered together unto him, so that [c]he
went into a ship, and sat; and the
whole multitude stood on the shore.
3 And he spake many things unto
them in parables, saying, Behold, a
sower went forth to sow;
4 And when he sowed, some *seeds*
fell by the way side, and the fowls
came and devoured them up:

38 [g]ch. 16.1; 1 Cor. 1.22
39 [h]Isa. 57.3; John 4.48
40 [i]Jon. 1.17
41 [j]Luke 11.32
[k]Jer. 3.11; Ezek. 16.51
[l]Jon. 3.5
[m]Isa. 9.6
42 [n]1 Ki. 10.1; 2 Chr. 9.1
[o]Col. 2.2-3
43 [p]Luke 11.24
[q]Job 1.7; 1 Pet. 5.8
45 [r]Heb. 6.4; 2 Pet. 2.20
46 [s]Mark 3.31; Luke 8.19
[t]Mark 6.3; Gal. 1.19
50 [u]ch. 25.40-45; Heb. 2.11
CHAPTER 13
1 [a]Mark 4.1
2 [b]Gen. 49.10; Luke 8.4
[c]Luke 5.3
5 [d]Ezek. 11.19
6 [e]Col. 2.7
8 [f]Gen. 26.12
9 [g]Mark 4.9
11 [h]ch. 11.25; Col. 1.26
12 [i]ch. 25.29; Luke 19.26
14 [j]Isa. 6.9; 2 Cor. 3.14
15 [k]Zech. 7.11; Heb. 5.11
16 [l]ch. 16.17; 2 Cor. 4.6
17 [m]Heb. 11.13; 1 Pet. 1.10
18 [n]Mark 4.14; Luke 8.11
19 [o]2 Cor. 2.11
20 [p]Isa. 58.2; John 5.35
21 [q]ch. 11.6; 2 Tim. 1.15
22 [r]ch. 19.23; 2 Tim. 4.10
[s]Jer. 4.3

5 Some fell upon [d]stony places,
where they had not much earth: and
forthwith they sprung up, because they
had no deepness of earth:
6 And when the sun was up, they
were scorched; and because they had
no [e]root, they withered away.
7 And some fell among thorns; and
the thorns sprung up, and choked them:
8 But other fell into good ground, and
brought forth fruit, some [f]an hundredfold, some sixtyfold, some thirtyfold.
9 Who [g]hath ears to hear, let him
hear.
10 And the disciples came, and said
unto him, Why speakest thou unto
them in parables?
11 He answered and said unto them,
Because [h]it is given unto you to know
the mysteries of the kingdom of heaven,
but to them it is not given.
12 For [i]whosoever hath, to him shall
be given, and he shall have more abundance: but whosoever hath not, from
him shall be taken away even that he
hath.
13 Therefore speak I to them in parables: because they seeing see not; and
hearing they hear not, neither do they
understand.
14 And in them is fulfilled the prophecy of E-sā'ias, which saith, By [j]hear-
ing ye shall hear, and shall not understand; and seeing ye shall see, and
shall not perceive:
15 For this people's heart is waxed
gross, and *their* ears [k]are dull of hearing, and their eyes they have closed; lest
at any time they should see with *their*
eyes, and hear with *their* ears, and
should understand with *their* heart, and
should be converted, and I should heal
them.
16 But [l]blessed *are* your eyes, for
they see: and your ears, for they hear.
17 For verily I say unto you, That
many [m]prophets and righteous *men*
have desired to see *those things* which
ye see, and have not seen *them;* and to
hear *those things* which ye hear, and
have not heard *them.*
18 ¶ Hear [n]ye therefore the parable
of the sower.
19 When any one heareth the word
of the kingdom, and understandeth *it*
not, then cometh [o]the wicked *one,* and
catcheth away that which was sown in
his heart. This is he which received
seed by the way side.
20 But he that received the seed into
stony places, the same is he that heareth the word, and anon with [p]joy receiveth it;
21 Yet hath he not root in himself,
but dureth for a while: for when tribulation or persecution ariseth because of
the word, by and by [q]he is offended.
22 He [r]also that received seed among
[s]the thorns is he that heareth the word;
and the care of this world, and the deceitfulness of riches, choke the word,
and he becometh unfruitful.
23 But he that received seed into the
good ground is he that heareth the word,
and understandeth *it;* which also bear-

eth fruit, and bringeth forth, some an hundredfold, some sixty, some thirty.

24 ¶ Another parable put he forth unto them, saying, The kingdom of heaven is likened unto a man which sowed good seed in his field:

25 But while men slept, [t]his enemy came and sowed tares among the wheat, and went his way.

26 But when the blade was sprung up, and brought forth fruit, then appeared the tares also.

27 So the servants of the householder came and said unto him, Sir, didst not thou sow good seed in thy field? from whence then hath it tares?

28 He said unto them, An enemy hath done this. The servants said unto him, Wilt thou then that we go and gather them up?

29 But he said, Nay; lest while ye gather up the tares, ye root up also the wheat with them.

30 Let both grow together until the harvest: and in the time of harvest I will say to the reapers, Gather ye together first the tares, and bind them in bundles to burn them: but [u]gather the wheat into my barn.

31 ¶ Another parable put he forth unto them, saying, [v]The kingdom of heaven is like to a grain of mustard seed, which a man took, and sowed in his field:

32 Which indeed is the least of all seeds: but when it is grown, it is the greatest among herbs, and becometh a tree, so that the birds of the air come and lodge in the branches thereof.

33 ¶ Another [w]parable spake he unto them; The kingdom of heaven is like unto leaven, which a woman took, and hid in three [1]measures of meal, till the whole was leavened.

34 All these things spake Jē'sus unto the multitude in parables; and without a parable spake he not unto them:

35 That it might be fulfilled which was spoken by the prophet, saying, [x]I will open my mouth in parables; [y]I will utter things which have been kept secret from the foundation of the world.

36 Then Jē'sus sent the multitude away, and went into the house: and his disciples came unto him, saying, Declare unto us the parable of the tares of the field.

37 He answered and said unto them, He that [z]soweth the good seed is the Son of man;

38 The [a]field is the world; the good seed are the children of the kingdom; but the tares are [b]the children of the wicked *one;*

39 The enemy that sowed them is the devil; [c]the harvest is the end of the world; and the reapers are the angels.

40 As therefore the tares are gathered and burned in the fire; so shall it be in the end of this world.

41 The Son of man shall send forth his angels, [d]and they shall gather out of his kingdom all [2]things that offend, and them which do iniquity;

42 And [e]shall cast them into a furnace of fire: there shall be wailing and gnashing of teeth.

43 Then [f]shall the righteous shine forth as the sun in the kingdom of their Father. Who hath ears to hear, let him hear.

44 ¶ Again, the kingdom of heaven is like unto treasure hid in a field; the which when a man hath found, he hideth, and for joy thereof goeth and [g]selleth all that he hath, and [h]buyeth that field.

45 ¶ Again, the kingdom of heaven is like unto a merchant man, seeking goodly pearls:

46 Who, when he had found [i]one pearl of great price, went and sold all that he had, and bought it.

47 ¶ Again, the kingdom of heaven is like unto a net, that was cast into the sea, and gathered [j]of every kind:

48 Which, when it was full, they drew to shore, and sat down, and gathered the good into vessels, but cast the bad away.

49 So shall it be at the end of the world: the angels shall come forth, and sever the wicked from among the just,

50 And shall cast them into the furnace of fire: there shall be wailing and gnashing of teeth.

51 Jē'sus saith unto them, Have ye understood all these things? They say unto him, Yea, Lord.

52 Then said he unto them, Therefore every scribe *which is* instructed unto the kingdom of heaven is like unto a man *that is* an householder, which bringeth forth out of his treasure [k]*things* new and old.

53 ¶ And it came to pass, *that* when Jē'sus had finished these parables, he departed thence.

54 And [l]when he was come into his own country, he taught them in their synagogue, insomuch that they were astonished, and said, Whence hath this *man* this wisdom, and *these* mighty works?

55 Is [m]not this the carpenter's son? is not his mother called Mā'rȳ? and [n]his brethren, [o]Jāmes, and Jō'sēs, and Sī'mon, and Jū'das?

56 And his sisters, are they not all with us? Whence then hath this *man* all these things?

57 And they [p]were offended in him. But Jē'sus said unto them, A [q]prophet is not without honour, save in his own country, and in his own house.

58 And [r]he did not many mighty works there because of their unbelief.

14 At that time [a]Hĕr'od the tetrarch heard of the fame of Jē'sus,

2 And said unto his servants, This is Jŏhn the Băp'tĭst; he is risen from the dead; and therefore mighty works [1]do shew forth themselves in him.

3 ¶ For [b]Hĕr'od had laid hold on Jŏhn, and bound him, and put *him* in prison for He-rō'dĭ-as' sake, his brother Phĭl'ĭp's wife.

4 For Jŏhn said unto him, [c]It is not lawful for thee to have her.

25 [t]Luke 10.19; 1 Pet. 5.8
30 [u]ch. 3.12; 2 Thess. 2.1
31 [v]Isa. 2.2-3; 2 Pet. 3.18
33 [w]Luke 13.20
[1]The word in the Greek is a measure containing about a peck and a half, wanting a little more than a pint
35 [x]Ps. 49.4; Ps. 78.2
[y]Rom. 16-25; Eph. 3.9
37 [z]Isa. 61.1
38 [a]Gen. 12.3; Mal. 1.11
[b]Gen. 3.13; 1 John 3.7-8-10
39 [c]Joel 3.13; Rev. 14.15
41 [d]ch. 24.31; 2 Pet. 2.1-2
[2]Or, scandals
42 [e]ch. 3.12; Rev. 20.10
43 [f]Prov. 4.18; Rev. 7.9
44 [g]Phil. 3.7
[h]Isa. 55.1; Rev. 3.18
46 [i]Prov. 2.4; Prov. 8.10
47 [j]ch. 22.10
52 [k]Song 7.13
54 [l]Deut. 18.15; Luke 4.16
55 [m]Isa. 49.7; Mark 6.3
[n]ch. 12.46
[o]Mark 15.40
57 [p]Ps. 22.6; ch. 26.31
[q]Luke 4.24; John 4.44
58 [r]Heb. 3.19;
CHAPTER 14
1 [a]Mark 6.14
2 [1]Or, are wrought by him
3 [b]Prov. 10.17
4 [c]Lev. 18.16

5 And when he would have put him
to death, he feared the multitude, [d]be-
cause they counted him as a prophet.
6 But when Hĕr′od's [e]birthday was
kept, the daughter of He-rō′dĭ-as danced
[2]before them, and pleased Hĕr′od.
7 Whereupon he promised with an
oath to give her whatsoever she would
ask.
8 And she, being before instructed
of her mother, said, Give me here Jŏhn
Băp′tĭst's head in a charger.
9 And the king was sorry: [f]neverthe-
less for the oath's sake, and them
which sat with him at meat, he commanded *it* to be given *her*.
10 And he sent, and beheaded Jŏhn
in the prison.
11 And his head was brought in a
charger, and given to the damsel: and
she brought *it* to her mother.
12 And his disciples came, and took
up the body, and buried it, and went
and told Jē′sus.
13 ¶ When [g]Jē′sus heard *of it*, he
departed thence by ship into a desert
place apart: and when the people had
heard *thereof*, they followed him on
foot out of the cities.
14 And Jē′sus went forth, and saw
a great multitude, and [h]was moved
with compassion toward them, and he
healed their sick.
15 ¶ And when it was evening, his
disciples came to him, saying, This is a
desert place, and the time is now past;
send the multitude away, that they
may go into the villages, and buy themselves victuals.
16 But Jē′sus said unto them, They
need not depart; [i]give ye them to eat.
17 And they say unto him, We have
here but five loaves, and two fishes.
18 He said, Bring them hither to me.
19 And he commanded the multitude to sit down on the grass, and took
the five loaves, and the two fishes, and
looking up to heaven, he [j]blessed, and
brake, and gave the loaves to *his* disciples, and the disciples to the multitude.
20 And they did all eat, and were
filled: and they took up of the fragments that remained twelve baskets
full.
21 And they that had eaten were
about five thousand men, beside women
and children.
22 ¶ And straightway Jē′sus constrained his disciples to get into a
ship, and to go before him unto the
other side, while he sent the multitudes away.
23 And [k]when he had sent the multitudes away, he went up into a mountain apart to pray: [l]and when the evening was come, he was there alone.
24 But the ship was now in the midst
of the sea, tossed with waves: for the
wind was contrary.
25 And in the fourth watch of the
night Jē′sus went unto them, walking
on the sea.
26 And when the disciples [m]saw him
walking on the sea, they were troubled,
saying, It is a spirit; and they cried out
for fear.
27 But straightway Jē′sus spake unto
them, saying, Be of good cheer; it is I; be
not afraid.
28 And Pē′tĕr answered him and
said, Lord, if it be thou, bid me come
unto thee on the water.
29 And he said, Come. And when
Pē′tĕr was come down out of the ship,
he walked on the water, to go to Jē′sus.
30 But when he saw the wind [3]bois-
terous, he was afraid; and beginning to
sink, he cried, saying, Lord, save me.
31 And immediately Jē′sus stretched
forth *his* hand, and caught him, and
said unto him, O thou of little faith,
wherefore [n]didst thou doubt?
32 And when they were come into
the ship, the [o]wind ceased.
33 Then they that were in the ship
came and worshipped him, saying, Of
a truth thou [p]art the Son of God.
34 ¶ And [q]when they were gone
over, they came into the land of Gĕn-
nĕs′a-rĕt.
35 And when the men of that place
had knowledge of him, they sent out
into all that country round about, and
brought unto him all that were diseased;
36 And besought him that they might
only touch the hem of his garment: and
as many as touched were made perfectly whole.

15 Then [a]came to Jē′sus scribes and
Phăr′ĭ-sees, which were of Je-ru′-
sa-lĕm, saying,
2 Why [b]do thy disciples transgress
[c]the tradition of the elders? for they
wash not their hands when they eat
bread.
3 But he answered and said unto
them, Why do ye also transgress the
commandment of God by your tradition?
4 For God commanded, saying, Honour [d]thy father and mother: and, [e]He
that curseth father or mother, let him
die the death.
5 But ye say, Whosoever shall say to
his father or *his* mother, [f]*It is* a gift, by
whatsoever thou mightest be profited
by me;
6 And honour not his father or his
mother, *he shall be free*. Thus have ye
made the commandment of God of
none effect by your tradition.
7 *Ye* [g]hypocrites, well did E-sā′ias
prophesy of you, saying,
8 This [h]people draweth nigh unto
me with their mouth, and honoureth
me with *their* lips; but their heart is far
from me.
9 But in vain they do worship me,
teaching [i]*for* doctrines the commandments of men.
10 ¶ And [j]he called the multitude,
and said unto them, Hear, and understand:
11 Not [k]that which goeth into the
mouth defileth a man; but that which
cometh out of the mouth, this defileth a
man.

5 [d]ch. 21.26; Luke 20.6
6 [e]Gen. 40.20 [2]in the midst
9 [f]Eccl. 5.2; Zech. 8.17; Tit. 1.16
13 [g]ch. 10.23; ch. 12.15; Mark 6.32; Luke 9.10; John 6.1-2
14 [h]Ps. 86.15; Ps. 111.4; Ps. 145.8; ch. 9.36; Mark 1.41; Luke 7.13; John 11.33-35; Heb. 2.17; Heb. 4.15; Heb. 5.2
16 [i]2 Ki. 4.42-43; Luke 3.11; John 13.29; 2 Cor. 8.2-3
19 [j]ch. 15.36; Acts 27.35
23 [k]ch. 6.6; Acts 6.4
[l]John 6.16
26 [m]Job 9.8; Isa. 43.16
30 [3]Or, strong
31 [n]ch. 8.26; John 20.25-27
32 [o]Ps. 107.29; John 6.18-21
33 [p]Ps. 2.7; Rom. 1.4
34 [q]Mark 6.53
CHAPTER 15
1 [a]Mark 7.1
2 [b]Mark 7.5
[c]Gal. 1.14; 1 Pet. 1.18
4 [d]Ex. 20.12; Eph. 6.2
[e]Ex. 21.17; Prov. 30.17
5 [f]Mark 7.11
7 [g]Mark 7.6
8 [h]Isa. 29.13; Ezek. 33.31
9 [i]Isa. 29.13; Tit. 1.14
10 [j]Mark 7.14
11 [k]Mark 7.15; Tit. 1.15

12 Then came his disciples, and said
unto him, Knowest thou that the Phăr'-
ĭ-sees were offended, after they heard
this saying?
13 But he answered and said, Every
[l]plant, which my heavenly Father hath
not planted, shall be rooted up.
14 Let [m]them alone: [n]they be blind
leaders of the blind. And if the blind
lead the blind, both shall fall into the
ditch.
15 Then [o]answered Pē'tēr and said
unto him, Declare unto us this parable.
16 And Jē'sus said, [p]Are ye also yet
without understanding?
17 Do not ye yet understand, that
whatsoever [q]entereth in at the mouth
goeth into the belly, and is cast out into
the draught?
18 But [r]those things which proceed
out of the mouth come forth from the
heart; and they defile the man.
19 For [s]out of the heart proceed evil
thoughts, murders, adulteries, fornications, thefts, false witness, blasphemies:
20 These are *the things* which defile
a man: but to eat with unwashen hands
defileth not a man.
21 ¶ Then Jē'sus went thence, and
departed into the coasts of Tȳre and
Sī'dŏn.
22 And, behold, a woman of Cā'-
năan came out of the same coasts, and
cried unto him, saying, Have mercy on
me, O Lord, *thou* son of Dā'vid; my
daughter is grievously vexed with a
devil.
23 But he answered her not a word.
And his disciples came and besought
him, saying, Send her away; for she
crieth after us.
24 But he answered and said, [t]I am
not sent but unto the lost sheep of the
house of Is'ra-el.
25 Then came she and worshipped
him, saying, Lord, help me.
26 But he answered and said, It is
not meet to take the children's bread,
and to cast *it* to [u]dogs.
27 And she said, Truth, Lord: yet the
dogs eat of the crumbs which fall from
their masters' table.
28 Then Jē'sus answered and said
unto her, O woman, great *is* thy faith:
be it unto thee even as thou wilt. And
her daughter was made whole from
that very hour.
29 And [v]Jē'sus departed from thence,
and came nigh [w]unto the sea of Găl'ĭ-
lee; and went up into a mountain, and
sat down there.
30 And [x]great multitudes came unto
him, having with them *those that were*
lame, blind, dumb, maimed, and many
others, and cast them down at Jē'sus'
feet; and he healed them:
31 Insomuch that the multitude wondered, when they saw the dumb to
speak, the maimed to be whole, the
lame to walk, and the blind to see: and
they glorified the God of Is'ra-el.
32 ¶ Then [y]Jē'sus called his disciples *unto him,* and said, I [z]have compassion on the multitude, because they
continue with me now three days, and

13 [l]John 15.2; 1 Cor. 3.12
14 [m]Hos. 4.14-17
[n]Isa. 9.16; Luke 6.39
15 [o]Mark 7.17
16 [p]ch. 16.9; Mark 7.18
17 [q]1 Cor. 6.13
18 [r]Prov. 6.12; Jas. 3.6
19 [s]Gen. 6.5; Mark 7.21
24 [t]Isa. 53.6; Acts 13.46
26 [u]Isa. 56.10-11; Rev. 32.15
29 [v]Mark 7.31
[w]ch. 4.18; Mark 1.16
30 [x]Isa. 35.5-6; Luke 7.22
32 [y]Mark 8.1
[z]Ps. 86.15; Heb. 5.2
33 [a]Num. 11.21-22; 2 Ki. 4.43
36 [b]ch. 14.19
[c]Deut. 8.10; Luke 22.19
37 [d]Ps. 103.1-5; Ps. 147.9
39 [e]Mark 8.10-11

CHAPTER 16
1 [a]ch. 12.38; 1 Cor. 1.22
3 [b]Gen. 49.10; Mic. 5.2
4 [c]Isa. 57.3
5 [d]ch. 15.37-38
6 [e]ch. 7.15
9 [f]ch. 14.17
10 [g]ch. 15.34
13 [h]Dan. 7.13;

have nothing to eat: and I will not send
them away fasting, lest they faint in
the way.
33 And [a]his disciples say unto him,
Whence should we have so much bread
in the wilderness, as to fill so great a
multitude?
34 And Jē'sus saith unto them, How
many loaves have ye? And they said,
Seven, and a few little fishes.
35 And he commanded the multitude to sit down on the ground.
36 And [b]he took the seven loaves
and the fishes, and [c]gave thanks, and
brake *them,* and gave to his disciples,
and the disciples to the multitude.
37 And they did all eat, [d]and were
filled: and they took up of the broken
meat that was left seven baskets full.
38 And they that did eat were four
thousand men, beside women and children.
39 And [e]he sent away the multitude, and took ship, and came into the
coasts of Măg'da-lȧ.

16 The [a]Phăr'ĭ-sees also with the
Săd'dū-çees came, and tempting
desired him that he would shew them a
sign from heaven.
2 He answered and said unto them,
When it is evening, ye say, *It will be*
fair weather: for the sky is red.
3 And in the morning, *It will be* foul
weather to day: for the sky is red and
lowring. O *ye* hypocrites, ye can discern the face of the sky; but can ye not
discern the [b]signs of the times?
4 A [c]wicked and adulterous generation seeketh after a sign; and there
shall no sign be given unto it, but the
sign of the prophet Jō'nas. And he left
them, and departed.
5 And [d]when his disciples were come
to the other side, they had forgotten to
take bread.
6 ¶ Then Jē'sus said unto them, Take
[e]heed and beware of the leaven of the
Phăr'ĭ-sees and of the Săd'dū-çees.
7 And they reasoned among themselves, saying, *It is* because we have
taken no bread.
8 *Which* when Jē'sus perceived, he
said unto them, O ye of little faith, why
reason ye among yourselves, because
ye have brought no bread?
9 Do [f]ye not yet understand, neither
remember the five loaves of the five
thousand, and how many baskets ye
took up?
10 Neither [g]the seven loaves of the
four thousand, and how many baskets
ye took up?
11 How is it that ye do not understand that I spake *it* not to you concerning bread, that ye should beware of the
leaven of the Phăr'ĭ-sees and of the
Săd'dū-çees?
12 Then understood they how that
he bade *them* not beware of the leaven
of bread, but of the doctrine of the
Phăr'ĭ-sees and of the Săd'dū-çees.
13 ¶ When Jē'sus came into the coasts
of Çæs-a-rē'ȧ Phĭ-lĭp'pī, he asked his
disciples, saying, [h]Whom do men say
that I the Son of man am?

14 And they said, [i]Some *say that thou art* Jŏhn the Băp'tĭst: [j]some, E-lī'ăs; and others, Jĕr-e-mī'as, or one of the prophets.

15 He saith unto them, But whom say ye that I am?

16 And Sī'mon Pē'tĕr answered and said, [k]Thou art the Chrīst, the Son of the living God.

17 And Jē'sus answered and said unto him, Blessed art thou, Sī'mon Bär-jō'nȧ: [l]for flesh and blood hath not revealed *it* unto thee, but [m]my Father which is in heaven.

18 And I say also unto thee, That [n]thou art Pē'tĕr, and [o]upon this rock I will build my church; and [p]the gates of hell shall not prevail against it.

19 And [q]I will give unto thee the keys of the kingdom of heaven: and whatsoever thou shalt bind on earth shall be bound in heaven: and whatsoever thou shalt loose on earth shall be loosed in heaven.

20 Then charged he his disciples that they should tell no man that he was Jē'sus the Chrīst.

21 ¶ From that time forth began Jē'sus to shew unto his disciples, how that he must go unto Je-ru̦'sa-lĕm, and suffer many things of the elders and chief priests and scribes, and be killed, and be raised again the third day.

22 Then Pē'tĕr took him, and began to rebuke him, saying, [1]Be it far from thee, Lord: this shall not be unto thee.

23 But he turned, and said unto Pē'tĕr, Get thee behind me, Sā'tan: thou [r]art an offence unto me: for thou savourest not the things that be of God, but those that be of men.

24 ¶ Then [s]said Jē'sus unto his disciples, If any *man* will come after me, let him deny himself, and take up his cross, and follow me.

25 For whosoever will save his life shall lose it: and whosoever will lose his life for my sake shall find it.

26 For what is a man profited, if he shall gain the whole world, and lose his own soul? or [t]what shall a man give in exchange for his soul?

27 For the Son of man shall come in the glory of his Father [u]with his angels; [v]and then he shall reward every man according to his works.

28 Verily I say unto you, There be some standing here, which shall not taste of death, till they see the Son of man coming in his [w]kingdom.

17 And [a]after six days Jē'sus taketh Pē'tĕr, Jāmes, and Jŏhn his brother, and bringeth them up into an high mountain apart,

2 And was transfigured before them: and his face did shine as the sun, and his raiment was white as the light.

3 And, behold, there appeared unto them [b]Mō'ses and E-lī'ăs talking with him.

4 Then answered Pē'tĕr, and said unto Jē'sus, Lord, it is good for us to be here: if thou wilt, let us make here three tabernacles; one for thee, and one for Mō'ses, and one for E-lī'ăs.

14 [i]ch. 3.1; ch. 14.2; Mark 1.4
[j]Mal. 4.5
16 [k]Ps. 2.7; ch. 14.33; Mark 8.29; Luke 9.20; John 6.69
17 [l]Eph. 2.8
[m]1 Cor. 2.10; Gal. 1.16
18 [n]John 1.42
[o]Isa. 28.16; 1 Cor. 3.11; Eph. 2.20; Rev. 21.14
[p]Isa. 54.17
19 [q]John 20.23
22 [1]Pity thyself
23 [r]Gen. 3.1-6; Deut. 25.16; ch. 4.10; Mark 8.33
24 [s]Acts 14.22; Rom. 8.17; 1 Thess. 3.3; 2 Tim. 3.12; Rev. 2.10
26 [t]Ps. 49.7-8; Mark 8.37
27 [u]Dan. 7.10; ch. 25.31; Zech. 14.15; Jude 14
[v]Job 34.11; Rev. 2.23
28 [w]Mark 9.1

CHAPTER 17
1 [a]Mark 9.2; Luke 9.28
3 [b]Rom. 3.21
5 [c]2 Pet. 1.17
[d]ch. 3.17; Luke 3.22
[e]Isa. 42.1
[f]Deut. 18.15; Heb. 12.25
6 [g]2 Pet. 1.18
10 [h]Mal. 4.5
11 [i]Mal. 4.6; Acts 3.21
12 [j]Mark 9.12
[k]ch. 14.3
14 [l]Luke 9.37
20 [m]ch. 21.21; 1 Cor. 13.2
22 [n]ch. 16.21; Luke 24.6-7
24 [o]Mark 9.33
[1]didrachma, in value fifteen pence; Ex. 30.13; Ex. 38.26

5 While [c]he yet spake, behold, a bright cloud overshadowed them: and behold a voice out of the cloud, which said, [d]This is my beloved Son, [e]in whom I am well pleased; [f]hear ye him.

6 And [g]when the disciples heard *it*, they fell on their face, and were sore afraid.

7 And Jē'sus came and touched them, and said, Arise, and be not afraid.

8 And when they had lifted up their eyes, they saw no man, save Jē'sus only.

9 And as they came down from the mountain, Jē'sus charged them, saying, Tell the vision to no man, until the Son of man be risen again from the dead.

10 And his disciples asked him, saying, [h]Why then say the scribes that E-lī'ăs must first come?

11 And Jē'sus answered and said unto them, E-lī'ăs truly shall first come, and restore [i]all things.

12 But [j]I say unto you, That E-lī'ăs is come already, and they knew him not, but have [k]done unto him whatsoever they listed. Likewise shall also the Son of man suffer of them.

13 Then the disciples understood that he spake unto them of Jŏhn the Băp'tĭst.

14 ¶ And [l]when they were come to the multitude, there came to him a *certain* man, kneeling down to him, and saying,

15 Lord, have mercy on my son: for he is lunatick, and sore vexed: for ofttimes he falleth into the fire, and oft into the water.

16 And I brought him to thy disciples, and they could not cure him.

17 Then Jē'sus answered and said, O faithless and perverse generation, how long shall I be with you? how long shall I suffer you? bring him hither to me.

18 And Jē'sus rebuked the devil; and he departed out of him: and the child was cured from that very hour.

19 Then came the disciples to Jē'sus apart, and said, Why could not we cast him out?

20 And Jē'sus said unto them, Because of your unbelief: for verily I say unto you, [m]If ye have faith as a grain of mustard seed, ye shall say unto this mountain, Remove hence to yonder place; and it shall remove; and nothing shall be impossible unto you.

21 Howbeit this kind goeth not out but by prayer and fasting.

22 ¶ And [n]while they abode in Găl'ĭ-lee, Jē'sus said unto them, The Son of man shall be betrayed into the hands of men:

23 And they shall kill him, and the third day he shall be raised again. And they were exceeding sorry.

24 ¶ And [o]when they were come to Ca-pĕr'na-ŭm, they that received [1]tribute *money* came to Pē'tĕr, and said, Doth not your master pay tribute?

25 He saith, Yes. And when he was come into the house, Jē'sus prevented

him, saying, What thinkest thou, Sī'-
mon? of whom do the kings of the
earth take custom or tribute? of their
own children, or of strangers?
26 Pē'tĕr saith unto him, Of strangers. Jē'sus saith unto him, Then are the
children free.
27 Notwithstanding, lest we should
[p]offend them, go thou to the sea, and
cast an hook, and take up the fish that
first cometh up; and when thou hast
opened his mouth, thou shalt find [2]a
piece of money: that take, and give
unto them for me and thee.

18 At [a]the same time came the disciples unto Jē'sus, saying, Who is
the greatest in the kingdom of heaven?
2 And Jē'sus called a little child unto
him, and set him in the midst of them,
3 And said, Verily I say unto you,
Except [b]ye be converted, and become
as little children, ye shall not enter into
the kingdom of heaven.
4 Whosoever [c]therefore shall humble himself as this little child, the same
is greatest in the kingdom of heaven.
5 And [d]whoso shall receive one such
little child in my name receiveth me.
6 But whoso shall offend one of these
little ones which believe in me, it were
better for him that a millstone were
hanged about his neck, and *that* he
were drowned in the depth of the sea.
7 ¶ Woe unto the world because of
offences! for [e]it must needs be that offences come; but [f]woe to that man by
whom the offence cometh!
8 Wherefore [g]if thy hand or thy foot
offend thee, cut them off, and cast
them from thee: it is better for thee to
enter into life halt or maimed, rather
than having two hands or two feet to
be cast into everlasting fire.
9 And if thine eye offend thee, pluck
it out, and cast *it* from thee: it is better
for thee to enter into life with one eye,
rather than having two eyes to be cast
into hell fire.
10 Take heed that ye despise not
one of these little ones; for I say unto
you, That in heaven their [h]angels do
always [i]behold the face of my Father
which is in heaven.
11 For the Son of man is come to
save that which was lost.
12 How [j]think ye? if a man have an
hundred sheep, and one of them be
gone astray, doth he not leave the
ninety and nine, and goeth into the
mountains, and seeketh that which is
gone astray?
13 And if so be that he find it, verily
I say unto you, he rejoiceth more of
that *sheep*, than of the ninety and nine
which went not astray.
14 Even so it is not the will of your
Father which is in heaven, that one of
these little ones should perish.
15 ¶ Moreover [k]if thy brother shall
trespass against thee, go and tell him
his fault between thee and him alone:
if he shall hear thee, thou [l]hast gained
thy brother.
16 But if he will not hear *thee, then*
take with thee one or two more, that
[m]in the mouth of two or three witnesses every word may be established.
17 And if he shall neglect to hear
them, tell *it* unto [n]the church: but if he
neglect to hear the church, let him be
unto thee as an [o]heathen man and a
publican.
18 Verily I say unto you, [p]Whatso-
ever ye shall bind on earth shall be
bound in heaven: and whatsoever ye
shall loose on earth shall be loosed in
heaven.
19 Again [q]I say unto you, That if
two of you shall agree on earth as
touching any thing that they shall ask,
[r]it shall be done for them of my Father
which is in heaven.
20 For where two or three are gathered together in my name, there [s]am I
in the midst of them.
21 ¶ Then came Pē'tĕr to him, and
said, Lord, how oft shall my brother
sin against me, and I forgive him? [t]till
seven times?
22 Jē'sus saith unto him, I say not
unto thee, Until seven times: but, [u]Un-
til seventy times seven.
23 ¶ Therefore is the kingdom of
heaven likened unto a certain king,
which would take account of his servants.
24 And when he had begun to reckon,
one was brought unto him, which owed
him ten thousand [1]talents.
25 But forasmuch as he had not to
pay, his lord commanded him to [v]be
sold, and his wife, and children, and all
that he had, and payment to be made.
26 The servant therefore fell down,
and [2]worshipped him, saying, Lord,
have patience with me, and I will pay
thee all.
27 Then the lord of that servant was
moved with compassion, and loosed
him, and forgave him the debt.
28 But the same servant went out,
and found one of his fellowservants,
which owed him an hundred [3]pence:
and he laid hands on him, and took
him by the throat, saying, Pay me that
thou owest.
29 And his fellowservant fell down
at his feet, and besought him, saying,
Have patience with me, and I will pay
thee all.
30 And he would not: but went and
cast him into prison, till he should pay
the debt.
31 So when his fellowservants saw
what was done, they were very sorry,
and came and told unto their lord all
that was done.
32 Then his lord, after that he had
called him, said unto him, O thou
wicked servant, I forgave thee all that
debt, because thou desiredst me:
33 Shouldest [w]not thou also have
had compassion on thy fellowservant,
even as I had pity on thee?
34 And his lord was wroth, and delivered him to the tormentors, till he
should pay all that was due unto him.
35 So [x]likewise shall my heavenly
Father do also unto you, if ye from

27 [p]Mark 12.17; [2]Or, a stater. It is half an ounce of silver, in value 2*s*. 6*d*. after 5*s*. the ounce

CHAPTER 18

1 [a]Mark 9.33

3 [b]Ps. 131.2

4 [c]ch. 11.29

5 [d]ch. 10.42

7 [e]Mark 9.42; [f]ch. 26.24

8 [g]ch. 5.29-30

10 [h]2 Ki. 19.35; [i]Esth. 1.14

12 [j]Luke 15.4

15 [k]Lev. 19.17; [l]Jas. 5.20

16 [m]Num. 35.30

17 [n]1 Tim. 5.20; [o]Rom. 16.17

18 [p]John 20.23

19 [q]ch. 5.24; [r]Jas. 5.16

20 [s]Ezek. 48.35

21 [t]Luke 17.4

22 [u]Col. 3.13

24 [1]A talent is 750 ounces of silver, which after five shillings the ounce is 187*l*. 10*s*

25 [v]Lev. 25.39

26 [2]Or, besought him

28 [3]The Roman penny is the eighth part of an ounce, which after five shillings the ounce is seven pence halfpenny; ch. 20.2

33 [w]Eph. 4.32

35 [x]Prov. 21.13

your hearts forgive not every one his
brother their trespasses.

19 And it came to pass, [a]*that* when
Jē'sus had finished these sayings, he departed from Găl'ĭ-lee, and
came into the coasts of Jū-dæ'ȧ beyond Jôr'dan;
2 And [b]great multitudes followed
him; and he healed them there.
3 ¶ The Phăr'ĭ-sees also came unto
him, tempting him, and saying unto
him, Is it lawful for a man to put away
his wife for every cause?
4 And he answered and said unto
them, Have ye not read, [c]that he which
made *them* at the beginning made
them male and female,
5 And said, [d]For this cause shall
a man leave father and mother, and
shall cleave to his wife: [e]and they
twain shall be one flesh?
6 Wherefore they are no more twain,
but one flesh. What therefore God
hath joined together, let not man put
asunder.
7 They say unto him, [f]Why did Mō'-
ses then command to give a writing of
divorcement, and to put her away?
8 He saith unto them, Mō'ses because of the hardness of your hearts
suffered you to put away your wives:
but [g]from the beginning it was not so.
9 And [h]I say unto you, Whosoever
shall put away his wife, except *it be* for
fornication, and shall marry another,
committeth adultery: and whoso marrieth her which is put away doth commit adultery.
10 ¶ His disciples say unto him, If
[i]the case of the man be so with *his*
wife, it is not good to marry.
11 But he said unto them, [j]All *men*
cannot receive this saying, save *they*
to whom it is given.
12 For there are some eunuchs,
which were so born from *their* mother's
womb: and there are some eunuchs,
which were made eunuchs of men: and
[k]there be eunuchs, which have made
themselves eunuchs for the kingdom of
heaven's sake. He that is able to receive
it, let him receive *it*.
13 ¶ Then [l]were there brought unto
him little children, that he should put
his hands on them, and pray: and the
disciples rebuked them.
14 But Jē'sus said, Suffer little children, and forbid them not, to come
unto me: for of [m]such is the kingdom
of heaven.
15 And he laid *his* hands on them,
and departed thence.
16 ¶ And, behold, one came and said
unto him, [n]Good Master, what good
thing shall I do, that I may have eternal
life?
17 And he said unto him, Why callest
thou me good? [o]*there is* none good but
one, *that is*, God: but if thou wilt enter
into life, keep the commandments.
18 He saith unto him, Which? Jē'-
sus said, Thou [p]shalt do no murder,
Thou shalt not commit adultery, Thou
shalt not steal, Thou shalt not bear
false witness,

CHAPTER 19
1 [a]Mark 10.1; John 10.40
2 [b]ch. 12.15
4 [c]Gen. 1.27; Mal. 2.15
5 [d]Gen. 2.24; Eph. 5.31
[e]1 Cor. 6.16; 1 Cor. 7.2
7 [f]Deut. 24.1
8 [g]Jer. 6.16
9 [h]ch. 5.32; 1 Cor. 7.10-11
10 [i]Gen. 2.18; 1 Tim. 5.11
11 [j]1 Cor. 7.2-7-9-17
12 [k]1 Cor. 7.32-34; 1 Cor. 9.5-15
13 [l]Mark 10.13; Luke 18.15
14 [m]ch. 18.3; 1 Pet. 2.1-2
16 [n]Luke 10.25
17 [o]1 Sam. 2.2
18 [p]Ex. 20.13; Deut. 5.17
19 [q]Lev. 19.3; Eph. 6.1-2
[r]Lev. 19.18
21 [s]Luke 12.33
23 [t]Job 31.24-28
26 [u]Gen. 18.14
27 [v]Mark 10.28
[w]Deut. 33.9
28 [x]2 Cor. 5.17
[y]Luke 22.28
30 [z]ch. 20.16

CHAPTER 20
2 [1]The Roman penny is the eighth part of an ounce, which after five shillings the ounce is seven pence halfpenny
8 [a]Acts 17.31

19 Honour [q]thy father and *thy*
mother: and, [r]Thou shalt love thy
neighbour as thyself.
20 The young man saith unto him,
All these things have I kept from my
youth up: what lack I yet?
21 Jē'sus said unto him, If thou wilt
be perfect, [s]go *and* sell that thou hast,
and give to the poor, and thou shalt
have treasure in heaven: and come *and*
follow me.
22 But when the young man heard
that saying, he went away sorrowful:
for he had great possessions.
23 ¶ Then said Jē'sus unto his disciples, Verily I say unto you, That a [t]rich
man shall hardly enter into the kingdom of heaven.
24 And again I say unto you, It is
easier for a camel to go through the
eye of a needle, than for a rich man to
enter into the kingdom of God.
25 When his disciples heard *it*, they
were exceedingly amazed, saying, Who
then can be saved?
26 But Jē'sus beheld *them*, and said
unto them, With men this is impossible; but with [u]God all things are
possible.
27 ¶ Then [v]answered Pē'tĕr and said
unto him, Behold, [w]we have forsaken
all, and followed thee; what shall we
have therefore?
28 And Jē'sus said unto them, Verily
I say unto you, That ye which have followed me, in [x]the regeneration when
the Son of man shall sit in the throne of
his glory, ye [y]also shall sit upon twelve
thrones, judging the twelve tribes of
Is'ra-el.
29 And every one that hath forsaken
houses, or brethren, or sisters, or father, or mother, or wife, or children, or
lands, for my name's sake, shall receive an hundredfold, and shall inherit
everlasting life.
30 But [z]many *that are* first shall be
last; and the last *shall be* first.

20 For the kingdom of heaven is
like unto a man *that is* an householder, which went out early in the
morning to hire labourers into his vineyard.
2 And when he had agreed with the
labourers for a [1]penny a day, he sent
them into his vineyard.
3 And he went out about the third
hour, and saw others standing idle in
the marketplace,
4 And said unto them; Go ye also
into the vineyard, and whatsoever is
right I will give you. And they went
their way.
5 Again he went out about the sixth
and ninth hour, and did likewise.
6 And about the eleventh hour he
went out, and found others standing
idle, and saith unto them, Why stand
ye here all the day idle?
7 They say unto him, Because no
man hath hired us. He saith unto them,
Go ye also into the vineyard; and whatsoever is right, *that* shall ye receive.
8 So when [a]even was come, the lord
of the vineyard saith unto his steward,

Call the labourers, and give them *their*
hire, beginning from the last unto the
first.
9 And when they came that *were*
hired about the eleventh hour, they received every man a penny.
10 But when the first came, they supposed that they should have received
more; and they likewise received every man a penny.
11 And when they had received *it,*
they murmured against the goodman
of the house,
12 Saying, These last [2]have wrought
but one hour, and thou hast made
them equal unto us, which have borne
the burden and heat of the day.
13 But he answered one of them,
and said, Friend, I do thee no wrong:
didst not thou agree with me for a
penny?
14 Take *that* thine *is,* and go thy
way: I will give unto this last, even as
unto thee.
15 Is [b]it not lawful for me to do what
I will with mine own? [c]Is thine eye
evil, because I am good?
16 So [d]the last shall be first, and the
first last: [e]for many be called, but few
chosen.
17 ¶ And [f]Jē'sus going up to Je-ru̧'-
sa-lĕm took the twelve disciples apart
in the way, and said unto them,
18 Behold, [g]we go up to Je-ru̧'sa-
lĕm; and the Son of man shall be betrayed unto the chief priests and unto
the scribes, and they shall condemn
him to death,
19 And [h]shall deliver him to the
Gĕn'tīles to mock, and to scourge, and
to crucify *him:* and the third day he
shall rise again.
20 ¶ Then [i]came to him [j]the mother
of Zĕb'e-dee's [k]children with her sons,
worshipping *him,* and desiring a certain thing of him.
21 And he said unto her, What wilt
thou? She saith unto him, Grant that
these my two sons [l]may sit, the one on
thy right hand, and the other on the
left in thy kingdom.
22 But Jē'sus answered and said, Ye
know not what ye ask. Are ye able to
drink of the [m]cup that I shall drink of,
and to be baptized with the [n]baptism
that I am baptized with? They say unto
him, We are able.
23 And he saith unto them, [o]Ye shall
drink indeed of my cup, and be baptized with the baptism that I am baptized with: but to sit on my right hand,
and on my left, is not mine to [p]give, but
it shall be given to them for whom it is
prepared of my Father.
24 And [q]when the ten heard *it,* they
were moved with indignation against
the two brethren.
25 But Jē'sus called them *unto him,*
and said, Ye know that the princes of
the Gĕn'tīles exercise dominion over
them, and they that are great exercise
authority upon them.
26 But [r]it shall not be so among you:
but whosoever [s]will be great among
you, let him be your minister;

12 [2]Or, have continued one hour only
15 [b]Rom. 9.21
[c]Deut. 15.9; Mark 7.22
16 [d]ch. 8.11-12; Mark 10.31
[e]ch. 7.13; 2 Thess. 2.13-14
17 [f]John 12.12
18 [g]ch. 13.21
19 [h]ch. 27.2; Acts 3.13
20 [i]Mark 10.35
[j]ch. 27.56; Mark 15.40
[k]ch. 4.21
21 [l]1 Ki. 2.19; Jas. 4.3
22 [m]Ps. 75.8; John 18.11
[n]Luke 12.50
23 [o]Acts 12.2; 2 Cor. 1.7
[p]ch. 25.34
24 [q]Luke 22.24
26 [r]1 Pet. 5.3
[s]ch. 23.11; Mark 10.43
27 [t]ch. 18.4
28 [u]John 13.4; Phil. 2.7
[v]Luke 22.27; John 13.14
[w]Job 33.24;
[x]ch. 26.28
29 [y]Mark 10.46
CHAPTER 21
1 [a]Mark 11.1;
[b]Zech. 14.4
3 [c]Ps. 24.1
[d]2 Cor. 8.9
4 [e]1 Ki. 1.33
6 [f]Mark 11.4
7 [g]2 Ki. 9.13
8 [h]Lev. 23.40
9 [i]Ps. 118.25;
[j]ch. 23.39
10 [k]ch. 2.3
11 [l]ch. 2.23
12 [m]Mal. 3.1-2;
[n]Deut. 14.25
13 [o]Isa. 56.7

27 And [t]whosoever will be chief
among you, let him be your servant:
28 Even [u]as the Son of man came
not to be ministered unto, but [v]to minister, and to [w]give his life a ransom
[x]for many.
29 And [y]as they departed from Jĕr'-
ĭ-chō, a great multitude followed him.
30 ¶ And, behold, two blind men sitting by the way side, when they heard
that Jē'sus passed by, cried out, saying, Have mercy on us, O Lord, *thou*
son of Dā'vid.
31 And the multitude rebuked them,
because they should hold their peace:
but they cried the more, saying, Have
mercy on us, O Lord, *thou* son of
Dā'vid.
32 And Jē'sus stood still, and called
them, and said, What will ye that I
shall do unto you?
33 They say unto him, Lord, that our
eyes may be opened.
34 So Jē'sus had compassion *on*
them, and touched their eyes: and immediately their eyes received sight,
and they followed him.

21

And [a]when they drew nigh unto
Je-ru̧'sa-lĕm, and were come to
Bĕth'pha-ġe, unto [b]the mount of Ŏl'-
ĭves, then sent Jē'sus two disciples,
2 Saying unto them, Go into the village over against you, and straightway
ye shall find an ass tied, and a colt with
her: loose *them,* and bring *them* unto
me.
3 And if any *man* say ought unto
you, ye shall say, The [c]Lord hath need
[d]of them; and straightway he will send
them.
4 All this was done, that it might
be fulfilled which was spoken by the
prophet, [e]saying,
5 Tell ye the daughter of Sī'ŏn, Behold, thy King cometh unto thee, meek,
and sitting upon an ass, and a colt the
foal of an ass.
6 And [f]the disciples went, and did
as Jē'sus commanded them,
7 And brought the ass, and the colt,
and put [g]on them their clothes, and
they set *him* thereon.
8 And a very great multitude spread
their garments in the way; others [h]cut
down branches from the trees, and
strawed *them* in the way.
9 And the multitudes that went before, and that followed, cried, saying, [i]Ho-săn'nȧ to the son of Dā'vid:
[j]Blessed *is* he that cometh in the name
of the Lord; Ho-săn'nȧ in the highest.
10 And [k]when he was come into Je-
ru̧'sa-lĕm, all the city was moved, saying, Who is this?
11 And the multitude said, This is
Jē'sus the [l]prophet of Năz'a-rĕth of
Găl'ĭ-lee.
12 ¶ And [m]Jē'sus went into the temple of God, and cast out all them that
sold and bought in the temple, and
overthrew the tables of the [n]money-
changers, and the seats of them that
sold doves,
13 And said unto them, It is written,
[o]My house shall be called the house of

prayer; but [p]ye have made it a den of
thieves.
14 And [q]the blind and the lame came
to him in the temple; and he healed
them.
15 And when the chief priests and
scribes saw the wonderful things that
he did, and the children crying in the
temple, and saying, Ho-săn′nȧ to [r]the
son of Dā′vid; they were sore displeased,
16 And said unto him, Hearest thou
what these say? And Jē′sus saith unto
them, Yea; have ye never read, [s]Out of
the mouth of babes and sucklings thou
hast perfected praise?
17 ¶ And he left them, and went out
of the city into [t]Bĕth′ă-nȳ; and he
lodged there.
18 Now in the morning as he returned into the city, he hungered.
19 And when he saw [1]a fig tree in
the way, he came to it, and found nothing thereon, but leaves only, and said
unto it, Let no fruit grow on thee
henceforward for ever. And presently
the fig tree withered away.
20 And when the disciples saw *it*,
they marvelled, saying, How soon is
the fig tree withered away!
21 Jē′sus answered and said unto
them, Verily I say unto you, [u]If ye have
faith, and [v]doubt not, ye shall not only
do this *which is done* to the fig tree,
[w]but also if ye shall say unto this mountain, Be thou removed, and be thou
cast into the sea; it shall be done.
22 And [x]all things, whatsoever ye
shall ask in prayer, believing, ye shall
receive.
23 ¶ And [y]when he was come into
the temple, the chief priests and the
elders of the people came unto him as
he was teaching, and said, [z]By what
authority doest thou these things? and
who gave thee this authority?
24 And [a]Jē′sus answered and said
unto them, I also will ask you one
thing, which if ye tell me, I in like wise
will tell you by what authority I do
these things.
25 The baptism of Jŏhn, whence was
it? from heaven, or of men? And they
reasoned with themselves, saying, If
we shall say, From heaven; he will say
unto us, Why did ye not then believe
him?
26 But if we shall say, Of men; we
fear the people; [b]for all hold Jŏhn as a
prophet.
27 And they answered Jē′sus, and
said, We cannot tell. And he said unto
them, Neither tell I you by what authority I do these things.
28 ¶ But what think ye? A *certain*
man had two sons; and he came to the
first, and said, Son, go work to day in
my vineyard.
29 He answered and said, I will not:
but afterward he repented, and went.
30 And he came to the second, and
said likewise. And he answered and
said, I go, sir: and went not.
31 Whether of them twain did the
will of *his* father? They say unto him,

[p]Jer. 7.11; Luke 19.46
14 [q]Isa. 35.5; Acts 3.1-9
15 [r]Isa. 11.1
16 [s]Ps. 8.2; ch. 11.25
17 [t]Mark 11.11; John 11.18
19 [1]one fig tree
21 [u]ch. 17.20; Luke 17.6
[v]Jas. 1.6
[w]1 Cor. 13.2
22 [x]ch. 7.7; 1 John 5.14
23 [y]Luke 20.1
[z]Ex. 2.14; Acts 7.27
24 [a]Job 5.13
26 [b]ch. 14.5; John 10.41-42
31 [c]Luke 7.29
32 [d]Isa. 35.8; ch. 3.1
[e]Luke 3.12
33 [f]Ps. 80.9; Luke 20.9
[g]ch. 25.14
34 [h]Song 8.11
35 [i]2 Chr. 24.21; Heb. 11.36
37 [j]ch. 3.17; Heb. 1.2
38 [k]Ps. 2.8; Heb. 1.2
[l]Ps. 2.2; Acts 4.27
39 [m]Acts 2.23
41 [n]Luke 20.16
[o]Deut. 4.26; Heb. 2.3
[p]Acts 13.46; Rom. 11.1
42 [q]Ps. 118.22; 1 Pet. 2.6-7
[r]1 Tim. 3.16
43 [s]ch. 8.12
44 [t]Isa. 8.14
[u]Ps. 2.9;
46 [v]John 7.40
CHAPTER 22
1 [a]Luke 14.16

The first. Jē′sus saith unto them, [c]Ver-
ily I say unto you, That the publicans
and the harlots go into the kingdom of
God before you.
32 For [d]Jŏhn came unto you in the
way of righteousness, and ye believed
him not: but [e]the publicans and the
harlots believed him: and ye, when ye
had seen *it*, repented not afterward,
that ye might believe him.
33 ¶ Hear another parable: [f]There
was a certain householder, which
planted a vineyard, and hedged it
round about, and digged a winepress
in it, and built a tower, and let it out to
husbandmen, [g]and went into a far
country:
34 And when the time of the fruit
drew near, he sent his servants to the
husbandmen, [h]that they might receive
the fruits of it.
35 And [i]the husbandmen took his
servants, and beat one, and killed another, and stoned another.
36 Again, he sent other servants
more than the first: and they did unto
them likewise.
37 But last of all [j]he sent unto them
his son, saying, They will reverence
my son.
38 But when the husbandmen saw
the son, they said among themselves,
[k]This is the heir; [l]come, let us kill him,
and let us seize on his inheritance.
39 And [m]they caught him, and cast
him out of the vineyard, and slew *him*.
40 When the lord therefore of the
vineyard cometh, what will he do unto
those husbandmen?
41 They [n]say unto him, [o]He will mis-
erably destroy those wicked men, [p]and
will let out *his* vineyard unto other husbandmen, which shall render him the
fruits in their seasons.
42 Jē′sus saith unto them, [q]Did ye
never read in the scriptures, The stone
which the builders rejected, the same
is become the head of the corner: this
is the Lord's doing, and it is [r]mar-
vellous in our eyes?
43 Therefore say I unto you, [s]The
kingdom of God shall be taken from
you, and given to a nation bringing
forth the fruits thereof.
44 And whosoever [t]shall fall on this
stone shall be broken: but on whomsoever it shall fall, [u]it will grind him to
powder.
45 And when the chief priests and
Phăr′ĭ-sees had heard his parables,
they perceived that he spake of them.
46 But when they sought to lay hands
on him, they feared the multitude, because they [v]took him for a prophet.

22 And Jē′sus answered [a]and spake
unto them again by parables, and
said,
2 The kingdom of heaven is like
unto a certain king, which made a marriage for his son,
3 And sent forth his servants to call
them that were bidden to the wedding:
and they would not come.
4 Again, he sent forth other servants, saying, Tell them which are

bidden, Behold, I have prepared my
dinner: [b]my oxen and *my* fatlings *are*
killed, and all things *are* ready: come
unto the marriage.
5 But they [c]made light of *it,* and
went their ways, one to his farm, another to his merchandise:
6 And [d]the remnant took his servants, and entreated *them* spitefully,
and slew *them.*
7 But when the king heard *thereof,*
he was wroth: and he sent forth [e]his
armies, and destroyed those murderers, and burned up their city.
8 Then saith he to his servants, The
wedding is ready, but they which were
bidden were [f]not worthy.
9 Go ye therefore into the highways,
and as many as ye shall find, bid to the
marriage.
10 So those servants went out into
the highways, and [g]gathered together
all as many as they found, both bad
and good: and the wedding was furnished with guests.
11 ¶ And when the king came in to
see the guests, he saw there a man
[h]which had not on a wedding garment:
12 And he saith unto him, Friend,
how camest thou in hither not having a wedding garment? And he [i]was
speechless.
13 Then said the king to the servants, Bind him hand and foot, and
take him away, and cast *him* [j]into
outer darkness; there shall be weeping
and gnashing of teeth.
14 For [k]many are called, but few *are*
chosen.
15 ¶ Then [l]went the Phăr'ĭ-sees, and
took counsel how they might entangle
him in *his* talk.
16 And they sent out unto him their
disciples with the He-rō'dĭ-ans, saying,
Master, we know that thou art true,
and teachest the way of God in truth,
neither carest thou for any *man:* for
thou regardest not the person of men.
17 Tell us therefore, What thinkest
thou? Is it lawful to give tribute unto
Çæ'sar, or not?
18 But Jē'sus perceived their wickedness, and said, Why tempt ye me, *ye*
hypocrites?
19 Shew me the tribute money. And
they brought unto him a [1]penny.
20 And he saith unto them, Whose *is*
this image and [2]superscription?
21 They say unto him, Çæ'sar's.
Then saith he unto them, [m]Render
therefore unto Çæ'sar the things which
are Çæ'sar's; and unto God the things
that are God's.
22 When they had heard *these words,*
they [n]marvelled, and left him, and went
their way.
23 ¶ The [o]same day came to him the
Săd'dū-çees, [p]which say that there is
no resurrection, and asked him,
24 Saying, Master, [q]Mō'ses said, If
a man die, having no children, his
brother shall marry his wife, and raise
up seed unto his brother.
25 Now there were with us seven
brethren: and the first, when he had
married a wife, deceased, and, having
no issue, left his wife unto his brother:
26 Likewise the second also, and the
third, unto the [3]seventh.
27 And last of all the woman died
also.
28 Therefore in the resurrection
whose wife shall she be of the seven?
for they all had her.
29 Jē'sus answered and said unto
them, Ye do err, [r]not knowing the
scriptures, nor the power of God.
30 For in the resurrection they neither marry, nor are given in marriage,
but [s]are as the angels of God in heaven.
31 But as touching the resurrection
of the dead, have ye not read that
which was spoken unto you by God,
saying,
32 I [t]am the God of Ā'brā-hăm, and
the God of Ī'saac, and the God of
Jā'cob? God is not the God of the dead,
but of the living.
33 And when the multitude heard
this, they [u]were astonished at his doctrine.
34 ¶ But when the Phăr'ĭ-sees had
heard that he had put the Săd'dū-çees
to silence, they were gathered together.
35 Then one of them, *which was* [v]a
lawyer, asked *him a question,* tempting him, and saying,
36 Master, which *is* the great commandment in the law?
37 Jē'sus said unto him, [w]Thou shalt
love the Lord thy God with all thy
heart, and with all thy soul, and with all
thy mind.
38 This is the first and great commandment.
39 And the second *is* like unto it,
[x]Thou shalt love thy neighbour as
thyself.
40 On [y]these two commandments
hang all the law and the prophets.
41 ¶ While [z]the Phăr'ĭ-sees were
gathered together, Jē'sus asked them,
42 Saying, What think ye of Christ?
whose son is he? They say unto him,
The son of Dā'vid.
43 He saith unto them, How then
doth Dā'vid [a]in spirit call him Lord,
saying,
44 The [b]LORD said unto my Lord,
Sit thou on my right hand, till I make
thine enemies thy footstool?
45 If Dā'vid then call him Lord, how
is he his son?
46 And [c]no man was able to answer
him a word, neither durst any *man*
from that day forth ask him any more
questions.

23

Then spake Jē'sus to the multitude, and to his disciples,
2 Saying, [a]The scribes and the Phăr'-
ĭ-sees sit in Mō'ses' seat:
3 All therefore whatsoever they bid
you observe, *that* observe and do; but
do not ye after their works: for [b]they
say, and do not.
4 For [c]they bind heavy burdens and
grievous to be borne, and lay *them* on
men's shoulders; but they *themselves*

4 [b]Prov. 9.2
5 [c]Ps. 81.11
6 [d]1 Thess. 2.14-15
7 [e]Isa. 10.5-7; Luke 19.27
8 [f]ch. 10.11; Acts 13.46
10 [g]ch. 13.38
11 [h]Zech. 3.3-4; Rev. 19.8
12 [i]Rom. 3.19
13 [j]ch. 8.12
14 [k]ch. 20.16
15 [l]Mark 12.13; Luke 20.20
19 [1]In value seven pence halfpenny; ch. 20.2
20 [2]Or, inscription
21 [m]ch. 17.25
22 [n]Job 5.13
23 [o]ch. 3.7
[p]Acts 23.8
24 [q]Gen. 38.8
26 [3]seven
29 [r]John 20.9
30 [s]Ps. 103.20
32 [t]Ex. 3.6-16
33 [u]ch. 7.28
35 [v]Luke 10.25
37 [w]Deut. 6.5
39 [x]Lev. 19.18
40 [y]ch. 7.12
41 [z]Mark 12.35
43 [a]2 Sam. 23.2
44 [b]Ps. 110.1
46 [c]Luke 14.6
CHAPTER 23
2 [a]Neh. 8.4-8
3 [b]Rom. 2.19
4 [c]Luke 11.46

will not move them with one of their fingers.

5 But [d]all their works they do for to be seen of men: [e]they make broad their phylacteries, and enlarge the borders of their garments,

6 And [f]love the uppermost rooms at feasts, and the chief seats in the synagogues,

7 And greetings in the markets, and to be called of men, Răb′bī, Răb′bī.

8 But [g]be not ye called Răb′bī: for one is your Master, *even* Christ; and all ye are brethren.

9 And call no *man* your father upon the earth: [h]for one is your Father, which is in heaven.

10 Neither be ye called masters: for one is your Master, *even* Christ.

11 But [i]he that is greatest among you shall be your servant.

12 And [j]whosoever shall exalt himself shall be abased; and he that shall humble himself shall be exalted.

13 ¶But [k]woe unto you, scribes and Phăr′ĭ-sees, hypocrites! for ye shut up the kingdom of heaven against men: for ye neither go in *yourselves,* neither suffer ye them that are entering to go in.

14 Woe unto you, scribes and Phăr′ĭ-sees, hypocrites! [l]for ye devour widows' houses, and for a pretence make long prayer: therefore ye shall receive the greater damnation.

15 Woe unto you, scribes and Phăr′ĭ-sees, hypocrites! for ye compass sea and land to make one proselyte, and when he is made, ye make him twofold more the child of hell than yourselves.

16 Woe unto you, [m]*ye* blind guides, which say, [n]Whosoever shall swear by the temple, it is nothing; but whosoever shall swear by the gold of the temple, he is a debtor!

17 *Ye* fools and blind: for whether is greater, the gold, [o]or the temple that sanctifieth the gold?

18 And, Whosoever shall swear by the altar, it is nothing; but whosoever sweareth by the gift that is upon it, he is [1]guilty.

19 *Ye* fools and blind: for whether *is* greater, the gift, or [p]the altar that sanctifieth the gift?

20 Whoso therefore shall swear by the altar, sweareth by it, and by all things thereon.

21 And whoso shall swear by the temple, sweareth by it, and [q]by him that dwelleth therein.

22 And he that shall swear by heaven, sweareth by [r]the throne of God, and by him that sitteth thereon.

23 Woe unto you, scribes and Phăr′ĭ-sees, hypocrites! [s]for ye pay tithe of mint and [2]anise and cummin, and [t]have omitted the weightier *matters* of the law, judgment, mercy, and faith: these ought ye to have done, and not to leave the other undone.

24 *Ye* blind guides, which strain at a gnat, and swallow a camel.

25 Woe unto you, scribes and Phăr′ĭ-sees, hypocrites! [u]for ye make clean the outside of the cup and of the platter, but within they are full of extortion and excess.

26 *Thou* blind Phăr′ĭ-see, cleanse first that *which* [v]*is* within the cup and platter, that the outside of them may be clean also.

27 Woe unto you, scribes and Phăr′ĭ-sees, hypocrites! [w]for ye are like unto whited sepulchres, which indeed appear beautiful outward, but are within full of dead *men's* bones, and of all uncleanness.

28 Even so ye also outwardly appear righteous unto men, but within ye are full of hypocrisy and iniquity.

29 Woe unto you, scribes and Phăr′ĭ-sees, hypocrites! because ye build the tombs of the prophets, and garnish the sepulchres of the righteous,

30 And say, If we had been in the days of our fathers, we would not have been partakers with them in the blood of the prophets.

31 Wherefore ye be witnesses unto yourselves, that [x]ye are the children of them which killed the prophets.

32 Fill [y]ye up then the measure of your fathers.

33 *Ye* serpents, *ye* [z]generation of vipers, how can ye escape the damnation of hell?

34 ¶ Wherefore, [a]behold, I send unto you prophets, and wise men, and scribes: and [b]*some* of them ye shall kill and crucify; and [c]*some* of them shall ye scourge in your synagogues, and persecute *them* from city to city:

35 That [d]upon you may come all the righteous blood shed upon the earth, [e]from the blood of righteous Ā′bel unto the blood of Zăch-a-rī′as son of Băr-a-chī′as, whom ye slew between the temple and the altar.

36 Verily I say unto you, All these things shall come upon this generation.

37 O Je-ru′sa-lĕm, Je-ru′sa-lĕm, *thou* that killest the prophets, and stonest them which are sent unto thee, how often would I [f]have gathered thy children together, even as a hen gathereth her chickens under *her* wings, and ye would not!

38 Behold, your house is left unto you desolate.

39 For I say unto you, Ye shall not see me henceforth, till ye shall say, [g]Blessed *is* he that cometh in the name of the Lord.

24 And [a]Jē′sus went out, and departed from the temple: and his disciples came to *him* for to shew him the buildings of the temple.

2 And Jē′sus said unto them, See ye not all these things? verily I say unto you, [b]There shall not be left here one stone upon another, that shall not be thrown down.

3 ¶ And as he sat upon the mount of Ŏl′ĭves, the disciples came unto him privately, saying, [c]Tell us, when shall these things be? and what *shall be* the sign of thy coming, and of the end of the world?

5 [d]ch. 6.1-2
[e]Num. 15.38; Deut. 22.12
6 [f]Mark 12.38; Luke 20.46
8 [g]Jas. 3.1
9 [h]Mal. 1.6
11 [i]ch. 20.26
12 [j]Job 22.29; Luke 18.14
13 [k]Isa. 33.14; Luke 11.52
14 [l]Ezek. 22.25; Tit. 1.11
16 [m]Isa. 56.10; ch. 15.14
[n]ch. 5.33
17 [o]Ex. 30.29
18 [1]Or, debtor, or, bound
19 [p]Ex. 29.37
21 [q]1 Ki. 8.13; Jas. 5.12
22 [r]Ps. 11.4; Rev. 4.2-3
23 [s]Luke 11.42
[2]anethon, dill
[t]1 Sam. 15.22; ch. 12.7
25 [u]Mark 7.4; Luke 11.39
26 [v]Isa. 55.7; Heb. 10.22
27 [w]Acts 23.3
31 [x]Acts 7.51; 1 Thess. 2.15
32 [y]Gen. 15.16
33 [z]ch. 3.7
34 [a]ch. 21.34;
[b]Acts 5.40;
[c]2 Cor. 11.24
35 [d]Rev. 18.24
[e]Gen. 4.8
37 [f]Deut. 32.11
39 [g]Ps. 118.26
CHAPTER 24
1 [a]Mark 13.1
2 [b]1 Ki. 9.7
3 [c]1 Thess. 5.1

4 And Jē'sus answered and said unto them, [d]Take heed that no man deceive you.

5 For [e]many shall come in my name, saying, I am Christ; and shall deceive many.

6 And ye shall hear of wars and rumours of wars: see that ye be not troubled: for all *these things* must come to pass, but the end is not yet.

7 For [f]nation shall rise against nation, and kingdom against kingdom: and there shall be famines, and pestilences, and earthquakes, in divers places.

8 All these *are* the beginning of sorrows.

9 Then [g]shall they deliver you up to be afflicted, and shall kill you: and ye shall be hated of all nations for my name's sake.

10 And then shall many [h]be offended, and shall betray one another, and shall hate one another.

11 And [i]many false prophets shall rise, and [j]shall deceive many.

12 And because iniquity shall abound, the love of many shall wax cold.

13 But [k]he that shall endure unto the end, the same shall be saved.

14 And this gospel of the kingdom [l]shall be preached in all the world for a witness unto all nations; and then shall the end come.

15 When ye therefore shall see the abomination of desolation, spoken of by [m]Dăn'iel the prophet, stand in the holy place, ([n]whoso readeth, let him understand:)

16 Then let them which be in Jū-dæ'ȧ flee into the mountains:

17 Let him which is on the house top not come down to take any thing out of his house:

18 Neither let him which is in the field return back to take his clothes.

19 And woe unto them that are with child, and to them that give suck in those days!

20 But pray ye that your flight be not in the winter, neither on the sabbath day:

21 For [o]then shall be great tribulation, such as was not since the beginning of the world to this time, no, nor ever shall be.

22 And except those days should be shortened, there should no flesh be saved: [p]but for the elect's sake those days shall be shortened.

23 Then if any man shall say unto you, Lo, here *is* Chrīst, or there; believe *it* not.

24 For [q]there shall arise false Chrīsts, and false prophets, and shall shew great signs and wonders; insomuch that, [r]if *it were* possible, they shall deceive the very elect.

25 Behold, I have told you before.

26 Wherefore if they shall say unto you, Behold, he is in the desert; go not forth: behold, *he is* in the secret chambers; believe *it* not.

27 For as the lightning cometh out of the east, and shineth even unto the west; so shall also the coming of the Son of man be.

28 For [s]wheresoever the carcase is, there will the eagles be gathered together.

29 ¶ Immediately [t]after the tribulation of those days [u]shall the sun be darkened, and the moon shall not give her light, and the stars shall fall from heaven, and the powers of the heavens shall be shaken:

30 And [v]then shall appear the sign of the Son of man in heaven: and [w]then shall all the tribes of the earth mourn, [x]and they shall see the Son of man coming in the clouds of heaven with power and great glory.

31 And [y]he shall send his angels [1]with a great sound of a trumpet, and they shall gather together his elect from the four winds, from one end of heaven to the other.

32 Now learn [z]a parable of the fig tree; When his branch is yet tender, and putteth forth leaves, ye know that summer *is* nigh:

33 So likewise ye, when ye shall see all these things, know that [2]it is near, *even* at the doors.

34 Verily I say unto you, [a]This generation shall not pass, till all these things be fulfilled.

35 Heaven [b]and earth shall pass away, but my words shall not pass away.

36 ¶ But [c]of that day and hour knoweth no *man,* no, not the angels of heaven, [d]but my Father only.

37 But as the days of Nō'e *were,* so shall also the coming of the Son of man be.

38 For [e]as in the days that were before the flood they were eating and drinking, marrying and giving in marriage, until the day that Nō'e entered into the ark,

39 And knew not until the flood came, and took them all away; so shall also the coming of the Son of man be.

40 Then shall two be in the field; the one shall be taken, and the other left.

41 Two *women shall be* grinding at the mill; the one shall be taken, and the other left.

42 ¶ Watch therefore: for ye know not what hour your Lord doth come.

43 But [f]know this, that if the goodman of the house had known in what watch the thief would come, he would have watched, and would not have suffered his house to be broken up.

44 Therefore be ye also ready: for in such an hour as ye think not the Son of man cometh.

45 [g]Who then is a faithful and wise servant, whom his lord hath made ruler over his household, to give them meat in due season?

46 [h]Blessed *is* that servant, whom his lord when he cometh shall find so doing.

47 Verily I say unto you, That he shall make him ruler over all his goods.

4 [d]Eph. 5.6; 1 John 4.1
5 [e]Jer. 14.14; Acts 5.36-37
7 [f]Isa. 19.2; Zech. 14.13
9 [g]Acts 4.2-3; Rev. 2.10-13
10 [h]2 Tim. 1.15; 2 Tim. 4.10-16
11 [i]Acts 20.29; Jude 4
[j]1 Tim. 4.1
13 [k]Heb. 3.6
14 [l]Rom. 10.18; Col. 1.6-23
15 [m]Dan. 9.27; Dan. 12.11
[n]Dan. 9.23
21 [o]Ps. 69.22-28; Joel 2.2
22 [p]Isa. 65.8-9; Zech. 14.2-3
24 [q]Deut. 13.1; Rev. 13.13
[r]Rom. 8.28; 1 Pet. 1.5
28 [s]Job 39.30
29 [t]Dan. 7.11
[u]Isa. 13.10; Rev. 6.12
30 [v]Dan. 7.13; Mark 13.4
[w]Zech. 12.12
[x]Rev. 1.7
31 [y]1 Cor. 15.52; 1 Thess. 4.16
[1]Or, with a trumpet, and a great voice
32 [z]Luke 21.29
33 [2]Or, he; Jas. 5.9
34 [a]ch. 16.28 ch. 23.36
35 [b]Ps. 102.26-27
36 [c]Acts 1.7;
[d]Zech. 14.7
38 [e]Gen. 6.3
43 [f]1 Thess. 5.6
45 [g]1 Cor. 4.2
46 [h]ch. 25.34

48 But and if that evil servant shall say in his heart, My lord delayeth his coming;

49 And shall begin to smite *his* fellowservants, and to eat and drink with the drunken;

50 The lord of that servant shall come in a day when he looketh not for *him,* and in an hour that he is not aware of,

51 And shall [3]cut him asunder, and appoint *him* [i]his portion with the hypocrites: there shall be weeping and gnashing of teeth.

CHAPTER 25

25 Then shall the kingdom of heaven be likened unto ten virgins, which took their lamps, and went forth to meet the [a]bridegroom.

2 And [b]five of them were wise, and five *were* foolish.

3 They that *were* foolish took their lamps, and took [c]no oil with them:

4 But the wise took oil in their vessels with their lamps.

5 While the bridegroom tarried, they [d]all slumbered and slept.

6 And at midnight [e]there was a cry made, Behold, the bridegroom cometh; go ye out to meet him.

7 Then all those virgins arose, and [f]trimmed their lamps.

8 And the foolish said unto the wise, Give us of your oil; for our lamps are [1]gone out.

9 But the wise answered, saying, *Not so;* lest there be not enough for us and you: but go ye rather to them that sell, and buy for yourselves.

10 And while they went to buy, the bridegroom came; and they that were ready went in with him to the marriage: and the [g]door was shut.

11 Afterward came also the other virgins, saying, [h]Lord, Lord, open to us.

12 But he answered and said, Verily I say unto you, [i]I know you not.

13 [j]Watch therefore, for ye know neither the day nor the hour wherein the Son of man cometh.

14 ¶ For [k]*the kingdom of heaven is* as [l]a man travelling into a far country, *who* called his own servants, and delivered unto them his goods.

15 And unto one he gave five [2]talents, to another two, and to another one; [m]to every man according to his several ability; and straightway took his journey.

16 Then he that had received the five talents went and [n]traded with the same, and made *them* other five talents.

17 And likewise he that *had received* two, he also gained other two.

18 But he that had received one went and digged in the earth, and hid [o]his lord's money.

19 After a long time the lord of those servants cometh, and reckoneth with them.

20 And so he that had received five talents came and brought other five talents, saying, Lord, thou deliveredst unto me five talents: behold, I have gained beside them five talents more.

21 His lord said unto him, Well done, *thou* good and faithful servant: thou hast been faithful over a few things, [p]I will make thee ruler over many things: enter thou into [q]the joy of thy lord.

22 He also that had received two talents came and said, Lord, thou deliveredst unto me two talents: behold, I have gained two other talents beside them.

23 His lord said unto him, Well done, good and faithful servant; thou hast been faithful over a few things, I will make thee ruler over many things: enter thou into the joy of thy lord.

24 Then he which had received the one talent came and said, Lord, I knew thee that thou art an hard man, reaping where thou hast not sown, and gathering where thou hast not strawed:

25 And I was afraid, and went and hid thy talent in the earth: lo, *there* thou hast *that is* thine.

26 His lord answered and said unto him, *Thou* wicked and slothful servant, thou knewest that I reap where I sowed not, and gather where I have not strawed:

27 Thou oughtest therefore to have put my money to the exchangers, and *then* at my coming I should have received mine own with usury.

28 Take therefore the talent from him, and give *it* unto him which hath ten talents.

29 For [r]unto every one that hath shall be given, and he shall have abundance: but from him that hath not shall be taken away even that which he hath.

30 And cast ye the unprofitable servant into outer darkness: there shall be weeping and gnashing of teeth.

31 ¶ When [s]the Son of man shall come in his glory, and all the holy angels with him, then shall he sit upon the throne of his glory:

32 And [t]before him shall be gathered all nations; and [u]he shall separate them one from another, as a shepherd divideth *his* sheep from the goats:

33 And he shall set the sheep on his right hand, but the goats on the left.

34 Then shall the King say unto them on his right hand, Come, ye blessed of my Father, [v]inherit the kingdom [w]prepared for you from the foundation of the world:

35 For [x]I was an hungred, and ye gave me meat: I was thirsty, and ye gave me drink: [y]I was a stranger, and ye took me in:

36 [z]Naked, and ye clothed me: I was sick, and ye visited me: [a]I was in prison, and ye came unto me.

37 Then shall the righteous answer him, saying, Lord, when saw we thee an hungred, and fed *thee?* or thirsty, and gave *thee* drink?

38 When saw we thee a stranger, and took *thee* in? or naked, and clothed *thee?*

51 [3]Or, cut him off
[i]Ps. 11.6; Luke 12.46

CHAPTER 25
1 [a]John 3.29; Rev. 21.2-9
2 [b]ch. 13.47; ch. 22.10
3 [c]2 Tim. 3.5
5 [d]Song 5.2; 1 Thess. 5.6
6 [e]Ps. 50.3-6; 1 Thess. 4.16
7 [f]Luke 12.35
8 [1]Or, going out
10 [g]Luke 13.25
11 [h]ch. 7.21
12 [i]Ps. 5.5; John 9.31
13 [j]ch. 24.42; Rev. 16.15
14 [k]Luke 19.12
[l]ch. 21.33
15 [2]A talent is 187*l.* 10*s*
[m]Rom. 12.6; Eph. 4.11
16 [n]Prov. 3.14; 1 Pet. 4.10
18 [o]Phil. 2.21
21 [p]ch. 24.47; Rev. 21.7
[q]Acts 2.28; 1 Pet. 1.8
29 [r]Luke 8.18; 2 Cor. 6.1
31 [s]Zech. 14.5; Rev. 1.7
32 [t]Rom. 14.10; Rev. 20.12
[u]Ps. 1.5
34 [v]Luke 12.32;
[w]1 Cor. 2.9
35 [x]Isa. 58.7;
[y]Heb. 13.2
36 [z]Jas. 2.15
[a]2 Tim. 1.16

39 Or when saw we thee sick, or in
prison, and came unto thee?
40 And the King shall answer and
say unto them, Verily I say unto you,
[b]Inasmuch as ye have done *it* unto one
of the least of these my brethren, ye
have done *it* unto me.
41 Then shall he say also unto them
on the left hand, [c]Depart from me,
ye cursed, into [d]everlasting fire, prepared for [e]the devil and his angels:
42 For I was an hungred, and ye
gave me no meat: I was thirsty, and ye
gave me no drink:
43 I was a stranger, and ye took me
not in: naked, and ye clothed me not:
sick, and in prison, and ye visited me
not.
44 Then shall they also answer him,
saying, Lord, when saw we thee an
hungred, or athirst, or a stranger, or
naked, or sick, or in prison, and did not
minister unto thee?
45 Then shall he answer them, saying, Verily I say unto you, [f]Inasmuch
as ye did *it* not to one of the least of
these, ye did *it* not to me.
46 And [g]these shall go away into
everlasting punishment: but the righteous into [h]life eternal.

26 And it came to pass, when Jē′sus
had finished all these sayings, he
said unto his disciples,
2 [a]Ye know that after two days is
the feast of the passover, and the Son
of man is betrayed to be crucified.
3 Then [b]assembled together the chief
priests, and the scribes, and the elders
of the people, unto the palace of the high
priest, who was called Cā′ia-phas,
4 And consulted that they might take
Jē′sus by subtilty, and kill *him*.
5 But they said, Not on the feast
day, lest there be an uproar among the
people.
6 ¶ Now [c]when Jē′sus was [d]in Bĕth′-
ă-nȳ, in the house of Sī′mon the leper,
7 There came unto him a woman
having an alabaster box of very precious ointment, and poured it on his
head, as he sat *at meat*.
8 But [e]when his disciples saw *it*,
they had indignation, saying, To what
purpose *is* this waste?
9 For this ointment might have been
sold for much, and given to the poor.
10 When Jē′sus understood *it*, he
said unto them, Why trouble ye the
woman? for she hath wrought a good
work upon me.
11 For [f]ye have the poor always
with you; but [g]me ye have not always.
12 For in that she hath poured this
ointment on my body, she did *it* for my
burial.
13 Verily I say unto you, [h]Whereso-
ever this gospel shall be preached in
the whole world, *there* shall also this,
that this woman hath done, be told for
a memorial of her.
14 ¶ [i]Then one of the twelve, called
[j]Jū′das Ĭs-căr′ĭ-ot, went unto the chief
priests,
15 And said *unto them*, [k]What will
ye give me, and I will deliver him unto
you? And they covenanted with him
for thirty pieces of silver.
16 And from that time he sought opportunity to betray him.
17 ¶ Now [l]the first *day* of the *feast of*
unleavened bread the disciples came to
Jē′sus, saying unto him, Where wilt
thou that we prepare for thee to eat the
passover?
18 And he said, Go into the city to
such a man, and say unto him, The
Master saith, My time is at hand; I will
keep the passover at thy house with
my disciples.
19 And the disciples did as Jē′sus
had appointed them; and they made
ready the passover.
20 Now when the even was come,
he sat down with the twelve.
21 And as they did eat, he said, Verily I say unto you, that one of you shall
betray me.
22 And they were exceeding sorrowful, and began every one of them to say
unto him, Lord, is it I?
23 And he answered and said, He
[m]that dippeth *his* hand with me in the
dish, the same shall betray me.
24 The Son of man goeth [n]as it is
written of him: but [o]woe unto that man
by whom the Son of man is betrayed! it
had been good for that man if he had
not been born.
25 Then Jū′das, which betrayed him,
answered and said, Master, is it I? He
said unto him, Thou hast said.
26 ¶ And as they were eating, [p]Jē′-
sus took bread, and [1]blessed *it*, and
brake *it*, and gave *it* to the disciples,
and said, Take, eat; [q]this is my body.
27 And he took the cup, and gave
thanks, and gave *it* to them, saying,
Drink ye all of it;
28 For [r]this is my blood [s]of the new
testament, which is shed [t]for many for
the remission of sins.
29 But I say unto you, I will not
drink henceforth of this fruit of the
vine, [u]until that day when I drink it
new with you in my Father's kingdom.
30 And [v]when they had sung an
[2]hymn, they went out into the mount of
Ŏl′ĭves.
31 Then saith Jē′sus unto them, [w]All
ye shall [x]be offended because of me
this night: for it is written, [y]I will smite
the shepherd, and the sheep of the
flock shall be scattered abroad.
32 But after I am risen again, [z]I will
go before you into Găl′ĭ-lee.
33 Pē′tẽr answered and said unto
him, Though all *men* shall be offended
because of thee, *yet* will I never be
offended.
34 Jē′sus said unto him, [a]Verily I
say unto thee, That this night, before
the cock crow, thou shalt deny me
thrice.
35 Pē′tẽr said unto him, Though I
should die with thee, yet will I not
deny thee. Likewise also said all the
disciples.
36 ¶ Then [b]cometh Jē′sus with them
unto a place called Gĕth-sĕm′a-ne, and

40 [b]Prov. 14.31; Heb. 6.10
41 [c]Ps. 6.8
[d]ch. 13.40
[e]2 Pet. 2.4; Jude 6
45 [f]Prov. 14.31; Acts 9.5
46 [g]Dan. 12.2; Rev. 20.10-15
[h]Rev. 3.21; Rev. 7.15

CHAPTER 26
2 [a]Mark 14.1; John 13.1
3 [b]Ps. 2.2; Acts 4.25
6 [c]Mark 14.3; John 12.3
[d]ch. 21.17
8 [e]John 12.4
11 [f]Deut. 15.11; John 12.8
[g]John 13.33; John 17.11
13 [h]Mark 13.10; Rom. 10.18
14 [i]Mark 14.10;
[j]ch. 10.4
15 [k]Zech. 11.12
17 [l]Ex. 12.6
23 [m]Ps. 41.9
24 [n]Gen. 3.15;
[o]ch. 18.7
26 [p]Luke 24.30;
[1]Many Greek copies have, gave thanks
[q]1 Cor. 10.16
28 [r]Ex. 24.8;
[s]Jer. 31.31
[t]Rom. 5.15
29 [u]Acts 10.41
30 [v]Mark 14.26
[2]Or, psalm
31 [w]John 16.32
[x]ch. 11.6
[y]Zech. 13.7
32 [z]ch. 28.7
34 [a]Luke 22.34
36 [b]John 18.1

saith unto the disciples, Sit ye here,
while I go and pray yonder.
37 And he took with him Pē'tēr and
[c]the two sons of Zēb'e-dee, and began
to be sorrowful and very heavy.
38 Then saith he unto them, [d]My
soul is exceeding sorrowful, even unto
death: tarry ye here, and [e]watch with
me.
39 And he went a little farther, and
fell on his face, and [f]prayed, saying,
[g]O my Father, if it be possible, [h]let this
cup pass from me: nevertheless [i]not as
I will, but as thou *wilt*.
40 And he cometh unto the disciples, and findeth them asleep, and
saith unto Pē'tēr, What, could ye not
watch with me one hour?
41 [j]Watch and pray, that ye enter
not into temptation: the spirit indeed *is*
willing, but the flesh *is* weak.
42 He went away again the second
time, and prayed, saying, O my Father,
if this cup may not pass away from me,
except I drink it, thy will be done.
43 And he came and found them
asleep again: for their eyes were heavy.
44 And he left them, and went away
again, and prayed the third time, saying the same words.
45 Then cometh he to his disciples,
and saith unto them, Sleep on now,
and take *your* rest: behold, the hour is
at hand, and the Son of man is betrayed into the hands of sinners.
46 Rise, let us be going: behold, he is
at hand that doth betray me.
47 ¶ And [k]while he yet spake, lo,
Jū'das, one of the twelve, came, and
with him a great multitude with swords
and staves, from the chief priests and
elders of the people.
48 Now he that betrayed him gave
them a sign, saying, Whomsoever I
shall kiss, that same is he: hold him
fast.
49 And forthwith he came to Jē'sus,
and said, Hail, master; [l]and kissed
him.
50 And Jē'sus said unto him, [3]Friend,
wherefore art thou come? Then came
they, and laid hands on Jē'sus, and
took him.
51 And, behold, [m]one of them which
were with Jē'sus stretched out *his* hand,
and drew his sword, and struck a servant of the high priest's, and smote off
his ear.
52 Then said Jē'sus unto him, [n]Put
up again thy sword into his place: [o]for
all they that take the sword shall perish with the sword.
53 Thinkest thou that I cannot now
pray to my Father, and he shall presently give me [p]more than twelve le-
gions of angels?
54 But how then shall [q]the scriptures be fulfilled, that thus it must be?
55 In that same hour said Jē'sus to
the multitudes, Are ye come out as
against a thief with swords and staves
for to take me? I sat daily with you
teaching in the temple, and ye laid no
hold on me.

37 [c]ch. 4.21
38 [d]Job 6.2-4; [e]1 Pet. 5.8
39 [f]Mark 14.36; [g]John 12.27 [h]ch. 20.22; [i]2 Sam. 15.26;
41 [j]Mark 13.33
47 [k]Mark 14.43
49 [l]2 Sam. 20.9
50 [3]Companion; Ps. 41.9; Ps. 55.13
51 [m]John 18.10
52 [n]1 Cor. 4.12 [o]Gen. 9.6
53 [p]2 Ki. 6.17
54 [q]Isa. 53.7
56 [r]Lam. 4.20; [s]John 18.15
57 [t]Mark 14.53
60 [u]1 Ki. 21.10; [v]Deut. 19.15
61 [w]ch. 27.40
63 [x]Isa. 53.7; [y]Lev. 5.1
64 [z]Ps. 110.1; [a]Ps. 110.1
65 [b]2 Ki. 18.37
66 [c]Lev. 24.16
67 [d]Num. 12.14; [e]Mic. 5.1; [4]Or, rods
68 [f]Mark 14.65
75 [g]2 Sam. 12.13
CHAPTER 27
1 [a]Ps. 2.2

56 But all this was done, that the
[r]scriptures of the prophets might be
fulfilled. Then [s]all the disciples forsook him, and fled.
57 ¶ And [t]they that had laid hold on
Jē'sus led *him* away to Cā'ia-phas the
high priest, where the scribes and the
elders were assembled.
58 But Pē'tēr followed him afar off
unto the high priest's palace, and went
in, and sat with the servants, to see the
end.
59 Now the chief priests, and elders,
and all the council, sought false witness against Jē'sus, to put him to
death;
60 But found none: yea, though
[u]many false witnesses came, *yet* found
they none. At the last came [v]two false
witnesses,
61 And said, This *fellow* said, [w]I am
able to destroy the temple of God, and
to build it in three days.
62 And the high priest arose, and
said unto him, Answerest thou nothing? what *is it which* these witness
against thee?
63 But [x]Jē'sus held his peace. And
the high priest answered and said unto
him, [y]I adjure thee by the living God,
that thou tell us whether thou be the
Chrīst, the Son of God.
64 Jē'sus saith unto him, Thou hast
said: nevertheless I say unto you,
[z]Hereafter shall ye see the Son of man
[a]sitting on the right hand of power,
and coming in the clouds of heaven.
65 Then the high priest [b]rent his
clothes, saying, He hath spoken blasphemy; what further need have we of
witnesses? behold, now ye have heard
his blasphemy.
66 What think ye? They answered
and said, [c]He is guilty of death.
67 Then [d]did they spit in his face,
and buffeted him; and [e]others smote
him with [4]the palms of their hands,
68 Saying, [f]Prophesy unto us, thou
Chrīst, Who is he that smote thee?
69 ¶ Now Pē'tēr sat without in the
palace: and a damsel came unto him,
saying, Thou also wast with Jē'sus of
Găl'ĭ-lee.
70 But he denied before *them* all,
saying, I know not what thou sayest.
71 And when he was gone out into
the porch, another *maid* saw him, and
said unto them that were there, This *fellow* was also with Jē'sus of Năz'a-rĕth.
72 And again he denied with an
oath, I do not know the man.
73 And after a while came unto *him*
they that stood by, and said to Pē'tēr,
Surely thou also art *one* of them; for
thy speech bewrayeth thee.
74 Then began he to curse and to
swear, *saying*, I know not the man.
And immediately the cock crew.
75 And Pē'tēr remembered the word
of Jē'sus, which said unto him, Before
the cock crow, thou shalt deny me
thrice. And he went out, and [g]wept
bitterly.

CHAPTER 27

27 When the morning was come, all
[a]the chief priests and elders of

the people took counsel against Jē'sus to put him to death:

2 And when they had bound him, they led *him* away, and [b]delivered him to Pŏn'tĭ-us Pī'late the governor.

3 ¶ Then [c]Jū'das, which had betrayed him, when he saw that he was condemned, repented himself, and brought again the thirty pieces of silver to the chief priests and elders,

4 Saying, I have sinned in that I have betrayed the innocent blood. And they said, What *is that* to us? see thou *to that*.

5 And he cast down the pieces of silver in the temple, [d]and departed, and went and hanged himself.

6 And the chief priests took the silver pieces, and said, It is not lawful for to put them into the treasury, because it is the price of blood.

7 And they took counsel, and bought with them the potter's field, to bury strangers in.

8 Wherefore that field was called, The field of blood, unto this day.

9 Then was fulfilled that which was spoken by Jĕr'e-mȳ the prophet, saying, [e]And they took the thirty pieces of silver, the price of him that was valued, [1]whom they of the children of Is'ra-el did value;

10 And gave them for the potter's field, as the Lord appointed me.

11 And Jē'sus stood before the governor: and [f]the governor asked him, saying, Art thou the King of the Jews? And Jē'sus said unto him, [g]Thou sayest.

12 And when he was accused of the chief priests and elders, [h]he answered nothing.

13 Then said Pī'late unto him, [i]Hearest thou not how many things they witness against thee?

14 And he answered him to never a word; insomuch that the governor marvelled greatly.

15 Now [j]at *that* feast the governor was wont to release unto the people a prisoner, whom they would.

16 And they had then a notable prisoner, called Ba-răb'bas.

17 Therefore when they were gathered together, Pī'late said unto them, Whom will ye that I release unto you? Ba-răb'bas, or Jē'sus which is called Chrīst?

18 For he knew that for [k]envy they had delivered him.

19 ¶ When he was set down on the judgment seat, his wife sent unto him, saying, Have thou nothing to do with that just man: for I have suffered many things this day in [l]a dream because of him.

20 But [m]the chief priests and elders persuaded the multitude that they should ask Ba-răb'bas, and destroy Jē'sus.

21 The governor answered and said unto them, Whether of the twain will ye that I release unto you? They said, Ba-răb'bas.

22 Pī'late saith unto them, What shall I do then with Jē'sus which is

2 [b]ch. 20.19; 1 Thess. 2.14
3 [c]Job 20.5; 2 Cor. 7.10
5 [d]2 Sam. 17.23; Acts 1.18
9 [e]Zech. 11.12
[1]Or, whom they bought of the children of Israel
11 [f]Mark 15.2; John 18.33
[g]John 18.37; 1 Tim. 6.13
12 [h]Isa. 53.7; 1 Pet. 2.23
13 [i]ch. 26.62; John 19.10
15 [j]Mark 15.6; Acts 25.9
18 [k]Acts 7.9
19 [l]Job 33.15
20 [m]Mark 15.11; Acts 3.14
24 [n]Deut. 21.6
25 [o]Num. 35.33; Acts 5.28
26 [p]Isa. 53.5; John 19.1
27 [2]Or, governor's house
28 [q]Luke 23.11
29 [r]Ps. 35.15-16
30 [s]Job 30.10;
[t]Mic. 5.1
31 [u]Isa. 53.7
32 [v]Num. 15.35;
[w]Mark 15.21
34 [x]Ps. 69.21
35 [y]Ps. 22.18
38 [z]Isa. 53.12
39 [a]Ps. 22.7
40 [b]ch. 26.61

called Chrīst? *They* all say unto him, Let him be crucified.

23 And the governor said, Why, what evil hath he done? But they cried out the more, saying, Let him be crucified.

24 ¶ When Pī'late saw that he could prevail nothing, but *that* rather a tumult was made, [n]he took water, and washed *his* hands before the multitude, saying, I am innocent of the blood of this just person: see ye *to it*.

25 Then answered all the people, and said, [o]His blood *be* on us, and on our children.

26 ¶ Then released he Ba-răb'bas unto them: and when [p]he had scourged Jē'sus, he delivered *him* to be crucified.

27 Then the soldiers of the governor took Jē'sus into the [2]common hall, and gathered unto him the whole band *of soldiers*.

28 And they stripped him, and [q]put on him a scarlet robe.

29 ¶ And [r]when they had platted a crown of thorns, they put *it* upon his head, and a reed in his right hand: and they bowed the knee before him, and mocked him, saying, Hail, King of the Jews!

30 And [s]they spit upon him, and took the reed, and [t]smote him on the head.

31 And after that they had mocked him, they took the robe off from him, and put his own raiment on him, [u]and led him away to crucify *him*.

32 And [v]as they came out, [w]they found a man of Çȳ-rē'ne, Sī'mon by name: him they compelled to bear his cross.

33 And when they were come unto a place called Gŏl'go-thȧ, that is to say, a place of a skull,

34 ¶ They [x]gave him vinegar to drink mingled with gall: and when he had tasted *thereof*, he would not drink.

35 And they crucified him, and parted his garments, casting lots: that it might be fulfilled which was spoken by the prophet, [y]They parted my garments among them, and upon my vesture did they cast lots.

36 And sitting down they watched him there;

37 And set up over his head his accusation written, THIS IS JĒ'SUS THE KING OF THE JEWS.

38 Then [z]were there two thieves crucified with him, one on the right hand, and another on the left.

39 ¶ And [a]they that passed by reviled him, wagging their heads,

40 And saying, [b]Thou that destroyest the temple, and buildest *it* in three days, save thyself. If thou be the Son of God, come down from the cross.

41 Likewise also the chief priests mocking *him*, with the scribes and elders, said,

42 He saved others; himself he cannot save. If he be the King of Is'ra-el, let him now come down from the cross, and we will believe him.

43 He [c]trusted in God; let him deliver him now, if he will have him: for he said, I am the Son of God.

44 The [d]thieves also, which were crucified with him, cast the same in his teeth.

45 Now [e]from the sixth hour there was darkness over all the land unto the ninth hour.

46 And about the ninth hour Jē′sus [f]cried with a loud voice, saying, Ē′lī, Ē′lī, lā′mȧ sā-bach-thā′nī? that is to say, [g]My God, my God, why hast thou forsaken me?

47 Some of them that stood there, when they heard *that*, said, This *man* calleth for E-lī′ăs.

48 And straightway one of them ran, and took a spunge, [h]and filled *it* with vinegar, and put *it* on a reed, and gave him to drink.

49 The rest said, Let be, let us see whether E-lī′ăs will come to save him.

50 ¶ Jē′sus, when he had cried again with a loud voice, yielded up the ghost.

51 And, behold, [i]the veil of the temple was rent in twain from the top to the bottom; and [j]the earth did quake, and the rocks rent;

52 And the graves were opened; and [k]many bodies of the saints which slept arose,

53 And came out of the graves after his resurrection, and went into the holy city, and appeared unto many.

54 Now [l]when the centurion, and they that were with him, watching Jē′sus, saw the earthquake, and those things that were done, they feared greatly, saying, Truly this was the Son of God.

55 And many women were there beholding afar off, [m]which followed Jē′sus from Găl′ĭ-lee, ministering unto him:

56 Among [n]which was Mā′rȳ Măg-da-lē′ne, and Mā′rȳ the mother of Jāmes and Jō′sēs, and the mother of Zĕb′e-dee's children.

57 When [o]the even was come, there came a rich man of Ăr-ĭ-mă-thæ′ȧ, named Jō′seph, who also himself was Jē′sus' disciple:

58 He went to Pī′late, and begged the body of Jē′sus. Then Pī′late commanded the body to be delivered.

59 And when Jō′seph had taken the body, he wrapped it in a clean linen cloth,

60 And [p]laid it in his own new tomb, which he had hewn out in the rock: and he rolled a great stone to the door of the sepulchre, and departed.

61 And there was Mā′rȳ Măg-da-lē′ne, and the other Mā′rȳ, sitting over against the sepulchre.

62 ¶ Now the next day, that followed the day of the preparation, the chief priests and Phăr′ĭ-sees came together unto Pī′late,

63 Saying, Sir, we remember that that [q]deceiver said, while he was yet alive, [r]After three days I will rise again.

64 Command therefore that the sepulchre be made sure until the third day, lest his disciples come by night, and steal him away, and say unto the people, He is risen from the dead: so the last error shall be worse than the first.

65 Pī′late said unto them, Ye have a watch: go your way, make *it* as sure as ye can.

66 So they went, and made the sepulchre sure, [s]sealing the stone, and setting a watch.

28 In the [a]end of the sabbath, as it began to dawn toward the first *day* of the week, came Mā′rȳ Măg-da-lē′ne [b]and the other Mā′rȳ to see the sepulchre.

2 And, behold, there [1]was a great earthquake: for [c]the angel of the Lord descended from heaven, and came and rolled back the stone from the door, and sat upon it.

3 His [d]countenance was like lightning, and his raiment white as snow:

4 And for fear of him the keepers did shake, and became as dead *men*.

5 And the angel answered and said unto the women, [e]Fear not ye: for I know that ye seek Jē′sus, which was crucified.

6 He is not here: for he is risen, as [f]he said. Come, see the place where the Lord lay.

7 And go quickly, and tell his disciples that he is risen from the dead; and, behold, he [g]goeth before you into Găl′ĭ-lee; there shall ye see him: lo, I have told you.

8 And they departed quickly from the sepulchre with fear and great joy; and did run to bring his disciples word.

9 ¶ And as they went to tell his disciples, behold, [h]Jē′sus met them, saying, All hail. And they came and held him by the feet, and worshipped him.

10 Then said Jē′sus unto them, Be not afraid: go tell [i]my brethren that they go into Găl′ĭ-lee, and there shall they see me.

11 ¶ Now when they were going, behold, some of the watch came into the city, and shewed unto the chief priests all the things that were done.

12 And when they were assembled with the elders, and had taken counsel, they gave large money unto the soldiers,

13 Saying, Say ye, His disciples came by night, and stole him *away* while we slept.

14 And if this come to the governor's ears, we will persuade him, and secure you.

15 So they took the money, and did as they were taught: and this saying is commonly reported among the Jews until this day.

16 ¶ Then the eleven disciples went away into Găl′ĭ-lee, into a mountain [j]where Jē′sus had appointed them.

17 And when they saw him, they worshipped him: but some doubted.

18 And Jē′sus came and spake unto them, saying, [k]All power is given unto me in heaven and in earth.

43 [c]Ps. 22.8
44 [d]Luke 23.39
45 [e]Isa. 50.3; Amos 8.9
46 [f]Heb. 5.7 [g]Ps. 22.1
48 [h]Ps. 69.21; John 19.29
51 [i]Ex. 26.31; 2 Chr. 3.14; Mark 15.38; Luke 23.45; Eph. 2.14-18; Heb. 6.19; Heb. 10.19-20 [j]Ex. 19.18; Ps. 18.7
52 [k]Ps. 68.20
54 [l]Ex. 20.18-19; Mark 15.39; Luke 23.47
55 [m]Luke 8.2
56 [n]Mark 15.40
57 [o]Mark 15.42; Luke 23.50; John 19.38
60 [p]Isa. 53.9
63 [q]Ps. 2.1-6; Luke 23.2; John 7.12; Acts 4.27-28; 2 Cor. 6.8 [r]ch. 16.21; ch. 17.23; ch. 20.19; ch. 26.61; Mark 8.31
66 [s]Dan. 6.17

CHAPTER 28
1 [a]ch. 12.1-2-5-8; Mark 16.1; Luke 23.54-56 [b]ch. 27.56
2 [1]Or, had been [c]Mark 16.5; Luke 24.4; John 20.12
3 [d]Dan. 10.6; ch. 17.2; Rev. 10.1; Rev. 18.1
5 [e]Rev. 1.17
6 [f]ch. 12.40; ch. 16.21; ch. 17.23; ch. 20.19
7 [g]ch. 26.32; Mark 16.7
9 [h]Mark 16.9; John 20.14; Rev. 1.17-18
10 [i]Rom. 8.29; Heb. 2.11
16 [j]ch. 26.32; Mark 15.41; Mark 16.7
18 [k]Dan. 7.13; Eph. 1.21; Phil. 2.9; 1 Pet. 3.22; Rev. 17.14

19 ¶ Go ye therefore, and [2]teach all
nations, baptizing them in the name of
the Father, and of the Son, and of the
Hō'lȳ Ghōst:
20 [l]Teaching them to observe all
things whatsoever I have commanded
you: and, lo, I am with you alway, *even*
unto the end of the world. Amen.

19 [2]Or, make disciples, or, Christians of all nations;
20 [l]Acts 2.42

THE GOSPEL ACCORDING TO

MARK

Life's Questions

Does Jesus expect me to suffer?
What proves that Jesus is the Messiah?
Can I be a believer in secret and not a part of the church?

God's Answers

As Rome began persecuting Christians in Rome after A.D. 60, God led John Mark to use his memories of service with Paul, Barnabas, and Peter to give the world a new kind of literature: a gospel of Jesus. This encouraged persecuted Christians who faced what Jesus had said they would; it sent Christians on mission to fish for people who would follow Jesus, and it assured believers that Jesus' promises remained true even as the years passed.

Mark shows: Jesus' authority in starting God's new age (1:1—3:6); despite evidence of His power and authority, old age leaders rejected Jesus (3:7—6:6); Jesus overcame opposition to gather a community of blessing (6:7—8:21); Jesus equipped the community to suffer and serve in the new age (8:22—10:52); Jesus' presence pronounced judgment on the old age headquarters in Jerusalem (11—13); the old age crucified Jesus, but God vindicated Him in resurrection (14—16).

Mark calls you to recognize Jesus as God's saving agent of the new age and follow Him even to death.

1 The beginning of the gospel of Jē'-
sus Chrīst, [a]the Son of God;
2 As it is written in the prophets,
[b]Behold, I send my messenger before
thy face, which shall prepare thy way
before thee.
3 The [c]voice of one crying in the wilderness, Prepare ye the way of the
Lord, make his paths straight.
4 Jŏhn did baptize in the wilderness, and preach the baptism of repentance [1]for the remission of sins.
5 And there went out unto him all
the land of Jū-dæ'ȧ, and they of Je-
ru'sa-lĕm, and were all baptized of him
in the river of Jôr'dan, confessing their
sins.
6 And Jŏhn was clothed with camel's hair, and with a girdle of a skin
about his loins; and he did eat [d]locusts
and wild honey;
7 And preached, saying, [e]There cometh one mightier than I after me, the
latchet of whose shoes I am not worthy
to stoop down and unloose.
8 I [f]indeed have baptized you with
water: but he shall baptize you [g]with
the Hō'lȳ Ghōst.
9 And [h]it came to pass in those
days, that Jē'sus came from Năz'a-
rĕth of Găl'ĭ-lee, and was baptized of
Jŏhn in Jôr'dan.
10 And [i]straightway coming up out
of the water, he saw the heavens
[2]opened, and the Spirit like a dove descending upon him:
11 And there came a voice from
heaven, *saying,* [j]Thou art my beloved
Son, in whom I am well pleased.
12 And [k]immediately the spirit driveth him into the wilderness.
13 And he was there in the wilderness forty days, tempted of Sā'tan; and
was with the wild beasts; [l]and the angels ministered unto him.
14 Now after that Jŏhn was put
in prison, Jē'sus came into Găl'ĭ-lee,
[m]preaching the gospel of the kingdom
of God,
15 And saying, [n]The time is fulfilled,
and the kingdom of God is at hand: repent ye, and believe the gospel.
16 Now [o]as he walked by the sea of
Găl'ĭ-lee, he saw Sī'mon and Ăn'drew
his brother casting a net into the sea:
for they were fishers.
17 And Jē'sus said unto them, Come
ye after me, and I will make you to
become fishers of men.
18 And straightway [p]they forsook
their nets, and followed him.
19 And [q]when he had gone a little
farther thence, he saw Jāmes the *son*
of Zēb'e-dee, and Jŏhn his brother,
who also were in the ship mending
their nets.
20 And straightway he called them:
and they left their father Zēb'e-dee in
the ship with the hired servants, and
went after him.
21 And [r]they went into Ca-pêr'na-
ŭm; and straightway on the sabbath
day he entered into the synagogue,
and taught.
22 And [s]they were astonished at his
doctrine: for he taught them as one
that had authority, and not as the
scribes.
23 And [t]there was in their synagogue a man with an unclean spirit;
and he cried out,
24 Saying, Let *us* alone; [u]what have
we to do with thee, thou Jē'sus of

CHAPTER 1
1 [a]Ps. 2.7; 1 John 4.15
2 [b]Mal. 3.1
3 [c]Isa. 40.3; John 1.15-23
4 [1]Or, unto
6 [d]Lev. 11.22
7 [e]Acts 13.25
8 [f]Acts 11.16; Acts 19.4
[g]Isa. 44.3; 1 Cor. 12.13
9 [h]Matt. 3.13; Luke 3.21
10 [i]John 1.32
[2]Or, cloven, or, rent
11 [j]Ps. 2.7; 2 Pet. 1.17
12 [k]Matt. 4.1; Luke 4.1
13 [l]Matt. 4.11
14 [m]Matt. 4.23
15 [n]Ps. 110.3
16 [o]Matt. 4.18
18 [p]Matt. 19.27
19 [q]Matt. 4.21
21 [r]Matt. 4.13
22 [s]Matt. 7.28
23 [t]Matt. 12.43
24 [u]2 Sam. 16.10

Nāz'a-rĕth? art thou come to destroy us? I know thee who thou art, the [v]Holy One of God.

25 And Jē'sus rebuked him, saying, Hold thy peace, and come out of him.

26 And when the unclean spirit [w]had torn him, and cried with a loud voice, he came out of him.

27 And they were all amazed, insomuch that they questioned among themselves, saying, What thing is this? what new doctrine *is* this? for with authority commandeth he even the unclean spirits, and they do obey him.

28 And immediately his fame spread abroad throughout all the region round about Găl'ĭ-lee.

29 And [x]forthwith, when they were come out of the synagogue, they entered into the house of Sī'mon and Ăn'drew, with Jāmes and Jŏhn.

30 But Sī'mon's wife's mother lay sick of a fever, and anon they tell him of her.

31 And he came and took her by the hand, and lifted her up; [y]and immediately the fever left her, and she ministered unto them.

32 And [z]at even, when the sun did set, they brought unto him all that were diseased, and them that were possessed with devils.

33 And all the city was gathered together at the door.

34 And he healed many that were sick of divers diseases, and cast out many devils; and [a]suffered not the devils [3]to speak, because they knew him.

35 And [b]in the morning, rising up a great while before day, he went out, and departed into a solitary place, and [c]there prayed.

36 And Sī'mon and they that were with him followed after him.

37 And when they had found him, they said unto him, All *men* seek for thee.

38 And he said unto them, [d]Let us go into the next towns, that I may preach there also: for [e]therefore came I forth.

39 And [f]he preached in their synagogues throughout all Găl'ĭ-lee, and [g]cast out devils.

40 And [h]there came a leper to him, beseeching him, and kneeling down to him, and saying unto him, If thou wilt, thou canst [i]make me clean.

41 And Jē'sus, [j]moved with compassion, put forth *his* hand, and touched him, and saith unto him, I will; be thou clean.

42 And as soon as he had spoken, immediately the leprosy departed from him, and he was cleansed.

43 And he straitly charged him, and forthwith sent him away;

44 And saith unto him, See thou say nothing to any man: but go thy way, shew thyself to the priest, and offer for thy cleansing those things [k]which Mō'ses commanded, for a testimony unto them.

45 But [l]he went out, and began to publish *it* much, and to blaze abroad the matter, insomuch that Jē'sus could no more openly enter into the city, but was without in desert places: [m]and they came to him from every quarter.

[v]Ps. 16.10; Jas. 2.19
26 [w]ch. 9.20
29 [x]Matt. 8.14; Luke 4.38
31 [y]Ps. 103.3
32 [z]Luke 4.40
34 [a]ch. 3.12; Acts 16.17 [3]Or, to say that they knew him
35 [b]Luke 4.42 [c]Ps. 69.1; Heb. 5.7
38 [d]Luke 4.43 [e]Isa. 61.1; John 17.4
39 [f]Matt. 4.23; 2 Tim. 4.2 [g]Gen. 3.15
40 [h]Num. 12.10-15; Luke 5.12 [i]Gen. 18.14; Jer. 32.17
41 [j]Heb. 2.17; Heb. 4.15
44 [k]Lev. 14.3-4-10; Luke 5.14
45 [l]Luke 5.15 [m]ch. 2.13

CHAPTER 2
1 [a]Matt. 9.1; Luke 5.18
2 [b]Isa. 61.1; Heb. 2.3
5 [c]Gen. 22.12; Heb. 4.13 [d]Ps. 103.3; Isa. 53.11
7 [e]Job 14.4
8 [f]1 Sam. 16.7
9 [g]Matt. 9.5
10 [h]Isa. 53.11
12 [i]Ps. 33.9
13 [j]Matt. 9.9
14 [k]Luke 5.27 [1]Or, at the place where the custom was received
15 [l]Matt. 9.10
16 [m]Isa. 65.5
17 [n]Matt. 9.12-13

2

And again [a]he entered into Ca-pêr'na-ŭm after *some* days; and it was noised that he was in the house.

2 And straightway many were gathered together, insomuch that there was no room to receive *them*, no, not so much as about the door: and he [b]preached the word unto them.

3 And they come unto him, bringing one sick of the palsy, which was borne of four.

4 And when they could not come nigh unto him for the press, they uncovered the roof where he was: and when they had broken *it* up, they let down the bed wherein the sick of the palsy lay.

5 When Jē'sus [c]saw their faith, he said unto the sick of the palsy, [d]Son, thy sins be forgiven thee.

6 But there were certain of the scribes sitting there, and reasoning in their hearts,

7 Why doth this *man* thus speak blasphemies? [e]who can forgive sins but God only?

8 And immediately [f]when Jē'sus perceived in his spirit that they so reasoned within themselves, he said unto them, Why reason ye these things in your hearts?

9 Whether [g]is it easier to say to the sick of the palsy, *Thy* sins be forgiven thee; or to say, Arise, and take up thy bed, and walk?

10 But that ye may know that [h]the Son of man hath power on earth to forgive sins, (he saith to the sick of the palsy,)

11 I say unto thee, Arise, and take up thy bed, and go thy way into thine house.

12 And [i]immediately he arose, took up the bed, and went forth before them all; insomuch that they were all amazed, and glorified God, saying, We never saw it on this fashion.

13 And [j]he went forth again by the sea side; and all the multitude resorted unto him, and he taught them.

14 And [k]as he passed by, he saw Lē'vī the *son* of Ăl-phæ'us sitting [1]at the receipt of custom, and said unto him, Follow me. And he arose and followed him.

15 And [l]it came to pass, that, as Jē'sus sat at meat in his house, many publicans and sinners sat also together with Jē'sus and his disciples: for there were many, and they followed him.

16 And when [m]the scribes and Phăr'ĭ-sees saw him eat with publicans and sinners, they said unto his disciples, How is it that he eateth and drinketh with publicans and sinners?

17 When Jē'sus heard *it*, he saith unto them, [n]They that are whole have no need of the physician, but they that are sick: I came not to call the righteous, but sinners to repentance.

18 And [o]the disciples of Jŏhn and of
the Phăr'ĭ-sees used to fast: and they
come and say unto him, Why do the
disciples of Jŏhn and of the Phăr'ĭ-sees
fast, but thy disciples fast not?
19 And Jē'sus said unto them, Can
the children of [p]the bridechamber fast,
while the [q]bridegroom is with them? as
long as they have the bridegroom with
them, they cannot fast.
20 But the days will come, when the
bridegroom shall be taken away from
them, and then shall they fast in those
days.
21 No man also seweth a piece of
[2]new cloth on an old garment: else the
new piece that filled it up taketh away
from the old, and the rent is made
worse.
22 And no man putteth new wine
into old bottles: else the new wine
doth burst the bottles, and the wine is
spilled, and the bottles will be marred:
but new wine must be put into new
bottles.
23 And [r]it came to pass, that he
went through the corn fields on the sabbath day; and his disciples began, as
they went, [s]to pluck the ears of corn.
24 And the Phăr'ĭ-sees said unto
him, Behold, why do they on the sabbath day that which is not lawful?
25 And he said unto them, Have ye
never read [t]what Dā'vid did, when he
had need, and was an hungred, he, and
they that were with him?
26 How he went into the house of
God in the days of A-bī'a-thär the
high priest, and did eat the shewbread,
[u]which is not lawful to eat but for the
priests, and gave also to them which
were with him?
27 And he said unto them, The sabbath was made for man, and not man
for the sabbath:
28 Therefore [v]the Son of man is
Lord also of the sabbath.

CHAPTER 3

3 And [a]he entered again into the
synagogue; and there was a man
there which had a withered hand.
2 And they watched him, whether
he would heal him on the sabbath day;
that they might accuse him.
3 And he saith unto the man which
had the withered hand, [1]Stand forth.
4 And he saith unto them, Is it lawful to do good on the sabbath days, or
to do evil? to save life, or to kill? But
they held their peace.
5 And when he had looked round
about on them with [b]anger, being
grieved for the [2]hardness of their
hearts, he saith unto the man, Stretch
forth thine hand. And he stretched *it*
out: and his hand was restored whole
as the other.
6 And [c]the Phăr'ĭ-sees went forth,
and straightway took counsel with [d]the
He-rō'dĭ-ans against him, how they
might destroy him.
7 But Jē'sus withdrew himself with
his disciples to the sea: and a great
multitude from Găl'ĭ-lee followed him,
[e]and from Jū-dæ'ȧ,
8 And from Je-ru̥'sa-lĕm, and from
I-du̥-mæ'ȧ, and *from* beyond Jôr'dan;
and they about Tȳre and Sī'dŏn, a
great multitude, when they had heard
what great things he did, came unto
him.
9 And he spake to his disciples, that
a small ship should wait on him because of the multitude, lest they should
throng him.
10 For he had healed many; insomuch that they [3]pressed upon him for
to touch him, as many as had plagues.
11 And [f]unclean spirits, when they
saw him, fell down before him, and
cried, saying, [g]Thou art the Son of
God.
12 And [h]he straitly charged them
that they should not make him known.
13 And [i]he goeth up into a mountain, and calleth *unto him* whom he
would: and they came unto him.
14 And he ordained twelve, that they
should be with him, and that he might
send them forth to preach,
15 And to have power to heal sicknesses, and to cast out devils:
16 And Sī'mon [j]he surnamed Pē'tẽr;
17 And Jāmes the *son* of Zēb'e-dee,
and Jŏhn the brother of Jāmes; and he
surnamed them Bō-ăn-ẽr'ġes, which
is, [k]The sons of thunder:
18 And Ăn'drew, and Phĭl'ĭp, and
Bär-thŏl'ŏ-mew, and Măt'thew, and
Thŏm'as, and Jāmes the *son* of Ăl-
phæ'us, and [l]Thăd-dæ'us, and Sī'mon
the Cā'năan-īte,
19 And Jū'das Ĭs-căr'ĭ-ot, which also
betrayed him: and they went [4]into an
house.
20 And the multitude cometh together again, [m]so that they could not
so much as eat bread.
21 And when his [5]friends heard *of it,*
they went out to lay hold on him: for
they said, He is beside himself.
22 ¶ And the scribes which came
down from Je-ru̥'sa-lĕm said, [n]He hath
Bēĕl'ze-bŭb, and by the prince of the
devils casteth he out devils.
23 And [o]he called them *unto him,*
and said unto them in parables, How
can Sā'tan cast out Sā'tan?
24 And if a kingdom be divided
against itself, that kingdom cannot
stand.
25 And if a house be divided against
itself, that house cannot stand.
26 And if Sā'tan rise up against himself, and be divided, he cannot stand,
but hath an end.
27 No [p]man can enter into a strong
man's house, and spoil his goods, except he will first bind the strong man;
and then he will spoil his house.
28 Verily [q]I say unto you, All sins
shall be forgiven unto the sons of
men, and blasphemies wherewith soever they shall blaspheme:
29 But he that shall blaspheme
against the Hō'lȳ Ghōst hath [r]never
forgiveness, but is in danger of eternal
damnation:
30 Because they said, He hath an unclean spirit.

18 [o]Matt. 9.14
19 [p]Song 1.4
[q]Ps. 45
21 [2]Or, raw, or, unwrought; Matt. 9.16
23 [r]Matt. 12.1;
[s]Deut. 23.25
25 [t]1 Sam. 21.6
26 [u]Ex. 25.30
28 [v]Matt. 12.8

CHAPTER 3

1 [a]Matt. 12.9
3 [1]Arise, stand forth in the midst; Dan. 6.10; Phil. 1.14
5 [b]1 Ki. 19.10; [2]Or, blindness
6 [c]Matt. 12.14
[d]Matt. 22.16
7 [e]Luke 6.17
10 [3]Or, rushed
11 [f]Matt. 8.31;
[g]Matt. 4.3-6;
12 [h]Matt. 12.16
13 [i]Matt. 10.1
16 [j]John 1.42
17 [k]Isa. 58.1
18 [l]Luke 6.16
19 [4]Or, home
20 [m]ch. 6.31
21 [5]Or, kinsmen; John 7.5; John 10.20
22 [n]Matt. 9.34
23 [o]Matt. 12.25
27 [p]Isa. 49.24
28 [q]Matt. 12.31
29 [r]Matt. 25.46

31 ¶ There [s]came then his brethren
and his mother, and, standing without,
sent unto him, calling him.
32 And the multitude sat about him,
and they said unto him, Behold, [t]thy
mother and thy brethren without seek
for thee.
33 And he answered them, saying,
Who is my mother, or my brethren?
34 And he looked round about on
them which sat about him, and said,
[u]Behold my mother and my brethren!
35 For whosoever shall do the will
of God, the same is my brother, and my
sister, and mother.

4

4 And [a]he began again to teach by
the sea side: and there was gathered unto him a great multitude, so
that he entered into a ship, and sat in
the sea; and the whole multitude was
by the sea on the land.
2 And he taught them many things
by parables, [b]and said unto them in
his doctrine,
3 Hearken; Behold, there went out a
sower to sow:
4 And it came to pass, as he sowed,
some fell by the way side, and the
fowls of the air came and devoured it
up.
5 And some fell on stony ground,
where it had not much earth; and immediately it sprang up, because it had
no depth of earth:
6 But when the sun was up, it was
scorched; and because it had no root, it
withered away.
7 And some fell among thorns, and
the thorns grew up, and choked it, and
it yielded no fruit.
8 And other fell on good ground,
and [c]did yield fruit that sprang up and
increased; and brought forth, some
thirty, and some sixty, and some an
hundred.
9 And he said unto them, He that
hath ears to hear, let him hear.
10 And when he was alone, they
that were about him with the twelve
[d]asked of him the parable.
11 And he said unto them, Unto you
it is given to know the [e]mystery of the
kingdom of God: but unto [f]them that
are without, all *these* things are done
in parables:
12 That [g]seeing they may see, and
not perceive; and hearing they may
hear, and not understand; lest at any
time they should be converted, and
their sins should be forgiven them.
13 And he said unto them, Know ye
not this parable? and how then will ye
know all parables?
14 ¶ The [h]sower soweth the word.
15 And these are they by the way
side, where the word is sown; but when
they have heard, [i]Sā'tan cometh immediately, and taketh away the word that
was sown in their hearts.
16 And these are they likewise which
are sown on stony ground; who, when
they have heard the word, immediately
receive it with gladness;
17 And have [j]no root in themselves,
and so endure but for a time: after-

31 [s]Matt. 12.46; Luke 8.19
32 [t]Matt. 13.55; John 7.3
34 [u]Deut. 33.9; Heb. 2.11
CHAPTER 4
1 [a]Matt. 13.1; Luke 8.4
2 [b]ch. 12.38
8 [c]John 15.5; Col. 1.6
10 [d]Prov. 2.1; Luke 8.9
11 [e]1 Cor. 2.10
[f]1 Cor. 1.18; 1 Tim. 3.7
12 [g]Isa. 6.9; Rom. 11.8
14 [h]Matt. 13.19
15 [i]2 Cor. 2.11
17 [j]Job 27.10
19 [k]Ps. 52.7
20 [l]Rom. 7.4
21 [m]Matt. 5.15; [1]The word in the original signifieth a less measure, as at Matt. 5.15
22 [n]Matt. 10.26
23 [o]Matt. 11.15
24 [p]1 John 4.1
[q]Matt. 7.2
25 [r]Matt. 13.12
26 [s]Matt. 3.2
29 [2]Or, ripe; Eph. 4.13
[t]Rev. 14.15
30 [u]Lam. 2.13
32 [v]Mal. 1.11
33 [w]Matt. 13.34
35 [x]Isa. 42.4

ward, when affliction or persecution
ariseth for the word's sake, immediately they are offended.
18 And these are they which are
sown among thorns; such as hear the
word,
19 And the cares of this world, and
[k]the deceitfulness of riches, and the
lusts of other things entering in, choke
the word, and it becometh unfruitful.
20 And these are they which are
sown on good [l]ground; such as hear
the word, and receive *it*, and bring
forth fruit, some thirtyfold, some sixty,
and some an hundred.
21 ¶ And [m]he said unto them, Is a
candle brought to be put under [1]a
bushel, or under a bed? and not to be
set on a candlestick?
22 For [n]there is nothing hid, which
shall not be manifested; neither was
anything kept secret, but that it should
come abroad.
23 If [o]any man have ears to hear, let
him hear.
24 And he said unto them, [p]Take
heed what ye hear: [q]with what measure ye mete, it shall be measured to
you: and unto you that hear shall more
be given.
25 For [r]he that hath, to him shall be
given: and he that hath not, from him
shall be taken even that which he hath.
26 ¶ And he said, [s]So is the kingdom
of God, as if a man should cast seed
into the ground;
27 And should sleep, and rise night
and day, and the seed should spring
and grow up, he knoweth not how.
28 For the earth bringeth forth fruit
of herself; first the blade, then the ear,
after that the full corn in the ear.
29 But when the fruit is [2]brought
forth, immediately [t]he putteth in the
sickle, because the harvest is come.
30 ¶ And he said, [u]Whereunto shall
we liken the kingdom of God? or with
what comparison shall we compare it?
31 *It is* like a grain of mustard seed,
which, when it is sown in the earth, is
less than all the seeds that be in the
earth:
32 But when it is sown, it [v]groweth
up, and becometh greater than all herbs,
and shooteth out great branches; so that
the fowls of the air may lodge under the
shadow of it.
33 And [w]with many such parables
spake he the word unto them, as they
were able to hear *it*.
34 But without a parable spake he
not unto them: and when they were
alone, he expounded all things to his
disciples.
35 And [x]the same day, when the
even was come, he saith unto them, Let
us pass over unto the other side.
36 And when they had sent away
the multitude, they took him even as
he was in the ship. And there were also
with him other little ships.
37 And there arose a great storm of
wind, and the waves beat into the ship,
so that it was now full.

38 And he was in the hinder part of the ship, asleep on a pillow: and they awake him, and say unto him, Master, carest thou not that we perish?

39 And he arose, and [y]rebuked the wind, and said unto the sea, Peace, be still. And the wind ceased, and there was a great calm.

40 And he said unto them, Why are ye so fearful? how is it that ye have no faith?

41 And they [z]feared exceedingly, and said one to another, What manner of man is this, that even the wind and the sea obey him?

5

And [a]they came over unto the other side of the sea, into the country of the Găd'a-rēnes.

2 And when he was come out of the ship, immediately there met him out of the tombs a man with an unclean spirit,

3 Who had *his* dwelling among the tombs; and no man could bind him, no, not with chains:

4 Because that he had been often bound with fetters and chains, and the chains had been plucked asunder by him, and the fetters broken in pieces: neither could any *man* tame him.

5 And always, night and day, he was in the mountains, and in the tombs, crying, and cutting himself with stones.

6 But when he saw Jē'sus afar off, he ran and [b]worshipped him,

7 And cried with a loud voice, and said, What have I to do with thee, Jē'sus, *thou* Son of the most high God? I adjure thee by God, that thou torment me not.

8 For he said unto him, Come out of the man, *thou* unclean spirit.

9 And he asked him, What *is* thy name? And he answered, saying, My name *is* Legion: for we are many.

10 And he besought him much that he would not send them away out of the country.

11 Now there was there nigh unto the mountains a great herd of [c]swine feeding.

12 And all the devils besought him, saying, Send us into the swine, that we may enter into them.

13 And forthwith Jē'sus [d]gave them leave. And the unclean spirits went out, and entered into the swine: and the herd ran violently down a steep place into the sea, (they were about two thousand;) and were choked in the sea.

14 And they that fed the swine fled, and told *it* in the city, and in the country. And they went out to see what it was that was done.

15 And they come to Jē'sus, and see him that was possessed with the devil, and had the legion, sitting, and clothed, and [e]in his right mind: and they were afraid.

16 And they that saw *it* told them how it befell to him that was possessed with the devil, and *also* concerning the swine.

17 And [f]they began to pray him to depart out of their coasts.

18 And when he was come into the ship, he [g]that had been possessed with the devil prayed him that he might be with him.

19 Howbeit Jē'sus suffered him not, but saith unto him, Go home to thy friends, and tell them how great things the Lord hath done for thee, and hath had compassion on thee.

20 And he departed, and [h]began to publish in De-căp'ŏ-lis how great things Jē'sus had done for him: and all *men* did marvel.

21 And [i]when Jē'sus was passed over again by ship unto the other side, much people gathered unto him: and he was nigh unto the sea.

22 And, [j]behold, there cometh one of the rulers of the synagogue, Ja-ī'rus by name; and when he saw him, he fell at his feet,

23 And besought him greatly, saying, My little daughter lieth at the point of death: *I pray thee,* come and lay thy hands on her, that she may be healed; and she shall live.

24 And *Jesus* went with him; and much people followed him, and thronged him.

25 And a certain woman, which [k]had an issue of blood twelve years,

26 And had suffered many things of many physicians, and had spent all that she had, and [l]was nothing bettered, but rather grew worse,

27 When she had heard of Jē'sus, came in the press behind, [m]and touched his garment.

28 For she said, If I may touch but his clothes, I shall be whole.

29 And [n]straightway the fountain of her blood was dried up; and she felt in *her* body that she was healed of that plague.

30 And Jē'sus, immediately knowing in himself that [o]virtue had gone out of him, turned him about in the press, and said, Who touched my clothes?

31 And his disciples said unto him, Thou seest the multitude thronging thee, and sayest thou, Who touched me?

32 And he looked round about to see her that had done this thing.

33 But the woman fearing and trembling, knowing what was done in her, came and fell down before him, and told him all the truth.

34 And he said unto her, Daughter, [p]thy faith hath made thee whole; go in peace, and be whole of thy plague.

35 While [q]he yet spake, there came from the ruler of the synagogue's *house certain* which said, Thy daughter is dead: why troublest thou the Master any further?

36 As soon as Jē'sus heard the word that was spoken, he saith unto the ruler of the synagogue, Be [r]not afraid, only believe.

37 And he suffered no man to follow him, save Pē'tĕr, and Jāmes, and Jŏhn the brother of Jāmes.

39 [y]Job 28.11; Job 38.11; Ps. 29.10; Ps. 65.5; Ps. 89.9; Ps. 93.4; Ps. 107.23-29; Ps. 135.5-6; Nah. 1.4; Matt. 8.24-27; ch. 9.25; Luke 4.39

41 [z]Ps. 33.8-9; Ps. 46.1-3; Isa. 43.2-3; John 6.19-20

CHAPTER 5

1 [a]Matt. 8.28; Luke 8.26

6 [b]Ps. 66.4; Phil. 2.10-11

11 [c]Lev. 11.7; Luke 15.15

13 [d]1 Ki. 22.22; Heb. 2.8

15 [e]Rom. 16.20; 1 John 3.8

17 [f]Gen. 26.16; 1 Cor. 2.14

18 [g]Ps. 116.12; Phil. 1.23

20 [h]Ex. 15.2; ch. 7.31

21 [i]Gen. 49.10; Matt. 9.1

22 [j]Matt. 9.18; Luke 13.14

25 [k]Lev. 15.25; Luke 8.43

26 [l]Ps. 108.12

27 [m]ch. 3.10; Acts 19.12

29 [n]Ex. 15.26; Luke 8.46-47

30 [o]Luke 6.19

34 [p]Matt. 9.22; Acts 14.9

35 [q]Luke 8.49

36 [r]Ps. 103.13; John 11.25-40

38 And he cometh to the house of the ruler of the synagogue, and seeth the tumult, and them that wept and wailed greatly.

39 And when he was come in, he saith unto them, Why make ye this ado, and weep? the damsel is not dead, but [s]sleepeth.

40 And they laughed him to scorn. But [t]when he had put them all out, he taketh the father and the mother of the damsel, and them that were with him, and entereth in where the damsel was lying.

41 And he took the damsel by the hand, and said unto her, Tăl'ĭ-thȧ cū'mī; which is, being interpreted, Damsel, I say unto thee, arise.

42 And [u]straightway the damsel arose, and walked; for she was *of the age* of twelve years. And they were astonished with a great astonishment.

43 And [v]he charged them straitly that no man should know it; and commanded that something should be given her to eat.

6 And [a]he went out from thence, and came into his own country; and his disciples follow him.

2 And when the sabbath day was come, he began to teach in the synagogue: and many hearing *him* were astonished, saying, [b]From whence hath this *man* these things? and what wisdom *is* this which is given unto him, that even such mighty works are wrought by his hands?

3 Is [c]not this the carpenter, the son of Mā'rȳ, [d]the brother of Jāmes, and Jō'sēs, and of Jū'dȧ, and Sī'mon? and are not his sisters here with us? And they [e]were offended at him.

4 But Jē'sus said unto them, [f]A prophet is not without honour, but in his own country, and among his own kin, and in his own house.

5 And [g]he could there do no mighty work, save that he laid his hands upon a few sick folk, and healed *them*.

6 And [h]he marvelled because of their unbelief. [i]And he went round about the villages, teaching.

7 ¶ And [j]he called *unto him* the twelve, and began to send them forth by two and two; and gave them power over unclean spirits;

8 And commanded them that they should take nothing for *their* journey, save a staff only; no scrip, no bread, no [1]money in *their* purse:

9 But [k]*be* shod with sandals; and not put on two coats.

10 And [l]he said unto them, In what place soever ye enter into an house, there abide till ye depart from that place.

11 And [m]whosoever shall not receive you, nor hear you, when ye depart thence, shake [n]off the dust under your feet for a testimony against them. [o]Verily I say unto you, It shall be more tolerable for Sŏd'om [2]and Go-mŏr'rhȧ in the day of judgment, than for that city.

12 And they went out, and preached that men should repent.

13 And they cast out many devils, [p]and anointed with oil many that were sick, and healed *them*.

14 And [q]king Hĕr'od heard *of him;* (for his name was spread abroad:) and he said, That Jŏhn the Băp'tĭst was risen from the dead, and therefore mighty works do shew forth themselves in him.

15 Others [r]said, That it is E-lī'ăs. And others said, That it is a prophet, or as one of the prophets.

16 But [s]when Hĕr'od heard *thereof,* he said, It is Jŏhn, whom I beheaded: he is risen from the dead.

17 For Hĕr'od himself had sent forth and laid hold upon Jŏhn, and bound him in prison for He-rō'dĭ-as' sake, his brother Phĭl'ĭp's wife: for he had married her.

18 For Jŏhn had said unto Hĕr'od, It [t]is not lawful for thee to have thy brother's wife.

19 Therefore He-rō'dĭ-as had [3]a quarrel against him, and would have killed him; but she could not:

20 For Hĕr'od [u]feared Jŏhn, knowing that he was a just man and an holy, and [4]observed him; and when he heard him, he did many things, and heard him gladly.

21 And [v]when a convenient day was come, that Hĕr'od [w]on his birthday made a supper to his lords, high captains, and chief *estates* of Găl'ĭ-lee;

22 And when the daughter of the said He-rō'dĭ-as came in, [x]and danced, and pleased Hĕr'od and them that sat with him, the king said unto the damsel, Ask of me whatsoever thou wilt, and I will give *it* thee.

23 And he sware unto her, Whatsoever [y]thou shalt ask of me, I will give *it* thee, unto the half of my kingdom.

24 And she went forth, and said unto her mother, What shall I ask? And she said, [z]The head of Jŏhn the Băp'tĭst.

25 And she came in straightway with haste unto the king, and asked, saying, I will that thou give me by and by in a charger the head of Jŏhn the Băp'tĭst.

26 And the king was exceeding sorry; *yet* for his oath's sake, and for their sakes which sat with him, he would not reject her.

27 And immediately the king sent [5]an executioner, and commanded his head to be brought: and he went and beheaded him in the prison,

28 And brought his head in a charger, and gave it to the damsel: and the damsel gave it to her mother.

29 And when his disciples heard *of it,* they came and [a]took up his corpse, and laid it in a tomb.

30 And [b]the apostles gathered themselves together unto Jē'sus, and told him all things, both what they had done, and what they had taught.

31 And [c]he said unto them, Come ye yourselves apart into a desert place, and rest a while: for there [d]were many

39 [s]Dan. 12.2 1 Thess. 5.10
40 [t]Acts 9.40
42 [u]Ps. 33.9
43 [v]Matt. 12.16

CHAPTER 6
1 [a]Matt. 13.54
2 [b]John 6.42
3 [c]Isa. 53.2-3; [d]Matt. 12.46; [e]Matt. 11.6
4 [f]Jer. 11.21
5 [g]Gen. 19.22
6 [h]Isa. 59.1-2-16 [i]Matt. 9.35
7 [j]Matt. 10.1
8 [1]The word signifieth a piece of brass money, in value somewhat less than a farthing, but here it is taken in general for money
9 [k]Acts 12.8
10 [l]Matt. 10.11
11 [m]Matt. 10.14 [n]Acts 13.51; [o]Heb. 10.31 [2]or
13 [p]Jas. 5.14
14 [q]Matt. 14.1
15 [r]Matt. 16.14
16 [s]Luke 3.19
18 [t]Lev. 18.16
19 [3]Or, an inward grudge
20 [u]Matt. 21.26 [4]Or, kept him, or, saved him
21 [v]Matt. 14.6 [w]Gen. 40.20
22 [x]Isa. 3.16
23 [y]Esth. 5.3-6
24 [z]verse 16
27 [5]Or, one of his guard
29 [a]1 Ki. 13.29-30
30 [b]Luke 9.10
31 [c]Matt. 14.13 [d]ch. 3.20

coming and going, and they had no lei-
sure so much as to eat.
32 And they departed into a desert
place by ship privately.
33 And the people saw them departing, and many knew him, and ran
afoot thither out of all cities, and out-
went them, and came together unto
him.
34 And Jē'sus, when he came out,
saw much people, and [e]was moved
with compassion toward them, because they were as sheep not having a
shepherd: and [f]he began to teach them
many things.
35 And [g]when the day was now far
spent, his disciples came unto him, and
said, This is a desert place, and now
the time *is* far passed:
36 Send them away, that they may
go into the country round about, and
into the villages, and buy themselves
bread: for they have nothing to eat.
37 He answered and said unto them,
Give ye them to eat. And they say unto
him, [h]Shall we go and buy two hundred [6]pennyworth of bread, and give
them to eat?
38 He saith unto them, How many
loaves have ye? go and see. And when
they knew, they say, [i]Five, and two
fishes.
39 And he commanded them to make
all sit down [j]by companies upon the
green grass.
40 And they sat down in ranks, by
hundreds, and by fifties.
41 And when he had taken the five
loaves and the two fishes, he looked up
to heaven, and [k]blessed, and brake the
loaves, and gave *them* to his disciples
to set before them; and the two fishes
divided he among them all.
42 And they did all eat, and were
filled.
43 And they took up twelve baskets
full of the fragments, and of the fishes.
44 And they that did eat of the loaves
were about five thousand men.
45 [l]And straightway he constrained
his disciples to get into the ship, and to
go to the other side before [7]unto Bĕth-
sā'ĭ-dȧ, while he sent away the people.
46 And when he had sent them away,
he departed into a mountain to pray.
47 [m]And when even was come, the
ship was in the midst of the sea, and he
alone on the land.
48 And he saw them toiling in row-
ing; for the wind was contrary unto
them: and about the fourth watch of
the night he cometh unto them, walking upon the sea, and [n]would have
passed by them.
49 But when they saw him walking
upon the sea, they supposed it had
been a spirit, and cried out:
50 For they all saw him, and were
troubled. And immediately he talked
with them, and saith unto them, Be of
good cheer: it is I; be not afraid.
51 And he went up unto them into
the ship; and the wind ceased: and
they were sore amazed in themselves
beyond measure, and wondered.
52 For [o]they considered not *the miracle* of the loaves: for [p]their heart was
hardened.
53 [q]And when they had passed over,
they came into the land of Gĕn-nĕs'a-
rĕt, and drew to the shore.
54 And when they were come out of
the ship, straightway they knew him,
55 And ran through that whole region round about, and began to carry
about in beds those that were sick,
where they heard he was.
56 And whithersoever he entered,
into villages, or cities, or country, they
laid the sick in the streets, and besought him that [r]they might touch if it
were but the border of his garment:
and as many as touched [8]him were
made whole.

7 Then [a]came together unto him
the Phăr'ĭ-sees, and certain of the
scribes, which came from Je-ru̥'sa-lĕm.
2 And when they saw some of his
disciples eat bread with [1]defiled, that is
to say, with unwashen, hands, they
found fault.
3 For the Phăr'ĭ-sees, and all the
Jews, except they wash *their* hands
[2]oft, eat not, holding the tradition of
the elders.
4 And *when they come* from the market, except they wash, they eat not.
And many other things there be, which
they have received to hold, *as* the washing of cups, and [3]pots, brasen vessels,
and of [4]tables.
5 [b]Then the Phăr'ĭ-sees and scribes
asked him, Why walk not thy disciples
according to the tradition of the elders,
but eat bread with unwashen hands?
6 He answered and said unto them,
Well hath E-sā'ias prophesied of you
hypocrites, as it is written, [c]This people honoureth me with *their* lips, but
their heart is far from me.
7 Howbeit in vain do they worship
me, teaching *for* doctrines the commandments of men.
8 For laying aside the commandment of God, ye hold the tradition of
men, *as* the washing of pots and cups:
and many other such like things ye do.
9 And he said unto them, Full well
ye [5d]reject the commandment of God,
that ye may keep your own tradition.
10 For Mō'ses said, [e]Honour thy father and thy mother; and, [f]Whoso curseth father or mother, let him die the
death:
11 But ye say, If a man shall say to
his father or mother, *It is* [g]Corban,
that is to say, a gift, by whatsoever
thou mightest be profited by me; *he
shall be free.*
12 And ye suffer him no more to do
ought for his father or his mother;
13 Making the word of God of none
effect through your tradition, which ye
have delivered: and many such like
things do ye.
14 ¶ And when he had called all the
people *unto him*, he said unto them,
Hearken unto me every one *of you*,
and understand:

34 [e]Ps. 86.15; Heb. 5.2
[f]Isa. 54.13; Luke 9.11
35 [g]Matt. 14.15; Luke 9.12
37 [h]Num. 11.13-22; John 6.7
[6]The Roman penny is seven pence halfpenny; Matt. 18.28
38 [i]Matt. 14.17; John 6.9
39 [j]1 Cor. 14.40
41 [k]1 Sam. 9.13; 1 Tim. 4.4-5
45 [l]Matt. 14.22; John 6.17
[7]Or, over against Bethsaida
47 [m]Matt. 14.23
48 [n]Luke 24.28
52 [o]Matt. 16.9-11;
[p]Jer. 17.9
53 [q]Matt. 14.34
56 [r]Matt. 9.20;
[8]Or, it
CHAPTER 7
1 [a]Matt. 15.1
2 [1]Or, common
3 [2]with the fist, or, diligently. Theophylact, up to the elbow
4 [3]Sextarius is about a pint and an half
[4]Or, beds
5 [b]Matt. 15.2
6 [c]Isa. 29.13
9 [5]Or, frustrate
[d]Isa. 24.5
10 [e]Ex. 20.12;
[f]Ex. 21.17
11 [g]Matt. 15.5

15 [h]There is nothing from without a man, that entering into him can defile him: but the things which come out of him, those are they that defile the man.

16 [i]If any man have ears to hear, let him hear.

17 [j]And when he was entered into the house from the people, his disciples asked him concerning the parable.

18 And he saith unto them, Are ye so without understanding also? Do ye not perceive, that whatsoever thing from without entereth into the man, *it* cannot defile him;

19 Because it entereth not into his heart, but into the belly, and goeth out into the draught, purging all meats?

20 And he said, That which cometh out of the man, that defileth the man.

21 [k]For from within, out of the heart of men, proceed evil thoughts, adulteries, fornications, murders,

22 Thefts, [6]covetousness, wickedness, deceit, lasciviousness, an evil eye, blasphemy, pride, foolishness:

23 All these evil things come from within, and defile the man.

24 ¶ [l]And from thence he arose, and went into the borders of Tȳre and Sī'dŏn, and entered into an house, and would have no man know *it:* but he could not be hid.

25 For a *certain* woman, whose young daughter had an unclean spirit, heard of him, and came and fell at his feet:

26 The women was a [7]Greek, a Sȳ-ro-phe-nĭ'çian by nation; and she besought him that he would cast forth the devil out of her daughter.

27 But Jē'sus said unto her, [m]Let the children first be filled: for it is not meet to take the children's bread, and to cast *it* unto the dogs.

28 And she answered and said unto him, Yes, Lord: yet the dogs under the table eat of the children's crumbs.

29 And he said unto her, For this saying go thy way; the devil is gone out of thy daughter.

30 And when she was come to her house, she found [n]the devil gone out, and her daughter laid upon the bed.

31 ¶ [o]And again, departing from the coasts of Tȳre and Sī'dŏn, he came unto the sea of Găl'ĭ-lee, through the midst of the coasts of De-căp'ŏ-lis.

32 And [p]they bring unto him one that was deaf, and had an impediment in his speech; and they beseech him to put his hand upon him.

33 And he took him aside from the multitude, and put his fingers into his ears, and [q]he spit, and touched his tongue;

34 And [r]looking up to heaven, [s]he sighed, and saith unto him, Eph'phā-thȧ, that is, Be opened.

35 [t]And straightway his ears were opened, and the string of his tongue was loosed, and he spake plain.

36 And [u]he charged them that they should tell no man: but the more he charged them, so much the more a great deal they published *it;*

37 And were beyond measure astonished, saying, He hath done all things well: he maketh both the deaf to hear, and the dumb to speak.

8 In those days [a]the multitude being very great, and having nothing to eat, Jē'sus called his disciples *unto him,* and saith unto them,

2 I have [b]compassion on the multitude, because they have now been with me three days, and have nothing to eat:

3 And if I send them away fasting to their own houses, they will faint by the way: for divers of them came from far.

4 And his disciples answered him, From whence [c]can a man satisfy these *men* with bread here in the wilderness?

5 [d]And he asked them, How many loaves have ye? And they said, Seven.

6 And he commanded the people to sit down on the ground: and he took the seven loaves, and [e]gave thanks, and brake, and gave to his disciples to set before *them;* and they did set *them* before the people.

7 And they had a few small fishes: and [f]he blessed, and commanded to set them also before *them.*

8 So they did eat, and were filled: and they took up of the broken *meat* that was left seven baskets.

9 And they that had eaten were about four thousand: and he sent them away.

10 ¶ And [g]straightway he entered into a ship with his disciples, and came into the parts of Dăl-ma-nū'thȧ.

11 [h]And the Phăr'ĭ-sees came forth, and began to question with him, seeking of him a sign from heaven, tempting him.

12 And he sighed deeply in his spirit, and saith, Why doth this generation seek after a sign? verily I say unto you, There shall no sign be given unto this generation.

13 And he left them, and entering into the ship again departed to the other side.

14 ¶ [i]Now *the disciples* had forgotten to take bread, neither had they in the ship with them more than one loaf.

15 [j]And he charged them, saying, Take heed, beware of the leaven of the Phăr'ĭ-sees, and *of* the leaven of Hĕr'od.

16 And they reasoned among themselves, saying, *It is* [k]because we have no bread.

17 And when Jē'sus knew *it,* he saith unto them, Why reason ye, because ye have no bread? [l]perceive ye not yet, neither understand? have ye your heart yet hardened?

18 Having eyes, see ye not? and having ears, hear ye not? and do ye not remember?

19 [m]When I brake the five loaves among five thousand, how many baskets full of fragments took ye up? They say unto him, Twelve.

20 And [n]when the seven among four thousand, how many baskets full of

15 [h]Acts 10.14-15; Tit. 1.15
16 [i]Matt. 11.15
17 [j]Matt. 15.15
21 [k]Gen. 6.5; Tit. 3.3
22 [6]covetousnesses, wickednesses
24 [l]Matt. 15.21
26 [7]Or, Gentile
27 [m]Matt. 7.6; Eph. 2.12
30 [n]Josh. 21.45; 1 John 3.8
31 [o]Matt. 15.29
32 [p]Matt. 9.32; Luke 11.14
33 [q]ch. 8.23; John 9.6
34 [r]ch. 6.41; [s]John 11.33-38
35 [t]Ps. 33.9
36 [u]Isa. 42.2

CHAPTER 8

1 [a]Matt. 15.32
2 [b]Ps. 86.15
4 [c]Num. 11.21-22
5 [d]Matt. 15.34
6 [e]Deut. 8.10
7 [f]Matt. 14.19
10 [g]Matt. 15.39
11 [h]Matt. 12.38
14 [i]Matt. 16.5
15 [j]Matt. 16.6
16 [k]Matt. 16.7
17 [l]Isa. 63.17
19 [m]Matt. 14.20
20 [n]Matt. 15.37

fragments took ye up? And they said, Seven.

21 And he said unto them, How is it that [o]ye do not understand?

22 ¶ And he cometh to Bĕth-sā'ĭ-dȧ; and they bring a blind man unto him, and besought him to touch him.

23 And he took the blind man by the hand, and led him out of the town; and when [p]he had spit on his eyes, and put his hands upon him, he asked him if he saw ought.

24 And he looked up, and said, I see men as trees, walking.

25 After that he put *his* hands again upon his eyes, and made him look up: and he was restored, and saw every man clearly.

26 And he sent him away to his house, saying, Neither go into the town, [q]nor tell *it* to any in the town.

27 ¶ [r]And Jē'sus went out, and his disciples, into the towns of Çæ̆s-a-rē'ȧ Phĭ-lĭp'pī: and by the way he asked his disciples, saying unto them, Whom do men say that I am?

28 And they answered, [s]Jŏhn the Băp'tĭst: but some *say,* E-lī'ăs; and others, One of the prophets.

29 And he saith unto them, But whom say ye that I am? And Pē'tēr answereth and saith unto him, [t]Thou art the Christ.

30 And [u]he charged them that they should tell no man of him.

31 And [v]he began to teach them, that the Son of man must suffer many things, and be rejected of the elders, and *of* the chief priests, and scribes, and be killed, and after three days rise again.

32 And he spake that saying openly. And Pē'tēr took him, and began to rebuke him.

33 But when he had turned about and looked on his disciples, he rebuked Pē'tēr, saying, Get thee behind me, Sā'tan: [w]for thou savourest not the things that be of God, but the things that be of men.

34 ¶ And when he had called the people *unto him* with his disciples also, he said unto them, [x]Whosoever will come after me, let him deny himself, and take up his cross, and follow me.

35 For [y]whosoever will save his life shall lose it; but whosoever shall lose his life for my sake and the gospel's, the same shall save it.

36 For what shall it profit a man, if he shall gain the whole world, and lose his own soul?

37 Or what shall a man give in exchange for his soul?

38 [z]Whosoever therefore shall be ashamed of me and of my words in this adulterous and sinful generation; of him also shall the Son of man be ashamed, when he cometh in the glory of his Father with the holy angels.

9 And he said unto them, [a]Verily I say unto you, That there be some of them that stand here, which shall not taste of death, till they have seen [b]the kingdom of God come with power.

2 ¶ [c]And after six days Jē'sus taketh *with him* Pē'tēr, and Jāmes, and Jŏhn, and leadeth them up into an high mountain apart by themselves: and he was transfigured before them.

3 And his raiment became shining, exceeding [d]white as snow; so as no fuller on earth can white them.

4 And there appeared unto them E-lī'ăs with Mō'ses: and they were talking with Jē'sus.

5 And Pē'tēr answered and said to Jē'sus, Master, it is good for us to be here: and let us make three tabernacles; one for thee, and one for Mō'ses, and one for E-lī'ăs.

6 For he wist not what to say; for they were sore afraid.

7 And there was [e]a cloud that overshadowed them: and a voice came out of the cloud, saying, This is my beloved Son: [f]hear him.

8 And suddenly, when they had looked round about, they saw no man any more, save Jē'sus only with themselves.

9 [g]And as they came down from the mountain, he charged them that they should tell no man what things they had seen, till the Son of man were risen from the dead.

10 And they kept that saying with themselves, questioning one with another what the rising from the dead should mean.

11 ¶ And they asked him, saying, Why say the scribes [h]that E-lī'ăs must first come?

12 And he answered and told them, E-lī'ăs verily cometh first, and restoreth all things; and [i]how it is written of the Son of man, that he must suffer many things, and [j]be set at nought.

13 But I say unto you, That [k]E-lī'ăs is indeed come, and they have done unto him whatsoever they listed, as it is written of him.

14 ¶ [l]And when he came to *his* disciples, he saw a great multitude about them, and the scribes questioning with them.

15 And straightway all the people, when they beheld him, were greatly amazed, and running to *him* saluted him.

16 And he asked the scribes, What question ye [1]with them?

17 And [m]one of the multitude answered and said, Master, I have brought unto thee my son, which hath a dumb spirit;

18 And wheresoever he taketh him, he [2]teareth him: and he foameth, and gnasheth with his teeth, and pineth away: and I spake to thy disciples that they should cast him out; and they could not.

19 He answereth him, and saith, O faithless generation, how long shall I be with you? how long shall I suffer you? bring him unto me.

20 And they brought him unto him: and [n]when he saw him, straightway the spirit tare him; and he fell on the ground, and wallowed foaming.

21 [o]ch. 6.52
23 [p]ch. 7.33
26 [q]Matt. 8.4; ch. 5.43
27 [r]Matt. 16.13; Luke 9.18
28 [s]Matt. 14.2
29 [t]Matt. 16.6; 1 John 5.1-6
30 [u]Matt. 16.20
31 [v]Matt. 16.21; Luke 9.22
33 [w]Rom. 8.7; 1 John 2.15-16
34 [x]Matt. 10.38; Gal. 6.14
35 [y]Matt. 10.39; Rev. 12.11
38 [z]Matt. 10.33

CHAPTER 9
1 [a]Matt. 16.28;
[b]Matt. 24.30
2 [c]Matt. 17.1
3 [d]Ps. 104.1-2
7 [e]Ex. 40.34;
[f]Heb. 1.1-2
9 [g]Matt. 17.9
11 [h]Mal. 4.5
12 [i]Gen. 3.15;
[j]Luke 23.11
13 [k]Matt. 11.14
14 [l]Matt. 17.14
16 [1]Or, among yourselves
17 [m]Matt. 17.14
18 [2]Or, dasheth him
20 [n]ch. 1.26

21 And he asked his father, How
long is it ago since this came unto him?
And he said, Of a child.
22 And ofttimes it hath cast him into
the fire, and into the waters, to destroy
him: but if thou canst do any thing,
have compassion on us, and help us.
23 Jē'sus said unto him, [o]If thou
canst believe, all things *are* possible to
him that believeth.
24 And straightway the father of
the child cried out, and said with
tears, Lord, I believe; [p]help thou mine
unbelief.
25 When Jē'sus saw that the people
came running together, he [q]rebuked
the foul spirit, saying unto him, *Thou*
dumb and deaf spirit, I charge thee,
come out of him, and enter no more
into him.
26 And *the spirit* cried, and rent him
sore, and came out of him: and he was
as one dead; insomuch that many said,
He is dead.
27 But Jē'sus took him by the hand,
and lifted him up; and he arose.
28 [r]And when he was come into the
house, his disciples asked him privately, Why could not we cast him out?
29 And he said unto them, This kind
can come forth by nothing, but by
prayer and fasting.
30 ¶ And they departed thence, and
passed through Găl'ĭ-lee; and he would
not that any man should know *it*.
31 [s]For he taught his disciples, and
said unto them, The Son of man is delivered into the hands of men, and they
shall kill him; and after that he is
killed, he shall rise the third day.
32 But they understood not that saying, and were afraid to ask him.
33 ¶ [t]And he came to Ca-pêr'na-ŭm:
and being in the house he asked them,
What was it that ye disputed among
yourselves by the way?
34 But they held their peace: [u]for by
the way they had disputed among themselves, who *should be* the greatest.
35 And he sat down, and called the
twelve, and saith unto them, [v]If any
man desire to be first, *the same* shall
be last of all, and servant of all.
36 And [w]he took a child, and set
him in the midst of them: and when he
had taken him in his arms, he said unto
them,
37 Whosoever shall receive one of
such children in my name, receiveth
me: and [x]whosoever shall receive me,
receiveth not me, but him that sent me.
38 ¶ [y]And Jŏhn answered him, saying, Master, we saw one casting out
devils in thy name, and he followeth
not us: and we forbad him, because he
followeth not us.
39 But Jē'sus said, Forbid him not:
[z]for there is no man which shall do a
miracle in my name, that can lightly
speak evil of me.
40 For [a]he that is not against us is
on our part.
41 [b]For whosoever shall give you a
cup of water to drink in my name, because ye belong to Chrĭst, verily I say
unto you, he shall not lose his reward.
42 [c]And whosoever shall offend one
of *these* little ones that believe in me, it
is better for him that a millstone were
hanged about his neck, and he were
cast into the sea.
43 [d]And if thy hand [3]offend thee, cut
it off: it is better for thee to enter into
life maimed, than having two hands to
go into hell, into the fire that never
shall be quenched:
44 [e]Where their worm dieth not,
and the fire is not quenched.
45 And if thy foot offend thee, cut it
off: it is better for thee to enter halt into
life, than having two feet to be cast into
hell, into the fire that never shall be
quenched:
46 Where their worm dieth not, and
the fire is not quenched.
47 And if thine eye offend thee,
[f]pluck it out: it is better for thee to enter into the kingdom of God with one
eye, than having two eyes to be cast
into hell fire:
48 Where their worm dieth not, and
the fire is not quenched.
49 For every one shall be salted with
fire, and [g]every sacrifice shall be salted
with salt.
50 [h]Salt *is* good: but if the salt have
lost his saltness, wherewith will ye season it? [i]Have salt in yourselves, and
[j]have peace one with another.

10

10 And [a]he arose from thence, and
cometh into the coasts of Jū-
dæ'ȧ by the farther side of Jôr'dan:
and the people resort unto him again;
and, as he was wont, he taught them
again.
2 ¶ [b]And the Phăr'ĭ-sees came to
him, and asked him, Is it lawful for a
man to put away *his* wife? tempting
him.
3 And he answered and said unto
them, What did Mō'ses command you?
4 And they said, [c]Mō'ses suffered to
write a bill of divorcement, and to put
her away.
5 And Jē'sus answered and said unto
them, [d]For the hardness of your heart
he wrote you this precept.
6 But from the beginning of the creation [e]God made them male and female.
7 [f]For this cause shall a man leave
his father and mother, and cleave to
his wife;
8 And they twain shall be one flesh:
so then they are no more twain, but
one flesh.
9 What therefore God hath joined together, let not man put asunder.
10 And in the house his disciples
asked him again of the same *matter*.
11 And he saith unto them, [g]Who-
soever shall put away his wife, and
marry another, committeth adultery
against her.
12 And if a woman shall put away
her husband, and be married to another, she committeth adultery.
13 ¶ [h]And they brought young children to him, that he should touch them:

23 [o]2 Chr. 20.20; Acts 14.9
24 [p]Luke 17.5; Heb. 12.2
25 [q]Zech. 3.2; 1 John 3.8
28 [r]Matt. 17.19
31 [s]Matt. 16.21; Luke 9.44
33 [t]Matt. 18.1
34 [u]Prov. 13.10
35 [v]Matt. 20.26-27
36 [w]Matt. 18.2
37 [x]Matt. 10.40
38 [y]Num. 11.28
39 [z]1 Cor. 12.3
40 [a]Matt. 12.30
41 [b]Matt. 10.42
42 [c]Matt. 18.6
43 [d]Deut. 13.6; [3]Or, cause thee to offend: and so verses 45-47
44 [e]Isa. 66.24
47 [f]Rom. 8.13
49 [g]Lev. 2.13
50 [h]Matt. 5.13; [i]Eph. 4.29; [j]Rom. 12.18

CHAPTER 10
1 [a]Matt. 19.1
2 [b]Matt. 19.3
4 [c]Deut. 24.1
5 [d]Deut. 9.6
6 [e]Gen. 1.27
7 [f]Gen. 2.24
11 [g]Matt. 5.32
13 [h]Matt. 19.13

and *his* disciples rebuked those that
brought *them*.
14 But when Jē'sus saw *it*, he was
much displeased, and said unto them,
Suffer the little children to come unto
me, and forbid them not: for [i]of such is
the kingdom of God.
15 Verily I say unto you, [j]Whoso-
ever shall not receive the kingdom of
God as a little child, he shall not enter
therein.
16 [k]And he took them up in his
arms, put *his* hands upon them, and
blessed them.
17 ¶ [l]And when he was gone forth
into the way, there came one running,
and kneeled to him, and asked him,
Good Master, what shall I do that I
may inherit eternal life?
18 And Jē'sus said unto him, Why
callest thou me good? *there is* none
good but one, *that is*, God.
19 Thou knowest the commandments, [m]Do not commit adultery, Do
not kill, Do not steal, Do not bear false
witness, Defraud not, Honour thy father and mother.
20 And he answered and said unto
him, Master, all these have I observed
from my youth.
21 Then Jē'sus beholding him loved
him, and said unto him, One thing thou
lackest: go thy way, [n]sell whatsoever
thou hast, and give to the poor, and
thou shalt have [o]treasure in heaven:
and come, take up [p]the cross, and follow me.
22 And he was sad at that saying,
and went away grieved: for he had
great possessions.
23 ¶ [q]And Jē'sus looked round about,
and saith unto his disciples, How hardly
shall they that have riches enter into the
kingdom of God!
24 And the disciples were astonished at his words. But Jē'sus answereth again, and saith unto them, Children, how hard is it for them [r]that trust
in riches to enter into the kingdom of
God!
25 It is easier for a camel to go
through the eye of a needle, than for a
rich man to enter into the kingdom of
God.
26 And they were astonished out of
measure, saying among themselves,
Who then can be saved?
27 And Jē'sus looking upon them
saith, With men *it is* impossible, but
not with God: for [s]with God all things
are possible.
28 ¶ [t]Then Pē'tēr began to say unto
him, Lo, we have left all, and have followed thee.
29 And Jē'sus answered and said,
Verily I say unto you, There is no man
that hath left house, or brethren, or sisters, or father, or mother, or wife, or
children, or lands, for my sake, and the
gospel's,
30 [u]But he shall receive an hundredfold now in this time, houses, and brethren, and sisters, and mothers, and children, and lands, with [v]persecutions;
and in the world to come eternal life.

14 [i]Matt. 18.4; 1 Pet. 2.2
15 [j]Matt. 18.3
16 [k]Gen. 48.14-16; Luke 2.28-34
17 [l]Matt. 19.16; Luke 18.18
19 [m]Ex. 20; Jas. 2.11
21 [n]Acts 2.44; [o]Matt. 6.19-20; [p]Acts 14.22
23 [q]Matt. 19.23
24 [r]Job 31.24
27 [s]Jer. 32.17
28 [t]Matt. 19.27
30 [u]2 Chr. 25.9; [v]Matt. 5.11-12
31 [w]Matt. 19.30
32 [x]Matt. 20.17; [y]ch. 8.31
35 [z]Matt. 20.20
39 [a]Acts 12.2
40 [b]Jas. 4.3
41 [c]Matt. 20.24
42 [d]Luke 22.25; [1]Or, think good
43 [e]Matt. 20.26-28
45 [f]Matt. 20.28; [g]Isa. 53.10
46 [h]Matt. 20.29
47 [i]Isa. 11.1

31 [w]But many *that are* first shall be
last; and the last first.
32 ¶ [x]And they were in the way going up to Je-ru̯'sa-lĕm; and Jē'sus went
before them: and they were amazed;
and as they followed, they were afraid.
[y]And he took again the twelve, and began to tell them what things should
happen unto him,
33 *Saying*, Behold, we go up to Je-
ru̯'sa-lĕm; and the Son of man shall be
delivered unto the chief priests, and
unto the scribes; and they shall condemn him to death, and shall deliver
him to the Gĕn'tīles:
34 And they shall mock him, and
shall scourge him, and shall spit upon
him, and shall kill him: and the third
day he shall rise again.
35 ¶ [z]And Jāmes and Jŏhn, the sons
of Zēb'e-dee, come unto him, saying,
Master, we would that thou shouldest
do for us whatsoever we shall desire.
36 And he said unto them, What
would ye that I should do for you?
37 They said unto him, Grant unto
us that we may sit, one on thy right
hand, and the other on thy left hand, in
thy glory.
38 But Jē'sus said unto them, Ye
know not what ye ask: can ye drink of
the cup that I drink of? and be baptized
with the baptism that I am baptized
with?
39 And they said unto him, We can.
And Jē'sus said unto them, Ye [a]shall
indeed drink of the cup that I drink of;
and with the baptism that I am baptized withal shall ye be baptized:
40 But to sit on my right hand and
on my left hand is not mine to give; but
it shall be [b]*given to them* for whom it
is prepared.
41 [c]And when the ten heard *it*, they
began to be much displeased with
Jāmes and Jŏhn.
42 But Jē'sus called them *to him*,
and saith unto them, [d]Ye know that
they which [1]are accounted to rule over
the Gĕn'tīles exercise lordship over
them; and their great ones exercise authority upon them.
43 [e]But so shall it not be among you:
but whosoever will be great among
you, shall be your minister:
44 And whosoever of you will be the
chiefest, shall be servant of all.
45 For even [f]the Son of man came
not to be ministered unto, but to minister, and [g]to give his life a ransom for
many.
46 ¶ [h]And they came to Jĕr'ĭ-chō:
and as he went out of Jĕr'ĭ-chō with
his disciples and a great number of
people, blind Băr-ti-mæ'us, the son
of Tī-mæ'us, sat by the highway side
begging.
47 And when he heard that it was
Jē'sus of Nāz'a-rĕth, he began to cry
out, and say, Jē'sus, *thou* [i]son of Dā'-
vid, have mercy on me.
48 And many charged him that he
should hold his peace: but he cried the
more a great deal, *Thou* son of Dā'vid,
have mercy on me.

49 And Jē′sus stood still, and commanded him to be called. And they call
the blind man, saying unto him, Be of
good comfort, rise; he calleth thee.
50 And he, casting away his garment, rose, and came to Jē′sus.
51 And Jē′sus answered and said
unto him, What wilt thou that I should
do unto thee? The blind man said unto
him, Lord, that I might receive my
sight.
52 And Jē′sus said unto him, Go
thy way; [j]thy faith hath [2]made thee
whole. And immediately [k]he received
his sight, and followed Jē′sus in the
way.
11 And [a]when they came nigh to Je-
rṳ′sa-lĕm, unto Bĕth′pha-ġe and
Bĕth′ă-nȳ, at the mount of [b]Ŏl′ĭves, he
sendeth forth two of his disciples,
2 And saith unto them, Go your way
into the village over against you: and
as soon as ye be entered into it, ye shall
find a colt tied, whereon never man
sat; loose him, and bring *him*.
3 And if any man say unto you, Why
do ye this? say ye that [c]the Lord hath
need of him; and straightway he will
send him hither.
4 And they went their way, and
found the colt tied by the door without
in a place where two ways met; and
they loose him.
5 And certain of them that stood
there said unto them, What do ye, loosing the colt?
6 And they said unto them even as
Jē′sus had commanded: and they let
them go.
7 And they brought the colt to Jē′-
sus, and cast their garments on him;
[d]and he sat upon him.
8 [e]And many spread their garments
in the way: and others cut down
branches off the trees, and strawed
them in the way.
9 And they that went before, and
they that followed, cried, [f]saying, Ho-
săn′nȧ; Blessed *is* he that cometh in
the name of the Lord:
10 Blessed *be* the kingdom of our father Dā′vid, that cometh in the name of
the Lord: [g]Ho-săn′nȧ in the highest.
11 [h]And Jē′sus entered into Je-rṳ′-
sa-lĕm, and into the temple: and when
he had looked round about upon all
things, and now the eventide was come,
he went out unto Bĕth′ă-nȳ with the
twelve.
12 ¶ And [i]on the morrow, when they
were come from Bĕth′ă-nȳ, he was
hungry:
13 [j]And seeing a fig tree afar off
having leaves, he came, if haply he
might find any thing thereon: and when
he came to it, he found nothing but
leaves; for the time of figs was not *yet*.
14 And Jē′sus answered and said
unto it, No man eat fruit of thee hereafter for ever. And his disciples heard
it.
15 ¶ [k]And they come to Je-rṳ′sa-
lĕm: and Jē′sus went into the temple,
and began to cast out them that sold
and bought in the temple, and overthrew the tables of the moneychangers, and the seats of them that sold
doves;
16 And would not suffer that any
man should carry *any* vessel through
the temple.
17 And he taught, saying unto them,
Is it not written, [l]My house shall be
called [1]of all nations the house of
prayer? but [m]ye have made it a den of
thieves.
18 And [n]the scribes and chief priests
heard *it*, and sought how they might
destroy him: for they feared him, because [o]all the people was astonished at
his doctrine.
19 And when even was come, he
went out of the city.
20 ¶ [p]And in the morning, as they
passed by, they saw the fig tree dried
up from the roots.
21 And Pē′tēr calling to remembrance saith unto him, Master, behold,
the fig tree which thou cursedst is withered away.
22 And Jē′sus answering saith unto
them, [2]Have faith in God.
23 For [q]verily I say unto you, That
whosoever shall say unto this mountain, Be thou removed, and be thou
cast into the sea; and shall not doubt in
his heart, but shall believe that those
things which he saith shall come to
pass; he shall have whatsoever he
saith.
24 Therefore I say unto you, [r]What
things soever ye desire, when ye pray,
believe that ye receive *them*, and ye
shall have *them*.
25 And when ye stand praying, [s]for-
give, if ye have ought against any: that
your Father also which is in heaven
may forgive you your trespasses.
26 But [t]if ye do not forgive, neither
will your Father which is in heaven forgive your trespasses.
27 ¶ And they come again to Je-
rṳ′sa-lĕm: [u]and as he was walking in
the temple, there come to him the chief
priests, and the scribes, and the elders,
28 And say unto him, By what authority doest thou these things? and
who gave thee this authority to do
these things?
29 And Jē′sus answered and said
unto them, I will also ask of you one
[3]question, and answer me, and I will
tell you by what authority I do these
things.
30 The baptism of Jŏhn, was *it* from
heaven, or of men? answer me.
31 And they reasoned with themselves, saying, If we shall say, From
heaven; he will say, Why then did ye
not believe him?
32 But if we shall say, Of men; they
feared the people: for [v]all *men* counted
Jŏhn, that he was a prophet indeed.
33 And they answered and said unto
Jē′sus, We cannot tell. And Jē′sus answering saith unto them, [w]Neither do I
tell you by what authority I do these
things.
12 And he began to speak unto
them by parables. A *certain* man

52 [j]Matt. 9.22
[2]Or, saved thee
[k]Isa. 29.18; Isa. 32.3; Isa. 35.5; Isa. 42.6-7; Isa. 43.8; ch. 8.22-26; Acts 26.18

CHAPTER 11
1 [a]Matt. 21.1; Luke 19.29; John 12.14
[b]Acts 1.12
3 [c]Acts 10.36; Heb. 1.2; Heb. 2.7-9
7 [d]1 Ki. 1.33; Zech. 9.9
8 [e]Matt. 21.8
9 [f]Ps. 118.26; Isa. 62.11; Matt. 21.9; Matt. 23.39; Luke 19.37-38; John 12.13
10 [g]Ps. 148.1
11 [h]Mal. 3.1; Matt. 21.12
12 [i]Matt. 21.18
13 [j]Matt. 21.19
15 [k]Matt. 21.12; Luke 19.45; John 2.14
17 [l]Isa. 56.7; Zech. 2.11
[1]Or, an house of prayer for all nations
[m]Jer. 7.11
18 [n]Matt. 21.45; Luke 19.47
[o]Matt. 7.28; Luke 4.32
20 [p]Matt. 21.19
22 [2]Or, Have the faith of God
23 [q]Matt. 17.20; Luke 17.6
24 [r]Matt. 7.7; Jas. 1.5-6
25 [s]Matt. 6.14; Col. 3.13
26 [t]Matt. 18.35
27 [u]Matt. 21.23; Luke 20.1
29 [3]Or, thing
32 [v]Matt. 3.5; ch. 6.20
33 [w]Job 5.13; 1 Cor. 3.19

planted [a]a vineyard, and set an hedge about *it*, and digged *a place for* the winefat, and built a tower, and let it out to husbandmen, and went into a far county.
2 And at the season he sent to the husbandmen a servant, that he might receive from the husbandmen of the fruit of the vineyard.
3 And they caught *him*, and beat him, and sent *him* away empty.
4 And again he sent unto them another servant; and at him they cast stones, and wounded *him* in the head, and sent *him* away shamefully handled.
5 And again he sent another; and him they killed, and many others; beating some, and [b]killing some.
6 Having yet therefore one son, his [c]wellbeloved, he sent him also last unto them, saying, They will reverence my son.
7 But those husbandmen said among themselves, This is [d]the heir; come, let us kill him, and the inheritance shall be ours.
8 And they took him, and [e]killed *him*, and cast *him* out of the vineyard.
9 What shall therefore the lord of the vineyard do? he will come and destroy the husbandmen, and will [f]give the vineyard unto others.
10 And have ye not read this scripture; [g]The stone which the builders rejected is become the head of the corner:
11 This was the Lord's doing, and [h]it is marvellous in our eyes?
12 And [i]they sought to lay hold on him, but feared the people: for they knew that he had spoken the parable against them: and they left him, and went their way.
13 ¶ [j]And they send unto him certain of the Phăr′ĭ-sees and of the Hē-rō′dĭ-ans, to catch him in *his* words.
14 And when they were come, they say unto him, Master, we know that thou art true, and carest for no man: for thou regardest not the person of men, but teachest the way of God in truth: Is it lawful to give tribute to Çæ′sar, or not?
15 Shall we give, or shall we not give? But he, knowing their hypocrisy, said unto them, Why tempt ye me? bring me [1]a penny, that I may see *it*.
16 And they brought *it*. And he saith unto them, Whose *is* this image and superscription? And they said unto him, Çæ′sar's.
17 And Jē′sus answering said unto them, Render to Çæ′sar the things that are Çæ′sar's, and to God the things that are God's. And they marvelled at him.
18 ¶ [k]Then come unto him the Săd′-dū-çees, [l]which say there is no resurrection; and they asked him, saying,
19 Master, [m]Mō′ses wrote unto us, If a man's brother die, and leave *his* wife *behind him*, and leave no children, that his brother should take his wife, and raise up seed unto his brother.
20 Now there were seven brethren: and the first took a wife, and dying left no seed.
21 And the second took her, and died, neither left he any seed: and the third likewise.
22 And the seven had her, and left no seed: last of all the woman died also.
23 In the resurrection therefore, when they shall rise, whose wife shall she be of them? for the seven had her to wife.
24 And Jē′sus answering said unto them, Do ye not therefore err, [n]because ye know not the scriptures, neither [o]the power of God?
25 For when they shall rise from the dead, they neither marry, nor are given in marriage; but [p]are as the angels which are in heaven.
26 And as touching the dead, that they rise: have ye not read in the book of Mō′ses, how in the bush God spake unto him, saying, [q]I *am* the God of Ā′bră-hăm, and the God of Ī′saac, and the God of Jā′cob?
27 He is not the God of the dead, but the God of the living: ye therefore do greatly err.
28 ¶ [r]And one of the scribes came, and having heard them reasoning together, and perceiving that he had answered them well, asked him, Which is the first commandment of all?
29 And Jē′sus answered him, The first of all the commandments *is*, [s]Hear, O Is′ra-el; the Lord our God is one Lord:
30 And thou shalt love the Lord thy God with all thy heart, and with all thy soul, and with all thy mind, and with all thy strength: this *is* the first commandment.
31 And the second *is* like, *namely* this, [t]Thou shalt love thy neighbour as thyself. There is none other commandment greater than these.
32 And the scribe said unto him, Well, Master, thou hast said the truth: for there is one God; [u]and there is none other but he:
33 And to love him with all the heart, and with all the understanding, and with all the soul, and with all the strength, and to love *his* neighbour as himself, [v]is more than all whole burnt offerings and sacrifices.
34 And when Jē′sus saw that he answered discreetly, he said unto him, Thou art not far from the kingdom of God. [w]And no man after that durst ask him *any question*.
35 ¶ [x]And Jē′sus answered and said, while he taught in the temple, How say the scribes that Chrīst is the son of Dā′vid?
36 For Dā′vid himself said [y]by the Hō′lȳ Ghōst, [z]The LORD said to my Lord, Sit thou on my right hand, till I make thine enemies thy footstool.
37 Dā′vid therefore himself calleth him Lord; and [a]whence is he *then* his son? And the common people heard him gladly.

CHAPTER 12
1 [a]Ps. 80.8; Luke 20.9
5 [b]2 Chr. 24.21; Heb. 11.36
6 [c]Ps. 2.7
7 [d]Ps. 2.8
8 [e]Acts 2.23
9 [f]Acts 28.23-28
10 [g]Ps. 118.22
11 [h]1 Tim. 3.16
12 [i]Matt. 21.45-46
13 [j]Matt. 22.15;
15 [1]In value sevenpence halfpenny
18 [k]Matt. 22.23;
[l]Acts 23.8
19 [m]Gen. 38.8
24 [n]Dan. 12.2;
[o]Gen. 18.14
25 [p]Matt. 22.30
26 [q]Ex. 3.6
28 [r]Matt. 22.35
29 [s]Deut. 6.4
31 [t]Lev. 19.18
32 [u]Deut. 4.39
33 [v]1 Sam. 15.22
34 [w]Matt. 22.46
35 [x]Luke 20.41
36 [y]2 Sam. 23.2;
[z]Ps. 110.1
37 [a]Rom. 1.3

38 ¶ And [b]he said unto them in his
doctrine, [c]Beware of the scribes, which
love to go in long clothing, and [d]love
salutations in the marketplaces,
39 And the chief seats in the synagogues, and the uppermost rooms at
feasts:
40 [e]Which devour widows' houses,
and for a pretence make long prayers:
these shall receive greater damnation.
41 ¶ [f]And Jē'sus sat over against the
treasury, and beheld how the people
cast [2]money [g]into the treasury: and
many that were rich cast in much.
42 And there came a certain poor
widow, and she threw in two [3]mites,
which make a farthing.
43 And he called *unto him* his disciples, and saith unto them, Verily I say
unto you, That [h]this poor widow hath
cast more in, than all they which have
cast into the treasury:
44 For all *they* did cast in of their
abundance; but she of her want did
cast in all that she had, [i]*even* all her
living.

13 And [a]as he went out of the temple,
one of his disciples saith unto him,
Master, see what manner of stones and
what buildings *are here!*
2 And Jē'sus answering said unto
him, Seest thou these great buildings?
[b]there shall not be left one stone upon
another, that shall not be thrown down.
3 And as he sat upon the mount of
Ŏl'ĭves over against the temple, Pē'tẽr
and Jāmes and Jŏhn and Ăn'drew
asked him privately,
4 [c]Tell us, when shall these things
be? and what *shall be* the sign when all
these things shall be fulfilled?
5 And Jē'sus answering them began
to say, [d]Take heed lest any *man* deceive you:
6 For many shall come in my name,
saying, I am Chrīst; and shall deceive
many.
7 And when ye shall hear of wars
and rumours of wars, be ye not troubled: for *such things* must needs be;
but the [e]end *shall* not *be* yet.
8 For nation shall rise against nation, and kingdom against kingdom:
and there shall be earthquakes in divers places, and there shall be famines
and troubles: these *are* the beginnings
of [1]sorrows.
9 ¶ But [f]take heed to yourselves: for
they shall deliver you up to councils;
and in the synagogues ye shall be
beaten: and ye shall be brought before
rulers and kings for my sake, for a testimony against them.
10 And [g]the gospel must first be published among all nations.
11 [h]But when they shall lead *you*,
and deliver you up, take no thought
beforehand what ye shall speak, neither do ye premeditate: but whatsoever shall be given you in that hour,
that speak ye: for it is not ye that
speak, [i]but the Hō'lȳ Ghōst.
12 Now [j]the brother shall betray the
brother to death, and the father the
son; and children shall rise up against
their parents, and shall cause them to
be put to death.
13 And ye shall be hated of all *men*
for my name's sake: but [k]he that shall
endure unto the end, the same shall be
saved.
14 ¶ [l]But when ye shall see the
abomination of desolation, [m]spoken of
by Dăn'iel the prophet, standing where
it ought not, (let him that readeth understand,) then [n]let them that be in Jū-
dæ'ȧ flee to the mountains:
15 And let him that is on the house
top not go down into the house, neither
enter *therein*, to take any thing out of
his house:
16 And let him that is in the field
not turn back again for to take up his
garment.
17 [o]But woe to them that are with
child, and to them that give suck in
those days!
18 And pray ye that your flight be
not in the winter.
19 [p]For *in* those days shall be affliction, such as was not from the beginning of the creation which God created
unto this time, neither shall be.
20 And except that the Lord had
shortened those days, no flesh should
be saved: but for the elect's sake, whom
he hath chosen, he hath shortened the
days.
21 [q]And then if any man shall say to
you, Lo, here *is* Chrīst; or, lo, *he is*
there; believe *him* not:
22 For false Chrīsts and false prophets shall rise, and shall shew signs and
wonders, to seduce, [r]if *it were* possible, even the elect.
23 But [s]take ye heed: behold, I have
foretold you all things.
24 ¶ [t]But in those days, after that
tribulation, the sun shall be darkened,
and the moon shall not give her light,
25 And the stars of heaven shall fall,
and the powers that are in heaven
shall be shaken.
26 [u]And then shall they see the Son
of man coming in the clouds with great
power and glory.
27 And then shall he send his angels, and shall gather together his elect
from the four winds, from the uttermost part of the earth to the uttermost
part of heaven.
28 Now learn a parable of the fig
tree; When her branch is yet tender,
and putteth forth leaves, ye know that
summer is near:
29 So ye in like manner, when ye
shall see these things come to pass,
know that it is nigh, *even* at the doors.
30 Verily I say unto you, that this
generation shall not pass, till all these
things be done.
31 Heaven and earth shall pass away:
but [v]my words shall not pass away.
32 ¶ But of that day and *that* hour
knoweth no man, no, not the angels
which are in heaven, neither the Son,
but the Father.
33 [w]Take ye heed, watch and pray:
for ye know not when the time is.

38 [b]ch. 4.2
[c]Matt. 23.1; Luke 20.46
[d]Luke 11.43
40 [e]Matt. 23.14
41 [f]Luke 21.1
[2]A piece of brass money, Matt. 10.9
[g]2 Ki. 12.9
42 [3]It is the seventh part of one piece of that brass money
43 [h]2 Cor. 8.12
44 [i]1 John 3.17
CHAPTER 13
1 [a]Matt. 24.1
2 [b]Luke 19.44
4 [c]Luke 21.7
5 [d]Jer. 29.8
7 [e]Jer. 4.27
8 [1]The word in the original importeth the pains of a woman in travail
9 [f]Matt. 10.17
10 [g]Matt. 24.14
11 [h]Ex. 24.12;
[i]Acts 2.4
12 [j]Mic. 7.6
13 [k]Dan. 12.12
14 [l]Matt. 24.15
[m]Dan. 9.27
[n]Luke 21.21
17 [o]Luke 23.29
19 [p]Deut. 28.15
21 [q]Deut. 13.1-3
22 [r]Matt. 24.24
23 [s]Matt. 7.15
24 [t]Dan. 7.10
26 [u]Dan. 7.13
31 [v]Num. 23.19
33 [w]Rom. 13.11

34 [x]*For the Son of man is* as a man taking a far journey, who left his house, and gave authority to his servants, and to every man his work, and commanded the porter to watch.
35 [y]Watch ye therefore: for ye know not when the master of the house cometh, at even, or at midnight, or at the cockcrowing, or in the morning:
36 Lest coming suddenly he find you sleeping.
37 And what I say unto you I say unto all, Watch.

14 After [a]two days was *the feast of* the passover, and of unleavened bread: and the chief priests and the scribes sought how they might take him by craft, and put *him* to death.
2 But they said, Not on the feast *day*, lest there be an uproar of the people.
3 ¶ [b]And being in Bĕth'ă-nȳ in the house of Sī'mon the leper, as he sat at meat, there came a woman having an alabaster box of ointment of [1]spikenard very precious; and she brake the box, and poured *it* on his head.
4 And there were some that had indignation within themselves, and said, Why was this waste of the ointment made?
5 For it might have been sold for more than three hundred [c]pence, and have been given to the poor. And they murmured against her.
6 And Jē'sus said, Let her alone; why trouble ye her? she hath wrought a good work on me.
7 [d]For ye have the poor with you always, and whensoever ye will ye may do them good: but me ye have not always.
8 She hath done what she could: she is come aforehand to anoint my body to the burying.
9 Verily I say unto you, Wheresoever this gospel shall be preached throughout the whole world, *this* also that she hath done shall be spoken of for a memorial of her.
10 ¶ [e]And Jū'das Ĭs-căr'ĭ-ot, one of the twelve, went unto the chief priests, to betray him unto them.
11 And when they heard *it*, they were glad, and promised to give him [f]money. And he sought how he might conveniently betray him.
12 ¶ [g]And the first day of unleavened bread, when they [2]killed the passover, his disciples said unto him, Where wilt thou that we go and prepare that thou mayest eat the passover?
13 And he sendeth forth two of his disciples, and saith unto them, Go ye into the city, and there shall meet you a man bearing a pitcher of water: follow him.
14 And wheresoever he shall go in, say ye to the goodman of the house, The Master saith, Where is the guestchamber, where I shall [h]eat the passover with my disciples?
15 And he will shew you a large upper room furnished *and* prepared: there make ready for us.
16 And his disciples went forth, and came into the city, and found as he had said unto them: and they made ready the passover.
17 [i]And in the evening he cometh with the twelve.
18 And as they sat and did eat, Jē'sus said, Verily I say unto you, One of you which eateth with me shall betray me.
19 And they began to be sorrowful, and to say unto him one by one, *Is* it I? and another *said, Is* it I?
20 And he answered and said unto them, *It is* one of the twelve, that dippeth with me in the dish.
21 [j]The Son of man indeed goeth, as it is written of him: but woe to that man by whom the Son of man is betrayed! good were it for that man if he had never been born.
22 ¶ [k]And as they did eat, Jē'sus took bread, and blessed, and brake *it*, and gave to them, and said, Take, eat: this is my body.
23 And he took the cup, and when he had given thanks, he gave *it* to them: and they all drank of it.
24 And he said unto them, This is [l]my blood of the new testament, which is shed for many.
25 Verily I say unto you, I will drink no more of the fruit of the vine, until that day that I drink it new in the kingdom of God.
26 ¶ [m]And when they had sung an [3]hymn, they went out into the mount of Ŏl'ĭves.
27 [n]And Jē'sus saith unto them, All ye shall be offended because of me this night: for it is written, [o]I will smite the shepherd, and the sheep shall be scattered.
28 But [p]after that I am risen, I will go before you into Găl'ĭ-lee.
29 But [q]Pē'tĕr said unto him, Although all shall be offended, yet *will* not I.
30 And Jē'sus saith unto him, Verily I say unto thee, That this day, *even* in this night, before the cock crow twice, thou shalt deny me thrice.
31 But he spake the more vehemently, If I should die with thee, I will not deny thee in any wise. Likewise also said they all.
32 [r]And they came to a place which was named Gĕth-sĕm'a-ne: and he saith to his disciples, Sit ye here, while [s]I shall pray.
33 And he taketh with him Pē'tĕr and Jāmes and Jŏhn, and began to be sore amazed, and to be very heavy;
34 And saith unto them, [t]My soul is exceeding sorrowful unto death: tarry ye here, and watch.
35 And he went forward a little, and fell on the ground, and prayed that, if it were possible, the hour might pass from him.
36 And he said, [u]Ăb'bȧ, Father, [v]all things *are* possible unto thee; take away this cup from me: [w]nevertheless not what I will, but what thou wilt.

34 [x]Matt. 25.14
35 [y]2 Pet. 3; Rev. 3.3
CHAPTER 14
1 [a]Ex. 12.6-20; Matt. 26.2
3 [b]Matt. 26.6; John 12.1-3
[1]Or, pure nard, or, liquid nard
5 [c]Matt. 18.28
7 [d]Deut. 15.11; John 12.8
10 [e]Matt. 10.4; Acts 1.16
11 [f]Zech. 11.12; Jude 11
12 [g]Matt. 26.17; Luke 22.7
[2]Or, sacrificed
14 [h]Ex. 12.6; Lev. 23.5
17 [i]Matt. 26.20; John 13.21
21 [j]Gen. 23.15; Zech. 13.7
22 [k]Matt. 26.26; 1 Cor. 10.4-16
24 [l]Ex. 24.8; Heb. 9.14
26 [m]Matt. 26.30
[3]Or, psalm
27 [n]Matt. 11.6; John 16.32
[o]Isa. 53.2-10; Zech. 13.7
28 [p]Matt. 16.21; ch. 16.7
29 [q]Prov. 3.5; Jer. 9.23-24
32 [r]Matt. 26.36; John 18.1
[s]Ps. 69
34 [t]Isa. 53.3-4-12
36 [u]Luke 24.49;
[v]Heb. 5.7
[w]John 5.30

37 And he cometh, and findeth them
sleeping, and saith unto Pē'tĕr, Sī'-
mon, sleepest thou? couldest not thou
watch one hour?
38 Watch ye and pray, lest ye enter
into temptation. [x]The spirit truly *is*
ready, but the flesh *is* weak.
39 And again he went away, and
prayed, and spake the same words.
40 And when he returned, he found
them asleep again, (for their eyes were
heavy,) neither wist they what to answer him.
41 And he cometh the third time,
and saith unto them, Sleep on now,
and take *your* rest: it is enough, [y]the
hour is come; behold, the Son of man
is betrayed into the hands of sinners.
42 [z]Rise up, let us go; lo, he that betrayeth me is at hand.
43 ¶ [a]And immediately, while he
yet spake, cometh Jū'das, one of the
twelve, and with him a great multitude
with swords and staves, from the chief
priests and the scribes and the elders.
44 And he that betrayed him had
given them a token, saying, Whomsoever I shall kiss, that same is he; take
him, and lead *him* away safely.
45 And as soon as he was come, he
goeth straightway to him, and saith,
[4b]Master, master; and [c]kissed him.
46 ¶ And they laid their hands on
him, and took him.
47 And one of them that stood by
drew a sword, and smote a servant of
the high priest, and cut off his ear.
48 [d]And Jē'sus answered and said
unto them, Are ye come out, as against
a thief, with swords and *with* staves to
take me?
49 I was daily with you in the temple
teaching, and ye took me not: but the
[e]scriptures must be fulfilled.
50 [f]And they all forsook him, and
fled.
51 And there followed him a certain
young man, having a linen cloth cast
about *his* naked *body;* and the young
men laid hold on him:
52 And he left the linen cloth, and
fled from them naked.
53 ¶ [g]And they led Jē'sus away to
the high priest: and with him were assembled all the chief priests and the
elders and the scribes.
54 And Pē'tĕr followed him afar off,
even into the palace of the high priest:
and he sat with the servants, and
warmed himself at the fire.
55 [h]And the chief priests and all the
council sought for witness against Jē'-
sus to put him to death; and [i]found
none.
56 For many bare [j]false witness
against him, but their witness agreed
not together.
57 And there arose certain, and bare
false witness against him, saying,
58 We heard him say, [k]I will destroy
this temple that is made with hands,
and within three days I will build another made without hands.
59 But neither so did their witness
agree together.

38 [x]Rom. 7.23; Gal. 5.17
41 [y]John 13.1
42 [z]Matt. 26.46; John 18.1-2
43 [a]Matt. 26.47; John 18.3
45 [4]Rabbi, Rabbi
[b]John 20.16
[c]2 Sam. 20.9
48 [d]Matt. 26.55; Luke 22.52
49 [e]Ps. 22.6; Luke 22.37
50 [f]Job 19.13-14; 2 Tim. 4.16
53 [g]Matt. 26.57; John 18.13
55 [h]Matt. 26.59
[i]Dan. 6.4; 1 Pet. 3.16
56 [j]Ps. 35.11; Prov. 19.5
58 [k]ch. 15.29
60 [l]Matt. 26.62
61 [m]Isa. 53.7
[n]Matt. 26.63
62 [o]Zech. 14.5
64 [p]Lev. 24.16
65 [q]Isa. 50.6
66 [r]Matt. 26.58
69 [s]Matt. 26.71
70 [t]Matt. 26.73;
[u]Judg. 12.6
71 [v]Prov. 29.25;
72 [5]Or, he wept abundantly, or, he began to weep
[w]Ezek. 7.16

CHAPTER 15
1 [a]Ps. 2.2
2 [b]Matt. 2.2;
[c]1 Tim. 6.13
3 [d]1 Pet. 2.23
4 [e]Matt. 26.62
5 [f]Isa. 53.7
6 [g]Matt. 27.15

60 [l]And the high priest stood up in
the midst, and asked Jē'sus, saying,
Answerest thou nothing? what *is it*
which these witness against thee?
61 But [m]he held his peace, and answered nothing. [n]Again the high priest
asked him, and said unto him, Art thou
the Chrīst, the Son of the Blessed?
62 And Jē'sus said, I am: [o]and ye
shall see the Son of man sitting on the
right hand of power, and coming in the
clouds of heaven.
63 Then the high priest rent his
clothes, and saith, What need we any
further witnesses?
64 Ye have heard the [p]blasphemy:
what think ye? And they all condemned
him to be guilty of death.
65 And some began to [q]spit on him,
and to cover his face, and to buffet
him, and to say unto him, Prophesy:
and the servants did strike him with
the palms of their hands.
66 ¶ [r]And as Pē'tĕr was beneath in
the palace, there cometh one of the
maids of the high priest:
67 And when she saw Pē'tĕr warm-
ing himself, she looked upon him, and
said, And thou also wast with Jē'sus of
Năz'a-rĕth.
68 But he denied, saying, I know
not, neither understand I what thou
sayest. And he went out into the porch;
and the cock crew.
69 [s]And a maid saw him again, and
began to say to them that stood by,
This is *one* of them.
70 And he denied it again. [t]And a
little after, they that stood by said
again to Pē'tĕr, Surely thou art *one* of
them: [u]for thou art a Găl-ĭ-læ'an, and
thy speech agreeth *thereto.*
71 But [v]he began to curse and to
swear, *saying,* I know not this man of
whom ye speak.
72 And the second time the cock
crew. And Pē'tĕr called to mind the
word that Jē'sus said unto him, Before
the cock crow twice, thou shalt deny
me thrice. And [5w]when he thought
thereon, he wept.

15

And [a]straightway in the morning the chief priests held a con-
sultation with the elders and scribes
and the whole council, and bound Jē'-
sus, and carried *him* away, and delivered *him* to Pī'late.
2 [b]And Pī'late asked him, Art thou
the King of the Jews? And he answering said unto him, [c]Thou sayest *it.*
3 And the chief priests accused him
of many things: but [d]he answered
nothing.
4 [e]And Pī'late asked him again, saying, Answerest thou nothing? behold
how many things they witness against
thee.
5 [f]But Jē'sus yet answered nothing;
so that Pī'late marvelled.
6 Now [g]at *that* feast he released
unto them one prisoner, whomsoever
they desired.
7 And there was *one* named Ba-
răb'bas, *which lay* bound with them
that had made insurrection with him,

who had committed murder in the
insurrection.
8 And the multitude crying aloud began to desire *him to do* as he had ever
done unto them.
9 But Pī'late answered them, saying, Will ye that I release unto you the
King of the Jews?
10 For he knew that the chief priests
had delivered him [h]for envy.
11 But [i]the chief priests moved the
people, that he should rather release
Ba-răb'bas unto them.
12 And Pī'late answered and said
again unto them, What will ye then
that I shall do *unto him* whom ye call
[j]the King of the Jews?
13 And they cried out again, Crucify
him.
14 Then Pī'late said unto them, Why,
what evil hath he done? And they cried
out the more exceedingly, Crucify him.
15 ¶ [k]And *so* Pī'late, willing to content the people, released Ba-răb'bas
unto them, and delivered Jē'sus, when
he had scourged *him,* to be crucified.
16 And the soldiers led him away
into the hall, called Præ-tō'rĭ-um; and
they call together the whole band.
17 And they clothed him with purple, and platted a crown of thorns, and
put it about his *head,*
18 And began to salute him, Hail,
King of the Jews!
19 And they smote him on the head
with a reed, and did spit upon him, and
bowing *their* knees worshipped him.
20 And when they had mocked him,
they took off the purple from him, and
put his own clothes on him, and led
him out to crucify him.
21 [l]And they compel one Sī'mon a
Çȳ-rē'nĭ-an, who passed by, coming
out of the country, the father of Ăl-ĕx-
ăn'dẽr and [m]Rụ'fus, to bear his cross.
22 [n]And they bring him unto the
place Gŏl'go-thȧ, which is, being interpreted, The place of a skull.
23 [o]And they gave him to drink
wine mingled with myrrh: but he received *it* not.
24 And when they had crucified him,
[p]they parted his garments, casting lots
upon them, what every man should
take.
25 And [q]it was the third hour, and
they crucified him.
26 And [r]the superscription of his accusation was written over, THE KING
OF THE JEWS.
27 And with him they crucify two
thieves; the one on his right hand, and
the other on his left.
28 And the scripture was fulfilled,
which saith, [s]And he was numbered
with the transgressors.
29 And [t]they that passed by railed
on him, wagging their heads, and saying, Ah, thou [u]that destroyest the temple, and buildest *it* in three days,
30 Save thyself, and come down
from the cross.
31 Likewise also the chief priests
mocking said among themselves with

10 [h]Acts 7.9-51; 1 John 3.12
11 [i]Matt. 27.20; Acts 3.14
12 [j]Ps. 2.6-7; Zech. 9.9
15 [k]Prov. 29.25; John 19.1-16
21 [l]Matt. 27.32; Luke 23.26
[m]Rom. 16.13
22 [n]John 19.17; Heb. 13.12
23 [o]Ps. 69.21
24 [p]Ps. 22.18; John 19.23
25 [q]Matt. 27.45; John 19.14
26 [r]Deut. 23.5
28 [s]Isa. 53.12; Luke 22.37
29 [t]Ps. 22.7; Ps. 35.15-16
[u]ch. 14.58; John 2.19
32 [v]1 Pet. 2.23
33 [w]Luke 23.44
34 [x]Ps. 22.1; Heb. 5.7
36 [y]Matt. 27.48; John 19.29
[z]Ps. 69.21
37 [a]Matt. 27.50; John 19.30
38 [b]Ex. 26.31-35; Heb. 10.19
39 [c]Deut. 32.31
40 [d]Luke 23.49
[e]Ps. 38.11
41 [f]Luke 8.2
42 [g]Matt. 27.57; John 19.38
43 [h]Ps. 25.2; Isa. 64.4
46 [i]Isa. 53.9
CHAPTER 16
1 [a]Matt. 28.1
[b]Luke 23.56
2 [c]John 20.1

the scribes, He saved others; himself
he cannot save.
32 Let Christ the King of Is'ra-el descend now from the cross, that we may
see and believe. And [v]they that were
crucified with him reviled him.
33 And [w]when the sixth hour was
come, there was darkness over the
whole land until the ninth hour.
34 And at the ninth hour Jē'sus cried
with a loud voice, saying, [x]E-lō'ī, E-
lō'ī, lā'mȧ sā-bach-thā'nī? which is, being interpreted, My God, my God, why
hast thou forsaken me?
35 And some of them that stood by,
when they heard *it,* said, Behold, he
calleth E-lī'ăs.
36 And [y]one ran and filled a spunge
full of vinegar, and put *it* on a reed,
and [z]gave him to drink, saying, Let
alone; let us see whether E-lī'ăs will
come to take him down.
37 [a]And Jē'sus cried with a loud
voice, and gave up the ghost.
38 And [b]the veil of the temple was
rent in twain from the top to the bottom.
39 ¶ And [c]when the centurion, which
stood over against him, saw that he so
cried out, and gave up the ghost, he
said, Truly this man was the Son of
God.
40 [d]There were also women looking
on [e]afar off: among whom was Mā'rȳ
Măg-da-lē'ne, and Mā'rȳ the mother
of Jāmes the less and of Jō'sēs, and
Sa-lō'me;
41 (Who also, when he was in Găl'-
ĭ-lee, [f]followed him, and ministered
unto him;) and many other women
which came up with him unto Je-rụ'sa-
lĕm.
42 ¶ [g]And now when the even was
come, because it was the preparation,
that is, the day before the sabbath,
43 Jō'seph of Ăr-ĭ-mă-thæ'ȧ, an honourable counsellor, which also [h]waited
for the kingdom of God, came, and
went in boldly unto Pī'late, and craved
the body of Jē'sus.
44 And Pī'late marvelled if he were
already dead: and calling *unto him* the
centurion, he asked him whether he
had been any while dead.
45 And when he knew *it* of the centurion, he gave the body to Jō'seph.
46 [i]And he bought fine linen, and
took him down, and wrapped him in
the linen, and laid him in a sepulchre
which was hewn out of a rock, and
rolled a stone unto the door of the
sepulchre.
47 And Mā'rȳ Măg-da-lē'ne and
Mā'rȳ *the mother* of Jō'sēs beheld
where he was laid.
16 And [a]when the sabbath was past,
Mā'rȳ Măg-da-lē'ne, and Mā'rȳ
the *mother* of Jāmes, and Sa-lō'me,
[b]had bought sweet spices, that they
might come and anoint him.
2 [c]And very early in the morning
the first *day* of the week, they came
unto the sepulchre at the rising of the
sun.

3 And they said among themselves, Who shall roll away the stone from the door of the sepulchre?

4 And when they looked, they saw that the stone was rolled away: for it was very great.

5 [d]And entering into the sepulchre, they saw a young man sitting on the right side, clothed in a long white garment; and they were affrighted.

6 [e]And he saith unto them, Be not affrighted: Ye seek Jē'sus of Nāz'a-rěth, which was crucified: he is [f]risen; he is not here: behold the place where they laid him.

7 But go your way, tell his disciples and Pē'tēr that he goeth before you into Găl'ĭ-lee: there shall ye see him, [g]as he said unto you.

8 And they went out quickly, and fled from the sepulchre; for they trembled and were amazed: [h]neither said they any thing to any *man;* for they were afraid.

9 ¶ Now when *Jesus* was risen early the first *day* of the week, [i]he appeared first to Mā'rȳ Măg-da-lē'ne, [j]out of whom he had cast seven devils.

10 *And* she went and told them that had been with him, as they mourned and wept.

11 [k]And they, when they had heard that he was alive, and had been seen of her, believed not.

12 ¶ After that he appeared in another form unto two of them, as they walked, and went into the country.

13 And they went and told *it* unto the residue: neither believed they them.

14 ¶ [l]Afterward he appeared unto the eleven as they sat [1]at meat, and upbraided them with their unbelief and hardness of heart, because they believed not them which had seen him after he was risen.

15 [m]And he said unto them, Go ye into all the world, [n]and preach the gospel to every creature.

16 [o]He that believeth and is baptized shall be saved: [p]but he that believeth not shall be damned.

17 And these signs shall follow them that believe; [q]In my name shall they cast out devils; [r]they shall speak with new tongues;

18 [s]They shall take up serpents; and if they drink any deadly thing, it shall not hurt them; [t]they shall lay hands on the sick, and they shall recover.

19 ¶ So then after the Lord had spoken unto them, he was received up into heaven, and [u]sat on the right hand of God.

20 And they went forth, and preached every where, the Lord working with *them,* and confirming the word with signs following. Amen.

5 [d]Luke 24.3
6 [e]Matt. 28.5
[f]John 2.19
7 [g]Matt. 26.32
8 [h]Matt. 28.8
9 [i]John 20.14
[j]Luke 8.2
11 [k]Luke 24.11
14 [l]Luke 24.36; 1 Cor. 15.5
[1]Or, together
15 [m]John 15.16
[n]Col. 1.23
16 [o]John 3.18-36; Acts 2.38; Acts 16.30; Rom. 10.9; 1 Pet. 3.21
[p]John 12.48
17 [q]Matt. 8.16; Luke 4.2-13; Acts 5.16
[r]Acts 2.4; Acts 10.46; Acts 19.6; 1 Cor. 12.10
18 [s]Acts 28.5
[t]Acts 9.17; Jas. 5.14
19 [u]Ps. 110.1; Heb. 1.3

THE GOSPEL ACCORDING TO

LUKE

Life's Questions

Who can we accept into God's church?
Who is the Holy Spirit?
What is my mission?

God's Answers

Probably about A.D. 65 God called a Gentile doctor to research and write two books about the mission Jesus left behind: Luke and Acts. Luke is a gospel seeking to show Gentiles and social outcasts their place in God's kingdom led by God's Spirit. Luke showed cultured Gentiles why they should repent and follow a Jewish teacher and what changes it meant for their lives when they did. He also shows the kingdom present and the kingdom coming.

Luke shows: Jesus fulfilled the expectations of Judaism (and the mission of the prophets but was rejected (1—4); Jesus' carried out His mission in faith, love, and forgiveness (5—7); God's kingdom offers awesome power to people of any social class who will believe but demands commitment unto death (8:1—9:50); the kingdom involves faithful ministry and witness to all people (9:51—13:21); the kingdom has surprising entrance requirements of repentance, total allegiance, and humble trust (13:22—19:27); Jesus exercised the authority of the divine king in face of rejection, betrayal, and death (19:28—22:6); Jesus died as the true Passover Lamb (22:7—23:56); Jesus' resurrection is the gate to faith and mission (ch. 24).

Luke invites all people to accept Christ's admission standards and join in His mission for all people, especially the poor and outcast.

1 Forasmuch as many have taken in hand to set forth in order a declaration of [a]those things which are most surely believed among us,

2 [b]Even as they delivered them unto us, which [c]from the beginning were eyewitnesses, and ministers of the word;

3 [d]It seemed good to me also, having had perfect understanding of all things from the very first, to write unto thee [e]in order, [f]most excellent The-ŏph'ĭ-lŭs,

4 [g]That thou mightest know the certainty of those things, wherein thou hast been instructed.

5 ¶ There was [h]in the days of Hĕr'-od, the king of Jū-dæ'ȧ, a certain priest named Zăch-a-rī'as, [i]of the course of A-bī'ȧ: and his wife *was* of the

CHAPTER 1
1 [a]John 20.31
2 [b]Heb. 2.3; [c]John 15.27
3 [d]1 Cor. 7.40
[e]Acts 11.4
[f]Acts 1.1
4 [g]John 20.31
5 [h]Matt. 2.1
[i]1 Chr. 24.10-19

daughters of Aâr'on, and her name
was E-lĭs'a-bĕth.
6 And they were both [j]righteous
before God, walking in all the commandments
and ordinances of the
Lord blameless.
7 And they had no child, because
that E-lĭs'a-bĕth was barren, and they
both were *now* well stricken in years.
8 And it came to pass, that while he
executed the priest's office before God
[k]in the order of his course,
9 According to the custom of the
priest's office, his lot was [l]to burn incense
when he went into the temple of
the Lord.
10 [m]And the whole multitude of the
people were praying without at the
time of incense.
11 And there appeared unto him an
angel of the Lord standing on the right
side of the altar of incense.
12 And when Zăch-a-rī'as saw *him*,
[n]he was troubled, and fear fell upon
him.
13 But the angel said unto him, Fear
not, Zăch-a-rī'as: for [o]thy prayer is
heard; and thy wife E-lĭs'a-bĕth shall
bear thee a son, and thou shalt call his
name Jŏhn.
14 And thou shalt have joy and gladness;
and many shall rejoice at his
birth.
15 For he shall be [p]great in the sight
of the Lord, and [q]shall drink neither
wine nor strong drink; and he shall be
filled with the Hō'ly̆ Ghōst, [r]even from
his mother's womb.
16 [s]And many of the children of
Is'ra-el shall he turn to the Lord their
God.
17 [t]And he shall go before him in
the spirit and power of E-lī'ăs, to turn
the hearts of the fathers to the children,
and the disobedient [1]to the wisdom
of the just; to make ready a people
prepared for the [u]Lord.
18 And Zăch-a-rī'as said unto the angel,
[v]Whereby shall I know this? for I
am an old man, and my wife well
stricken in years.
19 And the angel answering said
unto him, I am [w]Gā'brĭ-el, that stand
in the presence of God; and am sent to
speak unto thee, and to shew thee
these glad tidings.
20 And, behold, [x]thou shalt be dumb,
and not able to speak, until the day that
these things shall be performed, because
thou believest not my words,
which shall be fulfilled in their season.
21 And the people [y]waited for Zăch-a-rī'as,
and marvelled that he tarried
so long in the temple.
22 And when he came out, he could
not speak unto them: and they perceived
that he had seen a vision in the
temple: for he beckoned unto them,
and remained speechless.
23 And it came to pass, that, as soon
as [z]the days of his ministration were
accomplished, he departed to his own
house.

6 [j]1 Ki. 9.4; 2 Ki. 20.3; Ps. 119.6; Acts 24.16
8 [k]2 Chr. 8.14
9 [l]Ex. 30.7-8; 1 Sam. 2.28
10 [m]Lev. 16.17
12 [n]Dan. 10.8; Acts 10.4; Rev. 1.17
13 [o]1 Sam. 1.19
15 [p]Gen. 12.2; Josh. 4.14
[q]Num. 6.3; Judg. 13.4; ch. 7.33
[r]Jer. 1.5; Gal. 1.15
16 [s]Dan. 12.3
17 [t]Matt. 11.14
[1]Or, by
[u]1 Sam. 7.3; 1 Chr. 29.18; Ps. 10.17; Isa. 40.3
18 [v]Gen. 17.17
19 [w]Dan. 8.16
20 [x]Ezek. 3.26; Ezek. 24.27
21 [y]Num. 6.23
23 [z]2 Ki. 11.5
25 [a]Gen. 30.23
27 [b]Isa. 7.14
28 [2]Or, graciously accepted, or, much graced
31 [c]Gal. 4.4
32 [d]Phil. 2.10; 1 Tim. 6.15
[e]2 Sam. 7.11; Ps. 132.11; Isa. 9.6-7; Isa. 16.5; Jer. 23.5; Jer. 33.15-17
33 [f]Dan. 2.44; Dan. 7.14; Heb. 1.8
35 [g]Matt. 14.33; Rom. 1.4
37 [h]Gen. 18.14; Matt. 3.9
39 [i]Josh. 21.9
41 [j]Acts 6.3
42 [k]Judg. 5.24
45 [3]Or, which believed that there

24 And after those days his wife E-lĭs'a-bĕth
conceived, and hid herself
five months, saying,
25 Thus hath the LORD dealt with
me in the days wherein he looked on
me, to [a]take away my reproach among
men.
26 And in the sixth month the angel
Gā'brĭ-el was sent from God unto a
city of Găl'ĭ-lee, named Năz'a-rĕth,
27 To a virgin [b]espoused to a man
whose name was Jō'seph, of the house
of Dā'vid; and the virgin's name *was*
Mā'ry̆.
28 And the angel came in unto her,
and said, Hail, *thou that art* [2]highly
favoured, the Lord *is* with thee: blessed
art thou among women.
29 And when she saw *him*, she was
troubled at his saying, and cast in her
mind what manner of salutation this
should be.
30 And the angel said unto her, Fear
not, Mā'ry̆: for thou hast found favour
with God.
31 [c]And, behold, thou shalt conceive
in thy womb, and bring forth a son, and
shalt call his name JĒ'SUS.
32 He shall be [d]great, and shall be
called the Son of the Highest: and [e]the
Lord God shall give unto him the
throne of his father Dā'vid:
33 [f]And he shall reign over the house
of Jā'cob for ever; and of his kingdom
there shall be no end.
34 Then said Mā'ry̆ unto the angel,
How shall this be, seeing I know not a
man?
35 And the angel answered and said
unto her, The Hō'ly̆ Ghōst shall come
upon thee, and the power of the Highest
shall overshadow thee: therefore
also that holy thing which shall be
born of thee shall be called [g]the Son of
God.
36 And, behold, thy cousin E-lĭs'a-bĕth,
she hath also conceived a son in
her old age: and this is the sixth month
with her, who was called barren.
37 For [h]with God nothing shall be
impossible.
38 And Mā'ry̆ said, Behold the handmaid
of the Lord; be it unto me according
to thy word. And the angel departed
from her.
39 And Mā'ry̆ arose in those days,
and went into the hill country with
haste, [i]into a city of Jū'dȧ;
40 And entered into the house of
Zăch-a-rī'as, and saluted E-lĭs'a-bĕth.
41 And it came to pass, that, when E-lĭs'a-bĕth
heard the salutation of Mā'ry̆,
the babe leaped in her womb; and E-lĭs'a-bĕth
was filled [j]with the Hō'ly̆ Ghōst:
42 And she spake out with a loud
voice, and said, [k]Blessed *art* thou
among women, and blessed *is* the fruit
of thy womb.
43 And whence *is* this to me, that the
mother of my Lord should come to me?
44 For, lo, as soon as the voice of thy
salutation sounded in mine ears, the
babe leaped in my womb for joy.
45 And blessed *is* she [3]that believed:
for there shall be a performance of

those things which were told her from
the Lord.
46 And Mā'rȳ said, [l]My soul doth
magnify the Lord,
47 And my spirit hath rejoiced in
God my Saviour.
48 For [m]he hath regarded the low
estate of his handmaiden: for, behold,
from henceforth [n]all generations shall
call me blessed.
49 For he that is mighty hath done to
me great things; and holy *is* his name.
50 And [o]his mercy *is* on them that
fear him from generation to generation.
51 [p]He hath shewed strength with
his arm; [q]he hath scattered the proud
in the imagination of their hearts.
52 [r]He hath put down the mighty
from *their* seats, and exalted them of
low degree.
53 [s]He hath filled the hungry with
good things; and the rich he hath sent
empty away.
54 He hath holpen his servant Is'ra-
el, [t]in remembrance of *his* mercy;
55 [u]As he spake to our fathers, to
Ā'bră-hăm, and to his seed for ever.
56 And Mā'rȳ abode with her about
three months, and returned to her own
house.
57 Now E-lĭs'a-bĕth's full time came
that she should be delivered; and she
brought forth a son.
58 And her neighbours and her cous-
ins heard how the Lord had shewed
great mercy upon her; and they rejoiced with her.
59 And it came to pass, that [v]on the
eighth day they came to circumcise the
child; and they called him Zăch-a-
rī'as, after the name of his father.
60 And his mother answered and
said, Not *so;* but he shall be called
Jŏhn.
61 And they said unto her, There is
none of thy kindred that is called by
this name.
62 And they made signs to his father, how he would have him called.
63 And he asked for a writing table,
and wrote, saying, His name is Jŏhn.
And they marvelled all.
64 And his mouth was opened immediately, and his tongue *loosed,* and he
spake, and praised God.
65 And fear came on all that dwelt
round about them: and all these [4]say-
ings were noised abroad throughout
all the hill country of Jū-dæ'à.
66 And all they that heard [w]*them*
laid *them* up in their hearts, saying,
What manner of child shall this be!
And [x]the hand of the Lord was with
him.
67 And his father Zăch-a-rī'as [y]was
filled with the Hō'lȳ Ghōst, and prophesied, saying,
68 Blessed *be* the Lord God of Is'ra-
el; for he hath visited and redeemed
his people,
69 And hath raised up an horn of
salvation for us in the house of his servant Dā'vid;

46 [l]1 Sam. 2.1
48 [m]1 Sam. 1.11; Ps. 138.6
[n]Gen. 30.13; ch. 11.27
50 [o]Gen. 17.7; Ps. 85.9
51 [p]Ps. 98.1; Isa. 40.10
[q]Ps. 33.10; 1 Pet. 5.5
52 [r]1 Sam. 2.6; Ps. 113.6
53 [s]1 Sam. 2.5; Ezek. 34.29
54 [t]Ps. 98.3; Jer. 31.3-20
55 [u]Gen. 17.19; Gal. 3.16
59 [v]Gen. 17.12; Lev. 12.3
65 [4]Or, things
66 [w]ch. 2.19
[x]Acts 11.21
67 [y]Joel 2.28
70 [z]Jer. 23.5; Rom. 1.2
72 [a]Lev. 26.42
73 [b]Gen. 12.3; Heb. 6.13
74 [c]Rom. 6.18; Heb. 9.14
75 [d]Jer. 32.39; 2 Thess. 2.13
76 [e]Isa. 40.3
77 [5]Or, for
78 [6]Or, bowels of the mercy
[7]Or, sunrising, or, branch, Num. 24.17; Isa. 11.1
79 [f]Isa. 9.2

CHAPTER 2

1 [1]Or, enrolled in order to be taxed
2 [a]Acts 5.37
4 [b]Gen. 35.19; Matt. 2.6
[c]Matt. 1.16; ch. 1.27
7 [d]Matt. 1.25;
[e]Isa. 53.2
8 [2]Or, the night watches
10 [f]Gen. 12.3
11 [g]Isa. 7.14;
[h]Phil. 2.11

70 [z]As he spake by the mouth of his
holy prophets, which have been since
the world began:
71 That we should be saved from
our enemies, and from the hand of all
that hate us;
72 [a]To perform the mercy *promised*
to our fathers, and to remember his
holy covenant;
73 [b]The oath which he sware to our
father Ā'bră-hăm,
74 That he would grant unto us, that
we being delivered out of the hand of
our enemies might [c]serve him without
fear,
75 [d]In holiness and righteousness
before him, all the days of our life.
76 And thou, child, shalt be called
the prophet of the Highest: for [e]thou
shalt go before the face of the Lord to
prepare his ways;
77 To give knowledge of salvation
unto his people [5]by the remission of
their sins,
78 Through the [6]tender mercy of our
God; whereby the [7]dayspring from on
high hath visited us,
79 [f]To give light to them that sit in
darkness and *in* the shadow of death,
to guide our feet into the way of peace.
80 And the child grew, and waxed
strong in spirit, and was in the deserts
till the day of his shewing unto Is'ra-el.

2 And it came to pass in those days,
that there went out a decree from
Çæ'sar Au-gŭs'tus, that all the world
should be [1]taxed.
2 ([a]*And* this taxing was first made
when Çȳ-rē'nĭ-us was governor of
Sȳr'ĭ-à.)
3 And all went to be taxed, every
one into his own city.
4 And Jō'seph also went up from
Găl'ĭ-lee, out of the city of Nāz'a-rĕth,
into Jū-dæ'à, unto [b]the city of Dā'vid,
which is called Bĕth'lĕ-hĕm; ([c]because
he was of the house and lineage of
Dā'vid:)
5 To be taxed with Mā'rȳ his espoused wife, being great with child.
6 And so it was, that, while they were
there, the days were accomplished that
she should be delivered.
7 And [d]she brought forth her firstborn son, and wrapped him in swaddling clothes, and laid him in a [e]man-
ger; because there was no room for
them in the inn.
8 And there were in the same country shepherds abiding in the field, keeping [2]watch over their flock by night.
9 And, lo, the angel of the Lord
came upon them, and the glory of the
Lord shone round about them: and
they were sore afraid.
10 And the angel said unto them,
Fear not: for, behold, I bring you good
tidings of great joy, [f]which shall be to
all people.
11 [g]For unto you is born this day in
the city of Dā'vid a Saviour, [h]which is
Chrīst the Lord.
12 And this *shall be* a sign unto you;
Ye shall find the babe wrapped in
swaddling clothes, lying in a manger.

13 [i]And suddenly there was with the angel a multitude of the heavenly host praising God, and saying,

14 Glory to God in the highest, and on earth [j]peace, [k]good will toward men.

15 And it came to pass, as the angels were gone away from them into heaven, [3]the shepherds said one to another, Let us now go even unto Bĕth′lĕ-hĕm, and see this thing which is come to pass, which the Lord hath made known unto us.

16 And they came with haste, and found Mā′rȳ, and Jō′seph, and the babe lying in a manger.

17 And when they had seen *it*, they made known abroad the saying which was told them concerning this child.

18 And all they that heard *it* wondered at those things which were told them by the shepherds.

19 But Mā′rȳ kept all these things, and pondered *them* in her heart.

20 And the shepherds returned, glorifying and praising God for all the things that they had heard and seen, as it was told unto them.

21 [l]And when eight days were accomplished for the circumcising of the child, his name was called [m]JĒ′SUS, which was so named of the angel before he was conceived in the womb.

22 And when [n]the days of her purification according to the law of Mō′ses were accomplished, they brought him to Je-rụ′sa-lĕm, to present *him* to the Lord;

23 (As it is written in the law of the Lord, [o]Every male that openeth the womb shall be called holy to the Lord;)

24 And to offer a sacrifice according to that which is said in the law of the Lord, A pair of turtledoves, or two young pigeons.

25 And, behold, there was a man in Je-rụ′sa-lĕm, whose name *was* Sĭm′e-on; and the same man *was* just and devout, [p]waiting for the consolation of Is′ra-el: and the Hō′lȳ Ghōst was upon him.

26 And it was revealed unto him by the Hō′lȳ Ghōst, that he should not [q]see death, before he had seen the Lord's Chrīst.

27 And he came [r]by the Spirit into the temple: and when the parents brought in the child Jē′sus, to do for him after the custom of the law,

28 Then took he him up in his arms, and blessed God, and said,

29 Lord, [s]now lettest thou thy servant depart in peace, according to thy word:

30 For mine eyes [t]have seen thy salvation,

31 Which thou hast prepared before the face of all people;

32 [u]A light to lighten the Gĕn′tīles, and the glory of thy people Is′ra-el.

33 And Jō′seph and his mother marvelled at those things which were spoken of him.

34 And Sĭm′e-on blessed them, and said unto Mā′rȳ his mother, Behold, this *child* is set for the [v]fall and rising again of many in Is′ra-el; and for [w]a sign which shall be spoken against;

35 (Yea, [x]a sword shall pierce through thy own soul also,) that the [y]thoughts of many hearts may be revealed.

36 And there was one Ăn′nȧ, [z]a prophetess, the daughter of Phăn-ū′el, of the tribe of Ā′sēr: she was of a great age, and had lived with an husband seven years from her virginity;

37 And she *was* a widow of about fourscore and four years, which departed not from the temple, but served *God* with fastings and prayers [a]night and day.

38 And she coming in that instant gave thanks likewise unto the Lord, and spake of him to all them that [b]looked for redemption in [4]Je-rụ′sa-lĕm.

39 And when they had performed all things according to the law of the Lord, they returned into Găl′ĭ-lee, to their own city Nāz′a-rĕth.

40 And the child grew, and waxed strong in spirit, filled with wisdom: and the grace of God was upon him.

41 Now his parents went to Je-rụ′sa-lĕm [c]every year at the feast of the passover.

42 And when he was twelve years old, they went up to Je-rụ′sa-lĕm after the custom of the feast.

43 And when they had fulfilled the days, as they returned, the child Jē′sus tarried behind in Je-rụ′sa-lĕm; and Jō′seph and his mother knew not *of it*.

44 But they, supposing him to have been in the company, went a day's journey; and they sought him among *their* kinsfolk and acquaintance.

45 And when they found him not, they turned back again to Je-rụ′sa-lĕm, seeking him.

46 And it came to pass, that after three days they found him in the temple, sitting in the midst of the doctors, [d]both hearing them, and asking them questions.

47 And [e]all that heard him were astonished at his understanding and answers.

48 And when they saw him, they were amazed: and his mother said unto him, Son, why hast thou thus dealt with us? behold, thy father and I have sought thee sorrowing.

49 And he said unto them, How is it that ye sought me? wist ye not that I must be about [f]my Father's business?

50 And [g]they understood not the saying which he spake unto them.

51 And he went down with them, and came to Nāz′a-rĕth, and was subject unto them: but his mother [h]kept all these sayings in her heart.

52 And Jē′sus [i]increased in wisdom and [5]stature, and in favour with God and man.

3 Now in the fifteenth year of the reign of Tī-bē′rĭ-us Çæ′sar, Pŏn′tĭ-us Pī′late being governor of Jū-dæ′ȧ, and Hĕr′od being tetrarch of Găl′ĭ-lee, and his brother Phĭl′ĭp tetrarch of

13 [i]Gen. 28.12; Ps. 103.20; Dan. 7.10; Heb. 1.14
14 [j]Isa. 57.19; Col. 1.20
[k]Eph. 2.4-7; 2 Thess. 2.16; 1 John 4.9
15 [3]the men the shepherds
21 [l]Gen. 17.12; Lev. 12.3
[m]Matt. 1.21
22 [n]Lev. 12.2
23 [o]Ex. 13.2; Ex. 22.29; Num. 3.13
25 [p]Isa. 40.1
26 [q]Ps. 89.48; Heb. 11.5
27 [r]Acts 8.29; Rev. 1.10
29 [s]Gen. 46.30; Phil. 1.23; Rev. 14.13
30 [t]Gen. 49.18; 2 Sam. 23.1-5; Isa. 52.10; Acts 4.12
32 [u]Isa. 9.2; Acts 13.47
34 [v]Isa. 8.14; Hos. 14.9; Rom. 9.32; 1 Cor. 1.23; 2 Cor. 2.16; 1 Pet. 2.7-8
[w]Isa. 8.18; Matt. 26.65-67; Acts 28.22; 1 Pet. 2.12; 1 Pet. 4.14
35 [x]Ps. 42.10; John 19.25
[y]1 Cor. 11.19
36 [z]Ex. 15.20
37 [a]Acts 26.7
38 [b]Lam. 3.25-26; Mark 15.43; ch. 24.21
[4]Or, Israel
41 [c]Ex. 23.14-17; Deut. 16.1
46 [d]Isa. 11.1-4
47 [e]Matt. 7.28; Mark 1.22; John 7.15
49 [f]Ps. 40.8; John 4.34
50 [g]ch. 9.45; ch. 18.34
51 [h]Gen. 37.11; Dan. 7.28
52 [i]1 Sam. 2.26; Rom. 14.18
[5]Or, age

I-tu-ræ'à and of the region of Trăch-o-
nī'tis, and Lȳ-sā'nĭ-as the tetrarch of
Ăb-ĭ-lē'ne,
2 [a]Ăn'nas and Cā'ia-phas being the
high priests, the word of God came
unto Jŏhn the son of Zăch-a-rī'as in
the wilderness.
3 [b]And he came into all the country
about Jôr'dan, preaching the baptism
of repentance [c]for the remission of
sins;
4 As it is written in the book of the
words of E-sā'ias the prophet, saying,
[d]The voice of one crying in the wilderness, Prepare ye the way of the Lord,
make his paths straight.
5 Every valley shall be filled, and every mountain and hill shall be brought
low; and the crooked shall be made
straight, and the rough ways *shall be*
made smooth;
6 And [e]all flesh shall see the salvation of God.
7 Then said he to the multitude that
came forth to be baptized of him, [f]O
generation of vipers, who hath warned
you to flee from the wrath to come?
8 [g]Bring forth therefore fruits [1]wor-
thy of repentance, and begin not to say
within yourselves, We have Ā'brā-hăm
to *our* father: for I say unto you, That
God is able of these stones to raise up
children unto Ā'brā-hăm.
9 And now also the ax is laid unto
the root of the trees: [h]every tree therefore which bringeth not forth good
fruit is hewn down, and cast into the
fire.
10 And the people asked him, saying, [i]What shall we do then?
11 He answereth and saith unto
them, [j]He that hath two coats, let him
impart to him that hath none; and he
that hath meat, let him do likewise.
12 Then [k]came also publicans to be
baptized, and said unto him, Master,
what shall we do?
13 And he said unto them, [l]Exact no
more than that which is appointed you.
14 And the soldiers likewise demanded of him, saying, And what shall
we do? And he said unto them, [2]Do
violence to no man, [m]neither accuse
any falsely; and be content with your
[3]wages.
15 And as the people were [4]in expectation, and all men [5]mused in their
hearts of Jŏhn, whether he were the
Chrĭst, or not;
16 Jŏhn answered, saying unto *them*
all, [n]I indeed baptize you with water;
but one mightier than I cometh, the
latchet of whose shoes I am not worthy
to unloose: he shall baptize you with
[o]the Hō'lȳ Ghōst and with fire:
17 Whose fan *is* in his hand, and he
will throughly purge his floor, and
[p]will gather the wheat into his garner;
but the chaff he will burn with fire
unquenchable.
18 And many other things in his exhortation preached he unto the people.
19 But [q]Hĕr'od the tetrarch, being
reproved by him for He-rō'dĭ-as his
brother Phĭl'ĭp's wife, and for all the
evils which Hĕr'od had done,
20 Added yet this above all, that he
shut up Jŏhn in prison.
21 Now when all the people were
baptized, [r]it came to pass, that Jē'sus
also being baptized, and praying, the
heaven was opened,
22 And the Hō'lȳ Ghōst descended
in a bodily shape like a dove upon him,
and a voice [s]came from heaven, which
said, Thou art my beloved Son; in thee
I am well pleased.
23 And Jē'sus himself began to be
[t]about thirty years of age, being (as
was supposed) [u]the son of Jō'seph,
which was *the* [6]*son* of He'lī,
24 Which was *the son* of Măt'that,
which was *the son* of Lē'vī, which was
the son of Mĕl'chī, which was *the*
son of Jăn'nà, which was *the son* of
Jō'seph,
25 Which was *the son* of Măt-ta-
thī'as, which was *the son* of Ā'mos,
which was *the son* of Nā'um, which
was *the son* of Ĕs'lī, which was *the son*
of Năg'ge,
26 Which was *the son* of Mā'ath,
which was *the son* of Măt-ta-thī'as,
which was *the son* of Sĕm'e-ī, which
was *the son* of Jō'seph, which was *the*
son of Jū'dà,
27 Which was *the son* of Jo-ăn'nà,
which was *the son* of Rhē'sà, which
was *the son* of [7]Zo-rŏb'a-bĕl, which
was *the son* of Sa-lā'thĭ-el, which was
the son of Nē'rī,
28 Which was *the son* of Mĕl'chī,
which was *the son* of Ăd'dī, which was
the son of Cō'sam, which was *the son*
of Ĕl-mō'dăm, which was *the son* of
Er,
29 Which was *the son* of Jō'se, which
was *the son* of E-lĭ-ē'zēr, which was
the son of Jō'rim, which was *the son* of
Măt'that, which was *the son* of Lē'vī,
30 Which was *the son* of Sĭm'e-on,
which was *the son* of Jū'dà, which
was *the son* of Jō'seph, which was *the*
son of Jō'nan, which was *the son* of
E-lī'a-kĭm,
31 Which was *the son* of Mē'le-à,
which was *the son* of Mē'nan, which
was *the son* of Măt'ta-thà, which was
the son of [v]Nā'than, [w]which was *the*
son of Dā'vid,
32 [x]Which was *the son* of Jĕs'se,
which was *the son* of Ō'bed, which
was *the son* of Bō'ŏz, which was *the*
son of Săl'mŏn, which was *the son* of
Na-ăs'son,
33 Which was *the son* of A-mĭn'a-
dăb, which was *the son* of Ā'ram,
which was *the son* of Ĕs'rom, which
was *the son* of Phā'rēs, which was *the*
son of Jū'dà,
34 Which was *the son* of Jā'cob,
which was *the son* of Ī'saac, which
was *the son* of Ā'brā-hăm, [y]which was
the son of Thā'rà, which was *the son*
of Nā'chôr,
35 Which was *the son* of Sā'ruch,
which was *the son* of Rā'gau, which
was *the son* of Phā'lec, which was *the*

CHAPTER 3
2 [a]John 11.49; John 18.13; Acts 4.6
3 [b]Mal. 4.6; Matt. 3.1; Mark 1.4
[c]ch. 1.77
4 [d]Isa. 40.3; Matt. 3.3
6 [e]Ps. 98.2; Isa. 52.10
7 [f]Matt. 3.7
8 [g]Acts 26.20
[1]Or, meet for
9 [h]Matt. 3.10; John 15.2-6
10 [i]Acts 2.37
11 [j]Mark 14.5-8; John 13.29; Acts 10.2-31; 2 Cor. 8.14; 1 Tim. 6.18
12 [k]Matt. 21.32
13 [l]Mic. 6.8; ch. 19.8
14 [2]Or, Put no man in fear
[m]Ex. 23.1; Lev. 19.11
[3]Or, allowance
15 [4]Or, in suspense
[5]Or, reasoned, or, debated
16 [n]Matt. 3.11
[o]Prov. 1.23; Isa. 32.15; John 7.39; Acts 2.4
17 [p]Mic. 4.12
19 [q]Prov. 28.15-16; Mark 6.17
21 [r]Matt. 3.13; John 1.32
22 [s]2 Pet. 1.17
23 [t]Num. 4.3-35-39-47
[u]Matt. 13.55; John 6.42
[6]son-in-law
27 [7]It is uncertain whether Zorobabel and Salathiel are the same as those mentioned in Matt. 1.12-13- and 1 Chr. 3.17-19
31 [v]Zech. 12.12
[w]2 Sam. 5.14; 1 Chr. 3.5
32 [x]Ruth 4.18; 1 Chr. 2.10
34 [y]Gen. 11.24-26

son of Hē'bēr, which was *the son* of
Sā'lȧ,
36 [z]Which was *the son* of Ca-ī'-
nan, which was *the son* of Ăr-phăx'ăd,
[a]which was *the son* of Sĕm, which was
the son of Nō'e, which was *the son* of
Lā'mech,
37 Which was *the son* of Ma-thụ'sa-
lȧ, which was *the son* of Ē'nŏch, which
was *the son* of Jā'red, which was *the
son* of Ma-lē'le-el, which was *the son*
of Ca-ī'nan,
38 Which was *the son* of Ē'nos,
which was *the son* of Sĕth, which was
the son of Ăd'ăm, [b]which was *the son*
of God.
4 And [a]Jē'sus being full of the Hō'lȳ
Ghōst returned from Jôr'dan, and
[b]was led by the Spirit into the wilderness,
2 Being forty days [c]tempted of the
devil. And [d]in those days he did eat
nothing: and when they were ended,
he afterward hungered.
3 And the devil said unto him, If
thou be the Son of God, command this
stone that it be made bread.
4 And Jē'sus answered him, saying,
[e]It is written, That man shall not live
by bread alone, but by every word of
God.
5 And the devil taking him up into
an high mountain, shewed unto him all
the kingdoms of the world in a moment of time.
6 And the devil said unto him, All
this power will I give thee, and the
glory of them: for [f]that is delivered
unto me; and to whomsoever I will I
give it.
7 If thou therefore wilt [1]worship me,
all shall be thine.
8 And Jē'sus answered and said unto
him, Get thee behind me, Sā'tan: for [g]it
is written, Thou shalt worship the Lord
thy God, and him only shalt thou serve.
9 [h]And he brought him to Je-rụ'sa-
lĕm, and set him on a pinnacle of the
temple, and said unto him, If thou be
the Son of God, [i]cast thyself down
from hence:
10 For [j]it is written, He shall give his
angels charge over thee, to keep thee:
11 And in *their* hands they shall
bear thee up, lest at any time thou dash
thy foot against a stone.
12 And Jē'sus answering said unto
him, [k]It is said, Thou shalt not tempt
the Lord thy God.
13 And when the devil had ended all
the temptation, he [l]departed from him
[m]for a season.
14 ¶ [n]And Jē'sus returned in the
power of the Spirit into [o]Găl'ĭ-lee: and
there went out a fame of him through
all the region round about.
15 And he taught in their synagogues, being [p]glorified of all.
16 ¶ And he came to [q]Nāz'a-rĕth,
where he had been brought up: and, as
his custom was, [r]he went into the synagogue on the sabbath day, and stood
up for to read.
17 And there was delivered unto him
the book of the prophet E-sā'ias. And
when he had opened the book he found
the place where it was written,
18 [s]The Spirit of the Lord *is* upon
me, because he hath anointed me to
preach the gospel to the poor; he hath
sent me to heal the brokenhearted, to
preach deliverance to the captives, and
recovering of sight to the blind, to set
at liberty them that are bruised,
19 To preach the [t]acceptable year
of the Lord.
20 And he closed the book, and he
gave *it* again to the minister, and sat
down. And the eyes of all them that
were in the synagogue were fastened
on him.
21 And he began to say unto them,
This day is this scripture fulfilled in
your ears.
22 And all bare him witness, and
[u]wondered at the gracious words which
proceeded out of his mouth. And they
said, [v]Is not this Jō'seph's son?
23 And he said unto them, Ye will
surely say unto me this proverb, Physician, heal thyself: whatsoever we have
heard done in [w]Ca-pêr'na-ŭm, do also
here in [x]thy country.
24 And he said, Verily I say unto
you, No [y]prophet is accepted in his
own country.
25 But I tell you of a truth, [z]many
widows were in Is'ra-el in the days of
E-lī'ăs, when the heaven was shut up
three years and six months, when great
famine was throughout all the land;
26 But unto none of them was E-lī'ăs
sent, save unto Sa-rĕp'tȧ, *a city* of Sī'-
dŏn, unto a woman *that was* a widow.
27 [a]And many lepers were in Is'ra-
el in the time of Ĕl-ĭ-sē'us the prophet;
and none of them was cleansed, saving
Nā'a-man the Sȳr'ĭ-an.
28 And all they in the synagogue,
when they heard these things, were
filled with wrath,
29 And rose up, and thrust him out
of the city, and led him unto the [2]brow
of the hill whereon their city was
built, that they might cast him down
headlong.
30 But he [b]passing through the midst
of them went his way,
31 And [c]came down to Ca-pêr'na-
ŭm, a city of Găl'ĭ-lee, and taught them
on the sabbath days.
32 And they were astonished at his
doctrine: [d]for his word was with power.
33 ¶ [e]And in the synagogue there
was a man, which had a spirit of an
unclean devil, and cried out with a
loud voice,
34 Saying, [3]Let *us* alone; what have
we to do with thee, *thou* Jē'sus of
Nāz'a-rĕth? art thou come to destroy
us? I know thee who thou art; [f]the
Holy One of God.
35 And Jē'sus rebuked him, saying,
Hold thy peace, and come out of him.
And when the devil had thrown him in
the midst, he came out of him, and hurt
him not.
36 And they were all amazed, and
spake among themselves, saying, What
a word *is* this! for with authority and

36 [z]Gen. 11.12
[a]Gen. 5.6; Gen. 11.10
38 [b]Gen. 1.26-27; Isa. 64.8

CHAPTER 4
1 [a]Isa. 11.2; John 1.33
[b]1 Ki. 18.12; Acts 8.39
2 [c]Gen. 3.15; Heb. 2.18
[d]Ex. 34.28; 1 Ki. 19.8
4 [e]Ex. 23.25; Eph. 6.17
6 [f]John 12.31; Rev. 13.2-7
7 [1]Or, fall down before me
8 [g]Deut. 6.13; Deut. 10.20
9 [h]Matt. 4.5
[i]1 Pet. 5.8
10 [j]Ps. 91.11
12 [k]Deut. 6.16
13 [l]Jas. 4.7
[m]John 14.30; Heb. 4.15
14 [n]Matt. 4.12; John 4.43
[o]Acts 10.37
15 [p]Isa. 52.13
16 [q]Matt. 2.23
[r]Acts 13.14
18 [s]Isa. 42.1; Dan. 9.24
19 [t]Lev. 25.8; 2 Cor. 6.2
22 [u]Ps. 45.2
[v]John 6.42
23 [w]Matt. 4.13
[x]Matt. 13.54; Mark 6.1
24 [y]Matt. 13.57; John 4.44
25 [z]1 Ki. 17.9; Jas. 5.17
27 [a]2 Ki. 5.14
29 [2]Or, edge
30 [b]John 8.59; John 10.39
31 [c]Matt. 4.13; Mark 1.21
32 [d]Matt. 7.28-29; Tit. 2.15
33 [e]Mark 1.23
34 [3]Or, Away
[f]Ps. 16.10

power he commandeth the unclean spirits, and they come out.
37 [g]And the fame of him went out into every place of the country round about.
38 ¶ [h]And he arose out of the synagogue, and entered into Sī'mon's house. And Sī'mon's wife's mother was taken with a great fever; and they besought him for her.
39 And he stood over her, [i]and rebuked the fever; and it left her: and immediately she arose and ministered unto them.
40 ¶ [j]Now when the sun was setting, all they that had any sick with divers diseases brought them unto him; and he laid his hands on every one of them, and healed them.
41 [k]And devils also came out of many, crying out, and saying, Thou art Chrīst the Son of God. And [l]he rebuking *them* suffered them not [4]to speak: for they knew that he was Chrīst.
42 [m]And when it was day, he departed and went into a desert place: and the people sought him, and came unto him, and stayed him, that he should not depart from them.
43 And he said unto them, [n]I must preach the kingdom of God to other cities also: for therefore am I sent.
44 [o]And he preached in the synagogues of Găl'ĭ-lee.

5 And [a]it came to pass, that, as the people pressed upon him to hear the word of God, he stood by the lake of Gĕn-nĕs'a-rĕt,
2 And saw two ships standing by the lake: but the fishermen were gone out of them, and were washing *their* nets.
3 And he entered into one of the ships, which was Sī'mon's, and prayed him that he would thrust out a little from the land. And he sat down, and taught the people out of the ship.
4 Now when he had left speaking, he said unto Sī'mon, [b]Launch out into the deep, and let down your nets for a draught.
5 And Sī'mon answering said unto him, Master, we have toiled all the night, and have taken nothing: nevertheless at thy word I will let down the net.
6 And when they had this done, they inclosed a great multitude of fishes: and their net brake.
7 And they beckoned unto *their* partners, which were in the other ship, that they should come and help them. And they came, and filled both the ships, so that they began to sink.
8 When Sī'mon Pē'tĕr saw *it*, he fell down at Jē'sus' knees, saying, [c]Depart from me; for I am a sinful man, O Lord.
9 For he was astonished, and all that were with him, at the draught of the fishes which they had taken:
10 And so *was* also Jāmes, and Jŏhn, the sons of Zĕb'e-dee, which were partners with Sī'mon. And Jē'sus said unto Sī'mon, Fear not; [d]from henceforth thou shalt catch men.

37 [g]Mic. 5.4
38 [h]Matt. 8.14; Mark 1.29
39 [i]Ps. 103.3
40 [j]Matt. 8.16; Mark 1.32
41 [k]Mark 1.34
[l]Mark 1.25-34
[4]Or, to say that they knew him to be Christ
42 [m]Matt. 14.13; Mark 1.35
43 [n]Mark 1.14-15; Rom. 15.8
44 [o]Matt. 4.53

CHAPTER 5
1 [a]Matt. 4.18; Mark 1.16
4 [b]Matt. 17.27; John 21.6
8 [c]Judg. 13.22; Dan. 8.17
10 [d]Ezek. 47.9-10; Mark 1.17
11 [e]Matt. 4.20; Phil. 3.7-8
12 [f]Matt. 8.2; Mark 1.40
[g]Gen. 18.14; Heb. 7.25
14 [h]Matt. 8.4
[i]Lev. 13.1; Lev. 14.4-10-21-22
15 [j]Matt. 4.25; John 6.2
16 [k]Mark 14.23
18 [l]Matt. 9.2; Mark 2.3
20 [m]Matt. 9.2; Jas. 5.14-15
21 [n]Matt. 9.3; Mark 2.6-7
[o]Ex. 34.7
24 [p]Acts 5.31
25 [q]Ps. 103.1
27 [r]Matt. 9.9

11 And when they had brought their ships to land, [e]they forsook all, and followed him.
12 ¶ [f]And it came to pass, when he was in a certain city, behold a man full of leprosy: who seeing Jē'sus fell on *his* face, and besought him, saying, Lord, if thou wilt, thou canst [g]make me clean.
13 And he put forth *his* hand, and touched him, saying, I will: be thou clean. And immediately the leprosy departed from him.
14 [h]And he charged him to tell no man: but go, and shew thyself to the priest, and offer for thy cleansing, [i]according as Mō'ses commanded, for a testimony unto them.
15 But so much the more went there a fame abroad of him: [j]and great multitudes came together to hear, and to be healed by him of their infirmities.
16 ¶ [k]And he withdrew himself into the wilderness, and prayed.
17 And it came to pass on a certain day, as he was teaching, that there were Phăr'ĭ-sees and doctors of the law sitting by, which were come out of every town of Găl'ĭ-lee, and Jū-dæ'ȧ, and Je-ru̥'sa-lĕm: and the power of the Lord was *present* to heal them.
18 ¶ [l]And, behold, men brought in a bed a man which was taken with a palsy: and they sought *means* to bring him in, and to lay *him* before him.
19 And when they could not find by what *way* they might bring him in because of the multitude, they went upon the house top, and let him down through the tiling with *his* couch into the midst before Jē'sus.
20 And when he saw their faith, he said unto him, Man, [m]thy sins are forgiven thee.
21 [n]And the scribes and the Phăr'ĭ-sees began to reason, saying, Who is this which speaketh blasphemies? [o]Who can forgive sins, but God alone?
22 But when Jē'sus perceived their thoughts, he answering said unto them, What reason ye in your hearts?
23 Whether is easier, to say, Thy sins be forgiven thee; or to say, Rise up and walk?
24 But that ye may know that the [p]Son of man hath power upon earth to forgive sins, (he said unto the sick of the palsy,) I say unto thee, Arise, and take up thy couch, and go into thine house.
25 And immediately he rose up before them, and took up that whereon he lay, and departed to his own house, [q]glorifying God.
26 And they were all amazed, and they glorified God, and were filled with fear, saying, We have seen strange things to day.
27 ¶ [r]And after these things he went forth, and saw a publican, named Lē'vī, sitting at the receipt of custom: and he said unto him, Follow me.
28 And he left all, rose up, and followed him.

29 [s]And Lē'vī made him a great
feast in his own house: and [t]there was
a great company of publicans and of
others that sat down with them.
30 But their scribes and Phăr'ĭ-sees
murmured against his disciples, saying, Why do ye eat and drink with publicans and sinners?
31 And Jē'sus answering said unto
them, They that are whole need not a
physician; but they that are sick.
32 [u]I came not to call the righteous,
but sinners to repentance.
33 ¶ And they said unto him, [v]Why
do the disciples of Jŏhn fast often, and
make prayers, and likewise *the disciples* of the Phăr'ĭ-sees; but thine eat
and drink?
34 And he said unto them, Can ye
make the children of the bridechamber
fast, while the [w]bridegroom is with
them?
35 But the days will come, when the
bridegroom shall [x]be taken away from
them, and then shall they [y]fast in those
days.
36 ¶ [z]And he spake also a parable
unto them; No man putteth a piece of a
new garment upon an old; if otherwise, then both the new maketh a rent,
and the piece that was *taken* out of the
new agreeth not with the old.
37 And no man putteth new wine
into old bottles; else the new wine will
burst the bottles, and be spilled, and
the bottles shall perish.
38 But new wine must be put into
new bottles; and both are preserved.
39 No man also having drunk old
wine straightway desireth new: for he
saith, The old is better.

6

And [a]it came to pass on the second
sabbath after the first, that he went
through the corn fields; and his disciples plucked the ears of corn, and did
eat rubbing *them* in *their* hands.
2 And certain of the Phăr'ĭ-sees said
unto them, [b]Why do ye that which is
not lawful to do on the sabbath days?
3 And Jē'sus answering them said,
Have ye not read so much as this,
[c]what Dā'vid did, when himself was
an hungred, and they which were with
him;
4 How he went into the house of
God, and did take and eat the shewbread, and gave also to them that were
with him; [d]which it is not lawful to eat
but for the priests alone?
5 And he said unto them, That the
Son of man is Lord also of the sabbath.
6 [e]And it came to pass also on another sabbath, that he entered into the
synagogue and taught: and there was a
man whose right hand was withered.
7 And the scribes and Phăr'ĭ-sees
watched him, whether he would heal
on the sabbath day; that they might
find an accusation against him.
8 But he [f]knew their thoughts, and
said to the man which had the withered hand, Rise up, and stand forth in
the midst. And he arose and stood
forth.
9 Then said Jē'sus unto them, I will
ask you one thing; [g]Is it lawful on the
sabbath days to do good, or to do evil?
to save life, or to destroy *it*?
10 And looking round about upon
them all, he said unto the man, Stretch
forth thy hand. And he did so: and his
hand was restored whole as the other.
11 And they were filled with madness; and communed one with another
what they might do to Jē'sus.
12 [h]And it came to pass in those
days, that he went out into a mountain
to pray, and continued all night in
prayer to God.
13 ¶ And when it was day, he called
unto him his disciples: [i]and of them he
chose twelve, whom also he named
apostles;
14 Sī'mon, ([j]whom he also named
Pē'tĕr,) and Ăn'drew his brother, Jāmes
and Jŏhn, Phĭl'ĭp and Bär-thŏl'ŏ-mew,
15 Măt'thew and Thŏm'as, Jāmes the
son of Ăl-phæ'us, and Sī'mon called
Ze-lō'tēs,
16 And Jū'das [k]*the brother* of Jāmes,
and Jū'das Ĭs-căr'ĭ-ot, which also was
the traitor.
17 ¶ And he came down with them,
and stood in the plain, and the company of his disciples, [l]and a great multitude of people out of all Jū-dæ'à and
Je-ru'sa-lĕm, and from the sea coast of
Tȳre and Sī'dŏn, which came to hear
him, and to be healed of their diseases;
18 And they that were vexed with
unclean spirits: and they were healed.
19 And the whole multitude [m]sought
to touch him: for [n]there went virtue out
of him, and healed *them* all.
20 ¶ And he lifted up his eyes on his
disciples, and said, [o]Blessed *be ye*
poor: for yours is the kingdom of God.
21 [p]Blessed *are ye* that hunger now:
for ye shall be filled. [q]Blessed *are ye*
that weep now: for ye shall laugh.
22 [r]Blessed are ye, when men shall
hate you, and when they [s]shall separate you *from their company*, and shall
reproach *you*, and cast out your name
as evil, for the Son of man's sake.
23 [t]Rejoice ye in that day, and leap
for joy: for, behold, your reward *is*
great in heaven: for [u]in the like manner did their fathers unto the prophets.
24 [v]But woe unto you that are rich!
for [w]ye have received your consolation.
25 [x]Woe unto you that are full! for
ye shall hunger. [y]Woe unto you that
laugh now! for ye shall mourn and
weep.
26 [z]Woe unto you, when all men
shall speak well of you! for so did their
fathers to the false prophets.
27 ¶ [a]But I say unto you which hear,
Love your enemies, do good to them
which hate you.
28 Bless them that curse you, and
[b]pray for them which despitefully use
you.
29 [c]And unto him that smiteth thee
on the *one* cheek offer also the other;
[d]and him that taketh away thy cloke
forbid not *to take thy* coat also.

29 [s]Matt. 9.10; Mark 2.15
[t]ch. 15.1
32 [u]Matt. 9.13; 1 Tim. 1.15
33 [v]Matt. 9.14; Mark 2.18
34 [w]Matt. 22.2; Rev. 21.2
35 [x]Dan. 9.26; John 7.33
[y]Matt. 6.16-17; 2 Cor. 6.4-5
36 [z]Matt. 9.16-17; Mark 2.21-22
CHAPTER 6
1 [a]Matt. 12.1; Mark 2.23
2 [b]Ex. 20.10; Mark 2.24
3 [c]1 Sam. 21.6
4 [d]Ex. 29.23-33; Lev. 24.9
6 [e]Matt. 12.9; John 9.16
8 [f]1 Sam. 16.7; Rev. 2.23
9 [g]Matt. 12.12-13; John 7.23
12 [h]Matt. 14.23
13 [i]Matt. 10.1
14 [j]John 1.42
16 [k]Acts 1.13; Jude 1
17 [l]Matt. 4.25
19 [m]Matt. 14.36
[n]Mark 5.30
20 [o]Matt. 5.3; Jas. 2.5
21 [p]Isa. 55.1
[q]Isa. 61.3
22 [r]1 Pet. 2.19;
[s]John 16.2
23 [t]Acts 5.41;
[u]2 Ki. 6.31
24 [v]Amos 6.1;
[w]Matt. 6.2
25 [x]Isa. 65.13
[y]Prov. 14.13
26 [z]John 15.19
27 [a]Ex. 23.4
28 [b]ch. 23.34
29 [c]Matt. 5.39
[d]1 Cor. 6.7

30 [e]Give to every man that asketh of
thee; and of him that taketh away thy
goods ask *them* not again.
31 [f]And as ye would that men should
do to you, do ye also to them likewise.
32 [g]For if ye love them which love
you, what thank have ye? for sinners
also love those that love them.
33 And if ye do good to them which
do good to you, what thank have ye?
for sinners also do even the same.
34 [h]And if ye lend *to them* of whom
ye hope to receive, what thank have
ye? for sinners also lend to sinners, to
receive as much again.
35 But love ye your enemies, and do
good, and [i]lend, hoping for nothing
again; and your reward shall be great,
and [j]ye shall be the children of the
Highest: for [k]he is kind unto the unthankful and *to* the evil.
36 [l]Be ye therefore merciful, as your
Father also is merciful.
37 [m]Judge not, and ye shall not be
judged: condemn not, and ye shall not
be condemned: forgive, and ye shall be
forgiven:
38 [n]Give, and it shall be given unto
you; good measure, pressed down, and
shaken together, and running over,
shall men give into your [o]bosom. For
[p]with the same measure that ye mete
withal it shall be measured to you
again.
39 And he spake a parable unto
them, [q]Can the blind lead the blind?
shall they not both fall into the ditch?
40 The [r]disciple is not above his
master: but every one [1]that is perfect
shall be as his master.
41 [s]And why beholdest thou the
mote that is in thy brother's eye, but
perceivest not the beam that is in thine
own eye?
42 Either how canst thou say to thy
brother, Brother, let me pull out the
mote that is in thine eye, when thou
thyself beholdest not the beam that is
in thine own eye? Thou hypocrite,
[t]cast out first the beam out of thine
own eye, and then shalt thou see
clearly to pull out the mote that is in
thy brother's eye.
43 [u]For a good tree bringeth not
forth corrupt fruit; neither doth a corrupt tree bring forth good fruit.
44 For [v]every tree is known by his
own fruit. For of thorns men do not
gather figs, nor of a bramble bush
gather they [2]grapes.
45 [w]A good man out of the good treasure of his heart bringeth forth that
which is good; and an evil man out of
the evil treasure of his heart bringeth
forth that which is evil: for of the abundance of the heart his mouth speaketh.
46 ¶ [x]And why call ye me, Lord,
Lord, and do not the things which I
say?
47 [y]Whosoever cometh to me, and
heareth my sayings, and doeth them, I
will shew you to whom he is like:
48 He is like a man which built
an house, and digged deep, and laid
the foundation on a rock: and when
[z]the flood arose, the stream beat vehemently upon that house, and could not
shake it: for it was founded upon [a]a
rock.
49 But he that heareth, and doeth
not, is like a man that without a foundation built an house upon the earth;
against which the stream did beat vehemently, and immediately it fell; and
[b]the ruin of that house was great.

7 Now when he had ended all his sayings in the audience of the people,
he entered into Ca-pêr'na-ŭm.
2 And [a]a certain centurion's servant, who was dear unto him, was sick,
and ready to die.
3 And when he heard of Jē'sus, he
sent unto him the elders of the Jews,
beseeching him that he would come
and heal his servant.
4 And when they came to Jē'sus,
they besought him instantly, saying,
That he was worthy for whom he
should do this:
5 For he loveth our nation, and he
hath built us a synagogue.
6 Then Jē'sus went with them. And
when he was now not far from the
house, the centurion sent friends to
him, saying unto him, Lord, trouble
not thyself: for I am not worthy that
thou shouldest enter under my roof:
7 Wherefore neither thought I myself worthy to come unto thee: but say
in a word, and my servant shall be
healed.
8 For I also am a man set under authority, having under me soldiers, and
I say unto [1]one, Go, and he goeth; and
to another, Come, and he cometh; and
to my servant, Do this, and he doeth *it*.
9 When Jē'sus heard these things,
he marvelled at him, and turned him
about, and said unto the people that
followed him, I say unto you, I have
not found so great faith, no, not in
[b]Is'ra-el.
10 And they that were sent, returning to the house, found the servant
whole that had been sick.
11 ¶ And it came to pass the day after, that he went into a city called
Nā'in; and many of his disciples went
with him, and much people.
12 Now when he came nigh to the
gate of the city, behold, there was a
dead man carried out, the only son of
his mother, and she was a widow: and
much people of the city was with her.
13 And when the Lord saw her, he
[c]had compassion on her, and said unto
her, Weep not.
14 And he came and touched the
[2]bier: and they that bare *him* stood
still. And he said, Young man, I say
unto thee, [d]Arise.
15 And he that was dead sat up, and
began to speak. And he delivered him
to his mother.
16 [e]And there came a fear on all:
and they glorified God, saying, [f]That a
great prophet is risen up among us;
and, [g]That God hath visited his people.

30 [e]Deut. 15.7; Prov. 3.27
31 [f]Phil. 4.8
32 [g]Matt. 5.46
34 [h]Matt. 5.42
35 [i]Lev. 25.35; Prov. 14.20-21
[j]Matt. 5.45; 1 John 3.1
[k]Acts 14.17
36 [l]Matt. 5.48; Eph. 5.1-2
37 [m]Ezek. 16.52; Jas. 3.1
38 [n]Prov. 19.17
[o]Ps. 79.12
[p]Deut. 19.16-21; Mark 4.24
39 [q]Matt. 15.14
40 [r]Matt. 10.24; John 15.20
[1]Or, shall be perfected as his master
41 [s]Matt. 7.3
42 [t]Prov. 18.17
43 [u]Ps. 92.12-14; 2 Tim. 3.1-9
44 [v]Matt. 12.33
[2]a grape
45 [w]Rom. 8.5-8
46 [x]Mal. 1.6; Jas. 1.22
47 [y]Matt. 7.24
48 [z]Acts 14.22; 2 Tim. 3.12
[a]Ps. 125.1; Jude 1
49 [b]Job 8.13
CHAPTER 7
2 [a]Matt. 8.5
8 [1]this man
9 [b]Rom. 3.1-2
13 [c]Lam. 3.32
14 [2]Or, coffin
[d]1 Ki. 17.21
16 [e]ch. 1.65
[f]ch. 24.19;
[g]Ex. 4.31

17 And this rumour of him went forth
throughout all Jū-dæ'ȧ, and throughout
all the region round about.
18 [h]And the disciples of Jŏhn shewed
him of all these things.
19 ¶ And Jŏhn calling *unto him* two
of his disciples sent *them* to Jē'sus, saying, Art thou [i]he that should come? or
look we for another?
20 When the men were come unto
him, they said, Jŏhn Băp'tĭst hath sent
us unto thee, saying, Art thou he that
should come? or look we for another?
21 And in that same hour he cured
many of *their* infirmities and plagues,
and of evil spirits; and unto many *that*
were blind he gave sight.
22 [j]Then Jē'sus answering said unto
them, Go your way, and tell Jŏhn what
things ye have seen and heard; [k]how
that the blind see, the lame walk, the
lepers are cleansed, the deaf hear, the
dead are raised, [l]to the poor the gospel
is preached.
23 And blessed is *he*, whosoever
shall not be offended in me.
24 ¶ And [m]when the messengers of
Jŏhn were departed, he began to speak
unto the people concerning Jŏhn, What
went ye out into the wilderness for to
see? A reed shaken with the wind?
25 But what went ye out for to see?
A man clothed in soft raiment? Behold,
they which are gorgeously apparelled,
and live delicately, are in kings' courts.
26 But what went ye out for to see?
A prophet? Yea, I say unto you, and
much more than a prophet.
27 This is *he*, of whom it is written,
[n]Behold, I send my messenger before
thy face, which shall prepare thy way
before thee.
28 For I say unto you, Among those
that are born of women there is not a
greater prophet than Jŏhn the Băp'tĭst:
but he that is least in the kingdom of
God is greater than he.
29 And all the people that heard
him, and the publicans, justified God,
[o]being baptized with the baptism of
Jŏhn.
30 But the Phăr'ĭ-sees and lawyers
[3]rejected [p]the counsel of God [4]against
themselves, being not baptized of him.
31 ¶ And the Lord said, [q]Whereunto
then shall I liken the men of this generation? and to what are they like?
32 They are like unto children sitting
in the marketplace, and calling one to
another, and saying, We have piped
unto you, and ye have not danced; we
have mourned to you, and ye have not
wept.
33 For [r]Jŏhn the Băp'tĭst came neither eating bread nor drinking wine;
and ye say, He hath a devil.
34 The Son of man is come eating
and drinking; and ye say, Behold a
gluttonous man, and a winebibber, a
friend of publicans and sinners!
35 [s]But wisdom is justified of all her
children.
36 ¶ [t]And one of the Phăr'ĭ-sees
desired him that he would eat with

18 [h]Matt. 11.2
19 [i]Ezek 21.27; Ezek. 34.23-29; Dan. 9.24-26; Mic. 5.2; Hag. 2.7; Zech. 9.9; Mal. 3.1-3
22 [j]Matt. 11.4 [k]Isa. 29.18; Isa. 35.5; Isa. 42.6 [l]Isa. 61.1; Zeph. 3.12; ch. 4.18; Jas. 2.5
24 [m]Matt. 11.7
27 [n]Isa. 40.3; Mal. 3.1; ch. 1.16-17-76; John 1.23
29 [o]Matt. 3.5; ch. 3.12
30 [3]Or, frustrated [p]Acts 20.27 [4]Or, within themselves
31 [q]Matt. 11.16
33 [r]Matt. 3.4; ch. 1.15
35 [s]Matt. 11.19; 1 Cor. 1.23-24
36 [t]Matt. 26.6; John 11.2
37 [u]ch. 8.2
38 [v]Zech. 12.10
39 [w]ch. 15.2
41 [x]Matt. 18.28
42 [y]Ps. 32.1-5; Ps. 51.1-3; Ps. 103.3; Isa. 1.18; Isa. 43.25; Isa. 44.22; Dan. 9.18-19
44 [z]Gen. 18.4; 1 Tim. 5.10
45 [a]Gen. 29.11; Matt. 26.48-49; 1 Cor. 16.20
46 [b]Ps. 23.5; Ps. 45.7; Ps. 92.10; Eccl. 9.8
47 [c]1 Tim. 1.14
48 [d]Matt. 9.2; Mark 2.5
49 [e]Isa. 53.3; Matt. 9.3
50 [f]Matt. 9.22; Mark 5.34; ch. 8.48; ch. 18.42

CHAPTER 8
2 [a]Matt. 27.55-56 [b]Mark 16.9
4 [c]Matt. 13.2; Mark 4.1

him. And he went into the Phăr'ĭ-see's
house, and sat down to meat.
37 And, behold, a [u]woman in the
city, which was a sinner, when she
knew that *Jē'sus* sat at meat in the
Phăr'ĭ-see's house, brought an alabaster box of ointment,
38 And stood at his feet behind *him*
[v]weeping, and began to wash his feet
with tears, and did wipe *them* with the
hairs of her head, and kissed his feet,
and anointed *them* with the ointment.
39 Now when the Phăr'ĭ-see which
had bidden him saw *it*, he spake within
himself, saying, [w]This man, if he were
a prophet, would have known who and
what manner of woman *this is* that toucheth him: for she is a sinner.
40 And Jē'sus answering said unto
him, Sī'mon, I have somewhat to say
unto thee. And he saith, Master, say
on.
41 There was a certain creditor which
had two debtors: the one owed five hundred [x]pence, and the other fifty.
42 And when they had nothing to
pay, he frankly [y]forgave them both.
Tell me therefore, which of them will
love him most?
43 Sī'mon answered and said, I suppose that *he*, to whom he forgave most.
And he said unto him, Thou hast rightly
judged.
44 And he turned to the woman,
and said unto Sī'mon, Seest thou this
woman? I entered into thine house,
thou gavest me no [z]water for my feet:
but she hath washed my feet with
tears, and wiped *them* with the hairs of
her head.
45 Thou gavest me no [a]kiss: but this
woman since the time I came in hath
not ceased to kiss my feet.
46 [b]My head with oil thou didst not
anoint: but this woman hath anointed
my feet with ointment.
47 [c]Wherefore I say unto thee, Her
sins, which are many, are forgiven; for
she loved much: but to whom little is
forgiven, *the same* loveth little.
48 And he said unto her, [d]Thy sins
are forgiven.
49 And they that sat at meat with
him began to say within themselves,
[e]Who is this that forgiveth sins also?
50 And he said to the woman, [f]Thy
faith hath saved thee; go in peace.

8 And it came to pass afterward, that
he went throughout every city and
village, preaching and shewing the
glad tidings of the kingdom of God:
and the twelve *were* with him,
2 And [a]certain women, which had
been healed of evil spirits and infirmities, Mā'rȳ called Măg-da-lē'ne, [b]out
of whom went seven devils,
3 And Jo-ăn'nȧ the wife of Chū'zȧ
Hĕr'od's steward, and Sṳ-săn'nȧ, and
many others, which ministered unto
him of their substance.
4 ¶ [c]And when much people were
gathered together, and were come to
him out of every city, he spake by a
parable:

5 A sower went out to sow his seed:
and as he sowed, some fell by the way
side; and it was trodden down, and the
fowls of the air devoured it.
6 And some fell upon a rock; and as
soon as it was sprung up, it withered
away, because it lacked moisture.
7 And some fell among thorns; and
the thorns sprang up with it, and
choked it.
8 And other fell on good ground,
and sprang up, and bare fruit an hundredfold. And when he had said these
things, he cried, He that hath ears to
hear, let him hear.
9 [d]And his disciples asked him, saying, What might this parable be?
10 And he said, Unto you it is given
to know the mysteries of the kingdom
of God: but to others in parables; [e]that
seeing they might not see, and hearing
they might not understand.
11 [f]Now the parable is this: The
[g]seed is the word of God.
12 Those by [h]the way side are they
that hear; then cometh [i]the devil, and
taketh away the word out of their
hearts, lest they should believe and be
saved.
13 They on the rock *are they,* which,
when they hear, receive the word with
joy; and these have no root, which for
a while believe, and in time of temptation fall away.
14 And that which fell among thorns
are they, which, when they have heard,
go forth, and are choked with cares
[j]and riches and pleasures of *this* life,
and bring no fruit to perfection.
15 But that on the good ground are
they, which in an honest and good
heart, having heard the word, keep *it,*
and [k]bring forth fruit with patience.
16 ¶ [l]No man, when he hath lighted
a candle, covereth it with a vessel, or
putteth *it* under a bed; but setteth *it* on
a candlestick, that they which enter in
may see the light.
17 [m]For nothing is secret, that shall
not be made manifest; neither *any
thing* hid, that shall not be known and
come abroad.
18 Take heed therefore how ye hear:
[n]for whosoever hath, to him shall be
given; and whosoever hath not, from
him shall be taken even that which he
[1]seemeth to have.
19 ¶ [o]Then came to him *his* mother
and his brethren, and could not come
at him for the press.
20 And it was told him *by certain*
which said, Thy mother and thy brethren stand without, desiring to see thee.
21 And he answered and said unto
them, My mother and my brethren are
these which hear the word of God, and
do it.
22 ¶ [p]Now it came to pass on a certain day, that he went into a ship with
his disciples: and he said unto them,
Let us go over unto the other side of
the lake. And they launched forth.
23 But as they sailed he fell asleep:
and there came down a storm of wind
on the lake; and they were filled *with
water,* and were in jeopardy.
24 And they came to him, and awoke
him, saying, Master, master, we perish.
Then he [q]arose, and rebuked the wind
and the raging of the water: and they
ceased, and there was a calm.
25 And he said unto them, Where is
your faith? And they being [r]afraid wondered, saying one to another, What
manner of man is this! for he commandeth even the winds and water,
and they obey him.
26 ¶ [s]And they arrived at the country of the Găd′a-rēnes, which is over
against Găl′ĭ-lee.
27 And when he went forth to land,
there met him out of the city a certain
man, which had devils long time, and
ware no clothes, neither abode in *any*
house, but in the tombs.
28 When he saw Jē′sus, he [t]cried
out, and fell down before him, and
with a loud voice said, What have I to
do with thee, Jē′sus, *thou* Son of God
most high? I beseech thee, torment me
not.
29 (For he had commanded the unclean spirit to come out of the man. For
oftentimes it had caught him: and he
was kept bound with chains and in fetters; and he brake the bands, and was
driven of the devil into the wilderness.)
30 And Jē′sus asked him, saying,
What is thy name? And he said, Legion: because many devils were entered into him.
31 And they besought him that he
would not command them to go out
[u]into the deep.
32 And there was there an [v]herd of
many swine feeding on the mountain:
and they besought him that he would
suffer them to enter into them. And
[w]he suffered them.
33 Then went the devils out of the
man, and entered into the swine: and
the herd ran violently down a steep
place into the lake, and were choked.
34 When they that fed *them* saw
what was done, they fled, and went and
told *it* in the city and in the country.
35 Then they went out to see what
was done; and came to Jē′sus, and
found the man, out of whom the devils
were departed, sitting at the feet of
Jē′sus, clothed, and in his right mind:
and they were afraid.
36 They also which saw *it* told them
by what means he that was possessed
of the devils was healed.
37 ¶ [x]Then the whole multitude of
the country of the Găd′a-rēnes round
about [y]besought him to depart from
them; for they were taken with great
fear: and he went up into the ship, and
returned back again.
38 Now [z]the man out of whom the
devils were departed besought him
that he might be with him: but Jē′sus
sent him away, saying,
39 Return to thine own house, and
shew how great things God hath done
unto thee. And he went his way, and
published throughout the whole city

9 [d]Matt. 13.10; Mark 4.10
10 [e]Isa. 6.9; Mark 4.12
11 [f]Matt. 13.18; Mark 4.14
[g]Acts 20.27-32; 1 Pet. 1.23
12 [h]Jas. 1.23-24
[i]2 Cor. 2.11; 2 Cor. 4.3
14 [j]Matt. 19.23; 1 Tim. 6.9-10; 2 Tim. 4.10
15 [k]2 Pet. 1.5-10
16 [l]Matt. 5.15; Mark 4.21; ch. 11.33; Phil. 2.15-16
17 [m]Eccl. 12.14; Mark 4.22
18 [n]Matt. 25.29; Mark 4.25
[1]Or, thinketh that he hath
19 [o]Matt. 12.46; Mark 3.31; John 7.5; Acts 1.14; 1 Cor. 9.5
22 [p]Matt. 8.23; Mark 4.35
24 [q]Job 28.11; Job 38.11; Ps. 29.10; Ps. 46.1; Ps. 65.7
25 [r]Ps. 33.8-9; Matt. 8.27; Mark 4.41; ch. 4.36; ch. 8.25
26 [s]Matt. 8.28; Mark 5.1
28 [t]Acts 16.16-17; Phil. 2.10-11
31 [u]Rev. 20.3
32 [v]Lev. 11.7; Deut. 14.8
[w]Job 1.12; Job 12.16; Rev. 20.7
37 [x]Matt. 8.34
[y]Deut. 5.25-26; 1 Sam. 6.20; 1 Sam. 16.4; 2 Sam. 6.9; Job 21.14; Mark 1.24; ch. 4.34
38 [z]Ps. 103.1; Ps. 116.12; Mark 5.18; ch. 18.43

how great things Jē'sus had done unto him.

40 And it came to pass, that, when Jē'sus was returned, the people *gladly* received him: for they were all waiting for him.

41 ¶ [a]And, behold, there came a man named Ja-ī'rus, and he was a ruler of the synagogue: and he fell down at Jē'sus' feet, and besought him that he would come into his house:

42 For he had one only daughter, about twelve years of age, and she lay a dying. But as he went the people thronged him.

43 ¶ [b]And a woman having an issue of blood twelve years, which had spent all her living upon physicians, neither could be healed of any,

44 Came behind *him*, and [c]touched the border of his garment: and immediately her issue of blood stanched.

45 And Jē'sus said, Who touched me? When all denied, Pē'tēr and they that were with him said, Master, the multitude throng thee and press *thee*, and sayest thou, Who touched me?

46 And Jē'sus said, Somebody hath touched me: for I perceive that [d]virtue is gone out of me.

47 And when the woman saw that she was not hid, she came trembling, and falling down before him, she declared unto him before all the people for what cause she had touched him, and how she was healed immediately.

48 And he said unto her, Daughter, be of good comfort: thy faith hath made thee whole; go in peace.

49 ¶ [e]While he yet spake, there cometh one from the ruler of the synagogue's *house*, saying to him, Thy daughter is dead; trouble not the Master.

50 But when Jē'sus heard *it*, he answered him, saying, Fear not: [f]believe only, and she shall be made whole.

51 And when he came into the house, he suffered no man to go in, save Pē'tēr, and Jāmes, and Jŏhn, and the father and the mother of the maiden.

52 And all wept, and bewailed her: but he said, Weep not; she is not dead, [g]but sleepeth.

53 And they laughed him to scorn, knowing that she was dead.

54 And he put them all out, and took her by the hand, and called, saying, Maid, [h]arise.

55 [i]And her spirit came again, and she arose straightway: and he commanded to give her meat.

56 And her parents were astonished: but [j]he charged them that they should tell no man what was done.

9 Then [a]he called his twelve disciples together, and [b]gave them power and authority over all devils, and to cure diseases.

2 And [c]he sent them to preach the kingdom of God, and to heal the sick.

3 [d]And he said unto them, Take nothing for *your* journey, neither staves, nor scrip, neither bread, neither money; neither have two coats apiece.

4 [e]And whatsoever house ye enter into, there abide, and thence depart.

5 [f]And whosoever will not receive you, when ye go out of that city, [g]shake off the very dust from your feet for a testimony against them.

6 And they departed, and went through the towns, preaching the gospel, and healing every where.

7 ¶ [h]Now Hĕr'od the tetrarch heard of all that was done by him: and he was perplexed, because that it was said of some, that Jŏhn was risen from the dead;

8 And of some, that E-lī'ăs had appeared; and of others, that one of the old prophets was risen again.

9 And Hĕr'od said, Jŏhn have I beheaded: but who is this, of whom I hear such things? [i]And he desired to see him.

10 ¶ [j]And the apostles, when they were returned, told him all that they had done. [k]And he took them, and went aside privately into a desert place belonging to the city called Bĕth-sā'ī-dȧ.

11 And the people, when they knew *it*, followed him: and he received them, and spake unto them of the kingdom of God, and healed them that had need of healing.

12 [l]And when the day began to wear away, then came the twelve, and said unto him, Send the multitude away, that they may go into the towns and country round about, and lodge, and get victuals: for we are here in a desert place.

13 But he said unto them, [m]Give ye them to eat. And they said, [n]We have no more but five loaves and two fishes; except we should go and buy meat for all this people.

14 For they were about five thousand men. And he said to his disciples, Make them sit down by fifties in a company.

15 And they did so, and made them all sit down.

16 Then he took the five loaves and the two fishes, and looking up to heaven, he blessed them, and brake, and gave to the disciples to set before the multitude.

17 And they [o]did eat, and were all filled: and there was taken up of fragments that remained to them twelve baskets.

18 ¶ [p]And it came to pass, as he was alone praying, his disciples were with him: and he asked them, saying, Whom say the people that I am?

19 They answering said, [q]Jŏhn the Băp'tĭst; but some *say*, E-lī'ăs; and others *say*, that one of the old prophets is risen again.

20 He said unto them, But whom say ye that I am? [r]Pē'tēr answering said, The Chrīst of God.

21 [s]And he straitly charged them, and commanded *them* to tell no man that thing;

22 Saying, [t]The Son of man must suffer many things, and be rejected of the elders and chief priests and

41 [a]Matt. 9.18; Mark 5.22
43 [b]Lev. 15.25; Matt. 9.20
44 [c]Mark 5.27-28; Acts 5.15; Acts 19.12
46 [d]Mark 5.30; ch. 5.17
49 [e]Mark 5.35
50 [f]2 Chr. 20.20; Mark 5.36; Rom. 4.17-20
52 [g]John 11.11-13
54 [h]ch. 7.14; John 11.43
55 [i]Ps. 33.9
56 [j]Matt. 8.4; Mark 5.43

CHAPTER 9
1 [a]Matt. 10.1; Mark 3.13 [b]Matt. 10.1; Mark 16.17-18; John 14.12; Acts 1.8; Acts 3.6
2 [c]Matt. 10.7-8; Mark 6.12; ch. 10.1-9
3 [d]Ps. 37.3; Matt. 10.9; Mark 6.8; ch. 10.4
4 [e]Matt. 10.11; Mark 6.10
5 [f]Matt. 10.14 [g]Acts 13.51
7 [h]Mark 6.14
9 [i]ch. 23.8
10 [j]Mark 6.30 [k]Matt. 14.13
12 [l]John 6.1-5
13 [m]2 Ki. 4.42-43 [n]Num. 11.22; Ps. 78.19-20
17 [o]Ps. 145.15-16
18 [p]Matt. 16.13
19 [q]Matt. 14.2
20 [r]Mark 8.29; John 1.41-49; John 6.69; Rom. 10.9; 1 John 4.14-15
21 [s]Matt. 16.20
22 [t]Matt. 16.21; Mark 8.31; ch. 18.31; ch. 24.6-7

scribes, and be slain, and be raised the
third day.
23 ¶ [u]And he said to *them* all, If any
man will come after me, let him deny
himself, and take up his cross daily,
and follow me.
24 For whosoever will save his life
shall lose it: but whosoever will lose
his life for my sake, the same shall
save it.
25 [v]For what is a man advantaged,
if he gain the whole world, and lose
himself, or be cast away?
26 [w]For whosoever shall be ashamed
of me and of my words, of him shall the
Son of man be ashamed, when he shall
come in his own glory, and *in his* Father's, and of the holy angels.
27 [x]But I tell you of a truth, there be
some standing here, which shall not
taste of death, till they see the kingdom
of God.
28 ¶ [y]And it came to pass about an
eight days after these [1]sayings, he took
Pē′tẽr and Jŏhn and Jāmes, and went
up into a mountain to pray.
29 And as he prayed, [z]the fashion of
his countenance was altered, and his
raiment *was* white *and* glistering.
30 And, behold, there talked with
him two men, which were Mō′ses and
[a]E-lī′ăs:
31 Who appeared in [b]glory, and
spake of his decease which he should
accomplish at Je-rṳ′sa-lĕm.
32 But Pē′tẽr and they that were
with him [c]were heavy with sleep: and
when they were awake, they saw his
glory, and the two men that stood with
him.
33 And it came to pass, as they departed from him, Pē′tẽr said unto Jē′-
sus, Master, it is good for us to be here:
and let us make three tabernacles; one
for thee, and one for Mō′ses, and one
for E-lī′ăs: not knowing what he said.
34 While he thus spake, there came
a cloud, and overshadowed them: and
they feared as they entered into the
cloud.
35 And there came a voice out of the
cloud, saying, [d]This is my beloved
Son: [e]hear him.
36 And when the voice was past,
Jē′sus was found alone. [f]And they
kept *it* close, and told no man in those
days any of those things which they
had seen.
37 ¶ [g]And it came to pass, that on
the next day, when they were come
down from the hill, much people met
him.
38 And, behold, a man of the company cried out, saying, Master, I beseech thee, look upon my son: for he is
mine only child.
39 And, lo, a spirit taketh him, and
he suddenly crieth out; and it teareth
him that he foameth again, and bruising him hardly departeth from him.
40 And I besought thy disciples to
cast him out; and they could not.
41 And Jē′sus answering said, O
faithless and perverse generation, how
long shall I be with you, and suffer
you? Bring thy son hither.
42 And as he was yet a coming, the
devil threw him down, and tare *him*.
And Jē′sus rebuked the unclean spirit,
and healed the child, and delivered
him again to his father.
43 ¶ And they were all amazed at the
mighty power of God. But while they
wondered every one at all things which
Jē′sus did, he said unto his disciples,
44 [h]Let these sayings sink down
into your ears: for the Son of man shall
be delivered into the hands of men.
45 [i]But they understood not this saying, and it was hid from them, that they
perceived it not: and they feared to ask
him of that saying.
46 ¶ [j]Then there arose a reasoning
among them, which of them should be
greatest.
47 And Jē′sus, perceiving the thought
of their heart, took a child, and set him
by him,
48 And said unto them, [k]Whoso-
ever shall receive this child in my
name receiveth me: and whosoever
shall receive me receiveth him that
sent me: [l]for he that is least among
you all, the same shall be great.
49 ¶ [m]And Jŏhn answered and said,
Master, we saw one casting out devils
in thy name; and we forbad him, because he followeth not with us.
50 And Jē′sus said unto him, Forbid
him not: for [n]he that is not against us is
for us.
51 ¶ And it came to pass, when the
time was come that [o]he should be received up, he stedfastly set his face to
go to Je-rṳ′sa-lĕm,
52 And sent messengers before his
face: and they went, and entered into a
village of the Sa-măr′ĭ-tans, to make
ready for him.
53 And [p]they did not receive him,
because his face was as though he
would go to Je-rṳ′sa-lĕm.
54 And when his disciples Jāmes
and Jŏhn saw *this*, they said, Lord, wilt
thou that we command fire to come
down from heaven, and consume them,
even as [q]E-lī′ăs did?
55 But he turned, and rebuked them,
and said, Ye know not what [r]manner
of spirit ye are of.
56 For [s]the Son of man is not come to
destroy men's lives, but to save *them*.
And they went to another village.
57 ¶ [t]And it came to pass, that, as
they went in the way, a certain *man*
said unto him, Lord, I will follow thee
whithersoever thou goest.
58 And Jē′sus said unto him, Foxes
have holes, and birds of the air *have*
nests; but the Son of man hath not
where to lay *his* head.
59 [u]And he said unto another, Follow me. But he said, Lord, suffer me
first to go and bury my father.
60 Jē′sus said unto him, Let the dead
bury their dead: but go thou and preach
the kingdom of God.
61 And another also said, Lord, [v]I
will follow thee; but let me first go bid

23 [u]Matt. 10.38; Mark 8.34; ch. 14.27
25 [v]Ps. 49.6-8; Matt. 16.26; Mark 8.36; Acts 1.18-25; Rev. 18.7-8
26 [w]Mark 8.38; 2 Tim. 2.12
27 [x]Matt. 16.28
28 [y]Matt. 17.1
[1]Or, things
29 [z]Ex. 34.29-35
30 [a]2 Ki. 2.11; Rom. 3.21
31 [b]Ps. 17.15; Phil. 3.21; Col. 3.4; 1 John 3.2
32 [c]Dan. 8.18; Matt. 26.40-43; ch. 22.45
35 [d]Matt. 3.17; John 12.28; 2 Pet. 1.16-17
[e]Ex. 23.21; Deut. 18.15-18
36 [f]Matt. 17.9
37 [g]Matt. 17.14
44 [h]Matt. 17.22
45 [i]Mark 9.32; ch. 2.50
46 [j]Matt. 18.1
48 [k]Mark 9.37; John 12.44
[l]Matt. 23.11-12
49 [m]Num. 11.28; Mark 9.38
50 [n]Matt. 12.30; ch. 11.23; 1 Cor. 12.3
51 [o]Mark 16.19; Acts 1.2
53 [p]John 4.4-9
54 [q]1 Ki. 18.38; 2 Ki. 1.10-12; Rev. 13.13
55 [r]Job 2.10; Rom. 10.2
56 [s]Matt. 9.13; John 3.17
57 [t]Matt. 8.19
59 [u]Matt. 8.21
61 [v]1 Ki. 19.20

them farewell, which are at home at
my house.
62 And Jē'sus said unto him, [w]No
man, having put his hand to the plow,
and looking back, is fit for the kingdom of God.

10

After these things the Lord appointed other seventy also, and
[a]sent them two and two before his face
into every city and place, whither he
himself would come.
2 Therefore said he unto them, [b]The
harvest truly *is* great, but the labourers
are few: [c]pray ye therefore the [d]Lord
of the harvest, that he would send
forth labourers into his harvest.
3 Go your ways: [e]behold, I send you
forth as lambs among wolves.
4 [f]Carry neither purse, nor scrip,
nor shoes: and [g]salute no man by the
way.
5 [h]And into whatsoever house ye enter, first say, Peace *be* to this house.
6 And if the son of peace be there,
your peace shall rest upon it: if not, it
shall turn to you again.
7 [i]And in the same house remain,
[j]eating and drinking such things as
they give: for [k]the labourer is worthy
of his hire. Go not [l]from house to
house.
8 And into whatsoever city ye enter,
and they receive you, eat such things
as are set before you:
9 [m]And heal the sick that are therein,
and say unto them, [n]The kingdom of
God is come nigh unto you.
10 But into whatsoever city ye enter,
and they receive you not, go your ways
out into the streets of the same, and
say,
11 [o]Even the very dust of your city,
which cleaveth on us, we do wipe off
against you: notwithstanding be ye
sure of this, that the kingdom of God is
come nigh unto you.
12 But I say unto you, that [p]it shall be
more tolerable in that day for Sŏd'om,
than for that city.
13 [q]Woe unto thee, Cho-rā'zin! woe
unto thee, Bĕth-sā'ĭ-dȧ! [r]for if the
mighty works had been done in Tȳre
and Sī'dŏn, which have been done in
you, they had a great while ago [s]re-
pented, sitting in sackcloth and ashes.
14 But it shall be more tolerable for
Tȳre and Sī'dŏn at the judgment, than
for you.
15 [t]And thou Ca-pêr'na-ŭm, which
art [u]exalted to heaven, [v]shalt be thrust
down to hell.
16 [w]He that heareth you heareth
me; and [x]he that despiseth you despiseth me; [y]and he that despiseth me
despiseth him that sent me.
17 ¶ And the seventy returned again
with joy, saying, Lord, even the devils
are subject unto us through thy name.
18 And he said unto them, [z]I beheld
Sā'tan as lightning fall from heaven.
19 Behold, [a]I give unto you power
to tread on serpents and scorpions,
and over all the power of the enemy:
and nothing shall by any means hurt
you.
20 Notwithstanding in this rejoice
not, that the spirits are subject unto
you; but rather rejoice, because [b]your
names are written in heaven.
21 ¶ [c]In that hour Jē'sus rejoiced in
spirit, and said, I thank thee, O Father,
Lord of heaven and earth, that thou
hast hid these things from [d]the wise
and prudent, and hast revealed them
unto babes: even so, Father; for so it
seemed good in thy sight.
22 [1][e]All things are delivered to me
of my Father: and [f]no man knoweth
who the Son is, but the Father; and
who the Father is, but the Son, and *he*
to whom the Son will reveal *him*.
23 ¶ And he turned him unto *his* disciples, and said privately, [g]Blessed *are*
the eyes which see the things that ye
see:
24 For I tell you, [h]that many prophets and kings have desired to see those
things which ye see, and have not seen
them; and to hear those things which
ye hear, and have not heard *them*.
25 ¶ And, behold, a certain lawyer
stood up, and tempted him, saying,
[i]Master, what shall I do to inherit eternal life?
26 He said unto him, What is written
in the law? how readest thou?
27 And he answering said, [j]Thou
shalt love the Lord thy God with all thy
heart, and with all thy soul, and with
all thy strength, and with all thy mind;
and [k]thy neighbour as thyself.
28 And he said unto him, Thou hast
answered right; this do, and [l]thou shalt
live.
29 But he, willing to [m]justify himself, said unto Jē'sus, And who is my
neighbour?
30 And Jē'sus answering said, A certain *man* went down from Je-ru'sa-lĕm
to Jĕr'ĭ-chō, and fell among thieves,
which stripped him of his raiment, and
wounded *him*, and departed, leaving
him half dead.
31 And by chance there came down
a certain priest that way: and when he
saw him, [n]he passed by on the other
side.
32 And likewise a Lē'vīte, when he
was at the place, came and looked *on*
him, and passed by on the other side.
33 But a certain [o]Sa-măr'ĭ-tan, as he
journeyed, came where he was: and
when he saw him, he had compassion
on him,
34 And went to *him*, and bound up
his wounds, pouring in oil and wine,
and set him on his own beast, and
brought him to an inn, and took care of
him.
35 And on the morrow when he departed, he took out two pence, and
gave *them* to the host, and said unto
him, Take care of him; and whatsoever thou spendest more, when I come
again, I will repay thee.
36 Which now of these three, thinkest thou, was neighbour unto him that
fell among the thieves?

62 [w]Heb. 6.4

CHAPTER 10

1 [a]Matt. 10.1
2 [b]ch. 10.2; John 4.35
[c]2 Thess. 3.1
[d]Jer. 3.15; 1 Cor. 12.28
3 [e]Matt. 10.16
4 [f]Matt. 10.9; ch. 9.3
[g]2 Ki. 4.29
5 [h]Matt. 10.12
7 [i]Matt. 10.11
[j]1 Cor. 10.27
[k]Matt. 10.10; 1 Cor. 9.4
[l]Eph. 5.15
9 [m]ch. 9.2
[n]Isa. 2.2; Tit. 2.11
11 [o]Matt. 10.14; Acts 13.51
12 [p]Lam. 4.6; Ezek. 16.48-50
13 [q]Matt. 11.21
[r]Ezek. 3.6
[s]Jon. 3.5
15 [t]Matt. 11.23
[u]Gen. 11.4; Isa. 14.13
[v]Ezek. 26.20
16 [w]John 13.20
[x]1 Thess. 4.8
[y]John 5.23
18 [z]John 12.31; Heb. 2.14
19 [a]Acts 28.5
20 [b]Ex. 32.32; Rev. 13.8
21 [c]Matt. 11.25
[d]1 Cor. 1.19
22 [1]Many ancient copies add these words, And turning to his disciples, he said
[e]Matt. 28.18;
[f]John 1.18
23 [g]Matt. 13.16
24 [h]1 Pet. 1.10
25 [i]Matt. 22.35
27 [j]Deut. 6.5;
[k]Lev. 19.18
28 [l]Lev. 18.5
29 [m]ch. 16.15
31 [n]Ps. 38.11
33 [o]John 4.9

37 And he said, He that shewed
mercy on him. Then said Jē'sus unto
him, Go, and do thou likewise.
38 ¶ Now it came to pass, as they
went, that he entered into a certain
village: and a certain woman named
Mär'thȧ received him into her house.
39 And she had a sister called Mā'ry̆,
which also sat at Jē'sus' feet, and heard
his word.
40 But Mär'thȧ was cumbered about
much serving, and came to him, and
said, Lord, dost thou not care that my
sister hath left me to serve alone? bid
her therefore that she help me.
41 And Jē'sus answered and said
unto her, Mär'thȧ, Mär'thȧ, thou art
careful and troubled about many things:
42 But one thing is needful: and
Mā'ry̆ hath chosen that good part,
which shall not be taken away from
her.

11 And it came to pass, that, as he
was praying in a certain place,
when he ceased, one of his disciples
said unto him, Lord, [a]teach us to pray,
as Jŏhn also taught his disciples.
2 And he said unto them, When ye
pray, say, [b]Our Father which art in
heaven, Hallowed be thy name. [c]Thy
kingdom come. Thy will be done, as in
heaven, so in earth.
3 Give us [1]day by day our daily
bread.
4 And forgive us our sins; for [d]we
also forgive every one that is indebted
to us. [e]And lead us not into temptation; but deliver us from evil.
5 And he said unto them, Which of
you shall have a friend, and shall go
unto him at midnight, and say unto
him, Friend, lend me three loaves;
6 For a friend of mine [2]in his journey
is come to me, and I have nothing to set
before him?
7 And he from within shall answer
and say, Trouble me not: the door is
now shut, and my children are with me
in bed; I cannot rise and give thee.
8 I say unto you, [f]Though he will
not rise and give him, because he is his
friend, yet because of his importunity
he will rise and give him as many as he
needeth.
9 [g]And I say unto you, Ask, and it
shall be given you; seek, and ye shall
find; knock, and it shall be opened
unto you.
10 For every one that asketh receiveth; and he that seeketh findeth;
and to him that knocketh it shall be
opened.
11 [h]If a son shall ask bread of any of
you that is a father, will he give him a
stone? or if *he ask* a fish, will he for a
fish give him a serpent?
12 Or if he shall ask an egg, will he
[3]offer him a scorpion?
13 If ye then, being evil, know how
to give good gifts unto your children:
how much more shall *your* heavenly
Father give the [i]Hō'ly̆ Spĭr'ĭt to them
that ask him?
14 ¶ [j]And he was casting out a devil,
and it was dumb. And it came to pass,

CHAPTER 11
1 [a]Ps. 10.17; Ps. 19.14; Rom. 8.26-27; 2 Cor. 3.5; Jas. 4.3; Jude 20
2 [b]2 Chr. 20.6; Ps. 11.4; Isa. 63.16; Matt. 5.16
[c]Isa. 11.9; Dan. 7.14
3 [1]Or, for the day
4 [d]Matt. 6.12-14; Eph. 4.32
[e]Matt. 6.13; ch. 22.46; 1 Cor. 10.13; Jas. 1.13; Rev. 3.10
6 [2]Or, out of his way
8 [f]ch. 18.1
9 [g]Ps. 50.15; Ps. 118.5; Jer. 33.3; Matt. 7.7; Mark 11.24; John 15.7; Jas. 1.6; 1 John 5.14
11 [h]Matt. 7.9
12 [3]give
13 [i]Isa. 44.3; Jas. 1.15
14 [j]Matt. 9.32
15 [k]Matt. 9.34
[4]Beelzebul
16 [l]Matt. 12.38
17 [m]Mark 3.24; Rev. 2.23
19 [n]Mark 9.38; ch. 9.49
20 [o]Ex. 8.19; Acts 2.22
21 [p]Matt. 12.29; 1 Pet. 5.8
22 [q]Isa. 9.6; Col. 2.15
23 [r]Matt. 12.30
24 [s]Matt. 12.43
26 [t]John 5.14; Heb. 6.4
27 [u]ch. 1.28-48
28 [v]Ps. 1.1; Rev. 22.14
29 [w]Matt. 12.38-39
30 [x]Jon. 1.17
31 [y]1 Ki. 10.1
[z]Isa. 9.6; Phil. 2.10
32 [a]Jon. 3.5

when the devil was gone out, the dumb
spake; and the people wondered.
15 But some of them said, [k]He casteth out devils through [4]Be-ĕl'ze-bŭb
the chief of the devils.
16 And others, tempting *him*, [l]sought
of him a sign from heaven.
17 [m]But he, knowing their thoughts,
said unto them, Every kingdom divided against itself is brought to desolation; and a house *divided* against a
house falleth.
18 If Sā'tan also be divided against
himself, how shall his kingdom stand?
because ye say that I cast out devils
through Be-ĕl'ze-bŭb.
19 And if I by Be-ĕl'ze-bŭb cast out
devils, by whom do [n]your sons cast
them out? therefore shall they be your
judges.
20 But if I [o]with the finger of God
cast out devils, no doubt the kingdom
of God is come upon you.
21 [p]When a strong man armed keepeth his palace, his goods are in peace:
22 But [q]when a stronger than he
shall come upon him, and overcome
him, he taketh from him all his armour
wherein he trusted, and divideth his
spoils.
23 [r]He that is not with me is against
me: and he that gathereth not with me
scattereth.
24 [s]When the unclean spirit is gone
out of a man, he walketh through dry
places, seeking rest; and finding none,
he saith, I will return unto my house
whence I came out.
25 And when he cometh, he findeth
it swept and garnished.
26 Then goeth he, and taketh *to him*
seven other spirits more wicked than
himself; and they enter in, and dwell
there: and [t]the last *state* of that man is
worse than the first.
27 ¶ And it came to pass, as he spake
these things, a certain woman of the
company lifted up her voice, and said
unto him, [u]Blessed *is* the womb that
bare thee, and the paps which thou
hast sucked.
28 But he said, Yea [v]rather, blessed
are they that hear the word of God,
and keep it.
29 ¶ [w]And when the people were
gathered thick together, he began to
say, This is an evil generation: they
seek a sign; and there shall no sign be
given it, but the sign of Jō'nas the
prophet.
30 For as [x]Jō'nas was a sign unto
the Nĭn'e-vītes, so shall also the Son of
man be to this generation.
31 [y]The queen of the south shall rise
up in the judgment with the men of this
generation, and condemn them: for
she came from the utmost parts of the
earth to hear the wisdom of Sŏl'o-mon;
and, behold, a [z]greater than Sŏl'o-
mon *is* here.
32 The men of Nĭn'e-ve shall rise up
in the judgment with this generation,
and shall condemn it: for [a]they repented at the preaching of Jō'nas; and,
behold, a greater than Jō'nas *is* here.

33 [b]No man, when he hath lighted a
candle, putteth *it* in a secret place, neither under a [c]bushel, but on a candlestick, that they which come in may see
the light.
34 [d]The light of the body is the eye:
therefore when thine eye is single, thy
whole body also is full of light; but
when *thine eye* is evil, thy body also *is*
full of darkness.
35 Take heed therefore that the light
which is in thee be not darkness.
36 If thy whole body therefore *be*
full of light, having no part dark, the
whole shall be full of light, as when
[5]the bright shining of a candle doth
give thee light.
37 ¶ And as he spake, a certain
Phăr'ĭ-see besought him to dine with
him: and he went in, and sat down to
meat.
38 And when the Phăr'ĭ-see saw *it*,
he marvelled that he had not first
washed before dinner.
39 [e]And the Lord said unto him,
Now do ye Phăr'ĭ-sees make clean the
outside of the cup and the platter; but
[f]your inward part is full of ravening
and wickedness.
40 *Ye* fools, did not he that made
that which is without make that which
is within also?
41 [g]But rather give alms [6]of such
things as ye have; and, behold, all
things are clean unto you.
42 [h]But woe unto you, Phăr'ĭ-sees!
for [i]ye tithe mint and rue and all manner of herbs, and pass over judgment
and the love of God: these ought ye to
have done, and not to leave the other
undone.
43 [j]Woe unto you, Phăr'ĭ-sees! for
ye love the uppermost seats in the synagogues, and greetings in the markets.
44 [k]Woe unto you, scribes and Phăr'-
ĭ-sees, hypocrites! [l]for ye are as graves
which appear not, and the men that
walk over *them* are not aware *of them*.
45 ¶ Then answered one of the lawyers, and said unto him, Master, thus
saying thou reproachest us also.
46 And he said, Woe unto you also,
ye lawyers! [m]for ye lade men with burdens grievous to be borne, and ye yourselves touch not the burdens with one
of your fingers.
47 [n]Woe unto you! for ye build the
sepulchres of the prophets, and your
fathers killed them.
48 Truly ye bear witness that ye allow the deeds of your fathers: [o]for
they indeed killed them, and ye build
their sepulchres.
49 Therefore also said the [p]wisdom
of God, [q]I will send them prophets and
apostles, and *some* of them they shall
slay and persecute:
50 That the blood of all the prophets, which was shed from the foundation of the world, may be required of
this generation;
51 [r]From the blood of Ā'bel unto the
of Zăch-a-rī'as, which perished
en the altar and the temple: ver-

33 [b]Matt. 5.15; ch. 8.16
[c]Matt. 5.15
34 [d]Ps. 119.18; Eph. 1.18
36 [5]a candle by its bright shining
39 [e]Matt. 23.25
[f]Gen. 6.5; Jas. 4.8
41 [g]Isa. 58.7; ch. 12.33
[6]Or, as you are able
42 [h]Matt. 23.23
[i]1 Sam. 15.22
43 [j]Matt. 23.6
44 [k]Matt. 23.27
[l]Ps. 5.9; Acts 23.3
46 [m]Matt. 23.4
47 [n]Matt. 23.29
48 [o]Acts 7.51-52
49 [p]Prov. 1.20
[q]Matt. 23.24
51 [r]Gen. 4.8
52 [s]Matt. 23.13
[7]Or, forbad
54 [t]Mark 12.13
CHAPTER 12
1 [a]Matt. 16.6; Mark 8.15
[b]Matt. 16.12; 1 Cor. 5.7-8
2 [c]Eccl. 12.14
4 [d]Isa. 8.12-13
5 [e]Ps. 9.17
6 [f]Matt. 10.29
[g]Acts 15.18
8 [h]1 Sam. 2.30
10 [i]Matt. 12.31-32
11 [j]Matt. 10.19
12 [k]Ex. 4.12
14 [l]John 18.36
15 [m]Prov. 28.16

ily I say unto you, It shall be required
of this generation.
52 [s]Woe unto you, lawyers! for ye
have taken away the key of knowledge: ye entered not in yourselves,
and them that were entering in ye
[7]hindered.
53 And as he said these things unto
them, the scribes and the Phăr'ĭ-sees
began to urge *him* vehemently, and to
provoke him to speak of many things:
54 Laying wait for him, and [t]seek-
ing to catch something out of his mouth,
that they might accuse him.

12 In [a]the mean time, when there
were gathered together an innumerable multitude of people, insomuch
that they trode one upon another, he
began to say unto his disciples first of
all, [b]Beware ye of the leaven of the
Phăr'ĭ-sees, which is hypocrisy.
2 [c]For there is nothing covered, that
shall not be revealed; neither hid, that
shall not be known.
3 Therefore whatsoever ye have
spoken in darkness shall be heard
in the light; and that which ye have
spoken in the ear in closets shall be
proclaimed upon the house tops.
4 [d]And I say unto you my friends,
Be not afraid of them that kill the body,
and after that have no more that they
can do.
5 But I will forewarn you whom ye
shall fear: Fear him, which after he
hath killed hath [e]power to cast into
hell; yea, I say unto you, Fear him.
6 Are not five sparrows sold for two
[f]farthings, and [g]not one of them is forgotten before God?
7 But even the very hairs of your
head are all numbered. Fear not therefore: ye are of more value than many
sparrows.
8 [h]Also I say unto you, Whosoever
shall confess me before men, him shall
the Son of man also confess before the
angels of God:
9 But he that denieth me before men
shall be denied before the angels of
God.
10 And [i]whosoever shall speak a
word against the Son of man, it shall
be forgiven him: but unto him that blasphemeth against the Hō'lў Ghōst it
shall not be forgiven.
11 [j]And when they bring you unto
the synagogues, and *unto* magistrates,
and powers, take ye no thought how or
what thing ye shall answer, or what ye
shall say:
12 [k]For the Hō'lў Ghōst shall teach
you in the same hour what ye ought to
say.
13 ¶ And one of the company said
unto him, Master, speak to my brother,
that he divide the inheritance with me.
14 And he said unto him, [l]Man, who
made me a judge or a divider over you?
15 And he said unto them, [m]Take
heed, and beware of covetousness: for a
man's life consisteth not in the abundance of the things which he possesseth.

16 And he spake a parable unto
them, saying, The ground of a certain
rich man brought forth plentifully:
17 And he thought within himself,
saying, What shall I do, because I have
no room where to bestow my fruits?
18 And he said, This will I do: I will
pull down my barns, and build greater;
and there will I bestow all my fruits
and my goods.
19 And I will say to my soul, [n]Soul,
thou hast much goods laid up for many
years; take thine ease, eat, drink, *and*
be merry.
20 But God said unto him, *Thou*
fool, this night [1]thy soul shall be required of thee: [o]then whose shall those
things be, which thou hast provided?
21 So *is* he that layeth up treasure
for himself, [p]and is not rich toward
God.
22 ¶ And he said unto his disciples,
Therefore I say unto you, [q]Take no
thought for you life, what ye shall eat;
neither for the body, what ye shall put
on.
23 The life is more than meat, and
the body *is more* than raiment.
24 Consider the ravens: for they neither sow nor reap; which neither have
storehouse nor barn; and [r]God feedeth
them: how much more are ye better
than the fowls?
25 And which of you with taking
thought can add to his stature one
cubit?
26 If ye then be not able to do
that thing which is least, why take ye
thought for the rest?
27 Consider the lilies how they grow:
they toil not, they spin not; and yet I say
unto you, that Sŏl′o-mon in all his glory
was not arrayed like one of these.
28 If then God so clothe the grass,
which is to day in the field, and to morrow is cast into the oven; how much
more *will he clothe* you, O ye of little
faith?
29 And seek not ye what ye shall
eat, or what ye shall drink, [2]neither be
ye of doubtful mind.
30 For all these things do the nations of the world seek after: and your
Father [s]knoweth that ye have need of
these things.
31 ¶ [t]But rather seek ye the kingdom of God; and [u]all these things shall
be added unto you.
32 Fear not, little flock; for [v]it is
your Father's good pleasure to give
you the kingdom.
33 [w]Sell that ye have, and give alms;
[x]provide yourselves bags which wax
not old, a treasure in the heavens that
faileth not, where no thief approach-
eth, neither moth corrupteth.
34 For where your treasure is, there
will your heart be also.
35 [y]Let your loins be girded about,
and [z]*your* lights burning;
36 And ye yourselves like unto men
that wait for their lord, when he will
return from the wedding; that when he
cometh and knocketh, they may open
unto him immediately.

19 [n]Prov. 27.1; 1 Cor. 15.32
20 [1]Or, do they require thy soul
[o]Ps. 39.6; Jer. 17.11
21 [p]Matt. 6.20; Jas. 2.5
22 [q]Matt. 6.25; Phil. 4.6
24 [r]Job 38.41; Ps. 147.9
29 [2]Or, live not in careful suspense
30 [s]2 Chr. 16.9; Phil. 4.19
31 [t]Matt. 6.33
[u]Rom. 8.31; 1 Tim. 4.8
32 [v]Matt. 11.25; 2 Thess. 1.11
33 [w]Matt. 19.21; Acts 2.45
[x]Matt. 6.20; 1 Tim. 6.19
35 [y]Eph. 6.14; 1 Pet. 1.13
[z]Matt. 5.16; Phil. 2.15
37 [a]Matt. 24.46; Rev. 14.13
39 [b]1 Thess. 5.2; Rev. 16.15
40 [c]Matt. 25.13; 2 Pet. 3.12-14
42 [d]Matt. 24.45-46; 1 Cor. 4.2
44 [e]1 Pet. 5.4
46 [3]Or, cut him off
47 [f]Num. 15.30; Jas. 4.17
48 [g]Lev. 5.17
50 [h]Matt. 20.22
[4]Or, pained
51 [i]Matt. 10.34
[j]Mic. 7.6
52 [k]Matt. 10.35
54 [l]Matt. 16.2

37 [a]Blessed *are* those servants,
whom the lord when he cometh shall
find watching: verily I say unto you,
that he shall gird himself, and make
them to sit down to meat, and will
come forth and serve them.
38 And if he shall come in the second watch, or come in the third watch,
and find *them* so, blessed are those
servants.
39 [b]And this know, that if the goodman of the house had known what
hour the thief would come, he would
have watched, and not have suffered
his house to be broken through.
40 [c]Be ye therefore ready also: for
the Son of man cometh at an hour
when ye think not.
41 ¶ Then Pē′tēr said unto him, Lord,
speakest thou this parable unto us, or
even to all?
42 And the Lord said, [d]Who then is
that faithful and wise steward, whom
his lord shall make ruler over his
household, to give *them their* portion
of meat in due season?
43 Blessed *is* that servant, whom his
lord when he cometh shall find so
doing.
44 Of a truth I say unto you, that [e]he
will make him ruler over all that he
hath.
45 But and if that servant say in his
heart, My lord delayeth his coming;
and shall begin to beat the menservants and maidens, and to eat and
drink, and to be drunken;
46 The lord of that servant will come
in a day when he looketh not for
him, and at an hour when he is not
aware, and will [3]cut him in sunder, and
will appoint him his portion with the
unbelievers.
47 And [f]that servant, which knew
his lord's will, and prepared not *him-*
self, neither did according to his will,
shall be beaten with many *stripes*.
48 [g]But he that knew not, and did
commit things worthy of stripes, shall
be beaten with few *stripes*. For unto
whomsoever much is given, of him
shall be much required: and to whom
men have committed much, of him
they will ask the more.
49 ¶ I am come to send fire on the
earth; and what will I, if it be already
kindled?
50 But [h]I have a baptism to be baptized with; and how am I [4]straitened
till it be accomplished!
51 [i]Suppose ye that I am come to
give peace on earth? I tell you, Nay;
[j]but rather division:
52 [k]For from henceforth there shall
be five in one house divided, three
against two, and two against three.
53 The father shall be divided against
the son, and the son against the father;
the mother against the daughter, and
the daughter against the mother; the
mother in law against her daughter in
law, and the daughter in law against her
mother in law.
54 ¶ And he said also to the people,
[l]When ye see a cloud rise out of the

west, straightway ye say, There cometh a shower; and so it is.
55 And when *ye see* [m]the south wind blow, ye say, There will be heat; and it cometh to pass.
56 [n]*Ye* hypocrites, ye can discern the face of the sky and of the earth; but how is it that ye do not discern [o]this time?
57 Yea, and why even of yourselves judge ye not what is right?
58 ¶ [p]When thou goest with thine adversary to the magistrate, [q]*as thou art* in the way, give diligence that thou mayest be delivered from him; lest he hale thee to the judge, and the judge deliver thee to the officer, and the officer cast thee into prison.
59 I tell thee, thou shalt not depart thence, till thou hast paid the very last [r]mite.

13

There were present at that season some that told him [a]of the Găl-ĭ-læ'ans, whose blood Pī'late had mingled with their sacrifices.
2 And Jē'sus answering said unto them, [b]Suppose ye that these Găl-ĭ-læ'ans were sinners above all the Găl-ĭ-læ'ans, because they suffered such things?
3 I tell you, Nay: but, except ye repent, ye shall all likewise perish.
4 Or those eighteen, upon whom the tower in Sĭ-lō'am fell, and slew them, think ye that they were [1]sinners above all men that dwelt in Je-ru̧'sa-lĕm?
5 I tell you, Nay: but, [c]except ye repent, ye shall all likewise perish.
6 ¶ He spake also this parable; [d]A certain *man* had a fig tree planted in his vineyard; and he came and sought fruit thereon, and found none.
7 Then said he unto the dresser of his vineyard, Behold, these [e]three years I come seeking fruit on this fig tree, and find none: cut it down; why cumbereth it the ground?
8 And he answering said unto him, Lord, [f]let it alone this year also, till I shall dig about it, and dung *it:*
9 And if it bear fruit, *well:* and if not, *then* after that thou shalt cut it down.
10 And he was teaching in one of the synagogues on the sabbath.
11 ¶ And, behold, there was a woman which had a spirit of infirmity eighteen years, and was bowed together, and could in no wise lift up *herself*.
12 And when Jē'sus saw her, he called *her to him,* and said unto her, Woman, thou art loosed from thine infirmity.
13 [g]And he laid *his* hands on her: and immediately she was made straight, and glorified God.
14 And the ruler of the synagogue [h]answered with indignation, because that Jē'sus had healed on the sabbath day, and said unto the people, [i]There are six days in which men ought to work: in them therefore come and be healed, and [j]not on the sabbath day.
15 The Lord then answered him, and said, *Thou* hypocrite, [k]doth not each one of you on the sabbath loose his ox or *his* ass from the stall, and lead *him* away to watering?
16 And ought not this woman, [l]being a daughter of Ā'bră-hăm, whom Sā'tan hath bound, lo, these eighteen years, be loosed from this bond on the sabbath day?
17 And when he had said these things, all his adversaries were ashamed: and all the people rejoiced for all the glorious things that were done by him.
18 ¶ [m]Then said he, Unto what is the kingdom of God like? and whereunto shall I resemble it?
19 It is like a grain of mustard seed, which a man took, and cast into his garden; and it grew, and waxed a great tree; and the fowls of the air lodged in the branches of it.
20 And again he said, Whereunto shall I liken the kingdom of God?
21 It is like leaven, which a woman took and hid in three [n]measures of meal, till the whole was leavened.
22 [o]And he went through the cities and villages, teaching, and journeying toward Je-ru̧'sa-lĕm.
23 Then said one unto him, Lord, are there few that be saved? And he said unto them,
24 ¶ [2]Strive to enter in at the strait gate: for [p]many, I say unto you, will seek to enter in, and shall not be able.
25 [q]When once the master of the house is risen up, and [r]hath shut to the door, and ye begin to stand without, and to knock at the door, saying, [s]Lord, Lord, open unto us; and he shall answer and say unto you, [t]I know you not whence ye are:
26 Then shall ye begin to say, [u]We have eaten and drunk in thy presence, and thou hast taught in our streets.
27 [v]But he shall say, I tell you, I know you not whence ye are; [w]depart from me, all *ye* workers of iniquity.
28 [x]There shall be weeping and gnashing of teeth, [y]when ye shall see Ā'bră-hăm, and Ī'saac, and Jā'cob, and all the prophets, in the kingdom of God, and you *yourselves* thrust out.
29 [z]And they shall come from the east, and *from* the west, and from the north, and *from* the south, and shall sit down in the kingdom of God.
30 [a]And, behold, there are last which shall be first, and there are first which shall be last.
31 ¶ The same day there came certain of the Phăr'ĭ-sees, saying unto him, Get thee out, and depart hence: for Hĕr'od will kill thee.
32 And he said unto them, Go ye, and tell that fox, Behold, I cast out devils, and I do cures to day and to morrow, and the third *day* [b]I shall be perfected.
33 Nevertheless I must walk to day, and to morrow, and the *day* following: for it cannot be that a prophet perish out of Je-ru̧'sa-lĕm.
34 [c]O Je-ru̧'sa-lĕm, Je-ru̧'sa-lĕm, which killest the prophets, and stonest them that are sent unto thee; how often

55 [m]Job 37.17
56 [n]1 Cor. 1.19-27
[o]ch. 19.42-44; Gal. 4.4
58 [p]Prov. 25.8
[q]Ps. 32.6; Isa. 55.6; Heb. 3.7-15
59 [r]Matt. 18.34; Mark 12.42; 2 Thess. 1.9
CHAPTER 13
1 [a]Acts 5.37
2 [b]Acts 28.4
4 [1]Or, debtors
5 [c]Ezek. 18.30
6 [d]Isa. 5.2
7 [e]Lev. 19.23; Rom. 2.4-5
8 [f]Ex. 32.11; Joel 2.17
13 [g]Ps. 103.3-5; Ps. 116.16-17
14 [h]John 5.15-16; Rom. 10.2
[i]Ex. 20.9
[j]Matt. 12.10; ch. 14.3
15 [k]ch. 14.5
16 [l]ch. 19.9
18 [m]Mark 4.30
21 [n]Matt. 13.33
22 [o]Matt. 9.35; Mark 6.6
24 [2]Strive as in agony
[p]John 7.34; Rom. 9.31
25 [q]Ps. 32.6; Isa. 55.6
[r]Matt. 25.10
[s]ch. 6.46
[t]Matt. 7.23
26 [u]Tit. 1.16
27 [v]Matt. 7.23
[w]Ps. 6.8
28 [x]Matt. 8.12
[y]Matt. 8.11
29 [z]Gen. 28.14; Isa. 49.6-12; Acts 2.39; Rev. 5.9
30 [a]Matt. 19.30; Mark 10.31
32 [b]Heb. 2.10
34 [c]2 Chr. 24.21-22; Neh. 9.26-27; Jer. 2.30

would I have gathered thy children together, as a hen *doth gather* her brood under *her* wings, and ye would not!

35 Behold, [d]your house is left unto you desolate: and verily I say unto you, [e]Ye shall not see me, until *the time* come when ye shall say, [f]Blessed *is* he that cometh in the name of the Lord.

14 And it came to pass, as he went into the house of one of the chief Phăr'ĭ-sees to eat bread on the sabbath day, that they watched him.

2 And, behold, there was a certain man before him which had the dropsy.

3 And Jē'sus answering spake unto the lawyers and Phăr'ĭ-sees, saying, [a]Is it lawful to heal on the sabbath day?

4 And they held their peace. And he took *him*, and healed him, and let him go;

5 And answered them, saying, [b]Which of you shall have an ass or an ox fallen into a pit, and will not straightway pull him out on the sabbath day?

6 And they could not answer him again to these things.

7 ¶ And he put forth a parable to those which were bidden, when he marked how they chose out the chief rooms; saying unto them,

8 When thou art bidden of any *man* to a wedding, sit not down in the highest room; lest a more honourable man than thou be bidden of him;

9 And he that bade thee and him come and say to thee, Give this man place; and thou begin with shame to take the lowest room.

10 [c]But when thou art bidden, go and sit down in the lowest room; that when he that bade thee cometh, he may say unto thee, Friend, go up higher: then shalt thou have worship in the presence of them that sit at meat with thee.

11 [d]For whosoever exalteth himself shall be abased; and he that humbleth himself shall be exalted.

12 ¶ Then said he also to him that bade him, When thou makest a dinner or a supper, call not thy friends, nor thy brethren, neither thy kinsmen, nor *thy* rich neighbours, lest they also bid thee again, and a recompence be made thee.

13 But when thou makest a feast, call [e]the poor, the maimed, the lame, the blind;

14 And thou shalt be blessed; for they cannot recompense thee: for thou shalt be [f]recompensed at the resurrection of the just.

15 ¶ And when one of them that sat at meat with him heard these things, he said unto him, [g]Blessed *is* he that shall eat bread in the kingdom of God.

16 [h]Then said he unto him, A certain man made a great supper, and bade many:

17 And [i]sent his servant at supper time to say to them that were bidden, Come; for all things are now ready.

18 And they all with one *consent* began to make excuse. The first said unto him, [j]I have bought a piece of ground, and I must needs go and see it: I pray thee have me excused.

19 And another said, I have bought five yoke of oxen, and I go to prove them: I pray thee have me excused.

20 And another said, I have married a wife, and therefore I cannot come.

21 So that servant came, and shewed his lord these things. Then the master of the house being angry said to his servant, [k]Go out quickly into the streets and lanes of the city, and bring in hither the poor, and the maimed, and the halt, and the blind.

22 And the servant said, Lord, it is done as thou hast commanded, and yet there is room.

23 And the lord said unto the servant, Go out into the highways and hedges, [l]and compel *them* to come in, that my house may be filled.

24 For I say unto you, [m]That none of those men which were bidden shall taste of my supper.

25 ¶ And there went great multitudes with him: and he turned, and said unto them,

26 [n]If any *man* come to me, [o]and hate not his father, and mother, and wife, and children, and brethren, and sisters, [p]yea, and his own life also, he cannot be my disciple.

27 And [q]whosoever doth not bear his cross, and come after me, cannot be my disciple.

28 For [r]which of you, intending to build a tower, sitteth not down first, and counteth the cost, whether he have *sufficient* to finish *it?*

29 Lest haply, after he hath laid the foundation, and is not able to finish *it*, all that behold *it* begin to mock him,

30 Saying, This man began to build, and was not able to finish.

31 Or what king, going to make war against another king, sitteth not down first, and consulteth whether he be able with ten thousand to meet him that cometh against him with twenty thousand?

32 Or else, while the other is yet a great way off, he sendeth [s]an ambassage, and desireth conditions of peace.

33 So likewise, whosoever [t]he be of you that forsaketh not all that he hath, he cannot be my disciple.

34 ¶ [u]Salt *is* good: but if the salt have lost his savour, wherewith shall it be seasoned?

35 It is neither fit for the land, nor yet for the dunghill; *but* men cast it out. He that hath ears to hear, let him hear.

15 Then [a]drew near unto him all the publicans and [b]sinners for to hear him.

2 And the Phăr'ĭ-sees and scribes murmured, saying, This man receiveth sinners, [c]and eateth with them.

3 ¶ And he spake this parable unto them, saying,

35 [d]Ps. 69.25; ch. 21.24
[e]Prov. 1.24-30; Hos. 3.5
[f]Ps. 118.26; John 12.13
CHAPTER 14
3 [a]Matt. 12.10
5 [b]Ex. 23.5; John 7.22-23
10 [c]Prov. 15.33; Prov. 18.12
11 [d]Job 22.29; 1 Pet. 5.5
13 [e]Neh. 8.10-12; Prov. 3.9-28
14 [f]Dan. 12.2; Acts 24.15
15 [g]Rev. 19.9
16 [h]Matt. 22.2
17 [i]Prov. 9.2-5
18 [j]Matt. 6.24; 2 Tim. 4.10
21 [k]Matt. 28.18-19; Acts 13.46
23 [l]Prov. 1.20; 2 Cor. 5.20
24 [m]Matt. 8.11-12; Heb. 3.19
26 [n]Deut. 13.6; Matt. 10.37
[o]Rom. 9.13
[p]Rev. 12.11
27 [q]Matt. 16.24; ch. 9.23
28 [r]Gen. 11.4-9; 1 Pet. 2.5
32 [s]Job 22.21
33 [t]Matt. 19.27-28
34 [u]Matt. 5.13
CHAPTER 15
1 [a]Matt. 9.10;
[b]Ezek. 18.23
2 [c]Acts 11.3

4 [d]What man of you, having an hundred sheep, if he [e]lose one of them,
doth not leave the ninety and nine in
the wilderness, and go after that which
is lost, until he find it?
5 And when he hath found *it*, he
layeth *it* on his shoulders, rejoicing.
6 And when he cometh home, he
calleth together *his* friends and neighbours, saying unto them, Rejoice with
me; for I have found my sheep [f]which
was lost.
7 I say unto you, that likewise joy
shall be in heaven over one sinner
that repenteth, [g]more than over ninety
and nine just persons, which need no
repentance.
8 ¶ Either what woman having ten
[1]pieces of silver, if she lose one piece,
doth not light a candle, and sweep the
house, and seek diligently till she find
it?
9 And when she hath found *it*, she
calleth *her* friends and *her* neighbours
together, saying, Rejoice with me; for I
have found the piece which I had lost.
10 Likewise, I say unto you, there is
joy in the presence of the angels of
God over one sinner that repenteth.
11 ¶ And he said, A certain man had
two sons:
12 And the younger of them said to
his father, Father, give me the portion
of goods that falleth *to me*. And he divided unto them [h]*his* living.
13 And not many days after the
younger son gathered all together, and
took his journey into [i]a far country,
and there wasted his substance with
riotous living.
14 And when he had spent all, there
arose a mighty famine in that land;
and he began to be in want.
15 And he went and joined himself
to a citizen of that country; and he sent
him into his fields to feed swine.
16 And he would fain have filled his
belly with the husks that the swine did
eat: and no man gave unto him.
17 And when he came to himself, he
said, How many hired servants of my
father's have bread enough and to
spare, and I perish with hunger!
18 I will [j]arise and go to my father, and will say unto him, Father, [k]I
have sinned against heaven, and before thee,
19 And am no more worthy to be
called thy son: make me as one of thy
hired servants.
20 And he arose, and came to his
father. But [l]when he was yet a great
way off, his father saw him, and had
compassion, and ran, and fell on his
neck, and kissed him.
21 And the son said unto him, Father, I have sinned against heaven,
[m]and in thy sight, and am no more worthy to be called thy son.
22 But the father said to his servants, Bring forth [n]the best robe, and
put *it* on him; and put a ring on his
hand, and shoes on *his* feet:
23 And bring hither the fatted calf,
and kill *it;* and let us eat, and be merry:
24 [o]For this my son was dead, and is
alive again; he was lost, and is found.
[p]And they began to be merry.
25 Now his elder son was in the field:
and as he came and drew nigh to the
house, he heard musick and dancing.
26 And he called one of the servants, and asked what these things
meant.
27 And he said unto him, Thy brother
is come; and thy father hath killed the
fatted calf, because he hath received
him safe and sound.
28 And he was angry, and would not
go in: therefore came his father out,
and intreated him.
29 And he answering said to *his* father, Lo, these many years do I serve
thee, neither transgressed I at any time
thy commandment: and [q]yet thou never
gavest me a kid, that I might make
merry with my friends:
30 But as soon as this thy son was
come, which hath devoured thy living
with harlots, thou hast killed for him
the fatted calf.
31 And he said unto him, Son, thou
art ever with me, and all that I have is
thine.
32 [r]It was meet that we should make
merry, and be glad: for this thy brother
was dead, and is alive again; and was
lost, and is found.

16 And he said also unto his disciples, There was a certain rich
man, which had a steward; and the
same was accused unto him that he
had wasted his goods.
2 And he called him, and said unto
him, How is it that I hear this of thee?
give an [a]account of thy stewardship;
for thou mayest be no longer steward.
3 Then the steward said within himself, What shall I do? for my lord
taketh away from me the stewardship:
I cannot dig; to beg I am ashamed.
4 I am resolved what to do, that,
when I am put out of the stewardship,
they may receive me into their houses.
5 So he called every one of his lord's
debtors *unto him*, and said unto the
first, How much owest thou unto my
lord?
6 And he said, An hundred [1]mea-
sures of oil. And he said unto him,
Take thy bill, and sit down quickly,
and write fifty.
7 Then said he to another, And how
much owest thou? And he said, An
hundred [2]measures of wheat. And he
said unto him, Take thy bill, and write
fourscore.
8 And the lord commended the unjust steward, because he had done
wisely: for the children of this world
are in their generation wiser than [b]the
children of light.
9 And I say unto you, [c]Make to
yourselves friends of the [3]mammon of
unrighteousness; that, when ye fail,
they may receive you into everlasting
habitations.
10 [d]He that is faithful in that which
is least is faithful also in much: and he

4 [d]Matt. 18.12
[e]1 Pet. 2.25
6 [f]1 Pet. 2.10-25
7 [g]Prov. 30.12; ch. 5.32
8 [1]Drachma, here translated a piece of silver, is the eighth part of an ounce, which cometh to sevenpence halfpenny, and is equal to the Roman penny
12 [h]Mark 12.44
13 [i]Ps. 81.12; Rom. 1.21
18 [j]2 Chr. 33.12-13; Lam. 3.40
[k]Lev. 26.40; 1 John 1.9
20 [l]Isa. 49.15; Eph. 2.13-17
21 [m]Ps. 51.4; 1 Cor. 8.12
22 [n]Isa. 61.10; Rev. 19.8
24 [o]Rom. 6.13; Col. 1.13
[p]Isa. 35.10
29 [q]Matt. 20.11-12
32 [r]Rom. 15.9-12
CHAPTER 16
2 [a]Eccl. 11.9-10; 1 Pet. 4.5
6 [1]The word Batus in the original containeth nine gallons three quarts. See Ezek. 45.10-11-14
7 [2]The word here interpreted a measure in the original containeth about fourteen bushels and a pottle
8 [b]John 12.36
9 [c]Dan. 4.27; [3]Or, riches
10 [d]Matt. 25.21

that is unjust in the least is unjust also in much.

11 If therefore ye have not been faithful in the unrighteous [4]mammon, who will commit to your trust the [e]true *riches?*

12 And if ye have not been faithful in that which is another man's, who shall give you that which is your own?

13 ¶ No [f]servant can serve two masters: for either he will hate the one, and love the other; or else he will hold to the one, and despise the other. Ye cannot serve God and mammon.

14 And the Phăr'ĭ-sees also, [g]who were covetous, heard all these things: and they derided him.

15 And he said unto them, Ye are they which [h]justify yourselves before men; but [i]God knoweth your hearts: for [j]that which is highly esteemed among men is abomination in the sight of God.

16 [k]The law and the prophets *were* until Jŏhn: since that time the kingdom of God is preached, and every man presseth into it.

17 [l]And it is easier for heaven and earth to pass, than one tittle of the law to fail.

18 [m]Whosoever putteth away his wife, and marrieth another, committeth adultery: and whosoever marrieth her that is put away from *her* husband committeth adultery.

19 ¶ There was a certain rich man, which was clothed in purple and fine linen, and fared sumptuously every day:

20 And there was a certain beggar named Lăz'a-rus, which was laid at his gate, [n]full of sores,

21 And desiring to be fed with the crumbs which fell from the rich man's table: moreover the dogs came and licked his sores.

22 And it came to pass, that the beggar died, and [o]was carried by the angels into [p]Ā'bră-hăm's bosom: the rich man also died, and was buried;

23 And in hell he lift up his eyes, being in torments, and seeth Ā'bră-hăm afar off, and Lăz'a-rus in his bosom.

24 And he cried and said, Father Ā'bră-hăm, have mercy on me, and send Lăz'a-rus, that he may dip the tip of his finger in water, and [q]cool my tongue; for I [r]am tormented in this flame.

25 But Ā'bră-hăm said, Son, [s]remember that thou in thy lifetime receivedst thy good things, and likewise Lăz'a-rus evil things: but now he is comforted, and thou art tormented.

26 And beside all this, between us and you there is a [t]great gulf fixed: so that they which would pass from hence to you cannot; neither can they pass to us, that *would come* from thence.

27 Then he said, I pray thee therefore, father, that thou wouldest send him to my father's house:

28 For I have five brethren; that he may testify unto them, lest they also come into this place of torment.

29 Ā'bră-hăm saith unto him, [u]They have Mō'ses and the prophets; let them hear them.

30 And he said, Nay, father Ā'bră-hăm: but if one went unto them from the dead, they will repent.

31 And he said unto him, If they hear not Mō'ses and the prophets, [v]neither will they be persuaded, though one rose from the dead.

17 Then said he unto the disciples, [a]It is impossible but that offences will come: but [b]woe *unto him,* through whom they come!

2 It were better for him that a millstone were hanged about his neck, and he cast into the sea, than that he should offend one of these little ones.

3 ¶ Take heed to yourselves: [c]If thy brother trespass against thee, [d]rebuke him; and if he repent, [e]forgive him.

4 And if he trespass against thee seven times in a day, and seven times in a day turn again to thee, saying, I repent; thou shalt forgive him.

5 And the apostles said unto the Lord, Increase our faith.

6 [f]And the Lord said, If ye had faith as a grain of mustard seed, ye might say unto this sycamine tree, Be thou plucked up by the root, and be thou planted in the sea; and it should obey you.

7 But which of you, having a servant plowing or feeding cattle, will say unto him by and by, when he is come from the field, Go and sit down to meat?

8 And will not rather say unto him, Make ready wherewith I may sup, and gird thyself, [g]and serve me, till I have eaten and drunken; and afterward thou shalt eat and drink?

9 Doth he thank that servant because he did the things that were commanded him? I trow not.

10 So likewise ye, when ye shall have done all those things which are commanded you, say, We are [h]unprofitable servants: we have done that which was our duty to do.

11 ¶ And it came to pass, [i]as he went to Je-ru'sa-lĕm, that he passed through the midst of Sa-mā'rĭ-à and Găl'ĭ-lee.

12 And as he entered into a certain village, there met him ten men that were lepers, [j]which stood afar off:

13 And they lifted up *their* voices, and said, Jē'sus, Master, have mercy on us.

14 And when he saw *them,* he said unto them, [k]Go shew yourselves unto the priests. And it came to pass, that, as they went, they were cleansed.

15 And one of them, when he saw that he was healed, turned back, and with a loud voice [l]glorified God,

16 And fell down on *his* face at his feet, giving him thanks: and he was [m]a Sa-măr'ĭ-tan.

17 And Jē'sus answering said, Were there not ten cleansed? but where *are* the nine?

11 [4]Or, riches
[e]Eph. 3.8; Rev. 3.18
13 [f]Matt. 6.24
14 [g]Matt. 23.14; Tit. 1.11
15 [h]Matt. 6.2-5-16; ch. 10.29
[i]1 Chr. 28.9; 2 Chr. 6.30; Ps. 7.9; Prov. 15.11
[j]1 Sam. 16.7; Jas. 4.4
16 [k]Matt. 11.12-13
17 [l]Ps. 102.26-27; Isa. 40.8; 1 Pet. 1.25
18 [m]1 Cor. 7.10
20 [n]Heb. 11.37
22 [o]Heb. 1.14; Jas. 2.5
[p]Matt. 8.11
24 [q]Zech. 14.12
[r]Isa. 66.24; Mark 9.44; Heb. 10.31
25 [s]Job 21.13; ch. 6.24
26 [t]2 Thess. 1.9
29 [u]Isa. 8.20; 2 Tim. 3.15
31 [v]John 12.10

CHAPTER 17
1 [a]Matt. 18.6-7; 1 Cor. 11.19
[b]Matt. 13.41-42; Rev. 2.14-15
3 [c]Matt. 18.15
[d]Lev. 19.17; Jas. 5.19
[e]1 Cor. 13.4; Col. 3.12
6 [f]Matt. 17.20; Mark 9.23
8 [g]ch. 12.37
10 [h]Job 22.3; Phile. 11
11 [i]ch. 9.51; John 4.4
12 [j]Lev. 13.46; Num. 5.2
14 [k]Lev. 13.2; Matt. 8.4
15 [l]Ps. 103.1
16 [m]2 Ki. 17.24; Acts 1.8

18 There are not found that returned to give glory to God, save this stranger.

19 [n]And he said unto him, Arise, go thy way: thy faith hath made thee whole.

20 ¶ And when he was demanded of the Phăr'ĭ-sees, when the kingdom of God should come, he answered them and said, The kingdom of God cometh not [1]with observation:

21 Neither shall they say, Lo here! or, lo there! for, behold, [o]the kingdom of God is [2]within you.

22 And he said unto the disciples, [p]The days will come, when ye shall desire to see one of the days of the Son of man, and ye shall not see *it*.

23 [q]And they shall say to you, See here; or, see there: [r]go not after *them*, nor follow *them*.

24 For as the lightning, that lighteneth out of the one *part* under heaven, shineth unto the other *part* under heaven; so shall also [s]the Son of man be in his day.

25 [t]But first must he suffer many things, and be rejected of this generation.

26 [u]And as it was in the days of Nō'e, so shall it be also in the days of the Son of man.

27 They did eat, they drank, they married wives, they were given in marriage, until the day that Nō'e entered into the ark, and the flood came, and destroyed them all.

28 [v]Likewise also as it was in the days of Lŏt; they did eat, they drank, they bought, they sold, they planted, they builded;

29 But the same day that Lŏt went out of Sŏd'om it rained fire and brimstone from heaven, and destroyed *them* all.

30 Even thus shall it be in the day when the Son of man [w]is revealed.

31 In that day, he [x]which shall be upon the house top, and his stuff in the house, let him not come down to take it away: and he that is in the field, let him likewise not return back.

32 [y]Remember Lŏt's wife.

33 [z]Whosoever shall seek to save his life shall lose it; and whosoever shall lose his life shall preserve it.

34 [a]I tell you, in that night there shall be two *men* in one bed; the one shall be taken, and the other shall be left.

35 Two *women* shall be grinding together; the one shall be taken, and the other left.

36 [3]Two *men* shall be in the field; the one shall be taken, and the other left.

37 And they answered and said unto him, [b]Where, Lord? And he said unto them, Wheresoever the body *is*, thither will the eagles be gathered together.

18

18 And he spake a parable unto them *to this end*, that men ought [a]always to pray, and not to faint;

2 Saying, There was [1]in a city a judge, which feared not God, neither regarded man:

3 And there was a widow in that city; and she came unto him, saying, Avenge me of mine adversary.

4 And he would not for a while: but afterward he said within himself, Though I fear not God, nor regard man;

5 [b]Yet because this widow troubleth me, I will avenge her, lest by her continual coming she weary me.

6 And the Lord said, Hear what the unjust judge saith.

7 And [c]shall not God avenge his own elect, which cry day and night unto him, though he bear long with them?

8 I tell you [d]that he will avenge them speedily. Nevertheless when the Son of man cometh, shall he find faith on the earth?

9 And he spake this parable unto certain [e]which trusted in themselves [2]that they were righteous, and despised others:

10 Two men went up into the temple to pray; the one a Phăr'ĭ-see, and the other a publican.

11 The Phăr'ĭ-see [f]stood and prayed thus with himself, [g]God, I thank thee, that I am not as other men *are*, extortioners, unjust, adulterers, or even as this publican.

12 I fast twice in the week, I give tithes of all that I possess.

13 And the publican, [h]standing afar off, would not lift up so much as *his* eyes unto heaven, but smote upon his breast, saying, God be merciful to me a sinner.

14 I tell you, this man went down to his house justified *rather* than the other: [i]for every one that exalteth himself shall be abased; and he that humbleth himself shall be exalted.

15 [j]And they brought unto him also infants, that he would touch them: but when *his* disciples saw *it*, they rebuked them.

16 But Jē'sus called them *unto him*, and said, [k]Suffer little children to come unto me, and forbid them not: for [l]of such is the kingdom of God.

17 Verily I say unto you, Whosoever shall not receive the kingdom of God as a little child shall in no wise enter therein.

18 [m]And a certain ruler asked him, saying, Good Master, what shall I do to inherit eternal life?

19 And Jē'sus said unto him, Why callest thou me good? none *is* good, save one, *that is*, God.

20 Thou knowest the commandments, [n]Do not commit adultery, Do not kill, Do not steal, Do not bear false witness, [o]Honour thy father and thy mother.

21 And he said, All these have I kept from my youth up.

22 Now when Jē'sus heard these things, he said unto him, Yet lackest thou one thing: [p]sell all that thou hast, and distribute unto the poor, and thou shalt have treasure in heaven: and come, follow me.

---

19 [n]Matt. 9.22; Mark 5.34
20 [1]Or, with outward shew
21 [o]Rom. 14.17; Col. 1.27
[2]Or, among you
22 [p]Matt. 9.15; John 17.12
23 [q]Matt. 24.23; ch. 21.8
[r]1 John 4.1
24 [s]1 Tim. 6.15
25 [t]ch. 9.22
26 [u]Gen. 7
28 [v]Gen. 19
30 [w]Matt. 24.3-27-30; Rev. 1.7
31 [x]Mark 13.15
32 [y]Gen. 19.26
33 [z]Matt. 16.25
34 [a]1 Thess. 4.17
36 [3]This verse is wanting in many Greek copies
37 [b]Job 39.30
CHAPTER 18
1 [a]Gen. 32.9-10; Col. 4.2
2 [1]in a certain city
5 [b]Judg. 16.16; ch. 11.8
7 [c]1 Sam. 24.12; 2 Thess. 1.6
8 [d]Heb. 10.37
9 [e]Prov. 30.12;
[2]Or, as being righteous
11 [f]Ps. 135.2
[g]Isa. 1.15;
13 [h]Ps. 40.12
14 [i]Job 22.29
15 [j]Matt. 19.13
16 [k]Prov. 8.17
[l]1 Cor. 14.20
18 [m]Matt. 19.16
20 [n]Ex. 20.12;
[o]Eph. 6.2
22 [p]Matt. 6.19

23 And when he heard this, he was
very sorrowful: for he was very rich.
24 And when Jē'sus saw that he was
very sorrowful, he said, [q]How hardly
shall they that have riches enter into
the kingdom of God!
25 For it is easier for a camel to go
through a needle's eye, than for a rich
man to enter into the kingdom of God.
26 And they that heard *it* said, Who
then can be saved?
27 And he said, [r]The things which
are impossible with men are possible
with God.
28 [s]Then Pē'tēr said, Lo, we have
left all, and followed thee.
29 And he said unto them, Verily I
say unto you, [t]There is no man that
hath left house, or parents, or brethren, or wife, or children, for the kingdom of God's sake,
30 [u]Who shall not receive manifold
more in this present time, and [v]in the
world to come life everlasting.
31 ¶ [w]Then he took *unto him* the
twelve, and said unto them, Behold, we
go up to Je-rụ'sa-lĕm, and all things
[x]that are written by the prophets concerning the Son of man shall be accomplished.
32 For [y]he shall be delivered unto
the Gĕn'tīles, and shall be mocked,
and spitefully entreated, and spitted
on:
33 And they shall scourge *him*, and
put him to death: and the third day he
shall rise again.
34 [z]And they understood none of
these things: and this saying was hid
from them, neither knew they the
things which were spoken.
35 ¶ [a]And it came to pass, that as he
was come nigh unto Jĕr'ĭ-chō, a certain
blind man sat by the way side begging:
36 And hearing the multitude pass
by, he asked what it meant.
37 And they told him, that Jē'sus of
Năz'a-rĕth passeth by.
38 And he cried, saying, Jē'sus, *thou*
son of Dā'vid, have mercy on me.
39 And they which went before rebuked him, that he should hold his
peace: but he cried so much the more,
Thou son of Dā'vid, have mercy on me.
40 And Jē'sus [b]stood, and commanded him to be brought unto him:
and when he was come near, he asked
him,
41 Saying, What wilt thou that I
shall do unto thee? And he said, Lord,
that I may receive my sight.
42 And Jē'sus said unto him, Receive thy sight: [c]thy faith hath saved
thee.
43 And immediately [d]he received
his sight, and followed him, [e]glorify-
ing God: and all the people when they
saw *it*, gave praise unto God.

19 And *Jē'sus* entered and passed
through [a]Jĕr'ĭ-chō.
2 And, behold, *there was* a man
named Zăc-chæ'us, which was the
chief among the publicans, and he was
rich.
3 And he sought to see Jē'sus who
he was; and could not for the press,
because he was little of stature.
4 And he ran before, and climbed up
into a sycomore tree to see him: for he
was to pass that *way*.
5 And when Jē'sus came to the place,
he looked up, and saw him, and said
unto him, Zăc-chæ'us, make haste, and
come down; for to day I must abide at
thy house.
6 And he made haste, and came
down, and received him joyfully.
7 And when they saw *it*, they all
murmured, saying, [b]That he was gone
to be guest with a man that is a sinner.
8 And Zăc-chæ'us stood, and said
unto the Lord; Behold, Lord, the half
of my goods I give to the poor; and if I
have taken any thing from any man
by [c]false accusation, [d]I restore *him*
fourfold.
9 And Jē'sus said unto him, This
day is salvation come to this house,
forsomuch as [e]he also is a son of
Ā'brā-hăm.
10 [f]For the Son of man is come to
seek and to save that which was lost.
11 And as they heard these things,
he added and spake a parable, because
he was nigh to Je-rụ'sa-lĕm, and because [g]they thought that the kingdom
of God should immediately appear.
12 [h]He said therefore, A certain nobleman went into a far country to receive for himself a kingdom, and to
return.
13 And he called his ten servants,
and delivered them ten [1]pounds, and
said unto them, Occupy till I come.
14 [i]But his citizens hated him, and
sent a message after him, saying, We
will not have this *man* to reign over us.
15 And it came to pass, that when he
was returned, having received the kingdom, then he commanded these servants to be called unto him, to whom he
had given the [2]money, that he might
know how much every man had gained
by trading.
16 Then came the first, saying, Lord,
thy pound hath gained ten pounds.
17 And he said unto him, Well, thou
good servant: because thou hast been
[j]faithful in a very little, have thou authority over ten cities.
18 And the second came, saying,
Lord, thy pound hath gained five
pounds.
19 And he said likewise to him, Be
thou also over five cities.
20 And another came, saying, Lord,
behold, *here is* thy pound, which I have
kept laid up in a napkin:
21 [k]For I feared thee, because thou
art an austere man: thou takest up that
thou layedst not down, and reapest
that thou didst not sow.
22 And he saith unto him, [l]Out of
thine own mouth will I judge thee,
thou wicked servant. [m]Thou knewest
that I was an austere man, taking up
that I laid not down, and reaping that I
did not sow:

24 [q]Deut. 6.10-12; Jas. 2.5
27 [r]Gen. 18.14; Zech. 8.6
28 [s]Matt. 19.27
29 [t]Deut. 33.9
30 [u]Job 42.10
[v]Rev. 2.17
31 [w]Matt. 16.31
[x]Ps. 22; Isa. 53
32 [y]Matt. 27.2; Acts 3.13
34 [z]Mark 9.32; John 10.6
35 [a]Matt. 20.29
40 [b]Heb. 2.17
42 [c]ch. 17.19
43 [d]Ps. 33.9; Isa. 35.5
[e]Ps. 103.1; 1 Pet. 2.9

CHAPTER 19
1 [a]Josh. 6.26; 1 Ki. 16.34
7 [b]Matt. 9.11; ch. 5.30
8 [c]ch. 3.14
[d]Ex. 22.1
9 [e]ch. 13.16 Gal. 3.7
10 [f]Matt. 9.13
11 [g]ch. 17.20
12 [h]Matt. 25.14
13 [1]Mina, here translated a pound, is twelve ounces and an half: which, according to five shillings the ounce, is three pounds two shillings and sixpence
14 [i]John 1.11
15 [2]silver
17 [j]ch. 16.10
21 [k]Ex. 20.19-20
22 [l]2 Sam. 1.16;
[m]Matt. 25.26

23 Wherefore then gavest not thou
my money into the bank, that at my
coming I might have required mine
own with usury?
24 And he said unto them that stood
by, Take from him the pound, and give
it to him that hath ten pounds.
25 (And they said unto him, Lord, he
hath ten pounds.)
26 For I say unto you, [n]That unto
every one which hath shall be given;
and from him that hath not, even that
he hath shall be taken away from him.
27 But those mine enemies, which
would not that I should reign over
them, bring hither, and slay *them* before me.
28 ¶ And when he had thus spoken,
[o]he went before, ascending up to Je-
ru͡'sa-lĕm.
29 [p]And it came to pass, when he
was come nigh to Bĕth'pha-ġe and
Bĕth'ă-nȳ, at the mount called *the
mount* of Ŏl'ĭves, he sent two of his
disciples,
30 Saying, Go ye into the village over
against *you;* in the which at your entering ye shall find a colt tied, whereon yet
never man sat: loose him, and bring
him hither.
31 And if any man ask you, Why do
ye loose *him?* thus shall ye say unto
him, [q]Because the Lord hath need of
him.
32 And they that were sent went
their way, and found even as he had
said unto them.
33 And as they were loosing the colt,
the owners thereof said unto them,
Why loose ye the colt?
34 And they said, The Lord hath
need of him.
35 And they brought him to Jē'sus:
[r]and they cast their garments upon the
colt, and they set Jē'sus thereon.
36 [s]And as he went, they spread
their clothes in the way.
37 And when he was come nigh,
even now at the descent of the mount of
Ŏl'ĭves, the whole multitude of the disciples began to rejoice and praise God
with a loud voice for all the mighty
works that they had seen;
38 Saying, [t]Blessed *be* the King that
cometh in the name of the Lord: [u]peace
in heaven, and glory in the highest.
39 And some of the Phăr'ĭ-sees from
among the multitude said unto him,
Master, rebuke thy disciples.
40 And he answered and said unto
them, I tell you that, if these should
hold their peace, [v]the stones would immediately cry out.
41 ¶ And when he was come near,
he beheld the city, and [w]wept over it,
42 Saying, If thou hadst known, even
thou, at least in this thy day, the things
which belong unto thy peace! but now
they are hid from thine eyes.
43 For the days shall come upon
thee, that thine enemies shall [x]cast a
trench about thee, and compass thee
round, and keep thee in on every side,
44 And [y]shall lay thee even with the
ground, and thy children within thee;
and [z]they shall not leave in thee one
stone upon another; because [a]thou
knewest not the time of thy visitation.
45 [b]And he went into the temple,
and began to cast out them that sold
therein, and them that bought;
46 Saying unto them, [c]It is written,
My house is the house of prayer: but
[d]ye have made it a den of thieves.
47 And he taught daily in the temple. But [e]the chief priests and the
scribes and the chief of the people
sought to destroy him,
48 And could not find what they
might do: for all the people [3]were very
attentive to hear him.

20 And [a]it came to pass, *that* on
one of those days, as he taught
the people in the temple, and preached
the gospel, the chief priests and the
scribes came upon *him* with the elders,
2 And spake unto him, saying, Tell
us, [b]by what authority doest thou these
things? or who is he that gave thee this
authority?
3 And he answered and said unto
them, I will also ask you one thing; and
answer me:
4 The baptism of Jŏhn, was it from
heaven, or of men?
5 And they reasoned with themselves, saying, If we shall say, From
heaven; he will say, Why then believed
ye him not?
6 But and if we say, Of men; all the
people will stone us: [c]for they be persuaded that Jŏhn was a prophet.
7 And they answered, [d]that they
could not tell whence *it was.*
8 And Jē'sus said unto them, [e]Nei-
ther tell I you by what authority I do
these things.
9 Then began he to speak to the
people this parable; [f]A certain man
planted a vineyard, and let it forth to
husbandmen, and went into a far country for a long time.
10 And at the season [g]he sent a servant to the husbandmen, that they
should give him of the fruit of the vineyard: but the husbandmen beat him,
and sent *him* away empty.
11 And again he sent another servant: and they beat him also, and entreated *him* shamefully, and sent *him*
away empty.
12 [h]And again he sent a third: and
they wounded him also, and cast *him*
out.
13 Then said the lord of the vineyard, What shall I do? I will send [i]my
beloved son: it may be they will reverence *him* when they see him.
14 But when the husbandmen saw
him, they reasoned among themselves,
saying, This is [j]the heir: come, let us
kill him, that the inheritance may be
ours.
15 So they cast him out of the vineyard, and [k]killed *him.* What therefore
shall the lord of the vineyard do unto
them?
16 He shall come and destroy these
husbandmen, and shall give the vine-

26 [n]Matt. 13.12; ch. 8.18
28 [o]Mark 10.32; ch. 9.51
29 [p]verse 37; Zech. 14.4; Matt. 21.1; Mark 11.1; John 8.1; Acts 1.12
31 [q]Ps. 50.10; Acts 10.36
35 [r]2 Ki. 9.13; Mark 11.7; John 12.14
36 [s]Matt. 21.8
38 [t]Ps. 118.26; Matt. 21.9; Mark 11.9; ch. 13.35; 1 Tim. 1.17
[u]ch. 2.14; Eph. 2.14
40 [v]Hab. 2.11
41 [w]Isa. 53.3; Hos. 11.8; John 11.35; Rom. 12.15
43 [x]Isa. 29.3-4; Jer. 6.3-6; ch. 21.20
44 [y]1 Ki. 9.7
[z]Mark 13.2; ch. 21.6
[a]Dan. 9.24; 1 Pet. 2.12
45 [b]Matt. 21.12; John 2.14
46 [c]Ps. 93.5; Isa. 56.7
[d]Jer. 7.11
47 [e]Mark 11.18; John 7.19
48 [3]Or, hanged on him

CHAPTER 20
1 [a]Matt. 21.23
2 [b]Acts 4.7
6 [c]Matt. 14.5; ch. 7.29
7 [d]Job 24.13; 2 Thess. 2.9-10
8 [e]Job 5.12-13
9 [f]Ps. 80.8; Jer. 2.21
10 [g]2 Ki. 17.13-14; Heb. 11.36
12 [h]Neh. 9.29-30
13 [i]Isa. 7.14; Gal. 4.4
14 [j]Ps. 2.6; Heb. 1.2
15 [k]John 19; 1 Cor. 2.8

yard to others. And when they heard
it, they said, God forbid.
17 And he beheld them, and said,
What is this then that is written, [l]The
stone which the builders rejected, the
same is become the head of the corner?
18 Whosoever shall fall upon that
stone shall be broken; but [m]on whomsoever it shall fall, it will grind him to
powder.
19 ¶ And the chief priests and the
scribes the same hour sought to lay
hands on him; and they feared the people: for they perceived that he had
spoken this parable against them.
20 [n]And they watched *him,* and sent
forth spies, which should feign themselves just men, that they might take
hold of his words, that so they might
deliver him unto the power and authority of the governor.
21 And they asked him, saying,
[o]Master, we know that thou sayest
and teachest rightly, neither acceptest
thou the person *of any,* but teachest the
way of God [1]truly:
22 Is it lawful for us to give tribute
unto Çæ'sar, or no?
23 But he perceived their craftiness,
and said unto them, Why tempt ye me?
24 Shew me a [p]penny. Whose image and superscription hath it? They
answered and said, Çæ'sar's.
25 And he said unto them, Render
therefore unto Çæ'sar the things which
be Çæ'sar's, and unto God the things
which be God's.
26 And they could not take hold of
his words before the people: and they
marvelled at his answer, and held their
peace.
27 ¶ [q]Then came to *him* certain
of the Săd'dū-çees, [r]which deny that
there is any resurrection: and they
asked him,
28 Saying, Master, [s]Mō'ses wrote
unto us, If any man's brother die, having a wife, and he die without children,
that his brother should take his wife,
and raise up seed unto his brother.
29 There were therefore seven brethren: and the first took a wife, and died
without children.
30 And the second took her to wife,
and he died childless.
31 And the third took her; and in
like manner the seven also: and they
left no children, and died.
32 Last of all the woman died also.
33 Therefore in the resurrection
whose wife of them is she? for seven
had her to wife.
34 And Jē'sus answering said unto
them, The children of this world marry,
and are given in marriage:
35 But they which shall be [t]ac-
counted worthy to obtain that world,
and the resurrection from the dead, neither marry, nor are given in marriage:
36 Neither can they die any more:
for [u]they are equal unto the angels;
and are the children of God, [v]being the
children of the resurrection.
37 Now that the dead are raised,
[w]even Mō'ses shewed at the bush,

17 [l]Ps. 118.22; 1 Pet. 2.7
18 [m]Isa. 8.15; Dan. 2.34-35
20 [n]Matt. 22.15
21 [o]Mark 12.14
[1]of a truth
24 [p]Matt. 18.28
27 [q]Matt. 16.1-6-12; Mark 12.18; Acts 4.1-2
[r]Acts 23.6
28 [s]Gen. 38.8; Deut. 25.5
35 [t]2 Thess. 1.5; Rev. 3.4
36 [u]Matt. 22.30; Mark 12.25; 1 Cor. 15.42-49-52; Rev. 7.9-12
[v]Rom. 8.23; 1 John 3.2
37 [w]Ex. 3.6; Acts 7.32
38 [x]Ps. 16.5-11; Rom. 4.17; Col. 3.3-4; Heb. 11.16
[y]Rom. 6.10-11; Rom. 14.7-9; 2 Cor. 13.4
41 [z]Isa. 9.6-7; Matt. 1.1; Mark 12.35; ch. 18.38
42 [a]Ps. 110.1; 1 Cor. 15.25
45 [b]Matt. 23.1; Mark 12.38
46 [c]Matt. 23.5
[d]ch. 11.43
47 [e]Matt. 23.14
[f]Matt. 11.22; Jas. 4.17

CHAPTER 21
1 [a]Mark 12.41
3 [b]Prov. 3.9; 2 Cor. 8.12
5 [c]Matt. 24.1; Mark 13.1
6 [d]1 Ki. 9.7; ch. 19.44
8 [e]Matt. 24.4; Rev. 12.9
[1]Or, and, The time
10 [f]Matt. 24.7
12 [g]Rev. 2.10
[h]Acts 4.3; Acts 5.18
[i]Acts 25.23
[j]1 Pet. 2.13

when he calleth the Lord the God of
Ā'bră-hăm, and the God of Ī'saac, and
the God of Jā'cob.
38 [x]For he is not a God of the dead,
but of the living: for [y]all live unto him.
39 ¶ Then certain of the scribes answering said, Master, thou hast well
said.
40 And after that they durst not ask
him any *question at all.*
41 And he said unto them, [z]How say
they that Christ is Dā'vid's son?
42 And Dā'vid himself saith in the
book of Psalms, [a]The LORD said unto
my Lord, Sit thou on my right hand,
43 Till I make thine enemies thy
footstool.
44 Dā'vid therefore calleth him Lord,
how is he then his son?
45 ¶ [b]Then in the audience of all the
people he said unto his disciples,
46 [c]Beware of the scribes, which desire to walk in long robes, and [d]love
greetings in the markets, and the highest seats in the synagogues, and the
chief rooms at feasts;
47 [e]Which devour widows' houses,
and for a shew make long prayers: the
same [f]shall receive greater damnation.

21 And he looked up, [a]and saw the
rich men casting their gifts into
the treasury.
2 And he saw also a certain poor
widow casting in thither two mites.
3 And he said, Of a truth I say unto
you, [b]that this poor widow hath cast in
more than they all:
4 For all these have of their abundance cast in unto the offerings of
God: but she of her penury hath cast in
all the living that she had.
5 ¶ [c]And as some spake of the temple, how it was adorned with goodly
stones and gifts, he said,
6 *As for* these things which ye behold, the days will come, in the which
[d]there shall not be left one stone upon
another, that shall not be thrown down.
7 And they asked him, saying, Master, but when shall these things be?
and what sign *will there be* when these
things shall come to pass?
8 And he said, [e]Take heed that ye be
not deceived: for many shall come in
my name, saying, I am *Christ;* [1]and the
time draweth near: go ye not therefore
after them.
9 But when ye shall hear of wars
and commotions, be not terrified: for
these things must first come to pass;
but the end *is* not by and by.
10 [f]Then said he unto them, Nation
shall rise against nation, and kingdom
against kingdom:
11 And great earthquakes shall be
in divers places, and famines, and pestilences; and fearful sights and great
signs shall there be from heaven.
12 [g]But before all these, they shall
lay their hands on you, and persecute *you,* delivering *you* up to the
synagogues, and [h]into prisons, [i]being
brought before kings and rulers [j]for
my name's sake.

13 And [k]it shall turn to you for a testimony.

14 [l]Settle *it* therefore in your hearts, not to meditate before what ye shall answer:

15 For I will give you a mouth and wisdom, [m]which all your adversaries shall not be able to gainsay nor resist.

16 [n]And ye shall be betrayed both by parents, and brethren, and kinsfolks, and friends; [o]and *some* of you shall they cause to be put to death.

17 [p]And ye shall be hated of all *men* for my name's sake.

18 But there shall not an hair of your head perish.

19 In your patience possess ye your souls.

20 [q]And when ye shall see Je-rṳ'sa-lĕm compassed with armies, then know that the desolation thereof is nigh.

21 Then let them which are in Jū-dæ'à flee to the mountains; and let them which are in the midst of it depart out; and let not them that are in the countries enter thereinto.

22 For these be the days of vengeance, that [r]all things which are written may be fulfilled.

23 But woe unto them that are with child, and to them that give suck, in those days! for there shall be great distress in the land, and wrath upon this people.

24 And they shall fall by the edge of the sword, and shall be led away captive into all nations: and Je-rṳ'sa-lĕm shall be trodden down of the Gĕn'tīles, [s]until the times of the Gĕn'tīles be fulfilled.

25 ¶ [t]And there shall be signs in the sun, and in the moon, and in the stars; and upon the earth distress of nations, with perplexity; the sea and the waves roaring;

26 Men's hearts failing them for fear, and for looking after those things which are coming on the earth: [u]for the powers of heaven shall be shaken.

27 And then shall they see the Son of man [v]coming in a cloud with power and great glory.

28 And when these things begin to come to pass, then look up, and lift up your heads; for your redemption draweth nigh.

29 [w]And he spake to them a parable; Behold the fig tree, and all the trees;

30 When they now shoot forth, ye see and know of your own selves that summer is now nigh at hand.

31 So likewise ye, when ye see these things come to pass, know ye that the kingdom of God is nigh at hand.

32 Verily I say unto you, This generation shall not pass away, till all be fulfilled.

33 Heaven and earth shall pass away: but my words shall not pass away.

34 ¶ And [x]take heed to yourselves, lest at any time your hearts be overcharged with surfeiting, and drunkenness, and cares of this life, and *so* that day come upon you unawares.

35 For [y]as a snare shall it come on all them that dwell on the face of the whole earth.

36 [z]Watch ye therefore, and [a]pray always, that ye may be accounted worthy to escape all these things that shall come to pass, and [b]to stand before the Son of man.

37 And [c]in the day time he was teaching in the temple; and [d]at night he went out, and abode in the mount that is called *the mount* of Ŏl'īves.

38 And all the people came early in the morning to him [e]in the temple, for to hear him.

22

Now [a]the feast of unleavened bread drew nigh, which is called the Passover.

2 And [b]the chief priests and scribes sought how they might kill him; for they feared the people.

3 ¶ [c]Then entered Sā'tan into Jū'das surnamed Ĭs-căr'ĭ-ot, being of the number of the twelve.

4 And he went his way, and communed with the chief priests and captains, how he might betray him unto them.

5 And they were glad, and [d]covenanted to give him money.

6 And he promised, and sought opportunity to betray him unto them [1]in the absence of the multitude.

7 ¶ [e]Then came the day of unleavened bread, when the passover must be killed.

8 And he sent Pē'tĕr and Jŏhn, saying, Go and prepare us the passover, that we may eat.

9 And they said unto him, Where wilt thou that we prepare?

10 And he said unto them, Behold, when ye are entered into the city, there shall a man meet you, bearing a pitcher of water; follow him into the house where he entereth in.

11 And ye shall say unto the goodman of the house, The Master saith unto thee, Where is the guestchamber, where I shall eat the passover with my disciples?

12 And he shall shew you a large upper room furnished: there make ready.

13 And they went, and found as he had said unto them: and they made ready the passover.

14 And when the hour was come, he sat down, and the twelve apostles with him.

15 And he said unto them, [2]With desire I have desired to eat this passover with you before I suffer:

16 For I say unto you, I will not any more eat thereof, [f]until it be fulfilled in the kingdom of God.

17 And he took the cup, and gave thanks, and said, Take this, and divide *it* among yourselves:

18 For [g]I say unto you, I will not drink of the fruit of the vine, until the kingdom of God shall come.

19 ¶ And he took bread, and gave thanks, and brake *it*, and gave unto them, saying, This is my body which is

13 [k]Phil. 1.28
14 [l]Matt. 10.19
15 [m]Acts 6.10
16 [n]Mic. 7.6
[o]Acts 7.59
17 [p]Matt. 10.22
20 [q]Matt. 24.15
22 [r]Dan. 9.26-27; Zech. 11.1
24 [s]Dan. 9.27; Rom. 11.25
25 [t]Isa. 13.10-13; Rev. 6.12-14
26 [u]Matt. 24.29
27 [v]Acts 1.11; Rev. 1.7
29 [w]Mark 13.28
34 [x]Rom. 13.13; 1 Pet. 4.7
35 [y]1 Thess. 5.2; Rev. 3.3
36 [z]Matt. 24.42; Rev. 16.15
[a]Eph. 6.18; 1 Thess. 5.17
[b]Ps. 1.5; Eph. 6.13
37 [c]John 8.1-2
[d]ch. 22.39
38 [e]Hag. 2.7; Mal. 3.1

CHAPTER 22
1 [a]Ex. 12.3-28; 1 Cor. 5.7-8
2 [b]Ps. 2.2; Acts 4.27
3 [c]Matt. 26.14; Mark 14.10
5 [d]Zech. 11.12; Jude 11
6 [1]Or, without tumult
7 [e]Matt. 26.17; Mark 14.12
15 [2]Or, I have heartily desired
16 [f]Acts 10.41; Rev. 19.9
18 [g]Matt. 26.29;

given for you: [h]this do in remembrance of me.

20 Likewise also the cup after supper, saying, [i]This cup *is* the new testament in my blood, which is shed for you.

21 ¶ [j]But, behold, the hand of him that betrayeth me *is* with me on the table.

22 And truly the Son of man goeth, [k]as it was determined: but woe unto that man by whom he is betrayed!

23 And they began to inquire among themselves, which of them it was that should do this thing.

24 ¶ [l]And there was also a strife among them, which of them should be accounted the greatest.

25 [m]And he said unto them, The kings of the Gĕn′tīles exercise lordship over them; and they that exercise authority upon them are called benefactors.

26 [n]But ye *shall* not *be* so: [o]but he that is greatest among you, let him be as the younger; and he that is chief, as he that doth serve.

27 For whether *is* greater, he that sitteth at meat, or he that serveth? *is* not he that sitteth at meat? but [p]I am among you as he that serveth.

28 Ye are they which have continued with me in [q]my temptations.

29 And [r]I appoint unto you a kingdom, as my Father hath appointed unto me;

30 That [s]ye may eat and drink at my table in my kingdom, [t]and sit on thrones judging the twelve tribes of Is′ra-el.

31 ¶ And the Lord said, Sī′mon, Sī′mon, behold, [u]Sā′tan hath desired *to have* you, that he may [v]sift *you* as wheat:

32 But [w]I have prayed for thee, that thy faith fail not: [x]and when thou art converted, strengthen thy brethren.

33 And he said unto him, Lord, I am ready to go with thee, both into prison, and to death.

34 [y]And he said, I tell thee, Pē′tēr, the cock shall not crow this day, before that thou shalt thrice deny that thou knowest me.

35 [z]And he said unto them, When I sent you without purse, and scrip, and shoes, lacked ye any thing? And they said, Nothing.

36 Then said he unto them, But now, he that hath a purse, let him take *it*, and likewise *his* scrip: and he that hath no sword, let him sell his garment, and buy one.

37 For I say unto you, that this that is written must yet be accomplished in me, [a]And he was reckoned among the transgressors: for the things concerning me have an end.

38 And they said, Lord, behold, here *are* two swords. And he said unto them, It is enough.

39 ¶ And he came out, and went, as he was wont, to the mount of Ŏl′ĭves; and his disciples also followed him.

19 [h]1 Cor. 11.24
20 [i]1 Cor. 10.16
21 [j]Ps. 41.9; Mic. 7.5-6; Mark 14.18; John 13.21-26
22 [k]Isa. 53; Dan. 9.24; Acts 2.23
24 [l]Mark 9.34; ch. 9.46
25 [m]Matt. 20.25
26 [n]1 Pet. 5.3
[o]ch. 9.48
27 [p]Matt. 20.28; Phil. 2.7
28 [q]Heb. 4.15
29 [r]Matt. 24.47; Jas. 2.5
30 [s]2 Sam. 9.9-10; Rev. 19.9
[t]Ps. 49.14; Rev. 2.26
31 [u]1 Pet. 5.8
[v]Amos 9.9
32 [w]John 17.9-11-15
[x]Ps. 51.13; John 21.15
34 [y]Matt. 26.34
35 [z]Matt. 10.9; ch. 9.3
37 [a]Isa. 53.12; Mark 15.28
40 [b]Matt. 6.13; Mark 14.38
42 [3]willing to remove
[c]John 6.38
43 [d]Matt. 4.11
44 [e]John 12.27
47 [f]2 Sam. 20.9
50 [g]Matt. 26.51; Mark 14.47
53 [h]John 12.27; Acts 2.23
54 [i]Matt. 26.57; Acts 8.32
[j]John 18.15
55 [k]Matt. 26.69; Mark 14.66
58 [l]Matt. 26.71; John 18.25

40 [b]And when he was at the place, he said unto them, Pray that ye enter not into temptation.

41 And he was withdrawn from them about a stone's cast, and kneeled down, and prayed,

42 Saying, Father, if thou be [3]willing, remove this cup from me: nevertheless [c]not my will, but thine, be done.

43 And there appeared [d]an angel unto him from heaven, strengthening him.

44 [e]And being in an agony he prayed more earnestly: and his sweat was as it were great drops of blood falling down to the ground.

45 And when he rose up from prayer, and was come to his disciples, he found them sleeping for sorrow,

46 And said unto them, Why sleep ye? rise and pray, lest ye enter into temptation.

47 ¶ And while he yet spake, behold a multitude, and he that was called Jū′das, one of the twelve, went before them, and drew near unto Jē′sus [f]to kiss him.

48 But Jē′sus said unto him, Jū′das, betrayest thou the Son of man with a kiss?

49 When they which were about him saw what would follow, they said unto him, Lord, shall we smite with the sword?

50 ¶ And [g]one of them smote the servant of the high priest, and cut off his right ear.

51 And Jē′sus answered and said, Suffer ye thus far. And he touched his ear, and healed him.

52 Then Jē′sus said unto the chief priests, and captains of the temple, and the elders, which were come to him, Be ye come out, as against a thief, with swords and staves?

53 When I was daily with you in the temple, ye stretched forth no hands against me: [h]but this is your hour, and the power of darkness.

54 ¶ [i]Then took they him, and led *him*, and brought him into the high priest's house. [j]And Pē′tēr followed afar off.

55 [k]And when they had kindled a fire in the midst of the hall, and were set down together, Pē′tēr sat down among them.

56 But a certain maid beheld him as he sat by the fire, and earnestly looked upon him, and said, This man was also with him.

57 And he denied him, saying, Woman, I know him not.

58 [l]And after a little while another saw him, and said, Thou art also of them. And Pē′tēr said, Man, I am not.

59 And about the space of one hour after another confidently affirmed, saying, Of a truth this *fellow* also was with him: for he is a Găl-ĭ-læ′an.

60 And Pē′tēr said, Man, I know not what thou sayest. And immediately, while he yet spake, the cock crew.

61 And the Lord turned, and looked
upon Pē'tēr. [m]And Pē'tēr remembered
the word of the Lord, how he had said
unto him, [n]Before the cock crow, thou
shalt deny me thrice.
62 And Pē'tēr went out, and [o]wept
bitterly.
63 ¶ And [p]the men that held Jē'sus
mocked him, and smote *him*.
64 And when they had blindfolded
him, they struck him on the face, and
asked him, saying, Prophesy, who is it
that smote thee?
65 And many other things blasphe-
mously spake they against him.
66 ¶ [q]And as soon as it was day,
[r]the elders of the people and the chief
priests and the scribes came together,
and led him into their council, saying,
67 [s]Art thou the Chrīst? tell us. And
he said unto them, If I tell you, ye will
not believe:
68 And if I also ask *you*, ye will not
answer me, nor let *me* go.
69 [t]Hereafter shall the Son of man
sit on the right hand of the power of
God.
70 Then said they all, Art thou then
the Son of God? And he said unto
them, Ye say that I am.
71 And they said, What need we any
further witness? for we ourselves have
heard of his own mouth.

23 And [a]the whole multitude of
them arose, and led him unto
Pī'late.
2 And they began to accuse him, saying, We found this *fellow* [b]perverting
the nation, and [c]forbidding to give tribute to Çæ'sar, saying [d]that he himself
is Chrīst a King.
3 [e]And Pī'late asked him, saying,
Art thou the King of the Jews? And he
answered him and said, Thou sayest *it*.
4 Then said Pī'late to the chief priests
and *to* the people, [f]I find no fault in this
man.
5 And they were the more fierce, saying, He stirreth up the people, teaching
throughout all Jew'rȳ, beginning from
Găl'ĭ-lee to this place.
6 When Pī'late heard of Găl'ĭ-lee,
he asked whether the man were a
Găl-ĭ-læ'an.
7 And as soon as he knew that he
belonged unto [g]Hĕr'od's jurisdiction,
he sent him to Hĕr'od, who himself
also was at Je-ru̧'sa-lĕm at that time.
8 ¶ And when Hĕr'od saw Jē'sus, he
was exceeding glad: for [h]he was desirous to see him of a long *season*, because [i]he had heard many things of
him; and he hoped to have seen some
miracle done by him.
9 Then he questioned with him in
many words; but he answered him
nothing.
10 And the chief priests and scribes
stood and vehemently accused him.
11 [j]And Hĕr'od with his men of war
set him at nought, and mocked *him*,
and arrayed him in a gorgeous robe,
and sent him again to Pī'late.
12 ¶ And the same day [k]Pī'late and
Hĕr'od were made friends together:

61 [m]Ezek. 16.63; Rev. 2.5
[n]John 13.38
62 [o]Isa. 66.2; 2 Cor. 7.10
63 [p]Ps. 69.1-21; Mark 14.65
66 [q]Matt. 27.1
[r]Ps. 2.1; Acts 4.26
67 [s]Matt. 26.63; John 10.24
69 [t]Ps. 110.1; Rev. 1.7
CHAPTER 23
1 [a]Matt. 27.2; John 18.28
2 [b]1 Ki. 21.10-13; 1 Pet. 3.16-18
[c]Matt. 17.27; Mark 12.17
[d]Mark 14.61-62;
3 [e]1 Tim. 6.13
4 [f]Matt. 27.19;
7 [g]ch. 3.1
8 [h]ch. 9.9
[i]Matt. 14.1;
11 [j]Isa. 53.3
12 [k]Acts 4.27
13 [l]Matt. 27.23
14 [m]Dan. 6.4
16 [n]Matt. 27.26
17 [o]Matt. 27.15
18 [p]Acts 3.14
24 [1]Or, assented
25 [q]Prov. 17.15
26 [r]Matt. 27.32
29 [s]ch. 21.23
30 [t]Isa. 2.19
31 [u]Prov. 11.31
32 [v]Isa. 53.12
33 [w]Matt. 27.33; [2]Or, The place of a skull

for before they were at enmity between themselves.
13 ¶ [l]And Pī'late, when he had called
together the chief priests and the rulers
and the people,
14 Said unto them, Ye have brought
this man unto me, as one that perverteth the people: and, behold, I, having examined *him* before you, have
[m]found no fault in this man touching
those things whereof ye accuse him:
15 No, nor yet Hĕr'od: for I sent you
to him; and, lo, nothing worthy of
death is done unto him.
16 [n]I will therefore chastise him,
and release *him*.
17 [o](For of necessity he must release one unto them at the feast.)
18 And [p]they cried out all at once,
saying, Away with this *man*, and release unto us Ba-răb'bas:
19 (Who for a certain sedition made
in the city, and for murder, was cast
into prison.)
20 Pī'late therefore, willing to release Jē'sus, spake again to them.
21 But they cried, saying, Crucify
him, crucify him.
22 And he said unto them the third
time, Why, what evil hath he done? I
have found no cause of death in him: I
will therefore chastise him, and let *him*
go.
23 And they were instant with loud
voices, requiring that he might be crucified. And the voices of them and of the
chief priests prevailed.
24 And Pī'late [1]gave sentence that it
should be as they required.
25 [q]And he released unto them him
that for sedition and murder was cast
into prison, whom they had desired;
but he delivered Jē'sus to their will.
26 [r]And as they led him away, they
laid hold upon one Sī'mon, a Çȳ-re'nĭ-
an, coming out of the country, and on
him they laid the cross, that he might
bear *it* after Jē'sus.
27 ¶ And there followed him a great
company of people, and of women,
which also bewailed and lamented him.
28 But Jē'sus turning unto them said,
Daughters of Je-ru̧'sa-lĕm, weep not
for me, but weep for yourselves, and
for your children.
29 [s]For, behold, the days are coming, in the which they shall say, Blessed
are the barren, and the wombs that
never bare, and the paps which never
gave suck.
30 [t]Then shall they begin to say to
the mountains, Fall on us; and to the
hills, Cover us.
31 [u]For if they do these things in a
green tree, what shall be done in the
dry?
32 [v]And there were also two other,
malefactors, led with him to be put to
death.
33 And [w]when they were come to
the place, which is called [2]Căl'vă-rȳ,
there they crucified him, and the malefactors, one on the right hand, and the
other on the left.

34 ¶ Then said Jē'sus, Father, [x]for-
give them; for [y]they know not what
they do. And [z]they parted his raiment,
and cast lots.
35 And [a]the people stood beholding. And the rulers also with them derided *him,* saying, He saved others; let
him save himself, if he be Chrīst, the
chosen of God.
36 And the soldiers also mocked
him, coming to him, and offering him
vinegar,
37 And saying, If thou be the king of
the Jews, save thyself.
38 [b]And a superscription also was
written over him in letters of Greek,
and Lăt'in, and Hē'brew, THIS IS THE
KING OF THE JEWS.
39 ¶ [c]And one of the malefactors
which were hanged railed on him, saying, If thou be Chrīst, save thyself and
us.
40 But the other answering [d]rebuked
him, saying, Dost not thou fear God, seeing thou art in the same condemnation?
41 And we indeed justly; for we receive the due reward of our deeds: but
this man hath done nothing amiss.
42 And he said unto Jē'sus, Lord, remember me when thou comest into
[e]thy kingdom.
43 And Jē'sus said unto him, Verily
I say unto thee, To day shalt thou be
with me in [f]paradise.
44 [g]And it was about the sixth hour,
and there was a darkness over all the
[3]earth until the ninth hour.
45 And the sun was darkened, and
[h]the veil of the temple was rent in the
midst.
46 ¶ And when Jē'sus had cried with
a loud voice, he said, [i]Father, into thy
hands I commend my spirit: [j]and having said thus, he gave up the ghost.
47 [k]Now when the centurion saw
what was done, he glorified God, saying, Certainly this was a righteous
man.
48 And all the people that came
together to that sight, beholding the
things which were done, smote their
breasts, and returned.
49 [l]And all his acquaintance, and
the women that followed him from Găl'-
ĭ-lee, stood afar off, beholding these
things.
50 ¶ [m]And, behold, *there was* a man
named Jō'seph, a counsellor; *and he
was* a good man, and a just:
51 (The same [n]had not consented to
the counsel and deed of them;) *he was*
of Ăr-ĭ-mă-thæ'ȧ, a city of the Jews:
[o]who also himself waited for the kingdom of God.
52 This *man* went unto Pī'late, and
begged the body of Jē'sus.
53 [p]And he took it down, and
wrapped it in linen, and laid it in
[q]a sepulchre that was hewn in stone,
wherein never man before was laid.
54 And that day was the preparation, and the sabbath drew on.
55 And the women also, [r]which came
with him from Găl'ĭ-lee, followed after,
and [s]beheld the sepulchre, and how his
body was laid.
56 And they returned, and [t]pre-
pared spices and ointments; and rested
the sabbath day [u]according to the
commandment.

24 Now [a]upon the first *day* of the
week, very early in the morning,
they came unto the sepulchre, [b]bring-
ing the spices which they had prepared, and certain *others* with them.
2 And they found the stone rolled
away from the sepulchre.
3 [c]And they entered in, and found
not the body of the Lord Jē'sus.
4 And it came to pass, as they were
much perplexed thereabout, [d]behold,
two men stood by them in shining garments:
5 And as they were afraid, and
bowed down *their* faces to the earth,
they said unto them, Why seek ye [1]the
living among the dead?
6 He is not here, but is risen: [e]re-
member how he spake unto you when
he was yet in Găl'ĭ-lee,
7 Saying, The Son of man must be
delivered into the hands of sinful men,
and be crucified, and the third day rise
again.
8 And [f]they remembered his words,
9 [g]And returned from the sepulchre, and told all these things unto the
eleven, and to all the rest.
10 It was Mā'rȳ Măg-da-lē'ne, and
[h]Jo-ăn'nȧ, and Mā'rȳ *the mother* of
Jāmes, and other *women that were*
with them, which told these things
unto the apostles.
11 And their words seemed to them
as idle tales, and they believed them
not.
12 [i]Then arose Pē'tĕr, and ran unto
the sepulchre; and stooping down, he
beheld the linen clothes laid by themselves, and departed, wondering in
himself at that which was come to
pass.
13 ¶ And, behold, two of them went
that same day to a village called Ĕm'-
ma-us, which was from Je-ru̇'sa-lĕm
about threescore furlongs.
14 And they [j]talked together of all
these things which had happened.
15 And it came to pass, that, while
they communed *together* and reasoned, [k]Jē'sus himself drew near, and
went with them.
16 But [l]their eyes were holden that
they should not know him.
17 And he said unto them, What
manner of communications *are* these
that ye have one to another, as ye
walk, and are sad?
18 And the one of them, [m]whose
name was Clē'-o-pas, answering said
unto him, Art thou only a stranger in
Je-ru̇'sa-lĕm, and hast not known the
things which are come to pass there in
these days?
19 And he said unto them, What
things? And they said unto him, Concerning Jē'sus of Năz'a-rĕth, [n]which
was a prophet [o]mighty in deed and
word before God and all the people:

34 [x]Matt. 5.44; 1 Pet. 2.20-23
[y]Acts 3.17; 1 Tim. 1.13
[z]Ps. 22.18; John 19.24
35 [a]Ps. 22.17
38 [b]John 19.19
39 [c]Matt. 27.44
40 [d]Eph. 5.11
42 [e]Heb. 1.3
43 [f]Rev. 2.7
44 [g]Matt. 27.45; [3]Or, land
45 [h]Matt. 27.51
46 [i]Ps. 31.5; [j]Phil. 2.8
47 [k]Matt. 27.54
49 [l]Ps. 38.11
50 [m]Matt. 27.57
51 [n]Gen. 37.21-22; [o]Gen. 49.18
53 [p]Matt. 27.59
[q]Isa. 53.9
55 [r]ch. 8.2
[s]Mark 15.47
56 [t]Mark 16.1
[u]Gen. 2.3

CHAPTER 24
1 [a]Matt. 28.1;
[b]ch. 23.56
3 [c]Mark 16.5
4 [d]Gen. 18.2
5 [1]Or, him that liveth
6 [e]Matt. 16.21
8 [f]John 2.22
9 [g]Matt. 28.8
10 [h]ch. 8.3
12 [i]John 20.3
14 [j]Deut. 6.7
15 [k]Matt. 18.20
16 [l]John 20.14
18 [m]John 19.25
19 [n]John 3.2;
[o]Acts 7.22

20 And [p]how the chief priests and
our rulers delivered him to be condemned to death, and have crucified
him.
21 But we trusted [q]that it had been
he which should have redeemed Is'ra-
el: and beside all this, to day is the
third day since these things were done.
22 Yea, and certain women also
of our company made us astonished,
which were early at the sepulchre;
23 And when they found not his
body, they came, saying, that they had
also seen a vision of angels, which said
that he was alive.
24 And certain of them which were
with us went to the sepulchre, and
found *it* even so as the women had
said: but him they saw not.
25 Then he said unto them, O fools,
and slow of heart to believe all that the
prophets have spoken:
26 [r]Ought not Christ to have suffered these things, and to enter into his
glory?
27 And beginning at [s]Mō'ses and
[t]all the prophets, he expounded unto
them in all the scriptures the things
concerning himself.
28 And they drew nigh unto the village, whither they went: and [u]he made
as though he would have gone further.
29 But they constrained him, saying, Abide with us: for it is toward evening, and the day is far spent. And he
went in to tarry with them.
30 And it came to pass, as he sat at
meat with them, he took bread, and
blessed *it,* and brake, and gave to
them.
31 And their eyes were opened, and
they knew him; and he [2]vanished out
of their sight.
32 And they said one to another,
Did not our heart burn within us, while
he talked with us by the way, and
while he opened to us the scriptures?
33 And they rose up the same hour,
and returned to Je-ru'sa-lĕm, and found
the eleven gathered together, and them
that were with them,
34 Saying, The Lord is risen indeed,
and [v]hath appeared to Sī'mon.
35 And they told what things *were*
done in the way, and how he was
known of them in breaking of bread.

20 [p]Acts 13.27
21 [q]Acts 1.6
26 [r]Ps. 22; Isa. 53; Acts 17.3; 1 Cor. 15.3-4; Phil. 2.6-11; Heb. 2.8-10; 1 Pet. 1.11
27 [s]Gen. 3.15; Gen. 22.18; Gen. 26.4; Gen. 49.10; Num. 21.9; Deut. 18.15 [t]Ps. 22; Ps. 132.11; Isa. 7.14; Isa. 9.6; Isa. 40.10; Isa. 50.6; Isa. 53; Jer. 23.5; Jer. 33.14; Ezek. 34.23; Ezek. 37.25; Dan. 9.24; Mic. 7.20; Mal. 3.1; Mal. 4.2; John 1.45
28 [u]Gen. 19.2; Gen. 32.26
31 [2]Or, ceased to be seen of them
34 [v]1 Cor. 15.5
43 [w]Acts 10.41
44 [x]Matt. 16.21
45 [y]Mark 9.31; Acts 16.14; 2 Cor. 4.6
47 [z]Dan. 9.24 [a]Gen. 12.3; Ps. 22.27; Isa. 49.6; Jer. 31.34; Hos. 2.23; Mic. 4.2; Mal. 1.11; Gal. 3.14
48 [b]John 15.27; Acts 1.22
49 [c]Isa. 44.3; Joel 2.28; Acts 2.1
51 [d]Eph. 1.20
53 [e]Acts 2.46

36 ¶ And as they thus spake, Jē'sus
himself stood in the midst of them, and
saith unto them, Peace *be* unto you.
37 But they were terrified and affrighted, and supposed that they had
seen a spirit.
38 And he said unto them, Why are
ye troubled? and why do thoughts arise
in your hearts?
39 Behold my hands and my feet,
that it is I myself: handle me, and see;
for a spirit hath not flesh and bones, as
ye see me have.
40 And when he had thus spoken,
he shewed them *his* hands and *his* feet.
41 And while they yet believed not
for joy, and wondered, he said unto
them, Have ye here any meat?
42 And they gave him a piece of a
broiled fish, and of an honeycomb.
43 [w]And he took *it,* and did eat before them.
44 And he said unto them, [x]These
are the words which I spake unto you,
while I was yet with you, that all things
must be fulfilled, which were written
in the law of Mō'ses, and *in* the prophets, and *in* the psalms, concerning me.
45 Then [y]opened he their understanding, that they might understand
the scriptures,
46 And said unto them, Thus it is
written, and thus it behoved Christ to
suffer, and to rise from the dead the
third day:
47 And that repentance and [z]remis-
sion of sins should be preached in his
name [a]among all nations, beginning
at Je-ru'sa-lĕm.
48 And [b]ye are witnesses of these
things.
49 ¶ [c]And, behold, I send the promise of my Father upon you: but tarry ye
in the city of Je-ru'sa-lĕm, until ye be
endued with power from on high.
50 ¶ And he led them out as far as to
Bĕth'ă-nȳ, and he lifted up his hands,
and blessed them.
51 [d]And it came to pass, while he
blessed them, he was parted from them,
and carried up into heaven.
52 And they worshipped him, and returned to Je-ru'sa-lĕm with great joy:
53 And were continually [e]in the temple, praising and blessing God. Amen.

THE GOSPEL ACCORDING TO

JOHN

Life's Questions

Why should I believe in Jesus?
How do I know what the truth is?
Does anyone love me?

God's Answers

Perhaps about A.D. 90 God let the elderly disciple John to give the churches near Ephesus he had so faithfully served information in writing that would lead people to believe that Jesus Christ is God's Son and so have life. John wrote the Gospel, three letters, and Revelation to help the church understand the way to be faithful in a world of persecution, ridicule, and religious competition.

John's Gospel used seven signs to show: Jesus the incarnate Word of God came as God's sacrificial lamb and Israel's King (ch. 1); miraculous signs show faith that Jesus reveals the way to life in God's love (2—12); the sacrifice on the cross and the resurrection show God's humble servant Jesus is the promised King of Israel (13—20); the church has a missionary and a pastoral task as it witnesses to Jesus (ch. 21).

John calls us to confess Jesus openly as the truth and life, to let Jesus feed us the truth we need, to complete the pastoral task by loving others and worshiping Him, and to follow the Holy Spirit in witnessing to others.

1 In the beginning [a]was the Word,
and the Word was with God, and
[b]the Word was God.
2 The same was in the beginning
with God.
3 All things were made by him; and
without him was not any thing made
that was made.
4 In him was life; and the life was
the light of men.
5 And [c]the light shineth in darkness; and the darkness comprehended
it not.
6 ¶ [d]There was a man sent from
God, whose name *was* Jŏhn.
7 The same came for a witness, to
bear witness of the Light, that all *men*
through him might believe.
8 [e]He was not that Light, but *was*
sent to bear witness of that Light.
9 [f]*That* was the true Light, which
lighteth every man that cometh into
the world.
10 He was in the world, and [g]the
world was made by him, and the world
knew him not.
11 [h]He came unto his own, and his
own received him not.
12 But [i]as many as received him, to
them gave he [1]power to become the
sons of GOD, *even* to them that believe
on his name:
13 Which were born, not of blood,
nor of the will of the flesh, nor of the
will of man, [j]but of God.
14 [k]And the Word [l]was made [m]flesh,
and dwelt among us, (and [n]we beheld
his glory, the glory as of the only begotten of the Father,) [o]full of grace and
truth.
15 ¶ Jŏhn bare witness of him, and
cried, saying, This was he of whom I
spake, He that cometh after me is preferred before me: [p]for he was before
me.
16 And of his [q]fulness have all we
received, and grace for grace.
17 For [r]the law was given by Mō'-
ses, *but* [s]grace and [t]truth came by
Jē'sus Chrīst.
18 [u]No man hath seen God at any
time; [v]the only begotten Son, which is
in [w]the bosom of the Father, he hath
declared *him*.
19 ¶ And this is the record of Jŏhn,
when the Jews sent priests and Lē'-
vītes from Je-ru'sa-lĕm to ask him,
Who art thou?
20 And he confessed, and denied
not; but confessed, I am not the Chrīst.
21 And they asked him, What then?
Art thou [x]E-lī'ăs? And he saith, [y]I am
not. Art thou [2]that prophet? And he answered, No.

CHAPTER 1
1 [a]Rev. 19.13
[b]Isa. 9.6;
Phil. 2.6
5 [c]ch. 3.19
6 [d]Mal. 3.1
8 [e]Acts 13.25
9 [f]Isa. 49.6
10 [g]Ps. 33.6;
1 Cor. 8.6
11 [h]Luke
19.14
12 [i]Isa. 56.5;
Rom. 8.15;
2 Pet. 1.4
[1]Or, the right,
or, privilege
13 [j]Deut.
30.6;
Jas. 1.18
14 [k]Matt.
1.20;
1 Tim. 3.16
[l]Rom. 1.3
[m]Heb. 2.14
[n]Isa. 40.5;
Matt. 17.2
[o]Col. 2.3
15 [p]Col. 1.17
16 [q]Eph. 1.6
17 [r]Ex. 20.1
[s]Rom. 5.21
[t]ch. 14.6
18 [u]Ex. 33.20
[v]1 John 4.9
[w]Prov. 8.30
21 [x]Mal. 4.5
[y]Luke 1.17
[2]Or, a
prophet
23 [z]Isa. 40.3
26 [a]Mal. 3.1
29 [b]Ex. 12.3;
Isa. 53.7;
1 Pet. 1.19;
Rev. 5.6
[c]1 Cor. 15.3;
Gal. 1.4; Heb.
1.3; Heb.
2.17; Heb.
9.28; 1 John
2.2;
Rev. 1.5
[3]Or, beareth
33 [d]ch. 14.26;
ch. 20.22;
Acts 1.5; Acts
2.4; Acts 4.8-
31; Acts 6.3-
5-8;
Acts 7.55
38 [4]Or,
abidest
39 [5]That was
two hours be-
fore night

22 Then said they unto him, Who art
thou? that we may give an answer to
them that sent us. What sayest thou of
thyself?
23 He said, I *am* the voice of one crying in the wilderness, Make straight
the way of the Lord, as [z]said the
prophet E-sā'ias.
24 And they which were sent were
of the Phăr'ĭ-sees.
25 And they asked him, and said
unto him, Why baptizest thou then, if
thou be not that Chrīst, nor E-lī'ăs, neither that prophet?
26 Jŏhn answered them, saying, I
baptize with water: [a]but there standeth one among you, whom ye know
not;
27 He it is, who coming after me
is preferred before me, whose shoe's
latchet I am not worthy to unloose.
28 These things were done in Bĕth-
ăb'ă-rȧ beyond Jôr'dan, where Jŏhn
was baptizing.
29 ¶ The next day Jŏhn seeth Jē'sus
coming unto him, and saith, Behold
[b]the Lamb of God, [c]which [3]taketh
away the sin of the world.
30 This is he of whom I said, After
me cometh a man which is preferred
before me: for he was before me.
31 And I knew him not: but that he
should be made manifest to Is'ra-el,
therefore am I come baptizing with
water.
32 And Jŏhn bare record, saying, I
saw the Spirit descending from heaven
like a dove, and it abode upon him.
33 And I knew him not: but he that
sent me to baptize with water, the
same said unto me, Upon whom thou
shalt see the Spirit descending, and remaining on him, [d]the same is he which
baptizeth with the Hō'lȳ Ghōst.
34 And I saw, and bare record that
this is the Son of God.
35 ¶ Again the next day after Jŏhn
stood, and two of his disciples;
36 And looking upon Jē'sus as he
walked, he saith, Behold the Lamb of
God!
37 And the two disciples heard him
speak, and they followed Jē'sus.
38 Then Jē'sus turned, and saw them
following, and saith unto them, What
seek ye? They said unto him, Răb'bī,
(which is to say, being interpreted,
Master,) where [4]dwellest thou?
39 He saith unto them, Come and
see. They came and saw where he
dwelt, and abode with him that day:
for it was [5]about the tenth hour.

40 One of the two which heard Jŏhn *speak*, and followed him, was Ăn'drew, Sī'mon Pē'têr's brother.

41 He first findeth his own brother [e]Sī'mon, and saith unto him, We have found the Mĕs-sī'as, which is, being interpreted, [6]the Chrĭst.

42 And he brought him to Jē'sus. And when Jē'sus beheld him, he said, Thou art Sī'mon the son of Jō'nȧ: thou shalt be called Çē'phas, which is by interpretation, [7]A stone.

43 ¶ The day following Jē'sus would go forth into Găl'ĭ-lee, and findeth Phĭl'ĭp, and saith unto him, Follow me.

44 Now [f]Phĭl'ĭp was of Bĕth-sā'ĭ-dȧ, the city of Ăn'drew and Pē'têr.

45 Phĭl'ĭp findeth [g]Na-thăn'a-el, and saith unto him, We have found him, of whom [h]Mō'ses in the law, and the [i]prophets, did write, Jē'sus of Năz'a-rĕth, the son of Jō'seph.

46 And Na-thăn'a-el said unto him, Can there any good thing come out of Năz'a-rĕth? Phĭl'ĭp saith unto him, Come and see.

47 Jē'sus saw Na-thăn'a-el coming to him, and saith of him, Behold an Ĭs'ra-el-īte indeed, in whom is no guile!

48 Na-thăn'a-el saith unto him, Whence knowest thou me? Jē'sus answered and said unto him, Before that Phĭl'ĭp called thee, when thou wast under the fig tree, I saw thee.

49 Na-thăn'a-el answered and saith unto him, Răb'bī, thou art the Son of God; thou art [j]the King of Is'ra-el.

50 Jē'sus answered and said unto him, Because I said unto thee, I saw thee under the fig tree, believest thou? thou shalt see greater things than these.

51 And he saith unto him, Verily, verily, I say unto you, [k]Hereafter ye shall see heaven open, and the angels of God ascending and descending upon [l]the Son of man.

2 And the third day there was a marriage in Cā'nȧ of Găl'ĭ-lee; and the mother of Jē'sus was there:

2 And both Jē'sus was called, and his disciples, to the marriage.

3 And when they wanted wine, the mother of Jē'sus saith unto him, They have no wine.

4 Jē'sus saith unto her, [a]Woman, what [b]have I to do with thee? [c]mine hour is not yet come.

5 His mother saith unto the servants, Whatsoever he saith unto you, do *it*.

6 And there were set there six waterpots of stone, [d]after the manner of the purifying of the Jews, containing two or three firkins apiece.

7 Jē'sus saith unto them, Fill the waterpots with water. And they filled them up to the brim.

8 And he saith unto them, Draw out now, and bear unto the governor of the feast. And they bare *it*.

9 When the ruler of the feast had tasted [e]the water that was made wine, and knew not whence it was: (but the servants which drew the water knew;) the governor of the feast called the bridegroom,

10 And saith unto him, Every man at the beginning doth set forth good wine; and when men have well drunk, then that which is worse: *but* thou hast kept the good wine until now.

11 This beginning of miracles did Jē'sus in [f]Cā'nȧ of Găl'ĭ-lee, [g]and manifested forth his glory; and his disciples believed on him.

12 ¶ After this he went down to Ca-pêr'na-ŭm, he, and his mother, and [h]his brethren, and his disciples: and they continued there not many days.

13 ¶ [i]And the Jews' passover was at hand, and Jē'sus went up to Je-ru̥'sa-lĕm,

14 [j]And found in the temple those that sold oxen and sheep and doves, and the changers of money sitting:

15 And when he had made a scourge of small cords, he drove them all out of the temple, and the sheep, and the oxen; and poured out the changers' money, and overthrew the tables;

16 And said unto them that sold doves, Take these things hence; make not [k]my Father's house an house of merchandise.

17 And his disciples remembered that it was written, [l]The zeal of thine house hath eaten me up.

18 ¶ Then answered the Jews and said unto him, What sign shewest thou unto us, seeing that thou doest these things?

19 Jē'sus answered and said unto them, [m]Destroy this temple, and in three days I will raise it up.

20 Then said the Jews, Forty and six years was this temple in building, and wilt thou rear it up in three days?

21 But he spake [n]of the temple of his body.

22 When therefore he was risen from the dead, [o]his disciples remembered that he had said this unto them; and they believed the scripture, and the word which Jē'sus had said.

23 ¶ Now when he was in Je-ru̥'sa-lĕm at the passover, in the feast *day*, many believed in his name, when they saw the miracles which he did.

24 But Jē'sus did not commit himself unto them, because he knew all *men*,

25 And needed not that any should testify of man: for [p]he knew what was in man.

3 There was a man of the Phăr'ĭ-sees, named Nĭc-o-dē'mus, a ruler of the Jews:

2 The same came to Jē'sus by night, and said unto him, Răb'bī, we know that thou art a teacher come from God: for [a]no man can do these miracles that thou doest, except [b]God be with him.

3 Jē'sus answered and said unto him, Verily, verily, I say unto thee, [c]Except a man be born [1]again, he cannot see the kingdom of God.

4 Nĭc-o-dē'mus saith unto him, How can a man be born when he is old? can he enter the second time into his mother's womb, and be born?

---

41 [e]Matt. 4.18
[6]Or, the Anointed
42 [7]Or, Peter
44 [f]ch. 12.21
45 [g]ch. 21.2
[h]Gen. 3.15; Deut. 18.15
[i]Ps. 16.9; Mal. 3.1
49 [j]Matt. 21.5; ch. 19.14-19
51 [k]Gen. 28.12
[l]Dan. 7.13

CHAPTER 2
4 [a]ch. 19.26
[b]2 Sam. 16.10; Gal. 2.5-6
[c]Eccl. 3.1; ch. 12.23
6 [d]Mark 7.3; Heb. 10.22
9 [e]ch. 4.46
11 [f]Josh. 19.28
[g]Deut. 5.24; ch. 1.14
12 [h]Matt. 12.46
13 [i]Ex. 12.14
14 [j]Matt. 21.12
16 [k]Ps. 93.5
17 [l]Ps. 69.9
19 [m]Matt. 26.61
21 [n]Matt. 26.61
22 [o]Luke 24.8
25 [p]1 Sam. 16.7

CHAPTER 3
2 [a]ch. 5.36;
[b]Acts 10.38
3 [c]ch. 1.13; [1]Or, from above

5 Jē'sus answered, Verily, verily, I
say unto thee, [d]Except a man be born
of water and *of* the Spirit, he cannot
enter into the kingdom of God.
6 That which is born of the flesh is
flesh; and that which is born of the
Spirit is spirit.
7 Marvel not that I said unto thee,
Ye must be born [2]again.
8 [e]The wind bloweth where it listeth, and thou hearest the sound thereof,
but canst not tell whence it cometh, and
whither it goeth: so is every one that is
born of the Spirit.
9 Nĭc-o-dē'mus answered and said
unto him, [f]How can these things be?
10 Jē'sus answered and said unto
him, Art thou a master of Is'ra-el, and
knowest not these things?
11 Verily, verily, I say unto thee, We
speak that we do know, and testify that
we have seen; and ye receive not our
witness.
12 If I have told you earthly things,
and ye believe not, how shall ye believe, if I tell you *of* heavenly things?
13 And [g]no man hath ascended up
to heaven, but he that came down from
heaven, *even* the Son of man which is
in heaven.
14 ¶ [h]And as Mō'ses lifted up the serpent in the wilderness, even so must
the Son of man be lifted up:
15 That whosoever believeth in him
should not perish, but have eternal life.
16 ¶ [i]For God so loved the world,
that he gave his only begotten Son, that
whosoever believeth in him should not
perish, but have everlasting life.
17 [j]For God sent not his Son into the
world to condemn the world; but that
the world through him might be saved.
18 ¶ [k]He that believeth on him is not
condemned: but he that believeth not is
condemned already, because he hath
not believed in the name of the only
begotten Son of God.
19 And this is the condemnation,
[l]that light is come into the world, and
men loved darkness rather than light,
because their deeds were evil.
20 For every one that doeth evil hateth the light, neither cometh to the light,
lest his deeds should be [3]reproved.
21 But he that doeth truth cometh to
the light, that his deeds may be made
manifest, that they are wrought in God.
22 ¶ After these things came Jē'sus
and his disciples into the land of Jū-
dæ'ȧ; and there he tarried with them,
[m]and baptized.
23 ¶ And Jŏhn also was baptizing in
Æ'non near to [n]Sā'lim, because there
was much water there: and they came,
and were baptized.
24 For [o]Jŏhn was not yet cast into
prison.
25 ¶ Then there arose a question between *some* of Jŏhn's disciples and the
Jews about purifying.
26 And they came unto Jŏhn, and
said unto him, Răb'bī, he that was with
thee beyond Jôr'dan, [p]to whom thou
barest witness, behold, the same baptizeth, and all *men* come to him.
27 Jŏhn answered and said, [q]A man
can [4]receive nothing, except it be given
him from heaven.
28 Ye yourselves bear me witness,
that I said, I am not the Chrīst, but
[r]that I am sent before him.
29 [s]He that hath the bride is the
bridegroom: but [t]the friend of the
bridegroom, which standeth and heareth him, rejoiceth greatly because of
the bridgroom's voice: this my joy
therefore is fulfilled.
30 [u]He must increase, [v]but I *must*
decrease.
31 [w]He that cometh from above [x]is
above all: [y]he that is of the earth is
earthly, and speaketh of the earth: [z]he
that cometh from heaven is above all.
32 And [a]what he hath seen and
heard, that he testifieth; and no man
receiveth his testimony.
33 He that hath received his testimony [b]hath set to his seal that God is
true.
34 [c]For he whom God hath sent
speaketh the words of God: for God
giveth not the Spirit [d]by measure *unto
him.*
35 [e]The Father loveth the Son, and
hath given all things into his hand.
36 [f]He that believeth on the Son
hath everlasting life: and he that believeth not the Son shall not see life;
but [g]the wrath of God abideth on him.
4 When therefore the Lord knew how
the Phăr'ĭ-sees had heard that Jē'-
sus made and baptized more disciples
than Jŏhn,
2 (Though Jē'sus himself baptized
not, but his disciples,)
3 He left Jū-dæ'ȧ, and departed again
into Găl'ĭ-lee.
4 And he must needs go through
Sa-mā'rĭ-ȧ.
5 Then cometh he to a city of Sa-
mā'rĭ-ȧ, which is called Sȳ'char, near
to the parcel of ground [a]that Jā'cob
gave to his son Jō'seph.
6 Now Jā'cob's well was there. Jē'-
sus therefore, being wearied with *his*
journey, sat thus on the well: *and* it
was about the sixth hour.
7 There cometh a woman of Sa-
mā'rĭ-ȧ to draw water: Jē'sus saith
unto her, Give me to drink.
8 (For his disciples were gone away
unto the city to buy meat.)
9 Then saith the woman of Sa-mā'-
rĭ-ȧ unto him, How is it that thou, being
a Jew, askest drink of me, which am a
woman of Sa-mā'rĭ-ȧ? for [b]the Jews
have no dealings with the Sa-măr'ĭ-
tans.
10 Jē'sus answered and said unto
her, If thou knewest [c]the gift of God,
and who it is that saith to thee, Give me
to drink; thou wouldest have asked of
him, and he would have given thee [d]liv-
ing water.
11 The woman saith unto him, Sir,
thou hast nothing to draw with, and
the well is deep: from whence then
hast thou that living water?
12 Art thou greater than our father
Jā'cob, which gave us the well, and

5 [d]Isa. 44.3-4; 1 Pet. 3.21
7 [2]Or, from above
8 [e]Eccl. 11.5; 1 Cor. 2.11
9 [f]ch. 6.52
13 [g]Prov. 30.4; Eph. 4.9
14 [h]Num. 21.9; ch. 8.28
16 [i]Luke 2.14; Tit. 3.4
17 [j]Luke 9.56; 1 John 4.14
18 [k]Rom. 8.1
19 [l]Isa. 5.20; ch. 1.4
20 [3]Or, discovered
22 [m]ch. 4.2
23 [n]Gen. 14.18; 1 Sam. 9.4
24 [o]Matt. 14.3; Luke 3.19-20
26 [p]ch. 1.34
27 [q]Heb. 5.4; Jas. 1.17 [4]Or, take unto himself
28 [r]Mal. 3.1; Luke 3.4-6
29 [s]Matt. 22.2; Rev. 21.9 [t]Song 5.1
30 [u]Isa. 9.7 [v]Phil. 3.8-9
31 [w]ch. 8.23 [x]Matt. 28.18; Rom. 9.5 [y]1 Cor. 15.47 [z]Eph. 1.21
32 [a]ch. 15.15
33 [b]2 Cor. 1.22
34 [c]ch. 7.16 [d]ch. 1.16; Col. 1.19
35 [e]Dan. 7.14
36 [f]Hab. 2.4; Rom. 1.17 [g]Gal. 3.10

CHAPTER 4
5 [a]Gen. 33.19; Josh. 24.32
9 [b]2 Ki. 17.24;
10 [c]Isa. 9.6; [d]Ex. 17.6;

drank thereof himself, and his children, and his cattle?
13 Jē'sus answered and said unto
her, Whosoever drinketh of this water
shall thirst again:
14 But [e]whosoever drinketh of the
water that I shall give him shall never
thirst; but the water that I shall give
him [f]shall be in him a well of water
springing up into everlasting life.
15 [g]The woman saith unto him, Sir,
give me this water, that I thirst not,
neither come hither to draw.
16 Jē'sus saith unto her, Go, call thy
husband, and come hither.
17 The woman answered and said, I
have no husband. Jē'sus said unto her,
Thou hast well said, I have no husband:
18 For thou hast had five husbands;
and he whom thou now hast is not thy
husband: in that saidst thou truly.
19 The woman saith unto him, Sir,
[h]I perceive that thou art a prophet.
20 Our fathers worshipped [i]in this
mountain; and ye say, that in [j]Je-rụ'sa-
lĕm is the place where men ought to
worship.
21 Jē'sus saith unto her, Woman, believe me, the hour cometh, [k]when ye
shall neither in this mountain, nor yet
at Je-rụ'sa-lĕm, worship the Father.
22 Ye worship [l]ye know not what:
we know what we worship: for [m]salva-
tion is of the Jews.
23 But the hour cometh, and now is,
when the true worshippers shall worship the Father in [n]spirit [o]and in truth:
for the Father seeketh such to worship
him.
24 [p]God *is* a Spirit: and they that
worship him must worship *him* in spirit
and in truth.
25 The woman saith unto him, I
know that [q]Mĕs-sī'as cometh, which is
called Chrīst: when he is come, he will
tell us all things.
26 Jē'sus saith unto her, [r]I that speak
unto thee am *he*.
27 ¶ And upon this came his disciples, and marvelled that he talked with
the woman: yet no man said, What
seekest thou? or, Why talkest thou
with her?
28 The woman then left her wa-
terpot, and went her way into the city,
and saith to the men,
29 Come, see a man, which told me
all things that ever I did: is not this the
Chrīst?
30 Then they went out of the city,
and came unto him.
31 ¶ In the mean while his disciples
prayed him, saying, Master, eat.
32 But he said unto them, I have
meat to eat that ye know not of.
33 Therefore said the disciples one
to another, Hath any man brought him
ought to eat?
34 Jē'sus saith unto them, [s]My meat
is to do the will of him that sent me,
and to finish his work.
35 Say not ye, There are yet four
months, and *then* cometh harvest? behold, I say unto you, Lift up your eyes,
and look on the fields; [t]for they are
white already to harvest.
36 [u]And he that reapeth receiveth
wages, and gathereth fruit unto life
eternal: that both he that soweth and
he that reapeth may rejoice together.
37 And herein is that saying true,
One soweth, and another reapeth.
38 I sent you to reap that whereon
ye bestowed no labour: [v]other men laboured, and ye are entered into their
labours.
39 ¶ [w]And many of the Sa-măr'ĭ-
tans of that city believed on him for the
saying of the woman, which testified,
He told me all that ever I did.
40 [x]So when the Sa-măr'ĭ-tans were
come unto him, they besought him that
he would tarry with them: and he
abode there two days.
41 [y]And many more believed because of his own word;
42 And said unto the woman, Now
we believe, not because of thy saying:
for [z]we have heard *him* ourselves, and
know that this is indeed the Chrīst,
[a]the Saviour of the world.
43 ¶ Now after two days he departed
thence, and went into Găl'ĭ-lee.
44 For [b]Jē'sus himself testified, that
a prophet hath no honour in his own
country.
45 Then when he was come into Găl'-
ĭ-lee, the Găl-ĭ-læ'ans received him,
[c]having seen all the things that he did
at Je-rụ'sa-lĕm at the feast: [d]for they
also went unto the feast.
46 So Jē'sus came again into Cā'nȧ
of Găl'ĭ-lee, [e]where he made the water
wine. And there was a certain [1]noble-
man, whose son was sick at Ca-pêr'-
na-ŭm.
47 When he heard that Jē'sus was
come out of Jŭ-dæ'ȧ into Găl'ĭ-lee, he
went unto him, and besought him that
he would come down, and heal his son:
for he was at the point of death.
48 Then said Jē'sus unto him, [f]Ex-
cept ye see signs and wonders, ye will
not believe.
49 The nobleman saith unto him,
Sir, come down ere my child die.
50 Jē'sus saith unto him, [g]Go thy
way; thy son liveth. And the man believed the word that Jē'sus had spoken
unto him, and he went his way.
51 And as he was now going down,
his servants met him, and told *him*, saying, Thy son liveth.
52 Then inquired he of them the
hour when he began to amend. And
they said unto him, Yesterday at the
seventh hour the fever left him.
53 So the father knew that *it was* at
the same hour, in the which Jē'sus said
unto him, Thy son liveth: and himself
[h]believed, and his whole house.
54 This *is* again the second miracle
that Jē'sus did, when he was come out
of Jŭ-dæ'ȧ into Găl'ĭ-lee.

5 After [a]this there was a feast of
the Jews; and Jē'sus went up to
Je-rụ'sa-lĕm.
2 Now there is at Je-rụ'sa-lĕm [b]by
the sheep [1]*market* a pool, which is

14 [e]ch. 6.35
[f]ch. 7.38
15 [g]Rom. 6.23; 1 John 5.20
19 [h]Luke 7.16
20 [i]Gen. 12.6; Judg. 9.7
[j]Deut. 12.5; 2 Chr. 7.12
21 [k]Mal. 1.11; 1 Tim. 2.8
22 [l]2 Ki. 17.29
[m]Isa. 2.3; Rom. 9.4-5
23 [n]ch. 14.17; Phil. 3.3
[o]ch. 1.17
24 [p]Acts 17.24-29; 2 Cor. 3.17
25 [q]Deut. 18.15; Dan. 9.24
26 [r]Matt. 16.20; Rom. 10.20-21
34 [s]Job 23.12; ch. 6.38
35 [t]Matt. 9.37
36 [u]Gen. 17
38 [v]Acts 10.43
39 [w]Gen. 49.10
40 [x]Gen. 32.26
41 [y]Gen. 49.10
42 [z]ch. 17.8;
[a]Isa. 49.6
44 [b]Matt. 13.57
45 [c]ch. 2.23
[d]Deut. 16.16
46 [e]ch. 2.1-11
[1]Or, courtier, or, ruler
48 [f]Num. 14.11
50 [g]Matt. 8.13
53 [h]Acts 16.34
CHAPTER 5
1 [a]Lev. 23.2
2 [b]Neh. 3.1
[1]Or, gate

called in the Hē′brew tongue [2]Be-thĕs′-
dȧ, having five porches.
3 In these lay a great multitude of
impotent folk, of blind, halt, withered,
waiting for the moving of the water.
4 For an angel went down at a certain season into the pool, and troubled
the water: whosoever then first after
the troubling of the water stepped in
was made whole of whatsoever disease he had.
5 And a certain man was there,
which had an infirmity thirty and eight
years.
6 When Jē′sus saw him lie, [c]and
knew that he had been now a long time
in that case, he saith unto him, [d]Wilt
thou be made whole?
7 The impotent man answered him,
Sir, I have no man, when the water is
troubled, to put me into the pool: but
while I am coming, another steppeth
down before me.
8 Jē′sus saith unto him, [e]Rise, take
up thy bed, and walk.
9 And immediately the man was
made whole, and took up his bed, and
walked: and on [f]the same day was the
sabbath.
10 ¶ The Jews therefore said unto
him that was cured, It is the sabbath
day: [g]it is not lawful for thee to carry
thy bed.
11 He answered them, He that made
me whole, the same said unto me,
Take up thy bed, and walk.
12 Then asked they him, What man
is that which said unto thee, Take up
thy bed, and walk?
13 And he that was healed wist not
who it was: for Jē′sus had conveyed
himself away, [3]a multitude being in
that place.
14 Afterward Jē′sus findeth him in
the temple, and said unto him, Behold,
thou art made whole: [h]sin no more,
lest a worse thing come unto thee.
15 The man departed, and told the
Jews that it was Jē′sus, which had
made him whole.
16 And therefore did the Jews persecute Jē′sus, and sought to slay him, because he had done these things on the
sabbath day.
17 ¶ But Jē′sus answered them, [i]My
Father worketh hitherto, and I work.
18 Therefore the Jews [j]sought the
more to kill him, because he not only
had broken the sabbath, but said also
that God was his Father, [k]making himself equal with God.
19 Then answered Jē′sus and said
unto them, Verily, verily, I say unto
you, [l]The Son can do nothing of himself, but what he seeth the Father do:
for what things soever he doeth, these
also doeth the Son likewise.
20 For [m]the Father loveth the Son,
and sheweth him all things that himself
doeth: and he will shew him greater
works than these, that ye may marvel.
21 For as the Father raiseth up the
dead, and quickeneth *them;* [n]even so
the Son quickeneth whom he will.
22 For the Father judgeth no man,
but [o]hath committed all judgment unto
the Son:
23 That all *men* should [p]honour the
Son, even as they honour the Father.
He that honoureth not the Son honoureth not the Father which hath sent
him.
24 Verily, verily, I say unto you, He
that heareth my word, and believeth
on him that sent me, hath everlasting
life, and shall not come into condemnation; [q]but is passed from death unto
life.
25 Verily, verily, I say unto you, The
hour is coming, and now is, when [r]the
dead shall hear the voice of the Son of
God: and they that hear shall live.
26 For as the Father hath [s]life in
himself; so hath he given to the Son to
have life in himself;
27 And hath given him authority to
execute judgment also, [t]because he is
the Son of man.
28 Marvel not at this: for the hour is
coming, in the which all that are in the
graves shall hear his voice,
29 [u]And shall come forth; [v]they that
have done good, unto the resurrection
of life; and they that have done evil,
unto the resurrection of damnation.
30 I can of mine own self do nothing: as I hear, I judge: and my judgment is just; because [w]I seek not mine
own will, but the will of the Father
which hath sent me.
31 [x]If I bear witness of myself, my
witness is not true.
32 ¶ There is another that beareth
witness of me; and I know that the witness which he witnesseth of me is true.
33 Ye sent unto Jŏhn, [y]and he bare
witness unto the truth.
34 But I receive not testimony from
man: but these things I say, that ye
might be saved.
35 He was a burning and [z]a shining
light: and [a]ye were willing for a season to rejoice in his light.
36 ¶ But [b]I have greater witness
than *that* of Jŏhn: for [c]the works
which the Father hath given me to finish, the same works that I do, bear witness of me, that the Father hath sent
me.
37 And the Father himself, which
hath sent me, [d]hath borne witness of
me. Ye have neither heard his voice at
any time, [e]nor seen his shape.
38 And ye have not his word abiding
in you: for whom he hath sent, him ye
believe not.
39 ¶ [f]Search the scriptures; for in
them ye think ye have eternal life: and
[g]they are they which testify of me.
40 And ye will not come to me, that
ye might have life.
41 [h]I receive not honour from men.
42 But I know you, that ye have not
the love of God in you.
43 I am come in my Father's name,
and ye receive me not: if another shall
come in his own name, him ye will
receive.

[2]That is, House of mercy
6 [c]Heb. 4.13 [d]Ps. 72.13; Isa. 55.1
8 [e]Matt. 9.6; Luke 5.24
9 [f]ch. 9.14
10 [g]Ex. 20.10; Luke 6.2
13 [3]Or, from the multitude that was
14 [h]Matt. 12.45; ch. 8.11
17 [i]Gen. 2.1-2; Acts 14.17
18 [j]ch. 7.19 [k]ch. 10.30; Phil. 2.6
19 [l]ch. 8.28; Eph. 3.9
20 [m]Matt. 3.17; 2 Pet. 1.17
21 [n]Luke 7.14; ch. 11.25
22 [o]Matt. 11.27; 1 Pet. 4.5
23 [p]Matt. 28.19; Rev. 5.8
24 [q]1 John 3.14
25 [r]Gal. 2.20; Rev. 3.1
26 [s]Acts 17.31
27 [t]Dan. 7.13
29 [u]1 Cor. 15.52 [v]Dan. 12.2; 1 Pet. 3.11
30 [w]Matt. 26.39
31 [x]Isa. 55.4; Rev. 3.14
33 [y]ch. 1.15
35 [z]2 Pet. 1.19 [a]Matt. 13.20; Mark 6.20
36 [b]1 John 5.9 [c]Matt. 11.4-5; ch. 3.2
37 [d]Matt. 3.17; 1 John 5.6 [e]Deut. 4.12; 1 John 4.12
39 [f]Isa. 8.20; Acts 17.11 [g]Deut. 18.15;
41 [h]1 Thess. 2.6

44 How can ye believe, which receive honour one of another, and seek not [l]the honour that *cometh* from God only?

45 Do not think that I will accuse you to the Father: [j]there is *one* that accuseth you, *even* Mō′ses, in whom ye trust.

46 For had ye believed Mō′ses, ye would have believed me: [k]for he wrote of me.

47 But if [l]ye believe not his writings, how shall ye believe my words?

6 After [a]these things Jē′sus went over the sea of Găl′ĭ-lee, which is *the sea* of Ti-bē′rĭ-as.

2 And a great multitude followed him, because they saw his miracles which he did on them that were diseased.

3 And Jē′sus went up into a mountain, and there he sat with his disciples.

4 [b]And the passover, a feast of the Jews, was nigh.

5 ¶ [c]When Jē′sus then lifted up *his* eyes, and saw a great company come unto him, he saith unto Phĭl′ĭp, Whence shall we buy bread, that these may eat?

6 And this he said to prove him: for he himself knew what he would do.

7 Phĭl′ĭp answered him, [d]Two hundred pennyworth of bread is not sufficient for them, that every one of them may take a little.

8 One of his disciples, Ăn′drew, Sī′mon Pē′têr's brother, saith unto him,

9 There is a lad here, which hath five barley loaves, and two small fishes: [e]but what are they among so many?

10 And Jē′sus said, Make the men sit down. Now there was much grass in the place. So the men sat down, in number about five thousand.

11 And Jē′sus took the loaves; and when he had [f]given thanks, he distributed to the disciples, and the disciples to them that were set down; and likewise of the fishes as much as they would.

12 When they were filled, he said unto his disciples, Gather up the fragments that remain, that nothing be lost.

13 Therefore they gathered *them* together, and filled twelve baskets with the fragments of the five barley loaves, which remained over and above unto them that had eaten.

14 Then those men, when they had seen the miracle that Jē′sus did, said, This is of a truth [g]that prophet that should come into the world.

15 ¶ When Jē′sus therefore perceived that they would come and take him by force, to make him a king, he departed again into a mountain himself alone.

16 [h]And when even was *now* come, his disciples went down unto the sea,

17 And entered into a ship, and went over the sea toward Ca-pêr′na-ŭm. And it was now dark, and Jē′sus was not come to them.

18 And the sea arose by reason of a great wind that blew.

19 So when they had rowed about five and twenty or thirty furlongs, they see Jē′sus walking on the sea, and drawing nigh unto the ship: and they were afraid.

20 But he saith unto them, It is I; be not afraid.

21 Then they willingly received him into the ship: and immediately the ship was at the land whither they went.

22 ¶ The day following, when the people which stood on the other side of the sea saw that there was none other boat there, save that one whereinto his disciples were entered, and that Jē′sus went not with his disciples into the boat, but *that* his disciples were gone away alone;

23 (Howbeit there came other boats from Ti-bē′rĭ-as nigh unto the place where they did eat bread, after that the Lord had given thanks:)

24 When the people therefore saw that Jē′sus was not there, neither his disciples, they also took shipping, and came to Ca-pêr′na-ŭm, seeking for Jē′sus.

25 And when they had found him on the other side of the sea, they said unto him, Răb′bī, when camest thou hither?

26 Jē′sus answered them and said, Verily, verily, I say unto you, Ye seek me, not because ye saw the miracles, but because ye did eat of the loaves, and were filled.

27 [1]Labour not for the meat which perisheth, but [i]for that meat which endureth unto everlasting life, which the Son of man shall give unto you: [j]for him hath God the Father sealed.

28 Then said they unto him, What shall we do, that we might work the works of God?

29 Jē′sus answered and said unto them, [k]This is the work of God, that ye believe on him whom he hath sent.

30 They said therefore unto him, [l]What sign shewest thou then, that we may see, and believe thee? what dost thou work?

31 [m]Our fathers did eat manna in the desert; as it is written, [n]He gave them bread from heaven to eat.

32 Then Jē′sus said unto them, Verily, verily, I say unto you, Mō′ses gave you not that bread from heaven; but my Father giveth you the true bread from heaven.

33 For the bread of God is he which cometh down from heaven, and giveth life unto the world.

34 Then said they unto him, Lord, evermore give us this bread.

35 And Jē′sus said unto them, I am the bread of life: [o]he that cometh to me shall never hunger; and he that believeth on me shall never thirst.

36 But I said unto you, That ye also have seen me, and believe not.

37 All that the Father giveth me shall come to me; and [p]him that cometh to me I will in no wise cast out.

38 For I came down from heaven, [q]not to do mine own will, [r]but the will of him that sent me.

44 [i]1 Sam. 2.30; Matt. 25.21-23; Luke 19.17; Rom. 2.29
45 [j]Rom. 2.12
46 [k]Gen. 3.15; Gen. 12.3; Deut. 18.15; Acts 26.22
47 [l]Luke 16.29-31
CHAPTER 6
1 [a]Matt. 14.15; Mark 6.35; Luke 9.10
4 [b]Ex. 12.21; Lev. 23.5-7; Num. 28.16; Deut. 16.1; ch. 2.13; ch. 5.1; ch. 11.55
5 [c]Matt. 14.14; Mark 6.35; Luke 9.12
7 [d]Num. 11.21-22; 2 Ki. 4.43; Matt. 15.32-33; Mark 6.37; Mark 8.4
9 [e]2 Ki. 4.43
11 [f]Ex. 23.25; 1 Tim. 4.5
14 [g]Gen. 49.10; Deut. 18.15-18; Isa. 7.14; Isa. 9.6; Matt. 11.3; ch. 1.21; ch. 4.19
16 [h]Matt. 14.23; Mark 6.47
27 [1]Or, Work not
[i]ch. 4.14; Rom. 6.23
[j]Matt. 3.17; 2 Pet. 1.17
29 [k]1 John 3.23
30 [l]Matt. 12.38; 1 Cor. 1.22
31 [m]Ex. 16.15; 1 Cor. 10.3
[n]Neh. 9.15; Rev. 2.17
35 [o]ch. 4.14; Rev. 22.17
37 [p]Job 8.20; 1 John 2.19
38 [q]Matt. 26.39; ch. 5.30
[r]Luke 22.42; ch. 5.30

39 And this is the Father's will which hath sent me, [s]that of all which he hath given me I should lose nothing, but should raise it up again at the last day.

40 And this is the will of him that sent me, [t]that every one which seeth the Son, and believeth on him, may have everlasting life: and I will raise him up at the last day.

41 The Jews then murmured at him, because he said, I am the bread which came down from heaven.

42 And they said, Is not this Jē′sus, the son of Jō′seph, whose father and mother we know? how is it then that he saith, I came down from heaven?

43 Jē′sus therefore answered and said unto them, Murmur not among yourselves.

44 No man can come to me, except the Father which hath sent me draw him: and I will raise him up at the last day.

45 [u]It is written in the prophets, And they shall be all taught of God. Every man therefore that hath heard, and hath learned of the Father, cometh unto me.

46 [v]Not that any man hath seen the Father, save [w]he which is of God, he hath seen the Father.

47 Verily, verily, I say unto you, [x]He that believeth on me hath everlasting life.

48 I am that bread of life.

49 Your fathers did eat manna in the wilderness, and are dead.

50 This is the bread which cometh down from heaven, that a man may eat thereof, and not die.

51 I am the living bread which came down from heaven: if any man eat of this bread, he shall live for ever: and [y]the bread that I will give is my flesh, which I will give for the life of the world.

52 The Jews therefore [z]strove among themselves, saying, [a]How can this man give us *his* flesh to eat?

53 Then Jē′sus said unto them, Verily, verily, I say unto you, Except [b]ye eat the flesh of the Son of man, and drink his blood, ye have no life in you.

54 Whoso eateth my flesh, and drinketh my blood, hath eternal life; and I will raise him up at the last day.

55 For my flesh is meat indeed, and my blood is drink indeed.

56 He that eateth my flesh, and drinketh my blood, [c]dwelleth in me, and I in him.

57 As the living Father hath sent me, and I live by the Father: so he that eateth me, even he shall live by me.

58 This is that bread which came down from heaven: not as your fathers did eat manna, and are dead: he that eateth of this bread shall live for ever.

59 These things said he in the synagogue, as he taught in Ca-pēr′na-ŭm.

60 [d]Many therefore of his disciples, when they had heard *this,* said, This is an hard saying; who can hear it?

61 When Jē′sus knew in himself that his disciples murmured at it, he said unto them, Doth this offend you?

62 [e]*What* and if ye shall see the Son of man ascend up where he was before?

63 [f]It is the spirit that quickeneth; the flesh profiteth nothing: the words that I speak unto you, *they* [g]are spirit, and *they* are life.

64 But there are some of you that believe not. For [h]Jē′sus knew from the beginning who they were that believed not, and who should betray him.

65 And he said, Therefore said I unto you, that no man can come unto me, except it were given unto him of my Father.

66 ¶ From that *time* many of his disciples [i]went back, and walked no more with him.

67 Then said Jē′sus unto the twelve, Will ye also go away?

68 Then Sī′mon Pē′tēr answered him, Lord, to whom shall we go? thou hast the words of eternal life.

69 And we believe and are sure that thou art that Chrīst, the Son of the living God.

70 Jē′sus answered them, Have not I chosen you twelve, and one of you is a devil?

71 He spake of Jū′das Ĭs-căr′ĭ-ot *the son* of Sī′mon: for he it was that should betray him, being one of the twelve.

7 After these things Jē′sus walked in Găl′ĭ-lee: for he would not walk in Jew′ry̆, [a]because the Jews sought to kill him.

2 [b]Now the Jews' feast of tabernacles was at hand.

3 His [c]brethren therefore said unto him, Depart hence, and go into Jū-dæ′ȧ, that thy disciples also may see the works that thou doest.

4 For *there is* no man *that* doeth any thing in secret, and he himself seeketh to be known openly. If thou do these things, shew thyself to the world.

5 For [d]neither did his brethren believe in him.

6 Then Jē′sus said unto them, [e]My time is not yet come: but your time is alway ready.

7 [f]The world cannot hate you; but me it hateth, [g]because I testify of it, that the works thereof are evil.

8 Go ye up unto this feast: I go not up yet unto this feast; [h]for my time is not yet full come.

9 When he had said these words unto them, he abode *still* in Găl′ĭ-lee.

10 ¶ But when his brethren were gone up, then went he also up unto the feast, not openly, but as it were in secret.

11 Then [i]the Jews sought him at the feast, and said, Where is he?

12 And [j]there was much murmuring among the people concerning him: for [k]some said, He is a good man: others said, Nay; but he deceiveth the people.

13 Howbeit no man spake openly of him for fear of the Jews.

39 [s]ch. 5.24; ch. 10.28; ch. 17.12; ch. 18.9; Col. 3.3; Jude 1
40 [t]ch. 4.14
45 [u]Isa. 54.13; Jer. 31.34; Mic. 4.2; Heb. 8.10
46 [v]ch. 1.18; ch. 5.37
[w]Matt. 11.27; Luke 10.22; ch. 1.18; ch. 7.29; 2 Cor. 4.6
47 [x]ch. 3.16
51 [y]Heb. 10.5-10
52 [z]ch. 7.43; ch. 9.16
[a]ch. 3.9
53 [b]Matt. 26.26
56 [c]Isa. 57.15; ch. 14.23; Rom. 8.9; 1 Cor. 3.16; 1 Cor. 6.17; 2 Cor. 6.16; Eph. 3.17; Eph. 5.30; 2 Tim. 1.14; 1 John 3.24; Rev. 3.20
60 [d]Matt. 11.6
62 [e]Mark 16.19; ch. 3.13; Acts 1.9; Eph. 4.8
63 [f]Rom. 8.2; 1 Cor. 15.45; 2 Cor. 3.6
[g]Ps. 119.50; Eph. 1.17; 1 Thess. 2.13; Heb. 4.12
64 [h]Matt. 9.4; ch. 2.24; ch. 13.11; Acts 15.18; Rev. 2.23
66 [i]Luke 9.62; Heb. 6.4-6; 1 John 2.19

CHAPTER 7
1 [a]ch. 5.16; ch. 17.1
2 [b]Lev. 23.34
3 [c]Matt. 12.46; Gal. 1.19
5 [d]Mark 3.21
6 [e]Eccl. 3.1-2; Acts 1.7
7 [f]ch. 15.19
[g]ch. 3.19
8 [h]ch. 8.20
11 [i]ch. 11.56
12 [j]ch. 9.16
[k]Matt. 21.46; ch. 6.14

14 ¶ Now about the midst of the
feast Jē′sus went up into the temple,
and taught.
15 [l]And the Jews marvelled, saying,
How knoweth this man [1]letters, having
never learned?
16 Jē′sus answered them, and said,
[m]My doctrine is not mine, but his that
sent me.
17 [n]If any man will do his will, he
shall know of the doctrine, whether it
be of God, or *whether* I speak of myself.
18 [o]He that speaketh of himself seeketh his own glory: but he that seeketh
his glory that sent him, the same is true,
and no unrighteousness is in him.
19 [p]Did not Mō′ses give you the
law, and *yet* none of you keepeth the
law? [q]Why go ye about to kill me?
20 The people answered and said,
[r]Thou hast a devil: who goeth about to
kill thee?
21 Jē′sus answered and said unto
them, I have done one work, and ye all
marvel.
22 [s]Mō′ses therefore gave unto you
circumcision; (not because it is of Mō′-
ses, [t]but of the fathers;) and ye on the
sabbath day circumcise a man.
23 If a man on the sabbath day receive circumcision, [2]that the law of
Mō′ses should not be broken; are ye
angry at me, because [u]I have made a
man every whit whole on the sabbath
day?
24 [v]Judge not according to the appearance, but judge righteous judgment.
25 Then said some of them of Je-
ru′sa-lĕm, Is not this he, whom they
seek to kill?
26 But, lo, he speaketh boldly, and
they say nothing unto him. Do the rulers know indeed that this is the very
Chrīst?
27 Howbeit we know this man
whence he is: but when Chrīst cometh,
no man knoweth whence he is.
28 Then cried Jē′sus in the temple
as he taught, saying, [w]Ye both know
me, and ye know whence I am: and [x]I
am not come of myself, but he that sent
me [y]is true, whom ye [z]know not.
29 But [a]I know him: for I am from
him, and he hath sent me.
30 Then they sought to take him:
but no man laid hands on him, because
his hour was not yet come.
31 And many of the people believed
on him, and said, When Chrīst cometh,
will he do more miracles than these
which this *man* hath done?
32 ¶ The Phăr′ĭ-sees heard that the
people murmured such things concerning him; and the Phăr′ĭ-sees and the
chief priests sent officers to take him.
33 Then said Jē′sus unto them, [b]Yet
a little while am I with you, and *then* I
go unto him that sent me.
34 Ye [c]shall seek me, and shall not
find *me:* and where I am, *thither* ye
cannot come.
35 Then said the Jews among themselves, Whither will he go, that we
shall not find him? will he go unto [d]the
dispersed among the [3]Gĕn′tīles, and
teach the Gĕn′tīles?
36 What *manner of* saying is this
that he said, Ye shall seek me, and
shall not find *me:* and where I am,
thither ye cannot come?
37 In the last day, that great *day* of
the feast, Jē′sus stood and cried, saying, [e]If any man thirst, let him come
unto me, and drink.
38 [f]He that believeth on me, as the
scripture hath said, [g]out of his belly
shall flow rivers of living water.
39 ([h]But this spake he of the Spirit,
which they that believe on him should
receive: for the Hō′lȳ Ghōst was not
yet *given;* because that Jē′sus was not
yet [i]glorified.)
40 ¶ Many of the people therefore,
when they heard this saying, said, Of a
truth this is [j]the Prophet.
41 Others said, [k]This is the Chrīst.
But some said, Shall Chrīst come out
of Găl′ĭ-lee?
42 [l]Hath not the scripture said, That
Chrīst cometh of the seed of Dā′vid,
and out of the town of Bĕth′lĕ-hĕm,
[m]where Dā′vid was?
43 So there was a division among
the people because of him.
44 And some of them would have
taken him; but no man laid hands on
him.
45 ¶ Then came the officers to the
chief priests and Phăr′ĭ-sees; and they
said unto them, Why have ye not
brought him?
46 The officers answered, Never man
spake like this man.
47 Then answered them the Phăr′ĭ-
sees, Are ye also deceived?
48 [n]Have any of the rulers or of the
Phăr′ĭ-sees believed on him?
49 But this people who knoweth not
the law are cursed.
50 Nĭc-o-dē′mus saith unto them,
([o]he that came [4]to Jē′sus by night, being one of them,)
51 [p]Doth our law judge *any* man, before it hear him, and know what he
doeth?
52 They answered and said unto
him, Art thou also of Găl′ĭ-lee? Search,
and look: for [q]out of Găl′ĭ-lee ariseth
no prophet.
53 And every man went unto his
own house.
8 Jē′sus went unto the mount of
Ŏl′ĭves.
2 And early in the morning he came
again into the temple, and all the people came unto him; and he sat down,
and taught them.
3 And the scribes and Phăr′ĭ-sees
brought unto him a woman taken in
adultery; and when they had set her in
the midst,
4 They say unto him, Master, this
woman was taken in adultery, in the
very act.
5 [a]Now Mō′ses in the law commanded us, that such should be stoned:
but what sayest thou?
6 This they said, tempting him, that
they might have to accuse him. But

15 [l]Matt. 13.54; Acts 2.7
[1]Or, learning
16 [m]ch. 3.31-34; Rev. 1.1
17 [n]Ps. 25.8-9-12; ch. 8.43
18 [o]ch. 5.41
19 [p]Acts 7.38
[q]Matt. 12.14; ch. 5.16
20 [r]ch. 8.48
22 [s]Gen. 17.12; Phil. 3.5
[t]Gen. 17.10
23 [2]Or, without breaking the law of Moses
[u]ch. 5.8
24 [v]Deut. 1.16; Jas. 2.1
28 [w]ch. 8.14
[x]ch. 5.43
[y]ch. 5.32; Rom. 3.4
[z]ch. 1.18
29 [a]Matt. 11.27; ch. 10.15
33 [b]ch. 13.33
34 [c]Hos. 5.6; ch. 8.21
35 [d]Isa. 11.12; 1 Pet. 1.1
[3]Or, Greeks
37 [e]Isa. 55.1; Rev. 3.20
38 [f]Deut. 18.15
[g]Isa. 12.3
39 [h]Isa. 44.3; Acts 2.17
[i]ch. 12.16
40 [j]Deut. 18.15; ch. 1.21
41 [k]ch. 4.42
42 [l]Ps. 132.11;
[m]1 Sam. 16.1
48 [n]1 Cor. 1.20
50 [o]ch. 3.2
[4]to him
51 [p]Deut. 1.17
52 [q]1 Ki. 17.1
CHAPTER 8
5 [a]Ex. 20.14

Jē´sus stooped down, and with *his* finger wrote on the ground, *as though he heard them not*.

7 So when they continued asking him, he lifted up himself, and said unto them, [b]He that is without sin among you, let him first cast a stone at her.

8 And again he stooped down, and wrote on the ground.

9 And they which heard *it*, [c]being convicted by *their own* conscience, went out one by one, beginning at the eldest, *even* unto the last: and Jē´sus was left alone, and the woman standing in the midst.

10 When Jē´sus had lifted up himself, and saw none but the woman, he said unto her, Woman, where are those thine accusers? hath no man condemned thee?

11 She said, No man, Lord. And Jē´sus said unto her, [d]Neither do I condemn thee: go, and sin no more.

12 ¶ Then spake Jē´sus again unto them, saying, I am the light of the world: he that followeth me shall not walk in darkness, but shall have the light of life.

13 The Phăr´ĭ-sees therefore said unto him, [e]Thou bearest record of thyself; thy record is not true.

14 Jē´sus answered and said unto them, Though I bear record of myself, *yet* my record is true: for I know whence I came, and whither I go; but [f]ye cannot tell whence I come, and whither I go.

15 [g]Ye judge after the flesh; [h]I judge no man.

16 And yet if I judge, my judgment is true: for [i]I am not alone, but I and the Father that sent me.

17 [j]It is also written in your law, that the testimony of two men is true.

18 I am one that bear witness of myself, and [k]the Father that sent me beareth witness of me.

19 Then said they unto him, Where is thy Father? Jē´sus answered, [l]Ye neither know me, nor my Father: [m]if ye had known me, ye should have known my Father also.

20 These words spake Jē´sus in [n]the treasury, as he taught in the temple: and [o]no man laid hands on him; for [p]his hour was not yet come.

21 Then said Jē´sus again unto them, I go my way, and [q]ye shall seek me, and shall die in your sins: whither I go, ye cannot come.

22 Then said the Jews, Will he kill himself? because he saith, Whither I go, ye cannot come.

23 And he said unto them, [r]Ye are from beneath; I am from above: [s]ye are of this world; I am not of this world.

24 I said therefore unto you, that ye shall die in your sins: [t]for if ye believe not that I am *he*, ye shall die in your sins.

25 Then said they unto him, Who art thou? And Jē´sus saith unto them, Even *the same* that I said unto you from the beginning.

7 [b]Deut. 17.7; Rom. 2.1
9 [c]1 Ki. 2.44; 1 John 3.20
11 [d]Luke 9.56; Rom. 13.4
13 [e]ch. 5.31
14 [f]ch. 7.28
15 [g]1 Sam. 16.7; ch. 7.24
[h]Luke 12.14; ch. 3.17
16 [i]ch. 14.10-11; ch. 16.32
17 [j]Deut. 17.6; Rev. 11.3
18 [k]ch. 5.37
19 [l]ch. 16.3
[m]ch. 14.7
20 [n]Mark 12.41
[o]ch. 7.30
[p]ch. 7.8
21 [q]ch. 13.33
23 [r]ch. 3.31
[s]ch. 15.19
24 [t]Mark 16.16
26 [u]ch. 7.28
[v]ch. 3.32
28 [w]ch. 3.14
[x]Rom. 1.4
[y]ch. 5.19-30
[z]ch. 3.11
29 [a]Isa. 49.1
[b]ch. 4.34
32 [c]Ps. 119.45
33 [d]Lev. 25.42
34 [e]1 Ki. 21.25
35 [f]Gal. 4.30
36 [g]Isa. 49.24
37 [h]ch. 7.19
39 [i]Matt. 3.9
[j]Rom. 2.28
41 [k]Isa. 63.16
42 [l]1 John 4.19
[m]ch. 1.14;
[n]ch. 5.43
43 [o]ch. 7.17
44 [p]Matt. 13.38
[q]2 Cor. 11.3

26 I have many things to say and to judge of you: but [u]he that sent me is true; and [v]I speak to the world those things which I have heard of him.

27 They understood not that he spake to them of the Father.

28 Then said Jē´sus unto them, When ye have [w]lifted up the Son of man, [x]then shall ye know that I am *he*, and [y]*that* I do nothing of myself; but [z]as my Father hath taught me, I speak these things.

29 And [a]he that sent me is with me: the Father hath not left me alone; [b]for I do always those things that please him.

30 As he spake these words, many believed on him.

31 Then said Jē´sus to those Jews which believed on him, If ye continue in my word, *then* are ye my disciples indeed;

32 And ye shall know the truth, and [c]the truth shall make you free.

33 ¶ They answered him, [d]We be Ā´brā-hăm's seed, and were never in bondage to any man: how sayest thou, Ye shall be made free?

34 Jē´sus answered them, Verily, verily, I say unto you, [e]Whosoever committeth sin is the servant of sin.

35 And [f]the servant abideth not in the house for ever: *but* the Son abideth ever.

36 [g]If the Son therefore shall make you free, ye shall be free indeed.

37 I know that ye are Ā´brā-hăm's seed; but [h]ye seek to kill me, because my word hath no place in you.

38 I speak that which I have seen with my Father: and ye do that which ye have seen with your father.

39 They answered and said unto him, [i]Ā´brā-hăm is our father. Jē´sus saith unto them, [j]If ye were Ā´brā-hăm's children, ye would do the works of Ā´brā-hăm.

40 But now ye seek to kill me, a man that hath told you the truth, which I have heard of God: this did not Ā´brā-hăm.

41 Ye do the deeds of your father. Then said they to him, We be not born of fornication; [k]we have one Father, *even* God.

42 Jē´sus said unto them, [l]If God were your Father, ye would love me: [m]for I proceeded forth and came from God; [n]neither came I of myself, but he sent me.

43 [o]Why do ye not understand my speech? *even* because ye cannot hear my word.

44 [p]Ye are of *your* father the devil, and the lusts of your father ye will do. He was a murderer from the beginning, and [q]abode not in the truth, because there is no truth in him. When he speaketh a lie, he speaketh of his own: for he is a liar, and the father of it.

45 And because I tell *you* the truth, ye believe me not.

46 Which of you convinceth me of sin? And if I say the truth, why do ye not believe me?

47 [r]He that is of God heareth God's
words: ye therefore hear *them* not, because ye are not of God.
48 Then answered the Jews, and
said unto him, Say we not well that
thou art a Sa-măr'ĭ-tan, and hast a
devil?
49 Jē'sus answered, I have not a
devil; but I honour my Father, and ye
do dishonour me.
50 And [s]I seek not mine own glory:
there is one that seeketh and judgeth.
51 Verily, verily, I say unto you, [t]If a
man keep my saying, he shall never
see death.
52 Then said the Jews unto him,
Now we know that thou hast a devil.
[u]Ā'bră-hăm is dead, and the prophets;
and thou sayest, If a man keep my saying, he shall never taste of death.
53 Art thou greater than our father
Ā'bră-hăm, which is dead? and the
prophets are dead: whom makest thou
thyself?
54 Jē'sus answered, If I honour myself, my honour is nothing: [v]it is my
Father that honoureth me; of whom ye
say, that he is your God:
55 Yet [w]ye have not known him; but
I know him: and if I should say, I know
him not, I shall be a liar like unto you:
but I know him, and keep his saying.
56 Your father Ā'bră-hăm [x]rejoiced
to see my day: [y]and he saw *it*, and was
glad.
57 Then said the Jews unto him,
Thou art not yet fifty years old, and
hast thou seen Ā'bră-hăm?
58 Jē'sus said unto them, Verily, verily, I say unto you, Before Ā'bră-hăm
was, [z]I am.
59 Then took they up stones to cast
at him: but Jē'sus hid himself, and
went out of the temple, going through
the midst of them, and so passed by.

9 And as *Jē'sus* passed by, he saw
a man which was blind from *his*
birth.
2 And his disciples asked him, saying, Master, [a]who did sin, this man, or
his parents, that he was born blind?
3 Jē'sus answered, Neither hath this
man sinned, nor his parents: [b]but that
the works of God should be made manifest in him.
4 [c]I must work the works of him
that sent me, while it is day: the night
cometh, when no man can work.
5 As long as I am in the world, [d]I am
the light of the world.
6 When he had thus spoken, [e]he
spat on the ground, and made clay of
the spittle, and he [1]anointed the eyes of
the blind man with the clay,
7 And said unto him, Go wash [f]in the
pool of Sĭ-lō'am, (which is by interpretation, Sent.) [g]He went his way therefore, and washed, and came seeing.
8 ¶ The neighbours therefore, and
they which before had seen him that
he was blind, said, Is not this he that
sat and begged?
9 Some said, This is he: others *said*,
He is like him: *but* he said, I am *he*.
10 Therefore said they unto him,
How were thine eyes opened?
11 He answered and said, A man
that is called Jē'sus made clay, and
anointed mine eyes, and said unto me,
Go to the pool of Sĭ-lō'am, and wash:
and I went and washed, and I received
sight.
12 Then said they unto him, Where
is he? He said, I know not.
13 ¶ They brought to the Phăr'ĭ-sees
him that aforetime was blind.
14 And it was the sabbath day when
Jē'sus made the clay, and opened his
eyes.
15 Then again the Phăr'ĭ-sees also
asked him how he had received his
sight. He said unto them, He put clay
upon mine eyes, and I washed, and do
see.
16 Therefore said some of the Phăr'-
ĭ-sees, This man is not of God, because
he keepeth not the sabbath day. Others said, [h]How can a man that is a sinner do such miracles? And [i]there was
a division among them.
17 They say unto the blind man
again, What sayest thou of him, that he
hath opened thine eyes? He said, [j]He is
a prophet.
18 But the Jews did not believe concerning him, that he had been blind,
and received his sight, until they called
the parents of him that had received
his sight.
19 And they asked them, saying, Is
this your son, who ye say was born
blind? how then doth he now see?
20 His parents answered them and
said, We know that this is our son, and
that he was born blind:
21 But by what means he now seeth,
we know not; or who hath opened his
eyes, we know not: he is of age; ask
him: he shall speak for himself.
22 These *words* spake his parents,
because [k]they feared the Jews: for the
Jews had agreed already, that if any
man did confess that he was Chrĭst, he
[l]should be put out of the synagogue.
23 Therefore said his parents, He is
of age; ask him.
24 Then again called they the man
that was blind, and said unto him,
[m]Give God the praise: we know that
this man is a sinner.
25 He answered and said, Whether
he be a sinner *or no*, I know not:
one thing I know, that, whereas I was
blind, now I see.
26 Then said they to him again, What
did he to thee? how opened he thine
eyes?
27 He answered them, I have told
you already, and ye did not hear:
wherefore would ye hear *it* again? will
ye also be his disciples?
28 Then they reviled him, and said,
Thou art his disciple; but we are Mō'-
ses' disciples.
29 We know that God spake unto
Mō'ses: *as for* this *fellow*, [n]we know
not from whence he is.
30 The man answered and said unto
them, [o]Why herein is a marvellous

47 [r]1 John 4.6
50 [s]ch. 5.41
51 [t]ch. 5.24
52 [u]Zech. 1.5
54 [v]ch. 16.14; Acts 3.13
55 [w]ch. 7.28
56 [x]Gen. 22.18; Luke 10.24; Gal. 3.8-16
[y]Heb. 11.13
58 [z]Ex. 3.14; Col. 1.17; Heb. 13.8; Rev. 1.8

CHAPTER 9
2 [a]Acts 28.4
3 [b]Matt. 11.5; ch. 11.4; Acts 4.21-22
4 [c]ch. 4.34; ch. 5.19-36; ch. 11.9; ch. 12.35; ch. 17.4
5 [d]Isa. 42.6; Isa. 49.6; Luke 2.32; ch. 1.5-9; ch. 3.19; ch. 8.12; Acts 13.47; 1 John 2.8
6 [e]Mark 7.33
[1]Or, spread the clay upon the eyes of the blind man
7 [f]Neh. 3.15; Isa. 8.6
[g]Ex. 4.11; 2 Ki. 5.14; Ps. 146.8; Isa. 29.18; Isa. 35.5; Isa. 42.7
16 [h]ch. 3.2
[i]Luke 12.51-53; ch. 7.12-43
17 [j]Deut. 18.15; ch. 4.19
22 [k]ch. 7.13; Acts 5.13
[l]ch. 12.42
24 [m]Josh. 7.19; 1 Sam. 6.5; Isa. 66.5; ch. 5.23
29 [n]ch. 1.10
30 [o]ch. 3.10

thing, that ye know not from whence he is, and *yet* he hath opened mine eyes.

31 Now we know that [p]God heareth not sinners: but if any man be a worshippper of God, and doeth his will, him he heareth.

32 Since the world began was it not heard that any man opened the eyes of one that was born blind.

33 If this man were not of God, he could do nothing.

34 They answered and said unto him, Thou wast altogether born in sins, and dost thou teach us? And they [2]cast him out.

35 Jē'sus heard that they had cast him out; and when he had found him, he said unto him, Dost thou believe on [q]the Son of God?

36 He answered and said, Who is he, Lord, that I might believe on him?

37 And Jē'sus said unto him, Thou hast both seen him, and [r]it is he that talketh with thee.

38 And he said, Lord, I believe. And he worshipped him.

39 ¶ And Jē'sus said, [s]For judgment I am come into this world, [t]that they which see not might see; and that they which see might be made blind.

40 And *some* of the Phăr'ĭ-sees which were with him heard these words, [u]and said unto him, Are we blind also?

41 Jē'sus said unto them, [v]If ye were blind, ye should have no sin: but now ye say, We see; therefore your sin remaineth.

10

Verily, verily, I say unto you, [a]He that entereth not by the door into the sheepfold, but climbeth up some other way, the same is a thief and a robber.

2 But he that entereth in by the [b]door is the shepherd of the sheep.

3 To him [c]the porter openeth; and the sheep hear his voice: and he calleth his own sheep by name, and leadeth them out.

4 And when he putteth forth his own sheep, he goeth before them, and the sheep follow him: for they know his voice.

5 [d]And a stranger will they not follow, but will flee from him: for they know not the voice of strangers.

6 This parable spake Jē'sus unto them: but they understood not what things they were which he spake unto them.

7 Then said Jē'sus unto them again, Verily, verily, I say unto you, I am [e]the door of the sheep.

8 [f]All that ever came before me are thieves and robbers: but the sheep did not hear them.

9 I am the door: by me if any man enter in, he shall be saved, and shall go in and out, and find pasture.

10 [g]The thief cometh not, but for to steal, and to kill, and to destroy: I am come that they might have life, and that they might have *it* more abundantly.

11 [h]I am the good shepherd: the good shepherd giveth his life for the sheep.

12 But he that is an hireling, and not the shepherd, whose own the sheep are not, seeth the wolf coming, and [i]leaveth the sheep, and fleeth: and the wolf catcheth them, and scattereth the sheep.

13 The hireling fleeth, because he is an hireling, and careth not for the sheep.

14 I am the good shepherd, and [j]know my *sheep*, and [k]am known of mine.

15 As the Father knoweth me, even so know I the Father: and I lay down my life for the sheep.

16 And [l]other sheep I have, which are not of this fold: them also I must bring, and they shall hear my voice; [m]and there shall be one fold, *and* one shepherd.

17 Therefore doth my Father love me, [n]because I lay down my life, that I might take it again.

18 No man taketh it from me, but I lay it down of myself. I have power to lay it down, and I have power to take it again. [o]This commandment have I received of my Father.

19 ¶ There was a division therefore again among the Jews for these sayings.

20 And many of them said, He hath a devil, and is mad; why hear ye him?

21 Others said, These are not the words of him that hath a devil. [p]Can a devil open the eyes of the blind?

22 ¶ And it was at Je-ru'sa-lĕm the feast of the dedication, and it was winter.

23 And Jē'sus walked in the temple [q]in Sŏl'o-mon's porch.

24 Then came the Jews round about him, and said unto him, How long dost thou [1]make us to doubt? If thou be the Chrīst, tell us plainly.

25 Jē'sus answered them, I told you, and ye believed not: the works that I do in my Father's name, they bear witness of me.

26 But [r]ye believe not, because ye are not of my sheep, as I said unto you.

27 My sheep hear my voice, and I know them, and they follow me:

28 And I give unto them eternal life; and they shall never perish, neither shall any *man* pluck them out of my hand.

29 [s]My Father, [t]which gave *them* me, is greater than all; and no *man* is able to pluck *them* out of my Father's hand.

30 [u]I and *my* Father are one.

31 Then the Jews took up stones again to stone him.

32 Jē'sus answered them, Many good works have I shewed you from my Father; for which of those works do ye stone me?

33 The Jews answered him, saying, For a good work we stone thee not; but for blasphemy; and because that thou, being a man, [v]makest thyself God.

---

31 [p]Job 27.9; Ps. 18.41; Ps. 34.15; Prov. 1.28; Prov. 15.29; Isa. 1.15; Jer. 11.11; Ezek. 8.18; Mic. 3.4; Zech. 7.13

34 [2]Or, excommunicated him

35 [q]Matt. 14.33; Mark 1.1; ch. 10.36; 1 John 5.13

37 [r]ch. 4.26

39 [s]ch. 5.22; ch. 3.17

[t]Matt. 13.13; Luke 2.34; 2 Cor. 2.16

40 [u]Rom. 2.19

41 [v]ch. 15.22

CHAPTER 10

1 [a]Isa. 56.10

2 [b]Acts 20.28; 1 Cor. 12.28

3 [c]1 Cor. 16.9; 1 Pet. 1.12

5 [d]Prov. 19.27; Col. 2.8

7 [e]Eph. 2.18; Heb. 10.19

8 [f]Jer. 23.1; Acts 5.36-37

10 [g]Matt. 7.15; 2 Pet. 2.1

11 [h]Isa. 40.11; 1 Pet. 2.25

12 [i]Zech. 11.16

14 [j]2 Tim. 2.19

[k]Isa. 53.6-7; 1 John 5.20

16 [l]Isa. 56.8

[m]Eph. 2.14

17 [n]Isa. 53.7; Heb. 2.9

18 [o]Acts 2.24

21 [p]Ex. 4.11; Isa. 35.5

23 [q]Acts 3.11

24 [1]Or, hold us in suspense

26 [r]ch. 8.47; 1 John 4.6

29 [s]ch. 14.28

[t]ch. 17.2-6

30 [u]Deut. 6.4; 1 John 1.3

33 [v]ch. 5.18; Phil. 2.6

34 Jē'sus answered them, [w]Is it not written in your law, I said, Ye are gods?

35 If he called them gods, [x]unto whom the word of God came, and the scripture cannot be broken;

36 Say ye of him, [y]whom the Father hath sanctified, and [z]sent into the world, Thou blasphemest; because I said, I am [a]the Son of God?

37 [b]If I do not the works of my Father, believe me not.

38 But if I do, though ye believe not me, believe the works: that ye may know, and believe, [c]that the Father *is* in me, and I in him.

39 Therefore they sought again to take him: but he escaped out of their hand,

40 And went away again beyond Jôr'dan into the place [d]where Jŏhn at first baptized; and there he abode.

41 And many resorted unto him, and said, Jŏhn did no miracle: [e]but all things that Jŏhn spake of this man were true.

42 [f]And many believed on him there.

11 Now a certain *man* was sick, *named* Lăz'a-rus, of Běth'ă-ny̆, the town of [a]Mā'ry̆ and her sister Mär'thȧ.

2 ([b]It was *that* Mā'ry̆ which anointed the Lord with ointment, and wiped his feet with her hair, whose brother Lăz'a-rus was sick.)

3 Therefore his sisters sent unto him, saying, Lord, behold, he whom thou lovest is sick.

4 When Jē'sus heard *that*, he said, This sickness is not unto death, but [c]for the glory of God, that the Son of God might be glorified thereby.

5 Now Jē'sus loved Mär'thȧ, and her sister, and Lăz'a-rus.

6 When he had heard therefore that he was sick, [d]he abode two days still in the same place where he was.

7 Then after that saith he to *his* disciples, Let us go into Jŭ-dæ'ȧ again.

8 *His* disciples say unto him, Master, [e]the Jews of late sought to stone thee; and goest thou thither again?

9 Jē'sus answered, Are there not twelve hours in the day? [f]If any man walk in the day, he stumbleth not, because he seeth the light of this world.

10 But [g]if a man walk in the night, he stumbleth, because there is no light in him.

11 These things said he: and after that he saith unto them, Our friend Lăz'a-rus [h]sleepeth; but I go, that I may awake him out of sleep.

12 Then said his disciples, Lord, if he sleep, he shall do well.

13 Howbeit Jē'sus spake of his death: but they thought that he had spoken of taking of rest in sleep.

14 Then said Jē'sus unto them plainly, Lăz'a-rus is dead.

15 And I am glad for your sakes that I was not there, to the intent ye may believe; nevertheless let us go unto him.

16 Then said Thŏm'as, which is called Dĭd'y̆-mus, unto his fellowdisciples, Let us also go, that we may die with him.

17 Then when Jē'sus came, he found that he had *lain* in the grave four days already.

18 Now Běth'ă-ny̆ was nigh unto Je-ru̦'sa-lĕm, [1]about fifteen furlongs off:

19 And many of the Jews came to Mär'thȧ and Mā'ry̆, to comfort them concerning their brother.

20 Then Mär'thȧ, as soon as she heard that Jē'sus was coming, went and met him: but Mā'ry̆ sat *still* in the house.

21 Then said Mär'thȧ unto Jē'sus, Lord, if thou hadst been here, my brother had not died.

22 But I know, that even now, [i]whatsoever thou wilt ask of God, God will give *it* thee.

23 Jē'sus saith unto her, Thy brother shall [j]rise again.

24 Mär'thȧ saith unto him, [k]I know that he shall rise again in the resurrection at the last day.

25 Jē'sus said unto her, I am [l]the resurrection, and the [m]life: [n]he that believeth in me, though he were dead, yet shall he live:

26 And whosoever liveth and believeth in me shall never die. Believest thou this?

27 She saith unto him, Yea, Lord: [o]I believe that thou art the Chrīst, the Son of God, which should come into the world.

28 And when she had so said, she went her way, and called Mā'ry̆ her sister secretly, saying, The Master is come, and calleth for thee.

29 As soon as she heard *that*, she arose quickly, and came unto him.

30 Now Jē'sus was not yet come into the town, but was in that place where Mär'thȧ met him.

31 The Jews then which were with her in the house, and comforted her, when they saw Mā'ry̆, that she rose up hastily and went out, followed her, saying, She goeth unto the grave to weep there.

32 Then when Mā'ry̆ was come where Jē'sus was, and saw him, she fell down at his feet, saying unto him, Lord, if thou hadst been here, my brother had not died.

33 When Jē'sus therefore saw her weeping, and the Jews also weeping which came with her, he groaned in the spirit, and [2]was troubled,

34 And said, Where have ye laid him? They said unto him, Lord, come and see.

35 [p]Jē'sus wept.

36 Then said the Jews, Behold how he loved him!

37 And some of them said, Could not this man, [q]which opened the eyes of the blind, have caused that even this man should not have died?

38 Jē'sus therefore again groaning in himself cometh to the grave. It was a cave, and a stone lay upon it.

39 Jē'sus said, Take ye away the stone. Mär'thȧ, the sister of him that

34 [w]Ps. 82.6
35 [x]Rom. 13.1
36 [y]ch. 6.27
[z]ch. 3.17
[a]Luke 1.35; ch. 9.35
37 [b]ch. 15.24
38 [c]ch. 14.10
40 [d]ch. 1.28
41 [e]ch. 1.29
42 [f]ch. 8.30

CHAPTER 11
1 [a]Luke 10.38
2 [b]Matt. 26.7; Mark 14.3; Luke 7.37; ch. 12.3
4 [c]ch. 9.3; Phil. 1.11; 1 Pet. 4.11-14
6 [d]ch. 10.40
8 [e]ch. 10.31
9 [f]Ps. 97.11; Prov. 4.18; ch. 9.4
10 [g]Job 38.15; Ps. 27.2; Prov. 4.18-19; Jer. 13.16; ch. 12.35; 1 John 2.11
11 [h]Deut. 31.16; Dan. 12.2; Matt. 9.24; Mark 5.39; Acts 7.60
18 [1]That is, about two miles
22 [i]Mark 9.23-24; ch. 9.31; Heb. 11.17-19
23 [j]Dan. 12.2; Phil. 3.21; 1 Thess. 4.14
24 [k]Luke 14.14; ch. 5.29
25 [l]ch. 5.21; Rom. 5.17-19; 1 Cor. 15.20-26
[m]Ps. 36.9; ch. 1.4; ch. 6.35; Acts 3.15; Rom. 8.2; Col. 3.4; 1 John 1.1-2
[n]ch. 3.36; 1 John 5.10
27 [o]Mal. 3.1; Matt. 11.3; Luke 7.19-20; ch. 4.42; 1 Tim. 1.15-16
33 [2]he troubled himself
35 [p]Isa. 53.3; Luke 19.41; Rom. 12.15; Heb. 4.15
37 [q]ch. 9.6

was dead, saith unto him, Lord, by this
time he stinketh: for he hath been *dead*
four days.
40 Jē′sus saith unto her, Said I not
unto thee, that, if thou wouldest believe, thou shouldest see the glory of
God?
41 Then they took away the stone
from the place where the dead was
laid. And Jē′sus lifted up *his* eyes, and
said, Father, I thank thee that thou
hast heard me.
42 And I knew that thou hearest me
always: but [r]because of the people
which stand by I said *it*, that they may
believe that thou hast sent me.
43 And when he thus had spoken,
he cried with a loud voice, Lăz′a-rus,
[s]come forth.
44 And he that was dead came forth,
bound hand and foot with graveclothes:
and [t]his face was bound about with a
napkin. Jē′sus saith unto them, Loose
him, and let him go.
45 Then many of the Jews which
came to Mā′rȳ, [u]and had seen the
things which Jē′sus did, believed on
him.
46 But some of them went their ways
to the Phăr′ĭ-sees, and told them what
things Jē′sus had done.
47 ¶ [v]Then gathered the chief priests
and the Phăr′ĭ-sees a council, and said,
[w]What do we? for this man doeth many
miracles.
48 If we let him thus alone, all *men*
will believe on him: and [x]the Rō′mans
shall come and take away both our
place and nation.
49 And one of them, *named* [y]Cā′ia-
phas, being the high priest that same
year, said unto them, Ye know nothing
at all,
50 [z]Nor consider that it is expedient
for us, that one man should die for the
people, and that the whole nation perish not.
51 And this spake he not of himself:
but being high priest that year, he
prophesied that Jē′sus should die for
that nation;
52 And [a]not for that nation only,
[b]but that also he should gather together in one the children of God that
were scattered abroad.
53 Then from that day forth they
took counsel together for to put him to
death.
54 Jē′sus [c]therefore walked no more
openly among the Jews; but went
thence unto a country near to the wilderness, into a city called [d]Ē′phră-ĭm,
and there continued with his disciples.
55 ¶ [e]And the Jews' passover was
nigh at hand: and many went out of the
country up to Je-ru′sa-lĕm before the
passover, to [f]purify themselves.
56 [g]Then sought they for Jē′sus, and
spake among themselves, as they stood
in the temple, [h]What think ye, that he
will not come to the feast?
57 Now both the chief priests and
the Phăr′ĭ-sees had given a commandment, that, if any man knew where he
were, he should shew *it*, that they
might take him.

12 Then Jē′sus six days before the
passover came to Bĕth′ă-nȳ,
[a]where Lăz′a-rus was which had been
dead, whom he raised from the dead.
2 [b]There they made him a supper;
and Mär′thȧ served: but Lăz′a-rus was
one of them that sat at the table with
him.
3 Then took [c]Mā′rȳ a pound of
ointment of spikenard, very costly,
and anointed the feet of Jē′sus, and
wiped his feet with her hair: and the
house was filled with the odour of the
ointment.
4 Then saith one of his disciples,
Jū′das Ĭs-căr′ĭ-ot, Sī′mon's *son*, which
should betray him,
5 Why was not this ointment sold
for three hundred pence, and given to
the poor?
6 This he said, not that he cared for
the poor; but because he was a thief,
and [d]had the bag, and bare what was
put therein.
7 Then said Jē′sus, Let her alone:
against the day of my burying hath she
kept this.
8 For [e]the poor always ye have with
you; but me ye have not always.
9 Much people of the Jews therefore
knew that he was there: and they came
not for Jē′sus' sake only, but that they
might see Lăz′a-rus also, whom he had
raised from the dead.
10 ¶ [f]But the chief priests consulted
that they might put Lăz′a-rus also to
death;
11 [g]Because that by reason of him
many of the Jews went away, and believed on Jē′sus.
12 ¶ [h]On the next day much people that were come to the feast, when
they heard that Jē′sus was coming to
Je-ru′sa-lĕm,
13 Took branches of palm trees, and
went forth to meet him, and cried, [i]Ho-
săn′nȧ: Blessed *is* the King of Ĭs′ra-el
that cometh in the name of the Lord.
14 And Jē′sus, when he had found a
young ass, sat thereon; as it is written,
15 [j]Fear not, daughter of Sī′ŏn: behold, thy King cometh, sitting on an
ass's colt.
16 These things [k]understood not his
disciples at the first: [l]but when Jē′sus
was glorified, [m]then remembered they
that these things were written of him,
and *that* they had done these things
unto him.
17 The people therefore that was
with him when he called Lăz′a-rus out
of his grave, and raised him from the
dead, bare record.
18 For this cause the people also
met him, for that they heard that he
had done this miracle.
19 The Phăr′ĭ-sees therefore said
among themselves, Perceive ye how ye
prevail nothing? behold, the world is
gone after him.
20 ¶ And there [n]were certain Greeks
among them, [o]that came up to worship
at the feast:

42 [r]ch. 12.30
43 [s]Deut. 32.39; 1 Sam. 2.6; Ps. 33.9; Luke 7.14; Acts 3.15; Rom. 4.17
44 [t]ch. 20.7
45 [u]ch. 2.23
47 [v]Ps. 2.2; Matt. 26.3; Mark 14.1; Luke 22.2
[w]ch. 12.19; Acts 4.16
48 [x]Dan. 9.26; Zech. 13.7-8
49 [y]Luke 3.2; ch. 18.14; Acts 4.6
50 [z]ch. 18.14
52 [a]Isa. 49.6; 1 John 2.2
[b]ch. 10.16; Acts 13.47; Gal. 3.28; Eph. 3.6; 1 Pet. 5.9
54 [c]ch. 4.1-3
[d]2 Chr. 13.19
55 [e]ch. 2.13
[f]Ex. 19.10; 1 Sam. 16.5; Job 1.5; Acts 24.18
56 [g]ch. 7.11
[h]Ps. 2

CHAPTER 12
1 [a]1 Sam. 2.6; Luke 7.14; ch. 11.1-43; Acts 3.15; Rom. 4.17
2 [b]Matt. 26.6; Mark 14.3
3 [c]Song 1.12; Luke 10.38-39; ch. 11.2
6 [d]Prov. 26.25; 1 Cor. 6.10; ch. 13.29; Eph. 5.5; Col. 3.5
8 [e]Deut. 15.11; Matt. 26.11; Mark 14.7
10 [f]Prov. 1.16; Luke 16.31
11 [g]Mark 15.10; ch. 11.45
12 [h]Luke 19.35
13 [i]Ps. 72.17-19; 1 Tim. 1.17
15 [j]Isa. 62.11; Zech. 9.9
16 [k]Luke 18.34
[l]ch. 7.39
[m]ch. 14.26
20 [n]Acts 17.4
[o]1 Ki. 8.41

21 The same came therefore to
Phĭl'ĭp, which was of Bĕth-sā'ĭ-dȧ of
Găl'ĭ-lee, and desired him, saying, Sir,
we would see Jē'sus.
22 Phĭl'ĭp cometh and telleth Ăn''-
drew: and again Ăn''drew and Phĭl'ĭp
tell Jē'sus.
23 ¶ And Jē'sus answered them, saying, [p]The hour is come, that the Son of
man should be glorified.
24 Verily, verily, I say unto you,
[q]Except a corn of wheat fall into the
ground and die, it abideth alone: but if
it die, it bringeth forth much fruit.
25 [r]He that loveth his life shall lose
it; and he that hateth his life in this
world shall keep it unto life eternal.
26 If any man serve me, let him follow me; and [s]where I am, there shall
also my servant be: if any man serve
me, him will *my* Father honour.
27 [t]Now is my soul troubled; and
what shall I say? Father, save me from
this hour: [u]but for this cause came I
unto this hour.
28 Father, glorify thy name. [v]Then
came there a voice from heaven, *saying,* I have both glorified *it,* and will
glorify *it* again.
29 The people therefore, that stood
by, and heard *it,* said that it thundered:
others said, An angel spake to him.
30 Jē'sus answered and said, [w]This
voice came not because of me, but for
your sakes.
31 Now is the judgment of this world:
now shall [x]the prince of this world be
cast out.
32 And I, if I be lifted up from the
earth, will draw [y]all *men* unto me.
33 This he said, signifying what
death he should die.
34 The people answered him, [z]We
have heard out of the law that Chrīst
abideth for ever: and how sayest thou,
The Son of man must be lifted up? who
is this Son of man?
35 Then Jē'sus said unto them, Yet a
little while [a]is the light with you. [b]Walk
while ye have the light, lest darkness
come upon you: for [c]he that walketh
in darkness knoweth not whither he
goeth.
36 While ye have light, believe in
the light, that ye may be the [d]children
of light. These things spake Jē'sus, and
departed, and did hide himself from
them.
37 ¶ But though he had done so
many miracles before them, yet they
believed not on him:
38 That the saying of E-sā'ias the
prophet might be fulfilled, which he
spake, [e]Lord, who hath believed our
report? and to whom hath the arm of
the Lord been revealed?
39 Therefore they could not believe,
because that E-sā'ias said again,
40 [f]He hath blinded their eyes, and
hardened their heart; that they should
not see with *their* eyes, nor understand
with *their* heart, and be converted, and
I should heal them.

23 [p]ch. 13.32
24 [q]1 Cor. 15.36
25 [r]Luke 9.24
26 [s]1 Thess. 4.17
27 [t]Luke 12.50; ch. 13.21
[u]Luke 22.53
28 [v]2 Pet. 1.17
30 [w]ch. 11.42
31 [x]Luke 10.18; ch. 14.30; Acts 26.18; 2 Cor. 4.4; Eph. 2.2; 1 John 3.8
32 [y]Rom. 5.18; Heb. 2.9
34 [z]2 Sam. 7.13; Ps. 89.36; Isa. 9.7; Dan. 2.44; Mic. 4.7
35 [a]Isa. 42.6; ch. 1.9
[b]Isa. 2.5; Jer. 13.16; ch. 1.5-9; Eph. 5.8
[c]ch. 11.10; 1 John 2.11
36 [d]Luke 16.8; Eph. 5.8; 1 Thess. 5.5
38 [e]Isa. 53.1; Rom. 10.16
40 [f]Isa. 6.9; Matt. 13.14
41 [g]Isa. 6.1; Heb. 11.13
43 [h]Matt. 6.2; Luke 16.15; Rom. 2.29
44 [i]Matt. 10.40; ch. 13.20
45 [j]ch. 14.9; Heb. 1.3
46 [k]ch. 3.19
47 [l]ch. 5.45
[m]ch. 3.17
48 [n]Luke 10.16
[o]Deut. 18.19; Mark 16.16
49 [p]ch. 8.38

CHAPTER 13
2 [a]Luke 22.3
3 [b]ch. 3.35; Heb. 2.8
4 [c]Luke 22.27
6 [1]he
[d]Matt. 3.14
8 [e]Ps. 51.2-7; Tit. 3.5
10 [f]2 Cor. 7.1; 1 Thess. 5.23
[g]ch. 15.3

41 [g]These things said E-sā'ias, when
he saw his glory, and spake of him.
42 ¶ Nevertheless among the chief
rulers also many believed on him; but
because of the Phăr'ĭ-sees they did not
confess *him,* lest they should be put out
of the synagogue:
43 [h]For they loved the praise of men
more than the praise of God.
44 ¶ Jē'sus cried and said, [i]He that
believeth on me, believeth not on me,
but on him that sent me.
45 And [j]he that seeth me seeth him
that sent me.
46 [k]I am come a light into the world,
that whosoever believeth on me should
not abide in darkness.
47 And if any man hear my words,
and believe not, [l]I judge him not: for
[m]I came not to judge the world, but to
save the world.
48 [n]He that rejecteth me, and receiveth not my words, hath one that
judgeth him: [o]the word that I have
spoken, the same shall judge him in
the last day.
49 For [p]I have not spoken of myself;
but the Father which sent me, he gave
me a commandment, what I should
say, and what I should speak.
50 And I know that his commandment is life everlasting: whatsoever I
speak therefore, even as the Father
said unto me, so I speak.

13 Now before the feast of the passover, when Jē'sus knew that his
hour was come that he should depart
out of this world unto the Father, having loved his own which were in the
world, he loved them unto the end.
2 And supper being ended, [a]the devil
having now put into the heart of Jū'das
Ĭs-căr'ĭ-ot, Sī'mon's *son,* to betray him;
3 Jē'sus knowing [b]that the Father
had given all things into his hands, and
that he was come from God, and went
to God;
4 [c]He riseth from supper, and laid
aside his garments; and took a towel,
and girded himself.
5 After that he poureth water into a
bason, and began to wash the disciples' feet, and to wipe *them* with the
towel wherewith he was girded.
6 Then cometh he to Sī'mon Pē'tēr:
and [1]Pē'tēr saith unto him, Lord, [d]dost
thou wash my feet?
7 Jē'sus answered and said unto
him, What I do thou knowest not now;
but thou shalt know hereafter.
8 Pē'tēr saith unto him, Thou shalt
never wash my feet. Jē'sus answered
him, [e]If I wash thee not, thou hast no
part with me.
9 Sī'mon Pē'tēr saith unto him, Lord,
not my feet only, but also *my* hands and
my head.
10 Jē'sus saith to him, [f]He that is
washed needeth not save to wash *his*
feet, but is clean every whit: and [g]ye
are clean, but not all.
11 For he knew who should betray
him; therefore said he, Ye are not all
clean.

12 So after he had washed their feet,
and had taken his garments, and was
set down again, he said unto them,
Know ye what I have done to you?
13 [h]Ye call me Master and Lord:
and ye say well; for *so* I am.
14 [i]If I then, *your* Lord and Master,
have washed your feet; [j]ye also ought
to wash one another's feet.
15 For [k]I have given you an example, that ye should do as I have done to
you.
16 [l]Verily, verily, I say unto you,
The servant is not greater than his
lord; neither he that is sent greater
than he that sent him.
17 [m]If ye know these things, happy
are ye if ye do them.
18 ¶ I speak not of you all: [n]I know
whom I have chosen: but that the scripture may be fulfilled, [o]He that eateth
bread with me hath lifted up his heel
against me.
19 [2]Now I tell you before it come,
that, when it is come to pass, ye may
believe that I am *he*.
20 [p]Verily, verily, I say unto you, He
that receiveth whomsoever I send receiveth me; and he that receiveth me
receiveth him that sent me.
21 [q]When Jē'sus had thus said, [r]he
was troubled in spirit, and testified,
and said, Verily, verily, I say unto you,
that [s]one of you shall betray me.
22 Then the disciples looked one on
another, doubting of whom he spake.
23 Now [t]there was leaning on Jē'-
sus' bosom one of his disciples, whom
Jē'sus loved.
24 Sī'mon Pē'tĕr therefore beckoned
to him, that he should ask who it should
be of whom he spake.
25 He then lying on Jē'sus' breast
saith unto him, Lord, who is it?
26 Jē'sus answered, He it is, to whom
I shall give a [3]sop, when I have dipped
it. And when he had dipped the sop, he
gave *it* to Jū'das Ĭs-căr'ĭ-ot, *the son* of
Sī'mon.
27 And [u]after the sop Sā'tan entered into him. Then said Jē'sus unto
him, That thou doest, do quickly.
28 Now no man at the table knew
for what intent he spake this unto him.
29 For some *of them* thought, because [v]Jū'das had the bag, that Jē'sus
had said unto him, Buy *those things*
that we have need of against the feast;
or, that he should give something to
the poor.
30 He then having received the sop
went immediately out: and it was night.
31 ¶ Therefore, when he was gone
out, Jē'sus said, Now is the Son of man
glorified, and [w]God is glorified in him.
32 [x]If God be glorified in him, God
shall also glorify him in himself, and
shall straightway glorify him.
33 Little children, yet a little while I
am with you. Ye shall seek me: and as I
said unto the Jews, Whither I go, ye
cannot come; so now I say to you.
34 [y]A new commandment I give
unto you, That ye love one another; as

13 [h]Luke 6.46; Phil. 2.11
14 [i]Luke 22.27
[j]Rom. 12.10; 1 Pet. 5.5
15 [k]Phil. 2.5; 1 Pet. 2.21
16 [l]Luke 6.40; ch. 15.20
17 [m]Jas. 1.25
18 [n]ch. 17.12; Rev. 2.23
[o]Ps. 41.9
19 [2]From henceforth
20 [p]Luke 10.16; Gal. 4.14
21 [q]Luke 22.21
[r]Matt. 26.38; Acts 17.16
[s]Acts 1.17; 1 John 2.19
23 [t]ch. 19.26; ch. 20.2
26 [3]Or, morsel
27 [u]Ps. 109.6; ch. 6.70
29 [v]ch. 12.6
31 [w]ch. 14.13; 1 Pet. 4.11
32 [x]ch. 17.1
34 [y]Lev. 19.18; 1 John 2.7
35 [z]Acts 2.46
36 [a]ch. 21.18; 2 Pet. 1.14
37 [b]Luke 22.33

CHAPTER 14
2 [a]2 Cor. 5.1; Rev. 3.12-21
[b]ch. 13.33
3 [c]Matt. 25.32-34; 2 Cor. 5.6-8
[d]ch. 12.26; 1 Thess. 4.17
6 [e]Matt. 11.27;
[f]ch. 1.17
[g]ch. 1.4
[h]ch. 10.9
7 [i]ch. 8.19
9 [j]Col. 1.15
10 [k]ch. 10.38;
[l]ch. 5.19
13 [m]Matt. 7.7-8
15 [n]Matt. 10.37
16 [o]Rom. 8.15
17 [p]Rom. 8.7

I have loved you, that ye also love one
another.
35 By this shall all *men* know that ye
are my disciples, if ye have [z]love one
to another.
36 ¶ Sī'mon Pē'tĕr said unto him,
Lord, whither goest thou? Jē'sus answered him, Whither I go, thou canst
not follow me now; but [a]thou shalt follow me afterwards.
37 Pē'tĕr said unto him, Lord, why
cannot I follow thee now? I will [b]lay
down my life for thy sake.
38 Jē'sus answered him, Wilt thou
lay down thy life for my sake? Verily,
verily, I say unto thee, The cock shall
not crow, till thou hast denied me
thrice.

14

Let not your heart be troubled:
ye believe in God, believe also in
me.
2 [a]In my Father's house are many
mansions: if *it were* not *so*, I would
have told you. [b]I go to prepare a place
for you.
3 And if I go and prepare a place for
you, [c]I will come again, and receive
you unto myself; that [d]where I am,
there ye may be also.
4 And whither I go ye know, and the
way ye know.
5 Thŏm'as saith unto him, Lord, we
know not whither thou goest; and how
can we know the way?
6 Jē'sus saith unto him, I am [e]the
way, [f]the truth, and [g]the life: [h]no man
cometh unto the Father, but by me.
7 [i]If ye had known me, ye should
have known my Father also: and from
henceforth ye know him, and have
seen him.
8 Phĭl'ĭp saith unto him, Lord, shew
us the Father, and it sufficeth us.
9 Jē'sus saith unto him, Have I been
so long time with you, and yet hast thou
not known me, Phĭl'ĭp? [j]he that hath
seen me hath seen the Father; and how
sayest thou *then*, Shew us the Father?
10 Believest thou not that [k]I am in
the Father, and the Father in me? the
words that I speak unto you [l]I speak
not of myself: but the Father that dwelleth in me, he doeth the works.
11 Believe me that I *am* in the Father, and the Father in me: or else believe me for the very works' sake.
12 Verily, verily, I say unto you, He
that believeth on me, the works that I
do shall he do also; and greater *works*
than these shall he do; because I go
unto my Father.
13 [m]And whatsoever ye shall ask in
my name, that will I do, that the Father
may be glorified in the Son.
14 If ye shall ask any thing in my
name, I will do *it*.
15 ¶ [n]If ye love me, keep my commandments.
16 And I will pray the Father, and
[o]he shall give you another Comforter,
that he may abide with you for ever;
17 *Even* the Spirit of truth; [p]whom
the world cannot receive, because it
seeth him not, neither knoweth him:

but ye know him; for he dwelleth with
you, [q]and shall be in you.
18 I will not leave you [1]comfortless:
I will come to you.
19 Yet a little while, and the world
seeth me no more; but [r]ye see me: [s]be-
cause I live, ye shall live also.
20 At that day ye shall know that [t]I
am in my Father, and ye in me, and I in
you.
21 [u]He that hath my commandments,
and keepeth them, he it is that loveth
me: and he that loveth me shall be loved
of my Father, and I will love him, and
will manifest myself to him.
22 Jū'das saith unto him, not Ĭs-
căr'ĭ-ot, Lord, how is it that thou wilt
manifest thyself unto us, and not unto
the world?
23 Jē'sus answered and said unto
him, If a man love me, he will keep my
words: and my Father will love him,
[v]and we will come unto him, and make
our abode with him.
24 He that loveth me not keepeth
not my sayings: and [w]the word which
ye hear is not mine, but the Father's
which sent me.
25 These things have I spoken unto
you, being *yet* present with you.
26 But [x]the Comforter, *which is* the
Hō'lȳ Ghōst, whom the Father will
send in my name, [y]he shall teach you
all things, and bring all things to your
remembrance, whatsoever I have said
unto you.
27 [z]Peace I leave with you, my peace
I give unto you: not as the world giveth,
give I unto you. Let not your heart be
troubled, neither let it be afraid.
28 Ye have heard how I said unto
you, I go away, and come *again* unto
you. If ye loved me, ye would rejoice,
because I said, I go unto the Father: for
[a]my Father is greater than I.
29 And now I have told you before it
come to pass, that, when it is come to
pass, ye might believe.
30 Hereafter I will not talk much
with you: [b]for the prince of this world
cometh, and [c]hath nothing in me.
31 But that the world may know that
I love the Father; and [d]as the Father
gave me commandment, even so I do.
Arise, let us go hence.
15 I AM the true vine, and my Father is the husbandman.
2 [a]Every branch in me that beareth
not fruit he taketh away: and every
branch that beareth fruit, he purgeth
it, that it may bring forth more fruit.
3 [b]Now ye are clean through the
word which I have spoken unto you.
4 [c]Abide in me, and I in you. As the
branch cannot bear fruit of itself, except it abide in the vine; no more can
ye, except ye abide in me.
5 I am the vine, ye *are* the branches:
He that abideth in me, and I in him, the
same bringeth forth much [d]fruit: for
[1]without me ye can do nothing.
6 [e]If a man abide not in me, he is
cast forth as a branch, and is withered;
and men gather them, and cast *them*
into the fire, and they are burned.

[q]1 John 2.27
18 [1]Or, orphans
19 [r]ch. 16.16
[s]1 Cor. 15.20
20 [t]ch. 10.38
21 [u]1 John 2.5
23 [v]Ps. 91.1; 1 John 2.24; Rev. 3.20
24 [w]ch. 7.16
26 [x]Luke 24.49
[y]1 John 2.27
27 [z]Phil. 4.7; Col. 3.15
28 [a]Isa. 9.6; 1 Cor. 11.3; Gal. 4.4; Phil. 2.6-8
30 [b]ch. 12.31
[c]2 Cor. 5.21; 1 John 3.5
31 [d]Phil. 2.8; Heb. 5.8

CHAPTER 15
2 [a]Matt. 15.13; Heb. 6.8
3 [b]ch. 13.10; 1 Pet. 1.22
4 [c]Eph. 2.21-22; 1 John 2.6
5 [d]Prov. 11.30; Phil. 4.13
[1]Or, severed from me
6 [e]Matt. 3.10; Heb. 6.4-6
8 [f]Matt. 5.16; Phil. 1.11
11 [g]ch. 16.24; 1 John 1.4
12 [h]1 Thess. 4.9; 1 Pet. 4.8
13 [i]Rom. 5.7; Eph. 5.2
15 [j]Gen. 18.17-19; Rom. 16.25-26
16 [k]1 John 4.10
[l]Mark 16.15
18 [m]1 John 3.1
19 [n]1 John 4.5
[o]ch. 17.14
20 [p]Ezek. 3.7
22 [q]ch. 9.41
[r]Rom. 1.20
[2]Or, excuse
23 [s]1 John 2.23
25 [t]Ps. 35.19; Ps. 69.4
26 [u]ch. 14.26; Acts 1.4
[v]1 John 5.6
27 [w]Acts 1.8; 2 Pet. 1.16

7 If ye abide in me, and my words
abide in you, ye shall ask what ye will,
and it shall be done unto you.
8 [f]Herein is my Father glorified, that
ye bear much fruit; so shall ye be my
disciples.
9 As the Father hath loved me, so
have I loved you: continue ye in my
love.
10 If ye keep my commandments, ye
shall abide in my love; even as I have
kept my Father's commandments, and
abide in his love.
11 These things have I spoken unto
you, that my joy might remain in you,
and [g]*that* your joy might be full.
12 [h]This is my commandment, That
ye love one another, as I have loved
you.
13 [i]Greater love hath no man than
this, that a man lay down his life for his
friends.
14 Ye are my friends, if ye do whatsoever I command you.
15 Henceforth I call you not servants; for the servant knoweth not
what his lord doeth: but I have called
you friends; [j]for all things that I have
heard of my Father I have made known
unto you.
16 [k]Ye have not chosen me, but I
have chosen you, and [l]ordained you,
that ye should go and bring forth fruit,
and *that* your fruit should remain: that
whatsoever ye shall ask of the Father
in my name, he may give it you.
17 These things I command you, that
ye love one another.
18 [m]If the world hate you, ye know
that it hated me before *it hated* you.
19 [n]If ye were of the world, the
world would love his own: but [o]be-
cause ye are not of the world, but I
have chosen you out of the world,
therefore the world hateth you.
20 Remember the word that I said
unto you, The servant is not greater
than his lord. If they have persecuted
me, they will also persecute you; [p]if
they have kept my saying, they will
keep yours also.
21 But all these things will they do
unto you for my name's sake, because
they know not him that sent me.
22 [q]If I had not come and spoken
unto them, they had not had sin: [r]but
now they have no [2]cloke for their sin.
23 [s]He that hateth me hateth my Father also.
24 If I had not done among them the
works which none other man did, they
had not had sin: but now have they
both seen and hated both me and my
Father.
25 But *this cometh to pass*, that the
word might be fulfilled that is written
in their law, [t]They hated me without a
cause.
26 [u]But when the Comforter is come,
whom I will send unto you from the
Father, *even* the Spirit of truth, which
proceedeth from the Father, [v]he shall
testify of me:
27 And [w]ye also shall bear witness,

because [x]ye have been with me from
the beginning.

16

These things have I spoken unto
you, that ye should not be offended.
2 They shall put you out of the synagogues: yea, the time cometh, [a]that
whosoever killeth you will think that
he doeth God service.
3 And [b]these things will they do
unto you, because they have not known
the Father, nor me.
4 But these things have I told you,
that when the time shall come, ye may
remember that I told you of them. And
these things I said not unto you at the
beginning, because I was with you.
5 But now I go my way to him that
sent me; and none of you asketh me,
Whither goest thou?
6 But because I have said these
things unto you, sorrow hath filled
your heart.
7 Nevertheless I tell you the truth; It
is expedient for you that I go away: for
if I go not away, the Comforter will not
come unto you; but [c]if I depart, I will
send him unto you.
8 And when he is come, he will [1]re-
prove the world of sin, and of righteousness, and of judgment:
9 [d]Of sin, because they believe not
on me;
10 [e]Of righteousness, because I go
to my Father, and ye see me no more;
11 [f]Of judgment, because [g]the prince
of this world is judged.
12 I have yet many things to say unto
you, but ye cannot bear them now.
13 Howbeit when he, the Spirit of
truth, is come, [h]he will guide you into
all truth: for he shall not speak of himself; but whatsoever he shall hear, *that*
shall he speak: and he will [i]shew you
things to come.
14 He shall glorify me: for he shall
receive of mine, and shall shew *it* unto
you.
15 [j]All things that the Father hath
are mine: therefore said I, that he shall
take of mine, and shall shew *it* unto
you.
16 A little while, and ye shall not see
me: and again, a little while, and ye
shall see me, because I go to the Father.
17 Then said *some* of his disciples
among themselves, What is this that
he saith unto us, A little while, and ye
shall not see me: and again, a little
while, and ye shall see me: and, Because I go to the Father?
18 They said therefore, What is this
that he saith, A little while? we cannot
tell what he saith.
19 Now Jē'sus knew that they were
desirous to ask him, and said unto
them, Do ye inquire among yourselves
of that I said, A little while, and ye
shall not see me: and again, a little
while, and ye shall see me?
20 Verily, verily, I say unto you, That
ye shall weep and lament, but the
world shall rejoice: and ye shall be sorrowful, but your sorrow shall be turned
into joy.
21 A woman when she is in travail hath sorrow, because her hour is
come: but as soon as she is delivered of
the child, she remembereth no more
the anguish, for joy that a man is born
into the world.
22 And ye now therefore have sorrow: but I will see you again, and
[k]your heart shall rejoice, and your joy
no man taketh from you.
23 And in that day ye shall ask me
nothing. [l]Verily, verily, I say unto you,
Whatsoever ye shall ask the Father in
my name, he will give *it* you.
24 Hitherto have ye asked nothing
in my name: ask, and ye shall receive,
that your joy may be full.
25 These things have I spoken unto
you in [2]proverbs: but the time cometh,
when I shall no more speak unto you in
[3]proverbs, but I shall shew you plainly
of the Father.
26 At that day ye shall ask in my
name: and I say not unto you, that I
will pray the Father for you:
27 [m]For the Father himself loveth
you, because ye have loved me, and
[n]have believed that I came out from
God.
28 [o]I came forth from the Father,
and am come into the world: again, I
leave the world, and go to the Father.
29 His disciples said unto him, Lo,
now speakest thou plainly, and speakest no [4]proverb.
30 Now are we sure that [p]thou knowest all things, and needest not that any
man should ask thee: by this [q]we believe that thou camest forth from God.
31 Jē'sus answered them, Do ye now
believe?
32 Behold, the hour cometh, yea, is
now come, that ye shall be scattered,
every man to [5]his own, and shall leave
me alone: and yet I am not alone, because the Father is with me.
33 These things I have spoken unto
you, that [r]in me ye might have peace.
[s]In the world ye shall have tribulation:
but be of good cheer; [t]I have overcome
the world.

17

These words spake Jē'sus, and
lifted up his eyes to heaven, and
said, Father, the hour is come; glorify
thy Son, that thy Son also may glorify
thee:
2 [a]As thou hast given him power
over all flesh, that he should give eternal life to as many [b]as thou hast given
him.
3 And [c]this is life eternal, that they
might know thee [d]the only true God,
and Jē'sus Chrīst whom thou hast sent.
4 I have glorified thee on the earth: I
have finished the work which thou
gavest me to do.
5 And now, O Father, glorify thou
me with thine own self with the glory
[e]which I had with thee before the
world was.
6 [f]I have manifested thy name unto
the men which thou gavest me out of
the world: thine they were, and thou
gavest them me; and they have kept
thy word.

[x]Luke 1.2

CHAPTER 16
2 [a]Acts 8.1
3 [b]Rom. 10.2; 1 Cor. 2.8; 1 Tim. 1.13
7 [c]Acts 2.33; Eph. 4.8
8 [1]Or, convince
9 [d]Acts 2.22; Rom. 3.9; Gal. 3.22
10 [e]Isa. 42.6-21; Dan. 9.24; Acts 2.32; 1 Cor. 1.30; Gal. 5.5
11 [f]Matt. 12.18-36; Acts 10.42; 1 Cor. 4.5; Heb. 6.2; Rev. 1.7
[g]Luke 10.18; ch. 12.31; Eph. 2.2
13 [h]ch. 14.26
[i]1 Tim. 4.1
15 [j]Matt. 11.27; ch. 17.10; Col. 1.19
22 [k]Luke 24.41; ch. 14.1-27; ch. 20.20; Acts 2.46; 1 Pet. 1.8
23 [l]ch. 14.13
25 [2]Or, parables
[3]Or, parables
27 [m]Heb. 12.6; Jude 20-21
[n]ch. 3.13
28 [o]ch. 13.3
29 [4]Or, parable
30 [p]ch. 21.17
[q]ch. 17.8
32 [5]Or, his own home
33 [r]Isa. 9.6; ch. 14.27; Col. 1.20
[s]Matt. 10.38; Rev. 3.19
[t]Isa. 49.24-25; 1 John 4.4

CHAPTER 17
2 [a]Ps. 2.6; Heb. 2.8
[b]ch. 6.37
3 [c]Isa. 53.11
[d]1 Cor. 8.4; 1 Thess. 1.9
5 [e]ch. 1.1; Heb. 1.3-10
6 [f]Ps. 22.22

7 Now they have known that all
things whatsoever thou hast given me
are of thee.
8 For I have given unto them the
words which thou gavest me; and they
have received *them,* and have known
surely that I came out from thee, and
they have believed that thou didst send
me.
9 I pray for them: [g]I pray not for the
world, but for them which thou hast
given me; for they are thine.
10 [h]And all mine are thine, and
thine are mine; and I am glorified in
them.
11 And now I am no more in the
world, but these are in the world, and
I come to thee. Holy Father, [i]keep
through thine own name those whom
thou hast given me, that they may be
one, [j]as we *are.*
12 While I was with them in the
world, [k]I kept them in thy name: those
that thou gavest me I have kept, and
[l]none of them is lost, [m]but the son of
perdition; [n]that the scripture might be
fulfilled.
13 And now come I to thee; and
these things I speak in the world, that
they might have my joy fulfilled in
themselves.
14 I have given them thy word; [o]and
the world hath hated them, because
they are not of the world, even as I am
not of the world.
15 I pray not that thou shouldest
take them out of the world, but [p]that
thou shouldest keep them from the
evil.
16 They are not of the world, even
as I am not of the world.
17 Sanctify them through thy truth:
thy word is truth.
18 As thou hast sent me into the
world, even so have I also sent them
into the world.
19 And [q]for their sakes I sanctify
myself, that they also might be [1]sancti-
fied through the truth.
20 Neither pray I for these alone,
but for them also which shall believe
on me through their word;
21 That they all may be one; as
[r]thou, Father, *art* in me, and I in thee,
that they also may be one in us: that
the world may believe that thou hast
sent me.
22 And the glory which thou gavest
me I have given them; [s]that they may
be one, even as we are one:
23 I in them, and thou in me, [t]that
they may be made [u]perfect in one; and
that the world may know that thou
hast sent me, and hast loved them, as
thou hast loved me.
24 [v]Father, I will that they also,
whom thou hast given me, be with me
where I am; that they may [w]behold my
glory, which thou hast given me: for
thou lovedst me before the foundation
of the world.
25 O righteous Father, the world
hath not known thee: but I have known
thee, and these have known that thou
hast sent me.

9 [g]1 John 5.19
10 [h]Rom. 8.30
11 [i]1 Pet. 1.5
[j]ch. 10.30
12 [k]ch. 6.39; ch. 10.28; Heb. 2.13
[l]ch. 18.9; 1 John 2.19
[m]Ps. 41.9; ch. 13.18
[n]Ps. 109.8; Acts 1.20
14 [o]1 John 3.13
15 [p]Gal. 1.4; 2 Thess. 3.3
19 [q]1 Cor. 1.30; 1 Thess 4.7; Heb. 10.10
[1]Or, truly sanctified
21 [r]ch. 10.38; Phil. 2.6; 1 John 5.7
22 [s]1 John 1.3
23 [t]Rom. 12.5; Gal. 3.28; Col. 3.14
[u]ch. 10.38; Heb. 12.23
24 [v]1 Thess. 4.17
[w]2 Cor. 3.18; 1 John 3.2
26 [x]Eph. 3.17
CHAPTER 18
1 [a]Luke 22.39
[b]2 Sam. 15.23
2 [c]Luke 21.37
3 [d]Matt. 26.47; Mark 14.43; Luke 22.47; Acts 1.16
9 [e]ch. 6.39; 1 Pet. 1.5; Jude 1
10 [f]Matt. 26.51; Mark 14.57; Luke 22.49
11 [g]Matt. 20.22
13 [h]Matt. 26.57
[i]Luke 3.2; Acts 4.6
[1]And Annas sent Christ bound unto Caiaphas the high priest
14 [j]Luke 3.2; ch. 11.50; Acts 4.6

26 And I have declared unto them
thy name, and will declare *it:* that the
love wherewith thou hast loved me
may be in them, and [x]I in them.

18 When Jē′sus had spoken these
words, he [a]went forth with his
disciples over the [b]brook Çē′drŏn,
where was a garden, into the which he
entered, and his disciples.
2 And Jū′das also, which betrayed
him, knew the place: [c]for Jē′sus ofttimes resorted thither with his disciples.
3 [d]Jū′das then, having received a
band *of men* and officers from the
chief priests and Phăr′ĭ-sees, cometh
thither with lanterns and torches and
weapons.
4 Jē′sus therefore, knowing all things
that should come upon him, went forth,
and said unto them, Whom seek ye?
5 They answered him, Jē′sus of Nāz′-
a-rěth. Jē′sus saith unto them, I am *he.*
And Jū′das also, which betrayed him,
stood with them.
6 As soon then as he had said unto
them, I am *he,* they went backward,
and fell to the ground.
7 Then asked he them again, Whom
seek ye? And they said, Jē′sus of
Nāz′a-rěth.
8 Jē′sus answered, I have told you
that I am *he:* if therefore ye seek me, let
these go their way:
9 That the saying might be fulfilled,
which he spake, [e]Of them which thou
gavest me have I lost none.
10 [f]Then Sī′mon Pē′tẽr having a
sword drew it, and smote the high
priest's servant, and cut off his right
ear. The servant's name was Măl′chus.
11 Then said Jē′sus unto Pē′tẽr, Put
up thy sword into the sheath: [g]the cup
which my Father hath given me, shall I
not drink it?
12 Then the band and the captain
and officers of the Jews took Jē′sus,
and bound him,
13 And [h]led him away to [i]Ăn′nas
first; for he was father in law to Cā′ia-
phas, which was the high priest that
same year.[1]
14 [j]Now Cā′ia-phas was he, which
gave counsel to the Jews, that it was
expedient that one man should die for
the people.
15 ¶ And Sī′mon Pē′tẽr followed
Jē′sus, and *so did* another disciple:
that disciple was known unto the high
priest, and went in with Jē′sus into the
palace of the high priest.
16 But Pē′tẽr stood at the door without. Then went out that other disciple,
which was known unto the high priest,
and spake unto her that kept the door,
and brought in Pē′tẽr.
17 Then saith the damsel that kept
the door unto Pē′tẽr, Art not thou also
one of this man's disciples? He saith, I
am not.
18 And the servants and officers
stood there, who had made a fire
of coals; for it was cold: and they
warmed themselves: and Pē′tẽr stood
with them, and warmed himself.

19 ¶ The high priest then asked Jē'-
sus of his disciples, and of his doctrine.
20 Jē'sus answered him, [k]I spake
openly to the world; I ever taught
in the synagogue, and in the temple,
whither the Jews always resort; and in
secret have I said nothing.
21 Why askest thou me? ask them
which heard me, what I have said unto
them: behold, they know what I said.
22 And when he had thus spoken,
one of the officers which stood by
[l]struck Jē'sus [2]with the palm of his
hand, saying, Answerest thou the high
priest so?
23 Jē'sus answered him, [m]If I have
spoken evil, bear witness of the evil:
but if well, why smitest thou me?
24 Now Ăn'nas had sent him bound
unto Cā'ia-phas the high priest.
25 And Sī'mon Pē'tēr stood and
warmed himself. [n]They said therefore
unto him, Art not thou also *one* of his
disciples? He denied *it*, and said, I am
not.
26 One of the servants of the high
priest, being *his* kinsman whose ear
Pē'tēr cut off, saith, Did not I see thee
in the garden with him?
27 Pē'tēr then denied again: and
[o]immediately the cock crew.
28 ¶ [p]Then led they Jē'sus from Cā'-
ia-phas unto [3]the hall of judgment: and
it was early; [q]and they themselves
went not into the judgment hall, lest
they should be defiled; but that they
might eat [r]the passover.
29 Pī'late then went out unto them,
and said, What accusation bring ye
against this man?
30 They answered and said unto
him, If he were not a malefactor, we
would not have delivered him up unto
thee.
31 Then said Pī'late unto them, Take
ye him, and judge him according to
your law. The Jews therefore said unto
him, It is not lawful for us to put any
man to death:
32 [s]That the saying of Jē'sus might
be fulfilled, which he spake, signifying
what death he should die.
33 Then Pī'late entered into the judgment hall again, and called Jē'sus, and
said unto him, Art thou the King of the
Jews?
34 Jē'sus answered him, Sayest thou
this thing of thyself, or did others tell it
thee of me?
35 Pī'late answered, Am I a Jew?
Thine own nation and the chief priests
have delivered thee unto me: what
hast thou done?
36 [t]Jē'sus answered, [u]My kingdom
is not of this world: if my kingdom
were of this world, then would my servants fight, that I should not be delivered to the Jews: but now is my kingdom not from hence.
37 Pī'late therefore said unto him,
Art thou a king then? Jē'sus answered,
Thou sayest that I am a king. To this
end was I born, and for this cause
came I into the world, that I should
[v]bear witness unto the truth. Every
one that [w]is of the truth heareth my
voice.
38 Pī'late saith unto him, What is
truth? And when he had said this, he
went out again unto the Jews, and
saith unto them, [x]I find in him no fault
at all.
39 But ye have a custom, that I
should release unto you one at the passover: will ye therefore that I release
unto you the King of the Jews?
40 [y]Then cried they all again, saying, Not this man, but Ba-răb'bas.
[z]Now Ba-răb'bas was a robber.

19 Then [a]Pī'late therefore took Jē'-
sus, and scourged *him*.
2 And the soldiers platted a crown
of thorns, and put *it* on his head, and
they put on him a purple robe,
3 And said, Hail, King of the Jews!
and they smote him with their hands.
4 Pī'late therefore went forth again,
and saith unto them, Behold, I bring
him forth to you, [b]that ye may know
that I find no fault in him.
5 Then came Jē'sus forth, wearing
the crown of thorns, and the purple
robe. And *Pī'late* saith unto them, Behold the man!
6 [c]When the chief priests therefore
and officers saw him, they cried out,
saying, Crucify *him*, crucify *him*. Pī'-
late saith unto them, Take ye him, and
crucify *him*: for I find no fault in him.
7 The Jews answered him, [d]We have
a law, and by our law he ought to die,
because [e]he made himself the Son of
God.
8 ¶ When Pī'late therefore heard
that saying, he was the more afraid;
9 And went again into the judgment
hall, and saith unto Jē'sus, Whence art
thou? [f]But Jē'sus gave him no answer.
10 Then saith Pī'late unto him,
Speakest thou not unto me? knowest
thou not that I have power to crucify
thee, and have power to release thee?
11 Jē'sus answered, [g]Thou couldest
have no power *at all* against me, except it were given thee from above:
therefore he that delivered me unto
thee hath the greater sin.
12 And from thenceforth Pī'late
sought to release him: but the Jews
cried out, saying, [h]If thou let this man
go, thou art not Çæ'sar's friend: [i]who-
soever maketh himself a king speaketh against Çæ'sar.
13 ¶ When Pī'late therefore heard
that saying, he brought Jē'sus forth,
and sat down in the judgment seat in a
place that is called the Pavement, but
in the Hē'brew, [1]Găb'ba-thȧ.
14 And [j]it was the preparation of
the passover, and about the sixth hour:
and he saith unto the Jews, Behold
your King!
15 But they cried out, Away with
him, away with *him*, crucify him. Pī'-
late saith unto them, Shall I crucify
your King? The chief priests answered,
[k]We have no king but Çæ'sar.
16 [l]Then delivered he him therefore
unto them to be crucified. And they
took Jē'sus, and led *him* away.

20 [k]Matt. 26.55; ch. 3.21
22 [l]Job 16.10; Isa. 50.6; Jer. 20.2; Mic. 5.1; Acts 23.2
[2]Or, with a rod
23 [m]Heb. 12.3
25 [n]Mark 14.69; Luke 22.58
27 [o]Matt. 26.74; Luke 22.60; ch. 13.38
28 [p]Matt. 27.2; Mark 15.1; Acts 3.13
[3]Or, Pilate's house
[q]Matt. 26.69; Mark 14.66; Acts 11.3
[r]Deut. 16.2
32 [s]Matt. 20.19; ch. 12.32-33
36 [t]1 Tim. 6.13
[u]Isa. 9.6; Dan. 2.44; Luke 12.14; 2 Cor. 10.4
37 [v]Isa. 55.4; Rev. 1.5
[w]ch. 8.47; 1 John 3.19
38 [x]Matt. 27.18-19-24; ch. 19.4-6
40 [y]Acts 3.14
[z]Luke 23.19

CHAPTER 19
1 [a]Isa. 50.6; Luke 18.33
4 [b]ch. 18.38; 2 Cor. 5.21
6 [c]Acts 3.13
7 [d]Lev. 24.16
[e]Matt. 26.65; ch. 5.18
9 [f]Isa. 53.7; Acts 8.32
11 [g]Gen. 45.7-8; Acts 2.23
12 [h]Luke 23.2
[i]Acts 17.7
13 [1]That is, elevated
14 [j]Matt. 27.62
15 [k]Gen. 49.10
16 [l]Matt. 27.26-31; Luke 23.24

17 And he bearing his cross [m]went
forth into a place called *the place* of a
skull, which is called in the Hē'brew
Gŏl'go-thȧ:
18 [n]Where they crucified him, and
two other with him, on either side one,
and Jē'sus in the midst.
19 ¶ And Pī'late wrote a title, and
put *it* on the cross. And the writing
was, JĒ'SUS OF NĂZ'A-RĔTH THE
KING OF THE JEWS.
20 This title then read many of the
Jews: for the place where Jē'sus was
crucified was nigh to the city: and it
was written in Hē'brew, *and* Greek,
and Lăt'in.
21 Then said the chief priests of the
Jews to Pī'late, Write not, The King of
the Jews; but that he said, I am King of
the Jews.
22 Pī'late answered, What I have
written I have written.
23 ¶ Then the soldiers, when they
had crucified Jē'sus, took his garments,
and made four parts, to every soldier a
part; and also *his* coat: now the coat
was without seam, [2]woven from the top
throughout.
24 They said therefore among themselves, Let us not rend it, but cast lots
for it, whose it shall be: that the scripture might be fulfilled, which saith,
[o]They parted my raiment among them,
and for my vesture they did cast lots.
These things therefore the soldiers did.
25 ¶ Now there stood by the cross of
Jē'sus his mother, and his mother's sister, Mā'rȳ the *wife* of [3]Clē'o-phas, and
Mā'rȳ Măg-da-lē'ne.
26 When Jē'sus therefore saw his
mother, and [p]the disciple standing by,
whom he loved, he saith unto his
mother, [q]Woman, behold thy son!
27 Then saith he to the disciple, Behold thy mother! And from that hour
that disciple took her [r]unto his own
home.
28 ¶ After this, Jē'sus knowing that
all things were now accomplished,
[s]that the scripture might be fulfilled,
saith, I thirst.
29 Now there was set a vessel full of
vinegar: and they filled a spunge with
vinegar, and put *it* upon hyssop, and
put *it* to his mouth.
30 When Jē'sus therefore had received the vinegar, he said, [t]It is finished: and he bowed his head, and
[u]gave up the ghost.
31 The Jews therefore, [v]because it
was the preparation, [w]that the bodies
should not remain upon the cross on
the sabbath day, (for that sabbath day
was [x]an high day,) besought Pī'late
that their legs might be broken, and
that they might be taken away.
32 Then came the soldiers, and brake
the legs of the first, and of the other
which was crucified with him.
33 But when they came to Jē'sus,
and saw that he was dead already,
they brake not his legs:
34 But one of the soldiers with a
spear pierced his side, and forthwith
[y]came there out blood and water.
35 [z]And he that saw *it* bare record,
and his record is true: and he knoweth
that he saith true, that ye might believe.
36 For these things were done, [a]that
the scripture should be fulfilled, A bone
of him shall not be broken.
37 And again another scripture saith,
[b]They shall look on him whom they
pierced.
38 ¶ [c]And after this Jō'seph of Ăr-ĭ-
mă-thæ'ȧ, being a disciple of Jē'sus,
but secretly [d]for fear of the Jews, besought Pī'late that he might take away
the body of Jē'sus: and Pī'late gave
him leave. He came therefore, and
took the body of Jē'sus.
39 And there came also [e]Nĭc-o-dē'-
mus, which at the first came to Jē'sus
by night, and brought [f]a mixture of
myrrh and aloes, about an hundred
pound *weight*.
40 Then took they the body of Jē'-
sus, and [g]wound it in linen clothes
with the spices, as the manner of the
Jews is to bury.
41 Now in the place where he was
crucified there was a garden; and in
the garden a [h]new sepulchre, wherein
was never man yet laid.
42 [i]There laid they Jē'sus therefore
because of the Jews' preparation *day;*
for the sepulchre was nigh at hand.

20 The [a]first *day* of the week cometh
Mā'rȳ Măg-da-lē'ne early, when
it was yet dark, unto the sepulchre, and
seeth the stone taken away from the
sepulchre.
2 Then she runneth, and cometh to
Sī'mon Pē'tēr, and to the [b]other disciple, whom Jē'sus loved, and saith unto
them, They have taken away the Lord
out of the sepulchre, and we know not
where they have laid him.
3 [c]Pē'tēr therefore went forth, and
that other disciple, and came to the
sepulchre.
4 So they ran both together: and the
other disciple did outrun Pē'tēr, and
came first to the sepulchre.
5 And he stooping down, *and looking in,* saw [d]the linen clothes lying; yet
went he not in.
6 Then cometh Sī'mon Pē'tēr following him, and went into the sepulchre,
and seeth the linen clothes lie,
7 And [e]the napkin, that was about
his head, not lying with the linen
clothes, but wrapped together in a
place by itself.
8 Then went in also that other disciple, which came first to the sepulchre,
and he saw, and believed.
9 For as yet they knew not the [f]scrip-
ture, that he must rise again from the
dead.
10 Then the disciples went away
again unto their own home.
11 ¶ [g]But Mā'rȳ stood without at the
sepulchre weeping: and as she wept,
she stooped down, *and looked* into the
sepulchre,
12 And seeth two angels in white sitting, the one at the head, and the other
at the feet, where the body of Jē'sus
had lain.

17 [m]Num. 15.36; 1 Ki. 21.13; Luke 23.33; Heb. 13.12
18 [n]Isa. 53.12; Dan. 9.26; Gal. 3.13
23 [2]Or, wrought
24 [o]Ps. 22.18; Matt. 27.35; Mark 15.24
25 [3]Or, Clo-pas
26 [p]ch. 13.23 [q]ch. 2.4
27 [r]Gen. 47.12; ch. 1.11
28 [s]Ps. 69.21
30 [t]ch. 17.4 [u]Matt. 20.28; Acts 7.60; Phil. 2.8; 1 Thess. 5.10
31 [v]Mark 15.42 [w]Deut. 21.23 [x]Ex. 12.18
34 [y]Zech. 13.1
35 [z]ch. 17.21-23; ch. 20.31; 1 John 1.1
36 [a]Ex. 12.46; Num. 9.12; Ps. 34.20
37 [b]Ps. 22.16; Zech. 12.10; Rev. 1.7
38 [c]Matt. 27.57; Mark 15.42; Luke 23.50 [d]Prov. 29.25; ch. 9.22
39 [e]ch. 3.1-2 [f]2 Chr. 16.14; Luke 23.56
40 [g]Acts 5.6
41 [h]2 Ki. 23.30; Isa. 22.16; Matt. 27.60; Luke 23.53
42 [i]Isa. 53.9

CHAPTER 20
1 [a]Matt. 28.1; Mark 16.1; Luke 24.1
2 [b]ch. 13.23
3 [c]Luke 24.12
5 [d]ch. 19.40
7 [e]ch. 11.44
9 [f]Ps. 16.10; Isa. 26.19; Matt. 16.21; Acts 2.25-32; 1 Cor. 15.4
11 [g]Mark 16.5

13 And they say unto her, Woman, why weepest thou? She saith unto them, Because they have taken away my Lord, and I know not where they have laid him.

14 [h]And when she had thus said, she turned herself back, and saw Jē′sus standing, and [i]knew not that it was Jē′sus.

15 Jē′sus saith unto her, Woman, why weepest thou? whom seekest thou? She, supposing him to be the gardener, saith unto him, Sir, if thou have borne him hence, tell me where thou hast laid him, and I will take him away.

16 Jē′sus saith unto her, Mā′rȳ. She turned herself, and saith unto him, [j]Răb-bō′nī; which is to say, Master.

17 Jē′sus saith unto her, Touch me not; for I am not yet ascended to my Father: but go to [k]my brethren, and say unto them, [l]I ascend unto my Father, and your Father; and *to* [m]my God, and your God.

18 [n]Mā′rȳ Măg-da-lē′ne came and told the disciples that she had seen the Lord, and *that* he had spoken these things unto her.

19 ¶ [o]Then the same day at evening, being the first *day* of the week, when the doors were shut where the disciples were assembled for fear of the Jews, came Jē′sus and stood in the midst, and saith unto them, Peace *be* unto you.

20 And when he had so said, he [p]shewed unto them *his* hands and his side. [q]Then were the disciples glad, when they saw the Lord.

21 Then said Jē′sus to them again, Peace *be* unto you: [r]as *my* Father hath sent me, even so send I you.

22 And when he had said this, he breathed on *them*, and saith unto them, Receive ye the Hō′lȳ Ghōst:

23 [s]Whose soever sins ye remit, they are remitted unto them; *and* whose soever *sins* ye retain, they are retained.

24 ¶ But Thŏm′as, one of the twelve, [t]called Dĭd′ȳ-mus, was not with them when Jē′sus came.

25 The other disciples therefore said unto him, We have seen the Lord. But he said unto them, Except I shall see in his hands the print of the nails, and put my finger into the print of the nails, and thrust my hand into his side, I will not believe.

26 ¶ And after eight days again his disciples were within, and Thŏm′as with them: *then* came Jē′sus, the doors being shut, and stood in the midst, and said, [u]Peace *be* unto you.

27 Then saith he to Thŏm′as, Reach hither thy finger, and behold my hands; and [v]reach hither thy hand, and thrust *it* into my side: and be not faithless, but believing.

28 And Thŏm′as answered and said unto him, [w]My Lord and my God.

29 Jē′sus saith unto him, Thŏm′as, because thou hast seen me, thou hast believed: [x]blessed *are* they that have not seen, and *yet* have believed.

30 ¶ [y]And many other signs truly did Jē′sus in the presence of his disciples, which are not written in this book:

31 [z]But these are written, that ye might believe that Jē′sus is the Chrīst, the Son of God; [a]and that believing ye might have life through his name.

21

After these things Jē′sus shewed himself again to the disciples at the sea of Ti-bē′rĭ-as; and on this wise shewed he *himself*.

2 There were together Sī′mon Pē′tẽr, and Thŏm′as called Dĭd′ȳ-mus, and [a]Na-thăn′a-el of Cā′nȧ in Găl′ĭ-lee, and [b]the *sons* of Zēb′e-dee, and two other of his disciples.

3 Sī′mon Pē′tẽr saith unto them, I go a fishing. They say unto him, We also go with thee. They went forth, and entered into a ship immediately; and that night they caught nothing.

4 But when the morning was now come, Jē′sus stood on the shore: but the disciples [c]knew not that it was Jē′sus.

5 Then [d]Jē′sus saith unto them, [1]Children, have ye any meat? They answered him, No.

6 And he said unto them, [e]Cast the net on the right side of the ship, and ye shall find. They cast therefore, and now they were not able to draw it for the multitude of fishes.

7 Therefore [f]that disciple whom Jē′sus loved saith unto Pē′tẽr, It is the Lord. Now when Sī′mon Pē′tẽr heard that it was the Lord, he girt *his* fisher's coat *unto him*, (for he was naked,) and [g]did cast himself into the sea.

8 And the other disciples came in a little ship; (for they were not far from land, but as it were two hundred cubits,) dragging the net with fishes.

9 As soon then as they were come to land, they [h]saw a fire of coals there, and fish laid thereon, and bread.

10 Jē′sus saith unto them, Bring of the fish which ye have now caught.

11 Sī′mon Pē′tẽr went up, and drew the net to land full of great fishes, an hundred and fifty and three: and for all there were so many, yet was not the net broken.

12 Jē′sus saith unto them, [i]Come *and* dine. And none of the disciples durst ask him, Who art thou? knowing that it was the Lord.

13 Jē′sus then cometh, and taketh bread, and giveth them, and fish likewise.

14 This is now [j]the third time that Jē′sus shewed himself to his disciples, after that he was risen from the dead.

15 ¶ So when they had dined, Jē′sus saith to Sī′mon Pē′tẽr, Sī′mon, *son* of Jō′nas, [k]lovest thou me more than these? He saith unto him, Yea, Lord; [l]thou knowest that I love thee. He saith unto him, [m]Feed my lambs.

16 He saith to him again the second time, Sī′mon, *son* of Jō′nas, lovest thou me? He saith unto him, Yea, Lord; thou knowest that I love thee. [n]He saith unto him, Feed my sheep.

14 [h]Matt. 28.9 [i]Luke 24.16-31; ch. 21.4
16 [j]Matt. 23.8-10; ch. 1.38-49
17 [k]Ps. 22.22; Matt. 28.10; Rom. 8.29; Heb. 2.11 [l]ch. 16.28; 1 Pet. 1.3 [m]Eph. 1.17
18 [n]Matt. 28.10; Luke 24.10
19 [o]Mark 16.14; Luke 24.36
20 [p]1 John 1.1 [q]ch. 16.22
21 [r]Isa. 61.1; Matt. 28.18; ch. 17.18-19; Heb. 3.1; 2 Tim. 2.2
23 [s]Matt. 16.19; Mark 2.5-10; Acts 2.38
24 [t]ch. 11.16
26 [u]Isa. 9.7; Mic. 5.5; Col. 1.20
27 [v]1 John 1.1
28 [w]Ps. 73.25-26; Luke 1.46-47; 1 Tim. 1.17
29 [x]2 Cor. 5.7; 1 Pet. 1.8
30 [y]ch. 21.25
31 [z]Luke 1.4; Rom. 15.4 [a]ch. 3.15-16; 1 Pet. 1.9

CHAPTER 21
2 [a]ch. 1.45 [b]Matt. 4.21
4 [c]ch. 20.14
5 [d]Ps. 37.3; Luke 24.41; Heb. 13.5 [1]Or, Sirs
6 [e]Luke 5.4-6-7
7 [f]ch. 13.23 [g]Song 8.7
9 [h]1 Ki. 19.6; Mark 8.3-9
12 [i]Acts 10.41
14 [j]ch. 20.19-26
15 [k]Matt. 26.33 [l]2 Ki. 20.3 [m]Acts 20.28; Eph. 4.11; 1 Tim. 4.16; 1 Pet. 5.2
16 [n]Heb. 13.20; 1 Pet. 2.25

17 He saith unto him [o]the third time,
Sī'mon, *son* of Jō'nas, lovest thou me?
Pē'tĕr was grieved because he said
unto him the third time, Lovest thou
me? And he said unto him, Lord, [p]thou
knowest all things; thou knowest that I
love thee. Jē'sus saith unto him, Feed
my sheep.
18 [q]Verily, verily, I say unto thee,
When thou wast young, thou gird-
edst thyself, and walkedst whither thou
wouldest: but when thou shalt be old,
thou shalt stretch forth thy hands, and
another shall gird thee, and carry *thee*
whither thou wouldest not.
19 This spake he, signifying [r]by
what death he should glorify God. And
when he had spoken this, he saith unto
him, Follow me.
20 Then Pē'tĕr, turning about, seeth
the disciple [s]whom Jē'sus loved following; which also leaned on his breast at
supper, and said, Lord, which is he
that betrayeth thee?
21 Pē'tĕr seeing him saith to Jē'sus,
Lord, and what *shall* this man *do?*
22 Jē'sus saith unto him, If I will
that he tarry [t]till I come, what *is* [u]*that*
to thee? follow thou me.
23 Then went this saying abroad
among the brethren, that that disciple
should not die: yet Jē'sus said not unto
him, He shall not die; but, If I will that
he tarry till I come, what *is that* to
thee?
24 This is the disciple which testifieth of these things, and wrote these
things: and [v]we know that his testimony is true.
25 And there are also many other
things which Jē'sus did, the which,
if they should be written every one,
[w]I suppose that even the world itself
could not contain the books that should
be written. Amen.

17 [o]ch. 13.38 [p]1 Sam. 16.7; 1 Chr. 28.9; 2 Chr. 6.30; Ps. 7.9; Jer. 11.20; Matt. 9.4; Mark 2.8; ch. 2.24-25; ch. 6.64;
18 [q]ch. 13.36;
19 [r]Phil. 1.20; 2 Pet. 1.14
20 [s]ch. 13.23-25; ch. 19.26
22 [t]Matt. 16.27; 1 Cor. 4.5; Rev. 2.25 [u]Deut. 29.29
24 [v]ch. 7.17; 3 John 12
25 [w]Amos 7.10

THE

ACTS OF THE APOSTLES

Life's Questions

Will the gospel really win out over all opposition?
How does the Holy Spirit work?
Should I expect the Spirit to work through me?

God's Answers

Luke completed the literary work God gave Him by describing the unhindered spread of the gospel from Jerusalem to Rome, from Jew to Gentile, from Jewish culture to Greek culture (see introduction to Luke). Luke assured Christians that the nature of the gospel was worth holding on to despite all opposition and that the Holy Spirit would lead them as they joined in God's mission.

Acts shows: God prepared the way for unhindered mission as the church waited and organized (ch. 1); the Spirit empowers the church for mission and to overcome persecution (2:1—8:4); God is not hindered by cultural barriers, organized opposition, physical barriers, racial barriers, or political persecution (8:5—12:25); God is not hindered by geographical boundaries as the gospel of salvation by grace through faith ignores ritual requirements (13:1—20:12); God is not hindered by human prisons and powerful governments (20:13—28:31).

Acts calls you to ask the Holy Spirit to show you God's mission opportunity for you and to lead you to overcome all opposition to that mission.

1 The former treatise have I made,
[a]O The-ŏph'ĭ-lŭs, of all that Jē'sus
began both to do and teach,
2 [b]Until the day in which he was
taken up, after that he through the
Hō'lȳ Ghōst had given commandments
unto the apostles whom he had chosen:
3 [c]To whom also he shewed himself
alive after his passion by many infalli-
ble proofs, being seen of them forty
days, and speaking of the things pertaining to the kingdom of God:
4 And, [1]being assembled together
with *them,* commanded them that they
should not depart from Je-rụ'sa-lĕm,
but wait for the promise of the Father,
[d]which, *saith he,* ye have heard of me.
5 [e]For Jŏhn truly baptized with water; [f]but ye shall be baptized with the
Hō'lȳ Ghōst not many days hence.
6 When they therefore were come
together, they asked of him, saying,
Lord, wilt thou at this time [g]restore
again the kingdom to Is'ra-el?
7 And he said unto them, [h]It is not
for you to know the times or the seasons, which the Father hath put in his
own power.
8 But ye shall receive [2]power, after
that the Hō'lȳ Ghōst is come upon you:
and ye shall be witnesses unto me both
in Je-rụ'sa-lĕm, and in all Jū-dæ'ȧ, and
in Sa-mā'rĭ-ȧ, and unto the uttermost
part of the earth.
9 [i]And when he had spoken these
things, while they beheld, he was taken
up; and a cloud received him out of
their sight.
10 And while they looked stedfastly
toward heaven as he went up, behold, two men stood by them [j]in white
apparel;
11 Which also said, Ye men of Găl'-
ĭ-lee, why stand ye gazing up into
heaven? this same Jē'sus, which is

CHAPTER 1
1 [a]Luke 1.3
2 [b]1 Tim. 3.16; Heb. 1.3
3 [c]Matt. 28.9-16-17; 1 Cor. 15.5
4 [1]Or, eating together with them [d]John 14.16
5 [e]ch. 11.16 [f]Joel 2.28-29
6 [g]Isa. 1.26
7 [h]Deut. 29.29
8 [2]Or, the power of the Holy Ghost coming upon you
9 [i]John 6.62
10 [j]ch. 10.3

taken up from you into heaven, [k]shall so come in like manner as ye have seen him go into heaven.

12 Then returned they unto Je-ru'sa-lĕm from the [l]mount called Ŏl'i-vĕt, which is from Je-ru'sa-lĕm a [m]sabbath day's journey.

13 And when they were come in, they went up [n]into an upper room, where abode both Pē'tĕr, and Jāmes, and Jŏhn, and Ăn'drew, Phĭl'ĭp, and Thŏm'as, Bär-thŏl'ō-mew, and Măt'thew, Jāmes *the son* of Ăl-phæ'us, and [o]Sī'mon Ze-lō'tēs, and [p]Jū'das *the brother* of Jāmes.

14 These all continued with one accord in prayer and supplication, with [q]the women, and Mā'rȳ the mother of Jē'sus, and with [r]his brethren.

15 ¶ And in those days Pē'tĕr stood up in the midst of the disciples, and said, (the number [s]of names together were about an hundred and twenty,)

16 Men *and* brethren, this scripture must needs have been fulfilled, [t]which the Hō'lȳ Ghōst by the mouth of Dā'vid spake before concerning Jū'das, [u]which was guide to them that took Jē'sus.

17 For [v]he was numbered with us, and had obtained part of [w]this ministry.

18 [x]Now this man purchased a field with [y]the reward of iniquity; and [z]falling headlong, he burst asunder in the midst, and all his bowels gushed out.

19 And it was known unto all the dwellers at Je-ru'sa-lĕm; insomuch as that field is called in their proper tongue, A-çĕl'da-mȧ, that is to say, The field of blood.

20 For it is written in the book of Psalms, [a]Let his habitation be desolate, and let no man dwell therein: and his [3]bishoprick let another take.

21 Wherefore of these men which have companied with us all the time that the Lord Jē'sus went in and out among us,

22 Beginning from the baptism of Jŏhn, unto that same day that he was taken up from us, must one be ordained [b]to be a witness with us of his resurrection.

23 And they appointed two, Jō'seph called Bär'sa-băs, who was surnamed Jŭs'tus, and Măt-thī'as.

24 And they prayed, and said, Thou, Lord, [c]which knowest the hearts of all *men,* shew whether of these two thou hast chosen,

25 That he may take part of this ministry and apostleship, from which Jū'das by transgression fell, that he might go to his own place.

26 And they gave forth their [d]lots; and the lot fell upon Măt-thī'as; and he was numbered with the eleven apostles.

2 And when [a]the day of Pĕn'te-cŏst was fully come, [b]they were all with one accord in one place.

2 And suddenly there came a sound from heaven as of a rushing mighty wind, and [c]it filled all the house where they were sitting.

3 And there appeared unto them cloven tongues like as of fire, and it sat upon each of them.

4 And [d]they were all filled with the Hō'lȳ Ghōst, and began [e]to speak with other tongues, as the Spirit gave them utterance.

5 And there were [f]dwelling at Je-ru'sa-lĕm Jews, devout men, out of every nation under heaven.

6 Now [1]when this was noised abroad, the multitude came together, and were [2]confounded, because that every man heard them speak in his own language.

7 And they were all amazed and marvelled, saying one to another, Behold, are not all these which speak Găl-ĭ-læ'ans?

8 And how hear we every man in our own tongue, wherein we were born?

9 Pär'thĭ-ans, and Mēdes, and Ē'lăm-ītes, and the dwellers in Mĕs-o-po-tā'mĭ-ȧ, and in Jū-dæ'ȧ, and [g]Căp-pa-dō'çĭ-ȧ, in Pŏn'tus, and Ā'siȧ,

10 Phrȳġ'ĭ-ȧ, and Pam-phȳl'ĭ-ȧ, in Ē'ġȳpt, and in the parts of Lĭb'ȳ-ȧ about Çȳ-rē'ne, and strangers of Rōme, Jews and [h]proselytes,

11 Crētes and A-rā'bĭ-ans, we do hear them speak in our tongues the wonderful works of God.

12 And they were all amazed, and were in doubt, saying one to another, What meaneth this?

13 [i]Others mocking said, These men are full of new wine.

14 ¶ But Pē'tĕr, standing up with the eleven, lifted up his voice, and said unto them, Ye men of Jū-dæ'ȧ, and all *ye* that dwell at Je-ru'sa-lĕm, be this known unto you, and hearken to my words:

15 For these are not drunken, as ye suppose, seeing it is *but* the third hour of the day.

16 But this is that which was spoken by the prophet Jō'el;

17 [j]And it shall come to pass in the last days, saith God, [k]I will pour out of my Spirit upon all flesh: and your sons and [l]your daughters shall prophesy, and your young men shall see visions, and your old men shall dream dreams:

18 And on my servants and on my handmaidens I will pour out in those days of my Spirit; [m]and they shall prophesy:

19 [n]And I will shew wonders in heaven above, and signs in the earth beneath; blood, and fire, and vapour of smoke:

20 [o]The sun shall be turned into darkness, and the moon into blood, before that great and notable day of the Lord come:

21 And it shall come to pass, *that* [p]whosoever shall call on the name of the Lord shall be saved.

22 Ye men of Is'ra-el, hear these words; Jē'sus of Năz'a-rĕth, a man approved of God among you [q]by miracles and wonders and signs, which

11 [k]Dan. 7.13; John 14.3; 1 Thess. 1.10; 2 Thess. 1.10; Rev. 1.7
12 [l]Zech. 14.4
[m]John 11.18
13 [n]ch. 9.37
[o]Luke 6.15
[p]Jude 1
14 [q]Luke 23.49
[r]Matt. 13.55
15 [s]Rev. 3.4
16 [t]Ps. 41.9; Mark 12.36; Heb. 3.7-8
[u]John 18.3
17 [v]Luke 6.16
[w]ch. 12.25
18 [x]Matt. 27.5
[y]2 Pet. 2.15
[z]Ps. 55.23
20 [a]Ps. 69.25
[3]Or, office, or, charge
22 [b]Heb. 2.3
24 [c]John 2.24; Heb. 4.13; Rev. 2.23
26 [d]Lev. 16.8

CHAPTER 2
1 [a]Lev. 23.15; Deut. 16.9
[b]ch. 1.14
2 [c]ch. 4.31
4 [d]Luke 4.1; John 14.26; ch. 1.5; ch. 6.3
[e]Mark 16.17; 1 Cor. 12.10
5 [f]Ex. 23.17
6 [1]when this voice was made
[2]Or, troubled in mind
9 [g]1 Pet. 1.1
10 [h]Ex. 12.48; Isa. 56.6
13 [i]1 Sam. 1.14
17 [j]Isa. 44.3; Ezek. 11.19; Joel 2.28; Zech. 12.10; John 7.38
[k]ch. 10.45
[l]ch. 21.9
18 [m]ch. 21.4; 1 Cor. 12.10
19 [n]Joel 2.30
20 [o]Isa. 13.10; Ezek. 32.7; Matt. 24.29; Rev. 6.12
21 [p]Rom. 10.13
22 [q]Heb. 2.4

God did by him in the midst of you, as
ye yourselves also know:
23 Him, [r]being delivered by the de-
terminate counsel and foreknowledge
of God, ye have taken, and by wicked
hands have crucified and slain:
24 [s]Whom God hath raised up, having loosed the pains of death: because
it was not possible that he should be
holden of it.
25 For Dā′vid speaketh concerning
him, [t]I foresaw the Lord always before
my face, for he is on my right hand,
that I should not be moved:
26 Therefore did my heart rejoice,
and my tongue was glad; moreover
also my flesh shall rest in hope:
27 Because thou wilt not leave my
soul in hell, neither wilt thou suffer
thine [u]Holy One to see corruption.
28 Thou hast made known to me the
ways of life; thou shalt make me full of
joy with thy countenance.
29 Men *and* brethren, [3]let me freely
speak unto you [v]of the patriarch Dā′-
vid, that he is both dead and buried,
and his sepulchre is with us unto this
day.
30 Therefore being a prophet, and
knowing that God had sworn with an
oath to him, that of [w]the fruit of his
loins, according to the flesh, he would
raise up Chrīst to sit on his throne;
31 He seeing this before spake of the
resurrection of Chrīst, [x]that his soul
was not left in hell, neither his flesh did
see corruption.
32 This Jē′sus hath God raised up,
[y]whereof we all are witnesses.
33 Therefore [z]being by the right
hand of God exalted, and [a]having received of the Father the promise of the
Hō′lȳ Ghōst, he hath [b]shed forth this,
which ye now see and hear.
34 For Dā′vid is not ascended into
the heavens: but he saith himself, [c]The
LORD said unto my Lord, Sit thou on
my right hand,
35 Until I make thy foes thy footstool.
36 Therefore let all the house of Is′-
ra-el know assuredly, that God [d]hath
made that same Jē′sus, whom ye have
crucified, both Lord and Chrīst.
37 ¶ Now when they heard *this*,
[e]they were pricked in their heart, and
said unto Pē′tēr and to the rest of the
apostles, Men *and* brethren, what shall
we do?
38 Then Pē′tēr said unto them, [f]Re-
pent, and be baptized every one of you
in the name of Jē′sus Chrīst for the
remission of sins, and ye shall receive
the gift of the Hō′lȳ Ghōst.
39 For the [g]promise is unto you, and
[h]to your children, and [i]to all that are
afar off, *even* as many as the Lord our
God shall call.
40 And with many other words did
he testify and exhort, saying, Save
yourselves from this untoward generation.
41 ¶ Then they that gladly received
his word were baptized: and the same
day there were added *unto them* about
three thousand souls.
42 [j]And they continued stedfastly
in the apostles' doctrine and fellowship, and in breaking of bread, and in
prayers.
43 And fear came upon every soul:
and [k]many wonders and signs were
done by the apostles.
44 And all that believed were together, and [l]had all things common;
45 And sold their possessions and
goods, and [m]parted them to all *men*, as
every man had need.
46 And they, continuing daily with
one accord [n]in the temple, and [o]break-
ing bread [4]from house to house, did eat
their meat with gladness and singleness of heart,
47 Praising God, and [p]having favour with all the people. And [q]the
Lord added to the church daily such as
should be saved.

3 Now Pē′tēr and Jŏhn went up together into the temple at the hour of
prayer, *being* the ninth *hour*.
2 And a certain man lame from his
mother's womb was carried, whom
they laid daily at the gate of the temple
which is called Beautiful, [a]to ask alms
of them that entered into the temple;
3 Who seeing Pē′tēr and Jŏhn about
to go into the temple asked an alms.
4 And Pē′tēr, fastening his eyes upon
him with Jŏhn, said, Look on us.
5 And he gave heed unto them, expecting to receive something of them.
6 Then Pē′tēr said, [b]Silver and gold
have I none; but such as I have give I
thee: [c]In the name of Jē′sus Chrīst of
Nāz′a-rĕth rise up and walk.
7 And he took him by the right hand,
and lifted *him* up: and immediately his
feet and ancle bones received strength.
8 And he [d]leaping up stood, and
walked, and entered with them into
the temple, walking, and leaping, and
praising God.
9 [e]And all the people saw him walking and praising God:
10 And they knew that it was he
which sat for alms at the Beautiful gate
of the temple: and they were filled with
wonder and amazement at that which
had happened unto him.
11 And as the lame man which was
healed held Pē′tēr and Jŏhn, all the
people ran together unto them in
the porch [f]that is called Sŏl′o-mon's,
greatly wondering.
12 ¶ And when Pē′tēr saw *it*, he answered unto the people, Ye men of
Is′ra-el, why marvel ye at this? or why
look ye so earnestly on us, [g]as though
by our own power or holiness we had
made this man to walk?
13 [h]The God of Ā′bră-hăm, and of
Ī′saac, and of Jā′cob, the God of our
fathers, [i]hath glorified his Son Jē′sus;
whom ye delivered up, and denied him
in the presence of Pī′late, when he was
determined to let *him* go.
14 But ye denied [j]the Holy One [k]and
the Just, and desired a murderer to be
granted unto you;

23 [r]Luke 24.44; ch. 4.28
24 [s]ch. 3.15; ch. 4.10; Rom. 4.24; 1 Cor. 6.14; 2 Cor. 4.14; Gal. 1.1; Eph. 1.20; Col. 2.12; 1 Thess. 1.10; Heb. 13.20; 1 Pet. 1.21
25 [t]Ps. 16.8
27 [u]Dan. 9.24; Luke 1.35
29 [3]Or, I may [v]ch. 13.36
30 [w]2 Sam. 7.13; Ps. 132.11; Luke 1.32; Rom. 1.3
31 [x]Ps. 16.10
32 [y]Luke 24.46-48; ch. 1.8; ch. 3.15
33 [z]ch. 5.31; Phil. 2.9; Heb. 10.12 [a]John 14.26; ch. 1.4 [b]ch. 10.45; Eph. 4.8
34 [c]Ps. 110.1; Heb. 1.13
36 [d]Ps. 2.1-6; 2 Thess. 1.7-10
37 [e]Zech. 12.10; Luke 3.10
38 [f]Matt. 3.2-8; 2 Cor. 7.10
39 [g]Rom. 9.8 [h]Joel 2.28 [i]Eph. 2.13
42 [j]Heb. 10.25
43 [k]Mark 16.17
44 [l]ch. 4.32
45 [m]Isa. 58.7
46 [n]Luke 24.53 [o]ch. 20.7 [4]Or, at home
47 [p]Rom. 14.18 [q]Rom. 8.30

CHAPTER 3
2 [a]John 9.8
6 [b]1 Pet. 4.10 [c]ch. 4.10
8 [d]Isa. 35.6
9 [e]ch. 4.21
11 [f]John 10.23; ch. 5.12
12 [g]2 Cor. 3.5
13 [h]ch. 5.30 [i]John 7.39; Phil. 2.9
14 [j]Ps. 16.10; ch. 2.27 [k]ch. 7.52; ch. 22.14

15 And killed the [1]Prince of life, whom God hath raised from the dead; whereof we are witnesses.

16 [l]And his name through faith in his name hath made this man strong, whom ye see and know: yea, the faith which is by him hath given him this perfect soundness in the presence of you all.

17 And now, brethren, I wot that [m]through ignorance ye did *it*, as *did* also your rulers.

18 But those things, which God before had shewed [n]by the mouth of all his prophets, that Chrīst should suffer, he hath so fulfilled.

19 ¶ Repent ye therefore, and be converted, that your sins may be blotted out, when the times of refreshing shall come from the presence of the Lord;

20 And he shall send Jē'sus Chrīst, which before was preached unto you:

21 [o]Whom the heaven must receive until the times of [p]restitution of all things, which God hath spoken by the mouth of all his holy prophets since the world began.

22 For Mō'ses truly said unto the fathers, [q]A prophet shall the Lord your God raise up unto you of your brethren, [r]like unto me; him shall ye hear in all things whatsoever he shall say unto you.

23 And it shall come to pass, *that* every [s]soul, which will not hear that prophet, shall be destroyed from among the people.

24 Yea, and all the prophets from Sām'u-el and those that follow after, as many as have spoken, have likewise foretold of these days.

25 [t]Ye are the children of the prophets, and of the covenant which God made with our fathers, saying unto Ā'bră-hăm, [u]And in thy seed shall all the kindreds of the earth be blessed.

26 Unto you first God, having raised up his Son Jē'sus, sent him to bless you, in turning away every one of you from his iniquities.

4 And as they spake unto the people, the priests, and the [1]captain of the temple, and the Săd'dū-çees, came upon them,

2 [a]Being grieved that they taught the people, and preached through Jē'sus the resurrection from the dead.

3 And they laid hands on them, and put *them* in hold unto the next day: for it was now eventide.

4 Howbeit many of them which heard the word believed; and the number of the men was about five thousand.

5 ¶ And it came to pass on the morrow, that their rulers, and elders, and scribes,

6 And [b]Ăn'nas the high priest, and Cā'ia-phas, and Jŏhn, and Ăl-ĕx-ăn'dẽr, and as many as were of the kindred of the high priest, were gathered together at Je-ru'sa-lĕm.

7 And when they had set them in the midst, they asked, [c]By what power, or by what name, have ye done this?

8 [d]Then Pē'tẽr, filled with the Hō'lў Ghōst, said unto them, Ye rulers of the people, and elders of Is'ra-el,

9 If we this day be examined of the good deed done to the impotent man, by what means he is made whole;

10 Be it known unto you all, and to all the people of Is'ra-el, [e]that by the name of Jē'sus Chrīst of Năz'a-rĕth, whom ye crucified, whom God raised from the dead, *even* by him doth this man stand here before you whole.

11 [f]This is the stone which was set at nought of you builders, which is become the head of the corner.

12 [g]Neither is there salvation in any other: for there is none other name under heaven given among men, whereby we must be saved.

13 ¶ Now when they saw the boldness of Pē'tẽr and Jŏhn, [h]and perceived that they were unlearned and ignorant men, they marvelled; and they took knowledge of them, that they had been with Jē'sus.

14 And beholding the man which was healed standing with them, they could say nothing against it.

15 But when they had commanded them to go aside out of the council, they conferred among themselves,

16 Saying, [i]What shall we do to these men? for that indeed a notable miracle hath been done by them *is* [j]manifest to all them that dwell in Je-ru'sa-lĕm; and we cannot deny *it*.

17 But that it spread no further among the people, let us straitly threaten them, that they speak henceforth to no man in this name.

18 And they called them, and commanded them not to speak at all nor teach in the name of Jē'sus.

19 But Pē'tẽr and Jŏhn answered and said unto them, [k]Whether it be right in the sight of God to hearken unto you more than unto God, judge ye.

20 [l]For we cannot but speak the things which [m]we have seen and heard.

21 So when they had further threatened them, they let them go, finding nothing how they might punish them, [n]because of the people: for all *men* glorified God for [o]that which was done.

22 For the man was above forty years old, on whom this miracle of healing was shewed.

23 ¶ And being let go, [p]they went to their own company, and reported all that the chief priests and elders had said unto them.

24 And when they heard that, they [q]lifted up their voice to God with one accord, and said, Lord, [r]thou *art* God, which hast made heaven, and earth, and the sea, and all that in them is:

25 Who by the mouth of thy servant Dā'vid hast said, [s]Why did the heathen rage, and the people imagine vain things?

26 The kings of the earth stood up, and the rulers were gathered together against the Lord, and against his Chrīst.

15 [1]Or, Author
16 [l]Matt. 9.22; 1 Pet. 1.21
17 [m]Luke 23.34; 1 Cor. 2.8; 1 Tim. 1.13
18 [n]Ps. 22; Isa. 50.6; Dan. 9.26; 1 Pet. 1.10
21 [o]ch. 1.11; Heb. 8.1
[p]Matt. 17.11
22 [q]Deut. 18.15; Luke 13.33; Luke 24.19
[r]Heb. 3.2-5
23 [s]Mark 16.16; John 3.18; ch. 13.38-41; Heb. 2.2-3
25 [t]Rom. 9.4-8; Gal. 3.26
[u]Gen. 12.3; Gal. 3.8

CHAPTER 4
1 [1]Or, ruler
2 [a]Neh. 2.10; Matt. 22.23; ch. 23.8
6 [b]Luke 3.2; John 11.49
7 [c]Ex. 2.14; Matt. 21.23; Mark 11.28; ch. 7.27
8 [d]Luke 12.11
10 [e]ch. 3.6
11 [f]Ps. 118.22; Isa. 28.16; Matt. 21.42
12 [g]Matt. 1.21; ch. 10.43; Rom. 3.24
13 [h]Matt. 11.25; 1 Cor. 1.27
16 [i]John 11.47; ch. 12.19
[j]ch. 3.9
19 [k]ch. 5.29; Gal. 1.10
20 [l]ch. 1.8
[m]ch. 22.15; 1 John 1.1
21 [n]Matt. 9.33; Matt. 21.26; Luke 20.6; ch. 5.26
[o]ch. 3.7-8
23 [p]ch. 12.12
24 [q]Ps. 55.16-17; Ps. 103.1; Jer. 20.13
[r]Ex. 20.11; Jer. 32.17
25 [s]Ps. 2.1

27 For of a truth against [t]thy holy
child Jē′sus, [u]whom thou hast anointed,
both Hĕr′od, and Pŏn′tĭ-us Pī′late, with
the Gĕn′tīles, and the people of Is′ra-el,
were gathered together,
28 [v]For to do whatsoever thy hand
and thy counsel determined before to
be done.
29 And now, Lord, behold their
threatenings: and grant unto thy servants, [w]that with all boldness they
may speak thy word,
30 By stretching forth thine hand to
heal; [x]and that signs and wonders
may be done [y]by the name of thy holy
child Jē′sus.
31 ¶ And when they had prayed,
[z]the place was shaken where they
were assembled together; and they
were all filled with the Hō′lȳ Ghōst,
and they spake the word of God with
boldness.
32 And the multitude of them that
believed [a]were of one heart and of one
soul: [b]neither said any *of them* that
ought of the things which he possessed
was his own; but they had all things
common.
33 And with [c]great power gave the
apostles [d]witness of the resurrection
of the Lord Jē′sus: and [e]great grace
was upon them all.
34 [f]Neither was there any among
them that lacked: [g]for as many as
were possessors of lands or houses
sold them, and brought the prices of
the things that were sold,
35 And laid *them* down at the apostles' feet: [h]and distribution was made
unto every man according as he had
need.
36 And Jō′sēs, who by the apostles
was surnamed Bär′na-bās, (which is,
being interpreted, The son of consolation,) a Lē′vīte, *and* of the country of
Çȳ′prus,
37 [i]Having land, sold *it*, and brought
the money, and laid *it* at the apostles'
feet.

5 But a certain man named Ăn-a-
nī′as, with Săp-phī′rȧ his wife, sold
a possession,
2 [a]And kept back *part* of the price,
his wife also being privy *to it*, and
brought a certain part, and laid *it* at
the apostles' feet.
3 [b]But Pē′tēr said, Ăn-a-nī′as, why
hath [c]Sā′tan filled thine heart [1]to lie to
the Hō′lȳ Ghōst, and to keep back *part*
of the price of the land?
4 Whiles it remained, was it not thine
own? and after it was sold, was it not in
thine own power? why hast thou conceived this thing in thine heart? thou
hast not lied unto men, but unto God.
5 And Ăn-a-nī′as hearing these
words [d]fell down, and gave up the
ghost: and great fear came on all them
that heard these things.
6 And the young men arose, [e]wound
him up, and carried *him* out, and buried
him.
7 And it was about the space of
three hours after, when his wife, not
knowing what was done, came in.

27 [t]Heb. 7.26
[u]Isa. 61.1; John 10.36
28 [v]ch. 2.23
29 [w]Isa. 58.1; Ezek. 2.6; ch. 19.8; Eph. 6.19
30 [x]ch. 5.12
[y]ch. 3.6-16
31 [z]ch. 2.2-4
32 [a]Rom. 15.5; Phil. 1.27; 1 Pet. 3.8
[b]ch. 2.44
33 [c]Mark 16.20; 1 Thess. 1.5; Heb. 2.4
[d]ch. 1.22
[e]ch. 2.47
34 [f]1 John 3.17
[g]ch. 2.45
35 [h]ch. 6.1
37 [i]Prov. 3.9; 1 Tim. 6.19

CHAPTER 5
2 [a]Josh. 7.1; 1 Tim. 6.10
3 [b]Num. 30.2; Eccl. 5.4
[c]1 Ki. 22.21-22; Jas. 4.7
[1]Or, to deceive
5 [d]Num. 14.37
6 [e]John 19.40
9 [f]Deut. 6.16; Heb. 3.8-9
12 [g]Mark 16.15-20; Heb. 2.4
[h]ch. 3.11
13 [i]John 9.22
[j]ch. 2.47
15 [2]Or, in every street
[k]Matt. 9.21; Matt. 14.36
16 [l]Mark 16.17
17 [m]John 11.47-49; ch. 4.1-2
[3]Or, envy
18 [n]Luke 21.12
19 [o]Ps. 34.7; Heb. 1.14
20 [p]Jer. 7.2; John 6.68
21 [q]ch. 4.5-6
24 [r]Luke 22.4; ch. 4.1

8 And Pē′tēr answered unto her, Tell
me whether ye sold the land for so
much? And she said, Yea, for so much.
9 Then Pē′tēr said unto her, How is
it that ye have agreed together [f]to
tempt the Spirit of the Lord? behold,
the feet of them which have buried thy
husband *are* at the door, and shall
carry thee out.
10 Then fell she down straightway
at his feet, and yielded up the ghost:
and the young men came in, and found
her dead, and, carrying *her* forth, buried *her* by her husband.
11 And great fear came upon all the
church, and upon as many as heard
these things.
12 ¶ And [g]by the hands of the apostles were many signs and wonders
wrought among the people; ([h]and they
were all with one accord in Sŏl′o-
mon's porch.
13 And [i]of the rest durst no man
join himself to them: [j]but the people
magnified them.
14 And believers were the more
added to the Lord, multitudes both of
men and women.)
15 Insomuch that they brought forth
the sick [2]into the streets, and laid *them*
on beds and couches, [k]that at the least
the shadow of Pē′tēr passing by might
overshadow some of them.
16 There came also a multitude *out*
of the cities round about unto Je-ru̧′sa-
lĕm, bringing [l]sick folks, and them
which were vexed with unclean spirits: and they were healed every one.
17 ¶ [m]Then the high priest rose up,
and all they that were with him, (which
is the sect of the Săd′dū-çees,) and
were filled with [3]indignation,
18 [n]And laid their hands on the
apostles, and put them in the common
prison.
19 But [o]the angel of the Lord by
night opened the prison doors, and
brought them forth, and said,
20 Go, stand and speak in the temple to the people [p]all the words of this
life.
21 And when they heard *that*, they
entered into the temple early in the
morning, and taught. [q]But the high
priest came, and they that were with
him, and called the council together,
and all the senate of the children of
Is′ra-el, and sent to the prison to have
them brought.
22 But when the officers came, and
found them not in the prison, they returned, and told,
23 Saying, The prison truly found
we shut with all safety, and the keepers standing without before the doors:
but when we had opened, we found no
man within.
24 Now when the high priest and
[r]the captain of the temple and the
chief priests heard these things, they
doubted of them whereunto this would
grow.
25 Then came one and told them,
saying, Behold, the men whom ye put

in prison are standing in the temple, and teaching the people.

26 Then went the captain with the officers, and brought them without violence: [s]for they feared the people, lest they should have been stoned.

27 And when they had brought them, they set *them* before the council: and the high priest asked them,

28 Saying, [t]Did not we straitly command you that ye should not teach in this name? and, behold, ye have filled Je-ru'sa-lĕm with your doctrine, [u]and intend to bring this man's [v]blood upon us.

29 ¶ Then Pē'tĕr and the *other* apostles answered and said, [w]We ought to obey God rather than men.

30 The God of our fathers raised up Jē'sus, whom ye slew and [x]hanged on a tree.

31 [y]Him hath God exalted with his right hand *to be* [z]a Prince and [a]a Saviour, [b]for to give repentance to Is'ra-el, and forgiveness of sins.

32 And [c]we are his witnesses of these things; and *so is* also the Hō'lȳ Ghōst, whom God hath given to them that obey him.

33 ¶ When they heard *that,* they were cut *to the heart,* and took counsel to slay them.

34 Then stood there up one in the council, a Phăr'ĭ-see, named [d]Ga-mā'-lĭ-el, a doctor of the law, had in reputation among all the people, and commanded to put the apostles forth a little space;

35 And said unto them, Ye men of Is'ra-el, take heed to yourselves what ye intend to do as touching these men.

36 For before these days rose up Theū'das, boasting himself to be somebody; to whom a number of men, about four hundred, joined themselves: who was slain; and all, as many as [4]obeyed him, were scattered, and brought to nought.

37 After this man rose up Jū'das of Găl'ĭ-lee in the [e]days of the taxing, and drew away much people after him: he also perished; and all, *even* as many as obeyed him, were dispersed.

38 And now I say unto you, Refrain from these men, and let them alone: [f]for if this counsel or this work be of men, it will come to nought:

39 [g]But if it be of God, ye cannot overthrow it; lest haply ye be found even [h]to fight against God.

40 And to him they agreed: and when they had called the apostles, [i]and beaten *them,* they commanded that they should not speak in the name of Jē'sus, and let them go.

41 ¶ And they departed from the presence of the council, [j]rejoicing that they were counted worthy to suffer shame for his name.

42 And daily in the temple, and in every house, they ceased not to teach and preach Jē'sus Chrīst.

6 And in those days, [a]when the number of the disciples was multiplied, there arose a murmuring of the [b]Grē'çians against the Hē'brews, because their widows were neglected [c]in the daily ministration.

2 Then the twelve called the multitude of the disciples *unto them,* and said, [d]It is not reason that we should leave the word of God, and serve tables.

3 Wherefore, brethren, [e]look ye out among you seven men of honest report, full of the Hō'lȳ Ghōst and wisdom, whom we may appoint over this business.

4 But we [f]will give ourselves continually to prayer, and to the ministry of the word.

5 ¶ And the saying pleased the whole multitude: and they chose Stē'phen, [g]a man full of faith and of the Hō'lȳ Ghōst, and [h]Phĭl'ĭp, and Prŏch'o-rus, and Nicā'nor, and Tī'mon, and Păr'me-năs, and Nĭc'o-lăs a proselyte of Ăn'tĭ-ŏch:

6 Whom they set before the apostles: and [i]when they had prayed, [j]they laid *their* hands on them.

7 And [k]the word of God increased; and the number of the disciples multiplied in Je-ru'sa-lĕm greatly; and a great company [l]of the priests were obedient to the faith.

8 And Stē'phen, full of faith and power, did great wonders and miracles among the people.

9 ¶ Then there arose certain of the synagogue, which is called *the synagogue* of the Lĭb'ĕr-tīnes, and Çȳ-rē'nĭ-ans, and Ăl-ĕx-ăn'drĭ-ans, and of them of Çi-lĭ'çiȧ and of Ā'siȧ, disputing with Stē'phen.

10 And [m]they were not able to resist the wisdom and the spirit by which he spake.

11 [n]Then they suborned men, which said, We have heard him speak blasphemous words against Mō'ses, and *against* God.

12 And they stirred up the people, and the elders, and the scribes, and came upon *him,* and caught him, and brought *him* to the council,

13 And set up false witnesses, which said, This man ceaseth not to speak blasphemous words against this holy place, and the law:

14 [o]For we have heard him say, that this Jē'sus of Năz'a-rĕth shall [p]destroy this place, and shall change the [1]customs which Mō'ses delivered us.

15 And all that sat in the council, looking stedfastly on him, saw his face as it had been the face of [q]an angel.

7 Then said the high priest, Are these things so?

2 And he said, Men, brethren, and fathers, hearken; The God of glory appeared unto our father Ā'bră-hăm, when he was in Mĕs-o-po-tā'mĭ-ȧ, before he dwelt in Chăr'ran,

3 And said unto him, Get thee out of thy country, and from thy kindred, and come into the land [a]which I shall shew thee.

4 Then [b]came he out of the land of the Chăl-dæ'ans, and dwelt in Chăr'ran: and from thence, when his father

26 [s]Matt. 14.5; Luke 20.6
28 [t]ch. 4.18
[u]ch. 2.23; ch. 3.15
[v]Matt. 23.35
29 [w]Gal. 1.10
30 [x]ch. 10.39; 1 Pet. 2.24
31 [y]ch. 2.33; Heb. 2.10
[z]Isa. 9.6; Rev. 1.5
[a]Matt. 1.21
[b]Eph. 1.7; Col. 1.14
32 [c]John 15.26
34 [d]ch. 22.3
36 [4]Or, believed
37 [e]Luke 2.1
38 [f]Ps. 127.1; Matt. 15.13
39 [g]Gen. 24.50; Rev. 17.14
[h]ch. 9.5
40 [i]Matt. 10.17; Luke 20.10
41 [j]Matt. 5.12; 1 Pet. 4.13
CHAPTER 6
1 [a]Ps. 72.16
[b]ch. 9.29
[c]ch. 4.35
2 [d]Ex. 18.17; 2 Tim. 2.4
3 [e]Deut. 1.13; 1 Tim. 3.7
4 [f]ch. 2.42
5 [g]ch. 9.31
[h]ch. 8.5
6 [i]Ps. 37.5; Phil. 4.6
[j]ch. 8.17; Heb. 6.2
7 [k]Col. 1.6; 2 Tim. 3.1
[l]John 12.42
10 [m]Isa. 54.17; Luke 21.15
11 [n]Matt. 26.15
14 [o]ch. 25.8
[p]Dan. 9.26; Matt. 24.2
[1]Or, rites
15 [q]Dan. 10.6
CHAPTER 7
3 [a]Gen. 12.1
4 [b]Gen. 11.31

was dead, he removed him into this
land, wherein ye now dwell.
5 And he gave him none inheritance
in it, no, not *so much as* to set his foot
on: [c]yet he promised that he would
give it to him for a possession, and to
his seed after him, when *as yet* he had
no child.
6 And God spake on this wise, [d]That
his seed should sojourn in a strange
land; and that they should bring them
into bondage, and entreat *them* evil
[e]four hundred years.
7 And the nation to whom they shall
be in bondage will I judge, said God:
and after that shall they come forth,
and [f]serve me in this place.
8 [g]And he gave him the covenant
of circumcision: [h]and so Ā'bră-hăm
begat Ī'saac, and circumcised him the
eighth day; [i]and Ī'saac *begat* Jā'-
cob; and [j]Jā'cob *begat* the twelve
patriarchs.
9 [k]And the patriarchs, moved with
envy, sold Jō'seph into Ē'ġy̆pt: [l]but
God was with him,
10 And delivered him out of all his
afflictions, [m]and gave him favour and
wisdom in the sight of Phā'raōh king
of Ē'ġy̆pt; and he made him governor
over Ē'ġy̆pt and all his house.
11 Now there came a dearth over all
the land of Ē'ġy̆pt and Chā'năan, and
great affliction: and our fathers found
no sustenance.
12 But when Jā'cob heard that there
was corn in Ē'ġy̆pt, he sent out our fathers first.
13 And at the second *time* Jō'seph
was made known to his brethren; and
Jō'seph's kindred was made known
unto Phā'raōh.
14 [n]Then sent Jō'seph, and called
his father Jā'cob to *him,* and all his
kindred, [o]threescore and fifteen souls.
15 So Jā'cob went down into Ē'ġy̆pt,
[p]and died, he, and our fathers,
16 And [q]were carried over into Sy̆'-
chem, and laid in [r]the sepulchre that
Ā'bră-hăm bought for a sum of money
of the sons of Ĕm'môr *the father* of
Sy̆'chem.
17 But when [s]the time of the promise drew nigh, which God had sworn to
Ā'bră-hăm, the people grew and multiplied in Ē'ġy̆pt,
18 Till another king arose, which
knew not Jō'seph.
19 The same dealt subtilly with our
kindred, and evil entreated our fathers, so that they cast out their young
children, to the end they might not live.
20 [t]In which time Mō'ses was born,
and [u]was [1]exceeding fair, and nourished up in his father's house three
months:
21 And when he was cast out, Phā'-
raōh's daughter took him up, and nourished him for her own son.
22 And Mō'ses was learned in all
the wisdom of the E-ġy̆p'tians, and
was [v]mighty in words and in deeds.
23 [w]And when he was full forty
years old, it came into his heart to visit
his brethren the children of Is'ra-el.
24 And seeing one *of them* suffer
wrong, he defended *him,* and avenged
him that was oppressed, and smote the
E-ġy̆p'tian:
25 [2]For he supposed his brethren
would have understood how that God
by his hand would deliver them: but
they understood not.
26 And the next day he shewed himself unto them as they strove, and
would have set them at one again, saying, Sirs, ye are brethren; why do ye
wrong one to another?
27 But he that did his neighbour
wrong thrust him away, saying, [x]Who
made thee a ruler and a judge over us?
28 Wilt thou kill me, as thou diddest
the E-ġy̆p'tian yesterday?
29 [y]Then fled Mō'ses at this saying,
and was a stranger in the land of
Mā'dĭ-an, where he [z]begat two sons.
30 And when forty years were expired, there appeared to him in the wilderness of mount Sī'nȧ [a]an angel of
the Lord in a flame of fire in a bush.
31 When Mō'ses saw *it,* he wondered at the sight: and as he drew near
to behold *it,* the voice of the Lord came
unto him,
32 *Saying,* [b]I *am* the God of thy fathers, the God of Ā'bră-hăm, and the
God of Ī'saac, and the God of Jā'cob.
Then Mō'ses trembled, and durst not
behold.
33 [c]Then said the Lord to him, Put
off thy shoes from thy feet: for the
place where thou standest is holy
ground.
34 I have seen, I have seen the affliction of my people which is in Ē'ġy̆pt,
and I have heard their groaning, and
am come down to deliver them. And
now come, I will send thee into Ē'ġy̆pt.
35 This Mō'ses whom they refused,
saying, Who made thee a ruler and a
judge? the same did God send *to be* a
ruler and a deliverer [d]by the hand of
the angel which appeared to him in the
bush.
36 [e]He brought them out, after that
he had shewed wonders and signs in
the land of Ē'ġy̆pt, and in the Red sea,
[f]and in the wilderness forty years.
37 ¶ This is that Mō'ses, which said
unto the children of Is'ra-el, [g]A prophet
shall the Lord your God raise up unto
you of your brethren, [3]like unto me;
[h]him shall ye hear.
38 [i]This is he, that was in the church
in the wilderness with [j]the angel which
spake to him in the mount Sī'nȧ, and
with our fathers: [k]who received the
lively [l]oracles to give unto us:
39 To whom our fathers would not
obey, but thrust *him* from them, and in
their hearts turned back again into
Ē'ġy̆pt,
40 [m]Saying unto Aâr'on, Make us
gods to go before us: for *as for* this
Mō'ses, which brought us out of the
land of Ē'ġy̆pt, we wot not what is become of him.
41 And they made a calf in those
days, and offered sacrifice unto the

5 [c]Gen. 12.7; Ex. 6.7-8; Deut. 6.10; Neh. 9.8-24; Ps. 105.8-11
6 [d]Gen. 15.13; 1 Pet. 2.11
[e]Ex. 12.40; Gal. 3.17
7 [f]Ex. 3.12
8 [g]Gen. 17.9; Gal. 3.15-17
[h]Gen. 21.2; 1 Chr. 1.34; Matt. 1.2
[i]Gen. 25.26
[j]Gen. 29.31
9 [k]Gen. 37.4; Ps. 105.17
[l]Gen. 39.2
10 [m]Gen. 42.6; Gen. 45.8-9; 1 Sam. 2.30; Ps. 37.23; Prov. 8.15
14 [n]Gen. 45.9
[o]Gen. 46.27; Deut. 10.22
15 [p]Gen. 49.33; Ex. 1.6
16 [q]Gen. 50.25; Ex. 13.19
[r]Gen. 23.16
17 [s]Gen. 15.13
[t]Ex. 2.2
[u]Heb. 11.23
[1]Or, fair to God
22 [v]Luke 24.19
23 [w]Ex. 2.11
25 [2]Or, Now
27 [x]Luke 12.14
29 [y]Ex. 2.15
[z]Num. 12.1
30 [a]Gen. 48.16; Ex. 3.2; Isa. 63.9
32 [b]Gen. 50.24; Heb. 11.16
33 [c]Josh. 5.15
35 [d]Ex. 14.19; Num. 20.16
36 [e]Ex. 12.41; Ps. 78.12-13
[f]Ex. 16.1
37 [g]Deut. 18.15
[3]Or, as myself
[h]Matt. 17.5; ch. 3.24
38 [i]Ex. 19.3
[j]Isa. 63.9; Heb. 2.2
[k]Ex. 21.1; John 1.17
[l]Rom. 3.2
40 [m]Ex. 32.1

idol, and rejoiced in the works of their own hands.

42 Then [n]God turned, and gave them up to worship [o]the host of heaven; as it is written in the book of the prophets, [p]O ye house of Is'ra-el, have ye offered to me slain beasts and sacrifices *by the space of* forty years in the wilderness?

43 Yea, ye took up the tabernacle of Mō'lŏch, and the star of your god Rĕm'phan, figures which ye made to worship them: and I will carry you away beyond Băb'ȳ-lon.

44 Our fathers had the tabernacle of witness in the wilderness, as he had appointed, [4]speaking unto Mō'ses, [q]that he should make it according to the fashion that he had seen.

45 [r]Which also our fathers [5]that came after brought in with [6]Jē'sus into the possession of the Gĕn'tīles, whom God drave out before the face of our fathers, unto the days of Dā'vid;

46 [s]Who found favour before God, and [t]desired to find a tabernacle for the God of Jā'cob.

47 But Sŏl'o-mon built him an house.

48 Howbeit [u]the most High dwelleth not in temples made with hands; as saith the prophet,

49 [v]Heaven *is* my throne, and earth *is* my footstool: what house will ye build me? saith the Lord: or what *is* the place of my rest?

50 Hath not my hand made all these things?

51 ¶ Ye [w]stiffnecked and [x]uncircumcised in heart and ears, ye do always resist the Hō'lȳ Ghōst: as your fathers *did*, so *do* ye.

52 [y]Which of the prophets have not your fathers persecuted? and they have slain them which shewed before of the coming of [z]the Just One; of whom ye have been now the betrayers and murderers:

53 [a]Who have received the law by the disposition of angels, and have not kept *it*.

54 ¶ When they heard these things, they were cut to the heart, and they gnashed on him with *their* teeth.

55 But he, being full of the Hō'lȳ Ghōst, looked up stedfastly into heaven, and saw the glory of God, and Jē'sus standing on the right hand of God,

56 And said, Behold, [b]I see the heavens opened, and the [c]Son of man standing on the right hand of God.

57 Then they cried out with a loud voice, and stopped their ears, and ran upon him with one accord,

58 And [d]cast *him* out of the city, [e]and stoned *him*: and [f]the witnesses laid down their clothes at a young man's feet, whose name was Sąul.

59 And they stoned Stē'phen, calling upon *God*, and saying, Lord Jē'sus, [g]receive my spirit.

60 And he kneeled down, and cried with a loud voice, [h]Lord, lay not this sin to their charge. And when he had said this, he [i]fell asleep.

8 And [a]Sąul was consenting unto his death. And at that time there was a great persecution against the church which was at Je-rų'sa-lĕm; and [b]they were all scattered abroad throughout the regions of Jū-dæ'ȧ and Sa-mā'rĭ-ȧ, except the apostles.

2 And devout men carried Stē'phen *to his burial*, and [c]made great lamentation over him.

3 As for Sąul, [d]he made havock of the church, entering into every house, and haling men and women committed *them* to prison.

4 Therefore [e]they that were scattered abroad went every where preaching the word.

5 Then [f]Phĭl'ĭp went down to the city of Sa-mā'rĭ-ȧ, and preached Chrīst unto them.

6 And the people with one accord gave heed unto those things which Phĭl'ĭp spake, hearing and seeing the miracles which he did.

7 For [g]unclean spirits, crying with loud voice, came out of many that were possessed *with them*: and many taken with palsies, and that were lame, were healed.

8 And there was great joy in that city.

9 But there was a certain man, called Sī'mon, which beforetime in the same city [h]used sorcery, and bewitched the people of Sa-mā'rĭ-ȧ, [i]giving out that himself was some great one:

10 To whom they all gave heed, from the least to the greatest, saying, This man is the great power of God.

11 And to him they had regard, because that of long time he had bewitched them with sorceries.

12 But when they believed Phĭl'ĭp preaching the things [j]concerning the kingdom of God, and the name of Jē'sus Chrīst, they were baptized, both men and women.

13 Then Sī'mon himself [k]believed also: and when he was baptized, he continued with Phĭl'ĭp, and wondered, beholding the [1]miracles and signs which were done.

14 Now when the apostles which were at Je-rų'sa-lĕm heard that Sa-mā'rĭ-ȧ had received the word of God, they sent unto them Pē'tẽr and Jŏhn:

15 Who, when they were come down, prayed for them, [l]that they might receive the Hō'lȳ Ghōst:

16 (For [m]as yet he was fallen upon none of them: only [n]they were baptized in [o]the name of the Lord Jē'sus.)

17 Then [p]laid they *their* hands on them, and they received the Hō'lȳ Ghōst.

18 And when Sī'mon saw that through laying on of the apostles' hands the Hō'lȳ Ghōst was given, he offered them money,

19 Saying, Give me also this power, that on whomsoever I lay hands, he may receive the Hō'lȳ Ghōst.

20 But Pē'tẽr said unto him, Thy money perish with thee, because [q]thou hast thought that [r]the gift of God may be purchased with money.

42 [n]Ezek. 20.25; 2 Thess. 2.11 [o]Deut. 17.3; Jer. 19.13 [p]Amos 5.25
44 [4]Or, who spake [q]Ex. 25.40; Heb. 8.5
45 [r]Josh. 3.14 [5]Or, having received [6]That is, Joshua
46 [s]1 Sam. 15.28; Ps. 78.68-72 [t]1 Ki. 8.17
48 [u]2 Chr. 2.6; ch. 17.24-25
49 [v]Ps. 11.4; Rev. 3.21
51 [w]Isa. 48.4 [x]Ezek. 44.9
52 [y]2 Chr. 36.16; 1 Thess. 2.15 [z]ch. 3.14
53 [a]Ex. 20.1; Heb. 2.2
56 [b]Matt. 3.16 [c]Dan. 7.13
58 [d]Heb. 13.12 [e]Lev. 24.16 [f]Deut. 13.9
59 [g]Ps. 31.5
60 [h]Matt. 5.44; Luke 6.28 [i]1 Thess. 4.13; Rev. 14.13

CHAPTER 8
1 [a]ch. 7.58 [b]ch. 11.19
2 [c]2 Sam. 3.31
3 [d]1 Cor. 15.9; 1 Tim. 1.13
4 [e]Matt. 10.23
5 [f]ch. 6.5
7 [g]Matt. 10.1;
9 [h]ch. 13.6 [i]ch. 5.36
12 [j]ch. 1.3
13 [k]Luke 8.13 [1]signs and great miracles
15 [l]Matt. 18.19
16 [m]ch. 19.2 [n]Matt. 28.19; [o]ch. 10.48
17 [p]ch. 6.6
20 [q]2 Ki. 5.16; [r]ch. 2.38

21 Thou hast neither part nor lot in
this matter: for thy [s]heart is not right
in the sight of God.
22 Repent therefore of this thy wickedness, and pray God, [t]if perhaps the
thought of thine heart may be forgiven
thee.
23 For I perceive that thou art in
[u]the gall of bitterness, and *in* the bond
of iniquity.
24 Then answered Sī'mon, and said,
[v]Pray ye to the Lord for me, that none
of these things which ye have spoken
come upon me.
25 And they, when they had testified and preached the word of the
Lord, returned to Je-ru'sa-lĕm, and
preached the gospel in many villages
of the Sa-măr'ĭ-tans.
26 [w]And the angel of the Lord spake
unto Phĭl'ĭp, saying, Arise, and go toward the south unto the way that goeth
down from Je-ru'sa-lĕm unto Gā'zȧ,
which is desert.
27 And he rose and went: and, behold, [x]a man of Ē-thĭ-ō'pĭ-ȧ, an eunuch
of great authority under Căn'da-çē
queen of the Ē-thĭ-ō'pĭ-ans, who had
the charge of all her treasure, and [y]had
come to Je-ru'sa-lĕm for to worship,
28 Was returning, and sitting in his
chariot read E-sā'ias the prophet.
29 Then the Spirit said unto Phĭl'ĭp,
Go near, and join thyself to this chariot.
30 And Phĭl'ĭp ran thither to *him*,
and heard him read the prophet E-
sā'ias, and said, Understandest thou
what thou readest?
31 And he said, How can I, except
some man should guide me? And he
desired Phĭl'ĭp that he would come up
and sit with him.
32 The place of the scripture which
he read was this, [z]He was led as a
sheep to the slaughter; and like a lamb
dumb before his shearer, so opened he
not his mouth:
33 In his humiliation his judgment
was taken away: and who shall declare his generation? for his life is
taken from the earth.
34 And the eunuch answered Phĭl'ĭp,
and said, I pray thee, of whom speaketh the prophet this? of himself, or of
some other man?
35 Then Phĭl'ĭp opened his mouth,
[a]and began at the same scripture, and
preached unto him Jē'sus.
36 And as they went on *their* way,
they came unto a certain water: and
the eunuch said, See, *here is* water;
[b]what doth hinder me to be baptized?
37 And Phĭl'ĭp said, [c]If thou believest with all thine heart, thou mayest.
And he answered and said, [d]I believe
that Jē'sus Chrīst is the Son of God.
38 And he commanded the chariot
to stand still: and they went down both
into the water, both Phĭl'ĭp and the eunuch; and he baptized him.
39 And when they were come up out
of the water, [e]the Spirit of the Lord
caught away Phĭl'ĭp, that the eunuch
saw him no more: and he went on his
way rejoicing.
40 But Phĭl'ĭp was found [f]at A-zō'tus:
and passing through he preached in all
the cities, till he came to Çæs-a-rē'ȧ.

9 And [a]Saul, yet breathing out threatenings and slaughter against the
disciples of the Lord, went unto the
high priest,
2 And desired of him letters to Da-
măs'cus to the synagogues, that if he
found any [1]of this way, whether they
were men or women, he might bring
them bound unto Je-ru'sa-lĕm.
3 And [b]as he journeyed, he came
near Da-măs'cus: and suddenly there
shined round about him a light from
heaven:
4 And he fell to the earth, and heard
a voice saying unto him, Saul, Saul,
[c]why persecutest thou me?
5 And he said, [d]Who art thou, Lord?
And the Lord said, I am Jē'sus whom
thou persecutest: [e]*it is* hard for thee to
kick against the pricks.
6 And he trembling and astonished
said, Lord, [f]what wilt thou have me to
do? And the Lord *said* unto him, Arise,
and go into the city, and it shall be told
thee what thou must do.
7 And [g]the men which journeyed
with him stood speechless, hearing a
voice, but seeing no man.
8 And Saul arose from the earth; and
when his eyes were opened, he saw no
man: but they led him by the hand, and
brought *him* into Da-măs'cus.
9 And he was three days without
sight, and neither did eat nor drink.
10 ¶ And there was a certain disciple
at Da-măs'cus, named Ȧn-a-nī'as; and
to him said the Lord in a vision, Ȧn-a-
nī'as. And he said, Behold, I *am here*,
Lord.
11 And the Lord *said* unto him,
Arise, and go into the street which
is called Straight, and inquire in the
house of Jū'das for *one* called Saul, [h]of
Tär'sus: for, behold, he prayeth,
12 And hath seen in a vision a man
named Ȧn-a-nī'as coming in, and putting *his* hand on him, that he might
receive his sight.
13 Then Ȧn-a-nī'as answered, Lord,
I have heard by many of this man, how
much evil he hath done to thy saints at
Je-ru'sa-lĕm:
14 And here he hath authority from
the chief priests to bind all [i]that call on
thy name.
15 But the Lord said unto him, Go
thy way: for [j]he is a chosen vessel unto
me, to bear my name before [k]the Gĕn'-
tīles, and [l]kings, and the children of
Is'ra-el:
16 For [m]I will shew him how great
things he must suffer for my name's
sake.
17 [n]And Ăn-a-nī'as went his way,
and entered into the house; and putting his hands on him said, Brother
Saul, the Lord, *even* Jē'sus, that appeared unto thee in the way as thou
camest, hath sent me, that thou mightest receive thy sight, and [o]be filled
with the Hō'lȳ Ghōst.

21 [s]Prov. 6.16-18; Prov. 11.20; Isa. 44.20; Jer. 17.9; Rom. 8.7
22 [t]Isa. 55.7; Dan. 4.27; 2 Tim. 2.25
23 [u]Job 20.14; Heb. 12.15
24 [v]Gen. 20.7; Ex. 8.8; Num. 21.7; 1 Ki. 13.6; Jas. 5.16
26 [w]Ps. 91.11; Heb. 1.14
27 [x]Ps. 68.31; Isa. 43.3; Jer. 13.23; Zeph. 3.10
[y]Isa. 56.3-8; John 12.20
32 [z]Isa. 53.7; 1 Pet. 1.19
35 [a]Luke 24.27; 1 Pet. 1.11
36 [b]ch. 10.47
37 [c]Matt. 28.19; Mark 16.16
[d]Matt. 14.33; Rom. 10.10
39 [e]1 Ki. 18.12; 2 Cor. 12.2-4
40 [f]Zech. 9.6
CHAPTER 9
1 [a]ch. 8.3; 1 Tim. 1.13
2 [1]of the way
3 [b]ch. 22.6; 1 Cor. 15.8
4 [c]Matt. 25.40; Eph. 5.30
5 [d]1 Tim. 1.13
[e]ch. 5.39
6 [f]Luke 3.10; ch. 2.37
7 [g]Dan. 10.7; ch. 22.9
11 [h]ch. 21.39
14 [i]ch. 7.59; 2 Tim. 2.22
15 [j]ch. 13.2; 2 Tim. 1.11
[k]Rom. 1.5; 1 Tim. 2.7
[l]ch. 25.22
16 [m]Matt. 10.21-25; 2 Tim. 1.12
17 [n]ch. 22.12
[o]ch. 2.4

18 And immediately there fell from
his eyes as it had been scales: and he
received sight forthwith, and arose,
and was baptized.
19 And when he had received meat,
he was strengthened. [p]Then was Sa̧ul
certain days with the disciples which
were at Da-măs'cus.
20 And straightway he preached
Chrīst in the synagogues, [q]that he is
the Son of God.
21 But all that heard *him* were
amazed, and said; [r]Is not this he that
destroyed them which called on this
name in Je-ru̧'sa-lĕm, and came hither
for that intent, that he might bring
them bound unto the chief priests?
22 But Sa̧ul increased the more in
strength, [s]and confounded the Jews
which dwelt at Da-măs'cus, proving
that this is very Chrīst.
23 ¶ And after that many days were
fulfilled, [t]the Jews took counsel to kill
him:
24 But their laying await was known
of Sa̧ul. And they watched the gates
day and night to kill him.
25 Then the disciples took him by
night, and [u]let *him* down by the wall in
a basket.
26 And [v]when Sa̧ul was come to Je-
ru̧'sa-lĕm, he assayed to join himself to
the disciples: but they were all afraid
of him, and believed not that he was a
disciple.
27 [w]But Bär'na-bās took him, and
brought *him* to the apostles, and declared unto them how he had seen
the Lord in the way, and that he
had spoken to him, and how he had
preached boldly at Da-măs'cus in the
name of Jē'sus.
28 And he was with them coming in
and going out at Je-ru̧'sa-lĕm.
29 And he spake [x]boldly in the name
of the Lord Jē'sus, and disputed against
the [y]Grē'çians: [z]but they went about to
slay him.
30 *Which* when the brethren knew,
they brought him down to Caes-a-re'a,
and sent him forth to Tär'sus.
31 [a]Then had the churches rest
throughout all Jū-dæ'ȧ and Găl'ĭ-lee
and Sa-mā'rĭ-ȧ, and were edified; and
walking in the fear of the Lord, and in
the comfort of the Hō'lȳ Ghōst, were
multiplied.
32 ¶ And it came to pass, as Pē'tēr
passed [b]throughout all *quarters,* he
came down also to the saints which
dwelt at Lȳd'dȧ.
33 And there he found a certain man
named Æ'ne-ăs, which had kept his
bed eight years, and was sick of the
palsy.
34 And Pē'tēr said unto him, Æ'ne-
ăs, [c]Jē'sus Chrīst maketh thee whole:
arise, and make thy bed. And he arose
immediately.
35 And all that dwelt at Lȳd'dȧ and
[d]Sā'ron saw him, and [e]turned to the
Lord.
36 ¶ Now there was at Jŏp'pȧ a certain disciple named Tăb'i-thȧ, which
by interpretation is called [2]Dôr'cas:

19 [p]ch. 26.20
20 [q]ch. 8.37
21 [r]Matt. 13.54-57; ch. 3.10; Gal. 1.13
22 [s]ch. 18.28
23 [t]ch. 23.12
25 [u]Josh. 2.15; 1 Sam. 19.12
26 [v]ch. 22.17; Gal. 1.17
27 [w]ch. 4.36
29 [x]Eph. 6.19
[y]ch. 6.1
[z]2 Cor. 11.26
31 [a]Ps. 119.165
32 [b]ch. 8.14
34 [c]Matt. 8.3; John 2.11; ch. 3.6
35 [d]1 Chr. 5.16
[e]ch. 11.21
36 [2]Or, Doe, or, Roe
[f]Prov. 31.31; John 15.5-8; 1 Tim. 2.10; Tit. 3.8; Heb. 13.21; Jas. 1.27
37 [g]ch. 1.13
38 [3]Or, be grieved
40 [h]Matt. 9.25
[i]1 Ki. 17.19-23; 2 Ki. 4.32-36; ch. 7.60
[j]Mark 5.41; John 11.43
42 [k]John 11.45
43 [l]Josh. 19.46; 2 Chr. 2.16; Ezra 3.7; Jon. 1.3
[m]ch. 10.6
CHAPTER 10
2 [a]Gen. 18.19; Josh. 24.15; ch. 8.2
3 [b]ch. 11.13
[c]Ps. 34.7; ch. 5.19; ch. 11.13; Heb. 1.14
4 [d]2 Chr. 7.15; Ps. 65.2; Ps. 102.17; Rev. 5.8
6 [e]ch. 9.43
[f]John 7.17; ch. 9.6
9 [g]Ps. 55.17; 1 Thess. 5.17
11 [h]Ezek. 1.1; Rev. 19.11

this woman was full [f]of good works
and almsdeeds which she did.
37 And it came to pass in those days,
that she was sick, and died: whom
when they had washed, they laid *her* in
[g]an upper chamber.
38 And forasmuch as Lȳd'dȧ was
nigh to Jŏp'pȧ, and the disciples had
heard that Pē'tēr was there, they sent
unto him two men, desiring *him* that
he would not [3]delay to come to them.
39 Then Pē'tēr arose and went with
them. When he was come, they brought
him into the upper chamber: and all
the widows stood by him weeping,
and shewing the coats and garments
which Dôr'cas made, while she was
with them.
40 But Pē'tēr [h]put them all forth,
and [i]kneeled down, and prayed; and
turning *him* to the body [j]said, Tăb'i-
thȧ, arise. And she opened her eyes:
and when she saw Pē'tēr, she sat up.
41 And he gave her *his* hand, and
lifted her up, and when he had called
the saints and widows, presented her
alive.
42 And it was known throughout all
Jŏp'pȧ; [k]and many believed in the
Lord.
43 And it came to pass, that he tarried many days in [l]Jŏp'pȧ with one
[m]Sī'mon a tanner.

10 There was a certain man in Çæs-
a-rē'ȧ called Côr-nē'lius, a centurion of the band called the Ităl'ian
band,
2 [a]A devout *man,* and one that feared
God with all his house, which gave
much alms to the people, and prayed to
God alway.
3 [b]He saw in a vision evidently about
the ninth hour of the day an [c]angel of
God coming in to him, and saying unto
him, Côr-nē'lius.
4 And when he looked on him, he
was afraid, and said, What is it, Lord?
And he said unto him, [d]Thy prayers
and thine alms are come up for a memorial before God.
5 And now send men to Jŏp'pȧ, and
call for *one* Sī'mon, whose surname is
Pē'tēr:
6 He lodgeth with one [e]Sī'mon a tanner, whose house is by the sea side: [f]he
shall tell thee what thou oughtest to
do.
7 And when the angel which spake
unto Côr-nē'lius was departed, he
called two of his household servants,
and a devout soldier of them that
waited on him continually;
8 And when he had declared all
these things unto them, he sent them
to Jŏp'pȧ.
9 ¶ On the morrow, as they went on
their journey, and drew nigh unto the
city, Pē'tēr went up upon the house top
to pray about [g]the sixth hour:
10 And he became very hungry, and
would have eaten: but while they made
ready, he fell into a trance,
11 And [h]saw heaven opened, and a
certain vessel descending unto him, as

it had been a great sheet knit at the
four corners, and let down to the earth:
12 Wherein were all manner of fourfooted beasts of the earth, and wild
beasts, and creeping things, and fowls
of the air.
13 And there came a voice to him,
Rise, Pē'tēr; kill, and eat.
14 But Pē'tēr said, Not so, Lord; [i]for
I have never eaten any thing that is
common or unclean.
15 And the voice *spake* unto him
again the second time, [j]What God hath
cleansed, *that* call not thou common.
16 This was done thrice: and the vessel was received up again into heaven.
17 Now while Pē'tēr doubted in himself what this vision which he had seen
should mean, behold, the men which
were sent from Côr-nē'lius had made
inquiry for Sī'mon's house, and stood
before the gate,
18 And called, and asked whether
Sī'mon, which was surnamed Pē'tēr,
were lodged there.
19 ¶ While Pē'tēr thought on the vision, [k]the Spirit said unto him, Behold,
three men seek thee.
20 [l]Arise therefore, and get thee
down, and go with them, doubting
nothing: for I have sent them.
21 Then Pē'tēr went down to the
men which were sent unto him from
Côr-nē'lius; and said, Behold, I am
he whom ye seek: what *is* the cause
wherefore ye are come?
22 And they said, Côr-nē'lius the
centurion, a just man, and one that feareth God, and [m]of good report among
all the nation of the Jews, was warned
from God by an holy angel to send for
thee into his house, and to hear words
of thee.
23 Then called he them in, and
lodged *them*. And on the morrow Pē'-
tēr went away with them, and certain brethren from Jŏp'pȧ accompanied him.
24 And the morrow after they entered into Çæs-a-rē'ȧ. And Côr-nē'lius
waited for them, and had called together his kinsmen and near friends.
25 And as Pē'tēr was coming in,
Côr-nē'lius met him, and fell down at
his feet, and worshipped *him*.
26 But Pē'tēr took him up, saying,
[n]Stand up; I myself also am a man.
27 And as he talked with him, he
went in, and found many that were
come together.
28 And he said unto them, Ye know
how [o]that it is an unlawful thing for a
man that is a Jew to keep company, or
come unto one of another nation; but
[p]God hath shewed me that I should not
call any man common or unclean.
29 Therefore came I *unto you* without gainsaying, [q]as soon as I was sent
for: I ask therefore for what intent ye
have sent for me?
30 And Côr-nē'lius said, Four days
ago I was fasting until this hour; and at
the ninth hour I prayed in my house,
and behold, [r]a man stood before me
[s]in bright clothing,

14 [i]Lev. 11.4; Rom. 10.2
15 [j]Matt. 15.11; Tit. 1.15
19 [k]ch. 8.29; Rev. 22.17
20 [l]Matt. 28.19; ch. 15.7
22 [m]ch. 22.12
26 [n]Ex. 34.14; Rev. 14.7
28 [o]John 4.9; Gal. 2.12
[p]ch. 15.8; Eph. 3.6
29 [q]Gal. 1.16
30 [r]ch. 1.10
[s]Gen. 18.2; Luke 24.4
31 [t]Dan. 10.12
[u]Prov. 14.31; Heb. 6.10
34 [v]Deut. 10.17; 1 Pet. 1.17
35 [w]ch. 15.9; Eph. 2.13
36 [x]Isa. 57.19; Col. 1.20
[y]Dan. 7.14; Rev. 17.14
38 [z]Luke 4.18; Heb. 1.9
[a]John 1; Col. 2.9
41 [b]John 14.17
[c]John 21.13
42 [d]Matt. 28.19; ch. 4.19-20
[e]John 5.22
[f]Rom. 14.9
43 [g]Isa. 53.11
CHAPTER 11
1 [a]Gen. 49.10

31 And said, Côr-nē'lius, [t]thy prayer
is heard, [u]and thine alms are had in
remembrance in the sight of God.
32 Send therefore to Jŏp'pȧ, and call
hither Sī'mon, whose surname is Pē'-
tēr; he is lodged in the house of *one*
Sī'mon a tanner by the sea side: who,
when he cometh, shall speak unto thee.
33 Immediately therefore I sent to
thee; and thou hast well done that thou
art come. Now therefore are we all
here present before God, to hear all
things that are commanded thee of
God.
34 ¶ Then Pē'tēr opened *his* mouth,
and said, [v]Of a truth I perceive that
God is no respecter of persons:
35 But [w]in every nation he that feareth him, and worketh righteousness, is
accepted with him.
36 The word which *God* sent unto
the children of Is'ra-el, [x]preaching
peace by Jē'sus Chrīst: ([y]he is Lord of
all:)
37 That word, *I say*, ye know, which
was published throughout all Jū-dæ'ȧ,
and began from Găl'ĭ-lee, after the baptism which Jŏhn preached;
38 How [z]God anointed Jē'sus of
Nāz'a-rĕth with the Hō'lȳ Ghōst and
with power: who went about doing
good, and healing all that were oppressed of the devil; [a]for God was with
him.
39 And we are witnesses of all things
which he did both in the land of the
Jews, and in Je-ru'sa-lĕm; whom they
slew and hanged on a tree:
40 Him God raised up the third day,
and shewed him openly;
41 [b]Not to all the people, but unto
witnesses chosen before of God, *even*
to us, [c]who did eat and drink with him
after he rose from the dead.
42 And [d]he commanded us to preach
unto the people, and to testify [e]that it is
he which was ordained of God *to be* the
Judge [f]of quick and dead.
43 [g]To him give all the prophets witness, that through his name whosoever believeth in him shall receive remission of sins.
44 ¶ While Pē'tēr yet spake these
words, the Hō'lȳ Ghōst fell on all them
which heard the word.
45 And they of the circumcision
which believed were astonished, as
many as came with Pē'tēr, because
that on the Gĕn'tīles also was poured
out the gift of the Hō'lȳ Ghōst.
46 For they heard them speak with
tongues, and magnify God. Then answered Pē'tēr,
47 Can any man forbid water, that
these should not be baptized, which
have received the Hō'lȳ Ghōst as well
as we?
48 And he commanded them to be
baptized in the name of the Lord. Then
prayed they him to tarry certain days.
11 And the apostles and brethren
that were in Jū-dæ'ȧ heard that
the [a]Gĕn'tīles had also received the
word of God.

2 And when Pē'tẽr was come up to
Je-ru̧'sa-lĕm, [b]they that were of the circumcision contended with him,
3 Saying, [c]Thou wentest in to men
uncircumcised, and didst eat with them.
4 But Pē'tẽr rehearsed *the matter*
from the beginning, and expounded *it*
[d]by order unto them, saying,
5 [e]I was in the city of Jŏp'på praying: and in a trance I saw a vision, A
certain vessel descend, as it had been a
great sheet, let down from heaven by
four corners; and it came even to me:
6 Upon the which when I had fastened mine eyes, I considered, and saw
fourfooted beasts of the earth, and
wild beasts, and creeping things, and
fowls of the air.
7 And I heard a voice saying unto
me, Arise, Pē'tẽr; slay and eat.
8 But I said, [f]Not so, Lord: for nothing common or unclean hath at any
time entered into my mouth.
9 But the voice answered me again
from heaven, What God hath cleansed,
that call not thou common.
10 And this was done three times:
and all were drawn up again into
heaven.
11 And, behold, immediately there
were three men already come unto the
house where I was, sent from Çæs-a-
rē'à unto me.
12 And [g]the spirit bade me go with
them, nothing doubting. Moreover
[h]these six brethren accompanied me,
and we entered into the man's house:
13 [i]And he shewed us how he had
seen an angel in his house, which
stood and said unto him, Send men to
Jŏp'på, and call for Sī'mon, whose surname is Pē'tẽr;
14 Who shall tell thee words,
whereby thou and all thy house shall
be saved.
15 And as I began to speak, the
Hō'lȳ Ghōst fell on them, [j]as on us at
the beginning.
16 Then remembered I the word of
the Lord, how that he said, [k]Jŏhn indeed baptized with water; but [l]ye shall
be baptized with the Hō'lȳ Ghōst.
17 [m]Forasmuch then as God gave
them the like gift as *he did* unto us, who
believed on the Lord Jē'sus Chrīst;
[n]what was I, that I could withstand
God?
18 When they heard these things,
they held their peace, and glorified
God, saying, [o]Then hath God also to
the Gĕn'tīles granted repentance unto
life.
19 ¶ [p]Now they which were scattered abroad upon the persecution that
arose about Stē'phen travelled as far
as Phe-nī'çe, and Çȳ'prus, and Ăn'tĭ-
ŏch, preaching the word to none but
unto the Jews only.
20 And some of them were men of
Çȳ'prus and Çȳ-rē'nē, which, when
they were come to Ăn'tĭ-ŏch, spake
unto [q]the Grē'çians, [r]preaching the
Lord Jē'sus.
21 And [s]the hand of the Lord was
with them: and a great number believed, and [t]turned unto the Lord.
22 ¶ Then tidings of these things
came unto the ears of the church which
was in Je-ru̧'sa-lĕm: and they sent forth
[u]Bär'na-bās, that he should go as far as
Ăn'tĭ-ŏch.
23 Who, when he came, and had
seen the grace of God, was glad, and
[v]exhorted them all, that with purpose
of heart they would [w]cleave unto the
Lord.
24 For he was a good man, and full
of the Hō'lȳ Ghōst and of faith: [x]and
much people was added unto the Lord.
25 Then departed Bär'na-bās to
[y]Tär'sus, for to seek Sa̧ul:
26 And when he had found him,
he brought him unto Ăn'tĭ-ŏch. And
it came to pass, that a whole year
they assembled themselves [1]with the
church, and taught much people. And
the disçiples were called Chrĭs'tians
first in Ăn'tĭ-ŏch.
27 ¶ And in these days came [z]proph-
ets from Je-ru̧'sa-lĕm unto Ăn'tĭ-ŏch.
28 And there stood up one of them
named [a]Ăg'ă-bŭs, and signified by the
spirit that there should be great dearth
throughout all the world: which came to
pass in the days of Cla̧u'dĭ-us Çæ'sar.
29 Then the disciples, every man according to his ability, determined to
send [b]relief unto the brethren which
dwelt in Jū-dæ'à:
30 Which also they did, and sent it
to the [c]elders by the hands of Bär'na-
bās and Sa̧ul.

12 Now about that time Hĕr'od the
king [1]stretched forth *his* hands
[a]to vex certain of the church.
2 And he killed Jāmes [b]the brother
of Jŏhn with the sword.
3 And because he saw it pleased the
Jews, he proceeded further to take
Pē'tẽr also. (Then were [c]the days of
unleavened bread.)
4 And [d]when he had apprehended
him, he put *him* in prison, and delivered *him* to four quaternions of soldiers to keep him; intending after Easter to bring him forth to the people.
5 Pē'tẽr therefore was kept in prison:
but [2]prayer was made without ceasing
of the church unto God for him.
6 And when Hĕr'od would have
brought him forth, the same night Pē'-
tẽr was sleeping between two soldiers,
bound with two chains: and the keepers before the door kept the prison.
7 And, behold, [e]the angel of the
Lord came upon *him*, and a light shined
in the prison: and he smote Pē'tẽr on
the side, and raised him up, saying,
Arise up quickly. And his chains fell off
from *his* hands.
8 And the angel said unto him, Gird
thyself, and bind on thy sandals. And
so he did. And he saith unto him, Cast
thy garment about thee, and follow
me.
9 And he went out, and followed
him; and [f]wist not that it was true

2 [b]Gal. 2.12
3 [c]ch. 10.28
4 [d]Luke 1.3
5 [e]ch. 10.9
8 [f]Ezek. 4.14
12 [g]John 16.13; ch. 15.7
[h]ch. 10.23
13 [i]ch. 10.30
15 [j]ch. 2.4
16 [k]Matt. 3.11; Mark 1.8; Luke 3.16; John 1.26; ch. 1.5
[l]Isa. 44.3; Joel 2.28
17 [m]Matt. 20.14-15; ch. 15.8-9
[n]Job 9.12-14; Dan. 4.35; ch. 10.47
18 [o]Rom. 10.12
19 [p]ch. 8.1
20 [q]ch. 6.1
[r]ch. 8.5-35; Eph. 3.8
21 [s]Luke 1.66
[t]ch. 9.35
22 [u]ch. 9.27
23 [v]ch. 13.43; Jude 3
[w]Deut. 10.20; 1 Cor. 15.58; Gal. 2.20; Col. 2.6
24 [x]ch. 2.41-47; ch. 4.4; ch. 5.14; ch. 9.31
25 [y]ch. 9.30
26 [1]Or, in the church
27 [z]ch. 2.17; 1 Cor. 12.28; Eph. 4.11
28 [a]ch. 21.10
29 [b]Rom. 15.26; 1 Cor. 16.1; 2 Cor. 9.1; Gal. 2.10
30 [c]1 Pet. 5.1

CHAPTER 12
1 [1]Or, began
[a]Matt. 10.17; John 15.20-21
2 [b]Matt. 4.21
3 [c]Ex. 12.14
4 [d]John 21.18
5 [2]Or, instant and earnest prayer was made
7 [e]Ps. 34.7; Isa. 37.36; ch. 5.19; Heb. 1.14
9 [f]Ps. 126.1

which was done by the angel; but
thought [g]he saw a vision.
10 When they were past the first
and the second ward, they came unto
the iron gate that leadeth unto the city;
[h]which opened to them of his own accord: and they went out, and passed on
through one street; and forthwith the
angel departed from him.
11 And when Pē'tẽr was come to
himself, he said, Now I know of a
surety, that [i]the Lord hath sent his angel, and [j]hath delivered me out of the
hand of Hĕr'od, and *from* all the expectation of the people of the Jews.
12 And when he had considered *the
thing*, [k]he came to the house of Mā'rȳ
the mother of [l]Jŏhn, whose surname
was Märk; where many were gathered
together praying.
13 And as Pē'tẽr knocked at the
door of the gate, a damsel came [3]to
hearken, named Rhō'dȧ.
14 And when she knew Pē'têr's
voice, she opened not the gate for gladness, but ran in, and told how Pē'tẽr
stood before the gate.
15 And they said unto her, Thou art
mad. But she constantly affirmed that
it was even so. Then said they, [m]It is
his angel.
16 But Pē'tẽr continued knocking:
and when they had opened *the door*,
and saw him, they were astonished.
17 But he, beckoning unto them with
the hand to hold their peace, declared
unto them how the Lord had brought
him out of the prison. And he said, Go
shew these things unto Jāmes, and to
the brethren. And he departed, and
went into another place.
18 Now as soon as it was day, there
was no small stir among the soldiers,
what was become of Pē'tẽr.
19 And when Hĕr'od had sought for
him, and found him not, he examined
the keepers, and commanded that *they*
should be put to death. And he went
down from Jū-dæ'ȧ to Çǽs-a-rē'ȧ, and
there abode.
20 ¶ And Hĕr'od [4]was highly displeased with them of Tȳre and Sī'dŏn:
but they came with one accord to
him, and, having made Blăs'tus [5]the
king's chamberlain their friend, desired peace; because [n]their country
was nourished by the king's *country*.
21 And upon a set day Hĕr'od, arrayed in royal apparel, sat upon his
throne, and made an oration unto them.
22 And the people gave a shout, *saying*, [o]*It is* the voice of a god, and not of
a man.
23 And immediately the angel of the
Lord [p]smote him, because [q]he gave
not God the glory: and he was eaten of
worms, and gave up the ghost.
24 ¶ But [r]the word of God grew and
multiplied.
25 And Bär'na-bās and Sąul returned
from Je-rų'sa-lĕm, when they had fulfilled *their* [6]ministry, and [s]took with
them Jŏhn, whose surname was Märk.

13

Now there were [a]in the church
that was at Ăn'tĭ-ŏch certain

[g]ch. 10.3
10 [h]ch. 16.26
11 [i]Ps. 34.7;
[j]Job 5.19;
12 [k]ch. 4.23
[l]ch. 13.5
13 [3]Or, to ask who was there
15 [m]Gen. 48.16
20 [4]Or, bare an hostile mind, intending war
[5]that was over the king's bedchamber
[n]1 Ki. 5.9
22 [o]Jude 16
23 [p]Ex. 12.12-23-29;
[q]Lev. 10.3
24 [r]Isa. 55.11
25 [6]Or, charge
[s]ch. 15.37
CHAPTER 13
1 [a]ch. 14.26
[b]ch. 9.27
[c]Rom. 16.21
[1]Or, Herod's foster-brother
2 [d]Num. 8.14;
[e]Matt. 9.38
4 [f]ch. 4.36
5 [g]ch. 12.25
8 [h]Ex. 7.11
9 [2]That is, Destroyer
[3]That is, Worker
10 [i]Matt. 13.38
11 [j]Ex. 9.3
13 [k]ch. 15.38
15 [l]Luke 4.16
[m]Heb. 13.22
18 [4]etropophoresen, perhaps for etrophophoresen, bore, or, fed them as a nurse beareth, or, feedeth her child, Ex. 19.4; Deut. 1.31; Deut. 32.11-12; Isa. 46.3-4; Isa. 63.9; Hos. 11.3 according to the LXX. and so Chrysostom

prophets and teachers; as [b]Bär'na-bās,
and Sĭm'e-on that was called Nī'ġer,
and [c]Lų'çius of Çȳ-rē'ne, and Măn'a-
ĕn, [1]which had been brought up with
Hĕr'od the tetrarch, and Sąul.
2 As they ministered to the Lord,
and fasted, the Hō'lȳ Ghōst said, [d]Sep-
arate me Bär'na-bās and Sąul for the
work [e]whereunto I have called them.
3 And when they had fasted and
prayed, and laid *their* hands on them,
they sent *them* away.
4 ¶ So they, being sent forth by the
Hō'lȳ Ghōst, departed unto Se-leū'-
çĭ-ȧ; and from thence they sailed to
[f]Çȳ'prus.
5 And when they were at Săl'a-mis,
they preached the word of God in the
synagogues of the Jews: and they had
also [g]Jŏhn to *their* minister.
6 And when they had gone through
the isle unto Pā'phos, they found a certain sorcerer, a false prophet, a Jew,
whose name *was* Bär-jē'sus:
7 Which was with the deputy of the
country, Sẽr'ġĭ-us Pąu'lus, a prudent
man; who called for Bär'na-bās and
Sąul, and desired to hear the word of
God.
8 But [h]Ĕl'ȳ-măs the sorcerer (for so
is his name by interpretation) withstood them, seeking to turn away the
deputy from the faith.
9 Then [2]Sąul, (who also *is called*
[3]Pąul,) filled with the Hō'lȳ Ghōst, set
his eyes on him,
10 And said, O full of all subtilty and
all mischief, [i]*thou* child of the devil,
thou enemy of all righteousness, wilt
thou not cease to pervert the right
ways of the Lord?
11 And now, behold, [j]the hand of the
Lord *is* upon thee, and thou shalt be
blind, not seeing the sun for a season.
And immediately there fell on him a
mist and a darkness; and he went about
seeking some to lead him by the hand.
12 Then the deputy, when he saw
what was done, believed, being astonished at the doctrine of the Lord.
13 Now when Pąul and his company loosed from Pā'phos, they came
to Pẽr'gȧ in Pam-phȳl'ĭ-ȧ: and [k]Jŏhn
departing from them returned to Je-
rų'sa-lĕm.
14 ¶ But when they departed from
Pẽr'gȧ, they came to Ăn'tĭ-ŏch in Pi-
sĭd'ĭ-ȧ, and went into the synagogue
on the sabbath day, and sat down.
15 And [l]after the reading of the law
and the prophets the rulers of the synagogue sent unto them, saying, *Ye* men
and brethren, if ye have [m]any word of
exhortation for the people, say on.
16 Then Pąul stood up, and beckoning with *his* hand said, Men of Is'ra-el,
and ye that fear God, give audience.
17 The God of this people of Is'ra-el
chose our fathers, and exalted the people when they dwelt as strangers in the
land of Ē'ġȳpt, and with an high arm
brought he them out of it.
18 And about the time of forty years
[4]suffered he their manners in the wilderness.

19 And when he had destroyed seven nations in the land of Chā'năan, he divided their land to them by lot.

20 And after that he gave *unto them* judges about the space of four hundred and fifty years, until Săm'u-el the prophet.

21 And afterward they desired a king: and God gave unto them Sąul the son of Çĭs, a man of the tribe of Bĕn'ja-min, by the space of forty years.

22 And [n]when he had removed him, he raised up unto them Dā'vid to be their king; to whom also he gave testimony, and said, I have found Dā'vid the *son* of Jĕs'se, a man after mine own heart, which shall fulfil all my will.

23 [o]Of this man's seed hath God according [p]to *his* promise raised unto Is'ra-el [q]a Saviour, Jē'sus:

24 When Jŏhn had first preached before his coming the baptism of repentance to all the people of Is'ra-el.

25 And as Jŏhn fulfilled his course, he said, Whom think ye that I am? I am not *he*. But, behold, there cometh one after me, whose shoes of *his* feet I am not worthy to loose.

26 Men *and* brethren, children of the stock of Ā'bră-hăm, and whosoever among you feareth God, to you is the word of this salvation sent.

27 For they that dwell at Je-rụ'sa-lĕm, and their rulers, [r]because they knew him not, nor yet the voices of the prophets which are read every sabbath day, they have fulfilled *them* in condemning *him*.

28 And though they found no cause of death *in him*, yet desired they Pī'late that he should be slain.

29 And when they had fulfilled all that was written of him, they took *him* down from the tree, and laid *him* in a sepulchre.

30 [s]But God raised him from the dead:

31 And [t]he was seen many days of them which came up with him from Găl'ĭ-lee to Je-rụ'sa-lĕm, who are his witnesses unto the people.

32 And we declare unto you glad tidings, how that [u]the promise which was made unto the fathers,

33 God hath fulfilled the same unto us their children, in that he hath raised up Jē'sus again; as it is also written in the second psalm, [v]Thou art my Son, this day have I begotten thee.

34 And as concerning that he raised him up from the dead, *now* no more to return to corruption, he said on this wise, I will give you the sure [5]mercies of Dā'vid.

35 Wherefore he saith also in another *psalm*, [w]Thou shalt not suffer thine Holy One to see corruption.

36 For Dā'vid, [6]after he had served his own generation by the will of God, fell on sleep, and was laid unto his fathers, and saw corruption:

37 But he, whom God raised again, saw no corruption.

38 ¶ Be it known unto you therefore, men *and* brethren, that [x]through this man is preached unto you the forgiveness of sins:

39 And [y]by him all that believe are justified from all things, from which ye could not be justified by the law of Mō'ses.

40 Beware therefore, lest that come upon you, which is spoken of in [z]the prophets;

41 Behold, ye despisers, and wonder, and perish: for I work a work in your days, a work which ye shall in no wise believe, though a man declare it unto you.

42 And when the Jews were gone out of the synagogue, the Gĕn'tīles besought that these words might be preached to them the [7]next sabbath.

43 Now when the congregation was broken up, many of the Jews and religious proselytes followed Pąul and Bär'na-bās: who, speaking to them, persuaded them to continue in [a]the grace of God.

44 ¶ And the next sabbath day came almost the whole city together to hear the word of God.

45 But when the Jews saw the multitudes, they were filled with envy, and [b]spake against those things which were spoken by Pąul, contradicting and blaspheming.

46 Then Pąul and Bär'na-bās waxed bold, and said, [c]It was necessary that the word of God should first have been spoken to you: but [d]seeing ye put it from you, and judge yourselves unworthy of everlasting life, lo, we turn to the Gĕn'tīles.

47 For so hath the Lord commanded us, *saying*, [e]I have set thee to be a light of the Gĕn'tīles, that thou shouldest be for salvation unto the ends of the earth.

48 And when the Gĕn'tīles heard this, they were glad, and glorified the word of the Lord: [f]and as many as were ordained to eternal life believed.

49 And the word of the Lord was published throughout all the region.

50 But the Jews stirred up the devout and honourable women, and the chief men of the city, and [g]raised persecution against Pąul and Bär'na-bās, and expelled them out of their coasts.

51 [h]But they shook off the dust of their feet against them, and came unto I-cō'nĭ-um.

52 And the disciples [i]were filled with joy, and with the Hō'lȳ Ghōst.

14

And it came to pass in I-cō'nĭ-um, that they went both together into the synagogue of the Jews, and so spake, that a [a]great multitude both of the Jews and also of the Greeks believed.

2 But the unbelieving Jews stirred up the Gĕn'tīles, and made their minds evil affected against the brethren.

3 Long time therefore abode they speaking boldly in the Lord, [b]which gave testimony unto the word of his

22 [n]Hos. 13.11
23 [o]Ps. 132.11; Rom. 1.3
[p]2 Sam. 7.12
[q]Rom. 11.26
27 [r]1 Cor. 2.8
30 [s]Matt. 28.6; Heb. 13.20
31 [t]1 Cor. 15.5
32 [u]Gen. 3.15; Gal. 3.16
33 [v]Ps. 2.7; Heb. 5.5
34 [5]tahosia, holy, or, just things: which word the LXX. both in the place of Isa. 55.3, and in many others, use for that which is in the Hebrew, mercies
35 [w]Ps. 16.10
36 [6]Or, after he had in his own age served the will of God
38 [x]Dan. 9.24; Col. 1.14
39 [y]Isa. 53.11; Heb. 10.22
40 [z]Hab. 1.5
42 [7]in the week between, or, in the sabbath between
43 [a]ch. 11.23
45 [b]ch. 18.6
46 [c]Matt. 10.6;
[d]Ex. 32.10
47 [e]Isa. 42.6
48 [f]ch. 2.47
50 [g]Matt. 5.12
51 [h]Luke 9.5
52 [i]Matt. 5.12
CHAPTER 14
1 [a]Isa. 11.11
3 [b]Mark 16.20

grace, and granted signs and wonders
to be done by their hands.
4 But the multitude of the city was
divided: and part held with the Jews,
and part with the apostles.
5 And when there was an assault
made both of the Gĕn'tīles, and also of
the Jews with their rulers, [c]to use
them despitefully, and to stone them,
6 They were ware of *it,* and [d]fled
unto Lȳs'trȧ and Dẽr'be, cities of Lȳc-
a-ō'nĭ-ȧ, and unto the region that lieth
round about:
7 And there they preached the gospel.
8 ¶ [e]And there sat a certain man at
Lȳs'trȧ, impotent in his feet, being a
cripple from his mother's womb, who
never had walked:
9 The same heard Pa̧ul speak: who
stedfastly beholding him, and [f]perceiv-
ing that he had faith to be healed,
10 Said with a loud voice, [g]Stand upright on thy feet. And he leaped and
walked.
11 And when the people saw what
Pa̧ul had done, they lifted up their
voices, saying in the speech of Lȳc-a-
ō'nĭ-ȧ, [h]The gods are come down to us
in the likeness of men.
12 And they called Bär'na-bās, Jū'-
pĭ-tẽr; and Pa̧ul, Mẽr-cū'rĭ-us, because
he was the chief speaker.
13 Then the priest of Jū'pĭ-tẽr, which
was before their city, brought oxen and
garlands unto the gates, [i]and would
have done sacrifice with the people.
14 *Which* when the apostles,
Bär'na-bās and Pa̧ul, heard *of,* [j]they
rent their clothes, and ran in among
the people, crying out,
15 And saying, Sirs, why do ye these
things? [k]We also are men of like passions with you, and preach unto you
that ye should turn from [l]these vanities [m]unto the living God, [n]which
made heaven, and earth, and the sea,
and all things that are therein:
16 [o]Who in times past suffered all
nations to walk in their own ways.
17 [p]Nevertheless he left not himself
without witness, in that he did good,
and [q]gave us rain from heaven, and
fruitful seasons, filling our hearts with
food and gladness.
18 And with these sayings scarce restrained they the people, that they had
not done sacrifice unto them.
19 ¶ [r]And there came thither *certain*
Jews from Ăn'tĭ-ŏch and I-cō'nĭ-um,
who persuaded the people, [s]and, having stoned Pa̧ul, drew *him* out of the
city, supposing he [t]had been dead.
20 Howbeit, as the disciples stood
round about him, he rose up, and came
into the city: and the next day he departed with Bär'na-bās to Dẽr'be.
21 And when they had preached the
gospel to that city, and [1]had taught
many, they returned again to Lȳs'trȧ,
and *to* I-cō'nĭ-um, and Ăn'tĭ-ŏch,
22 Confirming the souls of the disciples, *and* exhorting them to continue in
the faith, and that [u]we must through
much tribulation enter into the kingdom of God.
23 And when they had [v]ordained
them elders in every church, and had
prayed with fasting, they commended
them to the Lord, on whom they believed.
24 And after they had passed
throughout Pi-sĭd'ĭ-ȧ, they came to
Pam-phȳl'ĭ-ȧ.
25 And when they had preached the
word in Pẽr'gȧ, they went down into
Ăt'tā'lĭ-ȧ:
26 And thence sailed to Ăn'tĭ-ŏch,
[w]from whence they had been recommended to the grace of God for the
work which they fulfilled.
27 And when they were come, and
had gathered the church together, they
rehearsed all that God had done with
them, and how he had [x]opened the
door of faith unto the Gĕn'tīles.
28 And there they abode long time
with the disciples.

15 And [a]certain men which came
down from Jū-dæ'ȧ taught the
brethren, *and said,* [b]Except ye be circumcised [c]after the manner of Mō'ses,
ye cannot be saved.
2 When therefore Pa̧ul and Bär'na-
bās had no small dissension and dis-
putation with them, they determined
that [d]Pa̧ul and Bär'na-bās, and certain other of them, should go up to Je-
ru̧'sa-lĕm unto the apostles and elders
about this question.
3 And [e]being brought on their way
by the church, they passed through
Phe-nī'çe and Sa-mā'rĭ-ȧ, [f]declaring
the conversion of the Gĕn'tīles: and
they caused great joy unto all the
brethren.
4 And when they were come to Je-
ru̧'sa-lĕm, they were received of the
church, and *of* the apostles and elders,
and they declared all things that God
had done with them.
5 But there [1]rose up certain of the
sect of the Phăr'ĭ-sees which believed,
saying, That it was needful to circumcise them, and to command *them* to
keep the law of Mō'ses.
6 ¶ And the apostles and elders came
together for to consider of this matter.
7 And when there had been much
disputing, Pē'tẽr rose up, and said unto
them, Men *and* brethren, ye know how
that a good while ago God made choice
among us, that the Gĕn'tīles by my
mouth should hear the word of the gospel, and believe.
8 And God, [g]which knoweth the
hearts, bare them witness, [h]giving
them the Hō'lȳ Ghōst, even as *he did*
unto us;
9 [i]And put no difference between us
and them, [j]purifying their hearts by
faith.
10 Now therefore why tempt ye God,
[k]to put a yoke upon the neck of the
disciples, which neither our fathers nor
we were able to bear?
11 But [l]we believe that through the
grace of the Lord Jē'sus Chrīst we
shall be saved, even as they.

5 [c]1 Thess. 2.14-16; 2 Tim. 3.11
6 [d]Matt. 10.23; ch. 16.1-2; 2 Tim. 3.11
8 [e]John 5.5; ch. 3.2
9 [f]Matt. 8.10; Mark 1.40-41
10 [g]Isa. 35.6
11 [h]ch. 28.6
13 [i]Dan. 2.46
14 [j]Matt. 26.65
15 [k]Jas. 5.17; Rev. 19.10
[l]Jer. 14.22; 1 Cor. 8.4
[m]1 Thess. 1.9
[n]Rev. 14.7
16 [o]Ps. 81.12; 1 Pet. 4.3
17 [p]ch. 17.27; Rom. 1.20
[q]Lev. 26.4; Matt. 5.45
19 [r]ch. 13.45
[s]2 Cor. 11.25
[t]2 Cor. 1.8
21 [1]had made many disciples
22 [u]Matt. 10.38; 2 Tim. 2.11
23 [v]Tit. 1.5
26 [w]ch. 13.1-3
27 [x]1 Cor. 16.9; Rev. 3.8

CHAPTER 15
1 [a]Gal. 2.12
[b]John 7.22; Phil. 3.2
[c]Gen. 17.10
2 [d]Gal. 2.1
3 [e]Rom. 15.24; 1 Cor. 16.6
[f]ch. 14.27
5 [1]Or, rose up, said they, certain
8 [g]1 Chr. 28.9; Rev. 2.23
[h]Luke 4.18; Heb. 1.9
9 [i]Rom. 10.11
[j]ch. 10.43; 1 Pet. 1.22
10 [k]Matt. 23.4; Gal. 5.1
11 [l]Isa. 53.11; Eph. 1.7

12 ¶ Then all the multitude kept silence, and gave audience to Bär'na-
bās and Pa̧ul, declaring what miracles
and wonders God had wrought among
the Gĕn'tīles by them.
13 ¶ And after they had held their
peace, [m]Jāmes answered, saying, Men
and brethren, hearken unto me:
14 Sĭm'e-on hath declared how God
at the first did visit the Gĕn'tīles, to
take out of them a people for his name.
15 And to this agree the [n]words of
the prophets; as it is written,
16 [o]After this I will return, and will
build again the tabernacle of Dā'vid,
which is fallen down; and I will build
again the ruins thereof, and I will set it
up:
17 That the residue of men might
seek after the Lord, and all the Gĕn'-
tīles, upon whom my name is called,
saith the Lord, who doeth all these
things.
18 Known unto God are all his works
from the beginning of the world.
19 Wherefore my sentence is, that we
trouble not them, which from among
the Gĕn'tīles [p]are turned to God:
20 But that we write unto them, that
they abstain [q]from pollutions of idols,
and [r]*from* fornication, and *from* things
strangled, [s]and *from* blood.
21 For Mō'ses of old time hath in every city them that preach him, [t]being
read in the synagogues every sabbath
day.
22 Then pleased it the apostles and
elders, with the whole church, to send
chosen men of their own company
to Ăn'tĭ-ŏch with Pa̧ul and Bär'na-
bās; *namely,* Jū'das surnamed [u]Bär'-
sa-bās, and Sī'las, chief men among
the brethren:
23 And they wrote *letters* by them
after this manner; The apostles and elders and brethren *send* greeting unto
the brethren which are of the Gĕn'tīles
in Ăn'tĭ-ŏch and Sȳr'ĭ-ȧ and Çi-lĭ'çiȧ:
24 Forasmuch as we have heard,
that [v]certain which went out from us
have troubled you with words, subvert-
ing your souls, saying, *Ye must* be circumcised, and keep the law: to whom
we gave no *such* commandment:
25 It seemed good unto us, being
assembled with one accord, to send
chosen men unto you with our beloved
Bär'na-bās and Pa̧ul,
26 [w]Men that have hazarded their
lives for the name of our Lord Jē'sus
Chrīst.
27 We have sent therefore Jū'das
and Sī'las, who shall also tell *you* the
same things by [2]mouth.
28 For it seemed good to [x]the Hō'lȳ
Ghōst, and to us, to lay upon you no
greater burden than these necessary
things;
29 [y]That ye abstain from meats offered to idols, and [z]from blood, and
from things strangled, and from fornication: from which if ye keep yourselves, ye shall do well. Fare ye well.
30 So when they were dismissed,
they came to Ăn'tĭ-ŏch: and when they
had gathered the multitude together,
they delivered the epistle:
31 *Which* when they had read, they
rejoiced for the [3]consolation.
32 And Jū'das and Sī'las, being
[a]prophets also themselves, [b]exhorted
the brethren with many words, and
confirmed *them.*
33 And after they had tarried *there*
a space, they were let [c]go in peace
from the brethren unto the apostles.
34 Notwithstanding it pleased Sī'las
to abide there still.
35 [d]Pa̧ul also and Bär'na-bās continued in Ăn'tĭ-ŏch, teaching and preaching the word of the Lord, with many
others also.
36 ¶ And some days after Pa̧ul said
unto Bär'na-bās, Let us go again and
visit our brethren [e]in every city where
we have preached the word of the
Lord, *and see* how they do.
37 And Bär'na-bās determined to
take with them [f]Jŏhn, whose surname
was Märk.
38 But Pa̧ul thought not good to take
him with them, [g]who departed from
them from Pam-phȳl'ĭ-ȧ, and went not
with them to the work.
39 And the contention was so sharp
between them, that they departed asunder one from the other: and so Bär'-
na-bās took Märk, and sailed unto
Çȳ'prus;
40 And Pa̧ul chose Sī'las, and departed, being recommended by the
brethren unto the grace of God.
41 And he went through Sȳr'ĭ-ȧ and
Çi-lĭ'çiȧ, confirming the churches.

16 Then came he to [a]Dĕr'be and
Lȳs'trȧ: and, behold, a certain
disciple was there, [b]named Ti-mō'the-
ŭs, the son of a certain woman, which
was a Jew'ess, and believed; but his
father *was* a Greek:
2 Which [c]was well reported of by
the brethren that were at Lȳs'trȧ and
I-cō'nĭ-um.
3 Him would Pa̧ul have to go forth
with him; and [d]took and circumcised
him because of the Jews which were in
those quarters: for they knew all that
his father was a Greek.
4 And as they went through the cities, they delivered them the decrees for
to keep, [e]that were ordained of
the apostles and elders which were at
Je-ru̧'sa-lĕm.
5 And [f]so were the churches established in the faith, and increased in
number daily.
6 Now when they had gone throughout Phrȳg'ĭ-ȧ and the region of Gā-
lā'tiȧ, and were forbidden of the Hō'lȳ
Ghōst to preach the word in Ā'siȧ,
7 After they were come to Mȳs'iȧ,
they assayed to go into Bi-thȳn'ĭ-ȧ: but
the Spirit suffered them not.
8 And they passing by Mȳs'iȧ came
down to [g]Trō'ăs.
9 And a [h]vision appeared to Pa̧ul in
the night; There stood a man of Măç-e-
dō'nĭ-ȧ, and prayed him, saying, Come
over into Măç-e-dō'nĭ-ȧ, and help us.

13 [m]ch. 12.17
15 [n]Isa. 11.10
16 [o]Isa. 54.1-5; Hos. 3.5; Amos 9.11; Mic. 5.2
19 [p]1 Thess. 1.9
20 [q]Gen. 35.2; Ex. 20.3; Ezek. 20.30; 1 Cor. 8.1; Rev. 10.20
[r]1 Cor. 6.9; Col. 3.5; 1 Thess. 4.3; 1 Pet. 4.3
[s]Gen. 9.4; Lev. 3.17; 1 Sam. 14.32
21 [t]ch. 13.15
22 [u]ch. 1.23
24 [v]Jer. 23.16; Gal. 2.4; Tit. 1.10; 1 John 2.19
26 [w]Judg. 5.18; ch. 13.50; 1 Cor. 15.30; 2 Cor. 11.23-26; Phil. 2.29-30
27 [2]word
28 [x]John 16.13
29 [y]ch. 21.25; Rev. 2.14
[z]Lev. 17.14
31 [3]Or, exhortation
32 [a]ch. 13.1; 1 Cor. 12.28
[b]ch. 14.22
33 [c]1 Cor. 16.11; Heb. 11.31
35 [d]ch. 13.1
36 [e]ch. 14.1
37 [f]ch. 12.12; Col. 4.10; 2 Tim. 4.11; Phile. 24
38 [g]ch. 13.13

CHAPTER 16
1 [a]Matt. 10.23; ch. 14.6; 2 Tim. 3.11
[b]ch. 19.22; Rom. 16.21; 1 Cor. 4.17; 2 Tim. 1.2
2 [c]ch. 6.3; 2 Tim. 3.15
3 [d]1 Cor. 9.20; Gal. 2.3
4 [e]ch. 15.28
5 [f]ch. 15.41; Jude 20-21
8 [g]2 Cor. 2.12; 2 Tim. 4.13
9 [h]Num. 12.6; 2 Cor. 12.1-4

10 And after he had seen the vision, immediately we endeavoured to go [i]into Măç-e-dō'nĭ-ȧ, assuredly gathering that the Lord had called us for to preach the gospel unto them.

11 Therefore loosing from Trō'ăs, we came with a straight course to Săm-o-thrā'çiȧ, and the next *day* to Ne-ăp'o-lis;

12 And from thence to [j]Phĭ-lĭp'pī, which is [1]the chief city of that part of Măç-e-dō'nĭ-ȧ, *and* a colony: and we were in that city abiding certain days.

13 And on the [2]sabbath we went out of the city by a river side, where prayer was wont to be made; and we sat down, and spake unto the women which resorted *thither*.

14 ¶ And a certain woman named Lȳd'ĭ-ȧ, a seller of purple, of the city of [k]Thȳ-a-tī'rȧ, which worshipped God, heard *us:* whose [l]heart the Lord opened, that she attended unto the things which were spoken of Pa̧ul.

15 And when she was baptized, and her household, she besought *us*, saying, If ye have judged me to be [m]faithful to the Lord, come into my house, and abide *there*. And [n]she constrained us.

16 ¶ And it came to pass, as we went to prayer, a certain damsel [o]possessed with a spirit [3]of divination met us, which brought her masters [p]much gain by soothsaying:

17 The same followed Pa̧ul and us, and cried, saying, These men are the servants of the most high God, which shew unto us the way of salvation.

18 And this did she many days. But Pa̧ul, [q]being grieved, turned and said to the spirit, I command thee in the name of Jē'sus Chrīst to come out of her. [r]And he came out the same hour.

19 ¶ And [s]when her masters saw that the hope of their gains was gone, [t]they caught Pa̧ul and Sī'las, and [u]drew *them* into the [4]marketplace unto the rulers,

20 And brought them to the magistrates, saying, These men, being Jews, [v]do exceedingly trouble our city,

21 And teach customs, which are not lawful for us to receive, neither to observe, being Rō'mans.

22 And the multitude rose up together against them: and the magistrates rent off their clothes, [w]and commanded to beat *them*.

23 [x]And when they had laid many stripes upon them, they cast *them* into prison, charging the jailor to keep them safely:

24 Who, having received such a charge, thrust them into the inner prison, and made their feet fast in the [y]stocks.

25 ¶ And at midnight Pa̧ul and Sī'las prayed, and [z]sang praises unto God: and the prisoners heard them.

26 [a]And suddenly there was a great earthquake, so that the foundations of the prison were shaken: and immediately [b]all the doors were opened, and every one's bands were loosed.

27 And the keeper of the prison awaking out of his sleep, and seeing the prison doors open, he drew out his sword, and would have killed himself, supposing that the prisoners had been fled.

28 But Pa̧ul cried with a loud voice, saying, [c]Do thyself no harm: for we are all here.

29 Then he called for a light, and sprang in, and came trembling, and fell down before Pa̧ul and Sī'las,

30 And brought them out, and said, [d]Sirs, what must I do to be saved?

31 And they said, [e]Believe on the Lord Jē'sus Chrīst, and thou shalt be saved, and thy house.

32 And they spake unto him the word of the Lord, and to all that were in his house.

33 And he took them the same hour of the night, and washed *their* stripes; and was baptized, he and all his, straightway.

34 And when he had brought them into his house, [f]he set meat before them, and [g]rejoiced, believing in God with all his house.

35 And when it was day, the magistrates sent the serjeants, saying, Let those men go.

36 And the keeper of the prison told this saying to Pa̧ul, The magistrates have sent to let you go: now therefore depart, and go in peace.

37 But Pa̧ul said unto them, They have beaten us openly uncondemned, [h]being Rō'mans, and have cast *us* into prison; and now do they thrust us out privily? nay verily; but let them come themselves and fetch us out.

38 And the serjeants told these words unto the magistrates: and they feared, when they heard that they were Rō'mans.

39 And they came and besought them, and brought *them* out, and [i]desired *them* to depart out of the city.

40 And they went out of the prison, and entered into *the house of* Lȳd'ĭ-ȧ: and when they had seen the brethren, they [j]comforted them, and departed.

17

Now when they had passed through Ăm-phĭp'o-lis and Ăp-ŏl-lō'nĭ-ȧ, they came to Thĕs-sa-lo-nī'cȧ, where was a synagogue of the Jews:

2 And Pa̧ul, as his manner was, went [a]in unto them, and three sabbath days reasoned with them out of the scriptures,

3 Opening and alleging, [b]that Chrīst must needs have suffered, and risen again from the dead; and that this Jē'sus, [1]whom I preach unto you, is Chrīst.

4 [c]And some of them believed, and consorted with Pa̧ul and [d]Sī'las; and of the devout Greeks a great multitude, and of the chief women not a few.

5 ¶ But the Jews which believed not, moved with envy, took unto them certain lewd fellows of the baser sort, and gathered a company, and set all the city on an uproar, and assaulted the

10 [i]2 Cor. 2.13
12 [j]Phil. 1.1 [1]Or, the first
13 [2]sabbath day
14 [k]Rev. 2.18 [l]Ps. 110.3; Eph. 1.17
15 [m]Gal. 6.10 [n]Gen. 19.3; Luke 24.29
16 [o]1 Sam. 28.7 [3]Or, of Python [p]ch. 19.24
18 [q]Mark 1.25-34 [r]Mark 16.17
19 [s]ch. 19.25; Phil. 3.19 [t]2 Cor. 6.5 [u]Matt. 10.18 [4]Or, court
20 [v]1 Ki. 18.17; ch. 17.6
22 [w]2 Cor. 6.5
23 [x]Luke 21.12; Eph. 3.1-13
24 [y]Ps. 105.18; Jer. 20.2
25 [z]ch. 5.41; Col. 1.24
26 [a]Matt. 28.2; ch. 4.31 [b]ch. 5.19
28 [c]Ex. 20.13
30 [d]Luke 3.10; ch. 2.37
31 [e]Isa. 45.22; 1 John 5.10
34 [f]Luke 5.29 [g]1 Sam. 2.1; 1 Pet. 1.6-8
37 [h]ch. 22.25
39 [i]Matt. 8.34 Luke 5.8
40 [j]Ps. 51.12-13; 1 Thess. 3.2-3

CHAPTER 17
2 [a]Luke 4.16
3 [b]Ps. 22; [1]Or, whom, said he, I preach
4 [c]ch. 28.24 [d]ch. 15.22-27-32-40

house of [e]Jā′son, and sought to bring
them out to the people.
6 And when they found them not,
they drew Jā′son and certain brethren
unto the rulers of the city, crying,
[f]These that have turned the world upside down are come hither also;
7 Whom Jā′son hath received: and
these all [g]do contrary to the decrees of
Çæ′sar, [h]saying that there is another
king, *one* Jē′sus.
8 And they troubled the people and
the rulers of the city, when they heard
these things.
9 And when they had taken security
of Jā′son, and of the other, they let
them go.
10 ¶ And [i]the brethren immediately
sent away Pąul and Sī′las by night
unto Be-rē′ȧ: who coming *thither* went
into the synagogue of the Jews.
11 These were more noble than those
in Thĕs-sa-lo-nī′cȧ, in that they received
the word with all readiness of mind, and
[j]searched the scriptures daily, whether
those things were so.
12 Therefore many of them believed;
also of honourable women which were
Greeks, and of men, not a few.
13 But when the Jews of Thĕs-sa-lo-
nī′cȧ had knowledge that the word of
God was preached of Pąul at Be-rē′ȧ,
[k]they came thither also, and stirred up
the people.
14 [l]And then immediately the brethren sent away Pąul to go as it were to
the sea: but Sī′las and Ti-mō′the-ŭs
abode there still.
15 And they that conducted Pąul
brought him unto Ăth′ĕns: and [m]re-
ceiving a commandment unto Sī′las
and Ti-mō′the-ŭs for to come to him
with all speed, they departed.
16 ¶ Now while Pąul waited for them
at Ăth′ĕns, [n]his spirit was stirred in
him, when he saw the city [2]wholly
given to idolatry.
17 Therefore disputed he in the synagogue with the Jews, and with the devout persons, and in the market daily
with them that met with him.
18 Then certain philosophers of the
Ĕp-ĭ-cū-rē′ans, and of the Stō′icks, en-
countered him. And some said, What
will this [3]babbler say? other some, He
seemeth to be a setter forth of strange
gods: because he preached unto them
Jē′sus, and the resurrection.
19 And they took him, and brought
him unto [4]Ăr-ĕ-ŏp′a-gus, saying, May
we know what this new doctrine,
whereof thou speakest, *is?*
20 For thou bringest certain strange
things to our ears: we would know
therefore what these things mean.
21 (For all the Ăth-ē′nĭ-ans and
strangers which were there spent their
time in nothing else, but either to tell,
or to hear some new thing.)
22 ¶ Then Pąul stood in the midst of
[5]Märs′ hill, and said, *Ye* men of Ăth′-
ĕns, I perceive that in all things ye are
[o]too superstitious.
23 For as I passed by, and beheld
your [6]devotions, I found an altar with

5 [e]Rom. 16.21
6 [f]1 Ki. 18.17
7 [g]Ezra 4.12 [h]Luke 23.2; 1 Pet. 2.15
10 [i]ch. 9.25
11 [j]Isa. 34.16; Luke 16.29
13 [k]Luke 11.52; 1 Thess. 2.15
14 [l]Matt. 10.23
15 [m]ch. 18.5
16 [n]Ex. 32.19-20; 2 Pet. 2.8 [2]Or, full of idols
18 [3]Or, base fellow
19 [4]Or, Mars' hill. It was the highest court in Athens
22 [5]Or, the court of the Areopagites [o]Jer. 50.38
23 [6]Or, gods that ye worship [p]Ps. 147.20; Eph. 2.12
24 [q]Ps. 146.5-6; Heb. 1.1-2 [r]Matt. 11.25 [s]ch. 7.48
25 [t]Ps. 50.8 [u]Num. 16.22; Dan. 4.35
26 [v]Deut. 30.20 [w]Deut. 32.8
27 [x]Rom. 1.20 [y]1 Ki. 8.27; Jer. 23.24
28 [z]1 Sam. 25.29; [a]Tit. 1.12
29 [b]Isa. 40.18
30 [c]Rom. 3.25 [d]Luke 24.47
31 [e]Rom. 2.16 [7]Or, offered faith
34 [f]Rom. 11.5

CHAPTER 18

2 [a]1 Cor. 16.19
3 [b]1 Cor. 4.12
5 [c]ch. 17.14 [d]Job 32.18; [1]Or, is the Christ
6 [e]1 Pet. 4.4 [f]Matt. 10.14 [g]Ezek. 33.4 [h]Ezek. 3.18 [i]ch. 28.28

this inscription, [p]TO THE UNKNOWN
GOD. Whom therefore ye ignorantly
worship, him declare I unto you.
24 [q]God that made the world and all
things therein, seeing that he is [r]Lord
of heaven and earth, [s]dwelleth not in
temples made with hands;
25 Neither is worshipped with men's
hands, [t]as though he needed any thing,
seeing [u]he giveth to all life and breath,
and all things;
26 And [v]hath made of one blood all
nations of men for to dwell on all the
face of the earth, and hath determined
the times before appointed, and [w]the
bounds of their habitation;
27 [x]That they should seek the Lord,
if haply they might feel after him, and
find him, [y]though he be not far from
every one of us:
28 For [z]in him we live, and move,
and have our being; [a]as certain also of
your own poets have said, For we are
also his offspring.
29 Forasmuch then as we are the offspring of God, [b]we ought not to think
that the Godhead is like unto gold, or
silver, or stone, graven by art and
man's device.
30 And [c]the times of this ignorance
God winked at; but [d]now commandeth
all men every where to repent:
31 Because he hath appointed a day,
in the which [e]he will judge the world
in righteousness by *that* man whom he
hath ordained; *whereof* he hath [7]given
assurance unto all *men,* in that he hath
raised him from the dead.
32 ¶ And when they heard of the resurrection of the dead, some mocked:
and others said, We will hear thee
again of this *matter.*
33 So Pąul departed from among
them.
34 [f]Howbeit certain men clave unto
him, and believed: among the which
was Dī-ŏ-nỹs′ius the Ăr-ĕ-ŏp′a-gīte,
and a woman named Dăm′a-rĭs, and
others with them.

18 After these things Pąul departed
from Ăth′ĕns, and came to Cŏr′-
inth;
2 And found a certain Jew named
[a]Ă′qųĭ-lȧ, born in Pŏn′tus, lately come
from Ĭt′a-lỹ, with his wife Prĭs-çĭl′lȧ; (because that Cląu′dĭ-us had commanded
all Jews to depart from Rōme:) and
came unto them.
3 And because he was of the same
craft, he abode with them, [b]and
wrought: for by their occupation they
were tentmakers.
4 And he reasoned in the synagogue
every sabbath, and persuaded the Jews
and the Greeks.
5 And [c]when Sī′las and Ti-mō′the-
ŭs were come from Măç-e-dō′nĭ-ȧ, Pąul
was [d]pressed in the spirit, and testified
to the Jews *that* Jē′sus *was* [1]Chrĭst.
6 And [e]when they opposed themselves, and blasphemed, [f]he shook *his*
raiment, and said unto them, [g]Your
blood *be* upon your own heads; [h]I *am*
clean: [i]from henceforth I will go unto
the Gĕn′tīles.

7 ¶ And he departed thence, and
entered into a certain *man's* house,
named Jŭs'tus, *one* that worshipped
God, whose house joined hard to the
synagogue.
8 [j]And Crĭs'pus, the chief ruler of
the synagogue, believed on the Lord
with all his house; and many of the Co-
rĭn'thĭ-ans hearing believed, and were
baptized.
9 Then [k]spake the Lord to Pạul in
the night by a vision, Be not afraid, but
speak, and hold not thy peace:
10 [l]For I am with thee, and no man
shall set on thee to hurt thee: for I have
much people in this city.
11 And he [2]continued *there* a year
and six months, teaching the word of
God among them.
12 ¶ And when Găl'lĭ-ō was the deputy of A-chā'iȧ, the Jews made insurrection with one accord against Pạul,
and brought him to the judgment seat,
13 Saying, This *fellow* persuadeth
men to worship God contrary to the
law.
14 And when Pạul was now about to
open *his* mouth, Găl'lĭ-ō said unto the
Jews, [m]If it were a matter of wrong or
wicked lewdness, O *ye* Jews, reason
would that I should bear with you:
15 But if it be a question of words
and names, and *of* your law, look ye *to*
it; for I will be no judge of such *mat-*
ters.
16 And he drave them from the judgment seat.
17 Then all the Greeks took [n]Sŏs'-
the-nēs, the chief ruler of the synagogue, and beat *him* before the judgment seat. And Găl'lĭ-ō cared for none
of those things.
18 ¶ And Pạul *after this* tarried *there*
yet a good while, and then took his
leave of the brethren, and sailed thence
into Șỳr'ĭ-ȧ, and with him Prĭs-çĭl'lȧ
and Ā'quĭ-lȧ; having [o]shorn *his* head in
[p]Çĕn'-chrĕ-ȧ: for he hạd a vow.
19 And he came to Ĕph'ĕ-sŭs, and
left them there: but he himself entered
into the synagogue, and reasoned with
the Jews.
20 When they desired *him* to tarry
longer time with them, he consented
not;
21 But bade them farewell, saying,
[q]I must by all means keep this feast
that cometh in Je-rụ'sa-lĕm: but I will
return again unto you, [r]if God will.
And he sailed from Ĕph'ĕ-sŭs.
22 And when he had landed at Çæs-
a-rē'ȧ, and gone up, and saluted the
church, he went down to Ăn'tĭ-ŏch.
23 And after he had spent some time
there, he departed, and went over *all*
the country of [s]Gā-lā'tiȧ and Phrỳ-
g'ĭ-ȧ in order, [t]strengthening all the
disciples.
24 ¶ [u]And a certain Jew named A-
pŏl'los, born at Ăl-ĕx-ăn'drĭ-ȧ, an eloquent man, *and* mighty in the scriptures, came to Ĕph'ĕ-sŭs.
25 This man was instructed in the
way of the Lord; and being [v]fervent in
the spirit, he spake and taught dili-

8 [j]1 Cor. 1.14
9 [k]ch. 23.11
10 [l]Isa. 41.10; Jer. 1.18; Matt. 28.20; Rom. 8.31
11 [2]sat there
14 [m]ch. 23.29; ch. 25.11-19
17 [n]1 Cor. 1.1
18 [o]Num. 6.18; ch. 21.24; 1 Cor. 9.20
[p]Rom. 16.1
21 [q]ch. 19.21
[r]Matt. 26.39; 1 Cor. 4.19; Heb. 6.3
23 [s]Gal. 1.2
[t]Isa. 35.3; Dan. 11.1; 1 Thess. 3.2
24 [u]1 Cor. 1.12; Tit. 3.13
25 [v]Rom. 12.11
[w]ch. 19.3
27 [x]John 1.12; 1 Cor. 3.6
28 [y]Luke 24.26-46; ch. 9.22; 1 Cor. 15.3-4; Gal. 3.1
[3]Or, is the Christ
[z]Gen. 49.10; Deut. 18.15; Ps. 16.9-10; Isa. 7.14; Mic. 5.2; Mal. 3.1

CHAPTER 19
1 [a]1 Cor. 1.12
2 [b]1 Sam. 3.7; ch. 8.16; 1 Cor. 6.19
3 [c]ch. 18.25
4 [d]Matt. 3.11; Mark 1.4-12; ch. 1.5
5 [e]ch. 8.12-16; Rom. 6.3; Gal. 3.27
6 [f]ch. 6.6; 2 Tim. 1.6
[g]ch. 2.4
8 [h]Luke 4.16
[i]ch. 1.3
9 [j]2 Tim. 1.15; 2 Pet. 2.2
[k]ch. 9.2
10 [l]ch. 20.31
11 [m]Mark 16.20
12 [n]2 Ki. 4.29
13 [o]Matt. 12.27
[p]Mark 9.38

gently the things of the Lord, [w]know-
ing only the baptism of Jŏhn.
26 And he began to speak boldly in
the synagogue: whom when Ā'quĭ-lȧ
and Prĭs-çĭl'lȧ had heard, they took
him unto *them,* and expounded unto
him the way of God more perfectly.
27 And when he was disposed to
pass into A-chā'iȧ, the brethren wrote,
exhorting the disciples to receive him:
who, when he was come, [x]helped them
much which had believed through
grace:
28 For he mightily convinced the
Jews, *and that* publickly, [y]shewing by
the scriptures that Jē'sus [3z]was Chrīst.
19 And it came to pass, that, while
[a]A-pŏl'los was at Cŏr'inth, Pạul
having pạssed through the upper coasts
came to Ĕph'ĕ-sŭs: and finding certain
disciples,
2 He said unto them, Have ye received the Hō'lỳ Ghōst since ye believed? And they said unto him, [b]We
have not so much as heard whether
there be any Hō'lỳ Ghōst.
3 And he said unto them, Unto what
then were ye baptized? And they said,
[c]Unto Jŏhn's baptism.
4 Then said Pạul, [d]Jŏhn verily baptized with the baptism of repentance,
saying unto the people, that they should
believe on him which should come after
him, that is, on Chrīst Jē'sus.
5 When they heard *this,* they were
baptized [e]in the name of the Lord
Jē'sus.
6 And when Pạul had [f]laid *his* hands
upon them, the Hō'lỳ Ghōst came on
them; and [g]they spake with tongues,
and prophesied.
7 And all the men were about
twelve.
8 [h]And he went into the synagogue,
and spake boldly for the space of
three months, disputing and persuading the things [i]concerning the kingdom of God.
9 But [j]when divers were hardened,
and believed not, but spake evil [k]of
that way before the multitude, he departed from them, and separated the
disciples, disputing daily in the school
of one Tỳ-răn'nus.
10 And [l]this continued by the space
of two years; so that all they which
dwelt in Ā'siȧ heard the word of the
Lord Jē'sus, both Jews and Greeks.
11 And [m]God wrought special miracles by the hands of Pạul:
12 [n]So that from his body were
brought unto the sick handkerchiefs
or aprons, and the diseases departed
from them, and the evil spirits went
out of them.
13 ¶ [o]Then certain of the vagabond
Jews, exorcists, [p]took upon them to
call over them which had evil spirits
the name of the Lord Jē'sus, saying,
We adjure you by Jē'sus whom Pạul
preacheth.
14 And there were seven sons of *one*
Sçē'vȧ, a Jew, *and* chief of the priests,
which did so.

15 And the evil spirit answered and said, [q]Jē′sus I know, and Paul I know; but who are ye?

16 And the man in whom the evil spirit was leaped on them, and overcame them, and prevailed against them, so that they fled out of that house naked and wounded.

17 And this was known to all the Jews and Greeks also dwelling at Ĕph′ĕ-sŭs; and [r]fear fell on them all, and the name of the Lord Jē′sus was magnified.

18 And many that believed came, and [s]confessed, and shewed their deeds.

19 Many of them also which [t]used curious arts brought their books together, and burned them before all *men:* and they counted the price of them, and found *it* fifty thousand *pieces* of silver.

20 [u]So mightily grew the word of God and prevailed.

21 ¶ [v]After these things were ended, Paul [w]purposed in the spirit, when he had passed through Măç-e-dō′nĭ-ȧ and A-chā′iȧ, to go to Je-ru′sa-lĕm, saying, After I have been there, [x]I must also see Rōme.

22 So he sent into Măç-e-dō′nĭ-ȧ two of [y]them that ministered unto him, Ti-mō′the-ŭs and [z]E-răs′tus; but he himself stayed in Ā′siȧ for a season.

23 And [a]the same time there arose no small stir about [b]that way.

24 For a certain *man* named De-mē′trĭ-us, a silversmith, which made silver shrines for Di-ăn′ȧ, brought [c]no small gain unto the craftsmen;

25 Whom he called together with the workmen of like occupation, and said, Sirs, ye know that by this craft [d]we have our wealth.

26 Moreover ye see and hear, that not alone at Ĕph′ĕ-sŭs, but almost throughout all Ā′siȧ, this Paul hath persuaded and turned away much people, saying that [e]they be no gods, which are made with hands:

27 So that not only this our craft is in danger to be set at nought; but also that the temple of the great goddess Di-ăn′ȧ should be despised, and her magnificence should be destroyed, whom all Ā′siȧ and the world worshippeth.

28 And when they heard *these sayings,* they were full of wrath, and cried out, saying, [f]Great *is* Di-ăn′ȧ of the Ē-phē′sians.

29 And the whole city was filled with confusion: and having caught [g]Gā′ius and [h]Ăr-ĭs-tär′chus, men of Măç-e-dō′nĭ-ȧ, Paul's companions in travel, they rushed with one accord into the theatre.

30 And when Paul would have entered in unto the people, the disciples suffered him not.

31 And certain of the chief of [i]Ā′siȧ, which were his friends, sent unto him, desiring *him* that he would not adventure himself into the theatre.

32 Some therefore cried one thing, and some another: for the assembly was confused; and the more part knew not wherefore they were come together.

33 And they drew Ăl-ĕx-ăn′dẽr out of the multitude, the Jews putting him forward. And [j]Ăl-ĕx-ăn′dẽr beckoned with the hand, and would have made his defence unto the people.

34 But when they knew that he was a Jew, all with one voice about the space of two hours cried out, Great *is* Di-ăn′ȧ of the Ē-phē′sians.

35 And when the townclerk had appeased the people, he said, *Ye* men of Ĕph′ĕ-sŭs, what man is there that knoweth not how that the city of the Ē-phē′sians is [1]a worshipper of the great goddess Di-ăn′ȧ, and of the *image* which fell down from Jū′pĭ-tẽr?

36 Seeing then that these things cannot be spoken against, ye ought to be quiet, and to do nothing rashly.

37 For ye have brought hither these men, which are neither robbers of churches, nor yet blasphemers of your goddess.

38 Wherefore if De-mē′trĭ-us, and the craftsmen which are with him, have a matter against any man, [2]the law is open, and there are deputies: let them implead one another.

39 But if ye inquire any thing concerning other matters, it shall be determined in a [3]lawful assembly.

40 For we are in danger to be called in question for this day's uproar, there being no cause whereby we may give an account of this concourse.

41 [k]And when he had thus spoken, he dismissed the assembly.

20 And after the uproar was ceased, Paul called unto *him* the disciples, and embraced *them,* [a]and departed for to go into Măç-e-dō′nĭ-ȧ.

2 And when he had gone over those parts, and had given them much exhortation, he came into Greece,

3 And *there* abode three months. And [b]when the Jews laid wait for him, as he was about to sail into Sўr′ĭ-ȧ, he purposed to return through Măç-e-dō′nĭ-ȧ.

4 And there accompanied him into Ā′siȧ Sŏp′a-tẽr of Be-rē′ȧ; and of the Thĕs-sa-lō′nĭ-ans, [c]Ăr-ĭs-tär′chus and Se-cŭn′dus; and [d]Gā′ius of Dẽr′be, and [e]Ti-mō′the-ŭs; and of Ā′siȧ, [f]Tўch′ĭ-cŭs and [g]Trŏph′ĭ-mŭs.

5 These going before tarried for us at Trō′ăs.

6 And we sailed away from Phĭ-lĭp′pī after [h]the days of unleavened bread, and came unto them [i]to Trō′ăs in five days; where we abode seven days.

7 And upon [j]the first *day* of the week, when the disciples came together [k]to break bread, Paul preached unto them, ready to depart on the morrow; and continued his speech until midnight.

8 And there were many lights [l]in the upper chamber, where they were gathered together.

15 [q]Matt. 8.29; ch. 16.17
17 [r]Luke 1.65; ch. 2.43
18 [s]Lev. 16.21-22; Matt. 3.6
19 [t]1 Sam. 28.7-9; ch. 8.9-11
20 [u]Isa. 55.11; 2 Thess. 3.1
21 [v]Rom. 15.25; Gal. 2.1
[w]ch. 20.22
[x]ch. 23.11; Rom. 15.24
22 [y]ch. 13.5
[z]Rom. 16.23; 2 Tim. 4.20
23 [a]2 Cor. 1.8
[b]ch. 9.2
24 [c]ch. 16.16-19
25 [d]Prov. 15.27;
26 [e]1 Chr. 16.26;
28 [f]Hab. 2.18-19;
29 [g]Rom. 16.23;
[h]ch. 20.4;
31 [i]ch. 16.6;
33 [j]1 Tim. 1.20;
35 [1]the temple keeper
38 [2]Or, the court days are kept
39 [3]Or, ordinary
41 [k]Prov. 15.1;
CHAPTER 20
1 [a]1 Cor. 16.5;
3 [b]ch. 9.23;
4 [c]ch. 27.2;
[d]ch. 19.29
[e]ch. 16.1
[f]Eph. 6.21;
[g]ch. 21.29;
6 [h]Ex. 12.14;
[i]ch. 16.8;
7 [j]John 20.1;
[k]Luke 22.19;
8 [l]ch. 1.13

9 And there sat in a window a certain young man named Eū′ty̆-chus, being fallen into a deep sleep: and as Pa̤ul
was long preaching, he sunk down
with sleep, and fell down from the third
loft, and was taken up dead.
10 And Pa̤ul went down, and [m]fell on
him, and embracing *him* said, [n]Trou-
ble not yourselves; for his life is in him.
11 When he therefore was come up
again, and had broken bread, and
eaten, and talked a long while, even till
break of day, so he departed.
12 And they brought the young man
alive, and were not a little comforted.
13 ¶ And we went before to ship,
and sailed unto Ăs′sŏs, there intending
to take in Pa̤ul: for so had he appointed, minding himself to go afoot.
14 And when he met with us at
Ăs′sŏs, we took him in, and came to
Mĭt-y̆-lē′ne.
15 And we sailed thence, and came
the next *day* over against Chī′os: and
the next *day* we arrived at Sā′mos, and
tarried at Tro-gy̆l′lĭ-um; and the next
day we came to Mī-lē′tus.
16 For Pa̤ul had determined to sail
by Ĕph′ĕ-sŭs, because he would not
spend the time in Ā′siȧ: for [o]he hasted,
if it were possible for him, [p]to be at Je-
ru̥′sa-lĕm [q]the day of Pĕn′te-cŏst.
17 ¶ And from Mī-lē′tus he sent to
Ĕph′ĕ-sŭs, and [r]called the elders of the
church.
18 And when they were come to
him, he said unto them, Ye know,
[s]from the first day that I came into
Ā′siȧ, after what manner I have been
with you at all seasons,
19 Serving the Lord with all humility of mind, and with many tears, and
temptations, which befell me by the lying in wait of the Jews:
20 *And* how I kept back nothing
that was profitable *unto you,* but have
shewed you, and have taught you publickly, and from house to house,
21 [t]Testifying both to the Jews, and
also to the Greeks, [u]repentance toward God, and faith toward our Lord
Jē′sus Chrīst.
22 And now, behold, [v]I go bound in
the spirit unto Je-ru̥′sa-lĕm, not knowing the things that shall befall me
there:
23 Save that [w]the Hō′ly̆ Ghōst witnesseth in every city, saying that bonds
and afflictions [1]abide me.
24 But [x]none of these things move
me, neither count I my life dear unto
myself, [y]so that I might finish my
course with joy, [z]and the ministry,
[a]which I have received of the Lord
Jē′sus, to testify the gospel of the grace
of God.
25 And now, behold, [b]I know that ye
all, among whom I have gone preaching the kingdom of God, shall see my
face no more.
26 Wherefore I take you to record
this day, that I *am* [c]pure from the
blood of all *men.*
27 For I have not shunned to declare
unto you all [d]the counsel of God.
28 ¶ [e]Take heed therefore unto yourselves, and to all the flock, over the
which the [f]Hō′ly̆ Ghōst hath made you
overseers, to feed the church of God,
[g]which he hath purchased [h]with his
own blood.
29 For I know this, that after my departing [i]shall grievous wolves enter in
among you, not sparing the flock.
30 Also [j]of your own selves shall
men arise, speaking perverse things,
to draw away disciples after them.
31 Therefore watch, and remember,
that [k]by the space of three years I
ceased not to warn every one night
and day with tears.
32 And now, brethren, I commend
you to God, and [l]to the word of his
grace, which is able [m]to build you up,
and to give you [n]an inheritance among
all them which are sanctified.
33 [o]I have coveted no man's silver,
or gold, or apparel.
34 Yea, ye yourselves know, [p]that
these hands have ministered unto my
necessities, and to them that were with
me.
35 I have shewed you all things,
[q]how that so labouring ye ought to
support the weak, and to remember
the words of the Lord Jē′sus, how he
said, [r]It is more blessed to give than to
receive.
36 ¶ And when he had thus spoken,
he kneeled down, and prayed with
them all.
37 And they all wept sore, and [s]fell
on Pa̤ul's neck, and kissed him,
38 Sorrowing most of all for the
words which he spake, that they should
see his face no more. And they accompanied him unto the ship.

21 And it came to pass, that after we
were gotten from them, and had
launched, we came with a straight
course unto Cō′ŏs, and the *day* following unto Rhōdes, and from thence unto
Păt′a-rȧ:
2 And finding a ship sailing over
unto Phe-nĭ′çiȧ, we went aboard, and
set forth.
3 Now when we had discovered Çȳ′-
prus, we left it on the left hand, and
sailed into Sy̆r′ĭ-ȧ, and landed at Tȳre:
for there the ship was to unlade her
burden.
4 And finding disciples, we tarried
there seven days: [a]who said to Pa̤ul
through the Spirit, that he should not
go up to Je-ru̥′sa-lĕm.
5 And when we had accomplished
those days, we departed and went our
way; and they all brought us on our
way, with wives and children, till *we
were* out of the city: and [b]we kneeled
down on the shore, and prayed.
6 And when we had taken our leave
one of another, we took ship; and they
returned [c]home again.
7 And when we had finished *our*
course from Tȳre, we came to Ptŏl-e-
mā′is, and saluted the brethren, and
abode with them one day.
8 And the next *day* we that were of
Pa̤ul's company departed, and came

10 [m]1 Ki. 17.21; 2 Ki. 4.34
[n]Matt. 9.24; ch. 9.40
16 [o]ch. 21.4-12
[p]ch. 24.17
[q]ch. 2.1; 1 Cor. 16.8
17 [r]1 Tim. 4.14
18 [s]ch. 18.19
21 [t]ch. 18.5
[u]Mark 1.15; Rom. 2.4
22 [v]ch. 19.21
23 [w]ch. 9.16; 2 Tim. 2.12
[1]Or, wait for me
24 [x]Rom. 8.35; 2 Cor. 4.16
[y]1 Cor. 9.24-27; 2 Tim. 4.7
[z]ch. 1.17; Tit. 1.3
[a]Gal. 1.1
25 [b]Rom. 15.23
26 [c]2 Cor. 7.2; 1 Thess. 2.10
27 [d]Matt. 28.20; Eph. 1.11
28 [e]1 Tim. 4.16; 1 Pet. 5.2
[f]ch. 13.2; 1 Tim. 4.14
[g]Eph. 1.7; Rev. 5.9
[h]Heb. 9.14
29 [i]Matt. 7.15; 2 Pet. 2.1
30 [j]1 John 2.19
31 [k]ch. 19.10
32 [l]Heb. 13.9
[m]John 17.17;
[n]ch. 26.18;
33 [o]1 Sam. 12.3;
34 [p]ch. 18.3;
35 [q]Rom. 15.1;
[r]Ps. 41.1;
37 [s]Gen. 45.14

CHAPTER 21
4 [a]ch. 20.23
5 [b]ch. 9.40
6 [c]John 1.11

unto Çǣs-a-rē'ȧ: and we entered into
the house of Phĭl'ĭp [d]the evangelist,
[e]which was *one* of the seven; and
abode with him.
9 And the same man had four daughters, virgins, [f]which did prophesy.
10 And as we tarried *there* many
days, there came down frǫm Jū-dǣ'ȧ a
certain prophet, named [g]Ăg'ă-bŭs.
11 And when he was come unto us,
he took Pąul's girdle, and bound his
own hands and feet, and said, Thus
saith the Hō'lȳ Ghōst, [h]So shall the
Jews at Je-rų'sa-lĕm bind the man that
owneth this girdle, and shall deliver
him into the hands of the Gĕn'tīles.
12 And when we heard these things,
both we, and they of that place, besought him not to go up to Je-rų'sa-lĕm.
13 Then Pąul answered, [i]What
mean ye to weep and to break mine
heart? [j]for I am ready not to be bound
only, but also to die at Je-rų'sa-lĕm for
the name of the Lord Jē'sus.
14 And when he would not be persuaded, we ceased, saying, [k]The will
of the Lord be done.
15 And after those days we took up
our carriages, and went up to Je-rų'sa-
lĕm.
16 There went with us also *certain*
of the disciples of Çǣs-a-rē-ȧ, and
brought with them one Mnā'son of
Çȳ'prus, an old disciple, with whom
we should lodge.
17 [l]And when we were come to Je-
rų'sa-lĕm, the brethren received us
gladly.
18 And the *day* following Pąul went
in with us unto [m]Jāmes; and all the
elders were present.
19 And when he had saluted them,
[n]he declared particularly what things
God had wrought among the Gĕn'tīles
[o]by his ministry.
20 And when they heard *it*, they glorified the Lord, and said unto him,
Thou seest, brother, how many thousands of Jews there are which believe;
and they are all [p]zealous of the law:
21 And they are informed of thee,
that thou [q]teachest all the Jews which
are among the Gĕn'tīles to forsake
Mō'ses, saying that they ought not to
circumcise *their* children, neither to
walk after the customs.
22 What is it therefore? the multitude must needs come together: for
they will hear that thou art come.
23 Do therefore this that we say to
thee: We have four men which have a
vow on them;
24 Them take, and purify thyself
with them, and be at charges with
them, that they may [r]shave *their* heads:
and all may know that those things,
whereof they were informed concerning thee, are nothing; but *that* thou thyself also walkest orderly, and [s]keepest
the law.
25 As touching the Gĕn'tīles which
believe, [t]we have written *and* concluded that they observe no such thing,
save only that they keep themselves
from *things* offered to idols, and from
blood, and from strangled, and from
fornication.
26 Then Pąul took the men, and the
next day purifying himself with them
[u]entered into the temple, [v]to signify
the accomplishment of the days of purification, until that an offering should
be offered for every one of them.
27 And when the seven days were
ąlmost ended, the Jews which were of
Ā'siȧ, when they saw him in the temple, stirred up all the people, and [w]laid
hands on him,
28 Crying out, Men of Is'ra-el, help:
[x]This is the man, that teacheth all *men*
every where against the people, and
the law, and this place: and further
brought Greeks also into the temple,
and hath polluted this holy place.
29 (For they had seen before with
him in the city [y]Trŏph'ĭ-mŭs an E-
phē'sian, whom they supposed that
Pąul had brought into the temple.)
30 And all the city was moved, and
the people ran together: and they took
Pąul, and drew him out of the temple:
and forthwith the doors were shut.
31 And as they went about to kill
him, tidings came unto the chief captain of the band, that all Je-rų'sa-lĕm
was in an uproar.
32 [z]Who immediately took soldiers
and centurions, and ran down unto
them: and when they saw the chief captain and the soldiers, they left beating
of Pąul.
33 Then the chief captain came near,
and took him, and [a]commanded *him* to
be bound with two chains; and demanded who he was, and what he had
done.
34 And some cried one thing, some
another, among the multitude: and
when he could not know the certainty
for the tumult, he commanded him to
be carried into the castle.
35 And when he came upon the
stairs, so it was, that he was borne
of the soldiers for the violence of the
people.
36 For the multitude of the people
followed after, crying, [b]Away with
him.
37 And as Pąul was to be led into the
castle, he said unto the chief captain,
May I speak unto thee? Who said,
Canst thou speak Greek?
38 Art not thou that [1]E-gȳp'tian,
which before these days madest an
uproar, and leddest out into the wilderness four thousand men that were
murderers?
39 But Pąul said, [c]I am a man *which*
am a Jew of Tär'sus, *a city* in Çi-lĭ'çiȧ,
a citizen of no mean city: and, I beseech thee, [d]suffer me to speak unto
the people.
40 And when he had given him licence, Pąul stood on the stairs, and
beckoned with the hand unto the people. And when there was made a great
silence, he spake unto *them* in the
Hē'brew tongue, saying,

8 [d]Eph. 4.11; 2 Tim. 4.5
[e]ch. 6.5
9 [f]Joel 2.28; ch. 2.17
10 [g]ch. 11.28
11 [h]Eph. 3.1
13 [i]Isa. 3.15; ch. 20.24
[j]Rom. 8.35; 2 Cor. 4.10; Col. 1.24; 2 Tim. 4.6
14 [k]Gen. 43.14; 1 Sam. 3.18; Matt. 26.42
17 [l]ch. 15.4
18 [m]ch. 15.13; Gal. 1.19; Jas. 1.1
19 [n]ch. 11.4; ch. 14.27; Rom. 15.18; 1 Cor. 3.5-9; Col. 1.28-29
[o]ch. 1.17
20 [p]ch. 22.3; Rom. 10.2; Gal. 1.14
21 [q]ch. 6.14; Gal. 5.1
24 [r]Num. 6.2-13; ch. 18.18
[s]1 Cor. 9.20
25 [t]Gen. 9.4; Lev. 17.14; 1 Cor. 5.1-9; 1 Thess. 4.3; Heb. 13.4
26 [u]ch. 24.18
[v]Num. 6.13
27 [w]Mark 10.30; Luke 21.12; ch. 4.3; ch. 5.18; Rom. 8.35; 2 Cor. 4.9; 1 Thess. 2.14-16; 2 Tim. 3.12
28 [x]Matt. 5.11; Luke 6.22; Luke 11.49; Luke 21.12; John 15.20; ch. 6.13; ch. 16.20; ch. 17.6; 1 Cor. 4.12; 1 Pet. 2.12
29 [y]ch. 20.4; 2 Tim. 4.20
32 [z]ch. 12.6; ch. 23.27
33 [a]ch. 20.23; ch. 28.20
36 [b]Luke 23.18; ch. 22.22
38 [1]This Egyptian rose A.D 55
39 [c]ch. 9.11; 2 Tim. 2.9
[d]1 Pet. 3.15

22

Men, [a]brethren, and fathers, hear ye my defence *which I make* now unto you.

2 (And when they heard that he spake in the Hē'brew tongue to them, they kept the more silence: and he saith,)

3 [b]I am verily a man *which am* a Jew, born in Tär'sus, *a city* in Çi-lĭ'çiȧ, yet brought up in this city [c]at the feet of [d]Ga-mā'lĭ-el, *and* taught [e]according to the perfect manner of the law of the fathers, and [f]was zealous toward God, [g]as ye all are this day.

4 [h]And I persecuted this way unto the death, binding and delivering into prisons both men and women.

5 As also the high priest doth bear me witness, and [i]all the estate of the elders: [j]from whom also I received letters unto [k]the brethren, and went to Da-măs'cus, to bring them which were there bound unto Je-ru̧'sa-lĕm, for to be punished.

6 And [l]it came to pass, that, as I made my journey, and was come nigh unto Da-măs'cus about noon, suddenly there shone from heaven a great light round about me.

7 And I fell unto the ground, and heard a voice saying unto me, Sa̧ul, Sa̧ul, why persecutest thou me?

8 And I answered, Who art thou, Lord? And he said unto me, I am Jē'sus of Nāz'a-rĕth, whom thou persecutest.

9 And [m]they that were with me saw indeed the light, and were afraid; but they heard not the voice of him that spake to me.

10 And I said, What shall I do, Lord? And the Lord said unto me, Arise, and go into Da-măs'cus; and there it shall be told thee of all things which are appointed for thee to do.

11 And when I could not see for the glory of that light, being led by the hand of them that were with me, I came into Da-măs'cus.

12 And [n]one Ăn-a-nī'as, a devout man according to the law, [o]having a good report of all the [p]Jews which dwelt *there,*

13 Came unto me, and stood, and said unto me, Brother Sa̧ul, receive thy sight. And the same hour I looked up upon him.

14 And he said, [q]The God of our fathers [r]hath chosen thee, that thou shouldest know his will, and [s]see [t]that Just One, and [u]shouldest hear the voice of his mouth.

15 [v]For thou shalt be his witness unto all men of [w]what thou hast seen and heard.

16 And now why tarriest thou? arise, and be baptized, [x]and wash away thy sins, [y]calling on the name of the Lord.

17 And [z]it came to pass, that, when I was come again to Je-ru̧'sa-lĕm, even while I prayed in the temple, I was in a trance;

18 And saw him saying unto me, [a]Make haste, and get thee quickly out of Je-ru̧'sa-lĕm: for they will not receive thy testimony concerning me.

19 And I said, Lord, [b]they know that I imprisoned and [c]beat in every synagogue them that believed on thee:

20 [d]And when the blood of thy martyr Stē'phen was shed, I also was standing by, and [e]consenting unto his death, and kept the raiment of them that slew him.

21 And he said unto me, Depart: [f]for I will send thee far hence unto the Gĕn'tīles.

22 And they gave him audience unto this word, and *then* lifted up their voices, and said, [g]Away with such a *fellow* from the earth: for it is not fit that [h]he should live.

23 And as they cried out, and cast off *their* clothes, and threw dust into the air,

24 The chief captain commanded him to be brought into the castle, and bade that he should be examined by scourging; that he might know wherefore they cried so against him.

25 And as they bound him with thongs, Pa̧ul said unto the centurion that stood by, [i]Is it lawful for you to scourge a man that is a Rō'man, and uncondemned?

26 When the centurion heard *that,* he went and told the chief captain, saying, Take heed what thou doest: for this man is a Rō'man.

27 Then the chief captain came, and said unto him, Tell me, art thou a Rō'man? He said, Yea.

28 And the chief captain answered, With a great sum obtained I this freedom. And Pa̧ul said, But I was *free* born.

29 Then straightway they departed from him which should have [1]examined him: and the chief captain also was afraid, after he knew that he was a Rō'man, and because he had bound him.

30 On the morrow, because he would have known the certainty wherefore he was accused of the Jews, he loosed him from *his* bands, and [j]commanded the chief priests and all their council to appear, and brought Pa̧ul down, and set him before them.

23

And Pa̧ul, earnestly beholding the council, said, Men *and* brethren, [a]I have lived in all good conscience before God until this day.

2 And the high priest Ăn-a-nī'as commanded them that stood by him [b]to smite him on the mouth.

3 Then said Pa̧ul unto him, God shall smite thee, *thou* whited wall: for sittest thou to judge me after the law, and [c]commandest me to be smitten contrary to the law?

4 And they that stood by said, Revilest thou God's high priest?

5 Then said Pa̧ul, [d]I wist not, brethren, that he was the high priest: for it is written, [e]Thou shalt not speak evil of the ruler of thy people.

6 But when Pa̧ul perceived that the one part were Săd'dū-çees, and the other Phăr'ĭ-sees, he cried out in the council, Men *and* brethren, [f]I am a

CHAPTER 22
1 [a]ch. 7.2
3 [b]ch. 9.30; Phil. 3.5
[c]Deut. 33.3; Luke 8.35
[d]ch. 5.34
[e]ch. 26.5
[f]2 Sam. 21.2; Phil. 3.6
[g]Rom. 10.2
4 [h]ch. 8.3; 1 Tim. 1.13
5 [i]Luke 22.66; ch. 4.5
[j]ch. 9.2
[k]Rom. 9.3
6 [l]ch. 26.12
9 [m]Dan. 10.7
12 [n]ch. 9.17
[o]ch. 10.22
[p]1 Tim. 3.7
14 [q]ch. 3.13; ch. 5.30
[r]John 15.16; Tit. 1.1
[s]1 Cor. 9.1
[t]ch. 3.14; 1 John 1.1
[u]1 Cor. 11.23; Gal. 1.12
15 [v]ch. 23.11
[w]ch. 26.16
16 [x]ch. 2.38; Heb. 10.22
[y]ch. 2.21; Rom. 10.13
17 [z]2 Cor. 12.2
18 [a]Matt. 10.17
19 [b]ch. 8.3
[c]Matt. 10.17
20 [d]ch. 7.58
[e]Luke 11.48; Rom. 1.32
21 [f]ch. 13.2; 2 Tim. 1.11
22 [g]ch. 21.36
[h]ch. 25.24
25 [i]ch. 16.37
29 [1]Or, tortured him
30 [j]Matt. 10.17; Luke 21.12

CHAPTER 23
1 [a]ch. 24.16; 1 Pet. 3.16
2 [b]1 Ki. 22.24 John 18.22
3 [c]Lev. 19.35
5 [d]ch. 24.17
[e]Ex. 22.28
6 [f]Phil. 3.5

Phăr'ĭ-see, the son of a Phăr'ĭ-see: [g]of the hope and resurrection of the dead I am called in question.

7 And when he had so said, there arose a dissension between the Phăr'ĭ-sees and the Săd'dū-çees: and the multitude was divided.

8 [h]For the Săd'dū-çees say that there is no resurrection, neither angel, nor spirit: but the Phăr'ĭ-sees confess both.

9 And there arose a great cry: and the scribes *that were* of the Phăr'ĭ-sees' part arose, and strove, saying, [i]We find no evil in this man: but [j]if a spirit or an angel hath spoken to him, [k]let us not fight against God.

10 And when there arose a great dissension, the chief captain, fearing lest Pa̤ul should have been pulled in pieces of them, commanded the soldiers to go down, and to take him by force from among them, and to bring *him* into the castle.

11 And [l]the night following the Lord stood by him, and said, Be of good cheer, Pa̤ul: for as thou hast testified of me in Je-rṳ'sa-lĕm, so must thou bear witness also at Rōme.

12 And when it was day, [m]certain of the Jews banded together, and bound themselves [1][n]under a curse, saying that they would neither eat nor drink till they had killed Pa̤ul.

13 And they were more than forty which had made this conspiracy.

14 And they came to the chief priests and elders, and said, We have bound ourselves under a great curse, that we will eat nothing until we have slain Pa̤ul.

15 Now therefore ye with the council signify to the chief captain that he bring him down unto you to morrow, as though ye would inquire something more perfectly concerning him: and we, or ever he come near, are ready to kill him.

16 And [o]when Pa̤ul's sister's son heard of their lying in wait, he went and entered into the castle, and told Pa̤ul.

17 Then [p]Pa̤ul called one of the centurions unto *him,* and said, Bring this young man unto the chief captain: for he hath a certain thing to tell him.

18 So he took him, and brought *him* to the chief captain, and said, Pa̤ul the prisoner called me unto *him,* and prayed me to bring this young man unto thee, who hath something to say unto thee.

19 Then the chief captain took him by the hand, and went *with him* aside privately, and asked *him,* What is that thou hast to tell me?

20 And he said, [q]The Jews have agreed to desire thee that thou wouldest bring down Pa̤ul to morrow into the council, as though they would inquire somewhat of him more perfectly.

21 But do not thou yield unto them: for there [r]lie in wait for him of them more than forty men, which have bound themselves with an oath, that they will neither eat nor drink till they have killed him: and now are they ready, looking for a promise from thee.

22 So the chief captain *then* let the young man depart, and charged *him, See thou* tell no man that thou hast shewed these things to me.

23 And he called unto *him* two centurions, saying, Make ready two hundred soldiers to go to Çæ̆s-a-rē'ȧ, and horsemen threescore and ten, and [2]spearmen two hundred, at the third hour of the night;

24 And provide *them* beasts, that they may set Pa̤ul on, and bring *him* safe unto Fē'lĭx the governor.

25 And he wrote a letter after this manner:

26 Cla̤u'dĭ-us Lȳs'ias unto the most excellent governor Fē'lĭx *sendeth* greeting.

27 [s]This man was taken of the Jews, and should have been killed of them: then came I with an army, and rescued him, having understood that he was a Rō'man.

28 [t]And when I would have known the cause wherefore they accused him, I brought him forth into their council:

29 Whom I perceived to be accused [u]of questions of their law, [v]but to have nothing laid to his charge worthy of death or of bonds.

30 And when it was told me how that the Jews laid wait for the man, I sent straightway to thee, and [w]gave commandment to his accusers also to say before thee what *they had* against him. Farewell.

31 Then the soldiers, as it was commanded them, to̤ok Pa̤ul, and brought *him* by night to Ăn-tĭp'a-trĭs.

32 On the morrow they left the horsemen to go with him, and returned to the castle:

33 Who, when they came to [x]Çæ̆s-a-rē'ȧ, and delivered the epistle to the governor, presented Pa̤ul also before him.

34 And when the governor had read *the letter,* he asked of what province he was. And when he understood that *he was* of [y]Çĭ-lĭ'çiȧ;

35 I [z]will hear thee, said he, when thine accusers are also come. And he commanded him to be kept in [a]Hĕr'-od's judgment hall.

24 And after [a]five days [b]Ăn-a-nī'as the high priest descended with the elders, and *with* a certain orator *named* Tĕr-tŭl'lus, who informed the governor against Pa̤ul.

2 And when he was called forth, Tĕr-tŭl'lus began to accuse *him,* saying, [c]Seeing that by thee we enjoy great quietness, and that very worthy deeds are done unto this nation by thy providence,

3 We accept *it* always, and in all places, most noble Fē'lĭx, with all thankfulness.

4 Notwithstanding, that I be not further tedious unto thee, I pray thee that thou wouldest hear us of thy clemency a few words.

[g]ch. 24.15-21; ch. 28.20

8 [h]Matt. 22.23; Mark 12.18; Luke 20.27

9 [i]Prov. 16.7; Luke 23.4

[j]ch. 22.7

[k]ch. 5.39; ch. 11.17

11 [l]Ps. 46.1; Isa. 41.10; ch. 2.25; ch. 18.9

12 [m]Isa. 8.9-10; ch. 25.3; Rom. 8.31
[1]Or, with an oath of execration

[n]1 Sam. 3.17; 2 Sam. 3.9; 1 Ki. 2.23; Matt. 26.74

16 [o]Job 5.13; Prov. 21.30

17 [p]Matt. 8.8-9; ch. 22.26

20 [q]ch. 20.3

21 [r]Ps. 10.9; Prov. 1.16; Isa. 59.7; Mic. 7.2; ch. 9.23-24; ch. 14.5-6; 2 Cor. 11.26-32-33

23 [2]Or, archers, or, javelin casters

27 [s]verse 10; ch. 20.23; ch. 21.33

28 [t]ch. 22.30

29 [u]ch. 18.15; ch. 24.5-6

[v]Ps. 27.12; ch. 26.31

30 [w]ch. 24.8

33 [x]ch. 8.40, A city on the north west of Canaan

34 [y]ch. 6.9

35 [z]ch. 24.1

[a]Matt. 27.27

CHAPTER 24

1 [a]ch. 21.27

[b]ch. 23.2-30-35

2 [c]Ps. 12.2; Ps. 55.21

5 [d]For we have found this man [1]*a*
pestilent *fellow,* and a mover of sedition among all the Jews throughout the
world, and a ringleader of the sect of
the Năz'a-rēnes:
6 [e]Who also hath gone about to profane the temple: whom we took, and
would [f]have judged according to our
law.
7 [g]But the chief captain Lȳs'ias came
upon us, and with great violence took
him away out of our hands,
8 [h]Commanding his accusers to
come unto thee: by examining of whom
thyself mayest take knowledge of all
these things, whereof we accuse him.
9 And the Jews also assented, saying that these things were so.
10 Then Pa̧ul, after that the governor had beckoned unto him to speak,
answered, Forasmuch as I know that
thou hast been of many years [2]a judge
unto this nation, I do the more cheer-
fully answer for myself:
11 Because that thou mayest understand, that there are yet but twelve
days since I went up to Je-ru̧'sa-lĕm
[i]for to worship.
12 [j]And they neither found me in
the temple disputing with any man, neither raising up the people, neither in
the synagogues, nor in the city:
13 Neither can they prove the things
whereof they now accuse me.
14 But this I confess unto thee, that
after [k]the way which they call heresy,
so worship I the [l]God of my fathers,
believing all things which are written
in [m]the law and in the prophets:
15 And [n]have hope toward God,
which they themselves also allow,
[o]that there shall be a resurrection of
the dead, both of the just and unjust.
16 And [p]herein do I exercise myself,
to have always a conscience void of
offence toward God, and *toward* men.
17 Now after many years [q]I came to
bring alms to my nation, and offerings.
18 [r]Whereupon certain Jews from
Ā'siȧ found me purified in the tem
ple, neither with multitude, nor with
tumult.
19 [s]Who ought to have been here
before thee, and object, if they had
ought against me.
20 Or else let these same *here* say, if
they have found any evil doing in me,
while I stood before the council,
21 Except it be for this one voice, that
I cried standing among them, [t]Touch-
ing the resurrection of the dead I am
called in question by you this day.
22 And when Fē'lĭx heard these
things, having more perfect knowledge of *that* way, he deferred them,
and said, When Lȳs'ias the chief captain shall come down, I will know the
uttermost of your matter.
23 And he commanded a centurion
to keep Pa̧ul, and to let *him* have liberty, and [u]that he should forbid none of
his acquaintance to minister or come
unto him.
24 And after certain days, when
Fē'lĭx came with his wife Dru̧-sĭl'lȧ,
which was a Jew'ess, he sent for Pa̧ul,
and heard him concerning the faith in
Chrīst.
25 And as he reasoned of righteousness, temperance, and judgment to
come, Fē'lĭx trembled, and answered,
Go thy way for this time; when I have a
convenient season, I will call for thee.
26 He hoped also that [v]money should
have been given him of Pa̧ul, that he
might loose him: wherefore he sent for
him the oftener, and communed with
him.
27 But after two years Pôr'çĭ-us Fĕs'-
tus came into Fē'lĭx' room: and Fē'lĭx,
[w]willing to shew the Jews a pleasure,
left Pa̧ul bound.

25

Now when Fĕs'tus was come
into the province, after three
days he ascended from Çæ̆s-a-rē'ȧ to
Je-ru̧'sa-lĕm.
2 [a]Then the high priest and the chief
of the Jews informed him against Pa̧ul,
and besought him,
3 And desired favour against him,
that he would send for him to Je-ru̧'sa-
lĕm, [b]laying wait in the way to kill
him.
4 But Fĕs'tus answered, that Pa̧ul
should be kept at Çæ̆s-a-rē'ȧ, and that
he himself would depart shortly *thither.*
5 Let them therefore, said he, which
among you are able, go down with *me,*
and accuse this man, [c]if there be any
wickedness in him.
6 And when he had tarried among
them [1]more than ten days, he went
down unto Çæ̆s-a-rē'ȧ; and the next
day sitting on the judgment seat commanded Pa̧ul to be brought.
7 And when he was come, the Jews
which came down from Je-ru̧'sa-lĕm
stood round about, [d]and laid many
and grievous complaints against Pa̧ul,
which they could not prove.
8 While he answered for himself,
[e]Neither against the law of the Jews,
neither against the temple, nor yet
against Caesar, have I offended any
thing at all.
9 But Fĕs'tus, [f]willing to do the Jews
a pleasure, answered Pa̧ul, and said,
Wilt thou go up to Je-ru̧'sa-lĕm, and
there be judged of these things before
me?
10 Then said Pa̧ul, I stand at Çæ'-
sar's judgment seat, where I ought to
be judged: to the Jews have I done no
wrong, as thou very well knowest.
11 [g]For if I be an offender, or have
committed any thing worthy of death, I
refuse not to die: but if there be none of
these things whereof these accuse me,
no man may deliver me unto them. [h]I
appeal unto Çæ'sar.
12 Then Fĕs'tus, when he had conferred with the council, answered, Hast
thou appealed unto Çæ'sar? unto Çæ'-
sar shalt thou go.
13 And after certain days king A-
grĭp'pȧ and Bĕr-nī'çe came unto Çæ̆s-
a-rē'ȧ to salute Fĕs'tus.
14 And when they had been there
many days, Fĕs'tus declared Pa̧ul's

5 [d]Matt. 5.11; Mark 10.30; Luke 11.49; John 15.20; 1 Pet. 2.12
[1]a plague
6 [e]ch. 21.28
[f]John 18.31
7 [g]ch. 21.33
8 [h]ch. 23.30
10 [2]Felix was made procurator over Judea A.D 53
11 [i]ch. 21.26
12 [j]ch. 25.8
14 [k]Ps. 119.46; ch. 9.2
[l]Ex. 3.15; 2 Tim. 1.3
[m]Luke 16.16; 2 Cor. 1.20
15 [n]ch. 23.6
[o]Dan. 12.2; Rev. 20.12
16 [p]ch. 23.1
17 [q]ch. 11.29; Gal. 2.10
18 [r]ch. 21.26
19 [s]ch. 23.30
21 [t]ch. 23.6
23 [u]ch. 27.3
26 [v]Ex. 23.8; 1 Tim. 6.10
27 [w]Ex. 23.2; ch. 25.9
CHAPTER 25
2 [a]ch. 24.1
3 [b]Ps. 37.32-33; ch. 23.12
5 [c]1 Sam. 24.11-12; ch. 18.14
6 [1]Or, as some copies read, no more than eight or ten days
7 [d]Esth. 3.8; 1 Pet. 4.14-16
8 [e]ch. 6.13
9 [f]Deut. 27.19; Jas. 2.6-9
11 [g]ch. 18.14
[h]Prov. 14.8; Eph. 5.15

cause unto the king, saying, [i]There is a certain man left in bonds by Fē'lĭx:

15 About whom, when I was at Je-rṳ'sa-lĕm, the chief priests and the elders of the Jews informed *me*, desiring *to have* judgment against him.

16 To whom I answered, It is not the manner of the Rō'mans to deliver any man to die, before that he which is accused have the accusers face to face, and have licence to answer for himself concerning the crime laid against him.

17 Therefore, when they were come hither, without any delay on the morrow I sat on the judgment seat, and commanded the man to be brought forth.

18 Against whom when the accusers stood up, they brought none accusation of such things as I supposed:

19 [j]But had certain questions against him of their own superstition, and of one Jē'sus, which was dead, whom Pa̤ul affirmed to be alive.

20 And because [2]I doubted of such manner of questions, I asked *him* whether he would go to Je-rṳ'sa-lĕm, and there be judged of these matters.

21 But when Pa̤ul had appealed to be reserved unto the [3]hearing of Au-gŭs'tus, I commanded him to be kept till I might send him to Çæ'sar.

22 Then [k]A-grĭp'pȧ said unto Fĕs'tus, I would also hear the man myself. To morrow, said he, thou shalt hear him.

23 And on the morrow, when A-grĭp'pȧ was come, and Bĕr-nī'çe, with [l]great pomp, and was entered into the place of hearing, with the chief captains, and principal men of the city, at Fĕs'tus' commandment Pa̤ul was brought forth.

24 And Fĕs'tus said, King A-grĭp'pȧ, and all men which are here present with us, ye see this man, about whom all the multitude of the Jews have dealt with me, both at Je-rṳ'sa-lĕm, and *also* here, crying that he ought [m]not to live any longer.

25 But when I found that [n]he had committed nothing worthy of death, and that he himself hath appealed to Au-gŭs'tus, I have determined to send him.

26 Of whom I have no certain thing to write unto my lord. Wherefore I have brought him forth before you, and specially before thee, O king A-grĭp'pȧ, that, after examination had, I might have somewhat to write.

27 For it seemeth to me unreasonable to send a prisoner, and not withal to signify the crimes *laid* against him.

26 Then A-grĭp'pȧ said unto Pa̤ul, Thou art permitted to speak for thyself. Then Pa̤ul stretched forth the hand, and answered for himself:

2 I think myself happy, king A-grĭp'pȧ, because I shall answer for myself this day before thee touching all the things whereof I am accused of the Jews:

3 Especially *because I know* thee to be [1a]expert in all customs and questions

14 [i]ch. 24.27
19 [j]ch. 18.15; ch. 23.29; 1 Cor. 1.18; 1 Cor. 2.14
20 [2]Or, I was doubtful how to inquire hereof
21 [3]Or, judgment
22 [k]ch. 9.15; ch. 26.1
23 [l]Eccl. 1.2; Jas. 1.11; 1 Pet. 1.24
24 [m]ch. 22.22
25 [n]Matt. 27.19-24; Mark 15.14; Luke 23.4; John 18.38; 2 Cor. 5.21; 1 Pet. 2.22

CHAPTER 26

3 [1]a knower
[a]Deut. 17.14-20; ch. 25.26
5 [b]ch. 22.3; Gal. 1.13; Phil. 3.5
6 [c]Gen. 3.15; Deut. 18.15; 2 Sam. 7.12; Ps. 132.11; Isa. 4.2; Ezek. 21.7; Dan. 9.24; Mal. 3.1; ch. 13.32; Rom. 15.8
7 [d]Jas. 1.1
[2]night and day
[e]Phil. 3.11
8 [f]Dan. 12.2
9 [g]John 16.2; 1 Tim. 1.13
10 [h]ch. 8.3
[i]ch. 22.5
11 [j]ch. 22.19
12 [k]ch. 9.3
16 [l]ch. 22.15; 2 Cor. 3.5-6; Col. 1.25; Gal. 1.12; 1 Tim. 1.12
17 [m]ch. 9.15; ch. 18.6; Rom. 1.5; Gal. 1.15-16; 1 Tim. 2.7; 2 Tim. 1.11
18 [n]Isa. 35.5; Luke 1.79
[o]2 Cor. 6.14; Eph. 4.18; Col. 1.13; 1 Pet. 2.9
[p]1 John 3.5
[q]Luke 1.77
[r]Eph. 1.11
[s]ch. 20.32
20 [t]ch. 9.20

which are among the Jews: wherefore I beseech thee to hear me patiently.

4 My manner of life from my youth, which was at the first among mine own nation at Je-rṳ'sa-lĕm, know all the Jews;

5 Which knew me from the beginning, if they would testify, that after [b]the most straitest sect of our religion I lived a Phăr'ĭ-see.

6 And now I stand and am judged for the hope of [c]the promise made of God unto our fathers:

7 Unto which *promise* [d]our twelve tribes, instantly serving *God* [2]day and night, [e]hope to come. For which hope's sake, king A-grĭp'pȧ, I am accused of the Jews.

8 Why should it be thought a thing incredible with you, that God should [f]raise the dead?

9 [g]I verily thought with myself, that I ought to do many things contrary to the name of Jē'sus of Năz'a-rĕth.

10 [h]Which thing I also did in Je-rṳ'sa-lĕm: and many of the saints did I shut up in prison, having received authority [i]from the chief priests; and when they were put to death, I gave my voice against *them*.

11 [j]And I punished them oft in every synagogue, and compelled *them* to blaspheme; and being exceedingly mad against them, I persecuted *them* even unto strange cities.

12 [k]Whereupon as I went to Da-măs'cus with authority and commission from the chief priests,

13 At midday, O king, I saw in the way a light from heaven, above the brightness of the sun, shining round about me and them which journeyed with me.

14 And when we were all fallen to the earth, I heard a voice speaking unto me, and saying in the Hē'brew tongue, Sa̤ul, Sa̤ul, why persecutest thou me? *it is* hard for thee to kick against the pricks.

15 And I said, Who art thou, Lord? And he said, I am Jē'sus whom thou persecutest.

16 But rise, and stand upon thy feet: for I have appeared unto thee for this purpose, [l]to make thee a minister and a witness both of these things which thou hast seen, and of those things in the which I will appear unto thee;

17 Delivering thee from the people, and *from* the Gĕn'tīles, [m]unto whom now I send thee,

18 [n]To open their eyes, *and* [o]to turn *them* from darkness to light, and [p]*from* the power of Sā'tan unto God, [q]that they may receive forgiveness of sins, and [r]inheritance among them which are [s]sanctified by faith that is in me.

19 Whereupon, O king A-grĭp'pȧ, I was not disobedient unto the heavenly vision:

20 But [t]shewed first unto them of Da-măs'cus, and at Je-rṳ'sa-lĕm, and throughout all the coasts of Jū-dæ'ȧ, and *then* to the Gĕn'tīles, that they

should repent and turn to God, and do
[u]works meet for repentance.
21 For these causes [v]the Jews caught
me in the temple, and went about to kill
me.
22 Having therefore obtained help
of God, I continue unto this day, witnessing both to small and great, saying
none other things than those [w]which
the prophets and [x]Mō′ses did say
should come:
23 [y]That Chrīst should suffer, *and*
[z]that he should be the first that should
rise from the dead, and [a]should shew
light unto the people, and to the Gĕn′-
tīles.
24 And as he thus spake for himself,
Fĕs′tus said with a loud voice, Pa̧ul
[b]thou art beside thyself; much learning doth make thee mad.
25 But he said, I am not mad, most
noble Fĕs′tus; but speak forth the words
of truth and soberness.
26 For the king knoweth of these
things, before whom also I speak freely:
for I am persuaded that none of these
things are hidden from him; for this
thing was not done in a corner.
27 King A-grĭp′pȧ, believest thou the
prophets? I know that thou believest.
28 Then A-grĭp′pȧ said unto Pa̧ul,
Almost thou persuadest me to be a
Chrĭs′tian.
29 And Pa̧ul said, [c]I would to God,
that not only thou, but also all that
hear me this day, were both almost,
and altogether such as I am, except
these bonds.
30 And when he had thus spoken,
the king rose up, and the governor,
and Bĕr-nī′çe, and they that sat with
them:
31 And when they were gone aside,
they talked between themselves, saying, [d]This man doeth nothing worthy
of death or of bonds.
32 Then said A-grĭp′pȧ unto Fĕs′tus,
This man might have been set at liberty, [e]if he had not appealed unto
Çæ′sar.
27 And when [a]it was determined
that we should sail into Ĭt′a-lȳ,
they delivered Pa̧ul and certain other
prisoners unto *one* named Jū′lius, a
centurion of Au-gŭs′tus′ band.
2 And entering into a ship of Ăd-ra-
mȳt′tĭ-um, we launched, meaning to
sail by the coasts of Ā′siȧ; *one* [b]Ār-ĭs-
tär′chus, a Măç-e-dō′nĭ-an of Thĕs-sa-
lo-nī′cȧ, being with us.
3 And the next *day* we touched at
Sī′dŏn. And Jū′lius [c]courteously entreated Pa̧ul, and gave *him* liberty to
go unto his friends to refresh himself.
4 And when we had launched from
thence, we sailed under Çȳ′prus, because the winds were contrary.
5 And when we had sailed over the
sea of Çi-lĭ′çiȧ and Pam-phȳl′ĭ-ȧ, we
came to Mȳ′rȧ, *a city* of Lȳ′çiȧ.
6 And there the centurion found a
ship of Ăl-ĕx-ăn′drĭ-ȧ sailing into Ĭt′a-
lȳ; and he put us therein.
7 And when we had sailed slowly
many days, and scarce were come
over against Cnī′dus, the wind not suffering us, we sailed under [1]Crēte, over
against Săl-mō′ne;
8 And, hardly passing it, came unto
a place which is called The fair havens; nigh whereunto was the city *of*
La-sē′ȧ.
9 Now when much time was spent,
and when sailing was now dangerous,
because [2]the fast was now already
past, Pa̧ul admonished *them*,
10 And said unto them, Sirs, I perceive that this voyage will be with
[3]hurt and much damage, not only of
the lading and ship, but also of our
lives.
11 Nevertheless the centurion believed the master and the owner of the
ship, more than those things which
were spoken by Pa̧ul.
12 And because the haven was not
commodious to winter in, the more
part advised to depart thence also, if
by any means they might attain [4][d]to
Phe-nī′çe, *and there* to winter; *which is*
an haven of Crēte, and lieth toward the
south west and north west.
13 And when the south wind blew
softly, supposing that they had obtained *their* purpose, loosing *thence*,
they sailed close by Crēte.
14 But not long after there [5]arose
against it a tempestuous wind, called
[6]Eū-rŏc′lȳ-don.
15 And when the ship was caught,
and could not bear up into the wind,
we let *her* drive.
16 And running under a certain island which is called Cla̧u′dȧ, we had
much work to come by the boat:
17 Which when they had taken up,
they used helps, undergirding the ship;
and, fearing lest they should fall into
the quicksands, strake sail, and so
were driven.
18 And we being exceedingly tossed
with a tempest, the next *day* they lightened the ship;
19 And the third *day* [e]we cast out
with our own hands the tackling of the
ship.
20 And when neither sun nor stars
in many days appeared, and no small
tempest lay on *us*, all hope that we
should be saved was then taken away.
21 But after long abstinence Pa̧ul
stood forth in the midst of them, and
said, Sirs, ye should have hearkened
unto me, and not have loosed from
Crēte, and to have gained this harm
and loss.
22 And now I exhort you to be of
good cheer: for there shall be no loss of
any man's life among you, but of the
ship.
23 [f]For there stood by me this night
the angel of God, whose I am, and
[g]whom I serve,
24 Saying, [h]Fear not, Pa̧ul; thou
must be brought [i]before Çæ′sar: and,
lo, God hath [j]given thee all them that
sail with thee.
25 Wherefore, sirs, be of good cheer:
[k]for I believe God, that it shall be even
as it was told me.

[u]Isa. 55.7; Matt. 3.8
21 [v]ch. 21.30
22 [w]Rom. 3.21 [x]John 5.46
23 [y]Ps. 22; Isa. 53 [z]Ps. 16.8-11; 1 Cor. 15.20; Col. 1.18; Rev. 1.5 [a]Isa. 42.6
24 [b]2 Ki. 9.11; 1 Cor. 1.23
29 [c]1 Cor. 7.7
31 [d]ch. 23.9; ch. 25.25
32 [e]ch. 25.11
CHAPTER 27
1 [a]ch. 25.12-25
2 [b]ch. 19.29; ch. 20.4; Col. 4.10
3 [c]ch. 28.16
7 [1]Or, Candy, a large island in the Mediterranean
9 [2]The fast was on the tenth day of the seventh month
10 [3]Or, injury
12 [4]Not Phenicia, the country on the north west of Canaan [d]ch. 11.19; ch. 21.2
14 [5]Or, beat [6]A north east wind
19 [e]Jon. 1.5
23 [f]Ps. 25.14; Amos 3.7; ch. 5.19; ch. 23.11; Heb. 1.13-14 [g]Ps. 143.12; Dan. 3.28; John 12.26; Rom. 1.9; Rom. 6.22; 2 Tim. 1.3
24 [h]Isa. 41.10-14; Isa. 43.1 [i]ch. 19.21; ch. 23.11; ch. 25.11 [j]Gen. 18.23-32; Gen. 19.29; Job 42.8
25 [k]Num. 23.19; 2 Chr. 20.20; Luke 1.45; 2 Tim. 1.12; Tit. 1.2

26 Howbeit [l]we must be cast upon a certain island.

27 But when the fourteenth night was come, as we were driven up and down in Ȧ′drĭ-ȧ, about midnight the shipmen deemed that they drew near to some country;

28 And sounded, and found *it* twenty fathoms: and when they had gone a little further, they sounded again, and found *it* fifteen fathoms.

29 Then fearing lest we should have fallen upon rocks, they cast four anchors out of the stern, and wished for the day.

30 And as the shipmen were about to flee out of the ship, when they had let down the boat into the sea, under colour as though they would have cast anchors out of the foreship,

31 Pa̤ul said to the centurion and to the soldiers, Except these abide in the ship, ye cannot be saved.

32 Then the soldiers cut off the ropes of the boat, and let her fall off.

33 And while the day was coming on, Pa̤ul besought *them* all to take meat, saying, This day is the fourteenth day that ye have tarried and continued fasting, having taken nothing.

34 Wherefore I pray you to take *some* meat: for this is for your health: for [m]there shall not an hair fall from the head of any of you.

35 And when he had thus spoken, he took bread, and [n]gave thanks to God in presence of them all: and when he had broken *it*, he began to eat.

36 Then were they all of good cheer, and they also took *some* meat.

37 And we were in all in the ship two hundred threescore and sixteen [o]souls.

38 And when they had eaten enough, they lightened the ship, and [p]cast out the wheat into the sea.

39 And when it was day, they knew not the land: but they discovered a certain creek with a shore, into the which they were minded, if it were possible, to thrust in the ship.

40 And when they had [7]taken up the anchors, they committed *themselves* unto the sea, and loosed the rudder bands, and hoised up the mainsail to the wind, and made toward shore.

41 And falling into a place where two seas met, [q]they ran the ship aground; and the forepart stuck fast, and remained unmoveable, but the hinder part was broken with the violence of the waves.

42 And the soldiers' counsel [r]was to kill the prisoners, lest any of them should swim out, and escape.

43 But the centurion, [s]willing to save Pa̤ul, kept them from *their* purpose; and commanded that they which could swim should cast *themselves* first *into the sea*, and get to land:

44 And the rest, some on boards, and some on *broken pieces* of the ship. And so it came to pass, that they escaped [t]all safe to land.

26 [l]ch. 28.1
34 [m]1 Ki. 1.52; Matt. 10.30; Luke 12.7
35 [n]1 Sam. 9.13; Matt. 15.36; Mark 8.6; John 6.11; Rom. 14.6
37 [o]ch. 2.41; Rom. 13.1; 1 Pet. 3.20
38 [p]Job 2.4; Matt. 6.25
40 [7]Or, cut the anchors, they left them in the sea, etc
41 [q]2 Cor. 11.25
42 [r]Prov. 1.16; Eccl. 9.3; Isa. 59.7; Mark 15.15-20; Rom. 3.15
43 [s]Ps. 34.17-19; Prov. 16.7; ch. 23.10; 2 Pet. 2.9
44 [t]Ps. 107.30

CHAPTER 28
1 [1]Or, Malta [a]ch. 27.26
2 [b]Lev. 19.18-34; ch. 27.3; Rom. 1.14; 1 Cor. 14.11; Col. 3.11; Heb. 13.1-2
4 [c]Luke 13.2; John 9.2
5 [d]Num. 21.9; Ps. 91.13; Mark 16.18; Luke 10.19; Rev. 9.3-4
6 [e]ch. 8.10; ch. 10.25; ch. 12.22; Rev. 22.8-9
8 [f]1 Ki. 17.20-22; ch. 9.40 [g]Matt. 8.8; Mark 6.5; Mark 7.32; Luke 4.40; ch. 19.11; 1 Cor. 12.9-28
10 [h]Matt. 15.6; 1 Tim. 5.17
16 [i]Gen. 39.21; ch. 24.23
17 [j]ch. 24.12; ch. 25.8 [k]Judg. 15.13; ch. 21.33

28

And when they were escaped, then they knew that the island was called [1][a]Mĕl′ĭ-tȧ.

2 And the [b]barbarous people shewed us no little kindness: for they kindled a fire, and received us every one, because of the present rain, and because of the cold.

3 And when Pa̤ul had gathered a bundle of sticks, and laid *them* on the fire, there came a viper out of the heat, and fastened on his hand.

4 And when the barbarians saw the *venomous* beast hang on his hand, they said among themselves, No [c]doubt this man is a murderer, whom, though he hath escaped the sea, yet vengeance suffereth not to live.

5 And he shook off the beast into the fire, and [d]felt no harm.

6 Howbeit they looked when he should have swollen, or fallen down dead suddenly: but after they had looked a great while, and saw no harm come to him, they changed their minds, and [e]said that he was a god.

7 In the same quarters were possessions of the chief man of the island, whose name was Pŭb′lĭ-us; who received us, and lodged us three days courteously.

8 And it came to pass, that the father of Pŭb′lĭ-us lay sick of a fever and of a bloody flux: to whom Pa̤ul entered in, and [f]prayed, and [g]laid his hands on him, and healed him.

9 So when this was done, others also, which had diseases in the island, came, and were healed:

10 Who also honoured us with many [h]honours; and when we departed, they laded *us* with such things as were necessary.

11 And after thre̤e months we departed in a ship of Ăl-ĕx-ăn′drĭ-ȧ, which had wintered in the isle, whose sign was Căs′tŏr and Pŏl′lṳx.

12 And landing at Sy̆r′a-cūse, we tarried *there* three days.

13 And from thence we fetched a compass, and came to Rhē′gĭ-um: and after one day the south wind blew, and we came the next day to Pū-tē′o-lī:

14 Where we found brethren, and were desired to tarry with them seven days: and so we went toward Rōme.

15 And from thence, when the brethren hea̤rd of us, they came to meet us as far as Ȧp′pĭ-ī forum, and The three taverns: whom when Pa̤ul saw, he thanked God, and took courage.

16 And when we came to Rōme, the centurion delivered the prisoners to the captain of the guard: but [i]Pa̤ul was suffered to dwell by himself with a soldier that kept him.

17 And it came to pass, that after three days Pa̤ul called the chief of the Jews together: and when they were come together, he said unto them, Men *and* brethren, [j]though I have committed nothing against the people, or customs of our fathers, yet was I [k]delivered prisoner from Je-rṳ′sa-lĕm into the hands of the Rō′mans.

18 Who, [l]when they had examined me, would have let *me* go, because there was no cause of death in me.

19 But when the Jews spake against *it*, [m]I was constrained to appeal unto Çæ′sar; not that I had ought to accuse my nation of.

20 For this cause therefore have I called for you, to see *you*, and to speak with *you*: because that [n]for the hope of Is′ra-el I am bound with [o]this chain.

21 And they said unto him, We neither received letters out of Jū-dæ′á concerning thee, neither any of the brethren that came shewed or spake any harm of thee.

22 But we desire to hear of thee what thou thinkest: for as concerning this sect, we know that every where [p]it is spoken against.

23 And when they had appointed him a day, there came many to him into *his* lodging; [q]to whom he expounded and testified the kingdom of God, persuading them concerning Jē′sus, [r]both out of the law of Mō′ses, and *out of* the prophets, from morning till evening.

24 And [s]some believed the things which were spoken, and some believed not.

18 [l]ch. 22.24; ch. 24.10; ch. 25.8
19 [m]ch. 25.11; ch. 26.32
20 [n]ch. 26.6-7 [o]ch. 26.29; Eph. 3.1; Eph. 4.1; Eph. 6.20; 2 Tim. 1.16; Phile. 10.13
22 [p]Luke 2.34; ch. 24.5; 1 Pet. 2.12
23 [q]Luke 24.27; ch. 17.2-3; [r]ch. 26.6
24 [s]ch. 13.48-50; ch. 14.4; ch. 18.6-8;
26 [t]Isa. 6.9; Jer. 5.21; Ezek. 12.2; Matt. 13.14; Mark 4.12;
27 [u]Isa. 44.18
28 [v]Matt. 21.41;
31 [w]Eph. 6.19

25 And when they agreed not among themselves, they departed, after that Pa̧ul had spoken one word, Well spake the Hō′lȳ Ghōst by E-sā′ias the prophet unto our fathers,

26 Saying, [t]Go unto this people, and say, Hearing ye shall hear, and shall not understand; and seeing ye shall see, and not perceive:

27 [u]For the heart of this people is waxed gross, and their ears are dull of hearing, and their eyes have they closed; lest they should see with *their* eyes, and hear with *their* ears, and understand with *their* heart, and should be converted, and I should heal them.

28 Be it known therefore unto you, that the salvation of God is sent [v]unto the Gĕn′tīles, and *that* they will hear it.

29 And when he had said these words, the Jews departed, and had great reasoning among themselves.

30 And Pa̧ul dwelt two whole years in his own hired house, and received all that came in unto him,

31 [w]Preaching the kingdom of God, and teaching those things which concern the Lord Jē′sus Chrīst, with all confidence, no man forbidding him.

THE LETTER OF PAUL TO THE

ROMANS

Life's Questions

Am I really a sinner?
How does God treat sinners?
What does God want me to do about my sin?

God's Answers

About A.D. 34 God changed a zealous Jewish rabbi from a persecutor of the church to its leading missionary. Paul founded churches throughout Asia Minor and Greece, but he aroused so much opposition from the Jews that they had him arrested. An appeal to Rome gave him boat passage to Italy and a Roman prison. Wherever He went, he preached the free gospel of Christ's grace and wrote letters to strengthen churches. About A.D. 55 he wrote the church at Rome to prepare them for his coming and to show them the essential elements of Christian faith.

Romans shows: the righteousness of God the power of salvation revealed in Jesus are needed because all people live under the power of sin (1:1—3:20); God provides righteousness to those who make faith commitments to Jesus Christ as Lord (3:21—4:25); salvation in Christ results in a victorious new life (5—8); God is faithful in all His promises, especially those to the Jews (9—11); God's saving mercy summons believers to a totally changed way of life (12—16).

Romans invites you to examine who you are in light of God's love, His wrath, His promises, and His expectations.

1 Pa̧ul, a servant of Jē′sus Chrīst, [a]called *to be* an apostle, [b]separated unto the gospel of God,

2 ([c]Which he had promised afore by his prophets in the holy scriptures,)

3 Concerning his Son Jē′sus Chrīst our Lord, which was made of the seed of Dā′vid according to the flesh;

4 And [1]declared *to be* the Son of God with power, according [d]to the spirit of holiness, by the resurrection from the dead:

5 By whom [e]we have received grace and apostleship, [2]for obedience to the

CHAPTER 1
1 [a]Acts 9.15; [b]Acts 9.15
2 [c]Tit. 1.2
4 [1]determined [d]Heb. 9.14;
5 [e]Eph. 3.8 [2]Or, to the obedience of faith [f]Acts 9.15;
8 [g]Phil. 1.3 [h]1 Thess. 1.8
9 [3]Or, in

faith among all nations, [f]for his name:

6 Among whom are ye also the called of Jē′sus Chrīst:

7 To all that be in Rōme, beloved of God, called *to be* saints: Grace to you and peace from God our Father, and the Lord Jē′sus Chrīst.

8 First, [g]I thank my God through Jē′sus Chrīst for you all, that [h]your faith is spoken of throughout the whole world.

9 For God is my witness, whom I serve [3]with my spirit in the gospel of

his Son, that without ceasing I make
mention of you always in my prayers;
10 Making request, if by any means
now at length I might have a prosperous journey [i]by the will of God to
come unto you.
11 For I long to see you, that [j]I may
impart unto you some spiritual gift, to
the end ye may be established;
12 That is, that I may be comforted
together [4]with you by the mutual faith
both of you and me.
13 Now I would not have you ignorant, brethren, that [k]oftentimes I purposed to come unto you, (but [l]was let
hitherto,) that I might have some fruit
[5]among you also, even as among other
Gĕn'tīles.
14 [m]I am debtor both to the Greeks,
and to the Bär-bā'rĭ-ans; both to the
wise, and to the unwise.
15 So, as much as in me is, I am
ready to preach the gospel to you that
are at Rōme also.
16 For [n]I am not ashamed of the gospel of Chrīst: for [o]it is the power of
God unto salvation to every one that
believeth; to the Jew first, and also to
the Greek.
17 For [p]therein is the righteousness
of God revealed from faith to faith: as
it is written, [q]The just shall live by
faith.
18 [r]For the wrath of God is revealed
from heaven against all ungodliness
and unrighteousness of men, [s]who
hold the truth in unrighteousness;
19 Because [t]that which may be
known of God is manifest [6]in them; for
[u]God hath shewed *it* unto them.
20 For [v]the invisible things of him
from the creation of the world are
clearly seen, being understood by the
things that are made, *even* his eternal
power and Godhead; [7]so that they are
without excuse:
21 Because that, when they knew
God, they glorified *him* not as God,
[w]neither were thankful; but [x]became
vain in their imaginations, and their
foolish heart was darkened.
22 [y]Professing themselves to be wise,
they became fools,
23 And changed the glory of the un-
corruptible [z]God into an image made
like to corruptible man, and to birds,
and fourfooted beasts, and creeping
things.
24 [a]Wherefore God also gave them
up to uncleanness through the lusts of
their own hearts, [b]to dishonour their
own bodies [c]between themselves:
25 Who changed [d]the truth of God
[e]into a lie, and worshipped and served
the creature [8]more than the Creator,
who is blessed for ever. Amen.
26 For this cause God gave them up
into [f]vile affections: for even their
women did change the natural use into
that which is against nature:
27 And likewise also the men, leaving the natural use of the woman,
burned in their lust one toward another; men with men working that
which is unseemly, and receiving in
themselves that recompence of their error which was meet.
28 And even as they did not like [9]to
retain God in *their* knowledge, God
gave them over to [10]a reprobate mind,
to do those things [g]which are not
convenient;
29 Being filled with all unrighteousness, fornication, wickedness, covetousness, maliciousness; full of envy,
murder, debate, deceit, malignity; whis-
perers,
30 Backbiters, haters of God, despiteful, proud, boasters, inventors of
evil things, disobedient to parents,
31 Without understanding, cove-
nantbreakers, [11]without natural affection, implacable, unmerciful:
32 Who knowing the judgment of
God, that they which commit such
things are worthy of death, not only do
the same, but [12]have pleasure in them
that do them.

2 Therefore thou art inexcusable, O
man, whosoever thou art that judgest: for wherein thou judgest another,
thou condemnest thyself; for thou that
judgest doest the same things.
2 But we are sure that the judgment
of God is [a]according to truth against
them which commit such things.
3 And [b]thinkest thou this, O man,
that judgest them which do such things,
and doest the same, that thou shalt escape the judgment of God?
4 Or despisest thou [c]the riches of his
goodness and forbearance and [d]long-
suffering; [e]not knowing that the goodness of God leadeth thee to repentance?
5 But after thy hardness and impenitent heart [f]treasurest up unto thyself
wrath against the day of wrath and
revelation of the righteous judgment of
God;
6 [g]Who will render to every man according to his deeds:
7 [h]To them who by patient continuance in well doing seek for glory and
honour and immortality, eternal life:
8 But [i]unto them that are contentious, and do not obey the truth, but
obey unrighteousness, indignation and
wrath,
9 Tribulation and anguish, upon every soul of man that doeth evil, of the
Jew [j]first, and also of the [1]Gen'tile;
10 [k]But glory, honour, and peace, to
every man that worketh good, to the
Jew first, and also to the [2]Gentile:
11 For there is [l]no respect of persons with God.
12 For as many as have sinned without law shall also perish without law:
and as many as have sinned in the law
shall be judged by the law;
13 (For [m]not the hearers of the law
are just before God, but the doers of
the law shall be justified.
14 For when the Gĕn'tīles, which
have not the law, do by nature the
things contained in the law, these,
having not the law, are a law unto
themselves:
15 Which shew the work of the law
written in their hearts, [3]their conscience

10 [i]Jas. 4.15
11 [j]ch. 15.29
12 [4]Or, in you
13 [k]ch. 15.23
[l]Acts 16.7; 1 Thess. 2.18
[5]Or, in you
14 [m]Ps. 40.9; Mark 8.38
16 [n]Ps. 40.9-10; 2 Tim. 1.8
[o]ch. 10.17; 2 Cor. 10.4
17 [p]ch. 3.21
[q]Hab. 2.4; Heb. 10.38
18 [r]Acts 17.30; ch. 2.5-6
[s]Job 24.13
19 [t]Acts 14.17
[6]Or, to them
[u]John 1.9
20 [v]Ps. 19.1
[7]Or, that they may be
21 [w]Ps. 106.13
[x]Gen. 6.5
22 [y]Jer. 10.14
23 [z]Isa. 40.18
24 [a]Ps. 81.12;
[b]1 Cor. 6.18;
[c]Lev. 18.22
25 [d]1 Thess. 1.9
[e]Isa. 44.20;
[8]Or, rather
26 [f]Jude 10
28 [9]Or, to acknowledge
[10]Or, a mind void of judgment
[g]Eph. 5.4
31 [11]Or, unsociable
32 [12]Or, consent with them

CHAPTER 2
2 [a]Gen. 18.25
3 [b]Prov. 11.21
4 [c]Ps. 86.5;
[d]Ex. 34.6
[e]2 Pet. 3.9
5 [f]Jas. 5.3
6 [g]Ps. 62.12
7 [h]2 Cor. 4.17
8 [i]Isa. 3.11
9 [j]1 Pet. 4.17
[1]Greek
10 [k]Ps. 112.6-9;
[2]Greek
11 [l]Deut. 10.17
13 [m]Deut. 30.12-14
15 [3]Or, the conscience witnessing with them

also bearing witness, and *their* thoughts
[4]the mean while accusing or else excus-
ing one another;)
16 [n]In the day when God shall judge
the secrets of men [o]by Jē'sus Chrīst
according to my gospel.
17 Behold, [p]thou art called a Jew,
and [q]restest in the law, [r]and makest
thy boast of God,
18 And [s]knowest *his* will, and [5]ap-
provest the things that are more excellent, being instructed out of the law;
19 And art confident that thou thyself art a guide of the blind, a light of
them which are in darkness,
20 An instructor of the foolish, a
teacher of babes, [t]which hast the form
of knowledge and of the truth in the
law.
21 [u]Thou therefore which teachest
another, teachest thou not thyself? thou
that preachest a man should not steal,
dost thou steal?
22 Thou that sayest a man should
not commit adultery, dost thou commit
adultery? thou that abhorrest idols,
[v]dost thou commit sacrilege?
23 Thou that makest thy boast of the
law, through breaking the law dishon-
ourest thou God?
24 For the name of God is blasphemed among the Gĕn'tīles through
you, as it is [w]written.
25 [x]For circumcision verily profiteth, if thou keep the law: but if thou be
a breaker of the law, thy circumcision
is made uncircumcision.
26 Therefore [y]if the uncircumcision
keep the righteousness of the law, shall
not his uncircumcision be counted for
circumcision?
27 And shall not uncircumcision
which is by nature, if it fulfil the law,
[z]judge thee, who by the letter and circumcision dost transgress the law?
28 For [a]he is not a Jew, which is one
outwardly; neither *is that* circumcision, which is outward in the flesh:
29 But he *is* a Jew, [b]which is one
inwardly; and [c]circumcision *is that* of
the heart, [d]in the spirit, *and* not in the
letter; whose praise *is* not of men, but
of God.

3 What advantage then hath the Jew?
or what profit *is there* of circumcision?
2 Much every way: chiefly, because
that [a]unto them were committed the
oracles of God.
3 For what if [b]some did not believe?
[c]shall their unbelief make the faith of
God without effect?
4 [d]God forbid: yea, let [e]God be true,
but [f]every man a liar; as it is written,
[g]That thou mightest be justified in thy
sayings, and mightest overcome when
thou art judged.
5 But if our unrighteousness commend the righteousness of God, what
shall we say? *Is* God unrighteous who
taketh vengeance? ([h]I speak as a man)
6 God forbid: for then [i]how shall
God judge the world?
7 For if the truth of God hath more
abounded through my lie unto his
glory; why yet am I also judged as a
sinner?
8 And not *rather,* (as we be slander-
ously reported, and as some affirm
that we say,) [j]Let us do evil, that good
may come? whose damnation is just.
9 What then? are we better *than
they*? No, in no wise: for we have before [1k]proved both Jews and Gĕn'tīles,
that [l]they are all under sin;
10 As it is written, [m]There is none
righteous, no, not one:
11 There is none that understandeth, there is none that seeketh after
God.
12 They are all gone out of the way,
they are together become unprofitable:
there is none that doeth good, no, not
one.
13 [n]Their throat *is* an open sepulchre; with their tongues they have
used deceit; [o]the poison of asps *is* under their lips:
14 [p]Whose mouth *is* full of cursing
and bitterness:
15 [q]Their feet *are* swift to shed
blood:
16 Destruction and misery *are* in
their ways:
17 And the way of peace have they
not known:
18 [r]There is no fear of God before
their eyes.
19 Now we know that what things
soever the law saith, it saith to them
who are under the law: that [s]every
mouth may be stopped, and [t]all the
world may become [2]guilty before God.
20 Therefore [u]by the deeds of the
law there shall no flesh be justified in
his sight: for [v]by the law *is* the knowledge of sin.
21 But now [w]the righteousness of
God without the law is manifested, being witnessed by the law [x]and the
prophets;
22 Even the righteousness of God
which is [y]by faith of Jē'sus Chrīst unto
all and upon all them that believe: for
[z]there is no difference:
23 For [a]all have sinned, and come
short of the glory of God;
24 Being justified freely [b]by his grace
through the redemption that is in Chrīst
Jē'sus:
25 Whom God hath [3]set forth [c]*to
be* a propitiation through faith in his
blood, to declare his righteousness for
the [4]remission of sins that are past,
through the forbearance of God;
26 To declare, *I say,* at this time his
righteousness: that he might be just,
and the justifier of him which believeth in Jē'sus.
27 [d]Where *is* boasting then? It is ex-
cluded. By what law? of works? Nay:
but by the law of faith.
28 Therefore we conclude [e]that a
man is justified by faith without the
deeds of the law.
29 *Is he* the God of the Jews only? *is
he* not also of the Gĕn'tīles? Yes, of the
Gĕn'tīles also:

[4]Or, between themselves
16 [n]Rev. 20.12
[o]John 5.22
17 [p]ch. 9.6
[q]Mic. 3.11
[r]John 8.41
18 [s]Deut. 4.8
[5]Or, triest the things that differ
20 [t]2 Tim. 3.5
21 [u]Matt. 23.3
22 [v]Mal. 3.8
24 [w]2 Sam. 12.14; Isa. 52.5
25 [x]Gal. 5.3
26 [y]Acts 10.34
27 [z]Matt. 12.41
28 [a]Matt. 3.9; Rev. 2.9
29 [b]1 Pet. 3.4
[c]Phil. 3.3; Col. 2.11
[d]ch. 7.6; 2 Cor. 3.6

CHAPTER 3
2 [a]Deut. 4.7
3 [b]Heb. 4.2
[c]Num. 23.19
4 [d]Job 40.8
[e]John 3.33
[f]Ps. 62.9
[g]Ps. 51.4
5 [h]Gal. 3.15
6 [i]Gen. 18.25; Ps. 9.8
8 [j]ch. 5.20
9 [1]charged
[k]ch. 1.28
[l]Gal. 3.22
10 [m]Ps. 14.1
13 [n]Ps. 5.9
[o]Ps. 140.3
14 [p]Ps. 10.7
15 [q]Prov. 1.16
18 [r]Ps. 36.1;
19 [s]Ezek. 16.63
[t]ch. 2.2
[2]Or, subject to the judgment of God
20 [u]Ps. 143.2;
[v]ch. 7.7
21 [w]Isa. 45.24;
[x]1 Pet. 1.10
22 [y]ch. 4
[z]Col. 3.11
23 [a]Gal. 3.22
24 [b]Matt. 20.28
25 [3]Or, foreordained
[c]Lev. 16.15;
[4]Or, passing over
27 [d]1 Cor. 1.29
28 [e]Gal. 2.16

30 Seeing *it is* one God, which shall
justify the circumcision by faith, and
uncircumcision through faith.
31 Do we then make void the law
through faith? God forbid: yea, we establish the law.

4 What shall we say then that Ā'brā-
hăm our father, as pertaining to the
flesh, hath found?
2 For if Ā'brā-hăm were justified by
works, he hath *whereof* to glory; but
not before God.
3 For what saith the scripture?
[a]Ā'brā-hăm believed God, and it was
counted unto him for righteousness.
4 Now [b]to him that worketh is the
reward not reckoned of grace, but of
debt.
5 But to him that worketh not, but
believeth on him that justifieth [c]the
ungodly, his faith is counted for righteousness.
6 Even as Dā'vid also describeth the
blessedness of the man, unto whom
God [d]imputeth righteousness without
works,
7 *Saying,* [e]Blessed *are* they whose
iniquities are forgiven, and whose sins
are covered.
8 Blessed *is* the man to whom the
Lord will not impute sin.
9 *Cometh* this blessedness then upon
the circumcision *only,* or upon the uncircumcision also? for we say that faith
was reckoned to Ā'brā-hăm for righteousness.
10 How was it then reckoned? when
he was in circumcision, or in uncircumcision? Not in circumcision, but in
uncircumcision.
11 And [f]he received the sign of circumcision, a seal of the righteousness
of faith which *he had yet* being uncircumcised: that [g]he might be the father
of all them that believe, though they
be not circumcised; that righteousness
might be imputed unto them also:
12 And the father of circumcision to
them who are not of the circumcision
only, but who also walk in the steps of
that faith of our father Ā'brā-hăm,
which *he had* being *yet* uncircumcised.
13 For the promise, that he should
be the [h]heir of the world, *was* not to
Ā'brā-hăm, or to his seed, through the
law, but through the righteousness of
faith.
14 For [i]if they which are of the law
be heirs, faith is made void, and the
promise made of none effect:
15 Because the law worketh wrath:
for where no law is, *there is* no transgression.
16 Therefore *it is* of faith, that *it
might be* [j]by grace; to the end the
promise might be sure to all the seed;
not to that only which is of the law, but
to that also which is of the faith of
Ā'brā-hăm; [k]who is the father of us
all,
17 (As it is written, I have made thee
a father of many nations,) [1]before him
whom he believed, *even* God, [l]who
quickeneth the dead, and calleth those
[m]things which be not as though they
were.
18 Who against hope believed in
hope, that he might become the father
of many nations, according to that
which was spoken, [n]So shall thy seed
be.
19 And being not weak in faith, [o]he
considered not his own body now dead,
when he was about an hundred years
old, neither yet the deadness of Sā'-
rah's womb:
20 He staggered not at the promise of God through unbelief; but was
strong in faith, giving glory to God;
21 And being fully persuaded that,
what he had promised, he was able
also to perform.
22 And therefore it was imputed to
him for righteousness.
23 Now [p]it was not written for his
sake alone, that it was imputed to him;
24 But for us also, to whom it shall
be imputed, if we believe [q]on him that
raised up Jē'sus our Lord from the
dead;
25 [r]Who was delivered for our offences, and was raised again for our
justification.

5 Therefore being justified by faith,
we have [a]peace with God through
our Lord Jē'sus Chrīst:
2 [b]By whom also we have access by
faith into this grace [c]wherein we stand,
[d]and rejoice in hope of the glory of
God.
3 And not only *so,* but [e]we glory in
tribulations also: knowing that tribulation worketh patience;
4 And patience, experience; and experience, hope:
5 [f]And hope maketh not ashamed;
[g]because the love of God is shed abroad
in our hearts by the Hō'lȳ Ghōst which
is given unto us.
6 For when we were yet without
strength, [1]in due time Chrīst died for
the ungodly.
7 For scarcely for a righteous man
will one die: yet peradventure for a
good man some would even dare to
die.
8 But [h]God commendeth his love toward us, in that, while we were yet sinners, Chrīst died for us.
9 Much more then, being now justified [i]by his blood, we shall be saved
[j]from wrath through him.
10 For if, when we were enemies,
[k]we were reconciled to God by the
death of his Son, much more, being reconciled, we shall be saved [l]by his life.
11 And not only *so,* but we also joy
in God through our Lord Jē'sus Chrīst,
by whom we have now received the
[2]atonement.
12 Wherefore, as [m]by one man sin
entered into the world, and death by
sin; and so death passed upon all men,
[3]for that all have sinned:
13 (For until the law sin was in the
world: but [n]sin is not imputed when
there is no law.
14 Nevertheless death reigned from
Ăd'ăm to Mō'ses, even over them that

CHAPTER 4
3 [a]Gen. 15.6; Gal. 3.6; Jas. 2.23
4 [b]ch. 11.6; ch. 9.32
5 [c]Josh. 24.2; Acts 13.39; Gal. 2.16
6 [d]Jer. 23.6; Dan. 9.24; 1 Cor. 1.30; 2 Cor. 5.19; 2 Pet. 1.1; Rev. 5.9
7 [e]Ps. 32.1-2
11 [f]Gen. 17.10
[g]Luke 19.9; John 8.39
13 [h]Gen. 12.3; Gal. 3.29
14 [i]Gal. 3.18
16 [j]ch. 3.24; Col. 3.11
[k]ch. 9.8
17 [1]Or, like unto him
[l]ch. 8.11; Eph. 2.1; 1 Tim. 6.13
[m]1 Cor. 1.28; 1 Pet. 2.10
18 [n]Gen. 15.5
19 [o]Heb. 11.11
23 [p]2 Tim. 3.16
24 [q]Acts 13.30; 1 Pet. 1.21
25 [r]Isa. 53.5; Heb. 9.28; 1 Pet. 3.18; 1 John 1.7

CHAPTER 5
1 [a]Isa. 32.17; John 16.33; Col. 1.20
2 [b]John 10.9; Heb. 10.19
[c]1 Cor. 15.1
[d]Ps. 16.9-11; Heb. 3.6
3 [e]Matt. 5.11; Phil. 2.17
5 [f]Phil. 1.20
[g]Matt. 22.36-37; Heb. 8.10
6 [1]Or, according to the time
8 [h]John 15.13; 1 Pet. 3.18
9 [i]1 John 1.7
[j]1 Thess. 1.10
10 [k]2 Cor. 5.18
[l]John 14.19
11 [2]Or, reconciliation
12 [m]Ezek. 18.4
[3]Or, in whom
13 [n]1 John 3.4

had not sinned after the similitude of Ăd'ăm's transgression, who is the figure of him that was to come.

15 But not as the offence, so also *is* the free gift. For if through the offence of one many be dead, much more the grace of God, and the gift by grace, *which is* by one man, Jē'sus Chrīst, hath abounded [o]unto many.

16 And not as *it was* by one that sinned, *so is* the gift: for the judgment *was* by one to condemnation, but the free gift *is* of many offences unto justification.

17 For if [4]by one man's offence death reigned by one; much more they which receive abundance of grace and of the gift of righteousness shall reign in life by one, Jē'sus Chrīst.)

18 Therefore as [5]by the offence of one *judgment came* upon all men to condemnation; even so [6]by the righteousness of one *the free gift came* [p]upon all men unto justification of life.

19 For as by one man's disobedience many were made sinners, so by the obedience of one shall many be made righteous.

20 Moreover [q]the law entered, that the offence might abound. But where sin abounded, grace did much [r]more abound:

21 That as sin hath reigned unto death, even so might grace reign through righteousness unto eternal life by Jē'sus Chrīst our Lord.

6 What shall we say then? Shall we continue in sin, that grace may abound?

2 God forbid. How shall we, that are [a]dead to sin, live any longer therein?

3 Know ye not, that [b]so many of us as [1]were baptized into Jē'sus Chrīst [c]were baptized into his death?

4 Therefore we are [d]buried with him by baptism into death: that [e]like as Chrīst was raised up from the dead by the glory of the Father, [f]even so we also should walk in newness of life.

5 [g]For if we have been planted together in the likeness of his death, we shall be also *in the likeness* of *his* resurrection:

6 Knowing this, that [h]our old man is crucified with *him,* that [i]the body of sin might be destroyed, that henceforth we should not serve sin.

7 For he that is dead is [2]freed from sin.

8 Now [j]if we be dead with Chrīst, we believe that we shall also live with him:

9 Knowing that [k]Chrīst being raised from the dead dieth no more; death hath no more dominion over him.

10 For in that he died, he died unto sin once: but in that he liveth, he liveth unto God.

11 Likewise reckon ye also yourselves to be dead indeed unto sin, but [l]alive unto God through Jē'sus Chrīst our Lord.

12 [m]Let not sin therefore reign in your mortal body, that ye should obey it in the lusts thereof.

15 [o]Isa. 53.11; Heb. 9.28
17 [4]Or, by one offence
18 [5]Or, by one offence [6]Or, by one righteousness [p]John 12.32; Heb. 2.9
20 [q]John 15.22; Gal. 3.19 [r]Luke 7.47; 1 Tim. 1.14
CHAPTER 6
2 [a]ch. 3.19-20; 1 Pet. 2.24
3 [b]Col. 3.3; 1 Pet. 2.24 [1]Or, are [c]1 Cor. 15.29
4 [d]Col. 2.12 [e]1 Cor. 6.14 [f]2 Cor. 5.17; 1 Pet. 4.1
5 [g]Eph. 2.5-6; Phil. 3.10
6 [h]Gal. 2.20 [i]Col. 2.11
7 [2]justified
8 [j]2 Cor. 5.1; 2 Tim. 2.11
9 [k]Rev. 1.18
11 [l]Gal. 2.19
12 [m]Eph. 4.22
13 [3]arms, or, weapons
14 [n]Ps. 130.7-8; Heb. 8.10
15 [o]1 Cor. 9.21
17 [4]whereto ye were delivered
18 [p]Luke 1.74-75; 1 Pet. 2.16
20 [5]to righteousness
23 [q]Gen. 2.17; [r]John 3.14
CHAPTER 7
2 [a]Matt. 19.6
3 [b]Matt. 5.32
4 [c]ch. 6.14; [d]Hos. 2.19
5 [1]passions [e]ch. 6.21
6 [2]Or, being dead to that [f]Ezek. 11.19
7 [g]ch. 3.20

13 Neither yield ye your members *as* [3]instruments of unrighteousness unto sin: but yield yourselves unto God, as those that are alive from the dead, and your members *as* instruments of righteousness unto God.

14 For [n]sin shall not have dominion over you: for ye are not under the law, but under grace.

15 What then? shall we sin, [o]because we are not under the law, but under grace? God forbid.

16 Know ye not, that to whom ye yield yourselves servants to obey, his servants ye are to whom ye obey; whether of sin unto death, or of obedience unto righteousness?

17 But God be thanked, that ye were the servants of sin, but ye have obeyed from the heart that form of doctrine [4]which was delivered you.

18 Being then [p]made free from sin, ye became the servants of righteousness.

19 I speak after the manner of men because of the infirmity of your flesh: for as ye have yielded your members servants to uncleanness and to iniquity unto iniquity; even so now yield your members servants to righteousness unto holiness.

20 For when ye were the servants of sin, ye were free [5]from righteousness.

21 What fruit had ye then in those things whereof ye are now ashamed? for the end of those things *is* death.

22 But now being made free from sin, and become servants to God, ye have your fruit unto holiness, and the end everlasting life.

23 For [q]the wages of sin *is* death; but [r]the gift of God *is* eternal life through Jē'sus Chrīst our Lord.

7 Know ye not, brethren, (for I speak to them that know the law,) how that the law hath dominion over a man as long as he liveth?

2 For [a]the woman which hath an husband is bound by the law to *her* husband so long as he liveth; but if the husband be dead, she is loosed from the law of *her* husband.

3 So then [b]if, while *her* husband liveth, she be married to another man, she shall be called an adulteress: but if her husband be dead, she is free from that law; so that she is no adulteress, though she be married to another man.

4 Wherefore, my brethren, ye also are become [c]dead to the law by the body of Chrīst; that ye should be [d]married to another, *even* to him who is raised from the dead, that we should bring forth fruit unto God.

5 For when we were in the flesh, the [1]motions of sins, which were by the law, did work in our members [e]to bring forth fruit unto death.

6 But now we are delivered from the law, [2]that being dead wherein we were held; that we should serve [f]in newness of spirit, and not *in* the oldness of the letter.

7 What shall we say then? *Is* the law sin? God forbid. Nay, [g]I had not known sin, but by the law: for I had not known

[3]lust, except the law had said, [h]Thou
shalt not covet.
8 But [i]sin, taking occasion by the
commandment, wrought in me all manner of concupiscence. For [j]without the
law sin *was* dead.
9 For I was alive without the law
once: but when the commandment
came, sin revived, and I died.
10 And the commandment, [k]which
was ordained to life, I found *to be* unto
death.
11 For sin, taking occasion by the
commandment, deceived me, and by it
slew *me*.
12 Wherefore [l]the law *is* holy, and
the commandment holy, and just, and
good.
13 Was then that which is good made
death unto me? God forbid. But sin,
that it might appear sin, working death
in me by that which is good; that sin by
the commandment might become exceeding sinful.
14 For we know that the law is spiritual: but I am carnal, [m]sold under sin.
15 For that which I do I [4]allow not:
for [n]what I would, that do I not; but
what I hate, that do I.
16 If then I do that which I would
not, I consent unto the law that *it is*
good.
17 Now then it is no more I that do it,
but sin that dwelleth in me.
18 For I know that [o]in me (that is, in
my flesh,) dwelleth no good thing: for
to will is present with me; but *how* to
perform that which is good I find not.
19 For the good that I would I do
not: but the evil which I would not, that
I do.
20 Now if I do that I would not, it
is no more I that do it, but sin that
dwelleth in me.
21 I find then a law, that, when I
would do good, evil is present with me.
22 For I [p]delight in the law of God
after [q]the inward man:
23 But I see another law in my members, warring against the law of my
mind, and bringing me into captivity to
the law of sin which is in my members.
24 O wretched man that I am! who
shall deliver me from [5]the body of this
death?
25 I thank God through Jē'sus Chrīst
our Lord. So then with the mind I myself serve the law of God; but with the
flesh the law of sin.

8

There *is* therefore now no condemnation to them which are in Chrīst
Jē'sus, who [a]walk not after the flesh,
but after the Spirit.
2 For [b]the law of [c]the Spirit of life in
Chrīst Jē'sus hath made me free from
the law of sin and death.
3 For [d]what the law could not do, in
that it was weak through the flesh,
God sending his own Son in the likeness of sinful flesh, and [1]for sin, condemned sin in the flesh:
4 That the righteousness of the law
might be fulfilled in us, who walk not
after the flesh, but after the Spirit.

[3]Or, concu-
piscence
[h]Ex. 20.17;
Mic. 2.2;
Eph. 5.3
8 [i]ch. 4.15
[j]1 Cor. 15.56
10 [k]Lev. 18.5;
2 Cor. 3.7
12 [l]Ps. 19.8;
1 Tim. 1.8
14 [m]1 Ki.
21.20-25
15 [4]know
[n]Gal. 5.17
18 [o]Gen. 8.21
22 [p]Job
23.12;
Heb. 8.10
[q]2 Cor. 4.16
24 [5]Or, this
body of death
CHAPTER 8
1 [a]Gal. 5.16
2 [b]John 8.36;
Gal. 2.19
[c]1 Cor. 15.45;
2 Cor. 3.6
3 [d]Heb. 7.18
[1]Or, by a sac-
rifice for sin
5 [e]1 Cor.
2.15;
Gal. 5.22
6 [2]the mind-
ing of the
flesh
[3]the minding
of the Spirit
7 [4]the mind-
ing of the
flesh
9 [f]1 Cor. 3.16
[g]John 3.34;
1 Pet. 1.11
11 [h]Isa.
26.19;
Eph. 2.5
[5]Or, because
of his Spirit
13 [i]ch. 6.21-
22;
Gal. 6.8
15 [j]Heb. 2.15
[k]2 Tim. 1.7;
1 John 4.18
[l]Isa. 56.5;
Gal. 4.5-6
16 [m]2 Cor.
1.22;
Eph. 1.13
17 [n]Matt.
25.21;
Gal. 4.7
18 [o]2 Cor.
4.17;
1 Pet. 1.6-7
19 [p]2 Pet.
3.13
[q]1 John 3.2
20 [r]Gen. 3.19
22 [6]Or, every
creature
[s]Jer. 12.11
23 [t]2 Cor. 5.5
[u]Luke 20.36
24 [v]Heb. 11.1

5 For they that are after the flesh do
mind the things of the flesh; but they
that are after the Spirit [e]the things of
the Spirit.
6 For [2]to be carnally minded *is* death;
but [3]to be spiritually minded *is* life and
peace.
7 Because [4]the carnal mind *is* enmity against God: for it is not subject
to the law of God, neither indeed can
be.
8 So then they that are in the flesh
cannot please God.
9 But ye are not in the flesh, but in
the Spirit, if so be that [f]the Spirit of
God dwell in you. Now if any man
have not [g]the Spirit of Chrīst, he is
none of his.
10 And if Chrīst *be* in you, the body
is dead because of sin; but the Spirit *is*
life because of righteousness.
11 But if the Spirit of him that raised
up Jē'sus from the dead dwell in you,
[h]he that raised up Chrīst from the
dead shall also quicken your mortal
bodies [5]by his Spirit that dwelleth in
you.
12 Therefore, brethren, we are debtors, not to the flesh, to live after the
flesh.
13 For [i]if ye live after the flesh, ye
shall die: but if ye through the Spirit do
mortify the deeds of the body, ye shall
live.
14 For as many as are led by the
Spirit of God, they are the sons of God.
15 For [j]ye have not received the
spirit of bondage again [k]to fear; but ye
have received the [l]Spirit of adoption,
whereby we cry, Ăb'bȧ, Father.
16 [m]The Spirit itself beareth witness with our spirit, that we are the
children of God:
17 And if children, then heirs; [n]heirs
of God, and joint-heirs with Chrīst; if so
be that we suffer with *him*, that we may
be also glorified together.
18 For I reckon that [o]the sufferings
of this present time *are* not worthy *to*
be compared with the glory which
shall be revealed in us.
19 For [p]the earnest expectation of
the creature waiteth for the [q]manifes-
tation of the sons of God.
20 For [r]the creature was made subject to vanity, not willingly, but by reason of him who hath subjected *the*
same in hope,
21 Because the creature itself also
shall be delivered from the bondage of
corruption into the glorious liberty of
the children of God.
22 For we know that [6]the whole creation [s]groaneth and travaileth in pain
together until now.
23 And not only *they*, but ourselves
also, which have [t]the firstfruits of the
Spirit, even we ourselves groan within
ourselves, [u]waiting for the adoption,
to wit, the redemption of our body.
24 For we are saved by hope: but
[v]hope that is seen is not hope: for what
a man seeth, why doth he yet hope for?

25 But if we hope for that we see not, *then* do we with patience wait for *it*.

26 Likewise the Spirit also helpeth our infirmities: for [w]we know not what we should pray for as we ought: but [x]the Spirit itself maketh intercession for us with groanings which cannot be uttered.

27 And [y]he that searcheth the hearts knoweth what *is* the mind of the Spirit, [7]because he maketh intercession for the saints [z]according to *the will of* God.

28 And we know that [a]all things work together for good to them that love God, to them [b]who are the called according to *his* purpose.

29 For whom [c]he did foreknow, [d]he also did predestinate [e]*to be* conformed to the image of his Son, [f]that he might be the firstborn among many brethren.

30 Moreover whom he did predestinate, them he also [g]called: and whom he called, them he also justified: [h]and whom he justified, them he also glorified.

31 What shall we then say to these things? If God *be* for us, who *can be* against us?

32 He that spared not his own Son, but delivered him up for us all, how shall he not with him also freely give us all things?

33 Who shall lay any thing to the charge of God's elect? [i]*It is* God that justifieth.

34 Who *is* he that condemneth? *It is* Chrīst that died, yea rather, that is risen again, who is even at the right hand of God, [j]who also maketh intercession for us.

35 Who shall separate us from the love of Chrīst? *shall* tribulation, or distress, or persecution, or famine, or nakedness, or peril, or sword?

36 As it is written, [k]For thy sake we are killed all the day long; we are accounted as sheep for the slaughter.

37 [l]Nay, in all these things we are more than conquerors through him that loved us.

38 For I am persuaded, that neither death, nor life, nor angels, nor [m]principalities, nor powers, nor things present, nor things to come,

39 Nor height, nor depth, nor any other creature, shall [n]be able to separate us from the love of God, which is in Chrīst Jē'sus our Lord.

9 I say the truth in Chrīst, I lie not, my conscience also bearing me witness in the Hō'lȳ Ghōst,

2 That I have great heaviness and continual sorrow in my heart.

3 For [a]I could wish that myself were [1]accursed from Chrīst for my brethren, my kinsmen according to the flesh:

4 [b]Who are Īs'ra-el-ītes; [c]to whom *pertaineth* the adoption, and [d]the glory, and the [2]covenants, and the giving of the law, and the service *of God*, and [e]the promises;

5 Whose *are* the fathers, and of whom as concerning the flesh Chrīst *came*, [f]who is over all, God blessed for ever. Amen.

6 Not as though the word of God hath taken none effect. For [g]they *are* not all Is'ra-el, which are of Is'ra-el:

7 [h]Neither, because they are the seed of Ā'brā-hăm, *are they* all children: but, In [i]Ī'saac shall thy seed be called.

8 That is, They which are the children of the flesh, these *are* not the children of God: but the children of the promise are counted for the seed.

9 For this *is* the word of promise, [j]At this time will I come, and Sā'rah shall have a son.

10 And not only *this;* but when [k]Re-bĕc'că also had conceived by one, *even* by our father Ī'saac;

11 (For *the children* being [l]not yet born, neither having done any good or evil, that the purpose of God according to election might stand, not of works, but of him that calleth;)

12 It was said unto her, The [3]elder shall serve the [4]younger.

13 As it is written, [m]Jā'cob have I loved, but Ē'sau have I hated.

14 What shall we say then? [n]*Is there* unrighteousness with God? God forbid.

15 For he saith to Mō'ses, [o]I will have mercy on whom I will have mercy, and I will have compassion on whom I will have compassion.

16 [p]So then *it is* not of him that willeth, nor of him that runneth, but of God that sheweth mercy.

17 For the scripture saith unto Phā'-raōh, [q]Even for this same purpose have I raised thee up, that I might shew my power in thee, and that my name might be declared throughout all the earth.

18 Therefore hath he mercy on whom he will *have mercy,* and whom he will he hardeneth.

19 Thou wilt say then unto me, Why doth he yet find fault? For [r]who hath resisted his will?

20 Nay but, O man, who art thou that [5][s]repliest against God? [t]Shall the thing formed say to him that formed *it,* Why hast thou made me thus?

21 Hath not the [u]potter power over the clay; of the same lump to make [v]one vessel unto honour, and another unto dishonour?

22 *What* if God, willing to shew *his* wrath, and to make his power known, endured with much longsuffering [w]the vessels of wrath [6]fitted to destruction:

23 And that he might make known the riches of his glory on the vessels of mercy, which he had afore prepared unto glory,

24 Even us, whom he hath called, not of the Jews only, but also of the Gĕn'tīles?

25 As he saith also in Ō'see, [x]I will call them my people, which were not my people; and her beloved, which was not beloved.

26 [y]And it shall come to pass, *that* in the place where it was said unto them, Ye *are* not my people; there shall

26 [w]Matt. 20.22 [x]Zech. 12.10; Eph. 6.18
27 [y]1 Thess. 2.4; Rev. 2.23 [7]Or, that [z]1 John 5.14
28 [a]Gen. 50.20; 2 Cor. 4.17 [b]2 Tim. 1.9
29 [c]Ps. 1.6; 2 Tim. 2.19 [d]Eph. 1.5 [e]John 17.22 [f]Col. 1.18
30 [g]Eph. 4.4; Heb. 9.15 [h]1 Cor. 6.11
33 [i]Isa. 50.8; Gal. 3.8
34 [j]Isa. 53.12; Heb. 7.25
36 [k]Ps. 44.22
37 [l]1 John 5.4
38 [m]Col. 1.16;
39 [n]John 10.28

CHAPTER 9
3 [a]Ex. 32.32 [1]Or, separated
4 [b]Deut. 7.6; [c]Deut. 14.1 [d]Ps. 63.2 [2]Or, testaments [e]Acts 13.32
5 [f]Ps. 45.6
6 [g]Gal. 6.16
7 [h]Gal. 4.23 [i]Gen. 21.12
9 [j]Gen. 17.21
10 [k]Gen. 25.21
11 [l]Eph. 1.4
12 [3]Or, greater [4]Or, lesser
13 [m]Deut. 21.15
14 [n]Gen. 18.25
15 [o]Ex. 33.19
16 [p]Ps. 115.3
17 [q]Ex. 9.16
19 [r]Job 9.12
20 [5]Or, answerest again, or, disputest with God [s]Job 33.13 [t]Isa. 29.16
21 [u]Jer. 18.6 [v]2 Tim. 2.20
22 [w]1 Thess. 5.9 [6]Or, made up
25 [x]Hos. 2.23
26 [y]Hos. 1.10

they be called the children of the living God.

27 E-sā'ias also crieth concerning Is'ra-el, [z]Though the number of the children of Is'ra-el be as the sand of the sea, a remnant shall be saved:

28 For he will finish [7]the work, and cut *it* short in righteousness: [a]because a short work will the Lord make upon the earth.

29 And as E-sā'ias said before, [b]Except the Lord of Săb'a-ŏth had left us a seed, [c]we had been as Sŏd'om-ȧ, and been made like unto Go-mŏr'rhȧ.

30 What shall we say then? That the Gĕn'tīles, which followed not after righteousness, have attained to righteousness, even the righteousness which is of faith.

31 But Is'ra-el, which followed after the law of righteousness, [d]hath not attained to the law of righteousness.

32 Wherefore? Because *they sought it* not by faith, but as it were by the works of the law. For [e]they stumbled at that stumblingstone;

33 As it is written, [f]Behold, I lay in Sī'ŏn a stumblingstone and rock of offence: and whosoever believeth on him shall not be [8]ashamed.

10 Brethren, my heart's desire and prayer to God for Is'ra-el is, that they might be saved.

2 For I bear them record [a]that they have a zeal of God, but not according to knowledge.

3 For they being ignorant of [b]God's righteousness, and going about to establish their own [c]righteousness, have not [d]submitted themselves unto the righteousness of God.

4 For [e]Chrīst *is* the end of the law for righteousness to every one that believeth.

5 For Mō'ses describeth the righteousness which is of the law, [f]That the man which doeth those things shall live by them.

6 But the righteousness which is of faith speaketh on this wise, [g]Say not in thine heart, Who shall ascend into heaven? (that is, to bring [h]Chrīst down *from above*:)

7 Or, Who shall descend into the deep? (that is, to [i]bring up Chrīst again from the dead.)

8 But what saith it? The word is nigh thee, *even* in thy mouth, and in thy heart: that is, the word of faith, which we preach;

9 That if thou shalt confess with thy mouth the Lord Jē'sus, and shalt believe in thine heart that God hath raised him from the dead, thou shalt be saved.

10 For with the heart man believeth unto righteousness; and with the mouth confession is made unto salvation.

11 For the scripture saith, [j]Whosoever believeth on him shall not be ashamed.

12 For [k]there is no difference between the Jew and the Greek: for [l]the same Lord over all [m]is rich unto all that call upon him.

13 [n]For whosoever shall call upon the name of the Lord shall be saved.

14 How then shall they call on him in whom they have not believed? and how shall they believe in him of whom they have not heard? and how shall they hear without [o]a preacher?

15 And how shall they preach, except they be sent? as it is written, [p]How beautiful are the feet of them that preach the gospel of peace, and bring glad tidings of good things!

16 But [q]they have not all obeyed the gospel. For E-sā'ias saith, [r]Lord, who hath believed [1]our [2]report?

17 So then faith *cometh* by hearing, and hearing by the word of God.

18 But I say, Have they not heard? Yes verily, [s]their sound went into all the earth, and their words unto the ends of the world.

19 But I say, Did not Is'ra-el know? First Mō'ses saith, [t]I will provoke you to jealousy by *them that are* no people, *and* by a [u]foolish nation I will anger you.

20 But E-sā'ias is very bold, and saith, [v]I was found of them that sought me not; I was made manifest unto them that asked not after me.

21 But to Is'ra-el he saith, All day long I have stretched forth my hands unto a disobedient and gainsaying people.

11 I say then, [a]Hath God cast away his people? God forbid. For [b]I also am an Ĭs'ra-el-īte, of the seed of Ā'bră-hăm, *of* the tribe of Bĕn'ja-min.

2 God hath not cast away his people which [c]he foreknew. Wot ye not what the scripture saith [1]of E-lī'ăs? how he maketh intercession to God against Is'ra-el, saying,

3 [d]Lord, they have killed thy prophets, and digged down thine altars; and I am left alone, and they seek my life.

4 But what saith the answer of God unto him? I have reserved to myself seven thousand men, who have not bowed the knee to *the image of* Bā'al.

5 [e]Even so then at this present time also there is a remnant according to the election of grace.

6 And [f]if by grace, then *is it* no more of works: otherwise grace is no more grace. But if *it be* of works, then is it no more grace: otherwise work is no more work.

7 What then? [g]Is'ra-el hath not obtained that which he seeketh for; but the [h]election hath obtained it, and the rest were [2][i]blinded

8 (According as it is written, [j]God hath given them the spirit of [3]slumber, [k]eyes that they should not see, and ears that they should not hear;) unto this day.

9 And Dā'vid saith, [l]Let their table be made a snare, and a trap, and a stumblingblock, and a recompence unto them:

10 Let their eyes be darkened, that they may not see, and bow down their back alway.

27 [z]Isa. 10.22
28 [7]Or, the account
[a]Isa. 28.22
29 [b]Isa. 1.9; Lam. 3.22
[c]Isa. 13.19
31 [d]Gal. 5.4
32 [e]Luke 2.34; 1 Cor. 1.23
33 [f]Ps. 118.22; 1 Pet. 2.6-8
[8]Or, confounded

CHAPTER 10
2 [a]2 Ki. 10.16; Phil. 3.6
3 [b]Ps. 71.15-16-19; 2 Pet. 1.1
[c]Phil. 3.9
[d]Heb. 10.29
4 [e]Matt. 5.17; Gal. 3.24
5 [f]Lev. 18.5
6 [g]Deut. 30.12
[h]Heb. 8.1
7 [i]ch. 4.25; Rev. 1.18
11 [j]Isa. 28.16
12 [k]Acts 15.9
[l]Acts 10.36
[m]Eph. 1.7
13 [n]Joel 2.32
14 [o]Tit. 1.3
15 [p]Isa. 52.7
16 [q]Heb. 4.2
[r]John 12.38
[1]the hearing of us
[2]Or, preaching
18 [s]Ps. 19.4
19 [t]Deut. 32.21
[u]Tit. 3.3
20 [v]Isa. 65.1

CHAPTER 11
1 [a]1 Sam. 12.22;
[b]Acts 22.3
2 [c]ch. 8.29
[1]in Elias
3 [d]1 Ki. 19.10
5 [e]ch. 9.27
6 [f]Deut. 9.4-5
7 [g]ch. 10.3
[h]John 10.28;
[2]Or, hardened
[i]2 Cor. 3.14
8 [j]Isa. 29.10;
[3]Or, remorse
[k]Deut. 29.4
9 [l]Ps. 69.22

11 I say then, Have they stumbled that they [m]should fall? God forbid: but *rather* [n]through their fall salvation *is come* unto the Gĕn'tīles, for to provoke them to jealousy.

12 Now if the fall of them *be* the riches of the world, and the [4]diminishing of them the riches of the Gĕn'tīles; how much more their [o]fulness?

13 For I speak to you Gĕn'tīles, inasmuch as [p]I am the apostle of the Gĕn'tīles, I magnify mine office:

14 If by any means I may provoke to emulation *them which are* my flesh, and [q]might save some of them.

15 For if the casting away of them *be* the reconciling of the world, what *shall* the receiving *of them be,* but life from the dead?

16 For if [r]the firstfruit *be* holy, the lump *is* also *holy:* and if the root *be* holy, so *are* the branches.

17 And if [s]some of the branches be broken off, [t]and thou, being a wild olive tree, wert graffed in [5]among them, and with them partakest of the root and fatness of the olive tree;

18 [u]Boast not against the branches. But if thou boast, thou bearest not the root, but the root thee.

19 Thou wilt say then, The branches were broken off, that I might be graffed in.

20 Well; because of unbelief they were broken off, and thou standest by faith. [v]Be not highminded, but [w]fear:

21 For if God spared not the natural branches, *take heed* lest he also spare not thee.

22 Behold therefore the goodness and severity of God: on them which fell, severity; but toward thee, goodness, [x]if thou continue in *his* goodness: otherwise [y]thou also shalt be cut off.

23 And they also, [z]if they abide not still in unbelief, shall be graffed in: for God is able to graff them in again.

24 For if thou wert cut out of the olive tree which is wild by nature, and wert graffed contrary to nature into a good olive tree: how much more shall these, which be the natural *branches,* be graffed into their own olive tree?

25 For I would not, brethren, that ye should be ignorant of this mystery, lest ye should be wise in your own conceits; that [6]blindness in part is happened to Is'ra-el, [a]until the fulness of the Gĕn'tīles be come in.

26 And so [b]all Is'ra-el shall be saved: as it is written, [c]There shall come out of Sī'ŏn the Deliverer, and shall turn away ungodliness from Jā'cob:

27 [d]For this *is* my covenant unto them, when I shall take away their sins.

28 As concerning the gospel, *they are* enemies for your sakes: but as touching the election, *they are* [e]beloved for the fathers' sakes.

29 For the gifts and calling of God *are* [f]without repentance.

30 For as ye in times past have not [7]believed God, yet have now obtained mercy through their unbelief:

31 Even so have these also now not [8]believed, that through your mercy they also may obtain mercy.

32 For God hath [9]concluded them all in unbelief, that he might have mercy upon all.

33 O the depth of the riches both of the wisdom and knowledge of God! how unsearchable *are* his judgments, and his ways past finding out!

34 [g]For who hath known the mind of the Lord? or who hath been his counsellor?

35 Or [h]who hath first given to him, and it shall be recompensed unto him again?

36 For of him, and through him, and to him, *are* all things: to whom *be* glory for ever. Amen.

12 I beseech you therefore, brethren, by the mercies of God, that ye [a]present your bodies [b]a living sacrifice, holy, acceptable unto God, *which is* your reasonable service.

2 And [c]be not conformed to this world: but [d]be ye transformed by the renewing of your mind, that ye may [e]prove what *is* that good, and acceptable, and perfect, will of God.

3 For I say, through the grace given unto me, to every man that is among you, not to think *of himself* more highly than he ought to think; but to think [1]soberly, according as God hath dealt [f]to every man the measure of faith.

4 For as we have many members in one body, and all members have not the same office:

5 So [g]we, *being* many, are one body in Chrīst, and every one members one of another.

6 [h]Having then gifts differing [i]according to the grace that is given to us, whether prophecy, *let us prophesy* according to the proportion of faith;

7 Or ministry, *let us wait* on *our* ministering: or [j]he that teacheth, on teaching;

8 Or [k]he that exhorteth, on exhortation: he that [2]giveth, *let him do it* [3]with simplicity; [l]he that ruleth, with diligence; he that sheweth mercy, with cheerfulness.

9 *Let* love be without dissimulation. [m]Abhor that which is evil; cleave to that which is good.

10 *Be* kindly affectioned one to another [4]with brotherly love; in honour preferring one another;

11 Not slothful in business; [n]fervent in spirit; serving the Lord;

12 [o]Rejoicing in hope; [p]patient in tribulation; continuing instant in prayer;

13 [q]Distributing to the necessity of saints; [r]given to hospitality.

14 [s]Bless them which persecute you: bless, and curse not.

15 Rejoice with them that do rejoice, and weep with them that weep.

16 *Be* of the same mind one toward another. Mind not high things, but [5]condescend to men of low estate. Be not wise in your own conceits.

11 [m]Ezek. 18.23
[n]Acts 13.46
12 [4]Or, decay, or, loss
[o]Isa. 11.11-12-16
13 [p]Acts 9.15
14 [q]1 Cor. 7.16
16 [r]Lev. 23.10
17 [s]Jer. 11.16
[t]Eph. 2.12
[5]Or, for them
18 [u]1 Cor. 10.12
20 [v]ch. 12.16
[w]Phil. 2.12
22 [x]1 Cor. 15.2;
[y]John 15.2
23 [z]2 Cor. 3.16
25 [6]hardness
[a]Luke 21.24
26 [b]Isa. 60.15;
[c]Ps. 14.7
27 [d]Jer. 31.31
28 [e]Deut. 9.5
29 [f]Num. 23.19
30 [7]Or, obeyed
31 [8]Or, obeyed
32 [9]Or, shut them all up together
34 [g]Isa. 40.13
35 [h]Job 35.7

CHAPTER 12
1 [a]1 Cor. 6.13
[b]Heb. 10.20
2 [c]John 7.7;
[d]Eph. 1.18;
[e]Eph. 5.10-17
3 [1]to sobriety
[f]1 Cor. 12.7
5 [g]Eph. 1.23
6 [h]1 Cor. 12.4-11;
[i]1 Cor. 12.10
7 [j]Gal. 6.6
8 [k]Acts 15.32;
[2]Or, imparteth
[3]Or, liberally
[l]Acts 20.28
9 [m]Amos 5.15
10 [4]Or, in the love of the brethren
11 [n]Rev. 3.15
12 [o]Heb. 3.6
[p]Heb. 10.36
13 [q]Heb. 6.10
[r]Heb. 13.2
14 [s]1 Pet. 3.9
16 [5]Or, be contented with mean things

17 Recompense to no man evil for evil. Provide things honest in the sight of all men.

18 If it be possible, as much as lieth in you, live peaceably with all men.

19 Dearly beloved, avenge not yourselves, but *rather* give place unto wrath: for it is written, [t]Vengeance *is* mine; I will repay, saith the Lord.

20 [u]Therefore if thine enemy hunger, feed him; if he thirst, give him drink: for in so doing thou shalt heap coals of fire on his head.

21 [v]Be not overcome of evil, but overcome evil with good.

13 Let every soul [a]be subject unto the higher powers. For [b]there is no power but of God: the powers that be are [1]ordained of God.

2 Whosoever therefore resisteth the power, resisteth the ordinance of God: and they that resist shall receive to themselves damnation.

3 [c]For rulers are not a terror to good works, but to the evil. Wilt thou then not be afraid of the power? [d]do that which is good, and thou shalt have praise of the same:

4 For he is the minister of God to thee for good. But if thou do that which is evil, be afraid; for he beareth not the sword in vain: for he is the minister of God, a revenger to *execute* wrath upon him that doeth evil.

5 Wherefore [e]*ye* must needs be subject, not only for wrath, but also for conscience sake.

6 For for this cause pay ye tribute also: for they are God's ministers, attending continually upon this very thing.

7 [f]Render therefore to all their dues: tribute to whom tribute *is due;* custom to whom custom; [g]fear to whom fear; honour to whom honour.

8 Owe no man any thing, but to love one another: for [h]he that loveth another hath fulfilled the law.

9 For this, Thou shalt not commit adultery, Thou shalt not kill, Thou shalt not steal, Thou shalt not bear false witness, Thou shalt not covet; and if *there be* any other commandment, it is briefly comprehended in this saying, namely, [i]Thou shalt love thy neighbour as thyself.

10 Love worketh no ill to his neighbour: therefore love *is* the fulfilling of the law.

11 And that, knowing the time, that now *it is* high time [j]to awake out of sleep: for now *is* our salvation nearer than when we believed.

12 The night is far spent, the day is at hand: let us therefore cast off the works of darkness, and [k]let us put on the armour of light.

13 [l]Let us walk [2]honestly, as in the day; not in rioting and drunkenness, not in chambering and wantonness, [m]not in strife and envying.

14 But [n]put ye on the Lord Jē'sus Chrīst, and [o]make not provision for the flesh, to *fulfil* the lusts *thereof.*

19 [t]Deut. 32.35
20 [u]Prov. 25.21
21 [v]1 Pet. 2.21

CHAPTER 13
1 [a]1 Cor. 7.21; Tit. 3.1
[b]Prov. 8.15; John 19.11
[1]Or, ordered
3 [c]2 Sam. 23.3; Ps. 94.20
[d]1 Pet. 3.13
5 [e]Eccl. 8.2
7 [f]Luke 20.25
[g]Lev. 19.3; Eph. 6.5
8 [h]Matt. 7.12
9 [i]Lev. 19.18; Gal. 5.14
11 [j]1 Cor. 15.34
12 [k]Eph. 6.13
13 [l]Phil. 4.8
[2]Or, decently
[m]Phil. 2.3; 1 Pet. 2.1-2
14 [n]Gal. 3.27
[o]Gal. 5.16

CHAPTER 14
1 [a]Job 4.3; Matt. 12.20
[1]Or, not to judge his doubtful thoughts
2 [b]1 Cor. 10.25
3 [c]Col. 2.16
4 [d]1 Cor. 4.4-5
5 [e]Gal. 4.10
[2]Or, fully assured
6 [3]Or, observeth
[f]1 Cor. 10.31
7 [g]1 Cor. 6.19
9 [h]2 Cor. 5.15
[i]Acts 10.36
10 [j]Matt. 25.31
11 [k]Isa. 45.23
12 [l]Matt. 12.36
13 [m]1 Cor. 8.9
14 [n]Tit. 1.15
[4]common
[o]1 Cor. 8.7
[5]common
15 [6]according to charity
16 [p]ch. 12.17
17 [q]1 Cor. 8.8
18 [r]2 Cor. 8.21
19 [s]Ps. 34.14
[t]1 Cor. 14.12
20 [u]Acts 10.15

14 Him that [a]is weak in the faith receive ye, *but* [1]not to doubtful disputations.

2 For one believeth that he [b]may eat all things: another, who is weak, eateth herbs.

3 Let not him that eateth despise him that eateth not; and [c]let not him which eateth not judge him that eateth: for God hath received him.

4 [d]Who art thou that judgest another man's servant? to his own master he standeth or falleth. Yea, he shall be holden up: for God is able to make him stand.

5 [e]One man esteemeth one day above another: another esteemeth every day *alike.* Let every man be [2]fully persuaded in his own mind.

6 He that [3]regardeth the day, regardeth *it* unto the Lord; and he that regardeth not the day, to the Lord he doth not regard *it.* He that eateth, eateth to the Lord, for [f]he giveth God thanks; and he that eateth not, to the Lord he eateth not, and giveth God thanks.

7 For [g]none of us liveth to himself, and no man dieth to himself.

8 For whether we live, we live unto the Lord; and whether we die, we die unto the Lord: whether we live therefore, or die, we are the Lord's.

9 For [h]to this end Chrīst both died, and rose, and revived, that he might be [i]Lord both of the dead and living.

10 But why dost thou judge thy brother? or why dost thou set at nought thy brother? for [j]we shall all stand before the judgment seat of Chrīst.

11 For it is written, [k]*As* I live, saith the Lord, every knee shall bow to me, and every tongue shall confess to God.

12 So then [l]every one of us shall give account of himself to God.

13 Let us not therefore judge one another any more: but judge this rather, that [m]no man put a stumblingblock or an occasion to fall in *his* brother's way.

14 I know, and am persuaded by the Lord Jē'sus, [n]that *there is* nothing [4]unclean of itself: but [o]to him that esteemeth any thing to be [5]unclean, to him *it is* unclean.

15 But if thy brother be grieved with *thy* meat, now walkest thou not [6]charitably. Destroy not him with thy meat, for whom Chrīst died.

16 [p]Let not then your good be evil spoken of:

17 [q]For the kingdom of God is not meat and drink; but righteousness, and peace, and joy in the Hō'lȳ Ghōst.

18 For he that in these things serveth Chrīst [r]*is* acceptable to God, and approved of men.

19 [s]Let us therefore follow after the things which make for peace, and things wherewith [t]one may edify another.

20 For meat destroy not the work of God. [u]All things indeed *are* pure; but *it is* evil for that man who eateth with offence.

21 *It is* good neither to eat flesh, nor
to drink wine, nor *any thing* whereby
thy brother stumbleth, or is offended,
or is made weak.
22 Hast thou faith? have *it* to thyself
before God. Happy *is* he that condemneth not himself in that thing which he
alloweth.
23 And he that [7]doubteth is damned
if he eat, because *he eateth* not of faith:
for [v]whatsoever *is* not of faith is sin.
15 We [a]then that are strong ought
to bear the [b]infirmities of the
weak, and not to please ourselves.
2 [c]Let every one of us please *his*
neighbour for *his* good [d]to edification.
3 For even Chrīst pleased not himself; but, as it is written, [e]The reproaches of them that reproached thee
fell on me.
4 For [f]whatsoever things were written aforetime were written for our
learning, that we through patience and
comfort of the scriptures might have
hope.
5 [g]Now the God of patience and consolation grant you to be likeminded one
toward another [1]according to Chrīst
Jē'sus:
6 That ye may with one mind *and*
one mouth glorify God, even the Father of our Lord Jē'sus Chrīst.
7 Wherefore receive ye one another,
[h]as Chrīst also received us to the glory
of God.
8 Now I say that [i]Jē'sus Chrīst was
a minister of the circumcision for the
truth of God, [j]to confirm the promises
made unto the fathers:
9 And [k]that the Gĕn'tīles might glorify God for *his* mercy; as it is written,
[l]For this cause I will confess to thee
among the Gĕn'tīles, and sing unto thy
name.
10 And again he saith, [m]Rejoice, ye
Gĕn'tīles, with his people.
11 And again, [n]Praise the Lord, all
ye Gĕn'tīles; and laud him, all ye
people.
12 And again, E-sā'ias saith, [o]There
shall be a root of Jĕs'se, and he that
shall rise to reign over the Gĕn'tīles; in
him shall the Gĕn'tīles trust.
13 Now the God of hope fill you with
all joy and peace in believing, that
ye may abound in hope, through the
power of the Hō'lȳ Ghōst.
14 And [p]I myself also am persuaded
of you, my brethren, that ye also are full
of goodness, [q]filled with all knowledge,
able also to admonish one another.
15 Nevertheless, brethren, I have
written the more boldly unto you in
some sort, as putting you in mind, [r]be-
cause of the grace that is given to me of
God,
16 That [s]I should be the minister of
Jē'sus Chrīst to the Gĕn'tīles, ministering the gospel of God, that the [2]offer-
ing up of the Gĕn'tīles might be acceptable, being sanctified by the Hō'lȳ
Ghōst.
17 I have therefore whereof I may
glory through Jē'sus Chrīst in [t]those
things which pertain to God.
18 For I will not dare to speak of any
of those things [u]which Chrīst hath not
wrought by me, [v]to make the Gĕn'tīles
obedient, by word and deed,
19 [w]Through mighty signs and wonders, by the power of the Spirit of God;
so that from Je-ru'sa-lĕm, and round
about unto Ĭl-lȳr'ĭ-cŭm, I have fully
preached the gospel of Chrīst.
20 Yea, so have I strived to preach
the gospel, not where Chrīst was
named, [x]lest I should build upon another man's foundation:
21 But as it is written, [y]To whom
he was not spoken of, they shall see:
and they that have not heard shall
understand.
22 For which cause also [z]I have
been [3]much hindered from coming to
you.
23 But now having no more place in
these parts, and [a]having a great desire
these many years to come unto you;
24 Whensoever I take my journey
into Spāin, I will come to you: for I
trust to see you in my journey, [b]and to
be brought on my way thitherward by
you, if first I be somewhat filled [4]with
your *company*.
25 But now [c]I go unto Je-ru'sa-lĕm
to minister unto the saints.
26 For [d]it hath pleased them of Măç-
e-dō'nĭ-ȧ and A-chā'iȧ to make a certain contribution for the poor saints
which are at Je-ru'sa-lĕm.
27 It hath pleased them verily; and
their debtors they are. For if the Gĕn'-
tīles have been made partakers of their
spiritual things, [e]their duty is also to
minister unto them in carnal things.
28 When therefore I have performed
this, and have sealed to them [f]this fruit,
I will come by you into Spāin.
29 [g]And I am sure that, when I come
unto you, I shall come in the [h]fulness
of the blessing of the gospel of Chrīst.
30 Now I beseech you, brethren, for
the Lord Jē'sus Chrīst's sake, and [i]for
the love of the Spirit, [j]that ye strive
together with me in *your* prayers to
God for me;
31 [k]That I may be delivered from
them that [5]do not believe in Jū-dæ'ȧ;
and that my service which *I have* for
Je-ru'sa-lĕm may be accepted of the
saints;
32 That I may come unto you with
joy [l]by the will of God, and may with
you be [m]refreshed.
33 Now the God of peace *be* with
you all. Amen.
16 I commend unto you Phē'be our
sister, which is a servant of the
church which is at [a]Çĕn'chrĕ-ȧ:
2 [b]That ye receive her in the Lord,
as becometh saints, and that ye assist
her in whatsoever business she hath
need of you: for she hath been a suc-
courer of many, and of myself also.
3 Greet [c]Prĭs-çĭl'lȧ and Ā'quĭ-lȧ my
helpers in Chrīst Jē'sus:
4 Who have for my life laid down
their own necks: unto whom not only I

23 [7]Or, discerneth and putteth a difference between meats; or, staggers [v]Tit. 1.15
CHAPTER 15
1 [a]Gal. 6.1 [b]ch. 14.1
2 [c]Phil. 2.4-5 [d]ch. 14.19
3 [e]Ps. 69.9
4 [f]2 Tim. 3.16
5 [g]Ex. 34.6; [1]Or, after the example of
7 [h]ch. 5.2
8 [i]Matt. 15.24; [j]ch. 3.3;
9 [k]John 10.16; [l]Ps. 18.49
10 [m]Deut. 32.43
11 [n]Ps. 117.1
12 [o]Isa. 9.6-7
14 [p]2 Pet. 1.12; [q]1 Cor. 8.1
15 [r]Isa. 49.1-5
16 [s]Gal. 2.7-9 [2]Or, sacrificing
17 [t]Heb. 5.1
18 [u]Acts 14.27; [v]Mark 16.20
19 [w]Acts 1.8
20 [x]2 Cor. 10.13
21 [y]Isa. 52.15
22 [z]ch. 1.13 [3]Or, many ways, or, oftentimes
23 [a]Acts 19.21
24 [b]Acts 15.3 [4]with you
25 [c]Acts 24.17
26 [d]1 Cor. 16.1
27 [e]1 Cor. 9.11
28 [f]Phil. 4.17
29 [g]ch. 1.11 [h]Eph. 3.8
30 [i]Phil. 2.1 [j]2 Cor. 1.11
31 [k]2 Thess. 3.2 [5]Or, are disobedient
32 [l]Jas. 4.15 [m]2 Cor. 7.13
CHAPTER 16
1 [a]Acts 18.18
2 [b]Matt. 25.40
3 [c]Acts 18.2

give thanks, but also all the churches
of the Gĕn'tīles.
5 Likewise *greet* [d]the church that is
in their house. Salute my wellbeloved
E-pæ̆n'e-tus, who is [e]the firstfruits of
A-chā'iȧ unto Chrīst.
6 Greet Mā'rȳ, who [f]bestowed much
labour on us.
7 Salute Ăn-dro-nī'cus and Jū'nĭȧ,
my kinsmen, and my fellowprisoners,
who are of note among the apostles,
who also [g]were in Chrīst before me.
8 Greet Ăm'plĭ-as my beloved in the
Lord.
9 Salute Ur'bane, our helper in
Chrīst, and Stā'chȳs my beloved.
10 Salute A-pĕl'les approved in
Chrīst. Salute them which are of Ăr-ĭs-
tŏ-bū'lus' [1]*household.*
11 Salute He-rō'dĭ-on my kinsman.
Greet them that be of the [2]*household* of
När-çĭs'sus, which are in the Lord.
12 Salute Trȳ-phē'nȧ and Trȳ-phō'-
sȧ, who labour in the Lord. Salute the
beloved Pĕr'sis, which laboured much
in the Lord.
13 Salute Ru̧'fus [h]chosen in the Lord,
and his mother and mine.
14 Salute A-sȳn'crĭ-tus, Phlē'gon,
Hĕr'mas, Păt'ro-băs, Hĕr'mēs, and the
brethren which are with them.
15 Salute Phĭ-lŏl'o-gus, and Jū'liȧ,
Nē're-us, and his sister, and O-lȳm'-
pas, and all the saints which are with
them.
16 [i]Salute one another with an holy
kiss. The churches of Chrīst salute
you.
17 Now I beseech you, brethren,
mark them [j]which cause divisions and
offences contrary to the doctrine which
ye have learned; and [k]avoid them.
18 For they that are such serve not
our Lord Jē'sus Chrīst, but [l]their own
belly; and [m]by good words and fair
speeches deceive the hearts of the
simple.
19 For your obedience is come
abroad unto all *men.* I am glad therefore on your behalf: but yet I would
have you [n]wise unto that which is
good, and [3]simple concerning evil.
20 And the God of peace shall [4]bruise
Sā'tan under your feet shortly. The
grace of our Lord Jē'sus Chrīst *be* with
you. Amen.
21 [o]Ti-mō'the-ŭs my workfellow,
and [p]Lu̧'çius, and [q]Jā'son, and [r]So-
sĭp'a-tĕr, my kinsmen, salute you.
22 I Tĕr'tius, who wrote *this* epistle,
salute you in the Lord.
23 Gā'ius [s]mine host, and of the
whole church, saluteth you. [t]E-răs'tus
the chamberlain of the city saluteth
you, and Quär'tus a brother.
24 [u]The grace of our Lord Jē'sus
Chrīst *be* with you all. Amen.
25 Now to him that is of power to
stablish you [v]according to my gospel,
and the preaching of Jē'sus Chrīst,
[w]according to the revelation of the
mystery, [x]which was kept secret since
the world began,
26 But [y]now is made manifest, and
by the scriptures of the prophets, according to the commandment of the
everlasting God, made known to all nations for the obedience of faith:
27 To God only wise, *be* glory
through Jē'sus Chrīst for ever. Amen.

5 [d]1 Cor. 16.19; Col. 4.15; [e]1 Cor. 16.15
6 [f]1 Tim. 5.10
7 [g]Gal. 1.22
10 [1]Or, friends
11 [2]Or, friends
13 [h]Eph. 1.4
16 [i]1 Thess. 5.26
17 [j]Acts 15; Phil. 3.2; Col. 2.8; [k]1 Cor. 5.9
18 [l]Isa. 56.10-12; [m]Col. 2.4; 2 Pet. 2.3
19 [n]Matt. 10.16 [3]Or, harmless
20 [4]Or, tread
21 [o]Acts 16.1; [p]Acts 13.1 [q]Acts 17.5 [r]Acts 20.4
23 [s]1 Cor. 1.14 [t]Acts 19.22; 2 Tim. 4.20
24 [u]1 Thess. 5.28
25 [v]ch. 2.16 [w]Eph. 3.3-5; Col. 1.27; [x]1 Cor. 2.7
26 [y]2 Tim. 1.10

THE FIRST LETTER OF PAUL TO THE

CORINTHIANS

Life's Questions

Why do members of my church not agree with one another?
Does God expect me to have total faithfulness in marriage?
Am I supposed to have a spiritual gift?

God's Answers

About A.D. 55 God led Paul to answer questions the church at Corinth was raising and to deal with problems the church faced. Paul dealt strongly with factions in the church, immorality, differences of opinion about worship and morals, doubts about the resurrection, and questions about spiritual gifts.

Paul taught: the church should be unified around the message of the cross (1—4); believers are free and called to reject all temptations to immorality (5—6); both devotion to marriage and celibacy are Christian callings (ch. 7); Christian freedom is no excuse to cause others to disobey what they think God wants (8:1—11:1); worship with wrong motives and actions can bring God's judgment (11:2—34); spiritual gifts are given to honor Christ, unify the church in ministry, show Christ's love, and bring order to worship (12—14); the resurrection of Christ is essential to Christian faith and the guarantee of personal resurrection (ch. 15); be faithful in helping the poor and in serving Christ (ch. 16).

First Corinthians calls you to exercise your spiritual gifts in love for Christ and His church so the church can give a unified witness to an unbelieving world.

1 Paul, called *to be* an apostle of
Jē'sus Chrīst through the will of
God, and [a]Sŏs'the-nēs *our* brother,
2 Unto the church of God which is at
Cŏr'inth, to them that [b]are sanctified
in Chrīst Jē'sus, [c]called *to be* saints,
with all that in every place call upon
the name of Jē'sus Chrīst [d]our Lord,
[e]both theirs and ours:
3 Grace *be* unto you, and peace,
from God our Father, and *from* the
Lord Jē'sus Chrīst.

CHAPTER 1
1 [a]Acts 18.17
2 [b]John 17.19; [c]Rom. 1.7; [d]ch. 8.6 [e]Rom. 3.22

4 I thank my God always on your
behalf, for the grace of God which is
given you by Jē'sus Chrīst;
5 That in every thing ye are enriched by him, [f]in all utterance, and *in*
all knowledge;
6 Even as [g]the testimony of Chrīst
was confirmed in you:
7 So that ye come behind in no gift;
waiting for the [1]coming of our Lord
Jē'sus Chrīst:
8 [h]Who shall also confirm you unto
the end, [i]*that ye may be* blameless in
the day of our Lord Jē'sus Chrīst.
9 [j]God *is* faithful, by whom ye were
called unto [k]the fellowship of his Son
Jē'sus Chrīst our Lord.
10 Now I beseech you, brethren, by
the name of our Lord Jē'sus Chrīst,
that ye all speak the same thing, and
that there be no [2]divisions among you;
but *that* ye be perfectly joined together in the same mind and in the
same judgment.
11 For it hath been declared unto me
of you, my brethren, by them *which
are of the house* of Chlō'e, that there
are contentions among you.
12 Now this I say, [l]that every one of
you saith, I am of Pa̤ul; and I of [m]A-
pŏl'los; and I of [n]Çē'phas; and I of
Chrīst.
13 [o]Is Chrīst divided? was Pa̤ul crucified for you? or were ye baptized in
the name of Pa̤ul?
14 I thank God that I baptized none
of you, but [p]Crĭs'pus [q]and Gā'ius;
15 Lest any should say that I had
baptized in mine own name.
16 And I baptized also the household of [r]Stĕph'a-năs: besides, I know
not whether I baptized any other.
17 [s]For Chrīst sent me not to baptize, but to preach the gospel: not with
wisdom of [3]words, lest the cross of
Chrīst should be made of none effect.
18 For the preaching of the cross
is to [t]them that perish [u]foolishness;
but unto us which are saved it is the
[v]power of God.
19 For it is written, [w]I will destroy
the wisdom of the wise, and will bring
to nothing the understanding of the
prudent.
20 [x]Where *is* the wise? where *is* the
scribe? where *is* the disputer of this
world? hath [y]not God made foolish the
wisdom of this world?
21 [z]For after that in the wisdom of
God the world by wisdom knew not
God, it pleased God by the foolishness
of preaching to save them that believe.
22 For the [a]Jews require a sign, and
the Greeks seek after wisdom:
23 But we preach Chrīst crucified,
[b]unto the Jews a stumblingblock, and
unto the Greeks foolishness;
24 But unto them which are called,
both Jews and Greeks, Chrīst [c]the
power of God, and [d] the wisdom of
God.
25 [e]Because the foolishness of God
is wiser than men; and the weakness of
God is stronger than men.

5 [f]2 Cor. 8.7
6 [g]Acts 18.5; ch. 2.1-2
7 [1]revelation
8 [h]2 Thess. 3.3
[i]1 Thess. 5.23
9 [j]Num. 23.19; Heb. 10.23
[k]John 15.4
10 [2]schisms
12 [l]ch. 3.4
[m]Acts 18.24
[n]John 1.42
13 [o]2 Cor. 11.4
14 [p]Acts 18.8
[q]Rom. 16.23
16 [r]ch. 16.15
17 [s]Acts 26.17
[3]Or, speech
18 [t]2 Cor. 2.15
[u]Acts 17.18
[v]Rom. 1.16
19 [w]Isa. 29.14
20 [x]Isa. 33.18
[y]2 Sam. 15.31; Rom. 1.22
21 [z]Luke 10.21
22 [a]Luke 11.16
23 [b]Isa. 8.14; Matt. 11.6
24 [c]Rom. 1.4
[d]Col. 2.3
25 [e]2 Cor. 4.7
26 [f]John 7.48
27 [g]Ps. 8.2; Matt. 11.25
28 [h]Rom. 4.17
[i]ch. 2.6
31 [j]Jer. 9.23

CHAPTER 2
1 [a]ch. 1.17
2 [b]Gal. 6.14; Phil. 3.8
3 [c]Acts 18.1
[d]2 Cor. 10.1
4 [e]2 Pet. 1.16
[1]Or, persuasible
5 [2]be
[f]2 Cor. 4.7
6 [g]Eph. 4.13
7 [h]Rom. 16.25
8 [i]Acts 13.27
9 [j]Isa. 64.4
10 [k]Matt. 16.17
11 [l]Jer. 17.9
[m]Rom. 11.33
12 [n]Rom. 8.15
13 [o]2 Pet. 1.16
14 [p]Matt. 16.23

26 For ye see your calling, brethren,
how that [f]not many wise men after the
flesh, not many mighty, not many noble, *are called:*
27 But [g]God hath chosen the foolish
things of the world to confound the
wise; and God hath chosen the weak
things of the world to confound the
things which are mighty;
28 And base things of the world, and
things which are despised, hath God
chosen, *yea,* and [h]things which are
not, [i]to bring to nought things that are:
29 That no flesh should glory in his
presence.
30 But of him are ye in Chrīst Jē'sus,
who of God is made unto us wisdom,
and righteousness, and sanctification,
and redemption:
31 That, according as it is written,
[j]He that glorieth, let him glory in the
Lord.

2 And I, brethren, when I came to
you, [a]came not with excellency of
speech or of wisdom, declaring unto
you the testimony of God.
2 For I determined not to know any
thing among you, [b]save Jē'sus Chrīst,
and him crucified.
3 And [c]I was with you [d]in weakness,
and in fear, and in much trembling.
4 And my speech and my preaching
[e]*was* not with [1]enticing words of man's
wisdom, but in demonstration of the
Spirit and of power:
5 That your faith should not [2]stand
in the wisdom of men, but [f]in the
power of God.
6 Howbeit we speak wisdom among
them [g]that are perfect: yet not the wisdom of this world, nor of the princes of
this world, that come to nought:
7 But we speak the wisdom of God
in a mystery, *even* the hidden *wisdom,*
[h]which God ordained before the world
unto our glory:
8 [i]Which none of the princes of this
world knew: for had they known *it,*
they would not have crucified the Lord
of glory.
9 But as it is written, [j]Eye hath not
seen, nor ear heard, neither have entered into the heart of man, the things
which God hath prepared for them
that love him.
10 But [k]God hath revealed *them*
unto us by his Spirit: for the Spirit
searcheth all things, yea, the deep
things of God.
11 For what man knoweth the things
of a man, [l]save the spirit of man which
is in him? [m]even so the things of God
knoweth no man, but the Spirit of God.
12 Now we have received, not the
spirit of the world, but [n]the spirit which
is of God; that we might know the
things that are freely given to us of
God.
13 [o]Which things also we speak,
not in the words which man's wisdom
teacheth, but which the Hō'lȳ Ghōst
teacheth; comparing spiritual things
with spiritual.
14 [p]But the natural man receiveth
not the things of the Spirit of God: for

they are foolishness unto him: [q]nei-
ther can he know *them,* because they
are spiritually discerned.
15 [r]But he that is spiritual [3]judgeth
all things, yet he himself is [4]judged of
no man.
16 [s]For who hath known the mind
of the Lord, that he [5]may instruct him?
[t]But we have the mind of Chrīst.
3 And I, brethren, could not speak
unto you as unto spiritual, but as
unto carnal, *even* as unto babes in
Chrīst.
2 I have fed you with [a]milk, and not
with meat: for hitherto ye were not
able *to bear it,* neither yet now are ye
able.
3 For ye are yet carnal: for whereas
there is among you envying, and strife,
and [1]divisions, are ye not carnal, and
walk [2]as men?
4 For while one saith, I am of Pa̧ul;
and another, I *am* of A-pŏl′los; are ye
not carnal?
5 Who then is Pa̧ul, and who *is* A-
pŏl′los, but ministers by whom ye believed, [b]even as the Lord gave to every
man?
6 [c]I have planted, [d]A-pŏl′los watered; but God [e]gave the increase.
7 So then neither is he that planteth
any thing, neither he that watereth;
but God that giveth the increase.
8 Now he that planteth and he that
watereth are one: [f]and every man shall
receive his own reward according to
his own labour.
9 For [g]we are labourers together
with God: ye are God's [3]husbandry, *ye
are* [h]God's building.
10 According to the grace of God
which is given unto me, as a wise mas-
terbuilder, I have laid [i]the foundation,
and another buildeth thereon. But [j]let
every man take heed how he buildeth
thereupon.
11 For other foundation can no man
lay than [k]that is laid, which is Jē′sus
Chrīst.
12 Now if any man build upon this
foundation gold, silver, precious stones,
wood, hay, stubble;
13 Every man's work shall be made
manifest: for the day [l]shall declare it,
because it [4]shall be revealed by fire;
and the fire shall try every man's work
of what sort it is.
14 If any man's work abide which
he hath built thereupon, he shall receive a reward.
15 If any man's work shall be burned,
he shall suffer loss: but he himself shall
be saved; [m]yet so as by fire.
16 Know ye not that ye are the temple of God, and *that* the Spirit of God
dwelleth in you?
17 If any man [5]defile the temple of
God, him shall God destroy; for the
[n]temple of God is holy, which *temple*
ye are.
18 Let no man deceive himself. If
any man among you seemeth to be
wise in this world, let him become a
fool, that he may be wise.
19 For the wisdom of this world is
foolishness with God. For it is written, [o]He taketh the wise in their own
craftiness.
20 And again, [p]The Lord knoweth
the thoughts of the wise, that they are
vain.
21 Therefore let no man glory in
men. For [q]all things are yours;
22 Whether Pa̧ul or A-pŏl′los, or Çē′-
phas, or the world, or life, or death, or
things present, or things to come; all
are yours;
23 And [r]ye are Chrīst's; [s]and Chrīst
is God's.
4 Let a man so account of us, as of the
ministers of Chrīst, [a]and stewards
of the mysteries of God.
2 Moreover it is required in stewards, that a man be found faithful.
3 But with me it is a very small thing
that I should be judged of you, or of
man's [1]judgment: yea, I judge not mine
own self.
4 For I know nothing by myself; yet
am I not hereby justified: but he that
judgeth me is the Lord.
5 [b]Therefore judge nothing before
the time, until the Lord come, who
both will bring to light the hidden
things of darkness, and will make manifest the counsels of the hearts: and
[c]then shall every man have praise of
God.
6 And these things, brethren, I have
in a figure transferred to myself and
to A-pŏl′los for your sakes; [d]that ye
might learn in us not to think *of men*
above that which is written, that no
one of you be puffed up for one against
another.
7 For who [2]maketh thee to differ
from another? and [e]what hast thou
that thou didst not receive? now if thou
didst receive *it,* why dost thou glory, as
if thou hadst not received *it?*
8 Now ye are full, [f]now ye are rich,
ye have reigned as kings without us:
and I would to God ye did reign, that
we also might reign with you.
9 For I think that God hath set forth
us [3]the apostles last, [g]as it were appointed to death: for [h]we are made a
[4]spectacle unto the world, and to angels, and to men.
10 We *are* [i]fools for Chrīst's sake,
but ye *are* wise in Chrīst; [j]we *are*
weak, but ye *are* strong; ye *are* honourable, but we *are* despised.
11 Even unto this present hour we
both hunger, and thirst, and are naked,
and are [k]buffeted, and have no certain
dwellingplace;
12 [l]And labour, working with our
own hands: [m]being reviled, we bless;
being persecuted, we suffer it:
13 Being defamed, we intreat: we
are made as the filth of the world, *and
are* the offscouring of all things unto
this day.
14 I write not these things to shame
you, but as my beloved sons I warn
you.
15 For though ye have ten thousand
instructors in Chrīst, yet *have ye* not

[q]Rom. 8.5; Jude 19
15 [r]Prov. 28.5; Col. 1.9
[3]Or, discerneth
[4]Or, discerned
16 [s]Job 15.8; Rom. 11.34
[5]shall
[t]Ps. 25.14; John 15.15

CHAPTER 3
2 [a]Heb. 5.13; 1 Pet. 2.2
3 [1]Or, factions
[2]according to man
5 [b]Rom. 12.3
6 [c]Acts 18.4
[d]Acts 19.1
[e]Isa. 55.10
8 [f]Ps. 62.12
9 [g]Acts 15.4
[3]Or, tillage
[h]Zech. 6.12-13
10 [i]Rom. 15.20
[j]1 Pet. 4.11
11 [k]Isa. 28.16
13 [l]1 Pet. 1.7
[4]is revealed
15 [m]Jude 23
17 [5]Or, destroy
[n]Heb. 3.1
19 [o]Job 5.13
20 [p]Ps. 94.11
21 [q]2 Cor. 4.5
23 [r]John 17.9-10;
[s]ch. 8.6

CHAPTER 4
1 [a]Matt. 13.11
3 [1]day
5 [b]Matt. 7.1;
[c]Rom. 2.29
6 [d]Rom. 12.3
7 [2]distinguisheth thee
[e]John 3.27
8 [f]Rev. 3.17
9 [3]Or, us the last apostles, as
[g]Ps. 44.22;
[h]Eph. 6.12;
[4]theatre
10 [i]Matt. 5.11;
[j]2 Cor. 13.9
11 [k]Acts 23.2
12 [l]Acts 18.3;
[m]Matt. 5.44

many fathers: for [n]in Chrīst Jē′sus I
have begotten you through the gospel.
16 Wherefore I beseech you, [o]be ye
followers of me.
17 For this cause have I sent unto
you Ti-mō′the-ŭs, [p]who is my beloved
son, and faithful in the Lord, who shall
bring you into remembrance of my
ways which be in Chrīst, as I teach every where in every church.
18 Now some are puffed up, as
though I would not come to you.
19 [q]But I will come to you shortly, if
the Lord will, and will know, not the
speech of them which are puffed up,
but the power.
20 For [r]the kingdom of God *is* not in
word, but in power.
21 What will ye? shall I come unto
you with a rod, or in love, and *in* the
spirit of meekness?

5 It is reported commonly *that there*
is fornication among you, and such
fornication as is not so much as [a]named
among the Gĕn′tīles, [b]that one should
have his [c]father's wife.
2 And ye are puffed up, and have
not rather mourned, that he that hath
done this deed might be taken away
from among you.
3 [d]For I verily, as absent in body,
but present in spirit, have [1]judged already, as though I were present, *con-*
cerning him that hath so done this
deed,
4 In the name of our Lord Jē′sus
Chrīst, when ye are gathered together,
and my spirit, [e]with the power of our
Lord Jē′sus Chrīst,
5 [f]To deliver such an one unto Sā′-
tan for the destruction of the flesh, that
the spirit may be saved in the day of
the Lord Jē′sus.
6 Your glorying *is* not good. Know
ye not that [g]a little leaven leaveneth
the whole lump?
7 Purge out therefore the old leaven,
that ye may be a new lump, as ye
are unleavened. For even [h]Chrīst our
[i]passover [2]is sacrificed for us:
8 Therefore [j]let us keep [3]the feast,
[k]not with old leaven, neither with the
leaven of malice and wickedness; but
with the unleavened *bread* of sincerity
and truth.
9 I wrote unto you in an epistle [l]not
to company with fornicators:
10 Yet not altogether with the fornicators of this world, or with the covetous, or extortioners, or with idolaters;
for then must ye needs go [m]out of the
world.
11 But now I have written unto you
not to keep company, [n]if any man that
is called a brother be a fornicator, or
covetous, or an idolater, or a railer, or
a drunkard, or an extortioner; with
such an one [o]no not to eat.
12 For what have I to do to judge
[p]them also that are without? do not ye
judge them that are within?
13 But them that are without God
[q]judgeth. Therefore put away from
among yourselves that wicked person.

6 Dare any of you, having a matter
against another, go to law before
the unjust, and not before the saints?
2 Do ye not know that [a]the saints
shall judge the world? and if the world
shall be judged by you, are ye unworthy to judge the smallest matters?
3 Know ye not that we shall [b]judge
angels? how much more things that
pertain to this life?
4 If then ye have judgments of things
pertaining to this life, set them to judge
who are least esteemed in the church.
5 I speak to your shame. Is it so, that
there is not a wise man among you?
no, not one that shall be able to judge
between his brethren?
6 But brother goeth to law with
brother, and that before the unbelievers.
7 Now therefore there is utterly a
fault among you, because ye go to
law one with another. [c]Why do ye not
rather take wrong? why do ye not rather
suffer yourselves to be defrauded?
8 Nay, ye do wrong, and defraud,
[d]and that *your* brethren.
9 Know ye not that [e]the unrighteous
shall not inherit the kingdom of God?
Be not deceived: neither fornicators,
nor idolaters, nor adulterers, nor ef-
feminate, nor abusers of themselves
with mankind,
10 Nor thieves, nor covetous, nor
drunkards, nor revilers, nor extortioners, shall inherit the kingdom of God.
11 And such were some of you: [f]but
ye are washed, but ye are sanctified,
but ye are justified in the name of the
Lord Jē′sus, and by the Spirit of our
God.
12 [g]All things are lawful unto me,
but all things are not [1]expedient: all
things are lawful for me, but I will not
be brought under the power of any.
13 Meats for the belly, and the belly
for meats: but God shall destroy both it
and them. Now the body *is* not for fornication, but [h]for the Lord; [i]and the
Lord for the body.
14 And [j]God hath both raised up the
Lord, and will also raise up us [k]by his
own power.
15 Know ye not that your bodies are
the members of Chrīst? shall I then
take the members of Chrīst, and make
them the members of an harlot? God
forbid.
16 What? know ye not that he which
is joined to an harlot is one body? for
[l]two, saith he, shall be one flesh.
17 [m]But he that is joined unto the
Lord is one spirit.
18 Flee fornication. Every sin that
a man doeth is without the body; but
he that committeth fornication sinneth
[n]against his own body.
19 What? [o]know ye not that your
body is the temple of the Hō′lȳ Ghōst
which is in you, which ye have of God,
[p]and ye are not your own?
20 For [q]ye are bought with a price:
therefore [r]glorify God in your body,
and in your spirit, which are God's.

15 [n]Rom. 15.20; Jas. 1.18
16 [o]ch. 11.1
17 [p]Acts 19.22; 1 Tim. 1.2
19 [q]Acts 19.21
20 [r]1 Thess. 1.5

CHAPTER 5
1 [a]Eph. 5.3
[b]Deut. 27.20
[c]2 Cor. 7.12
3 [d]Col. 2.5
[1]Or, determined
4 [e]Matt. 18.18; 2 Cor. 2.10
5 [f]Ps. 109.6; 1 Tim. 1.20
6 [g]Gal. 5.9
7 [h]Isa. 53.7; Rev. 5.6
[i]Ex. 12.5-6; Rev. 5.6-9
[2]Or, is slain
8 [j]Ex. 12.15
[3]Or, holy day
[k]Deut. 16.3
9 [l]2 Cor. 6.14
10 [m]John 17.15
11 [n]Matt. 18.17; 2 John 10
[o]Gal. 2.12
12 [p]Mark 4.11
13 [q]Eccl. 12.14

CHAPTER 6
2 [a]Ps. 49.14
3 [b]2 Pet. 2.4
7 [c]Prov. 20.22
8 [d]1 Thess. 4.6
9 [e]Isa. 3.11
11 [f]John 13.10
12 [g]ch. 10.23
[1]Or, profitable
13 [h]1 Thess. 4.3
[i]Eph. 5.23
14 [j]Acts 2.24;
[k]Eph. 1.19
16 [l]Gen. 2.24
17 [m]John 17.21
18 [n]Rom. 1.24
19 [o]2 Cor. 6.16
[p]Rom. 14.7
20 [q]Gal. 3.13;
[r]Matt. 5.16

7 Now concerning the things whereof
ye wrote unto me: *It is* good for a
man not to touch a woman.
2 Nevertheless, [a]*to avoid* fornication, let every man have his own wife,
and let every woman have her own
husband.
3 [b]Let the husband render unto the
wife due benevolence: and likewise
also the wife unto the husband.
4 The wife hath not power of her
own body, but the husband: and likewise also the husband hath not power
of his own body, but the wife.
5 Defraud ye not one the other, except *it be* with consent for a time,
that ye may give yourselves to fasting
and prayer; and come together again,
that [c]Sā'tan tempt you not for your
incontinency.
6 But I speak this by permission,
[d]*and* not of commandment.
7 For [e]I would that all men were
[f]even as I myself. But [g]every man hath
his proper gift of God, one after this
manner, and another after that.
8 I say therefore to the unmarried
and widows, [h]It is good for them if
they abide even as I.
9 But [i]if they cannot contain, let
them marry: for it is better to marry
than to burn.
10 And unto the married I command,
yet not I, but the Lord, [j]Let not the wife
depart from *her* husband:
11 But and if she depart, let her remain unmarried, or be reconciled to
her husband: and let not the husband
put away *his* wife.
12 But to the rest speak I, not the
Lord: If any brother hath a wife that
believeth not, and she be pleased to
dwell with him, let him not put her
away.
13 And the woman which hath an
husband that believeth not, and if he
be pleased to dwell with her, let her not
leave him.
14 For the unbelieving husband is
sanctified by the wife, and the unbelieving wife is sanctified by the husband:
else [k]were your children unclean; but
now are they holy.
15 But if the unbelieving depart, let
him depart. A brother or a sister is not
under bondage in such *cases:* but God
hath called us [1]to peace.
16 For what knowest thou, O wife,
whether thou shalt [l]save *thy* husband?
or [2]how knowest thou, O man, whether
thou shalt save *thy* wife?
17 But as God hath distributed to every man, as the Lord hath called every
one, so let him walk. And [m]so ordain I
in all churches.
18 Is any man called being circumcised? let him not become uncircumcised. Is any called in uncircumcision?
[n]let him not be circumcised.
19 [o]Circumcision is nothing, and uncircumcision is nothing, but [p]the keeping of the commandments of God.
20 [q]Let every man abide in the same
calling wherein he was called.
21 [r]Art thou called *being* a servant?
care not for it: but if thou mayest be
[s]made free, use *it* rather.
22 For he that is called in the Lord,
being a servant, is the Lord's [3]freeman:
likewise also he that is called, *being*
free, is [t]Chrīst's servant.
23 [u]Ye are bought with a price; be
not ye the servants of men.
24 Brethren, let every man, wherein
he is called, therein abide with God.
25 Now concerning virgins [v]I have
no commandment of the Lord: yet I
give my judgment, as one [w]that hath
obtained mercy of the Lord [x]to be
faithful.
26 I suppose therefore that this is
good for the present [4]distress, *I say,*
that *it is* good for a man so to be.
27 Art thou bound unto a wife? seek
not to be loosed. Art thou loosed from
a wife? seek not a wife.
28 But and if thou marry, thou hast
not sinned; and if a virgin marry, she
hath not sinned. Nevertheless such
shall have trouble in the flesh: but I
spare you.
29 But [y]this I say, brethren, the time
is short: it remaineth, that both they
that have wives be as though they had
none;
30 And they that weep, as though
they wept not; and they that rejoice, as
though they rejoiced not; and they that
buy, as though they possessed not;
31 And they that use this world, as
not [z]abusing *it:* for [a]the fashion of this
world passeth away.
32 But I would have you without
carefulness. [b]He that is unmarried careth for the things [5]that belong to the
Lord, how he may please the Lord:
33 But he that is married careth for
the things that are of the world, how he
may please *his* wife.
34 There is difference *also* between
a wife and a virgin. The unmarried
woman [c]careth for the things of the
Lord, that she may be holy both in
body and in spirit: but she that is married careth for the things of the world,
how she may please *her* husband.
35 And this I speak for your own
profit; not that I may cast a snare upon
you, but for that which is comely, and
that ye may attend upon the Lord without distraction.
36 But if any man think that he be-
haveth himself uncomely toward his
virgin, if she pass the flower of *her* age,
and need so require, let him do what
he will, he sinneth not: let them marry.
37 Nevertheless he that standeth
stedfast in his heart, having no necessity, but hath power over his own will,
and hath so decreed in his heart that
he will keep his virgin, doeth well.
38 [d]So then he that giveth *her* in
marriage doeth well; but he that giveth
her not in marriage doeth better.
39 [e]The wife is bound by the law as
long as her husband liveth; but if her
husband be dead, she is at liberty to be
married to whom she will; only in the
Lord.

CHAPTER 7
2 [a]Prov. 5.19
3 [b]Ex. 21.10; 1 Pet. 3.7
5 [c]2 Cor. 11.3
6 [d]2 Cor. 8.8
7 [e]Acts 26.29
[f]ch. 9.5
[g]Matt. 19.12; ch. 12.11
8 [h]verse 26
9 [i]1 Tim. 5.14
10 [j]Jer. 3.20; Mal. 2.14-16; Matt. 5.32; Matt. 19.6; Mark 10.11-12; Luke 16.18
14 [k]Mal. 2.15
15 [1]in peace
16 [l]Jas. 5.19-20; 1 Pet. 3.1
[2]what
17 [m]2 Cor. 11.28
18 [n]Acts 15.1-5-19-24-28; Gal. 5.2
19 [o]Gal. 6.15; Col. 3.11
[p]1 Sam. 15.22; Jer. 7.22-23; Matt. 5.19; John 15.14; 1 John 2.3; Rev. 22.14
20 [q]Eph. 4.1; 2 Thess. 3.11
21 [r]Gal. 3.28
[s]Isa. 58.6
22 [3]made free
[t]Gal. 5.13; Eph. 6.6; 1 Pet. 2.16
23 [u]Lev. 25.42; 1 Pet. 1.18
25 [v]2 Cor. 8.8-10
[w]1 Tim. 1.16
[x]ch. 4.2
26 [4]Or, necessity
29 [y]Matt. 24.13; Rom. 13.12; Phil. 4.5; Heb. 10.25; 1 Pet. 4.7
31 [z]ch. 9.18
[a]Ps. 39.6; Jas. 4.14
32 [b]1 Tim. 5.5
[5]of the Lord
34 [c]Luke 10.40
38 [d]Heb. 13.4
39 [e]Rom. 7.2

40 But she is happier if she so abide, after my judgment: and I think also that I have the Spirit of God.

8 Now [a]as touching things offered unto idols, we know that we all have [b]knowledge. Knowledge puffeth up, but charity edifieth.

2 And [c]if any man think that he knoweth any thing, he knoweth nothing yet as he ought to know.

3 But if any man love God, [d]the same is known of him.

4 As concerning therefore the eating of those things that are offered in sacrifice unto idols, we know that [e]an idol *is* nothing in the world, [f]and that *there is* none other God but one.

5 For though there be that are [g]called gods, whether in heaven or in earth, (as there be gods many, and lords many,)

6 But [h]to us *there is but* one God, the Father, [i]of whom *are* all things, and we [1]in him; and [j]one Lord Jē'sus Chrīst, [k]by whom *are* all things, and we by him.

7 Howbeit *there is* not in every man that knowledge: for some with conscience of the idol unto this hour eat *it* as a thing offered unto an idol; and their conscience being weak is defiled.

8 But meat commendeth us not to God: for neither, if we eat, [2]are we the better; neither, if we eat not, [3]are we the worse.

9 But take heed lest by any means this [4]liberty of yours become a stumblingblock to them that are weak.

10 For if any man see thee which hast knowledge sit at meat in the idol's temple, shall not the conscience of him which is weak be [5]emboldened to eat those things which are offered to idols;

11 And through thy knowledge shall the weak brother perish, for whom Chrīst died?

12 But [l]when ye sin so against the brethren, and wound their weak conscience, ye sin against Chrīst.

13 Wherefore, if meat make my brother to offend, I will eat no flesh while the world standeth, lest I make my brother to offend.

9 [a]Am I not an apostle? am I not free? have [b]I not seen Jē'sus Chrīst our Lord? are not ye my work in the Lord?

2 If I be not an apostle unto others, yet doubtless I am to you: for [c]the seal of mine apostleship are ye in the Lord.

3 Mine answer to them that do examine me is this,

4 [d]Have we not power to eat and to drink?

5 Have we not power to lead about a sister, a [1]wife, as well as other apostles, and *as* [e]the brethren of the Lord, and [f]Çē'phas?

6 Or I only and Bär'na-bās, [g]have not we power to forbear working?

7 Who [h]goeth a warfare any time at his own charges? who [i]planteth a vineyard, and eateth not of the fruit thereof? or who [j]feedeth a flock, and eateth not of the milk of the flock?

8 Say I these things as a man? or saith not the law the same also?

9 For it is written in the law of Mō'ses, [k]Thou shalt not muzzle the mouth of the ox that treadeth out the corn. Doth God take care for oxen?

10 Or saith he *it* altogether for our sakes? For our sakes, no doubt, *this* is written: that [l]he that ploweth should plow in hope; and that he that thresheth in hope should be partaker of his hope.

11 [m]If we have sown unto you spiritual things, *is it* a great thing if we shall reap your carnal things?

12 If others be partakers of *this* power over you, *are* not we rather? [n]Nevertheless we have not used this power; but suffer all things, lest we should hinder the gospel of Chrīst.

13 [o]Do ye not know that they which minister about holy things [2]live *of the things* of the temple? and they which wait at the altar are partakers with the altar?

14 Even so [p]hath the Lord ordained [q]that they which preach the gospel should live of the gospel.

15 But I have used none of these things: neither have I written these things, that it should be so done unto me: for *it were* better for me to die, than that any man should make my glorying void.

16 For though I preach the gospel, I have nothing to glory of: for necessity is laid upon me; yea, woe is unto me, if I preach not the gospel!

17 For if I do this thing willingly, I have a reward: but if against my will, [r]a dispensation *of the gospel* is committed unto me.

18 What is my reward then? *Verily* that, when I preach the gospel, I may make the gospel of Chrīst without charge, that I abuse not my power in the gospel.

19 For though I be free from all *men*, yet have [s]I made myself servant unto all, [t]that I might gain the more.

20 And [u]unto the Jews I became as a Jew, that I might gain the Jews; to them that are under the law, as under the law, that I might gain them that are under the law;

21 [v]To them that are without law, as without law, ([w]being not without law to God, but under the law to Chrīst,) that I might gain them that are without law;

22 [x]To the weak became I as weak, that I might gain the weak: I am made all things to all *men*, that I might by all means save some.

23 And this I do for the gospel's sake, that I might be partaker thereof with *you*.

24 Know ye not that they which run in a race run all, but one receiveth the prize? [y]So run, that ye may obtain.

25 And every man that [z]striveth for the mastery is temperate in all things. Now they *do it* to obtain a corruptible crown; but we [a]an incorruptible.

26 I therefore so run, [b]not as uncertainly; so fight I, not as one that beateth the air:

CHAPTER 8
1 [a]Acts 15.20
[b]Rom. 14.14
2 [c]Gal. 6.3; 1 Tim. 6.4
3 [d]Ex. 33.12; Gal. 4.9
4 [e]Isa. 41.24
[f]Deut. 3.39; Mark 12.29
5 [g]John 10.34
6 [h]Mal. 2.10; Eph. 4.6
[i]Acts 17.28; Rom. 11.36
[1]Or, for him
[j]Matt. 11.27; Phil. 2.11
[k]John 1.3; Heb. 1.2
8 [2]Or, have we the more
[3]Or, have we the less
9 [4]Or, power
10 [5]edified
12 [l]Matt. 25.40; Acts 9.4

CHAPTER 9
1 [a]1 Tim. 2.7
[b]Acts 9.3
2 [c]2 Cor. 3.2
4 [d]2 Thess. 3.9
5 [1]Or, woman
[e]Matt. 13.55; Gal. 1.19
[f]Matt. 8.14
6 [g]Acts 18.3
7 [h]2 Cor. 10.4
[i]Deut. 20.6; Prov. 27.18
[j]John 21.15; 1 Pet. 5.2
9 [k]Deut. 25.4
10 [l]2 Tim. 2.6
11 [m]Matt. 10.10; Rom. 15.27
12 [n]2 Cor. 11.7
13 [o]Lev. 6.16
[2]Or, feed
14 [p]Luke 10.7
[q]Gal. 6.6; 1 Tim. 5.17
17 [r]Gal. 2.7; Phil. 1.17
19 [s]Gal. 5.13
[t]Matt. 18.15; 1 Pet. 3.1
20 [u]Acts 16.3
21 [v]Rom. 2.12
[w]Matt. 5.17-20
22 [x]Rom. 15.1
24 [y]Matt. 10.22
25 [z]1 Tim. 6.12
[a]Jas. 1.12
26 [b]2 Cor. 5.1

27 But I keep under my body, and bring *it* into subjection: lest that by any means, when I have preached to others, I myself should be [c]a castaway.

10

Moreover, brethren, I would not that ye should be ignorant, how that all our fathers were under [a]the cloud, and all passed through [b]the sea;

2 And were all baptized unto Mō'ses in the cloud and in the sea;

3 And did all eat the same [c]spiritual meat;

4 And did all drink the same [d]spiritual drink: for they drank of that spiritual Rock that [1]followed them: and that Rock was Chrīst.

5 But with many of them God was not well pleased: for they were overthrown in the wilderness.

6 Now these things were [2]our examples, to the intent we should not lust after evil things, as they also lusted.

7 Neither be ye idolaters, as *were* some of them; as it is written, [e]The people sat down to eat and drink, and rose up to play.

8 Neither let us commit fornication, as some of them committed, and [f]fell in one day three and twenty thousand.

9 Neither let us tempt Chrīst, as [g]some of them also tempted, and were destroyed of serpents.

10 Neither murmur ye, as some of them also murmured, and were destroyed of the destroyer.

11 Now all these things happened unto them for [3]ensamples: and [h]they are written for our admonition, [i]upon whom the ends of the world are come.

12 Wherefore let him that thinketh he standeth take heed lest he fall.

13 There hath no temptation taken you but such as is [4]common to man: but God *is* faithful, [j]who will not suffer you to be tempted above that ye are able; but will with the temptation also [k]make a way to escape, that ye may be able to bear *it*.

14 Wherefore, my dearly beloved, flee from idolatry.

15 I speak as to wise men; judge ye what I say.

16 [l]The cup of blessing which we bless, is it not the communion of the blood of Chrīst? [m]The bread which we break, is it not the communion of the body of Chrīst?

17 For [n]we *being* many are one bread, *and* one body: for we are all partakers of that one bread.

18 Behold [o]Is'ra-el after the flesh: [p]are not they which eat of the sacrifices partakers of the altar?

19 What say I then? that the idol is any thing, or that which is offered in sacrifice to idols is any thing?

20 But *I say*, that the things which the Gĕn'tīles [q]sacrifice, they sacrifice to devils, and not to God: and I would not that ye should have fellowship with devils.

21 [r]Ye cannot drink the cup of the Lord, and [s]the cup of devils: ye cannot be partakers of the Lord's table, and of the table of devils.

22 Do we provoke the Lord to jealousy? [t]are we stronger than he?

23 All things are lawful for me, but all things are not expedient: all things are lawful for me, but all things edify not.

24 [u]Let no man seek his own, but every man another's *wealth*.

25 [v]Whatsoever is sold in the shambles, *that* eat, asking no question for conscience sake:

26 For the earth *is* the Lord's, and the fulness thereof.

27 If any of them that believe not bid you *to a feast*, and ye be disposed to go; [w]whatsoever is set before you, eat, asking no question for conscience sake.

28 But if any man say unto you, This is offered in sacrifice unto idols, eat not [x]for his sake that shewed it, and for conscience sake: for [y]the earth *is* the Lord's, and the fulness thereof:

29 Conscience, I say, not thine own, but of the other: for [z]why is my liberty judged of another *man's* conscience?

30 For if I by [5]grace be a partaker, why am I evil spoken of for that for which I give thanks?

31 [a]Whether therefore ye eat, or drink, or whatsoever ye do, do all to the glory of God.

32 Give none offence, neither to the Jews, nor to the [6]Gĕn'tīles, nor to the church of God:

33 Even as I please all *men* in all *things*, not seeking mine own profit, but the *profit* of many, that they may be saved.

11

Be [a]ye followers of me, even as I also *am* of Chrīst.

2 Now I praise you, brethren, that ye remember me in all things, and [b]keep the [1]ordinances, as I delivered *them* to you.

3 But I would have you know, that [c]the head of every man is Chrīst; and [d]the head of the woman *is* the man; and [e]the head of Chrīst *is* God.

4 Every man praying or prophesying, having *his* head covered, dishonoureth his head.

5 But [f]every woman that prayeth or prophesieth with *her* head uncovered dishonoureth her head: for that is even all one as if she were [g]shaven.

6 For if the woman be not covered, let her also be shorn: but if it be [h]a shame for a woman to be shorn or shaven, let her be covered.

7 For a man indeed ought not to cover *his* head, forasmuch as [i]he is the image and glory of God: but the woman is the glory of the man.

8 For [j]the man is not of the woman; but the woman of the man.

9 Neither was the man created for the woman; but the woman for the man.

10 For this cause ought the woman [k]to have [2]power on *her* head [l]because of the angels.

11 Nevertheless [m]neither is the man without the woman, neither the woman without the man, in the Lord.

[c]Jer. 6.30
CHAPTER 10
1 [a]Ex. 13.21; Isa. 63.11
[b]Ex. 14.22
3 [c]Ex. 16.15; Deut. 8.3
4 [d]Ex. 17.6; Rev. 22.17
[1]Or, went with them
6 [2]our figures
7 [e]Ex. 32.6
8 [f]Num. 25.1
9 [g]Ex. 17.2-7; Ps. 78.18-56
11 [3]Or, types
[h]Rom. 15.4
[i]Heb. 10.25
13 [4]Or, moderate
[j]Ex. 13.7-21; 2 Pet. 2.9
[k]Gen. 19.20-21
16 [l]Matt. 26.26
[m]Acts 2.42
17 [n]Rom. 12.5
18 [o]Rom. 4.12
[p]Lev. 3.3
20 [q]Deut. 32.17
21 [r]2 Cor. 6.15
[s]Deut. 32.38
22 [t]Job 9.4
24 [u]Rom. 15.1
25 [v]1 Tim. 4.4
27 [w]Luke 10.7
28 [x]ch. 8.10
[y]Deut. 10.14
29 [z]Rom. 14.16
30 [5]Or, thanksgiving
31 [a]Zech. 7.6
32 [6]Greeks
CHAPTER 11
1 [a]Eph. 5.1-2
2 [b]ch. 7.17
[1]Or, traditions
3 [c]Rom. 14.9;
[d]Gen. 3.16
[e]John 4.34
5 [f]Acts 21.9
[g]Deut. 21.12
6 [h]Num. 5.18
7 [i]Gen. 1.26
8 [j]Gen. 2.21
10 [k]Gen. 24.65
[2]That is, a covering, in sign that she is under the power of her husband
[l]Eccl. 5.6
11 [m]Gal. 3.28

12 For as the woman *is* of the man,
even so *is* the man also by the woman;
[n]but all things of God.
13 Judge in yourselves: is it comely
that a woman pray unto God uncovered?
14 Doth not even nature itself teach
you, that, if a man have long hair, it is a
shame unto him?
15 But if a woman have long hair, it
is a glory to her: for *her* hair is given
her for a [3]covering.
16 But [o]if any man seem to be contentious, we have no such custom, neither the churches of God.
17 Now in this that I declare *unto*
you I praise *you* not, that ye come together not for the better, but for the
worse.
18 For first of all, when ye come together in the church, [p]I hear that there
be [4]divisions among you; and I partly
believe it.
19 For [q]there must be also [5]heresies
among you, [r]that they which are approved may be made manifest among
you.
20 When ye come together therefore into one place, [6]*this* is not to eat
the Lord's supper.
21 For in eating every one taketh before *other* his own supper: and one is
hungry, and [s]another is drunken.
22 What? have ye not houses to eat
and to drink in? or [t]despise ye the
church of God, and shame [7]them that
have not? What shall I say to you?
shall I praise you in this? I praise *you*
not.
23 For [u]I have received of the Lord
that which also I delivered unto you,
That the Lord Jē'sus the *same* night in
which he was betrayed took bread:
24 And when he had given thanks,
he brake *it*, and said, Take, eat: this is
my body, which is broken for you: this
do [8]in remembrance of me.
25 After the same manner also *he*
took the cup, when he had supped, saying, This cup is [v]the new testament in
my blood: this do ye, as oft as ye drink
it, in remembrance of me.
26 For as often as ye eat this bread,
and drink this cup, [9]ye do shew the
Lord's death [w]till he come.
27 [x]Wherefore whosoever shall eat
this bread, and drink *this* cup of the
Lord, unworthily, shall be guilty of the
body and blood of the Lord.
28 But [y]let a man examine himself,
and so let him eat of *that* bread, and
drink of *that* cup.
29 For he that eateth and drinketh
unworthily, eateth and drinketh [10]damnation to himself, not discerning the
Lord's body.
30 For this cause many *are* weak and
sickly among you, and many sleep.
31 For [z]if we would judge ourselves,
we should not be judged.
32 But when we are judged [a]we are
chastened of the Lord, that we should
not be condemned with the world.
33 Wherefore, my brethren, when
ye come together to eat, tarry one for
another.
34 And if any man hunger, let him
eat at home; that ye come not together unto [11]condemnation. And the
rest [b]will I set in order when [c]I come.

12 Now [a]concerning spiritual *gifts*,
brethren, I would not have you
ignorant.
2 Ye know [b]that ye were Gĕn'tīles,
carried away unto these dumb idols,
even as ye were led.
3 Wherefore I give you to understand, [c]that no man speaking by the
Spirit of God calleth Jē'sus [1]accursed:
and [d]*that* no man can say that Jē'sus
is the Lord but by the Hō'lȳ Ghōst.
4 Now [e]there are diversities of gifts,
but [f]the same Spirit.
5 And there are differences of [2]administrations, but the same Lord.
6 And there are diversities of operations, but it is the same God [g]which
worketh all in all.
7 [h]But the manifestation of the Spirit
is given to every man to profit withal.
8 For to one is given by the Spirit
[i]the word of wisdom; to another [j]the
word of knowledge by the same Spirit;
9 [k]To another faith by the same
Spirit; to another [l]the gifts of healing
by the same Spirit;
10 [m]To another the working of miracles; to another [n]prophecy; [o]to another discerning of spirits; to another
[p]*divers* kinds of tongues; to another
the interpretation of tongues:
11 But all these worketh that one
and the selfsame Spirit, [q]dividing to
every man severally [r]as he will.
12 For as the body is one, and hath
many members, and all the members
of that one body, being many, are one
body: [s]so also *is* Chrīst.
13 For [t]by one Spirit are we all baptized into one body, [u]whether *we be*
Jews or [3]Gĕn'tīles, whether *we be* bond
or free; and [v]have been all made to
drink into one Spirit.
14 For the body is not one member,
but many.
15 If the foot shall say, Because I am
not the hand, I am not of the body; is it
therefore not of the body?
16 And if the ear shall say, Because I
am not the eye, I am not of the body; is
it therefore not of the body?
17 If the whole body *were* an eye,
where *were* the hearing? If the whole
were hearing, where *were* the smelling?
18 But now hath God set the members every one of them in the body, as
it hath pleased him.
19 And if they were all one member,
where *were* the body?
20 But now *are they* many members, yet but one body.
21 And the eye cannot say unto the
hand, I have no need of thee: nor again
the head to the feet, I have no need of
you.
22 Nay, much more those members
of the body, which seem to be more
feeble, are necessary:

12 [n]Prov. 16.4; ch. 8.6
15 [3]Or, veil
16 [o]1 Tim. 6.4
18 [p]ch. 1.10
[4]Or, schisms
19 [q]Luke 17.1
[5]Or, sects
[r]Luke 2.35
20 [6]Or, ye cannot eat
21 [s]Jude 12
22 [t]Lev. 19.30; Ps. 89.7
[7]Or, them that are poor
23 [u]Gal. 1.1
24 [8]Or, for a remembrance
25 [v]Heb. 9.15
26 [9]Or, shew ye
[w]Acts 1.11; Heb. 9.28
27 [x]Num. 9.10
28 [y]2 Cor. 13.5
29 [10]Or, judgment
31 [z]1 John 1.9
32 [a]Heb. 12.5
34 [11]Or, judgment
[b]Tit. 1.5
[c]ch. 4.19

CHAPTER 12
1 [a]ch. 14.1
2 [b]Eph. 2.11
3 [c]Mark 9.39
[1]Or, anathema
[d]Matt. 16.17
4 [e]Heb. 2.4
[f]Eph. 4.4
5 [2]Or, ministeries
6 [g]Eph. 1.23
7 [h]Rom. 12.6
8 [i]Gen. 41.38-39;
[j]2 Cor. 8.7
9 [k]Matt. 17.19
[l]Mark 16.18
10 [m]Gal. 3.5
[n]Rom. 12.6
[o]1 John 4.1
[p]Acts 2.4
11 [q]Rom. 12.6-8;
[r]John 3.8
12 [s]Gal. 3.16
13 [t]Isa. 44.3-5;
[u]Gal. 3.28;
[3]Greeks
[v]John 6.63

23 And those *members* of the body,
which we think to be less honourable,
upon these we [4]bestow more abundant
honour; and our uncomely *parts* have
more abundant comeliness.
24 For our comely *parts* have no
need: but God hath tempered the body
together, having given more abundant
honour to that *part* which lacked:
25 That there should be no [5]schism
in the body; but *that* the members
should have the same care one for
another.
26 And whether one member suffer,
all the members suffer with it; or one
member be honoured, all the members
rejoice with it.
27 Now [w]ye are the body of Christ,
and members in particular.
28 And [x]God hath set some in the
church, first [y]apostles, secondarily
[z]prophets, thirdly teachers, after that
miracles, then gifts of healings, [a]helps,
[b]governments, [6]diversities of tongues.
29 *Are* all apostles? *are* all prophets? *are* all teachers? *are* all [7]workers
of miracles?
30 Have all the gifts of healing? do all
speak with tongues? do all interpret?
31 But [c]covet earnestly the best gifts:
and yet shew I unto you a more excellent way.

13 Though I speak with the tongues
of men and of angels, and have
not [a]charity, I am become *as* sounding
brass, or a tinkling cymbal.
2 And though I have *the gift* [b]*of*
prophecy, and understand all mysteries, and all knowledge; and though I
have all faith, [c]so that I could remove
mountains, and have not charity, I am
nothing.
3 And [d]though I bestow all my goods
to feed *the poor*, and though I give my
body to be burned, and have not charity, it profiteth me nothing.
4 [e]Charity suffereth long, *and* is kind;
charity envieth not; charity [1]vaunteth
not itself, is not puffed up,
5 [f]Doth not behave itself unseemly,
[g]seeketh not her own, is not easily provoked, thinketh no evil;
6 [h]Rejoiceth not in iniquity, but [i]re-
joiceth [2]in the truth;
7 [j]Beareth all things, believeth all
things, hopeth all things, endureth all
things.
8 Charity never faileth: but whether
there be prophecies, they shall fail;
whether *there be* tongues, they shall
cease; whether *there be* knowledge, it
shall vanish away.
9 [k]For we know in part, and we
prophesy in part.
10 But [l]when that which is perfect is
come, then that which is in part shall
be done away.
11 When I was a child, I spake as a
child, I understood as a child, I [3]thought
as a child: but when I became a man, I
put away childish things.
12 For [m]now we see through a glass,
[4]darkly; but then [n]face to face: now I
know in part; but then shall I know
even as also I am known.

23 [4]Or, put on
25 [5]Or, division
27 [w]Rom. 12.5; Eph. 4.12
28 [x]Eph. 4.11 [y]Eph. 2.20 [z]Acts 13.1; Rom. 12.6 [a]Num. 11.17 [b]Rom. 12.8; Heb. 13.17 [6]Or, kinds
29 [7]Or, powers
31 [c]ch. 14.1

CHAPTER 13
1 [a]Matt. 25.45; Rom. 14
2 [b]Matt. 7.22 [c]Luke 17.6
3 [d]Matt. 6.1-2
4 [e]1 Pet. 4.8 [1]Or, is not rash
5 [f]Phil. 4.8 [g]Rom. 14.12-15; Phil. 2.4
6 [h]Ps. 10.3; Rom. 1.32 [i]2 John 4 [2]Or, with the truth
7 [j]Gal. 6.2
9 [k]ch. 8.2; 1 Tim. 6.4
10 [l]Isa. 54.13; John 6.45
11 [3]Or, reasoned
12 [m]2 Cor. 3.18; Phil. 3.12 [4]in a riddle [n]Matt. 18.10
13 [o]Matt. 22.38-39

CHAPTER 14
1 [a]Lev. 19.18; Eph. 5.2 [b]ch. 12.30-31 [c]Num. 11.25; Rom. 12.6
2 [d]Acts 2.4; Acts 10.46 [1]heareth [e]Matt. 13.11
3 [f]Rom. 15.4
7 [g]Job 21.11-12 [2]Or, tunes
9 [3]significant [h]ch. 9.26
12 [4]of spirits
13 [i]ch. 12.10
15 [j]Eph. 5.19 [k]Ps. 47.7
16 [l]ch. 11.24

13 And now abideth faith, hope,
charity, these three; [o]but the greatest
of these *is* charity.

14 Follow after [a]charity, [b]and desire spiritual *gifts*, [c]but rather
that ye may prophesy.
2 For he that [d]speaketh in an *unknown* tongue speaketh not unto men,
but unto God; for no man [1]under-
standeth *him*; howbeit in the spirit he
speaketh [e]mysteries.
3 But he that prophesieth [f]speaketh
unto men *to* edification, and exhortation, and comfort.
4 He that speaketh in an *unknown*
tongue edifieth himself; but he that
prophesieth edifieth the church.
5 I would that ye all spake with
tongues, but rather that ye prophesied:
for greater *is* he that prophesieth than
he that speaketh with tongues, except
he interpret, that the church may receive edifying.
6 Now, brethren, if I come unto you
speaking with tongues, what shall I
profit you, except I shall speak to you
either by revelation, or by knowledge,
or by prophesying, or by doctrine?
7 And even things without life giving sound, whether [g]pipe or harp, except they give a distinction in the
[2]sounds, how shall it be known what is
piped or harped?
8 For if the trumpet give an uncertain sound, who shall prepare himself
to the battle?
9 So likewise ye, except ye utter by
the tongue words [3]easy to be understood, how shall it be known what is
spoken? for ye shall [h]speak into the
air.
10 There are, it may be, so many
kinds of voices in the world, and none
of them *is* without signification.
11 Therefore if I know not the meaning of the voice, I shall be unto him
that speaketh a barbarian, and he that
speaketh *shall be* a barbarian unto me.
12 Even so ye, forasmuch as ye are
zealous [4]of spiritual *gifts*, seek that
ye may excel to the edifying of the
church.
13 Wherefore let him that speaketh
in an *unknown* tongue pray that [i]he
may interpret.
14 For if I pray in an *unknown*
tongue, my spirit prayeth, but my understanding is unfruitful.
15 What is it then? I will pray with
the spirit, and I will pray with the understanding also: [j]I will sing with the
spirit, and I will sing [k]with the understanding also.
16 Else when thou shalt bless with
the spirit, how shall he that occupieth
the room of the unlearned say Amen
[l]at thy giving of thanks, seeing he understandeth not what thou sayest?
17 For thou verily givest thanks well,
but the other is not edified.
18 I thank my God, I speak with
tongues more than ye all:
19 Yet in the church I had rather
speak five words with my understanding, that *by my voice* I might teach

others also, than ten thousand words
in an *unknown* tongue.
20 Brethren, [m]be not children in understanding: howbeit in malice [n]be
ye children, but in understanding be
[5]men.
21 [o]In the law it is [p]written, With
men of other tongues and other lips
will I speak unto this people; and yet
for all that will they not hear me, saith
the Lord.
22 Wherefore tongues are for a sign,
not to them that believe, but to them
that believe not: but prophesying *serveth* not for them that believe not, but
for them which believe.
23 If therefore the whole church be
come together into one place, and all
speak with tongues, and there come in
those that are unlearned, or unbelievers, [q]will they not say that ye are mad?
24 But if all prophesy, and there
come in one that believeth not, or *one*
unlearned, he is convinced of all, he is
judged of all:
25 And thus are the secrets of his
heart made manifest; and so falling
down on *his* face he will worship God,
and report [r]that God is in you of a
truth.
26 How is it then, brethren? when
ye come together, every one of you
hath a psalm, [s]hath a doctrine, hath a
tongue, hath a revelation, hath an interpretation. [t]Let all things be done
unto edifying.
27 If any man speak in an *unknown*
tongue, *let it be* by two, or at the most
by three, and *that* by course; and let
one interpret.
28 But if there be no interpreter, let
him keep silence in the church; and let
him speak to himself, and to God.
29 Let the prophets speak two or
three, and let the other judge.
30 If *any thing* be revealed to another that sitteth by, [u]let the first hold
his peace.
31 [v]For ye may all prophesy one by
one, that all may learn, and all may be
comforted.
32 And [w]the spirits of the prophets
are subject to the prophets.
33 For God is not *the author* of [6]con-
fusion, but of peace, [x]as in all churches
of the saints.
34 [y]Let your women keep silence in
the churches: for it is not permitted
unto them to speak; but [z]*they are commanded* to be under obedience, as also
saith the [a]law.
35 And if they will learn any thing,
let them ask their husbands at home:
for it is a shame for women to speak in
the church.
36 What? came the word of God
[b]out from you? or came it unto you
only?
37 [c]If any man think himself to be a
prophet, or spiritual, let him acknowledge that the things that I write unto
you are the commandments of the
Lord.
38 But if any man be ignorant, let
him be ignorant.
39 Wherefore, brethren, [d]covet to
prophesy, and forbid not to speak with
tongues.
40 Let all things be done decently
and in order.
15 Moreover, brethren, I declare
unto you the gospel which I
preached unto you, which also ye have
received, and [a]wherein ye stand;
2 [b]By which also ye are saved, if ye
[1]keep in memory [2]what I preached
unto you, unless [c]ye have believed in
vain.
3 For I delivered unto you first of all
that which I also received, how that
Chrīst died for our sins [d]according to
the scriptures;
4 And that he was buried, and that
he rose again the third day [e]according
to the scriptures:
5 [f]And that he was seen of Çē′phas,
then [g]of the twelve:
6 After that, he was seen of above
five hundred brethren at once; of whom
the greater part remain unto this present, but some are fallen asleep.
7 After that, he was seen of Jāmes;
then [h]of all the apostles.
8 [i]And last of all he was seen of me
also, as of [3]one born out of due time.
9 For I am the least of the apostles,
that am not meet to be called an apostle, because [j]I persecuted the church of
God.
10 But [k]by the grace of God I am
what I am: and his grace which *was
bestowed* upon me was not in vain; but
[l]I laboured more abundantly than they
all: [m]yet not I, but the grace of God
which was with me.
11 Therefore whether *it were* I or
they, so we preach, and so ye believed.
12 Now if Chrīst be preached that he
rose from the dead, how say some
among you that there is no resurrection of the dead?
13 But if there be no resurrection of
the dead, [n]then is Chrīst not risen:
14 And if Chrīst be not risen, then *is*
our preaching vain, and your faith *is*
also vain.
15 Yea, and we are found false witnesses of God; because we have testified of God that he raised up Chrīst:
whom he raised not up, if so be that the
dead rise not.
16 For if the dead rise not, then is
not Chrīst raised:
17 And if Chrīst be not raised, you
faith *is* vain; [o]ye are yet in your sins.
18 Then they also which are fallen
asleep in Chrīst are perished.
19 If [p]in this life only we have hope
in Chrīst, we are of all men most
miserable.
20 But now [q]is Chrīst risen from the
dead, *and* become [r]the firstfruits of
them that slept.
21 For [s]since by man *came* death,
by [t]man *came* also the resurrection of
the dead.
22 For as in Ăd′ăm all die, even so in
Chrīst shall all be made alive.

20 [m]Ps. 119.99; Matt. 11.25; Rom. 16.19; Heb. 5.12
[n]Matt. 18.3; 1 Pet. 2.2
[5]perfect, or, of a ripe age
21 [o]John 10.34
[p]Isa. 28.11
23 [q]Hos. 9.7; Acts 2.13
25 [r]Isa. 45.14; Zech. 8.23
26 [s]ch. 12.8-9
[t]Rom. 14.19; Eph. 4.12
30 [u]1 Thess. 5.19
31 [v]Deut. 33.10; Eccl. 12.9; Rom. 12.7
32 [w]1 John 4.1
33 [6]tumult, or, unquietness
[x]ch. 11.16
34 [y]1 Tim. 2.11
[z]ch. 11.3; Eph. 5.22; 1 Pet. 3.1
[a]Gen. 3.16
36 [b]Isa. 2.3
37 [c]Luke 10.16
39 [d]ch. 12.31
CHAPTER 15
1 [a]Rom. 5.2
2 [b]Rom. 1.16
[1]Or, hold fast
[2]by what speech
[c]Gal. 3.4
3 [d]Ps. 22.15; Isa. 53.5; Dan. 9.26; 1 Pet. 2.24
4 [e]Ps. 2.7; Isa. 53.10; Hos. 6.2
5 [f]Luke 24.34
[g]John 20.19
7 [h]Acts 1.3
8 [i]Acts 9.4
[3]Or, an abortive
9 [j]Acts 8.3
10 [k]Eph. 4.7
[l]2 Cor. 11.23
[m]Gal. 2.8
13 [n]1 Thess. 4.14
17 [o]Rom. 4.25
19 [p]2 Tim. 3.12
20 [q]1 Pet. 1.3
[r]Acts 26.23
21 [s]Rom. 5.12
[t]John 11.25

23 But [u]every man in his own order:
Chrīst the firstfruits; afterward they
that are Chrīst's at his coming.
24 Then *cometh* the end, when he
shall have delivered up [v]the kingdom
to God, even the Father; when he shall
have put down all rule and all authority and power.
25 For he must reign, [w]till he hath
put all enemies under his feet.
26 [x]The last enemy *that* shall be destroyed *is* death.
27 For he [y]hath put all things under
his feet. But when he saith all things
are put under *him, it is* manifest that
he is excepted, which did put all things
under him.
28 [z]And when all things shall be
subdued unto him, then [a]shall the Son
also himself be subject unto him that
put all things under him, that God may
be all in all.
29 Else what shall they do which are
baptized for the dead, if the dead rise
not at all? why are they then baptized
for the dead?
30 And [b]why stand we in jeopardy
every hour?
31 I protest by [4]your rejoicing which
I have in Chrīst Jē'sus our Lord, [c]I die
daily.
32 If [5]after the manner of men [d]I
have fought with beasts at Ĕph'ĕ-sŭs,
what advantageth it me, if the dead
rise not? [e]let us eat and drink; for to
morrow we die.
33 Be not deceived: evil communications corrupt good manners.
34 [f]Awake to righteousness, and sin
not; [g]for some have not the knowledge
of God: I speak *this* to your shame.
35 But some *man* will say, [h]How are
the dead raised up? and with what
body do they come?
36 *Thou* fool, [i]that which thou
sowest is not quickened, except it die:
37 And that which thou sowest, thou
sowest not that body that shall be, but
bare grain, it may chance of wheat, or
of some other *grain:*
38 But [j]God giveth it a body as it
hath pleased him, and to every seed his
own body.
39 All flesh *is* not the same flesh: but
there is one *kind of* flesh of men, another flesh of beasts, another of fishes,
and another of birds.
40 *There are* also celestial bodies,
and bodies terrestrial: but the glory of
the celestial *is* one, and the *glory* of the
terrestrial *is* another.
41 *There is* one glory of the sun, and
another glory of the moon, and another glory of the stars: for *one* star
differeth from *another* star in glory.
42 [k]So also *is* the resurrection of the
dead. It is sown in corruption: it is
raised in incorruption:
43 [l]It is sown in dishonour; it is
raised in glory: it is sown in weakness;
it is raised in power:
44 It is sown a natural body; it is
raised a spiritual body. There is a natural body, and there is a spiritual body.

23 [u]1 Thess. 4.15
24 [v]Dan. 7.14; Eph. 5.27
25 [w]Ps. 110.1; Heb. 1.13
26 [x]Heb. 2.14
27 [y]Matt. 28.18; 1 Pet. 3.22
28 [z]Matt. 13.41; Eph. 1.10; [a]John 14.28; ch. 11.3
30 [b]2 Cor. 11.26
31 [4]Some read, our [c]Acts 20.23;
32 [5]Or, to speak after the manner of men [d]2 Cor. 1.8 [e]Isa. 22.13
34 [f]Eph. 5.14 [g]1 Thess. 4.5
35 [h]Ezek. 37.3
36 [i]John 12.24
38 [j]Ps. 104.14
42 [k]Dan. 12.3;
43 [l]Phil. 3.21
45 [m]Gen. 2.7 [n]Rom. 5.14 [o]John 5.21
47 [p]Gen. 2.7 [q]Gen. 3.19 [r]Isa. 9.6
48 [s]Phil. 3.20
49 [t]Gen. 5.3 [u]Rom. 8.29
50 [v]Matt. 16.17
51 [w]1 Thess. 4.15 [x]Phil. 3.21
52 [y]Matt. 24.31
53 [z]2 Cor. 5.4
54 [a]Rev. 20.14
55 [b]Hos. 13.14 [6]Or, hell
56 [c]Rom. 3.19
57 [d]Rom. 7.25 [e]Ps. 98.1
58 [f]2 Chr. 15.7 [g]Ps. 19.11

CHAPTER 16

1 [a]Acts 11.29
2 [b]Luke 24.1
3 [c]2 Cor. 8.19 [1]gift
5 [d]Acts 19.21
6 [e]Acts 15.3

45 And so it is written, The first man
Ăd'ăm [m]was made a living soul; [n]the
last Ăd'ăm *was made* [o]a quickening
spirit.
46 Howbeit that *was* not first which
is spiritual, but that which is natural;
and afterward that which is spiritual.
47 [p]The first man *is* of the earth,
[q]earthy: the second man *is* the Lord
[r]from heaven.
48 As *is* the earthy, such *are* they
also that are earthy: [s]and as *is* the
heavenly, such *are* they also that are
heavenly.
49 And [t]as we have borne the image
of the earthy, [u]we shall also bear the
image of the heavenly.
50 Now this I say, brethren, that
[v]flesh and blood cannot inherit the
kingdom of God; neither doth corruption inherit incorruption.
51 Behold, I shew you a mystery;
[w]We shall not all sleep, [x]but we shall
all be changed,
52 In a moment, in the twinkling of
an eye, at the last trump: [y]for the trumpet shall sound, and the dead shall be
raised incorruptible, and we shall be
changed.
53 For this corruptible must put on
incorruption, and [z]this mortal *must*
put on immortality.
54 So when this corruptible shall
have put on incorruption, and this mortal shall have put on immortality, then
shall be brought to pass the saying that
is written, [a]Death is swallowed up in
victory.
55 [b]O death, where *is* thy sting? O
[6]grave, where *is* thy victory?
56 The sting of death *is* sin; and [c]the
strength of sin *is* the law.
57 [d]But thanks *be* to God, which
giveth us [e]the victory through our
Lord Jē'sus Chrīst.
58 Therefore, my beloved brethren,
[f]be ye stedfast, unmoveable, always
abounding in the work of the Lord,
forasmuch as ye know [g]that your labour is not in vain in the Lord.

16

Now concerning [a]the collection
for the saints, as I have given order to the churches of Gā-lā'tiȧ, even
so do ye.
2 [b]Upon the first *day* of the week let
every one of you lay by him in store, as
God hath prospered him, that there be
no gatherings when I come.
3 And when I come, [c]whomsoever
ye shall approve by *your* letters, them
will I send to bring your [1]liberality
unto Je-ru'sa-lĕm.
4 And if it be meet that I go also,
they shall go with me.
5 Now I will come unto you, [d]when I
shall pass through Măç-e-dō'nĭ-ȧ: for I
do pass through Măç-e-dō'nĭ-ȧ.
6 And it may be that I will abide,
yea, and winter with you, that ye may
[e]bring me on my journey whithersoever I go.
7 For I will not see you now by the
way; but I trust to tarry a while with
you, if the Lord permit.

8 But I will tarry at Ĕph'ĕ-sŭs until Pĕn'te-cŏst.

9 For [f]a great door and effectual is opened unto me, and [g]*there are* many adversaries.

10 Now if Ti-mō'the-ŭs come, see that he may be with you without fear: for [h]he worketh the work of the Lord, as I also *do*.

11 [i]Let no man therefore despise him: but conduct him forth in peace, that he may come unto me: for I look for him with the brethren.

12 As touching *our* brother [j]A-pŏl'los, I greatly desired him to come unto you with the brethren: but his will was not at all to come at this time; but he will come when he shall have convenient time.

13 Watch ye, stand fast in the faith, quit you like men, be strong.

14 Let all your things be done with charity.

15 I beseech you, brethren, (ye know the house of Stĕph'a-năs, that it is the firstfruits of A-chā'iȧ, and *that* they have addicted themselves to the ministry of the saints,)

16 That ye submit yourselves unto such, and to every one that helpeth with *us*, and laboureth.

17 I am glad of the coming of Stĕph'a-năs and Fôr-tū-nā'tus and A-chā'i-cus: [k]for that which was lacking on your part they have supplied.

18 [l]For they have refreshed my spirit and yours: therefore acknowledge ye them that are such.

19 [m]The churches of Ā'siȧ salute you. Ă'quĭ-lȧ and Prĭs-çĭl'lȧ salute you much in the Lord, [n]with the church that is in their house.

20 All the brethren greet you. Greet ye one another with an holy kiss.

21 The salutation of *me* Pạul with mine own hand.

22 If any man love nọt the Lord Jē'sus Chrīst, [o]let him be Ăn-ăth'e-mȧ [p]Mär'an-ā'thȧ.

23 The grace of our Lord Jē'sus Chrīst *be* with you.

24 My love *be* with you all in Chrīst Jē'sus. Amen.

9 [f]Acts 14.27; Rev. 3.8 [g]Acts 19.9
10 [h]Rom. 16.21; Phil. 2.19-22
11 [i]Luke 10.16
12 [j]Acts 18.24; ch. 1.12
17 [k]2 Cor. 11.9
18 [l]Col. 4.8
19 [m]Acts 16.6; Acts 19.10; Rev. 1.4-11 [n]Rom. 16.5; Phile. 2
22 [o]Gal. 1.8-9; Heb. 10.26 [p]Jude 14-15

THE SECOND LETTER OF PAUL TO THE

CORINTHIANS

Life's QUESTIONS

What is the preacher's job?
What should a preacher preach about?
Why is the preacher involved in so much social work?

God's Answers

About A. D. 57 Paul's troubles with the church at Corinth demanded that he defend himself and the work of preachers and show what a minister's job was all about. Ministry did not make one preacher better than another but joined all in sharing Christ's sufferings and proclaiming His message of reconciliation.

Second Corinthians shows: ministry may comfort or discipline but must be done in love, forgiveness, sincerity, and integrity (1—2); ministry ignores present suffering in light of resurrection hope and Christ's love leading to preaching the message of reconciliation (3—7); ministry encourages stewardship to provide help for the poor and needy (8—9); Paul's ministry offered an example to others of devotion to the church and willingness to suffer in God's cause (10—13).

Second Corinthians encourages you to minister for Christ in devotion to God, stewardship for others, and in willingness to suffer that all may be reconciled to God.

1 Pạul, an apostle of Jē'sus Chrīst by the will of God, and Tĭm'o-thȳ *our* brother, unto the church of God which is at Cŏr'inth, [a]with all the saints which are in all A-chā'iȧ:

2 [b]Grace *be* to you and peace from God our Father, and *from* the Lord Jē'sus Chrīst.

3 [c]Blessed *be* God, even the Father of our Lord Jē'sus Chrīst, [d]the Father of mercies, and the God of all comfort;

4 [e]Who comforteth us in all our tribulation, that we may be able to comfort them which are in any trouble, by the comfort wherewith we ourselves are comforted of God.

5 For as [f]the sufferings of Chrīst abound in us, so our consolation also aboundeth by Chrīst.

6 And whether we be afflicted, [g]*it is* for your consolation and salvation, which [1]is effectual in the enduring of the same sufferings which we also suffer: or whether we be comforted, *it is* for your consolation and salvation.

7 And our hope of you *is* stedfast, knowing, that [h]as ye are partakers of the sufferings, so *shall ye be* also of the consolation.

8 For we would not, brethren, have you ignorant of [i]our trouble which came to us in Ā'siȧ, that we were pressed out of measure, above strength, insomuch that we despaired even of life:

9 But we had the [2]sentence of death in ourselves, that we should not [j]trust in ourselves, but in God which raiseth the dead:

10 [k]Who delivered us from so great a death, and doth deliver: in whom we trust that he will yet deliver *us;*

CHAPTER 1
1 [a]Col. 1.2
2 [b]Phil. 1.2
3 [c]Eph. 1.3 [d]Ex. 34.6
4 [e]2 Thess. 2.16
5 [f]Acts 9.4; Phil. 1.20
6 [g]ch. 4.15 [1]Or, is wrought
7 [h]Rom. 8.17
8 [i]Acts 19.23
9 [2]Or, answer [j]Jer. 17.5-7; Heb. 11.19
10 [k]1 Sam. 7.12

11 Ye also [l]helping together by
prayer for us, that [m]for the gift *be-*
stowed upon us by the means of many
persons thanks may be given by many
on our behalf.
12 For our rejoicing is this, the testimony of our conscience, that in simplicity and [n]godly sincerity, [o]not with
fleshly wisdom, but by the grace of
God, we have had our conversation in
the world, and more abundantly to
you-ward.
13 For we write none other things
unto you, than what ye read or acknowledge; and I trust ye shall acknowledge even to the end;
14 As also ye have acknowledged us
in part, [p]that we are your rejoicing,
even as [q]ye also *are* ours in the day of
the Lord Jē'sus.
15 And in this confidence [r]I was
minded to come unto you before, that
ye might have [s]a second [3]benefit;
16 And to pass by you into Măç-e-
dō'nĭ-ȧ, and [t]to come again out of Măç-
e-dō'nĭ-ȧ unto you, and of you to be
brought on my way toward Jū-dæ'ȧ.
17 When I therefore was thus
minded, did I use lightness? or the
things that I purpose, do I purpose [u]ac-
cording to the flesh, that with me there
should be yea yea, and nay nay?
18 But *as* God *is* true, our [4]word toward you was not yea and nay.
19 For [v]the Son of God, Jē'sus Chrīst,
who was preached among you by us,
even by me and [w]Sĭl-vā'nus and Tĭ-
mō'the-ŭs, was not yea and nay, but in
him was yea.
20 [x]For all the promises of God in
him *are* yea, and in him Amen, unto
the glory of God by us.
21 Now he which stablisheth us with
you in Chrīst, and [y]hath anointed us, *is*
God;
22 Who [z]hath also sealed us, and
[a]given the earnest of the Spirit in our
hearts.
23 Moreover I call God for a record
upon my soul, [b]that to spare you I
came not as yet unto Cŏr'inth.
24 Not for that we have dominion
over your faith, but are helpers of your
joy: for [c]by faith ye stand.

2

But I determined this with myself,
[a]that I would not come again to you
in heaviness.
2 For if I make you sorry, who is he
then that maketh me glad, but the
same which is made sorry by me?
3 And I wrote this same unto you,
lest, when I came, I should have sorrow from them of whom I ought to rejoice; [b]having confidence in you all,
that my joy is *the joy* of you all.
4 For out of much affliction and anguish of heart I wrote unto you with
many tears; not [c]that ye should be
grieved, but that ye might know the
love which I have more abundantly
unto you.
5 But [d]if any have caused grief, he
hath not [e]grieved me, but in part: that I
may not overcharge you all.
6 Sufficient to such a man *is* this
[1]punishment, which *was inflicted* [f]of
many.
7 [g]So that contrariwise ye *ought*
rather to forgive *him,* and comfort *him,*
lest perhaps such a one should be swallowed up with overmuch sorrow.
8 Wherefore I beseech you that ye
would confirm *your* love toward him.
9 For to this end also did I write,
that I might know the proof of you,
whether ye be obedient in all things.
10 To whom ye forgive any thing, I
forgive also: for if I forgave any thing,
to whom I forgave *it,* for your sakes
forgave I it [2]in the person of Chrīst;
11 Lest [h]Sā'tan should get an advantage of us: for we are not ignorant of
his devices.
12 Furthermore, [i]when I came to
Trō'ăs to *preach* Chrīst's gospel, and a
door was opened unto me of the Lord,
13 I had no rest in my spirit, because
I found not Tī'tus my brother: but taking my leave of them, I went from
thence into Măç-e-dō'nĭ-ȧ.
14 Now thanks *be* unto God, which
always causeth us to triumph in Chrīst,
and maketh manifest the savour of his
knowledge by us in every place.
15 For we are unto God a sweet savour of Chrīst, in them that are saved,
and in them that perish:
16 To the one *we are* the savour of
death unto death; and to the other the
savour of life unto life. And who *is* sufficient for these things?
17 For we are not as many, which
[3]corrupt the word of God: but as of sincerity, but as of God, in the sight of
God speak we [4]in Chrīst.

3

Do [a]we begin again to commend
ourselves? or need we, as some *oth-*
ers, [b]epistles of commendation to you,
or *letters* of commendation from you?
2 [c]Ye are our epistle written in our
hearts, known and read of all men:
3 *Forasmuch as ye are* manifestly declared to be the epistle of Chrīst [d]minis-
tered by us, written not with ink, but
with the Spirit of the living God; not
[e]in tables of stone, but [f]in fleshy tables
of the heart.
4 And such trust have we through
Chrīst to God-ward:
5 [g]Not that we are sufficient of ourselves to think any thing as of ourselves; but [h]our sufficiency *is* of God;
6 Who also hath made us able ministers of [i]the new testament; not [j]of the
letter, but of the spirit: for [k]the letter
killeth, [l]but the spirit [1]giveth life.
7 But if the ministration of death,
written *and* engraven in stones, was
glorious, so that the children of Is'ra-el
could not stedfastly behold the face of
Mō'ses for the glory of his countenance; which *glory* was to be done
away:
8 How shall not [m]the ministration
of the spirit be rather glorious?
9 For if the ministration of condemnation *be* glory, much more doth the
ministration [n]of righteousness exceed
in glory.

11 [l]Rom. 15.30; Phil. 1.19; Phile. 22
[m]ch. 4.15
12 [n]ch. 2.17
[o]1 Cor. 2.4
14 [p]ch. 5.12
[q]Phil. 2.16
15 [r]1 Cor. 4.19
[s]Rom. 1.11
[3]Or, grace
16 [t]1 Cor. 16.5
17 [u]ch. 10.2
18 [4]Or, preaching
19 [v]Mark 1.1; Luke 1.35; Acts 9.20
[w]Acts 18.5
20 [x]Ps. 72.17; Isa. 7.14; Rom. 15.8-9
21 [y]1 John 2.20-27
22 [z]Eph. 4.30; 2 Tim. 2.19; Rev. 2.17
[a]Eph. 1.14
23 [b]1 Cor. 4.21
24 [c]Rom. 11.20

CHAPTER 2
1 [a]ch. 12.20
3 [b]Gal. 5.10
4 [c]ch. 7.8-9
5 [d]1 Cor. 5.1
[e]Gal. 4.12
6 [1]Or, censure
[f]1 Tim. 5.20
7 [g]Gal. 6.1; Heb. 12.12
10 [2]Or, in the sight
11 [h]Eph. 6.11-12; 1 Pet. 5.8
12 [i]Acts 16.8; Acts 20.6
17 [3]Or, deal deceitfully with
[4]Or, of

CHAPTER 3
1 [a]ch. 5.12
[b]Acts 18.27
2 [c]1 Cor. 9.2
3 [d]1 Cor. 3.5
[e]Ex. 24.12
[f]Ps. 40.8; Ezek. 11.19
5 [g]John 15.5
[h]1 Cor. 15.10
6 [i]Matt. 26.28; Heb. 8.6-8
[j]Rom. 2.27
[k]Rom. 3.20; Gal. 3.10
[l]Rom. 8.2
[1]Or, quickeneth
8 [m]Gal. 3.5
9 [n]Rom. 1.17

10 For even that which was made
glorious had no glory in this respect,
by reason of the glory that excelleth.
11 For if that which is done away
was glorious, much more that which
remaineth *is* glorious.
12 Seeing then that we have such
hope, we use great [2]plainness of speech:
13 And not as Mō'ses, [o]*which* put a
vail over his face, that the children of
Is'ra-el could not stedfastly look to
[p]the end of that which is abolished:
14 But [q]their minds were blinded:
for until this day remaineth the same
vail untaken away in the reading of the
old testament; which *vail* is done away
in Chrīst.
15 But even unto this day, when
Mō'ses is read, the vail is upon their
heart.
16 Nevertheless [r]when it shall turn
to the Lord, [s]the vail shall be taken
away.
17 Now the Lord is that Spirit: and
where the Spirit of the Lord *is*, there *is*
liberty.
18 But we all, with open face beholding [t]as in a glass the glory of the Lord,
[u]are changed into the same image
from glory to glory, *even* as [3]by the
Spirit of the Lord.

4 Therefore seeing we have this ministry, as we have received mercy,
we faint not;
2 But have renounced the hidden
things of [1]dishonesty, not walking in
craftiness, [a]nor handling the word of
God deceitfully; but by manifestation
of the truth commending ourselves to
every man's conscience in the sight of
God.
3 But if our gospel be hid, [b]it is hid
to them that are lost:
4 In whom [c]the god of this world
[d]hath blinded the minds of them which
believe not, lest the light of the glorious
gospel of Chrīst, [e]who is the image of
God, should shine unto them.
5 For we preach not ourselves, but
Chrīst Jē'sus the Lord; and [f]ourselves
your servants for Jē'sus' sake.
6 For God, [g]who commanded the
light to shine out of darkness, [2]hath
[h]shined in our hearts, to *give* [i]the light
of the knowledge of the glory of God in
the face of Jē'sus Chrīst.
7 But we have this treasure in
[j]earthen vessels, [k]that the excellency
of the power may be of God, and not of
us.
8 *We are* troubled on every side, yet
not distressed; *we are* perplexed, but
[3]not in despair;
9 Persecuted, but not forsaken; cast
down, but not destroyed;
10 [l]Always bearing about in the
body the dying of the Lord Jē'sus,
[m]that the life also of Jē'sus might be
made manifest in our body.
11 For we which live are alway delivered unto death for Jē'sus' sake, that
the life also of Jē'sus might be made
manifest in our mortal flesh.
12 So then death worketh in us, but
life in you.
13 We having the same spirit of faith,
according as it is written, [n]I believed,
and therefore have I spoken; we also
believe, and therefore speak;
14 Knowing that he which raised up
the Lord Jē'sus shall raise up us also
by Jē'sus, and shall present *us* with
you.
15 For all things *are* for your sakes,
that the abundant grace might through
the thanksgiving of many redound to
the glory of God.
16 For which cause we faint not; but
though our outward man perish, yet
the inward *man* is renewed day by
day.
17 For our light affliction, which is
but for a moment, worketh for us a far
more exceeding *and* eternal weight of
glory;
18 While we look not at the things
which are seen, but at the things which
are not seen: for the things which are
seen *are* temporal; but the things which
are not seen *are* eternal.

5 For we know that if [a]our earthly
house of *this* tabernacle were dissolved, we have [b]a building of God, an
house not made with hands, eternal in
the heavens.
2 For in this [c]we groan, earnestly
desiring to be clothed upon with our
house which is from heaven:
3 If so be that [d]being clothed we
shall not be found naked.
4 For we that are in *this* tabernacle
do groan, being burdened: not for that
we would be unclothed, but [e]clothed
upon, that mortality might be swallowed up of life.
5 Now [f]he that hath wrought us for
the selfsame thing *is* God, who also
[g]hath given unto us the earnest of the
Spirit.
6 Therefore *we are* always confident, knowing that, whilst we are at
home in the body, we are absent from
the Lord:
7 (For [h]we walk by faith, not by
sight:)
8 We are confident, *I say*, and [i]will-
ing rather to be absent from the body,
and to be present with the Lord.
9 Wherefore we [1]labour, that,
whether present or absent, we may be
accepted of him.
10 For we must all appear before the
judgment seat of Chrīst; [j]that every
one may receive the things *done* in *his*
body, according to that he hath done,
whether *it be* good or bad.
11 Knowing therefore the terror of
the Lord, we persuade men; but we are
made manifest unto God; and I trust
also are made manifest in your con-
sciences.
12 For we commend not ourselves
again unto you, but give you occasion
to glory on our behalf, that ye may
have somewhat to *answer* them which
glory [2]in appearance, and not in heart.
13 For [k]whether we be beside ourselves, *it is* to God: or whether we be
sober, *it is* for your cause.

12 [2]Or, boldness
13 [o]Ex. 34.33
[p]Rom. 10.4; Gal. 3.23
14 [q]Isa. 6.10
16 [r]Rom. 11.23
[s]Isa. 25.7
18 [t]ch. 4.4-6
[u]John 17.17; Rom. 8.29
[3]Or, of the Lord the Spirit

CHAPTER 4
2 [1]shame
[a]1 Thess. 2.3-5
3 [b]Isa. 6.9
4 [c]John 12.31; Eph. 6.12
[d]Isa. 6.10; Matt. 13.4
[e]John 1.18; Phil. 2.6
5 [f]1 Cor. 9.19
6 [g]Gen. 1.3
[2]is he who hath
[h]2 Pet. 1.19
[i]Ps. 27.1; Isa. 2.5; Eph. 5.8-14
7 [j]ch. 5.1
[k]1 Cor. 2.5; Eph. 1.19-20
8 [3]Or, not altogether without help, or, means
10 [l]Gal. 6.17; Phil. 3.10
[m]Rom. 8.17; 1 Pet. 4.13
13 [n]Ps. 116.10

CHAPTER 5
1 [a]2 Pet. 1.13
[b]Phil. 3.21; Heb. 11.10
2 [c]Rom. 8.23
3 [d]Rev. 3.18
4 [e]1 Cor. 15.53
5 [f]Isa. 29.23
[g]Rom. 8.23; Eph. 1.14
7 [h]Deut. 12.9; Rom. 8.24-25; 1 Cor. 13.12; 1 Pet. 1.8-9
8 [i]Phil. 1.23
9 [1]Or, endeavour
10 [j]Rev. 22.12
12 [2]in the face
13 [k]ch. 11.1

14 For the love of Chrīst constraineth us; because we thus judge, that [l]if
one died for all, then were all dead:
15 And *that* he died for all, [m]that
they which live should not henceforth
live unto themselves, but unto him
which died for them, and rose again.
16 [n]Wherefore henceforth know we
no man after the flesh: yea, though we
have known Chrīst after the flesh, [o]yet
now henceforth know we *him* no more.
17 Therefore if any man *be* in Chrīst,
[3]*he is* a new creature: [p]old things are
passed away; behold, all things are become new.
18 And all things *are* of God, who
hath reconciled us to himself by Jē'sus
Chrīst, and hath given to us the ministry of reconciliation;
19 To wit, that [q]God was in Chrīst,
reconciling the world unto himself, not
imputing their trespasses unto them;
and hath [4]committed unto us the word
of reconciliation.
20 Now then we are [r]ambassadors
for Chrīst, as though God did beseech
you by us: we pray *you* in Chrīst's
stead, be ye reconciled to God.
21 For [s]he hath made him *to be* sin
for us, who [t]knew no sin; that we
might be made [u]the righteousness of
God in him.

6 We then, *as* [a]workers together *with*
him, beseech *you* also [b]that ye receive not the grace of God in vain.
2 (For he saith, [c]I have heard thee in
a time accepted, and in the day of salvation have I succoured thee: behold,
now *is* the accepted time; behold, now
is the day of salvation.)
3 [d]Giving no offence in any thing,
that the ministry be not blamed:
4 But in all *things* [1]approving ourselves [e]as the ministers of God, in
much patience, in afflictions, in necessities, in distresses,
5 In stripes, in imprisonments, [2]in
tumults, in labours, in watchings, in
fastings;
6 By pureness, by knowledge, by
longsuffering, by kindness, by the Hō'lȳ
Ghōst, by love unfeigned,
7 By the word of truth, by [f]the power
of God, by [g]the armour of righteousness on the right hand and on the left,
8 By honour and dishonour, by evil
report and good report: as deceivers,
and *yet* true;
9 As unknown, and [h]*yet* well known;
[i]as dying, and, behold, we live; [j]as chastened, and not killed;
10 As sorrowful, yet alway rejoicing; as poor, yet making many rich; as
having nothing, and *yet* possessing all
things.
11 O *ye* Co-rĭn'thĭ-ans, our mouth is
open unto you, our heart is enlarged.
12 Ye are not straitened in us, but
[k]ye are straitened in your own bowels.
13 Now for a recompence in the
same, (I speak as unto *my* children,) be
ye also enlarged.
14 [l]Be ye not unequally yoked together with unbelievers: for [m]what fellowship hath righteousness with un-

14 [l]Isa. 53.6; 1 John 2.1-2
15 [m]1 Pet. 4.2
16 [n]Matt. 12.50
[o]John 6.63
17 [3]Or, let him be
[p]Isa. 65.17; Rev. 21.5
19 [q]Isa. 43.25; 1 John 2.1-2
[4]put in us
20 [r]Job 33.23; Eph. 6.20
21 [s]Isa. 53.6-9; 1 Pet. 2.22
[t]Isa. 53.9; Heb. 7.26
[u]Jer. 23.6; Phil. 3.9

CHAPTER 6
1 [a]1 Cor. 3.9; ch. 5.20
[b]Heb. 12.15
2 [c]Isa. 49.8
3 [d]1 Cor. 9.12
4 [1]commending
[e]1 Cor. 4.1
5 [2]Or, in tossings to and fro
7 [f]Acts 11.21; Heb. 2.4
[g]2 Tim. 4.7
9 [h]ch. 5.11
[i]1 Cor. 4.9
[j]Ps. 118.18
12 [k]ch. 12.15
14 [l]Ex. 34.16; Deut. 7.2-3
[m]1 Sam. 5.2; Eph. 5.7
16 [n]1 Pet. 2.5
[o]Lev. 26.12; Zech. 8.8
17 [p]Isa. 52.11; Rev. 18.4
18 [q]Jer. 31.1-9; Rev. 21.7

CHAPTER 7
1 [a]1 John 3.3
4 [b]1 Cor. 1.4
[c]Phil. 2.17
5 [d]ch. 2.13
[e]ch. 4.8
[f]Deut. 32.25
6 [g]2 Thess. 2.16
8 [h]ch. 2.4
9 [1]Or, according to God
10 [i]2 Sam. 12.13;
[j]Gen. 4.13
11 [k]Jer. 50.4-5

righteousness? and what communion
hath light with darkness?
15 And what concord hath Chrīst
with Bē'lĭ-al? or what part hath he that
believeth with an infidel?
16 And what agreement hath the
temple of God with idols? for [n]ye are
the temple of the living God; as God
hath said, [o]I will dwell in them, and
walk in *them;* and I will be their God,
and they shall be my people.
17 [p]Wherefore come out from among
them, and be ye separate, saith the
Lord, and touch not the unclean *thing:*
and I will receive you,
18 [q]And will be a Father unto you,
and ye shall be my sons and daughters, saith the Lord Almighty.

7 Having [a]therefore these promises,
dearly beloved, let us cleanse ourselves from all filthiness of the flesh
and spirit, perfecting holiness in the
fear of God.
2 Receive us; we have wronged no
man, we have corrupted no man, we
have defrauded no man.
3 I speak not *this* to condemn *you:*
for I have said before, that ye are in our
hearts to die and live with *you.*
4 Great *is* my boldness of speech toward you, [b]great *is* my glorying of
you: [c]I am filled with comfort, I am
exceeding joyful in all our tribulation.
5 For, [d]when we were come into
Măç-e-dō'nĭ-ȧ, our flesh had no rest,
but we [e]were troubled on every side;
[f]without *were* fightings, within *were*
fears.
6 Nevertheless [g]God, that comforteth those that are cast down, comforted us by the coming of Tī'tus;
7 And not by his coming only, but
by the consolation wherewith he was
comforted in you, when he told us your
earnest desire, your mourning, your
fervent mind toward me; so that I rejoiced the more.
8 For though I made you sorry with
a letter, I do not repent, [h]though I did
repent: for I perceive that the same
epistle hath made you sorry, though *it*
were but for a season.
9 Now I rejoice, not that ye were
made sorry, but that ye sorrowed to
repentance: for ye were made sorry [1]af-
ter a godly manner, that ye might receive damage by us in nothing.
10 For [i]godly sorrow worketh repentance to salvation not to be repented
of: [j]but the sorrow of the world worketh death.
11 For behold this selfsame thing,
that ye [k]sorrowed after a godly sort,
what carefulness it wrought in you,
yea, *what* clearing of yourselves, yea,
what indignation, yea, *what* fear, yea,
what vehement desire, yea, *what* zeal,
yea, *what* revenge! In all *things* ye
have approved yourselves to be clear
in this matter.
12 Wherefore, though I wrote unto
you, *I did it* not for his cause that had
done the wrong, nor for his cause that
suffered wrong, but that our care for

you in the sight of God might appear
unto you.
13 Therefore we were comforted in
your comfort: yea, and exceedingly
the more joyed we for the joy of Tī'tus,
because his spirit [l]was refreshed by
you all.
14 For if I have boasted any thing to
him of you, I am not ashamed; but as
we spake all things to you in truth,
even so our boasting, which *I made* before Tī'tus, is found a truth.
15 And his [2]inward affection is more
abundant toward you, whilst he remembereth [m]the obedience of you all,
how with fear and trembling ye received him.
16 I rejoice therefore that [n]I have
confidence in you in all *things*.

8 Moreover, brethren, [1]we do you to
wit of the grace of God bestowed on
the churches of Măç-e-dō'nĭ-ȧ;
2 How that in a great trial of affliction the abundance of their joy and
[a]their deep poverty abounded unto the
riches of their [2]liberality.
3 For to *their* power, I bear record,
yea, and beyond *their* power *they were*
willing of themselves;
4 Praying us with much intreaty that
we would receive the gift, and *take
upon us* [b]the fellowship of the ministering to the saints.
5 And *this they did*, not as we hoped,
but first [c]gave their own selves to the
Lord, and unto us by the will of God.
6 Insomuch that [d]we desired Tī'tus,
that as he had begun, so he would also
finish in you the same [3]grace also.
7 Therefore, as [e]ye abound in every
thing, in faith, and utterance, and
knowledge, and *in* all diligence, and *in*
your love to us, *see* [f]that ye abound in
this grace also.
8 [g]I speak not by commandment,
but by occasion of the forwardness of
others, and to prove the sincerity of
your love.
9 For ye know the grace of our Lord
Jē'sus Chrīst, [h]that, though he was
rich, yet for your sakes he became
poor, that ye through his poverty might
be rich.
10 And herein [i]I give *my* advice: for
[j]this is expedient for you, who have
begun before, not only to do, but also
to be [4]forward a year ago.
11 Now therefore perform the doing
of it; that as *there was* a readiness to
will, so *there may be* a performance
also out of that which ye have.
12 For [k]if there be first a willing
mind, *it is* accepted according to that a
man hath, *and* not according to that he
hath not.
13 For *I mean* not that other men be
eased, and ye burdened:
14 But by an equality, *that* now at
this time your abundance *may be a supply* for their want, that their abundance also may be *a supply* for your
want: that there may be equality:
15 As it is written, [l]He that *had gathered* much had nothing over; and he
that *had gathered* little had no lack.

13 [l]Rom. 15.32; 1 Cor. 16.18
15 [2]bowels
[m]ch. 2.9; Phil. 2.12
16 [n]Phile. 8-21
CHAPTER 8
1 [1]we must inform you
2 [a]Mark 12.44
[2]simplicity
4 [b]Acts 11.29; ch. 9.1
5 [c]1 Sam. 1.28; Heb. 13.16
6 [d]ch. 12.18
[3]Or, gift
7 [e]1 Cor. 1.5
[f]Ps. 112.9; ch. 9.8
8 [g]1 Cor. 7.6
9 [h]Matt. 8.20; Phil. 2.6-7
10 [i]1 Cor. 7.25
[j]Prov. 19.17; Matt. 10.42
[4]willing
12 [k]Mark 12.43-44; Luke 21.3
15 [l]Ex. 16.18
18 [m]ch. 12.18
19 [n]1 Cor. 16.3
[5]Or, gift
[o]ch. 4.15
20 [p]Eph. 5.15
21 [q]Prov. 3.4; Phil. 4.8
22 [6]Or, he hath
23 [r]Phil. 2.25
CHAPTER 9
1 [a]Acts 11.29; 1 Cor. 16.1
2 [b]ch. 8.19
[c]ch. 8.24
[d]ch. 8.10
3 [e]ch. 8.6-17
5 [1]blessing
[2]Or, which hath been so much spoken of before
6 [f]Prov. 11.24; Heb. 6.10
7 [g]Deut. 15.7
[h]Ex. 25.2;
8 [i]Ps. 84.11;
9 [j]Ps. 112.9

16 But thanks *be* to God, which put
the same earnest care into the heart of
Tī'tus for you.
17 For indeed he accepted the exhortation; but being more forward, of his
own accord he went unto you.
18 And we have sent with him [m]the
brother, whose praise *is* in the gospel
throughout all the churches;
19 And not *that* only, but who was
also [n]chosen of the churches to travel
with us with this [5]grace, which is administered by us [o]to the glory of the
same Lord, and *declaration of* your
ready mind:
20 [p]Avoiding this, that no man
should blame us in this abundance
which is administered by us:
21 [q]Providing for honest things, not
only in the sight of the Lord, but also in
the sight of men.
22 And we have sent with them our
brother, whom we have oftentimes
proved diligent in many things, but
now much more diligent, upon the
great confidence which [6]*I have* in you.
23 Whether *any do inquire* of Tī'tus,
he is my partner and fellowhelper concerning you: or our brethren *be inquired of, they are* [r]the messengers of
the churches, *and* the glory of Chrīst.
24 Wherefore shew ye to them, and
before the churches, the proof of your
love, and of our boasting on your
behalf.

9 For as touching [a]the ministering to
the saints, it is superfluous for me
to write to you:
2 For I know [b]the forwardness of
your mind, [c]for which I boast of you to
them of Măç-e-dō'nĭ-ȧ, that [d]A-chā'iȧ
was ready a year ago; and your zeal
hath provoked very many.
3 [e]Yet have I sent the brethren, lest
our boasting of you should be in vain
in this behalf; that, as I said, ye may be
ready:
4 Lest haply if they of Măç-e-dō'nĭ-ȧ
come with me, and find you unprepared, we (that we say not, ye) should
be ashamed in this same confident
boasting.
5 Therefore I thought it necessary to
exhort the brethren, that they would
go before unto you, and make up beforehand your [1]bounty, [2]whereof ye
had notice before, that the same might
be ready, as *a matter of* bounty, and
not as *of* covetousness.
6 [f]But this *I say*, He which soweth
sparingly shall reap also sparingly;
and he which soweth bountifully shall
reap also bountifully.
7 Every man according as he purposeth in his heart, *so let him give;*
[g]not grudgingly, or of necessity: for
[h]God loveth a cheerful giver.
8 [i]And God *is* able to make all grace
abound toward you; that ye, always
having all sufficiency in all *things*,
may abound to every good work:
9 (As it is written, [j]He hath dispersed abroad; he hath given to the
poor: his righteousness remaineth for
ever.

10 Now he that [k]ministereth seed to the sower both minister bread for *your* food, and multiply your seed sown, and increase the fruits of your [l]righteousness;)

11 Being enriched in every thing to all [3]bountifulness, [m]which causeth through us thanksgiving to God.

12 For the administration of this service not only supplieth the want of the saints, but is abundant also by many thanksgivings unto God;

13 Whiles by the experiment of this ministration they [n]glorify God for your professed subjection unto the gospel of Chrīst, and for *your* liberal [o]distribution unto them, and unto all *men;*

14 And by their prayer for you, which long after you for the exceeding grace of God in you.

15 Thanks *be* unto God [p]for his unspeakable gift.

10 Now [a]I Pąul myself beseech you by the meekness and gentleness of Chrīst, who [1]in presence *am* base among you, but being absent am bold toward you:

2 But I beseech *you,* [b]that I may not be bold when I am present with that confidence, wherewith I think to be bold against some, which [2]think of us as if we walked according to the flesh.

3 For though we walk in the flesh, we do not war after the flesh:

4 ([c]For the weapons of our warfare *are* not carnal, but mighty [3]through God [d]to the pulling down of strong holds;)

5 [e]Casting down [4]imaginations, and every high thing that exalteth itself against the knowledge of God, and bringing into captivity every thought to the obedience of Chrīst;

6 [f]And having in a readiness to revenge all disobedience, when [g]your obedience is fulfilled.

7 Do ye look on things after the outward appearance? [h]If any man trust to himself that he is Chrīst's, let him of himself think this again, that, as he *is* Chrīst's, even so *are* [i]we Chrīst's.

8 For though I should boast somewhat more of our authority, which the Lord hath given us for edification, and not for your destruction, I should not be ashamed:

9 That I may not seem as if I would terrify you by letters.

10 For *his* letters, [5]say they, *are* weighty and powerful; but [j]*his* bodily presence *is* weak, and *his* [k]speech contemptible.

11 Let such an one think this, that, such as we are in word by letters when we are absent, such *will we be* also in deed when we are present.

12 [l]For we dare not make ourselves of the number, or compare ourselves with some that commend themselves; but they measuring themselves by themselves, and comparing themselves among themselves, [6]are not wise.

13 But we will not boast of things without *our* measure, but according to the measure of the [7]rule which God hath distributed to us, a measure to reach even unto you.

14 For we stretch not ourselves beyond *our measure,* as though we reached not unto you: [m]for we are come as far as to you also in *preaching* the gospel of Chrīst:

15 Not boasting of things without *our* measure, *that is,* [n]of other men's labours; but having hope, when your faith is increased, that we shall be [8]enlarged by you according to our rule abundantly,

16 To preach the gospel in the *regions* beyond you, *and* not to boast in another man's [9]line of things made ready to our hand.

17 [o]But he that glorieth, let him glory in the Lord.

18 For [p]not he that commendeth himself is approved, but [q]whom the Lord commendeth.

11 Would to God ye could bear with me a little in [a]*my* folly: and indeed [1]bear with me.

2 For I am [b]jealous over you with godly jealousy: for [c]I have espoused you to one husband, [d]that I may present *you* [e]*as* a chaste virgin to Chrīst.

3 But I fear, lest by any means, as [f]the serpent beguiled Ēve through his subtilty, so your minds [g]should be corrupted from the simplicity that is in Chrīst.

4 For if he that cometh preacheth another Jē'sus, whom we have not preached, or *if* ye receive another spirit, which ye have not received, or [h]another gospel, which ye have not accepted, ye might well bear [2]with *him.*

5 For I suppose I was not a whit behind the very chiefest apostles.

6 But though *I be* rude in speech, yet not [i]in knowledge; but we have been throughly made manifest among you in all things.

7 Have I committed an offence [j]in abasing myself that ye might be exalted, because I have preached to you the gospel of God freely?

8 I robbed other churches, taking wages *of them,* to do you service.

9 And when I was present with you, and wanted, [k]I was chargeable to no man: for that which was lacking to me [l]the brethren which came from Măç-e-dō'nĭ-á supplied: and in all *things* I have kept myself [m]from being burdensome unto you, and *so* will I keep *myself.*

10 [n]As the truth of Chrīst is in me, [3]no man shall stop me of this boasting in the regions of A-chā'ia.

11 Wherefore? [o]because I love you not? God knoweth.

12 But what I do, that I will do, [p]that I may cut off occasion from them which desire occasion; that wherein they glory, they may be found even as we.

13 For such *are* false apostles, deceitful workers, transforming themselves into the apostles of Chrīst.

14 And no marvel; for Sā'tan himself is transformed into [q]an angel of light.

10 [k]Gen. 1.11-12; Isa. 55.10 [l]Hos. 10.12; Matt. 6.1
11 [3]simplicity, or, liberality [m]ch. 4.15
13 [n]Matt. 5.16 [o]Heb. 13.16
15 [p]Jas. 1.17

CHAPTER 10

1 [a]Isa. 42.2 [1]Or, in outward appearance
2 [b]1 Cor. 4.21 [2]Or, reckon
4 [c]Eph. 6.13 [3]Or, to God [d]Jer. 1.10
5 [e]1 Cor. 1.19 [4]Or, reasonings
6 [f]ch. 13.2 [g]ch. 7.15
7 [h]1 Cor. 14.37 [i]ch. 11.23
10 [5]saith he [j]Gal. 4.13 [k]1 Cor. 1.17
12 [l]ch. 5.12 [6]Or, understand it not
13 [7]Or, line
14 [m]1 Cor. 9.1
15 [n]Rom. 15.20 [8]Or, magnified in you
16 [9]Or, rule
17 [o]Isa. 65.16; Jer. 9.24
18 [p]Luke 13.14 [q]Rom. 2.29

CHAPTER 11

1 [a]ch. 5.13 [1]Or, ye do bear with me
2 [b]Gal. 4.17 [c]Hos. 2.19 [d]Col. 1.28 [e]Lev. 21.13
3 [f]Gen. 3.4; [g]1 Tim. 1.3;
4 [h]Gal. 1.7-8 [2]Or, with me
6 [i]Eph. 3.4
7 [j]Acts 18.3
9 [k]Acts 20.33 [l]Phil. 4.10 [m]ch. 12.14
10 [n]Rom. 9.1 [3]this boasting shall not be stopped in me
11 [o]ch. 7.3
12 [p]1 Cor. 9.12
14 [q]Rev. 12.9

15 Therefore *it is* no great thing if
his ministers also be transformed as
the ministers of righteousness; [r]whose
end shall be according to their works.
16 I say again, Let no man think me
a fool; if otherwise, yet as a fool [4]re-
ceive me, that I may boast myself a
little.
17 That which I speak, [s]I speak *it*
not after the Lord, but as it were foolishly, [t]in this confidence of boasting.
18 [u]Seeing that many glory after
the flesh, I will glory also.
19 For ye suffer fools gladly, seeing
ye *yourselves* are wise.
20 For ye suffer, [v]if a man bring you
into bondage, if a man devour *you*, if a
man take *of you*, if a man exalt himself,
if a man smite you on the face.
21 I speak as concerning reproach,
[w]as though we had been weak. Howbeit whereinsoever any is bold, (I speak
foolishly,) I am bold also.
22 Are they Hē′brews? [x]so *am* I.
Are they Īs′ra-el-ītes? so *am* I. Are they
the seed of Ā′brā-hăm? so *am* I.
23 Are they ministers of Chrīst? (I
speak as a fool) I *am* more; [y]in labours
more abundant, [z]in stripes above measure, in prisons more frequent, in
deaths oft.
24 Of the Jews five times received I
[a]forty *stripes* save one.
25 Thrice was I [b]beaten with rods,
[c]once was I stoned, thrice I [d]suffered
shipwreck, a night and a day I have
been in the deep;
26 *In* journeyings often, *in* perils of
waters, *in* perils of robbers, [e]*in* perils
by *mine own* countrymen, [f]*in* perils by
the heathen, *in* perils in the city, *in* perils in the wilderness, *in* perils in the
sea, *in* perils among false brethren;
27 In weariness and painfulness, in
watchings often, [g]in hunger and thirst,
in fastings often, in cold and nakedness.
28 Beside those things that are without, that which cometh upon me daily,
[h]the care of all the churches.
29 Who is weak, and I am not weak?
who is offended, and I burn not?
30 If I must needs glory, I will glory
of the things which concern mine
infirmities.
31 The God and Father of our Lord
Jē′sus Chrīst, [i]which is blessed for
evermore, knoweth that I lie not.
32 [j]In Da-măs′cus the governor under Ăr′e-tas the king kept the city of
the Dăm′as-çēnes with a garrison, desirous to apprehend me:
33 And through a window in a basket was I let down by the wall, and
escaped his hands.

12 It is not expedient for me doubtless to glory. [1]I will come to visions and revelations of the Lord.
2 I knew a man [a]in Chrīst above
fourteen years ago, (whether in the
body, I cannot tell; or whether out of
the body, I cannot tell: God knoweth;)
such an one [b]caught up to the third
heaven.
3 And I knew such a man, (whether
in the body, or out of the body, I cannot
tell: God knoweth;)
4 How that he was caught up into
[c]paradise, and heard unspeakable
words, which it is not [2]lawful for a man
to utter.
5 Of such an one will I glory: [d]yet of
myself I will not glory, but in mine infirmities.
6 For [e]though I would desire to
glory, I shall not be a fool; for I will say
the truth: but *now* I forbear, lest any
man should think of me above that
which he seeth me *to be*, or *that* he
heareth of me.
7 And lest I should be exalted above
measure through the abundance of the
revelations, there was given to me a
[f]thorn in the flesh, [g]the messenger of
Sā′tan to buffet me, lest I should be
exalted above measure.
8 [h]For this thing I besought the Lord
thrice, that it might depart from me.
9 And he said unto me, [i]My grace is
sufficient for thee: for my strength is
made perfect in weakness. Most gladly
therefore will I rather glory in my infirmities, [j]that the power of Chrīst may
rest upon me.
10 Therefore [k]I take pleasure in infirmities, in reproaches, in necessities, in persecutions, in distresses for
Chrīst's sake: [l]for when I am weak,
then am I strong.
11 I am become a fool in glorying;
ye have compelled me: for I ought to
have been commended of you: for [m]in
nothing am I behind the very chiefest
apostles, though I be nothing.
12 [n]Truly the signs of an apostle
were wrought among you in all patience, in signs, and wonders, and
mighty deeds.
13 [o]For what is it wherein ye were
inferior to other churches, except *it be*
that [p]I myself was not burdensome to
you? forgive me this wrong.
14 [q]Behold, the third time I am ready
to come to you; and I will not be burdensome to you: for [r]I seek not yours, but
you: [s]for the children ought not to lay
up for the parents, but the parents for
the children.
15 And [t]I will very gladly spend and
be spent for [3]you; though [u]the more
abundantly I love you, the less I be
loved.
16 But be it so, [v]I did not burden you:
nevertheless, being crafty, I caught you
with guile.
17 [w]Did I make a gain of you by any
of them whom I sent unto you?
18 [x]I desired Tī′tus, and with *him* I
sent a brother. Did Tī′tus make a gain
of you? walked we not in the same
spirit? *walked we* not in the same
steps?
19 [y]Again, think ye that we excuse
ourselves unto you? [z]we speak before
God in Chrīst: [a]but *we do* all things,
dearly beloved, for your edifying.
20 For I fear, lest, when I come, I
shall not find you such as I would, and
that [b]I shall be found unto you such

15 [r]Jer. 29.32; Phil. 3.19
16 [4]Or, suffer
17 [s]1 Cor. 7.6
[t]ch. 9.4
18 [u]Jer. 9.23-24; Phil. 3.3
20 [v]Gal. 2.4
21 [w]1 Cor. 1.17; Gal. 4.13
22 [x]Rom. 11.1
23 [y]1 Cor. 15.10
[z]Acts 9.16
24 [a]Deut. 25.3
25 [b]Acts 16.22; ch. 6.5
[c]Acts 14.19
[d]Acts 27.41
26 [e]Acts 9.23; Acts 21.31
[f]Acts 19.23
27 [g]1 Cor. 4.11
28 [h]Acts 20.18; Rom. 1.14
31 [i]Rom. 9.5
32 [j]Acts 9.24

CHAPTER 12
1 [1]For I will come
2 [a]Rom. 16.7; Gal. 1.22
[b]Acts 22.17
4 [c]Luke 23.43
[2]Or, possible
5 [d]ch. 11.30
6 [e]ch. 10.8
7 [f]Ezek. 28.24;
[g]Luke 13.16
8 [h]Deut. 3.23
9 [i]Eccl. 7.18;
[j]Matt. 28.18-20
10 [k]Rom. 5.3;
[l]ch. 13.4
11 [m]1 Cor. 3.4-7
12 [n]Rom. 15.18
13 [o]1 Cor. 1.7
[p]1 Cor. 9.12
14 [q]ch. 13.1
[r]Acts 20.33
[s]1 Cor. 4.14
15 [t]Phil. 2.17;
[3]your souls
[u]ch. 6.12
16 [v]ch. 11.9
17 [w]ch. 7.2
18 [x]ch. 8.6
19 [y]ch. 5.12
[z]Rom. 9.1
[a]1 Cor. 10.33
20 [b]1 Cor. 4.21

as ye would not: lest *there be* debates,
envyings, wraths, strifes, backbitings,
whisperings, swellings, tumults:
21 *And* lest, when I come again, my
God [c]will humble me among you, and
that I shall bewail many which have
sinned already, and have not repented
of the uncleanness and [d]fornication
and lasciviousness which they have
committed.
13 This *is* [a]the third *time* I am coming to you. [b]In the mouth of two
or three witnesses shall every word be
established.
2 [c]I told you before, and foretell
you, as if I were present, the second
time; and being absent now I write to
them [d]which heretofore have sinned,
and to all other, that, if I come again, I
will not spare:
3 Since ye seek a proof of Chrīst
[e]speaking in me, which to you-ward is
not weak, but is mighty [f]in you.
4 [g]For though he was crucified
through weakness, yet [h]he liveth by
the power of God. For [i]we also are
weak [1]in him, but we shall live with
him by the power of God toward you.
5 [j]Examine yourselves, whether ye
be in the faith; prove your own selves.
Know ye not your own selves, [k]how
that Jē'sus Chrīst is in you, except ye
be [l]reprobates?
6 But I trust that ye shall know that
we are not reprobates.
7 Now I pray to God that ye do no
evil; not that we should appear approved, but that ye should do that
which is honest, though [m]we be as
reprobates.
8 For we can do nothing against the
truth, but for the truth.
9 For we are glad, [n]when we are
weak, and ye are strong: and this also
we wish, [o]*even* your perfection.
10 Therefore I write these things being absent, lest being present [p]I should
use sharpness, according to the power
which the Lord hath given me to edification, and not to destruction.
11 Finally, brethren, farewell. Be perfect, be of good comfort, [q]be of one
mind, live in peace; and the God of love
[r]and peace shall be with you.
12 Greet one another with an holy
kiss.
13 All the saints salute you.
14 The grace of the Lord Jē'sus
Chrīst, and the love of God, and the
communion of the Hō'lȳ Ghōst, *be*
with you all. Amen.

21 [c]ch. 2.1-4
[d]1 Cor. 5.1
CHAPTER 13
1 [a]ch. 12.14
[b]Num. 35.30
2 [c]ch. 10.2
[d]ch. 12.21
3 [e]Matt. 10.20
[f]1 Cor. 9.2
4 [g]Phil. 2.7-8
[h]Rom. 6.4
[i]ch. 10.3
[1]Or, with him
5 [j]1 Cor. 11.28
[k]John 17.23; Rom. 8.10
[l]1 Cor. 9.27
7 [m]ch. 6.9
9 [n]1 Cor. 4.10
[o]1 Thess. 3.10
10 [p]Tit. 1.13
11 [q]Rom. 12.16; 1 Pet. 3.8
[r]Rom. 15.33; Heb. 13.20-21

THE LETTER OF PAUL TO THE

GALATIANS

Life's Questions

How can I earn salvation?
What requirements does God make for my life with Him?
What is the Spirit-filled life?

God's Answers

Perhaps about A.D. 48 Paul wrote a church in Asia Minor defining the Christian gospel against claims made by preachers who wanted the gospel to include more Jewish elements. Paul lifted legalistic requirements from believers and told them to live the life the Spirit led them to lead in faith commitment to Christ.

Galatians shows: God gives salvation through faith in Christ without requiring slavery to any legalistic actions that would give reason for boasting (1:1—5:12); salvation through faith leads to freedom to serve all people in love as the Spirit leads (5:13—6:10); boasting comes not from human accomplishments but from the new creation Christ makes you (6:11—18).

Galatians frees you to live in the Spirit and not worry about pleasing people by obeying human traditions and religious laws.

1 Pa̤ul, an apostle, (not of men, neither by man, but [a]by Jē'sus Chrīst,
and God the Father, who raised him
from the dead;)
2 And all the brethren [b]which are
with me, [c]unto the churches of Gā-
lā'tia̤:
3 [d]Grace *be* to you and peace from
God the Father, and *from* our Lord
Jē'sus Chrīst,
4 [e]Who gave himself for our sins,
that he might deliver us [f]from this present evil world, according to the will of
God and our Father:
5 To whom *be* glory for ever and
ever. Amen.
6 I marvel that ye are so soon removed from him that called you into
the grace of Chrīst unto another gospel:
7 [g]Which is not another; but there
be some [h]that trouble you, and would
pervert the gospel of Chrīst.
8 But though [i]we, or an angel from
heaven, preach any other gospel unto
you than that which we have preached
unto you, let him be accursed.
9 As we said before, so say I now
again, If any *man* preach any other gospel unto you [j]than that ye have received, let him be accursed.
10 For [k]do I now [l]persuade men, or
God? or [m]do I seek to please men? for
if I yet pleased men, I should not be the
servant of Chrīst.
11 [n]But I certify you, brethren, that
the gospel which was preached of me
is not after man.

CHAPTER 1
1 [a]Acts 9.6
2 [b]Phil. 2.22
[c]1 Cor. 16.1
3 [d]1 Cor. 1.3
4 [e]1 John 2.2
[f]Isa. 65.17; John 15.19
7 [g]2 Cor. 11.4
[h]Acts 15.1
8 [i]1 Cor. 16.22
9 [j]Deut. 4.2; Rev. 22.18
10 [k]1 Thess. 2.4
[l]1 John 3.19
[m]Jas. 4.4
11 [n]1 Cor. 15.1

12 For I neither received it of man, neither was I taught *it,* but [o]by the revelation of Jē′sus Chrīst.

13 For ye have heard of my conversation in time past in the Jews' religion, how that [p]beyond measure I persecuted the church of God, and [q]wasted it:

14 And profited in the Jews' religion above many my [1]equals in mine own nation, [r]being more exceedingly zealous [s]of the traditions of my fathers.

15 But when it pleased God, [t]who separated me from my mother's womb, and called *me* by his grace,

16 [u]To reveal his Son in me, that I might preach him among the heathen; immediately I conferred not with [v]flesh and blood:

17 Neither went I up to Je-ru′sa-lĕm to them which were apostles before me; but I went into A-rā′bĭ-ȧ, and returned again unto Da-măs′cus.

18 Then after three years I [2]went up to Je-ru′sa-lĕm to see Pē′tẽr, and abode with him fifteen days.

19 But [w]other of the apostles saw I none, save [x]Jāmes the Lord's brother.

20 Now the things which I write unto you, behold, before God, I lie not.

21 [y]Afterwards I came into the regions of Sȳr′ĭ-ȧ and Çi-lĭ′çiȧ;

22 And was unknown by face unto the churches of Jū-dæ′ȧ which were in Chrīst:

23 But they had heard only, That he which persecuted us in times past now preacheth the faith which once he destroyed.

24 And they glorified God in me.

2 Then fourteen years after [a]I went up again to Je-ru′sa-lĕm with Bär′-na-bās, and took Tī′tus with *me* also.

2 And I went up by revelation, [b]and communicated unto them that gospel which I preach among the Gĕn′tīles, but [1]privately to them which were of reputation, lest by any means [c]I should run, or had run, in vain.

3 But neither Tī′tus, who was with me, being a Greek, was compelled to be circumcised:

4 And that because of false brethren unawares brought in, who came in privily to spy out our [d]liberty which we have in Chrīst Jē′sus, [e]that they might bring us into bondage:

5 To whom we gave place by subjection, no, not for an hour; that the truth of the gospel might continue with you.

6 But of these [f]who seemed to be somewhat, (whatsoever they were, it maketh no matter to me: [g]God accepteth no man's person:) for they who seemed *to be somewhat* in [h]conference added nothing to me:

7 But contrariwise, [i]when they saw that the gospel of the uncircumcision [j]was committed unto me, as *the gospel* of the circumcision *was* unto Pē′tẽr;

8 (For he that wrought effectually in Pē′tẽr to the apostleship of the circumcision, [k]the same was mighty in me toward the Gĕn′tīles:)

9 And when Jāmes, Çē′phas, and Jŏhn, who seemed to be [l]pillars, perceived [m]the grace that was given unto me, they gave to me and Bär′na-bās the right hands of fellowship; that we *should go* unto the heathen, and they unto the circumcision.

10 Only *they would* that we should remember the poor; [n]the same which I also was forward to do.

11 [o]But when Pē′tẽr was come to Ăn′tĭ-ŏch, I withstood him to the face, because he was to be blamed.

12 For before that certain came from Jāmes, [p]he did eat with the Gĕn′tīles: but when they were come, he withdrew and separated himself, fearing them which were of the circumcision.

13 And the other Jews dissembled likewise with him; insomuch that Bär′-na-bās also was carried away with their dissimulation.

14 But when I saw that they walked not uprightly according to [q]the truth of the gospel, I said unto Pē′tẽr before *them* all, [r]If thou, being a Jew, livest after the manner of Gĕn′tīles, and not as do the Jews, why compellest thou the Gĕn′tīles to live as do the Jews?

15 [s]We *who are* Jews by nature, and not [t]sinners of the Gĕn′tīles,

16 [u]Knowing that a man is not justified by the works of the law, but [v]by the faith of Jē′sus Chrīst, even we have believed in Jē′sus Chrīst, that we might be justified by the faith of Chrīst, and not by the works of the law: for [w]by the works of the law shall no flesh be justified.

17 But if, while we seek to be justified by Chrīst, we ourselves also are found [x]sinners, *is* therefore Chrīst the minister of sin? God forbid.

18 For if I build again the things which I destroyed, I make myself a transgressor.

19 For I [y]through the law [z]am dead to the law, that I might [a]live unto God.

20 I am [b]crucified with Chrīst: nevertheless I live; yet not I, but Chrīst liveth in me: and the life which I now live in the flesh [c]I live by the faith of the Son of God, who loved me, and gave himself for me.

21 I do not frustrate the grace of God: for [d]if righteousness *come* by the law, then Chrīst is dead in vain.

3 O foolish Ga-lā′tians, [a]who hath bewitched you, that ye should not obey the truth, [b]before whose eyes Jē′sus Chrīst hath been evidently set forth, crucified among you?

2 This only would I learn of you, Received ye [c]the Spirit by the works of the law, [d]or by the hearing of faith?

3 Are ye so foolish? [e]having begun in the Spirit, are ye now made perfect by [f]the flesh?

4 [g]Have ye suffered [1]so many things in vain? if *it be* yet in vain.

5 He therefore [h]that ministereth to you the Spirit, and worketh miracles among you, *doeth he it* by the works of the law, or by the hearing of faith?

12 [o]Rom. 16.25; 1 Pet. 1.20
13 [p]1 Tim. 1.13
[q]Acts 8.3
14 [1]equals in years
[r]Phil. 3.6
[s]Jer. 9.14; Mark 7.5
15 [t]Isa. 49.1-5; Acts 9.15
16 [u]2 Cor. 4.6
[v]Matt. 16.17
18 [2]Or, returned
19 [w]1 Cor. 9.5
[x]Matt. 13.55; Mark 6.3
21 [y]Acts 9.30

CHAPTER 2
1 [a]Acts 15.2
2 [b]Acts 19.21
[1]Or, severally
[c]1 Cor. 9.26; Phil. 2.16
4 [d]John 8.31-36;
[e]ch. 4.3-9
6 [f]ch. 6.3
[g]Acts 10.34;
[h]2 Cor. 12.11
7 [i]Acts 13.46
[j]1 Thess. 2.4
8 [k]Acts 9.15
9 [l]Matt. 16.18;
[m]Rom. 1.5
10 [n]Acts 11.30
11 [o]Acts 15.35
12 [p]Acts 10.28
14 [q]Eccl. 7.20
[r]Acts 11.3
15 [s]Acts 15.10
[t]Matt. 9.11
16 [u]Acts 13.38
[v]Rom. 1.17;
[w]Ps. 143.2
17 [x]Rom. 15.8
19 [y]Rom. 3.19-20;
[z]Rom. 6.14
[a]Rom. 14.7-8
20 [b]Rom. 6.6
[c]2 Cor. 5.15
21 [d]Heb. 7.11

CHAPTER 3
1 [a]ch. 5.7
[b]1 Cor. 1.23
2 [c]Acts 2.38;
[d]Rom. 10.16
3 [e]ch. 4.9
[f]Heb. 7.16
4 [g]2 John 8
[1]Or, so great
5 [h]2 Cor. 3.8

6 Even as Ā'brā-hăm believed God, and it was [2]accounted to him for righteousness.

7 Know ye therefore that [i]they which are of faith, the same are the children of Ā'brā-hăm.

8 And the scripture, foreseeing that God would justify the heathen through faith, preached before the gospel unto Ā'brā-hăm, *saying,* [j]In thee shall all nations be blessed.

9 So then they which be of faith are blessed with faithful Ā'brā-hăm.

10 For as many as are of the works of the law are under the curse: for it is written, [k]Cursed *is* every one that continueth not in all things which are written in the book of the law to do them.

11 But that no man is justified by the law in the sight of God, *it is* evident: for, [l]The just shall live by faith.

12 And [m]the law is not of faith: but, [n]The man that doeth them shall live in them.

13 Chrīst hath redeemed us from the curse of the law, being made a curse for us: for it is written, [o]Cursed *is* every one that hangeth on a tree:

14 [p]That the blessing of Ā'brā-hăm might come on the Gĕn'tīles through Jē'sus Chrīst; that we might receive [q]the promise of the Spirit through faith.

15 Brethren, I speak after the manner of men; [r]Though *it be* but a man's [3]covenant, yet *if it be* confirmed, no man disannulleth, or addeth thereto.

16 Now to Ā'brā-hăm and his seed were the promises made. He saith not, And to seeds, as of many; but as of one, And to thy seed, which is [s]Chrīst.

17 And this I say, *that* the covenant, that was confirmed before of God in Chrīst, the law, [t]which was four hundred and thirty years after, cannot disannul, [u]that it should make the promise of none effect.

18 For if [v]the inheritance *be* of the law, [w]*it is* no more of promise: but God gave *it* to Ā'brā-hăm by promise.

19 Wherefore then *serveth* the law? [x]It was added because of transgressions, till the seed should come to whom the promise was made; *and it was* [y]ordained by angels in the hand [z]of a mediator.

20 Now a mediator is not *a mediator* of one, [a]but God is one.

21 *Is* the law then against the promises of God? God forbid: for if there had been a law given which could have given life, verily righteousness should have been by the law.

22 But the scripture hath concluded all under sin, that the promise by faith of Jē'sus Chrīst might be given to them that believe.

23 But before faith came, we were kept under the law, shut up unto the faith which should afterwards be revealed.

24 Wherefore [b]the law was our schoolmaster *to bring us* unto Chrīst, [c]that we might be justified by faith.

25 But after that faith is come, we are no longer under a schoolmaster.

26 For ye [d]are all the children of God by faith in Chrīst Jē'sus.

27 For as many of you as have been baptized into Chrīst have put on Chrīst.

28 [e]There is neither Jew nor Greek, there is neither bond nor free, there is neither male nor female: for ye are all [f]one in Chrīst Jē'sus.

29 And [g]if ye *be* Chrīst's, then are ye Ā'brā-hăms's seed, and [h]heirs according to the promise.

4 Now I say, *That* the heir, as long as he is a child, differeth nothing from a servant, though he be lord of all;

2 But is under tutors and governors until the time appointed of the father.

3 Even so we, when we were children, [a]were in bondage under the [1]elements of the world:

4 But [b]when the fulness of the time was come, God sent forth his Son, [c]made of a woman, [d]made under the law,

5 [e]To redeem them that were under the law, [f]that we might receive the adoption of sons.

6 And because ye are sons, God hath sent forth the Spirit of his Son into your hearts, crying, Ăb'bȧ, Father.

7 Wherefore thou art no more a servant, but a son; [g]and if a son, then an heir of God through Chrīst.

8 Howbeit then, [h]when ye knew not God, [i]ye did service unto them which by nature are no gods.

9 But now, [j]after that ye have known God, or rather are known of God, [k]how turn ye [2]again to [l]the weak and beggarly [3]elements, whereunto ye desire again to be in bondage?

10 [m]Ye observe days, and months, and times, and years.

11 I am afraid of you, lest I have bestowed upon you labour in vain.

12 Brethren, I beseech you, be as [n]I *am;* for I *am* as ye *are:* ye have not injured me at all.

13 Ye know how [o]through infirmity of the flesh I preached the gospel unto you [p]at the first.

14 And my temptation which was in my flesh ye despised not, nor rejected; but received me [q]as an angel of God, [r]*even* as Chrīst Jē'sus.

15 [4]Where is then the blessedness ye spake of? for I bear you record, that, if *it had been* possible, ye would have plucked out your own eyes, and have given them to me.

16 Am I therefore become your enemy, because I tell you the truth?

17 They [s]zealously affect you, *but* not well; yea, they would exclude [5]you, that ye might affect them.

18 But *it is* good to be zealously affected always in *a* good *thing,* and not only when I am present with you.

19 My [t]little children, of whom I travail in birth again until Chrīst be formed in you,

20 I desire to be present with you now, and to change my voice; for [6]I stand in doubt of you.

6 [2]Or, imputed
7 [i]John 8.39
8 [j]Gen. 12.3
10 [k]Deut. 27.26
11 [l]Hab. 2.4
12 [m]Rom. 4.4 [n]Lev. 18.5
13 [o]Deut. 21.23
14 [p]Rom. 4.9 [q]Isa. 32.15
15 [r]Heb. 9.17 [3]Or, testament
16 [s]1 Cor. 12.12
17 [t]Ex. 12.40 [u]Rom. 4.13-14
18 [v]Rom. 8.17 [w]Rom. 4.14
19 [x]John 15.22; [y]Acts 7.53; [z]Ex. 20.19
20 [a]Rom. 3.29
24 [b]Matt. 5.17 [c]Acts 13.39
26 [d]John 1.12
28 [e]Rom. 10.12 [f]John 10.16
29 [g]Gen. 21.10; [h]Rom. 8.17

CHAPTER 4
3 [a]Col. 2.8; [1]Or, rudiments
4 [b]Gen. 49.10; [c]John 1.14; [d]Matt. 5.17
5 [e]Matt. 20.28; [f]John 1.12
7 [g]Rom. 8.16
8 [h]Eph. 2.12 [i]Rom. 1.25
9 [j]1 Cor. 8.3 [k]Col. 2.20 [2]Or, back [l]Heb. 7.18 [3]Or, rudiments
10 [m]Rom. 14.5
12 [n]ch. 6.14
13 [o]1 Cor. 2.3 [p]ch. 1.6
14 [q]2 Sam. 19.27 [r]Matt. 10.40
15 [4]Or, What was then
17 [s]Rom. 10.2 [5]Or, us
19 [t]1 Cor. 4.15
20 [6]Or, I am perplexed for you

21 Tell me, ye that desire to be under the law, do ye not hear the law?
22 For it is written, that Ā'bră-hăm had two sons, [u]the one by a bondmaid, [v]the other by a freewoman.
23 But he *who was* of the bondwoman [w]was born after the flesh; [x]but he of the freewoman *was* by promise.
24 Which things are an allegory: for these are the two [7]covenants; the one from the mount [8]Sī'nāi, which gendereth to bondage, which is Ā'gär.
25 For this Ā'gär is mount Sī'nāi in A-rā'bĭ-ȧ, and [9]answereth to Je-ru'sa-lĕm which now is, and is in bondage with her children.
26 But [y]Je-ru'sa-lĕm which is above is free, which is the mother of us all.
27 For it is written, [z]Rejoice, *thou* barren that bearest not; break forth and cry, thou that travailest not: for the desolate hath many more children than she which hath an husband.
28 Now we, brethren, as Ī'saac was, are [a]the children of promise.
29 But as then [b]he that was born after the flesh persecuted him *that was born* after the Spirit, even so *it is* now.
30 Nevertheless what saith [c]the scripture? Cast out the bondwoman and her son: for [d]the son of the bondwoman shall not be heir with the son of the freewoman.
31 So then, brethren, we are not children of the bondwoman, but of the free.

5 Stand fast therefore in [a]the liberty wherewith Chrīst hath made us free, and be not entangled again [b]with the yoke of bondage.
2 Behold, I Paul say unto you, that [c]if ye be circumcised, Chrīst shall profit you nothing.
3 For I testify again to every man that is circumcised, [d]that he is a debtor to do the whole law.
4 [e]Chrīst is become of no effect unto you, whosoever of you are justified by the law; [f]ye are fallen from grace.
5 For we through the Spirit [g]wait for the hope of righteousness by faith.
6 For [h]in Jē'sus Chrīst neither circumcision availeth any thing, nor uncircumcision; but [i]faith which worketh by love.
7 Ye [j]did run well; [1]who did hinder you that ye should not obey the truth?
8 This persuasion *cometh* not of him that calleth you.
9 A little leaven leaveneth the whole lump.
10 [k]I have confidence in you through the Lord, that ye will be none otherwise minded: but [l]he that troubleth you [m]shall bear his judgment, whosoever he be.
11 [n]And I, brethren, if I yet preach circumcision, [o]why do I yet suffer persecution? then is [p]the offence of the cross ceased.
12 [q]I would they were even cut off [r]which trouble you.
13 For, brethren, ye have been called unto liberty; only [s]*use* not liberty for

22 [u]Gen. 16.15
[v]Gen. 21.2
23 [w]Rom. 9.7-8
[x]Gen. 18.10
24 [7]Or, testaments
[8]Sins
25 [9]Or, is in the same rank with
26 [y]Isa. 2.2
27 [z]Isa. 54.1
28 [a]Rom. 4.16
29 [b]Gen. 21.9
30 [c]ch. 3.8
[d]John 8.35

CHAPTER 5
1 [a]John 8.32;
[b]Acts 15.10
2 [c]Acts 15.1
3 [d]ch. 3.10
4 [e]Rom. 9.31
[f]Heb. 12.15
5 [g]Rom. 8.24
6 [h]Col. 3.11
[i]1 Thess. 1.3
7 [j]1 Cor. 9.24
[1]Or, who did drive you back?
10 [k]2 Cor. 8.22
[l]ch. 1.7
[m]2 Cor. 10.6
11 [n]ch. 6.12
[o]1 Cor. 15.30
[p]1 Cor. 1.23
12 [q]1 Cor. 5.13
[r]Acts 15.1
13 [s]1 Pet. 2.16
14 [t]Lev. 19.18
16 [u]Rom. 6.12
[2]Or, fulfil not
17 [v]Rom. 7.23
[w]Rom. 7.15
[3]Or, passions

CHAPTER 6
1 [1]Or, although
[a]1 Cor. 2.15
[b]2 Thess. 3.15
[c]1 Cor. 7.5
2 [d]Rom. 15.1
[e]John 13.14
3 [f]Rom. 12.3
[g]2 Cor. 3.5
4 [h]2 Cor. 13.5
[i]Luke 18.11
5 [j]Rom. 2.6
6 [k]Rom. 15.27
7 [l]1 Cor. 6.9
[m]Job 13.9
[n]Luke 16.25
8 [o]Jas. 3.18
9 [p]2 Thess. 3.13
[q]Matt. 24.13
10 [r]John 9.4
[s]1 Tim. 6.18

an occasion to the flesh, but by love serve one another.
14 For all the law is fulfilled in one word, *even* in this; [t]Thou shalt love thy neighbour as thyself.
15 But if ye bite and devour one another, take heed that ye be not consumed one of another.
16 *This* I say then, [u]Walk in the Spirit, and [2]ye shall not fulfil the lust of the flesh.
17 For [v]the flesh lusteth against the Spirit, and the Spirit against the flesh: and these are contrary the one to the other: [w]so that ye cannot do the things that ye would.
18 But if ye be led of the Spirit, ye are not under the law.
19 Now the works of the flesh are manifest, which are *these;* Adultery, fornication, uncleanness, lasciviousness,
20 Idolatry, witchcraft, hatred, variance, emulations, wrath, strife, seditions, heresies,
21 Envyings, murders, drunkenness, revellings, and such like: of the which I tell you before, as I have also told *you* in time past, that they which do such things shall not inherit the kingdom of God.
22 But the fruit of the Spirit is love, joy, peace, longsuffering, gentleness, goodness, faith,
23 Meekness, temperance: against such there is no law.
24 And they that are Chrīst's have crucified the flesh with the [3]affections and lusts.
25 If we live in the Spirit, let us also walk in the Spirit.
26 Let us not be desirous of vain glory, provoking one another, envying one another.

6 Brethren, [1]if a man be overtaken in a fault, ye [a]which are spiritual, restore such an one [b]in the spirit of meekness; considering thyself, [c]lest thou also be tempted.
2 [d]Bear ye one another's burdens, and so fulfil [e]the law of Chrīst.
3 For [f]if a man think himself to be something, when [g]he is nothing, he deceiveth himself.
4 But [h]let every man prove his own work, and then shall he have rejoicing in himself alone, and [i]not in another.
5 For [j]every man shall bear his own burden.
6 [k]Let him that is taught in the word communicate unto him that teacheth in all good things.
7 [l]Be not deceived; [m]God is not mocked: for [n]whatsoever a man soweth, that shall he also reap.
8 For he that soweth to his flesh shall of the flesh reap corruption; but he that soweth to [o]the Spirit shall of the Spirit reap life everlasting.
9 And [p]let us not be weary in well doing: for in due season we shall reap, [q]if we faint not.
10 [r]As we have therefore opportunity, [s]let us do good unto all *men*, espe-

cially unto them who are of [t]the household of faith.
11 Ye see how large a letter I have
written unto you with mine own hand.
12 As many as desire to make a fair
shew in the flesh, they constrain you to
be circumcised; only lest they should
[u]suffer persecution for the cross of
Christ.
13 For neither they themselves who
are circumcised keep the law; but desire to have you circumcised, that they
may glory in your flesh.
14 But God forbid that I should glory,
save in the cross of our Lord Jē'sus
Christ, [2]by whom the world is crucified
unto me, and I unto the world.
15 For in Christ Jē'sus neither circumcision availeth any thing, nor uncircumcision, but [v]a new creature.
16 And as many as walk according
to this rule, peace *be* on them, and
mercy, and upon [w]the Is'ra-el of God.
17 From henceforth let no man trouble me: for [x]I bear in my body the
marks of the Lord Jē'sus.
18 Brethren, the grace of our Lord
Jē'sus Christ *be* with your spirit. Amen.

[t]Eph. 2.19
12 [u]Phil. 3.18
14 [2]Or, whereby
15 [v]2 Cor. 5.17; Eph. 2.10
16 [w]Ps. 73.1; Ps. 125.5; ch. 3.7-9
17 [x]Col. 1.24

THE LETTER OF PAUL TO THE

EPHESIANS

Life's Questions

How far can I live like the world and still be a Christian?
Are some Christians automatically better and more important than I am?
How can I experience Christian victory?

God's Answers

About 60 A.D. while in prison in Rome, Paul wrote the church at Ephesus and its neighboring churches to give them a manual for Christian living showing how the church could be unified with each member reaching the potential God intended.

Ephesians shows: God's purpose in Christ creating a unified church based on God's grace (1—3) and God's purposes in the church creating a community filled with His Spirit and practicing His faith in boldness (4—6).

Ephesians calls you to work boldly for unity in Christ's church.

1 Paul, an apostle of Jē'sus Christ by
the will of God, to the saints which
are at Ĕph'ĕ-sŭs, [a]and to the faithful in
Christ Jē'sus:
2 [b]Grace *be* to you, and peace, from
God our Father, and *from* the Lord
Jē'sus Christ.
3 [c]Blessed *be* the God and Father
of our Lord Jē'sus Christ, who hath
blessed us with all spiritual blessings
in heavenly [1]*places* in Christ:
4 According as [d]he hath chosen us
in him [e]before the foundation of the
world, that we should [f]be holy and
without blame before him in love:
5 [g]Having predestinated us unto
[h]the adoption of children by Jē'sus
Christ to himself, [i]according to the
good pleasure of his will,
6 [j]To the praise of the glory of his
grace, [k]wherein he hath made us accepted in [l]the beloved.
7 [m]In whom we have redemption
through his blood, the forgiveness of
sins, according to [n]the riches of his
grace;
8 Wherein he hath abounded toward
us in all wisdom and prudence;
9 [o]Having made known unto us the
mystery of his will, according to his
good pleasure [p]which he hath purposed in himself:
10 That in the dispensation of [q]the
fulness of times [r]he might gather together in one [s]all things in Christ, both
which are in [2]heaven, and which are
on earth; *even* in him:
11 [t]In whom also we have obtained
an inheritance, being predestinated according to [u]the purpose of him who
worketh all things after the counsel of
his own will:
12 [v]That we should be to the praise
of his glory, [w]who first [3]trusted in
Christ.
13 In whom ye also *trusted*, after
that ye heard the word of truth, the
gospel of your salvation: in whom also
after that ye believed, [x]ye were sealed
with that holy Spirit of promise,
14 [y]Which is the earnest of our inheritance [z]until the redemption of [a]the
purchased possession, unto the praise
of his glory.
15 Wherefore I also, after I heard of
your faith in the Lord Jē'sus, and love
unto all the saints,
16 Cease not to give thanks for you,
making mention of you in my prayers;
17 That the God of our Lord Jē'sus
Christ, the Father of glory, [b]may give
unto you the spirit of wisdom and revelation in the knowledge of him:
18 [c]The eyes of your understanding
being enlightened; that ye may know
what is the hope of his calling, and
what the riches of the glory of his inheritance in the saints,
19 And what *is* the exceeding greatness of his power to us-ward who believe, [d]according to the working of his
mighty power,
20 Which he wrought in Christ, when
he raised him from the dead, and set

CHAPTER 1
1 [a]Col. 1.2
2 [b]Tit. 1.4
3 [c]Ps. 72.17
[1]Or, things
4 [d]1 Pet. 1.2
[e]1 Pet. 1.20
[f]Luke 1.75
5 [g]Rom. 8.29
[h]John 1.12
[i]Luke 12.32
6 [j]Isa. 43.21
[k]Rom. 3.24
[l]Matt. 17.5
7 [m]Heb. 9.12
[n]Rom. 3.24
9 [o]Col. 1.26
[p]2 Tim. 1.9
10 [q]Zech. 13.1; Heb. 9.10
[r]1 Cor. 3.22
[s]Phil. 2.9
[2]the heavens
11 [t]Rom. 8.17
[u]Isa. 46.10
12 [v]2 Thess. 2.13
[w]Jas. 1.18
[3]Or, hoped
13 [x]2 Cor. 1.22
14 [y]2 Cor. 5.5
[z]Rom. 8.23
[a]Acts 20.28
17 [b]Col. 1.9
18 [c]Acts 26.18
19 [d]Col. 1.29

him at his own right hand in the heavenly *places*,
21 [e]Far above all principality, and
power, and might, and dominion, and
every name that is named, not only in
this world, but also in that which is to
come:
22 And [f]hath put all *things* under
his feet, and gave him [g]*to be* the head
over all *things* to the church,
23 [h]Which is his body, the fulness of
him [i]that filleth all in all.
2 And [a]you *hath he quickened,* who
were dead in trespasses and sins;
2 [b]Wherein in time past ye walked
according to the course of this world,
according to the prince of the power of
the air, the spirit that now worketh in
[c]the children of disobedience:
3 [d]Among whom also we all had our
conversation in times past in [e]the lusts
of our flesh, fulfilling [1]the desires of
the flesh and of the mind; and [f]were by
nature the children of wrath, even as
others.
4 But God, [g]who is rich in mercy,
for his great love wherewith he loved
us,
5 [h]Even when we were dead in
sins, hath [i]quickened us together with
Chrīst, ([2]by grace ye are saved;)
6 And hath raised *us* up together,
and made *us* sit together in heavenly
places in Chrīst Jē'sus:
7 That in the ages to come he might
shew the exceeding riches of his grace
in *his* kindness toward us through
Chrīst Jē'sus.
8 For by grace are ye saved [j]through
faith; and that not of yourselves: [k]*it is*
the gift of God:
9 [l]Not of works, lest any man should
boast.
10 For we are his workmanship, created in Chrīst Jē'sus unto good works,
[m]which God hath before [3]ordained
that we should walk in them.
11 Wherefore remember, that ye *being* in time past Gĕn'tīles in the flesh,
who are called Uncircumcision by that
which is called [n]the Circumcision in
the flesh made by hands;
12 [o]That at that time ye were without Chrīst, [p]being aliens from the commonwealth of Is'ra-el, and strangers
from [q]the covenants of promise, [r]hav-
ing no hope, [s]and without God in the
world:
13 [t]But now in Chrīst Jē'sus ye who
sometimes were far off are made nigh
by the blood of Chrīst.
14 For [u]he is our peace, who hath
made both one, and hath broken down
the middle wall of partition *between
us;*
15 Having abolished [v]in his flesh
the enmity, *even* the law of commandments *contained* in ordinances; for to
make in himself of twain one [w]new
man, *so* making peace;
16 And that he might reconcile both
unto God in one body by the cross, having [x]slain the enmity [4]thereby:
17 And came [y]and preached peace
to you which were afar off, and to
them that were nigh.
18 For through him we both have access by one Spirit unto the Father.
19 Now therefore ye are no more
strangers and foreigners, but fellow-
citizens with the saints, and of the
household of God;
20 And are built [z]upon the foundation of the [a]apostles and prophets,
Jē'sus Chrīst himself being the [b]chief
corner *stone;*
21 In whom all the building fitly
framed together groweth unto an holy
temple in the Lord:
22 In whom ye also are builded
together for [c]an habitation of God
through the Spirit.
3 For this cause I Paul, [a]the prisoner
of Jē'sus Chrīst [b]for you Gĕn'tīles,
2 If ye have heard of [c]the dispensation of the grace of God [d]which is
given me to you-ward:
3 How that by revelation [e]he made
known unto me the mystery; (as I
wrote [1]afore in few words,
4 Whereby, when ye read, ye may
understand my knowledge [f]in the mystery of Chrīst)
5 [g]Which in other ages was not
made known unto the sons of men, as
it is now revealed unto his holy apostles and prophets by the Spirit;
6 That the Gĕn'tīles should be fel-
lowheirs, and of the same body, and
[h]partakers of his promise in Chrīst by
the gospel:
7 Whereof I was made a minister,
according to the gift of the grace of
God given unto me by [i]the effectual
working of his power.
8 Unto me, who am less than the
least of all saints, is this grace given,
that I should preach among the Gĕn'-
tīles [j]the unsearchable riches of Chrīst;
9 And to make all *men* see what *is*
the fellowship of the mystery, [k]which
from the beginning of the world hath
been hid in God, [l]who created all
things by Jē'sus Chrīst:
10 [m]To the intent that now [n]unto
the principalities and powers in heavenly *places* [o]might be known by the
church the manifold wisdom of God,
11 According to the eternal purpose
which he purposed in Chrīst Jē'sus our
Lord:
12 In whom we have boldness and
access with confidence by the faith of
him.
13 Wherefore I desire that ye faint
not at my tribulations for you, which is
your glory.
14 For this cause I bow my knees
unto the Father of our Lord Jē'sus
Chrīst,
15 Of whom [p]the whole family in
heaven and earth is named,
16 That he would grant you, [q]ac-
cording to the riches of his glory, [r]to be
strengthened with might by his Spirit
in [s]the inner man;

21 [e]Phil. 2.9; Heb. 1.4
22 [f]Matt. 28.18
[g]Heb. 2.7
23 [h]Rom. 12.5
[i]John 1.14-16; Col. 3.11

CHAPTER 2
1 [a]John 5.24
2 [b]1 John 5.19
[c]Col. 3.6
3 [d]Tit. 3.3
[e]Gal. 5.16
[1]the wills
[f]Ps. 51.5; Luke 15.21
4 [g]Rom. 10.12
5 [h]Rom. 5.6
[i]Rom. 6.4
[2]Or, by whose grace
8 [j]Rom. 4.16;
[k]John 6.44
9 [l]Rom. 3.20
10 [m]ch. 1.4
[3]Or, prepared
11 [n]Rom. 2.28
12 [o]Col. 1.21
[p]John 10.16
[q]Rom. 9.4-8
[r]1 Thess. 4.13
[s]Gal. 4.8
13 [t]John 10.16
14 [u]Mic. 5.5
15 [v]Col. 1.22
[w]2 Cor. 5.17
16 [x]Rom. 6.6;
[4]Or, in himself
17 [y]Isa. 57.19
20 [z]Matt. 16.18
[a]1 Cor. 12.28
[b]Ps. 118.22
22 [c]John 17.23

CHAPTER 3
1 [a]Acts 21.33
[b]2 Tim. 2.10
2 [c]Rom. 1.5
[d]Acts 9.15;
3 [e]Rom. 16.25
[1]Or, a little before
4 [f]1 Cor. 4.1
5 [g]Acts 10.28
6 [h]Gal. 3.14
7 [i]Rom. 15.18
8 [j]John 1.16
9 [k]Rom. 16.25
[l]Ps. 33.6
10 [m]1 Pet. 1.12
[n]1 Pet. 3.22
[o]1 Cor. 2.7
15 [p]Phil. 2.9
16 [q]Phil. 4.19
[r]Job 23.6;
[s]Rom. 7.22

17 [t]That Chrīst may dwell in your hearts by faith; that ye, being rooted and grounded in love,

18 May be able to comprehend with all saints [u]what *is* the breadth, and length, and depth, and height;

19 And to know the love of Chrīst, which passeth knowledge, that ye might be filled [v]with all the fulness of God.

20 Now unto him that is able to do exceeding abundantly above all that we ask or think, according to the power that worketh in us,

21 [w]Unto him *be* glory in the church by Chrīst Jē′sus throughout all ages, world without end. Amen.

4 I therefore, the prisoner [1]of the Lord, beseech you that ye [a]walk worthy of the vocation wherewith ye are called,

2 [b]With all lowliness and meekness, with longsuffering, forbearing one another in love;

3 Endeavouring to keep the unity of the Spirit [c]in the bond of peace.

4 [d]*There is* one body, and one Spirit, even as ye are called in one hope of your calling;

5 [e]One Lord, one faith, [f]one baptism,

6 [g]One God and Father of all, who *is* above all, and [h]through all, and in you all.

7 But unto every one of us is given grace according to the measure of the gift of Chrīst.

8 Wherefore he saith, [i]When he ascended up on high, [j]he led [2]captivity captive, and gave gifts unto men.

9 [k](Now that he ascended, what is it but that he also descended first into the lower parts of the earth?

10 He that descended is the same also [l]that ascended up far above all heavens, that he might [3]fill all things.)

11 [m]And he gave some, apostles; and some, prophets; and some, evangelists; and some, pastors and teachers;

12 For the perfecting of the saints, for the work of the ministry, [n]for the edifying of [o]the body of Chrīst:

13 Till we all come [4]in the unity of the faith, [p]and of the knowledge of the Son of God, unto a perfect man, unto the measure of the [5]stature of the fulness of Chrīst:

14 That we *henceforth* be no more children, tossed to and fro, and carried about with every [q]wind of doctrine, by the sleight of men, *and* cunning craftiness, whereby they lie in wait to deceive;

15 But [6]speaking the truth in love, may grow up into him in all things, which is the head, *even* Chrīst:

16 [r]From whom the whole body fitly joined together and compacted by that which every joint supplieth, according to the effectual working in the measure of every part, maketh increase of the body unto the edifying of itself in love.

17 This I say therefore, and testify in the Lord, that ye henceforth walk not as other Gĕn′tīles walk, in the vanity of their mind,

18 Having the understanding darkened, [s]being alienated from the life of God through the ignorance that is in them, because of the [7]blindness of their heart:

19 [t]Who being past feeling have given themselves over unto lasciviousness, to work all uncleanness with greediness.

20 But ye have not so learned Chrīst;

21 If so be that ye have heard him, and have been taught by him, as the truth is in Jē′sus:

22 That ye put off concerning the former conversation the old man, which is corrupt according to the deceitful lusts;

23 And [u]be renewed in the spirit of your mind;

24 And that ye put on the new man, which after God is created in righteousness and [8]true holiness.

25 Wherefore putting away lying, speak every man truth with his neighbour: for we are members one of another.

26 Be ye angry, and sin not: let not the sun go down upon your wrath:

27 [v]Neither give place to the devil.

28 Let him that stole steal no more: but rather let him labour, working with *his* hands the thing which is good, that he may have [9]to give to him that needeth.

29 Let no corrupt communication proceed out of your mouth, but that which is good [10]to the use of edifying, that it may minister grace unto the hearers.

30 And [w]grieve not the holy Spirit of God, whereby ye are sealed unto the day of redemption.

31 Let all bitterness, and wrath, and anger, and clamour, and evil speaking, be put away from you, with all malice:

32 And be ye kind one to another, tenderhearted, forgiving one another, even as God for Chrīst's sake hath forgiven you.

5 Be [a]ye therefore followers of God, as dear children;

2 And [b]walk in love, as Chrīst also hath loved us, and hath given himself for us an offering and a sacrifice to God [c]for a sweetsmelling savour.

3 But fornication, and all uncleanness, or covetousness, let it not be once named among you, as becometh saints;

4 Neither filthiness, nor foolish talking, nor jesting, [d]which are not convenient: but rather giving of thanks.

5 For this ye know, that no whoremonger, nor unclean person, nor covetous man, who is an idolater, [e]hath any inheritance in the kingdom of Chrīst and of God.

6 [f]Let no man deceive you with vain words: for because of these things cometh the wrath of God upon the children of [1]disobedience.

7 Be not ye therefore partakers with them.

17 [t]John 14.23
18 [u]Rom. 10.3
19 [v]John 1.16
21 [w]1 Tim. 1.17

CHAPTER 4
1 [1]Or, in the Lord
[a]Col. 1.10
2 [b]Gal. 5.22
3 [c]John 13.34
4 [d]Rom. 12.5
5 [e]1 Cor. 8.6
[f]Heb. 6.6
6 [g]Ps. 83.18; Mal. 2.10
[h]Rom. 11.36
8 [i]Ps. 68.18
[j]Col. 2.15
[2]Or, a multitude of captives
9 [k]John 3.13
10 [l]Acts 1.9; Heb. 4.14; Heb. 7.26; Heb. 8.1
[3]Or, fulfil
11 [m]ch. 2.20
12 [n]Rom. 14.19
[o]ch. 1.23
13 [4]Or, into the unity
[p]Col. 2.2
[5]Or, age
14 [q]Matt. 11.7
15 [6]Or, being sincere
16 [r]Col. 2.19
18 [s]Acts 26.18; ch. 2.12; Gal. 4.8; 1 Thess. 4.5
[7]Or, hardness
19 [t]Rom. 1.24
23 [u]Rom. 8.6; 1 Pet. 1.22-23
24 [8]Or, holiness of truth
27 [v]Acts 5.3; Jas. 4.7
28 [9]Or, to distribute
29 [10]Or, to edify profitably
30 [w]Ps. 78.40; Rom. 8.23

CHAPTER 5
1 [a]Lev. 11.45; ch. 4.32
2 [b]John 13.34
[c]Gen. 8.21; Lev. 1.9
4 [d]Rom. 1.28
5 [e]Rev. 22.15
6 [f]Jer. 29.8; Matt. 24.4
[1]Or, unbelief

8 [g]For ye were sometimes darkness,
but now [h]*are ye* light in the Lord: walk
as [i]children of light:
9 (For the fruit of the Spirit *is* in
all goodness and righteousness and
truth;)
10 [j]Proving what is acceptable unto
the Lord.
11 And [k]have no fellowship with
the unfruitful works of darkness, but
rather [l]reprove *them*.
12 For it is a shame even to speak of
those things which are done of them in
secret.
13 But [m]all things that are [2]reproved
are made manifest by the light: for
whatsoever doth make manifest is
light.
14 Wherefore [3]he saith, [n]Awake thou
that sleepest, and [o]arise from the dead,
and Chrīst shall give thee light.
15 See then that ye walk circum-
spectly, not as fools, but as wise,
16 Redeeming the time, because the
days are evil.
17 [p]Wherefore be ye not unwise,
but [q]understanding [r]what the will of
the Lord *is*.
18 And be not drunk with wine,
wherein is excess; but be filled with
the Spirit;
19 Speaking to yourselves [s]in psalms
and hymns and spiritual songs, singing
and making melody in your heart to the
Lord;
20 [t]Giving thanks always for all
things unto God and the Father in the
name of our Lord Jē'sus Chrīst;
21 [u]Submitting yourselves one to
another in the fear of God.
22 [v]Wives, submit yourselves unto
your own husbands, as unto the Lord.
23 For the husband is the head of
the wife, even as Chrīst is the head of
the church: and he is the saviour of the
body.
24 Therefore as the church is subject unto Chrīst, so *let* the wives *be* to
their own husbands in every thing.
25 Husbands, love your wives, even
as Chrīst also loved the church, and
gave himself for it;
26 That he might sanctify and cleanse
it [w]with the washing of water [x]by the
word,
27 That he might present it to himself a glorious church, not having spot,
or wrinkle, or any such thing; but that
it should be holy and without blemish.
28 So ought men to love their wives
as their own bodies. He that loveth his
wife loveth himself.
29 For no man ever yet hated his
own flesh; but nourisheth and cherisheth it, even as the Lord the church:
30 For we are members of his body,
of his flesh, and of his bones.
31 For this cause shall a man leave
his father and mother, and shall be
joined unto his wife, and they two shall
be one flesh.
32 This is a great mystery: but I speak
concerning Chrīst and the church.

8 [g]Isa. 9.2
[h]John 8.12; 1 John 2.9
[i]Luke 16.8
10 [j]Ps. 19.7-11; Rom. 14.18; Phil. 1.10; Heb. 12.28
11 [k]Job 24.13-17
[l]Lev. 19.17
13 [m]Heb. 4.13
[2]Or, discovered
14 [3]Or, it
[n]Isa. 60.1
[o]Ezek. 37.4-10; John 5.25; Rom. 6.4-5; ch. 2.5
17 [p]Col. 4.5
[q]Rom. 12.2
[r]1 Thess. 4.3
19 [s]Jas. 5.13
20 [t]Job 1.21
21 [u]Phil. 2.3
22 [v]Gen. 3.16
26 [w]John 3.5; Heb. 10.22
[x]John 15.3

CHAPTER 6
1 [a]Prov. 23.22; Luke 2.51
2 [b]Ex. 20.12; Deut. 5.16; Matt. 15.4
4 [c]Col. 3.21
[d]Gen. 18.19
8 [e]Rom. 2.6
9 [f]Col. 4.1
[1]Or, moderating
[2]Some read, both your and their Master
[g]1 Pet. 1.17
11 [h]Rom. 13.12
12 [3]blood and flesh
[i]Rom. 8.38
[j]John 12.31
[4]Or, wicked spirits
[5]Or, heavenly, as. ch. 1.3
13 [6]Or, having overcome all
14 [k]Isa. 59.17
15 [l]Isa. 52.7
16 [m]1 John 5.4
17 [n]Heb. 4.12; Rev. 1.16
18 [o]Phil. 1.4
20 [7]Or, in a chain
[8]Or, thereof
[p]1 Thess. 2.2
21 [q]Acts 20.4

33 Nevertheless let every one of you
in particular so love his wife even as
himself; and the wife *see* that she reverence *her* husband.

6 Children, [a]obey your parents in the
Lord: for this is right.
2 [b]Honour thy father and mother;
(which is the first commandment with
promise;)
3 That it may be well with thee, and
thou mayest live long on the earth.
4 And, [c]ye fathers, provoke not your
children to wrath: but [d]bring them up
in the nurture and admonition of the
Lord.
5 Servants, be obedient to them that
are *your* masters according to the flesh,
with fear and trembling, in singleness
of your heart, as unto Chrīst;
6 Not with eyeservice, as menpleasers; but as the servants of Chrīst, doing
the will of God from the heart;
7 With good will doing service, as to
the Lord, and not to men:
8 [e]Knowing that whatsoever good
thing any man doeth, the same shall he
receive of the Lord, whether *he be*
bond or free.
9 And, ye [f]masters, do the same
things unto them, [1]forbearing threaten-
ing: knowing that [2]your Master also is
in heaven; [g]neither is there respect of
persons with him.
10 Finally, my brethren, be strong in
the Lord, and in the power of his
might.
11 [h]Put on the whole armour of God,
that ye may be able to stand against the
wiles of the devil.
12 For we wrestle not against [3]flesh
and blood, but against [i]principalities,
against powers, against [j]the rulers of
the darkness of this world, against
[4]spiritual wickedness in [5]high *places*.
13 Wherefore take unto you the
whole armour of God, that ye may be
able to withstand in the evil day, and
[6]having done all, to stand.
14 Stand therefore, having your loins
girt about with truth, and [k]having on
the breastplate of righteousness;
15 [l]And your feet shod with the
preparation of the gospel of peace;
16 Above all, taking [m]the shield of
faith, wherewith ye shall be able to
quench all the fiery darts of the wicked.
17 And take the helmet of salvation,
and [n]the sword of the Spirit, which is
the word of God:
18 Praying always with all prayer
and supplication in the Spirit, and
watching thereunto with all perseverance and [o]supplication for all saints;
19 And for me, that utterance may
be given unto me, that I may open my
mouth boldly, to make known the mystery of the gospel,
20 For which I am an ambassador
[7]in bonds: that [8]therein [p]I may speak
boldly, as I ought to speak.
21 But that ye also may know my
affairs, *and* how I do, [q]Tўch'ĭ-cŭs, a
beloved brother and faithful minister
in the Lord, shall make known to you
all things:

22 Whom I have sent unto you for the same purpose, that ye might know our affairs, and *that* he might comfort your hearts.
23 Peace *be* to the brethren, and love with faith, from God the Father and the Lord Jē'sus Chrīst.
24 Grace *be* with all them that love our Lord Jē'sus Chrīst [9]in sincerity. Amen.

24 [9]Or, with incorruption

THE LETTER OF PAUL TO THE

PHILIPPIANS

Life's Questions

Where can I find joy?
Why am I suffering for Christ?
How do I know who is teaching the truth and who is not?

God's Answers

About A.D. 62 from a Roman prison Paul sounded his most exuberant note of joy. He wrote his partners in ministry at Philippi and encouraged them in their ministry. Paul thanked them for sending a gift to help his ministry and thanked God for the encouragement he drew from them in adverse circumstances.

Philippians shows: God can create a joy of partnership in ministry even under difficult circumstances (1:1—26); a pastor has concerns for a church's consistency, courage, unity, obedience, problems, and temptations (1:27—4:1); and a pastor encourages a church to practice reconciliation while experiencing Christ's joy (4:2—23).

Philippians calls you to joy in the faith no matter what your circumstances and to partnership in the gospel with other believers.

1 Paul and Ti-mō'the-ŭs, the servants of Jē'sus Chrīst, to all the saints in Chrīst Jē'sus which are at Phĭ-lĭp'pī, with the [1]bishops and deacons:
2 Grace *be* unto you, and peace, from God our Father, and *from* the Lord Jē'sus Chrīst.
3 [a]I thank my God upon every [2]remembrance of you,
4 Always in every prayer of mine for you all making request with joy,
5 [b]For your fellowship in the gospel from the first day until now;
6 Being confident of this very thing, that he which hath begun [c]a good work in you [3]will perform *it* until the day of Jē'sus Chrīst:
7 Even as it is meet for me to think this of you all, because [4]I have you in my heart; inasmuch as both in [d]my bonds, and in the defence and confirmation of the gospel, [e]ye all are [5]partakers of my grace.
8 For God is my record, how greatly I long after you all in the bowels of Jē'sus Chrīst.
9 And this I pray, [f]that your love may abound yet more and more in knowledge and *in* all [6]judgment;
10 That [g]ye may [7]approve things that [8]are excellent; [h]that ye may be sincere and without offence till the day of Chrīst;
11 Being filled with the fruits of righteousness, [i]which are by Jē'sus Chrīst, unto the glory and praise of God.
12 But I would ye should understand, brethren, that the things *which happened* unto me have fallen out rather unto the furtherance of the gospel;
13 So that my bonds [9]in Chrīst are manifest [j]in all [10]the palace, and [11]in all other *places;*
14 And many of the brethren in the Lord, waxing confident by my bonds, are much more bold to speak the word without fear.
15 Some indeed preach Chrīst even of envy and [k]strife; and some also of good will:
16 The one preach Chrīst of contention, not sincerely, supposing to add affliction to my bonds:
17 But the other of love, knowing that I am set for the defence of the gospel.
18 What then? notwithstanding, every way, whether in pretence, or in truth, Chrīst is preached; and I therein do rejoice, yea, and will rejoice.
19 For I know that this shall turn to my salvation [l]through your prayer, and the supply of [m]the Spirit of Jē'sus Chrīst,
20 According to my earnest expectation and *my* hope, that [n]in nothing I shall be ashamed, but *that* with all boldness, as always, *so* now also Chrīst shall be magnified in my body, whether *it be* by life, or by death.
21 For to me to live *is* Chrīst, and to die *is* gain.
22 But if I live in the flesh, this *is* the fruit of my labour: yet what I shall choose I wot not.
23 For [o]I am in a strait betwixt two, having a desire to [p]depart, and to be with Chrīst; which is far better:
24 Nevertheless to abide in the flesh *is* more needful for you.
25 And having this confidence, I know that I shall abide and continue with you all for your furtherance and joy of faith;
26 That your rejoicing may be more abundant in Jē'sus Chrīst for me by my coming to you again.

CHAPTER 1
1 [1]Or, overseers
3 [a]Col. 1.3 [2]Or, mention
5 [b]2 Cor. 8.1
6 [c]John 6.29 [3]Or, will finish it
7 [4]Or, ye have me in your heart [d]Eph. 3.1 [e]ch. 4.14 [5]Or, partakers with me of grace
9 [f]Phile. 6 [6]Or, sense
10 [g]Rom. 12.2 [7]Or, try [8]Or, differ [h]Acts 24.16
11 [i]John 15.4
13 [9]Or, for Christ [j]ch. 4.22 [10]Or, Caesar's court [11]Or, to all others
15 [k]ch. 2.3
19 [l]2 Cor. 1.11 [m]Rom. 8.9; 1 Pet. 1.11
20 [n]Rom. 5.5
23 [o]2 Cor. 5.8 [p]Luke 2.29-30

27 Only let your conversation be as
it becometh the gospel of Chrīst: that
whether I come and see you, or else be
absent, I may hear of your affairs, that
ye stand fast in one spirit, with one
mind striving together for the faith of
the gospel;
28 And in nothing terrified by your
[q]adversaries: which is to them an evident token of perdition, [r]but to you of
salvation, and that of God.
29 For unto you it is given in the behalf of Chrīst, [s]not only to believe on
him, but also to suffer for his sake;
30 [t]Having the same conflict
[u]which ye saw in me, and now hear *to
be* in me.

2 If *there be* therefore any consolation in Chrīst, if any comfort of
love, [a]if any fellowship of the Spirit, if
any bowels and mercies,
2 [b]Fulfil ye my joy, [c]that ye be
likeminded, having the same love, *being* of one accord, of one mind.
3 [d]*Let* nothing *be done* through
strife or vainglory; but [e]in lowliness of
mind let each esteem other better than
themselves.
4 [f]Look not every man on his own
things, but every man also on the
things of others.
5 [g]Let this mind be in you, which
was also in Chrīst Jē'sus:
6 Who, [h]being in the form of God,
[i]thought it not robbery to be equal
with God:
7 [j]But made himself of no reputation, and took upon him the form [k]of a
servant, and [l]was made in the [1]like-
ness of men:
8 And being found in fashion as a
man, he humbled himself, and became
[m]obedient unto death, even the death
of the cross.
9 Wherefore God also [n]hath highly
exalted him, and [o]given him a name
which is above every name:
10 [p]That at the name of Jē'sus every
knee should bow, of *things* in heaven,
and *things* in earth, and *things* under
the earth;
11 And [q]*that* every tongue should
confess that Jē'sus Chrīst *is* Lord, to
the glory of God the Father.
12 Wherefore, my beloved, as ye
have always obeyed, not as in my presence only, but now much more in my
absence, work out your own salvation
with fear and trembling.
13 For [r]it is God which worketh in
you both to will and to do of *his* good
pleasure.
14 Do all things without murmurings and disputings:
15 That ye may be blameless and
[2]harmless, the sons of God, without rebuke, in the midst of a crooked and perverse nation, among whom [3]ye shine as
lights in the world;
16 Holding forth the word of life;
that I may rejoice in the day of Chrīst,
that I have not run in vain, neither laboured in vain.
17 Yea, and if I be [4]offered upon the
sacrifice and service of your faith, I
joy, and rejoice with you all.
18 For the same cause also do ye
joy, and rejoice with me.
19 [5]But I trust in the Lord Jē'sus to
send Tĭ-mō'the-ŭs shortly unto you,
that I also may be of good comfort,
when I know your state.
20 For I have no man [6]likeminded,
who will naturally care for your state.
21 For all seek their own, not the
things which are Jē'sus Chrīst's.
22 But ye know the proof of him,
that, as a son with the father, he hath
served with me in the gospel.
23 Him therefore I hope to send presently, so soon as I shall see how it will
go with me.
24 But I trust in the Lord that I also
myself shall come shortly.
25 Yet I supposed it necessary to send
to you [s]E-păph-ro-dī'tus, my brother,
and companion in labour, and fellowsoldier, [t]but your messenger, and [u]he
that ministered to my wants.
26 For he longed after you all, and
was full of heaviness, because that ye
had heard that he had been sick.
27 For indeed he was sick nigh unto
death: but God had mercy on him; and
not on him only, but on me also, lest I
should have sorrow upon sorrow.
28 I sent him therefore the more
carefully, that, when ye see him again,
ye may rejoice, and that I may be the
less sorrowful.
29 Receive him therefore in the Lord
with all gladness; and [7]hold such in
reputation:
30 Because for the work of Chrīst he
was nigh unto death, not regarding his
life, [v]to supply your lack of service toward me.

3 Finally, my brethren, rejoice in the
Lord. To write the same things to
you, to me indeed *is* not grievous, but
for you *it is* safe.
2 [a]Beware of dogs, beware of evil
workers, [b]beware of the concision.
3 For we are [c]the circumcision,
[d]which worship God in the spirit, and
rejoice in Chrīst Jē'sus, and have no
confidence in the flesh.
4 Though I might also have confidence in the flesh. If any other man
thinketh that he hath whereof he might
trust in the flesh, I more:
5 Circumcised the eighth day, of the
stock of Is'ra-el, *of* the tribe of Bĕn'ja-
min, an Hē'brew of the Hē'brews; as
touching the law, [e]a Phăr'ĭ-see;
6 [f]Concerning zeal, [g]persecuting
the church; touching the righteousness
which is in the law, blameless.
7 But what things were gain to me,
those I counted loss for Chrīst.
8 Yea doubtless, and I count all
things *but* loss [h]for the excellency of
the knowledge of Chrīst Jē'sus my
Lord: for whom I have suffered the
loss of all things, and do count them
but dung, that I may win Chrīst,
9 And be found in him, not having
[i]mine own righteousness, which is of

28 [q]Isa. 41.10; Matt. 10.28; Heb. 13.5
[r]Matt. 5.10-12
29 [s]Acts 5.41; Eph. 2.8
30 [t]Col. 2.1
[u]Acts 16.19

CHAPTER 2
1 [a]2 Cor. 13.14
2 [b]John 3.29
[c]1 Pet. 3.8
3 [d]Rom. 13.13; Jas. 3.14
[e]Isa. 66.2; Eph. 5.21
4 [f]1 Cor. 10.24
5 [g]John 13.15
6 [h]Isa. 9.6; John 1.1-2; Heb. 1.3
[i]John 5.18
7 [j]Ps. 22.6; Dan. 9.26
[k]Isa. 42.1; Matt. 12.18
[l]John 1.14; Gal. 4.4
[1]Or, habit
8 [m]Heb. 12.2
9 [n]Ps. 2.6-12; Luke 10.22
[o]Heb. 1.4
10 [p]Isa. 45.23
11 [q]John 13.13
13 [r]Heb. 13.21
15 [2]Or, sincere
[3]Or, shine ye
17 [4]poured forth
19 [5]Or, Moreover
20 [6]Or, so dear unto me
25 [s]ch. 4.18
[t]2 Cor. 8.23
[u]ch. 4.18
29 [7]Or, honour such
30 [v]1 Cor. 16.17; ch. 4.10

CHAPTER 3
2 [a]Gal. 5.15; Rev. 22.15
[b]Rom. 2.28; Gal. 5.2
3 [c]Deut. 10.16; Rom. 2.29
[d]Mal. 1.11; Jude 20
5 [e]Acts 23.6
6 [f]Acts 22.3; Gal. 1.13
[g]Acts 8.3
8 [h]Isa. 53.11; John 17.3
9 [i]Ps. 143.2; Isa. 64.6

the law, but [j]that which is through the faith of Chrīst, the righteousness which is of God by faith:

10 That I may know him, and the power of his resurrection, and [k]the fellowship of his sufferings, being made conformable unto his death;

11 If by any means I might [l]attain unto the resurrection of the dead.

12 Not as though I had already [m]attained, either were already [n]perfect: but I follow after, if that I may apprehend that for which also I am apprehended of Chrīst Jē'sus.

13 Brethren, I count not myself to have apprehended: but *this* one thing *I do*, forgetting those things which are behind, and reaching forth [o]unto those things which are before,

14 [p]I press toward the mark for the prize of [q]the high calling of God in Chrīst Jē'sus.

15 Let us therefore, as many [r]as be [s]perfect, be thus minded: and if in any thing ye be otherwise minded, God shall reveal even this unto you.

16 Nevertheless, whereto we have already attained, let us walk by the same rule, let us mind the same thing.

17 Brethren, be followers together of me, and mark them which walk so as [t]ye have us for an ensample.

18 (For many walk, of whom I have told you often, and now tell you even weeping, *that they are* the enemies of the cross of Chrīst:

19 Whose end *is* destruction, whose God *is their* belly, and *whose* glory *is* in their shame, who mind earthly things.)

20 For [u]our conversation is in heaven; from whence also we [v]look for the Saviour, the Lord Jē'sus Chrīst:

21 [w]Who shall change our vile body, that it may be fashioned like unto his glorious body, according [x]to the working whereby he is able even to subdue all things unto himself.

4 Therefore, my brethren dearly beloved and longed for, [a]my joy and crown, so stand fast in the Lord, *my* dearly beloved.

2 I beseech Eū-ō'dĭ-as, and beseech Sȳn'tȳ-chē, that they be of the same mind in the Lord.

3 And I intreat thee also, true yokefellow, help those women which [b]laboured with me in the gospel, with Clĕm'ĕnt also, and *with* other my fellowlabourers, whose names *are* in [c]the book of life.

4 Rejoice in the Lord alway: *and* again I say, Rejoice.

5 Let your moderation be known unto all men. [d]The Lord *is* at hand.

6 [e]Be careful for nothing; but in every thing by prayer and supplication with thanksgiving let your requests be made known unto God.

7 And [f]the peace of God, which passeth all understanding, shall keep your hearts and minds through Chrīst Jē'sus.

8 Finally, brethren, whatsoever things are true, whatsoever things *are* [1]honest, whatsoever things *are* just, whatsoever things *are* pure, whatsoever things *are* lovely, whatsoever things *are* of good report; if *there be* any virtue, and if *there be* any praise, think on these things.

9 Those things, which ye have both learned, and received, and heard, and seen in me, do: and the God of peace shall be with you.

10 But I rejoiced in the Lord greatly, that now at the last [g]your care of me [2]hath flourished again; wherein ye were also careful, but ye lacked opportunity.

11 Not that I speak in respect of want: for I have learned, in whatsoever state I am, [h]*therewith* to be content.

12 [i]I know both how to be abased, and I know how to abound: every where and in all things I am instructed both to be full and to be hungry, both to abound and to suffer need.

13 I can do all things [j]through Chrīst which strengtheneth me.

14 Notwithstanding ye have well done, that [k]ye did communicate with my affliction.

15 Now ye Phĭ-lĭp'pĭ-ans know also, [l]that in the beginning of the gospel, when I departed from Măç-e-dō'nĭ-ȧ, [m]no church communicated with me as concerning giving and receiving, but ye only.

16 [n]For even in Thĕs-sa-lo-nī'cȧ ye sent once and again unto my necessity.

17 Not because I desire a gift: but I desire [o]fruit that may abound to your account.

18 But [3]I have all, and abound: I am full, having received [p]of E-păph-ro-dī'tus the things *which were sent* from you, an odour of a sweet smell, [q]a sacrifice acceptable, wellpleasing to God.

19 But my God [r]shall supply all your need according to his riches in glory by Chrīst Jē'sus.

20 Now unto God and our Father *be* glory for ever and ever. Amen.

21 Salute every saint in Chrīst Jē'sus. The brethren which are with me greet you.

22 All the saints salute you, [s]chiefly they that are of Çæ'sar's household.

23 The grace of our Lord Jē'sus Chrīst *be* with you all. Amen.

[j]Gal. 2.16; 2 Pet. 1.1
10 [k]1 Pet. 4.13
11 [l]Luke 20.35
12 [m]1 Tim. 6.12
[n]Heb. 12.23
13 [o]Heb. 6.1
14 [p]Heb. 12.1
[q]Rom. 9.23-24
15 [r]1 Cor. 2.6
[s]Gal. 5.10
17 [t]Ps. 37.37;
20 [u]Col. 3.1-3
[v]1 Cor. 1.7; 1 Thess. 1.10
21 [w]Ps. 17.15;
[x]Isa. 63.1; Matt. 28.18; Eph. 1.19

CHAPTER 4
1 [a]2 Cor. 1.14
3 [b]Acts 18.2; Rom. 16.3;
[c]Ex. 32.32; Ps. 69.28; Dan. 12.1; Luke 10.20; Rev. 3.5; Rev. 13.8
5 [d]Matt. 24.48-50; Heb. 10.25; Jas. 5.8-9; 1 Pet. 4.7
6 [e]Ps. 55.22; Prov. 16.3; Matt. 6.25; Luke 12.22;
7 [f]Num. 6.26; Isa. 26.3; John 14.27; Rom. 5.1
8 [1]Or, venerable
10 [g]2 Cor. 11.9
[2]Or, is revived
11 [h]1 Tim. 6.6
12 [i]1 Cor. 4.11
13 [j]John 15.5
14 [k]ch. 1.7
15 [l]Acts 11.15
[m]2 Cor. 11.8
16 [n]2 Thess. 3.8
17 [o]Rom. 15.28
18 [3]Or, I have received all
[p]ch. 2.25
[q]Heb. 13.16
19 [r]Ps. 23.1
22 [s]ch. 1.13

THE LETTER OF PAUL TO THE

COLOSSIANS

Life's Questions

Why does the church talk so much about Jesus?
What do I have to do be live like a Christian?
Are not other religions just as good as Christ's?

God's Answers

About A.D. 60 from a Roman prison Paul wrote a church he apparently never visited. His friend and fellow minister Epaphras told Paul of false teachers troubling the church with claims that Jesus was not the divine Son Paul taught that He was and that certain things had to be added to faith for salvation. Paul reacted strongly with a letter upholding Jesus as all sufficient for salvation.

Colossians shows: Christ is supreme in creation, in salvation, and in the church (1:1—2:5); false teachers demand practices that do not lead to salvation or freedom from sin (2:6—3:4); and believers must let Christ cleanse their lives to bring unity and joy in worship, service, family life, and prayer (3:5—4:6).

Colossians calls you to acknowledge Jesus as sufficient to provide all you need in salvation and in daily life.

1 Pa̧ul, an apostle of Jē'sus Chrīst by
the will of God, and Ti-mō'the-ŭs
our brother,
2 To the saints [a]and faithful brethren in Chrīst which are at Co-lŏs'se:
Grace *be* unto you, and peace, from
God our Father and the Lord Jē'sus
Chrīst.
3 We give thanks to God and the Father of our Lord Jē'sus Chrīst, praying
always for you,
4 [b]Since we heard of your faith in
Chrīst Jē'sus, and of [c]the love *which*
ye have to all the saints,
5 For the hope [d]which is laid up for
you in heaven, whereof ye heard before in the word of the truth of the
gospel;
6 Which is come unto you, [e]as *it is*
in all the world; and [f]bringeth forth
fruit, as *it doth* also in you, since the
day ye heard *of it,* and knew [g]the
grace of God in truth:
7 As ye also learned of [h]Ĕp'a-phrăs
our dear fellowservant, who is for you
a faithful minister of Chrīst;
8 Who also declared unto us your
love in the Spirit.
9 [i]For this cause we also, since the
day we heard *it,* do not cease to
pray for you, and to desire that ye
might be filled with the [j]knowledge of
his will in all wisdom and spiritual
understanding;
10 [k]That ye might walk worthy of
the Lord [l]unto all pleasing, [m]being
fruitful in every good work, and increasing in the knowledge of God;
11 Strengthened with all might, according to his glorious power, unto
all patience and longsuffering [n]with
joyfulness;
12 [o]Giving thanks unto the Father,
which hath made us meet to be partakers of [p]the inheritance of the saints
in light:
13 Who hath delivered us from [q]the
power of darkness, [r]and hath trans-

CHAPTER 1
2 [a]Eph. 6.21
4 [b]Eph. 1.15
[c]Heb. 6.10
5 [d]Matt. 5.12;
1 Pet. 1.4
6 [e]Matt.
24.14
[f]John 15.16
[g]Ps. 110.3;
1 Pet. 5.12
7 [h]Phile. 23
9 [i]Eph. 1.15
[j]Rom. 12.2
10 [k]1 Thess.
2.12
[l]1 Thess. 4.1
[m]John 15.16
11 [n]Acts 5.41
12 [o]Eph. 5.20
[p]Rom. 8.17;
Eph. 1.11
13 [q]Heb. 2.14
[r]2 Pet. 1.11
[1]the Son of
his love
15 [s]John
14.9;
Heb. 1.3
[t]Ps. 89.27;
Rev. 3.14
16 [u]John 1.3;
[v]Rom. 11.36
17 [w]John
17.5
18 [x]John
11.25;
[2]Or, among
all
19 [y]Matt.
28.18
20 [3]Or, mak-
ing peace
21 [4]Or, by
your mind in
wicked
works
24 [z]Phil. 3.10
[a]Eph. 1.23

lated *us* into the kingdom of [1]his dear
Son:
14 In whom we have redemption
through his blood, *even* the forgiveness of sins:
15 Who is [s]the image of the invisible
God, [t]the firstborn of every creature:
16 For [u]by him were all things created, that are in heaven, and that are in
earth, visible and invisible, whether
they be thrones, or dominions, or principalities, or powers: all things were
created [v]by him, and for him:
17 [w]And he is before all things, and
by him all things consist.
18 And he is the head of the body,
the church: who is the beginning, [x]the
firstborn from the dead; that [2]in all
things he might have the preeminence.
19 For it pleased *the Father* that [y]in
him should all fulness dwell;
20 And, [3]having made peace through
the blood of his cross, by him to reconcile all things unto himself; by him, *I*
say, whether *they be* things in earth, or
things in heaven.
21 And you, that were sometime
alienated and enemies [4]in *your* mind
by wicked works, yet now hath he
reconciled
22 In the body of his flesh through
death, to present you holy and unblameable and unreproveable in his
sight:
23 If ye continue in the faith
grounded and settled, and *be* not
moved away from the hope of the gospel, which ye have heard, *and* which
was preached to every creature which
is under heaven; whereof I Pa̧ul am
made a minister;
24 Who now rejoice in my sufferings for you, and fill up [z]that which is
behind of the afflictions of Chrīst in
my flesh for [a]his body's sake, which is
the church:
25 Whereof I am made a minister,
according to the dispensation of God

which is given to me for you, [5]to fulfil
the word of God;
26 *Even* [b]the mystery which hath
been hid from ages and from generations, but now is made manifest to his
saints:
27 To whom God would make known
what *is* the riches of the glory of this
mystery among the Gĕn'tīles; which is
Chrīst [6]in you, the hope of glory:
28 Whom we preach, warning every
man, and teaching every man in all wisdom; that we may present every man
perfect in Chrīst Jē'sus:
29 Whereunto I also labour, striving
according to his working, which worketh in me mightily.
2 For I would that ye knew what
great [1]conflict I have for you, and
for them at La-ŏd-ĭ-çē'ȧ, and *for* as
many as have not seen my face in the
flesh;
2 [a]That their hearts might be comforted, being knit together in love, and
unto all [b]riches of the full assurance of
understanding, to the acknowledge-
ment of the mystery of God, and of the
Father, and of Chrīst;
3 [2]In whom are hid all the treasures
of wisdom and knowledge.
4 And this I say, lest any man should
beguile you with enticing words.
5 For though I be absent in the flesh,
yet am I with you in the spirit, joying
and beholding your order, and the
stedfastness of your faith in Chrīst.
6 As ye have therefore received
Chrīst Jē'sus the Lord, *so* walk ye in
him:
7 Rooted and built up in him, and
stablished in the faith, as ye have
been taught, abounding therein with
thanksgiving.
8 [c]Beware lest any man spoil you
through philosophy and vain deceit, after [d]the tradition of men, after the [3]ru-
diments of the world, and not after
Chrīst.
9 For [e]in him dwelleth all the fulness of the Godhead bodily.
10 [f]And ye are complete in him,
[g]which is the head of all principality
and power:
11 In whom also ye are [h]circum-
cised with the circumcison made without hands, in putting off the body of
the sins of the flesh by the circumcision of Chrīst:
12 [i]Buried with him in baptism,
wherein also ye are risen with *him*
through [j]the faith of the operation of
God, who hath raised him from the
dead.
13 And you, being dead in your sins
and the uncircumcision of your flesh,
hath he quickened together with him,
having forgiven you all trespasses;
14 Blotting out the handwriting of
ordinances that was against us, which
was contrary to us, and took it out of
the way, nailing it to his cross;
15 *And* [k]having spoiled principalities and powers, he made a shew of
them openly, triumphing over them [4]in
it.

25 [5]Or, fully to preach the word of God
26 [b]Rom. 16.25
27 [6]Or, among you
CHAPTER 2
1 [1]Or, fear, or, care
2 [a]2 Cor. 1.6
[b]2 Pet. 3.18
3 [2]Or, Wherein
8 [c]Jer. 29.8; Rom. 16.17; Heb. 13.9
[d]Matt. 15.2; Gal. 1.14
[3]Or, elements
9 [e]Isa. 7.14; Matt. 1.23; John 1.14; 1 Tim. 3.16
10 [f]John 1.16
[g]1 Pet. 3.22
11 [h]Jer. 4.4
12 [i]Rom. 6.4
[j]Eph. 3.7
15 [k]Gen. 3.15; Eph. 4.8
[4]Or, in himself
16 [l]Rom. 14.3
[5]Or, for eating and drinking
[6]Or, in part
[m]Rom. 14.5; Gal. 4.10
17 [n]Heb. 8.5
18 [7]Or, judge against you
[8]being a voluntary in humility
20 [9]Or, elements
23 [10]Or, punishing, or, not sparing
CHAPTER 3
1 [a]Eph. 2.6
[b]Matt. 6.33
2 [1]Or, mind
3 [c]Gal. 2.20
[d]John 3.16
4 [e]1 John 3.2
[f]John 11.25
[g]1 Cor. 15.43
8 [h]Jas. 1.21
9 [i]Lev. 19.11
10 [j]Rom. 12.2
[k]Eph. 2.10
11 [l]Gal. 3.28
[m]Eph. 1.23
12 [n]1 Pet. 1.2
[o]Gal. 5.22; Phil. 2.1
13 [2]Or, complaint
14 [p]Rom. 13.8

16 Let no man therefore [l]judge you
[5]in meat, or in drink, or [6]in respect [m]of
an holyday, or of the new moon, or of
the sabbath *days:*
17 [n]Which are a shadow of things to
come; but the body *is* of Chrīst.
18 Let no man [7]beguile you of your
reward [8]in a voluntary humility and
worshipping of angels, intruding into
those things which he hath not seen,
vainly puffed up by his fleshly mind,
19 And not holding the Head, from
which all the body by joints and bands
having nourishment ministered, and
knit together, increaseth with the increase of God.
20 Wherefore if ye be dead with
Chrīst from the [9]rudiments of the world,
why, as though living in the world, are
ye subject to ordinances,
21 (Touch not; taste not; handle not;
22 Which all are to perish with the
using;) after the commandments and
doctrines of men?
23 Which things have indeed a shew
of wisdom in will worship, and humility, and [10]neglecting of the body; not in
any honour to the satisfying of the
flesh.
3 If ye then [a]be risen with Chrīst,
[b]seek those things which are above,
where Chrīst sitteth on the right hand
of God.
2 Set your [1]affection on things above,
not on things on the earth.
3 [c]For ye are dead, [d]and your life is
hid with Chrīst in God.
4 [e]When Chrīst, *who is* [f]our life,
shall appear, then shall ye also appear
with him [g]in glory.
5 Mortify therefore your members
which are upon the earth; fornication, uncleanness, inordinate affection,
evil concupiscence, and covetousness,
which is idolatry:
6 For which things' sake the wrath
of God cometh on the children of
disobedience:
7 In the which ye also walked some
time, when ye lived in them.
8 [h]But now ye also put off all these;
anger, wrath, malice, blasphemy, filthy
communication out of your mouth.
9 [i]Lie not one to another, seeing
that ye have put off the old man with
his deeds;
10 And have put on the new *man,*
which [j]is renewed in knowledge after
the image of him that [k]created him:
11 Where there is neither [l]Greek
nor Jew, circumcision nor uncircumcision, Bär-bā'rĭ-an, Scy̆th'ĭ-an, bond
nor free: [m]but Chrīst *is* all, and in all.
12 Put on therefore, [n]as the elect of
God, holy and beloved, [o]bowels of mercies, kindness, humbleness of mind,
meekness, longsuffering;
13 Forbearing one another, and forgiving one another, if any man have a
[2]quarrel against any: even as Chrīst
forgave you, so also *do* ye.
14 And above all these things [p]*put
on* charity, which is the bond of perfectness.

15 And let [q]the peace of God rule
in your hearts, [r]to the which also ye
are called [s]in one body; and be ye
thankful.
16 [t]Let the word of Chrĭst dwell in
you richly in all wisdom; teaching and
admonishing one another in psalms
and hymns and spiritual songs, singing [u]with grace [v]in your hearts to the
Lord.
17 And [w]whatsoever ye do in word
or deed, *do* all in the name of the Lord
Jē'sus, giving [x]thanks to God and the
Father by him.
18 Wives, submit yourselves unto
your own husbands, as it is fit in the
Lord.
19 Husbands, love *your* wives, and
be not bitter against them.
20 Children, obey *your* [y]parents in
all things: for this is well pleasing unto
the Lord.
21 [z]Fathers, provoke not your children *to anger*, lest they be discouraged.
22 Servants, obey in all things *your*
masters according to the flesh; not
with eyeservice, as menpleasers; but
in singleness of heart, fearing God:
23 And whatsoever ye do, do *it* heartily, as to the Lord, and not unto men;
24 Knowing that of the Lord ye shall
receive the reward of the inheritance:
for ye serve the Lord Chrĭst.
25 But he that doeth wrong shall receive for the wrong which he hath done:
and there is no respect of persons.
4 [a]Masters, give unto *your* servants
that which is just and equal; knowing that ye also have a Master in
heaven.
2 [b]Continue in prayer, and watch in
the same with thanksgiving;
3 [c]Withal praying also for us, that
God would [d]open unto us a door of
utterance, to speak [e]the mystery of
Chrĭst, [f]for which I am also in bonds:
4 That I may make it manifest, as I
ought to speak.
5 [g]Walk in wisdom toward them
that are without, redeeming the time.
6 Let your speech *be* alway [h]with
grace, [i]seasoned with salt, [j]that ye
may know how ye ought to answer every man.
7 All my state shall Tȳch'ĭ-cŭs declare unto you, *who is* a beloved brother,
and a faithful minister and fellowservant in the Lord:
8 Whom I have sent unto you for the
same purpose, that he might know
your estate, and comfort your hearts;
9 With [k]O'nĕs'i-mus, a faithful and
beloved brother, who is *one* of you.
They shall make known unto you all
things which *are done* here.
10 [l]Ăr-ĭs-tär'chus my fellowprisoner
saluteth you, and [m]Mär'cus, sister's son
to Bär'na-băs, (touching whom ye received commandments: if he come unto
you, receive him;)
11 And Jē'sus, which is called Jŭs'-
tus, who are of the circumcision. These
only *are my* fellowworkers unto the
kingdom of God, which have been a
comfort unto me.
12 [n]Ĕp'a-phrăs, who is *one* of you, a
servant of Chrĭst, saluteth you, always
[1]labouring fervently for you in prayers, that ye may stand [o]perfect and
[2]complete in all the will of God.
13 For I bear him record, that he
hath a great zeal for you, and them
that are in La-ŏd-ĭ-çē'ȧ, and them in
Hī-e-răp'o-lĭs.
14 [p]Luke, the beloved physician,
and [q]Dē'mas, greet you.
15 Salute the brethren which are in
La-ŏd-ĭ-çē'ȧ, and Nȳm'phas, and the
church which is in his house.
16 And when [r]this epistle is read
among you, cause that it be read also
in the church of the La-ŏd-ĭ-çē'ans;
and that ye likewise read the *epistle*
from La-ŏd-ĭ-çē'ȧ.
17 And say to [s]Ăr-chĭp'pus, Take
heed to [t]the ministry which thou hast
received in the Lord, that thou fulfil it.
18 The salutation by the hand of me
Paul. [u]Remember my bonds. Grace *be*
with you. Amen.

15 [q]Ps. 29.11; Isa. 26.3; Phil. 4.7
[r]1 Cor. 7.15
[s]Eph. 2.16
16 [t]Jer. 15.16; 2 Tim. 3.15-17
[u]Eph. 5.19
[v]ch. 4.6
17 [w]1 Cor. 10.31
[x]Eph. 5.20; ch. 2.7
20 [y]Prov. 23.22; Luke 2.51; Eph. 6.1
21 [z]Eph. 6.4
CHAPTER 4
1 [a]Lev. 19.13; Mal. 3.5; Eph. 6.9
2 [b]Luke 18.1; Eph. 6.18
3 [c]2 Thess. 3.1
[d]1 Cor. 16.9
[e]Matt. 13.11
[f]Phil. 1.7
5 [g]Eph. 5.15
6 [h]Eccl. 10.12
[i]Mark 9.50
[j]1 Pet. 3.15
9 [k]Phile. 10
10 [l]Acts 19.29; Acts 20.4; Phile. 24
[m]Acts 15.37
12 [n]ch. 1.7
[1]Or, striving
[o]Matt. 5.48
[2]Or, filled
14 [p]Luke 1.3; Acts 1.1
[q]Phile. 24
16 [r]1 Thess. 5.27
17 [s]Phile. 2
[t]1 Tim. 4.6
18 [u]Heb. 13.3

THE FIRST LETTER OF PAUL TO THE

THESSALONIANS

Life's Questions

Is Jesus really coming again?
Why should I endure such a hard life and witness for Jesus?
Can I trust any preacher?

God's Answers

About 50 A.D. Paul write to the church at Thessalonica to help them understand why Jesus had not returned and what they should look for. He showed them reasons to stay faithful in a hostile world.

First Thessalonians shows: the church is founded on faith, hope, and love (ch. 1); love and sincerity not personal greed motivate Christian witness (ch. 2); a true minister sacrifices self for love of the church and teaches the church to do the same (3:1—4:12); believers have assurance of resurrection with Christ without knowing all details (4:13—5:11); and the church has care for each other, respect for leaders, and commitment to the faithful God (5:12—28).

First Thessalonians calls you to sacrifice yourself in faith, hope, and love for Christ and His church as you wait for His promised and guaranteed return.

1 Pa̧ul, and [a]Sĭl-vā'nus, and Ti-mō'-
the-ŭs, unto the church of the Thĕs-
sa-lō'nĭ-ans *which is* [b]in God the Father and *in* the Lord Jē'sus Chrīst:
Grace *be* unto you, and peace, from
God our Father, and the Lord Jē'sus
Christ.
2 We give thanks to God always for
you all, making mention of you in our
prayers;
3 Remembering without ceasing
your work of [c]faith, [d]and labour of
love, and patience of hope in our Lord
Jē'sus Chrīst, in the sight of God and
our Father;
4 Knowing, brethren [1]beloved, [e]your
election of God.
5 For [f]our gospel came not unto you
in word only, but also in power, and
[g]in the Hō'lȳ Ghōst, [h]and in much assurance; as [i]ye know what manner of
men we were among you for your
sake.
6 And ye became followers of us,
and of the Lord, having received the
word in much affliction, with joy of the
Hō'lȳ Ghōst:
7 So that ye were ensamples to
all that believe in Măç-e-dō'nĭ-ȧ and
A-chā'iȧ.
8 For from you [j]sounded out the
word of the Lord not only in Măç-e-
dō'nĭ-ȧ and A-chā'iȧ, but also in every
place your faith to God-ward is spread
abroad; so that we need not to speak
any thing.
9 For they themselves shew of us
what manner of entering in we had
unto you, and how ye turned to God
from idols to serve the living and true
God;
10 And [k]to wait for his Son [l]from
heaven, whom he raised from the dead,
even Jē'sus, which delivered us [m]from
the wrath to come.
2 For yourselves, brethren, know our
entrance in unto you, that it was not
in vain:
2 But even after that we had suffered
before, and were shamefully entreated,
as ye know, at [a]Phĭ-lĭp'pī, we were
bold in our God [b]to speak unto you the
gospel of God with much contention.
3 For our exhortation *was* not of deceit, nor of uncleanness, nor in guile:
4 But as [c]we were allowed of God
[d]to be put in trust with the gospel, even
so we speak; not as pleasing men, but
God, [e]which trieth our hearts.
5 For neither at any time used we
flattering words, as ye know, nor a
cloke of covetousness; God *is* witness:
6 [f]Nor of men sought we glory, neither of you, nor *yet* of others, when we
might have [1]been burdensome, as the
apostles of Chrīst.
7 But we were gentle among you,
even as a nurse cherisheth her children:
8 So being affectionately desirous
of you, we were willing [g]to have imparted unto you, not the gospel of God
only, but also our [h]own souls, because
ye were dear unto us.
9 For ye remember, brethren, our labour and travail: for labouring night
and day, [i]because we would not be
chargeable unto any of you, we
preached unto you the gospel of God.
10 Ye *are* witnesses, and God *also*,
how holily and justly and unblameably
we behaved ourselves among you that
believe:
11 As ye know how we exhorted
and comforted and charged every one
of you, as a father *doth* his children,
12 [j]That ye would walk worthy of
God, who hath called you unto his kingdom and glory.
13 For this cause also thank we God
without ceasing, because, when ye received the word of God which ye heard
of us, ye received *it* [k]not *as* the word of
men, but as it is in truth, the word of
God, which effectually worketh also in
you that believe.
14 For ye, brethren, became followers [l]of the churches of God which in
Jū-dæ'ȧ are in Chrīst Jē'sus: for [m]ye
also have suffered like things of your
own countrymen, [n]even as they *have*
of the Jews:
15 Who both killed the Lord Jē'sus,
and [o]their own prophets, and have
[2]persecuted us; and they please not
God, and are contrary to all men:
16 [p]Forbidding us to speak to the
Gĕn'tīles that they might be saved, [q]to
fill up their sins alway: [r]for the wrath
is come upon them to the uttermost.
17 But we, brethren, being taken
from you for a short time in presence,
not in heart, endeavoured the more
abundantly to see your face with great
desire.
18 Wherefore we would have come
unto you, even I Pa̧ul, once and again;
but [s]Sā'tan hindered us.
19 For what *is* our hope, or joy, or
crown of [3]rejoicing? *Are* not even ye in
the presence of our Lord Jē'sus Chrīst
[t]at his coming?
20 For ye are our glory and joy.
3 Wherefore when we could no longer
forbear, [a]we thought it good to be
left at Ăth'ĕns alone;
2 And sent [b]Ti-mō'the-ŭs, our
brother, and minister of God, and our
fellowlabourer in the gospel of Chrīst,
to establish you, and to comfort you
concerning your faith:
3 [c]That no man should be moved by
these afflictions: for yourselves know
that [d]we are appointed thereunto.
4 [e]For verily, when we were with
you, we told you before that we should
suffer tribulation; even as it came to
pass, and ye know.
5 For this cause, when I could no
longer forbear, I sent to know your
faith, [f]lest by some means the tempter
have tempted you, and [g]our labour be
in vain.
6 [h]But now when Ti-mō'the-ŭs came
from you unto us, and brought us good
tidings of your faith and charity, and
that ye have good remembrance of us

CHAPTER 1
1 [a]2 Thess. 1.1; 1 Pet. 5.12
[b]John 14.23
3 [c]John 6.29; Gal. 5.6; ch. 3.6
[d]Heb. 6.10
4 [1]Or, beloved of God, your election
[e]Col. 3.12
5 [f]1 Cor. 2.4
[g]2 Cor. 6.6
[h]Heb. 2.3
[i]2 Thess. 3.7
8 [j]Rom. 10.18
10 [k]Rom. 2.7; Phil. 3.20; Rev. 1.7
[l]Acts 1.11
[m]1 Thess. 5.9

CHAPTER 2
2 [a]Acts 16.22
[b]Acts 17.2
4 [c]1 Cor. 4.15-16
[d]Tit. 1.3
[e]Prov. 17.3
6 [f]John 5.41
[1]Or, used authority
8 [g]Rom. 1.11
[h]2 Cor. 12.15
9 [i]2 Cor. 11.9
12 [j]Gal. 5.16; 1 Pet. 1.15
13 [k]Matt. 10.40; Heb. 4.12
14 [l]Gal. 1.22
[m]Acts 17.5
[n]Heb. 10.33
15 [o]Matt. 5.12; Acts 7.52
[2]Or, chased us out
16 [p]Luke 11.52; Acts 17.5
[q]Gen. 15.16
[r]Matt. 24.6
18 [s]Rom. 1.13
19 [3]Or, glorying
[t]ch. 3.13; Rev. 1.7

CHAPTER 3
1 [a]Acts 17.15
2 [b]Rom. 16.21
3 [c]Ps. 112.6; Eph. 3.13
[d]Acts 14.22; Acts 20.23
4 [e]Acts 20.24
5 [f]1 Cor. 7.5
[g]Gal. 2.2
6 [h]Acts 18.1

always, desiring greatly to see us, [i]as
we also *to see* you:
7 Therefore, brethren, we were comforted over you in all our affliction and
distress by your faith:
8 For now we live, if ye [j]stand fast in
the Lord.
9 For what thanks can we render to
God again for you, for all the joy wherewith we joy for your sakes before our
God;
10 [k]Night and day praying exceedingly that we might see your face, and
might perfect that which is lacking in
your faith?
11 Now God himself and our Father,
and our Lord Jē'sus Chrīst, [1]direct our
way unto you.
12 And the Lord make you to increase and abound in love one toward
another, and toward all *men*, even as
we *do* toward you:
13 To the end he may stablish your
hearts unblameable in holiness before
God, even our Father, at the coming of
our Lord Jē'sus Chrīst [l]with all his
saints.
4 Furthermore then we [1]beseech you,
brethren, and [2]exhort *you* by the
Lord Jē'sus, that as ye have received of
us how ye ought to walk and [a]to please
God, *so* ye would abound more and
more.
2 For ye know what commandments
we gave you by the Lord Jē'sus.
3 For this is [b]the will of God, *even*
your sanctification, that ye should abstain from fornication:
4 [c]That every one of you should
know how to possess his vessel in sanctification and honour;
5 Not in the lust of concupiscence,
even as the Gĕn'tīles [d]which know not
God:
6 [e]That no *man* go beyond and [3]de-
fraud his brother [4]in *any* matter: because that the Lord *is* the avenger of
all such, as we also have forewarned
you and testified.
7 For God hath not called us unto
uncleanness, [f]but unto holiness.
8 [g]He therefore that [5]despiseth, despiseth not man, but God, [h]who hath
also given unto us his holy Spirit.
9 But as touching brotherly love ye
need not that I write unto you: for [i]ye
yourselves are taught of God [j]to love
one another.
10 And indeed ye do it toward all
the brethren which are in all Măç-e-
dō'nĭ-ȧ: but we beseech you, brethren,
that ye increase more and more;
11 And that ye study to be quiet, and
to do your own business, and to work
with your own hands, as we commanded you;
12 That ye may walk honestly toward them that are without, and *that*
ye may have lack [6]of nothing.
13 But I would not have you to be
ignorant, brethren, concerning them
which are asleep, that ye sorrow not,
[k]even as others which have no hope.
14 For [l]if we believe that Jē'sus died
and rose again, even so them also
which sleep in Jē'sus will God bring
with him.
15 For this we say unto you [m]by the
word of the Lord, that we which are
alive *and* remain unto the coming of
the Lord shall not prevent them which
are asleep.
16 For [n]the Lord himself shall descend from heaven with a shout, with
the voice of the archangel, and with
the trump of God: and the dead in
Chrīst shall rise first:
17 Then we which are alive *and* remain shall be caught up together with
them [o]in the clouds, to meet the Lord
in the air: and so [p]shall we ever be
with the Lord.
18 Wherefore [7]comfort one another
with these words.
5 But of [a]the times and the seasons,
brethren, ye have no need that I
write unto you.
2 For yourselves know perfectly that
[b]the day of the Lord so cometh as a
thief in the night.
3 For when they shall say, Peace
and safety; then [c]sudden destruction
cometh upon them, as travail upon a
woman with child; and they shall not
escape.
4 [d]But ye, brethren, are not in darkness, that that day should overtake
you as a thief.
5 Ye are all [e]the children of light,
and the children of the day: we are not
of the night, nor of darkness.
6 Therefore let us not sleep, as *do*
others; but let us watch and be sober.
7 For [f]they that sleep sleep in the
night; and they that be drunken [g]are
drunken in the night.
8 But let us, who are of the day, be
sober, [h]putting on the breastplate of
faith and love; and for an helmet, the
hope of salvation.
9 For [i]God hath not appointed us to
wrath, but to obtain salvation by our
Lord Jē'sus Chrīst,
10 Who died for us, that, whether
we wake or sleep, we should live together with him.
11 Wherefore [1]comfort yourselves
together, and edify one another, even
as also ye do.
12 And we beseech you, brethren,
[j]to know them which labour among
you, and are over you in the Lord, and
admonish you;
13 And to esteem them very highly
in love for their work's sake. *And* be at
peace among yourselves.
14 Now we [2]exhort you, brethren,
warn them that are [3]unruly, comfort
the feebleminded, support the weak,
be patient toward all *men*.
15 [k]See that none render evil for
evil unto any *man;* but ever [l]follow
that which is good, both among yourselves, and to all *men*.
16 Rejoice evermore.
17 [m]Pray without ceasing.
18 In every thing give thanks: for
this is the will of God in Chrīst Jē'sus
concerning you.
19 [n]Quench not the Spirit.

[i]Phil. 1.8
8 [j]Phil. 4.1
10 [k]Acts 26.7
11 [1]Or, guide
13 [l]Zech. 14.5; Rev. 20.11

CHAPTER 4
1 [1]Or, request [2]Or, beseech
[a]Col. 1.10
3 [b]Rom. 12.2; Eph. 5.17
4 [c]Rom. 6.19
5 [d]Gal. 4.8; Eph. 2.12
6 [e]Lev. 19.11 [3]Or, oppress, or, overreach [4]Or, in the matter
7 [f]Lev. 11.44
8 [g]Luke 10.16 [5]Or, rejecteth [h]1 John 3.24
9 [i]Jer. 31.34; John 6.45 [j]John 13.34
12 [6]Or, of no man
13 [k]Lev. 19.28; 2 Sam. 12.20
14 [l]1 Cor. 15.13
15 [m]1 Ki. 13.17
16 [n]Matt. 24.30; Acts 1.11
17 [o]Acts 1.9; Rev. 11.12 [p]John 12.26; Rev. 21.3-4
18 [7]Or, exhort

CHAPTER 5
1 [a]Matt. 24.3; Acts 1.7
2 [b]Matt. 25.13; Rev. 3.3
3 [c]Ex. 15.9-10
4 [d]1 John 2.8
5 [e]Eph. 5.8
7 [f]Luke 21.34 [g]Acts 2.15
8 [h]Isa. 59.17
9 [i]Rom. 9.22
11 [1]Or, exhort
12 [j]Phil. 2.29
14 [2]Or, beseech [3]Or, disorderly
15 [k]Lev. 19.18; [l]Gal. 6.10
17 [m]Luke 18.1
19 [n]Ps. 78.40

20 [o]Despise not prophesyings.
21 [p]Prove all things; hold fast that
which is good.
22 [q]Abstain from all appearance of
evil.
23 And [r]the very God of peace sanctify you wholly; and *I pray God* your
whole spirit and soul and body [s]be preserved blameless unto the coming of
our Lord Jē'sus Chrīst.

20 [o]1 Cor. 14.1
21 [p]1 John 4.1
22 [q]Ex. 23.7
23 [r]Phil. 4.9
[s]1 Cor. 1.8
24 [t]1 Cor. 10.13
27 [4]Or, adjure

24 [t]Faithful *is* he that calleth you,
who also will do *it*.
25 Brethren, pray for us.
26 Greet all the brethren with an
holy kiss.
27 I [4]charge you by the Lord that
this epistle be read unto all the holy
brethren.
28 The grace of our Lord Jē'sus
Chrīst *be* with you. Amen.

THE SECOND LETTER OF PAUL TO THE

THESSALONIANS

Life's Questions

Has Christ already returned?
If Christ is coming, why should I work?
Is God just?

God's Answers

About 50 A.D., shortly after writing 1 Thessalonians, Paul wrote again to try to clear up misunderstanding about the second coming and to encourage the church.

Second Thessalonians shows: the church can be encouraged by its growth in faith, hope, and love and in knowing God is just (1:1—12); Christ has not come but will come to overcome all evil forces, giving the church encouragement to trust and obey Him (2:1—3:18).

Second Thessalonians calls you to trust God's justice and know that He will come again .

1 Paul, [a]and Sĭl-vā'nus, and Ti-mō'-
the-ŭs, unto the church of the Thĕs-
sa-lō'nĭ-ans [b]in God our Father and
the Lord Jē'sus Chrīst:
2 Grace unto you, and peace, from
God our Father and the Lord Jē'sus
Chrīst.
3 We are bound to thank God always
for you, brethren, as it is meet, because
that your faith [c]groweth exceedingly,
and the charity of every one of you all
toward each other aboundeth;
4 So that [d]we ourselves glory in you
in the churches of God [e]for your patience and faith [f]in all your persecutions and tribulations that ye endure:
5 *Which is* [g]a manifest token of the
righteous judgment of God, that ye
may be counted [h]worthy of the kingdom of God, for which ye also suffer:
6 [i]Seeing *it is* a righteous thing with
God to recompense tribulation to them
that trouble you;
7 And to you who are troubled [j]rest
with us, when the Lord Jē'sus shall be
revealed from heaven with [1]his mighty
angels,
8 [k]In flaming fire [2]taking vengeance
on them [l]that know not God, and that
obey not the gospel of our Lord Jē'sus
Chrīst:
9 Who shall be punished with everlasting destruction from the presence
of the Lord, and [m]from the glory of his
power;
10 When he shall come to be glorified in his saints, and to be admired in
all them that believe (because our testimony among you was believed) in that
day.
11 Wherefore also we pray always
for you, that our God would [3]count you
worthy of *this* calling, and fulfil all the

CHAPTER 1
1 [a]2 Cor. 1.19
[b]1 Thess. 1.1
3 [c]Job 17.9; Ps. 84.7
4 [d]2 Cor. 7.14
[e]1 Thess. 1.3
[f]1 Thess. 2.14
5 [g]Ps. 9.7-8; Ps. 33.5
[h]Luke 20.35, 36; Rev. 3.4
6 [i]Rev. 6.10
7 [j]Rev. 14.13
[1]the angels of his power
8 [k]Heb. 10.27; Rev. 21.8
[2]Or, yielding
[l]Ps. 79.6
9 [m]Deut. 33.2; Isa. 2.19
11 [3]Or, vouchsafe
12 [n]1 Pet. 1.7
CHAPTER 2
1 [a]Matt. 24.31
3 [b]2 Pet. 2.1;
[c]Isa. 37.23;
[d]John 17.12
4 [e]Isa. 14.13;
6 [1]Or, holdeth
7 [f]1 John 4.3
8 [g]Dan. 7.10
[h]Job 4.9;
[i]Heb. 10.27
9 [j]John 8.41;
[k]Deut. 13.1

good pleasure of *his* goodness, and the
work of faith with power:
12 [n]That the name of our Lord Jē'-
sus Chrīst may be glorified in you, and
ye in him, according to the grace of our
God and the Lord Jē'sus Chrīst.
2 Now we beseech you, brethren,
by the coming of our Lord Jē'sus
Chrīst, [a]and *by* our gathering together
unto him,
2 That ye be not soon shaken in
mind, or be troubled, neither by spirit,
nor by word, nor by letter as from us,
as that the day of Chrīst is at hand.
3 Let no man deceive you by any
means: for *that day shall not come,*
[b]except there come a falling away
first, and [c]that man of sin be revealed,
[d]the son of perdition;
4 Who opposeth and [e]exalteth himself above all that is called God, or that
is worshipped; so that he as God sitteth in the temple of God, shewing himself that he is God.
5 Remember ye not, that, when I
was yet with you, I told you these
things?
6 And now ye know what [1]with-
holdeth that he might be revealed in
his time.
7 For [f]the mystery of iniquity doth
already work: only he who now letteth
will let, until he be taken out of the
way.
8 And then shall that Wicked be revealed, [g]whom the Lord shall consume [h]with the spirit of his mouth, and
shall destroy [i]with the brightness of
his coming:
9 *Even him,* whose coming is [j]after
the working of Sā'tan with all power
and [k]signs and lying wonders,

10 And with all deceivableness of
unrighteousness in [l]them that perish;
because they received not the love of
the truth, that they might be saved.
11 And [m]for this cause God shall
send them strong delusion, [n]that they
should believe a lie:
12 That they all might be damned
who believed not the truth, but had
pleasure in unrighteousness.
13 But we are bound to give thanks
alway to God for you, brethren beloved of the Lord, because God hath
from the beginning chosen you to salvation through sanctification of the
Spirit and belief of the truth:
14 Whereunto he called you by our
gospel, to the obtaining of the glory of
our Lord Jē'sus Chrīst.
15 Therefore, brethren, stand fast,
and hold [o]the traditions which ye have
been taught, whether by word, or our
epistle.
16 Now our Lord Jē'sus Chrīst himself, and God, even our Father, [p]which
hath loved us, and hath given *us* everlasting consolation and good hope
through grace,
17 Comfort your hearts, and stablish
you in every good word and work.
3 Finally, brethren, pray for us, that
the word of the Lord [1]may have *free*
course, and be glorified, even as *it is*
with you:
2 And that we may be delivered
from [2]unreasonable and wicked men:
for all *men* have not faith.
3 But the Lord is faithful, who shall
stablish you, and [a]keep *you* from evil.
4 And we have confidence in the
Lord touching you, that ye both do and
will do the things which we command
you.
5 And [b]the Lord direct your hearts
into the love of God, and [3]into the patient waiting for Chrīst.
6 Now we command you, brethren,
in the name of our Lord Jē'sus Chrīst,
[c]that ye withdraw yourselves [d]from
every brother that walketh disorderly,
and not after the tradition which he
received of us.
7 For yourselves know how ye ought
to follow us: for we behaved not ourselves disorderly among you;
8 Neither did we eat any man's bread
for nought; but [e]wrought with labour
and travail night and day, that we
might not be chargeable to any of you:
9 [f]Not because we have not power,
but to make [g]ourselves an ensample
unto you to follow us.
10 For even when we were with
you, this we commanded you, [h]that if
any would not work, neither should
he eat.
11 For we hear that there are some
which walk among you [i]disorderly,
working not at all, but are busybodies.
12 Now them that are such we command and exhort by our Lord Jē'sus
Chrīst, [j]that with quietness they work,
and eat their own bread.
13 But ye, brethren, [4]be not weary in
well doing.
14 And if any man obey not our
word [5]by this epistle, note that man,
and have no company with him, that
he may be ashamed.
15 [k]Yet count *him* not as an enemy,
but admonish *him* as a brother.
16 Now the Lord of peace himself
give you peace always by all means.
The Lord *be* with you all.
17 The salutation of Paul with mine
own hand, which is the token in every
epistle: so I write.
18 The grace of our Lord Jē'sus
Chrīst *be* with you all. Amen.

10 [l] 2 Cor. 2.15
11 [m] 1 Ki. 22.22; Ezek. 14.9; Rom. 1.24
[n] Matt. 24.5
15 [o] ch. 3.6
16 [p] 1 John 4.10; Rev. 1.5
CHAPTER 3
1 [1] may run
2 [2] absurd
3 [a] Matt. 6.13
5 [b] 1 Ki. 8.58; Prov. 3.6; Matt. 22.37
[3] Or, the patience of Christ
6 [c] Rom. 16.17
[d] 1 Tim. 6.5; 2 John 10
8 [e] Acts 18.3; Acts 20.34; 1 Cor. 4.12
9 [f] Matt. 10.10
[g] 1 Pet. 5.3
10 [h] Gen. 3.19
11 [i] Isa. 56.10
12 [j] Rom. 12.11
13 [4] Or, faint not
14 [5] Or, signify that man by an epistle
15 [k] Lev. 19.17

THE FIRST LETTER OF PAUL TO

TIMOTHY

Life's Questions

What kind of life should I expect from church leaders?
Should a preacher play favorites in the congregation?
Why does the preacher always talk about money?

God's Answers

About A.D. 65 Paul wrote his young partner in ministry Timothy answering some basic questions about the work of the pastor. In Ephesus Timothy faced doctrinal, relational, personal, and financial problems.

First Timothy shows: spiritual leaders are stewards of the true gospel in face of threats from false teachers (ch. 1); spiritual leaders are persons of prayer leading the church in worship (ch. 2); spiritual leaders must meet spiritual and moral qualifications (ch. 3); spiritual leaders must be persons of integrity (ch. 4); spiritual leaders must show impartial concern for all church members and activities (5:1—6:2); spiritual leaders are devoted to the gospel and not to financial resources (6:3—21).

Second Timothy calls you to work in God's church as a spiritual leader with integrity, honesty, and commitment to God, not to materialistic goals.

1 Pąul, an apostle of Jē'sus Chrīst [a]by the commandment [b]of God our Saviour, and Lord Jē'sus Chrīst, [c]*which is* our hope;

2 Unto [d]Tĭm'o-thȳ, *my* own son in the faith: Grace, mercy, *and* peace, from God our Father and Jē'sus Chrīst our Lord.

3 As I besought thee to abide still at Ĕph'ĕ-sŭs, [e]when I went into Măç-e-dō'nĭ-ȧ, that thou mightest charge some [f]that they teach no other doctrine,

4 Neither give heed to fables and endless genealogies, which minister questions, rather than godly edifying which is in faith: *so do*.

5 Now [g]the end of the commandment is charity [h]out of a pure heart, and *of* a good conscience, and *of* faith unfeigned:

6 From which some [1]having swerved have turned aside unto vain jangling;

7 Desiring to be teachers of the law; understanding neither what they say, nor whereof they affirm.

8 But we know that [i]the law *is* good, if a man use it lawfully;

9 [j]Knowing this, that the law is not made for a righteous man, but for [k]the lawless and disobedient, for the ungodly and for sinners, for unholy and profane, for murderers of fathers and murderers of mothers, for manslayers,

10 For whoremongers, for them that defile themselves with mankind, for menstealers, for liars, for perjured persons, and if there be any other thing that is contrary to sound doctrine;

11 According to the glorious gospel of the blessed God, which was committed to my trust.

12 And I thank Chrīst Jē'sus our Lord, who hath enabled me, [l]for that he counted me faithful, [m]putting me into the ministry;

13 [n]Who was before a blasphemer, and a persecutor, and injurious: but I obtained mercy, because [o]I did *it* ignorantly in unbelief.

14 And the grace of our Lord was exceeding abundant with faith [p]and love which is in Chrīst Jē'sus.

15 This *is* a faithful saying, and worthy of all acceptation, that [q]Chrīst Jē'sus came into the world to save sinners; of whom I am chief.

16 Howbeit for this cause I obtained mercy, that in me first Jē'sus Chrīst might shew forth all longsuffering, for a pattern to them which should hereafter believe on him to life everlasting.

17 Now unto [r]the King eternal, immortal, [s]invisible, the only wise God, *be* honour and glory for ever and ever. Amen.

18 This charge I commit unto thee, son Tĭm'o-thȳ, [t]according to the prophecies which went before on thee, that thou by them mightest war a good warfare;

19 Holding faith, and a good conscience; which some having put away concerning faith have made shipwreck:

20 Of whom is [u]Hȳ-mĕ-næ'us and [v]Ăl-ĕx-ăn'dẽr; whom I have [w]delivered unto Sā'tan, that they may learn not to blaspheme.

2 I [1]exhort therefore, that, first of all, supplications, prayers, intercessions, *and* giving of thanks, be made for all men;

2 [a]For kings, and [b]*for* all that are in [2]authority; that we may lead a quiet and peaceable life in all godliness and honesty.

3 For this *is* [c]good and acceptable in the sight of God our Saviour;

4 [d]Who will have all men to be saved, [e]and to come unto the knowledge of the truth.

5 For *there is* one God, and one mediator between God and men, the man Chrīst Jē'sus;

6 Who gave himself a ransom for all, [3]to be testified [f]in due time.

7 Whereunto I am ordained a preacher, and an apostle, (I speak the truth in Chrīst, *and* lie not;) a teacher of the Gĕn'tīles in faith and verity.

8 I will therefore that men pray [g]every where, lifting up holy hands, without wrath and doubting.

9 In like manner also, that women adorn themselves in modest apparel, with shamefacedness and sobriety; not with [4]broided hair, or gold, or pearls, or costly array;

10 But (which becometh women professing godliness) with good works.

11 Let the woman learn in silence with all subjection.

12 But I suffer not a woman to teach, nor to usurp authority over the man, but to be in silence.

13 For Ȧd'ăm was first formed, then Ēve.

14 And Ăd'ăm was not deceived, but the woman being deceived was in the transgression.

15 Notwithstanding she shall be [h]saved in childbearing, if they continue in faith and charity and holiness with sobriety.

3 This *is* a true saying, If a man desire the office of a [a]bishop, he desireth a good work.

2 A bishop then must be blameless, the husband of one wife, vigilant, sober, [1]of good behaviour, given to hospitality, apt to teach;

3 [2]Not given to wine, no striker, not greedy of filthy lucre; but patient, not a brawler, not covetous;

4 [b]One that ruleth well his own house, having his children in subjection with all gravity;

5 (For if a man know not how to rule his own house, how shall he take care of the church of God?)

6 Not [3]a novice, lest being lifted up with pride he fall into the condemnation of the devil.

7 Moreover he must have a good report of them which are without; lest he fall into reproach and the snare of the devil.

CHAPTER 1
1 [a]Gal. 1.1
[b]ch. 2.3; ch. 4.10; Tit. 1.3; Jude 25
[c]Col. 1.27
2 [d]Acts 16.1
3 [e]Acts 20.1-3; Phil. 2.24
[f]Gal. 1.6-7
5 [g]Rom. 13.8; Gal. 5.14
[h]2 Tim. 2.22
6 [1]Or, not aiming at
8 [i]Rom. 7.12
9 [j]Gal. 3.19
[k]Rev. 21.8
12 [l]1 Cor. 7.25
[m]2 Cor. 3.5-6
13 [n]Acts 8.3; Acts 9.1; Phil. 3.6
[o]Luke 23.34; Acts 26.9
14 [p]Luke 7.47
15 [q]Matt. 9.13; Luke 19.10; Rom. 5.8
17 [r]Ps. 10.16; Ps. 45.6; Dan. 7.14; Matt. 6.13
[s]Rom. 1.23
18 [t]ch. 4.14
20 [u]2 Tim. 2.17
[v]2 Tim. 4.14
[w]Ps. 109.6; Matt. 18.17; Acts 26.18

CHAPTER 2
1 [1]Or, desire
2 [a]Jer. 29.7
[b]Rom. 13.1
[2]Or, eminent place
3 [c]Rom. 12.2
4 [d]Isa. 55.1-7; 2 Pet. 3.9
[e]John 17.3
6 [3]Or, a testimony;
[f]Gal. 4.4
8 [g]Mal. 1.11
9 [4]Or, plaited
15 [h]Gen. 3.15-16; Isa. 7.14

CHAPTER 3
1 [a]Acts 20.28; Phil. 1.1
2 [1]Or, modest
3 [2]Or, Not ready to quarrel, and offer wrong, as one in wine
4 [b]Josh. 24.15
6 [3]Or, one newly come to the faith

8 Likewise *must* the deacons *be*
grave, not doubletongued, not given to
much wine, not greedy of filthy lucre;
9 Holding the mystery of the faith in
a pure conscience.
10 And let these also first be proved;
then let them use the office of a deacon, being *found* blameless.
11 Even so *must their* wives *be*
grave, not slanderers, sober, faithful in
all things.
12 Let the deacons be the husbands
of one wife, ruling their children and
their own houses well.
13 For they that have [4]used the office of a deacon well purchase to themselves a good degree, and great boldness in the faith which is in Chrīst
Jē′sus.
14 These things write I unto thee,
hoping to come unto thee shortly:
15 But if I tarry long, that thou mayest know how thou oughtest to behave
thyself in the house of God, which is
the church of the living God, the pillar
and [5]ground of the truth.
16 And without controversy great is
the mystery of godliness: [c]God was
[6]manifest in the flesh, [d]justified in the
Spirit, [e]seen of angels, preached unto
the Gĕn′tīles, believed on in the world,
received up into glory.

4 Now the Spirit [a]speaketh expressly,
that [b]in the latter times some shall
depart from the faith, giving heed
[c]to seducing spirits, [d]and doctrines of
devils;
2 Speaking lies in hypocrisy; [e]hav-
ing their conscience seared with a hot
iron;
3 [f]Forbidding to marry, [g]*and commanding* to abstain from meats, which
God hath created [h]to be received with
thanksgiving of them which believe
and know the truth.
4 For [i]every creature of God *is* good,
and nothing to be refused, if it be received with thanksgiving:
5 For it is sanctified by the word of
God and prayer.
6 If thou put the brethren in remembrance of these things, thou shalt be a
good minister of Jē′sus Chrīst, [j]nour-
ished up in the words of faith and of
good doctrine, whereunto thou hast
attained.
7 But refuse profane and old wives'
fables, and exercise thyself *rather* unto
godliness.
8 For bodily exercise profiteth [1]lit-
tle: but godliness is profitable unto all
things, [k]having promise of the life that
now is, and of that which is to come.
9 This *is* a faithful saying and worthy of all acceptation.
10 For therefore we both labour and
suffer reproach, because we trust in
the living God, [l]who is the Saviour of
all men, specially of those that believe.
11 These things command and
teach.
12 [m]Let no man despise thy youth;
but be thou an example of the believers, in word, in conversation, in charity, in spirit, in faith, in purity.

13 [4]Or, ministered
15 [5]Or, stay
16 [c]Isa. 7.14; Mic. 5.2; Matt. 1.23; Phil. 2.6-8; 1 John 1.2
[6]manifested
[d]Matt. 3.16; John 1.32; 1 Pet. 3.18; 1 John 5.6
[e]Matt. 28.2; Luke 2.13; 1 Pet. 1.12

CHAPTER 4
1 [a]John 16.13
[b]1 Pet. 1.20
[c]2 Pet. 2.1
[d]Dan. 11.35
2 [e]Eph. 4.19
3 [f]Prov. 18.22
[g]1 Cor. 6.13
[h]Gen. 9.3
4 [i]Tit. 1.15
6 [j]Jer. 15.16
8 [1]Or, for a little time
[k]Ps. 37.4; Matt. 6.33
10 [l]Ps. 36.6; Acts 14.17
12 [m]Tit. 2.15
14 [n]2 Tim. 1.6
[o]ch. 1.18
[p]Acts 6.6; ch. 5.22
15 [2]Or, in all things
16 [q]Ezek. 33.9

CHAPTER 5
1 [a]Lev. 19.32
4 [1]Or, kindness
[b]Matt. 15.4; Eph. 6.1-2
6 [2]Or, delicately
8 [3]Or, kindred
9 [4]Or, chosen
10 [c]Acts 16.15
[d]Gen. 18.4; Luke 7.38
12 [e]Heb. 6.4-6
13 [f]2 Thess. 3.11
14 [g]1 Cor. 7.9
[h]2 Sam. 12.13; ch. 6.1
[5]for their railing
16 [i]Gen. 47.12; Matt. 15.4
17 [j]Rom. 12.8; Phil. 2.29
18 [k]Deut. 25.4
[l]Deut. 24.14; Luke 10.7

13 Till I come, give attendance to
reading, to exhortation, to doctrine.
14 [n]Neglect not the gift that is in
thee, which was given thee [o]by prophecy, [p]with the laying on of the hands
of the presbytery.
15 Meditate upon these things; give
thyself wholly to them; that thy profit-
ing may appear [2]to all.
16 Take heed unto thyself, and unto
the doctrine; continue in them: for in
doing this thou shalt both [q]save thyself, and them that hear thee.

5 Rebuke [a]not an elder, but intreat
him as a father; *and* the younger
men as brethren;
2 The elder women as mothers; the
younger as sisters, with all purity.
3 Honour widows that are widows
indeed.
4 But if any widow have children or
nephews, let them learn first to shew
[1]piety at home, and [b]to requite their
parents: for that is good and acceptable before God.
5 Now she that is a widow indeed,
and desolate, trusteth in God, and continueth in supplications and prayers
night and day.
6 But she that liveth [2]in pleasure is
dead while she liveth.
7 And these things give in charge,
that they may be blameless.
8 But if any provide not for his own,
and specially for those of his own
[3]house, he hath denied the faith, and is
worse than an infidel.
9 Let not a widow be [4]taken into the
number under threescore years old,
having been the wife of one man,
10 Well reported of for good works;
if she have brought up children, if she
have [c]lodged strangers, if she have
[d]washed the saints' feet, if she have
relieved the afflicted, if she have diligently followed every good work.
11 But the younger widows refuse:
for when they have begun to wax wanton against Chrīst, they will marry;
12 [e]Having damnation, because they
have cast off their first faith.
13 [f]And withal they learn *to be*
idle, wandering about from house to
house; and not only idle, but tattlers
also and busybodies, speaking things
which they ought not.
14 [g]I will therefore that the younger
women marry, bear children, guide the
house, [h]give none occasion to the adversary [5]to speak reproachfully.
15 For some are already turned aside
after Sā′tan.
16 [i]If any man or woman that believeth have widows, let them relieve
them, and let not the church be charged;
that it may relieve them that are widows
indeed.
17 [j]Let the elders that rule well be
counted worthy of double honour, especially they who labour in the word
and doctrine.
18 For the scripture saith, [k]Thou
shalt not muzzle the ox that treadeth
out the corn. And, [l]The labourer *is* worthy of his reward.

19 Against an elder receive not an accusation, but [6]before two or three witnesses.

20 [m]Them that sin rebuke before all, [n]that others also may fear.

21 I charge *thee* before God, and the Lord Jē'sus Chrīst, and the elect angels, that thou observe these things [7]without preferring one before another, doing nothing by partiality.

22 [o]Lay hands suddenly on no man, [p]neither be partaker of other men's sins: keep thyself pure.

23 Drink no longer water, but use a little wine for thy stomach's sake and thine often infirmities.

24 Some men's sins are open beforehand, going before to judgment; and some *men* they follow after.

25 Likewise also [q]the good works *of some* are manifest beforehand; and they that are otherwise cannot be hid.

6 Let as many [a]servants as are under the yoke count their own masters worthy of all honour, [b]that the name of God and *his* doctrine be not blasphemed.

2 And they that have believing masters, let them not despise *them,* [c]because they are brethren; but rather do *them* service, because they are [1]faithful and beloved, partakers of the benefit. These things teach and exhort.

3 If any man teach otherwise, and consent not to wholesome words, *even* the words of our Lord Jē'sus Chrīst, and to the doctrine which is according to godliness;

4 He is [2]proud, [d]knowing nothing, but [3]doting about questions and strifes of words, whereof cometh envy, strife, railings, evil surmisings,

5 [4]Perverse disputings of [e]men of corrupt minds, and destitute of the truth, [f]supposing that gain is godliness: [g]from such withdraw thyself.

6 But [h]godliness with contentment is great gain.

7 For [i]we brought nothing into *this* world, *and it is* certain we can carry nothing out.

8 And [j]having food and raiment let us be therewith content.

9 But [k]they that will be rich fall into temptation and a snare, and *into* many foolish and hurtful lusts, which drown men in destruction and perdition.

10 [l]For the love of money is the root of all evil: which while some coveted after, they have [5]erred from the faith, and pierced themselves through with many sorrows.

11 But thou, [m]O man of God, flee these things; and follow after righteousness, godliness, faith, love, patience, meekness.

12 [n]Fight the good fight of faith, [o]lay hold on eternal life, whereunto thou art also called, [p]and hast professed a good profession before many witnesses.

13 I give thee charge in the sight of God, [q]who quickeneth all things, and *before* Chrīst Jē'sus, [r]who before Pŏn'tĭ-us Pī'late witnessed a good [6]confession;

14 That thou keep *this* commandment without spot, unrebukeable, [s]until the appearing of our Lord Jē'sus Chrīst:

15 Which in his times he shall shew, *who is* [t]the blessed and only Potentate, [u]the King of kings, and Lord of lords;

16 Who [v]only hath immortality, dwelling in [w]the light which no man can approach unto; [x]whom no man hath seen, nor can see: [y]to whom *be* honour and power everlasting. Amen.

17 Charge them that are rich in this world, that they be not highminded, nor trust in [7]uncertain riches, but in the living God, who giveth us richly all things to enjoy;

18 That they do good, that they be rich in good works, ready to distribute, [8]willing to communicate;

19 Laying up in store for themselves a good foundation against the time to come, that they may lay hold on eternal life.

20 O Tĭm'o-thy̆, keep that which is committed to thy trust, avoiding profane *and* vain babblings, and oppositions of science falsely so called:

21 Which some professing have erred concerning the faith. Grace *be* with thee. Amen.

19 [6]Or, under
20 [m]Tit. 1.13
[n]Deut. 13.11
21 [7]Or, without prejudice
22 [o]ch. 4.14
[p]2 John 11
25 [q]1 Pet. 3.8-16

CHAPTER 6
1 [a]Tit. 2.9
[b]2 Sam. 12.14; Isa. 52.5
2 [c]Col. 4.1
[1]Or, believing
4 [2]Or, fool
[d]1 Cor. 8.2
[3]Or, sick
5 [4]Or, Gallings one of another
[e]2 Tim. 3.8
[f]Tit. 1.11
[g]Rom. 16.17
6 [h]Ps. 37.16; Luke 12.31-32
7 [i]Eccl. 5.15
8 [j]Gen. 28.20
9 [k]Matt. 13.22
10 [l]Ex. 23.8
[5]Or, been seduced
11 [m]Deut. 33.1
12 [n]Zech. 10.5; Eph. 6.10-18
[o]Phil. 3.12
[p]Heb. 13.23
13 [q]John 5.21
[r]Rev. 1.5
[6]Or, profession
14 [s]1 Thess. 3.13
15 [t]ch. 1.11
[u]Rev. 17.14
16 [v]John 5.26
[w]2 Chr. 5.14
[x]Ex. 33.20; Deut. 4.12; John 6.46
[y]Eph. 3.21;
17 [7]the uncertainty of riches
18 [8]Or, sociable

THE SECOND LETTER OF PAUL TO

TIMOTHY

Life's Questions

Can I trust the Bible?
How can I endure when everyone makes fun of my faith?
How can I avoid falling for the temptations of cult leaders?

God's Answers

About A.D. 67 Paul finished his writing ministry from a Roman prison probably waiting to be executed. He encouraged Timothy to endure persecution and ridicule from false teachers to remain faithful to Christ.

Second Timothy shows: a pastor should fearlessly endure suffering and avoid temptations to evil while exercising the gift of ministry (1:1—3:13); you can trust the Scriptures to lead you into mature faith (3:14—4:5); a faithful pastor looks forward to God's reward (4:6–22).

Second Timothy calls you to study God's Word and dedicate yourself to the ministry God gives you without worry what others think or how they treat you.

1 Paul, an apostle of Jē'sus Chrīst
by the will of God, according to
[a]the promise of life which is in Chrīst
Jē'sus,
2 To Tĭm'o-thȳ, *my* dearly beloved
son: Grace, mercy, *and* peace, from
God the Father and Chrīst Jē'sus our
Lord.
3 I thank God, whom I serve from
my forefathers with pure conscience,
that without ceasing I have remembrance of thee in my prayers night and
day;
4 Greatly desiring to see thee, being
mindful of thy tears, that I may be
filled with joy;
5 When I call to remembrance the
unfeigned faith that is in thee, which
dwelt first in thy grandmother Lō'is,
and [b]thy mother Eū'nĭçe; and I am persuaded that in thee also.
6 Wherefore I put thee in remembrance [c]that thou stir up the gift of
God, which is in thee by the putting on
of my hands.
7 For [d]God hath not given us the
spirit of fear; [e]but of power, and of
love, and of a sound mind.
8 [f]Be not thou therefore ashamed of
the testimony of our Lord, nor of me
his prisoner: but be thou partaker of
the afflictions of the gospel according
to the power of God;
9 Who hath saved us, and [g]called
us with an holy calling, [h]not according to our works, but [i]according to his
own purpose and grace, which was
given us in Chrīst Jē'sus [j]before the
world began,
10 But [k]is now made manifest by the
appearing of our Saviour Jē'sus Chrīst,
[l]who hath abolished death, and hath
brought life and immortality to light
through the gospel:
11 Whereunto I am appointed a
preacher, and an apostle, and a teacher
of the Gĕn'tīles.
12 For the which cause I also suffer
these things: nevertheless I am not
ashamed: for I know whom I have [1]be-
lieved, and am persuaded that he is
able to keep that which I have committed [m]unto him against that day.
13 [n]Hold fast [o]the form of sound
words, [p]which thou hast heard of me,
in faith and love which is in Chrīst
Jē'sus.
14 That good thing which was committed unto thee keep by the Hō'lȳ
Ghōst which dwelleth in us.
15 This thou knowest, that all they
which are in Ā'siȧ be turned away
from me; of whom are Phȳ-ġĕl'lus and
Hēr-mŏġ'e-nēs.
16 The Lord [q]give mercy unto the
house of Ŏn-e-sĭph'o-rus; [r]for he oft
refreshed me, and was not ashamed of
my chain:
17 But, when he was in Rōme, he
sought me out very diligently, and
found *me*.
18 The Lord grant unto him [s]that
he may find mercy of the Lord [t]in
that day: and in how many things
he [u]ministered unto me at Ĕph'ĕ-sŭs,
thou knowest very well.

2 Thou therefore, my son, [a]be strong
in the grace that is in Chrīst Jē'sus.
2 And the things that thou hast heard
of me [1]among many witnesses, [b]the
same commit thou to faithful men, who
shall be able to teach others also.
3 Thou therefore endure hardness,
as a good soldier of Jē'sus Chrīst.
4 [c]No man that warreth entangleth
himself with the affairs of *this* life; that
he may please him who hath chosen
him to be a soldier.
5 And if a man also strive for masteries, *yet* is he not crowned, except he
strive lawfully.
6 [2]The husbandman that laboureth
must be first partaker of the fruits.
7 Consider what I say; and the Lord
give thee understanding in all things.
8 Remember that Jē'sus Chrīst [d]of
the seed of Dā'vid [e]was raised from
the dead [f]according to my gospel:
9 Wherein I suffer trouble, as an evildoer, *even* unto bonds; but the word of
God is not bound.
10 Therefore I endure all things for
the elect's sakes, [g]that they may also
obtain the salvation which is in Chrīst
Jē'sus with eternal glory.
11 [h]*It is* a faithful saying: For [i]if we
be dead with *him,* we shall also live
with *him:*
12 [j]If we suffer, we shall also reign
with *him:* [k]if we deny *him,* he also will
deny us:
13 [l]If we believe not, *yet* he abideth
faithful: [m]he cannot deny himself.
14 Of these things put *them* in remembrance, [n]charging *them* before
the Lord [o]that they strive not about
words to no profit, *but* to the subvert-
ing of the hearers.
15 Study to shew thyself approved
unto God, a workman that needeth not
to be ashamed, rightly dividing the
word of truth.
16 But [p]shun profane *and* vain babblings: for they will increase unto more
ungodliness.
17 And their word will eat as doth a
[3]canker: of whom is [q]Hȳ-mĕ-næ'us
and Phī-lē'tus;
18 Who concerning the truth have
erred, [r]saying that the resurrection is
past already; and overthrow the faith
of some.
19 Nevertheless [s]the foundation of
God standeth [4]sure, having this seal,
The Lord [t]knoweth them that are his.
And, Let every one that nameth the
name of Chrīst depart from iniquity.

CHAPTER 1
1 [a]John 5.24-39-40; Heb. 9.15
5 [b]Acts 16.1
6 [c]1 Tim. 4.14
7 [d]Rom. 8.15
[e]Mic. 3.8; Luke 24.49
8 [f]Mark 8.38; Rom. 1.16
9 [g]Rom. 8.30; Heb. 3.1
[h]Tit. 3.5
[i]Rom. 8.28
[j]Eph. 1.4; 1 Pet. 1.20
10 [k]Eph. 1.9; 1 Pet. 1.20
[l]John 14.6
12 [1]Or, trusted
[m]Ps. 31.5;
13 [n]Heb. 10.23
[o]Rom. 2.20;
[p]ch. 2.2
16 [q]Matt. 5.7
[r]2 Cor. 7.13
18 [s]Matt. 25.34
[t]2 Thess. 1.10
[u]Heb. 6.10

CHAPTER 2
1 [a]Ps. 68.35
2 [1]Or, by
[b]1 Tim. 1.18
4 [c]1 Cor. 9.25
6 [2]Or, The husbandman, labouring first, must be partaker of the fruits
8 [d]Luke 1.32;
[e]1 Cor. 15.3-4
[f]Rom. 2.16
10 [g]2 Cor. 1.6
11 [h]1 Tim. 1.15
[i]Rom. 6.5-8
12 [j]1 Pet. 4.13
[k]Matt. 10.33
13 [l]Isa. 25.1;
[m]Num. 23.19
14 [n]1 Tim. 5.21;
[o]1 Tim. 1.4
16 [p]1 Tim. 4.7
17 [3]Or, gangrene
[q]1 Tim. 1.20
18 [r]1 Cor. 15.12
19 [s]Prov. 10.25;
[4]Or, steady
[t]Nah. 1.7

20 But in a great house there are not only vessels of gold and of silver, but also of wood and of earth; and some to honour, and some to dishonour.

21 If a man therefore purge himself from these, he shall be a vessel unto honour, sanctified, and meet for the master's use, *and* prepared unto every good work.

22 Flee also youthful lusts: but follow righteousness, faith, charity, peace, with them that call on the Lord out of a pure heart.

23 But foolish and unlearned questions avoid, knowing that they do gender strifes.

24 And the servant of the Lord must not strive; but be gentle unto all *men*, apt to teach, [5]patient,

25 In meekness instructing those that oppose themselves; if God peradventure will give them repentance to the acknowledging of the truth;

26 And *that* they may [6]recover themselves out of the snare of the devil, who are [7]taken captive by him at his will.

3 This know also, that [a]in the last days perilous times shall come.

2 For men shall be lovers of their own selves, covetous, boasters, proud, blasphemers, [b]disobedient to parents, unthankful, unholy,

3 Without natural affection, trucebreakers, [1]false accusers, incontinent, fierce, despisers of those that are good,

4 Traitors, heady, highminded, lovers of pleasures more than lovers of God;

5 Having a form of godliness, but [c]denying the power thereof: from such turn away.

6 For [d]of this sort are they which creep into houses, and lead captive silly women laden with sins, led away with divers lusts,

7 Ever learning, and never able [e]to come to the knowledge of the truth.

8 [f]Now as Jăn'nes and Jăm'bres withstood Mō'ses, so do these also resist the truth: men of corrupt minds, [2]reprobate concerning the faith.

9 But they shall proceed no further: for their folly shall be manifest unto all *men*, [g]as theirs also was.

10 But [3]thou hast fully known my doctrine, manner of life, purpose, faith, longsuffering, charity, patience,

11 Persecutions, afflictions, which came unto me [h]at Ăn'tĭ-ŏch, [i]at I-cō'nĭ-um, at Lȳs'trȧ; what persecutions I endured: but [j]out of *them* all the Lord delivered me.

12 Yea, and [k]all that will live godly in Chrīst Jē'sus shall suffer persecution.

13 But evil men and seducers shall wax worse and worse, deceiving, and being deceived.

14 But continue thou in the things which thou hast learned and hast been assured of, knowing of whom thou hast learned *them*;

15 And that from a child thou hast known the holy scriptures, which [l]are able to make thee wise unto salvation through faith which is in Chrīst Jē'sus.

16 [m]All scripture *is* given by inspiration of God, and *is* profitable for doctrine, for reproof, for correction, for instruction in righteousness:

17 [n]That the man of God may be perfect, [4]throughly furnished unto all good works.

4 I charge *thee* therefore before God, and the Lord Jē'sus Chrīst, who shall judge the quick and the dead at his appearing and his kingdom;

2 Preach the word; be instant in season, out of season; reprove, [a]rebuke, [b]exhort with all longsuffering and doctrine.

3 For the time will come when they will not endure [c]sound doctrine; but after their own lusts shall they heap to themselves teachers, having itching ears;

4 And they shall turn away *their* ears from the truth, and [d]shall be turned unto fables.

5 But watch thou in all things, endure afflictions, do the work of [e]an evangelist, [1]make full proof of thy ministry.

6 For I am now ready to be offered, and the time of my departure is at hand.

7 I have fought a good fight, I have finished *my* course, I have kept the faith:

8 Henceforth there is laid up for me [f]a crown of righteousness, which the Lord, the righteous judge, shall give me at that day: and not to me only, but unto all them also that love his appearing.

9 Do thy diligence to come shortly unto me:

10 For [g]Dē'mas hath forsaken me, [h]having loved this present world, and is departed unto Thĕs-sa-lo-nī'cȧ; Crĕs'çens to Gā-lā'tiȧ, Tī'tus unto Dăl-mā'ti-ȧ.

11 Only Lu̧ke is with me. Take [i]Märk, and bring him with thee: for he is profitable to me for the ministry.

12 And [j]Tȳch'ĭ-cŭs have I sent to Ĕph'ĕ-sŭs.

13 The cloke that I left at Trō'ăs with Cär'pus, when thou comest, bring *with thee*, and the books, *but* especially the parchments.

14 [k]Ăl-ĕx-ăn'dĕr the coppersmith did me much evil: [l]the Lord reward him according to his works:

15 Of whom be thou ware also; for he hath greatly withstood [2]our words.

16 At my first answer no man stood with me, but all *men* forsook me: [m]*I pray God* that it may not be laid to their charge.

17 [n]Notwithstanding the Lord stood with me, and strengthened me; that by me the preaching might be fully known, and *that* all the Gĕn'tīles might hear: and I was delivered [o]out of the mouth of the lion.

18 [p]And the Lord shall deliver me from every evil work, and will preserve *me* unto his heavenly kingdom: to whom *be* glory for ever and ever. Amen.

24 [5]Or, forbearing
26 [6]awake [7]taken alive

CHAPTER 3
1 [a]Jude 18
2 [b]Rom. 1.30
3 [1]Or, makebates
5 [c]Isa. 29.13; Ezek. 33.30-32
6 [d]Matt. 23.14
7 [e]1 Tim. 2.4
8 [f]Ex. 7.11 [2]Or, of no judgment
9 [g]Ex. 8.18; Ex. 9.11
10 [3]Or, thou hast been a diligent follower of
11 [h]Acts 13.14 [i]Acts 14.2 [j]Gen. 48.16; Job 5.19; Ps. 34.19; Jer. 1.19; Dan. 6.27
12 [k]Matt. 16.24; John 17.14; Acts 14.22
15 [l]Ps. 119.11; John 5.39-40; John 20.31; Acts 10.43
16 [m]2 Sam. 23.2; Mark 12.24; Luke 1.70; Acts 1.16; 2 Pet. 1.20
17 [n]1 Tim. 6.11 [4]Or, perfected

CHAPTER 4
2 [a]Tit. 1.13 [b]1 Tim. 4.13
3 [c]1 Tim. 1.10
4 [d]1 Tim. 1.4
5 [e]Acts 21.8 [1]Or, fulfil
8 [f]Rev. 2.10
10 [g]Col. 4.14; Phile. 24 [h]1 John 2.15
11 [i]Acts 12.25
12 [j]Acts 20.4
14 [k]Acts 19.33 [l]2 Sam. 3.39; Ps. 28.4
15 [2]Or, our preachings
16 [m]Acts 7.60
17 [n]Ps. 37.39-40; Matt. 10.19 [o]2 Pet. 2.9
18 [p]Ps. 121.7

19 Salute [q]Prĭs'çȧ and Ă'quĭ-lȧ, and
[r]the household of Ŏn-e-sĭph'o-rus.
20 [s]E-răs'tus abode at Cŏr'inth: but
[t]Trŏph'ĭ-mŭs have I left at Mī-lē'tum
sick.
21 Do thy diligence to come before
winter. Eū-bū'lus greeteth thee, and
Pū'dens, and Lī'nus, and Clạu'dĭ-ȧ,
and all the brethren.
22 The Lord Jē'sus Chrīst *be* with
thy spirit. Grace *be* with you. Amen.

19 [q]Acts 18.2
[r]ch. 1.16
20 [s]Acts 19.22
[t]Acts 20.4

THE LETTER OF PAUL TO

TITUS

Life's Questions

Does faith have anything to do with my politics?
Who can be a leader in the church?
How can I know who is teaching the truth?

God's Answers

About A.D. 66 Paul wrote his minister friend Titus to help him understand the pastor's role in the new churches. Paul showed him how to organize and teach in the church.

Titus shows: a minister must organize and provide leadership, especially opposing false teachings (ch. 1); ministers must train other leaders (ch. 2); and ministers must lead the church members to accept moral and civic responsibilities while waiting for eternal life (ch. 3).

Titus calls you to encourage your ministers in organizing and teaching your church and to find your civic and moral responsibilities.

1 Pạul, a servant of God, and an apostle of Jē'sus Chrīst, according to
the faith of God's elect, and [a]the acknowledging of the truth [b]which is after godliness;
2 [1]In hope of eternal life, which God,
that cannot lie, promised before [c]the
world began;
3 But hath in due times manifested
his word through preaching, which is
committed unto me [d]according to the
commandment of God our Saviour;
4 To [e]Tī'tus, *mine* own son after
the common faith: Grace, mercy, *and*
peace, from God the Father and the
Lord Jē'sus Chrīst our Saviour.
5 For this cause left I thee in Crēte,
that thou shouldest [f]set in order the
things that are [2]wanting, and [g]ordain
elders in every city, as I had appointed
thee:
6 If any be blameless, the husband
of one wife, having faithful children
not accused of riot or unruly.
7 For a bishop must be blameless, as
[h]the steward of God; not selfwilled,
not soon angry, [i]not given to wine, no
striker, not given to filthy lucre;
8 But a lover of hospitality, a lover of
[3]good men, sober, just, holy, temperate;
9 Holding fast the faithful word [4]as
he hath been taught, that he may be
able [j]by sound doctrine both to exhort
and to convince the gainsayers.
10 For there are many unruly and
vain talkers and deceivers, [k]specially
they of the circumcision:
11 Whose mouths must be stopped,
who subvert [l]whole houses, teaching
things which they ought not, for filthy
lucre's sake.
12 [m]One of themselves, *even* a
prophet of their own, said, The Crē'tī-
ans *are* alway liars, evil beasts, slow
bellies.
13 This witness is true. Wherefore
rebuke them sharply, that they may be
sound in the faith;
14 Not giving heed to Jew'ish fables,
and [n]commandments of men, that turn
from the truth.
15 Unto the pure all things *are* pure:
but unto them that are defiled and unbelieving *is* nothing pure; but even
their mind and conscience is defiled.
16 They profess that they know God;
but in works they deny *him*, being
abominable, and disobedient, and unto
every good work [5]reprobate.
2 But speak thou the things which become [a]sound doctrine:
2 That the aged men be [1]sober, grave,
temperate, sound in faith, in charity, in
patience.
3 [b]The aged women likewise, that
they be in behaviour as becometh [2]holi-
ness, not [3]false accusers, not given to
much wine, teachers of good things;
4 That they may teach the young
women to be [4]sober, to love their husbands, to love their children,
5 *To be* discreet, chaste, keepers at
home, good, [c]obedient to their own
husbands, that the word of God be not
blasphemed.
6 Young men likewise exhort to be
[5]sober minded.
7 [d]In all things shewing thyself a pattern of good works: in doctrine *shewing*
uncorruptness, gravity, [e]sincerity,
8 [f]Sound speech, that cannot be condemned; [g]that he that is of the contrary part may be ashamed, having no
evil thing to say of you.
9 *Exhort* servants to be obedient
unto their own masters, *and* to please
them well in all *things;* not [6]answering
again;
10 Not purloining, but shewing all
good fidelity; that they may adorn the
doctrine of God our Saviour in all
things.

CHAPTER 1
1 [a]2 Tim. 2.25
[b]1 Tim. 6.3
2 [1]Or, For
[c]2 Tim. 1.9; 1 Pet. 1.20
3 [d]Isa. 12.2; ch. 2.10-13
4 [e]2 Cor. 2.13
5 [f]1 Cor. 11.34
[2]Or, left undone
[g]Acts 14.23
7 [h]Matt. 24.45
[i]Lev. 10.9
8 [3]Or, good things
9 [4]Or, in teaching
[j]1 Tim. 1.10
10 [k]Acts 15.1
11 [l]Matt. 23.14
12 [m]Acts 17.28
14 [n]Isa. 29.13
16 [5]Or, void of judgment
CHAPTER 2
1 [a]1 Tim. 6.3
2 [1]Or, vigilant
3 [b]1 Pet. 3.3-4
[2]Or, holy women
[3]Or, makebates
4 [4]Or, wise
5 [c]Col. 3.18
6 [5]Or, discreet
7 [d]1 Pet. 5.3
[e]Eph. 6.24
8 [f]1 Tim. 6.3
[g]Neh. 5.9
9 [6]Or, gainsaying

11 For the grace of God that [7]bring-
eth salvation [h]hath appeared to all
men,
12 Teaching us [i]that, denying ungodliness and worldly lusts, we should
live soberly, righteously, and godly, in
this present world;
13 Looking for that blessed [j]hope,
and the glorious appearing of the great
God and our Saviour Jesus Christ;
14 Who gave himself for us, that
he might redeem us from all iniquity,
[k]and purify unto himself [l]a peculiar
people, zealous of good works.
15 These things speak, and exhort,
and rebuke with all authority. Let no
man despise thee.
3 Put them in mind to be subject to
principalities and powers, to obey
magistrates, [a]to be ready to every good
work,
2 To [b]speak evil of no man, to be no
brawlers, *but* gentle, shewing all meekness unto all men.
3 For we ourselves also were sometimes foolish, disobedient, deceived,
serving divers lusts and pleasures, living in malice and envy, hateful, *and*
hating one another.
4 But after that the kindness and
[1]love of God our Saviour toward man
appeared,
5 [c]Not by works of righteousness
which we have done, but according to
his mercy he saved us, by [d]the wash-

11 [7]Or, that bringeth salvation to all men, hath appeared
[h]Isa. 49.6
12 [i]Luke 1.75
13 [j]Acts 24.15
14 [k]Mal. 3.3; Matt. 3.12; Acts 15.9;
[l]Ex. 15.16

CHAPTER 3
1 [a]Heb. 13.21
2 [b]Eph. 4.31
4 [1]Or, pity
5 [c]Rom. 3.20;
[d]Matt. 3.11; John 3.3-5
6 [e]Ezek. 36.25;
[2]richly
9 [f]1 Tim. 1.4
10 [g]2 Cor. 13.2
[h]Matt. 18.17
11 [i]Matt. 25.26-28
12 [j]Acts 20.4
13 [k]Acts 18.24
14 [3]Or, profess honest trades
[l]Col. 1.10

ing of regeneration, and renewing of
the Hō'lȳ Ghōst;
6 [e]Which he shed on us [2]abundantly
through Jē'sus Chrīst our Saviour;
7 That being justified by his grace,
we should be made heirs according to
the hope of eternal life.
8 *This is* a faithful saying, and these
things I will that thou affirm constantly, that they which have believed
in God might be careful to maintain
good works. These things are good
and profitable unto men.
9 But [f]avoid foolish questions, and
genealogies, and contentions, and strivings about the law; for they are unprofitable and vain.
10 A man that is an heretick [g]after
the first and second admonition [h]reject;
11 Knowing that he that is such is
subverted, and sinneth, [i]being condemned of himself.
12 When I shall send Är'te-măs unto
thee, or [j]Tȳch'ĭ-cŭs, be diligent to come
unto me to Ni-cŏp'o-lĭs: for I have determined there to winter.
13 Bring Zē'nas the lawyer and [k]A-
pŏl'los on their journey diligently, that
nothing be wanting unto them.
14 And let ours also learn to [3]main-
tain good works for necessary uses,
that they be [l]not unfruitful.
15 All that are with me salute thee.
Greet them that love us in the faith.
Grace *be* with you all. Amen.

THE LETTER OF PAUL TO

PHILEMON

Life's Questions

Should I sacrifice what belongs to me for Christ and the church?
How can I help believers in need?
Can I forgive a person who has mistreated me?

God's Answers

About A.D. 60 Paul met a young man in a prison in Rome. Young Onesimus became a believer, but he had much to live down. He was a runaway slave and robber. Paul sent him back to his owner and master Philemon asking him as a fellow believer to accept Onesimus back as a son rather than as a slave.

Philemon shows: the meaning of one person's ministry (verses 1—7) and the new relationships created by faith in Christ (verses 8—25).

Philemon calls you to accept all believers as equal, to express gratitude for their ministry in the gospel, and to treat them fairly as God would.

1 Pa̤ul, [a]a prisoner of Jē'sus Chrīst,
and Tĭm'o-thȳ *our* brother, unto
Phĭ-lē'mon our dearly beloved, [b]and
fellowlabourer,
2 And to *our* beloved Ăpph'ĭ-ȧ, and
Är-chĭp'pus [c]our fellowsoldier, and to
[d]the church in thy house:
3 [e]Grace to you, and peace, from
God our Father and the Lord Jē'sus
Chrīst.
4 [f]I thank my God, making mention
of thee always in my prayers,
5 [g]Hearing of thy love and faith,
which thou hast toward the Lord Jē'-
sus, and toward all saints;
6 That the communication of thy
faith may become effectual by [h]the

CHAPTER 1
1 [a]Eph. 4.1
[b]Phil. 2.25
2 [c]Col. 4.17
[d]Rom. 16.5
3 [e]Eph. 1.2
4 [f]Phil. 1.3; 1 Thess. 1.2
5 [g]Eph. 1.15; 1 John 3.23
6 [h]Phil. 1.9
7 [i]2 Tim. 1.16
8 [j]2 Cor. 3.12
10 [k]Col. 4.9
[l]1 Cor. 4.15; Gal. 4.19

acknowledging of every good thing
which is in you in Chrīst Jē'sus.
7 For we have great joy and consolation in thy love, because the bowels
of the saints [i]are refreshed by thee,
brother.
8 Wherefore, [j]though I might be
much bold in Chrīst to enjoin thee that
which is convenient,
9 Yet for love's sake I rather beseech *thee,* being such an one as Pa̤ul
the aged, and now also a prisoner of
Jē'sus Chrīst.
10 I beseech thee for my [k]son O'nĕs'-
i-mus, whom [l]I have begotten in my
bonds:

11 Which in time past was to thee
unprofitable, but now profitable to thee
and to me:
12 Whom I have sent again: thou
therefore receive him, that is, mine
own bowels:
13 Whom I would have retained with
me, [m]that in thy stead he might have
ministered unto me in the bonds of the
gospel:
14 But without thy mind would I do
nothing; [n]that thy benefit should not
be as it were of necessity, but willingly.
15 [o]For perhaps he therefore departed for a season, that thou shouldest receive him for ever;
16 Not now as a servant, but above a
servant, [p]a brother beloved, specially
to me, but how much more unto thee,
[q]both in the flesh, and in the Lord?
17 If thou count me therefore [r]a partner, receive him as myself.

13 [m]Phil. 2.30
14 [n]2 Cor. 9.7
15 [o]Gen. 45.5-8
16 [p]Matt. 23.8; 1 Tim. 6.2
[q]Eph. 6.5-7; Col. 3.22
17 [r]2 Cor. 8.23
21 [s]2 Cor. 7.16
22 [t]Phil. 1.25
[u]Rom. 15.30-32; Jas. 5.16
23 [v]Col. 1.7
24 [w]Acts 12.12
[x]Acts 19.29
[y]Col. 4.14; 2 Tim. 4.11

18 If he hath wronged thee, or oweth
thee ought, put that on mine account;
19 I Pạul have written *it* with mine
own hand, I will repay *it:* albeit I do not
say to thee how thou owest unto me
even thine own self besides.
20 Yea, brother, let me have joy of
thee in the Lord: refresh my bowels in
the Lord.
21 [s]Having confidence in thy obedience I wrote unto thee, knowing that
thou wilt also do more than I say.
22 But withal prepare me also a lodging: for [t]I trust that [u]through your
prayers I shall be given unto you.
23 There salute thee [v]Ĕp'a-phrăs,
my fellowprisoner in Chrīst Jē'sus;
24 [w]Mär'cus, [x]Ăr-ĭs-tär'chus, Dē'-
mas, [y]Lụ'cas, my fellowlabourers.
25 The grace of our Lord Jē'sus
Chrīst *be* with your spirit. Amen.

THE LETTER TO THE

HEBREWS

Life's Questions

How is Jesus better than other religious leaders?
Why should I be loyal to Jesus when it costs me so much?
What kind of life does Jesus expect me to live?

God's Answers

God used someone whose name we do not know to write to a community of believers about whom we know nothing to encourage them not to give up their faith in face of false teachers who would lead them back to the safety of Judaism or in the face of government persecution which might demand their lives. The writer pointed to the greatness of Christ as the reason to persevere.

Hebrews shows: Jesus is God's ultimate revelation of Himself (1:1—2:4); Jesus is God's Son and our brother, who has atoned for our sins and helps us overcome temptations (2:5—18); Jesus provides a way of faith that assures and perseveres (3:1—4:13); Jesus the sinless high priest is the only source of salvation (4:14—5:10); Jesus the eternal high priest calls believers to spiritual maturity (5:11—6:20); Jesus the perfect sacrifice is the only priest believers need (7:1—10:39); Jesus the perfect example inspires believers to a life of faith and perseverance (11:1—12:29); and Jesus the unchanging Savior expects believers to live a life of love (ch. 13).

Hebrews calls you to endure all obstacles and temptations to follow Jesus in a life of love and persevering faith.

1 God, who at sundry times and [a]in
divers manners spake in time past
unto the fathers by the prophets,
2 Hath [b]in these last days [c]spoken
unto us by *his* Son, [d]whom he hath
appointed heir of all things, [e]by whom
also he made the worlds;
3 [f]Who being the brightness of *his*
glory, and the express image of his person, and [g]upholding all things by the
word of his power, when he had by
himself purged our sins, [h]sat down on
the right hand of the Majesty on high;
4 Being made so much better than
the angels, as [i]he hath by inheritance
obtained a more excellent name than
they.
5 For unto which of the angels said
he at any time, [j]Thou art my Son, this
day have I begotten thee? And again,
[k]I will be to him a Father, and he shall
be to me a Son?

CHAPTER 1
1 [a]Num. 12.6-8
2 [b]Gal. 4.4
[c]Matt. 13.11;
[d]Ps. 2.8;
[e]John 1.3
3 [f]John 14.9;
[g]Rev. 4.11
[h]Ps. 45.6
4 [i]Phil. 2.9
5 [j]Ps. 2.7
[k]Ps. 89.26
6 [1]Or, When he bringeth again
[l]Rom. 8.29
[m]Ps. 97.7;
7 [2]unto
[n]Ps. 104.4
8 [o]Ps. 45.6-7
[3]rightness, or, straightness
9 [p]Isa. 61.1

6 [1]And again, when he bringeth in
[l]the firstbegotten into the world, he
saith, [m]And let all the angels of God
worship him.
7 And [2]of the angels he saith, [n]Who
maketh his angels spirits, and his ministers a flame of fire.
8 But unto the Son *he saith,* [o]Thy
throne, O God, *is* for ever and ever: a
sceptre of [3]righteousness *is* the sceptre
of thy kingdom.
9 Thou hast loved righteousness, and
hated iniquity; therefore God, *even* thy
God, [p]hath anointed thee with the oil of
gladness above thy fellows.
10 And, Thou, Lord, in the beginning hast laid the foundation of the
earth; and the heavens are the works
of thine hands:
11 They shall perish; but thou remainest; and they all shall wax old as
doth a garment;

12 And as a vesture shalt thou fold
them up, and they shall be changed:
but thou art the same, and thy years
shall not fail.
13 But to which of the angels said he
at any time, Sit on my right hand, until
I make thine enemies thy footstool?
14 Are they not all ministering spirits, sent forth to minister for them who
shall be heirs of salvation?

2 Therefore we ought to give the more
earnest heed to the things which we
have heard, lest at any time we should
[1]let *them* slip.
2 For if the word spoken by angels
was stedfast, and every transgression
and disobedience received a just recompence of reward;
3 How shall we escape, if we neglect
so great [a]salvation; which at the first
began to be spoken by the Lord, and
was confirmed unto us by them that
heard *him;*
4 God also bearing *them* witness,
both with signs and wonders, and with
divers miracles, and [2]gifts of the Hō'lȳ
Ghōst, according to his own will?
5 For unto the angels hath he not
put in subjection the world to come,
whereof we speak.
6 But one in a certain place testified,
saying, [b]What is man, that thou art
mindful of him? or the son of man, that
thou visitest him?
7 Thou madest him [3]a little lower
than the angels; thou crownedst him
with glory and honour, and didst set
him over the works of thy hands:
8 Thou hast put all things in subjection under his feet. For in that he put
all in subjection under him, he left nothing *that is* not put under him. But now
we see not yet all things put under him.
9 But we see Jē'sus, who was made
a little lower than the angels [4]for the
suffering of death, crowned with glory
and honour; that he by the grace of
God should taste death for every man.
10 [c]For it became him, for whom
are all things, and by whom *are* all
things, in bringing many sons unto
glory, to make the captain of their salvation [d]perfect through sufferings.
11 For both he that sanctifieth and
they who are sanctified *are* all of one:
for which cause [e]he is not ashamed to
call them brethren,
12 Saying, [f]I will declare thy name
unto my brethren, in the midst of the
church will I sing praise unto thee.
13 And again, [g]I will put my trust in
him. And again, [h]Behold I and the children which God hath given me.
14 Forasmuch then as the children
are partakers of flesh and blood, he
[i]also himself likewise took part of the
same; [j]that through death he might destroy him that had the power of death,
that is, the devil;
15 And deliver them who [k]through
fear of death were all their lifetime subject to bondage.
16 For verily [5]he took not on *him the*
nature of angels; but he took on *him*
the seed of Ā'brā-hăm.
17 Wherefore in all things it behoved him [l]to be made like unto *his*
brethren, that he might be a merciful
and faithful high priest in things *per-*
taining to God, to make reconciliation
for the sins of the people.
18 [m]For in that he himself hath suffered being tempted, he is able to succour them that are tempted.

3 Wherefore, holy brethren, partakers
of the heavenly calling, consider
[a]the Apostle and High Priest of our profession, Chrīst Jē'sus;
2 Who was faithful to him that [1b]ap-
pointed him, as also [c]Mō'ses *was faith-*
ful in all his house.
3 For this *man* was counted worthy
of more glory than Mō'ses, inasmuch
as [d]he who hath builded the house
hath more honour than the house.
4 For every house is builded by some
man; but [e]he that built all things *is*
God.
5 And Mō'ses verily *was* faithful in
all his house, as a servant, [f]for a testimony of those things which were to be
spoken after;
6 But Chrīst as a son over his own
house; [g]whose house are we, [h]if we
hold fast the confidence and the rejoicing of the hope firm unto the end.
7 Wherefore (as [i]the Hō'lȳ Ghōst
saith, [j]To day if ye will hear his voice,
8 Harden not your hearts, as in the
provocation, in the day of temptation
in the wilderness:
9 When your fathers tempted me,
proved me, and saw my works forty
years.
10 Wherefore I was grieved with
that generation, and said, They do
alway err in *their* heart; and they have
not known my ways.
11 So I sware in my wrath, [2]They
shall not enter into my rest.)
12 Take heed, brethren, lest there be
in any of you an evil heart of unbelief,
in departing from the living God.
13 But exhort one another daily,
while it is called To day; lest any of you
be hardened through the deceitfulness
of sin.
14 For we are made partakers of
Chrīst, if we hold the beginning of our
confidence stedfast unto the end;
15 While it is said, To day if ye will
hear his voice, harden not your hearts,
as in the provocation.
16 [k]For some, when they had heard,
did provoke: howbeit not all that came
out of Ē'gȳpt by Mō'ses.
17 But with whom was he grieved
forty years? *was it* not with them that
had sinned, [l]whose carcases fell in the
wilderness?
18 And to whom sware he that they
should not enter into his rest, but to
them that believed not?
19 So we see that they could not enter in because of unbelief.

4 Let us therefore fear, lest, a promise being left *us* of entering into his
rest, any of you should seem to come
short of it.

CHAPTER 2
1 [1]run out as leaking vessels
3 [a]Isa. 45.17
4 [2]Or, distributions
6 [b]Ps. 8.4
7 [3]Or, a little while inferior to
9 [4]Or, by
10 [c]Prov. 16.4; Isa. 43.21; Luke 24.46
[d]ch. 6.20
11 [e]Matt. 28.10; John 20.17
12 [f]Ps. 22.22
13 [g]Ps. 18.2; Isa. 12.2
[h]Isa. 8.18; John 10.29
14 [i]John 1.14; Rom. 8.3
[j]Col. 2.15; 2 Tim. 1.10
15 [k]Job 33.24-28; Ps. 33.19; Luke 1.74
16 [5]he taketh not hold of angels, but of the seed of Abraham he taketh hold
17 [l]Phil. 2.7
18 [m]ch. 4.15; ch. 5.2

CHAPTER 3
1 [a]Matt. 15.24; 1 Tim. 3.15
2 [1]made
[b]1 Sam. 12.6
[c]Num. 12.7
3 [d]Zech. 6.12; Matt. 16.18
4 [e]Eph. 2.10
5 [f]Deut. 18.15-18-19
6 [g]Eph. 4.12; 1 Pet. 2.5
[h]Matt. 10.22
7 [i]2 Sam. 23.2; Acts 1.16
[j]Ps. 81.11; Isa. 55.3; Matt. 17.5
11 [2]If they shall enter
16 [k]Num. 14.2-4-11-24-30; Deut. 1.34
17 [l]Num. 14.22-29; Num. 26.65; Ps. 106.26

2 For unto us was the gospel
preached, as well as unto them: but [1]the
word preached did not profit them, [2]not
being mixed with faith in them that
heard *it*.
3 For we which have believed do enter into rest, as he said, [a]As I have
sworn in my wrath, if they shall enter
into my rest: although the works were
finished from the foundation of the
world.
4 For he spake in a certain place of
the seventh *day* on this wise, [b]And
God did rest the seventh day from all
his works.
5 And in this *place* again, If they
shall enter into my rest.
6 Seeing therefore it remaineth that
some must enter therein, [c]and they to
whom [3]it was first preached entered
not in because of unbelief:
7 Again, he limiteth a certain day,
saying in Dā'vid, To day, after so long
a time; as it is said, [d]To day if ye will
hear his voice, harden not your hearts.
8 For if [4]Jē'sus had given them rest,
then would he not afterward have
spoken of another day.
9 There remaineth therefore a [5]rest
to the people of God.
10 For he that is entered into his
rest, he also hath ceased from his own
works, as God *did* from his.
11 Let us labour therefore to enter
into that rest, lest any man fall after
the same example of [6]unbelief.
12 For the word of God *is* [e]quick,
and powerful, and sharper than any
[f]twoedged sword, piercing even to the
dividing asunder of soul and spirit, and
of the joints and marrow, and *is* [g]a dis-
cerner of the thoughts and intents of
the heart.
13 Neither is there any creature that
is not manifest in his sight: but all
things *are* naked and opened unto the
eyes of him with whom we have to do.
14 Seeing then that we have a great
high priest, that is passed into the heavens, Jē'sus the Son of God, let us hold
fast *our* profession.
15 For [h]we have not an high priest
which cannot be touched with the feeling of our infirmities; but [i]was in all
points tempted like as *we are*, [j]*yet*
without sin.
16 Let us therefore come boldly unto
the throne of grace, that we may obtain
mercy, and find grace to help in time of
need.
5 For every high priest taken from
among men is ordained for men in
things *pertaining* to God, [a]that he may
offer both gifts and sacrifices for sins:
2 Who [1]can have compassion on the
ignorant, and on them that are out of
the way; for that he himself also is compassed with infirmity.
3 And [b]by reason hereof he ought,
as for the people, so also for himself, to
offer for sins.
4 [c]And no man taketh this honour
unto himself, but he that is called of
God, as [d]*was* Aâr'on.

CHAPTER 4
2 [1]the word of hearing
[2]Or, because they were not united by faith to
3 [a]Ps. 95.11
4 [b]Gen. 2.2
6 [c]ch. 3.19
[3]Or, the gospel was first preached
7 [d]Ps. 95.7
8 [4]That is, Joshua
9 [5]Or, keeping of a sabbath
11 [6]Or, disobedience
12 [e]Isa. 49.2; [f]Rev. 1.16
[g]1 Cor. 14.24-25
15 [h]Isa. 53.3
[i]Luke 22.28
[j]Dan. 9.24

CHAPTER 5
1 [a]ch. 8.3-4
2 [1]Or, can reasonably bear with
3 [b]Lev. 4.3
4 [c]1 Sam. 13.9;
[d]Ex. 28.1
5 [e]John 8.54;
[f]Ps. 2.7
6 [g]Ps. 110.4
7 [h]John 17.1
[i]Ps. 22.1
[j]Matt. 26.53
[2]Or, for his piety
8 [k]Phil. 2.8
10 [l]ch. 6.20
13 [3]hath no experience
[m]Eph. 4.13
14 [4]Or, perfect
[5]Or, of an habit, or, perfection
[n]1 Cor. 2.14-15

CHAPTER 6
1 [1]Or, the word of the beginning of Christ
2 [a]Acts 19.4
[b]Acts 8.14
[c]Acts 17.31
[d]Acts 24.25
3 [e]1 Cor. 4.19
4 [f]Matt. 12.32;
[g]Matt. 7.22;
[h]John 4.10;
6 [i]ch. 10.29
7 [2]Or, for
10 [j]Matt. 10.42

5 [e]So also Chrīst glorified not himself to be made an high priest; but he
that said unto him, [f]Thou art my Son,
to day have I begotten thee.
6 As he saith also in another *place*,
[g]Thou *art* a priest for ever after the
order of Mĕl-chĭs'e-dĕc.
7 Who in the days of his flesh, when
he had [h]offered up prayers and supplications [i]with strong crying and tears
unto him [j]that was able to save him
from death, and was heard [2]in that he
feared;
8 Though he were a Son, yet learned
he [k]obedience by the things which he
suffered;
9 And being made perfect, he became the author of eternal salvation
unto all them that obey him;
10 Called of God an high priest [l]af-
ter the order of Mĕl-chĭs'e-dĕc.
11 Of whom we have many things to
say, and hard to be uttered, seeing ye
are dull of hearing.
12 For when for the time ye ought to
be teachers, ye have need that one
teach you again which *be* the first principles of the oracles of God; and are
become such as have need of milk, and
not of strong meat.
13 For every one that useth milk [3]*is*
unskilful in the word of righteousness:
for he is [m]a babe.
14 But strong meat belongeth to them
that are [4]of full age, *even* those who by
reason [5]of use have their senses exercised [n]to discern both good and evil.
6 Therefore leaving [1]the principles of
the doctrine of Chrīst, let us go on
unto perfection; not laying again the
foundation of repentance from dead
works, and of faith toward God,
2 [a]Of the doctrine of baptisms, [b]and
of laying on of hands, [c]and of resurrection of the dead, [d]and of eternal
judgment.
3 And this will we do, [e]if God permit.
4 For [f]*it is* impossible for those [g]who
were once enlightened, and have tasted
of [h]the heavenly gift, and were made
partakers of the Hō'lȳ Ghōst,
5 And have tasted the good word of
God, and the powers of the world to
come,
6 If they shall fall away, to renew
them again unto repentance; [i]seeing
they crucify to themselves the Son of
God afresh, and put *him* to an open
shame.
7 For the earth which drinketh in
the rain that cometh oft upon it, and
bringeth forth herbs meet for them [2]by
whom it is dressed, receiveth blessing
from God:
8 But that which beareth thorns and
briers *is* rejected, and *is* nigh unto cursing; whose end *is* to be burned.
9 But, beloved, we are persuaded
better things of you, and things that
accompany salvation, though we thus
speak.
10 For [j]God *is* not unrighteous to forget your work and labour of love, which
ye have shewed toward his name, in

that ye have ministered to the saints,
and do minister.
11 And we desire that every one of
you do shew the same diligence [k]to the
full assurance of hope unto the end:
12 That ye be not slothful, but followers of them who through faith and
patience [l]inherit the promises.
13 For when God made promise to
Ā'bră-hăm, because he could swear by
no greater, [m]he sware by himself,
14 Saying, Surely blessing I will
bless thee, and multiplying I will multiply thee.
15 And so, after he had patiently endured, he obtained the promise.
16 For men verily swear by the
greater: and [n]an oath for confirmation
is to them an end of all strife.
17 Wherein God, willing more abundantly to shew unto [o]the heirs of promise [p]the immutability of his counsel,
[3]confirmed *it* by an oath:
18 That by two immutable things, in
which *it was* impossible for God to lie,
we might have a strong consolation,
who have fled for refuge to lay hold
upon the hope [q]set before us:
19 Which [r]*hope* we have as an anchor of the soul, both sure and stedfast, [s]and which entereth into that
within the veil;
20 [t]Whither the forerunner is for us
entered, *even* Jē'sus, made an high
priest for ever after the order of Měl-
chĭs'e-dĕc.
7 For this [a]Měl-chĭs'e-dĕc, king of
Sā'lem, priest of the most high God,
who met Ā'bră-hăm returning from
the slaughter of the kings, and blessed
him;
2 To whom also Ā'bră-hăm gave a
tenth part of all; first being by interpretation King of righteousness, and after
that also King of Sā'lem, which is,
King of peace;
3 Without father, without mother,
[1]without descent, having neither beginning of days, nor end of life; but made
like unto the Son of God; abideth a
priest continually.
4 Now consider how great this man
was, [b]unto whom even the patriarch
Ā'bră-hăm gave the tenth of the spoils.
5 And verily [c]they that are of the
sons of Lē'vī, who receive the office of
the priesthood, have a commandment
to take tithes of the people according
to the law, that is, of their brethren,
though they come out of the loins of
Ā'bră-hăm:
6 But he whose [2]descent is not
counted from them received tithes of
Ā'bră-hăm, and blessed [d]him that had
the promises.
7 And without all contradiction the
less is blessed of the better.
8 And here men that die receive
tithes; but there he *receiveth them,* [e]of
whom it is witnessed that he liveth.
9 And as I may so say, Lē'vī also,
who receiveth tithes, payed tithes in
Ā'bră-hăm.
10 For he was yet in the loins of his
father, when Měl-chĭs'e-dĕc met him.

11 [k]Col. 2.2
12 [l]ch. 10.36
13 [m]Gen. 22.16
16 [n]Ex. 22.11
17 [o]ch. 11.9
[p]Job 23.13; Jas. 1.17
[3]interposed himself by an oath
18 [q]Isa. 27.5; ch. 12.1
19 [r]Ps. 130.7
[s]Lev. 16.15; ch. 9.7
20 [t]John 14.2-3; ch. 8.1
CHAPTER 7
1 [a]Gen. 14.18; ch. 5.6-10
3 [1]without pedigree
4 [b]Gen. 14.20
5 [c]Num. 18.21
6 [2]Or, pedigree
[d]Gen. 12.2; Gal. 3.16
8 [e]ch. 5.6
11 [f]Gal. 2.21; ch. 8.7
14 [g]Gen. 49.10; Rom. 1.3
17 [h]Ps. 110.4; ch. 5.6-10
18 [i]Rom. 8.3
19 [j]Acts 13.39; ch. 9.9
[3]Or, but it was the bringing in
[k]ch. 6.18
[l]Rom. 5.2
21 [4]Or, without swearing of an oath
[m]Ps. 110.4
24 [n]Isa. 9.6-7; ch. 13.8
[5]Or, which passeth not from one to another
25 [6]Or, evermore
[o]Isa. 53.12; 1 John 2.1
26 [p]Eph. 1.20
27 [q]Lev. 9.7;
[r]Lev. 16.15
[s]Rom. 6.10
28 [t]ch. 5.1-2
[u]ch. 2.10
[7]perfected
CHAPTER 8
1 [a]Col. 3.1

11 [f]If therefore perfection were by
the Le-vĭt'ĭ-cal priesthood, (for under it
the people received the law,) what further need *was there* that another priest
should rise after the order of Měl-
chĭs'e-dĕc, and not be called after the
order of Aâr'on?
12 For the priesthood being changed,
there is made of necessity a change also
of the law.
13 For he of whom these things are
spoken pertaineth to another tribe, of
which no man gave attendance at the
altar.
14 For *it is* evident that [g]our Lord
sprang out of Jū'dȧ; of which tribe Mō'-
ses spake nothing concerning priesthood.
15 And it is yet far more evident: for
that after the similitude of Měl-chĭs'e-
dĕc there ariseth another priest,
16 Who is made, not after the law of
a carnal commandment, but after the
power of an endless life.
17 For he testifieth, [h]Thou *art* a
priest for ever after the order of Měl-
chĭs'e-dĕc.
18 For there is verily a disannulling
of the commandment going before for
[i]the weakness and unprofitableness
thereof.
19 For [j]the law made nothing perfect, [3]but the bringing in of [k]a better
hope *did;* by the which [l]we draw nigh
unto God.
20 And inasmuch as not without an
oath *he was made priest:*
21 (For those priests were made
[4]without an oath; but this with an oath
by him that said unto him, [m]The Lord
sware and will not repent, Thou *art*
a priest for ever after the order of
Měl-chĭs'e-dĕc:)
22 By so much was Jē'sus made a
surety of a better testament.
23 And they truly were many priests,
because they were not suffered to continue by reason of death:
24 But this *man,* because he [n]con-
tinueth ever, hath [5]an unchangeable
priesthood.
25 Wherefore he is able also to save
them to [6]the uttermost that come unto
God by him, seeing he ever liveth [o]to
make intercession for them.
26 For such an high priest became
us, *who is* holy, harmless, undefiled,
separate from sinners, [p]and made
higher than the heavens;
27 Who needeth not daily, as those
high priests, to offer up sacrifice, [q]first
for his own sins, [r]and then for the people's: for [s]this he did once, when he
offered up himself.
28 For the law maketh [t]men high
priests which have infirmity; but the
word of the oath, which was since the
law, *maketh* the Son, [u]who is [7]conse-
crated for evermore.
8 Now of the things which we have
spoken *this is* the sum: We have
such an high priest, [a]who is set on the
right hand of the throne of the Majesty
in the heavens;

2 A minister [1]of the sanctuary, and
of [b]the true tabernacle, which the Lord
pitched, and not man.
3 For every high priest is ordained
to offer gifts and sacrifices: wherefore
[c]*it is* of necessity that this man have
somewhat also to offer.
4 For if he were on earth, he should
not be a priest, seeing that [2]there are
priests that offer gifts according to the
law:
5 Who serve unto the example and
[d]shadow of heavenly things, as Mō'-
ses was admonished of God when he
was about to make the tabernacle:
[e]for, See, saith he, *that* thou make all
things according to the pattern shewed
to thee in the mount.
6 But now [f]hath he obtained a more
excellent ministry, by how much also
he is the mediator of a better [3]cove-
nant, which was established upon better promises.
7 For if that first *covenant* had been
faultless, then should no place have
been sought for the second.
8 For finding fault with them, he
saith, [g]Behold, the days come, saith
the Lord, when I will make a new covenant with the house of Is'ra-el and with
the house of Jū'dah:
9 Not according to the covenant that
I made with their fathers in the day
when I took them by the hand to lead
them out of the land of Ē'ġy̆pt; because
they continued not in my covenant,
and I regarded them not, saith the
Lord.
10 For this *is* the covenant that I will
make with the house of Is'ra-el after
those days, saith the Lord; I will [4]put
my laws into their mind, and write
them [5]in their hearts: and [h]I will be to
them a God, and they shall be to me a
people:
11 And [i]they shall not teach every
man his neighbour, and every man his
brother, saying, Know the Lord: for all
shall know me, from the least to the
greatest.
12 For I will be merciful to their unrighteousness, and their sins and their
inquities will I remember no more.
13 In that he saith, A new *covenant*, he hath made the first old. Now
that which decayeth and waxeth old *is*
ready to vanish away.
9 Then verily the first *covenant* had
also [1]ordinances of divine service,
and a [a]worldly sanctuary.
2 [b]For there was a tabernacle made;
the first, wherein *was* the candlestick,
and [c]the table, and the shewbread;
which is called [2]the sanctuary.
3 [d]And after the second veil, the tabernacle which is called the Holiest of
all;
4 Which had the golden censer, and
the ark of the covenant overlaid round
about with gold, wherein *was* [e]the
golden pot that had manna, and [f]Aâr'-
on's rod that budded, and [g]the tables
of the covenant;

2 [1]Or, of holy things
[b]ch. 9.11
3 [c]Eph. 5.2
4 [2]Or, they are priests
5 [d]Col. 2.17
[e]Ex. 25.40; Num. 8.4
6 [f]ch. 7.22
[3]Or, testament
8 [g]Jer. 31.31
10 [4]give
[5]Or, upon
[h]Gen. 17.7-8; Zech. 8.8
11 [i]Isa. 54.13; 1 John 2.27

CHAPTER 9
1 [1]Or, ceremonies
[a]Ex. 25.8; Lev. 4.6
2 [b]Ex. 26.1
[c]Lev. 24.5
[2]Or, holy
3 [d]Ex. 40.3
4 [e]Ex. 16.33
[f]Num. 17.10
[g]Ex. 25.16; Deut. 10.2-5
5 [h]Lev. 16.2
6 [i]Num. 28.3; Dan. 8.11
7 [j]Ex. 30.10
8 [k]ch. 10.19
[l]John 14.6
9 [m]Gal. 3.21
10 [n]Rom. 14.17
[o]Lev. 11.25; Num. 19.7
[p]Eph. 2.15
[3]Or, rites, or, ceremonies
11 [q]ch. 10.1
[r]ch. 8.2
12 [s]Rev. 1.5
[t]Zech. 3.9
[u]Dan. 9.24
13 [v]Lev. 8.15
[w]Num. 19.2
14 [x]1 John 1.7
[y]Rom. 1.4; 1 Pet. 3.18
[z]Eph. 5.2
[4]Or, fault
[a]ch. 1.3
[b]ch. 6.1
[c]Luke 1.74
15 [d]1 Tim. 2.5
[e]1 Pet. 3.18
[f]ch. 3.1
16 [5]Or, be brought in
17 [g]Gal. 3.15
18 [h]Ex. 24.6
[6]Or, purified
19 [i]Ex. 24.5-8; Lev. 14.4
[7]Or, purple
20 [j]Ex. 24.8; 1 Pet. 1.2
21 [k]Ex. 29.12
22 [l]Lev. 17.11
23 [m]ch. 8.5

5 And [h]over it the cherubims of glory
shadowing the mercyseat; of which we
cannot now speak particularly.
6 Now when these things were thus
ordained, [i]the priests went always into
the first tabernacle, accomplishing the
service *of God*.
7 But into the second *went* the high
priest alone [j]once every year, not without blood, which he offered for himself, and *for* the errors of the people:
8 [k]The Hō'ly̆ Ghōst this signifying,
that [l]the way into the holiest of all was
not yet made manifest, while as the
first tabernacle was yet standing:
9 Which *was* a figure for the time
then present, in which were offered
both gifts and sacrifices, [m]that could
not make him that did the service perfect, as pertaining to the conscience;
10 *Which stood* only in [n]meats and
drinks, and [o]divers washings, [p]and
carnal [3]ordinances, imposed *on them*
until the time of reformation.
11 But Chrīst being come an high
priest [q]of good things to come, [r]by a
greater and more perfect tabernacle,
not made with hands, that is to say, not
of this building;
12 Neither by the blood of goats and
calves, but [s]by his own blood he entered in [t]once into the holy place, [u]hav-
ing obtained eternal redemption *for us*.
13 For if [v]the blood of bulls and of
goats, and [w]the ashes of an heifer
sprinkling the unclean, sanctifieth to
the purifying of the flesh:
14 How much more [x]shall the blood
of Chrīst, [y]who through the eternal
Spirit [z]offered himself without [4]spot
to God, [a]purge your conscience from
[b]dead works [c]to serve the living God?
15 [d]And for this cause he is the mediator of the new testament, [e]that by
means of death, for the redemption of
the transgressions *that were* under the
first testament, [f]they which are called
might receive the promise of eternal
inheritance.
16 For where a testament *is*, there
must also of necessity [5]be the death of
the testator.
17 For [g]a testament *is* of force after
men are dead: otherwise it is of no
strength at all while the testator liveth.
18 [h]Whereupon neither the first *testament* was [6]dedicated without blood.
19 For when Mō'ses had spoken every precept to all the people according
to the law, he took the blood of calves
and of goats, [i]with water, and [7]scarlet
wool, and hyssop, and sprinkled both
the book, and all the people,
20 Saying, [j]This *is* the blood of the
testament which God hath enjoined
unto you.
21 Moreover [k]he sprinkled with
blood both the tabernacle, and all the
vessels of the ministry.
22 And almost all things are by the
law purged with blood; and [l]without
shedding of blood is no remission.
23 *It was* therefore necessary that
[m]the patterns of things in the heavens
should be purified with these; but the

heavenly things themselves with better sacrifices than these.

24 For [n]Christ is not entered into the holy places made with hands, *which are* the figures of the true; but into heaven itself, now [o]to appear in the presence of God for us:

25 Nor yet that he should offer himself often, as the high priest entereth into the holy place every year with blood of others;

26 For then must he often have suffered since the foundation of the world: but now once [p]in the end of the world hath he appeared to put away sin by the sacrifice of himself.

27 [q]And as it is appointed unto men once to die, but after this the judgment:

28 So [r]Christ was once [s]offered to bear the sins of many; and unto them that look for him shall he [t]appear the second time without sin unto salvation.

10 For the law having [a]a shadow of good things to come, *and* not the very image of the things, can never with those sacrifices which they offered year by year continually make the comers thereunto perfect.

2 For then [1]would they not have ceased to be offered? because that the worshippers once purged should have had no more conscience of sins.

3 [b]But in those *sacrifices there is* a remembrance again *made* of sins every year.

4 For [c]*it is* not possible that the blood of bulls and of goats should take away sins.

5 Wherefore when he cometh into the world, he saith, [d]Sacrifice and offering thou wouldest not, but a body [2]hast thou prepared me:

6 In burnt offerings and *sacrifices* for sin thou hast had no pleasure.

7 Then said I, Lo, I come (in the volume of the book it is written of me,) to do thy will, O God.

8 Above when he said, Sacrifice and offering and burnt offerings and *offering* for sin thou wouldest not, neither hadst pleasure *therein;* which are offered by the law;

9 Then said he, Lo, I come to do thy will, O God. He taketh away the first, that he may establish the second.

10 [e]By the which will we are sanctified through the offering of the body of Jē'sus Christ once *for all.*

11 And every priest standeth [f]daily ministering and offering oftentimes the same sacrifices, which can never take away sins:

12 [g]But this man, after he had offered one sacrifice for sins for ever, sat down on the right hand of God;

13 From henceforth expecting [h]till his enemies be made his footstool.

14 For by one offering he hath perfected for ever them that are sanctified.

15 [i]*Whereof* the Hō'lȳ Ghōst also is a witness to us: for after that he had said before,

16 [j]This *is* the covenant that I will make with them after those days, saith the Lord, I will put my laws into their hearts, and in their minds will I write them;

17 [3]And their sins and iniquities will I remember no more.

18 Now where remission of these *is, there is* no more offering for sin.

19 Having therefore, brethren, [4]boldness to enter into the holiest by the blood of Jē'sus,

20 By [k]a new and living way, which he hath [5]consecrated for us, through the veil, that is to say, his flesh;

21 And *having* an high priest over [l]the house of God;

22 Let us draw near with a true heart [m]in full assurance of faith, having our hearts sprinkled from an evil conscience, and [n]our bodies washed with pure water.

23 Let us hold fast the profession of *our* faith without wavering; (for [o]he *is* faithful that promised;)

24 And let us consider one another to provoke unto love and to good works:

25 [p]Not forsaking the assembling of ourselves together, as the manner of some *is;* but exhorting *one another:* and [q]so much the more, as ye see [r]the day approaching.

26 For [s]if we sin wilfully [t]after that we have received the knowledge of the truth, there remaineth no more sacrifice for sins,

27 But a certain fearful looking for of judgment and [u]fiery indignation, which shall devour the adversaries.

28 He that despised Mō'ses' law died without mercy under two or three witnesses:

29 Of how much sorer punishment, suppose ye, shall he be thought worthy, who hath trodden under foot the Son of God, and [v]hath counted the blood of the covenant, wherewith he was sanctified, an unholy thing, [w]and hath done despite unto the Spirit of grace?

30 For we know him that hath said, [x]Vengeance *belongeth* unto me, I will recompense, saith the Lord. And again, [y]The Lord shall judge his people.

31 [z]*It is* a fearful thing to fall into the hands of the living God.

32 But [a]call to remembrance the former days, in which, after ye were illuminated, ye endured [b]a great fight of afflictions;

33 Partly, whilst ye were made a gazingstock both by reproaches and afflictions; and partly, whilst [c]ye became companions of them that were so used.

34 For ye had compassion of me in my bonds, and [d]took joyfully the spoiling of your goods, knowing [6]in yourselves that ye have in heaven a better and an enduring substance.

35 Cast not away therefore your confidence, which hath great recompence of reward.

36 [e]For ye have need of patience, that, after ye have done the will of God, [f]ye might receive the promise.

24 [n]ch. 6.20 [o]ch. 7.25; 1 John 2.1 **26** [p]1 Cor. 10.11; ch. 7.27 **27** [q]Gen. 3.19; Eccl. 3.20 **28** [r]Rom. 6.10 [s]Matt. 26.28; [t]Matt. 25.34

CHAPTER 10

1 [a]Col. 2.17 **2** [1]Or, they would have ceased to be offered, because, etc **3** [b]Lev. 16.21 **4** [c]Mic. 6.6 **5** [d]Ps. 40.6; [2]Or, thou hast fitted me **10** [e]John 17.19 **11** [f]Num. 28.3 **12** [g]Col. 3.1 **13** [h]Ps. 110.1 **15** [i]2 Pet. 1.21 **16** [j]Jer. 31.33 **17** [3]Some copies have, Then he said, And their **19** [4]Or, liberty **20** [k]Matt. 11.27; [5]Or, new made **21** [l]1 Tim. 3.15 **22** [m]Eph. 3.12; [n]Num. 19.13 **23** [o]1 Cor. 1.9 **25** [p]Acts 2.42 [q]Rom. 13.11 [r]2 Pet. 3.9 **26** [s]Num. 15.30; [t]2 Pet. 2.20 **27** [u]Ezek. 36.5 **29** [v]1 Cor. 11.29 [w]Matt. 12.31 **30** [x]Deut. 32.35 [y]Ps. 50.4 **31** [z]Isa. 33.14 **32** [a]Gal. 3.4 [b]Phil. 1.29-30 **33** [c]Phil. 1.7 **34** [d]Matt. 5.12 [6]Or, that ye have in yourselves, or, for yourselves **36** [e]Luke 21.19; [f]Col. 3.24

37 For [g]yet a little while, and [h]he that shall come will come, and will not tarry.

38 Now the just shall live by faith: but if *any man* draw back, my soul shall have no pleasure in him.

39 But we are not of them who draw back unto perdition; but of them that believe to the saving of the soul.

11 Now faith is the [1]substance of things hoped for, the evidence [a]of things not seen.

2 For by it the elders obtained a good report.

3 Through faith we understand that [b]the worlds were framed by the word of God, so that things which are seen were not made of things which do appear.

4 By faith [c]Ā'bel offered unto God a more excellent sacrifice than Cāin, by which he obtained witness that he was righteous, God testifying of his gifts: and by it he being dead [2]yet speaketh.

5 By faith [d]Ē'nŏch was translated that he should not see death; and was not found, because God had translated him: for before his translation he had this testimony, that he pleased God.

6 But [e]without faith *it is* impossible to please *him:* for he that cometh to God must believe that he is, and *that* he is a rewarder of them that diligently seek him.

7 By faith [f]Nō'ah, being warned of God of things not seen as yet, [3]moved with fear, prepared an ark to the saving of his house; by the which he condemned the world, and became heir of [g]the righteousness which is by faith.

8 By faith Ā'brā-hăm, when he was called to go out into a place which he should after receive for an inheritance, obeyed; and he went out, not knowing whither he went.

9 By faith he sojourned in the land of promise, as *in* a strange country, [h]dwelling in tabernacles with Ī'saac and Jā'cob, the heirs with him of the same promise:

10 For he looked for a city which hath foundations, [i]whose builder and maker *is* God.

11 Through faith also [j]Sā'rȧ herself received strength to conceive seed, and [k]was delivered of a child when she was past age, because she judged him faithful who had promised.

12 Therefore sprang there even of one, and [l]him as good as dead, *so many* as the stars of the sky in multitude, and as the sand which is by the sea shore innumerable.

13 These all died [4]in faith, not having received the promises, but [m]having seen them afar off, and were persuaded of *them,* and embraced *them,* and [n]confessed that they were strangers and pilgrims on the earth.

14 For they that say such things [o]declare plainly that they seek a country.

15 And truly, if they had been mindful of that *country* from whence they came out, they might have had opportunity to have returned.

16 But now they desire a better *country,* that is, an heavenly: wherefore God is not ashamed [p]to be called their God: for [q]he hath prepared for them a city.

17 By faith [r]Ā'brā-hăm, when he was tried, offered up Ī'saac: and he that had received the promises [s]offered up his only begotten *son,*

18 [5]Of whom it was said, [t]That in Ī'saac shall thy seed be called:

19 Accounting that God *was* able to raise *him* up, even from the dead; from whence also he received him in a figure.

20 By faith [u]Ī'saac blessed Jā'cob and Ē'saụ concerning things to come.

21 By faith Jā'cob, when he was a dying, [v]blessed both the sons of Jō'seph; and [w]worshipped, *leaning* upon the top of his staff.

22 By faith [x]Jō'seph, when he died, [6]made mention of the departing of the children of Is'ra-el; and gave commandment concerning his bones.

23 By faith [y]Mō'ses, when he was born, was hid three months of his parents, because they saw *he was* a proper child; and they were not afraid of the king's [z]commandment.

24 By faith Mō'ses, when he was come to years, refused to be called the son of Phā'raōh's daughter;

25 [a]Choosing rather to suffer affliction with the people of God, than to enjoy the pleasures of sin for a season;

26 Esteeming the reproach [7]of Chrīst greater riches than the treasures in Ē'ġy̆pt: for he had respect unto the recompence of the reward.

27 By faith [b]he forsook Ē'ġy̆pt, not fearing the wrath of the king: for he endured, as seeing him who is invisible.

28 Through faith [c]he kept the passover, and the sprinkling of blood, lest he that destroyed the firstborn should touch them.

29 By faith they passed through the Red sea as by dry *land:* which the Ē-ġy̆p'tians assaying to do were drowned.

30 By faith [d]the walls of Jĕr'ĭ-chō fell down, after they were compassed about seven days.

31 By faith [e]the harlot Rā'hăb perished not with them [8]that believed not, when she had received the spies with peace.

32 And what shall I more say? for the time would fail me to tell of [f]Gĕd'e-on, and *of* [g]Bā'rak, and *of* [h]Săm'son, and *of* [i]Jĕph'thā-e; *of* [j]Dā'vid also and [k]Sām'u-el, and *of* the prophets:

33 Who through faith subdued kingdoms, wrought righteousness, obtained promises, [l]stopped the mouths of lions,

34 [m]Quenched the violence of fire, [n]escaped the edge of the sword, [o]out of weakness were made strong, waxed valiant in fight, [p]turned to flight the armies of the aliens.

35 [q]Women received their dead raised to life again: and others were [r]tortured, not accepting deliverance; that they might obtain a better resurrection:

37 [g]Luke 18.8
[h]Heb. 2.3-4
CHAPTER 11
1 [1]Or, ground, or, confidence
[a]Rom. 8.24
3 [b]John 1.3
4 [c]Gen. 4.4
[2]Or, is yet spoken of
5 [d]Gen. 5.22
6 [e]John 3.18-36
7 [f]Gen. 6.13
[3]Or, being wary
[g]Rom. 3.22; Phil. 3.9
9 [h]Gen. 12.8
10 [i]Isa. 14.32
11 [j]Gen. 17.19
[k]Luke 1.36
12 [l]Rom. 4.19
13 [4]according to faith
[m]Gen. 49.10; Num. 24.17
[n]Gen. 47.9
14 [o]ch. 13.14
16 [p]Ex. 3.6-15
[q]Phil. 3.20
17 [r]Gen. 22.1
[s]Jas. 2.21
18 [5]Or, To
[t]Gen. 21.12
20 [u]Gen. 27.27
21 [v]Gen. 48.5
[w]Gen. 47.31
22 [x]Gen. 50.24; Ex. 13.19
[6]Or, remembered
23 [y]Ex. 2.2
[z]Ex. 1.16
25 [a]Ps. 84.10; Matt. 5.10-12
26 [7]Or, for Christ
27 [b]Ex. 10.29
28 [c]Ex. 12.21
30 [d]Josh. 6.20
31 [e]Jas. 2.25
[8]Or, that were disobedient
32 [f]Judg. 6.11
[g]Judg. 4.6
[h]Judg. 13.24
[i]Judg. 11.1
[j]1 Sam. 16.1
[k]1 Sam. 1.20
33 [l]1 Sam. 17.34
34 [m]Dan. 3.25
[n]1 Sam. 20.1;
[o]2 Ki. 20.7;
[p]1 Sam. 14.13
35 [q]1 Ki. 17.22;
[r]Acts 22.25

36 And others had trial of *cruel*
mockings and scourgings, yea, moreover [s]of bonds and imprisonment:
37 [t]They were stoned, they were
sawn asunder, were tempted, were
slain with the sword: [u]they wandered
about in sheepskins and goatskins; being destitute, afflicted, tormented;
38 (Of whom the world was not worthy:) they wandered in deserts, and *in*
mountains, and [v]*in* dens and caves of
the earth.
39 And these all, having obtained a
good report through faith, received not
the promise:
40 God having [9]provided some better thing for us, that they without us
should not be [w]made perfect.

12

12 Wherefore seeing we also are
compassed about with so great a
cloud of witnesses, let us lay aside every weight, and the sin which doth so
easily beset *us*, and let us run with patience the race that is set before us,
2 [a]Looking unto Jē'sus the [1]author
and finisher of *our* faith; [b]who for the
joy that was set before him endured
the cross, despising the shame, and [c]is
set down at the right hand of the
throne of God.
3 [d]For consider him that endured
such contradiction of sinners against
himself, [e]lest ye be wearied and faint
in your minds.
4 Ye have not yet resisted unto blood,
striving against sin.
5 And ye have forgotten the exhortation which speaketh unto you as unto
children, [f]My son, despise not thou the
chastening of the Lord, nor faint when
thou art rebuked of him:
6 For [g]whom the Lord loveth he
chasteneth, and scourgeth every son
whom he receiveth.
7 If ye endure chastening, God dealeth with you as with sons; for what son
is he whom the father chasteneth not?
8 But if ye be without chastisement,
[h]whereof all are partakers, then are ye
bastards, and not sons.
9 Furthermore we have had fathers
of our flesh which corrected *us*, and we
gave *them* reverence: shall we not
much rather be in subjection unto the
Father of spirits, and live?
10 For they verily for a few days
chastened *us* [2]after their own pleasure;
but he for *our* profit, [i]that *we* might be
partakers of his holiness.
11 Now no chastening for the present seemeth to be joyous, but grievous:
nevertheless afterward it yieldeth [j]the
peaceable fruit of righteousness unto
them which are exercised thereby.
12 Wherefore [k]lift up the hands
which hang down, and the feeble
knees;
13 And make [3]straight paths for your
feet, lest that which is lame be turned
out of the way; [l]but let it rather be
healed.
14 Follow peace with all *men*, and
holiness, [m]without which no man shall
see the Lord:
15 Looking diligently lest any man
[4]fail of the grace of God; [n]lest any root
of bitterness springing up trouble *you*,
and thereby many be defiled;
16 Lest there *be* any fornicator, or
profane person, as Ē'sau, [o]who for one
morsel of meat sold his birthright.
17 For ye know how that afterward,
[p]when he would have inherited the
blessing, he was rejected: for he found
no [5]place of repentance, though he
sought it carefully with tears.
18 For ye are not come unto [q]the
mount that might be touched, and that
burned with fire, nor unto blackness,
and darkness, and tempest,
19 And the sound of a trumpet, and
the voice of words; which *voice* they
that heard [r]intreated that the word
should not be spoken to them any
more:
20 (For they could not endure that
which was commanded, And if so much
as a beast touch the mountain, it shall
be stoned, or thrust through with a
dart:
21 And so terrible was the sight,
that Mō'ses said, I exceedingly fear
and quake:)
22 But ye are come [s]unto mount
Sī'ŏn, and [t]unto the city of the living
God, the heavenly Je-ru'sa-lĕm, [u]and
to an innumerable company of angels,
23 To the general assembly and
church of the firstborn, which are [6]writ-
ten in heaven, and to God the Judge of
all, and to the spirits of just men [v]made
perfect,
24 And to Jē'sus the mediator of the
new [7]covenant, and to [w]the blood of
sprinkling, that speaketh better things
[x]than *that of* Ā'bel.
25 See that ye refuse not him that
speaketh. For if they escaped not who
refused him [y]that spake on earth, much
more *shall not* we *escape*, if we turn
away from him that *speaketh* from
heaven:
26 [z]Whose voice then shook the
earth: but now he hath promised, saying, [a]Yet once more I shake not the
earth only, but also heaven.
27 And this *word*, Yet once more, signifieth [b]the removing of those things
that [8]are shaken, as of things that are
made, that those things which cannot
be shaken may remain.
28 Wherefore we receiving a kingdom which cannot be moved, [9]let us
have grace, whereby we may serve
God acceptably with reverence and
godly fear:
29 For [c]our God *is* a consuming fire.

13

13 Let brotherly love continue.
2 [a]Be not forgetful to entertain
strangers: for thereby [b]some have en-
tertained angels unawares.
3 [c]Remember them that are in bonds,
as bound with them; *and* them which
suffer adversity, as being yourselves
also in the body.
4 Marriage *is* honourable in all, and
the bed undefiled: but whoremongers
and adulterers God will judge.

36 [s]Gen. 39.20; Jer. 20.2
37 [t]1 Ki. 21.13; Acts 7.58
[u]2 Ki. 1.8
38 [v]1 Ki. 18.4
40 [9]Or, foreseen
[w]Rom. 11.26
CHAPTER 12
2 [a]2 Cor. 3.18
[1]Or, beginner
[b]1 Pet. 1.11
[c]Ps. 110.1
3 [d]John 15.20
[e]Gal. 6.9
5 [f]Job 5.17
6 [g]Ps. 94.12; Rev. 3.19
8 [h]Ps. 73.14
10 [2]Or, as seemed good, or, meet to them
[i]Lev. 19.2
11 [j]Jas. 3.18
12 [k]Job 4.3-4; Isa. 35.3
13 [3]Or, even
[l]Gal. 6.1
14 [m]Matt. 5.8
15 [4]Or, fall from
[n]Deut. 29.18
16 [o]Gen. 25.33
17 [p]Gen. 27.34
[5]Or, way to change his mind
18 [q]Ex. 19.12
19 [r]Ex. 20.19
22 [s]Gal. 4.26;
[t]Phil. 3.20
[u]Ps. 68.17
23 [6]Or, enrolled
[v]Phil. 3.12
24 [7]Or, testament
[w]Ex. 24.8;
[x]Gen. 4.10
25 [y]Num. 16
26 [z]Ex. 19.18
[a]Hag. 2.6
27 [b]Ps. 102.26;
[8]Or, may be shaken
28 [9]Or, let us hold fast
29 [c]Ex. 24.17
CHAPTER 13
2 [a]Gen. 19.2;
[b]Gen. 18.3
3 [c]Matt. 25.36

5 *Let your* conversation *be* without covetousness; *and be* content with
such things as ye have: for he hath
said, [d]I will never leave thee, nor forsake thee.
6 So that we may boldly say, [e]The
Lord *is* my helper, and I will not fear
what man shall do unto me.
7 Remember them which [1]have the
rule over you, who have spoken unto
you the word of God: whose faith
follow, considering the end of *their*
conversation.
8 Jē'sus Chrīst [f]the same yesterday,
and to day, and for ever.
9 Be not carried about with divers
and strange doctrines. For *it is* a good
thing that the heart be established with
grace; not with meats, which have not
profited them that have been occupied
therein.
10 [g]We have an altar, whereof they
have no right to eat which serve the
tabernacle.
11 For [h]the bodies of those beasts,
whose blood is brought into the sanctuary by the high priest for sin, are
burned without the camp.
12 Wherefore Jē'sus also, that he
might sanctify the people with his own
blood, [i]suffered without the gate.
13 Let us go forth therefore unto
him without the camp, bearing [j]his
reproach.
14 [k]For here have we no continuing
city, but we seek one to come.
15 By him therefore let us offer [l]the
sacrifice of praise to God continually,
that is, the fruit of *our* lips [2]giving
thanks to his name.
16 But to do good and to communicate forget not: for with such sacrifices
God is well pleased.
17 Obey them that [3]have the rule
over you, and submit yourselves: for
[m]they watch for your souls, as they
that must give account, that they may
do it with joy, and not with grief: for
that *is* unprofitable for you.
18 Pray for us: for we trust we have
a good conscience, in all things willing
to live honestly.
19 But I beseech *you* the rather to do
this, that I may be restored to you the
sooner.
20 Now the God of peace, that
brought again from the dead our Lord
Jē'sus, [n]that great shepherd of the
sheep, [o]through the blood of the everlasting [4]covenant,
21 Make you perfect in every good
work to do his will, [5]working in you
that which is wellpleasing in his sight,
through Jē'sus Chrīst; [p]to whom *be*
glory for ever and ever. Amen.
22 And I beseech you, brethren, suffer the word of exhortation: for I have
written a letter unto you in few words.
23 Know ye that [q]*our* brother Tĭm'-
o-thy̆ [r]is set at liberty; with whom, if
he come shortly, I will see you.
24 Salute all them that have the rule
over you, and all the saints. They of
Ĭt'a-ly̆ salute you.
25 Grace *be* with you all. Amen.

5 [d]Gen. 28.15; Deut. 31.6-8; Josh. 1.5; Ps. 37.25; Isa. 41.10-17
6 [e]Ps. 27.1
7 [1]Or, are the guides
8 [f]John 8.58; Eph. 4.5; ch. 1.12; Rev. 1.4
10 [g]1 Cor. 9.13
11 [h]Lev. 4.11
12 [i]John 19.17; Acts 7.58
13 [j]1 Pet. 4.14
14 [k]Mic. 2.10
15 [l]Lev. 7.12; Ps. 50.14
[2]confessing to
17 [3]Or, guide
[m]Ezek. 3.17
20 [n]Isa. 40.11; Ezek. 34.23; John 10.11
[o]Zech. 9.11; Matt. 26.28; Luke 22.20
[4]Or, testament
21 [5]Or, doing
[p]Gal. 1.5
23 [q]1 Thess. 3.2
[r]1 Tim. 6.12

THE LETTER OF

JAMES

Life's Questions

Which is the true religion , and which is fake?
Why do I have so many temptations and hardships?
What is the relationship between faith and good works?

God's Answers

James, the half brother of Jesus, wrote a troubled group of Jewish believers to help them understand how to distinguish true faith in Christ from insincere faith. He called on them to endure persecution to live out true religion.

James shows: trials and temptations develop true faith (1:1—2:15); faith is the starting point of true religion and leads to equal treatment for all people (1:16—2:26); true religion is known by its wise tongue (ch. 3); true religion shows itself in daily good works motivated by humility, not selfishness (4:1—5:12); true religion devotes itself to prayer for others and confession of sins (5:13—20).

James calls you to a life that shows the world true, humble, unselfish, loving religion.

1 Jāmes, [a]a servant of God and of the
Lord Jē'sus Chrīst, [b]to the twelve
tribes [c]which are scattered abroad,
greeting.
2 My brethren, count it all joy when
ye fall into divers temptations;
3 Knowing *this*, that the trying of
your faith worketh patience.
4 But let patience have *her* perfect
work, that ye may be perfect and entire, wanting nothing.
5 [d]If any of you lack wisdom, [e]let
him ask of God, that giveth to all *men*
liberally, and upbraideth not; and [f]it
shall be given him.
6 [g]But let him ask in faith, nothing
wavering. For he that wavereth is like
a wave of the sea driven with the wind
and tossed.
7 For let not that man think that he
shall receive any thing of the Lord.
8 A double minded man *is* unstable
in all his ways.
9 Let the brother of low degree [1]re-
joice in that he is exalted:

CHAPTER 1
1 [a]Matt. 10.3
[b]Acts 26.7
[c]John 7.35; Acts 2.5
5 [d]1 Ki. 3.9; Prov. 3.5-7
[e]Matt. 7.7;
[f]Jer. 29.12
6 [g]Matt. 21.22
9 [1]Or, glory

10 But the rich, in that he is made
low: because as the flower of the grass
he shall pass away.
11 For the sun is no sooner risen
with a burning heat, but it withereth
the grass, and the flower thereof falleth, and the grace of the fashion of it
perisheth: so also shall the rich man
fade away in his ways.
12 [h]Blessed *is* the man that endureth temptation: for when he is tried, he
shall receive [i]the crown of life, which
the Lord hath promised to them that
love him.
13 Let no man say when he is
tempted, I am tempted of God: for God
cannot be tempted with [2]evil, neither
tempteth he any man:
14 But every man is tempted, when
he is drawn away of his own lust, and
enticed.
15 Then when lust hath conceived,
it bringeth forth sin: and sin, when it is
finished, bringeth forth death.
16 Do not err, my beloved brethren.
17 Every good gift and every perfect
gift is from above, and cometh down
from the Father of lights, [j]with whom
is no variableness, neither shadow of
turning.
18 [k]Of his own will begat he us with
the word of truth, that we should be a
kind of [l]firstfruits of his creatures.
19 Wherefore, my beloved brethren,
let every man be swift to hear, slow to
speak, slow to wrath:
20 For the wrath of man worketh
not the righteousness of God.
21 Wherefore lay apart all filthiness
and superfluity of naughtiness, and
receive with meekness the engrafted
word, [m]which is able to save your
souls.
22 But be ye doers of the word, and
not hearers only, deceiving your own
selves.
23 For [n]if any be a hearer of the
word, and not a doer, he is like unto a
man beholding his natural face in a
glass:
24 For he beholdeth himself, and
goeth his way, and straightway forgetteth what manner of man he was.
25 But [o]whoso looketh into the perfect law of liberty, and continueth
therein, he being not a forgetful hearer,
but a doer of the work, [p]this man shall
be blessed in his [3]deed.
26 If any man among you seem to be
religious, and bridleth not his tongue,
but deceiveth his own heart, this man's
religion *is* vain.
27 Pure religion and undefiled before God and the Father is this, [q]To
visit the fatherless and widows in their
affliction, [r]*and* to keep himself unspot-
ted from the world.

2 My brethren, have not the faith of
our Lord Jē'sus Chrīst, [a]*the Lord* of
glory, with [b]respect of persons.
2 For if there come unto your [1]as-
sembly a man with a gold ring, in
goodly apparel, and there come in also
a poor man in vile raiment;

12 [h]Heb. 12.5; Rev. 3.19
[i]Matt. 25.34; Luke 22.28-30; 1 Pet. 5.4
13 [2]Or, evils
17 [j]Num. 23.19; Mal. 3.6
18 [k]John 1.13; 1 Cor. 4.15; 1 Pet. 1.23
[l]Jer. 2.3; Rev. 14.4
21 [m]Acts 13.26; Rom. 1.16; 1 Cor. 15.2; Eph. 1.13; Heb. 2.3; 1 Pet. 1.9
23 [n]Luke 6.47
25 [o]2 Cor. 3.18
[p]John 13.17
[3]Or, doing
27 [q]Isa. 1.16; 1 Tim. 1.5
[r]Ex. 23.2; Eph. 2.2

CHAPTER 2

1 [a]Acts 7.2; Phil. 2.9
[b]Lev. 19.15; Jude 16
2 [1]synagogue
3 [2]Or, well, or, seemly
5 [c]John 7.48
[3]Or, that
[d]Ex. 20.6; Luke 6.20
8 [e]Lev. 19.18; Matt. 22.39
10 [f]Deut. 27.26; Gal. 3.10
11 [4]Or, that law which said
[g]Ex. 20.13; Mark 10.19
13 [5]Or, glorieth
17 [6]by itself
18 [7]Some copies read, by thy works
19 [h]Matt. 8.29; Acts 16.17
20 [i]Gal. 5.6
21 [j]Gen. 22.9
22 [8]Or, Thou seest
23 [k]Gen. 15.6; Rom. 4.3
[l]2 Chr. 20.7; Isa. 41.8
25 [m]Heb. 11.31

3 And ye have respect to him that
weareth the gay clothing, and say unto
him, Sit thou here [2]in a good place; and
say to the poor, Stand thou there, or sit
here under my footstool:
4 Are ye not then partial in yourselves, and are become judges of evil
thoughts?
5 Hearken, my beloved brethren,
[c]Hath not God chosen the poor of this
world rich in faith, and heirs of [3]the
kingdom [d]which he hath promised to
them that love him?
6 But ye have despised the poor. Do
not rich men oppress you, and draw
you before the judgment seats?
7 Do not they blaspheme that worthy name by the which ye are called?
8 If ye fulfil the royal law according
to the scripture, [e]Thou shalt love thy
neighbour as thyself, ye do well:
9 But if ye have respect to persons,
ye commit sin, and are convinced of
the law as transgressors.
10 For whosoever shall keep the
whole law, and yet offend in one *point*,
[f]he is guilty of all.
11 For [4]he that said, [g]Do not commit
adultery, said also, Do not kill. Now if
thou commit no adultery, yet if thou
kill, thou art become a transgressor of
the law.
12 So speak ye, and so do, as they
that shall be judged by the law of
liberty.
13 For he shall have judgment without mercy, that hath shewed no mercy;
and mercy [5]rejoiceth against judgment.
14 What *doth it* profit, my brethren,
though a man say he hath faith, and
have not works? can faith save him?
15 If a brother or sister be naked,
and destitute of daily food,
16 And one of you say unto them,
Depart in peace, be *ye* warmed and
filled; notwithstanding ye give them
not those things which are needful to
the body; what *doth it* profit?
17 Even so faith, if it hath not works,
is dead, being [6]alone.
18 Yea, a man may say, Thou hast
faith, and I have works: shew me thy
faith [7]without thy works, and I will
shew thee my faith by my works.
19 Thou believest that there is one
God; thou doest well: [h]the devils also
believe, and tremble.
20 But wilt thou know, O vain man,
that [i]faith without works is dead?
21 Was not Ā'brā-hăm our father
justified by works, [j]when he had offered Ī'saac his son upon the altar?
22 [8]Seest thou how faith wrought
with his works, and by works was faith
made perfect?
23 And the scripture was fulfilled
which saith, [k]Ā'brā-hăm believed God,
and it was imputed unto him for righteousness: and he was called [l]the
Friend of God.
24 Ye see then how that by works a
man is justified, and not by faith only.
25 Likewise also [m]was not Rā'hăb
the harlot justified by works, when she

had received the messengers, and had
sent *them* out another way?
26 For as the body without the [9]spirit
is dead, so faith without works is dead
also.

3 My brethren, [a]be not many masters, [b]knowing that we shall receive the greater [1]condemnation.
2 For [c]in many things we offend all.
[d]If any man offend not in word, [e]the
same *is* a perfect man, *and* able also to
bridle the whole body.
3 Behold, we put bits in the horses'
mouths, that they may obey us; and we
turn about their whole body.
4 Behold also the ships, which
though *they be* so great, and *are* driven
of fierce winds, yet are they turned
about with a very small helm, whithersoever the governor listeth.
5 Even so the tongue is a little member, and boasteth great things. Behold, how great [2]a matter a little fire
kindleth!
6 And the tongue *is* a fire, a world of
iniquity: so is the tongue among our
members, that [f]it defileth the whole
body, and setteth on fire the [3]course of
nature; and it is set on fire of hell.
7 For every [4]kind of beasts, and of
birds, and of serpents, and of things in
the sea, is tamed, and hath been tamed
of [5]mankind:
8 But the tongue can no man tame; *it*
is an unruly evil, full of deadly poison.
9 Therewith bless we God, even the
Father; and therewith curse we men,
[g]which are made after the similitude
of God.
10 Out of the same mouth proceedeth blessing and cursing. My brethren,
these things ought not so to be.
11 Doth a fountain send forth at the
same [6]place sweet *water* and bitter?
12 Can the fig tree, my brethren,
bear olive berries? either a vine, figs?
so *can* no fountain both yield salt water and fresh.
13 [h]Who *is* a wise man and endued
with knowledge among you? let him
shew out of a good conversation his
works with meekness of wisdom.
14 But if ye have [i]bitter envying and
strife in your hearts, glory not, and lie
not against the truth.
15 [j]This wisdom descendeth not
from above, but *is* earthly, [7]sensual,
devilish.
16 For [k]where envying and strife
is, there *is* [8]confusion and every evil
work.
17 But [l]the wisdom that is from
above is first pure, then peaceable, gentle, *and* easy to be intreated, full of
mercy and good fruits, [9]without partiality, [m]and without hypocrisy.
18 [n]And the fruit of righteousness
is sown in peace of them that make
peace.

4 From whence *come* wars and [1]fight-
ings among you? *come they* not
hence, *even* of your [2]lusts that war in
your members?
2 Ye lust, and have not: ye [3]kill, and
desire to have, and cannot obtain: ye
fight and war, yet ye have not, because
[a]ye ask not.
3 [b]Ye ask, and receive not, [c]be-
cause ye ask amiss, that ye may consume *it* upon your [4]lusts.
4 Ye adulterers and adulteresses,
know ye not that [d]the friendship of the
world is enmity with God? [e]whosoever
therefore will be a friend of the world
is the enemy of God.
5 Do ye think that the scripture saith
in vain, [f]The spirit that dwelleth in us
lusteth [5]to envy?
6 But he giveth more grace. Wherefore he saith, [g]God resisteth the proud,
but giveth grace unto the humble.
7 Submit yourselves therefore to
God. [h]Resist the devil, and he will flee
from you.
8 [i]Draw nigh to God, and he will
draw nigh to you. Cleanse *your* hands,
ye sinners; and purify *your* hearts, *ye*
double minded.
9 Be afflicted, and mourn, and weep:
let your laughter be turned to mourning, and *your* joy to heaviness.
10 Humble yourselves in the sight of
the Lord, and he shall lift you up.
11 Speak not evil one of another,
brethren. He that speaketh evil of *his*
brother, and judgeth his brother, speaketh evil of the law, and judgeth the law:
but if thou judge the law, thou art not a
doer of the law, but a judge.
12 There is one lawgiver, [j]who is
able to save and to destroy: who art
thou that judgest another?
13 Go to now, ye that say, To day or
to morrow we will go into such a city,
and continue there a year, and buy and
sell, and get gain:
14 Whereas ye know not what *shall*
be on the morrow. For what *is* your
life? [6]It is even a vapour, that appeareth for a little time, and then van-
isheth away.
15 For that ye *ought* to say, If the
Lord will, we shall live, and do this, or
that.
16 But now ye rejoice in your boast-
ings: all such rejoicing is evil.
17 Therefore [k]to him that knoweth
to do good, and doeth *it* not, to him it is
sin.

5 Go to now, *ye* rich men, weep and
howl for your miseries that shall
come upon *you*.
2 Your riches are corrupted, and
your garments are motheaten.
3 Your gold and silver is cankered;
and the rust of them shall be a witness
against you, and shall eat your flesh as
it were fire. [a]Ye have heaped treasure
together for the last days.
4 Behold, [b]the hire of the labourers
who have reaped down your fields,
which is of you kept back by fraud,
crieth: and [c]the cries of them which
have reaped are entered into the ears
of the Lord of săb′a-ŏth.
5 Ye have lived in pleasure on the
earth, and been wanton; ye have nourished your hearts, as in a day of
slaughter.

26 [9]Or, breath

CHAPTER 3
1 [a]Matt. 23.8; 1 Pet. 5.3
[b]Luke 6.37
[1]Or, judgment
2 [c]1 Ki. 8.46; 1 John 1.8
[d]Ps. 34.13; 1 Pet. 3.10
[e]Matt. 12.37
5 [2]Or, wood
6 [f]Matt. 15.11-18-19-20; Mark 7.15-20-23
[3]wheel
7 [4]nature
[5]nature of man
9 [g]Gen. 1.26; 1 Cor. 11.7
11 [6]Or, hole
13 [h]Gal. 6.4
14 [i]Rom. 13.13
15 [j]Phil. 3.19
[7]Or, natural
16 [k]1 Cor. 3.3
[8]tumult, or, unquietness
17 [l]1 Cor. 2.6
[9]Or, without wrangling
[m]1 Pet. 1.22
18 [n]Matt. 5.9

CHAPTER 4
1 [1]Or, brawlings
[2]Or, pleasures
2 [3]Or, envy
[a]Ps. 10.4
3 [b]Job 27.9; Prov. 1.28
[c]Ps. 66.18
[4]Or, pleasures
4 [d]1 John 2.15
[e]John 15.19; Gal. 1.10
5 [f]Gen. 8.21
[5]Or, enviously
6 [g]Ps. 138.6; Luke 18.14
7 [h]Eph. 4.27; 1 Pet. 5.9
8 [i]Gen. 18.23; Hos. 6.1-2
12 [j]Matt. 10.28
14 [6]Or, For it is
17 [k]Luke 12.47; Rom. 1.20

CHAPTER 5
3 [a]Rom. 2.5
4 [b]Lev. 19.13; Mal. 3.5
[c]Gen. 4.10; Deut. 24.15

6 Ye have condemned *and* killed the just; *and* he doth not resist you.

7 [1]Be patient therefore, brethren, unto the coming of the Lord. Behold, the husbandman waiteth for the precious fruit of the earth, and hath long patience for it, until he receive [d]the early and latter rain.

8 Be ye also patient; stablish your hearts: [e]for the coming of the Lord draweth nigh.

9 [2]Grudge not one against another, brethren, lest ye be condemned: behold, the judge [f]standeth before the door.

10 [g]Take, my brethren, the prophets, who have spoken in the name of the Lord, for an example of suffering affliction, and of patience.

11 Behold, we count them happy which endure. Ye have heard of [h]the patience of Jōb, and have seen [i]the end of the Lord; that [j]the Lord is very pitiful, and of tender mercy.

12 But above all things, my brethren, [k]swear not, neither by heaven, neither by the earth, neither by any other oath: but let your yea be yea; and *your* nay, nay; lest ye fall into condemnation.

7 [1]Or, Be long patient, or, Suffer with long patience [d]Deut. 11.14
8 [e]Phil. 4.5
9 [2]Or, Groan, or, Grieve not [f]Matt. 24.33
10 [g]Matt. 5.12
11 [h]Job 1.21 [i]Job 42.10 [j]Ex. 34.6; Num. 14.18; Ps. 25.6-7; Dan. 9.9
12 [k]Matt. 5.34
14 [l]1 Tim. 5.17; [m]Mark 6.13
15 [n]Isa. 33.24
16 [o]Gen. 20.17
17 [p]1 Ki. 17.1 [3]Or, in his prayer
20 [q]1 Tim. 4.16 [r]Ps. 32.1

13 Is any among you afflicted? let him pray. Is any merry? let him sing psalms.

14 Is any sick among you? let him call for the [l]elders of the church; and let them pray over him, [m]anointing him with oil in the name of the Lord:

15 And the prayer of faith shall save the sick, and the Lord shall raise him up; [n]and if he have committed sins, they shall be forgiven him.

16 Confess *your* faults one to another, and pray one for another, that ye may be healed. [o]The effectual fervent prayer of a righteous man availeth much.

17 E-lī'ăs was a man subject to like passions as we are, and [p]he prayed [3]earnestly that it might not rain: and it rained not on the earth by the space of three years and six months.

18 And he prayed again, and the heaven gave rain, and the earth brought forth her fruit.

19 Brethren, if any of you do err from the truth, and one convert him;

20 Let him know, that he which converteth the sinner from the error of his way [q]shall save a soul from death, and [r]shall hide a multitude of sins.

THE FIRST LETTER OF

PETER

Life's Questions

Must I be isolated and lonely to be a Christian?
What assurance do I have that being faithful is worth what it costs?
What is the basic ethical principal for a Christian?

God's Answers

God called Peter to write to isolated believers suffering persecution in northern Asia Minor. They wanted to know what good they were doing themselves or anyone else by being faithful to Christ. Peter pointed to Christ's suffering as an example to encourage them.

First Peter shows: God's work in us (1:1—12); God's call to be the pure people of God maturing in love and salvation (1:13—2:10); the central principle of ethics: live to lead others to glorify God (2:11—3:12); you should endure suffering as Christ did and as God wills ((3:13—4:19); and each stage in life has special Christian responsibilities (ch. 5).

First Peter calls you to faithfulness to God in all stages and areas of life in response to Christ's example.

1 Pē'tēr, an apostle of Jē'sus Chrīst, to the strangers [a]scattered throughout Pŏn'tus, Gā-lā'tiȧ, Căp-pa-dō'çi-ȧ, Ā'siȧ, and Bi-thȳn'ĭ-ȧ,

2 Elect [b]according to the foreknowledge of God the Father, [c]through sanctification of the Spirit, unto obedience and sprinkling [d]of the blood of Jē'sus Chrīst: Grace unto you, and peace, be multiplied.

3 Blessed *be* the God and Father of our Lord Jē'sus Chrīst, which according to his [1]abundant mercy [e]hath begotten us again unto a lively hope [f]by the resurrection of Jē'sus Chrīst from the dead,

4 To an inheritance incorruptible, and undefiled, and that fadeth not away, reserved in heaven [2]for you,

CHAPTER 1
1 [a]John 7.35; Acts 2.5-9
2 [b]Rom. 8.29 [c]2 Thess. 2.13 [d]Heb. 10.22
3 [1]much [e]Jas. 1.18 [f]1 Thess. 4.14
4 [2]Or, for us.
5 [g]John 10.28
6 [h]Matt. 5.12; Rom. 12.12
7 [i]Ps. 66.10; Isa. 48.10
8 [j]1 John 4.20 [k]John 20.29
10 [l]Dan. 2.41; Zech. 6.12

5 [g]Who are kept by the power of God through faith unto salvation ready to be revealed in the last time.

6 [h]Wherein ye greatly rejoice, though now for a season, if need be, ye are in heaviness through manifold temptations:

7 That the trial of your faith, being much more precious than of gold that perisheth, though [i]it be tried with fire, might be found unto praise and honour and glory at the appearing of Jē'sus Chrīst:

8 [j]Whom having not seen, ye love; [k]in whom, though now ye see *him* not, yet believing, ye rejoice with joy unspeakable and full of glory:

9 Receiving the end of your faith, *even* the salvation of *your* souls.

10 [l]Of which salvation the prophets have inquired and searched diligently,

who prophesied of the grace *that*
should come unto you:
11 Searching what, or what manner
of time [m]the Spirit of Chrīst which was
in them did signify, when it testified
beforehand [n]the sufferings of Chrīst,
and the glory that should follow.
12 [o]Unto whom it was revealed, that
[p]not unto themselves, but unto us they
did minister the things, which are now
reported unto you by them that have
preached the gospel unto you with [q]the
Hō'lȳ Ghōst sent down from heaven;
[r]which things the angels desire to look
into.
13 Wherefore gird up the loins of
your mind, be sober, and hope [3]to the
end for the grace that is to be brought
unto you [s]at the revelation of Jē'sus
Chrīst;
14 As obedient children, not fashion-
ing yourselves according to the former
lusts in your ignorance:
15 But as he which hath called you
is holy, so be ye holy in all manner of
conversation;
16 Because it is written, [t]Be ye holy;
for I am holy.
17 And if ye call on the Father, who
without respect of persons judgeth according to every man's work, pass the
time of your [u]sojourning *here* in fear:
18 Forasmuch as ye know that ye
were not redeemed with corruptible
things, *as* silver and gold, from your
vain conversation [v]*received* by tradition from your fathers;
19 But [w]with the precious blood of
Chrīst, [x]as of a lamb without blemish
and without spot:
20 [y]Who verily was foreordained before the foundation of the world, but
was manifest [z]in these last times for
you,
21 Who by him do believe in God,
that raised him up from the dead, and
[a]gave him glory; that your faith and
hope might be in God.
22 Seeing ye have purified your souls
in obeying the truth through the Spirit
unto unfeigned love of the brethren, *see*
that ye love one another with a pure
heart fervently:
23 [b]Being born again, not of corruptible seed, but of incorruptible, [c]by the
word of God, which liveth and abideth
for ever.
24 [4]For all flesh *is* as grass, and all
the glory of man as the flower of grass.
The grass withereth, and the flower
thereof falleth away:
25 [d]But the word of the Lord endureth for ever. And this is the word
which by the gospel is preached unto
you.

2 Wherefore laying aside all malice,
and all guile, and hypocrisies, and
envies, and all evil speakings,
2 [a]As newborn babes, desire the sincere [b]milk of the word, that ye may
grow thereby:
3 If so be ye have [c]tasted that the
Lord *is* gracious.
4 To whom coming, *as unto* a living
stone, disallowed indeed of men, but
chosen of God, *and* precious,
5 [d]Ye also, as lively stones, [1]are
built up a spiritual house, [e]an holy
priesthood, to offer up [f]spiritual sacrifices, [g]acceptable to God by Jē'sus
Chrīst.
6 Wherefore also it is contained in
the scripture, [h]Behold, I lay in Sī'ŏn a
chief corner stone, elect, precious: and
he that believeth on him shall not be
confounded.
7 Unto you therefore which believe
he is [2]precious: but unto them which be
disobedient, [i]the stone which the builders disallowed, the same is made the
head of the corner,
8 [j]And a stone of stumbling, and a
rock of offence, *even to them* which
stumble at the word, being disobedient: [k]whereunto also they were appointed.
9 But ye *are* [l]a chosen generation,
[m]a royal priesthood, [n]an holy nation,
[3]a peculiar people; that ye should shew
forth the [4]praises of him who hath
called you out of darkness into his marvellous light:
10 [o]Which in time past *were* not a
people, but *are* now the people of God:
which had not obtained mercy, but
now have obtained mercy.
11 Dearly beloved, I beseech *you* as
strangers and pilgrims, abstain from
fleshly lusts, which war against the
soul;
12 Having your conversation honest
among the Gĕn'tīles: that, [5]whereas
they speak against you as evildoers,
they may by *your* good works, which
they shall behold, glorify God [p]in the
day of visitation.
13 Submit yourselves to every ordinance of man for the Lord's sake:
whether it be to the king, as supreme;
14 Or unto governors, as unto them
that are sent by him for the punishment of evildoers, and for the praise of
them that do well.
15 For so is the will of God, that with
well doing ye may put to silence the
ignorance of foolish men:
16 As free, and not [6]using *your* liberty for a cloke of maliciousness, but
as the servants of God.
17 [7]Honour all *men*. Love the brotherhood. Fear God. Honour the king.
18 Servants, *be* subject to *your* masters with all fear; not only to the good
and gentle, but also to the froward.
19 For this *is* [8]thankworthy, if a
man for conscience toward God endure grief, suffering wrongfully.
20 For what glory *is it*, if, when ye
be buffeted for your faults, ye shall
take it patiently? but if, when ye do
well, and suffer *for it*, ye take it patiently, this *is* [9]acceptable with God.
21 For even hereunto were ye called:
because Chrīst also suffered [10]for us,
leaving us an example, that ye should
follow his steps:
22 [q]Who did no sin, neither was
guile found in his mouth:

11 [m]Gal. 4.6; ch. 3.19; 2 Pet. 1.21
[n]Ps. 22.6; Isa. 53.3
12 [o]Dan. 12.9
[p]Heb. 11.39
[q]Acts 2.4
[r]Ex. 25.20; Eph. 3.10
13 [3]perfectly
[s]Luke 17.30
16 [t]Ex. 19.6; Lev. 11.44
17 [u]Gen. 47.9; Heb. 11.13
18 [v]Ezek. 20.18; ch. 4.3
19 [w]Matt. 26.28; Rev. 5.9
[x]Ex. 12.5; John 1.29
20 [y]Tit. 1.2-3; Rev. 13.8
[z]Gal. 4.4
21 [a]Phil. 2.9
23 [b]John 1.13; 1 John 3.9
[c]John 1.13
24 [4]Or, For that
25 [d]Isa. 40.8; Luke 16.17

CHAPTER 2
2 [a]Matt. 18.3
[b]1 Cor. 3.2
3 [c]Heb. 6.5
5 [d]Eph. 2.21
[1]Or, be ye built
[e]Isa. 66.21
[f]Hos. 14.2; Mal. 1.11
[g]Phil. 4.18
6 [h]Isa. 28.16
7 [2]Or, an honour
[i]Ps. 118.22; Luke 20.16-18
8 [j]Isa. 8.14; Luke 2.34
[k]Rom. 9.22
9 [l]Deut. 10.15
[m]Ex. 19.5-6; Rev. 5.10
[n]John 17.19
[3]Or, a purchased people
[4]Or, virtues
10 [o]Hos. 2.23
12 [5]Or, wherein
[p]Luke 19.44
16 [6]having
17 [7]Or, Esteem
19 [8]Or, thank
20 [9]Or, thank
21 [10]Some read, for you
22 [q]Isa. 53.9; Luke 23.41

23 [r]Who, when he was reviled, reviled not again; when he suffered, he
threatened not; but [11]committed *himself* to him that judgeth righteously:
24 Who his own self bare our sins in
his own body [12]on the tree, that we,
being dead to sins, should live unto
righteousness: [s]by whose stripes ye
were healed.
25 For [t]ye were as sheep going astray; but are now returned [u]unto the
Shepherd and Bishop of your souls.
3 Likewise ye wives, *be* in subjection
to your own husbands; that, if any
obey not the word, [a]they also may
without the word [b]be won by the conversation of the wives;
2 While they behold your chaste conversation *coupled* with fear.
3 [c]Whose adorning let it not be that
outward *adorning* of plaiting the hair,
and of wearing of gold, or of putting on
of apparel;
4 But *let it be* [d]the hidden man of
the heart, in that which is not corruptible, *even the ornament* of a meek and
quiet spirit, which is in the sight of God
of great price.
5 For after this manner in the old
time the holy women also, who trusted
in God, adorned themselves, being in
subjection unto their own husbands:
6 Even as Sā'rȧ obeyed Ā'brȧ-hăm,
[e]calling him lord: whose [1]daughters ye
are, as long as ye do well, and are not
afraid with any amazement.
7 Likewise, ye husbands, dwell with
them according to knowledge, giving
honour unto the wife, as unto the
weaker vessel, and as being heirs together of the grace of life; [f]that your
prayers be not hindered.
8 Finally, *be ye* all of one mind, having compassion one of another, [2]love
as brethren, *be* pitiful, *be* courteous:
9 Not rendering evil for evil, or railing for railing: but contrariwise blessing; knowing that ye are thereunto
called, [g]that ye should inherit a blessing.
10 For [h]he that will love life, and see
good days, let him refrain his tongue
from evil, and his lips that they speak
no guile:
11 Let him eschew evil, and do good;
let him seek peace, and ensue it.
12 For the eyes of the Lord *are* over
the righteous, [i]and his ears *are open*
unto their prayers: but the face of the
Lord *is* [3]against them that do evil.
13 [j]And who *is* he that will harm
you, if ye be followers of that which is
good?
14 [k]But and if ye suffer for righteousness' sake, happy *are ye:* and [l]be
not afraid of their terror, neither be
troubled;
15 But sanctify the Lord God in your
hearts: and [m]*be* ready always to *give*
an answer to every man that asketh
you a reason of the hope that is in you
with meekness and [4]fear:
16 Having a good conscience; that,
whereas they speak evil of you, as of
evildoers, they may be ashamed that
falsely accuse your good conversation
in Chrīst.
17 For *it is* better, if the will of God
be so, that ye [n]suffer for well doing,
than for evil doing.
18 For Chrīst also hath once suffered for sins, the just for the unjust,
that he might bring us to God, being
put to death [o]in the flesh, but [p]quick-
ened by the Spirit:
19 By [q]which also he went and
preached unto the spirits [r]in prison;
20 Which sometime were disobedient, when once the longsuffering of
God waited in the days of Nō'ah, while
[s]the ark was a preparing, [t]wherein
few, that is, eight souls were saved by
water.
21 [u]The like figure whereunto *even*
baptism doth also now save us (not the
putting away of the filth of the flesh,
but the answer of a good conscience
toward God,) by the resurrection of
Jē'sus Chrīst:
22 Who is gone into heaven, and [v]is
on the right hand of God; angels and
authorities and powers being made
subject unto him.
4 Forasmuch then as Chrīst hath suffered for us in the flesh, arm yourselves likewise with the same mind:
for [a]he that hath suffered in the flesh
hath ceased from sin;
2 That he no longer should live the
rest of *his* time in the flesh to the lusts
of men, but to the will of God.
3 For the time past of *our* life may
suffice us to have wrought the will
of the Gĕn'tīles, when we walked in
lasciviousness, lusts, excess of wine,
revellings, banquetings, and abominable idolatries:
4 Wherein they think it strange that
ye run not with *them* to the same excess of riot, speaking evil of *you:*
5 Who shall give account to him that
is ready [b]to judge the quick and the
dead.
6 For for this cause [c]was the gospel
preached also to them that are dead,
that they might be judged according to
men in the flesh, but live according to
God in the spirit.
7 But [d]the end of all things is at
hand: be ye therefore sober, and watch
unto prayer.
8 And above all things have fervent
charity among yourselves: for [e]charity
[1]shall cover the multitude of sins.
9 Use hospitality one to another
[f]without grudging.
10 As [g]every man hath received the
gift, *even so* minister the same one to
another, as good stewards of the manifold grace of God.
11 [h]If any man speak, *let him speak*
as the oracles of God; if any man minister, *let him do it* as of the ability which
God giveth: that [i]God in all things may
be glorified through Jē'sus Chrīst, [j]to
whom be praise and dominion for ever
and ever. Amen.
12 Beloved, think it not strange concerning the fiery trial which is to try

23 [r]Isa. 53.7 [11]Or, committed his cause
24 [12]Or, to [s]Isa. 53.5
25 [t]Isa. 53.6; Ps. 119.176; Matt. 10.6; Luke 15.4 [u]Ezek 34.23; John 10.11; Heb. 13.20

CHAPTER 3
1 [a]1 Cor. 7.16 [b]Matt. 18.15
3 [c]Isa. 3.16-24
4 [d]Ps. 45.13
6 [e]Gen. 18.12 [1]children
7 [f]Job 42.8; Matt. 5.23
8 [2]Or, loving to the brethren
9 [g]Matt. 25.34; Luke 12.32; Rev. 21.7
10 [h]Ps. 34.12
12 [i]John 9.31 [3]upon
13 [j]Prov. 16.7
14 [k]Matt. 5.10 [l]Isa. 8.12
15 [m]Ps. 119.46; Acts 4.8-12 [4]Or, reverence
17 [n]2 Tim. 3.12
18 [o]Col. 1.21 [p]Rom. 1.4
19 [q]Gen. 6.3; ch. 1.11-12; 2 Pet. 1.21 [r]Isa. 42.7
20 [s]Heb. 11.7 [t]2 Pet. 2.5
21 [u]Eph. 5.26
22 [v]Ps. 110.1; Heb. 1.3

CHAPTER 4
1 [a]Rom. 6.2-7; Gal. 5.24
5 [b]Acts 10.42; 2 Tim. 4.1
6 [c]ch. 3.19
7 [d]Matt. 24.13; Heb. 10.25
8 [e]Prov. 10.12; Jas. 5.20 [1]Or, will
9 [f]Deut. 15.7
10 [g]1 Cor. 4.7
11 [h]Jer. 23.22 [i]Eph. 5.20; ch. 2.5 [j]ch. 5.11; Rev. 1.6

you, as though some strange thing happened unto you:
13 But rejoice, inasmuch as [k]ye are
partakers of Christ's sufferings; that,
when his glory shall be revealed, ye
may be glad also with exceeding joy.
14 [l]If ye be reproached for the name
of Christ, happy *are ye;* for the [m]spirit
of glory and of God resteth upon you:
on their part he is evil spoken of, but
on your part he is glorified.
15 But let none of you suffer as a
murderer, or *as* a thief, or *as* an evildoer, or as a busybody in other men's
matters.
16 Yet if *any man suffer* as a Chris'-
tian, let him not be ashamed; [n]but let
him glorify God on this behalf.
17 For the time *is come* that [o]judg-
ment must begin at the house of God:
and [p]if *it* first *begin* at us, [q]what shall
the end *be* of them that obey not the
gospel of God?
18 [r]And if the righteous scarcely be
saved, where shall the ungodly and the
sinner appear?
19 Wherefore let them that suffer according to the will of God [s]commit the
keeping of their souls *to him* in well
doing, as unto a faithful Creator.

5 The elders which are among you I
exhort, who am also [a]an elder, and
[b]a witness of the sufferings of Christ,
and also [c]a partaker of the glory that
shall be revealed:
2 [d]Feed the flock of God [1]which
is among you, taking the oversight
thereof, not by constraint, but willingly; not for filthy lucre, but of a
ready mind;
3 Neither as [2]being lords over [e]*God's*
heritage, but being ensamples to the
flock.
4 And when [f]the chief Shepherd
shall appear, ye shall receive a crown
of glory that fadeth not away.
5 Likewise, ye younger, submit yourselves unto the elder. Yea, [g]all *of you* be
subject one to another, and be clothed
with humility: for God resisteth the
proud, and [h]giveth grace to the humble.
6 Humble yourselves therefore under the mighty hand of God, that he
may exalt you in due time:
7 [i]Casting all your care upon him;
for he careth for you.
8 Be sober, be vigilant; because your
adversary the devil, as a roaring lion,
walketh about, seeking whom he may
devour:
9 Whom resist stedfast in the faith,
knowing that the same afflictions are
accomplished in your brethren that
are in the world.
10 But the God of all grace, who
hath called us unto his eternal glory by
Christ Jē'sus, after that ye have suffered a while, make you perfect, stablish, strengthen, settle *you.*
11 To him *be* glory and dominion
for ever and ever. Amen.
12 [j]By Sĭl-vā'nus, a faithful brother
unto you, as I suppose, I have written
[k]briefly, exhorting, and testifying that
this is the true grace of God wherein ye
stand.
13 The *church that is* at [l]Băb'y̆-lon,
elected together with *you,* saluteth you;
and *so doth* [m]Mär'cus my son.
14 Greet ye one another with a kiss
of charity. Peace *be* with you all that
are in Christ Jē'sus. Amen.

13 [k]Rom. 8.17; 2 Cor. 1.7; Phil. 3.10; Col. 1.24; Rev. 1.9
14 [l]Matt. 5.11 [m]Matt. 10.20; 2 Cor. 12.9
16 [n]Acts 5.41
17 [o]Isa. 10.12; Jer. 25.29; Mal. 3.5 [p]Luke 23.31 [q]Luke 10.12
18 [r]Prov. 11.31
19 [s]Ps. 31.5; Luke 23.46

CHAPTER 5
1 [a]Phile. 9 [b]Luke 24.48; Acts 1.8 [c]Rom. 8.17; Rev. 1.9
2 [d]John 21.15 [1]Or, as much as in you is
3 [2]Or, overruling [e]Ps. 74.2
4 [f]Heb. 13.20
5 [g]Eph. 5.21; Phil. 2.3 [h]Ps. 34.18; Isa. 57.15
7 [i]Ps. 37.5; Matt. 6.25; Luke 12.11; Phil. 4.6
12 [j]2 Cor. 1.19 [k]Heb. 13.22
13 [l]Gen. 10.10; Rev. 17.5-18 [m]Acts 12.12

THE SECOND LETTER OF

PETER

Life's Questions

How do I grow as a believer?
How do I decide who is teaching the truth?
Why has Jesus not come back yet if He is coming?

God's Answers

Peter wrote again to the isolated Christians to encourage them to grow in their faith and to learn how to judge false teachers. He encouraged them by pointing to the true teaching of the second coming.

Second Peter shows: you should grow in Christ as God has given you all you need to do so (1:1—15); inspired Scripture helps you grow and is the standard by which to judge all teaching (1:16—21); false teachers do not teach Scripture but invent stories and doctrines while living immoral lives (ch. 2); hope comes because Christ will return to create new heavens and earth (ch. 3).

Second Peter calls you to study your Bible to know the truth and grow in Christ.

1 Sī'mon Pē'tĕr, a servant and an
apostle of Jē'sus Christ, to them
that have obtained [a]like precious
faith with us through the righteousness [1]of God and our Saviour Jē'sus
Christ:
2 Grace and peace be multiplied
unto you through the knowledge of
God, and of Jē'sus our Lord,
3 According as his divine power
hath given unto us all things that *per-*
tain unto life and godliness, [b]through

CHAPTER 1
1 [a]Acts 11.17; [1]of our God and Saviour
3 [b]John 17.3

the knowledge of him [c]that hath called
us [2]to glory and virtue:
4 [d]Whereby are given unto us exceeding great and precious promises:
that by these ye might be [e]partakers of
the divine nature, having escaped the
corruption that is in the world through
lust.
5 And beside this, giving all diligence, add to your faith virtue; and to
virtue [f]knowledge;
6 And to knowledge temperance;
and to temperance patience; and to patience godliness;
7 And to godliness brotherly kindness; and [g]to brotherly kindness charity.
8 For if these things be in you, and
abound, they make *you that ye shall*
neither *be* [3]barren nor unfruitful in the
knowledge of our Lord Jē'sus Chrīst.
9 But he that lacketh these things
[h]is blind, and cannot see afar off, and
hath forgotten that he was [i]purged
from his old sins.
10 Wherefore the rather, brethren,
give diligence [j]to make your calling
and election sure: for if ye do these
things, ye shall never fall:
11 [k]For so an entrance shall be ministered unto you abundantly into the
everlasting kingdom of our Lord and
Saviour Jē'sus Chrīst.
12 Wherefore I will not be negligent
to put you always in remembrance of
these things, though ye know *them*,
and be established in the present truth.
13 Yea, I think it meet, as long as I
am in this tabernacle, to stir you up by
putting *you* in remembrance;
14 [l]Knowing that shortly I must put
off *this* my tabernacle, even as [m]our
Lord Jē'sus Chrīst hath shewed me.
15 Moreover I will endeavor that ye
may be able after my decease to have
these things always in remembrance.
16 For we have not followed cun-
ningly devised fables, when we made
known unto you the power and coming of our Lord Jē'sus Chrīst, but were
eyewitnesses of his majesty.
17 For he received from God the Father honour and glory, when there
came such a voice to him from the excellent glory, [n]This is my beloved Son,
in whom I am well pleased.
18 And this voice which came from
heaven we heard, when we were with
him in [o]the holy mount.
19 We have also a more [p]sure word
of prophecy; whereunto ye do well
that ye take heed, as unto a light that
shineth in a dark place, until the day
dawn, and [q]the day star arise in your
hearts:
20 Knowing this first, that [r]no prophecy of the scripture is of any private
interpretation.
21 For [s]the prophecy came not [4]in
old time by the will of man: [t]but holy
men of God spake *as they were* moved
by the Hō'lȳ Ghōst.
2 But [a]there were false prophets also
among the people, even as [b]there
shall be false teachers among you,
who privily shall bring in damnable
heresies, even denying the Lord [c]that
bought them, and bring upon themselves swift destruction.
2 And many shall follow their [1]perni-
cious ways; by reason of whom the
way of truth shall be evil spoken of.
3 And through covetousness shall
they with feigned words make merchandise of you: whose judgment now
of a long time lingereth not, and their
damnation slumbereth not.
4 For if God spared not [d]the angels
[e]that sinned, but [f]cast *them* down to
hell, and delivered *them* into chains of
darkness, to be reserved unto judgment;
5 And spared not the old world, but
saved Nō'ah [g]the eighth *person*, a
preacher of righteousness, bringing
in the flood upon the world of the
ungodly;
6 And [h]turning the cities of Sŏd'om
and Go-mŏr'rhȧ into ashes condemned
them with an overthrow, making *them*
an ensample unto those that after
should live ungodly;
7 And delivered just Lŏt, vexed with
the filthy conversation of the wicked:
8 (For that righteous man dwelling
among them, in seeing and hearing,
vexed *his* righteous soul from day to
day with *their* unlawful deeds;)
9 [i]The Lord knoweth how to deliver
the godly out of temptations, and to
reserve the unjust unto the day of judgment to be punished:
10 But chiefly them that walk after
the flesh in the lust of uncleanness,
and despise [2]government. Presumptuous *are they*, selfwilled, they are not
afraid to speak evil of dignities.
11 Whereas [j]angels, which are
greater in power and might, bring not
railing accusation [3]against them before the Lord.
12 But these, [k]as natural brute beasts,
made to be taken and destroyed, speak
evil of the things that they understand
not; and shall utterly perish in their own
corruption;
13 [l]And shall receive the reward of
unrighteousness, *as* they that count it
pleasure [m]to riot in the day time. Spots
they are and blemishes, sporting themselves with their own deceivings while
[n]they feast with you;
14 Having eyes full of [4]adultery, and
that cannot cease from sin; beguiling
unstable souls: an heart they have exercised with covetous practices; cursed
children:
15 Which have forsaken the right
way, and are gone astray, following the
way of [o]Bā'laam *the son* of Bō'sŏr, who
loved the wages of unrighteousness;
16 But was rebuked for his iniquity:
the dumb ass speaking with man's voice
forbad the madness of the prophet.
17 These are wells without water,
clouds that are carried with a tempest;
to whom the mist of darkness is reserved for ever.
18 For when they speak great swelling *words* of vanity, they allure through

[c]1 Thess. 2.12; 2 Tim. 1.9; 1 Pet. 2.9
[2]Or, by
4 [d]2 Cor. 7.1
[e]Eph. 4.24; Heb. 12.10; 1 John 3.2
5 [f]Prov. 1.7; Hos. 4.6; 2 Cor. 6.4-6; 1 Pet. 3.7; ch. 3.18
7 [g]Gal. 6.10; 1 Thess. 3.12; 1 John 4.21
8 [3]idle
9 [h]1 John 2.9
[i]Eph. 5.26; Heb. 9.14; 1 John 1.7
10 [j]1 John 3.19
11 [k]2 Tim. 4.8
14 [l]Deut. 4.21
[m]John 21.18
17 [n]Matt. 3.17; Mark 1.11; Luke 3.22
18 [o]Gen. 28.16-17; Ex. 3.5; Acts 7.33
19 [p]Isa. 8.20
[q]2 Cor. 4.4-6; Rev. 2.28
20 [r]Rom. 12.6
21 [s]2 Tim. 3.16; 1 Pet. 1.11
[4]Or, at any time
[t]2 Sam. 23.2; Acts 1.16

CHAPTER 2
1 [a]Deut. 13.1
[b]Matt. 24.11
[c]1 Cor. 6.20; Heb. 10.29
2 [1]Or, lascivious ways, as some copies read
4 [d]Job 4.18
[e]John 8.44
[f]Luke 8.31
5 [g]Gen. 7.1; Heb. 11.7
6 [h]Gen. 19.24
9 [i]Ps. 34.17
10 [2]Or, dominion
11 [j]Jude 9
[3]Some read, against themselves
12 [k]Jer. 12.3
13 [l]Isa. 3.11; Phil. 3.19
[m]Rom. 13.13
[n]1 Cor. 11.20-21
14 [4]an adulteress
15 [o]Num. 22.5-7-21-23-28

the lusts of the flesh, *through much*
wantonness, those that [p]were [5]clean
escaped from them who live in error.
19 While they promise them [q]lib-
erty, they themselves are [r]the servants
of corruption: for of whom a man is
overcome, of the same is he brought in
bondage.
20 For [s]if after they [t]have escaped
the pollutions of the world through the
knowledge of the Lord and Saviour
Jē'sus Chrīst, they are again entangled
therein, and overcome, the latter end is
worse with them than the beginning.
21 For [u]it had been better for them
not to have known the way of righteousness, than, after they have known
it, to turn from the holy commandment
delivered unto them.
22 But it is happened unto them according to the true proverb, [v]The dog
is turned to his own vomit again; and
the sow that was washed to her wallow-
ing in the mire.
3 This second epistle, beloved, I now
write unto you; in *both* which [a]I
stir up your pure minds by way of
remembrance:
2 That ye may be mindful of the
words which were spoken before by
the holy prophets, [b]and of the commandment of us the apostles of the
Lord and Saviour:
3 [c]Knowing this first, that there shall
come in the last days scoffers, [d]walk-
ing after their own lusts,
4 And saying, [e]Where is the promise
of his coming? for since the fathers fell
asleep, all things continue as *they were*
from the beginning of the creation.
5 For this they willingly are ignorant of, that [f]by the word of God the
heavens were of old, and the earth
[1]standing out of the water and in the
water:
6 [g]Whereby the world that then was,
being overflowed with water, perished:
7 But the heavens and the earth,
which are now, by the same word
are kept in store, reserved unto [h]fire
against the day of judgment and perdition of ungodly men.

18 [p]Acts 2.40; ch. 1.4
[5]Or, for a little, or, a while, as some read
19 [q]Gal. 5.13; 1 Pet. 2.16
[r]John 8.34
20 [s]Matt. 12.45; Luke 11.26; Heb. 6.4
[t]ch. 1.4
21 [u]Luke 12.47; John 9.41
22 [v]Prov. 26.11
CHAPTER 3
1 [a]2 Tim. 1.6
2 [b]Jude 17
3 [c]1 Tim. 4.1;
[d]ch. 2.10
4 [e]Isa. 5.19; Matt. 24.48;
5 [f]Gen. 1.6; Ps. 33.6;
[1]consisting
6 [g]Gen. 7.11; ch. 2.5
7 [h]Matt. 25.41;
8 [i]Ps. 90.4
9 [j]Hab. 2.3
[k]Isa. 30.18;
[l]Ezek. 18.23
[m]Rom. 2.4
10 [n]Matt. 24.43;
[o]Matt. 24.35;
12 [2]Or, hasting the coming
[p]Ps. 50.3;
[q]Mic. 1.4
13 [r]Isa. 65.17
15 [s]Rom. 2.4; Eph. 1.7; Col. 1.27
16 [t]Rom. 8.19; 1 Cor. 15.24
17 [u]Eph. 4.14

8 But, beloved, be not ignorant of
this one thing, that one day *is* with the
Lord as a thousand years, and [i]a thousand years as one day.
9 [j]The Lord is not slack concerning
his promise, as some men count slackness; but [k]is longsuffering to us-ward,
[l]not willing that any should perish, but
[m]that all should come to repentance.
10 But [n]the day of the Lord will
come as a thief in the night; in the
which [o]the heavens shall pass away
with a great noise, and the elements
shall melt with fervent heat, the earth
also and the works that are therein
shall be burned up.
11 *Seeing* then *that* all these things
shall be dissolved, what manner *of per-*
sons ought ye to be in *all* holy conversation and godliness,
12 Looking for and [2]hasting unto
the coming of the day of God, wherein
the heavens being on fire shall [p]be dissolved, and the elements shall [q]melt
with fervent heat?
13 Nevertheless we, according to
his promise, look for [r]new heavens
and a new earth, wherein dwelleth
righteousness.
14 Wherefore, beloved, seeing that
ye look for such things, be diligent that
ye may be found of him in peace, without spot, and blameless.
15 And account *that* [s]the longsuffering of our Lord *is* salvation; even as
our beloved brother Pa̧ul also according to the wisdom given unto him hath
written unto you;
16 As also in all *his* epistles, [t]speak-
ing in them of these things; in which
are some things hard to be understood,
which they that are unlearned and unstable wrest, as *they do* also the other
scriptures, unto their own destruction.
17 Ye therefore, beloved, seeing ye
know *these things* before, [u]beware
lest ye also, being led away with the
error of the wicked, fall from your own
stedfastness.
18 But grow in grace, and *in* the
knowledge of our Lord and Saviour
Jē'sus Chrīst. To him *be* glory both
now and for ever. Amen.

THE FIRST LETTER OF

JOHN

Life's Questions

What is God like?
How can I witness in the world and not become like the world?
How do I know I am saved?

God's Answers

God led elderly John to write to churches he led and show them the central teachings of Christ as compared to false teachers they listened to. John pointed to the real human life of Christ, the fact He was not created as other humans, and to His expectation that we love Him as He is love.

First John shows: the Christian has fellowship with God through Christ, confesses sin, obeys Christ, and relates to other believers (1:1—2:14); the believer does not love the world and avoids antichrists (2:15—27); the Christian is becoming like Christ, not sinning, overcoming the world, and loving all God's children (2:28—4:21); and believers are assured of eternal life through Christ's gift and through their obedient love (ch. 5).

First John calls you to obedient love for Christ and for other Christians, thus gaining assurance of eternal life.

1 That [a]which was from the beginning, which we have heard, which we have seen with our eyes, [b]which we have looked upon, and [c]our hands have handled, of the [d]Word of life;

2 (For the life was manifested, and we have seen *it*, and bear witness, and shew unto you that eternal life, [e]which was with the Father, and was manifested unto us;)

3 That which we have seen and heard declare we unto you, that ye also may have fellowship with us: and truly [f]our fellowship *is* with the Father, and with his Son Jē'sus Chrīst.

4 And these things write we unto you, that your joy may be full.

5 This then is the message which we have heard of him, and declare unto you, that [g]God is light, and in him is no darkness at all.

6 If we say that we have fellowship with him, and walk in darkness, we lie, and do not the truth:

7 But if we walk in the light, as he is in the light, we have fellowship one with another, and the blood of Jē'sus Chrīst his Son cleanseth us from all sin.

8 [h]If we say that we have no sin, we deceive ourselves, and the truth is not in us.

9 [i]If we confess our sins, he is faithful and just to forgive us *our* sins, and to cleanse us from all unrighteousness.

10 If we say that we have not sinned, we make him a liar, and his word is not in us.

2 My little children, these things write I unto you, that ye sin not. And if any man sin, [a]we have an advocate with the Father, Jē'sus Chrīst the righteous:

2 And [b]he is the propitiation for our sins: and not for ours only, but [c]also for *the sins of* the whole world.

3 And hereby we do know that we know him, if we keep his commandments.

4 He that saith, I know him, and keepeth not his commandments, is a liar, and the truth is not in him.

5 But [d]whoso keepeth his word, in him verily is the love of God perfected: hereby know we that we are in him.

6 [e]He that saith he abideth in him [f]ought himself also so to walk, even as he walked.

7 Brethren, [g]I write no new commandment unto you, but an old commandment [h]which ye had from the beginning. The old commandment is the word which ye have heard from the beginning.

8 Again, [i]a new commandment I write unto you, which thing is true in him and in you: [j]because the darkness is past, and [k]the true light now shineth.

9 He that saith he is in the light, and hateth his brother, is in darkness even until now.

10 He that loveth his brother abideth in the light, and [l]there is none [1]occasion of stumbling in him.

11 But he that hateth his brother is in darkness, and [m]walketh in darkness, and knoweth not whither he goeth, because that darkness hath blinded his eyes.

12 I write unto you, little children, because [n]your sins are forgiven you for his name's sake.

13 I write unto you, fathers, because ye have known him [o]*that is* from the beginning. I write unto you, young men, because ye have overcome the wicked one. I write unto you, little children, because ye have known the Father.

14 I have written unto you, fathers, because ye have known him *that is* from the beginning. I have written unto you, young men, because [p]ye are strong, and [q]the word of God abideth in you, and ye have overcome the wicked one.

15 Love not the world, neither the things *that are* in the world. [r]If any man love the world, the love of the Father is not in him.

16 For all that *is* in the world, the lust of the flesh, [s]and the lust of the eyes, and the pride of life, is not of the Father, but is of the world.

17 And the world passeth away, and the lust thereof: but he that doeth the will of God [t]abideth for ever.

18 Little children, [u]it is the last time: and as ye have heard that [v]antichrist shall come, [w]even now are there many antichrists; whereby we know that it is the last time.

19 They went out from us, but they were not of us; for [x]if they had been of us, they would *no doubt* have continued with us: but *they went out,* that [y]they might be made manifest that they were not all of us.

20 But [z]ye have an unction [a]from the Holy One, and [b]ye know all things.

21 I have not written unto you because ye know not the truth, but because ye know it, and that no lie is of the truth.

22 Who is a liar but he that denieth that Jē'sus is the Chrīst? He is antichrist, that denieth the Father and the Son.

23 Whosoever denieth the Son, the same hath not the Father: *but* [c]*he that acknowledgeth the Son hath the Father also.*

24 Let that therefore abide in you, [d]which ye have heard from the beginning. If that which ye have heard from the beginning shall remain in you, [e]ye also shall continue in the Son, and in the Father.

CHAPTER 1
1 [a]Mic. 5.2
[b]2 Pet. 1.16
[c]Luke 24.39
[d]Rev. 19.13
2 [e]John 1.1-2
3 [f]John 15.4; 1 Cor. 1.9
5 [g]John 1.9; John 8.12; Rev. 1.5
8 [h]1 Ki. 8.46; Eccl. 7.20; Jas. 3.2
9 [i]Lev. 26.40-42; Ps. 32.5; Prov. 28.13

CHAPTER 2
1 [a]Rom. 8.34; 1 Tim. 2.5; Heb. 9.24
2 [b]Rom. 3.25; ch. 4.10
[c]John 1.29; John 4.42; 2 Cor. 5.18-21
5 [d]Tit. 2.11
6 [e]John 15.4
[f]Matt. 11.29
7 [g]2 John 5
[h]ch. 3.11
8 [i]John 13.34
[j]Rom. 13.12; Eph. 5.8
[k]John 1.9; John 8.12
10 [l]2 Pet. 1.10
[1]scandal
11 [m]John 12.35
12 [n]Luke 24.47; Acts 4.12
13 [o]ch. 1.1
14 [p]Eph. 6.10
[q]Jer. 31.33
15 [r]Matt. 6.24; Gal. 1.10
16 [s]Eccl. 5.11
17 [t]Ps. 125.1; Prov. 10.25
18 [u]Heb. 1.2
[v]2 Thess. 2.3
[w]Matt. 24.5
19 [x]Matt. 24.24; John 6.37
[y]1 Cor. 11.19
20 [z]Ps. 23.5; Isa. 44.3; Luke 4.18; Acts 10.38; Heb. 1.9
[a]Mark 1.24; Acts 3.14
[b]John 10.4-5
23 [c]John 14.7
24 [d]2 John 6
[e]John 15.9-10; ch. 1.3

25 [f]And this is the promise that he hath promised us, *even* eternal life.

26 These *things* have I written unto you concerning them that seduce you.

27 But the anointing which ye have received of him abideth in you, and [g]ye need not that any man teach you: but as the same anointing [h] teacheth you of all things, and is truth, and is no lie, and even as it hath taught you, ye shall abide in [2]him.

28 And now, little children, abide in him; that, when he shall appear, we may have confidence, and not be ashamed before him at his coming.

29 [i]If ye know that he is righteous, [3]ye know that every one that doeth righteousness is born of him.

3 Behold, what manner of love the Father hath bestowed upon us, that [a]we should be called the sons of God: therefore the world knoweth us not, [b]because it knew him not.

2 Beloved, now are we the sons of God, and [c]it doth not yet appear what we shall be: but we know that, when he shall appear, [d]we shall be like him; for [e]we shall see him as he is.

3 And every man that hath this hope in him purifieth himself, even as he is pure.

4 Whosoever committeth sin transgresseth also the law: for sin is the transgression of the law.

5 And ye know that he was manifested [f]to take away our sins; and [g]in him is no sin.

6 Whosoever abideth in him sinneth not: whosoever sinneth hath not seen him, neither known him.

7 Little children, let no man deceive you: [h]he that doeth righteousness is righteous, even as he is righteous.

8 [i]He that committeth sin is of the devil; for the devil sinneth from the beginning. For this purpose the Son of God was manifested, [j]that he might destroy the works of the devil.

9 [k]Whosoever is born of God doth not commit sin; for [l]his seed remaineth in him: and he cannot sin, because he is born of God.

10 In this the children of God are manifest, and the children of the devil: whosoever doeth not righteousness is not of God, neither he that loveth not his brother.

11 For this is the [1]message that ye heard from the beginning, [m]that we should love one another.

12 Not as [n]Cāin, *who* was of that wicked one, and slew his brother. And wherefore slew he him? Because his own works were evil, and his brother's righteous.

13 Marvel not, my brethren, if the world hate you.

14 We know that we have passed from death unto life, because we love the brethren. He that loveth not *his* brother abideth in death.

15 [o]Whosoever hateth his brother is a murderer: and ye know that [p]no murderer hath eternal life abiding in him.

25 [f]John 17.3
27 [g]John 14.26; Heb. 8.10
[h]John 16.13
[2]Or, it
29 [i]Acts 22.14
[3]Or, know ye

CHAPTER 3
1 [a]John 1.12
[b]John 15.18
2 [c]1 Cor. 2.9; 2 Cor. 4.17
[d]Ps. 17.15; Rom. 8.29
[e]Ps. 16.11; 2 Cor. 5.7
5 [f]Isa. 53.6-11; Heb. 1.3
[g]Isa. 53.9; 1 Pet. 2.22
7 [h]Ezek. 18.5
8 [i]Matt. 13.38
[j]Gen. 3.15; Luke 10.18
9 [k]ch. 5.18
[l]1 Pet. 1.23
11 [1]Or, commandment
[m]John 15.12
12 [n]Gen. 4.4
15 [o]Matt. 5.21; ch. 4.20
[p]1 Cor. 6.9-10; Rev. 21.8
16 [q]Rom. 5.8; Eph. 5.2-25
17 [r]Deut. 15.7; Luke 3.11
19 [s]John 18.37
[2]persuade
21 [t]Job 22.26
[u]Heb. 10.22
22 [v]Ps. 34.15; Mark 11.24
[w]John 8.29
24 [x]John 17.21
[y]Ezek. 37.27

CHAPTER 4
1 [a]Jer. 14.14; Jer. 23.21
[b]Matt. 24.5
2 [c]1 Cor. 12.3; ch. 5.1
3 [d]ch. 2.22; 2 John 7
4 [e]John 12.31; Eph. 2.2
5 [f]John 3.31
[g]John 15.19
6 [h]John 8.47; 2 Thess. 1.8
[i]Isa. 8.20
8 [j]Ex. 34.6-7
10 [k]John 15.16

16 [q]Hereby perceive we the love *of God*, because he laid down his life for us: and we ought to lay down *our* lives for the brethren.

17 But [r]whoso hath this world's good, and seeth his brother have need, and shutteth up his bowels *of compassion* from him, how dwelleth the love of God in him?

18 My little children, let us not love in word, neither in tongue; but in deed and in truth.

19 And hereby we know [s]that we are of the truth, and shall [2]assure our hearts before him.

20 For if our heart condemn us, God is greater than our heart, and knoweth all things.

21 [t]Beloved, if our heart condemn us not, [u]*then* have we confidence toward God.

22 And [v]whatsoever we ask, we receive of him, because we keep his commandments, [w]and do those things that are pleasing in his sight.

23 And this is his commandment, That we should believe on the name of his Son Jē'sus Chrīst, and love one another, as he gave us commandment.

24 And he that keepeth his commandments [x]dwelleth in him, and he in him. And [y]hereby we know that he abideth in us, by the Spirit which he hath given us.

4 Beloved, [a]believe not every spirit, but try the spirits whether they are of God: because [b]many false prophets are gone out into the world.

2 Hereby know ye the Spirit of God: [c]Every spirit that confesseth that Jē'sus Chrīst is come in the flesh is of God:

3 And [d]every spirit that confesseth not that Jē'sus Chrīst is come in the flesh is not of God: and this is that *spirit* of antichrist, whereof ye have heard that it should come; and even now already is it in the world.

4 Ye are of God, little children, and have overcome them: because greater is he that is in you, than [e]he that is in the world.

5 [f]They are of the world: therefore speak they of the world, [g]and the world heareth them.

6 We are of God: [h]he that knoweth God heareth us; he that is not of God heareth not us. Hereby know we [i]the spirit of truth, and the spirit of error.

7 Beloved, let us love one another: for love is of God; and every one that loveth is born of God, and knoweth God.

8 He that loveth not knoweth not God; for [j]God is love.

9 In this was manifested the love of God toward us, because that God sent his only begotten Son into the world, that we might live through him.

10 Herein is love, [k]not that we loved God, but that he loved us, and sent his Son *to be* the propitiation for our sins.

11 Beloved, if God so loved us, we ought also to love one another.

12 [l]No man hath seen God at any time. If we love one another, God dwelleth in us, and his love is perfected in us.
13 [m]Hereby know we that we dwell in him, and he in us, because he hath given us of his Spirit.
14 And [n]we have seen and do testify that [o]the Father sent the Son *to be* the Saviour of the world.
15 [p]Whosoever shall confess that Jē'sus is the Son of God, God dwelleth in him, and he in God.
16 And we have known and believed the love that God hath to us. God is love; and he that dwelleth in love dwelleth in God, and God in him.
17 Herein is [1]our love made perfect, that [q]we may have boldness in the day of judgment: [r]because as he is, so are we in this world.
18 There is no fear in love; but perfect love casteth out fear: because fear hath torment. He that feareth is not made perfect in love.
19 We love him, because he first loved us.
20 If a man say, I love God, and hateth his brother, he is a liar: for he that loveth not his brother whom he hath seen, how can he love God whom he hath not seen?
21 And [s]this commandment have we from him, That he who loveth God love his brother also.

5 Whosoever [a]believeth that [b]Jē'sus is the Chrīst is born of God: [c]and every one that loveth him that begat loveth him also that is begotten of him.
2 By this we know that we love the children of God, when we love God, and keep his commandments.
3 [d]For this is the love of God, that we keep his commandments: and [e]his commandments are not grievous.
4 For [f]whatsoever is born of God overcometh the world: and this is the victory that overcometh the world, *even* our faith.
5 Who is he that overcometh the world, but [g]he that believeth that Jē'sus is the Son of God?
6 This is he that came [h]by water and blood, *even* Jē'sus Chrīst; not by water only, but by water and blood. [i]And it is the Spirit that beareth witness, because the Spirit is truth.
7 [j]For there are three that bear record in heaven, the Father, [k]the Word, and the Hō'lȳ Ghōst: [l]and these three are one.
8 And there are three that bear witness in earth, the Spirit, and the water, and the blood: and these three agree in one.
9 If we receive [m]the witness of men, the witness of God is greater: [n]for this is the witness of God which he hath testified of his Son.
10 He that believeth on the Son of God [o]hath the witness in himself: he that believeth not God [p]hath made him a liar; because he believeth not the record that God gave of his Son.
11 And this is the record, that God hath given to us eternal life, and [q]this life is in his Son.
12 [r]He that hath the Son hath life; *and* he that hath not the Son of God hath not life.
13 [s]These things have I written unto you that believe on the name of the Son of God; [t]that ye may know that ye have eternal life, and that ye may believe on the name of the Son of God.
14 And this is the confidence that we have [1]in him, that, if we ask any thing according to his will, he heareth us:
15 And if we know that he hear us, whatsoever we ask, we know that we have the petitions that we desired of him.
16 If any man see his brother sin a sin *which is* not unto death, he shall ask, and [u]he shall give him life for them that sin not unto death. [v]There is a sin unto death: [w]I do not say that he shall pray for it.
17 All unrighteousness is sin: and there is a sin not unto death.
18 We know that whosoever is born of God sinneth not; but he that is begotten of God keepeth himself, and that wicked one toucheth him not.
19 *And* we know that we are of God, and the whole world lieth in wickedness.
20 And we know that the Son of God is come, and hath given us an understanding, that we may know him that is true, and we are in him that is true, *even* in his Son Jē'sus Chrīst. [x]This is the true God, and eternal life.
21 Little children, keep yourselves from idols. Amen.

12 [l]Ex. 33.20; 1 Tim. 6.16
13 [m]John 10.38
14 [n]John 1.14 [o]John 3.17
15 [p]Rom. 10.9
17 [1]love with us [q]Jas. 2.13; ch. 2.28 [r]ch. 3.3
21 [s]Lev. 19.18; Eph. 5.2; 1 Thess. 4.9

CHAPTER 5
1 [a]John 1.12 [b]ch. 2.22 [c]John 15.23
3 [d]John 14.15 [e]Mic. 6.8; Matt. 11.30
4 [f]John 16.33
5 [g]Rom. 7.25; 1 Cor. 15.57
6 [h]John 19.34 [i]John 15.26
7 [j]Isa. 48.16; Hag. 2.5-7 [k]John 1.1 [l]Deut. 6.4
9 [m]John 8.17 [n]Matt. 3.16
10 [o]Rom. 8.16; Gal. 4.6 [p]John 3.33
11 [q]John 1.4
12 [r]Heb. 3.14; ch. 2.23-24
13 [s]John 20.31 [t]ch. 1.1-2
14 [1]Or, concerning him
16 [u]Job 42.8 [v]Num. 15.30; 1 Sam. 2.25; Matt. 12.31-32; Mark 3.29; Luke 12.10; Heb. 6.4-6 [w]Jer. 7.16
20 [x]Isa. 9.6; Acts 20.28; Rom. 9.5

THE SECOND LETTER OF

JOHN

Life's Questions

Was Jesus really human like I am?
How can I tell if a person is a believer?
What is love?

God's Answers

John wrote the church again to help them know how to deal with false teachers who said Jesus was not really a human. He said to find people who did not think Jesus was human and who did not love as Jesus loved and have nothing to do with them.

Second John shows: love is the identifying mark of believers (1—6); deceitful teachers deny Jesus was human and should not be part of the church's fellowship (7—13).

Second John calls you to practice love as God commands and to reject false teachings.

1 The [a]elder unto the elect lady and her children, [b]whom I love in the truth; and not I only, but also all they that have known [c]the truth;

2 For the truth's sake, which dwelleth in us, and shall be with us for ever.

3 Grace [1]be with you, mercy, *and* peace, from God the Father, and from the Lord Jē'sus Chrīst, the Son of the Father, in truth and love.

4 I rejoiced greatly that I found of thy children [d]walking in truth, as we have received a commandment from the Father.

5 And now I beseech thee, lady, [e]not as though I wrote a new commandment unto thee, but that which we had from the beginning, [f]that we love one another.

6 And [g]this is love, that we walk after his commandments. This is the commandment, That, [h]as ye have heard from the beginning, ye should walk in it.

7 For many deceivers are entered into the world, who confess not that Jē'sus Chrīst is come in the flesh. This is a deceiver and an antichrist.

8 Look to yourselves, that we lose not those things which we have [2]wrought, but that we receive a full reward.

9 Whosoever transgresseth, and abideth not in the doctrine of Chrīst, hath not God. He that abideth in the doctrine of Chrīst, he hath both the Father and the Son.

10 If there come any unto you, and bring not this doctrine, receive him not into *your* house, [i]neither bid him God speed:

11 For he that biddeth him God speed is partaker of his evil deeds.

12 Having many things to write unto you, I would not *write* with paper and ink: but I trust to come unto you, and speak [3]face to face, that [4]our joy may be full.

13 The children of thy elect sister greet thee. Amen.

1 [a]1 Pet. 5.1 [b]1 John 3.18 [c]John 8.32; 2 Thess. 2.13; 1 Tim. 2.4; Heb. 10.26
3 [1]shall be
4 [d]3 John 3
5 [e]1 John 2.7 [f]John 15.12
6 [g]Rom. 13.8-9; 1 John 5.3 [h]1 John 1.3
8 [2]Or, gained: Some copies read, which ye have gained, but that ye receive, etc
10 [i]Rom. 16.17; 1 Cor. 5.11; 2 Tim. 3.5
12 [3]mouth to mouth [4]Or, your

THE THIRD LETTER OF

JOHN

Life's Questions

How should I treat other believers?
What does a little gossip hurt?
Who should be my examples?

God's Answers

John's final letter is a personal note to a pastor about another pastor who refused to accept other pastors but preferred to gossip about them. John commended those who gave hospitality to pastors they did not even know and condemned the gossiping pastor who wanted the headlines for himself.

Third John shows: believers should show hospitality and support for visiting Christians (see 1—8) but should not imitate or have anything to do with self-centered leaders who gossip about others but will not help them.

Third John calls you to warn Christian fellowship with other believers and warns you about selfishness, seeking personal glory, and gossiping about others.

1 The elder unto the wellbeloved [a]Gā'ius, whom I love [1]in the truth.

2 Beloved, I [2]wish above all things that thou mayest prosper and be in health, even as thy soul prospereth.

3 For I rejoiced greatly, when the brethren came and testified of the truth that is in thee, even as [b]thou walkest in the truth.

4 I have no greater joy than to hear that [c]my children walk in truth.

5 Beloved, thou doest faithfully whatsoever thou [d]doest to the brethren, and to strangers;

6 Which have borne witness of thy charity before the church: whom if thou bring forward on their journey [3]after a godly sort, thou shalt do well:

7 Because that for his name's sake they went forth, [e]taking nothing of the Gĕn'tīles.

8 We therefore ought to receive such, that we might be fellowhelpers to the truth.

9 I wrote unto the church: but Di-ŏt're-phēs, who loveth to have the preeminence among them, receiveth us not.

10 Wherefore, if I come, I will remember his deeds which he doeth, prating against us with malicious words: and not content therewith, neither doth he himself receive the brethren, and forbiddeth them that would, and casteth *them* out of the church.

11 Beloved, [f]follow not that which is evil, but that which is good. [g]He that doeth good is of God: but he that doeth evil hath not seen God.

12 De-mē'trĭ-us hath good report of all *men*, and of the truth itself: yea, and

1 [a]Acts 19.29; Rom. 16.23 [1]Or, truly
2 [2]Or, pray
3 [b]2 John 4
4 [c]1 Cor. 4.15
5 [d]Luke 12.42
6 [3]worthy of God
7 [e]1 Cor. 9.12-15; 2 Cor. 11.7
11 [f]Ps. 37.27; Isa. 1.16; John 10.27; 1 Cor. 4.16; Eph. 5.1; Phil. 3.17; Heb. 6.12 [g]1 John 2.29

we *also* bear record; [h]and ye know that our record is true.

13 I had many things to write, but I will not with ink and pen write unto thee:

14 But I trust I shall shortly see thee, and we shall speak [4]face to face. Peace *be* to thee. *Our* friends salute thee. Greet the friends by name.

12 [h]John 21.24
14 [4]mouth to mouth

THE LETTER OF
JUDE

Life's Questions

What is my responsibility to keep the church's teachings pure?
Is God going to judge the world and punish unbelievers?
How do I grow in the faith?

God's Answers

God used Jude, like James a half brother of Jesus, to warn the church about false teachers who acted immorally and led the church to reject Jesus as Lord. Jude demanded that believers enter into battle against false teachers by living lives of love, praying, and waiting for Jesus to come in judgment.

Jude shows: believers will fight for the faith against false teachers (1—4); judgment on unbelievers is sure (5—7); heretics are immoral, ungodly, and deny God's authority (8—19); and the faithful grow in Christ, pray in the Spirit, stay secure in God's love, minister to believers led astray by heretics, and wait for Jesus (20—25).

Jude calls you to Christian growth, love, faithfulness, and struggle for the pure doctrine.

1 Jūde, the servant of Jē'sus Chrīst, and [a]brother of Jāmes, to them that are sanctified by God the Father, and [b]preserved in Jē'sus Chrīst, *and* [c]called:

2 Mercy unto you, and peace, and love, be multiplied.

3 Beloved, when I gave all diligence to write unto you [d]of the common salvation, it was needful for me to write unto you, and exhort *you* that ye should earnestly contend for the faith which was once delivered unto the saints.

4 For there are certain men crept in unawares, [e]who were before of old ordained to this condemnation, ungodly men, turning [f]the grace of our God into lasciviousness, and [g]denying the only Lord God, and our Lord Jē'sus Chrīst.

5 I will therefore put you in remembrance, though ye once knew this, how that the Lord, having saved the people out of the land of Ē'ġy̆pt, afterward [h]destroyed them that believed not.

6 And [i]the angels which kept not their [1]first estate, but left their own habitation, he hath reserved in everlasting chains under darkness [j]unto the judgment of the great day.

7 Even as [k]Sŏd'om and Go-mŏr'rhȧ, and the cities about them in like manner, giving themselves over to fornication, and going after [2]strange flesh, are set forth for an example, suffering the vengeance of eternal fire.

8 Likewise also these *filthy* dreamers defile the flesh, despise dominion, and [l]speak evil of dignities.

9 Yet [m]Mī'chaĕl the archangel, when contending with the devil he disputed about the [n]body of Mō'ses, [o]durst not bring against him a railing accusation, but said, [p]The Lord rebuke thee.

10 But these speak evil of those things which they know not: but what they know naturally, as brute beasts, in those things they corrupt themselves.

11 Woe unto them! for they have gone in the way [q]of Cāin, and [r]ran greedily after the error of Bā'laam for reward, and perished [s]in the gainsaying of Cō're.

12 These are spots in your [t]feasts of charity, when they feast with you, feeding themselves without fear: clouds *they are* without water, [u]carried about of winds; trees whose fruit withereth, without fruit, twice dead, plucked up by the roots;

13 [v]Raging waves of the sea, foaming out their own shame; wandering stars, to whom is reserved the blackness of darkness for ever.

14 And Ē'nŏch also, [w]the seventh from Ăd'ăm, prophesied of these, saying, Behold, [x]the Lord cometh with ten thousands of his saints,

15 To execute judgment upon all, and to convince all that are ungodly among them of all their ungodly deeds which they have ungodly committed, and of all their hard *speeches* which ungodly sinners have spoken against him.

16 These are murmurers, complainers, walking after their own lusts; and their mouth speaketh great swelling *words*, [y]having men's persons in admiration because of advantage.

17 But, beloved, remember ye the words which were spoken before of the apostles of our Lord Jē'sus Chrīst;

18 How that they told you there should be mockers in the last time, who should walk after their own ungodly lusts.

19 These be they [z]who separate themselves, sensual, having not the Spirit.

1 [a]Luke 6.16; Acts 1.13
[b]John 17.11
[c]Rom. 1.7
3 [d]Tit. 1.4
4 [e]Rom. 9.21; 1 Pet. 2.8
[f]Tit. 2.11; Heb. 12.15
[g]2 Pet. 2.1; 1 John 2.22
5 [h]Num. 14.29; Heb. 3.17-19
6 [i]Matt. 8.29; 2 Pet. 2.4
[1]Or principality
[j]Rev. 20.10
7 [k]Deut. 29.23; 2 Pet. 2.6
[2]other
8 [l]Ex. 22.28
9 [m]Dan. 10.13; Rev. 12.7
[n]Deut. 34.6
[o]2 Pet. 2.11
[p]Zech. 3.2
11 [q]1 John 3.12
[r]Num. 22.7
[s]Num. 16.1
12 [t]1 Cor. 11.21
[u]Eph. 4.14
13 [v]Isa. 57.20
14 [w]Gen. 5.18
[x]Dan. 7.10; Heb. 11.5
16 [y]Prov. 28.21
19 [z]Prov. 18.1; Ezek. 14.7; Hos. 4.14; Heb. 10.25

20 But ye, beloved, [a]building up
yourselves on your most holy faith,
[b]praying in the Hō'lȳ Ghōst,
21 Keep yourselves in the love of
God, looking for the mercy of our Lord
Jē'sus Chrīst unto eternal life.
22 And of some have compassion,
making a difference:
23 And others [c]save with fear, [d]pull-
ing *them* out of the fire; hating even
[e]the garment spotted by the flesh.
24 [f]Now unto him that is able to
keep you from falling, and [g]to present
you faultless before the presence of his
glory with exceeding joy,
25 [h]To the only wise God our Saviour, *be* glory and majesty, dominion
and power, both now and ever. Amen.

20 [a]Col. 2.7; [b]Zech. 12.10 **23** [c]Rom. 11.14; [d]Amos 4.11 [e]Zech. 3.4-5 **24** [f]Eph. 3.20 [g]Col. 1.22 **25** [h]1 Tim. 1.17

THE

REVELATION TO JOHN

(The Apocalypse)

Life's Questions

How can I get hope to live by?
Will God ever get rid of all the evil in this world?
Does God expect me to be totally different from the world?

God's Answers

John's final book (see introduction to John) picked up the literary form of apocalyptic from Daniel and from Jewish writers between the Testaments to provide hope for a church suffering severe persecution from the Roman government about 95 A.D. John wrote letters to seven churches calling them to meet God's expectations and then painted a picture of Christ's great victory over all evil in the final judgment.

Revelation shows: the message comes directly from Jesus who holds the key to the future (ch. 1); Jesus calls His churches to persevere in doctrine, hope, rejection of false teachings, commitment, and morality (2:1—3:22); God is sovereign and rules the world (ch. 4); Christ the divine Redeemer deserves your praise (ch. 5); disasters will continue, but God will finally come in judgment (6:1—7:17); God will send a great tribulation on the earth (8:1—9:21); God's message will be heard and His kingdom revealed (10:1—11:19); Satan's war against Christ will fail (12:1—13:18); Christ will come to claim faithful believers but will execute vengeance on unbelievers (ch. 14); the last judgment will reveal God's justice (15—16); earthly powers who support the antichrist face God's just judgment (17:1—19:5); Christ;'s coming will bring a new heaven and a new earth (19:6—22:21).

Revelation calls you to persevere in obeying Christ and to be sure He will overcome all resistance and establish His kingdom.

1 The Revelation of Jē'sus Chrīst,
[a]which God gave unto him, to shew
unto his servants things which must
shortly come to pass; and [b]he sent and
signified *it* by his angel unto his servant Jŏhn:
2 Who bare record of the word of
God, and of the testimony of Jē'sus
Chrīst, and of all things [c]that he saw.
3 [d]Blessed *is* he that readeth, and
they that hear the words of this prophecy, and keep those things which are
written therein for the time *is* at hand.
4 Jŏhn to the seven churches which
are in Ā'siȧ: Grace *be* unto you, and
peace, from him [e]which is, and [f]which
was, and which is to come; and [g]from
the seven Spirits which are before his
throne;
5 And from Jē'sus Chrīst, [h]*who is*
the faithful witness, *and* the [i]first begotten of the dead, and [j]the prince of
the kings of the earth. Unto him [k]that
loved us, [l]and washed us from our sins
in his own blood,
6 And hath made us kings and priests
unto God and his Father; [m]to him *be*
glory and dominion for ever and ever.
Amen.
7 [n]Behold, he cometh with clouds;
and every eye shall see him, and [o]they
also which pierced him: and all kindreds of the earth shall wail because of
him. Even so, Amen.
8 [p]I am Ăl'phȧ and Ō'me-gȧ, the beginning and the ending, saith the Lord,
which is, and which was, and which is
to come, the Almighty.
9 I Jŏhn, who also am your brother,
and companion in tribulation, and [q]in
the kingdom and patience of Jē'sus
Chrīst, was in the isle that is called
Păt'mos, for the word of God, and for
the testimony of Jē'sus Chrīst.
10 [r]I was in the Spirit on [s]the Lord's
day, and heard behind me a great
voice, as of a trumpet,
11 Saying, I am Ăl'phȧ and Ō'me-gȧ,
the first and the last: and, What thou
seest, write in a book, and send *it* unto
the seven churches which are in Ā'siȧ;
unto Ēph'ĕ-sŭs, and unto Smȳr'nȧ, and
unto Pĕr'ga-mŏs, and unto Thȳ-a-tī'rȧ,
and unto Săr'dis, and unto Phĭl-a-dĕl'-
phĭ-ȧ, and unto La-ŏd-ĭ-çē'ȧ.
12 And I turned to see the voice that
spake with me. And being turned, [t]I
saw seven golden candlesticks;
13 And in the midst of the seven candlesticks [u]*one* like unto the Son of
man, [v]clothed with a garment down to

CHAPTER 1
1 [a]John 12.49 [b]ch. 22.16 **2** [c]1 John 1.1 **3** [d]Luke 11.28; ch. 22.7 **4** [e]Ex. 3.14; John 8.58; Col. 1.17; Jas. 1.17 [f]John 1.1 [g]Zech. 3.9 **5** [h]John 8.14 [i]Col. 1.18 [j]Eph. 1.20 [k]John 13.34 [l]Heb. 9.14 **6** [m]1 Tim. 6.16 **7** [n]Dan. 7.13 [o]Zech. 12.10 **8** [p]Isa. 41.4 **9** [q]Rom. 8.17 **10** [r]Acts 10.10 [s]Acts 20.7; 1 Cor. 16.2 **12** [t]Ex. 25.37; Zech. 4.2 **13** [u]Dan. 7.13 [v]Dan. 10.5

the foot, and girt about the paps with a
golden girdle.
14 His head and [w]*his* hairs *were*
white like wool, as white as snow; and
[x]his eyes *were* as a flame of fire;
15 [y]And his feet like unto fine brass,
as if they burned in a furnace; and [z]his
voice as the sound of many waters.
16 And he had in his right hand
seven stars: and [a]out of his mouth
went a sharp twoedged sword: [b]and
his countenance *was* as the sun shineth in his strength.
17 And [c]when I saw him, I fell at his
feet as dead. And [d]he laid his right
hand upon me, saying unto me, Fear
not; [e]I am the first and the last:
18 [f]*I am* he that liveth, and was
dead; and, behold, I am alive for evermore, Amen; and [g]have the keys of
hell and of death.
19 Write the things which thou hast
seen, and the things which are, and the
things which shall be hereafter;
20 The mystery of the seven stars
which thou sawest in my right hand,
and the seven golden candlesticks.
The seven stars are [h]the angels of the
seven churches: and the [i]seven candlesticks which thou sawest are the seven
churches.

2

Unto the angel of the church of
[a]Ēph'ĕ-sŭs write; These things saith
[b]he that holdeth the seven stars in his
right hand, who walketh in the midst of
the seven golden candlesticks;
2 [c]I know thy works, and thy labour, and thy patience, and how thou
canst not bear them which are evil:
and [d]thou hast tried them [e]which say
they are apostles, and are not, and hast
found them liars:
3 And hast borne, and hast patience,
and for my name's sake hast laboured,
and hast [f]not fainted.
4 Nevertheless I have *somewhat*
against thee, because thou hast left thy
first love.
5 Remember therefore from whence
thou art fallen, and repent, and do the
first works; [g]or else I will come unto
thee quickly, and will remove thy candlestick out of his place, except thou
repent.
6 But this thou hast, that thou hatest
the deeds of the Nĭc-o-lā'i-tanes, which
I also hate.
7 [h]He that hath an ear, let him hear
what the Spirit saith unto the churches;
To him that overcometh will I give [i]to
eat of [j]the tree of life, which is in the
midst of the paradise of God.
8 And unto the angel of the church
in Smy̆r'nȧ write; These things saith
[k]the first and the last, which was dead,
and is alive;
9 I know thy works, and tribulation,
and poverty, (but thou art [l]rich) and *I
know* the blasphemy of [m]them which
say they are Jews, and are not, but *are*
the synagogue of Sā'tan.
10 [n]Fear none of those things which
thou shalt suffer: behold, the devil
shall cast *some* of you into prison, that
ye may be tried; and ye shall have

14 [w]Dan. 7.9
[x]ch. 2.18
15 [y]Ezek. 1.7
[z]Ezek. 43.2
16 [a]Eph. 6.17; Heb. 4.12
[b]Acts 26.13
17 [c]Ezek. 1.28
[d]Dan. 8.18
[e]Isa. 41.4; Isa. 44.6
18 [f]Rom. 6.9
[g]Ps. 68.20; Isa. 22.22; Matt. 16.19; ch. 3.7; ch. 20.1
20 [h]Mal. 2.7
[i]Matt. 5.15; Phil. 2.15

CHAPTER 2
1 [a]Acts 19.1
[b]ch. 1.16
2 [c]Ps. 1.6; 1 Thess. 1.3; ch. 3.1-8-15
[d]1 John 4.1
[e]2 Cor. 11.13
3 [f]Gal. 6.9; Heb. 12.3-5
5 [g]Matt. 21.41; Mark 12.9; ch. 3.3
7 [h]Matt. 11.15; ch. 13.9
[i]ch. 22.2-14
[j]Gen. 2.9
8 [k]ch. 1.8
9 [l]Luke 12.21; Jas. 2.5
[m]Rom. 2.17
10 [n]Matt. 10.22
[o]Matt. 24.13; Mark 13.13
[p]Jas. 1.12
11 [q]ch. 13.9
[r]ch. 20.14
12 [s]ch. 1.16
[t]Josh. 5.13
13 [u]Lev. 17.7; Deut. 32.16-17
14 [v]Num. 25.1; 2 Pet. 2.15
[w]Acts 15.29
[x]1 Cor. 6.13
16 [y]Isa. 11.4
17 [z]ch. 3.12
18 [a]ch. 1.14
20 [b]1 Ki. 16.31
21 [c]Rom. 2.4
23 [d]1 Sam. 16.7; 1 Chr. 28.9; Ps. 7.9; Acts 1.24
[e]Ps. 62.12; Matt. 16.27; ch. 20.12
24 [f]2 Cor. 2.11; ch. 12.9
[g]Acts 15.28

tribulation ten days: [o]be thou faithful
unto death, and I will give thee [p]a
crown of life.
11 [q]He that hath an ear, let him hear
what the Spirit saith unto the churches;
He that overcometh shall not be hurt of
[r]the second death.
12 And to the angel of the church in
Pĕr'ga-mŏs write; These things saith
[s]he which hath [t]the sharp sword with
two edges;
13 I know thy works, and where
thou dwellest, *even* where Sā'tan's seat
is: and thou holdest fast my name, and
hast not denied my faith, even in those
days wherein Ăn'tĭ-pȧs *was* my faithful martyr, who was slain among you,
[u]where Sā'tan dwelleth.
14 But I have a few things against
thee, because thou hast there them
that hold the doctrine of [v]Bā'laam,
who taught Bā'lăc to cast a stumblingblock before the children of Ĭs'ra-el,
[w]to eat things sacrificed unto idols,
[x]and to commit fornication.
15 So hast thou also them that hold
the doctrine of the Nĭc-o-lā'i-tanes,
which thing I hate.
16 Repent; or else I will come unto
thee quickly, and [y]will fight against
them with the sword of my mouth.
17 He that hath an ear, let him hear
what the Spirit saith unto the churches;
To him that overcometh will I give to
eat of the hidden manna, and will give
him a white stone, and in the stone
[z]a new name written, which no man
knoweth saving he that receiveth *it*.
18 And unto the angel of the church
in Thy̆-a-tī'rȧ write; These things saith
the Son of God, [a]who hath his eyes
like unto a flame of fire, and his feet
are like fine brass;
19 I know thy works, and charity,
and service, and faith, and thy patience, and thy works; and the last *to
be* more than the first.
20 Notwithstanding I have a few
things against thee, because thou suf-
ferest that woman [b]Jĕz'e-bĕl, which
calleth herself a prophetess, to teach
and to seduce my servants to commit
fornication, and to eat things sacrificed unto idols.
21 And I gave her space [c]to repent
of her fornication; and she repented
not.
22 Behold, I will cast her into a bed,
and them that commit adultery with
her into great tribulation, except they
repent of their deeds.
23 And I will kill her children with
death; and all the churches shall know
that [d]I am he which searcheth the
reins and hearts: and [e]I will give unto
every one of you according to your
works.
24 But unto you I say, and unto the
rest in Thy̆-a-tī'rȧ, as many as have
not this doctrine, and which have not
[f]known the depths of Sā'tan, as they
speak; [g]I will put upon you none other
burden.
25 But that which ye have *already*
hold fast till I come.

26 And he that overcometh, and
keepeth [h]my works unto the end, [i]to
him will I give power over the nations:
27 [j]And he shall rule them with a
rod of iron; as the vessels of a potter
shall they be broken to shivers: even
as I received of my Father.
28 And I will give him [k]the morning
star.
29 He that hath an ear, let him hear
what the Spirit saith unto the churches.

3 And unto the angel of the church in
Sär′dis write; These things saith he
that hath the seven Spirits of God, and
the seven stars; I know thy works, that
thou hast a name, that thou livest,
[a]and art dead.
2 Be watchful, and strengthen the
things which remain, that are ready to
die: for I have not found thy works perfect before God.
3 Remember therefore how thou hast
received and heard, and hold fast, and
repent. [b]If therefore thou shalt not
watch, I will come on thee as a thief, and
thou shalt not know what hour I will
come upon thee.
4 Thou hast [c]a few names even in
Sär′dis which have not [d]defiled their
garments; and they shall walk with me
[e]in white: for they are worthy.
5 He that overcometh, the same
shall be clothed in white raiment; and I
will not [f]blot out his name out of the
[g]book of life, but [h]I will confess his
name before my Father, and before his
angels.
6 He that hath an ear, let him hear
what the Spirit saith unto the churches.
7 And to the angel of the church
in Phĭl-a-dĕl′phĭ-ȧ write; These things
saith [i]he that is holy, [j]he that is true,
he that hath [k]the key of Dā′vid, [l]he
that openeth, and no man shutteth;
and [m]shutteth, and no man openeth;
8 I know thy works: behold, I have
set before thee [n]an open door, and no
man can shut it: for thou hast a little
strength, and hast kept my word, and
hast not denied my name.
9 Behold, I will make them of the
synagogue of Sā′tan, which say they
are Jews, and are not, but do lie; behold, [o]I will make them to come and
worship before thy feet, and to know
that I have loved thee.
10 Because thou hast kept the word
of my patience, [p]I also will keep thee
from the hour of temptation, which
shall come upon all the world, to try
them that dwell upon the earth.
11 Behold, I come quickly: hold that
fast which thou hast, that no man take
thy crown.
12 Him that overcometh will I make
[q]a pillar in the temple of my God, and
he shall go no more out: and [r]I will
write upon him the name of my God,
and the name of the city of my God,
which is [s]new Je-ru̦′sa-lĕm, which cometh down out of heaven from my God:
[t]and *I will write upon him* my new
name.
13 He that hath an ear, let him hear
what the Spirit saith unto the churches.

26 [h]John 6.29
[i]Matt. 19.28;
Luke 22.29;
1 Cor. 6.3;
ch. 3.21
27 [j]Ps. 2.8-9;
Dan. 7.22;
ch. 19.15
28 [k]2 Pet.
1.19;
ch. 22.16

CHAPTER 3
1 [a]Luke
15.24-32; Eph.
2.1;
Col. 2.13
3 [b]Luke
12.39
4 [c]Acts 1.15
[d]Jude 23
[e]ch. 7.9-13
5 [f]Ex. 32.32;
Ps. 69.28
[g]Phil. 4.3;
ch. 21.27
[h]Matt. 10.32
7 [i]Acts 3.14
[j]1 John 5.20
[k]Isa. 22.22;
Luke 1.32;
ch. 1.18
[l]Matt. 16.19
[m]Job 12.14
8 [n]2 Cor. 2.12
9 [o]Isa. 49.23
10 [p]2 Pet. 2.9
12 [q]Gal. 2.9
[r]ch. 14.1
[s]Gal. 4.26;
ch. 21.2-10
[t]Isa. 65.15;
ch. 22.4
14 [1]Or, in La-
odicea
[u]2 Cor. 1.20
[v]Isa. 55.4;
ch. 22.6
[w]Prov. 8.22;
Col. 1.15
17 [x]Prov.
13.7;
Luke 1.53
18 [y]Isa. 55.1;
Matt. 13.44
[z]2 Cor. 5.3
19 [a]Deut. 8.5;
Heb. 12.5-6
20 [b]Song 5.2
[c]Luke 12.37
[d]John 14.23
21 [e]Matt.
19.28;
ch. 2.26

CHAPTER 4
2 [a]ch. 1.10
[b]Isa. 6.1;
Dan. 7.9
3 [c]Ezek. 1.28
5 [d]Ex. 37.23;
Zech. 4.2
6 [e]Ex. 38.8
[f]Ezek. 1.5
7 [g]Num. 2.2
8 [h]Isa. 6.2
[1]they have no
rest

14 And unto the angel of the church
[1]of the La-ŏd-ĭ-çē′ans write; These
things saith the [u]Amen, the faithful
and true [v]witness, the [w]beginning of
the creation of God;
15 I know thy works, that thou art
neither cold nor hot: I would thou wert
cold or hot.
16 So then because thou art luke-
warm, and neither cold nor hot, I will
spue thee out of my mouth.
17 Because thou sayest, [x]I am rich,
and increased with goods, and have
need of nothing; and knowest not that
thou art wretched, and miserable, and
poor, and blind, and naked:
18 I counsel thee [y]to buy of me gold
tried in the fire, that thou mayest be
rich; and [z]white raiment, that thou
mayest be clothed, and *that* the shame
of thy nakedness do not appear; and
anoint thine eyes with eyesalve, that
thou mayest see.
19 [a]As many as I love, I rebuke
and chasten: be zealous therefore, and
repent.
20 Behold, [b]I stand at the door, and
knock: [c]if any man hear my voice, and
open the door, [d]I will come in to him,
and will sup with him, and he with me.
21 To him that overcometh [e]will I
grant to sit with me in my throne, even
as I also overcame, and am set down
with my Father in his throne.
22 He that hath an ear, let him hear
what the Spirit saith unto the churches.

4 After this I looked, and, behold, a
door *was* opened in heaven: and the
first voice which I heard *was* as it were
of a trumpet talking with me; which
said, Come up hither, and I will shew
thee things which must be hereafter.
2 And immediately I [a]was in the
spirit: and, behold, [b]a throne was set
in heaven, and *one* sat on the throne.
3 And he that sat was to look upon
like a jasper and a sardine stone: [c]and
there was a rainbow round about the
throne, in sight like unto an emerald.
4 And round about the throne *were*
four and twenty seats: and upon the
seats I saw four and twenty elders sitting, clothed in white raiment; and
they had on their heads crowns of
gold.
5 And out of the throne proceeded
lightnings and thunderings and voices:
[d]and *there were* seven lamps of fire
burning before the throne, which are
the seven Spirits of God.
6 And before the throne *there was*
[e]a sea of glass like unto crystal: [f]and
in the midst of the throne, and round
about the throne, *were* four beasts full
of eyes before and behind.
7 [g]And the first beast *was* like a
lion, and the second beast like a calf,
and the third beast had a face as a
man, and the fourth beast *was* like a
flying eagle.
8 And the four beasts had each of
them [h]six wings about *him;* and *they*
were full of eyes within: and [1]they rest
not day and night, saying, Holy, holy,

holy, Lord God Almighty, which was, and is, and is to come.

9 And when those beasts give glory and honour and thanks to him that sat on the throne, who liveth for ever and ever,

10 The four and twenty elders fall down before him that sat on the throne, and worship him that liveth for ever and ever, and cast their crowns before the throne, saying,

11 Thou art worthy, O Lord, to receive glory and honour and power: for thou hast created all things, and for thy pleasure they are and were created.

5 And I saw in the right hand of him that sat on the throne [a]a book written within and on the backside, [b]sealed with seven seals.

2 And I saw a strong angel proclaiming with a loud voice, Who is worthy to open the book, and to loose the seals thereof?

3 And [c]no man in heaven, nor in earth, neither under the earth, was able to open the book, neither to look thereon.

4 And I wept much, because no man was found worthy to open and to read the book, neither to look thereon.

5 And one of the elders saith unto me, Weep not: behold, [d]the Lion of the tribe of Jū′dȧ, [e]the Root of Dā′vid, hath [f]prevailed to open the book, and to loose the seven seals thereof.

6 And I beheld, and, lo, in the midst of the throne, and of the four beasts, and in the midst of the elders, stood [g]a Lamb as it had been slain, having seven horns and [h]seven eyes, which are [i]the seven Spirits of God sent forth into all the earth.

7 And he came and took the book out of the right hand of him that sat upon the throne.

8 And when he had taken the book, the four beasts and four *and* twenty elders fell down before the Lamb, having every one of them [j]harps, and golden vials full of [1]odours, [k]which are the prayers of saints.

9 And [l]they sung a new song, saying, [m]Thou art worthy to take the book, and to open the seals thereof: for thou wast slain, and [n]hast redeemed us to God by thy blood [o]out of every kindred, and tongue, and people, and nation;

10 [p]And hast made us unto our God kings and priests: and we shall reign on the earth.

11 And I beheld, and I heard the voice of many angels round about the throne and the beasts and the elders: and the number of them was [q]ten thousand times ten thousand, and thousands of thousands;

12 Saying with a loud voice, Worthy is the Lamb that was slain to receive power, and riches, and wisdom, and strength, and honour, and glory, and blessing.

13 And [r]every creature which is in heaven, and on the earth, and under the earth, and such as are in the sea, and all that are in them, heard I saying, [s]Blessing, and honour, and glory, and power, *be* unto him that sitteth upon the throne, [t]and unto the Lamb for ever and ever.

14 And the four beasts said, Amen. And the four *and* twenty elders fell down and worshipped him that liveth for ever and ever.

6 And I saw when the Lamb opened one of the seals, and I heard, as it were the noise of thunder, one of the four beasts saying, Come and see.

2 And I saw, and behold [a]a white horse: [b]and he that sat on him had a bow; [c]and a crown was given unto him: and he went forth conquering, and to conquer.

3 And when he had opened the second seal, I heard the second beast say, Come and see.

4 [d]And there went out another horse *that was* red: and *power* was given to him that sat thereon to take peace from the earth, and that they should kill one another: and there was given unto him a great sword.

5 And when he had opened the third seal, I heard the third beast say, Come and see. And I beheld, and lo [e]a black horse; and he that sat on him had a pair of balances in his hand.

6 And I heard a voice in the midst of the four beasts say, [1]A measure of wheat for a penny, and three measures of barley for a penny; and [f]*see* thou hurt not the oil and the wine.

7 And when he had opened the fourth seal, I heard the voice of the fourth beast say, Come and see.

8 And I looked, and behold a pale horse: and his name that sat on him was Death, and Hell followed with him. And power was given [2]unto them over the fourth part of the earth, [g]to kill with sword, and with hunger, and with death, and [h]with the beasts of the earth.

9 And when he had opened the fifth seal, I saw under [i]the altar [j]the souls of them that were slain for the word of God, and for [k]the testimony which they held:

10 And they cried with a loud voice, saying, [l]How long, O Lord, holy and true, dost thou not judge and avenge our blood on them that dwell on the earth?

11 And white robes were given unto every one of them; and it was said unto them, [m]that they should rest yet for a little season, until their fellowservants also and their brethren, that should be killed as they *were*, should be fulfilled.

12 And I beheld when he had opened the sixth seal, [n]and, lo, there was a great earthquake; and the [o]sun became black as sackcloth of hair, and the moon became as blood;

13 And the stars of heaven fell unto the earth, even as a fig tree casteth her [3]untimely figs, when she is shaken of a mighty wind.

14 [p]And the heaven departed as a scroll when it is rolled together;

CHAPTER 5
1 [a]Ezek. 2.9
[b]Isa. 29.11; Dan. 12.4; ch. 6.1
3 [c]John 1.18
5 [d]Gen. 49.9-10; Heb. 7.14
[e]Isa. 11.1-10; Rom. 5.12; ch. 22.16
[f]Heb. 2.10
6 [g]Isa. 53.7; John 1.29; 1 Pet. 1.19; ch. 6.16
[h]Zech. 3.9
[i]ch. 4.5
8 [j]ch. 14.2
[1]Or, incense
[k]Ps. 141.2; ch. 8.3-4
9 [l]Ps. 33.3; Isa. 42.10; ch. 14.3
[m]ch. 4.11
[n]Matt. 26.28; Acts 20.28; Eph. 1.7; Heb. 9.12; 2 Pet. 2.1
[o]Dan. 4.1
10 [p]Ex. 19.6
11 [q]Ps. 68.17; Dan. 7.10; Heb. 12.22
13 [r]Phil. 2.10
[s]Eph. 3.21; 1 Tim. 1.17
[t]John 5.23

CHAPTER 6
2 [a]Zech. 6.3; ch. 19.11
[b]Ps. 45.4-5; LXX
[c]ch. 14.14
4 [d]Zech. 6.6
5 [e]Zech. 6.2
6 [1]The word *choenix* signifieth a measure containing one wine quart, and the twelfth part of a quart
[f]ch. 9.4
8 [2]Or, to him
[g]Jer. 15.2-3; Ezek. 5.17; Amos 4.10-12
[h]Lev. 26.22
9 [i]ch. 8.3
[j]ch. 20.4
[k]2 Tim. 1.8
10 [l]Gen. 4.10; Zech. 1.12
11 [m]Heb. 11.40
12 [n]ch. 16.18
[o]Joel 2.10; Matt. 24.29; Acts 2.20
13 [3]Or, green figs
14 [p]Isa. 34.4; Heb. 1.12

and [q]every mountain and island were
moved out of their places.
15 And the kings of the earth, and
the great men, and the rich men, and
the chief captains, and the mighty men,
and every bondman, and every free
man, [r]hid themselves in the dens and
in the rocks of the mountains;
16 And said to the mountains and
rocks, Fall on us, and hide us from the
face of him that sitteth on the throne,
and from the wrath of the Lamb:
17 [s]For the great day of his wrath is
come; [t]and who shall be able to stand?
7 And after these things I saw four
[a]angels standing on the four corners of the earth, [b]holding the four
winds of the earth, [c]that the wind
should not blow on the earth, nor on
the sea, nor on any tree.
2 And I saw another angel ascending from the east, having the seal of the
living God: and he cried with a loud
voice to the four angels, to whom it
was given to hurt the earth and the sea,
3 Saying, [d]Hurt not the earth, neither the sea, nor the trees, till we have
[e]sealed the servants of our God [f]in
their foreheads.
4 [g]And I heard the number of them
which were sealed: *and there were*
sealed [h]an hundred *and* forty *and* four
thousand of all the tribes of the children of Is'ra-el.
5 Of the tribe of Jū'dȧ *were* sealed
twelve thousand. Of the tribe of Reu̯'-
ben *were* sealed twelve thousand. Of
the tribe of Găd *were* sealed twelve
thousand.
6 Of the tribe of Ā'sẽr *were* sealed
twelve thousand. Of the tribe of Nĕp'-
tha-lĭm *were* sealed twelve thousand.
Of the tribe of Ma-năs'sēs *were* sealed
twelve thousand.
7 Of the tribe of Sĭm'e-on *were* sealed
twelve thousand. Of the tribe of Lē'vī
were sealed twelve thousand. Of the
tribe of Is'sa-char *were* sealed twelve
thousand.
8 Of the tribe of Zăb'u-lon *were*
sealed twelve thousand. Of the tribe of
Jō'seph *were* sealed twelve thousand.
Of the tribe of Bĕn'ja-min *were* sealed
twelve thousand.
9 After this I beheld, and, lo, [i]a great
multitude, which no man could number, [j]of all nations, and kindreds, and
people, and tongues, stood before the
throne, and before the Lamb, [k]clothed
with white robes, and palms in their
hands;
10 And cried with a loud voice, saying, [l]Salvation to our God [m]which
sitteth upon the throne, and unto the
Lamb.
11 [n]And all the angels stood round
about the throne, and *about* the elders
and the four beasts, and fell before the
throne on their faces, and worshipped
God,
12 [o]Saying, Amen: Blessing, and
glory, and wisdom, and thanksgiving,
and honour, and power, and might, *be*
unto our God for ever and ever. Amen.
13 And one of the elders answered,
saying unto me, What are these which
are arrayed in white robes? and whence
came they?
14 And I said unto him, Sir, thou
knowest. And he said to me, [p]These
are they which came out of great tribulation, and have [q]washed their robes,
and made them white in the blood of
the Lamb.
15 Therefore are they before the
throne of God, and serve him day and
night in his temple: and he that sitteth
on the throne shall [r]dwell among them.
16 [s]They shall hunger no more, neither thirst any more; [t]neither shall the
sun light on them, nor any heat.
17 For the Lamb which is in the
midst of the throne [u]shall feed them,
and shall lead them unto living fountains of waters: [v]and God shall wipe
away all tears from their eyes.
8 And when he had opened the seventh seal, there was silence in
heaven about the space of half an hour.
2 [a]And I saw the seven angels which
stood before God; [b]and to them were
given seven trumpets.
3 And another [c]angel came and
stood at the altar, having a golden censer; and there was given unto him
much [d]incense, that he should [1]offer *it*
with [e]the prayers of all saints upon
[f]the golden altar which was before the
throne.
4 And [g]the smoke of the incense,
which came with the prayers of the
saints, ascended up before God out of
the angel's hand.
5 And the angel took the censer, and
filled it with fire of the altar, and cast *it*
[2]into the earth: and [h]there were voices,
and thunderings, and lightnings, [i]and
an earthquake.
6 And the seven angels which had
the seven trumpets prepared themselves to sound.
7 The first angel sounded, [j]and there
followed hail and fire mingled with
blood, and they were cast [k]upon the
earth: and the third part [l]of trees was
burnt up, and all green grass was burnt
up.
8 And the second angel sounded,
and as it were a great mountain burning with fire was cast into the sea: and
the third part of the sea [m]became
blood;
9 And the third part of the creatures
which were in the sea, and had life,
died; and the third part of the ships
were destroyed.
10 And the third angel sounded, and
there fell a great star from heaven,
burning as it were a lamp, and it fell
upon the third part of the rivers, and
upon the fountains of waters;
11 And the name of the star is called
Wormwood: [n]and the third part of the
waters became wormwood; and many
men died of the waters, because they
were made bitter.
12 [o]And the fourth angel sounded,
and the third part of the sun was smitten, and the third part of the moon, and

[q]Jer. 3.23
15 [r]Isa. 2.19
17 [s]Isa. 13.6; Zeph. 1.14
[t]Ps. 76.7

CHAPTER 7
1 [a]Ps. 34.7; Dan. 6.22; Heb. 1.14
[b]Dan. 7.2
[c]ch. 9.4
3 [d]ch. 6.6; ch. 9.4
[e]Eph. 4.30; 2 Tim. 2.19; ch. 14.1
[f]ch. 22.4
4 [g]ch. 9.16
[h]Isa. 4.2-3; ch. 14.1
9 [i]Gen. 12.3; Gen. 22.17; Ps. 22.27; Isa. 2.2-3; Zech. 2.11; Rom. 11.25
[j]ch. 5.9
[k]ch. 3.5
10 [l]Ps. 3.8; Isa. 43.11; Jer. 3.23; Hos. 13.4; Zech. 9.9; Luke 3.6
[m]ch. 5.13
11 [n]ch. 4.6
12 [o]ch. 5.13
14 [p]Acts 14.22
[q]Isa. 1.18; ch. 1.5
15 [r]Isa. 4.5-6
16 [s]Isa. 49.10
[t]Ps. 121.6
17 [u]Ps. 23.1; John 10.11
[v]Isa. 25.8

CHAPTER 8
2 [a]Matt. 18.10; ch. 15.1
[b]2 Chr. 29.25-28
3 [c]Acts 7.30
[d]Eph. 5.2
[1]Or, add it to the prayers
[e]Luke 1.10; ch. 5.8
[f]Ex. 30.1
4 [g]Ps. 141.2
5 [2]Or, upon
[h]ch. 16.18
[i]2 Sam. 22.8
7 [j]Ezek. 38.22
[k]ch. 16.2
[l]Isa. 2.13
8 [m]Ezek. 14.19
11 [n]Ex. 15.23; Lam. 3.15
12 [o]Isa. 13.10; Amos 8.9

the third part of the stars; so as the third part of them was darkened, and the day shone not for a third part of it, and the night likewise.

13 And I beheld, [p]and heard an angel flying through the midst of heaven, saying with a loud voice, [q]Woe, woe, woe, to the inhabiters of the earth by reason of the other voices of the trumpet of the three angels, which are yet to sound!

9 And the fifth angel sounded, [a]and I saw a star fall from heaven unto the earth: and to him was given the key of [b]the bottomless pit.

2 And he opened the bottomless pit; [c]and there arose a smoke out of the pit, as the smoke of a great furnace; and the sun and the air were darkened by reason of the smoke of the pit.

3 And there came out of the smoke [d]locusts upon the earth: and unto them was given power, as the scorpions of the earth have power.

4 And it was commanded them [e]that they should not hurt [f]the grass of the earth, neither any green thing, neither any tree; but only those men which have not [g]the seal of God in their foreheads.

5 And to them it was given that they should not kill them, [h]but that they should be tormented five months: and their torment *was* as the torment of a scorpion, when he striketh a man.

6 And in those days [i]shall men seek death, and shall not find it; and shall desire to die, and death shall flee from them.

7 And [j]the shapes of the locusts *were* like unto horses prepared unto battle; [k]and on their heads *were* as it were crowns like gold, [l]and their faces *were* as the faces of men.

8 And they had hair as the hair of women, and [m]their teeth were as *the teeth* of lions.

9 And they had breastplates, as it were breastplates of iron; and the sound of their wings *was* as the sound of chariots of many horses running to battle.

10 And they had tails like unto scorpions, and there were stings in their tails: and their power *was* to hurt men five months.

11 [n]And they had a king over them, *which is* the angel of the bottomless pit, whose name in the Hē'brew tongue *is* A-băd'don, but in the Greek tongue hath *his* name [1]A-pŏll'yon.

12 [o]One woe is past; *and,* behold, there come two woes more hereafter.

13 And the sixth angel sounded, and I heard a voice from the four horns of the golden altar which is before God,

14 Saying to the sixth angel which had the trumpet, Loose the four angels which are bound [p]in the great river Eū-phrā'tēs.

15 And the four angels were loosed, which were prepared [2]for an hour, and a day, and a month, and a year, for to slay the third part of men.

16 And [q]the number of the army [r]of the horsemen *were* two hundred thousand thousand: [s]and I heard the number of them.

17 And thus I saw the horses in the vision, and them that sat on them, having breastplates of fire, and of jacinth, and brimstone: [t]and the heads of the horses *were* as the heads of lions; and out of their mouths issued fire and smoke and brimstone.

18 By these three was the third part of men killed, by the fire, and by the smoke, and by the brimstone, which issued out of their mouths.

19 For their power is in their mouth, and in their tails: [u]for their tails *were* like unto serpents, and had heads, and with them they do hurt.

20 And the rest of the men which were not killed by these plagues [v]yet repented not of the works of their hands, that they should not worship [w]devils, [x]and idols of gold, and silver, and brass, and stone, and of wood: which neither can see, nor hear, nor walk:

21 Neither repented they of their murders, nor of their sorceries, nor of their fornication, nor of their thefts.

10 And I saw another mighty angel come down from heaven, clothed with a cloud: [a]and a rainbow *was* upon his head, and [b]his face *was* as it were the sun, and [c]his feet as pillars of fire:

2 And he had in his hand a little book open: [d]and he set his right foot upon the sea, and *his* left *foot* on the earth,

3 And cried with a loud voice, as *when* a lion roareth: and when he had cried, [e]seven thunders uttered their voices.

4 And when the seven thunders had uttered their voices, I was about to write: and I heard a voice from heaven saying unto me, [f]Seal up those things which the seven thunders uttered, and write them not.

5 And the angel which I saw stand upon the sea and upon the earth lifted up his hand to heaven,

6 And sware by him that [g]liveth for ever and ever, who created heaven, and the things that therein are, and the earth, and the things that therein are, and the sea, and the things which are therein, [h]that there should be time no longer:

7 But [i]in the days of the voice of the seventh angel, when he shall begin to sound, the mystery of God should be finished, as he hath declared to his servants the prophets.

8 And the voice which I heard from heaven spake unto me again, and said, Go *and* take the little book which is open in the hand of the angel which standeth upon the sea and upon the earth.

9 And I went unto the angel, and said unto him, Give me the little book. And he said unto me, [j]Take *it,* and eat it up; and it shall make thy belly bitter,

13 [p]ch. 14.6
[q]ch. 9.12

CHAPTER 9
1 [a]Isa. 14.12; Luke 10.18; ch. 8.10
[b]Luke 8.31; ch. 17.8
2 [c]Joel 2.2-10
3 [d]Ex. 10.4
4 [e]ch. 6.6
[f]ch. 8.7
[g]Ex. 12.23; Ezek. 9.4; Eph. 4.30; ch. 7.3
5 [h]ch. 11.7
6 [i]Job 3.21; Isa. 2.19; Jer. 8.3; Hos. 10.8; Jon. 4.8; ch. 6.16
7 [j]Joel 2.4
[k]Nah. 3.17
[l]Dan. 7.8
8 [m]Joel 1.6
11 [n]John 12.31; Eph. 2.2; 2 Thess. 2.3-10
[1]That is to say, A destroyer
12 [o]ch. 8.13
14 [p]ch. 16.12
15 [2]Or, at
16 [q]Ps. 68.17; Dan. 7.10
[r]Ezek. 38.4
[s]ch. 7.4
17 [t]1 Chr. 12.8; Isa. 5.28
19 [u]Isa. 9.15
20 [v]Deut. 31.29; 2 Chr. 28.22; Jer. 5.3; Matt. 21.32; ch. 2.21
[w]Lev. 17.7; Deut. 32.17; Ps. 106.37; 1 Cor. 10.20
[x]Ps. 115.4; Dan. 5.23

CHAPTER 10
1 [a]Ezek. 1.28
[b]Matt. 17.2; ch. 1.16
[c]ch. 1.15
2 [d]Matt. 28.18
3 [e]ch. 8.5
4 [f]Dan. 8.26
6 [g]Jer. 10.10; ch. 4.9
[h]Dan. 12.7; ch. 16.17
7 [i]ch. 11.15
9 [j]Jer. 15.16; Ezek. 2.8

but it shall be in thy mouth sweet as
honey.
10 And I took the little book out of
the angel's hand, and ate it up; and it
was in my mouth sweet as honey: and
as soon as I had eaten it, my belly was
bitter.
11 And he said unto me, Thou must
prophesy again before many peoples,
and nations, and tongues, and kings.

11 And there was given me [a]a reed
like unto a rod: and the angel
stood, saying, [b]Rise, and measure the
temple of God, and the altar, and them
that worship therein.
2 But [c]the court which is without
the temple [1]leave out, and measure it
not; [d]for it is given unto the Gĕn'tīles:
and the holy city shall they [e]tread under foot [f]forty *and* two months.
3 And [2]I will give *power* unto my two
[g]witnesses, [h]and they shall prophesy
[i]a thousand two hundred *and* threescore days, clothed in sackcloth.
4 These are the [j]two olive trees, and
the two candlesticks standing before
the God of the earth.
5 And if any man will hurt them,
[k]fire proceedeth out of their mouth,
and devoureth their enemies: [l]and if
any man will hurt them, he must in this
manner be killed.
6 These [m]have power to shut heaven,
that it rain not in the days of their prophecy: and [n]have power over waters to
turn them to blood, and to smite the
earth with all plagues, as often as they
will.
7 And when they [o]shall have finished their testimony, [p]the beast that
ascendeth [q]out of the bottomless pit
shall make war against them, and shall
overcome them, and kill them.
8 And their dead bodies *shall lie* in
the street of [r]the great city, which spiritually is called Sŏd'om and Ē'gy̆pt,
[s]where also our Lord was crucified.
9 [t]And they of the people and kindreds and tongues and nations shall
see their dead bodies three days and
an half, [u]and shall not suffer their
dead bodies to be put in graves.
10 [v]And they that dwell upon the
earth shall rejoice over them, and make
merry, and shall send gifts one to another; because these two prophets tormented them that dwelt on the earth.
11 And after three days and an half
[w]the Spirit of life from God entered
into them, and they stood upon their
feet; and great fear fell upon them
which saw them.
12 And they heard a great voice
from heaven saying unto them, Come
up hither. [x]And they ascended up to
heaven [y]in a cloud; and their enemies
beheld them.
13 And the same hour was there a
great earthquake, [z]and the tenth part
of the city fell, and in the earthquake
were slain [3]of men seven thousand:
and the remnant were affrighted, and
gave glory to the God of heaven.
14 The second woe is past; *and,* behold, the third woe cometh quickly.

CHAPTER 11
1 [a]Ezek. 40.3; Zech. 2.1
[b]Num. 23.18
2 [c]Ezek. 40.17
[1]cast out
[d]2 Ki. 25.9; Luke 21.24
[e]Dan. 8.10
[f]ch. 13.5
3 [2]Or, I will give unto my two witnesses that they may prophesy
[g]ch. 6.9
[h]ch. 19.10
[i]ch. 12.6
4 [j]Ps. 52.8; Rom. 11.17
5 [k]2 Ki. 1.10; Hos. 6.5
[l]Num. 16.29
6 [m]1 Ki. 17.1; Jas. 5.16
[n]Ex. 7.19
7 [o]Luke 13.32
[p]ch. 13.1
[q]Dan. 7.21; Zech. 14.2
8 [r]ch. 14.8
[s]Heb. 13.12; ch. 18.24
9 [t]ch. 17.15
[u]Ps. 79.2-3
10 [v]ch. 12.12
11 [w]Ezek. 37.5-9-10-14
12 [x]Isa. 14.13
[y]Isa. 60.8
13 [z]ch. 14.7
[3]names of men
15 [a]Isa. 27.13
[b]Ps. 145.13
18 [c]Dan. 7.9;
[4]Or, corrupt
19 [d]Num. 4.5

CHAPTER 12
1 [1]Or, sign
[a]Isa. 60.19
2 [b]Isa. 53.11
3 [2]Or, sign
[c]ch. 17.3
[d]ch. 17.9
[e]ch. 13.1
4 [f]ch. 9.10
[g]ch. 17.18
[h]Dan. 8.10
[i]Ex. 1.16
5 [j]Ps. 2.9
6 [k]ch. 11.3
7 [l]Dan. 10.13
[m]ch. 20.2
9 [n]Luke 10.18
[o]Gen. 3.1;
[p]John 12.31
10 [q]ch. 11.15
[r]Job 1.9

15 And the seventh angel sounded;
[a]and there were great voices in heaven,
saying, The kingdoms of this world are
become *the kingdoms* of our Lord, and
of his Chrīst; [b]and he shall reign for
ever and ever.
16 And the four and twenty elders,
which sat before God on their seats,
fell upon their faces, and worshipped
God,
17 Saying, We give thee thanks, O
Lord God Almighty, which art, and
wast, and art to come; because thou
hast taken to thee thy great power, and
hast reigned.
18 And the nations were angry, and
thy wrath is come, [c]and the time of the
dead, that they should be judged, and
that thou shouldest give reward unto
thy servants the prophets, and to the
saints, and them that fear thy name,
small and great; and shouldest destroy
them which [4]destroy the earth.
19 And the temple of God was opened
in heaven, and there was seen in his temple [d]the ark of his testament; and there
were lightnings, and voices, and thunderings, and an earthquake, and great
hail.

12 And there appeared a great [1]won-
der in heaven; a [a]woman clothed
with the sun, and the moon under her
feet, and upon her head a crown of
twelve stars:
2 And she being with child cried,
[b]travailing in birth, and pained to be
delivered.
3 And there appeared another [2]won-
der in heaven; and behold a [c]great red
dragon, [d]having seven heads and ten
horns, [e]and seven crowns upon his
heads.
4 And [f]his tail drew the third part
[g]of the stars of heaven, [h]and did cast
them to the earth: and the dragon
stood before the woman which was
ready to be delivered, [i]for to devour
her child as soon as it was born.
5 And she brought forth a man child,
[j]who was to rule all nations with a rod
of iron: and her child was caught up
unto God, and *to* his throne.
6 And the woman fled into the wilderness, where she hath a place prepared of God, that they should feed her
there [k]a thousand two hundred *and*
threescore days.
7 And there was war in heaven: [l]Mī'-
chaĕl and his angels fought [m]against
the dragon; and the dragon fought and
his angels,
8 And prevailed not; neither was
their place found any more in heaven.
9 And [n]the great dragon was cast
out, [o]that old serpent, called the Dĕv'il,
and Sā'tan, which deceiveth the whole
world: [p]he was cast out into the earth,
and his angels were cast out with him.
10 And I heard a loud voice saying
in heaven, [q]Now is come salvation,
and strength, and the kingdom of our
God, and the power of his Chrīst: for
the accuser of our brethren is cast
down, [r]which accused them before
our God day and night.

11 And [s]they overcame him by the blood of the Lamb, and by the word of their testimony; [t]and they loved not their lives unto the death.

12 Therefore rejoice, *ye* heavens, and ye that dwell in them. [u]Woe to the inhabiters of the earth and of the sea! for the devil is come down unto you, having great wrath, [v]because he knoweth that he hath but a short time.

13 And when the dragon saw that he was cast unto the earth, he persecuted the woman which brought forth the man *child*.

14 [w]And to the woman were given two wings of a great eagle, that she might fly [x]into the wilderness, into her place, where she is nourished [y]for a time, and times, and half a time, from the face of the serpent.

15 And the serpent [z]cast out of his mouth water as a flood after the woman, that he might cause her to be carried away of the flood.

16 And the earth helped the woman, and the earth opened her mouth, and swallowed up the flood which the dragon cast out of his mouth.

17 And the dragon was wroth with the woman, [a]and went to make war with the remnant of her seed, which keep the commandments of God, and have [b]the testimony of Jē'sus Chrīst.

13 And I stood upon the sand of the sea, and saw [a]a beast rise up out of the sea, having seven heads and ten horns, and upon his horns ten crowns, and upon his heads the [1]name of blasphemy.

2 [b]And the beast which I saw was like unto a leopard, and his feet were as *the feet* of a bear, and his mouth as the mouth of a lion: and [c]the dragon gave him his power, and his seat, and great authority.

3 And I saw one of his heads as it were [2]wounded to death; and his deadly wound was healed: and [d]all the world wondered after the beast.

4 And they worshipped the dragon which gave power unto the beast: and they worshipped the beast, saying, [e]Who *is* like unto the beast? who is able to make war with him?

5 And there was given unto him [f]a mouth speaking great things and blasphemies; and power was given unto him [3]to continue [g]forty *and* two months.

6 And he opened his mouth in blasphemy against God, to blaspheme his name, [h]and his tabernacle, and them that dwell in heaven.

7 And it was given unto him [i]to make war with the saints, and to overcome them: and power was given him over all kindreds, and tongues, and nations.

8 And all that dwell upon the earth shall worship him, [j]whose names are not written in the book of life of the Lamb slain [k]from the foundation of the world.

9 If any man have an ear, let him hear.

11 [s]Rom. 8.37
[t]Luke 14.26
12 [u]ch. 8.13
[v]ch. 10.6
14 [w]Ex. 19.4
[x]ch. 17.3
[y]Dan. 7.25
15 [z]Isa. 59.19
17 [a]Gen. 3.15
[b]ch. 1.2-9

CHAPTER 13

1 [a]Dan. 7.2-7
[1]Or, names
2 [b]Dan. 7.6
[c]ch. 12.9
[2]slain
[d]2 Thess. 2.3
4 [e]ch. 18.18
5 [f]Dan. 7.8-11-25
[3]Or, to make war
[g]ch. 11.2
6 [h]John 1.14; Col. 2.9
7 [i]Dan. 7.21; ch. 11.7
8 [j]Ex. 32.32; Dan. 12.1; Luke 10.20; Phil. 4.3; ch. 3.5; ch. 21.27
[k]Eph. 1.4; 1 Pet. 1.19-20; ch. 5.6-13
10 [l]Isa. 14.2
[m]Gen. 9.6; Matt. 26.52
[n]Lam. 3.26; Heb. 12.3-4; ch. 14.12
13 [o]Deut. 13.1; Matt. 24.24; 2 Thess. 2.9; ch. 16.14
[p]1 Ki. 18.38; 2 Ki. 1.10
14 [q]2 Ki. 20.7
15 [4]breath
[r]ch. 20.4
16 [5]to give them
17 [s]ch. 14.11
[t]ch. 15.2
18 [u]Ps. 107.43; Hos. 14.9; ch. 21.17

CHAPTER 14

1 [a]Ex. 12.3; Isa. 53.7; 1 Pet. 1.19; ch. 5.6
[b]ch. 7.3
4 [c]2 Cor. 11.2
[1]were bought
[d]Jas. 1.18
5 [e]Ps. 32.2; Zeph. 3.13
[f]Eph. 5.27
6 [g]Matt. 28.19; Eph. 3.9; Tit. 1.2

10 [l]He that leadeth into captivity shall go into captivity: [m]he that killeth with the sword must be killed with the sword. [n]Here is the patience and the faith of the saints.

11 And I beheld another beast coming up out of the earth; and he had two horns like a lamb, and he spake as a dragon.

12 And he exerciseth all the power of the first beast before him, and causeth the earth and them which dwell therein to worship the first beast, whose deadly wound was healed.

13 And [o]he doeth great wonders, [p]so that he maketh fire come down from heaven on the earth in the sight of men,

14 And deceiveth them that dwell on the earth, by *the means of* those miracles which he had power to do in the sight of the beast; saying to them that dwell on the earth, that they should make an image to the beast, which had the wound by a sword, and [q]did live.

15 And he had power to give [4]life unto the image of the beast, that the image of the beast should both speak, [r]and cause that as many as would not worship the image of the beast should be killed.

16 And he causeth all, both small and great, rich and poor, free and bond, [5]to receive a mark in their right hand, or in their foreheads:

17 And that no man might buy or sell, save he that had the mark, or [s]the name of the beast, [t]or the number of his name.

18 [u]Here is wisdom. Let him that hath understanding count the number of the beast: for it is the number of a man; and his number *is* Six hundred threescore *and* six.

14 And I looked, and, lo, a [a]Lamb stood on the mount Sī'ŏn, and with him an hundred forty *and* four thousand, [b]having his Father's name written in their foreheads.

2 And I heard a voice from heaven, as the voice of many waters, and as the voice of a great thunder: and I heard the voice of harpers harping with their harps:

3 And they sung as it were a new song before the throne, and before the four beasts, and the elders: and no man could learn that song but the hundred *and* forty *and* four thousand, which were redeemed from the earth.

4 These are they which were not defiled with women; [c]for they are virgins. These are they which follow the Lamb whithersoever he goeth. These [1]were redeemed from among men, [d]*being* the firstfruits unto God and to the Lamb.

5 And [e]in their mouth was found no guile: for [f]they are without fault before the throne of God.

6 And I saw another angel fly in the midst of heaven, [g]having the everlasting gospel to preach unto them that dwell on the earth, and to every nation, and kindred, and tongue, and people,

7 Saying with a loud voice, Fear
God, and give glory to him; for the
hour of his judgment is come: [h]and
worship him that made heaven, and
earth, and the sea, and the fountains of
waters.
8 And there followed another angel,
saying, [i]Băb'ȳ-lon is fallen, is fallen,
that great city, because she made all
nations drink of the wine of the wrath
of her fornication.
9 And the third angel followed them,
saying with a loud voice, If any man
worship the beast and his image, and
receive *his* mark in his forehead, or in
his hand,
10 The same [j]shall drink of the wine
of the wrath of God, which is poured
out without mixture into the cup of his
indignation; and he shall be tormented
with fire and brimstone in the presence of the holy angels, and in the presence of the Lamb:
11 And [k]the smoke of their torment
ascendeth up for ever and ever: and
they have no rest day nor night, who
worship the beast and his image, and
whosoever receiveth the mark of his
name.
12 [l]Here is the patience of the saints:
[m]here *are* they that keep the commandments of God, and the faith of Jē'sus.
13 And I heard a voice from heaven
saying unto me, Write, [n]Blessed *are*
the dead [o]which die in the Lord [2]from
henceforth: Yea, saith the Spirit, [p]that
they may rest from their labours; and
their works do follow them.
14 And I looked, and behold a white
cloud, and upon the cloud *one* sat [q]like
unto the Son of man, having on his
head a golden crown, and in his hand a
sharp sickle.
15 And another angel came out of
the temple, crying with a loud voice to
him that sat on the cloud, [r]Thrust in
thy sickle, and reap: for the time is
come for thee to reap; for the harvest
[s]of the earth is [3]ripe.
16 And he that sat on the cloud
thrust in his sickle on the earth; and
the earth was reaped.
17 And another angel came out of
the temple which is in heaven, he also
having a sharp sickle.
18 And another angel came out from
the altar, [t]which had power over fire;
and cried with a loud cry to him that
had the sharp sickle, saying, [u]Thrust in
thy sharp sickle, and gather the clusters of the vine of the earth; for her
grapes are fully ripe.
19 And the angel thrust in his sickle
into the earth, and gathered the vine of
the earth, and cast *it* into [v]the great
winepress of the wrath of God.
20 And [w]the winepress was trodden
[x]without the city, and blood came out
of the winepress, even unto the horse
bridles, by the space of a thousand *and*
six hundred furlongs.

15 And I saw another sign in heaven,
great and marvellous, [a]seven angels having the seven last plagues; [b]for
in them is filled up the wrath of God.
2 And I saw as it were [c]a sea of
glass [d]mingled with fire: and them
that had gotten the victory over the
beast, [e]and over his image, and over
his mark, *and* over the number of his
name, stand on the sea of glass, having
the harps of God.
3 And they sing [f]the song of Mō'ses
the servant of God, and the song of the
Lamb, saying, [g]Great and marvellous
are thy works, Lord God Almighty;
[h]just and true *are* thy ways, thou King
of [1]saints.
4 [i]Who shall not fear thee, O Lord,
and glorify thy name? for *thou* only *art*
holy: for [j]all nations shall come and
worship before thee; for thy judgments
are made manifest.
5 And after that I looked, and, behold, [k]the temple of the tabernacle of
the testimony in heaven was opened:
6 And the seven angels came out of
the temple, having the seven plagues,
[l]clothed in pure and white linen, and
having their breasts girded with golden
girdles.
7 [m]And one of the four beasts gave
unto the seven angels seven golden vials full of the wrath of God, who liveth
for ever and ever.
8 And [n]the temple was filled with
smoke [o]from the glory of God, and
from his power; and no man was
able to enter into the temple, till the
seven plagues of the seven angels were
fulfilled.

16 And I heard a great voice out of
the temple saying to the seven
angels, Go your ways, and pour out the
vials of the wrath of God upon the
earth.
2 And the first went, and poured out
his vial [a]upon the earth; and [b]there fell
a noisome and grievous sore upon the
men [c]which had the mark of the beast,
and *upon* them which worshipped his
image.
3 And the second angel poured out
his vial upon the sea; and [d]it became
as the blood of a dead *man:* [e]and every
living soul died in the sea.
4 And the third angel poured out his
vial upon the rivers and fountains of
waters; and they became blood.
5 And I heard the angel of the waters say, [f]Thou art righteous, O Lord,
[g]which art, and wast, and shalt be, because thou hast judged thus.
6 For [h]they have shed the blood of
saints and prophets, [i]and thou hast
given them blood to drink; for they are
worthy.
7 And I heard another out of the altar say, Even so, Lord God Almighty,
[j]true and righteous *are* thy judgments.
8 And the fourth angel poured out
his vial upon the sun; and power was
given unto him to scorch men with fire.
9 And men were [1]scorched with great
heat, and blasphemed the name of God,
which hath power over these plagues:
[k]and they repented not to give him
glory.
10 And the fifth angel poured out his
vial [l]upon the seat of the beast; and his

7 [h]Ps. 33.6; Acts 14.15
8 [i]Isa. 21.9; ch. 17.5
10 [j]Ps. 75.8
11 [k]Isa. 34.10
12 [l]ch. 13.10
[m]ch. 12.17
13 [n]Eccl. 4.1-2
[o]1 Cor. 15.18; 1 Thess. 4.16
[2]Or, from henceforth saith the Spirit, Yea
[p]Isa. 57.1-2; ch. 6.11
14 [q]Dan. 7.13; ch. 1.13
15 [r]Matt. 13.39
[s]ch. 13.12
[3]Or, dried
18 [t]ch. 16.8
[u]Joel 3.13
19 [v]ch. 19.15
20 [w]Isa. 63.3; Lam. 1.15
[x]ch. 11.8; Heb. 13.12

CHAPTER 15
1 [a]ch. 16.1
[b]ch. 14.10
2 [c]ch. 4.6
[d]Matt. 3.11
[e]ch. 13.15
3 [f]Ex. 15.1
[g]Deut. 32.4
[h]Hos. 14.9
[1]Or, nations, or, ages
4 [i]Ex. 15.14; Jer. 10.7
[j]Isa. 66.23
5 [k]ch. 11.19; Num. 1.50
6 [l]Ex. 28.6
7 [m]ch. 4.6
8 [n]Ex. 40.34; 2 Chr. 5.14
[o]Deut. 33.2; Isa. 2.19

CHAPTER 16
2 [a]ch. 8.7
[b]Ex. 9.9
[c]ch. 13.16
3 [d]Ex. 7.17
[e]ch. 8.9
5 [f]Gen. 18.25; ch. 15.3
[g]ch. 1.4-8; ch. 4.8
6 [h]Matt. 23.34
[i]Isa. 49.26
7 [j]ch. 13.10; ch. 14.10
9 [1]Or, burned
[k]2 Chr. 28.22; Dan. 5.22
10 [l]ch. 13.2

kingdom was full of darkness; and
they gnawed their tongues for pain,
11 And blasphemed the God of
heaven because of their pains and
their sores, and repented not of their
deeds.
12 And the sixth angel poured out
his vial [m]upon the great river Eū-
phrā'tēs; [n]and the water thereof was
dried up, [o]that the way of the kings of
the east might be prepared.
13 And I saw three [p]unclean spirits
like frogs *come* out of the mouth of
[q]the dragon, and out of the mouth of
the beast, and out of the mouth of the
false prophet.
14 [r]For they are the spirits of devils, [s]working miracles, *which* go forth
unto the kings of the earth [t]and of
the whole world, to gather them to
[u]the battle of that great day of God
Almighty.
15 [v]Behold, I come as a thief. Blessed
is he that watcheth, and keepeth his garments, [w]lest he walk naked, and they
see his shame.
16 And he gathered them together
into a place called in the Hē'brew
tongue Ăr-ma-gĕd'don.
17 And the seventh angel poured
out his vial into the air; and there came
a great voice out of the temple of
heaven, from the throne, saying, [x]It is
done.
18 And there were voices, and thunders, and lightnings; and there was a
great earthquake, [y]such as was not
since men were upon the earth, so
mighty an earthquake, *and* so great.
19 And [z]the great city was divided
into three parts, and the cities of the
nations fell: and great Băb'ȳ-lon [a]came
in remembrance before God, [b]to give
unto her the cup of the wine of the
fierceness of his wrath.
20 And [c]every island fled away, and
the mountains were not found.
21 [d]And there fell upon men a great
hail out of heaven, *every stone* about
the weight of a talent: and men blasphemed God because of the plague of
the hail; for the plague thereof was exceeding great.

17 And there came [a]one of the seven
angels which had the seven vials,
and talked with me, saying unto me,
Come hither; I will shew unto thee the
judgment of [b]the great whore [c]that sitteth upon many waters:
2 With whom the kings of the earth
have committed fornication, and [d]the
inhabitants of the earth have been
made drunk with the wine of her
fornication.
3 So he carried me away in the
spirit [e]into the wilderness: and I saw a
woman sit [f]upon a scarlet coloured
beast, full of [g]names of blasphemy,
having seven heads and ten horns.
4 And the woman [h]was arrayed in
purple and scarlet colour, and [1]decked
with gold and precious stones and
pearls, [i]having a golden cup in her
hand full of abominations and filthiness of her fornication:
5 And upon her forehead *was* a
name written, [j]MYSTERY, BĂB'Ȳ-
LON [k]THE GREAT, [l]THE MOTHER
OF [2]HARLOTS AND ABOMINATIONS
OF THE EARTH.
6 And I saw the woman drunken
with the blood of the saints, and with
the blood of [m]the martyrs of Jē'sus:
and when I saw her, I wondered with
great admiration.
7 And the angel said unto me, Wherefore didst thou marvel? I will tell thee
the mystery of the woman, and of the
beast that carrieth her, which hath the
seven heads and ten horns.
8 The beast that thou sawest was,
and is not; and [n]shall ascend out of the
bottomless pit, and go into perdition:
and they that dwell on the earth shall
wonder, whose names were not written in the book of life from the foundation of the world, when they behold the
beast that was, and is not, and yet is.
9 And [o]here *is* the mind which hath
wisdom. [p]The seven heads are seven
mountains, on which the woman sitteth.
10 And there are seven kings: five
are fallen, and one is, *and* the other is
not yet come; and when he cometh, he
must continue a short space.
11 And the beast that was, and is
not, even he is the eighth, and is of the
seven, and goeth into perdition.
12 And [q]the ten horns which thou
sawest are ten kings, which have received no kingdom as yet; but receive
power as kings one hour with the beast.
13 These have [r]one mind, and shall
give their power and strength unto the
beast.
14 [s]These shall make war with the
Lamb, and the Lamb shall overcome
them: [t]for he is Lord of lords, and King
of kings: [u]and they that are with him
are called, and chosen, and faithful.
15 And he saith unto me, [v]The waters which thou sawest, where the
whore sitteth, [w]are peoples, and multitudes, and nations, and tongues.
16 And the ten horns which thou
sawest upon the beast, [x]these shall
hate the whore, and shall make her
desolate [y]and naked, [z]and shall eat
her flesh, and burn her with fire.
17 [a]For God hath put in their hearts
to fulfil his will, and to agree, and give
their kingdom unto the beast, [b]until
the words of God shall be fulfilled.
18 And the woman which thou saw-
est [c]is that great city, [d]which reigneth
over the kings of the earth.

18 And after these things I saw
another angel come down from
heaven, having great power; [a]and the
earth was lightened with his glory.
2 And he cried mightily with a strong
voice, saying, [b]Băb'ȳ-lon the great is
fallen, is fallen, and [c]is become the
habitation of devils, and the hold of every foul spirit, and [d]a cage of every unclean and hateful bird.
3 For all nations have drunk of the
wine of the wrath of her fornication,
and the kings of the earth have committed fornication with her, and the

12 [m]ch. 9.14 [n]Jer. 50.38 [o]Isa. 41.2
13 [p]1 John 4.1 [q]ch. 12.3
14 [r]1 Tim. 4.1 [s]2 Thess. 2.9 [t]Luke 2.1 [u]ch. 20.8
15 [v]Matt. 24.43; 1 Thess. 5.2 [w]2 Cor. 5.3
17 [x]ch. 21.6
18 [y]Dan. 12.1
19 [z]ch. 14.8 [a]ch. 18.5 [b]Isa. 51.17; ch. 14.10
20 [c]ch. 6.14
21 [d]ch. 11.19

CHAPTER 17

1 [a]ch. 15.1-6; ch. 16.1-17; ch. 21.9 [b]Nah. 3.4; ch. 19.2 [c]Jer. 51.13
2 [d]Jer. 51.7
3 [e]ch. 12.6 [f]ch. 12.3 [g]ch. 13.1
4 [h]ch. 18.12 [1]gilded [i]Jer. 51.7
5 [j]2 Thess. 2.7 [k]ch. 11.8 [l]ch. 18.9 [2]Or, fornications
6 [m]Acts 22.20; ch. 6.9
8 [n]ch. 11.7
9 [o]Ps. 107.43; Hos. 14.9; ch. 13.18 [p]ch. 13.1
12 [q]Dan. 7.20; Zech. 1.18
13 [r]Rom. 8.7
14 [s]ch. 16.14 [t]1 Tim. 6.15 [u]1 Pet. 2.9; ch. 14.4
15 [v]Isa. 8.7 [w]ch. 13.7
16 [x]Jer. 50.41 [y]Ezek. 16.37 [z]ch. 18.8
17 [a]Rom. 1.26 [b]ch. 10.7
18 [c]ch. 16.19 [d]ch. 12.4

CHAPTER 18

1 [a]2 Thess. 2.3
2 [b]Isa. 13.19; ch. 14.8; ch. 16.19 [c]Isa. 34.14 [d]Isa. 14.23; Mark 5.2-3

merchants of the earth are waxed
rich through the [1]abundance of her
delicacies.
4 And I heard another voice from
heaven, saying, [e]Come out of her, my
people, that ye be not partakers of her
sins, and that ye receive not of her
plagues.
5 [f]For her sins have reached unto
heaven, and God hath remembered
her iniquities.
6 [g]Reward her even as she rewarded
you, and double unto her double according to her works: in the cup which
she hath filled fill to her double.
7 [h]How much she hath glorified herself, and lived deliciously, so much torment and sorrow give her: for she saith
in her heart, I sit a [i]queen, and am no
widow, and shall see no sorrow.
8 Therefore shall her plagues come
in one day, death, and mourning, and
famine; and she shall be utterly burned
with fire: [j]for strong *is* the Lord God
who judgeth her.
9 And [k]the kings of the earth, who
have committed fornication and lived
deliciously with her, [l]shall bewail her,
and lament for her, when they shall
see the smoke of her burning,
10 Standing afar off for the fear of
her torment, saying, [m]Alas, alas that
great city Băb'ȳ-lon, that mighty city!
for in one hour is thy judgment come.
11 And [n]the merchants of the earth
shall weep and mourn over her; for
no man buyeth their merchandise any
more:
12 The merchandise of gold, and silver, and precious stones, and of pearls,
and fine linen, and purple, and silk, and
scarlet, and all [2]thyine wood, and all
manner vessels of ivory, and all manner vessels of most precious wood, and
of brass, and iron, and marble,
13 And cinnamon, and odours, and
ointments, and frankincense, and wine,
and oil, and fine flour, and wheat, and
beasts, and sheep, and horses, and chariots, and [3]slaves, and [o]souls of men.
14 And the fruits that thy soul lusted
after are departed from thee, and all
things which were dainty and goodly
are departed from thee, and thou shalt
find them no more at all.
15 The merchants of these things,
which were made rich by her, shall
stand afar off for the fear of her torment, weeping and wailing,
16 And saying, Alas, alas that great
city, that was clothed in fine linen,
and purple, and scarlet, and decked
with gold, and precious stones, and
pearls!
17 For in one hour so great riches
is come to nought. And [p]every shipmaster, and all the company in ships,
and sailors, and as many as trade by
sea, stood afar off,
18 [q]And cried when they saw the
smoke of her burning, saying, What
city is like unto this great city!
19 And [r]they cast dust on their heads,
and cried, weeping and wailing, saying,
Alas, alas that great city, wherein were
made rich all that had ships in the sea by
reason of her costliness! for in one hour
is she made desolate.
20 [s]Rejoice over her, *thou* heaven,
and *ye* holy apostles and prophets; for
[t]God hath avenged you on her.
21 And a mighty angel took up a
stone like a great millstone, and cast *it*
into the sea, saying, [u]Thus with violence shall that great city Băb'ȳ-lon be
thrown down, and shall be found no
more at all.
22 [v]And the voice of harpers, and
musicians, and of pipers, and trumpeters, shall be heard no more at all in
thee; and no craftsman, of whatsoever
craft *he be*, shall be found any more in
thee; and the sound of a millstone shall
be heard no more at all in thee;
23 And the light of a candle shall
shine no more at all in thee; [w]and the
voice of the bridegroom and of the
bride shall be heard no more at all
in thee: [x]for thy merchants were the
great men of the earth; [y]for by thy sorceries were all nations deceived.
24 And in her was found the blood
of prophets, and of saints, and of all
that [z]were slain upon the earth.

19

And after these things I heard a
great voice of much people in
heaven, saying, Ăl-le-lū'iȧ; [a]Salvation,
and glory, and honour, and power,
unto the Lord our God:
2 For true and righteous *are* his judgments: for he hath judged the great
whore, which did corrupt the earth with
her fornication, and [b]hath avenged the
blood of his servants at her hand.
3 And again they said, Ăl-le-lū'iȧ.
And [c]her smoke rose up for ever and
ever.
4 And [d]the four and twenty elders
and the four beasts fell down and worshipped God that sat on the throne, saying, [e]Amen; Ăl-le-lū'iȧ.
5 And a voice came out of the throne,
saying, [f]Praise our God, all ye his servants, and ye that fear him, both small
and great.
6 [g]And I heard as it were the voice of
a great multitude, and as the voice of
many waters, and as the voice of mighty
thunderings, saying, Ăl-le-lū'iȧ: for the
Lord God omnipotent reigneth.
7 Let us be [h]glad and rejoice, and
give honour to him: for [i]the marriage
of the Lamb is come, and his wife hath
made herself ready.
8 And [j]to her was granted that she
should be arrayed in fine linen, clean
and [1]white: [k]for the fine linen is the
righteousness of saints.
9 And he saith unto me, Write,
[l]Blessed *are* they which are called
unto the marriage supper of the Lamb.
And he saith unto me, These are the
true sayings of God.
10 And [m]I fell at his feet to worship
him. And he said unto me, [n]See *thou*
do it not: I am thy fellowservant, and
of thy brethren [o]that have the testimony of Jē'sus: worship God: for the
testimony of Jē'sus is the spirit of
prophecy.

3 [1]Or, power
4 [e]Gen. 19.12; Isa. 48.20; Jer. 50.8; 2 Cor. 6.17
5 [f]Gen. 4.10; Gen. 18.20; Jon. 1.2
6 [g]Ps. 137.8; Jer. 50.15; 2 Tim. 4.14; ch. 13.10
7 [h]Ezek. 28.2
[i]Isa. 47.7-8; Zeph. 2.15
8 [j]Jer. 50.34
9 [k]ch. 17.2
[l]Jer. 50.46
10 [m]Isa. 21.9; ch. 14.8
11 [n]Ezek. 27.27
12 [2]Or, sweet
13 [3]Or, bodies
[o]2 Pet. 2.3
17 [p]Isa. 23.14
18 [q]Ezek. 27.30
19 [r]1 Sam. 4.12; Job 2.12
20 [s]Judg. 5.31; Ps. 48.11; Ps. 58.10; Prov. 11.10; Isa. 44.23; Jer. 51.48; ch. 19.1-3
[t]Ps. 18.47; Isa. 26.21; Luke 11.49
21 [u]Jer. 51.64
22 [v]Isa. 24.8; Jer. 7.34
23 [w]Jer. 33.11
[x]Isa. 23.8
[y]2 Ki. 9.22; Nah. 3.4; ch. 17.2
24 [z]Jer. 51.49

CHAPTER 19
1 [a]Ps. 3.8; Matt. 6.13; ch. 4.11; ch. 7.10
2 [b]Deut. 32.43; ch. 6.10
3 [c]Isa. 34.10; ch. 14.11
4 [d]ch. 4.4
[e]Neh. 5.13
5 [f]Ps. 134.1
6 [g]Ezek. 1.24
7 [h]Isa. 44.23
[i]Matt. 22.2; 2 Cor. 11.2; Eph. 5.32
8 [j]Ps. 45.13
[1]Or, bright
[k]Ps. 132.9
9 [l]Luke 14.15
10 [m]ch. 22.8
[n]Acts 10.26
[o]1 John 5.10

11 And I saw heaven opened, and
behold a white horse; and he that sat
upon him *was* called [p]Faithful and
True, and [q]in righteousness he doth
judge and make war.
12 His eyes *were* as a flame of fire,
and on his head *were* many crowns;
[r]and he had a name written, that no
man knew, but he himself.
13 [s]And he *was* clothed with a vesture dipped in blood: and his name is
called [t]The Word of God.
14 And the armies *which were* in
heaven followed him upon white
horses, [u]clothed in fine linen, white
and clean.
15 And [v]out of his mouth goeth a
sharp sword, that with it he should
smite the nations: and [w]he shall rule
them with a rod of iron: and [x]he treadeth the winepress of the fierceness and
wrath of Almighty God.
16 And he hath on *his* vesture and
on his thigh a name written, [y]KING OF
KINGS, AND LORD OF LORDS.
17 And I saw an angel standing in
the sun; and he cried with a loud voice,
saying to all the fowls that fly in the
midst of heaven, [z]Come and gather
yourselves together unto the supper of
the great God;
18 That ye may eat the flesh of kings,
and the flesh of captains, and the flesh
of mighty men, and the flesh of horses,
and of them that sit on them, and the
flesh of all *men, both* free and bond,
both small and great.
19 [a]And I saw the beast, and the
kings of the earth, and their armies,
gathered together to make war against
him that sat on the horse, and against
his army.
20 And the beast was taken, and
with him the false prophet that wrought
miracles before him, with which he
deceived them that had received the
mark of the beast, and them that worshipped his image. [b]These both were
cast alive into a lake of fire burning
with brimstone.
21 And the remnant were slain with
the sword of him that sat upon the
horse, which *sword* proceeded out of
his mouth: and all the fowls were filled
with their flesh.

20 And I saw an angel come down
from heaven, [a]having the key of
the bottomless pit and a great chain in
his hand.
2 And he laid hold on [b]the dragon,
that old serpent, which is the Dĕv'il,
and Sā'tan, and bound him a thousand
years,
3 And cast him into the bottomless
pit, and shut him up, and [c]set a seal
upon him, [d]that he should deceive
the nations no more, till the thousand
years should be fulfilled: and after that
he must be loosed a little season.
4 And I saw [e]thrones, and they sat
upon them, and [f]judgment was given
unto them: and *I saw* [g]the souls of
them that were beheaded for the witness of Jē'sus, and for the word of
God, and [h]which had not worshipped
the beast, neither his image, neither
had received *his* mark upon their foreheads, or in their hands; and they lived
and [i]reigned with Chrīst a thousand
years.
5 But the rest of the dead lived not
again until the thousand years were finished. This *is* the first resurrection.
6 Blessed and holy *is* he that hath
part in the first resurrection: on such
[j]the second death hath no power, but
they shall be [k]priests of God and of
Chrīst, and shall reign with him a thousand years.
7 And when the thousand years are
expired, Sā'tan shall be loosed out of
his prison,
8 And shall go out [l]to deceive the
nations which are in the four quarters
of the earth, [m]Gŏg and Mā'gŏg, [n]to
gather them together to battle: the
number of whom *is* as the sand of the
sea.
9 [o]And they went up on the breadth
of the earth, and compassed the camp
of the saints about, and the beloved
city: and fire came down from God out
of heaven and devoured them.
10 And the devil that deceived them
was cast into the lake of fire and brimstone, where the beast and the false
prophet *are,* and shall be tormented
day and night for ever and ever.
11 And I saw a great white throne,
and him that sat on it, from whose face
[p]the earth and the heaven fled away;
[q]and there was found no place for
them.
12 And [r]I saw the dead, small and
great, stand before God; [s]and the books
were opened: and another [t]book was
opened, which is *the book* of life: and
the dead were judged out of those things
which were written in the books, [u]ac-
cording to their works.
13 And the sea gave up the dead
which were in it; and death and [1]hell
delivered up the dead which were in
them: and they were judged every man
according to their works.
14 And [v]death and hell were cast
into the lake of fire. This is the second
death.
15 And whosoever was not found
written in the book of life was cast into
the lake of fire.

21 And [a]I saw a new heaven and a
new earth: for the first heaven
and the first earth were passed away;
and there was no more [b]sea.
2 And I Jŏhn saw [c]the holy city,
new Je-rṳ'sa-lĕm, coming down from
God out of heaven, prepared [d]as a
bride adorned for her husband.
3 And I heard a great voice out of
heaven saying, Behold, [e]the tabernacle of God *is* with men, and he will
dwell with them, and they shall be his
people, and God himself shall be with
them, *and be* their God.
4 [f]And God shall wipe away all tears
from their eyes; and [g]there shall be no
more death, [h]neither sorrow, nor crying, neither shall there be any more

11 [p]John 14.6; ch. 3.14
[q]Isa. 11.4
12 [r]Isa. 9.6
13 [s]Isa. 63.2-3
[t]John 1.1
14 [u]Dan. 10.6; ch. 7.9
15 [v]Isa. 11.4; ch. 1.16
[w]Ps. 2.9; ch. 2.27
[x]Isa. 63.3; ch. 14.19-20
16 [y]Ps. 72; ch. 17.14
17 [z]Ezek. 39.17
19 [a]ch. 16.16
20 [b]Dan. 7.11; ch. 20.10

CHAPTER 20
1 [a]ch. 1.18
2 [b]2 Pet. 2.4; ch. 12.9
3 [c]Dan. 6.17
[d]Matt. 24.24; ch. 16.14
4 [e]Dan. 7.9-22-27; Luke 22.30
[f]1 Cor. 6.2-3
[g]ch. 6.9
[h]ch. 13.12
[i]Rom. 8.17
6 [j]ch. 21.8
[k]Isa. 61.6; ch. 5.10
8 [l]1 Pet. 5.8
[m]Ezek. 38.2
[n]ch. 16.14
9 [o]Isa. 8.8
11 [p]2 Pet. 3.7
[q]Dan. 2.35
12 [r]2 Cor. 5.10; 1 Thess. 4.15-17
[s]Dan. 7.10
[t]Ps. 69.28; Phil. 4.3
[u]Matt. 16.27; Rom. 2.6
13 [1]Or, the grave
14 [v]1 Cor. 15.26

CHAPTER 21
1 [a]Isa. 65.17; 2 Pet. 3.13
[b]Isa. 57.20
2 [c]Isa. 52.1; Heb. 11.10
[d]Isa. 54.5; 2 Cor. 11.2
3 [e]Lev. 26.11
4 [f]Isa. 25.8
[g]1 Cor. 15.26-54
[h]Isa. 35.10

pain: for the former things are passed
away.
5 And [i]he that sat upon the throne
said, [j]Behold, I make all things new.
And he said unto me, Write: for these
words are true and faithful.
6 And he said unto me, It is done. I
am Ăl′phȧ and Ō′me-gȧ, the beginning
and the end. [k]I will give unto him that
is athirst of the fountain of the water of
life freely.
7 He that [l]overcometh shall inherit
[1]all things; and [m]I will be his God, and
he shall be my son.
8 [n]But the fearful, and unbelieving,
and the abominable, and murderers,
and whoremongers, and sorcerers, and
idolaters, and all liars, shall have their
part in the lake which burneth with fire
and brimstone: which is the second
death.
9 And there came unto me one of
the seven angels which had the seven
vials full of the seven last plagues, and
talked with me, saying, Come hither, I
will shew thee the bride, the Lamb's
wife.
10 And he carried me away in the
spirit to a great and high mountain,
and shewed me [o]that great city, the
holy Je-ru̥′sa-lĕm, descending out of
heaven from God,
11 Having the glory of God: and her
light *was* like unto a stone most precious, even like a jasper stone, clear as
crystal;
12 And had a wall great and high,
and had twelve gates, and at the gates
twelve angels, and names written
thereon, which are *the names* of the
twelve tribes of the children of Is′ra-el:
13 On the east three gates; on the
north three gates; on the south three
gates; and on the west three gates.
14 And the wall of the city had
twelve foundations, and [p]in them the
names of the twelve apostles of the
Lamb.
15 And he that talked with me [q]had
a golden reed to measure the city, and
the gates thereof, and the wall thereof.
16 And the city lieth foursquare, and
the length is as large as the breadth:
and he measured the city with the reed,
twelve thousand furlongs. The length
and the breadth and the height of it are
equal.
17 And he measured the wall thereof,
an hundred *and* forty *and* four cubits,
according to the measure of a man, that
is, of the angel.
18 And the building of the wall of it
was *of* jasper: and the city *was* pure
gold, like unto clear glass.
19 [r]And the foundations of the wall
of the city *were* garnished with all manner of precious stones. The first foundation *was* jasper; the second, sapphire;
the third, a chalcedony; the fourth, an
emerald;
20 The fifth, sardonyx; the sixth,
sardius; the seventh, chrysolyte; the
eighth, beryl; the ninth, a topaz; the
tenth, a chrysoprasus; the eleventh, a
jacinth; the twelfth, an amethyst.

5 [i]ch. 4.2
[j]Isa. 43.19;
2 Cor. 5.17
6 [k]Isa. 12.3;
John 7.37;
ch. 22.17
7 [l]Rom. 8.17-32;
ch. 2.7-11
[1]Or, these things
[m]Zech. 8.8;
Rom. 8.15-17;
Heb. 8.10
8 [n]1 Cor. 6.9;
Eph. 5.5;
1 Tim. 1.9;
Heb. 12.14;
ch. 22.15
10 [o]Ezek. 48
14 [p]Matt. 10.2; Gal. 2.9;
Eph. 2.20;
ch. 18.20
15 [q]Zech. 2.1;
ch. 11.1
19 [r]Isa. 54.11
21 [s]ch. 22.2
22 [t]1 Ki. 8.27;
Isa. 66.1;
John 4.23;
1 Cor. 13.12
23 [u]Isa. 24.23
24 [v]Isa. 60.3;
Isa. 66.12
25 [w]Isa. 60.20
27 [x]Isa. 35.8
[y]Dan. 12.1;
Phil. 4.3; ch. 3.5; ch. 13.8;
ch. 20.12

CHAPTER 22
1 [a]Ps. 36.8;
Ezek. 47.1;
Zech. 14.8;
John 7.38-39
2 [b]Gen. 2.9;
Gen. 3.22;
ch. 2.7
[c]ch. 21.24
3 [d]Zech. 14.11; Matt. 25.41;
ch. 21.4
[e]Ps. 16.11;
Ezek. 48.35;
ch. 7.15-17
4 [f]Matt. 5.8;
1 Cor. 13.12;
1 John 3.2
5 [g]Ps. 36.9;
Ps. 84.11
[h]Dan. 7.27;
Rom. 5.17;
2 Tim. 2.12;
1 Pet. 1.3-4;
ch. 3.21
6 [i]Heb. 1.1
10 [j]Dan. 8.26;
Dan. 12.4-9
11 [k]Ezek. 3.27;
2 Tim. 3.13
12 [l]Isa. 40.10;
Matt. 16.27;
Rom. 2.6-11;
Rom. 14.12

21 And the twelve gates *were* twelve
pearls; every several gate was of one
pearl: [s]and the street of the city *was*
pure gold, as it were transparent glass.
22 [t]And I saw no temple therein: for
the Lord God Almighty and the Lamb
are the temple of it.
23 [u]And the city had no need of the
sun, neither of the moon, to shine in it:
for the glory of God did lighten it, and
the Lamb *is* the light thereof.
24 [v]And the nations of them which
are saved shall walk in the light of it:
and the kings of the earth do bring
their glory and honour into it.
25 And the gates of it shall not be
shut at all by day: for [w]there shall be
no night there.
26 And they shall bring the glory
and honour of the nations into it.
27 [x]And there shall in no wise enter
into it any thing that defileth, neither
whatsoever worketh abomination, or
maketh a lie: but they which are written in the Lamb's [y]book of life.

22 And he shewed me [a]a pure river
of water of life, clear as crystal,
proceeding out of the throne of God
and of the Lamb.
2 In the midst of the street of it, and
on either side of the river, *was there*
[b]the tree of life, which bare twelve
manner of fruits, *and* yielded her fruit
every month: and the leaves of the tree
were [c]for the healing of the nations.
3 And [d]there shall be no more curse:
[e]but the throne of God and of the Lamb
shall be in it; and his servants shall
serve him:
4 And [f]they shall see his face; and
his name *shall be* in their foreheads.
5 And there shall be no night there;
and they need no candle, neither light
of the sun; for [g]the Lord God giveth
them light: [h]and they shall reign for
ever and ever.
6 And he said unto me, These sayings *are* faithful and true: and the Lord
God of the [i]holy prophets sent his
angel to shew unto his servants the
things which must shortly be done.
7 Behold, I come quickly: blessed *is*
he that keepeth the sayings of the
prophecy of this book.
8 And I Jŏhn saw these things, and
heard *them*. And when I had heard
and seen, I fell down to worship before
the feet of the angel which shewed me
these things.
9 Then saith he unto me, See *thou*
do it not: for I am thy fellowservant,
and of thy brethren the prophets, and
of them which keep the sayings of this
book: worship God.
10 [j]And he saith unto me, Seal not
the sayings of the prophecy of this
book: for the time is at hand.
11 [k]He that is unjust, let him be unjust still: and he which is filthy, let him
be filthy still: and he that is righteous,
let him be righteous still: and he that is
holy, let him be holy still.
12 And, behold, I come quickly; and
[l]my reward *is* with me, to give every
man according as his work shall be.

13 [m]I am Ăl'phȧ and Ō'me-gȧ, the
beginning and the end, the first and
the last.
14 [n]Blessed *are* they that do his commandments, that they may have right
to the tree of life, and may enter in
through the gates into the city.
15 For without *are* dogs, and sorcerers, and whoremongers, and murderers, and idolaters, and whosoever
loveth and maketh a lie.
16 [o]I Jē'sus have sent mine angel to
testify unto you these things in the
churches. [p]I am the root and the offspring of Dā'vid, *and* [q]the bright and
morning star.
17 And the Spirit and the bride say,
Come. And let him that heareth say,
Come. [r]And let him that is athirst
come. And whosoever will, let him
take the water of life freely.
18 For I testify unto every man that
heareth the words of the prophecy of
this book, [s]If any man shall add unto
these things, God shall add unto him
the plagues that are written in this
book:
19 And if any man shall take away
from the words of the book of this
prophecy, [t]God shall take away his
part [1]out of the book of life, and out
of the holy city, and *from* the things
which are written in this book.
20 He which testifieth these things
saith, [u]Surely I come quickly. Amen.
Even so, come, Lord Jē'sus.
21 The grace of our Lord Jē'sus
Chrīst *be* with you all. Amen.

13 [m]Isa. 44.6
14 [n]Dan. 12.12
16 [o]1 Pet. 3.22
[p]Isa. 11.1; Jer. 23.5-6
[q]Num. 24.17; Zech. 6.12
17 [r]Isa. 55.1; John 4.14; John 7.37; ch. 21.6
18 [s]Deut. 4.2; Deut. 12.32; Prov. 30.6
19 [t]Ex. 32.33
[1]Or, from the tree of life
20 [u]Heb. 9.28

STUDY HELPS

Parables of Our Lord

PARABLE	OCCASION	LESSON	REFERENCES
The mote and beam	When reproving the Pharisees	Do not presume to judge others	Matt. 7:1-6; Luke 6:37-43
The two buildings	Sermon on the Mount	Discipleship demands obedience	Matt. 7:24-27; Luke 6:47-49
Children in the marketplace	Rejection by the Pharisees of John's baptism	Evil of a fault-finding disposition	Matt. 11:16-17; Luke 7:32
The two debtors	A Pharisee's self-righteous reflections	Love to Christ proportioned to grace received	Luke 7:41-43
The unclean spirit	The Scribes demand a miracle in the heavens	Hardening power of unbelief	Matt. 12:43-45; Luke 11:24-26
The rich man's meditation	Dispute of two brothers	Folly of reliance upon wealth	Luke 12:16-21
The barren fig tree	Tidings of the execution of certain Galileans	Danger in the unbelief of the Jewish people	Luke 13:6-9
The soils	Sermon on the seashore	God guarantees the harvest	Matt. 13:3-23; Mark 4:3-20; Luke 8:5-15
The tares	Sermon on the seashore	The final separation of righteousness and evil	Matt. 13:24-30, 36-43
The candle	To the disciples alone	Effect of good example	Matt. 5:15; Mark 4:21; Luke 8:16,11:33
The seed	Sermon on the seashore	Mysterious growth of the Kingdom	Mark 4:26-29
The grain of mustard seed	Sermon on the seashore	Small beginnings and growth of Christ's Kingdom	Matt. 13:31-32; Mark 4:31-32; Luke 13:19
The leaven	Sermon on the seashore	Kingdom's power to change	Matt. 13:33; Luke 13:21
The hidden treasure	To the disciples alone	Joy of the Kingdom	Matt. 13:44
The pearl of great price	To the disciples alone	Value of the Kingdom	Matt. 13:45-46
The net	To the disciples alone	Proclaim the Gospel to all	Matt. 13:47-50
The householder	To the disciples alone	Varied methods of teaching truth	Matt. 13:52

PARABLE	OCCASION	LESSON	REFERENCES
The marriage	To the disciples of John	Joyous response to Jesus	Matt. 9:15; Mark 2:19-20; Luke 5:34-35
The patched garment	To the disciples of John	The newness of Christ's message	Matt. 9:16; Mark 2:21; Luke 5:36
The wine bottles	To the disciples of John	The newness of Christ's message	Matt. 9:17; Mark 2:22; Luke 5:37
The harvest	Teaching disciples in Samaria	Need for true witnesses	Matt. 9:37-38; Luke 10:2
The adversary	Sermon on the Mount	Need of prompt repentance	Matt. 5:25-26; Luke 12:58-59
Two insolvent debtors	Peter's question	Need to forgive	Matt. 18:23-35
The good Samaritan	The lawyer's question	The golden rule for all	Luke 10:30-37
The three loaves	Disciples ask lesson in prayer	Effect of importunity in prayer	Luke 11:5-8
The true shepherd	Pharisees reject testimony of miracle	Christ, the only way to God	John 10:1-16
The strait gate	The question, Are there few that can be saved?	Difficulty of repentance	Matt. 7:13-14; Luke 13:24
The guests	Pharisee's Sabbath dinner	Chief places not to be usurped	Luke 14:7-11
The great banquet	Pharisee's Sabbath dinner	Salvation depends on proper response	Luke 14:16-24
The marriage supper	Pharisees seeking to arrest Jesus	Rejection of unbelievers	Matt. 22:2-9
The wedding garment	Pharisees seeking to arrest Jesus	Necessity of purity	Matt. 22:10-14
The tower	Multitudes surrounding Christ	Need of deliberation	Luke 14:28-30
The king going to war	Multitudes surrounding Christ	Need of deliberation	Luke 14:31-32
The lost sheep	Pharisees objected to His receiving the wicked	Christ's joy over sinner's salvation	Matt. 18:12-14; Luke 15:4-7
The lost coin	Pharisees objected to His receiving the wicked	Christ's joy over sinner's salvation	Luke 15:8-10
The prodigal son	Pharisees objected to His receiving the wicked	Christ's joy over sinner's salvation	Luke 15:11-32

PARABLE	OCCASION	LESSON	REFERENCES
The unjust steward	Teaching the disciples	Prudence in using power and possessions	Luke 16:1-9
The rich man and Lazarus	Derision of the Pharisees	Salvation not connected with wealth	Luke 16:19-31
The servant's duty	Teaching the disciples	Man's obedience	Luke 17:7-10
The importunate widow	Teaching the disciples	Perseverance in prayer	Luke 18:1-8
The Pharisee and the publican	Teaching the self-righteous	Humility in prayer	Luke 18:10-14
Laborers in the vineyard	Teaching the disciples	Attitude toward rewards	Matt. 20:1-16
The two sons	The chief priests demand His authority	Obedience better than words	Matt. 21:28-32
The talents	Teaching on last things	Stewardship is rewarded appropriately	Matt. 25:14-30; Luke 19:11-27
The wicked husbandman	The chief priests demand His authority	Rejection of the Jewish people	Matt. 21:33-44; Mark 12:1-12; Luke 20:9-18
The fig tree	Teaching on last things	Duty to watch for Christ's appearance	Matt. 24:32-33; Mark 13:28-29; Luke 21:29-31
The watching servants	Teaching on last things	Necessity of watchfulness	Luke 12:36-38
The watching householder	Teaching on last things	Duty to watch for Christ's appearance	Matt. 24:43-44; Luke 12:39-40
The man on a journey	Teaching on last things	Duty to watch for Christ's appearance	Mark 13:34
Character of two servants	Teaching on last things	Danger of unfaithfulness	Matt. 24:45-51; Luke 12:42-48
The ten virgins	Teaching on last things	Necessity of watchfulness	Matt. 25:1-12
The vine and branches	At the Last Supper	Disciples bear fruit	John 15:1-11

Miracles of Our Lord

MIRACLE	BIBLE PASSAGE			
Water turned to wine				John 2:1
Many healings	Matt. 4:23	Mark 1:32		
Healing of a leper	Matt. 8:1	Mark 1:40	Luke 5:12	
Healing of a Roman centurion's servant	Matt. 8:5		Luke 7:1	
Healing of Peter's mother-in-law	Matt. 8:14	Mark 1:29	Luke 4:38	
Calming of the storm at sea	Matt. 8:23	Mark 4:35	Luke 8:22	
Healing of the wild men of Gadara	Matt. 8:28	Mark 5:1	Luke 8:26	
Healing of a palsied man	Matt. 9:1	Mark 2:1	Luke 5:18	
Healing of a woman with a hemorrhage	Matt. 9:20	Mark 5:25	Luke 8:43	
Raising of Jairus' daughter	Matt. 9:23	Mark 5:22	Luke 8:41	
Healing of two blind men	Matt. 9:27			
Healing of a demon-possessed man	Matt. 9:32			
Healing of a man with a withered hand	Matt. 12:10	Mark 3:1	Luke 6:6	
Feeding of 5,000 people	Matt. 14:15	Mark 6:35	Luke 9:12	John 6:1
Walking on the sea	Matt. 14:22	Mark 6:47		John 6:16
Healing of the Syrophoenicians' daughter	Matt. 15:21	Mark 7:24		
Feeding of 4,000 people	Matt. 15:32	Mark 8:1		
Healing of an epileptic boy	Matt. 17:14	Mark 9:14	Luke 9:37	
Healing of two blind men at Jericho	Matt. 20:30			
Healing of a man with an unclean spirit		Mark 1:23	Luke 4:33	
Healing of a deaf, speechless man		Mark 7:31		
Healing of a blind man at Bethesda		Mark 8:22		
Healing of a blind Bartimaeus		Mark 10:46	Luke 18:35	
A miraculous catch of fish			Luke 5:4	John 21:1
Raising of a widow's son			Luke 7:11	
Healing of an infirm woman			Luke 13:11	
Healing of a man with the dropsy			Luke 14:1	
Healing of ten lepers			Luke 17:11	
Healing of Malchus' ear			Luke 22:50	
Healing of a nobleman's son				John 4:46
Healing of a lame man at Bethesda				John 5:1
Healing of a blind man				John 9:1
Raising of Lazarus				John 11:38

A Harmony of the Gospels

Event	Place	MATTHEW	MARK	LUKE	JOHN
	JESUS' EARLY YEARS				
Luke's prologue				1:1-4	
Pre-existence and genealogies		1:1-17		3:23-38	1:1-18
Birth of John the Baptist foretold	Jerusalem			1:5-23	
Annunciation to Mary	Nazareth			1:24-38	
Songs of Elizabeth and Mary	Judea			1:39-56	
Birth of John the Baptist	Judea			1:57-80	
Birth of Jesus	Bethlehem	1:18-25		2:1-21	
Presentation in the Temple	Jerusalem			2:22-39	
Visit of the Magi	Bethlehem	2:1-12			
Flight into Egypt		2:13-23			
Childhood and youth	Nazareth	2:23		2:39-52	
Jesus' First Passover	Jerusalem			2:41-50	
	SPECIAL PREPARATIONS				
Ministry of John the Baptist	Wilderness of Judea	3:1-12	1:1-8	3:1-18	1:19-28
Baptism of Jesus	Jordan	3:13-17	1:9-11	3:21-22	1:29-34
Temptation of Jesus	Wilderness of Judea	4:1-11	1:12, 13	4:1-13	
	JUDEAN MINISTRY				
First disciples won	Bethabara				1:35-51
First miracle: Wedding at Cana	Cana				2:1-12
First cleansing of the Temple	Jerusalem				2:13-25
First recorded discourse: Nicodemus	Jerusalem				3:1-21
First ministry in Judea begun	Judea				3:22-36
First converts in Samaria: Jacob's Well	Sychar				4:1-42
Healing of the nobleman's son	Capernaum				4:43-54
	THE GREAT GALILEAN MINISTRY				
Passover					5:1
Imprisonment of John the Baptist	Macherus	14:3-5	6:17-18	3:19-20	
Beginning of great Galilean ministry	Galilee	4:12	1:14, 15	4:14, 15	
Rejection at Nazareth	Nazareth			4:16-30	
Takes up residence at Capernaum	Capernaum	4:13-17		4:31	
Calls first disciples to follow Him	Capernaum	4:18-22	1:16-20	5:1-11	
Cure of demoniac in synagogue	Capernaum		1:21-28	4:31-37	

Event	Place	MATTHEW	MARK	LUKE	JOHN
Many miracles of healing	Capernaum Galilee	4:23-25 8:14-17	1:29-39	4:38-44	
Cure of a leper	Galilee	8:1-4	1:40-45	5:12-16	
Healing a paralytic	Capernaum	9:1-8	2:1-12	5:17-26	
Call of Matthew	Capernaum	9:9-17	2:13-22	5:27-39	
Healing at Pool of Bethsaida	Jerusalem				5:2-47
Man with withered hand	Capernaum	12:1-14	2:23-3:6	6:1-11	
Christ heals multitudes		12:15-21	3:7-12	6:17-19	
Appointing of the twelve apostles	Horns of Hattin	10:1-4	3:13-19	6:12-16	
The Sermon on the Mount	Horns of Hattin	Chs. 5-7		6:20-49	
Healing of the centurion's servant	Capernaum	8:5-13		7:1-10	
Raising of the widow's son	Nain			7:11-17	
John the Baptist sends messengers to Jesus	Galilee	11:2-19		7:18-35	
Warnings and invitations		11:20-30			
Anointing of Jesus by the penitent woman				7:36-50	
Another tour of Galilee	Galilee			8:1-3	
Demon controversy	Capernaum	12:22-45	3:20-30	11:14-36	
Visit of His mother and brethren	Capernaum	12:46-50	3:31-35	8:19-21	
Eight parables by the seaside	Capernaum	13:1-53	4:1-34	8:4-18	
Stilling of the tempest	Sea of Galilee	8:18-27	4:35-41	8:22-25	
Restoration of the demoniac	Gergesa	8:28-34	5:1-20	8:26-39	
Jairus' daughter raised; woman cured	Capernaum	9:18-26	5:21-43	8:40-56	
Cure of two blind and one dumb	Capernaum	9:27-34			
GREAT DEEDS AMID GREAT OPPOSITION					
Rejection at Nazareth	Nazareth	13:54-58	6:1-6	(4:16-30)	
The twelve sent out to preach	Galilee	9:35-11:1	6:6-13	9:1-6	
Death of John the Baptist	Macherus	14:1-12	6:14-29	9:7-9	
Feeding of the 5000	Bethsaida	14:13-21	6:30-46	9:10-17	6:1-15
Jesus walks on the water	Sea of Galilee	14:22-33	6:47-52		6:16-21
Heals many sick	Gennesaret	14:34-36	6:53-56		
Discourse on the bread of life	Capernaum				6:22-71
Eating with unwashed hands	Capernaum	15:1-20	7:1-23		
Heals daughter of Syrophoenician woman	Phoenicia	15:21-28	7:24-30		
Miracles of healing in					

Event	Place	Matthew	Mark	Luke	John
Decapolis	Decapolis	15:29-31	7:31-37		
Feeding the 4000	Decapolis	15:32-39	8:1-10		
Demand for a sign from heaven	Capernaum	16:1-12	8:11-21		
Blind man healed	Bethsaida		8:22-26		
Peter's great confession of faith	Near Caesarea-Philippi	16:13-20	8:27-30	9:18-21	
Jesus for the first time foretells His death	Near Caesarea-Philippi	16:21-28	8:31-9:1	9:22-27	
The transfiguration	Near Caesarea-Philippi	17:1-13	9:2-13	9:28-36	
Healing of the demoniac boy	Near Caesarea-Philippi	17:14-21	9:14-29	9:37-43	
Jesus again foretells His death	Galilee	17:22,23	9:30-32	9:43-45	
Temple tax		17:24-27			
Jesus and the children	Capernaum	18:1-14	9:33-50	9:46-50	
Unmerciful servant	Capernaum	18:15-35			
YEAR OF DEVELOPMENT					
At the Feast of Tabernacles	Jerusalem				7:1 to 10:21
The water of life	Jerusalem				7:37-39
Officers sent to arrest Him	Jerusalem				7:44-53
Discourse on light and freedom	Jerusalem				8:12-59
Healing of man born blind	Jerusalem				9:1-41
The Good Shepherd	Jerusalem				10:1-21
Returns to Galilee; final departure		19:1	10:1	9:51	
Repulsed by the Samaritans	Samaria			9:51-62	
The mission of the seventy	Perea			10:1-24	
Parable of the good Samaritan	Perea			10:25-37	
Discourse on prayer	Perea			11:1-13	
Answers attack of Pharisees	Perea			11:14-54	
The rich fool; the watchful servant	Perea			12:1-59	
Discourses: Galileans slain by Pilate; healing on Sabbath; parables of mustard seed and leaven; the narrow door; lament over Jerusalem				13:1-35	
Jesus the guest of Mary					

Event	Place	MATTHEW	MARK	LUKE	JOHN
and Martha	Bethany			10:38-42	
Feast of Dedication; discourses	Jerusalem				10:22-39
CULMINATION OF MIRACLES AND TEACHING					
Jesus retires beyond Jordan	Perea				10:40-42
Dines with a Pharisee	Perea			14:1-14	
Parable of the great supper	Perea			14:15-24	
Counting the cost of discipleship	Perea			14:25-35	
Parables of lost sheep and lost coin	Perea			15:1-10	
Parable of prodigal son	Perea			15:11-32	
Parable of the unjust steward	Perea			16:1-13	
Parable of the rich man and Lazarus	Perea			16:14-31	
Teachings on forgiveness	Perea			17:1-10	
Raising of Lazarus	Bethany				11:1-46
Retreat to Ephraim	Ephraim				11:47-57
The healing of the ten lepers	Samaria			17:11-19	
On the coming of the kingdom	Perea			17:20-37	
Parable of the importunate widow	Perea			18:1-8	
Parable of the Pharisee and publican	Perea			18:9-14	
Discourse about divorce	Perea	19:2-12	10:2-12		
Christ blesses little children	Perea	19:13-15	10:13-16	18:15-17	
The rich young man	Perea	19:16-30	10:17-31	18:18-30	
The laborers in the vineyard	Perea	20:1-16			
Jesus again predicts His death	Perea	20:17-19	10:32-34	18:31-34	
Ambitious request of James and John	Perea	20:20-28	10:35-45		
Healing two blind men (one being Bartimaeus)	Jericho	20:29-34	10:46-52	18:35-43	
Visit to Zaccheus the publican	Jericho			19:1-10	
Parable of the minas	Jericho			19:11-28	
THE LAST WEEK—MARCH 31 TO APRIL 7					
Jesus arrives at Bethany	Bethany				12:1
Anointing by Mary	Bethany	26:6-13	14:3-9		12:2-11
Triumphal Entry; visit to the Temple; return to Bethany	Jerusalem	21:1-11	11:1-11	19:29-44	12:12-19
Cursing of barren fig tree	Mt. of Olives	21:18-19	11:12-14		
Cleansing of the Temple				19:45-48	

Event	Place	Matthew	Mark	Luke	John
and return to Bethany	Jerusalem	21:12-17	11:15-19	21:37, 38	
THE LAST DAY OF PUBLIC TEACHING					
The fig tree withered; lesson on faith	Mt. of Olives	21:20-22	11:20-26		
Christ's authority challenged	The Temple	21:23-27	11:27-33	20:1-8	
Three parables of warning:					
The two sons	The Temple	21:28-32			
The wicked vine-growers	The Temple	21:33-46	12:1-12	20:9-19	
Marriage of the king's son	The Temple	22:1-14			
Three questions by Jewish rulers	The Temple	22:15-40	12:13-34	20:20-40	
Christ's unanswerable question	The Temple	22:41-46	12:35-37	20:41-44	
Woes against Scribes and Pharisees	The Temple	23:1-36	12:38-40	20:45-47	
Lamentation over Jerusalem	The Temple	23:37-39			
The widow's two coins	The Temple		12:41-44	21:1-4	
Greeks seeking Jesus	The Temple				12:20-36
Prophecy of the end of the age	Mt. of Olives	24:1-51	13:1-37	21:5-36	
Parable of the ten virgins	Mt. of Olives	25:1-13			
Parable of the talents	Mt. of Olives	25:14-30			
The last judgment	Mt. of Olives	25:31-46			
Conspiracy between the rulers and Judas	Jerusalem	26:1-5 26:14-16	14:1, 2 14:10-11	22:1-6	12:36*b*-50
THE LAST DAY WITH HIS DISCIPLES					
Preparation for the Passover	Jerusalem	26:17-20	14:12-17	22:7-14	
Strife for precedence	Jerusalem			22:24-30	
Jesus washes the disciples' feet	Jerusalem				13:1-20
The last supper	Jerusalem			22:15-18	
Jesus declares the betrayer; Judas goes out	Jerusalem	26:21-25	14:18-21	22:21-23	13:21-35
Institution of the Lord's Supper	Jerusalem	26:26-30	14:22-25	22:19, 20	1 Cor. 11
Jesus foretells the fall of Peter	Jerusalem			22:31-38	13:36-38
Christ's farewell discourses	Jerusalem				Chs. 14-16
Prayer of Jesus for the disciples	Jerusalem				17:1-26
Jesus goes forth; Peter's confidence	Jerusalem	26:30-35	14:26-31	22:39	18:1-3
The agony in the					

Event	Place	MATTHEW	MARK	LUKE	JOHN
Garden of Gethsemane	Mt. of Olives	26:36-46	14:32-42	22:40-46	
		THE LAST DAY			
Betrayal by Judas		26:47-50	14:43-45	22:47, 48	18:4-9
The arrest		26:50-56	14:46-52	22:49-53	18:10-12
		THE JEWISH TRIAL			
The trial before					
Annas	Jerusalem				18:13-15
Caiaphas	Jerusalem	26:57, 58	14:53, 54	22:54, 55	18:19-24
the Sanhedrin	Jerusalem	26:59-66	14:55-64		
Denials by Peter	Jerusalem	26:69-75	14:66-72	22:56-62	18:15-27
Mockery by enemies	Jerusalem	26:67, 68	14:65	22:63-65	
Legal meeting of Sanhedrin; Jesus condemned for blasphemy	Jerusalem	27:1, 2	15:1	22:66-71	
Death of Judas	Jerusalem	27:3-10		Acts 1:18, 19	
		THE ROMAN TRIAL			
Jesus before Pilate	Jerusalem	27:11-14	15:2-5	23:1-5	18:28-38
Jesus sent to Herod	Jerusalem			23:6-12	
Pilate seeks to release Jesus; people demand Barabbas	Jerusalem	27:15-23	15:6-14	23:13-23	18:38-40
Jesus condemned, scourged and mocked	Jerusalem	27:26-30	15:15-19	23:24, 25	19:1-3
Other attempts by Pilate to release Jesus	Jerusalem	27:24, 25			19:4-16
		THE CRUCIFIXION			
Jesus led away to be crucified	Jerusalem	27:31-38	15:20-28	23:26-32	19:16-18
The superscription	Jerusalem	27:37	15:26	23:38	19:19-22
First word from the cross: *"Father, forgive them"*	Jerusalem			23:33, 34	
Soldiers cast lots for garments	Jerusalem	27:35, 36	15:24	23:34	19:23, 24
Jews mock at Jesus on the cross	Jerusalem	27:39-44	15:29-32	23:35-37	
Second word from the cross: to the penitent thief	Jerusalem			23:39-43	
Third word: *"Woman, behold your son"*	Jerusalem				19:25-27
Darkness covers the land	Jerusalem	27:45	15:33	23:44, 45	
Fourth word: Cry of distress to God	Jerusalem	27:46, 47	15:34, 35		
Fifth word: *"I am thirsty"*	Jerusalem	27:48, 49	15:36		19:28, 29
Sixth word:					

Event	Place	MATTHEW	MARK	LUKE	JOHN
"It is finished"	Jerusalem				19:30
Seventh word: *"Into thy hands"*	Jerusalem			23:46	
Jesus dies; veil rent; earthquake	Jerusalem	27:50-56	15:37-41	23:45-49	19:30
Jesus is pierced in the side	Jerusalem				19:31-37
The burial	Jerusalem	27:57-61	15:42-47	23:50-56	19:38-42
THREE DAYS IN THE TOMB					
The watch at the tomb	Jerusalem	27:62-66			
RESURRECTION APPEARANCES					
The morning of the resurrection	Jerusalem	28:2-4			
Women come to the tomb	Jerusalem	28:1	16:1-4	24:1, 2	20:1
Mary Magdalene calls Peter and John	Jerusalem				20:2
The women at the tomb	Jerusalem	28:5-8	16:5-8	24:3-8	
Peter and John at the tomb	Jerusalem			24:12	20:3-10
Jesus appears to Mary Magdalene	Jerusalem		16:9-11		20:11-18
Jesus appears to the women	Jerusalem	28:9,10		24:9-11	
The guards report to the priests	Jerusalem	28:11-15			
The walk to Emmaus	Emmaus		16:12, 13	24:13-35	
Jesus appears to Peter	Jerusalem	1 Cor. 15:5		24:34	
Jesus appears to the apostles except Thomas	Jerusalem	1 Cor. 15:5	16:14	24:36-48	20:19-23
Jesus appears to all the apostles including Thomas	Jerusalem				20:24-29
Jesus appears to seven in Galilee	Sea of Galilee				21:1-23
Appears to over 500 at once	Sea of Galilee	28:16-20	16:15-18		1 Cor. 15:6
Jesus appears to James	Sea of Galilee				1 Cor. 15:7
Jesus appears to the apostles	Jerusalem			24:49	Acts 1:1-18
Jesus ascends to heaven	Bethany Mt. of Olives		16:19	24:50-53	Acts 1:9-12
The conclusions of Mark and John			16:20		20:30, 31 21:24, 25
BIRTH OF THE CHURCH					
Holy Spirit given at Pentecost	Jerusalem			Acts 2:1-11	
Jesus appears to Paul	Damascus			Acts 22:6-16	
Jesus appears to John	Patmos				Rev. 1:9-20

This section is adapted from The Gospels Paralleled, © Copyright 1942. Renewal, 1970. A.J. Holman Company.

CONCORDANCE

A

Abase
Ezek. 21:26 ... a him that is high
Phil. 4:12 .. I know . . . how to be a-ed

Abated
Gen. 8:3 ... the waters were a
Deut. 34:7 ... nor his natural force a

Abba
Mark 14:36 ... and he said, **A**, Father
Rom. 8:15 ... whereby we cry, **A**, Father
Gal. 4:6 ... crying, **A**, Father

Abhor
Job 19:19 ... friends a-ed me
Ps. 78:59 ... greatly a-ed Israel
Ps. 119:163 ... I hate and a lying
Prov. 24:24 ... nations shall a him
Is. 49:7 ... whom the nation a-eth
Rom. 12:9 ... a that which is evil

Abide
Ps. 15:1 ... shall a in thy tabernacle
Ps. 91:1 ... shall a under the shadow
Eccles. 1:4 ... the earth a-eth forever
Jer. 49:18 ... no man shall a there
Mal. 3:2 ... a the day of his coming
Luke 2:8 ... shepherds a-ing
Luke 19:5 ... I must a at thy house
Luke 24:29 ... a with us
John 3:36 ... wrath of God a-eth
John 5:38 ... not his word a-ing
John 8:35 ... the Son a-eth forever
John 15:4 ... **A** in me, and I in you
1 Cor. 3:14 ... if any man's work a
1 Cor. 7:8 ... they a even as I
1 Cor. 13:13 ... a-eth faith, hope,
1 Pet. 1:23 ... liveth and a-eth forever

Ability
Ezra 2:69 ... gave after their a
Acts 11:29 ... man according to his a
1 Pet. 4:11 ... a which God giveth

Able
Gen. 13:6 ... land was not a to bear
Deut. 16:17 . man shall give as he is a
1 Kin. 3:9 ... who is a to judge
Prov. 27:4 ... a to stand before envy
Matt. 3:9 ... God is a of these stones
Matt. 9:28 ... believe ye that I am a
Matt. 10:28 ... which is a to destroy
Matt. 20:22 ... a to drink of the cup
Luke 14:31 ... be a with ten thousand
John 10:29 ... no man is a to pluck
Acts 6:10 . not a to resist the wisdom
Rom. 8:39 ... a to separate us
1 Cor. 10:13 ... above that ye are a
2 Cor. 3:6 ... made us a ministers
Eph. 3:18 ... a to comprehend
Phil. 3:21 ... a even to subdue all
2 Tim. 2:2 ... a to teach others also
James 4:12 .. a to save and to destroy
Jude 24 ... a to keep you from falling
Rev. 5:3 ... a to open the book
Rev. 6:17 ... who shall be a to stand

Abode
Ex. 24:16 ... glory of the Lord a
Deut. 9:9 ... a in the mount forty days
John 1:32 ... it a upon him
John 8:44 ... a not in the truth
John 14:23 ... make our a with him
Acts 18:3 ... he a with them

Abolished
Eph. 2:15 ... a in his flesh the enmity
2 Tim. 1:10 ... who hath a death

Abominable
Deut. 14:3 ... not eat any a thing
Ps. 14:1 ... have done a works
Ps. 53:1 ... done a iniquity
Jer. 44:4 ... this a thing that I hate
Mic. 6:10 ... scant measure that is a
1 Pet. 4:3 ... walked in . . . a idolatries

Abomination
Gen. 46:34 ... shepherd is an a
Ex. 8:26 ... the a of the Egyptians
Deut. 7:26 ... bring an a . . . house
Deut. 29:17 . their a-s, and their idols
Ps. 88:8 ... hast made me an a
Prov. 3:32 ... froward is a to the Lord
Prov. 8:7 ... wickedness is an a
Is. 66:17 ... swine's flesh, and the a
Jer. 4:1 ... put away thine a-s
Ezek. 33:29 ... because of all their a-s
Dan. 12:11 ... a that maketh desolate
Luke 16:15 ... is a in the sight of God
Rev. 17:5 .. mother of harlots and a-s

Abound
Prov. 28:20 ... faithful man shall a
Rom. 15:13 ... that ye may a in hope
1 Cor. 15:58 . a-ing in the work of the
2 Cor. 1:5 ... sufferings of Christ a
Phil. 4:12 ... abased, and . . . how to a
1 Thess. 4:1 ... a more and more

Absent
1 Cor. 5:3 ... a in body, but present
2 Cor. 5:6 ... a from the Lord
2 Cor. 5:8 ... a from the body
2 Cor. 10:1 ... a am bold toward you

Abstain
Acts 15:20 ... a from pollutions
1 Thess. 5:22 .. a from all appearance
1 Tim. 4:3 ... a from meats
1 Pet. 2:11 ... a from fleshly lusts

Abundance
Deut. 28:47 ... for the a of all things
1 Kin. 18:41 ... sound of a of rain
Neh. 9:25 ... fruit trees in a
Ps. 52:7 . trusted in the a of his riches
Ps. 72:7 ... and a of peace so long
Ezek. 16:49 ... and a of idleness
Matt. 12:34 .. out of the a of the heart
Matt. 13:12 ... he shall have more a
Mark 12:44 ... did cast in of their a
Luke 12:15 ... consisteth not in the a
Rom. 5:17 ... receive a of grace
2 Cor. 12:7 ... the a of the revelations

Abundant
Ex. 34:6 ... a in goodness and truth
2 Cor. 7:15 ... affection is more a

Accept
Deut. 33:11 .. a the work of his hands
Job 13:8 ... will ye a his person
Prov. 18:5 .. not good to a the wicked
Luke 4:24 ... no prophet is a-ed
Rom. 15:31 ... be a-ed of the saints
2 Cor. 5:9 ... we may be a-ed of him
2 Cor. 6:2 ... now is the a-ed time
1 Tim. 1:15 ... worthy of all a-ation

Acceptable
Ps. 69:13 ... an a time
Is. 61:2 ... proclaim the a year
Eph. 5:10 ... proving what is a
Phil. 4:18 ... a sacrifice a
1 Tim. 2:3 ... this is good and a

Accomplished
Prov. 13:19 ... the desire a is sweet
Is. 40:2 ... her warfare is a
Luke 1:23 . of his ministration were a
John 19:28 ... all things are now a
1 Pet. 5:9 ... afflictions are a

Accord
Josh. 9:2 ... to fight . . . with one a
Acts 1:14 ... continued with one a
Acts 8:6 ... with one a gave heed
Phil. 2:2 . being of one a, of one mind

Accusation
Matt. 27:37 ... over his head his a
Luke 19:8 ... any man by false a
John 18:29 .. What a bring ye against

Accuse
Prov. 30:10 ... **A** not a servant
Matt. 27:12 ... a-d of the chief priests
John 5:45 ... I will a you to the Father
Acts 22:30 ... was a-d of the Jews
Titus 1:6 ... children not a-d of riot

Acknowledge
Ps. 32:5 ... I a-d my sin
Ps. 51:3 ... I a my transgressions
Prov. 3:6 ... In all thy ways a him
1 John 2:33 ... he that a-th the Son

Add
Deut. 4:2 ... not a unto the word
Ps. 69:27 ... a iniquity unto their
Is. 30:1 ... a sin to sin
Matt. 6:27 ... can a one cubit
Luke 12:31 ... shall be a-ed unto you
2 Pet. 1:5 ... a to your faith virtue
Rev. 22:18 . any man . . . a unto these

Adder
Gen. 49:17 ... an a in the path
Ps. 58:4 ... are like the deaf a
Ps. 91:13 ... tread upon the lion and a
Prov. 23:32 ... stingeth like an a

Administration
1 Cor. 12:5 ... are differences of a-s
2 Cor. 9:12 ... For the a of this service

Admonish
Rom. 15:14 ... a one another
Col. 3:16 ... a-ing one another
2 Thess. 3:15 ... a him as a brother
Heb. 8:5 ... Moses was a-ed of God

Admonition
1 Cor. 10:11 ... written for our a
Eph. 6:4 ... in the nurture and a
Titus 3:10 ... first and second a reject

Adoption
Rom. 8:15 ... received the spirit of a
Rom. 8:23 ... waiting for the a
Rom. 9:4 ... pertaineth the a
Gal. 4:5 ... receive the a of sons
Eph. 1:5 . predestinated as unto the a

Adorn
Is. 61:10 ... as a bride a-eth herself
Luke 21:5 ... a-ed with goodly stones
1 Tim. 2:9 ... women a themselves in
1 Pet. 3:3 ... a-ing . . . outward a-ing
Rev. 21:2 ... bride a-ed for her husband

Adulterer
Heb. 13:4 ... a-s God will judge

Adultery
Ex. 20:14 ... Thou shalt not commit a
Deut. 5:18 ... Neither . . . commit a
Matt. 5:28 ... committed a with her
Luke 18:20 ... Do not commit a
James 2:11 ... Do not commit a
2 Pet. 2:14 ... Having eyes full of a

Advantage
Luke 9:25 ... what is a man a-d
Rom. 3:1 ... a then hath the Jew
2 Cor. 2:11 ... Satan should get an a

Adversary
Ex. 23:22 ... an a unto thine a-ies
1 Kin. 11:14 ... Lord stirred up an a
Is. 50:8 ... who is mine a
Matt. 5:25 ... Agree with thine a
Luke 18:3 ... avenge me of mine a
1 Cor. 16:9 . and there are many a-ies
Phil. 1:28 ... terrified by your a-ies
Heb. 10:27 ... shall devour the a-ies
1 Pet. 5:8 ... because your a the devil

Adversity
2 Sam. 4:9 ... my soul out of all a
Prov. 17:17 ... brother is born for a
Prov. 24:10 ... faint in the day of a
Is. 30:20 ... give you the bread of a
Heb. 13:3 ... them which suffer a

Advise
Prov. 13:10 ... the well a-d is wisdom

Advocate
1 John 2:1 ... a with the father, Jesus

Afar
Jer. 23:23 ... and not a God a off
Matt. 26:58 . Peter followed him a off

Affection
Rom. 1:26..................up unto vile a-s
Rom. 12:10.......................kindly a-ed
Col. 3:2 ..Set your a on things above
Col. 3:5...........................inordinate a
1 Thess. 2:8 ..a-ately desirous of you
2 Tim. 3:3.............Without natural a

Afflict
Ps. 82:3 ....justice to the a-ed
Prov. 15:15 .days of the a-ed are evil
Is. 63:9 ..in . . . affliction he was a-ed
Nah. 1:12.........I will a thee no more
1 Tim. 5:10.......have relived the a-ed
James 5:13....is any among you a-ed

Affliction
Gen. 29:32....hath looked upon my a
Gen. 31:42......God hath seen mine a
Deut. 16:3...........even the bread of a
2 Chr. 20:9......cry unto thee in our a
2 Chr. 33:12..........when he was in a
Job 10:15 ....see thou mine a
Job 30:16 .days of a have taken hold
Job 36:15 ....the poor in his a
Ps. 25:18..............Look upon mine a
Is. 48:10................in the furnace of a
Jer. 16:19..my refuge in the day of a
Acts 20:23...bonds and a-s abide me
2 Cor. 2:4 ..out of much a . . . I wrote
2 Cor. 8:2............in a great trial of a
Phil. 1:16..........to add a to my bonds
James 1:27...fatherless . . . in their a

Afraid
Gen. 3:10.......a because I was naked
Ex. 3:6.................a to look upon God
Lev. 26:6 ....none shall make you a
Josh. 11:6..be not a because of them
Judg. 7:3.whosoever is fearful and a
Job 3:25.....which I was a of is come
Job 9:28......I am a of all my sorrows
Job 19:29 ....Be ye a of the sword
Ps. 27:1..............of whom shall I be a
Ps. 91:5........a for the terror by night
Ps. 112:7 ....not be a of evil tidings
Prov. 31:21............not a of the snow
Is. 51:12.be a of a man that shall die
Jer. 2:12.........................be horribly a
Mark 5:36.......Be not a, only believe
Mark 9:32......and were a to ask him
Luke 12:4.............a of them that kill
Gal. 4:11........................I am a of you
2 Pet. 2:10......are not a to speak evil

Afresh
Heb. 6:6......crucify . . . Son of God a

Aged
Job 12:20 ......understanding of the a
Job 15:10.....grayheaded, and very a
Job 32:9 ....neither do the a understand
Jer. 6:11 ..a with him . . . full of days
Titus 2:2, 3........a men be sober . . . a women

Agree
Matt. 5:25.....A with thine adversary
Matt. 18:19 ....if two of you shall a
Matt. 20:13.....a with me for a penny
Acts 15:15 ....to this a the words of
1 John 5:8...and these three a in one

Air
Gen. 1:26, 28..................fowl of the a
Deut. 4:17.....fowl that flieth in the a
2 Sam. 21:10.................birds of the a
Job 41:16.....no a can come between
Prov. 30:19 .way of an eagle in the a
1 Cor. 9:26.as one that beateth the a
1 Cor. 14:9 .ye shall speak into the a
Eph. 2:2prince of the power of the a
1 Thess. 4:17 .meet the Lord in the a

Alien
Ex. 18:3................a in a strange land
Deut. 14:21 ..mayest sell it unto an a
Job 19:15 ......I am an a in their sight
Ps. 69:8..............a unto my mother's children
Lam. 5:2..................our houses to a-s
Eph. 2:12.........................a-s from the commonwealth
Heb. 11:34..............armies of the a-s

Alienated
Eph. 4:18.........a from the life of God
Col. 1:21........that were sometimes a

Alive
Deut. 32:39.........I kill, and I make a
2 Kin. 5:7..........to kill and to make a
Luke 15:24....son was dead, and is a
Acts 1:3..................shewed himself a
Rom. 6:13...................................a from dead
1 Cor. 15:22.Christ . . . all be made a
Rev. 1:18...........I am a for evermore

Allegory
Gal. 4:24 ....which things are an a

Almighty
Gen. 17:1 ....I am the A God
Ex. 6:3...........by the name of God A
Job 11:7..............find out the A unto perfection
Job 29:5.........the A was yet with me
Job 37:23.A, we cannot find him out
Ps. 91:1 ....shadow of the A
Rev. 4:8 ....Lord God A
Rev. 11:17.....Lord God A, which art

Alms
Matt. 6:1...do not your a before men
Matt. 6:4 .....thine a may be in secret
Luke 12:33 ....Sell . . . and give a
Acts 10:2 ....which gave much a
Acts 24:17.........bring a to my nation

Alone
Gen. 2:18....Not good that man . . . a
Job 7:16....................................let me a
Matt. 4:4 ....man shall not live by bread a
Mark 14:6............................Let her a
Luke 9:18 ....as he was a praying
John 8:16.............................I am not a

Altar
Lev. 6:9.....................the fire of the a
Ps. 43:4 ....then will I go unto the a
Ezek. 6:4 . your a-s shall be desolate
Matt. 5:23........bring thy gift to the a
Matt. 23:19..............the gift, or the a
Rev. 9:13 .four horns of the golden a

Alway, Always
Gen. 6:3 ..my spirit shall not a strive
Deut. 14:23..fear the Lord thy God a
Matt. 28:20 ....lo, I am with you a
Mark 14:7...............me ye have not a
Phil 4:4.............rejoice in the Lord a

Am
Ex. 3:14............................I A that I A
Matt. 18:20.......there a I in the midst
1 Cor. 15:10......................I a what I a
Gal. 4:12 ....be as I a

Amazed
Is. 13:8 ....a one at another
Matt. 19:25..................exceedingly a
Mark 2:12...........a and glorified God
Mark 14:33..........began to be sore a
Luke 9:43 ..a at the mighty power of God
Acts 3:10 ....wonder and a-ment

Amen
Rev. 3:14....These things saith the A

Ancient
Dan. 7:9, 13, 22..................A of days

Angel
Gen. 24:7........send his a before thee
Ps. 78:25.........Man did eat a-s' food
Is. 63:9.....................a of his presence
Luke 20:36...........equal unto the a-s
Luke 22:43 ....an a . . . strengthening
John 20:12... two a-s in white sitting
Acts 6:15.........as . . . the face of an a
Acts 23:8..no resurrection, neither a
2 Cor. 11:14...............into an a of light
Col. 2:18.......and worshipping of a-s
Heb. 13:2..entertained a-s unawares
2 Pet. 2:4.......God spared not the a-s
Rev. 2:1, 8, 12............a of the church
Rev. 9:11........a of the bottomless pit

Anger
Gen. 49:7................Cursed be their a
Ex. 32:19............Moses' a waxed hot
Deut. 13:17 ....fierceness of his a
Neh. 9:17; Prov. 15:18.........slow to a
Ps. 30:5.....a endureth but a moment
Ps. 37:8.........................cease from a
Is. 5:25 ....a of the Lord kindled
Col. 3:21 ....provoke not . . . children to a

Angry
Gen. 18:30.........let not the Lord be a
Ps. 7:11......God is a with the wicked
Prov. 14:17 ....he that is soon a
Prov. 22:24........friendship with an a
Prov. 29:22...a man stirreth up strife
Jonah 4:4 .....Doest thou well to be a
Matt. 5:22..........is a with his brother
Eph 4:26............Be ye a, and sin not
Titus 1:7 ....not soon a

Anoint
Ps. 23:5 .thou a-est my head with oil
Ps. 105:15 ....touch not mine a-ed
Matt. 6:17..........fastest, a thine head
Mark 14:8 ....come to a my body
Mark 16:1.................come and a him
Luke 7:46.woman hath a-ed my feet
Acts 10:38..................God a-ed Jesus
2 Cor. 1:21..........hath a-ed us is God

Answer
Prov. 15:1........a soft a turneth away
Prov. 24:26 .lips that giveth a right a
Prov. 26:4, 5 ....A not a fool. A a fool
Eccles. 10:19 .money a-eth all things
Mic. 3:7 ....for there is no a of God
Matt. 26:62 ....A-est thou nothing
Luke 2:47....astonished at his . . . a-s
John 19:9 ....Jesus gave him no a
Col. 4:6..................how ye ought to a
1 Pet. 3:15 ....ready . . . to give an a
1 Pet. 3:21...................the a of a good conscience

Ant
Prov. 6:6..Go to the a, thou sluggard
Prov. 30:25........The a-s are a people

Antichrist
1 John 2:18, 22.a shall come. He is a
1 John 4:3........this is that spirit of a
2 John 7..............a deceiver and an a

Apostle
Matt. 10:2....names of the twelve a-s
Luke 11:49.............prophets and a-s
Rom. 1:1 ....called to be an a
Rom. 11:13 ....a of the Gentiles
1 Cor. 15:9......meet to be called an a
2 Cor. 12:11 ....very chiefest a-s
Gal. 1:19.other of the a-s saw I none
Gal. 2:8....a-ship of the circumcision
Eph. 4:11 ....he gave some, a-s
1 Tim. 2:7; 2 Tim. 1:11.........and an a

Apparel
1 Tim. 2:9........................in modest a
James 2:2........gold ring, in goodly a
1 Pet. 3:3 ....of putting on of a

Apple
Deut. 32:10; Ps. 17:8 ....a of his eye
Prov. 25:11 .....a-s of gold in pictures

Appoint
Ps. 79:11 ....those that a-ed to die
Is. 26:1 ....salvation will God a
Luke 22:29...I a unto you a kingdom
1 Thess. 5:9.......not a-ed us to wrath
Heb. 9:27 .a-ed unto men once to die

Approved
Acts 2:22 ....a man a of God
Rom. 14:18..acceptable . . . a of men
Rom. 16:10 ....a in Christ
2 Tim. 2:15..................shew thyself a

Archangel
1 Thess. 4:16 .with the voice of the a
Jude 9 ....Michael the a,

Arise
Ps. 3:7 ....**A**, O Lord; save me,
Luke 15:18..........will a and go to my father
Acts 22:16 ....**a**, and be baptized

Ark
Gen. 6:14..........an a of gopher wood
Ex. 2:3...............took for him an a of bulrushes
Ex. 37:1.made the a of shittim wood
Matt. 24:38....Noe entered into the a
Heb. 9:4 ....the a of the covenant
Rev. 11:19......the a of his testament

Arm
Deut. 33:27...........the everlasting **a**-s
Ps. 37:17 ....**a**-s of the wicked
Ps. 98:1...........**a** hath gotten him the victory
Mark 10:16...took them up in his **a**-s

Armour
Rom. 13:12.........put on the **a** of light
2 Cor. 6:7..by the **a** of righteousness
Eph. 6:11, 13.......the whole **a** of God

Array
Matt. 6:29.Solomon . . . not **a**-ed like
Rev. 7:13.What are these . . . **a**-ed in

Ascend
Ps. 24:3 ...who shall **a** into the hill of
Ps. 139:8...........If I **a** up into heaven
John 3:13...............no man hath **a**-ed
John 6:62 ....see the son of man **a** up
John 20:17 ....I **a** unto my Father
Rom. 10:6...Who shall **a** into heaven

Ashamed
Gen. 2:25....................and were not **a**
Ps. 25:2 ....let me not be **a**
Is. 24:23 ....and the sun **a**
Mark 8:38.shall the Son of man be **a**
Rom. 1:16.............not **a** of the gospel
2 Tim. 1:8.not . . . **a** of the testimony
Heb. 11:16.....not **a** to be called their
1 Pet. 4:16 ....let him not be **a**
1 John 2:28.........not be **a** before him

Ask
Judg. 18:5 ....**A** counsel . . . of God
1 Kin. 3:5.....**A** what I shall give thee
Ps. 2:8.........**A** of me, and I shall give
Is. 7:11.......**A** thee a sign of the Lord
Jer. 6:16.................**a** for the old paths
Zech. 10:1........**A** ye of the Lord rain
Matt. 5:42.......Give to him that **a**-eth
Matt. 7:7.**A** and it shall be given you
Matt. 21:22 .....whatsoever ye shall **a**
Luke 11:11.......If a son shall **a** bread
1 Cor. 10:25 ....**a**-ing no question
James 1:5......lack wisdom, let him **a**

Asleep
Judg. 4:21................for he was fast **a**
Matt. 26:40, 43....and findeth them **a**
Mark 4:38 .hinder part of the ship, **a**
Mark 14:40.........found them **a** again
Acts 7:60...he had said this, he fell **a**
1 Cor. 15:6..........but some are fallen **a**
1 Thess. 4:13, 15....them which are **a**

Ass
Num. 22:30..............am not I thine **a**
Prov. 26:3..................a bridle for the **a**
Jer. 22:19.......with the burial of an **a**
Zech. 9:9; Matt. 21:5..riding . . . an **a**
Matt. 21:2 ....ye shall find an **a** tied

Assembly
Lev. 23:36 ....it is a solemn **a**
Ps. 86:14...............**a**-ies of violent men
Ps. 111:1......................**a** of the upright
Acts 19:39..determined in a lawful **a**
Heb. 12:23 ....To the general **a**

Assurance
Is. 32:17 ....quietness and **a** for ever
Acts 17:31hath given **a** unto all men
Col. 2:2 ....full **a** of understanding
Heb. 6:11.full **a** of hope unto the end
Heb. 10:22.full **a** of faith, having our

Astray
Ps. 119:176 ..gone **a** like a lost sheep
Prov. 7:25..........go not **a** in her paths
Is. 53:6 ....like sheep have gone **a**
Matt. 18:13 ..and nine . . . went not **a**
1 Pet. 2:25 ....as sheep going **a**

Atonement
Lev. 23:27; 25:9 ....a day of **a**
Rom. 5:11 ....now received the **a**

Attain
Rom. 9:30 ....have **a**-ed to righteousness
Phil. 3:11 ......**a** unto the resurrection

Author
1 Cor. 14:33....not the **a** of confusion
Heb. 5:9.....the **a** of eternal salvation
Heb. 12:2 .**a** and finisher of our faith

Authority
Prov. 29:2 ....righteous are in **a**
Matt. 7:29............taught them as one having **a**
Matt. 8:9......For I am a man under **a**
Matt. 21:23......By what **a** doest thou
Luke 9:1 ......gave them power and **a**
Luke 20:8 ....by what **a** I do these
John 5:27 ......given him **a** to execute
1 Cor. 15:24 ....all rule and all **a**
1 Tim. 2:12..to usurp **a** over the man
Titus 2:15................rebuke with all **a**

Availeth
Gal. 5:6 ..neither circumcision **a** any
James 5:16 ......prayer of a righteous man **a** much

Avenge
2 Sam. 22:48 ...It is God that **a**-th me
Ps. 18:47..........It is God that **a**-th me
Jer. 5:9, 29..shall not my soul be **a**-d
Luke 18:3 ...**A** me of mine adversary
Rom. 12:19 ....**a** not yourselves
Rev. 18:20.............God hath **a**-d you

Awe
Ps. 4:4...........Stand in **a**, and sin not
Ps. 33:8..........of the world stand in **a**
Ps. 119:161.........standeth in **a** of thy word

Axe
2 Kin. 6:5 ..**a** head fell into the water
Jer. 51:20..........Thou art my battle **a**
Luke 3:9....the **a** is laid unto the root

B

Babe
Ex. 2:6 ....behold, the **b** wept
Ps. 8:2 ....out of the mouth of **b**-s
Matt. 11:25...revealed them unto **b**-s
Luke 1:41, 44.................the **b** leaped
1 Pet. 2:2.....................As newborn **b**-s

Back
2 Sam. 12:23 ....can I bring him **b**
Prov. 19:29 .stripes for the **b** of fools
Is. 50:6.....I gave my **b** to the smiters
Luke 9:62 .....man . . . looking **b** is fit
Heb. 10:38............if any man draw **b**

Backbite
Prov. 25:23.....................a **b**-ing tongue
Rom. 1:30............**B**-rs, haters of God
2 Cor. 12:20..................strifes, **b**-ings

Backslide
Prov. 14:14..the **b**-r in heart shall be
Jer. 3:14.........Turn, O **b**-ing children
Jer. 14:7 ....our **b**-ings are many
Jer. 31:22...........O thou **b**-ing daughter
Hos. 14:4.........I will heal their **b**-ing

Bad
Lev. 27:10 ..good for a **b**, or a **b** for a
Matt. 13:48 ....but cast the **b** away
Matt. 22:10 ..found, both **b** and good
2 Cor. 5:10...whether it be good or **b**

Balance
Lev. 19:36 ....Just **b**-s, just weights
Job 31:6...........weighed in an even **b**
Prov. 11:1; 20:23..................a false **b**
Is. 40:15 ....the small dust of the **b**
Mic. 6:11 ...pure with the wicked **b**-s
Rev. 6:5.......a pair of **b**-s in his hand

Balm
Gen. 43:11 .little **b** and a little honey
Jer. 8:22.........Is there no **b** in Gilead
Ezek. 27:17......honey, and oil, and **b**

Bands
Judg. 15:14.......his **b** loosed from off
Ps. 2:3 ....break their **b** asunder
Is. 58:6 .....loose the **b** of wickedness
Luke 8:29....................he brake the **b**
Acts 16:26............every one's **b** were loosed
Col. 2:19.....the body by joints and **b**

Baptism
Matt. 21:25...................The **b** of John
Mark 1:4 ....**b** of repentance
Rom. 6:4 ....buried with him by **b**
Eph 4:5 ....one Lord, one faith, one **b**
1 Pet. 3:21........**b** doth now also save

Baptize
Matt. 3:11; Mark 1:8; Luke 3:16..... **b** you with water . . . **b** with the Holy Ghost
John 1:25 ....Why **b**-st thou then, if
John 1:33 ..**b**-th with the Holy Ghost
John 3:26........the same **b**-th, and all men
1 Cor. 1:17....Christ sent me not to **b**

Baptized
Matt. 3:13.......................to be **b** of him
Matt. 20:22 ....that I am **b** with
Mark 1:8........have **b** you with water
Mark 10:39.........withal shall ye be **b**
Luke 3:21 ....all the people were **b**
John 4:2 ....Jesus himself **b** not
John 10:40 ....where John at first **b**
Acts 1:5..........**b** with the Holy Ghost
Acts 2:38................**b** every one of you
Acts 8:36...............hinder me to be **b**
Acts 18:8 ....believed, and were **b**
Rom. 6:3 ....**b** into Jesus Christ
1 Cor. 1:13 ......**b** in the name of Paul
1 Cor. 10:2 ....**b** unto Moses
1 Cor. 12:13...one Spirit are we all **b**
1 Cor. 15:29..........are **b** for the dead
Gal. 3:27..........................**b** into Christ

Barn
Matt. 6:26...reap, nor gather into **b**-s
Luke 12:18.............pull down my **b**-s

Barren
Gen. 11:30 ....Sarai was **b**
Gen. 29:31......................Rachel was **b**
Ex. 23:26..cast their young, nor be **b**
1 Sam. 2:5 ......the **b** hath born seven
Ps. 107:34.a fruitful land into **b**-ness
Luke 23:29 ....Blessed are the **b**
2 Pet. 1:8.neither be **b** nor unfruitful

Base
2 Sam. 6:22...be **b** in mine own sight
Job 30:8 ....children of **b** men
Is. 3:5 ....**b** against the honourable
Mal. 2:9 ....made you contemptible and **b**
Acts 17:5......lewd fellows of **b**-r sort
1 Cor. 1:28 ....**b** things of the world

Basket
Jer. 24:2 ......**b** had very naughty figs
Amos 8:1, 2 ....**b** of summer fruit
Matt. 14:20.remained twelve **b**-s full
Acts 9:25......let him down . . . in a **b**
2 Cor. 11:33.............**b** was I let down

Battle
1 Sam. 17:47.........the **b** is the Lord's
Ps. 18:39..............strength unto the **b**
Ps. 24:8 ....Lord mighty in **b**
Ps. 55:18.....soul in peace from the **b**
Eccles. 9:11 ...nor the **b** to the strong
Jer. 50:22....sound of **b** is in the land
Rev. 9:9 ....horses running to **b**

Beam
Matt. 7:5 ....cast out the **b** out of

Bear
2 Kin. 2:24 ....two she **b**-s
Prov. 17:12...**b** robbed of her whelps
Is. 11:7....cow and the **b** shall feed
Rev. 13:2.feet were as the feet of a **b**

Bear
Gen. 4:13....greater than I can **b**
Ex. 20:16 ....shalt not **b** false witness
Ps. 91:12....**b** thee up in their hands
Prov. 18:14....spirit who can **b**
Matt. 27:32.compelled to **b** his cross
Mark 10:19....Do not **b** false witness
John 1:7 .....to **b** witness of the Light
John 5:31....**b** witness of myself
John 15:4 ....branch cannot **b** fruit
John 15:8 ...**b** much fruit; so shall ye
John 15:27 ....ye also shall **b** witness
Acts 9:15 ....**b** my name before the Gentiles
Rom. 15:1 .....**b** the infirmities of the weak
1 Cor. 13:7....**B**-eth all things
Gal. 6:2 .**B** ye one another's burdens
Heb. 9:28....**b** the sins of many

Beast
Job 18:3 ....are we counted as **b**-s
Ps. 73:22 ....I was as a **b**
Luke 10:34....set him on his own **b**
1 Cor. 15:32 ...I have fought with **b**-s

Beautiful
Is. 52:7...How **b** upon the mountains
Matt. 23:27....indeed appear **b**
Acts 3:10....alms at the **B** gate
Rom. 10:15....How **b** are the feet

Beauty
1 Chr. 16:29 ....worship the Lord in the **b**
Job 40:10....with glory and **b**
Ps. 29:2....in the **b** of holiness
Prov. 20:29....**b** of old men

Bed
Deut. 3:11 .....**b**-stead was . . . of iron
1 Chr. 5:1....defiled his father's **b**
Ps. 63:6...remember thee upon my **b**
Prov. 7:17 ....perfumed my **b**
Is. 28:20....**b** is shorter than a man
Ezek. 23:17 ....into the **b** of love
Matt. 9:6....take up thy **b**
Mark 4:21 ....candle . . . under a **b**
Luke 11:7 .children are with me in **b**
Luke 17:34....two men in one **b**
Acts 9:33 .had kept his **b** eight years
Heb. 13:4 ....and the **b** undefiled
Rev. 2:22 ....cast her into a **b**

Beginning
Gen. 1:1 ....In the **b** God created
Job 8:7 ....thy **b** was small
Ps. 111:10....fear of the Lord is the **b**
Eccles. 7:8 ....the end . . . than the **b**
Mark 1:1 ....The **b** of the gospel
John 1:1 ....**b** was the Word
Rev. 21:6....the **b** and the end

Begotten
Ps. 2:7....this day have I **b** thee
Acts 13:33 .my Son . . . have I **b** thee
John 1:18 ....the only **b** Son
1 Pet. 1:3....**b** . . . unto a lively hope

Beguile
Gen. 3:13 ....The serpent **b**-d me
Gen. 29:25....hast thou **b**-d me
2 Cor. 11:3 ....serpent **b**-d Eve
Col. 2:4 ...lest any man should **b** you
2 Pet. 2:14 ....**b**-ing unstable souls

Behave
1 Sam. 18:5 ....**b**-d himself wisely
Ps. 101:2....I will **b** myself wisely
1 Cor. 13:5 ....Doth not **b** itself unseemly
1 Tim. 3:15...how thou oughtest to **b**

Believe
Gen. 15:6....he **b**-d in the Lord
2 Chr. 20:20....**b** in the Lord
Matt. 8:13...as thou hast **b**-d, so be it
Matt. 9:28 ....**B** ye that I am able
Matt. 21:22....in prayer, **b**-ing
Mark 9:24 .Lord, I **b**; help thou mine
Mark 15:32 ....we may see and **b**
John 3:18....that **b**-th on him is not
John 9:35....**b** on the Son of God
John 11:25....he that **b**-th in me
John 14:1 ..ye **b** in God, **b** also in me
John 16:31 ....Do ye now **b**
Rom. 4:24 ....**b** on . . . that raised up Jesus
Rom. 6:8we **b** that we shall also live
Rom. 10:16.who hath **b**-d our report
Rom. 15:13 ....with all joy . . . **b**-ing
1 Cor. 13:7...Beareth all things, **b**-th
Gal. 2:16..even we have **b**-d in Jesus
1 Thess. 4:14 .if we **b** that Jesus died
Heb. 4:3....which have **b**-d do enter
James 2:23 ....Abraham **b**-d God
1 John 5:1....Whosoever **b**-th that Jesus
1 John 5:10...**b**-th on the Son of God

Belly
Gen. 3:14 ...upon thy **b** shalt thou go
Judg. 3:21....thrust it into his **b**
Job 15:2.fill his **b** with the east wind
Prov. 18:20 ....**b** shall be satisfied
Ezek. 3:3....cause thy **b** to eat
Jonah 1:17 ....Jonah was in the **b** of
Luke 15:16....fain have filled his **b**
John 7:38 ....**b** shall flow rivers
Rom. 16:18 ....serve . . . their own **b**
Phil. 3:19 ....whose God is their **b**
Titus 1:12....evil beasts, slow **b**-s
Rev. 10:9 ....make thy **b** bitter

Beloved
Deut. 33:12...The **b** of the Lord shall
Ps. 127:2 ....he giveth his **b** sleep
Is. 5:1 ....a song of my **b**
Matt. 3:17....This is my **b** Son
Matt. 12:18..my **b**, in whom my soul
Rom. 12:19 ....Dearly **b**, avenge not
1 Cor. 4:14....as my **b** sons
Col. 3:12....elect of God, holy and **b**

Benefit
Ps. 68:19 ....daily loadeth us with **b**-s
Ps. 103:2 ....and forget not all his **b**-s
2 Cor. 1:15....have a second **b**
1 Tim. 6:2 ....partakers of the **b**

Bestow
Luke 12:17....where to **b** my fruits
John 4:38....ye **b**-ed no labour
1 Cor. 13:3 ..though I **b** all my goods
1 John 3:1 ...manner of love . . . hath **b**-ed

Betray
1 Chr. 12:17 ....to **b** me to mine enemies
Matt. 26:21....one of you shall **b** me
Matt. 27:4....**b**-ed the innocent blood
Mark 13:12 ....brother shall **b** the brother
John 18:2....Judas also, which **b**-ed him
1 Cor. 11:23 ...night in which he was **b**-ed

Better
1 Sam. 15:22obey is **b** than sacrifice
Ps. 118:8, 9....**b** to trust in the Lord
Prov. 8:11 ...wisdom is **b** than rubies
Prov. 17:1 ....**B** is a dry morsel
Eccles. 7:1....A good name is **b** than
Song 1:2 ....love is **b** than wine
Matt. 6:26....Are ye not much **b** then
Matt. 18:8....**b** for thee to enter into life
Mark 9:42.**b** for him that a millstone
Luke 5:39....The old is **b**
1 Cor. 7:9....**b** to marry
Heb. 8:6 ....a **b** covenant . . . **b** promises
Heb. 11:35 ....a **b** resurrection

Bewail
Judg. 11:37 ....and **b** my virginity
Luke 8:52 ....all wept, and **b**-ed her
2 Cor. 12:21 ....**b** many which have sinned

Beware
Ex. 23:21 ....**B** of him, and obey
Deut. 6:12 ....**b** lest thou forget the Lord
Matt. 7:15 ....**B** of false prophets
Matt. 10:17 ....But **b** of men
Mark 8:15....**b** of the leaven
Mark 12:38....**B** of the scribes
Luke 12:15 ....**b** of covetousness
Phil. 3:2.**B** of dogs, **b** of evil workers
Col. 2:8 ....**B** lest any man spoil you

Bid
Matt. 14:28....**b** me come unto thee
Matt. 22:3.call them that were **b**-den
Matt. 22.9....**b** to the marriage
Luke 9:61 ....let me first go **b** them
1 Cor. 10:27....that believe not **b** you
2 John 10...neither **b** him God speed

Bind
Gen. 37:7 ..**b**-ing sheaves in the field
Num. 30:2....oath to **b** his soul
Job 28:11....**b**-eth the floods
Prov. 3:3....**b** them about thy neck
Matt. 16:19....whatsoever . . . **b** on earth
Matt. 18:18 ....**b** on earth shall be bound
Mark 5:3....no man could **b** him

Bird
Gen. 7:14....every **b** of every sort
Deut. 14:11.all clean **b**-s ye shall eat
Job 41:5 ....play . . . as with a **b**
Ps. 124:7 .....**b** out of the snare of the
Song 2:2....time of the singing of **b**-s
Is. 16:2....**b** cast out of the nest
Hos. 9:11 ....shall fly away like a **b**
Amos 3:5....**b** fall in a snare
Matt. 8:20 ...**b**-s of the air have nests

Birth
Job 3:16 ...untimely **b** I had not been
Eccles. 7:1 ....than the day of one's **b**
Luke 1:14....rejoice at his **b**
John 9:1....blind from his **b**

Birthright
Gen. 25:31 ....Sell me this day thy **b**
1 Chr. 5:2....the **b** was Joseph's
Heb. 12:16 .....for . . . meat sold his **b**

Bishop
1 Tim. 3:2 .**b** then must be blameless
1 Pet. 2:25...Shepherd and **B** of your

Bitter
Ex. 12:8....**b** herbs they shall eat
Job 13:26....thou writest **b** things
Prov. 5:4....**b** as wormwood
Is. 5:20 ....**b** for sweet . . . sweet for **b**
Is. 22:4....I will weep **b**-ly
Matt. 26:75...went out and wept **b**-ly
James 3:14 ....**b** envying and strife

Bitterness
1 Sam. 15:32 ....**b** of death is past
Job 10:1 ....in the **b** of my soul
Rom. 3:14....mouth is full of . . . **b**
Eph. 4:31 ....all **b**, and wrath,
Heb. 12:15 ....lest any root of **b**

Blame
Gen. 43:9....bear the **b** for ever
2 Cor. 6:3....the ministry be not **b**-d
2 Cor. 8:20 ....no man should **b** us
Eph. 1:4....be holy and without **b**

Blameless
Gen. 44:10....ye shall be **b**
Luke 1:6 ....ordinances of the Lord **b**
1 Cor. 1:8 ....**b** in the day of our Lord
1 Thess. 5:23 ....soul and body . . . **b**
Titus 1:7 ....a bishop must be **b**
2 Pet. 3:14....without spot, and **b**

Blaspheme
Lev. 24:16**b**-th the name of the Lord
Ezek. 20:27.....your fathers have **b**-d
Matt. 9:3 ....This man **b**-th
Mark 3:29 .**b** against the Holy Ghost

Luke 22:65 ....other things **b**-ously
Acts 6:11 ......heard him speak **b**-ous
Rev. 16:9 ....**b** the name of God

Blasphemy
Matt. 12:31..All manner of sin and **b**
Matt. 15:19.out of the heart . . . **b**-ies
Matt. 26:65 ....ye have heard his **b**
Mark 7:22 ....evil eye, **b**, pride
Col. 3:8 ....wrath, malice, **b**

Blemish
Ex. 12:5 ....lamb shall be without **b**
2 Sam. 14:25...there was no **b** in you
Eph. 5:27 ....should be holy and without **b**
1 Pet. 1:19 ....a lamb without **b**
2 Pet. 2:13 ....spots they are and **b**-es

Bless
Gen. 1:22 ....And God **b**-ed them
Gen. 12:2.I will **b** thee and make thy
Gen. 28:3 ....God Almighty **b** thee
2 Sam. 7:29 ....please thee to **b** the house
Ps. 29:11 ......**b** his people with peace
Ps. 103:1 ....**B** the Lord, O my soul
Matt. 5:44 ....**b** them that curse you
Mark 14:22 .Jesus took bread and **b**-ed
1 Cor. 10:16cup of **b**-ing which we **b**
James 3:9 ....Therewith **b** we God

Blessed
Job 1:21...**b** be the name of the Lord
Prov. 31:28.....children . . . call her **b**
Matt. 5:3-10 ....**B** are the (they)
Luke 1:48..generations shall call me **b**
John 12:13 ....**B** is the King
Titus 2:13....Looking for that **b** hope
Rev. 14:13 ....**B** are the dead

Blessing
Gen. 12:2 ....thou shalt be a **b**
Gen. 27:36 ....taken away my **b**
Deut. 11:26......set before you . . . a **b**
Prov. 10:6 ..**B**-s are upon the head of
Ezek. 34:26 ....showers of **b**
Mal. 3:10 ....pour you out a **b**
Eph. 1:3......spiritual **b**-s in heavenly
1 Pet. 3:9 ....ye should inherit a **b**

Blind
Deut. 16:19 .....doth **b** the eyes of the wise
Job 29:15 ....I was eyes to the **b**
John 12:40...He hath **b**-ed their eyes
Rom. 2:19 ....a guide to the **b**
2 Cor. 3:14 .....their minds were **b**-ed
1 John 2:11...darkness hath **b**-ed his eyes

Blindness
2 Kin. 6:18.......Smite this people . . . with **b**
Rom. 11:25......**b** in part is happened
Eph. 4:18 ....the **b** of their heart

Blood
Gen. 4:10 .....voice of thy brother's **b**
Gen. 9:6..sheddeth man's **b** . . . his **b**
Gen. 49:11 ....in the **b** of grapes
Ps. 51:14 ....Deliver me from **b**-guiltiness
Ps. 55:23 ....**b**-y and deceitful men
Prov. 29:10 ....**b**-thirsty hate the upright
Is. 1:15 ....your hands are full of **b**
Is. 49:26 ...drunken with their own **b**
Matt. 16:17 ....flesh and **b** hath not
Matt. 26:28..my **b** . . . new testament
Matt. 27:4....betrayed the innocent **b**
John 6:55 ....my **b** is drink indeed
Acts 17:26.made of one **b** all nations
Acts 20:28...purchased with his own **b**
Rom. 3:25 ....through faith in his **b**
Rom. 5:9 ....justified by his **b**
1 Cor. 15:50 .....and **b** cannot inherit
Eph. 1:7....redemption through his **b**
1 John 1:7 ....**b** of Jesus Christ

1 John 5:6 ....but by water and **b**
Rev. 7:14.white in the **b** of the Lamb

Blot
Ex. 32:33 ....**b** out of my book
Ps. 51:1 ....**b** out my transgressions
Is. 43:25 ....I am he that **b**-eth out
Jer. 18:23 ....**b** out their sin
Col. 2:14 ..**B**-ing out the handwriting

Boast
2 Chr. 25:19 ....lifteth thee up to **b**
Ps. 44:8 ....In God we **b**
Prov. 27:1 ....**B** not thyself of tomorrow
Is. 10:15 ....Shall the ax **b** itself
James 4:16.ye rejoice in your **b**-ings

Bodies
Neh. 9:37 ....dominion over our **b**
Job 13:12 ....your **b** to **b** of clay
Jer. 31:40 ....valley of the dead **b**
Rom. 1:24 ....dishonour their own **b**
Rom. 8:11 ......quicken your mortal **b**
Rom. 12:1 .....present your **b** a living
Heb. 10:22 ....**b** washed with pure
Rev. 11:9 ....see their dead **b** three

Body
Job 19:26 ....worms destroy this **b**
Lam. 4:7 ....more ruddy in **b**
Matt. 6:22 .....light of the **b** is the eye
Matt. 10:28..destroy both soul and **b**
Matt. 26:26.....Take, eat; this is my **b**
Matt. 27:58 ....begged the **b** of Jesus
Luke 12:4 ....them that kill the **b**
Luke 22:19 ....This is my **b**
John 2:21 ....temple of his **b**
Rom. 8:10....**b** is dead because of sin
Rom. 8:23 ....redemption of our **b**
1 Cor. 6:20.......glorify God in your **b**
1 Cor. 9:27 ....I keep under my **b**
1 Cor. 13:3 .I give my **b** to be burned
1 Cor. 15:44.natural **b** . . . spiritual **b**
2 Cor. 5:8 ....be absent from the **b**
Gal. 6:17 ......bear in my **b** the marks
Eph. 4:4 ....There is one **b**
Phil. 1:20 ....magnified in my **b**
Phil. 3:21 ....change our vile **b**
Col. 1:18 ....he is the head of the **b**
Col. 3:15 ....ye are called in one **b**
1 Pet. 2:24 ....bare our sins in . . . **b**

Bold
Prov. 28:1...righteous are **b** as a lion
2 Cor. 11:21 .whereinsoever any is **b**
Eph. 3:12...In whom we have **b**-ness
Eph. 6:19 ....open my mouth **b**-ly
Heb. 4:16Let us therefore come **b**-ly
1 John 4:17 ....**b**-ness in the day

Bond
Eph. 4:3 ....Spirit in the **b** of peace
1 Cor. 12:13 ....we be **b** or free
Gal. 3:28 ..there is neither **b** nor free
Phil. 1:13....that my **b**-s in Christ are
Col. 3:14 ....is the **b** of perfectness
Rev. 13:16 .rich and poor, free and **b**

Bone
Gen. 2:23 .....This is now **b** of my **b**-s
Judg. 9:2 ....your **b** and your flesh
Job 10:11 ....fenced me with **b**-s
Job 19:20 ....**b** cleaveth to my skin
Ps. 6:2 ....heal me; for my **b**-s are vexed
Prov. 15:30 .....report maketh the **b**-s fat
Prov. 25:15 .....tongue breaketh the **b**
Ezek. 37:1 ..valley . . . was full of **b**-s
Matt. 23:27......full of dead men's **b**-s
Luke 24:39 .....hath not flesh and **b**-s
John 19:36 ....A **b** of him . . . not be broken

Book
Ex. 17:14 ....for a memorial in a **b**
Job 19:23 ....printed in a **b**
Ps. 69:28 ....blotted out of the **b**
Eccles. 12:12 .....many **b**-s . . . no end
Is. 34:16 .....out of the **b** of the Lord
Ezek. 2:9 ....roll of a **b** was therein
Mal. 3:16 ....a **b** of remembrance

Luke 4:17...when he had opened the **b**
Luke 20:42 ....in the **b** of Psalms
John 21:25 ......world . . . not contain the **b**-s
Phil. 4:3; Rev. 3:5; 22:19 ....**b** of life
Rev. 22:19 ....the words of the **b**

Born
Gen 15:3 ....one **b** in my house
Ex. 21:4 ......**b** him sons or daughters
Job 14:1 ....Man that is **b** . . . of few days
Prov. 17:17 ....brother is **b** for adversity
Is. 9:6 ....unto us a child is **b**
Matt. 2:1 ..Jesus was **b** in Bethlehem
John 3:3.....Except a man be **b** again
Acts 22:28 ....But I was free **b**
Gal. 4:29 ....**b** after the flesh
1 Pet. 1:23 ....**b** again, not of corruptible

Borrow
Deut. 15:6...thou shalt lend . . . not **b**
Ps. 37:21 ....wicked **b**-eth,
Prov. 22:7 ....**b**-er is servant to the
Matt. 5:42 ..him that would **b** of thee

Bottle
Matt. 9:17.put new wine into old **b**-s

Bottomless
Rev. 9:1 .....given the key of the **b** pit
Rev. 20:3 ....cast him into the **b** pit

Bought
1 Cor. 6:20.For ye are **b** with a price
2 Pet. 2:1 ....the Lord that **b** them

Bountiful
Ps. 13:6 ....he hath dealt **b**-ly
2 Cor. 9:6 ..soweth **b**-ly . . . reap also **b**-ly
2 Cor. 9:11.enriched . . . to all **b**-ness

Bow
Gen. 9:13 ..I do set my **b** in the cloud
Hos. 1:5 ...I will break the **b** of Israel

Bow
Ex. 20:5 ....Thou shalt not **b** down
Ps. 57:6 ....my soul is **b**-ed down
Is. 45:23 .unto me every knee shall **b**
John 19:30 ....**b**-ed his head
Eph. 3:14 ....I **b** my knees unto the Father
Phil. 2:10 ....every knee should **b**

Bramble
Judg. 9:14......all the trees unto the **b**
Is. 34:13.nettles and **b**-s in fortresses
Luke 6:44 ....not of a **b** bush gather they

Branch
Job 15:32 .....his **b** shall not be green
Prov. 11:28 ....shall flourish as a **b**
Is. 4:2 ......day shall the **b** of the Lord
John 15:2..every **b** that beareth fruit
John 15:6 ....cast forth as a **b**

Brand
Judg. 15:5 ....set the **b**-s on fire
Zech. 3:2..is not this a **b** plucked out

Brass
Gen. 4:22 ....artificer in **b** and iron
Num. 21:9 ....a serpent of **b**
Ps. 107:16 ....broken the gates of **b**
Matt. 10:9 ....gold, nor silver, nor **b**
1 Cor. 13:1 .....become as sounding **b**
Rev. 1:15 ....feet like unto fine **b**

Breach
Lev. 24:20 ....**B** for **b**, eye for eye
Ps. 60:2 ....heal the **b**-s thereof
Ps. 106:23 .stood before him in the **b**
Is. 58:12 ....repairer of the **b**

Bread
Gen. 3:19.sweat of thy face . . . eat **b**
Gen. 18:5 ....fetch a morsel of **b**
Deut. 8:3; Matt. 4:4....live by **b** alone
Deut. 16:8 .....shalt eat unleavened **b**
1 Kin. 17:6..brought him **b** and flesh

Ps. 102:9 .... eaten ashes like **b**
Prov. 9:17 .... **b** eaten in secret
Prov. 31:27 .... **b** of idleness
Eccles. 11:1 .... Cast thy **b** upon the waters
Matt. 4:3 .... stones be made **b**
Matt. 6:11 .... give us . . . our daily **b**
Mark 7:27.... to take, the children's **b**
Luke 11:11 .... if a son shall ask **b**

Breath
Gen. 2:7 .... his nostrils the **b** of life
Gen. 6:17 .... wherein is the **b** of life
Job 33:4..... **b** of the Almighty . . . life
Acts 17:25 .he giveth to all life and **b**

Breathe
Ps. 27:12 ...and such as **b** out cruelty
John 20:22 .... he **b**-d on them
Acts 9:1 .... and Saul, yet **b**-ing out

Breeches
Ex. 28:42 .**b** to cover their nakedness
Lev. 6:10 .shall put on his . . . linen **b**
Ezek. 44:18..shall have linen **b** upon

Brethren
Job 6:15 .My **b** have dealt deceitfully
Ps. 133:1 .... **b** to dwell together
Hos. 2:1 .... Say ye unto your **b**
Matt. 5:47..... if ye salute your **b** only
Matt. 12:46 .... mother . . . **b** stood
Matt. 23:8 .... and all ye are **b**
Matt. 25:40 .... least of these my **b**
Mark 12:20 .... there were seven **b**
Acts 7:2 .... Men, **b**, and fathers
1 Tim. 4:6 put the **b** in remembrance
1 Pet. 1:22 ....unfeigned love of the **b**
1 John 3:14 ....because we love the **b**

Brick
Ex. 5:7 .... no more straw to make **b**
Is. 9:10 .... the **b**-s are fallen

Bride
Is. 61:10 .... as a **b** adorneth
Is. 62:5 .... rejoiceth over the **b**
John 3:29 .... He that hath the **b**
Rev. 22:17 .... Spirit and the **b** say, Come

Bridechamber
Matt. 9:15.... children of the **b** mourn
Mark 2:19 .... children of **b** fast while
Luke 5:34 ..... make children of **b** fast

Bridegroom
Is. 61:10 .... as a **b** decketh himself
Jer. 7:34 .... the voice of the **b**
Matt. 9:15 long as the **b** is with them
Matt. 25:1 ...went forth to meet the **b**
John 3:29 .... hath the bride is the **b**

Bridle
2 Kin. 19:28..put . . . my **b** in thy lips
Ps. 32:9 ....must be held in with . . . **b**
Ps. 39:1 .I will keep my mouth with a **b**

Bridle
James 1:26...and **b**-th not his tongue
James 3:2....able also to **b** the whole body

Brimstone
Gen. 19:24 .... Sodom and . . . Gomorrah **b**
Is. 30:33 .... like a stream of **b**
Ezek. 38:22..... hail stones, fire and **b**
Luke 17:29 .... rained fire and **b**
Rev. 19:20 .... lake of fire burning with **b**

Broad
Job 36:16 .... strait into a **b** place
Ps. 119:96 .... commandment is exceeding **b**
Matt. 7:13 .**b** is the way, that leadeth

Broken
John 19:36....... bone of him shall not be **b**
1 Cor. 11:24....... body, which is **b** for you
Eph. 2:14..... **b** down the middle wall

Brook
Deut. 8:7.......... a land of **b**-s of water
Ps. 42:1...panteth after the water **b**-s
Prov. 18:4...... wisdom as a flowing **b**
John 18:1...... his disciples over the **b**

Brother
Ps. 50:20 .... speakest against thy **b**
Prov. 17:17 .... **b** is born for adversity
Prov. 18:24 ..sticketh closer than a **b**
Eccles. 4:8 .... neither child nor **b**
Matt. 12:50 .same is my **b**, and sister
1 Cor. 8:13 .... lest I make my **b** to offend
Gal. 1:19 .... James the Lord's **b**
1 John 2:9 ....He that . . . hateth his **b**

Brotherly
Rom. 12:10 .... with **b** love
Heb. 13:1 .... let **b** love continue
2 Pet. 1:7 .... godliness **b** kindness

Bruise
Gen. 3:15 .... **b** thy head, and thou shalt **b**
Jer. 30:12 .... Thy **b** is incurable
Matt. 12:20 .... **b**-d reed shall he not
Luke 4:18 .... at liberty them **b**-d
Rom. 16:20..**b** Satan under your feet

Build
Gen. 11:4 .... let us **b** us a city
Num. 23:1 ..... **B** me here seven altars
1 Sam. 2:35..will **b** him a sure house
1 Chr. 17:4 ..shalt not **b** me an house
Job 20:19 ...house which he **b**-ed not
Ps. 127:1 .... Except the Lord **b** the
Jer. 29:5 .... **B** ye houses, and dwell
Matt. 16:18 .... this rock will I **b** my
Acts 20:32 .... to **b** you up

Builders
2 Kin. 22:6.... Unto carpenters, and **b**
Ps. 118:22 ...... stone . . . the **b** refused
Matt. 21:42...stone . . . the **b** rejected
Acts 4:11 .... set at naught of you **b**

Building
1 Kin. 6:38 .... seven years in **b** it
1 Cor. 3:9 .... ye are God's **b**
2 Cor. 5:1 .... we have a **b** of God
Eph. 2:21 .the **b** fitly framed together

Burden
2 Sam. 15:33 .... be a **b** unto me
2 Kin. 9:25 .... Lord laid this **b**
Job 7:20 .... I am a **b** to myself
Ps. 55:22 ...Cast thy **b** upon the Lord
Jer. 23:34 .... The **b** of the Lord
Zech. 9:1 ....The **b** of the word of the
Matt. 11:30 .... my **b** is light
Matt. 20:12 ..borne the **b** and heat of
Gal. 6:5 .....man shall bear his own **b**

Burdensome
2 Cor. 11:9 kept myself from being **b**
2 Cor. 12:13, 14....... was not **b** to you
1 Thess. 2:6.......... might have been **b**

Buried
Gen. 15:15.......... **b** in a good old age
Ruth 1:17.......... and there will I be **b**
Eccles. 8:10.....so I saw the wicked **b**
Acts 2:29 .... he is both dead and **b**
Rom. 6:4 .... we are **b** with him
Col. 2:12 .... **B** with him in baptism

Bush
Ex. 3:2 .... the **b** burned with fire
Song 5:11 .... his locks are **b**-y
Mark 12:26 .in the **b** God spake unto
Acts 7:30....... in a flame of fire in a **b**

Bushel
Matt. 5:15.......... candle . . . under a **b**
Mark 4:21 .....put under a **b**, or a bed
Luke 11:33 .... neither under a **b**

Business
Deut. 24:5...... be charged with any **b**
Judg. 18:7 ....had no **b** with any man
Ps. 107:23 ..that do **b** in great waters
Prov. 22:29 .... man diligent in his **b**
Luke 2:49 .... must be about my Father's **b**

Acts 6:3 .... may appoint over his **b**
Rom. 12:11 .... not slothful in **b**
1 Thess. 4:11 .....study . . . to do your own **b**

Busybody
2 Thess. 3:11 .... but are **b**-ies
1 Tim. 5:13..... tattlers also, and **b**-ies
1 Pet. 4:15 .... a **b** in other men's matters

Byword
Deut. 28:37 .an astonishment . . . a **b**
1 Kin. 9:7..and a **b** among all people
Job 30:9 .... song, yea, I am their **b**

C

Calamity
2 Sam. 22:19; Ps. 18:18 ..day of my **c**
Ps. 57:1 ...until these **c**-s be overpast
Prov. 19:13 .... foolish son is the **c**
Prov. 27:10 .... in the day of the **c**

Calf
Gen. 18:7 .... fetch a **c** tender and
Is. 11:6 .... **c** and the young lion
Luke 15:23..bring hither the fatted **c**
Heb. 9:12....blood of goats and **c**-ves
Rev. 4:7 .... second beast like a **c**

Call
Gen. 4:26....men to **c** upon the name
Deut. 4:26....... **c** heaven and earth to
Ruth 1:20....... **C** me not Naomi, **c** me Mara
I Kin. 17:18 .... **c** my sin to remembrance
Ps. 4:1 .... Hear me when I **c**
Ps. 18:3 .... I will **c** upon the Lord
Is. 5:20...... **c** evil good, and good evil
Is. 7:14 .... **c** his name Immanuel
Jer. 3:19.......... shalt **c** me, My father
Matt. 9:13 .... not come to **c** the righteous
Luke 6:46 ..why **c** ye me, Lord, Lord
John 13:13......... Ye **c** me Master and Lord
Acts 10:15...that **c** not thou common
1 Pet. 1:17.......... if ye **c** on the Father

Calling
Rom. 11:29 .... gifts and **c** of God
1 Cor. 7:20.......... abide in the same **c**
2 Tim. 1:9....called us with an holy **c**
Heb. 3:1 .partakers of the heavenly **c**
2 Pet. 1:10 .make your **c** and election

Camel
Gen. 24:64 .... she lighted off the **c**
Matt. 19:24.......... easier for a **c** to go through
Matt. 23:24 .... swallow a **c**
Mark 1:6 .... clothed with **c**'s hair

Candle
Job 18:6.......... his **c** shall be put out
Ps. 18:28.......... thou wilt light my **c**
Prov. 20:27 .... **c** of the Lord
Matt. 5:15 .light a **c** and put it under
Rev. 22:5 .... they need no **c**

Candlestick
Ex. 25:31 .... a **c** of pure gold
1 King. 7:49........ the **c**-s of pure gold
2 Kin. 4:10 .... and a stool, and a **c**
Luke 8:16 .... setteth it on a **c**

Canker
2 Tim. 2:17 .... will eat as doth a **c**
James 5:3 .... your gold and silver is **c**-ed

Captive
Ps. 68:18 .... led captivity **c**
Jer. 13:17 ...... flock is carried away **c**
Luke 4:18 .preach deliverance to the **c**'s
Eph. 4:8 .... he led captivity **c**
2 Tim. 3:6.......... lead **c** silly women

Care
Ps. 142:4 ......no man **c**-d for my soul
Matt. 13:22 .... the **c** of this world
Mark 4:38 .... Master, **c**-st thou not

Luke 8:14 .... choked with c-s
John 12:6 .... he c-d for the poor
1 Cor. 9:9 .Doth God take c for oxen
1 Cor. 12:25 .... c one for another
1 Tim. 3:5 .... take c of the church
1 Pet. 5:7 .... Casting all your c

Careful
Phil. 4:6 .... Be c for nothing

Carnal
Rom. 8:6 ..to be c-ly minded is death
1 Cor. 9:11 ..shall reap your c things
2 Cor. 10:4 .... weapons . . . are not c

Carpenter
2 Sam. 5:11 .... c-s, and masons
2 Kin. 22:6 .... Unto c-s, and builders
Is. 44:13 .... c stretched out his rule
Zech. 1:20 .Lord shewed me four c-s
Matt. 13:55 .... not this the c's son
Mark 6:3 ..Is not this the c the son of

Carry
Is. 40:11 .... and c them in his bosom
Is. 53:4 .griefs, and c-ed our sorrows
Luke 10:4 .C neither purse, nor scrip
Luke 16:22 .... was c-ed by the angels
Heb. 13:9 .... Be not c-ed about

Cassia
Ex. 30:24 ...of c five hundred shekels
Ps. 45:8 ..thy garments smell of . . . c
Ezek. 27:19 .... c . . . in thy market

Cast
Gen. 21:10 .... C out this bondwoman
Gen. 37:20 .... c him into some pit
Ps. 51:11 .... C me not away from thy
Eccles. 11:1 .... C thy bread upon the
Matt. 7:5 .... first c out the beam
Luke 19:35 .... c their garments upon the
John 6:37 .... I will in no wise c out
Rom. 13:12 .... c off the works of darkness
1 Pet. 5:7 .... C-ing all your care upon him

Catch
Ps. 10:9 .... lieth in wait to c the poor
Mark 12:13 .... to c him in his words
Luke 5:10 .... thou shalt c men
John 10:12 .... wolf c-eth them

Cattle
Ps. 50:10 .... c upon a thousand hills
Ps. 104:14 .... grass to grow for the c

Cease
Gen. 8:22 .... summer and winter . . . not c
Deut. 15:11 .... poor shall never c
Ps. 37:8 .... C from anger
Ps. 46:9 .... He maketh wars to c
Prov. 23:4 .c from thine own wisdom
Luke 7:45 .... not c-d to kiss my feet
1 Cor. 13:8 ...be tongues, they shall c
1 Thess. 5:17 .... Pray without c-ing

Celestial
1 Cor. 15:40 ..there are also c bodies

Chaff
Ps. 1:4 .the c which the wind driveth
Is. 5:24 ....the flame consumeth the c
Matt. 3:12 .... burn up the c with

Chalcedony
Rev. 21:19 .... the third, a c

Chambering
Rom. 13:13 .not in c and wantonness

Change
Gen. 35:2 .... c your garments
Job 14:14 ..will I wait, till my c come
Job 17:12 ...they c the night into day
Jer. 13:23 ....the Ethiopian c his skin
Dan. 2:21 .... c-th the times and
Mal. 3:6 .... I am the Lord, I c not
Rom. 1:25 .... c-d the truth of God
1 Cor. 15:51 ...but we shall all be c-d
Phil. 3:21 .Who shall c our vile body

Charge
Lev. 8:35 .... keep the c of the Lord
Job 1:22 .... sinned not, nor c-d God
Ps. 91:11 .... give his angels c over
Matt. 4:6 ...He shall give his angels c
Mark 5:43 .... he c-d them straitly
Acts 7:60 ....lay not this sin to their c
1 Cor. 9:18 .... gospel of Christ without c
1 Tim. 5:21 .... I c thee before God

Charity
1 Cor. 13:1 .... and have not c
1 Cor. 14:1 .... Follow after c
Col. 3:14 .... all these things put on c
1 Tim. 1:5 .... the commandment is c out of
2 Tim. 2:22 .... righteousness, faith, c
1 Pet. 4:8 .c shall cover the multitude
3 John 6 .... borne witness of thy c

Chaste
2 Cor. 11:2 .present you as a c virgin
Titus 2:5 .... be discreet, c
1 Pet. 3:2 .... your c conversation

Chasten
Deut. 8:5 .... as a man c-eth his son
Ps. 38:1 ..c me in thy hot displeasure
Ps. 94:12 .... man whom thou c-est
Prov. 19:18 ..C thy son while there is
1 Cor. 11:32 .we are c-ed of the Lord
Heb. 12:6 ....the Lord loveth he c-eth

Chastise
Lev. 26:28 .... will c you seven times
1 Kin. 12:11 .... c-d you with whips
Luke 23:16 .... I will therefore c him
Heb. 12:8 .... if ye be without c-ment

Cheek
Job 16:10 .... smitten me upon the c
Is. 50:6 .... gave . . . my c-s to them
Joel 1:6 .... he hath the c teeth
Matt. 5:39 ..smite thee on thy right c

Cheer
Deut. 24:5 .... shall c up his wife
Judg. 9:13 .... which c-eth God and man
Prov. 15:13 .... c-ful countenance
Matt. 9:2 .Son, be of good c; thy sins
Matt. 14:27 .... Be of good c; it is I
John 16:33 .... of good c; I have overcome
Acts 23:11 .... Be of good c, Paul
2 Cor. 9:7 ....God loveth a c-ful giver

Chickens
Matt. 23:37 .as a hen gathereth her c

Chide
Ps. 103:9 .... He will not always c

Chief
1 Sam. 9:22 .... sit in the c-est place
Matt. 20:27 .... whosoever will be c among
Mark 10:44 .... the c-est shall be servant
Luke 22:26 .... he that is c doth serve
2 Cor. 11:5 .... whit behind the very c-est
1 Tim. 1:15 .... of whom I am c

Child
Gen. 21:8 .... the c grew
Prov. 22:6 .... Train up a c in the way
Prov. 23:13 .... correction from the c
Eccles. 4:8 .... neither c nor brother
Is. 9:6 .... unto us a c is born
Is. 11:6 .... a little c shall lead them
Jer. 31:20 .... Is he a pleasant c
Matt. 18:2 .... Jesus called a little c
1 Cor. 13:11 .I was a c, I spake as a c
2 Tim. 3:15 .... from a c thou hast known

Children
Gen. 3:16 .... sorrow . . . bring forth c
1 Sam. 16:11 .... Are here all thy c
Job 5:4 .... His c are far from safety
Ps. 103:13 .... as a father pitieth his c
Prov. 17:6 .C's c are the crown of old
Prov. 31:28 her c . . . call her blessed
Is. 30:9 .... lying c that will not hear
Is. 49:21 .... I have lost my c
Jer. 31:15 ..Rachel weeping for her c
Ezek. 18:2 ...c's teeth are set on edge
Matt. 18:3 .... and become as little c
Matt. 19:14 .... Suffer little c
John 12:36 .... may be the c of light
1 John 2:1 .... My little c these things
Rev. 2:23 .... kill her c with death

Choke
Matt. 13:22 .... riches, c the word
Mark 4:19 .... lusts of things . . . c the word
Luke 8:14 .... and are c-d with cares

Choose
Ex. 17:9 .... C us out men
Deut. 7:6 .... Lord . . . hath c-n thee
Josh. 24:15 ..c you this day whom ye
Ps. 119:30 .have c-n the way of truth
Is. 7:15 .... and c the good
Heb. 11:25 .... C-ing rather to suffer
1 Pet. 2:9 .... ye are a c-n generation

Christ
Matt. 16:16 ..Thou are the C, the Son
Luke 24:46 .... it behoved C to suffer
John 1:41 .... found the Messias . . . C
Acts 2:36 .Jesus . . . both Lord and C
Rom. 1:16 .... not ashamed . . . gospel of C
1 Cor. 1:23 .... we preach C crucified
Phil. 1:21 .... For me to live is C
Col. 3:4 .... C, who is our life
1 Thess. 4:16 .... dead in C shall rise
2 Thess. 2:2 ...the day of C is at hand
2 Thess. 3:5 .... patient waiting for C
2 John 9 .... not in the doctrine of C

Christian
Acts 11:26 .... called C-s first in
Acts 26:28 ...persuadest me to be a C
1 Pet. 4:16 .... any man suffer as a C

Church
Matt. 16:18 ..upon this rock . . . my c
Matt. 18:17 .... tell it unto the c
Acts 15:4 .... received of the c
1 Cor. 11:18 ...come together in the c
1 Cor. 14:35 .... women to speak in c
2 Cor. 11:8 .... I robbed other c-es
Eph. 5:23 .Christ is the head of the c
1 Tim. 3:5 .shall he take care of the c
Heb. 12:23 ...general assembly and c

Circumcise
Gen. 17:10 .... every man child . . . be c-d
Deut. 30:6 .... Lord . . . will c thine heart
Luke 1:59 .eighth day they came to c
Phil. 3:5 .... C-d the eighth day
Col. 2:11 .... In whom also ye are c-d

Citizen
Luke 15:15 .... joined himself to a c
Acts 21:39 .... a c of no mean city
Eph. 2:19 ..fellow-c-s with the saints

City
Gen. 4:17 .... builded a c . . . name of the c
Gen. 11:4 .... build us a c and a tower
Ps. 46:4 .... make glad the c of God
Ps. 127:1 .except the Lord keep the c
Eccles. 9:14 .... a little c and few men
Is. 1:26 .... The c of righteousness
Is. 19:18 .... The c of destruction
Matt. 21:10 .... all the c was moved
Luke 9:5 ....When ye go out of that c
Acts 7:58 .... cast him out of the c
Heb. 12:22 .... the c of the living God
Rev. 21:2 .... I John saw the holy c

Clay
Job 4:19 .... that dwell in houses of c
Job 33:6 .... formed out of the c
Is. 64:8 .... the c and thou our potter
Jer. 18:6 .... c in the potter's hand
Dan. 2:33 ...part of iron and part of c
John 9:6 .... made c . . . anointed
Rom. 9:21 .... potter power over the c

Clean
2 Kin. 5:12 ...may I not wash . . . and be **c**
Ps. 19:9.......The fear of the Lord is **c**
Ps. 24:4............He that hath **c** hands
Ps. 51:10 ....Create in me a **c** heart
Is. 1:16 ....Wash you, make you **c**
Matt. 8:3....................I will, be thou **c**
Matt. 23:25 ....make **c** the . . . cup
John 13:10 ....washed . . . is **c**

Cleanse
Ps. 19:12.........**c** thou me from secret faults
Matt. 8:3 ....his leprosy was **c**-d
Matt. 23:26 ....**c** first that which is within
Luke 4:27...........none . . . **c**-d, saving Naaman
Acts 10:15, 11:9..What God hath **c**-d
2 Cor. 7:1......**c** . . . from all filthiness
James 4:8..**C** your hands, ye sinners
1 John 1:7......blood of Jesus . . . **c**-th

Clear
Gen. 44:16.how shall we **c** ourselves
Num. 14:18 ....no means **c**-ing the guilty
2 Sam. 23:4....by **c** shining after rain
Ps. 51:4.........be **c** when thou judgest
Song 6:10 .as the moon, **c** as the sun
Matt. 7:5.......then shalt thou see **c**-ly
Rom. 1:20.....invisible things . . . **c**-ly seen
Rev. 22:1....water of life, **c** as crystal

Clefts
Song 2:14 ......art in the **c** of the rock
Is. 2:21.......go into the **c** of the rocks
Jer. 49:16 ......dwellest in the **c** of the rock

Cloke
Is. 59:17.............clad with zeal as a **c**
Matt. 5:40......let him have thy **c** also
1 Thess. 2:5 .nor a **c** of covetousness
2 Tim. 4:13.........**c** that I left at Troas
1 Pet. 2:16 ....**c** of maliciousness

Closet
Joel 2:16...and the bride out of her **c**
Matt. 6:6 .....prayest, enter into thy **c**
Luke 12:3.....spoken in the ear in **c**-s

Cloth
Matt. 9:16 ....of new **c** unto an old garment

Clothe
Ps. 93:1...........he is **c**-d with majesty
Matt. 6:30.............God so **c** the grass
Matt. 25:36.....Naked, and ye **c**-d me
Mark 15:17 ....**c**-d him with purple
Luke 7:25.A man **c**-d in soft raiment
Luke 12:28 ....God so **c** the grass
Rev. 3:5 ....shall be **c**-d in white

Clothes
Ex. 19:10..........let them wash their **c**
Deut. 29:5 .your **c** are not waxen old
Mark 5:28 ....If I may but touch his **c**
Mark 14:63.......high priest rent his **c**
Luke 2:7.............................swaddling
John 11:44....bound . . . with grave **c**

Cloud
Gen. 9:13 ....I do set my bow in the **c**
Ex. 13:21 ......by day in a pillar of a **c**
Ex. 14:24....pillar of fire and of the **c**
Ex. 24:15...........**c** covered the mount
Ps. 36:5 ....reacheth unto the **c**-s
Ps. 105:39 ....a **c** for a covering
Matt. 24:30.Son of . . . coming in the **c**-s
Mark 9:7 ...a voice came out of the **c**
Luke 12:54 ......see a **c** rise out of the west
Luke 21:27......in a **c** with power . . . glory
Acts 1:9 ..**c** received him out of their
1 Thess. 4:17......caught up . . . in the **c**-s
Jude 12 ...**c**-s they are without water
Rev. 1:7...behold he cometh with **c**-s

Cloven
Acts 2:3........**c** tongues like as of fire

Coal
Prov. 6:28........hot **c**-s and . . . not be burned
Prov. 25:22.heap **c**-s of fire upon his
Is. 6:6 ....a live **c** in his hand
Lam. 4:8 ...visage is blacker than a **c**
John 18:18 ...who had made a fire of **c**-s
John 21:9...fire of **c**-s there, and fish
Rom. 12:20 .....heap **c**-s of fire on his head

Coat
Gen. 3:21 ....Lord God make **c**-s of skins
Gen. 37:3 ....made . . . **c** of many colours
Lev. 16:4 ....put on the holy linen **c**
Matt. 5:40....any . . . take away thy **c**
Luke 9:3............neither have two **c**-s
John 21:7 ....girt his fisher's **c**

Cock
Matt. 26:34, 75 ......before the **c** crow
Mark 13:35 ....at the **c**-crowing

Cockatrice
Is. 11:8............child's hand on **c**' den
Is. 59:5..................they hatch **c**' eggs
Jer. 8:17....................will send . . . **c**-s

Cold
Gen. 8:22....**c** and heat, and summer
Job 24:7 ....no covering in the **c**
Job 37:9..................**c** out of the north
Prov. 25:13..**c** of snow in the time of
Prov. 25:25 ....**c** waters to a thirsty
Matt. 10:42 ....a cup of **c** water
Matt. 24:12...love of many . . . wax **c**
John 18:18..fire of coals; for it was **c**
2 Cor. 11:27.....in fastings often, in **c**
Rev. 3:15..thou are neither **c** nor hot

Collection
2 Chr. 24:6 ....bring the Lord **c** that Moses
1 Cor. 16:1..................**c** for the saints

Colt
Job 11:12.man . . . like a wild ass's **c**
Zech. 9:9.upon a **c** the foal of an ass
Matt. 21:2............an ass tied, and a **c**
John 12:15 ....king cometh . . . an ass's **c**

Come
Gen. 6:18 ....thou shalt **c** into the ark
Ps. 95:6 ....O **c** let us worship
Zech. 9:9......thy King **c**-th unto thee
Matt. 6:10...................thy kingdom **c**
Matt. 11:28......**C** unto me, all ye that
Mark 10:14...little children to **c** unto
Luke 21:27.......see Son of man **c**-ing
John 17:1 ....Father, the hour is **c**
Rev. 22:20 ..I **c** quickly . . . Even so **c**

Comely
1 Sam. 16:18..............and a **c** person
Ps. 33:1.....praise is **c** for the upright
Song 1:5 ....I am black, but **c**
Is. 53:2...he hath no form nor **c**-ness
1 Cor. 11:13 ....is it **c** that a woman pray

Comfort
Gen. 5:29...........This same shall **c** us
Gen. 18:5.....................**c** ye your hearts
Job 29:25 ....one that **c**-eth the mourners
Ps. 23:4....thy rod . . . staff they **c** me
Ps. 77:2 ...my soul refused to be **c**-ed
Song 2:5...................**c** me with apples
Is. 54:11.....afflicted . . . and not **c**-ed
Is. 61:2....................to **c** all that mourn
Lam. 1:21 ....there is none to **c** me
Matt. 5:4...that mourn . . . shall be **c**-ed
Matt. 9:22.....Daughter, be of good **c**
Luke 16:25 ..now he is **c**-ed, thou art
Acts 9:31..in the **c** of the Holy Ghost
Rom. 15:4 ....**c** of the scriptures
2 Cor. 1:3 ....and the God of all **c**
2 Cor. 7:4 ....I am filled with **c**
2 Cor. 7:13 ....were **c**-ed in your **c**
Phil. 2:1 ....if any **c** of love
1 Thess. 4:18 ....**c** one another
2 Thess. 2:17 ....**C** your hearts

Comforter
Job 16:2........miserable **c**-s are ye all
Eccles. 4:1 ....they had no **c**
Ps. 69:20.................looked . . . for **c**-s
Nah. 3:7........whence shall I seek **c**-s
John 14:16.shall give you another **C**

Comfortless
John 14:18 ....I will not leave you **c**

Coming
2 Sam. 3:25....going out and thy **c** in
Mal. 3:2 ....abide the day of his **c**
Matt. 24:30.......see the Son of man **c**
Matt. 26:64 ....**c** in the clouds of heaven
Luke 19:23 ....at my **c** I might have
John 5:25 ....hour is **c** and now is
1 Cor. 1:7..........for the **c** of our Lord
James 5:8 ....**c** of the Lord draweth nigh
2 Pet. 3:4...................promise of his **c**

Command
Luke 8:25....he **c**-eth even the winds
Luke 9:54 ....**c** fire . . . from heaven
John 15:14 .....do whatsoever I **c** you
Acts 17:30...........**c**-eth all men every where
1 Tim. 4:11These things **c** and teach

Commandment
Ex. 20:6 ....love me, and keep my **c**-s
Ex. 34:28...........tables . . . the ten **c**-s
Ps. 19:8..............**c** of the Lord is pure
Prov. 6:20 ....son, keep thy father's **c**
Eccles. 12:13......Fear God, and keep his **c**-s
Matt. 5:19.........one of these least **c**-s
Matt. 22:36 ....which is great **c**
Matt. 22:40 .two **c**-s hang all the law
John 14:15...........If ye love me, keep my **c**-s
John 15:10..............If ye keep my **c**-s
1 Tim. 1:5 ....end of the **c** is charity

Commit
Ex. 20:14......................not **c** adultery
Ps. 31:5.Into thine hand I **c** my spirit
Ps. 37:5 ......**C** thy way unto the Lord
Prov. 16:3 ....**C** thy works unto the Lord
Luke 12:48.....to whom men . . . **c**-ed much
Luke 18:20.............Do not **c** adultery
John 5:22 ......hath **c**-ed all judgment
John 8:34..........Whosoever **c**-eth sin
1 John 3:8.He that **c**-eth sin is of the

Common
Lev. 4:27 ....if . . . **c** people sin
Num. 16:29.........these men die the **c** death
Eccles. 6:1.There is an evil . . . it is **c**
Jer. 26:23 ....graves of the **c** people
Matt. 28:15.....saying is **c**-ly reported
Mark 12:37...the **c** people heard him
Acts 2:44............and had all things **c**
Acts 10:15 ....that call not thou **c**
1 Cor. 5:1................It is reported **c**-ly
Tit. 1:4 ....after the **c** faith
Jude 3............write unto you of the **c** salvation

Communicate
Gal. 6:6 ......**c** unto him that teacheth
1 Tim. 6:18........................willing to **c**
Heb. 13:16 ...do good and to **c** forget not

Communication
Matt. 5:37.....................**c** be, Yea, Yea
Luke 24:17.........What manner of **c**-s
1 Cor. 15:33.......evil **c**-s corrupt good
Eph. 4:29...Let no corrupt **c** proceed

Communion
1 Cor. 10:16 .c of the blood of Christ
2 Cor. 6:14 ......and what c hath light
2 Cor. 13:14........c of the Holy Ghost

Compassion
Ex. 2:6...................she had c on him
Ps. 86:15 ....a God full of c
Ps. 111:4 ....gracious and full of c
Matt. 9:36 ......moved with c on them
Matt. 15:32 ....I have c on the multitude
Luke 15:20..........his father . . . had c
Rom. 9:15 ......have c on whom I will have c
Heb. 5:2.........have c on the ignorant
1 Pet. 3:8.....having c one of another

Compel
Matt. 5:41 ....c thee to go a mile
Matt. 27:32 ....they c-ed to bear his cross
Luke 14:23 ....c them to come in

Complain
1 Sam. 1:16.......abundance of my c-t
Job 7:11......c in the bitterness of my
Ps. 144:14.......no c-ing in our streets
Jude 16.These are murmurers, c-ers

Comprehend
Job 37:5 ....things . . . we cannot c
Is. 40:12 ....c-ed the dust of the earth
John 1:5 ....darkness c-ed it not
Rom. 13:9.briefly c-ed in this saying

Conceit
Prov. 18:11 ....high wall in his own c
Prov. 26:5 ....fool wise in his own c
Rom. 11:25..be wise in your own c-s

Conceive
Num. 11:12...........Have I c-d all this
Job 15:35 ....They c mischief
Ps. 51:5 ...in sin did my mother c me
Is. 7:14..........virgin shall c and bear
Acts 5:4.........why hast thou c-d this thing
James 1:15...........when lust hath c-d

Concision
Phil. 3:2 ....beware of the c

Concord
2 Cor. 6:15 ..what c hath Christ with

Concupiscence
Rom. 7:8 ....all manner of c
Col. 3:5 ....evil c and covetousness
1 Thess. 4:5..........Not in the lust of c

Condemn
Job 9:20 ....own mouth shall c me
Prov. 12:2...wicked devices will he c
Is. 50:9 ....who is he that shall c
Mark 10:33 ....they shall c him to death
Luke 6:37.c not . . . shall not be c-ed
John 3:17 ..God sent not his Son . . . to c
Rom. 2:1................thou c-est thyself
Titus 2:8 ....speech, that cannot be c-ed
1 John 3:20........For if our heart c us

Condemnation
Luke 23:40 .....thou art in the same c
John 3:19....this is the c, that light is
Rom. 8:1 ..no c to them which are in
James 3:1.shall receive the greater c
James 5:12 ....lest ye fall into c

Condescend
Rom. 12:16 ....but c to men of low estate

Confection
Ex. 30:35...........c after the art of the
1 Sam. 8:13 ..daughters to be c-aries

Conferred
Acts 4:15 ..they c among themselves
Acts 25:12 .Festus c with the council
Gal. 1:16..........I c not with flesh and blood

Confess
Ps. 32:5 ....I will c my transgressions
Matt. 10:32............c me before men,
Mark 1:5 ......baptized . . . c-ing their sins
John 1:20 ..c-ed, and denied not; but c-ed
Acts 23:8 ....Pharisees c both
Rom. 10:9.........thou shalt c with thy mouth
Rom. 14:11........every tongue shall c
James 5:16.........C your faults one to
1 John 1:9........If we c our sins, he is

Confession
Josh. 71:9 ....and make c unto him
Rom. 10:10 ....with the mouth c is made
1 Tim. 6:13 ......Jesus . . . witnessed a good c

Confidence
Ps. 118:8...........than to put c in man
Prov. 3:26......the Lord shall be thy c
Eph. 3:12 ....with c by the faith
Phil. 3:3 ...and have no c in the flesh
Heb. 3:6.............if we hold fast the c

Confident
Ps. 27:3 ....in this will I be c
Prov. 14:16..the fool rageth, and is c
2 Cor. 5:6 .we are always c knowing
Phil. 1:6 ....Being c of this very thing

Confirmation
Phil. 1:7.defence and c of the gospel
Heb. 6:16......an oath for c is to them

Conform
Rom. 8:29 .....to be c-ed to the image
Rom. 12:2...be not c-ed to this world
Phil. 3:10..........made c-able unto his death

Confound
Gen. 11:7.................c their language
Ps. 22:5.......trusted . . . and were not c-ed
Is. 24:23.........the moon shall be c-ed
Acts 2:6.....came together, and were c-ed
1 Pet. 2:6.................shall not be c-ed

Confusion
Lev. 18:23 ....it is c
Job 10:15........................I am full of c
Ps. 71:1 ....let me never be put to c
Is. 45:16......................go to c together
Jer. 3:25.................our c covereth us
1 Cor. 14:33.....God is not the author of c
James 3:16 .....c and every evil work

Conquer
Rom. 8:37 ....more than c-ors
Rev. 6:2 .....went forth c-ing and to c

Conscience
John 8:9.....convicted by their own c
Acts 23:1....I have lived in all good c
Acts 24:16 ....a c void of offence
Rom. 2:15 ....their c also bearing witness
Rom. 13:5 ....wrath . . . for c sake
1 Cor. 8:7 ....their c being weak
1 Tim. 3:9 ....faith in a pure c
1 Tim. 4:2....c seared with a hot iron
Heb. 9:14....purge your c from dead works
Heb. 10:22......hearts sprinkled from evil c
1 Pet. 3:16.................Having a good c

Consecrate
Ex. 32:29 .C yourselves to day to the
Heb. 7:28...Son . . . c-d for evermore
Heb. 10:20 ...way, which he hath c-d

Consent
Prov. 1:10 ......entice thee, c thou not
Luke 14:18.......with one c began to make
Luke 23:51....not c-ed to the counsel
Acts 8:1.....Saul was c-ing unto his death

1 Tim. 6:3 ....c not to wholesome words

Consist
Luke 12:15..........man's life c-eth not
Col. 1:17...............by him all things c

Consolation
Job 15:11....Are the c-s of God small
Luke 6:24....ye have received your c
Acts 4:36 ....the son of c
Rom. 15:5.the God of patience and c
2 Cor. 1:6....for your c and salvation
Phil. 2:1 ....if there be . . . any c in Christ
2 Thess. 2:16..given us everlasting c
Heb. 6:18........might have a strong c

Constrain
Job 32:28 ..spirit within me c-eth me
2 Kin. 4:8..she c-ed him to eat bread
Luke 24:29.............but they c-ed him
2 Cor. 5:14....Love of Christ c-eth us
1 Pet. 5:2......not by c-t, but willingly

Consume
Gen. 41:30 ....famine shall c the land
Ex. 3:2 ....the bush was not c-ed
Deut. 4:24..............God is a c-ing fire
Deut. 5:25......this great fire will c us
Ps. 49:14 .beauty shall c in the grave
Ps. 90:7 ....we are c-d by thine anger
Luke 9:54 ..c them, even as Elias did
Gal. 5:15 ....heed that ye be not c-d
2 Thess. 2:8 .....shall c with the spirit

Contain
1 Kin. 8:27 ....heavens cannot c
Rom. 2:14.the things c-ed in the law
1 Cor. 7:9...cannot c, let them marry
1 Pet. 2:6 ....it is c-ed in the scripture

Contempt
Job 12:21......poureth c upon princes
Prov. 18:3 ....then cometh also c
Dan. 12:2 ..to shame and everlasting c
2 Cor. 10:10 .....and his speech c-ible

Contend
Job 40:2................that c-eth with the almighty
Is. 49:25 ....will c with him that c-eth
Is. 50:8..................who will c with me
Is. 57:16.....................I will not c forever
Jude 3 ....earnestly c for the faith
Jude 9.......when c-ing with the devil

Content
Gen. 37:27 ....his brethren were c
Mark 15:15.Pilate . . . to c the people
Luke 3:14 ....be c with your wages
Phil. 4:11...I have learned . . . to be c
1 Tim. 6:6...godliness with c-ment is
Heb. 13:5 ....be c with such things as ye

Contentious
Prov. 21:19..............a c and an angry woman
Rom. 2:8 ....them that are c do not obey
1 Cor. 11:6 ..if any man seem to be c

Contradiction
Heb. 7:7.without all c less is blessed
Heb. 12:3 .endured such c of sinners

Contrary
Lev. 26:21 ....if ye walk c unto me
Matt. 14:24..........for the wind was c
Rom. 11:24 ....graffed c to nature
Rom. 16:17 ....c to the doctrine
Gal. 5:17..........c the one to the other
1 Thess. 2:15 .....and are c to all men
1 Tim. 1:10..........c to sound doctrine

Contribution
Rom. 15:26 .certain c for poor saints

Contrite
Ps. 34:18.........saveth such of c spirit
Ps.51:17.........broken and a c heart
Is. 66:2.............poor and of a c spirit

Convenient
Prov. 30:8 ....feed me with food **c**
Jer. 40:4 ....seemeth good and **c**
Mark 6:21 ...when a **c** day was come
Mark 14:11 ....how he might **c**-ly betray
Acts 24:25 ....when I have a **c** season
Eph. 5:4.nor jesting, which are not **c**

Conversation
Ps. 50:23 ....ordereth his **c** aright
Gal. 1:13 ....have heard of my **c**
Eph. 4:22 ....concerning the former **c**
Phil. 1:27.............**c** be as it becometh
Heb. 13:5.**c** be without covetousness
James 3:13.......show out of a good **c**
1 Pet. 1:15.....holy in all manner of **c**
1 Pet. 2:12.......Having your **c** honest
2 Pet. 2:7...the filthy **c** of the wicked

Conversion
Acts 15:3.declaring the **c** of Gentiles

Convert
Ps. 19:7 ....perfect, **c**-ing the soul
Matt. 18:3 ....Except ye be **c**-ed
Acts 3:19.......Repent . . . and be **c**-ed
James 5:20...........he which **c**-eth the sinner

Cool
Gen. 3:8...walking . . . in the **c** of the day
Luke 16:24 ....and **c** my tongue

Copper
Ezra 8:27...........two vessels of fine **c**
2 Tim. 4:14 ....Alexander the **c**-smith

Copy
Deut. 17:18.write him a **c** of this law
Josh. 8:32..wrote there . . . a **c** of the law
Prov. 25:1 ...proverbs Hezekiah **c**-ed out

Corban
Mark 7:11 .if any man shall say, It is **C**

Corn
Gen. 41:5 ....seven ears of **c** came up
Lev. 2:14.....................green ears of **c**
2 Sam. 17:19............spread ground **c**
2 Kin. 4:42..full ears of **c** in the husk
Matt. 12:1 ....began to pluck the ears of **c**
Mark 4:28 .after that the full **c** in the
John 12:24...Except a **c** of wheat fall

Corner
Job 38:6............who laid the **c** stone thereof
Ps. 118:22......the head stone of the **c**
Prov. 7:12................in wait at every **c**
Is. 28:16....................precious **c** stone
Matt. 21:42 ..become the head of the **c**
Acts 10:11 ....knit at the four **c**-s
Eph. 2:20 ..Christ . . . being the chief **c**
Rev. 7:1 .....on the four **c** of the earth

Cornet
2 Sam. 6:5 ....on timbrels, and on **c**-s
1 Chr. 15:28........with sound of the **c**
Dan. 3:5 ....sound of the **c** flute, harp

Correct
Job 5:17....the man whom God **c**-eth
Prov. 3:12 ...the Lord loveth he **c**-eth
Prov. 29:17.........................**C** thy son,
Jer. 10:24 ...**c** me, but with judgment
2 Tim. 3:16 ....profitable . . . for **c**-ion

Corrupt
Gen. 6:11 ....The earth also was **c**
Ps. 14:1...They are **c** they have done
Prov. 25:26.................and a **c** spring
Matt. 6:19.........where moth and rust doth **c**
Matt. 7:17.......a **c** tree bringeth forth
1 Cor. 15:33 ..evil communications **c**
2 Cor. 7:2.........we have **c**-ed no man
Eph. 4:22.put off . . . old man, which is **c**
2 Tim. 3:8 ....men of **c** minds
James 5:2..........Your riches are **c**-ed

Corruptible
Rom. 1:23............made like to **c** man
1 Cor. 9:25 .do it to obtain a **c** crown
1 Cor. 15:53, 54 ....this **c** must put on
1 Pet. 1:23 ....not of **c** seed

Corruption
Lev. 22:25 ....their **c** is in them
Job 17:14..........**c** Thou art my father
Ps. 16:10; Acts 2:27........Holy One to see **c**
Rom. 8:21 ...delivered from bondage of **c**
1 Cor. 15:42 ....It is sown in **c**
Gal. 6:8 ....shall of the flesh reap **c**
2 Pet. 1:4 ....the **c** that is in the world
2 Pet. 2:19 ....are the servants of **c**

Cost, liness, ly
2 Sam. 24:24 ....which doth **c** me nothing
1 Kin. 5:17 ....**c'ly** stones, and hewed
John 12:3...........spikenard, very **c'ly**
1 Tim. 2:9 ......or pearls, or **c'ly** array
Rev. 18:19..by reason of her **c'liness**

Cottage
Is. 1:8 ....left as a **c** in a vineyard
Is. 24:20.....shall be removed like a **c**
Zeph. 2:6 ....shall be . . . **c**-s for shepherds

Council
Matt. 5:22 ....be in danger of the **c**
Matt. 10:17 .deliver you up to the **c**-s
Acts 5:27..........set them before the **c**
Acts 6:12 ...and brought him to the **c**

Counsel
Ex. 18:19..................I will give thee **c**
Ps. 1:1............walketh not in the **c** of
Ps. 33:11 ....**c** of the Lord standeth
Ps. 55:14 ....took sweet **c** together
Ps. 73:24 ....guide me with thy **c**
Prov. 11:14...........Where no **c** is, thy people
Prov. 19:20 ....Hear **c** and receive
Eccles. 8:2 ....I **c** thee to keep
Is. 28:29........................wonderful in **c**
Jer. 23:18..stood in the **c** of the Lord
Matt. 22:15..............took **c** . . . might entangle
Luke 7:30 ....reject the **c** of God
Acts 9:23.the Jews took **c** to kill him
1 Cor. 4:5 ....the **c**-s of the hearts
Eph. 1:11..after the **c** of his own will
Heb. 6:17..........immutability of his **c**
Rev. 3:18 ..I **c** thee to buy of me gold

Counseller, or
Prov. 11:14.....in the multitude of **c**-s
Is. 9:6 ..shall be called Wonderful, **C**
Mic. 4:9...................is thy **c** perished
Mark 15:43 ....an honourable **c**
Luke 23:50 ..man named Joseph, a **c**
Rom. 11:34 ...or who hath been his **c**

Count
Job 18:3...........are we **c**-ed as beasts
Ps. 44:22 ....**c**-ed as sheep for the
Prov. 17:28 ....his peace, is **c**-ed wise
Eccles. 7:27 ....**c**-ing one by one
Luke 14:28 ....and **c**-eth the cost, whether
Phil. 3:8 ....I **c** all things but loss
2 Pet. 3:9...as some men **c** slackness
James 5:11........**c** them happy which endure

Countenance
Gen. 4:6................why is thy **c** fallen
Num. 6:26...........The Lord lift up his **c**
1 Sam. 16:12......of a beautiful **c**, and
2 Sam. 14:27 ......a woman of a fair **c**
Ps. 4:6; 44:3; 89:15 ....light of thy **c**
Prov. 15:13 ....a cheerful **c**
Song 2:14...................thy **c** is comely
Dan. 1:15 ...their **c**-s appeared fairer
Matt. 6:16 .the hypocrites, of a sad **c**
Matt. 28:3....His **c** was like lightning
Rev. 1:16....**c** was as the sun shineth

Country
Gen. 12:1 ....Get thee out of thy **c**
Prov. 25:25...good news from a far **c**
Is. 8:9.......give ear, all ye of far **c**-ies
Matt. 2:12.departed into their own **c**
Matt. 21:33, 25:14 ...went into a far **c**
Luke 2:8...............were in the same **c** shepherds
Luke 15:13....his journey into a far **c**
John 4:44....no honours in his own **c**

Course
Judg. 5:20 ....stars in their **c**-s fought
1 Chr. 23:6.......divided them into **c**-s
Ezra 3:11 .....they sang together by **c**
Acts 20:24.....might finish my **c** with joy
2 Tim. 4:7..........I have finished my **c**
James 3:6.......setteth on fire the **c** of

Covenant
Gen. 6:18 ....will I establish my **c**
Num. 10:33 ..ark of the **c** of the Lord
2 Kin. 23:2 ....the book of the **c**
Job 31:1...I made a **c** with mine eyes
Ps. 25:10.......unto such as keep his **c**
Ps. 103:18........To such as keep his **c**
Acts 3:25.....**c** which God made with our
Gal. 4:24 ....these are the two **c**-s
Heb. 8:6 ....mediator of a better **c**
Heb. 13:20...blood of the everlasting **c**

Cover
Gen. 20:16 ....a **c**-ing of the eyes
Job 36:32 ....clouds he **c**-eth the light
Ps. 32:1...forgiven, whose sin is **c**-ed
Ps. 91:4 ....**c** thee with his feathers
Prov. 10:12......but love **c**-eth all sins
Is. 6:2 .....with twain he **c**-ed his face
Matt. 10:26...nothing **c**-ed, that shall
Luke 23:30 ....to the hills, **C** us
1 Cor. 11:4 ....having his head **c**-ed
1 Pet. 4:8 ....charity shall **c** the

Covet
Ex. 20:17 ....Thou shalt not **c**
Prov. 21:26....................**c**-eth greedily
Mic. 2:2 ....**c** fields, and take them
Acts 20:33...........have **c**-ed no man's silver
Rom. 13:9..................thou shalt not **c**
1 Cor. 12:31 ....**c** earnestly the best
1 Tim. 6:10......while some **c**-ed after

Covetous
Ps. 10:3..................and blesseth the **c**
1 Cor. 5:10 ....not altogether with the . . . **c**
Eph. 5:5............nor **c** man, who is an idolater
2 Tim. 3:2 ....lovers of their own selves, **c**

Covetousness
Ps. 119:36 ...Incline my heart . . . not to **c**
Mark 7:22 ....Thefts, **c**, wickedness
Luke 12:15...Take heed, and beware of **c**
1 Thess. 2:5.......................a cloak of **c**
Heb. 13:5.conversation be without **c**

Craftiness
Job 5:13...............wise in their own **c**
Luke 20:23.........he perceived their **c**
2 Cor. 4:2 ....not walking in **c**

Create
Gen. 1:1 ....**c**-d the heaven and the earth
Ps. 51:10..........**C** in me a clean heart
Is. 43:1 ....the Lord that **c**-ed thee
Is. 45:12 ....made the earth . . . **c**-ed man
Is. 57:19.........I **c** the fruits of the lips
Is. 65:17 ....**c** new heavens . . . new earth
Mal. 2:10.....hath not one God **c**-d us

Mark 13:19....God **c**-d unto this time
Eph. 2:10.............**c**-d in Christ Jesus
Eph. 3:9 ....**c**-d all things by Jesus
Eph. 4:24.......................God is **c**-d in righteousness
Col. 1:16..by him were all things **c**-d

Creation
Mark 10:6.....beginning of the **c** God made
Mark 13:19.......**c** which God created
2 Pet. 3:4..............beginning of the **c**

Creator
Eccles. 12:1......remember now thy **c**
Is. 40:28....**C** of the ends of the earth
Rom. 1:25.....the creature more than the **C**
1 Pet. 4:19...........as unto a faithful **C**

Creature
Gen. 1:21.every living **c** that moveth
Mark 16:15 ....preach the gospel to every **c**
2 Cor. 5:17..he is a new **c**: old things
1 Tim. 4:4.for every **c** of God is good
James 1:18 ....firstfruits of his **c**-s

Creditor
Deut. 15:2..........every **c** that lendeth
Is. 50:1 ....which of my **c**-s is it
Luke 7:41 ....certain **c** . . . had two debtors

Crew
Matt. 26:74...immediately the cock **c**
Mark 14:68 ....and the cock **c**
Luke 22:60..he yet spake, the cock **c**

Crib
Job 39:9 ....abide by thy **c**
Prov. 14:4........no oxen . . . **c** is clean
Is. 1:3 ....the ass his master's **c**

Crimson
2 Chr. 2:7 .in purple, and **c**, and blue
Is. 1:18 ...like **c** they shall be as wool
Jer. 4:30 ....clothest thyself with **c**

Cripple
Acts 14:8.**c** from his mother's womb

Crooked
Deut. 32:5..................perverse and **c** generation
Ps. 125:5 ....turn aside unto their **c** ways
Eccles. 1:15 ....**c** cannot be made straight
Luke 3:5.............the **c** shall be made straight
Phil. 2:15 ....**c** and perverse nation

Cross
Matt. 10:38 ....that taketh not his **c**
Matt. 27:40 ....come down from the **c**
John 19:17 ......he bearing his **c** went
John 19:25 ....stood by the **c** of Jesus
1 Cor. 1:17...........lest the **c** of Christ
1 Cor. 1:18....preaching of the **c** is to
Gal. 6:14 ....save in the **c** of our Lord
Eph. 2:16..........in one body by the **c**
Phil. 2:8..........even the death of the **c**
Phil. 3:18..enemies of the **c** of Christ
Col. 1:20 ......peace . . . blood of his **c**
Heb. 12:2 ...endured the **c**, despising

Crow
Matt. 26:34, 75.......before the cock **c**
Luke 22:34 .cock shall not **c** this day

Crown
Gen. 49:26 ....on the **c** of the head
Ps. 8:5................**c**-ed him with glory
Ps. 21:3..........settest a **c** of pure gold
Ps. 65:11.....Thou **c**-est the year with
Ps. 103:4 ....**c**-eth thee with loving
Prov. 12:4.......virtuous woman is a **c**
Prov. 14:18 ....are **c**-ed with knowledge
Prov. 14:24........**c** of the wise is their
Prov. 16:31.........hoary head is a **c** of glory
Prov. 17:6 .....children's children are the **c**

1 Cor. 9:25..to obtain a corruptible **c**
2 Tim. 4:8 ....a **c** of righteousness
Heb. 2:9.........see Jesus . . . **c**-ed with glory

Crucify
Matt. 20:19....mock . . . scourge . . . **c** him
Matt. 26:2 ....betrayed to be **c**-ed
Matt. 27:22................Let him be **c**-ed
Matt. 27:35...................they **c**-ed him
Matt. 28:5 ......Jesus, which was **c**-ed
Mark 13:15....cried out again, **C** him
1 Cor. 1:13......was Paul **c**-ed for you
1 Cor. 1:23 .....we preach Christ **c**-ed
2 Cor. 13:4 ...**c**-ed through weakness
Gal. 2:20 ....I am **c**-ed with Christ
Gal. 6:14 ....world is **c**-ed unto me
Heb. 6:6 ..**c** to themselves the Son of

Cruel, ty
Gen. 49:5 ....instruments of **c'ty**
Ps. 27:12......such as breathe out **c'ty**
Prov. 11:17.......he that is **c** troubleth
Prov. 27:4 ...Wrath is **c**, and anger is
Song 8:6....jealousy is **c** as the grave
Ezek. 34:4.....with **c'ty** have ye ruled

Crumbs
Matt. 15:27 ....dogs eat of the **c**
Mark 7:28 ....eat of the children's **c**

Cry
Gen. 4:10...thy brother's blood **c**-eth
Gen. 18:21.....according to the **c** of it
Lev. 13:45................shall **c**, Unclean, Unclean
Ps. 9:12 ....the **c** of the humble
Ps. 17:1 .....O Lord, attend unto my **c**
Ps. 27:7 ....Hear, O Lord, when I **c**
Ps. 130:1 .....Out of the depths have I **c**-ed
Prov. 8:1.............Doth not wisdom **c**
Is. 42:2..shall not **c** . . . nor cause his
Is. 42:14....**c** like a travailing woman
Matt. 3:3.one **c**-ing in the wilderness
Matt. 25:6............at midnight . . . a **c**
Mark 15:8 ....multitude **c**-ing aloud
Mark 15:37 ....**c**-ed with a loud voice
Rev. 21:4...neither sorrow, nor **c**-ing

Crystal
Job 28:17 ....gold and the **c** cannot
Ezek. 1:22 .....the colour of terrible **c**
Rev. 4:6.........sea of glass like unto **c**
Rev. 21:11.....jasper stone, clear as **c**

Cubit
Matt. 6:27.add one **c** unto his stature

Cummin
Matt. 23:23 ..of mint and anise and **c**

Cup
Ps. 23:5................my **c** runneth over
Ps. 116:13..................I will take the **c**
Prov. 23:31...........his colour in the **c**
Matt. 10:42 ....**c** of cold water only
Matt. 20:22..........able to drink of the **c**
Matt. 23:35..........the outside of the **c**
Matt. 26:27..........took the **c**, and gave thanks
Matt. 26:39....let this **c** pass from me
Mark 7:4 .....washing of **c**-s and pots
Luke 22:20 ....**c** is the new testament
John 18:11 ....the **c** which my Father
1 Cor. 10:16...........The **c** of blessing
1 Cor. 10:21 ....the **c** of devils

Cupbearer
1 Kin. 10:5 ...his ministers . . . his **c**-s
2 Chr. 9:4..........their apparel; his **c**-s
Neh. 1:11.........for I was the King's **c**

Curse
Gen. 3:14.............**c**-d above all cattle
Gen. 12:3............**c** him that **c**-th thee
Gen. 27:12...shall bring a **c** upon me
Lev. 19:14 ....shalt not **c** the deaf
Mal. 4:6 ....smite the earth with a **c**
Matt. 25:41 ..Depart from me, ye **c**-d
Mark 14:71 .began to **c** and to swear
Luke 6:28...........Bless them that **c** you
Acts 23:12..............bound under a **c**

Rom. 3:14.........mouth is full of **c**-ing
Rom. 12:14................bless, and **c** not
Gal. 3:13......redeemed us from the **c**
James 3:9...........therewith **c** we men

Custom
Gen. 31:35....**c** of women is upon me
Judg. 11:39 ....it was a **c** in Israel
Ezra 4:13 ....toll, tribute, and **c**
Matt. 9:9.....sitting at the receipt of **c**
Luke 4:16 ....as his **c** was
John 18:39 .a **c**, that I should release
Acts 28:17 ....**c**-s of our fathers
Rom. 13:7.........................**c** to whom **c**
1 Cor. 11:16..........we have no such **c**

Cut
Ex. 9:15 ....be **c** off from the earth
Judg. 1:6......**c** of his thumbs . . . toes
Ps. 12:3 ....shall **c** off all flattering
Ps. 90:6 ...in the evening it is **c** down
Prov. 10:31 ......froward tongue shall be **c**
Is. 45:2...**c** in sunder the bars of iron
Jer. 7:29 ....**C** off thine hair
Matt. 5:30 ..hand offend thee, **c** it off
Matt. 21:8 ...others **c** down branches
Matt. 24:51.........shall **c** him asunder
Mark 5:5 ...crying, and **c**-ing himself
Mark 14:47......................**c** off his ear
Acts 7:54.....they were **c** to the heart
Rom. 11:22 ...thou also shalt be **c** off

Cymbal
Ps. 150:5......upon the high sounding **c**-s
1 Cor. 13:1 ....sounding brass . . . tinkling **c**

D

Damnable
2 Pet. 2:1.....shall bring in **d** heresies

Damnation
Matt. 23:14 ....receive the greater **d**
Matt. 23:33 ....escape the **d** of hell
John 5:29 .unto the resurrection of **d**
Rom. 13:2 ....shall receive to themselves **d**
1 Cor. 11:29.....drinketh **d** to himself
2 Pet. 2:3........their **d** slumbereth not

Damned
Mark 16:16 ..believeth shall not be **d**
Rom. 14:23.......he that doubteth is **d**
2 Thess. 2:12 ....they all might be **d**

Damsel
Gen. 24:14.the **d** to whom I shall say
Matt. 14:11....head . . . given to the **d**
Mark 5:39................the **d** is not dead
John 18:17...the **d** that kept the door
Acts 12:13.**d** came . . . named Rhoda
Acts 16:16..certain **d** possessed with

Dance
Job 21:11 ....and their children **d**
Ps. 149:3.....Praise his name in the **d**
Ps. 150:4 ....with the timbrel and **d**
Eccles. 3:4 .....time to mourn . . . time to **d**
Lam. 5:15.**d** is turned into mourning
Matt. 11:17; Luke 7:32 ...ye have not **d**-d
Mark 6:22 ....came in, and **d**-d, and pleased
Luke 15:25 ....musick and **d**-ing

Danger
Matt. 5:22.......be in **d** of the judgment
Mark 3:29.in **d** of eternal damnation
Acts 19:27 ..our craft is in **d** to be set

Dare
Rom. 5:7...some would even **d** to die
Rom. 15:18 ....I will not **d** to speak
1 Cor. 6:1......**D** any of you, having a matter
2 Cor. 10:12 ....**d** not make ourselves

Dark
Ex. 10:15 ...that the land was **d**-ened
Job 12:25............They grope in the **d**
Job 24:16 ....In the **d** they dig

Job 38:2 ....that **d**-eneth counsel by words
Ps. 49:4; Prov. 1:6 ....**d** sayings
Is. 5:30 ....light is **d**-ened in the windows
Matt. 24:29 ....sun shall be **d**-ened
Luke 23:45 .sun was **d**-ened, and the veil
John 20:1 ....early, when it was yet **d**
Rom. 1:21 ..foolish heart was **d**-ened
Eph 4:18.........understanding **d**-ened
2 Pet. 1:19 ....shineth in a **d** place

Darkness
Gen. 1:2 ....**d** was upon the face
Deut. 5:22.thick **d** with a great voice
Deut. 28:29.....the blind gropeth in **d**
2 Sam. 22:10 .....**d** was under his feet
Eccles. 2:13 ...far as light excelleth **d**
Eccles. 2:14......the fool walketh in **d**
Is. 5:20 ....**d** for light . . . light for **d**
Matt. 6:23 ..Luke 11:34, body . . . full of **d**
Matt. 10:27 ....What I tell you in **d**
Luke 1:79 ..light to them that sit in **d**
Luke 23:44 ....**d** over all the earth
John 1:5 ....**d** comprehended it not
John 3:19 ...loved **d** rather than light
Acts 26:18 .turn them from **d** to light
Rom. 13:12 ....cast off the works of **d**
1 Cor. 4:5..............hidden things of **d**
2 Cor. 4:6 ....light to shine out of **d**
Col. 1:13 ....from the power of **d**
Heb. 12:18......unto blackness, and **d**
1 Pet. 2:9 ....out of **d** into . . . light
2 Pet. 2:4 ....into chains of **d**
1 John 1:5...........in him is no **d** at all
1 John 2:8.........because the **d** is past
1 John 2:11 ..**d** hath blinded his eyes
Rev. 16:10 ......kingdom was full of **d**

Dart
2 Sam. 18:14 .....took three **d**-s in his
Job 41:29 ....**D**-s are counted as stubble
Prov. 7:23..**d** strike through his liver
Eph. 6:16 ....fiery **d**-s of the wicked
Heb. 12:20 ...thrust through with a **d**

Dash
Ps. 2:9; Hos. 13:16 ..**d** them in pieces
Ps. 91:12; Matt. 4:6............**d** thy foot
Ps. 137:9 ....**d**-eth thy little ones

Dayspring
Job 38:12 .....the **d** to know his place
Luke 1:78.............the **d** from on high

Day star
2 Pet. 1:19.the **d** arise in your hearts

Dead
Gen. 23:3 ....stood up before his **d**
Lev. 19:28.........cuttings . . . for the **d**
Josh. 1:2 ....Moses my servant is **d**
1 Sam. 24:14 ....after a **d** dog
Ps. 31:12...........forgotten as a **d** man
Ps. 88:5 ....Free among the **d**
Ps. 115:17 ....**d** praise not the Lord
Prov. 21:16......congregation of the **d**
Eccles. 4:2......**d** which are already **d**
Eccles. 9:5........**d** know not anything
Jer. 22:10 ....Weep ye not for the **d**
Ezek. 24:17 ...make no mourning for the **d**
Matt. 8:22 ....let the **d** bury their **d**
Matt. 9:24..............maid is not **d**, but sleepeth
Matt. 22:32 ....not the God of the **d**
Luke 16:31......though one rose from the **d**
John 5:25..the **d** shall hear the voice
John 6:49....eat manna . . . and are **d**
John 11:44.he that was **d** came forth
Acts 10:42 ....Judge of quick and **d**
1 Cor. 15:12..........he rose from the **d**
1 Cor. 15:35 .....How are the **d** raised
1 Tim. 5:6...........is **d** while she liveth
2 Tim. 4:1 .judge the quick and the **d**
Heb. 11:4...he, being **d**, yet speaketh
James 2:17..if it hath not works, is **d**
James 2:20..faith without works is **d**

Rev. 1:5...........first begotten of the **d**
Rev. 14:13...............Blessed are the **d**
Rev. 20:13........the sea gave up the **d**

Deadly
1 Sam. 5:11 ....was a **d** destruction
Ps. 17:9 ....from my **d** enemies
Mark 16:18.if they drink any **d** thing
James 3:8 ....tongue . . . full of **d** poison
Rev. 13:3 ....his **d** wound was healed

Deaf
Ex. 4:11.who maketh the dumb, or **d**
Lev. 19:14...................not curse the **d**
Ps. 38:13..................But I, as a **d** man
Mic. 7:16 ....ears shall be **d**
Matt. 11:5...................................**d** hear
Mark 7:37 ....maketh both the **d** to hear

Deal
Gen. 24:49 ....if ye will **d** kindly
Ruth 1:8 .the Lord **d** kindly with you
Ps. 116:7....Lord hath **d**-t bountifully
Prov. 12:22..they that **d** truly are his
Luke 1:25.hath the Lord **d**-t with me
Luke 2:48 ......why hast thou thus **d**-t
John 4:9 ...Jews have no **d**-ings with
Acts 7:19..........The same **d**-t subtilly
Rom. 12:3 .....according as God hath **d**-t to
Heb. 12:7.God **d**-eth with you as . . . sons

Dearth
Gen. 41:54....seven years of **d** began
2 Chr. 6:28 ......there be **d** in the land
Neh. 5:3 ..buy corn, because of the **d**
Acts 7:11 .came a **d** over all the land

Death
Gen. 27:2 .know not the day of my **d**
Num. 16:29 ....these . . . die the common **d**
Num. 23:10 ....die the **d** of the righteous
Ruth 1:17 ......but **d** part thee and me
1 Kin. 2:26........thou are worthy of **d**
Job 3:21 ....long for **d** . . . cometh not
Job 38:17......gates of **d** been opened
Ps. 13:3 ......lest I sleep the sleep of **d**
Ps. 23:4 .....valley of the shadow of **d**
Ps. 89:48 ....man . . . shall not see **d**
Ps. 107:10........................shadow of **d**
Ps. 116:3.....sorrows of **d** compassed
Prov. 8:36.all . . . that hate me love **d**
Song 8:6................love is strong as **d**
Is. 25:8 ....swallow up **d** in victory
Jer. 8:3 .**d** . . . chosen rather than life
Jer. 21:8 ......of life, and the way of **d**
Ezek. 18:32; 33:11 ......no pleasure in the **d**
Matt. 15:4.................let him die the **d**
Luke 1:79 .....and in the shadow of **d**
John 4:47.....he was at the point of **d**
John 5:24..is passed from **d** unto life
Acts 2:24 ....loosed the pains of **d**
Rom. 8:6..to be carnally minded is **d**
Rom. 8:38 ....neither **d**, nor life
1 Cor. 15:21 .....since by man came **d**
1 Cor. 15:54..........**D** is swallowed up
1 Cor. 15:55 ..O **d**, where is thy sting
Phil. 1:20.....................by life, or by **d**
2 Tim. 1:10................Christ, who . . . abolished **d**
Heb. 2:9 ......taste of **d** for every man
James 5:20 ....save a soul from **d**
1 John 3:14 ..passed from **d** unto life
1 John 5:16 ....there is a sin unto **d**
Rev. 21:4 ....there shall be no more **d**

Debate
Prov. 25:9.........**D** thy cause with thy
Is. 58:4..................fast for strife and **d**
Rom. 1:29.....envy, murder, **d**, deceit
2 Cor. 12:20 ...there be **d**-s, envyings

Debt
1 Sam. 22:2...everyone that was in **d**
2 Kin. 4:7 ..sell the oil, and pay thy **d**

Matt. 6:12 ....forgive us our **d**-s
Matt. 18:27 ....and forgave him the **d**
Rom. 4:4.reckoned of grace, but of **d**

Debtor
Matt. 6:12 ....as we forgive our **d**-s
Luke 7:41 ....creditor which had two **d**-s
Rom. 1:14..............I am **d** both to the Greeks
Rom. 8:12 ....we are **d**-s, not to the flesh
Gal. 5:3 ....**d** to do the whole law

Deceit
Job 15:35.......their belly prepareth **d**
Job 31:5 ....my foot hath hasteth to **d**
Ps. 101:7 ....He that worketh **d**
Prov. 14:8 ....the folly of fools is **d**
Prov. 20:17..........Bread of **d** is sweet
Is. 53:9 .....neither . . . **d** in his mouth
Jer. 5:27............their houses full of **d**
Rom. 1:29................full of envy . . . **d**
Col. 2:8 ....philosophy and vain **d**
1 Thess. 2:3 ..exhortation was not of **d**

Deceitful
Gen. 34:13 ....answered . . . **d**-ly
Ps. 52:4......................O thou **d** tongue
Prov. 14:25...**d** witness speaketh lies
Jer. 17:9...heart is **d** above all things
Matt. 13:22 ....the **d**-ness of riches
2 Cor. 4:2 ....handling the . . . of God **d**-ly
2 Cor. 11:13..............false apostles, **d** workers
Heb. 3:13...through the **d**-ness of sin

Deceive
Gen. 31:7 ....your father hath **d**-d me
Deut. 11:16......your heart be not **d**-d
Lev. 6:2.........hath **d**-d his neighbour
1 Sam. 19:17..Why hast thou **d**-d me so
Matt. 24:4 ....Take heed that no . . . **d** you
Matt. 27:63.....remember . . . **d**-r said
1 Cor. 3:18.......Let no man **d** himself
2 Tim. 3:13 ....**d**-ing, and being **d**-d
James 1:22.....**d**-ing your own selves
1 John 1:8 ......no sin, we **d** ourselves

Declare
Gen. 41:24 ....none that could **d** it
Ex. 9:16....that my name may be **d**-d
Deut. 1:5 .began Moses to **d** this law
1 Chr. 16:24.**D** his glory . . . heathen
Job 38:4.........................**d**, if thou hast understanding
Ps. 2:7....................I will **d** the decree
Ps. 19:1 ..heavens **d** the glory of God
Is. 42:9.....................new things do I **d**
Matt. 13:36 .....**D** unto us the parable
John 1:18.begotten Son . . . hath **d**-d
Acts 13:32 ....we **d** unto you glad tidings
Acts 17:23 ....him **d** I unto you
1 Cor. 15:1....I **d** unto you the gospel
Heb. 2:12 ....I will **d** thy name

Decree
Job 28:26 ....made a **d** for the rain
Prov. 8:15.............................princes **d**
Is. 10:1 ....Woe . . . **d** unrighteous **d**-s
Jer. 5:22.............sea by a perpetual **d**
Dan. 3:10...Thou, O king, hast made a **d**
Luke 2:1 ...went out a **d** from Caesar
Acts 17:7..........contrary to the **d**-s of Caesar
1 Cor. 7:37 ...hath so **d**-d in his heart

Deed
Gen. 20:9.....thou hast done **d**-s unto me
1 Sam. 25:34 .....For in very **d**, as the Lord
Luke 11:48 ....allow the **d**-s of your fathers
Luke 24:19 .....a prophet mighty in **d**
John 3:19 ....their **d**-s were evil

Acts 7:22..................mighty in words and in **d**-s
Rom. 8:13........mortify the **d**-s of the body
Col. 3:17..............ye do in word or **d**
1 John 3:18.............in **d** and in truth

Deep
Gen. 1:2.............darkness was upon the **d**
Gen. 2:21.....God caused a **d** sleep to
Job 12:22.....He discovereth **d** things
Ps. 69:2.......I am come into **d** waters
Ps. 92:5........thy thoughts are very **d**
Prov. 8:28........the fountains of the **d**
Luke 5:4..........Launch out into the **d**
John 4:11.................and the well is **d**
Rom. 10:7....shall descend into the **d**
2 Cor. 8:2 .their **d** poverty abounded

Defence
Job 22:25.....Almighty shall be thy **d**
Ps. 7:10.........................My **d** is of God
Ps. 59:17.........................God is my **d**
Eccles. 7:12..................wisdom is a **d**
Acts 22:1.........................hear ye my **d**
Phil 1:17........for the **d** of the gospel

Defile
Lev. 18:24.......**D** not ye . . . in any of these
Is. 59:3 ....hands are **d**-ed with blood
Ezek. 9:7.........................**D** the house
Matt. 15:20.....things which **d** a man
Mark 7:2........eat bread with **d**-d . . . hands
John 18:28....lest they should be **d**-d
1 Cor. 3:17.man **d** the temple of God
1 Cor. 8:7..........conscience . . . is **d**-d
1 Tim. 1:10...........**d** themselves with mankind
Heb. 12:15........thereby many be **d**-d
James 3:6.......it **d**-th the whole body
Rev. 3:4................have not **d**-d their garments

Defraud
Lev. 19:13.shalt not **d** thy neighbour
Mark 10:19...........**D** not, Honour thy father
2 Cor. 7:2 ....we have **d**-ed no man
1 Thess. 4:6.......go beyond and **d** his

Delight
Num. 14:8.............If the Lord **d** in us
Deut. 10:15.........Lord had a **d** in thy fathers
Job 27:10 ..**d** himself in the almighty
Ps. 1:2.................his **d** is in the law
Ps. 37:4....**D** thy self also in the Lord
Ps. 40:8....................I **d** to do thy will
Ps. 51:16..**d**-est not in burnt offering
Prov. 12:22 ..that deal truly are his **d**
Is. 58:13..............call the sabbath a **d**
Mic. 7:18.because he **d**-eth in mercy
Rom. 7:22 ..For I **d** in the law of God

Deliver
Gen. 32:11...**D** me . . . from the hand
Ps. 18:2........The Lord is . . . my **d**-er
Ps. 22:20 .**D** my soul from the sword
Ps. 25:20..O keep my soul, and **d** me
Ps. 55:18........He . . . **d**-ed my soul in peace
Ps. 70:1.Make haste, O God, to **d** me
Prov. 23:14.........**d** his soul from hell
Matt. 6:13 ..into temptation, but **d** us
Matt. 20:19............shall **d** him to the Gentiles
Luke 4:17.**d**-ed unto him the book of
John 19:11 ....he that **d**-ed me unto thee
Rom. 4:25.was **d**-ed for our offences
Col. 1:13..........hath **d**-ed us from the power
Jude 3..faith . . . **d**-ed unto the saints

Deliverance
Gen. 45:7......to save . . . by a great **d**
Ps. 32:7...............with the songs of **d**
Luke 4:18....preach **d** to the captives
Heb. 11:35.tortured, not accepting **d**

Deny
Gen. 18:15 .Sarah **d**-ed . . . I laughed not
Josh. 24:27...........lest ye **d** your God
Matt. 10:33.....whosoever shall **d** me
Matt. 16:24.............let him **d** himself
Mark 14:30 ....thou shalt **d** me thrice
John 1:20......he confessed, and **d**-ed not
1 Tim. 5:8........he hath **d**-ed the faith
Titus 2:12.............**d**-ing ungodliness
2 Tim. 2:12...**d** him, he also will **d** us
2 Peter 2:1..........**d**-ing the Lord that bought
1 John 2:22..he that **d**-eth that Jesus
Jude 4.........**d**-ing the only Lord God
Rev. 2:13........hast not **d**-ed my faith

Depth
Ex. 15:5........**d**-s have covered them
Job 28:14........**d** saith, It is not in me
Ps. 33:7.................layeth up the **d** in storehouses
Ps. 77:16........**d**-s also were troubled
Ps. 130:1..Out of the **d**-s have I cried
Prov. 9:18..........are in the **d**-s of hell
Is. 7:11........in the **d**, or in the height
Matt. 18:6....drowned in the **d** of the sea
Mark 4:5.................had no **d** of earth
Rom. 8:39.......Nor height, nor **d**, nor any
Rom. 11:33........O the **d** of the riches
Eph. 3:18breadth, and length, and **d**
Rev. 2:24......known the **d**-s of Satan

Descend
Ex. 19:18.....Lord **d**-ed upon it in fire
Ex. 33:9.........cloudy pillar **d**-ed, and stood
Ex. 34:5..........Lord **d**-ed in the cloud
Matt. 3:16.....Spirit of God **d**-ing like
Matt. 7:25 .rain **d**-ed . . . floods came
Mark 15:32.Let Christ the king . . . **d**
Rom. 10:7.Who shall **d** into the deep
Eph. 4:10....He that **d**-ed is the same
1 Thess. 4:16.....Lord himself shall **d**
James 3:15....This wisdom **d**-eth not

Desire
Gen. 3:6..........tree to be **d**-d to make
Gen. 3:16..**d** shall be to thy husband
Deut. 14:26 ....whatsoever thy soul **d**-th
Judg. 8:24..would **d** a request of you
2 Chr. 15:15....sought him with . . . **d**
Job 36:20....................**D** not the night
Ps. 19:10 ......More to be **d**-d . . . than gold
Ps. 112:10.........**d** of the wicked shall
Ps. 140:8.......Grant not . . . **d**-s of the wicked
Ps. 145:16.....satisfiest the **d** of every
Prov. 11:23 ....**d** of the righteous is only
Prov. 13:19.**d** accomplished is sweet
Prov. 21:10...soul of the wicked **d**-th evil
Ezek. 24:21.............the **d** of your eyes
Hag. 2:7 ..**d** of all nations shall come
Matt. 13:17 ......have **d**-d to see those
Matt. 16:1 ......**d**-d him that he would
Mark 9:35.....If any man **d** to be first
Mark 11:24.things . . . ye **d**, when ye pray
Luke 10:24 .prophets . . . have **d**-d to see
Acts 13:7......**d**-d to hear the word of God
2 Cor. 5:2.........earnestly **d**-ing to be
2 Cor. 7:7 ..he told us your earnest **d**
Eph. 3:13..................I **d** that ye faint not
Col. 1:9........**d** that ye might be filled
1 Tim. 3:1..........he **d**-th a good work
Heb. 11:16..........now they **d** a better country
1 Pet. 2:2.........newborn babes, **d** the sincere

Desirous
Luke 23:8was **d** to see him of a long

Gal. 5:26................be **d** of vain glory
1 Thess. 2:8...affectionately **d** of you

Desolate
Ex. 23:29 ......lest the land become **d**
Lev. 26:22.your highways shall be **d**
Ps. 25:16.mercy upon me; for I am **d**
Ps. 143:4......my heart within me is **d**
Jer. 2:12...........................be ye very **d**
Ezek. 6:6 ....your altars . . . made **d**
Ezek. 35:3....I will make thee most **d**
Matt. 23:38 ..house is left unto you **d**
Acts 1:20..............his habitation be **d**
Gal. 4:27.............**d** hath many more children

Desolation
Lev. 26:31 ...your sanctuaries unto **d**
Josh. 8:28................a **d** unto this day
Ps. 46:8.........what **d**-s he hath made
Prov. 1:27................fear cometh as **d**
Is. 47:11...........**d** . . . come upon thee suddenly
Zeph. 1:15.a day of wasteness and **d**
Matt. 24:15.......the abomination of **d**

Despise
Gen. 25:34 ....Esau **d**-d his birthright
Lev. 26:15..........shall **d** my statutes
2 Sam. 6:16.she **d**-d him in her heart
Job 19:18 ......young children **d**-d me
Ps. 106:24........**d**-d the pleasant land
Prov. 1:7....**d** wisdom . . . instruction
Prov. 15:5..........fool **d**-th his father's
Jer. 4:30...........thy lovers will **d** thee
Matt. 6:24.hold to the one, and **d** the
Matt. 18:10...**d** not one of these little
Luke 10:16 .he that **d**-th you **d**-th me
Acts 13:41.........Behold, ye **d**-rs, and wonder
1 Cor. 11:22..**d** ye the church of God
1 Tim. 4:12 ..Let no man **d** thy youth
1 Thess. 4:8 ..that **d**-th, **d**-th not man
Heb. 12:2.the cross, **d**-ing the shame
James 2:6 ..But ye have **d**-d the poor

Destitute
Gen. 24:27.........not left **d** my master
Ps. 102:17.regard the prayer of the **d**
Ps. 141:8.............leave not my soul **d**
1 Tim. 6:5 ....minds . . . **d** of the truth
Heb. 11:37..............being **d**, afflicted
James 2:15 ......naked, and **d** of daily food

Destroy
Gen. 6:13.......I will **d** them with the earth
Gen. 18:23.thou also **d** the righteous
Deut. 4:31..not forsake thee, neither **d**
Job 6:9 ....please God to **d** me
Matt. 2:13 ..the young child to **d** him
Matt. 5:17.....not that I am come to **d**
Matt. 10:28 .....**d** both soul and body
Matt. 26:61 ....able to **d** the temple
Mark 1:24........art thou come to **d** us
Mark 14:58 ..I will **d** this temple that
Luke 17:27........flood came and **d**-ed them
John 2:19 ....**D** this temple, and in
John 10:10..........and to kill, and to **d**
1 Cor. 1:19.**d** the wisdom of the wise
1 Cor. 6:13 ....God shall **d** both it . . . them
Gal. 2:18.....again the things which I **d**-ed

Destruction
Job 26:6..............**d** hath no covering
Ps. 90:3..........Thou turnest man to **d**
Ps. 91:6 ..**d** that wasteth at noon day
Ps. 103:4 ..redeemeth thy life from **d**
Prov. 16:18........Pride goeth before **d**
Prov. 18:7......A fool's mouth is his **d**
Prov. 27:20.Hell and **d** are never full
Matt. 7:13 ....Broad is way . . . to **d**
Rom. 3:16............**D** . . . in their ways
Rom. 9:22 ..vessels of wrath fitted to **d**
2 Thess. 1:9.................punished with everlasting **d**

1 Tim. 6:9......which drown men in **d**
2 Pet. 2:1bring upon themselves . . . **d**

Devil
Lev. 17:7...............sacrifices unto **d**-s
Ps. 106:37....sons . . . daughters unto **d**-s
Matt. 4:1.........to be tempted of the **d**
Matt. 4:24 ....possessed with **d**-s
Matt. 9:32 ....possessed with a **d**
Luke 7:33............ye say, He hath a **d**
John 6:70.................one of you is a **d**
John 7:20.......................Thou hast a **d**
Acts 13:10 ....thou child of the **d**
1 Cor. 10:20........they sacrifice to **d**-s
Eph. 6:11...against the wiles of the **d**
2 Tim. 2:26..out of the snare of the **d**
James 2:19 ....**d**-s also believe . . . tremble
James 4:7 ...Resist the **d**, and he will flee
Rev. 12:9....old serpent, called the **D**

Dew
Gen. 27:28............give . . . of the **d** of heaven
Deut. 32:2 ....distill as the **d**
Judg. 6:37 .....**d** be on the fleece only
2 Sam. 1:21 ....let there be no **d**
Ps. 110:3........hast the **d** of thy youth
Prov. 19:12 .....is as **d** upon the grass
Song 5:2 ......my head is filled with **d**
Is. 18:4 ....a cloud of **d** in the heat
Dan. 4:15...wet with the **d** of heaven
Hos. 6:4.......your goodness is as . . . early **d**

Diamond
Ex. 28:18 ....a sapphire, and a **d**
Jer. 17:1 ....written . . . point of a **d**
Ezek. 28:13 .....**d**, the beryl, the onyx

Die
Gen. 2:17 ....eatest . . . thou shalt surely **d**
Gen. 6:17 ....everything . . . shall **d**
Gen. 30:1 ....Give me children, or else I **d**
Num. 23:10 .....Let me **d** the death of
Ruth 1:17 ...Where thou **d**-st, will I **d**
Job 14:14 .....If a man **d**, shall he live
Job 29:18.............I shall **d** in my nest
Ps. 104:29.**d**, and return to their dust
Ps. 118:17 ....I shall not **d**, but live
Prov. 10:21...........fools **d** for want of wisdom
Eccles. 3:2....to be born . . . time to **d**
Is. 22:13...eat . . . tomorrow we shall **d**
Is. 51:12.afraid of a man that shall **d**
Jer. 34:5 ....Thou shalt **d** in peace
Ezek. 18:4 ....soul that sinneth, it shall **d**
Jonah 4:8.better . . . to **d** than to live
Matt. 15:4......curseth . . . mother, let him **d**
Mark 14:31 ....If I should **d** with thee
John 11:26 ....believeth . . . shall never **d**
John 11:50.......one man . . . **d** for the people
1 Cor. 15:3.....Christ **d**-d for our sins
1 Cor. 15:22 ......For as in Adam all **d**
1 Thess. 4:14 ..believe that Jesus **d**-d

Diligence
Luke 12:58 ..give **d** that thou mayest
2 Tim. 4:9..Do thy **d** to come shortly
2 Pet. 1:5.....giving all **d**, add to your

Diligent
Deut. 4:9 ....keep thy soul **d**-ly
Prov. 10:4.........hand of the **d** maketh rich
Is. 21:7 ....he hearkened **d**-ly
Matt. 2:8 ...search **d**-ly for the young
Luke 15:8 .....seek **d**-ly till she find it
2 Cor. 8:22...have oftentimes proved **d**

Dip
Gen. 37:31 ....**d**-ed the coat in the blood
Lev. 4:6....priest shall **d** his finger in
Deut. 33:24 ....**d** his foot in oil
Matt. 26:23....He that **d**-eth his hand
Luke 16:24 ..**d** the tip of his finger in
John 13:26...............had **d**-ed the sop
Rev. 19:13 ....a vesture **d**-ed in blood

Direct
Num. 19:4....sprinkle . . . **d**-ly before
Ps. 5:3....morning will I **d** my prayer
Prov. 3:6............he shall **d** thy paths
Is. 40:13...**d**-ed the Spirit of the Lord
Ezek. 42:12way **d**-ly before the wall
1 Thess. 3:11..........Christ, **d** our way
2 Thess. 3:5 .Lord **d** your hearts into

Discern
2 Sam. 14:17.........to **d** good and bad
2 Sam. 19:35 ...can I **d** between good and
Ezra 3:13 ...not **d** the noise of . . . joy
Eccles. 8:5 .a wise man's heart **d**-eth
Matt. 16:3.....ye can **d** the face of the sky
1 Cor. 2:14..they are spiritually **d**-ed
1 Cor. 11:29 ....not **d**-ing the Lord's body
Heb. 4:12.....is a **d**-er of the thoughts
Heb. 5:14......to **d** both good and evil

Disciple
Is. 8:16....seal the law among my **d**-s
Matt. 9:14 ......came to him the **d**-s of John
Matt. 10:1....called . . . his twelve **d**-s
Matt. 10:24.....**d** is not . . . his master
Matt. 12:1 .his **d**-s were an hungered
Matt. 19:13......the **d**-s rebuked them
Matt. 21:1.....then sent Jesus two **d**-s
Matt. 26:26 ....gave it to the **d**-s
Luke 11:1 .....as John also taught his **d**-s
John 13:35 .know that ye are my **d**-s
John 19:26 ....**d** standing by, . . . he loved
John 20:19...the **d**-s were assembled
John 21:4......**d**-s knew not . . . it was Jesus
Acts 6:7 ....number of the **d**-s multiplied
Acts 14:22 ....the souls of the **d**-s

Discreet
Gen. 41:33 ....a man **d** and wise
Gen. 41:39...........none so **d** and wise
Mark 12:34............he answered **d**-ly
Titus 2:5 .To be **d**, chaste, keepers at

Discretion
Ps. 112:5.......guide his affairs with **d**
Prov. 1:4 ....subtilty . . . knowledge and **d**
Prov. 2:11 ....**D** shall preserve thee
Prov. 11:22 ......woman . . . without **d**
Is. 28:26 ....instruct him to **d**

Disease
Ex. 15:26...will put none of these **d**-s
1 Kin. 15:23.....old age he was **d**-d in
Job 30:18.................great force of my **d**
Ps. 41:8.....an evil **d** . . . cleaveth fast
Ps. 103:3 ....who healeth all thy **d**-s
Eccles. 6:2.........................it is an evil **d**
Matt. 4:23 .....all manner of **d** among
Matt. 14:35 ....all that were **d**-d
Mark 1:34 ....sick of divers **d**-s
Luke 9:1.......authority . . . to cure **d**-s
John 6:2 ....on them that were **d**-d

Dishonest
Ezek. 22:27.....................to get **d** gain
2 Cor. 4:2....the hidden things of **d**-y

Dishonour
Ps. 35:26 ..clothed with shame and **d**
Prov. 6:33 .wound and **d** shall he get
Mic. 7:6........the son **d**-eth the father
Rom. 1:24 ....to **d** their own bodies

1 Cor. 11:4 ...his head covered, **d**-eth
1 Cor. 15:43 ....It is sown in **d**
2 Tim. 2:20 ....honour, and some to **d**

Dismayed
Deut. 31:8 ....fear not, neither be **d**
2 Kin. 19:26 ....**d** and confounded
Is. 41:10....be not **d** . . . I am thy God
Jer. 10:2 ......**d** at the signs of heaven
Ezek. 3:9 .neither be **d** at their looks

Disobedience
Rom. 5:19 ....by one man's **d**
2 Cor. 10:6 ....revenge all **d**
Eph. 2:2 ....in the children of **d**

Disobedient
Luke 1:17...turn . . . **d** to the wisdom
Rom. 1:30 ....**d** to parents
Titus 3:3 ..were sometimes foolish, **d**
1 Pet. 2:7.........unto them which be **d**

Disorderly
2 Thess. 3:6....brother that walked **d**
2 Thess. 3:11........walk among you **d**

Dispute
Job 23:7 ....the righteous might **d**
Mark 9:33......What was it . . . ye **d**-d
Phil. 2:14 ..do . . . things without . . . **d**-ings
1 Cor. 1:20.........the **d**-r of this world
1 Tim. 6:5.....Perverse **d**-ings of men

Distaff
Prov. 31:19.......her hands hold the **d**

Distress
Gen. 35:3 ....in the day of my **d**
Deut. 2:9 ....**D** not the Moabites
Deut. 28:53 ....enemies shall **d** thee
Prov. 1:27..........when **d** and anguish cometh
Is. 25:4...............to the needy in his **d**
Is. 29:2......................Yet I will **d** Ariel
Lam. 1:20.........................for I am in **d**
Zeph. 1:17 ...I will bring **d** upon men
Luke 21:23 ......there shall be great **d**
1 Cor. 7:26 .....good for the present **d**
1 Thess. 3:7 ....and **d** by your faith

Distribute
Job 21:17 ....God **d**-th sorrows
Luke 18:22 ....**d** unto the poor
John 6:11................**d**-d to the disciples
Rom. 12:13.....**D**-ing to the necessity
1 Cor. 7:17 .....God hath **d**-d to every
2 Cor. 9:13 ....for your liberal **d**-ion

Ditch
2 Kin. 3:16...............valley full of **d**-es
Prov. 23:27............whore in a deep **d**
Matt. 15:14 .both shall fall into the **d**

Divide
Gen. 1:4.........God **d**-d the light from
Josh. 13:7 ....**d** this land for an
1 Kin. 3:25..**D** the living child in two
Prov. 16:19 ....**d** the spoil with the proud
Is. 53:12 ....will I **d** him a portion
Dan. 2:41 ..the kingdom shall be **d**-d
Matt. 25:32 .shepherd **d**-th his sheep
Luke 11:17...........Every kingdom **d**-d
Luke 15:12 ....he **d**-d unto them his living
2 Tim. 2:15 ...**d**-ing the word of truth

Divination
Num. 22:7 ....with the rewards of **d**
Jer. 14:14............a false vision and **d**
Ezek. 13:6.............vanity and lying **d**
Acts 16:16 ....with a spirit of **d**

Divine
Ezek. 13:9....................and that **d** lies
Mic. 3:11...prophets . . . **d** for money
Zech. 10:2 ....the **d**-rs have seen a lie
Heb. 9:1........ordinances of **d** service
2 Pet. 1:4...partakers of the **d** nature

Division
Ex. 8:23..........I will put a **d** between
John 7:43 ....there was a **d** among
Rom. 16:17....cause **d**-s and offenses

1 Cor. 1:10..........that there be no **d**-s
1 Cor. 3:3...........envying . . . and **d**-s

Divorce
Lev. 21:14 ...widow, or a **d**-d woman
Deut. 24:1, 3 ....a bill of **d**-ment
Jer. 3:8...............given her a bill of **d**
Matt. 5:31, 32 ....writing of **d**-ment

Doctor
Luke 2:46 ....in the midst of the **d**-s
Luke 5:17.....................**d**-s of the law
Acts 5:34.....Gamaliel, a **d** of the law

Doctrine
Deut. 32:2......My **d** shall drop as the rain
Job 11:4..........................My **d** is pure
Prov. 4:2.................I give you good **d**
Mark 1:22............astonished at his **d**
John 7:16 ..My **d** is not mine, but his
Acts 2:42................in the apostles' **d**
Rom. 16:17.............contrary to the **d**
Col. 2:22.commandments and **d**-s of
Eph. 4:14..................every wind of **d**
1 Tim. 4:6...........of faith and good **d**
2 Tim. 3:10 ....known my **d**
Titus 1:9...................able by sound **d**
Heb. 6:2............Of the **d** of baptisms
Rev. 2:24.as many as have not this **d**

Doer
Gen. 39:22 ....he was the **d** of it
2 Kin. 22:5..........the **d**-s of the work
Ps. 101:8..........cut off all wicked **d**-s
Rom. 2:13.the **d**-s of the law shall be
James 1:22.......be ye **d**-s of the word
James 4:11............not a **d** of the law

Dog
1 Sam. 17:43 ....Am I a **d**,
2 Sam. 3:8................Am I a **d**'s head
Ps. 22:16.....For **d**-s have compassed
Ps. 59:6...........make a noise like a **d**
Eccles. 9:4.......living **d** is better than
Is. 56:10...........they are all dumb **d**-s
Luke 16:21 ..the **d**-s came and licked
Phil. 3:2...........................Beware of **d**-s
Rev. 22:15...........For without are **d**-s

Doing
Ps. 66:5.........terrible in his **d** toward
Prov. 20:11............known by his **d**-s
Is. 1:16.put away the evil of your **d**-s
Matt. 21:42 ..is the Lord's **d**, and it is
Acts 10:38...........went about **d** good
Rom. 2:7 ....continuance in well **d**
2 Cor. 8:11..........perform the **d** of it
Gal. 6:9 ....not be weary in well **d**
Eph. 6:6..........**d** the will of God from
2 Thess. 3:13 ......not weary in well **d**
1 Pet. 2:15....that with well **d** ye may
1 Pet. 3:17.suffer . . . well **d** . . . evil **d**

Dominion
Gen. 1:26..them have **d** over the fish
Gen. 37:8..........shalt thou . . . have **d**
Job 25:2 ......**D** and fear are with him
Ps. 8:6 ...Thou madest him to have **d**
Ps. 49:14 ...upright shall have **d** over
Ps. 103:22 ....in all places of his **d**
Is. 26:13 ....beside thee have had **d**
Zech. 9:10 ....his **d** shall be from sea
Rom. 6:9.death hath no more **d** over
2 Cor. 1:24.....have **d** over your faith
Col. 1:16 ....or **d**-s, or principalities
1 Pet. 4:11 .to whom be praise and **d**
Rev. 1:6 ....be glory and **d** for ever

Door
Gen. 4:7....................sin lieth at the **d**
Gen. 6:16 .**d** of the ark shalt thou set
Gen. 18:1......................sat in the tent **d**
Ex. 12:7..............on the upper **d** post
Ex. 12:23 ...Lord will pass over the **d**
Judg. 4:20 .Stand in the **d** of the tent
2 Sam. 11:9..........Uriah slept at the **d**
Job 31:9 ....wait at my neighbour's **d**
Ps. 84:10 ....had rather be a **d** keeper
Ps. 141:3...........keep the **d** of my lips
Prov. 26:14..........................**d** turneth
Matt. 6:6 ..thou hast shut thy **d**, pray
Matt. 25:10...........buy . . . **d** was shut
Matt. 27:60 ....great stone to the **d**
John 10:9...........................I am the **d**
John 18:16..........Peter stood at the **d**
1 Cor. 16:9 ....a great **d** and effectual
James 5:9 ....judge standeth before the **d**
Rev. 3:8.....set before thee an open **d**
Rev. 4:1 ...a **d** was opened in heaven

Double
Gen. 43:12 ....take **d** money
2 Kin. 2:9 ....**d** portion of thy spirit
Ps. 12:2.........................with a **d** heart
Is. 40:2 ....**d** for all her sins
1 Tim. 5:17...be counted worthy of **d**

Doubt
Gen. 37:33...without **d** rent in pieces
Job 12:2..No **d** but ye are the people
Ps. 126:6 ......shall **d**-less come again
Is. 63:16....**d**-less thou art our Father
Matt. 14:31 ...wherefore didst thou **d**
Matt. 21:21..ye have faith, and **d** not
Matt. 28:17 ....but some **d**-ed
Luke 11:20........no **d** the kingdom of God
Luke 12:29.......neither be ye of **d**-ful
John 13:22 ....disciples looked . . . **d**-ing
Acts 10:20 ....go with them, **d**-ing nothing
Rom. 14:23.......that **d**-eth is damned
1 Cor. 9:2 ....yet **d**-less I am to you
1 Tim. 2:8 ...holy hands, without . . . **d**-ing

Dove
Gen. 8:8..............he sent forth a **d** from
Ps. 55:6...O that I had wings like a **d**
Song 1:15..............thou hast **d**'s eyes
Is. 38:14 ....I did mourn as a **d**
Matt. 3:16.Spirit . . . descending like a **d**
Matt. 10:16.serpents . . . harmless as **d**-s
John 1:32..........from heaven like a **d**

Dragon
Deut. 32:33.....wine . . . poison of **d**-s
Job 30:29 ....I am a brother to **d**-s
Ps. 91:13 .young lion and the **d** shalt
Ps. 148:7...Praise the Lord . . . ye **d**-s
Is. 51:9.............................wounded the **d**
Jer. 9:11 ..Jerusalem . . . a den of **d**-s
Rev. 20:2 ....the **d**, that old serpent

Draw
Gen. 24:13 ....come out to **d** water
Judg. 3:22 ....not **d** the dagger out
Ps. 69:18; 73:28.**D** nigh unto my soul
Prov. 20:5 ......man of understanding will **d**
Is. 12:3.....**d** water out of the wells of
Jer. 31:3...lovingkindness have I **d**-n
Luke 21:28....your redemption **d**-eth nigh
John 4:11 ....nothing to **d** with
John 12:32........lifted up . . . will **d** all men
Acts 11:10.**d**-n up again into heaven
Heb. 10:22 .Let us **d** near with a true
Heb. 10:38 ....if any man **d** back
James 2:6................**d** you before the judgment
James 4:8 ....**D** nigh to God . . . he will **d**

Dream
Gen. 20:3...........God came . . . in a **d**
Gen. 28:12 ....he **d**-ed . . . behold a ladder
Gen. 37:19 .Behold, this **d**-er cometh
Judg. 7:13 ..I **d**-ed a **d**, and lo, a cake
Job 20:8........................fly away as a **d**
Ps. 73:20..As a **d** when one awaketh
Ps. 126:1....we were like them that **d**
Is. 29:7 ....**d** of a night vision
Dan. 1:17 ...understanding in all . . . **d**-s
Joel 2:28.....your old men shall **d d**-s
Matt. 1:20 .appeared unto him in a **d**
Matt. 2:12 ....warned of God in a **d**
Matt. 27:19....suffered . . . things . . . in a **d**
Acts 2:17 ....your old men shall **d d**-s
Jude 8 ....these filthy **d**-ers defile

Drink
Gen. 35:14 ....poured a **d** offering
Lev. 10:9..Do not **d** wine or strong **d**
Num. 6:3 ...He . . . shall **d** no vinegar
Job 6:4.poison . . . **d**-eth up my spirit
Job 21:20 ....shall **d** of the wrath of
Ps. 16:4 .....their **d** offerings of blood
Ps. 80:5 ....givest them tears to **d**
Prov. 5:15....**D** waters . . . of . . . own cistern
Prov. 20:1 .Wine is mocker, strong **d**
Eccles. 9:7...**d** . . . wine with a merry heart
Is. 22:13 ....let us eat and **d**; for tomorrow
Is. 24:9...........strong **d** shall be bitter
Joel 1:5 .....howl, all ye **d**-ers of wine
Matt. 11:18 .neither eating nor **d**-ing
Matt. 25:35......................thirsty, and ye gave me **d**
Matt. 26:27 ....**D** ye all of it
Matt. 27:34.....gave him vinegar to **d**
John 6:55 ....my blood is **d** indeed
John 18:11 ......cup . . . shall I not **d** it
Rom. 12:20 ....if he thirst, give him **d**
1 Cor. 10:4.all **d** the same spiritual **d**
1 Cor. 10:21 ..Ye cannot **d** the cup of
1 Cor. 11:25 ....as oft as ye **d** it
Heb. 6:7 ......earth which **d**-eth in the rain

Drive
Gen. 4:14..........thou hast **d**-n me out
2 Kin. 9:20.**d**-ing is . . . **d**-ing of Jehu
Job 18:11 ......Terrors . . . shall **d** him
Ps. 1:4....which the wind **d**-eth away
Ps. 40:14 ..let them be **d**-n backward
Ps. 114:3...........Jordan was **d**-n back
Prov. 25:23 .....north wind **d**-th away rain
Mark 1:12.....Spirit **d**-th him into the
John 2:15 ....**d** them all out of the temple

Drop
Deut. 32:2 ......doctrine shall **d** as the rain
Job 36:27 ....small the **d**-s of water
Ps 65:11..............thy paths **d** fatness
Prov. 27:15.**d**-ing in a very rainy day
Eccles. 10:18 ....the house **d**-eth through
Song 4:11 ....**d** as the honeycomb
Is 40:15 ....nations are as a **d**
Is 45:8................**D** down, ye heavens
Luke 22:44.great **d**-s of blood falling

Drunk
Lev. 11:34.....all drink that may be **d**
Deut. 32:42.........mine arrows **d** with blood
Is. 29:9.........**d**-en, but not with wine
Is. 63:6.........make them **d** in my fury
Luke 5:39.............having **d** old wine
John 2:10 .....when men have well **d**,
Eph. 5:18.............be not **d** with wine
1 Thess. 5:7 ......are **d**-en in the night

Drunkard
Deut. 21:20...he is a glutton, and a **d**
Ps. 69:12 ....was the song of the **d**-s
Joel 1:5......Awake, ye **d**-s, and weep
1 Cor. 5:11 ....a railer, or a **d**

Drunkenness
Deut. 29:19.............to add **d** to thirst
Luke 21:34 ...overcharged with . . . **d**
Rom. 13:13 .....walk . . . not in rioting and **d**
Gal 5:21 .**d**, revellings, and such like

Dry
Gen. 1:9............let the **d** land appear
Ps. 63:1 ....in a **d** and thirsty land
Prov 17:1 ....Better is a **d** morsel
Is. 53:2....as a root out of a **d** ground

Jer. 4:11....**d** wind of the high places
Ezek. 37:4.....................O ye **d** bones,
Matt. 12:43...........walketh through **d** places
Mark 11:20..saw the fig tree **d**-ed up
Luke 23:31......what shall be done in the **d**

Due
Lev. 10:13 ..it is thy **d** . . . thy sons' **d**
Lev. 26:4 ...give you rain in **d** season
Ps. 104:27 ......their meat in **d** season
Prov. 15:23 ....word spoken in **d** season
Matt. 18:34...should pay all that was **d**
Luke 23:41.....**d** reward of our deeds
1 Cor. 15:8 ....born out of **d** time
Gal. 6:9.....in **d** season we shall reap
1 Tim. 2:6.....to be testified in **d** time

Dumb
Ex. 4:11 ..who maketh the **d**; or deaf
Ps. 39:2..............I was **d** with silence
Matt. 9:32....brought to him a **d** man
Mark 7:37.........deaf to hear . . . **d** to speak
Luke 1:20 ....thou shalt be **d**
1 Cor. 12:2 ....unto these **d**
2 Pet. 2:16...................**d** ass speaking

Dust
Gen. 2:7 ....Lord God formed man of the **d**
Gen. 3:14..................**d** shalt thou eat
Gen. 3:19...........**d** thou art . . . unto **d**
Gen. 13:16 ....as the **d** of the earth
1 Sam. 2:8......raiseth . . . poor out of the **d**
Job 30:19............I am become like **d**
Job 34:15 ......shall turn again unto **d**
Job 42:6 ..I . . . repent in **d** and ashes
Ps. 30:9..........Shall the **d** praise thee
Ps. 72:9........enemies shall lick the **d**
Ps. 103:14.............................we are **d**
Is. 26:19 ....sing, ye that dwell in **d**
Is. 40:15.........small **d** of the balance
Is. 65:25........**d** shall be the serpent's meat
Dan. 12:2 ....sleep in the **d**
Matt. 10:14 ...shake off the **d** of your feet
Luke 10:11.....the very **d** of your city
Acts 22:23..........threw **d** into the air
Rev. 18:19 ....cast **d** on their heads

Duty
Ex. 21:10................her **d** of marriage
Ezra 3:4 ....**d** of every day required
Eccles. 12:13 ......the whole **d** of man
Luke 17:10.....which was our **d** to do
Rom. 15:27...............their **d** is also to minister

Dwell
Gen. 4:20father of such as **d** in tents
Lev. 19:34 ...stranger that **d**-eth with
Deut. 12:11 ....cause his name to **d** there
1 Chr. 17:1.I **d** in an house of cedars
Ps. 5:4 .neither shall evil **d** with thee
Ps. 15:1 ..who shall **d** in thy holy hill
Ps. 23:6....**d** in the house of the Lord
Ps. 24:1 ....world, and they that **d** therein
Ps. 91:1.........He that **d**-eth . . . secret place
Prov. 21:9.......better to **d** in a corner
Is. 57:15..........**d** in the high and holy place
Matt. 12:45they enter in and **d** there
Luke 21:35.**d** on the face of . . . earth
John 1:38 ....where **d**-est thou
1 Cor. 4:11 ......have no certain **d**-ing place
Eph. 3:17..........Christ may **d** in your hearts
Col. 1:19 .in him should all fulness **d**
1 Tim. 6:16 ..**d**-ing in the light which no
2 Tim. 1:5.....................**d**-t first in thy
2 Pet. 2:8 ...righteousness man **d**-ing among
1 John 3:17......how **d**-eth the love of God
1 John 4:12................God **d**-eth in us

E

Eagle
Ex. 19:4.........bare you on **e**-s' wings
Deut. 28:49..........swift as the **e** flieth
Deut. 32:11 ......**e** stirring up her nest
Ps. 103:5............renewed like the **e**'s
Prov. 30:19......way of an **e** in the air
Lam. 4:19...........swifter than the **e**-s
Ezek. 10:14..............the face of an **e**
Obad. 4.............exalt thyself as the **e**
Matt. 24:28 ....**e**-s be gathered
Rev. 4:7 ......beast was like a flying **e**

Ear
Job 42:5 ....by the hearing of the **e**
Ps. 31:2.......Bow down thine **e** to me
Ps. 44:1.We have heard with our **e**-s
Ps. 94:9 ....He that planted the **e**
Ps. 115:6 ...have **e**-s, but . . . hear not
Prov. 18:15 ....**e** . . . seeketh knowledge
Prov. 20:12 .hearing **e** . . . seeing eye
Prov. 25:12 ....upon an obedient **e**
Is. 55:3..........................Incline your **e**
Matt. 10:27 .....what ye hear in the **e**,
Matt. 11:15..He that hath **e**-s to hear
Matt. 26:51 ....smote off his **e**
Mark 7:33 ....fingers into his **e**-s
1 Cor. 2:9 ......Eye . . . not seen, nor **e** heard
1 Cor. 12:16 ....if the **e** shall say
2 Tim. 4:3.............having itching **e**-s
Rev. 2:7....He that hath an **e**, let him

Early
Gen. 19:27 ....Abraham gat up **e**
1 Sam. 29:10....as soon as ye be up **e**
Ps. 46:5..God . . . help her . . . right **e**
Ps. 57:8............I myself will awake **e**
Mark 16:9....when Jesus was risen **e**
John 20:1.............Mary Magdalene **e**
James 5:7 .....receive the **e** and latter rain

Earnest
Luke 22:44..in . . . he prayed . . . **e**-ly
Luke 22:56 ......**e**-ly looked upon him
Rom. 8:19 ....**e** expectation of the creature
2 Cor. 1:22...given the **e** of the Spirit
2 Cor. 5:2.**e**-ly desiring to be clothed
Eph. 1:14 .....the **e** of our inheritance
Heb. 2:1......ought to give the more **e** heed
James 5:17 ....and he prayed **e**-ly

Earth
Gen. 1:1......created the heaven . . . **e**
Gen. 12:3............families of the **e** be blessed
Ex. 9:14.......none like me in all the **e**
Ex. 20:11 ...Lord made heaven and **e**
Lev. 6:28 ....**e**-en vessel
Deut. 32:1 ....hear, O, **e** the words
Josh. 2:11............heaven above . . . **e**
1 Sam. 2:10.......Lord shall judge . . . the **e**
1 Sam. 14:15.................the **e** quaked
1 Kin. 18:1 ....send rain upon the **e**
2 Kin. 5:15............no God in all the **e**
Job 5:10.Who giveth rain upon the **e**
Job 8:9 ....our days upon **e** are a shadow
Job 12:15 ....they overturn the **e**
Job 19:25...........latter day upon the **e**
Job 24:4 ....poor of the **e** hide themselves
Job 38:4.............laid the foundations of the **e**
Job 39:14 ....her eggs in the **e**
Ps. 2:2 .kings of the **e** set themselves
Ps. 12:6 ....in a furnace of **e**
Ps. 8:1.excellent is thy name in . . . **e**
Ps. 24:1................The **e** is the Lord's
Ps. 25:13 ....seed shall inherit the **e**
Ps. 37:11......meek shall inherit the **e**
Ps. 46:2......though the **e** be removed
Ps. 47:2.......great King over all the **e**
Ps. 65:9 ....Thou visitest the **e**, and
Ps. 72:6 .as showers that water the **e**
Ps. 85:11 ....Truth . . . spring out of the **e**
Ps. 98:3 ....ends of the **e** have seen
Prov. 2:22.....wicked . . . cut off from the **e**
Prov. 10:30....wicked . . . not inhabit the **e**
Prov. 30:21 ....the **e** is disquieted
Eccles. 12:7.........dust return to the **e**
Song 2:12 ....flowers appear on the **e**
Is. 1:2 ....give ear, O **e**
Is. 24:1 ......Lord maketh the **e** empty
Is. 34:1 ....let the **e** hear
Is. 49:6 ....salvation unto the end of the **e**
Is. 55:9................heavens are higher than the **e**
Is. 60:2.....darkness shall cover the **e**
Is. 61:11 ....the **e** bringeth forth her bud
Is. 66:1...............the **e** is my footstool
Jer. 19:1 .....get a potter's **e**-en bottle
Jer. 22:29.....O **e**, **e**, **e**, hear the word
Jer. 23:24..Do not I fill heaven and **e**
Jer. 50:23...........whole **e** cut asunder
Joel 3:16...heavens . . . **e** shall shake
Jonah 2:6 ....**e** with her bars was
Mic. 7:2.....................man is perished out of the **e**
Mic. 7:17 ....like worms of the **e**
Nah. 1:5 .**e** is burned at his presence
Hab. 2:20 ....let the **e** keep silence
Mal. 4:6 ....smite the **e** with a curse
Matt. 5:5 ....meek . . . shall inherit the **e**
Matt. 6:10 ....thy will be done in **e**
Matt. 6:19...............treasures upon **e**
Matt. 10:34.come to send peace on **e**
Matt. 11:25......Lord of heaven and **e**
Matt. 24:35.Heaven and **e** shall pass
Matt. 25:25......hid thy talent in the **e**
Matt. 27:51 ....and the **e** did quake
Matt. 28:18 ....power is given . . . in . . . **e**
Mark 4:5 ....had no depth of **e**
Luke 2:14 ....on **e** peace, good will
Luke 12:49.........to send fire on the **e**
Luke 18:8 ....find faith on the **e**
Luke 23:44....darkness over all the **e**
John 3:12 ....If I have told you **e**-ly
John 12:32.....be lifted up from the **e**
John 17:4 ....glorified thee on the **e**
Rom. 10:18 ....sound went into all the **e**
1 Cor. 15:47.the first man is of the **e**, **e**-y
2 Cor. 4:7.....treasure in **e**-en vessels
2 Cor. 5:1..........know that if our **e**-ly house
Eph. 6:3.....mayest live long on the **e**
Phil. 3:19 ....who mind **e**-ly things
Col. 3:2 ....not on things on the **e**
2 Tim. 2:20......also of wood and of **e**
Heb. 11:13 ....pilgrims on the **e**
Heb. 12:26.....voice then shook the **e**
James 3:15..........................but is **e**-ly
James 5:5 .lived in pleasure on the **e**
James 5:18 .**e** brought forth her fruit
2 Pet. 3:5**e** standing out of the water
1 John 5:8........three . . . witness in **e**
Rev. 1:5..prince of the kings of the **e**
Rev. 21:1.a new heaven and a new **e**

Earthquake
1 Kin. 19:11 .and after the wind an **e**
Is. 29:6 ....with **e**, and great noise
Amos 1:1 ....two years before the **e**
Matt. 24:7...shall be famines . . . and **e**-s
Matt. 28:2.............................a great **e**
Rev. 8:5.............lightnings, and an **e**

Ease
Ps. 25:13 .....His soul shall dwell at **e**

Is. 1:24..................I will **e** me of mine adversaries
Is. 32:9....11, ye women that are at **e**
Jer. 46:27 ....be in rest and at **e**
Ezek. 23:42 ....multitude being at **e**
Amos 6:1......Woe to them . . . at **e** in Zion
Matt. 9:5 ....whether is **e**-ier, to say
Matt. 19:24 ..It is **e**-ier for a camel to
Luke 12:19....take thine **e**, eat, drink
Luke 16:17........**e**-ier for heaven and earth
2 Cor. 8:13 ......that other men be **e**-d

East

Gen. 2:14 .....toward the **e** of Assyria
Gen. 3:24 .....**e** of the garden of Eden
Gen. 41:6 .....blasted with the **e** wind
Ex. 10:13.....Lord brought an **e** wind
Ex. 14:21 ....by a strong **e** wind
Num. 3:38...tabernacle toward the **e**
Judg. 6:3...........the children of the **e**
1 Kin. 4:30....wisdom . . . children of the **e**
Job 1:3...........greatest of all the men of the **e**
Job 15:2 ....belly with the **e** wind
Job 27:21 .**e** wind carrieth him away
Ps. 48:7.the ships . . . with an **e** wind
Ps. 103:12......far as the **e** is from the west
Is. 41:2......righteous man from the **e**
Is. 46:11.....ravenous bird from the **e**
Matt. 2:1 .came wise men from the **e**
Matt. 8:11......many shall come from the **e**
Matt. 24:27.lightning . . . out of the **e**
Rev. 7:2 .angel ascending from the **e**
Rev. 21:13 ....On the **e** three gates

Easter

Acts 12:4 ..after **E** to bring him forth

Eat

Gen. 2:16..........tree . . . thou mayest freely **e**
Gen. 3:1.......shall not **e** of every tree
Gen. 9:4........blood . . . shall ye not **e**
Ex. 2:20.........call him, that he may **e** bread
Ex. 12:4..man according to his **e**-ing
Lev. 6:16...with unleavened . . . **e**-en
Lev. 21:22......**e** the bread of his God
Num. 18:10 ....every male shall **e** it
Deut. 8:9 ..land wherein thou shalt **e**
Judg. 14:14.......Out of the **e**-er came forth
2 Chr. 30:18 ....yet did they **e** the passover
Job 5:5..Whose . . . the hungry **e**-eth
Job 6:6....Can . . . unsavoury be **e**-en
Ps. 22:26.meek . . . **e** and be satisfied
Ps. 78:25 ....man did **e** angels' food
Ps. 102:9 ....I have **e**-en ashes like bread
Ps. 128:2.**e** the labour of thine hands
Prov. 13:25 .....**e**-eth to the satisfying
Prov. 23:7....**E** and drink, saith he to
Prov. 27:18.........keepeth the fig tree shall **e**
Prov. 31:27 .....**e**-eth not the bread of
Eccles. 5:12 ....**e** little or much
Is. 3:14...............ye have **e**-en up the vineyard
Is. 7:15 ..Butter and honey shall he **e**
Is. 11:7..................**e** straw like the ox
Is. 22:13 ..**e** and drink; for tomorrow
Is. 55:1 ....come ye, buy, and **e**
Matt. 12:1.........pluck the ears . . . to **e**
Matt. 14:16 ....give ye them to **e**
Matt. 15:27.the dogs **e** of the crumbs
Matt. 26:26 .Take, **e**; this is my body
Mark 5:43...something . . . given her to **e**
Mark 7:5......**e** bread with unwashen
Luke 14:15...**e** bread . . . kingdom of God
Luke 15:23 .....let us **e**, and be merry
John 4:32..................I have meat to **e**
John 6:31...Our fathers did **e** manna
Acts 10:13......Rise, Peter; kill, and **e**
Rom. 14:2..........**e** all things . . . **e**-eth herbs
1 Cor. 10:3 ....**e** the same spiritual meat
2 Tim. 2:17 ....**e** as doth a canker
Heb. 13:10.....they have no right to **e**
James 5:3.**e** your flesh as it were fire
Rev. 2:7............to **e** of the tree of life

Edify

Acts 9:31 ....were **e**-ed
Rom. 14:19.wherewith . . . **e** another
1 Cor. 10:23.........but all things **e** not
Eph. 4:12.**e**-ing of the body of Christ
1 Tim. 1:4.....rather than godly **e**-ing

Effectual

1 Cor. 16:9...........great door and **e** is opened
Gal. 2:8.........he that wrought **e**-ly in Peter
Eph. 3:7........by the **e** working of his power
1 Thess. 2:13......which **e**-ly worketh
James 5:16...The **e** fervent prayer of

Elders

Ex. 24:9......seventy of the **e** of Israel
1 Sam. 15:30...honour me . . . before the **e**
Ps. 107:32 ....assembly of the **e**
Prov. 31:23 ....among the **e**
Matt. 15:2.....................tradition of the **e**
Acts 14:23..............**e** in every church
1 Tim 5:17.....Let the **e** that rule well
Heb. 11:2 ....the **e** obtained a good report
James 5:14 ....call for the **e**
Rev. 4:4 .....four and twenty **e** sitting

Elect

Is. 45:4 ....Israel mine **e**
Matt. 24:22 ....for the **e**'s sake
Luke 18:7.......God avenge his own **e**
Titus 1:1..........to the faith of God's **e**
1 Pet. 2:6.........a chief corner stone, **e**
2 John 1 ....The elder unto the **e** lady

Election

Rom. 9:11 ..purpose of . . . according to **e**
Rom. 11:5............................**e** of grace
1 Thess. 1:4..................your **e** of God
2 Pet. 1:10 ....your calling and **e** sure

End

Gen. 6:13....the **e** of all flesh is come
Ex. 23:16 ..in the **e** of the year, when
Num. 23:10...let my last **e** be like his
Deut. 8:16............good at thy latter **e**
Job 8:7 ....yet thy latter **e**
Job 16:3.Shall vain words have an **e**
Job 26:10 ....day and night come to an **e**
Job 42:12 ....the latter **e** of Job
Ps. 37:37 ..the **e** of that man is peace
Ps. 39:4 ....Lord, make me to know mine **e**
Ps. 102:27 .thy years shall have no **e**
Ps. 119:96.........an **e** of all perfection
Prov. 14:12...........................the **e** thereof
Eccles. 3:11....from the beginning to the **e**
Eccles. 4:8........no **e** of all his labour
Eccles. 4:16......no **e** of all the people
Eccles. 7:2 .....that is the **e** of all men
Eccles. 7:8 ..Better is the **e** of a thing
Eccles. 12:12..making . . . books . . . no **e**
Is. 9:7.........peace there shall be no **e**
Jer. 5:31 ....what will ye do in the **e**
Jer. 8:20..............the summer is **e**-ed
Lam. 1:9...................remembereth not her last **e**
Lam. 4:18................for our **e** is come
Hab. 2:3...........at the **e** it shall speak
Matt. 13:39 ....harvest is the **e** . . . world
Matt. 24:6............but the **e** is not yet
Matt. 24:14......then shall the **e** come
Matt. 26:58 ....Peter . . . sat . . . to see the **e**
Matt. 28:20....I am with you . . . unto the **e**
Luke 1:33 .....kingdom there shall be no **e**
Luke 21:9 ....**e** is not by and by
John 13:1 ..he loved them unto the **e**
John 18:37.........To this **e** was I born
Phil. 3:19 ......Whose **e** is destruction
1 Tim. 1:5 ....the **e** of the commandment
Heb. 6:8.......whose **e** is to be burned
Heb. 6:16 ....and **e** of all strife
James 5:11 .....have seen the **e** of the Lord
1 Pet. 1:9 ......Receiving the **e** of your
1 Pet. 4:7 ....the **e** of all things is at
2 Pet. 2:20 ....the latter **e** is worse
Rev. 2:26 .....keepeth my works unto the **e**
Rev. 21:6; 22:13.beginning and the **e**

Endure

Gen. 33:14 ..the children be able to **e**
Ex. 18:23.................shalt be able to **e**
Esther 8:6 ....can I **e** to see the evil
Job 8:15......hold it fast, but . . . not **e**
Job 31:23 .his highness I could not **e**
Ps. 9:7 ....Lord shall **e** for ever
Ps. 72:5 ....as long as the sun and moon **e**
Ps. 72:17 ...His name shall **e** for ever
Ps. 100:5.....................truth **e**-th to all generations
Ps. 135:13......name, O Lord, **e**-th for ever
Prov. 27:24......**e** to every generation
Ezek. 22:14 ....Can thine heart **e**
Matt. 24:13.............But he that shall **e**
John 6:27 .meat which **e**-th unto . . . life
Rom. 9:22 ....**e**-d with . . . longsuffering
1 Cor. 13:7.hopeth . . . **e**-th all things
Heb. 12:7................If ye **e** chastening
2 Tim. 2:3 ....therefore **e** hardness
James 1:12...Blessed is the man that **e**-th
1 Pet. 1:25 .word of the Lord **e**-th for
1 Pet. 2:19 ....for conscience . . . **e**

Enemy

Ex. 23:22 ....an **e** unto thine **e**-ies
Judg. 5:31 ....let all thine **e**-ies perish
1 Sam. 24:19 ..For if a man find his **e**
1 Kin. 21:20........found me, O mine **e**
Ps. 8:2......still the **e** and the avenger
Ps. 23:5 ....presence of mine **e**-ies
Ps. 38:19......But mine **e**-ies are lively
Ps. 72:9...his **e**-ies shall lick the dust
Ps. 119:98 ....than mine **e**-ies
Ps. 127:5 ....speak with the **e**-ies
Ps. 139:22 ....I count them mine **e**-ies
Prov. 16:7 ....even his **e**-ies to be at peace
Prov. 24:17.............Rejoice not when thine **e**
Prov. 27:6...............kisses of an **e** are deceitful
Is. 9:11 ....Lord . . . join his **e**-ies together
Jer. 15:11 .will cause the **e** to entreat
Mic. 7:6 ....**e**-ies . . . men of his . . . house
Matt. 5:43 ....hate thine **e**
Matt. 5:44...I say . . . Love your **e**-ies
Acts 13:10 ....thou **e** of all righteousness
Rom. 5:10 .**e**-ies, we were reconciled
Gal. 4:16.......Am I therefore become your **e**
Phil. 3:18....are the **e**-ies of the cross
2 Thess. 3:15 ..count him not as an **e**

Enter

Gen. 7:13 ....selfsame day **e**-ed Noah
Ps. 100:4 ....**E** into his gates with
Prov. 4:14 .....**E** not into the path . . . wicked
Prov. 18:6 ....lips **e** into contention
Is. 2:10 ....**E** into the rock, and hide thee

Ezek. 2:2 ....the spirit e-ed into me
Dan. 11:24........He shall e peaceably
Matt. 6:6 .when thou prayest, e unto
Matt. 7:13 ...E ye in at the strait gate
Matt. 18:3 .....not e into the kingdom
Matt. 25:21 ....e . . . joy of thy Lord
Matt. 26:41 ......e not into temptation
Luke 7:6.I am not . . . that thou . . . e
Luke 13:24Strive to e in at the strait
Luke 22:3.then e-d Satan into Judas
Luke 24:26 ....to e into his glory
John 10:1 .that e-eth not by the door
Acts 8:3 ....e-ing every house
Rom. 5:12.....as by one man sin e-ed into
Heb. 3:11......shall not e into my rest
Heb. 9:12 ....e-ed in once into holy place

Envy

Gen. 30:1 ....Rachel e-ied her sister
Job 5:2 ....and e slayeth the silly one
Ps. 37:1...........neither be thou e-ious
Ps. 73:3 ....I was e-ious at the foolish
Prov. 3:31..E thou not the oppressor
Prov. 23:17...........Let not . . . heart e sinners
Eccles. 4:4......for this a man is e-ied
Ezek. 35:11........according to thine e
Matt. 27:18 .for e they had delivered
Acts 7:9.....patriarchs, moved with e
Acts 13:45.............were filled with e
Rom. 1:29...full of e, murder, debate
Rom. 13:13 .....not in strife and e-ing
2 Cor. 12:20...lest there be . . . e-ings
Gal. 5:26 ....e-ing one another
Phil. 1:15......preach Christ even of e
1 Tim. 6:4...whereof cometh e, strife
Titus 3:3..........living in malice and e
James 3:14......bitter e-ing and strife

Equal

Job 28:17 ...gold . . . crystal cannot e
Ps. 17:2.............the things that are e
Prov. 26:7..legs of the lame . . . not e
Ezek. 18:25 .way of the Lord is not e
Matt. 20:12 ...hast made them e unto us
Luke 20:36 ....e unto the angels
John 5:18 ......making himself e with God
2 Cor. 8:14...........there may be e-ity
Phil. 2:6......not robbery to be e with God
Col. 4:1.........that which is just and e

Equity

Ps. 98:9.........judge . . . people with e
Ps. 99:4......................dost establish e
Prov. 2:9..Then . . . understand . . . e
Eccles. 2:21.......knowledge, and in e
Is. 11:4..reprove with e for the meek
Mic. 3:9 ....pervert all e
Mal. 2:6.....walked with me in peace and e

Err

Lev. 5:18.............ignorance wherein he e-ed
1 Sam. 26:21.the fool, and have e-ed
Ps. 95:10 .....people that do e in their
Prov. 10:17.....refuseth reproof e-eth
Is. 35:8........though fools, shall not e
Matt. 22:29......Ye do e, not knowing the
Mark 12:24 .....Do ye not therefore e
Heb. 3:10.........They do . . . e in their heart
James 1:16......Do not e, my beloved

Error

2 Sam. 6:7.............smote him for his e
Ps. 19:12 ....Who can understand his e-s
Is. 32:6.............iniquity . . . to utter e against
Jer. 10:15...........and the work of e-s
Matt. 27:64 .the last e shall be worse
James 5:20 ..sinner from the e of his

1 John 4:6......spirit of truth, and . . . of e
Jude 11......................the e of Balaam

Escape

Gen. 14:13 .....came one that had e-d
Gen. 19:17 .....E for thy life; look not
Josh. 8:22....let none . . . remain or e
Ezra 9:14.........no remnant nor e-ing
Job 19:20......e-d with the skin of my teeth
Prov. 19:5...speaketh lies shall not e
Eccles. 7:26.......whoso pleaseth God shall e
Is. 20:6........................how shall we e
Matt. 23:33 ..can ye e the damnation
Luke 21:36 ..be accounted worthy to e
John 10:39......but he e-d out of their
Rom. 2:3.......shalt e the judgment of God
1 Cor. 10:13 ....make a way to e
2 Pet. 1:4..having e-d the corruption

Espoused

2 Sam. 3:14 ....which I e to me
Matt. 1:18.....his mother Mary was e
Luke 1:27 ....a virgin e to a man
Luke 2:5 ....Mary his e wife
2 Cor. 11:2 ......e you to one husband

Establish

Gen. 6:18 ....I e my covenant
Deut. 28:9 ....e thee an holy people
Ps. 89:2 ....faithfulness shalt thou e
Ps. 93:2 ......Thy throne is e-ed of old
Prov. 20:18 .....Every purpose is e-ed
Is. 9:7..e it with judgment . . . justice
Is. 49:8...........................to e the earth
Jer. 10:12 ......he hath e-ed the world
Dan. 6:8.............O king, e the decree
Matt. 18:16.every word may be e-ed
Acts 16:5..churches e-ed in the faith
Rom. 3:31...............yea, we e the law
Heb. 13:9........the heart be e-ed with grace
2 Pet. 1:12 ..e-ed in the present truth

Estate

Ps. 136:23........................in our low e
Eccles. 1:16 ......I am come to great e
Eccles. 3:18.......e of the sons of men
Rom. 12:16................to men of low e
Col. 4:8...........he might know your e
Jude 6 ....kept not their first e

Esteem

Deut. 32:15..lightly e-ed the Rock of
Job 36:19............Will he e thy riches
Job 41:27......He e-eth irons as straw
Is. 29:16..be e-ed as the potter's clay
Is. 53:3....despised, and we e-ed him not
Luke 16:15..highly e-ed among men
Phil. 2:3 ......each e other better than
1 Thess. 5:13...to e them very highly
Heb. 11:26.......E-ing the reproach of Christ

Eternal

Deut. 33:27...the e God is thy refuge
Is. 60:15..make thee an e excellency
Matt. 25:46 ..the righteous into life e
Mark 3:29 ....is in danger of e damnation
Mark 3:29; 10:30 .....world to come e
John 3:15 .not perish, but have e life
John 4:36..gathereth fruit unto life e
John 6:54.eateth my flesh . . . hath e
John 10:28 .....I give unto them e life
John 17:3 ....this is life e
Acts 13:48.....were ordained to e life
Rom. 6:23......the gift of God is e life
2 Cor. 4:17.............e weight of glory
Eph. 3:11.............According to the e purpose
1 Tim. 6:12.............lay hold on e life
Titus 1:2...................In hope of e life
Heb. 5:9 .....the author of e salvation
Heb. 6:2......dead, and of e judgment
Heb. 9:12.........................e redemption

1 Pet. 5:10.called us unto his e glory
Jude 7 ....the vengeance of e fire

Evangelist

Acts 21:8 ....Philip the e
Eph. 4:11.....prophets; and some, e-s
2 Tim. 4:5.......................work of an e

Everlasting

Gen. 9:16 .remember the e covenant
Gen. 49:26 ....of the e hills
Ps. 24:7 ....be ye lift up, ye e doors
Ps. 90:2 .....from e to e, thou are God
Ps. 119:142..Thy . . . e righteousness
Ps. 145:13 ....Thy kingdom . . . e kingdom
Is. 9:6.e Father, The Prince of Peace
Hab. 3:6............the e mountains . . . scattered
Matt. 18:8 ....to be cast into e fire
Matt. 19:29 ....shall inherit e life
Matt. 25:46 ....e punishment
John 3:16 .not perish, but have e life
Rom. 16:26 ....of the e God
2 Thess. 1:9 ....with e destruction
1 Tim. 6:16...be honour and power e
Heb. 13:20...blood of the e covenant
Jude 6..he hath reserved in e chains
Rev. 14:6........having the e gospel to preach

Evil

Gen. 2:9 ....tree . . . of good and e
Ex. 32:14 ....Lord repented of the e
Deut. 22:14.........bring up an e name
Deut. 24:7 ...put e away from among
1 Sam. 25:21.requited me e for good
2 Kin. 6:33..........this e is of the Lord
Job 30:26 .....looked for good, then e
Job 35:12 ....pride of e man
Ps. 34:13......Keep thy tongue from e
Ps. 37:27 ....Depart from e
Ps. 51:4 ....done this e in thy sight
Ps. 91:10........There shall no e befall
Ps. 97:10 ....love the Lord, hate e
Ps. 121:7......preserve thee from all e
Prov. 3:7.......................depart from e
Prov. 13:21 ....E pursueth sinners
Prov. 16:27....................ungodly man diggeth up e
Eccles. 2:21 ...is vanity and a great e
Is 1:16............put away the e of your doings
Is 7:15..he may know to refuse the e
Is 59:7 ....Their feet run to e
Matt. 5:11 ....say all manner of e
Matt. 6:13.........but deliver us from e
Matt. 12:34 ....how can ye, being e
Matt. 27:23 ....what e hath he done
Luke 11:34..........when thine eye is e
John 18:23...If I have spoken e, bear
Rom. 12:17...Recompense . . . man e for e
Rom. 14:16........good be e spoken of
1 Cor. 13:5 ....thinketh no e
Phil. 3:2............Beware of dogs . . . e workers
1 Thess. 5:15 ....render e for e
1 Tim. 6:10 ....money . . . root of all e
Titus 1:12.........e beasts, slow bellies
1 Pet. 3:9..........Not rendering e for e
3 John 11 .follow not that which is e

Exalt

Ex. 15:2 .....father's God, and I will e
Ps. 34:3 ....let us e his name together
Ps. 99:5..........E ye the Lord our God
Prov. 14:34........Righteousness e-eth
Matt. 11:23............e-ed unto heaven
Luke 1:52 ....and e-ed them of low degree
Acts 5:31 ....Him hath God e-ed
2 Cor. 11:20 ....if a man e himself
Phil. 2:9 .....God . . . hath highly e-ed
James 1:9 ...rejoice in that he is e-ed
1 Pet. 5:6 ...that he may e you in due

Example

Matt. 1:19 ....make her a publick e
John 13:15 ......I have given you an e
1 Tim. 4:12 ....an e of the believers

James 5:10 ....for an e of suffering
1 Pet. 2:21 ....leaving us an e

Excellency
Deut. 33:26...........in his e on the sky
Eccles. 7:12 ..but the e of knowledge
Is. 35:2 ....see . . . e of our God
1 Cor. 2:1.came not with e of speech
2 Cor. 4:7 ..e of the power may be of God
Phil. 3:8 ....e of the knowledge of Christ

Excellent
Job 37:23 ....he is e in power
Ps. 8:1 ....how e is thy name
Ps. 36:7 ....How e is thy loving kindness
Ps. 148:13...........his name alone is e
Prov. 17:7 .E speech becometh not a
Is. 12:5 ......for he hath done e things
Hab. 1:4......obtained a more e name

Execute
Ex. 12:12.................I will e judgment
Num. 8:11 ..e the service of the Lord
1 Kin. 6:12 ....and e my judgments
2 Kin. 10:30.e-ing that which is right
Mark 6:27 ...the king sent an e-ioner
John 5:27 ....authority to e judgment

Exercise
Ps. 131:1.......neither do I e myself in
Jer. 9:24............Lord which e loving kindness
Matt. 20:25........Gentiles e dominion
1 Tim. 4:7 ....e thyself . . . unto godliness
Heb. 5:14.....e-ed to discern . . . good
2 Pet. 2:14.............e-d with covetous

Exhort
Luke 3:18.other things in his e-ation
Acts 13:15....any word of e-ation for
Rom. 12:8 .....he that e-th, on e-ation
1 Tim. 6:2..These things teach and e
2 Tim. 4:2 ...e with all long suffering
Titus 1:9............may be able . . . to e
Titus 2:15..speak, and e, and rebuke
Heb. 3:13 ....e one another daily
Heb. 10:25 ....e-ing one another: and

Expectation
Ps. 9:18........the e of the poor . . . not perish
Ps. 62:5 ....my e is from him
Prov. 10:28.......e of the wicked shall perish
Luke 3:15 .....as the people were in e
Rom. 8:19 ..earnest e of the creature

Expedient
John 16:7 ....e for you that I go
John 18:14 .....e that one man . . . die
1 Cor. 6:12..........all things are not e

Express
Num. 1:17..........e-ed by their names
1 Tim. 4:1 ....Spirit speaketh e-ly
Heb. 1:3..........e image of his person

Eye
Gen. 3:5 .....your e-s shall be opened
Ex. 21:24 ....E for e, tooth for tooth
Deut. 7:16..........e shall have no pity
Deut. 32:10 ....as the apple of his e
2 Kin. 6:17 ..I pray thee, open his e-s
Job 11:20.e-s of the wicked shall fail
Job 16:20 ...mine e poureth out tears
Job 17:7 ....Mine e also is dim
Job 24:15 ....No e shall see me
Job 28:21 ....it is hid from the e-s
Ps. 6:7 .Mine e is consumed because
Ps. 13:3 ....lighten mine e-s, lest I
Ps. 17:8 ....as the apple of the e
Ps. 19:8 ....enlightening the e-s
Ps. 32:8..will guide thee with mine e
Ps. 34:15.....e-s of the Lord are upon
Ps. 36:1 .....no fear of God before his e-s
Ps. 119:37.Turn away mine e-s from
Ps. 121:1 ..I will lift up mine e-s unto
Ps. 145:15 ...e-s of all wait upon thee
Prov. 3:7 ...not wise in thine own e-s
Prov. 10:10 ....winketh with the e
Prov. 22:9 ......that hath a bountiful e
Eccles. 6:9.Better . . . sight of the e-s
Is. 35:5............e-s of the blind . . . be opened
Is. 52:8 ....they shall see e to e
Jer. 9:1 ..mine e-s a fountain of tears
Lam. 2:11 ....Mine e-s do fail with tears
Ezek. 12:2 ......e-s to see, and see not
Hab. 1:13...............Thou are of purer e
Matt. 5:29...if thy right e offend thee
Matt. 7:3 .mote . . . in thy brother's e
Matt. 9:29.Then touched he their e-s
Matt. 13:16 ....blessed are your e-s
Matt. 20:15....Is thine e evil, because
Mark 10:25 ....e of a needle
Luke 2:30 ....e-s have seen thy salvation
Luke 16:23 ...in hell he lift up his e-s
Luke 24:31......their e-s were opened
John 4:35..................Lift up your e-s
John 9:6.........anointed the e-s of the blind
John 11:41 ......Jesus lifted up his e-s
1 Cor. 2:9....E hath not seen, nor ear
1 Cor. 15:52 .in the twinkling of an e
Gal 3:1 ....before whose e-s Jesus
Eph. 1:18 .e-s of your understanding
1 Pet. 3:12 .....For the e-s of the Lord
2 Pet. 2:14 ....Having e-s full of adultery
Rev. 1:7 ....and every e shall see him
Rev. 21:4.away all tears from . . . e-s

F

Fables
1 Tim. 1:4 ....Neither give heed to f
1 Tim. 4:7 ...profane and old wives' f
Titus 1:14 .....giving heed to Jewish f
2 Pet. 1:16 ....cunningly devised f

Face
Gen. 1:2 .darkness was upon the f of
Gen. 3:19..In the sweat of thy f shalt
Gen. 7:18 ....ark went upon the f of
Gen. 17:3 ....Abram fell on his f
Gen. 32:30.for I have seen God f to f
Ex. 33:11 ...Lord spake unto Moses f to f
Ex. 33:23 ....my f shall not be seen
Num. 6:25 ....The Lord make his f shine
Deut. 1:17 .....not be afraid of the f of man
2 Kin. 14:8.look one another in the f
Ezra 9:6.blush to lift up my f to thee
Job 33:26..he shall see his f with joy
Job 38:30 ....f of the deep is frozen
Ps. 13:1..long . . . hide thy f from me
Ps. 24:6...............................seek thy f
Ps. 34:16 ....f of the Lord is against
Ps. 67:1 .cause his f to shine upon us
Ps. 83:16 ......fill their f-s with shame
Ps. 84:9 ....look upon the f of thine
Prov. 27:19 ....f answereth to f
Eccles. 8:1.......man's wisdom maketh his f
Is. 25:8.wipe away tears from . . . f-s
Is. 50:6.....I hid not my f from shame
Jer. 5:3............f-s harder than a rock
Matt. 26:67 ....they spit in his f
Luke 1:76 .thou shalt go before the f
Luke 22:64 .they struck him on the f
Luke 24:5 ....bowed down their f-s
John 11:44.....his f was bound about
2 Cor. 3:18 ......with open f beholding
1 Pet. 3:12.......f of the Lord is against

Faith
Deut. 32:20.children in whom is no f
Hab. 2:4 .....the just shall live by his f
Matt. 6:30 .clothe you, O ye of little f
Matt. 9:2 ......Jesus seeing their f said
Matt. 15:28..O woman, great is thy f
Matt. 17:20 ...f as a grain of mustard
Matt. 23:23 ....law, judgment, mercy . . . f
Mark 4:40........is it that ye have no f
Mark 11:22...saith . . . Have f in God
Luke 7:50 ....Thy f hath saved thee
Luke 8:25 ....Where is your f
Luke 17:5..................Increase your f
Luke 18:8 ....shall he find f on the earth
Luke 22:32..............that thy f fail not
Acts 6:5........full of f and of the Holy Ghost
Acts 14:27.........opened the door of f
Acts 15:9 .purifying their hearts by f
Acts 20:21...f toward our Lord Jesus
Rom. 3:3.unbelief make the f of God
Rom. 4:14 ....f is made void
Rom. 5:1 ....being justified by f,
Rom. 10:17........f cometh by hearing
1 Cor. 13:2......though I have all f, so
1 Cor. 15:14 ....your f is also vain
1 Cor. 16:13 ....stand fast in the f
2 Cor. 13:5.....whether ye be in the f
Gal. 2:16.......by the f of Jesus Christ
Gal. 5:5...hope of righteousness by f
Gal. 5:22.......gentleness, goodness, f
Eph. 2:8.......................saved through f
Eph. 4:5 ....One Lord, one f, one baptism
Eph. 6:16..........taking the shield of f
Phil. 1:25.....furtherance and joy of f
Col. 2:5 ....stedfastness of your f in
1 Thess. 1:3..........................work of f
1 Thess. 5:8........breastplate of f and love
2 Thess. 1:3........that your f groweth
1 Tim. 1:2...........my own son in the f
1 Tim. 3:9 .mystery of the f in a pure
1 Tim. 4:1.....some shall depart from the f
1 Tim. 5:12...........cast off their first f
2 Tim. 4:7............................I have kept the f
Titus 1:13 ....be sound in the f
Titus 2:2 ....sound in f, in charity
Heb. 10:22 ....in full assurance of f
Heb. 11:1 ....f is the substance of
Heb. 12:2 ....author and finisher of our f
James 1:3...trying of your f worketh
James 2:1.have not the f of our Lord
1 Pet. 1:5 ....through f unto salvation
2 Pet. 1:5............add to your f virtue
Jude 20 ....your most holy f
Rev. 2:13 ...and hast not denied my f

Faithful
Num. 12:7 ....Moses . . . f in all mine house
Deut. 7:9 ....he is God, the f God
1 Sam. 2:35 ....will raise me up a f priest
2 Kin. 12:15 ....for they dealt f-ly
Neh. 9:8 ....foundest his heart f
Ps. 31:23 ...the Lord preserveth the f
Ps. 89:1 ....make known thy f-ness
Ps. 101:6...............Mine eyes . . . be f
Ps. 119:86 ....All thy commandments are f
Ps. 143:1 .....in thy f-ness answer me
Prov. 13:17.a f ambassador is health
Prov. 14:5......A f witness will not lie
Prov. 20:6 ....f man who can find
Prov. 27:6 ....F are the wounds
Is. 1:21 ....How is the f city become
Is. 11:5..f-ness the girdle of his reins
Jer. 23:28............speak my word f-ly
Matt. 24:45 ....a f and wise servant
Matt. 25:23 ....good and f servant
1 Cor. 1:9..................................God is f
Eph. 1:1 ....to the f in Christ Jesus
1 Thess. 5:24........F is he that calleth
1 Tim. 1:12 .for that he counted me f
1 Tim. 4:9...............This is a f saying
2 Tim. 2:2........commit thou to f men
Titus 1:6 ....having f children
Heb. 10:23 ..for he is f that promised
1 Pet. 4:19 ....as unto a f Creator
Rev. 1:5 .Christ, who is the f witness
Rev. 2:10...be thou f unto death, and
Rev. 19:11......was called F and True

Fall
Ps. 16:6 ....are f-en . . . in pleasant
Prov. 10:8, 10 ...a prating fool shall f
Prov. 16:18.haughty spirit before a f
Prov. 24:16........just man f-eth seven
Eccles. 11:3.......where the tree f-eth,
Is. 34:4....leaf f-eth off from the vine
Is. 40:30....young men shall utterly f
Ezek. 24:6 ....let no lot f upon it
Dan. 3:5........ye f down and worship
Dan. 11:26............shall f down slain
Mic. 7:8.............when I f, I shall rise
Matt. 7:27....and great was the f of it
Matt. 10:29shall not f on the ground
Matt. 12:11.........f into the pit on the
Matt. 15:14.........both shall f into the ditch
Luke 2:34.......set for the f and rising
Luke 8:13 ......in time of temptation f away
Rom. 11:12.........the f of them be the riches
Rom. 14:13......f in his brother's way
1 Cor. 10:12..........take heed lest he f
1 Cor. 15:6, 18............are f-en asleep
Gal. 5:4 ....ye are f-en from grace
1 Tim. 3:6........................he f into the condemnation
1 Tim. 3:7.......lest he f into reproach
1 Tim. 6:9........rich f into temptation
Heb. 4:11 ....lest any man f
Heb. 6:6 ....If they shall f away
Heb. 10:31 .....f into the hands of . . . God
James 1:2 ....ye f into divers temptations
2 Pet. 1:10..................ye shall never f
2 Pet. 3:17...................f from . . . own stedfastness

False
Ex. 20:16......shalt not bear f witness
Ex. 23:1 ......shalt not raise a f report
Ex. 23:7................far from a f matter
Ps. 119:104, 128....I hate every f way
Ps. 120:3......................thou f tongue
Prov. 6:19; 12:17; 14:5; 19:5 ....f witness
Prov. 11:1 ....A f balance is abomination
Prov. 17:4 ....heed to f lips
Zech. 10:2 ....diviners . . . told f dreams
Matt. 19:18............not bear f witness
Matt. 24:24.f Christs, and f prophets
Mark 13:22......................For f Christs
Luke 19:8..taken . . . by f accusation
2 Tim. 3:3 .trucebreakers, f accusers

Familiar
Lev. 19:31 ....that have f spirits
1 Sam. 28:7 ....f spirit at En-dor
Job 19:14.....f friends have forgotten
Ps. 41:9.................mine own f friend
Jer. 20:10..............all my f-s watched

Fan
Is. 30:24 ....shovel and with the f
Is. 41:16.................Thou shalt f them
Matt. 3:12 ......Whose f is in his hand

Fashion
Ex. 37:19.........after the f of almonds
Job 10:8....thine hands have . . . f-ed me
Job 31:15........did not one f us in the womb
Ps. 33:15..He f-eth their hearts alike
Is. 44:12 ....f-eth it with hammers
Is. 45:9...clay say to him that f-eth it
Mark 2:12 .We never saw it on this f
Luke 9:29 ...the f of his countenance
1 Cor. 7:31.....f of this world passeth
Phil. 2:8....being found in f as a man
1 Pet. 1:14..........not f-ing yourselves

Fast
Judg. 4:21............f asleep and weary
Ps. 33:9 ....he commanded, and it stood f
Ps. 38:2...............thine arrows stick f
Ps. 65:6.........setteth f the mountains
Prov. 4:13 ....f hold of instruction
Is. 58:3.....we f-ed . . . and thou seest not
Is. 58:4 ....ye f for strife and debate
Is. 58:5 ....wilt thou call this a f
Is. 58:6 ....is not this the f that I have
Joel 1:14...........Sanctify ye a f, call a
Zech. 7:5 ....did ye at all f unto me
Matt. 4:2.................had f-ed forty days
Matt. 6:16...when ye f, be not, as the
Matt. 6:18..appear not unto men to f
Mark 2:18.Pharisees f . . . disciples f not
Mark 2:19 ....children of the bridechamber f
Luke 18:12........I f twice in the week
Acts 13:3 ....had f-ed and prayed

Fat
Gen. 45:18.shall eat the f of the land
Prov. 11:25 ....liberal soul . . . made f
Prov. 13:4....diligent shall be made f
Prov. 15:30 ....report maketh the bones f
Is. 6:10 ....the heart of this people f
Is. 30:23.......shall be f and plenteous
Luke 15:23.......bring hither the f-ted calf

Father
Gen. 2:24.leave his f and his mother
Ex. 20:12..........Honour thy f and thy mother
Ex. 21:15......he that smiteth his f, or
Deut. 5:9 ....the iniquity of the f-s
2 Sam. 7:12...shalt sleep with thy f-s
Job 17:14.......................Thou art my f
Job 29:16 ....I was a f to the poor
Job 38:28 ....Hath the rain a f
Ps. 22:4...........Our f-s trusted in thee
Ps. 68:5..........A f of the fatherless, and
Ps. 89:26 ....Thou art my f, my God
Ps. 103:13 ....Like as a f pitieth his
Prov. 1:8 ....hear the instruction of thy f
Prov. 6:20 ....keep thy f-'s commandment
Prov. 10:1..wise son maketh a glad f
Is. 9:6..The everlasting F, the Prince
Is. 63:16 .....Doubtless thou art our F
Jer. 3:19 .....Thou shalt call me, My f
Mal. 2:10 ....Have we not all one f
Matt. 5:16 ....glorify your F . . . in heaven
Matt. 6:9.........F which art in heaven
Matt. 7:21........doeth the will of my f
Matt. 11:25..............I thank thee, O F
Matt. 11:26.....so, F: for so it seemed
Matt. 11:27 ....unto me of my F
Matt. 11:27...knoweth the Son, . . . F
Matt. 11:27.....neither knoweth . . . F
Matt. 26:29 ....with . . . my F-'s kingdom
Matt. 28:19 .....baptizing . . . name of the F
Mark 8:38...........cometh in the glory of his F
Mark 14:36 ....he said, Abba, F
Luke 2:49.be about my F-'s business
Luke 10:21..............I thank thee, O F
Luke 11:2.............Our F which art in heaven
Luke 15:18 ....arise and go to my f
Luke 23:34.......said Jesus, F, forgive them
Luke 23:46..F, . . . hands I commend
Luke 24:49 ....the promise of my F
John 2:16....make not my F-'s house
John 5:17.....My F worketh hitherto,
John 10:15 ....even so know I the F
John 14:2.................In my F-'s house
John 17:1 ....F, the hour is come;
1 Cor. 4:15.yet have ye not many f-s
2 Cor. 1:3F of mercies . . . God of all
Eph. 3:14I bow my knees unto the F
Eph. 6:4 ....f-s, provoke not your children
Phil. 2:11 ...to the glory of God the F
Heb. 1:5 ....I will be to him a F
Heb. 3:9 ..when your f-s tempted me
1 Pet. 1:3 ..Blessed be the God and F
2 Pet. 1:17.................from God the F
1 John 2:13 ....because ye . . . known the F
2 John 4 ....a commandment from the F
Jude 1....are sanctified by God the F
Rev. 1:6 ..priests unto God and his F

Fatherless
Ex. 22:22 .not afflict any widow, or f
Ps. 10:14 .thou art the helper of the f
Ps. 68:5 ....A father of the f
Hos. 14:3.in thee the f findeth mercy
James 1:27..............To visit the f and widows

Fault
Gen. 41:9 ....I do remember my f-s
Ex. 5:16 .the f is in thine own people
1 Sam. 29:3.I have found no f in him
Ps. 19:12.......................from secret f-s
Matt. 18:15 .....tell him his f between
Luke 23:4........I find no f in this man
1 Cor. 6:7 ....is utterly a f among you
Heb. 8:7.....covenant had been f-less
James 5:16...Confess your f-s one to
Jude 24..............to present you f-less
Rev. 14:5............without f before the throne

Favour
Gen. 18:3.I have found f in thy sight
Ruth 2:13................find f in thy sight
Ps. 112:5.............man sheweth f, and lendeth
Prov. 3:4..............So shalt thou find f
Jer. 16:13 ....will not shew you f
Luke 1:28...thou that are highly f-ed
Luke 1:30 ....hast found f with God
Luke 2:52 ......in f with God and man
Acts 7:46....Who found f before God

Fear
Gen. 9:2 ....f of you and the dread
Gen. 15:1 ......F not, Abram. I am thy
Gen. 26:24...f not, for I am with thee
Ex. 14:31 ....the people f-ed the Lord
Lev. 25:17 ...but thou shalt f thy God
Deut. 6:13...shalt f the Lord thy God
Deut. 25:18........and he f-ed not God
Deut. 31:8.................f not, neither be dismayed
Josh. 4:14....f-ed Moses, all the days
Josh. 22:25 ....cease from f-ing the Lord
Job 1:9..............Job f God for naught
Ps. 19:9 .....The f of the Lord is clean
Ps. 23:4.........I will f no evil: for thou
Ps. 25:12........what man . . . f-eth the Lord
Ps. 27:1 ....whom shall I f
Ps. 76:8 ....earth f-ed, and was still
Ps. 96:4...........be f-ed above all gods
Ps. 112:1 ....Blessed is the man that f-eth
Prov. 1:7.f of the Lord . . . beginning
Prov. 14:16.............A wise man f-eth
Prov. 24:21.................f thou the Lord
Eccles. 12:13 .....F God, and keep his
Song 3:8 ....of f in the night
Is. 59:19.they f the name of the Lord
Jer. 5:24 ....Let us now f the Lord
Matt. 8:26 ......Why are ye f-ful, O ye
Matt. 14:5.........he f-ed the multitude
Matt. 28:5 ....F not ye: for I know
Luke 1:30.F not, Mary: for thou hast
Luke 2:10 ...F not . . . behold, I bring you
Luke 12:32 ....F not, little flock
Luke 20:19 .and they f-ed the people
Luke 21:11.......f-ful sights and great signs
Luke 23:40.........Dost not thou f God
John 12:15 ...F not, daughter of Sion
Acts 5:26.....for they f-ed the people, lest
Acts 9:31 ....walking in the f of the Lord
Acts 13:26..whosoever . . . f-eth God
2 Tim. 1:7 ....given us the spirit of f

1 John 4:18........There is no **f** in love
Rev. 21:8 ...The **f**-ful, an unbelieving

Feast
Lev. 23:2 ....the **f**-s of the Lord
Deut. 16:16 ....the **f** of unleavened bread
2 Chr. 7:8.........kept the **f** seven days
Eccles. 10:19 ..**f** is made for laughter
Is. 1:14 ....appointed **f**-s my soul
Is. 25:6 ....**f** of wines on the lees
Amos 8:10 ....turn your **f**-s into mourning
Luke 20:46 ......the chief rooms at **f**-s
John 6:4.....a **f** of the Jews, was nigh
Acts 18:21 ...by all means keep this **f**
Jude 12 ...spots in your **f**-s of charity

Fed
Ex. 16:32.......**f** you in the wilderness
Ps. 37:3............verily thou shalt be **f**
Luke 16:21..desiring to be **f** with the
1 Cor. 3:2 ....I have **f** you with milk

Feeble
Job 4:4.......strengthened the **f** knees
Ps. 38:8 ....I am **f** and sore broken
Is. 35:3 ....confirm the **f** knees
Ezek. 7:17 ..All hands shall be **f**, and
Zech. 12:8 ...he that is **f** among them
1 Cor. 12:22...........seem to be more **f**
1 Thess. 5:14...comfort the **f**-minded
Heb. 12:12.........................the **f** knees

Feed
2 Sam. 5:2 ...shalt **f** my people Israel
1 Kin. 17:4 ...commanded the ravens to **f**
Job 24:20 ....worm shall **f** sweetly on
Ps. 49:14 ....death shall **f** on them
Prov. 30:8 ....**f** me with food
Is. 40:11 ...**f** his flock like a shepherd
Is. 49:26 ....I will **f** them that oppress
Jer. 3:15..........**f** you with knowledge
Ezek. 34:10........cease from **f**-ing the flock
Zeph. 3:13..........shall **f** and lie down
Matt. 6:26 ....heavenly Father **f**-eth
John 21:15 ....saith unto him, **F** my lambs
Acts 20:28 ....**f** the church of God
Rom. 12:20 ....thine enemy hunger, **f** him
1 Cor. 13:3 ....my goods to **f** the poor
1 Pet. 5:2 ...**F** the flock of God which

Feet
Ruth 3:8 ....a woman lay at his **f**
2 Sam. 22:37 ......so that my **f** did not slip
Ps. 8:6 ....put all things under his **f**
Ps. 22:16................pierced my hands and my **f**
Ps. 31:18 ....my **f** in a large room
Ps. 40:2......and set my **f** upon a rock
Ps. 66:9............not our **f** to be moved
Ps. 115:7........**f** . . . but they walk not
Ps. 119:105 ....a lamp unto my **f**
Ps. 122:2.......**f** shall stand within thy
Prov. 1:16 ....their **f** run to evil
Prov. 29:5 ...spreadeth a net for his **f**
Is. 3:16............a tinkling with their **f**
Is. 59:7 ....Their **f** run to evil
Jer. 13:16....your **f** stumble upon the
Jer. 18:22.............hid snares for my **f**
Jer. 38:22 ....**f** are sunk in the mire
Ezek. 1:7 ....their **f** were straight **f**
Matt. 18:8 ....two hands or two **f**
Mark 7:25.and came and fell at his **f**
Luke 7:38..stood at his **f** behind him
Luke 7:44.....washed my **f** with tears
Luke 8:35......sitting at the **f** of Jesus
Luke 10:39...........also sat at Jesus' **f**
Luke 24:39.........my hands and my **f**
Luke 24:40 ....hands and his **f**
John 11:2...wiped his **f** with her hair
John 12:3 ......anointed the **f** of Jesus
John 13:5 ....wash the disciples' **f**
John 13:14 ....wash one another's **f**
Rom. 3:15...**f** are swift to shed blood
Rom. 10:15 ....beautiful are the **f** of
Rev. 1:15 ....his **f** like unto fine brass
Rev. 13:2 .....**f** were as the **f** of a bear
Rev. 22:8.....before the **f** of the angel

Fellowship
Ps. 94:20 ....iniquity have **f** with thee
1 Cor. 10:20 ....should have **f** with devils
2 Cor. 6:14........**f** hath righteousness
Gal. 2:9 ....the right hand of **f**
Eph. 3:9 ....the **f** of the mystery
Eph. 5:11...........**f** with the unfruitful
1 John 1:3............ye also may have **f**
1 John 1:3.....our **f** is with the Father
1 John 1:7 ....**f** one with another

Female
Gen. 1:27 ....male and **f** created he
Gen. 6:19 ....they shall be male and **f**
Lev. 3:1 ......whether it be a male or **f**
Lev. 5:6.....a **f** from the flock, a lamb
Num. 5:3 ......male and **f** shall ye put
Deut. 4:16 ....likeness of male or **f**
Matt. 19:4 ......made them male and **f**
Mark 10:6 ....God made them male and **f**
Gal. 3:28 ....neither male nor **f**

Fervent
Acts 18:25 ....being **f** in the spirit
Rom. 12:11 ....**f** in spirit; serving
2 Cor. 7:7 .....your **f** mind toward me
Col. 4:12...........labouring **f**-ly for you
James 5:16 .....effectual **f** prayer of a
1 Pet. 4:8 ....have **f** charity among
2 Pet. 3:10 ....melt with the **f** heat

Fever
Deut. 28:22 ...consumption, and . . . **f**
Matt. 8:14 ..wife's mother . . . sick of a **f**
Luke 4:38 ...was taken with a great **f**
John 4:52 ....seventh hour the **f** left
Acts 28:8........lay sick of a **f** and of a

Few
1 Sam. 14:6......save by many or by **f**
Job 10:20..............Are not my days **f**
Ps. 109:8 ....Let his days be **f**
Eccles. 5:2..............let thy words be **f**
Ezek. 12:16 ....I will leave a **f** men
Matt. 9:37 ......but the labourers are **f**
Matt. 20:16 ....but **f** chosen
Matt. 25:21 ....faithful over a **f**
Luke 12:48........beaten with **f** stripes
Luke 13:23 .are there **f** that be saved
Acts 17:4............chief women not a **f**
Rev. 2:14........a **f** things against thee
Rev. 3:4............Thou hast a **f** names

Field
Gen. 2:5..............every plant of the **f**
Lev. 19:9 ....reap the corners of thy **f**
Deut. 20:19 ....tree of the **f** is man's
Ruth 2:3.....gleaned in the **f** after the
1 Kin. 11:29..two were alone in the **f**
Job 5:23 ..beasts of the **f** . . . at peace
Ps. 96:12 ....Let the **f** be joyful
Prov. 24:30..........the **f** of the slothful
Prov. 31:16 ....She considereth a **f**
Jer. 4:17 ....As keepers of a **f**
Jer. 26:18..............be plowed like a **f**
Jer. 32:44 ......shall buy **f**-s for money
Matt. 6:28.................the lilies of the **f**
Matt. 13:38 ....The **f** is the world
Matt. 27:10 ..gave them . . . potter's **f**
Luke 2:8..shepherds abiding in the **f**
Luke 15:15.........sent him into his **f**-s
John 4:35 ....look on the **f**-s
Acts 1:18.......................purchased a **f**

Fiery
Num. 21:6..........Lord sent **f** serpents
Dan. 3:6 ....a burning **f** furnace
Dan. 7:9 .throne was like the **f** flame
Eph. 6:16....the **f** darts of the wicked
Heb. 10:27..............and **f** indignation
1 Pet. 4:12........concerning the **f** trial

Fig
Gen. 3:7 ....they sewed **f** leaves
Deut. 8:8 ....and vines, and **f** trees
Judg. 9:11..............But the **f** tree said
Matt. 7:16..................or **f**-s of thistles
Matt. 21:19.the **f** tree withered away
Mark 11:13 ...a **f** tree afar off having
Mark 13:28 .....a parable of the **f** tree
Luke 6:44........men do not gather **f**-s
John 1:48 ....wast under the **f** tree
James 3:12 ....Can the **f** tree
Rev. 6:13.**f** tree casteth her untimely

Fight
Ex. 14:14.....The Lord shall **f** for you
1 Sam. 8:20.............and **f** our battles
Neh. 4:20...............God shall **f** for us
Ps. 35:1.**f** against them that **f** against
1 Tim. 6:12.........**F** the good **f** of faith
James 4:2 ....ye **f** and war

filth
2 Chr. 29:5......**f**-iness out of the holy
Job 15:16........abominable and **f**-y is man
Is. 4:4....Lord . . . washed away the **f**
Is. 28:8.........full of vomit and **f**-iness
Is. 64:6 ....are as **f**-y rags
Nah. 3:6................cast abominable **f**
2 Cor. 7:1 ....cleanse . . . from all **f**-iness
Col. 3:8.....**f**-y communication out of
Titus 1:11............for **f**-y lucre's sake
James 1:21.........lay apart all **f**-iness
1 Pet. 3:21 ....putting away of the **f**

Find
Gen. 32:5 ....**f** grace in thy sight
Num. 32:33 ....your sin will **f** you out
Deut. 4:29....thou shalt **f** him, if thou
Ruth 1:9 ..that ye may **f** rest, each of
Ruth 2:13..................Let me **f** favour
2 Sam. 15:25....I shall **f** favour in the
Job 11:7 ....searching **f** out God
Prov. 1:13......We shall **f** all precious
Prov. 3:4.**f** favour . . . understanding
Prov. 8:35...............**f**-eth me **f**-eth life
Prov. 18:22 .**f**-eth a wife **f**-eth a good
Song 5:8..................if ye **f** my beloved
Matt. 7:7.............seek, and ye shall **f**
Matt. 10:39.....that **f**-eth his life shall
Matt. 11:29......**f** rest unto your souls
Matt. 21:2.........ye shall **f** an ass tied
Mark 11:2...........ye shall **f** a colt tied
Mark 13:36............he **f** you sleeping
Mark 14:37.........**f**-eth them sleeping
Luke 2:12 ..shall **f** the babe wrapped
Luke 11:9...........seek, and ye shall **f**
Luke 15:8...........seek . . . till she **f** it
Luke 23:4 ......I **f** no fault in this man
John 10:9...........go in and out, and **f** pasture
John 18:38......**f** in him no fault at all
Acts 7:46 .....to **f** a tabernacle for the
Acts 23:9.....We **f** no evil in this man
Rom. 11:33 ...his ways past **f**-ing out
2 Cor. 9:4 ....**f** you unprepared
Rev. 18:14........shalt **f** them no more

Finger
Ex. 8:19 ....This is the **f** of God
Lev. 4:6............dip his **f** in the blood
Deut. 9:10..written with the **f** of God
1 Kin. 12:10....little **f** shall be thicker
1 Chr. 20:6 .....**f**-s and toes were four
Prov. 6:13 ....he teacheth with his **f**-s
Mark 7:33.....put his **f**-s into his ears
Luke 11:20........the **f** of God cast out
Luke 16:24 ....tip of his **f** in water
John 8:6 ...his **f** wrote on the ground
John 20:25 ....**f** into the print of the
John 20:27............Reach hither thy **f**

Finish
Gen. 2:1 ....heavens . . . earth were **f**-ed
Ex. 40:33 .....So Moses **f**-ed the work
2 Chr. 7:11 ..Solomon **f**-ed the house
John 4:34................and to **f** his work
John 17:4 ....I have **f**-ed the work
John 19:30...............he said, It is **f**-ed
Acts 20:24..I might **f** my course with
Rom. 9:28...............................**f** the work
Heb. 12:2....................the author and **f**-er
James 1:15 ....sin, when it is **f**-ed

Mark 5:37..suffered no man to f him
Mark 14:54....Peter f-ed him afar off
Luke 22:10 ....f him into the house
Luke 22:39 ....disciples also f-ed him
John 10:27..I know them, and they f me
John 18:15................Peter f-ed Jesus
Eph. 5:1...........Be ye . . . f-ers of God
1 Thess. 2:14....f-ers of the churches
Heb. 12:14........F peace with all men
1 Pet. 3:13.........f-ers of that which is good
3 John 11.......f not that which is evil
Rev. 14:4.are they which f the Lamb
Rev. 14:13.......their works do f them

Folly
Gen. 34:7.he had wrought f in Israel
Judg. 19:23......................do not this f
Prov. 14:18.........The simple inherit f
Prov. 15:21...................F is joy to him
Is. 9:17.........every mouth speaketh f
Jer. 23:13........seen f in the prophets

Food
Gen. 2:9 ....and good for f
Gen. 3:6.........the tree was good for f
Gen. 43:2....................buy us a little f
Lev. 3:11 ..the f of the offering made
Deut. 10:18.............giving him f and raiment
Job 38:41...............for the raven his f
Ps. 78:25 ....Man did eat angels' f
Ps. 136:25...Who giveth f to all flesh
Prov. 6:8.............her f in the harvest
Prov. 30:8...................feed me with f convenient
1 Tim. 6:8...........having f . . . content
James 2:15 ....destitute of daily f

Fool
1 Sam. 26:21........I have played the f
2 Sam. 3:33..Died Abner as a f dieth
Ps. 14:1 ..The f hath said in his heart
Prov. 1:7...f-s despise . . . instruction
Prov. 15:5......f despiseth his father's
Prov. 24:7...........Wisdom is too high for a f
Prov. 26:3 ....a rod for the f-'s back
Prov. 29:11 .A f uttereth all his mind
Eccles. 10:14 ....A f also is full of words
Hos. 9:7..................the prophet is a f
Matt. 5:22................shall say, Thou f
Matt. 23:17...............Ye f-s and blind
Luke 24:25 ..O f-s, and slow of heart
Rom. 1:22 ....wise, they became f-s
1 Cor. 3:18 ....let him become a f
1 Cor. 4:10 ....f-s for Christ's sake
Eph. 5:15 ....walk . . . not as f-s

Foolish
Gen. 31:28 ....hast now done f-ly
Deut. 32:6..........f people and unwise
Job 1:22 ....nor charged God f-ly
Job 5:3.............seen the f taking root
Ps. 5:5............f shall not stand in thy
Ps. 75:4...........................Deal not f-ly
Prov. 14:17 ..soon angry dealeth f-ly
Prov. 14:24.......f-ness of fools is folly
Prov. 15:2 ...mouth . . . poureth . . . f-ness
Prov. 24:9 .....thought of f-ness is sin
Lam. 2:14.......seen vain and f things
Matt. 25:8...........f said unto the wise
2 Cor. 11:21.......................I speak f-ly
1 Pet. 2:15 ....ignorance of f men

Foot
Ps. 91:12................dash thy f against
Ps. 121:3 .....suffer thy f to be moved
Prov. 3:23......thy f shall not stumble
Prov. 25:19 ....a f out of joint
Matt. 22:13 ....Bind him hand and f
Luke 4:11 ....dash thy f against
Rev. 10:2 ....right f upon the sea

Footstool
1 Chr. 28:2.........for the f of our God
Ps. 99:5 ....and worship at his f
Ps. 110:1 ....enemies thy f
Ps. 132:7 ......we will worship at his f
Is. 66:1 ....earth is my f
Mark 12:36 ....thine enemies thy f
James 2:3 ....or sit here under my f

Forbear
Ex. 23:5..and wouldest f to help him
Prov. 24:11..If thou f to deliver them
Prov. 25:15..by long f-ing is a prince
Jer. 20:9 ..was weary with f-ing, and
Ezek. 24:17............F to cry, make no mourning
Rom. 3:25 ....through the f-ance of God
1 Cor. 9:6 ....power to f working
2 Cor. 12:6...I f, lest any man should
Eph. 4:2 .....f-ing one another in love
Col. 3:13 ....F-ing one another, and
1 Thess. 3:1 ....when we could no longer f

Forbid
Gen. 44:7......God f that thy servants
1 Sam. 20:2 .he said unto him, God f
Matt. 19:14.f them not, to come unto
Mark 9:39.But Jesus said, F him not
Luke 18:16 ....f them not: for of such
Luke 23:2 ....f-ing to give tribute to
Acts 10:47.......Can any man f water,
1 Cor. 14:39 .and f not to speak with
1 Tim. 4:3 ....F-ing to marry, and

Forehead
Ex. 28:38......shall be upon Aaron's f
Lev. 13:42 ....bald head, or his bald f
1 Sam. 17:49.....stone sunk into his f
Jer. 3:3...........thou hadst a whore's f
Ezek. 3:8.......strong against their f-s
Ezek. 9:4 ....mark upon the f-s of the men
Ezek. 16:12 ......I put a jewel on thy f
Rev. 9:4 ...the seal of God in their f-s
Rev. 17:5.......upon her f was a name

Foreigner
Ex. 12:45..........f and a hired servant
Deut. 15:3 ....f thou mayest exact
Obad. 11 ....f-s entered into his gates
Eph. 2:19 .no more strangers and f-s

Forest
1 Kin. 7:2 .house of the f of Lebanon
Ps. 50:10..........every beast of the f is
Is. 10:18...consume the glory of his f
Is. 44:14.......among the trees of the f
Is. 56:9 ....all ye beasts in the f
Jer. 5:6..............lion out of the f shall
Jer. 21:14 ....kindle a fire in the f
Ezek. 15:2...among the trees of the f
Amos 3:4......Will a lion roar in the f

Forgave
Ps. 78:38 ....f their iniquity, and
Ps. 99:8 ....a God that f-st them
Matt. 18:27...........and f him the debt
Luke 7:42......he frankly f them both
Luke 7:43.............to whom he f most

Forget
Gen. 27:45.he f that which thou hast
Gen. 41:51.................me f all my toil
Deut. 4:9...........lest thou f the things
Deut. 6:12 ....lest thou f the Lord
Ps. 9:17......all the nations that f God
Ps. 13:1.......How long wilt thou f me
Ps. 74:23........F not the voice of thine
Ps. 88:12.................land of f-fulness
Ps. 119:176......f thy commandments
Prov. 3:1 ..My son, f not my law; but
Prov. 4:5 .get understanding: f it not
Prov. 31:5 ..they drink, and f the law
Is. 54:4 ....f the shame of thy youth
Jer. 2:32 ....maid f her ornaments
Jer. 23:27 ...cause my people to f my
Heb. 6:10.f your work and labour of
Heb. 13:2 ....f-ful to entertain strangers
Heb. 13:16.......to communicate f not
James 1:24.....f-teth what manner of man

Forgive
Gen. 50:17..........f the trespass of the
Ex. 32:32......................Wilt, f their sin
Num. 30:5...........the Lord shall f her
Ps. 25:18 ....and f all my sins
Ps. 86:5...............good and ready to f
Jer. 18:23.............f not their iniquity
Matt. 6:12 ....f us our debts, as we f
Matt. 9:5............Thy sins be f-n thee
Matt. 9:6..................on earth to f sins
Mark 2:7.......who can f sins but God
Mark 11:26 ....if ye do not f
Luke 6:37..........f, and ye shall be f-n
Luke 7:47........sins . . . many, are f-n
Luke 23:34........Jesus, Father, f them
2 Cor. 2:10......ye f any thing, I f also
Eph. 4:32 ....f-ing one another
Col. 2:13 ....f-n you all trespasses
1 John 1:9 ....just to f us our sins

Forgiveness
Ps. 130:4 ....there is f with thee
Mark 3:29...Holy Ghost hath never f
Acts 13:38...preached unto you the f
Acts 26:18 ....may receive f of sins
Eph. 1:7 ....f of sins, according to
Col. 1:14 ....even the f of sins

Forgotten
Gen. 41:30.....plenty . . . f in the land
Deut. 32:18...f God that formed thee
Job 19:14 ....friends have f me
Job 28:4 ....the waters f of the foot
Ps. 9:18.....needy . . . not always be f
Ps. 31:12...........I am f as a dead man
Ps. 77:9..............God f to be gracious
Jer. 2:32 ....my people have f me
Lam. 2:6.caused . . . sabbaths to be f
Ezek. 23:35 ....thou hast f me
Matt. 16:5............had f to take bread
Luke 12:6 ....is f before God

Form
Gen. 1:2........the earth was without f
Gen. 2:7.....God f-ed man of the dust
2 Sam. 14:20.............this f of speech
Job 33:6 ....f-ed out of the clay
Ps. 95:5 ....hands f-ed the dry land
Prov. 26:10...........that f-ed all things
Is. 45:7 ....I f the light, and create
Is. 53:2.................no f nor comeliness
Amos 4:13..that f-eth the mountains
Amos 7:1 ....he f-ed grasshoppers
Mark 16:12.....appeared in another f
Gal. 4:19 ..until Christ be f-ed in you
1 Tim. 2:13 .Adam . . . f-ed, then Eve

Fornication
Is. 23:17.........shall commit f with all
Matt. 15:19...murders, adulteries, f-s
Matt. 19:9 ....except it be for f
John 8:41............We be not born of f
1 Cor. 6:18............Flee f . . . f sinneth
1 Thess. 4:3.....should abstain from f
Rev. 2:20.......to commit f, and to eat
Rev. 17:2..................the wine of her f

Forsake
Deut. 4:31 ....he will not f thee
Josh. 1:5 ....not fail thee, nor f thee
2 Chr. 15:2..........if ye f him, he will f
Ezra 9:9.............God hath not f-n us
Job 6:14 ....f-th the fear of the
Ps. 22:1...God, why hast thou f-n me
Ps. 27:9..........leave me not, neither f
Ps. 27:10.father and my mother f me
Ps. 38:21 ....F me not, O God
Prov. 1:8.f not the law of thy mother
Prov. 2:17 ....f-th the guide of her youth
Prov. 3:3..........not mercy and truth f
Prov. 9:6...........F the foolish, and live
Is. 55:7 ....Let the wicked f his way
Jer. 5:7.......thy children have f-n me
Ezek. 9:9 ......Lord hath f-n the earth
Ezek. 20:8 ....f the idols of Egypt
Matt. 19:27........f-n all, and followed
Matt. 27:46...God, why hast thou f-n me
Mark 15:34...God, why hast thou f-n me
2 Cor. 4:9......Persecuted, but not f-n
Heb. 13:5.......never leave thee, nor f
2 Pet. 2:15 ....have f-n the right

Forsook
Deut. 32:15 ....then he f God
1 Kin. 12:8 ....he f the counsel
2 Chr. 12:1........f the law of the Lord
Matt. 26:56 .disciples f him, and fled
Mark 1:18 .f their nets, and followed
Luke 5:11 .....they f all, and followed
2 Tim. 4:16...............but all men f me
Heb. 11:27 ....By faith he f Egypt

Fortress
2 Sam. 22:2 ....my rock, and my f
Ps. 18:2 ....rock, and my f, and my
Ps. 91:2..............my refuge and my f
Is. 34:13 ....brambles in the f-es
Jer. 6:27 ..a tower and a f among my

Forty
Gen. 7:4..........the earth f days and f nights
Gen. 7:17.........f days upon the earth
Ex. 16:35 ....Israel did eat manna f years
Ex. 34:28.............f days and f nights
Num. 33:38...died there, in the f-ieth
Ps. 95:10 .F years long was I grieved
Matt. 4:2...............f days and f nights
Mark 1:13 ...in the wilderness f days
2 Cor. 11:24 ....f stripes save one

Fought
Num. 21:1.....then he f against Israel
Judg. 5:20 ....They f from heaven
2 Chr. 20:29 ....the Lord f against
1 Cor. 15:32.........I have f with beasts
2 Tim. 4:7 ....I have f a good fight
Rev. 12:7..........angels f . . . dragon f

Found
Gen. 2:20......there was not f an help meet
Gen. 6:8 .Noah f grace in the eyes of
Ex. 22:7.......................if the thief be f
Lev. 6:3 ...have f that which was lost
Deut. 17:2....If there be f among you
Judg. 14:18......not f out of my riddle
Ruth 2:10........Why have I f grace in thine
Job 28:12 ...where shall wisdom be f
Ps. 84:3the sparrow hath f an house
Prov. 25:16....Hast thou f honey? eat
Prov. 30:6 ....thou be f a liar
Eccles. 7:29............this only have I f
Song 3:1.sought him, but I f him not
Is. 51:3....joy and gladness shall be f
Jer. 15:16....Thy words were f, and I did
Dan. 5:27 ....balances, and art f wanting
Dan. 6:11..........and f Daniel praying
Mal. 2:6 ....iniquity was not f in his
Matt. 8:10............not f so great faith
Matt. 27:32...........f a man of Cyrene, Simon
Mark 11:4 ....and f the colt tied
Mark 14:40 ...he f them asleep again
Luke 2:46....they f him in the temple
Luke 15:6 ....I have f my sheep
Luke 24:2 .....f the stone rolled away
John 1:41 ......We have f the Messias
Acts 13:22 .I have f David the son of
1 Cor. 15:15.we are f false witnesses
Phil. 2:8..................being f in fashion
Rev. 18:24 ..in her was f the blood of

Foundation
Ex. 9:18.......f thereof even until now
2 Sam. 22:8.......f-s of heaven moved
Job 4:19..........whose f is in the dust,
Ps. 87:1 ....His f is in the holy mountains
Ps. 104:5 ....laid the f-s of the earth
Prov. 10:25...........is an everlasting f
Is. 28:16 ....corner stone, a sure f
Matt. 13:35 ...from the f of the world
Luke 6:48.....and laid the f on a rock
Rom. 15:20......upon another man's f
2 Tim. 2:19 ......the f of God standeth
Heb. 1:10 .hast laid the f of the earth
Heb. 6:1 ....the f of repentance

Founded
Ps. 24:2 .....he hath f it upon the seas
Prov. 3:19........by wisdom hath f the earth
Amos 9:6.......f his troop in the earth
Matt. 7:25 ....for it was f upon a rock

Fountain
Gen. 7:11 ....f-s of the great deep
Gen. 16:7...found her by a f of water
Ps. 36:9.........with thee is the f of life
Prov. 5:16....Let thy f-s be dispersed
Prov. 14:27......fear of the Lord is a f
Eccles. 12:6..........be broken at the f
Mark 5:29 ...f of her blood was dried
James 3:12...........no f both yield salt
Rev. 7:17 ....living f-s of water
Rev. 21:6 ....of the f of the water

Fowl
Gen. 1:20.....f that may fly above the
Gen. 6:7..thing, and the f-s of the air
Lev. 20:25 ....unclean f-s and clean
1 Kin. 4:23....fallowdeer and fatted f
Ps. 8:8 ....f of the air, and the fish
Ps. 148:10...creeping . . . and flying f
Jer. 9:10......the f of the heavens and the
Hos. 9:8 ....a share of a f
Matt. 6:26...Behold, the f-s of the air
Rev. 19:17 ....saying to all the f-s

Fox
Judg. 15:4.......caught three hundred f-es
Neh. 4:3.............if a f go up, he shall
Song 2:15.........the f-es, the little f-es
Ezek. 13:4 ....like the f-es in the deserts
Matt. 8:20...The f-es have holes, and
Luke 13:32........Go ye, and tell that f

Fragments
Matt. 14:20 ....took up of the f that
Mark 6:43 ....twelve baskets full of the f
John 6:12 ....Gather up the f

Frankincense
Ex. 30:34.....sweet spices with pure f
1 Chr. 9:29 ......the oil, and the f, and
Song 4:6........................to the hill of f
Matt. 2:11......gold, and f, and myrrh

Free
Gen. 2:16.garden . . . mayest f-ly eat
Ex. 21:11......go out f without money
Ps. 51:12....................with thy f spirit
Is. 58:6...............let the oppressed go f
Matt. 10:8 .f-ly . . . received, f-ly give
Matt. 17:26...Then are the children f
John 8:32.......truth shall make you f
Acts 22:28........obtained I this f-dom
Rom. 6:7...........he that is dead is f-d
Rom. 6:22.......being made f from sin
Rom. 8:2 ....f from the law
Gal. 5:1 ....Christ hath made us f
Eph. 6:8............................he be bond or f
Rev. 19:18..all men, both f and bond

Friend
Gen. 38:12 ....he and his f Hirah
Ex. 33:11 .a man speaketh unto his f
Judg. 14:20 ....he had used as his f
Ruth 2:13.........thou hast spoken f-ly
Job 16:20..................My f-s scorn me
Ps. 38:11.........My lovers . . . f-s stand aloof
Prov. 14:20 ....the rich hath many f-s
Prov. 17:17 .....A f loveth at all times
Prov. 18:24 ....a f that sticketh closer
Hos. 3:1.......................beloved of her f
Matt. 11:19...................f of publicans
Matt. 20:13......F, I do thee no wrong
John 15:13 ..lay down his life for his f-s
James 4:4 ....know ye not that the f-ship

Fruit
Gen. 1:11 ....f tree yielding f after
Gen. 3:6.....took of the f thereof, and
Ex. 21:22 ....her f depart from her
Lev. 25:19.........land shall yield her f
Lev. 27:30 .f of the tree, is the Lord's
Deut. 28:53.........f of thine own body
Ps. 1:3 ....bringeth forth his f in his
Ps. 92:14 ....bring forth f in old age
Prov. 11:30 ....f of the righteous
Song 4:16.....and eat his pleasant f-s
Is. 5:1..........................in a very f-ful hill
Jer. 6:19.even the f of their thoughts
Matt. 7:16 .....know them by their f-s
John 4:36 ....f unto life eternal
Rom. 7:4 ....bring forth f unto God
Col. 1:10.....f-ful in every good work
James 3:17 .....of mercy and good f-s

Frustrate
Ezra 4:5.....to f their purpose, all the
Is. 44:25...f-th the tokens of the liars
Gal. 2:21....do not f the grace of God

Fulfil
2 Chr. 36:21 ...f the word of the Lord
Ps. 20:5..........Lord f all thy petitions
Ps. 148:8..........stormy wind f-ing his word
Matt. 1:22.done that it might be f-ed
Matt. 5:17...not come to destroy, but to f
Luke 22:16.it be f-ed in the kingdom
Gal. 6:2 ....f the law of Christ
Col. 1:25 ...you, to f the word of God
Rev. 20:3......thousand years . . . f-ed

Full
Ps. 33:5.Earth is f of the goodness of
Ps. 73:10.................waters of a f cup
Is. 11:9...shall be f of the knowledge
Mic. 3:8.........f of power by the spirit
Matt. 23:27.....f of dead men's bones
Luke 4:1 ...being f of the Holy Ghost
Luke 11:34.......body also is f of light
John 1:14............f of grace and truth
Acts 2:13 ....men are f of new wine
1 Cor. 4:8 ...ye are f, now ye are rich
1 Cor. 10:26....Lord's, and the f-ness
1 John 1:4......that your joy may be f
Rev. 14:18 .....her grapes are f-y ripe

Fuller
2 Kin. 18:17.highway of the f-'s field
Mal. 3:2...................and like f-'s soap
Mark 9:3......no f . . . can white them

Furnace
Gen. 15:17...............smoking f, and a burning
Ps. 12:6 ....silver tried in a f
Is. 31:9............and his f in Jerusalem
Dan. 3:15 ..midst of a burning fiery f
Matt. 13:42 ....into a f of fire
Rev. 1:15 ....as they burned in a f

Furnish
Deut. 15:14.......f him liberally out of
Ps. 78:19.............God f a table in the
Prov. 9:2.......hath also f-ed her table
2 Tim. 3:17.f-ed unto all good works

Further
Phil. 1:12.........unto the f-ance of the gospel
Heb. 12:9 ....F-more we have had fathers

Fury
Gen. 27:44...........thy brother's f turn
Is. 27:4 ....F is not in me
Jer. 4:4 ....my f come forth like fire
Jer. 6:11 ....full of the f of the Lord
Jer. 30:23......Lord goeth forth with f
Ezek. 5:13.....cause my f to rest upon
Ezek. 19:12 ....plucked up in f
Mic. 5:15 ....anger and f upon the heathen

G

Gain
Judg. 5:19 ..they took no g of money
Prov. 3:14....g thereof than fine gold
Is. 33:15.............the g of oppressions
Ezek. 22:12.......hast greedily g-ed of
Ezek. 22:27............to get dishonest g
Dan. 11:39 ....divide the land for g

Matt. 16:26..shall **g** the whole world
Matt. 18:15......hast **g**-ed thy brother
Luke 9:25.....**g** the whole world, and lose
Acts 16:19........hope of their **g**-s was gone
Acts 19:24..brought no small **g** unto
1 Cor. 9:20....that I might **g** the Jews
2 Cor. 12:17....Did I make a **g** of you
1 Tim. 6:5.............supposing . . . **g** is godliness
James 4:13..................sell, and get **g**

Gall
Deut. 29:18..................beareth **g** and wormwood
Job 20:14................it is the **g** of asps
Ps. 69:21........gave me also **g** for my meat
Jer. 8:14...............water of **g** to drink
Lam. 3:19..the wormwood and the **g**
Amos 6:12....turned judgment into **g**
Matt. 27:34........vinegar . . . mingled with **g**
Acts 8:23..........in the **g** of bitterness

Garden
Gen. 2:8....the Lord God planted a **g**
Gen. 3:8...........God walking in the **g**
Gen. 3:10..I heard thy voice in the **g**
Deut. 11:10.................as a **g** of herbs
Song 6:11.....down into the **g** of nuts
Is. 1:8....a lodge in a **g** of cucumbers
Is. 58:11..............be like a watered **g**
Lam. 2:6................as if it were of a **g**
Joel 2:3........land is as the **g** of Eden
John 18:1......................where was a **g**
John 18:26......not I see thee in the **g**
John 19:41.in the **g** a new sepulchre
John 20:15..supposing him to be the **g**-er

Garment
Gen. 25:25....all over like an hairy **g**
Ex. 28:2......make holy **g**-s for Aaron
Ps. 22:18....part my **g**-s among them
Ps. 102:26................wax old like a **g**
Is. 59:17..............the **g**-s of vengeance
Dan. 7:9..........whose **g** was white as snow
Joel 2:13........heart and not your **g**-s
Matt. 9:20..touched the hem of his **g**
Matt. 22:11..had not on a wedding **g**
Mark 16:5.....man . . . a long white **g**
Luke 24:4..................two men . . . in shining **g**-s
Acts 12:8........Cast thy **g** about thee
Heb. 1:11.........wax old as doth as **g**
Rev. 1:13...........a **g** down to the foot

Garner
Ps. 144:13...That our **g**-s may be full
Joel 1:17.....the **g**-s are laid desolate
Matt. 3:12................wheat into the **g**

Garnish
Job 26:13..he hath **g**-ed the heavens
Matt. 23:29..and **g** the sepulchres of
Luke 11:25................swept and **g**-ed
Rev. 21:19.wall of the city were **g**-ed

Gate
Gen. 22:17...thy seed . . . possess the **g** of
Gen. 28:17......this is the **g** of heaven
Ex. 20:10.stranger . . . within thy **g**-s
Judg. 16:3.....took the doors of the **g**
Ps. 24:7.Lift up your heads, O ye **g**-s
Ps. 100:4........Enter into his **g**-s with
Is. 38:10.....go to the **g**-s of the grave
Matt. 7:13..Enter ye in at the strait **g**
Matt. 16:18..........**g**-s of hell shall not
Acts 12:14...Peter stood before the **g**

Gather
Ps. 26:9...............**G** not my soul with
Ps. 33:7...**g**-eth the waters of the sea
Is. 40:11.....**g** the lambs with his arm
Is. 66:18.....**g** all nations and tongues
John 4:36...........**g**-eth fruit unto life
John 6:12............**G** up the fragments
2 Thess. 2:1.**g**-ing together unto him
Rev. 14:19.**g**-ed the vine of the earth

Gave
Gen. 2:20..........Adam **g** names to all cattle
Gen. 3:12............she **g** me of the tree
Gen. 25:17..............he **g** up the ghost
Neh. 9:15.........**g**-st them bread from heaven
Job 1:21.Lord **g** . . . Lord hath taken
Ps. 21:4....He asked life . . . thou **g**-st
Ps. 68:11...................Lord **g** the word
Ps. 69:21.**g** me also gall for my meat
Ps. 69:21.........**g** me vinegar to drink
Ps. 77:1...........and he **g** ear unto me
Eccles 12:7...return unto God who **g**
Is. 50:6.....I **g** my back to the smiters
Matt. 10:1.............**g** them power . . . unclean
Matt. 15:36........**g** thanks, and brake them
Matt. 26:48....betrayed him **g** them a sign
Mark 8:6....and **g** thanks, and brake
Luke 7:44...**g**-st me no water for my feet
Luke 23:24.............Pilate **g** sentence
John 3:16.....**g** his only begotten son
John 13:26.........sop, he **g** it to Judas
John 19:30......................**g** up the ghost
Acts 12:23.....he **g** not God the glory
Rom. 1:28...............**g** them over to a reprobate
1 Cor. 3:6......but God **g** the increase
Eph. 1:22..**g** him to be the head over
1 Tim. 2:6..Who **g** himself a ransom

Generation
Gen. 2:4...are the **g**-s of the heavens
Deut. 1:35...not one . . . of this evil **g**
Ps. 90:1........dwelling place in all **g**-s
Ps. 100:5......truth endureth to all **g**-s
Matt. 3:7.......O **g** of vipers, who hath
Matt. 24:34........This **g** shall not pass
Luke 1:48........all **g**-s shall call me blessed
Luke 21:32......**g** shall not pass away
1 Pet. 2:9..............a chosen **g**, a royal

Gentile
Is. 66:19......my glory among the **G**-s
Luke 2:32......light to lighten the **G**-s
Acts 14:2......Jews stirred up the **G**-s
Rom. 2:9...Jew first . . . also of the **G**
Rom. 11:11...................salvation . . . unto the **G**-s
1 Cor. 12:13..........we be Jews or **G**-s
Rev. 11:2.......it is given unto the **G**-s

Gentle
Ps. 18:35.........thy **g**-ness hath . . . me great
2 Cor. 10:1................**g**-ness of Christ
1 Thess. 2:7....But we were **g** among you
2 Tim. 2:24......but be **g** unto all men
Titus 3:2...............no brawlers, but **g**
1 Pet. 2:18..not only to the good and **g**

Ghost
Gen. 25:8.....Then Abraham gave up the **g**
Job 3:11.Why did I not give up the **g**
Matt. 1:18...with child of the Holy **G**
Matt. 27:50.............cried . . . yielded up the **g**
Matt. 28:19...Son, and of the Holy **G**
Mark 1:8.............baptize you with the Holy **G**
Luke 1:15..be filled with the Holy **G**
Acts 2:4...all filled with the Holy **G**
2 Cor 13:14..........communion of the Holy **G**

Giant
Gen. 6:4..........................**g**-s in the earth
Deut. 3:13........called the land of **g**-s
1 Chr. 20:6.........was the son of the **g**
Job 16:14..runneth upon me like a **g**

Gift
Gen. 25:6.............Abraham gave **g**-s
Ex. 23:8........no **g**: for the **g** blindeth
Ps. 68:18...hast received **g**-s for men
Prov. 18:16.A man's **g** maketh room
Prov. 21:14.....A **g** in secret pacifieth
Is. 1:23......every one loveth **g**-s, and
Matt. 2:11.....presented unto him **g**-s
Matt. 5:23.....bring thy **g** to the altar
John 4:10........thou knewest the **g** of God
Acts 2:38......the **g** of the Holy Ghost
Rom. 6:23......**g** of God is eternal life
James 1:17.............good **g** and every perfect **g**

Girdle
Ex. 28:8...the curious **g** of the ephod
Ex. 28:40................make . . . **g**-s, and
Ex. 29:9.......shalt gird them with **g**-s
2 Kin. 1:8.......girt with a **g** of leather
Ps. 109:19..**g** wherewith he is girded
Is. 3:24..............instead of a **g** a rent
Jer. 13:1....Go and get thee a linen **g**
Matt. 3:4...leathern **g** about his loins
Rev. 1:13..........paps with a golden **g**

Give
Gen. 1:29......have **g**-n you every . . . seed
Ex. 20:12.land . . . Lord thy God **g**-th
Num. 6:26.......upon thee, and **g** thee peace
Ps. 29:11...Lord will **g** strength unto
Ps. 80:1................**G** ear, O Shepherd
Ps. 145:15..........**g**-st them their meat
Is. 9:6.............unto us as a son is **g**-n
Matt. 6:11.....**G** us this day our daily
Matt. 10:8...............................freely **g**
Matt. 16:19........**g** unto thee the keys
Matt. 26:9...........and **g**-n to the poor
Matt. 28:18.All power is **g**-n unto me
Mark 12:15...Shall we **g**, or . . . not **g**
Luke 1:77.**g** knowledge of salvation
Luke 6:38.........**G**, and it shall be **g**-n
Luke 11:9.....Ask, and it shall be **g**-n
Luke 22:19..my body . . . **g**-n for you
John 6:11...when he had **g**-n thanks
John 10:11...good shepherd **g**-th his life
John 14:27.....my peace I **g** unto you
Acts 20:35.more blessed to **g** than to
Rom. 12:20..if he thirst, **g** him drink
Rom. 14:6.....for he **g**-th God thanks
1 Cor. 3:10.........grace of God which is **g**-n
2 Cor. 12:7.was **g**-n to me a thorn in
Eph. 4:27........Neither **g** place to the devil
Eph. 5:20..........**G**-ing thanks always
James 4:6............**g**-th grace unto the humble
1 John 5:11.....hath **g**-n to us eternal life

Glad
Ex. 4:14.......he will be **g** in his heart
Num. 10:10.......in the day of your **g**-ness
Deut. 28:47.and with **g**-ness of heart
1 Chr. 16:31......Let the heavens be **g**
Ps. 16:9.my heart is **g**, and my glory
Ps. 32:11...................Be **g** in the Lord
Ps. 100:2.Serve the Lord with **g**-ness
Ps. 122:1.was **g** when they said unto me
Prov. 10:1.........wise son maketh a **g** father
Is. 16:10...And **g**-ness is taken away
Matt. 5:12.......................Rejoice, and be exceeding **g**
Luke 1:14.shalt have joy and **g**-ness
Luke 1:19.shew thee these **g** tidings
Luke 8:1.....**g** tidings of the kingdom
Acts 2:46....**g**-ness and singleness of heart
2 Cor. 11:19..For ye suffer fools **g**-ly

Glass
Job 37:18........as a molten looking **g**
Is. 3:23...........**g**-es, and the fine linen
1 Cor. 13:12.........through a **g** darkly
James 1:23......his natural face in a **g**
Rev. 4:6.......was a sea of **g** like unto

Glean
Lev. 19:10 ....not **g** thy vineyard
Ruth 2:8.Go not to **g** in another field
Ruth 2:15.......**g** even . . . the sheaves
Ruth 2:17 ....she **g**-ed in the field
Is. 17:6.......**g**-ing grapes shall be left
Jer. 49:9......leave some **g**-ing grapes

Glorify
Ps. 50:23.....offereth praise **g**-eth me
Ps. 86:12....**g** thy name for evermore
Is. 66:5 ....Let the Lord be **g**-ied
Matt. 5:16...........**g** your Father . . . in heaven
John 12:28...........Father, **g** thy name
John 13:31 ...is the Son of man **g**-ied
John 16:14....................He shall **g** me
John 17:1 ....**g** thy Son . . . **g** thee
Acts 13:48........**g**-ied the word of the Lord
1 Cor. 6:20..........**g** God in your body
Heb. 5:5.......Christ **g**-ied not himself

Glorious
Ex. 15:1 ....he hath triumphed **g**-ly
Neh. 9:5 ....blessed be thy **g** name
Ps. 87:3.**G** things are spoken of thee
Is. 49:5........**g** in the eyes of the Lord
2 Cor. 4:4...............**g** gospel of Christ
Phil. 3:21 ....like . . . his **g** body
1 Tim. 1:11...........the **g** gospel of the blessed

Glory
Gen. 31:1.....hath he gotten all this **g**
Ex. 16:7.............see the **g** of the Lord
Ex. 33:18......................shew me thy **g**
1 Chr. 16:24..............his **g** among the heathen
1 Chr. 29:11......the power, and the **g**
Job 19:9.............stripped me of my **g**
Job 29:20 ....My **g** was fresh in me
Ps. 8:1.........thy **g** above the heavens
Ps. 24:7.........King of **g** shall come in
Ps. 105:3.........**G** ye in his holy name
Prov. 16:31................hoary head . . . crown of **g**
Is. 6:3 ....earth is full of his **g**
Is. 35:2.....shall see the **g** of the Lord
Is. 66:19 ....my **g** among the Gentiles
Jer. 13:16..............Give **g** to the Lord
Ezek. 10:4.the **g** of the Lord went up
Hos. 4:7...change their **g** into shame
Matt. 6:29 ..Solomon in all his **g** was
Luke 2:9..**g** of the Lord shone round
Luke 2:14.....**G** to God in the highest
Luke 17:18........returned to give **g** to God
John 8:50 ....I seek not mine own **g**
Rom. 2:7 ....seek for **g** and honour
Rom. 3:23.......come short of the **g** of God
1 Cor. 5:6 ......Your **g**-ing is not good
Gal. 5:26....not be desirous of vain **g**
Heb. 2:7............crownedst . . . **g** and honour

Gnat
Matt. 23:24 ....which strain at a **g**

Go
Gen. 3:14.........thy belly shalt thou **g**
Ex. 5:1.....Let my people **g**, that they
Ex. 33:14...My presence shall **g** with
Ruth 1:16..............thou **g**-est, I will **g**
2 Kin. 2:23 ....**G** up, thou bald head
Ps. 122:1...Let us **g** into the house of
Prov. 4:14.....**g** not in the way of evil
Prov. 6:6.**G** to the ant, thou sluggard
Eccles. 9:7.**G** thy way, eat thy bread
Matt. 2:8 ......**G** and search diligently
Matt. 28:19.........**G** ye therefore, and teach
Mark 16:15....**G** ye into all the world
Luke 22:8.............**G** and prepare . . . passover
John 9:7..............**G**, wash in the pool
John 14:2...I **g** to prepare a place for
John 14:5.......not whither thou **g**-est
Heb. 6:1 ..let us **g** on unto perfection

Goat
Ex. 26:7 ....curtains of **g**-s' hair
Lev. 3:12...........if his offering be a **g**
Num. 15:27.he shall bring a she **g** of
1 Sam. 19:13 ......a pillow of **g**-s' hair
Dan. 8:5.....the **g** had a notable horn
Matt. 25:32...........sheep from the **g**-s
Heb. 9:13....blood of bulls and of **g**-s

God
Gen. 1:1 ...**G** created the heaven and
Gen. 1:2.......Spirit of **G** moved upon
Gen. 1:3.....**G** said, Let there be light
Gen. 1:27..............**G** created man in his
Gen. 2:3...**G** blessed the seventh day
Gen. 17:1 ....I am the Almighty **G**
Gen. 31:50 ..**G** is witness betwixt me
Ex. 3:15............... and the **G** of Jacob
Ex. 20:2 .I am the Lord thy **G**, which
Ex. 20:5 ..Lord thy **G** am a jealous **G**
Lev. 25:17..but thou shalt fear thy **G**
Deut. 6:5.............love the Lord thy **G**
Deut. 10:17...........your **G**, is **G** of **g**-s
Deut. 20:18.against the Lord your **G**
Deut. 33:27....eternal **G** is thy refuge
Ruth 1:16..................and thy **G** my **G**
2 Sam. 16:16 ....**G** save the King
2 Sam. 22:3......**G** of my rock; in him will
2 Sam. 22:32........is **G**, save the Lord
1 Kin. 2:23 .**G** do so to me, and more
1 Kin. 18:21 .if the Lord be **G**, follow
2 Kin. 5:7...Am I **G**, to kill and make
1 Chr. 13:10 ..there he died before **G**
Job 40:9......Hast thou an arm like **G**
Ps. 7:1 ....**G**, in thee do I put my trust
Ps. 14:1 ....heart, There is no **G**
Ps. 16:1 ....Preserve me, O **G**
Ps. 46:1.**G** is our refuge and strength
Ps. 46:5 .**G** is in the midst of her; she
Ps. 49:7 ...give to **G** a ranson for him
Ps. 67:1...**G** be merciful unto us, and
Ps. 67:6......**G**, even our own **G**, shall
Ps. 70:1 .Make haste, O **G**, to deliver
Ps. 86:10 ....thou art **G** alone
Ps. 145:1 ...I will extol thee, my **G**, O
Prov. 30:5 ...Every word of **G** is pure
Eccles. 5:2 ....**G** is in heaven
Is. 44:8 ....Is there a **G** beside me
Is. 53:4....stricken, smitten of **G**, and
Jer. 23:23 .a **G** at hand . . . **G** afar off
Ezek. 37:27.......I will be their **G**, and
Dan. 2:47...............your **G** is a **G** of **g**-s
Hos. 11:9 ....for I am **G**, and not man
Matt. 2:12....warned of **G** in a dream
Matt. 3:16.......he saw the Spirit of **G**
Matt. 4:3 ....If thou be the Son of **G**
Matt. 5:9......called the children of **G**
Matt. 22:37 ....shalt love the Lord thy **G**
Matt. 27:46....My **G**, my **G**, why hast
Matt. 27:54.....this was the Son of **G**
Mark 10:9 .....**G** hath joined together
Mark 11:22................Have faith in **G**
Mark 16:19 ......sat on the right hand of **G**
Luke 2:14..Glory to **G** in the highest
Luke 12:28.....**G** so clothed the grass
Luke 18:16........such is the kingdom of **G**
Luke 23:40 ....Dost not thou fear **G**
John 3:16.**G** so loved the world, that
John 3:17......**G** sent not his Son into
John 4:24...............................**G** is a Spirit
John 14:1 ..believe in **G**, believe also
John 20:17........to my **G**, and your **G**
Acts 10:40 ....Him **G** raised up the third
Acts 12:22.................the voice of a **g**
Acts 17:24.....**G** that made the world and
Rom. 1:25............truth of **G** into a lie
Rom. 8:14.......they are the sons of **G**
1 Cor. 15:57 ...thanks be to **G**, which
2 Cor. 3:3..........Spirit of the living **G**
Gal. 5:21....inherit the kingdom of **G**
Gal. 6:7 ....**G** is not mocked
Eph. 1:3 ....Blessed be the **G** and Father
Eph. 4:6 ....One **G** and Father of all
Phil. 4:7....peace of **G** which passeth
Col. 1:15......image of the invisible **G**
Titus 2:11 ...grace of **G** that bringeth
Heb. 12:29.......**G** is a consuming fire
1 Pet. 4:10..........manifold grace of **G**
2 Pet. 1:21 ....holy men of **G** spake
1 John 3:20......**G** is greater than our
1 John 4:12.......No man hath seen **G**
2 John 10....neither bid him **G** speed
Rev. 7:17.........**G** shall wipe away all tears
Rev. 11:17 ....O Lord **G** Almighty
Rev. 17:17 ....words of **G** . . . fulfilled

Godhead
Acts 17:29......the **G** is like unto gold
Rom. 1:20...his eternal power and **G**
Col. 2:9..........fulness of the **G** bodily

Godliness
1 Tim. 2:2...........in all **g** and honesty
1 Tim. 3:16.great is the mystery of **g**
1 Tim. 4:8 ....but **g** is profitable
1 Tim. 6:6 ....**g** with contentment
2 Tim. 3:5..............having a form of **g**
2 Pet. 1:7......to **g** brotherly kindness

Godly
Ps. 12:1 ....for the **g** man ceaseth
2 Cor. 1:12................simplicity and **g** sincerity
2 Cor. 7:10 ....**g** sorrow worketh
Heb. 12:28 ....with reverence and **g** fear
2 Pet. 2:9..............deliver the **g** out of

Gods
Gen. 3:5.shall be as **g** knowing good
Ex. 20:3...have no other **g** before me
Judg. 5:8 ....They chose new **g**
Is. 37:12....**g** of the nations delivered
Jer. 22:9......and worshipped other **g**
Dan. 2:47 ......your God is a God of **g**
Gal. 4:8.................by nature are no **g**

Going
Job 1:7 ....**g** to and fro in the earth
Ps. 121:8......shall preserve thy **g** out
Mic. 5:2...whose **g**-s forth have been
Matt. 26:46................Rise, let us be **g**
Mark 10:32 ...way **g** up to Jerusalem
1 Pet. 2:25 ....as sheep **g** astray
Jude 7 ....**g** after strange flesh

Gold
Gen. 2:12 ....**g** of that land is good
Ex. 3:22 ....and jewels of **g**
Job 31:24..If I have made **g** my hope
Ps. 19:10 ....yea, than much fine **g**
Ps. 72:15 ....of the **g** of Sheba
Prov. 16:16 .....better . . . get wisdom than **g**
Prov. 25:11 ....apples of **g** in pictures
Lam. 4:1 ...How is the **g** become dim
Zech. 9:3 ....fine **g** as the mire
Matt. 10:9...neither **g**, nor silver, nor
Acts 3:6......Silver and **g** have I none
Acts 20:33 ..coveted no man's silver, or **g**
James 2:2 ....man with a **g** ring
James 5:3....**g** and silver is cankered
1 Pet. 1:7.....more precious than of **g**
Rev. 3:18......buy of me **g** tried in the

Good
Gen. 1:4..........the light, that it was **g**
Gen. 50:20 ....God meant it unto **g**
Lev. 27:10.......................a **g** for a bad
Deut. 31:6.strong and of a **g** courage
Job 7:7 ....eye shall no more see **g**
Ps. 106:1 ..give thanks . . . for he is **g**
Ps. 136:1 .....for he is **g** . . . his mercy
Prov. 22:1 ...**g** name . . . to be chosen
Prov. 25:25 ....**g** news from a far country
Is. 39:8 ......**G** is the word of the Lord
Jer. 33:11.....Lord is **g**; for his mercy
Amos 5:14..........Seek **g**, and not evil
Matt. 3:10..bringeth not forth **g** fruit
Matt. 9:2....be of **g** cheer; thy sins be
Matt. 13:45..........seeking **g**-ly pearls
Matt. 19:16................**G** Master, what
Matt. 25:23 .....**g** and faithful servant

Mark 9:50......Salt is **g**, but if the salt
Luke 6:27...do **g** to them which hate
Luke 10:42...hath chosen that **g** part
Luke 18:19....Why callest thou me **g**
John 10:14.........I am the **g** shepherd
Acts 23:1.....lived in all **g** conscience
Rom. 2:10.................every man that worketh **g**
Rom. 12:21......overcome evil with **g**
Rom. 16:18.........by **g** words and fair
Gal. 6:10.........................do **g** unto all
Phil. 4:8...........things are of **g** report
2 Thess. 2:16...**g** hope through grace
1 Tim. 6:12..Fight the **g** fight of faith
James 1:17....Every **g** gift and every
1 Pet. 3:11.......eschew evil, and do **g**

Goodman
Prov. 7:19....For the **g** is not at home
Matt. 24:43.if the **g** of the house had

Goodness
Ex. 33:19........my **g** pass before thee
2 Chr. 6:41............saints rejoice in **g**
Ps. 23:6......**g** and mercy shall follow
Ps. 25:7........remember . . . for thy **g**' sake
Ps. 31:19...how great is thy **g**, which
Prov. 20:6..........every one his own **g**
Zech. 9:17........For how great is his **g**
Rom. 11:22.....**g** and severity of God
Gal. 5:22..............gentleness, **g**, faith
2 Thess. 1:11..good pleasure of his **g**

Goods
Job. 20:28........his **g** shall flow away
Matt. 12:29..................and spoil his **g**
Luke 12:19.........hast much **g** laid up
Luke 19:8...half of my **g** I give to the
Rev. 3:17.rich, and increased with **g**

Gospel
Matt. 4:23........the **g** of the Kingdom
Matt. 11:5..........have the **g** preached
Mark 16:15......preach the **g** to every
Luke 4:18...preach the **g** to the poor
Rom. 1:16.............I am not ashamed of the **g**
Rom. 10:16........not all obeyed the **g**
Rom. 15:29..........blessing of the **g** of Christ
2 Cor. 10:14..........preaching the **g** of Christ
2 Cor. 11:4.........................or another **g**
Gal. 1:7..........pervert the **g** of Christ
Eph. 1:13............**g** of your salvation
Eph. 6:15.......................the **g** of peace
Phil. 1:5................fellowship in the **g**
Col. 1:23........from the hope of the **g**
1 Pet. 4:17...........that obey not the **g**
Rev. 14:6................the everlasting **g**

Government
Is. 9:6......**g** . . . be upon his shoulder
Is. 22:21...............thy **g** into his hand
1 Cor. 12:28...........**g**-s, diversities of tongues
2 Pet. 2:10....................and despise **g**

Governor
Matt. 2:6....come a **G**, that shall rule
Matt. 27:11.Jesus stood before the **g**
Acts 7:10.he made him **g** over Egypt
James 3:4.withersoever the **g** listeth

Grace
Gen. 6:8Noah found **g** in the eyes of
Ex. 33:12....also found **g** in my sight
Esther 2:17..........she obtained **g** and favour
Ps. 45:2........**g** is poured into thy lips
Luke 2:40.....the **g** of God was upon him
John 1:16.........received, and **g** for **g**
Rom. 1:5...............by whom we have received **g**
Rom. 5:2.....this **g** wherein we stand
Rom. 16:20..The **g** of our Lord Jesus
2 Cor. 9:8............make all **g** abound
2 Cor. 12:9.............My **g** is sufficient
1 Thess. 1:1........**G** be upon you, and peace
2 Thess. 2:16....good hope through **g**
Philem. 25..........**g** of our Lord Jesus
Heb. 4:16....................the throne of **g**
James 4:6..giveth **g** unto the humble
2 Pet. 3:18........grow in **g**, and in the

Gracious
Gen. 43:29...God be **g** unto thee, my son
Ex. 33:19..........**g** to whom I will be **g**
Neh. 9:31...art a **g** and merciful God
Ps. 77:9...........God forgotten to be **g**
Ps. 111:4...........Lord is **g** and full of
Ps. 112:4.is **g** and full of compassion
Ps. 119:29.......grant me thy law **g**-ly
Amos 5:15Lord God of hosts will be **g**
Luke 4:22..wondered at the **g** words
1 Pet. 2:3.....tasted that the Lord is **g**

Grandmother
2 Tim. 1:5.....dwelt first in thy **g** Lois

Grape
Is. 18:5............the sour **g** is ripening
Jer. 31:29............have eaten a sour **g**
Matt. 7:16..men gather **g**-s of thorns
Luke 6:44....bramble . . . gather they **g**-s

Grass
Gen. 1:11.......the earth bring forth **g**
Num. 22:4............ox licketh up the **g**
Ps. 102:11..and I am withered like **g**
Ps. 103:15......man, his days are as **g**
Prov. 27:25...tender **g** sheweth itself
Is. 37:27..............**g** on the housetops
Is. 40:6..........................All flesh is **g**
Is. 40:7...The **g** withereth, the flower
Dan. 5:21...fed him with **g** like oxen
Matt. 6:30.God so clothe the **g** of the
1 Pet. 1:24..........all flesh is as **g**, and

Grave
Ps. 30:3..brought . . . soul from the **g**
Ps. 49:15......from the power of the **g**
Song 8:6....jealousy is cruel as the **g**
Ezek. 37:12.........I will open your **g**-s
Matt. 27:52.and the **g**-s were opened
John 11:17.....lain in the **g** four days
John 12:17..........Lazarus out of his **g**
1 Cor. 15:55...**g**, where is thy victory
Rev. 11:9........bodies to be put in **g**-s

Graven
Ex. 20:4..........make unto thee any **g** image
Ex. 32:16...of God, **g** upon the tables
Lev. 26:1...you no idols nor **g** image
Ps. 97:7......they that serve **g** images
Jer. 50:38..........the land of **g** images
Acts 17:29.................stones, **g** by art

Gray
Gen. 42:38..........**g** hairs with sorrow
Deut. 32:25..with the man of **g** hairs
Hos. 7:9...**g** hairs are here and there

Grayheaded
1 Sam. 12:2.................I am old and **g**
Job. 15:10........**g** and very aged men
Ps. 71:18...also when I am old and **g**

Great
Gen. 1:16...two **g** lights . . . **g**-er light
Gen. 12:2..........will make of thee a **g** nation
Gen. 15:1.....thy exceeding **g** reward
Ex. 18:11...............**g**-er than all gods
Ex. 32:30..........Ye have sinned a **g** sin
Deut. 1:17........small as well as the **g**
1 Chr. 16:25............For **g** is the Lord
Ps. 48:1....**G** is the Lord, and greatly
Ps. 57:10............mercy is **g** unto the heavens
Matt. 2:10.rejoiced with exceeding **g**
Matt. 4:16.........darkness saw **g** light
Matt. 5:12............**g** is your reward in heaven
Matt. 7:27......................**g** was the fall of it
Matt. 11:11.......not risen a **g**-er than John
Matt. 15:28.....................**g** is thy faith
Luke 2:10.........good tidings of **g** joy
Luke 6:23...........your reward is **g** in heaven
Luke 22:44...............**g** drops of blood
John 5:20........**g**-er works than these
John 15:13....**G**-er love hath no man
1 Cor. 13:13.**g**-est of these is charity
Rev. 8:10....fell a **g** star from heaven
Rev. 15:3...**G** and marvelous are thy
Rev. 21:3......I heard a **g** voice out of

Greedy
Ps. 17:12...a lion that is **g** of his prey
Prov. 15:27..........He that is **g** of gain
Is. 56:11.....................they are **g** dogs
1 Tim. 3:8...........not **g** of filthy lucre

Greek
Luke 23:38.............**G**, and Latin, and Hebrew
Acts 16:1........but his father was a **G**
Acts 21:37..........Canst thou speak **G**
Gal. 3:28...........neither Jew nor **G**
Rev. 9:11..................in the **G** tongue

Green
Gen. 1:30........every **g** herb for meat
Job 8:16..........He is **g** before the sun
Ps. 23:2......to lie down in **g** pastures

Grew
Gen. 21:8...........the child **g**, and was
Ex. 1:12.more they multiplied and **g**
1 Sam. 2:21.......Samuel **g** before the Lord
2 Sam. 5:10......David went on and **g** great
Mark 4:7.thorns **g** up, and choked it
Luke 2:40..................And the child **g**
Acts 12:24...........word of God **g** and multiplied
Acts 19:20.....mightily **g** the word of God

Grief
Gen. 26:35..Which were a **g** of mine
Job 2:13.....that his **g** was very great
Ps. 31:10.........my life is spent with **g**
Prov. 17:25...foolish son is a **g** to his
Is. 17:11.........a heap in the day of **g**
Is. 53:4.................hath borne our **g**-s
Jer. 45:3.hath added **g** to my sorrow
Heb. 13:17..with joy, and not with **g**

Grieve
Gen. 6:6..........it **g**-d him at his heart
Gen. 45:5.be not **g**-d, nor angry with
Ps. 78:40.......and **g** him in the desert
Ps. 95:10.Forty years long was I **g**-d
Amos 6:6.............are not **g**-d for the affliction
Mark 3:5...........**g**-d for the hardness
John 21:17..................Peter was **g**-d
2 Cor. 2:5.he hath not **g**-d me, but in
Eph. 4:30..........**G** not the holy Spirit
Heb. 3:10............I was **g**-d with that generation

Grind
Eccles. 12:3................the **g**-ers cease
Eccles. 12:4......sound of the **g**-ing is
Is. 3:15..........**g** the faces of the poor
Is. 47:2....Take the millstones, and **g**
Matt. 24:41...women . . . **g**-ing at the mill

Groan
Ex. 2:24..........God heard their **g**-ing
John 11:33......**g**-ed in the spirit, and
Acts 7:34.....I have heard their **g**-ing
Rom. 8:22..........**g**-eth and travaileth
Rom. 8:26....**g**-ings which cannot be
2 Cor. 5:2.......in this we **g**, earnestly

Ground
Gen. 2:5...was not a man to till the **g**
Gen. 2:7.......man of the dust of the **g**
Gen. 2:9........of the **g** made the Lord
Gen. 4:2...........................a tiller of the **g**
Gen. 8:21..will not again curse the **g**
1 Sam. 3:19....his words fall to the **g**
Job 5:6....trouble spring out of the **g**
Ps. 89:44....his throne down to the **g**
Is. 3:26.....desolate . . . sit upon the **g**

Jer. 4:3 ....Break up your fallow **g**
Hos. 10:12 ....break up your fallow **g**
Matt. 13:8 ....other fell into good **g**
Mark 4:5 ...And some fell on stony **g**
Luke 14:18.have bought a piece of **g**
John 8:6.....his finger wrote on the **g**
John 9:6...................he spat on the **g**
Acts 7:33.......thou standest is holy **g**
Eph. 3:17......rooted and **g**-ed in love

Grove
Gen. 21:33.......Abraham planted a **g**
Ex. 34:13.......and cut down their **g**-s
1 Kin. 15:13 ....made an idol in a **g**
2 Kin. 17:10......**g**-s in every high hill
2 Chr. 19:3 ..hast taken away the **g**-s
2 Chr. 33:19....set up **g**-s and graven
Mic. 5:14..........will pluck up thy **g**-s

Grow
Ps. 90:5.....like grass which **g**-eth up
Ps. 147:8 ....who maketh grass to **g**
Is. 11:1 ....Branch shall **g** out of his
Hos. 14:5 ....he shall **g** as the lily
Mal. 4:2.....**g** up as calves of the stall
Matt. 6:28 ....lilies . . . how they **g**
Eph. 4:15 .**g** up into him in all things
1 Pet. 2:2 ....that ye may **g** thereby
2 Pet. 3:18........**g** in grace, and in the

Grudge
Lev. 19:18..............any **g** against the children
2 Cor. 9:7 ....not **g**-ingly, or of
James 5:9 ....**G** not one against another
1 Pet. 4:9....to another without **g**-ing

Guide
Ps. 48:14.........our **g** even unto death
Ps. 112:5 ....**g** his affairs with discretion
Prov. 23:19 .**g** thine heart in the way
Is. 58:11....And the Lord shall **g** thee
Mic. 7:5.......ye not confidence in a **g**
Matt. 23:16.....unto you, ye blind **g**-s
Luke 1:79..........**g** our feet . . . way of peace
Acts 8:31 ....some man should **g** me
Rom. 2:19............art a **g** of the blind
1 Tim. 5:14.........bear children, **g** the house

Guile
Ex. 21:14...............to slay him with **g**
Ps. 32:2.....whose spirit there is no **g**
Ps. 34:13.....thy lips from speaking **g**
John 1:47..................in whom is no **g**
2 Cor. 12:16........I caught you with **g**
1 Pet. 2:1 ....all malice, and all **g**
1 Pet. 2:22 .....neither was **g** found in
1 Pet. 3:10 ....lips that speak no **g**
Rev. 14:5 .their mouth was found no **g**

Guiltless
Ex. 20:7......Lord will not hold him **g**
Num. 5:31 ....the man be **g** from iniquity
Num. 32:22.......be **g** before the Lord
2 Sam. 3:28.I and my kingdom are **g**
1 Kin. 2:9 ....hold him not **g**
Matt. 12:7 ..not have condemned the **g**

Guilty
Gen. 42:21 ....**g** concerning our brother
Lev. 6:4 ....he hath sinned, and is **g**
Num. 35:31..murderer, which is **g** of
Ezek. 22:4......become **g** in thy blood
Matt. 26:66................He is **g** of death
Rom. 3:19........become **g** before God
1 Cor. 11:27.**g** of the body and blood
James 2:10....one point, he is **g** of all

H

Habitation
Deut. 26:15.......Look down from thy holy **h**
Ps. 71:3 ....Be thou my strong **h**
Prov. 3:33 ..blesseth the **h** of the just
Is. 34:13 ....be an **h** of dragons
Jer. 21:13 ....enter into our **h**-s
Luke 16:9............into everlasting **h**-s
Acts 1:20 ....Let his **h** be desolate
Rev. 18:2 ...is become the **h** of devils

Hail
Ex. 9:18..........rain a very grievous **h**
Job 38:22.........the treasures of the **h**
Ps. 105:32 ....gave them **h** for rain
Ps. 148:8........Fire, and **h**; snow, and
Mark 15:18.......**H**, King of the Jews!
Rev. 8:7 ....**h** and fire mingled with

Hair
1 Sam. 14:45....not one **h** of his head
2 Sam. 14:26.....weighed the **h** of his
Dan. 3:27.....nor was an **h** . . . singed
Matt. 5:36.........one **h** white or black
Matt. 10:30.**h**-s . . . are all numbered
Mark 1:6 ....clothed with camel's **h**
John 11:2 ..wiped his feet with her **h**
1 Cor. 11:14......if a man have long **h**
1 Pet. 3:3 ....plaiting the **h**

Hallowed
Ex. 20:11..........sabbath day, and **h** it
Lev. 12:4..she shall touch no **h** thing
1 Sam. 21:6.priest gave him **h** bread
Matt. 6:9.......heaven, **H** be thy name

Halt
Gen. 32:31 ....**h**-ed upon his thigh
1 Kin. 18:21 ....**h** ye between two opinions
Matt. 18:8.better . . . enter into life **h**
Luke 14:21..........maimed, and the **h**
John 5:3.................blind, **h**, withered

Hand
Gen. 24:2.........thy **h** under my thigh
Ex. 17:12.......Moses' **h**-s were heavy
Ex. 21:24............**h** for **h**, foot for foot
Ex. 33:22..........cover thee with my **h**
Num. 11:23 .....Lord's **h** waxed short
Deut. 15:8 ....open thine **h** wide
1 Sam. 5:11 ....**h** of God was very heavy
1 Sam. 26:18............evil is in mine **h**
2 Kin. 19:18 ....work of men's **h**-s
Job 2:6..........Behold, he is in thine **h**
Job 31:27....mouth hath kissed my **h**
Ps. 16:8 ....he is at my right **h**
Ps. 22:16........pierced my **h**-s . . . feet
Ps. 24:4............clean **h**-s, and a pure
Ps. 26:10........right **h** is full of bribes
Ps. 31:5 ....Into thine **h** I commit
Prov. 3:16...left **h** riches and honour
Prov. 10:4.......dealeth with a slack **h**
Prov. 24:33 ....little folding of the **h**-s
Eccles. 9:10..........thy **h** findeth to do
Eccles. 11:6 ......withhold not thine **h**
Is. 1:12...........required this at your **h**
Is. 6:6 ....having a live coal in his **h**
Is. 19:4........into the **h** of a cruel lord
Is. 40:12 ....waters in the hollow of his **h**
Ezek. 37:1.............**h** of the Lord was upon me
Dan. 4:35 ....none can stay his **h**
Mic. 7:3............do evil with both **h**-s
Matt. 3:2..kingdom of heaven is at **h**
Matt. 5:30 ....right **h** offend thee
Matt. 6:3 ....let not thy left **h** know
Matt. 12:13 ....Stretch forth thine **h**
Matt. 18:8 ....thy **h** or thy foot offend
Matt. 22:44 ....Sit thou on my right **h**
Mark 16:19 ......on the right **h** of God
Luke 9:62 ....put his **h** to the plow
John 20:27 ....reach hither thy **h**
2 Cor. 5:1 ...house not made with **h**-s
1 Tim. 2:8 ....lifting up holy **h**-s
Heb. 1:13 ....Sit on my right **h**
Rev. 1:3 ....for the time is at **h**

Handful
Eccles. 4:6 ....Better . . . **h** with quietness
Jer. 9:22........**h** after the harvestman

Handmaid
Ps. 86:16........save the son of thine **h**
Luke 1:38...Behold the **h** of the Lord

Hang
Deut. 21:22and thou **h** him on a tree
Deut. 28:66 ..thy life shall **h** in doubt
Job 26:7 ....**h**-eth the earth upon nothing
Ps. 137:2.....**h**-ed our harps upon the willows
Matt. 27:5...................went and **h**-ed
Acts 5:30.ye slew and **h**-ed on a tree

Happy
Job 5:17 ......**h** is the man whom God
Ps. 144:15 ....**H** is that people
Prov. 3:13 .**H** is the man that findeth
Mal. 3:15 ....now we call the proud **h**
John 13:17 ...**h** are ye if you do them
1 Cor. 7:40 ....**h**-ier if she so abide
James 5:11 ....count them **h**

Hard
Gen. 18:14.....any thing too **h** for the Lord
2 Kin. 2:10.........hast asked a **h** thing
2 Chr. 9:1.Solomon with **h** questions
Prov. 13:15 ......way of transgressors is **h**
Jer. 32:27.......any thing too **h** for me
Matt. 25:24............thou art an **h** man
John 6:60.............This is an **h** saying
Acts 9:5.....**h** for thee to kick against
Heb. 5:11 .....say, and **h** to be uttered
2 Pet. 3:16............**h** to be understood

Harden
Ex. 4:21 ....but I will **h** his heart
Deut. 15:7 ......shalt not **h** thine heart
Job 6:10 ....**h** myself in sorrow
Ps. 95:8....................**H** not your heart
Prov. 21:29 .....wicked man **h**-eth his face
Mark 6:52 ...for their heart was **h**-ed
John 12:40....blinded their eyes, and **h**-ed
Acts 19:9 ....But when divers were **h**-ed

Hardness
Job 38:38............dust groweth into **h**
Mark 3:5....grieved for the **h** of their
Mark 16:14...unbelief and **h** of heart
Rom. 2:5.......**h** and impenitent heart
2 Tim. 2:3 ....endure **h**, as a good

Harm
1 Sam. 26:21.........no more do thee **h**
2 Kin. 4:41 ....no **h** in the pot
Ps. 105:15.........do my prophets no **h**
Matt. 10:16.................**h**-less as doves
Acts 27:21 ......gained this **h** and loss
Phil. 2:15..........blameless and **h**-less
Heb. 7:26........holy, **h**-less, undefiled
1 Pet. 3:13..who is he that will **h** you

Harp
Gen. 4:21 .....handle the **h** and organ
1 Chr. 25:3.........prophesied with a **h**
Job 30:31 ..**h** . . . turned to mourning
Ps. 33:2..........Praise the Lord with **h**
Ps. 137:2 ....hanged our **h**-s upon the
Ps. 150:3.......with the psaltery and **h**
Rev. 14:2 ....harping with their **h**-s

Harvest
Gen. 8:22.......seedtime and **h** . . . not cease
Ex. 23:16 .....feast of **h**, the firstfruits
Prov. 6:8.gathereth her food in the **h**
Prov. 10:5 ....he that sleepeth in **h**
Prov. 25:13 .cold of snow . . . time of **h**
Prov. 26:1......as rain in **h**, so honour
Is. 18:4 .....cloud of dew . . . heat of **h**
Jer. 8:20.......**h** is past, the summer is
Joel 3:13 ....for the **h** is ripe
Matt. 9:37 ....**h** truly is plenteous
Matt. 13:30 ....grow together until the **h**
Luke 10:2...........The **h** truly is great

John 4:35 ....white ready to **h**
Rev. 14:15 ....**h** of the earth is ripe

Hate

Ex. 20:5....generation of them that **h**
Lev. 19:17.....shalt not **h** thy brother
Deut. 19:11 ....any man **h** his neighbour
Ps. 97:10 ....love the Lord, **h** evil
Ps. 119:163 ....I **h** and abhor lying
Prov. 1:22 .....and fools **h** knowledge
Prov. 8:13 ......froward mouth, do I **h**
Prov. 13:24 ..spareth his rod **h**-th his
Prov. 15:10 ....that **h**-th reproof shall die
Eccles. 3:8.........love, and a time to **h**
Is. 1:14..your . . . feasts my soul **h**-th
Amos 5:15....**H** the evil, and love the
Mic. 3:2.......**h** the good, and love the evil
Matt. 5:44 ...good to them that **h** you
Matt. 6:24.....either he will **h** the one
Matt. 24:10..and shall **h** one another
Luke 6:22.......when men shall **h** you
John 7:7............**h** you; but me it **h**-th
John 14:26 ....**h** not his father, and mother
John 15:18 ....If the world **h** you
Eph. 5:29 .ever yet **h**-d his own flesh
1 John 3:15 ....Whosoever **h**-th his brother

Hatred

Ps. 25:19...........hate me with cruel **h**
Ps. 139:22 ..hate them with perfect **h**
Prov. 10:12.........**H** stirreth up strifes
Prov. 15:17............a stalled ox and **h**
Eccles. 9:6 ......their love, and their **h**
Gal. 5:20 ......**h**, variance, emulations

Haughty

2 Sam. 22:28 ......eyes are upon the **h**
Ps. 131:1 ....my heart is not **h**
Prov. 16:18 ....**h** spirit before a fall
Prov. 21:24 ....Proud and **h** scorner
Is. 2:17..**h**-ness of men . . . made low
Mic. 2:3 ....neither shall ye go **h**-ly

Head

Gen. 3:15............it shall bruise thy **h**
2 Kin. 6:5 ....axe **h** fell into the water
Ps. 24:7............Lift up your **h**-s, O ye
Ps. 118:22.........**h** stone of the corner
Prov. 25:22 ...coals of fire upon his **h**
Eccles. 2:14 ..man's eyes are in his **h**
Jer. 18:16.....................and wag his **h**
Matt. 5:36....................swear by thy **h**
Matt. 14:8..............Give me . . . John Baptist's **h**
Matt. 27:39 ....wagging their **h**-s
Mark 12:10 ....the **h** of the corner
Luke 21:18 ....not an hair of your **h**
Luke 21:28 ...up, and lift up your **h**-s
John 13:9...also my hands and my **h**
Acts 21:24 .they may shave their **h**-s
1 Cor. 11:3..**h** of every man is Christ
Eph. 1:22..................**h** over all things
Eph. 5:23...........Christ is the **h** of the church
1 Pet. 2:7....made the **h** of the corner
Rev. 1:14...**h** and his hairs are white

Heal

Ex. 15:26.....the Lord that **h**-eth thee
Num. 12:13...........**H** her now, O God
Deut. 32:29....alive; I wound, and I **h**
2 Kin. 2:21 .I have **h**-ed these waters
2 Chr. 7:14..........and will **h** their land
Ps. 6:2...O Lord, **h** me; for my bones
Ps. 147:3 ...**h**-eth the broken in heart
Is. 53:5...........his stripes we are **h**-ed
Jer. 3:22......will **h** your backslidings
Jer. 17:14 .....**h** me . . . I shall be **h**-ed
Jer. 30:13 ....no **h**-ing medicines
Hos. 14:4....I will **h** their backsliding
Matt 4:23 ....**h**-ing all manner of sickness
Matt 10:8 ....**H** the sick
Mark 3:2............would **h** him on the sabbeth
Mark 3:15 ......power to **h** sicknesses
Luke 4:18 .....to **h** the brokenhearted
Luke 4:23...........Physician, **h** thyself
Luke 9:2.....of God, and to **h** the sick
Luke 9:11 ....**h**-ed them . . . need of
1 Cor. 12:9..gifts of **h** . . . same spirit
James 5:16 ..pray . . . that ye may be **h**-ed
Rev. 22:2......the **h**-ing of the nations

Heap

Gen. 31:46.....stones, and made an **h**
Ex. 15:8 ....floods . . . upright as an **h**
Deut. 32:23 ...**h** mischiefs upon them
Job 27:16.........though he **h** up silver
Ps. 39:6..................he **h**-eth up riches
Prov. 25:22 ....**h** coals of fire upon
Is. 25:2.................made of a city an **h**
2 Tim. 4:3 ..**h** to themselves teachers
James 5:3.............have **h**-ed treasure

Hear

Ex. 20:19.....Speak . . . and we will **h**
Deut. 6:4.......**H**, O Israel: the Lord is
1 Kin. 8:30 ....**h** thou in heaven
Job 27:9................Will God **h** his cry
Job 35:13 ....God will not **h** vanity
Ps. 4:1 ....**H** me when I call, O God
Ps. 65:2...........thou that **h**-est prayer
Ps. 135:17 ....ears, but they **h** not
Prov. 20:12..**h**-ing ear . . . seeing eye
Is. 28:14.........**h** the word of the Lord
Ezek. 37:4 ......dry bones, **h** the word
Matt. 10:27 .**h** in the ear, that preach
Matt. 11:15 ....ears to **h**, let him **h**
Matt. 13:13 ....**h**-ing they **h** not
Matt. 15:10 ....**H** and understand
Matt. 17:5.....I am well pleased; **h** ye him
Mark 4:24 ....Take heed what ye **h**
Mark 7:37............................the deaf to **h**
John 5:24......He that **h**-eth my word
John 6:60 ....who can **h** it
John 10:3..and the sheep **h** his voice
John 12:47.......any man **h** my words
Acts 7:37 ......like unto me; him . . . **h**
Acts 17:32 ....We will **h** thee again
Rom. 10:17 .....faith cometh by **h**-ing
Rom. 11:8.......................ears that they should not **h**
Heb. 5:11.seeing ye are dull of **h**-ing
James 1:19 ..every man be swift to **h**
Rev. 3:20..........if any man **h** my voice

Heard

Gen. 3:10...**h** thy voice in the garden
Ps. 10:17 .**h** the desire of the humble
Is. 65:19 ....voice of weeping . . . no more **h**
Jer. 31:15 ....voice was **h** in Ramah
Ezek. 1:24.**h** the noise of their wings
Matt. 6:7..**h** for their much speaking
Luke 1:13...................thy prayer is **h**
Acts 4:4 ..which **h** the word believed
Acts 19:10 .dwelt in Asia **h** the word
1 Cor. 2:9 ....Eye . . . not seen, nor ear **h**
2 Cor. 12:4 ......**h** unspeakable words
Eph. 1:13 ....ye **h** the word of truth
Phil. 4:9..learned, and received, and **h**
Rev. 10:4 .....I **h** a voice from heaven

Heart

Gen. 8:21......imagination of man's **h**
Ex. 4:21..................I will harden his **h**
Judg. 5:16........great searchings of **h**
Judg. 16:25.........their **h**-s were merry
1 Sam. 10:9.God gave him another **h**
1 Sam. 13:14 ..a man after his own **h**
1 Sam. 16:7 ....Lord looketh on the **h**
1 Kin. 3:9............an understanding **h**
1 Kin. 15:3 ....his **h** was not perfect
1 Chr. 28:9 ....serve him with a perfect **h**
2 Chr. 17:6............his **h** was lifted up
Job 23:16..........God maketh my **h** soft
Job 29:13 ....caused the widow's **h** to sing
Job 41:24 ....**h** is as firm as a stone
Ps. 4:7...............put gladness in my **h**
Ps. 9:1 ....O Lord, with my whole **h**
Ps. 12:2 ....and with a double **h**
Ps. 15:2 ...speaketh the truth in his **h**
Ps. 17:3 .....Thou hast proved mine **h**
Ps. 19:14 ....the meditation of my **h**
Ps. 22:14 ....my **h** is like wax
Ps. 27:3 ....my **h** shall not fear
Ps. 38:10 ....My **h** panteth
Ps. 44:21 ....knoweth the secrets of the **h**
Ps. 51:10........Create in me a clean **h**
Ps. 51:17......broken and a contrite **h**
Ps. 111:1.praise . . . with my whole **h**
Ps. 119:11.word have I hid in mine **h**
Prov. 4:23 ....keep thy **h** . . . all diligence
Prov. 12:20 ....Deceit is in the **h**
Prov. 16:5.........one that is proud in **h**
Prov. 17:22.merry **h** doeth good like
Prov. 23:7 .thinketh in his **h**, so is he
Prov. 23:26 .My son, give me thine **h**
Prov. 25:20 ....singeth songs to a heavy **h**
Eccles. 8:5 ..wise man's **h** discerneth
Eccles. 11:9 ....let thy **h** cheer thee
Is. 35:4.say to them . . . of a fearful **h**
Is. 47:10.......thou hast said in thine **h**
Jer. 11:20 ...triest the reins and the **h**
Jer. 17:9.........**h** is deceitful above all
Jer. 17:10....I, the Lord, search the **h**
Jer. 24:7.give them an **h** to know me
Ezek. 11:19 ......stony **h** . . . **h** of flesh
Ezek. 18:31 ....make you a new **h**
Ezek. 21:7 ....every **h** shall melt
Ezek. 44:7, 9 ....uncircumcised in **h**
Joel 2:13 ..rend your **h**, and not your
Mal. 4:6.......turn the **h** of the fathers
Matt. 5:8....Blessed are the pure in **h**
Matt. 6:21 ...treasure is . . . your **h** be
Matt. 11:29 ....meek and lowly in **h**
Matt. 12:34 ....abundance of the **h**
Matt. 15:8.........their **h** is far from me
Matt. 19:8...the hardness of your **h**-s
Mark 12:30 ....love the Lord . . . all thy **h**
Luke 2:19 ....pondered them in her **h**
Luke 2:51 ..all these sayings in her **h**
Luke 24:25 ....slow of **h** to believe all
John 14:1 ......not your **h** be troubled
Acts 2:37 ....pricked in their **h**
Acts 7:54 ....they were cut to the **h**
Rom. 8:27..he that searcheth the **h**-s
Rom. 10:10 ....with the **h** man believeth
2 Cor. 3:3 ....fleshy tables of the **h**
2 Cor. 6:11 ....our **h** is enlarged
2 Cor. 9:7..........he purposeth in his **h**
Eph. 3:17 ....Christ may dwell in your **h**-s
Eph. 5:19 ..making melody in your **h**
Eph. 6:5.........in singleness of your **h**
Phil. 4:7.....keep your **h**-s and minds
Col. 3:22 ....but in singleness of **h**
2 Thess. 3:5.......Lord direct your **h**-s
Heb. 4:12.....................intents of the **h**
Heb. 10:22 ...draw near with a true **h**
James 1:26 ....deceiveth his own **h**
2 Pet. 1:19.day star arise in your **h**-s

Heat

Gen. 8:22....cold and **h**, and summer
Gen. 18:1 ....in the **h** of the day
Deut. 29:24 ....**h** of this great anger
Eccles. 4:11........two lie together . . . have **h**
Matt. 20:12 .burden and **h** of the day
2 Pet. 3:10 ....melt with fervent **h**
Rev. 16:9 ....scorched with great **h**

Heathen

Lev. 26:33 ..scatter you among the **h**
Ps. 2:1...................Why do the **h** rage
Ps. 102:15 ...**h** shall fear . . . the Lord
Matt. 6:7 .....repetitions, as the **h** do
Acts 4:25............Why did the **h** rage
Gal. 1:16 ....preach him among the **h**

Heaven

Gen. 1:1 ....God created the **h**
Gen. 1:8.....God . . . the firmament **H**
Gen. 28:17...........this is the gate of **h**
Ex. 20:22 ......talked with you from **h**
Deut. 33:13 ....precious things of **h**

1 Kin. 8:27 ......the **h** and **h** of **h**-s . . . contain
Job 11:8 ....It is as high as **h**
Ps. 19:1.**h**-s declare the glory of God
Ps. 103:11..**h** is high above the earth
Eccles. 5:2........God is in **h**, and thou
Is. 14:12 ....art thou fallen from **h**
Is. 65:17 .....new **h**-s and a new earth
Jer. 7:18 ....cakes to the queen of **h**
Jer. 23:24.....Do I not fill **h** and earth
Ezek. 32:8 ..All the bright lights of **h**
Mal. 3:10 ....open you the windows of **h**
Matt. 5:3 ..theirs is the kingdom of **h**
Matt. 5:12..great is your reward in **h**
Matt. 6:9 ....Father which art in **h**
Matt. 6:14.your **h**-ly Father will also
Matt. 10:7 ...kingdom of **h** is at hand
Matt. 16:19 ....keys . . . kingdom of **h**
Mark 13:31....**H** and earth shall pass
Luke 10:20 ..your names are written in **h**
Luke 15:18.....have sinned against **h**
John 3:12......I tell you of **h**-ly things
John 3:13 ..Son of man which is in **h**
1 Cor. 15:47..........second man is . . . from **h**
2 Cor. 12:2...caught up to the third **h**
Gal. 1:8 ..or an angel from **h**, preach
Eph. 6:9 ....Master also is in **h**
Phil. 3:20.....our conversation is in **h**
Heb. 12:23 ....written in **h**
James 5:12...swear not, neither by **h**
Rev. 21:1 ....I saw a new **h**

Heel
Gen. 3:15 ....thou shalt bruise his **h**
Gen. 25:26 ......took hold on Esau's **h**
Gen. 49:17 ..that biteth the horse **h**-s
Ps. 41:9.....lifted up his **h** against me

Height
Job 22:12 ......God in the **h** of heaven
Rom. 8:39................Nor **h**, nor depth

Heir
Matt. 21:38 ....This is the **h**; come
Rom. 8:17 ....then **h**-s; **h**-s of God
Gal. 4:7.......**h** of God through Christ
James 2:5.....and **h**-s of the kingdom

Hell
Deut. 32:22 ...burn unto the lowest **h**
2 Sam. 22:6.sorrows of **h** compassed
Job 26:6 ....**H** is naked before him
Ps. 16:10.........not leave my soul in **h**
Ps. 86:13..my soul from the lowest **h**
Ps. 139:8..........if I make my bed in **h**
Prov. 5:5............steps take hold on **h**
Prov. 27:20 ....**H** and destruction
Ezek. 32:21....................speak to him out of . . . **h**
Amos 9:2 ......Though they dig into **h**
Jonah 2:2 ....out of the belly of **h**
Hab. 2:5 .....enlargeth his desire as **h**
Matt. 5:22 ....in danger of **h** fire
Matt. 10:28 ......destroy . . . body in **h**
Matt. 16:18.gates of **h** . . . not prevail
Matt. 23:15..............more the child of **h**
Luke 16:23.....in **h** he lift up his eyes
Acts 2:31..........soul was not left in **h**
James 3:6.tongue . . . set on fire of **h**
2 Pet. 2:4 ....cast them down to **h**
Rev. 1:18 ....have the keys of **h**

Helmet
1 Sam. 17:5....an **h** of brass upon his
Is. 59:17....................an **h** of salvation
Eph. 6:17 ....take the **h** of salvation

Help
Gen. 2:18..............an **h** meet for him
2 Chr. 20:9 ....thou wilt hear and **h**
Job 6:13 ....Is not my **h** in me
Ps. 33:20...........our **h** and our shield
Ps. 46:1......very present **h** in trouble
Ps. 121:1 .....hills . . . whence cometh my **h**
Is. 41:6..................**h**-ed every one his neighbour
Is. 41:13...........Fear not; I will **h** thee
Matt. 15:25.........................Lord **h** me
Mark 9:24 ....**h** thou mine unbelief
2 Cor. 1:11.**h**-ing together by prayer
Heb. 4:16..grace to **h** in time of need

Helper
Job 30:13 ....they have no **h**
Ps. 10:14 ....the **h** of the fatherless
Ps. 30:10.............Lord, be thou my **h**
Ps. 54:4..........................God is mine **h**
Rom. 16:3 ......my **h**-s in Christ Jesus
Heb. 13:6........................Lord is my **h**

Heritage
Ex. 6:8 ....give it you for an **h**
Ps. 16:6....................I have a goodly **h**
Ps. 127:3...children . . . **h** of the Lord
1 Pet. 5:3 ....lords over God's **h**

Hid
Gen. 3:8...........Adam and his wife **h**
Job 38:30 ....waters are **h** as with a
Ps. 69:5 ....sins are not **h** from thee
Is. 50:6 ....**h** not my face from shame
Matt. 13:44.........treasure **h** in a field
Matt. 25:25..**h** thy talent in the earth
Matt. 4:22 ....For there is nothing **h**
John 8:59...................Jesus **h** himself
1 Cor. 2:7 .....even the **h**-den wisdom
Col. 3:3.......your life is **h** with Christ

Hide
Gen. 18:17 ..Shall I **h** from Abraham
Job 14:13 ....**h** me in the grave
Job 20:12..........**h** it under his tongue
Ps. 27:5.........time of trouble . . . **h** me
Ps. 27:9 ..**H** not thy face far from me
Is. 2:10....................**h** thee in the dust
Is. 3:9 ....their sin . . . they **h** it not
Jer. 38:14 ....**h** nothing from me
James 5:20........**h** a multitude of sins

High
Job 11:8..............It is as **h** as heaven
Job 22:12...the stars, how **h** they are
Ps. 62:9......men of **h** degree are a lie
Ps. 91:14...............I will set him on **h**
Ps. 103:11 ....heaven is **h** above the
Prov. 24:7.Wisdom is too **h** for a fool
Mark 5:7........Son of the most **h** God
Mark 11:10 ......Hosanna in the **h**-est
Luke 2:14 ..Glory to God in the **h**-est
Rom. 12:16............Mind not **h** things
Phil. 3:14 ....prize of the **h** calling
Heb. 3:1............Apostle and **H** Priest

Hill
Gen. 49:26 ....of the everlasting **h**-s
Ps. 15:1 ....dwell in thy holy **h**
Ps. 24:3.Who shall ascend into the **h**
Ps. 50:10.cattle upon a thousand **h**-s
Ps. 121:1 ....lift up mine eyes unto the **h**-s
Is. 5:1....vineyard in a very fruitful **h**
Matt. 5:14.......city that is set on an **h**
Luke 4:29 ......unto the brow of the **h**

Hinder
Job 11:10....................who can **h** him
1 Cor. 9:12....we should **h** the gospel
Gal. 5:7................who did **h** you that ye
1 Thess. 2:18 ....but Satan **h**-ed us
1 Pet. 3:7 ...your prayers be not **h**-ed

Hire
Gen. 30:18.God hath given me my **h**
Mic. 3:11 ....priests . . . teach for **h**
Luke 10:7.............labourer is worthy of his **h**
Luke 15:19 ....as one of thy **h**-ed servants

Hold
Ex. 20:7 ....not **h** him guiltless
Judg. 18:19.......................**H** thy peace
Job 6:24.........and I will **h** my tongue
Job 27:6...........righteousness I **h** fast
Ps. 119:117.....................**H** thou me up
Prov. 4:13.Take fast **h** of instruction
Is. 41:13.....God will **h** thy right hand
Matt. 6:24............he will **h** to the one
Mark 7:8.........**h** the tradition of men
Phil. 2:16......**H**-ing forth the word of
1 Thess. 5:21.......**h** fast that which is good
1 Tim. 1:19.................**H**-ing faith . . .
1 Tim. 6:12 ....lay **h** on eternal life
Titus 1:9..........**H**-ing fast the faithful word

Hole
Is. 11:8 ....play on the **h** of the asp
Matt. 8:20....................foxes have **h**-s

Holiness
Ex. 15:11 ....like thee, glorious in **h**
Ex. 28:36............................**H** to the Lord
1 Chr. 16:29...........in the beauty of **h**
Ps. 29:2 ....in the beauty of **h**
Ps. 47:8.................the throne of his **h**
Ps. 93:5 ....**h** becometh thine house
Is. 35:8...........be called The way of **h**
Jer. 31:23 ....and mountain of **h**
Rom. 6:22.......have your fruit unto **h**
2 Cor. 7:1.......perfecting **h** in the fear
1 Thess. 3:13 .....hearts unblameable in **h**
1 Tim. 2:15.....faith . . . charity and **h**
Heb. 12:10 ....partakers of his **h**

Holy
Ex. 3:5........the place . . . is **h** ground
Ex. 20:8 .....sabbath day, to keep it **h**
Lev. 20:7 ..be ye **h**, for I am the Lord
Deut. 7:6 ....thou art an **h** people
1 Sam. 2:2 ....none **h** as the Lord
2 Kin. 4:9 .....this is an **h** man of God
1 Chr. 16:10..Glory ye in his **h** name
Ps. 11:4.........Lord is in his **h** temple
Ps. 16:10....suffer thine **H** One to see
Ps. 99:9 ....worship at his **h** hill
Ps. 145:21 ....bless his **h** name
Is. 6:3 ....**H**, **h**, **h**, is the Lord
Hab. 2:20.......Lord is in his **h** temple
Matt. 7:6 ......give not that which is **h**
Mark 6:20 ....a just man and an **h**
Luke 1:49 ....**h** is his name
Luke 4:34..............the **H** One of God
John 17:11..**H** Father, keep . . . thine own
Acts 2:27 ....thine **H** One
Rom. 12:1............a living sacrifice, **h**
Rom. 16:16 ....with an **h** kiss
1 Cor. 3:17 .....the temple of God is **h**
1 Cor. 7:34 ......**h** both in body and in spirit
Eph. 1:4.......be **h** and without blame
Col. 1:22..............**h** and unblameable
1 Tim. 2:8 ....lifting up **h** hands
2 Tim. 1:9 ....called us with an **h** calling
2 Tim. 3:15 ....hast known the **h** scriptures

Holy Ghost
Matt. 1:20............in her is of the **H G**
Matt. 3:11 .baptize you with the **H G**
Matt. 12:31..........................blasphemy against the **H G**
Luke 3:22....................**H G** descended
Luke 4:1 ....full of the **H G**
Luke 12:12.........**H G** shall teach you
John 14:26.....Comforter . . . the **H G**
John 20:22 ....Receive ye the **H G**
Acts 2:4..........all filled with the **H G**
Acts 2:38...............the gift of the **H G**
Acts 7:51....do always resist the **H G**
Acts 10:38 ..the **H G** and with power
Acts 19:2..Have ye received the **H G**
Rom. 9:1.............witness in the **H G**
1 Cor. 2:13 ..which the **H G** teacheth

Holy Spirit
Luke 11:13........give the **H S** to them
Eph. 1:13.............that **h S** of promise
Eph. 4:30..grieve not the **H S** of God
1 Thess. 4:8 ....given unto his **h S**

Honest
Luke 8:15 ....an **h** and good heart
Acts 6:3 ....seven men of **h** report
Rom. 12:17..**h** in the sight of all men
Rom. 13:13 ....Let us walk **h**-ly, as in
2 Cor. 8:21 .....Providing for **h** things
2 Cor. 13:7 ....do that which is **h**
Phil. 4:8 ......whatsoever things are **h**

Ill
Rom. 13:10...........Love worketh no i

Image
Gen. 1:26 ..Let us make man in our i
Gen. 9:6 ....i of God made he man
Ex. 20:4 ...not make . . . any graven i
Matt. 22:20........i and superscription
1 Cor. 11:7 .....the i and glory of God
Col. 1:15..........i of the invisible God

Imagination
Gen. 8:21 ....i of man's heart is evil
Deut. 31:21..............for I know their i
Jer. 3:17 ....i of their evil heart
Rom. 1:21....become vain in their i-s
2 Cor. 10:5 ....Casting down i-s

Imagine
Ps. 2:1.........the people i a vain thing
Ps. 21:11 ....i-d a mischievous device
Zech. 7:10..i evil against his brother
Acts 4:25 ....people i vain things

Immortality
1 Cor. 15:53 ......mortal must put on i
1 Tim. 6:16...........Whom only hath i
2 Tim. 1:10 ....brought life and i to

Impossible
Matt. 19:26 ....With men this is i
Luke 1:37 ....with God nothing shall be i
Heb. 6:18 ....it was i for God to lie
Heb. 11:6 ....without faith it is i to

Impute
2 Sam. 19:19 ....Let not my lord i iniquity
Rom. 4:6 .....God i-eth righteousness
Rom. 5:13 ....sin is not i-ed
2 Cor. 5:19.not i-ing their trespasses

Incline
Josh. 24:23 ....i your heart unto the Lord
Ps. 119:36 ....I my heart unto thy
Prov. 2:18..........her house i-eth unto death
Is. 37:17................I thine ear, O Lord

Incorruptible
1 Cor. 9:25.corruptible . . . but we an i
1 Cor. 15:52.....dead shall be raised i
1 Pet. 1:4 ....To an inheritance i

Increase
Deut. 14:22.....................tithe all the i
Ps. 62:10 .riches i, set not your heart
Ps. 67:6...............the earth yield her i
Eccles. 1:18....i-eth knowledge, i-eth
Luke 2:52.........Jesus i-ed in wisdom
1 Cor. 3:6.............but God gave the i
2 Cor. 10:15............your faith is i-ed
Col. 1:10 ...i-ing in the knowledge of God

Indignation
Ps. 69:24.Pour out thine i upon them
Is. 30:27 ....his lips are full of i
Jer. 15:17 ..thou hast filled me with i
Nah. 1:6..who can stand before his i
Matt. 20:24...........were moved with i
Luke 13:14 ....answered with i
Heb. 10:27....of judgment and fiery i

Infirmity
Matt. 8:17.........himself took our i-es
Luke 13:12 ....art loosed from thine i
John 5:5 ..an i thirty and eight years
Rom. 15:1 ..bear the i-es of the weak
2 Cor. 12:9....................I rather glory in mine i-es
Gal. 4:13 ....through i of the flesh
1 Tim. 5:23 ....and thine often i-es
Heb. 4:15 ....feeling of our i-es

Inherit
Gen. 15:7....give thee this land to i it
Ex. 32:13.............they shall i it for ever
Judg. 11:2 ....i in our father's house
Ps. 37:11 ....meek shall i the earth
Prov. 3:35 ....The wise shall i glory
Prov. 14:18 ....The simple i folly
Is. 54:3 ....shall i the Gentiles
Matt. 5:5 ...meek . . . shall i the earth
Matt. 19:29 .....shall i everlasting life
Matt. 25:34 .i the Kingdom prepared
Luke 10:25 ....do to i eternal life
1 Cor. 6:9 .....shall not i the kingdom
1 Cor. 15:50....................corruption i in corruption
Rev. 21:7.........overcometh shall i all things

Inheritance
Ex. 34:9.................take us for thine i
Deut. 4:20.......unto him a people of i
Ps. 2:8 ....give . . . heathen for thine i
Ps. 28:9 ....and bless thine i
Ps. 94:14........neither will he forsake his i
Prov. 13:22 ...man leaveth an i to his
Eccles. 7:11 .....Wisdom is good with an i
Mark 12:7.............the i shall be ours
Acts 7:5 ....he gave him none i
Eph. 1:11 ....In whom . . . we . . . obtained an i
1 Pet. 1:4 ....an i incorruptible

Iniquity
Lev. 16:22.......shall bear . . . all their i-es
Deut. 5:9.visiting the i of the fathers
Deut. 32:4...........a God . . . without i
Job 13:26........possess the i-es of my youth
Ps. 25:11 ....pardon mine i, for it is
Ps. 32:5............mine i have I not hid
Ps. 51:5 .I was shapen in i and in sin
Ps. 51:9 ....blot out all mine i-es
Prov. 22:8....that soweth i shall reap
Is. 1:4................a people laden with i
Is. 31:2........help of them that work i
Is. 53:5....he was bruised for our i-es
Jer. 31:30 ....shall die for his own i
Ezek. 18:30...i shall not be your ruin
Ezek. 33:8................shall die in his i
Matt. 24:12 ...because i shall abound
Luke 13:27 ....depart . . . all ye workers of i
1 Cor. 13:6......Rejoiceth not in i, but
Titus 2:14 ....redeem us from all i
James 3:6 ..tongue is . . . a world of i

Innocent
Ex. 23:7.............the i . . . slay thou not
Job 4:7....who ever perished, being i
Job 22:19.........i laugh them to scorn
Prov. 6:17 ....hands that shed i blood
Is. 59:7 ...make haste to shed i blood
Matt. 27:4.have betrayed the i blood
Matt. 27:24.......I am i of the blood of

Inquire
Gen. 25:22 ....went to i of the Lord
Ex. 18:15 ..come unto me to i of God
1 Sam. 17:56 ....I thou whose son
Ps. 78:34...............i-d early after God
Prov. 20:25....after vows to make i-y
Ezek. 14:3 .....should I be i-d of at all
Matt. 2:7.Herod . . . i-d . . . diligently
Luke 22:23 ....to i among themselves
Acts 19:39 ....but if ye i any thing
1 Pet. 1:10 ....the prophets have i-d

Instruct
Deut. 4:36...........that he might i thee
Neh. 9:20....thy good spirit to i them
Ps. 32:8...I will i thee and teach thee
Prov. 16:22 ....i-ion of fools is folly
Matt. 13:52 ....i-ed unto the kingdom
Rom. 2:18...being i-ed out of the law
1 Cor. 4:15.....ten thousand i-ers in Christ
2 Tim. 3:16 ....for i-ion in righteousness

Integrity
Gen. 20:5 ....i of my heart
Job 2:3...............he holdeth fast his i
Ps. 26:1 ....have walked in mine i
Prov. 19:1 .poor that walketh in his i
Prov. 20:7 ..just man walketh in his i

Intercession
Is. 53:12..........i for the transgressors
Rom. 8:26..Spirit . . . maketh i for us
1 Tim. 2:1.......prayers, i-s . . . thanks
Heb. 7:25 ....ever liveth to make i

Intreat
Ex. 8:8 ....I the Lord, that he may
Ruth 1:16 ....I me not to leave thee
1 Kin. 13:6 ....I now the face of the Lord
Ps. 45:12 ....shall i thy favour
1 Tim. 5:1.................i him as a father
James 3:17 ....and easy to be i-ed

Iron
Deut. 3:11 ....a bedstead of i
Judg. 1:19........they had chariots of i
2 Kin. 6:6 ....the i did swim
Job 19:24..........graven with an i pen
1 Tim. 4:2............seared with a hot i

J

Jealous
Ex. 20:5.....Lord thy God am a j God
Ex. 34:14 ....name is J, is a j God
Num. 5:14 .....spirit of j-y come upon
Josh. 24:19 ...holy God; he is a j God
1 Kin. 19:10..........very j for the Lord
Prov. 6:34.....j-y is the rage of a man
Song 8:6.......j-y is cruel as the grave
Nah. 1:2 ....God is j
Rom. 10:19......provoke you to j-y by them
2 Cor. 11:2 ....j . . . with godly j-y

Join
Is. 5:8....woe, unto them that j house
Matt. 19:6 ....what . . . God . . . j-ed together
1 Cor. 1:10.....perfectly j-ed together
1 Cor. 6:17.....he that is j-ed unto the Lord
Eph. 5:31 .shall be j-ed unto his wife

Joint
Ps. 22:14 ....my bones are out of j
Rom. 8:17......and j-heirs with Christ

Journey
Matt. 10:10 ....Nor scrip for your j
Mark 13:34 ....man taking a far j
Luke 9:3 ......Take nothing for your j
Luke 15:13 ....his j into a far country
Acts 1:12.................a sabbath day's j
2 Cor. 11:26.In j-ings, often, in perils

Joy
Ezra 3:12 ....shouted aloud for j
Job 29:13.widow's heart to sing for j
Job 33:26 .....shall see his face with j
Ps. 66:1...........Make a j-ful noise unto
Ps. 126:5 .sow in tears shall reap in j
Prov. 17:21.father of a fool hath no j
Eccles. 9:7..........eat thy bread with j
Is. 52:9....................Break forth into j
Joel 1:12 ....j is withered away
Matt. 25:21 ....enter thou into the j of
Luke 15:7...j shall be in heaven over
John 15:11 ..that your j might be full
Acts 20:24 ....finish my course with j
Rom. 14:17 ..and j in the Holy Ghost
Gal. 5:22..........Spirit is love, j, peace
Phil. 2:2 ....Fulfill ye my j
James 1:2 ..count it all j when ye fall
1 John 1:4......that your j may be full

Judge
Gen. 18:25.........the J of all the earth
Matt. 7:1...............J not . . . be not j-d
Matt. 7:2 ......judgment ye j . . . be j-d
John 7:24........j righteous judgments
John 7:51.............our law j any man
John 12:47 ...came not to j the world
Acts 10:42 ....J of quick and dead
Heb. 12:23 ....God the J of all

Judgment
Gen. 18:19 ....to do justice and j
Ex. 12:12........................I will execute j
Lev. 18:4 ....Ye shall do my j-s
Deut. 1:17 ....the j is God's
Deut. 16:19..............shalt not wrest j

L

Labour
Ex. 20:9............Six days shalt thou l
Job 9:29.............why then I l in vain
Ps. 127:1...they l in vain that build it
Ps. 128:2.......eat the l of thine hands
Prov. 14:23.......In all l there is profit
Prov. 23:4.................L not to be rich
Eccles. 2:22.......hath man of all his l
Eccles. 4:9....good reward for their l
Eccles. 5:12........sleep of a l-ing man
Matt. 11:28......Come . . . all ye that l
John 6:27 ..L not for the meat which
Rom. 16:12............who l in the Lord
1 Cor. 15:10..I l-ed more abundantly
1 Cor. 15:58........your l is not in vain
Gal. 4:11.........bestowed . . . l in vain
Eph. 4:28...rather let him l, working
Phil. 1:22..................the fruit of my l
1 Thess. 1:3....work of faith, and l of
Heb. 4:11.....l therefore to enter into

Lack
Prov. 28:27................poor shall not l
Matt. 19:20.......................what l I yet
Mark 10:21.........one thing thou l-est
1 Thess. 4:12..may have l of nothing
James 1:5......If any of you l wisdom

Laid
Luke 12:19.........l up for many years
John 11:34.......Where have ye l him
Acts 20:3............Jews l wait for him
2 Tim. 4:8...........l up for me a crown
1 John 3:16............he l down his life

Lamb
Gen. 22:8 .....God will provide . . . a l
Is. 40:11..........gather the l-s with his
Is. 53:7............as a l to the slaughter
Is. 65:25......wolf and the l shall feed
Luke 10:3..........send you forth as l-s
John 1:29..........Behold the L of God
John 21:15.......................Feed my l-s
Acts 8:32...........like a l dumb before
1 Pet. 1:19..........a l without blemish

Lamp
1 Sam. 3:3.............l of God went out
2 Sam. 22:29.............For thou art my l
Ps. 119:105........Thy word is a l unto
Matt. 25:8.....for our l-s are gone out

Land
Gen. 1:9...............let the dry l appear
Job 28:13...........in the l of the living
Ps. 37:29...righteous . . . inherit the l
Ps. 88:12..........the l of forgetfulness
Matt. 27:45....darkness over all the l
Acts 4:37...................Having l, sold it

Language
Gen. 11:1........whole earth was one l
Ps. 19:3.........There is no speech or l
Acts 2:6................speak in his own l

Last
Gen. 49:1......befall you in the l days
Is. 44:6.................first, and I am the l
Matt. 12:45..........l state of that man
Matt. 19:30...first . . . l, and the l . . . first
Luke 11:26...........l state of that man
John 6:39.......raise it . . . at the l day
1 Cor. 15:45.the l Adam was made a
1 Cor. 15:52....an eye, at the l trump
1 Pet. 1:5..........revealed in the l time
Rev. 1:17........I am the first and the l

Law
Josh. 1:8.......This book of the l shall
2 Kin. 22:8....found the book of the l
Ps. 19:7..........l of the Lord is perfect
Prov. 1:8........forsake not . . . l of thy mother
Prov. 28:7......keepeth the l is a wise
Prov. 29:18.......keepeth the l, happy
Matt. 5:17....not . . . come to destroy the l
Matt. 7:12.......the l and the prophets
John 7:51..........our l judge any man
John 19:7..a l, and by our l he ought
Rom. 2:14.....having not the l, are a l
Rom. 4:15..........the l worketh wrath
Rom. 13:10............Love . . . fulfilling of the l
1 Cor. 6:7....go to l one with another
Gal. 3:24.......l was our schoolmaster
Gal. 5:23....against such there is no l
Gal. 6:2..........so fulfill the l of Christ
Titus 3:9....avoid . . . strivings about the l
Heb. 7:19......l made nothing perfect
James 1:25.....the perfect l of liberty

Lay
Num. 12:11.......l not the sin upon us
Ps. 4:8.................l me down in peace
Prov. 10:14.................Wise men l up knowledge
Matt. 6:19.......L not up . . . treasures
John 10:15................I l down my life
Acts 7:60...........l not this sin to their
Heb. 6:2..................l-ing on of hands
1 Pet. 2:1..........l-ing aside all malice

Lead
Ps. 23:2.........l-eth me beside the still
Ps. 27:11............l me in a plain path
Ps. 25:5......................L me in thy truth
Is. 11:6........a little child shall l them
Matt. 6:13....l us not into temptation
Matt. 15:14.........the blind l the blind

Learn
Deut. 31:13............l to fear the Lord
Prov. 1:5...............will increase l-ing
Is. 1:17..............................L to do well
Is. 2:4............neither shall they l war
Matt. 11:29..............................l of me
Acts 26:24.much l-ing . . . make thee mad
Rom. 15:4.were written for our l-ing
Eph. 4:20........ye have so l-ed Christ
2 Tim. 3:7...........................Ever l-ing
Heb. 5:8..........Yet l-ed he obedience

Least
Matt. 5:19.of these l commandments
Matt. 5:19...........l in the kingdom of
Luke 16:10.faithful in that which is l
1 Cor. 15:9.I am the l of the apostles

Leave
Gen. 2:24...........man l his father . . . mother
Ruth 1:16......Intreat me not to l thee
Ps. 16:10............not l my soul in hell
Matt. 19:5...........l father and mother
John 14:27............Peace I l with you
John 16:28......................I l the world
Heb. 13:5........I will never l thee, nor

Leaven
Matt. 13:33.kingdom . . . is like unto l
Matt. 16:6..................beware of the l
Luke 13:21...........................It is like l
1 Cor. 5:6.............a little l leaveneth
1 Cor. 5:7..........Purge out . . . the old l

Leopard
Is. 11:6........l shall lie down with the
Jer. 13:23.......skin, or the l his spots
Hos. 13:7................as a l by the way
Rev. 13:2.................was like unto a l

Less
Gen. 1:16...........l-er light to rule the
Eph. 3:8.............I am l than the least

Liar
Job 24:25.........who will make me a l
John 8:55............be a l like unto you
Rom. 3:4.God be true . . . every man a l
1 John 5:10...God hath made him a l

Liberty
Lev. 25:10......proclaim l throughout
Ps. 119:45...........And I will walk at l
Is. 61:1......proclaim l to the captives
Luke 4:18.............set at l . . . bruised
Rom. 8:21..glorious l of the children
2 Cor. 3:17...of the Lord is, there is l
Gal. 2:4.......................to spy out our l
Gal. 5:13..ye have been called unto l
James 1:25...into the perfect law of l
1 Pet. 2:16....using your l for a cloak

Lie
Ps. 23:2......l down in green pastures
Eccles. 4:11.............if two l together
Acts 5:3..Satan filled thine heart to l
Rom. 1:25..........truth of God into a l
Col. 3:9.............L not one to another
1 Tim. 4:2 .speaking l-s in hypocrisy
Heb. 6:18......impossible for God to l

Life
Gen. 2:7.........nostrils the breath of l
Ex. 21:23..........thou shalt give l for l
Deut. 30:19........set before you l and death
Job 10:1.....My soul is weary of my l
Ps. 16:11..........shew me the path of l
Ps. 36:9.with thee is the fountain of l
Ps. 133:3............even l for evermore
Prov. 4:13...keep her, for she is thy l
Prov. 8:35...........findeth me findeth l
Jer. 21:8..set before you the way of l
Dan. 12:2..................awake, some to everlasting l
Matt. 6:25.take no thought for your l
Matt. 10:39 ..loseth his l for my sake
Matt. 16:25......save his l shall lose it
Matt. 19:16.that I may have eternal l
Matt. 20:28 .his l a ransom for many
Mark 8:35........save his l shall lose it
Mark 10:17.......may inherit eternal l
Luke 12:15.....man's l consisteth not
Luke 12:23.....the l is more than meat
Luke 18:30.......to come l everlasting
John 4:36..............fruit into l eternal
John 5:24..............from death unto l
John 6:35.............I am the bread of l
John 10:11.giveth his l for the sheep
John 11:25.....resurrection, and the l
John 12:25..........He that loveth his l
John 14:6.....way, the truth, and the l
John 15:13.......lay down his l for his
John 17:3.......................this is l eternal
John 20:31 .have l through his name
Acts 3:15...........killed the Prince of l
Rom. 6:4...........walk in newness of l
Rom. 6:23.......gift of God is eternal l
2 Cor. 3:6.........but the spirit giveth l
Gal. 6:8........Spirit reap l everlasting
Phil. 2:16........................the word of l
Phil. 4:3...names are in the book of l
Col. 3:4................Christ, who is our l
1 Tim. 2:2.....a quiet and peaceable l
Titus 3:7...................hope of eternal l
James 1:12.....receive the crown of l
1 John 1:1.................of the Word of l
1 John 5:12 .that hath the Son hath l
Rev. 2:10.........give thee a crown of l
Rev. 13:8......written in the book of l

Lift
Gen. 13:14.........L up now thine eyes
Ps. 24:7.L up your heads, O ye gates
Ps. 121:1......l up mine eyes unto the hills
Is. 2:4............not l up sword against
Luke 18:13 .l up so much as his eyes
John 3:14.......Son of man be l-ed up
1 Tim. 3:6...being l-ed up with pride
James 4:10.......and he shall l you up

Light
Gen. 1:3.........Let there be l . . . was l
Ps. 4:6......l of thy countenance upon
Ps. 27:1..........my l and my salvation
Ps. 119:105.............a l unto my path
Prov. 4:18..........path . . . as shining l
Is. 2:5....................let us walk in the l
Is. 8:20...............there is no l in them
Is. 60:1.........Arise, shine; for thy l is
Jer. 31:35....giveth the sun for a l by
Mic. 7:9..........bring me forth to the l
Matt. 5:14...Ye are the l of the world
Matt. 5:15.Neither do men l a candle
Matt. 6:22......l of the body is the eye
Matt. 11:30.................my burden is l

Luke 2:32 ....l to lighten the Gentiles
Luke 16:8 ....the children of l
John 1:7........to bear witness of the l
John 1:9 ....That was the true L
John 8:12.......I am the l of the world
John 12:35.Walk while ye have the l
1 Cor. 4:5 ....bring to l the hidden
2 Cor. 4:4......l of the glorious gospel
Eph. 5:8 ....walk as children of l
1 John 1:7 ..if we walk in the l, as he

Likeness
Gen. 1:26 ....in our image, after our l
Ex. 20:4 .or any l of any thing that is
Deut. 4:16............l of male or female
Rom. 8:3.....................l of sinful flesh
Phil. 2:7 ....made in the l of men

Lily
Song 2:1 ....the l of the valleys
Hos. 14:5 ....he shall grow as the l
Matt. 6:28 ....Consider the l-es

Lion
Gen. 49:9............Judah is a l's whelp
1 Sam. 17:37 ..out of the paw of the l
Prov. 28:1 ....are bold as a l
Eccles. 9:4.........living dog . . . dead l
1 Pet. 5:8 ......the devil, as a roaring l
Rev. 9:8...................as the teeth of l-s

Lips
Ex. 6:12 ....of uncircumcised l
Ps. 31:18.......lying l be put to silence
Ps. 51:15.....................open thou my l
Is. 6:5.....................a man of unclean l
Is. 28:11 ....with stammering l
Matt. 15:8.honoureth me with their l
Rom. 13:3 ....poison . . . under their l
1 Pet. 3:10.l that they speak no guile

Little
Ps. 8:5 ....l lower than the angels
Ps. 37:16.........l that a righteous man
Prov. 6:10......l sleep, a l slumber, a l
Prov. 15:16 ....l with fear of the Lord
Prov. 16:8 ....Better is a l with
Is. 11:6............l child shall lead them
Is. 28:10...........here a l, and there a l
Matt. 6:30....................O ye of l faith
Matt. 18:3 ....become as l children
Luke 7:47 ....l is forgiven . . . loveth l
Luke 12:32 ....Fear not, l flock
Luke 18:16 ....Suffer l children to
John 7:33......Yet a l while am I with
Heb. 2:7.....a l lower than the angels
James 3:5.........tongue is a l member

Live
Gen. 3:22 ....eat, and l forever
Gen. 42:18....................This do, and l
Deut. 8:3.............not l by bread only
Job 7:16.............I would not l always
Job 19:25 ....my redeemer l-eth
Ps. 119:175 ....Let my soul l
Is. 55:3.....hear, and your soul shall l
Hab. 2:4 ....just shall l by his faith
Matt. 4:4 ....not l by bread alone
Luke 10:28 ..this do, and thou shalt l
Luke 20:38..............for all l unto him
John 11:25 .were dead, yet shall he l
Rom. 1:17 ....just shall l by faith
Rom. 8:12 ....to l after the flesh
Rom. 14:8....we l, we l unto the Lord
2 Cor. 5:15.not . . . l unto themselves
Phil. 1:21 ....to me to l is Christ
James 4:15 ..the Lord will, we shall l

Living
Gen. 2:7 ....man became a l soul
Deut. 5:26.............voice of the l God
Job 28:13..............in the land of the l
Dan. 6:26.....................he is the l God
Matt. 16:16..................Son of the l God
John 4:10.....have given thee l water
John 6:51..................I am the l bread
John 7:38.................rivers of l water
Rom. 12:1 ....bodies a l sacrifice
1 Cor. 15:45 ....Adam was made a l soul
2 Cor. 6:16 ....temple of the l God
Titus 3:3 ....l in malice and envy
Rev. 7:17..unto l fountains of waters

Loaves
Matt. 14:17 ....five l, and two fishes
Mark 6:52............the miracle of the l

Locust
Ex. 10:13 ...east wind brought the l-s
Prov. 30:27 ....The l-s have no king
Matt. 3:4 ....his meat was l-s

Lodge
Ruth 1:16 ....thou l-est, I will l
1 Tim. 5:10................if she have l-ed strangers

Loins
Eph. 6:14 ....l girt about with truth
1 Pet. 1:13gird up the l of your mind

Long
Job 3:21 ....Which l for death
Ps. 84:2 ....soul l-eth, yea, even
Prov. 3:2 ....l life, and peace shall
Matt. 23:14 ..pretence make l prayer
1 Cor. 11:14........if a man have l hair
Eph. 6:3 ....live l on the earth
Rev. 6:10 ....How l, O Lord

Longsuffering
Num. 14:18.....Lord is l, and of great
Ps. 86:15 ....l, and plenteous
2 Cor. 6:6 ....by l, by kindness
2 Tim. 4:2 ....all l and doctrine

Look
Gen. 19:17 ....l not behind thee
Ex. 3:2 ....l-ed . . . the bush burned
Ex. 3:6 ....afraid to l upon God
2 Sam. 11:2 ....beautiful to l upon
Esther 1:11..........she was fair to l on
Job 30:26........I l-ed for good . . . evil
Job 35:5..............L unto the heavens
Prov. 6:17 .....proud l, a lying tongue
Prov. 23:31..........L not thou upon
Eccles. 12:3 ......l out of the windows
Song 1:6.......................L not upon me
Is. 22:4 ....L away from me
Matt. 11:3...........do we l for another
Matt. 14:19 .....l-ing up to heaven, he
Luke 2:38 ...that l-ed for redemption
Luke 9:62 ......plough, and l-ing back
John 4:35 ....l on the fields
John 7:52 ....Search, and l: for out of
Acts 6:3 ....l ye out . . . seven men
Phil. 2:4 ....L not every man
Phil. 3:20............we l for the Saviour
2 Pet. 3:13 ....l for new heavens
Rev. 14:1 ....I l-ed, and, lo, a Lamb

Loose
Deut. 25:9.......l his shoe from off his
Ps. 116:16...thou hast l-ed my bonds
Eccles. 12:6 ....the silver cord be l-ed
Matt. 16:19 ....l on earth . . . l-ed in
Luke 19:30..colt . . . l him, and bring
Acts 2:24 ....l-ed the pains of death

Lord
Gen. 2:4..........L God made the earth
Gen. 4:1......gotten a man from the L
Gen. 21:1 ....L visited Sarah
Deut. 4:35 ....that the L he is God
Deut. 6:4....................L our God is one L
Deut. 10:17........L of l-s, a great God
Josh. 3:5..........................L will do wonders
Ruth 2:4 ....L be with you . . . L bless
1 Sam. 3:18 ....it is the L: let him do
Ps. 8:1........O L our L, how excellent
Ps. 23:1 ....the L is my shepherd
Ps. 100:3 ....Know ye that the L he is
Ps. 110:1 .....said unto my L, Sit thou
Ps. 123:3...Have mercy upon us, O L
Ezek. 13:9know that I am the L God
Matt. 7:21 ....one that saith . . . L, L
Mark 9:24.......L, I believe; help thou
Mark 12:29..........L our God is one L
Luke 4:18.Spirit of the L is upon me
Luke 22:33 ....L, I am ready to go
John 13:13.Ye call me Master and L
John 20:13....have taken away my L
John 20:28............My L and my God
Acts 2:36...........crucified, both L and
Acts 8:24 ....Pray ye to the L
Rom. 10:9 .....confess . . . the L Jesus
2 Cor. 13:14.......grace of the L Jesus
Eph. 4:5 ....One L, one faith, one
Eph. 5:17.....what the will of the L is
Phil. 2:11 .... Christ is L
Col. 3:24.....for ye serve the L Christ
Heb. 12:5.......the chastening of the L
Rev. 1:10..........Spirit of the L's day
Rev. 4:8........Holy, holy, holy, L God
Rev. 22:20....Even so, come, L Jesus

Lose
Eccles. 3:6 ....time to get . . . time to l
Matt. 16:25 ....save his life shall l it
Matt. 16:25 ....l his life for my sake
Mark 9:41........shall not l his reward

Lost
Lev. 6:3.........found that which was l
Ps. 119:176 ....astray like a l sheep
Matt. 5:13 ....salt have l his savour
Matt. 18:11 .....save that which was l
Luke 15:24 .....he was l, and is found

Lot
Lev. 16:8 ....other l for the scapegoat
Ps. 22:18.....cast l-s upon my vesture
Prov. 1:14......Cast in thy l among us
Jonah 1:7..........the l fell upon Jonah
Luke 17:32 ....Remember L's wife
John 19:24 ....not rend it, but cast l-s
Acts 1:26......the l fell upon Matthias
Acts 8:21.....neither part nor l in this

Love
Gen. 29:20 ....the l he had to her
Deut. 6:5.l the Lord thy God with all
Ps. 31:23 ....O l the Lord, all ye his
Prov. 3:12 ...Lord l-eth he correcteth
Prov. 8:17 ....I l them that l me
Prov. 12:1 ....l-eth instruction l-eth
Prov. 17:17..........A friend l-eth at all
Eccles. 3:8 .....A time to l, and a time
Amos 5:15.....Hate the evil, and l the
Zech. 8:17...................l no false oath
Matt. 5:44...................L your enemies
Matt. 6:24 ......hate the one, and l the
Matt. 22:39.....l thy neighbour as thy
Luke 6:27 ....L your enemies
John 3:16 ....God so l-ed the world
John 13:35.......have l one to another
John 15:13......greater l hath no man
2 Cor. 9:7 .God l-eth a cheerful giver
Eph. 5:2.......And walk in l, as Christ
Col. 3:19 ......Husbands, l your wives
1 Tim. 6:10......l of money is the root
Titus 2:4....................l their husbands
Heb. 13:1.....Let brotherly l continue
1 John 4:7...........let us l one another
Jude 21 ....Keep . . . in the l of God
Rev. 2:4 ....thou hast left thy first l

Low
1 Sam. 2:7..bringeth l, and lifteth up
Job 40:12..proud . . . and bring him l
Matt. 11:29......I am meek and l-ly in
Rom. 12:16...condescend to men of l
Phil. 2:3..................in l-liness of mind

Lucre
1 Sam. 8:3 ....turned aside after l
1 Tim. 3:3 ....not greedy of filthy l

Lump
1 Cor. 5:6.......Leaveneth the whole l
1 Cor. 5:7 ......that ye may be a new l

Lust
Matt. 5:28...looketh on a woman to l
Mark 4:19.............l-s of other things
1 John 2:16..l of the flesh . . . l of the
Jude 16...walking after their own l-s

Lying
Ps. 119:163............I hate and abhor l
Prov. 12:22 ...L lips are abomination
Eph. 4:25.....................putting away l

M

Made
Gen. 1:7 ....God m the firmament
Ex. 4:11 ...Who hath m man's mouth
Job 17:6.......................m me a byword

Ps. 8:5 ....**m** him a little lower
Ps. 119:73 ......Thy hands have **m** me
Prov. 20:9.....have **m** my heart clean
Eccles. 7:29..............God hath **m** man
Matt. 9:22 ...faith hath **m** thee whole
John 1:3 ...All things were **m** by him
John 5:6.........Wilt thou be **m** whole
2 Cor. 5:21......**m** him to be sin for us
Eph. 3:7 ....Whereof I was **m**
Heb. 6:4 ......**m** partakers of the Holy

Magnify
Job 7:17 ....man . . . shouldest **m** him
Ps. 34:3...........O **m** the Lord with me
Is. 42:21 ....he will **m** the law
Luke 1:46..My soul doth **m** the Lord
Phil. 1:20.........Christ . . . **m**-ed in my
Acts 19:17................Jesus was **m**-ed

Maid
Ex. 22:16.............if a man entice a **m**
Prov. 30:19...way of a man with a **m**
Jer. 2:32 ......**m** forget her ornaments
Luke 8:54 ....saying, **M** arise

Maiden
Judg. 19:24.here is my daughter a **m**
Job 41:5............bind him for thy **m**-s

Majesty
Ps. 93:1..............he is clothed with **m**
Heb. 1:3 ....right hand of the **m**
Jude 25..glory and **m**, dominion and

Make
Gen. 1:26...........Let us **m** man in our
Gen. 2:18.....**m** him an help meet for
Ex. 20:4.......**m** unto thee any graven
Ex. 20:25 ....**m** me an altar of stone
Eccles. 12:12 ....**m**-ing many books
Matt. 3:3 ....**m** his paths straight
Matt. 4:19 ....**m** you fishers of men
Luke 11:39.....**m** clean the outside of
Luke 19:5 ..Zacchaeus, **m** haste, and
John 1:23..**M** straight the way of the
Heb. 13:21 ....**M** you perfect in every

Maker
Job 35:10...........Where is God my **m**
Is. 17:7 ....man look to his **M**
Is. 54:5..........thy **M** is thine husband
Heb. 11:10 ....builder and **m** is God

Male
Gen. 5:2.....**M** and female created he
Gen. 34:25 ....and slew all the **m**-s
Matt. 19:4.made them **m** and female
Gal. 3:28 ....neither **m** nor female

Malice
Eph. 4:31...........from you, with all **m**
Col. 3:8 ....anger, wrath, **m**
1 Pet. 2:1................laying aside all **m**

Man
Gen. 1:26 ....Let us make **m**
Gen. 3:22...**m** is become as one of us
1 Sam. 16:17 ....Provide me now a **m**
2 Kin. 5:8 ....Elisha the **m** of God
Job 5:7....Yet **m** is born unto trouble
Job 14:1..**M** that is born of a woman
Job 33:12........God is greater than **m**
Ps. 1:1.Blessed is the **m** that walketh
Ps. 37:37 ....Mark the perfect **m**
Prov. 3:4...in the sight of God and **m**
Eccles. 12:13 .....the whole duty of **m**
Matt. 4:4....**M** shall not live by bread
Matt. 6:24 ....No **m** can serve two
Matt. 8:20..Son of **m** hath not where
Matt. 26:2 ..the Son of **m** is betrayed
Mark 2:27.......not **m** for the sabbath
Mark 10:25.........for a rich **m** to enter
Luke 6:45......a good **m** . . . an evil **m**
John 1:6..............a **m** sent from God
John 3:4How can a **m** be born when
John 19:5 ....Behold the **m**
Rom. 13:8 ....Owe no **m** anything
1 Cor. 15:21............by **m** came death
2 Cor. 12:2........I knew a **m** in Christ
Gal. 6:4 ....every **m** prove his own
Col. 3:9 ....put off the old **m**
James 1:8...........double minded **m** is
1 John 2:1.........................if any **m** sin

Manifest
John 9:3...works of God . . . made **m**
John 17:6 ....**m**-ed thy name
Rom. 8:19.......**m**-ation of the sons of
Rom. 10:20......................I was made **m**
Col. 1:26..............but now is made **m**
1 Tim. 3:16 ...God was **m** in the flesh

Manifold
Neh. 9:27.............according to thy **m**
Ps. 104:24........how **m** are thy works
Eph. 3:10 ....**m** wisdom of God

Manner
Matt. 5:11....say all **m** of evil against
Matt. 6:9......After this **m** . . . pray ye
1 Cor. 15:33............corrupt good **m**-s
Gal. 3:15 ...speak after the **m** of men

Mantle
1 Kin. 19:19.......cast his **m** upon him
Job 1:20 ....arose and rent his **m**

Many
Gen. 37:3................coat of **m** colours
1 Kin. 11:1 ....Solomon loved **m**
Job 13:23 ....**m** are my iniquities
Prov. 14:20...the rich hath **m** friends
Song 8:7 ....**M** waters cannot quench
Jer. 14:7........our backslidings are **m**
Matt. 7:22....**M** will say to me in that
Matt. 22:14 ......**m** are called, but few
Luke 7:47.......Her sins, which are **m**
Luke 21:8.**m** shall come in my name
John 14:2..................are **m** mansions
Acts 2:43 ....**m** wonders and signs
Rom. 12:4...**m** members in one body

Mark
Gen. 4:15.....Lord set a **m** upon Cain
Ps. 37:37...............**M** the perfect man
Phil. 3:14.............press toward the **m**
Rev. 14:9..........his **m** in his forehead
Rev. 19:20....................**m** of the beast

Marriage
Ex. 21:10 ....and her duty of **m**
Matt. 22:30............nor are given in **m**
John 2:1 ....there was a **m** in Cana
Heb. 13:4........**M** is honourable in all
Rev. 19:7.....................**m** of the Lamb

Marry
Matt. 5:32.......**m** her that is divorced
Matt. 19:9.....**m** another, committeth
Mark 12:25 ..they neither **m**, nor are
1 Cor. 7:9....better to **m** than to burn
1 Tim. 5:11 ....younger women **m**

Marvel
Ex. 34:10.........................I will do **m**-s
Matt. 8:10....Jesus heard it, he **m**-led
Luke 1:63......John . . . they **m**-led all
John 3:7 .**M** not that I said unto thee

Master
Job 3:19 ...servant is free from his **m**
Jonah 1:6.......So the ship-**m** came to
Matt. 6:24 ....can serve two **m**-s
Matt. 8:19..........**M**, I will follow thee
Matt. 17:24.......Doth not your **m** pay
Matt. 23:8...........one is your **M**, even
Matt. 26:25............................**M**, is it I
Mark 9:5.......**M**, it is good to be here
John 13:13....Ye call me **M** and Lord
Eph. 6:5....to them that are your **m**-s
James 3:1 ....be not many **m**-s

Matter
Gen. 30:15 ....Is it a small **m**
Ex. 23:7 .Keep . . . far from a false **m**
Job 19:28..the root of the **m** is found
Prov. 16:20........handleth a **m** wisely
Mark 1:45 ....blaze abroad the **m**
1 Cor. 6:2 ..to judge the smallest **m**-s

Mean
Josh. 4:21.........What **m** these stones
Prov. 22:29 .not stand before **m** men
Matt. 9:13 ....learn what that **m**-eth
Acts 17:20 ....what these things **m**
1 Cor. 14:11 ....not the **m**-ing of the

Means
Ex. 34:7.......by no **m** clear the guilty

Matt. 5:26 ....shalt by no **m** come out
1 Cor. 8:9 ..lest by any **m** this liberty

Measure
Gen. 18:6........three **m**-s of fine meal
Deut. 25:15 ....just **m** shalt thou have
2 Kin. 7:1 .**m** of fine flour be sold for
Ps. 80:5 ......tears to drink in great **m**
Matt. 7:2...and with what **m** ye mete
Matt. 13:33 .hid in three **m**-s of meal
2 Cor. 11:23..........in stripes above **m**
Rev. 21:16 ......**m**-ed the city with the reed

Meat
Gen. 1:29 ....it shall be for **m**
Gen. 27:4...........make me savoury **m**
Ps. 69:21gave me also gall for my **m**
Ps. 145:15.................**m** in due season
Matt. 3:4 ......**m** was locusts and wild
Matt. 6:25 ....the life more than **m**
Matt. 25:35 ....and ye gave me **m**
Luke 12:42..........portion of **m** in due
Luke 24:41 ....have ye here any **m**
John 4:34 ...My **m** is to do the will of
John 6:55...For my flesh is **m** indeed
1 Cor. 6:13...............**M**-s for the belly

Meddle
2 Chr. 25:19 ....**m** to thine hurt
2 Chr. 35:21 ....**m**-ing with God
Prov. 20:3 ...every fool will be **m**-ing

Mediator
Gal. 3:19 ....in the hand of a **m**
1 Tim. 2:5..**m** between God and men
Heb. 8:6.........**m** of a better covenant
Heb. 12:24........Jesus the **m** of a new

Meditate
Gen. 24:63..........Isaac went out to **m**
Ps. 1:2 .law doth he **m** day and night
Ps. 19:14 ....**m**-ion of my heart
1 Tim. 4:15........**M** upon these things

Meek
Num. 12:3....man Moses was very **m**
Ps. 37:11.....**m** shall inherit the earth
Ps. 147:6...........Lord lifteth up the **m**
Matt. 5:5 ....Blessed are the **m**
Matt. 11:29 ......for I am **m** and lowly
Matt. 21:5......**m**, and sitting upon an
1 Cor. 4:21......in the spirit of **m**-ness
Gal. 5:23............**M**-ness, temperance
Eph. 4:2...........lowliness and **m**-ness
1 Tim. 6:11.....love, patience, **m**-ness
1 Pet. 3:4 ....a **m** and quiet spirit

Melody
Is. 23:16...make sweet **m**, sing many
Is. 51:3..................and the voice of **m**
Eph. 5:19.....making **m** in your heart

Melt
Josh. 2:11 ....our hearts did **m**
Judg. 5:5.........mountains **m**-ed from
Ps. 97:5................hills **m**-ed like wax
Is. 64:2 ....the **m**-ing fire burneth

Member
Matt. 5:29 ..one of thy **m**-s . . . perish
1 Cor. 6:15 ....the **m**-s of Christ
1 Cor. 12:12 ....hath many **m**-s
1 Cor. 12:14 ....body is not one **m**
James 3:5 ......the tongue is a little **m**

Memorial
Ex. 3:15 ....**m** unto all generations
Ex. 17:14........Write this for a **m** in a
Josh. 4:7........stones shall be for a **m**
Matt. 26:13 ....told for a **m** of her
Acts 10:4 ....thine alms . . . for a **m**

Men
Gen. 6:1 ....**m** began to multiply
1 Sam. 4:9......quit yourselves like **m**
Job 11:3.........lies make **m** hold their
Job 32:9.......Great **m** are not always
Ps. 82:7 ....But ye shall die like **m**
Is. 46:8 ....and shew yourselves **m**
Matt. 10:17.......................beware of **m**
Mark 1:17 ....become fishers of **m**
Luke 20:4 ....from heaven, or of **m**
Rom. 6:19.......after the manner of **m**

1 Thess. 2:4....not as pleasing **m**, but
Jude 16..........having **m**'s persons in

Mention
Ps. 71:16....................make **m** of thy
Is. 63:7..**m** the lovingkindness of the
Rom. 1:9.**m** of you . . . in my prayers

Merchant
Gen. 23:16 ....money with the **m**
1 Kin. 10:28 ...**m**-s received the linen
Hos. 12:7......He is a **m**, the balances
Rev. 18:3............**m**-s of the earth are

Merciful
Ex. 34:6...Lord God, **m** and gracious
2 Sam. 22:26 ......wilt shew thyself **m**
Ps. 67:1.God be **m** unto us, and bless
Prov. 11:17...The **m** man doeth good
Matt. 5:7................Blessed are the **m**
Luke 18:13.........be **m** to me a sinner

Mercy
Ex. 33:19 .**m** on whom I will shew **m**
2 Sam. 24:14.....for his **m**-s are great
Ezra 3:11.....his **m** endureth for ever
Ps. 6:2.......Have **m** upon me, O Lord
Ps. 89:1 ....I will sing of thy **m**-s
Matt. 5:7 ....for they shall obtain **m**
Rom. 12:1.............by the **m**-s of God
Eph. 2:4..........God, who is rich in **m**

Merry
Judg. 16:25 ....their hearts were **m**
Prov. 15:15 ....**m** heart hath a
Prov. 17:22 .**m** heart doeth good like
Eccles. 8:15.....eat . . . drink . . . be **m**
Luke 12:19 ....eat, drink, and be **m**
Luke 15:29.make **m** with my friends
James 5:13 ....Is any man **m**

Messenger
2 Kin. 6:32 .**m** cometh, shut the door
Matt. 11:10......my **m** before thy face
2 Cor. 12:7.................the **m** of Satan

Midnight
Ruth 3:8............it came to pass at **m**
Ps. 119:62 ....At **m** I will arise to give
Matt. 25:6 ....at **m** there was a cry
Acts 16:25..........at **m** Paul and Silas

Midst
Gen. 1:6..........in the **m** of the waters
Prov. 30:19 ..ship in the **m** of the sea
Matt. 10:16.sheep in the **m** of wolves
Matt. 18:20 .....there am I in the **m** of
Luke 24:36..Jesus . . . stood in the **m**
John 20:26.in the **m**, and said, Peace

Might
Gen. 49:3 ....my firstborn, my **m**
Deut. 6:5..............and with all thy **m**
Judg. 5:31 ....goeth forth in his **m**
Judg. 6:14................Go in this thy **m**
Is. 40:29........to them that have no **m**
Zech. 4:6.....Not by **m**, nor by power
Col. 1:29...........worketh in me **m**-ily

Mighty
Gen. 10:9..**m** hunter before the Lord
Deut. 10:17..a great God, a **m**, and a
2 Sam. 1:19 ......how are the **m** fallen
Ps. 24:8.....strong and **m**, **m** in battle
Ps. 89:13.............Thou hast a **m** arm
Is. 63:1 ....**m** to save
Jer. 32:18.........the Great, the **M** God
Mark 6:5..could there do no **m** work
Luke 9:43 ....the **m** power of God
Luke 24:19....prophet **m** in deed and
Acts 18:24...........**m** in the scriptures
2 Cor. 13:3.................but is **m** in you
Eph. 1:19 ....working of his **m** power
1 Pet. 5:6.............the **m** hand of God

Milk
Gen. 49:12 ....teeth white with **m**
Ex. 3:8........land flowing with **m** and
Judg. 4:19..she opened a bottle of **m**
Job 10:10 ....poured me out as **m**
Prov. 30:33 ..churning of **m** bringeth
1 Cor. 3:2 ....have fed you with **m**
Heb. 5:12 .....such as have need of **m**
1 Pet. 2:2..the sincere **m** of the word

Mind
Lev. 24:12.....................**m** of the Lord
Ps. 31:12 ......as a dead man out of **m**
Prov. 29:11 .....fool uttereth all his **m**
Is. 46:8.................bring it again to **m**
Hab. 1:11 ...Then shall his **m** change
Mark 5:15.............and in his right **m**
Acts 28:6..............changed their **m**-s
Rom. 1:28 ....over to a reprobate **m**
Rom. 8:7.carnal **m** is enmity against
1 Cor. 1:10 .joined . . . in the same **m**
2 Cor. 8:12.there be first a willing **m**
2 Cor. 13:11 ....be of one **m**, live in
Phil. 2:2.............one accord, of one **m**
Phil. 2:3....in lowliness of **m** let each
1 Tim. 6:5............men of corrupt **m**-s
James 1:8...........A double **m**-ed man
1 Pet. 3:8...............be ye all of one **m**

Minister
Ezra 7:24 ...**m**-s of this house of God
Is. 61:6 ..call you the **M**-s of our God
Matt. 20:26 ....let him be your **m**
Luke 1:2 ....and **m**-s of the word
2 Cor. 11:23...Are they **m**-s of Christ
Eph. 3:7.....Whereof I was made a **m**
1 Tim. 4:6.........be a good **m** of Jesus

Ministry
Hos. 12:10 ....**m** of the prophets
Acts 6:4.............to the **m** of the word
2 Cor. 5:18...........**m** of reconciliation
Eph. 4:12.........for the work of the **m**
Col. 4:17............Take heed to the **m**
2 Tim. 4:5...make full proof of thy **m**
Heb. 8:6..............a more excellent **m**

Miracle
John 2:11 ....beginning of **m**-s did
John 10:41 ....John did no **m**
John 11:47.......man doeth many **m**-s
Acts 15:12.......**m**-s and wonders God
1 Cor. 12:10 ....the working of **m**-s

Mischief
Job 15:35 ....They conceive **m**
Ps. 52:2......Thy tongue deviseth **m**-s
Prov. 6:18........swift in running to **m**
Prov. 24:16..wicked shall fall into **m**
Acts 13:10 ....all subtilty and all **m**

Misery
Job 3:20 ..light given to him . . . in **m**
Prov. 31:7.remember his **m** no more
Eccles. 8:6 ....**m** of man is great
Rom. 3:16....and **m** are in their ways

Mock
2 Kin. 2:23......children . . . **m**-ed him
Prov. 14:9.......Fools make a **m** at sin
Prov. 20:1 ....Wine is a **m**-er
Matt. 27:29......before him, and **m**-ed
Gal. 6:7 ....God is not **m**-ed

Moment
Num. 16:21 .....consume them in a **m**
Job 34:20 ....In a **m** shall they die
Ps. 30:5..his anger endureth but a **m**
1 Cor. 15:52....**m**, in the twinkling of

Money
2 Kin. 5:26...Is it a time to receive **m**
Eccles. 7:12.................**m** is a defence
Eccles. 10:19...........**m** answereth all
Jer. 32:25.....Buy thee the field for **m**
Matt. 21:12..............the **m**-changers
Matt. 22:19....shew me the tribute **m**
Mark 6:8 ....no **m** in their purse
Luke 19:23 ....my **m** into the bank
Acts 8:20......Thy **m** perish with thee

Moon
Gen. 37:9.......**m** and the eleven stars
Josh. 10:12..thou, **M**, in the valley of
Job 31:26....**m** walking in brightness
Ps. 136:9.........**m** and stars to rule by
Is. 1:13 ....new **m**-s and sabbaths
Joel 2:31...........and the **m** into blood
Matt. 24:29 ....**m** shall not give her
Luke 21:25.....signs in the sun . . . **m**
Acts 2:20 ....and the **m** into blood

Morning
Ex. 8:20..........Rise up early in the **m**
Job 38:7 ....**m** stars sang together
Ps. 55:17 ....and **m**, and at noon
Ps. 139:9 ......take the wings of the **m**
Eccles. 11:6....In the **m** sow thy seed
Joel 2:2 ....**m** spread upon the
Mark 16:2 ....in the **m**, the first day
Rev. 22:16 ....the bright and **m** star

Mortal
Job 4:17....shall **m** man be more just
Rom. 6:12 ....reign in your **m** body
Rom. 8:11 .....quicken your **m** bodies
1 Cor. 15:53....................**m** . . . put on
2 Cor. 4:11 ...manifest in our **m** flesh

Mother
Gen. 2:24...................his father . . . **m**
Gen. 3:20 ....the **m** of all living
Gen. 17:16 ....she shall be a **m** of
Ex. 20:12 ....thy father and thy **m**
Job 17:14....................Thou art my **m**
Ezek. 16:44...............the **m**, so is her
Hos. 2:2 ....Plead with your **m**
Matt. 12:48..Who is my **m**? and who
John 19:27 ....Behold thy **m**
Heb. 7:3 ..Without father, without **m**

Mourn
Gen. 37:35 ..into the grave . . . **m**-ing
Is. 61:2 ....to comfort all that **m**
Matt. 5:4......Blessed are they that **m**
Luke 6:25 ...for ye shall **m** and weep
James 4:9.............be turned to **m**-ing

Mouth
Ex. 4:11.....Who hath made man's **m**
Deut. 17:6.....the **m** of two witnesses
Judg. 7:6 ....their hand to their **m**
Job 8:21 ....fill thy **m** with laughing
Job 15:6.....own **m** condemneth thee
Job 29:10............to the roof of . . . **m**
Ps. 8:2......Out of the **m** of babes and
Ps. 19:14........Let the words of my **m**
Ps. 39:1.......keep my **m** with a bridle
Ps. 55:21 ....words of his **m** were
Ps. 71:15..........My **m** shall shew forth
Prov. 13:3 ....that keepeth his **m**
Eccles. 5:2 ....Be not rash with thy **m**
Matt. 13:35...open my **m** in parables
Luke 21:15 ....give you a **m** and
Acts 3:21..**m** of all his holy prophets
Titus 1:11 ....Whose **m**-s must be
James 3:3.put bits in the horses' **m**-s

Move
Gen. 1:2 .Spirit of God **m**-d upon the
1 Sam. 1:13.............only her lips **m**-d
Jer. 4:24 ....all the hills **m**-d lightly
Matt. 9:36...........**m**-d with compassion
Mark 1:41 ....Jesus, **m**-d with
John 5:3.........the **m**-ing of the water
Acts 17:28.......in him we live, and **m**
2 Pet. 1:21.....**m**-d by the Holy Ghost

Multiply
Gen. 1:22 ....Be fruitful, and **m**
Ex. 32:13 ....I will **m** your seed
Dan. 4:1 ......Peace be **m**-ed unto you

Multitude
Gen. 16:10....not be numbered for **m**
Ex. 23:2 ......not follow a **m** to do evil
Job 32:7 ....**m** of years . . . teach
Prov. 24:6...............**m** of counsellors
Matt. 14:15 ....send the **m** away
James 5:20................hide a **m** of sins
1 Pet. 4:8 ....cover a **m** of sins

Murder
Ps. 10:8.........doth he **m** the innocent
Matt. 19:18 ....Thou shalt do no **m**
Rom. 1:29......full of envy, **m**, debate
Gal. 5:21 ....**m**-s, drunkenness

Murderer
Num. 35:16 ....**m** shall . . . be put to
John 8:44.....a **m** from the beginning
Acts 28:4................this man is a **m**
1 John 3:15.hateth his brother is a **m**

Murmur
Ex. 17:3 .people **m**-ed against Moses
Is. 29:24 ....that **m**-ed . . . learn

John 6:43...**M** not among yourselves
Phil. 2:4..........Do . . . without **m**-ings

Musick
1 Sam. 18:6....with instruments of **m**
Luke 15:25.he heard **m** and dancing

Muzzle
Deut. 25:4........not **m** the ox when he
1 Cor. 9:9.not **m** the mouth of the ox

Myrrh
Gen. 43:11 ...spices, and **m**, and nuts
Song 5:13...............sweet smelling **m**
Matt. 2:11 ....frankincense and **m**
John 19:39 ...mixture of **m** and aloes

Mystery
Matt. 13:11 ....**m**-s of the kingdom
1 Cor. 2:7 ....wisdom of God in a **m**
1 Cor. 13:2 ...and understand all **m**-s
Eph. 6:19............the **m** of the gospel
1 Tim. 3:9 ....the **m** of the faith

N

Nail
Judg. 4:21............took a **n** of the tent
Dan. 4:33........his **n**-s like bird claws
John 20:25 ....the print of the **n**-s

Naked
Gen. 2:25 ....they were both **n**
Job 1:21..**N** came I out . . . and **n** . . .
Matt. 25:36......**N**, and ye clothed me
Heb. 4:13....................all things are **n**

Name
Gen. 3:20 ....called his wife's **n** Eve
Ex. 20:7...........**n** of the Lord thy God
Deut. 29:20....................blot out his **n**
Job 1:21...................the **n** of the Lord
Ps. 8:1.............how excellent is thy **n**
Ps. 18:49 ....sing praises unto thy **n**
Ps. 72:17.His **n** shall endure for ever
Ps. 102:15........fear the **n** of the Lord
Prov. 22:1........good **n** is rather to be
Is. 48:2 ....Lord of hosts is his **n**
Is. 57:15 ....whose **n** is Holy
Matt. 6:9...............Hallowed by thy **n**
Matt. 10:22 ....for my **n**'s sake
Matt. 18:5 ....little child in my **n**
Mark 5:9.My **n** is Legion: for we are
Luke 21:8 .many shall come in my **n**
John 15:16...ye shall ask . . . in my **n**
Acts 3:16 ....through faith in his **n**
Acts 4:12.............none other **n** under
Eph. 1:21 ....every **n** that is **n**-ed
Phil. 2:9.....**n** which is above every **n**
Phil. 4:3 ...whose **n**-s are in the book

Nation
Gen. 12:2.......make of thee a great **n**
Ps. 33:12....Blessed . . . **n** whose God
Is. 2:4 ....**n** shall not lift up sword
Is. 18:2........a **n** scattered and peeled
Matt. 24:7.........**n** shall rise against **n**
Matt. 28:19 ..Go . . . and teach all **n**-s
John 11:50 ...that the whole **n** perish
Acts 2:5..devout men, out of every **n**
Gal. 3:8..........shall all **n**-s be blessed
Phil. 2:15 ..a crooked and perverse **n**

Natural
Deut. 34:7 ......nor his **n** force abated
Rom. 1:31............without **n** affection
1 Cor. 15:44.........It is sown a **n** body

Nature
Rom. 1:26 .....that which is against **n**
1 Cor. 11:14..............Doth not even **n**
Heb. 2:16 ....on him the **n** of angels
2 Pet. 1:4....partakers of the divine **n**

Near
Ex. 19:22..which come **n** to the Lord
Ps. 22:11 ....for trouble is **n**
Prov. 27:10.......a neighbour that is **n**
Joel 3:14 ....day of the Lord is **n**
Heb. 10:22..draw **n** with a true heart

Need
Matt. 6:8....what things ye have **n** of
Matt. 9:12 ....be whole **n** not a
Matt. 21:3 ..The Lord hath **n** of them
Luke 10:42 ......But one thing is **n**-ful
1 Cor. 12:21.......hand, I have no **n** of
Phil. 4:19.................supply all your **n**
Heb. 4:16 ....help in time of **n**
1 John 3:17.seeth his brother have **n**
Rev. 3:17................have **n** of nothing

Needy
Ps. 9:18 ....**n** . . . not always be
Ps. 40:17 ....But I am poor and **n**
Ps. 72:13...........spare the poor and **n**
Is. 14:30 ....**n** shall lie down in safety

Neighbour
Lev. 19:18....thou shalt love thy **n** as
Hab. 2:15 ....that giveth his **n** drink
Matt. 5:43 ....Thou shalt love thy **n**
Luke 10:29 ....And who is my **n**
Heb. 8:11........teach every man his **n**

Nest
Deut. 32:11 ....eagle stirreth up her **n**
Jer. 49:16 .thy **n** as high as the eagle
Obad. 4.....set thy **n** among the stars
Matt. 8:20 ...birds of the air have **n**-s

Never
Lev. 6:13.......fire . . . it shall **n** go out
Deut. 15:11.poor shall **n** cease out of
Job 3:16....infants which **n** saw light
Ps. 31:1 ....let me **n** be ashamed
Matt. 7:23 ....I **n** knew you
John 4:14.....of the water . . . **n** thirst
John 7:46........**N** man spake like this
John 8:51 ....shall **n** see death
Heb. 13:5 ....I will **n** leave thee

New
Ps. 33:3.........Sing unto him a **n** song
Eccles. 1:9 .no **n** thing under the sun
Is. 65:17 ......**n** heavens and a **n** earth
Ezek. 11:19.put a **n** spirit within you
Matt. 26:28.blood of the **n** testament
John 13:34........A **n** commandment I
2 Cor. 5:17 ....he is a **n** creature
Eph. 4:24 ....put on the **n** man
Rev. 21:1...........**n** heaven . . . **n** earth

Nigh
Deut. 4:7..............who hath God so **n**
Ps. 145:18 ...**n** unto all them that call
Eph. 2:13......made **n** by the blood of
James 4:8.Draw **n** to God . . . draw **n**

Night
Gen. 1:5.....the darkness he called **N**
Ex. 13:21 ....by **n** in a pillar of fire
Josh. 1:8.meditate therein day and **n**
Job 17:12 ....change the **n** into day
Ps. 19:2...................**n** unto **n** sheweth
Ps. 91:5 ......afraid for the terror by **n**
Is. 21:11....Watchman, what of the **n**
Luke 2:8.watch over their flock by **n**
John 9:4........the **n** cometh, when no
Rom. 13:12 ....The **n** is far spent
1 Thess. 5:2............as a thief in the **n**

Noise
Ex. 32:17 ....**n** of war in the camp
Ps. 66:1 ....Make a joyful **n** unto God
2 Pet. 3:10 .pass away with a great **n**
Rev. 6:1 ....the **n** of thunder

Nothing
Job 6:21 ....now ye are **n**
Job 26:7....hangeth the earth upon **n**
Ps. 49:17 ....he shall carry **n** away
Prov. 13:7 ....himself rich, yet hath **n**
Lam. 1:12 ....Is it **n** to you, all ye that
Mark 14:60............Answerest thou **n**
Luke 6:35 ...lend, hoping for **n** again
John 15:5.....without me ye can do **n**
1 Cor. 4:4 ....I know **n** by myself
Gal. 6:3 .be something, when he is **n**
Phil. 4:6 ....Be careful of **n**
James 1:4 ....perfect and entire, wanting **n**

Number
Gen. 15:5...stars, if thou be able to **n**
Num. 1:3.......**n** them by their armies
2 Sam. 24:4 .to **n** the people of Israel
Job 14:16............thou **n**-est my steps
Ps. 139:18 ...more in **n** than the sand
Matt. 10:30 ....hairs . . . are all **n**-ed

Nurse
Gen. 35:8........Deborah Rebekah's **n**
Ex. 2:7 .....a **n** of the Hebrew women
Num. 11:12..............as a **n**-ing father
1 Thess. 2:7 .....as a **n** cherisheth her

O

Oak
2 Sam. 18:10 ....hanged in an **o**
Is. 1:30...........an **o** whose leaf fadeth
Amos 2:9....he was strong as the **o**-s

Oath
Gen. 26:3 ....I will perform the **o**
Josh. 2:20........will be quit of thine **o**
Zech. 8:17 ....love no false **o**
Matt. 5:33.........perform . . . thine **o**-s

Obedience
Rom. 16:26 ....for the **o** of faith
2 Cor. 10:5 ....to the **o** of Christ
Heb. 5:8 ....yet learned he **o** by the
1 Pet. 1:2 ....unto **o** and sprinkling of

Obedient
Deut. 4:30 ....be **o** unto his voice
Prov. 25:12.wise reprover upon an **o**
Is. 1:19 ....If ye be willing and **o**
2 Cor. 2:9........whether ye be **o** in all
Phil. 2:8 ....**o** unto death
Titus 2:5 .....**o** to their own husbands
1 Pet. 1:14.....................As **o** children

Obey
Ex. 19:5 ....if ye will **o** my voice
Deut. 11:27 ....if ye **o** the commandments
1 Sam. 15:22..............**o** is better than
Matt. 8:27 ....and the sea **o** him
Acts 5:29 ......**o** God rather than men
Eph. 6:1 .....Children, **o** your parents
Heb. 11:8 ....By faith Abraham . . . **o**-ed
Heb. 13:17 ....**O** them that have the

Observe
Gen. 37:11 ....his father **o**-ed the
Prov. 23:26.let thine eyes **o** my ways
Eccles. 11:4...He that **o**-eth the wind
Matt. 28:20....Teaching them to **o** all
Mark 10:20 ....have I **o**-ed from my
Gal. 4:10 ....Ye **o** days, and months

Occasion
Judg. 9:33.do . . . as thou shalt find **o**
Jer. 2:24 ...in her **o** who can turn her
Rom. 14:13 ..**o** to fall in his brother's
Gal. 5:13 ....use not liberty for an **o**
1 Tim. 5:14 ....give none **o** to the

Offence
Is. 8:14..................a rock of **o** to both
Matt. 16:23 ....Satan: thou art an **o**
Matt. 18:7.....Woe . . . because of **o**-s
Acts 24:16.........conscience void of **o**
1 Cor. 10:32.......................Give none **o**
Phil. 1:10 .....without **o** till the day of
1 Pet. 2:8 ....and a rock of **o**

Offend
Job 34:31..........I will not **o** any more
Matt. 5:29...right eye **o** thee, pluck it
Mark 14:27 ....All shall be **o**-ed
Luke 17:2 ....**o** one of these little
James 3:2...For in many things we **o**

Offer
Judg. 5:2 ..willingly **o**-ed themselves
Ps. 50:14...**O** unto God thanksgiving
Mal. 1:8 ....**o** the blind . . . **o** the lame
Matt. 5:24 ....come and **o** thy gift
Luke 6:29.......check **o** also the other
1 Cor. 8:1........things **o**-ed unto idols
Phil. 2:17...............I be **o**-ed upon the
Heb. 9:14..**o**-ed himself without spot

Office
Ps. 109:8 ..and let another take his **o**
Rom. 12:4 ....members . . . not the same **o**
1 Tim. 3:1.....desire the **o** of a bishop

1 Tim. 3:10 ......use the **o** of a deacon
Heb. 7:5 ....**o** of the priesthood

Often
Prov. 29:1 ....being **o** reproved
Luke 13:34 .**o** would I have gathered
1 Cor. 11:26 ....For as **o** as ye eat this
1 Tim. 5:23 ....thine **o** infirmities

Oil
Ex. 25:6 ....**O** for the light
Job 29:6...rock poured me out rivers of **o**
Ps. 23:5.....anointest my head with **o**
Ps. 45:7...........with the **o** of gladness
Ps. 55:21 ...words were softer than **o**
Ps. 104:15 ....**o** to make his face
Matt. 25:8 ....Give us of your **o**
Luke 10:34.....pouring in **o** and wine
Rev. 6:6 .hurt not the **o** and the wine

Ointment
Ps. 133:2 ....like precious **o** upon
Matt. 26:7 ....alabaster box . . . precious **o**
Luke 7:46....anointed my feet with **o**
John 12:5....Why was not this **o** sold

Old
Gen. 15:15 .....buried in a good **o** age
Gen. 44:20 ....child of his **o** age
Ruth 1:12..too **o** to have an husband
1 Sam. 12:2...........**o** and grayheaded
Job 42:17 .....being **o** and full of days
Prov. 20:29 ....beauty of **o** men is the
Matt. 5:21 ......said by them of **o** time
Matt. 9:16 ....new cloth unto an **o**
Matt. 9:17 ....new wine into **o** bottles
John 3:4...man be born when he is **o**
Rom. 6:6.........our **o** man is crucified
1 Cor. 5:7.Purge out . . . the **o** leaven
2 Cor. 5:17..........**o** things are passed
Col. 3:9 ....put off the **o** man
Rev. 12:9.**o** serpent, called the Devil

One
Deut. 6:4 ......Lord our God is **o** Lord
Matt. 19:5.........they twain shall be **o** flesh
John 10:30......I and my Father are **o**
John 17:21.............they all may be **o**
Eph. 4:4 ....**o** Spirit . . . **o** hope
1 Tim. 2:5 ......**o** God, and **o** mediator
James 4:12..........There is **o** lawgiver

Open
Gen. 3:5........your eyes shall be **o**-ed
Ps. 51:15..............Lord, **o** thou my lips
Prov. 27:5.....**O** rebuke is better than
Is. 42:7 ....To **o** the blind eyes
Ezek. 16:63...never **o** thy mouth any
Matt. 7:7 .knock, and it shall be **o**-ed
Matt. 20:33......our eyes may be **o**-ed
Luke 13:25 ......Lord, Lord, **o** unto us
Luke 24:32 ....he **o**-ed to us the scriptures
John 1:51.........ye shall see heaven **o**
Rev. 4:1......door was **o**-ed in heaven
Rev. 5:2 ....Who is worthy to **o** the

Oppress
Lev. 25:14 ....shall not **o** one another
Hos. 12:7....merchant . . . loveth to **o**
Acts 10:38...all that were **o**-ed of the
James 2:6 ......Do not rich men **o** you

Ordain
1 Chr. 17:9...**o** a place for my people
Ps. 8:3 ....stars, which thou hast **o**-ed
Mark 3:14.......**o**-ed twelve, that they
John 15:16.......chosen you, and **o**-ed
1 Tim. 2:7 ....I am **o**-ed a preacher

Order
Judg. 13:12 ....How shall we **o** the
2 Kin. 20:1 ....Set thine house in **o**
Titus 1:5 ....set in **o** the things
Heb. 5:6 ....the **o** of Melchisedec

Ordinance
Job 38:33 ....the **o**-s of heaven
Mal. 3:7....gone away from mine **o**-s
Rom. 13:2 ....resisteth the **o** of God
Eph. 2:15..commandments . . . in **o**-s

Col. 2:14 ....the handwriting of **o**-s
1 Pet. 2:13...Submit . . . to every **o** of

Out
Num. 32:23 ..your sin will find you **o**
Prov. 4:23 ....**o** of it are the issues
Matt. 12:34.....**o** of the abundance of
2 Tim. 4:2 ....in season, **o** of season

Outward
1 Sam. 16:7.......on the **o** appearance
Rom. 2:28 ....**o** in the flesh
2 Cor. 4:16.............our **o** man perish

Overcome
Jer. 23:9.......man whom wine hath **o**
John 16:33............I have **o** the world
Rom. 12:21.................Be not **o** of evil
1 John 2:13......ye have **o** the wicked

Overtake
Amos 9:10 ....evil shall not **o** . . . us
Gal. 6:1............man be **o**-n in a fault
1 Thess. 5:4..day . . . **o** you as a thief

Overthrow
Ex. 23:24 ....shalt utterly **o** them
Prov. 18:5.......**o** the righteousness in
Acts 5:39.........of God, ye cannot **o** it
2 Tim. 2:18..........**o** the faith of some

Owe
Matt. 18:28......Pay me that thou **o**-st
Rom. 13:8..........**O** no man any thing
Philem. 19 ...**o**-st unto me even thine

Own
1 Chr. 29:14 ....of thine **o** have we
Prov. 14:10........heart knoweth his **o**
John 1:11 ...unto his **o** . . . **o** received
John 10:3........calleth his **o** sheep by
Acts 2:6 ....speak in his **o** language
1 Tim. 5:8 ..any provide not for his **o**
2 Pet. 3:3..walking after their **o** lusts

Ox
Job 6:5 .loweth the **o** over his fodder
Prov. 7:22....**o** goeth to the slaughter
Prov. 15:17 ....stalled **o** and hatred
1 Tim. 15:18..........muzzle the **o** that

P

Pain
Ps. 25:18 ....mine affliction and my **p**
Ps. 116:3....**p**-s of hell gat hold upon
Acts 2:24.......loosed the **p**-s of death
Rev. 21:4..neither . . . be any more **p**

Pardon
Ex. 23:21..not **p** your transgressions
2 Chr. 30:18..good Lord **p** every one
Neh. 9:17..........art a God ready to **p**
Ps. 25:11......O Lord, **p** mine iniquity
Is. 55:7 ....he will abundantly **p**

Parents
Matt. 10:21.....rise up against their **p**
Luke 2:41....his **p** went to Jerusalem
Luke 18:29..house, or **p**, or brethren
John 9:2 ...did sin, this man, or his **p**
Rom. 1:30................disobedient to **p**
2 Cor. 12:14.....for the **p** . . . **p** for the
Eph. 6:1.............Children, obey your **p**
2 Tim. 3:2 ....disobedient to **p**,

Part
Ps. 22:18.........**p** my garments among
Matt. 27:35....and **p**-ed his garments
Luke 10:42 ....that good **p**
Luke 11:39 ....inward **p** is full of
John 13:8 ....hast no **p** with me
Acts 8:21 ....neither **p** nor lot

Partaker
Ps. 50:18........been **p** with adulterers
Matt. 23:30 ...not have been **p**-s with
1 Cor. 9:10 ...should be **p** of his hope
Eph. 5:7......Be not . . . **p**-s with them
Heb. 3:1 ..**p**-s of the heavenly calling
Heb. 3:14 ....made of **p**-s of Christ
Heb. 6:4...........**p**-s of the Holy Ghost
2 Pet. 1:4......**p**-s of the divine nature

Pass
Prov. 4:15 ....Avoid it, **p** not by it

Matt. 26:39.....let this cup **p** from me
John 5:24..**p**-ed from death unto life
2 Cor. 5:17.old things are **p**-ed away
Rev. 21:1.first earth were **p**-ed away

Past
Deut. 4:32 ....the days that are **p**
Song 2:11.....the winter is **p**, the rain
Jer. 8:20.harvest is **p**, the summer is
Rom. 11:33 ....ways **p** finding out

Pastors
Jer. 3:15 ....will give you **p**
Jer. 10:21........**p** are become brutish
Eph. 4:11..and some, **p** and teachers

Path
Gen. 49:17 ....an adder in the **p**
Ps. 16:11..........shew me the **p** of life
Ps. 119:105 ....a light unto my **p**
Prov. 4:18 ....**p** of the just . . . shining
Matt. 3:3 ....make his **p**-s straight

Patience
Matt. 18:26 ....Have **p** with me
Luke 21:19........In your **p** possess ye
Rom. 5:3 ....tribulation worketh **p**
Rom. 15:4 ....**p** and comfort
Col. 1:11 ....all **p** and longsuffering
2 Thess. 1:4........for your **p** and faith
James 1:4 ...**p** have her perfect work
James 5:11.....................the **p** of Job

Patient
Rom. 12:12......hope; **p** in tribulation
2 Thess. 3:5........**p** waiting for Christ
1 Tim. 3:3 ....**p** not a brawler
James 5:8 ....Be ye also **p**; stablish

Peace
Gen. 15:15........go to thy fathers in **p**
Lev. 26:6.......I will give **p** in the land
Num. 6:26........countenance . . . give thee **p**
Ps. 4:8.....................lay me down in **p**
Ps. 34:14...........seek **p**, and pursue it
Ps. 119:165.Great **p** have they which
Ps. 147:14...maketh **p** in thy borders
Prov. 3:17 ....all her paths are **p**
Prov. 16:7...his enemies be at **p** with
Eccles. 3:8..time of war . . . time of **p**
Is. 9:6...........Father, The Prince of **P**
Is. 52:7 ......tidings, that publisheth **p**
Is. 57:19 .....**P**, **p** to him that is far off
Jer. 6:14.......**P**, **p**; when there is no **p**
Matt. 10:34........I came not to send **p**
Mark 9:50 ..have **p** one with another
Luke 2:14 ....on earth **p**, good will
John 14:27..**P** I leave with you, my **p**
John 20:19....saith . . . **P** be unto you
Acts 18:9 ..speak, and hold not thy **p**
Rom. 15:33.the God of **p** be with you
1 Cor. 7:15 ...God hath called us to **p**
Gal. 5:22 ....fruit of the Spirit is . . . **p**
Eph. 2:14..........................For he is our **p**
Phil. 4:7 ......**p** of God, which passeth
Heb. 12:14.......follow **p** with all men
James 2:16 ....Depart in **p**
1 Pet. 5:14 ....**P** be with you all

People
Ex. 6:7 ....take you to me for a **p**
Ruth 1:16 ....thy **p** shall be my **p**
Ps. 2:1 ....**p** imagine a vain thing
Ps. 100:3we are his **p**, and the sheep
Prov. 11:14...no counsel is, the **p** fall
Prov. 29:18 ....no vision, the **p** perish
Matt. 1:21.save not **p** from their sins
Mark 7:6..........**p** honoureth me with
John 11:50.man should die for the **p**

Perceive
Deut. 29:4 ....given you an heart to **p**
Mark 2:8..........Jesus **p**-d in his spirit
Luke 6:41 ...**p**-st not the beam that is
Luke 8:46........I **p** that virtue is gone
John 12:19 ....**P** ye how ye prevail
Acts 10:34 ....**p** that God is no
1 John 3:16.......**p** we the love of God

Perfect
Deut. 32:4..He is the Rock, his work is **p**
Ps. 19:7 ....law of the Lord is **p**

Matt. 5:48 ... Be ye therefore **p**
1 Cor. 13:10 .when that which is **p** is
2 Cor. 12:9 ... strength . . . **p** in weakness
James 1:4 .patience have her **p** work
James 1:25 ... **p** law of liberty
1 John 4:17 ... our love made **p**

Perish
Num. 17:12 ... we die, we **p**, we all **p**
Job 34:15 ...All flesh shall **p** together
Ps. 1:6 ... way of the ungodly shall **p**
Matt. 8:25 ... Lord, save us: we **p**
Matt. 18:14 ... little ones should **p**
2 Pet. 3:9 ... not willing that any should **p**

Persecute
Job 19:22 ... Why do ye **p** me as God
Ps. 7:1 .save me from all them that **p**
Ps. 143:3 ...enemy hath **p**-ed my soul
Matt. 5:11 ... revile you, and **p** you
John 15:20 ... if they have **p**-d me
Acts 9:4 ... Saul, why **p**-st thou me
1 Cor. 4:12 ... we bless; being **p**-d
2 Cor. 4:9 ... **P**-d, but not forsaken

Person
Deut. 1:17 ... shall not respect **p**-s
Ps. 15:4 ... a vile **p** is contemned
Ps. 26:4 ... have not sat with vain **p**-s
Matt. 22:16 ... regardest not the **p** of
Rom. 2:11 ... no respect of **p**-s with
Jude 16 ... having men's **p**-s in

Persuade
Prov. 25:15 ... a prince **p**-d
Matt. 28:14 ... we will **p** him, and
Acts 26:28 ... Almost thou **p**-st me
Rom. 14:14 ... am **p**-d by the Lord
Heb. 6:9 ... **p**-d better things of you

Perverse
Deut. 32:5 ... **p** and crooked
Job 6:30 ... taste discern **p** things
Prov. 4:24 ... **p** lips put far from thee
Prov. 23:33 ...heart . . . utter **p** things
Acts 20:30 ... speaking **p** things
Phil. 2:15 ... a crooked and **p** nation

Pervert
Job 8:3 ... Doth God **p** judgment
Luke 23:14 ... one that **p**-eth the
Gal. 1:7 ... **p** the gospel of Christ

Petition
1 Sam. 1:17.God . . . grant thee thy **p**
1 Kin. 2:16 ... I ask one **p** of thee
Ps. 20:5 ... the Lord fulfill all thy **p**-s
Dan 6:7 ..shall ask a **p** of any God or

Physician
Jer. 8:22 ..Gilead; is there no **p** there
Matt. 9:12 ... be whole need not a **p**
Luke 4:23 ... **P**, heal thyself
Col. 4:14 ... Luke, the beloved **p**

Piece
1 Sam. 2:36 ... that I may eat a **p** of
2 Sam. 11:21 ..cast a **p** of a millstone
Zech. 11:12 ... for my price thirty **p**-s
Matt. 9:16 ... **p** of new cloth
Luke 24:42 ... a **p** of a broiled fish

Pierce
Ps. 22:16 .they **p**-d my hands . . . feet
Prov. 12:18 ... the **p**-ings of a sword
Zech. 12:10 ... whom they have **p**
Luke 2:35 ... **p** through thy own soul
John 19:34 .with a spear **p**-d his side

Pillar
Gen. 19:26 ... she became a **p** of salt
Job 26:11.The **p**-s of heaven tremble
Prov. 9:1 ... hewn out her seven **p**-s
Gal. 2:9 .John, who seemed to be **p**-s
1 Tim. 3:15 ... **p** and ground of the

Pillow
Gen 28:18 ... stone . . . for his **p**-s
1 Sam. 19:13 ..**p** of goats' hair for his
Mark 4:38 ... asleep on a **p**

Piped
1 Kin. 1:40 ... people **p** with pipes

Matt. 11:17 ... We have **p** unto you
1 Cor. 14:7 ... known what is **p** or

Pit
Gen. 14:10 ... full of slime-**p**-s
Gen. 37:20 ... cast him into some **p**
Ex. 21:33 ...shall open a **p** . . . dig a **p**
Job 33:18 ... his soul from the **p**

Pitcher
Gen. 24:14 ... Let down thy **p**, I pray
Judg. 7:16 ... lamps within the **p**-s
Eccles. 12:6 ... **p** be broken at the
Mark 14:13 ... man bearing a **p**

Pity
Deut. 7:16 ... eye shall have no **p**
Job 19:21 ... Have **p** upon me, have **p**
Ps. 103:13 ..father **p**-ieth his children
Prov. 19:17 ... hath **p** upon the poor
Matt. 18:33 ... I had **p** on thee

Place
Gen. 1:9 ... gathered . . . one **p**
Ex. 3:5 ... **p** . . . thou standest is holy
Judg. 18:10 ... **p** where there is no
Job 9:6 ... earth out of her **p**
Ps. 24:3 ... stand in his holy **p**
Prov. 15:3 ... Lord . . . in every **p**
Matt. 26:36 ...a **p** called Gethsemane
Matt. 27:33.Golgotha . . . **p** of a skull
Matt. 28:6 ... **p** where the Lord lay
Luke 4:17 ... **p** where it was written
John 14:2 ..go to prepare a **p** for you
John 18:2 ... Judas . . . knew the **p**
Eph. 4:27.Neither give **p** to the devil
2 Pet. 1:19 ... light . . . in a dark **p**
Rev. 20:11 ..was found no **p** for them

Plague
Gen. 12:17 ... Lord **p**-ed Pharaoh
Lev. 13:2 ... like the **p** of leprosy
Mark 5:29 ..she was healed of that **p**
Rev. 16:21 ... the **p** of the hail
Rev. 21:9 ... the seven last **p**-s

Plain
Gen. 19:17 ..neither stay . . . all the **p**
Ps. 27:11 ... lead me in a **p** path
Prov. 15:19 ... righteous is made **p**
Hab. 2:2 ... make it **p** upon tables
Mark 7:35 ... and he spake **p**

Plainly
Deut. 27:8 ... write all the word . . . **p**
Ezra 4:18 ... hath been **p** read
Is. 32:4 ... shall be ready to speak **p**
John 16:25.shew you **p** of the Father

Plant
Gen. 2:8 ... God **p**-ed a garden
Deut. 6:11 ...trees, which thou **p**-edst
Job 14:9 ... boughs like a **p**
Ps. 1:3 ... tree **p**-ed by the rivers
Eccles. 3:2.a time to **p**, and a time to
Is. 51:16 ... that I may **p** the heavens
Is. 53:2 ... grow up . . . as a tender **p**
Matt. 15:13 ..**p** . . . Father hath not **p**-ed
Mark 12:1 ... certain man **p**-ed
Luke 17:6 ... be thou **p**-ed in the sea
1 Cor. 3:6 ... I have **p**-ed, Apollos

Play
Ex. 32:6 ... and rose up to **p**
2 Sam. 10:12 ... **p** the men for our
Ps. 33:3 ... **p** skillfully with a loud
Is. 11:8 ... **p** on the hole of the asp

Plead
Job 9:19 ... set me a time to **p**
Ps. 43:1 ... Judge me . . . and **p** my
Is. 1:17 ... **p** for the widow
Jer. 2:9 ... I will yet **p** with you

Pleasant
Gen. 2:9 ... every . . . **p** to the sight
2 Sam. 1:23 ... lovely and **p** in their
Ps. 133:1 ... **p** it is for brethren to
Prov. 9:17 .bread eaten in secret is **p**
Prov. 16:24 ... **P** words are as
Ezek. 33:32 ...one that hath a **p** voice
Dan. 10:3 ... I ate no **p** bread

Please
1 Kin. 3:10 ...the speech **p**-d the Lord
Prov. 16:7 ... man's ways **p** the Lord
Matt. 3:17 ... in whom I am well **p**-d
John 8:29 ... those things that **p** him
Rom. 15:1 ... not to **p** ourselves
Rom. 15:3 ... Christ **p**-d not himself
1 Cor. 7:33 ... how he may **p** his wife
1 Cor. 10:5 ... God was not well **p**-d
Heb. 13:16.sacrifices God is well **p**-d

Pleasure
Job 36:11 ... and their years in **p**-s
Ps. 16:11 .there are **p**-s for evermore
Ps. 51:18 ... Do good in thy good **p**
Ps. 149:4 Lord taketh **p** in his people
Eccles. 5:4 ... he hath no **p** in fools
Is. 53:10 .**p** of the Lord shall prosper
Luke 8:14 ...cares and riches and **p**-s
Luke 12:32 ...Father's good **p** to give
2 Cor. 12:10 ... take **p** in infirmities
Heb. 11:25 ... **p**-s of sin for a season
James 5:5 ... lived in **p** on the earth

Plenteous
Gen. 41:34 ... seven **p** years
Is. 30:23 ..earth . . . shall be fat and **p**
Matt. 9:37 ... harvest truly is **p**

Plenty
Gen. 41:29 ... seven years of great **p**
Prov. 3:10 .thy barns be filled with **p**
Joel 2:26 ... And ye shall eat in **p**

Plow
Deut. 22:10 .not **p** with an ox and an
Job 4:8 ... they that **p** iniquity
Is. 2:4 ... their swords into **p**-shares
Joel 3:10 ... **p**-shares into swords
Luke 9:62 ... put his hand to the **p**

Pluck
Ex. 4:7 ... **p**-ed it out of his bosom
Ps. 25:15 ... **p** my feet out of the net
Matt. 5:29 ... offend thee, **p** it out
Mark 2:23 ... to **p** the ears of corn
Luke 17:6 ... **p**-ed up by the root
John 10:28 ... **p** them out of my hand

Poison
Deut. 32:24 ... with the **p** of serpents
Deut. 32:33 .wine is the **p** of dragons
Ps. 140:3 ... adders' **p** is under their

Ponder
Prov. 4:26 ... **P** the path of thy feet
Prov. 5:6 ... **p** the path of life
Luke 2:19 ... **p**-ed them in her heart

Poor
1 Sam. 2:8 ... raiseth . . . **p** out of the
2 Sam. 12:4 ...took the **p** man's lamb
Job 5:16 ... so the **p** hath hope
Ps. 40:17 ... I am **p** and needy, yet
Ps. 69:33 ... the Lord heareth the **p**
Prov. 13:7 ...is that maketh himself **p**
Is. 3:15 ... grind the faces of the **p**
Matt. 5:3 ... Blessed are the **p** in
Matt. 26:11 ... ye have the **p** always
Mark 10:21 ... and give to the **p**
Luke 19:8 ...my goods I give to the **p**
1 Cor. 13:3 ... my goods to feed the **p**
2 Cor. 8:9 ... your sakes he became **p**
James 2:5 ...God chosen the **p** of this

Portion
Gen. 31:14 ... any **p** or inheritance
Deut. 32:9 ... Lord's **p** is his people
2 Kin. 2:9 ... double **p** of thy spirit
2 Chr. 10:16 ... What **p** have we in
Ps. 119:57 ... Thou art my **p**, O Lord
Dan. 1:8 ... the **p** of the king's meat
Matt. 24:51 ... **p** with the hypocrites
Luke 15:12 ... **p** of goods that falleth

Possess
Gen. 24:60 ... thy seed **p** the gate
Job 7:3 ..made to **p** months of vanity
Matt. 4:24 ... **p**-ed with devils
Luke 18:12 ... tithes of all that I **p**

Possession
Gen. 17:8 ... for an everlasting **p**
Gen. 34:10 ... and get you **p**-s therein
Ps. 44:3 ... land in **p** by their own

Prov. 28:10 .....have good things in **p**
Matt. 19:22.........for he had great **p**-s
Acts 2:45.....sold their **p**-s and goods

Possible
Matt. 19:26 ....God all things are **p**
Matt. 26:39..........**p**, let this cup pass
Luke 18:27 ....are **p** with God
Rom. 12:18.......If it be **p**, as much as

Pour
1 Sam. 1:15 ....**p**-ed out my soul
Job 10:10 ....**p**-ed me out as milk
Job 29:6 ....rock **p**-ed me out rivers
Joel 2:28.**p** out my spirit . . . all flesh
Matt. 26:7............**p**-ed it on his head
John 2:15.......**p**-ed out the changers'
Acts 10:45 .**p**-ed out the gift . . . Holy
Rev. 16:2 ....**p**-ed out his vial

Power
Ex. 15:6............become glorious in **p**
Deut. 8:18 ....thee **p** to get wealth
2 Sam. 22:33 ....my strength and **p**
1 Chr. 29:11 ....the **p**, and the glory
Ps. 37:35 .seen the wicked in great **p**
Ps. 49:15.......from the **p** of the grave
Prov. 3:27 .....**p** of thine hand to do it
Eccles. 8:8........**p** in the day of death
Hab. 2:9.delivered from the **p** of evil
Matt. 6:13 ..kingdom, and the **p**, and
Matt. 9:6 ....**p** on earth to forgive
Mark 9:1 ....God come with **p**
Mark 13:26 ....clouds with great **p**
Mark 14:62.....on the right hand of **p**
Luke 1:35........**p** of the Highest shall
Luke 4:6.....All this **p** will I give thee
Luke 5:24.............Son of man hath **p**
Luke 12:5...............**p** to cast into hell
Luke 22:69..........right hand the **p** of
John 1:12 ....**p** to become the sons of
John 10:18...**p** to lay it down . . . **p** to
John 17:2....................**p** over all flesh
Acts 1:8........ye shall receive **p**, after
Acts 8:10..This man is the great **p** of
Rom. 1:4 ....Son of God with **p**
Rom. 9:21........potter **p** over the clay
Rom. 13:1..................no **p** but of God
1 Cor. 1:24 ....Christ the **p** of God
1 Cor. 5:4**p** of our Lord Jesus Christ
1 Cor. 9:18..............I abuse not my **p**
Eph. 1:21.........all principality, and **p**
Eph. 2:2......prince of the **p** of the air
Col. 1:13 ....from the **p** of darkness
1 Pet. 3:22 ....**p**-s being made subject
Jude 25......majesty, dominion and **p**

Praise
Ex. 15:11........................fearful in **p**-s
Judg. 5:2 ....**P** ye the Lord
Ps. 22:25 ....My **p** shall be of thee
Ps. 89:5.........the heavens shall **p** thy
Prov. 27:21 ....so is a man to his **p**
John 9:24 ....Give God the **p**
Rom. 2:29.......whose **p** is not of men
2 Cor. 8:18 ..whose **p** is in the gospel
Phil. 4:8....................if there be any **p**

Pray
Gen. 20:7 ....he shall **p** for thee
1 Sam. 7:5..........I will **p** for you unto
1 Sam. 12:23...sin . . . in ceasing to **p**
Job 21:15........what profit . . . if we **p**
Ps. 55:17 ..morning . . . noon, will I **p**
Is. 45:20 ....**p** unto a god . . . cannot
Matt. 5:44..........................**p** for them
Matt. 6:6 ....**p** to thy Father
Matt. 14:23...........mountain apart to **p**
Matt. 26:41.......Watch, and **p**, that ye
Mark 11:24 ....when ye **p**, believe
Luke 11:1............Lord, teach us to **p**
Luke 18:1......men ought always to **p**
John 14:16 ....I will **p** the Father
1 Cor. 14:14 ....**p** in an unknown
Col. 1:9 ......do not cease to **p** for you
1 Thess. 5:17.........**P** without ceasing
James 5:13...........afflicted? let him **p**

Prayer
1 Kin. 8:45 ....in heaven their **p**
Neh. 11:17 ....thanksgiving in **p**
Ps. 4:1 ....hear my **p**
Ps. 55:1 ....Give ear to my **p**
Is. 56:7 ....called an house of **p**
Matt. 17:21........not out but by **p** and
Matt. 21:22..whatsoever . . . ask in **p**
Luke 6:12.....continued all night in **p**
Luke 19:46.My house . . . house of **p**
Rom. 12:12 ...continuing instant in **p**
1 Cor. 7:5............................fasting and **p**
Col. 4:2 .....Continue in **p**, and watch
1 Pet. 3:7....your **p**-s be not hindered

Preach
Is. 61:1 ....anointed me to **p** good
Matt. 4:17 ....Jesus began to **p**
Matt. 11:5 .....poor . . . gospel **p**-ed to
Mark 1:4 ....**p** the baptism of
Mark 1:39..**p**-ed in their synagogues
Mark 16:15 ......**p** the gospel to every
Luke 4:43.........**p** the kingdom of God
Acts 5:42....teach and **p** Jesus Christ
Acts 17:3..Jesus, whom I **p** unto you
1 Cor. 1:23 ......We **p** Christ crucified
2 Tim. 4:2.......**P** the word; be instant
1 Pet. 3:19 ....**p**-ed unto the spirits

Preacher
Eccles. 1:1 ....The words of the **P**
Rom. 10:14 ....hear without a **p**
1 Tim. 2:7 ....I am ordained a **p**
2 Pet. 2:5 ....**p** of righteousness

Preaching
Matt. 3:1 ....**p** in the wilderness
Acts 8:4.......every where **p** the word
Rom. 16:25..............**p** of Jesus Christ
1 Cor. 1:18 ..**p** of the cross is to them
1 Cor. 15:14..........then is our **p** vain

Precious
1 Sam. 3:1....word of the Lord was **p**
Ps. 116:15..**P** in the sight of the Lord
Prov. 3:15............more **p** than rubies
Is. 13:12..man more **p** than fine gold
Matt. 26:7 .....box of very **p** ointment
1 Pet. 1:7 ....more **p** than of gold that

Prepare
1 Sam. 7:3.....................**p** your hearts
Ps. 23:5 ....**p**-st a table before me
Ps. 57:6 ....**p**-d a net for my steps
Is. 40:3 ....**P** ye the way of the Lord
Jonah 1:17....................**p**-d a great fish to
Matt. 25:34.the kingdom **p**-d for you
John 14:2 ....I go to **p** a place for you

Presence
Ex. 33:14 .....My **p** shall go with thee
Ps. 23:5 ....**p** of mine enemies
Ps. 95:2 ....before his **p** with
Is. 64:2 ....tremble at thy **p**
Luke 13:26.eaten and drunk in thy **p**
Rev. 14:10.........in the **p** of the Lamb

Present
Ps. 46:1 ....a very **p** help in trouble
Luke 2:22 ....to **p** him to the Lord
John 14:25........being yet **p** with you
Rom. 12:1 ....**p** your bodies a living
1 Cor. 5:3.......................but **p** in spirit
Col. 1:22.................................**p** you holy and
Jude 24.....**p** you faultless before the

Preserve
Deut. 6:24............he might **p** us alive
Ps. 16:1.........**P** me, O God; for in thee
Ps. 86:2 ....**P** my soul; for I am holy
Prov. 2:11......Discretion shall **p** thee
Luke 17:33 ....lose his life shall **p** it
1 Thess. 5:23.**p**-d blameless unto the

Press
Mark 2:4 ....unto him for the **p**
Luke 6:38.good measure, **p**-ed down
Phil. 3:14 ....I **p** toward the mark

Prevail
Gen. 7:20..................did the waters **p**
1 Sam. 2:9 ....shall no man **p**
Ps. 65:3 ....Iniquities **p** against me
Matt. 16:18............of hell shall not **p**

Prey
Ps. 76:4 ....than the mountains of **p**
Is. 10:2 ....widows may be their **p**
Jer. 38:2.......shall have his life for a **p**
Ezek. 22:25 ....lion ravening the **p**

Price
Lev. 25:16 ....diminish the **p**
Deut. 23:18...................the **p** of a dog
Prov. 31:10.her **p** is far above rubies
Zech. 11:12 ..**p** thirty pieces of silver
Matt. 13:46.........one pearl of great **p**
Acts 5:2.........kept back part of the **p**
1 Cor. 6:20 ....ye are bought with a **p**

Pride
Prov. 13:10 ....by **p** cometh contention
Prov. 16:18 .**P** . . . before destruction
1 John 2:16 ....and the **p** of life

Priest
Gen. 14:18....**p** of the most high God
Ex. 19:6....................a kingdom of **p**-s
1 Sam. 2:35..raise me up a faithful **p**
2 Chr. 15:3........without a teaching **p**
Ps. 110:4.**p** . . . order of Melchizedek
Is. 24:2 ....people, so with the **p**
Ezek. 44:21 ....**p** drink wine
Matt. 8:4...........shew thyself to the **p**
Heb. 2:17......................faithful high **p**
Heb. 3:1 .....High **P** of our profession

Prince
Ex. 2:14........a **p** and a judge over us
Is. 9:6..................................**P** of Peace
Matt. 9:34.............the **p** of the devils
John 12:31............the **p** of this world
Acts 3:15 ....killed the **P** of life
Acts 5:31......to be a **P** and a Saviour
Eph. 2:2 ......**p** of the power of the air

Principality
Rom. 8:38...nor **p**-s, nor powers, nor
Eph. 1:21 ......above all **p**, and power

Prison
Judg. 16:21 .did grind in the **p** house
Ps. 142:7........Bring my soul out of **p**
Matt. 4:12 ....John was cast into **p**
Matt. 14:10 ..beheaded John in the **p**
Acts 5:19 ....Lord . . . opened the **p**
Acts 16:27..keeper of the **p** awaking

Prisoner
Ps. 102:20..............groaning of the **p**
Ps. 146:7 ....The Lord looseth the **p**-s
Eph. 3:1...Paul, the **p** of Jesus Christ

Proceed
Deut. 8:3 ..word that **p**-eth out of the
Matt. 4:4.that **p**-eth out of the mouth
Mark 7:21...........heart of man, **p** evil
John 15:26.......which **p**-eth from the

Proclaim
Ex. 33:19 ......**p** the name of the Lord
Is. 61:1 ....**p** liberty to the captives
Is. 61:2 ....**p** the acceptable year of
Jer. 34:15.....**p**-ing liberty every man
Luke 12:3 ..**p**-ed upon the housetops

Profane
Lev. 20:3 ....to **p** my holy name
Ezek. 22:8 ....hast **p**-d my sabbaths
Matt. 12:5...priests . . . **p** the sabbath
2 Tim. 2:16.......**p** and vain babblings

Profess
Rom. 1:22......**P**-ing themselves to be
Titus 1:16 ....**p** that they know God
Heb. 10:23.hold fast the **p**-ion of our

Profit
Gen. 37:26......What **p** is it if we slay
Prov. 14:23 ....In all labour there is **p**
Is. 48:17...God . . . teacheth thee to **p**
Jer. 7:8....lying words, that cannot **p**
Jer. 16:19......things . . . there is no **p**
Matt. 16:26...For what is a man **p**-ed
Mark 7:11 .thou mightest be **p**-ed by
1 Tim. 4:8.........bodily exercise **p**-eth
2 Tim. 3:16..........**p**-able for doctrine

Promise
Num. 14:34 .....know my breach of **p**
Acts 2:33 ....**p** of the Holy Ghost
Acts 26:6.......................the hope of the **p**
Gal. 3:14 ....might receive the **p**

Eph. 6:2..first commandment with **p**
2 Tim. 1:1..........**p** of life . . . in Christ
Titus 1:2**p**-d before the world began
Heb. 10:23 ....he is faithful that **p**-d
2 Pet. 1:4........great and precious **p**-s

Prophecy
Dan. 9:24.....seal up the vision and **p**
1 Cor. 13:2............I have the gift of **p**
2 Pet. 1:19......a more sure word of **p**
Rev. 19:10...testimony . . . spirit of **p**

Prophesy
1 Sam. 10:11 ....**p**-ed among the
1 Chr. 25:3......who **p**-ed with a harp
Is. 30:10....**P** not unto us right things
Ezek. 37:4...........**P** upon these bones
Joel 2:28 .....sons . . . daughters . . . **p**
Matt. 7:22...we not **p**-ed in thy name
1 Cor. 13:9......part, and we **p** in part
1 Thess. 5:20........Despise not **p**-ings

Prophet
Gen. 20:7 ....for he is a **p**
Deut. 18:18...I will raise them up a **p**
Judg. 4:4 ....Deborah, a **p**-ess
1 Kin. 20:35......of the sons of the **p**-s
Is. 9:15 ....the **p** that teacheth lies
Ezek. 13:3..Woe unto the foolish **p**-s
Amos. 7:14....neither was I a **p**'s son
Matt. 1:22 ...was spoken . . . by the **p**
Matt. 5:12.....persecuted they the **p**-s
Matt. 10:41 ....**p** . . . receive a **p**'s
Matt. 13:57..**p** is not without honour
Matt. 21:11..Jesus the **p** of Nazareth
Luke 4:24......No **p** is accepted in his
Luke 6:23..their fathers unto the **p**-s
Luke 7:28 ....greater **p** than John the
John 1:21.....................Art thou that **p**
John 4:19..perceive that thou art a **p**
John 7:52.out of Galilee ariseth no **p**
Acts 13:6 ....sorcerer, a false **p**
Acts 13:15..........of the law and the **p**
1 Cor. 14:37.man think himself . . . **p**
Eph. 4:11.......apostles; and some **p**-s
Heb. 1:1 ..unto the fathers by the **p**-s

Prosper
Gen. 39:3 ....all that he did to **p**
1 Cor. 16:2......as God hath **p**-ed him

Prosperity
Job 15:21 ....**p** the destroyer shall
Ps. 73:3........saw the **p** of the wicked
Prov. 1:32 ....**p** of fools . . . destroy

Proud
Ps. 12:3.........tongue that speaketh **p**
Prov. 6:17...A **p** look, a lying tongue
Is. 13:11.arrogancy of the **p** to cease
Jer. 50:32.....**p** shall stumble and fall
Rom. 1:30.......despiteful, **p**, boasters
1 Tim. 6:4.......is **p**, knowing nothing
James 4:6 ....God resisteth the **p**

Prove
Ex. 20:20..........God is come to **p** you
Luke 14:19.oxen, and I go to **p** them
Rom. 12:2 ....**p** what is that good
2 Cor. 8:8 ....**p** the sincerity of your
2 Cor. 13:5 ....**p** your own selves

Proverb
1 Kin. 9:7 ....a **p** and a byword
Jer. 24:9....reproach and a **p**, a taunt
John 16:29............and speakest no **p**
2 Pet. 2:22.....according to the true **p**

Provide
Gen. 22:8 .God will **p** himself a lamb
1 Sam. 16:17 ...**P** me now a man that
Matt. 10:9..**P** neither gold, nor silver
1 Tim. 5:8 ....if any **p** not for his own

Provision
Ps. 132:15 .....abundantly bless her **p**
Dan. 1:5....daily **p** of the king's meat
Rom. 13:14 .make not **p** for the flesh

Provoke
Ex. 23:21...obey his voice, **p** him not
Job 12:6..they that **p** God are secure
Prov. 20:2.**p**-th him to anger sinneth
Rom. 10:19 ...I will **p** you to jealousy

1 Cor. 13:5 ....is not easily **p**-d
Eph. 6:4 ....**p** not your children

Prudent
Prov. 12:16 ...**p** man covereth shame
Prov. 19:14...**p** wife is from the Lord
Jer. 49:7 ....perished from the **p**
1 Cor. 1:19....understanding of the **p**

Psalms
1 Chr. 16:9 ....sing **p** unto him
Ps. 95:2 ....joyful noise . . . with **p**
Luke 20:42......saith in the book of **P**
Luke 24:44 ..in the **p**, concerning me

Publican
Matt. 5:46 ....even the **p**-s the same
Matt. 10:3 ....and Matthew the **p**
Matt. 11:19.friend of **p**-s and sinners
Luke 18:13 ...the **p**, standing afar off

Pull
Gen. 8:9 .**p**-ed her in unto him in the
Ps. 31:4 ....**P** me out of the net
Jer. 12:3 ....**p** them out like sheep
Matt. 7:4.**p** out the mote out of thine
Luke 12:18...I will **p** down my barns
Luke 14:5 .**p** him out on the Sabbath
Jude 23 .....**p**-ing them out of the fire

Punish
Prov. 22:3........passion, and are **p**-ed
Is. 13:11 .....**p** the world for their evil
Acts 26:11 ....And I **p**-ed them oft

Punishment
Gen. 4:13........**p** is greater than I can
Job 19:29 ....the **p**-s of the sword
Matt. 25:46 .go . . . into everlasting **p**
2 Cor. 2:6 ....Sufficient . . . is this **p**

Purchase
Gen. 49:32 ....The **p** of the field
Ruth 4:10....have I **p**-d to be my wife
Acts 8:20......gift of God . . . **p**-d with
Acts 20:28 ....**p**-d with his own blood

Pure
2 Sam. 22:27...the **p** . . . shew thyself **p**
Job 11:4 ....My doctrine is **p**
Ps. 12:6.........words of the Lord are **p**
Ps. 24:4.........clean hands . . . **p** heart
Prov. 30:5.....Every word of God is **p**
Is. 1:25.....p-ly purge away thy dross
Matt. 5:8...Blessed are the **p** in heart
Phil. 4:8 ......whatsoever things are **p**
1 Tim. 1:5 .....charity out of a **p** heart
Titus 1:15................**p** all things are **p**
James 1:27 .**P** religion and undefiled

Purge
Ps. 51:7 ....**P** me with hyssop
Ps. 79:9 ....**p** away our sins
Is. 1:25 ....**p** away thy dross
Matt. 3:12 ....throughly **p** his floor
1 Cor. 5:7.....**P** out . . . the old leaven
2 Pet. 1:9...........**p**-d from his old sins

Purpose
Ezra 4:5................to frustrate their **p**
Job. 33:17.withdraw man from his **p**
Prov. 15:22 ....**p**-s are disappointed
Jer. 49:20...........**p**-s, that he hath **p**-d
Acts 26:16 ....appeared unto thee for this **p**
Rom. 8:28..............according to his **p**
Eph. 3:11 ....eternal **p** which he **p**-d

Pursue
Gen. 31:36........so hotly **p**-d after me
Lev. 26:17 ..flee when none **p**-th you
Job 30:15........**p** my soul as the wind
Ps. 34:14.............seek peace, and **p** it

Put
Gen. 3:15 ......**p** enmity between thee
Ex. 23:1 ....**p** not thine hand with the
Josh. 1:18........he shall be **p** to death
Job 18:6......his candle shall be **p** out
Job 38:36......**p** wisdom in the inward
Ps. 40:3...**p** a new song in my mouth
Is. 52:1..**p** on thy beautiful garments

Matt. 1:19 ....**p** her away privily
Matt. 5:31 ....shall **p** away his wife
Matt. 19:6.......let not man **p** asunder
Mark 4:21 ....**p** under a bushel
Luke 9:62...**p** his hand to the plough
Rom. 13:14....**p** ye on the Lord Jesus
1 Cor. 13:11 ..**p** away childish things
1 Cor. 15:53 ....**p** on immortality
Eph. 4:24...............**p** on the new man
Eph. 6:11 ......**P** on the whole armour

Q

Queen
1 Kin. 10:1...................the **q** of Sheba
Esther 1:9.Vashti the **q** made a feast
Matt. 12:42..The **q** of the south shall
Acts 8:27.................Candace **q** of the

Quench
Ps. 104:11 ....wild asses **q** their thirst
Song 8:7 ....Many waters cannot **q**
Is. 42:3...smoking flax shall he not **q**
Mark 9:43 ....never shall be **q**-ed
1 Thess. 5:19.............**Q** not the Spirit

Question
1 Kin. 10:1..prove him with hard **q**-s
Mark 8:11..........began to **q** with him
Mark 11:29..............ask of you one **q**
1 Cor. 10:25........no **q** for conscience
1 Tim. 6:4 ....**q**-s and strifes of words

Quicken
Ps. 119:88...........**Q** me . . . thy loving
John 5:21 ....Son **q**-eth whom he will
Rom. 8:11 ....**q** your mortal bodies
1 Pet. 3:18 ....**q**-ed by the Spirit

Quickly
Gen. 18:6............Make ready **q** three
Eccles. 4:12.......cord is not **q** broken
John 13:27.......That thou doest, do **q**
Rev. 3:11 ....Behold, I come **q**

Quiet
2 Chr. 14:1........land was **q** ten years
Job 21:23 ....wholly at ease and **q**
Eccles. 9:17 ....men are heard in **q**
Is. 7:4.............................be **q**; fear not
Acts 19:36 ...ye ought to be **q**, and to
1 Tim. 2:2 .....lead a **q** and peaceable

Quietness
Judg. 8:28......country was in **q** forty
Prov. 17:1 ....dry morsel, and **q**
Eccles. 4:6.............an handful with **q**
Acts 24:2 ...by thee we enjoy great **q**

Quit
Josh. 2:20 ....be **q** of thine oath
1 Sam. 4:9 ......**q** yourselves like men
1 Cor. 16:13..........**q** you like men, be

R

Race
Ps. 19:5............strong man to run a **r**
Eccles. 9:11 ....**r** is not to the swift

Rage
Ps. 2:1 ....Why do the heathen **r**
Prov. 6:34 .jealousy is the **r** of a man
Prov. 20:1..........strong drink is **r**-ing

Raiment
Deut. 8:4 ....Thy **r** waxed not old
Is. 63:3 ....I will stain all my **r**
Matt. 3:4 ....his **r** of camel's hair
Matt. 6:25meat, and the body than **r**
Matt. 28:3 ....his **r** white as snow
Luke 23:34 ....they parted his **r**

Rain
Gen. 7:12.**r** was upon the earth forty
Ex. 16:4 ......**r** bread from heaven for
Lev. 26:4 ....give you **r** in due season
Prov. 25:14 ....wind without **r**
Song 2:11.winter is past . . . **r** is over
Matt. 5:45 ......**r** on the just . . . unjust
Matt. 7:25 ....And the **r** descended
Heb. 6:7 ...earth . . . drinketh in the **r**

Raise
Ex. 23:1 ....not **r** a false report
Deut. 18:18........**r** them up a Prophet

Acts 10:43 ....shall receive **r** of sins
Heb. 9:22...shedding of blood is no **r**

Remnant
Deut. 3:11 ....of the **r** of giants
Jer. 6:9.........glean the **r** . . . as a vine
Matt. 22:6......the **r** took his servants
Rom. 11:5.............**r** according to the
Rev. 19:21 ....**r** were slain with the

Remove
Gen. 8:13.**r**-d . . . covering of the ark
1 Kin. 15:12 ....**r**-d all the idols
2 Kin. 18:4 .....He **r**-d the high places
Job 24:2 ....Some **r** the landmarks
Ps. 46:2 ....earth be **r**-d
Ps. 103:12 ......**r**-d our transgressions
Is. 24:20 ....be **r**-d like a cottage
Matt. 21:21 ....Be thou **r**-d
Luke 22:42 ....**r** this cup from me
1 Cor. 13:2 ....I could **r** mountains

Rend
Eccles. 3:7 ..time to **r** . . . time to sew
Is. 64:1..........wouldest **r** the heavens
Joel 2:13..................And **r** your heart
Matt. 7:6...........turn again and **r** you
John 19:24 ....Let us not **r** it, but cast

Render
Deut. 32:41 ....will **r** vengeance to
Ps. 94:2 ....**r** a reward to the proud
Prov. 24:12 ....**r** to every man
Matt. 22:21 .....**R** . . . unto Caesar the
Rom. 13:7........**R** . . . to all their dues
1 Cor. 7:3....husband **r** unto the wife
1 Pet. 3:9...........not **r**-ing evil for evil

Renew
Ps. 51:10 ....**r** a right spirit within
Ps. 103:5...........youth is **r**-ed like the
Rom. 12:2............**r**-ing of your mind
2 Cor. 4:16...inward man is **r**-ed day
Col. 3:10...................which is **r**-ed in
Titus 3:5.......**r**-ing of the Holy Ghost

Rent
1 Kin. 11:30........**r** it in twelve pieces
1 Kin. 19:11 ....wind **r** the mountains
Job 1:20.Job arose, and **r** his mantle
Is. 3:24............instead of a girdle a **r**
Matt. 27:51 ..veil of the temple was **r**

Repay
Deut. 7:10 ....**r** him to his face
Luke 10:35 .come again, I will **r** thee
Rom. 12:19.....I will **r**, saith the Lord
Philem. 19..........own hand, I will **r** it

Repent
Gen. 6:6 ....**r**-ed the Lord . . . made
Ex. 13:17 ......people **r** when they see
1 Sam. 15:35..........and the Lord **r**-ed
Job 42:6.......................**r** in dust and ashes
Ezek. 18:30...**R**, and turn yourselves
Matt. 3:2 ....**R** ye: for the kingdom of
Mark 1:15 ....**r** ye, and believe the
Mark 6:12.............that men should **r**
Luke 13:3.....except ye **r**, ye shall all
Luke 15:7 ....one sinner that **r**-eth
Acts 2:38.............**R**, and be baptized
Acts 3:19 ......**R** . . . and be converted
Acts 26:20 .should **r** and turn to God
2 Cor. 7:10................not to be **r**-ed of

Repentance
Matt. 3:8 ....fruits meet for **r**
Matt. 3:11..............with water unto **r**
Mark 1:4....................the baptism of **r**
Mark 2:17..................but sinners to **r**
Luke 24:47 ...**r** and remission of sins
2 Cor. 7:10 ..godly sorrow worketh **r**
Heb. 6:1....laying . . . foundation of **r**
2 Pet. 3:9...........all should come to **r**

Report
Prov. 15:30...........good **r** maketh the
Is. 53:1 ....Who hath believed our **r**
Acts 6:3..........seven men of honest **r**
Acts 16:2 ....well **r**-ed of by the
Phil. 4:8.............things are of good **r**
1 Tim. 5:10.......Well **r**-ed of for good
Heb. 11:39 ....obtained a good **r**

Reproach
Gen. 30:23 ....taken away my **r**
Job 27:6 ....my heart shall not **r** me
Ps. 15:3 ....**r** against his neighbour
Ps. 44:13 ....makest us a **r** to our
Ps. 74:10 ..long shall the adversary **r**
Ps. 119:39................Turn away my **r**
Prov. 14:34....sin is a **r** to any people
Is. 51:7 ....fear ye not the **r** of men
Jer. 24:9 ....be a **r** and a proverb
Ezek. 5:14 ......a **r** among the nations
Hos. 12:14 ....his **r** shall his Lord
Rom. 15:3........**r**-es of them that **r**-ed
1 Tim. 4:10 .both labour and suffer **r**
1 Pet. 4:14..........**r**-ed for the name of

Reproof
Job 26:11.............astonished at his **r**
Ps. 38:14......whose mouth are no **r**-s
Prov. 1:30.............despised all my **r**
Prov. 15:5 ......regardeth **r** is prudent
Prov. 15:10 ....hateth **r** shall die
Prov. 29:15....rod and **r** give wisdom
2 Tim. 3:16......for doctrine, for **r**, for

Reprove
Job 13:10 ....He will surely **r** you
Prov. 9:8.......**R** not a scorner, lest he
Prov. 29:1.....often **r**-d hardeneth his
Jer. 2:19 .....backslidings shall **r** thee
John 16:8 ....**r** the world of sin
Eph. 5:11.................but rather **r** them
2 Tim. 4:2..**r**, rebuke, exhort with all

Request
Judg. 8:24.....would desire a **r** of you
Neh. 2:4..........what dost thou make **r**
Job 6:8...........that I might have my **r**
Rom. 1:10 ....Making **r**, if by any
Phil. 4:6.let your **r**-s be made known

Require
Gen. 9:5...blood of your lives will I **r**
Deut. 10:12....what doth . . . God **r** of
Ps. 10:13 ....Thou wilt not **r** it
Prov. 30:7 ...things have I **r**-d of thee
Is. 1:12 .....hath **r**-d this at your hand
Mic. 6:8..........doth the Lord **r** of thee
Luke 12:20....thy soul shall be **r**-d of
Luke 19:23.**r**-d mine own with usury
1 Cor. 1:22......................Jews **r** a sign
1 Cor. 4:2 ....it is **r** in stewards

Reserved
Gen. 27:36.....not **r** a blessing for me
Judg. 21:22......**r** not to each man his
1 Pet. 1:4 ....**r** in heaven for you
Jude 6............**r** in everlasting chains

Resist
Matt. 5:39...............That ye **r** not evil
Luke 21:15.......able to gainsay nor **r**
Acts 6:10....not able to **r** the wisdom
Acts 7:51.....ye do always **r** the Holy
Rom. 13:2........**r**-eth the power, **r**-eth
James 4:6 ....God **r**-eth the proud
James 4:7.....**R** the devil, and he will

Respect
Gen. 4:4 ....Lord had **r** unto Abel
Lev. 19:15 ...**r** the person of the poor
Prov. 28:21 ..have **r** of persons is not
Is. 17:7......have **r** to the Holy One of
Acts 10:34.God is no **r**-er of persons
Rom. 2:11..no **r** of persons with God
Heb. 11:26.....**r** unto the recompence

Rest
Gen. 2:2..he **r**-ed on the seventh day
Gen. 49:15....he saw that **r** was good
Ex. 23:12 ....seventh day thou shalt **r**
Josh. 1:13.Lord . . . hath given you **r**
Josh. 14:15........land had **r** from war
Job 3:17 ....there the weary be at **r**
Ps. 37:7.........**R** in the Lord, and wait
Prov. 14:33........Wisdom **r**-eth in the
Prov. 29:17..son . . . shall give thee **r**
Is. 11:2..spirit of the Lord . . . **r** upon
Is. 14:3..give thee **r** from thy sorrow
Is. 57:2 ....shall **r** in their beds
Jer. 6:16.............find **r** for your souls
Lam. 5:5....we labour, and have no **r**
Hab. 3:16........**r** in the day of trouble

Matt. 11:28........and I will give you **r**
Matt. 26:45....sleep on . . . take you **r**
Luke 11:24 ....dry places, seeking **r**
2 Cor. 2:13......I had no **r** in my spirit
Heb. 3:11 ....not enter into my **r**
1 Pet. 4:2 ....live the **r** of his time in

Restore
Gen. 20:7 ....**r** the man his wife
2 Sam. 12:6 ....**r** the lamb fourfold
Ps. 23:3 ..he **r**-th my soul: he leadeth
Jer. 30:17 ....will **r** health unto thee
Matt. 17:11 ....first come, and **r** all
Mark 3:5......his hand was **r**-d whole
Luke 19:8 ....I **r** him fourfold

Restrain
Gen. 8:2..rain from heaven was **r**-ed
Job 15:8 ....dost thou **r** wisdom
Ezek. 31:15...............I **r**-ed the floods
Acts 14:18..........scarce **r**-ed they the

Resurrection
Luke 14:14 ....at the **r** of the just
Luke 20:27...deny that there is any **r**
John 11:25.............the **r**, and the life
Acts 24:15.....shall be a **r** of the dead
1 Cor. 15:13................if there be no **r**
Phil. 3:11 ....attain unto the **r**
Heb. 11:35.....might obtain a better **r**
1 Pet. 1:3............lively hope by the **r**
Rev. 20:5..................This is the first **r**

Return
Gen. 3:19 ......thou **r** unto the ground
Gen. 8:3 ......waters **r**-ed from off the
Gen. 32:9 ....**R** unto thy country, and
Gen. 43:18.......money . . . **r**-ed in our
Ex. 14:28 ....waters **r**-ed, and covered
Deut. 30:2 ...**r** unto the Lord thy God
Ruth 1:16........**r** from following after
2 Sam. 1:22 ...sword of Saul **r**-ed not
1 Kin. 20:26 ....at the **r** of the year
1 Kin. 22:17 ....**r** every man . . . in
Job 1:21..........naked shall I **r** thither
Job 33:25 ..**r** to the days of his youth
Prov. 26:27 .stone, it will **r** upon him
Eccles. 12:2 ....clouds **r** after the rain
Is. 10:21 ....The remnant shall **r**
Is. 38:8..............sun **r**-ed ten degrees
Is. 55:11................not **r** unto me void
Jer. 3:22 ..**R**, ye backsliding children
Jer. 4:1 ....Lord, **r** unto me
Jer. 23:20..............the Lord shall not **r**
Ezek. 16:55...**r** to their former estate
Hos. 2:7...........**r** to my first husband
Joel 2:14 ....if he will **r** and repent
Matt. 10:13....let your peace **r** to you
Matt. 12:44......I will **r** into my house
Luke 2:39 ....they **r**-ed into Galilee
Luke 4:14 ....**r**-ed in the power of the
Luke 10:17 ....the seventy **r**-ed again
Luke 24:9 ....**r**-ed from the sepulchre
Acts 13:34 ....no more to **r** to
1 Pet. 2:25 ....now **r**-ed unto the

Reveal
Job 20:27.heaven shall **r** his iniquity
Prov. 11:13 ..talebearer **r**-eth secrets
Is. 40:5 .glory of the Lord . . . be **r**-ed
Is. 53:1 ....arm of the Lord **r**-ed
Dan. 2:47..........couldest **r** this secret
Matt. 11:25......**r**-ed them unto babes
Matt. 16:17......blood hath not **r**-ed it
Luke 17:30 ....Son of man is **r**-ed
Rom. 8:18 ....glory . . . be **r**-ed in us
1 Cor. 3:13..........shall be **r**-ed by fire
Gal. 1:16..............To **r** his Son in me
2 Thess. 2:3 ..that man of sin be **r**-ed
1 Pet. 1:5 ....be **r**-ed in the last time

Revelation
Rom. 16:25 ....the **r** of the mystery
1 Cor. 14:6 ....speak to you . . . by **r**
Gal. 1:12.......by the **r** of Jesus Christ
Gal. 2:2 ....And I went up by **r**
Eph. 1:17........spirit of wisdom and **r**
Rev. 1:1 ....the **R** of Jesus Christ

Revenge
Jer. 15:15 .....**r** me of my persecutors
Nah. 1:2 ....the Lord **r**-th
2 Cor. 10:6 ....to **r** all disobedience

Reverence
Lev. 19:30..........and **r** my sanctuary
2 Sam. 9:6 .fell on his face, and did **r**
Ps. 89:7..........................to be had in **r**
Matt. 21:37..........They will **r** my son
Eph. 5:33.......wife . . . **r** her husband
Heb. 12:28...............**r** and godly fear

Revile
Matt. 5:11.......when men shall **r** you
Matt. 27:39............passed by **r**-d him
Mark 15:32.....crucified with him **r**-d
Acts 23:4..........**R**-st thou God's high
1 Pet. 2:23.....Who, when he was **r**-d

Reward
Gen. 15:1.........thy exceeding great **r**
Gen. 44:4................**r**-ed evil for good
Deut. 10:17......persons, nor taketh **r**
2 Sam. 3:39.....Lord . . . **r** the doer of
Job 7:2.......hireling . . . **r** of his work
Ps. 58:11...........a **r** for the righteous
Ps. 94:2.........render a **r** to the proud
Prov. 24:20.........no **r** to the evil man
Eccles. 4:9.....good **r** for their labour
Is. 1:23..................followeth after **r**-s
Is. 5:23..........justify the wicked for **r**
Is. 45:13................not for price nor **r**
Is. 62:11...................his **r** is with him
Mic. 7:3.............judge asketh for a **r**
Matt. 5:12..great is your **r** in heaven
Matt. 6:2................They have their **r**
Matt. 10:42............no wise lose his **r**
Acts 1:18..field with the **r** of iniquity
1 Cor. 3:8......shall receive his own **r**
1 Tim. 5:18.............is worthy of his **r**
2 John 8................we receive a full **r**
Rev. 22:12................my **r** is with me

Rich
Gen. 13:2..........Abram was very **r** in
Ex. 30:15..........**r** shall not give more
Ps. 49:2......low and high, **r** and poor
Prov. 18:23.the **r** answereth roughly
Prov. 23:4.............Labour not to be **r**
Eccles. 10:20..............curse not the **r**
Jer. 9:23.....**r** man glory in his riches
Matt. 19:23.**r** man shall hardly enter
Luke 1:53.........**r** he hath sent empty
Luke 6:24....woe unto you that are **r**
Luke 16:1........There was a certain **r**
Luke 18:23.............for he was very **r**
Rom. 10:12..**r** unto all that call upon
1 Cor. 4:8................full, now ye are **r**
Eph. 2:4........God, who is **r** in mercy
Col. 3:16..word . . . dwell in you **r**-ly
1 Tim. 6:18..........be **r** in good works
James 1:11.......the **r** man fade away
Rev. 13:16..........**r** and poor, free and

Riches
1 Kin. 3:11.....neither . . . asked **r** for
Job 36:19.esteem thy **r**? no, not gold
Ps. 62:10...if **r** increase, set not your
Prov. 3:16.....left hand **r** and honour
Prov. 13:7........poor, yet hath great **r**
Prov. 22:1.to be chosen than great **r**
Prov. 23:5......**r** . . . make themselves
Prov. 30:8........neither poverty nor **r**
Is. 45:3.......hidden **r** of secret places
Jer. 9:23.........rich man glory in his **r**
Mark 10:24.............trust in **r** to enter
Luke 8:14...choked with cares and **r**
2 Cor. 8:2............**r** of their liberality
Eph. 1:7..................the **r** of his grace
Eph. 3:8......unsearchable **r** of Christ
1 Tim. 6:17...nor trust in uncertain **r**
James 5:2.........Your **r** are corrupted

Right
Gen. 24:48..........led me in the **r** way
Deut. 21:17.........**r** of the firstborn is
Deut. 32:4....God . . . just and **r** is he
2 Kin. 10:15....Is thine heart **r**, as my
Job 34:6.....Should I lie against my **r**
Ps. 17:1................Hear the **r**, O Lord
Ps. 19:8......statutes of the Lord are **r**
Ps. 51:10..renew a **r** spirit within me
Ps. 119:75..........thy judgments are **r**
Prov. 4:11..............led thee in **r** paths
Prov. 14:12...a way which seemeth **r**
Prov. 24:26..........lips that giveth a **r**
Is. 41:13.....God will hold thy **r** hand
Jer. 17:11.getteth riches . . . not by **r**
Ezek. 18:5........which is lawful and **r**
Hos. 14:9.......ways of the Lord are **r**
Matt. 5:29.....................**r** eye offend thee
Matt. 22:44.....Sit thou on my **r** hand
Matt. 26:64...on the **r** hand of power
Mark 5:15.................and in his **r** mind
Luke 22:50...............cut off his **r** ear
John 21:6.........the **r** side of the ship
Acts 8:21.................thy heart is not **r**
Gal. 2:9...........**r** hands of fellowship
2 Pet. 2:15...........forsaken the **r** way
Rev. 22:14............**r** to the tree of life

Righteous
Gen. 18:23......................destroy the **r**
Ex. 9:27........Lord is **r**, and I and my
Ex. 23:7.........innocent and **r** slay thou
Num. 23:10......die the death of the **r**
1 Sam. 24:17.Thou art more **r** than I
Job 4:7........where were the **r** cut off
Ps. 11:5............The Lord trieth the **r**
Ps. 33:1...Rejoice in the Lord, O ye **r**
Ps. 37:16........little that a **r** man hath
Ps. 55:22.....suffer the **r** to be moved
Ps. 119:137..........**R** art thou, O Lord
Prov. 2:20.......keep the paths of the **r**
Prov. 11:28.........**r** shall flourish as a
Prov. 13:5...........**r** man hateth lying
Prov. 16:13..**R** lips are the delight of
Eccles. 3:17.....God shall judge the **r**
Is. 53:11...my **r** servant justify many
Jer. 23:5.........unto David a **r** Branch
Dan. 9:14....God is **r** in all his works
Amos 2:6............sold the **r** for silver
Matt. 9:13........not come to call the **r**
Matt. 13:43.....shall the **r** shine forth
Luke 23:47......Certainly this was a **r**
John 7:24................judge **r** judgment
Rom. 3:10............none **r**, no, not one
1 Tim. 1:9......law is not made for a **r**
James 5:16............prayer of a **r** man
1 Pet. 4:18..........**r** scarcely be saved

Righteousness
Gen. 15:6..........counted to him for **r**
Job 27:6.............................My **r** I hold fast
Job 29:14....I put on **r**, and it clothed
Ps. 17:15.............behold thy face in **r**
Ps. 23:3.leadeth me in the paths of **r**
Ps. 97:6............heavens declare his **r**
Ps. 111:3........his **r** endureth for ever
Prov. 11:19................**r** tendeth to life
Prov. 14:34..........**R** exalteth a nation
Prov. 16:8.......Better is a little with **r**
Is. 32:1...........a king shall reign in **r**
Is. 45:8...................skies pour down **r**
Is. 48:18.....**r** as the waves of the sea
Is. 51:5....My **r** is near; my salvation
Is. 59:17......put on **r** as a breastplate
Jer. 33:15......Branch of **r** to grow up
Ezek. 33:13............trust to his own **r**
Dan. 12:3...................turn many to **r**
Hos. 10:12.....Sow to yourselves in **r**
Matt. 5:6......hunger and thirt after **r**
Matt. 5:20...........I shall exceed the **r**
Acts 13:10.devil, thou enemy of all **r**
Rom. 4:3.......counted unto him for **r**
Rom. 4:22..........imputed to him for **r**
Rom. 5:18.....by the **r** of one the free
2 Cor. 6:14......fellowship hath **r** with
Gal. 2:21............if **r** come by the law
Gal. 3:6..........accounted to him for **r**
Eph. 4:24..........created in **r** and true
Eph. 6:14............the breastplate of **r**
1 Tim. 6:11..follow after **r**, godliness
2 Tim. 4:8...........for me a crown of **r**
Heb. 7:2.......interpretation King of **r**
Heb. 12:11....the peaceable fruit of **r**
1 Pet. 3:14.......ye suffer for **r**-s' sake

Riot
Prov. 23:20........**r**-ous eaters of flesh
Luke 15:13.......substance with **r**-ous
Titus 1:6..................not accused of **r**
2 Pet. 2:13....pleasure to **r** in the day

Ripe
Gen. 40:10.....brought forth **r** grapes
Ex. 22:29..............first of thy **r** fruits
Rev. 14:15....harvest of the earth is **r**
Rev. 14:18.......her grapes are fully **r**

Rise
Gen. 19:2..............ye shall **r** up early
Josh. 12:1...........the **r**-ing of the sun
Job 9:7...........the sun, and it **r**-th not
Ps. 27:3.......war should **r** against me
Ps. 35:11.....False witnesses did **r** up
Ps. 86:14....proud are **r**-n against me
Ps. 113:3.....**r**-ing of the sun unto the
Prov. 31:15.......**r**-th . . . while it is yet
Is. 32:9...**R** up, ye women . . . at ease
Is. 60:1.........glory of the Lord is **r**-n
Ezek. 7:11......Violence is **r**-n up into
Matt. 11:11.....not **r**-n a greater than
Matt. 14:2....Baptist . . . **r**-n from the
Matt. 20:19..........third day he shall **r**
Matt. 24:7...........nation . . . **r** against
Mark 12:25......shall **r** from the dead
Mark 13:12............**r** up against their
Mark 16:6.....he is **r**-n; he is not here
Luke 5:23....................**R** up and walk
Luke 12:54....cloud **r** out of the west
Luke 22:46...........**r** and pray, lest ye
Luke 24:34....The Lord is **r**-n indeed
Acts 10:13........**R**, Peter; kill, and eat
1 Cor. 15:13.....then is Christ not **r**-n
Col. 3:1....ye then be **r**-n with Christ
1 Thess. 4:16...dead in Christ shall **r**

River
Gen. 2:10..........a **r** went out of Eden
Josh. 1:4......great **r**, the **r** Euphrates
Job 40:23......................drinketh up a **r**
Ps. 1:3.....planted by the **r**-s of water
Ps. 46:4.......a **r**, the streams whereof
Ps. 137:1..........By the **r**-s of Babylon
Is. 11:15....shake his hand over the **r**
Is. 32:2.....**r**-s of water in a dry place
Jer. 2:18.....drink the waters of the **r**
Lam. 2:18.....tears run down like a **r**
John 7:38......flow **r**-s of living water
Rev. 22:1.........pure **r** of water of life

Roar
Job 4:10......................**r**-ing of the lion
Job 37:4.............After it a voice **r**-eth
Jer. 25:30........The Lord shall **r** from
1 Pet. 5:8...........devil, as a **r**-ing lion

Rob
Lev. 26:22......**r** you of your children
Prov. 22:22..................**R** not the poor
Prov. 28:24...Whoso **r**-eth his father
Is. 10:2.......they may **r** the fatherless
Mal. 3:8................Will a man **r** God?
2 Cor. 11:8.......I **r**-ed other churches

Robber
Job 12:6...tabernacles of **r**-s prosper
Jer. 7:11.............become a den of **r**-s
John 10:1.......same is a thief and a **r**
John 18:40.............Barabbas was a **r**
Acts 19:37..................**r**-s of churches

Robe
1 Sam. 24:4...off the skirt of Saul's **r**
Is. 61:10..........the **r** of righteousness
Matt. 27:28......put on him a scarlet **r**
Luke 15:22......Bring forth the best **r**
John 19:2.......put on him a purple **r**
Rev. 7:14.........have washed their **r**-s

Rock
Ex. 17:6...........thou shalt smite the **r**
Ex. 33:22.........thee in a clift of the **r**
Num. 20:11.rod he smote the **r** twice
Deut. 32:4.........................He is the **R**
1 Sam. 2:2............any **r** like our God
2 Sam. 22:2..............The Lord is my **r**
Ps. 27:5.......shall set me up upon a **r**
Ps. 31:3......art my **r** and my fortress
Prov. 30:19............a serpent upon a **r**
Is. 8:14..........................for a **r** of offence
Is. 51:1...........**r** whence ye are hewn
Matt. 7:24....built his house upon a **r**
Matt. 16:18..upon this **r** . . . build my
Mark 15:46..sepulchre . . . hewn . . .
a **r**
Luke 8:6................some fell upon a **r**
Rom. 9:33..........................**r** of offence

Rod
Ex. 4:4..........became a **r** in his hand
Ex. 7:12.......Aaron's **r** swallowed up
Num. 17:8......**r** or Aaron . . . budded
2 Sam. 7:14...chasten him with the **r**
Ps. 23:4.**r** and thy staff they comfort
Prov. 13:24...spareth his **r** hateth his
Is. 11:1.......**r** out of the stem of Jesse
Ezek. 20:37..........to pass under the **r**
Heb. 9:4.....Aaron's rod that budded
Rev. 19:15.rule them with a **r** of iron

Roll
Is. 34:4.heavens . . . **r**-ed together as
Jer. 36:2.......Take thee a **r** of a book
Matt. 28:2..**r**-ed back the stone from
Mark 16:3.shall **r** us away the stone

Roof
Gen. 19:8.under the shadow of my **r**
2 Sam. 11:2........from the **r** he saw a
Job 29:10.......to the **r** of their mouth
Mark 2:4..uncovered the **r** where he

Room
Gen. 6:14...........**r**-s shalt thou make
Ps. 31:8.........set my feet in a large **r**
Matt. 23:6.....uppermost **r**-s at feasts
Luke 2:7.......no **r** for them in the inn
Luke 14:8.sit not down . . . highest **r**
Acts 1:13.....went up into an upper **r**
1 Cor. 14:16..........**r** of the unlearned

Root
Job 18:14....confidence shall be **r**-ed
Job 19:28.............the **r** of the matter
Ps. 80:9...........cause it to take deep **r**
Is. 53:2.............**r** out of a dry ground
Jer. 12:2.................they have taken **r**
Matt. 3:10.........axe is laid unto the **r**
Mark 4:6...........had no **r**, it withered
Luke 17:6...........plucked up by the **r**
Rom. 11:16.................if the **r** be holy
Eph. 3:17.**r**-ed and grounded in love
1 Tim. 6:10.money is the **r** of all evil

Rose
Song 2:1............I am the **r** of Sharon
Is. 35:1....desert . . . blossom as the **r**

Rose
Josh. 3:16....waters . . . **r** up upon an
Luke 16:31.....though one **r** from the
Rom. 14:9.....Christ both died, and **r**

Round
Jos. 6:3........go **r** about the city once
2 Sam. 5:9...built **r** about from Millo
Rev. 4:3.rainbow **r** about the throne

Ruin
Prov. 26:28.............flattering mouth worketh **r**
Is. 23:13.................he brought it to **r**
Luke 6:49..**r** of that house was great
Acts 15:16.....will build again the **r**-s

Rule
Gen. 1:16.....**r** the day . . . **r** the night
Judg. 8:22...................**R** thou over us
Prov. 8:16.................By me princes **r**
Prov. 25:28..no **r** over his own spirit
Matt. 2:6..............**r** my people Israel
Mark 10:42..........**r** over the Gentiles
Gal. 6:16.....walk according to this **r**
Col. 3:15........peace of God **r** in your
1 Tim. 3:5.........not how to **r** his own
Rev. 2:27...**r** them with a rod of iron

Ruler
Ps. 2:2........**r**-s take counsel together
Prov. 6:7......no guide, overseer, or **r**
Is. 22:3...All thy **r**-s are fled together
Matt. 9:18................came a certain **r**
Matt. 24:45.......**r** over his household
John 3:1.Nicodemus, a **r** of the Jews
Eph. 6:12...the **r**-s of the darkness of

Rumour
Ezek. 7:26................**r** shall be upon **r**
Matt. 24:6.........wars and **r**-s of wars
Luke 7:17...........**r** of him went forth

Run
Lev. 15:13.....bathe his flesh in **r**-ing
2 Kin. 4:22.may **r** to the man of God
2 Chr. 16:9.eyes of the Lord **r** to and
Ps. 23:5..................my cup **r**-eth over
Prov. 1:16..............their feet **r** to evil
Prov. 6:18...feet . . . **r**-ing to mischief
Is. 40:31.............**r**, and not be weary
Ezek. 32:14...........rivers to **r** like oil
Matt. 9:17............the wine **r**-eth out
1 Cor. 9:24..................**r** in a race **r** all
Gal. 2:2.................**r**, or had **r**, in vain
Gal. 5:7..........................Ye did **r** well
Heb. 12:1.....**r** with patience the race

Rust
Matt. 6:19...moth and **r** doth corrupt
James 5:3............the **r** . . . shall be a

S

Sabbath
Ex. 16:26..seventh day, which is the **s**
Ex. 20:8.......Remember the **s** day, to
Ex. 31:15........seventh is the **s** of rest
Lev. 25:8.number seven **s**-s of years
Lev. 26:2...........Ye shall keep my **s**-s
Num. 15:32...gathered sticks upon **s**
Deut. 5:12..............Keep the **s** day to
Matt. 12:8......Lord even of the **s** day
Matt. 28:1.............In the end of the **s**
Mark 2:27.........**s** was made for man
Mark 3:4.........do good on the **s** days
John 19:31.....**s** day was an high day
Acts 1:12................a **s** day's journey

Sackcloth
Esther 4:1...........put on **s** with ashes
Job 16:15.......sewed **s** upon my skin
Dan. 9:3.....fasting, and **s**, and ashes
Matt. 11:21.......repented . . . in **s** and ashes

Sacrifice
Gen. 31:54.Jacob offered **s** upon the
Ex. 12:27.....**s** of the Lord's passover
Is. 43:23....honoured me with thy **s**-s
Jer. 46:10.........God of hosts hath a **s**
Hos. 6:6.....desired mercy, and not **s**
Matt. 9:13.......have mercy, and not **s**
Acts 7:41........offered **s** unto the idol
Rom. 12:1........your bodies a living **s**
Heb. 9:26.....put away sin by the **s** of
Heb. 11:4.....a more excellent **s** than
Heb. 13:16.........such **s**-s God is well

Safe
2 Sam. 18:29.Is the young man . . . **s**
Ezek. 34:27....shall be **s** in their land
Phil. 3:1..................but for you it is **s**

Safely
Lev. 26:5...........dwell in your land **s**
Prov. 3:23.............walk in thy way **s**
Mark 14:44.............lead him away **s**

Saints
Deut. 33:2....with ten thousands of **s**
1 Sam. 2:9........keep the feet of his **s**
Ps. 37:28..............forsaketh not his **s**
Ps. 89:5...............congregation of the **s**
Matt. 27:52.bodies of the **s** . . . arose
Rom. 1:7.........................called to be **s**
Rom. 8:27........intercession for the **s**
1 Cor. 6:2......**s** shall judge the world
Phil. 1:1........all the **s** in Christ Jesus
1 Thess. 3:13......Christ with all his **s**
Rev. 14:12...............patience of the **s**
Rev. 20:9...............the camp of the **s**

Sake
Gen. 8:21.........curse the ground . . . man's **s**
1 Sam. 12:22...for his great name's **s**
Ps. 23:3.....................for his name's **s**
Ps. 44:22.........for thy **s** are we killed
Ps. 115:1....................for thy truth's **s**
Matt. 16:25........lose his life for my **s**
Luke 6:22....................Son of man's **s**
Luke 18:29.........kingdom of God's **s**
John 13:37................my life for thy **s**
Rom. 8:36.thy **s** we are killed all the
Rom. 13:5................for conscience **s**
1 Cor. 9:23.........do for the gospel's **s**
2 Cor. 8:9......for your **s**-s he became
1 Tim. 5:23.wine for thy stomach's **s**
Titus 1:11..............for filthy lucre's **s**
2 John 2....................For the truth's **s**

Salt
Job 6:6.................be eaten without **s**
Matt. 5:13..............the **s** of the earth
Mark 9:50..........................**S** is good
Col. 4:6.....................seasoned with **s**
James 3:12...yield **s** water and fresh

Salvation
Gen. 49:18..waited for thy **s**, O Lord
Deut. 32:15.............the Rock of his **s**
Job 13:16.........He also shall be my **s**
Ps. 3:8.....**S** belongeth unto the Lord
Ps. 27:1.................my light and my **s**
Ps. 68:20.......our God is the God of **s**
Ps. 98:3...........seen the **s** of our God
Ps. 116:13................take the cup of **s**
Ps. 119:155.**S** is far from the wicked
Is. 33:2............our **s** . . . time of trouble
Is. 49:6.....**s** unto the end of the earth
Is. 52:7.......................that publisheth **s**
Is. 56:1.......................**s** is near to come
Jonah 2:9...................**S** is of the Lord
Luke 2:30..........eyes have seen thy **s**
Luke 3:6.flesh shall see the **s** of God
Luke 19:9......is **s** come to this house
Acts 4:12..Neither . . . **s** in any other
Acts 16:17.........unto us the way of **s**
Rom. 1:16.........power of God unto **s**
Rom. 11:11...........**s** is come unto the
2 Cor. 6:2.....................in the day of **s**
2 Cor. 7:10.worketh repentance to **s**
Eph. 6:17...........................helmet of **s**
Phil. 2:12..........work out your own **s**
1 Thess. 5:9......obtain **s** by our Lord
2 Tim. 3:15....make thee wise unto **s**
Heb. 1:14.......who shall be heirs of **s**
Heb. 2:3..........we neglect so great **s**
Heb. 9:28..............without sin unto **s**
1 Pet. 1:5............through faith unto **s**
Rev. 7:10.**S** to our God which sitteth
Rev. 12:10..........Now is come **s**, and

Same
2 Sam. 5:7.........**s** is the city of David
Ps. 102:27......But thou art the **s**, and
Matt. 5:46...even the publicans the **s**
Luke 2:8.in the **s** country shepherds
John 1:2........**s** was in the beginning
Rom. 10:12......**s** Lord over all is rich
Heb. 13:8........**s** yesterday . . . to day

Sanctify
Gen. 2:3......seventh day, and **s**-ied it
Ex. 13:2...**S** unto me all the firstborn
Deut. 5:12..Keep the sabbath day to **s** it
Is. 29:23..........they shall **s** my name
John 17:17..........**S** them through thy
Rom. 15:16..**s**-ied by the Holy Ghost
1 Cor. 7:14...is **s**-ied by the husband
1 Thess. 5:23.......God of peace **s** you
Jude 1..........**s**-ied by God the Father

Sanctuary
Ex. 25:8...........let them make me a **s**
Ps. 73:17......I went into the **s** of God
Ps. 150:1..............Praise God in his **s**
Is. 60:13...beautify the place of my **s**
Jer. 51:51......**s**-s of the Lord's house
Dan. 8:14.......shall the **s** be cleansed
Heb. 8:2...............A minister of the **s**

Sand
Gen. 32:12....seed as the **s** of the sea
Job 29:18.multiply my days as the **s**
Matt. 7:26.built his house upon the **s**

Sat
Gen. 18:1.....**s** in the tent door in the
Ex. 2:15.............he **s** down by a well
Job 2:8.......**s** down among the ashes
Jonah 4:5.........booth, and **s** under it
Matt. 9:10..................Jesus **s** at meat
Matt. 26:20...**s** down with the twelve
Mark 16:19.....**s** on the right hand of
Luke 7:15.......he that was dead **s** up
Luke 10:39..Mary . . . **s** at Jesus' feet

Satan
Job 1:6 ......S came also among them
Zech. 3:2 ....Lord rebuke thee, O S
Matt. 4:10 ....Get thee hence, S
Matt. 12:26 ....S cast out S
Matt. 16:23 ....Get thee behind me, S
Mark 1:13...forty days, tempted of S
Luke 10:18......beheld S . . . fall from
Luke 22:3.........entered S into Judas
Acts 5:3.........why hath S filled thine heart
2 Cor. 2:11.................S should get an
1 Thess. 2:18 ....but S hindered us
1 Tim. 1:20.....have delivered unto S
Rev. 3:9..........of the synagogue of S
Rev. 12:9.......called the Devil, and S
Rev. 20:7 ....S . . . loosed out of his

Satisfied
Lev. 26:26 ....eat, and not be s
Job 27:14...shall not be s with bread
Ps. 22:26 ......meek shall eat and be s
Prov. 12:11....tilleth his land . . . be s
Prov. 27:20..eyes of man are never s
Joel 2:26.........eat in plenty, and be s

Satisfy
Ps. 91:16 ....long life will I s him
Prov. 6:30 ....steal to s his soul
Mark 8:4.........man s these men with

Save
Gen. 14:24.......S only that which the
Ps. 18:31 .....s the Lord . . . s our God
Matt. 11:27 ......man the Father, s the
Luke 18:19..........none is good, s one
2 Cor. 11:24 ....forty stripes s one

Save
Deut. 28:29.........no man shall s thee
1 Sam. 10:27....How shall this man s us
Ps. 6:4 .....s me for thy mercies' sake
Ps. 28:9.........S thy people, and bless
Ps. 86:2....s thy servant that trusteth
Prov. 20:22 ....and he shall s thee
Is. 35:4 ....God . . . will come and s
Is. 63:1 ....mighty to s
Jer. 42:11...............with you to s you
Ezek. 18:27................s his soul alive
Matt. 1:21......s his people from their
Matt. 16:25........s his life shall lose it
Matt. 18:11 ......s that which was lost
Luke 23:35.s himself, if he be Christ
John 12:27.....Father, s me from this
Acts 27:43 ......centurion, willing to s
1 Cor. 7:16....s thy husband . . . s thy
1 Tim. 1:15 ....world to s sinners
James 1:21 ....able to s your souls
James 4:12...........to s and to destroy
James 5:15...prayer of faith . . . s the

Saved
Ps. 44:7 ....s us from our enemies
Jer. 8:20 ......ended, and we are not s
Matt. 19:25...........Who then can be s
Mark 16:16 ......is baptized shall be s
Luke 1:71............s from our enemies
Luke 7:50......faith hath s thee; go in
John 3:17..........through him . . . be s
John 10:9 ....enter in, he shall be s
Acts 4:12 ....whereby we must be s
Acts 16:30......what must I do to be s
Rom. 5:10 ....we shall be s by his life
Rom. 8:24 ....For we are s by hope
Eph. 2:5 ....by grace ye are s
2 Tim. 1:9.....hath s us, and called us

Saviour
2 Sam. 22:3...............my refuge, my s
Is. 19:20 ....he shall send them a s
Is. 43:11 ....beside me there is no s
Is. 49:26 ....I the Lord am thy S
Luke 2:11.....a S, which is Christ the
John 4:42..Christ, the S of the world
Eph. 5:23........he is the s of the body
2 Tim. 1:10 ....our S Jesus Christ
Titus 2:13 ....God and our S Jesus
2 Pet. 1:11 ....our Lord and S Jesus

Savour
Gen. 8:21 ......Lord smelled a sweet s
Joel 2:20 ....his ill s shall come up
Matt. 5:13 ....salt have lost his s
2 Cor. 2:15 ....a sweet s of Christ

Saw
Gen. 1:4 ..God s the light, that it was
Job 29:11.when the eye s me, it gave
Ps. 114:3 ....The sea s it, and fled
Is. 59:16 ......s that there was no man
Dan. 4:5 ....I s a dream
Matt. 2:11 ....s the young child
Mark 1:10 ....s the heavens opened
John 1:48...................fig tree, I s thee

Say
Ex. 3:13 ......what shall I s unto them
Job 33:32 ..If thou hast anything to s
Job 37:19 ..Teach us what we shall s
Ps. 106:48.let all the people s, Amen
Prov. 3:28 .S not unto thy neighbour
Is. 58:9 ....he shall s, Here I am
Matt. 7:22 .....will s to me in that day
Matt. 16:13 ....Whom do men s that I
Luke 7:40...somewhat to s unto thee
Luke 17:21...Neither shall they s, Lo
1 John 1:8.........s that ye have no sin
Rev. 22:17 ...Spirit . . . bride s, Come

Saying
Gen. 37:11 .his father observed the s
Ps. 49:13 .posterity approve their s-s
Ps. 78:2...............utter dark s-s of old
Luke 18:34.this s was hid from them
John 6:60.................This is an hard s
John 8:51 ....If a man keep my s
1 Tim. 1:15...........This is a faithful s

Scarlet
Gen. 38:28.upon his hand a s thread
Ex. 25:4.........blue, and purple, and s
Is. 1:18 ....your sins be as s
Nah. 2:3 ....valiant men are in s
Matt. 27:28 ....put on him a s robe
Rev. 17:3 .....upon a s coloured beast

Scatter
Job 18:15 ....brimstone . . . s-ed upon
Job 38:24 ...s-eth the east wind upon
Ps. 92:9 .workers of iniquity . . . s-ed
Prov. 11:24...There is that s-eth, and
Is. 18:7 ....a people s-ed and peeled
Jer. 23:1.......destroy and s the sheep
Matt. 26:31.....the flock shall be s-ed

Scourge
Job 5:21...............the s of the tongue
Matt. 20:19 ....mock . . . s, and to crucify
Matt. 27:26..when he had s-ed Jesus
John 2:15.....made a s of small cords
Heb. 12:6 ....s-eth every son

Scribe
Neh. 8:4.......Ezra the s stood upon a
Matt. 2:4 ....chief priests and s-s
Matt. 23:13 ....woe . . . s-s and
Mark 1:22 ....and not as the s-s
Mark 12:38 ....Beware of the s-s
1 Cor. 1:20.........wise? where is the s

Scripture(s)
Dan. 10:21 ......noted in the s of truth
Matt. 21:42 ..ye never read in the s-s
Matt. 22:29 .err, not knowing the s-s
Mark 14:49 ..the s-s must be fulfilled
Luke 4:21 ....day is this s fulfilled
Luke 24:32....he opened to us the s-s
John 5:39 ....Search the s-s; for in
John 10:35 ....s cannot be broken
John 20:9........For . . . knew not the s
Acts 18:24 ....mighty in the s-s
Rom. 4:3 ....For what saith the s
2 Tim. 3:15..hast known the holy s-s

Sea
Gen. 1:10 ....waters called he S-s
Ex. 10:19 ....cast them into the Red s
2 Sam. 17:11 .....sand that is by the s
Job 7:12 ....Am I a s, or a whale
Ps. 24:2 ....founded it upon the s-s
Ps. 65:5 ....are afar off upon the s
Ps. 146:6......s, and all that therein is
Is. 11:9.......as the waters cover the s
Is. 57:20...........are like the troubled s
Jer. 25:22.........isles . . . beyond the s
Nah. 1:4.................He rebuketh the s
Matt. 8:26...........the winds and the s
Matt. 14:26 ....walking on the s
2 Cor. 11:26.............in perils in the s
Rev. 4:6 ....was a s of glass
Rev. 21:1 ....there was no more s

Seal
1 Kin. 21:8.........s-ed them with his s
Song 8:6 ....as a s upon thine heart
Is. 29:11 ....a book that is s-ed
Rom. 4:11 ....s of the righteousness
2 Cor. 1:22 .....Who hath also s-ed us
Eph. 1:13...s-ed with that holy Spirit
Rev. 5:1................s-ed with seven s-s
Rev. 9:4..s of God in their foreheads

Search
Job 11:7...........by s-ing find out God
Ps. 139:23...S me . . . know my heart
Jer. 17:10.........I the Lord s the heart
John 5:39.......S the scriptures; for in
John 7:52...........................S, and look
Acts 17:11 ..s-ed the scriptures daily

Season
Gen. 1:14 .....be for signs, and for s-s
Lev. 26:4 ....give you rain in due s
Job 5:26.............corn cometh in his s
Ps. 104:27 ....their meat in due s
Eccles. 3:1 ....every thing there is a s
Dan. 2:21.changeth the times . . . s-s
John 5:35 ....willing for a s to rejoice
Acts 1:7.to know the times of the s-s
Acts 24:25....................when I have a convenient s
Gal. 6:9 ....in due s we shall reap
Col. 4:6 .....with grace, s-ed with salt
2 Tim. 4:2...........instant in s, out of s

Seat
Ex. 25:17 ....a mercy s of pure gold
1 Sam. 4:18.from off the s backward
Ps. 1:1 ....in the s of the scornful
Ezek. 28:2 ....I sit in the s of God
Rom. 14:10.the judgment s of Christ

Second
Gen. 1:8........................were the s day
Matt. 22:39 ....s is like unto it
1 Cor. 15:47 ....s man is the Lord
Rev. 2:11 ....hurt of the s death

Secret
Deut. 27:15 ......putteth it in a s place
Job 11:6..............shew thee the s-s of
Job 15:8...............heard the s of God
Job 40:13...............bind their faces in s
Ps. 19:12 ....cleanse . . . me from s
Ps. 44:21 ....knoweth the s-s of the
Ps. 91:1........s place of the most high
Prov. 9:17 ....bread eaten in s
Prov. 21:14..........A gift in s pacifieth
Prov. 27:5......rebuke is better than s
Song 2:14..........s places of the stairs
Is. 19...........I have not spoken in s
Matt. 6:4.........thine alms may be in s
Luke 8:17..................For nothing is s
Rom. 2:16 .....God shall judge the s-s
Rom. 16:25.....kept s since the world

See
Ex. 33:20 ....no man s me, and live
Job 9:11 ....by me, and I s him not
Job 19:26 ....my flesh shall I s God
Ps. 16:10....Holy One to s corruption
Ps. 34:8...........s that the Lord is good
Ps. 49:19......They shall never s light
Ps. 66:5 ....and s the works of God
Song 7:12 .....us s if the vine flourish
Is. 29:18 ....the blind shall s
Is. 35:2 ....s the glory of the Lord
Jer. 2:31....s ye the word of the Lord
Ezek. 12:2 ....eyes to s, and s not
Joel 2:28 ..young men shall s visions
Matt. 5:16....may s your good works
Matt. 11:8 ....went ye out for to s
Matt. 16:28.............s the Son of man
Luke 8:10 ....s-ing the night not s
Luke 17:23 ....S here; or, s there
John 4:29....and s a man, which told
John 16:16...little while . . . not s me
1 Cor. 13:12...........s through a glass,

Heb. 12:14...no man shall s the Lord
1 John 3:2......we shall s him as he is

Seed
Gen. 1:11....................herb yielding s
Gen. 8:22.............s-time and harvest
Lev. 26:16.....................sow your s in
Eccles. 11:6..........morning sow thy s
Is. 55:10..............give s to the sower
Is. 65:9...bring forth a s out of Jacob
Matt. 13:22..........s among the thorns
Matt. 13:31...to a grain of mustard s
Luke 8:5..sower went out to sow his s
Luke 8:11.........s is the word of God

Seek
Deut. 4:29............s the Lord thy God
2 Chr. 7:14.........pray, and s my face
Job 7:21...shalt s me in the morning
Ps. 24:6.....generation of them that s
Ps. 34:14.........s peace, and pursue it
Ps. 63:1...................early will I s thee
Prov. 8:17...s me early shall find me
Eccles. 7:25.............to s out wisdom
Is. 34:16.........S ye out of the book of
Is. 55:6..S ye the Lord while he may
Ezek. 34:12......will I s out my sheep
Ezek. 34:16......s that which was lost
Dan. 9:3....................s by prayer and
Hos. 10:12......it is time to s the Lord
Amos 5:4....S ye me . . . and ye shall
Matt. 6:33.......s ye first the kingdom
Matt. 7:7..............s, and ye shall find
Mark 8:12..generation s after a sign
Luke 11:10........he that s-eth findeth
John 5:30.........I s not mine own will
John 8:50.............one that s-eth and
Acts 10:21...........I am he whom ye s
1 Cor. 13:5.............s-eth not her own
Gal. 1:10...........do I s to please men

Seem
1 Sam. 8:23......S-eth it to you a light
Prov. 14:12....s-eth right unto a man
Matt. 11:26.....s-ed good in thy sight
1 Cor. 3:18.....s-eth to be wise in this
James 1:26..............s to be religious

Seen
Gen. 32:30.............s God face to face
Job 5:3........s the foolish taking root
Is. 6:5................eyes have s the King
Matt. 2:2...........s his star in the east
Luke 2:30..eyes have s thy salvation
Rom. 8:24.......hope . . . s is not hope
1 Cor. 2:9....................Eye hath not s
Heb. 11:1.....evidence of things not s

Sell
Gen. 25:31....S me . . . thy birthright
2 Kin. 4:7..Go, s the oil, and pay thy
Prov. 23:23.....Buy the truth, and s it
Matt. 19:21...go and s that thou hast

Send
Gen. 24:7......S his angel before thee
Is. 6:8........................Here I am; s me
Matt. 5:45.s-eth rain on the just and
Matt. 9:38........s forth labourers into
Luke 12:49...........s fire on the earth

Sent
Gen. 8:7, 8.s forth a raven . . . a dove
Is. 48:16..God, and his Spirit, hath s
Matt. 10:5.........These twelve Jesus s
Luke 4:18........................s me to heal
Acts 13:4..s forth by the Holy Ghost
Gal. 4:4...............God s forth his Son
1 John 4:9....s his only begotten Son

Separate
Gen. 13:9..........s thyself, I pray thee
Num. 6:3............s himself from wine
Acts 13:2...S me Barnabas and Saul
Rom. 8:35.........s us from the love of

Sepulchre
Is. 22:16................hewed thee out a s
Matt. 23:27.........like unto whited s-s
John 19:41.garden a new s, wherein
John 20:11......stood without at the s

Serpent
Gen. 3:1.................s was more subtil
Ex. 7:12.....rod, and they became s-s
Num. 21:9.............made a s of brass
Prov. 23:32...............it biteth like a s
Matt. 7:10...........will he give him a s
Mark 16:18......they shall take up s-s
John 3:14..........Moses lifted up the s
2 Cor. 11:3.................s beguiled Eve
Rev. 12:9.........old s, called the Devil

Servant
Gen. 9:25...........a s of s-s shall he be
Ex. 14:31........Lord, and his s Moses
1 Sam. 3:9.............Speak, Lord . . . s
Job 1:8.............considered my s Job
Job 4:18...........put no trust in his s-s
Ps. 31:16......face to shine upon thy s
Prov. 22:7...........borrower is s to the
Matt. 25:21...........good and faithful s
Luke 2:29.........thy s depart in peace
Gal. 4:7...........no more a s, but a son
Col. 3:22.S-s, obey in all things your

Serve
Deut. 6:13.....fear the Lord . . . and s
Josh. 22:5..s him with all your heart
Ps. 2:11..............S the Lord with fear
Ps. 100:2...S the Lord with gladness
Jer. 5:19.........so shall ye s strangers
Matt. 4:10........him only shalt thou s
Matt. 6:24.............No man can s two
John 12:26...............If any man s me
Rom. 12:11...in spirit; s-ing the Lord
Gal. 5:13.........by love s one another
Titus 3:3..........s-ing divers lusts and

Service
Jer. 22:13......useth his neighbour's s
Rom. 12:1..........is your reasonable s
Phil. 2:30..........supply your lack of s
Heb. 9:6.accomplishing the s of God

Set
Gen. 4:15............s a mark upon Cain
Lev. 17:10.............s my face against
Deut. 30:19........s before you life and
Ps. 8:1..............s thy glory above the
Ps. 40:2...........s my feet upon a rock
Song 8:6...S me as a seal upon thine
Is. 38:1...........S thine house in order
Jer. 5:26......s a trap, they catch men
Matt. 5:14............city . . . s on an hill
Acts 13:47..........s thee to be a light
Rom. 14:10...s at nought thy brother
Col. 3:2....S your affection on things
James 3:6...............is s on fire of hell

Seven
Gen. 29:20..Jacob served s years for
Ps. 119:164.S times a day do I praise
Prov. 9:1.....Wisdom . . . her s pillars
Is. 4:1.....s women shall take hold of
Dan. 9:25.....Prince shall be s weeks
Zech. 4:2..............s pipes . . . s lamps
Matt. 12:45.........s other spirits more
Matt. 18:21..forgive him? till s times
Acts 6:3.........s men of honest report
Rev. 1:4.........John to the s churches
Rev. 1:12.........s golden candlesticks
Rev. 3:1......................s Spirits of God
Rev. 15:1..s angels . . . s last plagues

Shadow
Gen. 19:8.......under the s of my roof
1 Chr. 29:15...our days . . . are as a s
Ps. 17:8.......under the s of thy wings
Ps. 23:4.........valley of the s of death
Ps. 91:1....................s of the almighty
Song 2:17........day break . . . s-s flee
Col. 2:17...........a s of things to come
Heb. 8:5.............s of heavenly things
James 1:17.........neither s of turning

Shake
Lev. 26:36........... sound of a s-n leaf
Job 16:4...............s mine head at you
Is. 13:13............s the heavens . . . earth
Matt. 10:14.........s off the dust of your
Matt. 11:7...a reed s-n with the wind
Luke 6:38.........pressed down . . . s-n

Shame
Ex. 32:25..............naked unto their s
Ps. 4:2................turn my glory into s
Ps. 83:16..........Fill their faces with s
Prov. 12:16.................man covereth s
Prov. 19:26........a son that causeth s
Is. 54:4........forget the s of thy youth
Zeph. 3:5..........unjust knoweth no s
Acts 5:41...............worthy to suffer s
1 Cor. 11:6.........s for a woman to be
1 Cor. 14:35.s for women to speak in
Phil. 3:19.................glory is in their s

Sharp
Prov. 27:17.............Iron s-eneth iron
Heb. 4:12........s-er . . . any twoedged sword

Shave
Judg. 16:19.......s off the seven locks
2 Sam. 10:4.........s-d . . . half of their
Is. 7:20..........Lord s with a razor that
1 Cor. 11:6.....woman to be shorn or s-n

Shed
Gen. 9:6......man shall his blood be s
Matt. 26:28.my blood . . . s for many
Luke 22:20.blood, which is s for you
Rom. 3:15....feet are swift to s blood

Sheep
Gen. 4:2........Abel was a keeper of s
29:9....Rachel . . . with her father's s
Num. 27:17.............s which have no
1 Sam. 16:19..David . . . is with the s
Job 31:20.warmed . . . fleece of my s
Ps. 44:22..........as s for the slaughter
Ps. 100:3.............the s of his pasture
Ps. 119:176...........astray like a lost s
Is. 53:6.All we like s . . . gone astray
Is. 53:7.............s before her shearers
Jer. 12:3................s for the slaughter
Matt. 9:36.......s having no shepherd
Matt. 15:24.......lost s of the house of
Matt. 25:32....divideth his s from the
Matt. 26:31..........................s of the flock
John 10:3.calleth his own s by name
John 10:27.........My s hear my voice
John 21:16..........................Feed my s
Heb. 13:20....great shepherd of the s
1 Pet. 2:25.....were as s going astray

Shepherd
Gen. 46:34.......................every s is an
Num. 27:17.............which have no s
Ps. 23:1....................The Lord is my s
Is. 40:11...........feed his flock like a s
Ezek. 34:5........because there is no s
Ezek. 37:24.........all shall have one s
Zeph. 2:6....................cottages for s-s
Zech. 11:16.............I will raise up a s
Matt. 9:36.........as sheep having no s
Matt. 26:31.............I will smite the s
Luke 2:8.........s-s abiding in the field
John 10:11.................I am the good s
1 Pet. 2:25......unto the S and Bishop

Shew
Gen. 12:1......a land that I will s thee
Esther 1:11.........s the people . . . her
Job 11:6.............s thee the secrets of
Ps. 25:4.........S me thy ways, O Lord
Prov. 18:24...must s himself friendly
Dan. 2:2...........s the king his dream
John 14:8....................s us the Father
Acts 26:23.....s light unto the people

Shield
Gen. 15:1.............Abram: I am thy s
2 Sam. 22:3.he is my s, and the horn
Ps. 28:7...........my strength and my s
Eph. 6:16...........taking the s of faith

Shine
Num. 6:25........make his face s upon
Ps. 104:15....oil to make his face to s
Prov. 4:18..s-th more and more unto
Is. 60:1..........Arise, s; for thy light is
Matt. 5:16............Let your light so s
Matt. 13:43.............righteous s forth
Luke 24:4.................men . . . in s-ing
John 1:5..........light s-th in darkness

2 Cor. 4:4 gospel should s unto them
2 Pet. 1:19 ....light that s-th in a dark
1 John 2:8 ....true light now s-th

Shoe
Ex. 12:11 ....your s-s on your feet
Deut. 33:25........s-s shall be iron and
Amos 2:6 ....poor for a pair of s-s
Mark 1:7 ...latchet of whose s-s I am
Acts 7:33......Put off thy s-s from thy

Shone
Ex. 34:29...........the skin of his face s
2 Kin. 3:22 ....sun s upon the water
Luke 2:9 ...glory of the Lord s round
Acts 22:6 ....s from heaven a great

Shoot
1 Sam. 20:20 .....I will s three arrows
Ps. 64:4 ....s in secret at the perfect
Mark 4:32 ..s-eth out great branches

Shore
Matt. 13:2...multitude stood on the s
John 21:4...........Jesus stood on the s
Acts 21:5.......kneeled down on the s

Short
Num. 11:23 ......Lord's hand waxed s
Ps. 89:47 ....how s my time is
Rom. 3:23............come s of the glory
Rom. 9:28 ....s work will the Lord
1 Cor. 7:29......brethren, the time is s

Shout
Ex. 32:18......them that s for mastery
Josh. 6:16...............Joshua said . . . S
Ps. 5:11...........let them ever s for joy
Ps. 47:5 ....God is gone up with a s
Ps. 78:65 ......s-eth by reason of wine
1 Thess. 4:16.....descend . . . with a s

Shower
Deut. 32:2.......the s-s upon the grass
Job 24:8 ....wet with the s-s
Luke 12:54 ye say, There cometh a s

Shut
Gen. 7:16................the Lord s him in
Job 38:8..........who s up the sea with
Song 4:12...a spring s up, a fountain
Jer. 36:5..........I am s up; I cannot go
Dan. 6:22 ....hath s the lions' mouths
Dan. 12:4.......Daniel, s up the words
Matt. 23:13 ....s up the kingdom of
Acts 5:23......prison truly found we s
Gal. 3:23 ....s up unto the faith
Rev. 21:25 ...gates of it shall not be s

Sick
Prov. 13:12.......Hope . . . maketh the heart s
Song 2:5.................for I am s of love
Matt. 25:36.....I was s, and ye visited
Mark 2:17.................. .they that are s
John 11:2.......brother Lazarus was s
James 5:14 ....Is any s among you
James 5:15...prayer of faith . . . save the s

Sickle
Deut. 16:9 .....to put the s to the corn
Joel 3:13.........Put ye in the s, for the
Rev. 14:15 .Thrust in thy s, and reap

Sickness
Deut. 7:15.take away from thee all s
Matt. 4:23.....healing all manner of s
Mark 3:15....have power to heal s-es
John 11:4.....This s is not unto death

Side
Ex. 32:26.......Who is on the Lord's s
Ps. 118:6........................Lord is on my s
Matt. 13:4......seeds fell by the way s
John 19:34........a spear pierced his s
John 20:20 ....his hands and his s
2 Cor. 4:8...........troubled on every s

Sight
Gen. 18:3 have found favour in thy s
Ruth 2:13 ....find favour in thy s
Job 19:15.......I am an alien in their s
Ps. 90:4 ....thousand years in thy s
Matt. 11:5 ....blind receive their s
Matt. 20:34 ....their eyes received s
Luke 4:18 ....recovering of s to the
Luke 21:11 ....fearful s-s and great
Acts 22:13 ....Saul, receive thy s
2 Cor. 5:7.......walk by faith, not by s
Rev. 4:3 .....in s like unto an emerald

Sign
Ex. 31:13 ....a s between me and you
Is. 7:11 ....Ask thee a s of the Lord
Is. 55:13 ....for an everlasting s
Ezek. 14:8 ....make him a s and a
Matt. 12:38 ....we would see a s from
Matt. 24:3 ......be the s of thy coming
Mark 13:22 ....shew s-s and wonders
1 Cor. 1:22.........the Jews require a s
2 Thess. 2:9 ...with all power and s-s
Rev. 15:1....saw another s in heaven

Silence
Eccles. 3:7.................a time to keep s
Jer. 8:14............God hath put us to s
Amos 5:13.........prudent shall keep s
1 Cor. 14:28 ......keep s in the church
1 Cor. 14:34 ....your women keep s
Rev. 8:1...........there was s in heaven

Silver
Prov. 16:16 ....to be chosen than s
Prov. 25:11 ....of gold in pictures of s
Eccles. 5:10 ....loveth s shall not be
Is. 1:22 ....Thy s is become dross
Is. 39:2................s . . . gold . . . spices
Amos 2:6......sold the righteous for s
Zech. 11:12....price thirty pieces of s
Matt. 26:15........for thirty pieces of s
Acts 3:6 ....S and gold have I none
Acts 20:33 ....coveted no man's s
James 5:3......gold and s is cankered

Sin
Gen. 4:7 ....s lieth at the door
Gen. 18:20 ....their s is very grievous
Ex. 32:30........Ye have s-ed a great s
Job 2:10 ...did not Job s with his lips
Ps. 25:7 Remember not the s-s of my
Ps. 79:9...............purge away our s-s
Prov. 10:12 ....love covereth all s-s
Is. 1:18 ....s-s be as scarlet
Is. 30:1 ....they may add s to s
Jer. 51:5...........s against the Holy One
Matt. 1:21......his people from . . . s-s
Matt. 12:31.........All manner of s . . .
Matt. 18:21 ....brother s against me
Matt. 26:28...for the remission of s-s
Mark 2:7.....forgive s-s but God only
Luke 11:4..............forgive us our s-s
John 1:29....taketh away the s of the
John 8:7..............He that is without s
John 8:11 ....go and s no more
Acts 22:16 ....wash away thy s-s
Acts 26:18 receive forgiveness of s-s
Rom. 5:12 ...s entered into the world
Rom. 6:23...........wages of s is death
Rom. 14:23................not of faith is s
1 Cor. 15:3 ....Christ died for our s-s
1 Cor. 15:56...........sting of death is s
2 Cor. 5:21 ..s for us, who knew no s
James 5:20 ....hide a multitude of s-s
1 Pet. 2:22.......Who did no s, neither
1 John 1:8 .we say that we have no s
1 John 1:9.........If we confess our s-s
1 John 2:1.....any man s, we have an
1 John 3:4...s in the transgression of
1 John 5:16...There is a s unto death
1 John 5:17.All unrighteousness is s
Rev. 1:5........washed us from our s-s

Sinful
Is. 1:4 .....Ah s nation, a people laden
Mark 8:38........................s generation
Luke 5:8 ....for I am a s man, O Lord
Rom. 8:3 ....the likeness of s flesh

Sing
Ex. 15:1............I will s unto the Lord
2 Sam. 22:50 ....s praises unto thy
Job 29:13..widow's heart to s for joy
Ps. 33:3 ....S unto him a new song
Ps. 100:2.......his presence with s-ing
Prov. 29:6 ....righteous doth s and
Is. 5:1....s to my well beloved a song
1 Cor. 14:15.....I will s with the spirit
Col. 3:16 .....s-ing with grace in your
James 5:13..merry? let him s psalms

Sinned
Deut. 1:41....have s against the Lord
Job 1:22...............In all this Job s not
Ps. 51:4 ....thee only, have I s
Luke 15:18 ....s against heaven
Rom. 3:23 ...s, and come short of the
Rom. 5:12 ....for that all have s
1 John 1:10....say that we have not s

Sinner
Ps. 1:1 ......standeth in the way of s-s
Prov. 1:10.................if s-s entice thee
Eccles. 9:18 ....one s destroyeth
Matt. 9:10...............publicans and s-s
Matt. 9:13.........but s-s to repentance
Luke 15:7 ....one s that repenteth
Luke 18:13.........be merciful to me a s
John 9:31 ....God heareth not s-s
Rom. 5:8 ....while we were yet s-s
1 Tim. 1:15....Jesus came . . . to save s-s

Sister
Job 17:14...art my mother, and my s
Prov. 7:4.......wisdom, Thou art my s
Matt. 12:50..is my brother, and my s
Luke 10:39.........had a s called Mary
Rom. 16:1........unto you Phebe our s

Sit
Ruth 3:18 ....S still, my daughter
1 Kin. 22:19 ....Lord s-ing on his
Ps. 1:1 .s-teth in the seat . . . scornful
Ps. 110:1 .....S thou at my right hand
Ps. 127:2...........................to s up late
Ezek. 28:2 ....I s in the seat of God
Matt. 9:9...s-ing at receipt of custom
Matt. 21:5..meek, and s-ing upon an
Matt. 26:36 ....S ye here, while I go
Matt. 27:61 .....s-ing over against the
Luke 8:35 ...s-ing at the feet of Jesus
John 12:15 ....s-ing on an ass's colt
Acts 8:28.............s-ing in his chariot

Skin
Ex. 34:29........the s of his face shone
Job 2:4 ....S for s, yea, all that a
Job 19:20 .My bone cleaveth to my s
Jer. 13:23 ......Ethiopian change his s
Mark 1:6......a girdle of a s about his

Sky
Job 37:18 ....spread out the s
Matt. 16:2, 3 ....for the s is red
Luke 12:56..discern the face of the s
Heb. 11:12 ....as the stars of the s

Slain
Gen. 4:23...s a man to my wounding
1 Sam. 18:7 ....Saul hath s his
Luke 9:22 ..s . . . raised the third day
Rev. 5:12..................Lamb that was s

Slaughter
Ps. 44:22.................as sheep for the s
Is. 53:7.....................as a lamb to the s
Rom. 8:36 ....as sheep for the s
James 5:5 ....as in a day of s

Slay
Gen. 4:14.........findeth me shall s me
Job 13:15.Though he s me, yet will I
Ps. 34:21........Evil shall s the wicked
John 5:16 ....Jesus, and sought to s
Acts 11:7........Arise, Peter; s and eat

Sleep
Gen. 2:21 ..deep s to fall upon Adam
Deut. 31:16 ....s with thy fathers
Ps. 76:6...................cast into a dead s
Prov. 3:24...........thy s shall be sweet
Prov. 6:10...........Yet a little s, a little
Prov. 20:13........Love not s, lest thou
Jer. 31:26 ....my s was sweet
Matt. 9:24 ....not dead, but s-eth
Matt. 26:45.S on now, and take your
Mark 13:36 ....he find you s-ing
John 11:11.Our friend Lazarus s-eth
Acts 20:9 ....fallen into a deep s
1 Cor. 15:51 ....We shall not all s

1 Thess. 4:14 ...also which s in Jesus
1 Thess. 5:10..whether we wake or s

Slew
Gen. 4:8.Abel his brother, and s him
Ex. 13:15........Lord s all the firstborn
1 Sam. 17:50 ...Phillistine, and s him
Matt. 2:16................s all the children
Acts 10:39.....s and hanged on a tree

Sling
Judg. 20:16...........s stones at an hair
1 Sam. 17:40....his s was in his hand

Slothful
Prov. 18:9...........that is s in his work
Matt. 25:26......wicked and s servant
Heb. 6:12..................That ye be not s

Slow
Ex. 4:10.......s of speech . . . s tongue
Ps. 103:8...s to anger, and plenteous
Prov. 16:32........He that is s to anger
James 1:19......s to speak, s to wrath

Slumber
Ps. 121:3........keepeth thee will not s
Prov. 6:10........a little sleep, a little s
Is. 5:27............none shall s nor sleep
Matt. 25:5.......they all s-ed and slept
Rom. 11:8..given them the spirit of s

Small
Deut. 25:13 .weights, a great and a s
2 Sam. 7:19..........s thing in thy sight
Job 8:7...............thy beginning was s
Mark 8:7.......they had a few s fishes

Smell
Gen. 27:27......s of my son is as the s
Ps. 115:6......noses . . . but they s not
Song 2:13...........grape give a good s
Is. 3:24...................instead of sweet s

Smite
Ex. 7:17..............I will s with the rod
Ex. 12:12................s all the firstborn
Ps. 121:6....sun . . . not s thee by day
Prov. 19:25........S a scorner, and the
Jer. 18:18........s him with the tongue
Matt. 5:39..s thee on thy right cheek
Matt. 26:31........I will s the shepherd
Acts 23:3........God shall s thee, thou
2 Cor. 11:20.................if a man s you

Smoke
Gen. 15:17.....behold a s-ing furnace
Ps. 102:3...days are consumed like s
Prov. 10:26................as s to the eyes
Matt. 12:20.....s-ing flax shall he not

Smooth
Gen. 27:11..............and I am a s man
1 Sam. 17:40.chose him five s stones
Ps. 55:21..words . . . s-er than butter
Is. 30:10.........speak unto us s things
Luke 3:5.......rough ways . . . made s

Smote
Ex. 7:20.s the waters . . . in the river
Num. 20:11..........he s the rock twice
Num. 22:23.............Balaam s the ass
Matt. 26:51................and s off his ear
Luke 18:13.............s upon his breast
Acts 12:23....angel of the Lord s him

Snare
Ex. 10:7........this man be a s unto us
Job 18:8.............he walketh upon a s
Ps. 91:3........from the s of the fowler
Prov. 7:23..........bird hasteth to the s
Rom. 11:9.....their table be made a s
2 Tim. 2:26...out of the s of the devil

Snow
Num. 12:10..........leprous, white as s
Ps. 51:7.........I shall be whiter than s
Prov. 25:13....cold of s in the time of
Prov. 26:1...................As s in summer
Is. 1:18....scarlet . . . be as white as s
Matt. 28:3.......his raiment white as s
Rev. 1:14......like wool, as white as s

Sober
Rom. 12:3.......................to think s-ly
1 Thess. 5:6................watch and be s
Titus 2:2..........aged men be s, grave
1 Pet. 5:8...................Be s, be vigilant

Sojourn
Gen. 26:3....S in this land, and I will
Ex. 12:48..stranger shall s with thee
Is. 23:7.............carry her afar off to s
Acts 7:6...............s in a strange land
1 Pet. 1:17.....time of your s-ing here

Sold
Gen. 25:33..................s his birthright
Gen. 45:4....brother, whom ye s into
Lev. 25:23..land . . . not be s for ever
Joel 3:3..............................s a girl for wine
Matt. 10:29...............sparrows s for a
Matt. 13:46.....went and s all that he
Acts 5:1........his wife, s a possession

Soldier
Mark 15:16.....s-s led him away into
Luke 23:36.the s-s also mocked him
Acts 28:16......with a s that kept him
2 Tim. 2:3...........as a good s of Jesus

Somewhat
Luke 7:40...I have s to say unto thee
Rev. 2:4............I have s against thee

Son
Gen. 6:2................s-s of God saw the
Gen. 22:2........Take now thy s, thine only s
Gen. 37:33.................It is my s's coat
Deut. 8:5..as a man chasteneth his s
Ps. 2:7..........................Thou art my S
Ps. 8:4.....s of man, that thou visitest
Prov. 10:1........wise s maketh a glad
Prov. 17:25........A foolish s is a grief
Is. 7:14.........virgin shall . . . bear a s
Is. 14:12.....Lucifer, s of the morning
Is. 60:4...thy s-s shall come from far
Ezek. 2:1...S of man, stand upon thy
Dan. 7:13.........one like the S of man
Hos. 11:1....called my s out of Egypt
Matt. 3:17.........This is my beloved S
Matt. 11:27....no man knoweth the S
Matt. 13:55..............the carpenter's s
Matt. 16:16..........S of the living God
Matt. 22:42......Christ? whose s is he
Matt. 26:63..the Christ, the S of God
Matt. 27:43..................I am the S of God
Mark 5:7......S of the most high God
Mark 14:61........the S of the Blessed
Luke 1:31..bring forth a s, and shalt
Luke 2:7......................her firstborn s
Luke 4:22.........Is not this Joseph's s
Luke 15:11.certain man had two s-s
Luke 15:24..........this my s was dead
John 1:18...................only begotten S
John 4:50....Go thy way; thy s liveth
John 5:21....the S quickeneth whom
John 6:42.this Jesus, the s of Joseph
John 14:13.........be glorified in the S
John 19:26......Woman, behold thy s
Rom. 8:32........spared not his own S
Gal. 4:7..................but a s; and if a s
2 Thess. 2:3............the s of perdition
Heb. 6:6.crucify . . . S of God afresh
Rev. 21:7.......be his God . . . be my s

Song
Ex. 15:2......The Lord is my strength and s
Job 30:9...................now am I their s
Ps. 33:3..........Sing unto him a new s
Ps. 137:4...How . . . sing the Lord's s
Prov. 25:20.......singeth s-s . . . heavy
Song 1:1...........................The s of s-s
Is. 5:1.....sing to my well beloved a s
Ezek. 33:32............as a very lovely s
Eph. 5:19.....hymns and spiritual s-s

Soon
Job 32:22.....maker would s take me
Ps. 37:2..............s be cut down like the
Matt. 21:20.s is the fig tree withered

Sore
Gen. 20:8..............men were s afraid
Job 5:18....maketh s, and bindeth up
Matt. 17:15......lunatick, and s vexed
Luke 16:21...came and licked his s-s

Sorrow
Gen. 3:16........greatly multiply thy s
Gen. 42:38............with s to the grave
1 Sam. 1:15...woman of a s-ful spirit
Job 21:17..........God distributeth s-s
Job 41:22.............s is turned into joy
Ps. 18:4..s-s of death compassed me
Ps. 127:2.............eat the bread of s-s
Prov. 15:13........by s of the heart the
Eccles. 1:18.knowledge increaseth s
Eccles. 7:3..S is better than laughter
Is. 14:3........give thee rest from thy s
Is. 35:10........s and sighing shall flee
Is. 53:3...........................a man of s-s
Jer. 8:18.....comfort myself against s
Lam. 1:12..................s like unto my s
Matt. 26:38......My soul is exceeding s-ful
Mark 13:8........the beginnings of s-s
2 Cor. 7:10......s worketh repentance

Sort
Gen. 6:19...two of every s shalt thou
Deut. 22:11......garment of divers s-s

Sought
Ex. 2:15.................he s to slay Moses
Ex. 33:7.every one which s the Lord
2 Chr. 16:12.......he s not to the Lord
Eccles. 2:3...I s in mine heart to give
Matt. 2:20......s the young child's life
Matt. 21:46......s to lay hands on him
Luke 2:44.............s him among their
Luke 19:3.................he s to see Jesus
Rom. 9:32..................s it not by faith

Soul
Gen. 2:7.........man became a living s
Gen. 12:13....my s shall live because
Lev. 4:2.........................if a s shall sin
Deut. 4:29.......all thy heart and . . . s
Judg. 16:16..s was vexed unto death
1 Sam. 18:1.knit with the s of David
Job 10:1......My s is weary of my life
Job 19:2...........long will ye vex my s
Job 33:30.......back his s from the pit
Ps. 16:10..........not leave my s in hell
Ps. 23:3..................He restoreth my s
Ps. 42:1.........panteth my s after thee
Ps. 62:1........my s waiteth upon God
Ps. 63:1..........my s thirsteth for thee
Ps. 103:1........Bless the Lord, O my s
Prov. 24:12......he that keepeth thy s
Is. 55:3.....hear, and your s shall live
Jer. 31:12..s . . . as a watered garden
Jer. 38:16.Lord . . . that made us this s
Ezek. 18:4.s that sinneth, it shall die
Matt. 10:28........not able to kill the s
Matt. 11:29.....find rest unto your s-s
Matt. 16:26.world, and lose his own s
Luke 1:46...s doth magnify the Lord
Luke 12:19.say to my s, S, thou hast
John 12:27......Now is my s troubled
Acts 4:32.......one heart and of one s
Rom. 13:1.......Let every s be subject
1 Thess. 5:23...spirit and s and body
Heb. 4:12.dividing . . . of s and spirit
Heb. 6:19..........as an anchor of the s
Heb. 10:39........to the saving of the s
James 1:21....is able to save your s-s
1 Pet. 2:11...which war against the s
Rev. 16:3..........every living s died in

Sound
1 Kin. 18:41...s of abundance of rain
Job 15:21.....dreadful s is in his ears
Prov. 2:7............layeth up s wisdom
Prov. 3:21...................Keep s wisdom
Jer. 25:10................s of the millstones
Jer. 50:22.....s of battle is in the land
Joel 2:1...........s an alarm in my holy
Acts 2:2..........came a s from heaven
Rom. 10:18..s went into all the earth
1 Cor. 13:1.....become as s-ing brass
1 Tim. 1:10.....contrary to s doctrine
2 Tim. 1:13..........the form of s words
Titus 1:13.........may be s in the faith
Rev. 1:15................s of many waters
Rev. 8:7..............The first angel s-ed

South
Gen. 24:62......dwelt in the s country
Job 37:9...Out of the s . . . whirlwind
Eccles. 11:3......tree fall toward the s
Matt. 12:42 ....queen of the s
Acts 27:13......the s wind blew softly

Sow
Gen. 47:23...........Ye shall s the land
Lev. 26:16...........s your seed in vain
Job 4:8....iniquity, and s wickedness
Ps. 126:5 .....s in tears . . . reap in joy
Prov. 22:8....s-eth iniquity shall reap
Eccles. 11:4........the wind shall not s
Eccles. 11:6 ..the morning s thy seed
Is. 32:20........that s beside all waters
Is. 55:10.....may give seed to the s-er
Jer. 4:3...............s not among thorns
Matt. 6:26.....fowls . . . for they s not
Matt. 13:3............s-er went forth to s
Luke 12:24...........neither s nor reap
Luke 19:21.......reapest that . . . didst not s
1 Cor. 9:11......s-n unto you spiritual
1 Cor. 15:42...........s-n in corruption
1 Cor. 15:44..........s-n a natural body
2 Cor. 9:6..He which s-eth sparingly
Gal. 6:7.......whatsoever a man s-eth
James 3:18 ....is s-n in peace

Space
Gen. 29:14..........abode . . . the s of a
Lev. 25:30............the s of a full year
Rev. 2:21.........I gave her s to repent

Spake
Gen. 8:15 ....God s unto Noah
Job 2:13.......none s a word unto him
Ps. 33:9 ....he s, and it was done
Jonah 2:10 ....Lord s unto the fish
Mal. 3:16 ....Lord s often one to
Matt. 13:34....s Jesus . . . in parables
Mark 3:9............he s to his disciples
John 7:46Never man s like this man
Acts 19:6 ....and s with tongues
1 Cor. 13:11.........................I s as a child
1 Cor. 14:5that ye all s with tongues
2 Pet. 1:21.......s as they were moved

Spare
Ps. 72:13 ....s the poor and needy
Ps. 78:50..........s-d not their soul from
Prov. 13:24.....s-th his rod hateth his
Is. 9:19 ....no man shall s his brother
Mal. 3:17 ....s them as a man s-th his
Acts 20:29............not s-ing the flock
Rom. 8:32 ....s-d not his own Son
Rom. 11:21 ....s not the natural
2 Cor. 9:6.........which soweth s-ingly
2 Cor. 13:2.I come again, I will not s
2 Pet. 2:4 ....God s-d not the angels

Speak
Gen. 18:32 ....s yet but this once
Deut. 9:4....S not thou in thine heart
Job 11:5............oh that God would s
Job 17:5..s-eth flattery to his friends
Job 33:14 .God s-eth once, yea twice
Job 41:3 ....s soft words unto thee
Ps. 41:5....Mine enemies s evil of me
Prov. 23:9 .S not in the ears of a fool
Eccles. 3:7 ....silence, and a time to s
Is. 40:2...................S ye comfortably
Zeph. 3:13 ....do iniquity, nor s lies
Matt. 10:19....how or what ye shall s
Mark 13:11.......not ye that s, but the
Mark 16:17 ....shall s with new
Luke 1:20 ....dumb, and not able to s
Luke 6:26 .....men shall s well of you
John 3:11.......We s that we do know
John 16:13 ....shall not s of himself
Acts 2:4 ....began to s with other
Rom. 3:5 ....(I s as a man)
1 Cor. 2:7....we s the wisdom of God
1 Cor. 13:1.....I s with the tongues of
Eph. 6:20.........boldly, as I ought to s
Titus 3:2 ....s evil of no man
James 1:19..slow to s, slow to wrath
James 4:11.S not evil one of another
1 Pet. 4:11......If any man s, let him s
2 Pet. 2:18.....s great swelling words

Spear
Josh. 8:18.....Stretch out the s that is
1 Sam. 26:7............his s stuck in the
2 Sam. 1:6.....Saul leaned upon his s
Is. 2:4.....their s-s into pruninghooks
John 19:34..with a s pierced his side

Speech
Gen. 11:1 ......one language . . . one s
Ex. 4:10 ....but I am slow of s
Job 13:17 ....Hear diligently my s
Job 37:19........we cannot order our s
Song 4:3.....................thy s is comely
Mark 7:32.....an impediment in his s
Rom. 16:18.good words, and fair s-s
2 Cor. 11:6........though I be rude in s
Col. 4:6 ....s be always with grace

Speed
1 Sam. 20:38.Make s, haste, stay not
Ezra 6:12...........let it be done with s
Ps. 31:2..........................deliver me s-ily
Luke 18:8..he will avenge them s-ily

Spend
Job 21:13 ....s their days in wealth
Is. 55:2................................do ye s money
2 Cor. 12:15..I will very gladly s and

Spent
Ps. 31:10 ....my life is s with grief
Mark 5:26..............s all that she had
Luke 24:29 ....the day is far s
Rom. 13:12 ....The night is far s

Spice
Ex. 35:28.........s, and oil for the light
Song 8:2............to drink of s-d wine
John 19:40.linen clothes with the s-s

Spies
Gen. 42:9..............................Ye are s
Luke 20:20 ....sent forth s
Heb. 11:31 .....she had received the s

Spirit
Gen. 1:2....the S of God moved upon
Ex. 31:3.filled him with the s of God
Judg. 9:23............God sent an evil s
1 Sam. 1:15.woman of a sorrowful s
2 Kin. 2:9......double portion of thy s
Job 27:3 ....s of God is in my nostrils
Ps. 31:5.Into thine . . . I commit my s
Ps. 51:10 ..renew a right s within me
Prov. 16:18....haughty s before a fall
Eccles. 3:21 ....s of man . . . goeth
Eccles. 7:8patient in s . . . proud in s
Is. 11:2...s of wisdom . . . knowledge
Is. 32:15.............s be poured upon us
Is. 57:15............contrite and humble s
Is. 61:1.....S of the Lord God is upon
Ezek. 3:12.......................s took me up
Ezek. 11:19...put a new s within you
Joel 2:28 ..pour out my s . . . all flesh
Mic. 3:8............full of power by the s
Matt. 3:16............S of God descending
Matt. 5:3.....Blessed are the poor in s
Matt. 10:1..............against unclean s-s
Mark 1:10 .S like a dove descending
Mark 14:38 ..s truly is ready, but the
Luke 4:18 ..S of the Lord is upon me
John 3:5 ..born of water and of the s
John 4:24.............................God is a S
John 14:17...........Even the S of truth
Acts 2:17.......I will pour out of my S
Rom. 2:29......in the s, and not in the
Rom. 8:1...............walk . . . after the S
1 Cor. 3:16.S of God dwelleth in you
1 Cor. 5:3.......absent . . . present in s
1 Cor. 12:4........gifts, but the same S
2 Cor. 3:6....of the letter, but of the s
Gal. 5:16.........................Walk in the S
Gal. 5:22 .....fruit of the S is love, joy
Eph. 1:13........that holy S of promise
Eph. 2:18 ...access by one S unto the
Eph. 4:4............one body, and one S
Phil. 1:27 ....stand fast in one s
Col. 2:5 ....am I with you in the s
1 Thess. 5:19...............Quench not the S
Heb. 4:12 ..dividing . . . of soul and s
James 2:26.......body without the s is
1 Pet. 4:6...according to God in the s
1 John 5:6......S that beareth witness
1 John 5:8.................s, and the water
Rev. 1:10...........I was in the S on the
Rev. 3:1........that hath the seven s of
Rev. 22:17...The S and the Bride say

Spiritual
Hos. 9:7..................the s man is mad
Rom. 8:6 ......to be s-ly minded is life
Rom. 15:27 ....partakers of their s
1 Cor. 14:1 ....desire s gifts
Eph. 1:3 ....blessed us . . . s blessings
Eph. 5:19...............hymns and s songs
1 Pet. 2:5 ....are built up a s house

Spit
Job 30:10 ...spare not to s in my face
Matt. 26:67.............they s in his face
Matt. 27:30 ....and they s upon him
Mark 8:23........when he had s on his
Mark 14:65 .some began to s on him
John 9:6 ....made clay of the s-tle

Spoil
Gen. 49:27 ....he shall divide the s
Song 2:15 ....foxes, that s the vines
Ezek. 25:7 ....will deliver thee for a s
Col. 2:8 ..Beware lest any man s you

Spoken
Ps. 62:11 ....God hath s once; twice
Ps. 87:3............Glorious things are s
Prov. 25:11...........word fitly s is like
John 12:49......I have not s of myself
Heb. 1:2............s unto us by his Son

Spot
Gen. 30:32 ..speckled and s-ed cattle
Num. 19:2 ....red heifer without s
Song 4:7 ....there is no s in thee
Jer. 13:23 ....the Leopard his s-s
Eph. 5:27 ....not having s, or wrinkle
Heb. 9:14......offered . . . without s to God
1 Pet. 1:19......blemish and without s
Jude 23.....garment s-ed by the flesh

Spread
Gen. 33:19....where he had s his tent
Ex. 9:29 .....I will s abroad my hands
Is. 19:8...........s nets upon the waters
Is. 33:23 ....could not s the sail
Joel 2:2.....................morning s upon the
Matt. 21:8......s their garments in the
Mark 1:28.............his fame s abroad
Luke 19:36.......S their clothes in the

Spring
Judg. 19:25..........the day began to s
Ps. 85:11.Truth . . . s out of the earth
Ps. 92:7...........wicked s as the grass
Song 4:12..........s shut up, a fountain
Is. 58:11 ....like a s of water
John 4:14........of water s-ing up into
Heb. 12:15 ....root of bitterness s-ing

Stablish
Ps. 119:38 ....S thy word unto thy
Rom. 16:25 ....s you according
2 Thess. 2:17......s you in every good
James 5:8 ....s your hearts

Staff
Gen. 38:18 ....thy s that is in thine
Ps. 23:4...........thy rod and thy s they
Is. 14:5....broken the s of the wicked
Ezek. 4:16 ....break the s of bread
Mark 6:8 ....save a s only

Stand
Josh. 10:12.....................Sun, s thou still
Job 8:15........house, but it shall not s
Ps. 1:5.......ungodly shall not s in the
Ps. 130:3............O Lord, who shall s
Is. 40:8 ....word of our God shall s
Is. 50:8 ....let us s together
Jer. 6:16....S ye in the ways, and see
Jer. 35:19 ......man to s before me for
Ezek. 2:1.......Son of man, s upon thy
Nah. 1:6......s before his indignation
Matt. 12:25 ....house divided . . . shall not s
Mark 11:25..........ye s praying, forgive
John 1:26.........s-eth one among you

Acts 1:11.....why s ye gazing up into
Acts 7:33.....where thou s-est is holy
Rom. 5:2......this grace wherein we s
1 Cor. 16:13............s fast in the faith
2 Cor. 1:24..................for by faith ye s
Eph. 6:14......S . . . having your loins
2 Tim. 2:19..foundation of God s-eth
Rev. 3:20........Behold, I s at the door
Rev. 20:12.......dead . . . s before God

Star
Gen. 1:16...........he made the s-s also
Num. 24:17...............a S out of Jacob
Job 38:7 ..morning s-s sang together
Ps. 136:9......moon and s-s to rule by
Jer. 31:35.......s-s for a light by night
Matt. 2:2...........seen his s in the east
Matt. 24:29.............s-s shall fall from
Rev. 1:16...........right hand seven s-s
Rev. 8:10...............fell a great s from
Rev. 8:11........s is called Wormwood
Rev. 22:16.......bright and morning s

Stature
Num. 13:32........are men of a great s
Matt. 6:27...........one cubit unto his s
Luke 2:52..increased in wisdom and s
Luke 19:3.................he was little of s

Statute
Gen. 26:5.....commandments, my s-s
Ps. 19:8........s-s of the Lord are right
Ps. 119:12.................teach me thy s-s
Ezek. 5:7.have not walked in my s-s

Stay
Gen. 19:17.......s thou in all the plain
1 Sam. 20:38....Make speed, haste, s
Ps. 18:18...............the Lord was my s
Song 2:5................S me with flagons
Is. 3:1 ....s of bread . . . s of water
Dan. 4:35...........none can s his hand
Hag. 1:10......heaven . . . is s-ed from

Stead
Gen. 30:2...................Am I in God's s
Num. 32:14.risen up in your father's s
Deut. 2:23..........and dwelt in their s
2 Cor. 5:20.we pray you in Christ's s

Steal
Gen. 31:27 ....and s away from me
Ex. 20:15.................Thou shalt not s
Deut. 5:19..........Neither shalt thou s
Deut. 24:7....If a man be found s-ing
Prov. 30:9.................I be poor, and s
Matt. 6:19 ....break through and s
Matt. 19:18..............Thou shalt not s
Mark 10:19 ....Do not kill, Do not s
Eph. 4:28...........that stole s no more

Stedfast
Job 11:15 ....thou shalt be s
Acts 1:10.............looked s-ly toward
1 Cor. 7:37.....standeth s in his heart
1 Cor. 15:58 ....be ye s
Col. 2:5................s-ness of your faith

Steps
1 Kin. 10:19......The throne had six s
Job 14:16.........thou numberest my s
Prov. 5:5........her s take hold on hell
Rom. 4:12.walk in the s of that faith
1 Pet. 2:21.......ye should follow his s

Steward
Gen. 43:19 ....s of Joseph's house
Luke 12:42...........faithful and wise s
Luke 16:2 ...an account of thy s-ship
1 Cor. 4:1 ....s-s of the mysteries of

Stick
2 Kin. 6:6..he cut down a s, and cast
Job 33:21...................bones . . . s out
Ezek. 37:16................take thee one s
Prov. 18:24...........s-eth closer than s

Still
Gen. 41:21...they were s ill favoured
Josh. 10:12...Sun, stand thou s upon
2 Kin. 7:4.......if we sit s here, we die
Ps. 23:2................beside the s waters
Ps. 65:7....s-eth the noise of the seas

Jer. 8:14....................Why do we sit s
Hab. 3:11........sun and moon stood s
Mark 4:39.........................Peace, be s

Sting
Prov. 23:32 ....s-eth like an adder
1 Cor. 15:55......death, where is thy s

Stir
Deut. 32:11..eagle s-reth up her nest
Prov. 10:12 ..Hatred s-reth up strifes
Prov. 15:1..............words s up anger
Prov. 28:25......proud heart s-reth up
Prov. 29:22 ....angry man s-reth up
Is. 42:13..........he shall s up jealousy
Acts 14:2..Jews s-ed up the Gentiles

Stole
Gen. 31:19 ....Rachel had s-en the
2 Sam. 15:6.Absalom s the hearts of

Stone
Gen. 29:3.....s from the well's mouth
Ex. 4:25 ......Zipporah took a sharp s
Ex. 20:25 ....not build it of hewn s
Ex. 34:1 ......hew thee two tables of s
Lev. 20:2............shall s him with s-s
Deut. 8:9......land whose s-s are iron
Deut. 9:9.....to receive the tables of s
1 Sam. 17:49..took . . . a s, and slang
2 Kin. 12:12 ....and hewers of s
2 Chr. 34:11.buy hewn s, and timber
Job 14:19...........waters wear the s-s
Job 28:2.brass is molten out of the s
Job 41:24.........heart is as firm as a s
Ps. 91:12 ....dash thy foot against a s
Ps. 118:22........s . . . builders refused
Is. 28:16 ..a precious corner s, a sure
Is. 57:6 ....smooth s-s of the stream
Ezek. 11:19.take the s-y heart out of
Ezek. 20:32........to serve wood and s
Dan. 2:34.........s was cut out without
Amos 5:11 .....built houses of hewn s
Hab. 2:11..s shall cry out of the wall
Matt. 4:3.....these s-s be made bread
Matt. 7:9.........bread . . . give him a s
Matt. 13:5.Some fell upon s-y places
Matt. 21:42.....s . . . builders rejected
Matt. 27:60........a great s to the door
Matt. 28:2................rolled back the s
Mark 12:4...........at him they cast s-s
Luke 19:44.........one s upon another
Luke 22:41................about a s's cast
John 2:6.................six waterpots of s
John 8:7 ....first cast a s at her
Acts 7:59...............they s-ed Stephen
2 Cor. 3:3................not in tables of s
Eph. 2:20..................the chief corner s
1 Pet. 2:8.......................s of stumbling
Rev. 2:17.......will give him a white s

Stood
Gen. 18:2 ....three men s by him
Num. 22:22.....angel . . . s in the way
Deut. 31:15.pillar of the cloud s over
Amos 7:7 ....Lord s upon a wall
Matt. 2:9......s over where the young
Luke 4:16.....................s up for to read
Luke 24:36...Jesus . . . s in the midst
John 19:25....s by the cross of Jesus
John 20:11.................Mary s without
John 21:4...........Jesus s on the shore
Acts 21:40...........Paul s on the stairs
Rev. 5:6.......s a Lamb as it had been
Rev. 13:1.s upon the sand of the sea

Stop
1 Kin. 18:44..........the rain s thee not
Job 5:16 ...iniquity s-peth her mouth
Ps. 63:11.......speak lies shall be s-ped
Prov. 21:13 ....Whoso s-peth his ears
Rom. 3:19 ....mouth may be s-ped
2 Cor. 11:10......s me of this boasting

Store
Gen. 26:14............great s of servants
Amos 3:10.............s up violence and
1 Cor. 16:2..................lay by him in s
1 Tim. 6:19 ....Laying up in s for

Storm
Job 21:18...chaff . . . s carrieth away
Is. 25:4.................a refuge from the s

Ezek. 38:9.ascend and come like a s
Mark 4:37.....arose a great s of wind

Straight
Ps. 5:8 ....make thy way s before
Eccles. 1:15..........crooked cannot be made s
Is. 40:3 ....make s . . . a highway
Matt. 3:3..................make his paths s
Luke 3:5.....crooked shall be made s
John 1:23.......Make s the way of the
Acts 9:11 ......street which is called S

Straightway
1 Sam. 9:13 ....ye shall s find him
Matt. 3:16 ....went up s out of the
Matt. 4:20...................s left their nets
Matt. 21:2.s ye shall find an ass tied
Luke 12:54.s ye say, there cometh a
Luke 14:5.s pull him out . . . sabbath
Acts 9:20 ....s he preached Christ

Strait
2 Sam. 24:14............I am in a great s
Is. 49:20 ....place is too s for me
Matt. 7:13 ....enter ye in at the s gate

Strange
Gen. 35:2...........Put away the s gods
Ex. 2:22...............stranger in a s land
1 Kin. 11:1 ....Solomon . . . many s
Ezra 10:2.............have taken s wives
Job 19:17 ....breath is s to my wife
Prov. 22:14....mouth of s women is a
Ezek. 3:5 ....people of a s speech
Luke 5:26............seen s things today
Heb. 13:9........divers and s doctrines
1 Pet. 4:12..think it not s concerning
Jude 7....................going after s flesh

Stranger
Gen. 15:13...........a s in a land that is
Ex. 20:10....s that is within thy gates
Ex. 22:21.....................neither vex a s
Deut. 10:19...Love ye therefore the s
Ruth 2:10....................seeing I am a s
Prov. 5:20.embrace the bosom of a s
Is. 1:7.s-s devour it in your presence
Jer. 22:3.........do no violence to the s
Matt. 25:35 .....I was a s, and ye took
John 10:5..know not the voice of s-s
Eph. 2:19 ....ye are no more s-s
Heb. 13:2....................to entertain s-s

Straw
Gen. 24:25.......both s and provender
Ex. 5:7.......................s to make bricks
Job 41:27 ....esteemeth iron as s
Is. 11:7.........lion . . . eat s like the ox

Street
Gen. 19:2 ....abide in the s all night
Is. 59:14...........truth is fallen in the s
Jer. 37:21 .bread out of the baker's s
Nah. 2:4.............shall rage in the s-s
Matt. 6:5........in the corners of the s-s
Acts 9:11 ..s which is called Straight
Rev. 21:21 ....s of the city was pure

Strength
Gen. 4:12.not . . . yield . . . thee her s
Ex. 15:2 ..The Lord is my s and song
Deut. 33:25.....days, so shall thy s be
Judg. 16:6..wherein thy great s lieth
1 Sam. 28:20.............was no s in him
2 Sam. 22:33.God is my s and power
Job 6:12..........Is my s the s of stones
Job 21:23 ....one dieth in his full s
Ps. 18:2..........................my God, my s
Ps. 19:14.............Lord, my s, and my
Ps. 28:7..Lord is my s and my shield
Ps. 46:1 ....God is our refuge and s
Prov. 10:29 ....way of the Lord is s
Prov. 31:3 ....not thy s unto women
Eccles. 9:16.Wisdom is better than s
Is. 26:4 ....Jehovah is everlasting s
Is. 30:7.................Their s is to sit still
Is. 41:1 ....people renew their s
Hab. 3:19 ....The Lord God is my s
Mark 12:30 .mind, and with all thy s
1 Cor. 15:56 ....s of sin is the law
Rev. 1:16.............sun shineth in his s

Strengthen
Deut. 3:28 ....encourage him, and s
Judg. 16:28.........s me, I pray . . . this
1 Sam. 23:16 ....s-ed his hand in God
Is. 35:3.............S ye the weak hands
Luke 22:32 ....s thy brethren
Col. 1:11..............S-ed with all might
1 Pet. 5:10.........stablish, s settle you

Stretch
Ex. 9:15.....now I will s out my hand
Job 38:5 ....s-ed the line upon it
Ps. 68:31...s out her hands unto God
Is. 3:16....walk with s-ed forth necks
Is. 28:20..........than that a man can s
Is. 44:13.carpenter s-eth out his rule
Jer. 10:12..........s-ed out the heavens
Matt. 12:13...........S forth thine hand
2 Cor. 10:14.........we s not ourselves

Stricken
Judg. 5:26.......s through his temples
Is. 1:5.Why should ye be s any more
Is. 53:4.......did esteem his s, smitten
Luke 1:7.......both . . . well s in years

Strife
Ps. 106:32...............at the waters of s
Prov. 10:12......Hatred stirreth up s-s
Prov. 16:28....froward man soweth s
Prov. 20:3.......a man to cease from s
Rom. 13:13.......not in s and envying
1 Cor. 3:3..................s, and divisions
Gal. 5:20..............wrath, s, seditions
James 3:16...where envying and s is

Strike
Ex. 12:22.......s the lintel and the two
Prov. 22:26one of them that s hands
1 Tim. 3:3...........to wine, no s-r, not

String
Ps. 11:2..........their arrow upon the s
Ps. 33:2........an instrument of ten s-s
Hab. 3:19.....................singer . . . s-ed
Mark 7:35...........s of his tongue was

Stripes
Deut. 25:3...Forty s he may give him
Prov. 19:29.....s for the back of fools
Luke 12:47....be beaten with many s
2 Cor. 11:24..............forty s save one
1 Pet. 2:24.by whose s ye are healed

Strive
Prov. 3:30.S not with a man without
Luke 13:24...........S to enter in at the
1 Cor. 9:25.........s-th for the mastery
2 Tim. 2:5...........also s for masteries

Strong
Lev. 10:9.................wine nor s drink
Deut. 31:6.Be s and of good courage
Judg. 14:18...what is s-er than a lion
1 Sam. 4:9.Be s, and quit yourselves
Ps. 19:5...............s man to run a race
Ps. 24:8.........The Lord s and mighty
Prov. 20:1................s drink is raging
Prov. 31:6....s drink unto him that is
Song. 8:6................love is s as death
Is. 5:11........they may follow s drink
Jer. 20:7.............thou are s-er than I
Jer. 50:34............Their Redeemer is s
Ezek. 30:21.........s to hold the sword
Joel 3:10.................weak say, I am s
Luke 2:40.child . . . waxed s in spirit
1 Cor. 4:10..we are weak, but ye are s
2 Cor. 12:10....am weak, then am I s
Eph. 6:10.....................be s in the Lord
Heb. 11:34....weakness were made s

Study
Eccles. 12:12..much s is a weariness
1 Thess. 4:11.............ye s to be quiet
2 Tim. 2:15.............S to shew thyself

Stumble
Prov. 3:23............thy foot shall not s
Jer. 50:32.............most proud shall s
Dan. 11:19......................shall s and fall
1 Pet. 2:8...........which s at the word

Subject
Luke 2:51.........and was s unto them
Rom. 8:20........was made s to vanity
1 Cor. 9:27.body, and bring it into s-ion
2 Cor. 9:13.......s-ion unto the gospel
Eph. 5:24.......church is s unto Christ
Heb. 2:8......all things in s-ion under
Heb. 12:9......in s-ion unto the Father
1 Pet. 2:18.........be s to your masters
1 Pet. 3:1...............s-ion to your own
1 Pet. 3:22.....being made s unto him
1 Pet. 5:5.................s one to another

Substance
Gen. 7:23..............every living s was
Prov. 3:9..Honour the Lord with thy s
Luke 15:13............wasted his s with riotous

Such
Gen. 4:20..........of s as dwell in tents
Ps. 107:10...........S as sit in darkness
Ps. 139:6..............S knowledge is too
Prov. 11:20..s as are upright in their
Matt. 19:14..........s is the kingdom of
Mark 4:18............s as hear the word
Acts 3:6.........s as I have given I thee
2 Cor. 3:12..................we have s hope
Heb. 13:16....s sacrifices God is well

Suddenly
Deut. 7:4..............and destroy thee s
Mark 13:36......coming s he find you
Acts 2:2...........s there came a sound
1 Tim. 5:22..Lay hands s on no man

Suffer
Job 24:11..........................and s thirst
Matt. 3:15................S it to be so now
Matt. 19:14.......S little children, and
Mark 8:31.Son of man must s many
Luke 24:46......it behoved Christ to s
Acts 2:27......s thine Holy One to see
1 Cor. 9:12.....................but s all things
1 Cor. 13:4...Charity s-eth long, and
1 Tim. 2:12...s not a woman to teach
2 Tim. 2:12.......If we s, we shall also
1 Pet. 2:21......Christ also s-ed for us
1 Pet. 4:13.........partakers of Christ's s-ings

Sufficient
Prov. 25:16..........eat so much as is s
Matt. 6:34..S unto the day is the evil
2 Cor. 12:9......My grace is s for thee

Summer
Gen. 8:22.......heat, and s and winter
Ps. 74:17......hast made s and winter
Prov. 26:1.As snow in s, and as rain
Zech. 14:8.s and in winter shall it be
Matt. 24:32.....ye know that s is nigh

Sun
Ex. 16:21...................the s waxed hot
Josh. 10:12.............S, stand thou still
Ps. 84:11...........God is a s and shield
Ps. 104:19..........s knoweth his going
Ps. 121:6.....s shall not smite thee by
Eccles. 1:9.no new thing under the s
Is. 60:19.s shall be no more thy light
Ezek. 32:7...cover the s with a cloud
Amos 8:9.........s to go down at noon
Matt. 5:45...........maketh his s to rise
Luke 21:25......shall be signs in the s
1 Cor. 15:41.......is one glory of the s
Eph. 4:26.........s go down upon your
Rev. 12:1.woman clothed with the s
Rev. 22:5...........neither light of the s

Supper
Mark 6:21...birthday made a s to his
Luke 14:16.........certain man made a great s
John 13:4.He riseth from s, and laid
1 Cor. 11:20....not to eat the Lord's s
Rev. 19:9.....marriage s of the Lamb

Supplications
1 Sam. 13:12......not made s unto the
Dan. 9:3........seek by prayer and s-s
Acts 1:14.........accord in prayer and s

Sure
Num. 32:23...s your sin will find you
Ps. 19:7.....testimony of the Lord is s
Is. 22:23............as a nail in a s place
Matt. 27:66......made the sepulchre s
John 6:69...s that thou art the Christ
2 Pet. 1:10........calling and election s

Surely
Gen. 2:17..eatest . . . thou shalt s die
Gen. 28:16..........S the Lord is in this
Num. 14:23.........S they shall not see
Ps. 23:6..........S goodness and mercy
Is. 53:4.....S he hath borne our griefs
Mark 14:70....S thou art one of them
Luke 1:1..things . . . most s believed
Rev. 22:20...............S I come quickly

Swallow
Num. 16:34.....Lest the earth s us up
Job 6:3...........my words are s-ed up
Ps. 84:3.........the s a nest for herself
Prov. 26:2...............as the s by flying
Is. 25:8..............s up death in victory
Jonah 1:17...great fish to s up Jonah
Matt. 23:24.........gnat, and s a camel
1 Cor. 15:54.........Death is s-ed up in

Swear
Gen. 50:5................father made me s
Lev. 19:12.not s by my name falsely
Num. 30:2..............s an oath to bind
Is. 45:23...........every tongue shall s
Zech. 5:3.....one that s-eth . . . be cut
Matt. 5:34......S not at all; neither by
Matt. 23:18...whosoever s-eth by the
Mark 14:71..began to curse and to s
James 5:12..........all things . . . s not

Sweet
Gen. 8:21....Lord smelled a s savour
Prov. 3:24...........thy sleep shall be s
Prov. 9:17...........Stolen waters are s
Is. 43:24...........bought me no s cane
2 Cor. 2:15..........a s savour of Christ
James 3:11............s water and bitter

Swell
Num. 5:21..............and thy belly to s
Deut. 8:4..........neither did thy foot s
2 Pet. 2:18.........great s-ing words of

Swift
Deut. 28:49.........s as the eagle flieth
Job 7:6.........My days are s-er than a
Prov. 6:18...s in running to mischief
Eccles. 9:11..........race is not to the s
Rom. 3:15...................s to shed blood
James 1:19..............man be s to hear

Swine
Prov. 11:22...........gold in a s's snout
Matt. 7:6..cast ye . . . pearls before s
Mark 5:11.....great herd of s feeding
Luke 15:15....into his fields to feed s

Sword
Gen. 27:40....by thy s shalt thou live
Ex. 5:3........pestilence, or with the s
Judg. 7:18.........s of the Lord, and of
2 Sam. 2:26.....Shall the s devour for
Ps. 64:3.....whet their tongue like a s
Prov. 5:4........sharp as a twoedged s
Is. 2:4.beat their s-s into plowshares
Jer. 15:2.......as are for the s, to the s
Hos. 1:7.save them by bow, nor by s
Mic. 4:3.beat . . . s-s into plowshares
Matt. 10:34.......not . . . peace, but a s
Matt. 26:51.....drew his s, and struck
Eph. 6:17......................s of the Spirit
Rev. 1:16.....................sharp twoedged s

Synagogue
Matt. 12:9...........he went into their s
Matt. 13:54.....taught them in their s
John 16:2.........put you out of the s-s
John 18:20.........I ever taught in the s
Acts 9:20..preached Christ in the s-s
Rev. 2:9..........but are the s of Satan

T

Tabernacle
Ex. 26:1 ....t with ten curtains
Ps. 61:4................I will abide in thy t
Matt. 17:4...........make here three t-s
2 Pet. 1:14.....I must put off this my t
Rev. 21:3...........t of God is with men

Table
Ex. 24:12 ....give thee t-s of stone
Ex. 31:18...................t-s of testimony
Ps. 23:5 ....preparest a t before me
Matt. 21:12 ....t-s of the moneychangers
Mark 7:28 .....dogs under the t eat of
John 2:15 ....and overthrew the t-s
Acts 6:2 ..word of God, and serve t-s
2 Cor. 3:3 ....fleshy t-s of the heart

Take
Gen. 3:22.......t also of the tree of life
Ex. 20:7...not t the name of the Lord
Ex. 34:9 .....t us for thine inheritance
Deut. 1:13 ....T you wise men
Job 5:13.......................t-th the wise in
Ps. 116:13 ....t the cup of salvation
Prov. 4:13..T fast hold of instruction
Prov. 7:18..................t our fill of love
Song 2:15......................T us the foxes
Is. 4:1.......seven women . . . t hold of
Hos. 1:2............Go t unto thee a wife
Mic. 2:4 ...t up a parable against you
Matt. 5:40 ....t away thy coat
Matt. 6:25.T no thought for your life
Matt. 11:29.......T my yoke upon you
Matt. 26:26 ....T, eat; this is my body
Mark 2:9 ....Arise, t up thy bed
Mark 10:21............t up the cross and
Mark 13:33 .....T ye heed, watch and
Luke 9:3.T nothing for your journey
John 1:29 .....t-th away the sin of the
John 7:30 ....they sought to t him
John 11:39.........T ye away the stone
Acts 1:9..........................he was t-n up
1 Cor. 11:24...T, eat: this is my body
Eph. 6:16 ......t-ing the shield of faith
Rev. 10:9................T it, and eat it up

Tale
Ex. 5:18...........deliver the t of bricks
Ezek. 22:9 .....carry t-s to shed blood

Talk
1 Sam. 2:3.T no more so . . . proudly
Job 15:3 ....with unprofitable t
Prov. 24:2.......their lips t of mischief
Eph. 5:4............nor foolish t-ing, nor
Titus 1:10....vain t-ers and deceivers

Tarry
Gen. 19:2 ....t all night, and wash
Matt. 26:38 ....t ye here, and watch
1 Tim. 3:15....................But if I t long

Taste
Job 34:3 ....as the mouth t-th meat
Prov. 24:13 ....sweet to thy t
Matt. 16:28 ....shall not t of death
Heb. 2:9 ....t death for every man
Heb. 6:4 ....t-d of the heavenly gift

Taught
Ps. 71:17.....hast t me from my youth
Is. 54:13.....children . . . t of the Lord
Matt. 7:29 ....t them as one having
Mark 4:2...he t them . . . by parables
Luke 19:47 ....t daily in the temple
John 8:28 .....as my Father hath t me
1 Thess. 4:9........t of God to love one

Tax
2 Kin. 23:35 ....he t-ed the land
Luke 2:1 ....all the world should be t-ed
Acts 5:37 ....in the days of the t-ing

Teach
Ex. 4:12 ...t thee what thou shalt say
Deut. 4:9.......................t them thy sons
Job 37:19 ......T us what we shall say
Ps. 25:4.........................t me thy paths
Ps. 27:11.........T me thy way, O Lord
Is. 28:9 .Whom shall he t knowledge
Matt. 15:9 ....t-ing for doctrines
Matt. 28:19...Go . . . and t all nations
Luke 11:1 ....Lord, t us to pray
Luke 12:12 ....Holy Ghost shall t you
Acts 1:1 ....began both to do and t
Acts 15:35 ...t-ing and preaching the
1 Cor. 11:14...........nature itself t you
1 Tim. 1:3.............t no other doctrine
1 Tim. 2:12 ..suffer not a woman to t
Rev. 2:20 ....t and to seduce my

Teacher
1 Chr. 25:8 ....the t as the scholar
John 3:2 ....art a t come from God
Eph. 4:11 ....some, pastors and t-s
1 Tim. 2:7 ....t of the Gentiles
2 Tim. 4:3 ......heap to themselves t-s
Titus 2:3.................t-s of good things

Tear
Ps. 7:2 ....t my soul like a lion
Ezek. 13:20...t them from your arms
Luke 9:39...............t-eth him that me

Tears
2 Kin. 20:5...............I have seen thy t
Job 16:20 ......mine eye poureth out t
Ps. 80:5 ..t to drink in great measure
Ps. 126:5 ....sow in t shall reap in joy
Eccles. 4:1..............t of such as were
Is. 25:8.............God will wipe away t
Luke 7:38 ....wash his feet with t
Rev. 7:17 ..God shall wipe away all t

Teeth
Gen. 49:12 ....t white with milk
Job 13:14.........take my flesh in my t
Job 41:14...........................his t are terrible
Ps. 57:4........t are spears and arrows
Jer. 31:29.................t are set on edge
Amos 4:6....given you cleanness of t
Matt. 8:12 .weeping and gnashing of t

Tell
Gen. 15:5.....................and t the stars
Ex. 19:3..........t the children of Israel
Ps. 101:7 ....he that t-eth lies shall
Dan. 2:36 .....will t the interpretation
Joel 1:3.........T ye your children of it
Matt. 8:4 ....See thou t no man
Matt. 26:63..........t us . . . thou be the
Luke 13:32 ....Go ye, and t that fox
John 8:45 ....I t you the truth
John 18:34 ....others t it thee
2 Cor. 12:2 .....in the body, I cannot t

Tempest
Amos 1:14 ....t in the day of the
Jonah 1:4..........a mighty t in the sea
Acts 27:18..................tossed with a t
Heb. 12:18................darkness, and t
2 Pet. 2:17..clouds . . . carried with a t

Temple
1 Sam. 1:9.......seat by a post of the t
2 Sam. 22:7.......my voice out of his t
Neh. 6:11 .....go into the t to save his
Ps. 11:4.............Lord is in his holy t
Jer. 7:4......t of the Lord, The t of the
Matt. 4:5...................pinnacle of the t
Matt. 12:6 ....one greater than the t
Mark 14:58 ....t . . . made with hands
Luke 23:45 ....veil of the t was rent
John 2:19......................Destroy this t
John 2:21 ....the t of his body
Acts 7:48.................dwelleth not in t-s
2 Cor. 6:16 .....ye are the t of . . . God
2 Thess. 2:4 ....God sitteth in the t
Rev. 21:22.God . . . the Lamb are the t

Tempt
Ex. 17:2..wherefore do ye t the Lord
Deut. 6:16 .....Ye shall not t the Lord
Luke 4:2 .forty days t-ed of the devil
Acts 5:9..............t the Spirit of the Lord
1 Cor. 10:13not suffer you to be t-ed
1 Thess. 3:5.....the tempter have t-ed
Heb. 4:15 ....t-ed like as we are
James 1:13 .God cannot be t-ed with

Temptations
Ps. 95:8.........................in the day of t
Matt. 6:13................lead us not into t
Matt. 26:41 ....enter not into t
1 Cor. 10:13 ....hath no t taken you
James 1:12 ....man that endureth t
2 Pet. 2:9....deliver the godly out of t

Ten
Gen. 31:7 ....changed my wages t
Num. 14:22 ...tempted me . . . t times
Deut. 10:4........the t commandments
Ps. 33:2..........t thousand at thy right
Song 5:10 ....chiefest among t
Ezek. 45:14......t baths are an homer
Matt. 25:1........likened unto t virgins
Luke 15:8.....having t pieces of silver
Luke 17:17...............Were there not t
Heb. 7:2....Abraham gave a t-th part

Tender
Deut. 32:2 ....small rain upon the t
2 Sam. 23:4 ......t grass springing out
2 Kin. 22:19 ....thine heart was t
1 Chr. 22:5.....my son is young and t
Ps. 25:6...............Remember . . . thy t
Prov. 27:25......t grass sheweth itself
Is. 53:2 ....grow up . . . as a t plant
Luke 1:78 ....t mercy of our God
Eph. 4:32.....t-hearted, forgiving one

Tent
Gen. 4:20 ....of such as dwell in t-s
Gen. 18:1 ....he sat in the t door
Gen. 25:27...................dwelling in t-s
Num. 24:5.........goodly are thy t-s, O
Ps. 84:10......in the t-s of wickedness
Song 1:8....beside the shepherds' t-s

Terrible
Deut. 8:15......great and t wilderness
Judg. 13:6...........angel of God, very t
Neh. 1:5..............the great and t God
Song 6:4 .t as an army with banners
Joel 2:31 ...great and the t day of the

Terror
Lev. 26:16.............appoint over you t
Deut. 32:25 ....sword without . . . t
Job 24:17.t-s of the shadow of death
Rom. 13:3........not a t to good works
2 Cor. 5:11 ....the t of the Lord

Testament
Matt. 26:28.....my blood of the new t
Luke 22:20 ....This cup is the new t
2 Cor. 3:6........ministers of the new t
2 Cor. 3:14 ....reading of the old t
Rev. 11:19...................the ark of his t

Testify
Deut. 19:18 ..t-ied falsely against his
2 Sam. 1:16 ....mouth hath t-ied
Is. 59:12 ....our sins t against us
John 3:11.................t that we have seen
Acts 2:40.many other words did he t
Acts 20:24....................to t the gospel
Gal. 5:3 ....t again to every man
1 Pet. 5:12 ......t-ing that this the true

Testimony
Ex. 16:34.........laid it up before the T
Ex. 25:16 ....put into the ark the t
Ex. 31:18 ....two tables of t
Lev. 16:13 ....seat that is upon the t
Ps. 19:7...............t of the Lord is sure
Is. 8:16.....Bind up the t, seal the law
Matt. 8:4................the gift . . . for a t
John 8:17 .....the t of two men is true
1 Cor. 1:6 .t of Christ was confirmed
2 Tim. 1:8.....ashamed of the t of our
Rev. 19:10 ....t of Jesus is the spirit

Thank
1 Chr. 16:7...this psalm to t the Lord
Ps. 100:4..................be t-ful unto him
Matt. 11:25 ....I t thee, O Father
Luke 6:32....................what t have ye
Luke 18:11 ....God, I t thee, that I am
2 Thess. 1:3 ..bound to t God always

Thanks
1 Chr. 16:34...O give t unto the Lord

Matt. 15:36............gave **t**, and brake
Matt. 26:27.took the cup, and gave **t**
Luke 22:19....took bread, and gave **t**
Rom. 14:6...........for he giveth God **t**
1 Cor. 15:57...But **t** be to God, which
Eph. 1:16..............Cease not to give **t**
1 Thess. 3:9.what **t** can we render to
1 Thess. 5:18.....In every thing give **t**

Thanksgiving
Lev. 7:12 ....If he offer it for a **t**
Ps. 26:7..................with the voice of **t**
Ps. 100:4..Enter into his gates with **t**
1 Tim. 4:3..........to be received with **t**
Rev. 7:12 ....and **t**, and honour

Theirs
Gen. 15:13 ....a land that is not **t**
2 Chr. 18:12 ....be like one of **t**
Matt. 5:3.**t** is the kingdom of heaven
1 Cor. 1:2 .Christ . . . both **t** and ours

Then
Ex. 15:1 ....**T** sang Moses and the
Mark 13:26 ..**t** shall they see the Son
1 Cor. 13:12 ....**t** face to face
2 Cor. 12:10 ....**t** am I strong

There
Gen. 1:3.......Let **t** be light: and **t** was
Matt. 2:13........be thou **t** until I bring
Matt. 24:23.....Lo, here is Christ, or **t**
Rev. 21:25............shall be no night **t**

Therefore
Gen. 2:24 ....**t** shall a man leave his
Matt. 6:9 ....this manner **t** pray ye
Mark 1:38...............for **t** came I forth
1 Cor. 5:7.Purge out **t** the old leaven

Thief
Job 24:14............in the night is as a **t**
Is. 1:23 ....and companions of **t**-s
Joel 2:9 ....enter . . . windows like a **t**
Matt. 6:19.......**t**-s break through and
Matt. 21:13 ....made it a den of **t**-s
Mark 15:27.him they crucify two **t**-s
Luke 10:30...........and fell among **t**-s
John 10:10 ...**t** cometh not, but for to
1 Thess. 5:2............as a **t** in the night

Thine
Gen. 22:2....thy son, **t** only son Isaac
Ex. 4:4 .....Put forth **t** hand, and take
Matt. 6:13.................**t** is the kingdom
Luke 15:31 ....all that I have is **t**
Luke 22:42 ....not my will, but **t**, be

Thing
Gen. 15:1.After these **t**-s the word of
Job 42:2 ....thou canst do every **t**
Ps. 8:6 ....all **t**-s under his feet
Ps. 92:1 ....good **t** to give thanks
Eccles. 1:9....no new **t** under the sun
Eccles. 3:1 ..every **t** there is a season
Is. 12:5 ....hath done excellent **t**-s
Matt. 19:26...God all **t**-s are possible
Matt. 21:24............will ask you one **t**
Mark 10:21...........One **t** thou lackest
Luke 2:19 ......Mary kept all these **t**-s
Luke 10:42 ....But one **t** is needful
John 14:14......ask any **t** in my name
Acts 2:44.............had all **t**-s common
Phil. 3:13 ....this one **t** I do
Phil. 4:8.................think on these **t**-s
James 3:10 ......**t**-s ought not so to be

Think
Gen. 40:14 ....**t** on me when it shall
Prov. 23:7......as he **t**-eth in his heart
Matt. 5:17..........**t** not that I am come
John 5:39.....ye **t** ye have eternal life
Rom. 12:3 ....but to **t** soberly
1 Cor. 13:5.......................**t**-eth no evil
Gal. 6:3.....**t** himself to be something
Phil. 4:8 ....**t** on these things

Third
Matt. 16:21 .....raised again the **t** day
Luke 24:21 ..to day is the **t** day since
1 Cor. 15:4....he rose again the **t** day
2 Cor. 12:2............caught up to the **t**

Thirst
Ex. 17:3..people **t**-ed there for water
Ps. 42:2 ....My soul **t**-eth for God
Prov. 25:25 .cold waters to a **t**-y soul
Is. 29:8 .....when a **t**-y man dreameth
Is. 49:10 ....shall not hunger nor **t**
Is. 65:13 .....drink, but ye shall be **t**-y
Matt. 5:6 ....**t** after righteousness
Matt. 25:35 .....I was **t**-y, and ye gave
John 4:13 ..drinketh . . . shall **t** again
John 6:35 .believeth . . . shall never **t**
John 19:28............Jesus . . . saith, I **t**
2 Cor. 11:27..............in hunger and **t**

Thirty
Ex. 21:32................**t** shekels of silver
Num. 20:29 ......mourned for Aaron **t**
Zech. 11:12 ....price **t** pieces of silver
Matt. 26:15 ....for **t** pieces of silver
Luke 3:23 .began to be about **t** years

Thorn
Gen. 3:18 ....**T**-s also and thistles
Job 41:2.....bore . . . through with a **t**
Prov. 15:19 ....as an hedge of **t**-s
Song 2:2 ....a lily among **t**-s
Jer. 12:13 ....sown wheat . . . reap **t**-s
Matt. 7:16 ....gather grapes of **t**-s
Matt. 13:7...........some fell among **t**-s
Matt. 27:29......platted a crown of **t**-s
John 19:5...wearing the crown of **t**-s
2 Cor. 12:7...................a **t** in the flesh

Thought
Gen. 50:20 ....**t** evil against me
Job 21:27 ....I know your **t**-s, and the
Ps. 94:11 ......knoweth the **t**-s of man
Is. 55:8 ....my **t**-s are not your **t**-s
Matt. 6:25 ....Take no **t** for your life
Matt. 9:4 ......Jesus knowing their **t**-s
Matt. 15:19 ......heart proceed evil **t**-s
Luke 24:38....**t**-s arise in your hearts
1 Cor. 3:20 .....knoweth the **t**-s of the
1 Cor. 13:11..........child, I **t** as a child

Thousand
Lev. 26:8 ....put ten **t** to flight
Ps. 84:10..a day . . . is better than a **t**
Ps. 91:7......**t** shall fall . . . ten **t** at thy
Song 5:10..........chiefest among ten **t**
Is. 30:17...........One **t** shall flee at the
Is. 60:22 ...little one shall become a **t**
Dan. 7:10 ....ten **t** times ten **t** stood
Mark 6:44.......were about five **t** men
Mark 8:9 ....were about four **t**
1 Cor. 4:15 ....ten **t** instructors in
2 Pet. 3:8..............**t** years as one day

Three
Gen. 6:10 ..Noah begat **t** sons, Shem
Job 2:11 ....Job's **t** friends
Ps. 90:10....are **t**-score years and ten
Prov. 30:15............**t** things . . . never
Eccles. 4:12 ....and a **t**-fold cord
Dan. 6;10 ......his knees **t** times a day
Jonah 1:17....fish **t** days and **t** nights
Matt. 12:40....**t** days . . . nights in the
Matt. 17:4 ...make here **t** tabernacles
Matt. 18:20 ......two or **t** are gathered
Matt. 27:63 ......After **t** days I will rise
Luke 2:46......after **t** days they found
Luke 10:36 ......Which now of these **t**
John 2:19 ....**t** days I will raise it up
Acts 2:41 ....about **t** thousand souls
Acts 9:9..............**t** days without sight

Threw
2 Sam. 16:13 ......**t** stones at him, and
Mark 12:42.widow . . . **t** in two mites
Luke 9:42................devil **t** him down
Acts 22:23 ....**t** dust into the air

Thrice
Matt. 26:34 ....shalt deny me **t**
2 Cor. 11:25 .....**T** was I beaten . . . **t** I

Throat
Ps. 69:3..............crying: my **t** is dried
Prov. 23:2.............put a knife to thy **t**
Matt. 18:28 ......and took him by the **t**
Rom. 3:13.......**t** is an open sepulchre

Throne
1 Kin. 22:19 ....Lord sitting on his **t**
Ps. 11:4 ....Lord's **t** is in heaven
Ps. 93:2...........**t** is established of old
Is. 66:1 ....The heaven is my **t**
Matt. 5:34 ....for it is God's **t**
Acts 7:49 ....Heaven is my **t**
Heb. 1:8 ......Thy **t** . . . is for ever and
Heb. 4:16..boldly unto the **t** of grace
Rev. 20:11 ....I saw a great white **t**

Through
Gen. 12:6........Abraham passed **t** the
Ex. 14:16..........**t** the midst of the sea
Num. 15:27 ....soul sin **t** ignorance
Eccles. 10:18.**t** idleness of the hands
Is. 43:2........**t** the waters . . . **t** the fire
Matt. 19:24 ...camel . . . **t** the eye of a
Luke 6:1 ....went **t** the corn fields
John 3:17.........world **t** him might be
Acts 10:43 ......**t** his name whosoever
Rom. 1:8 ....thank my God **t** Jesus
1 Cor. 13:12 ....see **t** a glass, darkly
Gal. 4:7 ....heir of God **t** Christ
Eph. 2:8...............are ye saved **t** faith
Phil. 4:13 ....do all things **t** Christ

Thunder
Ex. 9:23 ....Lord sent **t** and hail
2 Sam. 22:14.Lord **t**-ed from heaven
Is. 29:6................Lord of hosts with **t**
Mark 3:17 ...Boanerges . . . The sons of **t**
Rev. 14:2......as the voice of a great **t**

Tidings
2 Kin. 7:9 ....day is a day of good **t**
Is. 52:7........feet that bringeth good **t**
Luke 2:10 ....good **t** of great joy
Rom. 10:15.......glad **t** of good things
1 Thess. 3:6 ....good **t** of your faith

Time
Gen. 4:3..........in process of **t** it came
Judg. 15:1 ....**t** of wheat harvest
Job 7:1 ....appointed **t** to man upon
Ps. 41:1 ....deliver him in **t** of trouble
Ps. 89:47................how short my **t** is
Prov. 25:13 ....snow in **t** of harvest
Eccles. 7:17 ....die before thy **t**
Eccles. 9:12 ....knoweth not his **t**
Song 2:12 .. .**t** of the singing of birds
Hos. 10:12 ......it is **t** to seek the Lord
Amos 5:13 ....for it is an evil **t**
Matt. 26:18...................My **t** is at hand
Luke 4:11.......lest at any **t** thou dash
John 7:6 ....My **t** is not yet come
1 Cor. 7:29......................the **t** is short
Gal. 4:2......**t** appointed of the Father
1 Tim. 2:6............be testified in due **t**
Jude 18 ....mockers in the last **t**
Rev. 1:3 ....the **t** is at hand
Rev. 10:6...........there should be **t** no

Times
Ps. 9:9 ....refuge in **t** of trouble
Ps. 31:15 ....My **t** are in thy hand
Matt. 16:3 ..discern the signs of the **t**
Acts 1:7....know the **t** or the seasons
Gal. 4:10 ....observe days . . . and **t**
Rev. 12:14 ......time, and **t**, and half a

Tithe
Gen. 14:20 ....he gave him **t**-s of all
Lev. 27:30............all the **t** of the land
Num. 18:26 ....a tenth part of the **t**
Deut. 12:17...............the **t** of thy corn
Deut. 14:22..............**t** all the increase
Matt. 23:23...pay **t** of mint and anise
Luke 18:12 ....**t**-s of all that I possess
Heb. 7:5 ....take **t**-s of the people
Heb. 7:8 ....men that die receive **t**-s

Token
Gen. 9:12 ....the **t** of the covenant
Ex. 12:13 .....blood shall be . . . for a **t**
Mark 14:44..........had given them a **t**

Told
Luke 2:18 ...**t** them by the shepherds
John 4:39 ....**t** me all that ever I did
John 14:2.not so, I would have **t** you

Tongue
Gen. 10:5...........every one after his **t**
Job 6:30 ....is there iniquity in my **t**
Job 29:10.......**t** cleaved to the roof of

Ps. 5:9 ....they flatter with their t
Ps. 34:13 ....Keep thy t from evil
Ps. 57:4 ....their t a sharp sword
Ps. 140:3.............sharpened their t-s
Prov. 6:17 ....proud look, a lying t
Prov. 12:18......t of the wise is health
Prov. 15:4...Wholesome t is a tree of
Prov. 25:15 .soft t breaketh the bone
Jer. 9:8 ....Their t is as an arrow
Amos 6:10....shall he say, Hold thy t
Mark 16:17.shall speak with new t-s
Luke 16:24 ....water, and cool my t
Acts 2:4 ....to speak with other t-s
Rom. 14:11 ....every t shall confess
1 Cor. 13:1 ...with the t-s of men and
1 Cor. 14:4..speaketh . . . unknown t
1 Cor. 14:39......not to speak with t-s
Phil. 2:11.............every t . . . confess
James 3:5 ....t is a little member
1 Pet. 3:10 ....refrain his t from evil
Rev. 5:9............every kindred, and t

Tooth
Ex. 21:24..............Eye for eye, t for t
Deut. 19:21 ......t for t, hand for hand
Matt. 5:38................................t for a t

Top
Gen. 28:12..t of it reached to heaven
Ex. 19:20......................t of the mount
Heb. 11:21 ....leaning upon the t

Torment
Luke 8:28 ......beseech thee, t me not
Luke 16:23 ....hell . . . being in t-s
1 John 4:18 ....because fear hath t
Rev. 9:5 ....was as the t of a scorpion

Toss
Job 7:4..I am full of t-ings to and fro
Ps. 109:23......I am t-ed up and down
Eph. 4:14............t-ed to and fro, and
James 1:6......with the wind and t-ed

Touch
Gen. 3:3 ....neither shall ye t it
Ex. 19:12 ....or t the border of it
Lev. 5:2...............t any unclean thing
Job 5:19......there shall no evil t thee
Job 19:21 .hand of God hath t-ed me
Matt. 9:21 ....but t his garment
Mark 5:30 ....Who t-ed my clothes
1 Cor. 7:1 ....not to t a woman
Col. 2:21 .... (T not, taste not)

Tower
Gen. 11:4 ....build us a city and a t
2 Sam. 22:3 ....my high t, and my
Ps. 48:12................tell the t-s thereof
Matt. 21:33......................and built a t

Transgress
Num. 14:41 ....t the commandment
Josh. 7:11...............t-ed my covenant
Jer. 2:8 ....pastors also t-ed against
Luke 15:29.........neither t-ed I at any

Transgression
Num. 14:18..forgiving iniquity and t
1 Sam. 24:11 ....neither evil nor t
Job 13:23......make me to know my t
Job 14:17 .My t is sealed up in a bag
Job 33:9............I am clean without t
Ps. 39:8 ...Deliver me from all my t-s
Ps. 51:3...........I acknowledge my t-s
Is. 53:5 ..he was wounded for our t-s
Rom. 4:15 ......no law is, there is no t
1 John 3:4 ....sin is the t of the law

Transgressor
Ps. 37:38 ...the t-s shall be destroyed
Ps. 51:13 ....teach t-s thy ways
Prov. 13:15............way of t-s is hard
Mark 15:28 ....numbered with the t-s
James 2:11art become a t of the law

Travail
Gen. 38:27...........in the time of her t
Job 15:20.......wicked man t-eth with
Ps. 48:6.................as of a woman in t
Eccles. 2:26 .....the sinner he giveth t
Is. 42:14........cry like a t-ing woman
Gal. 4:19...........t in birth again until
Rev. 12:2 ....being with child cried, t-ing

Tread
Deut. 25:4 ...ox . . . t-eth out the corn
Job 24:11 ....t their winepresses
Is. 16:10.......t-ers shall t out no wine
Is. 41:25.........as the potter t-eth clay
Amos 5:11 ......t-ing is upon the poor
Luke 10:19 ....power to t on serpents
1 Tim. 5:18..muzzle the ox that t-eth
Rev. 19:15..........t-eth the winepress

Treasure
Ex. 19:5 ....be a peculiar t unto me
Deut. 33:19 ....t-s hid in the sand
Prov. 10:2 ...T-s of wickedness profit
Job 38:22the t-s of the snow . . . hail
Is. 33:6 ....fear of the Lord is his t
Matt. 6:21.where your t is, there will
Matt. 13:44..................t hid in a field
Matt. 19:21 ....thou shalt have t in
Col. 2:3 ....hid all the t-s of wisdom

Tree
Gen. 1:11 ....fruit t yielding fruit
Gen. 2:9...the t of life . . . knowledge
Deut. 21:22 ......thou hang him on a t
Judg. 9:8.t-s went forth . . . to anoint
Job 40:21 ...lieth under the shady t-s
Ps. 1:3 ....t planted by the rivers
Prov. 3:18..................She is a t of life
Prov. 27:18 .....keepeth the fig t shall
Is. 40:20 ....a t that will not rot
Is. 55:12..........t-s . . . shall clap their
Mic. 4:4 ....vine and under his fig t
Matt. 7:17...........good t . . . corrupt t
Matt. 12:33 ....t is known by his fruit
Luke 19:4 ....climbed . . . a sycamore
John 1:50 ....saw thee under the fig t
Rev. 2:7..................eat of the t of life

Tremble
Deut. 20:3........fear not, and do not t
Judg. 5:4 .earth t-d, and the heavens
Job 26:11 ....pillars of heaven t
Phil. 2:12.............with fear and t-ing
James 2:19.devils also believe, and t

Trespass
Ex. 22:9...............For all manner of t
Ezra 10:2 ....t-ed against our God
Matt. 6:14 ....forgive men their t-es
Matt. 18:15........brother . . . t against
Eph. 2:1 ....dead in t-es and sins
Col. 2:13 ....forgiven you all t-es

Tribe
Gen. 49:28....these are the twelve t-s
Num. 1:4............be a man of every t
Ps. 122:4...............the t-s of the Lord
Matt. 24:30...........all the t-s of earth
Luke 22:30....judging the twelve t-es

Tribulation
Deut. 4:30 ....When thou art in t
1 Sam. 26:24 ...deliver me out of all t
Matt. 24:21 ....then shall be great t
Rom. 5:3 ....t worketh patience
Rom. 12:12.........in hope; patient in t
Eph. 3:13..............faint not at my t-s
2 Thess. 1:6.....t to them that trouble

Tribute
Gen. 49:15 ....a servant unto t
Num. 31:28.....levy a t unto the Lord
Ezra 7:24 ....to impose toll, t, or
Matt. 17:24 .....not your master pay t
Matt. 22:19 .....Shew me the t money
Luke 20:22................give t to Caesar
Rom. 13:7.............t to whom t is due

Tried
2 Sam. 22:31 ....word of the Lord is t
Ps. 12:6 ....as silver t in a furnace
Is. 28:16a t stone, a . . . corner stone
1 Pet. 1:7 ....be t with fire
Rev. 3:18 ....gold t in the fire

Trouble
2 Kin. 19:3 ....This day is a day of t
Ps. 27:5.....time of t he shall hide me
Ps. 77:4.....so t-d that I cannot speak
Ps. 138:7 ....I walk in the midst of t
Is. 22:5 ....For it is a day of t
Is. 33:2..salvation . . . in the time of t
Matt. 26:10.......Why t ye the woman
Luke 24:38 ....Why are ye t-d
John 5:4 ....t-ing of the water
John 12:27...............Now is my soul t-d
2 Cor. 4:8 ...We are t-d on every side
1 Pet. 3:14 ....neither be t-d

True
Gen. 42:11 ....we are t men
1 Kin. 22:16 ....but that which is t
Ps. 119:160....................Thy word is t
Matt. 22:16........know that thou art t
Luke 16:11..............trust the t riches
John 1:9 ....That was the t Light
John 6:32 ....giveth you the t bread
John 8:17 .testimony of two men is t
Rom. 3:4...........................let God be t
Phil. 4:8 ....whatsoever things are t
Titus 1:13 ....This witness is t
Rev. 3:14 ....faithful and t witness

Truly
Deut. 14:22 .....t tithe all the increase
Ps. 62:1........T my soul waiteth upon
Prov. 12:22...They that deal t are his
Matt. 9:37........harvest t is plenteous
Mark 14:38 ....spirit t is ready
Acts 1:5..John t baptized with water

Trumpet
Ex. 19:16 ....the voice of the t
Is. 27:13 ....great t shall be blown
Matt. 6:2 ....alms, do not sound a t
1 Cor. 14:8...........t give an uncertain

Trust
Judg. 9:15 ..put your t in my shadow
2 Sam. 22:3...................in him will I t
Job 8:14......t shall be a spider's web
Ps. 4:5 ....put your t in the Lord
Prov. 11:28 ...t-eth in his riches shall
Jer. 7:4 ....T ye not in lying words
Mic. 7:5 ....T ye not in a friend
Mark 10:24 ....them that t in riches
1 Tim. 4:10............t in the living God
Heb. 2:13 ....put my t in him
Heb. 13:18 ....t we have a good

Truth
Gen. 42:16........there be any t in you
Deut. 32:4 ....a God of t
Ps. 15:2....speaketh the t in his heart
Prov. 23:23........Buy the t, and sell it
Is. 39:8..........peace and t in my days
Matt. 15:27.......T, Lord, yet the dogs
Luke 4:25....................I tell you of a t
John 1:14..............full of grace and t
John 8:32.........t shall make you free
John 14:6.......way, the t, and the life
Gal. 2:5.........the t of the gospel might
2 Tim. 2:15 .....dividing the word of t
1 John 1:8.................the t is not in us

Try
1 Cor. 3:13....fire shall t every man's
James 1:3 ....t-ing of your faith
1 John 4:1 ....t the spirits whether

Turn
Ruth 1:12 ......T again, my daughters
2 Kin. 17:13 ....T ye from your evil
Job 23:13.....................who can t him
Ps. 80:3 ....T us again, O God
Is. 53:6......t-ed every one to his own
Jer. 26:3....t every man from his evil
Matt. 5:39 ..cheek, t to him the other
Acts 17:6 ....t-ed the world upside
2 Tim. 3:5...............from such t away
1 Tim. 5:15......t-ed aside after Satan
James 1:17 ..neither shadow of t-ing

Twelve
Gen. 35:22..the sons of Jacob were t
Matt. 10:1....called . . . his t disciples
Mark 3:14 ....he ordained t
Luke 2:42 ...when he was t years old
John 11:9..............t hours in the day
Rev. 12:1 ....crown of t stars

Twice
Gen. 41:32...doubled unto Pharaoh t

Num. 20:11 ....he smote the rock **t**
Mark 14:30....before the cock crow **t**

Two
Gen. 1:16.....God made **t** great lights
Ex. 31:18...........**t** tables of testimony
Eccles. 4:9 ....**T** are better than one
Matt 6:24 ....No man can serve **t**
Matt 18:19.....**t** of you shall agree on
Luke 17:35 ....**T** women shall be
1 Cor. 6:16.....**t** . . . shall be one flesh
Gal. 4:24....these are the **t** covenants

U

Unawares
Gen. 31:20...........Jacob stole away **u**
Heb. 13:2 ....entertained angels **u**

Unbelief
Matt. 17:20............Because of your **u**
Mark 9:24 ....help thou mine **u**

Unbelievers
Luke 12:46............portion with the **u**
1 Cor. 14:23...............unlearned, or **u**
2 Cor. 6:14.....yoked together with **u**

Unclean
Lev. 5:2..........soul touch any **u** thing
Job 14:4.........clean thing out of an **u**
Is. 6:5 ....a man of **u** lips
Matt. 10:1 .....power against **u** spirits
Mark 5:13 ....**u** spirits went out
Luke 9:42...........rebuked the **u** spirit
Acts 10:14 ....that is common or **u**
Rom. 14:14............nothing **u** of itself
1 Thess. 4:7 .....called us unto **u**-ness
Rev. 16:13...three **u** spirits like frogs

Undefiled
Ps. 119:1 ......Blessed are the **u** in the
Heb. 13:4 ....and the bed **u**
James 1:27 ....Pure religion and **u**

Under
Gen. 1:9............waters **u** the heaven
Matt. 5:15.................put it **u** a bushel
John 1:50.......saw thee **u** the fig tree
Rom. 3:9.................they are all **u** sin
Eph. 1:22............all things **u** his feet
1 Pet. 5:6..**u** the mighty hand of God

Understand
Gen. 11:7 ....not **u** one another's
Is. 6:9 ....Hear ye . . . but **u** not
Dan. 8:17 ....U, O son of man
Matt. 15:10 ....Hear, and **u**
Luke 24:45.....might **u** the scriptures
John 8:43 ....Why do ye not **u** my

Understanding
Ex. 36:1........Lord put wisdom and **u**
1 Kin. 3:12 ......a wise and an **u** heart
Job 17:4..........hid their heart from **u**
Prov. 2:2 ....apply thine heart to **u**
Is. 27:11 ....a people of no **u**
Matt. 15:16............also yet without **u**
Luke 24:45............opened he their **u**
1 Cor. 14:20 ....be not children in **u**
Phil. 4:7 ....peace . . . passeth all **u**
2 Tim. 2:7.......Lord give thee **u** in all

Understood
Ps. 81:5............language that I **u** not
1 Cor. 13:11 ....I **u** as a child

Unfruitful
Matt. 13:22..........and he becometh **u**
1 Cor. 14:14 ..my understanding is **u**
2 Pet. 1:8............**u** in the knowledge

Ungodly
Ps. 1:1......not in the counsel of the **u**
Rom. 5:6...........Christ died for the **u**
Jude 18...........after their own **u** lusts

Unjust
Prov. 29:27 ....**u** man is an
Matt. 5:45....on the just and on the **u**
Acts 24:15.both of the just and the **u**

Unknown
Acts 17:23....................To The **U** God
1 Cor. 14:2, 4, 14, 19 ....**u** tongue
Gal. 1:22 ....was **u** by face

Unprofitable
Job 15:3 ....reason with **u** talk
Luke 17:10...........We are **u** servants
Rom. 3:12......are together become **u**
Heb. 13:17 ....for that is **u** for you

Unrighteous
Ex. 23:1 ....to be an **u** witness
Lev. 19:15 ....Ye shall do no **u**-ness
Is. 55:7 ....**u** man his thoughts
Luke 16:11 ....faithful in the **u**
Rom. 3:5 ....Is God **u**
1 Cor. 6:9........**u** shall not inherit the
Heb. 6:10........God is not **u** to forget
2 Pet. 2:13........the reward of **u**-ness
1 John 5:17........................all **u** is sin

Unwise
Deut. 32:6 .....O foolish people and **u**
Hos. 13:13 ....He is an **u** son
Rom. 1:14........the wise, and to the **u**
Eph. 5:17..........................be ye not **u**

Upper
Ex. 12:7 ....**u** door post of the houses
Luke 22:12...large **u** room furnished
Acts 1:13..........went into an **u** room
Acts 19:1.........passed through the **u**

Upright
2 Sam. 22:26 ....wilt shew thyself **u**
Job 1:8............perfect and an **u** man
Ps. 15:2 ....He that walketh **u**-ly
Prov. 10:9........walketh **u**-ly walketh
Mic. 7:2 ....is none **u** among men
Acts 14:10 ....Stand **u** on thy feet

Use
Matt. 5:44..which despitefully **u** you
2 Cor. 3:12 ....**u** great plainness of
Gal. 5:13 ....**u** not liberty for an
1 Tim. 5:23.......**u** a little wine for thy

Usury
Lev. 25:36......Take thou no **u** of him
Deut. 23:20 ....mayest lend upon **u**
Ps. 15:5 ....putteth not out . . . to **u**
Prov. 28:8 ....**u** and unjust gain
Matt. 25:27.............mine own with **u**

Utter
Judg. 5:12...awake, awake, **u** a song
1 Kin. 20:42 ....appointed to **u**
Job 15:5..mouth **u**-eth thine iniquity
Ps. 119:171 ....lips shall **u** praise
Prov. 14:5.....false witness will **u** lies
Jer. 1:16.........I will **u** my judgments
1 Cor. 14:9.....**u** by the tongue words

Utterance
Acts 2:4.....as the Spirit gave them **u**
2 Cor. 8:7................faith, and **u**, and
Col. 4:3.......open unto us a door of **u**

Utterly
Is. 2:18..........idols he shall **u** abolish
1 Cor. 6:7.......is **u** a fault among you
2 Pet. 2:12 ....shall **u** perish in their
Rev. 18:8.........be **u** burned with fire

V

Vail
Gen. 24:65......therefore she took a **v**
Ex. 34:33 ....he put a **v** on his face
Lev. 4:6...........the **v** of the sanctuary
2 Cor. 3:13 ....put a **v** over his face

Vain
Ex. 5:9 ....not regard **v** words
Lev. 26:16............sow your seed in **v**
2 Kin. 18:20 ....but they are but **v**
Ps. 2:1..........people imagine a **v** thing
Is. 45:18 ....he created it not in **v**
Matt. 6:7 ....use not **v** repetitions
Rom. 1:21 .....**v** in their imaginations
1 Cor. 15:14 .then is our preaching **v**
Gal. 2:21 ....Christ is dead in **v**
Eph. 5:6....deceive you with **v** words
Phil. 2:3.......through strife or **v**-glory
James 1:26....this man's religion is **v**

Valley
Josh. 10:12.Moon, in the **v** of Ajalon
2 Kin. 3:16............Make this **v** full of
Ps. 23:4..............the **v** of the shadow
Song 2:1 ....and the lily of the **v**-s
Jer. 31:40.....the whole **v** of the dead
Ezek. 37:1.**v** which was full of bones
Joel 3:14 ....the **v** of decision
Luke 3:5 ....Every **v** shall be filled

Vanity
Job 7:16 ....my days are **v**
Ps. 24:4........lifted up his soul unto **v**
Eccles. 1:2 ....**V** of **v**-s . . . all is **v**
Jer. 2:5 ....have walked after **v**
Eph. 4:17........walk, in the **v** of their

Veil
Matt. 27:51.**v** of the temple was rent
Heb. 6:19 ....that within the **v**
Heb. 9:3................after the second **v**

Vengeance
Gen. 4:15 .....**v** shall be taken on him
Deut. 32:35 ....To me belongeth **v**
Ps. 94:1 ...God, to whom **v** belongeth
Is. 34:8..........The day of the Lord's **v**
Heb. 10:30 ....**V** belongeth unto me
Jude 7 ....**v** of eternal fire

Verily
Ex. 31:13......**V** my sabbaths ye shall
Ps. 37:3.................**v** thou shalt be fed
Is. 45:15 ....**V** thou art a God that
John 1:51.............**V**, **v** I say unto you

Very
Gen. 1:31.........behold, it was **v** good
1 Sam. 5:11..........hand of God was **v**
Ps. 46:1 ......**v** present help in trouble
Is. 16:6 ....he is **v** proud
Ezek. 33:32 ....a **v** lovely song
Matt. 15:28...whole from that **v** hour
Mark 16:2......**v** early in the morning
Luke 12:7....the **v** hairs of your head
Acts 9:22 ....that this is **v** Christ
2 Cor. 11:5............**v** chiefest apostles
1 Thess. 5:23 ....the **v** God of peace
James 5:11..........the Lord is **v** pitiful

Vessel
Ex. 7:19 .**v**-s of wood . . . **v**-s of stone
Num. 5:17 ....water in an earthen **v**
2 Kin. 4:3 .....borrow thee **v**-s abroad
Ps. 31:12 ....I am like a broken **v**
Matt. 25:4...wise took oil in their **v**-s
Acts 9:15...................he is a chosen **v**
Rom. 9:22.........................**v**-s of wrath
2 Cor. 4:7......treasure in earthen **v**-s
2 Tim. 2:21 ....be a **v** unto honour
Rev. 2:27..........as the **v**-s of a potter

Vesture
Gen. 41:42 ....in **v**-s of fine linen
Ps. 22:18 ....cast lots upon my **v**
Matt. 27:35....my **v** did they cast lots

Vex
Job 19:2..........long will ye **v** my soul
Is. 63:10.................**v**-ed his holy Spirit
Matt. 15:22 ....**v**-ed with a devil
Luke 6:18 ..**v**-ed with unclean spirits
2 Pet. 2:8.......**v**-ed his righteous soul

Victory
2 Sam. 23:10Lord wrought a great **v**
1 Chr. 29:11........the glory, and the **v**
Is. 25:8............swallow up death in **v**
1 Cor. 15:54 ..Death is swallowed up in **v**
1 John 5:4 ......**v** that overcometh the
Rev. 15:2 ....the **v** over the beast

Vile
1 Sam. 3:13 ....his sons made themselves **v**
Job 40:4 ....I am **v**; what shall I
Rom. 1:26...............unto **v** affections
Phil. 3:21 ....change our **v** body

Vine
Gen. 40:9 ....a **v** was before me
Ps. 128:3.wife shall be as a fruitful **v**
Is. 36:16......eat ye every one of his **v**
Jer. 2:21 ....planted thee a noble **v**
Mal. 3:11...........your **v** cast her fruit
Matt. 26:29.....drink . . . fruit of the **v**
John 15:1 ....I am the true **v**

Vinegar
Ruth 2:14 ......dip thy morsel in the v
Prov. 10:26 ....As v to the teeth
Matt. 27:48 ..spunge . . . filled it with v

Vineyard
Gen. 9:20.............and he planted a v
1 Kin. 21:1...........Naboth . . . had a v
Is. 1:8....................as a cottage in a v
Jer. 12:10 ....have destroyed my v
Matt. 20:4 ....Go ye also into the v

Violence
Gen. 6:11 ....earth was filled with v
Ps. 55:9..........v and strife in the city
Jer. 22:3 ....do no v to the stranger
Luke 3:14 ....Do v to no man
Heb. 11:34 .....Quenched the v of fire

Violent
Ps. 18:48 .....delivered me from the v
Prov. 16:29................v man enticeth
Matt. 8:32 ......swine ran v-ly down a

Viper
Job 20:16...v's tongue shall slay him
Matt. 3:7 ....O generation of v-s
Acts 28:3.....came a v out of the heat

Virgin
Ex. 22:17..................the dowry of v-s
Jer. 31:13 ....v rejoice in the dance
Matt. 1:23..........v shall be with child
Matt. 25:1 ....likened unto ten v-s
Luke 1:27.....the v's name was Mary
1 Cor. 7:28......................if a v marry
2 Cor. 11:2..........a chaste v to Christ

Virtue
Ruth 3:11 ....thou art a v-ous woman
Prov. 12:4 ..v-ous woman is a crown
Phil. 4:8....................if there be any v
2 Pet. 1:5............to your faith v . . . v

Vision
Gen. 15:1 ....came to Abram in a v
Job 20:8.................as a v of the night
Prov. 29:18.........Where there is no v
Lam. 2:9 ......find no v from the Lord
Dan. 2:19....revealed . . . in a night v
Joel 2:28 .....young men shall see v-s
Hab. 2:2......Write the v, and make it
Acts 2:17.....young men shall see v-s
2 Cor. 12:1 ....come to v-s and

Visit
Gen. 50:24.......God will surely v you
Ex. 20:5 ....v-ing the iniquity of the
Ps. 8:4..................that thou v-est him
Matt. 25:36 ....sick, and ye v-ed me
Luke 1:68......v-ed and redeemed his
James 1:27.........v the fatherless and

Voice
Gen. 3:8........heard the v of the Lord
Deut. 4:30 ......be obedient unto his v
Josh. 6:10...............noise with your v
2 Sam. 19:35 ....v of singing men
1 Kin. 19:12 ......the fire a still small v
Eccles. 5:3 ....a fool's v is known
Song 2:12.............the v of the turtle
Is. 28:23 .Give ye ear, and hear my v
Is. 40:3......v of him that crieth in the
Dan. 4:31 ....fell a v from heaven
Matt. 2:18 ....Rama was there a v
Matt. 3:17 ....lo a v from heaven
Mark 9:7......v came out of the cloud
Luke 3:4.....................v of one crying
John 5:25...........v of the Son of God
Acts 10:13......came a v to him, Rise,
Heb. 12:26.....v then shook the earth
Rev. 3:20 ....if any man hear my v
Rev. 5:11 ....heard the v of many

Void
Gen. 1:2 ....without form, and v
Ps. 119:126.......have made v thy law
Is. 55:11 ....not return unto me v
Rom. 4:14 ....faith is made v

Vomit
Job 20:15 ....shall v them up again
Prov. 26:11 .....dog returneth to his v
Jonah 2:10 ....it v-ed out Jonah

W

Wages
Gen. 29:15..........what shall thy w be
Ex. 2:9.............I will give thee thy w
Lev. 19:13 ....w of him that is hired
Luke 3:14.....be content with your w
John 4:36...that reapeth receiveth w
2 Pet. 2:15 ....w of unrighteousness

Wail
Esther 4:3...and weeping, and w-ing
Matt. 13:42....w-ing and gnashing of
Mark 5:38......wept and w-ed greatly

Wait
Gen. 49:18......w-ed for thy salvation
Josh. 8:4...................ye shall lie in w
2 Kin. 5:2 ......she w-ed on Naaman's
Job 14:14......appointed time will I w
Ps. 27:14 W on the Lord . . . w, I say,
Ps. 37:34....W on the Lord, and keep
Prov. 1:18.lay w for their own blood
Is. 26:8 .Lord, have we w-ed for thee
Is. 30:18 ....will the Lord w
Dan. 12:12 ..Blessed is he that w-eth
Hos. 6:9..as . . . robbers w for a man
Mic. 7:2 ....all lie in w for blood
Mark 15:43.....w-ed for the kingdom
Luke 12:36 ....men that w for their
John 5:3 w-ing for the moving of the
Acts 10:7 ....that w-ed on him
Rom. 8:23......w-ing for the adoption
1 Cor. 1:7.....w-ing for the coming of
Gal. 5:5..................w for the hope of
Eph. 4:14......they lie in w to deceive

Walk
Gen. 3:8 .....God w-ing in the garden
Gen. 5:24........Enoch w-ed with God
Ex. 14:29............w-ed upon dry land
Lev. 26:3 ....If ye w in my statutes
Josh. 18:8.......Go and w through the
Job 18:8.........he w-eth upon a snare
Job 22:14 ....w-eth in the circuit of
Ps. 1:1.....w-eth not in the counsel of
Ps. 15:2........He that w-eth uprightly
Ps. 23:4..w through the valley of the
Prov. 28:18.....w-eth uprightly . . . be
Eccles. 2:14...fool w-eth in darkness
Is. 2:3 ....we will w in his paths
Is. 2:5 ....w in the light of the Lord
Is. 9:2..people that w-ed in darkness
Jer. 9:14 .w-ed after the imagination
Ezek. 36:12 .....cause men to w upon
Hos. 11:10......They shall w after the
Joel 2:8 ....w every one in his path
Amos 3:3 ....Can two w together,
Mic. 6:8...to w humbly with thy God
Nah. 2:5.......shall stumble in their w
Zeph. 1:17 .....shall w like blind men
Mal. 2:6 ....w-ed with me in peace
Matt. 9:5...........................Arise, and w
Matt. 14:29 ......he w-ed on the water
Mark 1:16........he w-ed by the sea of
John 6:19 ......Jesus w-ing on the sea
Acts 3:6..........................rise up and w
Rom. 6:4 ....w in newness of life
Rom. 8:1...........w not after the flesh
2 Cor. 4:2 ....w-ing in craftiness
2 Cor. 5:7 .....w by faith, not by sight
Gal. 5:16 ....W in the Spirit
Eph. 4:1 ....w worthy of the vocation
Eph. 5:2 ......w in love, as Christ also
Col. 2:6.........................so w ye in him
Col. 4:5...........................W in wisdom
1 Thess. 2:12 ....w worthy of God
1 Pet. 5:8.........devil . . . w-eth about,
1 John 2:6 ..so to w, even as he w-ed
Jude 16...w-ing after their own lusts
Rev. 3:4......shall w with me in white
Rev. 21:24.saved shall w in the light

Wall
Ex. 14:22 waters were a w into them
Josh. 2:15........she dwelt upon the w
2 Kin. 20:2...turned his face to the w
Neh. 4:6.....................So built we the w
Ps. 18:29........have I leaped over a w
Prov. 18:11...........high w in his own
Ezek. 12:5....Dig thou through the w
Joel 2:9............shall run upon the w
Amos 7:7 .....w made by a plumbline
Hab. 2:11 ....shall cry out of the w
Acts 9:25.down by the w in a basket
Heb. 11:30 ......the w-s of Jericho fell
Rev. 21:12 ....had a w great and high

Wander
Gen. 21:14.....w-ed in the wilderness
Job 15:23 .....w-eth abroad for bread
Ps. 55:7 ....then would I w far off
Prov. 27:8 ....bird . . . w-eth from her
Lam 4:14.......have w-ed as blind men
Jude 13 ....w-ing stars, to whom is

Want
Job 30:3 ....For w and famine they
Ps. 23:1 ....shepherd; I shall not w
Prov. 10:21 ....fools die for w of
Is. 34:16 ....none shall w her mate
Luke 15:14 ....he began to be in w
John 2:3 ....when they w-ed wine
James 1:4 ....w-ing nothing

War
Ex. 13:17.....repent when they see w
Num. 21:14...........book of the w-s of
Deut. 24:5 ....not go out to w
Ps. 46:9 ....maketh w-s to cease
Ps. 55:21 ....w was in his heart
Eccles. 3:8...a time of w . . . of peace
Is. 2:4..neither . . . learn w any more
Is. 21:15 ....the grievousness of w
Dan. 9:26...........the w of desolations
Matt. 24:6 .....w-s . . . rumours of w-s
Rom. 7:23 .w-ring against the law of
1 Cor. 9:7 ...Who goeth a w-fare any
2 Cor. 10:3 ...do not w after the flesh
2 Cor. 10:4 ....weapons of our w-fare
James 4:1 ....whence come w-s
1 Pet. 2:11 .which w against the soul
Rev. 12:7 ....there was w in heaven

Warm
Is. 47:14.............not be a coal to w at
Mark 14:54 ..w-ed himself at the fire
John 18:25.......Peter stood and w-ed
James 2:16.......be ye w-ed and filled

Warn
2 Kin. 6:10....God told him and w-ed
Acts 20:31 ......ceased not to w every
1 Thess. 5:14 ....w them that are
Heb. 11:7.............being w-ed of God

Wash
Gen. 18:4..........w your feet, and rest
2 Sam. 11:2 ....saw a woman w-ing
2 Kin. 5:10 ....Go and w in Jordan
Job 9:30..w myself with snow water
Ps. 51:2 ....W me . . . from mine
Song 5:12....eyes . . . w-ed with milk
Is. 1:16.........W you, make you clean
Ezek. 16:9........w-ed away thy blood
Matt. 6:17..........................w thy face
Matt. 15:2....w not their hands when
Mark 7:4 ......except they w, they eat
Luke 7:44 ....w-ed my feet with tears
Luke 11:38..first w-ed before dinner
John 9:7 Go, w in the pool of Siloam
Acts 22:16 ....and w away thy sins
1 Cor. 6:11 ....ye are w-ed
1 Tim. 5:10............she have w-ed the
Heb. 10:22 .....bodies w-ed with pure
Rev. 1:5 ....w-ed us from our sins

Waste
Lev. 26:31 ....will make your cities w
Job 14:10.man dieth, and w-th away
Ps. 79:7......laid w his dwelling place
Is. 5:6...........................I will lay it w
Is. 23:14.........your strength is laid w
Nah. 3:7 ....Nineveh is laid w
Luke 15:13..there w-d his substance
Gal. 1:13 ..church of God, and w-d it

Watch
Ex. 14:24 ....in the morning w
2 Kin. 11:5...............keepers of the w
2 Chr. 23:6....keep the w of the Lord
Job 7:12 ....settest a w over me
Matt. 24:42.........W wherefore: for ye
Matt. 25:13........W wherefore: for ye
Matt. 26:40 ..could ye not w with me

Luke 2:8 .keeping w over their flock
Acts 20:31 ....Therefore W, and
1 Cor. 16:13...W ye, stand fast in the
2 Cor. 11:27 ....in w-ings often
Heb. 13:17.......they w for your souls
1 Pet. 4:7 ....and w unto prayer
Rev. 16:15...Blessed is he that w-eth

Water
Gen. 1:2 ......upon the face of the w-s
Ex. 2:10.........drew him out of the w
Deut. 8:7............land of brooks of w
Judg. 5:4 ....clouds also dropped w
2 Sam. 14:14...........as w split on the
1 Kin. 13:22...Eat no bread . . . drink no w
2 Kin. 3:11 .w on the hands of Elijah
Job 9:30...wash myself with snow w
Job 11:16........as w-s that pass away
Job 14:19....The w-s wear the stones
Ps. 1:3 ......planted by the rivers of w
Ps. 22:14 ....poured out like w
Ps. 23:2.................beside the still w-s
Ps. 46:3 ....w-s . . . roar and be
Prov. 5:15.........w-s out of thine own
Prov. 20:5.....heart . . . is like deep w
Eccles. 11:1..thy bread upon the w-s
Is. 1:30 ....garden that hath no w
Is. 11:9.........as the w-s cover the sea
Is. 19:5 .....w-s shall fail from the sea
Is. 32:2 ......rivers of w in a dry place
Jer. 2:13....the fountain of living w-s
Jer. 8:14 ....w of gall to drink
Dan. 1:12.........pulse to eat, and w to
Matt. 3:11...........baptize you with w
Matt. 10:42...little ones a cup of cold w
Luke 7:44 .....gavest me no w for my feet
John 3:5.....man be born of w and of
John 4:10 ....given thee living w
Acts 1:5.....John . . . baptized with w
Acts 8:36 ..See, here is w; what doth
1 Cor. 3:6 ......planted, Appolos w-ed
James 3:11 ....sweet w and bitter
2 Pet. 3:5 ...out of the w and in the w
1 John 5:6 ....that came by w and
Rev. 22:17....take the w of life freely

Waves
2 Sam. 22:5 ...w of death compassed
Job 9:8 ....treadeth . . . w of the sea
Mark 4:37 ....w beat into the ship
Jude 13 ....Raging w of the sea

Wax
Gen. 26:13..And the man w-ed great
Ex. 16:21.......when the sun w-ed hot
1 Sam. 3:2 ....eyes began to w dim
Job 6:17 ....time they w warm
Ps. 22:14.................my heart is like w
Is. 50:9.................w old as a garment
Matt. 24:12.......love of many shall w
Luke 2:40.........child grew, and w-ed
2 Tim. 3:13...seducers shall w worse
Heb. 11:34.........w-ed valiant in fight

Way
Gen. 3:24............w of the tree of life
Num. 20:17..go by the king's high w
Deut. 8:6................to walk in his w-s
2 Sam. 22:33 ....he maketh my w
2 Kin. 17:13 ..Turn ye from your evil w-s
Ezra 8:21 ....seek of him a right w
Job 3:23 ....a man whose w is hid
Ps. 1:6............the w of the righteous
Ps. 18:30 ....God, his w is perfect
Ps. 25:8...........teach sinners in the w
Prov. 3:17 ....w-s are w-s of
Prov. 6:6 .....ant . . . consider her w-s
Prov. 7:27.Her house is the w to hell
Is. 2:3 ....he will teach us of his w-s
Is. 26:7 ...w of the just is uprightness
Is. 30:21 ..This is the w, walk ye in it
Is. 40:3Prepare ye the w of the Lord
Jer. 6:16............where is the good w
Jer. 12:1 .....w of the wicked prosper
Lam. 3:40..searched and try our w-s
Nah. 1:3 .... his w in the whirlwind
Hab. 3:6 ....his w-s are everlasting
Mal. 3:1......prepare the w before me
Matt. 7:13 ....broad is the w
Matt. 15:32....lest they faint in the w
Mark 1:3......Prepare ye the w of the
Luke 1:79 ....into the w of peace
John 1:23 .straight the w of the Lord
John 14:6 .I am the w, the truth, and
Acts 9:2 ....found any of this w
Acts 9:27 ....seen the Lord in the w
Rom. 3:17.w of peace . . . not known
1 Cor. 4:17 ....w-s which be in Christ
1 Cor. 12:31 ....a more excellent w
James 1:8 ....unstable in all his w-s
James 5:20 ...from the error of his w
2 Pet. 2:15 ....forsaken the right w
Jude 11...........gone in the w of Cain

Weak
Judg. 16:17 ....I shall become w
2 Chr. 15:7 ..let not your hands be w
Is. 14:10 ....also become w as we
Joel 3:10..............w say, I am strong
Mark 14:38............but the flesh is w
Acts 20:35.....ought to support the w
Rom. 4:19...........being not w in faith
1 Cor. 1:27 ......w things of the world
1 Cor. 4:10 ....we are w, but ye are
1 Thess. 5:14...............support the w

Weakness
1 Cor. 1:25........w of God is stronger
1 Cor. 2:3.with you in w, and in fear
1 Cor. 15:43 ....it is sown in w
2 Cor. 12:9 .strength is . . . perfect in w
Heb. 11:34 ....out of w were made

Wealth
Deut. 8:18...................power to get w
2 Chr. 1:11..........not asked riches, w
Ezra 9:12 ....nor seek their . . . w
Job. 21:13 ....spend their days in w
Ps. 49:6 ....that trust in their w
Prov. 13:11 ....W gotten by vanity

Weapon
2 Chr. 23:10...........his w in his hand
Neh. 4:17...........other hand held a w
Job 20:24 ....flee from the iron w
Eccles. 9:18 ...Wisdom is better than w-s
2 Cor. 10:4 ....w-s of our warfare

Wear
Ex. 18:18 ...Thou wilt surely w away
Dan. 7:25 ....w out the saints of the
Matt. 11:8...........that w soft clothing
Luke 9:12 ....day began to w away
John 19:5.Jesus . . . w-ing the crown

Weary
Gen. 27:46 ....I am w of my life
2 Sam. 17:2 .while he is w and weak
Job 3:17...........there the w be at rest
Prov. 25:17 ....lest he be w of thee
Eccles. 12:12 ....a w-ness of the flesh
Jer. 6:11 ....w with holding in
Hab. 2:13 ....w themselves for very
John 4:6 ....w-ed with his journey
2 Cor. 11:27 ....In w-ness and
Gal. 6;9 ....not be w in well doing

Week
Gen. 29:27..Fulfil her w, and we will
Ex. 34:22 .....observe the feast of w-s
Dan. 9:24..................Seventy w-s are
Matt. 28:1 ....first day of the w
Luke 18:12 ....fast twice in the w

Weep
Gen. 43:30 ......he sought where to w
Num. 11:13 ....for they w unto me
Deut. 34:8 ....days of w-ing and mourning
1 Sam. 1:8 ....why w-est thou
Neh. 8:9 ....mourn not, nor w
Job 16:16 ....face is foul with w-ing
Ps. 6:8 ..heard the voice of my w-ing
Eccles. 3:4 ...A time to w, and a time
Is. 22:4 ....I will w bitterly
Jer. 9:1 ....might w day and night
Matt. 2:18.........Rachel w-ing for her
Mark 5:39..................this ado, and w
Luke 6:21 ....Blessed are ye that w
John 11:31...........unto the grave to w
Rom. 12:15.............do rejoice, and w
Rev. 5:5...W not: behold, the Lion of

Weigh
Gen. 23:16 .....Abraham w-ed . . . the
1 Sam. 2:3 ..by him actions are w-ed
Job 6:2 .....Oh that my grief were . . . w-ed
Ps. 58:2 ....w the violence of your
Prov. 16:2.the Lord w-eth the spirits
Is. 26:7 ....w the path of the just

Weight
Gen. 24:22 ....of half a shekel w
Lev. 19:36......Just balances, just w-s
Deut. 25:15 ....a perfect and just w
Ezek. 4:16 ....shall eat bread by w
Mic. 6:11 ....bag of deceitful w-s
2 Cor. 4:17 ....eternal w of glory
Heb. 12:1 .....let us lay aside every w

Well
Deut. 4:40 ....that it may go w with
1 Sam. 9:10 ....W said
2 Sam. 17:21......they came up out of the w
2 Kin. 3:19 ....stop all w-s of water
Ps. 48:13....Mark ye w her bulwarks
Eccles. 8:13............not be w with the
Song 4:15...........a w of living waters
Is. 1:17...........................Learn to do w
Jonah 4:4 .Doest thou w to be angry
Matt. 3:17 ..in whom I am w pleased
Mark 7:37......hath done all things w
John 4:6 ....Jacob's w was there
Acts 15:29 ....shall do w. Fare ye w
Rom. 2:7 ......continuance in w doing
Gal. 5:7 ....Ye did run w
1 Tim. 3:4 ....ruleth w his own house
Heb. 13:16...........sacrifices God is w

Wept
Ex. 2:6 ....behold, the babe w
Matt. 26:75...............went out, and w
Luke 7:32...........................ye have not w
Luke 19:41.....beheld the city, and w
John 11:35...............................Jesus w
Rev. 5:4.........................And I w much

Whale
Gen. 1:21 ....God created great w-s
Job. 7:12 ....Am I a sea, or a w
Ezek. 32:2..............as a w in the seas
Matt. 12:40 ....three nights in the w's

Whatsoever
Gen. 31:16......W God hath said unto
Job 37:12 ....do w he commandeth
Ps. 1:3........w he doeth shall prosper
Eccles. 9:10....W thy hand findeth to
Jer. 1:7 ....w I command thee
Matt. 7:12 ....w ye would that men
Luke 12:3............w ye have spoken
John 11:22....w thou wilt ask of God
Rom. 14:23 ....w is not of faith
1 Cor. 10:31 .....w ye do, do all to the
Gal. 6:7 ....w a man soweth
Eph. 6:8.........w good thing any man
Phil. 4:8 ....w things are true
Col. 3:17.....w ye do in word or deed

Wheat
Gen. 30:14 ..in the days of w harvest
Ex. 34:22 ....firstfruits of w harvest
Deut. 8:8........A land of w, and barley
1 Sam. 12:17 ....Is it not w harvest to
Job 31:40 .thistles grow instead of w
Matt. 3:12.........gather his w into the
Luke 22:31 ....he may sift you as w
John 12:24......corn of w fall into the
Rev. 6:6....measure of w for a penny

Wheel
Ps. 83:13 ...God, make them like a w
Prov. 20:26 ....bringeth the w over
Ezek. 1:16......w in the middle of a w

Whelp
Gen. 49:9..............Judah is a lion's w
Deut. 33:22..............Dan is a lion's w
Jer. 51:38 ....shall yell as lion's w-s
Nah. 2:11 ....the lion's w

Where
Gen. 3:9 ..... **W** art thou
Ruth 1:17 ..... **W** thou diest, will I die
Ps. 42:3 ..... **W** is thy God
Prov. 29:18 ..... **W** there is no vision
Is. 19:12 ..... **w** are thy wise men
Matt. 2:2 ..... **W** is he that is born
Luke 8:25 ..... **W** is your faith
John 8:19 ..... **W** is thy Father
John 11:34 ..... **W** have ye laid him
Rom. 4:15 ..... **w** no law is
1 Cor. 1:20 ..... **W** is the wise

Whip
1 Kin. 12:11 ..chastised you with **w**-s
Nah. 3:2 ..... The noise of a **w**

Whirlwind
2 Kin. 2:1 ..... into heaven by a **w**
Job 37:9 ..... Out of the south cometh . . . **w**
Ps. 58:9 ..... away as with a **w**
Is. 17:13 ...rolling thing before the **w**
Jer. 4:13 ..... chariots shall be as a **w**
Hos. 8:7 ..... they shall reap the **w**

Whisper
Prov. 16:28 ..... **w**-er separateth
2 Cor. 12:20 ..... **w**-ings, swellings,

White
Gen. 49:12 ..... teeth **w** with milk
Num. 12:10 ..... leprous, **w** as snow
Ps. 51:7 ..... shall be **w**-r than snow
Is. 1:18 ....they shall be as **w** as snow
Dan. 7:9 ..... garment was **w** as snow
Luke 9:29 ..... raiment was **w** and
John 4:35 ..... **w** already to harvest
Acts 23:3 ..... thou **w**-d wall
Rev. 6:2 ..... behold a **w** horse

Whither
Gen. 28:15 ....all places **w** thou goest
Ex. 21:13 ..... place **w** he shall flee
Ruth 1:16 ..... **w** thou goest, I will go
1 Sam. 27:10 ..... **W** have ye made a
Ps. 139:7 ..... **W** shall I go from thy
John 8:21 ..... **w** I go, ye cannot come

Whole
Gen. 2:6 ..... watered the **w** face
2 Sam. 1:9 ..... my life is yet **w** in me
Job 5:18 ..... his hands make **w**
Matt. 6:22 ..... **w** body . . . full of light
Luke 5:31 ..... **w** need not a physician
John 5:6 ..... Wilt thou be made **w**
Acts 9:34 ..... Christ maketh thee **w**
1 Cor. 5:6 ..... leaveneth the **w** lump
Eph. 6:11 ..... the **w** armour of God
1 John 2:2 ..... sins of the **w** world

Whomsoever
Matt. 26:48.**W** I shall kiss, that same
Luke 12:48 ..... unto **w** much is given
Acts 8:19 ..... on **w** I lay hands
1 Cor. 16:3 ..... **w** ye shall approve

Wicked
Gen. 38:7..**w** in the sight of the Lord
Lev. 20:17 ..... it is a **w** thing
Deut. 23:9 ...keep thee from every **w**
2 Sam. 24:17 ..... I have done **w**-ly
Job 10:15 ..... If I be **w**, woe unto me
Job 11:20 ..... eyes of the **w** shall fail
Ps. 7:11 ..... God is angry with the **w**
Prov. 4:19 ..... way of the **w** is as
Prov. 10:30 ....**w** shall not inhabit the
Prov. 11:7 ..... When a **w** man dieth
Prov. 13:9..lamp of the **w** . . . put out
Eccles. 7:17 ..... Be not over much **w**
Is. 53:9 ....made his grave with the **w**
Ezek. 3:18 ..... warn the **w** from his **w**
Dan. 12:10 ..... **w** shall do **w**-ly
Matt. 12:45 ..... this **w** generation
Acts 2:23 ..... **w** hands have crucified
2 Thess. 2:8 ..... shall that **W** be
1 John 2:13 ..... overcome the **w** one

Wickedness
Gen. 6:5 ..... the **w** of man was great
Job 4:8 ..... plow iniquity, and sow **w**
Ps. 5:9 ....their inward part is very **w**
Prov. 4:17 ..... they eat the bread of **w**
Is. 9:18 ..... **w** burneth as the fire
Ezek. 3:19 ..... turn not from his **w**
Hos. 10:13 ..... Ye have plowed **w**
Matt. 22:18 ..Jesus perceived their **w**
Acts 8:22 ..... Repent . . . of this thy **w**
Eph. 6:12 ..spiritual **w** in high places
1 John 5:19 ...whole world lieth in **w**

Wide
Deut. 15:8 ..... open thine hand **w**
Job 29:23 ..... opened their mouth **w**
Ps. 104:25 ..... this great and **w** sea
Jer. 22:14 ..... build me a **w** house
Nah. 3:13 ..... shall be set **w** open
Matt. 7:13 ..... for **w** is the gate

Widow
Gen. 38:11 ..... Remain a **w** at thy
Ex. 22:22...Ye shall not afflict any **w**
Lev. 21:14 ..... A **w**, or a divorced
2 Sam. 14:5.I am indeed a **w** woman
Job 22:9 ..... sent **w**-s away empty
Ps. 68:5 ..... and a judge of the **w**-s
Is. 1:17 ..... plead for the **w**
Matt. 23:14 ....ye devour **w**-s' houses
Mark 12:43 ..... **w** hath cast more in
Luke 18:5 ..... this **w** troubleth me
1 Tim. 5:3...Honour **w**-s that are **w**-s

Wife
Gen. 2:24 ..... shall cleave unto his **w**
Ex. 20:17 ..... thy neighbour's **w**
Lev. 18:15 ..... she is thy son's **w**
Job 31:10 ..... let my **w** grind unto
Prov. 18:22 ..... findeth a **w** findeth a
Eccles. 9:9 ..Live joyfully with the **w**
Mark 1:30 ..... Simon's **w**'s mother
Luke 17:32 ..... Remember Lot's **w**
1 Cor. 7:2 ..... man have his own **w**
Eph. 5:23.husband . . . head of the **w**
1 Tim. 3:2 ..... the husband of one **w**
1 Pet. 3:7 ..giving honour unto the **w**

Wild
Gen. 16:12 ..... he will be a **w** man
Ps. 104:11 ..... **w** asses quench their
Is. 5:2 ..... brought forth **w** grapes
Jer. 50:39 ..... **w** beasts of the desert
Mark 1:6 ..... did eat locusts and **w**
Acts 10:12 ....**w** beasts, and creeping

Wilderness
Gen. 16:7.fountain of water in the **w**
Ex. 14:11 ..... away to die in the **w**
Deut. 29:5 ..... forty years in the **w**
Prov. 21:19...better to dwell in the **w**
Is. 40:3.voice . . . that crieth in the **w**
Matt. 3:3 ....voice . . . crying in the **w**
Mark 1:13..there in the **w** forty days
1 Cor. 10:5 ..... overthrown in the **w**
Heb. 3:8..day of temptation in the **w**
Rev. 12:6 ..... woman fled into the **w**

Will
Ps. 40:8 ..... delight to do thy **w**
Matt. 6:10 ..... Thy **w** be done
Matt. 7:21 .doeth the **w** of my Father
Mark 3:35 ..... shall do the **w** of God
Luke 2:14 ..... peace, good **w** toward
Luke 22:42 ..... not my **w**, but thine
John 1:13 ..... **w** of the flesh . . . **w** of
John 4:34 ..... **w** of him that sent me
Rom. 12:2 ..... and perfect, **w** of God
1 Cor. 4:19 ..... if the Lord **w**
Eph. 5:17 ..what the **w** of the Lord is
Phil. 2:13 ..... both to **w** and to do
James 4:15....If the Lord **w**, we shall

Willing
Gen. 24:5 ..... will not be **w** to follow
Ex. 35:5 ..... is of a **w** heart
Is. 1:19 ..... If ye be **w** and obedient
Matt. 26:41 ..... spirit indeed is **w**
Luke 22:42 ..... Father, if thou be **w**
2 Pet. 3:9 ...not **w** that any . . . perish

Win
2 Chr. 32:1 ..... to **w** them for himself
Prov. 11:30....he that **w**-neth souls is
Phil. 3:8 ..... that I may **w** Christ

Wind
Gen. 8:1.God made a **w** to pass over
2 Kin. 3:17 ..... Ye shall not see **w**
Ps. 1:4 ..... chaff which the **w** driveth
Prov. 11:29 ..... shall inherit the **w**
Eccles. 5:16 ..... laboured for the **w**
Is. 7:2 .....trees . . . moved with the **w**
Jer. 22:22 ..... **w** . . . eat up all thy
Ezek. 37:9...Come from the four **w**-s
Hos. 8:7 ..... they have sown the **w**
Matt. 7:25 .floods came . . . **w**-s blew
Mark 4:41 ...**w** and the sea obey him
Luke 8:24 ..... rebuked the **w**
Acts 2:2 ..... as of a rushing mighty **w**
Eph. 4:14 ..... every **w** of doctrine
James 3:4 ..... driven of fierce **w**-s
Jude 12 ..... carried about of **w**-s
Rev. 6:13 ..... shaken of a mighty **w**

Window
Gen. 7:11 ..... **w**-s of heaven were
2 Kin. 7:2 ..... make **w**-s in heaven
Is. 60:8 ..... as the doves to their **w**-s

Wine
Gen. 9:24 ....Noah awoke from his **w**
Ex. 29:40 ..... part of an hin of **w**
Lev. 10:9 ..... Do not drink **w**
1 Sam. 1:14 ..... put away thy **w** from
Ps. 60:3 ..... the **w** of astonishment
Prov. 3:10 ..... burst out with new **w**
Song 1:2 ..... thy love is better than **w**
Jer. 35:6 ..... We will drink no **w**
Matt. 9:17 ..... new **w** into old bottles
Mark 15:23 ...**w** mingled with myrrh
Luke 10:34 ..... pouring in oil and **w**
John 2:9 ..... water that was made **w**
Acts 2:13 ..... men are full of new **w**
Eph. 5:18 ..... be not drunk with **w**
1 Tim. 3:3 ..... Not given to **w**
Rev. 6:6 ....hurt not the oil and the **w**

Wings
Ex. 19:4 ..... bare you on eagles' **w**
Deut. 32:11 ...beareth them on her **w**
Ruth 2:12 ...under whose **w** thou are
Job 39:13 ..... goodly **w** unto the
Ps. 17:8 ..under the shadow of thy **w**
Is. 6:2 ..... each one had six **w**
Ezek. 1:6 ..... every one had four **w**
Zech 5:9 ..... wind was in their **w**
Mal. 4:2 ..... with healing in his **w**
Matt. 23:37 ..... chickens under her **w**
Luke 13:34 ....her brood under her **w**

Wipe
2 Kin. 21:13 ..... as a man **w**-th a dish
Prov. 6:33....reproach . . . not be **w**-d
Is. 25:8 ..... God will **w** away tears
John 11:2 .**w**-d his feet with her hair
Rev. 21:4 ..... shall **w** away all tears

Wisdom
Ex. 28:3 ..... filled with the spirit of **w**
1 Kin. 2:6 .Do . . . according to thy **w**
1 Chr. 22:12 ..... the Lord give thee **w**
Ps. 51:6 ..... make me to know **w**
Prov. 1:7 ..... fools despise **w**
Prov. 4:5...Get **w**, get understanding
Eccles. 7:12 ..... **w** giveth life
Jer. 9:23 ..... wise man glory in his **w**
Mic. 6:9 ..... man of **w** shall see thy
Matt. 11:19 ..... **w** is justified of her
Luke 2:52 ..... increased in **w** and
Luke 21:15 .give you a mouth and **w**
1 Cor. 1:17 ..... not with **w** of words
2 Cor. 1:12 ..... not with fleshly **w**
James 1:5 ..... If any of you lack **w**
Rev. 13:18 ..... Here is **w**

Wise
Gen. 3:6 ..... tree . . . to make one **w**
Ex. 23:8 ..... gift blindeth the **w**
Job 17:10 ..... cannot find one **w** man
Ps. 19:7 ..... making **w** the simple
Prov. 3:7 .....not **w** in thine own eyes
Is. 19:12 ..... where are thy **w** men
Matt. 2:1 .came **w** men from the east
Matt. 10:16 ..... **w** as serpents
Luke 10:21 ..these things from the **w**
Acts 7:6 ..... God spake on this **w**
Rom. 1:14 ..... **w**, and to the unwise
1 Cor. 3:18 ..... that he may be **w**
Eph. 5:15 ..... not as fools, but as **w**
2 Tim. 3:15 ..... **w** unto salvation
James 3:13 ..... Who is a **w** man

Withdraw
1 Sam. 14:19 ....**W** thine hand
Job 9:13.....God will not **w** his anger
Prov. 25:17........**W** thy foot from thy
Joel 2:10.....stars . . . **w** their shining
2 Thess. 3:6..................**w** yourselves
1 Tim. 6:5 ....from such **w** thyself

Wither
Ps. 1:3................leaf also shall not **w**
Ps. 37:2.......and **w** as the green herb
Is. 19:6.........reeds and flags shall **w**
Matt. 13:6...no root, they **w**-ed away
Mark 3:1...man . . . had a **w**-ed hand
Jude 12.........trees whose fruit **w**-eth

Withhold
Gen. 23:6 ....shall **w** from thee
Job 22:7............**w**-en bread from the
Prov. 11:26..........He that **w**-eth corn

Within
Gen. 9:21 ....uncovered **w** his tent
Ps. 51:10...renew a right spirit **w** me
Prov. 22:18............keep them **w** thee
Ezek. 11:19.........a new spirit **w** you
Matt. 23:26 ..that which is **w** the cup
Mark 7:23 ..evil things come from **w**
Luke 17:21.......kingdom of God is **w**
Acts 5:23............we found no man **w**
1 Cor. 5:12.....Judge them that are **w**
2 Cor. 7:5......fightings, **w** were fears
Rev. 5:1 ......throne a book written **w**

Without
Gen. 1:2.earth was **w** form, and void
2 Chr. 15:3........been **w** the true God
Job 5:9....................things **w** number
Job 8:11 ....rush grow up **w** mire
Prov. 1:20..............Wisdom crieth **w**
Is. 10:4...**W** me they shall bow down
Is. 52:3................redeemed **w** money
Hos. 7:11.....like a silly dove **w** heart
Matt. 10:29..................**w** your Father
Matt. 13:57.prophet is not **w** honour
Mark 14:58.................made **w** hands
John 1:3 ....**w** him was not any thing
John 8:7.....................He that is **w** sin
Rom. 3:28...............faith **w** the deeds
1 Cor. 11:11 ....man **w** the woman
2 Cor. 7:5 ....**w** were fightings
Eph. 2:12........time ye were **w** Christ
Col. 2:11......................made **w** hands
1 Thess. 5:17 ....Pray **w** ceasing
1 Tim. 6:14 ....commandment **w** spot
Heb. 7:3 ....**W** father, **w** mother, **w**
James 2:20......faith **w** works is dead
1 Pet. 1:19 ......**w** blemish and **w** spot
2 Pet. 2:17.............are wells **w** water
Jude 12 ......**w** fear . . . **w** water . . . **w**

Witness
Gen. 31:48...**w** between me and thee
Ex. 20:16.........shalt not bear false **w**
Deut. 4:26...call heaven and earth to **w**
Judge. 11:10 ..Lord be **w** between us
Job 16:19 ....my **w** is in heaven
Ps. 89:37............faithful **w** in heaven
Prov. 6:19...........false **w** that speaketh
Is. 19:20...........for a sign and for a **w**
Matt. 19:18...............not bear false **w**
John 1:7..........to bear **w** of the Light
Acts 26:22...**w**-ing both to small and
Rom. 1:9..................For God is my **w**
1 Cor. 15:15 ..we are found false **w**-s
Titus 1:13 ....This **w** is true
Heb. 10:15.....Holy Ghost also is a **w**
1 John 5:9 ....receive the **w** of men
Rev. 1:5.......Christ . . . the faithful **w**

Wives
Deut. 17:17...............Neither shall he multiply **w**
Ezra 10:2 ....have taken strange **w**
Eph. 5:22 ....**W**, submit yourselves
1 Tim. 4:7.........................old **w**' fables
1 Pet. 3:1.............**w**, be in subjection

Woe
Num. 21:29.............**W** to thee, Moab
Prov. 23:29 ..Who hath **w**? who hath
Is. 6:5..........................said I, **W** is me
Jer. 4:13.........**W** unto us! for we are
Matt. 11:21 ...**W** unto thee, Chorazin
Mark 14:21 .**w** to that man by whom
Rev. 8:13 .**W**, **w**, **w**, to the inhabiters

Wolf
Gen. 49:27 ....shall ravin as a **w**
Is. 65:25 ...**w** and the lamb shall feed
Jer. 5:6....................**w** of the evenings
Matt. 7:15...they are ravening **w**-ves

Woman
Gen. 2:23 ....she shall be called **W**
Ex. 2:9 ....**w** took the child
Deut. 22:5..................man put on a **w**'s
Ruth 3:11 ....thou art a virtuous **w**
Job 14:1 ....Man that is born of a **w**
Prov. 11:16.......gracious **w** retaineth
Prov. 12:4 ....virtuous **w** is a crown
Matt. 5:28 ....looketh on a **w** to lust
Matt. 15:28.....O **w**, great is thy faith
Luke 10:38..............certain **w** named
John 4:7..............**w** of Samaria to draw
John 8:4.......**w** was taken in adultery
Acts 9:36 ..**w** was full of good works
1 Cor. 7:1......a man not to touch a **w**
1 Cor. 7:2..**w** have her own husband
Gal. 4:4.............his Son, made of a **w**
1 Tim. 2:11 ....Let the **w** learn in
Rev. 12:1.......**w** clothed with the sun

Womb
Gen. 25:23.Two nations are in thy **w**
Ex. 13:2 ..whatsoever openeth the **w**
Num. 12:12.......out of his mother's **w**
Deut. 7:13 .....bless the fruit of thy **w**
Ruth 1:11 ....more sons in my **w**
Job 1:21 ...Naked . . . my mother's **w**
Prov. 30:16 ....the barren **w**
Is. 44:2.........formed thee from the **w**
Luke 1:41.........babe leaped in her **w**
John 3:4 ..enter . . . into his mother's **w**
Acts 3:2 ....from his mother's **w**

Women
Gen. 31:35...custom of **w** is upon me
1 Kin. 11:1 .....loved many strange **w**
Prov. 31:3....not thy strength unto **w**
Song 1:8......O thou fairest among **w**
Matt. 24:41.Two **w** shall be grinding
Mark 15:40 ...also **w** looking on afar
Luke 1:28.blessed art thou among **w**
1 Tim. 2:9......**w** adorn themselves in
Titus 2:4............young **w** to be sober
1 Pet. 3:5.....................the holy **w** also

Wonder
Deut. 4:34 ....by signs, and by **w**-s
Job 9:10.............**w**-s without number
Is. 9:6 .....name shall be called **W**-ful
Jer. 4:9....................the prophets shall **w**
Dan. 6:27....signs and **w**-s in heaven
Matt. 15:31 ....the multitude **w**-ed
Acts 2:11......the **w**-ful works of God
Rom. 15:19......mighty signs and **w**-s
Rev. 12:1 ....a great **w** in heaven
Rev. 13:3 ....and all the world **w**-ed

Wondrous
1 Chr. 16:9 ....of all his **w** works
Job 37:14 ....the **w** works of God
Ps. 71:17.......I declared thy **w** works
Ps. 72:18....who only doeth **w** things
Joel 2:26 ....dealt **w**-ly with you

Wood
Gen. 6:14.............an ark of gopher **w**
2 Sam. 18:8............**w** devoured more
1 Chr. 16:33...trees of the **w** sing out
2 Chr. 2:16 ....we will cut **w** out of
Neh. 8:4......stood upon a pulpit of **w**
Ps. 83:14.......As the fire burneth a **w**
Prov. 26:20.....Where no **w** is . . . the
Jer. 7:18.........The children gather **w**
Lam. 5:4...........our **w** is sold unto us
Ezek. 24:10....Heap on **w**, kindle the
1 Cor. 3:12....stones, **w**, hay, stubble
Rev. 18:12 ....of most precious **w**

Wool
Deut. 22:11 ....**w**-len and linen
Judg. 6:37...a fleece of **w** in the floor
Ps. 147:16......He giveth snow like **w**
Is. 1:18...................they shall be as **w**
Ezek. 44:17........no **w** . . . come upon
Heb. 9:19 ....scarlet **w**, and hyssop
Rev. 1:14 ...his hairs were white like **w**

Word
Gen. 15:1 ....**w** of the Lord . . . unto
Gen. 30:34 ....according to thy **w**
Ex. 20:1 ....God spake all these **w**-s
Lev. 10:7..........according to the **w** of
Num. 30:2...he shall not break his **w**
Deut. 5:5 ....shew you the **w** of the
Josh. 24:26.....wrote these **w**-s in the
1 Sam. 3:1.............**w** of the Lord was
Ezra 6:11 .whosoever shall alter this **w**
Job 2:13....none spake a **w** unto him
Job 6:25...how forcible are right **w**-s
Ps. 12:6 .**w**-s of the Lord are pure **w**-s
Ps. 19:14 ....Let the **w**-s of my mouth
Prov. 15:1 ....grievous **w**-s stir up
Prov. 15:23 ....**w** spoken in due
Eccles. 5:2............Let thy **w**-s be few
Jer. 5:13 ....the **w** is not in them
Mal. 1:1 ....The burden of the **w**
Matt. 4:4.....every **w** that proceedeth
Matt. 8:8 ....speak the **w** only
Matt. 12:36 .....every idle **w** that men
Mark 4:14 ....sower soweth the **w**
Mark 7:13....**w** of God of none effect
Luke 1:2................ministers of the **w**
Luke 4:4 ....but by every **w** of God
Luke 4:32 ....his **w** was with power
Luke 4:36 ....What a **w** is this
John 1:1...........beginning was the **W**
John 1:14..............**W** was made flesh
John 6:68 ....the **w**-s of eternal life
Acts 2:41 ....his **w** were baptized
Acts 6:7........the **w** of God increased
Rom. 10:8.......**w** is nigh thee . . . **w** of
1 Cor. 1:17...not with wisdom of **w**-s
2 Cor. 4:2 ....**w** of God deceitfully
Gal. 5:14 ......law is fulfilled in one **w**
Eph. 5:6...deceive you with vain **w**-s
Col. 3:16....Let the **w** of Christ dwell
2 Thess. 2:17 ....you in every good **w**
1 Tim. 4:5........sanctified by the **w** of
1 Tim. 5:17 ....who labour in the **w**
2 Tim. 2:15....dividing the **w** of truth
Titus 1:9 ....Holding fast the . . . **w**
Heb. 2:2 ....**w** spoken by angels
Heb. 4:12 ....**w** of God is quick
James 1:22 ....be ye doers of the **w**
1 Pet. 1:23.....**w** of God, which liveth
1 John 1:1 ...handled, of the **w** of life
Jude 16..................great swelling **w**-s
Rev. 19:13 .....is called The **w** of God

Work
Gen. 2:2...................God ended his **w**
Ex. 20:9......Six days . . . do all thy **w**
Deut. 4:28........the **w** of men's hands
1 Sam. 14:6.....the Lord will **w** for us
1 Chr. 23:4.......**w** of the house of the
2 Chr. 15:7................your **w** shall be
Job 7:2..........for the reward of his **w**
Ps. 9:1...shew . . . thy marvelous **w**-s
Ps. 62:12 ......man according to his **w**
Prov. 11:18..........**w**-eth a deceitful **w**
Prov. 16:3 ....Commit thy **w**-s . . . the
Eccles. 7:13...Consider the **w** of God
Eccles. 11:5 ..knowest not the **w**-s of
Is. 10:12....Lord . . . performed . . . **w**
Hab. 1:5.....I will **w** a **w** in your days
Matt. 5:16 ....see your good **w**-s
Mark 6:5 ....there do no mighty **w**
Luke 13:14................men ought to **w**
John 5:17......**w**-eth hitherto, and I **w**
John 6:28......might **w** the **w**-s of God
John 9:4 ..**w** the **w**-s of him that sent
Acts 5:38............or this **w** be of men
Rom. 2:15.......shew the **w** of the law
Rom. 8:28 ....things **w** together for
1 Cor. 3:13 ....man's **w** . . . made
Gal. 5:19.............**w**-s of the flesh are
Eph. 2:9......Not of **w**-s, lest any man
Eph. 4:12....for the **w** of the ministry

Phil. 2:12..w out your own salvation
Col. 1:10......fruitful in every good w
1 Tim. 6:18..........be rich in good w-s
2 Tim. 4:5.............w of an evangelist
Titus 3:1........ready to every good w
James 1:4.patience have her perfect w
James 2:18.........my faith by my w-s
1 John 3:8.......destroy the w-s of the
Rev. 2:2.......I know thy w-s, and thy
Rev. 14:13..their w-s do follow them

Workers
Ps. 5:5...........hatest all w of iniquity
1 Cor. 12:29.................w of miracles
2 Cor. 6:1.....We then, as w together
Phil. 3:2..................beware of evil w

Working
Ezek. 46:1...........shut the six w days
Mark 16:20.....the Lord w with them
1 Cor. 4:12.....w with our own hands

Workman
Ex. 38:23................and a cunning w
Matt. 10:10..w is worthy of his meat
Eph. 2:10........For we are his w-ship

World
2 Sam. 22:16....foundations of the w
Prov. 8:26..........of the dust of the w
Is. 14:21........fill . . . the w with cities
Matt. 5:14...Ye are the light of the w
Matt. 12:32.......this w . . . w to come
Mark 10:30.....w to come eternal life
Luke 16:8........the children of this w
John 1:10.......He was in the w . . . w was made by him . . . w knew him
John 3:16............God so loved the w
John 4:42.................Saviour of the w
John 6:33......giveth light unto the w
John 8:12.......I am the light of the w
Acts 17:6.turned the w upside down
Rom. 5:12.......sin entered into the w
1 Cor. 1:28.........base things of the w
1 Cor. 2:12......not the spirit of the w
2 Cor. 7:10.sorrow of the w worketh
Eph. 3:21......all ages, w without end
1 Tim. 6:17......that are rich in this w
2 Tim. 4:10........loved this present w
Heb. 6:5.....powers of the w to come
James 1:27......unspotted from the w
2 Pet. 2:5..........spared not the old w
1 John 2:15..............Love not the w
1 John 2:17........the w passeth away

Worm
Job 7:5.My flesh is clothed with w-s
Job 24:20.....w shall feed sweetly on
Is. 14:11.........and the w-s cover thee
Jon. 4:7................God prepared a w
Mark 9:44...Where their w dieth not
Acts 12:23..........he was eaten of w-s

Wormwood
Deut. 29:18..that beareth gall and w
Prov. 5:4..........her end is bitter as w
Rev. 8:11............the star is called W

Worship
Gen. 22:5................go yonder and w
Ex. 34:14..........shalt w no other god
2 Chr. 29:28..the congregation w-ed
Ps. 29:2..w the Lord in the beauty of
Mic. 5:13.w the work of thine hands
Matt. 2:2.......and are come to w him
Matt. 4:10.shalt w the Lord thy God
John 4:20.place where men ought to w
Phil. 3:3...............w God in the spirit
Rev. 4:10..w him that liveth for ever

Worthy
Gen. 32:10.....I am not w of the least
Deut. 17:6..........................w of death
1 Sam. 26:16..............ye are w to die
1 Kin. 1:52......will shew himself a w
Matt. 3:11..shoes I am not w to bear
Matt. 10:10.......workmen is w of his
Luke 3:8.........fruits w of repentance
Luke 10:7....labourer is w of his hire
Eph. 4:1........walk w of the vocation
1 Thess. 2:12......ye would walk w of
1 Tim. 1:15.........w of all acceptation
Heb. 11:38........the world was not w
Rev. 5:2..Who is w to open the book

Wound
Deut. 32:39.................I w, and I heal
Job 34:6................my w is incurable
Ps. 147:3............bindeth up their w-s
Prov. 23:29..hath w-s without cause
Is. 53:5..w-ed for our transgressions
Jer. 30:17...........heal thee of thy w-s
Luke 10:34......and bound up his w-s
Acts 19:16...fled . . . naked and w-ed

Wrapped
1 Kin. 19:13.w his face in his mantle
Matt. 27:59.........w it in a clean linen
Mark 15:46..........w him in the linen
Luke 2:7............w him in swaddling
John 20:7...napkin . . . w together in a place by itself

Wrath
Gen. 39:19............his w was kindled
Job 5:2......w killeth the foolish man
Ps. 37:8..............................forsake w
Prov. 12:16........fool's w is presently
Prov. 14:29........He that is slow to w
Eccles. 5:17.......much sorrow and w
Is. 54:8...........a little w I hid my face
Matt. 3:7......flee from the w to come
John 3:36.........the w of God abideth
Rom. 2:5.......w against the day of w
Eph. 2:3..................the children of w
Eph. 4:26.sun go down upon your w
Col. 3:6...................w of God cometh
1 Thess. 5:9....not appointed us to w
James 1:19.slow to speak, slow to w
Rev. 6:16.....from the w of the Lamb

Write
Prov. 3:3...w them upon the table of
Hab. 2:2...W the vision, and make it
Mark 10:4....w a bill of divorcement
John 19:21....W not, The King of the
1 Tim. 3:14........things w I unto thee
Heb. 10:16........minds will I w them
1 John 2:8....new commandment I w
2 John 12..not w with paper and ink

Writing
Ex. 32:16...........w was the w of God
2 Chr. 2:11...king . . . answered in w
Dan. 5:8...........could not read the w
Matt. 5:31..........a w of divorcement
Luke 1:63...........asked for a w table
John 5:47........ye believe not his w-s

Written
Ex. 31:18....w with the finger of God
Mal. 3:16........book of remembrance was w
Matt. 2:5..........it is w by the prophet
John 19:22..What I have w I have w
Acts 1:20....w in the book of Psalms
Rom. 2:15.........law w in their hearts
Philem. 19.w it with mine own hand
Rev. 13:8.....not w in the book of life
Rev. 17:5.....forehead was a name w

Wrong
Gen. 16:5.............My w be upon thee
Jer. 22:3......do no w, do no violence
Matt. 20:13.....Friend, I do thee no w
Acts 7:26......ye do w one to another
1 Cor. 6:7..........ye not rather take w
2 Cor. 7:2.......we have w-ed no man

Wrote
Ex. 24:4.........Moses w all the words
Mark 12:19............Master, Moses w
John 8:6.......finger w on the ground
Rom. 16:22.........Tertius, who w this
2 John 5....I w a new commandment
3 John 9.............I w unto the church

Wrought
Gen. 34:7......he had w folly in Israel
1 Sam. 14:45....hath w with God this
Is. 26:12...........w all our works in us
Jer. 18:3.......w a work on the wheels
Matt. 20:12...........have w but one hour
Mark 14:6.......w a good work on me
John 3:21............they are w in God
Acts 18:3....abode with them, and w
Rom. 15:18.Christ hath not w by me
Gal. 2:8............w effectually in Peter
2 Thess. 3:8.........w with labour and

Y

Yea
Lev. 35:35..............y, though he be a
Ps. 23:4.....Y, though I walk through
Prov. 8:19........gold, y than fine gold
Matt. 5:37....communication be, Y, y
2 Cor. 1:17..........there should be y y
Heb. 11:36.......y, moreover of bonds
James 5:12...........but let your y be y
1 Pet. 5:5.......................Y, all of you be
Rev. 14:13.............Y, saith the Spirit

Year
Gen. 7:11.six hundredth y of Noah's
Ex. 13:10....in his season from y to y
1 Sam. 7:16.........went from y to y in
2 Sam. 14:26...y's end that he polled
Job 10:5....are thy y-s as man's days
Ps. 90:4......thousand y-s in thy sight
Prov. 4:10y-s of thy life . . . be many
Is. 61:2........acceptable y of the Lord
Jer. 11:23...........y of their visitation
Joel 2:25................y-s that the locust
Matt. 2:16.......two y-s old and under
Luke 3:23....to be about thirty y-s of
Gal. 4:10.months, and times, and y-s
Rev. 9:15...........day . . . month . . . y

Yesterday
Ex. 5:14............making brick both y
Heb. 13:8.......the same y, and to day

Yet
Gen. 7:4...................For y seven days
Deut. 9:29.......Y they are thy people
Judg. 7:4........people are y too many
Job 13:15............y will I trust in him
Dan. 11:35.....y for a time appointed
Jonah 3:4................Y forty days, and
Matt. 15:17........not ye y understand
Matt. 19:20....................what lack I y
Mark 12:6..........y therefore one son
Luke 24:44....while I was y with you
John 2:4.....mine hour is not y come
Rom. 5:6..............y without strength
1 Cor. 7:10........y not I, but the Lord
2 Cor. 4:8..................y not distressed
Heb. 11:7...........things not seen as y
1 John 3:2....y appear what we shall

Yield
Gen. 1:11............the herb y-ing seed
Num. 17:8...........blossoms, and y-ed
Ps. 67:6..............earth y her increase
Eccles. 10:4........y-ing pacifeth great
Mark 4:8..........y fruit that sprang us
Rom. 6:13..............Neither y ye your
Heb. 12:11.y-eth the peaceable fruit
James 3:12......both y salt water and

Yoke
Gen. 27:40..break his y from off thy
1 Sam. 14:14...y of oxen might plow
Is. 9:4......broken the y of his burden
Jer. 27:2....Make thee bonds and y-s
Lam. 1:14......y of my transgressions
Matt. 11:29.......Take my y upon you
2 Cor. 6:14..unequally y-ed together
Gal. 5:1...........with the y of bondage
1 Tim. 6:1.servants as are under the y

Young
Ex. 23:26...shall nothing cast their y
Lev. 4:3...y bullock without blemish
Deut. 32:11........fluttereth over her y
Ruth 2:9........not charged the y men
Ps. 37:25.....been y, and now am old
Is. 11:7.y ones . . . lie down together
Ezek. 17:4.............top of his y twigs
Matt. 2:9.........where the y child was
John 21:18..When thou wast y, thou
Acts 2:17......y men shall see visions
Titus 2:4...........y women to be sober
1 John 2:13.............I write . . . y men

Younger
Gen. 25:23......elder shall serve the **y**
Luke 15:13...........**y** son gathered all
1 Tim. 5:11 .But the **y** widows refuse
1 Pet. 5:5......ye **y**, submit yourselves

Yours
Gen. 45:20 ......good . . . of Egypt is **y**
Josh. 2:14....Our life for **y**, if ye utter
2 Chr. 20:15..........battle is not **y**, but
Luke 6:20 ...**y** is the kingdom of God
John 15:20........they will keep **y** also
1 Cor. 3:21 ....for all things are **y**
2 Cor. 12:14.for I seek not **y**, but you

Yourselves
Gen. 18:4...........rest **y** under the tree
Ex. 19:12 ....Take heed to **y**
Lev. 11:44 ....sanctify **y**
Josh. 24:22 ....witnesses against **y**
2 Chr. 29:31 ....consecrated **y**
Jer. 37:9........................Deceive not **y**
Hos. 10:12 ....Sow to **y** in
Mark 9:50.....................Have salt in **y**
Acts 20:10.....................Trouble not **y**
Rom. 6:13................yield **y** unto God
2 Cor. 13:5..........................Examine **y**
Eph. 5:19 ....Speaking to **y** in psalms
1 Thess. 5:13 ....be at peace among **y**
1 John 5:21 ....keep **y** from idols
Jude 21.....Keep **y** in the love of God

Youth
Gen. 8:21.......heart is evil from his **y**
Num. 30:16.......................yet in her **y**
Judg. 8:20.....because he was yet a **y**
Job 33:25 .return to the days of his **y**
Ps. 25:7..............not the sins of my **y**
Prov. 5:18........with the wife of thy **y**
Eccles. 11:9.........Rejoice . . . in thy **y**
Is. 40:30........Even the **y**-s shall faint
Jer. 3:4 ....art the guide of my **y**
Jer. 31:19.bear the reproach of my **y**
Matt. 19:20...........kept from my **y** up
Acts 26:4 ....life from my **y**
1 Tim. 4:12...Let no man despise thy **y**
2 Tim. 2:22 ....Flee also **y**-ful lusts

Z

Zeal
2 Kin. 10:16.....see my **z** for the Lord
Ps. 119:139.My **z** hath consumed me
Is. 59:17 ....clad with **z** as a cloak
John 2:17.........**z** of thine house hath
Rom. 10:2..................have a **z** of God
Col. 4:13 ....he hath a great **z** for you

Zealous
Num. 25:11......he was **z** for my sake
Acts 21:20...................all **z** of the law
1 Cor. 14:12...........**z** of spiritual gifts
Gal. 4:17 ....They **z**-ly affect you
Titus 2:14 ....**z** of good works
Rev. 3:19 .be **z** therefore, and repent

Is There Any Hope?

The future is uncertain.
Families are falling apart.
Drugs are ruining cities and schools.
Disease is killing out people.

Is There Any Hope?

Can we have peace and joy in our hearts?
Can we have fulfillment in life?
Can we have power and strength to live meaningful lives?
Does anyone really care?

YES! Here's Hope for you: JESUS Cares for YOU.

"Now the God of hope fill you with all joy and peace in believing, that ye may abound in hope, through the power of the Holy Ghost" (Romans 15:13).

Read these verses in the Bible to see the road to hope, the road to Jesus and His care for you.

The road to hope has four stops. You must make each one.

1. Power

You need power to have hope. Only one Power is capable of giving you hope. The Bible tells us God has that power.

"*I am not ashamed of the gospel of Christ: for it is the power of God unto salvation to everyone that believeth*" (Romans 1:16).

2. Change

The release of God's power results in change. The Bible's word for change is repentance. This means allowing God to change the direction of your life.

"The goodness of God leadeth thee to repentance" (Romans 2:4).

Why, you ask, is change necessary? The Bible identifies a universal problem that makes change necessary for all of us. This universal problem the Bible calls sin. Sin means "missing the mark." You sin when you fail to meet God's standard for how you ought to live your life.

"*All have sinned, and come short of the glory of God*" (Romans 3:23).

3. God's Love

God is not pleased with us as we are because we are sinners. Still God loves us and wants to help you.

"*God commendeth His love toward us, in that, while we were yet sinners, Christ died for us*" (Romans 5:8).

Unfortunately, your sin carries the penalty of death, both physical and eternal.

God is willing to forgive you by accepting Jesus as your substitute. His death on the cross paid the penalty for your sin. His resurrection from the dead provides you eternal life.

"*The wages of sin is death, but the gift of God is eternal life through Christ Jesus our Lord*" (Romans 6:23).

4. Your Commitment

Commitment means to:

Repent = Turn away from sin to follow God's new direction for your life.

Believe = Trust Jesus as your substitute

Confess = Acknowledge Jesus as the supreme authority over your life.

Call = Ask Him for forgiveness, eternal life, and hope.

> *"If thou shalt confess with thy mouth the Lord Jesus, and shalt believe in thine heart that God hath raised Him from the dead, thou shalt be saved....For whosoever shall call upon the name of the Lord shall be saved"* (Romans 10:9,13).

5. Your Response

Read the following prayer, and see if it expresses the desire of your heart.

Dear God, I know that Jesus is Your Son and that He died on the cross and was raised from the dead. Because I have sinned and need forgiveness, I ask Jesus to come into my heart. I am willing to change the direction of my life by acknowledging Jesus as my Lord and Savior, and by turning away from my sins. Thank You for giving me forgiveness, eternal life, and hope. In Jesus' name, amen."

Use this prayer if it expresses your feelings, or pray a similar prayer in your own words, committing your life to Jesus and asking Him for His gift of eternal life.

6. Your Statement of Faith

Fill in the blanks in the following statement:

1. Because Jesus ____________________ on the cross and ________________________ from the dead, forgiveness and eternal life are possible.

2. Because I trusted Jesus to be my ____________________ and ________________, the direction of my life will change. I now have hope.

3. I have eternal life and will go to heaven when I die. (check one)

___ I Know ___ I am not sure.

7. My Record of Salvation

On ________________________________, I ______________________________
(date) (name)

gave my life to Jesus. Now I want to tell ___________________ what Jesus did for me.

Witnessed by: ____

8. My Next Steps

I will begin reading my Bible and praying each day.

I will join ____ Church.

I will be baptized.

I will tell others about my experience with Jesus.

I will join a Bible study class.

PLATE I
AGE OF THE PATRIARCHS
The Ancient World
Abraham's Journey
Kilometers 0 100 200 300 400 500
Statute Miles 0 100 200 300
Black Sea
Caspian Sea
Upper Sea
(Great Sea, Mediterranean Sea)
Lower Sea
(Persian Gulf)
Red Sea
MYCENAEANS
Aegean Sea
Troy
Assuwa
Lesbos
Kios
Samos
Hermes River
Maeander River
Athens
Mycenae
Pylos
Cyclades
Arzawa
MINOANS
Cnossus
CRETE
Rhodes
HITTITE EMPIRE
Hattusa
Kanish
Taurus Mts.
Kizzuwatna
Carchemish
Alalakh
Aleppo
Ebla
Ugarit
Hamath
CYPRUS
Arvad
Gebal
Berytus
Sidon
Damascus
Tyre
Acco
Hazor
Dor
Shechem
Joppa
Bethel
Jerusalem
Jericho
Gaza
Hebron
Beersheba
Haran
Mari
Euphrates River
Nineveh
Calah
ASSYRIA
Asshur
Nuzi
Tigris River
Zagros Mts.
Ecbatana
MADAI
Lake Van
Lake Urmai
+ Mt Ararat
Sippar
Cuthah
Akkad
Babylon
Kish
Nippur
Isin
BABYLONIA
SUMER
Lagash
Larsa
Erech
Ur
ELAM
Susa
Ancient Coastline
PUT
LIBYA
Sahara Desert
Nile Delta
Tanis, Zoan
Lower Egypt
Memphis
On
SINAI PENINSULA
Nile River
EGYPT
Amarna
Upper Egypt
Ernie Couch CONSULTX

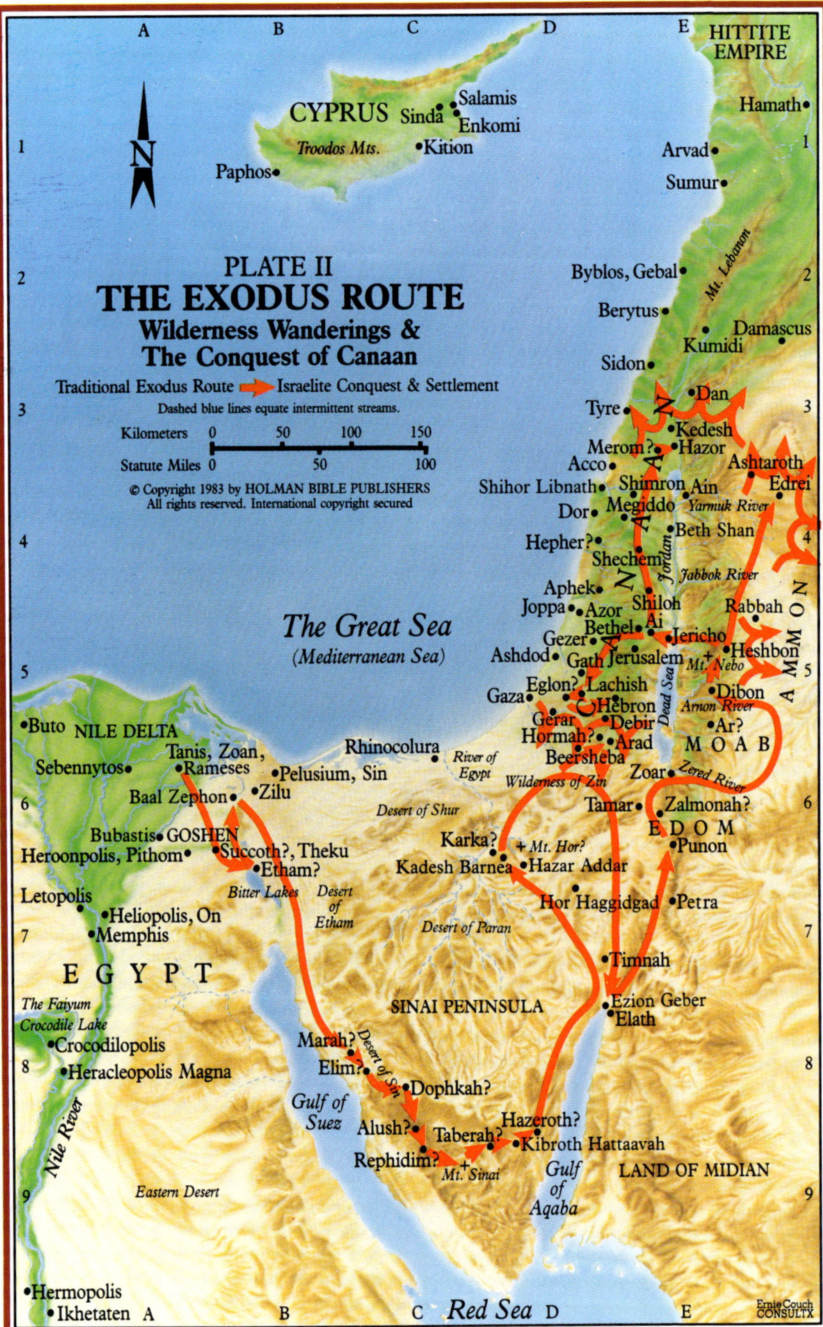
PLATE II
THE EXODUS ROUTE
Wilderness Wanderings &
The Conquest of Canaan
Traditional Exodus Route
Israelite Conquest & Settlement
Dashed blue lines equate intermittent streams.
Kilometers 0 50 100 150
Statute Miles 0 50 100
© Copyright 1983 by HOLMAN BIBLE PUBLISHERS
All rights reserved. International copyright secured
HITTITE EMPIRE
CYPRUS
Salamis
Sinda
Enkomi
Troodos Mts.
Kition
Paphos
Hamath
Arvad
Sumur
Byblos, Gebal
Mt. Lebanon
Berytus
Damascus
Kumidi
Sidon
Dan
Tyre
Kedesh
Merom?
Hazor
Acco
Ashtaroth
Edrei
Shihor Libnath
Shimron
Ain
Yarmuk River
Dor
Megiddo
Beth Shan
Hepher?
Shechem
Jordan
Jabbok River
CANAAN
Aphek
Joppa
Azor
Shiloh
Rabbah
AMMON
Bethel
Ai
Gezer
Jericho
Heshbon
Ashdod
Gath
Jerusalem
Mt. Nebo
The Great Sea
(Mediterranean Sea)
Eglon?
Lachish
Dead Sea
Gaza
Dibon
Hebron
Arnon River
Gerar
Debir
Ar?
Hormah?
Arad
MOAB
Beersheba
Zoar
Zered River
Wilderness of Zin
Tamar
Zalmonah?
EDOM
Punon
Buto
NILE DELTA
Sebennytos
Tanis, Zoan,
Rameses
Rhinocolura
River of Egypt
Pelusium, Sin
Baal Zephon
Zilu
Desert of Shur
Bubastis
GOSHEN
Heroonpolis, Pithom
Succoth?, Theku
Etham?
Karka?
Mt. Hor?
Kadesh Barnea
Hazar Addar
Bitter Lakes
Desert of Etham
Hor Haggidgad
Petra
Letopolis
Heliopolis, On
Memphis
Desert of Paran
Timnah
EGYPT
Ezion Geber
Elath
SINAI PENINSULA
The Faiyum
Crocodile Lake
Crocodilopolis
Heracleopolis Magna
Marah?
Desert of Sin
Elim?
Dophkah?
Gulf of Suez
Alush?
Taberah?
Hazeroth?
Kibroth Hattaavah
Rephidim?
Mt. Sinai
Gulf of Aqaba
LAND OF MIDIAN
Nile River
Eastern Desert
Hermopolis
Ikhetaten
Red Sea
Ernie Couch CONSULTX

PLATE III
THE TWELVE TRIBES IN CANAAN
c. 1200 - 1020 B.C.
The Twelve Tribes (DAN)
The Empire of David and Solomon
c. 1000 - 925 B.C.
Extent of Empire
Dashed blue lines equate intermittent streams.
Kilometers 0 10 20 30 40
Statute Miles 0 10 20 30
© Copyright 1983 by
HOLMAN BIBLE PUBLISHERS
All rights reserved.
International copyright secured.
The Great Sea
(Mediterranean Sea)
N
A B C D E
1 2 3 4 5 6 7 8 9
Sidon
SIDONIANS
Mt. Lebanon
Leontes River
Mt. Hermon
PHOENICIA
Tyre
DAN
Dan
Kedesh
Merom?
NAPHTALI
Hazor
ASHER
Acco
Kinnereth
Sea of Kinnereth
Mt. Carmel
Shihor Libnath
Achshaph?
Shimron
Yarmuk River
Ain?
ZEBULUN
Mt. Tabor
Jokneam
Dor
Ophrah?
Megiddo
ISSACHAR
Taanach
Mt. Gilboa
Beth Shan
Ginae
Pehel
Jordan River
Migdol
Dothan
MANASSEH
Hepher?
Plain of Sharon
MANASSEH
Tirzah
Succoth
Jabbok River
Shechem
GAD
Gath Rimmon
Aphek
Tappuah
Adam
Jogbehah
Joppa
Shiloh
Azor
EPHRAIM
Jazer?
AMMON
Bethel
Heshbon
DAN
Gibeon
Ai
Gilgal
Shittim
Kephirah
BENJAMIN
Jericho
Pisgah
Gezer
Jerusalem
Beth Jeshimoth
Mt. Nebo
PHILISTINES
Timnah
Ashdod
Beth Shemesh
Medeba
Bethlehem
Gath
REUBEN
Ashkelon
Zippor
Adullam
Libnah
Gedor
Kedemoth?
Lachish
JUDAH
Ataroth
Wilderness of Judah
Gaza
Eglon?
Hebron
Dead Sea
Dibon
Sharuhen?
En Gedi
Arnon River
Aroer
Deir el-Balah
Debir
Ziklag?
Yurza?
Gerar
Anab
Ar?
Raphia
Arad
MOAB
Beersheba
Hormah?
Eder
SIMEON
Zoar
Zered River
River of Egypt
Desert of Zin
EDOM
Ernie Couch CONSULTX

PLATE IV
THE DIVIDED KINGDOM
Judah and Israel
Dashed blue lines equate intermittent streams.
The Great Sea
(Mediterranean Sea)
ISRAEL
JUDAH
PHOENICIA
SIDONIANS
ARAM (Syrians)
PHILISTINES
AMMON
MOAB
EDOM
Sidon
Zarephath
Tyre
Mt. Lebanon
Leontes River
Mt. Hermon
Dan
Kedesh
Merom?
Bashan
Hazor
Acco
Kinnereth
Geshur
Ashtaroth
Sea of Kinnereth
Aphek
Mt. Carmel
Shihor Libnath
Achshaph?
Shimron
Yarmuk River
Ain?
Mt. Tabor
Havvoth Jair
Plain of Jezreel
Dor
Ophrah?
Lo Debar
Megiddo
Jezreel
Taanach
Mt. Gilboa
Beth Shan
Ginae
Jabesh Gilead
Migdol
Dothan
Tishbe
Hepher?
Socoh
Samaria
Jordan River
Tirzah
Zarethan
Mt. Ebal
Succoth
Mahanaim
Jabbok River
Plain of Sharon
Shechem
Gath Rimmon
Aphek
Tappuah
Adam
Jogbehah
Joppa
Azor
Gilead
Jazer?
Jabneel
Beth Horon
Bethel
Gilgal
Heshbon
Lod
Gibeon
Ai
Shittim
Kephirah
Jericho
Pisgah
Gezer
Ekron
Jerusalem
Beth Jeshimoth
Mt. Nebo
Timnah
Beth Shemesh
Ashdod
Bethlehem
Medeba
Gath
Ashkelon
Zippor
Adullam
Wilderness of Judah
Kedemoth?
Libnah?
Gedor
Ataroth
Lachish
Gaza
Eglon?
Hebron
Dead Sea
Dibon
Sharuhen?
Ziph
En Gedi
Arnon River
Aroer
Deir el-Balah
Debir
Ziklag?
Anab
Yurza?
Gerar
Ar?
Raphia
Arad
Beersheba
Hormah?
Eder
Kir Hareseth
Tamar
Valley of Salt
Zoar
Zered River
River of Egypt
Desert of Zin
Ernie Couch
CONSULTX
A B C D E
1 2 3 4 5 6 7 8 9
N

PLATE V
PALESTINE IN THE TIME OF JESUS
Dashed blue lines equate intermittent streams.
Kilometers 0 10 20 30 40
Statute Miles 0 10 20 30
© Copyright 1983 by HOLMAN BIBLE PUBLISHERS
All rights reserved. International copyright secured
A B C D E
1 2 3 4 5 6 7 8 9
N
The Great Sea
(Mediterranean Sea)
Sidon
ABILENE
SYRIA
PHOENICIA
Mt. Lebanon
Leontes River
Mt. Hermon
Tyre
Caesarea Philippi
Cadasa
Thella
Jamnith
Ecdippa
Sepph
Sogane
Ptolemais
GALILEE
Korazin
Bethsaida?
Gennesaret
Capernaum
Magdala
Sea of Galilee
Gergesa
Yarmuk River
Cana
Tiberias
Sepphoris
Ammathus
Hippos
Nazareth
Philoteria
Abel
Japhia
Gadara
Dor
Nain
Capercotnei, Kefar Otnay
Caesarea
Scythopolis
Pella
Narbata
Ginae
DECAPOLIS
Jordan River
Aenon?
SAMARIA
Agrippina?
Samaria
Gerasa
Sychar
Ragaba
Shechem
Ammathus
Jabbok River
Apollonia
Plan of Sharon
Coreae
Antipatris
Acrabeta
Tower of Aphek
Alexandrium
Zia
Gerasa
Joppa
Phasaelis
Gedora
Thamna
Archelaus
PEREA
Adida
Philadelphia
Lydda, Lod
Gophna
Ephraim
Bethennabris
Sappho
Ramah
Neara
Abila, Abel
Emmaus
Gabaon
Jericho
Livias, Julias, Beth-ramatha
Jamnia
Emmaus, Nicopolis
Jerusalem
Mt. of Olives
Ramat Rahel
Bethany
Qumran
Essene community
Bethletepha
Bethlehem
Hyrcania
Medeba
Ascalon
JUDEA
Herodium
Baaras
Beror Hayil
Betogabris
Tekoa
Machaerus
Anthedon
Belzedek?
Callirrhoe
Gaza
Hebron
Dibon
Adora
En Gedi
Dead Sea
Arnon River
Masada
Raphia
IDUMAEA
Arad
Areopolis
Beersheba
Malatha
En Boqeq
NABATEANS
Charachmoba
Elusa
Zoar
Zered River
Ernie Couch CONSULTX

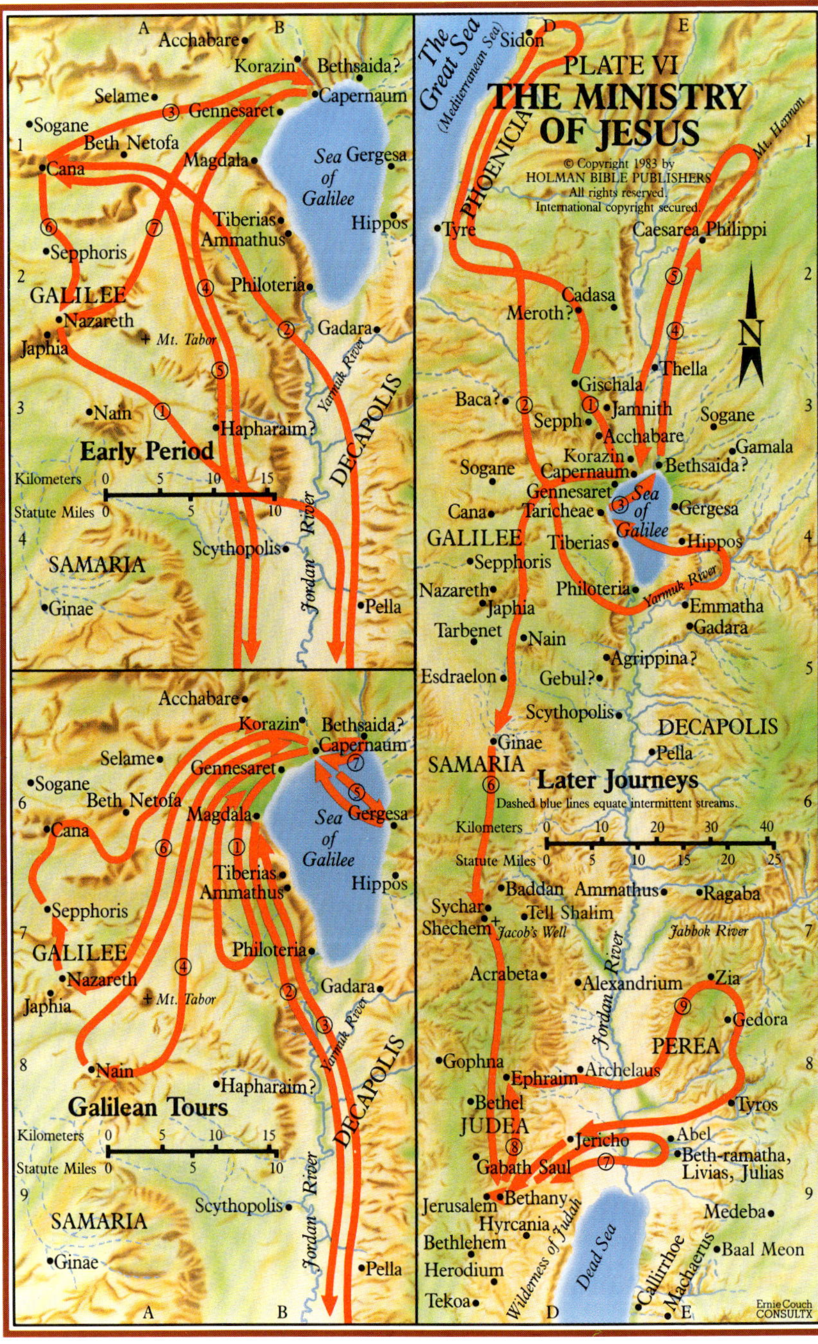

PLATE VI
THE MINISTRY OF JESUS
© Copyright 1983 by HOLMAN BIBLE PUBLISHERS
All rights reserved.
International copyright secured.
Early Period
Galilean Tours
Later Journeys
Dashed blue lines equate intermittent streams.
Kilometers
Statute Miles
The Great Sea (Mediterranean Sea)
PHOENICIA
GALILEE
SAMARIA
DECAPOLIS
PEREA
JUDEA
Sea of Galilee
Dead Sea
Jordan River
Yarmuk River
Jabbok River
Wilderness of Judah
Mt. Hermon
Mt. Tabor
Sidon
Tyre
Caesarea Philippi
Cadasa
Meroth?
Thella
Gischala
Baca?
Jamnith
Sepph.
Acchabare
Sogane
Gamala
Korazin
Capernaum
Bethsaida?
Gennesaret
Taricheae
Gergesa
Cana
Tiberias
Hippos
Sepphoris
Philoteria
Nazareth
Japhia
Emmatha
Gadara
Tarbenet
Nain
Agrippina?
Esdraelon
Gebul?
Scythopolis
Ginae
Pella
Selame
Beth Netofa
Magdala
Ammathus
Hapharaim?
Sychar
Shechem
Jacob's Well
Baddan
Tell Shalim
Ragaba
Acrabeta
Alexandrium
Zia
Gedora
Gophna
Ephraim
Archelaus
Bethel
Tyros
Jericho
Abel
Beth-ramatha, Livias, Julias
Gabath Saul
Jerusalem
Bethany
Hyrcania
Bethlehem
Herodium
Tekoa
Medeba
Baal Meon
Callirrhoe
Machaerus
Ernie Couch CONSULTX

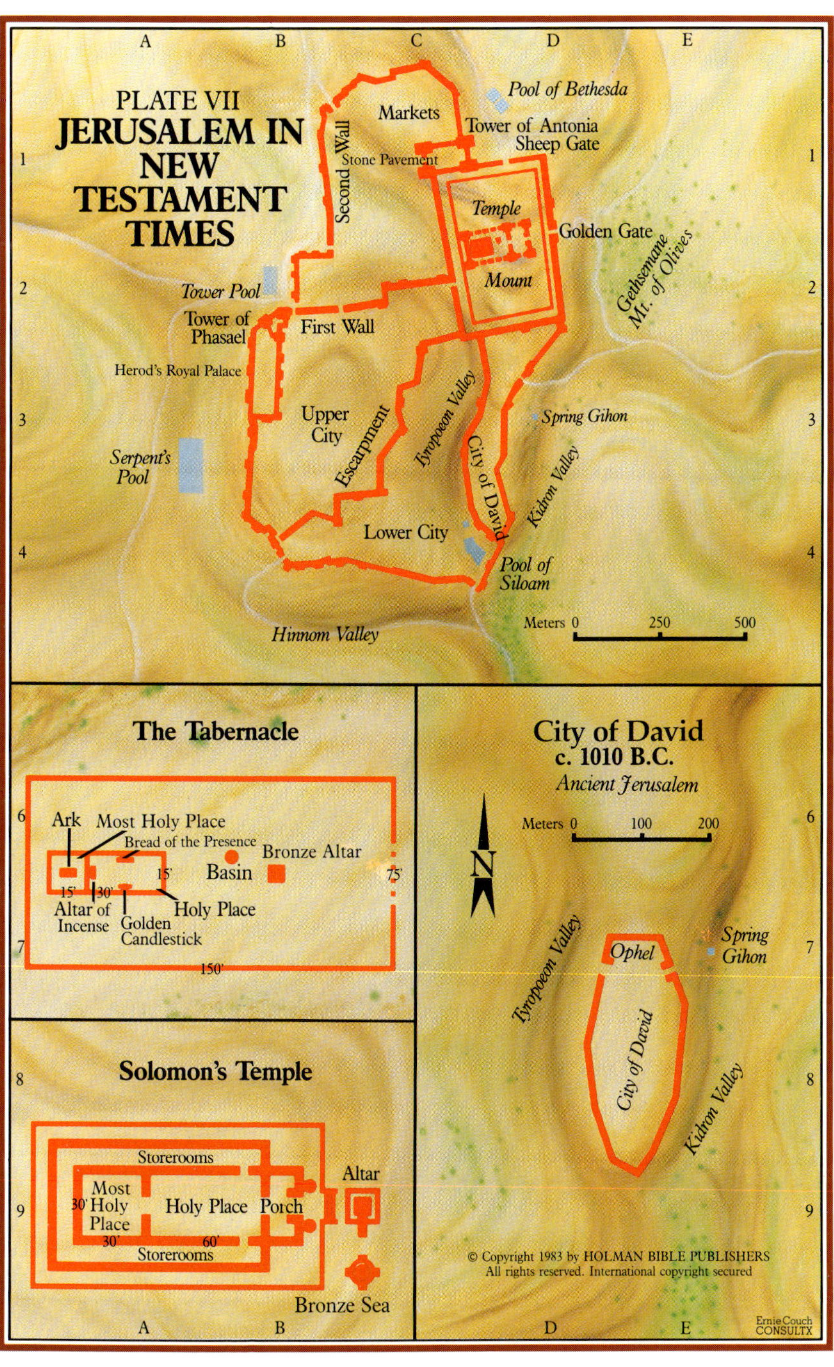
PLATE VII
JERUSALEM IN NEW TESTAMENT TIMES
A
B
C
D
E
1
2
3
4
Pool of Bethesda
Markets
Tower of Antonia
Sheep Gate
Second Wall
Stone Pavement
Temple
Mount
Golden Gate
Gethsemane
Mt. of Olives
Tower Pool
Tower of Phasael
First Wall
Herod's Royal Palace
Upper City
Escarpment
Tyropoeon Valley
City of David
Spring Gihon
Kidron Valley
Serpent's Pool
Lower City
Pool of Siloam
Hinnom Valley
Meters 0 250 500
The Tabernacle
6
7
Ark
Most Holy Place
Bread of the Presence
Bronze Altar
Basin
15'
15'
30'
75'
Altar of Incense
Golden Candlestick
Holy Place
150'
Solomon's Temple
8
9
Storerooms
Most Holy Place
30'
30'
Holy Place
60'
Porch
Altar
Storerooms
Bronze Sea
City of David
c. 1010 B.C.
Ancient Jerusalem
Meters 0 100 200
N
Tyropoeon Valley
Ophel
Spring Gihon
City of David
Kidron Valley
Ernie Couch CONSULTX

PLATE VIII
PAUL'S MISSIONARY JOURNEYS
First
Second
Third
To Rome
The Seven Churches of Asia
© Copyright 1983 by HOLMAN BIBLE PUBLISHERS
All rights reserved. International copyright secured
ITALIA
Rome
Three Taverns?
Forum of Appius
(Appii Forum)
Tarracina
Puteoli
Neapolis
Pompey
Paestum
Buxetum
Brundisium
Tarentum
Sybaris
Croton
Tyrrhenian Sea
Adriatic Sea
Panormus
Messana
Rhegium
SICILY
Mt. Etna
Catania
Agrigentum
Syracuse
Malta
(Melita)
ILLYRICUM
MOESIA
Dyrrhachium
Scupi
Philippopolis
THRACE
MACEDONIA
Philippi
Amphipolis
Neapolis
Apollonia
Pella
Berea
Thessalonica
Mt. Olympus
Thessaly
Larissa
Epirus
Dodona
Corcyra
Nicopolis
Actium
ACHAIA
Delphi
Patrae
Corinth
Athens
Cenchrea
Elis
Olympia
Pylos
Sparta
Samothrace
Imbros
Lemnos
Aegean Sea
Cyclades
Black Sea
Byzantium
Cyzicus
Abydos
Troas
Assos
Mysia
Adramyttium
Mytilene
Lesbos
Kios
Pergamum
Thyatira
Sardis
Smyrna
Philadelphia
Ephesus
Laodicia
Hermus R.
Maeander R.
Colosse
Samos
Patmos
Miletus
Halicarnassus
Cos
Cnidus
Rhodes
RHODES
Xanthus
Patara
Myra
LYCIA
ASIA
Phrygia
Pisidia
Antioch
Lycaonia
Iconium
Lystra
Derbe
Perga
Attalia
PAMPHYLIA
Nicaea
Prusa
Dorylaeum
Cotiaeum
Pessinus
Gordium
Heraclea
Amastris
BITHYNIA & PONTUS
Paphlagonia
Gangra
Ancyra
GALATIA
Tavium
Amisus
CAPPADOCIA
Archelaus
CILICIA
Cilician Gates
Tarsus
Issus
Soli
Seleucia
Antioch
Seleucia
Pieria
SYRIA
Salamis
CYPRUS
Paphos
Tripolis
Berytus
Sidon
Tyre
Ptolemais
Caesarea
Joppa
Jordan
Jerusalem
Gaza
Cydonia
Cnossus
CRETE
Fair Havens
Lasea
The Great Sea
Mediterranean Sea
Kilometers 0 100 200 300
Statute Miles 0 100 200
Oea
Leptis Magna
AFRICA
Greater Syrtis
Cyrene
CYRENAICA
LIBYA
Sahara Desert
Alexandria
Canopus
Nile Delta
EGYPT
Heliopolis
Memphis
Pelusium
Sinai
Ernie Couch
CONSULTX